# Acronyms, Initialisms & Abbreviations Dictionary

# Gale's publications in the acronyms and abbreviations field include:

## *Acronyms, Initialisms & Abbreviations Dictionary* series:

***Acronyms, Initialisms & Abbreviations Dictionary*** (Volume 1). A guide to acronyms, initialisms, abbreviations, and similar contractions, arranged alphabetically by abbreviation.

***New Acronyms, Initialisms & Abbreviations*** (Volume 2). An interedition supplement in which terms are arranged both by abbreviation and by meaning.

***Reverse Acronyms, Initialisms & Abbreviations Dictionary*** (Volume 3). A companion to Volume 1 in which terms are arranged alphabetically by meaning of the acronym, initialism, or abbreviation.

## *Acronyms, Initialisms & Abbreviations Dictionary Subject Guide* series:

***Computer & Telecommunications Acronyms*** (Volume 1). A guide to acronyms, initialisms, abbreviations, and similar contractions used in the field of computers and telecommunications in which terms are arranged alphabetically both by abbreviation and by meaning.

***Business Acronyms*** (Volume 2). A guide to business-oriented acronyms, initialisms, abbreviations, and similar contractions in which terms are arranged alphabetically both by abbreviation and by meaning.

## *International Acronyms, Initialisms & Abbreviations Dictionary* series:

***International Acronyms, Initialisms & Abbreviations Dictionary*** (Volume 1). A guide to foreign and international acronyms, initialisms, abbreviations, and similar contractions, arranged alphabetically by abbreviation.

***New International Acronyms, Initialisms & Abbreviations*** (Volume 2). An interedition supplement in which terms are arranged alphabetically both by abbreviation and by meaning.

***Reverse International Acronyms, Initialisms & Abbreviations Dictionary*** (Volume 3). A companion to Volume 1, in which terms are arranged alphabetically by meaning of the acronym, initialism, or abbreviation.

## *Periodical Title Abbreviations* series:

***Periodical Title Abbreviations: By Abbreviation*** (Volume 1). A guide to abbreviations commonly used for periodical titles, arranged alphabetically by abbreviation.

***Periodical Title Abbreviations: By Title*** (Volume 2). A guide to abbreviations commonly used for periodical titles, arranged alphabetically by title.

***New Periodical Title Abbreviations*** (Volume 3). An interedition supplement in which terms are arranged alphabetically both by abbreviation and by title.

ISSN 0270-4404

# Acronyms, Initialisms & Abbreviations Dictionary

*A Guide to More Than 520,000 Acronyms, Initialisms, Abbreviations, Contractions, Alphabetic Symbols, and Similar Condensed Appellations*

Covering: Aerospace, Associations, Banking, Biochemistry, Business, Data Processing, Domestic and International Affairs, Economics, Education, Electronics, Genetics, Government, Information Technology, Investment, Labor, Law, Medicine, Military Affairs, Periodicals, Pharmacy, Physiology, Politics, Religion, Science, Societies, Sports, Technical Drawings and Specifications, Telecommunications, Trade, Transportation, and Other Fields

**Sixteenth Edition**

**1992**

**Volume 1**

**Part 2**

**G-O**

Jennifer Mossman,
*Editor*

Pamela Dear
Prindle LaBarge
Ellen Paré,
*Associate Editors*

*Senior Editor:* Donna Wood
*Editor:* Jennifer Mossman

*Associate Editors:* Pamela Dear, Prindle LaBarge, Ellen Paré
*Assistant Editors:* Yvonne Y. Lee, Alice M. Walsh

*Contributing Editors:* Leland G. Alkire, Jr., Mildred Hunt, Edwin B. Steen, Miriam M. Steinert

*Data Entry Supervisor:* Benita L. Spight
*Data Entry Associate:* Merrie Ann Carpenter

*Production Manager:* Mary Beth Trimper
*Production Assistant:* Mary Winterhalter
*Art Director:* Arthur Chartow
*Keyliners:* C.J. Jonik, Yolanda Y. Latham

*Supervisor of Systems and Programming:* Theresa A. Rocklin
*Programmers:* Charles Beaumont, David Trotter



The paper used in this publication meets the minimum requirements of American National Standard for Information Sciences—Permanence Paper for Printed Library Materials, ANSI Z39.48-1984.™




835 Penobscot Building
Detroit, MI 48226-4094

Library of Congress Catalog Card Number 84-643188
ISBN 0-8103-5077-7 (Volume 1 Complete)
ISBN 0-8103-5099-8 (Part 1: A-F only)
ISBN 0-8103-5352-0 (Part 2: G-O only)
ISBN 0-8103-5353-9 (Part 3: P-Z only)
ISSN 0270-4404

Printed in the United States of America

Published simultaneously in the United Kingdom
by Gale Research International Limited
(An affiliated company of Gale Research Inc.)

# Contents

# User's Guide

The following examples illustrate the possible elements of entries in *AIAD*:

| |
|---|
| 1 2 3 4 5<br>**FATAC**....Force Aerienne Tactique [*Tactical Air Force*] [*French*] (NATG)<br><br>6 7<br>**MMT**...*Multiple-Mirror Telescope [Mount Hopkins, AZ]* [*Jointly operated by Smithsonian Institution and the University of Arizona*] [*Astronomy*]<br>8 |

1 Acronym, Initialism, or Abbreviation

2 Meaning or Phrase

3 English translation

4 Language (for non-English entries)

5 Source code (Allows you to verify entries or find additional information. Decoded in the List of Selected Sources)

6 Location or Country of origin (Provides geographic identifiers for airports, colleges and universities, libraries, military bases, political parties, radio and television stations, and others)

7 Sponsoring organization

8 Subject category (Clarifies entries by providing appropriate context)

The completeness of a listing is dependent upon both the nature of the term and the amount of information provided by the source. If additional information becomes available during future research, an entry is revised.

### Arrangement of Entries

Acronyms, initialisms, and abbreviations are arranged alphabetically in letter-by-letter sequence. Spacing, punctuation, and capitalization are not considered. If the same term has more than one meaning, the various meanings are subarranged in word-by-word sequence.

Should you wish to eliminate the guesswork from acronym formation and usage, a companion volume could help. *Reverse Acronyms, Initialisms and Abbreviations Dictionary* contains essentially the same entries as *AIAD*, but arranges them alphabetically by meaning, rather than by acronym or initialism.

# List of Selected Sources

Each of the print sources included in the following list contributed at least 50 terms. It would be impossible to cite a source for every entry in *Acronyms, Initialisms, and Abbreviations Dictionary (AIAD)* becuase the majority of terms are sent by outside contributors, are uncovered through independent research by the editorial staff, or surface as miscellaneous broadcast or print media references.

For sources used on an ongoing basis, only the latest edition is listed. For most of the remaining sources, the edition that was used is cited. The editors will provide further information about these sources upon request.

Unless further described in an annotation, the publications listed here contain no additional information about the acronym, initialism, or abbreviation cited in *AIAD*.

(AABC) *Catalog of Abbreviations and Brevity Codes.* Washington, DC: U.S. Department of the Army, 1981. [Use of source began in 1969]

(AAG) *Aerospace Abbreviations Glossary.* Report Number AG60-0014. Prepared by General Dynamics/Astronautics. San Diego: 1962.

(ADA) *The Australian Dictionary of Acronyms and Abbreviations.* 2nd ed. Compiled by David J. Jones. Leura, NSW, Australia: Second Back Row Press Pty. Ltd., 1981.

(AFIT) *Compendium of Authenticated Systems and Logistics.* Washington, DC: Air Force Institute of Technology. [Use of source began in 1984]

(AFM) *Air Force Manual of Abbreviations.* Washington, DC: U.S. Department of the Air Force, 1975. [Use of source began in 1969]

(AIA) *Aviation Insurance Abbreviations, Organisations and Institutions.* By M.J. Spurway. London: Witherby & Co. Ltd., 1983.

(APTA) *Australian Periodical Title Abbreviations.* Compiled by David J. Jones. Leura, NSW, Australia: Second Back Row Press Pty. Ltd., 1985.

(ARC) *Agricultural Research Centres: A World Directory of Organizations and Programmes.* 2 vols. Edited by Nigel Harvey. Harlow, Essex, England: Longman Group, 1983; distributed in the U.S. by Gale Research Inc., Detroit.

> A world guide to official, educational, industrial, and independent research centers which support research in the fields of agriculture, veterinary medicine, horticulture, aquaculture, food science, forestry, zoology, and botany.

(ASF) *Guide to Names and Acronyms of Organizations, Activities, and Projects.* Food and Agriculture Organization of the United Nations. Fishery Information, Data, and Statistics Service and U.S. National Oceanic and Atmospheric Administration. Aquatic Sciences and Fisheries Information System Reference Series, Number 10, 1982. n.p.

(BIB) *Bibliotech.* Ottawa, Canada: National Library of Canada, 1988-89.

(BJA) *Biblical and Judaic Acronyms.* By Lawrence Marwick. New York: Ktav Publishing House, Inc., 1979.

(BUR) *Computer Acronyms and Abbreviations Handbook.* Tokyo: Burroughs Co. Ltd., 1978.

(BYTE) *Byte: The Small Systems Journal.* Peterborough, NH: McGraw- Hill Information Systems, Inc., 1987-89.

(CAAL) *CAAL COMOPTEVFOR Acronym and Abbreviation List.* Norfolk, VA: (CAAL-U) Operational Test and Evaluation Force, 1981.

(CB) *Centres & Bureaux: A Directory of Concentrations of Effort, Information and Expertise.* Edited by Lindsay Sellar. Beckenham, Kent, England: CBD Research Ltd., 1987.

A guide to British organizations which include the words "centre" or "bureau" in their names. Entries include name and address; telephone and telex numbers; chief official; and a description of the purposes, activities, and services of the organization.

(CED) *Current European Directories.* 2nd ed. Edited by G.P. Henderson, Beckenham, Kent, England: CBD Research, 1981; distributed in U.S. by Gale Research Inc., Detroit.

(CET) *Communications-Electronics Terminology.* AFM 11-1. Vol. 3 U.S. Department of the Air Force, 1973.

(CINC) *A CINCPAC Glossary of Commonly Used Abbreviations and Short Titles.* By Ltc. J.R. Johnson. Washington, DC: 1968.

(CMD) *Complete Multilingual Dictionary of Computer Terminology.* Compiled by Georges Nania. Chicago: National Textbook Co., 1984.

Computer-related terms in Spanish, French, Italian, Portuguese, and English. Indexes in French, Italian, Spanish, and Portuguese are also provided.

(CNC) *American National Standard Codes for the Representation of Names of Countries, Dependencies, and Areas of Special Sovereignty for Information Interchange.* U.S. National Bureau of Standards. Washington, DC: Government Printing Office, 1986. [Use of source began in 1977]

These standard codes, approved by the International Organization for Standardization and the American National Standards Institute, are used in the international interchange of data in many fields.

(CRD) *Computer-Readable Databases: A Directory and Data Sourcebook.* 6th ed. Edited by Kathleen Young Marcaccio. Detroit: Gale Research Inc., 1990.

A guide to online databases, offline files available in various magnetic formats, and CD-ROM files. Entries include producer name, address, telephone number, description of coverage, vendors, and contact person.

(CSR) *Computer Science Resources: A Guide to Professional Literature.* Edited by Darlene Myers. White Plains, NY: Knowledge Industry Publications, Inc., 1981.

Covers several types of computer-related literature including journals, technical reports, directories, dictionaries, handbooks, and university computer center newsletters. Five appendices cover career and salary trends in the computer industry, user group acronyms, university computer libraries, and trade fairs and shows.

(CTT) *Corporate TrendTrac.* Edited by A. Dale Timpe. Detroit: Gale Research Inc., 1988-89.

Covers mergers and acquisitions, stock exchange listings and suspensions, company name changes, bankruptcies, liquidations, and reorganizations.

(DAS) *Dictionary of Abbreviations and Symbols.* By Edward Frank Allen. London: Cassell and Co. Ltd.

(DBQ) *A Dictionary of British Qualifications.* London: Kogan Page Ltd., 1985.

(DCTA) *Dictionary of Commercial Terms and Abbreviations.* By Alan E. Branch. London: Witherby & Co. Ltd., 1984.

(DEN) *Dictionary of Electronics and Nucleonics.* By L.E.C. Hughes, R.W.B. Stephens, and L.D. Brown. New York: Barnes & Noble, 1969.

(DHSM) *Dictionary of Health Services Management.* 2nd ed. By Thomas C. Timmreck. Owings Mills, MD: Rynd Communications, 1987.

(DIT) *Dictionary of Informatics Terms in Russian and English.* By G.S. Zhdanov, E.S. Kolobrodov, V.A. Polushkin, and A.I. Cherny. Moscow: Nauka, 1971.

(DLA) *Bieber's Dictionary of Legal Abbreviations.* 3rd ed. By Mary Miles Prince. Buffalo, NY: William S. Hein & Co., 1988.

(DMA) *Dictionary of Military Abbreviations: British, Empire, Commonwealth.* By. B.K.C. Scott. Hastings, East Sussex, England: Tamarisk Books, 1982.

(DS) *Dictionary of Shipping International Trade Terms and Abbreviations.* 3rd ed. By Alan E. Branch. London: Witherby & Co. Ltd., 1986.

(DSA) *Dictionary of Sigla and Abbreviations to and in Law Books before 1607.* By William Hamilton Bryson. Charlottesville, VA: University Press of Virginia, 1975.

(DSUE) *A Dictionary of Slang and Unconventional English.* 8th ed. By Eric Partridge. New York: Macmillan Publishing Co., 1984.

(EA) *Encyclopedia of Associations.* 25th ed. Vol. 1, National Organizations of the U.S. Edited by Deborah M. Burek. Detroit: Gale Research Inc., 1990. (and supplement, 1991) [Use of source began in 1960]

A guide to trade, professional, and other nonprofit associations that are national and international in scope and membership and that are headquartered in the United States. Entries include name and address; telephone and telex number; chief official; and a description of the purpose, activities, and structure of the organization.

(EAAP) *Encyclopedia of Associations: Association Periodicals.* 3 vols. Edited by Denise M. Allard and Robert C. Thomas. Detroit: Gale Research Inc., 1987.

A directory of publications issued by all types of national nonprofit organizations in the United States. Entries include title and organization name, address, telephone number; description of periodical, frequency of publication, and price.

(EAIO) *Encyclopedia of Associations: International Organizations.* 24th ed. Edited by Kenneth Estell. Detroit: Gale Research Inc., 1990. [Use of source began in 1985]

A guide to trade, professional, and other nonprofit associations that are national or international in scope and membership and that are headquartered outside the United States. Entries include name and address; principal foreign language name; telephone and telex number; chief official; and a description of the purpose, activities, and structure of the organization.

(ECON) *The Economist.* London: The Economist Newspaper Ltd., 1991. [Use of source began in 1988]

(EGAO) *Encyclopedia of Government Advisory Organizations.* 6th ed. Edited by Denise M. Allard and Donna Batten. Detroit: Gale Research Inc., 1988 [Use of source began in 1975]

A reference guide to permanent, continuing, and ad hoc U.S. presidential advisory committees, interagency committees, and other government-related boards, panels, task forces, commissions, conferences, and other similar bodies serving in a consultative, coordinating, advisory, research, or investigative capacity. Entries include name and address, telephone number, designated federal employee, history, recommendation and findings of the committee, staff size, publications, and subsidiaries. Also includes indexes to personnel, reports, federal agencies, presidential administration, and an alphabetical and keyword index.

(EY) *The Europa Year Book 1987: A World Survey.* London: Europa Publications Ltd., 1987. distributed in U.S. by Gale Research Inc., Detroit.

An annual survey containing detailed information about the political, economic, statistical, and commercial situation of the regions and countries covered.

(FAAC) *Contractions Handbook.* Changes. U.S. Department of Transportation. Federal Aviation Administration, 1985. [Use of source began in 1969]

(FAAL) *Location Identifiers.* U.S. Department of Transportation. Federal Aviation Administration. Air Traffic Service, 1982.

(FEA) *The Far East and Australasia 1987.* 18th ed. London: Europa Publications Ltd., 1986; distributed in U.S. by Gale Research Inc., Detroit.

Annual survey containing detailed information about the political, economic, statistical, and commercial situation of the regions and countries covered.

(GEA) *Government Economic Agencies of the World: An International Directory of Governmental Organisations Concerned with Economic Development and Planning.* A Keesing's Reference Publication. Edited by Alan J. Day. Harlow, Essex, England: Longman Group Ltd., 1985; distributed in U.S. by Gale Research Inc., Detroit.

Covers over 170 countries and territories. Two introductory sections for each area cover economic data and prevailing economic and political conditions. Individual entries provide title, address, and names of chief officials of each agency. Current activities and financial structure of each agency are also detailed. An index of agency officials is provided.

(GPO) *Style Manual.* Washington, DC: Government Printing Office, 1984. Terms are included in Chapter 24, Foreign Languages.

(GRD) *Government Research Directory.* 5th ed. Edited by Kay Gill and Susan E. Tufts. Detroit: Gale Research Inc., 1989. (and supplement, 1989)

A descriptive guide to U.S. government research and development centers, institutes, laboratories, bureaus, test facilities, experiment stations, data collection and analysis centers, and grants management and research coordinating offices in agriculture, business, education, energy, engineering, environment, the humanities, medicine, military science, and basic applied sciences.

(IBMDP) *IBM Data Processing Glossary.* 6th ed. White Plains, NY: IBM Corp., 1977.

(ICAO) *Aircraft Type Designators.* 13th ed. International Civil Aviation Organization, August, 1981.

(ICDA) *Designators for Aircraft Operating Agencies, Aeronautical Authorities and Services.* 49th ed. International Civil Aviation Organization, June 1982.

Document also includes telephony designators and postal and telegraphic addresses of government civil aviation authorities.

(ICLI) *Location Indicators.* 51st ed. International Civil Aviation Organization, February 1987.

Document also contains addresses of flight information centers.

(IEEE) *IEEE Standard Dictionary of Electrical and Electronics Terms.* Edited by Frank Jay. New York: The Institute of Electrical and Electronics Engineers, Inc., 1977, 1984.

Includes definitions for thousands of electrical and electronics terms. Each entry includes a numeric source code.

(IID) *Information Industry Directory.* 11th ed. Edited by Bradley J. Morgan. Detroit: Gale Research Inc., 1991 (and supplement, 1991).

An international guide to computer-readable databases, database producers, and publishers, online vendors and time-sharing companies, telecommunications networks, and many other information systems and services. Entries include name and address, telephone number, chief official, and a detailed description of the purpose and function of the system or service.

(ILCA) *Index to Legal Citations and Abbreviations.* By Donald Raistrick. Abingdon, Oxfordshire, England: Professional Books Ltd., 1981.

(IMH) *International Marketing Handbook.* 2nd ed. Edited by Frank Bair. Detroit: Gale Research Inc., 1985.

An in-depth guide to commercial and trade data on 142 countries of the world. Features include a list of European trade fairs and a report on growth markets in Western Europe.

(INF) *Infantry.* Fort Benning, GA: U.S. Army Infantry Training School, 1989. [Use of source began in 1983]

(IRC) *International Research Centers Directory 1988-89.* 4th ed. Edited by Darren L. Smith. Detroit: Gale Research Inc., 1988.

A world guide to government, university, independent, nonprofit, and commercial research and development centers, institutes, laboratories, bureaus, test facilities, experiment stations, and data collection and analysis centers, as well as foundations, councils, and other organizations which support research.

(IRUK) *Industrial Research in the United Kingdom.* 12th ed. Harlow, Essex, England: Longman Group UK Ltd., 1987.

A guide to all groups conducting or funding research relevant to British industrial development. Entries include name, address, telephone and telex numbers; chief officials; and scope of activities.

(IT) *Information Today: The Newspaper for Users and Producers of Electronic Information Services.* Medford, NJ: Learned Information Inc., 1988-89.

(ITD) *International Tradeshow Directory.* 5th ed. Frankfurt am Main: M + A Publishers for Fairs, Exhibitions and Conventions Ltd., 1989.

A guide to trade fairs and exhibitions throughout the world. Entries include event name, dates, frequency, location,description of purpose, profile of exhibitors and attendees.

(IYR) *The 1989-92 International Yacht Racing Rules.* London: International Yacht Racing Union, 1989.

(KSC) *A Selective List of Acronyms and Abbreviations.* Compiled by the Documents Department, Kennedy Space Center Library, 1971, 1973.

(LCCP) *MARC Formats for Bibliographic Data.* Appendix II. Washington, DC: Library of Congress, 1982.

(LCLS) *Symbols of American Libraries.* 13th ed. Washington, DC: Catalog Management and Publication Division, Library of Congress, 1985. [Use of source began in 1980]

(MCD) *Acronyms, Abbreviations, and Initialisms.* Compiled by Carl Lauer. St. Louis: McDonnell Douglas Corp., 1989 [Use of source began in 1969]

(MDG) *Microcomputer Dictionary and Guide.* By Charles J. Sippl. Champaign, IL: Matrix Publishers, Inc., 1975.

A listing of definitions for over 5,000 microelectronics terms. Seven appendices.

(MENA) *The Middle East and North Africa 1987.* 33rd ed. London: Europa Publications Ltd., 1986; distributed in U.S. by Gale Research Inc., Detroit.

An annual survey containing detailed information about the political, economic, statistical, and commercial situation of the regions and countries covered.

(MSA) *Military Standard Abbreviations for Use on Drawings, and in Specifications, Standards, and Technical Documents.* MIL-STD-12D. U.S. Department of Defense, 1981. [Use of source began in 1975]

(MSC) *Annotated Acronyms and Abbreviations of Marine Science Related Activities.* 3rd ed. Revised by Charlotte M. Ashby and Alan R. Flesh. Washington, DC: U.S. Department of Commerce. National Oceanographic and Atmospheric Administration. Environmental Data Service. National Oceanographic Data Center, 1976, 1981.

(MUGU) *The Mugu Book of Acronyms and Abbreviations.* Management Engineering Office, Pacific Missile Range, California, 1963, 1964.

(NASA) *Space Transportation System and Associated Payloads: Glossary, Acronyms, and Abbreviations.* Washington, DC: U.S. National Aeronautics and Space Administration, 1985.

(NATG) *Glossary of Abbreviations Used in NATO Documents.* AAP 15, n.p., 1979. [Use of source began in 1976]

(NG) *NAVAIR Glossary of Unclassified Common-Use Abbreviated Titles and Phrases.* NAVAIRNOTE 5216 AIR-6031, n.p., July 1969.

(NLC) *Symbols of Canadian Libraries.* 12th ed. National Library of Canada. Minister of Supply and Services Canada, 1987.

(NOAA) *NOAA Directives Manual.* 66-13 Acronyms. 1977.

(NQ) *NASDAQ Company Directory.* New York: National Association of Securities Dealers Inc., 1990. [Use of source began in 1983]

Entries include company name, SIC code, contact person's name, title, address, and telephone number.

(NRCH) *A Handbook of Acronyms and Initialisms.* Washington, DC: U.S. Nuclear Regulatory Commission. Division of Technical Information and Document Control, 1985.

(NVT) *Naval Terminology.* NWP3. Rev. B. U.S. Department of the Navy. Office of the Chief of Naval Operations, 1980 [Use of source began in 1974]

Includes a section on definitions of naval terminology.

(OAG) *Official Airline Guide Worldwide Edition.* Oak Brook, IL: Official Airlines Guide, Inc., 1984. [Use of source began in 1975]

(OCD) *Oxford Classical Dictionary.* 2nd ed. Edited by N.G. Hammond and H.H. Scullard. London: Oxford University Press, 1970.

(OCLC) *OCLC Participating Institutions Arranged by OCLC Symbol.* Dublin, OH: OCLC, 1981.

(OICC) *Abbreviations and Acronyms.* Des Moines, IA: Iowa State Occupational Information Coordinating Committee, 1986.

(OLDSS) *Online Database Search Services Directory.* 2nd ed. Edited by Doris Morris Maxfield. Detroit: Gale Research Inc., 1988.

Provides detailed descriptions of the online information retrieval services offered by libraries, private information firms, and other organizations in the United States and Canada. Entries include name and address, telephone number, and key contact, as well as online systems accessed, frequently searched databases, and access hardware.

(PCM) *PC Magazine.* New York: Ziff-Davis Publishing Co., 1989. [Use of source began in 1987]

(PD) *Political Dissent: An International Guide to Dissident, Extra-Parliamentary, Guerrilla and Illegal Political Movements.* A Keesing's Reference Publication. Compiled by Henry W. Degenhardt. Edited by Alan J. Day. Harlow, Essex, England: Longman Group, 1983; distributed in U.S. by Gale Research Inc., Detroit.

Includes the history and aims of approximately 1,000 organizations, with details of their leaderships.

(PPE) *Political Parties of Europe.* 2 vols. Edited by Vincent E. McHale. The Greenwood Historical Encyclopedia of the World's Political Parties. Westport, CT: Greenwood Press, 1983.

One of a series of reference guides to the world's significant political parties. Each guide provides concise histories of the political parties of a region and attempts to detail the evolution of ideology, changes in organization, membership, leadership, and each party's impact upon society.

(PPW) *Political Parties of the World.* 2nd ed. A Keesing's Reference Publication. Compiled and edited by Alan J. Day and Henry W. Degenhardt. Harlow, Essex, England: Longman Group, 1980, 1984; distributed in U.S. by Gale Research Inc., Detroit.

Covers historical development, structure, leadership, membership, policy, publications, and international affiliations. For each country, an overview of the current political situation and constitutional structure is provided.

(RCD) *Research Centers Directory.* 14th ed. Edited by Peter D. Dresser and Karen Hill. Detroit: Gale Research Inc., 1989 (and supplement, 1990). [Use of source began in 1986]

A guide to university-related and other nonprofit research organizations carrying on research in agriculture, astronomy and space sciences, behavioral and social sciences, computers and mathematics, engineering and technology, physical and earth sciences and regional and area studies.

(RDA) *Army RD and A Magazine.* Alexandria, VA: Development, Engineering, and Acquisition Directorate, Army Materiel Command, 1989. [Use of source began in 1979]

(ROG) *Dictionary of Abbreviations.* By Walter T. Rogers. London: George Allen & Co. Ltd., 1913; reprinted by Gale Research Inc., 1969.

(SDI) *Report to the Congress on the Strategic Defense Initiative.* U.S. Department of Defense. Strategic Defense Initiative Organization, April 1987.

(SEIS) *Seismograph Station Codes and Characteristics.* Geological Survey. Circular 791. By Barbara B. Poppe, Debbi A. Naab, and John S. Derr. Washington, DC: U.S. Department of the Interior, 1978.

(SPSG) *Security Owner's Stock Guide.* New York: Standard & Poor's Corp., 1991. [Use of source began in 1988]

(TEL) *Telephony's Dictionary.* 2nd ed. By Graham Langley. Chicago: Telephony Publishing Corp., 1986.

Includes definitions for U.S. and international telecommunications terms. Ten appendices.

(TSPED) *Trade Shows and Professional Exhibits Directory.* 2nd ed. Edited by Robert J. Elster. Detroit: Gale Research Inc., 1987. [Use of source began in 1986]

A guide to scheduled events providing commercial display facilities including conferences, conventions, meetings, fairs and festivals, etc. Entries include name of trade show; sponsor name, address, and telephone number; attendance figures; principal exhibits; special features; publications; and date and location of shows.

(TSSD) *Telecommunications Systems and Services Directory.* 4th ed. (and supplement) Edited by John Krol. Detroit: Gale Research Inc., 1989. [Use of source began in 1985]

An international descriptive guide to telecommunications organizations, systems, and services. Entries include name and address, telephone number, chief official, and a description of the purposes, technical structure, and background of the service or system.

# Acronyms, Initialisms & Abbreviations Dictionary

## G-O

# G

**G** ... Air Force Training Category [*12 training periods and zero days active duty training per year*]

**G** ... Air [*or Army*] National Guard [*Military aircraft identification prefix*] (FAAC)

**G** ... Application for Writ of Error Granted [*Legal term*] (DLA)

**G** ... Ciba-Geigy AG [*Switzerland*] [*Research code symbol*]

**G** ... Conductance [*Symbol*] [*IUPAC*]

**G** ... Federal Republic of Germany [*IYRU nationality code*] (IYR)

**G** ... Fire Control [*JETDS nomenclature*]

**G** ... Gain

**G** ... Gale [*Meteorology*]

**G** ... Gale's English Exchequer Reports [*A publication*] (DLA)

**G** ... Galliot [*Ship's rigging*] (ROG)

**G** ... Gambia [*Country in West Africa*] (ROG)

**G** ... Game

**G** ... Games Played [*Sports statistics*]

**G** ... Gamma

**G** ... Gamut [*Music*] (ROG)

**G** ... Gandulphus [*Flourished, 1160-85*] [*Authority cited in pre-1607 legal work*] (DSA)

**G** ... Ganglion [*Medicine*]

**G** ... Ganz [*White Blot*] [*Rorschach*] [*Psychology*]

**G** ... Gaon (BJA)

**G** ... Gap in Cell Cycle [*Cytology*]

**G** ... Garage

**G** ... [*Johannes*] Garcias Hispanus [*Flourished, 13th century*] [*Authority cited in pre-1607 legal work*] (DSA)

**(g)** ... Gas [*Chemistry*]

**G** ... Gas Oil

**g** ... Gastralia [*Osteology*]

**G** ... Gastrin [*Biochemistry*]

**G** ... Gate [*Electronics*]

**g** ... Gauche [*Chemical conformation*]

**G** ... Gauche [*Left*] [*French*]

**G** ... Gauge

**G** ... Gauss [*Unit of magnetic flux density*] [*Preferred unit is T, Telsa*]

**G** ... Gear (AAG)

**G** ... Ge'ez (BJA)

**G** ... Gelaendegaengig [*Having cross-country mobility*] [*German military - World War II*]

**G** ... Geld [*Monetary unit*] [*German*]

**G** ... Gelding [*Thoroughbred racing*]

**g** ... Gemeisamer Faktor [*General Factor*] [*Rorschach*] [*Psychology*]

**G** ... Gemini Airline [*British*]

**G** ... [*Dominicus de Sancto*] Geminiano [*Flourished, 1407-09*] [*Authority cited in pre-1607 legal work*] (DSA)

**G** ... Gender

**G** ... General

**G** ... General Audiences [*All ages admitted*] [*Movie rating*]

**G** ... General Duties [*Ranking title*] [*British Women's Royal Naval Service*]

**G** ... General Factor (ADA)

**G** ... General Intelligence

**G** ... General List [*Navy*] [*British*]

**G** ... General Procedures

**G** ... General-Purpose Freight Container (DCTA)

**G** ... General Staff Branch [*Army*] [*British*]

**G** ... Generalist [*Ecology*]

**G** ... Generalized Feeder [*Ichthyology*]

**G** ... Generally Labeled [*Radioactive compounds*]

**G** ... Generating Item [*Military*]

**G** ... Generators, Power [*JETDS nomenclature*] [*Military*] (CET)

**G** ... Genitive [*Case*] [*Grammar*]

**g** ... Genome [*Genetics*]

**G** ... Geography [*Secondary school course*] [*British*]

**G** ... Geonic (BJA)

**G** ... George [*Phonetic alphabet*] [*Royal Navy*] [*World War I*] [*Pre-World War II*] [*World War II*] (DSUE)

**G** ... George (King of England) (DLA)

**G** ... Georgia State Library, Atlanta, GA [*Library symbol*] [*Library of Congress*] (LCLS)

**G** ... Georgics [*of Vergil*] [*Classical studies*] (OCD)

**G** ... Gericht [*Court*] [*German*] (ILCA)

**G** ... German [*or Germanic*]

**G** ... Germanischer Lloyd [*Shipping*] (ROG)

**G** ... Germano-Slavica [*A publication*]

**G** ... Gerontology [*American Occupational Therapy Association*]

**G** ... Geschichte [*History*] [*German*] (ILCA)

**G** ... Gesetz [*Law*] [*German*] (ILCA)

**G** ... Ghost

**G** ... Giant Slalom [*In Olympics event, Super-G*]

**G** ... Gibbs Energy [*Symbol*] [*IUPAC*]

**G** ... Gibbs Function [*Preferred term is Gibbs Energy*]

**G** ... Gids [*A publication*]

**G** ... Giemsa [*Method*] [*Chromosome stain*]

**G** ... Gift Tax (DLA)

**G** ... Giga [*A prefix meaning multiplied by $10^9$ SI symbol*]

**G** ... Gilbert [*A unit of magnetomotive force*]

**G** ... Gilbertus [*Flourished, 13th century*] [*Authority cited in pre-1607 legal work*] (DSA)

**G** ... Gilt [*Bookbinding*]

**G** ... Gingival [*Dentistry*]

**G** ... Girder [*Technical drawings*]

**G** ... Girl About Town [*A publication*]

**G** ... Girls School [*British*]

**G** ... Giro [*Money Order*] [*Spanish*]

**G** ... Givenchy [*Couturier*]

**G** ... Gladstonian [*Politics, 1868-1894*] [*British*] (ROG)

**G** ... Glass (AAG)

**G** ... Glider

**G** ... Glimpse [*Optics*]

**G** ... Globulin

**G** ... Gloom

**G** ... Glucinium [*Also, Gl*] [*Old name for chemical element beryllium*]

**G** ... Glucose [*Also, Glc, GLUC*] [*A sugar*]

**G** ... Glycine [*One-letter symbol; see Gly*] [*An amino acid*]

**G** ... Glycogen [*Biochemistry*]

**G** ... Goal [*A position in lacrosse, soccer, hockey, etc.*]

**G** ... Goat [*Veterinary medicine*]

**G** ... Gofredus de Trano [*Deceased, 1245*] [*Authority cited in pre-1607 legal work*] (DSA)

**G** ... Gold

**G** ... Gold Inlay [*Dentistry*]

**G** ... Goldcorp Investments Ltd. [*Toronto Stock Exchange symbol*]

**G** ... Golf [*Phonetic alphabet*] [*International*] (DSUE)

**G** ... Gonidial [*With reference to colonies of bacteria*]

**G** ... Good [*Condition*] [*Antiquarian book trade, numismatics, etc.*]

**G** ... Good Skiing Conditions

**G** ... Gourde [*Monetary unit*] [*Haiti*]

**G** ... Government

**G** ... Government Expenditure [*Economics*]

**G** ... Grade (ADA)

**g** ... Graft (Polymer) [*Organic chemistry*]

**G** ... Grain

**g** ... Gram

**G** ... Grammar School [*British*]

**G** ... Grand [*Slang term for 1,000 dollars*]

**G** ... Grand-Orgue [*Great Organ*] [*Music*]

**G** ... Granite

**G** ... Granted [*Legal term*] (ILCA)

**G** ... Granular

**G** ... Graphed [*Quilting*]

**G** ... Graphite

**G** ... Grass [*Botany*]

**G** ... Gravel

**G** ... Gravida [*Obstetrics*]

**G** ... Gravity [*or the force or acceleration produced by it*]

**G** ... Great

**G** ... Greek

**G** ... Green
**G** ... Greenhouse Plant [*Botany*]
**G** ... Greenwich Meridian [*Upper branch*]
**g** ... Greenwich Meridian [*Lower branch*]
**G** ... Greenwich Time
**G** ... Gregarious [*Biology*]
**G** ... Gregorowski's Reports of the High Court [*A publication*] (DLA)
**G** ... Greyhound Dial Corp. [*NYSE symbol*] (SPSG)
**G** ... Grid [*Electronics*]
**G** ... Grog [*i.e., entitled to draw a daily rum ration and doing so*] [*See also, T, UA*] [*Obsolete*] [*Navy*] [*British*]
**G** ... Grondwet [*Constitution*] [*Netherlands*] (ILCA)
**G** ... Gros [*Large*] [*French*]
**G** ... Groschen [*Monetary unit*] [*Austria*]
**G** ... Gross [*Leukemia antigen*] [*Immunochemistry*]
**G** ... Groszy [*Monetary unit*] [*Poland*]
**G** ... Ground
**G** ... Ground Foraging [*Ecology*]
**G** ... Ground, General [*JETDS nomenclature*]
**G** ... Ground Swell
**G** ... Grounded [*Electronics*]
**G** ... Group [*Data processing*]
**G** ... [*Sir George*] Grove [*When used in identifying Beethoven's compositions, refers to cataloging of his works by musicologist Grove*]
**G** ... Growth [*Business term*]
**G** ... Grumman American Aviation [*ICAO aircraft manufacturer identifier*] (ICAO)
**G** ... Gruppenfuehrer [*Squad Leader*] [*German military - World War II*]
**G** ... Guanine [*Also, Gua*] [*Biochemistry*]
**G** ... Guanosine [*One-letter symbol; see Guo*]
**G** ... Guarani [*Monetary unit*] [*Paraguay*]
**G** ... Guard [*Position in football, basketball, etc.*]
**G** ... Guardian
**G** ... Guardian [*A publication*]
**G** ... Guarnerius [*Irnerius*] [*Flourished, 1113-18*] [*Authority cited in pre-1607 legal work*] (DSA)
**G** ... Gucci [*Designer*]
**G** ... Guide
**G** ... Guided Tour [*On a bus*] [*British*]
**G** ... Guido de Baysio [*Deceased, 1313*] [*Authority cited in pre-1607 legal work*] (DSA)
**G** ... Guido de Suzaria [*Deceased, 1293*] [*Authority cited in pre-1607 legal work*] (DSA)
**G** ... Guilder [*Modification of gulden*] [*Monetary unit*] [*Netherlands*]
**G** ... Guillelmus de Tocco [*Authority cited in pre-1607 legal work*] (DSA)
**G** ... Guilty
**G** ... Guinea [*Monetary unit*] [*Obsolete*] [*Great Britain*]
**G** ... Guirsh [*Monetary unit*] [*Saudi Arabia*]
**G** ... Guitar [*Music*]
**G** ... Guizzardinus [*Deceased, 1222*] [*Authority cited in pre-1607 legal work*] (DSA)
**G** ... Gulden [*Monetary unit*] [*Netherlands*]
**G** ... Gules [*Heraldry*]
**G** ... Gulf [*Maps and charts*]
**G** ... Gun
**g** ... Gunnery [*Navy*] [*British*]
**G** ... Gusts [*Meteorology*] (FAAC)
**G** ... Gutter Ball [*Bowling*]
**G** ... Gynoecium [*Botany*]
**G** ... Gyromagnetic Ratio
**G** ... Halls (Noncommercial) [*Public-performance tariff class*] [*British*]
**G** ... HMV [*His Master's Voice*], Gramophone Co. [*Record label*] [*Great Britain, Europe, etc.*]
**G** ... Longitude
**G** ... Obstetrics and Gynaecology [*Medical Officer designation*] [*British*]
**G** ... Permanently Grounded [*Aircraft classification letter*]
**G** ... Promoted to Glory [*Salvation Army*]
**G** ... Ranger [*Army skill qualification identifier*] (INF)
**G** ... Reports of the High Court of Griqualand [*1882-1910*] [*South Africa*] [*A publication*] (DLA)
**G** ... Shear Modulus [*Symbol*] [*IUPAC*]
**g** ... Statistical Weight [*Symbol*] [*IUPAC*]
**G** ... Surface Attack [*Missile mission symbol*]
**G** ... Telegraph [*JETDS nomenclature*]
**G** ... Teletype [*JETDS nomenclature*]
**G** ... Unit of Acceleration [*Military*]
**G** ... United Kingdom [*Aircraft nationality and registration mark*] (FAAC)
**G** ... Units of Gravitational Force (NASA)
**G** ... Weight [*Symbol*] [*IUPAC*]
**G** ... Workout from Starting Gate [*Horse racing*]
**G1** ... Government Current Expenditure [*Economics*]
**G-1** ... Personnel Section [*of an Army or Marine Corps division general staff, or Marine brigade or aircraft wing general staff; also, the officer in charge of this section*]
**G2** ... Government Capital Expenditure [*Economics*]
**G-2** ... Military Intelligence Section [*of an Army or Marine Corps division general staff, or Marine brigade or aircraft wing general staff; also, the officer in charge of this section*]
**G3** ... Gadolinium, Gallium, Garnet
**G3** ... [*The*] Godfather Part III [*Motion picture*]
**G-3** ... Operations and Training Section [*of an Army or Marine Corps division general staff or Marine brigade or aircraft wing general staff; also, the officer in charge of this section*]
**G-4** ... Logistics Section [*of an Army or Marine Corps division general staff, or Marine brigade or aircraft wing general staff; also, the officer in charge of this section*]
**4-G** ... Selective Service Class [*for Registrant Exempt from Service During Peace (Surviving Son or Brother)*]
**G-5** ... Civil Affairs Section [*of an Army division or brigade general staff; the officer in charge of this section*]
**G5** ... Group of Five [*United States, Japan, West Germany, France, and Britain*]
**G-7** ... Group of Seven [*United States, Japan, West Germany, France, Britain, Italy, and Canada*]
**9G** ... Ghana [*Aircraft nationality and registration mark*] (FAAC)
**G10** ... Group of Ten [*United States, Japan, West Germany, France, Britain, Italy, Canada, Sweden, Holland, Belgium, and Switzerland*] [*There are actually eleven member countries*]
**4G's** ... Glycosaminoglycans, Glycoproteins, and Glycolipids Group [*Informal name for organization that later became Society for Complex Carbohydrates*]
**G (Spot)** ... Graefenberg Spot [*Gynecology*]
**G (Suit)** ... Antigravity Suit [*Air Force clothing for supersonic flight*]
**GA** ... Atlanta Public Library, Atlanta, GA [*Library symbol*] [*Library of Congress*] (LCLS)
**GA** ... Decisions of General Appraisers [*United States*] [*A publication*] (DLA)
**GA** ... Gabon [*ANSI two-letter standard code*] (CNC)
**GA** ... Gain of Antenna (IEEE)
**GA** ... Galatians [*New Testament book*]
**Ga** ... Galileo Number
**GA** ... Gallic
**Ga** ... Gallium [*Chemical element*]
**GA** ... Gamblers Anonymous (EA)
**GA** ... Games Ahead [*Baseball*]
**Ga** ... Gandulphus [*Flourished, 1160-85*] [*Authority cited in pre-1607 legal work*] (DSA)
**GA** ... Gardens for All [*Later, National Association for Gardening*] (EA)
**GA** ... Garin Arava (EA)
**GA** ... Garrison Adjutant [*Military*] [*British*]
**GA** ... Garrison Artillery [*British military*] (DMA)
**GA** ... Garuda Indonesian Airways PT [*ICAO designator*] (FAAC)
**GA** ... Gas or Air [*Transportation*]
**G and A** ... Gas and Air [*Medicine*]
**GA** ... Gas Amplification
**GA** ... Gas Analysis (NRCH)
**GA** ... Gasoline Stowage and Fuel System Man [*Navy*]
**GA** ... Gastric Analysis
**GA** ... Gate
**GA** ... Gated Attenuation [*Data processing*]
**GA** ... Gauge (AAG)
**GA** ... Gauge Man [*Navy*]
**GA** ... Gazette Archeologique [*A publication*]
**GA** ... Gear Assembly
**GA** ... Geistige Arbeit [*A publication*]
**GA** ... Gelbray Association [*Later, GI*] (EA)
**GA** ... Gemini Agena [*NASA*] (KSC)
**GA** ... General Accounting (AAG)
**GA** ... General Activities (ADA)
**G & A** ... General and Administrative
**GA** ... General Agent [*Insurance*]
**GA** ... General Alert (NATG)
**GA** ... General Anesthesia [*Medicine*]
**GA** ... General Appearance [*Medicine*]
**GA** ... General Appraisers' Decisions [*A publication*] (DLA)
**GA** ... General of the Army (AABC)
**GA** ... General Arrangement (MCD)
**GA** ... General Assembly
**GA** ... General Assignment (ADA)
**GA** ... General Assistance [*A form of public charity*]
**GA** ... General Atomics [*Division of General Dynamics Corp.*]
**GA** ... General Attention [*Medicine*]
**GA** ... General Automation, Inc. [*AMEX symbol*]
**GA** ... General Average [*Insurance*]
**GA** ... General Avia SpA [*Italy*] [*ICAO aircraft manufacturer identifier*] (ICAO)
**GA** ... General Aviation (EA)
**GA** ... Genetic Algorithm [*Data processing*]
**GA** ... Gentisic Acid [*Analgesic drug*]
**GA** ... Geografiska Annaler [*A publication*]
**GA** ... Geographical Abstracts [*A publication*]

**GA**............ [*The*] Geographical Association [*British*]
**GA**............ Geographischer Anzeiger [*A publication*]
**GA**............ Geological Abstracts
**GA**............ Geologists' Association [*British*]
**GA**............ Geometrical Acoustics
**GA**............ Georgia [*Postal code*] (AFM)
**GA**............ Georgia Railroad Co. [*AAR code*]
**GA**............ Georgia Reports [*A publication*]
**GA**............ Georgia Supreme Court Reports [*A publication*] (DLA)
**GA**............ Geotechnical Abstracts [*A publication*]
**GA**............ German Army (NATG)
**GA**............ Germanistische Abhandlungen [*A publication*]
**GA**............ Germanistische Arbeitshefte [*A publication*]
**GA**............ Gesammelte Abhandlungen [*A publication*] (BJA)
**GA**............ Gesellschaft fuer Arzneipflanzenforschung [*Society for Medicinal Plant Research*] (EA)
**GA**............ Gestational Age [*Medicine*]
**GA**............ Getting Along [*Psychological testing*]
**GA**............ Giant Axon [*Neurology*]
**GA**............ Gibberellic Acid [*Also,* $GA_3$ *Plant growth hormone*]
**GA**............ Gimbal Angle (KSC)
**GA**............ Gimbal Assembly
**ga**............ Ginger Ale
**GA**............ Gingivoaxial [*Dentistry*]
**GA**............ Gland Anlage
**GA**............ Glide Angle [*Aviation*]
**GA**............ Global Address
**GA**............ Global Assessment [*Psychiatric evaluation test*]
**GA**............ Global Auto [*Data processing*]
**GA**............ Glos Anglii [*A publication*]
**GA**............ Glucoamylase [*An enzyme*]
**GA**............ Glucuronic Acid [*Also, GlcUA*] [*Biochemistry*]
**GA**............ Glutamic Acid [*See also Glu*] [*An amino acid*]
**GA**............ Glutaraldehyde [*Biochemistry*]
**GA**............ Gnomes Anonymous [*New Malden, Surrey, England*] (EA)
**GA**............ Go Ahead [*or resume sending*] [*Communications*]
**GA**............ Go Around (MCD)
**GA**............ Goals Against [*Hockey*]
**GA**............ Government Agency (AAG)
**GA**............ Government Architect (ADA)
**GA**............ Governmental Affairs (DLA)
**GA**............ Grade Age [*Education*]
**GA**............ Graduate in Agriculture
**GA**............ Graduate Assistant
**G/A**............ Grains per Anther [*Botany*]
**GA**............ Gramicidin A [*Antibiotic*]
**GA**............ Grand Admiral [*Freemasonry*] (ROG)
**GA**............ Grand Almoner [*Freemasonry*]
**GA**............ Grand Architect [*Freemasonry*]
**GA**............ Grand Award [*Record label*]
**GA**............ Grands Arrets de la Jurisprudence Civile [*A publication*] (ILCA)
**GA**............ Grant Aid [*Military*] (AFM)
**GA**............ Grant Application [*Job Training and Partnership Act*] (OICC)
**GA**............ Grant Award [*Job Training and Partnership Act*] (OICC)
**GA**............ Granulocyte Agglutination [*Hematology*]
**GA**............ Granulomatous Angiitis [*Medicine*]
**GA**............ Graphic Ammeter (MSA)
**GA**............ Graphic Artists Guild (EA)
**GA**............ Graphic Arts Monthly [*A publication*]
**GA**............ Grapple Adapter [*Nuclear energy*] (NRCH)
**GA**............ Great Artists [*A publication*]
**GA**............ Greenhouse Annual [*Horticulture*] (ROG)
**GA**............ Gross Asset [*Business term*]
**G-A**............ Ground-to-Air [*Communications, weapons*] (MSA)
**GA**............ Ground Attack [*Military*]
**GA**............ Ground Attacker Aircraft
**GA**............ Guanosine Triphosphatase Activating [*Biochemistry*]
**GA**............ Guardian Angels (EA)
**GA**............ Guardian Association (EA)
**GA**............ Guessed Average
**GA**............ Gunlayer Armourer [*British military*] (DMA)
**GA**............ Gut-Associated [*Medicine*]
**GA**............ Gypsum Association (EA)
**GA**............ Gyrate Atrophy [*Medicine*]
**GA**............ Gyro Assembly (NASA)
**GA**............ L-Glutamic [*acid*] and L-Alanine [*Copolymer*]
**GA**............ Tabun [*Nerve gas*] [*Army symbol*]
**$GA_3$**............ Gibberellin $A_3$ [*Also, GA*] [*Plant growth hormone*]
**GAA**............ Atlanta College of Art Library, Atlanta, GA [*OCLC symbol*] (OCLC)
**GAA**............ Atlanta School of Art, Atlanta, GA [*Library symbol*] [*Library of Congress*] (LCLS)
**GAA**............ Atlantic Air [*Newton, CT*] [*FAA designator*] (FAAC)
**GAA**............ Gaelic Athletic Association
**GAA**............ Gain Adjuster Adapter
**GAA**............ Gale Auto Annual [*A publication*]
**GaA**............ Gallium Arsenide [*Semiconductor*]
**GAA**............ Gay AA (EA)
**GAA**............ Gay Activists' Alliance [*Defunct*]
**GAA**............ Gene Amplification and Analysis Series [*Elsevier Book Series*] [*A publication*]
**GAA**............ General Account of Advances
**GAA**............ General Agency Agreement [*Navy*] (AABC)
**GAA**............ General Aviation Association [*Australia*]
**GaA**............ Georgia Appeals Reports [*A publication*] (DLA)
**GAA**............ Gift Association of America (EA)
**GAA**............ Girls Athletic Association [*Local school affiliates of National Girls Athletic Association*] [*Defunct*]
**GAA**............ Gospel and the Age Series [*A publication*]
**GAA**............ Grand National Resources, Inc. [*Vancouver Stock Exchange symbol*]
**GAA**............ Grandparents Association of America (EA)
**GAA**............ Graphic Arts Abstracts [*A publication*]
**GAA**............ Gravure Association of America (EA)
**GAA**............ Grenfell Association of America (EA)
**GAA**............ Ground-Aided Acquisition
**GAA**............ Ground Area Attainable
**GAA**............ GTO [*Gran Torismo Omologato*] Association of America (EA)
**GAA**............ Skrifter Utgivna av Kungliga. Gustav Adolfs Akademien [*A publication*]
**GAABA**..... Gas Abstracts [*A publication*]
**GAAC**........ Gastroenterology. Abstracts and Citations [*A publication*]
**GAAC**........ Graphic Arts Advertisers Council [*Later, GAAEC*]
**GA Admin Comp** ... Official Compilation of the Rules and Regulations of the State of Georgia [*A publication*] (DLA)
**GAAE**........ Graphic Arts Association Executives (EA)
**GAAEC**..... Graphic Arts Advertisers and Exhibitors Council [*Defunct*] (EA)
**GAAG**........ Guerrilla Art Action Group
**GAAGA**..... Gas Age [*A publication*]
**GA Ag Coll** ... Georgia State College of Agriculture. Publications [*A publication*]
**GA Ag Exp** ... Georgia. Agricultural Experiment Station. Publications [*A publication*]
**GA Agric Exp Stn Annu Rep** ... Georgia. Agricultural Experiment Station. Annual Report [*A publication*]
**GA Agric Exp Stn Bienn Rep** ... Georgia. Agricultural Experiment Stations. Biennial Report [*A publication*]
**GA Agric Exp Stn Bull** ... Georgia. Agricultural Experiment Station. Bulletin [*A publication*]
**GA Agric Exp Stn Circ** ... Georgia. Agricultural Experiment Station. Circular [*A publication*]
**GA Agric Exp Stn Field Crops Variety Trials** ... Georgia. Agricultural Experiment Stations. Field Crops Variety Trials [*A publication*]
**GA Agric Exp Stn Field Crops Var Trials** ... Georgia. Agricultural Experiment Stations. Field Crops Variety Trials [*A publication*]
**GA Agric Exp Stn Leafl** ... Georgia. Agricultural Experiment Station. Leaflet [*A publication*]
**GA Agric Exp Stn Mimeogr Ser** ... Georgia. Agricultural Experiment Station. Mimeograph Series [*A publication*]
**GA Agric Exp Stn Res Bull** ... Georgia. Agricultural Experiment Station. Research Bulletin [*A publication*]
**GA Agric Exp Stn Res Rep** ... Georgia. Agricultural Experiment Station. Research Report [*A publication*]
**GA Agric Exp Stn Tech Bull** ... Georgia. Agricultural Experiment Station. Technical Bulletin [*A publication*]
**GA Agric Res** ... Georgia Agricultural Research [*A publication*]
**GA Agric Res GA Exp Stn** ... Georgia Agricultural Research. Georgia Experiment Stations [*A publication*]
**GA Agr Res** ... Georgia Agricultural Research. University of Georgia [*A publication*]
**GAAO**........ Ansongo [*Mali*] [*ICAO location identifier*] (ICLI)
**GAAP**........ Gateway Army Ammunition Plant
**GAAP**........ Generally Accepted Accounting Principles [*or Procedures*]
**GA App**...... Georgia Appeals Reports [*A publication*] (DLA)
**GA App (NS)** ... Georgia Appeals Reports [*A publication*] (DLA)
**GAARS**...... Global Atmospheric and Aerosol Radiation Study
**GAART**..... Government Astronomy Administration Round Table
**GaAs**......... Gallium Arsenide [*Semiconductor*] (IEEE)
**GAAS**........ Generally Accepted Auditing Standards
**GAAS**........ German Association for American Studies (EAIO)
**GaAsP**....... Gallium Arsenide Phosphide [*Semiconductor*] (IEEE)
**GAATS**...... Gander Automated Air Traffic System
**GAATV**..... Gemini Atlas/Agena Target Vehicle [*NASA*] (MCD)
**GAB**........... Gabbs [*Nevada*] [*Seismograph station code, US Geological Survey*] [*Closed*] (SEIS)
**GAB**........... Gabbs, NV [*Location identifier*] [*FAA*] (FAAL)
**GAB**........... Gabbs Resources Ltd. [*Vancouver Stock Exchange symbol*]
**GAB**........... Gabelli Equity Trust, Inc. [*NYSE symbol*] (SPSG)
**GAB**........... Gable
**GAB**........... Gabon [*ANSI three-letter standard code*] (CNC)
**GAB**........... Gendall Air Ltd. [*North Battleford, SK, Canada*] [*FAA designator*] (FAAC)
**GAB**........... General Adjustment Bureau [*Insurance*]
**GAB**........... General Arrangements to Borrow [*United Nations*] (EY)
**GAB**........... Geoppinger Akademische Beitraege [*A publication*]
**GAB**........... Gifts and Decorative Accessories [*A publication*]
**GAB**........... Gospel Association for the Blind (EA)

**GAB** .......... Government Affairs Branch [*European Theater of Operations*] [*World War II*]
**GAB** .......... Graphic Adapter Board
**GAB** .......... Grievance and Appeals Board [*Australia*]
**GAB** .......... Group Announcement Bulletin [*Defense Documentation Center*]
**GABA** ........ Gamma-Aminobutyric Acid [*Biochemistry*]
**GA Bar J**.... Georgia Bar Journal [*A publication*]
**Gabb Cr Law** ... Gabbett's Criminal Law [*A publication*] (DLA)
**Gabb Stat L** ... Gabbett. Abridgment of Statute Law [*1812-18*] [*A publication*] (ILCA)
**GABD** ........ Bandiagara [*Mali*] [*ICAO location identifier*] (ICLI)
**GABD** ........ Gauge Board
**GABF**......... Bafoulabe [*Mali*] [*ICAO location identifier*] (ICLI)
**GABG** ........ Bougouni [*Mali*] [*ICAO location identifier*] (ICLI)
**GABH** ........ Georgia Baptist Hospital, Medical Library, Atlanta, GA [*Library symbol*] [*Library of Congress*] (LCLS)
**GABH-N** ... Georgia Baptist Hospital, School of Nursing, Atlanta, GA [*Library symbol*] [*Library of Congress*] (LCLS)
**GABHS** ..... Group A Beta-Hemolytic Streptococcus [*Pathology*]
**GA B J** ....... Georgia Bar Journal [*A publication*]
**GABOB** ..... Gamma-Amino-beta-hydroxybutyric Acid [*Pharmacology*]
**GABPAG**... Annales Geologiques de la Peninsule Balkanique [*A publication*]
**GABR** ........ Bourem [*Mali*] [*ICAO location identifier*] (ICLI)
**Gabr Roman** ... [*Antonius*] Gabrielius (Romanus) [*Deceased, 1555*] [*Authority cited in pre-1607 legal work*] (DSA)
**GABS**......... Bamako/Senou [*Mali*] [*ICAO location identifier*] (ICLI)
**GA Bus**....... Georgia Business [*A publication*]
**GA Bus Law** ... Georgia Business Lawyer (DLA)
**GABV** ........ Bamako [*Mali*] [*ICAO location identifier*] (ICLI)
**GAC**........... Armstrong State College, Savannah, GA [*OCLC symbol*] (OCLC)
**GAC** .......... Clark College, Atlanta, GA [*Library symbol*] [*Library of Congress*] (LCLS)
**GAC**........... Galvanized Aircraft
**GAC**........... Geac Computer Corp. Ltd. [*Toronto Stock Exchange symbol*]
**GAC**........... General Advisory Committee [*to the AEC, later, the Energy Research and Development Administration*]
**GAC**........... General Agency Check [*Army*]
**GAC**........... General Average Certificate [*Business term*] (DS)
**GAC**........... Gimbal Angle Change
**GAC**........... Gimbal Angle Controller
**GAC**........... Global Area Coverage [*Meteorology*]
**GAC**........... Goodyear Aerospace Corporation
**GAC**........... Government Accountants Journal [*A publication*]
**GAC**........... Government Advisory Committee on International Book and Library Programs [*Terminated, 1977*] (EGAO)
**GAC**........... Grand Assistant Conductor [*Freemasonry*] (ROG)
**GAC**........... Granular Activated Carbon
**GAC**........... Grilled American Cheese Sandwich
**GAC**........... Gross Available Capacity [*Electronics*] (IEEE)
**GAC**........... Ground Attitude Control (MCD)
**GAC**........... Group Access Capabilities [*Library automation*]
**GAC**........... Grumman Aerospace Corporation [*of Grumman Corp.*]
**G Ac** .......... Guillelmus de Accursio [*Deceased, 1314*] [*Authority cited in pre-1607 legal work*] (DSA)
**GAC**........... Gustavus Adolphus College [*St. Peter, MN*]
**Gac AVDA** ... Gaceta de AVDA [*A publication*]
**GACC** ........ Atlanta Chamber of Commerce, Atlanta, GA [*Library symbol*] [*Library of Congress*] (LCLS)
**GACC** ........ Great American Communications Co. [*NASDAQ symbol*] (NQ)
**G Accad Med Torino** ... Giornale. Accademia di Medicina di Torino [*A publication*]
**GACCC**...... Coca-Cola Company, Technical Information Services, Atlanta, GA [*Library symbol*] [*Library of Congress*] (LCLS)
**GACCLC** ... Cooperative College Library Center, Inc., Atlanta, GA [*Library symbol*] [*Library of Congress*] (LCLS)
**Gac Colmen** ... Gaceta del Colmenar [*A publication*]
**GACDC** ..... Center for Disease Control, Main Library, Atlanta, GA [*Library symbol*] [*Library of Congress*] (LCLS)
**GACDC-FP** ... Center for Disease Control, Family Planning Evaluation Division, Atlanta, GA [*Library symbol*] [*Library of Congress*] (LCLS)
**Gaceta Mat I** ... Gaceta Matematica. Primera Serie [*Madrid*] [*A publication*]
**Gac Farm** ... Gaceta Farmaceutica [*A publication*]
**GACHA**..... Georgia Automated Clearing House Association
**GACI** ......... Geographic Area Code Index [*Bureau of Census*]
**GACIA**....... Guidance and Control Information [*DoD*] (MCD)
**GACIAC**.... Guidance and Control Information Analysis Center [*Chicago, IL*] [*DoD*] [*Also, an information service or system*]
**GACL** ........ Crawford W. Long Memorial Hospital, Atlanta, GA [*Library symbol*] [*Library of Congress*] (LCLS)
**Gac Mat (Madrid)** ... Gaceta Matematica (Madrid) [*A publication*]
**Gac Med** .... Gaceta Medica [*A publication*]
**Gac Med Bol** ... Gaceta Medica Boliviana [*A publication*]
**Gac Med Car** ... Gaceta Medica de Caracas [*A publication*]
**Gac Med Caracas** ... Gaceta Medica de Caracas [*A publication*]
**Gac Med Catalana** ... Gaceta Medica Catalana [*A publication*]
**Gac Med Esp** ... Gaceta Medica Espanola [*A publication*]
**Gac Med (Guayaquil)** ... Gaceta Medica (Guayaquil) Ecuador [*A publication*]
**Gac Med Lima** ... Gaceta Medica de Lima [*A publication*]
**Gac Med Mex** ... Gaceta Medica de Mexico [*A publication*]
**Gac Med Norte Bilbao** ... Gaceta Medica del Norte Bilbao [*A publication*]
**Gac Med Quir Bol** ... Gaceta Medico-Quirurgica de Bolivia [*A publication*]
**Gac Med Urug** ... Gaceta Medica del Uruguay [*A publication*]
**Gac Med Zool** ... Gaceta de Medicina Zoologica [*A publication*]
**GACNA**..... Graphic Arts Council of North America (EA)
**Gac Num**.... Gaceta Numismatica [*A publication*]
**GACo**......... Coca-Cola Co., Marketing Information Center, Atlanta, GA [*Library symbol*] [*Library of Congress*] (LCLS)
**GACO**........ GardenAmerica Corporation [*NASDAQ symbol*] (NQ)
**GACOD**..... Graefe's Archive for Clinical and Experimental Ophthalmology [*A publication*]
**GA Code** .... Code of Georgia [*A publication*] (DLA)
**GA Code Ann** ... Georgia Code, Annotated [*A publication*] (DLA)
**GA Code Ann (Harrison)** ... Code of Georgia, Annotated (Harrison) [*A publication*]
**GA Code Ann (Michie)** ... Official Code of Georgia, Annotated (Michie) [*A publication*]
**GA Comp R & Regs** ... Official Compilation of the Rules and Regulations of the State of Georgia [*A publication*]
**G/A Con** .... General Average Contribution [*Marine insurance*] (DS)
**GA Const**... Georgia Constitution [*A publication*] (DLA)
**GACP** ........ Gunner's Accuracy Control Panel (MCD)
**Gac Per Med Cirug** ... Gaceta Peruana de Medicina y Cirugia [*A publication*]
**Gac Propr Ind** ... Gaceta de la Propriedad Industrial [*A publication*]
**GA & CS**.... Ground Acquisition and Command Station (MCD)
**GACS**......... Gun Alignment and Control System (MCD)
**Gac San Mil** ... Gaceta de Sanidad Militar [*A publication*]
**GACSU**...... Singapore Government Administrative and Clerical Services' Union
**GACT** ........ GAC Liquidating Trust [*NASDAQ symbol*] (NQ)
**GACT** ........ Generally Available Control Technology [*Environmental chemistry*]
**GACT** ........ Graphic Analysis and Correlation Terminal (MCD)
**GACTAI**.... General Arbitration Council of the Textile and Apparel Industries (EA)
**GACTD2** ... Glossary of Acarological Terminology/Glossaire de la Terminologie Acarologique [*A publication*]
**GACTI**....... General Arbitration Council of the Textile Industry [*Later, GACTAI*] (EA)
**GACU**........ Ground Air Conditioning Unit (MCD)
**GACU**........ Ground Avionics Cooling Unit
**Gac Vet (B Aires)** ... Gaceta Veterinaria (Buenos Aires) [*A publication*]
**GAD**........... Gadabout (DSUE)
**GAD**........... Gadsden [*Alabama*] [*Airport symbol*] (OAG)
**GAD**........... Gallium Arsenide Diode
**GAD**........... General Anthropology Division (EA)
**GAD**........... Germersheim Army Depot (MCD)
**GAD**........... Gladstone Resources [*Vancouver Stock Exchange symbol*]
**GAD**........... Glutamate Acid Decarboxylase [*An enzyme*]
**GAD**........... Glutamate Decarboxylase [*An enzyme*]
**GAD**........... Government Actuary's Department
**GAD**........... Government Archives Division [*National Archives of Canada*] [*Information service or system*] (IID)
**GAD**........... Graduate Assistantship Directory [*A publication*]
**GAD**........... Grand Alliance for Democracy [*Philippines*] [*Political party*]
**GAD**........... Grants Administration Division [*Environmental Protection Agency*]
**GAD**........... Great American Dream
**GAD**........... Guards' Armoured Division [*Military unit*] [*British*]
**GAD**........... Guide to American Directories [*A publication*]
**GADA**........ Dioila [*Mali*] [*ICAO location identifier*] (ICLI)
**GA Dec** ...... Georgia Decisions [*A publication*] (DLA)
**GA Dec (Dudley)** ... Dudley's Georgia Reports [*A publication*] (DLA)
**GADEF**...... Groupement des Associations Dentaires Francophones [*Group of Francophone Dentists' Associations*] [*Paris, France*] (EAIO)
**G/A Dep** .... General Average Deposit [*Marine insurance*] (DS)
**GA Dep Mines Min Geol Geol Surv Bull** ... Georgia. Department of Mines, Mining, and Geology. Geological Survey. Bulletin [*A publication*]
**GA Dep Mines Min Geol Geol Surv Circ** ... Georgia. Department of Mines, Mining, and Geology. Geological Survey. Circular [*A publication*]
**GA Dep Mines Mining Geol Geol Surv Bull** ... Georgia. Department of Mines, Mining, and Geology. Geological Survey. Bulletin [*A publication*]
**GA Dep Nat Resour Geol Water Resour Div Inf Circ** ... Georgia. Department of Natural Resources. Geologic and Water Resources Division. Information Circular [*A publication*]
**GADES**...... Gun Air Defense Effectiveness Study (MCD)
**GADH** ....... Gastric Alcohol Dehydrogenase [*An enzyme*]
**GADIP**....... Greater Achievement for Disadvantaged Ipswich People [*Australia*]
**GADL**........ Ground-to-Air Data Link
**GADNA**..... Gduei Noar [*Youth Battalions*] [*Israel*]
**GADNPH** ... Glycolic Aldehyde Dinitrophenylhydrazone [*Organic chemistry*]
**GADO**........ General Aviation District Office [*FAA*]
**GADP**........ Gongola Agricultural Development Project [*Nigeria*] (ECON)

**GADPS**...... Graphic Automatic Data Processing System (MCD)
**GADR**........ Guided Air Defense Rocket
**GADS**........ Gate-Assignment and Display System [*United Air Lines, Inc.*]
**GADS**........ Geographic and Alphanumeric Display System (MCD)
**GADS**........ Gonococcal Arthritis/Dermatitis Syndrome [*Medicine*]
**GADS**........ Goose Air Defense Sector
**GADSCO**.. Gages Documentation Scheduling Committee
**GADT**........ Ground/Air Defense Threat (MCD)
**GADZ**........ Douentza [*Mali*] [*ICAO location identifier*] (ICLI)
**gae**............. Gaelic (Scots) [*MARC language code*] [*Library of Congress*] (LCCP)
**GAE**........... Gallic Acid Equivalent [*Wine analysis*]
**GAE**........... GAO [*General Accounting Office*] Denver Regional Office, Denver, CO [*OCLC symbol*] (OCLC)
**GAE**........... Gaslite Petroleum [*Vancouver Stock Exchange symbol*]
**GAE**........... General Administrative Expense [*A budget appropriation title*]
**GAE**........... General Air Express
**GAE**........... General American English
**GAE**........... General Analytical Evaluation
**GAE**........... Gibbs Adsorption Equation [*Physical chemistry*]
**GAE**........... Graphic Arts Employers of America (EA)
**GAE**........... Grupos Armados Espanoles [*Armed Spanish Groups*] [*Political party*] (PD)
**GAE**........... Gunner Aiming Error (MCD)
**GAE-BPH**... Georgia State Department of Education, Division of Public Library, Library for the Blind and Physically Handicapped, Atlanta, GA [*Library symbol*] [*Library of Congress*] (LCLS)
**GAEC**........ Goodyear Aircraft and Engineering Corporation
**GAEC**........ Greek Atomic Energy Commission
**GAEC**........ Grumman Aircraft Engineering Corporation [*Later, Grumman Corp.*]
**GAeF**.......... Gesellschaft fuer Aerosolforschung [*Association for Aerosol Research*] (EAIO)
**GAEI**......... Equifax, Inc., Atlanta, GA [*Library symbol*] [*Library of Congress*] (LCLS)
**GAEL**......... Gaelic [*Language, etc.*]
**GAELIC**.... Grumman Aerospace Engineering Language for Instructional Checkout
**GAENA**..... Gas Engineer [*A publication*]
**GA Engineer**... Georgia Engineer [*A publication*]
**GAEO**........ Galileo Electro-Optics Corp. [*NASDAQ symbol*] (NQ)
**GAE-P**....... Georgia State Department of Education, Division of Public Library Services, Atlanta, GA [*Library symbol*] [*Library of Congress*] (LCLS)
**GAES**......... Gas Appliance Engineers Society [*Later, ASGE*] (EA)
**GAESDA**... Graphic Arts Equipment and Supply Dealers Association (EA)
**GAF**........... GAF Corp. [*Formerly, General Aniline & Film Corp.*] [*NYSE symbol*] (SPSG)
**GAF**........... GAO [*General Accounting Office*] Boston Regional Office, Boston, MA [*OCLC symbol*] (OCLC)
**GAf**............ Geneve-Afrique [*A publication*]
**GAF**........... German Air Force [*German Luftwaffe*]
**GAF**........... Government Affairs Foundation [*Defunct*] (EA)
**GAF**........... Government Aircraft Facilities
**GAF**........... Grafton, ND [*Location identifier*] [*FAA*] (FAAL)
**GAF**........... Growth of the American Family [*A study*]
**GAFA**........ German-American Football Association [*Later, CSL*]
**GAFADS**... German Air Force Air Defense School (MCD)
**GAFB**......... George Air Force Base [*California*] (MCD)
**GAFB**......... Goodfellow Air Force Base [*Texas*]
**GAFB**......... Griffiss Air Force Base [*New York*]
**GAFC**......... Fulton County Court House, Atlanta, GA [*Library symbol*] [*Library of Congress*] (LCLS)
**GAFD**........ Faladie [*Mali*] [*ICAO location identifier*] (ICLI)
**GAFD**........ Guild of American Funeral Directors [*Defunct*]
**GAFD**........ United States Food and Drug Administration, Atlanta, GA [*Library symbol*] [*Library of Congress*] (LCLS)
**GAFET**...... Gallium Arsenide Field-Effect Transistor (MCD)
**GAFG**........ General Aviation Flight Guide [*British*] (AIA)
**GAFIA**....... German Armed Forces Intelligence Agency (MCD)
**GAFL**......... Fulton County Law Library, Atlanta, GA [*Library symbol*] [*Library of Congress*] (LCLS)
**GAFM**....... Fulton County Medical Society, Atlanta, GA [*Library symbol*] [*Library of Congress*] (LCLS)
**GA For Res Counc Annu Rep**... Georgia. Forest Research Council. Annual Report [*A publication*]
**GA For Res Counc Rep**... Georgia. Forest Research Council. Report [*A publication*]
**GA For Res Pap**... Georgia Forest Research Paper [*A publication*]
**GA For Res Pap GA For Res Counc**... Georgia Forest Research Paper. Georgia Forest Research Council [*A publication*]
**GAFPG**...... General Aviation Facilities Planning Group
**GAFR**......... Federal Reserve Bank of Atlanta, Research Library, Atlanta, GA [*Library symbol*] [*Library of Congress*] (LCLS)
**GAFS**......... Gentile Air Force Station [*Ohio*]
**GAFS**......... United States Forest Service, Atlanta, GA [*Library symbol*] [*Library of Congress*] (LCLS)
**GAFSC**...... Fernbank Science Center, Atlanta, GA [*Library symbol*] [*Library of Congress*] (LCLS)
**GAFSC**...... German Air Force Southern Command (MCD)
**GAFTA**....... Grain and Food Trade Association [*British*]
**GAFTAC**... German Air Force Tactical Air Command (MCD)
**GAFTO**..... Germany Air Force Technical Order (MCD)
**GAFW**....... United States Fish and Wildlife Service, Atlanta, GA [*Library symbol*] [*Library of Congress*] (LCLS)
**GAG**........... Gage, OK [*Location identifier*] [*FAA*] (FAAL)
**GAG**........... Gallant Gold Mines Ltd. [*Vancouver Stock Exchange symbol*]
**GAG**........... GAO [*General Accounting Office*] Philadelphia Regional Office, Philadelphia, PA [*OCLC symbol*] (OCLC)
**GAG**........... Geo Abstracts. G [*A publication*]
**GAG**........... Glycosaminoglycan [*Biochemistry*]
**GAG**........... Glyoxal Bis(guanylhydrazone) [*Organic chemistry*]
**GAG**........... Goeppinger Arbeiten zur Germanistik [*A publication*]
**GAG**........... Grand Aleph Godol (BJA)
**GAG**........... Graphic Artists Guild (EA)
**GAG**........... Gross Available Generation [*Electronics*] (IEEE)
**GAG**........... Gross Gradability [*Truck specification*]
**GAG**........... Ground-to-Air-to-Ground [*Aviation*]
**GAGB**........ General Association of General Baptists (EA)
**GAGDT**..... Ground-to-Air-to-Ground Data Terminal [*Air Force*] (MCD)
**GAGE**........ Gerontology and Geriatrics Education [*A publication*]
**GAGE**........ Global Atmospheric Gases Experiment [*Environmental science*]
**GAGEA**..... Gakujutsu Geppo [*A publication*]
**GA Geol Surv Bull**... Georgia. Geological Survey. Bulletin [*A publication*]
**GA Geol Surv Circ**... Georgia. Geological Survey. Circular [*A publication*]
**GA Geol Survey Bull Circ**... Georgia Geological Survey. Bulletin. Circular [*A publication*]
**GA Geol Surv Inf Circ**... Georgia. Geological Survey. Information Circular [*A publication*]
**GA Geol Water Resour Div Inf Circ**... Georgia. Geologic and Water Resources Division. Information Circular [*A publication*]
**GAGF**........ Graphic Artists Guild Foundation (EA)
**GAGI**......... Goethe Institute, German Culture Institute, Atlanta, GA [*Library symbol*] [*Library of Congress*] (LCLS)
**GAGK**........ Graphic Arts Guidance Kit
**GAGL**........ Aguelhoc [*Mali*] [*ICAO location identifier*] (ICLI)
**GAGM**....... Georgia Mental Health Institute, Atlanta, GA [*Library symbol*] [*Library of Congress*] (LCLS)
**GAGM**....... Goundam [*Mali*] [*ICAO location identifier*] (ICLI)
**GAGO**........ Gao [*Mali*] [*ICAO location identifier*] (ICLI)
**GAGP**........ Georgia Power Co., Atlanta, GA [*Library symbol*] [*Library of Congress*] (LCLS)
**GAGR**........ Courma-Rharous [*Mali*] [*ICAO location identifier*] (ICLI)
**GAGR**........ Georgia Retardation Center, Atlanta, GA [*Library symbol*] [*Library of Congress*] (LCLS)
**G Agr**......... Giornale di Agricoltura [*A publication*]
**G Agr Domen**... Giornale di Agricoltura Domenica [*A publication*]
**GA GSB**..... Georgia. Geological Survey. Bulletin [*A publication*]
**GAGTh**...... Gammon Theological Seminary, Atlanta, GA [*Library symbol*] [*Library of Congress*] (LCLS)
**GAH**.......... Games at Home [*Baseball*]
**GAH**.......... Gayndah [*Australia*] [*Airport symbol*] (OAG)
**GAH**.......... Grand American Handicap [*Shooting competition*]
**GAH**.......... Wren's Nest [*Joel Chandler Harris Home*], Atlanta, GA [*Library symbol*] [*Library of Congress*] (LCLS)
**GAHAD**..... Genshiryoku Anzen Hakusho [*A publication*]
**GAHB**........ Hombori [*Mali*] [*ICAO location identifier*] (ICLI)
**GAHEDG**... Geologische Abhandlungen Hessen [*A publication*]
**GAHF**........ Grapple Adapter Handling Fixture [*Nuclear energy*] (NRCH)
**GAHGAJ**.. Geografiska Annaler. Series B. Human Geography [*A publication*]
**GAHH**....... Good American Helping Hands (EA)
**GAHi**......... Atlanta Historical Society, Atlanta, GA [*Library symbol*] [*Library of Congress*] (LCLS)
**GA His Q**... Georgia Historical Quarterly [*A publication*]
**GA Hist Q**... Georgia Historical Quarterly [*A publication*]
**GA Hist Quart**... Georgia Historical Quarterly [*A publication*]
**GA Hist Soc Coll**... Georgia Historical Society. Collections [*A publication*]
**GAHM**...... High Museum of Art, Atlanta, GA [*Library symbol*] [*Library of Congress*] (LCLS)
**GAHQ**....... Georgia Historical Quarterly [*A publication*]
**GAHR**........ Georgia Department of Human Resources, Atlanta, GA [*Library symbol*] [*Library of Congress*] (LCLS)
**GAI**............ Gaithersburg, MD [*Location identifier*] [*FAA*] (FAAL)
**GAI**............ Gate Alarm Indicator [*RADAR*]
**GAI**............ Gay American Indians (EA)
**GAI**............ General Accounting Instructions
**GAI**............ Geophysical Associates International
**GAI**............ Gibbs Adsorption Isotherm [*Physical chemistry*]
**GAI**............ Gilbert Associates, Incorporated
**GAI**............ Gli Archivi Italiani [*A publication*]
**GAI**............ [*A*] Glossary of the Aramaic Inscriptions [*A publication*] (BJA)
**GAI**............ Governmental Affairs Institute [*Later, VPS*] (EA)
**GAI**............ Grand Auto, Incorporated [*AMEX symbol*] (SPSG)
**GAI**............ Guaranteed Annual Income
**GAIA**......... Graphic Arts Industries Association
**GAIC**......... Gallium Arsenide Integrated Circuit [*Computer chip*]
**GAIF**.......... General Assembly of International Sports Federations [*Later, GAISF*] (EA)
**GAIF**.......... Gimbal Angle Information Failure

**GAIFC** ....... Gene Autry International Fan Club (EA)
**GAIFZ** ....... General Authority for Arab and Foreign Investment and Free Zones [*Egypt*] (IMH)
**GAIGD** ...... Genshiryoku Anzen Iinkai Geppo [*A publication*]
**Gaii** ........... Gaii Institutionum Commentarii [*Gaius' Institutes*] [*A publication*] (DLA)
**Gai Inst** ...... Gaius, Institutiones [*Second century AD*] [*Classical studies*] (OCD)
**GAILL** ....... Groupement des Allergologistes et Immunologistes de Langues Latines [*Latin Languages Speaking Allergists - LLSA*] (EAIO)
**GAIN** ......... Gas Appliance Improvement Network
**GAIN** ......... Gifted Advocacy Information Network (EA)
**GAIN** ......... Graphic Aids for Investigating Networks [*NASA*] (NASA)
**GAINS** ....... Gimballess Analytic Inertial Navigation System
**GAINS** ....... Growth and Income Security [*Finance*]
**GAINS** ....... Guaranteed Annual Income System
**GA Inst Technol Eng Exp Sta Bull** ... Georgia Institute of Technology. Engineering Experiment Station. Bulletin [*A publication*]
**GA Inst Technol Eng Exp Stn Circ** ... Georgia Institute of Technology. Engineering Experiment Station. Circular [*A publication*]
**GA Inst Technol Eng Exp Stn Rep** ... Georgia Institute of Technology. Engineering Experiment Station. Report [*A publication*]
**GA Inst Technol Eng Exp Stn Repr** ... Georgia Institute of Technology. Engineering Experiment Station. Reprints [*A publication*]
**GA Inst Technol Eng Exp Stn Spec Rep** ... Georgia Institute of Technology. Engineering Experiment Station. Special Reports [*A publication*]
**GA Inst Technol Environ Resour Cent ERC (Rep)** ... Georgia Institute of Technology. Environmental Resources Center. ERC (Report) [*A publication*]
**GA Inst Technol Ser Nucl Eng** ... Georgia Institute of Technology. Series in Nuclear Engineering [*A publication*]
**Gai S** .......... Gai Saber. Revista de l'Escola Occitana [*A publication*]
**GAIS** .......... Gallium Arsenide Illuminator System
**GAIS** .......... General Aviation Inspection Aids Summary [*FAA*]
**GAISF** ....... General Association of International Sports Federations [*Formerly, GAIF*] (EA)
**GAISO** ....... Gam-Anon International Service Office (EA)
**GAISSAR** ... Gilbert Associates, Incorporated, Standard Safety Analysis Report [*Nuclear energy*] (NRCH)
**GAIT** ......... Government and Industry Team
**GAIT** ......... [*The*] Langer Biomechanics Group, Inc. [*Deer Park, NY*] [*NASDAQ symbol*] (NQ)
**GAITh** ....... Interdenominational Theological Center, Atlanta, GA [*Library symbol*] [*Library of Congress*] (LCLS)
**GAIU** ......... Graphic Arts International Union [*Later, GCIU*]
**Gaius** .......... Gaius' Institutes [*A publication*] (DLA)
**Gaius Inst** .. Gaius' Institutes [*A publication*] (DLA)
**GAJ** ........... Atlanta Junior College, Atlanta, GA [*Library symbol*] [*Library of Congress*] (LCLS)
**GAJ** ........... Gaseous Axisymmetric Jet
**GAJ** ........... General-Anzeiger fuer die Gesamten Interessen des Judentums [*Berlin*] [*A publication*]
**GAJ** ........... Guild of Agricultural Journalists
**GAJ** ........... Yamagata [*Japan*] [*Airport symbol*] (OAG)
**GAJC** ......... Jimmy Carter Library, Atlanta, GA [*Library symbol*] [*Library of Congress*] (LCLS)
**GA J Int & Comp L** ... Georgia Journal of International and Comparative Law [*A publication*]
**GA J Internat and Comparative Law** ... Georgia Journal of International and Comparative Law [*A publication*]
**GA J Int'l & Comp L** ... Georgia Journal of International and Comparative Law [*A publication*]
**GA J Sci** ..... Georgia Journal of Science [*A publication*]
**GAK** ........... Gakona, AK [*Location identifier*] [*FAA*] (FAAL)
**GAK** ........... Galactokinase [*Also, GALK*] [*An enzyme*]
**GAKA** ........ Kenieba [*Mali*] [*ICAO location identifier*] (ICLI)
**GAKL** ........ Kidal [*Mali*] [*ICAO location identifier*] (ICLI)
**GAKM** ....... Ke-Macina [*Mali*] [*ICAO location identifier*] (ICLI)
**GAKN** ........ Kolokani [*Mali*] [*ICAO location identifier*] (ICLI)
**GAKO** ........ Koutiala [*Mali*] [*ICAO location identifier*] (ICLI)
**GAKS** ......... Gesammelte Aufsaetze zur Kulturgeschichte Spaniens [*A publication*]
**GAKT** ........ Kita [*Mali*] [*ICAO location identifier*] (ICLI)
**Gakujutsu Hokoku Bull Fac Agric Kagoshima Univ** ... Gakujutsu Hokoku. Bulletin. Faculty of Agriculture. Kagoshima University [*A publication*]
**Gakujutsu Hokoku Bull Utsunomiya Univ** ... Gakujutsu Hokoku. Bulletin of the College of Agriculture. Utsunomiya University [*A publication*]
**Gakujutsu Hokoku Tokushu Spec Bull** ... Gakujutsu Hokoku Tokushu. Special Bulletin [*A publication*]
**Gakujutsu Kenkyu Hokoku Res Bull Obihiro Univ** ... Gakujutsu Kenkyu Hokoku. Research Bulletin. Obihiro University [*A publication*]
**Gakujutsu Kenkyu Hokoku Res Rep Kochi Univ Nogaku** ... Gakujutsu Kenkyu Hokoku. Research Reports. Kochi University Nogaku [*A publication*]
**GAKY** ........ Kayes [*Mali*] [*ICAO location identifier*] (ICLI)
**GAl** ............ Albany Public Library, Albany, GA [*Library symbol*] [*Library of Congress*] (LCLS)
**GAL** ........... Galactic (KSC)
**Gal** ............ Galactose [*A sugar*]
**Gal** ............ Galatians [*New Testament book*]
**GAL** ........... Galaxy [*A publication*]
**Gal** ............ Galen [*Second century AD*] [*Classical studies*] (OCD)
**GAL** ........... Galena [*Alaska*] [*Airport symbol*] (OAG)
**GAL** ........... Galerazamba [*Colombia*] [*Seismograph station code, US Geological Survey*] (SEIS)
**gal** ............. Galileo [*Unit of acceleration*]
**gal** ............. Galla [*MARC language code*] [*Library of Congress*] (LCCP)
**GAL** ........... Gallery
**Gal** ............ Gallison's United States Circuit Court Reports [*A publication*] (DLA)
**GAL** ........... Gallium Arsenide LASER
**GAL** ........... Gallon (AAG)
**GAL** ........... Gallons of Fuel [*"Energy equivalent" abbreviation - biomass agriculture and conversion*] [*Fuel chemistry*]
**GAL** ........... Gallop [*Music*] (ROG)
**GAL** ........... Gallup Public Library, Gallup, NM [*OCLC symbol*] (OCLC)
**GAL** ........... Gallus-adeno-like [*Avian virus*]
**GAL** ........... Galoob [*Lewis*] Toys, Inc. [*NYSE symbol*] (SPSG)
**gal** ............. Galvanized Iron (ADA)
**GAL** ........... Galveston Resources Ltd. [*Toronto Stock Exchange symbol*] [*Vancouver Stock Exchange symbol*]
**GAL** ........... Galway [*County in Ireland*] (ROG)
**GAL** ........... Gas-Analysis Laboratory [*NASA*]
**GAL** ........... General Administration Letter (OICC)
**GAL** ........... General Aircraft Ltd. [*Australia*]
**GAL** ........... General George A. Lincoln [*World War II*]
**GAL** ........... Generic Array Logic [*Data processing*]
**GA L** .......... Georgia Law Review [*A publication*]
**GA L** .......... Georgia Lawyer [*A publication*] (DLA)
**GA L** .......... Georgia Sessions Laws [*A publication*] (DLA)
**GAL** ........... Gimbal Angle Loss
**GAL** ........... Graphics Application Language (BYTE)
**GAL** ........... Grupos Armados Libertarios [*Armed Libertarian Groups*] [*Spain*] [*Political party*] (PD)
**Gal** ............ Gualcosius [*Flourished, 11th-12th century*] [*Authority cited in pre-1607 legal work*] (DSA)
**GAL** ........... Guaranteed Access Level [*Foreign Trade*]
**GAL** ........... Guggenheim Aeronautical Laboratory [*California Institute of Technology*]
**GAL** ........... Guild of American Luthiers (EA)
**GAL** ........... Guinea Airways Limited
**GALA** ........ Galagraph Ltd. [*NASDAQ symbol*] (NQ)
**GALA** ........ Gaming and Liquor Authority [*Australian Capital Territory*]
**GALA** ........ Gay and Lesbian Atheists (EA)
**GALA** ........ Graphic Arts Literature Abstracts [*A publication*]
**GALAC** ...... Gay and Lesbian Association of Choruses (EA)
**Gal Act** ....... Galenica Acta [*A publication*]
**GA Law R** .. Georgia Law Review [*A publication*]
**GA Law Reporter** ... Georgia Law Reporter [*A publication*] (DLA)
**GA Laws** .... Georgia Laws [*A publication*]
**GALB** ......... Galbanum [*Agum*] [*Pharmacology*] (ROG)
**Galb** ........... Galbraith's Reports [*9-11 Florida*] [*A publication*] (DLA)
**GAlb** .......... Gjurmime Albanologijike [*A publication*]
**Galb & M** ... Galbraith and Meek's Reports [*9-12 Florida*] [*A publication*] (DLA)
**Galb & M (Fla)** ... Galbraith and Meek's Reports [*9-12 Florida*] [*A publication*] (DLA)
**Galbraith** ... Galbraith's Reports [*9-12 Florida*] [*A publication*] (DLA)
**GalC** ........... Galactocerebroside [*Biochemistry*]
**GALCIT** .... Graduate Aeronautical Laboratories - California Institute of Technology [*Research center*] (RCD)
**Gal Clin** ...... Galicia Clinica [*A publication*]
**GAlD** .......... Dougherty County Court House, Albany, GA [*Library symbol*] [*Library of Congress*] (LCLS)
**GALD** ........ Greatest Axial Linear Dimension
**Gal & Dav** .. Gale and Davison's English Queen's Bench Reports [*1841-43*] [*A publication*] (DLA)
**Gale** ........... Gale on Easements [*A publication*] (DLA)
**GALE** ......... Galerias de Arte y Salas de Exposiciones [*Ministerio de Cultura*] [*Spain*] [*Information service or system*] (CRD)
**Gale** ........... Gale's English Exchequer Reports [*A publication*] (DLA)
**Gale** ........... Gale's New Forest Decisions [*England*] [*A publication*] (DLA)
**GALE** ......... Gaseous and Liquid Effluent [*Nuclear energy*] (NRCH)
**GALE** ......... Genesis of Atlantic Tropical Lows Experiment [*National Oceanic and Atmospheric Administration*]
**Gale & D** .... Gale and Davison's English Queen's Bench Reports [*1841-43*] [*A publication*] (DLA)
**Gale & Dav** ... Gale and Davison's English Queen's Bench Reports [*1841-43*] [*A publication*] (DLA)
**Gale & D (Eng)** ... Gale and Davison's English Queen's Bench Reports [*1841-43*] [*A publication*] (DLA)
**Gale Eas** ..... Gale on Easements [*A publication*] (ILCA)
**Gale's St** ..... Gale's Statutes [*A publication*] (DLA)
**Gale Stat** .... Gale's Statutes [*A publication*] (DLA)
**Gale & Whatley Easem** ... Gale and Whatley [*later, Gale*] on Easements [*A publication*] (DLA)

**Gale & Wh Eas** ... Gale and Whatley [*later, Gale*] on Easements [*A publication*] (ILCA)
**GALF**......... Groupement des Acousticiens de Langue Francaise [*Group of French-Speaking Acousticians*] (EA)
**GAL/(FT D)** ... Gallons per Foot per Day
**GAL/(FT² D)** ... Gallons per Square-Foot per Day
**GAL/H**...... Gallons per Hour (MCD)
**GAL/(HP H)** ... Gallons per Horsepower-Hour
**Gali**........... Galileo [*A publication*]
**GA Libn**..... Georgia Librarian [*A publication*]
**GA Librn**.... Georgia Librarian [*A publication*]
**Galicia Clin** ... Galicia Clinica [*A publication*]
**GA LJ**........ Georgia Law Journal [*A publication*] (DLA)
**GAlJC**........ Albany Junior College, Albany, GA [*Library symbol*] [*Library of Congress*] (LCLS)
**GALK**........ Galactokinase [*Also, GAK*] [*An enzyme*]
**GALL**......... Gallae [*Nut Galls*] [*Pharmacology*] (ROG)
**GALL**......... Gallery (MSA)
**Gall**............ Gallison's United States Circuit Court Reports [*A publication*] (DLA)
**GALL**......... Gallon
**GALL**......... Galloway [*District in Scotland*] (ROG)
**Gallagher**... Gallagher Report [*A publication*]
**Gall Biol Act** ... Gallica Biologica Acta [*A publication*]
**Gall CCR**... Gallison's United States Circuit Court Reports [*A publication*] (DLA)
**Gall Cr Cas** ... Gallick's Reports (French Criminal Cases) [*A publication*] (DLA)
**Galleon**....... Galleon. Bulletin of the Society for Colonial History [*A publication*]
**Gallerie Grandi Opere Sotter** ... Gallerie e Grandi Opere Sotterranee [*A publication*]
**G Allevatori** ... Giornale degli Allevatori [*Italy*] [*A publication*]
**Gallia F**...... Gallia. Fouilles et Monuments Archeologiques en France Metropolitaine [*A publication*]
**Gallia Pr Hist** ... Gallia Prehistoire [*A publication*]
**Galligrassevil** ... Gallimard, Grasset, and Le Sevil [*French publishers*]
**Gall Int L**... Gallaudet on International Law [*A publication*] (DLA)
**Gallison**...... Gallison's United States Circuit Court Reports [*A publication*] (DLA)
**Gallison's Rep** ... Gallison's United States Circuit Court Reports [*A publication*] (DLA)
**Gallup Rep** ... Gallup Report [*A publication*]
**Gallup Rept** ... Gallup Report [*A publication*]
**Gallup Rpt** ... Gallup Report [*A publication*]
**GALLY**...... Gallery (ROG)
**GAL/MIN** ... Gallons per Minute
**GalN**.......... Galactosamine [*Biochemistry*]
**GalNac**....... N-Acetylgalactosamine
**GALOVAL** ... Grappling and Lock-On Validation
**GALPAT**... Galloping Pattern Memory
**GALPBX**... Geologie Alpine [*A publication*]
**Galpin S J** ... Galpin Society. Journal [*A publication*]
**Galpin Soc** ... Galpin Society. Journal [*A publication*]
**Galpin Soc J** ... Galpin Society. Journal [*A publication*]
**Galp Soc J** ... Galpin Society. Journal [*A publication*]
**GA LR**........ Georgia Law Review [*A publication*]
**GA L Rep**... Georgia Law Reporter [*A publication*] (DLA)
**GA L Rev**... Georgia Law Review [*A publication*]
**GAL/S**........ Gallons per Second
**GALS**......... General Aerodynamic Lifting Surface (KSC)
**GALS**......... Generalized Assembly Line Simulator [*General Motors Corp.*]
**GAlSC**....... Albany State College, Albany, GA [*Library symbol*] [*Library of Congress*] (LCLS)
**GALSFC**.... Ginger Alden "Lady Superstar" Fan Club (EA)
**GALT**......... Galactotransferase [*Cell strain deficient in galactose-1-phosphate uridyltransferase*]
**GALT**......... Gut-Associated Lymphoid Tissue [*Medicine*]
**GALV**........ Galvanic [*or Galvanized*]
**GALV**........ Galvanometer
**GALV**........ GalVest, Inc. [*NASDAQ symbol*] (NQ)
**GALV**........ Galveston [*Texas*]
**GALV**........ Gibbon Ape Leukemia Virus
**GALVA**...... Galvano [*France*] [*A publication*]
**Galvano Tec** ... Galvano Tecnica [*Later, Galvanotecnica & Processi al Plasma*] [*A publication*]
**Galvanotec Processi Plasma** ... Galvanotecnica e Processi al Plasma [*A publication*]
**GALVI**....... Galvanized Iron
**GALVND**.. Galvannealed
**GALVNM** ... Galvanometer
**GALVS**...... Galvanized Steel
**GALV TND** ... Galvanized or Tinned [*Freight*]
**GALVWG** ... Gemini Agena Launch Vehicle Working Group [*NASA*] (KSC)
**GALW**........ Galway [*County in Ireland*]
**GALX**........ Galaxy Cheese Co. [*NASDAQ symbol*] (NQ)
**GALY**........ Galley (MSA)
**GAM**.......... GAM. Bulletin du Groupe d'Acoustique Musicale [*A publication*]
**GAM**.......... Gambell [*Alaska*] [*Airport symbol*] (OAG)
**Gam**........... Gambit [*A publication*]
**GAM**.......... Gameness (DSUE)
**GAM**.......... Gamin Resources, Inc. [*Vancouver Stock Exchange symbol*]
**GAM**.......... Gamma (NASA)
**GAM**.......... Gamma [*A publication*]
**Gam**........... Gamma Biologicals, Inc.
**GAM**.......... Gamut [*Music*] (ROG)
**GAM**.......... General Accounting Office, Los Angeles Region, Los Angeles, CA [*OCLC symbol*] (OCLC)
**GAM**.......... General Aeronautical Material
**GAM**.......... General American Investors Co., Inc. [*NYSE symbol*] (SPSG)
**GAM**.......... Georgia Motor Trucking Association [*STAC*]
**GAM**.......... Global Asset Management [*Commercial firm*] [*British*] (ECON)
**GAM**.......... Globe and Mail Data Base [*Info Globe*] [*Information service or system*] (CRD)
**GAM**.......... Graduate Aerospace Mechanical Engineering
**GAM**.......... Grants Administration Manual [*HEW*]
**GAM**.......... Graphics Access Method (BUR)
**GAM**.......... Ground-to-Air Missile (AAG)
**GAM**.......... Groupement des Associations Meunieres des Pays de la CEE [*Flour Milling Associations Group of the EEC Countries*] (EAIO)
**GAM**.......... Grupo de Apoyo Mutuo [*Group for Mutual Support*] [*Guatemala*] [*Political party*]
**GAM**.......... Grupo de Apoyo Mutuo [*Group for Mutual Support*] [*Mexico*] [*Political party*]
**GAM**.......... Guaranteed Annual Minimum
**GAM**.......... Guest Aerovias Mexico, SA
**GAM**.......... Guided Aircraft Missile [*Obsolete*]
**GAM**.......... Morehouse College, Atlanta, GA [*Library symbol*] [*Library of Congress*] (LCLS)
**GAMA**....... Game Manufacturers Association (EA)
**GAMA**....... Gas Appliance Manufacturers Association (EA)
**GAMA**....... General Aviation Manufacturers Association (EA)
**GAMA**....... Graphics-Assisted Management Application [*Data processing*] (BUR)
**GAMA**....... Groupe d'Analyse Macroeconomique Appliquee [*Group for Applied Macroeconomic Analysis*] [*University of Paris - Nanterre*] [*Information service or system*] (IID)
**GAMA**....... Guitar and Accessory Manufacturers Association [*Formerly, NAMMM*]
**GAMA**....... Markala [*Mali*] [*ICAO location identifier*] (ICLI)
**GAMARTA** ... Metropolitan Atlanta Rapid Transit Authority, Atlanta, GA [*Library symbol*] [*Library of Congress*] (LCLS)
**GAMAS**.... Gamma Activation Materials Assay System [*Mobile laboratory*]
**GAMAS**.... General Atomic Material Assay System [*Nuclear energy*] (NRCH)
**GAMAS**.... Gulf Atomic Mobile Assay System
**GAMB**....... Gambro, Inc. [*NASDAQ symbol*] (NQ)
**GAMB**....... Mopti/Barbe [*Mali*] [*ICAO location identifier*] (ICLI)
**GAMB**....... Morris Brown College, Atlanta, GA [*Library symbol*] [*Library of Congress*] (LCLS)
**Gamba**........ [*Petrus Andreas*] Gambarus [*Deceased, 1528*] [*Authority cited in pre-1607 legal work*] (DSA)
**Gamb & Barl** ... Gamble and Barlow's Digest [*Ireland*] [*A publication*] (DLA)
**GAMBIT**... Gate-Modulated Bipolar Transistor (MCD)
**Gamboa**...... Gamboa's Introduction to Philippine Law [*A publication*] (DLA)
**Gamboa Philippine Law** ... Gamboa's Introduction to Philippine Law [*A publication*] (DLA)
**GAMBOG** ... Gambogia [*Gamboge*] [*Pharmacology*] (ROG)
**GAMC**....... General Agents and Managers Conference of NALU [*Washington, DC*] (EA)
**GAMD**....... Gallium Arsenide Microwave Diode
**GAME**....... Game-A-Tron Corp. [*NASDAQ symbol*] (NQ)
**GAMECOIN** ... Game Conservation International (EA)
**Game Conservancy Annu Rev** ... Game Conservancy Annual Review [*A publication*]
**Game Res Assoc Annu Rep** ... Game Research Association. Annual Report [*A publication*]
**Game Res Rep Colo Div Wildl** ... Game Research Report. Colorado Division of Wildlife [*A publication*]
**GAMET**.... Gyro Accelerometer Misalignment Erection Test
**GAMETAG** ... Global Atmospheric Measurements Experiment on Tropospheric Aerosols and Gases [*National Science Foundation*]
**Gamete Res** ... Gamete Research [*United States*] [*A publication*]
**GAmG**........ Georgia Southwestern College, Americus, GA [*Library symbol*] [*Library of Congress*] (LCLS)
**GAMHTE** ... General Association of Municipal Health and Technical Experts (EA)
**GAMI**........ Great American Management & Investment, Inc. [*NASDAQ symbol*] (NQ)
**GAMIg**...... Goat Anti-Mouse Immunoglobulin [*Immunology*]
**GA Mineral Newsletter** ... Georgia Mineral Newsletter [*A publication*]
**GA Miner Newsl** ... Georgia Mineral Newsletter [*A publication*]
**GAMIS**...... Graphic Arts Marketing Information Service (EA)
**GAMK**....... Martin Luther King, Jr., Memorial Center, Atlanta, GA [*Library symbol*] [*Library of Congress*] (LCLS)
**GAMK**....... Menaka [*Mali*] [*ICAO location identifier*] (ICLI)
**GAMLOGS** ... Gamma Ray Logs (IEEE)

**GAMM**...... Gesellschaft fuer Angewandte Mathematik und Mechanik [*Association for Applied Mathematics and Mechanics*] [*Federal Republic of Germany*]
**GAMM**...... Gimbal Angle Matching Monitor
**GAM-M** .... Morehouse College, School of Medicine, Atlanta, GA [*Library symbol*] [*Library of Congress*] (LCLS)
**GAMMA**... [*A*] programming language (CSR)
**GAMMA**... Gay and Married Men's Association [*Victoria, Australia*]
**GAMMA**... Guitar and Accesories Music Marketing Association (EA)
**GAMMA**... Guns and Magnetic Material Alarm [*Weapon-detecting device to prevent skyjacking*]
**Gamma Field Symp** ... Gamma Field Symposia [*A publication*]
**GAMO**....... Gamogen, Inc. [*NASDAQ symbol*] (NQ)
**GAMO**....... Ground and Amphibious Military Operations [*Army*]
**GAMP**....... Global Atmospheric Measurements Program [*National Science Foundation*]
**GAMP**....... Guided Antiarmor Mortar Projectile (INF)
**GAMR**....... Great American Resources, Inc. [*NASDAQ symbol*] (NQ)
**GAMRA**.... Graphic Arts Manufacturers' Representative Association
**GAMS**....... Groupement pour l'Avancement des Methodes Spectroscopiques et Physio-Chimiques d'Analyse [*Group for the Advancement of Spectroscopic Methods and Physicochemical Analysis*] [*Information service or system*] (IID)
**GAMSA**.... Glutamylaminomethylsulfonic Acid [*Biochemistry*]
**GAMSA**.... Management Science America, Inc., Atlanta, GA [*Library symbol*] [*Library of Congress*] (LCLS)
**GAM/SP**... Graphics Access Method/System Product [*IBM Corp.*]
**GAMU**....... Mercer University, Atlanta, GA [*Library symbol*] [*Library of Congress*] (LCLS)
**GAMU-P**... Mercer University, Southern School of Pharmacy, Atlanta, GA [*Library symbol*] [*Library of Congress*] (LCLS)
**GAN**........... Gandalf Technologies, Inc. [*Toronto Stock Exchange symbol*]
**Gan**............. Gandulphus [*Flourished, 1160-85*] [*Authority cited in pre-1607 legal work*] (DSA)
**GAN**........... GAO [*General Accounting Office*] Norfolk Regional Office, Virginia Beach, VA [*OCLC symbol*] (OCLC)
**GAN**........... Garan, Inc. [*AMEX symbol*] (SPSG)
**GAN**........... Generalized Activity Network (IEEE)
**GAN**........... Generating and Analyzing Networks [*Data processing*]
**GAN**........... Goldfields Air Navigation [*Australia*]
**GAN**........... Greenwich Apparent Noon (ROG)
**GAN**........... Ground Attack Night (MCD)
**GAN**........... Groupe des Assurances Nationales [*France*] (EY)
**GAN**........... Guidance and Navigation
**GAN**........... Gyro-Compass Automatic Navigation [*System*] (RDA)
**GAN**........... Net Gradability [*Truck specification*]
**Ganatra**...... Ganatra's Criminal Cases [*India*] [*A publication*] (DLA)
**GANBEO**.. Gas-Netz-Beobachtung [*German*]
**GANC**........ Groupe d'Action Nationale Camerounaise [*Cameroonian National Action Group*]
**GAND**........ Gandalf Technologies, Inc. [*NASDAQ symbol*] (NQ)
**Gand**.......... Gandulphus [*Flourished, 1160-85*] [*Authority cited in pre-1607 legal work*] (DSA)
**GANDALF** ... General Alpha-Numeric Direct Access Library Facility [*Search system*]
**Gane**........... Eastern District Court Reports [*South Africa*] [*A publication*] (DLA)
**GANEFO**.. Games of the New Emerging Forces [*A counter-attraction to the Olympic Games*] [*Indonesia*]
**GANESI**.... Gas-Netz-Simulation [*German*]
**G Anest Stomatol** ... Giornale di Anestesia Stomatologica [*A publication*]
**GANF**........ Ganfield [*England*]
**GANF**........ Niafunke [*Mali*] [*ICAO location identifier*] (ICLI)
**GANG**........ Ganglion [*Medicine*]
**GANGQ**..... Gas-Netz-Simulation for Gas Quality [*German*]
**GANH**....... Northside Hospital, Atlanta, GA [*Library symbol*] [*Library of Congress*] (LCLS)
**Ganita**........ Ganita Bharat Ganita Parisad [*Lucknow*] [*A publication*]
**GANK**........ Nara/Keibane [*Mali*] [*ICAO location identifier*] (ICLI)
**GANMA**.... Gann Monograph [*A publication*]
**Gann**.......... Gann Japanese Journal of Cancer Research [*A publication*]
**GANNET**.. General Administrative Network [*Computer linkup*] [*British*]
**Gann Mon** ... Gann Monographs [*A publication*]
**Gann Monogr** ... Gann Monograph [*A publication*]
**Gann Monogr Cancer Res** ... Gann Monograph on Cancer Research [*A publication*]
**Gannon Coll Chem J** ... Gannon College. Chemistry Journal [*A publication*]
**GANO**....... [*The*] Georgia Northern Railway Co. [*AAR code*]
**GANPAC**.. German American National Political Action Committee (EA)
**GANPRODA** ... Gas-Netz-Simulation mit Prozess-Daten [*German*]
**GANR**........ Nioro [*Mali*] [*ICAO location identifier*] (ICLI)
**GANSAT**... Gannett Satellite Information Network
**Gantt Dig**... Gantt's Digest of Arkansas Statutes [*A publication*] (DLA)
**Gantts Dig**... Gantt's Digest of Arkansas Statutes [*A publication*] (DLA)
**GA Nurse**... Georgia Nursing [*A publication*]
**GAO**........... GARP Activities Office [*Marine science*] (MSC)
**GAO**........... General Accounting Office [*of the US government*]
**GAO**........... General Accounting Office, Technical Information Sources and Service, Washington, DC [*OCLC symbol*] (OCLC)
**GAO**........... General Administrative Order
**GAO**........... General Agricultural Officer [*Ministry of Agriculture, Fisheries, and Food*] [*British*]
**GAO**........... General Alert Order (NATG)
**GAO**........... Glycolic Acid Oxidase [*An enzyme*]
**GAO**........... Government Accounting Office (MCD)
**GAO**........... Guantanamo [*Cuba*] [*Airport symbol*] (OAG)
**GAOC**........ Oglethorpe University, Atlanta, GA [*Library symbol*] [*Library of Congress*] (LCLS)
**GAO/CED** ... General Accounting Office/Community and Economic Development Division
**GAOF**........ Gummed All Over Flap [*Envelopes*]
**GAO/FGMSD** ... General Accounting Office/Financial and General Management Studies Division
**GAO/FPCD** ... General Accounting Office/Federal Personnel and Compensation Division
**GAO (Gen Accounting Office) R** ... GAO (General Accounting Office) Review [*A publication*]
**GAOHP**..... General Alliance of Operative House Painters [*A union*] [*British*]
**GAO/LCD** ... General Accounting Office/Logistics and Communications Division
**GAO Let Rep** ... General Accounting Office Letter Report [*A publication*] (DLA)
**GA Oper**.... Georgia Operator [*A publication*]
**GAO/PSAD** ... General Accounting Office/Procurement and Systems Acquisition Division
**GAOR**........ General Accounting Office Review
**GAOR**........ General Assembly Including the Reports of the Meetings, the Annexes to Those Records, and the Supplements. Official Reports [*A publication*]
**GAOR**........ General Assembly Official Record [*United Nations*] [*A publication*] (DLA)
**GAO Rev**... GAO [*General Accounting Office*] Review [*A publication*]
**GAOTU**..... Grand Architect of the Universe [*Freemasonry*] (ROG)
**GAOW**...... General Accounting Office, Washington
**GAP**........... Atlanta Public Library, Atlanta, GA [*OCLC symbol*] (OCLC)
**GAP**........... Atlanta Public Schools, Professional Library, Atlanta, GA [*Library symbol*] [*Library of Congress*] (LCLS)
**GAP**........... GAP [*Group for the Advancement of Psychiatry*] Report [*A publication*]
**GAP**........... Garmisch-Partenkirchen [*Federal Republic of Germany*] [*Seismograph station code, US Geological Survey*] (SEIS)
**GAP**........... Gastric and Peptic Ulcer [*A laboratory test kit*] [*Medicine*]
**GAP**........... Gemeinsamer Ausbildung Plan [*Training plan*] [*German*] (INF)
**GAP**........... General Antenna Package [*COMSAT*]
**GAP**........... General Application Plan (AFIT)
**GAP**........... General Assembly Program [*Data processing*]
**GAP**........... General and Practical Energy Information Data Base (MCD)
**GAP**........... Geographic Applications Program [*United States Geological Survey*] (IID)
**GAP**........... Ghetto Arts Program [*Later, Urban Arts Corps*] (EA)
**GAP**........... Glyceraldehyde Phosphate [*Biochemistry*]
**GAP**........... GnRH [*Gonadotropin Releasing Hormone*] Associated Peptide [*Endocrinology*]
**GAP**........... GOAL [*Ground Operations Aerospace Language*] Automatic Procedure [*NASA*] (NASA)
**GAP**........... Goodyear Associative Processor [*Data processing*]
**GAP**........... Government Accountability Project (EA)
**GAP**........... Government Aircraft Plant
**GAP**........... Government of Alberta Publications [*Alberta Public Affairs Bureau*] [*Canada*] [*Information service or system*] (CRD)
**GAP**........... Grant Air Program [*DoD*] (MCD)
**GAP**........... Graphics Adapter Processor [*Baytec*]
**GAP**........... Graphics Application Program
**GAP**........... Great Atlantic & Pacific Tea Co., Inc. [*NYSE symbol*] (SPSG)
**GAP**........... Greater Access to Publishing [*British*]
**GAP**........... Greenwood, Archer, and Pine [*Major streets in Tulsa, OK*] [*In musical group "The GAP Band"*]
**GAP**........... Group for the Advancement of Psychiatry (EA)
**GAP**........... Group for Aquatic Primary Productivity [*ICSU*]
**GAP**........... Group Attainment Program
**GAP**........... Growth-Associated Protein [*Cytochemistry*]
**GAP**........... Grupo de Auto-Defensa [*Self-Defense Group*] [*Uruguay*] [*Political party*] (PD)
**GAP**........... Guanosine Triphosphatase Activating Protein [*Biochemistry*]
**GAP**........... Guided Antitank Projectile (MCD)
**GAP**........... Gusap [*Papua New Guinea*] [*Airport symbol*] [*Obsolete*] (OAG)
**GAPA**........ Greek American Progressive Association (EA)
**GAPA**........ Ground-to-Air Pilotless Aircraft [*Early US test missiles*]
**GAPAN**..... Guide to Air Pilots and Air Navigation [*A publication*]
**GAPAN**..... Guild of Air Pilots and Air Navigators (MCD)
**GAPCE**..... General Assembly of the Presbyterian Church of England (DAS)
**Ga-PD**....... Gallium Arsenide Phosphide Photodiode
**GAPDH**..... Glyceraldehydephosphate Dehydrogenase [*Also, GPDH*] [*An enzyme*]
**GAPE**........ General Aviation Pilot Education [*Safety project*]
**GAPE**........ Ground Anchor Placement Equipment

**GAPh**......... Southern School of Pharmacy, Mercer University, Atlanta, GA [*Library symbol*] [*Library of Congress*] (LCLS)
**GAPHYOR** ... Gaz-Physique-Orsay Database [*Universite de Paris-Sud*] [*Information service or system*]
**GAPie**........ Piedmont Hospital, Atlanta, GA [*Library symbol*] [*Library of Congress*] (LCLS)
**GAPL**......... Group Assembly Parts List (MCD)
**GAPP**......... Geometric Arithmetic Parallel Processor [*Data processing*]
**GAPR**......... Great American Partners [*San Diego, CA*] [*NASDAQ symbol*] (NQ)
**GA Prac**..... Stand's Georgia Practice [*A publication*] (DLA)
**GAPS**......... Government Accountability Property System (MCD)
**GAPSALS** ... Give a Pint, Save a Life Society [*World War II organization which encouraged donating blood*]
**GAPSAT** ... Gap-Filler Satellite [*RADAR*] (NVT)
**GAPSATCOM** ... Gap-Filler Satellite Communication System (MCD)
**GA PSC**..... Georgia Public Service Commission Reports [*A publication*] (DLA)
**GAPSF**...... Government Agricultural Policy and Services for Farmers [*British*]
**GAPT**......... Graphical Automatically Programmed Tools [*Data processing*]
**GAQ**.......... Gao [*Mali*] [*Airport symbol*] (OAG)
**GAQ**.......... Good Average Quality (ADA)
**GAR**.......... Galling Report on Italy [*A publication*]
**GAR**.......... GAO [*General Accounting Office*] San Francisco Regional Office, San Francisco, CA [*OCLC symbol*] (OCLC)
**GAR**.......... Garage
**GAR**.......... Garaina [*Papua New Guinea*] [*Airport symbol*] (OAG)
**Gar**............ [*Johannes*] Garcias Hispanus [*Flourished, 13th century*] [*Authority cited in pre-1607 legal work*] (DSA)
**GAR**.......... Garden Lake Resources [*Vancouver Stock Exchange symbol*]
**GAR**.......... Garm [*USSR*] [*Seismograph station code, US Geological Survey*] (SEIS)
**GAR**.......... Garrison (MUGU)
**GAR**.......... General Adverse Reaction [*Noise*]
**GaR**.......... Georgia Reports [*A publication*] (DLA)
**GA R**.......... Georgia Review [*A publication*]
**G-Ar**.......... Georgia State Department of Archives and History, Atlanta, GA [*Library symbol*] [*Library of Congress*] (LCLS)
**GAR**.......... German Army
**GAR**.......... Gimbal Angle Rate
**GAR**.......... Gimbal Angle Readout
**GAR**.......... Glass Accumulation Rate [*Oceanography*]
**GAR**.......... Global Atmospheric Research (NOAA)
**GAR**.......... Goat Anti-Rabbit [*Also, GARb*] [*Immunology*]
**GAR**.......... Golden Age Records [*Record label*]
**GAR**.......... Golden Carriage-Aire [*Paso Robles, CA*] [*FAA designator*] (FAAC)
**GAR**.......... Government Authorized Representative
**GAR**.......... Grand Army of the Republic (GPO)
**GAR**.......... Graphics Action Request (MCD)
**GAR**.......... Growth Analysis and Review (BUR)
**GAR**.......... Gruppi Armati Radicali per il Comunismo [*Armed Radical Groups for Communism*] [*Italy*] (PD)
**GAR**.......... Guided Aircraft Rocket
**GAR**.......... Guided Antiarmor Rocket
**GARAD**..... Gastrointestinal Radiology [*A publication*]
**GArb**......... Geistige Arbeit [*A publication*]
**GARb**......... Goat Anti-Rabbit [*Also, GAR*] [*Immunology*]
**GARB**......... Green, Amber, Red, Blue [*Priority of the airways*]
**GARB**......... Guided Antiradiation Bomb
**GARBC**...... General Association of Regular Baptist Churches (EA)
**GARBD**..... Garboard [*Naval architecture*]
**GARC**......... Graphic Arts Research Center [*Later, T & E Center*] [*Rochester Institute of Technology*]
**GARC**......... Great Atlantic Radio Conspiracy (EA)
**GARC**......... Retail Credit Co., Atlanta, GA [*Library symbol*] [*Library of Congress*] (LCLS)
**G Arch**....... Graduate in Architecture
**Garcia de Orta (Lisb)** ... Garcia de Orta (Lisbon) [*A publication*]
**Garcia de Orta Ser Bot** ... Garcia de Orta. Serie de Botanica [*Lisbon*] [*A publication*]
**Garcia de Orta Ser Estud Agron** ... Garcia de Orta. Serie de Estudos Agronomicos [*Lisbon*] [*A publication*]
**Garcia de Orta Ser Geol** ... Garcia de Orta. Serie de Geologia [*A publication*]
**Garcia de Orta Ser Zool** ... Garcia de Orta. Serie de Zoologia [*Lisbon*] [*A publication*]
**GARC Newsl** ... GARC [*Graphic Arts Research Center*] Newsletter [*A publication*]
**Garc Orta**... Garcia de Orta [*A publication*]
**GARD**......... Denning Mobile Robotics, Inc. [*NASDAQ symbol*] (NQ)
**GARD**......... Gamma Atomic Radiation Detector
**GARD**......... Gardener (ROG)
**GARD**......... General Address Reading Devices [*Data processing*]
**GARD**......... General Aviation Recovery Device
**GARD**......... Gimbal Angle Runaway Detector
**GARD**......... Graphic Analyzer of Resistance Defects
**GARD**......... Grumman-Alderson Research Dummy [*Aircraft ejection seats*]
**Gard Abstr** ... Gardener's Abstracts [*A publication*]
**GARDAE** .. Gathers Alarms, Reports, Displays, and Evaluates
**Gard Bull (Singapore)** ... Gardens Bulletin (Singapore) [*A publication*]
**Gard Chron** ... Gardeners' Chronicle and Gardening Illustrated [*A publication*]
**Gard Chron Am** ... Gardeners' Chronicle of America [*A publication*]
**Gard Chron (Lond)** ... Gardeners' Chronicle (London) [*A publication*]
**Gard Digest** ... Garden Digest [*A publication*]
**Garden & F** ... Garden and Forest [*A publication*]
**Gardenhire** ... Gardenhire's Reports [*14, 15 Missouri*] [*A publication*] (DLA)
**Garden History Soc Newsletter** ... Garden History Society. Newsletter [*A publication*]
**Garden Is** ... Garden Island [*A publication*] (APTA)
**Garden J R Hortic Soc** ... Garden. Journal of the Royal Horticultural Society [*A publication*]
**Gard Ev**...... Garde on Evidence [*1830*] [*A publication*] (DLA)
**Gard & Home B** ... Garden and Home Builder [*A publication*]
**Gard Illustr** ... Gardening Illustrated [*A publication*]
**Gard J**........ Garden Journal [*A publication*]
**Gard J NY Bot Gard** ... Garden Journal. New York Botanical Garden [*A publication*]
**Gard M**...... Garden Magazine [*A publication*]
**Gardn PC**... Gardner's Peerage Case, Reported by Le Marchant [*A publication*] (DLA)
**Gard NY Rep** ... Gardenier's New York Reporter [*A publication*] (DLA)
**Gard NY Rept** ... Gardenier's New York Reporter [*A publication*] (DLA)
**Gard NY Rptr** ... Gardenier's New York Reporter [*A publication*] (DLA)
**Gard Pl**....... Garde's First Principles of Pleading [*A publication*] (DLA)
**GA Rep**...... Georgia Reports [*A publication*] (DLA)
**GA Rep Ann** ... Georgia Reports, Annotated [*A publication*] (DLA)
**GA Rev**....... Georgia Review [*A publication*]
**GAREX**...... Ground Aviation Radio Exchange System (MCD)
**GARF**......... Graphic Arts Research Foundation (EA)
**GARF**......... Guam Acoustic Range Facility [*Military*] (CAAL)
**GARG**........ Gargarisma [*Gargle*] [*Pharmacy*]
**GARGAR** .. Gargarisma [*Gargle*] [*Pharmacy*] (ROG)
**GARGG**..... Goat Antiserum to Rabbit Gamma-Globulin [*Immunology*]
**GARH**........ Georgia Regional Hospital at Atlanta, Atlanta, GA [*Library symbol*] [*Library of Congress*] (LCLS)
**GARI**......... Goat Anti-Rabbit Immunoglobulin [*Immunochemistry*]
**GARI**......... Groupe d'Action Revolutionnaire Internationaliste [*International Revolutionary Action Group*] [*France*] [*Political party*] (PD)
**GARI**......... Grupo de Accion Revolucionaria Internacional [*International Revolutionary Action Group*] [*Spain*] [*Political party*]
**GARIA7**..... Ghana. Animal Research Institute. Annual Report [*A publication*]
**GARIOA** ... Government and Relief in Occupied Areas [*Post-World War II*]
**Garkreba**.... Garantie- und Kreditbank [*Guaranty and Credit Bank*] [*German Democratic Republic*]
**GARL**........ Group Action Request Lists
**GARMI**...... General Aviation Radio Magnetic Indicator
**GArmO**..... Group Armaments Officer [*British military*] (DMA)
**GARN**........ Garnet Resources Corp. [*NASDAQ symbol*] (NQ)
**GARN**........ Garnish [*Automotive engineering*]
**GARN**........ Garnishee Order (DCTA)
**GARP**........ Global Atmospheric Research Program [*Terminated*] [*National Science Foundation*]
**GARP Publ Ser** ... GARP [*Global Atmospheric Research Programme*] Publications Series [*A publication*]
**GARS**......... Geological Applications of Remote Sensing
**GARS**......... Grand Assistant Recording Scribe [*Freemasonry*] (ROG)
**GART**........ Gartner Group, Inc. [*Stamford, CT*] [*NASDAQ symbol*] (NQ)
**Gartenbauwiss** ... Gartenbauwissenschaft [*A publication*]
**Garten u Kleintierz C (Imker)** ... Garten und Kleintierzucht. C (Imker) [*A publication*]
**G Arterioscir** ... Giornale della Arteriosclerosi [*A publication*]
**Gart Landschaft Landscape Archit Plann** ... Garten Landschaft. Landscape Architecture Planning [*A publication*]
**GAS**........... Autonomous Anarchist Groups [*Spanish*] (PD)
**GAS**........... Galena Air Service [*Galena, AK*] [*FAA designator*] (FAAC)
**GAS**........... Gallipolis, OH [*Location identifier*] [*FAA*] (FAAL)
**GAS**........... Gallium Arsenide [*Semiconductor*]
**GAS**........... Garissa [*Kenya*] [*Airport symbol*] (OAG)
**GAS**........... Gas Acquisition System
**GAS**........... Gas-Insulated Switchgear
**GAS**........... Gas. Maandblad voor de Gasindustrie [*A publication*]
**GAS**........... Gasoline (AFM)
**GAS**........... Gastroenterology [*Medicine*]
**GAS**........... Gauss [*Later, GTT*] [*Federal Republic of Germany*] [*Geomagnetic observatory code*]
**GAS**........... General Adaptation Syndrome [*Medicine*]
**GAS**........... General Air Staff (NATG)
**GAS**........... General Aptitude Series [*Test*]
**GAS**........... General Automotive Support
**GAS**........... General Aviation Simulator [*Data processing*] [*NASA*]
**GAS**........... Generalized Arteriosclerosis [*Medicine*]
**GAS**........... Generalized Audit Software [*Data processing*]
**GAS**........... German-American Studies [*A publication*]
**GAS**........... Get Away Special (MCD)
**GAS**........... Giant Air Shower
**GAS**........... Giant Attribute Survey
**GAS**........... Glass Art Society (EA)
**GAS**........... Global Analysis Systems [*Information service or system*] (IID)

**GAS** .......... Global Assessment Scale [*Psychiatric evaluation test*]
**GAS** .......... Goal Attainment Scale
**GAS** .......... Goilala Air Services [*Australia*]
**GAS** .......... Government Accounting Service [*British*]
**GAS** .......... Government of American Samoa (MUGU)
**GAS** .......... Grand Annual Sojourner [*Freemasonry*] (ROG)
**GAS** .......... Gray Area Systems (MCD)
**GAS** .......... Group A Streptococci [*Medicine*]
**GAS** .......... Guild of All Saints [*British*] (ROG)
**GAS** .......... Guild of All Souls [*British*]
**GAS** .......... Gun Accessory System (MCD)
**GAS** .......... Gun Aiming Sensor (MCD)
**GAS** .......... Gunner's Auxiliary Sight (MCD)
**GAS** .......... NICOR, Inc. [*Formerly, Northern Illinois Gas Co.*] [*NYSE symbol*] (SPSG)
**GAS** .......... Southern Technical Institute, Marietta, GA [*OCLC symbol*] (OCLC)
**GASA** ........ Graphic Arts Suppliers Association (EA)
**GASAA**...... Gazzetta Sanitaria [*A publication*]
**Gas Abstr**... Gas Abstracts [*A publication*]
**Gas Age Rec Nat Gas** ... Gas Age Record and Natural Gas [*A publication*]
**GASB**......... Governmental Accounting Standards Board [*Stamford, CT*] (EA)
**GASBIINDO** ... Gabungan Serikat Buruh Islam Indonesia [*Federation of Indonesian Islamic Trade Unions*]
**GA SBJ**...... Georgia State Bar Journal [*A publication*]
**GASC**......... Gas-Analysis Sample Container [*Apollo*] [*NASA*]
**GASC**......... Georgia, Ashburn, Sylvester & Camilla R. R. [*AAR code*]
**GASC**......... Gurkha Army Service Corps [*British military*] (DMA)
**Gas de Cal** ... Gaspar de Calderinis [*Deceased, 1390*] [*Authority cited in pre-1607 legal work*] (DSA)
**Gas de Cald** ... Gaspar de Calderinis [*Deceased, 1390*] [*Authority cited in pre-1607 legal work*] (DSA)
**GAS Can**.... Get-Away-Special Cannister [*NASA*]
**Gas Chromat Abstr** ... Gas Chromatography Abstracts [*A publication*]
**Gas Chromatogr Int Sym** ... Gas Chromatography. International Symposium [*A publication*]
**Gas Chromatogr Proc Int Symp (Eur)** ... Gas Chromatography. Proceedings of the International Symposium (Europe) [*A publication*]
**GA Sch Technol State Eng Exp Stn Repr** ... Georgia. School of Technology. State Engineering Experiment Station. Reprint [*A publication*]
**Gas Consum** ... Future Gas Consumption of the US [*A publication*]
**Gas Counc (Gt Brit) Res Commun** ... Gas Council (Great Britain) Research Communications [*A publication*]
**GASDA** ..... Gasoline and Automotive Service Dealers Association (EA)
**Gas Dig**...... Gas Digest [*A publication*]
**GASDSAS** ... Gust Alleviation and Structural Dynamic Stability Augmentation [*Aviation*]
**Gas Eng** ..... Gas Engineer [*England*] [*A publication*]
**Gas Engine Manage** ... Gas Engineering and Management [*A publication*]
**Gas Eng Manage** ... Gas Engineering and Management [*A publication*]
**Gas Engng Mgmnt** ... Gas Engineering and Management [*A publication*]
**Gas Engng Mgmt** ... Gas Engineering and Management [*A publication*]
**Gaseous Air Pollut Plant Metab Proc Int Symp** ... Gaseous Air Pollutants and Plant Metabolism. Proceedings. International Symposium on Gaseous Air Pollutants and Plant Metabolism [*A publication*]
**Gaseous Dielectr Proc Int Symp** ... Gaseous Dielectrics. Proceedings. International Symposium on Gaseous Dielectrics [*A publication*]
**GASER**...... Gamma Ray LASER (NATG)
**GASERBUN** ... Gabungan SB2 Non-Vakcentral [*Federation of Non-Affiliated Trade Unions*] [*Indonesia*]
**GASES** ...... Gravity-Anchored Space Experiments Satellite (MCD)
**Gases Res Ind** ... Gases in Research and Industry [*A publication*]
**Gases Res Ind Gas Div CIG** ... Gases in Research and Industry. Commonwealth Industrial Gases Ltd. [*A publication*] (APTA)
**GASF** ......... Graphic Arts Sales Foundation (EA)
**GASFET**.... Gallium Arsenide Field-Effect Transistor
**GASG** ........ Segou [*Mali*] [*ICAO location identifier*] (ICLI)
**GASGASGAS** ... Gild of Ancient Suppliers of Gas Appliances, Skills, Gins, Accessories, and Substances (EA)
**GASGB**...... Gasgemeinschaft [*A publication*]
**GASH**........ Guanidine Aluminum Sulfate Hexahydrate [*Insecticide*]
**GASH**........ Guanidine Aluminum Sulfate Hydrate [*Ferroelectrics*]
**GASHD**..... Gazo Shindan [*A publication*]
**Gas Ind** ...... Gas Industries [*A publication*]
**Gas Ind (Leipzig)** ... Gas Industrie (Leipzig) [*A publication*]
**Gas Ind (London)** ... Gas Industry (London) [*A publication*]
**Gas Ind Manuf Gas Ed** ... Gas Industry. Manufactured Gas Edition [*A publication*]
**Gas Ind Nat Gas Ed** ... Gas Industry. Natural Gas Edition [*A publication*]
**Gas Inst News** ... Gas Institute News [*A publication*]
**Gas J**.......... Gas Journal [*A publication*]
**GASJ** ......... Saint Joseph's Infirmary, Atlanta, GA [*Library symbol*] [*Library of Congress*] (LCLS)
**GASK**......... Sikasso [*Mali*] [*ICAO location identifier*] (ICLI)
**GASKET** ... Graphic Surface Kinetics [*Computer program*] (KSC)
**GASL**......... General Activity Simulation Language [*Data processing*]
**GASL**......... General Applied Science Laboratory
**G As (London) Pr** ... Geologists' Association (London). Proceedings [*A publication*]
**GASM** ....... Graphic Arts Spray Manufacturers [*Defunct*] (EA)
**Gas Mag**.... Gas Magazine [*United States*] [*A publication*]
**GAS-MOP** ... Gulf of Alaska Mesoscale Oceanographic Processes
**GASN**........ San [*Mali*] [*ICAO location identifier*] (ICLI)
**GASO**........ Gasoline
**GASOHOL** ... Gasoline/Ethanol [*Automotive fuel*]
**Gas Oil Pwr** ... Gas and Oil Power [*A publication*]
**GASP**......... Galloping Acronyms Save Paper
**GASP**......... Gas Annulus Sizing Program
**GASP**......... Gas Properties [*NASA computer program*]
**GASP**......... General Activity Simulation Program [*Programming language*] [*1970*] [*Data processing*] (BUR)
**GASP**......... General All-Purpose Simulation Package [*McDonnell Douglas Automation Co.*] (MCD)
**GASP**......... General Assembly to Stop the Powerline (EA)
**GASP**......... Generalized Academic Simulation Program [*Data processing*] (IEEE)
**GASP**......... Generalized Aerospace Program (KSC)
**GASP**......... Generalized Antisymmetric Potential
**GASP**......... Gevic Arithmetic Simulation Program
**GASP**......... Global Atmospheric Sampling Program [*NASA*]
**GASP**......... Grand Accelerated Space Platform
**GASP**......... Graphic Applications Subroutine Package [*Data processing*] (BUR)
**GASP**......... Gravity-Assisted Space Probe [*NASA*]
**GASP**......... Greater [*name of city*] Alliance to Stop Pollution
**GASP**......... Grip, Aim, Stance, and Posture [*Golf*]
**GASP**......... Ground Avoidance Simulation Program (MCD)
**GASP**......... Group Against Smokers' Pollution (EA)
**Gaspar** ....... Gaspar's Small Cause Court Reports [*Bengal*] [*A publication*] (DLA)
**GASPBY** ... Geological Association of Canada. Special Paper [*A publication*]
**Gasp de Cald** ... Gaspar de Calderinis [*Deceased, 1390*] [*Authority cited in pre-1607 legal work*] (DSA)
**GASPE**...... Gated Spin Echo [*Nuclear magnetic resonance*]
**Gas (Phila)** ... Gas (Philadelphia) [*A publication*]
**GASPI** ....... Guidance Attitude Space Position Indicator (MCD)
**Gas Process Assoc Proc** ... Gas Processors Association. Proceedings [*A publication*]
**Gas Res Inst Dig** ... Gas Research Institute Digest [*A publication*]
**GASS**......... Generalized Assembly System [*Data processing*] (IEEE)
**GASS**......... Geomagnetic Airborne Survey System
**GASS**......... Gimbal Assembly Storage System
**GASS**......... Great American Shoe Store [*Advertising slogan of Kinney Shoe Corp.*]
**GASS**......... Great Analog Signal Saver
**GASS**......... Guidance Accuracy Study for SPRINT [*Missile*] [*Army*] (AABC)
**GASSAR** ... Gilbert Associates [*or General Atomic*] Standard Safety Analysis Report [*Nuclear energy*] (NRCH)
**Gas Sep Purif** ... Gas Separation and Purification [*A publication*]
**GASSER**.... Geographic Aerospace Search RADAR
**GASSP** ...... Gas Source Seismic Section Profiler
**GASSP** ...... Gas Subject Pilot [*Aviation*] (FAAC)
**Gas Supply Rev** ... Gas Supply Review [*A publication*]
**GAST**......... Gastronomia Espanola [*Ministerio de Cultura*] [*Spain*] [*Information service or system*] (CRD)
**GAST**......... Geraeteausgabestelle [*Equipment distributing point*] [*German military - World War II*]
**GASTA**...... Gimbal Angle Sequencing Transformation Assembly (KSC)
**GA St BJ** ... Georgia State Bar Journal [*A publication*]
**GASTDE**... Butterworths International Medical Reviews. Gastroenterology [*A publication*]
**GASTROC** ... Gastrocnemius [*Muscle*] [*Anatomy*]
**Gastroent** ... Gastroenterologia [*A publication*]
**Gastroent** ... Gastroenterology [*A publication*]
**Gastroenterol** ... Gastroenterologia [*A publication*]
**Gastroenterol Abstr & Cit** ... Gastroenterology. Abstracts and Citations [*A publication*]
**Gastroenterol Abstr Citations** ... Gastroenterology. Abstracts and Citations [*A publication*]
**Gastroenterol Annu** ... Gastroenterology Annual [*A publication*]
**Gastroenterol Clin Biol** ... Gastroenterologie Clinique et Biologique [*A publication*]
**Gastroenterol Endosc** ... Gastroenterological Endoscopy [*A publication*]
**Gastroenterol Jpn** ... Gastroenterologia Japonica [*A publication*]
**Gastroenterol Stoffwechsel** ... Gastroenterologie und Stoffwechsel [*A publication*]
**Gastroenty** ... Gastroenterology [*A publication*]
**Gastroin En** ... Gastrointestinal Endoscopy [*A publication*]
**Gastroint Endosc** ... Gastrointestinal Endoscopy [*A publication*]
**Gastrointest Endosc** ... Gastrointestinal Endoscopy [*A publication*]
**Gastrointest Radiol** ... Gastrointestinal Radiology [*A publication*]
**Gas Turb**.... Turbomachinery International [*A publication*]
**Gas Turb H** ... Turbomachinery International. Handbook [*A publication*]
**Gas Turbine Int** ... Gas Turbine International [*A publication*]

**GASU**........ Georgia State University, Atlanta, GA [*Library symbol*] [*Library of Congress*] (LCLS)
**GASU-L**.... Georgia State University, Law Library, Atlanta, GA [*Library symbol*] [*Library of Congress*] (LCLS)
**GA Sup**...... Georgia Reports, Supplement [*A publication*] (DLA)
**GA Supp**.... Georgia Reports, Supplement [*A publication*] (DLA)
**GAS/W**...... Gas Weld
**Gas Waerme Int**... Gas Waerme International [*A publication*]
**Gas Wld**..... Gas World [*A publication*]
**GASWOA**... Great American Station Wagon Owner's Association (EA)
**Gas World Gas J**... Gas World and Gas Journal [*A publication*]
**Gas Z Ration Energieanwend**... Gas. Zeitschrift fuer Rationelle Energieanwendung [*West Germany*] [*A publication*]
**GAt**........... Athens Regional Library, Athens, GA [*Library symbol*] [*Library of Congress*] (LCLS)
**GAT**........... Gate-Associated Transistor (MCD)
**GAT**........... Gateway Corp. ADR [*NYSE symbol*] (SPSG)
**GAT**........... Gelatin-Agglutination Test [*Clinical chemistry*]
**GAT**........... Gemini Agena Target [*NASA*]
**GAT**........... General Air Traffic [*Europe-Asia*]
**GAT**........... General Air Training
**GAT**........... General Analysis Technique
**GAT**........... General Aptitude Test [*Psychometrics*]
**GAT**........... General Aviation Trainer
**GAT**........... General Aviation Transponder
**GAT**........... Generalized Algebraic Translator [*Data processing*]
**GAT**........... Georgetown Automatic Translator [*Data processing*]
**GAT**........... Georgia Institute of Technology, Atlanta, GA [*Library symbol*] [*Library of Congress*] [*OCLC symbol*] (LCLS)
**GAT**........... Goodyear Atomic Corp. (KSC)
**GAT**........... Greenwich Apparent Time
**GAT**........... Ground-to-Air Transmitter
**GAT**........... Ground Attack Tactics [*for air delivery of weapons against a ground target*]
**GAT**........... Guinea Air Traders [*Australia*]
**$GAT_{10}d$**...... Glutamic Acid-Alanine-Tyrosine [*Biopolymer*]
**GATAC**..... General Assessment Tridimensional Analog Computer (IEEE)
**GATAE**...... Graphic Arts Trade Association Executives [*Later, GAAE*]
**GAtAR**....... United States Department of Agriculture, Russell Agriculture Research Center, Athens, GA [*Library symbol*] [*Library of Congress*] (LCLS)
**GATASWA**... Gestalt and Transactional Analysis Seminar, Western Australia
**GATB**........ General Aptitude Test Battery
**GATB**........ General Avionics Testbed [*Military*]
**GATB**........ Tombouctou [*Mali*] [*ICAO location identifier*] (ICLI)
**GATBY**...... General Aptitude Test Battery
**GATCO**..... Guild of Air Traffic Control Officers [*British*]
**GATD**........ Graphic Analysis of Three-Dimensional Data
**GATE**........ GARP [*Global Atmospheric Research Program*] Atlantic Tropical Experiment [*National Oceanic and Atmospheric Administration*]
**GATE**........ General Access Transportation Extention [*Telecommunications*] (TSSD)
**GATE**........ General-Purpose Automatic Test Equipment [*Army*] (RDA)
**GATE**........ Generalized Algebraic Translator Extended [*Data processing*]
**GATE**........ Graduate Aid to Employment (OICC)
**GATEOR**... Gas-Assisted Thermal-Enhanced Oil Recovery
**Gateway Med**... Gateway to Medicine [*A publication*]
**GATF**........ Graphic Arts Technical Foundation (EA)
**GATF Bull**... GATF [*Graphic Arts Technical Foundation*] Bulletin [*A publication*]
**GATF Envir Control Rept**... GATF [*Graphic Arts Technical Foundation*] Environmental Control Report [*A publication*]
**GATF Res Progr**... GATF [*Graphic Arts Technical Foundation*] Research Progress [*A publication*]
**GATF Res Prog Rep**... GATF [*Graphic Arts Technical Foundation*] Research Progress Report [*A publication*]
**GATF Tech Serv Inform**... GATF [*Graphic Arts Technical Foundation*] Technical Service Information [*A publication*]
**GATH**........ Gatha [*Language, etc.*] (ROG)
**Gath**........... [*The*] Gathering [*A publication*]
**GAThS**...... Theosophical Society, Atlanta, GA [*Library symbol*] [*Library of Congress*] (LCLS)
**GATN**........ Taoudenni [*Mali*] [*ICAO location identifier*] (ICLI)
**GATN (German-Am Trade News)**... GATN (German-American Trade News) [*A publication*]
**Gatooma Res Stn Annu Rep**... Gatooma Research Station. Annual Report [*A publication*]
**GATP**......... Ground Acceptance [*or Article*] Test Procedure (MCD)
**GATR**........ Great American Truck Racing (EA)
**GATR**........ Gross Average Tax Rate
**GATR**........ Ground-to-Air Transmitting-Receiving [*Station*]
**GATRI**....... Gamma Technology Research Irradiator (ADA)
**GATS**......... General Acceptance Test Software
**GATS**......... General Agreement on Trade in Services
**GATS**......... Guidance Acceptance Test Set
**GATS**......... Gulf Applied Technologies, Inc. [*NASDAQ symbol*] (NQ)
**GATS**......... Tessalit [*Mali*] [*ICAO location identifier*] (ICLI)
**GATT**........ Gate Assisted Turnoff Thyristor [*NASA*] (NASA)
**GATT**........ General Agreement on Tariffs and Trade [*Organization, and the concept it represents, concerned with adjustment of tariffs among 73 member nations*] [*See also AGTDC*] [*Switzerland*] [*Also, an information service or system*]
**GATT**........ General Agreement on Tariffs and Trade Bibliography [*A publication*]
**GATT**........ Ground-to-Air Transmitter Terminal
**GATTC**...... General Aviation Technical Training Conference
**GATU**........ Geophysical Automatic Tracker Unit
**GATV**........ Gemini Agena Target Vehicle [*NASA*]
**GATW**....... Gateway Federal Savings & Loan Association [*NASDAQ symbol*] (NQ)
**GATX**........ GATX Corp. [*Formerly, General American Transportation Corp.*]
**GAU**.......... Atlanta University, Atlanta, GA [*Library symbol*] [*Library of Congress*] (LCLS)
**GAu**........... Augusta-Richmond County Library, Augusta, GA [*Library symbol*] [*Library of Congress*] (LCLS)
**GAU**.......... Gauhati [*India*] [*Airport symbol*] (OAG)
**Gau**............ Gauss [*Unit of magnetic flux density*]
**GAU**.......... Gay Academic Union [*Defunct*] (EA)
**gau**............ Georgia [*MARC country of publication code*] [*Library of Congress*] (LCCP)
**GAU**.......... Glen Auden Resources Ltd. [*Toronto Stock Exchange symbol*]
**GAU**.......... Glucoamylase Unit [*Of hydrolytic enzyme activity*]
**GAU**.......... Grupos de Accion Unificadora [*Groups for Unified Action*] [*Uruguay*] (PD)
**GAU**.......... Gun Automatic (MCD)
**GAuA**......... Augusta College, Augusta, GA [*Library symbol*] [*Library of Congress*] (LCLS)
**GAuACH**... Augusta Chronicle-Herald, Augusta, GA [*Library symbol*] [*Library of Congress*] (LCLS)
**GAuAH**...... Aquinas High School, Augusta, GA [*Library symbol*] [*Library of Congress*] (LCLS)
**GAuAR**...... Academy of Richmond County, Augusta, GA [*Library symbol*] [*Library of Congress*] (LCLS)
**GAuBH**...... Butler High School, Augusta, GA [*Library symbol*] [*Library of Congress*] (LCLS)
**GAUGE**..... General Automation Users Group Exchange [*Defunct*] (EA)
**GAuJ**......... T. W. Josey High School, Augusta, GA [*Library symbol*] [*Library of Congress*] (LCLS)
**GAuL**......... Lucey C. Laney High School, Augusta, GA [*Library symbol*] [*Library of Congress*] (LCLS)
**GAuM**........ Medical College of Georgia, Augusta, GA [*Library symbol*] [*Library of Congress*] (LCLS)
**GA (UN)**.... General Assembly of the United Nations
**GAuP**......... Paine College, Augusta, GA [*Library symbol*] [*Library of Congress*] (LCLS)
**GAuRC**...... Richmond County Law Library, Augusta, GA [*Library symbol*] [*Library of Congress*] (LCLS)
**GAUSA**..... Georgian Association in USA (EA)
**GAUSD**..... Gasohol USA [*A publication*]
**GAUSS**...... [*A*] programming language [*Named after German mathematician Karl Friedrich Gauss, 1777-1855*] (CSR)
**GAUSS**...... Gravity Association for Universal Scientific Study
**Gauss Ges (Goettingen) Mitt**... Gauss Gesellschaft eV. (Goettingen). Mitteilungen [*A publication*]
**GAuU**......... University Hospital, Augusta, GA [*Library symbol*] [*Library of Congress*] (LCLS)
**GAuV-F**..... United States Veterans Administration Hospital, Forest Hills Division, Augusta, GA [*Library symbol*] [*Library of Congress*] (LCLS)
**GAuV-L**..... United States Veterans Administration Hospital, Lenwood Division, Augusta, GA [*Library symbol*] [*Library of Congress*] (LCLS)
**Gav**............ Gavroche [*A publication*]
**GAV**.......... Geschichte des Alten Vorderasien [*A publication*] (BJA)
**GAV**.......... Glen Avon [*California*] [*Seismograph station code, US Geological Survey*] (SEIS)
**GAV**.......... Gustavus, AK [*Location identifier*] [*FAA*] (FAAL)
**GAVA**........ Gavotto [*Gavotte*] [*Music*] (ROG)
**GAVA**........ United States Veterans Administration Hospital, Atlanta, GA [*Library symbol*] [*Library of Congress*] (LCLS)
**GAVEA**..... Galpin Society. Journal [*A publication*]
**Gavel**.......... Milwaukee Bar Association. Gavel [*A publication*]
**GA Vet**....... Georgia Veterinarian [*A publication*]
**Gav & H Rev St**... Gavin and Hord's Revised Indiana Statutes [*A publication*] (DLA)
**GAVRS**...... Ground Attitude Vertical Reference System [*Aviation*]
**GAW**.......... Gangaw [*Burma*] [*Airport symbol*] (OAG)
**GAW**.......... Gram Atomic Weight [*Chemistry*]
**GAW**.......... Guaranteed Annual Wage
**GAW**.......... Guided Atomic Warhead
**GAWAM**... Great American Wife and Mother [*Slang*]
**GA Water Qual Control Board Tech Rep**... Georgia. Water Quality Control Board. Technical Report [*A publication*]
**GAWF**....... General Arab Women Federation (EA)
**GAWR**....... Gross Axle Weight Rating [*Auto safety*]
**GAWS**....... German American World Society (EA)
**GAWS**....... Grandmothers of America in War Service [*World War II*]
**GAWTS**..... Genetic Amplification with Transverse Sequencing [*Genetics*]

**GAWTS**..... Genomic Amplification with Transcript Sequencing [*Genetics*]
**GAWU**....... General Agricultural Workers' Union [*Kenya*]
**GAWW**...... Woodrow Wilson College of Law, Atlanta, GA [*Library symbol*] [*Library of Congress*] (LCLS)
**GAX**.......... Gamba [*Gabon*] [*Airport symbol*] (OAG)
**GAX**.......... GAO [*General Accounting Office*] Seattle Regional Office, Seattle, WA [*OCLC symbol*] (OCLC)
**GAY**.......... Galvasay [*USSR*] [*Seismograph station code, US Geological Survey*] [*Closed*] (SEIS)
**Gay**............ Gay Liberation [*A publication*]
**GAY**.......... Government Accumulation Yard
**Gayana Bot** ... Gayana Botanica [*A publication*]
**Gayana Bot Misc** ... Gayana Botanica Miscelanea [*A publication*]
**Gayana Misc** ... Gayana Miscelanea [*A publication*]
**Gayana Zool** ... Gayana Zoologia [*A publication*]
**Gayarre**...... Gayarre's Annual Reports [*25-28 Louisiana*] [*A publication*] (DLA)
**GAYE**........ Yelimane [*Mali*] [*ICAO location identifier*] (ICLI)
**GAYIG**...... Gallium Substituted Yttrium Iron Garnet
**Gay Insrg**... Gay Insurgent [*A publication*]
**Gay L**......... Gay Literature [*A publication*]
**Gay (LA)**.... Gayarre's Annual Reports [*25-28 Louisiana*] [*A publication*] (DLA)
**Gay News**... Gay Community News [*A publication*]
**Gay Sun**..... Gay Sunshine [*A publication*]
**GAZ**.......... GAO [*General Accounting Office*] Atlanta Regional Office, Atlanta, GA [*OCLC symbol*] (OCLC)
**GAZ**.......... Gazette [*or Gazetteer*]
**GAZ**.......... General Allied Oil [*Vancouver Stock Exchange symbol*]
**GAZ**.......... Gesamtverzeichnis [*A publication*]
**GAZ**.......... Gesamtverzeichnis Auslaendischer Zeitschriften [*Cumulative List of Foreign Periodicals*]
**GAZ**.......... Globe, AZ [*Location identifier*] [*FAA*] (FAAL)
**GAZ**.......... Gruene Aktion Zukunft [*Green Action for the Future*] [*Federal Republic of Germany*] (PPW)
**Gaz**............ Weekly Law Gazette [*Ohio*] [*A publication*] (DLA)
**Gaz Agr (Angola)** ... Gazeta do Agricultor (Angola) [*A publication*]
**Gaz Apic**.... Gazette Apicole [*A publication*]
**Gaz Arch**.... Gazette Archeologique [*A publication*]
**Gaz Aujourd** ... Gaz d'Aujourd'hui [*A publication*]
**GAZ B**........ Gazette of Bankruptcy [*A publication*] (ROG)
**Gaz BA**....... Gazette des Beaux-Arts [*A publication*]
**Gaz Bank** ... Gazette of Bankruptcy [*A publication*] (DLA)
**Gaz Bank Dig** ... Gazzam's Digest of Bankruptcy Decisions [*A publication*] (DLA)
**Gaz Bankr** ... Gazette of Bankruptcy [*A publication*] (DLA)
**Gaz & BC Rep** ... Gazette and Bankrupt Court Reporter [*New York*] [*A publication*] (DLA)
**Gaz Bea-Art** ... Gazette des Beaux-Arts [*A publication*]
**Gaz Beaux-Arts** ... Gazette des Beaux-Arts [*A publication*]
**Gaz Chim It** ... Gazzetta Chimica Italiana [*A publication*]
**Gaz Chim Ital** ... Gazzetta Chimica Italiana [*A publication*]
**Gaz Clin**..... Gazeta Clinica [*A publication*]
**Gaz Clin (S Paulo)** ... Gazeta Clinica (Sao Paulo) [*A publication*]
**Gaz Com**.... Gazzetta Commerciale [*A publication*]
**Gaz Cukrow** ... Gazeta Cukrownicza [*A publication*]
**Gazdasag es Jogtud** ... Gazdasag es Jogtudomany [*A publication*]
**Gaz Egypt Paediatr Assoc** ... Gazette. Egyptian Paediatric Association [*A publication*]
**Gaz Egypt Soc Gynaecol Obstet** ... Gazette. Egyptian Society of Gynaecology and Obstetrics [*A publication*]
**Gazeta Agric Angola** ... Gazeta Agricola de Angola [*A publication*]
**Gazeta Cukrown** ... Gazeta Cukrownicza [*A publication*]
**Gazette**....... Law Society. Gazette [*A publication*]
**Gazette**....... Rhode Island Foreign Language Gazette [*A publication*]
**Gazette Univ WA** ... Gazette. University of Western Australia [*A publication*] (APTA)
**Gaz Fis**....... Gazeta di Fisica [*A publication*]
**Gaz Hebd Sc Med Bordeaux** ... Gazette Hebdomadaire des Sciences Medicales de Bordeaux [*A publication*]
**Gaz Hop Civ Mil** ... Gazette des Hopitaux Civils et Militaires [*A publication*]
**Gaz India** ... Gazette India [*A publication*]
**Gaz Inst Med Lab Sci** ... Gazette. Institute of Medical Laboratory Science [*A publication*]
**Gaz Kasr El Aini Fac Med** ... Gazette. Kasr El Aini Faculty of Medicine [*A publication*]
**Gaz LR**....... Gazette Law Reports [*New Zealand*] [*A publication*] (DLA)
**Gaz LR (NZ)** ... New Zealand Gazette Law Reports [*A publication*] (DLA)
**Gaz L Soc of Upper Can** ... Gazette. Law Society of Upper Canada [*A publication*] (DLA)
**Gaz Mat**..... Gazeta de Matematica [*A publication*]
**Gaz Mat Mat Inform** ... Gazeta Matematica Perfectionare Metodica si Metodologica in Matematica si Informatica [*A publication*]
**Gaz Mat Publ Lunara pentru Tineret** ... Gazeta Matematica Publicatie Lunara pentru Tineret [*A publication*]
**Gaz Mat Ser A** ... Societatea de Stiinte Matematice din RPR. Gazeta Matematica Publicatie pentru Studiul si Raspindirea Stiintelor Matematice. Seria A [*A publication*]
**Gaz Med**.... Gazettes Medicales [*A publication*]
**Gaz Med Algerie** ... Gazette Medicale de l'Algerie [*A publication*]
**Gaz Med Bahia** ... Gazeta Medica da Bahia [*A publication*]
**Gaz Med Fr** ... Gazette Medicale de France [*A publication*]
**Gaz Med Nantes** ... Gazette Medicale de Nantes [*A publication*]
**Gaz Med Orient** ... Gazette Medicale d'Orient [*A publication*]
**Gaz Med Paris** ... Gazette Medicale de Paris [*A publication*]
**Gaz Med Picardie** ... Gazette Medicale de Picardie [*A publication*]
**Gaz Med Port** ... Gazeta Medica Portuguesa [*A publication*]
**Gaz (Montrl)** ... Gazette (Montreal) [*A publication*]
**Gaz Mus**.... Gazeta Musical e de Todas las Artes [*A publication*]
**Gaz Num**.... Gazzettino Numismatico [*A publication*]
**Gazov Delo** ... Gazovoe Delo [*USSR*] [*A publication*]
**Gazov Khromatogr** ... Gazovaya Khromatografiya [*USSR*] [*A publication*]
**Gazov Promst** ... Gazovaya Promyshlennost [*A publication*]
**Gaz Pharm** ... Gazeta da Pharmacia [*A publication*]
**GAZS**......... Gesamtverzeichnis Auslaendischer Zeitschriften und Serien [*Cumulative List of Foreign Periodicals and Serials*]
**GAZT**........ Gemeinsamer Aussenzolltarif [*Common External Tariff*] [*German Democratic Republic*]
**Gaz Trav**.... Gazette du Travail [*A publication*]
**Gaz Uff**...... Gazzetta Ufficiale della Repubblica Italiana [*A publication*]
**Gaz Univ Newcastle** ... Gazette. University of Newcastle [*A publication*] (APTA)
**Gaz Univ Syd** ... Gazette. University of Sydney [*A publication*] (APTA)
**Gaz Univ WA** ... Gazette. University of Western Australia [*A publication*] (APTA)
**Gaz Univ Wits** ... Gazette. University of the Witwatersrand [*A publication*]
**Gaz WA Inst Tech** ... Gazette: Official Journal of the Western Australian Institute of Technology [*A publication*] (APTA)
**Gaz Woda Tech Sanit** ... Gaz Woda i Technika Sanitarna [*A publication*]
**Gaz Zan EA** ... Gazette for Zanzibar and East Africa [*A publication*] (ILCA)
**Gazz Chim Ital** ... Gazzetta Chimica Italiana [*A publication*]
**Gazz Clin Sped Civ Palermo** ... Gazzetta Clinica dello Spedale Civico di Palermo [*A publication*]
**Gazz Internaz Med** ... Gazzetta Internazionale di Medicina [*A publication*]
**Gazz Int Med Chir** ... Gazzetta Internazionale di Medicina e Chirurgia [*Italy*] [*A publication*]
**Gazz Med Ital** ... Gazzetta Medica Italiana [*A publication*]
**Gazz Med Ital Arch Sci Med** ... Gazzetta Medica Italiana. Archivio per le Scienze Mediche [*A publication*]
**Gazz Med Ital Prov Venete** ... Gazzetta Medica Italiana. Provincie Venete [*A publication*]
**Gazz Med Sicil** ... Gazzetta Medica Siciliana [*Italy*] [*A publication*]
**Gazz Osp Milano** ... Gazzetta degli Ospitali Milano [*A publication*]
**Gazz Sanit Edn Francaise** ... Gazzetta Sanitaria. Edition Francaise [*A publication*]
**Gazz Sanit (Engl Issue)** ... Gazzetta Sanitaria (English Issue) [*A publication*]
**Gazz Sicil Med e Chir** ... Gazzetta Siciliana di Medicina e Chirurgia d'Igiene e d'Interessi Professionali [*A publication*]
**Gazz Uff Repub Ital** ... Gazzetta Ufficiale della Repubblica Italiana [*A publication*]
**GB**............. G & B Automated Equipment Ltd. [*Toronto Stock Exchange symbol*]
**GB**............. Gain Bandwidth (DEN)
**GB**............. Galaxy Books [*Oxford University Press*]
**GB**............. Gall Bladder [*or a patient with an affliction of this organ*] [*Medicine*]
**GB**............. Games Behind [*Baseball*]
**GB**............. Ganzer Bogen [*Full Bow*] [*Music*]
**GB**............. Gardner's Books Ltd. [*British*]
**GB**............. Gemeinde Berlin (BJA)
**GB**............. Gemini B
**GB**............. General Background
**GB**............. General Board [*Military judicial or investigative body*]
**GB**............. General Bronze Corp. (MCD)
**GB**............. Geschichtsbetrachtung und Geschichtliche Ueberlieferung bei den Vorexilischen Propheten [*A publication*] (BJA)
**GB**............. Geschiedkundige Bladen [*A publication*]
**Gb**............. Gibbsite [*A mineral*]
**Gb**............. GigaBIT [*Binary Digit*] [*$10^9$ BITs*]
**GB**............. Gigabyte [*$10^9$ bytes*]
**Gb**............. Gilbert [*A unit of magnetomotive force*] (CET)
**gb**.............. Gilbert Islands [*gn (Gilbert and Ellice Islands) used in records cataloged before October 1978*] [*MARC country of publication code*] [*Library of Congress*] (LCCP)
**Gb**............. Gildeboek [*A publication*]
**GB**............. Ginzburg's Bible [*New Massoretico-Critical Text of the Hebrew Bible*] [*A publication*] (BJA)
**GB**............. Glass Bowl
**GB**............. Glide Bomb [*Air Force*]
**G & B**......... Gloucester and Bristol [*Diocese*] (ROG)
**GB**............. Gold Bond [*Bond payable in gold coin*]
**GB**............. [*The*] Golden Bough [*A publication*] (OCD)
**GB**............. Good-By [*Amateur radio*]
**GB**............. Goofball [*Barbiturate pill*]
**G & B**......... Gordon & Breach [*Publisher*] [*British*]
**GB**............. Gouvernementsblad van Suriname [*A publication*]
**GB**............. Governing Body
**G/B**........... Government Boat
**GB**............. Government Bunkers
**GB**............. Grab Bar [*Technical drawings*]
**G and B**...... Grafton and Belington Railroad [*Initialism refers to a settlement of Indians who lived near this railroad*]

**GB**............ Grain Bulletin [*A publication*]
**GB**............ Grand Bounce [*Suspension or dismissal*] [*Slang*]
**GB**............ Grassland Biome [*Ecological biogeographic study*]
**GB**............ Grazer Beitraege [*A publication*]
**GB**............ Great Books
**GB**............ Great Britain [*International automobile identification tag*]
**GB**............ Green Belt Act [*Town planning*] [*British*]
**GB**............ Greenhouse Biennial [*Horticulture*] (ROG)
**GB**............ Greenish Blue
**GB**............ Grid Bearing [*Navigation*]
**GB**............ Grid Bias (DEN)
**GB**............ Griffiths & Bedell's [*System of stud tramways*] [*British*] (ROG)
**GB**............ Grounded Base
**GB**............ Grundbuch [*Land Register*] [*German*] (ILCA)
**GB**............ Guaranteed Bond [*Business term*]
**GB**............ Guardbridge Papers [*Manufacturer*] [*British*]
**GB**............ Guardian Bancorp [*AMEX symbol*] (SPSG)
**GB**............ Guidebook
**GB**............ Guillain-Barre [*Syndrome*] [*Medicine*]
**GB**............ Gun Board [*British*]
**GB**............ Gun-Bus [*Gun-carrying plane*] [*Air Force*] [*British*]
**GB**............ Gunboat [*Naval*]
**GB**............ Sarin [*Nerve gas*] [*Army symbol*]
**GB**............ Transports Aereos da-Guines-Bissau [*Guinea*] [*ICAO designator*] (FAAC)
**GB**............ United Kingdom [*ANSI two-letter standard code*] (CNC)
**GB**............ Weekblad voor Gemeentebelangen [*A publication*]
**GBA**.......... Ganglionic-Blocking Agent [*Medicine*]
**GBA**.......... Gauribidanur Array [*India*] [*Seismograph station code, US Geological Survey*] (SEIS)
**GBA**.......... Gazette des Beaux-Arts [*A publication*]
**GBA**.......... Gesetzbuch der Arbeit [*Labor Code*] [*German Democratic Republic*]
**GBA**.......... Gingivobuccoaxial [*Dentistry*]
**GBA**.......... Give Better Address [*Communications*]
**GBA**.......... Global Alert System [*Vancouver Stock Exchange symbol*]
**GBA**.......... Governing Bodies Association [*Organization of school officials*] [*British*]
**GBA**.......... Grammatik des Biblische-Aramaeischen [*A publication*] (BJA)
**GBA**.......... Gross Building Area (ADA)
**GB & A**...... Grosvenor Barber and Associates (IID)
**GBA**.......... Grundbuchamt [*Land Registry*] [*German*] (ILCA)
**GBaB**......... Bainbridge Junior College, Bainbridge, GA [*Library symbol*] [*Library of Congress*] (LCLS)
**GB Aeronaut Res Counc Curr Pap** ... Great Britain. Aeronautical Research Council. Current Papers [*A publication*]
**GBAN**........ Gateway Bancorp, Inc. [*Staten Island, NY*] [*NASDAQ symbol*] (NQ)
**GBAO**........ Graham Bond Appreciators Organization (EA)
**GBAPS**...... Governing Bodies Association of Public Schools [*British*]
**GBaS**......... Southwest Georgia Regional Library, Bainbridge, GA [*Library symbol*] [*Library of Congress*] (LCLS)
**GBAT**........ Graduate Business Admission Test
**G Batteriol Immunol** ... Giornale di Batteriologia e Immunologia [*A publication*]
**G Batteriol Virol Immunol** ... Giornale di Batteriologia, Virologia, ed Immunologia [*A publication*]
**G Batteriol Virol Immunol Ann Osp Maria Vittoria Torino** ... Giornale di Batteriologia, Virologia, ed Immunologia. Annali dell'Ospedale Maria Vittoria di Torino [*A publication*]
**G Batteriol Virol Immunol Clin** ... Giornale di Batteriologia, Virologia, ed Immunologia. Annali dell'Ospedale Maria Vittoria di Torino. Parte 2. Sezione Clinica [*A publication*]
**G de Bay**..... Guido de Baysio [*Deceased, 1313*] [*Authority cited in pre-1607 legal work*] (DSA)
**GBAYA**..... Greate Bay Casino Cl A [*NASDAQ symbol*] (NQ)
**GBB**.......... Gay Books Bulletin [*A publication*]
**GBB**.......... General Banner Bearer [*Freemasonry*] (ROG)
**GBB**.......... Guild of British Butlers [*London, England*] (EAIO)
**GBBA**........ Glass Bottle Blowers Association of the United States and Canada [*Later, GPPAW*]
**GB/BHE**.... Gesamtdeutscher Block/Bund der Heimatvertriebenen und Entrechteten [*All-German Bloc/Association of Homeless and Disenfranchised*] (PPE)
**GBBS**......... Great Bay Bankshares, Inc. [*NASDAQ symbol*] (NQ)
**GBC**.......... Berry College, Mount Berry, GA [*OCLC symbol*] (OCLC)
**GBC**.......... General Binding Corp.
**GBC**.......... Gold-Braid Chaser [*Refers to a woman who dates only officers*] [*Slang*] [*British*] (DSUE)
**GBC**.......... Greenland Base Command
**GBC**.......... Ground-Based Computer
**GBC**.......... Guantanamo Bay [*Cuba*] [*Seismograph station code, US Geological Survey*] [*Closed*] (SEIS)
**GBCB**......... GBC Bancorp [*NASDAQ symbol*] (NQ)
**GBCC**........ GBC Closed Circuit TV Corp. [*NASDAQ symbol*] (NQ)
**GBCC**........ Great Britain Collectors Club (EA)
**GBCI**......... Glacier Bancorp, Inc. [*NASDAQ symbol*] (SPSG)
**GBCSCMC** ... General Board of Christian Social Concerns of the Methodist Church (EA)
**GBCW**....... Governing Body of the Church in Wales (DAS)
**GBD**.......... Gale's Business Directory [*A publication*]
**GBD**.......... Gamma Ray Burst Detector [*Instrumentation*]
**GBD**.......... General Board
**GBD**.......... Grain Boundary Dislocation
**GBD**.......... Great Bear Development [*Vancouver Stock Exchange symbol*]
**GBD**.......... Great Bend [*Kansas*] [*Airport symbol*] (OAG)
**GBDC**........ General Builders Corporation [*NASDAQ symbol*] (NQ)
**GB Dep Health Soc Secur Rep Public Health Med Subj** ... Great Britain. Department of Health and Social Security. Reports on Public Health and Medical Subjects [*A publication*]
**GB Dep Sci Ind Res Chem Res Spec Rep** ... Great Britain. Department of Scientific and Industrial Research. Chemical Research. Special Report [*A publication*]
**GB Dep Sci Ind Res Food Invest Board Spec Rep** ... Great Britain. Department of Scientific and Industrial Research. Food Investigation Board. Special Report [*A publication*]
**GB Dep Sci Ind Res Food Invest Tech Pap** ... Great Britain. Department of Scientific and Industrial Research. Food Investigation Board. Technical Paper [*A publication*]
**GB Dep Sci Ind Res For Prod Res Bull** ... Great Britain. Department of Scientific and Industrial Research. Forest Products Research Bulletin [*A publication*]
**GB Dep Sci Ind Res For Prod Res Spec Rep** ... Great Britain. Department of Scientific and Industrial Research. Forest Products Research Special Report [*A publication*]
**GB Dep Sci Ind Res Fuel Res** ... Great Britain. Department of Scientific and Industrial Research. Fuel Research. Publication [*A publication*]
**GB Dep Sci Ind Res Fuel Res Surv Pap** ... Great Britain. Department of Scientific and Industrial Research. Fuel Research. Survey Paper [*A publication*]
**GB Dep Sci Ind Res Fuel Res Tech Pap** ... Great Britain. Department of Scientific and Industrial Research. Fuel Research. Technical Paper [*A publication*]
**GB Dep Sci Ind Res Natl Build Stud Res Pap** ... Great Britain. Department of Scientific and Industrial Research. National Building Studies Research Paper [*A publication*]
**GB Dep Sci Ind Res Overseas Tech Rep** ... Great Britain. Department of Scientific and Industrial Research. Overseas Technical Report [*A publication*]
**GB Dep Sci Ind Res Road Note** ... Great Britain. Department of Scientific and Industrial Research. Road Note [*A publication*]
**GB Dep Sci Ind Res Road Res Lab Rep RRL** ... Great Britain. Department of Scientific and Industrial Research. Road Research Laboratory. Report RRL [*A publication*]
**GB Dep Sci Ind Res Torry Res Stn Annu Rep** ... Great Britain. Department of Scientific and Industrial Research. Torry Research Station. Annual Report [*A publication*]
**GB Dep Sci Ind Res Torry Tech Pap** ... Great Britain. Department of Scientific and Industrial Research. Torry Technical Paper [*A publication*]
**GB Dep Trade Ind Warren Spring Lab Rev** ... Great Britain. Department of Trade and Industry. Warren Spring Laboratory. Review [*A publication*]
**GB Digest**.. GB Digest (Girls' Brigade) [*A publication*] (APTA)
**GBDP**........ Giessener Beitraege zur Deutschen Philologie [*A publication*]
**GBDV**........ Gate Breakdown Voltage
**GBE**.......... Dame Grand Cross of the Order of the British Empire (ADA)
**GBE**.......... Gaborone [*Botswana*] [*Airport symbol*] (OAG)
**GBE**.......... Gilt Beveled Edges [*Bookbinding*]
**GBE**.......... Ginkgo Biloba Extract [*Biochemistry*]
**GBE**.......... Goal-Based Evaluation
**GBE**.......... Great Britain and the East [*A publication*]
**GBE**.......... Grubb & Ellis Co. [*NYSE symbol*] (SPSG)
**GBE**.......... Knight Grand Cross of the [*Order of the*] British Empire
**GBERL**...... Gulf Breeze Environmental Research Laboratory [*Environmental Protection Agency*] (MSC)
**GBF**.......... Geographic Base File [*Civil Defense*]
**GBF**.......... Grand Ballon [*France*] [*Seismograph station code, US Geological Survey*] [*Closed*] (SEIS)
**GBF**.......... Great Bear Foundation (EA)
**GBF**.......... Great Books Foundation (EA)
**GBF**.......... Ground-Based Field
**GBFEL**...... Ground Based Free Electron LASER Proposal
**GBFH**........ Georgia Bonded Fibers, Inc. [*NASDAQ symbol*] (NQ)
**GB For Comm Annu Rep For Comm** ... Great Britain. Forestry Commission. Annual Report of the Forestry Commissioners [*A publication*]
**GB For Comm Bookl** ... Great Britain. Forestry Commission. Booklet [*A publication*]
**GB For Comm Bull** ... Great Britain. Forestry Commission. Bulletin [*A publication*]
**GB For Comm For Rec** ... Great Britain. Forestry Commission. Forest Record [*A publication*]
**GB For Comm Leafl** ... Great Britain. Forestry Commission. Leaflet [*A publication*]
**GB For Comm Occas Pap** ... Great Britain. Forestry Commission. Occasional Paper [*A publication*]
**GB For Comm Rep For Res** ... Great Britain. Forestry Commission. Report on Forest Research [*A publication*]
**GB For Comm Res Dev Pap** ... Great Britain. Forestry Commission. Research and Development Paper [*A publication*]

**GB For Prod Res Board Bull** ... Great Britain. Forest Products Research Board. Bulletin [*A publication*]
**GB For Prod Res Bull** ... Great Britain. Forest Products Research Bulletin [*A publication*]
**GB For Prod Res Spec Rep** ... Great Britain. Forest Products Research Special Report [*A publication*]
**GBG**........... Galesburg [*Illinois*] [*Airport symbol*] (OAG)
**GBG**........... Garbage (MSA)
**GBG**........... Glycine-Rich Beta-Globulin [*Immunology*]
**GBG**........... Good Book Guide [*A publication*]
**GBG**........... Governor's Bodyguard [*British military*] (DMA)
**GBG**........... Greensboro [*Georgia*] [*Seismograph station code, US Geological Survey*] (SEIS)
**GBGPGS**... Groupe Bakounine-Gdansk-Paris-Guatemala-Salvador [*Bakunin-Gdansk-Paris-Guatemala-Salvador Group*] [*French*] (PD)
**GBGSA**...... Governing Body of Girls' Schools Association [*British*]
**GBH**........... Galbraith Lake, AK [*Location identifier*] [*FAA*] (FAAL)
**GBH**........... Gamma Benzene Hexachloride [*Also, BHC, HCH*] [*Insecticide*]
**GBH**........... Garbell Holdings Ltd. [*Toronto Stock Exchange symbol*]
**GBH**........... Gas Bath Heater [*Classified advertising*] (ADA)
**GBH**........... Grievous Body Harm
**GBH**........... Group Busy Hour [*Telecommunications*] (TEL)
**GBHA**........ Glyoxal Bis(o-hydroxyanil) [*An indicator*] [*Chemistry*]
**GBHP**........ Gross Brake Horsepower (MCD)
**GBHRG**..... Ground-Based Hypervelocity Rail Gun [*Military*] (SDI)
**GBI**............ Buffalo, NY [*Location identifier*] [*FAA*] (FAAL)
**GBI**............ Gabriel Resources, Inc. [*Vancouver Stock Exchange symbol*]
**GBI**............ Gesellschaft fuer Betriebswirtschaftliche Information mbH [*Society for Business Information*] [*Federal Republic of Germany*] [*Database producer*]
**GBI**............ Global Brain Ischemia
**GBI**............ Grace Bible Institute [*Nebraska*]
**GBI**............ Granada BioSciences [*AMEX symbol*] (SPSG)
**GBI**............ Grand Bahama Island (KSC)
**GB & I**........ Great Britain and Ireland
**GBI**............ Gridlays Bank International Zambia Ltd.
**GBI**............ Ground Backup Instrument (MUGU)
**GBI**............ Guanidinebenzimidazole [*Biochemistry*]
**GBII**........... GBI International Industries, Inc. [*West Babylon, NY*] [*NASDAQ symbol*] (NQ)
**GBII**........... Ground-Based Infrared Instrumentation
**GBIIS**......... Ground-Based Infrared Instrumentation System
**GB Inst Geol Sci Annu Rep** ... Great Britain. Institute of Geological Sciences. Annual Report [*A publication*]
**GB Inst Geol Sci Geomagn Bull** ... Great Britain. Institute of Geological Sciences. Geomagnetic Bulletin [*A publication*]
**GB Inst Geol Sci Miner Assess Rep** ... Great Britain. Institute of Geological Sciences. Mineral Assessment Report [*A publication*]
**GB Inst Geol Sci Miner Resour Consult Comm Miner Dossier** ... Great Britain. Institute of Geological Sciences. Mineral Resources Consultative Committee. Mineral Dossier [*A publication*]
**GB Inst Geol Sci Overseas Mem** ... Great Britain. Institute of Geological Sciences. Overseas Memoir [*A publication*]
**GB Inst Geol Sci Rep** ... Great Britain. Institute of Geological Sciences. Report [*A publication*]
**G Biochim** ... Giornale di Biochimica [*A publication*]
**G Biol Ind Agrar Aliment** ... Giornale di Biologia Industriale Agraria ed Alimentare [*A publication*]
**G Biol Med Sper** ... Giornale di Biologia e Medicina Sperimentale [*A publication*]
**GBiP**.......... German Books in Print [*A publication*]
**GBISAX**.... Godisnik na Bioloskog Instituta Univerziteta u Sarajevu [*A publication*]
**GBIU**......... Geoballistic Input Unit
**GBJ**........... Georgia Bar Journal [*A publication*]
**GBJ**........... Glass Bell Jar
**GBJ**........... Jersey [*Great Britain*]
**GBJ**........... Marie Galante [*French Antilles*] [*Airport symbol*] (OAG)
**GBK**........... Gbangbatok [*Sierra Leone*] [*Airport symbol*] (OAG)
**GBKG**......... Gentsche Bijdragen tot de Kunstgeschiedenis [*A publication*]
**GBKMA**.... Gesellschaft zur Bekampfung der Krebskrankheiten im Nordrhein-Westfalen. Mitteilungsdienst [*A publication*]
**GBL**........... Brandstoffen Visie. Vakblad voor de Mandel in Aardolieprodukten en Vaste Brandstoffen [*A publication*]
**GBL**........... Gable Mountain [*Washington*] [*Seismograph station code, US Geological Survey*] (SEIS)
**GBL**........... Games behind Leader [*Baseball*]
**GBL**........... Gamma Biologicals, Inc. [*AMEX symbol*] (SPSG)
**GBL**........... Gamma-Butyrolactone [*Organic chemistry*]
**GBL**........... General Bearing Line [*Navy*] (NVT)
**GBl**............ Gesetzblatt [*Gazette*] [*German*] (DLA)
**GBL**........... Goldenbell Resources, Inc. [*Toronto Stock Exchange symbol*] [*Vancouver Stock Exchange symbol*]
**GBL**........... Goulburn Island [*Australia*] [*Airport symbol*] [*Obsolete*] (OAG)
**GBL**........... Government Bill of Lading
**GBL**........... Ground-Based LASER (MCD)
**GBL**........... Guide to Baseball Literature [*A publication*]
**GBLADING** ... Government Bill of Lading
**GB Land Resour Dev Cent Land Resour Study** ... Great Britain. Land Resources Development Centre. Land Resource Study [*A publication*]
**GB Land Resour Div Land Resour Bibliogr** ... Great Britain. Land Resources Division. Land Resource Bibliography [*A publication*]
**GB Land Resour Div Land Resour Study** ... Great Britain. Land Resources Division. Land Resource Study [*A publication*]
**GBLD**........ General Building Products Corp. [*NASDAQ symbol*] (NQ)
**GBl II**......... Gesetzblatt der DDR. Teil II [*German Democratic Republic*] [*A publication*]
**GBLN**........ Goldenbell Resources, Inc. [*NASDAQ symbol*] (NQ)
**GBLOC**...... Government Bill of Lading Office Code (AFIT)
**GBM**.......... Gain Band Merit
**GBM**.......... Galilean Baptist Mission (EA)
**GBM**.......... Gelre. Bijdragen en Mededeelingen [*A publication*]
**GBM**.......... Gibraltar Mines Ltd. [*Toronto Stock Exchange symbol*] [*Vancouver Stock Exchange symbol*]
**GBM**.......... Glass-Bonded Mica
**GBM**.......... Glomerular Basement Membrane [*Medicine*]
**GBM**.......... Glycerine Ball Memory
**GBM**.......... Golden Book Magazine [*A publication*]
**GBM**.......... Granite Butte [*Montana*] [*Seismograph station code, US Geological Survey*] [*Closed*] (SEIS)
**GBM**.......... Grape Berry Moth
**GBM**.......... Greater Britain Movement [*British*]
**GBM**.......... Isle Of Man (Great Britain)
**GBMA**....... Golf Ball Manufacturers Association (EA)
**GBMA**....... Great Britain Ministry of Aviation
**GBMC**....... Grain Bin Manufacturers Council [*Later, GEMC*] (EA)
**GBMD**....... Global Ballistic Missile Defense
**GBMI**........ Ground-Based Midcourse Interceptor [*Military*] (SDI)
**GBMI**........ Guilty-but-Mentally-Ill [*Legal term*]
**GB Minist Agric Fish Food Bull** ... Great Britain. Ministry of Agriculture, Fisheries, and Food. Bulletin [*A publication*]
**GB Minist Agric Fish Food Dir Fish Res Fish Res Tech Rep** ... Great Britain. Ministry of Agriculture, Fisheries, and Food. Directorate of Fisheries Research. Fisheries Research. Technical Report [*A publication*]
**GB Minist Agric Fish Food Dir Fish Res Lab Leafl** ... Great Britain. Ministry of Agriculture, Fisheries, and Food. Directorate of Fisheries Research. Laboratory Leaflet [*A publication*]
**GB Minist Agric Fish Food Tech Bull** ... Great Britain. Ministry of Agriculture, Fisheries, and Food. Technical Bulletin [*A publication*]
**GB Minist Aviat Aeronaut Res Counc Curr Pap** ... Great Britain. Ministry of Aviation. Aeronautic Research Council. Current Papers [*A publication*]
**GB Minist Overseas Dev Land Resour Div Land Resour Bibliogr** ... Great Britain. Ministry of Overseas Development. Land Resources Division. Land Resource Bibliography [*A publication*]
**GB Minist Overseas Dev Land Resour Div Prog Rep** ... Great Britain. Ministry of Overseas Development. Land Resources Division. Progress Report [*A publication*]
**GB Minist Power Saf Mines Res Establ Res Rep** ... Great Britain. Ministry of Power. Safety in Mines Research Establishment. Research Report [*A publication*]
**GB Ministry Agric Fish Food Fish Lab Leafl New Ser** ... Great Britain. Ministry of Agriculture, Fisheries, and Food. Fisheries Laboratory Leaflet. New Series [*A publication*]
**GB Minist Technol For Prod Res Bull** ... Great Britain. Ministry of Technology. Forest Products Research. Bulletin [*A publication*]
**GB Minist Technol For Prod Res Spec Rep** ... Great Britain. Ministry of Technology. Forest Products Research. Special Report [*A publication*]
**GBM-rAb**.. Glomerular Basement Membrane-Reactive Antibodies [*Immunology*]
**GBN**........... Gila Bend, AZ [*Location identifier*] [*FAA*] (FAAL)
**GBN**........... Golden Band Resources [*Vancouver Stock Exchange symbol*]
**GB Nat Build Stud Res Pap** ... Great Britain. National Building Studies. Research Paper [*A publication*]
**GB Nat Build Stud Tech Pap** ... Great Britain. National Building Studies. Technical Paper [*A publication*]
**GB Nat Environ Res Counc News J** ... Great Britain. Natural Environment Research Council. News Journal [*A publication*]
**GB Nat Environ Res Counc Rep** ... Great Britain. Natural Environment Research Council. Report [*A publication*]
**GBNBA7**... Geologische Blaetter fuer Nordost-Bayern und Angrenzende Gebiete [*A publication*]
**GBNC**........ Guaranty Bancshares Corporation [*Shamokin, PA*] [*NASDAQ symbol*] (NQ)
**GBND**........ General Binding Corp. [*NASDAQ symbol*] (NQ)
**GBO**........... Goods in Bad Order
**GBOD**........ [*P.*] Gustave Brunet and [*Joseph*] Octave Delepierre [*Pseudonym also said to be a play on the French word "Gebeode"*]
**GBOIA**...... Giornale Botanico Italiano [*A publication*]
**GBOSBU**... Geobios [*Jodhpur*] [*A publication*]
**G Bot Ital**... Giornale Botanico Italiano [*A publication*]

**GBowdC**..... Bowdon College, Bowdon, GA [*Library symbol*] [*Library of Congress*] [*Obsolete*] (LCLS)
**GBP**.......... Gain-Bandwidth Product
**GBP**.......... Galactose-Binding Protein [*Biochemistry*]
**GBP**.......... Gas Bearing Part
**GBP**.......... Gastric Bypass [*Surgery*]
**GBP**.......... Global Asset Portfolio, Inc. [*AMEX symbol*] (CTT)
**GBP**.......... Glycophorin Binding Protein [*Biochemistry*]
**GBP**.......... Great Britain Pound [*Banking*]
**GBP**.......... Great British Public
**GBP**.......... Guinea-Bissau Peso [*Monetary unit*]
**GBPA**......... Gettysburg Battlefield Preservation Association [*Defunct*] (EA)
**GBPC**......... Gold Bondholders Protective Council (EA)
**GB Pest Infest Res Board Rep** ... Great Britain. Pest Infestation Research Board. Report [*A publication*]
**GBPS**......... GigaBIT [*Binary Digits*] per Second [*Transmission rate*] [*Data processing*] (TSSD)
**GBPUA6** ... Geological Bulletin. Punjab University [*A publication*]
**GBQMAL** ... Genie Biologique et Medical [*A publication*]
**GBR**.......... Gas-Cooled Breeder Reactor [*Nuclear energy*] (NRCH)
**GBR**.......... Gemengde Branche. Vakblad voor de Huishoudelijke en Luxe Artikelen, Glas, Porselein, Aardewerk, en Kunstnijverheid [*A publication*]
**GBR**.......... Give Better Reference [*Communications*]
**GBR**.......... Glass Bead Rating (MCD)
**GBR**.......... Glutathione Bicarbonate Ringer [*Solution mixture*]
**GBR**.......... Golden Bear Resources Ltd. [*Vancouver Stock Exchange symbol*]
**GBR**.......... Grain Boundary Relaxation
**GBR**.......... Great Barrier Reef [*Australia*] (ADA)
**GBR**.......... Great Barrington, MA [*Location identifier*] [*FAA*] (FAAL)
**GBR**.......... Ground-Based Radiometer
**GBR**.......... Gun, Bomb, and Rocket
**GBR**.......... United Kingdom [*ANSI three-letter standard code*] (CNC)
**GB R Aircr Establ Tech Rep** ... Great Britain. Royal Aircraft Establishment. Technical Report [*A publication*]
**GB Road Res Lab Road Note** ... Great Britain. Road Research Laboratory. Road Note [*A publication*]
**GB Road Res Lab Road Tech Pap** ... Great Britain. Road Research Laboratory. Road Research Technical Paper [*A publication*]
**GBRP**......... General Bending Response Program [*Computer*] [*Navy*]
**GBRP**......... Giessener Beitraege zur Romanischen Philologie [*A publication*]
**GBru**......... Brunswick Regional Library, Brunswick, GA [*Library symbol*] [*Library of Congress*] (LCLS)
**GBruJC**..... Brunswick Junior College, Brunswick, GA [*Library symbol*] [*Library of Congress*] (LCLS)
**GBS**.......... Gall Bladder Series [*Radiography*]
**GBS**.......... Gallbladder Stone [*Medicine*]
**GBS**.......... Gas Bearing System (KSC)
**GBS**.......... Gas Bioassay System [*NASA*]
**GBS**.......... George Bernard Shaw [*Irish-born playwright, 1856-1950*]
**GBS**.......... Glasgow Bibliographical Society [*A publication*]
**GBS**.......... Glycine-Buffered Saline [*Microbiology*]
**GBS**.......... Government Bureau of Standards
**GBS**.......... Grain Boundary Segregation [*Metallurgy*]
**GBS**.......... Granular Boundary Segregation [*Petrology*]
**GBS**.......... Great Big Star [*in the movies*]
**G & BS**...... Greek and Byzantine Studies [*A publication*]
**GBS**.......... Ground-Based Scanner
**GBS**.......... Ground-Based Software (MCD)
**GBS**.......... Ground Beacon System (MCD)
**GBS**.......... Group B Streptococci [*Medicine*]
**GBS**.......... Guillain-Barre Syndrome [*Medicine*]
**GBSCA**...... Greater Blouse and Skirt Contractors Association [*Later, GBSUA*] (EA)
**GBSFI**....... Guillain-Barre Syndrome Foundation International (EA)
**GBSM**........ Graduate of the Birmingham School of Music [*British*] (DBQ)
**GBSM**........ Guild of Better Shoe Manufacturers
**GB Soil Surv Engl Wales Annu Rep** ... Great Britain. Soil Survey of England and Wales. Annual Report [*A publication*]
**GB Soil Surv Spec Surv** ... Great Britain. Soil Survey. Special Survey [*A publication*]
**GBSR**........ Graphite-Moderated Boiling and Superheating Reactor
**GBSS**........ Gey's Balanced Salt Solution [*Medium*] [*Cell culture*]
**GBSSG**...... Guillain-Barre Syndrome Support Group [*Later, GBSFI*] (EA)
**GBSSGI**..... Guillain-Barre Syndrome Support Group International [*Later, GBSFI*] (EA)
**GBST**........ Grassi Block Substitution Test [*Psychology*]
**GBSUA**...... Greater Blouse, Skirt, and Undergarment Association (EA)
**GBT**.......... Der Babylonische Talmud [*Goldschmidt*] [*A publication*] (BJA)
**GBT**.......... Generalized Burst Trapping
**GBT**.......... Graded Base Transistor
**GBT**.......... Great Bustard Trust [*An association*] (EA)
**GBT**.......... Ground-Based Telemetry
**GBT**.......... Gunboat
**GBTBC**...... Graham Brothers Truck and Bus Club (EA)
**GBTI**......... Gray-Body Temperature Index [*for thermal ecology of lizards*]
**GBTS**......... Gold Beaters' Trade Society [*A union*] [*British*]
**GBU**.......... Geschichtsbetrachtung und Geschichtliche Ueberlieferung bei den Vorexilischen Propheten [*A publication*] (BJA)
**GBU**.......... Glide Bomb Unit [*Air Force*] (MCD)
**GBU**.......... Groupes Bibliques Universitaires [*University Biblical Groups*] [*Canada*]
**GBU**.......... Guided Bomb Unit (MCD)
**GBV**.......... Gate Breakdown Voltage
**GBV**.......... Gibb River [*Australia*] [*Airport symbol*] [*Obsolete*] (OAG)
**GBV**.......... Globe Ball Valve
**GBV**.......... Green Bank [*West Virginia*] [*Seismograph station code, US Geological Survey*] (SEIS)
**GBVCAG**... Giornale di Batteriologia, Virologia, ed Immunologia. Annali dell'Ospedale Maria Vittoria di Torino. Parte II. Sezione Clinica [*A publication*]
**GBVID**....... Giornale di Batteriologia, Virologia, ed Immunologia [*A publication*]
**GBviz**........ Gall Bladder Visualization [*Medicine*]
**GBVMAC**... Giornale di Batteriologia, Virologia, ed Immunologia. Annali dell'Ospedale Maria Vittoria di Torino. Parte I. Sezione Microbiologia [*A publication*]
**GBW**.......... Good Bears of the World (EA)
**GBW**.......... Green Bay & Western Railroad Co. [*AAR code*]
**GB & W**..... Green Bay & Western Railroad Co.
**GBW**.......... Guild of Book Workers (EA)
**GB Warren Spring Lab Rep** ... Great Britain. Warren Spring Laboratory. Report [*A publication*]
**GB Warren Spring Lab Rev** ... Great Britain. Warren Spring Laboratory. Review [*A publication*]
**GB Water Resour Board Publ** ... Great Britain. Water Resource Board. Publication [*A publication*]
**GBX**.......... GBX Resources [*Vancouver Stock Exchange symbol*]
**GBY**.......... Giant Bay Resources Ltd. [*Toronto Stock Exchange symbol*]
**G-B-Y**........ God Bless You
**GBY**.......... Green Bay Aviation [*Green Bay, WI*] [*FAA designator*] (FAAC)
**GBYD**........ Banjul [*Gambia*] [*ICAO location identifier*] (ICLI)
**GBYL**......... Giant Bay Resources Ltd. [*NASDAQ symbol*] (NQ)
**GBZ**.......... Gibraltar
**GBZ**.......... Great Barrier [*New Zealand*] [*Seismograph station code, US Geological Survey*] (SEIS)
**GBZ**.......... Great Barrier Island [*Australia*] [*Airport symbol*] (OAG)
**GBZ**.......... Tampa, FL [*Location identifier*] [*FAA*] (FAAL)
**GBZUA**..... Gidrobiologicheskii Zhurnal [*A publication*]
**GBZUAM** ... Gidrobiologicheskii Zhurnal [*A publication*]
**GC**............. Gain Control
**GC**............. Galactic Center
**GC**............. Galactocerebroside [*Biochemistry*]
**GC**............. Galvanized Corrugated [*Metal industry*]
**GC**............. Game Conservancy [*British*]
**GC**............. Ganglion Cell [*Medicine*]
**GC**............. Garbage Collection [*Slang*] [*Data processing*]
**GC**............. Garrison Company [*British military*] (DMA)
**GC**............. Gas Chromatograph [*or Chromatography*]
**GC**............. Gas Council [*British*]
**GC**............. Gastrocnemius [*A muscle*]
**GC**............. Gavel Clubs (EA)
**GC**............. Gel Chromatography
**GC**............. General Circular
**GC**............. General Code [*A publication*] (DLA)
**GC**............. General Condition [*Medicine*]
**GC**............. General Contractor [*Technical drawings*]
**GC**............. General Control
**GC**............. General Counsel
**GC**............. General Cover [*Insurance*]
**GC**............. General Cueing
**GC**............. Generative Cell [*Botany*]
**GC**............. Generic Code (AFM)
**GC**............. Geneva Convention Relative to Protection of Civilian Persons in Time of War [*Army*] (AABC)
**GC**............. Gentleman Cadet [*British*]
**GC**............. Geopolitical Code [*Military*] (AFIT)
**GC**............. George Cross [*British*]
**GC**............. Geriatric Care
**GC**............. Germinal Center [*Immunochemistry*]
**Gc**............. Gigacycle [*Measurement*]
**GC**............. Gimbal Case (KSC)
**GC**............. Gin Cocktail [*Slang*]
**GC**............. Girls' College (ADA)
**GC**............. Glass Capillary
**GC**............. Glassy Carbon
**GC**............. Gliding Club [*British*] (ADA)
**GC**............. Glucocorticoid [*Endocrinology*]
**GC**............. Gnome Club (EA)
**GC**............. Gold Coast [*Later, Ghana*] (ROG)
**GC**............. Golden Companions [*An association*] (EA)
**GC**............. Goldsmith's College [*London, England*]
**GC**............. Golf Club
**GC**............. Gonococcal [*Clinical chemistry*]
**GC**............. Gonorrhea Case [*Medical slang*]
**G & C**......... Gonville and Caius College [*Cambridge University*] (ROG)

**gc**............... Good Condition [*Doll collecting*]
**GC**............... Good Conduct [*Military decoration*]
**G & C**........ Goodrich and Clincher (ROG)
**GC**............... Government Communications (TEL)
**GC**............... Government Contractor
**GC**............... Government Contribution
**GC**............... Governors' Conference
**Gc**............... Gradational, Calcareous [*Soil*]
**GC**............... Graham Center [*An association*] (EA)
**GC**............... Graham County Railroad Co. [*AAR code*]
**GC**............... Grain Count [*Measurement of cell labeling*]
**GC**............... Grain Cubic (DS)
**GC**............... Grand Canyon [*Arizona*]
**GC**............... Grand Chancellor
**GC**............... Grand Chaplain
**GC**............... Grand Chapter
**GC**............... Grand Commander
**GC**............... Grand Conductor
**GC**............... Grand Council [*Freemasonry*] (ROG)
**GC**............... Grand Cross
**GC**............... Grantsmanship Center (EA)
**GC**............... Granular Cast [*Medicine*]
**GC**............... Granulocyte Cytotoxic [*Hematology*]
**GC**............... Granulosa Cells [*Cytology*]
**GC**............... Graphic Communications Weekly [*A publication*]
**GC**............... Graphics Conferencing (MCD)
**GC**............... Great Central Railway [*British*] (ROG)
**GC**............... Great Churchmen [*A publication*]
**GC**............... Great Circle
**GC**............... Greek Church (ROG)
**GC**............... Green Currency [*EEC*]
**GC**............... Greenland Cruiser
**GC**............... Grid Course [*Navigation*]
**GC**............... Grolier Club (EA)
**GC**............... Ground Control (AFM)
**GC**............... Grounded Collector
**GC**............... Group Captain
**GC**............... Group Cohesiveness [*Psychological testing*]
**Gc**............... Group-Specific Component [*A serum group*]
**GC**............... Groupe de Chasse [*French aircraft fighter unit*] [*World War II*]
**GC**............... [*Stephen*] Grover Cleveland [*US president, 1837-1908*]
**GC**............... Guanine, Cytosine [*Type*] [*Biochemistry*]
**GC**............... Guidance Computer
**G & C**........ Guidance and Control [*Military*] (CAAL)
**GC**............... Guidance Control [*NASA*] (NASA)
**GC**............... Gun Camera (MCD)
**GC**............... Gun Captain
**GC**............... Gun Carriage
**GC**............... Gun Control
**GC**............... Gyro Compass
**GC**............... Gyro Control
**GC**............... Lignes Nationales Aeriennes [*Congo*] [*ICAO designator*] (FAAC)
**GCA**........... Gain Control Amplifier
**GCA**........... Garden Centers of America (EA)
**GCA**........... Garden Club of America (EA)
**GCA**........... Gauge Control Analyzer
**GCA**........... GCA Corp. [*NYSE symbol*] (SPSG)
**GCA**........... Genealogy Club of America (EA)
**GCA**........... General Claim Agent
**GCA**........... General Combining Ability
**GCA**........... General Control Approach
**GCA**........... Geophysics Corporation of America
**GCA**........... Giant Cell Arteritis [*Medicine*]
**GCA**........... Girls Clubs of America [*Later, GI*] (EA)
**GCA**........... Glass Crafts of America [*Defunct*] (EA)
**GCA**........... Glen Canyon [*Arizona*] [*Seismograph station code, US Geological Survey*] (SEIS)
**GCA**........... Global Citizens Association [*Quebec, PQ*] (EAIO)
**GCA**........... Gold Clause Agreement [*Shipping*] (DS)
**GCA**........... Golf Course Association (EA)
**GCA**........... Grains Council of Australia
**GCA**........... Graphic Communications Association (EA)
**GCA**........... Green Coffee Association of New York City (EA)
**GCA**........... Greeting Card Association (EA)
**GCA**........... Greyhound Club of America (EA)
**GCA**........... Ground-Controlled Aircraft (AFM)
**GCA**........... Ground-Controlled Apparatus [*RADAR*]
**GCA**........... Ground-Controlled Approach [*for lateral and vertical guidance of landing aircraft through use of ground RADAR and radio communications*]
**GCA**........... Grounded Cathode Amplifier
**GCA**........... Group Capacity Analysis [*or Assessment*]
**GCA**........... Guacamayas [*Colombia*] [*Airport symbol*] (OAG)
**GCA**........... Guidance Control and Adapter Section (MCD)
**GC & A**...... Guidance, Control, and Airframe
**GCA**........... Guidance and Control Assembly (NG)
**G de Ca**...... Guillelmus de Cabriano [*Deceased, 1201*] [*Authority cited in pre-1607 legal work*] (DSA)
**GCA**........... Gun Control Act [*1968*]
**GCA**........... Gunite Contractors Association (EA)
**GCA**........... Gyro Control Assembly
**GCAA**........ Golf Coaches Association of America (EA)
**GCACAK**... Geochimica et Cosmochimica Acta [*A publication*]
**GCA-CTS**... Ground-Controlled Approach - Controller Training System (MCD)
**GCAD**........ Granite City Army Depot (AABC)
**GCai**........... Roddenbery Memorial Library, Cairo, GA [*Library symbol*] [*Library of Congress*] (LCLS)
**GCAJS**...... Gratz College. Annual of Jewish Studies [*A publication*]
**G de Cal**..... Gaspar de Calderinis [*Deceased, 1390*] [*Authority cited in pre-1607 legal work*] (DSA)
**GCAL**........ General Councillor at Large [*Library Association of Australia*]
**GCAL**........ Gram Calorie
**GCAM**....... Groupement de la Caisse des Depots Automatisation pour le Management [*Bank Group for Automation in Management*] [*Information service or system*] (IID)
**GCA of NO**... Green Coffee Association of New Orleans (EA)
**GCanS**....... Sequoyah Regional Library, Canton, GA [*Library symbol*] [*Library of Congress*] (LCLS)
**GCAP**........ Generalized Circuit Analysis Program (IEEE)
**GCAP**........ Gold Co. of America [*NASDAQ symbol*] (NQ)
**G/Capt**....... Group Captain [*British military*] (DMA)
**GCarrS**...... Southwire Co., Carrollton, GA [*Library symbol*] [*Library of Congress*] (LCLS)
**GCarrWG**... West Georgia College, Carrollton, GA [*Library symbol*] [*Library of Congress*] (LCLS)
**GCAS**......... Ground Collision Avoidance System [*Army*]
**GCASD**...... Geochimica et Cosmochimica Acta. Supplement [*A publication*]
**GCAT**........ Guidance and Control Analysis Team [*Space Flight Operations, NASA*]
**GCatO**....... Group Catering Officer [*British military*] (DMA)
**GCB**........... Dame Grand Cross of the Order of the Bath [*British*] (ADA)
**GCB**........... Gas. Zeitschrift fuer Rationelle Energieanwendung [*A publication*]
**GCB**........... Generator Control Breaker
**GCB**........... German Convention Bureau (EA)
**GCB**........... Ghana Commercial Bank
**GCB**........... Ghanian Cocoa Butter
**GCB**........... Gonococcal Base [*Broth*] [*Growth medium*]
**GCB**........... Good Conduct Badge [*British*]
**GCB**........... Graphitized Carbon Black
**GCB**........... Gravity Cutback (NRCH)
**GCB**........... Guthrie, C. B., Tariff Bureau Inc., Washington DC [*STAC*]
**GCB**........... Knight Grand Cross of the [*Order of the*] Bath [*British*]
**GCBA**........ Golf Course Builders of America (EA)
**GCBC**........ Goucher College Babylonian Collection (BJA)
**GCBI**.......... Godisnjak Centra za Balkanoloska Ispitivanja [*A publication*]
**GCBK**........ Great Country Bank [*Ansonia, CT*] [*NASDAQ symbol*] (NQ)
**GCBM**........ Gas Chromatography in Biology and Medicine [*British*]
**GCBR**........ Gas-Cooled Breeder Reactor [*Nuclear energy*]
**GCBS**......... General Council of British Shipping
**GCBS**......... Ground-Control Bombing System (NG)
**GCC**........... Coca-Cola Co., Business Information, Atlanta, GA [*OCLC symbol*] (OCLC)
**GCC**........... Garden Cat Club (EA)
**GCC**........... General Cinema Corporation [*Chestnut Hill, MA*]
**GCC**........... General Commission on Chaplains and Armed Forces Personnel [*Later, NCMAF*] (EA)
**GCC**........... Georgian Court College [*Lakewood, NJ*]
**GCC**........... Giannini Controls Corporation (AAG)
**GCC**........... Gillette [*Wyoming*] [*Airport symbol*] (OAG)
**GCC**........... Girton College [*Cambridge University*] (DAS)
**GCC**........... Global Competitiveness Council (EA)
**GCC**........... Goddard Communications Center [*NASA*]
**GCC**........... Goddard Computing Center [*NASA*]
**GCC**........... Goebel Collectors' Club [*Later, MIHC*] (EA)
**GCC**........... Gogebic Community College [*Ironwood, MI*]
**GCC**........... Golden Concord Mining [*Vancouver Stock Exchange symbol*]
**GCC**........... Gonville and Caius College [*Cambridge University*] (ROG)
**GCC**........... Good Counsel College [*New York*]
**GCC**........... Government Contract Committee [*Later, OFCCP*] [*Department of Labor*]
**GCC**........... Graduated Combat Capability [*Military*]
**GCC**........... Grand Canyon College [*Phoenix, AZ*]
**GCC**........... Granite Creek [*California*] [*Seismograph station code, US Geological Survey*] (SEIS)
**GCC**........... Graphic Control Center [*Touch-activated CRT display*]
**GCC**........... Greenfield Community College [*Massachusetts*]
**GCC**........... Ground Calcium Carbonate [*Inorganic chemistry*]
**GCC**........... Ground Communications Controller
**GCC**........... Ground Communications Coordinator [*NASA*] (NASA)
**GCC**........... Ground Computer Controller
**GCC**........... Ground-Control Center
**GCC**........... Group Change Control
**GCC**........... Group Control Center (MCD)
**GCC**........... Grove City College [*Pennsylvania*]
**GCC**........... Guidance Checkout Computer
**GCC**........... Guidance and Control Computer
**G & CC**....... Guidance and Control Coupler (KSC)

**GCC**.......... Gulf Cooperation Council [*Consists of Saudi Arabia, Bahrain, Kuwait, Oman, Qatar, and the United Arab Emirates*]
**GCC**.......... Gun Control Console [*Military*] (CAAL)
**GCCA**........ G-Cat Class Association (EA)
**GCCA**........ Gambling Chip Collectors Association (EA)
**GCCA**........ Graphic Communications Computer Association [*Printing Industries of America*] [*Later, GCA*]
**GCCA**........ Greater Clothing Contractors Association (EA)
**GCCA**........ Greeting Card and Calendar Association [*British*]
**GCCA Newsletter** ... GCCA [*Graduate Careers Council of Australia*] Newsletter [*A publication*] (APTA)
**GCCC**........ Canarias [*Canary Islands*] [*ICAO location identifier*] (ICLI)
**GCCC**........ General Computer Corporation [*Twinsburg, OH*] [*NASDAQ symbol*] (NQ)
**GCCC**........ Ground-Control Computer Center (MCD)
**GCCG**........ German Colonies Collectors Group (EA)
**GCCNPIP** ... General Conference Committee of the National Poultry Improvement Plan [*Department of Agriculture*] (EGAO)
**GCCO**........ Ground-Control Checkout (MCD)
**GCCS**........ Geneva Convention on the Continental Shelf (NOAA)
**GCCS**........ Government Code and Cypher School [*Later, GCHQ*] [*Sometimes facetiously translated as Golf, Chess, and Cheese Society*] [*British*]
**GCCU**........ Grand Council of the Cree (of Quebec) Update [*A publication*]
**GCCVF**...... Golden Concord Mining [*NASDAQ symbol*] (NQ)
**GCCW**....... United Gas, Coke, and Chemical Workers of America [*Later, OCAW*]
**GCD**.......... DeKalb Community College, Clarkston, GA [*OCLC symbol*] (OCLC)
**GCD**.......... Gain Control Driver (CET)
**GCD**.......... General and Complete Disarmament
**GCD**.......... Gold Coupling Dendrite
**GCD**.......... Golden Cadillac Resources Ltd. [*Vancouver Stock Exchange symbol*]
**GCD**.......... Good Conduct Discharge
**GCD**.......... Graphic Codepoint Definition [*Telecommunications*]
**GCD**.......... Great Circle Distance
**GCD**.......... Greatest Common Denominator
**GCD**.......... Greatest Common Divisor
**GCD**.......... Gyro-Compass, Desired Cluster Orientation (MCD)
**GCDC**........ Gold Coast Divisional Court Reports [*A publication*] (DLA)
**GCDC**........ Grace Cancer Drug Center [*Roswell Park Memorial Institute*] [*Research center*] (RCD)
**GCDC**........ Ground Checkout Display and Control [*NASA*] (NASA)
**GCDCS**...... Ground Checkout Display and Control System (MCD)
**GC Div C** ... Selected Judgments of the Divisional Courts [*Ghana*] [*A publication*] (DLA)
**GC Div Ct**.. Gold Coast Selected Judgments of the Divisional Courts [*A publication*] (DLA)
**GCDU**........ Grupo de Convergencia Democratica en Uruguay [*Group of Democratic Convergence in Uruguay*] (EA)
**GCE**.......... Commission for Geographical Education (EA)
**GCE**.......... General Certificate of Education [*British*]
**GCE**.......... Glassy Carbon Electrode
**GCE**.......... Great Canadian Cider [*Vancouver Stock Exchange symbol*]
**GCE**.......... Greenwood Cotton Exchange (EA)
**GCE**.......... Ground Checkout Equipment [*Aerospace*] (AAG)
**GCE**.......... Ground Communications Equipment
**GCE**.......... Ground-Control Equipment
**GCEBT**...... Galveston Cotton Exchange and Board of Trade (EA)
**GC-EC**....... Gas Chromatography with Electron Capture
**GCECEE**... Groupement des Caisses d'Epargne de la CEE [*Savings Bank Group of the European Economic Community*]
**GCEG**........ Grid-Controlled Electron Gun
**GCEI**......... Gold C Enterprises, Incorporated [*NASDAQ symbol*] (NQ)
**GCEOS**...... Group Contribution Equation of State
**GCEP**........ Gas Centrifuge Enrichment Plant [*Department of Energy*]
**GCEP**........ Governing Council for Environmental Programs [*United Nations*]
**G & CEP**.... Guidance and Control Equipment Performance (KSC)
**GCER**........ General Ceramics, Inc. [*Haskell, NJ*] [*NASDAQ symbol*] (NQ)
**GCESq**....... Geodetic Communications and Electronics Squadron [*Air Force*] (AFM)
**G-CEU**....... General Certified End User [*Department of Commerce export license*]
**GCF**.......... Generation Control Function [*Telecommunications*] (TEL)
**GCF**.......... Greatest Common Factor
**GCF**.......... Greenhouse Crisis Foundation (EA)
**GCF**.......... Gross Capacity Factor (IEEE)
**GCF**.......... Ground Command Facility
**GCF**.......... Ground Communications Facility [*NASA*]
**GCFAP**...... Guidance and Control Flight Analysis Program [*Aerospace*]
**GCFBR**...... Gas-Cooled Fast Breeder Reactor
**GCFC**........ Glen Campbell Fan Club (EA)
**GCFC**........ Gold Coast Full Court Selected Judgments [*A publication*] (DLA)
**GCFC**........ Gulf Coast Fisheries Center
**GCF-CS**..... Ground Communications Facility - Communications Switcher [*NASA*]
**GCFI**......... Giornale Critico della Filosofia Italiana [*A publication*]
**GCFI**......... Gulf and Caribbean Fisheries Institute (EA)
**GC-FID**...... Gas Chromatography with Flame Ionization Detection
**GCFLH**...... Grand Cross of the French Legion of Honour
**GCFR**........ Gas-Cooled Fast Reactor
**GCFRE**...... Gas-Cooled Fast Reactor Experiment (IEEE)
**GCFT**........ Gonorrhea Complement Fixation Test [*Medicine*]
**GC/FTIR**... Gas Chromatography plus Fourier Transform Infrared Spectrometry
**GC Full Ct** ... Gold Coast Full Court Selected Judgments [*A publication*] (DLA)
**GCFV**........ Puerto Del Rosario/Fuerteventura [*Canary Islands*] [*ICAO location identifier*] (ICLI)
**GCG**.......... Gorham Collectors' Guild (EA)
**GCG**.......... Grand Captain General [*Freemasonry*]
**GCG**.......... Grand Captain of the Guard [*Freemasonry*]
**GCG**.......... Gravity-Controlled Gyro
**GCG**.......... Ground Command Guidance
**GCG**.......... Guardian Capital Group Ltd. [*Toronto Stock Exchange symbol*]
**GCG**.......... Guatemala City [*Guatemala*] [*Seismograph station code, US Geological Survey*] [*Closed*] (SEIS)
**GCG**.......... Guidance Control Group [*Military*]
**GCG**.......... Gyro Control Gunsight
**GCGC**........ Golden Cycle Gold Corporation [*NASDAQ symbol*] (NQ)
**GCGGA**..... Gulf Coast Association of Geological Societies. Field Trip Guidebook [*A publication*]
**GCGI**......... Geneve Capital Group, Incorporated [*NASDAQ symbol*] (NQ)
**GCGS**........ Gravity-Controlled Gyro System
**G CH**......... [*The*] Gardeners' Chronicle [*A publication*] (ROG)
**GCH**.......... Gas Collection Header (NRCH)
**GCH**.......... Generalized Continuum Hypothesis [*Logic*]
**GCH**.......... Germinal Center Hyperplasia [*Medicine*]
**GCH**.......... Gigacharacters
**GCH**.......... Global Community Health
**GCH**.......... Glucocorticoid Hormone [*Endocrinology*]
**GCH**.......... Golden Chance Resources, Inc. [*Vancouver Stock Exchange symbol*]
**GCH**.......... Grand Captain of the Host [*Freemasonry*]
**GCH**.......... Grand Chapter of Harodim [*Freemasonry*]
**GCH**.......... Guidance Capsule Handling
**GCH**.......... Knight Grand Cross of the Guelphic Order of Hanover [*British*]
**GCHC**........ Gulf Coast Hydroscience Center [*Department of the Interior*] [*National Space Technology Laboratories Station, MS*] (GRD)
**GCHI**......... Hierro [*Canary Islands*] [*ICAO location identifier*] (ICLI)
**G Chim Appl** ... Giornale di Chimica Applicata [*A publication*]
**G Chim Ind** ... Giornale di Chimica Industriale [*A publication*]
**G Chim Ind Appl** ... Giornale di Chimica Industriale ed Applicata [*A publication*]
**GCHQ**....... Government Communications Headquarters [*British*]
**GCHR**........ Guatemala Committee for Human Rights (EAIO)
**GCHWR**.... Gas-Cooled, Heavy-Water-Moderated Reactor [*Nuclear energy*] (NRCH)
**GCHX**........ Ground Cooling Heat Exchanger [*NASA*] (NASA)
**GCI**........... Gannett Company, Incorporated [*NYSE symbol*] (SPSG)
**GCI**........... Gas Chromatograph Intoximeter [*Measure-of-intoxication test for drunk drivers*]
**GCI**........... General Capital Increase [*Banking*]
**GCI**........... General Communication, Incorporated [*Anchorage, AK*] [*Telecommunications*] (TSSD)
**GCI**........... Generalized Communication Interface
**GCI**........... Genie Climatique International (EA)
**GCI**........... Getty Conservation Institute [*Database producer*] (IID)
**GCI**........... Globetrotter Communications, Inc. [*NASDAQ symbol*]
**GCI**........... Gnostic Concepts, Incorporated [*San Mateo, CA*] [*Database producer*] [*Information service or system*] [*Telecommunications*] (TSSD)
**GCI**........... Grand China Resources Ltd. [*Vancouver Stock Exchange symbol*]
**GCI**........... Graphic Communications, Incorporated [*Data processing*]
**GCI**........... Gray Cast Iron
**GCI**........... Ground Clearance Intercept [*System similar to US commercial RADAR for ground control of aircraft*] [*North Vietnam*]
**GCI**........... Ground-Controlled Interception [*RADAR*]
**GCI**........... Groupe des Communications Informatiques [*Computer Communications Group*] [*Canada*]
**GCI**........... Guernsey [*Channel Islands*] [*Airport symbol*] (OAG)
**GCI**........... Gulf Communications, Incorporated [*Melbourne, FL*] [*Telecommunications service*] (TSSD)
**GCIA**........ Granite Cutters' International Association [*Later, Tile, Marble, Terrazzo, Finishers, Shopworkers, and Granite Cutters International Union*]
**GCIC**......... German Chamber of Industry and Commerce (DS)
**GCIC**......... Gifted Children's Information Centre [*British*] (CB)
**GCIC**......... Groupement Cinematographique International de Conciliation (EA)
**GCIE**......... Knight Grand Commander of the [*Order of the*] Indian Empire [*British*]
**GCIL**......... Ground-Control Interface Logic (MCD)
**GCILC**....... Ground-Control Interface Logic Controller (MCD)
**GCILU**....... Ground-Control Interface Logic Unit (MCD)
**GCIP**......... Guidance Correction Input Panel
**GC/IR**....... Gas Chromatography/Infrared

**GCIRC**....... Glass Container Industry Research Corporation [*An association*] (EA)
**GCIRC**....... Groupe Consultatif International de Recherche sur le Colza [*International Consultative Research Group on Rape Seed*] (EAIO)
**GCIS**.......... Ground-Control Intercept Squadron
**GCISD**....... Guidance, Control, and Information Systems Division [*NASA*]
**GCITNG**.... Ground-Control Intercept Training (NVT)
**GCIU**......... Graphic Communications International Union (EA)
**GCJB**......... Guidance Checkout Junction Box
**GCK**........... Garden City [*Kansas*] [*Airport symbol*] (OAG)
**GCK**........... Glomerulocystic Kidney [*Nephrology*]
**GCK**........... Grid-Controlled Klystron
**GCK**........... Grocka [*Yugoslavia*] [*Geomagnetic observatory code*]
**GCKP**......... Grand Commander of the Knights of Saint Patrick
**GCL**........... Columbia Theological Seminary, Decatur, GA [*OCLC symbol*] (OCLC)
**GCL**........... Galactic Center Lobe
**GCL**........... Ganglion Cell Layer [*Neuroanatomy*]
**GCL**........... Gas-Cooled Loop [*Nuclear energy*] (NRCH)
**GCL**........... Generic Control Language [*Data processing*] (TEL)
**GCL**........... Grand Cross (of the Order) of Leopold (ROG)
**GCL**........... Great Cameron Lake Resources, Inc. [*Vancouver Stock Exchange symbol*]
**GCL**........... Ground-Control Landing
**GCL**........... Ground Coolant Loop (MCD)
**GCL**........... Guidance Control Laboratory (AAG)
**GCL**........... Guide to Computing Literature [*A publication*] (IT)
**GCL**........... Guild of Catholic Lawyers (EA)
**GCL**........... Gulf Canada Limited [*UTLAS symbol*]
**GCLA**........ La Palma [*Canary Islands*] [*ICAO location identifier*] (ICLI)
**GCLC**......... Greater Cincinnati Library Consortium [*Library network*]
**GCLCS**...... Groundcrew Liquid Cooling System
**GCLH**........ Knight Grand Cross of the Legion of Honour [*British*]
**G Clin Med**... Giornale di Clinica Medica [*A publication*]
**G Clin Med (Bologna)**... Giornale di Clinica Medica (Bologna) [*A publication*]
**GC LISP**.... Golden Common LISP [*List Processor*] [*Artificial intelligence language*]
**GCLLM**..... Groupement Canadien des Locataires des Logements Municipaux [*Canadian Organization of Public Housing Tenants*]
**GCLP**......... Gran Canaria [*Canary Islands*] [*ICAO location identifier*] (ICLI)
**GC/LRMS**... Gas Chromatography/Low Resolution Mass Spectrometry
**GCLWD**.... Gulf Coast Low Water Datum
**GCM**.......... Gay Christian Movement [*British*]
**GCM**.......... General Circulation Model [*Data processing*] [*Meteorology*]
**GCM**.......... General Counsel's Memorandum [*Internal Revenue Service*]
**GCM**.......... General Court-Martial
**GCM**.......... General George C. Marshall [*World War II*]
**GCM**.......... Generator Coordinate Method [*Physics*]
**GCM**.......... Global Circulation Model [*National Center for Atmospheric Research*]
**GCM**.......... Global Climate Model
**GCM**.......... Good Company Man [*Theater term*] (DSUE)
**GCM**.......... Good Conduct Medal [*Military decoration*]
**GCM**.......... Grand Cayman [*West Indies*] [*Airport symbol*] (OAG)
**GCM**.......... Great Central Mines [*Vancouver Stock Exchange symbol*]
**GCM**.......... Greatest Common Measure
**GCM**.......... Greatest Common Multiple (ADA)
**GCM**.......... Ground-Control Message (MCD)
**G/CM²**....... Grams per Square Centimeter
**G/CM³**....... Grams per Cubic Centimeter
**GCMA**....... General Court-Martial Authority
**GCMA**....... Government Contract Management Association of America (EA)
**GCMAPA**... Gay Caucus of Members of the American Psychiatric Association [*Later, AGLP*] (EA)
**GCMC**....... Good Conduct Medal Clasp
**GCMCA**.... General Court-Martial Convening Authority [*DoD*]
**GCMDL**.... Good Conduct Medal [*Military decoration*] (AABC)
**GCMF**....... George C. Marshall Foundation (EA)
**GCMG**....... Dame Grand Cross of the Order of Saint Michael and Saint George [*British*] (ADA)
**GCMG**....... Knight Grand Cross of St. Michael and St. George [*Facetiously translated "God Calls Me God"*] [*British*]
**GCMI**........ Glass Container Manufacturers Institute [*Later, GPI*] (EA)
**GCMJ**........ General Court-Martial Jurisdiction
**GCMO**....... General Court-Martial Order
**GCMP**....... General Court-Martial Prisoner
**GCMP**....... Greater Cleveland Mathematics Program [*Education*]
**GCMPC**..... General Chairman-Member Pickwick Club [*From "The Pickwick Papers" by Charles Dickens*]
**GCMPS**..... Gyro Compass
**GCMR**....... Ground-Control Message Request (MCD)
**GCMRF**..... George C. Marshall Research Foundation (EA)
**GCMRGlc**... Global Cerebral Metabolic Rate for Glucose [*Brain research*]
**GCMRJS**... Great Central Midland [*or Metropolitan*] Joint Stock [*Railroad*] [*British*] (ROG)
**GC/MS**...... Gas Chromatography/Mass Spectrometry
**GCMSC**..... George C. Marshall Space Flight Center [*Also known as MSFC*] [*NASA*]
**GCMSFC**.. George C. Marshall Space Flight Center [*Also known as MSFC*] [*NASA*]
**GCMU**....... Glazed Concrete Masonry Units [*Technical drawings*]
**GCN**........... Gauge Code Number
**GCN**........... Gay Community News [*A publication*] (APTA)
**GCN**........... General Cinema Corp. [*NYSE symbol*] (SPSG)
**GCN**........... Giant Cerebral Neuron [*Brain anatomy*]
**GCN**........... Gold Canyon Mines, Inc. [*Vancouver Stock Exchange symbol*]
**GCN**........... Government Computer News [*A publication*]
**GCN**........... Grand Canyon [*Arizona*] [*Airport symbol*] (OAG)
**GCN**........... Greenwich Civil Noon
**GCN**........... Ground Communications Network
**GCN**........... Ground-Control Network [*NASA*] (NASA)
**GCNA**........ Guild of Carillonneurs in North America (EA)
**GCNA**........ Guild of Carillonneurs in North America. Bulletin [*A publication*]
**GCNED**..... Government Computer News [*A publication*]
**GcNM**........ GCN/Microfilm, Boston, MA [*Library symbol*] [*Library of Congress*] (LCLS)
**GC-NPD**.... Gas Chromatography-Nitrogen Phosphorus Detector
**GCNPP**...... Gay Community News Prisoner Project [*An association*] (EA)
**GCNPP**...... Greene County Nuclear Power Plant (NRCH)
**GCNR**........ Gas Core Nuclear Rocket
**GCO**........... Columbus College, Library, Columbus, GA [*OCLC symbol*] (OCLC)
**GCO**........... GENESCO, Inc. [*NYSE symbol*] (SPSG)
**GCO**........... Georgetown College Observatory (MCD)
**GCO**........... Glenco International Corp. [*Vancouver Stock Exchange symbol*]
**GCO**........... Governor's Commissioned Officer [*British military*] (DMA)
**GCO**........... Ground Checkout [*NASA*] (NASA)
**GCO**........... Ground Cutout
**GCO**........... Guidance Control Officer (AAG)
**GC & O**...... Guidance, Control, and Ordnance
**GCO**........... Gun Control Officer [*Navy*]
**GCOC**........ Gun Control Officer Console [*Military*] (CAAL)
**GCocM**...... Middle Georgia College, Cochran, GA [*Library symbol*] [*Library of Congress*] (LCLS)
**GColu**......... W. C. Bradley Memorial Library, Columbus, GA [*Library symbol*] [*Library of Congress*] (LCLS)
**GCoiuC**...... Columbus College, Columbus, GA [*Library symbol*] [*Library of Congress*] (LCLS)
**GColuGS**... Church of Jesus Christ of Latter-Day Saints, Genealogical Society Library, Macon Branch, Columbus, GA [*Library symbol*] [*Library of Congress*] (LCLS)
**GCom**......... Grand Commander [*or Commandery*] [*Freemasonry*]
**GCOM**....... Gray Communications Systems, Inc. [*NASDAQ symbol*] (NQ)
**GCON**........ Grand Cross, Order of the Niger [*British*]
**GConT**....... Monastery of the Holy Ghost, Conyers, GA [*Library symbol*] [*Library of Congress*] (LCLS)
**G Coop**....... [*George*] Cooper's English Chancery Reports [*A publication*] (DLA)
**G Cooper**.... [*George*] Cooper's English Chancery Reports [*A publication*] (DLA)
**G Cooper (Eng)**... [*George*] Cooper's English Chancery Reports [*A publication*] (DLA)
**GCOR**........ Gencor Industries, Inc. [*NASDAQ symbol*] (NQ)
**GCOS**........ General Comprehensive Operating Supervisor [*Data processing*]
**GCOS**........ General Computer Operational System [*NASA*]
**GCOS**........ Great Canadian Oil Sands Ltd.
**GCOS**........ Great Canadian Sands News [*A publication*]
**GCOS**........ Ground Computer Operating System [*NASA*] (NASA)
**GCP**........... Generalized Computer Program
**GCP**........... Good Clinical Practice [*Medicine*]
**GCP**........... Government Contracts Program [*George Washington University Law Center*] (DLA)
**GCP**........... Grancamp Resources [*Vancouver Stock Exchange symbol*]
**GCP**........... Graphics Control Program [*IBM Corp.*] (PCM)
**GCP**........... Green Circle Program (EA)
**GCP**........... Guidance Checkout [*or Control*] Package (NG)
**GCP**........... Guild of Catholic Psychiatrists [*Later, National Guild of Catholic Psychiatrists*] (EA)
**GCPA**........ Grammatik des Christlich-Palaestinischen Aramaeisch [*A publication*] (BJA)
**GCPD**........ Grade Crossing Protection Device
**GCPPD**...... Global Committee of Parliamentarians on Population and Development (EA)
**GCPPI**....... Gifted Children's Pen Pals International (EA)
**GCPR**........ General Ceiling Price Regulation (DLA)
**GCPS**......... Gigacycles per Second (MUGU)
**GCPS**......... Ground Claims Processing System
**GCPS**......... Group Claims Processing System [*McAuto*]
**GCQ**........... Group Climate Questionnaire [*Occupational therapy*]
**GCQBD**..... Geo-Heat Center. Quarterly Bulletin [*A publication*]
**GCR**........... Gain Control Range
**GCR**........... Galactic Cosmic Radiation [*or Ray*]
**GCR**........... Galvanocutaneous Reaction
**GCR**........... Gamma Cosmic Ray [*Geophysics*]

**GCR** .......... Gas-Cooled Reactor
**GCR** .......... Gaylord Container Corp. Class A [*AMEX symbol*] (SPSG)
**GCR** .......... General Cargo Rates [*Business term*]
**GCR** .......... General Commodity Rate [*Shipping*] (DS)
**GCR** .......... General Competition Rules [*Motorcycle racing*] [*Australia*]
**GCR** .......... General Component Reference (IEEE)
**GCR** .......... Geneva Consultants Registry [*Alpha Systems Resource*] [*Database*]
**GCR** .......... German Canadian Review [*A publication*]
**GCR** .......... Glencair Resources, Inc. [*Toronto Stock Exchange symbol*]
**GCR** .......... Glomerular Complement Receptor [*Immunology*]
**GCR** .......... Glucose Consumption Rate
**GCR** .......... Glucuronidase [*An enzyme*]
**GCR** .......... Glycinecresol Red [*An indicator*] [*Chemistry*]
**GCR** .......... Gold Coast Regiment [*British military*] (DMA)
**GCR** .......... Grand Central Rocket Co. (AAG)
**GCR** .......... Grandparents'/Children's Rights (EA)
**GCR** .......... Gray-Component Replacement [*Color reproduction technology*]
**GCR** .......... Grayling Creek [*Montana*] [*Seismograph station code, US Geological Survey*] (SEIS)
**GCR** .......... Great Central Railway [*British*]
**GCR** .......... Grignard's Chemical Reaction
**GCR** .......... Ground-Controlled RADAR
**GCR** .......... Group Coded Recording [*Data processing*] (BUR)
**GCR** .......... Guerrilleros de Cristo Rey [*Warriors of Christ and King*] [*Revolutionary Group*] [*Spain*]
**GCRA** ........ Gas-Cooled Reactor Associates (NRCH)
**GCRA** ........ Giant Chinchilla Rabbit Association (EA)
**GCRA** ........ Golden Corral Realty Corp. [*Raleigh, NC*] [*NASDAQ symbol*] (NQ)
**GCRC** ........ General Clinical Research Center [*Scripps Clinic and Research Foundation*] [*Research center*]
**GCRC** ........ General Clinical Research Center [*Stanford University*] [*Research center*] (RCD)
**GCRC** ........ General Clinical Research Center [*University of Alabama in Birmingham*] [*Research center*] (RCD)
**GCRC** ........ General Clinical Research Center [*University of Virginia*] [*Research center*] (RCD)
**GCRCPB** ... General Clinical Research Center Program Branch [*National Institutes of Health*]
**GCRE** ........ Gas-Cooled Reactor Experiment (NRCH)
**GCRF** ........ Greensboro Civil Rights Fund (EA)
**GCRG** ........ Giant Cell Reparative Granuloma [*Oncology*]
**GCRG** ........ Gun Carriage
**GCRI** .......... Georgetown Clinical Research Institute [*FAA*]
**GCRI** .......... German Carpet Research Institute [*See also TFI*] (EAIO)
**GCRI** .......... Gillette Company Research Institute
**G Crit Filosof Ital** ... Giornale Critico della Filosofia Italiana [*A publication*]
**GCRL** .......... Gulf Coast Research Laboratory [*Ocean Springs, MS*]
**GCRO** ........ General Council and Register of Osteopaths Ltd. [*British*]
**GCRP** ......... Galactic Cosmic Ray Particle
**GCRR** ........ Arrecife/Lanzarote [*Canary Islands*] [*ICAO location identifier*] (ICLI)
**GCRRAE** ... Glasshouse Crops Research Institute. Annual Report [*A publication*]
**GCRV** ........ Ground Cruising Recreational Vehicle [*Owosso Motor Car Company*] [*Owosso, MI*]
**GCS** ........... Die Griechische Christliche Schriftsteller der Ersten Drei Jahrhunderten [*A publication*]
**GCS** ........... Gas Cylinder System
**GCS** ........... Gate-Controlled Switch
**GCS** ........... GCS Air Service [*Galion, OH*] [*FAA designator*] (FAAC)
**GCS** ........... General Communication Subsystem [*Data processing*]
**GCS** ........... General Computer Systems, Inc.
**GCS** ........... Generator Control Switch (MCD)
**GCS** ........... Geostationary Communications Satellite [*WARC*]
**GCS** ........... Gifted Child Society (EA)
**Gc/s** ........... Gigacycles per Second [*IEEE*]
**GCS** ........... Glasgow Coma Score [*Medicine*]
**GCS** ........... Golden Crown Resources Ltd. [*Vancouver Stock Exchange symbol*]
**GCS** ........... Golf Collectors' Society (EA)
**GCS** ........... Government Contractors Subcontractors
**GCS** ........... Grand Commander (of the Order) of Spain (ROG)
**GCS** ........... Graphic Compatibility System
**GCS** ........... Graphics Compatibility Standard [*For image processing*]
**GCS** ........... Ground Command System
**GCS** ........... Ground Communications System
**GCS** ........... Ground-Control Station (MCD)
**G & CS** ....... Guidance and Control System
**GCS** ........... Guidance Cutoff Signal [*NASA*] (NASA)
**GCS** ........... Gyroless Control System
**GCS** ........... Portland, ME [*Location identifier*] [*FAA*] (FAAL)
**GCSA** ......... Galloway Cattle Society of America (EA)
**GCSA** ......... Gross Cell-Surface Antigen [*Immunology*]
**GCSAA** ...... Golf Course Superintendents Association of America (EA)
**GCSC** ......... Guidance Control and Sequencing Computer
**GCSE** ......... General Certificate of Secondary Education [*British*]
**Gc/sec** ........ Gigacycles per Second [*AIP*]
**G-CSF** ........ Granulocyte-Colony Stimulating Factor [*Hematology*]
**GCSF** ......... Gulf, Colorado & Santa Fe Railway Co. [*AAR code*]
**GC & SF** .... Gulf, Colorado & Santa Fe Railway Co.
**GCSG** ........ Knight Grand Cross of St. Gregory the Great [*British*]
**GCSI** .......... Knight Grand Commander of the [*Order of the*] Star of India [*British*]
**GCSM** ....... Glandless Cottonseed Meal [*Animal feed*]
**GCSM** ....... Ground Composite Signal Mixer
**GCSRW - UMC** ... General Commission on the Status and Role of Women - United Methodist Church (EA)
**GCSS** ......... Global Communications Satellite System
**GCSS** ......... Ground-Controlled Space System
**GCSS** ......... Knight Grand Cross of St. Sylvester [*British*]
**GCStJ** ........ Bailiff Grand Cross of [*the Order of*] Saint John of Jerusalem [*British*] (ADA)
**GCStJ** ........ Dame Grand Cross of [*the Order of*] Saint John of Jerusalem [*British*] (ADA)
**GCStJ** ........ Knight Grand Cross of [*the Order of*] St. John of Jerusalem [*British*]
**GCSU** ........ Government Clerical Services' Union [*Ceylon*]
**GCSV** ......... Groundnut Chlorotic Spot Virus
**GCSW** ........ Graduate Certificate of Social Work
**GCT** ........... Coca-Cola Co., Technical Information Services, Atlanta, GA [*OCLC symbol*] (OCLC)
**GCT** ........... General Classification Test [*Military*]
**GCT** ........... Gesture Comprehension Test [*Occupational therapy*]
**GCT** ........... Giant Cell Tumor [*Oncology*]
**GCT** ........... Glass Cloth Tape
**GCT** ........... Government Competitive Testing
**GCT** ........... Grand Cadence de Tir [*Self-propelled howitzer*] (RDA)
**GCT** ........... Graphics Communications Terminal
**GCT** ........... Great Circle Track
**GCT** ........... Greenwich Civil Time
**GCT** ........... Greenwich Conservatory Time
**GCT** ........... Ground Checkout and Test [*Aerospace*]
**GCT** ........... Guidance Command Test
**GCT** ........... Guidance Computer Test
**GCT** ........... Gun Control Tower [*British military*] (DMA)
**GCTA** ........ Ground Commanded [*or Controlled*] Television Assembly [*Apollo*] [*NASA*]
**GCTC** ........ Giant Cell Tumor Cells [*A cell line*]
**GCTE** ......... Guidance Computer Test Equipment
**GCTF** ......... Gold Coast Territorial Force [*British military*] (DMA)
**GCTS** ......... Gas Component Test Stand (MCD)
**GCTS** ......... Ground Communications Tracking Systems
**GCTS** ......... Tenerife-Reina Sofia [*Canary Islands*] [*ICAO location identifier*] (ICLI)
**GCU** ........... General Control Unit (MCD)
**GCU** ........... Generator Control Unit [*NASA*] (NASA)
**GCU** ........... Generator/Converter Unit
**GCU** ........... Gold Canyon Resources [*Vancouver Stock Exchange symbol*]
**GCU** ........... Ground Checkout Unit [*Aerospace*] (MCD)
**GCU** ........... Ground-Control Unit (AAG)
**GCU** ........... Ground Cooling Unit [*NASA*] (NASA)
**GCU** ........... Guidance and Control Unit (NATG)
**GCU** ........... Guidance Coupler Unit
**G de Cu** ...... Guillelmus de Cuneo [*Deceased, 1335*] [*Authority cited in pre-1607 legal work*] (DSA)
**GCU** ........... Gunner's Control Unit
**GCU** ........... Gyro Coupling Unit (KSC)
**GCuA** ......... Andrew College, Cuthbert, GA [*Library symbol*] [*Library of Congress*] (LCLS)
**GCUUSA** .. Greek Catholic Union of the USA (EA)
**GCV** ........... Chattahoochee Valley Regional Library, Columbus, GA [*OCLC symbol*] (OCLC)
**GCV** ........... Gaseous Oxygen Control Valve (NASA)
**GCV** ........... Gross Caloric Value
**GCV** ........... Leakesville, MS [*Location identifier*] [*FAA*] (FAAL)
**GCVO** ........ Dame Grand Cross of the Royal Victorian Order [*British*] (ADA)
**GCVO** ........ Knight Grand Cross of the Royal Victorian Order [*British*]
**GCW** .......... Coca-Cola Co., Law Library, Atlanta, GA [*OCLC symbol*] (OCLC)
**GCW** .......... [*The*] Garden City Western Railway Co. [*AAR code*]
**GCW** .......... Generative Cell Wall [*Botany*]
**GCW** .......... Global Chart of the World [*Air Force*]
**GCW** .......... Glomerular Capillary Wall [*Anatomy*]
**GCW** .......... Grand Coulee [*Washington*] [*Seismograph station code, US Geological Survey*] [*Closed*] (SEIS)
**GCW** .......... Graphic Communications Weekly [*A publication*]
**GCW** .......... Gridiron Club of Washington, DC (EA)
**GCW** .......... Gross Combination Weight [*for tractor and loaded trailer*]
**GCWDA** .... Gulf Coast Waste Disposal Authority [*Governmental industrial waste disposal system*]
**GCWIU** ..... General Cigarette Workers' Industrial Union [*British*]
**GCWM** ...... General Conference on Weights and Measures
**GCWOD** .... Graphic Communications World [*A publication*]
**GCWR** ....... Global Congress of the World's Religions (EA)
**GCWR** ....... Gross Combination Weight Rating [*Environmental Protection Agency*]
**GCXO** ........ Tenerife [*Canary Islands*] [*ICAO location identifier*] (ICLI)
**GCY** ........... General Cybernetics Corp. [*Vancouver Stock Exchange symbol*]

**GCY** .......... German-Canadian Yearbook [*Deutschkanadisches Jahrbuch*] [*A publication*]
**GCY** .......... Glen Cove [*New York*] [*Seismograph station code, US Geological Survey*] (SEIS)
**GCY** .......... Greeneville, TN [*Location identifier*] [*FAA*] (FAAL)
**GD**.............. Channel Aviation Ltd. [*Great Britain*] [*ICAO designator*] (FAAC)
**GD**.............. DeKalb County Library System, Regional Service-Rockdale and Newton Counties, Decatur, GA [*Library symbol*] [*Library of Congress*] (LCLS)
**GD**.............. Diganglioside [*Chemistry*]
**Gd** .............. Gadolinium [*Chemical element*]
**G & D**......... Gale and Davison's English Queen's Bench Reports [*1841-43*] [*A publication*] (DLA)
**GD**.............. Gaol Delivery [*Legal*] [*British*] (ROG)
**GD**.............. Gap Detector
**GD**.............. Gas Drainage
**GD**.............. Gate Driver
**GD**.............. Gave Delivery
**GD**.............. Gear Down [*Aviation*]
**GD**.............. Gel Destainer [*Analytical chemistry*]
**GD**.............. Gel Dryer [*Chromatography*]
**GD**.............. General Delivery
**GD**.............. General Design (AAG)
**GD**.............. General Development
**GD**.............. General Diagram
**GD**.............. General Discharge
**GD**.............. General Dispensary [*Military*]
**GD**.............. General Duty
**GD**.............. General Dynamics Corp. [*NYSE symbol*] (SPSG)
**GD**.............. Geographic Digest [*A publication*] [*British*]
**GD**.............. Geographic Distribution
**GD**.............. Gestational Day
**GD**.............. Giornale Dantesco [*A publication*]
**GD**.............. Glass Door (ADA)
**GD**.............. Global Data Systems [*Vancouver Stock Exchange symbol*]
**GD**.............. Global Digest [*A publication*]
**GD**.............. Glow Discharge [*Photovoltaic energy systems*]
**GD**.............. Glutamate Dehydrogenase [*An enzyme*]
**GD**.............. Glutaraldehyde-Dichromate [*Fixative*]
**GD**.............. Glyceryl Distearate [*Organic chemistry*]
**GD**.............. God Damn
**GD**.............. Gold (FAAC)
**GD**.............. Golden Dawn [*In occult society name, Hermetic Order of the Golden Dawn*]
**GD**.............. Gonadal Dysgenesis [*Endocrinology*]
**GD**.............. Good
**GD**.............. Good [*Track condition*] [*Thoroughbred racing*]
**GD**.............. Good Delivery [*Business term*]
**Gd** .............. Government Expenditure [*Economics*]
**GD**.............. Grade [*Technical drawings*]
**GD**.............. Graduate in Divinity
**GD**.............. Grand Deacon [*Freemasonry*]
**GD**.............. Grand Division
**GD**.............. Grand Duchess [*or Duke*]
**GD**.............. Grand Duchy
**GD**.............. Granddaughter
**GD**.............. Grandes Decisions de la Jurisprudence Administrative [*A publication*] (ILCA)
**GD**.............. Graphic Demand Meter
**GD**.............. Graphic Display
**GD**.............. Grave's Disease [*Endocrinology*]
**GD**.............. Gravimetric Density
**Gd** .............. Greenside Darter [*Ichthyology*]
**GD**.............. Greenwich Date
**GD**.............. Grenada [*ANSI two-letter standard code*] (CNC)
**gd**............... Grenada [*MARC country of publication code*] [*Library of Congress*] (LCCP)
**GD**.............. Gross Debt [*Business term*]
**G & D**......... Grosset & Dunlap [*Publisher*]
**GD**.............. Ground
**GD**.............. Ground Detector (MSA)
**GD**.............. Grouping Distance [*Industrial engineering*]
**GD**.............. Grove Dictionary of Music and Musicians [*A publication*]
**GD**.............. Grown Diffused
**GD**.............. Guard (AABC)
**GD**.............. Guardian [*London*] [*A publication*]
**GD**.............. Gudermannian Amplitude
**GD**.............. Gundeck
**GD**.............. Gunnery Division [*British military*] (DMA)
**GD**.............. Guntersville Dam [*TVA*]
**G and D**...... Guts and Determination (DSUE)
**GD**.............. Nerve Gas [*US Chemical Corps symbol*]
**GD**.............. Soman [*Nerve gas*] [*Army symbol*]
**GDA**........... Galvo-Drive Amplifier
**GD/A** ......... General Dynamics/Astronautics
**GDA**........... Gimbal Drive Actuator [*or Assembly*] (KSC)
**GDA**........... Global Data Area
**GDA**........... Goldera Resources, Inc. [*Vancouver Stock Exchange symbol*]
**Gda**............ Granddaughter
**GDA**........... Gun Damage Assessment (NVT)
**GDA**........... Gun-Defended Area
**GDAA**......... Gift and Decorative Accessories Association of America [*Later, GAA*] (EA)
**GDahN** ...... North Georgia College, Dahlonega, GA [*Library symbol*] [*Library of Congress*] (LCLS)
**GDAIS**....... Atlanta Information Services, Decatur, GA [*Library symbol*] [*Library of Congress*] (LCLS)
**GDAJA**...... Journal. Georgia Dental Association [*A publication*]
**GDal** .......... Dalton Regional Library, Dalton, GA [*Library symbol*] [*Library of Congress*] (LCLS)
**GDanH** ...... Heritage Papers, Danielsville, GA [*Library symbol*] [*Library of Congress*] (LCLS)
**Gdansk Tow Nauk Rozpr Wydz** ... Gdanskie Towarzystwo Naukowe Rozparawy Wydzialu [*Poland*] [*A publication*]
**GDAP** ........ GEOS [*Geodetic Earth-Orbiting Satellite*] Data Adjustment Program
**GDAS** ........ Ground Data Acquisition System
**GDAU**........ General Data Acquisition Unit (MCD)
**GDB**........... Geometric Database (MCD)
**GdB**............ Giornale di Bordo. Mensile di Storia, Letteratura, ed Arte [*A publication*]
**GDB**........... Global Database
**GDB**........... Guide Dogs for the Blind (EA)
**GDBMS**..... Generalized Data Base Management Systems [*Air Force*]
**GDBS**......... Generalized Database System (NASA)
**GDC**........... Columbia Theological Seminary, Decatur, GA [*Library symbol*] [*Library of Congress*] (LCLS)
**GDC**........... Garage Door Council (EA)
**GDC**........... Gas Discharge Counter
**GDC**........... Gas Displacement Chromatography
**GDC**........... Gel Dryer with Clamps [*Chromatography*]
**GDC**........... Gel Drying Cart [*Chromatography*]
**GDC**........... General DataComm Industries, Inc. [*NYSE symbol*] (SPSG)
**GDC**........... General Dental Council [*British*]
**GDC**........... General Design Criteria (NRCH)
**GDC**........... General Development Corporation (AAG)
**GDC**........... General [*Purpose*] Digital Computer
**GD/C** ......... General Dynamics/Convair
**GDC**........... General Dynamics Corporation
**GDC**........... Geocentric Dust Cloud
**GDC**........... Geodetic Data Center [*Environmental Science Services Administration*]
**GDC**........... Geological Data Center [*University of California, San Diego*] (IID)
**GDC**........... Geomagnetic Data Center [*National Oceanic and Atmospheric Administration*]
**GDC**........... Geophysical Data Center
**GDC**........... Gettysburg College, Gettysburg, PA [*OCLC symbol*] (OCLC)
**GDC**........... Governmental Defence Council [*British*]
**GDC**........... Grand-Dad's Day Council [*Defunct*] (EA)
**GDC**........... Grand Deacon of Ceremonies [*Freemasonry*] (ROG)
**GDC**........... Granduc Mines Ltd. [*Toronto Stock Exchange symbol*] [*Vancouver Stock Exchange symbol*]
**GDC**........... Graphic Display Console (MCD)
**GDC**........... Gross Dependable Capacity [*Electronics*] (IEEE)
**GDC**........... Groupe des Democrates Camerounais [*Cameroonian Democratic Group*]
**GDC**........... Guidance Data Converter [*Aerospace*] (AAG)
**GDC**........... Gun Direction Computer
**GDC**........... Gyro Display Coupler (MCD)
**GDC**........... Society of Graphic Designers of Canada (EAIO)
**GDCA**......... Great Dane Club of America (EA)
**GDCH**......... Glycerol Dichlorohydrin [*Organic chemistry*]
**GDCI**.......... Gypsum Drywall Contractors International [*Later, AWCI*]
**GDCR**......... Glacial Debris Conjugate Region [*Oceanography*]
**GDCS** ......... Government Documents Catalog Service [*Information service or system*] (IID)
**GD/CV** ...... General Dynamics/Convair Division (MCD)
**GDCX**......... Growth Development Corp. [*NASDAQ symbol*] (NQ)
**GDD**........... DeKalb Historical Society, Decatur, GA [*Library symbol*] [*Library of Congress*] (LCLS)
**GDD**........... Geddes Resources Ltd. [*Toronto Stock Exchange symbol*]
**GdD** ............ Gegenwart der Dichtung [*A publication*]
**GDD**........... Group Display Device (MCD)
**GDDL**......... Graphical Data Definition Language
**GDDM**........ Graphical Data Display Manager [*Data processing*]
**GDDQ** ........ Group Dimensions Descriptions Questionnaire [*Psychology*]
**GDDS**......... Gamma Dose Detector System
**GDDTD**..... Gesetzblatt der Deutschen Demokratischen Republik. Teil 1 [*A publication*]
**GDE**........... Beaumont, TX [*Location identifier*] [*FAA*] (FAAL)
**GDE**........... Generalized Data Entry (ADA)
**GDE**........... Gibbs-Duhem Equation [*Physical chemistry*]
**GDE**........... Gilt Deckled Edge [*Bookbinding*]
**GDE**........... Gode [*Ethiopia*] [*Airport symbol*] (OAG)
**GDE**........... Golden Dawn Explorations Ltd. [*Vancouver Stock Exchange symbol*]
**GDE**........... Gourde [*Monetary unit*] [*Haiti*]
**GDE**........... Graduate Diploma in Educational Studies
**GDE**........... Graduate Diploma in Extension (ADA)
**GDE**........... Ground Data Equipment [*Electronics*]

**GDE**........ Guide [*or Guided*] (MSA)
**GD/EB**....... General Dynamics/Electric Boat Division (KSC)
**GDemP**...... Piedmont College, Demorest, GA [*Library symbol*] [*Library of Congress*] (LCLS)
**G-Dest**........ General Destination
**GDEU**........ Guidance Digital Evaluation Unit
**GDEX**........ Gold Express Corp. [*Spokane, WA*] [*NASDAQ symbol*] (NQ)
**GDF**........... Gas Dynamic Facility [*Air Force*]
**GDF**........... Geographic Data File [*LPC, Inc.*] [*Information service or system*] (IID)
**GDF**........... Gibraltar Defence Force [*British military*] (DMA)
**GDF**........... Goldfarb Corp. [*Toronto Stock Exchange symbol*]
**GDF**........... Ground Decommutation Facility
**GDF**........... Ground Defense Forces
**GDF**........... Ground Diverted Force [*Military*] (CINC)
**GDF**........... Group Distributing Frames
**GDF**........... Guyanese Defense Force
**GDFB**........ Guide Dog Foundation for the Blind [*Also known as Second Sight Guiding Eyes - Guide Dog Foundation*] (EA)
**GDFF**......... Geographic Distribution of Federal Funds Information System [*Comptroller General of the United States*]
**GD/FW**...... General Dynamics/Fort Worth (KSC)
**GDFY**........ Godfrey Co. [*NASDAQ symbol*] (NQ)
**GDG**........... Gas Discharge Gauge
**GD(G)**........ General Duties (Ground) [*British military*] (DMA)
**GDG**........... Generation Data Group [*Data processing*] (BUR)
**GDG**........... Golden Glory [*Vancouver Stock Exchange symbol*]
**GDG**........... Group Display Generator
**GdG**........... Grundlagen der Germanistik [*A publication*]
**GDGA**........ Garment Dyers Guild of America (EA)
**GD/GA**...... General Dynamics/General Atomic (KSC)
**GDGIP**...... Gas-Driven Gyro Inertial Platform [*Aerospace*] (AAG)
**GDH**.......... DeKalb General Hospital, Decatur, GA [*Library symbol*] [*Library of Congress*] (LCLS)
**GDH**.......... Glutamate Dehydrogenase [*An enzyme*]
**GDH**.......... Godhavn [*Greenland*] [*Seismograph station code, US Geological Survey*] (SEIS)
**GDH**.......... Godhavn [*Greenland*] [*Geomagnetic observatory code*]
**GDH**.......... Goldsearch, Inc. [*Vancouver Stock Exchange symbol*]
**GDH**.......... Gonadotropic Hormone [*Endocrinology*]
**GDH**.......... Goods on Hand (DS)
**GDH**.......... Grand Ducal Highness (ROG)
**GDH**.......... Ground Data Handling
**GDH**.......... Growth and Differentiation Hormone [*Endocrinology*]
**GDHC**........ Ground Data Handling Centre [*Canada*]
**Gd House**... Good Housekeeping [*A publication*]
**GDHS**........ Ground Data Handling System (MCD)
**GDHSE**..... Guardhouse (AABC)
**GDHSWT**... General Dynamics High-Speed Wind Tunnel
**GdI**............ Giornale d'Italia [*A publication*]
**GDI**............ God Damned Independent [*College slang for student not affiliated with a fraternity or sorority*]
**GDI**............ Graphic Display Interface (MCD)
**GDI**............ Graphics Device Interface
**GDI**............ Ground Detector Indicator
**GDI**............ New York, NY [*Location identifier*] [*FAA*] (FAAL)
**GDI**............ Sammlung der Griechischen Dialektinschriften [*A publication*] (OCD)
**GDIAN**...... Guardian (ROG)
**GDIC**......... General Devices, Incorporated [*NASDAQ symbol*] (NQ)
**GDIFS**....... Gray and Ductile Iron Founders' Society [*Later, Iron Castings Society - ICS*]
**GdIG**.......... Gadolinium Iron Garnet (IEEE)
**GDIKAN**... Gifu Daigaku Igakubu Kiyo [*A publication*]
**GdiM**......... Giornale di Metafisica [*A publication*]
**GDIP**......... Gale Directory of International Publications [*A publication*]
**GDIP**......... General Defense Intelligence Program [*DoD*]
**GDIPP**....... General Defense Intelligence Proposed Program [*DoD*] (MCD)
**GDIS**......... Gier-Dunkle Integrating Sphere
**GDKKD2**... Annual Report. Faculty of Education. Gunma University. Art, Technology, Health, and Physical Education and Science of Human Living Series [*A publication*]
**GDKTA**..... Genshi Doryoku Kenkyukai Teirei Kenkyukai Nenkai Hokokusho [*A publication*]
**GDKYA7**... Annual Report. Faculty of Education. Gunma University. Art and Technology Series [*A publication*]
**GDL**.......... Gas Dynamic LASER
**GDL**.......... Gas Dynamics Laboratory
**GDL**.......... Gladstone-Dale Law
**GDL**.......... Glass Delay Line
**GDL**.......... Glass Development LASER
**GDL**.......... Global Data Link
**GDL**.......... Glow-Discharge Lamp [*Spectrometry*]
**GDL**.......... Glucono-delta-Lactone [*Organic chemistry*]
**GDL**.......... Graphic Display Library
**GDL**.......... Guadalajara [*Mexico*] [*Airport symbol*] (OAG)
**GDL**.......... Takeoff Guide Light [*Aviation*] (FAAC)
**GDLK**........ Grid Leak
**GDLS**........ General Dynamics [*Corp.*] Land Systems Division
**GDLS**........ Glow-Discharge Lamp Source [*Spectrometry*]
**GDLS**........ Graduate Diploma in Library Science (ADA)
**GDM**.......... Gads Danske Magasin [*A publication*]
**GDM**.......... Gardner, MA [*Location identifier*] [*FAA*] (FAAL)
**GdM**........... Gazzetta del Mezzogiorno [*A publication*]
**GDM**.......... General Development Map [*or Model*]
**GDM**.......... Geodetic Distance Measurement
**GDM**.......... Gestational Diabetes Mellitus [*Medicine*]
**GDM**.......... Ghana Democratic Movement [*Political party*] (EY)
**GDM**.......... Gibraltar Democratic Movement (PPE)
**GDM**.......... Global Data Manager
**GDM**.......... Goldome FSB [*NYSE symbol*] (SPSG)
**GDM**.......... Grenada Democratic Movement (EAIO)
**GDM**.......... Grid-Dip Modulator
**GDM**.......... Guidance Design Manager (MCD)
**GdmCl**........ Guanidinium Chloride [*Biochemistry*]
**GDME**........ Glycol Dimethyl Ether [*Organic chemistry*]
**GDMK**........ GoodMark Foods, Inc. [*Raleigh, NC*] [*NASDAQ symbol*] (NQ)
**GDML**........ Gas Dynamic Mixing LASER [*Navy*]
**GDMO**...... General Duties Medical Officer
**GDMS**....... Generalized Data Management System [*Data processing*] (BUR)
**GDMS**....... Geographic Data Management System [*Data processing*]
**GDMS**....... Glow-Discharge Mass Spectroscopy [*or Spectrometry*]
**GDN**.......... Garden
**GDN**.......... Gdansk [*Poland*] [*Airport symbol*] (OAG)
**GDN**.......... Giant Descending Neuron [*Neurology*]
**GDN**.......... Glycol Dinitrate [*Organic chemistry*]
**GDN**.......... Golden News Resources Corp. [*Vancouver Stock Exchange symbol*]
**Gdn**............ Guanidine [*Biochemistry*]
**GDN**.......... Guardian
**GDNC**........ Guidance (MSA)
**GDNCE**..... Guidance (AFM)
**Gdng Ill**...... Gardening Illustrated [*A publication*]
**Gdn J NY Bot Gdn**... Garden Journal. New York Botanical Garden [*A publication*]
**GDNS**........ Gardens (MCD)
**Gdns Bull**... Gardens Bulletin [*A publication*]
**Gdns Bull (Singapore)**... Gardens Bulletin (Singapore) [*A publication*]
**GDO**.......... Garage Door Opener (NG)
**GDO**.......... General Development Order [*Town and country planning*] [*British*]
**GDO**.......... Grid-Dip Oscillator
**GDO**.......... Gross Domestic Output [*Economics*]
**GDO**.......... Guasdualito [*Venezuela*] [*Airport symbol*] (OAG)
**GDO**.......... Guidance Officer (KSC)
**GDO**.......... Gun Direction Officer (NATG)
**GDOA**........ Graphic Data Output Area (CMD)
**GDOC**........ University of Guelph Document Holdings [*Database*] [*No longer available online*]
**GDOES**..... Glow-Discharge Optical Emission Spectroscopy
**GDOP**........ Geometric Degradation of Position [*Aerospace*]
**GDOP**........ Geometric Dilution of Precision
**GDoS**......... South Georgia College, Douglas, GA [*Library symbol*] [*Library of Congress*] (LCLS)
**GDP**........... Gaede Diffusion Pump
**GDP**........... Gale Directory of Publications [*Later, GDPBM*] [*A publication*]
**GDP**........... Gaseous Discharge Principle
**GDP**........... General Defense Plan [*Formerly, EDP*] [*NATO*] (NATG)
**GDP**........... General Development Plan (MUGU)
**GDP**........... Generalized Distributor Program [*Data processing*]
**GDP**........... Generalized Documentation Processor (NASA)
**GDP**........... Generalized Drawing Primitive
**GDP**........... Gesamtdeutsche Partei [*All-German Party*] [*Federal Republic of Germany*] (PPE)
**GDP**........... Goal-Directed Programming
**GDP**........... Golden Pond Resources [*Vancouver Stock Exchange symbol*]
**GDP**........... Government Data Publications [*Information service or system*] (IID)
**GDP**........... Graphic Display Processor
**GDP**........... Grid Driving Power
**GDP**........... Gross Domestic Product [*Economics*]
**GDP**........... Grounded into Double Plays [*Baseball*]
**GDP**........... Guadalupe Pass, TX [*Location identifier*] [*FAA*] (FAAL)
**GDP**........... Guanosine Diphosphate [*Biochemistry*]
**GDP**........... Gun Defence Position [*Navy*] [*British*]
**GDP**........... Gun Director Pointer [*Naval gunnery*]
**GDPA**........ General Dental Practitioner's Association [*British*]
**GDPBM**.... Gale Directory of Publications and Broadcast Media [*Formerly, GDP*] [*A publication*]
**GDP(CL)**... Gun Director Pointer (Cross Leveler) [*Naval gunnery*]
**GD/PD**...... General Dynamics, Pomona Division
**GDP(L)**...... Gun Director Pointer (Leveler) [*Naval gunnery*]
**GDPMan**... Guanosine Diphosphomannose [*Biochemistry*]
**GDP(P)**...... Gun Director Pointer (Pointer) [*Naval gunnery*]
**GDPS**......... Global Data Processing System [*World Meteorological Organization*]
**GDPS**......... Government Document Publishing Service
**GDP(SS)**.... Gun Director Pointer (Sight Setter) [*Naval gunnery*]
**GDP(T)**...... Gun Director Pointer (Trainer) [*Naval gunnery*]

**GDQ** .......... Golden Dragon Resources [*Vancouver Stock Exchange symbol*]
**GDQ** .......... Gondar [*Ethiopia*] [*Airport symbol*] (OAG)
**GDQ** .......... Ministry of Transport, Government of Quebec [*Canada*] [*FAA designator*] (FAAC)
**GDQF** ........ Graphical Display and Query Facility [*IBM Corp.*]
**GDR** .......... Gaol Delivery Roll (ROG)
**GDR** .......... Gaucher's Disease Registry [*Superseded by National Gaucher Foundation - NGF*] (EA)
**GDR** .......... Geodetic Data Reduction
**GDR** .......... Geophysical Data Record
**GDR** .......... German Democratic Republic [*East Germany*]
**GDR** .......... Giant Dipole Resonance
**GDR** .......... Graphic Depth Recorder
**GDR** .......... Grid Dead Reckon [*Military*] (CAAL)
**GDR** .......... Guard Rail (AAG)
**GDRC** ........ Gyro Drift Rate Compensation
**GDROA** ...... Gidroaeromehanika [*A publication*]
**GDS** .......... Agnes Scott College, Decatur, GA [*Library symbol*] [*Library of Congress*] (LCLS)
**GDS** .......... Gas Dynamic System
**GDS** .......... Gel Drying System [*Chromatography*]
**GDS** .......... Gendis, Inc. [*Toronto Stock Exchange symbol*]
**GDS** .......... General Data Stream [*Data processing*]
**GDS** .......... General Declassification Schedule (MCD)
**GDS** .......... General Disposal Schedule [*Australia*]
**GDS** .......... Geodetic Data Site
**GDS** .......... Gesell Developmental Schedules [*Education*]
**GDS** .......... Glenmore Distilleries Co. [*AMEX symbol*] (SPSG)
**GDS** .......... Global Deterioration Scale [*Medicine*]
**GDS** .......... Glow-Discharge Spectrometry
**GDS** .......... GNC [*Guidance and Navigation Computer*] Dynamic Simulator [*NASA*] (NASA)
**GDS** .......... Going Down Swinging [*A publication*] (APTA)
**GDS** .......... Goldstone, CA [*Spaceflight tracking and data network*] [*NASA*] (NASA)
**GDS** .......... Goods
**GDS** .......... Graphic Data System
**GDS** .......... Graphic Design System
**GDS** .......... Graphic Display Segment
**GDS** .......... Graphical Display System [*Station control and data acquisition*] (IEEE)
**GDS** .......... Great Dark Spot [*Image on Neptune*] [*Astronomy*]
**GDS** .......... Ground Data System
**GDS** .......... Ground Display System
**Gds** .......... Guards [*British military*] (DMA)
**GDS** .......... Overheidsdocumentatie. Orgaan voor Documentatie en Administratieve Organisatie der Overheid [*A publication*]
**GDSA** ........ Goal-Directed Serial Alternation
**GDSBFC** ... Good Day Sunshine Beatles Fan Club (EA)
**GDSC** ........ Graduate Diploma in Social Communication (ADA)
**GDSCC** ...... Goldstone Deep Space Communications Complex [*NASA*]
**GDSD** ........ Ground Data Systems Divsion [*NASA*] (NASA)
**GDSL** ......... Graduate Diploma in School Librarianship (ADA)
**GDSM** ........ Ground Data Systems Manager (MCD)
**GDSM** ........ Guardsman [*Military*]
**GDSN** ........ Global Digital Seismograph Network [*Earthquake study*]
**GDSO** ........ Ground Data Systems Officer (MCD)
**GDSSR** ...... GDSD [*Ground Data Systems Division*] Staff Support Room [*NASA*] (NASA)
**GDT** .......... Gas Decay Tank (NRCH)
**GDT** .......... Gas Discharge Tube
**GD/T** ......... General Dynamics/Telecommunications
**GDT** .......... Geographic Data Technology, Inc. [*Information service or system*] (IID)
**GD & T** ...... Geometric Dimensioning and Tolerancing
**GDT** .......... Global Descriptor Table [*Data processing*]
**GDT** .......... Grand Turk [*British West Indies*] [*Airport symbol*] (OAG)
**GDT** .......... Graphic Display Terminal
**GDT** .......... Ground Data Terminal
**GDTI** ......... General Database Technology [*NASDAQ symbol*] (NQ)
**Gd Times** ... Good Times [*A publication*]
**GDTL** ........ Graduate Diploma in Teacher Librarianship (ADA)
**GDTS** ......... Gliding Deceleration Technology System
**GDU** .......... Garbage Disposal Unit (ADA)
**GDU** .......... Glendale Resources, Inc. [*Vancouver Stock Exchange symbol*]
**GDU** .......... Graphic Display Unit
**GDU** .......... Guide Dog Users (EA)
**GDunGS** .... Church of Jesus Christ of Latter-Day Saints, Genealogical Society Library, Sandy Springs Georgia Branch, Dunwoody, GA [*Library symbol*] [*Library of Congress*] (LCLS)
**G Dur** ......... Guillelmus Durandi [*Deceased, 1296*] [*Authority cited in pre-1607 legal work*] (DSA)
**G Duran** ..... Guillelmus Durandi [*Deceased, 1296*] [*Authority cited in pre-1607 legal work*] (DSA)
**GDuV** ......... United States Veterans Administration Center, Dublin, GA [*Library symbol*] [*Library of Congress*] (LCLS)
**GDV** .......... General Development Corp. [*NYSE symbol*] (SPSG)
**GDV** .......... Geomagnetic Daily Variations
**GDV** .......... Gesamtverband der Deutschen Versicherungswirtschaft eV [*Insurance association*] [*Federal Republic of Germany*] (EY)
**GDV** .......... Glendive [*Montana*] [*Airport symbol*] (OAG)
**GDVMA** .... Gidravlicheskie Mashiny [*A publication*]
**GdVP** ......... Grossdeutsche Volkspartei [*Pan-German People's Party*] [*Austria*] [*Political party*] (PPE)
**GDW** .......... Gladwin, MI [*Location identifier*] [*FAA*] (FAAL)
**GDW** .......... Golden West Financial Corp. [*NYSE symbol*] (SPSG)
**GDW** .......... Goldwest Resources Ltd. [*Vancouver Stock Exchange symbol*]
**GDWDA** .... Glaciological Data. World Data Center A [*A publication*]
**GDWDCA** ... Glaciological Data. World Data Center A [*A publication*]
**GDWND** ... Gradient Wind (NOAA)
**GDX** .......... Genovese Drug Stores, Inc. [*AMEX symbol*] (SPSG)
**GDX** .......... Goldstone, California [*Spaceflight Tracking and Data Network*] [*NASA*]
**GDX** .......... Grandex Resources Ltd. [*Vancouver Stock Exchange symbol*]
**GDX** .......... Gun Direction Exercise [*British military*] (DMA)
**GDX** .......... Upperville, VA [*Location identifier*] [*FAA*] (FAAL)
**GDXM** ....... Goldex Mines Ltd. [*NASDAQ symbol*] (NQ)
**GDY** .......... Grundy, VA [*Location identifier*] [*FAA*] (FAAL)
**GDYL** ........ Great Dictionary of the Yiddish Language [*Columbia University Department of Linguistics*] [*Information service or system*] (IID)
**GDYN** ........ Geodynamics Corp. [*Santa Barbara, CA*] [*NASDAQ symbol*] (NQ)
**GE** ............. Federal Republic of Germany [*West Germany*] [*NATO*] (AFM)
**GE** ............. Garrison Engineer [*British military*] (DMA)
**GE** ............. Garrison Extracts [*Army*]
**GE** ............. Gas Ejection [*Opening*] [*Technical drawings*]
**GE** ............. Gas Examiner [*British*]
**GE** ............. Gastroenterology [*Medicine*]
**GE** ............. Gastroenterostomy [*Medicine*]
**GE** ............. Gateway Exchange [*Telecommunications*]
**GE** ............. Gauge
**GE** ............. Gaussian Elimination (IEEE)
**Ge** ............. Gecelinus [*Zenzelinus de Cassanis*] [*Deceased, 1334*] [*Authority cited in pre-1607 legal work*] (DSA)
**Ge** ............. Gegenwart [*A publication*]
**GE** ............. Gel Electrophoresis [*Analytical chemistry*]
**Ge** ............. [*Dominicus de Sancto*] Geminiano [*Flourished, 1407-09*] [*Authority cited in pre-1607 legal work*] (DSA)
**GE** ............. General Election
**GE** ............. General Electric Co. [*NYSE symbol*] (SPSG)
**GE** ............. General Examination
**GE** ............. General Expenses
**GE** ............. Gentamicin [*Antibacterial compound*] [*Generic form*]
**Ge** ............. [*Albericus*] Gentilis [*Deceased, 1611*] [*Authority cited in pre-1607 legal work*] (DSA)
**GE** ............. Geoscience Electronics (MCD)
**GE** ............. German Cargo Services [*ICAO designator*] (FAAC)
**Ge** ............. Germanium [*Chemical element*]
**GE** ............. Germany (NATG)
**ge** ............. Germany, East [*MARC country of publication code*] [*Library of Congress*] (LCCP)
**GE** ............. Gilbert Islands [*ANSI two-letter standard code*] [*Obsolete*] (CNC)
**GE** ............. [*The*] Gilgamesh Epic and Old Testament Parallels [*A publication*] (BJA)
**GE** ............. Gilt Edges [*Bookbinding*]
**GE** ............. Gimbal Electronics
**GE** ............. Giornale degli Economisti e Annali di Economia [*A publication*]
**Ge** ............. Gli Ebrei nell'Alto Medioevo [*A publication*]
**GE** ............. Gnome Engine [*Hovercraft*]
**GE** ............. Good Evening [*Amateur radio*]
**GE** ............. Grand Earl [*Freemasonry*] (ROG)
**GE** ............. Grand East [*Freemasonry*] (ROG)
**GE** ............. Grand Encampment [*Freemasonry*]
**GE** ............. Grand Expert [*Freemasonry*] (ROG)
**GE** ............. Grand Ezra [*Freemasonry*] (ROG)
**G/E** ........... Granulocyte-Erythroid (Ratio) [*Hematology*]
**G/E** ........... Graphite Epoxy (NASA)
**GE** ............. Gravissimam Educationis [*Declaration on Christian Education*] [*Vatican II document*]
**GE** ............. Great Educators [*A publication*]
**GE** ............. Great Exuma [*Bahama Islands*]
**GE** ............. Greater than or Equal To [*FORTRAN*]
**GE** ............. Gross Earnings [*Business term*]
**G & E** ........ Ground and Environmental (KSC)
**GE** ............. Ground Equipment
**GE** ............. Grounded Emitter
**GE** ............. Group Engineer
**GE** ............. Group of Experts (NATG)
**GE** ............. Gyro Error
**GE** ............. Transportes Aereos da Portuguesa [*Portugal*] [*ICAO designator*] [*Obsolete*] (FAAC)
**GEA** ........... Farbenfabriken Bayer [*Germany*] [*Research code symbol*]
**GEA** ........... General Electric-ARSD, Sunnyvale, CA [*OCLC symbol*] (OCLC)

**GEA**.......... Georgia Air Freight [*Atlanta, GA*] [*FAA designator*] (FAAC)
**GEA**.......... German East Africa [*Obsolete*] (ROG)
**GEA**.......... Global Education Associates (EA)
**GEA**.......... Gravure Engravers Association (EA)
**GEA**.......... Greater East Asia [*Used by Japanese in such terms as War of Greater East Asia and Greater East Asia Co-Prosperity Sphere*] [*World War II*]
**GEA**.......... Noumea [*New Caledonia*] Magenta Airport [*Airport symbol*] (OAG)
**GEAAE**...... Groupement Europeen des Artistes des Ardennes et de l'Eifel [*European Group of Artists of the Ardennes and the Eifel*] (EAIO)
**GEAB**........ Geophysical Abstracts [*A publication*]
**GEADGE**.. German Air Defense Ground Environment
**GEAEA**...... Geomagnetizm i Aeronomiya [*A publication*]
**GEAG**........ General Electric Airborne Guidance (AAG)
**GEANS**...... Gimbaled Electrostatic-Gyro Aircraft Navigation System [*Air Force*]
**GEAP**......... General Electric Atomic Power [*or Products*]
**GEAP**......... Groupe Europeen d'Administration Publique [*European Group of Public Administration - EGPA*] [*Brussels, Belgium*] (EAIO)
**GEAPS**...... Grain Elevator and Processing Society (EA)
**GEARA**..... Georgia Agricultural Research [*A publication*]
**Gear Landl & T**... Gear on Landlord and Tenant [*A publication*] (DLA)
**GEASA**...... Geofizika i Astronomiya Informatsionnyi Byulleten [*A publication*]
**GEASCOP**... General Asymptotic Composition Program [*Data processing*]
**GE/ASD**.... General Electric/Apollo Support Division (KSC)
**GEAU**........ Groupe d'Etudes et d'Actions Urbaines [*Canada*]
**GEAV**........ Guidance Error Analysis Vehicles [*Air Force*]
**GEB**........... Chefmagazin fuer Kleinbetriebe und Mittelbetriebe [*A publication*]
**GEB**........... Geboren [*Born*] [*German*]
**GEB**........... Gebrueder [*Brothers*] [*German*]
**GEB**........... Gebunden [*Bound*] [*Publishing*] [*German*]
**GEB**........... General Engine Bulletin
**GEB**........... Gerber Products Co. [*NYSE symbol*] (SPSG)
**GEB**........... Guiding Eyes for the Blind (EA)
**GEBA**........ Government Excess Baggage Authorization
**GEBAAX**... Geologica Bavarica [*A publication*]
**GEBAD2**... Geologica Balcanica [*A publication*]
**GEBCO**..... General Bathymetric Chart of the Oceans [*International Hydrographic Bureau*]
**Gebrauchs**... Gebrauchsgraphik [*A publication*]
**Gebrauchs Novum**... Gebrauchsgraphik Novum [*A publication*]
**GEBSAJ**.... Geobios [*Lyon*] [*A publication*]
**Geburtsh Fr**... Geburtshilfe und Frauenheilkunde [*A publication*]
**Geburtshilfe Frauenheilkd**... Geburtshilfe und Frauenheilkunde [*A publication*]
**Geburtshilfe Fraunheilkd**... Geburtshilfe und Frauenheilkunde [*A publication*]
**GEC**........... Galactose Elimination Capacity
**GEC**........... Gaseous Electronics Conference
**GEC**........... Geauga County Public Library, Chardon, OH [*OCLC symbol*] (OCLC)
**GEC**........... GEICO Corporation [*NYSE symbol*] (SPSG)
**GEC**........... General Electric Company
**GEC**........... General Electrodynamics Corporation (MCD)
**GEC**........... General Equipment Command [*Army*]
**GEC**........... Geneva Executives Club (EA)
**GEC**........... Government Employees Council [*Later, PED*] (EA)
**GEC**........... Graphic Export Center [*Netherlands*]
**GEC**........... Ground Environment Complex (MCD)
**GECA**........ Government Employees' Compensation Act [*1908*]
**GECAL**...... General Electric Credit Auto Lease, Inc.
**GEC At Energy Rev**... GEC [*General Electric Company*] Atomic Energy Review [*A publication*]
**GECC**........ Gasoline Engine, Close-Coupled
**GECC**........ Government Employees Clinic Center [*British*]
**GECCMSEF**... Group to Establish Criteria for Certifying Munitions Systems to Electromagnetic Fields [*DoD*] (RDA)
**GECECS**... General Electric Chemical Engineering Calculation System
**Gecel**.......... Gecelinus [*Zenzelinus de Cassanis*] [*Deceased, 1334*] [*Authority cited in pre-1607 legal work*] (DSA)
**GECHB**..... Geochemistry [*Nagoya*] [*A publication*]
**GECHD**..... Geochronique [*A publication*]
**GEC J**........ GEC [*General Electric Company*] Journal [*A publication*]
**GEC J Sci & Technol**... GEC [*General Electric Company*] Journal of Science and Technology [*A publication*]
**GECM**....... GENICOM Corp. [*Waynesboro, VA*] [*NASDAQ symbol*] (NQ)
**GECO**........ General Aero Products Corporation [*Copiague, NY*] [*NASDAQ symbol*] (NQ)
**GECO**........ Guidance Engine Cutoff [*NASA*] (KSC)
**GECOM**.... Generalized Compiler [*Data processing*]
**G Economisti**... Giornale degli Economisti e Annali di Economia [*A publication*]
**GECOS**...... General Comprehensive Operating Supervisor [*Data processing*]
**GECOS**...... General Comprehensive Operating System
**GEC Telecommun**... GEC [*General Electric Company*] Telecommunications [*A publication*]
**GECX**........ Gulf Exploration Consultants, Inc. [*NASDAQ symbol*] (NQ)
**GED**........... Gasoline Engine Driven
**Ged**............ Gedaagde [*Defendant*] [*Netherlands*] (ILCA)
**GED**........... Gedampft [*Muted*] [*Music*]
**GED**........... Gedeh [*Java*] [*Seismograph station code, US Geological Survey*] [*Closed*] (SEIS)
**GED**........... General Educational Development [*Test*]
**GED**........... General Energy Development Ltd. [*NYSE symbol*] (SPSG)
**GED**........... General Equivalency Diploma [*For nongraduates*]
**GED**........... Geo-Data International [*Vancouver Stock Exchange symbol*]
**GED**........... Georgetown, DE [*Location identifier*] [*FAA*] (FAAL)
**GED**........... Global Engineering Documents [*Santa Ana, CA*] [*Information service or system*]
**GED**........... Government Electronics Division
**GED**........... Group on Electronic Devices
**GED**........... Gunn Effect Device
**GEDAC**..... General Electric Detection and Automatic Correction (NASA)
**GEDEAL**... Gesundheitswesen und Desinfektion [*A publication*]
**GEDED**..... General Dentistry [*A publication*]
**GEDI**......... General Educational Development Institute (EA)
**GEDI**......... Groupe d'Etudes en Developpement International [*International Development Studies Group*] [*Canada*]
**GEDID2**.... Gerbil Digest [*A publication*]
**GEDMAB**... Geoderma [*A publication*]
**GEdO**......... Group Education Officer [*British military*] (DMA)
**GEDP**........ General Educational Development Program [*Army*] (AABC)
**GEDPD**..... Gallaudet Encyclopedia of Deaf People and Deafness [*A publication*]
**Gedrag & Gezond**... Gedrag und Gezondheid [*A publication*]
**Gedrag T P**... Gedrag-Tijdschrift voor Psychologie [*A publication*]
**GEDT**........ General Educational Development Test
**GEDY**........ Genetic Dynamics Corp. [*NASDAQ symbol*] (NQ)
**GEE**........... Geehi [*Australia*] [*Seismograph station code, US Geological Survey*] [*Closed*] (SEIS)
**GEE**........... General Evaluation Equipment
**GEE**........... Geneseo, NY [*Location identifier*] [*FAA*] (FAAL)
**GEE**........... Group for Environmental Education
**GEEIA**....... Ground Electronics Engineering Installation Agency [*Air Force*]
**GEEK**........ Geomagnetic Electrokinetograph [*Equipment for exploring ocean depths*]
**GEEN**........ Genetic Engineering, Inc. [*NASDAQ symbol*] (NQ)
**GEE/NA**.... Nova Americana. Giulio Einaudi Editore [*A publication*]
**Ge Engr**...... Geological Engineer
**GEEP**......... General Electric Electronic Processor
**GEESE**...... General Electric Electronic System Evaluator
**GEF**........... Gauss Error Function [*Mathematics*]
**Gef**............. Gefaells [*Revenue*] [*German*]
**GEF**........... Gel Electrofocusing [*Analytical chemistry*]
**GEF**........... General Electric Co. and Fanuc Automation Corp.
**GEF**........... Gonadotropin Enhancing Factor [*Endocrinology*]
**GEF**........... Gradient Elution Fractionation
**GEF**........... Gravure Education Foundation (EA)
**GEF**........... Greenville, FL [*Location identifier*] [*FAA*] (FAAL)
**GEF**........... Ground Equipment Failure [*Air Force*]
**GEF**........... Nicholas-Applegate Group [*NYSE symbol*] (SPSG)
**GEFA**........ Gulf-European Freight Association [*Defunct*] (EA)
**GEFAP**...... Groupement Europeen des Associations Nationales des Fabricants de Pesticides [*European Group of National Pesticide Manufacturer' Associations*] [*Common Market*]
**GEFDU**..... Groupe Europeen des Femmes Diplomees des Universites [*University Women of Europe - UWE*] (EA)
**GEFO**........ Geoforum [*A publication*]
**GEFP**......... Guild of Ethical Funeral Practice (EA)
**GEFR**......... George Eliot Fellowship Review [*A publication*]
**GEFRC**...... General File/Record Control [*Honeywell, Inc.*]
**GEFS**......... General Electric Flame Site (MUGU)
**GEFT**......... Group Embedded Figure Test [*Education*]
**GEG**........... Gamma Eta Gamma [*Fraternity*]
**GEG**........... Gegechkori [*USSR*] [*Seismograph station code, US Geological Survey*] [*Closed*] (SEIS)
**GEG**........... Geluid en Omgeving [*A publication*]
**GEG**........... Grace Energy Corp. [*NYSE symbol*] (SPSG)
**GEG**........... Grange Gold Corp. [*Vancouver Stock Exchange symbol*]
**GEG**........... Gun Evaluation Group [*Military*] (CAAL)
**GEG**........... Spokane [*Washington*] [*Airport symbol*] (OAG)
**GEGAS**...... General Electric Gas [*Process*]
**Gegenbaurs Morphol Jahrb**... Gegenbaurs Morphologisches Jahrbuch [*A publication*]
**Geg G S Erz**... Gegenwartskunde Gesellschaft Staat Erziehung [*A publication*]
**GEGIA**....... Geneeskundige Gids [*A publication*]
**GEGR**........ General Grant National Memorial
**GEGS**......... General Electric Guidance System [*Aerospace*] (AAG)
**Geh**............ Gehalt [*Contents*] [*German*] (ILCA)
**Geh**............ Geheimrat [*Privy Councillor*] [*German*] (ILCA)
**GEH**........... George Eastman House [*Rochester, NY*]
**GEHAD**..... Gekkan Haikibutsu [*A publication*]
**GEHEA7**... Gentes Herbarum [*A publication*]
**GEHF**........ Government Employees Health Fund [*Australia*]

**GEHIA** ...... Gencho Hiroshima Igaku [*A publication*]
**GEHL** ........ Gehl Co. [*NASDAQ symbol*] (NQ)
**GEI** ............ Geisinger Medical Center, Medical Library, Danville, PA [*OCLC symbol*] (OCLC)
**G & EI** ........ Gilbert and Ellice Islands (ILCA)
**GEI** ............ Graphics Engine Interface [*Data processing*]
**GEI** ............ Graymoor Ecumenical Institute (EA)
**GEI** ............ Grenlock Energy, Incorporated [*Vancouver Stock Exchange symbol*]
**GEI** ............ Gruppo Esponenti Italiani (EA)
**GEICO** ...... Government Employees Insurance Company
**GEII** ........... Great Eastern International, Incorporated [*Denver, CO*] [*NASDAQ symbol*] (NQ)
**GEINA** ...... Gesundheits-Ingenieur [*A publication*]
**GEIR** .......... GPETE End Item Replacement (NVT)
**GEIRD** ....... Gendai Iryo [*A publication*]
**GEIS** .......... GE [*General Electric Co.*] Information Services [*Information service or system*] (IID)
**GEIS** .......... Generalized Environmental Impact Statement
**GEIS** .......... Generic Environmental Impact Statement [*or Study*] [*Nuclear energy*] (NRCH)
**GEISA** ....... Gestion et Etude des Informations Spectroscopiques Atmospheriques [*Database*] [*Laboratoire de Meteorologie Dynamique du CNRS*] [*French*] [*Information service or system*] (CRD)
**GEISCO** .... General Electric Information Services Company [*General Electric Co.*] [*Software manufacturer*] [*Information service or system*] [*Telecommunications*] (IID)
**GEISHA** .... Geodetic Inertial Survey and Horizontal Alignment (IEEE)
**GEISHA** .... Gun Electron-Induced Semiconductor Hybrid Amplifier
**GeistLeb** .... Geist und Leben [*Wuerzburg*] [*A publication*]
**GEJ** ............ Gaseous Ejection (KSC)
**GEJAA** ...... Geologisches Jahrbuch [*A publication*]
**GEJAA5** .... Geologisches Jahrbuch [*A publication*]
**GEJBA8** .... Geologisches Jahrbuch. Beihefte [*A publication*]
**GEJO** ......... Geographical Journal [*A publication*]
**GEJOBE** ... Geochemical Journal [*A publication*]
**GEJODG** ... Geomicrobiology Journal [*A publication*]
**GE & JR** .... Great Eastern & Joint Railway [*British*] (ROG)
**GEK** ........... Ganes Creek, AK [*Location identifier*] [*FAA*] (FAAL)
**GEK** ........... Geomagnetic Electrokinetograph [*Equipment for exploring ocean depths*]
**GEKYA** ...... Gensen-Kyo [*A publication*]
**GEL** ........... Gelatin
**GEL** ........... Gelco Corp. [*NYSE symbol*] (SPSG)
**GEL** ........... General Electric Laboratory
**GEL** ........... General Emulation Language
**GEL** ........... Gilbert Islands [*ANSI three-letter standard code*] [*Obsolete*] (CNC)
**GEL** ........... Golden Eagle Airlines [*Redding, CA*] [*FAA designator*] (FAAC)
**GEL** ........... Goldenlode Resources Ltd. [*Vancouver Stock Exchange symbol*]
**GEL** ........... Groupement Europeen de Lymphologie [*European Lymphology Group - ELG*] [*Brussels, Belgium*] (EAIO)
**GEL** ........... Guaranteed Employment Level
**GEL** ........... Santo Angelo [*Brazil*] [*Airport symbol*] (OAG)
**GELAC** ...... Georgia Division, Lockheed Aircraft Corporation
**GELAP** ...... General Electric Computer Analysis Program
**GELC** ......... Groupe des Editeurs de Livres de la CEE [*Book Publishers Group of EEC*] (EAIO)
**Gelcap** ........ Gelatin-Coated Capsule [*Pharmacy*]
**GELD** ........ [*Dr. Karl F.*] Geldner [*German Oriental scholar, 1852-1929*] (ROG)
**Geldart** ....... Geldart and Maddock's English Chancery Reports [*6 Maddock's Reports*] [*A publication*] (DLA)
**Geld & M** ... Geldart and Maddock's English Chancery Reports [*6 Maddock's Reports*] [*A publication*] (DLA)
**Geld & O** .... Nova Scotia Decisions, by Geldert and Oxley [*A publication*] (DLA)
**Geld & Ox** ... Nova Scotia Decisions, by Geldert and Oxley [*A publication*] (DLA)
**Geld & R** .... Geldert and Russell's Nova Scotia Reports [*A publication*] (DLA)
**GELFAC** ... Gel Frontal Analysis Chromatography
**Gel and Glue Res Assoc** ... Gelatin and Glue Research Association [*A publication*]
**GELIS** ....... Ground Emitter Location and Identification System [*Army*]
**GELIS-H** ... Ground Emitter Location and Identification System - High [*Army*]
**Gell** ............ [*Aulus*] Gellius [*Roman author, second century AD*] [*Classical studies*] (OCD)
**GEL QUAV** ... Gelatina Quavis [*In Any Kind of Jelly*] [*Pharmacy*] (ROG)
**GELTSPAP** ... Group of Experts on Long-Term Scientific Policy and Planning [*UNESCO*]
**GEM** .......... Gas Energy Management
**GEM** .......... Gas Energy Management [*British*]
**GEM** .......... Gas Exchange Module [*Cell culture*]
**Gem** ........... Gemara (BJA)
**Gem** ........... Geminatae (BJA)
**gem** ............ Geminate [*Chemistry*]
**Gem** ........... Gemini [*Constellation*]
**GEM** .......... General Epitaxial Monolith (IEEE)
**GEM** .......... Generic Experiment Module
**GEM** .......... Genetically Engineered Microorganism
**GeM** ........... Geographical Magazine [*A publication*]
**gem** ............ Germanic [*MARC language code*] [*Library of Congress*] (LCCP)
**GEM** .......... GeV Electron Microtron [*Atomic accelerator*] [*Proposed*]
**GEM** .......... Giant Earth Mover [*Machine*]
**GEM** .......... Goddard Earth Model [*NASA*]
**GEM** .......... Government-Education-Medical
**GEM** .......... Graduated [*or Growing*] Equity Mortgage
**GEM** .......... Graff Electronic Machines Ltd. [*British*]
**GEM** .......... Graphics Environment Manager [*Data processing*]
**GEM** .......... Ground Effect Machine (NG)
**GEM** .......... Ground Electronics Maintenance
**GEM** .......... Groupes Evangile et Mission [*Institute of the Heart of Jesus - IHJ*] (EA)
**GEM** .......... Growing Equity Mortgage
**GEM** .......... Guidance Evaluation Missile
**GEM** .......... Gulf Energy & Minerals Co.
**GEM** .......... Gun Effectiveness Model
**GEM** .......... Gunn Effect Material
**GEM** .......... Gyro Energy & Minerals Corp. [*Vancouver Stock Exchange symbol*]
**GEM** .......... Miami, FL [*Location identifier*] [*FAA*] (FAAL)
**GEM** .......... National Consortium for Graduate Degrees for Minorities in Engineering (EA)
**GEMA** ....... Geographical Magazine [*A publication*]
**GEMA** ....... Grain Equipment Manufacturers Association (EA)
**GE/MAC** ... General Electric Measurement and Control
**GEMAGS** ... General Electric Magnetically Anchored Gravity System
**GEMAS** ..... Groupement Europeen des Maisons d'Alimentation et d'Approvisionnement a Succursales [*European Group of Food and Provision Chain Stores*] [*Common Market*] [*Brussels, Belgium*]
**Gematol Pereliv Krovi** ... Gematologiya i Perelivanie Krovi [*A publication*]
**Gematol Pereliv Krovi Resp Mezhved Sb** ... Gematologiya i Perelivanie Krovi Respublikanskoi Mezhvedomstvennyi Sbornik [*A publication*]
**Gematol Transfuziol** ... Gematologiya i Transfuziologiya [*A publication*]
**GEMBAN** ... Getreide Mehl und Brot [*A publication*]
**GEMC** ....... Geriatric & Medical Centers, Inc. [*NASDAQ symbol*] (NQ)
**GEMCO** .... Global Electronic Markets Company [*Joint venture of Citicorp and McGraw-Hill, Inc. to provide computerized buying, selling, shipping, and insuring services for commodities traders*]
**GEMCOS** ... Generalized Message Control System (BUR)
**GEMEE2** ... Genitourinary Medicine [*A publication*]
**Gemeinsames Amtsbl A** ... Gemeinsames Amtsblatt. Ausgabe A [*West Germany*] [*A publication*]
**Gemeinsames Amtsbl Landes Baden-Wuerttemb A** ... Gemeinsames Amtsblatt des Landes Baden-Wuerttemberg. Ausgabe A [*A publication*]
**Gemeinsames Ministerialbl A** ... Gemeinsames Ministerialblatt A [*A publication*]
**GEMGA4** .. Geological Magazine [*A publication*]
**GEMH** ....... Gemcraft, Inc. [*Houston, TX*] [*NASDAQ symbol*] (NQ)
**Gemi** .......... Gemini [*Constellation*]
**Gemi** .......... Geminiano [*Flourished, 1407-09*] [*Authority cited in pre-1607 legal work*] (DSA)
**GEMIA** ...... Geologie en Mijnbouw [*A publication*]
**GEMIAA** ... Geologie en Mijnbouw [*A publication*]
**GEML** ........ Melilla [*Spain*] [*ICAO location identifier*] (ICLI)
**GEMM** ...... Generalized Electronics Maintenance Model
**GEMM** ...... Generic Missile Model (MCD)
**GEMM** ...... Gilt-Edged Market Maker [*London Stock Exchange*] [*England*]
**GEMM** ...... Granulocyte, Erythroid, Macrophage, Megakaryocyte [*Hematology*]
**GEMMA** ... Gilt-Edged Market Makers' Association [*London Stock Exchange*] [*England*]
**Gemmol Soc Jap J** ... Gemmological Society of Japan Journal [*A publication*]
**GEMMS** .... Geophysical Exploration Manned Mobile Submersible
**GEMMSS** ... Ground Emplaced Mine Scattering System [*Military*] (RDA)
**GEMO** ....... Ground Electronic Maintenance Officer [*NASA*] (NG)
**Gemol (Sao Paulo)** ... Gemologia. Associacao Brasileira de Gemologia e Mineralogia (Sao Paulo) [*A publication*]
**GEMP** ....... Government Energy Management Program [*Australia*]
**GEMS** ........ Electronic Specialty Products, Inc. [*NASDAQ symbol*] (NQ)
**GEMS** ........ General Education Management System [*Data processing*] (IEEE)
**GEMS** ........ General Electric Manufacturing Simulator (IEEE)
**GEMS** ........ General Energy and Materials Balance System [*Data processing*] [*Chemical engineering*]
**GEMS** ........ General Equipment Maintenance System [*Software*] [*Diagonal Data Corp.*] [*Automotive engineering*]
**GEMS** ........ Generalized Evaluation Model Simulator [*NASA*]
**GEMS** ........ Geostationary European Meteorological Satellite
**GEMS** ........ German Mass Spectrometer
**GEMS** ........ Global Environment Monitoring System [*UNEP*] [*Database producer*] (IID)

**GEMS**........ Graphical Exposure Modeling System [*For estimating pollutants*]
**GEMS**........ Ground Emplaced Mine Scattering System [*Military*] (AABC)
**GEMS**........ Growth, Economy, Management, and Customer Satisfaction [*Procedure for establishing management goals*]
**GEMSA**..... Guanidinoethylmercaptosuccinic Acid [*Biochemistry*]
**GeMSAEC** ... General Medical Sciences and Atomic Energy Commission
**GEMSERVICE** ... Global Electronic Mail Service [*Electronic Mail Corp. of America*] [*Old Greenwich, CT*] [*Telecommunications*] (TSSD)
**Gems Gemol** ... Gems and Gemology. Gemological Institute of America [*A publication*]
**GEMSI**...... Group of Experts on Methods, Standards, and Intercalibration [*Oceanography*] (MSC)
**GEMSIP** ... Gemini Stability Improvement Program [*NASA*]
**GEMSS**..... Ground Emplaced Mine Scattering System [*Military*] (RDA)
**Gem State News Lett** ... Gem State News Letter [*A publication*]
**Gem State RN News Lett** ... Gem State RN News Letter [*Idaho*] [*A publication*]
**GEMU**....... German Economic and Monetary Union
**Gen**............ Gecelinus [*Zenzelinus de Cassanis*] [*Deceased, 1334*] [*Authority cited in pre-1607 legal work*] (DSA)
**GEN**.......... GEN. Government Equipment News [*A publication*] (APTA)
**Gen**............ Genava [*A publication*]
**GEN**.......... Gender
**GEN**.......... Genealogy
**GEN**.......... General (AABC)
**GEN**.......... General Electric Network [*Data processing*]
**GEN**.......... Generate
**GEN**.......... Generation (MSA)
**GEN**.......... Generator [*Data processing*] (AAG)
**GEN**.......... Generic
**Gen**............ Genesis [*Old Testament book*]
**GEN**.......... Genetics
**GEN**.......... Geneva [*City in Switzerland*]
**GEN**.......... Genital
**GEN**.......... Genitive [*Case*] [*Grammar*]
**GEN**.......... Genoa [*Italy*] [*Seismograph station code, US Geological Survey*] [*Closed*] (SEIS)
**GEN**.......... GenRad, Inc. [*NYSE symbol*] (SPSG)
**GEN**.......... Genuine (ADA)
**GEN**.......... Genus [*Biology*]
**GEN**.......... Gerin, Inc. [*Toronto Stock Exchange symbol*]
**GEN**.......... Gilgamesh, Enkidu, and the Netherworld (BJA)
**GEN**.......... Greater Lenora Resources Corp. [*Toronto Stock Exchange symbol*] [*Vancouver Stock Exchange symbol*]
**GEN**. ......... Oslo [*Norway*] Ardermoen Airport [*Airport symbol*] (OAG)
**Gen Abr Cas Eq** ... General Abridgment of Cases in Equity [*Equity Cases Abridged*] [*1677-1744*] [*A publication*] (DLA)
**Gen An**....... De Generatione Animalium [*of Aristotle*] [*Classical studies*] (OCD)
**Gen Appl Entomol** ... General and Applied Entomology [*A publication*]
**Gen Arm** .... Generals of the Army and the Air Force and Admirals of the Navy [*A publication*]
**GENB**........ [*The*] Genesee Brewing Co., Inc. [*NASDAQ symbol*] (NQ)
**GENBANK** ... Genetic Sequences Databank [*Intelligenetics, Inc.*] [*Information service or system*] (IID)
**GENC**........ General Electric Nose Cone [*Aerospace*] (AAG)
**GEN CAR** ... General Cargo [*Shipping*] (DS)
**Gen C Endoc** ... General and Comparative Endocrinology [*A publication*]
**GENCHEM** ... General Chemical Indicators [*Database*] [*Probe Economics, Inc.*] [*Information service or system*] (CRD)
**Gen Chim**... Genie Chimique [*Chemical Engineering Science*] [*A publication*]
**Gen Comp Endocr** ... General and Comparative Endocrinology [*A publication*]
**Gen Comp Endocrinol** ... General and Comparative Endocrinology [*A publication*]
**Gen Comp Endocrinol Suppl** ... General and Comparative Endocrinology. Supplement [*A publication*]
**GENCONV** ... Geneva Conventions [*Military*] (NVT)
**Gen Corr** .... De Generatione et Corruptione [*of Aristotle*] [*Classical studies*] (OCD)
**Gen Cytochem Methods** ... General Cytochemical Methods [*A publication*]
**GEND**........ Generated Data File [*Data processing*]
**GENDARME** ... Generalized Data Reduction, Manipulation, Evaluation
**GEN DEL** ... General Delivery
**Gen Dent**.... General Dentistry [*A publication*]
**GENDEP**... General Depot [*Military*]
**GENDET**... General Detail [*Coast Guard*]
**Gen Dig**...... General Digest [*A publication*] (DLA)
**Gen Dig NS** ... General Digest, New Series [*A publication*] (DLA)
**GENDIS**.... General Distribution [*Pentagon security classification code*]
**GENDISP** ... General Dispensary [*Military*]
**GENDYN** ... General Dynamics
**GENEA3** ... Genetica [*The Hague*] [*A publication*]
**GENEAL**... Genealogy
**GENEAL MAG** ... Genealogical Magazine [*A publication*]
**Genealogical Period Annu Index** ... Genealogical Periodical Annual Index [*A publication*]
**Genealog Mag** ... Genealogists' Magazine [*A publication*]
**Geneal Per Ind** ... Genealogical Periodical. Annual Index [*A publication*]
**Gene Anal T** ... Gene Analysis Techniques [*A publication*]
**Gene Anal Tech** ... Gene Analysis Techniques [*A publication*]
**Geneesk** ..... Geneeskunde [*A publication*]
**Geneesk Courant** ... Geneeskundige Courant voor het Koningrijk der Nederlanden [*A publication*]
**Geneeskd** ... Geneeskunde [*A publication*]
**Geneeskd Gids** ... Geneeskundige Gids [*A publication*]
**Geneeskd Sport** ... Geneeskunde en Sport [*A publication*]
**Geneesk Tijdschr Nederl-Indiee** ... Geneeskundig Tijdschrift voor Nederlandsch-Indiee [*A publication*]
**Geneesk Tijdschr Ned Indie** ... Geneeskundig Tijdschrift voor Nederlandsch-Indiee [*A publication*]
**Gen Elec R** ... General Electrical Review [*A publication*]
**Gen Electr Co Ltd J Sci Technol** ... General Electric Company Limited. Journal of Science and Technology [*A publication*]
**Gen Electr Rev** ... General Electric Review [*A publication*]
**Gen El Rev** ... General Electric Review [*A publication*]
**Gen Eng**..... General Engineer [*United Kingdom*] [*A publication*]
**GENENG**.. Generalized Engine [*Data processing*]
**Gen Eng Trans** ... General Engineering Transactions [*Australia*] [*A publication*]
**General Ed** ... General Education [*A publication*]
**General Topology and Appl** ... General Topology and Its Applications [*A publication*]
**GENESCO** ... General Shoe Corporation [*Acronym now official name of firm*]
**GENESIS** ... [*A*] programming language [*1978*] (CSR)
**GENESIS** ... Generation Simulation System [*Power systems*]
**GENESYS** ... General Engineering System
**GENESYS** ... Graduate Engineering Education System
**GENET**...... Genetics
**Genet**......... Genetics [*A publication*]
**Genet Abstr** ... Genetics Abstracts [*A publication*]
**Genet Agr**... Genetica Agraria [*A publication*]
**Genet Agrar** ... Genetica Agraria [*A publication*]
**Genet Biokhim Immunokhim Osobo Opasnykh Infekts** ... Genetika Biokhimiya i Immunokhimiya Osobo Opasnykh Infektsii [*A publication*]
**Genet Biokhim Immunokhim Osobo Opasnykh Infektsii** ... Genetika Biokhimiya i Immunokhimiya Osobo Opasnykh Infektsii [*A publication*]
**Genet Biol Drosophila** ... Genetics and Biology of Drosophila [*A publication*]
**Genet Cell Technol** ... Genetic and Cellular Technology [*A publication*]
**Genet Eng Biotechnol Yearb** ... Genetic Engineering and Biotechnology Yearbook [*A publication*]
**Genet Eng Lett** ... Genetic Engineering Letter [*A publication*]
**Genet Eng News** ... Genetic Engineering News [*A publication*]
**Genet Epidemiol** ... Genetic Epidemiology [*A publication*]
**Genet Iber** ... Genetica Iberica [*A publication*]
**Genetics Suppl** ... Genetics. Supplement [*United States*] [*A publication*]
**Genet Lect** ... Genetics Lectures [*A publication*]
**Genet Maps** ... Genetic Maps [*A publication*]
**GENETOX** ... Genetic Toxicity [*Database*] [*Environmental Protection Agency*] [*Information service or system*] (CRD)
**Genet Physiol Note Inst Paper Chem** ... Genetics and Physiology Notes. Institute of Paper Chemistry [*A publication*]
**Genet Physiol Notes** ... Genetics and Physiology Notes [*A publication*]
**Genet Plant Breed** ... Genetics and Plant Breeding [*A publication*]
**Genet Pol** ... Genetica Polonica [*A publication*]
**Genet Princ Perspect** ... Genetics; Principles and Perspectives [*A publication*]
**Genet Psych** ... Genetic Psychology Monographs [*A publication*]
**Genet Psychol Mon** ... Genetic Psychology Monographs [*A publication*]
**Genet Psychol Monog** ... Genetic Psychology Monographs [*A publication*]
**Genet Psychol Monogr** ... Genetic Psychology Monographs [*A publication*]
**Genet Res**... Genetical Research [*A publication*]
**Genet Sel**.... Genetika i Selektsiya [*A publication*]
**Genet Sel Azerb** ... Genetika i Selektsiia v Azerbaidzhan [*A publication*]
**Genet Selektsiya** ... Genetika i Selektsiya [*A publication*]
**Genet Sel Evol** ... Genetique, Selection, Evolution [*A publication*]
**Genet Sel Genet Plant Breed** ... Genetika i Selektsiia. Genetics and Plant Breeding [*A publication*]
**Genet Sinica** ... Genetica Sinica [*Peking*] [*A publication*]
**Genet Slecht** ... Genetika a Slechteni [*A publication*]
**Genet Slechteni** ... Genetika a Slechteni [*A publication*]
**Genet Soc Gen Psychol Monogr** ... Genetic, Social, and General Psychology Monographs [*A publication*]
**Genet Technol News** ... Genetic Technology News [*A publication*]
**Geneve-Afr** ... Geneve-Afrique [*A publication*]
**Gen Fish Counc Mediterr Sess Rep** ... General Fisheries Council for the Mediterranean. Session Report [*A publication*]
**GENG**........ Gasoline Engine
**GENG**........ General Genetics Corp. [*NASDAQ symbol*] (NQ)
**GENGA**..... Geologiya Nefti i Gaza [*A publication*]
**Geng Kenk** ... Gengo Kenkyu [*Journal. Linguistic Society of Japan*] [*A publication*]
**Gen Heterocycl Chem Ser** ... General Heterocyclic Chemistry Series [*A publication*]
**Gen Hosp Psychiatry** ... General Hospital Psychiatry [*A publication*]
**GENI**......... Genetics Institute, Inc. [*Cambridge, MA*] [*NASDAQ symbol*] (NQ)

**GENI** ......... Global Energy Network International
**Gen Iber** ..... Genetica Iberica [*A publication*]
**GEnie** ......... General Electric Network for Information Exchange [*General Electric Co.*] [*Online information service*] (IID)
**GENIE** ....... General Information Environment [*Data Dynamics, Inc.*] [*Portland, OR*] [*Telecommunications service*] (TSSD)
**GENIE** ....... General Information Extractor
**Genie Biol Med** ... Genie Biologique et Medical [*A publication*]
**Genie Chim** ... Genie Chimique [*Chemical Engineering Science*] [*France*] [*A publication*]
**Genie Civ** ... Genie Civil [*A publication*]
**Genie Ind** ... Genie Industrial [*France*] [*A publication*]
**Gen Index** .. General Index [*A publication*]
**Gen Index Publ Reports** ... General Index to Published Reports. Mineral Resources Group [*A publication*]
**GENIP** ....... Geographic Education National Implementation Project [*National Geographic Society*]
**GENISYS** ... General Inferencing System
**GENIT** ....... Genitalia [*Medicine*]
**GENIT** ....... Genitive [*Case*] [*Grammar*]
**Genitourin Med** ... Genitourinary Medicine [*A publication*]
**GENL** ........ General
**GEN L** ....... General Licence [*British*] (ROG)
**GENL** ........ Genetic Laboratories, Inc. [*NASDAQ symbol*] (NQ)
**GENLED** ... General Ledger
**Gen Ling** .... General Linguistics [*A publication*]
**Gen Linguis** ... General Linguistics [*A publication*]
**GENLY** ...... Generally (ROG)
**Gen M As Que J** ... General Mining Association of the Province of Quebec. Journal [*A publication*]
**GENMISH** ... US Military Mission with the Iranian Gendarmerie
**GENMO** .... Generalissimo [*Commander-in-Chief*] [*Spanish*] (ROG)
**GENMOD** ... General Model (RDA)
**Gen Mot Corp Res Lab Res Publ** ... General Motors Corporation. Research Laboratories. Research Publication [*A publication*]
**Gen Mot Eng J** ... General Motors Engineering Journal [*United States*] [*A publication*]
**Gen Newsl Natl Res Counc (Can) Div Mech Eng** ... General Newsletter. National Research Council (Canada). Division of Mechanical Engineering [*A publication*]
**gen nov** ....... Genus Novum [*New Genus*] [*Biology*]
**Gen Ord Ch** ... General Orders of the English High Court of Chancery [*A publication*] (DLA)
**GENOS** ..... Generate Operating System [*Computer program*]
**GENOT** ..... General Notice
**Gen Pharm** ... General Pharmacology [*A publication*]
**Gen Pharmacol** ... General Pharmacology [*A publication*]
**Gen Physiol Biophys** ... General Physiology and Biophysics [*A publication*]
**Gen Pract Clin** ... General Practice Clinics [*A publication*]
**Gen Practnr (Lond)** ... General Practitioner (London) [*A publication*]
**GENPRL** ... General Precision Laboratory
**Gen Psych Mon** ... Genetic Psychology Monographs [*A publication*]
**Gen Pub** ..... General Publication [*A publication*]
**GENR** ........ Generate (AABC)
**GenR** .......... Genesis Rabbah (BJA)
**GENRA8** .... Genetical Research [*A publication*]
**GenRabb** .... Genesis Rabbah (BJA)
**Gen Rad Exp** ... General Radio Experimenter [*A publication*]
**GENRB** ..... Genie Rural [*A publication*]
**Gen Relat G** ... General Relativity and Gravitation [*A publication*]
**Gen Relativ and Gravitation** ... General Relativity and Gravitation [*A publication*]
**Gen Relativ Gravitation** ... General Relativity and Gravitation [*A publication*]
**Gen Relativity Gravitation** ... General Relativity and Gravitation [*A publication*]
**GENREP** ... General Reports [*Military*]
**Gen Rep Dep Archit Sci Syd Univ** ... General Report. Department of Architectural Science. University of Sydney [*A publication*] (APTA)
**Gen Rep Minist Mines Prov Que** ... General Report. Minister of Mines. Province of Quebec [*A publication*]
**Gen Repos** ... General Repository [*A publication*]
**Gen Res** ...... Genetical Research [*A publication*]
**Gen Rur** ...... Genio Rurale [*A publication*]
**GENS** ........ General Soviet [*Later, A Group*] [*Division of National Security Agency*]
**GENS** ........ Genetic Systems Corp. [*NASDAQ symbol*] (NQ)
**GENSA** ...... Journal. Georgia Entomological Society [*A publication*]
**GENSAL** ... Generic Structure Language
**Gen Sci Index** ... General Science Index [*A publication*]
**Gen Sci Q** ... General Science Quarterly [*A publication*]
**GENSER** ... General Service [*Military*] (MCD)
**GENSER** ... General Services Intelligence [*Military*] (CAAL)
**Gen Ser Colo State Agr Exp Sta** ... General Series. Colorado State University. Agricultural Experiment Station [*A publication*]
**GENSESS** ... General Sessions (ADA)
**GENSH** ...... Generate Shell [*Data processing*] (PCM)
**GENSIT** ... General Situation [*Military*] (NVT)
**GENSUP** ... General Support [*Army*]
**GENSURG** ... General Surgery (AABC)
**GENSV** ...... General Service [*Military*]
**Gen Syst** ..... General Systems [*A publication*]
**Gen Syst** ..... General Systems Bulletin [*A publication*]
**GENT** ........ General Technologies Group Ltd. [*NASDAQ symbol*] (NQ)
**Gen T** ......... General Term (DLA)
**GENT** ........ Gentamicin [*Antibacterial compound*]
**GENT** ........ Gentleman
**GENTAE** ... Genetics [*A publication*]
**Gen Tech Rep FPL US Dep Agric For Serv For Prod Lab** ... General Technical Report FPL. United States Department of Agriculture. Forest Service. Forest Products Laboratory [*A publication*]
**Gen Tech Rep FPL US For Prod Lab (Madison Wis)** ... General Technical Report FPL. United States. Forest Products Laboratory (Madison, Wisconsin) [*A publication*]
**Gen Tech Rep RM Rocky Mt For Range Exp Stn US For Serv** ... General Technical Report. RM. Rocky Mountain Forest and Range Experiment Station. United States Forest Service [*A publication*]
**GENTEL** ... General Telephone & Electronics Corp.
**Gentes Herb** ... Gentes Herbarum [*A publication*]
**Gent Herb** ... Gentes Herbarum [*A publication*]
**Gent M** ....... Gentleman's Magazine [*A publication*]
**Gent M ns** ... Gentleman's Magazine. New Series [*A publication*]
**GENTN** ..... Gentleman [*or Gentlemen*] (ROG)
**GENU** ........ General Nutrition, Inc. [*NASDAQ symbol*] (NQ)
**Gen View Cr L** ... Stephen's General View of the Criminal Law [*2nd ed.*] [*1890*] [*A publication*] (DLA)
**GENVST** ... General Public Visiting [*Navy*] (NVT)
**GENY** ........ General Energy Resources & Technology Corp. [*NASDAQ symbol*] (NQ)
**GENY** ........ Generally
**GENZ** ........ Genzyme Corp. [*Boston, MA*] [*NASDAQ symbol*] (NQ)
**GEO** ........... Genetically Engineered Organism
**GEO** ........... Geographic
**GEO** ........... Geographic Division [*Census*] (OICC)
**GEO** ........... Geologist
**GEO** ........... Geophysical Report [*Oil industry term*] (DSUE)
**GEO** ........... Georgetown [*Guyana*] [*Airport symbol*] (OAG)
**GEO** ........... Georgetown [*District of Columbia*] [*Seismograph station code, US Geological Survey*] (SEIS)
**Geo** ............. Georgetown Law Journal [*A publication*]
**GEO** ........... Georgetown, OH [*Location identifier*] [*FAA*] (FAAL)
**GEO** ........... Georgia [*Obsolete*] (ROG)
**Geo** ............. Georgia Reports [*A publication*] (DLA)
**geo** .............. Georgian [*MARC language code*] [*Library of Congress*] (LCCP)
**GEO** ........... Geoscience Electronics (MCD)
**GEO** ........... Geostationary Earth Orbit
**GEO** ........... Geosynchronous Earth Orbit
**GEO** ........... Geotech Capital [*Vancouver Stock Exchange symbol*]
**GEO** ........... Geothermal Resources International, Inc. [*AMEX symbol*] (SPSG)
**GEO** ........... Glosa Education Organisation (EAIO)
**Ge O** ........... Graecolatina et Orientalia [*A publication*]
**GeoAb** ........ Geographical Abstracts [*A publication*]
**Geo Abs & Indexes** ... Geo Abstracts and Indexes [*A publication*]
**Geo Abstr** ... Geographical Abstracts [*A publication*]
**Geo Abstr B Climatol Hydrol** ... Geo Abstracts. B. Climatology and Hydrology [*A publication*]
**Geo Abstr C Econ Geog** ... Geo Abstracts. C. Economic Geography [*A publication*]
**Geo Abstr D Soc Hist Geog** ... Geo Abstracts. D. Social and Historical Geography [*A publication*]
**Geo Abstr E Sedimentology** ... Geo Abstracts. E. Sedimentology [*A publication*]
**Geo Abstr F Reg Com Plan** ... Geo Abstracts. F. Regional and Community Planning [*A publication*]
**Geo Abstr G Remote Sensing Photogram Cartogr** ... Geo Abstracts. G. Remote Sensing, Photogrammetry, and Cartography [*A publication*]
**Geo-Archeologia** ... Geo-Archeologia. Periodico dell'Associazione Geo-Archeologica Italiana [*A publication*]
**GEOBASE** ... Geographic Cross-Reference Data [*Claritas LP*] [*Information service or system*] (CRD)
**GEOBD2** ... Geobotany [*A publication*]
**Geobot Inst Rubel Veroeff** ... Geobotanisches Institut Rubel Veroeffentlichungen [*A publication*]
**GEOCD** ..... Geochimica [*English Translation*] [*A publication*]
**GEOCEIVER** ... Geodetic Receiver
**Geoch Cos A** ... Geochimica et Cosmochimica Acta [*A publication*]
**Geoch Cosm A** ... Geochimica et Cosmochimica Acta [*A publication*]
**GEOCHEM** ... Geochemical
**Geochem Geochem Methods Data** ... Geochemie. Geochemical Methods and Data [*A publication*]
**Geochem Int** ... Geochemistry International [*A publication*]
**Geochem J** ... Geochemical Journal [*A publication*]
**Geochem J (Geochem Soc Jap)** ... Geochemical Journal (Geochemical Society of Japan) [*A publication*]
**Geochem J (Nagoya)** ... Geochemical Journal (Nagoya) [*A publication*]
**Geochem J (Tokyo)** ... Geochemical Journal (Tokyo) [*A publication*]
**Geochem News** ... Geochemical News [*A publication*]

**Geochem Soc India Bull** ... Geochemical Society of India. Bulletin [*A publication*]
**Geochim Cosmochim Acta** ... Geochimica et Cosmochimica Acta [*A publication*]
**Geochim et Cosmochim Acta** ... Geochimica et Cosmochimica Acta [*A publication*]
**Geochim Cosmochim Acta Suppl** ... Geochimica et Cosmochimica Acta. Supplement [*A publication*]
**Geo Coop** ... [*George*] Cooper's English Chancery Cases Tempore Eldon [*A publication*] (DLA)
**GEOD**........ Geodesy [*Science of measuring the earth*] (ROG)
**GEOD**........ Geodetic
**GEOD**........ Geodyne Resources, Inc. [*NASDAQ symbol*] (NQ)
**Geod Aerophotogr (USSR)** ... Geodesy and Aerophotography [*Later, Geodesy, Mapping, and Photogrammetry*] (USSR) [*A publication*]
**Geodaet Geophys Veroeffentlichungen Reihe III** ... Geodaetische und Geophysikalische Veroeffentlichungen. Reihe III [*A publication*]
**Geodaet Inst Medd** ... Geodaetisk Institut. Meddelelse [*A publication*]
**Geod Darb** ... Geodezijos Darbai [*Lithuanian SSR*] [*A publication*]
**Geod E** ....... Geodetic Engineer
**Geo Dec**...... Georgia Decisions [*A publication*] (DLA)
**Geodes Mapp Photogramm** ... Geodesy, Mapping, and Photogrammetry [*A publication*]
**GEODIAL** ... Geoscience Data Index for Alberta [*Alberta Research Council*] [*Information service or system*] (IID)
**Geo Dig**...... George's Mississippi Digest [*A publication*] (DLA)
**Geod Inst (Den) Medd** ... Geodaetisk Institut (Denmark). Meddelelse [*A publication*]
**Geod Inst Medd** ... Geodaetisk Institut. Meddelelse [*A publication*]
**Geod Inst Skr** ... Geodaetisk Institut. Skrifter [*A publication*]
**GeoDIS**...... Geographic Districting Information System for Maryland [*Maryland State Department of State Planning*] [*Baltimore*] [*Information service or system*] (IID)
**Geod Kartogr** ... Geodezia es Kartografia [*A publication*]
**Geod Kartogr Aerofotos** ... Geodeziia, Kartografiia, i Aerofotos'emka [*Ukrainian SSR*] [*A publication*]
**Geod Kartogr (Budap)** ... Geodezia es Kartografia (Budapest) [*A publication*]
**Geod Kartogr Obzor** ... Geodeticky a Kartograficky Obzor [*A publication*]
**Geod Mapp Photogramm** ... Geodesy, Mapping, and Photogrammetry [*A publication*]
**Geod Mapp Photogramm Engl Transl** ... Geodesy, Mapping, and Photogrammetry. English Translation [*A publication*]
**Geod Soc Jap J** ... Geodetic Society of Japan. Journal [*A publication*]
**GEODSS**... Ground-Based Electro-Optical Deep Space Surveillance [*Satellite-tracking network*]
**Geoexplor** .. Geoexploration [*A publication*]
**Geoexplor Monogr** ... Geoexploration Monographs [*A publication*]
**GEOF** ........ Geoforum [*A publication*]
**GEOFILE** ... Geographic File [*DoD*]
**Geofis Int**... Geofisica International [*A publication*]
**Geofis Met** ... Geofisica e Meteorologia [*A publication*]
**Geofis Meteorol** ... Geofisica e Meteorologia [*A publication*]
**Geofis Pura Appl** ... Geofisica Pura e Applicata [*Italy*] [*A publication*]
**Geofis Pur Appl** ... Geofisica Pura e Applicata [*A publication*]
**GEOFIZ**.... Geosciences Information Center [*Federal Institute for Geosciences and Natural Resources*] [*Information service or system*] (IID)
**Geofiz App** ... Geofizicheskaya Apparatura [*USSR*] [*A publication*]
**Geofiz Appar** ... Geofizicheskaya Apparatura [*A publication*]
**Geofiz Astron Inf Byull** ... Geofizika i Astronomiya Informatsionnyi Byulleten [*Ukrainian SSR*] [*A publication*]
**Geofiz Byull** ... Geofizicheskii Byulleten [*USSR*] [*A publication*]
**Geofiz Geol Naft** ... Geofizyka i Geologia Naftowa [*Poland*] [*A publication*]
**Geofiz Issled** ... Geofizicheskie Issledovaniya [*A publication*]
**Geofiz Issled Reshenii Geol Zadach Vost Sib** ... Geofizicheskie Issledovaniya pri Reshenii Geologicheskikh Zadach v Vostochnoi Sibri [*A publication*]
**Geofiz Koeslemenyek** ... Geofizikae Koeslemenyek [*A publication*]
**Geofiz Kozl** ... Geofizikai Koezlemenyek [*A publication*]
**Geofiz Kozlemenyek** ... Geofizikai Koezlemenyek [*A publication*]
**Geofiz Metody Razved Arkt** ... Geofizicheskie Metody Razvedki v Arktike [*A publication*]
**Geofiz Priborostr** ... Geofizicheskoe Priborostroenie [*A publication*]
**Geofiz Razved** ... Geofizicheskaya Razvedka [*A publication*]
**Geofiz Sb**.... Geofizicheskii Sbornik [*A publication*]
**Geofiz Sb Akad Nauk Ukr SSR Inst Geofiz** ... Geofizicheskii Sbornik. Akademiya Nauk Ukrainskoi SSR. Institut Geofiziki [*Ukrainian SSR*] [*A publication*]
**Geofiz Sb (Kiev)** ... Geofizicheskii Sbornik (Kiev) [*Ukrainian SSR*] [*A publication*]
**Geofiz Sb (Sverdlovsk)** ... Geofizicheskii Sbornik (Sverdlovsk) [*A publication*]
**Geofiz Zh** ... Geofizicheskii Zhurnal [*Ukrainian SSR*] [*A publication*]
**Geof Koezl** ... Geofizikai Koezlemenyek [*A publication*]
**Geof Publ** ... Geofysiske Publikasjoner [*A publication*]
**Geofys Publ** ... Geofysiske Publikasjoner [*A publication*]
**Geofys Sb**... Geofysikalni Sbornik [*A publication*]
**GEOG**........ Geografia [*A publication*]
**Geog**........... Geographia [*of Ptolemy*] [*Classical studies*] (OCD)
**GEOG**........ Geography (AFM)
**Geog Annaler** ... Geografiska Annaler [*A publication*]
**Geog Bul**.... Geographical Bulletin [*A publication*]
**Geog Gesell Hamburg Mitt** ... Geographische Gesellschaft in Hamburg. Mitteilungen [*A publication*]
**Geog Ges Muenchen Jber** ... Geographische Gesellschaft in Muenchen. Jahresbericht [*A publication*]
**Geog J**........ Geographical Journal [*A publication*]
**Geog Jnl**..... Geographical Journal [*A publication*]
**Geog M**...... Geographical Magazine [*A publication*]
**Geog Mag**.. Geographical Magazine [*A publication*]
**Geog Map Div Bull** ... Geography and Map Division Bulletin [*Special Libraries Association*] [*A publication*]
**GEOGNOS** ... Geognosy [*A knowledge of the structure of the earth*] (ROG)
**Geog Phys et Quat** ... Geographie Physique et Quaternaire [*A publication*]
**Geogr**......... Geographia [*A publication*]
**Geogr**......... Geographica [*A publication*]
**Geog R**....... Geographical Review [*A publication*]
**Geogr**......... Geography [*A publication*]
**Geogr A**...... Geografiska Annaler [*A publication*]
**Geogr Abstr** ... Geographical Abstracts [*A publication*]
**Geogr Anal** ... Geographical Analysis [*A publication*]
**Geogr Ann** ... Geografiska Annaler [*A publication*]
**Geogr Ann B** ... Geografiska Annaler. Series B. Human Geography [*A publication*]
**Geogr Annlr** ... Geografiska Annaler [*A publication*]
**Geogr Ann Ser B Hum Geogr** ... Geografiska Annaler. Series B. Human Geography [*A publication*]
**GEOGRAPHY** ... George Emerson's Old Grandmother Rode a Pig Home Yesterday [*Mnemonic guide for spelling "geography"*]
**Geogr B**...... Geographical Bulletin [*A publication*]
**Geogr Ber**... Geographische Berichte [*A publication*]
**Geogr Can** ... Geographe Canadien [*A publication*]
**Geogr Cas**.. Geografiske Casopis [*A publication*]
**Geog Rdsch** ... Geographische Rundschau [*A publication*]
**Geogr Ed**.... Geographical Education [*A publication*]
**Geogr Educ** ... Geographical Education [*A publication*] (APTA)
**Geog Rev**.... Geographical Review [*A publication*]
**Geogr Ezheg Geogr Ova Lit SSR** ... Geografiya Ezhegodnogo Geograficheskogo Obshchestva Litovskoi SSR [*A publication*]
**Geogr Geol Meded Physiogr Geol Reeks Geogr Inst (Utrecht)** ... Geographische en Geologische Mededelingen, Physiographisch Geologische Reeks, Geographisch Instituut (Utrecht) [*A publication*]
**Geogr Ges Hamb Mitt** ... Geographische Gesellschaft in Hamburg. Mitteilungen [*A publication*]
**Geogr Glas** ... Geografski Glasnik [*A publication*]
**Geogr Glasn** ... Geografski Glasnik [*A publication*]
**Geogr Helv** ... Geographica Helvetica [*A publication*]
**Geog R Ind** ... Geographical Review of India [*A publication*]
**Geogr Inf**.... Geographische Informationen [*A publication*]
**Geogr J**...... Geographical Journal [*A publication*]
**Geogr Jb**.... Geographisches Jahrbuch [*A publication*]
**Geogr Jber Oesterr** ... Geographischer Jahresbericht aus Oesterreich [*A publication*]
**Geogr J (Lond)** ... Geographical Journal (London) [*A publication*]
**Geogr Journ** ... Geographical Journal [*A publication*]
**Geogr Knowl (Peking)** ... Geographical Knowledge (Peking) [*A publication*]
**Geogrl Abstr** ... Geographical Abstracts [*A publication*]
**Geogrl J**..... Geographical Journal [*A publication*]
**Geogrl Rev** ... Geographical Review [*A publication*]
**Geogr Mag (Lond)** ... Geographical Magazine (London) [*A publication*]
**Geogr Med** ... Geographia Medica [*A publication*]
**Geogr Metrastis** ... Geografinis Metrastis [*A publication*]
**Geogr Ovo SSSR Dokl** ... Geograficheskoe Obshchestvo SSSR Doklady [*A publication*]
**Geogr Pol** ... Geographia Polonica [*A publication*]
**Geogr Pregl** ... Geografski Pregled [*A publication*]
**Geogr R**...... Geographical Review [*A publication*]
**Geogr Raka Turkm** ... Geografiya Raka v Turkmenii [*A publication*]
**Geogr Rdsch** ... Geographische Rundschau [*A publication*]
**Geogr Rev** .. Geographical Review [*A publication*]
**Geogr Rev Jap** ... Geographical Review of Japan [*A publication*]
**Geogr Rev (New York)** ... Geographical Review (New York) [*A publication*]
**Geogr RI**.... Geographical Review of India [*A publication*]
**Geogr Rundsch** ... Geographische Rundschau [*A publication*]
**Geogr Sb**.... Geograficeskij Sbornik [*A publication*]
**Geogr Sb Penz Otd Geogr O-va SSSR** ... Geograficheskii Sbornik Penzenskogo Otdeleniya Geograficheskogo Obshchestva SSSR [*A publication*]
**Geogr Shk** ... Geografiya v Shkole [*USSR*] [*A publication*]
**Geogr Stud** ... Geographical Studies [*A publication*]
**Geogr TB** ... Geographisches Taschenbuch [*A publication*]
**Geogr Teach** ... Geography Teacher [*A publication*] (APTA)
**Geogr Tjds** ... Geografisch Tijdschrift [*A publication*]
**Geog Rund** ... Geographische Rundschau [*A publication*]
**Geogr Vestn** ... Geografski Vestnik [*A publication*]
**Geogr Z**...... Geographische Zeitschrift [*A publication*]
**Geog Soc Chicago B** ... Geographic Society of Chicago. Bulletin [*A publication*]
**Geog Soc Phila** ... Geographical Society of Philadelphia. Bulletin [*A publication*]

**Geog Soc Phila B** ... Geographical Society of Philadelphia. Bulletin [*A publication*]
**GEOG T** .... Geographical Teacher [*A publication*] (ROG)
**Geog Tidsskr** ... Geografisk Tidsskrift [*A publication*]
**Geog Z** ....... Geographische Zeitschrift [*A publication*]
**GEOHAH** ... Geologi [*Helsinki*] [*A publication*]
**Geo Heat Cent Q Bull** ... Geo-Heat Center. Quarterly Bulletin [*United States*] [*A publication*]
**Geo-Heat Util Center Q Bull** ... Geo-Heat Utilization Center. Quarterly Bulletin [*A publication*]
**Geo-Heat Util Cent Q Bull** ... Geo-Heat Utilization Center. Quarterly Bulletin [*United States*] [*A publication*]
**GEOI** ......... Georesources, Incorporated [*NASDAQ symbol*] (NQ)
**GEOIM** ..... Geodaetisk Institut. Meddelelse [*A publication*]
**GEOIS** ....... Geodaetisk Institut. Skrifter [*A publication*]
**GEOIS** ....... Geographic Information System [*Data processing*]
**Geo J** ......... Geo Journal [*A publication*]
**GEOJA** ...... Geophysical Journal. Royal Astronomical Society [*A publication*]
**GEOJDQ** .. Geojournal [*A publication*]
**GEOK** ........ Geokinetics, Inc. [*NASDAQ symbol*] (NQ)
**Geokhim** .... Geokhimiya [*A publication*]
**Geokhim Akad Nauk SSSR** ... Geokhimiya Akademiya Nauk SSSR [*A publication*]
**Geokhim Issled** ... Geokhimicheskie Issledovaniya [*A publication*]
**Geokhim Metody Poiskakh Razved Rudn Mestorozhd** ... Geokhimicheskie Metody pri Poiskakh i Razvedke Rudnykh Mestorozhdenii [*A publication*]
**Geokhim Metody Poiskov Nefti Gaza** ... Geokhimicheskie Metody Poiskov. Nefti i Gaza [*A publication*]
**Geokhim Mineral Petrol** ... Geokhimiya, Mineralogiya, i Petrologiya [*A publication*]
**Geokhim Rudoobraz** ... Geokhimiya i Rudoobrazovanie [*A publication*]
**Geokhim Sb** ... Geokhimicheskii Sbornik [*A publication*]
**GeoL** .......... Geographica (Lisbon) [*A publication*]
**Geol** ........... Geologie [*A publication*]
**Geol** ........... Geologija [*A publication*]
**GEOL** ........ Geology (AFM)
**Geol Abh Hessen** ... Geologische Abhandlungen Hessen [*A publication*]
**Geol Abstr** ... Geological Abstracts [*A publication*]
**Geol Alp** ..... Geologie Alpine [*A publication*]
**Geol Anagoriseis Ekthesis** ... Geologikai Anagnoriseis Ekthesis [*A publication*]
**Geol An Balk Poluostrva** ... Geolshki Anali Balkanskoga Poluostrva [*A publication*]
**Geol Appl Idrogeol** ... Geologia Applicata e Idrogeologia [*A publication*]
**Geol Appl Prospect Miniere** ... Geologie Appliquee et Prospection Miniere [*A publication*]
**Geol Assoc Can** ... Geological Association of Canada [*A publication*]
**Geol Assoc Canada Proc** ... Geological Association of Canada. Proceedings [*A publication*]
**Geol Assoc Can Cordilleran Sect Programme Abstr** ... Geological Association of Canada. Cordilleran Section. Programme and Abstracts [*A publication*]
**Geol Assoc Can Spec Pap** ... Geological Association of Canada. Special Paper [*A publication*]
**Geol Assoc (Lond) Proc** ... Geologists' Association (London). Proceedings [*A publication*]
**Geol Atlas PA** ... Geologic Atlas of Pennsylvania [*A publication*]
**GEOLB** ...... Geologues [*A publication*]
**Geol Balc** .... Geologica Balcanica [*A publication*]
**Geol Balc (Sofia)** ... Geologica Balcanica. Bulgarska Akademiya ne Naukite (Sofia) [*A publication*]
**Geol Bauwes** ... Geologie und Bauwesen [*A publication*]
**Geol Bav** ..... Geologica Bavarica [*A publication*]
**Geol Bavarica** ... Geologica Bavarica [*A publication*]
**Geol Beih** ... Geologie. Beihefte [*A publication*]
**Geol Bl** ....... Geologische Blaetter fuer Nordost-Bayern und Angrenzende Gebiete [*A publication*]
**Geol Bl Nordost-Bayern** ... Geologische Blaetter fuer Nordost-Bayern und Angrenzende Gebiete [*A publication*]
**Geol Bl Nordost-Bayern Angrenzende Geb** ... Geologische Blaetter fuer Nordost-Bayern und Angrenzende Gebiete [*A publication*]
**Geol Bull Natl Geol Surv China** ... Geological Bulletin. National Geological Survey of China [*People's Republic of China*] [*A publication*]
**Geol Bull Punjab Univ** ... Geological Bulletin. Punjab University [*A publication*]
**Geol Bull Soc Belge Geol** ... Geologie. Bulletin de la Societe Belge de Geologie [*A publication*]
**Geol Bull Univ Peshawar** ... Geological Bulletin. University of Peshawar [*A publication*]
**Geol Center Research Ser** ... Geological Center. Research Series [*A publication*]
**Geol Colomb** ... Geologia Colombiana [*A publication*]
**Geol Correl** ... Geological Correlation [*Paris*] [*A publication*]
**Geol E** ........ Geological Engineer
**Geol Explor Min BC** ... Geology. Exploration and Mining in British Columbia [*A publication*]
**Geol Foeren St Foerh** ... Geologiska Foereningens i Stockholm. Foerhandlingar [*A publication*]
**Geol Foeren Stockh Foerh** ... Geologiska Foereningens i Stockholm. Foerhandlingar [*A publication*]
**Geol Foer Stockh Foerh** ... Geologiska Foereningens i Stockholm. Foerhandlingar [*A publication*]
**Geol Fr** ....... Geologie de la France [*A publication*]
**Geol Geofiz** ... Geologiya i Geofizika [*A publication*]
**Geol i Geofiz** ... Geologiya i Geofizika [*A publication*]
**Geol Geofiz Meletai** ... Geologikai kai Geofizikai Meletai [*A publication*]
**Geol Geokhim** ... Geologiya i Geokhimiya [*A publication*]
**Geol Geokhim Goryuch Iskop** ... Geologiya i Geokhimiya Goryuchikh Iskopaemykh [*Ukrainian SSR*] [*A publication*]
**Geol Geokhim Goryuch Iskop Akad Nauk Ukr SSR** ... Geologiya i Geokhimiya Goryuchikh Iskopaemykh Akademiya Nauk Ukrainskoy SSR [*A publication*]
**Geol Geokhim Goryuch Kopalin Akad Nauk Ukr RSR** ... Geologiya i Geokhimiya Goryuchikh Kopalin Akademiya Nauk Ukrain'skoi RSR [*A publication*]
**Geol Geokhim Mestorozhd Tverd Goryuch Iskop** ... Geologiya i Geokhimiya Mestorozhdenii Tverdykh Goryuchikh Iskopaemykh [*A publication*]
**Geol Geokhim Neft Gazov Mestorozhd** ... Geologiya i Geokhimiya Neftyanskh i Gazovykh Mestorozhdenii [*A publication*]
**Geol Glas** ... Geoloski Glasnik [*Yugoslavia*] [*A publication*]
**Geol Glas Posebna Izd** ... Geoloski Glasnik. Posebna Izdanja [*A publication*]
**Geol Glas (Titograd Yugosl)** ... Geoloski Glasnik (Titograd, Yugoslavia) [*A publication*]
**Geol Hung** ... Geologica Hungarica [*A publication*]
**Geol Hung Ser Palaeontol** ... Geologica Hungarica. Series Palaeontologica [*A publication*]
**Geo Lib** ...... George on Libel [*1812*] [*A publication*] (DLA)
**Geol Invest Ser Geol Surv Pak Interim Geol Rep** ... Geological Investigation Series. Geological Survey of Pakistan. Interim Geological Report [*A publication*]
**Geol Izuch SSR** ... Geologicheskaya Izuchennost SSR [*A publication*]
**Geol J** .......... Geological Journal [*A publication*]
**Geo LJ** ....... Georgetown Law Journal [*A publication*]
**Geol Jahrb** ... Geologisches Jahrbuch [*A publication*]
**Geol Jahrb Beih** ... Geologisches Jahrbuch. Beihefte [*A publication*]
**Geol Jahrb Hessen** ... Geologisches Jahrbuch Hessen [*A publication*]
**Geol Jahrb Reihe A** ... Geologisches Jahrbuch. Reihe A. Allgemeine und Regionale Geologie BR Deutschland und Nachbargebiete, Tektonik, Stratigraphie, Palaeontologie [*A publication*]
**Geol Jahrb Reihe B** ... Geologisches Jahrbuch. Reihe B. Regionale Geologie Ausland [*A publication*]
**Geol Jahrb Reihe C** ... Geologisches Jahrbuch. Reihe C. Hydrogeologie, Ingenieurgeologie [*West Germany*] [*A publication*]
**Geol Jahrb Reihe D** ... Geologisches Jahrbuch. Reihe D. Mineralogie, Petrographie, Geochemie, Lagerstaettenkunde [*A publication*]
**Geol Jahrb Reihe E** ... Geologisches Jahrbuch. Reihe E. Geophysik [*West Germany*] [*A publication*]
**Geol Jahrb Reihe E Geophys** ... Geologisches Jahrbuch. Reihe E. Geophysik [*A publication*]
**Geol Jahrb Reihe F Bodenk** ... Geologisches Jahrbuch. Reihe F. Bodenkunde [*A publication*]
**Geol Jahrbuch Ser B** ... Geologisches Jahrbuch. Series B [*A publication*]
**Geol Jahrbuch Ser D** ... Geologisches Jahrbuch. Series D [*A publication*]
**Geol Jb** ....... Geologisches Jahrbuch [*A publication*]
**Geol J (Liverpool)** ... Geological Journal (Liverpool) [*A publication*]
**Geol J Queen Mary Coll** ... Geological Journal of Queen Mary College [*A publication*]
**Geol Lit SSSR Bibliogr Yezhegodnik** ... Geologicheskaya Literatura SSSR Bibliograficheskiy Yezhegodnik [*A publication*]
**Geol M** ....... Geological Magazine [*A publication*]
**Geol Mag** ... Geological Magazine [*A publication*]
**Geol Map Deputy Minist Miner Resour (Saudi Arabia)** ... Geologic Map. Deputy Ministry for Mineral Resources (Kingdom of Saudi Arabia) [*A publication*]
**Geol Map Miner Resour Summ North Carolina Geol Surv** ... Geology Map and Mineral Resources Summary. North Carolina Geological Survey [*A publication*]
**Geol Map Miner Resour Summ (State Tennessee)** ... Geologic Map and Mineral Resources. Summary (State of Tennessee) [*A publication*]
**Geol Map Montana Bur Mines Geol** ... Geologic Map. Montana Bureau of Mines and Geology [*A publication*]
**Geol Mediter** ... Geologie Mediterraneenne [*A publication*]
**Geol Mem Geol Surv China Ser A** ... Geological Memoirs. Geological Survey of China. Series A [*A publication*]
**Geol Mem Geol Surv China Ser B** ... Geological Memoirs. Geological Survey of China. Series B [*A publication*]
**Geol Mestorozhd Redk Elem** ... Geologiya Mestorozhdenii Redkikh Elementov [*A publication*]
**Geol Metal** ... Geologia y Metalurgia [*Bolivia*] [*A publication*]
**Geol Metal Bol** ... Geologia e Metalurgia. Boletim [*A publication*]
**Geol Metal (San Luis Potosi)** ... Geologia y Metalurgia (San Luis Potosi) [*A publication*]
**Geol Metal (Sao Paulo)** ... Geologia e Metalurgia (Sao Paulo) [*A publication*]
**Geol Met Bol** ... Geologia e Metalurgia. Boletim. Escola Politecnica. Universidade de Sao Paulo [*A publication*]

**Geol Metod Tekh Razved Lab Rab** ... Geologiya. Metodika i Tekhnika Razvedki. Laboratornye Raboty [*A publication*]
**Geol Mijnb** ... Geologie en Mijnbouw [*A publication*]
**Geol Mijnbouw** ... Geologie en Mijnbouw [*A publication*]
**Geol Mineral** ... Geologiya i Mineralogiya [*A publication*]
**Geol Min Metall Soc India Q J** ... Geological, Mining, and Metallurgical Society of India. Quarterly Journal [*A publication*]
**Geol Min Metall Soc Liberia Bull** ... Geological, Mining, and Metallurgical Society of Liberia. Bulletin [*A publication*]
**Geol Min Met Soc Liberia Bull** ... Geological, Mining, and Metallurgical Society of Liberia. Bulletin [*A publication*]
**Geol Mitt** ... Geologische Mitteilungen [*A publication*]
**Geol Morya** ... Geologiya Morya [*A publication*]
**Geol Nefti** .. Geologiya Nefti [*A publication*]
**Geol Nefti Gaza** ... Geologiya Nefti i Gaza [*A publication*]
**Geol Nefti i Gaza** ... Geologiya Nefti i Gaza [*A publication*]
**Geol Nefti Gaza Sev Vostoka Evr Chasti SSSR** ... Geologiya Nefti i Gaza Severo-Vostoka Evropeiskoi Chasti SSSR [*A publication*]
**Geol Notes Local Details 1:10000 Sheets Inst Geol Sci** ... Geological Notes and Local Details for 1:10,000 Sheets. Institute of Geological Sciences [*Keyworth*] [*A publication*]
**GEOLOC** .. Geographical Location [*Military*] (AABC)
**Geologie Mijnb** ... Geologie en Mijnbouw [*A publication*]
**Geologists' Assoc (London) Proc** ... Geologists' Association (London). Proceedings [*A publication*]
**Geology Club Puerto Rico Bull** ... Geology Club of Puerto Rico. Bulletin [*A publication*]
**Geol Palaeontol** ... Geologica et Palaeontologica [*A publication*]
**Geol Palaeontol Southeast Asia** ... Geology and Palaeontology of Southeast Asia [*A publication*]
**Geol Pap Carleton Univ Dep Geol** ... Geological Paper. Carleton University. Department of Geology [*A publication*]
**Geol Pap Geol Surv Malaysia** ... Geological Papers. Geological Survey of Malaysia [*A publication*]
**Geol Pap Miner Resour Div (Manitoba)** ... Geological Paper. Mineral Resources Division (Manitoba) [*A publication*]
**Geol Poberezh'ya Dna Chern Azovskogo Morei Predelakh Ukr SSR** ... Geologiya Poberezh'ya i Dna Chernogo i Azovskogo Morei v Predelakh Ukrainskoi SSR [*A publication*]
**Geol Poiski Razved Nerudn Polezn Iskop** ... Geologiya, Poiski, i Razvedka Nerudnykh Poleznykh Iskopaemykh [*A publication*]
**Geol Polezn Iskop Urala** ... Geologiya i Poleznye Iskopaemye Urala [*A publication*]
**Geol Polezn Iskop Zapadn Kaz** ... Geologiya i Poleznye Iskopaemye Zapadnogo Kazakhstana [*A publication*]
**Geol Pr**....... Geologicke Prace [*A publication*]
**Geol Prace Zpr** ... Geologicke Prace. Zpravy [*A publication*]
**Geol Pr (Bratisl)** ... Geologicke Prace (Bratislava) [*A publication*]
**Geol Pruzkum** ... Geologicky Pruzkum [*A publication*]
**Geol Razpr Porocila** ... Geologija. Razprave in Porocila [*Ljubljana*] [*A publication*]
**Geol Razved Gazov Gazokondens Mestorozhd** ... Geologiya i Razvedka Gazovykh i Gazokondensatnykh Mestorozhdenii [*A publication*]
**Geol Rep Dep Nat Resour (Queb)** ... Geological Reports. Department of Natural Resources (Quebec) [*A publication*]
**Geol Rep Hiroshima Univ** ... Geological Report. Hiroshima University [*A publication*]
**Geol Rep Miner Resour Div (Manitoba)** ... Geological Report. Mineral Resources Division (Manitoba) [*A publication*]
**Geol Rep Shimane Univ** ... Geological Reports. Shimane University [*A publication*]
**Geol Rep State Alaska Dep Nat Resour** ... Geologic Report. State of Alaska Department of Natural Resources [*A publication*]
**Geol Rev (Beijing)** ... Geological Review (Beijing) [*A publication*]
**Geol Rom** ... Geologica Romana [*A publication*]
**Geol Roman** ... Geologica Romana [*A publication*]
**Geol Rud Mestorozhd** ... Geologiya Rudnykh Mestorozhdenii [*A publication*]
**Geol Rudn Mestorozhd** ... Geologiya Rudnykh Mestorozhdenii [*A publication*]
**Geol Rudonosn Yuga Ukr** ... Geologiya i Rudonosnost Yuga Ukrainy [*A publication*]
**Geol Rundsch** ... Geologische Rundschau [*A publication*]
**Geol Rundschau** ... Geologische Rundschau [*A publication*]
**Geol S Am B** ... Geological Society of America. Bulletin [*A publication*]
**Geol Sb (Lvov)** ... Geologicheskii Sbornik (Lvov) [*A publication*]
**Geol Sbornik** ... Geologicheskii Sbornik [*A publication*]
**Geol Sb (Tiflis)** ... Geologicheskii Sbornik (Tiflis) [*A publication*]
**Geol Sb Vses Inst Nauchno Tekhnol Inf** ... Geologicheskii Sbornik Vsesoyuznogo Instituta Nauchno Tekhnologicheskoi Informatsii [*A publication*]
**Geol Sect Bull Libya Minist Ind** ... Geological Section. Bulletin. Libya Ministry of Industry [*A publication*]
**Geol Soc Am Abstr Programs** ... Geological Society of America. Abstracts with Programs [*A publication*]
**Geol Soc Am Annu Meet Field Trip Guideb** ... Geological Society of America. Annual Meeting. Field Trip Guidebook [*A publication*]
**Geol Soc Am Bull** ... Geological Society of America. Bulletin [*A publication*]
**Geol Soc Am Cordilleran Sect Annu Meet Guideb** ... Geological Society of America. Cordilleran Section. Annual Meeting Guidebook [*A publication*]
**Geol Soc Amer Bull** ... Geological Society of America. Bulletin [*A publication*]
**Geol Soc Amer Eng Geol Case Hist** ... Geological Society of America. Engineering Geology Case Histories [*A publication*]
**Geol Soc America Abs with Programs** ... Geological Society of America. Abstracts with Programs [*A publication*]
**Geol Soc America Spec Paper** ... Geological Society of America. Special Papers [*A publication*]
**Geol Soc Amer Mem** ... Geological Society of America. Memoir [*A publication*]
**Geol Soc Amer Spec Pap** ... Geological Society of America. Special Paper [*A publication*]
**Geol Soc Am Map Chart Ser** ... Geological Society of America. Map and Chart Series [*A publication*]
**Geol Soc Am Mem** ... Geological Society of America. Memoir [*A publication*]
**Geol Soc Am Microform Publ** ... Geological Society of America. Microform Publication [*A publication*]
**Geol Soc Am Proc** ... Geological Society of America. Proceedings [*A publication*]
**Geol Soc Am Southeast Sect Guideb** ... Geological Society of America. Southeastern Section Guidebook [*A publication*]
**Geol Soc Am Spec Pap** ... Geological Society of America. Special Paper [*A publication*]
**Geol Soc Am Spec Pap (Reg Stud)** ... Geological Society of America. Special Paper (Regional Studies) [*A publication*]
**Geol Soc Australia J** ... Geological Society of Australia. Journal [*A publication*]
**Geol Soc Bull** ... Geological Society of America. Bulletin [*A publication*]
**Geol Soc China Proc** ... Geological Society of China. Proceedings [*A publication*]
**Geol Soc Egypt Annu Meet Abstr** ... Geological Society of Egypt. Annual Meeting. Abstracts [*A publication*]
**Geol Soc Finl Bull** ... Geological Society of Finland. Bulletin [*A publication*]
**Geol Soc Greece Bull** ... Geological Society of Greece. Bulletin [*A publication*]
**Geol Soc India Bull** ... Geological Society of India. Bulletin [*A publication*]
**Geol Soc India J** ... Geological Society of India. Journal [*A publication*]
**Geol Soc India Jour** ... Geological Society of India. Journal [*A publication*]
**Geol Soc India Mem** ... Geological Society of India. Memoir [*A publication*]
**Geol Soc Iraq J** ... Geological Society of Iraq. Journal [*A publication*]
**Geol Soc Jam J** ... Geological Society of Jamaica. Journal [*A publication*]
**Geol Soc Jap J** ... Geological Society of Japan. Journal [*A publication*]
**Geol Soc Korea J** ... Geological Society of Korea. Journal [*A publication*]
**Geol Soc Lond J** ... Geological Society of London. Journal [*A publication*]
**Geol Soc Lond Misc Pap** ... Geological Society of London. Miscellaneous Paper [*A publication*]
**Geol Soc (Lond) Newsl** ... Geological Society. Newsletter (London) [*A publication*]
**Geol Soc London Mem** ... Geological Society of London. Memoirs [*A publication*]
**Geol Soc Lond Q J** ... Geological Society of London. Quarterly Journal [*A publication*]
**Geol Soc Lond Spec Rep** ... Geological Society of London. Special Report [*A publication*]
**Geol Soc Malays Bull** ... Geological Society of Malaysia. Bulletin [*A publication*]
**Geol Soc Malays Newsl** ... Geological Society of Malaysia. Newsletter [*A publication*]
**Geol Soc NJ Rept** ... Geological Society of New Jersey. Report [*A publication*]
**Geol Soc Norfolk Bull** ... Geological Society of Norfolk. Bulletin [*A publication*]
**Geol Soc NZ Newsl** ... Geological Society of New Zealand. Newsletter [*A publication*]
**Geol Soc Oregon Country News Letter** ... Geological Society of the Oregon Country. News Letter [*A publication*]
**Geol Soc Philipp J** ... Geological Society of the Philippines. Journal [*A publication*]
**Geol Soc Proc** ... Geological Society of America. Proceedings [*A publication*]
**Geol Soc S Afr Congr Abstr** ... Geological Society of South Africa. Congress Abstracts [*A publication*]
**Geol Soc S Afr Q News Bull** ... Geological Society of South Africa. Quarterly News Bulletin [*A publication*]
**Geol Soc S Afr Spec Publ** ... Geological Society of South Africa. Special Publication [*A publication*]
**Geol Soc S Afr Trans** ... Geological Society of South Africa. Transactions [*A publication*]
**Geol Soc So Africa Trans** ... Geological Society of South Africa. Transactions and Proceedings [*A publication*]
**Geol Soc Zimbabwe Spec Publ** ... Geological Society of Zimbabwe. Special Publication [*A publication*]
**Geol SSSR** ... Geologiya SSSR [*A publication*]
**Geol Str Poleznye Iskop Kalmytskoi ASSR** ... Geologicheskoe Stroenie i Poleznye Iskopaemye Kalmytskoi ASSR [*A publication*]
**Geol Sudetica** ... Geologia Sudetica [*A publication*]
**Geol Sudetica (Warsaw)** ... Geologia Sudetica (Warsaw) [*A publication*]
**Geol Surv Br Guiana Bull** ... Geological Survey of British Guiana. Bulletin [*A publication*]
**Geol Surv Bull Tasmania** ... Tasmania. Geological Survey. Bulletin [*A publication*] (APTA)
**Geol Surv Can Bull** ... Geological Survey of Canada. Bulletin [*A publication*]
**Geol Surv Can Econ Geol Rep** ... Geological Survey of Canada. Economic Geology Report [*A publication*]
**Geol Surv Can Mem** ... Geological Survey of Canada. Memoir [*A publication*]

**Geol Surv Can Pap** ... Geological Survey of Canada. Paper [*A publication*]
**Geol Surv Ceylon Mem** ... Geological Survey of Ceylon. Memoir [*A publication*]
**Geol Surv Circ** ... Geological Survey Circular [*A publication*]
**Geol Surv Den III Ser** ... Geological Survey of Denmark. III Series [*A publication*]
**Geol Surv Den II Ser** ... Geological Survey of Denmark. II Series [*A publication*]
**Geol Surv Den Rep** ... Geological Survey of Denmark. Report [*A publication*]
**Geol Surv Den Ser A** ... Geological Survey of Denmark. Serie A [*A publication*]
**Geol Surv Den Ser B** ... Geological Survey of Denmark. Serie B [*A publication*]
**Geol Surv Den Yearb** ... Geological Survey of Denmark. Yearbook [*A publication*]
**Geol Surv Dep (Jam) Bull** ... Geological Survey Department (Jamaica, West Indies). Bulletin [*A publication*]
**Geol Surv Dep (Jam West Indies) Occas Pap** ... Geological Survey Department (Jamaica, West Indies). Occasional Paper [*A publication*]
**Geol Surv Finl Bull** ... Geological Survey of Finland. Bulletin [*A publication*]
**Geol Surv GA Bull** ... Geological Survey of Georgia. Bulletin [*A publication*]
**Geol Surv GB Mem Geol Surv (Scotl)** ... Geological Survey of Great Britain. Memoirs of the Geological Survey (Scotland) [*A publication*]
**Geol Surv Greenland Rep** ... Geological Survey of Greenland. Report [*A publication*]
**Geol Surv Guyana Bull** ... Geological Survey of Guyana. Bulletin [*A publication*]
**Geol Surv India Misc Publ** ... Geological Survey of India. Miscellaneous Publication [*A publication*]
**Geol Surv India News** ... Geological Survey of India. News [*A publication*]
**Geol Surv Iran Rep** ... Geological Survey of Iran. Report [*A publication*]
**Geol Surv Irel Bull** ... Geological Survey of Ireland. Bulletin [*A publication*]
**Geol Surv Isr Bull** ... Geological Survey of Israel. Bulletin [*A publication*]
**Geol Surv Jap Hydrogeol Maps Jap** ... Geological Survey of Japan. Hydrogeological Maps of Japan [*A publication*]
**Geol Surv Jap Rep** ... Geological Survey of Japan. Report [*A publication*]
**Geol Surv Jpn Rep** ... Geological Survey of Japan. Report [*A publication*]
**Geol Surv Kenya Bull** ... Geological Survey of Kenya. Bulletin [*A publication*]
**Geol Surv Kenya Rep** ... Geological Survey of Kenya. Report [*A publication*]
**Geol Surv Korea Tech Pap** ... Geological Survey of Korea. Technical Paper [*A publication*]
**Geol Surv Malays Annu Rep** ... Geological Survey of Malaysia. Annual Report [*A publication*]
**Geol Surv Malays Dist Mem** ... Geological Survey of Malaysia. District Memoir [*A publication*]
**Geol Surv Malays Geol Pap** ... Geological Survey of Malaysia. Geological Papers [*A publication*]
**Geol Surv Nigeria Bull** ... Geological Survey of Nigeria. Bulletin [*A publication*]
**Geol Surv NSW Bull** ... Geological Survey of New South Wales. Bulletin [*A publication*]
**Geol Surv NSW Geol Surv Rep** ... Geological Survey of New South Wales. Geological Survey Report [*A publication*]
**Geol Surv of NSW Miner Ind NSW** ... Geological Survey of New South Wales. Department of Mines. The Mineral Industry of New South Wales [*A publication*]
**Geol Surv NSW Miner Ind NSW** ... New South Wales. Geological Survey. Mineral Industry of New South Wales [*A publication*] (APTA)
**Geol Surv NSW Rep** ... Geological Survey of New South Wales. Geological Survey Report [*A publication*]
**Geol Surv Pap Tas Dep Mines** ... Geological Survey Paper. Department of Mines. Tasmania [*A publication*] (APTA)
**Geol Surv Queensl Pub** ... Geological Survey of Queensland. Publication [*A publication*] (APTA)
**Geol Surv Queensl Publ** ... Geological Survey of Queensland. Publication [*A publication*]
**Geol Surv Queensl Rep** ... Geological Survey of Queensland. Report [*A publication*] (APTA)
**Geol Surv Rep Dep Mines (NSW)** ... Geological Survey Report. Department of Mines (New South Wales) [*A publication*]
**Geol Surv Sierra Leone Bull** ... Geological Survey of Sierra Leone. Bulletin [*A publication*]
**Geol Surv Tanzania Bull** ... Geological Survey of Tanzania. Bulletin [*A publication*]
**Geol Surv Uganda Mem** ... Geological Survey of Uganda. Memoir [*A publication*]
**Geol Surv Uganda Rep** ... Geological Survey of Uganda. Report [*A publication*]
**Geol Surv Victoria Bull** ... Geological Survey of Victoria. Bulletin [*A publication*]
**Geol Surv Victoria Mem** ... Geological Survey of Victoria. Memoir [*A publication*]
**Geol Surv W Aust Bull** ... Geological Survey of Western Australia. Bulletin [*A publication*]
**Geol Surv West Aust Bull** ... Western Australia. Geological Survey. Bulletin [*A publication*] (APTA)
**Geol Surv West Malaysia Dist Mem** ... Geological Survey of West Malaysia. District Memoir [*A publication*]
**Geol Surv Wyo Bull** ... Geological Survey of Wyoming. Bulletin [*A publication*]
**Geol Surv Wyo C Resour Ser** ... Geological Survey of Wyoming. County Resource Series [*A publication*]
**Geol Surv Wyo Mem** ... Geological Survey of Wyoming. Memoir [*A publication*]
**Geol Surv Wyo Prelim Rep** ... Geological Survey of Wyoming. Preliminary Report [*A publication*]
**Geol Surv Wyo Rep Invest** ... Geological Survey of Wyoming. Report of Investigations [*A publication*]
**Geol Tec**..... Geologia Tecnica [*A publication*]
**Geol Tutkimuslaitos Geotek Julk** ... Geologinen Tutkimuslaitos. Geoteknillisia Julkaisuja [*A publication*]
**Geol Ultriectina** ... Geologica Ultriectina [*A publication*]
**Geol Ver S-Afr Kwart Nuusbull** ... Geologiese Vereniging van Suid-Afrika. Kwartaallikse Nuusbulletin [*A publication*]
**Geol Vjesn (Zagreb)** ... Geoloski Vjesnik (Zagreb) [*A publication*]
**Geol Zakaspiya** ... Geologiya Zakaspiya [*A publication*]
**Geol Zb**...... Geologicky Zbornik [*A publication*]
**Geol Zb Geol Carpathica** ... Geologicky Zbornik - Geologica Carpathica [*A publication*]
**Geol Zb Slov Akad Vied** ... Geologicky Zbornik - Geologica Carpathica. Slovenska Akademia Vied [*A publication*]
**Geol Zh**...... Geologicheskii Zhurnal [*Kiev*] [*A publication*]
**Geol Zh (Russ Ed)** ... Geologicheskii Zhurnal (Russian Edition) [*A publication*]
**Geol Zh (Ukr Ed)** ... Geologichnii Zhurnal (Ukrainian Edition) [*A publication*]
**GEOM**....... Geometry
**GEOMA**..... Geophysical Magazine [*Tokyo*] [*A publication*]
**GEOMAG** ... Geomagnetism
**Geomag Aer** ... Geomagnetizm i Aeronomiya [*A publication*]
**Geomagn and Aeron** ... Geomagnetism and Aeronomy (English Translation) [*A publication*]
**Geomagn Aeron** ... Geomagnetizm i Aeronomiya [*A publication*]
**Geomagn Aeron (USSR)** ... Geomagnetism and Aeronomy (USSR) [*A publication*]
**Geomagn Bull Inst Geol Sci** ... Geomagnetic Bulletin. Institute of Geological Sciences [*A publication*]
**Geomagn Ser Earth Phys Branch** ... Geomagnetic Series. Earth Physics Branch [*A publication*]
**GEOMAN** ... Global Energy Operations & Management Co.
**Geo-Mar Let** ... Geo-Marine Letters [*A publication*]
**Geo Mason UL Rev** ... George Mason University. Law Review [*A publication*]
**GEOMD**.... Geomimet [*A publication*]
**Geom Dedicata** ... Geometriae Dedicata [*A publication*]
**Geomech Comput Progm** ... Geomechanics Computing Programme [*A publication*] (APTA)
**Geomicrobiology J** ... Geomicrobiology Journal [*A publication*]
**Geomorph Abstr** ... Geomorphological Abstracts [*A publication*]
**GEON**........ Gyro Erected Optical Navigation
**GEONAMES** ... Geologic Names of the United States [*US Geological Survey*] [*Information service or system*] (IID)
**GEONAV**.. Geographic Navigation [*Navy*] (CAAL)
**GEOP**........ General Emergency Operations Plan (CINC)
**GEOPA7**... Geologicke Prace [*Bratislava*] [*A publication*]
**GEOPAUSE** ... Geodetic Satellite in Polar Geosynchronous Orbit [*NASA*] (NASA)
**GEOPHYS** ... Geophysical
**Geophys**..... Geophysics [*A publication*]
**Geophys Abstr** ... Geophysical Abstracts [*A publication*]
**Geophys Arb Mitt Meteorol Astrophys** ... Geophysikalische Arbeiten sowie Mitteilungen aus Meteorologie und Astrophysik [*A publication*]
**Geophys Astrophys Fluid Dyn** ... Geophysical and Astrophysical Fluid Dynamics [*A publication*]
**Geophys and Astrophys Fluid Dyn** ... Geophysical and Astrophysical Fluid Dynamics [*A publication*]
**Geophys Astrophys Monogr** ... Geophysics and Astrophysics Monographs [*A publication*]
**Geophys Case Histories** ... Geophysical Case Histories [*A publication*]
**Geophys Fluid Dyn** ... Geophysical Fluid Dynamics [*A publication*]
**Geophys Geol** ... Geophysik und Geologie [*A publication*]
**Geophys Inst Fac Sci Tokyo Univ Geophys Notes Suppl** ... Geophysical Institute. Faculty of Science. Tokyo University. Geophysical Notes. Supplement [*A publication*]
**Geophys J** ... Geophysical Journal [*A publication*]
**Geophys Jour** ... Geophysical Journal [*A publication*]
**Geophys J R** ... Geophysical Journal. Royal Astronomical Society [*A publication*]
**Geophys J R Astronom Soc** ... Geophysical Journal. Royal Astronomical Society [*A publication*]
**Geophys J R Astron Soc** ... Geophysical Journal. Royal Astronomical Society [*A publication*]
**Geophys J R Astr Soc** ... Geophysical Journal. Royal Astronomical Society [*A publication*]
**Geophys Mag** ... Geophysical Magazine [*A publication*]
**Geophys Mag (Tokyo)** ... Geophysical Magazine (Tokyo) [*A publication*]
**Geophys Mem (Lond)** ... Geophysical Memoirs (London) [*A publication*]
**Geophys Monogr** ... Geophysical Monograph [*A publication*]

**Geophys Monogr Am Geophys Union** ... Geophysical Monograph. American Geophysical Union [*A publication*]
**Geophys Norv** ... Geophysica Norvegica [*A publication*]
**Geophys Note (Tokyo)** ... Geophysical Note (Tokyo) [*A publication*]
**Geophys Prospect** ... Geophysical Prospecting [*A publication*]
**Geophys Prospecting** ... Geophysical Prospecting [*A publication*]
**Geophys Prospect (The Hague)** ... Geophysical Prospecting (The Hague) [*A publication*]
**Geophys R B** ... Geophysical Research Bulletin [*A publication*]
**Geophys Res Bull** ... Geophysical Research Bulletin [*A publication*]
**Geophys Res Lett** ... Geophysical Research Letters [*A publication*]
**Geophys Res Pap** ... Geophysical Research Papers [*A publication*]
**Geophys R L** ... Geophysical Research Letters [*A publication*]
**Geophys Soc Tulsa Proc** ... Geophysical Society of Tulsa. Proceedings [*A publication*]
**Geophys Space Data Bull** ... Geophysics and Space Data Bulletin [*A publication*]
**Geophys Surv** ... Geophysical Surveys [*A publication*]
**Geophys Tecton Abstr** ... Geophysics and Tectonics Abstracts [*A publication*]
**Geopp**......... Geopposserde [*Defendant*] [*Netherlands*] [*Legal term*] (DLA)
**Geo-Process** ... Geo-Processing [*A publication*]
**GEOQ**........ Geos. Canada Department of Energy, Mines, and Resources [*A publication*]
**GeoR**.......... Geographical Review [*A publication*]
**Geo R**......... Georgia Review [*A publication*]
**GEORAD**.. Geographical Review [*A publication*]
**GEOREF**... Geographic Reference System [*Civil Defense*]
**GEOREF**... Geological Reference File [*American Geological Institute*] [*Bibliographic database*] [*Information service or system*] (IID)
**Geo Rep**..... Georgia Reports [*A publication*] (DLA)
**GEOREQ**.. Relocation Request [*Code*] [*Military*] (MCD)
**Geo Rev**...... Georgia Law Review [*A publication*]
**GEORG**..... Georgics [*Poetry*] (ROG)
**GEORGE**.. General Organizational Environment [*Data processing*] (BUR)
**George**........ George's Reports [*30-39 Mississippi*] [*A publication*] (DLA)
**George Partn** ... George on Partnership [*A publication*] (DLA)
**Georget Law** ... Georgetown Law Journal [*A publication*]
**Georget LJ** ... Georgetown Law Journal [*A publication*]
**GEORGETN** ... Georgetown (ROG)
**Georgetown Dent J** ... Georgetown Dental Journal [*A publication*]
**Georgetown Law J** ... Georgetown Law Journal [*A publication*]
**Georgetown LJ** ... Georgetown Law Journal [*A publication*]
**Georgetown Med Bull** ... Georgetown Medical Bulletin [*A publication*]
**Georgetown Univ Sch Dent Mirror** ... Georgetown University. School of Dentistry. Mirror [*A publication*]
**George Wash** ... George Washington Law Review [*A publication*]
**George Washington J Internat Law and Econ** ... George Washington Journal of International Law and Economics [*A publication*]
**George Washington Law R** ... George Washington Law Review [*A publication*]
**George Washington Univ Bull** ... George Washington University. Bulletin [*A publication*]
**George Wash L Rev** ... George Washington Law Review [*A publication*]
**George Wash Univ Bull** ... George Washington University. Bulletin [*A publication*]
**Georgia**...... Georgia Reports [*A publication*] (DLA)
**Georgia BJ** ... Georgia Bar Journal [*A publication*]
**Georgia J Int Comp L** ... Georgia Journal of International and Comparative Law [*A publication*]
**Georgia Law Rep** ... Georgia Law Reporter [*A publication*]
**Georgia L Rev** ... Georgia Law Review [*A publication*]
**Georgia R**... Georgia Review [*A publication*]
**Georgia Rep** ... Georgia Reports [*A publication*] (DLA)
**Georgia St BJ** ... Georgia State Bar Journal [*A publication*]
**Georgikon Delt** ... Georgikon Deltion [*A publication*]
**Georg Nat**.. Georgius Natta [*Flourished, 1477-95*] [*Authority cited in pre-1607 legal work*] (DSA)
**Georgr et Rech** ... Geographie et Recherche [*A publication*]
**GEOS**........ Geodetic Earth-Orbiting Satellite
**GEOS**........ Geodetic Observation Satellite
**GEOS**........ Geodynamic Experimental Ocean Satellite
**GEOS**........ Geos Corp. [*NASDAQ symbol*] (NQ)
**GEOS**........ Geoscope [*A publication*]
**GEOS**........ Geosynchronous Earth Observation System (IEEE)
**GEOS**........ Graphic Environment Operating System [*Commodore 64*]
**GEOSAR**... Geosynchronous Synthetic Aperture RADAR (IEEE)
**GEOSAT**... Geodesy Satellite
**Geosat**........ Geodetic Satellite
**GEOSCAN** ... Ground-Based Electronic Omnidirectional Satellite Communications Antenna
**Geosci Abstr** ... Geoscience Abstracts [*A publication*]
**Geosci Can** ... Geoscience Canada [*A publication*]
**Geosci Doc** ... Geoscience Documentation [*A publication*]
**Geoscience Abs** ... Geoscience Abstracts [*A publication*]
**Geoscience Inf Soc Proc** ... Geoscience Information Society. Proceedings [*A publication*]
**Geosci Man** ... Geoscience and Man [*A publication*]
**Geosci Stud** ... Geoscience Studies [*Japan*] [*A publication*]
**GEOSECS** ... Geochemical Ocean Sections Study [*Submarine ocean exploration by US for International Decade of Ocean Exploration*]
**GEOSEPS** ... Geosynchronous Solar Electric Propulsion Stage [*NASA*] (NASA)
**GEO/SIT**... Geographical Situation (MCD)
**GEOSS**...... Geophysical Survey System [*Naval Oceanographic Office*]
**GeoSSR**..... Georgian Soviet Socialist Republic
**Geostandards Newsl** ... Geostandards Newsletter [*A publication*]
**Geostand Newsl** ... Geostandards Newsletter [*A publication*]
**GEOTA**..... Geotimes [*A publication*]
**GEOTAJ**... Geotimes [*A publication*]
**Geotech Abstr** ... Geotechnical Abstracts [*A publication*]
**Geotech Eng** ... Geotechnical Engineering [*A publication*]
**Geotechniq** ... Geotechnique [*A publication*]
**Geotech Test J** ... Geotechnical Testing Journal [*A publication*]
**Geotecton**... Geotectonics [*A publication*]
**Geotek Julk** ... Geoteknillisia Julkaisuja [*A publication*]
**Geoteknisk Inst Bull** ... Geoteknisk Institut. Bulletin [*A publication*]
**Geotekton**.. Geotektonika [*A publication*]
**Geotekton Forsch** ... Geotektonische Forschungen [*A publication*]
**Geotektonika Tektonofiz Geodinamika** ... Geotektonika, Tektonofizika, i Geodinamika [*A publication*]
**Geotektonische Forsch** ... Geotektonische Forschungen [*A publication*]
**Geotherm**... Geothermics [*A publication*]
**Geotherm Energy** ... Geothermal Energy [*A publication*]
**Geotherm Energy Mag** ... Geothermal Energy Magazine [*A publication*]
**Geotherm Energy Update** ... Geothermal Energy Update [*A publication*]
**Geotherm Hot Line** ... Geothermal Hot Line [*A publication*]
**Geotherm Rep** ... Geothermal Report [*A publication*]
**Geotherm Rep Miner Resour Dep (Fiji)** ... Geothermal Report. Mineral Resources Department (Fiji) [*A publication*]
**Geotherm Resour Counc Spec Rep** ... Geothermal Resources Council. Special Report [*A publication*]
**Geotherm Resour Counc Trans** ... Geothermal Resources Council. Transactions [*People's Republic of China*] [*A publication*]
**Geotherm Technol** ... Geothermal Technology [*Japan*] [*A publication*]
**GEOU**........ Graphics Entity and Operation Unification [*Data processing*]
**Geo Wash J Int L** ... George Washington Journal of International Law and Economics [*A publication*]
**Geo Wash J Intl L and Econ** ... George Washington Journal of International Law and Economics [*A publication*]
**Geo Wash L Rev** ... George Washington Law Review [*A publication*]
**Geowiss Unserer Zeit** ... Geowissenschaften in Unserer Zeit [*A publication*]
**GEOX**........ Geonex Corp. [*St. Petersburg, FL*] [*NASDAQ symbol*] (NQ)
**GEP**........... Gastroenteropancreatic System [*Medicine*]
**GEP**........... Geological Echo Profiler [*Oceanography*] (MSC)
**GEP**........... Goddard Experimental Package [*NASA*]
**GEP**........... Graduate English Papers [*A publication*]
**GEP**........... Great Pacific Resources [*Vancouver Stock Exchange symbol*]
**GEP**........... Grolier Electronic Publishing, Inc. [*Information service or system*] (IID)
**GEP**........... Gross Energy Product
**GEP**........... Grosshandels-Einkaufspreis [*Wholesale Purchasing Price*] [*German*]
**GEP**........... Ground Effects Phenomenon
**GEP**........... Ground Entry Point (NVT)
**GEP**........... Group Employment Plan (MCD)
**GEP**........... Gulf Environmental Measurements Program (MCD)
**GEP**........... Minneapolis, MN [*Location identifier*] [*FAA*] (FAAL)
**GEPA**......... General Education Provisions Act [*1970*]
**GEPAC**...... General Electric Process Automation Computer
**GEPAC**...... General Electric Programmable Automatic Comparator [*or Computer*]
**GEPACDE** ... Geographical Paper. Canada Department of Environment [*A publication*]
**GEPB**......... Grievance and Employment Policy Board [*Army*]
**GEPC**......... German External Property Control Commission [*Minden*] [*Allied German Occupation Forces*]
**GEPCA**...... GP. Journal of the American Academy of General Practice [*A publication*]
**GEPDS**...... General Electric Process Design System
**GEPE**......... GATE [*GARP Atlantic Tropical Experiment*] Equatorial Profiling Experiment [*Marine science*] (MSC)
**GEPE**......... Groupe d'Etudes Politiques Europeennes (EA)
**GEPEXS**... General Electric Parts Explosion System
**GEpFAR**.... Federal Archives and Records Center, General Services Administration, Atlanta Region, East Point, GA [*Library symbol*] [*Library of Congress*] (LCLS)
**GEPGA**...... Gepgyartastechnologia [*Hungary*] [*A publication*]
**GEPI**......... Gestioni e Partecipazioni Industriali [*Industrial Management and Participation*] [*Italian government-sponsored agency to aid ailing companies*]
**GEPL**......... General Equipment and Packaging Laboratory [*Army*]
**GEPLACEA** ... Grupo de Paises Latinoamericanos y del Caribe Exportadores de Azucar [*Group of Latin American and Caribbean Sugar Exporting Countries - GLACSEC*] (EAIO)
**GEPURS**... General Electric General Purpose
**GEPVP**...... Groupement Europeen des Producteurs de Verre Plat [*European Group of Flat Glass Manufacturers*] (EAIO)
**GEQ**........... Moline, IL [*Location identifier*] [*FAA*] (FAAL)

**GER**.......... Gardiner Resources [*Vancouver Stock Exchange symbol*]
**GER**.......... Gastroesophageal Reflux [*See also GERD*] [*Medicine*]
**GER**.......... General Engineering Research
**GeR**.......... Gengogaku Ronso [*A publication*]
**Ger**.......... Gerard Pucelle [*Deceased, 1184*] [*Authority cited in pre-1607 legal work*] (DSA)
**GER**.......... Geriatrics
**Ger**.......... Gerim (BJA)
**GER**.......... German [*Language, etc.*]
**ger**.......... German [*MARC language code*] [*Library of Congress*] (LCCP)
**GER**.......... German Economic Review [*A publication*]
**Ger**.......... Germania [*A publication*]
**Ger**.......... Germanistik [*A publication*]
**GER**.......... Germany
**GER**.......... Germany Fund, Inc. [*NYSE symbol*] (SPSG)
**GER**.......... Gerontology [*American Occupational Therapy Association*]
**GER**.......... Gerund
**GER**.......... Goodyear Engineering Report (MCD)
**GER**.......... Great Eastern Railway [*British*]
**GER**.......... Guilde Europeenne du Raid [*European Expedition Guild - EEG*] (EAIO)
**GER**.......... Nueva Gerona [*Cuba*] [*Airport symbol*] (OAG)
**GERA**........ Guard's Expense in Returning Absentee [*Army*]
**GerAE**........ German Antarctic Expedition [*1901-03,1911-12,1938-39*]
**GERBIL**.... Great Education Reform Bill [*British*]
**Gerbil Dig**.. Gerbil Digest [*A publication*]
**Ger Bundesanst Bodenforsch Geol Jahrb Beih** ... Germany. Bundesanstalt fuer Bodenforschung und Geologische Landesaemter. Geologisches Jahrbuch. Beiheft [*A publication*]
**Ger Chem Eng** ... German Chemical Engineering [*A publication*]
**Ger Chem Engng** ... German Chemical Engineering [*A publication*]
**Gercke Norden** ... Gercke und Norden. Einleitung in die Altertumswissenschaft [*A publication*]
**GERD**........ Gastroesophageal Reflux Disease [*Medicine*]
**GERDAT**... Groupement d'Etudes et de Recherche pour le Developpement de l'Agronomie Tropicale [*Group for the Study and Research of Tropical Agronomy*] [*International Cooperation Center of Agricultural Research for Development*] [*Information service or system*] (IID)
**GEREA**...... General Electric Review [*A publication*]
**Ger Ec Bul** ... Economic Bulletin (Germany) [*A publication*]
**Ger Econ Re** ... German Economic Review [*A publication*]
**GERED**...... Geothermal Report [*A publication*]
**GerefTTS**... Gereformeerd Theologisch Tijdschrift [*Kampen*] [*A publication*]
**GEREP**...... Generalized Equipment Reliability Evaluation Procedure
**Gereq**.......... Gerequireerde [*Defendant*] [*Netherlands*] (ILCA)
**Gerfaut Rev Sci Belge Ornithol** ... Gerfaut. Revue Scientifique Belge d'Ornithologie [*A publication*]
**GERG**........ Groupe Europeen de Recherches Gazieres [*European Gas Research Group*] (EAIO)
**GERIA**....... Geriatrics [*A publication*]
**GERIAT**.... Geriatrics
**Geriatric Nurs** ... Geriatric Nursing [*A publication*]
**Geriatr Nurs** ... Geriatric Nursing [*A publication*]
**Geriatr Nurs (Lond)** ... Geriatric Nursing (London) [*A publication*]
**GERIAZ**.... Geriatrics [*A publication*]
**GERIS**....... Graphic Expression Reading Improvement System
**GERL**......... Golgi-Associated Endoplasmic Reticulum Lysosomes
**Gerlands Beitr Geophys** ... Gerlands Beitraege zur Geophysik [*A publication*]
**Ger Life L**.. German Life and Letters [*A publication*]
**Ger Life Lett** ... German Life and Letters [*A publication*]
**Ger L & L**... German Life and Letters [*A publication*]
**GERM**....... German [*Language, etc.*] (ROG)
**Germ**.......... Germania [*of Tacitus*] [*Classical studies*] (OCD)
**GERM**....... Ground Effect Research Machine
**GERMA**.... Groupe d'Etude des Ressources Maritimes [*Universite du Quebec a Rimouski*] [*Canada*] [*Research center*]
**German**...... Germanicus [*15BC-19AD*] [*Classical studies*] (OCD)
**German Chem Engng** ... German Chemical Engineering [*A publication*]
**German Econ R** ... German Economic Review [*A publication*]
**German Fct** ... Facts and Figures (Germany) [*A publication*]
**German Int** ... German International [*A publication*]
**German Internat** ... German International [*A publication*]
**German Med Monthly** ... German Medical Monthly [*A publication*]
**German Q**.. German Quarterly [*A publication*]
**German TN** .. German American Trade News [*A publication*]
**German Yb Int'l L** ... German Yearbook of International Law [*A publication*] (DLA)
**GERMD**.... German Mining [*A publication*]
**GERMDF**... German Ministry of Defense
**GERME**..... Groupe d'Etude en Regulation Metabolique [*University of Quebec at Rimouski*] [*Research center*] (RCD)
**Ger Med**..... German Medicine [*A publication*]
**Ger Med Mon** ... German Medical Monthly [*A publication*]
**Germfask**... Grant, Edge, Robinson, Mead, French, Ackley, Shephard, and Knaggs [*Founders of a town in Michigan's Upper Peninsula that derived its name from the initial letters of their surnames*]
**GermJud**.... Germania Judaica [*A publication*] (BJA)
**GermL**........ Germanistische Linguistik [*A publication*]
**Germn Tb Q** ... German Tribune Quarterly Review [*A publication*]
**Germ R**....... Germanic Review [*A publication*]
**Germ-Rom Monat** ... Germanisch-Romanische Monatsschrift [*A publication*]
**Germ Stud Newsl** ... German Studies Newsletter [*A publication*]
**GERNDJ**... Gerontology [*A publication*]
**GERNORSEA** ... German Naval Forces, North Sea Subarea [*NATO*] (NATG)
**Ger Note**.... Germanic Notes [*A publication*]
**GERO**........ GE [*General Electric Co.*] Robot
**GERO**........ George Rogers Clark National Historical Park
**GERO**........ Global Environmental Research Organization
**GEROA**..... Gerontologia [*A publication*]
**GEROAJ**... Gerontologia [*Basel*] [*A publication*]
**Gerodontolo** ... Gerodontology [*A publication*]
**Gerontol**..... Gerontologist [*A publication*]
**GERONTOL** ... Gerontology
**Gerontol Abstr** ... Gerontological Abstracts [*A publication*]
**Gerontol Clin** ... Gerontologia Clinica [*Later, Gerontology*] [*A publication*]
**Gerontol Ext Lect** ... Gerontology Extension Lectures [*A publication*]
**Gerontol Geriatr Educ** ... Gerontology and Geriatrics Education [*A publication*]
**Ger Plast**.... German Plastics [*West Germany*] [*A publication*]
**Ger Q**......... German Quarterly [*A publication*]
**Ger Quart**... German Quarterly [*A publication*]
**GERR**........ Government Employee Relations Report [*A publication*]
**Ger Rev**...... Germanic Review [*A publication*]
**Ger Rom Mon** ... Germanisch-Romanische Monatsschrift [*A publication*]
**GERSIS**..... General Electric Range Safety Instrumentation System [*Aerospace*]
**Ger Slav**..... Germano-Slavica [*A publication*]
**Ger S R**...... German Studies Review [*A publication*]
**Ger St Rev** ... German Studies Review [*A publication*]
**GERT**......... Graphical Evaluation and Review Technique
**Ger Tekh**.... Germanskaya Tekhnika [*A publication*]
**Ger Tit**....... Gerard's Titles to Real Estate [*A publication*] (DLA)
**GERTS**...... General Electric Radio [*or Range*] Tracking System [*Aerospace*]
**GERTS**...... General Electric Remote Terminal Supervisor
**GERTS**...... General Electric Remote Terminal System (IEEE)
**GERUA**..... Geologische Rundschau [*A publication*]
**GERV**........ General Electric Reentry Vehicle [*Aerospace*] (AAG)
**Ger Zent Geol Inst Abh** ... Germany. Zentrales Geologisches Institut. Abhandlungen [*A publication*]
**Ger Zent Geol Inst Jahrb Geol** ... Germany. Zentrales Geologisches Institut. Jahrbuch fuer Geologie [*A publication*]
**Ger Zentrales Geol Inst Wiss-Tech Informationsdienst** ... Germany. Zentrales Geologisches Institut. Wissenschaftlich-Technischer Informationsdienst [*A publication*]
**GES**............ General Educational Services Corp.
**GES**............ General Electric Semiconductor
**GES**............ General Santos [*Philippines*] [*Airport symbol*] (OAG)
**GES**............ Generic Environmental Statement [*Nuclear energy*] (NRCH)
**GES**............ Genesis Resource Corp. [*Vancouver Stock Exchange symbol*]
**GES**............ Genisco Technology Corp. [*AMEX symbol*] (SPSG)
**GES**............ Gesellschaft [*Company*] [*German*]
**GES**............ Gilt-Edged Securities [*Business term*]
**GES**............ Glucose Electrolyte Solution [*Medicine*]
**GES**............ Goddard Experiment Support System [*NASA*] (MCD)
**GES**............ Gold Exchange of Singapore (DS)
**GES**............ Gold Exchange Standard
**GES**............ Goliath Edison Screw
**GES**............ Gordon, E. S., Joplin MO [*STAC*]
**GES**............ Government Economic Service [*British*]
**GES**............ Government Evacuation Scheme [*British*] [*World War II*]
**GES**............ Ground Electronic System
**GES**............ Ground Entry Station (MCD)
**GES**............ Ground Equipment System
**GES**............ Group Encounter Survey
**GES**............ Group Environment Scale [*Personality development test*] [*Psychology*]
**GES**............ Groupe d'Etudes Sartriennes (EAIO)
**GESAANP/NW** ... GE [*General Electric Co.*] Stockholders' Alliance Against Nuclear Power/Nuclear Weapons (EA)
**Ges Abh**..... Gesammelte Abhandlungen zur Roemischen Religions- und Stadtgeschichte [*A publication*] (OCD)
**GESAC**...... General Electric Self-Adaptive Control System
**Gesammelte Abh Dtsch Lederinst (Freiberg)** ... Gesammelte Abhandlungen. Deutsches Lederinstitut (Freiberg) [*A publication*]
**Gesammelte Abh Kenn Kohle** ... Gesammelte Abhandlungen zur Kenntnis der Kohle [*A publication*]
**Gesammelte Ber Betr Forsch Ruhrgas Ag** ... Gesammelte Berichte aus Betrieb und Forschung der Ruhrgas Aktiengesellschaft [*West Germany*] [*A publication*]
**GESAMP**.. Group of Experts on the Scientific Aspects of Marine Pollution [*ICSU*] (EAIO)
**Gesamtverzeichnis Oesterreichischer Diss** ... Gesamtverzeichnis Oesterreichischer Dissertationen [*A publication*]
**GESB**......... General Export Services Branch [*Department of Trade*] [*British*]
**GesB**.......... Hebraeisches und Aramaeisches Handwoerterbuch ueber das Alte Testament [*W. Gesenius and F. Buhl*] [*A publication*] (BJA)

**GESBA** ...... Geologicky Zbornik [*Bratislava, Czechoslovakia*] [*A publication*]
**GESBAJ** .... Geologicky Zbornik [*A publication*]
**Ges Bekampf Krebskr Nordrhein-Westfalen Mitteilungdienst** ... Gesellschaft zur Bekampfung der Krebskrankheiten im Nordrhein-Westfalen. Mitteilungsdienst [*West Germany*] [*A publication*]
**GESBT** ...... Generic Expert System Building Tool
**GESC** ......... Government EDP [*Electronic Data Processing*] Standards Committee [*Canada*]
**Gesch** ......... Geschichte [*of Germanicus*] [*Classical studies*] (OCD)
**GESCH** ...... Geschichte [*History*] [*German*]
**Gesch Ges** .. Geschichte und Gesellschaft [*A publication*]
**Gesch Wiss Unterr** ... Geschichte in Wissenschaft und Unterricht [*A publication*]
**gesch Wm** .. Geschuetzte Warenmarke [*Patented Trademark*] [*German*]
**GESCO** ...... General Electric Supply Corporation
**Ges Dtsch Metallhuetten- und Bergleute Schr** ... Gesellschaft Deutscher Metallhuetten- und Bergleute. Schriften [*A publication*]
**Ges Dtsch Naturforsch Aerzte Wiss Konf** ... Gesellschaft Deutscher Naturforscher und Aerzte. Wissenschaftliche Konferenz [*A publication*]
**Gesell Erdk Leipz Mitt** ... Gesellschaft fuer Erdkunde zu Leipzig. Mitteilungen [*A publication*]
**Gesell f Kieler Stadtgesch Mitt** ... Gesellschaft fuer Kieler Stadtgeschichte. Mitteilungen [*A publication*]
**Gesell Kieler Stadtgesch Mitt** ... Gesellschaft fuer Kieler Stadtgeschichte. Mitteilungen [*A publication*]
**GESEM** ..... Groupement Europeen des Sources d'Eaux Minerales Naturelles [*European Group ofNatural Mineral Water Sources*] (EAIO)
**Ges Erdk Berlin Verh Zs** ... Gesellschaft fuer Erdkunde zu Berlin. Verhandlungen. Zeitschrift [*A publication*]
**Gesetzblatt Dtsch Demokr Repub** ... Gesetzblatt der Deutschen Demokratischen Republik [*East Germany*] [*A publication*]
**Gesetzbl Baden-Wuerttemb** ... Gesetzblatt fuer Baden-Wuerttemberg [*A publication*]
**Gesetzbl DDR Teil I** ... Gesetzblatt der Deutschen Demokratischen Republik. Teil 1 [*German Democratic Republic*] [*A publication*]
**Gesetz- Verordnungsbl Land Hessen Teil 1** ... Gesetz- und Verordnungsblatt fuer das Land Hessen. Teil 1 [*A publication*]
**Ges Geol Bergbaustud Oesterr Mitt** ... Gesellschaft der Geologie- und Bergbaustudenten in Oesterreich. Mitteilungen [*A publication*]
**Ges Geol Bergbaustud Wien Mitt** ... Gesellschaft der Geologie- und Bergbaustudenten in Wien. Mitteilungen [*A publication*]
**Ges Gesch & Bibliog Brauwes Jahrb** ... Gesellschaft fuer die Geschichte und Bibliographie des Brauwesens. Jahrbuch [*Berlin*] [*A publication*]
**GESH** ........ Grain Effect Screenless Halftone [*Printing technique*]
**GESHA** ..... Genden Shiryo [*A publication*]
**GESHUA** .. General Electric Six Hundred Users' Association [*Later, HLSUA*] [*Data processing*]
**Ges-Ing** ...... Gesundheits-Ingenieur [*A publication*]
**GESKAC** ... Genetika i Selektsiya [*A publication*]
**GESLB** ...... Genetika a Slechteni [*A publication*]
**GESLBG** ... Genetika a Slechteni [*A publication*]
**GESMO** .... General Environmental Statement for Mixed Oxide Fuel
**Gesn** ........... Gesnerus [*A publication*]
**Ges Naturf Freund Berlin Szb** ... Gesellschaft Naturforschender Freunde zu Berlin. Sitzungsberichte [*A publication*]
**Ges Naturkd Wuerttemb Jahresh** ... Gesellschaft fuer Naturkunde in Wuerttemberg. Jahreshefte [*A publication*]
**Ges Naturw Marburg Schrift** ... Gesellschaft zur Befoerderung der Gesammten Naturwissenschaften zu Marburg. Schriften [*A publication*]
**GESO** ........ Group Equipment Staff Officer [*British military*] (DMA)
**GESOC** ...... General Electric Satellite Orbit Control [*Aerospace*]
**GESP** ......... General Extrasensory Perception [*Parapsychology*]
**Ges Reaktorsicherh Ber GRS-S** ... Gesellschaft fuer Reaktorsicherheit. Bericht GRS-S [*West Germany*] [*A publication*]
**Ges Schr** ..... Gesammelte Schriften [*A publication*] (OCD)
**GesStud** ..... Gesammelte Studien [*A publication*] (BJA)
**GEST** ......... Gas Explosive Simulation Technique [*Air Force*]
**GEST** ......... Gemini Slowscan Television [*NASA*]
**GEST** ......... General Systems Theory
**GEST** ......... Gestational [*Pediatrics*]
**Gest** ........... Gestion [*A publication*]
**GEST** ......... Gestorben [*Died*] [*German*]
**GEST** ......... Guest Supply, Inc. [*NASDAQ symbol*] (NQ)
**GESTA** ...... Gesetzgebungsstand [*Database*] [*Deutscher Bundestag*] [*German*] [*Information service or system*] (CRD)
**GESTAPO** ... Geheime Staats Polizei [*Secret State Police*] [*Germany*]
**GESTAPU** ... Gerkang, September, Tigapuluh [*See also GESTOK*] [*Plot against the government of Indonesia beginning on September 30, 1965*]
**GESTOK** ... Gerkang Oktober [*See also GESTAPU*] [*Plot against the government of Indonesia which began on September 30, 1965 and continued into October*]
**Gesunde Pfl** ... Gesunde Pflanzen [*A publication*]
**Gesunde Pflanz** ... Gesunde Pflanzen [*A publication*]
**Gesundhd** ... Gesundheitsdienst [*A publication*]
**Gesundheitsfuehr Dtsch Volkes** ... Gesundheitsfuehrung des Deutschen Volkes [*A publication*]
**Gesundheits-Ing** ... Gesundheits-Ingenieur [*A publication*]
**Gesundheitswes Desinfekt** ... Gesundheitswesen und Desinfektion [*A publication*]
**Gesundh Fuers** ... Gesundheitsfuersorge [*A publication*]
**Gesundh-Ing** ... Gesundheits-Ingenieur [*A publication*]
**Gesundh Wohlf** ... Gesundheit und Wohlfahrt [*A publication*]
**Gesund-Ing** ... Gesundheits-Ingenieur [*A publication*]
**Gesund-Ing Haustech-Bauphys-Umwelttech** ... Gesundheits-Ingenieur. Haustechnik-Bauphysik-Umwelttechnik [*A publication*]
**Gesun Wohlfahrt** ... Gesundheit und Wohlfahrt [*A publication*]
**GET** ........... Gas, Electric, Telephones [*of GET, Inc., a consumer group*]
**GET** ........... Gastric Emptying Time [*Medicine*]
**GET** ........... Generator Environmental Tester
**GET** ........... Geografisch Tijdschrift. Nieuwe Reeks [*A publication*]
**GET** ........... Geraldton [*Australia*] [*Airport symbol*] (OAG)
**Get** ............. Geteilt [*Divided*] [*Music*]
**GET** ........... Graduate Employment and Training [*British*]
**GET** ........... Ground Elapsed Time [*Aerospace*]
**GET** ........... Ground Entry Terminal (MCD)
**GETA** ........ General Equipment Test Activity [*Army*]
**GETA** ........ Government Employees Training Act [*1966*]
**GETAB** ...... General Electric BWR [*Boiling Water Reactor*] Thermal Analysis Branch (NRCH)
**GE/TAC** .... General Electric Telemetering and Control (IEEE)
**GETC** ......... Gemtec Corp. [*NASDAQ symbol*] (NQ)
**GETD** ......... Geografisk Tidsskrift [*A publication*]
**GETE** ......... Geotel, Inc. [*NASDAQ symbol*] (NQ)
**GETEL** ...... General Electric Test Engineering Language [*Data processing*] (IEEE)
**Geterog Katal** ... Geterogennyi Kataliz. Trudy Mezhdunarodnogo Simpoziuma po Geterogennomu Katalizu [*A publication*]
**GETh** ......... [*The*] Epic of Gilgamesh [*R. C. Thompson*] [*A publication*] (BJA)
**GETI** .......... Ground Elapsed Time of Ignition [*Aerospace*] (KSC)
**GETIL** ........ Ground Elapsed Time of Landing
**GETIS** ........ Ground Environment Technical Installation System [*NATO*] (NATG)
**GETLO** ...... Obtain by Local Purchase [*Military*]
**GETMA** .... Getreide und Mehl [*A publication*]
**GETMA** .... Obtain by Local Manufacture [*Military*]
**GETO** ........ Ground Equipment Turn Off (KSC)
**GETOL** ...... General Electric Training Operational Logic [*Data processing*] (IEEE)
**GETOL** ...... Ground Effect Takeoff and Landing
**GETR** ......... General Electric Test Reactor
**Getreide Mehl Brot** ... Getreide Mehl und Brot [*A publication*]
**Getriebe Mot Antriebselem** ... Getriebe Motoren Antriebselemente [*A publication*]
**GETS** ......... General Track Simulation [*NASA*] (KSC)
**GETS** ......... Ground Equipment Test Set
**GETSCO** ... General Electric Technical Services Company (NRCH)
**GETT** ......... German Tactical Truck (MCD)
**GETT** ......... Gettysburg National Military Park
**GETT** ......... Grants Equal to Taxes
**Getty Mus J** ... J. Paul Getty Museum. Journal [*A publication*]
**Getuig** ........ Getuigenis [*Roermond/Maaseik*] (BJA)
**GETY** ......... Gettysburg Railroad Co. [*AAR code*]
**Getz F** ......... Getz's Forms in Conveyancing [*A publication*] (DLA)
**GEU** ........... Emory University, Atlanta, GA [*Library symbol*] [*Library of Congress*] (LCLS)
**GEU** ........... Geothermal Energy Update [*A publication*]
**GEU** ........... Grossesse Extra-Uterine [*Medicine*]
**GEU-B** ....... Emory University, School of Business Administration, Atlanta, GA [*Library symbol*] [*Library of Congress*] (LCLS)
**GEU-D** ....... Emory University, School of Dentistry, Atlanta, GA [*Library symbol*] [*Library of Congress*] (LCLS)
**GEU-L** ....... Emory University, Lamar School of Law, Atlanta, GA [*Library symbol*] [*Library of Congress*] (LCLS)
**GEU-LS** ..... Emory University, Division of Librarianship, Atlanta, GA [*Library symbol*] [*Library of Congress*] (LCLS)
**GEU-M** ...... Emory University, A. W. Calhoun Medical Library, Atlanta, GA [*Library symbol*] [*Library of Congress*] (LCLS)
**GEU-T** ....... Emory University, Candler School of Theology, Atlanta, GA [*Library symbol*] [*Library of Congress*] (LCLS)
**GEU-Y** ....... Emory University, Yerkes Primate Research Center, Atlanta, GA [*Library symbol*] [*Library of Congress*] (LCLS)
**GEV** ........... Gallivare [*Sweden*] [*Airport symbol*] (OAG)
**GeV** ........... Giga Electron Volt
**GEV** ........... Ground Effect Vehicle
**GEV** ........... Groundnut Eyespot Virus
**GEVIC** ....... General Electric Variable Increment Computer
**GEVJA** ...... Geoloski Vjesnik [*A publication*]
**GEVJAO** ... Geoloski Vjesnik [*Zagreb*] [*A publication*]
**GEVST** ...... Gordon Environmental Studies Laboratory [*University of Montana*] [*Research center*] (RCD)
**GEW** .......... Gas, Electricity, Water [*Department of Employment*] [*British*]
**GeW** .......... Germanica Wratislaviensia [*A publication*]
**GEW** .......... Gewoya [*Papua New Guinea*] [*Airport symbol*] (OAG)

**GEW** .......... Glazed Earthenware
**GEWA** ....... George Washington Birthplace National Monument
**Gew A** ........ Gewerbearchiv [*A publication*]
**GEWAD5**.. Gewasbescherming [*A publication*]
**GEWED** .... Gewerbearchiv [*A publication*]
**Gewerbliche Rdsch** ... Gewerbliche Rundschau [*A publication*]
**Gewerbl Rechtsschutz Urheberrecht** ... Gewerblicher Rechtsschutz und Urheberrecht [*A publication*]
**Gewerk MH** ... Gewerkschaftliche Monatshefte [*A publication*]
**Gewerk Prax** ... Gewerkschaftliche Praxis [*A publication*]
**Gewerk Rd** ... Gewerkschaftliche Rundschau [*A publication*]
**Gewerkschaftliche Mhefte** ... Gewerkschaftliche Monatshefte [*A publication*]
**Gewerkschaftl Mh** ... Gewerkschaftliche Monatshefte [*A publication*]
**Gewerksch Monatsh** ... Gewerkschaftliche Monatshefte [*A publication*]
**Gewerksch Rundsch** ... Gewerkschaftliche Rundschau [*A publication*]
**Gew MH**.... Gewerkschaftliche Monatshefte [*A publication*]
**Gew Mon H** ... Gewerkschaftliche Monatshefte [*A publication*]
**GewO** ......... Gewerbeordnung [*Trade Regulation Law*] [*German*] (ILCA)
**GEWP** ....... George Washington Memorial Parkway [*National Park Service designation*]
**Gew St G**.... Gewerbesteuergesetz [*A publication*]
**GEX** .......... Gas Exchange
**GEX** .......... Government Employees Exchange
**GEX** .......... Granges Exploration Ltd. [*Toronto Stock Exchange symbol*]
**GEXA** ........ GEXA Gold Corp. [*NASDAQ symbol*] (NQ)
**GEY** .......... Getty Resources Ltd. [*Toronto Stock Exchange symbol*]
**GEY** .......... Greybull, WY [*Location identifier*] [*FAA*] (FAAL)
**Geyer DT** ... Geyer's Dealer Topics [*A publication*]
**Geyer OD**... Geyer's Office Dealer [*A publication*]
**GEYPA**...... Geologicky Pruzkum [*A publication*]
**GEYSD**...... Geyser [*A publication*]
**GEZ** .......... Garretson - Elmendorf - Zinov, Architects and Engineers [*San Francisco, CA*] [*Telecommunications service*] (TSSD)
**GEZ** .......... General Electric Canada, Inc. [*Toronto Stock Exchange symbol*]
**GEZ** .......... Gosudarstvennoe Knigoizdatelstvo [*State Publishing House*] [*USSR*]
**GEZERD**... Alfarbandishe Gezelshaft far Ainordenen Yidn af Erd in FSSR [*A publication*] (BJA)
**GEZHD**..... Geofizicheskii Zhurnal [*A publication*]
**Gezira Res Stn Substn Annu Rep** ... Gezira Research Station and Substations. Annual Report [*A publication*]
**GF** ............. French Guiana [*ANSI two-letter standard code*] (CNC)
**GF** ............. G and A Factor
**GF** ............. Gain Factor [*Data processing*]
**GF** ............. Galvanized Steel Fastenings
**GF** ............. Games Finished [*Baseball*]
**GF** ............. Gap Filler [*RADAR*]
**GF** ............. Garage Forecourts [*Public-performance tariff class*] [*British*]
**GF** ............. Gas Filled (MSA)
**GF** ............. Gas-Freeing System
**GF** ............. Gaudeamus Foundation (EAIO)
**GF** ............. Gauge Factor (MCD)
**GF** ............. Gelatinous Fiber [*Botany*]
**GF** ............. Generator Field
**GF** ............. Generic Failure
**GF** ............. Gentleman Friend
**G & F**......... Georgia & Florida R. R.
**GF** ............. Georgia & Florida R. R. [*AAR code*]
**GF** ............. Germfree [*Medicine*]
**GF** ............. Girl Friend [*Slang*]
**GF** ............. Girl Friends (EA)
**GF** ............. Glaciofluvial Soil [*Agronomy*]
**GF** ............. Glass Factor [*Tissue culture*]
**GF** ............. Glass Fiber
**GF** ............. Globular-Fibrous [*Biochemistry*]
**GF** ............. Glomerular Filtrate [*Medicine*]
**GF** ............. Gluten-Free [*Diet*]
**GF** ............. Goals For [*Hockey*]
**GF** ............. Gold Field
**GF** ............. Goldfinch [*Ornithology*]
**GF** ............. Goldflow (AFM)
**GF** ............. Gonococcus Filus [*A microorganism*]
**GF** ............. Gordon Fraser [*Publisher*] [*British*]
**GF** ............. Gorilla Foundation (EA)
**GF** ............. Government Form
**GF** ............. Governmental Finance [*A publication*]
**GF** ............. Grafiskt Forum [*A publication*]
**GF** ............. Grand Fleet [*British military*] (DMA)
**GF** ............. Grandfather
**GF** ............. Grayson Foundation [*Later, GJC*] (EA)
**GF** ............. Great Fire [*of London, 1666*]
**GF** ............. Greensward Foundation (EA)
**GF** ............. Grinding Fixture (MCD)
**GF** ............. Ground Face [*Technical drawings*]
**GF** ............. Ground Fog [*Meteorology*]
**GF** ............. Ground Foraging [*Ecology*]
**GF** ............. Ground Forces [*Military*]
**GF** ............. Group of Fourteen [*NATO countries minus France*] (NATG)
**GF** ............. Growth Fraction [*Endocrinology*]
**GF** ............. Gulf Aviation Ltd. [*Great Britain*] [*ICAO designator*] (FAAC)
**GF** ............. Gunnery Flight
**GF** ............. New Germany Fund [*NYSE symbol*] (SPSG)
**GFA** .......... Federal Aviation Administration, Southern Region, East Point, GA [*OCLC symbol*] (OCLC)
**GFA** .......... Gasket Fabricators Association (EA)
**GFA** .......... General Fitness Assessment
**GFA** .......... General Forestry Assistance
**GFA** .......... General Freight Agent
**GFA** .......... Giddens Family Associates (EA)
**GFA** .......... Gideon Family Association (EA)
**GFA** .......... Glial Fibrillary Acidic Protein [*Also, GFAP*] [*Biochemistry*]
**GFA** .......... Gloucester Fisheries Association (EA)
**GFA** .......... Gold Filled Association (EA)
**GFA** .......... Good Fair Average [*Insurance*]
**GFA** .......... Goodenow Family Association (EA)
**GFA** .......... Government-Furnished Ammunition (MCD)
**GFA** .......... Government-Furnished Articles (KSC)
**GFA** .......... Grain Futures Administration [*Superseded by Commodity Exchange Administration, 1936*]
**GFA** .......... Great Falls, MT [*Location identifier*] [*FAA*] (FAAL)
**GFA** .......... Gross Floor Area (ADA)
**GFA** .......... Guitar Foundation of America (EA)
**GF & A**....... Gulf Florida & Alabama Railway
**GFA** .......... Gunfire Area
**GFAA** ........ Game Fishing Association of Australia
**GFAA** ........ Graphite-Furnace Atomic Absorption [*Spectroscopy*] [*Physics*]
**GFAAS**...... Graphite Furnace Atomic Absorption Spectroscopy [*Physics*]
**GFAC**......... Ground Forward Air Controller (MCD)
**GFAE**......... Government-Furnished Aeronautical Equipment (AFM)
**GFAE**......... Government-Furnished Aerospace Equipment
**GFAE**......... Government-Furnished Aircraft Equipment
**GFAEL**...... Government-Furnished Aeronautical Equipment List (MCD)
**GFAM** ....... Graphics Flutter Analysis Methods [*Data processing*]
**GFAP**......... Glial Fibrillary Acidic Protein [*Also, GFA*] [*Biochemistry*]
**G Farm Chim** ... Giornale di Farmacia Chimica e Scienze Affini [*A publication*]
**G Farm Chim Sci Affini** ... Giornale di Farmacia Chimica e Scienze Affini [*A publication*]
**GFAVO** ..... Grossfeuerungsanlagen Verordnung [*Regulations for Large Boilers*] [*Federal Republic of Germany*]
**GFB** .......... GF Corp. [*Formerly, GF Business Equipment, Inc.*] [*NYSE symbol*] (SPSG)
**GFB** .......... Go for Broke [*Slang*]
**GFB** .......... Government Facilities Brochure
**GFB** .......... Government-Furnished Baseline
**GFB** .......... Gustav Freytag Blaetter [*A publication*]
**GFBA**......... Graduate Fellowships for Black Americans (EA)
**GFBI**.......... Grand Fleet Battle Instructions [*British military*] (DMA)
**GFbIS**........ United States Army, Infantry School, Fort Benning, GA [*Library symbol*] [*Library of Congress*] (LCLS)
**GFBN** ........ Bonthe [*Sierra Leone*] [*ICAO location identifier*] (ICLI)
**GFBO** ........ Grand Fleet Battle Orders [*British military*] (DMA)
**GfBV**.......... Gesellschaft fuer Bedrohte Voelker [*Society for Threatened Peoples*] (EAIO)
**GFC** .......... Gas-Filled Counter
**GFC** .......... Gas Filter Correlation [*NASA*] (KSC)
**GFC** .......... Gas Frontal Chromatography
**GFC** .......... Gel Filtration Chromatography
**GFC** .......... General Failure Criteria
**GFC** .......... Genstar Financial Corporation [*Toronto Stock Exchange symbol*]
**GFC** .......... George Fox College [*Oregon*]
**GFC** .......... Get Fresh Crew [*Rap recording group*]
**GFC** .......... Gibraltar Financial Corporation [*NYSE symbol*] (SPSG)
**GFC** .......... Glass Filter Covers
**GFC** .......... Goldwing Flyers Club (EA)
**GFC** .......... Grand Falls Central Railway Co. Ltd. [*AAR code*]
**GFC** .......... Graphite Fiber Composite
**GFC** .......... Gulf Coast Aviation, Inc. [*Gulfport, MS*] [*FAA designator*] (FAAC)
**GFC** .......... Gun Feed Control (MCD)
**GFCB**......... Ground Fault Circuit Breaker [*Electronics*]
**GFCC**......... Guarantee Financial Corporation of California [*NASDAQ symbol*] (NQ)
**GFCC**......... Gun Fire Control Computer [*Military*] (CAAL)
**GFCCAH**... FAO [*Food and Agriculture Organization of the United Nations*] General Fisheries Council for the Mediterranean. Circular [*A publication*]
**GFCE**......... Government-Furnished Capital Equipment (MCD)
**GFCES** ...... Glider Flight Control Electronics Subsystem
**GFCF** ........ Gross Fixed Capital Formation
**GFCG** ........ Government Fluidic Coordinating Group
**GFCI**.......... Gay Fathers Coalition International [*Later, GLPCI*] (EA)
**GFCI**.......... Ground Fault Circuit Interrupter [*Electronics*]
**GFCM** ....... General Fisheries Council for the Mediterranean [*Rome, Italy*]
**GF/CM²** .... Gram Force per Square Centimeter
**GFCO** ........ Good Faith Charitable Organization (EA)
**GFCR**......... Gas Filter Correlation Radiometer [*NASA*]
**GFCS** ......... Gaseous Flowmeter Calibration Stand
**GFCS** ......... Gunfire Control System
**GFCSMT** .. Generalized Fire-Control System Maintenance Trainer [*Spacecraft*] [*Navy*]

**GFCS SATSIM** ... Gun Fire Control System Satellite Simulation [*Military*] (CAAL)
**GFCT**......... Greenwich Finance Corp. [*NASDAQ symbol*] (NQ)
**GFD**.......... Gallons per Square-Foot per Day
**GFD**.......... Gap-Filler Data [*RADAR*]
**GFD**.......... Gemini Food Corp. [*Toronto Stock Exchange symbol*]
**GFD**.......... General Freight Department
**GFD**.......... General Functional Description [*Military*] (AABC)
**GFD**.......... Geophysical Fluid Dynamics Laboratory [*National Oceanic and Atmospheric Administration*]
**Gfd**.......... Geschichtsfreund [*A publication*]
**GFD**.......... Glucose-Free Dialysate [*Nephrology*]
**GFD**.......... Gluten-Free Diet
**GFD**.......... Gone for the Day
**GFD**.......... Government-Furnished Data (NASA)
**GFD**.......... Government-Furnished Documentation (KSC)
**GFD**.......... Greenfield, IN [*Location identifier*] [*FAA*] (FAAL)
**GFD**.......... Ground Forces Training Devices (Provisional) [*Army*] (RDA)
**GFD**.......... Group Finance Department
**GFD**.......... Guilford Mills, Inc. [*NYSE symbol*] (SPSG)
**GFDC**......... Group Fire Distribution Center [*Army*] (AABC)
**GFDD**......... Gunfire Detection Device
**GFDEP**...... Ground Fog Estimated ____ Feet Deep [*Meteorology*] (FAAC)
**GFDL**......... Geophysical Fluid Dynamics Laboratory [*National Oceanic and Atmospheric Administration*] [*Princeton, NJ*]
**GFDNA**..... Grain and Feed Dealers National Association [*Later, NGFA*] (EA)
**GFDS**......... Goldfields Flying Doctor Service [*Australia*]
**GFE**.......... Gays for Equality
**GFE**.......... Gibbs Free Energy [*Physical chemistry*]
**GFE**.......... Government-Furnished Equipment
**GFE**.......... Gross Feasibility Estimator (MCD)
**GFEC**......... Gulf Energy Corporation [*NASDAQ symbol*] (NQ)
**GFE & D**.... Government-Furnished Equipment and Data
**GFEL**......... Government-Furnished Equipment List (MCD)
**GFE & M**... Government-Furnished Equipment and Material (NRCH)
**GFEM**........ Graphics Finite Element Module [*McDonnell-Douglas Automation Corp.*]
**GFER**......... Government-Furnished Equipment Records
**GFERC**...... Grand Forks Energy Research Center [*Energy Research and Development Administration*]
**GFERR**...... Government-Furnished Equipment Requirements Request
**GFETC**...... Grand Forks Energy Technology Center [*Later, University of North Dakota Energy Research Center*] [*Department of Energy*] (GRD)
**GFF**.......... Geologiska Foereningens i Stockholm. Foerhandlingar [*A publication*]
**GFF**.......... Glass-Fiber Filter [*Separation technology*]
**GFF**.......... Government-Furnished Facilities (MCD)
**GFF**.......... Granolithic Finish Floor [*Technical drawings*]
**GFF**.......... Graphic Firing Fan [*Weaponry*] (INF)
**GFF**.......... Griffith [*Australia*] [*Airport symbol*] (OAG)
**GFF**.......... Grillparzer Forum Forchtenstein [*A publication*]
**GFFAR**...... Guided Folding-Fin Aircraft Rocket
**GFFC**........ Gibb Family Friendship Club (EA)
**GFFD**......... Gross Failed Fuel Detector [*Nuclear energy*] (NRCH)
**GFF (Geol Foren Stockholm Forhandl)** ... GFF (Geologiska Foreningen i Stockholm Forhandlingar) [*A publication*]
**GFFIL**........ Groupement Francais des Fournisseurs d'Information en Ligne [*French Association of Online Information Providers*] [*Paris*] [*Information service or system*] (IID)
**GFF Mitt** ... Mitteilungen der Gesellschaft zur Foerderung der Forschung an der Eidgenoessischen Technischen Hochschule [*A publication*]
**GFFNS**...... Godisnjak Filozofskog Fakulteta u Novom Sadu [*A publication*]
**GFG**.......... Geographical Field Group [*British*]
**GFG**.......... Glare Free Gloss [*Paper*]
**GFG**.......... [*The*] Good Food Guide [*A publication*] [*British*]
**GFG**.......... Governor's Foot Guard
**GFG**.......... Grafton Group Ltd. [*Toronto Stock Exchange symbol*]
**GFG**.......... Leesburg, VA [*Location identifier*] [*FAA*] (FAAL)
**GFGC**........ Great Falls Gas Company [*Great Falls, MT*] [*NASDAQ symbol*] (NQ)
**GFgC**......... United States Army, Civil Affairs School, Fort Gordon, GA [*Library symbol*] [*Library of Congress*] (LCLS)
**GFGF**......... Group Fore Golf Foundation (EA)
**GFGK**........ Gbangbatok [*Sierra Leone*] [*ICAO location identifier*] (ICLI)
**GFgML**...... United States Army, Medical Library, Fort Gordon, GA [*Library symbol*] [*Library of Congress*] (LCLS)
**GFgMP**...... United States Army, Military Police School, Fort Gordon, GA [*Library symbol*] [*Library of Congress*] (LCLS)
**GFgS**.......... United States Army, Special Services Library, Fort Gordon, GA [*Library symbol*] [*Library of Congress*] (LCLS)
**GFgSS**....... United States Army, Southeastern Signal School, Fort Gordon, GA [*Library symbol*] [*Library of Congress*] (LCLS)
**GFH**.......... Glucose-Free Hanks [*Solution*] [*Cell incubation medium*]
**GFH**.......... Group Financial Holdings Pty. Ltd. [*Australia*]
**GFHA**........ Hastings [*Sierra Leone*] [*ICAO location identifier*] (ICLI)
**GFHR**........ Gas-Filled Hydrophobic Region
**GFI**............ Gap-Filler Input [*RADAR*]
**GFI**............ Gas Flow Indicator [*NASA*]
**GFI**............ Giornale Critico della Filosofia Italiana [*A publication*]
**GFI**............ Global Finance Information [*Information service or system*] (IID)
**GFI**............ Gmelin Formula Index [*Gmelin-Institut fuer Anorganische Chemie und Grenzgebiete*] [*Federal Republic of Germany*] [*Information service or system*] (CRD)
**GFI**............ Government Final Inspection
**GFI**............ Government Free Issue (AABC)
**GFI**............ Government-Furnished Information
**GFI**............ Government-Owned Financial Institution (ADA)
**GFI**............ Graham-Field Health [*AMEX symbol*] (SPSG)
**GFI**............ Greyvest Financial Services, Inc. [*Toronto Stock Exchange symbol*]
**GFI**............ Ground Fault Interrupter [*Electronics*]
**GFI**............ Guided Fault Isolation
**G Fis**.......... Giornale di Fisica [*A publication*]
**G Fis Sanit** ... Giornale di Fisica Sanitaria e Protezione Contro le Radiazioni [*A publication*]
**G Fis Sanit Protez Contro Radiaz** ... Giornale di Fisica Sanitaria e Protezione Contro le Radiazioni [*A publication*]
**G Fis Sanit Prot Radiaz** ... Giornale di Fisica Sanitaria e Protezione Contro le Radiazioni [*A publication*]
**G Fis Soc Ital Fis** ... Giornale di Fisica. Societa Italiana di Fisica [*Italy*] [*A publication*]
**GFIT**.......... Glass-Fiber Insulation Tubing
**GFIV**.......... Generation 5 Technology, Inc. [*NASDAQ symbol*] (NQ)
**GFK**........... Grand Forks [*North Dakota*] [*Airport symbol*] (OAG)
**GFK**........... Grand Forks Mines [*Vancouver Stock Exchange symbol*]
**GFKB**......... Kabala [*Sierra Leone*] [*ICAO location identifier*] (ICLI)
**GFKE**......... Kenema [*Sierra Leone*] [*ICAO location identifier*] (ICLI)
**GFL**............ Geoffrion, Leclerc, Inc. [*Toronto Stock Exchange symbol*]
**GFL**............ Glens Falls, NY [*Location identifier*] [*FAA*] (FAAL)
**GFL**............ Glossary Function List
**GFL**............ Government-Furnished List
**GFL**............ Ground Fire Locator
**GFL**............ Guide to Football Literature [*A publication*]
**GFLA**......... [*The*] Growth Fund of Florida, Inc. [*NASDAQ symbol*] (NQ)
**GFLAAL** ... Gesellschaft zur Foerderung der Literatur aus Afrika, Asien, und Lateinamerika (EAIO)
**GFLD**......... Generator Field
**GFLL**.......... Freetown/Lungi [*Sierra Leone*] [*ICAO location identifier*] (ICLI)
**GFLOPS**.... Giga Floating Operations per Second [*Data processing*]
**GFLS**.......... Ground Fire Locating System
**GFLU**......... General Federation of Labor Unions [*Syria*]
**GFM**........... Glass-Fiber Material
**GFM**........... Goldfinch Mineral Ltd. [*Vancouver Stock Exchange symbol*]
**GFM**........... Government-Furnished Material
**GFM**........... Government-Furnished Missile
**GFM**........... Greyhound Food Management
**GFM**........... Marktforschung [*A publication*]
**GFMA**........ Gold-Filled Manufacturers Association [*Later, GFA*] (EA)
**GFmA**........ United States Army, Fort McPherson Post Library, Fort McPherson, GA [*Library symbol*] [*Library of Congress*] (LCLS)
**GFMD**........ Gold Film Mercury Detector [*Spectrometry*]
**GFME**........ Government-Furnished Missile Equipment (AAG)
**GFMP**........ Marampa [*Sierra Leone*] [*ICAO location identifier*] (ICLI)
**GFMS**........ Gaseous Flow Measuring System
**GFMS**........ Generalized File Maintenance System (ADA)
**GFMVT**..... General Foods Moisture Vapor Transmission
**GFN**........... Global Futures Network [*Bombay, India*] (EA)
**GFN**........... Grafton [*New York*] [*Seismograph station code, US Geological Survey*] [*Closed*] (SEIS)
**GFN**........... Grafton [*Australia*] [*Airport symbol*] (OAG)
**GFO**........... Bartica [*Guyana*] [*Airport symbol*] (OAG)
**GFO**........... Gap-Filler Output [*RADAR*]
**GFO**........... Gas-Fired Oven
**GFO**........... General Freight Office
**GFO**........... German Foreign Office [*British*] [*World War II*]
**GFOA**........ Government Finance Officers Association of United States and Canada (EA)
**G Foeren Stockholm Foerh** ... Geologiska Foereningens i Stockholm. Foerhandlingar [*A publication*]
**GFoF**.......... Fort Valley State College, Fort Valley, GA [*Library symbol*] [*Library of Congress*] (LCLS)
**GForsT**...... Tift College, Forsyth, GA [*Library symbol*] [*Library of Congress*] (LCLS)
**GFP**............ Gas Flow Programmer [*Chromatography*]
**GF & P**....... Gases, Fluids, and Propellants [*NASA*] (NASA)
**GFP**............ Geheime Feldpolizei [*Secret Police*] [*German*]
**GFP**............ General Forecasting Program (BUR)
**GFP**............ General Foreign Policy [*A publication*]
**GFP**............ Generalized File Processor
**GFP**............ Generations for Peace (EA)
**GFP**............ Glass-Fiber Pulling [*Materials processing*]
**GFP**............ Government Full Period (FAAC)
**GFP**............ Government-Funded Procurement
**GFP**............ Government-Funded Program

**GFP**........... Government-Furnished Parts (AFM)
**GFP**........... Government-Furnished Property
**GFP**........... Ground Fine Pitch (AIA)
**GFPBBD**... Groupement Francais des Producteurs de Bases et Banques de Donnees [*French Federation of Data Base Producers*] [*Information service or system*] (IID)
**GFPIAW**... Ghana. Council for Scientific and Industrial Research. Forest Products Research Institute. Annual Report [*A publication*]
**GFPL**......... Government-Furnished Property List (MCD)
**GFPM**........ Gas Fission Products Monitor
**GFPO**........ Grand Forks Project Office [*Terminated*] [*Grand Forks, ND*] [*Department of Energy*] (GRD)
**GFPO**........ Port Loko [*Sierra Leone*] [*ICAO location identifier*] (ICLI)
**GFP & S**..... Government-Furnished Property and Services (MSA)
**GFQ**........... Austin, TX [*Location identifier*] [*FAA*] (FAAL)
**GFR**........... Federal Reserve Bank of Atlanta, Atlanta, GA [*OCLC symbol*] (OCLC)
**GFR**........... Gap-Filler RADAR
**GFR**........... Gas-Filled Rectifier
**GFR**........... General Flight Rules [*CAB*] [*A publication*] (DLA)
**GFR**........... General Functional Requirements
**GFR**........... Geotechnical Fabrics Report [*A publication*] (EAAP)
**GFR**........... German Federal Republic [*West Germany*]
**GFR**........... Glass-Fiber Reinforced
**GFR**........... Glass and Fiber Resin
**GFR**........... Glomerular Filtration Rate [*Nephrology*]
**GFR**........... Government Facilities Request (AAG)
**GFR**........... Government Flight Representative
**GFR**........... Groenten en Fruit [*A publication*]
**G de Fr**....... Guillelmus de Ferreriis [*Deceased, 1295*] [*Authority cited in pre-1607 legal work*] (DSA)
**GFRC**......... Glass Fiber Reinforced Concrete
**GFRHS**...... Germans-from-Russia Heritage Society (EA)
**GF/RP**....... Gap-Filler/Reporting Post [*RADAR*]
**GFRP**......... Glass-Fiber-Reinforced Plastic [*Also, GlFRP*]
**GFRP**......... Graphite-Fiber-Reinforced Plastic [*Also, GrFRP*] (NASA)
**GFRRA**...... Georgia. Forest Research Council. Report [*A publication*]
**GFRS**......... Ground Forces Replacement Service [*World War II*]
**GFRT**......... Gas-Filled Rectifying Tube
**GFS**........... Fernbank Science Center, Atlanta, GA [*OCLC symbol*] (OCLC)
**GFS**........... Girls' Friendly Society of the USA (EA)
**GFS**........... Goffs, CA [*Location identifier*] [*FAA*] (FAAL)
**GFS**........... Government Finance Statistics Yearbook [*A publication*]
**GFS**........... Government-Furnished Services (KSC)
**GFS**........... Government-Furnished Software (NASA)
**GFS**........... Gower Federal Service [*Rocky Mountain Mineral Law Foundation*] [*Information service or system*] (CRD)
**GFS**........... Grand Financial Scribe [*Freemasonry*] (ROG)
**GFS**........... Guernsey Freight Services [*British*]
**GFS**........... Gulfstream Airlines, Inc. [*South Windsor, CT*] [*FAA designator*] (FAAC)
**GFS**........... Gunfire Support (NVT)
**GFSA**......... Goldfish Society of America (EA)
**GFSE**......... Government-Furnished Support Equipment (MCD)
**GFSFA**...... Geologiska Foereningens i Stockholm. Foerhandlingar [*A publication*]
**GFSFA4**.... Geologiska Foereningens i Stockholm. Foerhandlingar [*A publication*]
**GFsH**......... United States Army, Fort Stewart/Hunter AAF Library, Fort Stewart, GA [*Library symbol*] [*Library of Congress*] (LCLS)
**GFSL**......... Gaffsail [*Ship's rigging*] (ROG)
**GFSM**........ Government-Furnished Surplus Material (MCD)
**GFSP**......... Government-Furnished Support Property (KSC)
**GFSR**......... General Function System Requirement
**GFSRA**...... Giornale di Fisica Sanitaria e Protezione Contro le Radiazioni [*A publication*]
**GFSS**......... Gunfire Support Ship
**GFST**......... Ground Fuel Start Tank (AAG)
**GFSUSA**... Girls' Friendly Society of the USA (EA)
**GFSY**......... Government Finance Statistics [*International Monetary Fund*] [*Information service or system*] (CRD)
**GFT**........... Glass Fabric Tape
**GFT**........... (Glucopyranosyl)fluorothymine [*Biochemistry*]
**GFT**........... Graphic Firing Table [*Weaponry*] (NATG)
**GFT**........... Green Forest Lumber Corp. [*Toronto Stock Exchange symbol*]
**G/FT²**........ Grams per Square Foot
**GFTA**......... Goldman-Fristoe Test of Articulation [*Education*]
**GFTC-ER**.. General Freight Traffic Committee - Eastern Railroads
**GFTNAX**... Ghana. Council for Scientific and Industrial Research. Forest Products Research Institute. Technical Newsletter [*A publication*]
**GFTO**........ Tongo [*Sierra Leone*] [*ICAO location identifier*] (ICLI)
**GFTU**........ General Federation of Trade Unions [*Various countries*]
**GFU**........... Glazed Facing Units [*Technical drawings*]
**GFUT**........ Ground Fuel Ullage Tank (AAG)
**GFV**........... Fort Valley State College, Fort Valley, GA [*OCLC symbol*] (OCLC)
**GFV**........... Goldfever Resources Ltd. [*Vancouver Stock Exchange symbol*]
**GfV**........... Gueterfernverkehr [*Carriage of Goods*] [*German*] [*Business term*] (ILCA)
**GFV**........... Guided Flight Vehicle
**GFW**.......... Druk en Werk [*A publication*]
**GFW**.......... General Flight Work
**GFW**.......... Gesellschaft fuer Weltraumforschung [*Society for Space Research*] [*Germany*]
**G-F-W**........ Goldman-Fristoe-Woodcock Test of Auditory Discrimination [*Education*]
**GFW**.......... Goodman Fielder Wattie Ltd. [*Australia*]
**GFW**.......... Gram Formula Weight [*Chemistry*]
**GFW**.......... Great French Writers [*A publication*]
**GFW**.......... Ground-Fault Warning (IEEE)
**GFWC**....... General Federation of Women's Clubs (EA)
**GFWJ**........ Gesellschaft zur Foerderung der Wissenschaft des Judentums [*A publication*]
**GFX**........... Grandfield, OK [*Location identifier*] [*FAA*] (FAAL)
**GFX**........... PLM Equipment Growth Fund LP [*AMEX symbol*] (SPSG)
**GFY**........... Government Fiscal Year (MCD)
**GFY**........... Grootfontein [*South-West Africa*] [*Airport symbol*] (OAG)
**GFY**........... PLM Equipment Growth Fund II LP [*AMEX symbol*] (SPSG)
**GFYE**......... Yengema [*Sierra Leone*] [*ICAO location identifier*] (ICLI)
**GFZ**........... Greenfield, IA [*Location identifier*] [*FAA*] (FAAL)
**GFZSA**...... Geofizicheskii Sbornik. Akademiya Nauk Ukrainskoi SSR. Institut Geofiziki [*A publication*]
**GG**............. Air London [*Great Britain*] [*ICAO designator*] (FAAC)
**GG**............. Galloping Gourmet [*TV program*]
**GG**............. Gamma Globulin [*Medicine*]
**GG**............. Gas Generator (AAG)
**GG**............. Gatling Gun
**GG**............. Geist und Gestalt [*A publication*]
**G & G**......... Gems & Gemology [*A publication*] (EAAP)
**GG**............. Gender Gap [*Refers to women's tendency to vote for Democratic over Republican candidates, a phenomenon noticed by pollsters beginning with the 1980 election*]
**GG**............. Generator Gas [*System*] [*Nuclear energy*] (NRCH)
**GG**............. Gestalt und Gedanke [*A publication*]
**GG**............. Gewehrgranate [*Rifle Grenade*] [*German military - World War II*]
**Gg**.............. Gigagram
**GG**............. Glass Glover [*Commercial firm*] [*British*]
**Gg**.............. Glucagon [*Endocrinology*]
**GG**............. Glycylglycine [*Organic chemistry*]
**GG**............. Goal Gradient [*Psychology*]
**GG**............. Golden Gloves Association of America [*Later, GGA of A*]
**GG**............. Golden Goose [*A publication*]
**G & G**......... Goldsmith and Guthrie's Appeals Reports [*Missouri*] [*A publication*] (DLA)
**GG**............. Government Girl
**GG**............. Government Grade [*Followed by a number, 1-18; National Security Agency Employee Grade*]
**GG**............. Governor General
**GG**............. Grand Guardian [*Freemasonry*]
**GG**............. Gravity Gradient (KSC)
**GG**............. Great Gatsby [*Describes clothing style modeled after the type worn by characters in F. Scott Fitzgerald's novel, "The Great Gatsby"*]
**GG**............. Great Gross [*144 dozen*] [*Also, GGR*]
**GG**............. Grenadier Guards [*Military*] [*British*]
**GG**............. Groove Gauge
**G-G**........... Ground-to-Ground [*Communications, weapons, etc.*] (MSA)
**GG**............. Ground Guidance [*Aerospace*] (AAG)
**GG**............. Ground Gunner [*Air Force*] [*British*]
**GG**............. Grounded Grid [*Valve*] (DEN)
**GG**............. Grundgesetz [*Basic law of the Federal Republic of Germany*] (DLA)
**GG**............. Gutenberg Gesellschaft (EA)
**G & G**......... Gyandoh and Griffiths. Sourcebook of the Constitutional Law of Ghana [*A publication*] (ILCA)
**GGA**.......... Gale Global Access [*Also, GGAEA*]
**GGA**.......... Girl Guides Association [*British*]
**GGA**.......... Goettingische Gelehrte Anzeiger [*A publication*]
**GGA**.......... Golden Glacier [*Vancouver Stock Exchange symbol*]
**GGA**.......... Good Gardeners' Association [*British*]
**GGA**.......... Grounded Grid Amplifier
**GGA**.......... Group Gross Assets (ADA)
**GGA**.......... Gulf General Atomic [*Commercial firm*]
**GGAA**........ Golden Gloves Association of America [*Later, GGA of A*] (EA)
**GGA of A**... Golden Gloves Association of America (EA)
**GGaB**........ Brenau College, Gainsville, GA [*Library symbol*] [*Library of Congress*] (LCLS)
**GGAB**........ Ghana Geographical Association. Bulletin [*A publication*]
**GGAEA**..... Gale Global Access, Encyclopedia of Associations [*Also, GGA*]
**GGAR**........ Gas-Guided Aircraft Rocket
**GGASA**..... Geologiya i Geofizika [*A publication*]
**GGBB**........ Bambadinca [*Guinea-Bissau*] [*ICAO location identifier*] (ICLI)
**GGBE**........ Bedanda [*Guinea-Bissau*] [*ICAO location identifier*] (ICLI)
**GGBF**........ Bafata [*Guinea-Bissau*] [*ICAO location identifier*] (ICLI)
**GGBG**........ Governor-General's Bodyguard [*British military*] (DMA)
**GGBI**......... Bissora [*Guinea-Bissau*] [*ICAO location identifier*] (ICLI)

**GGBO**........ Bolama [*Guinea-Bissau*] [*ICAO location identifier*] (ICLI)
**GGBU**........ Bubaque [*Guinea-Bissau*] [*ICAO location identifier*] (ICLI)
**GGC**........... General Grand Chapter [*Freemasonry*]
**GGC**........... Georgia College, Milledgeville, GA [*OCLC symbol*] (OCLC)
**GGC**........... Georgia Gulf Corporation [*NYSE symbol*] (SPSG)
**GGC**........... Golden Gate College [*California*]
**GGC**........... Grey Goose Corporation Ltd. [*Toronto Stock Exchange symbol*]
**GGC**........... Ground Guidance Computer [*Aerospace*]
**GGC**........... Gun Group Commander [*British military*] (DMA)
**GGCC**........ Cacine [*Guinea-Bissau*] [*ICAO location identifier*] (ICLI)
**GGCF**........ Cufar [*Guinea-Bissau*] [*ICAO location identifier*] (ICLI)
**GGCG**........ Cantchungo [*Guinea-Bissau*] [*ICAO location identifier*] (ICLI)
**GGCST**...... Gleb-Goldstein Color Sorting Test [*Psychology*]
**GGCT**........ Catio [*Guinea-Bissau*] [*ICAO location identifier*] (ICLI)
**GGCV**........ Caravela [*Guinea-Bissau*] [*ICAO location identifier*] (ICLI)
**GGD**........... Gold Bridge Development [*Vancouver Stock Exchange symbol*]
**GGD**........... Great Granddaughter
**GGD**........... Gregory Downs [*Australia*] [*Airport symbol*] [*Obsolete*] (OAG)
**GGDC**........ G. G. Drayton Club (EA)
**GGE**........... Gauge
**GGE**........... Generalized Glandular Enlargement [*Medicine*]
**GGE**........... Georgetown, SC [*Location identifier*] [*FAA*] (FAAL)
**GGE**........... Golden Group Explorations, Inc. [*Vancouver Stock Exchange symbol*]
**GGE**........... Gospelrama Gospel Expo [*An association*] (EA)
**GGE**........... Gradient Gel Electrophoresis
**GGE**........... Ground Guidance Equipment [*Aerospace*]
**G Genio Civ** ... Giornale del Genio Civile [*A publication*]
**G Geol (Bologna)** ... Giornale di Geologia (Bologna) [*A publication*]
**G Geol Mus Geol Bologna Ann** ... Giornale di Geologia. Museo Geologico di Bologna. Annali [*A publication*]
**GGEP**........ Empada [*Guinea-Bissau*] [*ICAO location identifier*] (ICLI)
**G Gerontol** ... Giornale di Gerontologia [*A publication*]
**G Gerontol Suppl** ... Giornale di Gerontologia. Supplemento [*A publication*]
**GGF**........... Glass and Glazing Federation [*British*]
**GGF**........... Glial Growth Factor [*Biochemistry*]
**GGF**........... Global Government Plus Fund Ltd. [*Toronto Stock Exchange symbol*]
**GGF**........... Global Growth & Income Fund, Inc. [*NYSE symbol*] (SPSG)
**GGF**........... Granges-Gontardes [*France*] [*Seismograph station code, US Geological Survey*] [*Closed*] (SEIS)
**GGF**........... Grant, NE [*Location identifier*] [*FAA*] (FAAL)
**GGF**........... Ground Gained Forward [*Aerial photography*]
**GGFA**........ Geografiska Annaler. Series A [*A publication*]
**GGFC**........ Girl Groups Fan Club (EA)
**GGFC**........ Girl Groups - Rock 'n' Roll - Fan Club (EA)
**GGFC**........ Go Go's Fan Club (EA)
**GGFO**........ Formosa [*Guinea-Bissau*] [*ICAO location identifier*] (ICLI)
**GGFR**........ Farim [*Guinea-Bissau*] [*ICAO location identifier*] (ICLI)
**G/G/FRIS** ... Gal/Guy Fridays [*Classified advertising*]
**GGFU**........ Fulacunda [*Guinea-Bissau*] [*ICAO location identifier*] (ICLI)
**GGG**........... Gadolinium, Gallium, Garnet [*Also, G3*] [*Substrate for magnetic film*]
**GGG**........... Goat Gamma-Globulin [*Immunology*]
**GGG**........... Graco, Inc. [*NYSE symbol*] (SPSG)
**GGG**........... Gummi Guttae Gambiae [*Gamboge*] [*Pharmacology*] (ROG)
**GGG**........... Gunnar Gold, Inc. [*Toronto Stock Exchange symbol*]
**GGG**........... Longview [*Texas*] [*Airport symbol*] (OAG)
**GGGA**........ Galinhas [*Guinea-Bissau*] [*ICAO location identifier*] (ICLI)
**GGGB**........ Gabu [*Guinea-Bissau*] [*ICAO location identifier*] (ICLI)
**GGGG**........ 4G Data Systems, Inc. [*NASDAQ symbol*] (NQ)
**GG Hb**........ Grafschaft Glatzer Heimatblaetter [*A publication*]
**GGHP**........ General Grand High Priest [*Freemasonry*]
**GGHP**........ Governor-General's Honorary Physician [*Australia*]
**GGHVA4**... Geographica Helvetica [*A publication*]
**GGHY-A**.... Geography [*A publication*]
**GGHYAD** ... Geography [*A publication*]
**GGIA**......... Granite Grit Institute of America (EA)
**GGJO-A**.... Geographical Journal [*A publication*]
**GGK**........... Gaigokugo Gaigoku Bungaku Kenkyu [*A publication*]
**GGKGA**..... Godishnik na Sofiiskiya Universitet. Geologo-Geografski Fakultet. Kniga 1. Geologiya [*A publication*]
**GGI**........... Geografski Glasnik [*A publication*]
**GGL**........... Gerle Gold Limited [*Vancouver Stock Exchange symbol*]
**GGL**........... Gissing, Glen L., Evansville WI [*STAC*]
**GGL**........... Gravity-Gradient Libration [*Damper*]
**GGL**........... Ground Glass
**GGL**........... Guild of Guide Lecturers [*British*]
**GGL**........... Titusville, FL [*Location identifier*] [*FAA*] (FAAL)
**GGIF**......... Federal Law Enforcement Training Center, Glynco, GA [*Library symbol*] [*Library of Congress*] (LCLS)
**GGM**........... Geographici Graeci Minores [*A publication*] (OCD)
**GGM**........... Glitter Gold Mines [*Vancouver Stock Exchange symbol*]
**GGM**........... Gravity Gradiometer Mission [*NASA*]
**GGM**........... Ground-to-Ground Missile
**GGMA**........ Glassine and Greaseproof Manufacturers Association [*Later, API*] (EA)
**GGMA**........ Government Gold Mining Areas
**GGMA-A**... Geographical Magazine [*A publication*]
**GGMK**........ Great, Grand Master Key [*Locks*] (ADA)
**GGMMA**... Gabriel Garcia Moreno Memorial Association (EA)
**G & G (MO)** ... Goldsmith and Guthrie's Appeals Reports [*Missouri*] [*A publication*] (DLA)
**GGMS**........ Mansoa [*Guinea-Bissau*] [*ICAO location identifier*] (ICLI)
**GGMWA**... Grace of God Movement for the Women of America [*Later, GGMWW*] (EA)
**GGMWW** ... Grace of God Movement for the Women of the World (EA)
**GGN**........... Gagnoa [*Ivory Coast*] [*Airport symbol*] (OAG)
**GGNI**......... Governor-General of Northern Ireland (DAS)
**GGNRA**..... Golden Gate National Recreation Area Advisory Commission [*National Park Service*] [*San Francisco, CA*] (EGAO)
**GGNRACAC** ... Golden Gate National Recreation Area Advisory Commission [*National Park Service*] [*San Francisco, CA*] (EGAO)
**GGNS**........ Genus, Inc. [*NASDAQ symbol*] (CTT)
**GGNS**........ Grand Gulf Nuclear Station (NRCH)
**GGNTAS**... Glasgow Naturalist [*A publication*]
**GGO**........... Glavnaya Geofizicheskaya Observatory [*Main Geophysical Observatory*] [*USSR*]
**GGO**........... Governor-General's Order [*British military*] (DMA)
**GGO**........... Greater Greensboro [*North Carolina*] Open [*Golf tournament*]
**GGO**........... Guiglo [*Ivory Coast*] [*Airport symbol*] (OAG)
**GGOV**........ Bissau/Oswaldo Vieira International [*Guinea-Bissau*] [*ICAO location identifier*] (ICLI)
**GGP**........... Gas-Gathering Pipeline
**GGP**........... George Resources Co. [*Vancouver Stock Exchange symbol*]
**GGP**........... Golden Gate Productions [*San Francisco, CA*] [*Telecommunications*] (TSSD)
**GGP**........... Good Gay Poets (EA)
**GGP**........... Gross Global Product
**GGP**........... Logansport, IN [*Location identifier*] [*FAA*] (FAAL)
**GGPA**........ Graduate Grade-Point Average [*Higher education*]
**GGPC**........ Pecixe [*Guinea-Bissau*] [*ICAO location identifier*] (ICLI)
**GGPF**......... Glial Growth Promoting Factor [*Neurology*]
**GGPI**......... Pedagogical Institute in Gorki. Transactions [*A publication*]
**GGPL**......... Glycine, Glycine Phenylalanine, Leucine [*A synthetic peptide*]
**GGPR**........ Pirada [*Guinea-Bissau*] [*ICAO location identifier*] (ICLI)
**GGR**........... Gallagher Explorations Ltd. [*Vancouver Stock Exchange symbol*]
**GGR**........... Geology and Geophysics. Academy of Sciences (USSR) [*A publication*]
**GGR**........... Geschichte der Griechischen Religion [*A publication*] (OCD)
**GGR**........... Goed Geraakt [*A publication*]
**GGR**........... Great Gross [*144 dozen*] [*Also, GG*]
**GGR**........... [*G.*] Greene's Iowa Reports [*1847-54*] [*A publication*] (DLA)
**GGR**........... Ground Gunnery Range
**G Gracch**.... Gaius Gracchus [*of Plutarch*] [*Classical studies*] (OCD)
**GGraG**........ Gracewood State School and Hospital, Gracewood, GA [*Library symbol*] [*Library of Congress*] (LCLS)
**G Greene (Iowa)** ... [*G.*] Greene's Iowa Reports [*1847-54*] [*A publication*] (DLA)
**GGriEx**...... University of Georgia, Experiment Station, Griffin, GA [*Library symbol*] [*Library of Congress*] (LCLS)
**GGS**........... Gates-Gaudin-Schuhmann [*Particle size distribution*]
**GGS**........... Girls' Grammar School (ADA)
**GG or S**...... Glands, Goiter, or Stiffness [*Medicine*]
**GGS**........... Global Geospace Study [*Proposed*] [*United States, Japan, and Europe*]
**GGS**........... Gobernador Gregores [*Argentina*] [*Airport symbol*] (OAG)
**GGS**........... Graphic Generator System
**GGS**........... Gravity-Gradient Satellite
**GGS**........... Gravity-Gradient Sensor
**GGS**........... Great Grandson
**GGS**........... Ground Gained Sideways [*Aerial photography*]
**GGS**........... Ground Guidance System [*Aerospace*] (AAG)
**GGSA**........ German Genealogical Society of America (EA)
**GGSD**........ Sao Domingos [*Guinea-Bissau*] [*ICAO location identifier*] (ICLI)
**GGSE**......... Gravity-Gradient Stabilization Experiment
**GGSM**........ Graduate Diploma of the Guildhall School of Music [*British*] (DBQ)
**GGSP**......... Giant-to-Giant Interneuron Synaptic Potential [*Neurochemistry*]
**GGSPFWFH** ... Goose and Gander, Society for the Preservation of First Wives and First Husbands (EA)
**GGT**........... Gamma-Glutamyltransferase [*Also, GGTP, GT*] [*An enzyme*]
**GGT**........... George Town [*Bahamas*] [*Airport symbol*] (OAG)
**GGT**........... Georgetown, NY [*Location identifier*] [*FAA*] (FAAL)
**GGT**........... Gravity-Gradient Torque
**GGT**........... Greater Temagami [*Vancouver Stock Exchange symbol*]
**GGTI-A**..... Geografisk Tidsskrift [*A publication*]
**GGTP**........ Gamma-Glutamyl Transpeptidase [*Also, GGT, GT*] [*An enzyme*]
**GGTS**........ Gravity-Gradient Test Satellite [*NASA*]
**GGTT**........ Tite [*Guinea-Bissau*] [*ICAO location identifier*] (ICLI)
**GGU**........... Giant Gastric Ulcer [*Medicine*]
**GGUALE**.. Golden Gate University Advanced Legal Education Program (DLA)
**GGUB**........ Groenlands Geologiske Undersoegelse. Bulletin [*A publication*]

**GGUMP**.... Groenlands Geologiske Undersoegelse. Miscellaneous Papers [*A publication*]
**GGUN** ....... Uno [*Guinea-Bissau*] [*ICAO location identifier*] (ICLI)
**GGUR**........ Groenlands Geologiske Undersoegelse. Rapport [*A publication*]
**GGUY**........ [*The*] Good Guys, Inc. [*NASDAQ symbol*] (NQ)
**GGV**.......... Gabriel Gonzalez Videla [*Antarctica*] [*Seismograph station code, US Geological Survey*] [*Closed*] (SEIS)
**GGV**.......... Gas Generator Valve (KSC)
**GGV**.......... Kwigillingok, AK [*Location identifier*] [*FAA*] (FAAL)
**GGVR**........ Varela [*Guinea-Bissau*] [*ICAO location identifier*] (ICLI)
**GGW**.......... Glasgow [*Montana*] [*Airport symbol*] (OAG)
**GGX**.......... Golden Gate Explorations [*Vancouver Stock Exchange symbol*]
**GGY**.......... Clanton, AL [*Location identifier*] [*FAA*] (FAAL)
**GGY**.......... Greentree Energy [*Vancouver Stock Exchange symbol*]
**GGZ**.......... Akron, OH [*Location identifier*] [*FAA*] (FAAL)
**GH**............ Gaseous Hydrogen (KSC)
**GH**............ Gate House (NRCH)
**G & H**........ Gavin and Hord's Indiana Statutes [*A publication*] (DLA)
**GH**............ Gelbe Hefte [*A publication*]
**GH**............ Gemini Hatch [*NASA*]
**GH**............ General Hospital [*Initialism also refers to a TV program*]
**GH**............ General Host Corp. [*NYSE symbol*] (SPSG)
**GH**............ George Horne [*Refers to old news*] [*Slang*] (DSUE)
**GH**............ Ghana [*ANSI two-letter standard code*] (CNC)
**gh**............ Ghana [*MARC country of publication code*] [*Library of Congress*] (LCCP)
**GH**............ Ghana Airways Ltd. [*ICAO designator*] (FAAC)
**G & H**........ Gibbs & Hill, Inc. (NRCH)
**GH**............ Gilt Head [*Bookbinding*] (ROG)
**GH**............ Glasgow Herald [*A publication*]
**GH**............ Gmelin's Handbuch der Anorganischen Chemie [*A publication*]
**GH**............ Good Housekeeping [*A publication*]
**G-H**........... Goodenough-Harris Drawing Test [*Education*]
**GH**............ Government House [*Canada*]
**GH**............ Gray Herbarium [*Harvard University*] [*Cambridge, MA*]
**GH**............ Grid Heading [*Navigation*]
**GH**............ Ground Handling [*Aerospace*]
**GH**............ Growth Hormone [*Somatotrophin*] [*Also, SH, STH*] [*Endocrinology*]
**GH**............ Guardhouse
**GH**............ Guest House
**GH**............ Gure Herria [*A publication*]
**$GH_2$**........... Gaseous Hydrogen [*NASA*] (KSC)
**GHA**.......... Gas, Wasser, Abwasser. Schweizerische Monatszeitschrift fuer Gasfoerderung und Siedlungswasserwirtschaft [*A publication*]
**GH d A**....... Genealogisches Handbuch des Adels [*A publication*]
**GHA**.......... General Housekeeping Area [*NASA*] (NASA)
**GHA**.......... Georgia Hospital Association [*Atlanta*] (TSSD)
**GHA**.......... Georgia Southwestern College, Americus, GA [*OCLC symbol*] (OCLC)
**GHA**.......... Gesneriad Hybridizers Association (EA)
**GHA**.......... Ghana [*ANSI three-letter standard code*] (CNC)
**GHA**.......... Ghardaia [*Algeria*] [*Airport symbol*] (OAG)
**GHA**.......... Glashutten [*Austria*] [*Seismograph station code, US Geological Survey*] (SEIS)
**GHA**.......... Goeteborgs Hogskolas Arsskrift [*A publication*]
**GHA**.......... Golden Hat Resources [*Vancouver Stock Exchange symbol*]
**GHA**.......... Grassland Husbandry Adviser [*Ministry of Agriculture, Fisheries, and Food*] [*British*]
**GHA**.......... Green Hills Aviation Ltd. [*Kirksville, MO*] [*FAA designator*] (FAAC)
**GHA**.......... Greenwich Hour Angle
**GHA**.......... Ground Hazard Area (MUGU)
**GHA**.......... Gyro Header Assembly
**GHAA**........ Group Health Association of America (EA)
**GhAF**......... Ghanaian Air Force
**GHAF**........ Grosvenor House Antiques Fair [*British*] (ITD)
**GHAMS**.... Greenwich Hour Angle of Mean Sun
**Ghana**........ [*C. C.*] Ghana. Current Cases [*1965-1971*] [*A publication*] (DLA)
**Ghana Anim Res Inst Annu Rep** ... Ghana. Animal Research Institute. Annual Report [*A publication*]
**Ghana B Theol** ... Ghana Bulletin of Theology [*A publication*]
**Ghana Bull Theol** ... Ghana Bulletin of Theology [*A publication*]
**Ghana Counc Sci Ind Res For Prod Res Inst Tech Newsl** ... Ghana. Council for Scientific and Industrial Research. Forest Products Research Institute. Technical Newsletter [*A publication*]
**Ghana CSIR For Prod Res Inst Annu Rep** ... Ghana. Council for Scientific and Industrial Research. Forest Products Research Institute. Annual Report [*A publication*]
**Ghana CSIR For Prod Res Inst Tech Newsl** ... Ghana. Council for Scientific and Industrial Research. Forest Products Research Institute. Technical Newsletter [*A publication*]
**Ghana Fish Res Unit Inf Rep** ... Ghana. Fishery Research Unit. Information Report [*A publication*]
**Ghana Fish Res Unit Mar Fish Res Rep** ... Ghana. Fishery Research Unit. Marine Fishery Research Reports [*A publication*]
**Ghana Fmr** ... Ghana Farmer [*A publication*]
**Ghana For J** ... Ghana Forestry Journal [*A publication*]
**Ghana J Agric Sci** ... Ghana Journal of Agricultural Science [*A publication*]
**Ghana J Sci** ... Ghana Journal of Science [*A publication*]
**Ghana J Sociol** ... Ghana Journal of Sociology [*A publication*]
**Ghana Libr J** ... Ghana Library Journal [*A publication*]
**Ghana LRC** ... Ghana Law Reform Commission (DLA)
**Ghana Med J** ... Ghana Medical Journal [*A publication*]
**Ghana Nurse** ... Ghanaian Nurse [*A publication*]
**Ghana Soc S** ... Ghana Social Science Journal [*A publication*]
**GHAT**........ Goettinger Handkommentar zum Alten Testament (1917-1922) [*A publication*]
**GHAT**........ Ground Handling and Transportation [*Aerospace*] (KSC)
**GHATS**..... Greenwich Hour Angle of True Sun
**GHB**.......... Gamma-Hydroxybutyric Acid [*Organic chemistry*]
**GHb**.......... Glycohemoglobin [*Biochemistry, medicine*]
**GHB**.......... Glycosylated Hemoglobin [*Clinical chemistry*]
**GHB**.......... Governor's Harbour [*Bahamas*] [*Airport symbol*] (OAG)
**GHB**.......... Heileman [*G.*] Brewing Co., Inc. [*NYSE symbol*] (SPSG)
**GHBA**........ Galiceno Horse Breeders Association (EA)
**GHBUD**..... Gl. Haustechnik, Bauphysik, Umwelttechnik [*A publication*]
**GHC**.......... Gating Half-Cycle [*Data processing*]
**GHC**.......... Generalized Hyperbolic Class
**GHC**.......... Gold Hill [*California*] [*Seismograph station code, US Geological Survey*] (SEIS)
**GHC**.......... Grays Harbor College [*Washington*]
**GHC**.......... Great Harbour Cay [*Bahamas*] [*Airport symbol*] (OAG)
**GHC**.......... Greyhound Computer of Canada Ltd. [*Toronto Stock Exchange symbol*]
**GHC**.......... Ground Half Coupling (KSC)
**GHC**.......... Guidance Heater Control
**GHCl**......... Guanidine Hydrochloride [*Organic chemistry*]
**GHCR**........ Gross Henle Chromoreaction [*Clinical chemistry*]
**GHCS**........ Good Housekeeping Check Sheet (AAG)
**GHD**.......... Growth Hormone Deficiency [*Endocrinology*]
**GHDBAX**.. Glasnik Khemijskog Drushtva [*Beograd*] [*A publication*]
**GHDV**........ Gasoline-Engine Heavy-Duty Vehicle
**GHE**.......... Gable House Estates Ltd. [*British*]
**GHE**.......... Garachine [*Panama*] [*Airport symbol*] (OAG)
**GHE**.......... Gaseous Helium (KSC)
**GHE**.......... Gauss Hypergeometric Equation [*Mathematics*]
**GHE**.......... Gibbs-Helmholtz Equation [*Physical chemistry*]
**GHE**.......... Ginn, Herbert E., South Portland ME [*STAC*]
**GHE**.......... Golden Hemlock [*Vancouver Stock Exchange symbol*]
**GHE**.......... Ground Handling Equipment [*Aerospace*]
**G Heb**........ Gospel of the Hebrews [*Apocryphal work*]
**GHEF**........ Givat Haviva Educational Foundation (EA)
**GHER**........ Greater Heritage Corp. [*NASDAQ symbol*] (NQ)
**GHF**.......... Gauss Hypergeometric Function [*Mathematics*]
**GHF**.......... Gradient Heating Facility
**GHF**.......... Grassland Heritage Foundation (EA)
**GHF**.......... Growth Hormone Transcription Factor [*Endocrinology*]
**GHFC**........ Gebhardt-Heriot Foundation for All Cats (EA)
**GHFC**........ Gunilla Hutton Fan Club (EA)
**GHFF**........ George Hamilton IV and Friends [*Defunct*] (EA)
**GHG**.......... Galactic Hitchhiker's Guild (EA)
**GHG**.......... [*The*] Good Hotel Guide [*A publication*] [*British*]
**GHG**.......... Governor's Horse Guard
**GHG**.......... Grosshandelsgesellschaft [*Wholesale Business Establishment*] [*German*]
**GHH**.......... Galveston, Houston & Henderson Railroad Co. [*AAR code*]
**GHi**........... Georgia Historical Society, Savannah, GA [*Library symbol*] [*Library of Congress*] (LCLS)
**GHI**........... German Historical Institute (EA)
**GHI**........... GHI Mortgage Investors [*Vancouver Stock Exchange symbol*]
**GHI**........... Gilbert Hill [*Idaho*] [*Seismograph station code, US Geological Survey*] [*Closed*] (SEIS)
**GHI**........... Group Health Insurance [*British*]
**GHIA**......... Genealogical and Heraldic Institute of America (EA)
**GHJ**.......... Gastonia, NC [*Location identifier*] [*FAA*] (FAAL)
**GHJ**.......... George Herbert Journal [*A publication*]
**GHJSA**...... Ghana Journal of Science [*A publication*]
**GHJSAC**... Ghana Journal of Science [*A publication*]
**GHK**.......... Greyhawk Resources Ltd. [*Vancouver Stock Exchange symbol*]
**GHK**.......... Grosshandelskontor [*Wholesale Business Office*] [*German*]
**GHK**.......... Handkommentar zum Alten Testament (Goettingen) [*A publication*] (BJA)
**GHL**.......... George Henry Lewes [*Initials used as pseudonym*]
**GHL**.......... Good Harvest Line (DS)
**GHL**.......... [*A*] Grammar of the Hurrian Language [*A publication*] (BJA)
**GHL**.......... Greyhound Lines of Canada Ltd. [*Toronto Stock Exchange symbol*]
**GHL**.......... Guardhouse Lawyer [*Military slang*]
**GH/LCD**... Guest-Host/Liquid Crystal Display [*Telecommunications*] (TEL)
**GHLI**......... Guilford-Holley L Inventory [*Psychology*]
**GHLID**...... Geothermal Hot Line [*A publication*]
**GHM**.......... Centerville, TN [*Location identifier*] [*FAA*] (FAAL)
**GHM**.......... Going-Home Money
**GHM**.......... Graham Corp. [*AMEX symbol*] (SPSG)
**GHM**.......... Guaranteed Hourly Minimum
**GHME**........ Gott Hilf Mir Elenden [*God Help Miserable Me*] [*German*] [*Motto of Eleonore, Electress of Brandenburg (1583-1607)*]
**GHMI**........ Generalized Human-Machine Interface (MCD)

**GHMJA** ..... Ghana Medical Journal [*A publication*]
**GHMJAY** ... Ghana Medical Journal [*A publication*]
**GHN** .......... Generalized Hypertrophic Neuropathy
**GHN** .......... Ghana Navy
**GHN** .......... Goldhaven Resources Ltd. [*Vancouver Stock Exchange symbol*]
**GHN** .......... Groupe Hygiene Naturelle [*European Natural Hygiene Society - ENHS*] (EAIO)
**GHO** .......... General Homes Corp. [*NYSE symbol*] (SPSG)
**GHO** .......... Greater Hartford [*Connecticut*] Open [*Golf tournament*]
**Ghose Mort** ... Ghose on Mortgages in India [*A publication*] (DLA)
**GHOST** ..... Global Horizontal Sounding Technique [*Meteorology*]
**GHOST** ..... Golf Head Optical Speed Trap [*Golf self-improvement program*]
**GHP** .......... Gas High Pressure
**GHP** .......... Grand High Priest [*Freemasonry*]
**GHP** .......... Great Hungarian Plain [*Geology*]
**GHP** .......... Greater Hartford Process [*An association*] (EA)
**GHP** .......... Greenwich Hospital Pension [*British military*] (DMA)
**GHPADP** .. Geologica Hungarica. Series Palaeontologica [*A publication*]
**GHPR** ........ Gliding Horse and Pony Registry (EA)
**GHQ** .......... General Headquarters [*Military*]
**GHQ** .......... General Health Questionnaire [*Personality development test*] [*Psychology*]
**GHQ** .......... Georgia Historical Quarterly [*A publication*]
**GHQAF** ..... General Headquarters Air Force
**GHQC** ....... GH [*General Hospital*] Questionnaire Club (EA)
**GHR** .......... Golden Hope Resources, Inc. [*Vancouver Stock Exchange symbol*]
**GHREA** ..... Guy's Hospital Reports [*A publication*]
**GH-RF** ....... Growth Hormone Releasing Factor [*Somatoliberin*] [*Also, GH-RH, GRF*] [*Endocrinology*]
**GHRF** ........ Guardians of Hydrocephalus Research Foundation (EA)
**GH-RH** ...... Growth Hormone Releasing Hormone [*Somatoliberin*] [*Also, GH-RF, GRF*] [*Endocrinology*]
**GH-RIF** ..... Growth Hormone Release Inhibiting Factor [*Also, GH-RIH, GRIF, SRIF, SS*] [*Endocrinology*]
**GH-RIH** .... Growth Hormone Release Inhibiting Hormone [*Also, GH-RIF, GRIF, SRIF, SS*] [*Endocrinology*]
**GHRKA** ..... Genshiryoku Heiwa Riyo Kenkyu Seika Hokokusho [*A publication*]
**GHRP** ........ Growth Hormone Releasing Peptide [*Endocrinology*]
**GHRS** ........ Goddard High-Resolution Spectrograph
**GHRSP** ...... Guatemalan Health Rights Support Project (EA)
**GHR/USA** ... Guatemalan Human Rights Commission/USA (EA)
**GHS** .......... Garden History Society [*British*]
**GHS** .......... General Household Survey [*Office of Population Census and Surveys*] [*British*]
**GHS** .......... Getchell Resources, Inc. [*Vancouver Stock Exchange symbol*]
**GHS** .......... Gilroy Hot Springs [*California*] [*Seismograph station code, US Geological Survey*] (SEIS)
**GHS** .......... Ground Handling System [*Aerospace*] (AAG)
**GHS** .......... Grunberg Hydrofoil System
**GHSG** ........ Guest Housing [*Army*] (AABC)
**GHSI** ......... GHS, Inc. [*Formerly, Global Health Systems, Inc.*] [*NASDAQ symbol*] (NQ)
**GHSV** ........ Gas Hour Space Velocity [*Chemical engineering*]
**GHT** .......... Gas World [*A publication*]
**GHT** .......... Ghat [*Libya*] [*Airport symbol*] (OAG)
**GHT** .......... Goeteborgs Handelstidning [*A publication*]
**GHT** .......... Golden Hour Tango
**GHT** .......... Goldhurst Resources [*Vancouver Stock Exchange symbol*]
**GHU** .......... Gualeguaychu [*Argentina*] [*Airport symbol*] (OAG)
**GHV** .......... Golden Hind Ventures Ltd. [*Vancouver Stock Exchange symbol*]
**GHVL** ........ Groot Hertog von Luxemberg [*Grand Duke of Luxemburg*] [*Numismatics*] (ROG)
**GHW** ......... Garrison Hill [*Washington*] [*Seismograph station code, US Geological Survey*] (SEIS)
**GHW** ......... General Housewares Corp. [*NYSE symbol*] (SPSG)
**GHW** ......... Guaranteed Hourly Wage
**GHWP** ....... Greenhouse Warming Potential [*Environmental chemistry*]
**GHWS** ....... Gas Hot Water Service [*Classified advertising*] (ADA)
**GHX** .......... Galveston-Houston Co. [*NYSE symbol*] (SPSG)
**GHX** .......... Graham, TX [*Location identifier*] [*FAA*] (FAAL)
**GHX** .......... Ground Heat Exchanger
**GHYD** ....... General Hydrocarbons of Minnesota [*NASDAQ symbol*] (NQ)
**GHz** ........... Gigahertz [*1,000 megahertz*]
**GHZ** ........... Golden Horizon [*Vancouver Stock Exchange symbol*]
**GI** .............. Air Guinee [*Guinea*] [*ICAO designator*] (FAAC)
**GI** .............. Galvanized Iron
**GI** .............. Garden Island [*Australia*] (ADA)
**GI** .............. Gastrointestinal [*Medicine*]
**GI** .............. Gazette d'Israel [*Tunis*] [*A publication*]
**GI** .............. Gelbray International (EA)
**GI** .............. Gemeinschaft der Ikonenfreunde [*Society of Friends of Icons - SFI*] (EAIO)
**GI** .............. Genealogical Institute (EA)
**GI** .............. General Index
**GI** .............. General Indulgence (ROG)
**GI** .............. General Inspection [*Military*] (AABC)
**GI** .............. General Instruments
**GI** .............. General Issue
**GI** .............. Generic Identifier [*Telecommunications*] (TEL)
**GI** .............. Genesis Information (EA)
**GI** .............. Genesis Institute [*An association*] (EA)
**GI** .............. Geodesic Isotensoid (IEEE)
**GI** .............. Geographically Impossible (ADA)
**GI** .............. Geophysical Institute [*University of Alaska, Fairbanks*] [*Research center*]
**GI** .............. Gerson Institute (EA)
**GI** .............. Gesundheits-Ingenieur [*A publication*]
**GI** .............. Giant Industries [*NYSE symbol*] (SPSG)
**GI** .............. Giant Interneurons [*Neurology*]
**GI** .............. Gibraltar [*ANSI two-letter standard code*] (CNC)
**gi** ............... Gibraltar [*MARC country of publication code*] [*Library of Congress*] (LCCP)
**GI** .............. Gideons International (EA)
**Gi** ............... Gilbert [*A unit of magnetomotive force*]
**GI** .............. Gill
**GI** .............. Gingival Index [*Dentistry*]
**GI** .............. Girls, Inc. (EA)
**GI** .............. Globin Insulin
**GI** .............. Glomus intraradices [*A fungus*]
**GI** .............. Glossaria Interpretum [*Elsevier Book Series*] [*A publication*]
**GI** .............. Goethe Institute (EA)
**GI** .............. Gold Institute [*Also known as L'Institut de l'Or*] (EA)
**GI** .............. Government of India
**GI** .............. Government and Industrial (IEEE)
**GI** .............. Government Initiated (IEEE)
**GI** .............. Government Issue [*Army*]
**GI** .............. Grassroots International (EA)
**GI** .............. Gray Iron (MSA)
**GI** .............. Gray's Inn [*London*] [*One of the Inns of Court*]
**GI** .............. Great Indulgence
**GI** .............. Green Island [*Plant pathology*]
**GI** .............. Greenpeace International (EA)
**GI** .............. Gross Income
**GI** .............. Gross Investment
**GI** .............. Group Insurance
**GI** .............. Growth and Income [*Business term*]
**GI** .............. Growth Index
**GI** .............. Growth Inhibiting
**GI** .............. Guidance Inventory [*Psychology*]
**GI** .............. Guided Imagery [*Psychology*]
**Gi** ............... Guido de Suzaria [*Deceased, 1293*] [*Authority cited in pre-1607 legal work*] (DSA)
**GI** .............. Gunner Instructor [*Navy*] [*British*]
**GI** .............. Gyro International (EA)
**GI** .............. Royal Glasgow Institute of Fine Arts [*Scotland*]
**GI** .............. Soldier [*Slang, probably from Government Issue*]
**GI (Bill)** ..... Veterans Benefits Act, Public Law 345, 1944
**GI (Insurance)** ... Popular name for US Government Life Insurance [*Available to military personnel in World War II*]
**GIA** ............ Garden Industry of America [*Inactive*] (EA)
**GIA** ............ Garuda Indonesian Airways Ltd.
**GIA** ............ Gemological Institute of America (EA)
**GIA** ............ General Industry Applications (MCD)
**GIA** ............ General International Agreement [*Legal term*] (DLA)
**GIA** ............ Geophysical Institute, University of Alaska [*Alaska*] [*Seismograph station code, US Geological Survey*] [*Closed*] (SEIS)
**GIA** ............ Goodwill Industries of America (EA)
**GIA** ............ GPC [*General Purpose Computer*] Interface Adapter (NASA)
**GIA** ............ Grants-in-Aid
**GIA** ............ Group Interaction Analysis
**GIA** ............ Gummed Industries Association (EA)
**GIABS** ....... Gastrointestinal Absorption Database [*Environmental Protection Agency*] [*Information service or system*] (CRD)
**GIAC** ......... General Industry Advisory Committee
**GIAD** ......... Independent Group of Dance Artists [*Spanish*]
**GIAKF** ....... Goldale Investments [*NASDAQ symbol*] (NQ)
**GIAM** ........ Global Impacts of Applied Microbiology [*International conferences*]
**GIANT** ...... Genealogical [*or Geological*] Information and Name Tabulating System [*Data processing*] (IEEE)
**GIANT** ...... General Information and Analysis Tool
**GIANT** ...... Geographic Intelligence and Topographic System
**GIANT** ...... Graphic Interactive Analytic Network Technique (MCD)
**GIANTS** .... Greater Independent Association of National Travel Services (EA)
**GIAO** ........ Gauge-Invariant Atomic Orbital [*NASA*]
**GIAR** ......... Grants-in-Aid of Research
**GIAT** ......... Groupement Industriel des Armements Terrestres [*Land Based Industrial Group*] [*French*]
**Giauq El** ..... Giauque's Election Laws [*A publication*] (DLA)
**GIB** ........... General Information Booklet [*Navy*]
**GIB** ........... General Instruction Book
**Gib** ............ Gibbon's Reports, New York Surrogate Court [*A publication*] (DLA)
**GIB** ........... Gibilmanna [*Sicily*] [*Seismograph station code, US Geological Survey*] (SEIS)

**GIB** ........ Gibraltar [*Gibraltar*] [*Airport symbol*] (OAG)
**GIB** ........ Gibraltar
**GIB** ........ Gibraltar [*ANSI three-letter standard code*] (CNC)
**GIB** ........ Gibson [*C. R.*] Co. [*AMEX symbol*] (SPSG)
**GIB** ........ Good in Bed (DSUE)
**GIB** ........ Gulf International Bank [*Middle East*]
**GIB** ........ Guy in the Back [*Copilot*] [*Air Force slang*]
**Gib Aids** ..... Gibson's Aids to the Examinations [*A publication*] (DLA)
**GIBAIR** ..... Gibraltar Airways Ltd.
**Gibbon** ....... Gibbon on Nuisances [*A publication*] (DLA)
**Gibbon Rom Emp** ... Gibbon's History of the Decline and Fall of the Roman Empire [*A publication*] (DLA)
**Gibbons** ...... Gibbon's Reports, New York Surrogate Court [*A publication*] (DLA)
**Gibbons (NY)** ... Gibbon's Reports, New York Surrogate Court [*A publication*] (DLA)
**Gibb Rom Emp** ... Gibbon's History of the Decline and Fall of the Roman Empire [*A publication*] (DLA)
**Gibbs** .......... Gibbs' Reports [*2-4 Michigan*] [*A publication*] (DLA)
**Gibbs F** ...... Gibbs' Practical Forms [*A publication*] (DLA)
**Gibbs' Jud Chr** ... Gibbs' Judicial Chronicle [*A publication*] (DLA)
**GIBBSSAR** ... Gibbs & Hill, Inc., Standard Safety Analysis Report [*Nuclear energy*] (NRCH)
**Gibb Sur** ..... Gibbon's Reports, New York Surrogate Court [*A publication*] (DLA)
**Gibb Surr** ... Gibbon's Reports, New York Surrogate Court [*A publication*] (DLA)
**GIBCA** ....... General International Business Contracting Associates [*Arab*]
**Gib Civ L** .... Gibbons on the Civil Law [*A publication*] (DLA)
**Gib Cod** ...... Gibson's Codex Juris Ecclesiastia Anglicani [*A publication*] (DLA)
**Gib Cont** ..... Gibbons on Contracts [*A publication*] (DLA)
**Gib Dec** ...... Gibson's Scottish Decisions [*A publication*] (DLA)
**Gib Dil** ....... Gibbon's Dilapidations and Nuisances [*2nd ed.*] [*1849*] [*A publication*] (DLA)
**Gib Fix** ....... Gibbon's Law of Fixtures [*1836*] [*A publication*] (DLA)
**GIBG** ......... Gibson Greetings, Inc. [*NASDAQ symbol*] (NQ)
**GIBH** ......... Gibson-Homans Co. [*NASDAQ symbol*] (NQ)
**Gi Biochim** ... Giornale di Biochimica [*A publication*]
**GIBIS** ........ Graphical IBIS [*Issue-Based Information System*] [*Data processing*] (BYTE)
**Gib Lim** ...... Gibbons' Lex Temporis, Limitations and Prescription [*A publication*] (DLA)
**Gib LN** ....... Gibson's Law Notice [*1882-84*] [*A publication*] (DLA)
**Gib Lynd** .... Gibson's Memoir of Lord Lyndhurst [*A publication*] (DLA)
**GIBMED** ... Gibraltar Mediterranean Command [*NATO*] (NATG)
**Gib & Na Eq Jur** ... Gibbons and Nathans' Equitable Jurisdiction of County Courts [*A publication*] (DLA)
**Gib Nui** ...... Gibbons' Dilapidations and Nuisances [*2nd ed.*] [*1849*] [*A publication*] (DLA)
**Gibridnye Vycisl Masiny i Kompleksy** ... Gibridnye Vychislitel'nye Mashiny i Kompleksy [*A publication*]
**GIBS** .......... Guy in the Backseat [*Copilot*] [*Air Force slang*]
**Gibs Camd** ... Gibson's Edition of Camden's Britannia [*A publication*] (DLA)
**Gibs Code** .. Gibson's Codex [*A publication*] (DLA)
**Gibs LN** ..... Gibson's Law Notes [*1882-84*] [*A publication*] (DLA)
**Gibson** ........ (Gibson of) Durie's Decisions, Scotch Court of Session [*1621-42*] [*A publication*] (DLA)
**GIC** ........... Galit Resource Corp. [*Vancouver Stock Exchange symbol*]
**GIC** ........... General Improvement Contractors Association (EA)
**GIC** ........... General Industries Corporation [*Burma*] (DS)
**GIC** ........... General Input/Output Channel
**GIC** ........... Generalized Immittance [*or Impedance*] Converter (IEEE)
**GIC** ........... Geomagnetically Induced Current
**GIC** ........... German Information Center [*Information service or system*] (EISS)
**GIC** ........... Gids [*A publication*]
**GIC** ........... Global Interdependence Center (EA)
**GIC** ........... Goods in Custody (ADA)
**GIC** ........... Graphite Intercalation Compound [*Inorganic chemistry*]
**GIC** ........... Guaranteed Income Contract
**GIC** ........... Guaranteed Investment Contract
**GIC** ........... Guilde Internationale des Cooperatrices
**GIC** ........... Gulf Intercoastal Conference
**GICC** ......... Government-Industry Coordinating Committee
**GICCD7** .... Giornale Italiano di Chimica Clinica [*A publication*]
**GICG** ......... Glaze Icing [*Aviation*] (FAAC)
**GICL** .......... Gila Cliff Dwellings National Monument
**GICLDC** .... GI Civil Liberties Defense Committee
**GICLDY** .... Ginecologia Clinica [*A publication*]
**GICLE** ....... Institute of Continuing Legal Education in Georgia [*University of Georgia School of Law*] (DLA)
**GICORP** .... Government-Industry Cooperative Oyster Research Program
**GICQA** ....... Gifted Child Quarterly [*A publication*]
**GICR** .......... Goodwin Institute for Cancer Research [*Nova University*] [*Research center*] (RCD)
**GID** ........... Gastrointestinal Dialysis [*Medicine*]
**GID** ........... General Installation Dolly
**GID** ........... Gesellschaft fuer Information und Dokumentation mbH [*Society for Information and Documentation*] [*Information service or system*] (IID)
**GID** ........... Gitega [*Burundi*] [*Airport symbol*] (OAG)
**GID** ........... Guilde International du Disque [*Record label*] [*France*]
**GIDAD** ...... Gijutsu Daijesuto [*A publication*]
**GIDAP** ....... Guidance Inertial Data Analysis Program
**GIDAS** ....... Geoanomaly Interactive Data Analysis System (MCD)
**GIDE** ......... [*The*] Sportsman's Guide, Inc. [*Golden Valley, MN*] [*NASDAQ symbol*] (NQ)
**GIDEP** ....... Government-Industry Data Exchange Program [*Formerly, IDEP*] [*Navy*] [*Information service or system*]
**GID-IZ** ...... GID [*Gesellschaft fuer Information und Dokumentation*]-Informationszentrum fuer Informationswissenschaft und -Praxis [*GID Information Center for Information Science and Information Work*] [*Society for Information and Documentation*] [*Information service or system*] (IID)
**GIDL** ......... Giddings & Lewis, Inc. [*NASDAQ symbol*] (NQ)
**GIDP** ......... Gale International Directory of Publications [*A publication*]
**GIDP** ......... Grounded into Double Plays [*Baseball*]
**Gidravl Gidrotekh** ... Gidravlika i Gidrotekhnika [*A publication*]
**Gidroaeromeh i Teor Uprogosti** ... Gidroaeromehanika i Teorija Uprugosti [*A publication*]
**Gidrobiol Zh** ... Gidrobiologicheskii Zhurnal [*A publication*]
**Gidrobiol Zh Akad Nauk Ukr SSR** ... Gidrobiologicheskij Zhurnal Akademiya Nauk Ukrainskoj SSR [*A publication*]
**Gidrobiol Zh Hydrobiol J** ... Gidrobiologicheskii Zhurnal/Hydrobiological Journal [*A publication*]
**Gidrodin Bol'shikh Skorostei** ... Gidrodinamika Bol'shikh Skorostei [*A publication*]
**Gidrodin Teploobmen** ... Gidrodinamika i Teploobmen [*A publication*]
**Gidrogeol Gidrogeokhim** ... Gidrogeologiya i Gidrogeokhimiya [*A publication*]
**Gidrogeol Karstoved** ... Gidrogeologiya i Karstoverdenie [*A publication*]
**Gidrogeol Sb** ... Gidrogeologicheskii Sbornik [*A publication*]
**Gidrokhim Mater** ... Gidrokhimicheskiye Materialy [*A publication*]
**Gidroliz Lesokhim Promysh** ... Gidroliznaya i Lesokhimicheskaya Promyshlennost [*A publication*]
**Gidrol Lesohim Prom** ... Gidroliznaja i Lesohimiceskaja Promyshlennost [*A publication*]
**Gidromekh** ... Akademiya Nauk Ukrainskoi SSR. Institut Gidromekhaniki. Gidromekhanika [*A publication*]
**Gidromet Azerb Kasp Morya** ... Gidrometeorologiya Azerbaidzhana i Kaspiiskogo. Morya [*A publication*]
**Gidroprivod Gidropnevmoavtomatika** ... Gidroprivod Gidropnevmoavtomatika [*A publication*]
**Gidrotekh Melior** ... Gidrotekhnika i Melioratsiya [*A publication*]
**Gidrotekh Stroit** ... Gidrotekhnicheskoe Stroitel'stvo [*A publication*]
**Gids** ........... De Gids [*A publication*]
**GIE** ........... Constructeur. Vaktijdschrift voor het Werktuigbouwkundig Construeren naar Functie, Vorm, en Kostprijs [*A publication*]
**GIE** ........... Galapagos Islands [*Ecuador*] [*Seismograph station code, US Geological Survey*] (SEIS)
**GIE** ........... Glycerinisopropylidene Ether [*Organic chemistry*]
**GIE** ........... Ground Instrumentation Equipment
**GIEA** ......... German-American Information and Education Association (EA)
**GIEE** .......... Graduate of the Institute of Electrical Engineers [*British*] (DAS)
**GIEK** .......... Guarantee Institute for Export Credits [*Norway*]
**GIENDG** ... Giornale Italiano di Entomologia [*A publication*]
**GIER** .......... General Industrial Equipment Reserve
**GIERB** ....... Giesserei-Rundschau [*A publication*]
**GIESA** ....... Giesserei [*West Germany*] [*A publication*]
**Giess** .......... Giesserei [*A publication*]
**Giessener Abh Agr WirtForsch Eur Ostens** ... Giessener Abhandlungen zur Agrar- und Wirtschaftsforschung des Europaeischen Ostens [*A publication*]
**Giessener Geol Schr** ... Giessener Geologische Schriften [*A publication*]
**Giessener Schriftenr Tierz Haustiergenet** ... Giessener Schriftenreihe Tierzucht und Haustiergenetik [*A publication*]
**Giesserei-Erfah** ... Giesserei-Erfahrungsaustausch [*A publication*]
**Giesserei Maschinenbau Ztg** ... Giesserei und Maschinenbau Zeitung [*A publication*]
**Giesserei-Rundsch** ... Giesserei-Rundschau [*Austria*] [*A publication*]
**GIEUS** ....... Guide to International Education in the US [*A publication*]
**GIF** ............ General Insurance Fund [*Federal Housing Administration*]
**GIF** ............ Gesellschaft fuer Informationsmarkt-Forschung [*Society for Information-Market Research*] [*Database producer*] (IID)
**Gif** ............. Giffard's English Vice-Chancellors' Reports [*65-66 English Reprint*] [*A publication*] (DLA)
**GIF** ............ Gifu [*Japan*] [*Seismograph station code, US Geological Survey*] (SEIS)
**GIF** ............ Giornale Italiano di Filologia [*A publication*]
**GIF** ............ Graphics Interchange Format [*Computer technology*]
**GIF** ............ Gravito-Inertial Force
**GIF** ............ Guardian International Income Fund Units [*Toronto Stock Exchange symbol*]
**GIF** ............ Gulf It to FORTRAN [*Translator*] [*Data processing*]
**GIF** ............ Guy in the Front Seat [*Pilot*] [*Slang*] (DSUE)
**GIF** ............ Winter Haven, FL [*Location identifier*] [*FAA*] (FAAL)
**GIFA** .......... General Iron Fitters Association [*A union*] [*British*]

**GIFAP**....... Groupement International des Associations Nationales de Fabricants de Produits Agrochimiques [*International Group of National Associations of Manufacturers of Agrochemical Products*] (EAIO)
**GIFC**.......... Gilligan's Island Fan Club (EA)
**Giff**............. Giffard's English Vice-Chancellors' Reports [*65-66 English Reprint*] [*A publication*] (DLA)
**Giff (Eng)**... Giffard's English Vice-Chancellors' Reports [*65-66 English Reprint*] [*A publication*] (DLA)
**Giff & H**..... Giffard and Hemming's English Chancery Reports [*A publication*] (DLA)
**GIFFI**......... Group Inventory for Finding Interests [*Educational test*]
**GIFS**.......... Generalized Interrelated Flow Simulation (IEEE)
**GIFS**.......... Gray Iron Founders Society (EA)
**GIFS**.......... Guggenheim Institute of Flight Structures (MUGU)
**GIFT**.......... Gamete Intrafallopian Transfer [*Fertilization technique*]
**GIFT**.......... Gas-Insulated Flow Tube (NRCH)
**GIFT**.......... General Internal FORTRAN Translator [*Data processing*] (IEEE)
**GIFT**.......... Glasgow International Freight Terminal [*Scotland*] (DS)
**GIFT**.......... Group Inventory for Finding Creative Talent [*Educational test*]
**Gift Child**... Gifted Child Quarterly [*A publication*]
**Gift Ch Q**... Gifted Child Quarterly [*A publication*]
**Gifted Child Q**... Gifted Child Quarterly [*A publication*]
**GIFTPOOL**... Datenbank ueber Gifte und Vergiftungen [*Databank for Poisons and Poisoning*] [*German*]
**Gig**............. De Gigantibus [*Philo*] (BJA)
**GIG**............ Gesellschaft fuer Internationale Geldgeschichte (EAIO)
**GIG**............ Gigi Resources Ltd. [*Vancouver Stock Exchange symbol*]
**GIG**............ Gluten Intolerance Group [*Later, GIGNA*] (EA)
**GIG**............ Rio De Janeiro [*Brazil*] [*Airport symbol*] (OAG)
**GIG**............ Scottsbluff, NE [*Location identifier*] [*FAA*] (FAAL)
**GIGA**......... Giga-Tronics, Inc. [*NASDAQ symbol*] (NQ)
**Gig i Epidemiol**... Gigiena i Epidemiologiia [*A publication*]
**GIGI**.......... Gamma Inspection of Grain Integrity
**GIGL**......... Gale Information Guide Library [*Publication series*]
**G Ig Med Prev**... Giornale di Igiene e Medicina Preventiva [*A publication*]
**GIGNA**...... Gluten Intolerance Group of North America (EA)
**Gig Naselennykh Mest**... Gigiena Naselennykh Mest [*Ukrainian SSR*] [*A publication*]
**Gig Nasel Mest Resp Mezhved Sb**... Gigiena Naselennykh Mest Respublikanskoi Mezhvedomstvennyi Sbornik [*A publication*]
**GIGO**......... Garbage In, Garbage Out [*Data processing*]
**Gig Primen Polim Mater Izdelii Nikh**... Gigiena Primeneniya Polimernykh Materialov i Izdelii iz Nikh [*A publication*]
**Gig Primen Toksikol Pestits Klin Otravlenii**... Gigiena Primeneniya. Toksikologiya, Pestitsidov, i Klinika Otravlenii [*A publication*]
**GIGS**.......... Gemini Inertial Guidance System [*NASA*] (KSC)
**GIGS**.......... Gravity-Gradient Test Satellite
**Gig San**...... Gigiena i Sanitariya [*A publication*]
**Gig Sanit**.... Gigiena i Sanitariya [*A publication*]
**GIGTA7**..... Gigiena Truda Respublikanskii Mezhvedomstvennyi Sbornik [*A publication*]
**Gig Toksikol Pestitsi Klin Otravlenii**... Gigiena i Toksikologiya Pestitsidov i Klinika Otravlenii [*A publication*]
**Gig Tr**........ Gigiena Truda [*Ukrainian SSR*] [*A publication*]
**Gig Tr Prof Patol Est SSR**... Gigiena Truda i Professional'naya Patologiya v Estonskoi SSR [*Estonian SSR*] [*A publication*]
**Gig Tr Prof Zabol**... Gigiena Truda i Professional'nye Zabolevaniya [*A publication*]
**Gig Tr Resp Mezhved Sb**... Gigiena Truda Respublikanskii Mezhvedomstvennyi Sbornik [*A publication*]
**GIH**............ Gastrointestinal Hormone [*Endocrinology*]
**GIH**............ Groupe International Hachette [*France*]
**GIH**............ United States Geological Survey, Water Resources Division, Helena, MT [*OCLC symbol*] (OCLC)
**Giho Res Dev Headquarters Jpn Defense Agency**... Giho. Research and Development Headquarters. Japan Defense Agency [*A publication*]
**GII**............. Gastrointestinal Infection [*Medicine*]
**GII**............. Greiner Engineering, Inc. [*AMEX symbol*] (SPSG)
**GII**............. Guillevin International, Inc. [*Toronto Stock Exchange symbol*]
**G-II**........... Gulfstream II [*Shuttle training aircraft*] [*NASA*] (NASA)
**GIID**........... GENSER Integration Information Display (MCD)
**GIII**........... G-III Apparel Group Ltd. [*NASDAQ symbol*] (NQ)
**GIIP**........... Groupement International de l'Industrie Pharmaceutique des Pays de la CEE [*International Pharmaceutical Industry Group for the EEC Countries*]
**GIIR**........... Government Idle Industrial Reserve (AAG)
**GIIV**........... Gated Image Intensifier Viewer
**GIJUA**....... Gijutsu [*A publication*]
**GIK**............ Glucose, Insulin, and Potassium [*Solution*] [*Medicine*]
**GIL**............ Gaseous Ion LASER
**Gil**............. Gilbert [*A unit of magnetomotive force*]
**Gil**............. Gilbert's Cases in Law and Equity [*A publication*] (DLA)
**Gil**............. Gilbert's English Chancery Reports [*1705-27*] [*A publication*] (DLA)
**Gil**............. Gilfillan's Reports [*1-20 Minnesota*] [*A publication*] (DLA)
**GIL**............ Gilley Airways Corp. [*Glen Falls, NY*] [*FAA designator*] (FAAC)
**Gil**............. Gilman's Reports [*6-10 Illinois*] [*A publication*] (DLA)
**Gil**............. Gilmer's Virginia Reports [*21 Virginia*] [*A publication*] (DLA)
**GIL**............ Gilmore Creek [*Alaska*] [*Seismograph station code, US Geological Survey*] (SEIS)
**GIL**............ Green Indicating Lamp
**GIL**............ Group Investment-Linked (ADA)
**Gil**............. Guillelmus Durandi [*Deceased, 1296*] [*Authority cited in pre-1607 legal work*] (DSA)
**GIL**............ United States Geological Survey, Metairie, LA [*OCLC symbol*] (OCLC)
**GILB**.......... Gilbert Associates, Inc. [*NASDAQ symbol*] (NQ)
**Gilb**........... Gilbert's Cases in Law and Equity [*A publication*] (DLA)
**Gilb**........... Gilbert's English Chancery Reports [*1705-27*] [*A publication*] (DLA)
**Gilb Bank**... Gilbert on Banking [*A publication*] (DLA)
**Gilb Cas**..... Gilbert's Cases in Law and Equity [*A publication*] (DLA)
**Gilb Cas L & Eq**... Gilbert's Cases in Law and Equity [*A publication*] (DLA)
**Gilb Cas L & Eq (Eng)**... Gilbert's Common Pleas [*93 English Reprint*] [*A publication*] (DLA)
**Gilb Ch**...... Gilbert's English Chancery Reports [*1705-27*] [*A publication*] (DLA)
**Gilb Com Pl**... Gilbert's Common Pleas [*93 English Reprint*] [*A publication*] (DLA)
**Gilb CP**...... Gilbert's Common Pleas [*93 English Reprint*] [*A publication*] (DLA)
**Gilb Debt**... Gilbert on the Action of Debt [*A publication*] (DLA)
**Gilb Dev**..... Gilbert's Law of Devises [*A publication*] (DLA)
**Gilb Dis**...... Gilbert on Distress and Replevin [*A publication*] (DLA)
**Gilb Ej**........ Gilbert on Ejectments [*A publication*] (DLA)
**Gilb Eq**....... Gilbert's English Equity Reports [*25 English Reprint*] [*1705-27*] [*A publication*] (DLA)
**Gilb Eq (Eng)**... Gilbert's English Equity Reports [*25 English Reprint*] [*1705-27*] [*A publication*] (DLA)
**Gilb Eq Rep**... Gilbert's English Equity Reports [*1705-27*] [*A publication*] (DLA)
**Gilbert Ev**.. Gilbert's Law of Evidence [*A publication*] (DLA)
**Gilbert Uses by Sugd**... Gilbert's Uses and Trusts by Sugden [*A publication*] (DLA)
**Gilb Ev**....... Gilbert's Law of Evidence [*A publication*] (DLA)
**Gilb Ex**....... Gilbert's Executions [*A publication*] (DLA)
**Gilb Exch**... Gilbert's English Exchequer Reports [*A publication*] (DLA)
**Gilb Exch Pr**... Gilbert's History and Practice of the Exchequer [*A publication*] (DLA)
**Gilb For Rom**... Gilbert's Forum Romanum [*A publication*] (DLA)
**Gilb Forum Rom**... Gilbert's Forum Romanum [*A publication*] (DLA)
**Gilb Hist CP**... Gilbert's History of Common Pleas [*A publication*] (DLA)
**Gilb KB**...... Gilbert's Cases in Law and Equity [*A publication*] (DLA)
**Gilb Lex Pr**... Gilbert's Lex Praetoria [*A publication*] (DLA)
**Gilb PC**...... Gilbert's Common Pleas [*93 English Reprint*] [*A publication*] (DLA)
**Gilb Rem**.... Gilbert's Remainders [*A publication*] (DLA)
**Gilb Rents**... Gilbert's Treatise on Rents [*A publication*] (DLA)
**Gilb Rep**..... Gilbert's English Chancery Reports [*1705-27*] [*A publication*] (DLA)
**Gilb Repl**.... Gilbert on Replevin [*A publication*] (DLA)
**Gilb RR**...... Gilbert's Railway Law of Illinois [*A publication*] (DLA)
**Gilb Ten**..... Gilbert on Tenures [*A publication*] (DLA)
**Gilb Uses**... Gilbert on Uses and Trusts [*A publication*] (DLA)
**Gilchr**......... Gilchrist's Local Government Cases [*A publication*] (DLA)
**Gild**............ Gildersleeve's Reports [*New Mexico*] [*A publication*] (DLA)
**GILD**.......... Guilford Industries, Inc. [*NASDAQ symbol*] (NQ)
**Gildersleeve**... Gildersleeve's Reports [*New Mexico*] [*A publication*] (DLA)
**Gildersleeve (N Mex)**... Gildersleeve's Reports [*New Mexico*] [*A publication*] (DLA)
**Gildr**.......... Gildersleeve's Reports [*New Mexico*] [*A publication*] (DLA)
**Gil Dur**....... Guillelmus Durandi [*Deceased, 1296*] [*Authority cited in pre-1607 legal work*] (DSA)
**Gil & Fal**.... Gilmour and Falconer's Cases, Scotch Court of Session [*A publication*] (DLA)
**Gilfillan**...... Gilfillan's Reports [*1-20 Minnesota*] [*A publication*] (DLA)
**Gilg**............ Gilgames (BJA)
**GILL**.......... Gillingham [*Municipal borough in England*]
**Gill**............ Gill's Maryland Court of Appeals Reports [*1843-51*] [*A publication*] (DLA)
**Gillett Cr Law**... Gillett's Treatise on Criminal Law and Procedure in Criminal Cases [*A publication*] (DLA)
**Gillett Mem Lect**... Gillett Memorial Lecture [*A publication*]
**Gill & J**...... Gill and Johnson's Maryland Reports [*A publication*] (DLA)
**Gill and J (Maryland)**... Gill and Johnson's Maryland Reports [*A publication*] (DLA)
**Gill & J (MD)**... Gill and Johnson's Maryland Reports [*A publication*] (DLA)
**Gill & Johns**... Gill and Johnson's Maryland Reports [*A publication*] (DLA)
**Gill (MD)**... Gill's Maryland Reports [*A publication*] (DLA)
**Gill Pol Rep**... Gill's Police Court Reports [*Boston, MA*] [*A publication*] (DLA)
**GILM**........ Gil-Med Industries, Inc. [*NASDAQ symbol*] (NQ)
**Gilm**.......... Gilman's Reports [*6-10 Illinois*] [*A publication*] (DLA)
**Gilm**.......... Gilmer's Virginia Reports [*21 Virginia*] [*A publication*] (DLA)

**Gilm** .......... Gilmour's Reports, Scotch Court of Session [*A publication*] (DLA)
**Gilman** ....... Gilman's Reports [*6-10 Illinois*] [*A publication*] (DLA)
**Gilm Dig** .... Gilman's Illinois and Indiana Digest [*A publication*] (DLA)
**Gilmer** ........ Gilmer's Virginia Reports [*21 Virginia*] [*1820-21*] [*A publication*] (DLA)
**GILMER** ... Guardian of Impressive Letters and Master of Excellent Replies
**Gilmer (VA)** ... Gilmer's Virginia Reports [*21 Virginia*] [*A publication*] (DLA)
**Gilm & F** .... Gilmour and Falconer's Decisions, Scotch Court of Session [*1961-66*] [*A publication*] (DLA)
**Gilm & Fal** ... Gilmour and Falconer's Decisions, Scotch Court of Session [*1961-66*] [*A publication*] (DLA)
**Gilm & Falc** ... Gilmour and Falconer's Reports, Scotch Court of Session [*A publication*] (DLA)
**Gilm (Ill)** .... Gilman's Reports [*6-10 Illinois*] [*A publication*] (DLA)
**Gil (Minn)** ... Gilfillan's Edition [*1-20 Minnesota*] [*A publication*] (DLA)
**GILN** ......... Glosa International Language Network (EAIO)
**Gilp** ............ Gilpin's United States District Court Reports [*A publication*] (DLA)
**Gilp Opin** ... Gilpin's Opinions of the United States Attorneys-General [*A publication*] (DLA)
**GIM** ........... Gaining Inventory Managers (AFM)
**GIM** ........... Geldermann Investment Management [*Finance*] [*British*]
**GIM** ........... Generalized Information Management [*Language*]
**GIM** ........... Glashow-Iliopoulos-Maiani [*Theory in particle physics*]
**GIM** ........... Glass Insulation Material
**GIM** ........... Grace's Insect [*Growth*] Medium [*Microbiology*]
**GIM** ........... Gruppe Internationale Marxisten [*International Marxist Group*] [*Federal Republic of Germany*] [*Political party*] (PPW)
**GIM** ........... Gulf International Minerals [*Vancouver Stock Exchange symbol*]
**GIM** ........... Templeton Global Income [*NYSE symbol*] (SPSG)
**Gima** .......... Grupo Independente de Macau [*Independent Group of Macao*] [*Political party*] (PPW)
**GIMB** ......... Gimbal (KSC)
**GI Mech E** ... Graduate of the Institution of Mechanical Engineers [*British*]
**GIMI** .......... Graduate of the Institute of the Motor Industry [*British*] (DBQ)
**GIMIC** ....... Guard Ring Isolated Monolithic Integrated Circuit
**GIMLDG** ... Giornale Italiano di Medicina del Lavoro [*A publication*]
**GIMMIS** ... G-I Manpower Management Information System
**GIMP** ......... Gimbal Positioning
**GIMPY** ...... Growing, Improving, Maturing - Puppy of the Year [*Canine award*]
**GIMRADA** ... Geodesy, Intelligence, and Mapping Research and Development Agency [*Army*]
**GIMS** ......... Graduates of Italian Medical Schools (EA)
**GIMS** ......... Ground Identification of Missions in Space
**GIMT** ......... Gott Ist Mein Teil [*God Is My Portion*] [*German*] [*Motto of Friedrich IV, Duke of Liegnitz (1552-96)*]
**GIMT** ......... Gott Ist Mein Trost [*God Is My Comfort*] [*German*] [*Motto of Anna, Duchess of Wohlau (1561-1616); August, Duke of Braunschweig-Wolfenbuttel (1579-1666); Karl III, Duke of Munsterberg and Oels (d. 1617); August, Duke of Saxony-Lauenburg (1577-1656)*]
**GIMTB4** .... Italian Journal of Chest Diseases [*A publication*]
**GIMU** ......... Gimballess Inertial Measuring Unit
**GIN** ............ Galilean Resources Corp. [*Vancouver Stock Exchange symbol*]
**GIN** ............ Gimbaled Integral Nozzle
**GIN** ............ Global Information Network (EA)
**GIN** ............ Guinea [*ANSI three-letter standard code*] (CNC)
**GIN** ............ Stromboli-Ginostra [*Italy*] [*Seismograph station code, US Geological Survey*] (SEIS)
**GINA** ......... Graphical Interactive NMR Analysis [*Data processing*]
**GInd** .......... Guide to Indian Periodical Literature [*A publication*]
**GINDB** ...... Genie Industrial [*A publication*]
**G Indian Per Lit** ... Guide to Indian Periodical Literature [*A publication*]
**Ginecol Bras** ... Ginecologia Brasileira [*A publication*]
**Ginecol Obstet (Lima)** ... Ginecologia y Obstetricia (Lima) [*A publication*]
**Ginecol Obstet Mex** ... Ginecologia y Obstetricia de Mexico [*A publication*]
**Ginekol Pol** ... Ginekologia Polska [*A publication*]
**Ginekol Pol Supl** ... Ginekologia Polska. Suplement [*A publication*]
**GINETEX** ... Groupement International d'Etiquetage pour l'Entretien des Textiles [*International Association for Textile Care Labelling*] [*Barcelona, Spain*] (EA)
**GING** ......... Gingiva [*Gum*] [*Latin*]
**GINGA** ...... Gas Industry. Natural Gas Edition [*A publication*]
**GINI** .......... Gazette International Networking Institute (EA)
**GINNI** ....... Generic Interactive Neural Network Interpreter
**GINNIE MAE** ... Government National Mortgage Association [*See also GNMA*]
**GINO** ......... Graphical Input/Output
**GINO-F** ..... Graphical Input and Output in FORTRAN [*GST Computer Systems Ltd.*] [*Software package*] [*Data processing*] [*British*]
**G Inst** ......... Institutes of Gaius [*Roman law*] [*A publication*]
**GInstM** ...... Graduate of the Institute of Marketing [*British*] (DBQ)
**GIO** ............ Gas Identification Officer
**GIO** ............ Giocossamente [*Humorously*] [*Music*] (ROG)
**GIO** ............ Golden Trio Minerals [*Vancouver Stock Exchange symbol*]
**GIO** ............ Government Information Organization [*Later, NAGC*]
**GIO** ............ Group Intelligence Officer [*British military*] (DMA)
**GIO** ............ Guaranteed Insurability Option
**GIOA** ......... Gregorian Institute of America [*Record label*]
**GIOC** ......... Generalized Input/Output Controller [*Data processing*] (IEEE)
**GIOP** ......... General-Purpose Input/Output Processor [*Data processing*]
**GIOR** ......... GPETE Initial Outfitting Requirement [*Military*] (CAAL)
**Gior Clin Med** ... Giornale di Clinica Medica [*A publication*]
**Gior Geront** ... Giornale di Gerontologia [*A publication*]
**Gior Internaz Sc Med** ... Giornale Internazionale delle Scienze Mediche [*A publication*]
**Gior Ital Mal Esot e Trop ed Ig Colon** ... Giornale Italiano di Malattie Esotiche e Tropicali ed Iglene Coloniale [*A publication*]
**Gior Ital Mal Ven** ... Giornale Italiano delle Malattie Veneree e della Pelle [*A publication*]
**Gior Lett Italia** ... Giornale di Letterati d'Italia [*A publication*]
**Gior Med Prat** ... Giornale di Medicina Practica [*A publication*]
**Gior Med R Esercito** ... Giornale Medico del Regio Esercito e della Regia Marina [*A publication*]
**Gior Med Vet** ... Giornale di Medicina Veterinaria [*A publication*]
**Giornale Econ** ... Giornale Economico [*A publication*]
**Giornale Economisti e Ann Econ** ... Giornale degli Economisti e Annali di Economia [*A publication*]
**Giorn Econom Ann Econom** ... Giornale degli Economisti e Annali di Economia [*A publication*]
**Giorn Fil Ferr** ... Giornale Filologico Ferrarese [*A publication*]
**Giorn It Fil** ... Giornale Italiano di Filologia [*A publication*]
**Giorn Mat Battaglini** ... Giornale di Matematiche di Battaglini [*A publication*]
**Giorn Mat Battaglini 6** ... Giornale di Matematiche di Battaglini. Serie 6 [*Naples*] [*A publication*]
**Giorn Stor Lunig** ... Giornale Storico della Lunigiana [*A publication*]
**Gior R Accad Med Torino** ... Giornale della Reale Accademia di Medicina di Torino [*A publication*]
**Gior R Soc Ital Ig** ... Giornale della Reale Societa Italiana d'Igiene [*A publication*]
**Gior Sc Lett ed Arti Sicilia** ... Giornale di Scienze, Lettere, ed Arti per la Sicilia [*A publication*]
**Gior Storico** ... Giornale Storico della Letteratura Italiana [*A publication*]
**GIP** ............ Galvanized Improved Plow [*Steel*]
**GIP** ............ Garden Island Prison [*Australia*] [*World War II*] (DSUE)
**GIP** ............ Gastric [*or Gastrin*] Inhibitory Principle [*or Polypeptide*] [*Medicine*]
**GIP** ............ Gaussian Image Point [*Optics*]
**GIP** ............ General Implementation Plan
**GIP** ............ General Insertion Protein [*Genetics*]
**GIP** ............ Gileppe [*Belgium*] [*Seismograph station code, US Geological Survey*] (SEIS)
**GIP** ............ Glazed Imitation Parchment
**GIP** ............ Great Indian Peninsular R. R.
**GIP** ............ Great Irish Painter [*Reference to Jack B. Yeats, ca. 1905*]
**GIP** ............ Gross Internal Product
**GIP** ............ Gunnery Improvement Program [*Military*] (CAAL)
**GIPD** ......... B. F. Goodrich Institute for Personnel Development
**GIPEIE** ...... Groupe International Postal d'Echanges d'Information et d'Experience [*International Group for the Exchange of Information and Experience among Postal Savings Institutions - IGEIEPSI*] (EAIO)
**Giperton Bolezn Ateroskler Koron Nedostatochn** ... Gipertonicheskaya Bolezn Ateroskleroz i Koronarnaya Nedostatochnost [*A publication*]
**GI/PI** ......... General Inspection/Procurement Inspection (MCD)
**GIPLA** ....... Giornale dei Pollicoltori [*A publication*]
**GIPME** ...... Global Investigation of Pollution in the Marine Environment [*National Science Foundation*]
**GIPND** ...... General Information Programme-UNISIST [*Universal System for Information in Science and Technology*] Newsletter [*A publication*]
**GIPOA** ...... Ginekologia Polska [*A publication*]
**GIPOA3** .... Ginekologia Polska [*A publication*]
**GIPPSDOC** ... Gippsland Database [*Australia*]
**GIPPSLD** .. Gippsland [*Australia*] (ROG)
**GIPS** .......... Government Imprinted Penalty Stationery Society (EA)
**GIPS** .......... Ground Information Processing System
**GIPSB** ....... Giornale Italiano di Psicologia [*A publication*]
**GIPSE** ....... Gravity Independent Photosynthetic Gas Exchanger
**GIPSY** ....... Generalized Information Processing System
**GIPXA** ....... Giessereipraxis [*A publication*]
**GIQ** ............ Giant Imperial Quart [*of beer*]
**GIR** ............ Glucose Infusion Rate [*Physiology*]
**GIR** ............ Golden Lion Resources Ltd. [*Vancouver Stock Exchange symbol*]
**GIR** ............ Resource Appraisal Group Library, United States Geological Survey, Denver, CO [*OCLC symbol*] (OCLC)
**GIRA** ......... Gallups Island Radio Association (EA)
**GIRA** ......... Group Individual Retirement Account
**GIRA** ......... Groupement Independant de Reflexion et d'Action [*Independent Grouping of Reflection and Action*] [*Central Africa*] (PD)
**GIRAFFE** ... Graphic Interface for Finite Elements [*Graphics data processing*]

**GIRAS**....... Geographic Information Retrieval and Analysis System [*Department of the Interior*]
**GIRAST**.... Groupe Interdisciplinaire de Recherche pour l'Amelioration des Situations de Travail [*University of Quebec at Rimouski*] [*Canada*] [*Research center*] (RCD)
**GIRD**......... General Incentive for Research and Development [*Canada*]
**GIRD**......... Good Industrial Relations Directors [*Meetings sponsored by Master Printers of America*]
**GIRD**......... Grants for Industry Research and Development [*Australia*]
**GIRD**......... Ground Integration Requirements Document (MCD)
**GIRGV**...... Groupe International des Ressources Genetiques Vegetales [*International Board for Plant Genetic Resources - IBPGR*] (EA)
**GIRL**.......... Generalized Information Retrieval Language [*US Defense Nuclear Agency*]
**GIRL**.......... Graph Information Retrieval Language [*1970*] [*Data processing*] (CSR)
**GIRLS**....... General Indexing in Reciprocal Lattice Space (KSC)
**GIRLS**....... Generalized Information Retrieval and Listing System
**GIRLS**....... Global Interrogation Recording and Location System (MCD)
**GIRM**........ Generalized Internal Reference Method [*Statistical procedure*]
**GIRMS**...... Geographical Inter-University Resource Management Seminar
**GIRO**......... General Instructions for Routing and Reporting Officers
**GIROQ**...... Groupe Interuniversitaire des Recherches Oceanographiques du Quebec [*Interuniversity Group for Oceanographic Research of Quebec*] [*Laval University*] [*Canada*] [*Research center*] (RCD)
**GIRS**.......... Gallaudet Information Retrieval Service
**GIRS**.......... Gimballess Inertial Reference System
**GIRSO**....... Groupement International pour la Recherche Scientifique en Stomatologie et Odontologie [*International Group for Scientific Research on Stomato-Odontology*] (EA)
**GIRSS**....... General Information Retrieval System Simulation
**GIRSTERM**... Groupe Interdisciplinaire de Recherche Scientifique et Appliquee en Terminologie [*INFOTERM*]
**Gir WC**...... Girard's Will Case Report [*A publication*] (DLA)
**GIS**............ Gastrointestinal Series [*Radiology*]
**GIS**............ General Installation Subcontractor
**GIS**............ General Mills, Inc. [*NYSE symbol*] (SPSG)
**GIS**............ Generalized Information System [*IBM Corp.*]
**GIS**............ Generalized Inquiry System [*Data processing*]
**GIS**............ Geographic Information Systems [*Fish and Wildlife Service*] (IID)
**GIS**............ Geological Information Systems [*University of Oklahoma*] [*Information service or system*] (IID)
**GIS**............ Geoscience Information Society (EA)
**GIS**............ Gids op Maatschappelijk Gebied. Tijdschrift voor Syndicale, Culturele, en Sociale Problemen [*A publication*]
**GIS**............ Gisborne [*New Zealand*] [*Airport symbol*] (OAG)
**GIS**............ Gismondine [*A zeolite*]
**GIS**............ Gissar [*USSR*] [*Seismograph station code, US Geological Survey*] [*Closed*] (SEIS)
**GIS**............ Global Information Services, Inc. [*Flushing, NY*] [*Telecommunications*] (TSSD)
**GIS**............ Global Ionospheric Studies
**GIS**............ Global Issues [*Program*] [*Department of State*]
**GIS**............ Golden Iskut Resources [*Vancouver Stock Exchange symbol*]
**GIS**............ Grand Inside Sentinel [*Freemasonry*] (ROG)
**GIS**............ Grant Information System [*Oryx Press*] (IID)
**GIS**............ Graphic Input System
**GIS**............ Greatness Is Simplicity [*See also SIG*]
**GIS**............ Guaranteed Income Stream [*UAW program included in the union's 1982 contract with General Motors Corp.*]
**GIS**............ Guaranteed Income Supplement [*Program*] [*Canada*]
**GIS**............ Guidance Information System [*Houghton Mifflin Co.*] [*Information service or system*] (IID)
**GIS**............ Guild of the Infant Saviour (EA)
**GIS**............ Guild for Infant Survival [*Later, ICIS*]
**GIS**............ United States Department of the Interior, United States Geological Survey, Reston, VA [*OCLC symbol*] (OCLC)
**GISA**.......... Government in the Sunshine Act [*1976*]
**GISAA**........ Gigiena i Sanitariya [*A publication*]
**GISAAA**...... Gigiena i Sanitariya [*A publication*]
**GISAT**........ Ground Identification of Satellites (MCD)
**GISC**.......... Government Information Services Committee [*Special Libraries Association*]
**GISC**.......... Grail International Student Center [*Defunct*] (EA)
**GISE**.......... Generalized Integrated Square Error [*Aeronautics*]
**GI Sec**........ General Inspectorate Section [*European Theater of Operations*] [*World War II*]
**GISGE**....... Good Intent Society of Galvanizers and Enamellers [*A union*] [*British*]
**GISH**......... Gish Biomedical, Inc. [*NASDAQ symbol*] (NQ)
**GISL**.......... Graphic Imaging Specification Language [*Printing technology*]
**GISMO**..... General Interpretative System for Matrix Operations [*Data processing system used in engineering*] [*Navy*]
**GISP**.......... Grain Income Stabilization Plan
**GISP**.......... Greenland Ice Sheet Project [*National Science Foundation*]
**GISPA**........ Geoscience Information Society. Proceedings [*A publication*]
**GISPA**........ Guide to International Scientific Publications and Associations [*A publication*]
**GI for SS**.... Goddard Institute for Space Studies [*NASA*]
**GISS**.......... Goddard Institute for Space Studies [*NASA*]
**GISSI**......... Gruppo Italiano per lo Studio della Streptochinasi nell'Infarto [*Italy*]
**Gissing N**... Gissing Newsletter [*A publication*]
**GIST**.......... GARP International Sea Trial [*National Science Foundation*]
**GIST**.......... Gochnour Idiom Screening Test
**GIT**............ Gastrointestinal Tract [*Medicine*]
**GIT**............ General Information Test
**GIT**............ Georgia Institute of Technology [*Atlanta*]
**GIT**............ Gilgit [*Pakistan*] [*Geomagnetic observatory code*]
**GIT**............ Gitano Group, Inc. [*NYSE symbol*] (CTT)
**Git**............ Gittin (BJA)
**GIT**............ Glas- und Instrumenten Technik Fachzeitschrift fuer das Laboratorium [*A publication*]
**GIT**............ Graduate Institute of Technology [*University of Arkansas at Little Rock*] [*Research center*] (RCD)
**GIT**............ Graph Isomorphism Tester
**GIT**............ Grease Interceptor Trap
**GIT**............ [*The*] Great Ideas Today [*A publication*]
**GIT**............ Grit Resources, Inc. [*Vancouver Stock Exchange symbol*]
**GIT**............ Grooved for Iron Tongues
**GIT**............ Group Inclusive Tour [*Airline fare*]
**G Ital Anest Analg**... Giornale Italiano di Anestesia e di Analgesia [*A publication*]
**G Ital Anestesiol**... Giornale Italiano di Anestesiologia [*A publication*]
**G Ital Cardiol**... Giornale Italiano di Cardiologia [*A publication*]
**G Ital Chemioter**... Giornale Italiano di Chemioterapia [*A publication*]
**G Ital Chir**... Giornale Italiano di Chirurgia [*A publication*]
**G Ital Dermatol**... Giornale Italiano di Dermatologia [*Later, Giornale Italiano di Dermatologia e Venereologia*] [*A publication*]
**G Ital Dermatol Minerva Dermatol**... Giornale Italiano di Dermatologia Minerva Dermatologica [*A publication*]
**G Ital Dermatol Venereol**... Giornale Italiano di Dermatologia e Venereologia [*A publication*]
**G Ital Mal Torace**... Giornale Italiano delle Malattie del Torace [*A publication*]
**G Ital Mal Torace Suppl**... Giornale Italiano delle Malattie del Torace. Supplemento [*A publication*]
**G Ital Med Lav**... Giornale Italiano di Medicina del Lavoro [*A publication*]
**G Ital Oftalmol**... Giornale Italiano di Oftalmologia [*A publication*]
**G Ital Patol Sci Affini**... Giornale Italiano di Patologia e di Scienze Affini [*A publication*]
**G Ital Tuberc**... Giornale Italiano della Tubercolosi [*A publication*]
**G Ital Tuberc Mal Torace**... Giornale Italiano della Tubercolosi e delle Malattie del Torace [*A publication*]
**GITC**.......... Government of Israel Trade Center (EA)
**GITEA**....... GIT [*Glas- und Instrumenten-Technik*] Fachzeitschrift fuer das Laboratorium [*West Germany*] [*A publication*]
**GIT Fachz Lab**... Glas- und Instrumenten Technik Fachzeitschrift fuer das Laboratorium [*A publication*]
**GIT Fachz Lab Suppl**... GIT [*Glas- und Instrumenten-Technik*] Fachzeitschrift fuer das Laboratorium. Supplement [*A publication*]
**GITG**......... Ground Interface Technical Group [*NASA*] (NASA)
**GITI**.......... Government Issue Technical Inspection (INF)
**GIT Labor Med**... GIT [*Glas- und Instrumenten-Technik*] Labor-Medizin [*A publication*]
**GITP**.......... Ground Integration Test Program (KSC)
**GIT/SCID**... Studies in Comparative International Development. Georgia Institute of Technology [*A publication*]
**GIT Suppl**... GIT [*Glas- und Instrumenten-Technik*] Supplement [*A publication*]
**GITT**.......... Glucose Insulin Tolerance Test [*Medicine*]
**GITU**......... Gastrointestinal Transcription Unit [*Medicine*]
**Gitut'yun Texnika**... Gitut'yun ew Texnika [*A publication*]
**GIU**........... General Intelligence Unit [*US, London*]
**GIU**........... Geoballistic Input Unit
**GIU**........... Guidance Integration Unit (MCD)
**GIUAC**...... Geophysical Institute. University of Alaska. Contribution Series [*A publication*]
**GIUAG R**.. Geophysical Institute. University of Alaska. UAG Report Series [*A publication*]
**GIUK**......... Greenland-Iceland-United Kingdom [*NATO naval defense line*]
**Giur Compl Cass Civ**... Giurisprudenza Completa della Corte Suprema di Cassazione. Civile [*A publication*]
**Giur Cost**.... Giurisprudenza Costituzionale [*A publication*]
**Giur Imp Reg Negoz**... Giurisprudenza delle Imposte Dirette di Registro e di Negoziazione [*A publication*]
**Giust Civ**.... Giustizia Civile [*A publication*]
**Giust Pen**... Giustizia Penale [*A publication*]
**GIV**........... Given
**Givaudan Flavor**... Givaudan Flavorist [*A publication*]
**GIVE**.......... Government's Involvement in Volunteer Efforts Programs
**GIVS**.......... Goodwill Industries Volunteer Services (EA)
**GIW**........... Glass-Insulated Wire
**GIW**........... Greenwood, SC [*Location identifier*] [*FAA*] (FAAL)
**GIW**........... Gulf Intracoastal Waterway
**GIWG**........ Ground Interface Working Group
**GIWW**........ Gulf Intracoastal Waterway

**GIY** ............ Glamorgan Imperial Yeomanry [*British military*] (DMA)
**G18 IYRA** ... Geary 18 International Yacht Racing Association (EA)
**GIZ** ............ Gizan [*Saudi Arabia*] [*Airport symbol*] (OAG)
**GIZ** ............ Gizo [*Solomon Islands*] [*Seismograph station code, US Geological Survey*] (SEIS)
**GIZ** ............ Marshfield, WI [*Location identifier*] [*FAA*] (FAAL)
**GIZH** ......... Gosudarstvennyi Institut Zhurnalistiki
**GJ** ............. British Guiana General Jurisdiction (Official Gazette) [*1899-*] [*A publication*] (ILCA)
**GJ** ............. Gap Junction [*Cytology*]
**GJ** ............. Gas Journal [*A publication*]
**GJ** ............. General Journal [*Accounting*]
**GJ** ............. Geographical Journal [*A publication*]
**GJ** ............. German Jewish (BJA)
**GJ** ............. Germania Judaica (BJA)
**GJ** ............. Gigajoule
**G & J** ......... Gill and Johnson's Maryland Court of Appeals Reports [*1829-42*] [*A publication*] (DLA)
**GJ** ............. Gill and Johnson's Maryland Reports [*A publication*] (DLA)
**G & J** ......... Glyn and Jameson's English Bankruptcy Reports [*1821-28*] [*A publication*] (DLA)
**GJ** ............. Goldreich-Julian [*PULSAR theory*]
**GJ** ............. Graduate Jeweller
**GJ** ............. Grand Jury
**GJ** ............. Grapefruit Juice [*Restaurant slang*]
**GJ** ............. Greenwich & Johnsonville Railway Co. [*AAR code*]
**GJ** ............. Group Junction (MCD)
**GJ** ............. Grown Junction (IEEE)
**G + J** ......... Gruner + Jahr AG & Co. [*Magazine publisher*] [*Federal Republic of Germany*]
**GJ** ............. Gutenberg-Jahrbuch [*A publication*]
**GJ** ............. Transportes Aereos SA [*Guatemala*] [*ICAO designator*] (FAAC)
**GjA** ............ Gjurmime Albanologjike [*Prishtina*] [*A publication*]
**GJASA** ...... Ghana Journal of Agricultural Science [*A publication*]
**GJASAF** .... Ghana Journal of Agricultural Science [*A publication*]
**GJb** ........... Geographisches Jahrbuch [*A publication*]
**G Jb** .......... Gutenberg-Jahrbuch [*A publication*]
**GJC** ........... Gainesville Junior College [*Later, Cooke County Junior College*] [*Texas*]
**GJC** ........... Grayson-Jockey Club Research Foundation (EA)
**GJCFC** ....... George Jones Country Fan Club (EA)
**GJCHD** ..... Gesuido Jigyo Chosahi Hokoku [*A publication*]
**GJD** .......... Global Jewish Database [*Bar-Ilan University*] [*Information service or system*] (CRD)
**GJD** .......... Grand Junior Deacon [*Freemasonry*]
**GJE** ........... Gauss-Jordan Elimination (IEEE)
**GJF** ........... Greensboro Justice Fund (EA)
**GJFC** ......... George Jones Fan Club (EA)
**GJG** .......... Augusta College, Augusta, GA [*OCLC symbol*] (OCLC)
**GJHEDB** ... Geologisches Jahrbuch Hessen [*A publication*]
**GJI** ............ Ghetto Job Information [*US Employment Service*] [*Department of Labor*]
**GJL** ........... Geographical Journal (London) [*A publication*]
**GJL** ........... Jijel [*Algeria*] [*Airport symbol*] (OAG)
**G & J (MD)** ... Gill and Johnson's Maryland Reports [*A publication*] (DLA)
**G & Jo** ........ Gill and Johnson's Maryland Reports [*A publication*] (DLA)
**GJO** .......... Grand Junction Office [*Department of Energy*] [*Grand Junction, CO*]
**GJO** .......... Greater Jacksonville [*Florida*] Open [*Golf tournament*]
**GJOA** ........ G. J. Orphan & Associates [*Telecommunications service*] (TSSD)
**G & John** .... Gill and Johnson's Maryland Reports [*A publication*] (DLA)
**GJOUD** ..... Geophysical Journal [*A publication*]
**GJP** ........... Galactic Jupiter Probe [*NASA*]
**GJP** ........... Grand Jury Project (EA)
**GJP** ........... Graphic Job Processor (MCD)
**GJPA** ........ Grammatik des Juedisch-Palaestinischen Aramaeisch [*A publication*] (BJA)
**GJR** ........... Gjogur [*Iceland*] [*Airport symbol*] (OAG)
**GJS** ........... Ghana Journal of Sociology [*A publication*]
**GJSCD** ...... Georgia Journal of Science [*A publication*]
**GJT** ........... Grand Junction [*Colorado*] [*Airport symbol*] (OAG)
**GJTA** ........ Goldsmiths' and Jewellers' Trade Association [*A union*] [*British*]
**GJV** ........... Geschichte des Juedischen Volkes im Zeitalter Jesu Christi [*A publication*] (BJA)
**GJW** .......... Grand Junior Warden [*Freemasonry*]
**GJW** .......... Great Jurists of the World, by Sir John MacDonnel and Edward Manson [*1913*] [*A publication*] (DLA)
**GK** ............ Gazeta Krakowska [*A publication*]
**GK** ............ Gengo Kenkyu [*Journal. Linguistic Society of Japan*] [*A publication*]
**GK** ............ Geodezija i Kartografija [*A publication*]
**GK** ............ Geographenkalender (BJA)
**G f K** .......... Gesellschaft fuer Konsumforschung [*A publication*]
**GK** ............ Ginze Kedem (BJA)
**GK** ............ Goethe-Kalender [*A publication*]
**GK** ............ Gottesdienst und Kirchenmusik [*A publication*]
**GK** ............ Grand King [*Freemasonry*]
**GK** ............ Granular Kidney [*Medicine*] (ROG)
**GK** ............ Greek
**GK** ............ Guy America Airways, Inc. [*ICAO designator*] (FAAC)
**GK** ............ Hebraeische Grammatik Voellig Umgearbeitet [*Gesenius and E. Kautzsch*] [*A publication*] (BJA)
**GK-101** ...... N-Monochloroglycine [*Dental caries treatment named for patent holders, Goldman and Kronman*]
**GKA** .......... Garter King of Arms
**GKA** .......... Goroka [*Papua New Guinea*] [*Seismograph station code, US Geological Survey*] [*Closed*] (SEIS)
**GKA** .......... Goroka [*Papua New Guinea*] [*Airport symbol*] (OAG)
**GKA** .......... Grounded Kathode Amplifier
**GKa** .......... Hebraeische Grammatik Voellig Umgearbeitet [*Gesenius and E. Kautzsch*] [*A publication*] (BJA)
**GKABL** ...... George Khoury Association of Baseball Leagues (EA)
**GKAEA** ..... Geodeziia, Kartografiia, i Aerofotos'emka [*A publication*]
**GKAR** ........ Gesetz ueber Kassenarztrecht [*A publication*]
**GKB** .......... Garantie- und Kreditbank [*Guaranty and Credit Bank*] [*German Democratic Republic*]
**GKBZH** ..... Glowna Komisja Badania Zbrodni Hitlerowskich [*A publication*] (BJA)
**GKB Zt** ...... GKB [*Graz-Koeflacher Eisenbahn und Bergbaugesellschaft*] Zeitung fuer Eisenbahn und Bergbau [*A publication*]
**GKC** .......... Gilbert Keith Chesterton [*British journalist and author*]
**GKC** .......... Gold King Construction [*Vancouver Stock Exchange symbol*]
**GKC** .......... Gold King River [*Alaska*] [*Seismograph station code, US Geological Survey*] (SEIS)
**GKC** .......... Hebrew Grammar Gesenius, Kautzsch, Cowley [*A publication*] (BJA)
**GKCI** ......... Gold King Consolidated, Inc. [*NASDAQ symbol*] (NQ)
**GKCS** ........ G. K. Chesterton Society (EA)
**GKF** .......... Florence, SC [*Location identifier*] [*FAA*] (FAAL)
**GKF** .......... Grope Kunstfuehrer [*A publication*]
**GKG** .......... Grundlagenstudien aus Kybernetik und Geisteswissenschaft [*A publication*]
**GKG** .......... Grundriss der Kirchengeschichte [*A publication*]
**GKH** .......... G. K. Hall Co. [*Publisher*]
**GKI** ........... General Kinetics, Incorporated
**GKI** ........... Glon Kristy Resources [*Vancouver Stock Exchange symbol*]
**GKIE** ......... General Kinetics, Inc. [*Rockville, MD*] [*NASDAQ symbol*] (NQ)
**GKJ** ........... Kennesaw College, Marietta, GA [*OCLC symbol*] (OCLC)
**GKJ** ........... Meadville, PA [*Location identifier*] [*FAA*] (FAAL)
**GKL** ........... Great Keppel Island [*Australia*] [*Airport symbol*] (OAG)
**GKLL** ......... Garage Keeper's Legal Liability [*Insurance*]
**GKN** .......... Guest, Kean & Nettlefolds [*Steel-forging company*] [*British*]
**GKN** .......... Gulkana [*Alaska*] [*Airport symbol*] (OAG)
**GKN** .......... Gulkana, AK [*Location identifier*] [*FAA*] (FAAL)
**GKNHS** ...... Golden Key National Honor Society (EA)
**GKO** .......... Gosudarstvennyi Komitet Oborony [*State Defense Committee*] [*USSR*] [*World War II*]
**GkOd** ......... Greek Odeon [*Record label*]
**GK Oe D** .... Gesamtkommentar Oeffentliches Dienstrecht [*A publication*]
**GKPSAT** ... Ginekologia Polska. Suplement [*A publication*]
**GKQ** .......... Newark, NJ [*Location identifier*] [*FAA*] (FAAL)
**GKR** .......... Goddard Kay Rogers Ltd. [*British*]
**GKR** .......... Golden Knight Resources, Inc. [*Toronto Stock Exchange symbol*] [*Vancouver Stock Exchange symbol*]
**GKRV** ........ Golden Knight Resources, Inc. [*Vancouver, BC*] [*NASDAQ symbol*] (NQ)
**GKS** .......... Gesamtverzeichnis der Kongressschriften [*Union List of Conference Proceedings*] [*Deutsches Bibliotheksinstitut*] [*Federal Republic of Germany*] [*Information service or system*] (CRD)
**GKS** .......... Grand Keeper of the Seals [*Freemasonry*]
**GKS** .......... Graphical Kernel System [*International Standards Organization*] [*Data processing*]
**GKSBA** ...... Geokhimicheskii Sbornik [*A publication*]
**GKSHA** ..... Gijutsu Kenkyusho Shoho [*A publication*]
**GKSR** ........ G & K Services, Inc. [*NASDAQ symbol*] (NQ)
**GKT** .......... Gasket [*Technical drawings*]
**GKT** .......... Goldteck Mines Ltd. [*Toronto Stock Exchange symbol*]
**GKT** .......... Kaffee und Tee Markt [*A publication*]
**GKTW** ....... Give Kids the World (EA)
**GKV** .......... Gesamtverband Kunststoffverarbeitende Industrie eV [*Federal Republic of Germany*] (EY)
**GKVVH** ..... Goeteborgs Kungliga Vetenskaps-och Vitterhets-Samhaelles Handlingar [*A publication*]
**GKWW** ...... Gespraechskreis Wissenschaft und Wirtschaft [*A publication*]
**GKY** .......... Golden Key Resources Ltd. [*Vancouver Stock Exchange symbol*]
**Gl** ............. Galatians [*New Testament book*] (BJA)
**GL** ............ Galeries Lafayette [*Department store*] [*Paris, France*]
**Gl** ............. Galleon [*Spanish vessel*] (DS)
**GL** ............ Gallon (MCD)
**Gl** ............. Galvanized [*Metallurgy*]
**GL** ............ Gas LASER
**GL** ............ Gate Leads (IEEE)
**GL** ............ Gauge Length
**GL** ............ Gazette des Lettres [*A publication*]
**GL** ............ Geist und Leben [*A publication*]
**GL** ............ General Laws [*A publication*] (DLA)

**GL** .......... General Ledger (AABC)
**GL** .......... General Letter
**GL** .......... General Liability [*Insurance*]
**GL** .......... General Licence to Officiate [*Church of England in Australia*]
**GL** .......... General Linear [*Group theory, mathematics*]
**GL** .......... General Linguistics [*A publication*]
**GL** .......... General List [*Navy*] [*British*] (DMA)
**GL** .......... Generator Lorry [*British*]
**GL** .......... Genius Loci [*Genius of the Place*] [*Latin*] (ROG)
**GL** .......... Germanischer Lloyd [*German ship classification society*] (DS)
**GL** .......... Gill [*Unit of weight*]
**GL** .......... Gilt Leaves [*Bookbinding*] (ROG)
**GL** .......... Gilt Lines [*Bookbinding*] (ROG)
**GL** .......... Gimbal Limit Prearming Inhibiting Signal
**GL** .......... Giornale della Libreria [*A publication*]
**GL** .......... Glabella [*Anatomy*] (ROG)
**GL** .......... Glacier (ROG)
**GL** .......... Gladstonian Liberal [*British*] (ROG)
**gl** .......... Gland
**Gl** .......... Glasnik [*A publication*]
**GL** .......... Glass
**GL** .......... Glaucolacustrine Soil [*Agronomy*]
**GL** .......... Glaze
**Gl** .......... Gleaver's Reports [*Jamaica*] [*A publication*] (ILCA)
**GL** .......... Glebe [*Ecclesiastical*] (ROG)
**GL** .......... Global Learning (EA)
**GL** .......... Global Utility Fund [*NYSE symbol*] (SPSG)
**Gl** .......... Globe [*A publication*]
**Gl** .......... Globigerina [*Quality of the bottom*] [*Nautical charts*]
**Gl** .......... Globus (BJA)
**GL** .......... Gloria [*Glory*] [*Latin*]
**Gl** .......... Gloss (DSA)
**Gl** .......... Glossa [*A publication*]
**GL** .......... Glossary (ROG)
**Gl** .......... Glotta [*A publication*]
**Gl** .......... Glucinium [*Also, G*] [*Old name for chemical element beryllium*]
**GL** .......... Glycosphingolipid [*Biochemistry*]
**GL** .......... Go Long [*Investment term*]
**GL** .......... Gold Lease (ADA)
**GL** .......... Gothic Letter
**GL** .......... Grade Line
**GL** .......... Graduate in Law
**G/L** .......... Grams per Liter
**GL** .......... Grand Larceny
**GL** .......... Grand Lodge [*Freemasonry*]
**GL** .......... Grand Lot
**GL** .......... Great Lakes [*Vessel load line mark*]
**GL** .......... Great Lakes Forest Products Ltd. [*Toronto Stock Exchange symbol*]
**GL** .......... Greater London [*England*]
**GL** .......... Greatest Length
**GL** .......... Green Library [*See also BVM*] [*Saint Egreve, France*] (EAIO)
**GL** .......... Green Light (MSA)
**GL** .......... Greenland [*ANSI two-letter standard code*] (CNC)
**gl** .......... Greenland [*MARC country of publication code*] [*Library of Congress*] (LCCP)
**GL** .......... Grenade Launcher (AABC)
**GL** .......... Grid Leak
**GL** .......... Gronlandsfly Ltd. [*Denmark*] [*ICAO designator*] (FAAC)
**GL** .......... Gross Line [*Insurance*]
**GL** .......... Ground Level
**GL** .......... Guild Library [*Church of Scotland*] [*A publication*]
**GL** .......... Guitar and Lute [*A publication*]
**GL** .......... Gun Lay [*or Laying*] [*RADAR*]
**GL** .......... Gun Laying RADAR
**GL** .......... Gun Licence [*British*] (DAS)
**GL** .......... Gunnery Lieutenant [*British military*] (DMA)
**GL** .......... L-Glutamic [*acid*] and L-Lysine [*Copolymer*]
**GL** .......... Lanier Lake Regional and Gwinnett County Library, Lawrenceville, GA [*Library symbol*] [*Library of Congress*] (LCLS)
**4GL** .......... Fourth-Generation Language [*Computer language*]
**GLA** .......... Gamma-Linoleic Acid [*Organic chemistry*]
**GLA** .......... Gamma-Linolenic Acid
**GLa** .......... Gazette de Lausanne [*A publication*]
**GLA** .......... General Laboratory Associates
**GLA** .......... General Learning Ability
**GLA** .......... General Ledger Account (AFM)
**GLA** .......... General Library Assistant [*Australia*]
**GLA** .......... General Lighthouse Authority [*British*]
**GLA** .......... Gingivolinguoaxial [*Dentistry*]
**GLA** .......... Glamis [*California*] [*Seismograph station code, US Geological Survey*] (SEIS)
**Gla** .......... [*Rannulf de*] Glanvill's Tractatus de Legibus [*A publication*] (DSA)
**GLA** .......... Glasgow [*Scotland*] [*Airport symbol*] (OAG)
**GLA** .......... Glass [*Automotive engineering*]
**GLA** .......... Gold Star Resources, Inc. [*Vancouver Stock Exchange symbol*]
**GLA** .......... Great Lakes Aviation Ltd. [*Spencer, IA*] [*FAA designator*] (FAAC)
**GLA** .......... Gross Leasable Area
**GLA** .......... Group Life Assurance [*British*]
**GLA** .......... Groupe de Liberation Armee [*Armed Liberation Group*] [*Guadeloupe*] (PD)
**GLA** .......... Guadeloupe Liberation Army
**GLA** .......... Gulkana, AK [*Location identifier*] [*FAA*] (FAAL)
**GLA** .......... Gust Load Alleviation [*Aviation*]
**GLAAD** .......... Gay and Lesbian Alliance Against Defamation (EA)
**GLAADS** .......... Gun Low-Altitude Air Defense System (NASA)
**Gla Bi** .......... Glasul Bisericii [*A publication*]
**GLAC** .......... Gay and Lesbian Association of Choruses (EA)
**GLAC** .......... General Ledger Account Code
**GLAC** .......... Glacial
**GLAC** .......... Glacier National Park
**Glacier Nat History Assoc Special Bull** ... Glacier Natural History Association. Special Bulletin [*A publication*]
**GLACSEC** ... Group of Latin American and Caribbean Sugar Exporting Countries [*See also GEPLACEA*] [*Mexico City, Mexico*] (EAIO)
**GLAD** .......... Gladiator Fighter Aircraft [*British*] (DSUE)
**GLAD** .......... Gladiolus (DSUE)
**GLAD** .......... GLOTRAC [*Global Tracking*] Adjustment
**GLAD** .......... Government and Legal Affairs Division [*American Occupational Therapy Association*]
**GLAD** .......... Greater London Association for the Disabled. Quarterly [*A publication*]
**GLAD** .......... Grenade Launcher Attachment Development (MCD)
**GLAD** .......... Group Learning about Drugs
**GLADB** .......... Gladiolus [*A publication*]
**GLADIS** .......... Ground-LASER Attack Designator/Identification System (MCD)
**GLADS** .......... Gun Low-Altitude Air Defense System
**GLAG** .......... Ginzburg-Landau-Abrikosov-Gorkov [*Superconductivity theory*]
**GLagC** .......... La Grange College, La Grange, GA [*Library symbol*] [*Library of Congress*] (LCLS)
**GLagCM** ... Callaway Mills Co., Technical Library, LaGrange, GA [*Library symbol*] [*Library of Congress*] (LCLS)
**GLAIU** .......... Gledaliski List Akademije za Igralsko Umetnost [*A publication*]
**GLAKES** ... Great Lakes (MUGU)
**GLAL** .......... German Life and Letters [*A publication*]
**GLAM** .......... Glamorganshire [*County in Wales*]
**GLAM** .......... Glamour [*or Glamourous*] (DSUE)
**GLAM** .......... Greying, Leisured, Affluent, and Married [*Lifestyle classification*] [*British*]
**Glamorgan Hist** ... Glamorgan Historian [*A publication*]
**GLAMS** .......... Glamorganshire [*County in Wales*]
**GLANCE** ... Global Lightweight Airborne Navigation Computer Equipment
**Glan El Cas** ... Glanville's English Election Cases [*A publication*] (DLA)
**Glan LLB** ... Glanville's De Legibus et Consuetudinibus Angliae [*A publication*] (DLA)
**Glanv** .......... Glanville's De Legibus et Consuetudinibus Angliae [*A publication*] (DLA)
**Glanv El Cas** ... Glanville's English Election Cases [*A publication*] (DLA)
**Glanvil** .......... Glanville's De Legibus et Consuetudinibus Angliae [*A publication*] (DLA)
**GLAPPAR** ... General Ledger, Accounts Payable, and Accounts Receivable [*Accounting*]
**GLARE** .......... Ground-Level Attack, Reconnaissance, and Electronic Countermeasures (MCD)
**GLARP** .......... Grupo Latinoamericano de Rehabilitacion Profesional [*Latin American Vocational Rehabilitation Group*] [*Bogata, Colombia*] (EAIO)
**Glas** .......... Glascock's Reports in All the Courts of Ireland [*A publication*] (DLA)
**GLAS** .......... Glasgow [*Scotland*]
**Glas** .......... Glasnik [*A publication*]
**Glas Appar** ... Glas und Apparat [*A publication*]
**Glasc** .......... Glascock's Reports in All the Courts of Ireland [*A publication*] (DLA)
**Glas Casop Poljopriv Vodopriv Vet Sumar AKMO** ... Glasnik Casopis za Poljoprivredu Vodoprivredu. Veterinarstvo i Sumarstvo AKMO [*A publication*]
**Glascock** .......... Glascock's Reports in All the Courts of Ireland [*A publication*] (DLA)
**Glas-Email-Keramo-Tech** ... Glas-Email-Keramo-Technik [*West Germany*] [*A publication*]
**Glas Em Ker** ... Glas-Email-Keramo-Technik [*A publication*]
**Glasers Ann** ... Glasers Annalen [*A publication*]
**Glasers Ann ZEV** ... Glasers Annalen ZEV [*Zeitschrift fuer Eisenbahnwesen und Verkehrstechnik*] [*A publication*]
**GLASG** .......... Glasgow [*Scotland*] (ROG)
**Glasg Dent J** ... Glasgow Dental Journal [*A publication*]
**Glasg Med J** ... Glasgow Medical Journal [*A publication*]
**Glasg Nat** ... Glasgow Naturalist [*A publication*]
**GlasgOrTrans** ... Glasgow University. Oriental Society. Transactions [*Glasgow*] [*A publication*]
**Glasgow AJ** ... Glasgow Archaeological Journal [*A publication*]
**Glasgow Archaeol J** ... Glasgow Archaeological Journal [*A publication*]
**Glasgow Arch J** ... Glasgow Archaeological Journal [*A publication*]

**Glasgow Art R** ... Glasgow Art Gallery and Museums Association. Review [*A publication*]
**Glasgow Med J** ... Glasgow Medical Journal [*A publication*]
**Glasgow Nat** ... Glasgow Naturalist [*A publication*]
**Glasg Univ Publ** ... Glasgow University. Publications [*A publication*]
**Glas Hem Drus (Beograd)** ... Glasnik Hemijskog Drustva (Beograd) [*A publication*]
**Glas Hem Drus Kralj Jugosl** ... Glasnik Hemijskog Drustva Kraljevine Jugoslavije [*A publication*]
**Glas Hemicara Technol Bosne Hercegovine** ... Glasnik Hemicara i Technologa Bosne i Hercegovine [*Yugoslavia*] [*A publication*]
**Glas Hem Technol Bosne Hercegovine** ... Glasnik Hemicara i Technologa Bosne i Hercegovine [*A publication*]
**Glas Hochvak Tech** ... Glas- und Hochvakuum Technik [*A publication*]
**Glas Hochv Techn** ... Glas- und Hochvakuum Technik [*A publication*]
**Glas-Instrum-Tech** ... Glas-Instrument-Technik [*West Germany*] [*A publication*]
**Glas Khem Drush (Beogr)** ... Glasnik Khemijskog Drushtva (Beograd) [*A publication*]
**GLASLA** ... Great Lakes - St. Lawrence Association
**Glas Mat**.... Glasnik Matematicki [*A publication*]
**Glas Mat-Fiz Astron** ... Glasnik Matematicko-Fizicki i Astronomski [*Yugoslavia*] [*A publication*]
**Glas Math J** ... Glasgow Mathematical Journal [*A publication*]
**Glas Mat Ser III** ... Glasnik Matematicki. Serija III [*A publication*]
**Glasn**.......... Glasnik [*A publication*]
**Glasn Biol Sekc Hrv Prir Dr** ... Glasnik. Bioloske Sekcije. Hrvatsko Prirodoslovno Drustvo [*A publication*]
**Glasn Hem Drust (Beogr)** ... Glasnik Hemijskog Drustva (Beograd) [*A publication*]
**Glasnik Mat Ser III** ... Glasnik Matematicki. Serija III. Drustvo Matematicara i Fizicara SR Hrvatske. [*A publication*]
**Glasnik Sumar Fak Univ Beogradu** ... Glasnik Sumarskog Fakulteta Univerzitet u Beogradu [*A publication*]
**Glasnik Tsentral Khig Zavoda (Beograd)** ... Glasnik Tsentralnogo Khigiyenskog Zavoda (Beograd) [*A publication*]
**Glas Prir Muz Beogradu Ser A** ... Glasnik Prirodnjackog Muzeja u Beogradu. Serija A. Mineralogija, Geologija, Paleontologija [*A publication*]
**Glas Prir Muz Beogradu Serija A** ... Glasnik Prirodnjackog Muzeja u Beogradu. Serija A. Mineralogija, Geologija, Palentologija [*Yugoslavia*] [*A publication*]
**Glas Prir Muz Srp Zemlje Ser A** ... Glasnik Prirodnjackog Muzeja Srpske Zemlje. Serija A. Mineralogiya, Geologija, Paleontologija [*A publication*]
**Glas Repub Zavoda Zast Prir Prir Muz Titogradu** ... Glasnik Republickog Zavoda za Zastitu Prirode i Prirodnjackog Muzeja Titogradu [*A publication*]
**GLASS** ...... Geodetic LASER Survey System
**GLASS** ...... Germanium-Lithium Argon Scanning System (NRCH)
**Glass** .......... Glassworks [*A publication*]
**GlasSAN** ... Glas. Srpska Akademija Nauka [*A publication*]
**Glass Aust** ... Glass in Australia [*A publication*] (APTA)
**Glass Ceram** ... Glass and Ceramics [*A publication*]
**Glass and Ceram** ... Glass and Ceramics [*A publication*]
**GLASSEX** ... Glass Technology and Fabrication Exhibition (TSPED)
**Glassf Ev**.... Glassford on Evidence [*A publication*] (DLA)
**Glasshouse Crops Res Inst Annu Rep** ... Glasshouse Crops Research Institute. Annual Report [*A publication*]
**Glass Ind**.... Glass Industry [*A publication*]
**Glass Int** .... Glass International [*A publication*]
**Glas Srp Akad Nauka** ... Glas. Srpska Akademija Nauka i Umetnosti Odeljenje Medicinskih Nauka [*A publication*]
**Glas Srp Akad Nauka Umet Od Prir Mat Nauka** ... Glas. Srpska Akademija Nauka i Umetnosti Odeljenje Prirodno-Matematickikh Nauka [*A publication*]
**Glas Srp Akad Nauk Umet Od Med Nauk** ... Glas. Srpska Akademija Nauka i Umetnosti Odeljenje Medicinskih Nauka [*A publication*]
**Glas Srpska Akad Nauka Umet Od Prir-Mat Nauka** ... Glas. Srpska Akademija Nauka i Umetnosti Odeljenje Prirodno-Matematickikh Nauka [*A publication*]
**Glass Tech** ... Glass Technology [*A publication*]
**Glass Technol** ... Glass Technology [*A publication*]
**Glas Sumske Pokuse** ... Glasnik za Sumske Pokuse [*A publication*]
**GLAS & SW** ... Glasgow & South-Western [*Railway*] [*Scotland*] (ROG)
**Glass Wkrs News** ... Glass Workers News [*A publication*]
**Glastech Ber** ... Glastechnische Berichte [*A publication*]
**Glastek Tidskr** ... Glasteknisk Tidskrift [*Sweden*] [*A publication*]
**Glastek Tidskrift** ... Glasteknisk Tidskrift [*A publication*]
**GLAT**......... Government Lot Acceptance Test [*Military*] (CAAL)
**GLAU** ........ General Labourers' Amalgamated Union [*British*]
**Glaube 2 Welt** ... Glaube in der 2 Welt [*A publication*]
**GLAUD4**... Glaucoma [*A publication*]
**Glaxo Vol**... Glaxo Volume [*A publication*]
**GLB** ........... Gas [*or Grease*] Lubricated Bearing
**GLB** ........... Girls' Life Brigade [*British*]
**GLB** ........... Glass in Barrels [*Freight*]
**GLB** ........... Glass Block (AAG)
**GLB** ........... Great Lakes Freight Bureau Inc., Cleveland OH [*STAC*]
**GLBA**......... Glacier Bay National Monument
**GLBC**......... Great Lakes Bancorp, a Federal Savings Bank [*NASDAQ symbol*] (NQ)
**GLBC**......... Great Lakes Basin Commission [*Terminated, 1981*] (EGAO)
**GLBCAK**... Gleanings in Bee Culture [*A publication*]
**GLBM** ....... Ground-Launched Ballistic Missile
**GLBO** ........ Glenbow [*A publication*]
**GLBS**......... Globes [*Freight*]
**GLBU** ........ Buchanan [*Liberia*] [*ICAO location identifier*] (ICLI)
**GLC** ........... Galactic Resources Ltd. [*Toronto Stock Exchange symbol*] [*Vancouver Stock Exchange symbol*] [*AMEX symbol*]
**GLC** ........... Gas-Liquid Chromatography [*Analytical chemistry*]
**GLC** ........... Gate Leakage Current
**GLC** ........... Gay and Lesbian Caucus (EA)
**GLC** ........... General Learning Corporation [*of Time, Inc.*]
**GLC** ........... Generator Line Contractor (NASA)
**GLC** ........... German Language Club (EA)
**GLC** ........... Glaucoma
**GLC** ........... Global LORAN Navigation Chart [*Air Force*]
**GLC** ........... Glossari di Lingua Contemporanea [*A publication*]
**Glc**............. Glucose [*Also, G, GLUC*] [*A sugar*]
**GLC** ........... Great Lakes Club (EA)
**GLC** ........... Great Lakes Commission (EA)
**GLC** ........... Great Little Car [*Mazda Motors of America*]
**GLC** ........... Greater London Council [*Information service or system*] (IID)
**GLC** ........... Philadelphia, PA [*Location identifier*] [*FAA*] (FAAL)
**GLCA** ........ Gallery of Living Catholic Authors [*Defunct*] (EA)
**GLCA** ........ Glen Canyon National Recreation Area
**GlcA**........... Gluconic Acid [*Biochemistry*]
**GLCA** ........ Great Lakes Colleges Association (EA)
**GLCM** ....... Graduate Diploma of the London College of Music [*British*] (DBQ)
**GLCM** ....... Ground-Launched Cruise Missile [*Pronounced "glick-em"*]
**GLCM** ....... Robertsport/Cape Mount [*Liberia*] [*ICAO location identifier*] (ICLI)
**GlcN**........... Glucosamine [*Biochemistry*]
**GLCN** ........ Gold Coin Mining, Inc. [*NASDAQ symbol*] (NQ)
**GLCNA** ...... German Lutheran Conference of North America (EA)
**GlcNac**....... N-Acetylglucosamine
**GLCP**......... Harper/Cape Palmas [*Liberia*] [*ICAO location identifier*] (ICLI)
**GlcUA**........ Glucuronic Acid [*Also, GA*] [*Biochemistry*]
**GLD** ........... Cases in the Griqualand West Local Division of the Supreme Court [*1910-46*] [*South Africa*] [*A publication*] (DLA)
**GLD** ........... Gas Leak Detector
**GLD** ........... General Learning Disability
**GLD** ........... Glide Slope [*Aviation*] (NASA)
**GLD** ........... Glider
**GLD** ........... Gold (MSA)
**GLD** ........... Golden [*Colorado School of Mines*] [*Colorado*] [*Seismograph station code, US Geological Survey*] (SEIS)
**GLD** ........... Goodland [*Kansas*] [*Airport symbol*] (OAG)
**GLD** ........... Gould, Inc. [*NYSE symbol*] (SPSG)
**GLD** ........... Gross Logical Design
**GLD** ........... Ground-LASER Designators (RDA)
**GLD** ........... Guild
**Gld** ............ Guilder [*Modification of gulden*] [*Monetary unit*] [*Netherlands*]
**GLDA** ........ Gay and Lesbian Democrats of America (EA)
**GLDC** ........ Golden Enterprises, Inc. [*NASDAQ symbol*] (NQ)
**GLDF**......... Gold Fields of South Africa Ltd. [*NASDAQ symbol*] (NQ)
**GLDMS**..... Groupe de Liaison de Docimologues en Milieu Scolaire [*Canada*]
**gldn** ............ Golden [*Philately*]
**GLD PLTD** ... Gold Plated [*Freight*]
**GLDR** ........ Glider (FAAC)
**GLDR** ........ Gold Reserve Corp. [*NASDAQ symbol*] (NQ)
**GLDR** ........ Groupe Liberal, Democratique, et Reformateur (EAIO)
**GLDS**......... Gemini Launch Data System [*NASA*] (MCD)
**GLDT** ........ Gas LASER Discharge Tube
**GLE** ........... Gainesville, TX [*Location identifier*] [*FAA*] (FAAL)
**GLE** ........... GLE Resources Ltd. [*Vancouver Stock Exchange symbol*]
**GLE** ........... Gleason Corp. [*NYSE symbol*] (SPSG)
**GLE** ........... Glenmuick [*New Zealand*] [*Seismograph station code, US Geological Survey*] [*Closed*] (SEIS)
**GLE** ........... Government-Loaned Equipment (MSA)
**GLE** ........... Grade Level Equivalent [*Educational testing*]
**GLE** ........... Ground-Level Event [*Geophysics*]
**GLE** ........... Ground Liaison Element (MCD)
**GLEAM**..... Graphic Layout and Engineering Aid Method
**Glean Bee Cult** ... Gleanings in Bee Culture [*A publication*]
**Gleanings**... Gleanings in Bee Culture [*A publication*]
**Gleanings Bee Cult** ... Gleanings in Bee Culture [*A publication*]
**GLECS** ...... Groupe Linguistique d'Etudes Chamito-Semitiques. Comptes Rendus [*A publication*]
**GLEDIC** .... Great Lakes Environmental Information Center [*Ann Arbor, MI*]
**GLEEP** ...... Graphite Low-Energy Experimental Pile [*Nuclear reactor*] [*British*]
**GLEF** ......... Geothermal Loop Experimental Facility [*Department of Energy*]
**GLEIS** ....... Great Lakes Environmental Information Sharing

**GLEN** ........ Global Environmental Corp. [*NASDAQ symbol*] (NQ)
**Gl Ency** ...... Globe Encyclopaedia [*A publication*] (ROG)
**GLENDAL** ... Glendalough [*Valley in Ireland*] (ROG)
**Glendale Law R** ... Glendale Law Review [*A publication*]
**Glendale L Rev** ... Glendale Law Review [*A publication*]
**Glen High** .. Glen's Highway Laws [*A publication*] (DLA)
**Glenn** ......... Glenn's Annual Reports [*16-18 Louisiana*] [*A publication*] (DLA)
**Glen Pub H** ... Glen on the Public Health Laws [*A publication*] (DLA)
**Glen Reg** .... Glen on Registration of Births and Deaths [*A publication*] (DLA)
**GLEP** ......... Group for Lunar Exploration and Planning (MCD)
**GLERL** ...... Great Lakes Environmental Research Laboratory [*Ann Arbor, MI*] [*National Oceanic and Atmospheric Administration*] (GRD)
**GLERR** ...... Great Lakes Ecosystem Restoration and Rehabilitation [*Canada*] (ASF)
**GLET** ......... Government Logistics Evaluation and Testing (MCD)
**GLF** ............ Gaussian Lens Formula [*Optics*]
**GLF** ............ Gay Liberation Front
**GLF** ............ General Telephone Company of Florida [*NYSE symbol*] (SPSG)
**GLF** ............ Generalized Lambda Family [*Statistics*]
**GLF** ............ Glass Fiber [*Technical drawings*]
**GLF** ............ Golfito [*Costa Rica*] [*Airport symbol*] (OAG)
**GLF** ............ Great Lakes Fisheries Laboratory, Ann Arbor, MI [*OCLC symbol*] (OCLC)
**GLF** ............ Gulf (FAAC)
**GLF** ............ McGill University, Law Library [*UTLAS symbol*]
**GLFALSK** ... Gulf of Alaska [*FAA*] (FAAC)
**GLFC** ......... Georganne LaPiere Fan Club (EA)
**GLFC** ......... Ginger Lynn Fan Club (EA)
**GLFC** ......... Gloria Loring Fan Club (EA)
**GLFC** ......... Great Lakes Fishery Commission [*Canada and United States*] (NOAA)
**GLFC** ......... Guiding Light Fan Club (EA)
**GLFCAL** ...... Gulf of California (FAAC)
**GLFDCC** ... Great Lakes Fish Disease Control Committee [*Canada*] (ASF)
**GLFL** ......... Great Lakes Fishery Laboratory [*Department of the Interior*] (GRD)
**GLFM** ........ Gulf Mirror [*A publication*]
**GLFMEX** .. Gulf of Mexico [*FAA*] (FAAC)
**GLFRB** ...... Great Lakes Fisheries Research Branch [*Canadian Department of Fisheries and Oceans*] [*Research center*] (RCD)
**GLFRC** ...... Great Lakes Forest Research Centre [*Environment Canada*] [*Research center*] (RCD)
**GlFRP** ........ Glass-Fiber-Reinforced Plastic [*Also, GFRP*]
**GLFS** ......... Great Lakes Federal Savings & Loan Association [*NASDAQ symbol*] (NQ)
**GLFSTLAWR** ... Gulf of St. Lawrence [*FAA*] (FAAC)
**GLFT** ......... Gulf Times [*A publication*]
**GLG** ........... Glamis Gold Ltd. [*Toronto Stock Exchange symbol*]
**GLG** ........... Glengyle [*Australia*] [*Airport symbol*] (OAG)
**GLG** ........... La Grange College, La Grange, GA [*OCLC symbol*] (OCLC)
**GLGE** ......... Greenville/Sinoe [*Liberia*] [*ICAO location identifier*] (ICLI)
**GLGSA** ...... Geologist [*New York*] [*A publication*]
**GLGV** ........ Glamis Gold Ltd. [*NASDAQ symbol*] (NQ)
**GLGYB** ...... Geology [*A publication*]
**GLGYBA** ... Geology [*Boulder*] [*A publication*]
**GlH** ............ Glass Hill [*A publication*]
**GLH** ........... Glue Line Heating
**GLH** ........... Go Like Hell [*In model name Omni GLH, proposed for Dodge car designed by Carroll Shelby*]
**GLH** ........... Greenville [*Mississippi*] [*Airport symbol*] (OAG)
**GLH** ........... Gwent Local History [*A publication*]
**GLHA** ........ Great Lakes Harbor Association (EA)
**GLH-S** ....... Goes Like Hell - Some More [*In model "GLH-S," Dodge car designed by Carroll Shelby*] [*Facetious translation: "Goes Like Hell - Squared"*]
**GLHS** ........ Great Lakes Historical Society (EA)
**GLHS** ........ Ground-Launched HELLFIRE System (MCD)
**GLHSC** ...... Gay and Lesbian History on Stamps Club (EA)
**GLI** ............ Gamma LINAC Instrumentation
**GLI** ............ Glass Industry [*A publication*]
**GLI** ............ Glen Innes [*Australia*] [*Airport symbol*] (OAG)
**GLI** ............ Glider
**GLI** ............ Global Income Plus Fund, Inc. [*NYSE symbol*] (CTT)
**GLI** ............ Glucagon-Like Immunoreactivity [*or Immunoreactant*] [*Endocrinology*]
**GLI** ............ Grandma Lee's, Incorporated [*Toronto Stock Exchange symbol*]
**GLI** ............ Gurkha Light Infantry [*British military*] (DMA)
**GLIAC** ....... Great Lakes Intercollegiate Athletic Conference
**GLIB** ......... Government Libraries in Belconnen [*Australia*]
**GliBad** ........ Glider Badge [*Military decoration*]
**GLIC** .......... General Ledger Identification Code (AFM)
**GLICF** ........ Grandma Lee's, Incorporated [*NASDAQ symbol*] (NQ)
**GLIJ** .......... Greater London Intelligence Journal [*A publication*]
**GLIM** ........ General Linear Modeling Program [*Data processing*]
**GLIMPCE** ... Great Lakes International Multidisciplinary Program on Crustal Evolution [*Geophysics*]
**Glimp Kash Cult** ... Glimpses of Kashmir Culture [*A publication*]
**GLIMPSE** ... Global Limb Photometric Scanning Experiment (MCD)
**GLIN** .......... Georgia Library Information Network [*Library network*]
**GLINT** ........ Global Intelligence (IEEE)
**GLINT** ........ Gospel Literature International (EA)
**GLIP** .......... Glide and Skip [*Bombing mission*]
**GLIPAR** .... Guide Line Identification Program for Antimissile Research [*ARPA*]
**GLIPAR** .... Guidelines for Investigation, Planning, and Research
**GLIS** .......... Gleaner Life Insurance Society [*Adrian, MI*] (EA)
**GLIS** .......... Glissando [*Gliding*] [*Music*] (ROG)
**GLIS** .......... Government Library and Information Service [*Tasmania, Australia*]
**GLISA** ....... Government Losses in Shipment Act [*1937*]
**GLISCAC** ... Government Library and Information Service Computer Applications Committee [*Australia*]
**Gliss** ........... Glissando [*Gliding*] [*Music*]
**GLit** ............ Gazeta Literara [*A publication*]
**GLITCH** .... Goblin Loose in the Computer Hut [*Data processing*]
**GLJ** ............ Gates LearJet Corp. [*AMEX symbol*] (SPSG)
**Gl & J** ......... Glyn and Jameson's English Bankruptcy Reports [*1821-28*] [*A publication*] (DLA)
**GLK** ........... Golden Lake Resources Ltd. [*Vancouver Stock Exchange symbol*]
**GLK** ........... Great Lakes Chemical Corp. [*NYSE symbol*] (SPSG)
**GLK** ........... Northaire [*Davisburg, MI*] [*FAA designator*] (FAAC)
**GLKPA** ...... Gidroliznaya i Lesokhimicheskaya Promyshlennost [*A publication*]
**GLL** ........... General Leaseholds Limited [*Toronto Stock Exchange symbol*]
**GLL** ........... German Life and Letters [*A publication*]
**GL & L** ....... German Life and Letters [*A publication*]
**GLL** ........... Gilgames and the Land of the Living (BJA)
**GLL** ........... Gill, CO [*Location identifier*] [*FAA*] (FAAL)
**GLL** ........... Great Lakes Laboratory [*State University College at Buffalo*] [*Research center*] (RCD)
**GLL** ........... GULL, Inc. [*AMEX symbol*] (SPSG)
**GLL** ........... McGill University Library [*UTLAS symbol*]
**GLLB** ......... Buchanan [*Liberia*] [*ICAO location identifier*] (ICLI)
**GLLD** ......... Ground-LASER Locator Designator (MCD)
**GLLD-E** ..... Ground-LASER Locator Designator-Evaluator (MCD)
**GLLD-TNS** ... Ground-LASER Locator Designator-Thermal Night Sight (MCD)
**GLLD/VLLD** ... Ground-LASER Locator Designator/Vehicular LASER Locator Designator (MCD)
**GLLKA** ...... Great Lakes Lighthouse Keepers Association (EA)
**GLLM** ....... German Language and Literature Monographs [*A publication*]
**GLLNS** ...... German Life and Letters. New Series [*A publication*]
**GLLO** ........ Great Lakes Licensed Officers' Organization
**GLM** .......... Generalized Lagrangian Multiplier [*Military*] (AFIT)
**GLM** .......... Generalized Linear Model [*Statistics*]
**GLM** .......... Gilmore [*Alaska*] [*Also, GLN*] [*Seismograph station code, US Geological Survey*] (SEIS)
**GLM** .......... Global Marine, Inc. [*NYSE symbol*] (SPSG)
**GLM** .......... Government-Loaned Material
**GLM** .......... Graduated Length Method [*of learning to ski*] [*Later, Accelerated Length Method*]
**GLM** .......... Grand Livre du Mois [*Best-selling book of the month*] [*French*]
**GLM** .......... Graphics Lathe Module [*McDonnell-Douglas Automation Co.*]
**GLM** .......... Great Lakes Megalopolis [*Proposed name for possible "super-city" formed by growth and mergers of other cities*]
**GLM** .......... Growth-Limiting Medium [*For microorganisms*]
**GLM** .......... McGill University, Medical Library [*UTLAS symbol*]
**GLMA** ....... Glassmaster Co. [*NASDAQ symbol*] (NQ)
**GLMA** ....... Great Lakes Mink Association (EA)
**GLMC** ....... Gay and Lesbian Media Coalition (EA)
**GLMC** ....... Monrovia City [*Liberia*] [*ICAO location identifier*] (ICLI)
**GLMDD** .... GIT [*Glas- und Instrumenten-Technik*] Labor-Medizin [*A publication*]
**GLMI** ........ Great Lakes Maritime Institute (EA)
**GLMMM** .. Grand Lodge of Mark Master Masons [*Freemasonry*]
**GLMMS** .... Groupement Latin et Mediterraneen de Medecine du Sport [*Latin and Mediterranean Group for Sport Medicine - LMGSM*] (EAIO)
**GLMR** ....... Monrovia/Spriggs Payne [*Liberia*] [*ICAO location identifier*] (ICLI)
**GlmRS** ....... Glutaminyl-RNA Synthetase [*An enzyme*]
**Gl M Sar** .... Glasnik Zemaljskog Muzeja u Sarajevu [*A publication*]
**GLMWC** ... Great Lakes and Marine Waters Center [*University of Michigan*] [*Research center*] (RCD)
**GLN** .......... Gilmore [*Alaska*] [*Also, GLM*] [*Seismograph station code, US Geological Survey*] (SEIS)
**GLN** .......... Glen
**GLN** .......... Glenayre Electronics Ltd. [*Toronto Stock Exchange symbol*]
**GLN** .......... Glenfed, Inc. [*NYSE symbol*] (SPSG)
**Gln** ............ Glutamine [*or Glu($NH_2$)*] [*Also, Q*] [*An amino acid*]
**GLNA** ....... Nimba [*Liberia*] [*ICAO location identifier*] (ICLI)
**GlnRS** ....... Glutamine-Transfer Ribonucleic Acid Synthetase
**GLNTC** ..... Great Lakes Naval Training Center
**GLO** .......... Clovis, NM [*Location identifier*] [*FAA*] (FAAL)
**GLO** .......... General Land Office [*Became part of Bureau of Land Management, 1946*]

**GLO**........... Get the Lead Out [*Of GLO week, sponsored by American Oil Co.*]
**Glo**............. Global
**GLO**........... Global Ocean Carriers Ltd. [*AMEX symbol*] (CTT)
**GLO**........... Globe Ocean Carriers Ltd. [*AMEX symbol*] (CTT)
**GLO**........... Gloucester [*British depot code*]
**GLO**........... Gloucester [*Massachusetts*] [*Seismograph station code, US Geological Survey*] (SEIS)
**GLO**........... Glyoxalase [*An enzyme*]
**GLO**........... Goddard Launch Operations [*NASA*]
**GLO**........... Graecolatina et Orientalia [*A publication*]
**G LO**.......... Grand Lodge [*Freemasonry*] (ROG)
**GLO**........... Ground Liaison Officer [*Military*]
**GLO**........... Ground Logistics Operations [*NASA*] (KSC)
**GLO**........... Guaiacol-Linoleic Acid Hydroperoxide Oxidoreductase [*An enzyme*]
**GLO**........... Gunnery Liaison Officer [*Navy*]
**GLO**........... GVN [*Government of Vietnam*] Liaison Officer
**GLO**........... L-Gulanolactone Oxidase [*An enzyme*]
**GLO**........... Ultra Glow Cosmetics [*Vancouver Stock Exchange symbol*]
**Gloag & Henderson** ... Gloag and Henderson's Introduction to the Law of Scotland [*7th ed.*] [*1968*] [*A publication*] (DLA)
**GLOAS**...... German Liaison Office for the Armament Sector [*Military*]
**GLOB**........ Globular
**GLOB**........ Globulin
**Global Anal Pure Appl Adv** ... Global Analysis Pure and Applied. Advanced [*A publication*]
**Global Atmos Res Programme Publ Ser** ... Global Atmospheric Research Programme. Publications Series [*A publication*]
**Global Commun** ... Global Communications [*A publication*]
**Global One** ... Global 2000. Report to the President. Volume 1 [*United States*] [*A publication*]
**Global Two** ... Global 2000. Report to the President. Volume 2 [*United States*] [*A publication*]
**GLOBE**...... Global Lending and Overseas Banking Evaluator [*Chase Econometrics*] [*Database*]
**GLOBECOM** ... Global Communications System [*Air Force*]
**Globe Mail Rep Bus Globe Mail Ltd** ... Globe and Mail Report on Business. Globe and Mail Limited [*A publication*]
**GLOC**........ Ground Line of Communications (AFM)
**GLOCK**..... Glockenspiel [*Music*]
**GLOCOM** ... Global Communications System [*Air Force*]
**GLOL**........ Golay Logic Operating Language
**GLOM**....... Gross Lift-Off Mass [*NASA*] (KSC)
**GLOMB**.... Glide Bomb [*Air Force*]
**GLOMEX** ... Global Oceanographic and Meteorological Experiment [*Marine science*] (MSC)
**GLOMR**.... Global Low-Orbiting Message Relay [*Satellite*]
**GLONASS** ... Global Navigation Satellite System [*Military*]
**GLOP**........ Gevic Logic Operation Program
**GLOPAC**... Gyroscopic Low-Power Attitude Control
**Gl Ord**........ Glossa Ordinaria [*A publication*] (DSA)
**GLORIA**.... Geological Long-Range Inclined ASDIC
**GLOS**........ Glossary
**GLOS**........ Gloucestershire [*County in England*]
**GLOS**........ Gun Line of Site [*Tank*] [*Army*]
**GLOSS**...... Global Ocean Surveillance System (IEEE)
**GLOSS**...... Glossary
**Glossary Acarol Terminol** ... Glossary of Acarological Terminology [*A publication*]
**Gloss Lat**.... Glossaria Latina [*A publication*] (OCD)
**GLOSTER** ... Gloucester [*City in England*] (ROG)
**GLOTRAC** ... Global Tracking [*RADAR*]
**GLOUC**..... Gloucester [*City in England*] (ROG)
**GLOUC**..... Gloucestershire [*County in England*] (ROG)
**GLOUC R** ... Gloucestershire Regiment [*Military*] [*British*] (ROG)
**GLOUCS**... Gloucestershire [*County in England*]
**Glov Mun Cor** ... Glover's Municipal Corporations [*A publication*] (DLA)
**GLOW**....... Global RADAR for Ocean Waves
**Glow**.......... Glow International [*A publication*]
**GLOW**....... Gross Lift-Off Weight [*NASA*]
**GLOW**....... Ground Lift-Off Weight [*NASA*] (NASA)
**GLOXAC**... Gloxinian [*A publication*]
**GLP**........... Gastrointestinal and Liver Physiology [*A publication*]
**GLP**........... Gelled Liquid Propellant
**GLP**........... General Layout Plan (NATG)
**GLP**........... GOAL [*Ground Operations Aerospace Language*] Language Processor (MCD)
**GLP**........... Golden Princess [*Vancouver Stock Exchange symbol*]
**GLP**........... Golpazari [*Turkey*] [*Also, GPA*] [*Seismograph station code, US Geological Survey*] (SEIS)
**GLP**........... Good Laboratory Practice [*FDA*]
**GLP**........... Gospel Light Publications [*British*]
**GLP**........... Gould Investors LP [*AMEX symbol*] (SPSG)
**GLP**........... Government-Lent Property (NG)
**GLP**........... Greek Literary Papyri [*A publication*] (OCD)
**GLP**........... Gross Lawyer Product [*Term for measurement of the income of attorneys*]
**GLP**........... Guadeloupe [*ANSI three-letter standard code*] (CNC)
**GLP**........... Guide Line Paper [*of Washington Standardization Officers*] [*Military*]
**GLPA**......... Gay and Lesbian Press Association (EA)
**GLPA**......... Great Lakes Pilotage Administration [*Department of Transportation*]
**GLP-AACR** ... Gibraltar Labour Party - Association for the Advancement of Civil Rights [*Political party*] (PPW)
**GLPAAG**... Glass Packer [*A publication*]
**GLPC**......... Gas-Liquid Partition Chromatography
**GLPCI**....... Gay and Lesbian Parents Coalition International (EA)
**GLPG**......... Glow Plug
**GLPIAC**.... Great Lakes Physical Information Analysis Center
**GLPP**......... Glucose, Post Prandial [*Clinical chemistry*]
**GLPR**......... Goldstone Predict [*Orbit identification*] [*NASA*]
**GLPU**........ Gasline Planning Update. Northwest Alaska Pipeline Company. Manpower and Impact Planning Department [*A publication*]
**GLQ**........... Golden Adit Resources [*Vancouver Stock Exchange symbol*]
**GLQ**........... Greater-than-Lot Quantities
**GLR**........... Garcia Lorca Review [*A publication*]
**GLR**........... Gaylord, MI [*Location identifier*] [*FAA*] (FAAL)
**GLR**........... Gazette Law Reports [*New Zealand*] [*A publication*] (DLA)
**GLR**........... General Line Rate [*Advertising*]
**GLR**........... Georgia Law Review [*A publication*]
**GLR**........... Ghana Law Reports [*A publication*]
**GLR**........... Gladiator Resources Ltd. [*Vancouver Stock Exchange symbol*]
**GLR**........... Glass LASER Rod
**GLR**........... Graphic Level Recorder
**GLR**........... Grolier, Inc. [*NYSE symbol*] (SPSG)
**GLR**........... Groom Lake Road [*Nevada*] [*Seismograph station code, US Geological Survey*] (SEIS)
**GLR**........... Gujarat Law Reporter [*A publication*]
**GLR**........... McGill University Rare Books [*UTLAS symbol*]
**GLRB**......... Monrovia/Roberts International [*Liberia*] [*ICAO location identifier*] (ICLI)
**GLRBAT**... Great Britain. Land Resources Division. Land Resource Bibliography [*A publication*]
**GLRC**......... Gas-Liquid Radiochromatography [*Analytical chemistry*]
**GLRE**......... Geniki Laiki Rizospastiki Enosis [*General Union of Populists and Radicals*] [*Greek*] (PPE)
**GLRev**........ Great Lakes Review [*A publication*]
**GLR (NZ)**.. Gazette Law Reports [*New Zealand*] [*A publication*] (DLA)
**GLRS**......... Geodynamics LASER Ranging System [*NASA*]
**GLRSAC**... Great Britain. Land Resources Development Centre. Land Resource Study [*A publication*]
**GLRSHLD** ... Glare Shield (MCD)
**GLS**............ Galveston [*Texas*] [*Airport symbol*] (OAG)
**GLS**............ Gaylord Circulation Control System [*Information service or system*] (IID)
**GLS**............ General Lighting Service
**GLS**............ General Line School
**GLS**............ Generalized Least Squares [*Statistics*]
**GLS**............ Giles [*Australia*] [*Seismograph station code, US Geological Survey*] (SEIS)
**GLS**............ Glide Slope [*Aviation*] (MSA)
**GLS**............ Golden Shield Resources Ltd. [*Toronto Stock Exchange symbol*] [*Vancouver Stock Exchange symbol*]
**GLS**............ Graduate Library School
**GLS**............ Grand Lodge of Scotland [*Freemasonry*]
**GLS**............ Great Lakes Screw
**GLS**............ Green LASER System
**GLS**............ Ground Launch Sequence [*or Sequencer*] (NASA)
**GLS**............ Gypsy Lore Society, North American Chapter (EA)
**GLSA**......... General Ledger Subsidiary Account (AFM)
**GLSA**......... General Livestock Agent
**GLSA**......... Gray Line Sightseeing Assòciation [*Commercial firm*] (EA)
**GLSA**......... Great Lakes Seaplane Association (EA)
**GlSAN**........ Glas. Srpska Akademija Nauka [*A publication*]
**GLSBG**...... Great Lakes Sugar Beet Growers (EA)
**GLSDA6**.... Geologia Sudetica [*Warsaw*] [*A publication*]
**GLSE**......... Generalized Weighted Least Squares Estimates [*Statistics*]
**GLSECT**.... Ground Liaison Section [*Military*] [*British*]
**GLSFC**....... Great Lakes Sport Fishing Council (EA)
**GLSGW**..... Glasgow [*Scotland*]
**GLSK**......... Sanniquellie [*Liberia*] [*ICAO location identifier*] (ICLI)
**GLSM**........ Gold Life Saving Medal [*Military decoration*]
**GLSNG-L** ... Gledaliski List Slovenskega Narodnega Gledalisca v Ljubljane [*A publication*]
**GLSNG-M** ... Gledaliski List Slovenskega Narodnega Gledalisca v Mariboru [*A publication*]
**GLSOA**...... Great Lakes Ship Owners Association (EA)
**GLSPA8**.... Glasnik za Sumske Pokuse [*A publication*]
**GLSS**......... Ground-Launch Support System (MCD)
**GLST**......... Sasstown [*Liberia*] [*ICAO location identifier*] (ICLI)
**GLSTM**...... Graduate of the London School of Tropical Medicine (DAS)
**GLT**........... Gas LASER Tube
**GLT**........... General Labor and Trades
**GLT**........... Gilt [*Bookbinding*] (ROG)
**GLT**........... Gladstone [*Australia*] [*Airport symbol*] (OAG)
**GLT**........... Glass Lined Tubing
**GLT**........... Glatfelter [*P. H.*] Co. [*AMEX symbol*] (SPSG)
**GLT**........... Golden Lion Tamarin [*South American monkey*]
**GLT**........... Greeting Letter Telegram (ADA)

**GLT** .......... Gridded Line of Thrust (MCD)
**GLT** .......... Ground-LASER Tracking
**GLT** .......... Guide Light (AAG)
**GL(T)** .......... Gun-Laying (Turret) (DEN)
**GLTMC** ..... Golden Lion Tamarin Management Committee (EA)
**GlTN** .......... Glomerulo-Tubulo-Nephritis [*Medicine*]
**GLTN** .......... Guillotine (MSA)
**GLTN** .......... Tchien [*Liberia*] [*ICAO location identifier*] (ICLI)
**GLTX** .......... Goldtex, Inc. [*NASDAQ symbol*] (NQ)
**GLU** .......... Gambia Labour Union
**GLU** .......... General Logic Unit [*Computer chip*]
**GLU** .......... Global Land Use [*NASA*]
**Glu** .......... Glutamic Acid [*Also, E, GA*] [*An amino acid*]
**GLU** .......... Great Lakes United (EA)
**GLU** .......... Green Lake Resources Ltd. [*Vancouver Stock Exchange symbol*]
**GLU** .......... Gruene Liste Umweltschutz [*Green List Ecology*] [*Federal Republic of Germany*] (PPE)
**GLUC** .......... Glucose [*Also, G, Glc*] [*A sugar*]
**GLUCEPTATE** ... Glucoheptonate [*Organic chemistry*] [*USAN*]
**Glueckauf-Forschungsh** ... Glueckauf-Forschungshefte [*A publication*]
**Glu(NH$_2$)** ... Glutamine [*or Gln*] [*Also, Q*] [*An amino acid*]
**GLV** .......... Gemini Launch Vehicle [*NASA*]
**GLV** .......... Globe Valve (AAG)
**GLV** .......... Golden Vale Explorations Corp. [*Vancouver Stock Exchange symbol*]
**GLV** .......... Golovin [*Alaska*] [*Airport symbol*] (OAG)
**GLV** .......... Gross Leukemia Virus
**GLVA** .......... Voinjama [*Liberia*] [*ICAO location identifier*] (ICLI)
**GLVOAK** .. Glaxo Volume [*A publication*]
**GLVS** .......... Galveston Resources Ltd. [*NASDAQ symbol*] (NQ)
**GLW** .......... Corning, Inc. [*NYSE symbol*] [*Wall Street slang name: "Glow Worm"*] (SPSG)
**GLW** .......... Glasgow, KY [*Location identifier*] [*FAA*] (FAAL)
**GLW** .......... Gunnery Lieutenant's Writer [*British military*] (DMA)
**GLWB** .......... Glazed Wallboard [*Technical drawings*]
**GLWDA** .... Great Lakes Waterways Development Association (EA)
**GLX** .......... Galela [*Indonesia*] [*Airport symbol*] (OAG)
**GLX** .......... Glaxo Holdings PLC [*NYSE symbol*] (SPSG)
**Glx** .......... Glutamic Acid [*or Glutamine*] [*Also, Z*] [*An amino acid*]
**GLX** .......... Goldex Mines Ltd. [*Toronto Stock Exchange symbol*]
**GLX** .......... McGill University RECON [*UTLAS symbol*]
**GLXI** .......... Glenex Industries, Inc. [*NASDAQ symbol*] (NQ)
**GLY** .......... Clinton, MO [*Location identifier*] [*FAA*] (FAAL)
**GLY** .......... Galaxy Minerals, Inc. [*Toronto Stock Exchange symbol*]
**gly** .......... Glycinate [*Organic chemistry*]
**Gly** .......... Glycine [*Also, G*] [*An amino acid*]
**GLY** .......... Glycol (KSC)
**GLY** .......... Gully (ADA)
**GLYC** .......... Glycerin
**GLYCEROPH** ... Glycerophophas [*Pharmacy*] (ROG)
**GLYCN** ..... Glycerine
**Glyc in W** ... Glycerin in Water [*Medicine*] (DHSM)
**GLYCYRRH** ... Glycyrrhiza [*Licorice*] [*Pharmacology*] (ROG)
**Gly-IPC** .... Glycinergic Interplexiform Cell [*Physiology*]
**GLYME** ..... Ethylene Glycol Dimethyl Ether [*Also, DME,EGDE*] [*Organic chemistry*]
**Glyn & J** ..... Glyn and Jameson's English Bankruptcy Reports [*1821-28*] [*A publication*] (DLA)
**Glyn & Jam** ... Glyn and Jameson's English Bankruptcy Reports [*1821-28*] [*A publication*] (DLA)
**Glyn & J (Eng)** ... Glyn and Jameson's English Bankruptcy Reports [*1821-28*] [*A publication*] (DLA)
**Glynn Wat Pow** ... Glynn on Water Powers [*A publication*] (DLA)
**Glyph Jon H** ... Glyph. Johns Hopkins Textual Studies [*A publication*]
**GLYPNIR** ... [A] programming language [*1970*] (CSR)
**GlyR** .......... Glycine Receptor [*Organic chemistry*]
**GLYT** .......... Genlyte Group, Inc. [*NASDAQ symbol*] (NQ)
**GLZ** .......... Glaze (MSA)
**GLZ** .......... Great Lakes Group, Inc. [*Toronto Stock Exchange symbol*]
**GLZD** .......... Glazed
**GM** .......... Aerocenter [*Sweden*] [*ICAO designator*] (FAAC)
**GM** .......... Gabexate Mesilate [*A proteolytic enzyme inhibitor*]
**GM** .......... Gainesville Midland Railroad Co. [*AAR code*]
**G/M** .......... Gallons per Minute
**gm** .......... Gambia [*MARC country of publication code*] [*Library of Congress*] (LCCP)
**GM** .......... Gambia [*ANSI two-letter standard code*] (CNC)
**Gm** .......... Gamma [*Subgroup of IgG*] [*Immunology*]
**GM** .......... Gandhi Marg [*A publication*]
**GM** .......... Gas Meter
**GM** .......... Gaseous Mixture (MSA)
**GM** .......... Gastric Mucosa [*Medicine*]
**GM** .......... Gay Male [*Classified advertising*]
**GM** .......... Gazeta Musical [*A publication*]
**G-M** .......... Geiger-Mueller [*Radiation counter*]
**GM** .......... General Maintenance [*Army*]
**GM** .......... General Maintenance Aptitude Area [*Military*] (AFIT)
**GM** .......... General Manager
**GM** .......... General Medicine
**GM** .......... General Meetings [*Quakers*]
**GM** .......... General Merchandise
**GM** .......... General Merit [*Military*]
**GM** .......... General Mortgage [*Bond*]
**GM** .......... General Motors Corp. [*NYSE symbol*] [*Toronto Stock Exchange symbol*] (SPSG)
**G & M** .......... General and Municipal
**GM** .......... Gentamicin [*Antibacterial compound*]
**GM** .......... Gentil Membre [*Guest of Club Mediterranee, a vacation cooperative*]
**GM** .......... Gentleman's Magazine [*A publication*]
**GM** .......... Geographical Magazine [*A publication*]
**GM** .......... Geometric Mean
**GM** .......... George Medal [*British*]
**GM** .......... Giant Melanoma [*Oncology*]
**gm** .......... Gigameter
**GM** .......... Gill-Morrell [*Valve oscillator*] (DEN)
**GM** .......... Giornale di Metafisica [*A publication*]
**G & M** .......... Girth and Mirth (EA)
**GM** .......... Global Marketplace
**GM** .......... Gluteus Medius [*Anatomy*]
**GM** .......... Gold Medal
**GM** .......... Gold Medallist (DAS)
**GM** .......... Golf Course Operations and Management Programs [*Association of Independent Colleges and Schools specialization code*]
**GM** .......... Good Mason [*Freemasonry*] (ROG)
**GM** .......... Good Morning [*Amateur radio*]
**GM** .......... Gopher Music Notes [*A publication*]
**GM** .......... Gradient Mixer [*Chromatography*]
**GM** .......... Grail Movement (EA)
**GM** .......... Gram
**GM** .......... Gramophone Motor (DEN)
**GM** .......... Grand Mal [*Epilepsy*]
**GM** .......... Grand Marshal [*Freemasonry*] (ROG)
**GM** .......... Grand Master [*Freemasonry*]
**GM** .......... Grand Medal [*Ghana*]
**GM** .......... Grand Minister [*Freemasonry*] (ROG)
**GM** .......... Grand Multiparity [*Obstetrics*]
**GM** .......... Grandmother
**G/M** .......... Granulocyte/Macrophage [*Ratio*] [*Hematology*]
**GM** .......... Gravitational Mass
**GM** .......... Great Musicians [*A publication*]
**GM** .......... Greater Manchester [*County in England*]
**GM** .......... Greenwich Meridian
**G-M** .......... Grid-to-Magnetic Angle [*Navigation*] (INF)
**GM** .......... Grid Modulation
**GM** .......... Grog Money [*British military*] (DMA)
**GM** .......... Gross Motor
**GM** .......... Ground Malfunction
**GM** .......... Ground Mode
**GM** .......... Group Mark [*Data processing*]
**GM** .......... Group Mobile (CINC)
**GM** .......... Group MODEM (MCD)
**GM** .......... Guam [*IYRU nationality code*] (IYR)
**GM** .......... Guard Mail
**GM** .......... Guided Missile
**G & M** .......... Gulf & Mississippi Railroad
**GM** .......... Gun-Laying Mark I [*RADAR*]
**GM** .......... Gun Mount [*Military*] (CAAL)
**GM** .......... Gunmetal
**GM** .......... Gunner's Mate [*Navy rating*]
**GM** .......... Gypsy Moths [*An association*] (EA)
**GM** .......... Metacentric Height [*Naval architecture*]
**GM** .......... Monosialoganglioside [*Chemistry*]
**Gm** .......... Mutual Conductance
**GM** .......... Swedair i Vaxjo AB [*Sweden*] [*ICAO designator*] (FAAC)
**GM** .......... Washington Memorial Library, Middle Georgia Regional Library, Macon, GA [*Library symbol*] [*Library of Congress*] (LCLS)
**GM1** .......... Gunner's Mate, First Class [*Navy rating*]
**GM2** .......... Gunner's Mate, Second Class [*Navy rating*]
**GM3** .......... Gunner's Mate, Third Class [*Navy rating*]
**GMA** .......... Game Manufacturers Association (EA)
**GMA** .......... Gas Metal Arc
**GMA** .......... Gemena [*Zaire*] [*Airport symbol*] (OAG)
**GMA** .......... Gen State Airlines [*Hayden Lake, ID*] [*FAA designator*] (FAAC)
**GMA** .......... General Maintenance Aptitude [*Military*] (MCD)
**GMA** .......... General Mental Ability
**GMA** .......... Geomechanics Abstracts [*Rock Mechanics Information Service*] [*Bibliographic database*] [*British*]
**GMA** .......... Giant Molecular Association [*Galactic science*]
**GMA** .......... Gilt Market Analysis [*MMS International*] [*Information service or system*] (CRD)
**GMA** .......... Glycidyl Methacrylate [*Organic chemistry*]
**GMA** .......... Glycol Methacrylate [*Organic chemistry*]
**GMA** .......... Good Morning America [*Television program*]
**GMA** .......... Gospel Music Association (EA)
**GMA** .......... Government Modification Authorization (AAG)
**GMA** .......... Graduate Management Association [*Australia*]

**GMA**.......... Granite Mountain [*Alaska*] [*Seismograph station code, US Geological Survey*] (SEIS)
**GMA**.......... Grocery Manufacturers of America (EA)
**GM/A**........ Ground Meat/Analyzer [*USDA*]
**GMA**.......... Growth and Maturation Activity [*Biochemistry*]
**GMA**.......... Guided Missile Ammunition (AABC)
**GMA**.......... Whitefield, NH [*Location identifier*] [*FAA*] (FAAL)
**GMAA**....... Agadir/Inezgane [*Morocco*] [*ICAO location identifier*] (ICLI)
**GMAA**....... Gold Mining Association of America
**GMAC**....... Gaining Motor Air Command (MCD)
**GMAC**....... Gas Metal Arc Cutting [*Welding*]
**GMAC**....... General Motors Acceptance Corporation
**GMAC**....... Genetic Manipulation Advisory Committee [*Australia*]
**GMAC**....... Graduate Management Admission Council [*Los Angeles, CA*] (EA)
**GMAD**....... General Motors Allison Division
**GMAD**....... General Motors Assembly Division
**GMAG**....... Genetic Manipulation Advisory Group [*British*]
**G Mag**........ Geological Magazine [*A publication*]
**GMAIC**..... Guided Missile and Aerospace Intelligence Committee (AFM)
**GMAJCOM**... Gaining Major Command [*Military*] (AFM)
**GMAL**....... General Electric Macro Assembly Language (NASA)
**G Mal Infett Parassit**... Giornale di Malattie Infettive e Parassitarie [*A publication*]
**GMAMA**... Gemeinsames Amtsblatt. Ausgabe A [*A publication*]
**GMAP**....... General Macroassembly Program [*Honeywell, Inc.*]
**GMAP**....... Generalized Macroprocessor
**GMARA**.... Geomagnetism and Aeronomy [*English Translation*] [*A publication*]
**GMarC**...... Cobb County-Marietta Public Library, Marietta, GA [*Library symbol*] [*Library of Congress*] (LCLS)
**GMarK**...... Kennesaw College, Marietta, GA [*Library symbol*] [*Library of Congress*] (LCLS)
**GMarLG**.... Lockheed-Georgia Co., Scientific and Technical Information Department, Marietta, GA [*Library symbol*] [*Library of Congress*] (LCLS)
**GMarS**....... Southern Technical Institute, Marietta, GA [*Library symbol*] [*Library of Congress*] (LCLS)
**GMAS**....... Glovers' Mutual Aid Society [*A union*] [*British*]
**GMAS**....... Ground Munitions Analysis Study (AABC)
**GMASI**...... Graduate Member of the Ambulance Service Institute [*British*] (DBQ)
**GMAT**....... Graduate Management Admission Test
**GMAT**....... Greenwich Mean Astronomical Time
**GMAT**....... Tan-Tan/Plage Blanche [*Morocco*] [*ICAO location identifier*] (ICLI)
**GMATS**..... General Motors Air Transport System
**GMAW**...... Gas Metal Arc Welding
**GMAW-P**... Gas Metal Arc Welding - Pulsed Arc
**GMAW-S**.. Gas Metal Arc Welding - Short Circuiting Arc
**GMAX**....... Graphics Multi-Axis Module [*McDonnell-Douglas Automation Co.*]
**GMAZ**....... Zagora [*Morocco*] [*ICAO location identifier*] (ICLI)
**GMB**.......... Gambela [*Ethiopia*] [*Airport symbol*] (OAG)
**GMB**.......... Gambia [*ANSI three-letter standard code*] (CNC)
**GMB**.......... General Mortgage Bond
**GMB**.......... Glass Microballoon (MCD)
**GMB**.......... Global Management Bureau
**GMB**.......... Good Merchantable Brand [*Business term*]
**GMB**.......... Good Morning Britain [*Early morning television program*] [*ITV*] [*British*]
**GMB**.......... Grand Master of the Bath [*British*]
**GMB**.......... Green Mountain Boy [*Pseudonym used by Henry Stevens*]
**GMB**.......... Guided Missile Brigade [*Army*]
**GMBATU**... General Municipal Boilermakers' and Allied Trades Union [*British*]
**GMBE**....... Grand Master of the Order of the British Empire (EY)
**GMBF**........ Gastric Mucosal Blood Flow [*Medicine*]
**GmbH**........ Gesellschaft mit Beschraenkter Haftung [*Limited Liability Company*] [*German*]
**GmbH & CoKG**... Gesellschaft mit Beschraenkter Haftung und Kommanditgesellschaft [*Combined Limited Partnership and Limited Liability Company*] [*German*]
**GmbHG**..... Gesetz Betreffend der Gesellschaft mit Beschraenkter Haftung [*Law Governing Limited Liability Company*] [*German*] (ILCA)
**GMBL**....... Gimbal (AAG)
**GMBS**........ Glenn Miller Birthplace Society (EA)
**GMC**.......... Ganglion Mother Cell [*Cytology*]
**GMC**.......... General Medical Council [*British*]
**GmC**........... General Microfilm Co., Cambridge, MA [*Library symbol*] [*Library of Congress*] (LCLS)
**GMC**.......... General Military Course (AFM)
**GMC**.......... General Monte Carlo Code [*Data processing*]
**GMC**.......... General Motors Corporation
**GMC**.......... Georgia Military College [*Milledgeville*]
**GMC**.......... Geostar Mining Corp. [*Vancouver Stock Exchange symbol*]
**GMC**.......... Germanic [*Language, etc.*]
**GMC**.......... Gerner-Mathisen Chartering AS [*Norway*] (DS)
**GMC**.......... Giant Molecular Cloud [*Cosmology*]
**GMC**.......... Gordon Military College [*Georgia*]
**GMC**.......... Grivet Monkey Cell Line
**GMC**.......... Gross Maximum Capacity [*Electronics*] (IEEE)
**GMC**.......... Ground Mobile Cenetheodolite
**GMC**.......... Ground Movement Controller
**GMC**.......... Groundwater Management Caucus (EA)
**GMC**.......... Gruen Marketing Corporation [*AMEX symbol*] (SPSG)
**GMC**.......... Guaranteed Mortgage Certificate [*Federal Home Loan Mortgage Corp.*]
**GMC**.......... Guard-Cell Mother Cell [*Botany*]
**GMC**.......... Guided Missile Control (AAG)
**GMC**.......... Gun Motor Carriage
**GMC**.......... Gunner's Mate, Chief [*Navy rating*]
**GMC**.......... Middle Georgia College, Cochran, GA [*OCLC symbol*] (OCLC)
**GMCB**....... Gunner's Mate, Construction Battalion [*Navy rating*]
**GMCBA**.... Gunner's Mate, Construction Battalion, Armorer [*Navy rating*]
**GMCBP**..... Gunner's Mate, Construction Battalion, Powderman [*Navy rating*]
**GMCC**....... General Magnaplate Corporation [*NASDAQ symbol*] (NQ)
**GMCC**....... Geophysical Monitoring for Climatic Change [*National Oceanic and Atmospheric Administration*]
**GMCC**....... Ground Mobile Command Center
**GMCF**....... Goddard Mission Control Facility [*NASA*] (KSC)
**GMCF**....... Guided Missile Control Facility (AAG)
**GMCI**........ Giftware Manufacturers' Credit Interchange (EA)
**GMCL**....... Ground Measurements Command List (MCD)
**GMCM**...... Guided Missile Countermeasure [*NATO*]
**GMCM**...... Gunner's Mate, Master Chief [*Navy rating*]
**GMCO**....... Guided Missile Control Officer (AAG)
**GMCR**....... Globe Mackay Cable and Radio Corp. [*Philippines*] [*Telecommunications*] (TSSD)
**GMCS**....... Gunner's Mate, Senior Chief [*Navy rating*]
**GM-CSA**... Granulocyte-Macrophage Colony-Stimulating Activity [*Hematology*]
**GM-CSF**.... Granulocyte-Macrophage Colony-Stimulating Factor [*Biochemistry*]
**GMCT**....... Giftware Manufacturers Credit Interchange (EA)
**GMCY**....... Grant-Makers for Children and Youth (EA)
**GMD**.......... General Management Directive
**GMD**.......... General Marine Distress
**GMD**.......... Geometric Mean Distance
**GMD**.......... Geometrodynamics
**GMD**.......... Gesellschaft fuer Mathematik und Datenverarbeitung [*Society for Mathematics and Data Processing*] [*Federal Republic of Germany*] [*Information service or system*] (IID)
**GMD**.......... Government Maintenance Depot (MCD)
**GMD**.......... Ground Meteorological Detector [*or Device*]
**GMDA**....... Golf Manufacturers and Distributors Association (EA)
**GMDA**....... Groundwater Management Districts Association (EA)
**GMDA**....... Group Method of Determining Arguments [*Equation*]
**GMDC**....... General Merchandise Distributors Council [*Colorado Springs, CO*] (EA)
**GMDCB4**.. Geographia Medica [*A publication*]
**GMDD**....... Guided Missile Development Division [*NASA*] (KSC)
**GMDEP**.... Guided Missile Data Exchange Program [*Navy*]
**GMDH**...... Group Method of Data Handling [*Mathematical technique*]
**GMDIL**..... General Motors Distribution Ireland Limited [*Dublin, Ireland*]
**GMD-IZ**.... GMD-Informationszentrum fuer Informationswissenschaft und -Praxis [*GMD Information Center for Information Science and Information Work*] [*Information service or system*] (EISS)
**GMDP**....... Guaranteed Minimum Delivery Price (ADA)
**GMDRL**.... General Motors Defense Research Laboratory (MCD)
**GMDS**....... German Military Documents Section [*of AGO, Army*] [*World War II*]
**GM Dud**..... Dudley's Georgia Reports [*A publication*] (DLA)
**GM Dudl**.... Dudley's Georgia Reports [*A publication*] (DLA)
**GME**.......... Gelatine Manufacturers of Europe (EAIO)
**GME**.......... General Microelectronics
**GME**.......... Generic Macro Expander [*Telecommunications*] (TEL)
**GME**.......... German Minimum Economy [*Allied German Occupation Forces*]
**GME**.......... Gilt Marbled Edges [*Bookbinding*]
**GME**.......... Gimbal Mounted Electronics (KSC)
**GME**.......... Glimmer Resources, Inc. [*Vancouver Stock Exchange symbol*]
**GME**.......... Globe Microphone Evaluation
**GME**.......... Gmelinite [*A zeolite*]
**GME**.......... Graduate Medical Education [*Program*] [*Army*]
**GME**.......... Greater Middle East
**GME**.......... Green, M. E., Jefferson City MO [*STAC*]
**GME**.......... Guided Missile Evaluator
**GMECH**.... General Mechanic (FAAC)
**GMED**....... [*The*] GMI Group, Inc. [*NASDAQ symbol*] (NQ)
**G Med Mil**... Giornale di Medicina Militare [*A publication*]
**GMEFC**..... Golden Memories of Elvis Fan Club (EA)
**GMEL**....... Groupement des Mathematiciens d'Expression Latine [*Group of Mathematicians of Romance Languages - GMRL*] (EAIO)
**GMEM**...... GPC [*General Purpose Computer*] Memory (NASA)
**GMENAC**... Graduate Medical Education National Advisory Committee [*Department of Health and Human Services*]
**GME-PC**... General Motors Europe - Passenger Cars [*Switzerland*]

**GMET** ....... General Metal & Abrasives Co. [*Romulus, MI*] [*NASDAQ symbol*] (NQ)
**GMET** ....... Graphical Munitions Effects Tables (MCD)
**GMET** ....... Gun Metal
**G Metaf**...... Giornale di Metafisica [*A publication*]
**GMetO** ...... Group Meteorological Officer [*British military*] (DMA)
**GMEVALU** ... Guided Missile Evaluation Unit (MUGU)
**GMEX** ....... Garcia's of Scottsdale [*NASDAQ symbol*] (NQ)
**GMF** .......... Galactic Magnetic Field
**GMF** .......... General Motors Corp. and Fanuc Ltd. [*In company name GMF Robotics Corp.*]
**GMF** .......... Generalized Mainline Framework [*Data processing*]
**GMF** .......... Glass Manufacturers Federation
**GMF** .......... Glass Microfilter
**GMF** .......... Glial Maturation Factor [*Biochemistry*]
**GMF** .......... Ground Mobile Forces [*Military*] (RDA)
**GMF** .......... Ground Monitor Facility (MCD)
**GMF** .......... Guided Missile Facilities (NG)
**GMF** .......... Milwaukee, WI [*Location identifier*] [*FAA*] (FAAL)
**GMFA** ........ Ouezzane [*Morocco*] [*ICAO location identifier*] (ICLI)
**GMFC** ....... Gary Morris Fan Club (EA)
**GMFC** ....... Guided Missile Fire Control
**GMFCS** ..... Guided Missile Fire Control System (NG)
**GMFD** ....... Germania Bank FSB [*NASDAQ symbol*] (NQ)
**GMFF**........ Fes/Saiss [*Morocco*] [*ICAO location identifier*] (ICLI)
**GMFI**......... Ifrane [*Morocco*] [*ICAO location identifier*] (ICLI)
**GMFJ** ........ Ghana Movement of Freedom and Justice [*Political party*]
**GMFK** ....... Er-Rachidia [*Morocco*] [*ICAO location identifier*] (ICLI)
**GMFM** ...... Meknes/Bassatine [*Morocco*] [*ICAO location identifier*] (ICLI)
**GMFMC** ... Gulf of Mexico Fishery Management Council (MSC)
**GMFN** ....... Nador/Taouima [*Morocco*] [*ICAO location identifier*] (ICLI)
**GMFO** ....... Oujda/Angads [*Morocco*] [*ICAO location identifier*] (ICLI)
**GMFP**........ Guided Missile Firing Panel
**GMFRBP** .. Ghana. Fishery Research Unit. Marine Fishery Research [*A publication*]
**GMFS**........ Ground Mobile Forces/Tactical Satellite Communications Program
**GMFSC** ..... Ground Mobile Forces Satellite Communications (MCD)
**GMFT**........ Touahar [*Morocco*] [*ICAO location identifier*] (ICLI)
**GMF/TACSAT** ... Ground Mobile Forces/Tactical Satellite Communications (MCD)
**GMFU** ...... Fes/Sefrou [*Morocco*] [*ICAO location identifier*] (ICLI)
**GMFZ** ....... Taza [*Morocco*] [*ICAO location identifier*] (ICLI)
**GMG**.......... Gott Mein Gut [*God Is My Good*] [*German*] [*Motto of Karl, Margrave of Baden-Durlach (1529-77); Ernst Friedrich, (1560-1604)*]
**GMG**.......... Grenade Machine Gun [*Military*]
**GMG**.......... Gross Maximum Generation [*Electronics*] (IEEE)
**GMG**.......... Gunner's Mate, Guns [*Navy rating*]
**GMGB** ....... Guards Machine Gun Battalion [*British military*] (DMA)
**GMGR** ....... Guards Machine Gun Regiment [*British military*] (DMA)
**GMGRU**.... Guided Missile Group (MUGU)
**GMGS** ....... Guided Missile General Support (MCD)
**GMGW**...... Geraghty & Miller, Inc. [*NASDAQ symbol*] (NQ)
**GMGZA** .... Gas Magazine [*A publication*]
**GMH** ......... General Motors-Holden's Ltd. [*Australia*] (ADA)
**GMH** ......... Georgia Mental Health Institute, Atlanta, GA [*OCLC symbol*] (OCLC)
**gmh** ............ German, Middle High [*MARC language code*] [*Library of Congress*] (LCCP)
**GMH** ......... Greenville, KY [*Location identifier*] [*FAA*] (FAAL)
**GMHC**....... Gay Men's Health Crisis (EA)
**GMHC**....... Grease Monkey Holding Corp. [*NASDAQ symbol*] (NQ)
**GMHE**....... General Motors Hughes Electronics Corp.
**GMI** ........... Galtaco, Inc. [*Toronto Stock Exchange symbol*]
**GMI** ........... Garnes Mountain [*Idaho*] [*Seismograph station code, US Geological Survey*] (SEIS)
**GMI** ........... Gasmata [*Papua New Guinea*] [*Airport symbol*] (OAG)
**GMI** ........... Gelatin Manufacturers Institute of America (EA)
**GMI** ........... Gemini Fund, Inc. [*NYSE symbol*] (SPSG)
**GMI** ........... General Medical Intelligence (MCD)
**GMI** ........... General Mills, Incorporated, Minneapolis, MN [*OCLC symbol*] (OCLC)
**GMI** ........... Global Marine, Inc. (NOAA)
**GMI** ........... Goddard Management Instruction [*NASA*]
**g/mi**........... Gram per Mile [*Automotive engineering*]
**GMI** ........... Guarantee Material Inspection (MCD)
**GMI** ........... Guaranteed Minimum Income (ADA)
**GMIA** ........ Gelatin Manufacturers Institute of America (EA)
**GMIC** ........ General Microelectronics Corporation [*NASDAQ symbol*] (NQ)
**GMIC** ........ Graphic Memory Interface Controller [*Computer chip*]
**G Microbiol** ... Giornale di Microbiologia [*A publication*]
**GMIE** ........ Grand Master of the Order of the Indian Empire [*British*]
**GMI-EMI** ... General Motors Institute - Engineering and Management Institute [*Flint, MI*]
**GMIF**......... Gandhi Memorial International Foundation (EA)
**GMII** ......... Guaranteed Market Index Investment [*Canada*]
**GMiM** ....... Georgia Military College, Milledgeville, GA [*Library symbol*] [*Library of Congress*] (LCLS)
**GMI Mech E** ... Graduate Member of the Institution of Mechanical Engineers [*British*]
**GMIP** ........ General Motors Improvement Project [*Investigating team sponsored by consumer-advocate Ralph Nader*]
**GMIS**......... Generalized Management Information System
**GMIS**......... Government Management Information Sciences (EA)
**GMI Short Pap Oreg Dep Geol Miner Ind** ... GMI Short Paper. Oregon Department of Geology and Mineral Industries [*A publication*]
**GMit** .......... Germanistische Mitteilungen. Zeitschrift des Belgischen Germanisten- und Deutschlehrerverbandes [*A publication*]
**GMiW**........ Georgia College, Milledgeville, GA [*Library symbol*] [*Library of Congress*] (LCLS)
**GMJ** .......... Macon Junior College, Macon, GA [*Library symbol*] [*Library of Congress*] (LCLS)
**GMJC**........ Green Mountain Junior College [*Vermont*]
**GMJSU**..... Gems, Minerals, and Jewelry Study Unit (EA)
**GMK**.......... Gold Mark Minerals [*Vancouver Stock Exchange symbol*]
**GMK**.......... Grand Master Key [*Locks*] (ADA)
**GMK**.......... Green Monkey Kidney Cell
**GMK**.......... Gyromagnetic Kompass
**GMKP** ....... Grand Master of the Knights of St. Patrick
**GML**.......... Galvanometer-Mirror Lightbeam
**GML**.......... General Measurement Loop (MCD)
**GML**.......... Generalized Markup Language [*Data processing*]
**GML**.......... Glycerol Monolaurate [*Food-grade lipid*] [*Pharmacology*]
**GML**.......... Gold Maple Leaf [*Canadian coin*]
**GML**.......... Gold-Medal Resources Limited [*Vancouver Stock Exchange symbol*]
**GML**.......... Goldrich Maritime Line (DS)
**GML**.......... Gorgas Memorial Laboratory [*Panama*] [*Research center*] (RCD)
**GML**.......... Grand Master's Lodge [*Freemasonry*] (ROG)
**GML**.......... Graphic Machine Language
**GML**.......... Guided Missile Launcher (NG)
**GML**.......... Mercer University, Law Library, Macon, GA [*OCLC symbol*] (OCLC)
**GMLDG**.... Garnish Molding [*Mechanical engineering*]
**GMLS**........ Guided Missile Launching System
**GMM**......... General Methods of Moments [*Statistics*]
**GMM**......... Goldsmith Minerals [*Vancouver Stock Exchange symbol*]
**GM-M** ....... Gram Meter
**GMM**......... Graphics Mill Module [*McDonnell-Douglas Corp.*]
**GMM**......... Gunner's Mate, Missile [*Navy rating*]
**GMM**......... Mercer University, Macon, GA [*Library symbol*] [*Library of Congress*] (LCLS)
**GMM**......... Mercer University, School of Medicine, Macon, GA [*OCLC symbol*] (OCLC)
**GMMA**...... Gas Meter Makers' Association [*A union*] [*British*]
**GMMA**...... Gloucester Master Mariners Association (EA)
**GMMA**...... Golda Meir Memorial Association (EA)
**GMMB**...... Ben Slimane [*Morocco*] [*ICAO location identifier*] (ICLI)
**GMMC**...... Casablanca/ANFA [*Morocco*] [*ICAO location identifier*] (ICLI)
**GMMD**...... Beni-Mellal [*Morocco*] [*ICAO location identifier*] (ICLI)
**GMME**...... Rabat/Sale [*Morocco*] [*ICAO location identifier*] (ICLI)
**GMMEA** ... Gaceta Medica de Mexico [*A publication*]
**GMMF**...... Sidi Ifni [*Morocco*] [*ICAO location identifier*] (ICLI)
**GMMG**...... Grand Master of the Order of St. Michael and St. George [*British*]
**GMMI**....... Essaouira [*Morocco*] [*ICAO location identifier*] (ICLI)
**GMMJ** ...... El Jadida [*Morocco*] [*ICAO location identifier*] (ICLI)
**GMMK**...... Khouribga [*Morocco*] [*ICAO location identifier*] (ICLI)
**GMM-L**..... Mercer University, School of Law, Macon, GA [*Library symbol*] [*Library of Congress*] (LCLS)
**GMMM**..... Casablanca [*Morocco*] [*ICAO location identifier*] (ICLI)
**GMMN** ..... Casablanca/Mohamed V [*Morocco*] [*ICAO location identifier*] (ICLI)
**GMMO** ..... Taroudant [*Morocco*] [*ICAO location identifier*] (ICLI)
**GMMR**...... General Mobilization Material Readiness [*DoD*]
**GMMRI** .... Georgia Mining and Mineral Research Institute [*Georgia Institute of Technology*] [*Research center*] (RCD)
**GMMS** ...... Safi [*Morocco*] [*ICAO location identifier*] (ICLI)
**GMMT**...... Casablanca/Tit-Mellil [*Morocco*] [*ICAO location identifier*] (ICLI)
**GMMX**...... Marrakech/Menara [*Morocco*] [*ICAO location identifier*] (ICLI)
**GMMY**...... Kenitra/Tourisme [*Morocco*] [*ICAO location identifier*] (ICLI)
**GMMZ**...... Quarzazate [*Morocco*] [*ICAO location identifier*] (ICLI)
**GMN** ......... Gorman [*TACAN station*] (MCD)
**GMN** ......... Gorman, CA [*Location identifier*] [*FAA*] (FAAL)
**GMN** ......... Greenman Brothers, Inc. [*AMEX symbol*] (SPSG)
**GMN** ......... Greenwich Mean Noon (ROG)
**GM & N**..... Gulf Mobile & Northern Railroad
**GMNA**....... Glutamyl(methoxy)naphthylamide [*Biochemistry*]
**GmNE**........ Graphic Microfilm of New England, Waltham, MA [*Library symbol*] [*Library of Congress*] (LCLS)
**GmNY**........ Graphic Microfilm Corp., Valley Stream, NY [*Library symbol*] [*Library of Congress*] (LCLS)

**GMO** ......... Gadolinium Molybdate
**GMO** ......... Genetically Manipulated Organism [*Biochemistry*]
**GMO** ......... Gill-Morrell Oscillator
**GMO** ......... Glyceryl Monooleate [*Organic chemistry*]
**GMO** ......... Groupe de Travail Charge de la Mise en Oeuvre de l'Information et de la Statistique Juridique [*Implementation Work Group on Justice Information and Statistics - IWG*] [*Canada*]
**GMO** ......... Guided Missile Officer
**GMO** ......... Gulf, Mobile & Ohio Railroad [*Later, Illinois Central Gulf Railroad*] [*AAR code*]
**GM & O**..... Gulf, Mobile & Ohio Railroad [*Later, Illinois Central Gulf Railroad*]
**GMoC**........ Colquitt-Thomas Regional Library, Moultrie, GA [*Library symbol*] [*Library of Congress*] (LCLS)
**GMOCU**.... Guided Missile Operation and Control Unit
**GMODC**.... General Motors Overseas Distribution Corporation
**G de Mon**... Guillelmus de Monte Lauduno [*Deceased, 1343*] [*Authority cited in pre-1607 legal work*] (DSA)
**GMOND**... Gewerkschaftliche Monatshefte [*A publication*]
**G de Mon Lau** ... Guillelmus de Monte Lauduno [*Deceased, 1343*] [*Authority cited in pre-1607 legal work*] (DSA)
**G de Mon Laud** ... Guillelmus de Monte Lauduno [*Deceased, 1343*] [*Authority cited in pre-1607 legal work*] (DSA)
**GMOO**...... Guided Missile Operations Officer (AAG)
**GMorGE**.... Genealogical Enterprises, Morrow, GA [*Library symbol*] [*Library of Congress*] (LCLS)
**GMP**.......... Garrison Military Police [*British*]
**GMP**.......... Gay Men's Press [*GMP is now the name of the company*]
**GMP**.......... Gemini Management Panel [*NASA*] (KSC)
**GMP**.......... General Management Plan [*National Park Service*]
**GMP**.......... General Matrix Program
**GMP**.......... General Medical Problem
**GMP**.......... Glycomacropeptide [*Biochemistry*]
**GMP**.......... Good Management Practice
**GMP**.......... Good Manufacturing Practice
**GMP**.......... Grand Master of the Order of St. Patrick
**GMP**.......... Granule Membrane Protein
**GMP**.......... Grass-Model Polygraph
**GMP**.......... Green Mountain Power Corp. [*NYSE symbol*] (SPSG)
**GMP**.......... Guanosine Monophosphate [*Biochemistry*]
**GMP**.......... Guaranteed Minimum Pension [*British*]
**GMP**.......... Guaranteed Minimum Price
**GMP**.......... Guide to Microforms in Print [*A publication*]
**GMP**.......... Gurkha Military Police [*British military*] (DMA)
**GMPA**....... General Material and Petroleum Activity [*NCAD*] [*Army*] (MCD)
**GMPC**....... Green Mountain Power Corporation (NRCH)
**GMPI**........ Guilford-Martin Personnel Inventory [*Psychology*]
**GMPMA**... General Material and Petroleum Management Agency (MCD)
**GMPPAW**... Glass, Molders, Pottery, Plastics, and Allied Workers International Union (EA)
**GMPR**....... General Maximum Price Regulation [*World War II*]
**GMPS**........ Great Masters in Painting and Sculpture [*A publication*]
**GMQ**......... Geomaque Explorations Ltd. [*Toronto Stock Exchange symbol*]
**GMQ**......... Good Marketable Quality [*Business term*]
**GMR**.......... Gambier Island [*French Polynesia*] [*Airport symbol*] (OAG)
**GMR**.......... General Mobilization Reserves [*DoD*]
**GMR**.......... General Modular Redundancy
**GMR**.......... General Motors Research
**GMR**.......... Geometric Mean Radii
**GMR**.......... Graphics Metafile Resources [*Data processing*]
**GMR**.......... Gromer Aviation, Inc. [*Versailles, MO*] [*FAA designator*] (FAAC)
**GMR**.......... Ground Mapping RADAR
**GMR**.......... Ground Mobile RADAR
**GMR**.......... Ground Movement RADAR [*Military*]
**GMR**.......... Group Medical Report
**GMR**.......... Grupo Marxista Revolucionario [*Marxist Revolutionary Group*] [*Portuguese*] [*Political party*] (PPE)
**GMRAO**.... General Mobilization Reserve Acquisition Objective [*DoD*]
**GMRC**....... Green Mountain Railroad Corporation [*AAR code*]
**GMRD**....... Guards Motorized Rifle Division (MCD)
**GMRD**....... Guided Missile Range Division [*NASA*] (KSC)
**GMRL**....... General Motors Corp. Research Laboratories [*Warren, MI*]
**GMRL**....... Grain Marketing Research Laboratory [*Department of Agriculture*] [*Manhattan, KS*] (GRD)
**GMRL**....... Group of Mathematicians of Romance Languages [*See also GMEL*] [*Coimbra, Portugal*] (EAIO)
**GMRLA**.... Research Publication. General Motors Corporation. Research Laboratories [*A publication*]
**GMRMO**... General Mobilization Reserve Materiel Objective [*DoD*]
**GMRMR**... General Mobilization Reserve Materiel Requirement [*DoD*]
**GMROI**..... Gross Margin Return on Investment [*Air carrier designation symbol*]
**GMRS**....... General Mobile Radio Service [*Telecommunications*] (TSSD)
**GMRS**....... General Mobilization Reserve Stock [*DoD*]
**GMRSO**.... General Mobilization Reserve Stockage Objective [*DoD*]
**GMRT**....... Gates MacGinitie Reading Test [*Educational test*]
**GMRWG**... Guided Missile Relay Working Group [*Navy*]
**GMS**.......... Gabriel Marcel Society (EA)
**GMS**.......... Gas Measurement System
**GMS**.......... Gelatin Matrix System
**GMS**.......... Gemeentestem; Weekblad, aan de Belangen van de Gemeente in Nederland Gewijd [*A publication*]
**GMS**.......... Gemini Mission Simulator [*NASA*]
**GMS**.......... General Maintenance System [*Data processing*] (BUR)
**GMS**.......... General Material Services
**GMS**.......... General Medical Services [*British*]
**GM & S**...... General Medicine and Surgery
**GMS**.......... General Military Science
**GMS**.......... General Milk Sales [*An association*] [*Inactive*] (EA)
**GMS**.......... Generation Management Station
**GMS**.......... Geophysical Monitoring Satellite [*DoD, NOAA*]
**GMS**.......... George MacDonald Society [*Lincoln, England*] (EAIO)
**GMS**.......... Geostationary Meteorological Satellite [*Japan*]
**GMS**.......... Giant Motor Synapse [*Anatomy*]
**GMS**.......... Gichner Mobile Shelters (MCD)
**GMS**.......... Gilbert M. Smith Herbarium [*Stanford University*] [*Pacific Grove, CA*]
**GMS**.......... Glen Miller Society (EAIO)
**GMS**.......... Glyceryl Monostearate [*Organic chemistry*]
**GMS**.......... Gomori's Methenamine Silver [*A biological stain*]
**G/MS**......... Graphics and/or Media Specialist
**GMS**.......... Gravitational Mass Sensor
**GMS**.......... Gravity Measuring System
**GMS**.......... Ground Maintenance Support
**GMS**.......... Ground Mapping [*or Marking*] System
**GMS**.......... Group Membership Scores [*Psychometrics*]
**GMS**.......... Guardian-Morton Shulman Precious Metals, Inc. [*Toronto Stock Exchange symbol*] [*Vancouver Stock Exchange symbol*]
**GMS**.......... Guidance Monitor Set [*Aerospace*] (AAG)
**GMS**.......... Guided Missile School [*Dam Neck, VA*]
**GMS**.......... Guided Missile Simulator [*Military*] (CAAL)
**GMS**.......... Guided Missile System
**GMS**.......... Master Construction Specification [*Canada*]
**GMS**.......... Morehouse College, School of Medicine, Atlanta, GA [*OCLC symbol*] (OCLC)
**GMSA**....... General Motors South African
**GMSA**....... German Minesweeping Administration [*Allied German Occupation Forces*]
**GMSA**....... Seaman Apprentice, Gunner's Mate, Striker [*Navy rating*]
**GM Search** ... General Motors Research Laboratories. Search [*A publication*]
**GMSED**..... GBF Monograph Series [*A publication*]
**GMSER**..... Guided Missile Service Report (NG)
**GMSFC**..... George Marshall Space Flight Center [*Huntsville, AL*] (IEEE)
**GMSI**......... Gateway Medical Systems, Incorporated [*Atlanta, GA*] [*NASDAQ symbol*] (NQ)
**GMSI**......... Grand Master of the Order of the Star of India [*British*]
**GMSIA**...... Guided Missile System, Intercept-Aerial (MCD)
**GMSK**....... Gaussian Filtered Minimum Shift Keying (MCD)
**G/MSL**...... Guided Missile
**GMSL**........ Sidi Slimane [*Morocco*] [*ICAO location identifier*] (ICLI)
**GMSLL**..... Georgetown University. Monograph Series on Languages and Linguistics [*A publication*]
**GMSN**....... Seaman, Gunner's Mate, Striker [*Navy rating*]
**GMSO**....... German Mine Supplies Organization [*Allied German Occupation Forces*]
**G M Soc Am Univ Y Bk** ... Geological and Mining Society of American Universities. Year Book and Directory [*A publication*]
**GMSQUAD** ... Guided Missile Squadron (MUGU)
**GMSR**....... Guided Missile Service Record
**GMSR**....... Gulf & Mississippi Corp. [*Columbus, MS*] [*NASDAQ symbol*] (NQ)
**GMSR**....... Gunner's Mate, Ship Repair [*Navy rating*] [*Obsolete*]
**GMSRON** ... Guided Missile Service Squadron (MUGU)
**GMSRP**..... Gunner's Mate, Ship Repair, Powderman [*Navy rating*] [*Obsolete*]
**GMSS**........ Graphical Modeling and Simulation System
**GMST**........ General Military Subjects Test
**GMST**........ Glossary of Merchant Ship Types (MCD)
**GMSTS**..... Guided Missile System Test Set (NATG)
**GMSU**....... General Maritime Stevedores' Union [*Philippines*]
**GMSU**....... Guided Missile Service Unit [*Air Force*]
**GMSW**....... Gross Maximum Shipping Weight
**GMT**.......... Gas Missile Tube
**GMT**.......... GATX Corp. [*Formerly, General American Transportation Corp.*] [*NYSE symbol*] (SPSG)
**GMT**.......... Geiger-Mueller Tube
**GMT**.......... Gemini Technology, Inc. [*Toronto Stock Exchange symbol*] [*Vancouver Stock Exchange symbol*]
**GMT**.......... General Machine Test [*Data processing*] (BUR)
**GMT**.......... General Military Training (AFM)
**GMT**.......... Generalized Multitasking
**GMT**.......... Geomarine Technology
**GMT**.......... Geometric Mean Titer [*Analytical chemistry*]
**GMT**.......... Glass-Mat Reinforced Thermoplastic [*Automotive engineering*]
**GMT**.......... Government Maturity Test (MCD)
**GMT**.......... Greenwich Mean [*or Meridian*] Time
**GMT**.......... Guided Missile Target (NG)
**GMT**.......... Guided Missile Trainer

**GMT** .......... Gunner's Mate, Technician [*Navy rating*]
**GMTA** ....... Al Hoceima/Cote Du Rif [*Morocco*] [*ICAO location identifier*] (ICLI)
**GMtbC**....... Berry College, Mount Berry, GA [*Library symbol*] [*Library of Congress*] (LCLS)
**GMTC** ....... Chief Gunner's Mate, Technician [*Navy rating*]
**GMTC** ....... Glutamate Manufacturers Technical Committee (EA)
**GMTCM** ... Master Chief Gunner's Mate, Technician [*Navy rating*]
**GMTCS**..... Senior Chief Gunner's Mate, Technician [*Navy rating*]
**Gmtebest**.... Gemeentebestuur Maandschrift der Vereeniging van Nederlandsche Gemeenten [*A publication*]
**GMTF**........ Gay Media Task Force (EA)
**GMTF**........ Geometric Modulation Transfer Function (MCD)
**GMTI** ........ Gemini Technology, Inc. [*NASDAQ symbol*] (NQ)
**GMTI** ........ Ground Moving Target Indicator
**GMTN**....... Tetouan/Sania R'Mel [*Morocco*] [*ICAO location identifier*] (ICLI)
**GMTO**....... General Military Training Office
**GMTOA**.... Green Mountain Textile Overseers Association (EA)
**GMTR**....... Guided Missile Test Round [*Military*] (CAAL)
**GMTRB**..... General Military Training Review Board (AFM)
**GMTRY** .... Geometry (MSA)
**GMTS**........ Guided Missile Test Set (AFM)
**GMTSA**...... Gunner's Mate, Technician, Seaman Apprentice [*Navy rating*]
**GMTSN** .... Gunner's Mate, Technician, Seaman [*Navy rating*]
**GMTT** ....... Tanger/Boukhalf [*Morocco*] [*ICAO location identifier*] (ICLI)
**GMTTR**..... Geometric Mean Time to Repair [*Military*] (CAAL)
**GMTU**....... Guided Missile Training Unit [*Navy*]
**GMtvB**....... Brewton-Parker College, Mount Vernon, GA [*Library symbol*] [*Library of Congress*] (LCLS)
**GMU** ......... George Mason University [*Virginia*]
**GMU** ......... Gospel Missionary Union (EA)
**GMU** ......... Granite Mountain [*Utah*] [*Seismograph station code, US Geological Survey*] (SEIS)
**GMU** ......... Greenville, SC [*Location identifier*] [*FAA*] (FAAL)
**GMU** ......... Guided Missile Unit
**GMU** ......... Mercer University, Macon, GA [*OCLC symbol*] (OCLC)
**GMU LR** ... George Mason University. Law Review [*A publication*]
**GMU L Rev** ... George Mason University. Law Review [*A publication*]
**GMUS**....... Guildhall Museum [*London*]
**GMusRNCM(Hons)** ... Graduate in Music of the Royal Northern College of Music [*British*] (DBQ)
**GMV**.......... Galinsoga Mosaic Virus
**GMV**.......... Generalized Minimum Variance [*Control technology*]
**GMV**.......... Gram Molecular Volume [*Chemistry*]
**GMV**.......... Grand Master of the Vails [*Freemasonry*]
**GMV**.......... Guaranteed Minimum Value
**GMVDC**.... Gay Men's VD Clinic (EA)
**GMVLS**..... Guided Missile Vertical Launch System [*Canadian Navy*]
**GMW**......... General Microwave Corp. [*AMEX symbol*] (SPSG)
**GMW**......... Gold Mountain [*Washington*] [*Seismograph station code, US Geological Survey*] (SEIS)
**GMW**......... Gram Molecular Weight [*Chemistry*]
**GMW**......... Guevara-McInteer-Wageman
**GMW**......... Wesleyan College, Macon, GA [*Library symbol*] [*Library of Congress*] (LCLS)
**GMWA**...... Gospel Music Workshop of America (EA)
**GMWS** ...... Guided Missile Weapon System [*Military*] (CAAL)
**GMWU**...... General and Municipal Workers' Union [*British*]
**GMXC**....... GMX Communications, Inc. [*NASDAQ symbol*] (NQ)
**GMZ**.......... Bowie, TX [*Location identifier*] [*FAA*] (FAAL)
**GMZFO** .... Gouvernement Militaire de la Zone Francaise d'Occupation [*Military Government of the French Zone of Occupation*] [*of Germany*]
**GN** ............ Compagnie Nationale Air Gabon [*Gabon*] [*ICAO designator*] (FAAC)
**GN** ............ Gain (NASA)
**GN** ............ Ganglion Nodosum [*Neurology*]
**GN** ............ Gathering of Nations (EA)
**GN** ............ Gaylactic Network [*An association*] (EA)
**GN** ............ Geldgeschichtliche Nachrichten [*A publication*]
**GN** ............ General Note (MSA)
**Gn** ............. Genesis [*Old Testament book*]
**GN** ............ Georgia Music News [*A publication*]
**GN** ............ German
**GN** ............ Germanic Notes [*A publication*]
**gn** .............. Gilbert and Ellice Islands [*Tuvalu*] [*gb (Gilbert Islands) or tu (Tuvalu) used in records cataloged after October 1978*] [*MARC country of publication code*] [*Library of Congress*] (LCCP)
**GN** ............ Girls Nation (EA)
**GN** ............ Glomerular Nephritis [*Medicine*]
**G:N** ........... Glucose:Nitrogen [*Ratio*]
**Gn** ............. Gnomon [*A publication*]
**GN** ............ Golden Nematode [*A worm*]
**GN** ............ Golden Number [*Number used to fix the date of Easter*]
**GN** ............ Golden Titan Resources [*Vancouver Stock Exchange symbol*]
**GN** ............ Goldneck Summer Squash
**Gn** ............. Gonadotropin [*Endocrinology*]
**GN** ............ Good Night [*Amateur radio*]
**Gn** ............. Gradational, Non-Calcareous [*Soil*]
**GN** ............ Graduate Nurse
**G in N** ........ Graduate in Nursing
**GN** ............ Grain (MCD)
**GN** ............ Gram-Negative [*Also, GRN*] [*Microbiology*]
**GN** ............ Grand National [*Automobile racing*]
**GN** ............ Grand Nehemiah [*Freemasonry*] (ROG)
**GN** ............ Grandnephew (ADA)
**GN** ............ Grandniece (ADA)
**GN** ............ Green [*Maps and charts*]
**GN** ............ Ground Nester [*Ornithology*]
**GN** ............ Guanine Nucleotide [*Biochemistry*]
**G & N**......... Guidance and Navigation [*System*] [*Apollo*] [*NASA*]
**GN** ............ Guide-Number [*Photography*]
**GN** ............ Guinea [*ANSI two-letter standard code*] (CNC)
**GN** ............ Gun[*s*] [*Freight*]
**$GN_2$**.......... Gaseous Nitrogen [*NASA*]
**GN's**.......... Global Negotiations
**GNA**.......... Gainsco, Inc. [*AMEX symbol*] (SPSG)
**GNA**.......... Gay Nurses' Alliance (EA)
**GNA**.......... Genossenschafts Forum. Raiffeisenrundschau und Blaetter fuer Genossenschaftswesen [*A publication*]
**GNA**.......... Ghana News Agency
**GNA**.......... Gnangara [*Australia*] [*Geomagnetic observatory code*]
**GNA**.......... Granada Exploration Corp. [*Vancouver Stock Exchange symbol*]
**GNA**.......... Grants Pass, OR [*Location identifier*] [*FAA*] (FAAL)
**GNA**.......... Graphics Network Architecture
**GNA**.......... Graysonia, Nashville & Ashdown Railroad Co. [*AAR code*]
**GNA**.......... Great Northern Airlines, Inc. [*Anchorage, AK*] [*FAA designator*] (FAAC)
**GNAACBJA** ... Greater North American Aviculturist and Color Bred Judges Association [*Formerly, GNACBJA*] (EA)
**GNACBJA** ... Greater North American Color-Bred Judge Association [*Later, GNAACBJA*] (EA)
**GNADS**..... Gimbaled Night and Day Sight
**GNAGS**..... Ground Adjutant General Section [*World War II*]
**GNAMAP** ... Gigiena Naselennykh Mest Respublikanskoi Mezhvedomstvennyi Sbornik [*A publication*]
**GNAS** ........ Grand National Archery Society [*British*]
**G Nas** ......... Guillelmus Naso [*Flourished, 1220-34*] [*Authority cited in pre-1607 legal work*] (DSA)
**GNAT**........ General Numerical Analysis of Transport [*Computer program*]
**GNATS**...... General Noise and Tonal System (NVT)
**GNATS**...... General Nonlinear Analysis of Two-Dimensional Structures [*Computer program*]
**GNavO**....... Group Navigation Officer [*British military*] (DMA)
**GNB**.......... Gambia News Bulletin [*A publication*]
**GNB**.......... Good News Bible [*Today's English Version*] [*A publication*] (BJA)
**GNB**.......... Good News Broadcaster [*A publication*]
**GNB**.......... Gram-Negative Bacillus [*Microbiology*]
**GNB**.......... Granby, CO [*Location identifier*] [*FAA*] (FAAL)
**GNB**.......... Granby Resources Ltd. [*Vancouver Stock Exchange symbol*]
**GNB**.......... Grenoble [*France*] [*Airport symbol*] (OAG)
**GNB**.......... Guinea-Bissau [*ANSI three-letter standard code*] (CNC)
**GNBC**........ Glendale Bancorporation [*NASDAQ symbol*] (NQ)
**GNBM**....... Gram-Negative Bacillary Meningitis [*Medicine*]
**GNC**.......... General Nautical Chart [*Navy*]
**GNC**.......... General Nursing Care [*Medicine*]
**GNC**.......... General Nursing Council
**GNC**.......... General Nutrition [*NYSE symbol*] (SPSG)
**GNC**.......... Geologic Names Committee [*US Geological Survey*]
**GNC**.......... Global Navigation Chart [*Military*]
**GNC**.......... Goddard Network Control [*NASA*] (MCD)
**GNC**.......... Graphic Numerical Control [*Deltacam Systems Ltd.*] [*Software package*] [*British*] (MCD)
**GNC**.......... Guidance and Navigation Computer [*NASA*] (KSC)
**GNC**.......... Guidance, Navigation, and Control (NASA)
**GN & C** ...... Guidance, Navigation, and Control (MCD)
**GNC**.......... Seminole, TX [*Location identifier*] [*FAA*] (FAAL)
**GNCAM**.... Glia-Neuron Cell Adhesion Molecule [*Cytology*]
**GNCBA** ..... Ginecologia Brasileira [*A publication*]
**GNCBA2** ... Ginecologia Brasileira [*A publication*]
**GNCCA** ..... Grand National Curling Club of America
**GNCEW**.... General Nursing Council for England and Wales
**GNCFTS** ... GN & C [*Guidance, Navigation, and Control*] Flight Test Station (MCD)
**GNCIS**....... Guidance, Navigation, and Control Integration Simulator (NASA)
**GNCM**....... General Communication, Inc. [*NASDAQ symbol*] (NQ)
**G & N Coop** ... G & N Cooperator (Gippsland and Northern Cooperative) [*A publication*] (APTA)
**GNCS** ........ Guidance, Navigation, and Control System (MCD)
**GNCTS**...... GN & C [*Guidance, Navigation, and Control*] Test Station (MCD)
**GND** .......... Grandview Resources, Inc. [*Toronto Stock Exchange symbol*] [*Vancouver Stock Exchange symbol*]
**GND** .......... Grenada [*Windward Islands*] [*Airport symbol*] (OAG)
**GND** .......... Ground (AAG)
**GND** .......... Grounded [*Electricity*] [*Electronics*]

**GND** .......... North Georgia College, Stewart Library, Dahlonega, GA [*OCLC symbol*] (OCLC)
**GNDBiH** ... Godisnjak Naucnog Drustva Nr Bosne i Hercegovine [*A publication*]
**GNDCG** ..... Ground Forces Commanding General [*World War II*]
**GNDCK** ..... Ground Check [*Aviation*]
**GND C/O** .. Ground Checkout [*NASA*] (NASA)
**GNDCON** ... Ground Control
**GNDFG** ..... Ground Fog [*Meteorology*] (FAAC)
**GNDI** ......... Gross National Disposable Income [*Economics*]
**GNDR** ........ Gander Mountain, Inc. [*Wilmot, WI*] [*NASDAQ symbol*] (NQ)
**GNDW** ...... Grandview Resources, Inc. [*Vancouver, BC*] [*NASDAQ symbol*] (NQ)
**GNE** ........... Gane Energy Corp. Ltd. [*Toronto Stock Exchange symbol*]
**GNE** ........... Genentech, Inc. [*NYSE symbol*] (SPSG)
**GNE** ........... Gross National Effluent
**GNE** ........... Gross National Expenditure
**GNE** ........... Guidance and Navigation Electronics (KSC)
**GNE** ........... Guidance and Navigation Equipment
**GNEC** ......... General Nuclear Engineering Corporation (MCD)
**GNEHAU** ... Great Britain. Ministry of Agriculture, Fisheries, and Food. National Agricultural Advisory Service. Experimental Husbandry Farms and Experimental Horticulture Stations. Progress Report [*A publication*]
**GNEM** ....... Global Network for Environmental Monitoring [*Defunct*] (EA)
**GNESIT** .... Greater New England Society of Inhalation Therapists
**GNET** ........ Games Network, Inc. [*NASDAQ symbol*] (NQ)
**G Neuropsichiatr Eta Evol** ... Giornale di Neuropsichiatria dell'Eta Evolutiva [*A publication*]
**GNEX** ........ Genex Corp. [*NASDAQ symbol*] (NQ)
**GNF** ........... Gannett Newspaper Foundation
**GNF** ........... Granada Foods [*AMEX symbol*] (SPSG)
**GNFC** ......... Graceland News Fan Club (EA)
**GNFMS** ..... Gaseous Nitrogen Flow Measuring System
**GNG** .......... Gaussian Noise Generator [*Electronics*]
**GNG** .......... Generation Gather Group [*Data processing*]
**GNG** .......... Golden Nugget, Inc. [*NYSE symbol*] (SPSG)
**GNG** .......... Gooding, ID [*Location identifier*] [*FAA*] (FAAL)
**GNG** .......... Granger Resources Corp. [*Vancouver Stock Exchange symbol*]
**GNGCS** ..... Ground Forces Chief of Staff [*World War II*]
**GNGDC** ..... Ground Forces Deputy Chief of Staff [*World War II*]
**GNGPS** ...... Ground Forces Plans Section [*World War II*]
**GNGS** ........ Genoa Nuclear Generating Station (NRCH)
**GNGSE** ..... Ground Forces Secretariat [*World War II*]
**GNH** .......... Grand National Hunt [*British*]
**GNI** ............ Genco Industry, Inc. [*Vancouver Stock Exchange symbol*]
**GNI** ............ Grand Isle, LA [*Location identifier*] [*FAA*] (FAAL)
**GN of I** ....... Great Northern of Ireland [*Railway*] (ROG)
**GNI** ............ Great Northern Iron Ore Properties [*NYSE symbol*] (SPSG)
**GNI** ............ Gross National Income [*Economics*]
**GNIB** ......... Guatemala News and Information Bureau (EA)
**GNIC** ......... Gay News Information and Communication Network [*Information service or system*] (IID)
**GNIC** ......... Guaranty National Corporation [*NASDAQ symbol*] (NQ)
**GNID** ......... Gram-Negative Intracellular Diplococci [*Microbiology*]
**GNIS** ......... Geographic Names Information System [*US Geological Survey*] [*Information service or system*]
**GNJ** ........... Lexington, KY [*Location identifier*] [*FAA*] (FAAL)
**GNKAA5** ... Genetika [*A publication*]
**GNKEAH** ... Gifu Daigaku Nogakubu Kenkyu Hokoku [*A publication*]
**GNKNA** ...... Genshi Nenryo Kosha Nempo [*A publication*]
**GNL** ........... Gemco National, Inc. [*AMEX symbol*] (SPSG)
**GNL** ........... General
**GNL** ........... General Aviation, Inc. [*Greenville, TN*] [*FAA designator*] (FAAC)
**GNL** ........... Georgia Nuclear Laboratory [*AEC*]
**GNL** ........... Great National Land [*Vancouver Stock Exchange symbol*]
**GNLTD** ...... Granulated (MSA)
**GNM** ......... Genetron Marine, Inc. [*Vancouver Stock Exchange symbol*]
**GNM** ......... Golden [*New Mexico*] [*Seismograph station code, US Geological Survey*] (SEIS)
**GNM** ......... Good News Mission (EA)
**GNM** ......... Guanambi [*Brazil*] [*Airport symbol*] (OAG)
**GNMA** ....... Government National Mortgage Association [*Nickname: Ginnie Mae*]
**GNMR** ....... Genmar Industries, Inc. [*Minneapolis, MN*] [*NASDAQ symbol*] (NQ)
**GNMS** ....... Gaseous Nitrogen Measuring System
**GNN** .......... Giant North Resources Ltd. [*Vancouver Stock Exchange symbol*]
**GNN** .......... Great Northern Nekoosa Corp. [*NYSE symbol*] (SPSG)
**GNN** .......... Gunnerudssatern [*Sweden*] [*Seismograph station code, US Geological Survey*] (SEIS)
**GNNED** ..... General Newsletter. National Research Council (Canada). Division of Mechanical Engineering [*A publication*]
**GNO** .......... Golden North Resource Corp. [*Toronto Stock Exchange symbol*] [*Vancouver Stock Exchange symbol*]
**Gnom** ......... Gnomon [*Munich*] [*A publication*] (BJA)
**GNOMAC** ... Greater New Orleans Microform Cooperative [*Library network*]
**Gnomon** ...... Kritische Zeitschrift fuer die Gesamte Klassische Altertumswissenschaft [*Berlin, Germany*] [*A publication*] (DLA)
**G-NORM** .. Grounded - Not Operationally Ready Maintenance (MCD)
**G-NORS** .... Grounded - Not Operationally Ready Supply (MCD)
**GNOS** ........ Goddard Network Operations Support [*NASA*] (KSC)
**GNOX** ........ Golden North Resource Corp. [*Vancouver, BC*] [*NASDAQ symbol*] (NQ)
**GNOZ** ........ Grease Nozzle
**GNP** ........... Gas, Nonpersistent
**GNP** ........... Gerontological Nurse Practitioner
**GNP** ........... Graphics Nesting Processor (MCD)
**GNP** ........... Graphics Nesting Program (MCD)
**GNP** ........... Grenada National Party [*Political party*] (PPW)
**GNP** ........... Gross National Product [*Economics*]
**GNP** ........... Tulsa, OK [*Location identifier*] [*FAA*] (FAAL)
**GNP & BR** ... Great Northern Piccadilly & Brompton Railway [*British*] (ROG)
**GNPC** ........ Global Navigation and Planning Chart [*Military*]
**GNpN** ........ Norman Junior College, Norman Park, GA [*Library symbol*] [*Library of Congress*] (LCLS)
**GNPP** ........ Ginna Nuclear Power Plant (NRCH)
**GNPP** ........ Great Nigeria People's Party [*Political party*] (PPW)
**GNQ** .......... Equatorial Guinea [*ANSI three-letter standard code*] (CNC)
**GNR** ........... Gaseous Nuclear Rocket
**GNR** ........... General Roca [*Argentina*] [*Airport symbol*] (OAG)
**GNR** ........... Global Natural Resources, Inc. [*NYSE symbol*] (SPSG)
**GNR** ........... Great Northern Railway
**GNR** ........... Gunner (AFM)
**GNRA** ........ Gateway National Recreation Area [*New York*] [*Department of the Interior*]
**GNRA** ........ Government National Railway Association [*Proposed*] [*Nickname: Ginnie Rae*]
**GNRA** ........ Grand National Racing Association (EA)
**GNRB** ........ Grid Navigational Reference Beacon [*Navy*] (CAAL)
**GNRE** ........ Gross National Recreation Experience [*Refers to cost of recreation in relation to gross national product*]
**GnRF** ......... Gonadotropin-Releasing Factor [*Also, GnRH, LH-RF, LH-RH, LH-RH/FSH-RH, LRF, LRH*] [*Endocrinology*]
**GnRH** ........ Gonadotropin-Releasing Hormone [*Also, GnRF, LH-RF, LH-RH, LH-RH/FSH-RH, LRF, LRH*] [*Endocrinology*]
**GNRP** ........ General Neighborhood Renewal Plan
**GNRY** ........ Great Northern Railway
**GNRY** ........ Gunnery (AFM)
**GNS** ........... Gannett News Service
**GNS** ........... Gazette Numismatique Suisse [*A publication*]
**GNS** ........... General Naval Staff [*NATO*] (NATG)
**G/NS** .......... Glucose in Normal Saline [*Medicine*]
**GNS** ........... Glutamine Synthetase [*Also, GS*] [*An enzyme*]
**GNS** ........... Grain Neutral Spirits [*Alcohol*]
**GNS** ........... Gram-Negative Sensitivity [*to antibiotics*]
**GNS** ........... Grand National Sportsman [*Car racing division*]
**GNS** ........... Great North of Scotland Railway (ROG)
**GNS** ........... Griffin's Nautical Series [*A publication*]
**GNS** ........... Guidance and Navigation System
**GNS** ........... Guineas [*Monetary unit*] [*Obsolete*] [*Great Britain*]
**GNSH** ........ Grey Nuns of the Sacred Heart [*Roman Catholic religious order*]
**GNSHD** ..... Gendai No Shinryo [*A publication*]
**GNSI** ......... Guild of Natural Science Illustrators (EA)
**GNSM** ....... Graduate of the Northern School of Music [*Obsolete*] [*British*] (DBQ)
**GNSO** ........ Goddard Network Support Operations [*King's College*] [*Wilkes-Barre, PA*] [*NASA*] (KSC)
**GNSP** ......... Gross National Sports Product [*Economics*]
**GNSR** ........ Great North of Scotland Railway
**GNsS** ......... Grammatik der Neusyrischen Sprache [*A publication*] (BJA)
**GNST** ........ Glossary of Naval Ship Types (MCD)
**GNT** ........... General Naval Training [*British military*] (DMA)
**GNT** ........... Grant Exploration [*Vancouver Stock Exchange symbol*]
**GNT** ........... Grants, NM [*Location identifier*] [*FAA*] (FAAL)
**GNT** ........... Great Northern Telegraph Co. [*Denmark*] [*Telecommunications*] (TEL)
**GNT** ........... Green Tree Acceptance, Inc. [*NYSE symbol*] (SPSG)
**GNT** ........... Ground Test [*NASA*] (KSC)
**GNTAA** ..... Ganita [*India*] [*A publication*]
**GNTC** ........ Girls' Naval Training Corps [*British*]
**GNTE** ........ Granite Co-Operative Bank [*North Quincy, MA*] [*NASDAQ symbol*] (NQ)
**GNTGD** ..... Gensan Nenji Taikai Gijiroku [*A publication*]
**GNTKAC** .. Genetik [*A publication*]
**GNTO** ........ Greek National Tourist Organization (EA)
**GNTP** ........ Graduate Nurse Transition Program
**GNTR** ........ Generator (FAAC)
**GNTSA** ...... Genetics. Supplement [*A publication*]
**GNTUD** ..... Geologiya i Neftegazonosnost Turkmenistana [*A publication*]
**GNTX** ........ Gentex Corp. [*NASDAQ symbol*] (NQ)
**GNU** .......... Golden Rule Resources Ltd. [*Toronto Stock Exchange symbol*]
**GNU** .......... Goodnews Bay [*Alaska*] [*Airport symbol*] (OAG)
**GNUC** ........ [*The*] GNI Group, Inc. [*NASDAQ symbol*] (NQ)
**GNV** ........... Gainesville [*Florida*] [*Airport symbol*]

**GNV**.......... Geneva Steel Class A [*NYSE symbol*] (SPSG)
**GNV**.......... Genoveva Resources, Inc. [*Vancouver Stock Exchange symbol*]
**GNV**.......... Glycinenaphthol Violet [*An indicator*] [*Chemistry*]
**GNVA**........ Genova, Inc. [*NASDAQ symbol*] (NQ)
**GNVN**........ Government of North Vietnam
**GNW**......... Greenwell Resources Corp. [*Vancouver Stock Exchange symbol*]
**GNWF**....... GNW Financial Corp. [*NASDAQ symbol*] (CTT)
**GNWP**....... Gross National Waste Product Forum (EA)
**GNWR**....... Genessee & Wyoming Railroad Co. [*AAR code*]
**GNX**.......... Genex Resources [*Vancouver Stock Exchange symbol*]
**GNY**.......... Fort Jay, NY [*Location identifier*] [*FAA*] (FAAL)
**GNY**.......... German Navy
**GNYCFS**... Greater New York Council for Foreign Students [*Later, English in Action*]
**GNYO**........ Guild of New York Opera [*Record label*]
**GNZ**.......... Gisborne [*New Zealand*] [*Seismograph station code, US Geological Survey*] (SEIS)
**GNZ**.......... Government of New Zealand
**GO**............ Canada - Transport Canada [*Canada*] [*ICAO designator*] (ICDA)
**GO**............ Collins Industries, Inc. [*AMEX symbol*] (SPSG)
**go**............. Gabon [*MARC country of publication code*] [*Library of Congress*] (LCCP)
**GO**............ Galactose Oxidase [*An enzyme*]
**GO**............ Garrison Orders [*British military*] (DMA)
**GO**............ Gas Operated (ADA)
**G & O**........ Gas and Oxygen [*Medicine*]
**GO**............ Gasoffizier [*Gas Officer*] [*German military - World War II*]
**GO**............ Gaussian Orbitals [*Atomic physics*]
**GO**............ General Obligation [*Bond*] [*Business term*]
**GO**............ General Office [*or Officer*] [*Military*]
**GO**............ General Order
**GO**............ General Organization [*Identification card used at Madison Square Garden*]
**GO**............ Generale Occidentale [*Commercial firm*]
**GO**............ Generalized Operations (MCD)
**GO**............ Generaloberst [*Full General*] [*German military - World War II*]
**GO**............ Generated Output
**GO**............ Genius Operator Advertising Data Bank [*Gert Richter*] [*Federal Republic of Germany*] [*Information service or system*] (CRD)
**GO**............ Gentil Organisateur [*Genial Host*] [*Employee of Club Mediterranee, a vacation cooperative*]
**GO**............ Geometry-Optimized [*Calculations*]
**GO**............ Global Options (EA)
**GO**............ Global Outreach [*An association*] (EA)
**GO**............ Glucose Oxidase [*Also, glu ox, GOD*] [*An enzyme*]
**Go**............. Godecke AG [*Germany*] [*Research code symbol*]
**Go**............. Goebel's Probate Court Cases [*Ohio*] [*A publication*] (DLA)
**GO**............ Goethite [*A mineral*]
**Go**............. Gofredus de Trano [*Deceased, 1245*] [*Authority cited in pre-1607 legal work*] (DSA)
**GO**............ Goniometer [*JETDS nomenclature*] [*Military*] (CET)
**GO**............ Gothic [*Language, etc.*] (ROG)
**GO**............ Government Obligation [*Economics*]
**GO**............ Government Operations Committee [*US Senate*]
**GO**............ Government Owned
**GO**............ Graduate Opportunities [*British*]
**GO**............ Grand Orator [*Freemasonry*]
**GO**............ Grand Organist [*Freemasonry*] (ROG)
**GO**............ Grand Orient [*Freemasonry*] (ROG)
**GO**............ Graphitic Oxide
**GO**............ Great Organ [*Music*]
**GO**............ Ground Out [*Baseball*]
**GO**............ Group Officer [*British military*] (DMA)
**G-O**........... Grumman Olson [*Grumman Corp.*]
**GO**............ Guest Option [*Hotel plan, Hilton hotels*]
**GO**............ Gummed Only [*Envelopes*]
**GO**............ Gunn Oscillator
**GO**............ Gunnery Officer [*Navy*] [*British*]
**GO**............ Gurkha Officer [*British military*] (DMA)
**GOA**.......... General Operating Agency
**GOA**.......... Generalized Osteoarthritis [*Medicine*]
**GOA**.......... Genoa [*Italy*] [*Airport symbol*] (OAG)
**GOA**.......... Glacier-Ocean-Atmosphere [*Global system used for modelling*]
**G & OA**...... Glycerine and Oleochemicals Association (EA)
**GOA**.......... Goa [*Panjim*] [*India*] [*Seismograph station code, US Geological Survey*] (SEIS)
**GOA**.......... Golden Seal Resources Ltd. [*Vancouver Stock Exchange symbol*]
**GOA**.......... Government of Australia (CINC)
**GOA**.......... Government-Owned Aircraft
**GOA**.......... Group, Operations Analysis [*Air Force*] (MCD)
**GOA**.......... Gun Owners of America (EA)
**GOA**.......... Gyro Output Amplifier
**GOAA**........ American Adventure, Inc. [*Formerly, Great Outdoor American Adventure, Inc.*] [*NASDAQ symbol*] (NQ)
**GOAD**........ Group of Ancient Drama
**GOAL**........ Goal Systems International, Inc. [*NASDAQ symbol*] (NQ)
**GOAL**........ Ground Operations Aerospace Language [*Data processing*] [*NASA*]
**GOAL**........ Ground Operations Assembly Language [*Data processing*]
**GOALS**...... General Operations and Logistics Simulation [*Boeing*]
**GOALS**...... General Optronics Line of Sight Atmospheric Lightwave Communication System [*General Optronics Corp.*] [*Edison, NJ*] [*Telecommunications service*] (TSSD)
**GOALS**...... Generalized Officer Assignment On-Line System [*Navy*] (NVT)
**GOALS**...... Goal-Oriented Approach to Life Cycle Software
**GOAM**....... Government-Owned and Maintained [*Telecommunications*] (TEL)
**GOAR**........ Ground Observer Aircraft Recognition [*Army*]
**GOAS**........ Guidance Optical Alignment Shelter (KSC)
**GOASEX**... Gulf of Alaska SEASAT Experiment [*National Oceanic and Atmospheric Administration*]
**GOAT**........ Gerber Oscillogram Amplitude Translator
**GOAT**........ Goes Over All Terrain [*Vehicle*]
**GOATS**...... Group Operational Access Tester System [*AT & T*]
**GOB**.......... General Officers Branch [*Air Force*]
**GOB**.......... General Order of Battle
**GOB**.......... Glass Oceanographic Buoy
**GOB**.......... Gobble (DSUE)
**GOB**.......... Goldbrae Development Ltd. [*Vancouver Stock Exchange symbol*]
**GOB**.......... Good Ordinary Brand [*Business term*]
**GOB**.......... Government of Burma (CINC)
**GOB**.......... Ground Order of Battle (AFM)
**GOBAB**..... Gamma-Hydroxy-beta-aminobutyric Acid [*Pharmacology*]
**GOBEP**...... Generalized One-Boson Exchange Potential
**GOBI**......... Growth Monitoring, Oral Rehydration, Breastfeeding, and Immunization [*Program*] [*UNICEF plan to reduce child mortality in Third World countries*]
**GOBILS**.... Government Bill of Lading System
**GOC**.......... Gas-Oil Contact
**GOC**.......... Gas-Operated Core
**GOC**.......... General Officer Commanding [*Navy*]
**GOC**.......... General Operating Committee
**GOC**.......... General Optical Council [*British*]
**GOC**.......... Glas Owners Club (EA)
**GOC**.......... Glycidoxycoumarin [*Biochemistry*]
**GOC**.......... Gora [*Papua New Guinea*] [*Airport symbol*] (OAG)
**GOC**.......... Government Operations Committee
**GOC**.......... Grafisch Orgaan [*A publication*]
**GOC**.......... Greatest Overall Coefficient (TEL)
**GOC**.......... Griffith Observatory [*California*] [*Seismograph station code, US Geological Survey*] (SEIS)
**GOC**.......... Ground Observer Corps
**GOC**.......... Ground Operations Coordinator [*NASA*] (NASA)
**GOC**.......... Group Operations Center (NATG)
**GOC**.......... Guaranteed One Coat [*Brand of house paint*]
**GOC**.......... Gulf Canada Corporation [*Formerly, Gulf Oil Canada Ltd.*] [*AMEX symbol*] [*Vancouver Stock Exchange symbol*] (SPSG)
**GOC**.......... Gunnery Officer's Console [*Army*] (AABC)
**GOCA**........ Geoscience Canada [*A publication*]
**GOCA**........ Ground Operations Control Area [*NASA*] (NASA)
**GOCAP**..... Graphic Output Circuit Analysis Program
**GOCC**........ GARP Operational Control Center [*Marine science*] (MSC)
**GOCC**........ GATE [*GARP Atlantic Tropical Experiment*] Operational Control Centre [*Marine science*] (MSC)
**GOC-in-C**.. General Officer Commanding-in-Chief [*British*]
**GOCC**........ General Order of the Commander-in-Chief [*British military*] (DMA)
**GOCC**........ Geodetic Operations Control Center [*NASA*]
**GOCESS**... Government-Operated Civil Engineering Supply Store
**GOCHEM**... Gulf Oil Chemicals Co.
**GOCI**......... General Operator-Computer Interaction (IEEE)
**GOCI**......... Graham Owners Club International (EA)
**GOCO**........ Golden Oil Company [*NASDAQ symbol*] (NQ)
**GOCO**........ Government-Owned/Commercial-Operated [*Facility*] (AFIT)
**GO/CO**...... Government-Owned/Contractor-Operated [*Facility*] (NG)
**GOCOM**.... General Officer Command [*US Army Reserve*] (AABC)
**GOCR**........ Gated-Off Controlled Rectifier
**GOCRM**.... General Officer Commanding Royal Marines [*British*]
**GOD**.......... Generation of Diversity [*Immunology*]
**GOD**.......... Glucose Oxidase [*Also, glu ox, GO*] [*An enzyme*]
**God**........... Godisnik na Sofijskiya Universitet. Istorikofilologiceski Fakultet [*A publication*]
**God**........... Gofredus de Trano [*Deceased, 1245*] [*Authority cited in pre-1607 legal work*] (DSA)
**GOD**.......... Golden Sceptre Resources [*Toronto Stock Exchange symbol*] [*Vancouver Stock Exchange symbol*]
**GOD**.......... Government-Owned Depot
**GODAS**..... Graphically Oriented Design and Analysis System [*Data processing*]
**God Balk Isp**... Godisnjak Centra za Balkanoloska Ispitivanja [*A publication*]
**Godb (Eng)**... Godbolt's English King's Bench Reports [*78 English Reprint*] [*A publication*] (DLA)
**God Biol Inst Univ Sarajevu**... Godisnjak Bioloskog Instituta Univerziteta u Sarajevu [*A publication*]

**GODD**....... Goddard Industries, Inc. [*NASDAQ symbol*] (NQ)
**Goddard**..... Goddard on Easements [*A publication*] (DLA)
**Godd Ease**... Goddard on Easements [*A publication*] (DLA)
**Godd Easem**... Goddard on Easements [*A publication*] (DLA)
**God Durzh Politekh (Sofiya)**... Godishnik na Durzhavna ta Politekhnika (Sofiya) [*A publication*]
**GODE**........ Gulf Organization for Development in Egypt
**Godefroi**..... Godefroi's Law of Trusts and Trustees [*A publication*] (DLA)
**Godef & Sh RC**... Godefroi and Shortt on Railway Companies [*A publication*] (DLA)
**Godef Trust**... Godefroi's Law of Trusts and Trustees [*A publication*] (DLA)
**God Energoproekt**... Godisnik na Energoproekt [*A publication*]
**Godey**......... Godey's Lady's Book [*A publication*]
**GodFFNS**.. Godisnjak Filozofskog Fakulteta u Novom Sadu [*A publication*]
**God Inzh Stroit Inst**... Godishnik na Inzhenerno-Stroitelniya Institut [*A publication*]
**Godis Ekon Fak (Skopje)**... Godisnik na Ekonomski ot Fakultet (Skopje) [*A publication*]
**Godisen Zb Zemjod-Fak Univ Skopje Ovostarstvo**... Godisen Zbornik na Zemjodelsko-Sumarskiot. Fakultet na Univerzitetot Skopje Ovostarstvo [*A publication*]
**Godisen Zb Zemjod-Sum Fak Univ (Skopje)**... Godisen Zbornik na Zemjodelsko-Sumarskiot. Fakultet na Univerzitetot (Skopje) [*A publication*]
**Godishnik Vissh Khimikotekhn Inst (Burgas)**... Godishnik na Visshiya Khimikotekhnologicheski Institut (Burgas, Bulgaria) [*A publication*]
**Godishnik Vissh Ped Inst Shumen Prirod-Mat Fak**... Godishnik na Visshiya Pedagogicheski Institut v Shumen. Prirodo-Matematicheski Fakultet [*A publication*]
**Godishnik Vissh Uchebn Zaved Prilozhna Mat**... Godishnik na Visshite Uchebni Zavedeniya. Prilozhna Matematika [*A publication*]
**Godishnik Vissh Uchebn Zaved Tekhn Fiz**... Godishnik na Visshite Uchebni Zavedeniya. Seriya Tekhnicheski Fizika [*A publication*]
**Godishnik Vissh Uchebn Zaved Tekhn Mekh**... Godishnik na Visshite Uchebni Zavedeniya. Seriya Tekhnicheski Mekhanika [*A publication*]
**Godisnik Viss Himikotehn Inst (Burgas)**... Godisnik na Vissija Himikotehnologiceski Institut (Burgas) [*A publication*]
**Godisnik Viss Inz-Stroitel Inst**... Godisnik na Vissija Inzerno-Stroitelnija Institut [*A publication*]
**Godisnik Viss Ped Inst Sumen Prirod-Mat Fak**... Godisnik na Vissija Pedagogiceski Institut v Sumen Prirodo-Matematiceski Fakultet [*A publication*]
**Godisnik Viss Tehn Ucebn Zaved Fiz**... Godisnik na Vissite Tehniceski Ucebni Zavedenija. Fizika [*A publication*]
**Godisnik Viss Tehn Ucebn Zaved Mat**... Godisnik na Vissite Tehniceski Ucebni Zavedenija. Matematika [*A publication*]
**Godisnik Viss Tehn Ucebn Zaved Prilozna Meh**... Godisnik na Vissite Tehniceski Ucebni Zavedenija Prilozna Mehanika [*A publication*]
**Godisnik Viss Ucebn Zaved Prilozna Mat**... Godisnik na Vissite Ucebni Zavedenija. Prilozna Matematika [*A publication*]
**Godisnik Viss Ucebn Zaved Tehn Fiz**... Godisnik na Vissite Ucebni Zavedenija. Tehniceski Fizika [*A publication*]
**Godisnjak Pomorskog Muz Kotoru**... Godisnjak Pomorskog Muzeja u Kotoru [*A publication*]
**God Khim Tekhnol Inst**... Godishnik na Khimiko Tekhnologicheskiya Institut [*A publication*]
**God Mash Elektrotekh Inst**... Godishnik na Mashino Elektrotekhnicheskiya Institut [*A publication*]
**God Med Akad (Sofia)**... Godishnik na Meditsinkata Akademiya "Vulko Chervenkov" (Sofia) [*A publication*]
**God Minniya Nauchnoizsled Inst**... Godishnik na Minniya Nauchnoizsledovatelski Institut [*A publication*]
**God Nauchnoizsled Inst Khim Prom**... Godishnik na Nauchnoizsledovatelskiya Institut po Khimicheska Promishlennost [*A publication*]
**God Nauchnoizsled Inst Koksokhim Neftoprerab**... Godishnik na Nauchnoizsledovatelskiya Institut po Koksokhimiya i Neftoprerabotvane [*A publication*]
**God Nauchnoizsled Inst Metal Obogat**... Godishnik na Nauchnoizsledovatelskiya Institut po Metalurgiya i Obogatyatvane [*A publication*]
**God Nauchnoizsled Inst Neftoprerab Neftokhim**... Godishnik na Nauchnoizsledovatelskiya Institut po Neftoprerabotvane i Neftokhimiya [*A publication*]
**God Nauchnoizsled Inst Tekhnol Izsled Gorivata**... Godishnik na Nauchnoizsledovatelskiya Institut za Tekhnolozhki Izsledovaniya na Gorivata [*A publication*]
**God Nauchnoizsled Inst Tsvetna Metal (Plovdiv)**... Godishnik na Nauchnoizsledovatelskiya Institut po Tsvetna Metalurgiya (Plovdiv) [*Bulgaria*] [*A publication*]
**God Nauchnoizsled Proekt Inst Rudodobiv Obogat**... Godishnik na Nauchnoizsledovatelskiya i Proektantski Institut za Rudodobiv i Obogatyavane [*A publication*]
**Godo**........... Godolphin on Admiralty Jurisdiction [*A publication*] (DLA)
**Godo**........... Godolphin's Abridgment of Ecclesiastical Law [*A publication*] (DLA)
**Godo**........... Godolphin's Orphan's Legacy [*A publication*] (DLA)
**Godo**........... Godolphin's Repertorium Canonicum [*A publication*] (DLA)
**Godol**.......... Godolphin's Orphan's Legacy [*A publication*] (DLA)
**Godolph Adm Jur**... Godolphin on Admiralty Jurisdiction [*2nd ed.*] [*1685*] [*A publication*] (DLA)
**Godolph Ecc Law**... Godolphin's Ecclesiastical Law [*A publication*] (DLA)
**Godolph Leg**... Godolphin's Orphan's Legacy [*A publication*] (DLA)
**Godolph Orph Leg**... Godolphin's Orphan's Legacy [*A publication*] (DLA)
**Godolph Rep Can**... Godolphin's Repertorium Canonicum [*A publication*] (DLA)
**GODORT**... Government Documents Round Table [*American Library Association*]
**GODORT DTTP**... GODORT [*Government Documents Round Table*] Documents to the People [*A publication*]
**GODORT ETF**... GODORT [*Government Documents Round Table*] Education Task Force
**GODORT FDTF**... GODORT [*Government Documents Round Table*] Federal Documents Task Force
**GODORT IDTF**... GODORT [*Government Documents Round Table*] International Documents Task Force
**GODORT MRGITF**... GODORT [*Government Documents Round Table*] Machine-Readable Government Information Task Force
**GODORT SLDTF**... GODORT [*Government Documents Round Table*] State and Local Documents Task Force
**God Otchet Durzh Zemled Opitna Kontrolna Stn (Sofia)**... Godishen Otchet. Durzhavna Zemledelska Opitna i Kontrolna Stantsiya (Sofia) [*A publication*]
**GOD-POD**... Glucose Oxidase-Peroxidase [*Also, PGO*] [*Enzyme mixture*]
**GODS**........ Geniuses of Distinction Society [*Later, SGD*] (EA)
**God Selskostop Akad George Dimitrov**... Godishnik na Selskostopanskata Akademiya "Georgi Dimitrov" Sofia [*A publication*]
**God Selskostop Akad (Sofia) Agron Fak**... Godishnik na Selskostopanskata Akademiya "Georgi Dimitrov" (Sofia) Agronomicheski Fakultet [*A publication*]
**God Selskostop Akad (Sofia) Lesotekh Fak**... Godishnik na Selskostopanskata Akademiya "Georgi Dimitrov" (Sofia). Lesotekhnicheski Fakultet [*A publication*]
**GODSEP**... Guidance and Orbit Determination for Solar Electric Propulsion [*NASA*]
**God Sofii Univ Agron Fak**... Godishnik na Sofiiskiya Universitet. Agronomicheski Fakultet [*A publication*]
**God Sofii Univ Agron Lesovud Fak**... Godishnik na Sofiiskiya Universitet. Agronomo Lesovudski Fakultet [*A publication*]
**God Sofii Univ Biol Fak**... Godisnik na Sofiiskiya Universitet. Biologicheski Fakultet [*A publication*]
**God Sofii Univ Biol Fak Kn I Zool Fiziol Biokhim Zhivotn**... Godishnik na Sofiiskiya Universitet. Biologicheski Fakultet. Kniga 1. Zoologiya, Fiziologiya, i Biokhimiya na Zhivotnite [*A publication*]
**God Sofii Univ Biol Geol Geogr Fak**... Godishnik na Sofiiskiya Universitet. Biologo-Geologo-Geografski Fakultet [*A publication*]
**God Sofii Univ Biol-Geol-Geogr Fak Kn I Biol**... Godishnik na Sofiiskiya Universitet. Biologo-Geologo-Geografski Fakultet. Kniga I. Biologiya [*A publication*]
**God Sofii Univ Biol-Geol-Geogr Fak Kn I Biol (Bot)**... Godishnik na Sofiiskiya Universitet. Biologo-Geologo-Geografski Fakultet. Kniga I. Biologiya (Botanika) [*A publication*]
**God Sofii Univ Biol-Geol-Geogr Fak Kn I Biol (Zool)**... Godishnik na Sofiiskiya Universitet. Biologo-Geologo-Geografski Fakultet. Kniga I. Biologiya (Zoologiya) [*A publication*]
**God Sofii Univ Fiz Fak**... Godishnik na Sofiiskiya Universitet. Fizicheski Fakultet [*Bulgaria*] [*A publication*]
**God Sofii Univ Fiz Mat Fak**... Godishnik na Sofiiskiya Universitet. Fiziko-Matematicheski Fakultet [*A publication*]
**God Sofii Univ Geol Geogr Fak**... Godishnik na Sofiiskiya Universitet. Geologo-Geografski Fakultet [*A publication*]
**God Sofii Univ Khim Fak**... Godishnik na Sofiiskiya Universitet. Khimicheski Fakultet [*A publication*]
**God Sofii Univ Kliment Okhridski Biol Fak**... Godishnik na Sofiiskiya Universitet Kliment Okhridski Biologicheski Fakultet [*A publication*]
**God Sofii Univ Lesovud Fak**... Godishnik na Sofiiskiya Universitet. Lesovuden Fakultet [*A publication*]
**God Sofii Univ Med Fak**... Godishnik na Sofiiskiya Universitet. Meditsinski Fakultet [*A publication*]
**God Sofii Univ Prir Mat Fak**... Godishnik na Sofiiskiya Universitet. Prirodo-Matematicheski Fakultet [*A publication*]
**God Sof Un**... Godishnik na Sofiiskiya Universitet [*A publication*]
**God Sof Univ**... Godishnik na Sofiiskiya Universitet [*A publication*]
**Godson**....... Godson's Mining Commissioner's Cases [*Ontario*] [*A publication*] (DLA)
**Gods Pat**.... Godson on Patents [*2nd ed.*] [*1840*] [*A publication*] (DLA)
**GodSU**....... Godisnik na Sofijskiya Universitet. Fakultet po Slavjanski Filologii [*A publication*]
**God Sumar Inst (Skopje)**... Godisnik. Sumarski Institut (Skopje) [*A publication*]
**God Vissh Inst Arkhit Stroit (Sofiya)**... Godishnik na Visshiya Institut po Arkhitektura i Stroitelstvo (Sofiya) [*A publication*]
**God Vissh Inzh Stroit Inst**... Godishnik na Visshiya Inzhenerno-Stroitelen Institut [*A publication*]

**God Vissh Khimikotekhnol Inst** ... Godishnik na Visshiya Khimikotekhnologicheski Institut [*Bulgaria*] [*A publication*]
**God Vissh Khimikotekhnol Inst Sofia** ... Godishnik na Visshiya Khimikotekhnologicheski Institut Sofia [*A publication*]
**God Vissh Khim-Tekhnol Inst (Burgas Bulg)** ... Godishnik na Visshiya Khimiko-Tekhnologicheski Institut (Burgas, Bulgaria) [*A publication*]
**God Vissh Mash Elektrotekh Inst** ... Godishnik na Visshiya Mashino-Elektrotekhnicheski Institut [*A publication*]
**God Vissh Minno-Geol Inst (Sofia)** ... Godishnik na Visshiya Minno-Geolozhki Institut (Sofia) [*A publication*]
**God Vissh Tekh Uchebni Zaved Mekh** ... Godishnik na Visshite Tekhnicheski Uchebni Zavedeniya. Prilozhna Mekhanika [*A publication*]
**God Vissh Tekh Uchebn Zaved Prilozh Mekh** ... Godishnik na Visshite Tekhnicheski Uchebni Zavedeniya. Prilozhna Mekhanika [*A publication*]
**God Vissh Uchebni Zaved Tekh Fiz** ... Godishnik na Visshite Uchebni Zavedeniya. Tekhnicheska Fizika [*A publication*]
**God Vissh Uchebn Zaveden Ser Tekh Fiz** ... Godishnik na Visshite Uchebni Zavedeniya. Seriya Tekhnicheska Fizika [*Bulgaria*] [*A publication*]
**God Vissh Uchebn Zaved Prilozh Mat** ... Godishnik na Visshite Uchebni Zavedeniya. Prilozhna Matematika [*A publication*]
**God Vojnomed Akad** ... Godisnjak Vojnomedicinske Akademije [*Beograd*] [*A publication*]
**God Zb Annu Biol** ... Godishen Zbornik Annuaire. Biologie [*A publication*]
**God Zb Biol Biol Fak Univ Kiril Metod Skopje** ... Godishen Zbornik Biologija Bioloshki Fakultet na Univerzitetot Kiril i Metodij Skopje [*A publication*]
**God Zb Biol Prir-Mat Fak Univ Kiril Metodij Skopje** ... Godishen Zbornik Biologija Priridno-Matematichki. Fakultet na Univerzitetot Kiril i Metodij Skopje [*A publication*]
**God Zb Filoz Fak Univ Skopje Prir Mat Oddel** ... Godisen Zbornik na Filozofski ot Fakultet na Univerzitetot vo Skopje. Prirodno-Matematicki Oddel [*A publication*]
**God Zb Med Fak Skopje** ... Godishen Zbornik na Meditsinskiot. Fakultet vo Skopje [*A publication*]
**God Zbor Skopje** ... Godisen Zbornik na Filozofskiot Fakultet na Universitetot vo Skopje [*A publication*]
**God Zbor Zemjodel Sumar Fak Univ Skopje** ... Godisen Zbornik ka Zemjodelsko-Sumarskiot. Fakultet na Univerzitetot Skopje [*A publication*]
**God Zb Prir Mat Fak Univ (Skopje)** ... Godisen Zbornik. Prirodno-Matematicki. Fakultet na Univerzitetot (Skopje) [*A publication*]
**God Zb Prir Mat Fak Univ (Skopje) Mat Fiz Hem** ... Godisen Zbornik. Prirodno-Matematicki. Fakultet na Univerzitetot (Skopje) Matematika, Fizika, i Hemija [*A publication*]
**God Zb Sumar Fak Univ (Skopje)** ... Godisen Zbornik na Sumarskiot. Fakultet na Univerzitetot (Skopje) [*A publication*]
**God Zb Zemjod Sumar Fak Univ Skopje Sumar** ... Godisen Zbornik na Zemjodelsko-Sumarskiot. Fakultet na Univerzitetot Skopje. Sumarstvo [*A publication*]
**God Zb Zemjod Sumar Fak Univ Skopje Zemjod** ... Godisen Zbornik na Zemjodelsko-Sumarskiot. Fakultet na Univerzitetot Skopje. Zemjodelstvo [*A publication*]
**GOE** ........ Gas, Oxygen, Ether [*Anesthesiology*]
**GOE** ........ General Operating Expenses (MCD)
**GOE** ........ General Ordination Examination
**GOE** ........ Geodome Resources Ltd. [*Toronto Stock Exchange symbol*] [*Vancouver Stock Exchange symbol*]
**Goe** ........ Goethe. Vierteljahresschrift der Goethe-Gesellschaft [*A publication*]
**GOE** ........ Gonalia [*Papua New Guinea*] [*Airport symbol*] (OAG)
**GOE** ........ Government-Owned Equipment (MCD)
**GOE** ........ Ground Operational Equipment [*NASA*]
**Goeb** ........ Goebel's Probate Court Cases [*Ohio*] [*A publication*] (DLA)
**Goebel** ........ Goebel's Probate Reports [*Ohio*] [*A publication*] (DLA)
**Goebel (Ohio)** ... Goebel's Probate Court Cases [*Ohio*] [*A publication*] (DLA)
**Goebel's Rep** ... Goebel's Probate Reports [*Ohio*] [*A publication*] (DLA)
**GOED** ........ Geodome Resources Ltd. [*NASDAQ symbol*] (NQ)
**GOE for OAO** ... Ground Operational Equipment for the Orbiting Astronomical Observatory [*NASA*] (MUGU)
**GOE/RPIE** ... Ground Operational Equipment/Real Property Installed Equipment [*NASA*] (AFM)
**GOES** ........ Geostationary Operational Environmental Satellite [*National Oceanic and Atmospheric Administration*]
**GOES** ........ Geosynchronous Operational Environmental Satellite [*NASA*] (NASA)
**GOES** ........ Geosynchronous Orbiting Earth Satellite
**GOES/DCP** ... Geostationary Operational Environmental Satellite Data Collection Platform (MSC)
**Goeteborgs K Vetensk-o Vitterhets Samh Handl** ... Goeteborgs Kungliga Vetenskaps-och Vitterhets-Samhaelles Handlingar [*A publication*]
**Goethe-Al** .. Goethe-Almanach [*A publication*]
**Goethe-Jahr** ... Goethe-Jahrbuch [*A publication*]
**Goethe-Jahrb** ... Goethe-Jahrbuch [*A publication*]
**Goett Arb Geol Palaeontol** ... Goettinger Arbeiten zur Geologie und Palaeontologie [*A publication*]
**Goett Florist Rundbriefe** ... Goettinger Floristische Rundbriefe [*A publication*]
**Goettinger Wirtsch Sozialwissensch Stud** ... Goettinger Wirtschafts- und Sozialwissenschaftliche Studien [*A publication*]
**Goetting J Naturw** ... Goettingisches Journal der Naturwissenschaften [*A publication*]
**Goett Jahrb** ... Goettinger Jahrbuch [*A publication*]
**Goett Misz** ... Goettinger Miszellen Beitraege zur Aegyptologischen Diskussion [*A publication*]
**Goett Nachr** ... Nachrichten. Gesellschaft der Wissenschaften zu Goettingen [*A publication*]
**Gof** ........ Gofredus de Trano [*Deceased, 1245*] [*Authority cited in pre-1607 legal work*] (DSA)
**GOF** ........ Golden Fleece [*A publication*]
**GOF** ........ Good Old Friday [*Slang*]
**GOF** ........ Goodness of Fit (MCD)
**GOF** ........ Government-Owned Facility
**GOF** ........ Governmental Finance [*A publication*]
**GOF** ........ San Angelo, TX [*Location identifier*] [*FAA*] (FAAL)
**GOFAR** ..... Global Ocean Floor Analysis and Research [*Navy*]
**GOFC** ........ Great Oaks Financial Corp. [*NASDAQ symbol*] (NQ)
**GOFS** ........ Global Ocean Flux Study [*Federal government*]
**GOG** ........ GEOSECS Operations Group [*Marine science*] (MSC)
**GOG** ........ Golden Tag Resources [*Vancouver Stock Exchange symbol*]
**GOG** ........ Gynecologic Oncology Group (EA)
**GOGG** ........ Ziguinchor [*Senegal*] [*ICAO location identifier*] (ICLI)
**GOGK** ........ Kolda [*Senegal*] [*ICAO location identifier*] (ICLI)
**GO/GO** ...... Government-Owned/Government-Operated [*Facility*]
**GOGO** ........ Nutri-Products, Inc. [*NASDAQ symbol*] (NQ)
**Gog Or** ........ Goguet's Origin of Laws [*A publication*] (DLA)
**GOGS** ........ Cap Skirring [*Senegal*] [*ICAO location identifier*] (ICLI)
**GOH** ........ Garments on Hangers [*Shipping*]
**goh** ........ German, Old High [*MARC language code*] [*Library of Congress*] (LCCP)
**GOH** ........ German Order of Harugari
**GOH** ........ Godthaab [*Denmark*] [*Airport symbol*]
**GOH** ........ Goliath Gold Mines Ltd. [*Toronto Stock Exchange symbol*] [*Vancouver Stock Exchange symbol*]
**GOH** ........ Goods on Hand (DS)
**GOH** ........ Nuuk [*Greenland*] [*Airport symbol*] (OAG)
**GOI** ........ Fort Knox, KY [*Location identifier*] [*FAA*] (FAAL)
**GOI** ........ Gearhart Industries, Inc. [*Formerly, Gearhart-Owen Industries, Inc.*] [*NYSE symbol*] (SPSG)
**GOI** ........ General Oriental Investments Ltd. [*Vancouver Stock Exchange symbol*]
**GOI** ........ Goa [*India*] [*Airport symbol*] (OAG)
**GOI** ........ Government of Indonesia
**GOI** ........ Government of Iran
**GOI** ........ Government of Israel (MCD)
**GOI** ........ Government-Owned Installation
**GOI** ........ Group Operations Instruction [*British military*] (DMA)
**GOI** ........ Gun Owners, Incorporated (EA)
**GOIC** ........ Gulf Organization for Industrial Consulting [*Doha, Qatar*] (EAIO)
**GOIFE** ....... Government of Israel Furnished Equipment (MCD)
**Goir Fr Co** ... Goirand's French Code of Commerce [*A publication*] (DLA)
**GOJ** ........ Blytheville, AR [*Location identifier*] [*FAA*] (FAAL)
**GOJ** ........ Government of Japan (CINC)
**GOK** ........ God Only Knows [*Facetious diagnosis for a puzzling medical case*]
**GOK** ........ Government of Korea
**GOK** ........ Guthrie, OK [*Location identifier*] [*FAA*] (FAAL)
**GOL** ........ General Operating Language [*Data processing*] (IEEE)
**GOL** ........ Goal-Oriented Language
**GOL** ........ Gold Beach, OR [*Location identifier*] [*FAA*] (FAAL)
**GOL** ........ Golden [*Bergen Park*] [*Colorado*] [*Seismograph station code, US Geological Survey*] (SEIS)
**GOL** ........ Golden Gate University. Law Review [*A publication*]
**GOL** ........ Goldlund Mines Ltd. [*Toronto Stock Exchange symbol*]
**GOL** ........ Guinness Overseas Limited [*British*]
**Gold** ........ Goldesborough's [*or Gouldsborough's*] English King's Bench Reports [*A publication*] (DLA)
**GOLD** ........ Graphic Online Language [*Data processing*] (IEEE)
**GOLD** ........ Great Eastern Mines Ltd. [*NASDAQ symbol*] (NQ)
**GOLDBERG** ... Generally Operational Linear Digit-Controlled Biphase Electrical Retardance Gate [*IBM Corp.*]
**Gold Bull** .... Gold Bulletin [*A publication*]
**Gold Coast** ... Judgments of the Full Court, Privy Council, and Divisional Courts, Gold Coast [*A publication*] (DLA)
**Gold Coast Geol Surv Bull** ... Gold Coast Geological Survey. Bulletin [*A publication*]
**Golden Bk** ... Golden Book Magazine [*A publication*]
**Golden Gate L Rev** ... Golden Gate Law Review [*A publication*]
**Golden Gate UL Rev** ... Golden Gate University. Law Review [*A publication*]
**Goldes** ........ Goldesborough's [*or Gouldsborough's*] English King's Bench Reports [*A publication*] (DLA)
**Gold Fleece** ... Golden Fleece [*A publication*]
**Gold & G** .... Goldsmith and Guthrie's Appeals Reports [*Missouri*] [*A publication*] (DLA)
**Gold K** ........ Goldene Keyt [*A publication*]
**Gold Placer Deposits Foot East Cordillera Bolivia** ... Gold Placer Deposits at the Foot of the Eastern Cordillera of Bolivia [*A publication*]

**Goldschmidt Inf** ... Goldschmidt Informiert [*A publication*]
**Golds Eq** .... Goldsmith's Doctrine and Practice of Equity [*6th ed.*] [*1871*] [*A publication*] (DLA)
**Goldsmiths J Gemm** ... Goldsmiths Journal and Gemmologist [*A publication*]
**Golf** .......... Olfactory G Protein [*Physiology*]
**GOLF** ........ S2 Golf, Inc. [*NASDAQ symbol*] (NQ)
**Golf Course Rep** ... Golf Course Reporter [*A publication*]
**Golf Dig** ..... Golf Digest [*A publication*]
**Golf Dig Mag** ... Golf Digest Magazine [*A publication*]
**Golf Mag**.... Golf Magazine [*A publication*]
**Gol Gate LR** ... Golden Gate University. Law Review [*A publication*]
**GOLKAR** .. Sekber Golongan Karya [*Joint Secretariat of Functional Groups*] [*Indonesia*] [*Political party*] (PPW)
**GOLPH**..... Giannetti On-Line Psychosocial History [*Personality development test*] [*Psychology*]
**GOLPS**...... Greek Orthodox Ladies Philoptochos Society (EA)
**GOM** ......... God's Own Medicine [*Also, God's Medicine*] [*Morphine*] [*Slang*]
**GOM** ......... Golden Eye Minerals [*Vancouver Stock Exchange symbol*]
**GOM** ......... Goma [*Zaire*] [*Airport symbol*] (OAG)
**Gom**............ [*Ludovicus*] Gomez [*Deceased, 1553*] [*Authority cited in pre-1607 legal work*] (DSA)
**GOM** ......... Government of Malaysia (CINC)
**GOM** ......... Government-Owned Material
**GOM** ......... Grand Old Man [*A venerated man, especially in a specific field. Originally referred to William Gladstone, 1809-98, British statesman and prime minister, who was also sometimes known to his detractors as "Grand Old Muddler"*] [*See also HOM*]
**GOM** ......... Gulf of Mexico [*Also, GLFMEX*]
**GOM** ......... KSC [*Kennedy Space Center*] Ground Operations Manager at DFRC [*Hugh L. Dryden Flight Research Center*] or WSMR [*White Sands Missile Range*] (NASA)
**GOM** ......... Macon Junior College, Macon, GA [*OCLC symbol*] (OCLC)
**GOMA**....... General Officer Money Allowance [*Military*] (AABC)
**GOMA**....... Good Outdoor Manners Association (EA)
**GOMAB**.... Goriva i Maziva [*A publication*]
**GOMAC**.... Government Microcircuit Applications Conference
**GOMAC**.... Groupement des Opticiens du Marche Commun [*Common Market Opticians' Group*] [*Paris, France*]
**GOMALCO** ... Gobel O'Malley Company [*Entertainer George Gobel's firm; O'Malley is business manager*]
**Gomal Univ J Res** ... Gomal University. Journal of Research [*A publication*]
**Gome**.......... [*Antonius*] Gomez [*Flourished, 16th century*] [*Authority cited in pre-1607 legal work*] (DSA)
**GOMER**.... Get Out of My Emergency Room [*Used as a noun in reference to an elderly, chronically ill patient*]
**GOMMS**... Ground Operations and Material Management System (MCD)
**GOMR**....... Global Ozone Monitoring Radiometer
**GOMR & R** ... Government-Owned Material Repair and Reimbursement (MCD)
**GOMS**....... Ground Operations Management System [*NASA*] (NASA)
**gon**............. Gondi [*MARC language code*] [*Library of Congress*] (LCCP)
**GON** .......... Gonococcal Ophthalmia Neonatorum [*Medicine*]
**GON** .......... New London [*Connecticut*] [*Airport symbol*] (OAG)
**GONAAR** ... Forest Science [*Sofia*] [*A publication*]
**GOND** ....... Gondola
**GONE**........ Plastigone Technologies, Inc. [*NASDAQ symbol*] (NQ)
**GONG** ....... Global Oscillations Network Group [*National Science Foundation*]
**GONG** ....... Groupe d'Organisation Nationale Guadeloupeenne [*Guadeloupe*] (PD)
**GONIO**...... Goniometer [*RADAR instrument*] (DSUE)
**Gon LR** ...... Gonzaga Law Review [*A publication*]
**GONT**........ Government on Taiwan
**Gonzaga L Rev** ... Gonzaga Law Review [*A publication*]
**Gonz L Rev** ... Gonzaga Law Review [*A publication*]
**Gonz Pub Lab L Rep** ... Gonzaga Special Report. Public Sector Labor Law [*A publication*] (DLA)
**GOO** .......... Generalized Overhauser Orbitals [*Atomic physics*]
**GOO** .......... Get Oil Out (EA)
**GOO** .......... Goldsil Resources Ltd. [*Toronto Stock Exchange symbol*] [*Vancouver Stock Exchange symbol*]
**GOO** .......... Goondiwindi [*Australia*] [*Airport symbol*] (OAG)
**GOO** .......... Goosecreekite [*A zeolite*]
**GOO** .......... Ground Observer Organization (NATG)
**GOO** .......... Ground Operation Order (NATG)
**GOO** .......... Group Operations Order [*British military*] (DMA)
**GOOD** ....... Diourbel [*Senegal*] [*ICAO location identifier*] (ICLI)
**GOOD** ....... Goody Products, Inc. [*NASDAQ symbol*] (NQ)
**Good Apple** ... Good Apple Newspaper [*A publication*]
**GOOD-B'YE** ... God Be with You (ROG)
**GOOD EGGS** ... Geriatric Order of Old Dolls Who Encourage the Generation Gap Singlemindedly [*Tongue-in-cheek teachers' organization*]
**Good Ev** ..... Goodeve's Law of Evidence [*India*] [*A publication*] (DLA)
**Goodeve** ..... Goodeve on Real Property [*1883-1906*] [*A publication*] (DLA)
**Good Farming Quart** ... Good Farming Quarterly [*A publication*]
**Goodfellow** ... Goodfellow Review of Crafts [*A publication*]
**Good Gard** ... Good Gardening [*A publication*]
**Good Govt** ... Good Government [*A publication*]
**Good H**....... Good Housekeeping [*A publication*]
**Good House** ... Good Housekeeping [*A publication*]
**Good Housekeep** ... Good Housekeeping [*A publication*]
**Good Pat** .... Goodeve's Abstract of Patent Cases [*1785-1883*] [*England*] [*A publication*] (DLA)
**Good Pkg** ... Good Packaging [*A publication*]
**Good Pr**...... Goodwin's Probate Practice [*A publication*] (DLA)
**Goodrich** .... BF Goodrich Co. Economic and Business Facts and Forecasts [*A publication*]
**Goodrich-Amram** ... Goodrich-Amram Procedural Rules Service [*A publication*] (DLA)
**Good Ry C** ... Goodeve on Railway Companies and Passengers [*A publication*] (DLA)
**Good & Wood** ... Full Bench Rulings, Edited by Goodeve and Woodman [*Bengal*] [*A publication*] (DLA)
**GOOFC** ..... Grand Ole Opry Fan Club (EA)
**GOOG** ....... Linguere [*Senegal*] [*ICAO location identifier*] (ICLI)
**GOOK** ....... Kaolack [*Senegal*] [*ICAO location identifier*] (ICLI)
**GOOMBY** ... Get Out of My Backyard [*Slang*]
**GOONS**..... Guild of One Name Studies [*Organization to link people with a common surname for the study of family history*] [*British*]
**GOOO** ....... Dakar [*Senegal*] [*ICAO location identifier*] (ICLI)
**GOOS**........ Gunnery Officers Ordnance School
**GOOSE** ..... Waysgoose [*Country fair*] (ROG)
**GOOV** ....... Dakar [*Senegal*] [*ICAO location identifier*] (ICLI)
**GOOY** ....... Dakar/Yoff [*Senegal*] [*ICAO location identifier*] (ICLI)
**GOP**........... General Operational Plot
**GOP**........... General Outpost [*Army*] (AABC)
**GOP**........... Girls' Own Paper [*A publication*]
**GOP**........... Gold Point Resources [*Vancouver Stock Exchange symbol*]
**GOP**........... Gorakhpur [*India*] [*Airport symbol*] (OAG)
**GOP**........... Government-Owned Property
**GOP**........... Government of the Philippines (CINC)
**GOP**........... Graham-McCormick Oil & Gas Partnership [*AMEX symbol*] (SPSG)
**GOP**........... Grand Old Party [*The Republican Party*]
**GOP**........... Grille Opening Panel [*Automotive engineering*]
**GOP**........... Ground Observer Post
**GOP**........... Ground Operations Panel [*NASA*] (NASA)
**GOPAL** ..... GOP [*Grand Old Party*] Women's Political Action League (EA)
**GOPARS**... Government-Operated Parts Store
**GOPE** ........ Government-Owned Plant Equipment
**GOPG**........ Ground Operations Planning Group [*NASA*] (NASA)
**GOPIRB**.... General Officer Product Improvement Review Board
**GOPITS** .... Grand Offertory Procession in the Sky [*Corporate sobriquet used by novelist William X. Kienzle*]
**GOPL** ........ General Outpost Line [*Army*]
**GOPOA**..... Gas and Oil Power [*A publication*]
**GOPR** ........ General Officers' Protocol Roster
**GOQ** ......... Golmud [*China*] [*Airport symbol*] (OAG)
**GOQS**........ General On-Line Query System (MCD)
**GOR**........... Gained Output Ratio (IEEE)
**GOR**........... Gas-Oil Ratio (IEEE)
**GOR**........... General Ocean Research [*Navy ship symbol*]
**GOR**........... General Officer Review (MCD)
**GOR**........... General Operating Room
**GOR**........... General Operational Requirement
**GOR**........... General Overruling Regulation [*Office of Price Stabilization*] (DLA)
**GOR**........... Golden Range Resources, Inc. [*Toronto Stock Exchange symbol*]
**GOR**........... Goldstack Resources [*Vancouver Stock Exchange symbol*]
**GOR**........... Gordian. Internationale Zeitschrift fuer Lebensmittel und Lebensmitteltechnologie [*A publication*]
**GOR**........... Gordon Jewelry Corp. [*NYSE symbol*] (SPSG)
**GOR**........... Gore [*Ethiopia*] [*Airport symbol*] (OAG)
**GOR**........... Gori [*USSR*] [*Seismograph station code, US Geological Survey*] (SEIS)
**GOR**........... Ground Operations Review (MCD)
**GOR**........... Gun Operations Room [*British military*] (DMA)
**GOR**........... Gurkha Other Rank [*Military*] [*British*]
**GORABE**... GO. Revista de Atualizacao em Ginecologia e Obstetricia [*A publication*]
**Gord Dec**.... Gordon on the Law of Decedents in Pennsylvania [*A publication*] (DLA)
**Gord Dig** .... Gordon's Digest of United States Laws [*A publication*] (DLA)
**GORD HIGHRS** ... Gordon Highlanders [*Military*] [*British*] (ROG)
**Gordian Int Z Lebensm Lebensmitteltechnologie** ... Gordian. Internationale Zeitschrift fuer Lebensmittel und Lebensmitteltechnologie [*A publication*]
**Gordon** ....... Gordon's Reports [*24-26 Colorado and 10-13 Colorado Appeals*] [*A publication*] (DLA)
**Gord Tr** ...... Gordon's Treason Trials [*A publication*] (DLA)
**Gore-B Comp** ... Gore-Brown on Companies [*43rd ed.*] [*1977*] [*A publication*] (DLA)
**GOREDCO** ... Gulf Oil Real Estate Development Company
**GO Rev Atualizacao Ginecol Obstet** ... GO. Revista de Atualizacao em Ginecologia e Obstetricia [*A publication*]
**GORF** ........ Goddard Optical Research Facility [*Goddard Space Flight Center*] [*NASA*]

**GORG**........ General Officers Review Group [*Air Force*]
**Gorg**........... Gorgias [*483-376BC*] [*Classical studies*] (OCD)
**G Org**......... Grand-Orgue [*Great Organ*] [*Music*]
**G ORG**....... Great Organ [*Music*]
**GORID**....... Ground Optical Recorder for Intercept Determination
**GORK**........ God Only Really Knows [*Facetious diagnosis for a puzzling medical case*]
**Gor'k Gos Nauchno Issled Inst Gig Tr Profbolezn Tr** ... Gor'kovskii Gosudarstvennyi Nauchno-Issledovatel'skii Institut Gigieny Truda i Profboleznei. Trudy [*A publication*]
**Gor'kov Gos Univ Ucen Zap** ... Gor'kovskii Gosudarstvennyi Universitet. Ucenye Zapiski [*A publication*]
**Gor'k Skh Inst Tr** ... Gor'kovskii Sel'skokhozyaistvennyi Institut. Trudy [*A publication*]
**Gor Let**....... Goriski Letnik Zbornik Goriskega Muzeja [*A publication*]
**Gorn Elektromekh Avtom** ... Gornaya Elektromekhanika i Avtomatika [*A publication*]
**Gorn Mash Avtom** ... Gornye Mashiny i Avtomatika [*A publication*]
**Gorn Odkrywkowe** ... Gornictwo Odkrywkowe [*A publication*]
**Gorno-Obogat Delo** ... Gorno-Obogatitel'noe Delo [*A publication*]
**Gorno-Obogat Zh** ... Gorno-Obogatitel'nyi Zhurnal [*A publication*]
**Gorn Zh**..... Gornyi Zhurnal [*A publication*]
**Gorn Zh (Mos)** ... Gornyi Zhurnal (Moscow) [*A publication*]
**GORP**........ Ground Operational [*or Operations*] Requirements Plan [*NASA*]
**GORP**........ Ground Operations Review Panel [*NASA*] (NASA)
**Gor R**.......... Gordon Review [*A publication*]
**GORS**........ Ground Observation Reporting System
**GORS**........ Ground Observer RF [*Radio Frequency*] System [*NASA*] (NASA)
**Gorsko Stop** ... Gorsko Stopanstvo [*Bulgaria*] [*A publication*]
**Gorskostop Nauka** ... Gorskostopanska Nauka [*A publication*]
**Gorskostop Nauka For Sci** ... Gorskostopanska Nauka. Forest Science [*A publication*]
**Gorskostop Nauka Izv Akad Selskostop Nauke** ... Gorskostopanska Nauka Izvestiya na Akademiiata na Selskostopankite Nauke [*A publication*]
**GORT**........ Gray Oral Reading Tests
**GORT-R**..... Gray Oral Reading Tests - Revised [*Educational test*]
**GORX**........ Graphite Oxidation from Reactor Excursion [*Engineering computer code*]
**Goryuchie Slantsy Khim Tekhnol** ... Goryuchie Slantsy. Khimiya i Tekhnologiya [*A publication*]
**Goryuch Slantsy Khim Tekhnol** ... Goryuchie Slantsy. Khimiya i Tekhnologiya [*Estonian SSR*] [*A publication*]
**Goryuch Slantsy (Moscow)** ... Goryuchie Slantsy (Moscow) [*A publication*]
**Goryuch Slantsy (Tallinn)** ... Goryuchie Slantsy (Tallinn) [*Estonian SSR*] [*A publication*]
**GOS**........... Gaekwad's Oriental Series [*A publication*]
**GOS**........... General Operating Specification [*Air Materiel Command*] (AAG)
**GOS**........... General Overhaul Specification
**GOS**........... Geodetic Optical System
**GOS**........... Global Observing Systems [*Weather*]
**GOS**........... Golden State Resources [*Vancouver Stock Exchange symbol*]
**GOS**........... Gosford [*Australia*] [*Airport symbol*] [*Obsolete*] (OAG)
**GOS**........... Gossip (DSUE)
**GOS**........... Government of Singapore (CINC)
**GOS**........... Government of Spain
**GOS**........... Government of Sweden (MCD)
**GOS**........... Grade of Service
**GOS**........... Grand Outside Sentinel [*Freemasonry*] (ROG)
**GOS**........... Graphics Operating System [*Tektronix*]
**GOS**........... Ground Operations System (MCD)
**GOS**........... Group Operating Services (NRCH)
**GOS**........... Group and Organization Studies [*A publication*]
**GOS**........... Lakeview, OR [*Location identifier*] [*FAA*] (FAAL)
**GOSC**........ General Officer Steering Committee [*Military*] (MCD)
**GOSD**........ Goinsiday [*A publication*]
**Gosf**............ Gosford's Manuscript Reports, Scotch Court of Session [*A publication*] (DLA)
**GOSH**........ Graphical Operating System Hack [*Data processing*]
**GOSH**........ Oshkosh B'Gosh, Inc. [*Oshkosh, WI*] [*NASDAQ symbol*] (NQ)
**Gos Inst Prikl Khim Tr** ... Gosudarstvennyi Institut Prikladnoi Khimii Trudy [*A publication*]
**GOSIP**....... Government Open Systems Implementation Protocol [*Telecommunications*]
**GOSM**....... Matam/Ouro Sogui [*Senegal*] [*ICAO location identifier*] (ICLI)
**Gos Nauchno Issled Energ Inst Im G M Krzhizhanovskogo Sb Tr** ... Gosudarstvennyi Nauchno-Issledovatel'skii Energeticheskii Institut Imeni G. M. Krzhizhanovskogo Sbornik Trudov [*A publication*]
**Gos Nauchno Issled Inst Keram Promsti Tr** ... Gosudarstvennyi Nauchno-Issledovatel'skii Institut Keramicheskoi Promyshlennosti Trudy [*A publication*]
**Gos Nauchno Issled Rentgeno Radiol Inst Tr** ... Gosudarstvennyi Nauchno-Issledovatel'skii Rentgeno-Radiologicheskii Institut Trudy [*A publication*]
**GOSP**........ Gas-Oil Separation Plant
**GOSP**........ Golden Spike National Historic Site
**GOSP**........ Gospel (ROG)
**GOSP**........ Podor [*Senegal*] [*ICAO location identifier*] (ICLI)
**Gosp Delo**.. Gospital'noe Delo [*A publication*]
**GOSPLAN** ... Gosudarstvennaja Planovaja Komissija [*Central Planning Commission*] [*USSR*]
**Gospod Miesna** ... Gospodarka Miesna [*A publication*]
**Gospod Paliwami Energ** ... Gospodarka Paliwami i Energia [*A publication*]
**Gospod Wodna** ... Gospodarka Wodna [*A publication*]
**Gosp Planowa** ... Gospodarka Planowa [*A publication*]
**GOSR**........ Richard Toll [*Senegal*] [*ICAO location identifier*] (ICLI)
**GOSS**......... Gossamer Hat [*Tall hat*] (ROG)
**GOSS**......... Ground Operational [*or Operations*] Support System [*NASA*]
**GOSS**......... Saint Louis [*Senegal*] [*ICAO location identifier*] (ICLI)
**GOSSIP**..... Government Open Systems Inter-Connection Procurement Policy [*Australia*]
**GOSSTCOMP** ... Global Sea Surface Temperature Computation
**GOSSTRAKH** ... Gosudarstvennoe Strakhovanie [*State insurance*] [*USSR*]
**GOST**........ Goddard Satellite Tracking [*NASA*] (MCD)
**GOST**........ Gossudarstvenny Obstschessojusny Standart [*All-Union State Standard*] [*USSR*]
**GOST**........ Guidance Optics and Sighting
**GOSTA**...... Gorsko Stopanstvo [*A publication*]
**G Ostet Ginecol** ... Giornale di Ostetricia e Ginecologia [*A publication*]
**Gos Vses Nauchno Issled Inst Tsem Promsti Nauchn Soobshch** ... Gosudarstvennyi Vsesoyuznyi Nauchno-Issledovatel'skii Institut Tsementnoi Promyshlennosti Nauchnye Soobshcheniya [*A publication*]
**Gos Vses Proektn Nauchno Issled Inst Tsem Promsti Tr** ... Gosudarstvennyi Vsesoyuznyi Proektnyi i Nauchno-Issledovatel'skii Institut Tsementnoi Promyshlennosti Trudy [*A publication*]
**GOT**.......... Glutamic-Oxaloacetic Transaminase [*Also, AAT, ASAT, AST*] [*An enzyme*]
**GOT**.......... Goldbelt Mines [*Vancouver Stock Exchange symbol*]
**GOT**.......... Goteborg [*Sweden*] [*Seismograph station code, US Geological Survey*] [*Closed*] (SEIS)
**GOT**.......... Gothenburg [*Sweden*] [*Airport symbol*] (OAG)
**got**............. Gothic [*MARC language code*] [*Library of Congress*] (LCCP)
**GOT**.......... Gottschalks, Inc. [*NYSE symbol*] (SPSG)
**GOT**.......... Government-Owned Terminal
**GOTA**........ Gotabanken [*Bank*] [*Sweden*]
**GOTA**........ Green Olive Trade Association (EA)
**GOTB**........ Bakel [*Senegal*] [*ICAO location identifier*] (ICLI)
**G/OTBSR** ... Gas/Oil Tax Block Summary Record [*IRS*]
**GOTCO**...... Gulf Oil Trading Company
**Goteb Ethnogr Mus** ... Goteborgs Ethnographical Museum [*A publication*]
**Goteb K Vetensk Vitter Hets-Samh Handl Sjatte Foljden Ser B** ... Goteborgs Kungliga Vetenskaps och Vitter Hets-Samhalles Handlingar Sjatte Foljden. Series B [*A publication*]
**Goteb Naturhist Mus Arstryck** ... Goteborgs Naturhistoriska Museum Arstryck [*A publication*]
**Goteborg Univ Naturgeogr Inst Rapp** ... Goteborg Universitet. Naturgeografiska Institutionen. Rapport [*A publication*]
**GOTG**........ Government of the Gambia
**Goth**........... De Bello Gothico [*of Procopius*] [*Classical studies*] (OCD)
**GOTH**....... Gothic [*Language, etc.*]
**GotHA**....... Goteborgs Hogskolas Arsskrift [*Gothenburg*] [*A publication*] (BJA)
**Gothenburg Stud Phys** ... Gothenburg Studies in Physics [*A publication*]
**Goth SE**..... Gothenburg Studies in English [*A publication*]
**GOTK**........ Geotek Industries, Inc. [*NASDAQ symbol*] (NQ)
**GOTK**........ Kedougou [*Senegal*] [*ICAO location identifier*] (ICLI)
**GOTL**........ Gotaas-Larsen Shipping Corp. [*NASDAQ symbol*] (NQ)
**Gotlaendskt Arkiv** ... Gotlaendskt Arkiv [*A publication*]
**GOTN**........ Niokolo Koba [*Senegal*] [*ICAO location identifier*] (ICLI)
**GOTOH**.... Go to Heaven [*Name of missionary, "Professor Gotoh," for Worldwide Church of God*]
**G/OTPSR** ... Gas/Oil Tax Program Summary Record [*IRS*]
**GOTR**........ Greek Orthodox Theological Review [*A publication*] (BJA)
**GOTRAN**.. Load and Go FORTRAN [*Data processing*]
**GOTS**........ Gravity-Oriented Test Satellite [*NASA*]
**GOTS**........ Simenti [*Senegal*] [*ICAO location identifier*] (ICLI)
**GOTT**........ Gott Corp. [*NASDAQ symbol*] (NQ)
**GOTT**........ Tambacounda [*Senegal*] [*ICAO location identifier*] (ICLI)
**Gott Abh**.... Abhandlungen der Kungliga. Gessellschaft der Wissenschaften zu Goettingen [*A publication*]
**Gott Anz**..... Goettingischer Gelehrte Anzeigen [*A publication*] (OCD)
**Gottesdienst Km** ... Gottesdienst und Kirchenmusik [*A publication*]
**Gottesd u Kir** ... Gottesdienst und Kirchenmusik [*A publication*]
**GOTTEX**... Gottlieb Textiles
**Gott Nachr** ... Nachrichten von der Gesellschaft der Wissenschaften zu Goettingen [*A publication*] (OCD)
**Gottschall**.. Gottschall's Dayton Superior Court Reports [*Ohio*] [*A publication*] (DLA)
**GOTU**........ Glider Operational Training Unit [*British military*] (DMA)
**GOU**.......... Garoua [*Cameroon*] [*Airport symbol*] (OAG)
**GOU**.......... Grupo de Oficiales Unidos [*Group of United Officers*] [*Argentina*]
**GOU**.......... Gulf Canada Resources Ltd. [*AMEX symbol*] [*Toronto Stock Exchange symbol*]
**GOU**.......... Oglethorpe University, Atlanta, GA [*OCLC symbol*] (OCLC)
**Gouc Col Se** ... Goucher College Series [*A publication*]

**Goud Pand** ... Goudsmit's Pandects [*Roman law*] [*A publication*] (DLA)
**GOULB** ..... Goulburn [*Australia*] (ROG)
**Goulcae J Educ** ... Goulcae Journal of Education (Goulburn College of Advanced Education) [*A publication*] (APTA)
**Gould** ......... Gouldsborough's English King's Bench Reports [*A publication*] (DLA)
**Gould League NSW Notes** ... Gould League of Bird Lovers of New South Wales. Notes [*A publication*] (APTA)
**Gould Pl** ..... Gould on the Principles of Pleading in Civil Actions [*A publication*] (DLA)
**Gouldsb** ...... Gouldsborough's English King's Bench Reports [*A publication*] (DLA)
**Gouldsb (Eng)** ... Gouldsborough's English King's Bench Reports [*A publication*] (DLA)
**Gould's Dig** ... Gould's Arkansas Digest of Laws [*A publication*] (DLA)
**Gould Sten Rep** ... Gould's Stenographic Reporter [*Monographic Series*] [*Albany, NY*] [*A publication*] (DLA)
**Gould & T** .. Gould and Tucker's Notes on Revised Statutes of United States [*A publication*] (DLA)
**Gould Wat** ... Gould on Waters [*A publication*] (DLA)
**Gour** .......... Gourick's Patent Digest [*1889-91*] [*A publication*] (DLA)
**Gourl Gen Av** ... Gourlie on General Average [*A publication*] (DLA)
**GOV** .......... Generator Output Voltage
**GOV** .......... Global Government Plus Fund, Inc. [*NYSE symbol*] (SPSG)
**GOV** .......... Golden Dividend Resources [*Vancouver Stock Exchange symbol*]
**GOV** .......... Govalkot [*India*] [*Seismograph station code, US Geological Survey*] [*Closed*] (SEIS)
**GOV** .......... Gove [*Australia*] [*Airport symbol*] (OAG)
**GOV** .......... Govern (ROG)
**GOV** .......... Government
**GOV** .......... Government Executive [*A publication*]
**GOV** .......... Governor (AFM)
**GOVAD** ...... Golden Fleece [*A publication*]
**Gov Agric Res Cent Ghent Act Rep** ... Government Agricultural Research Centre. Ghent. Activity Report [*A publication*]
**GOVAIRAUTHOUT** ... Travel via Government Aircraft Authorized Outside CONUS [*Military*]
**GOVAIRAUTHVATL** ... Travel via Government Aircraft Authorized Outside CONUS Where Available [*Military*]
**GOVAIRDIR** ... Travel via Government Aircraft Is Directed Where Necessary [*Military*]
**GOVAIRDIROUT** ... Travel via Government Aircraft Is Directed Outside CONUS [*Military*]
**GOVAIRDIRVAIL** ... Travel via Government Aircraft Is Directed Outside CONUS Where Available [*Military*]
**GOVAIRPRI** ... Travel via Government Aircraft Outside CONUS Class _____ Priority Certified [*Military*]
**GOVCOMLAIRAUTH** ... Travel via Government and/or Commercial Aircraft Authorized Where Necessary to Expedite Completion of Duty [*Military*]
**GOVD** ........ Governed (ROG)
**Gov Data Syst** ... Government Data Systems [*United States*] [*A publication*]
**Govea** ......... [*Antonius*] Goveanus [*Deceased, 1565*] [*Authority cited in pre-1607 legal work*] (DSA)
**Governmental Fin** ... Governmental Finance [*A publication*]
**Governmental Research Bul (Fla)** ... Governmental Research Bulletin (Florida) [*A publication*]
**Gov Finance** ... Governmental Finance [*A publication*]
**GOVG** ........ Governing (MSA)
**GOVMAR** ... Governor, Marshall Islands
**Gov Metall Lab Repub S Afr Rep** ... Government Metallurgical Laboratory. Republic of South Africa. Report [*A publication*]
**GOVN** ....... Govern (ROG)
**Gov Pest Infest Lab Annu Rep** ... Government Pest Infestation Laboratory. Annual Report [*A publication*]
**Gov Publ Rev** ... Government Publications Review [*A publication*]
**Gov Pub R** ... Government Publications Review [*A publication*]
**Govr** .......... Governor
**Gov Relat Note** ... Government Relations Note [*A publication*]
**Gov Rep Announce** ... Government Reports Announcements [*A publication*]
**Gov Rep Announce Index** ... Government Reports Announcements and Index [*A publication*]
**Gov Reports Announce & Index** ... Government Reports Announcements and Index [*A publication*]
**GOVS** ........ Governments Division [*Census*] (OICC)
**GOV STD** ... Government Standards
**GOVT** ........ Government (AFM)
**GOVT** ........ Government [*Boston*] [*A publication*]
**Govt Col Econ J** ... Government College Economic Journal [*A publication*]
**Gov't Cont Rep** ... Government Contracts Reporter [*Commerce Clearing House*] [*A publication*] (DLA)
**Govt Cont Rep CCH** ... Government Contracts Reports. Commerce Clearing House [*A publication*]
**Govt Data Sys** ... Government Data Systems [*A publication*]
**Gov't Empl Rel Rep** ... Government Employee Relations Report [*A publication*]
**Govt Empl Rel Rep BNA** ... Government Employee Relations Report. Bureau of National Affairs [*A publication*]
**Govt Fin** ..... Governmental Finance [*A publication*]
**Govt Fin R** ... Government Finance Review [*A publication*]
**Govt Gaz W Aust** ... Government Gazette. Western Australia [*A publication*]
**GOVTL** ..... Governmental
**GOVTLAIRNOREUR** ... Commander, Allied Air Forces, Northern Europe
**Govt & Oppos** ... Government and Opposition [*A publication*]
**Govt Oppos** ... Government and Opposition [*A publication*]
**Govt and Opposition** ... Government and Opposition [*A publication*]
**Govt Publns** ... Government Publications [*England*] [*A publication*]
**Govt Pubns R** ... Government Publications Review [*A publication*]
**Govt Pubns Rev** ... Government Publications Review [*A publication*]
**Govt Pubns R (Pt A)** ... Government Publications Review (Part A) [*A publication*]
**Govt Pub R** ... Government Publications Review [*A publication*]
**Govt Pub Rev** ... Government Publications Review [*A publication*]
**GOVTRANSDIROUT** ... Travel via Government Transportation Directed Outside CONUS [*Military*]
**GOVTRANSDIRVAIL** ... Travel via Government Transportation Directed Outside CONUS Where Available [*Military*]
**Govt Rep Announce Index** ... Government Reports Announcements and Index [*A publication*]
**Govt Rept Announc** ... Government Reports Announcements and Index [*A publication*]
**Govt Stand** ... Government Standard [*A publication*]
**Govt Union R** ... Government Union Review [*A publication*]
**Govt Union Rev** ... Government Union Review [*A publication*]
**GOW** ......... Gowganda Resources, Inc. [*Toronto Stock Exchange symbol*] [*Vancouver Stock Exchange symbol*]
**Gow** ........... Gow's English Nisi Prius Cases [*171 English Reprint*] [*A publication*] (DLA)
**GOW** ......... Grand Old Woman [*England's Queen Victoria*]
**GOW** ......... Gunnery Officer's Writer [*Navy*] [*British*]
**Gower B** ...... Gower Birds [*A publication*]
**GOWEX** .... Geometry of the Wake Experiment [*Military*] (MCD)
**GOWG** ...... Ground Operations Working Group (MCD)
**GOWGF** .... Gowganda Resources, Inc. [*NASDAQ symbol*] (NQ)
**GOWMA** ... Gulf Oil Wholesale Marketers Association (EA)
**Gow NP** ...... Gow's English Nisi Prius Cases [*171 English Reprint*] [*A publication*] (DLA)
**Gow NP (Eng)** ... Gow's English Nisi Prius Cases [*171 English Reprint*] [*A publication*] (DLA)
**Gow Part** .... Gow on Partnerships [*A publication*] (DLA)
**GOX** .......... Galaxy Oil Co. [*AMEX symbol*] (SPSG)
**GOX** .......... Gaseous Oxygen
**GOX** .......... Greenville, SC [*Location identifier*] [*FAA*] (FAAL)
**GOY** .......... Gorny [*USSR*] [*Seismograph station code, US Geological Survey*] [*Closed*] (SEIS)
**GOY** .......... GWE [*Global Weather Experiment*] Operational Year [*Marine science*] (MSC)
**GOYA** ........ Get Off Your After-End [*Slang*] [*Bowdlerized version*]
**GOYA** ........ Greek Orthodox Youth of America [*Later, GOYAL*] (EA)
**GOYAL** ..... Greek Orthodox Young Adult League (EA)
**GOZ** .......... Gorna Orjachovica [*Bulgaria*] [*Airport symbol*] (OAG)
**Goza** .......... [*Ludovicus*] Gozzadini [*Deceased, 1536*] [*Authority cited in pre-1607 legal work*] (DSA)
**Gozad** ......... [*Ludovicus*] Gozzadini [*Deceased, 1536*] [*Authority cited in pre-1607 legal work*] (DSA)
**Gozd Vestn** ... Gozdarski Vestnik [*A publication*]
**Goz Klin Bul** ... Goz Klinigi Bulteni [*A publication*]
**GP** ............. Albania [*License plate code assigned to foreign diplomats in the US*]
**GP** ............. Ciba-Geigy AG [*Switzerland*] [*Research code symbol*]
**GP** ............. Du Pont [*E. I.*] De Nemours & Co., Inc. [*Research code symbol*]
**GP** ............. Galactic Plane [*Astronomy*]
**GP** ............. Galactic Probe
**GP** ............. Gallbladder Patient
**GP** ............. Galley Proof (ADA)
**GP** ............. Gallup Poll
**GP** ............. Galvanized Pipe [*Technical drawings*]
**GP** ............. Galvanized Plain [*Metal industry*]
**GP** ............. Games Played [*Sports statistics*]
**GP** ............. Gang Punch [*Data processing*]
**G/P** ............ Ganhos e Perdas [*Profit and Loss*] [*Business term*] [*Portuguese*]
**GP** ............. Gas, Persistent
**GP** ............. Gas-Plasma [*Computer display panel*]
**GP** ............. Gas Pressure (MUGU)
**GP** ............. Gastric Pressure [*Physiology*]
**GP** ............. Gastroplasty [*Medicine*]
**GP** ............. Gemini Airlines Ltd. [*Ghana*] [*ICAO designator*] (FAAC)
**GP** ............. General Paralysis [*or Paresis*] [*Medicine*]
**GP** ............. General Pause [*Music*]
**GP** ............. General Plant Telephone [*Nuclear energy*] (NRCH)
**GP** ............. General Practice [*A publication*]
**GP** ............. General Practitioner [*of medicine*]
**GP** ............. General Preferred Tariff [*Canada*]
**GP** ............. General Principles [*FBI standardized term*]
**GP** ............. General Processor
**GP** ............. General Product (BUR)
**GP** ............. General Protection [*Data processing*] (BYTE)
**GP** ............. General Provision
**GP** ............. General Public [*Merchandising slang*]
**GP** ............. General Publication (KSC)

**GP** ............. General Purpose
**GP** ............. Generalized Programming [*Data processing*]
**GP** ............. Genesis Project (EA)
**GP** ............. Genetic Prediabetes [*Endocrinology*]
**GP** ............. Geographic Point
**GP** ............. Geographical Pole
**GP** ............. Geographical Position
**GP** ............. Geometric Progression
**GP** ............. Georgia-Pacific Corp. [*NYSE symbol*] (SPSG)
**GP** ............. Germinable Propagule [*Botany*]
**GP** ............. Geuzenpenning Munt- en Penningkundig Nieuws [*A publication*]
**GP** ............. Giant Pulse
**GP** ............. Gimbal Package
**GP** ............. Gimbal Platform (AAG)
**GP** ............. Gimbal Point
**GP** ............. Giornale dei Poeti [*A publication*]
**GP** ............. Girard-Point [*Virus*]
**GP** ............. Girls' PROUT [*Progressive Utilization Theory*] (EA)
**GP** ............. Glia Precursor [*Biochemistry*]
**GP** ............. Glide Path [*Aviation*]
**GP** ............. Gliomatosis Peritonei [*Oncology*]
**GP** ............. Globus Pallidus [*Brain anatomy*]
**GP** ............. Gloria Patri [*Glory to the Father*] [*Latin*]
**GP** ............. Glucose Phosphate [*Biochemistry*]
**GP** ............. Glycerophosphate [*Biochemistry*]
**GP** ............. Glycogen Phosphorylase [*An enzyme*]
**GP** ............. Glycolyl Phthalate [*Organic chemistry*]
**GP** ............. Glycoprotein
**GP** ............. Goal Post
**GP** ............. Goal Programming
**GP** ............. Going Public [*Investment term*]
**GP** ............. Gold Points [*Investment term*]
**GP** ............. Government Property
**GP** ............. Gozo Party [*Malta*] [*Political party*] (PPE)
**GP** ............. Grace Period [*Business term*]
**GP** ............. Graded Program
**GP** ............. Graduate in Pharmacy [*British*] (ROG)
**GP** ............. Gram-Positive [*Also, GRP*] [*Microbiology*]
**GP** ............. Grand Passion
**GP** ............. Grand Patron [*Freemasonry*]
**GP** ............. Grand Prelate [*Freemasonry*]
**GP** ............. Grand Prix
**GP** ............. Grand Pursuivant [*Freemasonry*] (ROG)
**GP** ............. Grandmothers for Peace (EA)
**GP** ............. Graphics Processor
**GP** ............. Grass Pollen [*Immunology*]
**GP** ............. Gratitude Patient [*A nonpaying patient*] [*Medical slang*]
**GP** ............. Gravitational Redshift Space Probe [*Also, GRAVR*]
**GP** ............. Gray Panthers (EA)
**GP** ............. Great Peoples [*A publication*]
**GP** ............. Great Portland Street [*London*] (DSUE)
**GP** ............. Great Primer
**G/P** ............. Green Phone [*NASA*] (KSC)
**GP** ............. Greenhouse Perennial [*Horticulture*] (ROG)
**GP** ............. Gregorios ho Palamas [*A publication*]
**GP** ............. Gross Premium [*Insurance*] (AIA)
**GP** ............. Gross Profit [*Business term*]
**GP** ............. Ground Pneumatic (AAG)
**GP** ............. Ground-Protective [*Relay*]
**GP** ............. Ground Rods [*JETDS nomenclature*] [*Military*] (CET)
**GP** ............. Group (AFM)
**GP** ............. Groupe de Paris [*Paris Group*] [*Saint Cloud, France*] (EAIO)
**GP** ............. Growing Point [*A publication*]
**GP** ............. Guadeloupe [*ANSI two-letter standard code*] (CNC)
**gp** ............. Guadeloupe [*MARC country of publication code*] [*Library of Congress*] (LCCP)
**GP** ............. Guidance Package
**GP** ............. Guided Projectile [*Military*] (CAAL)
**GP** ............. Guinea Pig
**GP** ............. Guitar Player [*A publication*]
**GP** ............. Gulden Passer [*A publication*]
**GP** ............. Gun Pointer [*Naval gunnery*]
**GP** ............. Gutter Pair [*Philately*]
**GP** ............. GWEN [*Ground Wave Emergency Network*] Project (EA)
**GP** ............. Gyro Package
**GP** ............. Parental Guidance Suggested [*Later, PG*] [*All ages admitted*] [*Movie rating*]
**G1P** ............. Glucose-1-phosphate [*Biochemistry*]
**GP (Gas)** .... Persistent Chemical Agent Gas
**GPA** ........... Ciba-Geigy Corp. [*Research code symbol*]
**GPA** ........... Gas Pressure Activator (MCD)
**GPA** ........... Gas Processors Association (EA)
**GPA** ........... Gay Press Association [*Later, GLPA*] (EA)
**GPA** ........... General Passenger Agent
**GPA** ........... General Public Assistance [*A form of public charity*]
**GPA** ........... General Purchasing Agency [*Allied German Occupation Forces*]
**GPA** ........... General-Purpose Amplifier
**GPA** ........... General-Purpose Analysis (IEEE)
**GPA** ........... General-Purpose Array
**G PA** .......... Geology of Pennsylvania [*A publication*]
**GPA** ........... Geschichte der Perser und Araber zur Zeit der Sasaniden [*A publication*] (BJA)
**GPa** ........... Gigapascal [*SI unit of pressure*]
**G & PA** ....... Girls and Physical Activity National Newsletter [*A publication*]
**GPA** ........... Global Program on AIDS [*Acquired Immune Deficiency Syndrome*] [*WHO*]
**GPA** ........... Glycerine Producers Association (EA)
**GPA** ........... Glycophorin A [*Biochemistry*]
**GPA** ........... Golpazari [*Turkey*] [*Also, GLP*] [*Seismograph station code, US Geological Survey*] (SEIS)
**GPA** ........... Government Property Administration (MCD)
**GPA** ........... Grade-Point Average [*Education*]
**GPA** ........... Graduation Pledge Alliance [*An association*] (EA)
**GPA** ........... Grandparents Anonymous (EA)
**GPA** ........... Graphical PERT [*Program Evaluation and Review Technique*] Analog [*Data processing*] (IEEE)
**GPA** ........... Graphics Philately Association (EA)
**GPA** ........... Graphics Preparatory Association (EA)
**GPA** ........... Green Party of Australia [*Political party*] (ADA)
**GPA** ........... Green Peach Aphid [*Entomology*]
**GPA** ........... Ground Plane Antenna
**GPA** ........... Grounded Plate Amplifier
**GPA** ........... Group Practice Association [*Medicine*]
**GPA** ........... Guidance Platform Assembly [*Military*] (AABC)
**GPA** ........... Guidance Positioning Assembly
**GPA** ........... Guide to the Performing Arts [*A publication*]
**GPA** ........... Guinea Pig Albumin
**GPA** ........... Guinness Peat Aviation [*Commercial firm*] [*British*]
**GPA** ........... Gulfcoast Pulpwood Association (EA)
**GPA** ........... United States Government Printing Office - Serials, Alexandria, VA [*OCLC symbol*] (OCLC)
**GPAA** ......... Gold Prospectors Association of America (EA)
**GPAC** ......... General-Purpose Analog Computer (DEN)
**GPAC** ......... Great Plains Agricultural Council (EA)
**GPAD** ......... Gallons per Acre per Day [*Irrigation*]
**GPAD** ......... Graphics Program for Aircraft Design
**GPAK** ......... Graphic Packaging Corp. [*NASDAQ symbol*] (NQ)
**G Pal Abh** .. Geologische und Paleontologische Abhandlungen [*A publication*]
**GPAM** ....... Graduated-Payment Adjustable Mortgage
**GPAR** ........ General Parametrics Corp. [*Berkeley, CA*] [*NASDAQ symbol*] (NQ)
**GPAS** ......... General Performance Appraisals System
**GPAS** ......... General-Purpose Airborne Simulator
**GPAT** ......... General-Purpose Automatic Test [*Air Force*]
**GPATE** ....... General-Purpose Automatic Test Equipment [*Army*] (MSA)
**GPATS** ....... General-Purpose Automatic Test Station
**GPATS** ....... General-Purpose Automatic Test System [*Air Force*]
**GPAX** ........ Grow Ventures Corp. [*NASDAQ symbol*] (NQ)
**GPB** ........... General Purchasing Board
**GPB** ........... General-Purpose Buffer
**GPB** ........... Geon Process Butadiene
**GPB** ........... Glossopharyngeal Breathing
**GPB** ........... Glucose Phosphorylase B [*An enzyme*]
**GPB** ........... Glycoprotein B [*Biochemistry*]
**GPB** ........... Government Patents Board [*Functions transferred to Secretary of Commerce, 1961*]
**GP-B** .......... Gravity Probe-B [*Experiment to test Einstein's Theory of General Relativity*]
**GPB** ........... Pittsburgh, PA [*Location identifier*] [*FAA*] (FAAL)
**GPBIM** ....... General-Purpose Buffer Interface Module [*Data processing*] (MCD)
**GPBP** ......... Guinea Pig Myelin Basic Protein [*Immunochemistry*]
**GPBS** ......... Gas Pressure Bending System
**GPBTO** ...... General-Purpose Barbed Tape Obstacle [*Army*] (RDA)
**GPC** ........... Gallons per Capita
**GPC** ........... Gandhi Peace Center (EA)
**GPC** ........... Gastrointestinal Pathology Club [*Later, GPS*] (EA)
**GPC** ........... Gauge Pressure Control
**GPC** ........... Gay People at Columbia [*Later, CGLA*] (EA)
**GPC** ........... Gel Permeation Chromatography
**GPC** ........... General People's Congress [*or Committee*] [*Libya*] [*Political party*] (PPW)
**GPC** ........... General Peripheral Controller
**GPC** ........... General Physical Condition [*Medicine*]
**GPC** ........... General-Purpose Carrier [*Military*]
**GPC** ........... General-Purpose Computer
**GPC** ........... General Purposes Committee [*British*] (DCTA)
**GPC** ........... Genuine Parts Company [*NYSE symbol*] (SPSG)
**GPC** ........... Geocentric Pendulum Control
**GPC** ........... Georgia Peanut Commission (EA)
**GPC** ........... Ghana Publishing Company
**GPC** ........... Giant Papillary Conjunctivitis [*Ophthalmology*]
**GPC** ........... Giant Piston Core [*Geology*]
**GPC** ........... Global Plotting Chart [*Air Force*]
**GPC** ........... Glycerylphosphorylcholine [*Biochemistry*]
**GPC** ........... Golay Pneumatic Cell
**GPC** ........... Government Paint Committee [*Australia*]
**GPC** ........... Grande Prairie Regional College Library [*UTLAS symbol*]
**GPC** ........... Grass Pollen Count [*Immunology*]
**GPC** ........... Gross Profit Contribution

**GPC** .......... Ground Power Contactor
**GPC** .......... Guinea Pig Complement [*Immunochemistry*]
**GPC** .......... Gulf Publishing Company
**GPC** .......... Gypsum-Plaster Ceiling [*Technical drawings*]
**GPCA** ........ General-Purpose Communications Adapter
**GPCA** ........ Golf Products and Components Association (EA)
**GPCA** ........ Great Pyrenees Club of America (EA)
**Gp Capt**...... Group Captain [*British military*] (DMA)
**GPCB**......... GOAL [*Ground Operations Aerospace Language*] Program Control Block (MCD)
**GPCD** ........ Gallons per Capita per Day
**GPC-ERR** ... General Passenger Committee - Eastern Railroads [*Defunct*] (EA)
**GPCI**.......... Geographic Practice Cost Index [*Medicare*]
**GPCK**......... Guardian Packaging Corp. [*NASDAQ symbol*] (NQ)
**GPCL**.......... General-Purpose Closed Loop [*Nuclear energy*] (NRCH)
**GPCO** ........ Global Perspective Country Outlooks [*Global Perspective, Inc.*] [*Information service or system*] (CRD)
**GPCOC** ..... General-Purpose Central Office Concentrator [*Telecommunications*]
**GPCP**......... General-Purpose Contouring Program
**GPCP**......... Generalized Process Control Programming [*Data processing*] (IEEE)
**GPCP**......... Global Precipitation Chemistry Project [*Study of rain properties*]
**GPCP**......... Great Plains Conservation Program
**GPCR**......... Gas-to-Particle Conversion Rate [*Physics*]
**GPCR**......... Great Proletarian Cultural Revolution [*People's Republic of China*]
**GPCT**......... George Peabody College for Teachers [*Later, George Peabody College for Teachers of Vanderbilt University*] [*Tennessee*]
**GPD** ........... Gallons per Day
**GPD** ........... General Passenger Department
**GPD** ........... General Police Duties [*British military*] (DMA)
**GPD** ........... General-Purpose Data
**GPD** ........... General-Purpose Discipline [*IBM Corp.*]
**GPD** ........... Generals for Peace and Disarmament [*Ittervoort, Netherlands*] (EAIO)
**GPD** ........... Gimbal Position Display (KSC)
**GPD** ........... Glucose-6-phosphate Dehydrogenase [*Also, G6PD, G6PDH*] [*An enzyme*]
**GPD** ........... Glycerophosphate Dehydrogenase
**GPD** ........... Grams per Denier
**GPD** ........... Greenpond [*New Jersey*] [*Seismograph station code, US Geological Survey*] (SEIS)
**G6PD** ......... Glucose-6-phosphate Dehydrogenase [*Also, GPD, G6PDH*] [*An enzyme*]
**GPDC** ........ General-Purpose Digital Computer
**GPDH**........ Glycerolphosphate Dehydrogenase [*An enzyme*]
**G6PDH**...... Glucose-6-phosphate Dehydrogenase [*Also, GPD, G6PD*] [*An enzyme*]
**GPDM** ....... Geopotential Decameter [*Telecommunications*] (TEL)
**GPDS**......... General-Purpose Display System
**GPDSC**...... Girl's Public Day School Company [*British*] (ROG)
**GPDST** ...... Girls' Public Day School Trust [*British*]
**GPDU**........ Groupe de Planification des Derives Urbaines [*Canada*]
**GPDW** ....... Gypsum Dry Wall [*Technical drawings*]
**GPE** ........... Gas Power Exchange
**GPE** ........... General-Purpose English (ADA)
**GPE** ........... General-Purpose Equipment
**GPE** ........... General-Purpose Evaporator [*Nuclear energy*] (NRCH)
**GPE** ........... Geometric Position Error (MCD)
**Gp E** ........... Geophysical Engineer
**GPE** ........... Georgia Power Co. [*NYSE symbol*] (SPSG)
**GPE** ........... Global Perspectives in Education (EA)
**GPE** ........... Golden Pheasant [*Vancouver Stock Exchange symbol*]
**GPE** ........... Government Preliminary Evaluation (MCD)
**GPE** ........... Grammaire du Palmyrenien Epigraphique [*A publication*] (BJA)
**GPE** ........... Los Angeles, CA [*Location identifier*] [*FAA*] (FAAL)
**Gp Engr** ..... Geophysical Engineer
**GPEP**......... General Professional Education of the Physician [*Panel report*] [*Association of American Medical Colleges*]
**GPER**......... General Plant Equipment Requirements
**GPERF** ...... Ground Passive Electronic Reconnaissance Facility
**GPerfArts** .. Guide to the Performing Arts [*A publication*]
**GPES** ......... Ground Proximity Extraction System
**G Pet** .......... Gospel of Peter [*Apocryphal work*]
**GPETE** ...... General-Purpose Electronic Test Equipment (NVT)
**GPF**............ Gallons per Flush [*Plumbing*]
**GPF**............ Gandhi Peace Foundation (EAIO)
**GPF**............ Gas Proof (AABC)
**GPF**............ General Protection Fault [*Computer programming*] (BYTE)
**GPF**............ General-Purpose Forces
**GPF**............ Generalized Production Function [*Industrial economics*]
**GPF**............ Grains per Foot
**GPF**............ Grande Puissance Filloux [*World War II*]
**GPF**............ Granulocytosis-Promoting Factor [*Hematology*]
**GPF**............ Groove between Parallel Folds
**GPF**............ Guardian Pacific Rim Corp. [*Toronto Stock Exchange symbol*]
**GPF**............ Guinea Pig Fibrinogen
**GPFC**.......... Galaxy Patrol Fan Club (EA)
**GPFC**.......... Gene Pitney Fan Club (EA)
**GPFC**.......... General-Purpose Function Code (NVT)
**GPFL**.......... Group Flashing [*Navigation signal lights*]
**GPFU**.......... Gas Particulate Filter Unit (MCD)
**GPG**............ General Planning Group
**GPG**............ Grains per Gallon [*Unit of measure for water hardness*]
**GPG**............ Grande Portage [*Vancouver Stock Exchange symbol*]
**GPG**............ Guinness Peat Group [*British*]
**GPGG**......... Guinea Pig Gamma Globulin [*Immunochemistry*]
**GPGL**.......... General-Purpose Graphic Language [*Data processing*] (IEEE)
**GPH**............ Gallons per Hour
**G Ph**........... Graduate in Pharmacy
**GPH**............ Graphite (MSA)
**GPH**............ Grenzpolizeihelfer [*Border Police Aide*] [*German*]
**GPHA**......... Great Plains Historical Association [*Later, IGP*] (EA)
**GPHF** ......... General Pulaski Heritage Foundation (EA)
**GPHMG**.... General-Purpose Heavy Machine Gun (MCD)
**GPHP** ......... Give Peace Holiday Project (EA)
**GPHS** ......... General-Purpose Heat Source [*Nuclear energy*]
**GPHSC**...... Group Project for Holocaust Survivors and Their Children (EA)
**GPHTAR** .. Geophytology [*A publication*]
**GPHW**....... Gay Public Health Workers Caucus [*Later, LGCPHW*] (EA)
**GPHY**......... General Physics Corp. [*NASDAQ symbol*] (NQ)
**GPI** ............ General Paralysis of the Insane [*Literal translation, but also medical slang for eccentricity*]
**GPI** ............ General Patents Index [*A publication*]
**GPI** ............ General Periodicals Index [*Information Access Co.*] [*Information service or system*] (CRD)
**GPI** ............ General Precision, Incorporated
**GPI** ............ General-Purpose Interface
**GPI** ............ General-Purpose Inverter (KSC)
**GPI** ............ Gimbal Position Indicator (KSC)
**GPI** ............ Gingival-Periodontal Index [*Dentistry*]
**GPI** ............ Glass Packaging Institute (EA)
**GPI** ............ Glide Path Indicator [*Aviation*] (NATG)
**GPI** ............ Glucophosphate Isomerase [*An enzyme*]
**GPI** ............ Glycosyl-Phosphatidylinositol [*Biochemistry*]
**GPI** ............ Gordon Personal Inventory [*Psychology*]
**GPI** ............ Government Preliminary Inspection (MCD)
**GPI** ............ Grain Products Irradiator [*Nuclear energy*]
**GPI** ............ Graphics Programming Interface [*IBM Corp.*] (PCM)
**GPI** ............ Great Pacific Industries, Inc. [*Toronto Stock Exchange symbol*] [*Vancouver Stock Exchange symbol*]
**GPI** ............ Grocery Prices Index [*British*]
**GPI** ............ Ground Point of Impact
**GPI** ............ Ground Point of Intercept (AFM)
**GPI** ............ Ground Position Indicator [*Dead-reckoning computer*]
**GPI** ............ Guapi [*Colombia*] [*Airport symbol*] (OAG)
**GPI** ............ Guardsman Products, Incorporated [*NYSE symbol*] (SPSG)
**GPIA**.......... General-Purpose Interface Adapter (IEEE)
**GPIA**.......... Generic Pharmaceutical Industry Association (EA)
**GPIB**.......... General-Purpose Interface Bus [*Data processing*]
**GPIC**.......... General-Purpose Intercomputer [*Test*] (NVT)
**GPID** .......... Guidance Package Installation Dolly [*Polaris missile*]
**GPIN** .......... Groupement Professionnel de l'Industrie Nucleaire [*Also known as NIC*] [*Belgium*]
**GPIO** .......... General-Purpose Input/Output [*Data processing*]
**GPIP**.......... Glide Path Intercept Point [*Aviation*]
**GPIS**.......... Gemini Problem Investigation Status [*NASA*] (IEEE)
**GPIX**.......... Globus Growth Group, Inc. [*NASDAQ symbol*] (NQ)
**GPJ**............ Great Peace Journey [*Sweden*] (EAIO)
**GPJ**............ Great Plains Journal [*A publication*]
**GP J Am Acad Gen Pract** ... GP. Journal of the American Academy of General Practice [*A publication*]
**GPK** ........... Goldpac Investments Ltd. [*Vancouver Stock Exchange symbol*]
**GPKA** ......... Guinea Pig Kidney Absorption (Test) [*Clinical chemistry*]
**GPKD** ......... General-Purpose Keyboard and Display Control [*Data processing*] (MDG)
**GPKT**.......... Grand Priory of the Knights of the Temple [*Freemasonry*]
**GPL** ........... Gallahad Petroleum [*Vancouver Stock Exchange symbol*]
**GPL** ........... General Precision Laboratory
**GPL** ........... General Price Level (ADA)
**GPL** ........... General-Purpose Laboratory (KSC)
**GPL** ........... General-Purpose Language [*Data processing*] (CSR)
**GPL** ........... General-Purpose Loop [*Nuclear energy*] (NRCH)
**GPL** ........... Generalized Programming Language [*Data processing*]
**GPL** ........... Geographic Position Locator [*Navigation*]
**GPL** ........... Giant Pulse LASER
**GPL** ........... Gimbal Pickoff Loop
**GPL** ........... GOAL [*Ground Operations Aerospace Language*] Processing Language (MCD)
**GPL** ........... Gravatom Projects Ltd. [*British*] (IRUK)
**GPL** ........... Group Processing Logic (TEL)
**GPL** ........... Guapiles [*Costa Rica*] [*Airport symbol*] (OAG)
**GPL** ........... Guymon Public Library, Guymon, OK [*OCLC symbol*] (OCLC)
**GPL** ........... Gypsum Lathe [*Technical drawings*]
**GPLA**.......... General Price Level Accounting (ADA)

**GPLAD**...... German Plastics [*A publication*]
**GPLAN**...... Generalized Database Planning System
**GPLD**........ Government Property Lost or Damaged [*or Destroyed*]
**GPLE**......... Global Program Line Editor [*Beagle Bros.*]
**GPLI**.......... Group-Page-Line-Inserts (MCD)
**GPLP**......... General-Purpose Linear Programming [*Data processing*] (IEEE)
**GPLRG**...... Gay Parents Legal and Research Group [*Defunct*] (EA)
**GPLS**......... Giant Pulse LASER System
**GPLY**......... Gingivoplasty [*Dentistry*]
**GPM**.......... Gallons per Mile
**GPM**.......... Gallons per Minute
**GPM**.......... Gas Plasma Monitor
**GPM**.......... General Preventive Medicine
**GPM**.......... General-Purpose Macrogenerator [*Data processing*] (IEEE)
**GPM**.......... General-Purpose Maneuver
**GPM**.......... General-Purpose Missile
**GPM**.......... Genetic Psychology Monographs [*A publication*]
**GPM**.......... Geopotential Meter
**GPM**.......... Georgia Southern College, Statesboro, GA [*OCLC symbol*] (OCLC)
**GPM**.......... Gepanzerte Pioniermaschine [*Armored Engineer Vehicle*] [*General Electric Co.*] [*German*] (MCD)
**GPM**.......... Goettinger Predigt-Meditationen [*A publication*] (BJA)
**GPM**.......... Gradient Pump Module
**GPM**.......... Graduated Payment Mortgage [*Sometimes referred to as "Jeep"*]
**GPM**.......... Grams per Mile
**GPM**.......... Grand Past Master [*Freemasonry*]
**GPM**.......... Grand Prairie, TX [*Location identifier*] [*FAA*] (FAAL)
**GPM**.......... Graphics Postprocessor Module [*McDonnell-Douglas Corp.*]
**GPM**.......... Ground Potential Model [*Physics*]
**GPM**.......... Groups [*of code transmitted*] per Minute [*or Message*] [*Telecommunications*]
**GPM**.......... Gunnery Prize Money [*British military*] (DMA)
**GPMA**....... Gasoline Pump Manufacturers Association (EA)
**GPMAL**..... Gravida, Para, Multiple Births, Abortions, Live Births [*Obstetrics*]
**GPMC**....... Grocery Products Manufacturers of Canada [*See also FCPA*]
**GPMC**....... Group and Pension Marketing Conference [*LIMRA*]
**GPME**....... Gas-Porous Membrane Electrode [*Electrochemistry*]
**GPME**....... General-Purpose Mission Equipment (NASA)
**GPMF**....... Gram Parsons Memorial Foundation (EA)
**GPMFGND**... Great Peace March for Global Nuclear Disarmament (EA)
**GPMG**....... General-Purpose Machine Gun [*Military*]
**GPMGAD**... Geophysical Monograph [*A publication*]
**GPMM**....... Guild of Professional Model Makers [*Australia*]
**GPMMA**... Grain Processing Machinery Manufacturers Association (EA)
**GPMOA3**.. Genetic Psychology Monographs [*A publication*]
**GPMS**........ General-Purpose Microprogram Simulator [*Data processing*] (IEEE)
**GPMS**........ General-Purpose Multiplex System [*Aviation*]
**GPMS**........ Gross Performance Measuring System [*Air Force*]
**GPN**........... Garden Point [*Australia*] [*Airport symbol*] (OAG)
**GPN**........... General Performance Number
**GPN**........... Glass Plate Negative
**GPN**........... Gold-Pan Resources, Inc. [*Vancouver Stock Exchange symbol*]
**GPN**........... Government Packet Network [*Canada*]
**GPN**........... Graduate Practical Nurse
**GPNCO**..... Great Pacific Navigation Co. Ltd. (DS)
**G Pneumol**... Giornale di Pneumologia [*A publication*]
**GPNITL**.... Great Plains National Instructional Television Library
**GPNOA**..... Geophysica Norvegica [*A publication*]
**GPO**........... Gemini Program [*or Project*] Office [*NASA*] (KSC)
**GPO**........... General Pico [*Argentina*] [*Airport symbol*] (OAG)
**GPO**........... General Post Office [*British*] [*Defunct*]
**GPO**........... General Practitioner Obstetrician
**GPO**........... General-Purpose Oscilloscope
**GPO**........... General-Purpose Outlet (ADA)
**GPO**........... General-Purpose Output [*Space Flight Operations Facility, NASA*]
**GPO**........... Genprobe Tech [*Vancouver Stock Exchange symbol*]
**GPO**........... Giant Group Ltd. [*NYSE symbol*] (SPSG)
**GPO**........... Government Pharmaceutical Organization [*Thailand*] (DS)
**GPO**........... Government Printing Office
**GPO**........... Granulopoietin [*Hypothetical substance*] [*Hematology*]
**GPO**........... Gross Product Originating [*Department of Transportation*]
**GPO**........... Guaranteed Purchase Option [*Insurance*]
**GPO**........... Gun Position Officer (NATG)
**GPO**........... Gunner's Primary Optics (MCD)
**GPO**........... Library of Congress, Government Printing Office [*Source file*] [*UTLAS symbol*]
**GPO**........... Portland, OR [*Location identifier*] [*FAA*] (FAAL)
**GPO**........... United States Government Printing Office, Alexandria, VA [*OCLC symbol*] (OCLC)
**GPOA**........ Guild of Prescription Opticians of America [*Later, OAA*] (EA)
**GPOA**........ Gun Position Officer's Assistant [*British military*] (DMA)
**GPOB**........ Government Printing Office Bookstore (OICC)
**GPOCC**..... Group Occulting Lights [*Navigation signal*]
**Gp Offr**...... Group Officer [*British military*] (DMA)
**G Pollicolt**... Giornale dei Pollicoltori [*A publication*]
**GPOND**..... GPO [*Government Printing Office*] Newsletter [*A publication*]
**GPO Newsl**... GPO [*Government Printing Office*] Newsletter [*United States*] [*A publication*]
**G by Pos**..... Games by Position [*Baseball*]
**GPOS**........ General-Purpose Operating System
**GPP**........... General Plant Project
**GPP**........... General Purchasing Power [*Accounting*]
**GPP**........... General-Purpose Programming [*Data processing*]
**GPP**........... Giant Pacific Petroleums, Inc. [*Vancouver Stock Exchange symbol*]
**GPP**........... Glycosylated Plasma Protein [*Clinical chemistry*]
**GPP**........... Goal Programming Problem
**GPP**........... Gordon Personal Profile [*Psychology*]
**GPP**........... Gross Primary Productivity
**GPP**........... Ground Power Panel
**GPP**........... Gyro Pitch Position
**GPPA**......... Government Patent Policy Act [*1981*]
**GPPAW**..... Glass, Pottery, Plastics, and Allied Workers International Union (EA)
**GPPB**......... Gemini Program Planning Board [*NASA*] (KSC)
**GPPB**......... Government Procurement Practices Board [*Proposed*]
**GPPEDP**... Genetics; Principles and Perspectives [*A publication*]
**GPP-I**......... Gordon Personal Profile and Inventory [*Personality development test*] [*Psychology*]
**GPPL**......... Gypsum Plaster [*Technical drawings*]
**GPPQ**......... General-Purpose Psychiatric Questionnaire
**GPPRA**...... Geophysical Prospecting [*A publication*]
**GPPS**......... General Provisions Policy Statement (MCD)
**GPPT**......... Group Personality Projective Test [*Psychology*]
**GPPX**......... Giant Pacific Petroleum, Inc. [*NASDAQ symbol*] (NQ)
**GPQ**........... Carrollton, GA [*Location identifier*] [*FAA*] (FAAL)
**GPQ**........... Great Plains Quarterly [*A publication*]
**GPR**........... General-Purpose RADAR (MCD)
**GPR**........... General-Purpose Radiometer
**GPR**........... General-Purpose Receiver
**GPR**........... General-Purpose Register [*Data processing*] (MDG)
**GPR**........... General-Purpose Relay
**GPR**........... General-Purpose Representative
**GPR**........... Genio Populi Romani [*To the Genius of the Roman People*] [*Latin*]
**GPR**........... Glider Pilot Regiment [*Military unit*] [*British*]
**GPR**........... Golden Pyramid Resources, Inc. [*Vancouver Stock Exchange symbol*]
**GPR**........... Government Plant Representative
**GPR**........... Gran Premio Romeo [*Alfa Romeo race car*] [*Italian*]
**GPR**........... Ground-Penetrating RADAR
**GPRA**........ Gouvernement Provisoire de la Republique Algerienne [*Provisional Government of the Algerian Republic*]
**GPRA**........ Government Public Relations Association [*Defunct*]
**GPrag**......... Germanistica Pragensia [*A publication*]
**GPRC**......... Geophysical and Polar Research Center [*University of Wisconsin*]
**GPRF-G**..... General-Purpose Rocket Furnace - Gradient
**GPRF-I**...... General-Purpose Rocket Furnace - Isothermal
**GPRG**........ Gadsden Purchase Refund Group [*Formerly, PRI*] [*Defunct*] (EA)
**GPRID**....... Geologiya, Poiski, i Razvedka Nerudnykh Poleznykh Iskopaemykh [*A publication*]
**GPRMC**..... Groupement des Plastiques Renforces et Materiaux Composites [*Organization of Reinforced Plastics and Composite Materials*] (EAIO)
**GPRN**........ GOAL [*Ground Operations Aerospace Language*] Test Procedure Release Notice [*NASA*] (NASA)
**GPRO**........ Gen-Probe, Inc. [*NASDAQ symbol*] (NQ)
**GPRR**........ General-Purpose Radio Receiver
**G & P RR Laws**... Gregg and Pond's Railroad Laws of the New England States [*A publication*] (DLA)
**GPRS**......... General Parent Ring System [*Proposed chemical classification*]
**GPRS**......... General Plumbing & Roofing Services [*Commercial firm*] [*British*]
**GPRT**......... General-Purpose Radio Transmitter
**GPRT**......... Guanine Phosphoribosyltransferase [*An enzyme*]
**GPS**........... Galapagos Islands [*Ecuador*] [*Airport symbol*] (OAG)
**GPS**........... Gallons per Second
**GPS**........... Gap, Inc. [*Formerly, Gap Stores, Inc.*] [*NYSE symbol*] (SPSG)
**GPS**........... Gastrointestinal Pathology Society (EA)
**GPS**........... Gauge Pressure Switch
**GPS**........... General Problem Solver [*Data processing*]
**GPS**........... General Process Simulator
**GPS**........... General Processing Subsystem (MCD)
**GPS**........... General-Purpose Shelter
**GPS**........... Generality and Problem Solving
**GPS**........... Generalized Preference Scheme [*Tariff policy*]
**GPS**........... Generic Processing System [*Data processing*] (TEL)
**GPS**........... Germany Philatelic Society (EA)
**GPS**........... GigaBIT [*Binary Digits*] per Second [*Transmission rate*] [*Data processing*]
**GPS**........... Global Positioning Satellite
**GPS**........... Global Positioning System [*Formerly, NAVSTAR*] [*Air Force*]
**GPS**........... Global Precision System
**GPS**........... Government Paper Specification Standards

**GPS**........... Grams per Second
**GPS**........... Grand Past Sojourner [*Freemasonry*] (ROG)
**GPS**........... Grand Principal Sojourner [*Freemasonry*]
**GPS**........... Graphic Programming Services [*Data processing*] (IBMDP)
**GPS**........... Ground Plane Simulator
**GPS**........... Ground Power Supply [*NASA*] (NASA)
**GPS**........... Ground Processing Simulation (MCD)
**GPS**........... Ground Processing System [*Aviation*]
**GPS**........... Ground Proximity Sensor
**GPS**........... Groups of Pulses per Second (DEN)
**GPS**........... Guidance Power Supply
**GPS**........... Guinea Pig Serum
**GPS**........... Guinea Pig Spleen
**GPS**........... Gunner's Primary Sight (MCD)
**GPS**........... Gyroscope Parameter Shift
**GPSA**......... Gas Processors Suppliers Association (EA)
**GPSC**......... Gas Proportional Scintillation Counters [*Spectroscopy*]
**GPSC**......... Guinea Pig Spinal Cord
**GPSCS**....... General-Purpose Satellite Communication System (MCD)
**GPSDIC**.... General-Purpose Scientific Document Image Code [*System*] [*National Institute of Standards and Technology*]
**GPSDW**..... General-Purpose Scientific Document Writer [*National Institute of Standards and Technology*]
**GPSE**......... General-Purpose Simulation Environment [*Data processing*]
**GPSE**......... Gunner's Primary Sight Extension
**G Psichiatr Neuropatol**... Giornale di Psichiatria e di Neuropatologia [*A publication*]
**GPS NCC**.. Global Positioning System Network Control Center [*Air Force*] (MCD)
**GPSP**......... General-Purpose Signal Processor
**GPSP**......... General-Purpose Software Program [*Data processing*]
**GPS PC**...... Global Positioning System Program Contractor [*Air Force*] (MCD)
**GPSR**......... Glossaire des Patois de la Suisse Romande [*A publication*]
**GPSS**......... General [*or Generic*] Problem Statement Simulator
**GPSS**......... General Process Simulation Studies
**GPSS**......... General-Purpose Simulation System [*formerly, Systems Simulator*] [*IBM Corp.*] [*1961*] [*Data processing*]
**GPSS**......... Global Positioning Satellite System
**GPSSM**...... General-Purpose Surface-to-Surface Missile [*Army*]
**GPSU**......... Ground Power Supply Unit [*NASA*] (AAG)
**GPSVA**...... Geophysical Surveys [*A publication*]
**GPSX**......... General Parcel Service, Inc. [*NASDAQ symbol*] (NQ)
**GPT**........... Gallons per Ton
**GPT**........... Gas Phase Titration
**GPT**........... Gas Power Transfer (IEEE)
**GPT**........... GEC Plessey Telecommunications [*British*] (ECON)
**GPT**........... Gemini Pad Test [*NASA*] (KSC)
**GPT**........... General Perturbation Theory [*Nuclear science*]
**GPT**........... General Preferred Tariff [*Canada*]
**GPT**........... General-Purpose Tool
**GPT**........... General-Purpose Transport [*British military*] (DMA)
**GPT**........... Geometric and Positional Tolerance [*Drafting symbol*]
**GPT**........... Glass Precision Tubing
**GPT**........... Glass Probe Thermistor
**GPT**........... Glutamic-Pyruvic Transaminase [*Also, AAT, ALAT, ALT*] [*An enzyme*]
**GPT**........... Goldpost Resources, Inc. [*Toronto Stock Exchange symbol*]
**GPT**........... Goteborgs-Posten [*A publication*]
**GPT**........... Grayson Perceptualization Test [*Psychology*]
**GPT**........... Grid Pool Tank
**GPT**........... Guidance Position Tracking [*Aerospace*] (AAG)
**GPT**........... Gulfport/Biloxi [*Mississippi*] [*Airport symbol*] (OAG)
**GPT**........... Gypsum Tile [*Technical drawings*]
**GPTE**......... General-Purpose Test Equipment (MCD)
**GpTh**......... Group Therapy
**GPTI**......... General-Purpose Terminal Interchanges [*Airline communication system*] [*Raytheon Co.*]
**GPTKS**...... Glasnik Pravoslavne Tzrkve u Kraljevini Srbiji [*A publication*]
**GPTR**......... General-Purpose Tape Routine [*Data processing*] (PCM)
**GPTR**......... Guidance Power Temperature Regulator
**GPTS**......... Geomagnetic Polarity Timescale
**GPTU**......... Glass Painters' Trade Union [*British*]
**GPU**........... Gas Power Unit (MUGU)
**GPU**........... General Postal Union [*Later, UPU*]
**GPU**........... General Public Utilities Corp. [*NYSE symbol*] (SPSG)
**GPU**........... Generating Power Unit
**GPU**........... Gosudarstvennoe Politicheskoe Upravlenie [*Government Political Administration*] [*Soviet secret service organization, also known as OGPU*] [*Later, KGB*]
**GPU**........... Ground Power Unit
**GPU**........... Guinea Pig Unit [*Endocrinology*]
**GPUN**......... General Public Utilities Nuclear Corp. (NRCH)
**GPUR**......... GOAL [*Ground Operations Aerospace Language*] Test Procedure Update Request (MCD)
**GPUSA**...... Greenpeace USA (EA)
**GPV**........... General-Purpose Vehicle
**GPV**........... General-Purpose Vessel
**GPV**........... Gereformeerd Politiek Verbond [*Reformed Political League*] [*Netherlands*] [*Political party*] (PPE)
**GPV**........... Gyroscope Pickoff Voltage
**GPVB**......... General-Purpose Video Buffer
**GPVEH**..... General-Purpose Vehicle
**GPVJ**......... Gesellschaft pro Vindonissa. Jahresbericht [*A publication*]
**GPW**.......... Geneva Convention Relative to Treatment of Prisoners of War, 12 August 1949 [*Army*] (AABC)
**GPW**.......... Global Point Warning [*Military*]
**GPW**.......... Gold Power Resources Corp. [*Vancouver Stock Exchange symbol*]
**GPW**.......... Great Plains Wheat, Inc. (EA)
**GPW**.......... Green Pulse Width [*Instrumentation*]
**GPW**.......... Gypsum-Plaster Wall [*Technical drawings*]
**GPW 1929**... Geneva Convention Relative to Treatment of Prisoners of War, 27 July 1929 [*Army*]
**GPWD**....... General Political Warfare Department [*Military*]
**GPWM**...... Guild for the Promotion of Welsh Music (EAIO)
**GPWS**....... Ground Proximity Warning System [*FAA*]
**GPWU**....... Granite Polishers' and Workers' Union [*British*]
**GPX**........... Generalized Programming Extended [*Livermore Atomic Research Computer*] [*Sperry UNIVAC*]
**GPx**........... Glutathione Peroxidase [*An enzyme*]
**GPX**........... Greyhound Package Express
**GPY**........... Government Property Yard
**GPY**........... Gypsy Resources Ltd. [*Vancouver Stock Exchange symbol*]
**GPYSA**...... Geophysics [*A publication*]
**GPZ**........... Gebbies Pass [*New Zealand*] [*Seismograph station code, US Geological Survey*] (SEIS)
**GPZ**........... Grand Rapids [*Minnesota*] [*Airport symbol*] (OAG)
**GPZOA**..... GPz Owners of America [*Defunct*] (EA)
**GQ**............. Druk Air [*Bhutan*] [*ICAO designator*] (FAAC)
**GQ**............. Equatorial Guinea [*ANSI two-letter standard code*] (CNC)
**GQ**............. General Quarters [*General Alert*] [*Navy*]
**GQ**............. Gentlemen's Quarterly [*A publication*]
**GQ**............. German Quarterly [*A publication*]
**GQ**............. Grumman Corp. [*NYSE symbol*] (SPSG)
**GQ**............. North Korea [*License plate code assigned to foreign diplomats in the US*]
**GQ & A**...... General's Branch, Quarter Master's Branch, and Adjutant's Branch [*Main divisions of Staff Duties*] [*Military*] [*British*]
**GQA**........... Get Quick Answer [*Communications*]
**GQA**........... Give Quick Answer [*Communications*]
**GQA**........... Government Quality Assurance (NATG)
**GQE**........... Generalized Queue Entry [*Data processing*]
**GQE**........... Gilmore, AR [*Location identifier*] [*FAA*] (FAAL)
**GQG**........... Gallaudet College, Washington, DC [*OCLC symbol*] (OCLC)
**GQG**........... Grand Quartier-General [*French GHQ*]
**GQK**........... Gallaudet College, Kendall Demonstration School, Washington, DC [*OCLC symbol*] (OCLC)
**GQM**.......... Gallaudet College, Montessori School, Washington, DC [*OCLC symbol*] (OCLC)
**GQM**.......... Golden Queen Mining [*Vancouver Stock Exchange symbol*]
**GQMS**....... Garrison Quartermaster-Sergeant [*British military*] (DMA)
**GQNA**....... Aioun El Atrouss [*Mauritania*] [*ICAO location identifier*] (ICLI)
**GQNB**........ Boutilimit [*Mauritania*] [*ICAO location identifier*] (ICLI)
**GQNC**........ Tichitt [*Mauritania*] [*ICAO location identifier*] (ICLI)
**GQND**....... Tidjikja [*Mauritania*] [*ICAO location identifier*] (ICLI)
**GQNE**........ Bogue [*Mauritania*] [*ICAO location identifier*] (ICLI)
**GQNF**........ Kiffa [*Mauritania*] [*ICAO location identifier*] (ICLI)
**GQNH**....... Timbedra [*Mauritania*] [*ICAO location identifier*] (ICLI)
**GQNI**......... Nema [*Mauritania*] [*ICAO location identifier*] (ICLI)
**GQNJ**........ Akjoujt [*Mauritania*] [*ICAO location identifier*] (ICLI)
**GQNK**........ Kaedi [*Mauritania*] [*ICAO location identifier*] (ICLI)
**GQNL**........ Moudjeria/Letfotar [*Mauritania*] [*ICAO location identifier*] (ICLI)
**GQNM**...... Timbedra/Dahara [*Mauritania*] [*ICAO location identifier*] (ICLI)
**GQNN**....... Nouakchott [*Mauritania*] [*ICAO location identifier*] (ICLI)
**GQNR**........ Rosso [*Mauritania*] [*ICAO location identifier*] (ICLI)
**GQNS**........ Selibabi [*Mauritania*] [*ICAO location identifier*] (ICLI)
**GQNT**........ Tamchakett [*Mauritania*] [*ICAO location identifier*] (ICLI)
**GQNU**....... M'Bout [*Mauritania*] [*ICAO location identifier*] (ICLI)
**GQNV**........ Nouakchott [*Mauritania*] [*ICAO location identifier*] (ICLI)
**GQP**........... Gas Quenching Process
**GQPA**........ Atar [*Mauritania*] [*ICAO location identifier*] (ICLI)
**GQPF**........ F'Derick [*Mauritania*] [*ICAO location identifier*] (ICLI)
**GQPP**........ Nouadhibou [*Mauritania*] [*ICAO location identifier*] (ICLI)
**GQPT**........ Bir Moghrein [*Mauritania*] [*ICAO location identifier*] (ICLI)
**GQPZ**........ Zouerate [*Mauritania*] [*ICAO location identifier*] (ICLI)
**GQQ**........... Galion [*Ohio*] [*Airport symbol*] (OAG)
**GQR**........... Gauss Quadrature Rule
**GQR**........... Golden Quail Resources Ltd. [*Vancouver Stock Exchange symbol*]
**GQRV**........ Golden Quail Resources Ltd. [*NASDAQ symbol*] (NQ)
**GQW**.......... Denver, CO [*Location identifier*] [*FAA*] (FAAL)
**GQX**........... Goldquest Exploration, Inc. [*Toronto Stock Exchange symbol*]
**GR**............. Aurigny Air Services Ltd. [*Great Britain*] [*ICAO designator*] (FAAC)
**GR**............. Carnegie Library, Rome, GA [*Library symbol*] [*Library of Congress*] (LCLS)
**GR**............. Gambia Regiment [*British military*] (DMA)

**GR** ........ Gamma Ray [*or Roentgen*]
**GR** ........ Gas Ratio
**GR** ........ Gastric Resection [*Medicine*]
**GR** ........ Gear (MSA)
**GR** ........ Gear Ratio
**GR** ........ Geared Radial [*Aircraft engine*]
**G & R** ........ Geldert and Russell's Nova Scotia Reports [*A publication*] (DLA)
**GR** ........ Gemeenteraad [*A publication*]
**GR** ........ General Radio
**GR** ........ General Reader
**GR** ........ General Reconnaissance [*Marine Corps*]
**GR** ........ General Register [*Data processing*]
**GR** ........ General Relativity [*Physics*]
**GR** ........ General Research
**GR** ........ General Reserve
**GR** ........ Genesis Rabbah (BJA)
**GR** ........ Gentleman Rider [*Horsemanship*]
**GR** ........ Geographical Review [*A publication*]
**GR** ........ Georgia Review [*A publication*]
**GR** ........ Georgist Registry [*An association*] (EA)
**GR** ........ Georgius Rex [*King George*]
**GR** ........ Germ Ring [*Embryology*]
**GR** ........ German Reports (MCD)
**GR** ........ German Roach [*Immunology*]
**GR** ........ Germanic Review [*A publication*]
**GR** ........ Germanium Rectifier
**GR** ........ Girl's Realm [*A publication*]
**GR** ........ Glaxo Laboratories Ltd. [*Great Britain*] [*Research code symbol*]
**GR** ........ Gloucestershire Regiment [*Military unit*] [*British*]
**GR** ........ Glucocorticoid Receptor [*Endocrinology*]
**GR** ........ Glutathione Reductase [*An enzyme*]
**G-R** ........ Gnome-Rhone [*Aircraft engine*]
**GR** ........ Gold Reserve
**G-R** ........ Goldbarg-Rutenberg [*Enzyme unit*]
**GR** ........ Golden Rule [*Freemasonry*] (ROG)
**GR** ........ [*The*] Goodrich [*B. F.*] Co. [*NYSE symbol*] (SPSG)
**GR** ........ Gospel Recordings (EA)
**GR** ........ Government Regulation (AAG)
**GR** ........ Government Report (AAG)
**GR** ........ Government Reserve [*British*] (ADA)
**GR** ........ Government Responsibility (MCD)
**gr** ........ Government Revenue (MENA)
**GR** ........ Grab Rod (AAG)
**GR** ........ Grade (KSC)
**GR** ........ Gradual-Release [*Pharmacy*]
**GR** ........ Graduate
**GR** ........ Grain (KSC)
**GR** ........ Gram (KSC)
**GR** ........ Grammar
**GR** ........ Gramophone [*A publication*]
**GR** ........ Gran Rabinato (BJA)
**GR** ........ Grand [*Title*]
**GR** ........ Grand
**GR** ........ Grand Rapids, Michigan
**GR** ........ Grand Recorder [*Freemasonry*]
**GR** ........ Grand Registrar [*Freemasonry*] (ROG)
**GR** ........ Grande Revue [*A publication*]
**GR** ........ Grange [*or Manor, a religious residence*]
**GR** ........ Grant
**GR** ........ Grant Recipient [*Job Training and Partnership Act*] (OICC)
**Gr** ........ Grant's Jamaica Reports [*A publication*] (DLA)
**Gr** ........ Grant's Pennsylvania Cases [*A publication*] (DLA)
**Gr** ........ Grant's Upper Canada Chancery Reports [*A publication*] (DLA)
**GR** ........ Granular Snow [*Skiing condition*]
**GR** ........ Granum [*Grain*] [*Latin*]
**Gr** ........ Graphite
**Gr** ........ Grashof Number [*IUPAC*]
**Gr** ........ Grasp
**GR** ........ Grass (ROG)
**GR** ........ Grass Extract [*Immunology*]
**GR** ........ Grasse River R. R. Corp. [*AAR code*]
**GR** ........ Grave Record [*Genealogy*]
**GR** ........ Graves Registration [*Military*]
**GR** ........ Gravity
**GR** ........ Gray
**GR** ........ Gray [*Thoroughbred racing*]
**GR** ........ Great (MCD)
**GR** ........ Great Roll [*of the Pipe*] [*British*]
**GR** ........ Grecian (ROG)
**gr** ........ Greece [*MARC country of publication code*] [*Library of Congress*] [*IYRU nationality code*] (LCCP)
**GR** ........ Greece [*ANSI two-letter standard code*] (CNC)
**G a R** ........ Greece and Rome [*A publication*]
**G & R** ........ Greece and Rome [*A publication*]
**GR** ........ Greek
**GR** ........ Green (FAAC)
**Gr** ........ Greenleaf's Reports [*1-9 Maine*] [*A publication*] (DLA)
**Gr** ........ Green's Reports [*A publication*] (DLA)
**GR** ........ Grid Resistor
**GR** ........ Grid Return
**GR** ........ Grind (ADA)
**GR** ........ Grooved Roofing [*Lumber*]
**Gr** ........ Gros [*Gross*] [*Business term*] [*German*]
**gr** ........ Grosa [*Gross*] [*Business term*] [*Portuguese*]
**GR** ........ Gross
**GR** ........ Gross Rate [*Insurance*] (AIA)
**GR** ........ Gross Receipts [*Business term*]
**GR** ........ Gross Requirement (AABC)
**GR** ........ Gross Revenue [*Business term*]
**Gr** ........ Ground
**GR** ........ Ground Range
**GR** ........ Ground Rent (ROG)
**GR** ........ Ground Rule (MCD)
**GR** ........ Group
**GR** ........ Group Report
**GR** ........ Grove (ADA)
**GR** ........ Growth Rate [*Biology*]
**GR** ........ Guardrail
**GR** ........ Gulf Rijad Bank [*Bahrain*]
**GR** ........ Gulielmus Rex [*King William*]
**GR** ........ Gun Control RADAR [*Military*] (CAAL)
**GR** ........ Gunner
**GR** ........ Gunnery Range
**G n R** ........ Guns n' Roses [*Rock recording group*]
**GR** ........ Gurkha Rifles [*British military*] (DMA)
**GR** ........ Hail [*Aviation code*] (FAAC)
**GRA** ........ Fayetteville, NC [*Location identifier*] [*FAA*] (FAAL)
**GRA** ........ Gamma Ray Amplification
**GRA** ........ Girls Rodeo Association [*Later, WPRA*] (EA)
**Gra** ........ Glyceraldehyde [*Biochemistry*]
**GRA** ........ Government Reports Announcements [*Department of Commerce*] [*Database producer*]
**GRA** ........ Government Responsibility Action
**GRA** ........ Government Responsibility Authorized (MCD)
**GR-A** ........ Government Rubber-Acrylonitrile [*Synthetic rubber*]
**GRA** ........ Governmental Research Association (EA)
**GRA** ........ Grace [*W. R.*] & Co. [*NYSE symbol*] (SPSG)
**GRA** ........ Graduate Research Assistant
**Gra** ........ Graham's Reports [*98-107 Georgia*] [*A publication*] (DLA)
**Gra** ........ Grant [*Legal term*] (DLA)
**GRA** ........ Grant Aid [*Military*] (AABC)
**GRA** ........ Grass Roots Association (EA)
**Gra** ........ Gratianus [*Flourished, 1151-59*] [*Authority cited in pre-1607 legal work*] (DSA)
**Gra** ........ Gravida [*A publication*]
**GRA** ........ Gray (MSA)
**GRA** ........ Graz [*Steiermark*] [*Austria*] [*Seismograph station code, US Geological Survey*] [*Closed*] (SEIS)
**GRA** ........ Great American Airways [*Reno, NV*] [*FAA designator*] (FAAC)
**Gr A** ........ Groene Amsterdammer [*A publication*]
**GRA** ........ Growth Rate Adjustment [*Business term*]
**GRA** ........ Guild for Religious Architecture [*Later, IFRAA*]
**GRA** ........ Gyro Reference Assembly
**GRAAL** ........ Graph Algorithmic Language [*Data processing*]
**GRAB** ........ Galactic Radiation and Background (MCD)
**GRAB** ........ Galatic Radiation and Background
**GRAB** ........ Group Room Availability Bank [*Sheraton Corp.*]
**GRABS** ........ Giant Reusable Air Blast Simulator [*Air Force*]
**GRAC** ........ Grand Royal Arch Captain [*Freemasonry*]
**GRAC** ........ Grand Royal Arch Chapter [*Freemasonry*] (ROG)
**GRAC** ........ Groupe de Recherche sur les Attitudes Envers la Criminalite [*Canada*]
**GRACE** ........ Graphic Arts Composing Equipment
**GRACE** ........ Group Routing and Charging Equipment [*British*]
**GRACE** ........ Mrs. Gould's Residential Advisory Centre for the Elderly [*British*] (CB)
**Grace Hosp Bull** ... Grace Hospital. Bulletin [*A publication*]
**Grace Th J** ... Grace Theological Journal [*A publication*]
**GRACO** ........ Gray Company, Inc.
**GRAD** ........ General Recursive Algebra and Differentiation (IEEE)
**GRAD** ........ Generalized Remote Access Database
**GRAD** ........ Gradatim [*Gradually*] [*Pharmacy*]
**GRAD** ........ Gradient (AFM)
**GRAD** ........ Gradual
**Grad** ........ Graduate [*A publication*]
**GRAD** ........ Graduate (AFM)
**GRAD** ........ Graduate Resume Accumulation and Distribution [*Data processing*]
**GRADB** ........ Generalized Remote Access Database (IEEE)
**Gradbeni Vestn** ... Gradbeni Vestnik [*Yugoslavia*] [*A publication*]
**GradBHI** ........ Graduate of the British Horological Institute (DBQ)
**GRADD** ........ Graduate [*Canada*] [*A publication*]
**GradDipAcct** ... Graduate Diploma in Accounting
**GradDipActng** ... Graduate Diploma in Accounting
**GradDipAdmin** ... Graduate Diploma in Administration
**GradDipAdvAcctg** ... Graduate Diploma in Advanced Accounting
**GradDipAnalytChem** ... Graduate Diploma in Analytical Chemistry

**GradDipAppCommunications** ... Graduate Diploma in Applied Communications
**GradDipAppHist** ... Graduate Diploma in Applied History
**GradDipAppLing** ... Graduate Diploma in Applied Linguistics
**GradDipAppStats** ... Graduate Diploma in Applied Statistics
**GradDipAsianStudies** ... Graduate Diploma in Asian Studies
**GradDipAud** ... Graduate Diploma in Internal Auditing
**GradDipBldgProjMgt** ... Graduate Diploma in Building Project Management
**GradDipBusAdmin** ... Graduate Diploma in Business Administration
**GradDipBusComp** ... Graduate Diploma in Business Computing
**GradDipChildLit** ... Graduate Diploma in Children's Literature
**GradDipClinBiochem** ... Graduate Diploma in Clinical Biochemistry
**GradDipCmlComptg** ... Graduate Diploma in Commercial Computing
**GradDipCommDataProc** ... Graduate Diploma in Commercial Data Processing
**GradDipCommn** ... Graduate Diploma in Communication
**GradDipCommunicationMgt** ... Graduate Diploma in Communication Management
**GradDipCompContSys** ... Graduate Diploma in Computer Controlled Systems
**GradDipCompEng** ... Graduate Diploma in Digital Computer Engineering
**GradDipCompStud** ... Graduate Diploma in Computer Studies
**GradDipComptgSc** ... Graduate Diploma in Computing Science
**GradDipCouns** ... Graduate Diploma in Counselling
**GradDipCPPhty** ... Graduate Diploma in Cardio Pulmonary Physiotherapy
**GradDipDatAnal** ... Graduate Diploma in Data Analysis
**GradDipDemog** ... Graduate Diploma in Demography
**GradDipDesStud** ... Graduate Diploma in Design Studies
**GradDipDP** ... Graduate Diploma in Data Processing
**GradDipEc** ... Graduate Diploma in Economics
**GradDipEcDev** ... Graduate Diploma in Economics of Development
**GradDipEcHist** ... Graduate Diploma in Economic History
**GradDipEcmetrics** ... Graduate Diploma in Econometrics
**GradDipEd** ... Graduate Diploma in Education
**GradDipEdCouns** ... Graduate Diploma in Educational Counselling (ADA)
**GradDipEdStudies** ... Graduate Diploma in Educational Studies
**GradDipEmpRels** ... Graduate Diploma in Employment Relations
**GradDipEng-PlantMgnt** ... Graduate Diploma in Engineering - Plant Management
**GradDipEnv & MunEng** ... Graduate Diploma in Environmental and Municipal Engineering
**GradDipExerSportSc** ... Graduate Diploma in Exercise and Sport Sciences
**GradDipFilm & Tele in Ed** ... Graduate Diploma in Film and Television in Education
**GradDipFin** ... Graduate Diploma in Finance
**GradDipFineArt** ... Graduate Diploma in Fine Art
**GradDipGeol** ... Graduate Diploma for Science Teachers (Geology)
**GradDipGeront** ... Graduate Diploma in Gerontology
**GradDipHealthServMgmt** ... Graduate Diploma in Health Services Management
**GradDipHIM** ... Graduate Diploma in Health Information Management
**GradDipIndDes** ... Graduate Diploma in Industrial Design
**GradDipInfServ** ... Graduate Diploma in Information Services
**GradDipInfStudies** ... Graduate Diploma in Information Studies
**GradDipIntLaw** ... Graduate Diploma in International Law
**GradDipKnowlBasSys** ... Graduate Diploma in Knowledge Based Systems
**GradDipLandArch** ... Graduate Diploma in Landscape Architecture
**GradDipLandDatMan** ... Graduate Diploma in Land Data Management
**GradDipLD** ... Graduate Diploma in Landscape Design
**GradDipLegalPrac** ... Graduate Diploma in Legal Practice
**GradDipLeisureStud** ... Graduate Diploma in Leisure Studies
**GradDipLibInfStud** ... Graduate Diploma in Librarianship and Information Studies
**GradDipLibSc** ... Graduate Diploma in Library Science (ADA)
**GradDipLocalGovtEng** ... Graduate Diploma in Local Government Engineering
**GradDipLoc & AppHist** ... Graduate Diploma in Local and Applied History
**GradDipManipTh** ... Graduate Diploma in Manipulative Therapy
**GradDipMathMethods** ... Graduate Diploma in Mathematical Methods
**GradDipMgmt** ... Graduate Diploma in Management
**GradDipMinRes** ... Graduate Diploma in Mineral Resources
**GradDipMktg** ... Graduate Diploma in Marketing
**GradDipNurs** ... Graduate Diploma in Nursing
**GradDipNursStudies** ... Graduate Diploma in Nursing Studies
**GradDipNutr & Diet** ... Graduate Diploma in Nutrition and Dietetics
**GradDipOH & S** ... Graduate Diploma in Occupational Health and Safety
**GradDipOR** ... Graduate Diploma in Operations Research
**GradDipOrgDev** ... Graduate Diploma in Organisation Development
**GradDipPaedPhty** ... Graduate Diploma in Paediatric Physiotherapy
**GradDipProp** ... Graduate Diploma in Property
**GradDipPSM** ... Graduate Diploma in Public Sector Management
**GradDipPubEcPol** ... Graduate Diploma in Public Economic Policy
**GradDipPubLaw** ... Graduate Diploma in Public Law
**GradDipPubPol** ... Graduate Diploma in Public Policy
**GradDipQlty** ... Graduate Diploma in Quality
**GradDipQualTech** ... Graduate Diploma in Quality Technology
**GradDipRc** ... Graduate Diploma in Rehabilitation Counselling
**GradDipSc** ... Graduate Diploma in Science
**GradDipSEAsianStud** ... Graduate Diploma in Southeast Asian Studies
**GradDipSecStud** ... Graduate Diploma in Secretarial Studies
**GradDipStats** ... Graduate Diploma in Statistics
**GradDipSurFin** ... Graduate Diploma in Metal Finishing and Surface Protection
**GradDipSurvPrac** ... Graduate Diploma in Surveying Practice
**GradDipT** .. Graduate Diploma in Teaching (ADA)
**GradDipTax** ... Graduate Diploma in Taxation
**GradDipTchrLib** ... Graduate Diploma in Teacher Librarianship (ADA)
**GradDipTeachLib** ... Graduate Diploma in Teacher Librarianship
**GradDipTrans & Dist** ... Graduate Diploma in Transport and Distribution
**GradDipUEM** ... Graduate Diploma in Urban Estate Management
**GradDipUltr** ... Graduate Diploma in Ultrasonography
**GradDipUrb & RegPlan** ... Graduate Diploma in Urban and Regional Planning
**GradDipURP** ... Graduate Diploma in Urban and Regional Planning
**GradDip(VisArts)** ... Graduate Diploma in Visual Arts
**GradDipWeldTech** ... Graduate Diploma in Welding Technology
**GRADE** ..... Gestalt Recognition by Asymptotic Differential Equations
**Grade Teach** ... Grade Teacher [*A publication*]
**Gradevin Fak Rad (Sarajevo)** ... Gradevinski Fakultet. Radovi (Sarajevo) [*A publication*]
**Gradevinski Fak (Sarajevo) Rad** ... Gradevinski Fakultet (Sarajevo). Radovi [*A publication*]
**GRADEX**... Graded Exercise (NVT)
**Grad Fac Phil J** ... Graduate Faculty Philosophy Journal [*A publication*]
**Grad Fix**..... Grady on Fixtures [*A publication*] (DLA)
**Grad Hind Inh** ... Grady's Hindoo Law of Inheritance [*A publication*] (DLA)
**Grad Hind L** ... Grady's Manual of Hindoo Law [*A publication*] (DLA)
**GradIAE**.... Graduate of the Institution of Automobile Engineers [*British*]
**GradIElecIE** ... Graduate of the Institution of Electrical and Electronics Incorporated Engineers [*British*] (DBQ)
**Grad IERE** ... Graduate of the Institution of Electronic and Radio Engineers [*British*]
**GradIISec**.. Graduate of the Institute of Industrial Security [*British*] (DBQ)
**GradIMA**... Graduate Member of the Institute of Mathematics and Its Applications [*British*] (DBQ)
**GradIManf** ... Graduate Member of the Institute of Manufacturing [*British*] (DBQ)
**Grad I Mech E** ... Graduate of the Institution of Mechanical Engineers [*British*]
**GradIMF** ... Graduate of the Institute of Metal Finishing [*British*] (DBQ)
**GradIMS** ... Graduate of the Institute of Management Specialists [*British*] (DBQ)
**Gradinar Lozar Nauk** ... Gradinarska i Lozarska Nauka [*Horticulture and Viticultural Science*] [*A publication*]
**Gradinar Lozar Nauka** ... Gradinarska i Lozarska Nauka [*Horticulture and Viticultural Science*] [*A publication*]
**Gradinar Lozar Nauka Hortic Vitic Sci** ... Gradinarska i Lozarska Nauka/ Horticulture and Viticultural Science [*A publication*]
**Grad Ind Co** ... Grady's Indian Codes [*A publication*] (DLA)
**Grad Inst BE** ... Graduate Member of the Institute of British Engineers
**GradInstBTM** ... Graduate of the Institute of Business and Technical Management [*British*] (DBQ)
**GradInstNDT** ... Graduate of the British Institute of Non-Destructive Testing (DBQ)
**Grad Inst P** ... Graduate Member of the Institute of Physics and the Physical Society [*British*]
**GradInstPS** ... Graduate of the Institute of Purchasing and Supply [*British*] (DBQ)
**GradIOP**.... Graduate of the Institute of Printing [*British*] (DBQ)
**GradIPM** ... Graduate of the Institute of Personnel Management [*British*] (DBQ)
**GradIS** ....... Graduate Member of the Institute of Statisticians [*British*] (DBQ)
**GradISM** ... Graduate of the Institute of Supervisory Management [*British*] (DBQ)
**Gradja** ........ Gradja za Povijest Knjizevnosti Hrvatske [*A publication*]
**Gradjevin Fak (Sarajevo) Rad** ... Gradjevinski Fakultet (Sarajevo) Radovi [*A publication*]
**Grad MNDTS** ... Graduate Member of the Non-Destructive Testing Society of Great Britain
**GradNIH** ... Graduate of the National Institute of Hardware [*British*] (DBQ)
**GradPRI** .... Graduate of the Plastics and Rubber Institute [*British*] (DBQ)
**Grad Res Ed** ... Graduate Research in Education and Related Disciplines [*A publication*]
**Grad RIC** ... Graduate Member of the Royal Institute of Chemistry [*British*]
**GRADS**...... Generalized Remote Access Database System (IEEE)
**GRADS**...... Ground RADAR Aerial Delivery System (MCD)
**GradSCP** ... Graduate of the Society of Certified Professionals [*British*] (DBQ)
**Grad Sem J** ... Graduate Seminar Journal [*A publication*]
**GradSLAET** ... Graduate of the Society of Licensed Aircraft Engineers and Technologists [*British*] (DBQ)
**Grad Texts Math** ... Graduate Texts in Mathematics [*A publication*]
**GRADU**..... Gradual
**Graduate IElecIE** ... Graduate of the Institution of Electrical and Electronics Incorporated Engineers [*British*] (DBQ)
**Graduate Texts in Math** ... Graduate Texts in Mathematics [*A publication*]
**GradWeldI** ... Graduate of the Welding Institute [*British*] (DBQ)
**Grad Woman** ... Graduate Woman [*A publication*]
**GRAE** ........ Generally Regarded [*or Recognized*] as Effective [*Medicine*]

**GRAE**........ Gouvernement de la Republique de l'Angola en Exile [*Government of the Republic of Angola in Exile*]
**GRAE**........ Governo Revolucionario de Angola no Exilio [*Revolutionary Angolan Government-in-Exile*] [*Portuguese*] (PD)
**Graefes Arch Klin Exp Ophthalmol** ... Graefes Archiv fuer Klinische und Experimentelle Ophthalmologie [*A publication*]
**Graeffe's Arch Clin Exp Ophthalmol** ... Graeffe's Archive for Clinical and Experimental Ophthalmology [*A publication*]
**GR Aero S** ... Graduate of the Royal Aeronautical Society [*British*]
**GRAF**......... Graffiti [*Slang*] [*British*]
**GRAF**......... Graphic Addition to FORTRAN [*Data processing*]
**GRAFEM** ... Graphic Finite Element Modeling [*Software*] [*Automotive engineering*]
**Grafische Tech** ... Grafische Technik Dokumentationsdienst [*A publication*]
**Grafiska Forskningslab Medd** ... Grafiska Forskningslaboratoriets. Meddelande [*A publication*]
**Grafiska Forskningslab Projektrapp** ... Grafiska Forskningslaboratoriet. Projektrapport [*A publication*]
**Grafiske Hojskoles Smaskr** ... Grafiske Hojskoles Smaskrifter [*A publication*]
**GRAFMA** ... Grand Rapids Area Furniture Manufacturers Association (EA)
**GRAFTABL** ... Load Graphics Table [*Data processing*]
**Grafton**....... Smith's New Hampshire Reports [*A publication*] (DLA)
**Grahamstown Hist Soc Ann** ... Grahamstown Historical Society. Annals [*A publication*]
**Grah & W New Trials** ... Graham and Waterman on New Trials [*A publication*] (DLA)
**GRAI**......... Government Reports Announcements and Index [*Department of Commerce*] [*A publication*]
**GRA and I** ... Government Reports Announcements and Index [*A publication*]
**GRAID**...... Graphical Aid [*Data processing*]
**GRAIL**....... Genoa Resources and Investment Ltd. [*Australia*]
**Grain**.......... Grain de Sel [*A publication*]
**GRAIN**...... Graphics-Oriented Relational Algebraic Interpreter
**Grain Feed J Consol** ... Grain and Feed Journals Consolidated [*A publication*]
**Grain Feed Rev** ... Grain and Feed Review [*A publication*]
**Grainger J** ... Grainger Journal [*A publication*]
**Grain Prod News** ... Grain Producer News [*A publication*]
**Grains J**..... Grains Journal [*A publication*]
**Grain Trade Buyers Guide Manage Ref** ... Grain Trade Buyers Guide and Management Reference [*A publication*]
**GRAL**........ General (ROG)
**Gram**.......... De Grammaticis [*of Suetonius*] [*Classical studies*] (OCD)
**GRAM**....... Grammar
**Gram**.......... Gramophone [*Division of Record Corp. of America*] [*Record label*]
**GRAM**....... Granulocyte Activating Mediator [*Immunochemistry*]
**Gramm**....... [*Thomas*] Grammaticus [*Flourished, 16th century*] [*Authority cited in pre-1607 legal work*] (DSA)
**Gramm Lat** ... Grammatici Latini [*A publication*] (OCD)
**Gramm Rom Frag** ... Grammaticae Romana Fragmenta [*A publication*] (OCD)
**Gramo**........ Gramola [*Record label*] [*Belgium*]
**GRAMPA** ... General Analytical Model for Process Analysis (IEEE)
**GRAMPS**.. Graphics for the Multipicture System [*Computer graphics*]
**GRAMS**..... Generalized Reliability and Maintainability Simulator (MCD)
**GRAMS**..... Gramophone Records [*Music or sound effects*]
**GRAN**........ Bank of Granite Corp. [*Granite Falls, NC*] [*NASDAQ symbol*] (NQ)
**GRAN**........ Global Rescue Alarm Network [*Program*] [*Navy*]
**GRAN**........ Grandmother (DSUE)
**GRAN**........ Granite (MSA)
**GRAN**........ Granodize
**GRAN**........ Granulatus [*Granulated*] [*Pharmacy*]
**GRANADA** ... Grammatical Nonalgorithmic Data Description
**Grana Palynol** ... Grana Palynologica [*A publication*]
**GRAND AM** ... Grand Marnier and Amaretto
**Grand Canyon Nat History Assoc Bull** ... Grand Canyon Natural History Association. Bulletin [*A publication*]
**Grand Cou** ... Grand Coutumier de Normandie [*A publication*] (DLA)
**Grand Cout** ... Grand Coutumier de Normandie [*A publication*] (DLA)
**GRANDE**.. Gamma Ray and Neutrino Detector Experiment [*Proposed*] [*University of California, Irvine*]
**GRANDO** ... Grandioso [*Majestic*] [*Music*]
**Granger**...... Granger's State Reports [*22-23 Ohio*] [*A publication*] (DLA)
**GRANIS**.... Graphical Natural Inference System
**GRANITE** ... By Order of the Secretary of the Army. If the individual so desires and no military objections exist, the servicemember will be returned to the United States or territory of residence for emergency leave (AABC)
**GRANITE** ... Gamma Ray Astrophysics New Imaging Telescope
**Granite Mo** ... Granite Monthly [*A publication*]
**GRANL**..... Granulated
**Gran Mo**.... Granite Monthly [*A publication*]
**GRANO**..... Granolithic
**Granos Semilla Selec** ... Granos Semilla Selecta [*A publication*]
**Gran St M** ... Granite State Magazine [*Manchester, NH*] [*A publication*]
**Grant**......... Grant of Elchies' Scotch Session Cases [*A publication*] (DLA)
**Grant**......... Grant's Chancery Chamber Reports [*1850-65*] [*Upper Canada*] [*A publication*] (DLA)
**Grant**......... Grant's Jamaica Reports [*A publication*] (DLA)
**Grant**......... Grant's Pennsylvania Cases [*A publication*] (DLA)
**Grant**......... Grant's Upper Canada Chancery Reports [*A publication*] (DLA)
**Grant Bank** ... Grant on Banking [*A publication*] (DLA)
**Grant Cas**... Grant's Pennsylvania Cases [*A publication*] (DLA)
**Grant Cas (PA)** ... Grant's Pennsylvania Cases [*A publication*] (DLA)
**Grant Ch**.... Grant's Upper Canada Chancery Reports [*A publication*] (DLA)
**Grant Ch (Can)** ... Grant's Upper Canada Chancery Reports [*A publication*] (DLA)
**Grant Corp** ... Grant on Corporations [*A publication*] (DLA)
**Grant E & A** ... Grant's Error and Appeal Reports [*A publication*] (DLA)
**Grant Err & App** ... Grant's Error and Appeal Reports [*A publication*] (DLA)
**Grant Jamaica** ... Grant's Jamaica Reports [*A publication*] (DLA)
**Grant PA**.... Grant's Pennsylvania Cases [*A publication*] (DLA)
**Gra N Tr**.... Graham on New Trials [*A publication*] (DLA)
**Grants Mag** ... Grants Magazine [*A publication*]
**Grantsmanship Cent News** ... Grantsmanship Center. News [*A publication*]
**Grant's R** ... Grant's Jamaica Reports [*A publication*] (DLA)
**Grant UC**... Grant's Upper Canada Chancery Reports [*A publication*] (DLA)
**GRAO**........ Gamma Ray Astronomy Observatory
**GRAP**........ Greatest Response Amplitude Probability
**GRAPD**..... Greatest Response Amplitude Probability Data
**GRAPDEN** ... Graphic Data Entry Unit [*Data processing*]
**GRAPE**...... Gamma Ray Attenuation Porosity Evaluator
**GRAPE**...... Graphical Analysis of Program Execution [*Data processing*]
**GRAPH**..... Graphic
**GRAPH**..... Graphical Repair Discard Analysis Procedure Handbook
**Graph Arts Abstr** ... Graphic Arts Abstracts [*A publication*]
**Graph Arts Mon Print Ind** ... Graphic Arts Monthly and the Printing Industry [*A publication*]
**GRAPHDEN** ... Graphical Data Entry [*Data processing*] (MUGU)
**Graphic Arts Abstr** ... Graphic Arts Abstracts [*A publication*]
**Graphic Arts Bul** ... Graphic Arts Bulletin [*A publication*] (APTA)
**Graphic Arts Lit Abstr** ... Graphic Arts Literature Abstracts [*A publication*]
**Graphic Arts M** ... Graphic Arts Monthly [*A publication*]
**Graphic Arts Mon** ... Graphic Arts Monthly and the Printing Industry [*A publication*]
**Graphic Arts Prog** ... Graphic Arts Progress [*A publication*]
**Graphic Commun World** ... Graphic Communications World [*A publication*]
**Graphic Comm Wk** ... Graphic Communications Weekly [*A publication*]
**Graphic Sci** ... Graphic Science [*A publication*]
**Grap Just**... Grapel's Translation of the Institutes of Justinian [*A publication*] (DLA)
**GRAPO**..... Grupos de Resistencia Anti-Fascista Primero de Octubre [*October First Antifascist Resistance Groups*] [*Spain*] [*Political party*] (PPE)
**Gra Pr**........ Graham's Practice of the New York Supreme Court [*A publication*] (DLA)
**Grap Rom Law** ... Grapel's Sources of the Roman Civil Law [*A publication*] (DLA)
**GRAR**........ Government Report Authorization and Record (AAG)
**GRAR**........ Great American Recreation, Inc. [*McAfee, NJ*] [*NASDAQ symbol*] (NQ)
**GRAR**........ Grinding Arbor
**GRARD**..... Goddard Range and Range Data [*NASA*] (KSC)
**GRARE**..... Ground-Receiving and Analog Ranging Equipment [*AFSCF*] (MCD)
**GRARR**..... Goddard Range and Range Rate [*Tracking system*] [*NASA*]
**GRAS**......... Generally Recognized [*or Regarded*] as Safe [*FDA term*]
**GRAS**......... Ground Return Area Suppression (NATG)
**Grasas Aceit** ... Grasas y Aceites [*A publication*]
**Grasas Aceites** ... Grasas y Aceites [*A publication*]
**GRASER**... Gamma Ray Amplification by Stimulated Emission of Radiation
**GRASP**...... Gamma Ray Astronomy with Spectroscopy and Positioning
**GRASP**...... General Reduction and Analysis Support Package [*Military*] (CAAL)
**GRASP**...... General Resource Allocation and Selection Program [*NASA*] (KSC)
**GRASP**...... Generalized Read and Simulate Program
**GRASP**...... Generalized Reentry Application Simulation Program [*NASA*] (KSC)
**GRASP**...... Generalized Remote Acquisition and Sensor Processing
**GRASP**...... Generalized Retrieval and Storage Program [*Data processing*]
**GRASP**...... Generic RADAR Analysis and Synthesis Program
**GRASP**...... Graphic Service Program (IEEE)
**GRASP**...... Graphics-Augmented Structural Post-Processing [*Module*]
**GRASP Lab** ... General Robotics and Active Sensory Processing Laboratory [*University of Pennsylvania*] [*Research center*] (RCD)
**GRASR**...... General Railroad and Airline Stabilization Regulations [*A publication*] (DLA)
**GRASS**...... General Random Audit Sample Selection Technique [*Military*] (AFIT)
**GRASS**...... Generalized Reactor Analysis Subsystem
**GRASS**...... Germinating Ray Acoustics Simulation System (MCD)
**GRASS**...... Grassland Research and Serengeti Systems [*Model for simulation*]
**GRASS**...... Great Revolutionary American Standard System [*Book title*]
**GRASS**...... Ground-to-Air Scanner Surveillance

**Grass Forage Sci** ... Grass and Forage Science [*A publication*]
**Grass J Br Assoc Green Crop Driers** ... Grass: The Journal of the British Association of Green Crop Driers [*A publication*]
**Grassl Res Inst (Hurley) Annu Rep** ... Grassland Research Institute (Hurley). Annual Report [*A publication*]
**Grassl Res Inst (Hurley) Exp Prog** ... Grassland Research Institute (Hurley). Experiments in Progress [*A publication*]
**Grassl Res Inst (Hurley) Tech Rep** ... Grassland Research Institute (Hurley). Technical Report [*A publication*]
**Grassl Soc South Afr Proc** ... Grassland Society of Southern Africa. Proceedings [*A publication*]
**Grass R** ...... Grass Roots [*A publication*]
**GRAT** ........ Gratis [*Free*] [*Latin*] (ROG)
**Grat** ............ Grattan's Virginia Reports [*A publication*] (DLA)
**GRAT** ........ Gratuity (AABC)
**Grat** ............ [*Hieronymus*] Gratus [*Deceased, 1544*] [*Authority cited in pre-1607 legal work*] (DSA)
**Grat Act** ..... Gratiarum Actio [*of Ausonius*] [*Classical studies*] (OCD)
**GRATE** ...... Growth Rate [*Botany*]
**GRATIS** .... Generation, Reduction, and Training Input System (IEEE)
**Gratt** ........... Grattan's Virginia Supreme Court Reports [*1844-80*] [*A publication*] (DLA)
**Gratt (VA)** ... Grattan's Virginia Reports [*A publication*] (DLA)
**GratzCAJS** ... Gratz College. Annual of Jewish Studies [*A publication*]
**GRAUL** ..... Grand Rapids Area Union List of Serials [*Library network*]
**GRAV** ........ Gravid [*Pregnant*] [*Medicine*]
**GRAV** ........ Gravitational
**Grav De Jur Nat Gent** ... Gravina's De Jure Naturale Gentium, Etc. [*A publication*] (DLA)
**Graver Water Cond Co Tech Repr** ... Graver Water Conditioning Company. Technical Reprint [*A publication*]
**Graves** ........ Proceedings in English King's Council [*1392-93*] [*A publication*] (DLA)
**Gravin** ........ Gravina's Originum Juris Civilis [*A publication*] (DLA)
**Gravitatsiya Teor Otnositel'nosti** ... Gravitatsiya i Teoriya Otnositel'nosti [*USSR*] [*A publication*]
**GRAVR** ..... Gravitational Redshift Space Probe [*Also, GP*]
**Gra & Wat NT** ... Graham and Waterman on New Trials [*A publication*] (DLA)
**GRAY** ........ Grayhound Electronics, Inc. [*NASDAQ symbol*] (NQ)
**Gray** ........... Gray's Massachusetts Supreme Judicial Court Reports [*67-82 Massachusetts*] [*1854-60*] [*A publication*] (DLA)
**Gray** ........... Gray's Reports [*112-22 North Carolina*] [*A publication*] (DLA)
**Gray Att Pr** ... Gray's Country Attorney's Practice [*9th ed.*] [*1869*] [*A publication*] (DLA)
**Gray Forms** ... Graydon's Forms of Conveyance [*A publication*] (DLA)
**Graylands Ed News** ... Graylands Education News [*A publication*] (APTA)
**Gray (Mass)** ... Gray's Massachusetts Reports [*A publication*] (DLA)
**Gray Pant** ... Gray Panther Network [*A publication*]
**Gray Perpetuities** ... Gray's Rule Against Perpetuities [*A publication*] (DLA)
**GRAZ** ........ Grazioso [*Gracefully*] [*Music*]
**Graz Beitr** .. Grazer Beitraege [*A publication*]
**Grazer Phil Stud** ... Grazer Philosophische Studien [*A publication*]
**Grazhdanskaya Aviats** ... Grazhdanskaya Aviatsiya [*A publication*]
**Graz Landesmus Joanneum Abt Geol Palaeontol Bergbau Mitt** ... Graz. Landesmuseum Joanneum. Abteilung fuer Geologie, Palaeontologie, und Bergbau. Mitteilungen [*A publication*]
**Graz Landesmus Joanneum Abt Mineral Mitteilungsbl** ... Graz. Landesmuseum Joanneum. Abteilung fuer Mineralogie. Mitteilungsblatt [*A publication*]
**Graz Landesmus Joanneum Jahresber** ... Graz. Landesmuseum Joanneum. Jahresbericht [*A publication*]
**Graz Landesmus Joanneum Mus Bergbau Geol Tech Mitt** ... Graz. Landesmuseum Joanneum. Museum fuer Bergbau, Geologie, und Technik. Mitteilungen [*A publication*]
**GRAZO** ..... Grazioso [*Gracefully*] [*Music*]
**GRB** ........... Gamma Ray Burst
**GRB** ........... Garbo Industries [*Vancouver Stock Exchange symbol*]
**GRB** ........... Geophysics Research Board
**GRB** ........... Gerber Scientific, Inc. [*NYSE symbol*] (SPSG)
**GRB** ........... Government Reservation Bureau
**GRB** ........... Granatbuechse [*Antitank Grenade Rifle*] [*German*]
**GRB** ........... Granolithic Base
**GRB** ........... Green Bay [*Wisconsin*] [*Airport symbol*] (OAG)
**GRBC** ........ Goose Red Blood Cell
**GRBC** ........ GreatBanc, Inc. [*NASDAQ symbol*] (NQ)
**GRBDS** ...... Gyroscopes-Rate Bomb-Direction System (AAG)
**GRBF** ......... Generalized Radial Basis Function [*Mathematics*]
**GRBL** ......... Garble (FAAC)
**GRBM** ....... Global Range Ballistic Missile [*Air Force*]
**GRBM** ....... Greek, Roman, and Byzantine Monographs [*A publication*]
**GRBNKS** ... Grand Banks [*FAA*] (FAAC)
**GRBR** ........ Gerber Energy International, Inc. [*Denver, CO*] [*NASDAQ symbol*] (NQ)
**Gr Brice** ..... Green's Edition of Brice's Ultra Vires [*A publication*] (DLA)
**Gr Brit** ........ Great Britain
**GR & BS** .... Greek, Roman, and Byzantine Studies [*A publication*]
**GRBS** ......... Greek, Roman, and Byzantine Studies [*A publication*]
**GRBSA** ...... Greek, Roman, and Byzantine Scholarly Aids [*A publication*]
**GRBSC** ...... Greenland Bioscience. Meddelelser om Gronland [*A publication*]
**GRBUD** ..... Geophysical Research Bulletin [*A publication*]
**GRBX** ........ Gearbox
**GRC** ........... Gale Research Company [*Later, GRI*]
**GRC** ........... Garchy [*France*] [*Seismograph station code, US Geological Survey*] (SEIS)
**GRC** ........... Gearcase (MSA)
**GRC** ........... Gendarmerie Royale du Canada [*Royal Canadian Mounted Police - RCMP*]
**GRC** ........... General Railway Classification [*British*]
**GRC** ........... General Research Corporation [*Information service or system*] (IID)
**GRC** ........... Generation Review Committee [*Nuclear Regulatory Commission*] (NRCH)
**GRC** ........... Geographic Resources Center [*University of Missouri - Columbia*] [*Research center*] (RCD)
**GRC** ........... Geotechnical Research Centre [*McGill University*] [*Canada*] [*Research center*] (RCD)
**GRC** ........... Geothermal Resources Council (EA)
**GRC** ........... Gerontology Research Center [*Department of Health and Human Services*] [*Research center*]
**GRC** ........... Glass-Fiber Reinforced Concrete
**GRC** ........... Glenmary Research Center (EA)
**GRC** ........... Global Reference Code [*Developed by Smithsonian Institution*]
**GRC** ........... Gorman-Rupp Company [*AMEX symbol*] (SPSG)
**GRC** ........... Government of the Republic of China
**GRC** ........... Government Research Centers Directory [*Later, GRD*] [*A publication*]
**GRC** ........... Government Research Corporation [*Information service or system*] (IID)
**GRC** ........... Grand Cess [*Liberia*] [*Airport symbol*] (OAG)
**GRC** ........... Greece [*ANSI three-letter standard code*] (CNC)
**grc** ............. Greek, Ancient [*MARC language code*] [*Library of Congress*] (LCCP)
**GRC** ........... Greene County District Library, Xenia, OH [*OCLC symbol*] (OCLC)
**GRC** ........... Gross Replacement Cost (ADA)
**GRC** ........... Growth and Change [*A publication*]
**GRC** ........... Guard Ring Capacitor
**GRCA** ........ Glassfibre Reinforced Cement Association [*British*]
**GRCA** ........ Golden Retriever Club of America (EA)
**GRCA** ........ Grand Canyon National Park
**Gr Ca** .......... Grant's Cases [*A publication*] (DLA)
**Gr Capt** ...... Group Captain [*British military*] (DMA)
**Grc Bk Eco** ... Economic Bulletin. Commercial Bank of Greece [*A publication*]
**GRCD** ........ German Rhine Coordination Directorate [*Allied German Occupation Forces*]
**GRCDA** ..... Governmental Refuse Collection and Disposal Association (EA)
**GRC Genet Resour Commun** ... GRC. Genetic Resources Communication [*A publication*]
**GR CHAP** ... Grand Chapter [*Freemasonry*] (ROG)
**GRCHRSCHR** ... Die Griechische Christliche Schriftsteller der Ersten Drei Jahrhunderten (BJA)
**GRCM** ....... Graduate of the Royal College of Music [*British*]
**GRCO** ........ Gradco Systems, Inc. [*NASDAQ symbol*] (NQ)
**gr coup** ........ Grosses Coupures [*Large Denominations (of Currency)*] [*Business term*] [*French*]
**GR/CP** ....... Group Registration for Contributions to Periodicals [*US Copyright Office form*]
**GRCQ** ........ Grenfell Clinical Quarterly [*A publication*]
**GrCr** ........... Grande Croix (EY)
**GR/CS** ....... Guardrail/Common Sensor System [*Military*]
**GRCSCC** ... Golden Ring Council of Senior Citizens Clubs (EA)
**GRCSW** ..... Graduate Research Center of the Southwest [*Formerly, Southwest Center for Advanced Studies; later, University of Texas at Dallas*]
**GRCV** ........ Ground Cover [*Ecology*]
**GRCV** ........ Guard Receiver (MCD)
**GRD** ........... Geophysics Research Directorate [*US*]
**GRD** ........... Goldrich Resources, Inc. [*Vancouver Stock Exchange symbol*]
**GRD** ........... Government Research Directory [*A publication*]
**GRD** ........... Grading
**GRD** ........... Gramicidin [*Antimicrobial compound*]
**GR D** .......... Grand Duchess [*or Duke*] (ROG)
**GRD** ........... Greatest Response Data
**GRD** ........... Greenwood [*South Carolina*] [*Airport symbol*] (OAG)
**GRD** ........... Grenada [*ANSI three-letter standard code*] (CNC)
**GRD** ........... Grind (MSA)
**GRD** ........... Ground
**GRD** ........... Ground Detector
**GRD** ........... Ground Resolved Distance [*Satellite camera*]
**GRD** ........... Ground Rule Double [*Baseball*]
**Grd** ............. Ground Shells [*Quality of the bottom*] [*Nautical charts*]
**GRD** ........... Guaranteed
**GRD** ........... Guard
**GRDAU** ..... Granddaughter (ROG)
**GRDCUS** ... Gulf Range Drone Control Upgrade System
**GRDF** ........ Gypsum Roof Deck Foundation [*Later, NRDCA*] (EA)
**GRDL** ........ Geodetic Research and Development Laboratory [*Rockville, MD*] [*Department of Commerce*] (MSC)

**GRDL**........ Gradually (FAAC)
**GRDL**........ Griddle (MSA)
**GRDN**........ Garden (ADA)
**GRDND6**... Gerodontology [*A publication*]
**GR/D/O**.... Granddaughter Of [*Genealogy*]
**GRDSR**...... Geographically Referenced Data Storage and Retrieval System [*Canada*]
**GRDTN**..... Graduation (MSA)
**GRE**.......... Gamma Ray Experiment
**GRE**.......... Gamma Ray Explorer (NASA)
**GRE**.......... Generated Repeatable Exams [*Education*]
**GRE**.......... Glucocorticoid Responsive Element [*Endocrinology*]
**GRE**.......... Graduate Record Examination [*Higher education*]
**GRE**.......... Graduate Record Examinations Board (EA)
**GRE**.......... Graduate Reliability Engineering
**GRE**.......... Grant-Related Expenditure [*British*]
**GRE**.......... Graphite-Reinforced Epoxy
**gre**............ Greek, Modern [*MARC language code*] [*Library of Congress*] (LCCP)
**GRE**.......... Greenstone Resources Ltd. [*Toronto Stock Exchange symbol*]
**GRE**.......... Greenville, IL [*Location identifier*] [*FAA*] (FAAL)
**GRE**.......... Grenada [*Seismograph station code, US Geological Survey*] (SEIS)
**GRE**.......... Ground Reconnaissance Equipment
**GRE**.......... Ground Reconstruction Electronics [*Used in photographing moon*] [*NASA*]
**GRE**.......... Ground Reconstruction Equipment
**GRE**.......... Guardian Royal Exchange Assurance [*British*]
**GRE**.......... Gulf Resources & Chemical Corp. [*NYSE symbol*] (SPSG)
**GREA**........ Grant-Related Expenditure Assessments [*British*]
**GREAT**...... Geriatric Education and Training Act [*1985*]
**Great Basin Nat** ... Great Basin Naturalist [*A publication*]
**Great Basin Nat Mem** ... Great Basin Naturalist. Memoirs [*A publication*]
**Greater Milw Dent Bull** ... Greater Milwaukee Dental Bulletin [*A publication*]
**Greater St Louis Dent Soc Bull** ... Greater St. Louis Dental Society. Bulletin [*US*] [*A publication*]
**Great Lakes** ... Great Lakes Review [*A publication*]
**Great Lakes Entomol** ... Great Lakes Entomologist [*A publication*]
**Great Lakes Fish Comm Annu Rep** ... Great Lakes Fishery Commission. Annual Report [*A publication*]
**Great Lakes Fish Comm Tech Rep** ... Great Lakes Fishery Commission. Technical Report [*A publication*]
**Great Lakes Res Div Univ Mich Publ** ... Great Lakes Research Division. University of Michigan. Publication [*A publication*]
**Great Plains Agric Counc Publ** ... Great Plains Agricultural Council. Publication [*A publication*]
**Great Synag Cong J** ... Great Synagogue Congregational Journal [*A publication*] (APTA)
**Greav Cr L** ... Greaves. Criminal Consolidation [*2nd ed.*] [*1862*] [*A publication*] (DLA)
**Greaves**...... Judgments of the Windward Islands Court of Appeal [*1866-1904*] [*A publication*] (DLA)
**Greav Russ** ... Greaves' Edition of Russell on Crimes [*A publication*] (DLA)
**GREB**......... Galactic Radiation Experiment Background Satellite [*Navy transit satellite*]
**GRECC**...... Geriatric Research, Education, and Clinical Center [*Veterans Administration*]
**GRECE**...... Groupement de Recherche et d'Etudes pour la Civilisation Europeenne [*Research and Study Group for European Civilization*] [*France*] (PD)
**GRED**........ Generalized Random Extract Device [*Data processing*]
**GREDI**....... Groupe d'Etudes en Developpement International [*International Development Studies Group*] [*Canada*]
**GREE**......... General Requests for Ground-Based Electronics Equipment [*NASA*]
**Greece Bk** .. National Bank of Greece. Bulletin [*A publication*]
**Greece & Rome New Surv Class** ... Greece and Rome. New Surveys in the Classics [*A publication*]
**GRE & E Div** ... Graves Registration and Effects Division [*Military*]
**Greek Roman Byz Stud** ... Greek, Roman, and Byzantine Studies [*A publication*]
**Greek Rom B** ... Greek, Roman, and Byzantine Studies [*A publication*]
**Greek Rom & Byz Stud** ... Greek, Roman, and Byzantine Studies [*A publication*]
**Greek Stat** ... Monthly Statistical Bulletin (Greece) [*A publication*]
**Green** ......... Green's Reports [*A publication*] (DLA)
**GREEN** ..... Guild to Revive Exhausted Nurses
**Green Bag** .. Green Bag; A Legal Journal [*Boston*] [*A publication*] (DLA)
**Green BL** ... Green's Bankrupt Law [*A publication*] (DLA)
**Green Bri** ... Green's Edition of Brice's Ultra Vires [*A publication*] (DLA)
**Green Bull** ... Green Bulletin [*A publication*]
**Green C E** .. [*C. E.*] Greene. New Jersey Chancery Reports [*A publication*] (DLA)
**Green Ch**.... [*H. W.*] Green's New Jersey Chancery Reports [*2-4 New Jersey Equity*] [*A publication*] (DLA)
**Green Conv** ... Greenwood's Manual of Conveyancing [*9th ed.*] [*1897*] [*A publication*] (DLA)
**Green Cr** .... Green's Criminal Law [*England*] [*A publication*] (DLA)
**Green Cr Cas** ... Green's Criminal Cases [*A publication*] (DLA)
**Green Crim Reports** ... Criminal Law Reports, by Green [*United States*] [*A publication*] (DLA)
**Green Cr Law R** ... Green's Criminal Law Reports [*A publication*] (DLA)
**Green Cr L Rep** ... Green's Criminal Law Reports [*A publication*] (DLA)
**Green Cr Rep** ... Criminal Law Reports, by Green [*United States*] [*A publication*] (DLA)
**Green Cruise** ... Greenleaf's Edition of Cruise's Digest of Real Property [*A publication*] (DLA)
**Green Cts**... Greenwood on Courts [*A publication*] (DLA)
**Greene**........ [*G.*] Greene's Iowa Reports [*1847-54*] [*A publication*] (DLA)
**Greene**........ Greene's Reports [*7 New York Annotated Cases*] [*A publication*] (DLA)
**Greene G (Iowa)** ... [*G.*] Greene's Iowa Reports [*1847-54*] [*A publication*] (DLA)
**Green Ev**.... Greenleaf on Evidence [*A publication*] (DLA)
**Green Forms** ... Greening's Forms of Declarations, Pleadings, Etc. [*A publication*] (DLA)
**Green & H Conv** ... Greenwood and Horwood's Conveyancing [*A publication*] (DLA)
**Greenh Pub Pol** ... Greenhood's Doctrine of Public Policy in the Law of Contracts [*A publication*] (DLA)
**Greenh Sh** ... Greenhow's Shipping Law Manual [*A publication*] (DLA)
**Greenkeepers Rep** ... Greenkeepers Reporter [*A publication*]
**Greenl** ........ Greenleaf's Reports [*1-9 Maine*] [*A publication*] (DLA)
**Green L**...... [*J. S.*] Green's Law Reports [*13-15 New Jersey*] [*A publication*] (DLA)
**Greenland Geol Unders Bull** ... Greenland. Geologiske Undersoegelse. Bulletin [*A publication*]
**Greenland Geol Unders Rapp** ... Greenland. Geologiske Undersoegelse. Rapport [*A publication*]
**Greenl Cr**... Greenleaf's Edition of Cruise's Digest of Real Property [*A publication*] (DLA)
**Greenl Cruise** ... Greenleaf's Edition of Cruise's Digest of Real Property [*A publication*] (DLA)
**Greenl Cruise Real Prop** ... Greenleaf's Edition of Cruise's Digest of Real Property [*A publication*] (DLA)
**Greenl Ev**... Greenleaf on Evidence [*A publication*] (DLA)
**Greenl Geosci** ... Greenland Geoscience [*Denmark*] [*A publication*]
**Greenl Ov Cas** ... Greenleaf's Over-Ruled Cases [*A publication*] (DLA)
**Greenl Test Ev** ... Greenleaf on the Testimony of the Evangelists [*A publication*] (DLA)
**Green Mt**... Green Mountain [*A publication*]
**Green (NJ)** ... Green's New Jersey Law or Equity [*A publication*] (DLA)
**Green Ov Cas** ... Greenleaf's Over-Ruled Cases [*A publication*] (DLA)
**Green R**...... Greenfield Review [*A publication*]
**Green Rev** .. Green Revolution [*A publication*]
**Green Revol** ... Green Revolution [*A publication*]
**Green (RI)** ... Green's Reports [*Rhode Island*] [*A publication*] (DLA)
**Green Rom Law** ... Green's Outlines of Roman Law [*A publication*] (DLA)
**Green Sc Cr Cas** ... Green's Criminal Cases [*A publication*] (DLA)
**Green Sc Tr** ... Green's Scottish Trials for Treason [*A publication*] (DLA)
**Green Ship** ... Greenhow's Law of Shipowners [*A publication*] (DLA)
**Greenw Conv** ... Greenwood's Manual of Conveyancing [*9th ed.*] [*1897*] [*A publication*] (DLA)
**Greenw Cts** ... Greenwood on Courts [*A publication*] (DLA)
**Greenwich Time Rep** ... Greenwich Time Report [*A publication*]
**Greenw & M Mag Pol** ... Greenwood and Martin's Magistrates' Police Guide [*A publication*] (DLA)
**Greer** .......... Greer's Irish Land Acts, Leading Cases [*1872-1903*] [*A publication*] (DLA)
**GREF** ......... General Reserve Engineer Force [*British military*] (DMA)
**GREFICOR** ... Groupe de Recherche sur l'Efficacite Organisationnelle [*University of Quebec at Hull*] [*Research center*] (RCD)
**G/REG**....... Generator-Regulator [*Automotive engineering*]
**G REG** ....... Grand Registrar [*Freemasonry*] (ROG)
**GREG** ........ Gregorian (ROG)
**Greg** ........... Gregorianum [*A publication*]
**Greg** ........... Gregorowski's Reports of the High Court [*A publication*] (DLA)
**Greg** ........... [*Pope*] Gregory I [*Deceased, 604*] [*Authority cited in pre-1607 legal work*] (DSA)
**GregLA**...... Pontificiae Universitatis Gregorianae Liber Annuus [*Rome*] [*A publication*] (BJA)
**GRegO**....... Group Regiment Officer [*British military*] (DMA)
**Gregor**........ Gregoriusblad [*A publication*]
**Gregorowski** ... High Court Reports, Orange Free State [*A publication*] (DLA)
**GREI**.......... Groupe de Recherche en Enseignement Individualise [*Canada*]
**G Reichs-Mus Leiden Samm** ... Geologische Reichs-Museum in Leiden. Sammlungen [*A publication*]
**Grein Pr** ..... Greiner's Louisiana Practice [*A publication*] (DLA)
**GREL**......... General Real Estate Shares [*NASDAQ symbol*] (NQ)
**G Rel Per** ... Guide to Religious Periodicals [*A publication*]
**GREM** ....... Gremlin [*Refers to a person unskilled in skateboarding*] [*Slang*] [*British*] (DSUE)
**GREMAS** ... Genealogische Recherche mit Magnetband-Speicherung [*Organic chemistry coding system*]
**GREMEX** ... Goddard Research and Engineering Management Exercise [*NASA*]
**GREMF**..... Groupe de Recherche et d'Echange Multidisciplinaires Feministes [*Universite Laval, Quebec*] [*Canada*]
**GREN** ........ Great Eastern Energy & Development Corp. [*NASDAQ symbol*] (NQ)

**GREN**........ Grenade (AABC)
**Gren**.......... Grenier's Ceylon Reports [*A publication*] (DLA)
**Grenada Agric Dep Rep** ... Grenada Agricultural Department. Report [*A publication*]
**GRENDR**.. Grenadier (AABC)
**Grenier**....... Grenier's Ceylon Reports [*A publication*] (DLA)
**Grenoble Fac Sci Lab Geol Mem** ... Grenoble. Faculte des Sciences. Laboratoire de Geologie. Memoires [*A publication*]
**Grenoble Univ Lett Ann** ... Universite de Grenoble. Lettres-Droit. Annales [*A publication*]
**Grenoble Univ Sci Ann** ... Universite de Grenoble. Sciences-Medecine. Annales [*A publication*]
**Grenzgeb Med** ... Grenzgebiete der Medizin [*A publication*]
**GREP**......... Global Regular-Expression Purser [*Data processing*]
**GREPAT**... Greenland Patrol [*Navy*]
**G Rep Sask Res Counc Geol Div** ... G Report. Saskatchewan Research Council. Geology Division [*A publication*]
**GrEq** ......... [*H. W.*] Green's New Jersey Equity Reports [*A publication*] (DLA)
**GrEq** .......... Gresley's Equity Evidence [*A publication*] (DLA)
**GRER** ........ Greenstone Resources Ltd. [*NASDAQ symbol*] (NQ)
**Gre Rom Law** ... Greene's Outlines of Roman Law [*A publication*] (DLA)
**GRES**......... Gippsland Regional Environmental Study [*Australia*]
**GRES**......... Greatest Amount of Resources
**Gres EqEv** ... Gresley's Equity Evidence [*A publication*] (DLA)
**GRESLET** ... Groupe de Recherche en Semantique, Lexicologie, et Terminologie [*Universite de Montreal, Quebec*] [*Canada*]
**GRETA**...... Ground RADAR Emitter for Training Aviators [*Army*] (RDA)
**Gretton**....... Oxford Quarter Sessions Records [*Oxford Record Society, No. 16*] [*A publication*] (DLA)
**GrEv**........... Greenleaf on Evidence [*A publication*] (DLA)
**GREY** ........ Grey Advertising, Inc. [*NASDAQ symbol*] (NQ)
**Grey Deb**.... Grey's House of Commons Debates [*A publication*] (DLA)
**GRF** ........... Garbell Research Foundation (MCD)
**GRF** ........... Gelatin, Resorcinol, and Formaldehyde
**GRF** ........... Gerald Rudolf Ford [*US president, 1913-*]
**GRF** ........... Gesneriad Research Foundation (EA)
**GRF** ........... Golden Rule Foundation (EA)
**GRF** ........... Gonadotropin-Releasing Factor [*Also, GnRF, GnRH, LH-RF, LH-RH/FSH-RH, LRF, LRH*] [*Endocrinology*]
**GRF** ........... Graefenberg Array [*Erlangen*] [*Federal Republic of Germany*] [*Seismograph station code, US Geological Survey*] (SEIS)
**GRF** ........... Graficus; Onafhankelijk Weekblad voor de Grafische Industrie [*Rijswijk*] [*A publication*]
**GRF** ........... Grandfather
**GRF** ........... Grassland Research Foundation (EA)
**GRF** ........... Gravity Research Foundation (EA)
**GRF** ........... Group Repetition Frequency
**GRF** ........... Growth Hormone Releasing Factor [*Somatoliberin*] [*Also, GH-RF, GH-RH*] [*Endocrinology*]
**GRF** ........... Guaranty Reserve Fund
**GRF** ........... Tacoma/Fort Lewis, WA [*Location identifier*] [*FAA*] (FAAL)
**GR-FeSV**... Gardner-Rasheed Feline Sarcoma Virus
**GRFIA**....... Grinding and Finishing [*A publication*]
**GRFL**......... Gerald R. Ford Library
**GRFMA**..... Grand Rapids Furniture Market Association [*Inactive*] (EA)
**GRFO** ........ Gun Range-Finder Operator
**GrFRP** ....... Graphite-Fiber-Reinforced Plastic [*Also, GFRP*]
**GRFS**......... Greencastle Federal Savings Bank [*NASDAQ symbol*] (NQ)
**GRFTAV**... Gerfaut [*A publication*]
**GRFTAV**... Giervalk [*A publication*]
**GRFX**......... Grinding Fixture
**GRG**........... Den Haag. Maandblad van de Gemeente ('S-Gravenhage) [*A publication*]
**GRG**........... Gastroenterology Research Group [*Defunct*] (EA)
**GRG**........... Gearing (MSA)
**GRG**........... Generalized Reduced Gradient
**GRG**........... Glass-Fiber Reinforced Gypsum [*Substitute wood*]
**GRG**........... Gordetsky [*G.R.*] Telecommunications and General Management Consulting [*San Diego, CA*] [*Telecommunications*] (TSSD)
**Grg**............. Gorgias [*of Plato*] [*Classical studies*] (OCD)
**GRG**........... Graphical Rewriting Grammar
**GRG**........... Greenery Rehabilitation Group, Inc. [*NYSE symbol*] (SPSG)
**GRG**........... Gross Reserve Generation [*Electronics*] (IEEE)
**GRGE**........ Garage [*Classified Advertising*] (ADA)
**GRGE**........ Gorge [*Board on Geographic Names*]
**GRGE**........ Grudge Music Group, Inc. [*NASDAQ symbol*] (NQ)
**Gr Gesch**.... Griechische Geschichte [*A publication*] (OCD)
**GRGL**........ Groundwater Residue Guidance Level [*Environmental Protection Agency*]
**GRGS** ........ Ground Roll Guidance System (MCD)
**GRGSC**...... Greenland Geoscience. Meddelelser om Gronland [*A publication*]
**GRGSD** ..... Gesellschaft fuer Reaktorsicherheit. Bericht GRS-S [*A publication*]
**GRH** .......... Garuahi [*Papua New Guinea*] [*Airport symbol*] (OAG)
**GRH** .......... Gas Recycle Hydrogenation [*Petroleum engineering*]
**GRH** .......... Grahamstown [*South Africa*] [*Seismograph station code, US Geological Survey*] [*Closed*] (SEIS)
**GRH** .......... Gramm-Rudman-Hollings [*Law*]
**GRH** .......... GRC International [*NYSE symbol*] (SPSG)
**GRH** .......... Green Hills Aviation Ltd. [*Kirksville, MO*] [*FAA designator*] (FAAC)
**GRHKA**..... Grudnaya Khirurgiya [*A publication*]
**GRHQU** .... Gruppen-Hauptquartier [*Group Headquarters*] [*German military - World War II*]
**GRHS**........ Germans-from-Russia Heritage Society (EA)
**GRI**............ Gabriel Richard Institute (EA)
**GRI**............ Gale Research, Inc.
**GRI**............ Gallaudet Research Institute [*Gallaudet College*] [*Research center*] (RCD)
**GRI**............ Gas Research Institute (EA)
**GRI**............ Geographical Review of India [*A publication*]
**GR et I** ....... Georgius Rex et Imperator [*George, King and Emperor*]
**GRI**............ Geoscience Research Institute
**GRI**............ Gidley Research Institute [*Research center*] (RCD)
**GRI**............ Ginseng Research Institute (EA)
**GRI**............ Glider Developments, Inc. [*Vancouver Stock Exchange symbol*]
**Gri**.............. Glyceric Acid [*Biochemistry*]
**GRI**............ Gospel Recordings, Incorporated
**GRI**............ Government Reports Index [*Formerly, USGRDR-I*] [*Department of Commerce*]
**GR-I**........... Government Rubber-Isobutylene [*Synthetic rubber*]
**GRI**............ Government of the Ryukyu Islands
**GRI**............ Grand Island [*Nebraska*] [*Airport symbol*] (OAG)
**GRI**............ Grassland Research Institute [*Research center*] [*British*] (IRC)
**GRI**............ Grassroots International (EA)
**GRI**............ Gravure Research Institute [*Later, GAA*] (EA)
**GRI**............ Group Repetition Interval (IEEE)
**GRI**............ Groupe de Recherche et d'Intervention en Ideologie [*Universite du Quebec a Montreal*] [*Canada*]
**GRI**............ Guaranteed Retirement Income
**GRIB**.......... Gippsland Region Information Bank [*Australia*]
**GRIBAT**.... Graphics Interface Basic Acceptance Test (MCD)
**GRIC**.......... Graduate Member of the Royal Institute of Chemistry [*British*] (DBQ)
**GRID** ......... Gas Research Institute Digest [*Acronym is used as title of publication*] [*A publication*]
**GRID** ......... Gay-Related Immunodeficiency [*Also, AID, AIDS*] [*Medicine*]
**GRID** ......... Global Resource Information Data Base [*UNEP*] [*Nairobi, Kenya*] [*Information service or system*] (IID)
**GRID** ......... Global Resource Information Database [*NASA*]
**GRID** ......... Graphic Interactive Display (IEEE)
**GRID** ......... Graphic Reproduction by Integrated Design
**GRID** ......... Graphic Retrieval and Information Display (NASA)
**GRIDEQ**.... Groupe de Recherche en Developpement de l'Est du Quebec [*Canada*]
**GRIF**.......... Government Research Institute of Formosa
**GRIF**.......... Griffin Technology, Inc. [*NASDAQ symbol*] (NQ)
**GRIF**.......... Growth Hormone Release Inhibiting Factor [*Also, GH-RIF, GH-RIH, SRIF, SS*] [*Endocrinology*]
**Grif Cr**........ Griffith on Arrangements with Creditors [*A publication*] (DLA)
**Grif Ct Mar** ... Griffith on Military Law and Courts-Martial [*A publication*] (DLA)
**Grif Eq** ....... Griffith's Institutes of Equity [*A publication*] (DLA)
**GRIFF** ....... Groupe de Recherches Interdisciplinaires des Fertilisation des Forets [*Joint federal-provincial project*] [*Canada*]
**Griffin Pat Cas** ... Griffin's Patent Cases [*1866-87*] [*A publication*] (DLA)
**Griffin PC**.. Griffin's Abstract of Patent Cases [*England*] [*A publication*] (DLA)
**Griffin's Statist Monograph Ser** ... Griffin's Statistical Monograph Series [*A publication*]
**Griffith**....... Griffith's Reports [*1-5 Indiana Appeals and 117-132 Indiana*] [*A publication*] (DLA)
**Griff Pat Cas** ... Griffin's Patent Cases [*1866-87*] [*A publication*] (DLA)
**Grif Inst**..... Griffith's Institutes of Equity [*A publication*] (DLA)
**Grif Jud Acts** ... Griffith on the Judicature Acts [*A publication*] (DLA)
**Grif L Reg** ... Griffith's Law Register [*Burlington, NJ*] [*A publication*] (DLA)
**Grif Mar Wom** ... Griffith's Married Women's Property Act [*A publication*] (DLA)
**Grif Mil Law** ... Griffith on Military Law and Courts-Martial [*A publication*] (DLA)
**Grif Pat C** .. Griffin's Patent Cases [*1866-87*] [*A publication*] (DLA)
**Grif PC**....... Griffin's Patent Cases [*1866-87*] [*A publication*] (DLA)
**Grif PLC**.... Griffin's London Poor Law Cases [*1821-31*] [*A publication*] (DLA)
**Grif PL Cas** ... Griffith's London Poor Law Cases [*1821-31*] [*A publication*] (DLA)
**Grif Pr**....... Griffith's Practice [*A publication*] (DLA)
**Grif PRC**.... Griffith's Poor Rate Cases [*A publication*] (DLA)
**Grif PR Cas** ... Griffith's English Poor Rate Cases [*A publication*] (DLA)
**Grif St**........ Griffith's Stamp Duties [*A publication*] (DLA)
**GRIL**.......... Gale Research International Ltd.
**Grim Bank** ... Grimsey's Proceedings in Bankruptcy [*A publication*] (DLA)
**Grimke Ex** ... Grimke on Executors and Administrators [*A publication*] (DLA)
**Grimke Jus** ... Grimke's Justice [*A publication*] (DLA)
**Grimke PL** ... Grimke's Public Laws of South Carolina [*A publication*] (DLA)

**GRIN**......... Germplasm Resources Information Network [*Department of Agriculture*] [*Beltsville, MD*]
**GRIN**......... Graded Refractive-Index [*Optics*]
**GRIN**......... Gradient of Refractive Index [*Optics*]
**GRIN**......... Graphical Input [*Language*] [*Data processing*]
**GRIN**......... Great Plains [*AAR code*]
**GRIN-2**...... Graphical Interaction [*Language*] [*Data processing*]
**GRIN-A**..... Geographical Review of India [*A publication*]
**GRIND**...... Group Index (MCD)
**GRINDER**... Graphical Interactive Network Designer
**Grinding Finish**... Grinding and Finishing [*A publication*]
**Grindlays Bank R**... Grindlays Bank Review [*A publication*]
**GRI Newsl**... GRI [*Gravure Research Institute*] Newsletter [*A publication*]
**GRINS**....... General Retrieval Inquiry Negotiation Structure
**GRINS**....... Graphical Input of SMILES [*Simplified Molecular Line Editor System*] Input
**GR Insights**... Gas Research Insights [*A publication*]
**GRIP**.......... Gemini Reentry Integration Program [*NASA*]
**GRIP**.......... General Retrieval of Information Program [*Data processing*]
**GRIP**.......... Grandmet Information Processing [*British*]
**GRIP**.......... Graphics Interaction with Proteins [*Computer graphics*]
**GRIP**.......... Graphics Interactive Programming
**GRIP**.......... Graphics Interactive Programming Language [*McDonnell-Douglas Corp.*]
**GRIP**.......... Groupe de Recherche sur les Insectes Piqueurs [*University of Quebec at Trois-Rivieres*] [*Canada*] [*Research center*] (RCD)
**GRIP**.......... Guaranteed Recovery of Investment Principal [*Economics*]
**GRIPHOS**... General Retrieval and Information Processor for Humanities Oriented Studies
**Gripp Respir Virusn Infektsii**... Gripp i Respiratornye Virusnye Infektsii [*A publication*]
**GRIPS**....... Graphic Image Pagination System [*Penta Systems International*]
**GRIR**......... Groupe de Recherche et d'Intervention Regionales [*Universite du Quebec a Chicoutimi*] [*Canada*]
**GRIS**.......... Gamma-Ray Imaging Spectrometer
**GRIS**.......... Global Resources Information System
**GRIS**.......... Grisons [*Canton in Switzerland*] (ROG)
**GRIS**.......... Groupe de Recherche Interdisciplinaire en Sante [*Interdisciplinary Health Research Group - IHRG*] [*Universite de Montreal*] [*Canada*] [*Research center*]
**GRISAH**.... Groupe de Recherche et d'Intervention sur les Systemes d'Activities Humaines [*University of Quebec at Rimouski*] [*Research center*] (RCD)
**G Risic**....... Giornale di Risicoltura [*A publication*]
**GRISS**....... Golombok Rust Inventory of Sexual Satisfaction [*Test*] [*Psychology*]
**GRIST**....... Grazing-Incidence Solar Telescope
**Grisw**......... Griswold's Reports [*14-19 Ohio*] [*A publication*] (DLA)
**Griswold**..... Griswold's Reports [*14-19 Ohio*] [*A publication*] (DLA)
**Grisw Und**... Griswold's Fire Underwriter's Text-Book [*A publication*] (DLA)
**GRIT**.......... Graduated Reduction in Tensions [*Cold War term*]
**GRIT**.......... Grantor-Retained Income Trust [*Estate planning*]
**GRIT**.......... Grubb & Ellis Realty Income Trust [*San Francisco, CA*] [*NASDAQ symbol*] (NQ)
**GRITS**....... Gamma Ray Imaging Telescope System
**GRITS**....... Goddard Range [*and Range Rate*] Instrumentation Tracking System [*NASA*] (AAG)
**Grits Grinds (Worcester, Mass)**... Grits and Grinds (Worcester, Massachusetts) [*A publication*]
**GRJ**........... George [*South Africa*] [*Airport symbol*] (OAG)
**GRJ**........... Gorje [*Yugoslavia*] [*Seismograph station code, US Geological Survey*] [*Closed*] (SEIS)
**GRJC**......... Grand Rapids Junior College [*Michigan*]
**GRK**........... Gear Rack
**GRK**........... Golden Rock Resources Ltd. [*Vancouver Stock Exchange symbol*]
**GRK**........... Goroka [*Papua New Guinea*] [*Seismograph station code, US Geological Survey*] [*Closed*] (SEIS)
**GRK**........... Greek [*Language, etc.*]
**GRK**........... Killeen, TX [*Location identifier*] [*FAA*] (FAAL)
**GRL**........... General
**GRL**........... General Instrument Corp. [*NYSE symbol*] (SPSG)
**GRL**........... Geophysical Research Letters [*A publication*]
**GRL**........... Gerontology Research Center, Baltimore, MD [*OCLC symbol*] (OCLC)
**GRL**........... Goldenrod Resources & Technology, Inc. [*Vancouver Stock Exchange symbol*]
**GRL**........... Grain Research Laboratory [*Canadian Grain Commission*] [*Research center*] (RCD)
**GRL**........... Greenland [*ANSI three-letter standard code*] (CNC)
**GRL**........... Grille
**GRL**........... Grundrichtungslinie [*Base line, a gunnery term*] [*German military - World War II*]
**GRLH**........ Garland Reference Library of the Humanities [*A publication*]
**Gr LJ**......... Georgetown Law Journal [*A publication*]
**GrLR**.......... Great Lakes Review. A Journal of Midwest Culture [*A publication*]
**GRLS**......... Great River Library System [*Library network*]
**GRM**.......... Generalized Reed-Muller [*Codes*] (IEEE)
**GRM**.......... Generalized Report Module Program [*Data processing*]
**GRM**.......... Geopotential Research Mission [*NASA*]
**GRM**.......... Germanisch-Romanische Monatsschrift [*A publication*]
**GRM**.......... Global Range Missile [*Air Force*]
**GRM**.......... Grahamstown [*South Africa*] [*Seismograph station code, US Geological Survey*] (SEIS)
**GRM**.......... Grahamstown [*South Africa*] [*Geomagnetic observatory code*]
**GRM**.......... Gram (ADA)
**GRM**.......... Gramme [*Gram*] [*French*] (ROG)
**GRM**.......... Grand Marais, MN [*Location identifier*] [*FAA*] (FAAL)
**GRM**.......... Grandmother
**GRM**.......... Graziano, R. M., Washington DC [*STAC*]
**GRM**.......... Great Renunciation Movement (EA)
**GRM**.......... Groene Amsterdammer [*A publication*]
**GRM**.......... Gruppe Revolutionaerer Marxisten [*Group of Revolutionary Marxists*] [*Austria*] [*Political party*] (PPE)
**GRM**.......... Guarded Relay Multiplexer
**GRM**.......... Guidance Rate Measurement
**GRMAA**.... Geologiya Rudnykh Mestorozhdenii [*A publication*]
**GRMDA**.... German Medicine [*A publication*]
**GRMI**........ GRM Industries, Inc. [*NASDAQ symbol*] (NQ)
**GRMMA**... German Medical Monthly [*A publication*]
**G-R Mon**.... Germanisch-Romanische Monatsschrift [*A publication*]
**GRMS**....... Germanisch-Romanische Monatsschrift [*A publication*]
**GRMT**....... Grommet [*Automotive engineering*]
**GRN**........... General Re Corp. [*NYSE symbol*] (SPSG)
**Grn**............ Glycerone [*Biochemistry*]
**GRN**........... Gordon, NE [*Location identifier*] [*FAA*] (FAAL)
**Gr N**.......... Graduate Nurse
**GRN**........... Gram-Negative [*Also, GN*] [*Microbiology*]
**GRN**........... Granite [*Technical drawings*]
**GRN**........... Green (KSC)
**GRN**........... Greenville & Northern Railway Co. [*AAR code*]
**GRN**........... Greenwich Library, Greenwich, CT [*OCLC symbol*] (OCLC)
**GRN**........... Grenoble [*France*] [*Seismograph station code, US Geological Survey*] (SEIS)
**GRN**........... Grenoble Energy [*Vancouver Stock Exchange symbol*]
**GRNC**........ Group Number No Count [*Military communication*]
**GRNCA**..... Gerontologia Clinica [*A publication*]
**GRNCAK**.. Gerontologia Clinica [*A publication*]
**GRNCM**.... Graduate of the Royal Northern College of Music [*British*] (DBQ)
**GRND**........ Grand
**GRND**........ Ground (ADA)
**GRNDR**..... Grinder[*s*] [*Freight*]
**GRNL**........ Gay Rights National Lobby (EA)
**GRNL**........ Greenland Newsletter. Greenland Home Rule Information Service (Tusarliivik) [*A publication*]
**GRNR**........ [*The*] Grand River Railway Co. [*AAR code*]
**GRNR**........ Greinar [*A publication*]
**grnsh**.......... Greenish [*Philately*]
**GRNTA**..... Gerontologist [*A publication*]
**GRO**........... Gamma Ray Observatory [*NASA*] (EGAO)
**GRO**........... General Register Office [*British*]
**GRO**........... General Routine Order
**GRO**........... Gerona [*Spain*] [*Airport symbol*] (OAG)
**Gro**............. Glycerol [*Biochemistry*]
**GRO**........... Grandparents Rights Organization (EA)
**GRO**........... Graves Registration Officer [*Military*]
**GRO**........... Gross (MSA)
**Gro**............. Gross' Select Cases Concerning the Law Merchant [*Selden Society*] [*A publication*] (DLA)
**Gro**............. Grotius' Rights of War and Peace [*Many eds.*] [*1625-1901*] [*A publication*] (DLA)
**GRO**........... Ground Risks Only [*Insurance*] (AIA)
**GRO**........... Grove
**GRO**........... Grow Group, Inc. [*NYSE symbol*] (SPSG)
**GRO**........... Growth Investment Corp. [*Toronto Stock Exchange symbol*]
**GRO**........... Grozny [*USSR*] [*Seismograph station code, US Geological Survey*] (SEIS)
**GRO**........... Rota Island, TT [*Location identifier*] [*FAA*] (FAAL)
**GROBDM**... General Register Office for Births, Deaths, and Marriages [*A publication*] (DLA)
**Gro BP**....... Grotius. De Jure Belli et Pacis [*A publication*] (DLA)
**GROCAP**... Gross Capability Estimator [*Air Force*]
**Groc & Storekeeping News**... Grocery and Storekeeping News [*A publication*] (APTA)
**Gro De JB**... Grotius. De Jure Belli et Pacis [*A publication*] (DLA)
**Gro Dr**........ Grotius' Le Droit de la Guerre [*A publication*] (DLA)
**Groenlands Geol Unders Bull**... Groenlands Geologiske Undersoegelse. Bulletin [*A publication*]
**Groenlands Geol Unders Misc Pap**... Groenlands Geologiske Undersoegelse. Miscellaneous Papers [*A publication*]
**Groenlands Geol Undersoegelse Bull**... Groenlands Geologiske Undersoegelse. Bulletin [*A publication*]
**Groenl Geol Unders Rap**... Groenlands Geologiske Undersoegelse. Rapport [*A publication*]
**GROF**........ Groff Industries, Inc. [*NASDAQ symbol*] (NQ)
**GROFIS**.... Ground Forces Intelligence Study (MCD)

**Gro Ges & Verord** ... Grotofend's Gestze und Verordnungen [*A publication*] (DLA)
**GROJ** ........ Get Rid of Junk [*Garage sale sign*]
**GROKA** ..... Gornictwo Odkrywkowe [*A publication*]
**GROM**....... Groman Corp. [*NASDAQ symbol*] (NQ)
**GROM**....... Grommet (KSC)
**GROMAL** ... Geologica Romana [*A publication*]
**Gron** .......... Gronningen. Siglum for Tablets [*Leiden*] [*A publication*] (BJA)
**Grondboor Hamer** ... Grondboor en Hamer [*Nederlandse Geologische Vereniging Tijdschrift*] [*A publication*]
**GROOVE** .. Generated Real-Time Output Operations on Voltage-Controlled Equipment [*Data processing*]
**GROPAC**... Group Pacific
**Gro PC** ....... Grotius. De Jure Praedae Commentarius [*A publication*] (DLA)
**Gr Orth Th R** ... Greek Orthodox Theological Review [*A publication*]
**GrOrthTR** ... Greek Orthodox Theological Review [*Brookline, MA*] [*A publication*]
**Gros** .......... Generos [*Goods*] [*Business term*] [*Spanish*]
**GROS** ........ Grossman's, Inc. [*Braintree, MA*] [*NASDAQ symbol*] (NQ)
**Grosses Zool Prakt** ... Grosses Zoologisches Praktikum [*A publication*]
**Gross St** ..... Gross' Illinois Compiled Statutes [*A publication*] (DLA)
**GROT** ........ Grote [*or Grotius*] [*Literature*] (ROG)
**GROT** ........ Grotesque (ADA)
**GROT** ........ Grotto (ROG)
**Grot De Aequit** ... Grotius. De Aequitate [*A publication*] (DLA)
**Grot De JB** ... Grotius. De Jure Belli et Pacis [*A publication*] (DLA)
**Grot De JrB** ... Grotius. De Jure Belli et Pacis [*A publication*] (DLA)
**Grotius**....... Grotius. Latin Law [*A publication*] (DLA)
**Grotius De Jure Belli** ... Grotius. De Jure Belli et Pacis [*A publication*] (DLA)
**Grot Soc'y** .. Transactions. Grotius Society [*England*] [*A publication*] (DLA)
**Ground Eng** ... Ground Engineering [*A publication*]
**Ground Engng** ... Ground Engineering [*A publication*]
**Grounds Maint** ... Grounds Maintenance [*A publication*]
**Ground Wat** ... Ground Water Age [*A publication*]
**Ground Water Heat Pump J** ... Ground Water Heat Pump Journal [*A publication*]
**Ground Water Monit Rev** ... Ground Water Monitoring Review [*A publication*]
**Group Adv Psychiatry Rep** ... Group for the Advancement of Psychiatry. Report [*A publication*]
**Group Avan Mec Ind** ... Groupement pour l'Avancement de la Mecanique Industrielle [*A publication*]
**Group Fam Ther** ... Group and Family Therapy [*A publication*]
**Group Fr Dev Rech Aeronaut Bull GRA** ... Groupement Francais pour le Developpement des Recherches Aeronautiques. Bulletin du GRA [*A publication*]
**Group Health J** ... Group Health Journal [*A publication*]
**Group Legal Rev** ... Group Legal Review [*A publication*] (DLA)
**Group Organ Stud** ... Group and Organization Studies [*A publication*]
**Group Org Stud** ... Group and Organization Studies [*A publication*]
**Group Pract** ... Group Practice [*A publication*]
**Group Pract J** ... Group Practice Journal [*A publication*]
**Group Psych** ... Group Psychotherapy and Psychodrama [*Later, Group Psychotherapy, Psychodrama, and Sociometry*] [*A publication*]
**Group Psychother Psychodrama Sociometry** ... Group Psychotherapy, Psychodrama, and Sociometry [*A publication*]
**GROV** ........ Grove Bank for Savings [*NASDAQ symbol*] (NQ)
**Grove**.......... Grove's Dictionary of Music and Musicians [*A publication*]
**Grove Chron Mus Hist** ... Grove Chronology of Music History [*A publication*]
**GROW**....... Greater Opportunities through Work [*Proposed federal program*]
**GROW**....... Group Relations Ongoing Workshops
**Grow**.......... Growth [*A publication*]
**GROWBY** ... Green, Red, Orange, White, Blue, Yellow [*System devised by a military wife and used by the Army in commissaries of its European posts to indicate day on which packaged bread and rolls were baked. The twist ties on the packages are color-coded to represent the day, with Green indicating Monday, Red for Tuesday, etc., throughout the week.*]
**Grower Annu** ... Grower Annual [*A publication*]
**Growers' Dir Ill Crop Impr Ass** ... Growers' Directory. Illinois Crop Improvement Association [*A publication*]
**Growers' Handb Annu Proc** ... Growers' Handbook and Annual Proceedings. Ohio Vegetable and Potato Growers' Association [*A publication*]
**Growth Chan** ... Growth and Change [*A publication*]
**Growth Dev Aging** ... Growth, Development, and Aging [*A publication*]
**Grozn Neft** ... Groznenskii Neftyznik [*A publication*]
**Grozn Neft Inst Tr** ... Groznenskii Neftyanoi Institut. Trudy [*A publication*]
**GRP** ........... Gamma Ray Projector
**GRP** ........... Gastrin-Releasing Peptide [*Endocrinology*]
**GRP** ........... Gaussian Random Process [*Mathematics*]
**GRP** ........... Gelatin Rigidized Panel
**GRP** ........... Giant Reef Petroleums [*Vancouver Stock Exchange symbol*]
**GRP** ........... Glass-Reinforced Plastic [*or Polyester*]
**GRP** ........... Glucocorticoid Receptor Protein [*Biochemistry*]
**GRP** ........... Glucose Regulated Protein [*Biochemistry*]
**GRP** ........... Gram-Positive [*Also, GP*] [*Microbiology*]
**GR & P**....... Grand Rapids & Petoskey Railway
**GRP** ........... Granite Point, AK [*Location identifier*] [*FAA*] (FAAL)
**GRP** ........... Grant-Related Poundage [*British*]
**GRP** ........... Greatest Response Probability
**GrP** ............ Greenwood Publishing Corp., Westport, CT [*Library symbol*] [*Library of Congress*] (LCLS)
**GRP** ........... Gross Rating Point [*Television*]
**GRP** ........... Gross Regional Product
**GRP** ........... Ground Relay Panel [*Aerospace*] (AAG)
**GRP** ........... Group (KSC)
**GRP** ........... Group Reference Pilot [*Telecommunications*] (TEL)
**GRP** ........... Grundrichtungspunkt [*Base point, a gunnery term*] [*German military - World War II*]
**GRP** ........... Guardia Republicana [*Peru*]
**GRPC**......... Gulf Regional Planning Commission
**Grp Capt** ..... Group Captain [*British military*] (DMA)
**GRPCD**....... GraphiCommunicator [*A publication*]
**GRPENT**.... Grouped Enterprises Data Base [*Australian Bureau of Statistics*] [*Information service or system*] (CRD)
**GRPH** ........ Graphic (MSA)
**GRPH** ........ Graphic Industries, Inc. [*NASDAQ symbol*] (NQ)
**GRPHA** ..... Graphis [*A publication*]
**GRPI**.......... Greenwich Pharmaceuticals, Incorporated [*NASDAQ symbol*] (NQ)
**GRPJ** ......... Glass-Reinforced Plastic Joint
**GRPL**......... Grand Rapids Public Library [*Michigan*]
**GRPS**......... Glucose-Ringer-Phosphate Solution
**GRPSB** ...... Group Psychotherapy [*Later, Group Psychotherapy, Psychodrama, and Sociometry*] [*A publication*]
**GRQ**........... Goldrite Mining [*Vancouver Stock Exchange symbol*]
**GRQ**........... Groningen [*Netherlands*] [*Airport symbol*] (OAG)
**GRQU**........ Gran Quivira National Monument
**GR & R** ...... Gauge Repeatability and Reproducibility [*Materials testing*]
**GRR** ........... Gear Reduction Ratio [*Military*] (CAAL)
**GRR** ........... Geneva Radio Regulations
**GRR** ........... Georgetown Railroad Co. [*AAR code*]
**GRR** ........... Golden Rim Resources, Inc. [*Vancouver Stock Exchange symbol*]
**GRR** ........... Gorron [*France*] [*Seismograph station code, US Geological Survey*] (SEIS)
**GRR** ........... Government Research and Development Reports
**GRR** ........... Grand Rapids [*Michigan*] [*Airport symbol*] (OAG)
**GRR** ........... Greek Research Reactor
**GRR** ........... Green River Review [*A publication*]
**GRR** ........... GRI Corp. [*AMEX symbol*] (SPSG)
**GRR** ........... Guidance Reference Release (KSC)
**GRRC** ........ Government Regulations Review Committee [*Western Australia*]
**GRRC** ........ Gurkha Rifles Regimental Centre [*British military*] (DMA)
**GRREG** ..... Graves Registration [*Military*]
**GRRI** ......... Greenstone Rabasca Roberts, Inc. [*NASDAQ symbol*] (NQ)
**GRRL**......... Greenwood Holdings, Inc. [*NASDAQ symbol*] (NQ)
**Gr Rom Byz St** ... Greek, Roman, and Byzantine Studies [*A publication*]
**GRRR** ........ Lion Country Safari [*NASDAQ symbol*] (NQ)
**GRS** ........... Gamma Radiation Source
**GRS** ........... Gamma Radiation Spectrometer
**GRS** ........... Gamma Ray Spectrometer
**GRS** ........... Gamma Ray Spectrum
**GRS** ........... Gaseous RADWASTE System [*Nuclear energy*] (NRCH)
**GRS** ........... General Radio Service [*Canada*]
**GRS** ........... General Reconnaissance School [*British military*] (DMA)
**GRS** ........... General Records Schedules [*Military*] (AABC)
**GRS** ........... General Register Set/Stack [*Data processing*]
**GRS** ........... General Reporting System
**GRS** ........... General Revenue Sharing [*Office of Revenue Sharing*]
**GRS** ........... Generalized Retrieval System [*Data processing*]
**GRS** ........... Gereedschap [*A publication*]
**GRS** ........... German Dermatological Society (EAIO)
**GRS** ........... German Research Satellite [*NASA*]
**GRS** ........... Ghost Research Society (EA)
**GRS** ........... Golden Rule Society (EA)
**GRS** ........... Goris [*USSR*] [*Seismograph station code, US Geological Survey*] (SEIS)
**GR-S** .......... Government Rubber-Styrene [*Also, SBR*] [*Synthetic rubber*]
**GRS** ........... Graduate Rabbinical School (BJA)
**GRS** ........... Grand Recording Scribe [*Freemasonry*] (ROG)
**GRS** ........... Grandson (ROG)
**GRS** ........... Grass [*Maps and charts*]
**GRS** ........... Gratiam Resources [*Vancouver Stock Exchange symbol*]
**GRS** ........... Graves Registration Service [*Military*]
**GRS** ........... Gravity Reference Signal [*or System*]
**GRS** ........... Grease (MSA)
**GRS** ........... Great Red Spot [*on planet Jupiter*]
**GRS** ........... Grid Reference Ship [*Navy*] (NVT)
**GRS** ........... Grigori Rasputin Society (EA)
**GrS**............ Grosser Senat (DLA)
**GRS** ........... Groupe Revolution naire Socialiste [*Socialist Revolution Group*] [*Martinique*] [*Political party*] [*Political party*] (PPW)
**GRS** ........... Groupe Revolutionnaire Socialiste [*Socialist Revolution Group*] [*France*] [*Political party*]
**G & RS**....... Guidance and Reporting System [*Army*]

**GRS** .......... Gyro Reference System (AAG)
**GRS** .......... Shorter College, Rome, GA [*Library symbol*] [*Library of Congress*] (LCLS)
**GRSA**......... Germersheim Reserve Storage Activity (MCD)
**GRSA**......... Great Sand Dunes National Monument
**GRSC**......... Graduate of the Royal Society of Chemistry [*British*] (DBQ)
**GRSE**......... Gamma Ray Spectrometric Equipment
**GRS (Ges Reaktorsicherheit) Kurz-Inf Reihe A** ... GRS (Gesellschaft fuer Reaktorsicherheit). Kurz-Information. Reihe A [*A publication*]
**GRS (Ges Reaktorsicherheit) Kurz-Inf Reihe B** ... GRS (Gesellschaft fuer Reaktorsicherheit). Kurz-Information. Reihe B [*A publication*]
**GRS (Ges Reaktorsicherheit) Kurz-Inf Reihe C** ... GRS (Gesellschaft fuer Reaktorsicherheit). Kurz-Information. Reihe C [*A publication*]
**GRS (Ges Reaktorsicherheit) Kurz-Inf Reihe D** ... GRS (Gesellschaft fuer Reaktorsicherheit). Kurz-Information. Reihe D [*A publication*]
**GRS (Ges Reaktorsicherheit) Kurz-Inf Reihe E** ... GRS (Gesellschaft fuer Reaktorsicherheit). Kurz-Information. Reihe E [*A publication*]
**GRS (Ges Reaktorsicherheit) Kurz-Inf Reihe F** ... GRS (Gesellschaft fuer Reaktorsicherheit). Kurz-Information. Reihe F [*A publication*]
**GRS (Ges Reaktorsicherheit) Kurz-Inf Reihe G** ... GRS (Gesellschaft fuer Reaktorsicherheit). Kurz-Information. Reihe G [*A publication*]
**GRS (Ges Reaktorsicherheit) Kurz-Inf Reihe H** ... GRS (Gesellschaft fuer Reaktorsicherheit). Kurz-Information. Reihe H [*A publication*]
**GRS (Ges Reaktorsicherheit) Kurz-Inf Reihe K** ... GRS (Gesellschaft fuer Reaktorsicherheit) Kurz-Information. Reihe K [*A publication*]
**GRS (Ges Reaktorsicherheit) Transl Saf Codes Guides** ... GRS (Gesellschaft fuer Reaktorsicherheit) Translations. Safety Codes and Guides [*A publication*]
**GRSHFT**... Gearshaft (MSA)
**GRS Kurz-Inf Reihe J** ... GRS (Gesellschaft fuer Reaktorsicherheit). Kurz-Information. Reihe J [*West Germany*] [*A publication*]
**GRSLND**... Grassland (RDA)
**GRSM** ....... Graduate of the Royal Schools of Music [*British*]
**GRSM** ....... Great Smoky Mountains National Park [*Also, GSMNP*]
**GR/S/O**..... Grandson Of [*Genealogy*]
**GRSP**......... General Range Safety Plan [*NASA*]
**GRSP**......... Glass-Reinforced Structural Plastic
**GRSS**......... IEEE Geoscience and Remote Sensing Society (EA)
**Grssgdb**...... Grossgrundbesitzer [*Landed Proprietor*] [*German*]
**Grsshdlr**..... Grosshaendler [*Wholesale Dealer or Merchant*] [*German*]
**Grssind** ...... Grossindustrieller [*Wholesale Manufacturer or Industrial Magnate*] [*German*]
**GRST**......... Grist Mill Co. [*Lakeville, MN*] [*NASDAQ symbol*] (NQ)
**GR ST**........ Groom of the Stole [*British*]
**GRST**......... Gross Tons
**GrSt**........... Grundtvig Studier [*A publication*]
**GRSU** ........ Geography Remote Sensing Unit [*University of California, Santa Barbara*]
**GRT** .......... Gamma Ray Telescope
**GRT** .......... Gamma Ray Tube
**GRT** .......... General Reactor Technology (NRCH)
**GRT** .......... Government Rate Tender
**GRT** .......... Graduate Respiratory Therapist
**Grt**............. Grant's Pennsylvania Cases [*A publication*] (DLA)
**grt**.............. Graphic Technician [*MARC relator code*] [*Library of Congress*] (LCCP)
**GRT** .......... Graphic Technology, Inc. [*AMEX symbol*] (SPSG)
**GRT** .......... Gratio [*Tennessee*] [*Seismograph station code, US Geological Survey*] (SEIS)
**GRT** .......... Great (ROG)
**GRT** .......... Gross Registered Tons [*Navigation*]
**GRT** .......... Ground-Received Times [*Solar wind measurements*]
**GRT** .......... Ground Resistance Tester
**GRT** .......... GTC Transcontinental Group Ltd. [*Toronto Stock Exchange symbol*]
**Gr(T)**.......... Gunner (Torpedo) [*British military*] (DMA)
**GRT** .......... Tri-County Regional Library, Rome, GA [*Library symbol*] [*Library of Congress*] (LCLS)
**GRTA** ........ Government Reports and Topical Announcements [*Later, WGA*] [*National Technical Information Service*]
**GRTA** ........ Great American Federal Savings Bank [*NASDAQ symbol*] (NQ)
**GRTB**......... Great American Bancorp [*NASDAQ symbol*] (NQ)
**Grt Barrier Reef Comm Pap** ... Great Barrier Reef Committee. Heron Island Research Station. Papers [*A publication*] (APTA)
**Grt Bird**...... Great Speckled Bird [*A publication*]
**GRTC** ........ Green River Test Complex
**GRTC** ........ Groupe de Recherches pour les Transports au Canada [*Canadian Transportation Research Forum*]
**GRTE**......... Grand Teton National Park
**GRTG** ........ Granting
**GRTG** ........ Grating (MSA)
**GRTLKS** ... Great Lakes [*FAA*] (FAAC)
**GRTLS** ...... Glide Return to Landing Site (NASA)
**GRTLS** ...... Glide Return to Launch Site (MCD)
**GRTM** ....... Geared Roller Test Machine
**GRTM** ....... Gross Ton-Mile (ADA)
**GRTN** ........ Grid Return (MSA)
**GRTPEP** ... Australia. Commonwealth Scientific and Industrial Research Organisation. Groundwater Research. Technical Paper [*A publication*]
**GRTR** ........ Grater (MSA)
**GRTR** ........ Greater [*Freight*]
**GRTR** ........ [*The*] Greater New York Savings Bank [*NASDAQ symbol*] (NQ)
**GRTS**......... General Remote Terminal Supervisor
**GRTS**......... Geomagnetic Reversal Time Scale
**GRTS**......... Ground Tracking System (MCD)
**GRTSFC**.... Ginger Rogers: The Star Fan Club (EA)
**GRU**........... Geographische Rundschau; Zeitschrift fuer Schulgeographie [*A publication*]
**GRU**........... Glavnoe Razvedivatelnoe Upravlenie [*Chief Administration for Intelligence*] [*Division of the General Staff of the Soviet Army*] [*USSR*]
**GRU**........... Gold Ridge Resources [*Vancouver Stock Exchange symbol*]
**GRU**........... Grid Reference Unit [*Military*] (CAAL)
**GRU**........... Group
**GRU**........... Gruntal Financial Corp. [*NYSE symbol*] (SPSG)
**Gru**............. Grus [*Constellation*]
**GRU**........... Guidance Regulator Unit
**GRU**........... Gyroscope Reference Unit (MCD)
**GRUB**........ Grocery Update and Billing
**GRUCOM**... Group Commander
**Grudman**.... Gramm-Rudman-Hollings Bill [*Proposed deficit-reducing bill, 1985-1986*]
**Grudn Khir** ... Grudnaya Khirurgiya [*A publication*]
**Gruene Reihe Bundesminist Gesund Umweltschutz** ... Gruene Reihe des Bundesministeriums fuer Gesundheit und Umweltschutz [*A publication*]
**GrUff** ......... Grand Ufficiale [*Grand Officer*] (EY)
**GRUMB**.... Grumbalds [*England*]
**Grumpie**..... Grim Ruthless Upwardly Mobile Professional [*Lifestyle classification*]
**Grumpie**..... Grown-Up Mature Person [*Lifestyle classification*]
**GRUN**........ Gruene, Inc. [*NASDAQ symbol*] (NQ)
**GRUNCH**... Gross Universal Cash Heist [*Techno-economic term coined by Buckminster Fuller*]
**GRUND**..... Grundeigentum [*A publication*]
**Grundig Tech Inf** ... Grundig Technische Informationen [*A publication*]
**Grundkurs Math** ... Grundkurs Mathematik [*A publication*]
**Grundkurs Phys** ... Grundkurs Physik [*A publication*]
**Grund Kyber Geist** ... Grundlagenstudien aus Kybernetik und Geisteswissenschaft [*A publication*]
**Grundlagen Landtech** ... Grundlagen der Landtechnik [*A publication*]
**Grundlagen Math Inform** ... Grundlagen der Mathematik und Informatik [*A publication*]
**Grundlehren Math Wiss** ... Grundlehren der Mathematischen Wissenschaften [*A publication*]
**G Rundschau** ... Geologische Rundschau [*A publication*]
**Grundwissen Math** ... Grundwissen Mathematik [*A publication*]
**Grune Stadt Natur Grosstadt** ... Grune Stadt. Naturschutz in der Grossstadt [*A publication*]
**Gruppenpsyc** ... Gruppenpsychotherapie und Gruppendynamik [*A publication*]
**GRUR**........ Gewerblicher Rechtsschutz und Urheberrecht [*A publication*] (ILCA)
**GRUR Int**.. Gewerblicher Rechtsschutz und Urheberrecht, Internationaler Teil [*A publication*] (ILCA)
**GRUSL**...... Group Sail [*Navy*] (NVT)
**Gruzin Politehn Inst Trudy** ... Gruzinskii Politehniceskii Institut Imeni V. I. Lenina Trudy [*A publication*]
**Gruzl** .......... Gruzlica i Choroby Pluc [*A publication*]
**Gruz Skh Inst Nauchn Tr** ... Gruzinskii Sel'skokhozyaistvennyi Institut Nauchnye Trudy [*A publication*]
**Gruz Skh Inst Tr** ... Gruzinskii Sel'skokhozyaistvennyi Institut Trudy [*A publication*]
**GRV** .......... Grantsville, MD [*Location identifier*] [*FAA*] (FAAL)
**GRV** .......... Granville Island Brewing Co. Ltd. [*Vancouver Stock Exchange symbol*]
**GRV** .......... Graphite Rod Vaporization
**GRV** .......... Greenville [*Lake Wappapelo*] [*Missouri*] [*Seismograph station code, US Geological Survey*] [*Closed*] (SEIS)
**GRV** .......... Groove (KSC)
**GRV** .......... Grove
**GRVA** ........ Graphic Varmeter
**GRVD** ........ Grooved
**GRVG**........ Grooving
**GR VJ POND** ... Grana Sex Pondere [*Six Grains by Weight*] [*Pharmacy*] (ROG)
**GRVL** ........ Gravel
**GRVR** ........ Groover
**GRVS**......... Advanced Gravis Computer Technology Ltd.[*NASDAQ symbol*] (NQ)

**GRVXF**...... Grove Explorations Ltd. [*NASDAQ symbol*] (NQ)
**GRW**......... Galactic Radio Wave
**GRW**......... General Railway Warrants [*US Military Government, Germany*]
**GRW**......... Goodyear-Reston-Winthrop [*Publishing group*]
**GRW**......... Graciosa Island [*Azores*] [*Airport symbol*] (OAG)
**GRW**......... Greenwich [*United Kingdom*] [*Later, HAD*] [*Geomagnetic observatory code*]
**GRW**......... Greenwich Resources PLC [*Toronto Stock Exchange symbol*] [*Vancouver Stock Exchange symbol*]
**GRW**......... Greenwood, MS [*Location identifier*] [*FAA*] (FAAL)
**GRW**......... Griechischer Wirtschaftsdienst [*A publication*]
**GRWS**....... Gimbaled Reaction Wheel Scanner
**GRWT**....... Gross Weight
**GRX**.......... General Refractories Co. [*NYSE symbol*] (SPSG)
**GRX**.......... GR Foods, Inc. [*AMEX symbol*] (SPSG)
**GRX**.......... Granada [*Spain*] [*Airport symbol*] (OAG)
**GRY**.......... Gray (ADA)
**GRY**.......... Greymouth [*New Zealand*] [*Seismograph station code, US Geological Survey*] [*Closed*] (SEIS)
**GRY**.......... Greystoke Exploration [*Vancouver Stock Exchange symbol*]
**GRY**.......... Grimsey [*Iceland*] [*Airport symbol*] (OAG)
**GRYCC**...... Geraldton Region Youth Co-Ordinating Committee [*Australia*]
**grysh**.......... Grayish [*Philately*]
**GRZ**.......... Galapagos Rift Zone [*Marine science*] (MSC)
**GRZ**.......... Graz [*Austria*] [*Airport symbol*] (OAG)
**GRZ**.......... Growth and Change [*A publication*]
**GRZZAD**... Glasnik Republickog Zavoda za Zastitu Prirode i Prirodnjackog Muzeja Titogradu [*A publication*]
**G-S**............ Gallard-Schlesinger [*Chemical manufacturing corporation*]
**G/S**............ Gallons per Second
**GS**............. Galpin Society (EA)
**GS**............. Galvanized Steel [*Telecommunications*]
**GS**............. Games Started [*Baseball*]
**GS**............. Gap Separation
**GS**............. Gardner Syndrome [*Medicine*]
**GS**............. Gas Servicer (MCD)
**GS**............. Gas Sulfide [*Process for obtaining heavy water*]
**GS**............. Gasoline Supply
**GS**............. Gastric Shield [*Medicine*]
**GS**............. Gaudium et Spes [*Pastoral Constitution on the Church in the Modern World*] [*Vatican II document*]
**GS**............. Gauss [*Unit of magnetic flux density*] [*Preferred unit is T, Telsa*]
**GS**............. General and Aviation Services Ltd. [*Nigeria*] [*ICAO designator*] (FAAC)
**GS**............. General Schedule [*Federal employee job classification GS-1 to GS-18*]
**GS**............. General Secretary
**GS**............. General Semantics
**GS**............. General Service [*Literal translation, but used in sense of "excessively keen," or "overly acute"*] [*Army*] [*British*]
**GS**............. General Sessions
**GS**............. General Specials
**GS**............. General Speed [*Military*]
**GS**............. General Staff [*Military*]
**GS**............. General Statistics
**GS**............. General Strike
**GS**............. General Subjects (MCD)
**GS**............. General Superintendent
**GS**............. General Support [*Military*]
**GS**............. General Surgery
**GS**............. Gengo Seikatsu [*A publication*]
**GS**............. Geochemical Society (EA)
**GS**............. Geological Survey [*Department of the Interior*]
**GS**............. German Silver
**GS**............. Germanistische Studien [*A publication*]
**GS**............. Gerontological Society [*Later, GSA*] (EA)
**GS**............. Gesammelte Schriften [*A publication*]
**GS**............. Gesetzsammlung [*Collection of Statutes, Gazette*] [*German*] (ILCA)
**GS**............. Giant Slalom
**G & S**......... Gilbert and Sullivan
**GS**............. Gilbert's Syndrome [*Medicine*]
**GS**............. Gillette Co. [*NYSE symbol*] (SPSG)
**GS**............. Girl Scouts of the USA (EA)
**GS**............. Girls' School (ADA)
**GS**............. Glamour Stock [*Investment term*]
**GS**............. Gland Seal [*System*] [*Nuclear energy*] (NRCH)
**GS**............. Glazounov Society (EA)
**GS**............. Glide Slope [*Aviation*]
**GS**............. Gliding School [*British military*] (DMA)
**GS**............. Glomerular Sclerosis [*Medicine*]
**GS**............. Glucose and Saline [*Medicine*]
**GS**............. Glutamine Synthetase [*Also, GNS*] [*An enzyme*]
**GS**............. Glycolytic Substrate
**GS**............. Gold Standards
**GS**............. Golden Shamrock Resources Corp. [*Vancouver Stock Exchange symbol*]
**GS**............. Goudy Society (EA)
**GS**............. Government Security [*Business term*]
**GS**............. Government Service
**GS**............. Government Staffs [*British*]
**GS**............. Grab Sample [*Analytical technique*]
**GS**............. Grade System (AAG)
**GS**............. Grai si Suflet [*A publication*]
**G & S**......... Grai si Suflet [*A publication*]
**GS**............. Grammar School
**GS**............. Grand Scribe [*Freemasonry*]
**GS**............. Grand Secretary [*Freemasonry*]
**GS**............. Grand Sentinel [*Freemasonry*]
**GS**............. Grand Sentry [*Freemasonry*]
**GS**............. Grand Steward [*Freemasonry*]
**GS**............. Grandson
**GS**............. Graphics and Sound [*in Apple IIGS*] [*Apple Computer, Inc.*]
**G/S**............ Gravity per Second (KSC)
**GS**............. Great Seal [*British*]
**GS**............. Greenhouse Shrub [*Horticulture*] (ROG)
**GS**............. Grip Strength
**GS**............. Grocery Store
**GS**............. Gross Sales [*Business term*]
**GS**............. Gross Spread [*Business term*]
**G/S**............ Ground to Slant (MCD)
**GS**............. Ground Speed [*Aviation*]
**GS**............. Ground Stabilized (MUGU)
**GS**............. Ground Station [*Aerospace*] (AAG)
**GS**............. Ground System (MCD)
**GS**............. Group Selector [*Telecommunications*] (TEL)
**GS**............. Group Separator [*Data processing*]
**gs**.............. Group Specific [*Antigen*] [*Immunology*]
**GS**............. Group Structured [*Counseling group*]
**GS**............. Growth Stage
**GS**............. Growth Stock [*Investment term*]
**GS**............. Grupo Socialista [*Socialist Group*] [*Portugal*] [*Political party*] (PPE)
**GS**............. Guard Society (EA)
**GS**............. Guardship
**GS**............. Guidance Simulator
**GS**............. Guidance Station [*Aerospace*] (AAG)
**GS**............. Guidance System [*Aerospace*] (AAG)
**GS**............. Guide Slope (MUGU)
**GS**............. Guild of Surveyors [*Middlesex, England*] (EAIO)
**GS**............. Gum Skips [*Philately*]
**GS**............. Gungywamp Society (EA)
**GS**............. Gunnery School [*Air Force*]
**GS**............. Gunnery and Searchlight [*Control*] [*British*] [*World War II*]
**GS**............. Gunnery Sergeant
**GS**............. Gunnery Support
**GS**............. Gyrostabilizer
**GS**............. Pfizer Ltd. [*Great Britain*] [*Research code symbol*]
**GS**............. Pioneer Airlines Ltd. [*Ghana*] [*ICAO designator*] (FAAC)
**GS**............. Savannah Public and Chatham-Effingham-Liberty Regional Library, Savannah, GA [*Library symbol*] [*Library of Congress*] (LCLS)
**GSA**........... Armstrong State College, Savannah, GA [*Library symbol*] [*Library of Congress*] (LCLS)
**GSA**........... Garden Seed Association
**GSA**........... Garden State Airlines, Inc. [*Shrewsbury, NJ*] [*FAA designator*] (FAAC)
**GSA**........... Gardenia Society of America (EA)
**GSA**........... General Services Administration [*Washington, DC*]
**GSA**........... General Services Administration, Washington, DC [*OCLC symbol*] (OCLC)
**GSA**........... General Somatic Afferent [*Nerve*] [*Anatomy*]
**GSA**........... General Studies Association [*British*]
**GSA**........... General Support Announcement [*Public television*]
**GSA**........... General Syntax Analyzer [*Sperry UNIVAC*]
**GSA**........... Genetics Society of America (EA)
**GSA**........... Geographic Systems Analysis [*Information service or system*] (IID)
**GSA**........... Geological Society of America (EA)
**GSA**........... German Studies in America [*A publication*]
**GSA**........... Germanistic Society of America (EA)
**GSA**........... Gerontological Society of America (EA)
**GSA**........... Girl Scouts of America
**GSA**........... Girls' Schools Association [*British*]
**GSA**........... Glasgow School of Art [*Scotland*]
**GSA**........... Glass-Steagal Act [*1933*]
**GSA**........... Glide Slope Antenna [*Aviation*]
**GSA**........... Glutamatesemialdehyde [*Organic chemistry*]
**GSA**........... Goldfish Society of America (EA)
**GSA**........... Gourd Society of America [*Superseded by AGS*] (EA)
**GSA**........... Greenhouse Suppliers Association (EA)
**GSA**........... Gross Soluble Antigen
**GSA**........... Ground-Based Surface-to-Air (MCD)
**GSA**........... Ground Safety Approval (MUGU)
**GSA**........... Groundstar Resources Ltd. [*Vancouver Stock Exchange symbol*]
**GSA**........... Group-Specific Antigen [*Immunology*]
**GSA**........... Guild of Saint Alban
**GSA/ADTS**... General Services Administration/Automated Data and Telecommunications Services (OICC)

**GSA-BCA** ... General Services Administration - Board of Contract Appeals
**GSA-CPO** ... General Services Administration - Civilian Personnel Office
**GSA/FPRS** ... General Services Administration/Federal Property Resources Services (OICC)
**GSA/FSS** .. General Services Administration/Federal Supply Services (OICC)
**GSAI** ......... El Aaiun [*Western Sahara*] [*ICAO location identifier*] (ICLI)
**GSAI** ......... Giornale della Societa Asiatica Italiana [*A publication*]
**GSAKAK** ... Glas. Srpska Akademija Nauka i Umetnosti Odeljenje Prirodno-Matematickikh Nauka [*A publication*]
**GSAM** ....... Generalized Sequential Access Method [*Data processing*]
**GSAM** ....... Generalized Standard Addition Method [*Mathematics*]
**GSAMAQ** ... Geological Society of America. Memoir [*A publication*]
**GSA/NARS** ... General Services Administration/National Archives and Records Services [*Franklin D. Roosevelt Library*] [*Hyde Park, NY*] (OICC)
**GSA/OFR** ... General Services Administration/Office of the Federal Register (OICC)
**GSA-OP** .... General Services Administration - Office of Preparedness
**GSAP** ......... Gun Sight Aiming Point
**GSAPAZ** ... Geological Society of America. Special Paper (Regional Studies) [*A publication*]
**GSA-PBS** .. General Services Administration - Public Building Service
**GSAR** ......... General Services Acquisition Regulation
**GSARRTS** ... Generator, Starter, Alternator, Regulator, and Rectifier Test Stand (MCD)
**GSA Spec Pap (Reg Stud)** ... GSA [*Geological Society of America*] Special Paper (Regional Studies) [*A publication*]
**GSAT** ......... General Satellite (NASA)
**GSAT** ......... Gesammelte Studien zum Alten Testament [*A publication*] (BJA)
**GSAT** ......... Globesat Holding Corp. [*NASDAQ symbol*] (NQ)
**GS/ATE** .... General Support/Automatic Test Equipment (MCD)
**GS/ATSS** .. General Support/Automatic Test Support System (MCD)
**GSB** ........... Gastric Stress Bleeding [*Medicine*]
**GSB** ........... General Semantics Bulletin [*A publication*]
**GSB** ........... General Services Building [*Nuclear energy*] (NRCH)
**GSB** ........... General Stud Book [*Horses*]
**GSB** ........... Georgia State Bar Journal [*A publication*]
**GSB** ........... Gold Surface Barrier
**GSB** ........... Goldsboro, NC [*Location identifier*] [*FAA*] (FAAL)
**GSB** ........... Grand Standard Bearer [*Freemasonry*] (ROG)
**GSB** ........... Grand Sword-Bearer [*Freemasonry*]
**GSB** ........... Gypsum Sheathing Board [*Technical drawings*]
**GSBBAW** .. Godishnik na Sofiiskiya Universitet. Biologo-Geologo-Geografski Fakultet. Kniga I. Biologiya [*A publication*]
**GSBC** ......... Great Southern Bancorp [*NASDAQ symbol*] (NQ)
**GSBCA** ....... General Services Board of Contract Appeals
**GSBG** ......... Gonadal Steroid-Binding Globulin [*Medicine*]
**GSBI** ......... Gabungan Serikat Buruh Indonesia [*Federation of Indonesian Trade Unions*]
**GSBI** ......... Granite State Bankshares, Incorporated [*Keene, NH*] [*NASDAQ symbol*] (NQ)
**GSBIAJ** ..... Godishnik na Sofiiskiya Universitet. Biologicheski Fakultet [*A publication*]
**GSBK** ......... Germantown Savings Bank [*NASDAQ symbol*] (NQ)
**GSBR** ......... Gravel-Surface Built-Up Roof [*Technical drawings*]
**GSBZA2** .... Godishnik na Sofiiskiya Universitet. Biologicheski Fakultet. Kniga 1. Zoologiya, Fiziologiya, i Biokhimiya na Zhivotnite [*A publication*]
**GSC** ........... Galapagos Spreading Center [*Oceanography*]
**GSC** ........... Gas-Solid Chromatography
**GSC** ........... Gascoyne Junction [*Australia*] [*Airport symbol*] [*Obsolete*] (OAG)
**GSC** ........... Gelman Sciences, Inc. [*AMEX symbol*] (SPSG)
**GSC** ........... General Service Corps [*Military unit*] [*British*]
**GSC** ........... General Staff Corps [*Military*]
**GSC** ........... General Staff Council [*Military*] (AABC)
**GSC** ........... Genetically Significant Concentration [*Mutagenesis*]
**GSC** ........... Geodetic Spacecraft (AAG)
**GSC** ........... Geological Survey of Canada [*Marine science*] (MSC)
**GSC** ........... German Shippers Council (DS)
**GSC** ........... Giant Serotonin-Containing [*Neuron*]
**GSC** ........... Gland Seal Condenser [*Nuclear energy*] (NRCH)
**GSC** ........... Gland Steam Condenser [*Nuclear energy*] (NRCH)
**GSC** ........... Glenville State College [*West Virginia*]
**GSC** ........... Golden Star Resources Ltd. [*Toronto Stock Exchange symbol*]
**GSC** ........... Golden State Airlines, Inc. [*Burbank, CA*] [*FAA designator*] (FAAC)
**GSC** ........... Goldstone [*California*] [*Seismograph station code, US Geological Survey*] (SEIS)
**GSC** ........... Good Samaritan Coalition (EA)
**GSC** ........... Gravity Settling Culture
**GSC** ........... Great Southwest Corporation
**GSC** ........... Grid Spot Converter (NVT)
**GSC** ........... Ground Services Cart
**GSC** ........... Ground-Speed Continuing [*Aviation*]
**GSC** ........... Group Study Course
**GSC** ........... Group Switching Center [*British*] [*Telecommunications*] (TEL)
**GSC** ........... GSA [*General Services Administration*] Stock Catalog
**GSC** ........... Guidance Shipping Container
**GSC** ........... Guidance System Console [*Aerospace*] (AAG)
**GSCA** ......... Giant Schnauzer Club of America (EA)
**GSCA** ......... Gordon Setter Club of America (EA)
**GSCARNGARP** ... General Staff Committees on Army National Guard and Army Reserve Policy (AABC)
**G Sc B** ........ Geological and Scientific Bulletin [*A publication*]
**GSCB** ......... Geological Survey of Canada. Bulletin [*A publication*]
**GSC Bul** ..... Geological Survey of Canada. Bulletin [*A publication*]
**GSCC** ......... General Staff Consultative Committee [*Australia*]
**GSCC** ......... General Steel Casting Corporation
**GSCC** ......... Graphic Scanning Corporation [*NASDAQ symbol*] (NQ)
**GSCC** ......... Greater Siamese Cat Club (EA)
**GSCF** ......... Geriatric Sentence Completion Form [*Personality development test*] [*Psychology*]
**GSCG** ........ Ground Systems Coordination Group
**GSCI** ......... Ground Sound Control, Incorporated
**G Sci Med** ... Giornale di Scienze Mediche [*A publication*]
**GSCM** ....... Geological Survey of Canada. Memoir [*A publication*]
**GSCN** ........ Grantsmanship Center. News [*A publication*]
**GSCNY** ...... German Society of the City of New York (EA)
**GSCO** ....... Guidance Sustainer Cutoff [*Aerospace*] (AAG)
**GSCP** ......... Geological Survey of Canada. Paper [*A publication*]
**GSCT** ......... Goldstein-Scheerer Cube Test [*Psychology*]
**GSCT** ......... Guild of Sorting Clerks and Telegraphists [*A union*] [*British*]
**GSCU** ........ Ground Service [*or Support*] Cooling Unit (KSC)
**GSCW** ........ General Society of Colonial Wars (EA)
**GSCWPPC** ... Guam Stamp Club and Western Pacific Philatelic Collectors (EA)
**GSCX** ......... General Sciences Corp. [*NASDAQ symbol*] (NQ)
**GSD** ........... Gate Stealer Display (MCD)
**GSD** ........... Geistes- und Sozialwissenschaftliche Dissertationen [*A publication*]
**GSD** ........... General Supply Depot
**GSD** ........... General Support Division [*Air Force*]
**GSD** ........... General System Description [*Military*] (AABC)
**GSD** ........... General Systems Division [*IBM Corp.*]
**GSD** ........... Generating Significant Dose [*Nuclear energy*] (NRCH)
**GSD** ........... Generator Starter Drive
**GSD** ........... Generic Structure Diagram [*Telecommunications*] (TEL)
**GSD** ........... Genetic Sex Determination [*Biology*]
**GSD** ........... Genetically Significant Dosage [*X-Ray*]
**GSD** ........... Geometric Standard Deviation [*Statistics*]
**GSD** ........... Gesco Industries, Inc. [*Toronto Stock Exchange symbol*]
**GSD** ........... Glycogen Storage Disease [*Medicine*]
**GSD** ........... Grand Senior Deacon [*Freemasonry*]
**GSD** ........... Grid Sphere Drag [*DoD satellite*]
**GSD** ........... Ground Station Data
**GSDA** ........ Ground-Speed Drift Angle [*Aviation*] (NG)
**GSDB** ......... Geophysics and Space Data Bulletin [*A publication*] [*Air Force*]
**GSDBA** ....... Geophysics and Space Data Bulletin [*A publication*]
**GSDC** ......... Get Set Day Care Program [*Later, CDCP*] (EA)
**GSDCA** ...... German Shepherd Dog Club of America (EA)
**GSDCB** ...... Geoscience Documentation [*England*] [*A publication*]
**GSDF** ......... Ground Self-Defense Force [*Japan*]
**GSDFJ** ........ Ground Self-Defense Force Japan
**GSDL** ......... German Shepherd Dog League [*Australia*]
**GSDL** ......... Ground Software Development Laboratory [*NASA*] (NASA)
**GSDMA** .... Gornye, Stroitel'nye i Dorozhnye Mashiny [*A publication*]
**GSDN** ........ Garden Supply Dealers National (EA)
**GSDO** ........ General [*Aviation*] Safety District Office
**GSDS** ......... Goldstone Duplicate Standard [*Deep Space Instrumentation Facility*] [*NASA*]
**GSE** ........... General Somatic Efferent [*Nerve*] [*Anatomy*]
**GSE** ........... General Support Equipment [*Military*] (MUGU)
**GSE** ........... Geocentric Solar Ecliptic [*System*] [*NASA*]
**GSE** ........... Glutagen Sensitive Enteropathy [*Medicine*]
**GSE** ........... Gluten-Sensitive Enteropathy [*Medicine*]
**GSE** ........... Gothenburg Studies in English [*A publication*]
**GSE** ........... Graduate Student of English [*A publication*]
**GSE** ........... Ground Service Equipment [*Air Force*]
**GSE** ........... Ground Support Equipment [*Aviation*]
**GSE** ........... Group Support Equipment
**G SEC** ........ Grand Secretary [*Freemasonry*] (ROG)
**GSECP** ...... Ground Support Engineering Change Proposal [*Aerospace*] (AAG)
**GSED** ......... Ground Support Equipment Division [*Naval Air Engineering Center*]
**GSEE** ......... Geniki Synomospondia Ergaton Hellados [*General Confederation of Greek Labor*]
**GSEEI** ....... Ground Support Equipment End Item [*Military*]
**GSEF** ......... Ground Subsystem Evaluation Facility [*Army*] (RDA)
**GSEI** ......... Ground Support Equipment Illustration [*Military*] (MCD)
**GSEID** ....... Ground Support Equipment Illustration Data [*Military*] (MCD)
**GSEL** ......... Government Specified Equipment List [*Military*] (CAAL)
**GSEL** ......... Great South East Lines Pty. Ltd. (DS)
**GSEL** ......... Ground Support Equipment List [*NASA*] (NASA)
**GSEL** ......... Guidance System Evaluation Laboratory [*Military*] (CAAL)
**GSERD** ...... Ground Support Equipment Recommendation Data [*Military*] (MCD)

**GSES** Government-Sponsored Enterprises [*Federal National Mortgage Association, Student Loan Marketing Association, etc.*]
**GSETD** General Systems Engineering and Technical Direction
**GSEVD8** Genetique, Selection, Evolution [*A publication*]
**GSF** ACM Government Securities [*NYSE symbol*] (SPSG)
**GSF** Galactosemic Fibroblasts [*Medicine*]
**GSF** Galaxy Science Fiction [*A publication*]
**GSF** General Semantics Foundation (EA)
**GSF** General Supply Fund
**GSF** General Support Force [*Air Force*]
**GSF** Georgia Southern & Florida Railway Co. [*AAR code*]
**GS & F** Georgia Southern & Florida Railway Co.
**GSF** Global Strategy Fund [*British*]
**GSF** Grenade Safety Fuze
**GSF** Ground Support Facilities [*Later, MGE*] [*Aerospace*] (AAG)
**GSF** Ground Support Fighter (MCD)
**GSF** Gulf Sea Frontier
**GSFA** Genealogical Society of Flemish Americans (EA)
**GSFB** Geological Survey of Finland. Bulletin [*A publication*]
**GSFB** Great Southern Federal Savings Bank [*Savannah, GA*] [*NASDAQ symbol*] (NQ)
**GSFC** George Strait Fan Club (EA)
**GSFC** Goddard Space Flight Center [*NASA*] [*Greenbelt, MD*]
**GSFG** Group of Soviet Forces in Germany (NATG)
**GSFGB** Giessereiforschung [*A publication*]
**GSFLT** Graduate School Foreign Language Test
**GSFN** Galaxy Science Fiction Novels [*A publication*]
**GSFNAK** Geological Survey of Finland. Bulletin [*A publication*]
**GSFS** Great Science Fiction Stories [*A publication*]
**GSFSR** Ground Safety and Flight Safety Requirements (AAG)
**GSFU** Glazed Structural Facing Units [*Technical drawings*]
**GSG** Garment Salesmen's Guild of New York [*Later, AG*] (EA)
**GSG** General Support Group [*Army*] (AABC)
**GSG** Glasgow, MT [*Location identifier*] [*FAA*] (FAAL)
**GSG** Glass-Silicone-Glass [*Electronics*] (DEN)
**GSG** Grammar School for Girls (ADA)
**GSG** Grenzschutzgruppe [*Border Protection Group*] [*German*]
**GSG** Ground Systems Group [*Hughes Aircraft Co.*]
**GSGA** Geode Specialty Growers Association (EA)
**GSGMEQ** Genetic, Social, and General Psychology Monographs [*A publication*]
**GSGS** Geographical Section General Staff [*British*]
**GSH** Gas Space Heater
**GSH** Gas Surge Header [*Nuclear energy*] (NRCH)
**GSH** Glutathione [*Biochemistry*]
**GSH** Glutathione-SH [*Reduced glutathione*] [*Biochemistry*]
**GSH** Goshen, IN [*Location identifier*] [*FAA*] (FAAL)
**GSHL** General Shale Products Corp. [*NASDAQ symbol*] (NQ)
**GSHR** Gandhi Society for Human Rights (EA)
**GSHR** Grand Slam Home Runs [*Baseball*]
**G & Sh RR** Godefroi and Shortt's Law of Railway Companies [*A publication*] (DLA)
**GSHV** Ground Squirrel Hepatitis Virus
**GSI** General Safety Inspector [*Aviation*]
**GSI** General Service Infantry [*Army*]
**GSI** Generic Safety Issue (NRCH)
**GSI** Genetic Stock Identification [*Pisciculture*]
**GSI** Geographic Systems, Incorporated [*Information service or system*] (IID)
**GSI** Geophysical Service, Incorporated
**GSI** Gesneriad Society International (EA)
**GSI** Glide Slope Indicator [*Aviation*]
**GSI** Glide Speed Indicator
**GSI** Gonosomatic Indices
**GSI** Gordon Diagnostic System [*Attention deficit disorder test*]
**GSI** Government Source Inspection
**GSI** Grand Scale Integration (BUR)
**GSI** Graphic Structure Input
**GSI** Ground-Speed Indicator [*Aviation*] (MCD)
**GSI** Guild of Saint Ives (EA)
**G & SI** Gulf & Ship Island Railroad Co.
**GSIBAX** Geological Society of India. Bulletin [*A publication*]
**GSIC** Great Southwest Industries Corporation [*NASDAQ symbol*] (NQ)
**GSICO** Glaucoma Society of the International Congress of Ophthalmology (EA)
**GSID** Ground-Emplaced Seismic Intrusion Detector (NVT)
**GSIDC** Arab Gulf States Information Documentation Center [*Information service or system*] (IID)
**GSIdentBad** General Staff Identification Badge [*Military decoration*] (AABC)
**GSIFC** Gene Summers International Fan Club (EA)
**GSigsO** Group Signals Officer [*British military*] (DMA)
**GSIHS** Group for the Study of Irish Historic Settlement [*British*]
**GSIL** German Silver
**GSIL** Goldsil Mining & Milling, Inc. [*NASDAQ symbol*] (NQ)
**GSIO** General Staff Interpreter Officer [*Military*] [*British*]
**GSISEA** Government Service Insurance System Employees' Association [*Philippines*]
**GSIT** Group Shorr Imagery Test [*Personality development test*] [*Psychology*]
**GSIU** Ground Standard Interface Unit (MCD)
**GSJ** Galpin Society. Journal [*A publication*]
**G & S J** Gilbert and Sullivan Journal [*A publication*]
**GSJ** Gold Spring Resources [*Vancouver Stock Exchange symbol*]
**GSJBS** Goldsmiths', Silversmiths', and Jewellers' Benevolent Society [*British*]
**GSK** General Storekeeper [*Navy*]
**GSK** George Simon Kaufman [*American playwright, 1889-1961*]
**GSK** Glycogen Synthase Kinase [*An enzyme*]
**GSK** Gold Seeker Resources Ltd. [*Vancouver Stock Exchange symbol*]
**GSKT** Gasket (KSC)
**GSL** General Service Launch [*British military*] (DMA)
**GSL** Generalized Simulation Language [*Data processing*] (MDG)
**GSL** Generation Strategy Language [*Data processing*] (IEEE)
**GSL** Geographic Air Surveys Ltd. [*Edmonton, AB, Canada*] [*FAA designator*] (FAAC)
**GSL** Geographic Sciences Laboratory [*Fort Belvoir, VA*] [*United States Army Engineer Topographic Laboratories*] (GRD)
**GSL** Geographic Systems Laboratory [*US Army Engineer Topographic Laboratories*]
**GSL** Geophysical Sciences Laboratory [*New York University*]
**GSL** Georgia Department of Education, Atlanta, GA [*OCLC symbol*] (OCLC)
**Gsl** Germano-Slavica [*A publication*]
**GSL** Girls' Service League [*Later, YCL*] (EA)
**GSL** Glycosphingolipid [*Biochemistry*]
**GSL** Gold Cup Resources [*Vancouver Stock Exchange symbol*]
**GSL** Gorilla Sign Language (BYTE)
**GSL** Graduate Student Loan
**GSL** Great Salt Lake [*Utah*]
**GSL** Great Somalia League
**GSL** Ground Systems Laboratory
**GSL** Guaranteed Student Loan
**GSL** Medieval Studies in Memory of Gertrude Schoepperle Loomis [*A publication*]
**GSLABHF** Greater St. Louis Amateur Baseball Hall of Fame (EA)
**G Slav** Germano-Slavica [*A publication*]
**GSLB** Gold Star Lapel Button [*Military decoration*] (AABC)
**GSLG** German Studies Library Group (EAIO)
**GSLI** Giornale Storico della Letteratura Italiana [*A publication*]
**GSLL** Giornale Storico e Letterario della Liguria [*A publication*]
**GSLO** Gland Seal Leak Off [*Nuclear energy*] (NRCH)
**GSLP** Gibraltar Socialist Labour Party [*Political party*] (PPW)
**GSLP** Guaranteed Student Loan Program
**GSM** Garrison Sergeant-Major [*British*]
**GSM** General Sales Manager
**GSM** General Service Medal [*British*]
**GSM** General Situation Map [*Military*] (NATG)
**GSM** General Stores Material [*Navy*]
**GSM** General Support Maintenance (MCD)
**GSM** General Synod Measures (ILCA)
**GSM** Generalized Sequential Machine [*Data processing*]
**GSM** Generalized Sort/Merge [*Data processing*]
**GSM** Geocentric Solar Magnetospheric [*System*] [*NASA*]
**GSM** Geological Society of Malaysia (EAIO)
**GSM** Gibson Spiral Maze [*Psychology*]
**GSM** Gold Star Mothers
**GSM** Goldstream Resources Ltd. [*Vancouver Stock Exchange symbol*]
**GSM** Good Sound Merchantable
**GSM** Grams per Square Meter
**GSM** Graphics Schematics Module [*McDonnell-Douglas Corp.*]
**GSM** Graphics System Module
**GSM** Grass Mountain [*Washington*] [*Seismograph station code, US Geological Survey*] (SEIS)
**GSM** Ground Signal Mixer
**GSM** Ground Station Modules [*Communications*] [*Army*]
**GSM** Ground Support Maintenance (MCD)
**GSM** Group Scout Master [*Scouting*]
**GSM** Groupe Speciale Mobile [*European digital cellular radio standard*]
**GSM** Guild of Saint Matthew
**GSM** Guildhall School of Music [*London*]
**GSMA** Goldstone-SFOF [*Space Flight Operations Facility*] Microwave Assembly [*NASA*]
**GSMBBK** Geological Society of Malaysia. Bulletin [*A publication*]
**GSMBE** Gas-Source Molecular Beam Epitaxy [*Coating technology*]
**GSMD** General Society of Mayflower Descendants (EA)
**GSME** Ground Support Maintenance Equipment [*Aerospace*]
**GSMFC** Gulf States Marine Fisheries Commission
**GSMH** Gayri Safi Milli Hasili [*Gross National Product*] [*Turkish*]
**GSML** General Stores Material List
**GSML** Generalized Standard Markup Language [*Also, SGML*]
**GSMMBJ** Geological Survey of Malaysia. District Memoir [*A publication*]
**GSMNBM** Geological Society of Malaysia. Newsletter [*A publication*]
**GSMNP** Great Smoky Mountains National Park [*Also, GRSM*]
**GSMPAR** Geological Survey of Malaysia. Geological Papers [*A publication*]

**GSMS**........ Government Securities Management System [*The Bond Buyer, Inc.*] [*Information service or system*] (IID)
**GSMT**........ General Society of Mechanics and Tradesmen (EA)
**GSN**........... Gesneriad Saintpaulia News [*A publication*]
**GSN**........... Greenwich Sidereal Noon (ROG)
**GSN**........... Mount Gunson [*Australia*] [*Airport symbol*] (OAG)
**GSNA**........ Goethe Society of North America (EA)
**GSNB**........ Grant Street National Bank [*NASDAQ symbol*] (NQ)
**GSNC**........ General Steam Navigation Company [*British*]
**GSNCO**..... General Steam Navigation Company [*Shipping*] [*British*]
**GS News Tech Rep**... GS News Technical Report [*Japan*] [*A publication*]
**GSNS**........ Guidance Control and Navigation Subsystem
**GSO**........... General Salary Order [*United States*] (DLA)
**GSO**........... General Services Officer
**GSO**........... General Spin Orbitals [*Atomic physics*]
**GSO**........... General Staff Officer [*Military*]
**GSO**........... General Supply Office
**GSO**........... General Support Office
**GSO**........... Geo. S. Olive & Co. [*Telecommunications service*] (TSSD)
**GSO**........... Geosynchronous Orbit
**GSO**........... Graduate School of Oceanography [*University of Rhode Island*]
**GSO**........... Greensboro/High Point/Winston Salem [*North Carolina*] [*Airport symbol*]
**GSO**........... Ground Safety Office [*or Officer*] [*Air Force*]
**GSO**........... Ground-Speed Oscillator [*Aviation*]
**GSO**........... Ground Support Office [*or Officer*] [*Military*] (AFIT)
**GSO**........... Ground Support Office [*NASA*] (NASA)
**GSO**........... Ground Support Operations [*Aerospace*] (MCD)
**GSO**........... Ground Systems Operations (MCD)
**GSO**........... Growth Stock Outlook Trust, Inc. [*NYSE symbol*] (SPSG)
**GSO**........... GSR Goldsearch Resources [*Vancouver Stock Exchange symbol*]
**GSO**........... Gyro Storage Oven
**GSO**........... Olive [*Geo S.*] & Co. [*Indianapolis, IN*] (TSSD)
**GSoA**......... Gerontological Society of America (EA)
**GSOC**........ Gold Star Owners Club (EA)
**G Soc Am B**... Geological Society of America. Bulletin [*A publication*]
**G Soc Dublin J**... Geological Society of Dublin. Journal [*A publication*]
**G Soc Glas Tr**... Geological Society of Glasgow. Transactions [*A publication*]
**G Soc London Tr Pr Q J**... Geological Society of London. Transactions. Proceedings. Quarterly Journal [*A publication*]
**G Soc PA Tr**... Geological Society of Pennsylvania. Transactions [*A publication*]
**G Soc Tokyo J**... Geological Society of Tokyo. Journal [*A publication*]
**GSOF**......... Group 1 Software, Inc. [*NASDAQ symbol*] (NQ)
**GSOP**........ General Stock Ownership Plan
**GSOP**........ Guidance Systems Operation Plan [*NASA*] (KSC)
**GSOR**........ General Staff Operational Requirements [*Army*] (AABC)
**GSORD**..... Geological Survey Open-File Report [*United States*] [*A publication*]
**GSOST**...... Goldstein-Scheerer Object Sorting Test [*Psychology*]
**GSOWM**... Global Spectral Ocean Wave Model
**GSP**........... Galvanic Skin Potential [*Physiology*]
**GSP**........... Genealogical Society of Pennsylvania (EA)
**GSP**........... General Sea Harvest [*Vancouver Stock Exchange symbol*]
**GSP**........... General Semantic Problem (AAG)
**GSP**........... General Simulation Program [*Programming language*] (IEEE)
**GSP**........... General Strike for Peace
**GSP**........... General Strike Plan (NATG)
**GSP**........... General Syntactic Processor
**GSP**........... Generalised System of Preferences [*Foreign trade*]
**GSP**........... Generalized System of Tariff Preferences [*US Customs Service*]
**GSP**........... Geodetic Satellite Program
**GSP**........... German Society of Pennsylvania (EA)
**GSP**........... Girl Scouts of the Philippines
**GSP**........... Gladstone Stream [*New Zealand*] [*Seismograph station code, US Geological Survey*] (SEIS)
**GSP**........... Glasnik za Sumske Pokuse [*A publication*]
**GSP**........... Glycosylated Serum Protein
**GSP**........... Good-Service Pension [*Navy*] [*British*]
**GSP**........... Government Selected Price
**GSP**........... Government Sponsored Promotion (ADA)
**GSP**........... Government Standard Parts
**GSP**........... Graphic Subroutine Package [*Data processing*]
**GSP**........... Graphics System Processor [*Texas Instruments, Inc.*] [*Computer hardware*]
**GSP**........... Greenville/Spartanburg [*South Carolina*] [*Airport symbol*]
**GSP**........... Greer, SC [*Location identifier*] [*FAA*] (FAAL)
**GSP**........... Gross Social Product [*Economics*]
**GSP**........... Gross State Product (OICC)
**GSP**........... Ground Safety Plan (MUGU)
**GSP**........... Growth Fund of Spain [*NYSE symbol*] (SPSG)
**GSP**........... Guidance Signal Processor (KSC)
**GSP**........... Royal Geographical Society. Proceedings [*A publication*]
**GSPA**......... Gold Star Parents for Amnesty [*Defunct*] (EA)
**GSPA**......... Grain Sorghum Producers Association (EA)
**GSPC**......... Gas Scintillation Proportional Counter [*Instrumentation*]
**GSPCA**...... German Shorthaired Pointer Club of America (EA)
**GSPE**......... Groupe Socialiste du Parlement Europeen [*Socialist Group in the European Parliament - SGEP*] (EAIO)
**GSPGAF**... Geograficheskii Sbornik Penzenskogo Otdeleniya Geograficheskogo Obshchestva SSSR [*A publication*]
**GSPHCT**... Group Simplified Perturbed Hard Chain Theory [*Equation of state*]
**GSPO**......... Gemini Spacecraft Project Office [*NASA*] (MCD)
**GSPR**......... General Session of Peace Roll [*British*] [*Legal term*] (ROG)
**GSPR**......... GSA [*General Services Administration*] Procurement Regulations
**GSP-R**........ Guidance Signal Processor-Repeater (KSC)
**GSPS**......... Generating Station Protection System [*Nuclear energy*] (NRCH)
**GSPS**......... Guidance Spare Power Supply
**GSPTEK**.... Graphics Support Processor/Tektronix
**GSQ**........... Generalized Sinusoidal Quantity
**GSQ**........... Genus Equity Corp. [*Toronto Stock Exchange symbol*]
**GSQ**........... German Shepherd Quarterly [*A publication*]
**GSQC**......... Ground Surveillance Qualification Course [*Army*]
**GSQNA**..... Geological Society of South Africa. Quarterly News Bulletin [*A publication*]
**GSQT**......... Gun Ship Qualification Trials (MCD)
**GSR**........... Galvanic Skin Response [*Physiology*]
**GSR**........... Galvanic Stimulation Rate [*Physiology*]
**GSR**........... Gardo [*Somalia*] [*Airport symbol*] (OAG)
**GSR**........... General Service Recruit [*Navy*]
**GSR**........... General Staff Requirement [*British*] (RDA)
**GSR**........... General Support Reinforcing [*Army*] (AABC)
**GSR**........... General Systems Research Ltd. [*Vancouver Stock Exchange symbol*]
**GSR**........... Generalized Schartzman Reaction [*Medicine*]
**GSR**........... Geological Survey, Reston [*Virginia*] [*Seismograph station code, US Geological Survey*] (SEIS)
**gsr**............. Georgian Soviet Socialist Republic [*MARC country of publication code*] [*Library of Congress*] (LCCP)
**GSR**........... German Sanchez Ruiperez [*Founder and chairman of Anaya, a Spanish publishing enterprise*]
**GSR**........... Germanium Stack Rectifier
**GSR**........... Gland Steam Regulator [*Nuclear energy*] (NRCH)
**GSR**........... Glide Slope Receiver [*Aviation*]
**GSR**........... Global Shared Resources [*Data processing*] (IBMDP)
**GSR**........... Gongwer's State Reports [*Ohio*] [*A publication*] (DLA)
**GSR**........... Government Spares Release (MCD)
**GSR**........... Graphic Service Routines [*Data processing*] (MCD)
**GSR**........... Grid Space Relay
**GSR**........... Ground Service Relay (MCD)
**GSR**........... Ground-Speed Returning [*Aviation*]
**GSR**........... Ground Surveillance RADAR
**GSR**........... Group Selective Register
**GSR**........... Gun Sound Ranging [*An acoustic device*]
**GSRB**......... Glide Slope Reference Bar [*Aviation*]
**GSRED**...... Gas Supply Review [*A publication*]
**GSRI**.......... Great Swamp Research Institute (EA)
**GSRI**.......... Gulf South Research Institute
**GSRP**......... Gambian Socialist Revolutionary Party [*Political party*] (PD)
**GSRS**......... General Support Rocket System
**GSRS**......... Ground Surveillance RADAR System
**GSRTA**...... Giessereitechnik [*A publication*]
**GSRVC**...... Good Sam Recreational Vehicle Club (EA)
**GSS**........... Galvanized Steel Sheet [*Technical drawings*]
**GSS**........... Galvanized Steel Strand [*Telecommunications*] (TEL)
**GSS**........... Gamete Shedding Substance [*Endocrinology*]
**GSS**........... Gamma Scintillation System (MSA)
**GSS**........... Gamma Sigma Sigma (EA)
**GSS**........... General Service School [*Army*]
**GSS**........... General Social Survey [*National Opinion Research Center*]
**GSS**........... General Supply Schedule
**GSS**........... General Support System
**GSS**........... Geodetic Stationary Satellite
**GSS**........... George Sand Studies (EA)
**GSS**........... Gerontology Special Interest Section [*American Occupational Therapy Association*]
**GSS**........... Gerstmann-Staussler Syndrome [*Medicine*]
**GSS**........... Gilbert and Sullivan Society (EA)
**GSS**........... Global Surveillance System [*Air Force*]
**GSS**........... Gonad-Stimulating Substance [*Endocrinology*]
**GSS**........... Gossan Resources [*Vancouver Stock Exchange symbol*]
**GSS**........... Government Statistical Service [*British*]
**GSS**........... Graphic Support Software
**GSS**........... Gravity Sensors System [*Navigation*]
**GSS**........... Gray-Scale Sonography [*Medicine*]
**GSS**........... Ground Support Software [*NASA*] (NASA)
**GSS**........... Ground Support System [*Aerospace*] (AAG)
**GSS**........... Growth Space Station (KSC)
**GSS**........... Guidance System Simulator
**GSS**........... Rome, NY [*Location identifier*] [*FAA*] (FAAL)
**GSSA**......... General Support Service Area (MCD)
**GSSA**......... General Support Supply Activity (MCD)
**GSSA**......... Grassland Society of Southern Africa [*See also WVSA*] [*Howick, South Africa*] (EAIO)
**GSSA**......... Ground Support Systems Activation [*NASA*] (NASA)
**GSSC**......... Greater Super Six Club [*Inactive*] (EA)
**GSSC**......... Grenada Sunburst System Corp. [*NASDAQ symbol*] (NQ)

**GSSC** ........ Ground Support Simulation Computer [*Aerospace*] (KSC)
**GSSC** ........ Ground Support Systems Contractor [*NASA*] (NASA)
**GSSC** ........ Savannah State College, Savannah, GA [*Library symbol*] [*Library of Congress*] (LCLS)
**GSSF** ........ General Supply Stock Fund [*Air Force*] (AFM)
**GSSF** ........ Ground Special Security Forces
**GSSG** ........ Glutathione [*Oxidized*] [*Biochemistry*]
**GSSI** ........ Ground Support System Integration (MCD)
**GSSL** ........ Genoa, Savona, Spezia, or Leghorn [*Italian ports*] (DS)
**GSSLNCV** ... Genoa, Savona, Spezia, Leghorn, Naples, or Civita Vecchia [*Italian ports*] (DS)
**GSSO** ........ General Stores Supply Office
**GSSP** ........ Global Stratotype Section and Point [*Paleontology*]
**GSSPS** ....... Gravitationally Stabilized Solar Power System
**GSSq** ........ Geodetic Survey Squadron [*Air Force*] (AFM)
**GSSR** ........ General Salary Stabilization Regulations [*United States*] (DLA)
**GSSR** ........ Ground Support System Review [*Aerospace*] (AAG)
**GSSRPL** .... Guide to Social Science and Religion in Periodical Literature [*A publication*]
**GSSS** ........ Ground Support System Specification [*Aerospace*] (AAG)
**GSST** ........ Gatherer, Stitcher, Side Sewer, and Trimmer [*Publishing*]
**GSST** ........ Goldstein-Scheerer Stick Test [*Psychology*]
**GSSTFR** .... Gas-Solid-Solid Trickle Flow Reactor [*Chemical engineering*]
**GST** ........... Flying Boat [*Russian aircraft symbol*]
**GST** ........... Garter Stitch [*Knitting*] (ADA)
**GST** ........... Gas Surge Tank [*Nuclear energy*] (NRCH)
**GST** ........... General Screening Test
**GST** ........... General Service Test (NATG)
**GST** ........... General Service Truck [*British*]
**GST** ........... General Staff Target (NATG)
**GST** ........... General Staff with Troops [*Army*]
**GST** ........... General Systems Theory
**GST** ........... Generation-Skipping Transfer Tax
**GST** ........... Geographical Specialist Team [*Army*] (AABC)
**GSt** ............ Germanische Studien [*A publication*]
**GST** ........... Gesammelte Studien zum Alten Testament [*A publication*] (BJA)
**GST** ........... Glass Science and Technology [*Elsevier Book Series*] [*A publication*]
**GST** ........... Glazed Structural Tile [*Technical drawings*]
**GST** ........... Glutathione S-Transferase [*An enzyme*]
**GST** ........... Goods and Service Tax [*New Zealand*]
**GST** ........... Government Securities Trading [*Computer*]
**GST** ........... Government Steam Train [*British*]
**GST** ........... Graphic Stress Telethermometry [*Medicine*]
**GST** ........... Greenwich Sidereal [*or Standard*] Time
**GST** ........... Ground Sensor Terminal (AABC)
**GST** ........... Ground System Test [*NASA*] (NASA)
**GST** ........... Gunner Skills Test [*Army*] (INF)
**GST** ........... Gustavus [*Alaska*] [*Airport symbol*] (OAG)
**GS & TA** .... Ground Surveillance and Target Acquisition (IEEE)
**GSTA** ......... Ground Surveillance and Target Acquisition (MCD)
**G ST B** ....... Grand Standard Bearer [*Freemasonry*] (ROG)
**GSTC** ......... Gorham State Teachers College [*Merged with University of Maine*]
**GSTD** ......... Gold Standard, Inc. [*NASDAQ symbol*] (NQ)
**G STD B** .... Grand Standard Bearer [*Freemasonry*]
**GSTDN** ..... Ground Space Flight Tracking and Data Network [*NASA*] (NASA)
**GSTE** ......... Guidance System Test Equipment
**GSTF** ......... Ground Systems Test Flow [*NASA*] (NASA)
**GStG** ......... Georgia Southern College, Statesboro, GA [*Library symbol*] [*Library of Congress*] (LCLS)
**GSTHA4** ... Giessener Schriftenreihe Tierzucht und Haustiergenetik [*A publication*]
**GSTI** .......... Gerber Systems Technology, Incorporated [*NASDAQ symbol*] (NQ)
**GSTK** ......... Good Stuff to Know
**G Stor Let** .. Giornale Storico della Letteratura Italiana [*A publication*]
**GSTS** ......... German Student Travel Service
**GSTS** ......... Guidance System Test Set
**GSTS** ......... Gusts [*Meteorology*] (FAAC)
**GSTT** ......... Generation-Skipping Transfer Tax
**GSTU** ......... Guidance System Test Unit
**GStud** ........ Grudtvig Studier [*A publication*]
**GSTX** ......... Gibraltar Savings Association [*NASDAQ symbol*] (NQ)
**GSTY** ......... Gusty [*Meteorology*] (FAAC)
**GSU** .......... Gas Servicer Unit (MCD)
**GSU** .......... General Service Unit [*Marine Corps*]
**GSU** .......... General Support Unit [*Army*] (AABC)
**GSU** .......... Generator Step-Up Transformer [*Nuclear energy*] (NRCH)
**GSU** .......... Geographically Separated Units [*Military*] (AFM)
**GSU** .......... Georgia State University, Atlanta, GA [*OCLC symbol*] (OCLC)
**GSU** .......... Glazed Structural Unit [*Technical drawings*]
**GSU** .......... Godisnik na Sofijskiya Universitet. Filologiceski Fakultet [*A publication*]
**GSU** .......... Golden Seven Industry [*Vancouver Stock Exchange symbol*]
**GSU** .......... Governors State University [*Illinois*]
**GSU** .......... Grain Services Union
**GSU** .......... Gulf States Utilities Co. [*NYSE symbol*] (SPSG)
**GSUB** ........ Glazed Structural Unit Base [*Technical drawings*]
**GSUC** ........ Ground Stub-Up Connection [*Aerospace*] (AAG)
**GSUEG** ..... Governors State University Energy Group (EA)
**GSUF** ......... Godisnik na Sofijskiya Universitet. Filologiceski Fakultet [*A publication*]
**GSUFD6** .... Godishnik na Sofiiskiya Universitet. Kliment Okhridski Biologicheski Fakultet [*A publication*]
**GSUFZF** .... Godisnik na Sofijskiya Universitet. Fakultet po Zapadni Filologii [*A publication*]
**GSUG** ........ Gross Seasonal Unavailable Generation [*Electronics*] (IEEE)
**G SUPT** ..... Grand Superintendent [*Freemasonry*]
**GSUSA** ...... Gallipoli Society in the United States of America (EA)
**GSUSA** ...... General Staff, United States Army
**GSUSA** ...... Girl Scouts of the USA (EA)
**G de Suz** ..... Guido de Suzaria [*Deceased, 1293*] [*Authority cited in pre-1607 legal work*] (DSA)
**GSV** .......... Gas Sampling Valve
**GSV** .......... Globe Stop Valve
**GSV** .......... Golden Seville Resources Ltd. [*Vancouver Stock Exchange symbol*]
**GSV** .......... Governor Steam Valve (IEEE)
**GSV** .......... Ground-to-Surface Vessel [*RADAR*] (NATG)
**GSV** .......... Grumman Submersible Vehicle
**GSV** .......... Guided Space Vehicle [*Air Force*]
**GSVAD** ...... General Service Volunteer Aid Detachment [*British military*] (DMA)
**GSVC** ......... Generalized Supervisor Calls [*Data processing*] (IBMDP)
**GSVO** ........ Villa Cisneros [*Western Sahara*] [*ICAO location identifier*] (ICLI)
**GSVP** ......... Ground Support Verification Plan [*NASA*] (NASA)
**GSVT** ......... Ground System Validation Test (MCD)
**GSW** .......... General Service Wagon [*British military*] (DMA)
**G & SW** ...... Glasgow & South-Western [*Railway*] [*Scotland*]
**GSW** .......... Gold Star Wives of America (EA)
**GSW** .......... Grand Senior Warden [*Freemasonry*] (ROG)
**GS of W** ..... Grand Superintendent of Works [*Freemasonry*]
**GSW** .......... Great Southwest Railroad, Inc. [*AAR code*]
**GSW** .......... Ground Saucer Watch (EA)
**GSW** .......... GSW, Inc. [*Toronto Stock Exchange symbol*]
**GSW** .......... Gunshot Wound [*Medicine*]
**GSW 1812** ... General Society of the War of 1812 (EA)
**GSWA** ........ Gold Star Wives of America [*Later, GSW*] (EA)
**GSWA** ........ Gunshot Wound to the Abdomen
**GSWA** ........ International PEN - Centre of German-Speaking Writers Abroad (EAIO)
**G SWD B** ... Grand Sword Bearer [*Freemasonry*]
**GSwE** ......... Emanuel County Junior College, Swainsboro, GA [*Library symbol*] [*Library of Congress*] (LCLS)
**GSWR** ........ Galvanized Steel Wire Rope
**G & SWR** ... Glasgow & South-Western Railway [*Scotland*]
**GS-WRD** ... Geological Survey - Water Resources Division
**GSWT** ......... General Staff with Troops [*Army*]
**GSX** .......... General Signal Corp. [*NYSE symbol*] (SPSG)
**GSY** .......... Global Strategy Corp. [*Vancouver Stock Exchange symbol*]
**GSY** .......... Gulf Science Year [*1970*]
**GSYB** ......... [*The*] Girls' School Year Book [*A publication*] (ROG)
**GSYIH** ....... Gayrisafi Yurtici Hasila [*Gross Domestic Revenue*] [*Turkish*]
**GSYIM** ...... Gayrisafi Yurtici Mamulati [*Gross Domestic Product*] [*Turkish*]
**GSZ** .......... Golden Sitka Resources [*Vancouver Stock Exchange symbol*]
**GSZ** .......... Guernsey, WY [*Location identifier*] [*FAA*] (FAAL)
**G vs T** ........ Deceleration Units of Gravity versus Time (KSC)
**GT** ............. Gabbart [*Ship's rigging*] (ROG)
**G/T** ............ [*Antenna*] Gain-to-Noise Temperature Ratio
**GT** ............. Galactosyltransferase [*An enzyme*]
**GT** ............. Game Theory
**GT** ............. Gamma-Glutamyltransferase [*Also, GGT, GGTP*] [*An enzyme*]
**GT** ............. Gamow-Teller [*Transition*] [*Nuclear physics*]
**GT** ............. Garbage Truck
**GT** ............. Gas Tight
**GT** ............. Gas Turbine
**GT** ............. GB Airways Ltd. [*Great Britain*] [*ICAO designator*] (FAAC)
**GT** ............. Gel Tube [*Electrophoresis*]
**GT** ............. Gelling Temperature [*Analytical biochemistry*]
**GT** ............. Gemini-Titan [*NASA*]
**GT** ............. General Tariff (ADA)
**GT** ............. General Technical Aptitude Area
**GT** ............. General Test
**GT** ............. General Tool
**GT** ............. General Transport [*Military*]
**GT** ............. Generation Time [*Microbiology*]
**GT** ............. Genetic Therapy
**GT** ............. Gentleman Traveller
**GT** ............. Geografisk Tidsskrift [*A publication*]
**GT** ............. German Growth Trust [*Lloyds Bank International*]
**GT** ............. German Translation (MCD)
**GT** ............. Ghanaian Times [*A publication*]
**GT** ............. Gibraltar Airways Ltd. [*United Kingdom*] [*ICAO designator*] (ICDA)
**GT** ............. Gift Tax (DLA)

**GT** ........ Gifted and Talented [*Education*]
**GT** ........ Gilt
**GT** ........ Gilt Top [*Bookbinding*]
**G & T** ........ Gin and Tonic
**GT** ........ Glacial Till Soil [*Agronomy*]
**GT** ........ Glass Tube (DEN)
**GT** ........ Globe Thermometer
**GT** ........ Glucose Tolerance [*Medicine*]
**GT** ........ Glucose Transporter [*Biochemistry*]
**GT** ........ Glucose Turnover [*Physiology*]
**GT** ........ Glucuronosyltransferase [*An enzyme*]
**GT** ........ Glumitocin [*Endocrinology*]
**GT** ........ Glutamyl Transpeptidase [*An enzyme*]
**GT** ........ Glycotyrosine [*Biochemistry*]
**GT** ........ Gnomonic Tracking Chart [*Air Force*]
**GT** ........ Good Templar
**GT** ........ Good Tidings (EA)
**GT** ........ Goodyear Canada, Inc. [*Toronto Stock Exchange symbol*]
**GT** ........ [*The*] Goodyear Tire & Rubber Co. [*NYSE symbol*] (SPSG)
**GT** ........ Gopher Tape Armor [*Telecommunications*] (TEL)
**G & T** ........ Gould and Tucker's Notes on Revised Statutes of United States [*A publication*] (DLA)
**GT** ........ Gran Turismo [*Grand Touring*] [*Automotive term*]
**GT** ........ Grand Theft
**GT** ........ Grand Tiler [*Freemasonry*]
**GT** ........ Grand Treasurer [*Freemasonry*]
**G/T** ........ Granulation Time
**G/T** ........ Granulation Tissue
**GT** ........ Graphics Terminal
**GT** ........ Grease Trap (AAG)
**GT** ........ Great
**Gt** ........ Great Organ [*Music*]
**GT** ........ Great Thoughts [*A publication*] (ROG)
**GT** ........ Greater Than [*FORTRAN*]
**GT** ........ Greater Trochanter [*Anatomy*]
**GT** ........ Green Thumb (EA)
**GT** ........ Green Thumbs [*National Weather Service and Department of Agriculture Extension Service telecommunication system*]
**GT** ........ Greenwich Time
**GT** ........ Gross Ton [*or Tonnage*]
**GT** ........ Ground Team (MCD)
**GT** ........ Ground Test [*NASA*] (NASA)
**GT** ........ Ground Track
**GT** ........ Ground Transmit (AFM)
**GT** ........ Ground-Tree Foraging [*Ecology*]
**GT** ........ Group Technology
**GT** ........ Group Therapy
**GT** ........ Group Transformation
**GT** ........ Grout [*Technical drawings*]
**GT** ........ Guard of Tent [*Oddfellows*] (ROG)
**gt** ........ Guatemala [*MARC country of publication code*] [*Library of Congress*] (LCCP)
**GT** ........ Guatemala [*ANSI two-letter standard code*] (CNC)
**GT** ........ Guidance Transmitter (NVT)
**GT** ........ Gun Target (NVT)
**GT** ........ Gun Tractor [*British*]
**GT** ........ Gun Turret
**GT** ........ Gutta [*Drop of Liquid*] [*Pharmacy*]
**GT** ........ Gyro Torque (MCD)
**GT** ........ Journal of Geotechnical Engineering [*A publication*]
**GT** ........ Triganglioside [*Chemistry*]
**GT1** ........ Glycogenosis Type 1 [*Medicine*]
**GT's** ........ Globetrotters' Club (EAIO)
**GTA** ........ Gas Toxicity Analysis
**GTA** ........ Gas Tungsten Arc
**GTA** ........ Gay Theatre Alliance [*Defunct*] (EA)
**GTA** ........ Gear Train Analyzer
**GTA** ........ Gemini-Titan-Agena [*NASA*] (KSC)
**GTA** ........ Gene Transfer Agent [*Genetics*]
**GTA** ........ General Terms Agreement (MCD)
**GTA** ........ General Training Assistance (ADA)
**GTA** ........ Genetic Toxicology Association (EA)
**GTA** ........ German Teachers' Association [*British*]
**GTA** ........ Glass Tempering Association (EA)
**GTA** ........ Glycerol Triacetate [*Known as Triacetin*] [*Organic chemistry*]
**GTA** ........ Gospel Truth Association (EA)
**GTA** ........ Government Telecommunications Agency [*Canada*]
**GTA** ........ Graduate Teachers' Association [*A union*] [*British*]
**GTA** ........ Graduate Teaching Assistant
**GTA** ........ Grain Transportation Agency [*Winnipeg, MB*]
**GTA** ........ Gran Turisimo Americano [*In automobile name Pontiac Firebird GTA*]
**GTA** ........ Graphic Training Aid
**GTA** ........ Gravure Technical Association [*Later, GAA*] (EA)
**GTA** ........ Great American Bank SSB [*NYSE symbol*] (SPSG)
**GT & A** ........ Ground Test and Acceptance [*NASA*] (NASA)
**GTA** ........ Ground Test Access (MCD)
**GTA** ........ Ground Test Article [*NASA*] (NASA)
**GTA** ........ Ground Torquing Assembly (MCD)
**GTA** ........ Ground Training Aid [*Aerospace*] (AAG)
**GTA** ........ Group Training Association [*British*] (DCTA)
**GTA** ........ Groupement Technique de Assureurs du Canada [*Government Telecommunications Agency*] [*Canada*]
**GTA** ........ Guide Tube Assembly (NRCH)
**GTA** ........ Gutta [*Drop of Liquid*] [*Pharmacy*] (ROG)
**GTAA** ........ Groupe de Travail Inter Agences sur l'Afrique Australe [*Inter-Agency Working Group on Southern Africa - IAWGSA*] [*Canadian Council for International Cooperation*]
**GTAC** ........ Gas Tungsten Arc Cutting [*Welding*]
**GTAC** ........ General Technical Advisory Committee [*for fossil energy*] [*Energy Research and Development Administration*]
**GTAC** ........ Ground-to-Air Cycle
**GTA Dig** ........ GTA [*Grain Terminal Association*] Digest [*A publication*]
**GTAM** ........ Great American Corp. [*NASDAQ symbol*] (NQ)
**GTAO** ........ Graphic Training Aids Officer [*Army*]
**GTAV** ........ General Transport Administrative Vehicle
**GTAW** ........ Gas Tungsten Arc Weld [*or Welding*]
**GTAW-P** ........ Gas Tungsten Arc Welding - Pulsed Arc
**GTB** ........ Fort Drum, NY [*Location identifier*] [*FAA*] (FAAL)
**GTB** ........ General Tariff Bureau Inc. Lansing MI [*STAC*]
**GTB** ........ General Trade Books [*Publishing*]
**GTB** ........ Glycinethymol Blue [*An indicator*] [*Chemistry*]
**GTB** ........ Grand Traverse Bay, Michigan
**GTBA** ........ Gasoline-Grade Tertiary-Butyl Alcohol [*Organic chemistry*]
**Gt Basin Nat** ... Great Basin Naturalist [*A publication*]
**GT BR** ........ Great Britain (ROG)
**Gt Brit & East** ... Great Britain and the East [*A publication*]
**GTBWA** ........ Gartenbauwissenschaft [*A publication*]
**GTC** ........ Gain Time Control
**GTC** ........ Gas Turbine Compressor
**GTC** ........ General Teaching Council [*British*]
**GT & C** ........ General Terms and Conditions
**GTC** ........ General Transistor Corporation (AAG)
**GTC** ........ Girls' Training Corps [*British*] (DAS)
**GTC** ........ Global Tomorrow Coalition (EA)
**GTC** ........ Glycol Trim Console (MCD)
**GTC** ........ Golder, Thoma & Cressey [*Chicago, IL*] [*Telecommunications service*] (TSSD)
**GTC** ........ Good Till Canceled [*as in a brokerage order*]
**GTC** ........ Government Telegraph Code [*British*] [*World War II*]
**GTC** ........ Government Training Centre [*British*]
**GTC** ........ Grand Touring Coupe [*In automobile name Lincoln Mark VII GTC*]
**GTC** ........ Greater Toy Center (EA)
**GTC** ........ Ground Test Conductor (MCD)
**GTC** ........ Group for Technical Coordination [*Marine science*] (MSC)
**GTC** ........ Group Training Command [*Air Force*] [*British*]
**GTC** ........ Guidance Transfer Container
**GTC** ........ Guild of Television Cameramen [*British*] (EA)
**GTC** ........ Gulf Transport [*AAR code*]
**GTC** ........ Man, WV [*Location identifier*] [*FAA*] (FAAL)
**GTCC** ........ Greater-than-Class-C [*Radioactive waste level definition*]
**GTCH** ........ GTECH Corp. [*NASDAQ symbol*] (NQ)
**GTCL** ........ Graduate of Trinity College of Music, London
**GTCL** ........ Great Circle [*FAA*] (FAAC)
**GTCM** ........ Guaranty Commerce Corp. [*NASDAQ symbol*] (NQ)
**GTCP** ........ Gas Turbine Compressor and Power Unit (NG)
**GTCP** ........ General Telephone Call Processing
**GTCP** ........ Global Tropospheric Chemistry Program [*Federal government*]
**GTCS** ........ General Teaching Council for School [*British*]
**GTCU** ........ Ground Thermal Conditioning Unit [*NASA*] (NASA)
**GTD** ........ Gear Test Data
**GTD** ........ General Traffic Department
**GTD** ........ Geometrical Theory of Diffraction
**GTD** ........ Georgetown [*Delaware*] [*Seismograph station code, US Geological Survey*] (SEIS)
**GTD** ........ Graphic Tablet Display [*Data processing*] (IEEE)
**GTD** ........ Ground Target Detection
**GTD** ........ Guaranteed
**GTD** ........ Guards Tank Division (MCD)
**GTDHD** ........ Give the Devil His Due [*Slang*]
**GTDPL** ........ Generalized Top-Down Parsing Language
**GTDR** ........ General Technical Data Restricted
**GTDS** ........ Goddard Trajectory Determination System [*NASA*]
**GTE** ........ Gas Turbine Engine
**GTE** ........ General Telephone and Electronics [*Information service or system*] (IID)
**GT & E** ........ General Telephone & Electronics Corp.
**GTE** ........ General Telephone Equipment (MCD)
**GTE** ........ Geothermal Energy
**Gte** ........ Gerente [*Manager*] [*Spanish*] [*Business term*]
**GTE** ........ Gilt Top Edge [*Bookbinding*]
**GTE** ........ Global Tropospheric Experiment [*National Oceanic and Atmospheric Administration*]
**GTE** ........ Gothenburg, NE [*Location identifier*] [*FAA*] (FAAL)
**GTE** ........ Government Technology Event [*Australia*]
**GTE** ........ Government Trading Enterprises [*Australia*]
**GTE** ........ Groote Island [*Australia*] [*Airport symbol*] (OAG)
**GTE** ........ Ground Test Equipment
**GTE** ........ Ground Training Engine [*Military*] (AFIT)
**GTE** ........ Ground Transport Equipment (KSC)
**GTE** ........ Group Translating Equipment

**GTE** .......... GTE Corp. [*Formerly, General Telephone & Electronics Corp.*] [*NYSE symbol*] (SPSG)
**GTE** .......... Guidance Test Equipment
**GTEA** ........ Group Test Equipment Assembly
**GTE Auto** .. GTE [*General Telephone and Electronics Corp.*] Automatic Electric Technical Journal [*Later, GTE Automatic Electric World-Wide Communications Journal*] [*A publication*]
**GTE Autom Electr J** ... GTE [*General Telephone and Electronics Corp.*] Automatic Electric Technical Journal [*Later, GTE Automatic Electric World-Wide Communications Journal*] [*A publication*]
**GTE Autom Electr Tech J** ... GTE [*General Telephone and Electronics Corp.*] Automatic Electric Technical Journal [*Later, GTE Automatic Electric World-Wide Communications Journal*] [*A publication*]
**GTE Autom Electr World-Wide Commun J** ... GTE [*General Telephone and Electronics Corp.*] Automatic Electric World-Wide Communications Journal [*A publication*]
**GTED** ........ Gas Turbine Engine-Driven [*Generator*] (RDA)
**GTEE** ......... Guarantee
**GTEL** ......... GTE California, Inc. [*NASDAQ symbol*] (NQ)
**GT-ENDOR** ... General Triple-Electron Nuclear Double Resonance [*Spectroscopy*]
**GTEP** ......... General Telephone and Electronics Practice [*Telecommunications*] (TEL)
**GTETDS** ... Gas Turbine and Engine Type Designation System
**GTF** .......... Generalized Trace Facility [*Data processing*] (MCD)
**GTF** .......... Generalized Transformation Function
**GTF** .......... German Territorial Forces (MCD)
**GTF** .......... Glucose Tolerance Factor [*Medicine*]
**GTF** .......... Government Test Facility
**GTF** .......... Great Falls [*Montana*] [*Airport symbol*] (OAG)
**GTF** .......... GT Greater Europe Fund [*NYSE symbol*] (SPSG)
**GTF** .......... Guidance Test Fixture
**GTF** .......... Guilt Free Goodies [*Vancouver Stock Exchange symbol*]
**GTG** .......... Game-Tying Goals [*Hockey*]
**GTG** .......... Gas Turbine Generator
**GTG** .......... Gold Thioglucose
**GTG** .......... Golden Trend Energy [*Vancouver Stock Exchange symbol*]
**GTG** .......... Grantsburg, WI [*Location identifier*] [*FAA*] (FAAL)
**GTG** .......... Ground-to-Ground [*Communications, weapons, etc.*]
**GTGEEEPS** ... Groupe de Travail sur la Gestion de l'Energie dans les Etablissements d'Enseignement Post-Secondaire [*Postsecondary Education Task Force on Energy Management - PETFEM*] [*Canada*]
**GTGL** ........ Give the Gift of Literacy Foundation [*Duxbury, MA*]
**GTGS** ........ Gas Turbine Generator Set (AABC)
**GTGT** ........ Gun Target (AABC)
**GTH** .......... Gas Tight High Pressure (IEEE)
**GTH** .......... Genomic Thymus [*Genetics*]
**GTH** .......... Gonadotropic Hormone [*Endocrinology*]
**GTH** .......... Groton Minerals Ltd. [*Vancouver Stock Exchange symbol*]
**GTH** .......... Guthrie, TX [*Location identifier*] [*FAA*] (FAAL)
**G Thom** ...... Gospel of Thomas [*Apocryphal work*]
**GThT** ......... Gereformeerd Theologisch Tijdschrift [*Kampen*] [*A publication*]
**GT-HTGR** ... Gas Turbine High-Temperature Gas-Cooled Reactor [*Nuclear energy*] (NRCH)
**GTi** .......... Coastal Plains Regional Library, Tifton, GA [*Library symbol*] [*Library of Congress*] (LCLS)
**GTI** .......... General Transportation Importance
**GTI** .......... Glass Technical Institute [*Commercial firm*] (EA)
**GTI** .......... Glentech International Ltd. [*British*]
**GTI** .......... Grand Turk Island
**GTI** .......... Ground Test Instrumentation (MCD)
**GTI** .......... GTI Corp. [*AMEX symbol*] (SPSG)
**GTiA** ......... Abraham Baldwin Agricultural College, Tifton, GA [*Library symbol*] [*Library of Congress*] (LCLS)
**GTIC** ......... GTI Corporation [*NASDAQ symbol*] (NQ)
**GTiE** ......... Coastal Plains Experiment Station, Tifton, GA [*Library symbol*] [*Library of Congress*] (LCLS)
**GTIG** ......... Gamma Thermometer Interest Group [*Nuclear energy*] (NRCH)
**GTIP** ......... Ground Tilt Isolation Platform
**GTJ** .......... Gold Torch Resources [*Vancouver Stock Exchange symbol*]
**GTJ** .......... Grace Theological Journal [*A publication*]
**GTKRD** ..... Gan To Kagaku Ryoho [*A publication*]
**GTKTA** ...... Geotektonika [*A publication*]
**GTL** .......... Gas Transport LASER
**GTL** .......... Gas Turbine Laboratory [*MIT*] (MCD)
**GTL** .......... Gaseous Tritium Light [*Device*] [*Nuclear energy*] (NRCH)
**GTL** .......... Georgia Tech Language [*Data processing*] (CSR)
**GTL** .......... Government Test Laboratory (MSA)
**GTL** .......... Great Lakes Nickel Ltd. [*Toronto Stock Exchange symbol*]
**GTL** .......... Gun/Target Line [*Navy*] (NVT)
**Gt Lakes Ent** ... Great Lakes Entomologist [*A publication*]
**GTLS** ........ Gaseous Tritium Light Source [*Nuclear energy*] (MCD)
**GTM** .......... Abraham Baldwin Agricultural College, Tifton, GA [*OCLC symbol*] (OCLC)
**GTM** .......... Gas to Methanol [*Process developed by ICI*]
**GTM** .......... General Traffic Manager
**GTM** .......... Geometry Technology Module [*NASA*]
**GTM** .......... Getting the Message [*A reading program*]
**GTM** .......... Good This Month [*Business term*]
**GTM** .......... Ground Team Manager (MCD)
**GTM** .......... Ground Test Missile
**GTM** .......... Ground Test Motor (MCD)
**GTM** .......... Group Talk Microphone
**GTM** .......... Guatemala [*ANSI three-letter standard code*] (CNC)
**GTM** .......... Guild of Temple Musicians (EA)
**GTMA** ........ Gauge and Toolmakers Association [*United Kingdom*] (DS)
**GTMBAQ** ... Georgetown Medical Bulletin [*A publication*]
**GTMCA** .... Geothermics [*A publication*]
**GTMMM** .. Det Gamle Testament [*S. Michelet, S.Mowinckel, og N. Mersel*] [*Oslo*] [*A publication*] (BJA)
**GTMO** ........ Guantanamo Bay, Cuba
**GTMS** ........ Ground Target Marking System
**GTMV** ........ Gasoline-Tolerant Methanol Vehicle [*Chrysler Corp.*] [*Automotive engineering*]
**GTN** .......... Genetic Technology News [*A publication*]
**GTN** .......... Gestational Trophoblastic Neoplasia [*Medicine*]
**GTN** .......... Glomerulo-Tubulo-Nephritis [*Medicine*]
**GTN** .......... Glyceryl Trinitrate [*Also, NG, NTG*] [*Explosive, vasodilator*]
**GTN** .......... Gotenba [*Japan*] [*Seismograph station code, US Geological Survey*] [*Closed*] (SEIS)
**GTN** .......... Great Eastern Line [*Vancouver Stock Exchange symbol*]
**GTN** .......... Washington, DC [*Location identifier*] [*FAA*] (FAAL)
**GTNEEA** ... Genetic Technology News [*A publication*]
**GTNQA** ..... Geotechnique [*England*] [*A publication*]
**GTNR** ........ Gentner Electronics Corp. [*NASDAQ symbol*] (NQ)
**GTNW** ....... General Telephone Co. of the Northwest
**GTO** .......... Gate Turn Off [*Data processing*]
**GTO** .......... Gaussian-Type Orbitals [*Atomic physics*]
**GTO** .......... General Telecommunications Organization [*Oman*] [*Telecommunications service*] (TSSD)
**GTO** .......... Geostationary Transfer Orbit [*Space technology*]
**GTO** .......... Gigaton
**GTO** .......... Golgi Tendon Organ [*Anatomy*]
**GTO** .......... Gorontalo [*Indonesia*] [*Airport symbol*] (OAG)
**GTO** .......... Gran Torismo Omologato [*Grand Touring, Homologated*] [*Automotive engineering*] [*Italian*]
**GTO** .......... Graphics Text Organizer [*Data processing*]
**GTO** .......... Grenada Tourist Office (EA)
**GTO's** ........ Girls Together Outrageously [*or Organically*] [*Rock music group*]
**GTOL** ........ Ground Takeoff and Landing (AAG)
**GT ORM H** ... Great Ormond Street Hospital for Children [*British*] (ROG)
**GTOS** ........ Gantos, Inc. [*Grand Rapids, MI*] [*NASDAQ symbol*] (NQ)
**GTOW** ....... Gross Takeoff Weight [*of an aircraft*] [*Also, GTW*]
**GTP** .......... Gas Turbine Power Unit (NG)
**GTP** .......... General Test Plan (AAG)
**GTP** .......... Generate Target Position [*Military*] (CAAL)
**GTP** .......... Grand Touring Prototype [*Race car designation*]
**GTP** .......... Grand Trunk Pacific Railway
**GTP** .......... Great Northern Petroleums [*Vancouver Stock Exchange symbol*]
**GTP** .......... Great Trunk Pacific Railway [*British*] (ROG)
**GTP** .......... Green Tea Polyphenol [*Biochemistry*]
**GTP** .......... Ground Test Plan (MCD)
**GTP** .......... Ground Track Plotter
**GTP** .......... Group-Transfer Polymerization [*Du Pont process*] [*1983*]
**GTP** .......... Guanosine Triphosphate [*Biochemistry*]
**GTPase** ...... Guanosine Triphosphatase [*An enzyme*]
**GTPI** ......... Grupo de Trabajo para los Pueblos Indigenas [*Working Group Indigenous Peoples*] (EAIO)
**Gt Plains Jour** ... Great Plains Journal [*A publication*]
**GTPPA** ...... Gigiena Truda i Professional'naya Patologiya v Estonskoi SSR [*A publication*]
**GTPR** ......... Grand Trunk Pacific Railway
**GTPS** ......... Gas Turbine Power System
**GTPSS** ....... Ground Test Plan Summary Sheets (MCD)
**GTPT** ......... Geometrical and True Positioning Tolerance
**GTPU** ........ Gas Turbine Power Unit (MCD)
**GTPZA** ...... Gigiena Truda i Professional'nye Zabolevaniya [*A publication*]
**GTPZAB** ... Gigiena Truda i Professional'nye Zabolevaniya [*A publication*]
**GTR** .......... Columbus [*Mississippi*] [*Airport symbol*] (OAG)
**GTR** .......... Gantry Test Rack [*Aerospace*] (AAG)
**GTR** .......... Garter (MSA)
**GTR** .......... General Theory of Relativity
**GTR** .......... Golden Terrace Resource Corp. [*Toronto Stock Exchange symbol*]
**GTR** .......... Government Technical Report
**GTR** .......... Government Technical Representative
**GTR** .......... Government Transportation [*or Travel*] Request
**GTR** .......... Grand Trunk Railway
**GTR** .......... Granulocyte Turnover Rate [*Hematology*]
**GTR** .......... Greater (FAAC)
**GTR** .......... Greek Orthodox Theological Review [*A publication*]
**GTR** .......... Ground Test Reactor [*Air Force*]
**GT/R** ......... Guard Transmit/Receive (MCD)
**GTR** .......... Guitar [*Music*]
**GTR** .......... Guitar Review [*A publication*]

**GTR**.......... Gurkha Transport Regiment [*Military unit*] [*British*]
**GTRB**......... Gas Turbine
**GTRD**......... Greatest Total Resource Demand
**GTRE**......... Global Tape Recording Exchange (EA)
**GTRE**......... GranTree Corp. [*NASDAQ symbol*] (NQ)
**G TREAS**.. Grand Treasurer [*Freemasonry*] (ROG)
**GTRI**.......... Georgia Tech Research Institute [*Georgia Institute of Technology*] [*Research center*] (RCD)
**GTRO**......... Glyceryl Triricinoleate [*Organic chemistry*]
**GTRO**......... Golden Triangle Royalty & Oil, Inc. [*NASDAQ symbol*] (NQ)
**GTRP**......... General Transpose [*Data processing*]
**GTRR**......... Georgia Institute of Technology Research Reactor
**GTRR**......... Grand Trunk Railroad [*British*] (ROG)
**GTRWA**.... Gdanskie Towarzystwo Naukowe Rozparawy Wydzialu [*A publication*]
**GTRWDF**... US Forest Service. General Technical Report. WO [*A publication*]
**GTRY**......... Grand Trunk Railway
**GTS**........... Gas Turbine Starter (MCD)
**GTS**........... General Tabulation System
**GTS**........... General Technical Services, Inc. (MCD)
**GTS**........... General Test Support (MCD)
**GTS**........... General Theological Seminary [*New York, NY*]
**GTS**........... General Troubleshooting
**GTS**........... Geostationary Technology Satellite
**GTS**........... Germanistische Texte und Studien [*A publication*]
**GTS**........... Gettysburg Theological Studies [*A publication*]
**GTS**........... Gimbal Trim System
**GTS**........... Girls' Technical School (ADA)
**GTS**........... Glider Training School [*British military*] (DMA)
**GTS**........... Global Telecommunication System [*World Meteorological Organization*] (IID)
**GTS**........... Global Tracking Systems
**GTS**........... Global Treasury Services [*Barclays Bank*] [*British*]
**GTS**........... GN & C [*Guidance, Navigation and Control*] Test Station [*NASA*] (NASA)
**GTS**........... Golden Tech Resources Ltd. [*Vancouver Stock Exchange symbol*]
**GTS**........... Golden Treasury Series [*A publication*]
**GTS**........... Goldstone Tracking Station [*NASA*]
**GTS**........... Graphics Terminal Scheduler (MCD)
**GTS**........... Graphics Terminal Services
**GTS**........... Graphics Terminal System
**GTS**........... Greenwich Time Signal (DEN)
**GTS**........... Ground Telemetry Subsystem
**GTS**........... Ground Terminal System
**GTS**........... Ground Test Station
**GTS**........... Ground Tracking System (MCD)
**GTS**........... Group Teleconferencing System [*Telecommunications*]
**GTS**........... Group Training Scheme [*Australia*]
**GTS**........... Guam Tracking Station [*NASA*] (MCD)
**GTS**........... Guidance Test Set (AAG)
**GTS**........... Guinean Trawling Survey [*United Nations*]
**GTS**........... Gunnery Training School [*British military*] (DMA)
**GTS**........... Gyro Tilt Signal
**GTSA**......... German Telecommunications Statistics Agency
**GTSC**......... German Territorial Southern Command [*NATO*] (NATG)
**GTSC**......... GTS Corporation [*NASDAQ symbol*] (NQ)
**GTSF**......... Gifted and Talented Screening Form [*Educational test*]
**GTSF**......... Guidance Test and Simulation Facility
**GTSS**......... Gas Turbine Starting System (NG)
**GTSS**......... General Time Sharing System [*Data processing*]
**GTSTA**...... Gidrotekhnicheskoe Stroitel'stvo [*A publication*]
**GTSTD**...... Grid Test of Schizophrenic Thought Disorder [*Psychology*]
**GTSW**........ Greentree Software, Inc. [*NASDAQ symbol*] (NQ)
**GTT**........... Generated Target Tracking
**GTT**........... Geographical and Topographical Texts of the Old Testament [*A publication*] (BJA)
**GTT**........... Georgetown [*Australia*] [*Airport symbol*] (OAG)
**GTT**........... Gereformeerd Theologisch Tijdschrift [*A publication*]
**GTT**........... Glucose Tolerance Test [*Medicine*]
**GTT**........... Goettingen [*Federal Republic of Germany*] [*Geomagnetic observatory code*]
**GTT**........... Gone to Texas [*Sign on doors of New Englanders who had gone West, nineteenth century*]
**GTT**........... Gottingen [*Federal Republic of Germany*] [*Seismograph station code, US Geological Survey*] (SEIS)
**GTT**........... Grand Teton Industries, Inc. [*Vancouver Stock Exchange symbol*]
**GTT**........... Group Timing Technique [*Industrial engineering*]
**GTT**........... Guttae [*Drops of Liquid*] [*Pharmacy*]
**GTTC**......... Gulf Transportation Terminal Command
**GTTF**......... Gas Turbine Test Facility
**GT & TM**... General Traffic and Transportation Manager
**GTT QUIBUSD**... Guttis Quibusdam [*With Some Drops*] [*Pharmacy*] (ROG)
**GTTS**......... Gyro Transfer Table System
**GTU**........... Gamma Theta Upsilon (EA)
**GTU**........... Georgetown University, Medical Center Library, Washington, DC [*OCLC symbol*] (OCLC)
**GTU**........... Glycol Trim Unit (MCD)
**GTU**........... Graduate Theological Union, University of Saskatchewan [*UTLAS symbol*]
**GTU**........... Ground Test Unit
**GTU**........... Guidance Test Unit
**GTUC**......... Ghana Trades Union Congress
**GTUSIdentBad**... Guard, Tomb of the Unknown Soldier Identification Badge [*Military decoration*] (AABC)
**GTV**........... Galaxy Cablevision LP [*AMEX symbol*] (SPSG)
**GTV**........... Gas Toggle Valve
**GTV**........... Gate Valve (AAG)
**GTV**........... Ground Test Vehicle (KSC)
**GTV**........... Ground Transport Vehicle
**GTV**........... Growth Test Vehicle (MCD)
**GTV**........... Guidance [*or Guided*] Test Vehicle
**GTW**........... Good This Week [*Business term*]
**GTW**........... Gottwaldov [*Czechoslovakia*] [*Airport symbol*] (OAG)
**GTW**........... Grand Trunk Western Railroad Co. [*AAR code*]
**GTW**........... Gross Takeoff Weight [*of an aircraft*] [*Also, GTOW*]
**GTW**........... Gross Train Weight (DCTA)
**GTW**........... Guild of Travel Writers [*British*]
**GTWOD**.... Gas Turbine World [*A publication*]
**GTWT**......... Gridded Traveling-Wave Tube (MCD)
**GTWY**......... Gateway (MCD)
**GTWY**......... Gateway Financial Corp. [*NASDAQ symbol*] (NQ)
**GTX**........... Alma, MI [*Location identifier*] [*FAA*] (FAAL)
**GTX**........... General Tool Experimental (MCD)
**GTX**........... Gold Texas Resources Ltd. [*Vancouver Stock Exchange symbol*]
**GTX**........... Gran Turismo Experimental [*Grand Touring, Experimental*] [*Automotive term*]
**GTX**........... Grant Industries [*AMEX symbol*] (SPSG)
**GTX**........... Ground Transport Express [*Airport baggage computer*]
**GTY**........... Getty Petroleum Corp. [*NYSE symbol*] (SPSG)
**gty**............ Gritty [*Quality of the bottom*] [*Nautical charts*]
**Gty**............ Guaranty (DLA)
**GTY**........... Guaranty Trustco Ltd. [*Toronto Stock Exchange symbol*]
**GU**............. Empresa Guatemalteca de Aviacion "AVIATECA" [*Guatemala*] [*ICAO designator*] (FAAC)
**GU**............. Gasschutzunteroffizier [*Gas Noncommissioned Officer*] [*German military - World War II*]
**GU**............. Gastric Ulcer [*Medicine*]
**GU**............. Gear Up [*Aviation*]
**GU**............. Generations United (EA)
**GU**............. Generic Unit (TEL)
**GU**............. Genitourinary [*Medicine*]
**GU**............. Geographically Undesirable [*Slang*]
**GU**............. Georgetown University [*Washington, DC*]
**GU**............. Glycogenic Unit [*Medicine*]
**GU**............. Gonococcal Urethritis [*Medicine*]
**G & U**......... Grafe & Unzer [*Publisher*] [*German*]
**GU**............. Grafton & Upton Railroad Co. [*AAR code*]
**GU**............. Gravitational Ulcer [*Medicine*]
**GU**............. Guam [*ANSI two-letter standard code*] [*Postal code*] (CNC)
**gu**.............. Guam [*MARC country of publication code*] [*Library of Congress*] (LCCP)
**GU**............. Guanase [*An enzyme*]
**GU**............. Guarantee
**GU**............. Guatemala [*IYRU nationality code*] (IYR)
**GU**............. Guidance Unit
**Gu**.............. Guillelmus de Tocco [*Authority cited in pre-1607 legal work*] (DSA)
**GU**............. Guinea
**GU**............. Guitar Review [*A publication*]
**GU**............. Gules [*Heraldry*]
**GU**............. Gunner (ADA)
**GU**............. University of Georgia, Athens, GA [*Library symbol*] [*Library of Congress*] (LCLS)
**GUA**........... Goeteborgs Universitets Arsskrift [*A publication*]
**GUA**........... Guam [*Santa Rosa*] [*Mariana Islands*] [*Seismograph station code, US Geological Survey*] (SEIS)
**GUA**........... Guam [*Mariana Islands*] [*Geomagnetic observatory code*]
**Gua**............ Guanine [*Also, G*] [*Biochemistry*]
**gua**............ Guarani [*MARC language code*] [*Library of Congress*] (LCCP)
**GUA**........... Guatemala City [*Guatemala*] [*Airport symbol*] (OAG)
**GUA**........... Guidance Unit Assembly
**GUA**........... Guinea [*Monetary unit*] [*Obsolete*] [*Great Britain*] (ROG)
**GUA**........... International Guards Union of America
**GUA**........... University of Georgia, Athens, GA [*OCLC symbol*] (OCLC)
**GuaAF**........ Nieves M. Flores Memorial Library, Agana, Guam [*Library symbol*] [*Library of Congress*] (LCLS)
**GUAD**......... Guadeloupe (ROG)
**Gual**........... Gualcosius [*Flourished, 11th-12th century*] [*Authority cited in pre-1607 legal work*] (DSA)
**Gualc**.......... Gualcosius [*Flourished, 11th-12th century*] [*Authority cited in pre-1607 legal work*] (DSA)
**GUALO**...... General Union of Associations of Loom Overlookers [*British*] (DCTA)
**Guam Admin R**... Administrative Rules and Regulations of the Government of Guam [*A publication*] (DLA)
**Guam Ag Exp**... Guam Agricultural Experiment Station. Publications [*A publication*]

**Guam Civ Code** ... Guam Civil Code [*A publication*] (DLA)
**Guam Code Civ Pro** ... Guam Code of Civil Procedure [*A publication*] (DLA)
**Guam Gov't Code** ... Guam Government Code [*A publication*] (DLA)
**Guam Prob Code** ... Guam Probate Code [*A publication*] (DLA)
**GUAR**........ Guarantee (MSA)
**Guar**........... Guarnerius [*Irnerius*] [*Flourished, 1113-18*] [*Authority cited in pre-1607 legal work*] (DSA)
**GUARD**..... Government Employees United Against Discrimination [*An association*]
**GUARD**..... Guaranteed Assignment Retention Detailing [*Navy*] (NVT)
**GUARDS**.. Generalized Unified Ammunition Reporting Data System (MCD)
**GUARDSMAN** ... Guidelines and Rules for Data Systems Management (TEL)
**GUAREE**... Guarantee (ROG)
**GUAROR** ... Guarantor [*Legal term*] (ROG)
**GUASO**..... Guatemalan Solidarity Committee (EA)
**GUAT**........ Guatemala
**Guatem Indig** ... Guatemala Indigena [*A publication*]
**GuaU**.......... University of Guam, Agana, GU [*Library symbol*] [*Library of Congress*] (LCLS)
**GUB**........... Generalized Upper Bounding [*Data processing*]
**GUB**........... Government Union of Burma
**GUB**........... Greatest Upper Bound [*Data processing*]
**GUB**........... Guerrero Negro [*Mexico*] [*Airport symbol*]
**GUB**........... Law School Library, University of Georgia, Athens, GA [*OCLC symbol*] (OCLC)
**GUBA**........ Growing Up Born Again [*Pronounced "goobah"*] [*Book published by Fleming H. Revell Co.*]
**GUBGF**..... General Union of Bellhangers and Gas Fitters [*British*]
**GUBI**......... Gemeinschaft Unabhangiger Beratender Ingenieurbueros [*Association of German Consulting Engineers*]
**GUBL**........ Beyla [*Guinea*] [*ICAO location identifier*] (ICLI)
**GUBR**........ Gentleman Usher of the Black Rod [*British*] (ROG)
**GUBSMW** ... General Union of Braziers and Sheet Metal Workers [*British*]
**GUBTW**.... General Union of Bedding Trade Workers [*British*]
**GUBU**........ Grotesque, Unbelievable, Bizarre, Unprecedented [*Term coined by an Irish politician to describe certain incidents in Irish politics*]
**GUC**........... Good-until-Canceled Order [*Business term*]
**GUC**........... Groupe d'Union Camerounaise [*Group for Cameroonian Union*]
**GUC**........... Gunnison [*Colorado*] [*Airport symbol*] (OAG)
**GUC**........... Union Catalog of the Atlanta-Athens Area, Atlanta, GA [*OCLC symbol*] (OCLC)
**GUCCIAAC** ... General Union of Chambers of Commerce, Industry, and Agriculture for Arab Countries [*Beirut, Lebanon*] (EAIO)
**GUCCO**..... Guidance Computer Control Subsystem
**GUCJ**......... General Union of Carpenters and Joiners [*British*]
**GUCL**........ General-Use Consumable List [*Military*]
**GUCO**........ Guilford Courthouse National Military Park
**GUCOTROIS** ... Great, Unopposable Commandant of the Realm of Inextinguishable Sagacity [*Rank in Junior Woodchucks organization mentioned in Donald Duck comic by Carl Barks*]
**GUCP**........ Ground Umbilical Carrier Plate (MCD)
**GUCY**........ Conakry/Gbessia [*Guinea*] [*ICAO location identifier*] (ICLI)
**GUD**.......... Goundam [*Mali*] [*Airport symbol*] (OAG)
**GUD**.......... Guardian Resources Corp. [*Vancouver Stock Exchange symbol*]
**GUDD**....... Didi [*Guinea*] [*ICAO location identifier*] (ICLI)
**GU-De**....... University of Georgia, DeRenne Georgia Library, Athens, GA [*Library symbol*] [*Library of Congress*] (LCLS)
**Gude Pr**...... Gude. Practice of the Crown Side of the Court of King's Bench [*1828*] [*A publication*] (DLA)
**GUDSPA**... General Union Democratic Students and Patriotic Afghan (EA)
**GUE**........... University of Guelph [*UTLAS symbol*]
**GUER**........ Guerilla
**GUERAP**... General Unwanted Energy Rejection Analysis Program [*Air Force*]
**Guern Eq Jur** ... Guernsey's Key to Equity Jurisprudence [*A publication*] (DLA)
**Guern Ins**... Guernsey on Questions of Insanity [*A publication*] (DLA)
**Guern Mech L** ... Guernsey's Mechanics' Lien Laws of New York [*A publication*] (DLA)
**Guertler Bijout Metallwaren Ind** ... Guertler. Bijouterie und Metallwaren Industrie [*A publication*]
**Guetersloher Beitr** ... Guetersloher Beitraege zur Heimatund Landeskunde [*A publication*]
**GUF**........... French Guiana [*ANSI three-letter standard code*] (CNC)
**GUFA**........ Fria [*Guinea*] [*ICAO location identifier*] (ICLI)
**GUFEX**...... Gulf Underwater Flare Experiment [*Marine science*] (MSC)
**GUFH**........ Faranah/Badala [*Guinea*] [*ICAO location identifier*] (ICLI)
**GuG**........... Gestalt und Gedanke. Ein Jahrbuch [*A publication*]
**GUG**.......... Guari [*Papua New Guinea*] [*Airport symbol*] (OAG)
**GuGIC**....... Instituto de Nutricion de Centro America y Panama, Guatemala City, Guatemala [*Library symbol*] [*Library of Congress*] (LCLS)
**GuGIN**....... Instituto Centroamericano de Investigacion y Tecnologia Industrial, Guatemala City, Guatemala [*Library symbol*] [*Library of Congress*]
**GUGL**........ Gaoual [*Guinea*] [*ICAO location identifier*] (ICLI)
**GUGO**....... Banankoro/Gbenko [*Guinea*] [*ICAO location identifier*] (ICLI)
**GUGR**........ Gentleman Usher of the Green Rod [*British*] (ROG)
**GuGS**......... Universidad de San Carlos de Guatemala, Ciudad Universitaria, Guatemala City, Guatemala [*Library symbol*] [*Library of Congress*] (LCLS)
**GUH**.......... Gunnedah [*Australia*] [*Airport symbol*] (OAG)
**GUHA**....... General Unary Hypothesis Automation (IEEE)
**GUI**............ Gay Union International [*Paris, France*] (EAIO)
**GUI**............ Graphical User Interface [*Data processing*] (PCM)
**GUI**............ Guiana (ROG)
**Gui**............ Guido de Cumis [*Flourished, 13th century*] [*Authority cited in pre-1607 legal work*] (DSA)
**Gui**............ Guido de Suzaria [*Deceased, 1293*] [*Authority cited in pre-1607 legal work*] (DSA)
**Gui**............ Guillelmus de Accursio [*Deceased, 1314*] [*Authority cited in pre-1607 legal work*] (DSA)
**Gui**............ Guillelmus de Tocco [*Authority cited in pre-1607 legal work*] (DSA)
**GUI**............ Guiria [*Venezuela*] [*Airport symbol*] (OAG)
**GUI**............ Guitar [*Music*]
**GUIAC**...... Guaiacum [*Lignum Vitae*] [*Pharmacy*] (ROG)
**Gui de Cu**... Guillelmus de Cuneo [*Deceased, 1335*] [*Authority cited in pre-1607 legal work*] (DSA)
**GUID**......... Guidance (AAG)
**GUID**......... Guidon Oil & Gas Co. [*NASDAQ symbol*] (NQ)
**GUID**......... Kindia [*Guinea*] [*ICAO location identifier*] (ICLI)
**GUIDE**...... General Usage Inventory Director (MCD)
**GUIDE**...... Guidance for Users of Integrated Data Processing Equipment
**Guideb Annu Field Conf Mont Geol Soc** ... Guidebook. Annual Field Conference. Montana Geological Society [*A publication*]
**Guideb Geol Utah** ... Guidebook to the Geology of Utah [*A publication*]
**Guideb Ser Geol Inst (Bucharest)** ... Guidebook Series. Geological Institute (Bucharest) [*A publication*]
**Guide Indian Period Lit** ... Guide to Indian Periodical Literature [*A publication*]
**Guidel Med** ... Guidelines in Medicine [*A publication*]
**Guide Perform Arts** ... Guide to the Performing Arts [*A publication*]
**Guide Relig Period** ... Guide to Religious Periodicals [*A publication*]
**Guide Relig Semi Relig Period** ... Guide to Religious and Semi-Religious Periodicals [*A publication*]
**Guide Rev Books Hisp Am** ... Guide to Reviews of Books from and about Hispanic America [*A publication*]
**Guide Soc Sci Relig Period Lit** ... Guide to Social Science and Religion in Periodical Literature [*A publication*]
**Guidhall Stud London Hist** ... Guildhall Studies in London History [*A publication*]
**GUIDN**...... Guidance (AABC)
**GUIDO**...... Guidance and Navigation Officer [*NASA*]
**GUIDO**...... Guidance Officer [*NASA*] (NASA)
**Guid Pancir** ... Guido Pancirolus [*Deceased, 1599*] [*Authority cited in pre-1607 legal work*] (DSA)
**Guid Pancirol** ... Guido Pancirolus [*Deceased, 1599*] [*Authority cited in pre-1607 legal work*] (DSA)
**Guid Pap**.... Guido Papa [*Deceased, 1487*] [*Authority cited in pre-1607 legal work*] (DSA)
**Guid Spec Educ Bull** ... Guidance and Special Education Bulletin [*A publication*] (APTA)
**Guil Bene**... Guillelmus de Benedictis [*Flourished, 16th century*] [*Authority cited in pre-1607 legal work*] (DSA)
**Guild C Psych** ... National Guild of Catholic Psychiatrists. Bulletin [*A publication*]
**GUILDF**.... Guildford [*City in England*] (ROG)
**Guildhall Misc** ... Guildhall Miscellany [*A publication*]
**Guildhall S** ... Guildhall Studies in London History [*A publication*]
**Guild Law**.. Guild Lawyer [*National Lawyers' Guild*] [*New York Chapter*] [*A publication*] (DLA)
**Guild Nts**... Guild Notes [*A publication*]
**Guild Prac**... Guild Practitioner [*A publication*]
**Guild Q**...... National Lawyers Guild Quarterly [*A publication*] (DLA)
**Guilford Law Behav Ser** ... Guilford Law and Behavior Series [*A publication*]
**Guill**........... Guillelmus Durandi [*Deceased, 1296*] [*Authority cited in pre-1607 legal work*] (DSA)
**Guillel Bened** ... Guillelmus de Benedictis [*Flourished, 16th century*] [*Authority cited in pre-1607 legal work*] (DSA)
**Guill de Montelaud** ... Guillelmus de Monte Lauduno [*Deceased, 1343*] [*Authority cited in pre-1607 legal work*] (DSA)
**Guil Na**...... Guillelmus Naso [*Flourished, 1220-34*] [*Authority cited in pre-1607 legal work*] (DSA)
**GUIMARC** ... Guidelines Marketing Corporation
**GUIN**......... Guinea [*Monetary unit*] [*Obsolete*] [*Great Britain*] (ROG)
**GUISA**...... Guide to Scientific Instruments [*A publication*]
**Gui de Su**.... Guido de Suzaria [*Deceased, 1293*] [*Authority cited in pre-1607 legal work*] (DSA)
**Gui de Suz** ... Guido de Suzaria [*Deceased, 1293*] [*Authority cited in pre-1607 legal work*] (DSA)
**Gui de Suza** ... Guido de Suzaria [*Deceased, 1293*] [*Authority cited in pre-1607 legal work*] (DSA)
**Guit**........... Guitar [*Music*]
**Guitar R**..... Guitar Review [*A publication*]

**Guitarra** ..... Guitarra Magazine [*A publication*]
**Guitar Rev** ... Guitar Review [*A publication*]
**Guiz**........... Guizzardinus [*Deceased, 1222*] [*Authority cited in pre-1607 legal work*] (DSA)
**Guizot Rep Govt** ... Guizot's History of Representative Government [*A publication*] (DLA)
**GUJ** ........... Guaratingueta [*Brazil*] [*Airport symbol*] (OAG)
**guj** ............. Gujarati [*MARC language code*] [*Library of Congress*] (LCCP)
**Gujarat Agric Univ Res J** ... Gujarat Agricultural University. Research Journal [*A publication*]
**Gujarat Statist Rev** ... Gujarat Statistical Review [*A publication*]
**Guj Ind**....... Gujarat, India (ILCA)
**Guj L Rep**... Gujarat Law Reporter [*A publication*] (ILCA)
**Guj LT** ....... Gujarat Law Times [*A publication*]
**GUJRD**...... Gomal University. Journal of Research [*A publication*]
**GUK**.......... Guanylate Kinase [*An enzyme*]
**GUKE**........ Kerouane [*Guinea*] [*ICAO location identifier*] (ICLI)
**GUKR**........ Glavnoe Upravlenie Kontrrazvedkoi [*Chief Administration for Counter-intelligence*] [*of the Ministry of War*] [*USSR*] [*World War II*]
**GUKR**........ Kamsar/Kawass [*Guinea*] [*ICAO location identifier*] (ICLI)
**GUKU**........ Kissidougou [*Guinea*] [*ICAO location identifier*] (ICLI)
**GUL**........... Georgetown University, Law Library, Washington, DC [*OCLC symbol*] (OCLC)
**GUL**........... GSE [*Ground Support Equipment*] Utilization List [*NASA*] (NASA)
**Gul** ............ Guillelmus de Cuneo [*Deceased, 1335*] [*Authority cited in pre-1607 legal work*] (DSA)
**GUL**........... Gull Air [*South Yarmouth, MA*] [*FAA designator*] (FAAC)
**GUL**........... Gulmarg [*India*] [*Geomagnetic observatory code*]
**GU-L**.......... University of Georgia, Law Library, Athens, GA [*Library symbol*] [*Library of Congress*] (LCLS)
**GULAG**..... Glavnoe Upravlenie Ispravitel'no-Trudovykh Lagerei [*Main Administration of Corrective Labor Camps*] [*USSR*]
**GULB** ........ Labe/Tata [*Guinea*] [*ICAO location identifier*] (ICLI)
**GULC** ........ Glasgow University Language Centre [*University of Glasgow*] [*United Kingdom*] (CB)
**GULD**........ Goulds Pumps, Inc. [*NASDAQ symbol*] (NQ)
**Gulf Caribb Fish Inst Univ Miami Proc** ... Gulf and Caribbean Fisheries Institute. University of Miami. Proceedings [*A publication*]
**Gulf Coast Assoc Geol Socs Trans** ... Gulf Coast Association of Geological Societies. Transactions [*A publication*]
**Gulf Coast Cattlem** ... Gulf Coast Cattleman [*A publication*]
**GULFCOBASESERVUNIT** ... Gulf Coast Base Service Unit
**GULFCON** ... Gulf Control
**GULFNAVFACENGCOM** ... Gulf Division Naval Facilities Engineering Command
**Gulf Res Rep** ... Gulf Research Reports [*A publication*]
**GULFSEAFRON** ... Gulf Sea Frontier
**GULL** ........ Gull Laboratories, Inc. [*NASDAQ symbol*] (NQ)
**GULP** ........ General Utility Library Program [*Data processing*]
**GULP** ........ Grenada United Labour Party [*Political party*] (PPW)
**GULP** ........ Group Universal Life Program
**GUM** ......... General Utility Mechanic
**GUM** ......... Glavny Universalny Magazin [*Department store in USSR*]
**GUM** ......... Gosudarstvennyi Universal'nyi Magazin [*Government Department Store*] [*Moscow*]
**GUM** ......... Grand Unified Monopoles [*Cosmology*]
**GUM** ......... Guadalajara [*Mexico*] [*Seismograph station code, US Geological Survey*] (SEIS)
**GUM** ......... Guam [*ANSI three-letter standard code*] (CNC)
**GUM** ......... Guam Island [*Mariana Islands*] [*Airport symbol*] (OAG)
**GUM** ......... Guild Mortgage Investments, Inc. [*AMEX symbol*] (SPSG)
**GUM** ......... Gulderand Mining [*Vancouver Stock Exchange symbol*]
**GUM** ......... Gummi, Asbest, Kunststoffe. Internationale Unabhangige Fachzeitschrift [*A publication*]
**GUMA**....... Macenta [*Guinea*] [*ICAO location identifier*] (ICLI)
**Gummi Asbest Kunstst** ... Gummi, Asbest, Kunststoffe [*Later, Gummi, Fasern, Kunststoffe*] [*A publication*]
**Gummi Fasern Kunstst** ... Gummi, Fasern, Kunststoffe [*A publication*]
**Gummi Kunst** ... Gummi, Asbest, Kunststoffe [*Later, Gummi, Fasern, Kunststoffe*] [*A publication*]
**Gummi Kunst** ... Gummi, Fasern, Kunststoffe [*A publication*]
**GUMO** ...... Guam [*Mariana Islands*] [*Seismograph station code, US Geological Survey*] (SEIS)
**GUMP**....... Gas, Undercarriage, Mixture, and Prop [*Checkout procedure*]
**GUMSL**..... Georgetown University. Monograph Series on Languages and Linguistics [*A publication*]
**GUN** .......... Gundle Environmental Systems, Inc. [*AMEX symbol*] (SPSG)
**GUN** .......... Gunnery (MSA)
**GUN** .......... Gunsteel Resources, Inc. [*Vancouver Stock Exchange symbol*]
**GUN** .......... Montgomery, AL [*Location identifier*] [*FAA*] (FAAL)
**Gunby** ........ Gunby's District Court Reports [*1885*] [*Louisiana*] [*A publication*] (DLA)
**Gunby (LA)** ... Gunby's District Court Reports [*1885*] [*Louisiana*] [*A publication*] (DLA)
**Gunby's Dec** ... Gunby's District Court Reports [*1805*] [*Louisiana*] [*A publication*] (DLA)
**Gundry**....... Gundry. Manuscripts in Lincoln's Inn Library [*A publication*] (DLA)
**GUNEX**..... Gunnery Exercise [*Navy*] (NVT)
**Gunma J Libr Arts Sci** ... Gunma Journal of Liberal Arts and Science [*A publication*]
**Gunma J Med Sci** ... Gunma Journal of Medical Sciences [*A publication*]
**Gunma J Med Sci Suppl** ... Gunma Journal of Medical Sciences. Supplementum [*A publication*]
**Gunma Rep Med Sci** ... Gunma Reports of Medical Sciences [*A publication*]
**Gunma Symp Endocrinol** ... Gunma Symposia on Endocrinology [*A publication*]
**GUN MOLL** ... Gonif's Molly [*Thief's Girl*] [*Yiddish*]
**Gunn Tolls** ... Gunning on Tolls [*A publication*] (DLA)
**GUNR**........ Gunnar Gold Mining, Inc. [*NASDAQ symbol*] (NQ)
**GUNSGT**.. Gunnery Sergeant
**GUNSS**...... Gunnery Schoolship [*Navy*] (NVT)
**Gunton** ....... Gunton's Magazine [*A publication*]
**GUNZ**........ N,Zerekore/Konia [*Guinea*] [*ICAO location identifier*] (ICLI)
**GUO** .......... Georgetown, TX [*Location identifier*] [*FAA*] (FAAL)
**GUO** .......... Greater Union Organisation [*Australia*]
**Guo**............. Guanosine [*Also, G*] [*A nucleoside*]
**GUOK**........ Boke/Baralande [*Guinea*] [*ICAO location identifier*] (ICLI)
**GUOOF**..... Grand United Order of Odd Fellows (EA)
**GUP**........... Gallup [*New Mexico*] [*Airport symbol*] (OAG)
**GUP**........... Gas Under Pressure
**GUP**........... Georgetown University. Papers on Languages and Linguistics [*A publication*]
**GU-P**.......... Grifora Umbellata Polysaccharide [*Antineoplastic drug*]
**GU-P**.......... University of Georgia, School of Pharmacy, Athens, GA [*Library symbol*] [*Library of Congress*] (LCLS)
**GUPAC** ..... Gulf Permanent Assistance Committee [*Persian Gulf*]
**GUPH**....... Group for the Use of Psychology in History (EA)
**Guppie**........ Gay Urban Professional [*Lifestyle classification*]
**GUPPY**...... Greater Underwater Propulsive Power [*Type of submarine*]
**GUQ** .......... Guanare [*Venezuela*] [*Airport symbol*] (OAG)
**GUR**........... Alotau [*Papua New Guinea*] [*Airport symbol*] (OAG)
**GUR**........... Government Union Review [*A publication*]
**GUR**........... Ground under Repair
**GUR**........... Gulfstream Resources Canada Ltd. [*Toronto Stock Exchange symbol*]
**GURC** ........ Gulf Universities Research Consortium (EA)
**GURID** ...... Gazzetta Ufficiale della Repubblica Italiana [*A publication*]
**GURR**........ Gentleman Usher of the Red Rod [*British*] (ROG)
**GURS** ........ Kouroussa [*Guinea*] [*ICAO location identifier*] (ICLI)
**GURT** ........ Georgetown University. Round Table on Languages and Linguistics [*A publication*]
**Gurukula Kangri Vishwavidyalaya J Sci Res** ... Gurukula Kangri Vishwavidyalaya. Journal of Scientific Research [*A publication*]
**GUS** ........... Generic Update System [*Data processing*]
**GUS** ........... Generic User System [*Data processing*]
**GUS** ........... Genitourinary System [*Medicine*]
**GUS** ........... Give Up Smoking [*Health Education Council campaign*] [*British*]
**GUS** ........... Glucuronidase [*An enzyme*]
**GUS** ........... Great Universal Stores [*Mail-order firm*] [*British*]
**GUS** ........... Group Unit Simulator (MCD)
**GUS** ........... Gunflint Resources Ltd. [*Vancouver Stock Exchange symbol*]
**GUS** ........... Gusset (MSA)
**GUS** ........... Peru, IN [*Location identifier*] [*FAA*] (FAAL)
**GUSA** ........ Sangaredi [*Guinea*] [*ICAO location identifier*] (ICLI)
**GUSB** ........ Guided Unified S-Band (MCD)
**GUSB** ........ Sambailo [*Guinea*] [*ICAO location identifier*] (ICLI)
**GUSER**...... GCOS Security Module
**GUSI**.......... Siguiri [*Guinea*] [*ICAO location identifier*] (ICLI)
**GUSSIES**.. Great Universal Stores [*Mail-order firm*] [*British*]
**GUSTO** ...... Guidance Using Stable Tuning Oscillations
**GUSYA** ..... Gunma Symposia on Endocrinology [*A publication*]
**GuT**............ Geist und Tat [*A publication*]
**GUT**........... Grand Unified Theory [*Cosmology*]
**GUT**........... Gulf Titanium Ltd. [*Vancouver Stock Exchange symbol*]
**GUT**........... Gutter (MSA)
**GUT**........... Pittsburgh, PA [*Location identifier*] [*FAA*] (FAAL)
**Gut Brac**..... Guterbock's Bracton [*A publication*] (DLA)
**Guth L & T** ... Guthrie's Landlord and Tenant [*A publication*] (DLA)
**Guth Pr** ...... Guthrie's Principles of the Laws of England [*1843*] [*A publication*] (DLA)
**Guthrie**....... Guthrie's Reports [*33-83 Missouri Appeals*] [*A publication*] (DLA)
**Guthrie**....... Guthrie's Sheriff Court Cases [*1861-92*] [*Scotland*] [*A publication*] (DLA)
**Guthrie Bull** ... Guthrie Bulletin [*A publication*]
**Guth Sh Cas** ... Guthrie's Sheriff Court Cases [*1861-92*] [*Scotland*] [*A publication*] (DLA)
**Guth Sher Cas** ... Guthrie's Sheriff Court Cases [*1861-92*] [*Scotland*] [*A publication*] (DLA)
**Guth Tr Un** ... Guthrie on Trade Unions [*A publication*] (DLA)
**GUTS** ........ General Understanding on Trade in Services [*International trade*]
**GUTS** ........ Georgians Unwilling to Surrender [*Organization founded by former governor, Lester Maddox*]
**GUTS** ........ Ground Up-to-Space (MCD)
**GUTS** ........ Guerilla Urban Traffic System [*Refers to driving in Boston*]
**gutt**............. Goutte [*Drop*] [*Pharmacy*]

**GUTT** ........ Guttae [*Drops of Liquid*] [*Pharmacy*]
**GUTT** ........ Gutturi [*To the Throat*] [*Pharmacy*]
**GUTTAT**... Guttatim [*Drop by Drop*] [*Pharmacy*] (GPO)
**GUTT QUIBUSD** ... Guttis Quibusdam [*With a Few Drops*] [*Pharmacy*]
**GUU** .......... Grundarfjordur [*Iceland*] [*Airport symbol*] (OAG)
**GUUG** ....... Gross Unit Unavailable Generation [*Electronics*] (IEEE)
**GUV**........... Gerecht und Volkommen [*Correct and Complete*] [*German*]
**GUV**........... Guri [*Venezuela*] [*Seismograph station code, US Geological Survey*] (SEIS)
**GuV-Rechnung** ... Gewinn-und-Verlust-Rechnung [*Profit and Loss Statement*] [*German*]
**GU/WQ**..... Washington Quarterly. Georgetown University Center for Strategic and International Studies [*A publication*]
**GUXD**........ Kankan/Diankana [*Guinea*] [*ICAO location identifier*] (ICLI)
**GUXUD**..... Guangxue Xuebao [*A publication*]
**GUY**........... French Guiana Space Center
**GUY**........... Guyana [*ANSI three-letter standard code*] (CNC)
**GUY**........... Guymon, OK [*Location identifier*] [*FAA*] (FAAL)
**Guyana Geol Surv Dep Rep** ... Guyana. Geological Survey Department. Report [*A publication*]
**Guyana J Sci** ... Guyana Journal of Science [*A publication*]
**Guyana Minist Agric Nat Resour Agric Land Dev Ann Rep** ... Guyana. Ministry of Agriculture and Natural Resources. Agriculture and Land Development Departments. Annual Report [*A publication*]
**Guyana Minist Agric Nat Resour Geol Surv Dep Rep** ... Guyana. Ministry of Agriculture and Natural Resources. Geological Survey Department. Report [*A publication*]
**Guyana Mist Agric Nat Resourc Agric Land Dev Dep Annu Rep** ... Guyana. Ministry of Agriculture and Natural Resources. Agriculture and Land Development Departments. Annual Report [*A publication*]
**Guyana Sugar Exp Stn Bull** ... Guyana Sugar Experiment Station's Bulletin [*A publication*]
**Guy For Med** ... Guy's Forensic Medicine [*7th ed.*] [*1895*] [*A publication*] (DLA)
**Guy Med Jur** ... Guy's Medical Jurisprudence [*A publication*] (DLA)
**Guyot Inst Feod** ... Guyot's Instituts Feodales [*A publication*] (DLA)
**Guy Rep**..... Guy's Repertoire de la Jurisprudence [*A publication*] (DLA)
**Guy's Hosp Gaz** ... Guy's Hospital Gazette [*A publication*]
**Guy's Hosp Rep** ... Guy's Hospital Reports [*A publication*]
**GuZ**............ Geist und Zeit [*A publication*]
**G vs V**......... Deceleration Units of Gravity Versus Velocity (KSC)
**GV**............. Galvanized [*Technical drawings*]
**GV**............. Genital Vein
**GV**............. Gentian Violet [*Also, MRC*] [*A dye*]
**GV**............. Gigavolt
**GV**............. Gil Vicente [*A publication*]
**GV**............. Goerz-Visier [*Bomb sight manufactured by Goerz Co.*] [*German military - World War II*]
**GV**............. Goldfield Corp. [*AMEX symbol*] (SPSG)
**GV**............. Governor (DSUE)
**GV**............. Grande Vitesse [*French high-speed train*]
**GV**............. Granulosis Virus
**GV**............. Gravimetric Volume
**G-V** ........... Gravity-Velocity (MCD)
**GV**............. Great Value [*In automobile name Yugo GV*]
**GV**............. Green Valley [*Plant pathology*]
**GV**............. Grid Variation [*Navigation*]
**GV**............. Gross Virus [*Leukemogenesis*] [*Immunochemistry*]
**GV**............. Ground Visibility
**GV**............. Growth Vessel
**GV**............. Guard Vessel [*Nuclear energy*] (NRCH)
**gv**............... Guinea [*MARC country of publication code*] [*Library of Congress*] (LCCP)
**GV**............. Talair Pty. Ltd. [*New Guinea*] [*ICAO designator*] (FAAC)
**GVA**........... Gamewardens of Vietnam Association (EA)
**GVA**........... Gay Veterans Association (EA)
**GVA**........... General Visceral Afferent [*Neurology*]
**GVA**........... Geneva [*Switzerland*] [*Airport symbol*] (OAG)
**GVA**........... Geschichte Vorderasien bis zum Hellenismus [*A publication*] (BJA)
**GVA**........... Golden Nevada [*Vancouver Stock Exchange symbol*]
**GVA**........... Golden Nevada Resources, Inc. [*Toronto Stock Exchange symbol*]
**GVA**........... Goulburn Valley Airlines [*Australia*]
**GVA**........... GOX [*Gaseous Oxygen*] Vent Arm (NASA)
**GVA**........... Graphic Kilovolt-Ampere [*Meter*] (MSA)
**GVA**........... Groningsche Volksalmanach [*A publication*]
**GVA**........... Gyroscope Vibration Absorber
**GVA**........... Henderson, KY [*Location identifier*] [*FAA*] (FAAL)
**GVAC** ........ Amilcar Cabral International/Sal Island [*Cape Verde*] [*ICAO location identifier*] (ICLI)
**GVAC** ........ Graphic Video Attributes Controller [*Computer chip*]
**GVaS** ......... Valdosta State College, Valdosta, GA [*Library symbol*] [*Library of Congress*] (LCLS)
**GVB** ........... Generalized Valence Bond [*Physics*]
**GVB** ........... Geschriften van de Vereniging voor Belastingswetenschap [*A publication*]
**GVB** ........... Guaranteed Voltage Breakdown
**GVBA** ........ Boavista, Boavista Island [*Cape Verde*] [*ICAO location identifier*] (ICLI)
**GVBD**......... Germinal Vesicle Breakdown [*Cytology*]
**GVC**........... General Videotex Corporation
**GVC**........... Glazed Vitrified Clay
**GVC**........... Grand View College [*Iowa*]
**GVC**........... Graphics Vendor Control
**GVC**........... Guild Vector Colorimeter
**GVD**........... Group View Display (MCD)
**GVDSB**...... Government Data Systems [*A publication*]
**GVDSN** ..... Gott Verlaeszt die Seinen Nicht [*God Forsakes Not His Own*] [*German*] [*Motto of Dorothee, Duchess of Braunschweig-Wolfenbuttel (1607-34)*]
**GVE** ........... General Visceral Efferent [*Neurology*]
**GVE** ........... Gordonsville, VA [*Location identifier*] [*FAA*] (FAAL)
**GVE** ........... Group Value Engineering
**GVE** ........... Grove (ADA)
**GVEN** ........ Growth Ventures, Inc. [*Colorado Springs, CO*] [*NASDAQ symbol*] (NQ)
**G Veneto Sci Med** ... Giornale Veneto di Scienze Mediche [*A publication*]
**GVF** ........... Garnisonsverwendungsfaehig Feld [*Fit for Garrison Duty in the Field*] [*German military - World War II*]
**GVF** ........... Golden Valley Microwave Foods, Inc. [*NYSE symbol*] (SPSG)
**GVF** ........... Grazhdanskii Vozdushnyi Flot [*Civil Air Fleet*] [*USSR*]
**GVFM** ....... Francisco Mendes, Santiago Island [*Cape Verde*] [*ICAO location identifier*] (ICLI)
**GVG**........... Gamma-Vinyl-GABA [*Biochemistry*]
**GVG**........... Giving (FAAC)
**GVG**........... Grundriss der Vergleichenden Grammatik der Semitischen Sprachen [*A publication*] (BJA)
**GVGC** ........ Grand Valley Gas Co. [*NASDAQ symbol*] (NQ)
**GVGSS**...... Grundriss der Vergleichenden Grammatik der Semitischen Sprachen [*A publication*] (BJA)
**GVH** .......... Garnisonsverwendungsfaehig Heimat [*Fit for Garrison Duty in Zone of Interior*] [*German military - World War II*]
**GVH** .......... Government Vehicle (FAAC)
**GVH** .......... Graft Versus Host [*Immunology*]
**GVHBCIFC** ... Gene Vincent and His Blue Caps International Fan Club (EAIO)
**GVHD** ....... Graft-Versus-Host Disease [*Immunology*]
**GVHR**........ Graft-Versus-Host Reaction [*Immunology*]
**GVHRR**..... Geosynchronous Very-High-Resolution Radiometer
**GVI** ........... Gas Vent Institute [*Inactive*] (EA)
**GVI** ........... Green River [*Papua New Guinea*] [*Airport symbol*] (OAG)
**GVIAO** ...... Gross Value of Industrial and Agricultural Output
**GVidO** ...... Ohoopee Regional Library, Vidalia, GA [*Library symbol*] [*Library of Congress*] (LCLS)
**GVKIA**....... Godishnik na Visshiya Khimikotekhnologicheski Institut [*A publication*]
**GVL** ........... Gainesville, GA [*Location identifier*] [*FAA*] (FAAL)
**GVL** ........... Gold Vapor LASER [*Physics*]
**GVL** ........... Gold Ventures Ltd. [*Vancouver Stock Exchange symbol*]
**GVL** ........... Gravel (KSC)
**G/VLLD**.... Ground/Vehicular LASER Locator Designator (RDA)
**GVMA**....... Maio, Maio Island [*Cape Verde*] [*ICAO location identifier*] (ICLI)
**GVMDS** .... Ground Vehicle Mine Dispensing System [*Military*]
**GVMF** ....... Golden Valley Microwave Foods, Inc. [*NASDAQ symbol*] (NQ)
**GVMI** ........ GV Medical, Incorporated [*Minneapolis, MN*] [*NASDAQ symbol*] (NQ)
**GVMKD**.... Gibridnye Vychislitel'nye Mashiny i Kompleksy [*A publication*]
**GVMR**....... Gross Vehicle Mass Rating [*Load that a vehicle can carry*]
**GVMT**....... Mosteiros, Fogo Island [*Cape Verde*] [*ICAO location identifier*] (ICLI)
**GVN**........... Goodyear Video Network [*Training and motivational program*]
**GVN**........... Government of Vietnam
**GVO**........... Gaviota, CA [*Location identifier*] [*FAA*] (FAAL)
**GVO**........... Graeber-Verwaltungsoffizier [*Graves Registration Officer*] [*German military - World War II*]
**GVP** ........... Gesamtdeutsche Volkspartei [*All-German People's Party*] [*Federal Republic of Germany*] [*Political party*] (PPE)
**GVP** ........... Gravis Computer Peripherals, Inc. [*Vancouver Stock Exchange symbol*]
**GVP** ........... Greater Victoria Public Library [*UTLAS symbol*]
**GVP** ........... Group Visionary Productions, Inc. [*Studio City, CA*] [*Telecommunications*] (TSSD)
**GVPF**......... Guinea Pig Vascular Permeability Factor [*Biochemistry*]
**GVPR** ........ Praia/Praia, Santiago Island [*Cape Verde*] [*ICAO location identifier*] (ICLI)
**GVQ**........... Batavia, NY [*Location identifier*] [*FAA*] (FAAL)
**GVR**........... Glyn Valley Railway [*Formerly, E & GVR*] [*Wales*]
**GVR**........... Governador Valadares [*Brazil*] [*Airport symbol*] (OAG)
**GVR**........... Granville Resources, Inc. [*Vancouver Stock Exchange symbol*]
**GVR**........... Green Valley Road [*California*] [*Seismograph station code, US Geological Survey*] (SEIS)
**GVRAA** ..... Government Reports Announcements [*United States*] [*A publication*]
**GVS** ........... Government Vehicle Service [*Postal Service*]

**GVS** .......... Graniteville [*South Carolina*] [*Seismograph station code, US Geological Survey*] [*Closed*] (SEIS)
**GVS** .......... Ground Vibration Survey [*Aerospace*]
**GVSC** .......... Sal Oceanic Area Control Center [*Cape Verde*] [*ICAO location identifier*] (ICLI)
**GVSF** .......... Sao Felipe, Fogo Island [*Cape Verde*] [*ICAO location identifier*] (ICLI)
**GVSN** .......... Sao Nicolau, Sao Nicolau Island [*Cape Verde*] [*ICAO location identifier*] (ICLI)
**GV-SOLAS** ... Gesellschaft fuer Versuchstierkunde - Society of Laboratory Animal Science [*Birsfelden, Switzerland*] (EAIO)
**GVSU** .......... Grand Valley State University [*Michigan*]
**GVSV** .......... Sao Vicente, Sao Vicente Island [*Cape Verde*] [*ICAO location identifier*] (ICLI)
**GVT** .......... Dean Witter Government Income Trust SBI [*NYSE symbol*] (SPSG)
**GVT** .......... Gated Video Tracker
**GVT** .......... Glenvet Resources Ltd. [*Vancouver Stock Exchange symbol*]
**GVT** .......... Gravity Vacuum Tube System [*High-speed ground transportation*]
**GVT** .......... Greenville, TX [*Location identifier*] [*FAA*] (FAAL)
**GVT** .......... Ground Vibration Test [*Aerospace*] (MCD)
**GVTA** .......... Ground Vibration Test Article [*Aerospace*] (NASA)
**GVTKA** .......... Galvanotechnik [*A publication*]
**Gvt and Opposition** ... Government and Opposition [*A publication*]
**GVTY** .......... Gingivectomy [*Dentistry*]
**GVV** .......... Grangeville, ID [*Location identifier*] [*FAA*] (FAAL)
**GVW** .......... Grandview, MO [*Location identifier*] [*FAA*] (FAAL)
**GVW** .......... Gross Vehicle Weight (MCD)
**GVWR** .......... Gross Vehicle Weight Rating
**GVX** .......... Extra-Great Value [*In automobile name Yugo GVX*]
**GVX** .......... Gavle [*Sweden*] [*Airport symbol*] (OAG)
**GVX** .......... Grove Explorations Ltd. [*Vancouver Stock Exchange symbol*]
**GVX** .......... Gruver, TX [*Location identifier*] [*FAA*] (FAAL)
**GVY** .......... Green Valley Mine [*Vancouver Stock Exchange symbol*]
**GW** .......... Air Force Guide for Writing
**GW** .......... Cases in the Griqualand West Local Division of the Supreme Court [*1910-46*] [*South Africa*] [*A publication*] (DLA)
**GW** .......... Gambia Airways [*ICAO designator*] (FAAC)
**GW** .......... Game Winning [*Baseball*]
**GW** .......... General Warning
**GW** .......... General Will [*Collectivist theory of government*]
**GW** .......... Genesis West [*A publication*]
**GW** .......... George Washington [*US general and president, 1732-1799*]
**GW** .......... George Washington Law Review [*A publication*]
**GW** .......... George Washington University [*Washington, DC*]
**GW** .......... Germ Warfare
**GW** .......... Germanica Wratislaviensia [*A publication*]
**gw** .......... Germany, West [*MARC country of publication code*] [*Library of Congress*] (LCCP)
**GW** .......... Gigawatt
**GW** .......... Glauben und Wissen (BJA)
**GW** .......... Global Water (EA)
**G/W** .......... Glucose in Water [*Medicine*]
**GW** .......... Glycerine in Water [*Medicine*]
**GW** .......... Good Weekend [*A publication*]
**GW** .......... Good Words [*A publication*] (ROG)
**GW** .......... Grand Warder [*Freemasonry*]
**GW** .......... Great Writers [*A publication*]
**GW** .......... Grenzwache [*Frontier Guard*] [*German military - World War II*]
**GW** .......... Gross Weight (NG)
**GW** .......... Ground Waves (NATG)
**GW** .......... Groundwork for a Just World (EA)
**GW** .......... Growth [*Business term*]
**GW** .......... Guardian Weekly [*A publication*]
**GW** .......... Guerrilla Warfare (AABC)
**GW** .......... Guided Weapon [*Air Force*]
**GW** .......... Guided Wire [*British military*] (DMA)
**GW** .......... Guinea-Bissau [*ANSI two-letter standard code*] (CNC)
**G & W** .......... Gulf & Western Industries, Inc.
**GW** .......... Gymnasium und Wissenschaft [*A publication*]
**G2W** .......... Glaube in der 2. Welt [*Faith in the Second World - FSW*] [*Zollikon-Zurich, Switzerland*] (EAIO)
**GWA** .......... General Work Area [*NASA*] (NASA)
**GWA** .......... Gewerbearchiv. Zeitschrift fuer Gewerbeverwaltungsrecht und Wirtschaftsverwaltungsrecht [*A publication*]
**GWA** .......... Golden West Airlines [*Los Angeles, CA*] [*FAA designator*] (FAAC)
**GWA** .......... Grand Worthy Associate [*Freemasonry*] (ROG)
**GWA** .......... Greater Washington Investors, Inc. [*AMEX symbol*] (SPSG)
**GWA** .......... International PEN - Guatemalan Writers Abroad (EA)
**GWAA** .......... Garden Writers Association of America (EA)
**GWAA** .......... Golf Writers Association of America (EA)
**GWAD** .......... Great Warbirds Air Display [*British*]
**GWAH** .......... Global Women of African Heritage (EA)
**GWAI** .......... German Workshop on Artificial Intelligence [*A publication*]
**GWASA** .......... Gas, Wasser, Abwasser [*A publication*]
**GWasB** .......... Bartram Trail Regional Library, Washington, GA [*Library symbol*] [*Library of Congress*] (LCLS)
**GWAY** .......... Galway [*County in Ireland*] (ROG)
**GWAY** .......... Gateway Communications, Inc. [*Irvine, CA*] [*NASDAQ symbol*] (NQ)
**GWayC** .......... Waycross Junior College, Waycross, GA [*Library symbol*] [*Library of Congress*] (LCLS)
**GWAZB** .......... Gott Wende Alles zum Besten [*May God Turn Everything to the Best*] [*German*] [*Motto of Amoene Amalie, Princess of Anhalt (d. 1626)*]
**GWB** .......... Gesetz Gegen Wettbewerbsbeschrankungen [*German Law Against Restraint of Competition*] (DLA)
**GWB** .......... Glycosylated Whole Blood [*Clinical chemistry*]
**GWB** .......... Gypsum Wallboard [*Technical drawings*]
**GWBB** .......... Greenwood Bank of Bethel, Inc. [*NASDAQ symbol*] (NQ)
**GWBC** .......... Governor William Bradford Compact [*An association*] (EA)
**GWC** .......... Gardner-Webb College [*Boiling Springs, NC*]
**GWC** .......... George Williams College [*Downer's Grove, IL*]
**GWC** .......... Global Weather Central
**GWC** .......... Grand Worthy Chief [*Templars*] [*Freemasonry*] (ROG)
**GWC** .......... Great Whale River [*Quebec*] [*Seismograph station code, US Geological Survey*] [*Closed*] (SEIS)
**GWC** .......... Great Whale River [*Quebec*] [*Geomagnetic observatory code*]
**GWC** .......... Ground Water Council [*Defunct*]
**GWC** .......... Guard Well Capacitor
**GWC** .......... Omaha, NE [*Location identifier*] [*FAA*] (FAAL)
**GWC** .......... West Georgia College, Carrollton, GA [*OCLC symbol*] (OCLC)
**GWCA** .......... George Washington Carver National Monument
**GWCC** .......... Georgia World Congress Center
**GWCC** .......... GWC Corp. [*NASDAQ symbol*] (NQ)
**GW CHAP** ... Grand Worthy Chaplain [*Templars*] [*Freemasonry*] (ROG)
**GWCI** .......... Giftware Manufacturers' Credit Interchange [*Buffalo, NY*] (EA)
**GWCSA** .......... Greater World Christian Spiritualist Association (EA)
**GWCSWBD** ... Gunnery Weapon Control Switchboard
**GWCT** .......... Grand Worthy Chief Templar [*Templars*] [*Freemasonry*] (ROG)
**GWD** .......... Gaseous Waste Disposal [*System*] [*Nuclear energy*] (NRCH)
**GWD** .......... Grinding Wheel Dresser
**GWD** .......... Gwadar [*Pakistan*] [*Airport symbol*] (OAG)
**GWD** .......... South African Law Reports, Griqualand West Local Division [*A publication*] (DLA)
**GWDM** .......... Grand Worthy Deputy Marshal [*Templars*] [*Freemasonry*] (ROG)
**GWDRS** .......... Ground Winds Data Reduction System [*NASA*]
**GWe** .......... Gigawatt Electrical
**GWE** .......... Global Weather Experiment [*Marine science*] (MSC)
**GWE** .......... Glycerin and Water Enema [*Medicine*]
**GWE** .......... Gwelo [*Zimbabwe*] [*Airport symbol*] (OAG)
**GWEN** .......... Ground Wave Emergency Network
**GWeP** .......... West Point-Pepperell, Inc., West Point, GA [*Library symbol*] [*Library of Congress*] (LCLS)
**GWESF** .......... Guided Weapons and Electronics Support Facility [*Australia*]
**GWF** .......... Galveston Wharves [*AAR code*]
**GWF** .......... Gating Waveform
**GWF** .......... Graphik Visuelles Marketing [*A publication*]
**GWF** .......... Great Western Financial Corp. [*NYSE symbol*] (SPSG)
**GWF** .......... Lancaster, CA [*Location identifier*] [*FAA*] (FAAL)
**GWFN** .......... Global Weather Facsimile Network (MCD)
**GWG** .......... Game-Winning Goals [*Hockey*]
**GWG** .......... Gaussian Wave Group [*Physics*]
**GWG** .......... Gottes Wille Geschehe [*God's Will Be Done*] [*German*] [*Motto of Juliane Ursula, Margravine of Baden (d. 1614)*]
**GWG** .......... Gullwing Group (EA)
**GWGI** .......... Gullwing Group International (EA)
**GWh** .......... Gigawatt-Hour
**GWH** .......... Great Water Holt (EA)
**GWH** .......... Guided Warheads
**G & Wh Eas** ... Gale and Whatley [*later, Gale*] on Easements [*A publication*] (ILCA)
**GWHF** .......... George Williams Hooper Foundation [*Research center*] (RCD)
**GWHJD** .......... Ground Water Heat Pump Journal [*A publication*]
**GWI** .......... Galvanized Wrought Iron (ADA)
**GWI** .......... Government-Wide Index [*Later, USGRDR*]
**GWI** .......... Grinding Wheel Institute (EA)
**GWI** .......... Ground Water Institute (EA)
**G & WI** .......... Gulf & Western Industries, Inc.
**GWIBIT** .......... Guild of Washington Incompetent Bureaucratic Ideal Throatcutters [*An organization rumored to have been active in World War II*]
**GWIC** .......... Geothermal World Info Center [*Later, REIC*] (EA)
**GWIG** .......... Grand Worthy Inside Guard [*Templars*] [*Freemasonry*] (ROG)
**GWIGWO** ... Good Will In, Good Will Out [*Data processing*]
**Gwil** .......... Gwillim's Tithe Cases [*England*] [*1224-1824*] [*A publication*] (DLA)
**Gwill** .......... Gwillim's Tithe Cases [*England*] [*A publication*] (DLA)
**Gwill Bac Abr** ... Gwillim's Tithe Cases [*England*] [*A publication*] (DLA)
**Gwill T Cas** ... Gwillim's Tithe Cases [*England*] [*A publication*] (DLA)
**Gwill Ti Cas** ... Gwillim's Tithe Cases [*England*] [*A publication*] (DLA)
**Gwil Ti Cas** ... Gwillim's Tithe Cases [*England*] [*A publication*] (DLA)
**GWIN** .......... Goodwin Railroad, Inc. [*AAR code*]
**GWIRD** .......... Government-Wide Index to Research and Development
**GWJ** .......... Chicopee Falls, MA [*Location identifier*] [*FAA*] (FAAL)

**GWJ** .......... Glue Weld Joint
**GWJC** ........ Gardner-Webb Junior College [*Later, Gardner-Webb College*] [*North Carolina*]
**GWL** .......... George Washington University, Law Library, Washington, DC [*OCLC symbol*] (OCLC)
**GWL** .......... Great-West Life Assurance Co. [*Toronto Stock Exchange symbol*]
**GWL** .......... Grosswetterlage [*Meteorology*]
**GWL** .......... Gwalior [*India*] [*Airport symbol*] (OAG)
**GWL** .......... Reports of Cases Decided in the Supreme Court of South Africa (Griqualand West Local Division), by Kitchin [*A publication*] (DLA)
**GWLD** ....... South Africa Law Reports, Griqualand West Local Division [*A publication*] (DLA)
**GW LR** ...... George Washington Law Review [*A publication*]
**GWLRA** .... George Washington Law Review [*A publication*]
**GWM** ......... Gay White Male [*Classified advertising*]
**GWM** ......... George Washington University, Medical Library, Washington, DC [*OCLC symbol*] (OCLC)
**GWM** ......... Gewerkschaftliche Monatshefte [*A publication*]
**GWM** ......... Grand Worthy Marshal [*Templars*] [*Freemasonry*] (ROG)
**GWM** ......... Guam Tracking Station [*NASA*] (KSC)
**GWM** ......... Guaranteed Weekly Minimum
**GWMC** ...... Galvanized Ware Manufacturers Council (EA)
**GWMD** ...... Ground Water Management District
**GWMR** ...... Ground Water Monitoring Review [*A publication*]
**GW & MRJS** ... Great Western & Midland Railway Joint Stock [*British*] (ROG)
**GWMS** ...... Gas-Water Module Storage [*Nuclear energy*] (NRCH)
**GWMS** ...... Gaseous Waste Management System [*Nuclear energy*] (NRCH)
**GWN** ......... Goldwinn Resources Ltd. [*Vancouver Stock Exchange symbol*]
**G & W New Tr** ... Graham and Waterman on New Trials [*A publication*] (DLA)
**GWNRF** .... Goldwinn Resources Ltd. [*NASDAQ symbol*] (NQ)
**GWO** ......... General Watch Officer [*Army*] (AABC)
**GWO** ......... Great-West Lifeco, Inc. [*Toronto Stock Exchange symbol*]
**GWO** ......... Greenwood [*Mississippi*] [*Airport symbol*] (OAG)
**GWOA** ....... Guerrilla Warfare Operational Area [*Army*]
**GWOG** ...... Grand Worthy Outside Guard [*Templars*] [*Freemasonry*] (ROG)
**GWO & HP** ... Gas Wall Oven and Hot Plate [*Classified advertising*] (ADA)
**GWOX** ....... [*The*] Goodheart-Wilcox Co., Inc. [*NASDAQ symbol*] (NQ)
**GWP** .......... Gesellschaft fuer Wirtschaftspublizistik GmbH [*Society for Public Economics*] (IID)
**GWP** .......... Gift with Purchase
**GWP** .......... Government White Paper
**GWP** .......... Grand Worthy Patriarch [*Freemasonry*] (ROG)
**GWP** .......... Great Western Petroleum Corp. [*Vancouver Stock Exchange symbol*]
**GWP** .......... Gross World Product
**GWP** .......... Guided Writing Procedure [*Reading improvement method*]
**GWPCA** ..... German Wirehaired Pointer Club of America (EA)
**GWPS** ....... Gaseous Waste Processing System [*Nuclear energy*] (NRCH)
**GWpSO** ..... Group Weapons Staff Officer [*British military*] (DMA)
**GWPU** ....... General Workers Professional Unions [*Bulgaria*]
**GWQ** ......... GWR Resources [*Vancouver Stock Exchange symbol*]
**GWQ** ......... San Francisco, CA [*Location identifier*] [*FAA*] (FAAL)
**GWQAP** .... Government-Wide Quality Assurance Program
**GWQE** ....... General Water-Quality Engineering [*Survey*] [*Army*] (RDA)
**GWR** ......... General War Reserves [*Army*] (AABC)
**GWR** ......... Gill Withdrawal Reflex
**GWR** ......... [*The*] Great Western Railway Co. [*Prior to nationalization*] [*AAR code*]
**GWR** ......... Great World Resources [*Vancouver Stock Exchange symbol*]
**GWR** ......... Griqualand High Court Reports [*A publication*] (DLA)
**GWR** ......... Gwinner, ND [*Location identifier*] [*FAA*] (FAAL)
**GW-RBI** .... Game-Winning Run Batted In [*Baseball*]
**GWRI** ....... Ground Water Resources Institute [*Later, Ground Water Council*]
**GWRRA** .... Gold Wing Road Riders Association (EA)
**GWS** ......... Gar Wood Society (EA)
**GWS** ......... Gaseous Waste System [*Nuclear energy*] (NRCH)
**GWS** ......... GEEIA [*Ground Electronics Engineering Installation Agency*] Workload Schedule (AFM)
**GWS** ......... General War Subsystem (MCD)
**GWS** ......... Geneva Convention for the Amelioration of the Condition of the Wounded and Sick in Armed Forces in the Field, 12 August 1949 [*Army*] (AABC)
**GWS** ......... Glashow-Weinberg-Salam Theories [*Physics*]
**GWS** ......... Glenwood Springs, CO [*Location identifier*] [*FAA*] (FAAL)
**GWS** ......... Grand Worthy Scribe [*Templars*] [*Freemasonry*] (ROG)
**GWS** ......... Great West Steel Industries Ltd. [*Toronto Stock Exchange symbol*] [*Vancouver Stock Exchange symbol*]
**GWS** ......... Great Western Airlines, Inc. [*Tulsa, OK*] [*FAA designator*] (FAAC)
**GWS** ......... Great Western Society (EA)
**GWS** ......... Gun Weapon System [*Military*] (CAAL)
**GWS** ......... Gwil Industries, Inc. [*Toronto Stock Exchange symbol*] [*Vancouver Stock Exchange symbol*]
**GWS 1929** ... Geneva Convention for the Amelioration of the Condition of the Wounded and Sick in Armed Forces in the Field, 27 July 1929 [*Army*]
**GWS-A & L** ... Girl Watchers Society - Ankle and Leg Division
**GWSB** ....... Great Western Savings Bank [*NASDAQ symbol*] (NQ)
**GWSF** ....... Georgia Warm Springs Foundation [*Later, RWSF*] (EA)
**GWSH** ....... George Washington Corp. [*NASDAQ symbol*] (NQ)
**Gw Sh** ........ Gwynne on Sheriffs [*A publication*] (DLA)
**GWSI** ........ Great Western Systems, Incorporated [*NASDAQ symbol*] (NQ)
**GWSIP** ...... Gun Weapon System Improvement Program [*Military*] (CAAL)
**GWSR** ....... General Wage Stabilization Regulations [*United States*] (DLA)
**GWSRP** ..... Gun Weapon System Replacement Program (NVT)
**GWS Sea** ... Geneva Convention for the Amelioration of the Condition of the Wounded, Sick, and Shipwrecked Members of the Armed Forces at Sea, 12 August 1949 [*Army*] (AABC)
**GWSTV** ..... Golden West Subscription Television [*Cable TV programming service*]
**GWT** .......... Chicopee Falls, MA [*Location identifier*] [*FAA*] (FAAL)
**GWt** .......... Gigawatt Thermal
**GWT** .......... Glazed Wall Tile [*Technical drawings*]
**GWT** .......... Grand Worthy Templar [*Templars*] [*Freemasonry*] (ROG)
**GWT** .......... Gross Weight
**GWT** .......... Ground Winds Tower [*NASA*] (NASA)
**GWT** .......... GW Utilities Ltd. [*AMEX symbol*] [*Toronto Stock Exchange symbol*] [*Vancouver Stock Exchange symbol*] (SPSG)
**GWT** .......... Westerland [*West Germany*] [*Airport symbol*] (OAG)
**GWTA** ....... Gift Wrappings and Tyings Association [*Defunct*] (EA)
**GWTB** ....... Glazed Wall Tile Base [*Technical drawings*]
**GWTI** ........ Groundwater Technology, Incorporated [*Norwood, MA*] [*NASDAQ symbol*] (NQ)
**GW TREAS** ... Grand Worthy Treasurer [*Templars*] [*Freemasonry*] (ROG)
**GWTUF** .... Government Workers' Trade Union Federation [*Ceylon*]
**GWTW** ...... Gone with the Wind [*A novel by Margaret Mitchell; also, a motion picture*]
**GWU** .......... Gambia Workers' Union
**GWU** .......... General Workers Union [*Malta*]
**GWU** .......... George Washington University [*Washington, DC*]
**GWU** .......... Granite Workers' Union [*British*]
**GWU** .......... International Glove Workers' Union of America [*Later, ACTWU*]
**GWV** .......... Glendale, WV [*Location identifier*] [*FAA*] (FAAL)
**GWVA** ....... Great War Veterans' Association [*Canada*]
**GWVT** ....... Grand Worthy Vice Templar [*Templars*] [*Freemasonry*] (ROG)
**GWW** ......... Goldsboro, NC [*Location identifier*] [*FAA*] (FAAL)
**GWW** ......... Grainger, [*W. W.*] Inc. [*NYSE symbol*] (SPSG)
**GWW** ......... Guaranteed Weekly Wage
**GWWAA** ... GWF. Gas- und Wasserfach: Wasser/Abwasser [*A publication*]
**GWWS** ...... Gott Wirds Wohl Schaffen [*God Will Arrange*] [*German*] [*Motto of Dorothee Auguste, Duchess of Braunschweig (1577-1625)*]
**GWY** .......... Galway [*Ireland*] [*Airport symbol*]
**GWY** .......... Gateway Aviation Ltd. [*Edmonton, AB*] [*FAA designator*] (FAAC)
**GWY** .......... Goldways Resources [*Vancouver Stock Exchange symbol*]
**GWY** .......... Gwynedd-Mercy College, Gwynedd, PA [*OCLC symbol*] (OCLC)
**GX** ............. GEO International Corp. [*NYSE symbol*] (SPSG)
**GX** ............. Global International Airways [*ICAO designator*] (FAAC)
**GX** ............. Glycinxylidide [*Biochemistry*]
**Gx** ............. Graded Exercise
**GXA** ........... Gunn-Diode X-Band Amplifier
**GXD** ........... General X-Ray Diagnosis [*Medicine*]
**GXG** ........... Negage [*Angola*] [*Airport symbol*] (OAG)
**GXI** ............ Glenex Industries, Inc. [*Vancouver Stock Exchange symbol*]
**GXL** ........... Granges, Inc. [*AMEX symbol*] [*Toronto Stock Exchange symbol*] (SPSG)
**GXL** ........... Grinnell, IA [*Location identifier*] [*FAA*] (FAAL)
**GXM** .......... Gordex Minerals Ltd. [*Toronto Stock Exchange symbol*]
**GXM** .......... Medical College of Georgia, Augusta, GA [*OCLC symbol*] (OCLC)
**GXMN** ....... Gordex Minerals Ltd. [*NASDAQ symbol*] (NQ)
**G/XMTR** ... Guidance Transmitter (AAG)
**GXO** ........... Butler, PA [*Location identifier*] [*FAA*] (FAAL)
**GXQ** ........... Coyhaique [*Chile*] [*Airport symbol*]
**GXS** ........... Goldex Resources [*Vancouver Stock Exchange symbol*]
**GXSP** ......... Guierrezia Xylem Sap Potential [*Botany*]
**GXT** ........... Graded Exercise Testing
**GXU** ........... Wrightstown, NJ [*Location identifier*] [*FAA*] (FAAL)
**GXV** ........... Golden Exodus [*Vancouver Stock Exchange symbol*]
**GXY** ........... Galaxy Carpet Mills, Inc. [*AMEX symbol*] (SPSG)
**GXY** ........... Galaxy Industry Ltd. [*Vancouver Stock Exchange symbol*]
**GXY** ........... Greeley, CO [*Location identifier*] [*FAA*] (FAAL)
**GY** ............. Galley
**GY** ............. Galley-Yarn [*Crooked*] [*Slang*] [*British*] (DSUE)
**GY** ............. Gardan [*France*] [*ICAO aircraft manufacturer identifier*] (ICAO)
**GY** ............. GenCorp, Inc. [*NYSE symbol*] (SPSG)
**GY** ............. Germany

**GY**.............. Gray
**Gy**.............. Gray [*Symbol*] [*SI unit for absorbed dose acceleration*]
**GY**.............. Greenish Yellow
**GY**.............. Guaranty Trust Co. of Canada [*Toronto Stock Exchange symbol*]
**GY**.............. Guidance Year [*DoD*]
**gy**.............. Guyana [*MARC country of publication code*] [*Library of Congress*] (LCCP)
**GY**.............. Guyana [*ANSI two-letter standard code*] (CNC)
**GY**.............. Guyana Airways Corp. [*ICAO designator*] (FAAC)
**GY**.............. Gyroscope
**Gy**.............. Gyrus [*Brain anatomy*]
**GYA**............ Got Ya Again [*Initialism used as name of second successful phony event staged by Washington, DC, law enforcement agents posing as fences*] [*See PFF Inc*]
**GYA**............ Guayaramerin [*Bolivia*] [*Airport symbol*] (OAG)
**GyAR**.......... Rhein-Westfalische Technische Hochschule, Aachen, Germany [*Library symbol*] [*Library of Congress*] (LCLS)
**GyAsH**........ Hofbibliothek, Aschaffenburg, Germany [*Library symbol*] [*Library of Congress*] (LCLS)
**GYB**............ Giddings, TX [*Location identifier*] [*FAA*] (FAAL)
**GyBaA**........ Archiv des Kreises Asch, Fernleihe, Bayern, Federal Republic of Germany [*Library symbol*] [*Library of Congress*] (LCLS)
**GyBFU**........ Freie Universitaet (Berlin), Garystrasse, Berlin, Germany [*Library symbol*] [*Library of Congress*] (LCLS)
**GyBFU-P**.... Freie Universitaet (Berlin), Fachbereich Politische Wissenschaft, Bibliothek, Berlin, Germany [*Library symbol*] [*Library of Congress*] (LCLS)
**GyBiU**........ Universitat Bielfeld, Kurt Schumacher, Bielfeld, Germany [*Library symbol*] [*Library of Congress*] (LCLS)
**GyBochU**.... Ruhr-Universitat Bochum, Bochum, Germany [*Library symbol*] [*Library of Congress*] (LCLS)
**GyBoDB**...... Deutscher Bundestag, Abteilung Wissenschaftliche Dokumentation, Bonn, Germany [*Library symbol*] [*Library of Congress*] (LCLS)
**GyBoFE**...... Friedrich-Ebert-Stiftung, Archiv der Sozialen Demokratie, Bonn, Germany [*Library symbol*] [*Library of Congress*] (LCLS)
**GyBoFN**...... Friedrich-Naumann-Stiftung, Bonn, Germany [*Library symbol*] [*Library of Congress*] (LCLS)
**GyBoGI**...... Gesamtdeutsches Institut, Bonn, Germany [*Library symbol*] [*Library of Congress*] (LCLS)
**GyBraTU**.... Technische Universitat Carolo Wilhelmina zu Braunschweig, Braunschweig, Federal Republic of Germany [*Library symbol*] [*Library of Congress*] (LCLS)
**GyBrSU**...... Staatsbibliothek und Universitatsbibliothek, Breitenweg, Bremen, Germany [*Library symbol*] [*Library of Congress*] (LCLS)
**GyBrU**........ Universitaet Bremen, Bremen, Germany [*Library symbol*] [*Library of Congress*] (LCLS)
**GyBTU**........ Technische Universitat Berlin, Berlin, Germany [*Library symbol*] [*Library of Congress*] (LCLS)
**GYC**............ Glasgow Yeomanry Cavalry [*British military*] (DMA)
**GYC**............ Global Energy Ltd. [*Vancouver Stock Exchange symbol*]
**GYC**............ Greater Yellowstone Coalition (EA)
**GYC**............ Young Harris College, Young Harris, GA [*Library symbol*] [*Library of Congress*] (LCLS)
**GyDaD**........ Deutsches Kunststoff-Institut, Darmstadt, Germany [*Library symbol*] [*Library of Congress*] (LCLS)
**GyDaH**........ Hessische Landes- und Hochschulbibliothek, Darmstadt (Schloss), Germany [*Library symbol*] [*Library of Congress*] (LCLS)
**GyDaM**........ E. Merck AG, Darmstadt, Germany [*Library symbol*] [*Library of Congress*] (LCLS)
**GyDIZ**........ Institut fur Zeitungsforschung, Dortmund, Germany [*Library symbol*] [*Library of Congress*] (LCLS)
**GYDKA9**.... Gifu Yakka Daigaku Kiyo [*Annual Proceedings. Gifu Pharmaceutical University*] [*A publication*]
**GyDMA**...... Mikrofilmarchiv der Deutschsparchigen Presse e.V., Dortmund, Germany [*Library symbol*] [*Library of Congress*] (LCLS)
**GyDuiH**...... Gesamthochschulbibliothek Duisburg, Duisburg, Germany [*Library symbol*] [*Library of Congress*] (LCLS)
**GyDuU**........ Universitat Dusseldorf, Grabbeplatz, Dusseldorf, Germany [*Library symbol*] [*Library of Congress*] (LCLS)
**GYE**............ Glory Explorations [*Vancouver Stock Exchange symbol*]
**GYE**............ Guayaquil [*Ecuador*] [*Airport symbol*] (OAG)
**GyEU**.......... Friedrich-Alexander-Universitat zu Erlangen-Nurnberg, Erlangen, Germany [*Library symbol*] [*Library of Congress*] (LCLS)
**GyFmB**........ Beilstein-Institut, Frankfurt/Main, Germany [*Library symbol*] [*Library of Congress*] (LCLS)
**GyFmDB**.... Deutsche Bibliothek, Zeppelinallee, Frankfurt am Main, Germany [*Library symbol*] [*Library of Congress*] (LCLS)
**GyFmSU**.... Stadt u Universitatsbibliothek, Senckenbergische Bibliothek Fernleihe, Frankfurt/Main, Federal Republic of Germany [*Library symbol*] [*Library of Congress*] (LCLS)
**GYG**............ Grayling, MI [*Location identifier*] [*FAA*] (FAAL)
**GYG**............ Valdosta State College, Valdosta, GA [*OCLC symbol*] (OCLC)
**GyGiU**........ Justus Liebig Universitatsbibliothek Giessen, Giessen/Lahn, Federal Republic of Germany [*Library symbol*] [*Library of Congress*] (LCLS)
**GyGoN**........ Niedersachsische Staats- und Universitatsbibliothek, Gottingen, Germany [*Library symbol*] [*Library of Congress*] (LCLS)
**GYH**............ Greenville, SC [*Location identifier*] [*FAA*] (FAAL)
**GyHanM**.... Medizinische Hochschule, Karl Wiechert, Hannover-Kleefeld, Germany [*Library symbol*] [*Library of Congress*] (LCLS)
**GyHaS**........ Staats- und Universitatsbibliothek Hamburg, Hamburg, Germany [*Library symbol*] [*Library of Congress*] (LCLS)
**GyHeM**........ Max-Planck-Institut fuer Medizinisch Forschung, Heidelberg, Germany [*Library symbol*] [*Library of Congress*] (LCLS)
**GyHGU**........ University of Gottingen, Hannover, Germany [*Library symbol*] [*Library of Congress*] (LCLS)
**GyHoU**........ Universitat Hohenheim (Landwirtschaftliche Hochschule), Stuttgart-Hohenheim, Germany [*Library symbol*] [*Library of Congress*] (LCLS)
**GyHTIB**...... Universitaetsbibliothek der Technischen Universitaet Hannover und Technische Informationsbibliothek, Hannover, Federal Republic of Germany [*Library symbol*] [*Library of Congress*] (LCLS)
**GYIL**............ German Yearbook of International Law [*A publication*] (DLA)
**GyJuK**.......... Kernforschungsanlage Julich, Julich, Germany [*Library symbol*] [*Library of Congress*] (LCLS)
**GYK**............ Giant Yellowknife Mines Ltd. [*AMEX symbol*] [*Toronto Stock Exchange symbol*]
**GyKaU**.......... Universitat Trier-Kaiserslautern, Kaiserslautern, Germany [*Library symbol*] [*Library of Congress*] (LCLS)
**GyKG**............ Gesellschaft fuer Kernforschung mbH, Karlsruhe, Germany [*Library symbol*] [*Library of Congress*] (LCLS)
**GyKiU**.......... Christian-Albrechts Universitat Kiel, Kiel, Germany [*Library symbol*] [*Library of Congress*] (LCLS)
**GYM**............ General Yardmaster [*Railroading*]
**GYM**............ Guaymas [*Mexico*] [*Seismograph station code, US Geological Survey*] (SEIS)
**GYM**............ Guaymas [*Mexico*] [*Airport symbol*] (OAG)
**GYM**............ Guaymas, Mexico [*Remote site*] [*NASA*] (NASA)
**Gym**............ Gymnasium [*A publication*]
**GYM**............ Gymnasium
**GYM**............ Gymnastics (ADA)
**GyMB**.......... Boehringer Mannheim GmbH, Mannheim, Germany [*Library symbol*] [*Library of Congress*] (LCLS)
**GyMIZ**........ Institut fur Zeitgeschichte [*Institute of Modern History*], Munchen, Federal Republic of Germany [*Library symbol*] [*Library of Congress*] (LCLS)
**GyMLM**...... Ludwig Maxmilians Universitatsbibliothek Munchen, Munich, Federal Republic of Germany [*Library symbol*] [*Library of Congress*] (LCLS)
**GYMS**.......... Concept 90 Marketing, Inc. [*NASDAQ symbol*] (NQ)
**GYMSTIC**... Gymnastic [*Freight*]
**GyMuW**...... Westfalische Wilhelms-Universitat Munster, Munster, Germany [*Library symbol*] [*Library of Congress*] (LCLS)
**GYN**............ Goiania [*Brazil*] [*Airport symbol*] (OAG)
**GYN**............ Gynecology
**GYNAE**...... Gynaecology [*British*]
**GYNAEC**.. Gynaecologist [*or Gynaecology*] [*British*] (ADA)
**GYNAECOL**... Gynaecology [*British*]
**Gynaecol Endocr**... Journal of Gynaecological Endocrinology [*A publication*]
**Gynaekol Rundsch**... Gynaekologische Rundschau [*A publication*]
**GYNCLGY**... Gynecology
**GyNeA**........ Augustana Hochschule Bibliothek, Neuendettelsau, Federal Republic of Germany [*Library symbol*] [*Library of Congress*] (LCLS)
**Gynecol**...... Gynecology
**Gynecol Inv**... Gynecologic Investigation [*A publication*]
**Gynecol Invest**... Gynecologic Investigation [*A publication*]
**Gynecol Obstet**... Gynecologie et Obstetrique [*A publication*]
**Gynecol Obstet Invest**... Gynecologic and Obstetric Investigation [*A publication*]
**Gynecol Oncol**... Gynecologic Oncology [*A publication*]
**Gynecol Prat**... Gynecologie Pratique [*A publication*]
**GYNOA**...... Gynecologic Oncology [*A publication*]
**GyNU**.......... Friedrich-Alexander-Universitat zu Erlangen-Nurnberg, Abteilung fur Wirtschafts- und Socialwissenschaften, Nurnberg, Germany [*Library symbol*] [*Library of Congress*] (LCLS)
**GYNX**.......... Gynex, Inc. [*Des Plaines, IL*] [*NASDAQ symbol*] (NQ)
**GYOBA**...... Gynecologie et Obstetrique de Langue Francaise [*A publication*]
**Gyosai Geppo**... Gyosei Saiban Geppo [*A publication*]
**GYP**............ CGC, Inc. [*Toronto Stock Exchange symbol*]
**GYP**............ Gympie [*Australia*] [*Airport symbol*]
**GYP**............ Gypsum (KSC)
**GYP**............ Gyro Yaw Position
**GYPSY**........ General Image Processing System
**GYR**............ Gigayear [*A billion years*]
**GYR**............ Goodyear, AZ [*Location identifier*] [*FAA*] (FAAL)
**GYRO**.......... Gyrodyne Co. of America, Inc. [*NASDAQ symbol*] (NQ)
**GYRO**.......... Gyroscope (AAG)
**GYROCOMP**... Gyroscope Compassing
**GyRU**.......... Universitat Regensburg, Regensburg, Germany [*Library symbol*] [*Library of Congress*] (LCLS)
**Gy S**............ Gypsy Scholar [*A publication*]
**GySalS**........ Stadtbucherei Salzgitter, Joachim Campe, Salzgitter, Germany [*Library symbol*] [*Library of Congress*] (LCLS)

**GySaU** ....... Universitat des Saarlandes, Saarbrucken, Germany [*Library symbol*] [*Library of Congress*] (LCLS)
**GYSGT** ...... Gunnery Sergeant
**GySIA** ........ Institut fuer Auslandsbeziehungen, Stuttgart, Germany [*Library symbol*] [*Library of Congress*] (LCLS)
**GySU** ......... Universitat Stuttgart, Stuttgart, Germany [*Library symbol*] [*Library of Congress*] (LCLS)
**GySW** ........ Wuerttembergische Landesbibliothek, Konrad Adenauer, Stuttgart, Germany [*Library symbol*] [*Library of Congress*] (LCLS)
**GyTrU** ........ Universitat Trier-Kaiserslautern, Schneidershof, Trier, Germany [*Library symbol*] [*Library of Congress*] (LCLS)
**GyWitS** ...... Stadtbucherei Witten, Witten, Germany [*Library symbol*] [*Library of Congress*] (LCLS)
**GyWK** ........ Kalle Aktiengesellschaft, Litteraturabteilung, Wiesbaden-Biebrich, Germany [*Library symbol*] [*Library of Congress*] (LCLS)
**GyWoS** ...... Niedersachsische Staatsarchiv, Wolfenbuttel, Germany [*Library symbol*] [*Library of Congress*] (LCLS)
**GYY** ........... Gary, IN [*Location identifier*] [*FAA*] (FAAL)
**GZ** ............. Aerogulf Services Co. [*United Arab*] [*ICAO designator*] (FAAC)
**GZ** ............. Ganzfeld [*Whole Field*] [*ESP test*] [*German*]
**gz** ............. Gaza Strip [*MARC country of publication code*] [*Library of Congress*] (LCCP)
**GZ** ............. Gazeta Zydowska [*A publication*]
**GZ** ............. Geographische Zeitschrift [*A publication*]
**GZ** ............. Gigahertz [*1,000 megahertz*] [*Preferred form is GHz*] (MCD)
**GZ** ............. Girozentrale und Bank der Oesterreichischen Sparkassen Aktiengesellschaft [*Bank*] [*Vienna, Austria*]
**Gz** ............. Graetz Number [*Physics*]
**GZ** ............. Ground Zero [*An association*] (EA)
**GZ** ............. Ground Zero [*Atomic detonation*]
**Gz** ............. Guizzardinus [*Deceased, 1222*] [*Authority cited in pre-1607 legal work*] (DSA)
**GZA** ........... Alverno College, Milwaukee, WI [*OCLC symbol*] (OCLC)
**GZABA8** .... Annuaire de Biologie. Faculte des Sciences Naturelles. Universite Kiril. Metodij [*Skopje*] [*A publication*]
**GZAS** ......... Guilford-Zimmerman Aptitude Survey [*Test*]
**GZAS:GR** ... Guilford-Zimmerman Aptitude Survey: General Reasoning [*Test*]
**GZAS:NO** ... Guilford-Zimmerman Aptitude Survey: Numerical Operations [*Test*]
**GZAS:PS** ... Guilford-Zimmerman Aptitude Survey: Perceptual Speed [*Test*]
**GZAS:SO** .. Guilford-Zimmerman Aptitude Survey: Spatial Orientation [*Test*]
**GZAS:SV** .. Guilford-Zimmerman Aptitude Survey: Spatial Visualization [*Test*]
**GZAS:VC** .. Guilford-Zimmerman Aptitude Survey: Verbal Comprehension [*Test*]
**GZB** ........... Carroll College, Waukesha, WI [*OCLC symbol*] (OCLC)
**GZB** ........... Genossenschaftliche Zentralbank AG [*Bank*] [*Austria*]
**GZBBDG** ... Bioloshki Fakultet na Univerzitetot Kiril i Metodij Skopje Godishen Zbornik [*A publication*]
**GZC** ........... Carthage College, Kenosha, WI [*OCLC symbol*] (OCLC)
**GZD** ........... Milwaukee Public Library, Milwaukee, WI [*OCLC symbol*] (OCLC)
**GZE** ........... University of Wisconsin-Eau Claire, Eau Claire, WI [*OCLC symbol*] (OCLC)
**GZEA** ......... GZA GeoEnvironmental Technologies, Inc. (NQ)
**GZF** ........... Eau Claire Public Library, Eau Claire, WI [*OCLC symbol*] (OCLC)
**GZG** ........... Blackford, VA [*Location identifier*] [*FAA*] (FAAL)
**GZG** ........... Brown County Library, Green Bay, WI [*OCLC symbol*] (OCLC)
**GZG** ........... Gonzales Gold Mines Ltd. [*Vancouver Stock Exchange symbol*]
**GZH** ........... Gdanskie Zeszyty Humanistyczne [*A publication*]
**GZH** ........... University of Wisconsin-Madison, Health Sciences, Madison, WI [*OCLC symbol*] (OCLC)
**GZI** ............ University of Wisconsin-Madison, Instructional Materials Center, Madison, WI [*OCLC symbol*] (OCLC)
**GZII** ........... Guilford-Zimmerman Interest Inventory [*Vocational guidance test*]
**GZINB** ....... Bharat Ka Rajpatra [*A publication*]
**GZJ** ............ University of Wisconsin-Milwaukee, School of Library Science, Milwaukee, WI [*OCLC symbol*] (OCLC)
**GZK** ........... Oshkosh Public Library, Oshkosh, WI [*OCLC symbol*] (OCLC)
**GZL** ........... Gazelle Resources Limited [*Vancouver Stock Exchange symbol*]
**GZL** ........... University of Wisconsin-Madison, Law Library, Madison, WI [*OCLC symbol*] (OCLC)
**GZM** .......... Gaz Metropolitain, Inc. [*Toronto Stock Exchange symbol*]
**GZM** .......... Glasnik Zemaljskog Muzeja [*Subseries*] Etnologija [*A publication*]
**GZM** .......... University of Wisconsin-Madison, Madison, WI [*OCLC symbol*] (OCLC)
**GZMS** ........ Glasnik Zemaljskog Muzeja u Sarajevu [*A publication*]
**GZN** ........... Ground Zero [*Nevada*] [*Seismograph station code, US Geological Survey*] [*Closed*] (SEIS)
**GZN** ........... University of Wisconsin-Milwaukee, Milwaukee, WI [*OCLC symbol*] (OCLC)
**GZO** ........... Gizo [*Solomon Islands*] [*Airport symbol*] (OAG)
**GZO** ........... University of Wisconsin-Oshkosh, Oshkosh, WI [*OCLC symbol*] (OCLC)
**GZOB** ......... Glowna Zydowska Organizacja Bojowa [*A publication*] (BJA)
**GZP** ........... University of Wisconsin-Parkside, Kenosha, WI [*OCLC symbol*] (OCLC)
**GZPP** ......... Ground Zero Pairing Project (EA)
**GZQ** ........... Marquette University, Milwaukee, WI [*OCLC symbol*] (OCLC)
**GZR** ........... Golden Zone Resources [*Vancouver Stock Exchange symbol*]
**GZR** ........... Wisconsin Department of Public Instruction, Reference and Loan Library, Madison, WI [*OCLC symbol*] (OCLC)
**GZRC** ......... Ground Zero Resource Center (EA)
**GZS** ........... Gesellschaft fuer Zahlungssysteme [*International banking*] [*Federal Republic of Germany*]
**GZS** ........... Gozaisho [*Japan*] [*Seismograph station code, US Geological Survey*] [*Closed*] (SEIS)
**GZS** ........... Pulaski, TN [*Location identifier*] [*FAA*] (FAAL)
**GZS** ........... University of Wisconsin-Stout, Menomonie, WI [*OCLC symbol*] (OCLC)
**GZSRAA** ... Gezira Research Station and Substations. Annual Report [*A publication*]
**GZT** ........... Gaziantep [*Turkey*] [*Airport symbol*] (OAG)
**GZT** ........... Greenwich Zone Time
**GZT** ........... University of Wisconsin-Whitewater, Whitewater, WI [*OCLC symbol*] (OCLC)
**GZTS** ......... Guilford-Zimmerman Temperament Survey [*Psychology*]
**GZU** ........... University of Wisconsin-La Crosse, La Crosse, WI [*OCLC symbol*] (OCLC)
**GZV** ........... University of Wisconsin-Platteville, Platteville, WI [*OCLC symbol*] (OCLC)
**GZW** .......... University of Wisconsin-Green Bay, Green Bay, WI [*OCLC symbol*] (OCLC)
**GZX** ........... La Crosse Public Library, La Crosse, WI [*OCLC symbol*] (OCLC)
**GZX** ........... Peoria, IL [*Location identifier*] [*FAA*] (FAAL)
**GZY** ........... Wisconsin Interlibrary Loan Service, Madison, WI [*OCLC symbol*] (OCLC)

# H

H ........ Air Force Training Category

H ........ Altitude

H ........ Altitude Rate [*Symbol*] (NASA)

H ........ Atmospheric Head (AAG)

H ........ Bracco Industria Chimica [*Italy*] [*Research code symbol*]

h ........ Coefficient of Heat Transfer [*Symbol*] [*Thermodynamics*]

h ........ Dihydro [*As substituent on nucleoside*] [*Biochemistry*]

H ........ Enthalpy [*Symbol*] [*IUPAC*] (DEN)

H ........ Exposure [*Symbol*] [*IUPAC*]

h------ ........ French Union [*MARC geographic area code*] [*Library of Congress*] (LCCP)

H ........ Haber [*Credit*] [*Business term*] [*Spanish*]

h ........ Hacia [*Around*] [*Spanish*]

H ........ Haftarah (BJA)

H ........ Hagelkorn [*Hailstone*] [*Bomb*] [*German military - World War II*]

H ........ Haggai [*Freemasonry*]

H ........ Hail [*Meteorology*]

H ........ Haler [*Monetary unit*] [*Czechoslovakia*]

H ........ Half

H ........ Half-Word Designator [*Data processing*]

H ........ Hall

H ........ Halothane [*Also, HAL*] [*An anesthetic*]

H ........ Halt [*Data processing*] (MDG)

H ........ Hamiltonian Function [*Mathematics*]

H ........ Hamlet

H ........ Hamlyn Publishing [*British*]

H ........ Hand [*Music*]

H ........ Handily [*Horse racing*]

H ........ Handy's Ohio Reports [*12 Ohio Decisions*] [*A publication*] (DLA)

H ........ Harbor [*Maps and charts*]

H ........ Hard [*or Hardness*] [*Pencil leads*]

H ........ Hardness [*Of precious stones*]

H ........ Hardware [*Data processing*] (MDG)

H ........ Hardy [*Horticulture*]

H ........ Hare's English Chancery Reports [*A publication*] (DLA)

H ........ Harmonic Mean [*Psychology*]

h ........ Harmonized [*Apparent inconsistency explained and shown not to exist*] [*Used in Shepard's Citations*] [*Legal term*] (DLA)

H ........ Harper's Magazine [*A publication*]

H ........ Harrier (ROG)

H ........ Harry [*Phonetic alphabet*] [*Royal Navy*] [*World War I*] [*Pre-World War II*] (DSUE)

H ........ Has

H ........ Hassle [*Sweden*] [*Research code symbol*]

H ........ Hatch [*Technical drawings*]

H ........ Hauch [*Antigen*] [*Immunology*]

H ........ Haustus [*A Drink*] [*Pharmacy*]

H ........ Have (ROG)

H ........ Haven (ADA)

H ........ Haver [*Credit*] [*Business term*] [*Portuguese*]

H ........ Hawaii Reports [*A publication*] (DLA)

(H) ........ Hazardous [*Task classification*] [*NASA*] (NASA)

H ........ Hazardous Cargo [*Shipping*]

H ........ Haze [*Weather reports*]

H ........ Hazor (BJA)

H ........ Head [*Horse racing*]

H ........ Head [*Linguistics*]

H ........ Head, Hand, and Chest Sets [*JETDS nomenclature*] [*Military*] (CET)

H ........ Headquarters

H ........ Healthy

H ........ Hearing Power (ROG)

H ........ Heart [*Freemasonry*] (ROG)

H ........ Heart Trouble [*Classification system used by doctors on Ellis Island to detain, re-examine, and possibly deny entry to certain immigrants*]

H ........ Hearts (ADA)

H ........ Heartwood [*Forestry*]

H ........ Heat [*or Heater*]

H ........ Heaton Mint [*British*]

H ........ Heavy (AAG)

H ........ Heavy [*Chain*] [*Biochemistry, immunochemistry*]

H ........ Heavy Lift Cargo Airlines Ltd. [*British*]

H ........ Heavy Sea [*Navigation*]

H ........ Hebrew (BJA)

h ........ Hecto [*A prefix meaning multiplied by* $10^2$ *SI symbol*]

H ........ Heel [*Music*]

H ........ Heft [*Part*] [*German*]

H ........ Height

h ........ Height [*Symbol*] [*IUPAC*]

H ........ Heir

H ........ Helicopter [*When the second letter or only letter*] [*Designation for all US military aircraft*]

H ........ Helicopteros do Brasil SA [*Brazil*] [*ICAO aircraft manufacturer identifier*] (ICAO)

H ........ Helium [*Chemical symbol is He*] (AAG)

H ........ Helix

H ........ Helm Resources, Inc. [*AMEX symbol*] (SPSG)

H ........ Hemagglutinating [*Virology*]

H ........ Hematite [*A mineral*]

H ........ Hemic Subgroup [*Magnetite, chromite, hematite*] [*CIPW classification*] [*Geology*]

H ........ Hemin [*Hematology*]

H ........ Hence

H ........ Henry [*Symbol*] [*SI unit of inductance*]

H ........ Henry (King of England) (DLA)

H ........ Herb [*Botany*]

H ........ Herbivore

H ........ Heres [*Heir*] [*Legal term*] [*Latin*]

H ........ Hermes. Zeitschrift fuer Klassische Philologie [*A publication*]

H ........ Hermit

H ........ Heroin [*Slang*]

H ........ Hertzog's High Court Reports [*South Africa*] [*A publication*] (DLA)

H ........ Heterozygosity [*Cytology*]

H ........ Hettangian [*Geology*]

H ........ Hexadecimal (BUR)

H ........ Hic [*Here*] [*Latin*]

H ........ Hieroglyphics [*Freemasonry*] (ROG)

H ........ High

H ........ High Season [*Airline fare code*]

H ........ High-Viscosity Fuel

H ........ Hilary Term [*England*] [*Legal term*] (DLA)

H ........ Hilkoth (BJA)

H ........ Hill (ROG)

H ........ Hill's New York Reports [*A publication*] (DLA)

H ........ Hinged [*Philately*]

H ........ Hispania [*A publication*]

H ........ Hispanic

H ........ [*Laurentius*] Hispanus [*Deceased, 1248*] [*Authority cited in pre-1607 legal work*] (DSA)

H ........ Histamine [*Anesthesiology*]

H ........ Histidine [*One-letter symbol*]

H ........ Historiae [*of Sallust*] [*Classical studies*] (OCD)

H ........ Historical Re-Issue [*Record cataloging*]

H ........ History [*A publication*]

H ........ History [*Secondary school course*] [*British*]

H ........ Hits [*Baseball*]

H ........ [*Anthony von*] Hoboken [*When used in identifying Haydn's compositions, refers to cataloging of his works by musicologist Hoboken*]

H ........ Hoffmann [*Reflex*] [*Neurology*]

H ........ Holding [*Electronics*]

H ........ Holding Instructions Issued [*Aviation*] (FAAC)

H ........ Holiness (BJA)

H ........ Holland [*IYRU nationality code*] (IYR)

H ........ Holy

H ........ Holzknecht [*Unit*]

H ........ Home

- **H** ... Home Radio Beacon (FAAC)
- **H** ... Homobonus de Cremona [Deceased, 1272] [Authority cited in pre-1607 legal work] (DSA)
- **H** ... Homosexual
- **H** ... Honor
- **H** ... Honorary [Academic degree]
- **H** ... Hooker
- **H** ... Hope [Freemasonry] (ROG)
- **H** ... Hopper-Tainer [A form of container] [British] (DCTA)
- **h** ... Hora [Hour] [Latin]
- **H** ... Horizontal
- **H** ... Horizontal Force of the Earth's Magnetism [Amplitude of a tide]
- **H** ... Hormone [Endocrinology]
- **H** ... Horn
- **H** ... Horrific [Film certificate] [British]
- **H** ... Horse [Thoroughbred racing]
- **H** ... Hospital [Traffic sign] [British]
- **H** ... Hospital Plane [When suffixed to Navy plane designation]
- **H** ... Host [Freemasonry] (ROG)
- **H** ... Hostiensis [Deceased, 1271] [Authority cited in pre-1607 legal work] (DSA)
- **H** ... Hostile [Military]
- **H** ... Hot
- **H** ... Hotel [Phonetic alphabet] [International] (DSUE)
- **H** ... Hotel
- **H** ... Hour [Also, h]
- **H** ... House
- **H** ... House Bill [Legal term] (DLA)
- **H** ... House of Representatives
- **H** ... How [Phonetic alphabet] [World War II] (DSUE)
- **H** ... Howard's United States Supreme Court Reports [42-65 United States] [A publication] (DLA)
- **H** ... Hoy [Ship's rigging] (ROG)
- **H** ... Hoyre [Conservative Party] [Norway] [Political party] (PPE)
- **H** ... Hugolinus de Presbyteris [Flourished, 1197-1238] [Authority cited in pre-1607 legal work] (DSA)
- **H** ... Huguccio [Deceased, 1210] [Authority cited in pre-1607 legal work] (DSA)
- **H** ... Hull (ADA)
- **H** ... Human
- **H** ... Human Being [Rorschach] [Psychology]
- **H** ... [The] Humanitarian [A publication] (ROG)
- **H** ... Humidity
- **H** ... Hun-Stoffe [Mustard gas] [Formerly, HS] [Also, HD, HT, M]
- **H** ... Hundred
- **H** ... Hungary
- **H** ... Hurricane Evacuation - General [Military aircraft identification prefix] (FAAC)
- **H** ... Husband
- **H** ... Hussars [Military unit] [British]
- **H** ... Hydrant
- **H** ... Hydraulics (ADA)
- **H** ... Hydrodynamic Head
- **H** ... Hydrogen [Chemical element]
- **H** ... Hydrographic Survey [Navy] [British]
- **H** ... Hydrolysis
- **H** ... Hydroxydaunomycin [See also ADR, Adriamycin] [Antineoplastic drug]
- **H** ... Hygiene [Preventive and Industrial Medicine] [Medical Officer designation] [British]
- **H** ... Hyoscine [Organic chemistry]
- **H** ... Hypermetropia [Ophthalmology]
- **H** ... Hyperopia [Ophthalmology] (ROG)
- **H** ... Hyperplasia [Medicine]
- **H** ... Hypodermic
- **h** ... Hypotheque [Mortgage] [French]
- **H** ... Hypothesis
- **H** ... Instructor [Army skill qualification identifier] (INF)
- **H** ... Magnetizing Force [Symbol] (DEN)
- **H** ... Mustard Gas [Also, HD, HS, HT, M] [Poison Gas] [US Chemical Corps symbol]
- **H** ... Nondirectional Radio Homing Beacon [Navigation charts]
- **H** ... Officer Qualified at a School of Musketry [Military] [British] (ROG)
- **h** ... Planck Constant [Symbol] [IUPAC]
- **H** ... Regarding [JETDS nomenclature]
- **H** ... Restaurants, Cafes, and Hotel Lounges [Public-performance tariff class] [British]
- **H** ... Search/Rescue [When the first letter of a pair] [Designation for all US military aircraft]
- **H** ... Silo Stored [Missile launch environment symbol]
- **h** ... Small Increment [Mathematics] (ROG)
- **H** ... Total Energy (ROG)
- **$H_0$** ... Hubble's Constant [Astronomy]
- **H1** ... Haploid Cell Line 1
- **1-H** ... Selective Service Class [for Registrant Not Currently Subject to Processing for Induction]
- **H2** ... Hawaii (Kauai) [Spaceflight Tracking and Data Network] [NASA]
- **$H^2$** ... Hot and Heavy [In reference to a romance]
- **$H_3$** ... Tritium [Also, T] [Radioisotope of hydrogen]
- **4H** ... Head, Heart, Hands, and Health [As in 4H organizations]
- **$H_4$** ... Tetrahydro [Biochemistry]
- **H5** ... Henry V [Shakespearean work]
- **5H** ... Tanzania United Republic [Aircraft nationality and registration mark] (FAAC)
- **H8** ... Henry VIII [Shakespearean work]
- **9H** ... Malta [Aircraft nationality and registration mark] (FAAC)
- **1H4** ... Henry IV, Part I [Shakespearean work]
- **1H6** ... Henry VI, Part I [Shakespearean work]
- **2H4** ... Henry IV, Part II [Shakespearean work]
- **H24** ... Twenty-Four Hour [Continuous] Operation [Aviation]
- **2H6** ... Henry VI, Part II [Shakespearean work]
- **3H6** ... Henry VI, Part III [Shakespearean work]
- **H (Bomb)** ... Hydrogen Bomb
- **HA** ... Apogee Altitude (NASA)
- **HA** ... CASA [Construcciones Aeronauticas Sociedad Anonima] [Spain] [ICAO aircraft manufacturer identifier] (ICAO)
- **HA** ... Chem. Werke Albert [Germany] [Research code symbol]
- **HA** ... Habitual Abortion [Medicine]
- **Ha** ... Hahnium [Proposed name for chemical element 105]
- **HA** ... HAL, Inc. [AMEX symbol] (SPSG)
- **HA** ... Half Adder [Circuitry] (MSA)
- **Ha** ... Hallah (BJA)
- **H/A** ... Hand/Automatic [Nuclear energy] (NRCH)
- **HA** ... Handelsabgabe [Commercial Tax] [German]
- **HA** ... Handes Amsorya [A publication]
- **HA** ... Hardness Assurance (MSA)
- **HA** ... Hardy Annual [Horticulture] (ROG)
- **Ha** ... Hare's English Vice-Chancellors' Reports [66-68 English Reprint] [1841-53] [A publication] (DLA)
- **HA** ... Harmonie Associates (EA)
- **HA** ... Harness Assembly
- **Ha** ... Harpers [A publication]
- **Ha** ... Hartmann Number [IUPAC]
- **HA** ... Hatch Act [1887]
- **HA** ... Hatchway (DS)
- **HA** ... Hawaiian Airlines, Inc. [ICAO designator] (ICDA)
- **HA** ... Hazard Analysis (NASA)
- **HA** ... Hazardous Area
- **HA** ... Headache
- **HA** ... Headmasters [or Headmistresses] Association (EA)
- **HA** ... Headquarters Administration Division [Coast Guard]
- **H & A** ... Health and Accident [Insurance]
- **HA** ... Health Act (OICC)
- **HA** ... Healthy America [An association] [Defunct] (EA)
- **HA** ... Hearing Aid
- **HA** ... Heavy Artillery
- **HA** ... Heavy Atoms
- **HA** ... Hectare (AAG)
- **HA** ... Hectocotylized Arm
- **HA** ... Heeres-Atmer [Service Oxygen Breathing Apparatus] [German military - World War II]
- **HA** ... Hefte von Auschwitz (BJA)
- **HA** ... Heidelberger Abhandlungen [A publication]
- **HA** ... Height of Apogee
- **HA** ... Heir Apparent
- **HA** ... Hellenic Army (MCD)
- **HA** ... Helvetia Archaeologica [A publication]
- **HA** ... Hemadsorption [Hematology]
- **HA** ... Hemagglutination [Hematology]
- **HA** ... Hemolytic Anemia [Hematology]
- **HA** ... Henry Adams, Inc. [Baltimore, MD] (TSSD)
- **HA** ... Henson Associates [Television production company]
- **HA** ... Hepatitis Associated [Virus]
- **Ha** ... Hermathena [A publication]
- **HA** ... Heterophile Antibody [Immunochemistry]
- **HA** ... Heyden Antibiotic [Pharmacology]
- **HA** ... High Altitude
- **HA** ... High Angle
- **HA** ... High Authority of the ECSC [European Coal and Steel Community] (ILCA)
- **HA** ... Highways Act [British] (ILCA)
- **HA** ... Hiram Abiff [Freemasonry] (ROG)
- **HA** ... Historia Animalium [of Aristotle] [Classical studies] (OCD)
- **HA** ... Historical Abstracts [ABC-CLIO] [Information service or system] [A publication]
- **HA** ... Historical Association [London, England] (EAIO)
- **HA** ... Hoc Anno [This Year] [Latin]
- **HA** ... Hockey Association [British]
- **H/A** ... Holding Activity
- **HA** ... Holiness Army (ROG)
- **HA** ... Home Address
- **HA** ... Homesteaders Association (EA)
- **HA** ... Horse Artillery
- **HA** ... Horticultural Abstracts
- **HA** ... Hosanna Army (ROG)
- **HA** ... Hospice Association (EA)
- **HA** ... Hospital Academy (EA)
- **HA** ... Hospital Admission

**HA** ............ Hospital Apprentice [*Navy rating*]
**HA** ............ Hostile Aeroplane [*British military*] (DMA)
**HA** ............ Hot Air
**HA** ............ Hour Angle [*Navigation*]
**HA** ............ House Account [*Business term*]
**HA** ............ House Administration (DLA)
**HA** ............ Housing Allowance [*Military*]
**HA** ............ Housing Assistance [*HUD*]
**HA** ............ Housing Authority
**HA** ............ Hoverclub of America (EA)
**HA** ............ Huius Anni [*This Year's*] [*Latin*]
**HA** ............ Human Adaptability
**HA** ............ Human Argininosuccinate Lyase [*An enzyme*]
**HA** ............ Humic Acid [*Organic chemistry*]
**HA** ............ Humor Association (EA)
**HA** ............ Hungary [*Aircraft nationality and registration mark*] (FAAC)
**HA** ............ Hyaluronic Acid [*Biochemistry*]
**HA** ............ Hydrophone Allowance [*British military*] (DMA)
**HA** ............ Hydroxyapatite [*Also, HAP*] [*A mineral*]
**HA** ............ Hydroxylapatite [*Inorganic chemistry*]
**HA** ............ Hypermetropia, Absolute [*Ophthalmology*]
**HA** ............ Netherlands [*IYRU nationality code*] (IYR)
**HAA** .......... Haflinger Association of America (EA)
**HAA** .......... Haitian-American Association [*Defunct*]
**HAA** .......... Handbooks of Archaeology and Antiquities [*A publication*]
**HAA** .......... Handicapped Artists of America (EA)
**HAA** .......... Hands Across America (EA)
**HAA** .......... Hasvik [*Norway*] [*Airport symbol*] (OAG)
**HAA** .......... Head Access Area [*Nuclear energy*] (NRCH)
**HAA** .......... Hearing Aid Amplifier
**HAA** .......... Heater Amplifier Assembly
**HAA** .......... Heavy Antiaircraft Artillery
**HAA** .......... Height above Airport (AFM)
**HAA** .......... Helicopter Airline Association (EA)
**HAA** .......... Helicopter Association of America [*Later, HAI*] (EA)
**HAA** .......... Hemolytic Anemia Antigen [*Immunochemistry*]
**HAA** .......... Hepatitis Associated Antigen [*Clinical chemistry*]
**HAA** .......... Heptaminol Adenosinemonophosphate Amidate [*Biochemistry*]
**HAA** .......... High-Altitude Abort [*NASA*] (KSC)
**HAA** .......... High-Altitude Application
**HAA** .......... Hispanic American Almanac [*A publication*]
**HAA** .......... Historic Aircraft Association [*British*]
**HAA** .......... Hitotsubashi University. Hitotsubashi Academy. Annals [*A publication*]
**HAA** .......... Honduran-American Association (EA)
**HAA** .......... Horticulture Awareness Association (EA)
**HAA** .......... Hospital Activity Analysis [*British*]
**HAA** .......... Hotel Accountants Association of New York City (EA)
**HAA** .......... Houseboat Association of America (EA)
**HAA** .......... Housing Assistance Administration [*HUD*]
**HAA** .......... Human Asset Accounting (ADA)
**HAAA**........ Addis Ababa [*Ethiopia*] [*ICAO location identifier*] (ICLI)
**HAAB**........ Addis Ababa/Bole International [*Ethiopia*] [*ICAO location identifier*] (ICLI)
**HAAC**........ Housing Aid & Advice Centre [*England*]
**HAAC**........ Hydraulic Actuator Assembly Container
**HAAD** ....... Adaba [*Ethiopia*] [*ICAO location identifier*] (ICLI)
**HAAD** ....... High-Altitude Aircraft Detection
**HAADA**..... Horatio Alger Association of Distinguished Americans (EA)
**HAAFCE**... Headquarters, Allied Air Force, Central Europe [*NATO*]
**HAAFE** ..... Hawaiian Army and Air Force Exchange [*Military*]
**HAAG**........ Agordat [*Ethiopia*] [*ICAO location identifier*] (ICLI)
**HAA J** ....... HAA [*Herpetological Association of Africa*] Journal [*A publication*]
**HAAL**........ Addis Ababa/Liddetta [*Ethiopia*] [*ICAO location identifier*] (ICLI)
**HAALS**...... High-Accuracy Airborne Location System (MCD)
**HAAM**....... Arba Minch [*Ethiopia*] [*ICAO location identifier*] (ICLI)
**HAAO** ....... High-Altitude Airborne Observation
**HAAP**........ Hawthorne Army Ammunition Plant (MCD)
**HAAP**........ High-Altitude Air Pollution Program [*FAA*] (MCD)
**HAAP**........ Holston Army Ammunition Plant
**HAAP**........ Home-Based Advanced Assignment Program [*Military*]
**Ha App** ...... Appendix to Volume 10 of Hare's Vice-Chancellor's Reports [*England*] [*A publication*] (DLA)
**HAARS** ..... High-Altitude Airdrop Resupply System
**HAARS** ..... Hourly Attendance and Absence Reporting System [*Military*] (MCD)
**HAAS**........ Asmara App [*Ethiopia*] [*ICAO location identifier*] (ICLI)
**HAAT**........ Height above Average Terrain
**HAATC** ..... High-Altitude Air Traffic Control
**HAAW**....... Awash [*Ethiopia*] [*ICAO location identifier*] (ICLI)
**HAAW**....... Heavy Antitank/Assault Weapon [*Army*]
**HAAX**........ Axum [*Ethiopia*] [*ICAO location identifier*] (ICLI)
**HAAY**........ Asmara/Yohannes IV [*Ethiopia*] [*ICAO location identifier*] (ICLI)
**HAB**........... Habacuc [*Old Testament book*] [*Douay version*]
**Hab** ........... Habakkuk [*Old Testament book*]
**HAB**........... Habitat [*Dwelling*] (ROG)
**HAB**........... Habitation
**HAB**........... Habitual [*FBI standardized term*]
**HAB**........... Haboro [*Japan*] [*Seismograph station code, US Geological Survey*] [*Closed*] (SEIS)
**HAB**........... Hamburg Afrika Bank [*Hamburg Africa Bank*]
**HAB**........... Hamilton, AL [*Location identifier*] [*FAA*] (FAAL)
**HAB**........... Hazards Analysis Board [*Air Force*]
**HAB**........... Hear a Book [*Australia*]
**HAB**........... Hearing Aid Battery
**HAB**........... Heavy Assault Bridge
**HAB**........... High-Altitude Bombing [*Military*]
**HAB**........... Hiram Abiff [*Freemasonry*] (ROG)
**HAB**........... Historic American Buildings [*Survey*] [*Library of Congress*]
**HAB**........... Home Address Block
**HAB**........... Horizontal Assembly Building [*NASA*] (KSC)
**HAB**........... Horizontal Axis Bearing
**HAB**........... Hot Air Balloon
**HAB**........... Humanities Association. Bulletin [*A publication*]
**HAB**........... Hybrid Antibody [*Immunology*]
**HABA**........ Health and Beauty Aids [*Retailing*] (AABC)
**HABA**........ (Hydroxyazobenzene)benzoic Acid [*Also, HBABA*] [*Organic chemistry*]
**Habana Mus y Biblioteca Malacologia Circ** ... Habana Museo y Biblioteca de Malacologia. Circulares [*A publication*]
**Habana Mus y Biblioteca Zoologia Circ** ... Habana Museo y Biblioteca de Zoologia. Circulares [*A publication*]
**HABB**........ Bunno Bedele [*Ethiopia*] [*ICAO location identifier*] (ICLI)
**HABC**........ Baco [*Ethiopia*] [*ICAO location identifier*] (ICLI)
**HAB CORP** ... Habeas Corpus [*You Have the Body*] [*Legal*] [*Latin*] (ROG)
**HABD**........ Bahar Dar [*Ethiopia*] [*ICAO location identifier*] (ICLI)
**HABE**........ Beica [*Ethiopia*] [*ICAO location identifier*] (ICLI)
**HABE**........ Haber, Inc. [*NASDAQ symbol*] (NQ)
**HABF**........ Hepatic Artery Blood Flow
**HAB FAC POSS** ... Habere Facias Possessionem [*A writ to put the plaintiff in possession*] [*Latin*] [*Legal term*] (ROG)
**Hab Fa Poss** ... Habere Facias Possessionem [*A writ to put the plaintiff in possession*] [*Legal term*] [*Latin*]
**HAB FA SEIS** ... Habere Facias Seisenam [*A writ to put the plaintiff in actual possession*] [*Latin*] [*Legal term*] (ROG)
**HAB FA SEIS** ... Habere Facias Seisinam [*That You Cause to Have Seisin*] [*Latin*] [*Legal term*] (DLA)
**HABGT**..... Hutt Adaptation of the Bender-Gestalt Test
**HABI**......... Habitat [*A publication*]
**Habitat Aust** ... Habitat Australia [*A publication*]
**Habitat Int** ... Habitat International [*England*] [*A publication*]
**Habitat Vie Soc** ... Habitat et Vie Sociale [*A publication*]
**HABN**........ Haben Industries, Inc. [*NASDAQ symbol*] (NQ)
**HABP**........ Hypersonic Arbitrary Body Program [*NASA*]
**HABRA**..... Harvard Business Review [*A publication*]
**HABS**........ High-Altitude Bombsight (NATG)
**HABS**........ Historic American Buildings Survey [*Library of Congress*]
**HABT**........ Habeat [*Let Him Have*] [*Pharmacy*]
**HABT-A**.... Habitat [*A publication*]
**HABU**........ Bulchi [*Ethiopia*] [*ICAO location identifier*] (ICLI)
**HABY**........ Haberdashery (DSUE)
**HAC**.......... Hachijojima Island [*Japan*] [*Airport symbol*] (OAG)
**HAC**.......... Hachinohe [*Japan*] [*Seismograph station code, US Geological Survey*] (SEIS)
**HAC**.......... Haitian Air Corps
**HAC**.......... Handicapped Action Committee
**HAC**.......... Hawaii Aeronautics Commission (FAAC)
**HAC**.......... Heading Alignment Circle [*NASA*] (NASA)
**HAC**.......... Heading Alignment Cone [*NASA*] (NASA)
**HAC**.......... Heading Alignment Cylinder (MCD)
**HAC**.......... Headquarters Area Command [*Military*]
**HAC**.......... Health Advisory Council [*Generic term*] (DHSM)
**HAC**.......... Hearing Aid with Compression
**HAC**.......... Heating and Air Conditioning Journal [*A publication*]
**HAC**.......... Heavy-Aggregate Concrete (DEN)
**HAC**.......... Heavy Antitank Convoy
**HAC**.......... Heavy Attack Aircraft Commander
**HAC**.......... Helicopter Air Control [*Military*] (CAAL)
**HAC**.......... Helicopter Aircraft Commander (NVT)
**HAC**.......... Herbicide Assessment Commission
**HAC**.......... Hexamethylmelamine [*Altretamine*], Adriamycin, Cyclophosphamide [*Antineoplastic drug regimen*]
**HAC**.......... High-Acceleration Cockpit [*Air Force*]
**HAC**.......... High-Altitude Compensation [*Automotive engineering*]
**HAC**.......... High-Aluminous Concrete
**HAC**.......... Highway Action Coalition
**HAC**.......... Hines Administrative Center [*Veterans Administration*]
**HAC**.......... Historians of American Communism (EA)
**HAC**.......... Historical Atlas of Canada [*Project*]
**HAC**.......... Holland America Cruises [*Formerly, Holland-America Line*]
**HAC**.......... Honourable Artillery Company [*Military unit*] [*British*]
**HAC**.......... House Appropriations Committee [*US Congress*] (AAG)
**HAC**.......... Housing Assistance Council (EA)
**HAC**.......... Hover and Approach Coupler (MCD)
**HAC**.......... Hughes Aircraft Co.
**HAC**.......... Humanities Association of Canada [*See also ACH*]
**HAC**.......... Hydrogenated Amorphous Carbon [*Inorganic chemistry*]
**HACBS**...... Hibernian Australian Catholic Benefit Society

**HACC**........ Help and Action Coordinating Committee (EAIO)
**HACC**........ Home and Community Care Program [*Australia*]
**HACCA**..... Heating and Air Conditioning Contractor [*A publication*]
**HACCP**..... Hazard Analysis Critical Control Point [*Quality control*]
**HACE**........ High-Altitude Cerebral Edema [*Medicine*]
**HACEK**..... Hemophilus, Actinobacillus, Cardiobacterium, Eikenella, and Kingella [*Gram-negative bacilli*]
**Hacett B SS** ... Hacettepe Bulletin of Social Sciences and Humanities [*A publication*]
**Hacettepe Bull Med-Surg** ... Hacettepe Bulletin of Medicine-Surgery [*A publication*]
**Hacettepe Fen Muhendislik Bilimleri Derg** ... Hacettepe Fen ve Muhendislik Bilimleri Dergisi [*A publication*]
**Hacettepe Med J** ... Hacettepe Medical Journal [*A publication*]
**Hacettepe Muhendislik Bilimleri Derg** ... Hacettepe Fen ve Muhendislik Bilimleri Dergisi [*Turkey*] [*A publication*]
**HACH**....... Hach Co. [*NASDAQ symbol*] (NQ)
**HAChT**...... High-Affinity Choline Transport
**HACI**......... Hughes Aircraft Company, International Division
**Hacienda Publica Esp** ... Hacienda Publica Espanola [*A publication*]
**HACK**........ Hackney [*Borough of London*]
**Hack Gen Aw** ... Hackett on the Geneva Award Acts [*A publication*] (DLA)
**HACL**........ Harvard Air Cleaning Laboratory (NRCH)
**HACL**........ Hostility Adjective Check List [*Psychology*]
**HACLCS**... Harpoon Aircraft Command and Launch Control Set [*Missiles*] (NVT)
**HACLS**...... Harpoon Aircraft Command and Launch Subsystem [*Missiles*] (MCD)
**HAC NOCT** ... Hac Nocte [*Tonight*] [*Pharmacy*]
**HACOBU** ... Hawkesbury Agricultural College Old Boys Union [*Australia*]
**HACOM**.... Headquarters Area Command [*Military*]
**HACS**........ Hazard Assessment Computer System [*Coast Guard*]
**HACS**........ High-Angle Control System [*British military*] (DMA)
**HACS**........ Homeostatic Adaptive Control System
**HACS**........ Hyperactive Child Syndrome
**HACSG**..... Hyper Active Children's Support Group [*British*]
**HACT**........ High-Affinity Choline Transport
**HACUITEX** ... Habillement, Cuir, et Textile [*France*] (EY)
**HAD**.......... Casper, WY [*Location identifier*] [*FAA*] (FAAL)
**HAD**.......... Hadassah (BJA)
**Had**............ Haddington's Manuscript Reports, Scotch Court of Session [*A publication*] (DLA)
**Had**............ Hadley's Reports [*45-48 New Hampshire*] [*A publication*] (DLA)
**HAD**.......... Hadson Corp. [*NYSE symbol*] (SPSG)
**HAD**.......... Half Amplitude Duration [*Telecommunications*] (TEL)
**HAD**.......... Halmstad [*Sweden*] [*Airport symbol*] (OAG)
**HAD**.......... Handicappers for Accountable Democracy (EA)
**HAD**.......... Hardness Assurance Document
**HAD**.......... Hartland [*United Kingdom*] [*Geomagnetic observatory code*]
**HAD**.......... Hassan Addakhil Dam [*Morocco*] [*Seismograph station code, US Geological Survey*] (SEIS)
**HA or D**..... Havre, Antwerp, or Dunkirk [*Business term*]
**HAD**.......... Hawaii Air Defense
**HAD**.......... Heat-Activated Device (NRCH)
**HAD**.......... Helicopter Approach/Departure [*Military*] (CAAL)
**HAD**.......... Hemadsorption [*Hematology*]
**HAD**.......... Hexamethylmelamine, Adriamycin, Diamminedichloroplatinum [*Cisplatin*] [*Antineoplastic drug regimen*]
**HAD**.......... High-Accuracy Data [*System*] (MUGU)
**HAD**.......... High-Altitude Density [*Sounding rocket*]
**HAD**.......... High-Altitude Diagnostic [*Unit*] [*Rocket launcher*]
**HAD**.......... Horizontal Array of Dipoles
**HAD**.......... Hospital Administration [*or Administrator*]
**HADA**....... Hawaiian Defense Area
**HADAPS**... Hydrographic Automated Data Acquisitioning and Processing System (MCD)
**Hadashot Arch** ... Hadashot Archaeologioth [*A publication*]
**HADB**........ Dagabour [*Ethiopia*] [*ICAO location identifier*] (ICLI)
**HADB**........ High-Altitude Dive Bomb [*Military*]
**HADC**........ Dessie/Combolcha [*Ethiopia*] [*ICAO location identifier*] (ICLI)
**HADC**........ Holloman Air Development Center [*Air Force*]
**Had Chy Jur** ... Haddan's Administrative Jurisdiction of the Court of Chancery [*A publication*] (DLA)
**HADD**....... Dembidollo [*Ethiopia*] [*ICAO location identifier*] (ICLI)
**Hadd**.......... Haddington's Manuscript Reports, Scotch Court of Session [*A publication*] (DLA)
**HADD**....... Hawaiian Air Defense Division
**Haddington** ... Haddington's Manuscript Reports, Scotch Court of Session [*A publication*] (DLA)
**HADE**........ Hadson Europe, Inc. [*NASDAQ symbol*] (NQ)
**HA-DEC**.... Hour Angle-Declination [*Type of antenna mounting*]
**HADES**..... Hypersonic Air Data Entry System
**HADIZ**...... Hawaiian Air Defense Identification Zone
**HADL**........ Dallol [*Ethiopia*] [*ICAO location identifier*] (ICLI)
**Hadl**........... Hadley's Reports [*45-48 New Hampshire*] [*A publication*] (DLA)
**Hadley**....... Hadley's Reports [*45-48 New Hampshire*] [*A publication*] (DLA)
**Hadl Rom Law** ... Hadley's Introduction to the Roman Law [*A publication*] (DLA)
**HADM**...... Debre Marcos [*Ethiopia*] [*ICAO location identifier*] (ICLI)
**HADM**...... Heavy Atomic Demolition Munition [*Military*] (AABC)
**HADN**....... Danguilla [*Ethiopia*] [*ICAO location identifier*] (ICLI)
**HAD(N)**..... Head of Aircraft Department (Naval) [*British*]
**HADO**....... Dodola [*Ethiopia*] [*ICAO location identifier*] (ICLI)
**HADOPAD** ... High-Altitude Delayed Opening Parachute Actuation Device (MCD)
**HADOSS**.. HWWA-Dossiers [*Society for Business Information*] [*Information service or system*] (IID)
**HADR**........ Dire Dawa/Aba Tenna Dejazmatch Yilma [*Ethiopia*] [*ICAO location identifier*] (ICLI)
**Hadr**........... Hadrian [*of Scriptores Historiae Augustae*] [*Classical studies*] (OCD)
**HADR**........ Hughes Air Defense RADAR [*Military*]
**Hadronic J** ... Hadronic Journal [*A publication*]
**HADS**........ Hawaii Air Defense System
**HADS**........ Hypersonic Air Data Sensor (IEEE)
**HADT**........ Debre Tabor [*Ethiopia*] [*ICAO location identifier*] (ICLI)
**HADTS**..... High-Accuracy Data Transmission System (MUGU)
**HAE**........... Hannibal, MO [*Location identifier*] [*FAA*] (FAAL)
**HAE**........... Havasupai [*Arizona*] [*Airport symbol*] (OAG)
**HAE**........... Hereditary Angioneurotic Edema [*Medicine*]
**HAEC**........ Holarctic Ecology [*A publication*]
**HAEE**........ Harwell Atomic Energy Establishment
**HAEH**........ Horizontal Axis Electrical Hairspring
**HAEK**........ Historische. Archiv fuer die Erzbistum Koeln [*A publication*]
**HAEM**....... Haemolysis [*British*]
**HAEMA**.... Haematologica [*A publication*]
**HAEMAT** .. Haematocrit [*British*]
**HAEMATOL** ... Haematology [*British*]
**Haematol Bluttransfus** ... Haematologie und Bluttransfusion [*Haematology and Blood Transfusion*] [*A publication*]
**Haematol Lat** ... Haematologica Latina [*A publication*]
**HAEMORRH** ... Haemorrhage [*British*]
**HAEMP**.... High-Altitude Electromagnetic Pulse
**HAENE6**... Handbook of Endotoxin [*A publication*]
**HAER**........ Historic American Engineering Record [*Department of the Interior*]
**Haerterei-Tech Mitt** ... Haerterei-Technische Mitteilungen [*A publication*]
**Haerterei-Tech Waermebehandl** ... Haerterei-Technik und Waermebehandlung [*A publication*]
**Haert-Tech Mitt** ... Haerterei-Technische Mitteilungen [*A publication*]
**HAES**........ High-Altitude Effects Simulation [*Defense Nuclear Agency*]
**HAF**........... Haifa [*Israel*] [*Seismograph station code, US Geological Survey*] [*Closed*] (SEIS)
**HAF**........... Half Moon Bay, CA [*Location identifier*] [*FAA*] (FAAL)
**HAF**........... Headquarters, Air Force (AFM)
**HAF**........... Headquarters, Allied Forces
**HAF**........... Heavy Aircraft Fuel (MSA)
**HAF**........... Hebrew Arts Foundation (EA)
**HAF**........... Helicopter Assault Force (NVT)
**HAF**........... Hellenic Armed Forces (NATG)
**HAF**........... Helms Athletic Foundation [*Later, Citizens Savings Athletic Foundation*] (EA)
**HAF**........... High-Abrasion Furnace (IEEE)
**HAF**........... High-Altitude Fluorescence (IEEE)
**HAF**........... High-Altitude Fuze [*To activate weapons*]
**HAF**........... Human Antitumor Factor [*Biochemistry*]
**HAF**........... Hypersonic Aerothermaldynamic Facility
**HAFB**........ Heavy Assault Floating Bridge [*British military*] (DMA)
**HAFB**........ Holloman Air Force Base [*New Mexico*]
**HAFC**........ High-Altitude Forecast Center
**HAFC**........ Hoyt Axton Fan Club (EA)
**HAFE**........ Harpers Ferry National Historical Park
**HAFFB**...... Health Affairs [*A publication*]
**Haffkine Inst Annu Rep** ... Haffkine Institute. Annual Report [*A publication*]
**HAFID**...... Hydrogen Atmosphere Flame Ionization Detector
**HAFMED** ... Headquarters, Allied Forces, Mediterranean
**HAFN**........ Fincha [*Ethiopia*] [*ICAO location identifier*] (ICLI)
**HAFO**........ Home Accounting and Finance Office
**HAFS**........ Homosexuals Anonymous Fellowship Services (EA)
**HAFSE**...... Headquarters, Allied Forces, Southern Europe (NATG)
**HAFTB**...... Holloman Air Force Test Base [*New Mexico*] (AAG)
**Hag**............ Hagan's Reports [*Utah*] [*A publication*] (DLA)
**Hag**............ Hagan's Reports [*West Virginia*] [*A publication*] (DLA)
**Hag**............ Haggai [*Old Testament book*]
**Hag**............ Haggard's English Admiralty Reports [*A publication*] (DLA)
**Hag**............ Hagigah (BJA)
**HAG**.......... Helicopter Action Group (NVT)
**HAG**.......... High-Explosive Antiarmor Grenade [*Weaponry*] (MCD)
**HAG**.......... Hold for Arrival of Goods
**HAG**.......... Housing Association Grant [*British*]
**HAG**.......... Hydroxyaminoguanidine [*Biochemistry*]
**Hag Adm**.... Haggard's English Admiralty Reports [*A publication*] (DLA)
**Hagan**........ Hagan's Reports [*Utah*] [*A publication*] (DLA)
**HAGB**........ Goba [*Ethiopia*] [*ICAO location identifier*] (ICLI)
**HAG COM** ... Haga Comitum [*The Hague*] [*Imprint*] (ROG)
**Hag Con**..... Haggard's English Consistory Reports [*161 English Reprint*] [*A publication*] (DLA)

**Hag Ecc**...... Haggard's English Ecclesiastical Reports [*162 English Reprint*] [*A publication*] (DLA)
**HAGG**....... Heat-Aggregated Gamma Globulin [*Clinical chemistry*]
**HAGG**....... Hyperimmune Antivariola Gamma Globulin
**Hagg Adm**... Haggard's English Admiralty Reports [*A publication*] (DLA)
**Hagg Adm (Eng)**... Haggard's English Admiralty Reports [*161 English Reprint*] [*A publication*] (DLA)
**Hagg Con**... Haggard's English Consistory Reports [*161 English Reprint*] [*A publication*] (DLA)
**Hagg Cons**... Haggard's English Consistory Reports [*161 English Reprint*] [*A publication*] (DLA)
**Hagg Consist**... Haggard's English Consistory Reports [*161 English Reprint*] [*A publication*] (DLA)
**Hagg Consist (Eng)**... Haggard's English Consistory Reports [*161 English Reprint*] [*A publication*] (DLA)
**Hagg Ecc**.... Haggard's English Ecclesiastical Reports [*162 English Reprint*] [*A publication*] (DLA)
**Hagg Eccl**.. Haggard's English Ecclesiastical Reports [*162 English Reprint*] [*1827-33*] [*A publication*] (DLA)
**Hagg Eccl (Eng)**... Haggard's English Ecclesiastical Reports [*162 English Reprint*] [*A publication*] (DLA)
**HAGH**....... Ghinnir [*Ethiopia*] [*ICAO location identifier*] (ICLI)
**HAGL**........ Galadi [*Ethiopia*] [*ICAO location identifier*] (ICLI)
**HAGL**........ Handheld Grenade-Launcher
**HAGM**...... Gambella [*Ethiopia*] [*ICAO location identifier*] (ICLI)
**HAGN**....... Gondar [*Ethiopia*] [*ICAO location identifier*] (ICLI)
**Hagn & M**... Hagner and Miller's Reports [*2 Maryland Chancery*] [*A publication*] (DLA)
**Hagn & Mill**... Hagner and Miller's Reports [*2 Maryland Chancery*] [*A publication*] (DLA)
**HAGO**....... Gode [*Ethiopia*] [*ICAO location identifier*] (ICLI)
**HAGR**........ Gore [*Ethiopia*] [*ICAO location identifier*] (ICLI)
**HAGR**........ Hamilton Grange National Memorial
**HAGU**....... Gura [*Ethiopia*] [*ICAO location identifier*] (ICLI)
**Hague Ct Rep**... Hague Court Reports [*A publication*] (DLA)
**HAH**.......... Jacksonville, NC [*Location identifier*] [*FAA*] (FAAL)
**HAH**.......... Moroni [*Comoro Islands*] Hahaia Airport [*Airport symbol*] (OAG)
**HAHGG**.... Historiche Avonden. Uitgegeven door het Historiche Genootschap te Groningen ter Gelegenheid van Zijn Twintigjarig Bestaan [*A publication*]
**Ha Hinnuk Ham M**... Ha-Hinnuk Ham-Musiquali [*A publication*]
**HAHM**...... Debre Zeit/Harar Meda [*Ethiopia*] [*ICAO location identifier*] (ICLI)
**Hahnemann Symp**... Hahnemann Symposium [*A publication*]
**HAHR**....... Hispanic American Historical Review [*A publication*]
**HA(HS)**..... Hospital Apprentice, High School
**HAHS**........ Hossana [*Ethiopia*] [*ICAO location identifier*] (ICLI)
**HAHST**..... High-Altitude High-Speed Target [*Formerly, HAST*] (MCD)
**HAHT**...... Hypersonic Arc-Heated Tunnel [*Langley Research Center*] [*NASA*]
**HAHU**....... Humera [*Ethiopia*] [*ICAO location identifier*] (ICLI)
**hai**............. Haida [*MARC language code*] [*Library of Congress*] (LCCP)
**HAI**............ Haiwee [*California*] [*Seismograph station code, US Geological Survey*] [*Closed*] (SEIS)
**HAI**............ Hampton Industries, Inc. [*AMEX symbol*] (SPSG)
**HAI**............ Handwriting Analysts, International (EA)
**HAI**............ Health Action International (EA)
**HAI**............ Helicopter Association International (EA)
**HAI**............ Helicopter Attitude Indicator
**HAI**............ Hemagglutination Inhibition [*Immunochemistry*]
**HAI**............ Hepatic Artery Infusion [*Chemotherapy*]
**HAI**............ Hospital-Acquired Infection [*Medicine*]
**HAI**............ Hospital Audiences (EA)
**HAI**............ Hot Air Intake [*Automotive engineering*]
**HAI**............ Three Rivers, MI [*Location identifier*] [*FAA*] (FAAL)
**HAIC**......... Harwyn Industries Corp. [*NASDAQ symbol*] (NQ)
**HAIC**......... Hearing Aid Industry Conference [*Later, HIA*] (EA)
**HAIC**......... Hetero-Atom-in-Context
**HAID**......... Hand-Emplaced Acoustic Intrusion Detector (NVT)
**HAID**......... Hispanic Americans Information Directory [*A publication*]
**HAIDEX**... Hughes Artificial Intelligence Diagnostic Expert [*Hughes Aircraft Co.*] [*Army*]
**Hailes**......... Dalrymple (Lord Hailes). Decisions of the Scotch Court of Session [*1776-91*] [*A publication*] (DLA)
**Hailes Ann**... Hailes' Annals of Scotland [*A publication*] (DLA)
**Hailes Dec**... Hailes' Decisions, Scotch Court of Sessions [*A publication*] (DLA)
**Haile Selassie I Univ Dep Geol Annu Rep**... Haile Selassie I University. Department of Geology. Annual Report [*A publication*]
**Hain JP**...... Haine's Illinois Justice of the Peace [*A publication*] (DLA)
**HAIR**......... Help Alopecia International Research (EA)
**HAIRDS**.... High-Altitude Infrared Detecting Set (MCD)
**HAIRS**....... High-Altitude Test and Evaluation of Infrared Sources (MCD)
**HAISS**....... High-Altitude Infrared Sensor System
**HAIT**......... Haiti
**HAIT**......... Hash Algorithm Information Table
**HAJ**........... Hanover [*West Germany*] [*Airport symbol*] (OAG)
**HAJC**........ Hawaiian Area Joint Committee [*Military*] (CINC)
**HAJJ**.......... Jijiga [*Ethiopia*] [*ICAO location identifier*] (ICLI)
**HAJM**....... Jimma [*Ethiopia*] [*ICAO location identifier*] (ICLI)
**HAK**........... Adelanto, CA [*Location identifier*] [*FAA*] (FAAL)
**HAK**........... Haikou [*China*] [*Airport symbol*] (OAG)
**HAK**........... Hakodate [*Japan*] [*Seismograph station code, US Geological Survey*] (SEIS)
**HAK**........... Horizontal Access Kit (NASA)
**HAKASH**.. Hayl Kashish [*Elderly Army*] [*Israel*]
**HAKD**........ Kabre Dare [*Ethiopia*] [*ICAO location identifier*] (ICLI)
**HAKL**........ Kelafo [*Ethiopia*] [*ICAO location identifier*] (ICLI)
**HAKO**....... Hako Minuteman, Inc. [*NASDAQ symbol*] (NQ)
**HAKOD4**.. Bioscience and Industry [*A publication*]
**Hakone Symp Proc**... Hakone Symposium. Proceedings [*A publication*]
**Hal**............. Halakha (BJA)
**Hal**............. Halieuticon Liber [*of Ovid*] [*Classical studies*] (OCD)
**HAL**........... Halifax [*Nova Scotia*] [*Seismograph station code, US Geological Survey*] (SEIS)
**Hal**............. Hallah (BJA)
**HAL**........... Halliburton Co. [*NYSE symbol*] [*Toronto Stock Exchange symbol*] (SPSG)
**HAL**........... Haloperidol [*A tranquilizer*]
**HAL**........... Halothane [*Also, H*] [*An anesthetic*]
**HAL**........... Hamburg-Amerika Linie [*Hamburg-America Steamship Co.*]
**HAL**........... Handicapped Assistance Loan
**HAL**........... Harwell Automated Loans [*Library circulation system*]
**HAL**........... Hash Algorithm Library
**HAL**........... Hawaiian Airlines, Inc.
**HAL**........... Hazards Assessment Laboratory [*Colorado State University*] [*Research center*] (RCD)
**H-A-L**........ Head-Arm-Leg [*Medicine*]
**HAL**........... Heads-Up Audio-Vision Logistics [*NASA*]
**HAL**........... Height above Landing [*Area*]
**HA(L)**........ Helicopter Attack Squadron (Light) (CINC)
**HAL**........... Hemispheric Activation Level [*Data processing*] (BYTE)
**HAL**........... Hepatic Artery Ligation [*Medicine*]
**HAL**........... Heuristically-Programmed Algorithmic [*Name of computer in film, "2001: A Space Odyssey." Acronym is also considered to have been formed by combining the letters preceding IBM in the alphabet*]
**HAL**........... High-Order Articulated Language [*Data processing*] (MCD)
**HAL**........... High-Order Assembly Language [*Data processing*] (NASA)
**HAL**........... Highly Automated Logic [*Data processing*]
**HAL**........... Hindustan Aeronautics Limited
**HAL**........... Holding and Approach-to-Land [*Procedure*] [*Aviation*]
**HAL**........... Holland-America Line [*Later, Holland America Cruises*]
**HAL**........... Houston Aerospace Language [*NASA*] (NASA)
**HAL**........... Human Access Language [*Data processing*]
**HAL**........... Hypogastric Artery Ligation [*Medicine*]
**HAL**........... VCR [*Video Cassette Recorder*] device allowing programming via telephone [*Advanced Video Dynamics*]
**HALA**........ Awasa [*Ethiopia*] [*ICAO location identifier*] (ICLI)
**HALA**........ Hallamore Corp. [*NASDAQ symbol*] (NQ)
**Hal Anal**.... Hale's Analysis of the Law [*A publication*] (DLA)
**HALAT**..... Hebraeisches und Aramaeisches Lexikon zum Alten Testament [*Leiden*] (BJA)
**HALB**........ Halberton [*England*]
**Halbmon Literaturverz Fortschr Phys**... Halbmonatliches Literaturverzeichnis der Fortschrifte der Physik [*A publication*]
**Halc**........... Halcomb's Mining Cases [*England*] [*A publication*] (DLA)
**Hal Civ Law**... Hallifax's Analysis of the Civil Law [*A publication*] (DLA)
**Halc Min Cas**... Halcomb's Mining Cases [*England*] [*A publication*] (DLA)
**HALCON**... High-Altitude Long-Focus Convergent Mapping System
**Hal Const Hist**... Hallam's Constitutional History of England [*A publication*] (DLA)
**HALE**........ Haleakala National Park
**Hale**........... Hale's English Common Law [*A publication*] (DLA)
**Hale**........... Hale's Reports [*33-37 California*] [*A publication*] (DLA)
**HALE**........ High-Altitude, Long-Endurance [*Proposed unmanned reconnaissance drone*] [*Military*]
**HALEA**..... Harvey Lectures [*A publication*]
**Hale Anal**... Hale's Analysis of the Law [*A publication*] (DLA)
**Hale C L**.... Hale's History of the Common Law [*A publication*] (DLA)
**Hale Com Law**... Hale's History of the Common Law [*A publication*] (DLA)
**Hale Cr Prec**... Hale's Precedents in (Ecclesiastical) Criminal Cases [*1475-1640*] [*A publication*] (DLA)
**Hale De Jure Mar**... Hale's De Jure Maris, Appendix to Hall on the Sea Shore [*A publication*] (DLA)
**Hale De Port Mar**... Hale's De Portibus Maris [*A publication*] (DLA)
**Hale Ecc**..... Hale's English Ecclesiastical Reports [*1583-1736*] [*A publication*] (DLA)
**HALEF**...... Hale Resources Ltd. [*NASDAQ symbol*] (NQ)
**Hale Hist Eng Law**... Hale's History of the English Law [*A publication*] (DLA)
**Hale Jur HL**... Hale's Jurisdiction of the House of Lords [*1796*] [*A publication*] (DLA)
**Hale Parl**... Hale's History of Parliament [*2nd ed.*] [*1745*] [*A publication*] (DLA)
**Hale PC**..... Hale's Pleas of the Crown [*England*] [*A publication*] (DLA)
**Hale PC (Eng)**... Hale's Pleas of the Crown [*England*] [*A publication*] (DLA)
**Hale Prec**... Hale's Precedents in (Ecclesiastical) Criminal Cases [*1475-1640*] [*A publication*] (DLA)

**Hale's**......... Hale's Precedents in (Ecclesiastical) Criminal Cases [*1475-1640*] [*A publication*] (DLA)
**Hale Sug CM** ... Hale's Suggestion on Courts-Martial [*A publication*] (DLA)
**Hale Sum**... Hale's Summary of the Pleas of the Crown [*England*] [*A publication*] (DLA)
**Hal Ev**......... Halsted's Digest of the Law of Evidence [*A publication*] (DLA)
**HALFSEE** ... Headquarters, Allied Land Forces, Southeastern Europe
**Half-Yrly J Mysore Univ Sect B Sci Incl Med Eng** ... Half-Yearly Journal. Mysore University. Section B. Science Including Medicine and Engineering [*A publication*]
**Halh Gent L** ... Halhed's Code of Gentoo Laws [*A publication*] (DLA)
**Halifax Anal** ... Halifax' Analysis of the Roman Civil Law [*A publication*] (DLA)
**Hal Int Law** ... Halleck's International Law [*A publication*] (DLA)
**Halk**........... Halkerston's Compendium of Scotch Faculty Decisions [*A publication*] (DLA)
**Halk**........... Halkerston's Digest of the Scotch Marriage Law [*A publication*] (DLA)
**Halk**........... Halkerston's Latin Maxims [*A publication*] (DLA)
**Halk Comp** ... Halkerston's Compendium of Scotch Faculty Decisions [*A publication*] (DLA)
**Halk Dig**.... Halkerston's Digest of the Scotch Marriage Law [*A publication*] (DLA)
**Halk Lat Max** ... Halkerston's Latin Maxims [*A publication*] (DLA)
**Halk Max**.. Halkerston's Latin Maxims [*A publication*] (DLA)
**Halk Tech Terms** ... Halkerston's Technical Terms of the Law [*A publication*] (DLA)
**Hall**............ Decisions of the Water Courts [*1913-36*] [*South Africa*] [*A publication*] (DLA)
**HALL**......... Hall Financial Group, Inc. [*NASDAQ symbol*] (SPSG)
**Hall**............ Hallett's Reports [*1, 2 Colorado*] [*A publication*] (DLA)
**Hall**............ Hallmark [*Record label*] [*Canada*]
**Hall**............ Hall's New York Superior Court Reports [*A publication*] (DLA)
**Hall**............ Hall's Reports [*56, 57 New Hampshire*] [*A publication*] (DLA)
**HALL**......... Lalibela [*Ethiopia*] [*ICAO location identifier*] (ICLI)
**Hall Adm** ... Hall's Admiralty Practice and Jurisdiction [*A publication*] (DLA)
**Hall ALJ**.... Hall's American Law Journal [*A publication*] (DLA)
**Hallam**....... Hallam's Constitutional History of England [*A publication*] (DLA)
**Hall Am LJ** ... Hall's American Law Journal [*A publication*] (DLA)
**Hal Law**..... Halsted's New Jersey Law Reports [*6-12 New Jersey*] [*A publication*] (DLA)
**Hall Ch Pr** ... Halliday's Elementary View of Chancery Proceedings [*A publication*] (DLA)
**Hall Civ Law** ... Hallifax's Analysis of the Civil Law [*A publication*] (DLA)
**Hall (Col)**... Hallett's Reports [*1, 2 Colorado*] [*A publication*] (DLA)
**Hall Const Hist** ... Hallam's Constitutional History of England [*A publication*] (DLA)
**Hall Const L** ... Hall's Tracts on Constitutional Law [*A publication*] (DLA)
**(Halle) Beitr** ... Beitraege zur Geschichte der Deutschen Sprache und Literatur (Halle) [*A publication*]
**Halleck Int Law** ... Halleck's International Law [*A publication*] (DLA)
**Hall Emerig Mar Loans** ... Hall's Essay on Maritime Loans from the French of Emerigon [*A publication*] (DLA)
**Haller Mb** ... Haller Muenzblaetter [*A publication*]
**Hallesches Jahrb Mitteldtsh Erdgesch** ... Hallesches Jahrbuch fuer Mitteldeutsche Erdgeschichte [*A publication*]
**Hallett**........ Hallett's Reports [*1, 2 Colorado*] [*A publication*] (DLA)
**Halle Univ Wiss Z Gesellsch & Sprachw Reihe** ... Halle Universitaet. Wissenschaftliche Zeitschrift Gesellschafts und Sprachwissenschaftliche Reihe [*A publication*]
**Hall Hist**.... Hallam's Constitutional History of England [*A publication*] (DLA)
**Hallifax Anal (of Civil Law)** ... Hallifax's Analysis of the Civil Law [*A publication*] (DLA)
**Hallif CL**.... Hallifax's Analysis of the Civil Law [*A publication*] (DLA)
**Hall Int Law** ... Hall on International Law [*A publication*] (DLA)
**Hall Int Law** ... Halleck's International Law [*A publication*] (DLA)
**Hall J Criminal Law** ... [*Jerome*] Hall. General Principles of Criminal Law [*A publication*] (DLA)
**Hall Jour Jur** ... Journal of Jurisprudence (Hall's) [*A publication*] (DLA)
**Hall Law of W** ... Halleck's Law of War [*A publication*] (DLA)
**Hall LJ**...... Hall's American Law Journal [*A publication*] (DLA)
**Hall Marit Loans** ... Hall's Essay on Maritime Loans from the French of Emerigon [*A publication*] (DLA)
**Hall Mex Law** ... Hall's Laws of Mexico Relating to Real Property, Etc. [*A publication*] (DLA)
**Hall Neut**... Hall's Rights and Duties of Neutrals [*1874*] [*A publication*] (DLA)
**Hall NH**..... Hall's Reports [*56, 57 New Hampshire*] [*A publication*] (DLA)
**Hall (NY)**... Hall's New York Superior Court Reports [*A publication*] (DLA)
**HALLO**..... Hang Alle Laffe Landverraders Op [*Hang All Cowardly Traitors to Their Country*] [*Greeting for Dutch Nazis allegedly coined by the Netherlands people during World War II*]
**Hall Profits a Prendre** ... Hall's Treatise on the Law Relating to Profits a Prendre, Etc. [*A publication*] (DLA)
**Hall's Am LJ** ... Hall's American Law Journal [*A publication*] (DLA)
**Hall Shores** ... Hall's Rights in the Sea Shores [*A publication*] (DLA)
**Hall's J Jur** ... Journal of Jurisprudence (Hall's) [*A publication*] (DLA)
**Hall & T**..... Hall and Twell's English Chancery Reports [*47 English Reprint*] [*A publication*] (DLA)
**Hall & Tw**.. Hall and Twell's English Chancery Reports [*47 English Reprint*] [*A publication*] (DLA)
**Hall & Tw (Eng)** ... Hall and Twell's English Chancery Reports [*47 English Reprint*] [*A publication*] (DLA)
**HALLUC**... Hallucination
**Hal Min Law** ... Halleck's Mining Laws of Spain and Mexico [*A publication*] (DLA)
**HALO**........ Handling of Alarms with Logic [*Nuclear reactors*]
**HALO**........ High-Altitude Large Optics [*Air Force*] (MCD)
**HALO**........ High-Altitude, Low-Opening [*Parachute*]
**HALO**........ Hughes Automated Lunar Observer [*NASA*]
**Haloan**....... [*Gregorius*] Haloander [*Deceased, 1531*] [*Authority cited in pre-1607 legal work*] (DSA)
**HALOE**..... Halogen Occulation Experiment (MCD)
**HALON**..... Halogenated Hydrocarbon
**HALP**........ Husbands of Airline Pilots
**HAL-PC**.... Houston Area League of PC [*Personal Computer*] Users
**HALPRO**.. Halverson Project [*World War II plan to bomb Japan from China*]
**HALRA**..... Harvard Law Review [*A publication*]
**Hals**........... Halsted's New Jersey Law Reports [*6-12 New Jersey*] [*A publication*] (DLA)
**HAL/S**....... High-Order Assembly Language for Shuttle Flight Computer (MCD)
**HAL/S**....... High-Order Assembly Language for Spacelab Usage [*NASA*] (NASA)
**HALS**........ Hindered Amine Light Stabilizers [*for plastics*]
**HALS**........ Houston Area Library System [*Library network*]
**Halsbury**.... Halsbury's Law of England [*A publication*]
**Halsbury**.... Halsbury's Statutes of England [*A publication*] (DLA)
**Halsbury L Eng** ... Halsbury's Law of England [*A publication*]
**Halsbury's Laws** ... Halsbury's Law of England [*A publication*]
**Halsbury's S Is** ... Halsbury's Statutory Instruments [*A publication*] (DLA)
**Halsbury's Statutes** ... Halsbury's Statutes of England [*A publication*] (DLA)
**Hals Ch**...... Halsted's New Jersey Equity Reports [*A publication*] (DLA)
**Hals Eq**...... Halsted's New Jersey Equity Reports [*A publication*] (DLA)
**HALSIM**... Hardware Logic Simulator [*Data processing*] (IEEE)
**HALST**...... Halstead [*Urban district in England*]
**Halst**......... Halsted's New Jersey Equity Reports [*A publication*] (DLA)
**Halst**......... Halsted's New Jersey Law Reports [*6-12 New Jersey*] [*A publication*] (DLA)
**Halst Ch**.... Halsted's New Jersey Chancery Reports [*A publication*] (DLA)
**Halsted (NJ)** ... Halsted's New Jersey Chancery Reports [*A publication*] (DLA)
**Halst Ev**..... Halsted's Digest of the Law of Evidence [*A publication*] (DLA)
**HALT**........ Help Abolish Legal Tyranny [*In organization name HALT-ALR*] (EA)
**HALT**........ Holdup Alert - Local Transmission [*Bank robbery alarm system*]
**HALT**........ Hungry? Angry? Lonely? Tired? [*Slogan used by Alcoholics Anonymous members to determine whether their emotions are out of control to the point that they may be tempted to take a drink*]
**HALT-ALR** ... HALT - An Organization of Americans for Legal Reform (EA)
**Halton Bus Jnl** ... Halton Business Journal [*A publication*]
**Hal & Tw**... Hall and Twell's English Chancery Reports [*47 English Reprint*] [*A publication*] (DLA)
**HaLV**......... Hamster Leukemia Virus
**HAM**......... Hairy Anatomy Marine [*See also BAM*] [*Slang term for male marines*] [*Bowdlerized version*]
**HAM**......... Hamburg [*West Germany*] [*Airport symbol*] (OAG)
**HAM**......... Hamburg [*West Germany*] [*Seismograph station code, US Geological Survey*] (SEIS)
**HAM**......... Hamilton Aviation, Inc. [*Hamilton, OH*] [*FAA designator*] (FAAC)
**Ham**........... (Hamilton of) Haddington's Manuscript Cases, Scotch Court of Session [*A publication*] (DLA)
**Ham**........... Hamlet [*Shakespearean work*]
**Ham**........... Hammond's India and Burma Election Cases [*A publication*] (DLA)
**Ham**........... Hammond's Reports [*1-9 Ohio*] [*A publication*] (DLA)
**HAM**......... Hampshire College, Amherst, MA [*OCLC symbol*] (OCLC)
**HAM**......... Hardware Associative Memory [*Data processing*] (DIT)
**HAM**......... Hearing Aid Microphone
**HAM**......... Heavy Atom Method
**HAM**......... Heavy Automotive Maintenance
**HAM**......... Height Adjustment Maneuver (MCD)
**HAM**......... Hexamethylmelamine, Adriamycin, Melphalan [*Antineoplastic drug regimen*]
**HAM**......... Hexamethylmelamine, Adriamycin, Methotrexate [*Antineoplastic drug regimen*]
**HAM**......... Hierarchical Access Method
**HAM**......... High-Altitude Missile (MCD)
**HAM**......... High-Speed Automatic Monitor
**HAM**......... Hold and Modify [*Computer display mode*]
**HAM**......... Home Access Mortgage
**HAM**......... Home Amateur [*Radio*]

**HAM** ......... Honda of America Manufacturing
**HAM** ......... HTLV-1-Associated Myelopathy [*Medicine*]
**HAM** ......... Human Albumin Microsphere [*Clinical anesthesiology*]
**HAM** ......... Human Associative Memory
**HA & M**..... Hymns Ancient and Modern
**HAM** ......... Hymns Ancient and Modern
**HAM** ......... Hypoparathyroidism, Addison's Disease, and Musculocutaneous Candidiasis [*Medicine*]
**HAMAA**.... Harper's Magazine [*A publication*]
**HAMAD**.... Harvard Magazine [*A publication*]
**Ham A & O** ... Hamerton, Allen, and Otter's English Magistrates' Cases [*3 New Sessions Cases*] [*A publication*] (DLA)
**HAMB**....... Hambledon [*England*]
**HAMB**....... Hamburg [*West Germany*] (ROG)
**HAMB**....... Hamburger Hamlets, Inc. [*NASDAQ symbol*] (NQ)
**Hamb Beitr A** ... Hamburger Beitraege zur Archaeologie [*A publication*]
**Hamb Beitr Angew Mineral Kristallphys Petrog** ... Hamburger Beitraege zur Angewandten Mineralogie, Kristallphysik, und Petrogenese [*A publication*]
**Hamb Beitr Num** ... Hamburger Beitraege zur Numismatik [*A publication*]
**Hamb Geophys Einzelschriften** ... Hamburger Geophysikalische Einzelschriften [*A publication*]
**Hamb St u Z Nachr** ... Hamburger Steuer und Zoll-Nachrichten [*A publication*]
**Hamburg Geol Staatsinstitut Mitt** ... Hamburg Geologischen Staatsinstitut. Mitteilungen [*A publication*]
**Hamburg Jb Wirtsch- u Ges-Polit** ... Hamburger Jahrbuch fuer Wirtschafts- und Gesellschaftspolitik [*A publication*]
**Hamb Wirtsch** ... Hamburger Wirtschaft [*Mitteilungen der Handelskammer Hamburg*] [*A publication*]
**Hamb Wschr Ae Zahn Ae** ... Hamburger Wochenschrift fuer Aerzte und Zahnaerzte [*A publication*]
**Hamb Zool Staatsinst u Zool Mus Mitt** ... Hamburg. Zoologisches Staatsinstitut und Zoologisches Museum. Mitteilungen [*A publication*]
**HAMCHAM** ... Haitian-American Chamber of Commerce and Industry (EA)
**HAMCHAM** ... Honduran-American Chamber of Commerce [*See also CCHA*] (EA)
**HAMCO**.... HAWK [*Homing All the Way Killer*] Assembly and Missile Checkout (AAG)
**Ham Cont** .. Hammon on Contracts [*A publication*] (DLA)
**Ham Cust**... Hamel's Laws of the Customs [*A publication*] (DLA)
**HAM-D**..... Hamilton Psychiatric Rating Scale for Depression
**HAMD** ...... Helicopter Ambulance Medical Detachment
**Hamdard Islam** ... Hamdard Islamicus [*A publication*]
**Hamdard Med Dig** ... Hamdard Medical Digest [*A publication*]
**HAME**....... Mieso [*Ethiopia*] [*ICAO location identifier*] (ICLI)
**Hamel Cust** ... Hamel's Laws of the Customs [*A publication*] (DLA)
**Ham Fed** .... Hamilton's Federalist [*A publication*] (DLA)
**HAMG** ...... Hamilton Group Holdings, Inc. [*Phoenix, AZ*] [*NASDAQ symbol*] (NQ)
**HAMIA**..... Hasler-Mitteilungen [*A publication*]
**Hamilton**.... Hamilton on Company Law [*3 eds.*] [*1891-1910*] [*A publication*] (DLA)
**Hamilton**.... (Hamilton of) Haddington's Manuscript Cases, Scotch Court of Session [*A publication*] (DLA)
**Hamilton**.... Hamilton's American Negligence Cases [*A publication*] (DLA)
**Hamilton As J Pr** ... Hamilton Association. Journal and Proceedings [*A publication*]
**Hamilton Sc As J Pr** ... Hamilton Scientific Association. Journal and Proceedings [*A publication*]
**HAMIM**.... Hizbul Muslimin [*Islamic Front*] [*Political party*] [*Malaysia*] (FEA)
**Ham Ins**..... Hammond on Fire Insurance [*A publication*] (DLA)
**Ham Ins**..... Hammond on Insanity [*A publication*] (DLA)
**Ham Int** ..... Hamel's International Law [*A publication*] (DLA)
**Ham & J** .... Hammond and Jackson's Reports [*45 Georgia*] [*A publication*] (DLA)
**HAMJ** ....... Maji [*Ethiopia*] [*ICAO location identifier*] (ICLI)
**HAMK**....... Makale [*Ethiopia*] [*ICAO location identifier*] (ICLI)
**HAML**....... Hamilton Oil Corp. [*NASDAQ symbol*] (NQ)
**HAML**....... Masslo [*Ethiopia*] [*ICAO location identifier*] (ICLI)
**HamletR** .... Hamlet Review [*A publication*]
**Hamlin**...... Hamlin's Reports [*81-93 Maine*] [*A publication*] (DLA)
**Hamline LR** ... Hamline Law Review [*A publication*]
**Hamline L Rev** ... Hamline Law Review [*A publication*]
**HAMM** ..... Hammer Technologies, Inc. [*San Rafael, CA*] [*NASDAQ symbol*] (NQ)
**HAMM** ..... Metema [*Ethiopia*] [*ICAO location identifier*] (ICLI)
**Ham Mar Laws** ... Hammick's Marriage Laws [*2nd ed.*] [*1887*] [*A publication*] (DLA)
**HAMMARR** ... Hazardous Materials Management and Resource Recovery [*University of Alabama*] [*Research center*] (RCD)
**Hammersmith Cardiol Workshop Ser** ... Hammersmith Cardiology Workshop Series [*A publication*]
**Ham Mo Bul** ... Ham (Walter P.) and Company. Monthly Bulletin [*A publication*] (APTA)
**Hammond** .. Hammond's Reports [*36-45 Georgia*] [*A publication*] (DLA)
**Hammond** .. Hammond's Reports [*1-9 Ohio*] [*A publication*] (DLA)
**Hammond & Jackson** ... Hammond and Jackson's Reports [*45 Georgia*] [*A publication*] (DLA)
**HAMN**...... Mendi [*Ethiopia*] [*ICAO location identifier*] (ICLI)
**Ham NP**..... Hammond's Nisi Prius [*A publication*] (DLA)
**Ham O** ....... [*Charles*] Hammond's Reports [*Ohio*] [*A publication*] (DLA)
**HAMO** ...... Motta [*Ethiopia*] [*ICAO location identifier*] (ICLI)
**Ham OR** .... [*Charles*] Hammond's Reports [*Ohio*] [*A publication*] (DLA)
**HAMOTS** ... High-Altitude Multiple Object Tracking System [*Air Force*]
**HAMP**....... Hampstead [*Region of London*]
**HAMP**....... Hampton National Historic Site
**HAMP**....... High-Altitude Measurement Probe
**HAMP**....... Hop and Stamp [*Dance terminology*]
**Ham Part**... Hammond on Parties to Action [*A publication*] (DLA)
**Ham Parties** ... Hammond on Parties to Action [*A publication*] (DLA)
**HAMPBF** ... Hawaii. Agricultural Experiment Station. Miscellaneous Publication [*A publication*]
**Ham Pl**....... Hammond's Principles of Pleading [*1819*] [*A publication*] (DLA)
**HAMPS** .... Hampshire [*County in England*]
**HAMPS** .... Heavy Airborne Multipurpose System (MCD)
**Hamps Beekpr** ... Hampshire Beekeeper [*A publication*]
**Hamps Co Cas** ... Hampshire County Court Reports [*England*] [*A publication*] (DLA)
**HAMPS R** ... Hampshire Regiment [*Military unit*] [*British*] (ROG)
**Hampton**.... Hampton's Magazine [*A publication*]
**Hamp Tr**.... Hampson. Trustees [*2nd ed.*] [*1830*] [*A publication*] (DLA)
**HAMR**....... Mui River [*Ethiopia*] [*ICAO location identifier*] (ICLI)
**HAMS**....... Hardness Assurance Monitoring System (MCD)
**HAMS**....... Headquarters and Maintenance Squad
**HAMS**....... Hour Angle of the Mean Sun [*Navigation*]
**HAMS**....... Massawa [*Ethiopia*] [*ICAO location identifier*] (ICLI)
**HAMS**....... [*The*] Smithfield Companies, Inc. [*NASDAQ symbol*] (NQ)
**HAMSB** ..... Heidelberger Akademie der Wissenschaften. Mathematisch-Naturwissenschaftliche Klasse. Sitzungsberichte [*A publication*]
**HAMT**....... Human-Aided Machine Translation
**HAMT**....... Mizan Teferi [*Ethiopia*] [*ICAO location identifier*] (ICLI)
**HAMTC**..... Hanford [*Washington*] Atomic Metal Trades Council
**HAMTF** .... Hispanic American Ministries Task Force of JSAC [*Joint Strategy and Action Committee*] (EA)
**HaMuSV**... Harvey Murine Sarcoma Virus
**HAN** ......... Chandler, AZ [*Location identifier*] [*FAA*] (FAAL)
**HAN** ......... Hambro Resources, Inc. [*Vancouver Stock Exchange symbol*]
**Han** ............ Handy's Ohio Reports [*12 Ohio Decisions*] [*A publication*] (DLA)
**HAN** ......... Hanford [*Washington*] [*Seismograph station code, US Geological Survey*] (SEIS)
**Han** ............ Hannay's New Brunswick Reports [*12, 13 New Brunswick*] [*A publication*] (DLA)
**HAN** ......... Hanoi [*North Vietnam*] [*Airport symbol*] (OAG)
**HAN** ......... Hanover [*Former state in Germany*]
**Han** ............ Hansard's Book of Entries [*1685*] [*A publication*] (DLA)
**HAN** ......... Hanson Trust PLC [*NYSE symbol*] (SPSG)
**Han** ............ Hanson's Bankruptcy Reports [*1915-17*] [*A publication*] (DLA)
**HAN** ......... Health Activation Network [*Later, WHAN*] (EA)
**HAN** ......... Hex Aluminum Nut
**HAN** ......... Hyannis Aviation [*Hyannis, MA*] [*FAA designator*] (FAAC)
**HAN** ......... Hydroxylammonium Nitrate [*Component of liquid propellants*] [*Inorganic chemistry*]
**HAN** ......... Hyperplastic Alveolar Nodules [*Precancerous lesions in mice*]
**HANA** ....... Halibut Association of North America (EA)
**HANA** ....... Hana Biologics, Inc. [*NASDAQ symbol*] (NQ)
**HANA** ....... Helvetia Association of North America [*Defunct*] (EA)
**Hanb Pat**.... Hanbury's Judicial Error in the Law of Patents [*A publication*] (DLA)
**Hanb Us**..... Hanbury-Jones on Uses [*A publication*] (DLA)
**Hanc Conv** ... Hancock's System of Conveyancing [*Canada*] [*A publication*] (DLA)
**Hand** .......... Hand Book [*A publication*]
**HAND** ....... Handex Environmental Recovery, Inc. [*NASDAQ symbol*] (NQ)
**Hand** .......... Hand's Reports [*40-45 New York*] [*A publication*] (DLA)
**Hand** .......... Handy's Ohio Reports [*12 Ohio Decisions*] [*A publication*] (DLA)
**HAND** ....... Have a Nice Day
**HandAms**... Handes Amsorya [*Vienna*] (BJA)
**HANDB**..... Handbook
**Handball Mag** ... Handball Magazine [*A publication*]
**Handb Anxiety** ... Handbook of Anxiety [*A publication*]
**Handb Bakt Infekt Tieren** ... Handbuch der Bakteriellen Infektionen bei Tieren [*A publication*]
**Handb Endotoxin** ... Handbook of Endotoxin [*A publication*]
**Handb Exp Pharmak** ... Handbuch der Experimentellen [*A publication*]
**Handb Gk Myth** ... Handbook of Greek Mythology [*A publication*] (OCD)
**Handb Lebensmittelchemie** ... Handbuch der Lebensmittelchemie [*A publication*]
**Handb Mag** ... Handbook for Magistrates [*1853-55*] [*A publication*] (DLA)
**Handb Med Radiol** ... Handbuch der Medizinschen Radiologie [*West Germany*] [*A publication*]
**Handb Mineral** ... Handbuch der Mineralogie [*A publication*]

**Handbook Appl Math Guidebook** ... Handbook of Applicable Mathematics Guidebook [*A publication*]
**Handbooks in Econom** ... Handbooks in Economics [*A publication*]
**Handb Pflanzenanat** ... Handbuch der Pflanzenanatomie [*A publication*]
**Handb Pflernahr Dueng** ... Handbuch der Pflanzenernahrung und Duengung [*A publication*]
**Handb Phys** ... Handbuch der Physik [*A publication*]
**Handb Physiol** ... Handbook of Physiology [*A publication*]
**Handb Plant Cell Cult** ... Handbook of Plant Cell Culture [*A publication*]
**Handb Shock Trauma** ... Handbook of Shock Trauma [*A publication*]
**Handb South Aust Dep Mines Energy** ... Handbook. South Australia Department of Mines and Energy [*A publication*]
**Handb Spez Path Anat Haustiere (Ernst Joest)** ... Handbuch der Speziellen Pathologischen Anatomie der Haustiere (Ernst Joest) [*A publication*]
**Handb Urol** ... Handbuch der Urologie [*A publication*]
**Handb US Natn Bur Stand** ... Handbook. United States National Bureau of Standards [*A publication*]
**Handb Zool** ... Handbuch der Zoologie [*A publication*]
**Hand Ch P** ... Hand's Chancery Practice [*A publication*] (DLA)
**Hand Clin** .. Hand Clinics [*A publication*]
**Hand Cr Pr** ... Hand's Crown Practice [*A publication*] (DLA)
**HANDE**..... Hydrofoil Analysis and Design [*Data processing*]
**Han Deb**..... Hansard's Parliamentary Debates [*A publication*] (DLA)
**Handel Ind** ... Handel en Industrie [*A publication*]
**Handelingen Commissie Toponymie & Dialectologie** ... Handelingen. Koninklijke Commissie voor Toponymie en Dialectologie [*A publication*]
**Handelingen Ned Phonol Werkgemeenschap** ... Handelingen. Nederlandse Phonologische Werkgemeenschap [*A publication*]
**Handel Jb** .. Handel Jahrbuch [*A publication*]
**Handel Koll Geneeskd S-Afr** ... Handelinge. Kollege van Geneeskunde van Suid-Afrika [*A publication*]
**Handel Ned Nat Geneeskd Congr** ... Handelingen. Nederlands Natuur- en Geneeskundig Congres [*A publication*]
**Handel Oudheidkunde Mechelen** ... Handelingen. Koninklijke Kring voor Oudheidkunde. Letteren en Kunst van Mechelen Malines [*Belgium*] [*A publication*]
**Handelsblt** ... Handelsblatt [*Information service or system*] [*A publication*]
**Handel Voeding Ver Suidel** ... Handelinge. Voedingvereeniging van Suidelike Afrika [*A publication*]
**Handel Wewn** ... Handel Wewnetrzny [*A publication*]
**Handel Zagran** ... Handel Zagraniczy [*A publication*]
**Handes Amsorya** ... Handes Amsorya. Monatschrift fuer Armenische Philologie [*A publication*]
**Hand Fines** ... Hand on Fines and Recoveries [*A publication*] (DLA)
**Hand Gent** ... Handelingen der Maatschappij voor Geschiedenis en Oudheidkunde te Gent [*A publication*]
**HANDICP** ... Handicap
**HandKonCommTop-Dial** ... Handelingen. Koninklijke Commissie voor Toponymie en Dialectologie [*A publication*]
**Handl Conveying Autom** ... Handling, Conveying, Automation [*West Germany*] [*A publication*]
**Handl & Shipp** ... Handling and Shipping [*Later, Handling and Shipping Management*] [*A publication*]
**Handl Shipp Manage** ... Handling and Shipping Management [*A publication*]
**Handl & Shipp Mgt** ... Handling and Shipping Management [*A publication*]
**Hand Ned Jur V** ... Handelingen. Nederlandse Juristen-Vereeniging [*A publication*]
**HandNFc**... Handelingen. Nederlands Filologencongres [*A publication*]
**Hand Pat**.... Hand on Patents [*A publication*] (DLA)
**HANDS**..... High-Altitude Nuclear Detection Studies [*National Institute of Standards and Technology*]
**Hand Vl Fc** ... Handelingen. Vlaamse Filologencongres [*A publication*]
**Handweaver** ... Handweaver and Craftsman [*A publication*]
**Hand Wewn** ... Handel Wewnetrzny [*A publication*]
**Handw O**.... Handwerksordnung [*A publication*]
**Handy** ........ Handy's Ohio Reports [*12 Ohio Decisions*] [*A publication*] (DLA)
**Handyman** ... Family Handyman [*A publication*]
**Handy (Ohio)** ... Handy's Ohio Reports [*12 Ohio Decisions*] [*A publication*] (DLA)
**Handy R**..... Handy's Cincinnati Superior Court Reports [*Ohio*] [*A publication*] (DLA)
**HANE**........ Hereditary Angioneurotic Edema [*Medicine*]
**HANE**........ High-Altitude Nuclear Effects [*Study*]
**HANE**........ High-Altitude Nuclear Explosion
**Hane Cr Dig** ... Hanes' United States Digest of Criminal Cases [*A publication*] (DLA)
**Han Ent**..... Hansard's Book of Entries [*1685*] [*A publication*] (DLA)
**Hanes**......... Hanes' English Chancery [*A publication*] (DLA)
**HANES**..... Health and Nutrition Examination Survey [*Public Health Service*]
**Hanf**........... Hanford's Entries [*1685*] [*A publication*] (DLA)
**HANG** ....... Hawaiian Air National Guard (FAAC)
**HANG** ....... Neghelle [*Ethiopia*] [*ICAO location identifier*] (ICLI)
**Hang L**........ Hanging Loose [*A publication*]
**Han Guk J Genet Eng** ... Han Guk Journal of Genetic Engineering [*A publication*]
**Han'guk Sikp'un Kwhak Hoechi Korea J Food Sci Technol** ... Han'guk Sikp'un Kwahak Hoechi. Korean Journal of Food Science and Technology [*A publication*]
**Hanh Mar Wom** ... Hanhart on the Laws Relating to Married Women [*A publication*] (DLA)
**Han Hor**..... Hanover on the Law of Horses [*A publication*] (DLA)
**HANJ** ........ Nejjo [*Ethiopia*] [*ICAO location identifier*] (ICLI)
**HANK** ....... Hanks Seafood Company, Inc. [*NASDAQ symbol*] (NQ)
**HANK** ....... Nekemte [*Ethiopia*] [*ICAO location identifier*] (ICLI)
**HAN/LCD** ... Hybrid Assigned Nematic/Liquid Crystal Display (TEL)
**Hanm** ......... Lord Kenyon's English King's Bench Reports, Notes, Edited by Hanmer [*A publication*] (ILCA)
**Han Mar Wom** ... Hanhart on the Laws Relating to Married Women [*A publication*] (DLA)
**Hanmer**...... Lord Kenyon's English King's Bench Reports, Notes, Edited by Hanmer [*A publication*] (DLA)
**Hann** .......... Hannay's New Brunswick Reports [*12, 13 New Brunswick*] [*A publication*] (DLA)
**Hannah Dairy Res Inst Rep** ... Hannah Dairy Research Institute. Report [*A publication*]
**Hannah Res Inst Rep** ... Hannah Research Institute. Report [*A publication*]
**Han (NB)**... Hannay's New Brunswick Reports [*12, 13 New Brunswick*] [*A publication*] (DLA)
**Hanneton** ... [*Guillelmus*] Hannetonius [*Deceased, 1586*] [*Authority cited in pre-1607 legal work*] (DSA)
**Hann Rpfl** .. Hannoversche Rechtspflege [*A publication*]
**hANP**......... Human Atrial Natriuretic Peptide [*Biochemistry*]
**Han Prob** ... Hanson on the Probate and Legacy Acts [*A publication*] (DLA)
**HANS**........ Hansard [*Database*] [*Australia*]
**HANS**........ High-Altitude Navigation System
**Hans Al**...... Hansard on Aliens [*A publication*] (DLA)
**Hansard (C)** ... Hansard (Commons) [*A publication*]
**Hansard House Commons Off Rep** ... Hansard. House of Commons. Official Report [*Great Britain*] [*A publication*]
**Hansard (L)** ... Hansard (Lords) [*A publication*]
**Hansb** ........ Hansbrough's Reports [*76-90 Virginia*] [*A publication*] (DLA)
**HANSB** ....... Hanseniase [*A publication*]
**Hans Deb**... Hansard's Parliamentary Debates [*A publication*] (DLA)
**Hanseniase Resumos Not** ... Hanseniase. Resumos e Noticias [*A publication*]
**Hansenol Int** ... Hansenologia Internationalis [*A publication*]
**Hans Ent**.... Hansard's Book of Entries [*1685*] [*A publication*] (DLA)
**Hans G Bl**.. Hansische Geschichtsblaetter [*A publication*]
**Hans JV Bl** ... Hanseatisches Justizverwaltungsblatt [*A publication*]
**Hans Parl Deb** ... Hansard's Parliamentary Debates [*A publication*] (DLA)
**Hans Pr**...... Hanson on Probate Acts [*A publication*] (DLA)
**HAnt**.......... Hispania Antiqua [*A publication*]
**Hanta**......... Hanrei Taimuzu [*A publication*]
**Hant Ams** .. Hantes Amsoriay [*A publication*]
**HANTS**..... Hampshire [*County in England*]
**Hanzaigaku Zasshi (Acta Criminol Med Leg Jpn)** ... Hanzaigaku Zasshi (Acta Criminologiae et Medicinae Legalis Japonica) [*A publication*]
**HAO** .......... Hamilton, OH [*Location identifier*] [*FAA*] (FAAL)
**HAO** .......... Hardware Action Officer [*Military*] (AABC)
**HAO** .......... High-Altitude Observatory [*Boulder, CO*] [*National Center for Atmospheric Research*]
**HAO** .......... Hospitals, Administration, and Organizations [*British*]
**HAOA** ....... High Angle of Attack [*Combat aircraft*] [*Navy*]
**HAOC** ....... Haynes-Apperson Owners Club (EA)
**HAOC** ....... Hexaazaoctadecahydrocoronene [*Organic chemistry*]
**HAOG** ....... Handbuch der Altorientalischen Geisteskultur [*A publication*] (BJA)
**HAOS**........ Hydroxylamine-ortho-sulfonic Acid [*Organic chemistry*]
**HAOSS** ..... High-Altitude Orbital Space Station (IEEE)
**HAP**........... Hafnium Column Product [*Nuclear energy*] (NRCH)
**HAP**........... Hampshire Aircraft Parks [*British military*] (DMA)
**HAP**........... Happy Bay [*Australia*] [*Airport symbol*] (OAG)
**HAP**........... Hardware Allocation Panel
**HAP**........... Harwood Academic Publishers [*British*]
**HAP**........... Hazardous Air Pollutant
**HAP**........... Heading Axis Perturbation
**HAP**........... Health Alliance Plan
**HAP**........... Heat Shock Activator Protein [*Biochemistry*]
**HAP**........... Height Above Plate [*Roofing*]
**HAP**........... Heredopathia Atactica Polyneuritiformis [*Medicine*]
**HAP**........... Hersteller-Abgabepreis [*Producer Sales Price*] [*German*]
**HAP**........... High-Acid Column Product (NRCH)
**HAP**........... High-Altitude Platform
**HAP**........... High-Altitude Probe (AAG)
**HAP**........... Home Owners Assistance Program [*Military*] (AABC)
**HAP**........... Honeycomb Aluminum Panel
**HAP**........... Hook-Associated Protein [*Genetics*]
**HAP**........... Horizontal Axis Pivot
**HAP**........... Host-Associated Population [*Ecology*]
**HAP**........... Housing Assistance Program
**HAP**........... Hutch Apparel Ltd. [*Vancouver Stock Exchange symbol*]
**HAP**........... Hydrated Antimony Pentaoxide [*Inorganic chemistry*]
**HAP**........... Hydrolyzed Animal Protein [*Food technology*]
**HAP**........... Hydroxyacetophenone [*Organic chemistry*]
**HAP**........... Hydroxyapatite [*Also, HA*] [*A mineral*]
**HAP**........... Hydroxylamine Perchlorate [*Organic chemistry*]

**HAP**........... Hyperboloid Approximation Procedure
**HAP**........... Hyperpolarizing Afterpotential [*Electrophysiology*]
**HAP**........... Whitsunday Resort (Long Island) [*Australia*] [*Airport symbol*]
**HAPAB**..... Health Aspects of Pesticides Abstract Bulletin [*Environmental Protection Agency*]
**HAPCWS**... Holt-Atherton Pacific Center for Western Studies [*University of the Pacific*] [*Research center*] (RCD)
**HAPDAR**.. Hard Point Demonstration Array RADAR
**HAPDEC**.. Hard Point Decoys (MCD)
**HAPE**........ High-Altitude Pulmonary Edema
**HAPFF-EUR**... HAWK [*Homing All the Way Killer*] Project Field Facility - Europe (MCD)
**HAPG**........ Heidelberger Abhandlungen zur Philosophie und Ihrer Geschichte [*A publication*]
**HAPI**......... Harris and Paulson, Incorporated [*NASDAQ symbol*] (NQ)
**HAPI**......... Holding as Previously Instructed [*Aviation*] (FAAC)
**HAPI**......... Host Application Programming Interface
**HAP-NICA**... Humanitarian Assistance Project for Independent Agricultural Development in Nicaragua [*Defunct*] (EA)
**HAPO**........ Hanford Atomic Products Operations [*General Electric Co.*]
**HAPORTH**... Halfpennyworth [*British*] (ROG)
**H App**........ Heir Apparent (DAS)
**HAPP**........ High Air Pollution Potential
**HAPP**........ High-Altitude Pollution Project [*FAA*]
**HAPP**........ High-Altitude Powered Platforms (MCD)
**HAPPE**...... High-Altitude Particle Program Experiment [*NASA*]
**HAPPE**...... Honeywell Associative Parallel Processing Ensemble
**HAPPI**...... Household and Personal Products Industry [*A publication*]
**HAPS**........ Health Aspects of Pesticides
**HAPS**........ Historic Aircraft Preservation Society [*Australia*]
**HAPS**........ Houston Automatic Priority Spooling [*Data processing*] (NRCH)
**HAPS**........ Hydroxyalkylpropyl Sephadex [*Analytical biochemistry*]
**HAPTONG**... Haptong Tongsin [*Press agency*] [*South Korea*]
**HAPUB**..... High-Speed Arithmetic Processing Unit Board
**HAP-USA**... Handicapped Aid Program - USA (EA)
**HAQO**....... Hydroxyaminoquinoline Oxide [*Organic chemistry*]
**HAR**.......... Hamburger Akademische Rundschau [*A publication*]
**Har**............ Harari (BJA)
**HAR**.......... Harbor (AFM)
**HAR**.......... Harbor Advisory RADAR
**HAR**.......... Harbor Airlines [*Oak Harbor, WA*] [*FAA designator*] (FAAC)
**HAR**.......... Hardware Affiliated Representatives [*Defunct*] (EA)
**HAR**.......... Harford Community College, Bel Air, MD [*OCLC symbol*] (OCLC)
**HAR**.......... Harman International Industries, Inc. [*NYSE symbol*] (SPSG)
**HAR**.......... Harmonic
**Har**............ Harradine Group [*Australia*] [*Political party*]
**Har**............ Harrington's Delaware Reports [*A publication*] (DLA)
**Har**............ Harrington's Michigan Chancery Reports [*A publication*] (DLA)
**HAR**.......... Harrisburg, PA [*Location identifier*] [*FAA*] (FAAL)
**Har**............ Harrison's Condensed Louisiana Reports [*A publication*] (DLA)
**Har**............ Harrison's Michigan Chancery Reports [*A publication*] (DLA)
**Har**............ Harrison's Reports [*15-17, 23-29 Indiana*] [*A publication*] (DLA)
**HAR**.......... Hartford [*Connecticut*] [*Seismograph station code, US Geological Survey*] [*Closed*] (SEIS)
**HAR**.......... Harum [*Of These*] [*Pharmacy*] (ROG)
**HAR**.......... Harvard Journal on Legislation [*A publication*]
**HAR**.......... Hebrew Annual Review [*A publication*]
**HAR**.......... Heinemann, A. R., East Saint Louis IL [*STAC*]
**HAR**.......... Highway Advisory Radio [*Federal program*]
**HAR**.......... Home Address Register
**HAR**.......... Honorary Air Reserve [*Air Force*]
**HAR**.......... Horse of the Americas Registry (EA)
**HAR**.......... Hover Agility Rotor (RDA)
**HAR**.......... Humanities Association. Review [*A publication*]
**H-Ar**.......... Public Archives, Honolulu, HI [*Library symbol*] [*Library of Congress*] (LCLS)
**HARA**........ High-Altitude RADAR Altimeter [*NASA*]
**HARA**........ High-Assault Risk Area [*DoD*]
**HARAC**..... High-Altitude Resonance Absorption Calculation (IEEE)
**Har Alum Bull**... Harvard Alumni Bulletin [*A publication*]
**Har App**..... Hare's English Chancery Reports, Appendix to Vol. X [*A publication*] (DLA)
**HARAS**..... Hughes Active RADAR Augmentation System
**HARB**........ Harbor [*Maps and charts*] (ROG)
**H Arb G**..... Heimarbeitsgesetz [*A publication*]
**Harb & Nav C**... Harbors and Navigation Code [*A publication*] (DLA)
**Harbor Dent Log**... Harbor Dental Log [*A publication*]
**Harbour**..... Australian Coal, Shipping, Steel, and the Harbour [*A publication*] (APTA)
**Harbour & Shipp**... Harbour and Shipping [*A publication*]
**Har Bus R**... Harvard Business Review [*A publication*]
**Harc**........... Harcarse's Decisions, Scotch Court of Session [*1681-91*] [*A publication*] (DLA)
**HARC**........ HarCor Energy Co. [*NASDAQ symbol*] (NQ)
**HARC**........ Hester Adrian Research Centre [*University of Manchester*] [*British*] (CB)
**HARC**........ High-Altitude RADAR Controller
**HARCFT**... Harbor Craft
**Har Ch**....... Harrington's Michigan Chancery Reports [*A publication*] (DLA)
**Har Ch Pr**.. Harrison's Chancery Practice [*A publication*] (DLA)
**Har Chy**..... Harrington's Michigan Chancery Reports [*A publication*] (DLA)
**Har Civ Ri LR**... Harvard Civil Rights - Civil Liberties Law Review [*A publication*]
**HARCO**..... Hyperbolic Area Coverage [*Navigation*]
**Har Col Jur**... Hargrave's Collectanea Juridica [*1791-92*] [*A publication*] (DLA)
**Har Com**.... Harrison's Compilation of the Laws of New Jersey [*A publication*] (DLA)
**Har Com Proc**... Harrison's Common Law Procedure Act [*Canada*] [*A publication*] (DLA)
**Har Ct Mar**... Harwood's Practice of United States Naval Courts-Martial [*A publication*] (DLA)
**HARCVS**... Honorary Associate of the Royal College of Veterinary Surgeons [*British*]
**Hard**.......... Hardin's Kentucky Reports [*A publication*] (DLA)
**Hard**.......... Hardres' English Exchequer Reports [*145 English Reprint*] [*A publication*] (DLA)
**HARD**........ Horizontal Acoustic Range Depiction (NVT)
**Hard**.......... [*William*] Kelynge's English Chancery Reports [*A publication*] (DLA)
**Hard Eccl L**... Harding on Ecclesiastical Law [*A publication*] (DLA)
**Har Del**...... Harrington's Delaware Reports [*1-5 Delaware*] [*A publication*] (DLA)
**Hard El Pet**... Hardcastle on Election Petitions [*A publication*] (DLA)
**Hardes**....... Hardesty's Delaware Term Reports [*A publication*] (DLA)
**HARDEX**.. Harbor Defense Exercise [*Navy*] (NG)
**Har Dig**...... Harris' Georgia Digest [*A publication*] (DLA)
**Har Dig**...... Harrison's Digest of English Common Law Reports [*A publication*] (DLA)
**Hardin**........ Hardin's Kentucky Reports [*A publication*] (DLA)
**Hardin (KY)**... Hardin's Kentucky Reports [*A publication*] (DLA)
**HARDIS**.... Hotel and Restaurant Design and Interiors Exhibition [*British*] (ITD)
**HARDMAN**... Hardware-Manpower Program [*Navy*]
**Hardr**......... Hardres' English Exchequer Reports [*145 English Reprint*] [*1655 69*] [*A publication*] (DLA)
**Hardr (Eng)**... Hardres' English Exchequer Reports [*145 English Reprint*] [*A publication*] (DLA)
**Hardres**...... Hardres' English Exchequer Reports [*145 English Reprint*] [*A publication*] (DLA)
**HARDS**..... High-Altitude Radiation Detection System (MCD)
**Hard St L**... Hardcastle on Statutory Law [*A publication*] (DLA)
**Hard Tr M**... Hardingham on Trade Marks [*A publication*] (DLA)
**HARDTS**... High-Accuracy RADAR Data Transmission System (MUGU)
**Hardw**........ Cases Tempore Hardwicke, by Lee [*England*] [*A publication*] (DLA)
**Hardw**........ Cases Tempore Hardwicke, by Ridgeway [*England*] [*A publication*] (DLA)
**Hardware J**... Hardware Journal [*A publication*] (APTA)
**Hardware R**... Hardware Retailing [*A publication*]
**Hardware Trade J**... Hardware Trade Journal [*A publication*]
**Hardw Cas Temp**... Cases Tempore Hardwicke, by Lee and Hardwicke [*A publication*] (DLA)
**Hardw (Eng)**... Cases Tempore Hardwicke, by Lee [*England*] [*A publication*] (DLA)
**Hardw (Eng)**... Cases Tempore Hardwicke, by Ridgeway [*England*] [*A publication*] (DLA)
**Hardw NB**... Hardwicke's Note Books [*A publication*] (DLA)
**HARDWR**... Hardware [*Data processing*]
**Hare**.......... Hare's English Vice-Chancellors' Reports [*66-68 English Reprint*] [*1841-53*] [*A publication*] (DLA)
**HARE**........ Harrier, Inc. [*NASDAQ symbol*] (NQ)
**HARE**........ High-Altitude Ramjet Engine
**HARE**........ High-Altitude Recombination-Energy Propulsion (AAG)
**HARE**........ Humans Against Rabbit Exploitation (EA)
**HARE**........ Hydrazine Auxiliary Rocket Engine
**HAREA**..... Harefuah [*A publication*]
**Hare App**.... Hare's English Chancery Reports, Appendix to Vol. X [*A publication*] (DLA)
**Hare Const Law**... Hare's American Constitutional Law [*A publication*] (DLA)
**Hare Disc**... Hare on Discovery of Evidence [*A publication*] (DLA)
**Hare Elec**... Hare on Elections [*A publication*] (DLA)
**Hare (Eng)**... Hare's English Vice-Chancellors' Reports [*66-68 English Reprint*] [*1841-53*] [*A publication*] (DLA)
**Hare Ev**...... Hare on Discovery of Evidence [*A publication*] (DLA)
**Haref**......... Harefuah [*A publication*]
**Hare & W**.. Hare and Wallace's American Leading Cases [*A publication*] (DLA)
**Hare & Wallace Amer Leading Cases**... American Leading Cases, Edited by Hare and Wallace [*A publication*] (DLA)
**Hare & Wallace Lead Cases (Am)**... American Leading Cases, Edited by Hare and Wallace [*A publication*] (DLA)
**Hare & Wal LC**... American Leading Cases, Edited by Hare and Wallace [*A publication*] (DLA)

**Harg**........... Hargrave's State Trials [*A publication*] (DLA)
**Harg**........... Hargrove's Reports [*68-75 North Carolina*] [*A publication*] (DLA)
**HARG**........ Harper Group, Inc. [*NASDAQ symbol*] (NQ)
**Har & G**..... Harris and Gill's Maryland Reports [*A publication*] (DLA)
**HARG**........ High-Speed Autoradiography
**Harg & B Co Litt** ... Hargrave and Butler's Edition on Coke upon Littleton [*A publication*] (DLA)
**Harg Co Litt** ... Hargrave's Notes to Coke on Littleton [*A publication*] (DLA)
**Harg Coll Jur** ... Hargrave's Collectanea Juridica [*1791-92*] [*A publication*] (DLA)
**Harg Exer** ... Hargrave's Jurisconsult Exercitations [*A publication*] (DLA)
**Har & Gil**... Harris and Gill's Maryland Reports [*A publication*] (DLA)
**Har & Gill** ... Harris and Gill's Maryland Reports [*A publication*] (DLA)
**Harg Jur Arg** ... Hargrave's Juridical Arguments and Collections [*A publication*] (DLA)
**Harg Law Tracts** ... Hargrave's Law Tracts [*A publication*] (DLA)
**Harg LT**..... Hargrave's Law Tracts [*A publication*] (DLA)
**Hargrave & Butlers Notes on Co Litt** ... Hargrave and Butler's Notes on Coke upon Littleton [*A publication*] (DLA)
**Hargr Co Litt** ... Hargrave's Notes to Coke on Littleton [*A publication*] (DLA)
**Har & G Rep** ... Harris and Gill's Maryland Reports [*A publication*] (DLA)
**Hargrove**.... Hargrove's Reports [*68-75 North Carolina*] [*A publication*] (DLA)
**Harg State Tr** ... Hargrave's State Trials [*A publication*] (DLA)
**Harg St Tr** ... Hargrave's State Trials [*A publication*] (DLA)
**Harg Th**..... Hargrave on the Thellusson Act [*A publication*] (DLA)
**HARH**....... High-Altitude Retinal Hemorrhage [*Medicine*]
**Har Int LJ** ... Harvard International Law Journal [*A publication*]
**Hari Rao**.... Indian Income Tax Decisions [*A publication*] (DLA)
**HARIS**....... High-Altitude Radiological Instrumentation System
**Har & J**...... Harris and Johnson's Maryland Reports [*A publication*] (DLA)
**Har J Leg**... Harvard Journal on Legislation [*A publication*]
**Har & J (MD)** ... Harris and Johnson's Maryland Reports [*A publication*] (DLA)
**Har & John** ... Harris and Johnson's Maryland Court of Appeals Reports [*1800-26*] [*A publication*] (DLA)
**Har & Johns MD Rep** ... Harris and Johnson's Maryland Reports [*A publication*] (DLA)
**Har Just**..... Harris' Justinian [*A publication*] (DLA)
**HARK**........ Hardened Reentry Kill [*Air Force*]
**Harker Geol Soc J** ... Harker Geological Society. Journal [*A publication*]
**HARL**........ Harleysville Savings Association [*NASDAQ symbol*] (NQ)
**Harland**...... Manchester Court Leet Records [*A publication*] (DLA)
**HARL CBM** ... Harleian Collection, British Museum (DLA)
**Harl Hosp Bull** ... Harlem Hospital Bulletin [*A publication*]
**HARL MISC** ... Harleian Miscellany [*British*] (ROG)
**HARL MSS** ... Harleian Manuscripts [*British*] (ROG)
**HARLOT**.. Height [*Depth*] of Burst, Altitude of Targets, Resources, Location, Objectives, and Time [*Nuclear war games*]
**Har LR**....... Harvard Law Review [*A publication*]
**HARLS**...... Horse Antiserum to Rabbit Lymphocytes [*Immunology*]
**Harm**.......... Harmonica [*of Ptolemy*] [*Classical studies*] (OCD)
**Harm**.......... Harmonica [*of Aristoxenus*] [*Classical studies*] (OCD)
**Harm**.......... Harmon's Reports [*13-15 California*] [*A publication*] (DLA)
**Harm**.......... Harmon's Upper Canada Common Pleas Reports [*A publication*] (DLA)
**HARM**....... Harmony
**HARM**....... High-Acceleration Rocket-Missile
**HARM**....... High-Speed Anti-RADAR Missile
**HARM**....... Hypervelocity Antiradiation Missile (MCD)
**Harma**........ Harmannus [*Authority cited in pre-1607 legal work*] (DSA)
**Har & McH** ... Harris and McHenry's Maryland Reports [*A publication*] (DLA)
**Har and M'Hen** ... Harris and McHenry's Maryland Reports [*A publication*] (DLA)
**Harmon**...... Harmon's Upper Canada Common Pleas Reports [*A publication*] (DLA)
**Harmonika Jb** ... Harmonika-Jahrbuch [*A publication*]
**Harm Pens** ... Harmon's Manual of United States Pension Laws [*A publication*] (DLA)
**HARN**....... Harness (MSA)
**HARNG**..... Hawaii Army National Guard (CINC)
**Harokeach Haivri Heb Pharm (Sci Ed)** ... Harokeach Haivri. The Hebrew Pharmacist (Science Edition) [*A publication*]
**Harold L Lyon Arbor Lect** ... Harold L. Lyon Arboretum. Lecture [*A publication*]
**HAROTS**.. High-Accuracy RADAR Data Transmission System
**HARP**........ Halpern's AntiRADAR Point
**Harp**........... Harper's Magazine [*A publication*]
**Harp**........... Harper's South Carolina Equity Reports [*A publication*] (DLA)
**Harp**........... Harper's South Carolina Law Reports [*1823-30*] [*A publication*] (DLA)
**Harp**........... Harpocration [*Classical studies*] (OCD)
**HARP**........ Hazard Assessment of Rocket Propellants
**HARP**........ Heating, Air Conditioning, Refrigeration, Plumbing (ADA)
**HARP**........ Heimlich-Armstrong-Rieveschl-Patrick [*Heart pump for aerospace use*]
**HARP**........ High-Altitude Reconnaissance Platform
**HARP**........ High-Altitude Relay Point
**HARP**........ High-Altitude Research Program [*or Project*] [*Military*]
**HARP**........ High-Altitude Rocket Probe [*Army*]
**HARP**........ Hitachi Arithmetic Processor [*Data processing*] (IEEE)
**HARP**........ Home Renovation Advisory and Referral Project [*Victoria, Australia*]
**HARP**........ Hybrid Automated Reliability Predictor
**Harp Ad Util Poult J** ... Harper Adams Utility Poultry Journal [*A publication*]
**Harp B**....... Harper's Bazaar [*A publication*]
**Harp Baz**.... Harper's Bazaar [*A publication*]
**Harp Con Cas** ... Harper's Conspiracy Cases [*Maryland*] [*A publication*] (DLA)
**Har Pen Man** ... Harmon's Manual of United States Pension Laws [*A publication*] (DLA)
**Harp Eq**..... Harper's South Carolina Equity Reports [*A publication*] (DLA)
**Harp Eq (SC)** ... Harper's South Carolina Equity Reports [*A publication*] (DLA)
**Harper**....... Harper's Conspiracy Cases [*Maryland*] [*A publication*] (DLA)
**Harper**....... Harper's Magazine [*A publication*]
**Harper**....... Harper's South Carolina Equity Reports [*A publication*] (DLA)
**Harper**....... Harper's South Carolina Law Reports [*1823-30*] [*A publication*] (DLA)
**Harper Hosp Bull** ... Harper Hospital. Bulletin [*A publication*]
**Harper's Mag** ... Harper's New Monthly Magazine [*A publication*]
**Harp L**....... Harper's South Carolina Law Reports [*1823-30*] [*A publication*] (DLA)
**Harp L (SC)** ... Harper's South Carolina Law Reports [*1823-30*] [*A publication*] (DLA)
**Harp MM** ... Harper's Monthly Magazine [*A publication*]
**Harp N**....... Harp News [*A publication*]
**Har Prob**.... Harrison on Probate and Divorce [*A publication*] (DLA)
**HARPS**...... Hybrid AUTODIN Red Patch System (MCD)
**Harp W**...... Harper's Weekly [*A publication*]
**HARPY**..... Hydrofoil Advanced Research Study Program [*Navy*]
**Harr**........... Harrington's Delaware Reports [*1-5 Delaware*] [*A publication*] (DLA)
**Harr**........... Harrington's Michigan Chancery Reports [*A publication*] (DLA)
**Harr**........... Harris' Reports [*A publication*] (DLA)
**Harr**........... Harrison's Law Reports [*16-19 New Jersey*] [*A publication*] (DLA)
**Harr**........... Harrison's Reports [*15-17, 23-29 Indiana*] [*A publication*] (DLA)
**Harr Adv**.... Harris' Hints on Advocacy [*18th ed.*] [*1943*] [*A publication*] (DLA)
**Harr Ch**..... Harrington's Michigan Chancery Reports [*A publication*] (DLA)
**Harr Ch (Mich)** ... Harrington's Michigan Chancery Reports [*A publication*] (DLA)
**Harr Ch R** ... Harrington's Michigan Chancery Reports [*A publication*] (DLA)
**Harr & Cl Conv** ... Harris and Clarkson on Conveyancing, Etc. [*A publication*] (DLA)
**Harr Con LA R** ... Harrison's Condensed Louisiana Reports [*A publication*] (DLA)
**Harr Cr L**... Harris' Principles of the Criminal Law [*22nd ed.*] [*1973*] [*A publication*] (DLA)
**Harr (Del)** ... Harrington's Delaware Reports [*1-5 Delaware*] [*A publication*] (DLA)
**Harr Dig**.... Harrison's Digest of English Common Law Reports [*A publication*] (DLA)
**Har Resp**.... De Haruspicum Responso [*of Cicero*] [*Classical studies*] (OCD)
**Harr & G**.... Harris and Gill's Maryland Reports [*A publication*] (DLA)
**Harr (GA)** ... Harris' Georgia Digest [*A publication*] (DLA)
**Harr & H** ... Harrison and Hodgin's Upper Canada Municipal Reports [*1845-51*] [*A publication*] (DLA)
**Harr Hints** ... Harris' Hints on Advocacy [*18th ed.*] [*1943*] [*A publication*] (DLA)
**Harr & Hodg** ... Harrison and Hodgin's Upper Canada Municipal Reports [*1845-51*] [*A publication*] (DLA)
**Harring**...... Harrington's Delaware Reports [*1-5 Delaware*] [*A publication*] (DLA)
**Harring**...... Harrington's Michigan Chancery Reports [*A publication*] (DLA)
**Harring Ch (Mich)** ... Harrington's Michigan Chancery Reports [*A publication*] (DLA)
**Harrington** ... Harrington's Delaware Supreme Court Reports [*1832-55*] [*A publication*] (DLA)
**Harrington** ... Harrington's Michigan Chancery Reports [*A publication*] (DLA)
**Harris**........ Harris' Reports [*A publication*] (DLA)
**Harris County Physician** ... Harris County Physician Newsletter [*A publication*]
**Harris Dig** ... Harris' Georgia Digest [*A publication*] (DLA)
**Harris & G** ... Harris and Gill's Maryland Reports [*A publication*] (DLA)
**Harris & Gill's MD R** ... Harris and Gill's Maryland Reports [*A publication*] (DLA)
**Harris & J** ... Harris and Johnson's Maryland Reports [*A publication*] (DLA)
**Harrison**.... Harrison's Law Reports [*16-19 New Jersey*] [*A publication*] (DLA)

**Harrison** .... Harrison's Reports [*15-17, 23-29 Indiana*] [*A publication*] (DLA)
**Harrison Ch** ... Harrison's Chancery Practice [*A publication*] (DLA)
**Harrison Dig** ... Harrison's Digest of English Common Law Reports [*A publication*] (DLA)
**Harris & S** ... Harris and Simrall's Reports [*49-52 Mississippi*] [*A publication*] (DLA)
**Harris & Sim** ... Harris and Simrall's Reports [*49-52 Mississippi*] [*A publication*] (DLA)
**Harris & Simrall** ... Harris and Simrall's Reports [*49-52 Mississippi*] [*A publication*] (DLA)
**Harr & J** .... Harris and Johnson's Maryland Reports [*A publication*] (DLA)
**Harr & J (MD)** ... Harris and Johnson's Maryland Reports [*A publication*] (DLA)
**Harr Just** ... Harris' Translation of the Institute of Justinian [*A publication*] (DLA)
**Harr & M** ... Harris and McHenry's Maryland Reports [*A publication*] (DLA)
**Harr & McH** ... Harris and McHenry's Maryland Reports [*A publication*] (DLA)
**Harr & McHen** ... Harris and McHenry's Maryland Reports [*A publication*] (DLA)
**Harr & McH (MD)** ... Harris and McHenry's Maryland Reports [*A publication*] (DLA)
**Harr & M'H** ... Harris and McHenry's Maryland Reports [*A publication*] (DLA)
**Harr (Mich)** ... Harrington's Michigan Chancery Reports [*A publication*] (DLA)
**Harr Min** ... Harris on Titles to Mines [*A publication*] (DLA)
**Harr Mun Law** ... Harrison's Municipal Law of Ontario [*A publication*] (DLA)
**Harr NJ** ..... Harrison's Law Reports [*16-19 New Jersey*] [*A publication*] (DLA)
**Harr Prin** ... Harris' Principiae Primae Legum [*A publication*] (DLA)
**Harr Proc** ... Harrison's Common Law Procedure Act [*Canada*] [*A publication*] (DLA)
**Harr & R** .... Harrison and Rutherford's English Common Pleas Reports [*1865-66*] [*A publication*] (DLA)
**Harr Rom Law** ... Harris' Elements of Roman Law [*A publication*] (DLA)
**Harr & Ruth** ... Harrison and Rutherford's English Common Pleas Reports [*1865-66*] [*A publication*] (DLA)
**Harr & Sim** ... Harris and Simrall's Reports [*49-52 Mississippi*] [*A publication*] (DLA)
**Har & Ruth** ... Harrison and Rutherford's English Common Pleas Reports [*1865-66*] [*A publication*] (DLA)
**Harr & W** ... Harrison and Wollaston's English King's Bench Reports [*A publication*] (DLA)
**Harr & W (Eng)** ... Harrison and Wollaston's English King's Bench Reports [*A publication*] (DLA)
**Harr & Woll** ... Harrison and Wollaston's English King's Bench Reports [*A publication*] (DLA)
**HARS** ........ Heading Attitude Reference System (MCD)
**HARS** ........ Heavy Assault Rocket System (MCD)
**HARSAP** ... Harbor Survey Assistance Program [*Naval Oceanographic Office*]
**HarSemSer** ... Harvard Semitic Series [*Cambridge, MA*] [*A publication*]
**Hars Pr** ...... Harston's California Practice and Pleading [*A publication*] (DLA)
**Har St Tr** ... Hargrave's State Trials [*A publication*] (DLA)
**HART** ........ Cardiopulmonary Technologies, Inc. [*Syosset, NY*] [*NASDAQ symbol*] (NQ)
**HART** ........ Hardened Amplifier for Radiation Transients
**Hart** ........... Hartley's Digest of Texas Laws [*A publication*] (DLA)
**Hart** ........... Hartley's Reports [*4-10 Texas*] [*A publication*] (DLA)
**HART** ........ Hayden Analysis and Reporting Tool [*Data processing*]
**HART** ........ Hypervelocity Aircraft Rocket, Tactical
**Hart Bank** .... Hart's Bankrupt Law and Practice [*A publication*] (DLA)
**Hart Dig** .... Hartley's Digest of Texas Laws [*A publication*] (DLA)
**Hartfd Cou** ... Hartford Courant [*A publication*]
**Hartf Hosp Bull** ... Hartford Hospital. Bulletin [*A publication*]
**Hartford Hosp Bull** ... Hartford Hospital. Bulletin [*A publication*]
**Hartf Sem Rec** ... Hartford Seminary Record [*A publication*]
**Hartf Stud Ling** ... Hartford Studies in Linguistics [*A publication*]
**Hart & H** .... Hartley and Hartley's Reports [*11-21 Texas*] [*A publication*] (DLA)
**Hart Hartm** ... Hartmannus Hartmanni [*Deceased, 1586*] [*Authority cited in pre-1607 legal work*] (DSA)
**Har Theol Rev** ... Harvard Theological Review [*A publication*]
**Hartley** ....... Hartley's Reports [*4-10 Texas*] [*A publication*] (DLA)
**Hartley & Hartley** ... Hartley and Hartley's Reports [*11-21 Texas*] [*A publication*] (DLA)
**Hartley & Hartley Rep** ... Hartley and Hartley's Reports [*11-21 Texas*] [*A publication*] (DLA)
**Hartman Pist** ... Hartmannus Pistoris [*Deceased, 1601*] [*Authority cited in pre-1607 legal work*] (DSA)
**Hartm Pistor** ... Hartmannus Pistoris [*Deceased, 1601*] [*Authority cited in pre-1607 legal work*] (DSA)
**Hartm Tds** ... Hartman's Tijdschrift ter Beoefening van het Administratieve Recht [*A publication*]
**Hart Pist** .... Hartmannus Pistoris [*Deceased, 1601*] [*Authority cited in pre-1607 legal work*] (DSA)
**Hart Q** ........ Hartford Quarterly [*A publication*]
**Hart R** ........ Hartwick Review [*A publication*]
**HARTRAN** ... Hardwell FORTRAN [*Data processing*] (IEEE)
**HAR-TRU** ... Tennis-court surface material. Name derives from developer, H. A. Robinson, and from "true," referring to "bounce" qualities of the surface.
**HARTS** ...... Hardening Technology Studies Program (MCD)
**Hart-Tech Mitt** ... Harterei-Technische Mitteilungen [*West Germany*] [*A publication*]
**HARU** ........ Handbuch fuer Rundfunk und Fernsehen [*Handbook for Radio and Television*] [*NOMOS Datapool*] [*Database*]
**HARV** ........ Harassment Vehicle (MCD)
**HARV** ........ Harvard Group PLC [*NASDAQ symbol*] (NQ)
**HARV** ........ Harvard University [*Massachusetts*]
**Harv** ........... Harvard Vocarium [*Record label*]
**HARV** ........ Harvest
**Harv Ad** ..... Harvard Advocate [*A publication*]
**HARVAN** ... Harriman and Vance [*Code name for 1968 Paris peace talks on Vietnam, derived from the surnames of US negotiators W. Averell Harriman and Cyrus R. Vance*]
**Harvard A** ... Harvard Advocate [*A publication*]
**Harvard Archre Review** ... Harvard Architecture Review [*A publication*]
**Harvard BR** ... Harvard Business Review [*A publication*]
**Harvard Bsns R** ... Harvard Business Review [*A publication*]
**Harvard Bus R** ... Harvard Business Review [*A publication*]
**Harvard Bus Rev** ... Harvard Business Review [*A publication*]
**Harvard Civil Rights - Civil Liberties Law R** ... Harvard Civil Rights - Civil Liberties Law Review [*A publication*]
**Harvard Civil Rights L Rev** ... Harvard Civil Rights - Civil Liberties Law Review [*A publication*]
**Harvard Coll Mus Comp Zoology Bull** ... Harvard College. Museum of Comparative Zoology. Bulletin [*A publication*]
**Harvard Coll Mus CZ An Rp** ... Harvard College. Museum of Comparative Zoology. Annual Report [*A publication*]
**Harvard Coll Mus C Z B** ... Harvard College. Museum of Comparative Zoology. Bulletin [*A publication*]
**Harvard Coll Mus C Z Mem** ... Harvard College. Museum of Comparative Zoology. Memoirs [*A publication*]
**Harvard Ed R** ... Harvard Educational Review [*A publication*]
**Harvard Educ R** ... Harvard Educational Review [*A publication*]
**Harvard Engl Stud** ... Harvard English Studies [*A publication*]
**Harvard Environ Law Rev** ... Harvard Environmental Law Review [*A publication*]
**Harvard Environmental Law R** ... Harvard Environmental Law Review [*A publication*]
**Harvard Forest Bull** ... Harvard Forest. Bulletin [*A publication*]
**Harvard Internat Law J** ... Harvard International Law Journal [*A publication*]
**Harvard Int LJ** ... Harvard International Law Journal [*A publication*]
**Harvard J Asiat Stud** ... Harvard Journal of Asiatic Studies [*A publication*]
**Harvard J Law and Public Policy** ... Harvard Journal of Law and Public Policy [*A publication*]
**Harvard J on Legis** ... Harvard Journal on Legislation [*A publication*]
**Harvard J Legislation** ... Harvard Journal on Legislation [*A publication*]
**Harvard Law R** ... Harvard Law Review [*A publication*]
**Harvard Lib Bul** ... Harvard Library Bulletin [*A publication*]
**Harvard L Rev** ... Harvard Law Review [*A publication*]
**Harvard Med Alumni Bull** ... Harvard Medical Alumni Bulletin [*A publication*]
**Harvard Med Sch Health Let** ... Harvard Medical School. Health Letter [*A publication*]
**Harvard Mon Applied Sci** ... Harvard Monographs in Applied Science [*A publication*]
**Harvard Public Health Alumni Bull** ... Harvard Public Health Alumni Bulletin [*A publication*]
**Harvard Theol R** ... Harvard Theological Review [*A publication*]
**Harvard Univ B** ... Harvard University. Bulletin [*A publication*]
**Harvard Univ Bot Mus Leaflets** ... Harvard University. Botanical Museum Leaflets [*A publication*]
**Harvard Univ Dep Eng Publ** ... Harvard University. Department of Engineering. Publications [*A publication*]
**Harvard Univ Gray Herbarium Contr** ... Harvard University. Gray Herbarium. Contributions [*A publication*]
**Harvard Univ Harvard Soil Mech Ser** ... Harvard University. Harvard Soil Mechanics Series [*A publication*]
**Harvard Univ Mus Comp Zoology Bull** ... Harvard University. Museum of Comparative Zoology. Bulletin [*A publication*]
**Harvard Women's Law J** ... Harvard Women's Law Journal [*A publication*]
**Harv Asia** ... Harvard Journal of Asiatic Studies [*A publication*]
**Harv Books Biophys** ... Harvard Books in Biophysics [*A publication*]
**Harv Bus Re** ... Harvard Business Review [*A publication*]
**Harv Bus Rev** ... Harvard Business Review [*A publication*]
**Harv Bus World** ... Harvard Business World (DLA)
**Harv Civil Rights L Rev** ... Harvard Civil Rights - Civil Liberties Law Review [*A publication*]
**Harv Civ Rights - Civ Liberties Law Rev** ... Harvard Civil Rights - Civil Liberties Law Review [*A publication*]
**Harv Class Phil** ... Harvard Studies in Classical Philology [*A publication*]
**Harv CR-CLL** ... Harvard Civil Rights - Civil Liberties Law Review [*A publication*]
**Harv CR CL Law Rev** ... Harvard Civil Rights - Civil Liberties Law Review [*A publication*] (ILCA)

**Harv CR-CLL Rev** ... Harvard Civil Rights - Civil Liberties Law Review [*A publication*]
**HarvDBull** ... Harvard Divinity School. Bulletin [*Cambridge, MA*] [*A publication*]
**Harv Dent Alumni Bull** ... Harvard Dental Alumni Bulletin [*A publication*]
**Harv Div B** ... Harvard Divinity Bulletin [*A publication*]
**Harv East As Ser** ... Harvard East Asian Series [*A publication*]
**Harv Ed Rev** ... Harvard Educational Review [*A publication*] (DLA)
**Harv Educ Rev** ... Harvard Educational Review [*A publication*]
**Harv Edu Re** ... Harvard Educational Review [*A publication*]
**Harv Environ Law Rev** ... Harvard Environmental Law Review [*A publication*]
**Harv Env L Rev** ... Harvard Environmental Law Review [*A publication*] (DLA)
**Harv Envtl L Rev** ... Harvard Environmental Law Review [*A publication*]
**Harvester in Aust** ... Harvester in Australia [*A publication*] (APTA)
**Harvester Readings Hist Sci Philos** ... Harvester Readings in the History of Science and Philosophy [*Brighton*] [*A publication*]
**Harvest Q** .. Harvest Quarterly [*A publication*]
**Harvey Lect** ... Harvey Lectures [*A publication*]
**Harv For Annu Rep** ... Harvard Forest. Annual Report [*A publication*]
**Harv For Bull** ... Harvard Forest. Bulletin [*A publication*]
**Harv For Pap** ... Harvard Forest. Papers [*A publication*]
**Harv Grad M** ... Harvard Graduates' Magazine [*A publication*]
**Harv Int L J** ... Harvard International Law Journal [*A publication*]
**Harv Int'l L Club Bull** ... Harvard International Law Club. Bulletin [*A publication*] (DLA)
**Harv Int'l L Club J** ... Harvard International Law Club. Journal [*A publication*] (DLA)
**Harv Int'l LJ** ... Harvard International Law Journal [*A publication*]
**Harv J Asia** ... Harvard Journal of Asiatic Studies [*A publication*]
**Harv J Asiatic Stud** ... Harvard Journal of Asiatic Studies [*A publication*]
**Harv J Leg** ... Harvard Journal on Legislation [*A publication*]
**Harv J Legis** ... Harvard Journal on Legislation [*A publication*]
**Harv J on Legis** ... Harvard Journal on Legislation [*A publication*]
**Harv JL and Pub Poly** ... Harvard Journal of Law and Public Policy [*A publication*]
**Harv Law R** ... Harvard Law Review [*A publication*]
**Harv Law Rev** ... Harvard Law Review [*A publication*]
**HarvLB** ...... Harvard Library Bulletin [*A publication*]
**Harv Lib Bull** ... Harvard Library Bulletin [*A publication*]
**Harv Libr B** ... Harvard Library Bulletin [*A publication*]
**Harv Libr Bull** ... Harvard Library Bulletin [*A publication*]
**Harv L Lib Inf Bull** ... Harvard Law Library. Information Bulletin [*A publication*] (DLA)
**Harv L Rev** ... Harvard Law Review [*A publication*]
**Harv LS Bull** ... Harvard Law School Bulletin [*A publication*]
**Harv LS Rec** ... Harvard Law School. Record [*A publication*] (DLA)
**Harv Mag** .. Harvard Magazine [*A publication*]
**Harv Med Alumni Bull** ... Harvard Medical Alumni Bulletin [*A publication*]
**Harv Med Sch Health Lett** ... Harvard Medical School. Health Letter [*A publication*]
**Harv Mo** .... Harvard Monthly [*A publication*]
**Harv Pathophysiol Ser** ... Harvard Pathophysiology Series [*A publication*]
**Harv Public Health Alumni Bull** ... Harvard Public Health Alumni Bulletin [*A publication*]
**Harv R** ....... Harvard Review [*A publication*]
**Harv Ser Ukrain Stud** ... Harvard Series in Ukrainian Studies [*A publication*]
**Harv St** ...... Harvard Studies in Classical Philology [*A publication*]
**Harv St Cla** ... Harvard Studies in Classical Philology [*A publication*]
**Harv Stud** .. Harvard Studies in Classical Philology [*A publication*] (OCD)
**Harv Stud Class Philol** ... Harvard Studies in Classical Philology [*A publication*]
**Harv Theol** ... Harvard Theological Review [*A publication*]
**Harv Theol R** ... Harvard Theological Review [*A publication*]
**Harv Theol Rev** ... Harvard Theological Review [*A publication*]
**Harv Th R** ... Harvard Theological Review [*A publication*]
**HarvTR** ...... Harvard Theological Review [*Cambridge, MA*] [*A publication*]
**Harv Univ Mus Comp Zool Bull** ... Harvard University. Museum of Comparative Zoology. Bulletin [*A publication*]
**Harv Univ Mus Comp Zool Spec Occas Publ** ... Harvard University. Museum of Comparative Zoology. Special Occasional Publication [*A publication*]
**Harv Univ Sch Public Health Dean's Rep** ... Harvard University. School of Public Health. Dean's Report [*A publication*]
**Harv Women LJ** ... Harvard Women's Law Journal [*A publication*]
**Harv Women's LJ** ... Harvard Women's Law Journal [*A publication*] (DLA)
**Harv W Tax Ser** ... Harvard World Tax Series [*A publication*] (DLA)
**Har & W** .... Harrison and Wollaston's English King's Bench Reports [*A publication*] (DLA)
**HARW** ....... Harwich [*Municipal borough in England*]
**Har & Woll** ... Harrison and Wollaston's English King's Bench Reports [*A publication*] (DLA)
**Har Women LR** ... Harvard Women's Law Review [*A publication*]
**Haryana Agric Univ J Res** ... Haryana Agricultural University. Journal of Research [*A publication*]
**Haryana J Hort Sci** ... Haryana Journal of Horticulture Sciences [*A publication*]
**HARYOU-ACT** ... Harlem Youth Opportunities Unlimited - Associated Community Teams [*A kind of Peace Corps for Harlem area of New York City*]
**Harz Z** ........ Harz Zeitschrift [*A publication*]
**HAS** .......... Hail [*Saudi Arabia*] [*Airport symbol*] (OAG)
**HAS** .......... Hardened Aircraft Shelter [*British military*] (DMA)
**HAS** .......... Harold's Air Service [*Galena, AK*] [*FAA designator*] (FAAC)
**HAS** .......... Hasbro, Inc. [*AMEX symbol*] (SPSG)
**HAS** .......... Hastings [*New Zealand*] [*Seismograph station code, US Geological Survey*] [*Closed*] (SEIS)
**HAS** .......... Heading Altitude System
**HAS** .......... Health Advocacy Services [*AARP*]
**HAS** .......... Helical Antenna System
**HAS** .......... Helicopter Anti-Submarine
**HAS** .......... Helicopter Avionics System [*Air Force*]
**HAS** .......... Hellenic Affiliation Scale [*Psychology*]
**HAS** .......... High-Altitude Sampler
**HAS** .......... High-Angle Strafe
**HAS** .......... Highest Asymptomatic [*Dose*] [*Medicine*]
**HAS** .......... Holddown Alignment Support (NASA)
**HAS** .......... Holograph Assessment System
**HAS** .......... Horatio Alger Society (EA)
**HAS** .......... Hospital Adjustment Scale [*Psychology*]
**HAS** .......... Hospital Administrative Services
**HAS** .......... Hospital Advisory Service [*British*]
**HAS** .......... Hover Augmentation System
**HAS** .......... Human Albumin Solution [*Clinical chemistry*]
**HAS** .......... Hydraulic Actuation System (MCD)
**HAS** .......... Hydraulic Adjustable Speed
**HAS** .......... Hydrogen Actuation System (NASA)
**HAS** .......... Hydroxy-Aluminosilicate [*Inorganic chemistry*]
**HAS** .......... Hydroxylamine Acid Sulfate [*Inorganic chemistry*]
**HAS** .......... Hypertensive Arteriosclerotic [*Cardiology*]
**HAS** .......... Hypoxanthine and Azaserine [*Medium*]
**HASB** ........ Assab [*Ethiopia*] [*ICAO location identifier*] (ICLI)
**Hasb** .......... Hasbrouck's Reports [*Idaho*] [*A publication*] (DLA)
**HASC** ........ Headquarters, Air Service Command [*Air Force*]
**HASC** ........ Historical Automobile Society of Canada
**HASC** ........ House Armed Services Committee [*US Congress*] (AABC)
**HASC** ........ Hyderabad Army Service Corps [*British military*] (DMA)
**HASCI** ....... Human Applications Standard Computer Interface [*Keyboard*] (MCD)
**HASCO** ..... Haitian-American Sugar Company
**Has Con LQ** ... Hastings Constitutional Law Quarterly [*A publication*]
**HASD** ........ Sodo [*Ethiopia*] [*ICAO location identifier*] (ICLI)
**HASE** ........ Head Angulation Sighting Equipment [*British military*] (DMA)
**HASH** ........ Sheik Hussein [*Ethiopia*] [*ICAO location identifier*] (ICLI)
**H & ASHD** ... Hypertension and Arteriosclerotic Heart Disease [*Medicine*]
**Has Int and Comp LR** ... Hastings International and Comparative Law Review [*A publication*]
**HASIS** ....... House Armed Services Investigation Subcommittee [*US Congress*]
**HASJPL** .... H. Allen Smith Jet Propulsion Laboratory [*Former name, JPL, continues to be used as official name*] [*Name adopted in 1973 to honor retiring congressman*]
**Hask** .......... Haskell's Reports for United States Courts in Maine (Fox's Decisions) [*A publication*] (DLA)
**HASL** ........ Health and Safety Laboratory [*ERDA*]
**Hasler Mitt** ... Hasler-Mitteilungen [*A publication*]
**Hasler Rev** ... Hasler Review [*A publication*]
**Has LJ** ....... Hastings Law Journal [*A publication*]
**Hasl Med Jur** ... Haslam's Medical Jurisprudence [*A publication*] (DLA)
**HASO** ........ Assosa [*Ethiopia*] [*ICAO location identifier*] (ICLI)
**HASP** ........ High Altitude Sampling Plane
**HASP** ........ High-Altitude Sampling Program [*Air Force*]
**HASP** ........ High-Altitude Sounding Projectile
**HASP** ........ High-Altitude Space Platform
**HASP** ........ High-Level Automatic Scheduling Program (BUR)
**HASP** ........ Houston Automatic Spooling Priority System [*Data processing*]
**HASPA** ...... High-Altitude Superpressure Powered Aerostat [*Navy*]
**HASPID** .... House Armed Services Permanent Investigations Subcommittee [*US Congress*] (AAG)
**HASPS** ...... Hardened Array Solar Power System [*Military*]
**HASQ** ........ Hardware-Assisted Software Queue
**HASR** ........ Hauserman, Inc. [*NASDAQ symbol*] (NQ)
**HASR** ........ High-Altitude Sounding Rocket
**HASRD** ..... Health and Safety Research Division [*Oak Ridge National Laboratory*]
**HASSA** ...... Hassadeh [*A publication*]
**Hast** ........... Hastings' Reports [*69, 70 Maine*] [*A publication*] (DLA)
**HAST** ........ High-Altitude Selection Test [*British military*] (DMA)
**HAST** ........ High-Altitude Supersonic Target [*Later, HAHST*] (MCD)
**Hast Cen St** ... Hastings Center. Studies [*A publication*]
**Hast Cent Rpt** ... Hastings Center. Report [*A publication*]
**Hast Cent St** ... Hastings Center. Studies [*A publication*]
**Hast Const LQ** ... Hastings Constitutional Law Quarterly [*A publication*]
**Hast Deering News** ... Hastings Deering News [*A publication*] (APTA)
**HASTE** ...... Hazard Assessment System for Toxic Emissions [*Computer-based emergency management system*] [*Environmental Research & Technology*]
**HASTE** ...... Helicopter Assault Survivability in a Threat Environment (MCD)
**HASTI** ....... High-Altitude Strike Indicator

**Hastings Area Archaeol Pap** ... Hastings Area Archaeological Papers [*A publication*]
**Hastings Cent Rep** ... Hastings Center. Report [*A publication*]
**Hastings Cent Stud** ... Hastings Center. Studies [*A publication*]
**Hastings Const LQ** ... Hastings Constitutional Law Quarterly [*A publication*]
**Hastings Ctr Rept** ... Hastings Center. Report [*A publication*]
**Hastings E Suss Nat** ... Hastings and East Sussex Naturalist [*A publication*]
**Hastings Intl and Comp L Rev** ... Hastings International and Comparative Law Review [*A publication*]
**Hastings L J** ... Hastings Law Journal [*A publication*]
**Hast Int & Comp L Rev** ... Hastings' International and Comparative Law Review [*A publication*] (DLA)
**Hast Law J** ... Hastings Law Journal [*A publication*]
**Hast LJ**...... Hastings Law Journal [*A publication*]
**Hast Tr** ...... Trial of Warren Hastings [*A publication*] (DLA)
**HASVR** ..... High-Altitude Space Velocity RADAR (AAG)
**HASWA** ..... Health and Safety at Work Act [*British*]
**HAT**.......... Handbuch zum Alten Testament [*A publication*] (BJA)
**HAT**.......... Handelsblatt. Wirtschaftzeitung und Finanzzeitung [*A publication*]
**HAT**.......... Harbour Acceptance Trials [*Missile*] [*United Kingdom*]
**HAT**.......... Hardness Assurance Test
**Hat**............ Hatran (BJA)
**HAT**.......... Hatteras Income Securities, Inc. [*NYSE symbol*] (SPSG)
**HAT**.......... Hatteras, NC [*Location identifier*] [*FAA*] (FAAL)
**HAT**.......... Hawaiian Archives for Tsunamis
**HAT**.......... Heathlands [*Australia*] [*Airport symbol*] [*Obsolete*] (OAG)
**HAT**.......... Heavy Artillery Tractor [*British military*] (DMA)
**HAT**.......... Height above Runway Touchdown Zone Elevation [*Aviation*]
**HAT**.......... Height above Terrain
**HAT**.......... Helicopter Acquisition Test (MCD)
**HAT**.......... High-Altitude Target
**HAT**.......... High-Altitude Testing [*Sounding rocket*]
**HAT**.......... High-Altitude Transmitter
**HAT**.......... Highly Aphid Transmissible [*Plant pathology*]
**HAT**.......... Home Area Toll [*Telecommunications*] (TEL)
**HAT**.......... Horizontal Alidade Tie
**HAT**.......... Housing Action Trust [*British*] (ECON)
**HAT**.......... Hug-a-Tree and Survive (EA)
**HAT**.......... Hypoxanthine-Aminopterin-Thymidine [*Medium*] [*Biochemistry*]
**HATAA4**... Amino Acid and Nucleic Acid [*A publication*]
**HATACS**... Helicopter Air-to-Air Combat Simulation (MCD)
**HATCDS**... High-Altitude Terrain Contour Data Sensor (MSA)
**Hatcher's Kan Dig** ... Hatcher's Kansas Digest [*A publication*] (DLA)
**HATF** ........ Hydraulic Actuator Test Fixture
**HATFPEV** ... Hatfield Peverel [*England*]
**HATH** ....... Hathaway Corp. [*NASDAQ symbol*] (NQ)
**HATH** ....... Heterosexual Attitudes toward Homosexuality [*Scale*]
**HATLS**....... Hostile Artillery Positions (RDA)
**HATO**........ Handling Tool (AAG)
**HATO**........ Tendaho [*Ethiopia*] [*ICAO location identifier*] (ICLI)
**HATP** ........ Tippi [*Ethiopia*] [*ICAO location identifier*] (ICLI)
**HATR**........ Hazardous Air Traffic Report
**HATR**........ Horizontal Attenuated Total Reflection [*Spectroscopy*]
**HATRAC** .. Handover Transfer and Receiver Accept Change [*SAGE*]
**HATREMS** ... Hazardous and Trace Emissions System [*Environmental Protection Agency*]
**HATRON** ... Heavy Attack Squadron (MUGU)
**HATS** ........ Hardened Tactical Shelters
**Hats** ........... Hatsell's Parliamentary Precedents [*1290-1818*] [*A publication*] (DLA)
**HATS** ........ Head and Torso Simulator [*A dummy developed by British Telecommunications Ltd.*]
**HATS** ........ Heading, Altitude, True Airspeed [*Aviation*] (CAAL)
**HATS** ........ Helicopter Advanced Tactical System (MCD)
**HATS** ........ Helicopter Attack System
**HATS** ........ Helmut Attitude Tracking System (MCD)
**HATS** ........ Heuristic Automated Transportation System (MCD)
**HATS** ........ High-Accuracy Targeting Subsystem
**HATS** ........ High-Altitude Terrain Contour Data Sensor
**HATS** ........ High-Altitude Test Stand
**HATS** ........ Holden's Air Transport Services [*Australia*]
**HATS** ........ Hour Angle of the True Sun [*Navigation*]
**HATS** ........ Tessenei [*Ethiopia*] [*ICAO location identifier*] (ICLI)
**Hats Pr** ...... Hatsell's Parliamentary Precedents [*1290-1818*] [*A publication*] (DLA)
**Hats Prec**... Hatsell's Parliamentary Precedents [*1290-1818*] [*A publication*] (DLA)
**HATT**........ Hambros Advanced Technology Trust [*Hambros Bank of Britain*]
**Hatt**............ Hattusilis (BJA)
**HATU**........ Heavy Air Training Unit
**HATU**........ Heavy Attack Training Unit
**HATV**........ High-Altitude Test Vehicle
**Ha & Tw** .... Hall and Twell's English Chancery Reports [*1849-50*] [*A publication*] (DLA)
**HATWING** ... Heavy Attack Wing
**HATWINGLANT** ... Heavy Attack Wing, Atlantic Fleet
**HATWINGPAC** ... Heavy Attack Wing, Pacific Fleet
**HAU** .......... Haudompre [*France*] [*Seismograph station code, US Geological Survey*] (SEIS)
**HAU** .......... Haugesund [*Norway*] [*Airport symbol*] (OAG)
**HAU** .......... Haultain Resources Ltd. [*Vancouver Stock Exchange symbol*]
**hau** ............ Hausa [*MARC language code*] [*Library of Congress*] (LCCP)
**HAU** .......... Hebrew Actors Union (EA)
**HAU** .......... Helena, MT [*Location identifier*] [*FAA*] (FAAL)
**HAU** .......... Hemagglutination Unit [*Hematology*]
**HAU** .......... Horizontal Arithmetic Unit
**HAU** .......... Hybrid Arithmetic Unit
**HAUID**...... Han'guk Uikwahak [*A publication*]
**HAUND**.... Hannover Uni [*A publication*]
**HAUPTW** ... Hauptwerk [*Masterpiece*] [*German*]
**HAURBR**.. Encyclopedia of Urology [*A publication*]
**HAURIEND** ... Hauriendus [*To Be Drunk*] [*Pharmacy*] (ROG)
**Hausm**........ Hausmusik [*A publication*]
**Hausmitt Jos Schneider** ... Hausmitteilungen Jos Schneider [*A publication*]
**Hausmus**.... Hausmusik [*A publication*]
**HAUST** ..... Haustus [*A Drink*] [*Pharmacy*]
**Haus Tech** ... Haus Technik [*West Germany*] [*A publication*]
**Haustech Bauphys Umwelttech** ... Haustechnik, Bauphysik, Umwelttechnik [*A publication*]
**Haus Tech Essen Vortragsveroeff** ... Haus der Technik-Essen-Vortragsveroeffentlichungen [*A publication*]
**Haustech Rundsch** ... Haustechnische Rundschau [*West Germany*] [*A publication*]
**Haus Tech-Vortrag-Veroeff** ... Haus der Technik-Vortrags-Veroeffentlichungen [*A publication*]
**HAUST PURG** ... Haustus Purgans [*Purging Draught*] [*Pharmacy*] (ROG)
**Hausz VAW Erftwerk AG Alum** ... Hauszeitschrift der VAW und der Erftwerk AG fuer Aluminium [*A publication*]
**HAUT**........ Hautboy [*Oboe*]
**Haut**........... Heautontimorumenos [*of Terence*] [*Classical studies*] (OCD)
**HAUTA**..... Hautarzt [*Austria*] [*A publication*]
**HAV**.......... Havana [*Cuba*] [*Airport symbol*] (OAG)
**HAV**.......... Havering [*Borough in England*]
**HAV**.......... Haversine [*Mathematics*]
**HAV**.......... Havilah [*California*] [*Seismograph station code, US Geological Survey*] [*Closed*] (SEIS)
**Hav** ............ Haviland's Prince Edward Island Chancery Reports, by Peters [*1850-72*] [*Canada*] [*A publication*] (DLA)
**Hav** ............ Havildar [*British military*] (DMA)
**HAV**.......... Heavily Armed Vessels
**HAV**.......... Hepatitis A Virus
**HAV**.......... High-Accuracy Voltmeter
**HAV**.......... Hilprecht Anniversary Volume. Studies in Assyriology and Archaeology Dedicated to Hermann V. Hilprecht [*Leipzig*] [*A publication*] (BJA)
**HAV**.......... Hot Air Vulcanization
**HAVA**........ Harvard Industries, Inc. [*NASDAQ symbol*] (NQ)
**HAVAg**...... Hepatitis A Virus Antigen [*Immunochemistry*]
**Havana Bibl Nac R** ... Havana Biblioteca Nacional. Revista [*A publication*]
**Havana Univ Cienc Ser 4 Cienc Biol** ... Havana Universidad. Ciencias. Serie 4. Ciencias Biologicas [*A publication*]
**Havana Univ Cienc Ser 7 Geogr** ... Havana Universidad. Ciencias. Serie 7. Geografia [*A publication*]
**Havana Univ Cienc Ser 8 Invest Mar** ... Havana Universidad. Ciencias. Serie 8. Investigaciones Marinas [*A publication*]
**Havana Univ Tecnol Ser 10 Ing Hidraul** ... Havana Universidad. Tecnologia. Serie 10. Ingenieria Hidraulica [*A publication*]
**HAVC**........ Health Audiovisual On-Line Catalog [*Northeastern Ohio Universities*] [*Information service or system*] [*Defunct*]
**Hav Ch Rep** ... Haviland's Prince Edward Island Chancery Reports [*1850-72*] [*A publication*] (DLA)
**HAVEN**..... Help Addicts Voluntarily End Narcotics
**Havforskningsinst Skr** ... Havsforskningsinstituets Skrift [*A publication*]
**Havil** .......... Haviland's Prince Edward Island Reports [*A publication*] (DLA)
**Hav-Maj** .... Havildar-Major [*British military*] (DMA)
**HAVO** ....... Hawaii Volcanoes National Park
**HAVOC**..... Heritage and Videotex over the Country [*Australia*]
**HAVOC**..... Histogram Average Ogive Calculator
**Hav PEI**..... Haviland's Prince Edward Island Reports [*A publication*] (DLA)
**HAVREP**... Abridged Arrival Report [*Navy*] (NVT)
**HAVT**........ Hardness Assurance Verification Testing (MCD)
**HAVT**........ Haverty Furniture Companies, Inc. [*NASDAQ symbol*] (NQ)
**HAW** ......... Fargo, ND [*Location identifier*] [*FAA*] (FAAL)
**HAW** ......... Hafnium Column Waste [*Nuclear energy*] (NRCH)
**HAW** ......... Hawaii (KSC)
**Haw**........... Hawaii Reports [*A publication*]
**Haw**........... Hawaii Supreme Court Reports [*A publication*] (DLA)
**haw**............ Hawaiian [*MARC language code*] [*Library of Congress*] (LCCP)
**Haw**........... Hawarde's Star Chamber Cases [*A publication*] (DLA)
**Haw**........... Hawkins' Annual Reports [*19-24 Louisiana*] [*A publication*] (DLA)
**Haw**........... Hawkins' Pleas of the Crown [*England*] [*A publication*] (DLA)
**HAW** ......... Hawksbill Resources, Inc. [*Vancouver Stock Exchange symbol*]
**Haw**........... Hawley's Reports [*10-20 Nevada*] [*A publication*] (DLA)
**HAW** ......... Heavy Antiarmor Weapon

**HAW** ......... Heavy Antitank Weapon (INF)
**HAW** ......... Heavy Assault Weapon
**HAW** ......... Helicopter Assault Wave
**HAW** ......... High-Acid Waste [*Nuclear energy*] (NRCH)
**HAW** ......... Holidays and Anniversaries of the World [*A publication*]
**HAW** ......... Home All the Way [*Military*] (CAAL)
**HAWA**....... Hawaii
**Hawaii**........ Hawaii Reports [*A publication*] (DLA)
**Hawaii Ag Exp** ... Hawaii. Agricultural Experiment Station. Publications [*A publication*]
**Hawaii Agric Exp Stn Agric Econ Bull** ... Hawaii. Agricultural Experiment Station. Agricultural Economics Bulletin [*A publication*]
**Hawaii Agric Exp Stn Bienn Rep** ... Hawaii. Agricultural Experiment Station. Biennial Report [*A publication*]
**Hawaii Agric Exp Stn Bull** ... Hawaii. Agricultural Experiment Station. Bulletin [*A publication*]
**Hawaii Agric Exp Stn Circ** ... Hawaii. Agricultural Experiment Station. Circular [*A publication*]
**Hawaii Agric Exp Stn Misc Pub** ... Hawaii. Agricultural Experiment Station. Miscellaneous Publication [*A publication*]
**Hawaii Agric Exp Stn Misc Publ** ... Hawaii. Agricultural Experiment Station. Miscellaneous Publication [*A publication*]
**Hawaii Agric Exp Stn Prog Notes** ... Hawaii. Agricultural Experiment Station. Progress Notes [*A publication*]
**Hawaii Agric Exp Stn Res Bull** ... Hawaii. Agricultural Experiment Station. Research Bulletin [*A publication*]
**Hawaii Agric Exp Stn Res Rep** ... Hawaii. Agricultural Experiment Station. Research Report [*A publication*]
**Hawaii Agric Exp Stn Spec Publ** ... Hawaii. Agricultural Experiment Station. Special Publication [*A publication*]
**Hawaii Agric Exp Stn Tech Bull** ... Hawaii. Agricultural Experiment Station. Technical Bulletin [*A publication*]
**Hawaii Agric Exp Stn Tech Prog Rep** ... Hawaii. Agricultural Experiment Station. Technical Progress Report [*A publication*]
**Hawaiian For** ... Hawaiian Forester and Agriculturist [*A publication*]
**Hawaiian Rep** ... Hawaii Reports [*A publication*] (DLA)
**Hawaiian Vol Obs** ... Hawaiian Volcano Observatory [*A publication*]
**Hawaii B J** ... Hawaii Bar Journal [*A publication*]
**Hawaii BN** ... Hawaii Bar News [*A publication*] (DLA)
**Hawaii Bsn** ... Hawaii Business [*A publication*]
**Hawaii Bus** ... Hawaii Business [*A publication*]
**Hawaii Dent J** ... Hawaii Dental Journal [*A publication*]
**Hawaii Dist** ... United States District Court, District of Hawaii (DLA)
**Hawaii Div Hydrogr Bull** ... Hawaii. Division of Hydrography. Bulletin [*A publication*]
**Hawaii Div Water Land Dev Circ** ... Hawaii. Division of Water and Land Development. Circular [*A publication*]
**Hawaii Div Water Land Dev Rep** ... Hawaii. Division of Water and Land Development. Report [*A publication*]
**Hawaii Farm Sci** ... Hawaii Farm Science [*A publication*]
**Hawaii Food Process Hawaii Univ Coop Ext Serv** ... Hawaii Food Processor. Hawaii University. Cooperative Extension Service [*A publication*]
**Hawaii Inst Geophys Bienn Rep** ... Hawaii Institute of Geophysics. Biennial Report [*A publication*]
**Hawaii Inst Geophys Publ** ... Hawaii Institute of Geophysics. Publication [*A publication*]
**Hawaii J Hist** ... Hawaii Journal of History [*A publication*]
**Hawaii Lib Assn J** ... Hawaii Library Association. Journal [*A publication*]
**Hawaii Med J** ... Hawaii Medical Journal [*A publication*]
**Hawaii Med J Inter Isl Nurses Bull** ... Hawaii Medical Journal and Inter-Island Nurses' Bulletin [*A publication*]
**Hawaii Orchid J** ... Hawaii Orchid Journal [*A publication*]
**Hawaii Plant Mon** ... Hawaiian Planters' Monthly [*A publication*]
**Hawaii Plant Rec** ... Hawaiian Planters' Record [*A publication*]
**Hawaii Plrs' Rec** ... Hawaiian Planters' Record [*A publication*]
**Hawaii PUC Dec** ... Hawaii Public Utilities Commission Decisions [*A publication*] (DLA)
**Hawaii Rep** ... Hawaii Reports [*A publication*] (DLA)
**Hawaii Rev Stat** ... Hawaii Revised Statutes [*A publication*] (DLA)
**Hawaii Rules & Reg** ... Hawaii Rules and Regulations [*A publication*] (DLA)
**Hawaii Sess Laws** ... Session Laws of Hawaii [*A publication*] (DLA)
**Hawaii Shell News** ... Hawaiian Shell News [*A publication*]
**Hawaii Shell News (Honolulu)** ... Hawaiian Shell News (Honolulu) [*A publication*]
**Hawaii Sugar Plant Assoc Exp Stn Annu Rep** ... Hawaiian Sugar Planters' Association. Experiment Station. Annual Report [*A publication*]
**Hawaii Sugar Technol Rep** ... Hawaiian Sugar Technologists Reports [*A publication*]
**Hawaii Univ Coop Ext Serv Circ** ... Hawaii University. Cooperative Extension Service. Circular [*A publication*]
**Hawaii Univ Inst Geophys** ... Hawaii University. Institute of Geophysics. Report [*A publication*]
**Hawaii Univ Inst Geophys Contrib** ... Hawaii University. Institute of Geophysics. Contributions [*A publication*]
**Hawaii Univ Look Lab Oceanogr Eng Tech Rep** ... Hawaii University. Look Laboratory of Oceanographic Engineering. Technical Report [*A publication*]
**Hawaii Univ Sea Grant Prog Rep** ... Hawaii University. Sea Grant Program. Reports [*A publication*]
**Hawaii Univ Water Resour Res Cent Annu Rep** ... Hawaii University. Water Resources Research Center. Annual Report [*A publication*]
**Hawaii Univ Water Resour Res Cent Tech Rep** ... Hawaii University. Water Resources Research Center. Technical Report [*A publication*]
**Hawaii Uni Water Resour Cent Tech Rep** ... Hawaii University. Water Resources Research Center. Technical Report [*A publication*]
**Haw App**.... Hawaii Appellate Reports [*A publication*]
**Hawarde** .... Hawarde's Star Chamber Cases [*A publication*] (DLA)
**Hawarde St Ch** ... Hawarde's Star Chamber Cases [*A publication*] (DLA)
**Haw Ass**...... Hawes on Assignments [*A publication*] (DLA)
**HAWB**........ House Air Waybill [*Shipping*] (DS)
**HAWC**....... Homing and Warning Computer (MCD)
**HAWC**....... Wacca [*Ethiopia*] [*ICAO location identifier*] (ICLI)
**Haw Cr Rep** ... Hawley's American Criminal Reports [*A publication*] (DLA)
**HAWE**........ Hamburg-Wechsler Intelligence Test [*Psychology*]
**Hawes Jur** ... Hawes on Jurisdiction of Courts [*A publication*] (DLA)
**HAWFA**..... Hawaii Farm Science [*A publication*]
**Haw Fed**..... Hawaii Federal [*Legal term*] (DLA)
**HAWHA** ... Heart of America Walking Horse Association (EA)
**HAWIA**..... Hauswirtschaft und Wissenschaft [*A publication*]
**HAWIK**..... Hamburg-Wechsler-Intelligenztest fuer Kinder [*Hamburg-Wechsler Intelligence Test for Children*] [*Psychology*]
**HAWK**....... Have Alimony, Will Keep
**HAWK**....... Hawkesbury [*England*]
**Hawk** ......... Hawkins' Pleas of the Crown [*England*] [*A publication*] (DLA)
**HAWK**....... Hawks Industries, Inc. [*NASDAQ symbol*] (NQ)
**HAWK**....... Homing All the Way Killer [*Small missile*]
**Hawk Abr**.. Hawkins' Abridgment of Coke upon Littleton [*A publication*] (DLA)
**Hawk Coke Abr** ... Hawkins' Abridgment of Coke upon Littleton [*A publication*] (DLA)
**Hawk Co Litt** ... Hawkins' Coke upon Littleton [*A publication*] (DLA)
**Hawker Siddeley Tech Rev** ... Hawker Siddeley Technical Review [*A publication*]
**Hawkins**..... Hawkins' Annual Reports [*19-24 Louisiana*] [*A publication*] (DLA)
**Hawk PC** ... Hawkins' Pleas of the Crown [*England*] [*A publication*] (DLA)
**Hawk Pl Cr** ... Hawkins' Pleas of the Crown [*England*] [*A publication*] (DLA)
**Hawks**........ Hawks' North Carolina Reports [*A publication*] (DLA)
**Hawks (NC)** ... Hawks' North Carolina Reports [*A publication*] (DLA)
**Hawk Wills** ... Hawkins' Construction of Wills [*A publication*] (DLA)
**Hawl**.......... Hawley's Reports [*10-20 Nevada*] [*A publication*] (DLA)
**Hawl Cr R** ... Hawley's American Criminal Reports [*A publication*] (DLA)
**Hawley**....... Hawley's American Criminal Reports [*A publication*] (DLA)
**Hawley**....... Hawley's Reports [*10-20 Nevada*] [*A publication*] (DLA)
**Hawley's Crim Rep** ... Hawley's American Criminal Reports [*A publication*] (DLA)
**Hawn**.......... Hawaii Reports [*A publication*] (DLA)
**HAWP**....... Homing and Warning Programmer (MCD)
**HAWR**....... Helicopter Attack Warning RADAR (NVT)
**Haw Rep** ... Hawaii Reports [*A publication*] (DLA)
**Haw Rev Stat** ... Hawaii Revised Statutes [*A publication*] (DLA)
**HAWSEAFRON** ... Hawaiian Sea Frontier
**Haw Sess Laws** ... Session Laws of Hawaii [*A publication*] (DLA)
**HAWT**....... Horizontal Axis Wind Turbine [*Generator*] [*Also, HAWTG*] (MCD)
**HAWTADS** ... Helicopter All-Weather Target Acquisition and Designation System
**HAWTG**.... Horizontal Axis Wind Turbine Generator [*Also, HAWT*]
**Haw WC** ... Hawes' Will Case [*A publication*] (DLA)
**HAX**.......... Hafnium Column Extractant [*Nuclear energy*] (NRCH)
**HAX**.......... Helicopter Armored Experiment
**HAX**.......... Muskogee, OK [*Location identifier*] [*FAA*] (FAAL)
**HAY**.......... Haycock, AK [*Location identifier*] [*FAA*] (FAAL)
**HAY**.......... Hayes-Dana, Inc. [*Toronto Stock Exchange symbol*]
**Hay** ........... Hayes' Irish Exchequer Reports [*1830-32*] [*A publication*] (DLA)
**Hay** ........... Hayes' Reports [*Calcutta*] [*A publication*] (DLA)
**HAY**.......... Hayfield [*California*] [*Seismograph station code, US Geological Survey*] (SEIS)
**Hay** ........... Hay's High Court Appeals Reports [*1862-63*] [*Bengal, India*] [*A publication*] (DLA)
**Hay** ........... Hay's Poor Law Decisions [*1711-1859*] [*Scotland*] [*A publication*] (DLA)
**Hay** ........... Hay's Scotch Decisions [*A publication*] (DLA)
**Hay** ........... Haywood's North Carolina Reports [*A publication*] (DLA)
**Hay** ........... Haywood's Tennessee Reports [*A publication*] (DLA)
**Hay Acc**..... Hay's Decisions on Accidents and Negligence [*1860*] [*Scotland*] [*A publication*] (DLA)
**Hay (Calc)** ... Hay's Reports [*Calcutta*] [*A publication*] (DLA)
**Hay Dec**..... Hay's Decisions on Accidents and Negligence [*1860*] [*Scotland*] [*A publication*] (DLA)
**Haydn-Stud** ... Haydn-Studien [*A publication*]
**Haydn Yb**... Haydn Yearbook [*A publication*]
**Hay Eq**....... Haynes' Outlines of Equity [*5th ed.*] [*1880*] [*A publication*] (DLA)
**Hayes**......... Hayes' Irish Exchequer Reports [*1830-32*] [*A publication*] (DLA)
**Hayes Con Conv** ... Hayes' Concise Conveyancer [*A publication*] (DLA)

**Hayes Conv** ... Hayes on Conveyancing [*A publication*] (DLA)
**Hayes Cr & P** ... Hayes on Crimes and Punishments [*A publication*] (DLA)
**Hayes Exch** ... Hayes' Irish Exchequer Reports [*1830-32*] [*A publication*] (DLA)
**Hayes Exch (Ir)** ... Hayes' Irish Exchequer Reports [*1830-32*] [*A publication*] (DLA)
**Hayes Heirs** ... Hayes' Dispositions to Heirs in Tail, Etc. [*A publication*] (DLA)
**Hayes Intr** ... Hayes' Introduction to Conveyancing [*A publication*] (DLA)
**Hayes & J** .. Hayes and Jones' Irish Exchequer Reports [*1832-34*] [*A publication*] (DLA)
**Hayes & J (Ir)** ... Hayes and Jones' Irish Exchequer Reports [*1832-34*] [*A publication*] (DLA)
**Hayes & Jo** ... Hayes and Jones' Irish Exchequer Reports [*1832-34*] [*A publication*] (DLA)
**Hayes & Jon** ... Hayes and Jones' Irish Exchequer Reports [*1832-34*] [*A publication*] (DLA)
**Hayes & J Wills** ... Hayes and Jarman's Concise Forms of Wills [*18th ed.*] [*1952*] [*A publication*] (DLA)
**Hayes Lim** ... Hayes on Limitations as to Heirs of the Body, Etc. [*A publication*] (DLA)
**Hayes R Est** ... Hayes' Real Estate [*A publication*] (DLA)
**Hayes UD & T** ... Hayes' Law of Uses, Devises, and Trust [*A publication*] (DLA)
**Hay Exch**... Hayes' Irish Exchequer Reports [*1830-32*] [*A publication*] (DLA)
**Hay Exp**..... Hay on Expatriation [*A publication*] (DLA)
**Hayford**...... Gold Coast Native Institutions [*A publication*] (DLA)
**Haygaz Hayag Handes** ... Haygazean Hayagitagan Handes [*A publication*]
**Hay & H** .... Hayward and Hazelton's United States Circuit Court Reports [*District of Columbia*] [*A publication*] (DLA)
**Hay & Haz** ... Hayward and Hazelton's United States Circuit Court Reports [*District of Columbia*] [*A publication*] (DLA)
**Hay & J**...... Hayes and Jones' Irish Exchequer Reports [*A publication*] (DLA)
**Hay & Jo**.... Hayes and Jones' Irish Exchequer Reports [*1832-34*] [*A publication*] (DLA)
**Hay & M**.... Hay and Marriott's English Admiralty Reports [*A publication*] (DLA)
**Hay & Mar** ... Hay and Marriott's English Admiralty Reports [*A publication*] (DLA)
**Hay & Marr** ... Hay and Marriott's English Admiralty Reports [*A publication*] (DLA)
**Hay & M (Eng)** ... Hay and Marriott's English Admiralty Reports [*A publication*] (DLA)
**Hayn Ch Pr** ... Haynes' Chancery Practice [*1879*] [*A publication*] (DLA)
**Hayn Eq**..... Haynes' Outlines of Equity [*5th ed.*] [*1880*] [*A publication*] (DLA)
**Haynes Eq** ... Haynes' Outlines of Equity [*5th ed.*] [*1880*] [*A publication*] (DLA)
**Hayn Lead Cas** ... Haynes' Students' Leading Cases [*A publication*] (DLA)
**HAYOE7**... Ocean Research [*Seoul*] [*A publication*]
**Hay PL** ...... Hay's Poor Law Decisions [*1711-1859*] [*Scotland*] [*A publication*] (DLA)
**HAYR**........ Hayridge [*England*]
**HAYSTAQ** ... Have You Stored Answers to Questions? [*Data processing*]
**Hayw**.......... Haywood's North Carolina Reports [*A publication*] (DLA)
**Hayw**.......... Haywood's Tennessee Reports [*A publication*] (DLA)
**Hayw & H** ... Hayward and Hazelton's United States Circuit Court Reports [*District of Columbia*] [*A publication*] (DLA)
**Hayw & HDC** ... Hayward and Hazelton's United States Circuit Court Reports [*District of Columbia*] [*A publication*] (DLA)
**Hayw LR**.... Hayward's Law Register [*Boston*] [*A publication*] (DLA)
**Hayw Man** ... Haywood's Manual of the Statute Laws of North Carolina [*A publication*] (DLA)
**Hayw NC**... Haywood's North Carolina Reports [*A publication*] (DLA)
**Haywood Tenn Rep** ... Haywood's Tennessee Reports [*A publication*] (DLA)
**Hayw Tenn** ... Haywood's Tennessee Reports [*A publication*] (DLA)
**HAZ**........... Hazardous (KSC)
**HAZ**........... Heat-Affected Zone
**HAZ**........... Heat-Annealed Zone [*Metallurgy*]
**HAZAL**..... Hahameinu Zikhronam Livrakha [*Our Sages of Blessed Memory*] [*Hebrew*]
**HAZAN**..... Hazard Analysis
**Hazard Cargo Bull** ... Hazardous Cargo Bulletin [*A publication*]
**Hazard Mater Manage J** ... Hazardous Materials Management Journal [*A publication*]
**Hazardous Cargo Bull** ... Hazardous Cargo Bulletin [*A publication*]
**Hazards Bull** ... Hazards Bulletin [*A publication*]
**Hazard Waste** ... Hazardous Waste [*A publication*]
**Haz Bull**..... Hazards Bulletin [*A publication*]
**HAZCHEM** ... Hazardous Chemical
**HAZCON** ... Hazardous Condition (NVT)
**HAZEL**...... Homogeneous Assembly Zero Energy Level [*AERE*]
**HAZINF**.... Hazardous Chemicals Information and Disposal [*University of Alberta*] [*Canada*] [*Information service or system*] (CRD)
**HAZMACON** ... West Coast Hazardous Materials Management Conference (TSPED)
**HAZMAT** ... Hazardous Material
**HAZOP**..... Hazard and Operability [*Chemical engineering*]
**Haz PA Reg** ... Hazard's Pennsylvania Register [*A publication*] (DLA)
**Haz PA Reg (PA)** ... Hazard's Pennsylvania Register [*A publication*] (DLA)
**Haz P Reg** ... Hazard's Pennsylvania Register [*A publication*] (ILCA)
**Haz Reg**..... Hazard's Pennsylvania Register [*A publication*] (DLA)
**Haz Rev**..... Hazards Review [*A publication*]
**Haz & R M War** ... Hazlitt and Roche on Maritime Warfare [*A publication*] (DLA)
**Haz US Reg** ... Hazard's United States Register [*A publication*] (DLA)
**HAZWRAP** ... Hazardous Waste Remedial Action Program [*Oak Ridge National Laboratory*]
**HB**............. Belize Airways Ltd. [*ICAO designator*] (FAAC)
**HB**............. Bell Helicopter Co., Brantly Helicopter Corp., Brditschka [*Heinrich Brditschka Flugzeugbau*] [*ICAO aircraft manufacturer identifier*] (ICAO)
**HB**............. [*Henry*] Blackstone's English Common Pleas Reports [*1788-96*] [*A publication*] (DLA)
**HB**............. Brinell Hardness Number [*Also, BH, BHN, BHNo*]
**HB**............. Farbwerke Hoechst AG [*Germany*] [*Research code symbol*]
**Hb**............. Habakkuk [*Old Testament book*]
**HB**............. Half Bound [*Bibliography*]
**HB**............. Half Bow [*Music*] (ROG)
**HB**............. Half Breadth (AAG)
**HB**............. Halfback [*Football*]
**HB**............. Halk Bankasi [*Peoples Bank of Turkey*] [*See also THB*]
**HB**............. Hallelujah Band
**HB**............. Hampton & Branchville Railroad Co. [*AAR code*]
**HB**............. Handbook (NASA)
**HB**............. Handelsbeziehungen [*Trade Relations*] [*German*]
**HB**............. Handelsblatt [*Information service or system*] [*A publication*]
**HB**............. Handlebar (ROG)
**HB**............. Hard Black [*Pencil leads*]
**HB**............. Hard-Boiled [*Egg*]
**HB**............. Hardboard (ADA)
**HB**............. Hardy Biennial [*Horticulture*] (ROG)
**HB**............. Health Benefit
**HB**............. Health Board [*Ireland*]
**HB**............. Heart Block [*Medicine*]
**HB**............. Heat to Boiling Point [*Calorimetry*]
**HB**............. Heavy Barrel [*Rifles*]
**HB**............. Heavy Bombardment [*or Bomber*]
**HB**............. Hebraeische Bibliographie [*Berlin*] [*A publication*]
**Hb**............. Hebrew (BJA)
**Hb**............. Hemoglobin [*Biochemistry, medicine*]
**HB**............. Henricus Boich [*Flourished, 1320-30*] [*Authority cited in pre-1607 legal work*] (DSA)
**HB**............. Hepatitis B [*Medicine*]
**HB**............. Herba [*Herb*] [*Pharmacology*] (ROG)
**HB**............. Herders Bibelkommentar [*A publication*] (BJA)
**HB**............. Herri Batazuna [*Union of the People*] [*Spain*] [*Political party*] (PPE)
**HB**............. Het Boek [*A publication*]
**H-B**............ Hexadecimal-to-Binary [*Data processing*] (IEEE)
**HB**............. High Band (AAG)
**HB**............. High Bay (KSC)
**HB**............. High Boilers
**HB**............. Highways and Byways [*A publication*]
**HB**............. Hill-Burton [*Federal grant and loan program for construction and modernization of medical facilities*]
**HB**............. Hillenbrand Industries, Inc. [*NYSE symbol*] (SPSG)
**HB**............. Hinged Block [*British military*] (DMA)
**HB**............. His Beatitude [*or His Blessedness*]
**HB**............. His Bundle [*Cardiology*]
**HB**............. Historical Branch [*Army*]
**HB**............. Historical Bulletin [*A publication*]
**HB**............. Hit by Ball [*or Hit Batsman*] [*Baseball*]
**HB**............. Hold Breakfast [*Medicine*]
**HB**............. Holiness Band
**H & B**......... Holland & Barrett [*Grocery and health food shop chain*] [*British*]
**HB**............. Homing Beacon [*Aviation*]
**HB**............. Honey Bee
**HB**............. Honeywell-Bull
**HB**............. Horizontal Baffle (NRCH)
**HB**............. Horizontal Bands [*Navigation markers*]
**HB**............. Horizontal Bomber
**HB**............. Horizontal-Branch [*Astronomy*]
**HB**............. Hormone Binding [*Endocrinology*]
**HB**............. Horn Book [*A publication*]
**HB**............. Hose Bib (AAG)
**HB**............. Hot Boning [*Meat processing*]
**HB**............. House Bill [*In state legislatures*]
**HB**............. Housebreaking
**HB**............. Household Battalion [*British military*] (DMA)
**HB**............. Household Goods/Baggage
**HB**............. Housing Benefit [*British*]
**HB**............. Hub. Hay River [*A publication*]
**H & B**......... Hudson and Brooke's Irish King's Bench Reports [*1827-31*] [*A publication*] (DLA)
**HB**............. Human Behavior [*National Science Foundation project*]
**HB**............. Human Behavior [*A publication*]
**HB**............. Human Being [*Slang*]

**H & B**......... [*Alexander Von*] Humboldt and [*Aime*] Bonpland [*Naturalists who made a scientific journey to Central and South America from 1799 to 1804*] (ROG)
**HB**............. Huntington Beach [*California*]
**HB**............. Hybridoma [*Cytology*]
**HB**............. Liechtenstein [*Aircraft nationality and registration mark*] (FAAC)
**HB**............. Switzerland [*Aircraft nationality and registration mark*] (FAAC)
**HBA**........... Bible Atlas [*Hurblut*] [*A publication*] (BJA)
**HBA**........... General Hotel, Boarding House, and Apartments [*British*]
**HBA**........... Halley Bay [*Antarctica*] [*Seismograph station code, US Geological Survey*] [*Closed*] (SEIS)
**HBA**........... Handbook Art
**HBA**........... Handicapped Boaters Association (EA)
**HBA**........... Harrison Bay, AK [*Location identifier*] [*FAA*] (FAAL)
**HBA**........... Health and Beauty Aid [*Retailing*]
**HBA**........... Health Benefit Advisor [*CHAMPUS*]
**HbA**........... Hemoglobin, Adult [*Medicine*]
**HBA**........... Historiografia y Bibliografia Americanistas [*A publication*]
**HBA**........... Hobart [*Tasmania*] [*Airport symbol*] (OAG)
**HBA**........... Home Baking Association (EA)
**HBA**........... Home Base [*Military*] (NVT)
**HBA**........... Honest Ballot Association (EA)
**HBA**........... Horizontal Baffle Assembly [*Nuclear energy*] (NRCH)
**HBA**........... Host Bus Adapter [*Data processing*]
**HBA**........... Hydraulic and Boatyard Association [*A union*] [*British*]
**HBA**........... Hydrazinobenzoic Acid [*Organic chemistry*]
**HBA**........... Hydrogen-Bond Acceptor [*Chemistry*]
**HBAb**......... Hepatitis B Antibody [*Immunology*]
**HBABA**..... (Hydroxybenzeneazo)benzoic Acid [*Also, HABA*] [*Organic chemistry*]
**HBAg**......... Hepatitis B Antigen [*Immunology*]
**HBAH**....... Hydroxybenzoic Acid Hydrazide [*Reagent*]
**HBalt**......... Hispania (Baltimore) [*A publication*]
**HBAM**....... Historic Buildings and Ancient Monuments Act [*Town planning*] [*British*]
**HBAN**........ Huntington Bancshares, Inc. [*NASDAQ symbol*] (NQ)
**H-BAR**....... Heavy Barrel [*Rifles*]
**HbAT**......... Handbuch zum Alten Testament [*Tuebingen*] [*A publication*]
**HBAT**......... Having Been Assigned to This Organization [*or Headquarters*]
**HBAVS**...... Human Betterment Association for Voluntary Sterilization [*Later, AVS*] (EA)
**HBB**........... Historic Buildings Bureau [*British*]
**HBB**........... Hobbs, NM [*Location identifier*] [*FAA*] (FAAL)
**HBB**........... Hook-Basal Body [*Genetics*]
**HBB**........... Hospital Blood Bank
**HBBA**......... Bujumbura [*Burundi*] [*ICAO location identifier*] (ICLI)
**HBBD**......... Hydroxybenzylbutanediol [*Clinical chemistry*]
**HBBE**......... Gitega [*Burundi*] [*ICAO location identifier*] (ICLI)
**HBBIAD**.... Harvard Books in Biophysics [*A publication*]
**HBBK**......... Kiofi-Mosso [*Burundi*] [*ICAO location identifier*] (ICLI)
**HBBL**......... Hydroxybenzylbutyrolactone [*Clinical chemistry*]
**HBBL**......... Nyanza-Lac [*Burundi*] [*ICAO location identifier*] (ICLI)
**HBBM**....... Mugera [*Burundi*] [*ICAO location identifier*] (ICLI)
**HBBN**........ Nyakagunda [*Burundi*] [*ICAO location identifier*] (ICLI)
**HBBW**....... Hold Breakfast for Blood Work [*Medicine*]
**HBC**........... Hajji Baba Club (EA)
**HBC**........... Handbooks for Bible Classes [*A publication*]
**HBC**........... Handlebar Control [*Early automobiles*] (ROG)
**HBC**........... Health Benefit Card (ADA)
**HBC**........... Highamerica Balloon Club (EA)
**HBC**........... Historic Buildings Council [*British*]
**HBC**........... [*The*] History Book Club
**HBC**........... Homogeneous Boundary Condition
**HBC**........... Honeywell Business Computer [*or Compiler*]
**HBC**........... Horseshoe Bay [*British Columbia*] [*Seismograph station code, US Geological Survey*] [*Closed*] (SEIS)
**HBC**........... Hostage Bracelet Committee (EA)
**HBC**........... House Budget Committee
**HBC**........... Hudson's Bay Co. [*Facetious translations include "Here before Christ," "Here before Columbus," and "Hungry Belly Company."*]
**HBC**........... Hudson's Bay Co. [*Toronto Stock Exchange symbol*]
**HBC**........... Human Biology Council (EA)
**HBC**........... Hydrogen Bubble Chamber
**HBCAg**...... Hepatitis B Core Antigen [*Immunology*]
**HBCD**........ Hexabromocyclododecane [*Flame retardant*] [*Organic chemistry*]
**HBCI**......... Harmonia Bancorp, Inc. [*NASDAQ symbol*] (NQ)
**HBCN**........ Hazard Beacon (MSA)
**HbCO**........ Hemoglobin, Carboxy [*Biochemistry, medicine*]
**HBCU**........ Historically Black Colleges and Universities
**HBD**........... Detailhandel Magazine [*A publication*]
**HBd**........... Haarlemsch Bijdragen [*A publication*]
**HBD**........... Hardboard [*Technical drawings*]
**HBD**........... Harper's Bible Dictionary [*A publication*]
**HBD**........... Has Been Drinking [*Medical notation*]
**HBD**........... Hubbard, OH [*Location identifier*] [*FAA*] (FAAL)
**HBD**........... Hydrogen Bond Donor [*Solvent*]
**HBD**........... Hydroxybutyrate Dehydrogenase [*Also, HBDH*] [*An enzyme*]
**HBDC**........ Home Base Development Committee [*Navy*]
**HBDH**....... Hydroxybutyrate Dehydrogenase [*Also, HBD*] [*An enzyme*]
**HBDMA**.... Hat Block and Die Makers Association (EA)
**HBDMI**..... Historical Biographical Dictionaries Master Index [*A publication*]
**HBDR**........ Helicopter Battle Damage Repair (RDA)
**HBDS**........ Hypergraph-Based Data Structures
**HBDT**........ High BIT [*Binary Digit*] Density Tape [*Skylab*] [*NASA*]
**HBE**........... Hamilton Board of Education Schools [*UTLAS symbol*]
**HBE**........... His Bundle Electrogram [*Cardiology*]
**HBE**........... Honeybee, Inc. [*AMEX symbol*] (SPSG)
**HBeAg**....... Hepatitis B e Antigen [*Immunology*]
**HBED**........ Bis(hydroxybenzyl)ethylenediaminediacetic Acid [*Organic chemistry*]
**HBEF**......... Hubbard Brook Experimental Forest
**HBEN**........ High Byte Enable
**HBEN**........ Home Beneficial Corp. [*NASDAQ symbol*] (NQ)
**HBF**........... Hamilton Board of Education [*UTLAS symbol*]
**HBF**........... Harts Bluff [*South Carolina*] [*Seismograph station code, US Geological Survey*] (SEIS)
**HBF**........... Hauptbahnhof [*Main Railroad Station*] [*German*]
**HbF**........... Hemoglobin, Fetal [*Also, HgF*] [*Medicine*]
**HBF**........... Hepatic Blood Flow
**HBF**........... High Bleeding Frequency [*Medicine*]
**Hb d G**....... Handbuch der Deutschen Gegenwartsliteratur [*A publication*]
**HBG**........... Hattiesburg, MS [*Location identifier*] [*FAA*] (FAAL)
**HBG**........... Hope Brook Gold, Inc. [*Toronto Stock Exchange symbol*]
**HBG**........... Hospital Buyer's Guide [*A publication*]
**HBG**........... Hydroxybenzoylglycine [*Biochemistry*]
**HBG**........... (Hydroxybutyl)guanine [*Biochemistry*]
**Hb d G A**.... Handbuch der Gesamten Arbeitsmedizin [*A publication*]
**HBGF**......... Heparin-Binding Growth Factor [*Biochemistry*]
**HBGM**....... Home Blood Glucose Monitoring [*Medicine*]
**HBGM**....... Hypersonic Boost-Glide Missile
**HBH**........... Hobart Bay [*Alaska*] [*Airport symbol*] (OAG)
**HBHC**........ Hospital-Based Home Care
**Hb Hist St**... Handbuch der Historischen Staetten Deutschlands [*A publication*]
**HBI**............ Hemibody Irradiation [*Oncology*]
**HbI**............ Hemoglobin I [*Biochemistry*] [*Medicine*]
**HBI**............ Hindustan Bible Institute (EA)
**HBI**............ Hospital Bureau, Incorporated [*Formerly, HBSS*] (EA)
**HBI**............ Hot Biquetted Iron
**HBI**............ House-Breaking Implements [*British police term*]
**HBIG**......... Hepatitis B Immune Globulin [*Immunology*]
**HBII**.......... Houston Biomedical, Inc. [*NASDAQ symbol*] (NQ)
**Hb Inst Orth**... Handbook. Institute of Orthopaedics [*A publication*]
**HBITDG**... Handbuch der Bakteriellen Infektionen bei Tieren [*A publication*]
**HBJ**........... Harcourt, Brace, Jovanovich, Inc. [*Publishers*] [*NYSE symbol*] (SPSG)
**HBJ**........... High-Band Jammer (MCD)
**HBJ Mth**... HBJ [*Hypothec Bank of Japan*] Monthly [*A publication*]
**HBK**........... Habekacin [*Antibacterial*]
**HBK**........... Handbook
**HBK**........... Hardwood Bleached Kraft [*Pulp and paper technology*]
**HBK**........... Hartebeesthoek [*South Africa*] [*Geomagnetic observatory code*]
**HBk**........... Herders Bibelkommentar [*A publication*] (BJA)
**HBK**........... Hinchinbrook, AK [*Location identifier*] [*FAA*] (FAAL)
**HB Kr I**...... Hamburger Beitraege zur Philosophie des Kritischen Idealismus [*A publication*]
**H Bl**............ [*Henry*] Blackstone's English Common Pleas Reports [*1788-96*] [*A publication*] (DLA)
**HBL**........... Harbor Belt Line Railroad
**HBL**........... Heeresbetriebsstofflager [*Army Gasoline-Supply Depot*] [*German military - World War II*]
**H Bl**............ Historische Blaetter [*A publication*]
**HBL**........... Hofmannsthal Blaetter [*A publication*]
**HBL**........... Huntington Beach Public Library, Huntington Beach, CA [*OCLC symbol*] (OCLC)
**H Black**...... [*Henry*] Blackstone's English Common Pleas Reports [*1788-96*] [*A publication*] (DLA)
**HBLB**........ Horserace Betting Levy Board [*British*]
**H Bl (Eng)**... [*Henry*] Blackstone's English Common Pleas Reports [*1788-96*] [*A publication*] (DLA)
**H Bl HVB**... Heimatblaetter des Historischen Vereins Bamberg [*A publication*]
**HBLO**........ Home Base, Ledger Office [*British military*] (DMA)
**HBLV**........ Human B-Lymphotropic Virus
**HBM**.......... Die Haghe. Bijdragen en Mededeelingen [*A publication*]
**HBM**.......... Heavy Ballistic Missile
**HBM**.......... Held by Manufacturer
**HBM**.......... High-Beta Model (MCD)
**HBM**.......... His [*or Her*] Britannic Majesty
**HBM**.......... Hobart Mills [*California*] [*Seismograph station code, US Geological Survey*] (SEIS)
**HBM**.......... Horizontal Boring Mill
**HBM**.......... Hudson Bay Mining & Smelting Co. Ltd. [*Toronto Stock Exchange symbol*]
**HBM**.......... Hydraulic Bore-Hole Mining [*Coal*]
**HBMB**....... Holy Blossom Men's Bulletin [*A publication*]

**Hb Miet R** ... Handbuch des Gesamten Miet und Raumrechts [*A publication*]
**HBMS** ....... His [*or Her*] Britannic Majesty's Service
**HBMS** ....... His [*or Her*] Britannic Majesty's Ship (ROG)
**HBN** .......... Hamburger Beitraege zur Numismatik [*A publication*]
**HBN** .......... Hazard Beacon
**HB(N)** ........ Heavy Bomber (Night) [*British military*] (DMA)
**Hb Norg Byggforsk Inst** ... Handbok. Norges Byggforskningsinstitutt [*A publication*]
**HBO** .......... Health Benefits Organization [*Insurance*]
**H Bo** .......... Henricus Boich [*Flourished, 1320-30*] [*Authority cited in pre-1607 legal work*] (DSA)
**HBO** .......... Home Box Office [*Cable-television system*]
**HBO** .......... Horizontal-Branch Oscillation [*Astronomy*]
**HBO** .......... Humboldt, NE [*Location identifier*] [*FAA*] (FAAL)
**HBO** .......... Hyperbaric Oxygen [*Also, HPO, OHP*] [*Medicine*]
**$HbO_2$** .......... Hemoglobin, Oxy [*Biochemistry, medicine*]
**HBOC** ........ HBO & Company [*NASDAQ symbol*] (NQ)
**HBOI** ......... Harbor Branch Oceanographic Institution [*Fort Pierce, FL*]
**HbOr** ......... Handbuch der Orientalistik [*Leiden*] [*A publication*] (BJA)
**HBP** .......... Dauphin County Library System, Harrisburg, PA [*OCLC symbol*] (OCLC)
**HBP** .......... Hamilton Board of Education, Education Centre Library [*UTLAS symbol*]
**HBP** .......... Handbook Production
**HBP** .......... Held for Blueprint (MCD)
**HBP** .......... Hepatic Binding Protein [*Biochemistry*]
**HBP** .......... High Blood Pressure [*Medicine*]
**HbP** .......... Hilfsbuch des Pehlevi [*A publication*] (BJA)
**HBP** .......... Hit by Pitcher [*Baseball*]
**HBP** .......... Hospital Benefits Payment
**HBP** .......... Hydraulic Bench Press
**HBP** .......... Hydrocortisone(butyrate)propionate [*Endocrinology*]
**HbP** .......... Primitive [*Fetal*] Hemoglobin
**HBPA** ........ Horsemen's Benevolent and Protective Association (EA)
**Hb Palaeozool** ... Handbuch der Palaeozoologie [*A publication*]
**H-BPH** ...... Hawaii Regional Library for the Blind and Physically Handicapped, Honolulu, HI [*Library symbol*] [*Library of Congress*] (LCLS)
**HBPIC** ....... High Blood Pressure Information Center [*Public Health Service*] (IID)
**HBPP** ......... Humboldt Bay Power Plant (NRCH)
**Hb d Ps** ...... Handbuch der Psychologie [*A publication*]
**Hb Psych** ... Handbuch der Psychologie [*A publication*]
**HBR** .......... Haibara [*Japan*] [*Seismograph station code, US Geological Survey*] (SEIS)
**HBR** .......... Hansell's Bankruptcy Reports [*1915-17*] [*A publication*] (DLA)
**HBR** .......... Harbor [*Maps and charts*]
**HBR** .......... Harvard Business Review [*John Wiley & Sons, Inc.*] [*Bibliographic database*] [*A publication*]
**HBR** .......... Has Been Reviewed (AAG)
**HBR** .......... Heidelberger Beitraege zur Romanistik [*A publication*]
**HBR** .......... High BIT [*Binary Digit*] Rate (KSC)
**HBR** .......... Hobart, OK [*Location identifier*] [*FAA*] (FAAL)
**H & BR** ...... Hull & Barnsley Railway [*British*] (ROG)
**HBRACW** ... Has Been Reviewed and Concurred With (AAG)
**HBRI** ......... Hospital Bureau Research Institute [*Defunct*] (EA)
**H/BRK** ...... Hand Brake [*Automotive engineering*]
**Hbr Mr** ...... Harbor Master
**HBS** .......... Half Bar Symbology
**HBS** .......... Hanks Balanced Salt [*Solution*] [*Cell incubation medium*]
**HBS** .......... Harbor Boat Service [*Military*]
**HBS** .......... Harvard Business School
**HBS** .......... Harvard Business School, Boston, MA [*OCLC symbol*] (OCLC)
**HBS** .......... Havergal Brian Society (EAIO)
**HBS** .......... Heavy Bomber Support
**HBS** .......... Helicopter Blade Slap
**HbS** .......... Hemoglobin, Sickle [*Medicine*]
**HBS** .......... Henry Bradshaw Society [*British*]
**HBS** .......... Hepatitis B Surface Antigen [*Immunology*]
**HBS** .......... Herringbone Strutting [*Construction*]
**HBS** .......... Hoboken Shore Railroad [*AAR code*]
**HBS** .......... Honey Bee Spiroplasma [*Bacteriology*]
**HBS** .......... Hot Blade Stripper
**HBS** .......... Hyperkinetic Behavior Syndrome [*Medicine*]
**HBSA** ........ Health and Building Surveyors Association [*Australia*]
**HBSA** ........ Hjalmar Bergman Samfundet Arsbok [*A publication*]
**HBSA** ........ Hungarian Boy Scout Association (EA)
**Hb SAE** ..... Society of Automotive Engineers. Handbook [*A publication*]
**HBsAg** ....... Hepatitis B Surface Antigen [*Immunology*]
**HbSC** ......... Hemoglobin C Sickle Cell Disease [*Medicine*]
**HBSI** .......... Hamptons Bancshares, Inc. [*NASDAQ symbol*] (NQ)
**HBSMA** .... Hack and Band Saw Manufacturers Association of America
**HBSMAA** ... Hack and Band Saw Manufacturers Association of America (EA)
**HBSS** ......... Hanks Balanced Salt Solution [*Cell incubation medium*]
**HBSS** ......... Hospital Bureau of Standards and Supplies [*Later, HBI*]
**HBT** .......... Habeat [*Let Him Have*] [*Pharmacy*] (ROG)
**HBT** .......... Harbor Bay Telecommunications [*Alameda, CA*] (TSSD)
**HBT** .......... Heflex Bioengineering Test [*NASA*]
**HBT** .......... Herringbone Twill
**HBT** .......... Hobart Mills [*California*] [*Seismograph station code, US Geological Survey*] (SEIS)
**HBT** .......... Houston Belt & Terminal Railway Co. [*AAR code*]
**HB & T** ...... Houston Belt & Terminal Railway Co.
**HBT** .......... Human Brain Thromboplastin [*Clinical chemistry*]
**HBT** .......... Human Breast Tumor [*Type of cell line*]
**H & BT** ...... Huntingdon & Broad Top Railroad
**HBT** .......... Hydroxybenzotriazole [*Organic chemistry*]
**HBT** .......... Sand Point, AK [*Location identifier*] [*FAA*] (FAAL)
**$H_2BT$** .......... Hydrogen Breath Test
**HBTA** ........ HB [*Homeward Bound Ministries*] Tract Association (EA)
**HBTA** ........ Hutchinson Board of Trade Association (EA)
**HBTF-A** .... Habiter [*A publication*]
**HBU** .......... Aurora, OR [*Location identifier*] [*FAA*] (FAAL)
**HBU** .......... Houston Baptist University [*Texas*]
**HBUA** ........ Hungarian Baptist Union of America (EA)
**HBUF** ........ Homestyle Buffet, Inc. [*NASDAQ symbol*] (NQ)
**H Bull** ........ Heart Bulletin [*A publication*]
**HBV** .......... Harrisonburg [*Virginia*] [*Seismograph station code, US Geological Survey*] (SEIS)
**HBV** .......... Hebbronville, TX [*Location identifier*] [*FAA*] (FAAL)
**HBV** .......... Hepatitis B Virus
**HBV** .......... Hessische Blaetter fuer Volkskunde [*A publication*]
**HBV** .......... Honey Bee Venom [*Immunology*]
**HBVk** ......... Hessische Blaetter fuer Volkskunde [*A publication*]
**HBVP** ........ Hepatitis B Virus Polymerase [*An enzyme*]
**Hb d W** ...... Handbuch der Wirtschaftswissenschaften [*A publication*]
**HBW** .......... High-Speed Black and White [*Photography*]
**HBW** .......... Hillsboro, WI [*Location identifier*] [*FAA*] (FAAL)
**HBw** .......... Historische Burowelt [*A publication*]
**HBW** .......... Hot Bridgewire (KSC)
**HBW** .......... Wolf [*Howard B.*], Inc. [*AMEX symbol*] (SPSG)
**HBWA** ........ High-Band Warning Antenna (MCD)
**HBWR** ........ Halden Boiling Water Reactor [*Norway*] [*Nuclear energy*]
**HBWR** ........ High-Band Warning Receiver (MCD)
**HBY** .......... Hereby (ROG)
**HBZ** .......... Hamburger Beitraege zur Zeitgeschichte [*A publication*]
**HBZ** .......... Heber Springs, AR [*Location identifier*] [*FAA*] (FAAL)
**HbzAT** ....... Handbuch zum Alten Testament [*Tuebingen*] [*A publication*]
**HC** ............ Cargoman Ltd. [*Oman*] [*ICAO designator*] (FAAC)
**HC** ............ Command Chaplain [*AFSC*]
**HC** ............ Cross of Honour [*British military*] (DMA)
**HC** ............ Crystal Holder [*JETDS nomenclature*] [*Military*] (CET)
**HC** ............ Ecuador [*Aircraft nationality and registration mark*] (FAAC)
**HC** ............ Habeas Corpus [*You Have the Body*] [*Legal term*] [*Latin*] (DLA)
**HC** ............ Habitual Criminal
**HC** ............ Hague Convention
**HC** ............ Hair Cell [*Otology*]
**HC** ............ Half Calf
**HC** ............ Half-Caste (ADA)
**HC** ............ Half-Changes [*Statistics*]
**HC** ............ Half Chest
**HC** ............ Half Covered [*Marine insurance*] (ROG)
**H/C** .......... Hand Carry (KSC)
**HC** ............ Hand-Colored [*Photography*]
**HC** ............ Hand Control [*Technical drawings*]
**HC** ............ Hand Crank
**HC** ............ Hand Cut [*Envelopes*]
**HC** ............ Hand-Held Unit Chromatography
**HC** ............ Handbooks for the Clergy [*A publication*]
**HC** ............ Handicapped [*Medicine*]
**HC** ............ Handling Capacity (DEN)
**HC** ............ Hannibal Connecting R. R. [*AAR code*]
**HC** ............ Hard Copy [*Data processing*]
**HC** ............ Hardcore
**HC** ............ Hastings Center (EA)
**HC** ............ Hatz Club (EA)
**HC** ............ Hauling Class
**HC** ............ Hauling Code
**HC** ............ Haute-Contre [*Alto*] [*Music*]
**HC** ............ Head Circumference [*Medicine*]
**H & C** ........ Head and Cover (MSA)
**HC** ............ Headcount
**HC** ............ Headmaster Commander [*Navy*] [*British*]
**HC** ............ Headquarters Command [*Military*]
**HC** ............ Heal the Children (EA)
**HC** ............ Health Certificate [*British*] (ADA)
**HC** ............ Heat of Combustion (ROG)
**HC** ............ Heater Cord
**HC** ............ Heating Cabinet (AAG)
**HC** ............ Heating Coil (AAG)
**HC** ............ Heavy Chain [*Immunoglobulin*]
**HC** ............ Held Covered [*Insurance*]
**HC** ............ Helene Curtis Industries, Inc. [*NYSE symbol*] (SPSG)
**H/C** .......... Helicopter (NATG)
**HC** ............ Helicopter Combat (NVT)
**HC** ............ Helicopter Command (NVT)
**HC** ............ Helicopter Coordinator [*Military*] (CAAL)
**HC** ............ Helicopter Council
**HC** ............ Helium Circulation [*System*]

**HC** ............ Hellenisme Contemporain [*A publication*]
**HC** ............ Helminthosporium carbonum [*A toxin-producing fungus*]
**HC** ............ Helper Component [*Biology*]
**HC** ............ Hematopoietic Cell [*Hematology*]
**HC** ............ Hepatic Coma [*Medicine*]
**HC** ............ Heralds' College [*British*]
**H and C**...... Heroin and Cocaine (DSUE)
**HC** ............ Herzberg Continuum [*Spectral region*]
**HC** ............ Hessische Chronik [*A publication*]
**HC** ............ Heuristic Concepts (IEEE)
**HC** ............ Hexachloroethane [*Organic chemistry*]
**HC** ............ High Capacity
**HC** ............ High Carbon [*Steel*]
**HC** ............ High Church
**HC** ............ High Churchman [*British*] (ROG)
**HC** ............ High Commissioner
**HC** ............ High Compression
**HC** ............ High Conditioners [*Psychology*]
**HC** ............ High Conductivity [*Copper*]
**HC** ............ High Cost of Living
**HC** ............ High Court
**HC** ............ High Current
**HC** ............ Highland Cyclists [*British military*] (DMA)
**HC** ............ Highway Code [*A publication*] (DLA)
**HC** ............ Hippocampal
**HC** ............ Hire Car (ADA)
**HC** ............ Histamine Club [*Later, HRSNA*] (EA)
**HC** ............ Historical Commission
**HC** ............ Historical Cost (ADA)
**HC** ............ Historicky Casopis [*A publication*]
**HC** ............ Hockey Club
**H & C**......... Hoffmann & Campe [*Publisher*] [*Federal Republic of Germany*]
**HC** ............ Holding Coil (MSA)
**HC** ............ Holding Company [*Business term*]
**HC** ............ Holiday Camps [*Public-performance tariff class*] [*British*]
**HC** ............ Hollins Critic [*A publication*]
**HC** ............ Hollow Core [*Technical drawings*]
**HC** ............ Holy Communion
**HC** ............ Holy Cross
**HC** ............ Home Care
**HC** ............ Honor Contracts [*Insurance*]
**HC** ............ Honoris Causa [*For the Sake of Honor, Honorary*] [*Latin*]
**HC** ............ Horizontal Cell [*Eye anatomy*]
**HC** ............ Horn Call [*A publication*]
**Hc**............. Hornyhead Chub [*Ichthyology*]
**HC** ............ Hors Concours [*Not Competing*] [*French*]
**HC** ............ Hose Cart [*Early fire engines*] (ROG)
**HC** ............ Hose Clamp (MSA)
**HC** ............ Hospital Corps [*or Corpsman*] [*Navy*]
**HC** ............ Host Cell [*Parasitology*]
**HC** ............ Host Computer
**HC** ............ Host Country (NATG)
**HC** ............ Hot and Cold
**HC** ............ Hour Circle
**HC** ............ House Cable [*Telecommunications*] (TEL)
**HC** ............ House Call [*Medicine*]
**H of C**......... House of Commons [*British*]
**HC** ............ House of Commons [*British*]
**HC** ............ House of Correction
**HC** ............ Household Cavalry [*British*]
**HC** ............ Housing Census
**HC** ............ Hristianskoe Ctenie [*A publication*]
**HC** ............ Hroswitha Club (EA)
**HC** ............ Hug Club (EA)
**HC** ............ Humid Crepidations [*Medicine*] (ROG)
**HC** ............ Humidity Control
**HC** ............ Hungarian Congress (EA)
**HC** ............ Huntington's Chorea [*Medicine*]
**HC** ............ Hupmobile Club (EA)
**H & C**......... Hurlstone and Coltman's English Exchequer Reports [*A publication*] (DLA)
**HC** ............ Hyaline Casts [*Clinical chemistry*]
**HC** ............ Hybrid Computer [*for processing both analog and digital data*] (NASA)
**HC** ............ Hyderabad Contingent [*British military*] (DMA)
**HC** ............ Hydraulic Clean (MSA)
**HC** ............ Hydraulic Coupling (DCTA)
**HC** ............ Hydraulic Cylinder
**HC** ............ Hydrocarbon [*Organic chemistry*]
**HC** ............ Hydrocortisone [*Endocrinology*]
**HC** ............ Hydrogen Chloride (AABC)
**HC** ............ Hydrographic Center [*Defense Mapping Agency*]
**HC** ............ Hypatia Cluster (EA)
**HC** ............ Hysteresis Comparator
**HC** ............ Pechiney-Progil [*France*] [*Research code symbol*]
**HC** ............ Reports of the High Court of Griqualand West [*South Africa*] [*A publication*] (DLA)
**HC** ............ Screening Smoke [*Mixture*]
**HC4** ........... Helicopterborne Command and Control Communications Central
**HCA**........... Absent by Reason of Being Held by Civil Authorities [*Military*]
**HCA**........... Haitian Coalition on AIDS (EA)
**HCA**........... Handicapped Children's Allowance [*Australia*]
**HCA**........... Harness and Cable Assembly
**HCA**........... Head of Contracting Activity [*Military*] (AABC)
**HCA**........... Health Care Administration
**HCA**........... Heart Cell Aggregate [*Cytology*]
**HCA**........... Heisey Collectors of America (EA)
**HCA**........... Held by Civil Authorities
**HCA**........... Helicopter Club of America (EA)
**HC(A)**........ Helicopter Coordinator (Airborne) (NVT)
**HCA**........... Helvetica Chirurgica Acta [*A publication*]
**HCA**........... Hepatocellular Adenoma [*Medicine*]
**HCA**........... Heterocyclic Antidepressant [*Psychopharmaceutical*]
**HCA**........... Hexachloroacetone [*Organic chemistry*]
**HCA**........... High Court of Australia (DLA)
**HC of A**....... High Court of Australia (DLA)
**HCA**........... High Courts of Admiralty [*British*]
**HCA**........... Hispanic Computing Association (EA)
**HCA**........... Historic Cost Accounts [*London Stock Exchange*]
**HCA**........... Hobby Clubs of America (EA)
**HCA**........... Hobie Class Association (EA)
**HCA**........... Holy Childhood Association (EA)
**HCA**........... Horizon Crossing Ascending
**HCA**........... Hospital Caterers Association [*British*]
**HCA**........... Hospital Corporation of America [*NYSE symbol*] (SPSG)
**HCA**........... Human Component Analysis
**HCA**........... Hunter Club of America (EA)
**HCA**........... Hunting-Clan Air Transport Ltd.
**HCA**........... Hyderabad Contingent Artillery [*British military*] (DMA)
**HCA**........... Hydrocortisone Acetate [*Pharmacology*]
**HCA**........... Lake Havasu Air Service [*Lake Havasu City, AZ*] [*FAA designator*] (FAAC)
**HCAA**......... Hebrew Christian Alliance of America [*Later, MJAA*]
**HCACA**....... Helvetica Chimica Acta [*A publication*]
**HCAIEJ**....... Health Care Instrumentation [*A publication*]
**HCal**........... Hispania (Stanford, California) [*A publication*]
**HCAP**......... Handicapped
**H-CAP**........ Hexamethylmelamine, Cyclophosphamide, Adriamycin, Platinol [*Cisplatin*] [*Antineoplastic drug regimen*]
**HCAR**......... Historic Commands of the American Revolution (EA)
**HCAS**......... Highway Cost Allocation Study [*Also, FHCAS*]
**HCATA**....... Helvetica Chirurgica Acta [*A publication*]
**HCAUA**....... Handling, Conveying, Automation [*A publication*]
**HCB**........... Hard Convex Body [*Equation of state*]
**HCB**........... Heaviside-Campbell Bridge [*Electronics*]
**HCB**........... Hemisphere Cylinder Body
**HCB**........... Hexachlorobenzene [*Organic chemistry*]
**HCB**........... High Capability Buoy [*Marine science*] (MSC)
**HCB**........... High-Capacity Bomb
**HCB**........... Highland Cyclist Battalion [*British military*] (DMA)
**HCB**........... Hollow Concrete Block
**HCB**........... Hoopes Conductivity Bridge [*Electronics*]
**HCB**........... House of Commons Bill [*British*]
**HCB**........... Hungarian Credit Bank
**HCB**........... Hydrocortisone Butyrate [*Glucocorticoid*]
**HCBD**......... Hexachlorobutadiene [*Organic chemistry*]
**HCBI**.......... Health Conference for Business and Industry [*Defunct*]
**HCBP**......... Hexachlorobiphenyl [*Organic chemistry*]
**HCC**........... Harlem Cultural Council (EA)
**HCC**........... Hawaii Control Center [*Missiles*] (MUGU)
**HCC**........... Health Care Card (ADA)
**HCC**........... Health Care Corporation [*Proposed*] (DHSM)
**HCC**........... Health Coordinating Council
**HCC**........... Heliax Coaxial Cable
**HCC**........... Helicopter Control Center (NVT)
**HCC**........... Helicopter Coordination Center
**HCC**........... Hepatitis Contagiosa Canis [*Virus*]
**HCC**........... Hepatocellular Carcinoma [*Oncology*]
**HCC**........... Hereditary Colon Cancer
**HCC**........... Hibbing Community College, Hibbing, MN [*OCLC symbol*] (OCLC)
**HCC**........... History of Chief Complaint [*Medicine*]
**HCC**........... Hollow Copper Conductor
**HCC**........... Hollywood Comedy Club (EA)
**HCC**........... Holy Cross [*California*] [*Seismograph station code, US Geological Survey*] (SEIS)
**HCC**........... Holyoke Community College [*Massachusetts*]
**HCC**........... Home Care Coordinator [*Medicine*]
**HCC**........... Honda Car Club (EA)
**HCC**........... Honda Civic Club [*Later, H-I*] (EA)
**HCC**........... Honeycomb Corrugated Construction
**HCC**........... Hospital Conveyance Corps [*British military*] (DMA)
**HCC**........... Host Country Contributions [*Peace Corps*]
**HCC**........... Hubcap Collector's Club (EA)
**HCC**........... Hull Construction Certificate
**HCC**........... Hummel Collectors Club (EA)
**HCC**........... Humor Correspondence Club (EA)
**HCC**........... Hyderabad Contingent Cavalry [*British military*] (DMA)
**HCC**........... Hydraulic Cement Concrete
**HCC**........... Hydroxycholecalciferol [*Biochemistry*]

**HCCA**........ Health Care Consumers Association [*Australia*]
**HCCA**........ Heavy Construction Contractors Association
**HCCA**........ Horseless Carriage Club of America (EA)
**HCCAPS**... Helmet Compatible Communications/Aural Protection System
**HCCBE**...... Hungarian Central Committee for Books and Education (EA)
**HCCC**........ Computer Center [*Haverford College*] [*Research center*] (RCD)
**HCCC**........ HealthCare COMPARE Corp. [*NASDAQ symbol*] (NQ)
**HCCC**........ Helix Countercurrent Chromatography
**HCCG**........ Discharge [*from Military Service*] under Honorable Conditions, Convenience of Government
**HCCH**........ Hexachlorocyclohexane [*Organic chemistry*]
**HCCI**......... HCC Industries, Inc. [*NASDAQ symbol*] (NQ)
**HCCM**....... Discharge [*from Military Service*] under Honorable Conditions, Convenience of Man
**HCCM**....... High-Performance Common Channel Module [*Telecommunications*]
**HCCP**........ Hexachlorocyclopentadiene [*Also, HCP, HEX*] [*Organic chemistry*]
**HCCP**........ Honorary Certified Claims Professional
**HCD**.......... College of the Holy Cross, Worcester, MA [*OCLC symbol*] (OCLC)
**HCd**........... Hair Cadmium Level [*Medicine*]
**HCD**.......... Handcarried (AABC)
**HCD**.......... Heavy Chain Disease [*Protein*]
**HCD**.......... High-Current Density
**HCD**.......... High-Current Diode
**HCD**.......... Hoffman Core Driver
**HCD**.......... Hollow Cathode Discharge [*Spectrometry*]
**HCD**.......... Homologous Canine Distemper [*Antiserum*]
**HCD**.......... Horizon Crossing Descending
**HCD**.......... Horizontal Correlation Distance
**HCD**.......... Hot-Carrier Diode (IEEE)
**HCD**.......... Hutchinson, MN [*Location identifier*] [*FAA*] (FAAL)
**HCD**.......... Hydrocolloid Dressing [*Dermatology*]
**HCDA**........ Hydrodynamic Core Disruptive Accident [*Nuclear energy*] (NRCH)
**HCDA**........ Hypothetical Core Disruptive Accident [*Nuclear energy*]
**HCDD**........ Hexachlorodibenzodioxin [*Organic chemistry*]
**HCDE**........ Homothetic-Constant Differences of Elasticities of Substitution [*Statistics*]
**HCDP**........ Discharge [*from Military Service*] under Honorable Conditions, Dependency Existing Prior to Enlistment
**HCDR**........ Hours and Cost Detail Report
**HCE**.......... Haveth Childer Everywhere [*Key phrase in "Finnegan's Wake"*]
**HCE**.......... Here Comes Everybody [*Key phrase in "Finnegan's Wake"*]
**HCE**.......... Hic Conditus Est [*Here Lies Buried*] [*Latin*]
**HCE**.......... Hollow-Cathode Effect (IEEE)
**HCE**.......... Human-Caused Error
**HCE**.......... Humphrey Chimpden Earwicker [*Hero of "Finnegan's Wake"*]
**HCEA**........ Health Care Exhibitors Association (EA)
**HCEA**........ Holland Cheese Exporters Association [*Later, DDB*] (EA)
**HCEBT**...... Houston Cotton Exchange and Board of Trade [*Defunct*] (EA)
**HCED**........ Hand Controller Engage Driver (NASA)
**HCEE**........ Discharge [*from Military Service*] under Honorable Conditions, Expiration of Enlistment
**HCEEP**...... Handicapped Children's Early Education Programs
**HCEN**........ Home Centers [*NASDAQ symbol*] (SPSG)
**HCEX**........ High-Speed Color Exterior
**HCF**.......... Fluorocarbon without Chlorine (ECON)
**HCF**.......... Hardened Compact Fiber
**HCF**.......... Health Care Finder
**HCF**.......... Health Concepts IV, Inc. [*AMEX symbol*] (SPSG)
**HCF**.......... [*The*] Healthcare Forum (EA)
**HCF**.......... Heat Control Filter
**HCF**.......... Hebrew Christian Fellowship (EA)
**HCF**.......... Hebrew Culture Foundation (EA)
**HCF**.......... Height Correction Factor
**HCF**.......... High Carbohydrate, High Fiber [*Nutrition*]
**HCF**.......... High-Carbon Ferrochrome [*Metallurgy*]
**HCF**.......... High-Cycle Fatigue [*Rocket engine*]
**HCF**.......... Highest Common Factor [*Mathematics*]
**HCF**.......... HIM [*Hardware Interface Module*] Configuration File [*NASA*] (NASA)
**HCF**.......... Honorary Chaplain to the Forces [*British*]
**HCF**.......... Hood College, Frederick, MD [*OCLC symbol*] (OCLC)
**HCF**.......... Host Command Facility
**HCF**.......... Hungarian Cultural Foundation (EA)
**HCFA**........ Health Care Financing Administration [*HHS*]
**HCFAR**..... Health Care Financing Administration Rulings [*A publication*] (DLA)
**HCFA Rev**... Health Care Financing Review [*A publication*]
**HCFC**........ Helen Cornelius Fan Club (EA)
**HCFC**........ Hydrochlorofluorocarbon [*Organic chemistry*]
**HCFD**........ Hydrochemical Form Die [*Tool*] (AAG)
**HCFDS**...... Health Care Fund SBI [*NASDAQ symbol*] (NQ)
**HCFF**........ High-Capacity Fog Foam [*Navy*] (NVT)
**HCFMS**..... Holy Cross Foreign Mission Society (EA)
**HCFR**........ Health Care Financing Review [*A publication*] (DLA)
**HCF Rev**.... Health Care Financing Review [*A publication*] (DLA)
**HCFSG**...... Health Care Financing Study Group (EA)
**hCFU**......... Human Colony-Forming Unit [*Genetics*]
**HCG**.......... Griqualand High Court Reports [*A publication*] (DLA)
**HCG**.......... Hardware Character Generator
**HCG**.......... Hermanas Catequistas Guadalupanas [*Sister Catechists of Guadeloupe*] [*Roman Catholic women's religious order*]
**HCG**.......... Home Capital Group, Inc. [*Toronto Stock Exchange symbol*]
**HCG**.......... Horizontal Location of Center of Gravity
**HCG**.......... Human Chorionic Gonadotrophin [*Endocrinology*]
**HCGF**........ Haematopoietic Cell Growth Factor [*Biochemistry*]
**hCGRP**...... Human Calcitonin Gene-Related Peptide [*Biochemistry*]
**HCGS**........ Hope Creek Generating Station (NRCH)
**HCH**.......... Crossville, TN [*Location identifier*] [*FAA*] (FAAL)
**H-CH**......... Handy-Cap Horizons (EA)
**HCH**.......... Health-Chem Corp. [*AMEX symbol*] (SPSG)
**HCH**.......... Herbert Clark Hoover [*US president, 1874-1964*]
**HCH**.......... Hexachlorocyclohexane [*Also, BHC, GBH*] [*Insecticide*]
**H Ch A**....... Helvetica Chirurgica Acta [*A publication*]
**HCHC**........ High Carbon, High Chrome
**HChD**........ Diploma in Higher Chiropodial Theory of the Institute of Chiropodists [*British*] (DBQ)
**HCHED7**... Specialist Periodical Reports. Heterocyclic Chemistry [*A publication*]
**HCHF**........ High Carbohydrate, High Fiber [*Nutrition*]
**H CH F**...... Homme Cherche Femme [*Man Looking for Woman*] [*French*]
**HCHGC**..... Hollingworth Center for Highly Gifted Children (EA)
**Hchl**........... Hochland [*A publication*]
**HCHP**........ Health Care for the Homeless Program (EA)
**HCHS**........ Handicapped Children's Home Service [*Later, Easter Seal Home Service*] (EA)
**HCHY**........ Hovering Craft and Hydrofoil [*A publication*]
**HCI**........... Handgun Control, Incorporated (EA)
**HCI**........... Hardness-Critical Item (MSA)
**HCI**........... Hawthorne Communications, Incorporated
**HCI**........... HCI Holdings Ltd. [*Toronto Stock Exchange symbol*]
**HCI**........... Health Care International [*British*]
**HCI**........... Heritage Communications, Incorporated [*NYSE symbol*] (SPSG)
**HCI**........... Hierarchically Classified Index
**HCI**........... High-Current Inductor
**HCI**........... Home Center Institute (EA)
**HCI**........... Host Computer Interface
**HCI**........... Hughes Communications, Inc. [*Hughes Aircraft Co.*] [*Los Angeles, CA*]
**HCI**........... Human Cancer Immunology [*Elsevier Book Series*] [*A publication*]
**HCIA**......... Highlander Class International Association (EA)
**H & Cie**...... Hentsch & Compagnie [*Bank*] [*Switzerland*]
**HcIMP**...... Hydrocolloid Impression [*Dentistry*]
**HCIND5**.... Health Communications and Informatics [*A publication*]
**4-H Circ Univ MO Coll Agr Ext Serv** ... 4-H Circular. University of Missouri. College of Agriculture. Extension Service [*A publication*]
**HCIS**.......... House Committee on Internal Security [*Formerly, HUAC*] [*Dissolved, 1975*] [*US Congress*]
**HCITE**........ Horizontal Cargo Integration Test Equipment (MCD)
**HCJ**........... High Court of Justice
**HCJB**......... High Court Junior Beadle [*Ancient Order of Foresters*]
**HCJC**......... Henderson County Junior College [*Texas*]
**HCJC**......... Howard County Junior College [*Texas*]
**HC Jour**..... House of Commons Journals [*England*] [*A publication*] (DLA)
**HCJW**........ High Court Junior Woodward [*Ancient Order of Foresters*]
**HCL**........... Hairy Cell Leukemia [*Medicine*]
**HCL**........... Hard Contact Lens [*Ophthalmology*]
**HCL**........... Harpoon Check List [*Missiles*] (MCD)
**HCL**........... Helium Cadmium LASER
**HCL**........... High, Common, Low [*Relay*] (IEEE)
**HCL**........... High Cost of Living
**HCL**........... Hollow Cathode Lamp
**HCL**........... Horizontal Center Line
**HCL**........... Human Cultured Lymphoblastoid [*Cells*]
**HCL**........... Huron College [*UTLAS symbol*]
**HCL**........... Husson College, Bangor, ME [*OCLC symbol*] (OCLC)
**HCL**........... Hyderabad Contingent Lancers [*British military*] (DMA)
**HCl**........... Hydrochloric Acid
**HCl**........... Hydrogen Chloride [*Inorganic chemistry*]
**HCL**........... International Hod Carriers', Building and Common Laborers' Union of America [*Later, Laborers' International Union of North America*]
**HCLA**........ Hungarian Catholic League of America (EA)
**HCLD**........ Housing Construction and Land Development
**HCLE**........ Humanities Center for Liberal Education
**HCLF**......... Health Care Libraries Forum [*Association of Specialized and Cooperative Library Agencies*]
**HCLF**......... High Carbohydrate, Low Fiber [*Nutrition*]
**HCLF**......... Horizontal Cask Lifting Fixture [*Nuclear energy*] (NRCH)
**HCLIP**........ Harvard Computer-Aided Legal Instruction Project (DLA)
**HCLL**......... Homecall, Inc. [*NASDAQ symbol*] (NQ)
**HCLM**........ Health Care Labor Manual [*A publication*] (DLA)
**HC-LN**....... High Control/Low Nurturance [*Psychology*]
**HCLP**......... Home Conversion Loan Program [*Canada*]
**HCM**.......... Haitian Campaign Medal
**HCM**.......... Halifax Conservatory of Music

**HCM** .......... Harcum, VA [*Location identifier*] [*FAA*] (FAAL)
**HCM** .......... Hard Copy Module (NASA)
**HCM** .......... HARDMAN [*Hardware-Manpower Program*] Comparability Methodology [*Army*]
**HCM** .......... Health Care Management Review [*A publication*]
**HCM** .......... His [*or Her*] Catholic Majesty
**HCM** .......... Hundred Club of Massachusetts (EA)
**HCM** .......... Hydraulic Core Mock-Up [*Nuclear energy*] (NRCH)
**HCM** .......... Hypercalcemia of Malignancy [*Medicine*]
**HCM** .......... Hypertrophic Cardiomyopathy [*Cardiology*]
**HCMA** ....... Alula [*Somalia*] [*ICAO location identifier*] (ICLI)
**HCMA** ....... Hotel Credit Managers Association [*New York, NY*] (EA)
**HCMA** ....... Western Australian Health Care Museums Association [*Australia*]
**HCMB** ....... Baidoa [*Somalia*] [*ICAO location identifier*] (ICLI)
**HCMC** ....... Candala [*Somalia*] [*ICAO location identifier*] (ICLI)
**HCMC** ....... Ho Chi Minh City [*Vietnam*]
**HCMD** ....... Bardera [*Somalia*] [*ICAO location identifier*] (ICLI)
**HCME** ....... Eil [*Somalia*] [*ICAO location identifier*] (ICLI)
**HCME** ....... Hirsch Chemie Ltd. [*NASDAQ symbol*] (NQ)
**HCMF** ....... Bosaso [*Somalia*] [*ICAO location identifier*] (ICLI)
**HCMF** ....... Henry Clay Memorial Foundation (EA)
**HCMG** ....... Gardo [*Somalia*] [*ICAO location identifier*] (ICLI)
**HCMH** ....... Hargeisa [*Somalia*] [*ICAO location identifier*] (ICLI)
**HCMI** ....... Berbera [*Somalia*] [*ICAO location identifier*] (ICLI)
**HCMJ** ....... Lugh Ferrandi [*Somalia*] [*ICAO location identifier*] (ICLI)
**HCMK** ....... Kisimayu [*Somalia*] [*ICAO location identifier*] (ICLI)
**HCML** ....... El Bur [*Somalia*] [*ICAO location identifier*] (ICLI)
**HCMM** ...... Heat Capacity Map Mission [*NASA*]
**HCMM** ...... Heavy Capability Mapping Mission [*Satellite*]
**HCMM** ...... Mogadishu [*Somalia*] [*ICAO location identifier*] (ICLI)
**HCMMS** ... Health Care Material Management Society (EA)
**HCMN** ....... Belet Uen [*Somalia*] [*ICAO location identifier*] (ICLI)
**HCMO** ....... Obbia [*Somalia*] [*ICAO location identifier*] (ICLI)
**HCMP** ....... Las Anod [*Somalia*] [*ICAO location identifier*] (ICLI)
**HCMR** ....... Galcaio [*Somalia*] [*ICAO location identifier*] (ICLI)
**HCMR** ....... Health Care Management Review [*A publication*]
**HCMR** ....... Heat Capacity Mapping Radiometer [*NASA*]
**HCMS** ....... Discharge [*from Military Service*] under Honorable Conditions, Medical Survey
**HCMS** ....... Scusciuban [*Somalia*] [*ICAO location identifier*] (ICLI)
**HCMTS** ..... High-Capacity Mobile Telecommunications System (TEL)
**HCMU** ....... Discharge [*from Military Service*] under Honorable Conditions, under Age of Authorized Enlistment
**HCMU** ....... Erigavo [*Somalia*] [*ICAO location identifier*] (ICLI)
**HCMU** ....... Hebrew Cabinet Makers' Union [*British*]
**HCMV** ....... Burao [*Somalia*] [*ICAO location identifier*] (ICLI)
**HCMV** ....... Human Cytomegalovirus
**HCMW** ...... Discharge [*from Military Service*] under Honorable Conditions, Minor Enlisted Without Consent, under Eighteen at Time of Discharge
**HCMW** ...... United Hatters, Cap, and Millinery Workers International Union (EA)
**HCN** .......... Hart Crane Newsletter [*A publication*]
**HCN** .......... Health Care REIT, Inc. [*AMEX symbol*] (SPSG)
**HCN** .......... Health Communications Network [*Medical University of South Carolina*] [*Charleston*] [*Telecommunications*] (TSSD)
**HCN** .......... Hilton Communications Network [*Hilton Hotels Corp.*] [*Beverly Hills, CA*] [*Telecommunications service*] (TSSD)
**HCN** .......... Hydrocyanic Acid [*Inorganic chemistry*]
**HCN** .......... Hydrogen Cyanide [*Also, AC*] [*Inorganic chemistry*]
**HCN** .......... Hygienic Community Network (EA)
**HCO** .......... Hangar Control Officer [*Navy*]
**HCO** .......... Harvard College Observatory
**HCO** .......... Headquarters Catalog Office
**HCO** .......... Heavy Cycle Oil [*Petroleum technology*]
**HCO** .......... Helicopter Control Officer [*British military*] (DMA)
**HCO** .......... Higher Clerical Officer [*Civil Service*] [*British*]
**HCO** .......... Horizontal Control Operator [*Military*]
**HCO** .......... HUBCO, Inc. [*AMEX symbol*] (SPSG)
**HCOA** ........ Home Centers of America [*NASDAQ symbol*] (NQ)
**HCOC** ........ Honorary Colonel of the Corps [*Army*]
**HCompL** .... Hebrew Computational Linguistics [*A publication*]
**HCONN** .... Hose Connector
**H Con Res** ... House of Representatives Concurrent Resolution (DLA)
**HCOR** ........ Honorary Colonel of the Regiment
**HCORF** ...... Hi-Cor Resources Ltd. [*NASDAQ symbol*] (NQ)
**HCP** ........... Handicap
**HCP** ........... Handicap Race [*Horse racing*]
**HCP** ........... Handicapped Programs Review [*Australia*]
**HCP** ........... Hangar Control Position [*Navy*]
**HCP** ........... Harbor Control Post
**HCP** ........... Hard Copy Printer [*Data processing*]
**HCP** ........... Hardness-Critical Process (MSA)
**HCP** ........... Health Care Products, Inc. [*Toronto Stock Exchange symbol*]
**HCP** ........... Health Care Property Investors, Inc. [*NYSE symbol*] (SPSG)
**HCp** ........... Heat of Combustion (of an Element under Constant Pressure) (ROG)
**HCP** ........... Hexachlorocyclopentadiene [*Also, HCCP, HEX*] [*Organic chemistry*]
**HCP** ........... Hexachlorophene [*Germicide*]
**HCP** ........... Hexagonal Close-Packed [*Crystallography*]
**HCP** ........... Holiday Caravan Parks [*Public-performance tariff class*] [*British*]
**HCP** ........... Horizontal Candlepower
**H and CP** ... Hospital and Community Psychiatry [*A publication*]
**HCP** ........... Host Communications Processor
**HCP** ........... Hybrid Combustion Process (RDA)
**HCP** ........... Hydrazine Catalytic Plenum
**HCP** ........... Hydroxycalcium Phenoxide [*Organic chemistry*]
**HCP** ........... Hypervelocity Countermeasures Program
**HCPA** ........ Health Care Products, Inc. [*NASDAQ symbol*] (NQ)
**HCPAA** ..... Hungarian Catholic Priests' Association in America (EA)
**HCPDG** ..... Health Care Professionals Discussion Group [*American Occupational Therapy Association*]
**HCPNY** ..... Harbor Carriers of the Port of New York (EA)
**HCPS** ........ Horizontal Candlepower Seconds
**HCPT** ........ Hydroxycamptothecin [*Antineoplastic drug*]
**HCPTR** ...... Helicopter (CINC)
**HCPV** ........ Hydrocarbon Pore Volume [*Petroleum technology*]
**H/CQ** ........ Habitability/Crew Quarters (KSC)
**HCQ** .......... Halls Creek [*Australia*] [*Airport symbol*] [*Obsolete*] (OAG)
**HCQ** .......... Hot Carrier Quad
**H & CR** ...... Handling and Checkout Requirements
**HCR** ........... Hardware Check Routine
**HCR** ........... Hardware Correction Report
**HCR** ........... Haut-Commissaire des Nations Unies pour les Refugies [*United Nations High Commission for Refugees - UNHCR*] [*Switzerland*]
**HCR** ........... Hemin Controlled Repressor [*Biochemistry*]
**HCR** ........... High Chief Ranger [*Ancient Order of Foresters*]
**HCR** ........... High Court Reports, India [*A publication*] (DLA)
**HCR** ........... High Cross Range
**HCR** ........... Highway Contract Route
**HCR** ........... Holy Cross [*Alaska*] [*Airport symbol*] (OAG)
**HCR** ........... Horeca Info [*A publication*]
**HCR** ........... Hotel and Catering Review [*A publication*]
**HCR** ........... House Concurrent Resolution [*US Congress*]
**HCR** ........... Household Cavalry Regiment [*British military*] (DMA)
**HCr** ........... Houston's Delaware Criminal Cases [*A publication*] (DLA)
**HCR** ........... Hurricane Rescue Craft, Inc. [*Vancouver Stock Exchange symbol*]
**HCRC** ........ Hillsdale County Railroad Company, Inc. [*AAR code*]
**HCRC** ........ Hotel and Catering Research Centre [*British*] (IRUK)
**HCRCA** ..... Harvard Civil Rights - Civil Liberties Law Journal [*A publication*]
**HCRD** ........ Health Care Research Division [*Brooke Army Medical Center*]
**HCRE** ........ Homeopathic Council for Research and Education (EA)
**HCRE** ........ Human Communications Research [*A publication*]
**HCREF** ...... Health Care Research and Educational Foundation [*Later, AAMAREF*] (EA)
**HC Res** ...... House of Representatives Concurrent Resolution [*Legal term*] (DLA)
**H'CRIT** ...... Hematocrit [*Medicine*]
**HCRM** ........ Holocaust Curriculum Resources Material (BJA)
**HCRNWF** ... High Court Reports, North West Frontier [*A publication*] (DLA)
**HCRNWP** ... High Court Reports, Northwest Provinces [*India*] [*A publication*] (DLA)
**HCRO** ........ High Cross-Range Orbiter (KSC)
**HCRR** ........ Home Counties Reserve Regiment [*British military*] (DMA)
**HCRS** ........ Heritage Conservation Recreation Service [*Abolished, 1981, functions transferred to National Park Service*] [*Department of the Interior*]
**HCRW** ....... Hot and Cold Running Water
**HCRX** ........ Health Care & Retirement Corp. [*NASDAQ symbol*] (NQ)
**HCS** ........... Hammered Chainmakers' Society [*A union*] [*British*]
**HCS** ........... Handicapped Children's Services
**HCS** ........... Harris Consultive Services, Inc. [*Information service or system*] (IID)
**HCS** ........... Harvey Cushing Society [*Later, AANS*] (EA)
**HCS** ........... Hazard Communication Standard [*OSHA*]
**HCS** ........... Header Check Sequence [*Data processing*]
**HCS** ........... Health Care Supervisor [*A publication*]
**HCS** ........... Health Care Support [*System*] [*IBM Corp.*]
**HCS** ........... Helicopter Control Ship [*Navy*] (NVT)
**HCS** ........... Helium Circulator Seal (IEEE)
**HCS** ........... High-Carbon Steel
**HCS** ........... High Court Secretary [*Ancient Order of Foresters*]
**HCS** ........... Histochemical Society (EA)
**HCS** ........... Home Care Service [*New South Wales, Australia*]
**HCS** ........... Home Civil Servant [*British*]
**HCS** ........... Home Civil Service [*British*]
**HCS** ........... Home Run Control System [*Data processing*]
**HCS** ........... Homogeneous Computer System
**HCS** ........... Hospital Car Service
**HCS** ........... House Committee Substitute [*US Congress*]
**HCS** ........... HUD [*Housing and Urban Development*] Clearinghouse Service
**HCS** ........... Human Chorionic Somatomammotrophin [*Also, CGP, hcs, HPL*] [*Endocrinology*]

**HCS** .......... Human Cord Serum
**HCS** .......... Hummocky Cross-Stratification [*Sedimentology*]
**HCS** .......... Hundred Call Seconds [*Telecommunications*]
**HCS** .......... Hydrogen Control System (NRCH)
**HCS** .......... Hydromechanical Control System (KSC)
**HCS** .......... Membership Section for Health Care Systems [*An association*] (EA)
**HCSA** .......... Halogenated Cleaning Solvent Association (EA)
**HCSA** .......... Hexylcarbonate of Salicylic Acid [*Analgesic*]
**HCSA** .......... Hospital Consultants' and Specialists' Association [*British*] (DCTA)
**HCSA** .......... House Committee on Space and Astronautics [*US Congress*] (AAG)
**HCSB** .......... High Court Senior Beadle [*Ancient Order of Foresters*]
**HCSB** .......... Home & City Savings Bank [*Albany, NY*] [*NASDAQ symbol*] (NQ)
**HCSBC** .......... Historical Commission, Southern Baptist Convention (EA)
**HCSD** .......... Health Care Studies Division [*Academy of Health Sciences*] [*Army*]
**HCSDS** .......... High Capacity Satellite Digital Service [*AT & T*] (TSSD)
**HCSF** .......... Histamine-Producing Cell-Stimulating Factor [*Biochemistry*]
**HCSG** .......... Healthcare Services Group, Inc. [*NASDAQ symbol*] (NQ)
**HCSG** .......... Hyperactive Children's Support Group [*England*]
**HCSHT** .......... High-Carbon Steel, Heat-Treated
**HCSI** .......... Hughes Communications Services, Inc. (NASA)
**HCSL** .......... Hybrid Computation and Simulation Laboratory
**HCSLP** .......... Hungarian Committee of Socialist Labor Party [*Defunct*] (EA)
**HCSM** .......... Human Chorionic Somatomammotropin [*Endocrinology*]
**HCSM** .......... Mogadishu [*Somalia*] [*ICAO location identifier*] (ICLI)
**HCSR** .......... E. O. Hulburt Center for Space Research (MCD)
**HCSS** .......... Head Compartment Support Structure [*Nuclear energy*] (NRCH)
**HCSS** .......... Home and Colonial School Society [*British*]
**HCSS** .......... Hospital Computer Sharing System (IEEE)
**HCSTA** .......... Hastings Center. Studies [*A publication*]
**HCSW** .......... High Court Senior Woodward [*Ancient Order of Foresters*]
**HCT** .......... Hayes Center, NE [*Location identifier*] [*FAA*] (FAAL)
**HCT** .......... Heart-Circulation-Training [*Physical fitness*]
**HCT** .......... Heater Center Top
**HCT** .......... Hematocrit [*Medicine*]
**HCT** .......... High Commission Territories Corps [*Military unit*] [*British*]
**H Ct** .......... High Court
**HCT** .......... High Court Treasurer [*Ancient Order of Foresters*]
**HCT** .......... Hollow Cathode Tube
**HCT** .......... Hot Cathode Tube
**HCT** .......... Hull Collector Tank
**hCt** .......... Human Calcitonin [*Endocrinology*]
**HCT** .......... Human Chorionic Thyrotrophin [*Endocrinology*]
**HCT** .......... Hydraulic Components Test
**HCT** .......... Hydrochlorothiazide [*Drug*] [*Also, HCTZ, HCZ*] [*Organic chemistry*]
**HCTB** .......... Hotel and Catering Training Board [*British*]
**HCTDS** .......... High-Capacity Terrestrial Digital Service [*AT & T*] (TSSD)
**HCTL** .......... Healthcare Technologies Ltd. [*NASDAQ symbol*] (NQ)
**HCTLR** .......... High Commission Territories Reports [*Basutoland, Bechuanaland, and Swaziland*] [*A publication*] (DLA)
**HCTS** .......... House Call Tax Service
**HCTSS** .......... Health Care Technology Study Section [*HEW*] (EGAO)
**HCTZ** .......... Hydrochlorothiazide [*Drug*] [*Also, HCT, HCZ*] [*Organic chemistry*]
**HCU** .......... Harbor Clearance Unit [*Navy*] (NVT)
**HCU** .......... Harbor Control Unit
**HCU** .......... Hard Copy Unit
**HCU** .......... Heavy Conversion Unit [*British military*] (DMA)
**HCU** .......... Helicopter Control Unit (NVT)
**HCU** .......... Helium Charging Unit (AAG)
**HCU** .......... Homing Comparator Unit (AAG)
**HCU** .......... Homocystinuria [*Medicine*]
**HCU** .......... Horse Canyon [*Utah*] [*Seismograph station code, US Geological Survey*] (SEIS)
**HCU** .......... Hydraulic Charging Unit (NASA)
**HCU** .......... Hydraulic Control Unit [*Nuclear energy*] (NRCH)
**HCU** .......... Hydraulic Cycling Unit (AFM)
**HCUND** .......... Hospitality Committee for United Nations Delegations (EA)
**HCUS** .......... Discharge [*from Military Service*] under Honorable Conditions, Unsuitable
**HCUT** .......... Homfray Carpets Unit Trust [*Commercial firm*] [*British*]
**HCV** .......... Hand Control Valve (NRCH)
**HCv** .......... Heat of Combustion (of an Element under Constant Volume) (ROG)
**HCV** .......... Hepatitis C Virus
**HCV** .......... Hercules Ventures [*Vancouver Stock Exchange symbol*]
**HCV** .......... High Calorific Value [*of a fuel*]
**HCV** .......... Home Consumption Value [*Importation*] [*Philippines*] (IMH)
**HCV** .......... Hull Check Valve
**HCV** .......... Human Coronavirus
**HCV** .......... Hutchinson Cablevision [*British*]
**HCV** .......... Hydraulic Control Valve
**HCVC** .......... Historic Commercial Vehicle Club [*British*] (DCTA)
**HCVD** .......... Hypertensive Cardiovascular Disease [*Medicine*]
**HCVIS** .......... High Clouds Visible [*Meteorology*] (FAAC)
**HC Wkly Inf Bull** ... House of Commons Weekly Information Bulletin [*A publication*] (DLA)
**HCWO** .......... HCW Oil & Gas [*NASDAQ symbol*] (NQ)
**HCWSEN** ... Hammersmith Cardiology Workshop Series [*A publication*]
**HCY** .......... Cowley/Lovell/Byron, WY [*Location identifier*] [*FAA*] (FAAL)
**Hcy** .......... Homocysteine [*An amino acid*]
**HCZ** .......... Hydrochlorothiazide [*Drug*] [*Also, HCT, HCTZ*] [*Organic chemistry*]
**HCZ** .......... Hydrogen Convection Zone
**HD** .......... Air-Conditioning Apparatus [*JETDS nomenclature*] [*Military*] (CET)
**HD** .......... Air-Cushion Vehicle built by Hovercraft Development [*England*] [*Usually used in combination with numerals*]
**HD** .......... Half Duplex Transmission [*Data communication*] (CET)
**HD** .......... Hand (ROG)
**HD** .......... Hand-Drawn
**HD** .......... Hansen's Disease [*Leprosy*] [*Medicine*]
**HD** .......... Harbor Defense [*Military*]
**HD** .......... Hard (MSA)
**HD** .......... Hard Disk [*Data processing*]
**HD** .......... Hard-Drawn [*Metallurgy*]
**H & D** .......... Hardened and Dispersed (AFM)
**HD** .......... Hardware Design
**H-D** .......... Harley-Davidson
**HD** .......... Harmonic Distortion
**HD** .......... Harpsichord [*A publication*]
**HD** .......... Hawaiian Department [*Army*] [*World War II*]
**HD** .......... Head (AAG)
**HD** .......... Head Diameter
**Hd** .......... Headland [*Maps and charts*]
**HD** .......... Heard (ROG)
**HD** .......... Hearing Distance [*Medicine*]
**HD** .......... Heart Disease [*Medicine*]
**HD** .......... Heavy Distillate [*Fuel technology*]
**HD** .......... Heavy-Duty
**HD** .......... Hechos y Dichos [*A publication*]
**HD** .......... Helicopter Delivered
**HD** .......... Helicopter Director [*Military*] (CAAL)
**HD** .......... Hemidesmosome [*Cytology*]
**HD** .......... Hemodialysis [*Nephrology*]
**HD** .......... Hemodilution
**HD** .......... Hemolyzing Dose [*Medicine*]
**HD** .......... Henry Draper Catalogue [*Astronomy*]
**HD** .......... Herniated Disc [*Medicine*]
**H-D** .......... Hexadecimal-to-Decimal [*Data processing*] (IEEE)
**HD** .......... Hexagonal Domain Structure
**HD** .......... Hexanedione [*Organic chemistry*]
**HD** .......... Hierarchical Direct
**HD** .......... High Density
**HD** .......... High Dose [*Medicine*]
**HD** .......... High Drag [*Navy*] (NVT)
**HD** .......... High Dynamic
**HD** .......... Highland Division [*British military*] (DMA)
**HD** .......... Highly Desirable (KSC)
**HD** .......... Hilda Doolittle [*Initials used as pen name of American poet, 1886-1961*]
**HD** .......... Hip Disarticulation [*Medicine*]
**HD** .......... Historic Deerfield (EA)
**HD** .......... Historical Development
**HD** .......... Historical Division [*Air Force*]
**HD** .......... Hodgkin's Disease [*Medicine*]
**HD** .......... Hoessel und Winkler GmbH Luftverkehragesellschaft [*West Germany*] [*ICAO designator*] (FAAC)
**HD** .......... Hogshead
**H/D** .......... Holddown (AAG)
**HD** .......... Home Defence [*British*] [*World War II*]
**HD** .......... [*The*] Home Depot, Inc. [*NYSE symbol*] (SPSG)
**HD** .......... Homoeodomain [*Genetics*]
**HD** .......... Honorable Discharge [*Military*]
**HD** .......... Honorary Degree [*Freemasonry*] (ROG)
**HD** .......... Hora Decubitus [*At Bedtime*] [*Pharmacy*]
**HD** .......... Horizontal Drain
**HD** .......... Horizontal Drive
**HD** .......... Horse-Drawn
**HD** .......... Hourly Difference [*Navigation*]
**HD** .......... House Document
**HD** .......... Housing Debtline [*Telephone service*] [*British*]
**HD** .......... Housing Density
**HD** .......... Human Development [*A publication*]
**HD** .......... Human Development
**HD** .......... Humanitarian Deferment [*Military*]
**HD** .......... Humper Dears (EA)
**HD** .......... Hundred
**HD** .......... Huntington's Disease [*Medicine*]
**HD** .......... Hurel Dubois [*Societe de Construction des Avions Hurel Dubois*] [*France*] [*ICAO aircraft manufacturer identifier*] (ICAO)
**HD** .......... Hurricane Deck
**H & D** .......... Hurter and Driffield [*Chemists for whom H & D Curve and H & D Speed System are named*] (DEN)

**HD**.......... Hydralazine [*Antihypertensive drug*]
**HD**.......... Hydrogen Drain (MCD)
**H-D**.......... Hypothetico-Deductive
**HD**.......... Hypotonic Duodenogram [*Medicine*]
**H & D**.......... Lalor's Supplement to Hill and Denio's New York Reports [*A publication*] (DLA)
**HD**.......... Mustard Gas [*Also, H, HS, HT, M*] [*Poison gas*] [*US Chemical Corps symbol*]
**10HD**.......... Ten High-Day [*Telecommunications*]
**HDA**.......... Halopredone Diacetate [*Endocrinology*]
**HdA**.......... Handwoerterbuch des Deutschen Aberglaubens [*A publication*] (BJA)
**HDA**.......... Harding Lake [*Alaska*] [*Seismograph station code, US Geological Survey*] (SEIS)
**HDA**.......... Hardwood Distributors Association (EA)
**HDA**.......... Hawkesbury Diploma in Agriculture [*Australia*]
**HDA**.......... Head Disk Assembly
**HDA**.......... Headquarters, Department of the Army
**HDA**.......... Heavy-Duty Amplifier
**HDA**.......... Hexadecenyl Acetate [*Pheromone*] [*Organic chemistry*]
**HDA**.......... Hexanediamine [*or Hexamethylenediamine*] [*Organic chemistry*]
**HDA**.......... High-Density Acid
**HDA**.......... High Duty Alloys Ltd.
**HDA**.......... Higher Duties Allowance (ADA)
**HDA**.......... Holddown Arm (KSC)
**HDA**.......... Holistic Dental Association (EA)
**HDA**.......... Horizontal Danger Angle [*Navigation*]
**HDA**.......... Horticultural Dealers Association (EA)
**HDA**.......... Housekeeping Data Acquisition (MCD)
**HDA**.......... Housing and Development Administration [*New York City*]
**HDA**.......... Huldra Silver [*Vancouver Stock Exchange symbol*]
**HDA**.......... Hydroxydopamine [*Also, HDM, OHDA*] [*Biochemistry*]
**HDAC**.......... Dictionary of the Apostolic Church [*James Hasting*] [*A publication*] (BJA)
**HDAC**.......... Headache (KSC)
**HDAC**.......... Heavy-Duty Air Cylinder
**HDAg**.......... Hepatitis Delta Antigen [*Immunology*]
**HDAL**.......... Hexadecenal [*Pheromone*] [*Organic chemistry*]
**HDAM**.......... Hierarchical Direct Access Method [*Data processing*] (MCD)
**HDAP**.......... Heavy-Duty Automatic Press
**HDAS**.......... House Defense Appropriations Subcommittee [*US Congress*] (AAG)
**HDAS**.......... Hybrid Data Acquisition System
**HDAS**.......... Hydrographic Data Acquisition System
**HDATA**.......... Hydrogene Data [*National College of Chemistry of Paris*] [*France*] [*Information service or system*] (IID)
**HDATZ**.......... High-Density Air Traffic Zone
**HdAW**.......... Handbuch der Altertumswissenschaft [*A publication*] (BJA)
**HDB**.......... [*A*] Dictionary of the Bible [*James Hasting*] [*A publication*] (BJA)
**HDB**.......... Hamper, Deritend, Birmingham [*Pseudonym used by William Hamper*]
**HDB**.......... Herpes-Dissociated Buffer [*Medicine*]
**HDB**.......... High-Density Binary (TEL)
**HDB**.......... High-Density Bipolar Code [*Telecommunications*] (TEL)
**HDB**.......... Horizontal Dynamic Balancing
**HDB3**.......... High-Density Binary Three Level Signal (TEL)
**HDBA**.......... Horizontal Dynamic Balancing Adjustment
**HDBF**.......... Heavy Duty Business Forum (EA)
**HDBK**.......... Handbook (AFM)
**HDBLA2**.......... Hidrobiologia [*Bucharest*] [*A publication*]
**HDC**.......... Claremont Men's College, Claremont, CA [*OCLC symbol*] (OCLC)
**HDC**.......... Half Double Crochet
**HDC**.......... Harbor Defense Command [*Army*]
**HDC**.......... Harry Diamond Center [*Army*]
**HDC**.......... Hasselblad Data Camera (MCD)
**HDC**.......... Heavy-Duty Contractor (MCD)
**HDC**.......... Helicopter Direction Center
**HDC**.......... Hierarchical Distributed Control [*Data processing*]
**HDC**.......... High Dirt Capacity [*A type of filter*] [*Pall Trinity Micro Corp.*]
**HDC**.......... Histidine Decarboxylase [*An enzyme*]
**H in DC**.......... Holder in Due Course [*Owner or holder of a negotiable instrument at some future time*]
**HDC**.......... Holder in Due Course [*Owner or holder of a negotiable instrument at some future time*]
**HDC**.......... Holston Defense Corporation (MCD)
**HDC**.......... Hospital Data Center [*American Hospital Association*] [*Information service or system*] (IID)
**HDC**.......... Hough Development Corporation [*Cleveland*]
**HDC**.......... Housing Development Corporation (EA)
**HDC**.......... Hungarian Data Center (EA)
**HDC**.......... Hybrid Device Controller (NASA)
**HDC**.......... Hydrodynamic Chromatography
**HDCES**.......... Hot/Dry Clothing and Equipment System [*Army*] (INF)
**HDCG**.......... Dictionary of Christ and the Gospels [*James Hasting*] [*A publication*] (BJA)
**HDCG**.......... Honorable Discharge, Convenience of Government [*Military*]
**HDCM**.......... Honorable Discharge, Convenience of Man [*Military*]
**HDCO**.......... Hadco Corp. [*Salem, NH*] [*NASDAQ symbol*] (NQ)
**HDCR**.......... Hard Chromium
**HDCR(R) or (T)**... Higher Award in Radiodiagnosis or Radiotherapy, College of Radiographers [*British*] (DBQ)
**HDCS**.......... Human Diploid Cell Strains [*Immunology*]
**HDCV**.......... Human Diploid Cell Vaccine [*For rabies*]
**HDD**.......... Halogenated Dibenzodioxin [*Organic chemistry*]
**HDD**.......... Head-Down Display [*Aviation*]
**HDD**.......... Heavy-Duty Detergent
**HDD**.......... Heavy-Duty Diesel [*Vehicle*]
**HDD**.......... Heavy Duty Distribution [*A publication*]
**HDD**.......... High-Density Data (KSC)
**HDD**.......... Higher Dental Diploma [*British*]
**HDD**.......... Homopolar Disk Dynamo
**HDD**.......... Human Disorientation Device
**HDD**.......... Hyderabad [*Pakistan*] [*Airport symbol*] (OAG)
**HDDA**.......... Hexadecadienyl Acetate [*Pheromone*] [*Organic chemistry*]
**HDDA**.......... Hexanediol Diacrylate [*Also, HDODA*] [*Organic chemistry*]
**HDDP**.......... Honorable Discharge, Dependency Existing Prior to Enlistment [*Military*]
**HDDR**.......... High-Density Digital Recording
**HDDS**.......... High-Density Data System [*Data processing*]
**HDDS**.......... Honorable Discharge, Dependency Arising Since Enlistment [*Military*]
**HDDT**.......... High-Density Digital Tape
**HDDV**.......... Heavy-Duty Diesel Vehicle
**HDE**.......... Heavy Duty Engine [*Environmental Protection Agency*]
**HDE**.......... Holdrege, NE [*Location identifier*] [*FAA*] (FAAL)
**HDE**.......... Homogeneous Differential Equation
**HDEC**.......... Holocaust Documentation and Education Center (EA)
**HDED**.......... Heavy-Duty Enzyme Detergent
**HDEE**.......... Honorable Discharge, Expiration of Enlistment [*Military*]
**HDEG**.......... Union List of Higher Degree Theses in Australian Libraries [*University of Tasmania Library*] [*Australia*] [*Information service or system*] (CRD)
**HDeH**.......... Hawker De Havilland [*Australia*]
**HDeHV**.......... Hawker De Havilland Victoria [*Australia*]
**HDEP**.......... Haze Layer Estimated _____ Feet Deep [*Aviation*] (FAAC)
**HDEP**.......... High-Density Electronic Packaging
**HDES**.......... Hydrodynamic Equilibrium System [*For chromatography*]
**HDEU**.......... Heating and Domestic Engineers' Union [*British*]
**HDF**.......... Haitian Development Fund [*Later, MH*] (EA)
**HDF**.......... Halogenated Dibenzofuran [*Organic chemistry*]
**HDF**.......... Handle Door Fastener
**HDF**.......... Hartmann Dispersion Formula
**HDF**.......... Hereditary Disease Foundation (EA)
**HDF**.......... High-Density Flexible
**HDF**.......... High-Frequency Direction Finding [*Electronics*]
**HDF**.......... Horizontal Distributing Frame
**HDF**.......... Human Diploid Fibroblasts [*Cytology*]
**H/DF**.......... Human/Dolphin Foundation (EA)
**HDFP**.......... Hypertension Detection and Follow-Up Program [*NHLBI*]
**HDFRZ**.......... Hard Freeze [*Meteorology*] (FAAC)
**HDG**.......... Halsey Drug Co. [*AMEX symbol*] (CTT)
**HDG**.......... Heading (AFM)
**HDG**.......... Heavy-Duty Gasoline [*Vehicle*]
**HDG**.......... Hochdruck-Windkanal Goettingen [*Federal Republic of Germany*]
**HDG**.......... Hot Dip Galvanization
**HDGDD6**.......... Bulletin. Faculty of School Education. Hiroshima University. Part II [*A publication*]
**HDGH**.......... Hodgson Houses, Inc. [*New York, NY*] [*NASDAQ symbol*] (NQ)
**HDGHA**.......... Hiroshima Daigaku Genbaku Hoshano Igaku Kenkyusho Nenpo [*A publication*]
**HDGKDR**.......... Bulletin. Faculty of School Education. Hiroshima University. Part I [*A publication*]
**HDH**.......... Hemihydrate-Dihydrate [*Chemical technology*]
**HDH**.......... Histidinol Dehydrogenase [*An enzyme*]
**H-D-H**.......... [*Eddie*] Holland, [*Lamont*] Dozier, and [*Brian*] Holland [*Motown songwriters and producers*]
**HDH**.......... Howden [*D. H.*] & Co. Ltd. [*Toronto Stock Exchange symbol*]
**HDH**.......... Hydrogen Dehydrogenase [*An enzyme*]
**HDH**.......... Mokuleia, HI [*Location identifier*] [*FAA*] (FAAL)
**HDHD**.......... Hilf Du Heilige Dreifaltigkeit [*Help Thou Holy Trinity*] [*German*] [*Motto of Johann Georg I, Prince of Anhalt-Dessau (1567-1618)*]
**HD/HE**.......... Hospital Design/Hospital Equipment [*British*]
**HDHL**.......... High-Density Helicopter Landing [*Army*]
**HDHQ**.......... Hostility and Direction of Hostility Questionnaire [*Psychology*]
**HDHS**.......... Haul Down and Handling System [*Canadian Navy*]
**HD-HT**.......... Hemodilution Combined with Hypotension
**HDI**.......... Cleveland, TN [*Location identifier*] [*FAA*] (FAAL)
**HDI**.......... Harley-Davidson, Incorporated [*NYSE symbol*] (SPSG)
**HDI**.......... Hawaiian Development Irradiator [*AEC*]
**HDI**.......... Helicopter Direction Inbound [*Military*] (CAAL)
**HDI**.......... Hexamethylene Diisocyanate [*Organic chemistry*]
**HDI**.......... High-Density Interconnect
**HDI**.......... Horizontal Display Indicator (NG)
**HDI**.......... House Dress Institute (EA)
**HDI**.......... Household Disposable Income

**HDI**.......... Human Development Index [*Human Development Report*] [*United Nations Development Program*]
**HDI**.......... Human Development Institute
**HDIF**......... Heavy-Duty Industrial Filter
**HDIG**......... Hamilton Digital Controls, Inc. [*NASDAQ symbol*] (NQ)
**HDIP**......... Hazardous Duty Incentive Pay [*Air Force*] (AFM)
**HDIP**......... High-Dose Immunological Paralysis [*Medicine*]
**H Dip E**...... Higher Diploma in Education [*British*]
**HDIR**......... Heavy-Duty Industrial Relay
**H Dist Ct**... United States District Court, District of Hawaii (DLA)
**HDIV**......... Hughes Dynamic Imagery Viewer
**HDIZA**...... Medical Journal. Hiroshima University [*A publication*]
**HDK**.......... Hidaka [*Japan*] [*Seismograph station code, US Geological Survey*] (SEIS)
**HDKF**........ Handkerchief
**HDKKA**...... Hokkaido Daigaku Kogakubu Kenkyu Hokoku [*A publication*]
**HDL**.......... Handbuch der Deutschen Literaturgeschichte [*A publication*]
**Hdl**.......... Handel [*Trade*] [*German*]
**HDL**.......... Handel Society [*Record label*]
**HDL**.......... Handle (KSC)
**HDL**.......... Handleman Co. [*NYSE symbol*] (SPSG)
**HDL**.......... Hardware Description Language [*Data processing*]
**HDL**.......... Harry Diamond Laboratories [*Formerly, DOFL*] [*Army*] [*Adelphi, MD*]
**HDL**.......... Hidalgo County Library System, McAllen, TX [*OCLC symbol*] (OCLC)
**HDL**.......... High-Density Lipoprotein [*Biochemistry*]
**HDL**.......... Holdenville, OK [*Location identifier*] [*FAA*] (FAAL)
**HDL-C**...... High-Density Lipoprotein - Cell Surface Receptor [*Biochemistry*]
**HDLC**........ High-Density Lipoprotein Cholesterol [*Physiology*]
**HDLC**........ High-Level Data Link Control [*International Standards Organization*] [*Data communication*]
**HDLD**........ Heavy-Duty Liquid Detergent
**HDLE**........ Hurdle
**HDLG**........ Handling (AABC)
**Hdlg**.......... Handlung [*Store, Trading*] [*Business term*] [*German*]
**HDLP**........ Holdup [*FBI standardized term*]
**Hdlr**.......... Haendler [*Merchant*] [*German*]
**HDLR**........ Handler (AABC)
**HDLS**........ Headless (KSC)
**HDLW**....... Distance at Which a Watch Is Heard with Left Ear [*Medicine*]
**HDLYDQ**... Annual Research Reviews. Hodgkin's Disease and the Lymphomas [*A publication*]
**HDM**......... Haddam [*Connecticut*] [*Seismograph station code, US Geological Survey*] (SEIS)
**HDM**......... Hand-Deboned Meat
**HDM**......... Harmonic Distortion Meter (DEN)
**HDM**......... Hierarchical Development Method [*Data processing*]
**HDM**......... High-Density Microsome [*Cytology*]
**HDM**......... Hizbia Dighill e Mirifle [*Somali political party*]
**HDM**......... Hot Dark Matter [*Astronomy*]
**HDM**......... House Dust Mite
**HDM**......... Hudson & Manhattan [*AAR code*]
**HDM**......... Hydrodemetalation [*Petroleum refining*]
**HDM**......... Hydrodynamic Machining [*Manufacturing term*]
**HDM**......... Hydrodynamic Modulation
**HDM**......... Hydroxydopamine [*Also, HDA, OHDA*] [*Biochemistry*]
**HDMA**...... Hardwood Dimension Manufacturers Association [*Later, NDMA*] (EA)
**HDMA**...... Heavy Duty Manufacturers' Association
**HDMC**...... Helicopter Depot Maintenance Center (MCD)
**HDMCC**.... Howdy Doody Memorabilia Collectors Club (EA)
**HDMI**........ High-Density Multichip Interconnect [*Semiconductor packaging*]
**HDML**....... Harbor Defense Motor Launch [*NATO*] (NATG)
**HDMR**...... High-Density Moderated Reactor (IEEE)
**HDMR**...... High-Density Multitrack Recording (MCD)
**HDMS**....... High-Density Memory System
**HDMS**....... High-Density MODEM System [*Microcom*] [*Norwood, MA*] [*Data processing*]
**HDMS**....... Hizb Dastur Mustaghil Somalia [*Somali Independent Constitution Party*]
**HDMS**....... Honorable Discharge, Medical Survey [*Military*]
**HDMSW**.... High-Density Mach Shock Wave
**HDMTX**.... High Dose Methotrexate [*Antineoplastic drug regimen*]
**HDMTX-CF**... High-Dose Methotrexate-Citrovorum Factor [*Antineoplastic drug regimen*]
**HDMTX-LV**... High-Dose Methotrexate, Leucovorin [*Antineoplastic drug regimen*]
**HDMU**...... Honorable Discharge, under Age of Authorized Consent [*Military*]
**HDMW**..... Honorable Discharge, Minors Enlisted without Consent, under Eighteen at Discharge [*Military*]
**HDN**.......... Harden (KSC)
**HDN**.......... Hayden, CO [*Location identifier*] [*FAA*] (FAAL)
**HDN**.......... Hemolytic Disease of the Newborn [*Medicine*]
**Hdn**........... Herodianus [*Greek scholar, c. 200AD*] [*Classical studies*] (OCD)
**HDN**.......... Hildon Mining [*Vancouver Stock Exchange symbol*]
**HDN**.......... Hydrodenitrogenation [*of chemical compounds*]
**HDN**.......... Steamboat Springs [*Colorado*] [*Airport symbol*] [*Obsolete*] (OAG)
**hDNA**........ Deoxyribonucleic Acid, heteroduplex [*Biochemistry, genetics*]
**hDNA**........ Deoxyribonucleic Acid, Histone [*Biochemistry, genetics*]
**HDNA**....... Habonim Dror North America (EA)
**HDNA**....... Hinged Deoxyribonucleic Acid [*Biochemistry, genetics*]
**HDNPRSGR**... Headquarters Squadron Personnel Group
**HDNS**........ Hardness (MSA)
**HDNSW**.... High-Density Nuclear Shock Wave
**HDNT**....... Headnote
**HdO**........... Handbuch der Orientalistik [*Leiden*] [*A publication*] (BJA)
**HDO**.......... Helicopter Direction Outbound [*Military*] (CAAL)
**HDO**.......... Hondo, TX [*Location identifier*] [*FAA*] (FAAL)
**HDOC**....... Handy Dandy Orbital Computer (IEEE)
**HDOC**....... House Document
**HDODA**.... Hexanediol Diacrylate [*Also, HDDA*] [*Organic chemistry*]
**HDOL**........ Hexadecenol [*Pheromone*] [*Organic chemistry*]
**HDON**....... Henredon Furniture [*NASDAQ symbol*] (NQ)
**HDOP**........ Horizontal Dilution of Precision
**HDOS**........ Hard Disk Operating System
**HDOV**....... Hardover
**HDP**.......... Harpoon Data Processor [*Missiles*] (MCD)
**HDP**.......... Hearing Dog Project [*Later, HDRC*] (EA)
**HDP**.......... Hexose Diphosphate [*Biochemistry*]
**HDP**.......... Hiburd Properties [*Vancouver Stock Exchange symbol*]
**HDP**.......... High Detonation Pressure
**HDP**.......... High-Discharge Pressure (IEEE)
**HDP**.......... Holddown Post (NASA)
**HDP**.......... Horizontal Data Processing
**HDP**.......... Hydroxydimethylpyrimidine [*Organic chemistry*]
**HDPE**........ High-Density Polyethylene [*Plastics*]
**HDPPA**..... Housing Development and Public Participation Administration [*Turkey*] (ECON)
**H & D Pr**.... Holmes and Disbrow's Practice [*A publication*] (DLA)
**HDPS**........ High-Density Power Supply
**HDQ**.......... Headquarters [*Colorado*] [*Seismograph station code, US Geological Survey*] [*Closed*] (SEIS)
**HDQR**....... Headquarters
**HDQRS**..... Headquarters
**HDQTRS**.. Headquarters (NASA)
**HDR**.......... Hair's Daily Requirement [*Brand of shampoo*]
**HDR**.......... Hand Rail
**HDR**.......... Header [*Data processing*]
**HDR**.......... Header [*Automotive engineering*]
**HDR**.......... Heldor Industries, Inc. [*AMEX symbol*] (SPSG)
**HDR**.......... High Data Rate
**HDR**.......... High Data Register
**HDR**.......... High Definition RADAR
**HDR**.......... High-Density Recorder [*Deep Space Instrumentation Facility, NASA*]
**HDR**.......... Holddown and Release (AAG)
**HDR**.......... Home Dockyard Regulations [*Navy*] (MCD)
**HDR**.......... Hot Dry Rock [*Geothermal science*]
**HDRA**........ Heavy Duty Representatives Association (EA)
**HDRA**........ Henry Doubleday Research Association [*Coventry, England*] (EAIO)
**HDRA**........ High-Data-Rate Assembly (MCD)
**HDRANCE**... Hindrance (ROG)
**HDRC**........ Hearing Dog Resource Center (EA)
**HDREDU**... HLA and Disease Registry [*A publication*]
**HDRF**........ Heart Disease Research Foundation (EA)
**HDRL**........ High-Data-Rate LASER (MCD)
**HDRM**...... High-Data-Rate Multiplexer (MCD)
**HDRN**....... Hadron, Inc. [*NASDAQ symbol*] (NQ)
**HDRO**....... House Democratic Research Organization (EA)
**HDRP**........ HDR Power Systems, Inc. [*Columbus, OH*] [*NASDAQ symbol*] (NQ)
**HDRR**........ High-Data Rate Recorder
**HDRR**........ Holloman Development Research Report [*Air Force*] (MCD)
**HDRS**........ High-Data Rate Switch (MCD)
**HDRSS**...... High-Data-Rate Storage System [*or Subsystem*] [*NASA*] (MCD)
**HDRV**........ Human Diploid-Cell Rabies Vaccine
**HDRW**....... Distance at Which a Watch Is Heard with Right Ear [*Medicine*]
**HDS**........... Handicapped Driving Systems [*Burnsville, MN*]
**HDS**........... Hardware Description Sheet (NASA)
**HDS**........... Head of Defence Sales [*British*] (RDA)
**HDS**........... Head Set [*Telecommunications*] (TEL)
**HDS**........... Heads [*Automotive engineering*]
**HDS**........... Herdis International Canada, Inc. [*Vancouver Stock Exchange symbol*]
**HDS**........... Herniated Disc Syndrome [*Medicine*]
**HDS**........... Hills Department Stores, Inc. [*NYSE symbol*] (SPSG)
**HDS**........... Historical Data System [*Air Force*] (MCD)
**HDS**........... History of Dermatology Society (EA)
**HDS**........... Holographic Diffractive Structure [*Advanced Environmental Research Group*]
**HDS**........... Holy Days of Obligation [*Roman Catholicism*] (ROG)
**HDS**........... Hospital Discharge Survey [*Public Health Service*]
**HDS**........... Household Delivery Service [*British Post Office facility*] (DCTA)

**HDS** .......... Hybrid Development System
**HDS** .......... Hydrodesulfurization
**HDS** .......... Hydrogen Detection System
**HDS** .......... Office of Human Development Services [*Department of Health and Human Services*]
**HDSA** ........ Huntington's Disease Society of America (EA)
**HDSB** ........ Harvard Divinity School. Bulletin [*A publication*]
**HDSC** ........ Harpoon Data System Cabinet [*Missiles*] (MCD)
**HdSchm** ..... Head Schoolmaster [*Navy*] [*British*]
**HDSCS** ...... Hospital Disaster Support Communications System
**HD(S)E** ...... Home Defence Security Executive [*British*] [*World War II*]
**HDSHK** ..... Handshake [*Computers*] (MSA)
**HDS-NA** .... High Definition System for North America
**HDSP** ........ Hardship (AABC)
**HDST** ........ Headset (MCD)
**HDST** ........ Headstart [*Education*] (OICC)
**HDST** ........ High-Density Shock Tube (IEEE)
**HDSVLY** ... Hudson Valley [*FAA*] (FAAC)
**HDSW** ....... Handwoerterbuch der Sozialwissenschaft [*Dictionary of the Social Sciences*] [*A publication*]
**HDT** .......... Half Duplex Teletype (KSC)
**HDT** .......... Heat Deflection Temperature [*of plastics*]
**HDT** .......... Heat Distortion Temperature
**HDT** .......... Heavy Duty Truck [*Environmental Protection Agency*]
**Hdt** .......... Herodotus [*Greek historian, c. 484BC*] [*Classical studies*] (OCD)
**HDT** .......... Hi-Pot Dwell Time
**HDT** .......... Humboldt, TN [*Location identifier*] [*FAA*] (FAAL)
**HDTA** ........ High-Density Traffic Airport
**HDTMA** .... Heavy-Duty Truck Manufacturers Association (EA)
**HDTMA** .... Hexadecyltrimethylammonium
**HDTV** ........ High-Definition Television [*Offers wider-screen pictures with high resolution that improves their depth, clarity, and detail*]
**HDTYA** ..... Heredity [*England*] [*A publication*]
**HDU** .......... Heads-Up Display Unit [*Aviation*] (RDA)
**HDU** .......... Hemodialysis Unit [*Medicine*]
**HDU** .......... Home Defence Unit [*British military*] (DMA)
**HDU** .......... Hyde Park [*Utah*] [*Seismograph station code, US Geological Survey*] (SEIS)
**HDUE** ....... High Dynamic User Equipment
**HDV** .......... Health Department Victoria [*Australia*]
**HDV** .......... Heavy Duty Vehicle [*Environmental Protection Agency*]
**HDV** .......... Hepatitis Delta Virus
**HDV** .......... High-Definition Video
**HDV** .......... High-Dollar Value
**HDV** .......... Horse-Drawn Vehicle
**HDV** .......... Hydrodevanadization [*Petroleum technology*]
**HDV** .......... Hydrodynamic Voltammogram [*Electrochemistry*]
**HDVS** ........ High Definition Video System
**HDW** .......... Hardware [*Data processing*] (KSC)
**HDW** .......... Hearing Distance with Watch [*Medicine*]
**HDW** .......... High-Pressure Demineralized Water (NRCH)
**HDW** .......... Hydrodynamic Welding
**HDWC** ....... Hardware Cloth
**HDWD** ...... Hardwood
**HDWE** ....... Hardware
**HDWND** ... Headwind [*Aviation*] (FAAC)
**HDWS** ....... How Do We Stand?
**Hdwt** .......... Hundredweight
**HDW Werkztg** ... Howaldtswerke Deutsche Werft. Aktiengesellschaft. Hamburg und Kiel. Werkzeitung [*A publication*]
**HDX** .......... Half Duplex Transmission [*Data communication*]
**HDY** .......... Haadyai [*Thailand*] [*Airport symbol*] (OAG)
**HDY** .......... Heavy-Duty
**HDYN** ....... Healthdyne, Inc. [*NASDAQ symbol*] (NQ)
**HDZ** .......... Hrvatski Dijalektoloski Zbornik [*A publication*]
**HDZb** ........ Hrvatski Dijalektoloski Zbornik [*A publication*]
**HDZNV** ..... De Handschriften van de Dode Zee in Nederlandse Vertaling [*Amsterdam*] [*A publication*] (BJA)
**HE** ............ Handbooks in Economics [*Elsevier Book Series*] [*A publication*]
**HE** ............ Handling Equipment
**HE** ............ Hardware Evaluator [*NASA*]
**HE** ............ Hardware Executive
**HE** ............ Hare Express. Fort Good Hope [*A publication*]
**HE** ............ Hawaiian Electric Industries, Inc. [*NYSE symbol*] (SPSG)
**HE** ............ Hearing Examiner [*Also, ALJ*]
**HE** ............ Heat Engine
**HE** ............ Heat Exchanger
**HE** ............ Heavy Enamel (AAG)
**HE** ............ Heavy Equipment (AFM)
**HE** ............ [*The*] Hebrew [*A publication*] (BJA)
**HE** ............ Height of Eye [*Navigation*]
**HE** ............ Heinkel [*German aircraft type*] [*World War II*]
**HE** ............ Helio Aircraft Co. [*ICAO aircraft manufacturer identifier*] (ICAO)
**He** ............ Helium [*Chemical element*]
**H & E** ........ Hematoxylin and Eosin [*Biological stain*]
**HE** ............ Hematoxylin and Eosin [*Biological stain*]
**HE** ............ Hemicylindrical [*Leaf characteristic*] [*Botany*]
**H & E** ........ Hemorrhage and Exudate [*Medicine*]
**He** ............ Henceforth [*A publication*]
**HE** ............ Hepatic Encephalography [*Medicine*]
**HE** ............ Hepatic Encephalopathy [*Medicine*]
**HE** ............ Hepatic Extraction [*Endocrinology*]
**HE** ............ Hereditary Elliptocytosis [*Medicine*]
**H & E** ........ Heredity and Environment
**HE** ............ Hexane-Extractable Compound
**HE** ............ Hic Est [*Here Is, That is, or This is*] [*Latin*]
**HE** ............ High Efficiency
**HE** ............ High Energy (MCD)
**HE** ............ High-Energy Astrophysics (NASA)
**HE** ............ High Explosive (AAG)
**HE** ............ Highest Electroendosmosis [*Analytical biochemistry*]
**HE** ............ His Eminence
**HE** ............ His [*or Her*] Excellency
**HE** ............ Historia Ecclesiastica [*of Eusebius*] [*Classical studies*]
**HE** ............ Hoc Est [*That Is or This Is*] [*Latin*]
**HE** ............ Hollis & Eastern Railroad Co. [*AAR code*]
**HE** ............ Holy Empire [*Freemasonry*]
**HE** ............ Holy Eucharist
**HE** ............ Home Economics [*Secondary school course*] [*British*]
**HE** ............ Honda Engineering
**HE** ............ Horizontal Equivalent
**HE** ............ Horticultural Enterprise [*A publication*]
**HE** ............ Housekeeping Element (TEL)
**HE** ............ Human Engineering
**HE** ............ Human Enolase [*An enzyme*]
**HE** ............ Human Enteric [*Virology*]
**HE** ............ Human Events [*A publication*]
**HE** ............ Human Exposure Dose [*Medicine*]
**HE** ............ Hydraulics Engineer
**HE** ............ Hydrogen Embrittlement
**HE** ............ Hydrophone Effect [*Navy*] (NVT)
**HE** ............ Hydroxyecdysone [*Endocrinology*]
**HE** ............ Hygienic Effect
**HE** ............ Hygienic Electrician [*British*] (ROG)
**HE** ............ Hypogonadotrophic Eunuchoidism [*Medicine*]
**HE** ............ Trans European Airways [*Belgium*] [*ICAO designator*] (FAAC)
**HEA** .......... Centre des Hautes Etudes Americaines [*Paris*]
**HEA** .......... Health Education Authority [*British*]
**HEA** .......... Hemorrhagic Arteries [*Veterinary medicine*]
**HEA** .......... Herat [*Afghanistan*] [*Airport symbol*] [*Obsolete*] (OAG)
**HEA** .......... Higher Education Act [*1965*]
**HEA** .......... Horticultural Education Association [*British*]
**HEA** .......... Hot Electron Amplifier
**HEA** .......... Hydroxyethyl Acrylate [*Organic chemistry*]
**HEAA** ........ High-Explosive, Antiaircraft [*Weaponry*]
**HEAC** ........ Higher Education Administration Charge [*Australia*]
**HEAD** ........ Hand-Held Encryption and Authentication Device (RDA)
**Head** .......... Head's Tennessee Supreme Court Reports [*1858-59*] [*A publication*] (DLA)
**HEADA** ..... Headache [*A publication*]
**HEADCOM** ... Headquarters Command [*Military*]
**HEADE** ..... High Erucic Acid Development Effort
**Headline Ser** ... Headline Series [*A publication*]
**Head Neck Surg** ... Head and Neck Surgery [*A publication*]
**Head Nec Surg** ... Head and Neck Surgery [*A publication*]
**HEADSS** ... Helicopter Escort, Air Defense Suppression System
**Head Teachers' R** ... Head Teachers' Review [*A publication*]
**Head (Tenn)** ... Head's Tennessee Reports [*38-40 Tennessee*] [*A publication*] (DLA)
**HEAF** ........ Heavy End Aviation Fuel
**HEAHB** ..... Health [*A publication*]
**HEAL** ........ Health Education Assistance Loan [*Bureau of Health Professions*]
**HEAL** ........ Healthwatch, Inc. [*Broomfield, CO*] [*NASDAQ symbol*] (NQ)
**HEAL** ........ Human Ecology Action League (EA)
**Heal Ed Mon** ... Health Education Monographs [*A publication*]
**Heal JS Comp** ... Healy on Joint Stock Companies [*A publication*] (DLA)
**Heal Light** ... Healing Light [*A publication*]
**Heal Pews** ... Heale's Law of Church Pews [*A publication*] (DLA)
**HEALS** ...... Honeywell Error Analysis and Logging System
**HEALT** ...... Helicopter Employment and Assault Landing Table (NVT)
**HEALTH** .. Happiness, Energy, and Longevity through Health [*Title of 1979 film directed by Robert Altman*]
**Health** ........ Health Law in Canada [*A publication*]
**Health Aff** ... Health Affairs [*A publication*]
**Health Aff (Millwood)** ... Health Affairs (Millwood, Virginia) [*A publication*]
**Health Aff (Pa)** ... Health Affairs (Philadelphia) [*A publication*]
**Health Aspects Chem Saf Interim Doc** ... Health Aspects of Chemical Safety. Interim Document [*A publication*]
**Health Bul** ... Health Bulletin [*A publication*] (APTA)
**Health Bull** ... Health Bulletin [*A publication*]
**Health Bull (Edinb)** ... Health Bulletin (Edinburgh) [*A publication*]
**Healthcare** ... Healthcare Marketing Report [*A publication*]
**Health Care Can** ... Health Care in Canada [*A publication*]
**Health Care Dimen** ... Health Care Dimensions [*A publication*]
**Health Care Educ** ... Health Care Education [*A publication*]
**Health Care Financing R** ... Health Care Financing Review [*A publication*]

**Healthcare Financ Manage** ... Healthcare Financial Management [*A publication*]
**Health Care Financ Rev** ... Health Care Financing Review [*A publication*]
**Health Care Financ Trends** ... Health Care Financing Trends [*A publication*]
**Health Care Instrum** ... Health Care Instrumentation [*A publication*]
**Health Care Law Newsl** ... Health Care Law Newsletter [*A publication*]
**Health Care Manage Rev** ... Health Care Management Review [*A publication*]
**Health Care Mark Target Market** ... Health Care Marketer and Target Market [*A publication*]
**Health Care Newsl** ... Health Care Newsletter [*A publication*]
**Health Care Plan & Mkt** ... Health Care Planning and Marketing [*A publication*]
**Health Care Plann Market** ... Health Care Planning and Marketing [*A publication*]
**Health Care Secur Saf Manage** ... Health Care Security and Safety Management [*A publication*]
**Health Care Strateg Manage** ... Health Care Strategic Management [*A publication*]
**Health Care Superv** ... Health Care Supervisor [*A publication*]
**Health Care Syst** ... Health Care Systems [*A publication*]
**Health Care Wk** ... Health Care Week [*A publication*]
**Health Care Women Int** ... Health Care for Women, International [*A publication*]
**Healthc Comput Commun** ... Healthcare Computing and Communications [*A publication*]
**Healthc Executive** ... Healthcare Executive [*A publication*]
**Healthc Forum** ... Healthcare Forum Journal [*A publication*]
**Health Commun Inf** ... Health Communications and Informatics [*A publication*]
**Health Commun Informatics** ... Health Communications and Informatics [*A publication*]
**Healthc Online** ... Healthcare Online [*A publication*]
**Health Cost Manage** ... Health Cost Management [*A publication*]
**Healthc Prot Manage** ... Healthcare Protection Management [*A publication*]
**Health Ed** .. Health Education [*A publication*]
**Health Ed J** ... Health Education Journal [*A publication*]
**Health Educ** ... Health Education [*A publication*]
**Health Educ** ... Health Education Journal [*A publication*]
**Health Educ Assoc NSW Newsl** ... Health Education Association of New South Wales. Newsletter [*A publication*] (APTA)
**Health Educ Bull** ... Health Education Bulletin [*A publication*]
**Health Educ J** ... Health Education Journal [*A publication*]
**Health Educ Monogr** ... Health Education Monographs [*A publication*]
**Health Educ Q** ... Health Education Quarterly [*A publication*]
**Health Educ Rep** ... Health Education Reports [*A publication*]
**Health Foods Bus** ... Health Foods Business [*A publication*]
**Health Hyg** ... Health and Hygiene [*A publication*]
**Health Ind** ... Health Industry Today [*A publication*]
**Health Inspectors Conf** ... Annual Conference of Health Inspectors of New South Wales [*A publication*] (APTA)
**Health Insur Stat** ... Health Insurance Statistics [*United States Health, Education, and Welfare Department*] [*A publication*]
**Health Lab** ... Health Laboratory Science [*A publication*]
**Health Lab Sc** ... Health Laboratory Science [*A publication*]
**Health Lab Sci** ... Health Laboratory Science [*A publication*]
**Health Law Proj Libr Bull** ... Health Law Project Library Bulletin [*A publication*]
**Health L Can** ... Health Law in Canada [*A publication*]
**Health Libr Rev** ... Health Libraries Review [*A publication*]
**HEALTHLINE** ... Health Planning and Administration [*National Library of Medicine*] [*Database*]
**Health Manage Forum** ... Health Management Forum [*A publication*]
**Health Manage Q** ... Health Management Quarterly [*A publication*]
**Health Manpow Lit** ... Health Manpower Literature [*A publication*]
**Health Manpow Rep** ... Health Manpower Report [*Later, Health Planning and Manpower Report*] [*A publication*]
**Health Mark Q** ... Health Marketing Quarterly [*A publication*]
**Health & Med** ... Health and Medicine [*A publication*]
**Health Med Care Serv Rev** ... Health and Medical Care Services Review [*A publication*]
**Health Mkt Q** ... Health Marketing Quarterly [*A publication*]
**Health NSW** ... Health in New South Wales [*A publication*] (APTA)
**Health Officers J** ... Health Officers' Journal [*A publication*] (APTA)
**Health-PAC Bull** ... Health-PAC [*Policy Advisory Center*] Bulletin [*A publication*]
**Health Perspect** ... Health Perspectives [*Later, Consumer Health Perspectives*] [*A publication*]
**Health Perspect Issues** ... Health Perspectives and Issues [*A publication*]
**Health Phys** ... Health Physics [*A publication*]
**Health Phys (Tokyo)** ... Health Physics (Tokyo) [*A publication*]
**Health Plann Manpower Rep** ... Health Planning and Manpower Report [*A publication*]
**Health Plann Manpow Rep** ... Health Planning and Manpower Report [*A publication*]
**Health Policy Educ** ... Health Policy and Education [*A publication*]
**Health Policy Q** ... Health Policy Quarterly [*A publication*]
**Health Popul Perspect Issues** ... Health and Population Perspectives and Issues [*A publication*]
**Health Pract Physician Assist** ... Health Practitioner. Physician Assistant [*A publication*]
**Health Prog** ... Health Progress [*A publication*]
**Health Psychol** ... Health Psychology [*A publication*]
**Health Saf Bull** ... Health and Safety Bulletin [*A publication*]
**Health Saf Ind Commer** ... Health and Safety in Industry and Commerce [*A publication*]
**Health Saf Work** ... Health and Safety at Work [*A publication*]
**Health & SC** ... Health and Safety Code [*A publication*] (DLA)
**Health Serv** ... Health Services Report [*A publication*]
**Health Serv J** ... Health Service Journal [*A publication*]
**Health Serv Manager** ... Health Services Manager [*A publication*]
**Health Serv Manpow Rev** ... Health Services Manpower Review [*A publication*]
**Health Serv Rep** ... Health Service Reports [*A publication*]
**Health Serv Res** ... Health Services Research [*Chicago*] [*A publication*]
**Health Social Serv J** ... Health and Social Service Journal [*A publication*]
**Health Soc Serv J** ... Health and Social Service Journal [*A publication*]
**Health Soc Work** ... Health and Social Work [*A publication*]
**Health (US)** ... Health Crisis 2000 (United States) [*A publication*]
**Health Visit** ... Health Visitor [*A publication*]
**Health Welfare Stat** ... Health and Welfare Statistics [*A publication*]
**HEAO**........ High-Energy Astronomy Observatory [*Pronounced "hee-oh"*] [*NASA*]
**HEAP**........ Helicopter Extended Area Platform
**HEAP**........ High-Energy Aim Point [*Weaponry*] (MCD)
**HEAP**........ High-Explosive, Antipersonnel [*Weaponry*]
**HEAP**........ High-Explosive Armor-Piercing [*Weaponry*]
**HEAPS**...... Hawaiian Environmental Analysis and Prediction System (MUGU)
**HEAPS**...... Health Education and Promotion Information System [*Australia*]
**HEAR**........ El Arish/El Arish [*Egypt*] [*ICAO location identifier*] (ICLI)
**HEAR**........ Health Associated Representatives [*Later, HIRA*] (EA)
**HEAR**........ Hearing Education through Auditory Research [*In association name, HEAR Center*] (EA)
**HEAR**........ Hereafter (ROG)
**HEAR**........ High Erucic Acid Rapeseed [*Agricultural chemistry*]
**HEAR**........ Human Error Action Report [*NASA*] (KSC)
**Hear Aid J** ... Hearing Aid Journal [*A publication*]
**Heard Civ Pl** ... Heard's Civil Pleading [*A publication*] (DLA)
**Heard Cr Pl** ... Heard's Criminal Pleading [*A publication*] (DLA)
**Heard Cur Rep** ... Heard's Curiosities of the Law Reporters [*A publication*] (DLA)
**Heard Eq Pl** ... Heard's Equity Pleading [*A publication*] (DLA)
**Heard Lib & Sl** ... Heard on Libel and Slander [*A publication*] (DLA)
**Heard's Shortt Extr Rem** ... Heard's Edition of Shortt on Extraordinary Legal Remedies [*A publication*] (DLA)
**Hear Exam** ... Hearing Examiner [*Legal term*] (DLA)
**HEAR-FOUND** ... Hearing, Educational Aid and Research Foundation (EA)
**Hear Instrum** ... Hearing Instruments [*A publication*]
**Hearnshaw** ... Southampton Court Leet Records [*A publication*] (DLA)
**Hear Rehab Quart** ... Hearing Rehabilitation Quarterly [*A publication*]
**Hear Res**.... Hearing Research [*A publication*]
**HEARS**...... Higher Education Administration Referral Service [*Defunct*] (EA)
**Hearst's M** ... Hearst's Magazine [*A publication*]
**HEART**..... Hardened Electronics and Radiation Technology (MCD)
**HEART**..... Health Evaluation and Risk Tabulation (MCD)
**HEART**..... Household Employment Association for Reevaluation and Training [*Later, Personnel Resources*]
**HEART**..... Hydrometer Erosion and Recession Test (MCD)
**Heart Bull** ... Heart Bulletin [*A publication*]
**Heart Cent Bull St Francis Hosp (Roslyn NY)** ... Heart Center Bulletin. St. Francis Hospital (Roslyn, New York) [*A publication*]
**HEARTHFIRE** ... High-Energy Accelerator and Reactor for Thermonuclear Fusion with Ion Beams of Relativistic Energies
**Heart Lung** ... Heart and Lung. Journal of Critical Care [*A publication*]
**Heart and Lung** ... Heart and Lung. Journal of Critical Care [*A publication*]
**HEAS**........ Harvard East Asian Series [*A publication*]
**HEASDA** .. Home Economics Association of Seventh-Day Adventists (EA)
**HEAT**........ Asyut [*Egypt*] [*ICAO location identifier*] (ICLI)
**Heat**........... Heating and Ventilating Engineer [*A publication*]
**HEAT**........ High-Enthalpy Ablation Test
**HEAT**........ High Enthalpy Arc Tunnel [*NASA*]
**HEAT**........ High-Explosive, Antitank [*Weaponry*]
**HEAT**........ Human Erythrocyte Agglutination Test [*Hematology*]
**Heat Air Cond Contr** ... Heating and Air Conditioning Contractor [*A publication*]
**Heat Air Condit J** ... Heating and Air Conditioning Journal [*A publication*]
**Heat Air Condit Refrig** ... Heating, Air Conditioning, and Refrigeration [*A publication*]
**Heat and Air Cond J** ... Heating and Air Conditioning Journal [*A publication*]
**Heat Air Cond J** ... Heating and Air Conditioning Journal [*A publication*]
**Heat Air Cond Refrig** ... Heating, Air Conditioning, and Refrigeration [*A publication*]
**Heat Combust Equip News** ... Heating/Combustion Equipment News [*A publication*]
**Heat Eng**.... Heat Engineering [*A publication*]
**Heath**......... Heath's Reports [*36-40 Maine*] [*A publication*] (DLA)
**HEATH**...... Higher Education and the Handicapped [*An association*] (EA)
**Heath Max** ... Heath's Maxims [*A publication*] (DLA)
**Heating & Air Conditioning Jnl** ... Heating and Air Conditioning Journal [*A publication*]

**Heating Piping** ... Heating, Piping, and Air Conditioning [*A publication*]
**Heat Manage Pollut Control** ... Heat Management and Pollution Control [*Japan*] [*A publication*]
**HEAT-MP-T** ... High-Explosive Antitank, Multipurpose, Tracer [*Weaponry*] (MCD)
**Heat Pip Air Condit** ... Heating, Piping, and Air Conditioning [*A publication*]
**Heat Piping Air Cond** ... Heating, Piping, and Air Conditioning [*A publication*]
**Heat Pipng** ... Heating, Piping, and Air Conditioning [*A publication*]
**HEAT-T** .... High-Explosive Antitank-Tracer [*Weaponry*] (AABC)
**Heat Technol** ... Heat Technology [*A publication*]
**HEAT-TP-T** ... High-Explosive Antitank, Target Practice, Tracer [*Weaponry*] (MCD)
**Heat Transfer Eng** ... Heat Transfer Engineering [*A publication*]
**Heat Transfer Engng** ... Heat Transfer Engineering [*A publication*]
**Heat Transfer & Fluid Flow Dig** ... Heat Transfer and Fluid Flow Digest [*A publication*]
**Heat Transfer Fluid Mech Inst Prepr Pap** ... Heat Transfer and Fluid Mechanics Institute. Preprints of Papers [*A publication*]
**Heat Transfer - Japan Res** ... Heat Transfer. Japanese Research [*A publication*]
**Heat Transfer Jap Res** ... Heat Transfer. Japanese Research [*A publication*]
**Heat Transfer Jpn Res** ... Heat Transfer. Japanese Research [*A publication*]
**Heat Transfer Sov Res** ... Heat Transfer. Soviet Research [*A publication*]
**Heat Treat** ... Heat Treating [*A publication*]
**Heat Treat Forg** ... Heat Treating and Forging [*A publication*]
**Heat Treat Met** ... Heat Treatment of Metals [*A publication*]
**Heat Treat Met (China)** ... Heat Treatment of Metals (China) [*A publication*]
**Heat & Vent** ... Heating and Ventilating [*A publication*]
**Heat and Vent Eng** ... Heating and Ventilating Engineer [*A publication*]
**Heat Vent Eng** ... Heating and Ventilating Engineer [*A publication*]
**Heat Vent Eng J Air Cond** ... Heating and Ventilating Engineer and Journal of Air Conditioning [*A publication*]
**Heat Vent Engr** ... Heating and Ventilating Engineer [*A publication*]
**Heat & Vent Engr** ... Heating and Ventilating Engineer [*A publication*]
**Heat Vent News** ... Heating and Ventilating News [*A publication*]
**Heat Vent Rev** ... Heating and Ventilating Review [*A publication*]
**Heavy Met Environ Int Conf 4th** ... Heavy Metals in the Environment. International Conference. 4th [*A publication*]
**HEAVYPHOTORON** ... Heavy Photographic Squadron
**HEAX** ........ Alexandria [*Egypt*] [*ICAO location identifier*] (ICLI)
**HEB** .......... Hebraic [*Language, etc.*] (ROG)
**HEB** .......... Hebrew
**heb** ............ Hebrew [*MARC language code*] [*Library of Congress*] (LCCP)
**Heb** ........... Hebrews [*New Testament book*]
**HEB** .......... Heinemann Educational Books [*London, England*]
**HEB** .......... Hepar Embryonis Bovis [*Embryonic bovine liver cells used in tissue culture studies of viruses*] [*Medicine*]
**HEB** .......... Hollow Electron Beam
**Hebbel-Jahrb** ... Hebbel-Jahrbuch [*A publication*]
**HEBBLE** ... High-Energy Benthic Boundary Layer Experiment [*Oceanography*]
**HEBC** ........ Heavy Enamel Bonded Cotton [*Wire insulation*]
**HEBC** ........ Heritage Bankcorp, Inc. [*NASDAQ symbol*] (NQ)
**HEBD** ........ Hebdomada [*A Week*] [*Pharmacy*] (ROG)
**HEBDC** ..... Heavy Enamel Bonded Double Cotton [*Wire insulation*] (AAG)
**HEBDOM** ... Hebdomada [*A Week*] [*Pharmacy*]
**HEBDP** ..... Heavy Enamel Bonded Double Paper [*Wire insulation*] (AAG)
**HEBDS**...... Heavy Enamel Bonded Double Silk [*Wire insulation*] (AAG)
**HEBL** ........ Abu Simbel [*Egypt*] [*ICAO location identifier*] (ICLI)
**Heb Med J** ... Hebrew Medical Journal [*A publication*]
**HEBP** ........ Heavy Enamel Bonded Paper [*Wire insulation*]
**Heb Pharm** ... Hebrew Pharmacist [*A publication*]
**Hebr**........... Hebraic (BJA)
**HEBR** ........ Hebrew
**Hebrew Univ (Jerusalem)** ... Hebrew University (Jerusalem) [*A publication*]
**Hebrew U St** ... Hebrew University. Studies in Literature [*A publication*]
**Hebridean Nat** ... Hebridean Naturalist [*A publication*]
**HebrUCA** .. Hebrew Union College. Annual [*A publication*]
**HEBS**......... Heavy Enamel Bonded Silk [*Wire insulation*]
**HEBS**......... High-Energy Battery System
**HEBT** ........ High-Energy Beam Transport [*For protons*]
**Heb Tech Coll (Haifa) Sci Publ** ... Hebrew Technical College (Haifa). Scientific Publications [*A publication*]
**HEBUA** ..... Heart Bulletin [*A publication*]
**HEC**........... Ecole des Hautes Etudes Commerciales, Bibliotheque [*UTLAS symbol*]
**HEC**........... Hamster Embryonic Cell
**HEC**........... Hardened Electronic Component
**HEC**........... Harken Energy Co. [*NYSE symbol*] (SPSG)
**HEC**........... Hasselblad Electric Camera
**HEC**........... Heavy Enamel Single Cotton [*Wire insulation*] (AAG)
**Hec**............ Hecate [*A publication*]
**HEC**........... Hector, CA [*Location identifier*] [*FAA*] (FAAL)
**HEC**........... Hector Resources, Inc. [*Vancouver Stock Exchange symbol*]
**Hec**............ Hecuba [*of Euripides*] [*Classical studies*] (OCD)
**HEC**........... Hepatoma Cells [*Oncology*]
**HEC**........... High Emission Cathode
**HEC**........... High-Energy Chemistry
**HEC**........... Hodgin's Election Cases [*Ontario*] [*A publication*] (DLA)
**HEC**........... Hollerith Electronic Computer
**HEC**........... Human Economy Center (EA)
**HEC**........... Human Endometrial Cancer [*Oncology*]
**HEC**........... Human Endothelial Cell [*Cytology*]
**HEC**........... Human Enteric Coronavirus
**HEC**........... Human Environment Center (EA)
**HEC**........... Human Epithelial Cell [*Cytology*]
**HEC**........... Hydrologic Engineering Center [*Davis, CA*] [*Army*] (GRD)
**HEC**........... (Hydroxyethyl)cellulose [*Organic chemistry*]
**HEC**........... United States Department of Health and Human Services, Health Care Financial Administration, Baltimore, MD [*OCLC symbol*] (OCLC)
**HECA**......... Cairo/International [*Egypt*] [*ICAO location identifier*] (ICLI)
**HECAD**....... Human Engineering Computer-Aided Design [*Air Force*]
**HECC**......... Cairo [*Egypt*] [*ICAO location identifier*] (ICLI)
**HECC**......... Hailey Energy Corporation [*Abilene, TX*] [*NASDAQ symbol*] (NQ)
**HECC**......... Higher Education Coordinating Council of Metropolitan St. Louis [*Library network*]
**HECC**......... Hooker Electro-Chemical Company
**HECD**......... Hall Electrolytic Conductivity Detector [*Analytical instrumentation*]
**HECH**......... Hechinger Co. [*NASDAQ symbol*] (NQ)
**HECI**.......... Human-Interface Equipment Catalog Item (TEL)
**Heck Cas** ... Hecker's Cases on Warranty [*A publication*] (DLA)
**HECLINET** ... Health Care Literature Information Network [*Institut fuer Krankenhausbau*] [*Federal Republic of Germany*] [*Information service or system*] (IID)
**HE Cls B**.... Heating Coils in Bunkers [*on a ship*] (DS)
**HE Cls C**.... Heating Coils in Cargo Tanks [*on a ship*] (DS)
**HECMAR** ... Human Engineering Criteria for Maintenance and Repair [*GE, NASA*]
**HECP**......... Harbor Entrance Control Post [*Nautical charts*]
**HECRE**....... High-Energy Cosmic Ray Experiment [*Balloon flight*] [*NASA*]
**HECS**......... Higher Education Contribution Scheme [*Australia*]
**HECTO**....... Hectograph
**HECTOG**.. Hectogram
**HECTOL**... Hectoliter
**HECTOM** ... Hectometer [*100 meters*]
**HECTOR** .. Heated Experimental Carbon Thermal Oscillator Reactor [*British*]
**HECUA**...... Higher Education Consortium for Urban Affairs (EA)
**HECV**......... Heavy Enamel Cotton Varnish [*Wire insulation*]
**HECV**......... Helium Check Valve (MCD)
**HECV**......... Human Enteric Coronavirus
**HECVES**.... Harbor Entrance Control Vessel
**HED**........... Hall Effect Device
**HED**........... Haut-Einheits-Dosis [*Unit Skin Dose*]
**HED**........... Hazard Evaluation Division [*Environmental Protection Agency*]
**HED**........... Headquarters (CINC)
**HED**........... Health Devices [*A publication*]
**HED**........... Hedley Pacific Mining [*Vancouver Stock Exchange symbol*]
**HED**........... Herendeen Bay, AK [*Location identifier*] [*FAA*] (FAAL)
**HED**........... High-Energy Detector [*NASA*]
**HED**........... High-Explosive Delay [*Weaponry*] (MCD)
**HED**........... Historical Earthquake Data (NRCH)
**HED**........... Historical English Dictionary [*A publication*]
**HED**........... Horizontal Electrical Dipole (IEEE)
**HED**........... Human Engineering Data
**HED**........... Human Engineering Discrepancy [*Nuclear energy*] (NRCH)
**HED**........... Hydraulically Extendable Dipperstick [*for tractors*]
**HED**........... Hymnal-Epic Dialect (BJA)
**HEDC**......... Hasselblad Electric Data Camera
**HEDC**......... Heavy Enamel Double Cotton [*Wire insulation*]
**HEDCC**...... Human Error Data Control Center [*NASA*] (KSC)
**HEDCOM** ... Headquarters Command [*Military*]
**HEDCV**...... Heavy Enamel Double Cotton Varnish [*Wire insulation*] (AAG)
**HEDDS**...... Hawaii Educational Dissemination Diffusion System [*Hawaii State Department of Education*] [*Honolulu*] [*Information service or system*] (IID)
**HEDE**......... Heavy Engineering Development Establishment [*Australia*]
**Hedeselsk Tidsskr** ... Hedeselskabets Tidsskrift [*A publication*]
**HEDF**......... High Energy Density Facility [*Proposed site for testing nuclear bombs*]
**HEDGE**...... Human Factor Evaluation Data for General Equipment
**HEDGE**...... Human Factors Engineering Data Guide for Evaluation
**Hedges**...... Hedges' Reports [*2-6 Montana*] [*A publication*] (DLA)
**HEDI**......... High Endoatmospheric Defense Interceptor [*Military*] (RDA)
**HEDING**.... Hedingham [*England*]
**HEDJ**......... Health Education Journal [*London*] [*A publication*]
**HEDL**......... Hanford Engineering and Development Laboratory [*Richland, WA*] [*Department of Energy*]
**HEDO**........ Health Education [*Ottawa*] [*A publication*]
**HEDP**......... Hearing Ear Dog Program (EA)
**HEDP**......... High-Explosive Dual-Purpose [*Cartridge*] (RDA)
**HEDP**......... (Hydroxyethylidene)diphosphonic Acid [*Also, EHDP*] [*Organic chemistry*]
**HEDQ**........ Health Education Quarterly [*A publication*]
**HEdR**......... Harvard Educational Review [*A publication*]

**HEDRON** ... Headquarters Squadron [*Obsolete*]
**HEDRONFAIRWING** ... Headquarters Squadron Fleet Air Wing
**HEDS** ........ Heavy Enamel Double Silk [*Wire insulation*]
**HEDS** ........ High Endoatmospheric Defense System
**HEDS** ........ High-Explosive, Discarding Sabot [*Weaponry*] (AAG)
**HEDSUPPACT** ... Headquarters Support Activity
**HEDSV** ..... Heavy Enamel Double Silk Varnish [*Wire insulation*] (AAG)
**HEDT** ........ Health Edutech, Inc. [*Minneapolis, MN*] [*NASDAQ symbol*] (NQ)
**HEDTA** ..... Hydroxyethylenediaminetriacetic Acid [*Organic chemistry*]
**HEDU** ....... Health Educator. Newsletter [*A publication*]
**HEDW** ....... Health Education (Washington) [*A publication*]
**HEE** ........... Heerlen [*Netherlands*] [*Seismograph station code, US Geological Survey*] (SEIS)
**HEE** ........... Helena/West Helena, AR [*Location identifier*] [*FAA*] (FAAL)
**HEE** ........... Household Earnings and Expenditure
**HEEA** ........ Home Economics Education Association (EA)
**HEEB** ........ High-Energy Electrolyte Battery
**HEED** ........ High-Energy Electron Diffraction
**HEEDTA** .. (Hydroxyethyl)ethylenediaminetetracetate [*or -tetracetic*] Acid [*Organic chemistry*]
**HEEEL** ...... High-Energy Electronically Excited LASER
**HEEM** ....... Embaba [*Egypt*] [*ICAO location identifier*] (ICLI)
**HEEMA** .... Health Education Monographs [*A publication*]
**HEENA** ..... Heat Engineering [*Livingston, NJ*] [*A publication*]
**HEENT** ..... Head, Ears, Eyes, Nose, Throat
**HEEO** ........ High Electroendosmosis [*Analytical biochemistry*]
**HEEP** ........ Health Effects of Environmental Pollutants [*A publication*]
**HEEP** ........ Highway Engineering Exchange Program (EA)
**HEF** ........... Health Education Foundation (EA)
**HEF** ........... Hearth Electric Furnace
**HEF** ........... Heat-Curing Epoxy Film
**HEF** ........... High Energy Forming
**HEF** ........... High-Energy Fuel [*Air Force*]
**HEF** ........... High-Expansion Foam
**HEF** ........... Hispanic Energy Forum (EA)
**HEF** ........... Human Ecology Fund (EA)
**HEF** ........... Human Embryo Fibroblast [*A cell line*]
**HEF** ........... Hydroxyethylflurazepam [*Sedative*]
**HEF** ........... Manassas, VA [*Location identifier*] [*FAA*] (FAAL)
**HEFA** ........ Higher Education Facilities Act of 1963
**HEFC** ........ Higher Education Facilities Commission
**HEFG** ........ Hall Effect Function Generator
**HEFOA** ..... Hebezeuge und Foerdermittel [*A publication*]
**HEFT** ........ Heavy-Element Fission Tracer
**Hefte A Bern** ... Hefte des Archaeologischen Seminars der Universitaet Bern [*A publication*]
**Hefte Unfallheilkd** ... Hefte zur Unfallheilkunde [*A publication*]
**HEFTH** ..... Henceforth (ROG)
**Heft Unfallheilk** ... Hefte zur Unfallheilkunde [*West Germany*] [*A publication*]
**HEFU** ........ High-Energy Firing Unit [*Army*] (AABC)
**HEG** .......... Haftentschaedigungsgesetz [*A publication*] (BJA)
**HEG** .......... Hall Effect Generator
**HEG** .......... Handbook of Exploration Geochemistry [*Elsevier Book Series*] [*A publication*]
**HEG** .......... Heavy Enamel Single Glass [*Wire insulation*] (AAG)
**HEG** .......... Helium Gauge (MCD)
**HEG** .......... Hemgold Resources Ltd. [*Vancouver Stock Exchange symbol*]
**HEG** .......... Histioeosinophilic Granuloma [*Medicine*]
**HEG** .......... Jacksonville, FL [*Location identifier*] [*FAA*] (FAAL)
**Hegel-Jrbh** ... Hegel-Jahrbuch [*A publication*]
**Hegel-Stud** ... Hegel-Studien [*A publication*]
**HEGF** ........ High-Energy Gas Fracturing [*For freeing natural gas from rock*]
**HEGF** ........ Human Epidermal Growth Factor [*Biochemistry*]
**HEGIS** ....... Higher Education General Information Survey [*Office of Education*]
**HEGN** ....... Hurghada [*Egypt*] [*ICAO location identifier*] (ICLI)
**HEGR** ....... El-Gora [*Egypt*] [*ICAO location identifier*] (ICLI)
**HEGR** ....... High-Energy Gamma Ray
**HEGS** ........ Helicopter External Gondola System
**HEGV** ....... Helium Gauge Valve (MCD)
**HEH** .......... Heho [*Burma*] [*Airport symbol*] (OAG)
**HEH** .......... His [*or Her*] Exalted Highness [*Term applied only to personages of British India*]
**HEH** .......... (Hydroxyethyl)hydrazine [*Organic chemistry*]
**HEH** .......... Newark, OH [*Location identifier*] [*FAA*] (FAAL)
**HEHF** ........ Hanford Environmental Health Foundation [*Nuclear energy*]
**HEHO** ....... Herbert Hoover National Historic Site
**HEHUA** .... Herba Hungarica [*A publication*]
**HEHYDD** ... Health and Hygiene [*A publication*]
**HEI** ........... Handelsreiziger [*A publication*]
**HEI** ........... Hangar Engineering Item
**HEI** ........... Health Effects Institute [*Research center*] (RCD)
**HEI** ........... Health and Energy Institute (EA)
**HEI** ........... Heat Exchange Institute (EA)
**HEI** ........... HEICO Corp. [*AMEX symbol*] (SPSG)
**HEI** ........... Heidelberg [*Konigstuhl*] [*Federal Republic of Germany*] [*Seismograph station code, US Geological Survey*] (SEIS)
**HEI** ........... Heidelberg College, Tiffin, OH [*OCLC symbol*] (OCLC)
**HEI** ........... Hettinger, ND [*Location identifier*] [*FAA*] (FAAL)
**HEI** ........... High-Energy Ignition (KSC)
**HEI** ........... High-Explosive, Incendiary [*Weaponry*]
**HEI** ........... Higher Education Institution
**HEI** ........... Hospice Education Institute (EA)
**HEI** ........... Hourly Earnings Index (OICC)
**HEI** ........... House Ear Institute (EA)
**HEI** ........... Human Engineering Institute
**HEI** ........... Humidity-Electronic Indicator
**HEIAC** ...... Hydraulic Engineering Information Analysis Center [*Army Corps of Engineers*] (IID)
**HEIAS** ....... Human Engineering Information and Analysis Service [*Tufts University*]
**HEIB** ......... Home Economists in Business (EA)
**HEIC** ......... HEI Corporation [*NASDAQ symbol*] (NQ)
**HEIC** ......... Honourable East India Company [*British*]
**HE-ICM** .... High Explosive - Improved Conventional Ammunition
**HEICN** ...... Honourable East India Company Navy [*British military*] (DMA)
**HEICS** ....... Honourable East India Company's Service [*British*]
**HEIDA** ...... (Hydroxyethyl)iminodiacetic Acid [*Organic chemistry*]
**HEIDELB** ... Heidelberg [*City in Germany*] (ROG)
**Heidelberg Akad Wiss Math Naturwiss Kl Sitzungsber** ... Heidelberger Akademie der Wissenschaften. Mathematisch-Naturwissenschaftliche Klasse. Sitzungsberichte [*West Germany*] [*A publication*]
**Heidelberger Beitr Mineralogie u Petrographie** ... Heidelberger Beitrage zur Mineralogie und Petrographie [*A publication*]
**Heidelb Jahrb** ... Heidelberger Jahrbuecher [*A publication*]
**Heidelb Sci Libr** ... Heidelberg Science Library [*A publication*]
**Heidelb Taschenb** ... Heidelberger Taschenbuecher [*A publication*]
**HEIDI** ....... Higher Education Data Base [*Information service or system*] (EISS)
**HeidJb** ....... Heidelberger Jahrbuecher [*A publication*]
**Heid Sitzb** ... Heidelberger Akademie der Wissenschaften. Sitzungsberichte [*A publication*]
**HEIFER** .... High Frequency Relay (NVT)
**HEIG** ......... Handbook of Environmental Isotope Geochemistry [*Elsevier Book Series*] [*A publication*]
**HEII** .......... HEI, Incorporated [*NASDAQ symbol*] (NQ)
**Heil Gewuerz-Pflanz** ... Heil Gewuerz-Pflanzen [*A publication*]
**Heilpaedagog Forsch** ... Heilpaedagogische Forschung [*A publication*]
**Heilpaed For** ... Heilpaedagogische Forschung [*A publication*]
**Hein** ........... Heineccius. Elementa Juris Naturae et Gentium [*A publication*] (DLA)
**Hein** ........... William S. Hein and Co., Inc. [*Publisher*] (DLA)
**Heinecc Ant Rom** ... Heineccius. Antiquitatum Romanarum [*Roman Antiquities*] [*A publication*] (DLA)
**Heinecc de Camb** ... Heineccius. Elementa Juris Cambialis [*A publication*] (DLA)
**Heinecc Elem** ... Heineccius. Elementa Juris Civilis [*Elements of the Civil Law*] [*A publication*] (DLA)
**Heinec Elem Jur Camb** ... Heineccius. Elementa Juris Cambialis [*A publication*] (DLA)
**Heinec Elem Jur Civ** ... Heineccius. Elementa Juris Civilis [*Elements of the Civil Law*] [*A publication*] (DLA)
**HeineJ** ....... Heine-Jahrbuch [*A publication*]
**Heine-Jahrb** ... Heine-Jahrbuch [*A publication*]
**HEIP** ......... High-Explosive, Incendiary Plug [*Weaponry*] (NATG)
**HEIS** .......... High-Energy Ion Scattering Spectroscopy
**HEISD** ....... High-Explosive, Incendiary Self-Destroying [*Weaponry*] (NATG)
**Heisk** ......... Heiskell's Tennessee Supreme Court Reports [*1870-74*] [*A publication*] (DLA)
**Heisk (Tenn)** ... Heiskell's Tennessee Reports [*48-59 Tennessee*] [*A publication*] (DLA)
**HEIT** ......... High-Explosive, Incendiary [*Shell*] Traced [*i.e., fitted with tracer*] [*Weaponry*]
**HEITDISD** ... High-Explosive, Incendiary Tracer, Dark Ignition, Self-Destroying [*Weaponry*] (NATG)
**HEITSD** .... High-Explosive, Incendiary Tracer, Self-Destroying [*Weaponry*] (NATG)
**Heiz Lueft Haustech** ... Heizung, Lueftung, Haustechnik [*Later, HLH. Zeitschrift fuer Heizung, Lueftung, Klimatechnik, Haustechnik*] [*A publication*]
**Heizung-Lueftung Haustech** ... Heizung, Lueftung, Haustechnik [*Later, HLH. Zeitschrift fuer Heizung, Lueftung, Klimatechnik, Haustechnik*] [*West Germany*] [*A publication*]
**HEK** .......... Heavy Enamel Single Cellophane [*Wire insulation*] (AAG)
**HEK** .......... Hemingway, SC [*Location identifier*] [*FAA*] (FAAL)
**HEK** .......... Human Embryonic Kidney [*Type of cell line*]
**HEKB** ........ El Nakab/El Nakab [*Egypt*] [*ICAO location identifier*] (ICLI)
**HEKN** ........ Heekin Can, Inc. [*Cincinnati, OH*] [*NASDAQ symbol*] (NQ)
**HEKOD** ..... Herder Korrespondenz [*A publication*]
**HEL** .......... Handbooks of English Literature [*A publication*]
**Hel** ............ Helena [*of Gorgias*] [*Classical studies*] (OCD)
**Hel** ............ Helena [*of Euripides*] [*Classical studies*] (OCD)
**Hel** ............ Helicon [*A publication*]
**HEL** .......... Helicopter (AABC)
**Hel** ............ Heliodor [*Record label*] [*Great Britain*]
**hel** ............ Heliotrope [*Philately*]
**Hel** ............ Hellas-Jahrbuch [*A publication*]

**HEL**.......... Hellenic Resources [*Vancouver Stock Exchange symbol*]
**Hel**............ Hellenistic [*Period*]
**HEL**.......... Helsingfors [*Helsinki*] [*Finland*] [*Seismograph station code, US Geological Survey*] (SEIS)
**HEL**.......... Helsinki [*Finland*] [*Airport symbol*] (OAG)
**HEL**.......... Helvetia [*Switzerland*] (ROG)
**HEL**.......... Hen-Egg White Lysozyme [*Also, HEWL*] [*An enzyme*]
**HEL**.......... High-Energy LASER
**HEL**.......... History of English Law, Edited by W. Holdsworth [*A publication*] (DLA)
**HEL**.......... Home Equity Loan
**HEL**.......... Hugoniot Elastic Limit [*Thermodynamics*]
**HEL**.......... Human Embryonic Lung [*Type of cell line*]
**HEL**.......... Human Engineering Laboratory [*Aberdeen Proving Ground, MD*] [*Army*]
**HEL**.......... Human Erythroleukemia [*Type of cell line*]
**HEL**.......... Hydraulic Engineering Laboratory [*University of California at Berkeley*]
**HeLa**.......... Henrietta Lacks [*Pseudonym, Helen Lane*] [*Type of cell line*]
**HELAB**...... High-Energy LASER Assessment Board (MCD)
**HELABA**... Hessische Landesbank-Girozentrale [*Hessian National Bank*] [*Federal Republic of Germany*]
**HELAIRDET** ... Helicopter Air Detachment [*Canadian Navy*]
**HELANTISUBRON** ... Helicopter Antisubmarine Squadron [*Navy*]
**HELASRON** ... Helicopter Antisubmarine Squadron [*Navy*]
**HELAST**... Human Engineering Laboratory Armor Systems Test [*Army*] (RDA)
**HELB** ........ High-Energy LASER Beam
**HELB** ........ High-Energy Line Break [*Nuclear energy*] (NRCH)
**HELBAT**... Human Engineering Laboratories Battalion Artillery Test [*Army*]
**HELCAR**... Helicopter Collision Avoidance RADAR (NG)
**HELCIS** .... Helicopter Command Instrumentation System (MCD)
**HELCM** .... High-Energy LASER Countermeasures (MCD)
**HELCO** ..... Hartford Electric Light Company
**HELCOM** ... Baltic Marine Environment Protection Commission - Helsinki Commission (EAIO)
**HELCOS**... High-Energy LASER Component Servicing (MCD)
**HELDREF** ... Helen Dwight Reid Educational Foundation
**HELE** ........ Helen of Troy Corp. [*NASDAQ symbol*] (NQ)
**HELEN** ..... Hydrogenous Exponential Liquid Experiment [*British*]
**HELEX**...... Helium Extraction
**HELF**......... Human Embryonic Lung Fibroblasts [*Biochemistry*]
**HELFAST** ... Human Engineering Laboratory Forward Area Supply and Transfer [*Army*] (RDA)
**Helgolander Wiss Meeresunters Mar Invest** ... Helgolaender Wissenschaftliche Meeresuntersuchungen/Marine Investigations [*A publication*]
**Helgol Meeresunters** ... Helgolaender Meeresuntersuchungen [*A publication*]
**Helgol Wiss Meeresunters** ... Helgolaender Wissenschaftliche Meeresuntersuchungen [*A publication*]
**Helg W Meer** ... Helgolaender Wissenschaftliche Meeresuntersuchungen [*A publication*]
**HELHAT**.. Human Engineering Laboratory Helicopter Armament Test [*Army*] (RDA)
**HELI** ......... Helicopter (AFM)
**Helicop Wld** ... Helicopter World [*A publication*]
**Heli Intnl** ... Helicopter International [*A publication*]
**Helikon**...... Helikon. Revista di Tradizione e Cultura Classica dell'Universita di Messina [*A publication*]
**HELILEX** ... Helicopter Landing Exercise [*Amphibious*] [*Navy*] (NVT)
**Helinium**.... Helinium. Revue Consacree a l'Archeologie des Pays-Bas de la Belgique et du Grand Duche de Luxembourg [*A publication*]
**HELIOD** ... Heliodorus [*Greek writer, c. 200AD*] (ROG)
**Heliogab** .... Heliogabalus [*of Scriptores Historiae Augustae*] [*Classical studies*] (OCD)
**Helios**......... Helios - Joies de la Musique [*Record label*] [*France*]
**HELIOS**.... Heteropowered Earth-Launched Inter-Orbital Spacecraft (KSC)
**HELIP**....... HAWK [*Homing All the Way Killer*] European Limited Improvement Program [*NATO*]
**HELIPATH** ... Helicopter Position and Terrain Height
**HELIST** .... Human Engineering Laboratory Infantry System Test [*Army*] (RDA)
**HELITEAM** ... Helicopter Team
**HELITECH** ... International Helicopter Technology and Operations Conference and Exhibition [*British*] (ITD)
**Heli World** ... Helicopter World [*A publication*]
**Hell**........... Hellenica [*of Xenophon*] [*Classical studies*] (OCD)
**HELL**......... Higher Education Learning Laboratory (EA)
**Hell Adelphe** ... Hellenis Adelphe [*A publication*]
**HellasJB**.... Hellas-Jahrbuch [*A publication*]
**Hell Dicht**.. Hellenistische Dichtung in der Zeit des Kallimachos [*A publication*] (OCD)
**Hellen** ........ Hellenika [*Salonika*] [*A publication*]
**Hellenika Jb** ... Hellenika. Jahrbuch fuer die Freunde Griechenlands [*A publication*]
**Hellenika (S)** ... Hellenika (Salonika) [*A publication*]
**HELLFIRE** ... Heliborne LASER Fire and Forget [*Missile system*] [*Army*] (RDA)
**HELLFIRE/GLD** ... HELLFIRE [*Heliborne LASER Fire and Forget*]/ Ground LASER Designator [*Army*] (RDA)
**Hell Kteniatr** ... Hellenike Kteniatrike [*A publication*]
**Hell Mikrobiol Hygieinol Hetaireia Delt** ... Hellenike Mikrobiologike kai Hygieinologike Hetaireia Deltion [*A publication*]
**HELLOG** .. Human Engineering Laboratory Logistics [*Systems concept study*] (MCD)
**Hell Oxy**.... Hellenica Oxyrhynchia [*Classical studies*] (OCD)
**HELLP**...... Hemolysis, Elevated Liver Enzymes, and Low Platelet Count [*Clinical chemistry*]
**Hell Stomatol Chron** ... Hellenika Stomatologika Chronika [*A publication*]
**Hell Vet Med** ... Hellenic Veterinary Medicine [*A publication*]
**Helm**.......... Helm's Reports [*2-9 Nevada*] [*A publication*] (DLA)
**Helminth Abstr** ... Helminthological Abstracts [*A publication*]
**Helminthol** ... Helminthologia [*A publication*]
**HELMS**..... Helicopter Multifunction System
**HELN**........ Hubungan Ekonomi Luar Negeri [*Foreign Economic Relations*] [*Indonesian*]
**HELNAVS** ... Helicopter Navigation System (RDA)
**HELO**........ Helicopter (NG)
**HELO**........ High-Energy Liquid Oxidizer
**HELO**........ Hispanic Elected Local Officials (EA)
**HELOA**..... Helgolaender Wissenschaftliche Meeresuntersuchungen [*A publication*]
**HELOQUALS** ... Helicopter Qualifications [*Navy*] (NVT)
**HELORADE** ... Helicopter Operations in Selected RADAR Environment (MCD)
**HELOS**...... Highly Eccentric Lunar Occultation Satellite
**HELOSID** ... Helicopter-Delivered Seismic Intrusion Detector (NVT)
**HELOTNG** ... Helicopter Training (NVT)
**HELP**......... Harlem Eastside Lifesaving Program [*Television program*]
**HELP**......... Hawaii Early Learning Profile [*Child development test*] [*Psychology*]
**HELP**......... Health Education, Liaison, and Promotion [*South Australian Health Commission*]
**HELP**......... Health Education Library Program [*Library network*]
**HELP**......... Health and Energy Learning Project (EA)
**HELP**......... Health Evaluation and Learning Program
**HELP**......... Heat Escape Lessening Posture [*First aid technique*]
**HELP**......... Heavy Vehicle Electronic License Plate
**HELP**......... Helicopter Electronic Landing Path [*Army*]
**HELP**......... Helium Liquid Program [*NASA*]
**HELP**......... Help Establish Lasting Peace
**HELP**......... HELP, International [*Defunct*] (EA)
**HELP**......... Helping Early Leavers Program [*Australia*]
**HELP**......... Heroin Emergency Life Project
**HELP**......... Herpetics Engaged in Living Productively [*Later, Herpes Research Center*] (EA)
**HELP**......... High-Energy Lightweight Propellant
**HELP**......... Highly Extendable Language Processor [*Data processing*]
**HELP**......... Highway Emergency Locating Plan
**HELP**......... Home Education Livelihood Program [*New Mexico*]
**HELP**......... Home Emergency Ladies' Pal [*Book title*]
**HELP**......... Homophile Effort for Legal Protection [*An association*] [*Defunct*] (EA)
**HELP**......... Honeywell Equipment Lease Plan
**HELP**......... Hospital Equipment Loan Project
**HELP**......... Housewives Elect Lower Prices [*New York women's lobby group*]
**HELP**......... Howitzer Extended Life Program
**HELP**......... Hughes Emergency Locator Pack
**HELP**......... Student Aide Centers of America, Inc. [*Hauppauge, NY*] [*NASDAQ symbol*] (NQ)
**HELPIS**..... Higher Education Learning Programmes Information Service [*British Universities Film & Video Council*] [*Database*]
**Help Person Group** ... Helping Person in the Group [*A publication*]
**HELPR**...... Handbook of Electronic Parts Reliability
**HELPS**...... Handicapped Education Learner's Planning System [*Battelle Memorial Institute*] [*Information service or system*] (IID)
**HELPS**...... Health Environment Long-Range Planning Support [*A computer model*]
**HELPS**...... Helmet-Position Sensing System
**HELPS**...... Highway Emergency Locating Paging Service [*For motorist assistance*]
**HELRAS**... Helicopter Long-Range Acoustic Sensor [*Military*] (CAAL)
**HELRATS** ... High-Energy LASER RADAR Acquisition and Tracking System (MCD)
**HELREC**... Health Record
**HELRG**..... High-Energy LASER Review Group [*Terminated, 1977*] [*DoD*]
**HELS**......... High-Energy LASER System
**Helsingin Tek Korkeakoulu Tiet Julk** ... Helsingin Teknillinen Korkeakoulu Tieteellisia Julkaisuja [*A publication*]
**Helsinki Univ Technol Lab Phys Res Rep** ... Helsinki University of Technology. Laboratory of Physics. Research Report [*A publication*]
**Helsinki Univ Technol Res Pap** ... Helsinki University of Technology. Research Papers [*A publication*]
**HELST**...... Helston [*Municipal borough in England*]
**HELSTF**.... High-Energy LASER System Test Facility (MCD)
**HELSUPPRON** ... Helicopter Combat Support Squadron [*Navy*]
**HELTADS** ... High-Energy LASER Tactical Air Defense System

**HELTAS** ... High-Energy LASER Technology Applications Study (MCD)
**HELTRARON** ... Helicopter Training Squadron [*Navy*]
**Helv** ............ Ad Helviam [*of Seneca the Younger*] [*Classical studies*] (OCD)
**Helv A** ......... Helvetia Archaeologica [*A publication*]
**Helv Chim A** ... Helvetica Chimica Acta [*A publication*]
**Helv Chim Acta** ... Helvetica Chimica Acta [*A publication*]
**Helv Chir Acta** ... Helvetica Chirurgica Acta [*A publication*]
**Helv Chir Acta Suppl** ... Helvetica Chirurgica Acta. Supplementum [*A publication*]
**Helvet Arch** ... Helvetia Archaeologica [*A publication*]
**Helvetica Odontol Acta Suppl** ... Helvetica Odontologica Acta. Supplementum [*A publication*]
**Helv Med Acta** ... Helvetica Medica Acta [*A publication*]
**Helv Med Acta Suppl** ... Helvetica Medica Acta. Supplementum [*A publication*]
**Helv Odon A** ... Helvetica Odontologica Acta [*A publication*]
**Helv Odontol Acta** ... Helvetica Odontologica Acta [*A publication*]
**Helv Paed A** ... Helvetica Paediatrica Acta [*A publication*]
**Helv Paediat Acta** ... Helvetica Paediatrica Acta [*A publication*]
**Helv Paediatr Acta** ... Helvetica Paediatrica Acta [*A publication*]
**Helv Paediatr Acta Suppl** ... Helvetica Paediatrica Acta. Supplementum [*A publication*]
**Helv Phys A** ... Helvetica Physica Acta [*A publication*]
**Helv Phys Acta** ... Helvetica Physica Acta [*A publication*]
**Helv Phys Acta Suppl** ... Helvetica Physica Acta. Supplementum [*A publication*]
**Helv Physiol Pharmac Acta** ... Helvetica Physiologica et Pharmacologica Acta [*A publication*]
**Helv Physiol Pharmacol Acta** ... Helvetica Physiologica et Pharmacologica Acta [*A publication*]
**Helv Physiol Pharmacol Acta Suppl** ... Helvetica Physiologica et Pharmacologica Acta. Supplementum [*A publication*]
**HELWS** ..... High-Energy LASER Weapon System (MCD)
**HELX** ........ Helix Technology Corp. [*NASDAQ symbol*] (NQ)
**HELX** ........ Luxor [*Egypt*] [*ICAO location identifier*] (ICLI)
**HEM** .......... Hall Effect Multiplier
**HEM** .......... Handbook on Emergency Measures (NATG)
**HEM** .......... Hatchlike Experiment Module [*NASA*] (NASA)
**HEM** .......... Heat Exchanger Method (RDA)
**HEM** .......... Hematite [*A mineral*]
**HEM** .......... Hematology [*Medicine*] (DHSM)
**HEM** .......... Hemisphere
**HEM** .......... Hemlo Gold Mines, Inc. [*Toronto Stock Exchange symbol*] [*Vancouver Stock Exchange symbol*]
**HEM** .......... Hemolysis [*Medicine*]
**HEM** .......... HEPES-Buffered EMEM
**HEM** .......... Hitchhike Experiment Module (MCD)
**HEM** .......... Homogeneous Equilibrium Model (NRCH)
**HEM** .......... Hybrid Electromagnetic [*Wave*]
**HEM** .......... Hydroxyethylmorpholine [*Organic chemistry*]
**Hem** ........... Ons Hemecht [*A publication*]
**HEM** .......... Sparta, TN [*Location identifier*] [*FAA*] (FAAL)
**HEMA** ....... Health Education Media Association (EA)
**HEMA** ....... HemaCare Corp. [*Sherman Oaks, CA*] [*NASDAQ symbol*] (NQ)
**HEMA** ....... Hot Melt Equipment Manufacturers Association (EA)
**HEMA** ....... Hydroxyethyl Methacrylate [*Organic chemistry*]
**HEMAC** ..... Hybrid Electromagnetic Antenna Coupler
**HEMAEZ** ... Hematology [*New York*] [*A publication*]
**HEMAR** ..... Human Engineering Criteria for Maintenance and Repair [*GE, NASA*]
**HEMAT** .... Hematology [*Medicine*]
**hemat ab** .... Hematologic Abnormality [*Medicine*]
**Hematol** ..... Hematology [*Medicine*]
**Hematol Onc** ... Hematological Oncology [*A publication*]
**Hematol Oncol** ... Hematological Oncology [*A publication*]
**HEME** ....... Hemokinetics, Inc. [*NASDAQ symbol*] (NQ)
**HEME** ....... Hostile Electromagnetic Emission (MCD)
**HEME** ....... Hydroxyethyl Methyl (Cellulose) [*Organic chemistry*]
**HEMEA** .... Hemel en Dampkring [*A publication*]
**HEMEDC** ... Helgolaender Meeresuntersuchungen [*A publication*]
**HEMF** ....... Handling Equipment Maintenance Facility [*Charleston Naval Shipyard*]
**HEMI** ........ Hemiparalysis [*Medicine*]
**HEMI** ........ Hemiplegia [*Medicine*]
**HEMI** ........ Hemispherical [*Automotive engineering*]
**HEMI** ........ Hemispherical [*S-band antenna*]
**Hemijska Ind** ... Hemijska Industrija [*A publication*]
**Hem Ind** ..... Hemijska Industrija [*A publication*]
**Heming** ...... Hemingway's Mississippi Reports [*A publication*] (DLA)
**Heming (Miss)** ... Hemingway's Mississippi Reports [*A publication*] (DLA)
**HEMIS** ...... Hemisphere (AFM)
**Hemis** ........ Hemisphere [*A publication*] (APTA)
**HEMISEARCH** ... Hemispherical Search [*First frequency-scanning RADAR*] (MCD)
**HEMLAW** ... Helicopter Mounted LASER Weapon (MCD)
**HEMLOC** ... Health and Medical Libraries On-Line Catalogue [*Australian Commonwealth Department of Health*] [*Information service or system*] (ADA)
**HEMLOC** ... Heliborne Emitter Location/Countermeasures
**Hem & M** ... Hemming and Miller's English Vice-Chancellors' Reports [*A publication*] (DLA)
**HEMM** ...... Mersa-Matruh [*Egypt*] [*ICAO location identifier*] (ICLI)
**Hemmant** ... Hemmant's Select Cases in Exchequer Chamber [*Selden Society Publications, Vol. 51*] [*1377-1460*] [*A publication*] (DLA)
**Hem & M (Eng)** ... Hemming and Miller's English Vice-Chancellors' Reports [*A publication*] (DLA)
**Hem & Mill** ... Hemming and Miller's English Vice-Chancellors' Reports [*A publication*] (DLA)
**HEMMS** ... Hand-Emplaced Minefield Marking System (MCD)
**HEMO** ...... HemoTec, Inc. [*NASDAQ symbol*] (NQ)
**HEMOA** .... Hemostase [*A publication*]
**HEMOD** .... Hemoglobin [*A publication*]
**HEMOR** .... Hemorrhage [*Medicine*]
**Hemp** ......... Hempstead's Arkansas Reports [*A publication*] (DLA)
**Hemp** ......... Hempstead's United States Circuit Court Reports [*A publication*] (DLA)
**HEMP** ....... High-Altitude Electromagnetic Pulse (MCD)
**HEMPA** .... Hexamethylphosphoric Triamide [*Also, HMP, HMPA, HMPT, HPT*] [*Organic chemistry*] (MCD)
**HEMPAS** ... Hereditary Erythroblastic Multinuclearity Associated with a Positive Acidified-Serum Test [*Hematology*]
**HEMPE** .... Henry, Edward, Mary, Philip, Elizabeth [*Bacon's prophecy*]
**Hempst** ...... Hempstead's Arkansas Reports [*A publication*] (DLA)
**Hempst** ...... Hempstead's United States Circuit Court Reports [*A publication*] (DLA)
**HemR** ......... Hemingway Review [*A publication*]
**HEMT** ....... High Electron Mobility Transistor [*Data processing*]
**HEMTT** .... Heavy Expanded Mobility Tactical Truck [*Army*] (RDA)
**HEMT/UMHE** ... Higher Education Ministries Team/United Ministries in Higher Education (EA)
**HEMV** ....... Helium Manual Valve (MCD)
**HEMW** ...... Hybrid Electromagnetic Wave (MSA)
**HEN** .......... Harris Electronic News [*Service suspended*] [*Information service or system*] (IID)
**HEN** .......... Heat-Exchanger Network [*Chemical engineering*]
**HEN** .......... Hengchun [*Republic of China*] [*Seismograph station code, US Geological Survey*] (SEIS)
**HEN** .......... Henley International, Inc. [*AMEX symbol*] (SPSG)
**Hen** ........... Henricus Boich [*Flourished, 1320-30*] [*Authority cited in pre-1607 legal work*] (DSA)
**Hen** ........... Henry (King of England) (DLA)
**HEN** .......... Home Entertainment Network [*Cable-television system*]
**HENA** ........ Hemeroteca Nacional [*Database*] [*Ministerio de Cultura*] [*Spanish*] [*Information service or system*] (CRD)
**Hen Am Pl** ... Hening's American Pleader [*A publication*] (DLA)
**Hen Bl** ........ [*Henry*] Blackstone's English Common Pleas Reports [*1788-96*] [*A publication*] (DLA)
**Hen Bo** ....... Henricus Boich [*Flourished, 1320-30*] [*Authority cited in pre-1607 legal work*] (DSA)
**HEND** ....... Henderson Petroleum Corp. [*NASDAQ symbol*] (NQ)
**Hen For L** .. Henry on Foreign Law [*A publication*] (DLA)
**Hen Forms** ... Hennell's Forms [*A publication*] (DLA)
**HENG** ....... [*The*] Henley Group, Inc. [*NASDAQ symbol*] (NQ)
**HENILAS** ... Helicopter Night-Landing System
**Hen JP** ....... Hening's Virginia Justice of the Peace [*A publication*] (DLA)
**Hen LA Dig** ... Hennen's Louisiana Digest [*A publication*] (DLA)
**Hen Law** .... Hennepin Lawyer [*A publication*] (DLA)
**Hen & M** .... Hening and Munford's Virginia Supreme Court Reports [*1806-10*] [*A publication*] (DLA)
**Hen Man Cas** ... Henry's Manumission Cases [*A publication*] (DLA)
**Hen Max** .... Hening's Maxims [*A publication*] (DLA)
**Hen & Mun** ... Hening and Munford's Reports [*11-14 Virginia*] [*A publication*] (DLA)
**Hennepin Law** ... Hennepin Lawyer [*A publication*]
**HENP** ........ High Energy and Nuclear Physics Program [*Department of Energy*]
**HENRE** ..... High-Energy Neutron Reactions Experiment [*Nuclear energy*]
**Henric** ........ Henricus Boich [*Flourished, 1320-30*] [*Authority cited in pre-1607 legal work*] (DSA)
**Henry E Sigerist Suppl Bull Hist Med** ... Henry E. Sigerist Supplements. Bulletin of the History of Medicine [*A publication*]
**Henry Ford Hosp Med Bull** ... Henry Ford Hospital. Medical Bulletin [*A publication*]
**Henry Ford Hosp Med J** ... Henry Ford Hospital. Medical Journal [*A publication*]
**Henry Judg** ... Henry's Judgment in Ordwin V. Forbes [*A publication*] (DLA)
**Hen St** ........ Hening's Statutes [*Virginia*] [*A publication*] (DLA)
**Hent Forms** ... Hent's Forms and Use of Blanks in California [*A publication*] (DLA)
**HENV** ........ New Valley [*Egypt*] [*ICAO location identifier*] (ICLI)
**HEO** .......... High Earth Orbit (IEEE)
**HEO** .......... High-Energy Orbit [*NASA*] (NASA)
**HEO** .......... Higher Executive Officer [*Civil service*] [*British*]
**HEO** .......... Higher Executive Order
**HEO(A)** ..... Higher Executive Officer (Administration) [*Civil service*] [*British*]
**HEOB** ........ High-Energy Organic Battery
**HEOC** ........ Higher Education Opportunities Committee (EA)
**HEOD** ....... Hexachloroepoxyoctahydro-exo-endo-dimethanonaphthalene [*Dieldrin*] [*Insecticide*]

**HEOEBS**... High-Energy Organic Electrolyte Battery System
**Heohr Zb Lviv Vida Heohr Tov Ukr SSR** ... Heohragicheskyi Zbirnyk L'vivs'koho Vida Heohraficheskoho Tovarystva Ukrains'koho SSR [*A publication*]
**HEOP**........ Higher Equal Opportunity Program [*Education*]
**HEOS**........ Highly Eccentric [*or Elliptical*] Orbit Satellite
**HEOY**........ Handicapped Employee of the Year [*Award given to federal employees*] (RDA)
**HEP**.......... Hall Effect Probe
**HEP**.......... Hallwood Energy Corp. [*AMEX symbol*] (SPSG)
**HEP**.......... HEP [*Higher Education Publications*] Higher Education Directory [*A publication*]
**HEP**.......... Hepatic [*Pertaining to the liver*] [*Pharmacy*] (ROG)
**HEP**.......... Hepatoerythropoietic Porphyria [*Medicine*]
**HEP**.......... Heterogeneous Element Processor [*Data processing*] (RDA)
**HEP**.......... Hi-Peg Resources Ltd. [*Vancouver Stock Exchange symbol*]
**HEP**.......... High Egg Passage [*Rabies vaccine*]
**HEP**.......... High-Energy Particle
**HEP**.......... High-Energy Phosphate [*Biochemistry*]
**HEP**.......... High-Energy Physics
**HEP**.......... High-Energy Pulse
**HEP**.......... High-Explosive Plastic [*Weaponry*]
**HEP**.......... High-Explosive Plugged [*Weaponry*]
**HEP**.......... High School Equivalency Program
**HEP**.......... Higher Education Panel (EA)
**HEP**.......... Histamine Equivalent Prick Unit [*Immunology*]
**HEP**.......... Hole-Electron Pair
**HEP**.......... Hong Kong Economic Papers [*A publication*]
**HEP**.......... Human Engineering Plan
**HEp**.......... Human Epithelial [*Cells*]
**HEP**.......... Human Error Probability (IEEE)
**HEP**.......... Hydrazine Electrolysis Plenum
**HEP**.......... Hydroelectric Plant
**HEP**.......... Hydroelectric Power
**HEP**.......... Hydrogen Embrittlement Proof
**HEPA**........ High-Efficiency Particle Accumulator (NASA)
**HEPA**........ High-Efficiency Particulate Air [*Filter*]
**HEPAD**..... High-Energy Proton and Alpha Detector
**HEPADF**... Hepatology Research and Clinical Issues [*A publication*]
**HEPALIS** ... Higher Education Policy and Administration Library and Information Service
**HEPAP**...... High-Energy Physics Advisory Panel [*Department of Energy*] [*Washington, DC*] (EGAO)
**HEPAT**...... High-Explosive Plastic Antitank [*Weaponry*] (NATG)
**Hepato-Gastroenterol** ... Hepato-Gastroenterology [*A publication*]
**Hepatol (Amst)** ... Journal of Hepatology (Amsterdam) [*A publication*]
**Hepb**.......... Hepburn's Reports [*California*] [*A publication*] (DLA)
**Hepb**.......... Hepburn's Reports [*Pennsylvania*] [*A publication*] (DLA)
**HEPB**........ High-Energy Pipe Break [*Nuclear energy*] (NRCH)
**HEPCA**..... Heavy Engineering Projects Corporation of Australia
**HEPCA**..... House Employees Position Classification Act [*1964*]
**HEPCAT**... Helicopter Pilot Control and Training
**HE-PD**....... High-Explosive - Point Detonating [*Weaponry*] (MCD)
**HEPDEX**... High-Energy Proton Detection Experiment
**HEPDNP**.. High-Explosive, Point Detonating Nose Plug [*Weaponry*] (NATG)
**HEPES**...... Hydroxyethylpiperazineethanesulfonic Acid [*A buffer*]
**HEPIA**....... High Energy Physics Index [*A publication*]
**HEPL**........ High-Energy Physics Laboratory [*Stanford University*] (MCD)
**HEPM**....... Hispanic Employment Program Manager [*DoD*]
**HEPM**....... Human Embryonic Palatal Mesenchymal [*Type of cell line*]
**HEPP**........ High-Energy Particle Physics Group [*Florida State University*] [*Research center*] (RCD)
**HEPP**........ Northwest Association of Horticulturists, Entomologists, and Plant Pathologists [*Defunct*] (EA)
**HEPPS**...... Hydroxyethylpiperazinepropanesulfonic Acid [*A buffer*]
**HEPS**........ High-Energy Particle Spectrometer (MCD)
**HEPS**........ Port Said [*Egypt*] [*ICAO location identifier*] (ICLI)
**HEP-T**...... High-Explosive Plastic Tracer [*Weaponry*] (AABC)
**HEP-UP**.... High School Education Program at University of Pennsylvania
**HE-PX**....... High-Explosive Proximity Fuse [*Weaponry*] (MCD)
**HEQ**.......... Holyoke, CO [*Location identifier*] [*FAA*] (FAAL)
**HER**.......... Harvard Educational Review [*A publication*]
**Her**........... Haver [*Credit*] [*Business term*] [*Portuguese*]
**HER**.......... Health and Education Resources (EA)
**HER**.......... Heraklion [*Greece*] [*Airport symbol*] (OAG)
**Her**........... Herald [*Record label*] [*Great Britain*]
**HER**.......... Heraldry
**Her**........... Hercules [*Constellation*]
**her**........... Herero [*MARC language code*] [*Library of Congress*] (LCCP)
**HER**.......... Heres [*Heir*] [*Legal term*] [*Latin*]
**HER**.......... Heritage Petroleum [*Vancouver Stock Exchange symbol*]
**Her**........... Hermannus [*Authority cited in pre-1607 legal work*] (DSA)
**HER**.......... Hermanus [*South Africa*] [*Seismograph station code, US Geological Survey*] (SEIS)
**HER**.......... Hermanus [*South Africa*] [*Geomagnetic observatory code*]
**Her**........... Herne's Law of Charitable Uses [*A publication*] (DLA)
**Her**........... Herodian [*Period*]
**Her**........... Heroides [*of Ovid*] [*Classical studies*] (OCD)
**HER**.......... Hershey Foods Corp., Hershey, PA [*OCLC symbol*] (OCLC)
**HER**.......... High-Efficiency Radiator [*General Motors Corp.*] [*Automotive engineering*]
**HER**.......... High-Energy Ray
**HER**.......... High-Energy Rotor [*Helicopter*] [*Army*]
**HER**.......... HIM [*Hardware Interface Module*] Equipment Rack [*NASA*] (NASA)
**HER**.......... Horizontal Earth Rate
**HER**.......... Human EGF [*Epidermal Growth Factor*] Receptor [*Biochemistry*]
**HER**.......... Human Embryonic Retinoblast
**HER**.......... Human Error Rate
**HER**.......... Human Estrogen Receptor [*Endocrinology*]
**HER**.......... Hydrogen Evolution Reaction [*Metallurgy*]
**HER**.......... Hyperenvironmental RADAR
**Her**........... Quis Rerum Divinarum Heres [*Philo*] (BJA)
**HERA**........ Hadron-Elektron-Ring Anlage [*Hadron-Electron Ring Accelerator*] [*Germany*]
**HERA**........ Heritage Australia Information System [*Australian Heritage Commission*] [*Information service or system*] (IID)
**HERA**........ High-Explosive Rocket Assisted [*Weaponry*]
**HERA**........ Homemakers Equal Rights Association (EA)
**HERAC**..... Health and Environmental Research Advisory Committee [*Department of Energy*] [*Washington, DC*] (EGAO)
**Heracl**........ Heraclidae [*of Euripides*] [*Classical studies*] (OCD)
**Heraclid Pont** ... Heraclides Ponticus [*Fourth century BC*] [*Classical studies*] (OCD)
**Her Aconza** ... Henricus Acconzaioco [*Flourished, 1374-82*] [*Authority cited in pre-1607 legal work*] (DSA)
**HERALD**.. Harbor Echo Ranging and Listening Device
**HERALD**.. Highly Enriched Reactor, Aldermaston [*British*] (DEN)
**Herald Lib Sci** ... Herald of Library Science [*A publication*]
**Herald Research Bul** ... Herald Research Bulletin [*A publication*] (APTA)
**HERAP**..... Health and Environmental Risk Analysis Program [*Department of Energy*]
**HERAP**..... Human Error Research and Analysis Program (MCD)
**HERB**........ Herbalife International, Inc. [*NASDAQ symbol*] (NQ)
**HERB**........ Herbalist (ROG)
**Herb Abstr** ... Herbage Abstracts [*A publication*]
**Herbage Abstr** ... Herbage Abstracts [*A publication*]
**Herba Hung** ... Herba Hungarica [*A publication*]
**Herb Ant**.... Herbert's Antiquities of the Inns of Court, Etc. [*A publication*] (DLA)
**Herba Pol**... Herba Polonica [*A publication*]
**HERBIC**.... Herbicide
**HERB RECENT** ... Herbarium Recentium [*Of Fresh Herbs*] [*Pharmacy*]
**HERC**........ Health Economics Research Center [*University of Wisconsin - Madison*] [*Research center*] (RCD)
**Herc**........... Hercules [*Constellation*]
**HERC**........ Home Education Resource Center [*Inactive*] (EA)
**HERCA**..... Hercynia [*A publication*]
**Her Char U** ... Herne's Law of Charitable Uses [*A publication*] (DLA)
**Her Chat**.... Herman on Chattel Mortgages [*A publication*] (DLA)
**Hercul**........ [*Franciscus*] Herculanus [*Flourished, 16th century*] [*Authority cited in pre-1607 legal work*] (DSA)
**HERCULES** ... High-Energy Radiation Camera Using Light-Emitting Showers
**Hercynia Fachgeb Bot-Geogr-Geol Palaeontol-Zool** ... Hercynia fuer die Fachgebiete Botanik-Geographie-Geologie Palaeontologie-Zoologie [*A publication*]
**HERD**........ High-Explosives Research and Development (MCD)
**HerdCor**..... Herder Correspondence [*London/New York*] [*A publication*] (BJA)
**Herder Korresp** ... Herder Korrespondenz [*A publication*]
**HERDET**... Hereby Detached from Duty Assigned [*Military*]
**HerdKor**..... Herder-Korrespondenz [*Freiburg Im Breisgau*] [*A publication*] (BJA)
**HERE**........ Hastings' Encyclopaedia of Religion and Ethics [*A publication*] (BJA)
**HERE**........ Herefordshire [*County in England*]
**HERE**........ Hotel Employees and Restaurant Employees International Union (EA)
**HEREA**..... Hereditas [*A publication*]
**Hered**......... Hereditas [*A publication*]
**Hered**......... Heredity [*A publication*]
**HERED**..... Heredity
**HEREDITS** ... Hereditaments (ROG)
**HEREF**...... Herefordshire [*County in England*]
**Hereford J Sthn Afr** ... Hereford Journal of Southern Africa [*A publication*]
**Hereford Q** ... Hereford Quarterly [*A publication*] (APTA)
**HEREFORDS** ... Herefordshire [*County in England*]
**HEREFS** ... Herefordshire [*County in England*]
**Herenn Modest** ... Herennius Modestinus [*Flourished, 3rd century*] [*Authority cited in pre-1607 legal work*] (DSA)
**Her Est**....... Herman's Law of Estoppel [*A publication*] (DLA)
**Her Ex**....... Herman's Law of Executors [*A publication*] (DLA)
**HERF**........ Hazards of Electromagnetic Radiation to Fuel (TEL)
**HERF**........ High-Energy Rate Forging [*Metalworking*]
**HERF**........ High-Energy Rate Forming
**HERI**......... Heavy Oil/Enhanced Recovery Index [*Alberta Oil Sands Technology and Research Authority*] [*Information service or system*]

**HERI**......... Heritage. Monthly Newsletter. Alaska Office of History and Archaeology [*A publication*]
**HERI**......... Higher Education Research Institute [*University of California, Los Angeles*] [*Research center*]
**HERI**......... Home Economics Research Institute [*Iowa State University*] [*Research center*] (RCD)
**Herion Inf**.. Herion Informationen [*A publication*]
**HERJ**......... High-Explosive Ramjet [*Weaponry*]
**HERJ**......... Home Economics Research Journal [*A publication*]
**Her Jur**...... Heron's Jurisprudence [*1860*] [*A publication*] (DLA)
**HERL**......... Health Effects Research Laboratory [*Environmental Protection Agency*] [*Research Triangle Park, NC*] (GRD)
**Her Libr Sci** ... Herald of Library Science [*A publication*]
**Herm**.......... Hermand's Consistorial Decisions [*Scotland*] [*A publication*] (DLA)
**Herm**.......... Hermogenianus [*Flourished, 4th century*] [*Authority cited in pre-1607 legal work*] (DSA)
**HERMAN** ... Hierarchical Environmental Retrieval for Management and Networking [*Biological Information Service*] [*Riverside, CA*]
**Hermand**.... Hermand's Consistorial Decisions [*Scotland*] [*A publication*] (DLA)
**Herm Chat Mortg** ... Herman on Chattel Mortgages [*A publication*] (DLA)
**Her (Mel)**... Herald (Melbourne) [*A publication*]
**HERMES** ... Heavy Element and Radioactive Material Electromagnetic Separator [*British*]
**Herm Estop** ... Herman's Law of Estoppel [*A publication*] (DLA)
**Hermes Z Kl** ... Hermes. Zeitschrift fuer Klassische Philologie [*A publication*]
**Herm Ex'ns** ... Herman's Law of Executions [*A publication*] (DLA)
**HERMIES** ... Hostile Environment Robotic Machine Intelligence Experiment Series [*Oak Ridge National Laboratory*]
**Hermo**........ Hermogenianus [*Flourished, 4th century*] [*Authority cited in pre-1607 legal work*] (DSA)
**Her Mort** ... Herman on Mortgages of Real Estate [*A publication*] (DLA)
**Hermot**....... Hermotimus [*of Lucian*] [*Classical studies*] (OCD)
**Herm Schil** ... Hermannus Schildis [*Deceased, 1357*] [*Authority cited in pre-1607 legal work*] (DSA)
**Hermsdorfer Tech Mitt** ... Hermsdorfer Technische Mitteilungen [*A publication*]
**HERN**........ Hernia [*or Herniated*] [*Medicine*]
**HERN**........ Ras-Nasrani [*Egypt*] [*ICAO location identifier*] (ICLI)
**HERO**........ Hazards of Electromagnetic Radiation to Ordnance
**HERO**........ Health Education Resource Organization (EA)
**HERO**........ Heath Educational Robot [*Heath Co.*]
**HERO**........ Heritage Education and Review Organization (EA)
**HERO**........ Home Economics Related Occupations
**HERO**........ Hot Experimental Reaction of O Power [*Nuclear energy*]
**Herod**......... Herodas [*Third century BC*] [*Classical studies*] (OCD)
**HEROD**..... Herodotus [*Greek historian, c. 484BC*] [*Classical studies*] (ROG)
**HERODIAN** ... Herodianus [*Greek scholar, c. 200AD*] [*Classical studies*] (ROG)
**Herold**........ Der Herold. Vierteljahrsschrift fuer Heraldik, Genealogie, und Verwandte Wissenschaften [*A publication*]
**Heron (Engl Ed)** ... Heron (English Edition) [*A publication*]
**HERP**........ Hazards of Electromagnetic Radiation to Personnel (TEL)
**HERP**........ Health Education Reports [*A publication*]
**HERP**........ Herpetology
**HERP**........ Human Exposure Dose/Rodent Potency Dose [*Toxicology*]
**HERPET**... Herpetology (ADA)
**Herpetologi** ... Herpetologica [*A publication*]
**Herpetol Rev** ... Herpetological Review [*A publication*]
**Her Prec**...... Herne's Precedents [*A publication*] (DLA)
**HERR**........ Home Economics Research Reports
**HERS**........ Hardware Error Recovery System [*Sperry UNIVAC*]
**HERS**........ Health Education Research Service [*Department of Health and Human Services*]
**HERS**........ Health Evaluation and Referral Service
**HERS**........ Heritage Financial Services, Inc. [*Blue Island, IL*] [*NASDAQ symbol*] (NQ)
**HERS**........ Herself
**HERS**........ High-Energy-Range Spectrometer [*Instrumentation*]
**HERS**........ Higher Education Resource Services (EA)
**HERS**........ Home Economics Reading Service [*Recipe clipping service*]
**HERS**........ Home Emergency Response System
**HERS**........ Hysterectomy Educational Resources and Services Foundation (EA)
**HERS**........ National Heart Education Research Society (EA)
**HERSCP**... Hazardous Exposure Reduction and Safety Criteria Plan [*NASA*] (NASA)
**HERTF**...... Hertford [*City in England*] (ROG)
**HERTF**...... High-Energy Radiation Test Facility [*Military*]
**Hertford A** ... Hertfordshire Archaeology [*A publication*]
**Hertfordshire Arch** ... Hertfordshire Archaeology [*A publication*]
**Hertfordshire Archaeol** ... Hertfordshire Archaeology [*A publication*]
**Hertfordshire Archaeol Rev** ... Hertfordshire Archaeological Review [*A publication*]
**Hert Map Eur** ... Hertslet's Map of Europe [*A publication*] (DLA)
**Hert M & Serv** ... Hertslet on Master and Servant [*A publication*] (DLA)
**HERTS**...... Hertfordshire [*County in England*] (EY)
**Hert Treat** ... Hertslet's Treaties [*A publication*] (DLA)
**Hertzog**...... Hertzog's Reports of Transvaal High Court [*A publication*] (DLA)
**HERV**......... Human Endogenous Retrovirus
**HervTS**...... Hervormde Teologiese Studies [*Pretoria, South Africa*] [*A publication*] (BJA)
**HervTST**.... Hervormde Teologiese Studies [*Pretoria, South Africa*] [*A publication*] (BJA)
**Herz Kreisl** ... Herz Kreislauf [*A publication*]
**HES**........... Hamlet Evaluation Survey [*South Vietnam*]
**HES**........... Hanford Engineering Service [*Nuclear energy*] (NRCH)
**HES**........... Harvard English Studies [*A publication*]
**HES**........... Harvard Expedition to Samaria (BJA)
**HES**........... Head End Steering
**HES**........... Health Examination Survey [*NCHS*]
**HES**........... Healthcare Evaluation System [*National Planning Data Corp.*] [*Information service or system*] (CRD)
**HES**........... Heavy Enamel Single Silk [*Wire insulation*] (AAG)
**HES**........... Helium Emergency Supply
**HES**........... Hesiod [*Greek poet, c. 800BC*] [*Classical studies*] (ROG)
**HES**........... Hesston Corp. [*NYSE symbol*] (SPSG)
**HES**........... Hetastarch [*Biochemistry*]
**HES**........... Hic Est Sepultus [*Here Is Buried*] [*Latin*] (ROG)
**HES**........... High Early Strength Cement [*Technical drawings*]
**HES**........... High-Explosive Spotting [*Weaponry*]
**HES**........... Higher Elementary School (ADA)
**HES**........... History of Economics Society (EA)
**HES**........... History of Education Society (EA)
**HES**........... Homeowners Emergency Services, Inc.
**HES**........... Hughes Earth Station [*Aerospace*]
**HES**........... Hydroxyethyl Starch [*Plasma volume expander*]
**HES**........... Hypereosinophilic Syndrome [*Medicine*]
**HES**........... Lonely, AK [*Location identifier*] [*FAA*] (FAAL)
**HESB**......... Hahnemann Elementary School Behavior Rating Scale [*Test*]
**HESB**......... Hessische Bibliographie [*Database*] [*Arbeitsgemeinschaft Hessische Bibliographie*] [*German*] [*Information service or system*] (CRD)
**HESC**......... St. Catherine/St. Catherine [*Egypt*] [*ICAO location identifier*] (ICLI)
**HESCA**...... Health Sciences Communications Association (EA)
**HESD**......... High-Explosive, Self-Destroying [*Weaponry*] (NATG)
**HESD**......... Hospital Equipment and Supplies Directory [*A publication*]
**HESDEP**... Helicopter Sensor Development Program
**Hesdoerffers Monatsh Blumen Gartenfreunde** ... Hesdoerffers Monatshefte fuer Blumen- und Gartenfreunde [*A publication*]
**HESEA**...... Health Services Research [*A publication*]
**HESF**......... High-Energy Symmetric Fission
**HESH**......... High-Explosive, Squash Head [*Weaponry*] (NATG)
**HESI**.......... Hunter Environmental Services, Inc. [*NASDAQ symbol*] (NQ)
**HESN**......... Aswan [*Egypt*] [*ICAO location identifier*] (ICLI)
**HESO**......... High-Energy Solid Oxidizer
**HESO**......... Hospital Educational Services Officer [*Navy*]
**HESOD**..... Heizen mit Sonne [*A publication*]
**HESODAC** ... Helicopter SONAR Data Collection
**HESP**......... Health and Environmental Studies Program [*Department of Energy*] (IID)
**Hesp**........... Hesperia [*A publication*]
**HESP**......... High-Efficiency Solar Panel
**HESRE**...... Hamlet Evaluation System Monthly Report (MCD)
**HESS**......... High-Energy Squib Simulator [*NASA*] (NASA)
**HESS**......... History of Earth Sciences Society (EA)
**HESS**......... Human Engineering Systems Simulator [*Air Force*]
**Hess Aerztebl** ... Hessisches Aerzteblatt [*A publication*]
**Hess Biene** ... Hessische Biene [*A publication*]
**Hesse Landesamt Bodenforsch Notizblatt** ... Hesse Landesamt fuer Bodenforschung Notizblatt [*A publication*]
**HESSES**.... High-Energy Squib Simulators [*NASA*] (KSC)
**Hess Florist Briefe** ... Hessische Floristische Briefe [*A publication*]
**Hess Jb Landesgesch** ... Hessisches Jahrbuch fuer Landesgeschichte [*A publication*]
**Hess Lagerstaettenarch** ... Hessisches Lagerstaettenarchiv [*A publication*]
**HEST**......... HEAF Emergency Service Tanks
**HEST**......... High Explosives Simulation Technique
**HESTA**...... Health Employees' Superannuation Trust Australia
**HESV**......... Heavy Enamel Single Silk Varnish [*Wire insulation*] (AAG)
**HET**........... Health Education Technologies [*New York, NY*] (TSSD)
**HET**........... Health-Education Telecommunications [*HEW*]
**HET**........... Heavy Equipment Transporter
**HET**........... Henryetta, OK [*Location identifier*] [*FAA*] (FAAL)
**HET**........... Heterodyne (DEN)
**HET**........... Heterozygosity [*Cytology*]
**Het**............ Hetley's English Common Pleas Reports [*124 English Reprint*] [*A publication*] (DLA)
**HET**........... High-Energy Telescope [*Geophysics*]
**HET**........... High-Explosive [*Shell*] Traced [*i.e., fitted with tracer*] [*Weaponry*]
**HET**........... Higher Educational Test [*British military*] (DMA)
**HET**........... Hohhot [*China*] [*Airport symbol*] (OAG)
**HET**........... Horizontal Electrical Tunnel (NRCH)
**HET**........... Houston - ET [*Texas*] [*Seismograph station code, US Geological Survey*] [*Closed*] (SEIS)
**HET**........... Hudson-Essex Terraplane [*Australia*]

**HET** .......... Hydroxyethyl Terephthalate [*Organic chemistry*]
**HETAC** ..... Heavy Transport Aircraft [*Military*]
**HETB** ........ Heart of England Tourist Board (DCTA)
**HETC** ........ Heavy Equipment Test Chamber (MCD)
**HETC** ........ HETRA Computer and Commercial Industries, Inc. [*NASDAQ symbol*] (NQ)
**Het CP** ....... Hetley's English Common Pleas Reports [*124 English Reprint*] [*A publication*] (DLA)
**HETDI** ...... High-Explosive, Tracer, Dark Ignition [*Weaponry*] (NATG)
**HETE** ........ Hydroxyeicosatetraenoic Acid [*Biochemistry*]
**Het (Eng)** ... Hetley's English Common Pleas Reports [*124 English Reprint*] [*A publication*] (DLA)
**HETERO** .. Heterosexual (DSUE)
**HETEROG** ... Heterogeneous (ROG)
**Heterog Catal Proc Int Symp** ... Heterogeneous Catalysis. Proceedings. International Symposium [*A publication*]
**HETF** ........ Hill Engineering Test Facility [*Air Force*]
**Hetl** ........... Hetley's English Common Pleas Reports [*124 English Reprint*] [*A publication*] (DLA)
**HETM** ....... Hybrid Engineering Test Model (NASA)
**HETOC** ..... Hudson-Essex-Terraplane Owners Club (EA)
**HETP** ........ Head End Treatment Plant [*Nuclear energy*] [*British*]
**HETP** ........ Height Equivalent to a Theoretical Plate [*Chemical engineering*]
**HETP** ........ Hexaethyl Tetraphosphate [*Organic chemistry*]
**HETP** ........ Human Engineering Test Plan
**HETR** ........ El-Tor [*Egypt*] [*ICAO location identifier*] (ICLI)
**HETS** ......... Height Equivalent to a Theoretical Stage [*Chemical engineering*] (NRCH)
**HETS** ......... High-Efficiency Transfer Solution [*CINNA/BIOTECX International, Inc.*] [*Analytical biochemistry*]
**HETS** ......... High-Energy Telescope System [*Geophysics*]
**HETS** ......... High-Energy Transfer Stage
**HETS** ......... Hyperenvironmental Test Station [*or System*] [*Air Force*]
**Het Voice** ... Heterodoxical Voice [*A publication*]
**HEU** .......... Heulandite [*A zeolite*]
**HEU** .......... Highly Enriched Uranium [*Nuclear reactor technology*]
**HEU** .......... Hydroelectric Unit
**HEU** .......... Schenectady, NY [*Location identifier*] [*FAA*] (FAAL)
**Heubner Foundation Monograph Ser** ... Heubner Foundation Monograph Series [*A publication*]
**Heurtey Bull Inform** ... Heurtey Bulletin d'Informations. English Edition [*A publication*]
**HEUS** ........ High-Energy Upper Stage [*NASA*]
**HEV** .......... Health and Environment (AABC)
**HEV** .......... High-Walled Endothelial Venule [*Anatomy*]
**HEV** .......... Human Enteric Virus
**Hev** ............ Nahal Hever Caves (BJA)
**HEVA** ........ Hydrolyzed Ethylene-Vinyl Acetate [*Plastics technology*]
**HEVEA** ..... Heating and Ventilating [*A publication*]
**HEVN** ........ HE Ventures, Inc. [*NASDAQ symbol*] [*NASDAQ symbol*] (NQ)
**HEW** .......... Department of Health, Education, and Welfare [*Sometimes facetiously translated "Halls of Eternal Warfare"*] [*Later, HHS*]
**HEW** .......... Department of Health, Education, and Welfare. Publications [*A publication*]
**HEW** .......... Department of Health, Education, and Welfare, Washington, DC [*OCLC symbol*] (OCLC)
**HEW** .......... Hanford Engineering Works [*Nuclear energy*]
**HEW** .......... Houston, TX [*Location identifier*] [*FAA*] (FAAL)
**HEWE** ....... Heritage West. British Columbia's Leading Heritage Magazine [*A publication*]
**HEWH** ...... High-Explosive Warhead [*Weaponry*]
**HEWL** ....... Hen Egg White Lysozyme [*Also, HEL*] [*An enzyme*]
**Hewlett** ...... Hewlett-Packard Journal [*A publication*]
**Hewlett-Packard J** ... Hewlett-Packard Journal [*A publication*]
**HEWPR** .... Department of Health, Education, and Welfare [*Later, HHS*] Procurement Regulations
**HEX** ........... Handicapped Education Exchange [*Amateur Radio Research and Development Corp.*] [*Information service or system*] (IID)
**HEX** ........... Heat Exchanger (KSC)
**HEX** ........... Hemlo Explorations [*Vancouver Stock Exchange symbol*]
**HEX** ........... Hexachlorocyclopentadiene [*Also, HCCP, HCP*] [*Organic chemistry*]
**HEX** ........... Hexachord [*Music*] (ADA)
**HEX** ........... Hexadecimal [*System*]
**HEX** ........... Hexagon [*or Hexagonal*]
**HEX** ........... Hexamethylmelamine [*Altretamine*] [*Also, HMM, HXM*] [*Antineoplastic drug*]
**HEX** ........... Hexateuch (ROG)
**HEX** ........... Santo Domingo [*Dominican Republic*] [*Airport symbol*] (OAG)
**HEX-A** ....... Hexosaminidase-A
**Hexa-CAF** ... Hexamethylmelamine, Cyclophosphamide, Amethopterin [*Methotrexate*], Fluorouracil [*Antineoplastic drug regimen*]
**HEX-B** ....... Hexosominidase-B
**HEXE** ........ High Energy X-Ray Experiment
**HEXHD** ..... Hexagonal Head
**HEXX** ........ Heck's, Inc. [*NASDAQ symbol*] (NQ)
**HEY** ........... Ozark/Fort Rucker, AL [*Location identifier*] [*FAA*] (FAAL)
**Heyl Imp D** ... Heyl's United States Import Duties [*A publication*] (DLA)
**HEYM** ....... Herrold's Egg Yolk Medium [*For growing microorganisms*]
**HeythJ** ....... Heythrop Journal. A Quarterly Review of Philosophy and Theology [*Oxford*] [*A publication*]
**Heythrop** .... Heythrop Journal [*A publication*]
**Heythrop J** ... Heythrop Journal [*A publication*]
**Heyw Ca** .... Heywood's Table of Cases [*Georgia*] [*A publication*] (DLA)
**Heyw Co Ct** ... Heywood's County Courts Practice [*4th ed.*] [*1876*] [*A publication*] (DLA)
**Heyw Elec** ... Heywood on Elections [*A publication*] (DLA)
**Heywood & Massey** ... Heywood and Massey's Court of Protection Practice [*9th ed.*] [*1971*] [*A publication*] (DLA)
**HEZ** ........... Natchez [*Mississippi*] [*Airport symbol*] (OAG)
**Hez-PBAN** ... Heliothis Zea Pheromone Biosynthesis Activating Neuropeptide
**HF** ............. Dorsey Laboratories [*Research code symbol*]
**Hf** .............. Hafnium [*Chemical element*]
**HF** ............. Hageman Factor [*Factor XII*] [*Hematology*]
**HF** ............. Hale Foundation (EA)
**HF** ............. Half (AAG)
**HF** ............. Half Forward (ADA)
**HF** ............. Hamburger Fremdenblatt [*A publication*]
**HF** ............. Hammer Form (MCD)
**H/F** ........... Handling Fee [*Coupon redemption*]
**HF** ............. Handling Fixture (MCD)
**HF** ............. Handwriting Foundation
**HF** ............. Hankes Foundation (EA)
**HF** ............. Hanuman Foundation (EA)
**HF** ............. Hapag Lloyd Fluggesellschaft mbH [*ICAO designator*] (FAAC)
**HF** ............. Harassing Fire [*Military*] (AABC)
**HF** ............. Hard Failure
**HF** ............. Hard Filled [*Capsules*]
**HF** ............. Hard Firm [*Pencil leads*]
**HF** ............. Harry Franco [*Pseudonym used by Charles F. Briggs*]
**HF** ............. Hartree-Fock [*Orbitals*] [*Atomic structure*]
**HF** ............. Hay Fever [*Medicine*]
**HF** ............. Hazard Function
**HF** ............. Haze Filter [*Photography*]
**HF** ............. Hazelden Foundation (EA)
**HF** ............. Heart Failure [*Medicine*]
**HF** ............. Heat Flow [*Physiology*]
**HF** ............. Heavy Fuel [*Engine technology*]
**HF** ............. Heeresfahrzeug [*Army Vehicle*] [*German military - World War II*]
**HF** ............. Heidelberger Forschungen [*A publication*]
**HF** ............. Height Finder [*or Finding*] [*RADAR*]
**H of F** ........ Height of Fundus [*Obstetrics*]
**H/F** ........... Held For (AAG)
**HF** ............. Helper Factor [*Immunology*]
**HF** ............. Hemorrhagic Factor [*Medicine*]
**HF** ............. Hepatic Fat
**HF** ............. Hercules Furens [*of Euripides*] [*Classical studies*] (OCD)
**HF** ............. Heritage Foundation [*Washington, DC*] (EA)
**HF** ............. Hesperian Foundation (EA)
**HF** ............. High Fat [*Type of diet*]
**HF** ............. High Fidelity [*A publication*]
**HF** ............. High Foliage Forager [*Ecology*]
**HF** ............. High Food Density [*Ecology*]
**HF** ............. High Frequency [*Electronics*]
**HF** ............. High Frontier (EA)
**HF** ............. High Rate Forward
**HF** ............. Hippocampal Fissure [*Neuroanatomy*]
**HF** ............. Hlutafelag [*Joint-Stock Company*] [*Icelandic*] (CED)
**HF** ............. Hold Fire [*Military*]
**HF** ............. Holding Fixture (MSA)
**HF** ............. Hollow Fiber
**H-F** ........... Holstein-Friesian [*Cattle breed*]
**HF** ............. Holy Father (ROG)
**HF** ............. Holyearth Foundation (EA)
**HF** ............. Home Fleet [*Obsolete*] [*British*]
**HF** ............. Home Forces [*Military*] [*British*]
**HF** ............. Home Front
**HF** ............. Homeopathic Foundation [*Later, FHR*] (EA)
**H ou F** ....... Homme ou Femme [*Man or Woman*] [*French*]
**HF** ............. Hoosier Folklore [*A publication*]
**HF** ............. Horizontal Flight (NASA)
**HF** ............. Hot Firing (MCD)
**HF** ............. House of Fabrics, Inc. [*NYSE symbol*] (SPSG)
**HF** ............. House File (OICC)
**HF** ............. Hull Filter
**HF** ............. Human Factors
**HF** ............. Human Foreskin [*Anatomy*]
**HF** ............. Huna Forschunggesellschaft [*Huna Research Association - HRA*] [*Zurich, Switzerland*] (EAIO)
**HF** ............. Hundred Feet
**HF** ............. Husky Fever (The Musher's Monthly News. Insert in Northern News Report) [*A publication*]
**HF** ............. Hydrogen Fill (MCD)
**HF** ............. Hydrogen Fluoride [*Inorganic chemistry*] (AFM)
**HF** ............. Hyperfiltration (NASA)

**HF** ........ MBB-UH [*Messerschmitt-Boelkow-Blohm*] [*Federal Republic of Germany*] [*ICAO aircraft manufacturer identifier*] (ICAO)
**HF** ........ Wander AG [*Switzerland*] [*Research code symbol*]
**HFA** ........ Haifa [*Israel*] [*Airport symbol*] (OAG)
**HFA** ........ Hard Fibres Association (EA)
**HFA** ........ Hardened Flexible Array
**HFA** ........ Harmelink Family Association (EA)
**HFA** ........ [*The*] Harry Fox Agency
**HFA** ........ Hartshorn Family Association (EA)
**HFA** ........ Headquarters Field Army (NATG)
**HFA** ........ Heavy Field Artillery
**HFA** ........ Hexafluoroaceytlacetone [*Organic chemistry*]
**HFA** ........ High Flow Alarm (IEEE)
**HFA** ........ High-Frequency Accelerometer (NASA)
**HFA** ........ High-Frequency Antenna (KSC)
**HFA** ........ Hired Fishermen's Association [*A union*] [*British*]
**HFA** ........ Historical Farm Association (EA)
**HFA** ........ Hitchhikers for America (EA)
**HFA** ........ Homofolic Acid [*Biochemistry*]
**HFA** ........ Humane Farming Association (EA)
**HFA** ........ Hydrofluoroalkane [*Organic chemistry*]
**HFA** ........ Hydrogen-Fueled Aircraft
**HFAA** ........ Hardanger Fiddle Association of America (EA)
**HFAA** ........ High-Frequency Airborne Antenna
**HFAA** ........ Holstein-Friesian Association of America (EA)
**HFAC** ........ Human Factors Association of Canada
**HFAF** ........ Hawaii Foundation for American Freedoms (EA)
**HFAL** ........ Home Federal Savings Bank of Alabama [*NASDAQ symbol*] (NQ)
**HFAM** ........ Helicopter Familiarization (MCD)
**HFARA** ........ Honorary Foreign Associate of Royal Academy [*British*]
**HFAS** ........ High-Frequency Antenna System (KSC)
**HFAS** ........ Honeywell File Access System
**HFB** ........ Bouwhandel [*A publication*]
**HFB** ........ Hand Form Block (MSA)
**HFB** ........ Helium Filled Bubble [*For study of air flow*]
**HFB** ........ Heptafluorobutyrate [*or Heptafluorobutyric*] [*Organic chemistry*]
**HFB** ........ Hoosier Folklore Bulletin [*A publication*]
**HFBA** ........ Hebrew Free Burial Association (EA)
**HFBA** ........ Heptafluorobutyric Acid [*Organic chemistry*]
**HFBF** ........ Home Federal Bank of Florida FSB [*St. Petersburg, FL*] [*NASDAQ symbol*] (NQ)
**HFBI** ........ Heptafluorobutyrylimidazole [*Organic chemistry*]
**HFBR** ........ High Flux Beam Research Reactor [*Nuclear energy*]
**HFBT** ........ Helps for Bible Translators [*A publication*]
**HFBUP** ........ High-Frequency Backup Program [*Military*] (CAAL)
**HFC** ........ Hants Field Club and Archaeological Society [*A publication*]
**HFC** ........ Harpers Ferry Center [*National Park Service*] (GRD)
**HFC** ........ Heart Fan Club (EA)
**HFC** ........ Heat Flow and Convection (NASA)
**HFC** ........ High-Energy LASER Fire Control
**HFC** ........ High-Frequency Choke
**HFC** ........ High-Frequency Correction
**HFC** ........ High-Frequency Current
**HFC** ........ Higher Fire Control [*British military*] (DMA)
**HFC** ........ Holy Family College [*California, Pennsylvania, Wisconsin*]
**HFC** ........ Holy Family College, Philadelphia, PA [*OCLC symbol*] (OCLC)
**HFC** ........ Household Food Consumption
**HFC** ........ Human Factors Checklists [*Navy*]
**HFC** ........ Hydraulic Flight Control (NASA)
**HFC** ........ Hydrofluorocarbon [*Organic chemistry*]
**HFCA** ........ Holy Family Christian Association [*In 1983 movie "Zelig"*]
**HFCAA** ........ Hatters' Fur Cutters Association of America [*Formerly, HFCAUS*] (EA)
**HFCAUS** ........ Hatters' Fur Cutters Association of the United States [*Later, HFCAA*]
**HFCC** ........ Henry Ford Community College [*Dearborn, MI*]
**HFCE** ........ HFIR [*High-Flux Isotope Reactor*] Critical Experiment [*Nuclear energy*] (NRCH)
**HFCS** ........ Harpoon Fire Control System [*Missiles*] (MCD)
**HFCS** ........ High-Fructose Corn Sweetener [*or Syrup*]
**HFCT** ........ Hydraulic Flight Control Test (NASA)
**HFCUR** ........ High-Frequency Current
**HFCV** ........ Helium Flow Control Valve (KSC)
**HFCVD** ........ Hot Filament Chemical Vapor Deposition [*Coating technology*]
**HFD** ........ Halifax Developments Ltd. [*Toronto Stock Exchange symbol*]
**HFD** ........ Hartford, CT [*Location identifier*] [*FAA*] (FAAL)
**HFD** ........ Held for Detail
**HFD** ........ Helium Fill to Distribution Unit [*Aerospace*] (AAG)
**HFD** ........ Hereford [*British depot code*]
**HFD** ........ Herefordshire [*County in England*] (ROG)
**HFD** ........ HomeFed Corp. [*NYSE symbol*] (SPSG)
**HFD** ........ Horizon Flight Director [*Aircraft*]
**HFD** ........ Hospital Field Director [*Red Cross*]
**HFD** ........ Hot Form Die
**HFD** ........ Human Factor Division [*Air Research and Development Command*] [*Air Force*] (AAG)
**HFD** ........ Hydro-Form Die
**HFDA** ........ Hospital Food Directors Association
**HFDF** ........ High-Frequency Direction Finding [*Pronounced "huff duff"*] [*Electronics*]
**HFDF** ........ High-Frequency Distribution Frame (IEEE)
**HF/DF** ........ Hydrogen Fluoride/Deuterium Fluoride (MCD)
**HFDK** ........ Human Fetal Diploid Kidney [*Type of cell line*]
**HFDL** ........ Human Fetal Diploid Lung [*Type of cell line*]
**HFDS** ........ Hydrogen Fluid Distribution System (MCD)
**HFE** ........ Heat-Flow Electronics
**HFE** ........ Heat-Flow Experiment
**HFE** ........ Hefei [*China*] [*Airport symbol*] (OAG)
**HFE** ........ Helmholtz Free Energy
**HFE** ........ Hexafluorodiethyl Ether [*Convulsant*]
**HFE** ........ High Frequency Executive (NASA)
**HFE** ........ Hillside Energy [*Vancouver Stock Exchange symbol*]
**HFE** ........ Housing Finance Review [*A publication*]
**HFE** ........ Human Factors in Electronics (MCD)
**HFE** ........ Human Factors Engineering (AABC)
**HFE** ........ Human Factors Evaluation (MCD)
**HFE** ........ Pittsburgh, PA [*Location identifier*] [*FAA*] (FAAL)
**HFEA** ........ Human Factors Engineering Analysis [*or Assessment*] [*Army*] (RDA)
**HFED** ........ Heart Federal Savings & Loan Association [*NASDAQ symbol*] (NQ)
**HFEF** ........ High Flux Experimental Facility [*Nuclear energy*]
**HFEF** ........ Hot Fuel Examination Facility [*Nuclear energy*]
**HFET** ........ Hellmann-Feynmann Electrostatic Theorem [*Physics*]
**HFET** ........ Highway Fuel Economy Test [*Environmental Protection Agency*]
**HFET** ........ Home Federal Savings & Loan Association of Upper East Tennessee [*NASDAQ symbol*] (NQ)
**HFET** ........ Human Factors Engineering Testing (MCD)
**HFeU** ........ Hepatic Iron (Ferrum) Uptake [*Physiology*]
**HFF** ........ Health Affairs [*A publication*]
**HFF** ........ Heavy Freight Flight [*British military*] (DMA)
**HFF** ........ High Flight Foundation (EA)
**HFF** ........ High-Frequency Furnace
**HFF** ........ Hoffman, NC [*Location identifier*] [*FAA*] (FAAL)
**HFF** ........ Holly Farms Foods, Inc. [*NYSE symbol*] (SPSG)
**hFF** ........ Human Follicular Fluid [*Physiology*]
**HFF** ........ Human Foreskin Fibroblast [*A cell line*]
**HFF** ........ Hydraulic Fluid Filter
**HFF** ........ Hypervelocity Flow Field
**HFFC** ........ Hart Family Fan Club (EA)
**HFFC** ........ Helen Forrest Fan Club (EA)
**HFFF** ........ Djibouti/Ambouli [*Djibouti*] [*ICAO location identifier*] (ICLI)
**HFFF** ........ Hungarian Freedom Fighters Federation USA (EA)
**HFFF** ........ Hypervelocity Free Flight Facility
**HFFS** ........ HELLFIRE Fire and Forget Seeker [*Missile*]
**HFG** ........ Harmonic Frequency Generator
**HFG** ........ Heavy Free Gas (IEEE)
**HFG** ........ Human Factors Group
**HFGA** ........ Hall of Fame for Great Americans (EA)
**HFGA** ........ Home Federal Savings Bank of Georgia [*Gainesville, GA*] [*NASDAQ symbol*] (NQ)
**HFHC** ........ Heritage Financial Corporation [*NASDAQ symbol*] (NQ)
**HFHJA** ........ Henry Ford Hospital. Medical Journal [*A publication*]
**HFHT** ........ Handling Fixture - Hoist Tool (MCD)
**HFI** ........ Health First International (EA)
**HFI** ........ Helicopter Foundation International (EA)
**HFI** ........ Hereditary Fructose Intolerance [*Medicine*]
**HFI** ........ High Fidelity Institute
**HFI** ........ Hocker Federation International (EA)
**HFI** ........ Hudson Foods, Inc., Class A [*NYSE symbol*] (SPSG)
**HFI** ........ Hyperfine Interaction
**HFIAW** ........ International Association of Heat and Frost Insulators and Asbestos Workers (EA)
**HFIB** ........ Hexafluoroisobutylene [*Organic chemistry*]
**HFIC** ........ Harpoon Firing Interlock Closed [*Missiles*] (MCD)
**HFIC** ........ Home Furnishings Industry Committee [*Defunct*] (EA)
**HFID** ........ Heated Flame Ionization Detection [*Analytical chemistry*]
**HFIF** ........ Human Fibroblast Interferon [*Cytology*]
**HFIM** ........ High-Frequency Instruments and Measurements (IEEE)
**HFIN** ........ Horizon Financial Services, Inc. [*Beachwood, OH*] [*NASDAQ symbol*] (NQ)
**HFIP** ........ Hexafluoroisopropanol [*or Hexafluoroisopropyl*] [*Organic chemistry*]
**HFIR** ........ High Flux Isotope Reactor
**HFITR** ........ High-Field Ignition Test Reactor [*Nuclear energy*] (MCD)
**HFIW** ........ High-Frequency Induction Welding [*Manufacturing term*]
**HFJ** ........ High-Frequency Jammer
**HFJV** ........ High-Frequency Jet Ventilation [*Pulmonary ventilation*]
**HFK** ........ Holland Quarterly [*A publication*]
**HFL** ........ Helium Fill Line
**HFL** ........ Hesperia Fine Sandy Loam [*A soil type*]
**HFL** ........ Homestead Financial Corp. [*NYSE symbol*] (SPSG)
**HFL** ........ Human Factors Laboratory [*University of South Dakota*] [*National Institute of Standards and Technology*] [*Research center*]
**HFL** ........ Human Fetal Lung
**HFLA** ........ Handling Fixture - Line Accessory (MCD)

**HFLA** ........ Heritage Federal Savings & Loan Florida [*NASDAQ symbol*] (NQ)
**HFLD** ........ Handling Fixture - Line Dolly (MCD)
**HFLM** ........ Hydro Flame Corp. [*NASDAQ symbol*] (NQ)
**HFM** .......... Healthcare Financial Management [*A publication*]
**HFM** .......... Heavy Force Modernization [*Army*]
**HFM** .......... Held for Manufacturing
**HFM** .......... Held for Material
**HFM** .......... High-Field Magnetometer [*Instrumentation*]
**HFM** .......... Historisk-Filosofiske Meddelelser Udgivet af det Kongelinge Danske Videnskabernes Selskab [*A publication*]
**HFM** .......... Hold for Money [*Business term*]
**HFM** .......... Hollow Fiber Membrane (NASA)
**HFMA** ........ Healthcare Financial Management Association (EA)
**HFMA** ........ Hospital Financial Management Association [*Later, Healthcare Financial Management Association*] (EA)
**HFMD** ........ Home Federal Corp. [*NASDAQ symbol*] (NQ)
**HFMF** ........ Hone-Finish Monolithic Floor [*Technical drawings*]
**HFMKDVS** ... Historisk-Filosofiske Meddelelser Udgivet af det Kongelinge Danske Videnskabernes Selskab [*A publication*]
**HFMRA** .... Honorary Foreign Member of the Royal Academy
**HFMS** ........ Highway Fleet Management System (MCD)
**HFMS** ........ Human Factors Measurement System
**HFMU** ........ High-Fidelity Mock-Up [*NASA*] (NASA)
**HFN** .......... Hi-Fi News and Record Review [*A publication*]
**HFN** .......... Hofn [*Iceland*] [*Airport symbol*] (OAG)
**HFN** .......... Human Fibronectin [*Cytochemistry*]
**HFNO** ........ Home Federal Savings Bank [*NASDAQ symbol*] (NQ)
**HFO** .......... Half-Fare Order [*Aviation*] (FAAC)
**HFO** .......... Heavy Fuel Oil
**HFO** .......... Heavy Fuel Oils [*Database*] [*Department of Energy*]
**HFO** .......... Height Finder Operator (MUGU)
**HFO** .......... High-Frequency Oscillator
**HFO** .......... Honolulu, HI [*Location identifier*] [*FAA*] (FAAL)
**$H_4$folate** ...... Tetrahydrofolate [*Biochemistry*]
**HF & OR** .... Human Factors and Operations Research [*Army*] (MCD)
**HFORL** ...... Human Factors Operation Research Laboratory [*Air Force*]
**HFOX** ........ Home Federal Savings Bank [*NASDAQ symbol*] (NQ)
**HFP** .......... Hamdard Foundation Pakistan (EAIO)
**HFP** .......... Held for Planning (MCD)
**HFP** .......... Helical Flight Path
**HFP** .......... Helium Fuel-Tank Pressurization (AAG)
**HFP** .......... Hexafluoropropylene [*Organic chemistry*]
**HFP** .......... Highfield Property Investments Ltd. [*Toronto Stock Exchange symbol*]
**HFP** .......... Hostile Fire Pay [*Special pay for hazardous duty*] [*Military*] (AABC)
**HFP** .......... Hot Full Power [*Nuclear energy*] (NRCH)
**HFP** .......... Huon Forest Products [*Australia*]
**HFP** .......... Hybrid Fabrication Procedure (MCD)
**HFP** .......... Hypofibrinogenic Plasma
**HFPA** ........ Hollywood Foreign Press Association (EA)
**HFPA** ........ Home Fashions Products Association (EA)
**HFPCS** ...... Health Facilities Planning and Construction Service
**HFPO** ........ Hexafluoropropylene Oxide [*Organic chemistry*]
**HFPPV** ...... High-Frequency Positive Pressure Ventilation [*Medicine*]
**HFPR** ........ Handling Fixture - Production (MCD)
**HFPS** ........ Hay Fever Prevention Society
**HFPS** ........ High-Frequency Phase Shifter [*Telecommunications*]
**HFPS** ........ Home Fallout Protection Survey [*Formerly, EFPH*] [*Civil Defense*]
**HFPSI** ....... Human Factors Personnel Selection Inventory [*Interpersonal skills and attitudes test*]
**HFR** .......... Height Finder RADAR (CET)
**HFR** .......... High Fill Rate [*Valve*] [*Automotive engineering*]
**HFR** .......... High Flux Reactor [*Netherlands*] [*Nuclear energy*]
**HFR** .......... High Frequency of Recombination [*Medicine*]
**HFR** .......... High-Frequency Resistor
**HFR** .......... Hold for Release [*Business term*] (FAAC)
**HFR** .......... Human Factors Research
**HFRA** ........ High-Frequency Recovery Antenna (KSC)
**HFRA** ........ Honorary Fellow of the Royal Academy [*British*]
**HFRDF** ...... High-Frequency Repeater Distribution Frame (DEN)
**HFRE** ........ Hydraulic Fluid Replenishment Equipment
**HFRG** ........ High-Frequency Radio Group [*Military*] (CAAL)
**HFRO** ........ Hill Farming Research Organisation [*British*]
**HFRS** ........ Hemorrhagic Fever with Renal Syndrome [*Medicine*]
**HFRT** ........ High-Frequency Radio Transmitter
**HFRW** ........ High-Frequency Resistance Welding [*Manufacturing term*]
**HFRZ** ........ Halbfranzband [*Half-Calf Binding*] [*Publishing*] [*German*]
**HFS** .......... French Frigate Shoals, HI [*Location identifier*] [*FAA*] (FAAL)
**HFS** .......... Hagfors [*Sweden*] [*Seismograph station code, US Geological Survey*] (SEIS)
**HFS** .......... Harrison Fisher Society (EA)
**HFS** .......... Heat Flux Sensor
**HFS** .......... Heavy Flushing Spray
**HFS** .......... Hemifacial Spasm [*Medicine*]
**HFS** .......... Hierarchical File System [*Data processing*]
**HFS** .......... High-Frequency Stimulation [*Physiology*]
**HFS** .......... Holy Family Seminary [*Connecticut*]
**HFS** .......... Home Owners Savings Bank FSB [*NYSE symbol*] (SPSG)
**HFS** .......... Horizontal Flight Simulator (MCD)
**HFS** .......... Hostile Fire Simulator [*Military*] (MCD)
**HFS** .......... Human Factors Society (EA)
**HFS** .......... Human Factors Study
**HFS** .......... Hyperfine Structure
**HFS** .......... Hypothetical Future Samples [*Statistics*]
**HFSA** ........ Home Federal Savings Bank [*NASDAQ symbol*] (NQ)
**HFSA** ........ Hydrofluorsilicic Acid [*Inorganic chemistry*]
**HFSB** ........ Home Federal Savings Bank [*NASDAQ symbol*] (NQ)
**HFSC** ........ Human Fetal Spinal Cord
**HFSC** ........ Hyperfine Splitting Constant [*Spectroscopy*]
**HFSE** ........ High-Field-Strength Elements [*Geochemistry*]
**HFSF** ........ Home Federal Savings & Loan Association of San Francisco [*San Francisco, CA*] [*NASDAQ symbol*] (NQ)
**HFSG** ........ Healthcare Financing Study Group (EA)
**HFSH** ........ Human Follicle Stimulating Hormone [*Endocrinology*]
**HFSL** ........ Home Owners Savings Bank FSB [*NASDAQ symbol*] (NQ)
**HFSP** ........ Human Frontier Science Program [*An international effort, proposed by Japan in 1987*]
**HFSSB** ...... High-Frequency Single Sideband [*Telecommunications*]
**HFSSC** ...... High-Frequency Swept Spectrum Communications
**HFST** ........ Hearing-for-Speech Test
**HFST** ........ High-Flux Scram Trip [*Nuclear energy*] (IEEE)
**HFSU** ........ Heat Flux Sensing Unit
**HFSV** ........ High Flow Shutoff Valve
**HFT** .......... Hachette-Filipacchi Telematique [*Information service or system*] (EISS)
**HFT** .......... Hammerfest [*Norway*] [*Airport symbol*] (OAG)
**HFT** .......... Heavy Fire Team [*Military*]
**HFT** .......... Heft (ROG)
**HFT** .......... Heiney Family Tree (EA)
**HFT** .......... Held for Tooling
**HFT** .......... High-Frequency of Transduction [*Virology*]
**HFT** .......... Horizontal Flight Testing [*NASA*] (KSC)
**HFT** .......... Hot Functional Testing [*Nuclear energy*] (NRCH)
**HFTB** ........ Handling Fixture - Tow Bar (MCD)
**HFTE** ........ Human Factors Test and Evaluation [*Military*] (MCD)
**HFTF** ........ Horizontal Flight Test Facility [*NASA*] (NASA)
**HFTS** ........ Horizontal Flight Test Simulator [*NASA*] (NASA)
**HFTS** ........ Human Factors Trade Studies [*Navy*]
**HFU** .......... Heat-Flow [*or Flux*] Unit [*Nuclear energy*]
**HFU** .......... Heeres-Funkstelle [*Army Radio Station*] [*German military - World War II*]
**HFUR** ........ Hickory Furniture Co. [*NASDAQ symbol*] (NQ)
**$H_4$furan** ...... Tetrahydrofuran [*Organic chemistry*]
**HFV** .......... Helicopter Flight Vietnam [*Australia*]
**HFV** .......... High-Frequency Ventilation [*Medicine*]
**HFV** .......... Horizontal Flight Vector
**HFV** .......... Human Foamy Virus
**HFWA** ........ High-Frequency Wave Analyzer
**HFWE** ........ Having Fun with Elvis [*Fan club*] (EA)
**HFWF** ........ Hired Farm Working Force
**HFX** .......... Halifax City Regional Library [*UTLAS symbol*]
**HFX** .......... High-Frequency Transceiver [*or Transducer*]
**HG** ............ Airtouring Charter Ltd. [*ICAO designator*] (FAAC)
**HG** ............ Centreline Air Services Ltd. [*United Kingdom*] [*ICAO designator*] (ICDA)
**HG** ............ Die Hethitischen Gesetze. Documenta et Monumenta Orientis Antiqui 7 [*Leiden*] [*A publication*] (BJA)
**Hg** ............ Haggai [*Old Testament book*]
**HG** ............ Hammurabi's Gesetz (BJA)
**HG** ............ Hand Generator
**HG** ............ Hannoversche Geschichtsblaetter [*A publication*]
**HG** ............ Hard Gelatin [*Pharmacy*]
**H & G** ........ Harden and Grind [*Technical drawings*]
**HG** ............ Harmonic Generator
**H & G** ........ Harris and Gill's Maryland Court of Appeals Reports [*1826-29*] [*A publication*] (DLA)
**HG** ............ Having (ROG)
**H & G** ........ Headed and Gutted [*Fish processing*]
**HG** ............ Hectogram
**HG** ............ Heliogram
**HG** ............ Hemoglobin [*Biochemistry, medicine*]
**HG** ............ Heptadecapeptide Gastrin [*Endocrinology*]
**HG** ............ Herpes Gestationis [*Medicine*]
**HG** ............ Heschl's Gyrus [*Brain anatomy*]
**Hg** ............ Heterodera glycenes [*A nematode*]
**HG** ............ Hexylene Glycol [*Organic chemistry*]
**H & G** ........ Hicks & Greist [*Advertising agency*]
**HG** ............ High German [*Language, etc.*]
**HG** ............ High Glucose [*Clinical chemistry*]
**HG** ............ High Grain (NASA)
**HG** ............ Higher Grade
**HG** ............ His [*or Her*] Grace
**HG** ............ Holy Ghost
**H & G** ........ Home and Garden Bulletins [*A publication*]
**HG** ............ Home Guard [*British*]
**HG** ............ Homing Guidance (AAG)
**HG** ............ Horse Guards [*British*]
**HG** ............ Hotchkiss Gunner [*British military*] (DMA)
**H & G** ........ House and Garden [*A publication*]

**HG** ........ Housing Guaranty
**HG** ........ Hull Gauge
**HG** ........ Human Gonadotrophin [*Endocrinology*]
**HG** ........ Humanistisches Gymnasium [*A publication*]
**H & G** ........ Hurlstone and Gordon's English Exchequer Reports [*A publication*] (DLA)
**Hg** ........ Hydrargyrum [*Mercury*] [*Chemical element*]
**HG** ........ Hydrogen Gas [*System*] [*Nuclear energy*] (NRCH)
**HG** ........ Hydrogen Generator
**HG** ........ Hydrophilic Group [*Surfactant technology*]
**HG** ........ Hyperglycemic-Glycogenolytic [*Factor*] [*Endocrinology*]
**HG** ........ Hypertensive Group [*Cardiology*]
**HG** ........ Hypobranchial Gland
**HG** ........ Workout Handily from Gate [*Horse racing*]
**HG** ........ Yr Haul a'r Gengell [*A publication*]
**HGA** ........ Handweavers Guild of America (EA)
**HGA** ........ Hang Glider Association (EA)
**HGA** ........ Hargeisa [*Somalia*] [*Airport symbol*] (OAG)
**HGA** ........ Heat Generator Assembly (KSC)
**HGA** ........ Heptagonal Games Association (EA)
**HGA** ........ Hercules Graphics Adapter (PCM)
**HGA** ........ Hereditary Grand Almoner [*Freemasonry*]
**HGA** ........ High Gain Antenna
**HGA** ........ Hobby Greenhouse Association (EA)
**HGA** ........ Hobby Greenhouse Owners Association of America [*Defunct*] (EA)
**HGA** ........ Hobby Guild of America (EA)
**HGA** ........ Homogentisate [*Biochemistry*]
**HGA** ........ Hop Growers of America (EA)
**HGA** ........ Hotel Greeters of America [*Later, HMGI*]
**HGAA** ........ Hydride Generation Atomic Absorption [*Analytical chemistry*]
**HGAC** ........ High Gain Antenna Controller
**HGAMA** ........ Hidrotehnica Gospodarirea Apelor. Meteorologia [*A publication*]
**HGAS** ........ High Gain Antenna System (IEEE)
**HGB** ........ Handelsgesetzbuch [*Commercial Code*] [*German*] [*Legal term*] (DLA)
**HGB** ........ Hanford Gable Butte [*Washington*] [*Seismograph station code, US Geological Survey*] (SEIS)
**HGB** ........ Hansische Geschichtsblaetter [*A publication*]
**HGB** ........ Hemoglobin [*Biochemistry, medicine*]
**HGB** ........ Het Gildeboek. Tijdschrift voor Kerkelijke Kunst en Oudheidkunde [*A publication*]
**HGB** ........ Hot Gas Bonder
**HGB** ........ Household Goods Carriers' Bureau Agent, Arlington VA [*STAC*]
**HGBN** ........ Herringbone [*Electronics, engineering*]
**HGC** ........ Hanes Gweithwyr Cymru [*Welsh Labour History*] [*A publication*]
**HGC** ........ Hudson General Corporation [*AMEX symbol*] (SPSG)
**HGC** ........ Hypergolic Clean
**HGCB** ........ Household Goods Carriers' Bureau (EA)
**HG-CSF** ........ Human Granulocyte, Colony Stimulation Factor [*Hematology*]
**HGCU** ........ Heavy Glider Conversion Unit [*British military*] (DMA)
**HGD** ........ Hawthorne Gold [*Vancouver Stock Exchange symbol*]
**HGD** ........ High Grade Dysplasia [*Medicine*]
**HGD** ........ Hogshead
**HGD** ........ Hourglass Device [*Military decoration*] (AFM)
**HGD** ........ Hughenden [*Australia*] [*Airport symbol*] (OAG)
**HGDH** ........ His [*or Her*] Grand Ducal Highness
**HGDS** ........ Hazardous Gas Detection Systems (KSC)
**HGE** ........ Handling Ground Equipment
**HGE** ........ Hemorrhage [*Medicine*] (ROG)
**HGE** ........ Het Gilgamesj-Epos [*A publication*] (BJA)
**HGE** ........ Hinge [*Automotive engineering*]
**HGE** ........ Hybrid Geotempered Envelope [*Architecture*]
**HGE** ........ Hydraulic Grade Elevations (NRCH)
**HgF** ........ Hemoglobin, Fetal [*Also, HbF*] [*Medicine*]
**HGF** ........ Hemopoietic Growth Factor [*Hematology*]
**HGF** ........ Hepatocyte Growth Factor [*Biochemistry*]
**HGF** ........ Household Goods Forwarders Tariff Bureau, Washington DC [*STAC*]
**HGF** ........ Human Growth Foundation (EA)
**HGF** ........ Hyperglycemic-Glycogenolytic Factor [*Later, Glucagon*] [*Endocrinology*]
**HGFA** ........ Henry George Foundation of America (EA)
**HGFA** ........ Household Goods Forwarders Association of America [*Washington, DC*]
**HGG** ........ Hot Gas Generator
**HGG** ........ Hotelgewerbe und Gastgewerbe Rundschau. Unabhangiges Fachorgan fuer Gastronomie, Betriebstechnische, und Kuhltechnische Praxis und Gemeinschaftsverpflegung [*A publication*]
**HGG** ........ Human Gamma-Globulin [*Endocrinology*]
**HGGSEB** ........ Handelingen. Genootschap voor Geschiedenis Gesticht Onder de Benaming. Societe d'Emulation de Bruges [*A publication*]
**HGH** ........ Hangzhou [*China*] [*Airport symbol*] (OAG)
**HGH** ........ Hansische Geschichtsblaetter [*A publication*]
**HGH** ........ Historische Grammatik der Hebraeischen Sprache [*H. Bauer and P. Leander*] [*A publication*] (BJA)
**HGH** ........ Human Growth Hormone [*Also, hGH*] [*Endocrinology*]
**HGHGHG** ........ Hilf Gott, Hilf Gott, Hilf Gott [*God Help, God Help, God Help*] [*Motto of Sophie Elisabeth, Countess of Schwarzenburg (1565-1621)*]
**HGHR** ........ Highlander International Corp. [*NASDAQ symbol*] (NQ)
**HGI** ........ Henry George Institute (EA)
**HGIC** ........ Harleysville Group, Incorporated [*NASDAQ symbol*] (NQ)
**HGIS** ........ Healthgroup International [*NASDAQ symbol*] (NQ)
**HGJ** ........ Hongo [*Japan*] [*Seismograph station code, US Geological Survey*] (SEIS)
**HGKV** ........ Hefte fuer Geschichte, Kunst, und Volkskunde [*A publication*]
**HGL** ........ Hamilton Group Ltd. [*Toronto Stock Exchange symbol*]
**HGL** ........ Hauptgesellschaftsleitung [*Main Company Management*] [*German*]
**HGL** ........ Helgoland [*West Germany*] [*Airport symbol*] (OAG)
**HGL** ........ High Gain Link
**HGL** ........ High Go Low Test
**HGL** ........ Homach Gap Lathe
**HGLDS** ........ Highlands (MCD)
**HGM** ........ Harvard Graduates' Magazine [*A publication*]
**HGM** ........ Hectogram (ROG)
**HGM** ........ Hereditary Grand Master [*Freemasonry*] (ROG)
**HGM** ........ Hot Gas Manifold (NASA)
**HGMAA** ........ Hang Glider Manufacturers Association of America [*Defunct*] (EA)
**HGMCR** ........ Human Genetic Mutant Cell Repository
**HGMF** ........ High-Gradient Magnetic Filtration
**HGMGR** ........ Household Goods Military and Government Rate Tariff
**HGMM** ........ Hereditary Grand Master Mason [*Freemasonry*]
**HGMS** ........ Helicopter Gravity-Measuring System [*Naval Oceanographic Office*]
**HGMS** ........ High-Gradient Magnetic Separator (NRCH)
**HGMU** ........ Heavy Glider Maintenance Unit [*British military*] (DMA)
**HGMUS** ........ Horizontal Generator Mock-Up System [*NASA*]
**HGN** ........ Horizontal Gaze Nystagmus Test
**HGN** ........ Hypogastric Nerve [*Anatomy*]
**HGN** ........ Mae Hong Son [*Thailand*] [*Airport symbol*] (OAG)
**HG/NG** ........ Hydrogen Gas/Nitrogen Gas (NRCH)
**HGO** ........ Halsgerichtsordnung [*German*] (DSA)
**HGO** ........ Heavy Gas Oils [*Petroleum product*]
**HGO** ........ Hepatic Glucose Output [*Physiology*]
**HGO** ........ Hugo, CO [*Location identifier*] [*FAA*] (FAAL)
**HGO** ........ Korhogo [*Ivory Coast*] [*Airport symbol*] (OAG)
**HGP** ........ Hard Gas-Permeable [*Contact lenses*]
**HGP-OIMLA** ... Hindustani Ghadar Party-Organization of Indian Marxist-Leninists Abroad
**HGPRT** ........ Hypoxanthine-Guanine Phosphoribosyltransferase [*AO HPRT*] [*An enzyme*]
**HGPS** ........ High-Grade Plow Steel
**HGR** ........ Hagerstown [*Maryland*] [*Airport symbol*] (OAG)
**HGR** ........ Hangar (KSC)
**HGR** ........ Hanger
**HGR** ........ Haubitzgranate [*Howitzer Shell*] [*German military - World War II*]
**HGR** ........ High Group Receiving
**HGR** ........ High River Resources Ltd. [*Vancouver Stock Exchange symbol*]
**HGR** ........ Histoire Generale des Religions [*A publication*] (BJA)
**HGR** ........ Human Glucocorticoid Receptor [*Endocrinology*]
**HGRF** ........ Hot Gas Radiating Facility
**HGRF** ........ Human Growth-Hormone Releasing Factor [*Biochemistry*]
**HGR & SPTFAC** ... Hangar and Support Facility [*NASA*] (NASA)
**HGS** ........ Freetown [*Sierra Leone*] Hastings Airport [*Airport symbol*] (OAG)
**HGS** ........ Hagensborg Resources Ltd. [*Vancouver Stock Exchange symbol*]
**HGS** ........ Harvard Germanic Studies [*A publication*]
**HGS** ........ Hot Gas System
**HGS** ........ Hydrogen Gas Saver (MCD)
**HGS** ........ Hyperbolic Grid System
**HGSC** ........ Hoare Govett Small Companies Index [*British*]
**HGSD** ........ Heavy Gauge Solid Drawn [*Conduit*]
**HGSD News** ... Harvard Graduate School of Design. News [*A publication*]
**HGSE** ........ Harvard Graduate School of Education
**HGSE** ........ Hot Gas Soldering Equipment
**HGSEI** ........ Home and Garden Show Executives International [*Inactive*] (EA)
**HGSHS** ........ Harvard Group Scale of Hypnotic Susceptibility [*Psychology*]
**HGSW** ........ Heavy Gauge Screwed Welded [*Conduit*]
**HGSW** ........ Horn Gap Switch
**HGT** ........ Fort Hunter-Liggett (Jolon), CA [*Location identifier*] [*FAA*] (FAAL)
**HGT** ........ Height (KSC)
**HGT** ........ High Gelling Temperature [*Analytical biochemistry*]
**HGT** ........ High Group Transmitting
**HGT** ........ Household Goods Transportation Association, Washington DC [*STAC*]
**HGT** ........ Hydrostatic-Gauging Technology [*Engineering*]
**HGTA** ........ Honours Graduate Teachers' Association [*British*]
**HGTVC** ........ Hot Gas Thrust Vector Control
**HGU** ........ Horizon Gyroscope Unit [*Aviation*] (AIA)
**HGU** ........ Mount Hagen [*Papua New Guinea*] [*Airport symbol*] (OAG)

**HGUC** ........ Helsinki Guarantees for Ukraine Committee (EA)
**HGV** .......... Heavy Goods Vehicles
**HGV** .......... Highgrade Ventures [*Vancouver Stock Exchange symbol*]
**HGV** .......... Hydrogen Gas Valve (MCD)
**HGVT** ......... Horizontal Ground Vibration Test [*NASA*] (NASA)
**HGW** .......... Heat-Generative Radioactive Wastes [*Nuclear energy*]
**HGWS** ........ H. G. Wells Society (EA)
**HGX** .......... Lawrence, MA [*Location identifier*] [*FAA*] (FAAL)
**HGZG** ......... Hilf Gott zu Glueck [*May God Help Us to Fortune*] [*German*] [*Motto of Magdalene, Princess of Anhalt (1585-1657)*]
**HH** ............. Double Hard [*Pencil leads*]
**HH** ............. Extra Hard [*Pencil leads*]
**HH** ............. Fairchild/Republic [*ICAO aircraft manufacturer identifier*] (ICAO)
**HH** ............. Habitat for Humanity (EA)
**HH** ............. Haiti [*Aircraft nationality and registration mark*] (FAAC)
**HH** ............. Half Hard [*Metallurgy*]
**HH** ............. Half Hardy [*Horticulture*]
**H/H** ........... Half Height [*of an International Standards Organization container*] (DCTA)
**HH** ............. Halothane Hypoxia [*Medicine*]
**HH** ............. Hamish Hamilton [*Publisher*] [*British*]
**HH** ............. Hamizrah Hehadash [*Jerusalem*] [*A publication*] (BJA)
**HH** ............. Hampshire Hunt [*British*]
**HH** ............. Handelshochschule [*Commercial College*] [*German*]
**HH** ............. Handhole (AAG)
**HH** ............. Hands [*Units of measure, especially for the height of horses*]
**HH** ............. Hanging Handset [*Telecommunications*] (TEL)
**HH** ............. Happy Humpers (EA)
**HH** ............. Hard of Hearing
**H & H** ......... Harrison and Hodgin's Upper Canada Municipal Reports [*1845-51*] [*A publication*] (DLA)
**HH** ............. Hashomer Hatzair (EA)
**HH** ............. Haunt Hunters (EA)
**H/H** ........... Havre to Hamburg [*Shipping*]
**HH** ............. Hawaii State Library System, Honolulu, HI [*Library symbol*] [*Library of Congress*] (LCLS)
**HH** ............. Hayward and Hazelton's United States Circuit Court Reports [*District of Columbia*] [*A publication*] (DLA)
**HH** ............. Head, Head [*Coin-tossing possibility*]
**HH** ............. Head-to-Head [*Polymer structure*]
**HH** ............. Heavy Hinged [*Philately*]
**HH** ............. Heavy Hydrogen
**H to H** ........ Heel to Heel
**HH** ............. Heil Hitler [*Political organization*] [*British*]
**HH** ............. Helen Hunt Jackson [*American novelist, 1830-1885*] [*Initials used as pseudonym*]
**H-H** ............ Heli-Home [*Recreational vehicle*]
**HH** ............. Hemmets Haerold [*Record label*] [*Sweden*]
**H & H** ......... Hemoglobin and Hematocrit [*Clinical chemistry*]
**HH** ............. Here's Health [*Exhibition*] [*British*]
**HH** ............. Herman Hospital [*Houston, TX*]
**HH** ............. Hertfordshire Hunt [*British*] (ROG)
**HH** ............. Hiatal Hernia [*Medicine*]
**HH** ............. High-Powered, Nondirectional Radio Homing Beacon [*Navigation*]
**HH** ............. His [*or Her*] Highness
**HH** ............. His Holiness
**HH** ............. His Honour [*British*] (ADA)
**HH** ............. Historical Handbook
**HH** ............. Hodgson's Horse [*British military*] (DMA)
**HH** ............. Hold Harmless (OICC)
**HH** ............. Holidays for Humanity [*An association*] (EA)
**H & H** ......... Holland & Holland [*Custom gun maker*]
**H of H** ........ Holy of Holies [*Freemasonry*] (ROG)
**H u H** ......... Holzforschung und Holzverwertung [*A publication*]
**HH** ............. Home Help [*Medicine*]
**HH** ............. Home Radio Beacon - High Power (FAAC)
**HH** ............. Hommel AG [*Switzerland*] [*Research code symbol*]
**HH** ............. Homonymous Hemianopsia [*Ophthalmology*]
**H & H** ......... Hoofs and Horns [*A publication*] (APTA)
**HH** ............. Hooper Holmes, Inc. [*AMEX symbol*] (SPSG)
**H & H** ......... Horn and Hurlstone's English Exchequer Reports [*1838-39*] [*A publication*] (DLA)
**HH** ............. Hour Hand [*Clocks*] (ROG)
**H/H** ........... House to House (ADA)
**HH** ............. Household
**HH** ............. Hughes Helicopters (MCD)
**HH** ............. Human Hair [*Doll collecting*]
**HH** ............. Human Heredity [*A publication*]
**HH** ............. Humbert Humbert [*Character in Vladimir Nabokov's "Lolita"*]
**HH** ............. Hydroxyhexenal [*Organic chemistry*]
**HH** ............. Hyporeninemic Hypoaldosteronism [*Endocrinology*]
**HH** ............. Les Hieroglyphes Hittites [*A publication*] (BJA)
**HH** ............. Rotary-Wing Air-Sea-Rescue Aircraft [*Navy symbol*] (MUGU)
**HH** ............. Somali Airlines [*Somali Democratic Republic*] [*ICAO designator*] (FAAC)
**HHA** .......... Half-Hardy Annual [*Horticulture*] (ROG)
**H(Ha)** ........ Hare Tempore Wigram, Etc. [*1841-53*] [*A publication*] (DLA)
**HHA** .......... Hatton Heritage Association (EA)
**HHA** .......... Health Hazard Assessment [*Army*]
**HHA** .......... Hereditary Hemolytic Anemia [*Medicine*]
**HHA** .......... Hickory Handle Association (EA)
**HHA** .......... Historic House Association [*British*]
**HHA** .......... Home Health Agency
**HHA** .......... Hungarian Horse Association (EA)
**HHA** .......... Hydro Home Appliances Ltd. [*Formerly, Hemgold Resources Ltd.*] [*Vancouver Stock Exchange symbol*]
**HHA** .......... Hypothalamo-Hypophyseal-Adrenal [*Endocrinology*]
**HHAA** ........ Historic House Association of America (EA)
**HHAG** ........ Human Health Assessment Group [*Environmental Protection Agency*]
**HHALSA** .. Heritage Hills Area Library Services Authority [*Library network*]
**HHAR** ........ Health Hazard Assessment Report [*Army*]
**HHB** .......... Bernice Pauahi Bishop Museum, Honolulu, HI [*Library symbol*] [*Library of Congress*] (LCLS)
**HHB** .......... Half-Hardy Biennial [*Horticulture*] (ROG)
**HHB** .......... Happy Hours Brotherhood (EA)
**HHB** .......... Hattiesburg, MS [*Location identifier*] [*FAA*] (FAAL)
**HHB** .......... Headquarters and Headquarters Battery [*Army*]
**HHb** .......... Hemoglobin, Reduced [*Biochemistry, medicine*]
**HHBC** ......... Honourable Hudson's Bay Company [*Canada*]
**HHBLA** ...... Harper Hospital. Bulletin [*A publication*]
**HHBLG** ...... Hobby Horse Brigade of the Legion of Guardsmen (EA)
**HHBX** ......... HHB Systems, Inc. [*NASDAQ symbol*] (NQ)
**HHC** .......... Chatham College, Pittsburgh, PA [*OCLC symbol*] (OCLC)
**HHC** .......... Hammer Head Crane (NASA)
**HHC** .......... Handheld Computer
**HHC** .......... Harley Hummer Club (EA)
**HHC** .......... Headquarters and Headquarters Company [*Army*]
**HHC** .......... Higher Harmonic Control (MCD)
**HHC** .......... Highland Crow Resources Ltd. [*Toronto Stock Exchange symbol*] [*Vancouver Stock Exchange symbol*]
**HHC** .......... Honolulu Community College, Honolulu, HI [*Library symbol*] [*Library of Congress*] (LCLS)
**HHC** .......... Horizon Healthcare Corporation [*NYSE symbol*] (SPSG)
**HHC** .......... Hovercraft-Helicopter Carrier
**HHC** .......... Hughes Helicopter Company
**HHC** .......... New York City Health and Hospitals Corporation (EA)
**HHCA** ........ Home Health Care of America [*NASDAQ symbol*] (NQ)
**HHCC** ........ Higher Harmonic Circulation Control [*Rotor*] [*Navy*]
**hHCF** ......... Human Humoral Hypercalcemic Factor [*Oncology*]
**HHCL** ........ H-Hour Coordinating Line [*Army*] (AABC)
**HHCL** ........ Hale's History of the Common Law [*A publication*] (DLA)
**HHCL** ........ Howell Henry Chaldecott Lury [*Advertising agency*] [*British*]
**HHD** .......... Doctor of Honorary Humanities
**HHD** .......... Doctor of Humanities
**HHD** .......... Headquarters and Headquarters Detachment [*Army*] (AABC)
**HHD** .......... High Holy Days (BJA)
**HHD** .......... Hogshead
**HHD** .......... Hypertensive Heart Disease [*Medicine*]
**HHDN** ........ Hexachlorohexahydrodimethanonaphthalene [*Insecticide, commonly called Aldrin*]
**HHDS** ........ Hogsheads
**HHDW** ....... Heavy Handy Deadweight [*Scrap*] [*Shipping*]
**HHDWS** .... Heavy Handy Deadweight Scrap Iron [*Shipping*] (DS)
**HHE** .......... Helium to Heat Exchanger (AAG)
**HHE** .......... Hemiconvulsions, Hemiplegia, Epilepsy [*Medicine*]
**HHE** .......... Herringer-Hulster Effect
**HHE** .......... Household Economics Research Division [*of ARS, Department of Agriculture*]
**HHE** .......... Household Effects [*Insurance*]
**HHEC** ......... Hispanic Higher Education Coalition [*Inactive*] (EA)
**HHEFG** ...... Hughes Hall Effect Function Generator
**HHEG** ........ Hughes Hall Effect Generator
**HHE-P** ....... East-West Center, Population Institute, Honolulu, HI [*Library symbol*] [*Library of Congress*] (LCLS)
**HHES** ......... Hex Head Electrical Squib
**HHESD** ...... Population Division and Housing and Household Economics Statistics Division [*Bureau of the Census*] [*Also, an information service or system*] (IID)
**HHF** .......... Canadian, TX [*Location identifier*] [*FAA*] (FAAL)
**HHF** .......... Friends of the Library of Hawaii, Honolulu, HI [*Library symbol*] [*Library of Congress*] (LCLS)
**HHF** .......... Health for Haiti Foundation (EA)
**HHF** .......... Household Furniture [*Insurance*]
**HHF** .......... Hyper-High-Frequency (DEN)
**HHFA** ........ Housing and Home Finance Agency [*Terminated 1965, functions taken over by HUD*]
**HHFC** ........ H. H. Franklin Club (EA)
**HHFTH** ...... National Foundation for Happy Horsemanship for the Handicapped (EA)
**HH-G** ......... Hitchhiker (Goddard Space Flight Center) [*NASA*]
**HHG** .......... Household Goods [*Insurance*]
**HHGFAA** ... Household Goods Forwarders Association of America (EA)
**HHGP** ........ Harris & Harris Group, Inc. [*NASDAQ symbol*] (NQ)
**HHGR** ........ Helian Health Group, Inc. [*NASDAQ symbol*] (NQ)
**HHH** .......... Devine, TX [*Location identifier*] [*FAA*] (FAAL)
**HHH** .......... Harrison Horncastle Holdings [*Investment firm*] [*British*]
**HHH** .......... Hawaii Medical Library, Inc., Honolulu, HI [*Library symbol*] [*Library of Congress*] (LCLS)

**HHH**.......... Heritage Entertainment, Inc. [*AMEX symbol*] (SPSG)
**HHH**.......... Hilton Head Island [*South Carolina*] [*Airport symbol*] (OAG)
**HHH**.......... Hincherton Hayfever Helmet [*Clear plastic head-enclosing device that allegedly relieves hayfever symptoms*]
**HHH**.......... Holistic Health Havens (EA)
**HHH**.......... Hubert Horatio Humphrey [*American politician, 1911-1978*]
**HHH**.......... Triple Hard [*Pencil leads*]
**HHHA**....... Homemaker Home Health Aide (OICC)
**HHHC**....... Hanover Companies, Inc. [*New York, NY*] [*NASDAQ symbol*] (NQ)
**HHHCA**.... Journal. Oceanological Society of Korea [*South Korea*] [*A publication*]
**HHH-CRC** ... Hubert H. Humphrey Cancer Research Center [*Boston University*] [*Research center*] (RCD)
**HHHH**...... Head, Heart, Hands, and Health [*As in 4H organizations*]
**HHHHD**... Heh Hua Hsueh Yu Fang She Hua Hsueh [*A publication*]
**HHHHH**... Hilf, Himmlischer Herr, Hoechster Hort [*Help, Heavenly Father, Highest Treasure*] [*German*] [*Motto of Elisabeth, Duchess of Saxony-Coburg (1540-94)*]
**HHHMU**... Hydrazine Hand-Held Maneuvering Unit (MCD)
**HHHO**...... Hypotonia-Hypomentia-Hypogonadism-Obesity [*Medicine*]
**HHHPA**.... Hua Hsueh Hsueh Pao [*A publication*]
**HHI**.......... Ha-Hevra ha-Historit ha-Israelit [*Historical Society of Israel*] (EAIO)
**HHI**.......... Hampton Healthcare [*AMEX symbol*] (SPSG)
**HHI**.......... Harmony Heights [*Idaho*] [*Seismograph station code, US Geological Survey*] [*Closed*] (SEIS)
**HHI**.......... Harness Horsemen International (EA)
**HHI**.......... Hawaii County Library, Hilo, HI [*Library symbol*] [*Library of Congress*] (LCLS)
**HHi**.......... Hawaiian Historical Society, Honolulu, HI [*Library symbol*] [*Library of Congress*] (LCLS)
**HHI**.......... Histologic HCM [*Hypertrophic Cardiomyopathy*] Index
**HHI**.......... Homer Hoyt Institute
**HHI**.......... Horton Hydrocarbons, Incorporated [*Vancouver Stock Exchange symbol*]
**HHI**.......... Wahiawa, HI [*Location identifier*] [*FAA*] (FAAL)
**HHIC**........ Hilo College, Hilo, HI [*Library symbol*] [*Library of Congress*] (LCLS)
**HHI Geophys Data** ... Heinrich Hertz Institut Geophysical Data [*A publication*]
**HHIP**........ Hand-Held Information Processor
**HHIRF**...... Holifield Heavy Ion Research Facility [*Department of Energy*]
**HHI Sol Data** ... Heinrich Hertz Institut Solar Data [*A publication*]
**HHJ**.......... Hunt, Harold, Jr., Bala-Cynwyd PA [*STAC*]
**HHK**.......... Kapiolani Community College, Honolulu, HI [*Library symbol*] [*Library of Congress*] (LCLS)
**HHL**.......... Court of Session Cases, House of Lords [*Scotland*] [*A publication*] (DLA)
**HHL**.......... Haddon Hall Library [*A publication*]
**HHL**.......... Hollywood Hotline [*Information service or system*] (IID)
**HHLD**....... Household [*Marketing*]
**HHLH**....... Heaviest Heavy Lift Helicopter (MCD)
**HHLR**....... Hand-Held LASER Range-Finder [*Military*] (RDA)
**HHLR**....... Horace Hardy Lestor Reactor
**HHLRF**..... Hand-Held LASER Range-Finder [*Military*] [*British*] (INF)
**H + Hm**.... Compound Hypermetropic Astigmatism [*Ophthalmology*]
**HHM**........ Hawkes Hospital of Mount Carmel, Mount Carmel Medical Center Library, Columbus, OH [*OCLC symbol*] (OCLC)
**HHM**........ Health and Healing Ministries (EA)
**HH-M**....... Hitchhiker (Marshall Space Flight Center) [*NASA*]
**HHM**........ Humoral Hypercalcemia of Malignancy [*Medicine*]
**HHM**........ Hungry Horse [*Montana*] [*Seismograph station code, US Geological Survey*] (SEIS)
**HHM**........ Kotzebue, AK [*Location identifier*] [*FAA*] (FAAL)
**HHM**........ Sisters of the Holy Humility of Mary [*Roman Catholic religious order*]
**HHMC**...... Hawaiian Mission Children's Society, Honolulu, HI [*Library symbol*] [*Library of Congress*] (LCLS)
**HHMHDB** ... Hispanic Health and Mental Health Data Base [*National Institute of Mental Health*] [*Information service or system*] (CRD)
**HHMI**....... Howard Hughes Medical Institute
**HHMS**...... His Hellenic Majesty's Ship
**HHMU**...... Handheld Maneuvering Unit [*NASA*]
**HHN**......... Hahnemann Medical College and Hospital, Philadelphia, PA [*OCLC symbol*] (OCLC)
**HHN**......... Hot Hydrogen Nozzle
**HHN**......... Houthandel en Houtnijverheid. Algemeen Vakblad voor de Houthandel en de Houtnijverheid [*A publication*]
**HHNC**...... His Highness the Nizam's Cavalry [*British military*] (DMA)
**HHNK**...... Hyperosmolar Hyperglycemic Nonketotic (Coma) [*Also, NKHHC*] [*Medicine*]
**HHOC**...... Holistic Health Organizing Committee (EA)
**H Hol**....... Herald of Holiness [*A publication*]
**H & Home** ... House and Home [*A publication*]
**HHOT**...... H & H Oil Tool Co., Inc. [*NASDAQ symbol*] (NQ)
**HHP**......... Half-Hardy Perennial [*Horticulture*] (ROG)
**HHP**......... Head of Household Program [*IRS*]
**HHP**......... Hydraulic Hand Pump
**HHP**......... Pineapple Research Institute, Honolulu, HI [*Library symbol*] [*Library of Congress*] (LCLS)
**HHPA**....... Hexahydrophthalic Anhydride [*Organic chemistry*]
**HHPAA**..... Hospital Health Promotion Association of Australia
**HHPC**....... Hale's History of the Pleas of the Crown [*A publication*] (DLA)
**HHPC**....... Hand-Held Programmable Calculator (MCD)
**HHPLA**..... Herbert Hoover Presidential Library Association (EA)
**HHPRT**..... Human Hypoxanthine Phosphoribosyltransferase [*An enzyme*]
**HHR**......... Handheld RADAR (AABC)
**HHR**......... Hawthorne, CA [*Location identifier*] [*FAA*] (FAAL)
**HHR**......... High Reserve Resources [*Vancouver Stock Exchange symbol*]
**HHRSD**..... Helicopter Hauldown and Rapid Securing Device [*Military*] (CAAL)
**HHRV**....... Holistic Health Review [*A publication*]
**HHS**.......... Department of Health and Human Services [*Formerly, HEW*]
**HHS**.......... Hawaiian Sugar Planters' Association, Experiment Station, Honolulu, HI [*Library symbol*] [*Library of Congress*] (LCLS)
**H & HS**...... Headquarters and Headquarters Squadron [*Marine Corps*]
**HHS**.......... Hex Head Squib
**HHS**.......... Horse Hemolyzate Supernatant
**HHS**.......... Hospital and Health Services Administration [*A publication*]
**HHS**.......... Huguenot Historical Society (EA)
**HHS**.......... Hypothenar Hammer Syndrome [*Medicine*]
**HHS**.......... Society of Helpers of the Holy Souls [*Roman Catholic women's religious order*]
**HHSA**....... Home Health Services Association [*Later, HHSSA*] (EA)
**HHSA**....... Honolulu Star-Bulletin and Advertiser, Honolulu, HI [*Library symbol*] [*Library of Congress*] (LCLS)
**HHSB**....... Hahnemann High School Behavior Rating Scale [*Psychology*]
**HHSD**....... Holographic Horizontal Situation Display
**HHSI**........ High-Head Safety Injection [*Nuclear energy*] (NRCH)
**HHSSA**..... Home Health Services and Staffing Association (EA)
**HHSZYM** ... Hashomer Hatzair Socialist Zionist Youth Movement (EA)
**HHT**......... Headquarters and Headquarters Troop [*Army*] (AABC)
**HHT**......... Hereditary Hemorrhagic Telangiectasia [*Medicine*]
**HHT**......... Holland Historical Trust (EA)
**HHT**......... Homoharringtonine [*Antineoplastic drug*]
**HHT**......... Horn-Hellersberg Test [*Psychology*]
**HHT**......... Hurricane Hollow [*Tennessee*] [*Seismograph station code, US Geological Survey*] [*Closed*] (SEIS)
**HHT**......... Hush House Tiedown
**HHT**......... Hydroxyheptadecatrienoic Acid [*Organic chemistry*]
**HHTG**....... House Heating [*Freight*]
**HHTI**........ Hand-Held Thermal Imager [*Navy*] [*British*]
**HHTM**...... United States Army, Tripler Army Medical Center, Honolulu, HI [*Library symbol*] [*Library of Congress*] (LCLS)
**HHTPA**..... Hua Hsueh Tung Pao [*China*] [*A publication*]
**HHTTFS**.... Huddersfield Healders and Twisters Trade and Friendly Society [*A union*] [*British*] (DCTA)
**HHTV**....... Handheld Thermal Viewer (RDA)
**HHV**......... Handheld Viewer
**HHV**......... Help Hospitalized Veterans (EA)
**HHV**......... High Heat [*or Heating*] Value
**HHV**......... Human Herpes Virus
**HHW**........ High-Heat Waste (NRCH)
**HHW**........ Higher High Water [*Tides and currents*]
**HHW**........ Household Hazardous Waste
**HHWI**....... Higher High-Water Interval
**HHY**......... Savannah, TN [*Location identifier*] [*FAA*] (FAAL)
**HHYF**....... Harness Horse Youth Foundation (EA)
**HI**.............. Dominican Republic [*Aircraft nationality and registration mark*] (FAAC)
**HI**.............. Habitability Improvement [*Navy*] (NVT)
**HI**.............. Hamersley Iron Proprietary Ltd. [*Australia*]
**HI**.............. Handicap Introductions (EA)
**HI**.............. Handling Instructions (MCD)
**H and I**....... Harassment and Interdiction
**HI**.............. Harcost Industries
**HI**.............. Harold Institute (EA)
**HI**.............. Harvest Index [*Agronomy*]
**HI**.............. Hat Institute (EA)
**HI**.............. Hawaii [*Postal code*]
**HI**.............. Hawaii Reports [*A publication*] (DLA)
**HI**.............. Hawaiian Islands
**HI**.............. Health Inspector [*British military*] (DMA)
**HI**.............. Health Insurance
**HI**.............. Hearing Impaired (OICC)
**HI**.............. Heartland Institute [*Research center*] (RCD)
**HI**.............. Heat Index
**HI**.............. Heavily Included [*Colored gemstone grade*]
**HI**.............. Height Indicator (NVT)
**HI**.............. Hemagglutination Inhibition [*Immunochemistry*]
**Hi**.............. Hiburnium [*Supposed chemical element, discovered 1922*]
**HI**.............. Hic Iacet [*Here Lies*] [*Latin*]
**Hi**.............. Hid [*A publication*]
**HI**.............. Hideaways International [*Commercial firm*] (EA)
**HI**.............. High [*Data processing*] (AAG)
**HI**.............. High Impact
**HI**.............. High Intensity

**HI**.............. Hirth KG [*Federal Republic of Germany*] [*ICAO aircraft manufacturer identifier*] (ICAO)
**Hi**.............. Hispania [*A publication*]
**HI**.............. Hispanic Institute (EA)
**HI**.............. Histadruth Ivrith of America
**HI**.............. Historica Iberica [*A publication*]
**HI**.............. Holton Inter-Urban Railway Co. [*AAR code*]
**H-I**.............. Hondacar International (EA)
**HI**.............. Honeywell, Incorporated (NASA)
**HI**.............. Hong Kong Air International Ltd. [*ICAO designator*] (FAAC)
**HI**.............. Horizontal Interval
**HI**.............. Hospital Insurance
**HI**.............. Hostesses Internationales [*French dating service*]
**HI**.............. Hot Issue [*Investment term*]
**HI**.............. Household International, Inc. [*NYSE symbol*] (SPSG)
**HI**.............. Housing Improvement
**HI**.............. Hudson Institute (EA)
**HI**.............. Human Interest
**HI**.............. Humanities Index [*A publication*]
**HI**.............. Humidity Index
**HI**.............. Hybrid Index [*Botany*]
**HI**.............. Hydraulic Institute (EA)
**HI**.............. Hydriodic Acid [*Inorganic chemistry*]
**HI**.............. Hydrodynamic Interaction [*Chemistry*]
**HI**.............. Hydrogen Iodide [*Inorganic chemistry*]
**HI**.............. Hydronics Institute (EA)
**Hi**.............. Methemoglobin [*Symbol*] [*Medicine*]
**HI-12**.............. High Twelve International (EA)
**HIA**.............. Handkerchief Industry Association [*Defunct*] (EA)
**HIA**.............. Harrisburg International Airport (MCD)
**HIA**.............. Headwear Institute of America (EA)
**HIA**.............. Health Industries Association [*Later, HIMA*]
**HIA**.............. Hearing Industries Association (EA)
**HIA**.............. Heart Infusion Agar [*Medicine*]
**HIA**.............. Held [*or Hold*] in Abeyance [*Military*] (AFM)
**HIA**.............. Hemagglutination Inhibition Antibody [*Immunochemistry*]
**HIA**.............. Histadruth Ivrith of America (EA)
**HIA**.............. Hobby Industry Association of America
**HIA**.............. Holiday Corp. [*NYSE symbol*] (SPSG)
**HIA**.............. Horological Institute of America [*Later, AWI*]
**HIA**.............. Housing Industry Association
**HIA**.............. Whitehall, MT [*Location identifier*] [*FAA*] (FAAL)
**HIAA**.............. Health Insurance Association of America [*Washington, DC*] (EA)
**HIAA**.............. Hobby Industry Association of America (EA)
**HIAA**.............. Hydroxyindoleacetic Acid [*Organic chemistry*]
**HIAC**.............. Health Industry Advisory Committee [*Terminated, 1974*] (EGAO)
**HIAC**.............. High Accuracy [*RADAR*]
**HIAD**.............. Handbook of Instructions for Aircraft Designers
**HIADS**.............. Hawaiian Integrated Air Defense System
**HIAFSB**.............. Handbook of Instructions for Air Force Subsystem Designers
**HIAG**.............. Healthcare International Audit Group (EA)
**HIAGSE**.............. Handbook of Instructions for Aircraft Ground Support Equipment Designers
**HIAGSED**... Handbook of Instructions for Aircraft Ground Support Equipment Designers
**HIAI**.............. Housing Industries of America [*NASDAQ symbol*] (NQ)
**HIALS**.............. High-Intensity Approach Lighting System [*Airport runways*]
**HIALT**.............. High Altitude (MCD)
**HI/AMBBA**... Hair International/Associated Master Barbers and Beauticians of America (EA)
**HIAPSD**.............. Handbook of Instructions for Aerospace Personnel Subsystem Designers
**HIAR**.............. Hamburger Ibero-Amerikanische Reihe [*A publication*]
**HIARA**.............. Hail Insurance Adjustment and Research Association [*Later, NCIA*] (EA)
**HIAS**.............. Hebrew Immigrant Aid Society
**HIAS**.............. Heritage of Indian Art Series [*A publication*]
**HIASD**.............. Handbook of Instructions for Aerospace Systems Design
**HIAVED**... Handbook of Instructions for Aerospace Vehicle Equipment Design
**HIB**.............. Haemophilus Influenzae, Type B
**HIB**.............. Hawaiian Freight Tariff Bureau Inc., Maywood CA [*STAC*]
**HIB**.............. Hemophilus Influenzae Type B [*Medicine*]
**HIB**.............. Herring Industries Board [*British*]
**HIB**.............. Hibbing [*Minnesota*] [*Airport symbol*] (OAG)
**HIB**.............. Hibernia [*Ancient name for Ireland*] (ROG)
**HIB**.............. Hibernia Corp. Class A [*NYSE symbol*] (SPSG)
**HIB**.............. High-Impedance Bridge
**HIB**.............. Hoop-Iron Bond [*Construction*]
**HIBA**.............. Hawaiian International Billfish Association (EA)
**HIBA**.............. Hydroxyisobutyric Acid [*Organic chemistry*]
**HIBAC**.............. Health Insurance Benefits Advisory Council [*Department of Health and Human Services*] [*Inactive*]
**HIBAL**.............. High-Altitude Balloon
**Hibb**.............. Hibbard's Reports [*Opinions Attorneys-General*] [*A publication*] (DLA)
**Hibb**.............. Hibbard's Reports [*New Hampshire*] [*A publication*] (DLA)
**HibbJ**.............. Hibbert Journal [*A publication*]
**HIBC**.............. Hydrogen-Induced Blister Cracking [*Metallurgy*]
**HIBCC**.............. Health Industry Business Communications Council (EA)
**Hibernation Torpor Mamm Birds**... Hibernation and Torpor in Mammals and Birds [*A publication*]
**HIBEX**.............. High-Impulse Booster Experiments [*DARPA/Army*]
**HibJ**.............. Hibbert Journal [*A publication*]
**HIBR**.............. Huxley Institute for Biosocial Research (EA)
**HIBREL**.............. High-Brightness Relay [*Military*] (SDI)
**Hibridni Kukuruz Jugoslav**... Hibridni Kukuruz Jugoslavie [*A publication*]
**HIBT**.............. High-Interest Books for Teens [*A publication*]
**HIBT**.............. Howard Ink Blot Test [*Psychology*]
**HIC**.............. Habitat International Council [*The Hague, Netherlands*] (EAIO)
**HIC**.............. Hand Indicator Controller (NRCH)
**HIC**.............. Happy Irish Celebration
**HIC**.............. Hardware Indenture Code (KSC)
**HIC**.............. Head Injury Criteria [*Medicine*]
**HIC**.............. Health Insurance Claim Number [*Medicare*] (DHSM)
**HIC**.............. Health Insurance Council [*Later, Consumer and Professional Relations Division of HIAA*] (EA)
**HIC**.............. Health Issues Centre [*Australia*]
**HIC**.............. Heart Information Center
**HIC**.............. Heavy Industries Corporation [*Burma*] (DS)
**HIC**.............. Hemispheric Insurance Conference
**HIC**.............. Hickam Air Force Base, Hawaii [*NASA*] (NASA)
**HI-C**.............. High-Conversion Critical Experiment (IEEE)
**HIC**.............. High-Intensity Conflict [*Military*]
**HIC**.............. Higher Education and Research in the Netherlands [*A publication*]
**HIC**.............. Highly Indebted Country
**HIC**.............. Highly Ionized Cloud [*Galactic science*]
**HIC**.............. Hole-in-Corner [*Paper*] (DSUE)
**HIC**.............. Homosexual Information Center (EA)
**HIC**.............. Honduras Information Center (EA)
**HIC**.............. Hot Idle Compensation [*Automotive engineering*]
**HIC**.............. Hot Isostatic Compaction
**HIC**.............. Household and Industrial Chemical
**HIC**.............. Humidity Indicator Controller [*Aerospace*]
**HIC**.............. Hybrid Integrated Circuit
**HIC**.............. Hydrogen-Induced Cracking [*Metallurgy*]
**HIC**.............. Hydrographic Information Committee [*NATO*] (NATG)
**HIC**.............. Hydrologist in Charge (NOAA)
**HIC**.............. Hydrophobic Interaction Chromatography
**HIC**.............. White Cloud, MI [*Location identifier*] [*FAA*] (FAAL)
**HICA**.............. Honey Industry Council of America (EA)
**HICAP**.............. High-Capacity Projectile (NVT)
**HICAP**.............. High [*Altitude*] Combat Air Patrol (NVT)
**HICAPCOM**... High-Capacity Communication System
**HICAS**.............. High-Capacity Active Control Suspension [*Automotive engineering*]
**HICAT**.............. High-Altitude Clear Air Turbulence [*Aviation*]
**HICB**.............. Hong Kong Industrial & Commercial Bank
**H-ICDA**.............. International Classification of Diseases - Adopted Code for Hospitals
**HICES**.............. Heads of Independent Co-Educational Schools [*Australia*]
**HICF**.............. Health Insurance Claim Form
**HICHS**.............. Helicopter Internal Cargo Handling System
**Hick Ct Mar**... Hickman on Naval Courts-Martial [*A publication*] (DLA)
**Hickenia (Bol Darwinion)**... Hickenia (Boletin del Darwinion) [*A publication*]
**Hickory Task Force Rep Stheast For Exp Sta**... Hickory Task Force Report. Southeastern Forest Experiment Station [*A publication*]
**Hicks Ethics**... Hicks' Organization and Ethics of Bench and Bar [*A publication*] (DLA)
**Hicks Leg Research**... Hicks on Materials and Methods of Legal Research [*A publication*] (DLA)
**Hicks Men & Books**... Hicks on Men and Books Famous in the Law [*A publication*] (DLA)
**HICL**.............. Histoire des Idees et Critique Litteraire [*A publication*]
**HICLASS**... Hierarchical Classification [*Indexing*]
**HICLR**.............. Hastings International and Comparative Law Review [*A publication*]
**HICOG**.............. High Commissioner for Germany
**HICOM**.............. High Command
**HICOM**.............. High Commission [*or Commissioner*]
**HICOMRY**... High Commissioner of Ryukyu Islands
**HICOMSEVONET**... High Command Secure Voice Network [*Navy*] (NVT)
**HICOMTERPACIS**... High Commissioner Trust Territory, Pacific Islands
**HICS**.............. Hardened Intersite Cable System (CET)
**HICS**.............. Hierarchical Information Control System [*Japanese*]
**HICS**.............. Holt International Children's Services (EA)
**HICW**.............. History of the Canadian West [*A publication*]
**HID**.............. Hamer Butte [*Idaho*] [*Seismograph station code, US Geological Survey*] (SEIS)
**HID**.............. Hardware Installation Data (CAAL)
**HID**.............. Hardware Interface Device (NASA)
**HID**.............. Headache, Insomnia, Depression [*Syndrome*]
**HID**.............. Helium Ionization Detector [*Instrumentation*]
**HID**.............. Hierarchical Identification
**HID**.............. High-Impact Design (NRCH)
**HID**.............. High-Intensity Discharge [*Vapor lamp*]
**HID**.............. High-Iron Diamine

**HID**........... HIM [*Hardware Interface Module*] Interface Distributor (NASA)
**HID**........... Human Immune Deficiency [*Immunology*]
**HID**........... Hyperkinetic Impulse Disorder [*Medicine*]
**HIDA**......... Health Industry Distributors Association (EA)
**HIDA**......... Home Improvement Dealers Association of America (EA)
**HID-AB**..... High-Iron Diamine-Alcian Blue [*A biological stain*]
**HIDACZ**... High-Density Airspace Control Zone (MCD)
**HIDAD**...... Helicopter Insecticide Dispersal Apparatus, Dry (NG)
**HIDAF**...... Helicopter Insecticide Dispersal Apparatus, Fog (NG)
**HIDAL**...... Helicopter Insecticide Dispersal Apparatus, Liquid (NG)
**HIDAM**..... Hierarchical Indexed Direct Access Method [*Data processing*] (BUR)
**HIDAN**...... High-Density Air Navigation
**HIDB**......... Highlands and Islands Development Board [*Scotland*] (ECON)
**HIDE**......... Helicopter Integrated Direction Equipment
**HIDE**......... High-Absorption Integrated Defense Electromagnetic Warfare System
**HIDEC**...... Highly Integrated Digital Engine Control (MCD)
**HIDF**......... Horizontal Side of an Intermediate Distribution Frame [*Telecommunications*] (TEL)
**HIDI**......... Health-Care Instruments and Devices Institute [*State University of New York at Buffalo*] [*Research center*] (RCD)
**HIDKA**...... Hiroshima Daigaku Kogakubu Kenkyu Hokoku [*A publication*]
**HiD/LoD**... High-Density/Low-Density Tariff
**HIDM**........ High Information Delta Modulation [*Data processing*] (BUR)
**HIDRA**...... Hidrologiai Koczlocny [*A publication*]
**Hidrol Koezl**... Hidrologiai Koezloeny [*A publication*]
**Hidroteh Gospod Apelor Meteorol**... Hidrotehnica Gospodarirea Apelor. Meteorologia [*Romania*] [*A publication*]
**Hidroteh Melior Latv PSR**... Hidrotehnika un Melioracija Latvijas PSR [*A publication*]
**HIDTC**...... Hangar and Industrial Door Technical Council [*Defunct*] (MSA)
**HIE**........... Express. Daily Financial Newspaper [*Athens*] [*A publication*]
**HIE**........... Height Integration Equipment
**HIE**........... Help in Emergency (ADA)
**HIE**........... Hibernation Information Exchange [*Later, IHS*]
**HIE**........... Homelessness Information Exchange (EA)
**HIE**........... Whitefield, NH [*Location identifier*] [*FAA*] (FAAL)
**HIEAT**....... Highest Temperature Equaled for All Time [*Meteorology*] (FAAC)
**HIECA**...... High Energy Chemistry [*English Translation*] [*A publication*]
**HIEFM**...... Highest Temperature Equaled for the Month [*Meteorology*] (FAAC)
**HIEFSS**..... Hospital, Institution, and Educational Food Service Society [*Later, Dietary Managers Association - DMA*] (EA)
**Hier**........... Hieronymus [*Jerome*] [*348-420AD*] (BJA)
**HIER**......... Hierusolymo [*Jerusalem*] (ROG)
**Hier Gabr**... Hieronymus Gabrielius [*Deceased, 1587*] [*Authority cited in pre-1607 legal work*] (DSA)
**Hiero**.......... Hieroglyphics
**Hiero**.......... Hierophant [*A publication*]
**Hiero Cag**... Hieronymus Cagnolus [*Deceased, 1551*] [*Authority cited in pre-1607 legal work*] (DSA)
**Hiero Cagno**... Hieronymus Cagnolus [*Deceased, 1551*] [*Authority cited in pre-1607 legal work*] (DSA)
**Hieron**........ Hieronymus [*Jerome*] [*348-420AD*] (OCD)
**Hieron Cagno**... Hieronymus Cagnolus [*Deceased, 1551*] [*Authority cited in pre-1607 legal work*] (DSA)
**Hieron Gabriel**... Hieronymus Gabrielius [*Deceased, 1587*] [*Authority cited in pre-1607 legal work*] (DSA)
**Hieron Grat**... Hieronymus Gratus [*Deceased, 1544*] [*Authority cited in pre-1607 legal work*] (DSA)
**Hier Schurf**... Hieronymus Schurff [*Deceased, 1554*] [*Authority cited in pre-1607 legal work*] (DSA)
**Hier Torniel**... Hieronymus Torniellus [*Deceased, 1575*] [*Authority cited in pre-1607 legal work*] (DSA)
**HIES**.......... Hadassah Israel Education Services [*Jerusalem*]
**HIESE**....... Highest Temperature Equaled So Early [*Meteorology*] (FAAC)
**HIESL**....... Highest Temperature Equaled So Late [*Meteorology*] (FAAC)
**HIF**............ Health Information Foundation
**HIF**............ High-Impedance Follower
**HIF**............ Higher Integrative Functions [*Neurology*]
**HIF**............ Hocker International Federation (EA)
**H of IF**....... House of Ill Fame
**HIF**............ Human-Initiated Failure
**HIF**............ Ogden, UT [*Location identifier*] [*FAA*] (FAAL)
**HIFAM**..... High-Fidelity Amplitude Modulation (DEN)
**HIFAR**...... High Flux Australian Research Reactor [*Nuclear energy*] (DEN)
**HIFAR**...... High-Frequency Fixed Array RADAR
**HIFBS**....... Heat-Inactivated Fetal Bovine Serum [*Immunology*]
**HIFC**......... Hog Intrinsic Factor Concentrate
**HIFI**.......... HFIR [*High-Flux Isotope Reactor*] Irradiation Facility Improvement [*Nuclear energy*]
**HIFI**.......... High Fibre Biscuits [*British*]
**HI-FI**......... High-Fidelity [*Usually, in reference to home sound-reproducing equipment*]
**Hi Fi**.......... High Fidelity [*A publication*]
**Hi Fi**.......... High Fidelity/Musical America [*A publication*]
**HIFI**.......... High Fidelity Records [*Record label*]
**HIFI**.......... High-Intensity Food Irradiator
**Hi Fi/Mus Am**... High Fidelity/Musical America [*A publication*]
**Hi-Fi News Rec Rev**... Hi-Fi News and Record Review [*A publication*]
**HIFO**......... Highest In, First Out [*Accounting*]
**HIFOR**...... High-Level Forecast [*Meteorology*]
**HIFPA**....... Hispanic Institute for the Performing Arts (EA)
**HIFR**......... Helicopter In-Flight Refueling (NVT)
**HIFRAG**.... High Fragmentation (MCD)
**HIFS**.......... Hingham Institution for Savings [*NASDAQ symbol*] (CTT)
**HIFT**.......... Hardware Implemented Fault Tolerance
**HIG**............ Hartford Fire Insurance Co. [*NYSE symbol*] (SPSG)
**HIG**............ Hawaii Institute of Geophysics [*University of Hawaii*] [*Seismograph station code, US Geological Survey*] [*Research center*] (SEIS)
**HIG**............ Hermetically Sealed, Integrating Gyroscope
**HIG**............ Higginsville, MO [*Location identifier*] [*FAA*] (FAAL)
**HIG**............ High Input Grant [*Real estate*] [*Canada*]
**HIG**............ High-Integrating Gyroscope (KSC)
**HIG**............ Honeywell Integrating Gyro
**HIG**............ Hypervelocity Intercept Guidance
**HIGAD**...... High-Impulse Gun Airborne Demonstrator (MCD)
**HIGB**......... J. Higby's, Inc. [*NASDAQ symbol*] (NQ)
**HIGE**......... Hovering in Ground Effect [*Army*]
**HIGED**...... Handbook of Instructions for Ground Equipment Designers (MCD)
**Higgins**...... Higgins' Tennessee Court of Civil Appeals Reports [*A publication*] (DLA)
**Higg J Poet**... Higginson Journal of Poetry [*A publication*]
**HIGH**........ Highland Railway [*British*] (ROG)
**HIGH**........ Highland Superstores, Inc. [*NASDAQ symbol*] (NQ)
**HIGHB**...... Highbury College of Divinity [*British*] (ROG)
**High Bail**... Highmore on Bail [*A publication*] (DLA)
**HIGHCT**... Commonwealth Law Reports. Decisions of the High Court and Privy Council [*Database*] [*Australia*]
**High Ct**...... High Court Reports, Northwest Provinces [*India*] [*A publication*] (DLA)
**High Educ**... Higher Education [*A publication*]
**High Educ Abstr**... Higher Education Abstracts [*A publication*]
**High Educ R**... Higher Education Review [*A publication*]
**High Educ R & D**... Higher Education Research and Development [*A publication*]
**High Educ Rev**... Higher Education Review [*A publication*]
**High Energy Chem**... High Energy Chemistry [*A publication*]
**Higher Ed**.. Higher Education [*A publication*]
**Higher Ed J**... Higher Education Journal [*A publication*]
**Higher Ed R**... Higher Education Review [*A publication*]
**Higher Educ**... Higher Education [*A publication*]
**High Ex Rem**... High on Extraordinary Legal Remedies [*A publication*] (DLA)
**High Extr Leg Rem**... High on Extraordinary Legal Remedies [*A publication*] (DLA)
**HIGH GASSER**... High Geographic Aerospace Search RADAR
**High Inj**..... High on Injunctions [*A publication*] (DLA)
**HIGH LI**... Highland Light Infantry [*Military*] [*British*] (ROG)
**Highlights Agr Res**... Highlights of Agricultural Research. Alabama Agricultural Experiment Station [*A publication*]
**High Lun**.... Highmore on Lunacy [*A publication*] (DLA)
**High Mort**... Highmore on Mortmain [*A publication*] (DLA)
**HIG (Honolulu) HI**... Hawaii Institute of Geophysics (Honolulu). University of Hawaii [*A publication*]
**High Per T**... High Performance Textiles [*A publication*]
**High Polym**... High Polymers [*A publication*]
**High Polym (Jpn)**... High Polymers (Japan) [*A publication*]
**High Rec**.... High on the Law of Receivers [*A publication*] (DLA)
**HIGHRS**.... Highlanders [*British*]
**High Sch Chem Teach Mag**... High School Chemistry Teachers' Magazine [*A publication*]
**High Sch J**... High School Journal [*A publication*]
**High Speed Ground Transp J**... High Speed Ground Transportation Journal [*A publication*]
**High Speed Gr Transpn J**... High Speed Ground Transportation Journal [*A publication*]
**High-Speed Surf Craft**... High-Speed Surface Craft [*A publication*]
**Hight**.......... Hight's Reports [*57-58 Iowa*] [*A publication*] (DLA)
**High Tech**... High Technology [*A publication*]
**High Technol**... High Technology [*United States*] [*A publication*]
**High Temp**... High Temperature [*A publication*]
**High Temp High Pressures**... High Temperatures - High Pressures [*A publication*]
**High Temp R**... High Temperature USSR [*A publication*]
**High Temp S**... High Temperature Science [*A publication*]
**High Temp Sci**... High Temperature Science [*A publication*]
**High Temp Technol**... High Temperature Technology [*A publication*]
**Highw**........ Highway [*A publication*] (APTA)
**Highway Engr**... Highway Engineer [*A publication*]
**Highway Geol Symp Proc**... Highway Geology Symposium Proceedings [*A publication*]
**Highway User Q**... Highway User Quarterly [*A publication*]
**Highw Des Constr**... Highways Design and Construction [*A publication*]

**Highw Eng** ... Highway Engineer [*A publication*]
**Highw Eng Aust** ... Highway Engineering in Australia [*A publication*] (APTA)
**Highw Engng Aust** ... Highway Engineering in Australia [*A publication*] (APTA)
**Highw Engr** ... Highway Engineer [*A publication*]
**Highw Heavy Constr** ... Highway and Heavy Construction [*A publication*]
**Highw Public Wks** ... Highways and Public Works [*A publication*]
**Highw Public Works** ... Highways and Public Works [*A publication*]
**Highw Publ Wks** ... Highways and Public Works [*A publication*]
**Highw Rd Constr** ... Highways and Road Construction [*A publication*]
**Highw Res Abstr** ... Highway Research Abstracts [*A publication*]
**Highw Res Bd Nat Coop Highw Res Program Rep** ... Highway Research Board. National Cooperative Highway Research Program. Report [*A publication*]
**Highw Res Board Bull** ... Highway Research Board. Bulletin [*A publication*]
**Highw Res Board Bull Spec Rep** ... Highway Research Board. Bulletin. Special Reports [*A publication*]
**Highw Res Board Natl Coop Highw Res Program** ... Highway Research Board. National Cooperative Highway Research Program. Report [*A publication*]
**Highw Res Board Proc Annu Meet** ... Highway Research Board. Proceedings of the Annual Meeting [*A publication*]
**Highw Res Board Spec Rep** ... Highway Research Board. Special Report [*A publication*]
**Highw Res Bull** ... Highway Research Bulletin [*India*] [*A publication*]
**Highw Res Bull (New Delhi)** ... Highway Research Bulletin (New Delhi) [*A publication*]
**Highw Res News** ... Highway Research News [*A publication*]
**Highw Res Rec** ... Highway Research Record [*A publication*]
**Highw Road Const** ... Highways and Road Construction [*A publication*]
**Highw Road Constr Int** ... Highways and Road Construction International [*A publication*]
**Highws Transpn** ... Highways and Transportation [*A publication*]
**Highw Traff Engng** ... Highways of Traffic Engineering [*A publication*]
**Highw Transp** ... Highway Transport [*A publication*] (APTA)
**Highw Urban Mass Transp** ... Highway and Urban Mass Transportation [*United States*] [*A publication*]
**Hig Pat Dig** ... Higgins' Digest of Patent Cases [*1890*] [*A publication*] (DLA)
**HIGS** ......... Hypervelocity Interceptor Guidance Simulation
**HIGSED**.... Handbook of Instructions for Aircraft Ground Support Equipment Designers
**HIGSS** ....... Hypervelocity Intercept Guidance Simulator Study
**Hig Waterc** ... Higgins' Pollution and Obstruction of Watercourses [*1877*] [*A publication*] (DLA)
**HIH** ........... Greensboro, NC [*Location identifier*] [*FAA*] (FAAL)
**HIH** ........... His [*or Her*] Imperial Highness
**HIHAD** ..... Hanyang Idae Haksuljip [*A publication*]
**HIHAT**...... High-Resolution Hemispherical Reflector Antenna Technique
**HI-HICAT** ... High High-Altitude Clear Air Turbulence [*Aviation*]
**HIHOE**...... Hydrogen, Ions, Helium, Oxygen in the Exosphere (MUGU)
**HIHRC**...... Humanitas International Human Rights Committee (EA)
**HII** ............ Health Industries Institute (EA)
**HII** ............ Health Insurance Institute (EA)
**HII** ............ Healthcare International, Incorporated [*AMEX symbol*] (SPSG)
**HII** ............ Heard Island [*Heard Island*] [*Seismograph station code, US Geological Survey*] [*Closed*] (SEIS)
**HII** ............ High Input Impedance
**HIID** .......... Harvard Institute for International Development [*Harvard University*] [*Research center*] (RCD)
**HIID** .......... Heavy Ion-Induced Desorption [*Analytical chemistry*]
**HIIS**........... Honeywell Institute for Information Science (IEEE)
**HIISAP** ..... Industrija Secera [*A publication*]
**HIIYSP** ..... Himalayan International Institute of Yoga Science and Philosophy
**HIJ** ............ Hiroshima [*Japan*] [*Airport symbol*] (OAG)
**HIJ** ............ Sisters of the Holy Infant Jesus [*Roman Catholic religious order*]
**HIJMA**...... Hiroshima Journal of Medical Sciences [*A publication*]
**HIJMS** ...... His Imperial Japanese Majesty's Ship
**HIK**............ High Permittivity (DEN)
**HIK**............ Hikone [*Japan*] [*Seismograph station code, US Geological Survey*] (SEIS)
**HIK**............ Honolulu, HI [*Location identifier*] [*FAA*] (FAAL)
**HIKAA** ...... Hikaku Kagaku [*Japan*] [*A publication*]
**HIKEEV**.... Handbuch der Infusionstherapie und Klinischen Ernaehrung [*A publication*]
**Hikobia J Hiroshima Bot Club** ... Hikobia Journal of the Hiroshima Botanical Club [*A publication*]
**HIKYA** ...... Hinyokika Kiyo [*Japan*] [*A publication*]
**HIKYAJ** .... Acta Urologica Japonica [*A publication*]
**HIL**............ Great Bend, KS [*Location identifier*] [*FAA*] (FAAL)
**HIL**............ Hees International Bancorp, Inc. [*Toronto Stock Exchange symbol*]
**HIL**............ Helium Impurities Loop [*Nuclear energy*] (NRCH)
**HIL**............ High-Intensity Light
**Hil**............. Hilary Term [*England*] [*Legal term*] (DLA)
**HIL**............ Hillhaven Corp. [*AMEX symbol*] (SPSG)
**HIL**............ Hilo [*Hawaii*] [*Seismograph station code, US Geological Survey*] (SEIS)
**Hil Abr**....... Hilliard's American Law [*A publication*] (DLA)
**HILAC**....... Heavy-Ion Linear Accelerator [*Nuclear energy*]
**HILASD**.... Hard Link Arm Safe Device (MCD)
**HILAST** .... High-Altitude Large Area Surveillance Tactic [*Military*] (CAAL)
**HILAT**....... High-Latitude Research Satellite [*Defense Nuclear Agency*]
**HILC** ......... Hampshire Inter-Library Center [*Library network*]
**HILC** ......... High-Intermediate Level Cell [*Nuclear energy*] (NRCH)
**HILDCAA** ... High-Intensity, Long-Duration, Continuous Aurora Event, Activity [*Astrophysics*]
**Hild Ins**...... Hildyard on Insurance [*A publication*] (DLA)
**Hild Mar Ins** ... Hildyard's Marine Insurance [*A publication*] (DLA)
**Hil Elem Law** ... Hilliard's Elements of Law [*A publication*] (DLA)
**HILGA** ...... Hilgardia [*A publication*]
**Hilgardia Calif Agric Exp Stn** ... Hilgardia. California Agricultural Experiment Station [*A publication*]
**HILI**........... Heavy Ion, Light Ion
**Hill**............ Hill's New York Supreme Court Reports [*1841-44*] [*A publication*] (DLA)
**Hill**............ Hill's South Carolina Law Reports [*A publication*] (DLA)
**Hill Abr**...... Hilliard's Abridgment of Real Property Law [*A publication*] (DLA)
**Hill Am Jur** ... Hilliard's American Jurisprudence [*A publication*] (DLA)
**Hill Am Law** ... Hilliard's American Law [*A publication*] (DLA)
**Hill Bank** ... Hilliard on Bankruptcy and Insolvency [*A publication*] (DLA)
**Hill B & I** ... Hilliard on Bankruptcy and Insolvency [*A publication*] (DLA)
**Hill Ch** ....... Hill's Equity South Carolina Reports [*1833-37*] [*A publication*] (DLA)
**Hill Ch Pr** .. Hill's Chancery Practice [*A publication*] (DLA)
**Hill Cont**.... Hilliard on Contracts [*A publication*] (DLA)
**Hill & D** ..... Lalor's Supplement to Hill and Denio's New York Reports [*A publication*] (DLA)
**Hill & Den** ... Lalor's Supplement to Hill and Denio's New York Reports [*A publication*] (DLA)
**Hill & Den Supp** ... Lalor's Supplement to Hill and Denio's New York Reports [*A publication*] (DLA)
**Hill & D Supp** ... Hill and Denio's Lalor's Supplement [*New York*] [*A publication*] (DLA)
**Hill Elem Law** ... Hilliard's Elements of Law [*A publication*] (DLA)
**Hill Eq** ....... Hill's Equity South Carolina Reports [*1833-37*] [*A publication*] (DLA)
**Hill Eq (SC)** ... Hill's Equity South Carolina Reports [*1833-37*] [*A publication*] (DLA)
**Hill Fixt**..... Hill's Law of Fixtures [*A publication*] (DLA)
**Hilliard RP** ... Hilliard on Real Property [*A publication*] (DLA)
**Hill Ill Chy** ... Hill's Illinois Chancery Practice [*A publication*] (DLA)
**Hill Ill Com Law** ... Hill's Illinois Common Law Jurisdiction and Practice [*A publication*] (DLA)
**Hill Inj** ....... Hilliard on the Law of Injunctions [*A publication*] (DLA)
**Hill Lib & Law** ... Hill's Liberty and Law [*A publication*] (DLA)
**Hill Mor**..... Hilliard's Law of Mortgages [*A publication*] (DLA)
**Hill Mortg** ... Hilliard's Law of Mortgages [*A publication*] (DLA)
**Hill New Trials** ... Hilliard on New Trials [*A publication*] (DLA)
**Hill N Tr**.... Hilliard on New Trials [*A publication*] (DLA)
**Hill NY**...... Hill's New York Reports [*A publication*] (DLA)
**Hill NYR**.... Hill's New York Reports [*A publication*] (DLA)
**Hill Prob**.... Hill's Illinois Probate Jurisdiction and Practice [*A publication*] (DLA)
**Hill Real Prop** ... Hilliard on Real Property [*A publication*] (DLA)
**Hill & Redman** ... Hill and Redman's Law of Landlord and Tenant [*16th ed.*] [*1976*] [*A publication*] (DLA)
**Hill Rem** .... Hilliard on Remedies for Torts [*A publication*] (DLA)
**Hill Sales**... Hilliard on Sales of Personal Property [*A publication*] (DLA)
**Hill's Ann Codes & Laws** ... Hill's Annotated Codes and General Laws [*Oregon*] [*A publication*] (DLA)
**Hill's Ann St & Codes** ... Hill's Annotated General Statutes and Codes [*Washington*] [*A publication*] (DLA)
**Hill SC**....... Hill's Equity South Carolina Reports [*1833-37*] [*A publication*] (DLA)
**Hill SC**....... Hill's South Carolina Law Reports [*A publication*] (DLA)
**Hill's Code** ... Hill's Annotated Codes and General Laws [*Oregon*] [*A publication*] (DLA)
**Hill's Code** ... Hill's Annotated General Statutes and Codes [*Washington*] [*A publication*] (DLA)
**Hillside J Clin Psychiatry** ... Hillside Journal of Clinical Psychiatry [*A publication*]
**Hill Tax** ..... Hilliard on the Law of Taxation [*A publication*] (DLA)
**Hill Torts**... Hilliard on the Law of Torts [*A publication*] (DLA)
**Hill Tr**....... Hill on Trustees [*A publication*] (DLA)
**Hill Vend** ... Hilliard on the Law of Vendors [*A publication*] (DLA)
**Hillyer**........ Hillyer's Reports [*20-22 California*] [*A publication*] (DLA)
**HILNNEP** ... Health Information Library Network of Northeastern Pennsylvania [*Library network*]
**Hi Lo**......... High/Low Report [*A publication*]
**HILOW** ..... Health Information Libraries of Westchester [*Library network*]
**HILP**.......... Health Information Library Program [*Library network*]
**HILS**.......... High-Intensity Learning Systems
**Hil T** .......... Hilary Term [*England*] [*Legal term*] (DLA)
**Hilt**............ Hilton's New York Common Pleas Reports [*A publication*] (DLA)
**Hil Term 4 Will IV** ... Hilary Term 4, William IV [*A publication*] (DLA)

**Hilt (NY)** ... Hilton's New York Common Pleas Reports [*A publication*] (DLA)
**Hil Torts** .... Hilliard on the Law of Torts [*A publication*] (DLA)
**HIL VAC** ... Hilary Vacation [*British*] [*Legal term*] (DLA)
**HILY SITTGS** ... Hilary Sittings [*British*] [*Legal term*] (ROG)
**HIM** .......... Hardware Interface Module [*NASA*] (NASA)
**HIM** .......... Health Insurance Manual
**HIM** .......... Heavy Interdiction Missile
**HIM** .......... Helps International Ministries (EA)
**HIM** .......... Herald International Mailings Ltd. [*British*]
**HIM** .......... High Impact
**HIM** .......... High-Intensity Microphone
**HIM** .......... Hill Interaction Matrix [*Psychology*]
**HIM** .......... Himac Resources Ltd. [*Vancouver Stock Exchange symbol*]
**him** .......... Himachali [*MARC language code*] [*Library of Congress*] (LCCP)
**HIM** .......... Himeji [*Japan*] [*Seismograph station code, US Geological Survey*] (SEIS)
**HIM** .......... His [*or Her*] Imperial Majesty
**HiM** .......... Hispania (Madrid) [*A publication*]
**HIM** .......... Horizontal Impulse
**HIM** .......... Hot Ionized Medium [*Astrophysics*]
**HIM** .......... Human Individual Metamorphosis [*Flying saucer cult*]
**HIM** .......... Human Integrated Manufacturing
**HIMA** ........ Health Industry Manufacturers Association (EA)
**HIM-A** ....... Hill Interaction Matrix-A [*Personality development test*] [*Psychology*]
**Himachal J Agric Res** ... Himachal Journal of Agricultural Research [*A publication*]
**HIMAD** ..... High-to-Medium-Altitude Air Defense (AABC)
**HIMAG** ..... High-Mobility-Agility [*Test for combat vehicles*] (RDA)
**Himalayan Geol** ... Himalayan Geology [*A publication*]
**Himal R** ..... Himalayan Review [*A publication*]
**HIMAT** ..... Highly Maneuverable Aircraft Technology Testbed [*Rockwell International Corp.*] (MCD)
**HIMB** ........ Hawaii Institute of Marine Biology [*University of Hawaii*] [*Research center*] (RCD)
**HIMD** ........ Handbook of Instructions for Missile Designers
**HIMDD3** ... Hileia Medica [*A publication*]
**HIMG** ........ Health Images, Inc. [*Atlanta, GA*] [*NASDAQ symbol*] (NQ)
**HIMO** ........ High Mobility [*Vehicle analysis*] (MCD)
**HIMOWC** ... High-Mobility Weapons Carrier [*Army*] (MCD)
**HIMP** ........ High Impact
**Him Pra** ..... All India Reporter, Himachal Pradesh [*A publication*] (DLA)
**HIMR** ........ Handbook of Inspection Maintenance Requirements [*Navy*] (MCD)
**HIMR** ........ Hearing-Impaired Mentally Retarded
**HIMS** ........ Heavy Interdiction Missile System (MCD)
**HIMS** ........ Helicopter In-Flight Monitoring System [*Army*] (RDA)
**HIMS** ........ Himself
**HIMS** ........ Housing Information Management System
**HIMSEUR** ... HAWK [*Homing All the Way Killer*] Intensified Management System Europe Program [*Military*]
**HIMSS** ...... Healthcare Information and Management Systems Society (EA)
**HIMVF** ..... Himac Resources Ltd. [*NASDAQ symbol*] (NQ)
**HIN** .......... Chadron, NE [*Location identifier*] [*FAA*] (FAAL)
**HIN** .......... Heterotrophic Intestinal Nitrification [*Metabolism*]
**HIN** .......... Hidden Lake Gold Mines [*Vancouver Stock Exchange symbol*]
**HIN** .......... High Intensity
**HIN** .......... High-Intensity Noise
**HIN** .......... Hinchinbrook Island [*Alaska*] [*Seismograph station code, US Geological Survey*] (SEIS)
**hin** .......... Hindi [*MARC language code*] [*Library of Congress*] (LCCP)
**HIN** .......... Holocaust Information Network (EA)
**HIN** .......... Home Insurance Co. [*NYSE symbol*] (SPSG)
**HIN** .......... Hybrid Integrated Network [*Bell System*] [*Telecommunications*]
**HIN** .......... Hydrocarbon-Induced Nephropathy [*Medicine*]
**HINAA** ...... Hindustan Antibiotics Bulletin [*A publication*]
**HINAS** ...... Historic Naval Ships Association of North America (EA)
**HINASW** .. Historic Naval Ships of the World [*Later, HINAS*] (EA)
**Hincmar Epist** ... Hincmari Epistolae [*A publication*] (DLA)
**HIND** ......... Harvest Industries, Inc. [*NASDAQ symbol*] (NQ)
**Hind** .......... Hindustan
**HIND** ......... Hindustani [*Language, etc.*]
**Hind Antibiot Bull** ... Hindustan Antibiotics Bulletin [*A publication*]
**Hinde Ch Pr** ... Hinde's Modern Practice of the High Court of Chancery [*A publication*] (DLA)
**Hindemith Jb** ... Hindemith-Jahrbuch [*Annales Hindemith*] [*A publication*]
**Hind LJ** ..... Hindu Law Journal [*A publication*] (DLA)
**Hind LQ** ..... Hindu Law Quarterly [*A publication*] (DLA)
**Hind Pat** .... Hindmarch on Patents [*A publication*] (DLA)
**Hind Pr** ...... Hind's Practice [*A publication*] (DLA)
**Hindu Astronom Math Text Ser** ... Hindu Astronomical and Mathematical Text Series [*A publication*]
**Hindustan Antibiot Bull** ... Hindustan Antibiotics Bulletin [*A publication*]
**HINE** ......... Hines [*Edward*] Lumber Co. [*NASDAQ symbol*] (NQ)
**HINEKF** .... Hinekford [*England*]
**Hine & N Ass** ... Hine and Nicholas on Assignment of Life Policies [*A publication*] (DLA)
**Hine & N Dig** ... Hine and Nicholas. Insurance Digest [*A publication*] (DLA)
**Hines** .......... Hines' Reports [*83-96 Kentucky*] [*A publication*] (DLA)
**HINF** ......... Hypodermoclysis Infusion [*Medicine*]
**HING** ......... High-Intensity Noise Generator
**HINIL** ........ High-Noise-Immunity Logic (MCD)
**HINL** ......... History of Ideas Newsletter [*A publication*]
**HINS** ......... [*The*] Hanover Insurance Co. [*NASDAQ symbol*] (NQ)
**HINS** ......... Health Information Network Services [*Database search service*] (OLDSS)
**HINS** ......... Helicopter Integrated Navigation System [*Canadian Navy*]
**HINT** ......... High Intensity
**HINT** ......... Hinton [*Test*] [*Medicine*]
**HINT** ......... Housewares Industry News and Topics [*A publication*] (EAAP)
**HINTD** ...... Habitat International [*A publication*]
**HIO** .......... Hillsboro, OR [*Location identifier*] [*FAA*] (FAAL)
**HIO** .......... Hypoiodism [*Medicine*]
**HIOMT** ..... Hydroxyindole O-Methyltransferase [*Also, HOMT*] [*An enzyme*]
**HiOVIS** ..... Highly Interactive Optical Visual Information System [*Australia*]
**HIP** .......... Habitability Improvement Plan [*Navy*]
**HIP** .......... Hanford Isotopes Plant [*Nuclear energy*]
**HIP** .......... Hardware Interface Program (NASA)
**HIP** .......... Harpoon Indicator Panel [*Missiles*] (MCD)
**HIP** .......... HAWK [*Homing All the Way Killer*] Improvement Program
**HIP** .......... Health Insurance Plan
**HIP** .......... Hearing Impaired Peer
**HIP** .......... Help for Incontinent People (EA)
**HIP** .......... High-Impact Pressure
**HIP** .......... High-Intent Priority [*In the record business, a heavily promoted disk*]
**HIP** .......... High Internal Phase [*Emulsion chemistry*]
**HIP** .......... High-Potential Iron Protein
**HIP** .......... Highly Ionized Plasma
**HIP** .......... Hipotronics, Inc. [*AMEX symbol*] (SPSG)
**HIP** .......... Horizontal Injection Press
**HIP** .......... Hospital Improvement Project
**HIP** .......... Hospital Insurance Program
**HIP** .......... Hot Isostatically Pressed [*Materials processing*]
**HIP** .......... Housing Improvement Program [*Federal government*]
**HIP** .......... Howitzer Improvement Program
**HIP** .......... Hydrostatic Indifference Point
**HIP** .......... Hypnotic Induction Profile
**HIPA** ......... Health Insurance Persistency Award [*Later, HIQA*] [*LIMRA*]
**HIPA** ......... Home Improvement Products Association [*Defunct*] (EA)
**HIPAAS** .... High-Performance Advanced Attack Systems (MCD)
**HIPAC** ....... High-Performance Aircraft Cannon (MCD)
**HIPAC** ....... Hitachi Parametron Automatic Computer
**HIPAR** ....... High-Performance Precision Approach Control RADAR (MCD)
**HIPAR** ....... High-Power Acquisition RADAR (AAG)
**HIPC** ........ High Plains Corporation [*NASDAQ symbol*] (NQ)
**HIPE** ......... Hospital In-Patient Enquiry [*British*]
**HIPEG** ....... High-Performance External Gun
**HIPEHT** .... High-Performance Electrothermal Hydrazine Thruster (MCD)
**HIPERARC** ... High-Performance Archiheater (MCD)
**HI-PERF** ... High Performance [*Automotive engineering*]
**HIPERNAS** ... High-Performance Navigation System
**HIPERTHINO** ... High-Performance Throttleable Injector (KSC)
**HIPG** ......... Human Information Processing Group [*Princeton University*]
**HI-PI** ......... High-Performance Intercept
**HIPIR** ........ High-Power Illuminator RADAR [*Army*] (AABC)
**HIPO** ......... Hierarchy plus Input-Process-Output [*Data processing*]
**Hipo** .......... High-Potential Employee
**HIPO** ......... Highway Post Office [*Bus or truck equipped with mail distribution facilities*]
**HIPO** ......... Hilfspolizei [*Auxiliary Police*] [*German*]
**Hipo** .......... Hippolytus Marsilius [*Deceased, 1529*] [*Authority cited in pre-1607 legal work*] (DSA)
**HIPO** ......... Hospital Indicator for Physicians' Orders
**HIPOA** ....... High Polymers [*A publication*]
**HIPOT** ....... High Potential (KSC)
**HIPOTT** .... High-Potential Test (IEEE)
**HIPP** ......... Hippocrates [*Greek physician, 460? -377? BC*]
**Hipp** .......... Hippolytus [*of Euripides*] [*Classical studies*] (OCD)
**HIPPA** ....... Hippokrates [*A publication*]
**Hipparch** .... Hipparchus [*of Plato*] [*Classical studies*] (OCD)
**Hipp Bonacoss** ... Hippolytus Bonacossa [*Deceased, 1591*] [*Authority cited in pre-1607 legal work*] (DSA)
**HIPPO** ...... Hippodrome [*London*] (DSUE)
**HIPPO** ...... Hippopotamus (DSUE)
**Hippoc** ....... Hippocrates [*Greek physician, 460? -377? BC*] [*Classical studies*] (OCD)
**HIPPY** ....... Home Instruction Program for Preschool Youngsters [*Israel*]
**HIPR** ......... High Internal Phase Ratio
**HIPR** ......... High Pressure (KSC)
**HIPRES** .... High Pressure
**HIPRI** ........ High Priority (NG)
**Hip Riminal** ... Hippolytus Riminaldus [*Deceased, 1589*] [*Authority cited in pre-1607 legal work*] (DSA)
**HIPS** ......... Helmet Initiated Pointing System (MCD)

**HIPS**.......... High-Impact Polystyrene [*Plastics technology*]
**HIPS**.......... Hyperintense Proximal Scanning
**HIPSA**.......... Hallicrafters Incremental Power Spectrum Analyzer
**HIPSF**.......... High-Performance Space Feed
**HIPT**.......... Hi-Port Industries, Inc. [*NASDAQ symbol*] (NQ)
**HIQ**.......... Housing Intelligence Quotient
**HIQ**.......... New York, NY [*Location identifier*] [*FAA*] (FAAL)
**HIQA**.......... Health Insurance Quality Award [*Formerly, HIPA*] [*LIMRA*]
**HIR**.......... Hammersley Iron Proprietary Ltd. Railway [*Australia*] (DCTA)
**HIR**.......... Handbook of Inspection Requirements [*Navy*] (MCD)
**HIR**.......... Helicopter Instrument Rules
**HIR**.......... HELWS-Integrated RADAR
**HIR**.......... Hierarchy [*Data processing*]
**HIR**.......... Hilton Resource Corp. [*Vancouver Stock Exchange symbol*]
**HIR**.......... Hiram College, Hiram, OH [*OCLC symbol*] (OCLC)
**HIR**.......... Hiring (ROG)
**HIR**.......... Hiroshima [*Japan*] [*Seismograph station code, US Geological Survey*] (SEIS)
**HIR**.......... Hispanic Review [*A publication*]
**HIR**.......... Honiara [*Guadalcanal*] [*Airport symbol*] (OAG)
**HIR**.......... Horizontal Impulse Reaction (MSA)
**HIR**.......... Human Insulin Receptor [*Biochemistry*]
**HIR**.......... Hydrostatic Impact Rocket (NATG)
**HIRA**.......... Health Industry Representatives Association (EA)
**HIRAA**.......... Hiradastechnika [*Hungary*] [*A publication*]
**HIRAC**.......... High Random Access
**Hiradas-Tech** ... Hiradastechnika. Hiradastechnikai Tudomanyos Egyesulet Lapja [*A publication*]
**Hiradastech Ipari Kutatointez Kozl** ... Hiradastechnikai Ipari Kutatointezet Koezlemenyei [*A publication*]
**Hiradastech Ipari Kut Intez Koezl** ... Hiradastechnikai Ipari Kutato Intezet Koezlemenyei [*A publication*]
**Hiram Po R** ... Hiram Poetry Review [*A publication*]
**HIRAN**.......... High-Precision SHORAN (AAG)
**HIRC**.......... Head Injuries Rehabilitation Centre [*British*] (CB)
**HIRC**.......... Holy Innocents Reparation Committee (EA)
**HIRD**.......... High-Intensity Radiation Device
**HIRDAP**.......... Geological Report. Hiroshima University [*A publication*]
**HIRDL**.......... High-Intensity Radiation Development Laboratory [*Brookhaven National Laboratory*] [*Department of Energy*]
**HIRE**.......... Diversified Human Resources Group, Inc. [*Dallas, TX*] [*NASDAQ symbol*] (NQ)
**HIRE**.......... Help through Industry Retraining and Employment [*Program*] [*Department of Labor*]
**HI Rep**.......... Hawaiian Islands Reports [*A publication*] (DLA)
**HI-RES**.......... High Resolution [*Data processing*]
**HIRES**.......... Hypersonic In-Flight Refueling System
**HIREWIMP** ... High-Resolution Wind Measurement Program (MUGU)
**HIRF**.......... High-Intensity Reciprocity Failure
**HI and RH** ... His [*or Her*] Imperial and Royal Highness
**HIRI**.......... Home Improvement Research Institute (EA)
**HIRIA**.......... Hirosaki Igaku [*Japan*] [*A publication*]
**HIRIB**.......... Hifuka No Rinsho [*Japan*] [*A publication*]
**HIRIS**.......... High-Resolution Imaging Spectrometer
**HIRIV**.......... How Will Arrival Report Be Filed Concerning _____ [*Aviation*] (FAAC)
**HIRL**.......... High-Intensity Runway Lights [*Aviation*]
**HIRM**.......... High-Incidence Research Model (MCD)
**HIROA**.......... Hirosaki Daigaku Nogakubu Gakujutsu Hokoku [*A publication*]
**HiroBK**.......... Hiroshima Daigaku Bungakubu Kiyo [*A publication*]
**HIROP**.......... Hand-Held Infrared Controller Overpopulation [*Data processing*]
**Hirosaki Med J** ... Hirosaki Medical Journal [*A publication*]
**Hiroshima J Med Sci** ... Hiroshima Journal of Medical Sciences [*A publication*]
**Hiroshima J M Sc** ... Hiroshima Journal of Medical Sciences [*A publication*]
**Hiroshima Math J** ... Hiroshima Mathematical Journal [*A publication*]
**Hiroshima Med J** ... Hiroshima Medical Journal [*Japan*] [*A publication*]
**Hiroshima Univ Geol Rep** ... Hiroshima University Geological Report [*A publication*]
**Hiroshima Univ J Sci Ser C** ... Hiroshima University Journal of Science. Series C. Geology and Mineralogy [*A publication*]
**Hiros J Med** ... Hiroshima Journal of Medical Sciences [*A publication*]
**HIRRA**.......... Highway Research Record [*A publication*]
**HIRS**.......... Harker's Information Retrieval Systems [*Harker's Specialist Book Importers*] [*Information service or system*] (IID)
**HIRS**.......... High-Impulse Retrorocket System
**HIRS**.......... High-Resolution Infrared Radiation Sounder
**HIRS**.......... High Resolution Sciences, Inc. [*NASDAQ symbol*] (NQ)
**HIRSO**.......... High-Resolution Solar Optical Telescope
**HIRSS**.......... Hover Infrared Suppressor Subsystem
**HIRT**.......... High Reynolds Number Tunnel
**HIRUD**.......... Hirudo [*A Leech*] [*Pharmacy*] (ROG)
**HIS**.......... CIGNA High Income Shares [*NYSE symbol*] (SPSG)
**HIS**.......... Hardware Information System (MCD)
**HIS**.......... Hayman Island [*Australia*] [*Airport symbol*] (OAG)
**HIS**.......... Health Information Series [*Federal government*]
**HIS**.......... Health Information Services [*Department of Health and Human Services*]
**HIS**.......... Health Interview Survey [*National Institutes of Health*]
**HIS**.......... Heavy-Ion Source
**HIS**.......... Heiss Island [*USSR*] [*Geomagnetic observatory code*]
**HIS**.......... Heliborne Illumination System (CINC)
**HIS**.......... Hic Iacet Sepultus [*Here Lies Buried*] [*Latin*]
**HIS**.......... Hierarchical Intensive Search [*of the literature*]
**HIS**.......... High-Intensity Spectrometer
**HIS**.......... High-Interest Shipping (MCD)
**HIS**.......... High-Resolution Interferometer Spectrometer
**His**.......... Hispania [*A publication*]
**His**.......... Histidine [*An amino acid*]
**HIS**.......... Histogram Scanning
**HIS**.......... Historian [*or History*] (EY)
**HIS**.......... Hit Indicator System
**HIS**.......... Homogeneous Information Sets
**HIS**.......... Honeywell Information Systems, Inc. (IEEE)
**HIS**.......... Horwitz Information Services [*Information service or system*] (EISS)
**HIS**.......... Hospital Information System [*Data processing*]
**HIS**.......... Hospitality and Information Service (EA)
**HIS**.......... House Information Systems [*House of Representatives*] [*Washington, DC*]
**HIS**.......... Humanities in Society [*A publication*]
**HIS**.......... Hybrid Infrared Source
**HISA**.......... Hawaii International Services Agency
**HISA**.......... Headquarters and Installation Support Activity [*Army*] (AABC)
**HISAM**.......... Hardware Initiated Standalone Memory (NASA)
**HISAM**.......... Hierarchical Indexed Sequential Access Method [*Data processing*] (BUR)
**His Am Hist Rev** ... Hispanic American Historical Review [*A publication*]
**HISARS**.......... Hydrologic Information Storage and Retrieval System [*North Carolina State University*] [*Raleigh, NC*]
**HISC**.......... House Internal Security Committee
**HISDAM**.. Hierarchical Indexed Sequential Direct Access Method [*Data processing*]
**HISE**.......... High Interference Signaling Environment
**HISG**.......... Human Immune Serum Globulin [*Immunochemistry*]
**HISI**.......... Health Information Systems, Incorporated [*NASDAQ symbol*] (NQ)
**HISI**.......... Honeywell Information Systems, Incorporated
**HisJ**.......... Hispanic Journal [*A publication*]
**HisK**.......... Hispania (University of Kansas. Lawrence) [*A publication*]
**HisL**.......... Hispania (University of Kansas. Lawrence) [*A publication*]
**HISLA**.......... Revista Latinoamericana de Historia Economica y Social [*A publication*]
**His Med Ser** ... History of Medicine Series [*A publication*]
**His Outlook** ... Historical Outlook [*A publication*]
**HISP**.......... Heat-Inactivated Serum Pool [*Clinical chemistry*]
**Hisp**.......... Hispania [*Madrid*] [*A publication*]
**HisP**.......... Historia (Paris) [*A publication*]
**Hispa**.......... Hispavox [*Record label*] [*Spain*]
**HISPA**.......... International Association for the History of Physical Education and Sport [*Belgium*]
**Hispam**.......... Hispamerica. Revista de Literatura [*A publication*]
**Hisp Amer Hist Rev** ... Hispanic American Historical Review [*A publication*]
**Hispan Am H** ... Hispanic American Historical Review [*A publication*]
**Hispan Am Hist R** ... Hispanic American Historical Review [*A publication*]
**Hispan Am Rep** ... Hispanic American Report [*A publication*]
**Hispanic Am His R** ... Hispanic American Historical Review [*A publication*]
**Hispanic B** ... Hispanic Business [*A publication*]
**Hispanic Bus** ... Hispanic Business [*A publication*]
**Hispano**.......... Hispanofila [*Madrid*] [*A publication*]
**Hispan R**.......... Hispanic Review [*A publication*]
**Hispan Rev** ... Hispanic Review [*A publication*]
**HispCal**.......... Hispania (Stanford, California) [*A publication*]
**Hispl**.......... Hispanofila [*Madrid and Illinois*] [*A publication*]
**HispM**.......... Hispania (Madrid) [*A publication*]
**HISPOT**.......... High-Altitude Surveillance Platform for Over-the-Horizon Targeting (MCD)
**Hisp Press Ind** ... Hispanic Press Index [*A publication*]
**Hisp Rev**.......... Hispanic Review [*A publication*]
**His Q**.......... History Quarterly [*A publication*]
**HISRAN**.......... High-Precision SHORAN [*Short-Range Navigation*]
**HISS**.......... Helicopter Inflight Spray System (MCD)
**HISS**.......... Herpetological Information Search Systems
**HISS**.......... High-Intensity Sound Simulator
**HISS**.......... High-Intensity Sound System
**HISSG**.......... Healthcare Information Systems Sharing Group (EA)
**HISS News-J** ... HISS [*Herpetological Information Search Systems*] News-Journal [*A publication*]
**HIST**.......... High Input Shock Test
**HIST**.......... Histoire [*History*] [*French*] (ROG)
**HIST**.......... Histology (ADA)
**Hist**.......... Historia [*A publication*] (OCD)
**Hist**.......... Historiae [*of Tacitus*] [*Classical studies*] (OCD)
**Hist**.......... Historian [*A publication*]
**HIST**.......... Historian [*or History*] (AFM)
**Hist**.......... Historica [*A publication*]
**HIST**.......... Historical [*Linguistics*]
**Hist**.......... History [*A publication*]

**HIST**.......... Hospital In-Service Training
**HIST**.......... Hyderabad Imperial Service Troops [*British military*] (DMA)
**HistAb**....... Historical Abstracts [*A publication*]
**Hist Abstr**... Historical Abstracts [*A publication*]
**Hist Abstr Part A Mod Hist Abstr**... Historical Abstracts. Part A. Modern History Abstracts [*A publication*]
**Hist Abstr Part B Twent Century Abstr**... Historical Abstracts. Part B. Twentieth Century Abstracts [*A publication*]
**Hist Acad Roy Sc**... Histoire de l'Academie Royale des Sciences [*A publication*]
**Hist Afr**...... History in Africa [*A publication*]
**Hist Africa**... History in Africa [*A publication*]
**Hist Ag**....... Historia Agriculturae [*A publication*]
**Hist An**...... Historia Animalium [*of Aristotle*] [*Classical studies*] (OCD)
**Hist Anc Geog**... [A] History of Ancient Geography [*A publication*] (OCD)
**Hist Arkisto**... Historiallinen Arkisto [*A publication*]
**Hist Athen Const**... [A] History of the Athenian Constitution [*A publication*] (OCD)
**Hist Aug**..... Historia Augusta [*A publication*] (OCD)
**Hist Berwickshire Natur Club**... History. Berwickshire Naturalists' Club [*A publication*]
**Hist Bull**.... Historical Bulletin [*A publication*]
**Hist Can W**... History of the Canadian West [*A publication*]
**Hist Cas**..... Historicky Casopis [*A publication*]
**Hist Casopis**... Historicky Casopis [*A publication*]
**Hist Child Q**... History of Childhood Quarterly [*A publication*]
**Hist Conscr**... Quomodo Historia Conscribenda Sit [*of Lucian*] [*Classical studies*] (OCD)
**HISTDD**.... Histopathology [*Oxford*] [*A publication*]
**His Teach M**... History Teacher's Magazine [*A publication*]
**Hist Eccl**.... Historia Ecclesiastica [*of Eusebius*] [*Classical studies*] (OCD)
**Hist Ed R**.... History of Education Review [*A publication*]
**Hist Educ**.... History of Education [*A publication*]
**Hist Educ Jour**... History of Education Journal [*A publication*]
**Hist Educ Q**... History of Education Quarterly [*A publication*]
**Hist Eur Id**... History of European Ideas [*A publication*]
**Hist Euro Ideas**... History of European Ideas [*A publication*]
**Hist G**........ History of Greece [*A publication*] (OCD)
**Hist Gk Phil**... History of Greek Philosophy [*A publication*] (OCD)
**Hist of Greek Maths**... History of Greek Mathematics [*A publication*] (OCD)
**Hist Hosp**.. Historia Hospitalium. Mitteilungen der Deutschen Gesellschaft fuer Kranken-Hausgeschichte [*A publication*]
**Hist J**......... Historical Journal [*A publication*]
**Hist Jahrb**... Historisches Jahrbuch [*A publication*]
**Hist Jahrb Stadt Linz**... Historisches Jahrbuch der Stadt Linz [*A publication*]
**HistJb**........ Historisches Jahrbuch der Goerresgesellschaft [*A publication*]
**Hist Jb Graz**... Historisches Jahrbuch der Stadt Graz [*A publication*]
**Hist J Film**... Historical Journal of Film, Radio, and Television [*A publication*]
**Hist J FR & TV**... Historical Journal of Film, Radio, and Television [*A publication*]
**Hist Jnl F R & TV**... Historical Journal of Film, Radio, and Television [*A publication*]
**Hist Ju (Birmingham)**... Historical Journal (Birmingham) [*A publication*]
**Hist J West Mass**... Historical Journal of Western Massachusetts [*A publication*]
**HISTL**....... Historical
**HistL**.......... Historiographia Linguistica [*A publication*]
**Hist Learn Sci Finland**... History of Learning and Science in Finland [*A publication*]
**HISTLINE**... History of Medicine On-Line [*National Library of Medicine*] [*Bibliographic database*] (IID)
**Hist Ling**.... Historiographia Linguistica [*A publication*]
**Hist M**....... Historical Magazine [*Dawson's*] [*A publication*]
**Hist Mag**... Historical Magazine of the Protestant Episcopal Church [*A publication*]
**Hist Mag PE Ch**... Historical Magazine of the Protestant Episcopal Church [*A publication*]
**Hist Mag Protest Episc Church**... Historical Magazine of the Protestant Episcopal Church [*A publication*]
**Hist Med**.... History of Medicine [*A publication*]
**Hist Med Ser**... History of Medicine Series [*A publication*]
**Hist Med Vet**... Historia Medicinae Veterinariae [*A publication*]
**Hist Metall**... Historical Metallurgy [*A publication*]
**Hist Meth**.. Historical Methods [*A publication*]
**Hist Methods Newsl**... Historical Methods Newsletter [*A publication*]
**Hist Mex**.... Historia Mexicana [*A publication*]
**HISTN**....... Historian (AABC)
**Hist Nat**..... Histoire et Nature. Cahiers de l'Association pour l'Histoire des Sciences de la Nature [*A publication*]
**Hist News**.. Historical News [*New Zealand*] [*A publication*]
**Hist NH**..... Historical New Hampshire [*A publication*]
**Hist Num**.... Historia Numorum [*A publication*] (OCD)
**Histochemis**... Histochemistry [*A publication*]
**Histochem J**... Histochemical Journal [*A publication*]
**HISTOL**.... Histology
**Historia Math**... Historia Mathematica [*A publication*]
**Historia Sci**... Historia Scientiarum [*A publication*]
**Historia Z**.. Historia. Zeitschrift fuer Alte Geschichte [*A publication*]
**Historia Z Alt Gesch**... Historia. Zeitschrift fuer Alte Geschichte [*A publication*]
**History**....... History Workshop [*A publication*]
**History of Ed Soc Bull**... History of Education Society. Bulletin [*A publication*]
**History Rev**... History. Reviews of New Books [*A publication*]
**Hist Outl**.... Historical Outlook [*A publication*]
**Hist Papers**... Historical Papers [*A publication*]
**Hist Philos Life Sci (Pubbl Stn Zool Napoli Sect II)**... History and Philosophy of the Life Sciences (Pubblicazioni della Stazione Zoologica di Napoli. Section II) [*A publication*]
**Hist Philos Logic**... History and Philosophy of Logic [*A publication*]
**Hist Photo**... History of Photography [*A publication*]
**Hist Photog**... History of Photography [*A publication*]
**Hist of Photogr**... History of Photography [*A publication*]
**Hist Pl**........ Historia Plantarum [*of Theophrastus*] [*Classical studies*] (OCD)
**Hist Pol Ec**... History of Political Economy [*A publication*]
**Hist Pol Econ**... History of Political Economy [*A publication*]
**Hist Pol Economy**... History of Political Economy [*A publication*]
**Hist Polit**... History of Political Economy [*A publication*]
**Hist Polit Econ**... History of Political Economy [*A publication*]
**Hist Polit Thought**... History of Political Thought [*A publication*]
**Hist Pol Th**... History of Political Thought [*A publication*]
**Hist Pres**.... Historic Preservation [*A publication*]
**Hist Preser**... Historic Preservation [*A publication*]
**Hist Preservation**... Historic Preservation [*A publication*]
**HISTRAP**... Heavy Ion Storage Ring for Atomic Physics
**Hist Refl D**... Historical Reflections. Directions Series [*A publication*]
**Hist Reflec**... Historical Reflections/Reflexions Historiques [*A publication*]
**Hist Rel**...... History of Religions [*A publication*]
**Hist Relig**... History of Religions [*A publication*]
**Hist Rev**..... Historical Review (New Zealand) [*A publication*]
**Hist R New Bk**... History. Reviews of New Books [*A publication*]
**Hist Rom Rel**... Roemische Religions-Geschichte [*A publication*] (OCD)
**HISTRU**.... Hydraulic System Test and Repair Unit [*Army*] (MCD)
**Hist of Sci**.. History of Science [*A publication*]
**Hist Sci**...... History of Science [*A publication*]
**Hist Sci Med**... Histoire des Sciences Medicales [*A publication*]
**Hist Sci Ser**... History of Science Series [*A publication*]
**Hist Sc Soc Manit Tr**... Historical and Scientific Society of Manitoba. Transactions [*A publication*]
**Hist Ser Can Dep Agric**... Historical Series. Canada Department of Agriculture [*A publication*]
**Hist Soc**..... Histoire Sociale/Social History [*A publication*]
**Hist Soc Mont Contr**... Historical Society of Montana. Contributions [*A publication*]
**Hist Soc Q J**... Historical Society of Queensland. Journal [*A publication*] (APTA)
**Hist Soc Qld J**... Historical Society of Queensland. Journal [*A publication*] (APTA)
**Hist Soc Qld News**... Historical Society of Queensland. News Bulletin [*A publication*] (APTA)
**Hist Soc Sci Teach**... History and Social Science Teacher [*A publication*]
**Hist St Prob**... On the History of Statistics and Probability [*A publication*]
**Hist Stud**.... Historical Studies [*A publication*]
**Hist Stud**.... Historical Studies - Australia and New Zealand [*A publication*] (APTA)
**Hist Stud Aust NZ**... Historical Studies - Australia and New Zealand [*A publication*] (APTA)
**Hist Stud Austral**... Historical Studies - Australia and New Zealand [*A publication*]
**Hist Studies**... Historical Studies - Australia and New Zealand [*A publication*] (APTA)
**Hist Stud Phys Sci**... Historical Studies in the Physical Sciences [*A publication*]
**Hist & T**..... History and Theory [*A publication*]
**Hist Tchr**... History Teacher [*A publication*]
**Hist Teach**... History Teacher [*A publication*] (APTA)
**Hist Teach Assoc NSW Newsl**... History Teachers Association of New South Wales. Newsletter [*A publication*] (APTA)
**Hist Theor**... History and Theory [*A publication*]
**Hist Theory**... History and Theory [*A publication*]
**Hist and Theory**... History and Theory [*A publication*]
**Hist Tidskr**... Historisk Tidskrift [*A publication*]
**Hist Tidskr Finl**... Historisk Tidskrift foer Finland [*A publication*]
**Hist Tidssk**... Historisk Tidsskrift [*A publication*]
**Hist Today**... History Today [*A publication*]
**Hist Univ**... History of Universities [*A publication*]
**Hist Verein Oberpfalz & Regensburg Verh**... Historischer Verein fuer Oberpfalz und Regensburg. Verhandlungen [*A publication*]
**Hist Ver f d Grafsch Ravensberg Jahresber**... Historischer Verein fuer die Grafschaft Ravensberg zu Bielefeld. Jahresberichte [*A publication*]
**Hist Ver f Mittelfranken Jahresber**... Historischer Verein fuer Mittelfranken. Jahresberichte [*A publication*]
**Hist Ver Straubing**... Historischer Verein fuer Straubing und Umgebung [*A publication*]
**Hist Work S**... History Workshop Series [*A publication*]
**Hist Worksh**... History Workshop [*A publication*]
**Hist Workshop**... History Workshop [*A publication*]

**Hist Z**......... Historische Zeitschrift [*A publication*]
**Hist Ztsch** ... Historische Zeitschrift [*A publication*]
**HISXE**....... Heavy Ion-Induced Satellite X-Ray Emission [*Analytical chemistry*]
**HIT**........... Headline International Talent [*Commercial firm*]
**HIT**........... Health Indication Test [*Engine system*]
**HIT**........... HELWS-Integrated Tracker
**HIT**........... Hemagglutination Inhibition Test [*for pregnancy*] [*Medicine*]
**HIT**........... Hibernation Induction Trigger [*Biochemistry*]
**HIT**........... High Incidence Target [*Crime computer*]
**HIT**........... High-Interest Tracker (MCD)
**HIT**........... High-Isolation Transformer (IEEE)
**HIT**........... Histamine Inhalation Test [*Immunology*]
**HIT**........... History of Political Economy [*A publication*]
**HIT**........... Hitachi Ltd. [*NYSE symbol*] (SPSG)
**Hit**............ Hittite (BJA)
**HIT**........... Holtzman Inkblot Test [*Psychology*]
**HIT**........... Homing Interceptor Technology [*Navigation*] (IEEE)
**HIT**........... Housing Investment Trust [*AFL-CIO*]
**HIT**........... Houston International Teleport [*Houston, TX*] [*Telecommunications*] (TSSD)
**HIT**........... Hughes Improved Terminal [*Aviation*] (MCD)
**HIT**........... Hughes, Induced Turbulence
**HIT**........... Hypersonic Interference Technique
**HIT**........... Hypervelocity Impulse Tunnel (MCD)
**HITAB**....... High-Altitude Target and Background [*Program*] (MUGU)
**HITAC** ...... Hitachi Computer (DIT)
**Hitachi Rev** ... Hitachi Review [*A publication*]
**Hitachi Zosen Tech Rev** ... Hitachi Zosen Technical Review [*A publication*]
**HITAHR**... Hawaii Institute of Tropical Agriculture and Human Resources [*University of Hawaii*] [*Research center*] (RCD)
**Hitch Pr & Proc** ... Hitch's Practice and Procedure in the Probate Court of Massachusetts [*A publication*] (DLA)
**HITEA**....... High Temperature [*English Translation*] [*A publication*]
**HITEC**....... Health Information Technologies and Education Center [*University of Texas Health Science Center*] [*Houston, TX*] [*Data processing*]
**HITECC**.... Higher Introductory Technology and Engineering Conversion Courses [*Education*] [*British*]
**HITK** ......... HITK Corp. [*NASDAQ symbol*] (NQ)
**HITK** ......... Hungarologiai Intezet Tudomanyos Kozlemenyei [*A publication*]
**HITLS** ....... Hardware in the Loop Simulation [*Data processing*] (MCD)
**HIT and MISS** ... Hitler and Mussolini [*Slang*] (DSUE)
**HITMORE** ... Helicopter Installed Television Monitor and Recorder (MCD)
**HITMP**...... Highest Temperature (FAAC)
**Hitots J Econ** ... Hitotsubashi Journal of Economics [*A publication*]
**Hitotsubashi J Arts Sc** ... Hitotsubashi Journal of Arts and Sciences [*A publication*]
**Hitotsubashi J Arts Sci** ... Hitotsubashi Journal of Arts and Sciences [*A publication*]
**Hitotsubashi J Com Manag** ... Hitotsubashi Journal of Commerce and Management [*A publication*]
**Hitotsubashi J Commer Manage** ... Hitotsubashi Journal of Commerce and Management [*A publication*]
**Hitotsubashi J Commer and Mgt** ... Hitotsubashi Journal of Commerce and Management [*A publication*]
**Hitotsubashi J Econ** ... Hitotsubashi Journal of Economics [*A publication*]
**Hitotsubashi J Law and Politics** ... Hitotsubashi Journal of Law and Politics [*A publication*]
**Hitotsubashi JL & Pol** ... Hitotsubashi Journal of Law and Politics [*A publication*]
**Hitotsubashi J Social Studies** ... Hitotsubashi Journal of Social Studies [*A publication*]
**Hitotsubashi J Soc Stud** ... Hitotsubashi Journal of Social Studies [*A publication*]
**HITP** ......... High-Ignition-Temperature Propellant
**HITPRO**.... Hit Probability [*Military*] (MCD)
**HITP-SEAP** ... High-Ignition-Temperature Propellants Self-Extinguishing at Atmospheric Pressure [*Cartridge*] (RDA)
**HITS**.......... Handbook of Information Technology Standards [*A publication*]
**HITS**.......... Hargrave Information Technology Services [*Australia*]
**HITS**.......... HAWK [*Homing All the Way Killer*] Institutional Training System [*Military*] (RDA)
**HITS**.......... Hercules Integrated Telecommunications System [*Telecommunications*]
**HITS**.......... High Income Trust Securities [*Drexel Burnham Lambert, Inc.*]
**HITS**.......... High-Rate Multiplexer Input/Output Test System (NASA)
**HITS**.......... High-Speed Integrated Test System
**HITS**.......... Hobbyist's Interchange Tape Standard [*Data recording*]
**HITSA**....... High Temperature Science [*A publication*]
**Hitt Cod**..... Hittell's California Codes [*A publication*] (DLA)
**Hittell's Laws** ... Hittell's California General Laws [*A publication*] (DLA)
**hiu** ............. Hawaii [*MARC country of publication code*] [*Library of Congress*] (LCCP)
**HIU**............ Headseat Interface Unit (MCD)
**Hi-U**........... High-Usage [*Telecommunications*]
**HIU**............ Homing Instrumentation Unit (MCD)
**Hi Urb Mass Tran** ... Highway and Urban Mass Transportation [*A publication*]
**HiUS**.......... Hispania (USA) [*A publication*]
**HIUS** ......... Hispanic Institute in the United States [*Later, HI*] (EA)
**HIV**............ Helium Isolation Valve [*NASA*] (NASA)
**HIV**............ Human Immunodeficiency Virus
**HIVAC**...... High-Value Accounting Control
**HIVAC**...... High-Value Asset Control
**HIVAC**...... Human Immunodeficiency Virus Vaccine [*Medicine*]
**HIVOS**...... High-Vacuum Orbital Simulator
**HIVOS**...... Humanistisch Institut voor Ontwikkelings Samenwerking [*Humanistic Institute for Co-Operation with Developing Countries*] [*Hague, Netherlands*] (EAIO)
**HIV-1 PR** .. Human Immunodeficiency Virus-1 Protease [*An enzyme*]
**HIVT** ......... Health Insurance of Vermont, Inc. [*NASDAQ symbol*] (NQ)
**HIWD**........ Highwood Resources Ltd. [*NASDAQ symbol*] (NQ)
**HIWSC**...... Health Industry Wage and Salary Committee [*Terminated, 1974*] (EGAO)
**HIWSD** ..... Handbook of Instructions for Weapon Systems Designers
**HIX**............ Heat-Inactivated Muscle Extract
**HIX**............ Helix Systems Ltd. [*Vancouver Stock Exchange symbol*]
**HIX**............ Hopkinsville, KY [*Location identifier*] [*FAA*] (FAAL)
**HIXAT** ...... Highest Temperature Exceeded for All Time [*Meteorology*] (FAAC)
**HIXFM**...... Highest Temperature Exceeded for the Month [*Meteorology*] (FAAC)
**HIXSE**....... Highest Temperature Exceeded So Early [*Meteorology*] (FAAC)
**HIXSL**....... Highest Temperature Exceeded So Late [*Meteorology*] (FAAC)
**HIY**............ Hampshire Imperial Yeomanry [*British military*] (DMA)
**HIY**............ Hertfordshire Imperial Yeomanry [*British military*] (DMA)
**HIY**............ Holiday Institute of Yonkers (EA)
**HIZA** ......... Informationsdienst-AUSTAUSCH [*Information Service-EXCHANGE*] [*NOMOS Datapool*] [*Database*] (IID)
**HJ** ............. Air-Cushion Vehicle built by Hoverjak [*England*] [*Usually used in combination with numerals*]
**HJ** ............. Air-Cushion Vehicle built by Hoverjet [*Canada*] [*Usually used in combination with numerals*]
**HJ** ............. Air Haiti [*ICAO designator*] (FAAC)
**HJ** ............. Halt and Jump [*Data processing*] (BUR)
**H & J** ........ Harris and Johnson's Maryland Court of Appeals Reports [*1800-26*] [*A publication*] (DLA)
**H & J** ........ Hayes and Jones' Irish Exchequer Reports [*1832-34*] [*A publication*] (DLA)
**HJ** ............. Heilige Johannes [*Saint John*] [*German*] [*Freemasonry*]
**HJ** ............. Hepatojugular [*Reflex*] [*Medicine*]
**HJ** ............. Hibbert Journal [*A publication*]
**HJ** ............. Hic Jacet [*Here Lies*] [*Latin*]
**HJ** ............. High Jump
**HJ** ............. Hinge Jaw (MSA)
**HJ** ............. Historia Judaica [*A publication*]
**HJ** ............. Historisches Jahrbuch [*A publication*]
**HJ** ............. Holt-Jackson [*Commercial firm*] [*British*]
**HJ** ............. Honest John [*A type of short range, unguided Army rocket*]
**HJ** ............. Hose Jacket (KSC)
**H of J** ....... Hospitallers of Jerusalem [*Freemasonry*] (ROG)
**HJ** ............. Howell-Jolly [*Bodies*] [*Hematology*]
**H & J** ........ Hyphenation and Justification [*Typography*]
**HJ** ............. Station Open from Sunrise to Sunset [*ITU designation*] (CET)
**HJAS**......... Harry James Appreciation Society (EAIO)
**HJAS**......... Harvard Journal of Asiatic Studies [*A publication*]
**HJAS**......... Hitotsubashi Journal of Arts and Sciences [*A publication*]
**H Jb** .......... Handel Jahrbuch [*A publication*]
**HJb**............ Hebbel-Jahrbuch [*A publication*]
**HJB** .......... Hydrodynamic Journal Bearing
**HJC** .......... Hagerstown Junior College [*Maryland*]
**HJC** .......... Hansoms of John Clayton [*An association*] (EA)
**HJC** .......... Harcum Junior College [*Pennsylvania*]
**HJC** .......... Hibbing Junior College [*Later, Hibbing Community College*] [*Minnesota*]
**HJC** .......... Highland Junior College [*Kansas*]
**HJC** .......... Hinds Junior College [*Raymond, MS*]
**HJC** .......... Hitotsubashi Journal of Commerce and Management [*A publication*]
**HJC** .......... Holmes Junior College [*Goodman, MS*]
**HJC** .......... Holyoke Junior College [*Later, Holyoke Community College*] [*Massachusetts*]
**HJC** .......... Hutchinson Junior College [*Kansas*]
**HJCC**......... Honolulu Japanese Chamber of Commerce (EA)
**HJCPDU**... Hillside Journal of Clinical Psychiatry [*A publication*]
**HJD** .......... Heterojunction Device
**HJDRB5**.... Essays and Studies. Faculty of Hiroshima Jogakuin College [*A publication*]
**HJE** .......... Hitotsubashi Journal of Economics [*A publication*]
**HJE** .......... Hot Jet Exhaust
**H & J Forms** ... Hayes and Jarman's Concise Forms of Wills [*18th ed.*] [*1952*] [*A publication*] (DLA)
**HJH**........... Hebron, NE [*Location identifier*] [*FAA*] (FAAL)
**HJI** ........... Hachtmann, J. I., Newark NJ [*STAC*]
**HJIL**.......... Houston Journal of International Law [*A publication*] [*Also, an information service or system*] (IID)
**H & J Ir** ..... Hayes and Jones' Irish Exchequer Reports [*1832-34*] [*A publication*] (DLA)

**HJJ**........... Hachijojima [*Japan*] [*Seismograph station code, US Geological Survey*] (SEIS)
**Hj Kreis Hofgeismar** ... Heimatjahrbuch fuer den Kreis Hofgeismar [*A publication*]
**HJl**............ Hibbert Journal [*A publication*]
**HJL**........... Honest John Launcher [*See also HJ*] [*Army*]
**HJM**........... Akron-Canton, OH [*Location identifier*] [*FAA*] (FAAL)
**HJM**........... Hot Jet Model
**HJMSA**..... Journal. Mysore University. Section B. Science [*A publication*]
**H & John**... Harris and Johnson's Maryland Reports [*A publication*] (DLA)
**HJP**........... Hand Jewel Pusher
**HJP**........... Heat Jacketed Pump
**HJPP**......... Heat Jacketed Proportioning Pump
**HJR**........... Henry James Review [*A publication*]
**HJR**........... Hepatojugular Reflex [*Medicine*]
**HJR**........... Honest John Rocket [*See also HJ*] [*Army*]
**HJR**........... House Joint Resolution
**HJR**........... Khajuraho [*India*] [*Airport symbol*] (OAG)
**HJ Res**....... House Joint Resolution
**HJS**........... Hebrew Jewellers' Society [*A union*] [*British*]
**HJS**........... Helsingen Juutalainen Seurakunta [*Finland*] [*A publication*] (BJA)
**HJS**........... Hic Jacet Sepultus [*Here Lies Buried*] [*Latin*]
**HJSS**......... Hitotsubashi Journal of Social Studies [*A publication*]
**HJT**........... Head Joint [*Technical drawings*]
**HJud**......... Historia Judaica [*A publication*]
**HK**............ Colombia [*Aircraft nationality and registration mark*] (FAAC)
**HK**............ Handelskammer [*Chamber of Commerce*] [*German*]
**HK**............ Handkommentar zum Alten Testament [*Goettingen*] [*A publication*] (BJA)
**H-K**........... Hands to Knee [*Medicine*]
**HK**............ Hank [*Cotton*] (ROG)
**HK**............ Hauptwerk [*Masterpiece*] [*German*]
**HK**............ Hawker De Havilland Australia Pty. Ltd., Kaman Aircraft Corp. [*ICAO aircraft manufacturer identifier*] (ICAO)
**HK**............ Heater Kit
**HK**............ Heckler and Koch [*Machine gun*] (MCD)
**H-K**........... Heel to Knee
**HK**............ Helikopter Service A/S [*Norway*] [*ICAO designator*] (FAAC)
**HK**............ Heritage of Kansas [*A publication*]
**HK**............ Hevra Kaddisha (BJA)
**HK**............ Hexokinase [*An enzyme*]
**HK**............ High-Priority Key [*IRS*]
**H & K**........ Hill & Knowlton, Inc. [*Public relations firm*]
**HK**............ Hoeheres Kommando [*Higher Command*] [*German military - World War II*]
**hk**.............. Hong Kong [*MARC country of publication code*] [*Library of Congress*] (LCCP)
**HK**............ Hong Kong [*ANSI two-letter standard code*] (CNC)
**HK$**.......... Hong Kong Dollar [*Monetary unit*] (DS)
**HK**............ Hook
**HK**............ House of Keys [*Isle Of Man*]
**HK**............ Housekeeping
**HK**............ Hrvatsko Kolo [*A publication*]
**Hk**............. Hulk [*Nautical charts*]
**HK**............ Human Kidney
**H-K**........... Hunter-Killer [*Missile*] (MUGU)
**H-K**........... Hypoascorbemia-Kwashiorkor [*Orthomolecular medicine*]
**HK**............ Knoop Hardness Number
**HK**............ People's Liberation [*Revolutionary group*] [*Turkey*]
**HKA**.......... Blytheville, AR [*Location identifier*] [*FAA*] (FAAL)
**HKA**.......... Hand Knitting Association (EA)
**HKA**.......... Hong Kong Airways Ltd.
**HKAFO**..... Hip-Knee-Ankle-Foot Orthosis [*Medicine*]
**HKAM**....... Amboseli [*Kenya*] [*ICAO location identifier*] (ICLI)
**HKAO**....... Hip-Knee-Ankle Orthosis [*Medicine*]
**HkAT**........ Handkommentar zum Alten Testament [*Goettingen*] [*A publication*] (BJA)
**HKBA**........ Busia [*Kenya*] [*ICAO location identifier*] (ICLI)
**HKBC**........ Hongkong Bank of Canada
**HKBR**........ Bura [*Kenya*] [*ICAO location identifier*] (ICLI)
**HKBU**........ Bungoma [*Kenya*] [*ICAO location identifier*] (ICLI)
**HKC**.......... Henkel Corporation, Minneapolis, MN [*OCLC symbol*] (OCLC)
**HKC**.......... Hong Kong [*Hong Kong*] [*Seismograph station code, US Geological Survey*] (SEIS)
**HKC**.......... Hong Kong [*Hong Kong*] [*Geomagnetic observatory code*]
**HKC**.......... Shirley, NY [*Location identifier*] [*FAA*] (FAAL)
**HKCE**........ Hongkong Commodities Exchange
**HKCHDD**... Korean Journal of Mycology [*A publication*]
**HKCL**........ Hong Kong Container Line (DS)
**HKCSA**..... Hang K'ung Chih Shih [*A publication*]
**HKCTD**..... Handelingen. Koninklijke Commissie voor Toponymie en Dialectologie [*A publication*]
**HKD**.......... Hakodate [*Japan*] [*Airport symbol*] (OAG)
**HKDBK**..... Hokkaido Daigaku Bungakubu Kiyo [*A publication*]
**HK Econ Pap**... Hong Kong Economic Papers [*A publication*]
**HKEL**........ Eldoret [*Kenya*] [*ICAO location identifier*] (ICLI)
**HKEM**....... Embu [*Kenya*] [*ICAO location identifier*] (ICLI)
**HKES**........ Eliye Springs [*Kenya*] [*ICAO location identifier*] (ICLI)
**HKF**.......... Halbkettenfahrzeug [*Half-Track Vehicle*] [*German military - World War II*]
**HKF**.......... Hancock Fabrics, Inc. [*NYSE symbol*] (SPSG)
**HKF**.......... Handkerchief
**HKF**.......... Middletown, OH [*Location identifier*] [*FAA*] (FAAL)
**HKFE**........ Hong Kong Futures Exchange
**HKFG**........ Kalokol [*Kenya*] [*ICAO location identifier*] (ICLI)
**HKG**.......... Hochgeschwindigkeitskanal Goettingen [*Federal Republic of Germany*]
**HKG**.......... Hong Kong [*ANSI three-letter standard code*] (CNC)
**HKG**.......... Hong Kong [*Hong Kong*] [*Airport symbol*] (OAG)
**HKGA**........ Garissa [*Kenya*] [*ICAO location identifier*] (ICLI)
**HKGS**........ Church of Jesus Christ of Latter-Day Saints, Genealogical Society Library, Kaneohe Stake Branch, Kaneohe, HI [*Library symbol*] [*Library of Congress*] (LCLS)
**HKGT**........ Garba Tula [*Kenya*] [*ICAO location identifier*] (ICLI)
**HKH**.......... Chicago, IL [*Location identifier*] [*FAA*] (FAAL)
**HKHB**........ Homa Bay [*Kenya*] [*ICAO location identifier*] (ICLI)
**HKHO**........ Hola [*Kenya*] [*ICAO location identifier*] (ICLI)
**HKI**........... Helen Keller International (EA)
**HKI**........... Husiki [*Japan*] [*Seismograph station code, US Geological Survey*] (SEIS)
**HKIL**......... Hong Kong Islands Line (DS)
**HKIS**......... Isiolo [*Kenya*] [*ICAO location identifier*] (ICLI)
**HKK**.......... Hokitika [*New Zealand*] [*Airport symbol*] (OAG)
**HKKA**........ Kabarak [*Kenya*] [*ICAO location identifier*] (ICLI)
**HKKE**........ Keekorok [*Kenya*] [*ICAO location identifier*] (ICLI)
**HKKG**........ Kakamega [*Kenya*] [*ICAO location identifier*] (ICLI)
**HKKI**......... Kisumu [*Kenya*] [*ICAO location identifier*] (ICLI)
**HKKK**........ Helsingin Kauppakorkeakoulun Kirjasto [*Helsinki School of Economics Library*] [*Finland*] [*Information service or system*] (IID)
**HKKL**........ Kilaguni [*Kenya*] [*ICAO location identifier*] (ICLI)
**HKKR**........ Kericho [*Kenya*] [*ICAO location identifier*] (ICLI)
**HKKS**........ Kisii [*Kenya*] [*ICAO location identifier*] (ICLI)
**HKKT**........ Kitale [*Kenya*] [*ICAO location identifier*] (ICLI)
**HKL**.......... Haleakala [*Hawaii*] [*Seismograph station code, US Geological Survey*] (SEIS)
**HKL**.......... Hoyrekvinners Landsforbund [*Women's Organization of the Conservative Party*] [*Norway*] [*Political party*] (EAIO)
**HK Law R**... Hong Kong Law Review [*A publication*]
**HKLG**........ Lokitaung [*Kenya*] [*ICAO location identifier*] (ICLI)
**HKLJ**......... Hong Kong Law Journal [*A publication*] (DLA)
**HKLK**........ Lokichoggio [*Kenya*] [*ICAO location identifier*] (ICLI)
**HKLO**........ Lodwar [*Kenya*] [*ICAO location identifier*] (ICLI)
**HKLR**........ Hong Kong Law Reports [*A publication*] (DLA)
**HKLT**........ Loitokitok [*Kenya*] [*ICAO location identifier*] (ICLI)
**HKLU**........ Lamu [*Kenya*] [*ICAO location identifier*] (ICLI)
**HKLY**........ Loyengalani [*Kenya*] [*ICAO location identifier*] (ICLI)
**HKM**.......... Hypermetropic Keratomileusis [*Ophthalmology*]
**HKM**.......... Hypervelocity Kill Mechanism [*Air Force*]
**HKMA**....... Mandera [*Kenya*] [*ICAO location identifier*] (ICLI)
**HKMB**....... Marsabit [*Kenya*] [*ICAO location identifier*] (ICLI)
**HKME**........ [*The*] Keith Group of Companies, Inc. [*NASDAQ symbol*] (NQ)
**HKMG**....... Magadi [*Kenya*] [*ICAO location identifier*] (ICLI)
**HKMI**........ Maralal [*Kenya*] [*ICAO location identifier*] (ICLI)
**HKMK**....... Mulika [*Kenya*] [*ICAO location identifier*] (ICLI)
**HKML**........ Malindi [*Kenya*] [*ICAO location identifier*] (ICLI)
**HKMO**....... Mombasa/Moi International [*Kenya*] [*ICAO location identifier*] (ICLI)
**HKMR**....... Mackinnon Road [*Kenya*] [*ICAO location identifier*] (ICLI)
**HKMSC**.... Hong Kong Military Service Corps [*British military*] (DMA)
**HKMU**....... Makindu [*Kenya*] [*ICAO location identifier*] (ICLI)
**HKMY**....... Moyale [*Kenya*] [*ICAO location identifier*] (ICLI)
**HKN**.......... Harken Technologies, Inc. [*Vancouver Stock Exchange symbol*]
**HKN**.......... Hogen Kenkyu Nenpo [*A publication*]
**HKN**.......... Hoskins [*Papua New Guinea*] [*Airport symbol*] (OAG)
**HKNA**........ Nairobi/Jomo Kenyatta International [*Kenya*] [*ICAO location identifier*] (ICLI)
**HKNC**........ Nairobi [*Kenya*] [*ICAO location identifier*] (ICLI)
**HKNCDBYA**... Helen Keller National Center for Deaf-Blind Youths and Adults (EA)
**HKNI**......... Nyeri [*Kenya*] [*ICAO location identifier*] (ICLI)
**HKNK**........ Nakuru [*Kenya*] [*ICAO location identifier*] (ICLI)
**HKNO**........ Narok [*Kenya*] [*ICAO location identifier*] (ICLI)
**HKNT**........ Handkommentar zum Neuen Testament [*A publication*] (BJA)
**HKNV**........ Naivasha [*Kenya*] [*ICAO location identifier*] (ICLI)
**HKNW**....... Nairobi/Wilson [*Kenya*] [*ICAO location identifier*] (ICLI)
**HKNY**........ Nanyuki [*Kenya*] [*ICAO location identifier*] (ICLI)
**HKO**.......... Hip-Knee Orthosis [*Medicine*]
**HKOKD**..... Hakko Kogaku Kaishi [*A publication*]
**HKP**.......... Hidden Lake [*Pennsylvania*] [*Seismograph station code, US Geological Survey*] [*Closed*] (SEIS)
**HKP**.......... Hookup (MSA)
**HKP**.......... Kaanapali [*Hawaii*] [*Airport symbol*] (OAG)
**HKR**.......... Hallmark Resources [*Vancouver Stock Exchange symbol*]
**HKR**.......... Hong Kong Regiment [*British military*] (DMA)
**HKR**.......... Hooker [*Ship's rigging*] (ROG)
**HKRE**........ Nairobi/Eastleigh [*Kenya*] [*ICAO location identifier*] (ICLI)

**HKROD**..... Bulletin of Environmental Sciences [*South Korea*] [*A publication*]
**HKS**.......... Jackson, MS [*Location identifier*] [*FAA*] (FAAL)
**HKSA**........ East African School of Aviation [*Kenya*] [*ICAO location identifier*] (ICLI)
**HKSB**........ Samburu [*Kenya*] [*ICAO location identifier*] (ICLI)
**HKSC**........ Hong Kong Study Circle (EA)
**HKSRA**..... Hong Kong and Singapore Royal Artillery [*British military*] (DMA)
**HKSRGA**.. Hong Kong and Singapore Royal Garrison Artillery [*British military*] (DMA)
**HKSU**........ Hong Kong Seamen's Union
**HKT**.......... Hiram, King of Tyre [*Freemasonry*]
**HKT**.......... Hockley [*Texas*] [*Seismograph station code, US Geological Survey*] (SEIS)
**HKT**.......... Hollow Kathode Tube
**HKT**.......... Hong Kong Telecommunications Ltd. [*NYSE symbol*] (CTT)
**HKT**.......... Hot Kathode Tube
**HKT**.......... Phuket [*Thailand*] [*Airport symbol*] (OAG)
**HKTAG**..... Hong Kong Trade Advisory Group [*British Overseas Trade Board*] (DS)
**HKTSA**...... Haikan To Sochi [*A publication*]
**HKU**.......... Hong Kong University
**HkU**.......... University of Hong Kong, Hong Kong, Hong Kong [*UK*] [*Library symbol*] [*Library of Congress*] (LCLS)
**HKVC**........ Hong Kong Volunteer Corps [*British military*] (DMA)
**HKVO**........ Voi [*Kenya*] [*ICAO location identifier*] (ICLI)
**HKWJ**........ Wajir [*Kenya*] [*ICAO location identifier*] (ICLI)
**HKX**.......... Ellington Air Force Base, TX [*Location identifier*] [*FAA*] (FAAL)
**HKY**.......... Canstar Sports, Inc. [*Toronto Stock Exchange symbol*]
**HKY**.......... Hickory [*North Carolina*] [*Airport symbol*] (OAG)
**HKYSDK**... Bulletin. Korea Ocean Research and Development Institute [*A publication*]
**HKZ**.......... Minneapolis, MN [*Location identifier*] [*FAA*] (FAAL)
**HKZM**....... Handelingen. Koninklijke Zuidnederlandse Maatschappij voor Taal en Letterkunde en Geschiedenis [*A publication*]
**HL**............. Das Heilige Land (BJA)
**HL**............. Haiti Air Transport [*ICAO designator*] (FAAC)
**HL**............. Half-Life [*of radioactive elements*]
**hl**............. Halite [*CIPW classification*] [*Geology*]
**HL**............. Hand Lantern (AAG)
**HL**............. Hanging Loose [*A publication*]
**HL**............. Hard Labor
**HL**............. Hardline (MCD)
**HL**............. Harelip
**HL**............. Hariana Lancers [*British military*] (DMA)
**HL**............. Harvard Library Bulletin [*A publication*]
**HL**............. Haul (MSA)
**HL**............. Hawser Laid
**HL**............. Head Linesman [*Football*]
**HL**............. Headmaster-Lieutenant [*Navy*] [*British*]
**HL**............. Hearing Level
**HL**............. Hearing Loss
**H & L**........ Heart and Lungs [*Medicine*]
**HL**............. Heavy Lift
**HL**............. Hebrew Leader (BJA)
**HL**............. Hebrew Letters (BJA)
**HL**............. Hebrew Literature (BJA)
**HL**............. Hecla Mining Co. [*NYSE symbol*] (SPSG)
**HL**............. Hectoliter (GPO)
**HL**............. Heel Line (MSA)
**HL**............. Height-Length
**HL**............. Heilig [*Holy, Saint*] [*German*]
**HL**............. Heir-at-Law
**HL**............. Helium Level
**HL**............. Herpetologists' League (EA)
**HL**............. High Level
**H/L**........... High or Low
**HL**............. Highline (MSA)
**HL**............. Hill
**HL**............. Hinge Line [*Technical drawings*]
**HL**............. Histiocytic Lymphoma [*Oncology*]
**HL**............. Histocompatibility Locus [*Immunology*]
**HL**............. Historiographia Linguistica [*A publication*]
**HL**............. Hittite Laws (BJA)
**HL**............. Hoc Loco [*In This Place*] [*Latin*]
**Hl**............. Hochland [*A publication*]
**HL**............. Hodges-Lehmann Estimator [*Statistics*]
**HL**............. Hodgkin's Lymphoma [*Medicine*]
**HL**............. Honors List (ADA)
**HL**............. Horizontal Landing (KSC)
**HL**............. Horizontal Line
**HL**............. Host Language
**HL**............. Hot Line [*Alert system*] (AAG)
**HL**............. House of Lords [*British*]
**HL**............. House of Lords Cases (Clark) [*England*] [*A publication*] (DLA)
**HL**............. Howard League [*An association*] (EAIO)
**HL**............. Huius Loci [*Of This Place*] [*Latin*]
**HL**............. Human Lymphoid [*Immunology*]
**HL**............. Humanistica Lovaniensia [*A publication*]
**HL**............. Hyborean Legion (EA)
**HL**............. Hydrodynamics Laboratory [*MIT*] (MCD)
**HL**............. Hydrogen Line (MCD)
**HL**............. Hydrology Laboratory [*Department of Agriculture*] [*Information service or system*] (IID)
**H/L**........... Hydrophile/Lipophile [*Followed by a number*]
**HL**............. Hygienic Laboratory [*US*]
**HL**............. Hypermetropia, Latent [*Ophthalmology*]
**HL**............. Hypertrichosis Lanuginosa [*Medicine*]
**HL**............. [*Republic of*] Korea [*Aircraft nationality and registration mark*] (FAAC)
**HL**............. Law Reports, House of Lords, English and Irish Appeals [*1866-75*] [*A publication*] (DLA)
**HL**............. Mustard/Lewisite Mix [*Poisonous gas*] [*Army*]
**HL**............. VEB Deutsche Hydrierwerk, Rodleben [*East Germany*] [*Research code symbol*]
**HLA**.......... Hall's Lagoon [*Australia*] [*Seismograph station code, US Geological Survey*] [*Closed*] (SEIS)
**HLA**.......... Hat Leather Association (EA)
**HLA**.......... Heavy-Lift Airship (MCD)
**HLA**.......... Helicopter Loggers Association (EA)
**HLA**.......... High-Level Analog (MCD)
**HLA**.......... Histocompatibility Locus Antigens [*System*] [*Immunology*]
**HLA**.......... Historical Labor Applications [*Military*] (AFIT)
**HLA**.......... Homologous Leucocytic Antibodies
**HLA**.......... Horizontal Line Array (MCD)
**HL-A**......... Human Leukocyte- [*or Lymphocyte-*] Antigen [*System for recognizing foreign tissue*] [*Immunology*]
**HLA**.......... Human Life Amendment
**HLaB**........ Brigham Young University, Hawaii Campus, Laie, HI [*Library symbol*] [*Library of Congress*] (LCLS)
**HLAD**....... High-Level Air Defence [*Military*] [*British*]
**HLAD**....... Horse-Liver Alcohol Dehydrogenase [*Also, HLADH, HLALD*] [*An enzyme*]
**HLADH**..... Horse-Liver Alcohol Dehydrogenase [*Also, HLAD, HLALD*] [*An enzyme*]
**HLA Dis Regist**... HLA and Disease Registry [*A publication*]
**HLA/DZ**... Helicopter Landing Area/Drop Zone [*Military*] (MCD)
**HLA/DZS**... Helicopter Landing Area/Drop Zone Study [*Military*] (MCD)
**HLAF**........ High-Level Arithmetic Function
**HLaGS**...... Church of Jesus Christ of Latter-Day Saints, Genealogical Society Library, Laie Branch, Laie, HI [*Library symbol*] [*Library of Congress*] (LCLS)
**HLAHWG**... High Level Ad Hoc Working Group [*NATO*] (NATG)
**HLA J**........ Hawaii Library Association. Journal [*A publication*]
**HLAL**........ High-Level Assembly Language (MCD)
**HLALD**..... Horse-Liver Alcohol Dehydrogenase [*Also, HLAD, HLADH*] [*An enzyme*]
**HL-A LD**... Human Lymphocyte-Antigen Lymphocyte Defined [*Immunology*]
**H-LAND**... Headland (ADA)
**HLAS**........ Handbook of Latin American Studies
**HLAS**........ Hot Line Alert System
**HLASD**..... Hand-Link Arm Safe Device
**HL-A SD**... Human Lymphocyte-Antigen Serologically Defined [*Immunology*]
**HLB**.......... Batesville, IN [*Location identifier*] [*FAA*] (FAAL)
**HLB**.......... Federal Home Loan Bank Board, Accounts Payable, Washington, DC [*OCLC symbol*] (OCLC)
**HLB**.......... Harvard Library. Bulletin [*A publication*]
**HLB**.......... Historisches Literaturblatt [*A publication*]
**HLB**.......... Huntington Library. Bulletin [*A publication*]
**HLB**.......... Hydrophile-Lipophile Balance [*Surfactant technology*]
**HLB**.......... Hypotonic Lysis Buffer [*Analytical biochemistry*]
**HLBB**........ Home Loan Bank Board [*Federal agency*] (GPO)
**HLBFA**...... Heilberufe [*East Germany*] [*A publication*]
**HLBI**......... Human Lymphoblastoid Interferon [*Antineoplastic drug*]
**HLBR**........ Heel Breaster
**HLBRD**..... Halberd
**HLC**.......... HAWK [*Homing All the Way Killer*] Logistics Complex (MCD)
**HLC**.......... Hazleton Laboratories Corporation [*NYSE symbol*] (SPSG)
**HLC**.......... Headmaster Lieutenant-Commander [*Navy*] [*British*]
**HLC**.......... Heavy/Light Corps (MCD)
**HLC**.......... High-Level Cell [*Nuclear energy*] (NRCH)
**HLC**.......... Hill City, KS [*Location identifier*] [*FAA*] (FAAL)
**HLC**.......... Homeowner's Land Corporation [*Federal agency formed in 1932*] [*Investment term*]
**HLC**.......... Homogenized Leaf Curing [*Tobacco industry*]
**HLC**.......... House of Lords Cases (Clark) [*England*] [*A publication*] (DLA)
**HLC**.......... Human Lactation Center (EA)
**HLC**.......... Human Life Center (EA)
**HLCADS**... High-Level Container Airdrop System [*Army*] (RDA)
**HL Cas**...... House of Lords Cases (Clark) [*England*] [*A publication*] (DLA)
**HL Cas (Eng)**... House of Lords Cases [*A publication*] (DLA)
**HLC-ATC**... Heavy-Lift Helicopter Advanced Technology Component [*Program*] [*Army*] (RDA)
**HLCF**........ Hardened Launch Control Facility (MUGU)
**HLCF**........ Heat-Labile Citrororum Factor [*Biochemistry*]
**HLCF**........ Holy Land Conservation Fund (EA)
**HLCL**........ Helical

**HLCM**....... Holy Land Christian Mission (EA)
**HLCMI**..... Holy Land Christian Mission International [*Later, HLCM*] (EA)
**HLCO**........ Healthco International, Inc. [*Boston, MA*] [*NASDAQ symbol*] (NQ)
**HLCPS**...... Helical Compression
**HLCPTR**... Helicopter (MSA)
**HLCS**........ Heat Limiter Control Switch
**HLCS**........ High-Level Compaction Station [*Nuclear energy*] (NRCH)
**HLCV**........ Hot Leg Check Valve [*Nuclear energy*] (NRCH)
**HLD**.......... Doctor of Humane Letters
**HLD**.......... Hailar [*China*] [*Airport symbol*] (OAG)
**HLD**.......... Helium Leak Detector
**HLD**.......... Herniated Lumbar Disc [*Medicine*]
**HLD**.......... Hold (FAAC)
**HLD**.......... Holdings [*Online database field identifier*]
**HLD**.......... Hollywood Investments [*Vancouver Stock Exchange symbol*]
**HLD**.......... Hypersensitivity Lung Disease [*Medicine*]
**HLDA**........ Hold Acknowledge [*Data processing*]
**HLDC**........ High-Level Data Link Control (MCD)
**HLDDN**..... Holddown
**HLDG**........ Holding (MSA)
**HLDH**....... Heat-Stable Lactic Dehydrogenase [*Clinical chemistry*]
**HLDI**........ Highway Loss Data Institute (EA)
**HLDN**........ Holddown (MSA)
**HLDR**........ Holder
**HLDS**........ Hydrogen Leak Detection System (NASA)
**HLDS**........ Vermont-New Hampshire-New York Hospital Libraries [*Library network*]
**HLE**........... Hailey, ID [*Location identifier*] [*FAA*] (FAAL)
**HLE**........... Hale Resources Ltd. [*Toronto Stock Exchange symbol*]
**HLE**........... Halle [*German Democratic Republic*] [*Seismograph station code, US Geological Survey*] (SEIS)
**HLE**........... Hazleton Laboratories Europe Ltd. [*British*] (IRUK)
**HLE**........... Human Leucocyte Elastase [*An enzyme*]
**HLE**........... Hydrogen Line Emission
**HLEKT**...... Handbuch der Literaturgeschichte in Einzeldarstellungen. Kroeners Taschenausgabe [*A publication*]
**HLEXT**...... Helical Extension
**HLF**........... Half (FAAC)
**HLF**........... Hall's Legal Forms [*A publication*] (DLA)
**HLF**........... Heart and Lung Foundation [*Defunct*] (EA)
**HLF**........... Heat-Labile Factor
**HLF**........... Hidden Lake Formation [*Geology*]
**HLF**........... High Loss Ferrite
**HLF**........... Histoire Litteraire de la France [*A publication*]
**HLF**........... Holistic Life Foundation [*Later, Feathered Pipe Foundation*] (EA)
**HLF**........... Horizontal Line Frequency
**HLF**........... House Leadership Fund (EA)
**HLF**........... Hultsfred [*Sweden*] [*Airport symbol*] (OAG)
**HLF**........... Human Life Foundation (EA)
**HLF**........... Human Lung Fluid [*Medicine*]
**HLF**........... Hyperbolic LOFAR Fix [*Military*] (CAAL)
**HLFL**......... Buattifel [*Libya*] [*ICAO location identifier*] (ICLI)
**HLFM**........ Half-Moon
**HLFM**........ High-Level Flux Monitor
**HLG**........... Dr. John W. Tintera Memorial Hypoglycemia Lay Group (EA)
**HLG**........... HAWK [*Homing All the Way Killer*] Logistics Group (AABC)
**HLG**........... Heligoland [*Federal Republic of Germany*] [*Seismograph station code, US Geological Survey*] (SEIS)
**HLG**........... High-Level Group [*NATO*]
**HLG**........... Hollinger, Inc. [*Toronto Stock Exchange symbol*] [*Vancouver Stock Exchange symbol*]
**HLG**........... Homing Level Gauge
**HLG**........... Hot Leg [*Nuclear energy*]
**HLG**........... Housing and Local Government [*A publication*] (DLA)
**HLG**........... Wheeling, WV [*Location identifier*] [*FAA*] (FAAL)
**HLGC**........ Hannibal-La Grange College [*Missouri*]
**HLGL**........ Giallo/Warehouse 59 E [*Libya*] [*ICAO location identifier*] (ICLI)
**HLGS**........ Hot Line Gunsight System
**HLGT**........ Ghat [*Libya*] [*ICAO location identifier*] (ICLI)
**HLH**.......... Heavy-Lift Helicopter
**HLH**.......... Hertfordshire Light Horse [*British military*] (DMA)
**H & L & H**... HLH. Zeitschrift fuer Heizung, Lueftung, Klimatechnik, Haustechnik [*A publication*]
**HLH**.......... Human Luteinizing Hormone [*Endocrinology*]
**HLH**.......... Hypoplastic Left Heart [*Cardiology*]
**HLH**.......... Ulanhot [*China*] [*Airport symbol*] (OAG)
**HLH (Heiz Luftung Klimatech Haustech)**... HLH. Zeitschrift fuer Heizung, Lueftung, Klimatechnik, Haustechnik [*A publication*]
**HLHP**........ HLH Petroleum Corp. [*NASDAQ symbol*] (NQ)
**HLHS**........ Heavy-Lift Helicopter System
**HLHS**........ Hypoplastic Left-Heart Syndrome [*Medicine*]
**HLHZA**..... HLH. Heizung, Lueftung, Klimatechnik, Haustechnik [*A publication*]
**HLH Zeit Heizung Lueftung Klim Haustech**... HLH. Zeitschrift fuer Heizung, Lueftung, Klimatechnik, Haustechnik [*A publication*]
**HLH Z Heiz Lueft Klimatech Haustech**... HLH. Zeitschrift fuer Heizung, Lueftung, Klimatechnik, Haustechnik [*A publication*]
**HLI**............ Highland Light Infantry [*Military unit*] [*British*]
**HLI**............ Holly Springs, MS [*Location identifier*] [*FAA*] (FAAL)
**HLI**............ Holmium LASER Illuminator
**HLI**............ Hospital Literature Index [*A publication*]
**HLI**............ Host Language Interface
**HLI**............ Human Life International (EA)
**HLIC**......... Highland Light Infantry of Canada [*Military unit*]
**H/LIN**....... Head Lining [*Automotive engineering*]
**HLIV**......... High-Level Input Voltage
**HLIV**......... Hot Leg Isolation Valve [*Nuclear energy*] (NRCH)
**HLJ**........... All Seasons Air Pacific, Inc. [*Long Beach, CA*] [*FAA designator*] (FAAC)
**HLJ**........... Hastings Law Journal [*A publication*]
**HLJ**........... Hindu Law Journal [*A publication*] (DLA)
**HL Jour**..... House of Lords Journals [*England*] [*A publication*] (DLA)
**HLK**........... Haleakala [*Hawaii*] [*Seismograph station code, US Geological Survey*] (SEIS)
**HLK**........... Hanser Literatur-Kommentare [*A publication*]
**HLK**........... Hefte fuer Literatur und Kritik [*A publication*]
**HLK**........... Kauai Public Library Association, Linhue, HI [*Library symbol*] [*Library of Congress*] (LCLS)
**HLKF**........ Kufra [*Libya*] [*ICAO location identifier*] (ICLI)
**HLL**........... Hallett [*Antarctica*] [*Seismograph station code, US Geological Survey*] [*Closed*] (SEIS)
**HLL**........... Halley Resources Ltd. [*Vancouver Stock Exchange symbol*]
**HLL**........... Hebrew Language and Literature (BJA)
**HLL**........... High-Level Language [*Data processing*]
**HLL**........... Hill [*Board on Geographic Names*]
**HLLAPI**.... High-Level Application Program Interface [*Data processing*] (PCM)
**HLLB**......... Benghazi/Benina [*Libya*] [*ICAO location identifier*] (ICLI)
**HLLL**......... Tripoli [*Libya*] [*ICAO location identifier*] (ICLI)
**HLLO**........ Metega [*Libya*] [*ICAO location identifier*] (ICLI)
**HLLQ**........ El Beida/Labraq [*Libya*] [*ICAO location identifier*] (ICLI)
**HLLS**......... Sebha [*Libya*] [*ICAO location identifier*] (ICLI)
**HLLT**......... Tripoli/International [*Libya*] [*ICAO location identifier*] (ICLI)
**HLLV**........ Heavy-Lift Launch Vehicle [*Rocketry*] (MCD)
**HLLW**....... High-Level Liquid Waste [*Nuclear energy*]
**HLLWT**..... High-Level Liquid Waste Tank [*Nuclear energy*] (NRCH)
**HLM**.......... Hampshire Local Militia [*British military*] (DMA)
**HLM**.......... Harpoon Logic Module [*Missiles*] (MCD)
**HLM**.......... Helmville [*Montana*] [*Seismograph station code, US Geological Survey*] [*Closed*] (SEIS)
**HLM**.......... Henry Louis Mencken [*American author/critic*]
**HLM**.......... High-Latitude Mode
**HLM**.......... High-Level Meeting (DCTA)
**HLM**.......... High-Level Mixer
**HLM**.......... Holland, MI [*Location identifier*] [*FAA*] (FAAL)
**HLMB**....... Marsa Brega [*Libya*] [*ICAO location identifier*] (ICLI)
**HLME**....... Holmes [*D. H.*] Co. Ltd. [*NASDAQ symbol*] (NQ)
**HLMI**........ High-Load Melt Index [*Plastics*] [*Automotive engineering*]
**HLML**....... High-Level Microprogramming Language
**HLMR**....... Hunter-Leggitt Military Reservation (AABC)
**HLMT**....... Helmet (NASA)
**HLN**.......... Halton Reinsurance Co. Ltd. [*Toronto Stock Exchange symbol*]
**HLN**.......... Helena [*Montana*] [*Airport symbol*] (OAG)
**HLN**.......... Holnam, Inc. [*NYSE symbol*] (SPSG)
**HLN**.......... Hualilan [*Argentina*] [*Seismograph station code, US Geological Survey*] (SEIS)
**HLN**.......... Hyperplastic Liver Nodules [*Medicine*]
**HLNCC**..... High-Level Neutron Coincidence Counter [*Nuclear energy*] (NRCH)
**HLND**........ Highlands [*Board on Geographic Names*]
**HLNE**........ Hillsboro & North Eastern Railway Co. [*AAR code*]
**HLNF**........ Ras Lanouf V 40 [*Libya*] [*ICAO location identifier*] (ICLI)
**HLNFPF**... Human Life and Natural Family Planning Foundation (EA)
**HLNG**........ Headlining
**HLNL**........ Hydroxylysinonorleucine [*Biochemistry*]
**HLNR**........ Health Lawyers News Report [*A publication*] (DLA)
**HLO**.......... High-Latitude Operation
**HLO**.......... High-Level Override [*Nuclear energy*] (NRCH)
**HLO**.......... Horizontal Lockout
**HLON**....... Hon [*Libya*] [*ICAO location identifier*] (ICLI)
**HLOV**........ High-Level Output Voltage
**H/LP**......... Headlamp [*Automotive engineering*]
**HLP**........... Heavy-Lift Pontoon
**HLP**........... Hel [*Poland*] [*Geomagnetic observatory code*]
**HLP**........... Help File [*Data processing*]
**HLP**........... Helper
**HLP**........... Hilina Pali [*Hawaii*] [*Seismograph station code, US Geological Survey*] (SEIS)
**HLP**........... Home and Law Publishers [*British*]
**HLP**........... Hyperlipoproteinemia [*Medicine*]
**HLP**........... Hypersonic Local Pressure
**HLP**........... Jakarta [*Indonesia*] [*Airport symbol*] (OAG)
**HLPH**........ Holy Land Postal History [*A publication*]
**HLPI**......... High-Level Programming Interface
**HLPS**........ Heavy Lift Prepositioning Ship [*Navy*]
**HLQ**.......... Highly Luminous QUASAR [*Astronomy*]
**HLQ**.......... Huntington Library. Quarterly [*A publication*]
**HLQC**........ Hora Locoque Consuetis [*At the Usual Time and Place*] [*Latin*]

**HLQL**........ High-Level Query Language
**HLQS**........ Hora Locoque Solitis [*At the Usual Time and Place*] [*Latin*]
**HLR**........... Haifa Law Reports [*A publication*]
**HLR**........... Hand-Held LASER Range-Finder
**HLR**........... Harvard Law Review [*A publication*]
**HLR**........... Heart-Lung Resuscitation [*Medicine*]
**HLR**........... Helicopter LASER Range-Finder
**HLR**........... High-Level Representation
**HLR**........... High Level Resources Ltd. [*Vancouver Stock Exchange symbol*]
**HLR**........... Highland Ranch [*Colorado*] [*Seismograph station code, US Geological Survey*] [*Closed*] (SEIS)
**HLR**........... Holder (KSC)
**HLR**........... Houston Law Review [*A publication*] (ILCA)
**HLR**........... Killeen, TX [*Location identifier*] [*FAA*] (FAAL)
**HLRA**........ Dahra/Warehouse 32 [*Libya*] [*ICAO location identifier*] (ICLI)
**HLRA**........ Health Labour Relations Association [*Canada*]
**HL Rep**...... English House of Lords Reports [*A publication*] (DLA)
**HLRF**......... Jaref/Sirte [*ICAO location identifier*] (ICLI)
**HLRM**........ High-Level Radio Modulator
**HLRO**........ House of Lords Record Office [*British*] (DLA)
**HLRSC**...... Holland Lop Rabbit Specialty Club (EA)
**HLRV**........ Heavy Lift Research Vehicle [*Military*]
**HLS**........... Harvard Law School [*Massachusetts*]
**HLS**........... Harvard University, Cambridge, MA [*OCLC symbol*] (OCLC)
**HLS**........... Health Learning Systems
**HLS**........... Heavy-Lift System
**HLS**........... Heavy Logistics System
**HLS**........... Helicopter Landing Site [*Military*] (INF)
**HLS**........... High-Level Service [*Data processing*]
**HLS**........... Hills (MCD)
**HLS**........... Historiska och Litteraturhistoriska Studier [*A publication*]
**HLS**........... Hoc Loco Situs [*Laid in This Place*] [*Latin*]
**HLS**........... Holes (ADA)
**HLS**........... Holograph Letter Signed
**HLS**........... Horizontal Liquid Spring
**HLS**........... Hue, Lightness, and Saturation [*Color model*] (BYTE)
**HLS**........... Leather and Shoes [*A publication*]
**HlSAN**....... Helsingin Sanomat [*A publication*]
**HLSC**......... Helicopter Logistic Support Center (NVT)
**HLSCA**...... Health Laboratory Science [*A publication*]
**HL Sc App Cas** ... English Law Reports, House of Lords, Scotch and Divorce Appeal Cases [*1866-75*] [*A publication*] (DLA)
**HLSD**........ Essider [*Libya*] [*ICAO location identifier*] (ICLI)
**HLSD**........ Heel Sanding
**HLSE**......... High-Level, Single-Ended
**HLSP**......... Heitler-London-Slater-Pauling [*Method*] [*Physics*]
**HLSTO**....... Hailstones [*Meteorology*] (FAAC)
**HLSUA**...... Honeywell Large Systems Users Association (EA)
**HLSV**......... Helium Latching Solenoid Valve
**HLSW**....... High-Level Solidified Waste [*Nuclear energy*] (NRCH)
**HLT**........... Halt [*Data processing*] (MDG)
**HLT**........... Hamilton [*Australia*] [*Airport symbol*] (OAG)
**HLT**........... Heterodyne Look-Thru [*Telecommunications*] (TEL)
**HLT**........... High-Level Terminal (CAAL)
**HLT**........... Highly Leveraged Transaction [*Banking*]
**HLT**........... Hilton Hotels Corp. [*NYSE symbol*] (SPSG)
**HL & T**...... Hunter's Landlord and Tenant [*Scotland*] [*A publication*] (DLA)
**HLTA**........ Halt Acknowledge [*Data processing*]
**HLTD**........ Ghadames [*Libya*] [*ICAO location identifier*] (ICLI)
**HLTH**........ Health
**Hlth**............ Health [*A publication*]
**HLTH**........ Healthsource, Inc. [*NASDAQ symbol*] (NQ)
**Hlth Horiz** ... Health Horizon [*A publication*]
**Hlth Hyg Ho** ... Health and Hygiene in the Home [*A publication*]
**Hlth Inf Dig** ... Health Information Digest [*A publication*]
**Hlth Inf Dig Hot Count** ... Health Information Digest for Hot Countries [*A publication*]
**Hlth Instr Yb** ... Health Instruction Yearbook [*A publication*]
**Hlth Lab Sci** ... Health Laboratory Science [*A publication*]
**Hlth Ne**...... Health News [*A publication*]
**Hlth New**... Health News [*A publication*]
**Hlth PAC**... Health-PAC [*Policy Advisory Center*] Bulletin [*A publication*]
**Hlth Phys**.. Health Physics [*A publication*]
**Hlth Rght**... Health Rights News [*A publication*]
**Hlth Saf Exec Direct Inf and Advisory Services Transl** ... Health and Safety Executive Directorate of Information and Advisory Services. Translations [*England*] [*A publication*]
**Hlth Saf Monitor** ... Health and Safety Monitor [*A publication*]
**Hlth Saf at Work** ... Health and Safety at Work [*A publication*]
**Hlth Sch Ch** ... Health of the School Child [*A publication*]
**Hlth Serv** ... Health Services [*A publication*]
**Hlth Serv Res** ... Health Services Research [*A publication*]
**Hlth Soc Serv J** ... Health and Social Service Journal [*A publication*]
**Hlth Soc Wrk** ... Health and Social Work [*A publication*]
**Hlth Top**.... Health Topics [*A publication*]
**Hlth Yb**...... Health Yearbook [*A publication*]
**HLTL**......... High-Level Test Language
**HLTL**......... High-Level Transistor Logic
**HLTP**......... Hilltop (FAAC)
**HLTPA**...... Health Physics [*A publication*]
**HLTRF**...... Hospitality Lodging and Travel Research Foundation [*Also known as Research Foundation*] (EA)
**HLTTL**...... High-Level Transistor Translator Logic
**HLU**........... Houailou [*New Caledonia*] [*Airport symbol*] (OAG)
**HLU**........... House Logic Unit
**HLV**........... Hallsville, MO [*Location identifier*] [*FAA*] (FAAL)
**HLV**........... Heavy-Lift Vehicle
**HLV**........... Herpes-Like Virus
**HLVG**........ Das Heilige Land in Vergangenheit und Gegenwart [*A publication*] (BJA)
**HLW**.......... Halbleinwand [*Half-Bound Cloth*] [*Bookbinding*] [*German*]
**HLW**.......... Handbuch der Literaturwissenschaft [*Potsdam*] [*A publication*] (BJA)
**HLW**.......... Hattiesburg, Camp Shelby, MS [*Location identifier*] [*FAA*] (FAAL)
**HLW**.......... Helwan [*Egypt*] [*Seismograph station code, US Geological Survey*] (SEIS)
**HLW**.......... High-Level Waste [*Nuclear energy*]
**HLW**.......... Higher Low Water
**HLW**.......... Landbode; Hollands Landbouwweekblad [*A publication*]
**HLWC**....... High-Level Waste Calcination [*Nuclear energy*] (NRCH)
**HLWC**....... High-Level Waste Concentrate [*Nuclear energy*] (NRCH)
**HLWD**....... High-Level Waste Concentrator Distillate [*Nuclear energy*] (NRCH)
**HLWF**....... High-Level Waste Concentrator Feed [*Nuclear energy*] (NRCH)
**HLWI**........ Higher Low-Water Interval
**HL Wkly Inf Bull** ... House of Lords Weekly Information Bulletin [*A publication*] (DLA)
**HLW/OC**.. Hard Labor without Confinement
**HLWOG**.... High-Level Liquid Waste Off-Gas [*Nuclear energy*] (NRCH)
**HLWS**....... High-Level Waste Surge [*Nuclear energy*] (NRCH)
**HLX**........... Galax/Hillsville, VA [*Location identifier*] [*FAA*] (FAAL)
**HLX**........... Helix Circuits, Inc. [*Toronto Stock Exchange symbol*]
**HLXA**........ Helix Angle
**HLY**........... Haley Industries Ltd. [*Toronto Stock Exchange symbol*]
**HLY**........... Halley Bay [*United Kingdom*] [*Geomagnetic observatory code*]
**HLY**........... Holly Sugar Corp. [*NYSE symbol*] (SPSG)
**HLY**........... Valparaiso, FL [*Location identifier*] [*FAA*] (FAAL)
**HLYR**........ Haze Layer Aloft [*Aviation*] (FAAC)
**HLZ**........... Hamilton [*New Zealand*] [*Airport symbol*] (OAG)
**HLZ**........... Helicopter Landing Zone
**HLZA**........ Zella 74 [*Libya*] [*ICAO location identifier*] (ICLI)
**HLZBL**...... Holzblaeser [*Woodwind Instrument*] [*Music*]
**HLZL**........ Helicopter Landing Zone Locator
**HM**............ Air-Cushion Vehicle built by Hovermarine [*England*] [*Usually used in combination with numerals*]
**HM**............ Air-Cushion Vehicle built by Hovermarine [*US*] [*Usually used in combination with numerals*]
**HM**............ Air Seychelles [*Seychelles*] [*ICAO designator*] (FAAC)
**HM**............ Haagsch Maandblad [*A publication*]
**HM**............ Half Morocco
**HM**............ Hallmark
**HM**............ Hamarein Air [*United Arab Emirates*] [*ICAO designator*] (ICDA)
**HM**............ Hand Movement
**HM**............ Handmade
**HM**............ Hands of Mercy [*An association*] (EA)
**HM**............ Harbor Master
**HM**............ Hardness Maintenance (MSA)
**HM**............ Harmonic Mean [*Music*]
**HM**............ Harper's Magazine [*A publication*]
**H & M**........ Hay and Marriott's English Admiralty Reports [*A publication*] (DLA)
**HM**............ Head Motion [*Gravity*]
**HM**............ Headmaster [*or Headmistress*]
**HM**............ Healthy Male (ROG)
**HM**............ Heard Island and McDonald Islands [*ANSI two-letter standard code*] (CNC)
**hm**............. Heard Island and McDonald Islands [*MARC country of publication code*] [*Library of Congress*] (LCCP)
**HM**............ Heavy Maintenance [*Ordnance*]
**HM**............ Heavy Metal [*Rock music type*]
**HM**............ Heavy Mobile
**HM**............ Hectometer [*100 meters*]
**HM**............ Hejnat Mariacki [*A publication*]
**hm**............. Hematite [*CIPW classification*] [*Geology*]
**H & M**........ Hemming and Miller's English Vice-Chancellors' Reports [*A publication*] (DLA)
**H & M**........ Hening and Munford's Reports [*11-14 Virginia*] [*A publication*] (DLA)
**H/m**........... Henry per Meter
**HM**............ Hepatic Microcirculation [*Physiology*]
**HM**............ Heritage Manor (BJA)
**Hm**............ Hermes [*A publication*]
**HM**............ Hermeter Master [*Freemasonry*] (ROG)
**hM**............ Herrschende Meinung [*Prevailing Opinion*] [*German*] (ILCA)
**HM**............ High-Meaningfulness [*Psychology*]
**HM**............ High Molecular [*Weight*] [*Also, HMW*] [*Organic chemistry*]
**HM**............ Hinge Mount (MCD)
**HM**............ His [*or Her*] Majesty

**HM** ........... Hoc Mense [*In This Month*] [*Latin*]
**HM** ........... Hollow Metal [*Technical drawings*]
**HM** ........... Home (ROG)
**HM** ........... Home Mission
**HM** ........... Homestake Mining Co. [*NYSE symbol*] (SPSG)
**H & M**........ Hommes et Mondes [*A publication*]
**HM** ........... Hommes et Mondes [*A publication*]
**HM** ........... Homogenization Medium
**HM** ........... Honorary Member [*Freemasonry*] (ROG)
**HM** ........... Horizontal Meridian [*Optics, eye anatomy*]
**HM** ........... Horniman Museum [*London*]
**HM** ........... Hortus Musicus [*A publication*]
**HM** ........... Hoshen Mishpat, Shulhan 'Arukh (BJA)
**HM** ........... Hospital Corpsman [*Navy rating*]
**HM** ........... Hospitality Management [*A publication*]
**HM** ........... Houghton Mifflin Co. [*Publisher*]
**HM** ........... Hours, Minutes (ROG)
**HM** ........... House Magazine [*Australia*] [*A publication*]
**HM** ........... Housing Management [*HUD*]
**HM** ........... Huius Mensis [*This Month's*] [*Latin*]
**HM** ........... Huntingdon Militia [*British military*] (DMA)
**HM** ........... Hydatidiform Mole [*Gynecology*]
**HM** ........... Hydra Medium [*Culture medium*]
**HM** ........... Hydrogen MASER
**HM** ........... Hydrometeorological
**hm** ............ Hydroxymethyl [*As substituent on nucleoside*] [*Biochemistry*]
**HM** ........... Hyperimmune Mice
**Hm** ............ Manifest Hypermetropia [*Medicine*]
**HM** ........... Marine Helicopter Squadron
**HM** ........... Master of Humanities
**HM** ........... Sandoz [*Italy*] [*Research code symbol*]
**HM** ........... Sisters of the Humility of Mary [*Roman Catholic religious order*]
**HM1** .......... Hospital Corpsman, First Class [*Navy rating*]
**HM2** .......... Hospital Corpsman, Second Class [*Navy rating*]
**HM$^2$** .......... Square Hectometer
**HM3** .......... Hospital Corpsman, Third Class [*Navy rating*]
**HMA** ......... Hardwood Manufacturers Association (EA)
**Hma** .......... Harmona [*Record label*] [*Austria*]
**HMA** ......... Health Management Associates [*AMEX symbol*] (SPSG)
**HMA** ......... Helvetica Medica Acta [*A publication*]
**HMA** ......... High Memory Area [*Data processing*] (PCM)
**HMA** ......... His [*or Her*] Majesty's Airship
**HMA** ......... Hoist Manufacturers Association [*Later, HMI*] (EA)
**HMA** ......... Home Manufacturers Association [*Later, HMC*] (EA)
**HMA** ......... Home Mission Association [*Episcopalian*]
**HMA** ......... Hondo, TX [*Location identifier*] [*FAA*] (FAAL)
**HMA** ......... Hot Melt Adhesive
**HMA** ......... Hot Melt Applicator
**HMA** ......... Hydroxymethyladenine [*Biochemistry*]
**HMA** ......... Hypergol Maintenance Area (MCD)
**HMA** ......... Hyundai Motor America, Inc.
**HMA** ......... Marine Helicopter Squadron Attack (NVT)
**HMAA**........ Haitian Medical Association Abroad [*Later, AMHE*] (EA)
**HMAC**........ Hazardous Materials Advisory Council (EA)
**HMAC**........ Health Manpower Advisory Council
**HMAC**........ His [*or Her*] Majesty's Aircraft Carrier
**HMACA**.... Helvetica Medica Acta [*A publication*]
**HMACI**..... His [*or Her*] Majesty's Alkali and Clean Air Inspectorate [*British*] (DCTA)
**HMad** ........ Hispania (Madrid) [*A publication*]
**HMAF**....... His [*or Her*] Majesty's Armed Forces
**H MAJ:T**... Hans Majestaet [*His Majesty*] [*Swedish*]
**HMANA** ... Hawk Migration Association of North America (EA)
**HMAS**....... His [*or Her*] Majesty's Australian Ship
**HMAV**....... His [*or Her*] Majesty's Army Vessel [*British military*] (DMA)
**HMAZ**....... Home Federal Savings & Loan of Arizona [*NASDAQ symbol*] (NQ)
**HMB**.......... Garden City, KS [*Location identifier*] [*FAA*] (FAAL)
**HMB**.......... Haemophilus Maintenance Broth [*Microbiology*]
**HMB**.......... Hamburg [*New York*] [*Seismograph station code, US Geological Survey*] [*Closed*] (SEIS)
**HMB**.......... Hazara Mountain Battery [*British military*] (DMA)
**HMB**.......... Hermannsburger Missionsblatt [*A publication*]
**HMB**.......... Hexamethylbenzene [*Organic chemistry*]
**HMB**.......... Homatropine Methylbromide [*Anticholinergic*]
**HMB**.......... Hops Marketing Board [*British*]
**HMB**.......... Hughes Mining Barge [*Support vessel for Glomar Explorer*]
**HMB**.......... Hydroxy(methoxy)benzaldehyde [*Organic chemistry*]
**HMBA**........ Hebrew Master Bakers Association [*Inactive*] (EA)
**HMBA**........ Hexamethylene Bis(Acetamide) [*Organic chemistry*]
**HMBA**........ Hotel and Motel Brokers of America (EA)
**HMBA**........ Hydroxymethyl(methyl)benzanthracene [*Organic chemistry*]
**HMBCEE** ... Horace Mann Bond Center for Equal Education (EA)
**HMBDV**.... His [*or Her*] Majesty's Boom Defence Vessel
**H-MBP-H** ... Human-Mannose Binding Protein-H
**HMBS** ....... His [*or Her*] Majesty's British Ship
**HMC**.......... Halley Multicolor Camera [*Instrumentation*]
**HMC**.......... Hammerson Canada, Inc. [*Toronto Stock Exchange symbol*]
**HMC**.......... Hand-Mirror Cell [*Oncology*]
**HMC**.......... Head Masters' Conference [*British*]
**HMC**.......... Heroin, Morphine, and Cocaine [*Mixture*] [*Slang*]
**HMC**.......... His [*or Her*] Majesty's Council (ROG)
**HMC**.......... His [*or Her*] Majesty's Customs
**HmC** .......... Historian's Microfilm Company, Cazenovia, NY [*Library symbol*] [*Library of Congress*] (LCLS)
**HMC**.......... Historic Memorials Committee [*Australia*]
**HMC**.......... Historical Manuscripts Commission [*British*]
**HMC**.......... Holland Mills [*Quebec*] [*Seismograph station code, US Geological Survey*] [*Closed*] (SEIS)
**HMC**.......... Home Manufacturers Councils of NAHB [*National Association of Home Builders of the US*] (EA)
**HMC**.......... Honda Motor Company Ltd. [*NYSE symbol*] (SPSG)
**HMC**.......... Hospital Corpsman, Chief [*Navy rating*]
**HMC**.......... Houghton Mifflin Co., Boston, MA [*OCLC symbol*] (OCLC)
**HMC**.......... Housing Ministers Conference [*Australia*]
**HMC**.......... Howard Mold Count [*Food quality measure*]
**HMC**.......... Howitzer Motor Carriage
**HMC**.......... Hundred Million Club (EA)
**HMC**.......... Hungarian Management Center (ECON)
**HMC**.......... Hybrid Microcircuit (NASA)
**HMC**.......... (Hydroxymethyl)carboline [*Biochemistry*]
**HMC**.......... Hydroxymethylcystosine [*Organic chemistry*]
**HMC**.......... Hydroxypropyl(methyl)cellulose [*Synthetic food gum*] [*Organic chemistry*]
**HMC**.......... Hyoscine, Morphine, and Cactine [*Tablets*] [*Medicine*]
**HMC**.......... Hypergolic Maintenance and Checkout (NASA)
**HMCC**....... Hazardous Materials Control Committee [*General Motors Corp.*]
**HMCC**....... Houston Mission Control Center [*NASA*] (KSC)
**HMCC**....... Hypergolic Maintenance and Checkout Cell (NASA)
**HMC & E**.. His [*or Her*] Majesty's Customs and Excise [*British*] (DCTA)
**HMCF** ....... Hypergolic Maintenance and Checkout Facility [*NASA*] (NASA)
**H & McH**... Harris and McHenry's Maryland Court of Appeals Reports [*1785-99*] [*A publication*] (DLA)
**H & M Ch** ... Hemming and Miller's English Vice-Chancellors' Reports [*A publication*] (DLA)
**H & McHenry** ... Harris and McHenry's Maryland Reports [*A publication*] (DLA)
**HMCII** ...... Higher Military Command, Interior and Islands (MCD)
**HMCL**....... Hand-Mirror Cell Leukemia [*Oncology*]
**HMCM**...... Hospital Corpsman, Master Chief [*Navy rating*]
**HMCN** ...... His [*or Her*] Majesty's Canadian Navy
**HMCO** ...... Homestead Minerals Corporation [*NASDAQ symbol*] (NQ)
**HMCRI** ..... Hazardous Materials Control Research Institute (EA)
**HMCS** ....... His [*or Her*] Majesty's Canadian Ship
**HMCS** ....... His [*or Her*] Majesty's Civil Service
**HMCS** ....... His [*or Her*] Majesty's Colonial Steamer [*In use in 19th century*]
**HMCS** ....... Hoffman Modulation Contrast System
**HMCS** ....... Hospital Corpsman, Senior Chief [*Navy rating*]
**HMCV**....... Human Cytomegalovirus
**HMD** ......... Charlie Hammond's Flying Service, Inc. [*Houma, LA*] [*FAA designator*] (FAAC)
**HMD** ......... Hamada [*Japan*] [*Seismograph station code, US Geological Survey*] (SEIS)
**HMD** ......... Handbuch der Modernen Datenverarbeitung [*A publication*]
**HMD** ......... Heard Island and McDonald Islands [*ANSI three-letter standard code*] (CNC)
**HMD** ......... Helmet-Mounted Display
**HMD** ......... Heterodyne Matrix Detector
**HMD** ......... His [*or Her*] Majesty's Destroyer [*British military*] (DMA)
**HMD** ......... His [*or Her*] Majesty's Dockyard [*Navy*] [*British*]
**HMD** ......... His [*or Her*] Majesty's Drifter
**HMD** ......... Humid (MSA)
**HMD** ......... Hyaline Membrane Disease [*Later, RDS*] [*Medicine*]
**HMD** ......... Hydraulic Mean Depth
**HMD** ......... HydrazinomethylDOPA [*Biochemistry*]
**HMD** ......... Hydrostatic Motor-Driven
**HMDA** ...... Hexamethylenediamine [*Organic chemistry*]
**HMDA** ...... Home Mortgage Disclosure Act
**HMDAA**.... Hydroxymethyl Diacetone Acrylamide [*Organic chemistry*]
**HMDBA**.... Hollow Metal Door and Buck Association (EA)
**HMDDAH** ... Hamdard Medicus [*A publication*]
**HMDE**....... Hanging Mercury Drop Electrode [*Electrochemistry*]
**HMDF**....... Hollow Metal Door and Frame [*Technical drawings*]
**HMDF**....... Horizontal Side of Main Distribution Frame (TEL)
**HMDI**........ Hexamethylene Diisocyanate [*Organic chemistry*]
**HMDP**....... Hydroxymethylenediphosphonate [*Organic chemistry*]
**HMDS**....... Hexamethyldisiloxane [*Organic chemistry*]
**HMDS**....... Hospital Morbidity Data System
**HMDY** ...... Hemodynamics, Inc. [*Boca Raton, FL*] [*NASDAQ symbol*] (NQ)
**HMDZ**....... Hexamethyldisilazane [*Organic chemistry*]
**HME**.......... Hassi Messaoud [*Algeria*] [*Airport symbol*] (OAG)
**HME**.......... Health Media Education (EA)
**HME**.......... Heat, Massage, Exercise [*Medicine*]
**HME**.......... Historical Magazine of the Protestant Episcopal Church [*A publication*]
**HME**.......... Hull, Mechanical, Electrical [*Ship equipment*] [*Navy*]
**HMEA**....... Hatters Machinery and Equipment Association [*Defunct*] (EA)

**HMED**....... HiMEDICS, Inc. [*NASDAQ symbol*] (NQ)
**HMEED**.... Heavy Military Electronic Equipment Division [*General Electric Co.*] (AAG)
**HMEIA**..... Health Manpower Education Initiative Award
**HMENR**.... High Mountain Ecology Research Station (Finse, Norway) Reports [*A publication*]
**H Mex**........ Historia Mexicana [*A publication*]
**HMF**.......... Handbook of Military Forces (MCD)
**HMF**.......... Hastings Manufacturing Co. [*AMEX symbol*] (SPSG)
**HMF**.......... High Mach Flow
**HMF**.......... High Magnetic Field
**HMF**.......... His [*or Her*] Majesty's Forces
**HMF**.......... Horizontal Mating Facility [*NASA*] (KSC)
**HMF**.......... Hum Modulation Factor (DEN)
**HMF**.......... Hydroxymethylfuraldehyde [*Organic chemistry*]
**HMF**.......... Hypergol Maintenance Facility [*NASA*] (NASA)
**HMFF**........ Hoc Monumentum Fieri Fecit [*Caused This Monument to Be Made*] [*Latin*]
**HMFI**......... His [*or Her*] Majesty's Factory Inspectorate [*Department of Employment*] [*British*]
**HMFIHQ**... His [*or Her*] Majesty's Factory Inspectorate Headquarters [*Department of Employment*] [*British*]
**HMFR**........ Homefree Village Resorts, Inc. [*Denver, CO*] [*NASDAQ symbol*] (NQ)
**HMG**......... Hardware Message Generator [*Telecommunications*] (TEL)
**HMG**......... Harvard University, Gutman Library, Cambridge, MA [*OCLC symbol*] (OCLC)
**HMG**......... Heavy Machine Gun
**HMG**......... High Mobility Group [*of nonhistone proteins*] [*Biochemistry*]
**HMG**......... His [*or Her*] Majesty's Government
**HMG**......... HMG/Courtland Properties [*Formerly, Hospital Mortgage Group*] [*AMEX symbol*] (SPSG)
**HMG**......... Home-Made Gents [*Facetious interpretation of HMG, Her Majesty's Government*] (DSUE)
**HMG**......... Human Menopausal Gonadotrophin [*Endocrinology*]
**HMG**......... Hydroxymethylglutaryl [*Biochemistry*]
**HMGB**........ His [*or Her*] Majesty's Gunboat
**HMGF**........ High Modulus Glass Fiber
**HMGI**......... Hotel-Motel Greeters International (EA)
**HMGOG**... Handelingen der Maatschappij voor Geschiedenis en Oudheidkunde te Gent [*A publication*]
**HMH**......... Heintz, M. H., Chicago IL [*STAC*]
**HMH**......... His [*or Her*] Majesty's Household
**HMH**......... Home Hill [*Australia*] [*Airport symbol*]
**HMH**......... Marine Helicopter Squadron Heavy
**HMHB**...... Healthy Mothers, Healthy Babies (EA)
**HMHCY**... Hexamethyl Hexacyclen [*Organic chemistry*]
**HMHD**...... High Molecular Weight, High Density
**HMHF**....... Hydrophobic Microporous Hollow Fiber [*Membranes for chemical reactions*]
**HMHP**...... Hospital Management, Hospital Problems [*British*]
**HMHS**....... His [*or Her*] Majesty's Hospital Ship
**HMI**........... Handbook of Maintenance Instructions
**HMI**........... Hardware Monitor Interface
**HMI**........... Health-Mor, Incorporated [*AMEX symbol*] (SPSG)
**HMI**........... Hexamethyleneimine [*Trademark*] [*Celanese Corp.*]
**HMI**........... His [*or Her*] Majesty's Inspector
**HMI**........... Hoist Manufacturers Institute (EA)
**HMI**........... Horizontal Motion Index [*Printer technology*]
**HMI**........... Horticultural Marketing Inspectorate [*Ministry of Agriculture, Fisheries, and Food*] [*British*]
**HMI**........... House Magazine Institute [*Later, NY/IABC*]
**HMI**........... Human Machine Interface
**HMIC**........ Heinkel-Messerschmitt-Isetta Club (EA)
**HMIF**........ His [*or Her*] Majesty's Inspector of Factories (ROG)
**HMIMF**.... His [*or Her*] Majesty's Indian Military Forces
**HMIN**........ His [*or Her*] Majesty's Indian Navy
**HMIO**........ Haitian Migrant Interdiction Operation [*Haitian-US agreement, allowing US Coast Guard to board Haitian vessels on high seas*]
**HMIP**........ His [*or Her*] Majesty's Inspectorate of Pollution [*British*]
**HMIPI**....... His [*or Her*] Majesty's Industrial Pollution Inspectorate for Scotland (DCTA)
**HMIS**........ Hazardous Materials Identification System [*National Paint and Coating Association*]
**HMIS**........ Hazardous Materials Information System (MCD)
**HMIS**........ His [*or Her*] Majesty's Indian Ship [*British military*] (DMA)
**HMIS**........ His [*or Her*] Majesty's Inspector of Schools (ROG)
**HMIS**........ Hospital Management Information System
**HMJ**.......... Homer, IL [*Location identifier*] [*FAA*] (FAAL)
**HMK**......... Highmark Resources [*Vancouver Stock Exchange symbol*]
**HMK**......... Historiske Meddelelser om Staden Kobenhavn og dens Borgere [*A publication*]
**HML**.......... Hamilton [*Ontario*] [*Seismograph station code, US Geological Survey*] [*Closed*] (SEIS)
**HML**.......... Hammond Metallurgical Laboratory [*Yale*] (MCD)
**HML**.......... Harbor Motor Launch
**HML**.......... Hard Mobile Launcher [*Boeing Aerospace-Loral Defense Systems*]
**HML**.......... Hawaii Medical Library, Inc., Honolulu, HI [*OCLC symbol*] (OCLC)
**HML**.......... Heeresmunitionslager [*Army Ammunition Depot*] [*German military - World War II*]
**HML**.......... His [*or Her*] Majesty's Lieutenant
**HML**.......... Horace Mann League of the USA (EA)
**HML**.......... Houston Metals Corp. [*Vancouver Stock Exchange symbol*]
**HML**.......... Human Milk Lysozyme [*An enzyme*]
**HML**.......... Huntsman Marine Laboratory [*Canada*] (MSC)
**HML**.......... Marine Helicopter Squadron Light
**HMLC**....... High-Mobility Load Carrier [*British military*] (DMA)
**HMLR**....... His [*or Her*] Majesty's Land Registry
**HMLT**....... Hamlet
**HMM**........ Hamamatsu [*Japan*] [*Seismograph station code, US Geological Survey*] (SEIS)
**HMM**........ Hamilton, MT [*Location identifier*] [*FAA*] (FAAL)
**HMM**........ Hammond Manufacturing Co. Ltd. [*Toronto Stock Exchange symbol*]
**HMM**........ Hardware Multiply Module
**HMM**........ Heavy Meromyosin [*Biochemistry*]
**HMM**........ Hexamethylmelamine [*Altretamine*] [*Also, HEX, HXM*] [*Antineoplastic drug*]
**HMM**........ Hidden Markov Modeling [*Data processing*]
**HMM**........ Marine Helicopter Squadron Medium
**HMMA**..... Hydroxymethoxymandelic Acid [*Also, VMA*] [*Biochemistry*]
**HMMFC**... House Merchant Marine and Fisheries Committee
**H & M Mgmt**... Hotel and Motel Management [*A publication*]
**HMMHE**.. High-Mobility Materiel Handling Equipment [*Army*]
**HMML**...... His [*or Her*] Majesty's Motor Launch
**HMMMS**... His [*or Her*] Majesty's Motor Mine Sweeper
**HMMNL**... Handelingen en Mededeelingen. Maatschappij der Nederlandsche Letterkunde te Leiden [*A publication*]
**HMMS**...... HELLFIRE Modular Missile System
**HMMWV**... High-Mobility Multipurpose Wheeled Vehicle [*Nicknamed "hummer"*] [*Army*] (RDA)
**HMMWV-L**... High-Mobility Multipurpose Wheeled Vehicle - Lightweight
**HMN**......... Alamogordo, NM [*Location identifier*] [*FAA*] (FAAL)
**HMN**......... Heptamethylnonane [*Fuel*]
**HMN**......... Human
**HMNC**...... Harmonic (MSA)
**HMNZS**.... His [*or Her*] Majesty's New Zealand Ship
**HMO**......... H. Mason [*Oregon*] [*Seismograph station code, US Geological Survey*] (SEIS)
**HMO**......... Hardware Microcode Optimizer
**HMO**......... Health Maintenance Organization
**HMO**......... Heart Minute Output [*Cardiology*]
**HMO**......... Hermosillo [*Mexico*] [*Airport symbol*] (OAG)
**HMO**......... Honolulu Magnetic Observatory (CINC)
**HMO**......... Hueckel Molecular Orbital [*Atomic physics*]
**HMOA**...... HMO America, Inc. [*Chicago, IL*] [*NASDAQ symbol*] (NQ)
**HMOCS**.... His [*or Her*] Majesty's Overseas Civil Service
**HMOH**...... HealthAmerica Corp. [*NASDAQ symbol*] (NQ)
**HMOS**....... Health Maintenance Organization Service [*Public Health Service*]
**HMOS**....... High-Speed Metal-Oxide Semiconductor [*ROM*]
**HMOW**...... His [*or Her*] Majesty's Office of Works (ROG)
**HMP**.......... Handmade Paper
**HMP**.......... Harper's Magazine Press
**HMP**.......... Helmet-Mounted Pick-Offs (MCD)
**HMP**.......... Hexamethylphosphoramide [*or Hexamethylphosphoric Triamide*] [*Also, HEMPA, HMPA, HMPT, HPT*] [*Organic chemistry*]
**HMP**.......... Hexasodium Metaphosphate [*Inorganic chemistry*]
**HMP**.......... Hexose Monophosphate [*Biochemistry*]
**HMP**.......... High Melting Point
**HMP**.......... High-Methoxy Pectin [*Food technology*]
**HMP**.......... Hoc Monumentum Posuit [*He, or She, Erected This Monument*] [*Latin*]
**HMP**.......... Homenaje a Menendez Pidal [*A publication*]
**HMP**.......... Honda-Mrkos-Pajdusakova [*Comet*]
**HMP**.......... Hot Moist Packs [*Medicine*]
**HMP**.......... Humidity Monitoring Panel
**HMP**.......... Hydraulic Maintenance Panel (AAG)
**HMP**.......... Hydroxymethyl Hydroperoxide [*Organic chemistry*]
**HMP**.......... Hydroxymethyl(methyl)propanediol [*Organic chemistry*]
**HMP**.......... Hydrozene Monopropellant (MCD)
**HMPA**....... Hexamethylphosphoramide [*or Hexamethylphosphoric Triamide*] [*Also, HEMPA, HMP, HMPT, HPT*] [*Organic chemistry*]
**HMPCD9**.. Handchirurgie, Mikrochirurgie, Plastische Chirurgie [*A publication*]
**HMPEC**.... Historical Magazine of the Protestant Episcopal Church [*A publication*]
**HMPGTS**... His [*or Her*] Majesty's Procurator General and Treasury Solicitor
**HMPI**........ His [*or Her*] Majesty's Pollution Inspectorate [*British*] (DCTA)
**HMPMA**... Historical Motion Picture Milestones Association
**HMPP**....... Hexose Monophosphate Pathway [*Biochemistry*]
**HMPS**....... Hexose Monophosphate Shunt [*Biochemistry*]
**HMPSA**.... Hot Melt Pressure Sensitive Adhesive
**HMPT**....... Hexamethylphosphoric Triamide [*Also, HEMPA, HMP, HMPA, HPT*] [*Organic chemistry*]
**HMQ**......... Homer, LA [*Location identifier*] [*FAA*] (FAAL)

**HMQC**...... Heteronuclear Multiple-Quantum Coherence [*Physics*]
**HMQS**....... His [*or Her*] Majesty's Queensland Ship [*Australia*]
**HMR**......... Hamilton Ranch [*California*] [*Seismograph station code, US Geological Survey*] (SEIS)
**HMR**......... Hammer (MSA)
**HMR**......... Headquarters Modification Request [*Military*] (CAAL)
**HMR**......... Health Management Resources [*Diet program*]
**HMR**......... Histocytic Medullary Reticulosis [*Oncology*]
**HMR**......... HMR World Enterprise [*Vancouver Stock Exchange symbol*]
**HMR**......... Hoboken Manufacturers [*AAR code*]
**HMR**......... Hotel, Motel, Resort Database [*American Database Corp.*] [*Santa Barbara, CA*] [*Information service or system*] (IID)
**HMR**......... Human Milk Ribonuclease [*An enzyme*]
**hMR**......... Human Mineralocorticoid Receptor [*Endocrinology*]
**HMR**......... Hungry Mind Review [*A publication*]
**HMR**......... Hybrid Modular Redundancy
**HMRA**....... Hadassah Medical Relief Association (EA)
**HMRB**....... Hazardous Materials Regulation Board
**HMRI**........ Huntington Medical Research Institutes [*Huntington Memorial Hospital*] [*Research center*] (RCD)
**HMRL**....... His [*or Her*] Majesty's Royal Licence (ROG)
**HMRN**...... Hull Moulding Release Note
**H-mRNA**... Ribonucleic Acid, H-Chain Messenger [*Biochemistry, genetics*]
**HMRP**....... Hurricane Microseismic Research Problem [*Aerology*]
**HMRR**....... His [*or Her*] Majesty's Reserve Regiment [*British military*] (DMA)
**HMS**.......... Hammer Makers' Society [*A union*] [*British*]
**HMS**.......... Hanford Meteorology Surveys [*Nuclear energy*] (NRCH)
**HMS**.......... Hardened Memory System
**HMS**.......... Harmonic Multiplier Source
**HMS**.......... Harvard University Medical School, Countway Library of Medicine, Boston, MA [*OCLC symbol*] (OCLC)
**HMS**.......... Hazardous Materials Systems [*A publication*] (EAAP)
**HMS**.......... Hazards Monitoring System [*NASA*] (KSC)
**H & MS**..... Headquarters and Maintenance Squadron [*Marine Corps*]
**HMS**.......... Health Mobilization Series
**HMS**.......... Heavy Materiel Supply Units [*Military*]
**HMS**.......... Helmet-Mounted Sight [*Aviation*]
**HMS**.......... Hierarchical Memory Storage [*Data processing*]
**HMS**.......... His [*or Her*] Majesty's Service
**HMS**.......... His [*or Her*] Majesty's Ship
**HMS**.......... His [*or Her*] Majesty's Steamer
**HMS**.......... Historical Metallurgy Society [*London, England*] (EAIO)
**HMS**.......... History Memory System (MCD)
**HMS**.......... Hours, Minutes, Seconds
**HMSA**....... Hardware Manufacturers Statistical Association [*Later, BHMA*]
**HMSA**....... Hawk Mountain Sanctuary Association (EA)
**HMSA**....... Health Manpower Shortage Area
**HMSA**....... Historic Motor Sports Association (EA)
**HMSA**....... Hydroxymethanesulfonate [*Organic chemistry*]
**HMSAS**..... His [*or Her*] Majesty's South African Ship (DAS)
**HMSAS**..... His [*or Her*] Majesty's South Australian Ship
**HMSB**....... [*The*] Home Savings Bank [*NASDAQ symbol*] (NQ)
**HMS(BOE)**... Hazardous Materials Systems (Bureau of Explosives) (EA)
**HMSCDO**... Human Movement Science [*A publication*]
**HMSD**....... Homestead Holding Corp. [*NASDAQ symbol*] (NQ)
**HMSEDU**... History of Medicine Series [*A publication*]
**HM & SG**.. Hirshhorn Museum and Sculpture Garden [*Smithsonian Institution*]
**HMSL**....... Hemerdon Mining & Smelting Limited [*NASDAQ symbol*] (NQ)
**HMSM**...... Heavy Mortar, Smart Munition
**HMS/M**.... His [*or Her*] Majesty's Submarine
**HMSO**....... His [*or Her*] Majesty's Stationery Office
**HMSO**....... Honolulu Magnetic and Seismological Observatory
**HMSO Daily Lists**... Her Majesty's Stationery Office Daily Lists [*A publication*]
**HMSRR**.... Harpoon Missile Select Relay Rack [*Missiles*] (MCD)
**HMSS**....... Helmet-Mounted Sight Set
**HMSS**....... HMSS, Inc. [*NASDAQ symbol*] (NQ)
**HMSS**....... Hospital Management Systems Society [*Later, HIMSS*] (EA)
**HMT**......... Handwoerterbuch der Musikalischen Terminologie [*A publication*]
**HmT**......... Helminthosporium maydis race T [*A toxin-producing fungus*]
**HMT**......... Hemet, CA [*Location identifier*] [*FAA*] (FAAL)
**HMT**......... Hexamethoxytriphenylene [*Organic chemistry*]
**HMT**......... Hexamethylenetetramine [*Also, HMTA*] [*Organic chemistry*]
**HMT**......... HIMONT, Inc. [*NYSE symbol*] (SPSG)
**HMT**......... His [*or Her*] Majesty's Transport
**HMT**......... His [*or Her*] Majesty's Trawler
**HMT**......... His [*or Her*] Majesty's Troopship [*British military*] (DMA)
**HMT**......... His [*or Her*] Majesty's Tug [*British military*] (DMA)
**HMT**......... Histamine Methyltransferase [*An enzyme*]
**HMT**......... Human Metallothioneine [*Biochemistry*]
**HMT**......... Hydrazine Monopropellant Thruster
**HMTA**....... Hazardous Materials Transportation Act [*1975*]
**HMTA**....... Hexamethylenetetramine [*Also, HMT*] [*Organic chemistry*]
**HMTA**....... Hexamethylenetriamine [*Organic chemistry*]
**HMTC**....... Hazardous Materials Technical Center [*Rockville, MD*] [*DoD*] (GRD)
**HMTE**....... HealthMate, Inc. [*Northbrook, IL*] [*NASDAQ symbol*] (NQ)
**HMTGA4**... Helminthologia [*Bratislava*] [*A publication*]
**HMTS**....... His [*or Her*] Majesty's Telegraph Ship
**HMTSF**..... Hexamethylenetetraselenafulvalenium [*Organic chemistry*]
**HMTT**....... Hexamethyltrithiane [*Organic chemistry*]
**HMTT**....... High-Mobility Tactical Trucks (MCD)
**HMU**......... Hammond, LA [*Location identifier*] [*FAA*] (FAAL)
**HMU**......... Hardware Mockup (NASA)
**HMU**......... Hydraulic Mock-Up
**HMU**......... Hydromechanical Unit
**HMU**......... Hydroxymethyluracil [*Organic chemistry*]
**HMV**......... High Magnification Viewer
**HMV**......... His Master's Voice [*Phonograph records*]
**HMV**......... Holston Mountain, TN [*Location identifier*] [*FAA*] (FAAL)
**HMV**......... Hydrodynamically Modulated Voltammetry [*Analytical chemistry*]
**HMV**......... Hydrogen Manual Valve (MCD)
**H & M (VA)**... Hening and Munford's Reports [*11-14 Virginia*] [*A publication*] (DLA)
**HMW**........ High Molecular Weight [*Also, HM*] [*Organic chemistry*]
**HMWC**...... Health of Munition Workers Committee [*British*] [*World War I*]
**HMWC**...... High-Mobility Weapons Carrier [*Army*]
**HMWC/CSV**... High-Mobility Weapons Carrier/Combat Support Vehicle [*Army*] (MCD)
**HMW Jb**... HMW [*Heilmittelwerke*] Jahrbuch [*A publication*]
**HMWKa**... High Molecular Weight Kallikrein [*Biochemistry*]
**HMWP**...... High-Molecular-Weight Protein [*or Polypeptide*] [*Biochemistry*]
**HMX**......... Denver, CO [*Location identifier*] [*FAA*] (FAAL)
**HMX**......... Hartmarx Corp. [*NYSE symbol*] (SPSG)
**HMX**......... Heat, Massage, Exercise [*Medicine*]
**HMX**......... High-Melting Explosive [*Proprietary name for cyclotetramethylene tetramintriamine*]
**HMX**......... Marine Helicopter Experimental Squadron
**HMX-1**...... Marine Helicopter Experimental Squadron One [*Organized in 1947 for the development and study of helicopter tactics*]
**HMY**......... Heilig-Meyers Co. [*NYSE symbol*] (SPSG)
**HMY**......... High Modulus Yarn
**HMY**......... His [*or Her*] Majesty's Yacht [*Navy*] [*British*]
**HMY**......... Lexington, OK [*Location identifier*] [*FAA*] (FAAL)
**HMYB**....... Hinrichsen's Musical Year Book [*A publication*]
**HMZ**......... Helvetische Muenzen-Zeitung [*A publication*]
**HMZA**....... Hamburg in Zahlen [*A publication*]
**HN**............ Hadassah Newsletter [*New York*] [*A publication*]
**HN**............ Hamann Newsletter [*A publication*]
**Hn**............ Haven [*Maps and charts*]
**H & N**........ Head and Neck [*Medicine*]
**HN**............ Head Nurse
**HN**............ Hear Now [*An association*] (EA)
**HN**............ Hemagglutinin-Neuraminidase [*An enzyme*]
**HN**............ Hemingway Notes [*A publication*]
**hn**............ Henna [*Philately*]
**Hn**............ Henricus de Baila [*Flourished, 1169-70*] [*Authority cited in pre-1607 legal work*] (DSA)
**H & N**........ Here and Now [*A publication*]
**HN**............ Here and Now [*A publication*]
**HN**............ Heroes of the Nations [*A publication*]
**HN**............ Herpes Network (EA)
**hn**............ Heterogeneous Nuclear [*Biochemistry*]
**HN**............ Hexagonal Nut
**HN**............ High Foliage Nester [*Ecology*]
**HN**............ High Nitrogen [*Clinical chemistry*]
**HN**............ High Nutrition
**HN**............ Hindustan-Aeronautics Ltd. [*India*] [*ICAO aircraft manufacturer identifier*] (ICAO)
**HN**............ Hoc Nocte [*Tonight*] [*Pharmacy*]
**Hn**............ Hochschulnachrichten [*A publication*]
**H & N**........ Holmes and Narver, Inc. (NRCH)
**HN**............ Home Nursing
**HN**............ Honduras [*ANSI two-letter standard code*] (CNC)
**HN**............ Horn
**HN**............ Hospitalman [*Nonrated enlisted man*] [*Navy*]
**HN**............ Host Nation (AABC)
**HN**............ Host to Network [*Data processing*]
**HN**............ House Nigger [*Derogatory nickname for an obsequious black person*]
**H & N**........ Hum and Noise (DEN)
**HN**............ Human Nutrition Research Division [*of ARS, Department of Agriculture*]
**H & N**........ Hurlstone and Norman's English Exchequer Reports [*156, 158 English Reprint*] [*A publication*] (DLA)
**HN**............ [*The*] Hutchinson & Northern Railway Co. [*AAR code*]
**H of N**........ Hydrographer of the Navy [*British*]
**HN**............ Naturalis Historia [*of Pliny the Elder*] [*Classical studies*] (OCD)
**HN**............ Nitrogen Mustard [*Also, M, MBA, NM*] [*Antineoplastic drug, war-gas base*] [*Army symbol used with numerals, as HN1*]
**HN**............ NLM [*Nederlandse Luchtvaart Maatschappij*] City Hopper [*Netherlands*] [*ICAO designator*] (FAAC)

**HN** ........ Station Open from Sunset to Sunrise [*ITU designation*] (FAAC)
**HNA** ........ Chicago, IL [*Location identifier*] [*FAA*] (FAAL)
**HNA** ........ Hanamaki [*Japan*] [*Airport symbol*] [*Obsolete*] (OAG)
**HNA** ........ Harrison Narcotic Act
**HNA** ........ Henson Aviation, Inc. [*Hagerstown, MD*] [*FAA designator*] (FAAC)
**HNA** ........ Heparin Neutralizing Activity [*Medicine*]
**HNA** ........ Hierarchical Network Architecture
**HNA** ........ High Nickel Alloy
**HNA** ........ Hitachi Network Architecture
**HNA** ........ Hockey North America (EA)
**HNAB** ........ Hexanitroazobenzene [*Organic chemistry*]
**HNADC** ........ Honorary Naval Aide-de-Camp [*British*]
**HNAND8** .. Human Nutrition. Applied Nutrition [*A publication*]
**HNARMENTD** ... Hereinafter Mentioned [*Legal*] [*British*] (ROG)
**HNAT** ........ Hartford National Corp. [*NASDAQ symbol*] (NQ)
**HNB** ........ Hrvatska Narodna Banka [*Croatian National Bank*]
**HNB** ........ Huntingburg, IN [*Location identifier*] [*FAA*] (FAAL)
**HNB** ........ Hydroxynitrobenzyl [*Organic chemistry*]
**HNB** ........ New Britain General Hospital, Health Sciences Library, New Britain, CT [*OCLC symbol*] (OCLC)
**HNBA** ........ Hispanic National Bar Association (EA)
**HNBC** ........ Harleysville National Corporation [*Harleysville, PA*] [*NASDAQ symbol*] (NQ)
**HNBEFMENTD** ... Hereinbefore Mentioned [*Legal*] [*British*] (ROG)
**HNC** ........ Center for Disease Control, Atlanta, GA [*OCLC symbol*] (OCLC)
**HNC** ........ High National Council
**HNC** ........ Higher National Certificate [*British*]
**HNC** ........ Human Nutrition Center [*Oklahoma State University*] [*Research center*] (RCD)
**HNC** ........ Hypothalamo-Neurohypophyseal Complex [*Endocrinology*]
**HNCNDI** ... Human Nutrition. Clinical Nutrition [*A publication*]
**HNCO** ........ Henley Manufacturing Corp. [*NASDAQ symbol*] (NQ)
**HNCP** ........ Home National Corporation [*Milford, MA*] [*NASDAQ symbol*] (NQ)
**HND** ........ Handwierk [*A publication*]
**HND** ........ Higher National Diploma [*British*]
**HND** ........ Hinderliter Industries, Inc. [*AMEX symbol*] (SPSG)
**HND** ........ Honduras [*ANSI three-letter standard code*] (CNC)
**HND** ........ Hundred (FAAC)
**HND** ........ Huntsville Nuclear Division [*Army Corps of Engineers*] (RDA)
**HND** ........ State Historical Society of North Dakota, Bismarck, ND [*OCLC symbol*] (OCLC)
**HND** ........ Tokyo [*Japan*] Haneda Airport [*Airport symbol*] (OAG)
**HNDBK** ........ Handbook
**HNDI** ........ Hinderliter Industries, Inc. [*NASDAQ symbol*] (NQ)
**HNDKB** ........ Hyogo Noka Daigaku Kiyo [*A publication*]
**HNDLER** .. Handler (NASA)
**HNDP** ........ Handicap
**HNDRL** ........ Hand Rail
**HNDST** ........ Handset
**HNDT** ........ Holographic Nondestructive Testing
**HNDWL** ........ Handwheel
**HNE** ........ Harriman & Northeastern R. R. [*AAR code*]
**HNE** ........ HN Engineering, Inc. [*Burnaby, BC*] [*Telecommunications*] (TSSD)
**HNE** ........ Human Neutrophil Elastase [*An enzyme*]
**HNE** ........ Hydroxynonenal [*Biochemistry*]
**HNE** ........ National Institute of Environmental Health Sciences, Research Triangle Park, NC [*OCLC symbol*] (OCLC)
**HNE** ........ Tahneta Pass Lodge, AK [*Location identifier*] [*FAA*] (FAAL)
**HNEI** ........ Hawaii Natural Energy Institute [*University of Hawaii at Manoa*] [*Research center*] (RCD)
**HNET** ........ Houston Network Controller [*NASA*] (KSC)
**HNews** ........ Hemingway Newsletter [*A publication*]
**HNF** ........ Hepatocyte Nuclear Factor [*Biochemistry*]
**HNF1** ........ Hepatocyte Nuclear Factor 1 [*Genetics*]
**HNFBR** ........ Horn Fiber
**HNG** ........ Hanging (MSA)
**HNG** ........ Hienghene [*New Caledonia*] [*Airport symbol*] [*Obsolete*] (OAG)
**HNG** ........ Hilfsfonds fuer die Opfer der Nuernberger Gesetze [*A publication*] (BJA)
**HNG** ........ Hinge (MSA)
**HNG** ........ Hongo [*Japan*] [*Seismograph station code, US Geological Survey*] [*Closed*] (SEIS)
**HNGI** ........ Hospital Newspapers Group, Inc. [*NASDAQ symbol*] (NQ)
**HNGL** ........ Helium Neon Gas LASER
**HNGR** ........ Hangar (KSC)
**HNH** ........ Handy & Harman [*NYSE symbol*] (SPSG)
**HNH** ........ Hanover [*New Hampshire*] [*Seismograph station code, US Geological Survey*] (SEIS)
**H & NH** ........ Hartford & New Haven Railroad
**HNH** ........ Historical New Hampshire [*A publication*]
**HNH** ........ Hoonah [*Alaska*] [*Airport symbol*] (OAG)
**HNHIC** ........ Hepatic Nonheme Iron Content [*Physiology*]
**HNI** ........ Health News Institute [*Defunct*]
**HNI** ........ Holmes & Narver, Incorporated (MCD)
**HNI** ........ National Institutes of Health, Bethesda, MD [*OCLC symbol*] (OCLC)
**HNIC** ........ Head Nigger in Charge [*Slang*]
**HNIC** ........ Hockey Night in Canada [*Television program*]
**HNIL** ........ High-Noise-Immunity Logic
**HNIS** ........ Human Nutrition Information Service [*Hyattsville, MD*] [*Department of Agriculture*]
**HNK** ........ Hancock, NY [*Location identifier*] [*FAA*] (FAAL)
**HNK** ........ Hinchinbrook Island [*Australia*] [*Airport symbol*]
**HNK** ........ Ho Neos Koubaras [*A publication*]
**HNL** ........ Hadassah Newsletter [*New York*] [*A publication*]
**HNL** ........ Helium Neon LASER
**HNL** ........ Holden National Leasing Ltd. [*Australia*]
**HNL** ........ Holifield National Laboratory [*Later, Oak Ridge National Laboratory*]
**HNL** ........ Honolulu [*Hawaii*] [*Airport symbol*] (OAG)
**HNL** ........ Honolulu [*Hawaii*] [*Seismograph station code, US Geological Survey*] [*Closed*] (SEIS)
**HNL** ........ Hourly Noise Level
**HNL** ........ HUD [*Department of Housing and Urban Development*] Newsletter [*A publication*]
**HNLM** ........ High Noise-Level Margin
**HNM** ........ Hana [*Hawaii*] [*Airport symbol*] (OAG)
**HNM** ........ Hertzberg-New Method [*Standard periodical binding*]
**HNM** ........ Hexanitromannite [*Organic chemistry*]
**HNML** ........ Hindu Meal [*Airline notation*]
**HNMR** ........ High-Resolution Nuclear Magnetic Resonance
**HNMS** ........ Her Netherlands Majesty's Ship
**HNMS** ........ High NATO Military Structure (NATG)
**HNN** ........ Henderson, WV [*Location identifier*] [*FAA*] (FAAL)
**HNO** ........ Henderson, TX [*Location identifier*] [*FAA*] (FAAL)
**HNO** ........ HNO. Hals-, Nasen-, Ohren-Heilkunde [*A publication*]
**HNO** ........ Honcho Gold Mines, Inc. [*Vancouver Stock Exchange symbol*]
**HNO** ........ Hrvatski Narodni Odbor [*Croatian National Resistance*] [*Yugoslavia*] (PD)
**HNorv** ........ Humaniora Norvegica [*A publication*]
**HNO Weg Fac** ... HNO: Wegweiser fuer die Fachaerztliche Praxis [*Later, HNO. Hals-, Nasen-, Ohren-Heilkunde*] [*A publication*]
**HNP** ........ Haddam Neck Plant [*Nuclear energy*] (NRCH)
**HNP** ........ Hartsville Nuclear Plant (NRCH)
**HNP** ........ Harvard Negotiation Project
**HNP** ........ Herniated Nucleus Pulposus [*Medicine*]
**HNP** ........ Herstigte Nasionale Party [*Reconstituted National Party*] [*South Africa*] [*Political party*] (PPW)
**HNP** ........ High Needle Position [*on dial*]
**HNP** ........ Minneapolis, MN [*Location identifier*] [*FAA*] (FAAL)
**HNP** ........ Parklawn Health Library, Rockville, MD [*OCLC symbol*] (OCLC)
**HNPA** ........ Home Numbering Plan Area [*AT & T*]
**HNPF** ........ Hallam Nuclear Power Facility [*AEC*] [*Decommissioned*]
**HNQ** ........ Hydroxynaphthoquinone [*Organic chemistry*]
**HNR** ........ Harlan, IA [*Location identifier*] [*FAA*] (FAAL)
**HNR** ........ Heaston Resources Ltd. [*Vancouver Stock Exchange symbol*]
**HNR** ........ Hikone Ronso [*A publication*]
**HNR** ........ Honiara [*Solomon Islands*] [*Seismograph station code, US Geological Survey*] (SEIS)
**hnr** ........ Honoree [*MARC relator code*] [*Library of Congress*] (LCCP)
**HNRC** ........ USDA [*United States Department of Agriculture*] Human Nutrition Research Center on Aging at Tufts [*Tufts University*] [*Research center*] (RCD)
**hnRNA** ........ Ribonucleic Acid, Heterogeneous Nuclear [*Biochemistry, genetics*]
**hnRNP** ........ Ribonucleoprotein, Heterogeneous [*Biochemistry*]
**HNRS** ........ Honors (ADA)
**HNRY** ........ Henry Energy Corp. [*NASDAQ symbol*] (NQ)
**HNS** ........ Haines [*Alaska*] [*Airport symbol*] (OAG)
**HNS** ........ Hamilton Normal School
**HNS** ........ Head, Neck, and Shaft [*of a bone*] [*Osteology*]
**HNS** ........ Head and Neck Surgery [*Medical specialty*] (DHSM)
**HNS** ........ Hexanitrostilbene [*High explosive*]
**HNS** ........ Holy Name Society (EA)
**HNS** ........ Home Nursing Service [*Australia*]
**HNS** ........ Home Nursing Supervisor [*Red Cross*]
**HNS** ........ Host Nation Support [*Military*]
**HNSD** ........ Hansard (DCTA)
**HNSF** ........ Hungarian National Sports Federation (EA)
**HNSHA** ........ Hereditary Nonspherocytic Hemolytic Anemia [*Medicine*]
**HNSI** ........ Home Nutritional Services, Inc. [*NASDAQ symbol*] (NQ)
**HNSWA** ........ Health in New South Wales [*A publication*]
**HNSX** ........ Honeywell-NEC Supercomputers, Inc.
**HNT** ........ Handbuch zum Neuen Testament [*A publication*] (BJA)
**HNT** ........ National Center for Toxicological Research, Jefferson, AR [*OCLC symbol*] (OCLC)
**HNTG** ........ Hunting (MSA)
**HNTR** ........ Hunter International Trade Corp. [*Omaha, NE*] [*NASDAQ symbol*] (NQ)
**HNTSup** ........ Handbuch zum Neuen Testament. Supplement [*A publication*]
**HNV** ........ Has Not Voided [*Urology*]
**HNVS** ........ Hughes Night Vision System [*Aviation*]
**HNW** ........ Head, Nut, and Washer [*Construction*]

**HNW**......... Heeresnachrichtenwesen [*Army Communications System*] [*German military - World War II*]
**HNW**......... Hein-Werner Corp. [*AMEX symbol*] (SPSG)
**HNW**......... Placerville, CA [*Location identifier*] [*FAA*] (FAAL)
**HNY**......... Hamilton [*New York*] [*Seismograph station code, US Geological Survey*] (SEIS)
**HNY**......... Happy New Year
**HNY**......... Hennessy Resource Corp. [*Vancouver Stock Exchange symbol*]
**HNYCMB**... Honeycomb
**HNZ**......... Havelock North [*New Zealand*] [*Seismograph station code, US Geological Survey*] [*Closed*] (SEIS)
**HNZ**......... Heinz [*H. J.*] Co. [*NYSE symbol*] (SPSG)
**HO**............ Hale Observatories [*Formerly, Mount Palomar and Mount Wilson Observatories*]
**H-O**........... Half of 'O' Gauge [*Model railroading*]
**HO**............ Hand Orthosis [*Medicine*]
**HO**............ Hand Over (MCD)
**HO**............ Handbuch der Orientalistik [*A publication*]
**H/O**.......... Hard Over (KSC)
**HO**............ Harmonic Oscillator
**HO**............ Head Office
**HO**............ Heel Off Ground [*Medicine*]
**HO**............ Heterotopic Ossification [*Osteology*]
**HO**............ High Oblique [*Aerospace*]
**HO**............ High Output [*Automotive engineering*]
**HO**............ Hip Orthosis [*Medicine*]
**H/O**.......... History Of [*Medicine*]
**HO**............ History Office (MCD)
**Ho**............ Hochland [*A publication*]
**HO**............ Hoist
**HO**............ Hold [*Shipping*] (DS)
**HO**............ Holding Out [*Cashier fraud*]
**HO**............ Holdover [*Theater*]
**Ho**............ Holmium [*Chemical element*]
**HO**............ Holy Day of Obligation
**HO**............ Holy Orders (ROG)
**HO**............ Home Office [*British*]
**HO**............ Home Only [*British military*] (DMA)
**HO**............ Homeowners' [*Insurance*]
**Ho**............ Homobonus de Cremona [*Deceased, 1272*] [*Authority cited in pre-1607 legal work*] (DSA)
**ho**............. Honduras [*MARC country of publication code*] [*Library of Congress*] (LCCP)
**Ho**............ Hosea [*Old Testament book*] (BJA)
**Ho**............ Hostiensis [*Deceased, 1271*] [*Authority cited in pre-1607 legal work*] (DSA)
**HO**............ Hostilities Only [*Applied to men who joined for duration of war only*] [*Navy*] [*British*] [*World War II*]
**HO**............ Hotel (ROG)
**HO**............ Hours of Operation
**HO**............ House
**HO**............ House Officer
**HO**............ Houston Oil Trust UBI [*AMEX symbol*] (SPSG)
**HO**............ Human Organization [*A publication*]
**HO**............ Hydraulic Operator (NRCH)
**HO**............ Hydrogen-Oxygen [*NASA*] (NASA)
**HO**............ Hydrographic Office [*Terminated, 1963; later, NOO*] [*Navy*]
**ho**............. Hydroxy [*As substituent on nucleoside*] [*Also, oh*] [*Biochemistry*]
**HO**............ Hyperbaric Oxygen [*Medicine*]
**HO**............ Observation Helicopter
**HO**............ Service Available to Meet Operational Requirements [*Aviation code*] (FAAC)
**3HO**.......... Healthy-Happy-Holy Organization
**HOA**......... Hands Off - Automatic (AAG)
**HOA**......... Heavy Observation Aircraft
**HOA**......... Hechalutz Organization of America [*Defunct*] (EA)
**HOA**......... Home Owner Association
**HOA**......... Homeowners Assistance Fund, Defense [*DoD*]
**HOA**......... (Hydroxyethyl)oxamic Acid [*Organic chemistry*]
**HOACGA**... Heart of America Carnival Glass Association (EA)
**HOAGDS**... Annual Research Reviews. Hormones and Aggression [*A publication*]
**HOAI**........ Human Outreach and Advancement Institute
**HOAN**....... Hoan Products Ltd. [*NASDAQ symbol*] (NQ)
**HOAP**........ Home Ownership Assistance Program [*Farmers Home Administration*]
**HOAP**........ Housing Opportunity Assistance Program [*Federal Home Loan Bank Board*]
**HOAP-BLEO**... Hydroxydaunomycin [*Adriamycin*], Oncovin [*Vincristine*], ara-C [*Cytarabine*], Prednisone, Bleomycin [*Antineoplastic drug regimen*]
**Hoard's D**.. Hoard's Dairyman [*A publication*]
**Hoards Dairym**... Hoard's Dairyman [*A publication*]
**HoaRhLG**... Horse Anti-Rhesus Lymphocyte Globulin [*Immunology*]
**HOASAR**.. Helvetica Odontologica Acta. Supplementum [*A publication*]
**HOATS**..... Human Ovarian Antitumor Serum [*Antineoplastic compound*]
**HoaTTG**.... Horse Anti-Tetanus Toxoid Globulin [*Immunology*]
**HOB**......... Half-Octave Bandwidth
**HOB**......... Head of Bed [*Medicine*]
**HOB**......... Height [*Depth*] of Burst
**Hob**........... Hobart [*Tasmania, Australia*]
**Hob**........... Hobart's English King's Bench Reports [*80 English Reprint*] [*A publication*] (DLA)
**Hob**........... Hobbies [*A publication*]
**HOB**......... Hobbs [*New Mexico*] [*Airport symbol*] (OAG)
**HOB**......... Hobbs Public Library, Hobbs, NM [*OCLC symbol*] (OCLC)
**HOB**......... Homing on Offset Beacon
**Hobart**....... Hobart's English King's Bench Reports [*80 English Reprint*] [*A publication*] (DLA)
**Hobart (Eng)**... Hobart's English King's Bench Reports [*80 English Reprint*] [*A publication*] (DLA)
**Hobby Electron**... Hobby Electronics [*A publication*]
**HOBC**........ Howard BanCorp [*NASDAQ symbol*] (NQ)
**HOBE**........ Horseshoe Bend National Military Park
**HOBGI**...... Honorable Order of the Blue Goose, International [*West Bend, WI*] (EA)
**HOBIS**...... Hotel Billing Information System [*Telecommunications*] (TEL)
**HOBITS**.... Haifa On-line Bibliographic Text System [*University of Haifa Library*] [*Information service or system*] (IID)
**HOBN**....... Home Office Business Network [*Information service or system*] (EISS)
**HOBO**....... Homing Optical Bomb (MCD)
**Hobonus**..... Homobonus de Cremona [*Deceased, 1272*] [*Authority cited in pre-1607 legal work*] (DSA)
**HOBOS**..... Homing Bomb System [*Air Force*]
**HOBP**........ Hydroxy(octylidene)bis(phosphonic Acid) [*Organic chemistry*]
**Hob R**........ Hobart's English Common Pleas Reports [*80 English Reprint*] [*1613-25*] [*A publication*] (DLA)
**Hob R**........ Hobart's English King's Bench Reports [*80 English Reprint*] [*A publication*] (DLA)
**HOBS**........ High-Orbital Bombardment System (KSC)
**HOBS**........ Home and Office Banking Service [*Bank of Scotland*] (ECON)
**HOBS**........ Homing Bomb System [*Air Force*]
**HOBT**........ Hydroxybenzotriazole
**HOBY**........ Hugh O'Brian Youth Foundation (EA)
**HOBYAA**... Hugh O'Brian Youth Foundation Alumni Association (EA)
**HOC**......... Hands-On Component
**HOC**......... Heat of Combustion
**HOC**......... Heavy Oil Cracking [*Process*] [*Petroleum industry*]
**HOC**......... Height Overlap Coverage [*RADAR*]
**HOC**......... High Output Current
**HOC**......... Hillman Owners Club [*Lancing, Sussex, England*] (EAIO)
**HOC**......... Hillsboro, OH [*Location identifier*] [*FAA*] (FAAL)
**HOC**......... History of Coverage (MCD)
**HOC**......... Holly Corporation [*AMEX symbol*] (SPSG)
**HOC**......... House of Commons [*British*]
**HOC**......... Housing Officers Conference [*Australia*]
**HoC**.......... Hoven & Company, Bakersfield, CA [*Library symbol*] [*Library of Congress*] (LCLS)
**HOC**......... Human Ovarian Cancer [*Cytology*]
**HOC**......... Hurricane Operations Center (AFM)
**HOC**......... Hydrofoil Ocean Combatant
**HOC**......... Hydrophobic Organic Chemical [*Physical chemistry*]
**HOC**......... Hydroxycorticosteroid [*Endocrinology*]
**HOCA**....... Hurst/Olds Club of America (EA)
**HOCCU**..... Heavy Oil Catalytic Cracking Unit [*Petroleum refining*]
**Hochfrequenztech Elektroakust**... Hochfrequenztechnik und Elektroakustik [*East Germany*] [*A publication*]
**Hochl**......... Hochland [*A publication*]
**Hochschulb Math**... Hochschulbuecher fuer Mathematik [*A publication*]
**Hochschulb Phys**... Hochschulbuecher fuer Physik [*A publication*]
**Hochschulbuecher fuer Phys**... Hochschulbuecher fuer Physik [*A publication*]
**Hochschuldidaktik Naturwiss**... Hochschuldidaktik der Naturwissenschaften [*A publication*]
**Hochschullehrb Biol**... Hochschullehrbuecher fuer Biologie [*A publication*]
**HochschulSammlung Ingenieurwiss Datenverarbeitung**... HochschulSammlung Ingenieurwissenschaft Datenverarbeitung [*A publication*]
**HochschulSammlung Naturwiss Informat**... HochschulSammlung Naturwissenschaft Informatik [*A publication*]
**HochschulSammlung Naturwiss Math**... HochschulSammlung Naturwissenschaft Mathematik [*A publication*]
**HOCM**....... Hypertrophic Obstructive Cardiomyopathy [*Cardiology*]
**HOCUS**..... Hand or Computer Universal Simulation [*PE Computer Services Ltd.*] [*Software package*] [*British*]
**HOC VESP**... Hoc Vespere [*Tonight*] [*Pharmacy*]
**HOD**......... Head of Department
**HOD**......... Heat of Detonation
**HOD**......... Hebrew Order of David
**HOD**......... Hodeidah [*Yemen Arab Republic*] [*Airport symbol*] (OAG)
**Hod**........... Hodges' English Common Pleas Reports [*1835-37*] [*A publication*] (DLA)
**HOD**......... Hoffer-Osmond Diagnostic Test [*Psychology*]
**HOD**......... Holz-Zentralblatt. Unabhangiges Organ fuer die Forstwirtschaft und Holzwirtschaft [*A publication*]
**HOD**......... Home on Decoy [*Military*] (CAAL)
**HOD**......... Hyperbaric Oxygen Drenching
**HODA**....... Hawkfarm One Design Association (EA)
**HODAG**.... Housing Development Action Grant [*HUD*]
**HODCRA**... Hampton One-Design Class Racing Association (EA)

**Hodg** .......... Hodges' English Common Pleas Reports [*1835-37*] [*A publication*] (DLA)
**Hodg** .......... Hodgin's Election Cases [*Ontario*] [*A publication*] (DLA)
**Hodg Can Elec Cas** ... Hodgin's Canada Election Cases [*A publication*] (DLA)
**Hodg El**...... Hodgins' Upper Canada Election Cases [*A publication*] (DLA)
**Hodg El Cas** ... Hodgin's Election Cases [*Ontario*] [*A publication*] (DLA)
**Hodg El Cas (Ont)** ... Hodgin's Election Cases [*Ontario*] [*A publication*] (DLA)
**Hodge Presb Law** ... Hodge on Presbyterian Law [*A publication*] (DLA)
**Hodges**....... Hodges' English Common Pleas Reports [*1835-37*] [*A publication*] (DLA)
**Hodges (Eng)** ... Hodges' English Common Pleas Reports [*1835-37*] [*A publication*] (DLA)
**Hodg Ont Elect** ... Hodgin's Election Cases [*Ontario*] [*A publication*] (DLA)
**Hodg Ry**..... Hodges' Law of Railways [*A publication*] (DLA)
**HODI** ........ Homozygous Diabetes Insipidus [*A genetic variety of rat*]
**Hodowla Rosl** ... Hodowla Roslin [*A publication*]
**Hodowla Rosl Aklim Nasienn** ... Hodowla Roslin Aklimatyzacja i Nasiennictwo [*A publication*]
**HODS**........ Hydrographic Oceanographic Data Sheets (NG)
**HOE** .......... Height of Eye [*Navigation*]
**HoE**........... Ho Eranistes [*A publication*]
**HOE** .......... Hoechst-Roussel Pharmaceuticals, Inc. [*Research code symbol*]
**HOE** .......... Holographic Optical Element
**HOE** .......... Homerville, GA [*Location identifier*] [*FAA*] (FAAL)
**HOE** .......... Homing Overlay Experiment [*Ballistic missile defense*] (RDA)
**HOE** .......... Hydraulically Operated Equipment
**HOEC**........ Hoe [*R.*] & Company, Inc. [*NASDAQ symbol*] (NQ)
**HOECD2**... Holarctic Ecology [*A publication*]
**Hoefchenbr Wiss Prax** ... Hoefchen-Briefe fuer Wissenschaft und Praxis [*A publication*]
**Hoefl** .......... Hoeflich [*Respectfully*] [*Correspondence*] [*German*]
**Hoehle Wiss Beih** ... Hoehlankunde Wissenschaftliche Beihefte [*A publication*]
**Hoe Jb** ....... Hoelderlin-Jahrbuch [*A publication*]
**Hoesch Ber Forsch Entwickl Unserer Werke** ... Hoesch. Berichte aus Forschung und Entwicklung Unserer Werke [*A publication*]
**Hoesch Ber Forsch Entwickl Werke** ... Hoesch. Arbeitskreis Forschung und Entwicklung, Berichte aus Forschung und Entwicklung Unserer Werke [*A publication*]
**HOET**........ Heavy Oil Engine Tractor [*British*]
**HOF**.......... Hafuf [*Saudi Arabia*] [*Airport symbol*] (OAG)
**HOF**.......... Hall of Fame
**HOF**.......... Heat of Formation
**HoF**........... Height of Fundus [*Obstetrics*]
**HOF**.......... Hof [*Federal Republic of Germany*] [*Seismograph station code, US Geological Survey*] (SEIS)
**HOF**.......... Hofmann Industries, Inc. [*AMEX symbol*] (SPSG)
**HOF**.......... Home Office Facility
**HOF**.......... Homing Fixture (MCD)
**HOF**.......... House of Fraser [*Department store conglomerate*] [*British*]
**HOF**.......... St. Paul, MN [*Location identifier*] [*FAA*] (FAAL)
**HOFC**........ Hall and Oates Fan Club (EA)
**HOFC**........ Houston Oil Fields Company [*NASDAQ symbol*] (NQ)
**HOFCO**..... Horizontal Function Checkout (KSC)
**HOFD**........ Heterogeneous Opposed Flow Diffusion
**HOFF**........ Hoffmann [*Reflex*] [*Medicine*]
**Hoff**........... Hoffman's Land Cases, United States District Court [*A publication*] (DLA)
**Hoff**........... Hoffman's New York Chancery Reports [*A publication*] (DLA)
**Hoff Ch**...... Hoffman's New York Chancery Reports [*A publication*] (DLA)
**Hoff CR**...... Hoffman's New York Chancery Reports [*A publication*] (DLA)
**Hoff Dec**..... Hoffman's Decisions [*A publication*] (DLA)
**Hoff Ecc L** ... Hoffman's Ecclesiastical Law [*A publication*] (DLA)
**Hoff Land** .. Hoffman's Land Cases, United States District Court [*A publication*] (DLA)
**Hoff Land Cas** ... Hoffman's Land Cases, United States District Court [*A publication*] (DLA)
**Hoff LC**...... Hoffman's Land Cases, United States District Court [*A publication*] (DLA)
**Hoff L Cas** ... Hoffman's Land Cases, United States District Court [*A publication*] (DLA)
**Hoff Lead Cas** ... Hoffman's Leading Cases [*A publication*] (DLA)
**Hoff Leg St** ... Hoffman's Course of Legal Study [*A publication*] (DLA)
**HOFFM** .... Hereditary Order of the First Families of Massachusetts (EA)
**Hoffm**........ Hoffman's Land Cases, United States District Court [*A publication*] (DLA)
**Hoffm**........ Hoffman's New York Chancery Reports [*A publication*] (DLA)
**Hoffman Ch R** ... Hoffman's New York Chancery Reports [*A publication*] (DLA)
**Hoffman's Ch R** ... Hoffman's New York Chancery Reports [*A publication*] (DLA)
**Hoff Mast** .. Hoffman's Master in Chancery [*A publication*] (DLA)
**Hoff Mast Ch** ... Hoffman's Master in Chancery [*A publication*] (DLA)
**Hoffm Ch**... Hoffman's Land Cases, United States District Court [*A publication*] (DLA)
**Hoffm Ch**... Hoffman's New York Chancery Reports [*A publication*] (DLA)
**Hoffm Ch (NY)** ... Hoffman's New York Chancery Reports [*A publication*] (DLA)
**Hoffm Dec (F)** ... Hoffman's Decisions, United States District Court [*A publication*] (DLA)
**Hoffm Land Cas (F)** ... Hoffman's Land Cases, United States District Court [*A publication*] (DLA)
**Hoffm Ops (F)** ... Hoffman's Opinions, United States District Court [*A publication*] (DLA)
**Hoffm Rep Land Cases** ... Hoffman's Land Cases, United States District Court [*A publication*] (DLA)
**Hoff NY**..... Hoffman's New York Chancery Reports [*A publication*] (DLA)
**Hoff Op**...... Hoffman's Opinions [*A publication*] (DLA)
**Hoff Out**..... Hoffman's Legal Outlines [*A publication*] (DLA)
**Hoff Pr Rem** ... Hoffman's Provisional Remainders [*A publication*] (DLA)
**Hoff Pub P** ... Hoffman's Public Papers [*New York*] [*A publication*] (DLA)
**Hoff Ref**..... Hoffman on Referees [*A publication*] (DLA)
**Hof LR**....... Hofstra Law Review [*A publication*]
**Ho & For R** ... Home and Foreign Review [*A publication*]
**HOFR**........ Home of Franklin D. Roosevelt and Vanderbilt Mansion National Historic Sites
**HOFS**........ Hydrogen-Oxygen Fuel System [*NASA*]
**HOFSL**...... Home Office Forensic Science Laboratory [*British*]
**Hofstra Lab LF** ... Hofstra Labor Law Forum [*A publication*] (DLA)
**Hofstra Lab LJ** ... Hofstra Labor Law Journal [*A publication*] (DLA)
**Hofstra L Rev** ... Hofstra Law Review [*A publication*]
**Hofstra Univ Yrbk Bus** ... Hofstra University. Yearbook of Business [*A publication*]
**HOG**.......... Arkansas Traveler Airline [*Midway, AR*] [*FAA designator*] (FAAC)
**HOG**.......... Harley Owners' Group (EA)
**HOG**.......... Head End Off-Gas [*Nuclear energy*] (NRCH)
**HOG**.......... Head of Government (ADA)
**HOG**.......... Heavy Ordnance Gunship (NVT)
**HOG**.......... High Old Genius [*Slang*] [*British*]
**Hog**........... (Hogan of) Harcarse's Scotch Session Cases [*A publication*] (DLA)
**Hog**........... Hogan's Irish Rolls Court Reports [*A publication*] (DLA)
**HOG**.......... Holguin [*Cuba*] [*Airport symbol*] (OAG)
**HOG**.......... Homing Optical Guidance
**HOG**.......... Hondo Oil & Gas [*AMEX symbol*] (SPSG)
**Hogan**........ (Hogan of) Harcarse's Scotch Session Cases [*A publication*] (DLA)
**Hogan**........ Hogan's Irish Rolls Court Reports [*A publication*] (DLA)
**Hogan (Ir)** ... Hogan's Irish Rolls Court Reports [*A publication*] (DLA)
**Hogarth Ess** ... Hogarth Essays [*A publication*]
**HOGC**....... Handbook of Occupational Groups and Series of Classes
**HOGE**....... Hover-Out-of-Ground Environment
**HOGEN**.... Hold Off Generator (MSA)
**Hog Farm Manage** ... Hog Farm Management [*A publication*]
**HOGG**....... Hanger Orthopedic Group, Inc. [*NASDAQ symbol*] (NQ)
**Hogg**.......... Hogg's Instructor [*A publication*]
**Hog Kenk**... Hogaku Kenkyu [*A publication*]
**HOGN**....... Hogan Systems, Inc. [*NASDAQ symbol*] (NQ)
**Hog Prod**.... Hog Production [*A publication*]
**HOGS**........ Homing Optical Guidance System
**Hog St Tr**... Hogan's Pennsylvania State Trials [*A publication*] (DLA)
**Hogue**........ Hogue's Reports [*1-4 Florida*] [*A publication*] (DLA)
**HOH**.......... Haunt of Horror [*A publication*]
**HOH**.......... Head of Household [*IRS*]
**HOH**.......... Hereford Otter Hounds
**HOH**.......... Hohenheim [*Federal Republic of Germany*] [*Seismograph station code, US Geological Survey*] [*Closed*] (SEIS)
**HOH**.......... Houtwereld Vakblad Gewijd aan de Belangen van de Houthandel en van de Houtverwerkende Industrie [*A publication*]
**Hohenheimer Arb** ... Hohenheimer Arbeiten [*A publication*]
**HOHI**........ Handbook of Overhaul Instructions [*Navy*]
**HOHI**........ HOH Water Technology Corp. [*NASDAQ symbol*] (NQ)
**HOH of J**... Holy Order of the Hospital of Jerusalem [*Freemasonry*] (ROG)
**HOHP**........ Holocaust Oral History Project [*An association*] (EA)
**HOI**.......... Handbook of Inflammation [*Elsevier Book Series*] [*A publication*]
**HOI**.......... Handbook of Operating Instructions [*Navy*]
**HOI**.......... Handbook of Overhaul Instructions [*Navy*] (MCD)
**HOI**.......... Hao Island [*French Polynesia*] [*Airport symbol*] (OAG)
**HOI**.......... Headquarters Office Instruction
**HOI**.......... Headquarters Operating Instructions [*Air Force*] (AFM)
**HOI**.......... Hear O Israel (EA)
**HOI**.......... House of Issue [*Banking*]
**HoIg**.......... Horse Immunoglobulin [*Immunology*]
**HOIS**......... Hostile Intelligence Service [*Military*] (MCD)
**HOJ**.......... Home on Jamming
**HOJ**.......... Hope [*Jamaica*] [*Seismograph station code, US Geological Survey*] (SEIS)
**Hoja Divulgativa Campo Agric Exp (Valle Fuerte)** ... Hoja Divulgativa. Campo Agricola Experimental (Valle del Fuerte) [*A publication*]
**Hoja Tisiol** ... Hoja Tisiologica [*A publication*]
**HoJb**......... Hoelderlin-Jahrbuch [*A publication*]
**HOJO**........ Howard Johnson [*Restaurant chain*] [*Slang*]
**Hoj Tisiol**... Hoja Tisiologica [*A publication*]
**HOK**.......... Hellmuth, Obata & Kassabaum [*Architectural firm*]

**HOK**.......... Hohkeppel [*Federal Republic of Germany*] [*Seismograph station code, US Geological Survey*] (SEIS)
**HOK**.......... Hoko Exploration [*Vancouver Stock Exchange symbol*]
**HOK**.......... House of Keys [*Isle Of Man*]
**HOKBA**....... Hoken Butsuri [*A publication*]
**HOKDA**..... Hokkaido Daigaku Nogakubu Enshurin Kenkyu Hokoku [*A publication*]
**Hokkaido Forest Prod Res Inst Rept** ... Hokkaido Forest Products Research Institute. Reports [*A publication*]
**Hokkaido Geol Surv Rep** ... Hokkaido Geological Survey. Report [*A publication*]
**Hokkaido J Med Sci** ... Hokkaido Journal of Medical Science [*A publication*]
**Hokkaido J Orthop & Trauma Surg** ... Hokkaido Journal of Orthopedic and Traumatic Surgery [*A publication*]
**Hokkaido Math J** ... Hokkaido Mathematical Journal [*A publication*]
**Hokkaido Natl Agric Exp Stn Data** ... Hokkaido National Agricultural Experiment Station. Data [*A publication*]
**Hokkaido Natl Agric Exp Stn Rep** ... Hokkaido National Agricultural Experiment Station. Report [*A publication*]
**Hokkaido Natl Agric Exp Stn Soil Surv Rep** ... Hokkaido National Agricultural Experiment Station. Soil Survey Report [*A publication*]
**Hokkaido Univ Fac Sci J Ser 4** ... Hokkaido University. Faculty of Science. Journal. Series 4. Geology and Mineralogy [*A publication*]
**Hokkaido Univ Inst Low Temp Sci Low Temp Sci Ser A Phys Sci** ... Hokkaido University. Institute of Low Temperature Science. Low Temperature Science. Series A. Physical Sciences [*A publication*]
**Hokkaido Univ Med Libr Ser** ... Hokkaido University. Medical Library Series [*A publication*]
**Hokk Daig Juig Bu** ... Hokkaido Daigaku Juigaku Bu [*Japanese Journal of Veterinary Research*] [*A publication*]
**Hokoku Aichi-Ken Ringyo Shikenjo** ... Hokoku. Aichi-ken Ringyo Shikenjo [*A publication*]
**Hokoku Bull Akita Fruit Tree Exp Stn/Akita Kaju Shikenjo** ... Hokoku. Bulletin. Akita Fruit-Tree Experiment Station/Akita Kaju Shikenjo [*A publication*]
**Hokoku Bull Chugoku Natl Agric Exp Stn Ser E Environ Div** ... Hokoku. Bulletin. Chugoku National Agricultural Experiment Station. Series E. Environment Division [*A publication*]
**Hokoku Bull Kagoshima Tob Exp Stn/Kagoshima Tabako Shikenjo** ... Hokoku. Bulletin. Kagoshima Tobacco Experiment Station/Kagoshima Tabako Shikenjo [*A publication*]
**Hokoku Bull Natl Inst Agric Sci Ser A Phys and Stat** ... Hokoku. Bulletin. National Institute of Agricultural Sciences. Series A. Physics and Statistics [*A publication*]
**Hokoku Bull Tohoku Daigaku Nogaku Kenkyujo** ... Hokoku. Bulletin. Tohoku Daigaku Nogaku Kenkyujo [*A publication*]
**Hokoku Jap Tab Shikenjo Okayama/Bull Okayama Tob Exp Stn** ... Hokoku, Japan. Tabako Shikenjo Okayama/Bulletin. Okayama Tobacco Experiment Station [*A publication*]
**HOKSA**..... Hokkaido-Ritsu Kogyo Shikenjo Hokoku [*A publication*]
**HOL**.......... High- [*or Higher-*] Order Language [*Data processing*]
**HOL**.......... Higher Order Logic [*Data processing*]
**HOL**.......... Holiday (AFM)
**HOL**.......... Holiday Airlines, Inc. [*Morristown, NJ*] [*FAA designator*] (FAAC)
**HOL**.......... Holiday and Leave [*Military*] (NVT)
**HOL**.......... Hollinger Argus Ltd. [*Toronto Stock Exchange symbol*]
**HOL**.......... Hollow (MSA)
**HOL**.......... House of Lords [*British*]
**HOLA**........ Hispanic Organization of Latin Actors (EA)
**HOLA**........ Holco Mortgage Acceptance [*AMEX symbol*] (SPSG)
**HOLA**........ Home Owners' Loan Act of 1933
**Holarct Ecol** ... Holarctic Ecology [*A publication*]
**Holarctic Ecol** ... Holarctic Ecology [*Denmark*] [*A publication*]
**Holb Rev**.... Holborn Review [*A publication*]
**HOLC**........ High-Order Language Computer (NASA)
**HOLC**........ Home Owners' Loan Corporation [*Terminated, 1942*]
**Ho L Cas**.... Clark's House of Lords Cases [*1847-66*] [*England*] [*A publication*] (DLA)
**Holc Debt & Cr** ... Holcombe's Law of Debtor and Creditor [*A publication*] (DLA)
**Holc Eq Jur** ... Holcombe's Equity Jurisdiction [*A publication*] (DLA)
**Holc L Cas** ... Holcombe's Leading Cases of Commercial Law [*A publication*] (DLA)
**Hol Crit**...... Hollins Critic [*A publication*]
**HOLD**........ Holder Communications Corp. [*Tampa, FL*] [*NASDAQ symbol*] (NQ)
**Holderlin-Jahrb** ... Hoelderlin-Jahrbuch [*A publication*]
**Holdsw Hist EL** ... [*Sir W. S.*] Holdsworth's History of English Law [*A publication*] (DLA)
**Holdsworth** ... [*Sir W. S.*] Holdsworth's History of English Law [*A publication*] (DLA)
**HOLF**........ Helicopter Outlying Field
**HOLL**........ Holland
**Holl**............ Hollinshead's Reports [*1 Minnesota*] [*A publication*] (DLA)
**HOLLAND** ... Here Our Love Lives and Never Dies [*Correspondence*] (DSUE)
**Holland Shipbuild** ... Holland Shipbuilding [*Netherlands*] [*A publication*]
**Holland Shipbuild** ... Holland Shipbuilding and Marine Engineering [*Later, Holland Shipbuilding*] [*A publication*]
**Hollands Maandbl** ... Hollands Maandblad [*A publication*]
**Holl Comp Deeds** ... Holland on Composition Deeds [*A publication*] (DLA)
**Holld Info**.. Holland Info [*A publication*]
**Holl El Jur** ... Holland's Elements of Jurisprudence [*A publication*] (DLA)
**Hollinshead** ... Hollinshead's Reports [*1 Minnesota*] [*A publication*] (DLA)
**Holl Jur**..... Holland's Elements of Jurisprudence [*A publication*] (DLA)
**Holl Just**.... Holland's Institutes of Justinian [*A publication*] (DLA)
**Holloman Symp Primate Immunol Mol Genet** ... Holloman Symposium on Primate Immunology and Molecular Genetics [*A publication*]
**Hollow Sec** ... Hollow Section [*United Kingdom*] [*A publication*]
**Hollywood Q** ... Hollywood Quarterly [*A publication*]
**HOLM**....... Higher-Order Language Machine [*Data processing*] (KSC)
**Holm**.......... Holmes' Reports [*15-17 Oregon*] [*A publication*] (DLA)
**Holm**.......... Holmes' United States Circuit Court Reports [*A publication*] (DLA)
**Holm Com Law** ... Holmes on the Common Law [*A publication*] (DLA)
**Holmes**....... Holmes' United States Circuit Court Reports [*A publication*] (DLA)
**HOLMES** ... Home Office Large Major Enquiry System [*Computer system*] [*British*]
**Holm Statesman** ... Holmes' Statesman [*A publication*] (DLA)
**Holoand**..... [*Gregorius*] Haloander [*Deceased, 1531*] [*Authority cited in pre-1607 legal work*] (DSA)
**Ho Lords C** ... Clark's House of Lords Cases [*1847-66*] [*England*] [*A publication*] (DLA)
**Ho Lords Cas** ... Clark's House of Lords Cases [*1847-66*] [*England*] [*A publication*] (DLA)
**HOLSA**..... Health-Oriented Libraries of San Antonio [*Library network*]
**Holstein World** ... Holstein-Friesian World [*A publication*]
**HOLSW**.... Holsworthy [*England*]
**Holt**............ Holt's English Equity Reports [*1845*] [*A publication*] (DLA)
**Holt**............ Holt's English King's Bench Reports [*A publication*] (DLA)
**Holt**............ Holt's English Nisi Prius Reports [*A publication*] (DLA)
**Holt Adm**... Holt's English Admiralty Cases (Rule of the Road) [*1863-67*] [*A publication*] (DLA)
**Holt Adm Ca** ... Holt's English Admiralty Cases (Rule of the Road) [*1863-67*] [*A publication*] (DLA)
**Holt Adm Cas** ... Holt's English Admiralty Cases (Rule of the Road) [*1863-67*] [*A publication*] (DLA)
**Holt Eq**...... Holt's English Equity Reports [*1845*] [*A publication*] (DLA)
**Holthouse**.. Holthouse's Law Dictionary [*A publication*] (DLA)
**Holt KB**...... Holt's English King's Bench Reports [*A publication*] (DLA)
**Holt L Dic**... Holthouse's Law Dictionary [*A publication*] (DLA)
**Holt Lib**..... Holt on Libels [*A publication*] (DLA)
**Holt Nav**.... Holt on Navigation [*A publication*] (DLA)
**Holt NP**..... Holt's English Nisi Prius Reports [*A publication*] (DLA)
**Holt Reg**..... Holt on Registration of Title [*A publication*] (DLA)
**Holt R of R**... Holt's English Admiralty Cases (Rule of the Road) [*A publication*] (DLA)
**Holt Sh**...... Holt on Shipping [*A publication*] (DLA)
**Holt Shipp** ... Holt on Shipping [*A publication*] (DLA)
**Holtz Enc**... Holtzendorff. Encyclopadie der Rechtswissenschaft [*Encyclopedia of Jurisprudence*] [*A publication*] (DLA)
**HOLUA**..... Home Office Life Underwriters Association [*St. Louis, MO*] (EA)
**HOLUPK**.. Holiday, Upkeep [*Military*] (NVT)
**HOLW**....... Hollow
**HOLWG**.... High- [*or Higher-*] Order Language Working Group [*Data processing*] (RDA)
**HOLX**........ Holiday Airlines, Inc. [*Air carrier designation symbol*]
**Holy Name Mo** ... Holy Name Monthly [*A publication*] (APTA)
**HOLZ**........ Higher Order Laue Zone [*Crystal diffraction lines*]
**Holzf Holzv** ... Holzforschung und Holzverwertung [*A publication*]
**Holzforsch** ... Holzforschung [*A publication*]
**Holzforsch Holzverwert** ... Holzforschung und Holzverwertung [*A publication*]
**Holz Roh We** ... Holz als Roh- und Werkstoff [*A publication*]
**Holz Roh- Werkst** ... Holz als Roh- und Werkstoff [*A publication*]
**Holztechnol** ... Holztechnologie [*A publication*]
**Holz Zbl**..... Holz-Zentralblatt [*A publication*]
**HOM**......... Heartless Old Man [*Alternative sobriquet for William Gladstone, 1809-98, British statesman and prime minister, who was known to admirers as GOM, which see*]
**HOM**......... Hectometric Emissions [*Radio astronomy*]
**HOM**......... Homer [*Alaska*] [*Seismograph station code, US Geological Survey*] (SEIS)
**HOM**......... Homer [*Greek poet, c. 800BC*] [*Classical studies*] (ROG)
**HOM**......... Homer [*Alaska*] [*Airport symbol*] (OAG)
**Hom**........... Homiletics [*A publication*]
**HOM**......... Homily (ROG)
**HOM**......... Homing
**Hom**........... Homobonus de Cremona [*Deceased, 1272*] [*Authority cited in pre-1607 legal work*] (DSA)
**Hom**........... Homoptera [*Entomology*]
**HoM**.......... Howell Microfilms Co., College, MD [*Library symbol*] [*Library of Congress*] (LCLS)
**HOMA**...... Home Federal Savings & Loan of Atlanta [*NASDAQ symbol*] (NQ)

**HomBib** ...... Homiletica en Biblica [*The Hague*] [*A publication*] (BJA)
**Hombre y Cult** ... Hombre y Cultura [*A publication*]
**HOMC** ...... Homac, Inc. [*NASDAQ symbol*] (NQ)
**HOME** ...... Home Observation for Measurement of the Environment [*Child development test*] [*Psychology*]
**HOME** ...... Home Oncology Medical Extension [*A home treatment program*]
**HOME** ...... Home Oriented Maternity Experience [*Defunct*] (EA)
**HOME** ...... Home Ownership Made Easy Association (EA)
**Home** ......... Home's Manuscript Decisions, Scotch Court of Session [*A publication*] (DLA)
**HOME** ...... Homestead National Monument
**HOME** ...... Homeworkers Organized for More Employment (EA)
**HOME** ...... International American Homes, Inc. [*NASDAQ symbol*] (NQ)
**Home Auto** ... Home and Auto Buyer Guide [*A publication*]
**Home (Cl)** .. Clerk Home's Decisions, Scotch Court of Session [*1735-44*] [*A publication*] (DLA)
**Home (Clk)** ... Home's Manuscript Decisions, Scotch Court of Session [*A publication*] (DLA)
**Home Com N** ... Home Computer News [*A publication*]
**Home Ct of Sess** ... Home's Manuscript Decisions, Scotch Court of Session [*A publication*] (DLA)
**Home Ec Bul** ... Home Economics Bulletin [*A publication*] (APTA)
**Home Econ News** ... Home Economics News [*A publication*]
**Home Econ Newsl** ... Home Economics Newsletter [*A publication*]
**Home Econ Res J** ... Home Economics Research Journal [*A publication*]
**Home Energy Dig Wood Burn Q** ... Home Energy Digest and Wood Burning Quarterly [*A publication*]
**Home Finan** ... Savings and Home Financing Source Book 1984 [*A publication*]
**Home Gard** ... Home Garden [*Later, Family Handyman*] [*A publication*]
**Home Gdn Bull** ... Home and Garden Bulletins [*A publication*]
**Home Geog Mo** ... Home Geographic Monthly [*A publication*]
**Home H Dec** ... Home's Manuscript Decisions, Scotch Court of Session [*A publication*] (DLA)
**Home Health Care Serv Q** ... Home Health Care Services Quarterly [*A publication*]
**Home Healthc Nurse** ... Home Healthcare Nurse [*A publication*]
**Home Health J** ... Home Health Journal [*A publication*]
**Home Health Rev** ... Home Health Review [*A publication*]
**Home Improvements Jnl** ... Home Improvements Journal [*A publication*]
**Home Mag** ... Homemakers' Magazine [*A publication*]
**HOMEO** ... Homeopathy (ADA)
**Home Off Lib Bull** ... Home Office Library Bulletin [*A publication*]
**Home Off Res Bull** ... Home Office Research Bulletin [*A publication*]
**HOMEOP** ... Homeopathy [*Medicine*]
**Home Prog** ... Home Progress [*A publication*]
**HOMES** .... Homeowner-Mortgage Eurosecurities [*Salomon Brothers*] [*Real estate*]
**HOMES** .... Housing Operations Management System [*DoD*]
**HOMES** .... Huron, Ontario, Michigan, Erie, Superior [*Great Lakes*]
**Home Sci** ... Home Science [*A publication*] (APTA)
**Home Tech** ... Home Techniques [*A publication*]
**Home Video** ... Home Video Publisher [*A publication*]
**HOMF** ....... Home Federal Savings Bank [*NASDAQ symbol*] (NQ)
**HOMG** ...... Homeowners Group, Inc. [*NASDAQ symbol*] (NQ)
**HOMI** ........ Homicide (DLA)
**Homme Oiseau** ... Homme et l'Oiseau [*A publication*]
**Hommes et Migr** ... Hommes et Migrations [*A publication*]
**Hommes et Migr Doc** ... Hommes et Migrations. Documents [*A publication*]
**Homme Soc** ... Homme et Societe [*A publication*]
**Homme et Soc** ... Homme et Societe [*A publication*]
**Hommes Tech** ... Hommes et Techniques [*A publication*]
**Hommes et Techn** ... Hommes et Techniques [*A publication*]
**Homm O-Mer** ... Hommes d'Outre-Mer [*A publication*]
**Homm Techn** ... Hommes et Technique [*A publication*]
**HOMO** ...... Highest Occupied Molecular Orbital [*Atomic physics*]
**HOMO** ...... Homogenous
**HOMO** ...... Homosexual
**Homob** ....... Homobonus de Cremona [*Deceased, 1272*] [*Authority cited in pre-1607 legal work*] (DSA)
**HOMOCO** ... Homemakers & Mothers Cooperatives, Inc.
**HomoD** ...... Homo Dei. Przeglad Ascetyczno-Duszpasterski [*Warsaw/Wroclaw*] [*A publication*] (BJA)
**HOMOEO** ... Homoeopathy [*Medicine*]
**Homoeopath** ... Homoeopathic Digest [*A publication*]
**Homogeneous Catal Org Inorg Chem** ... Homogeneous Catalysis in Organic and Inorganic Chemistry [*A publication*]
**HOMOLAT** ... Homolateral [*Medicine*]
**HOMP** ....... Halifax Ocean Meeting Point
**Hom Past Rev** ... Homiletic and Pastoral Review [*A publication*]
**Hom R** ........ Homiletic Review [*A publication*]
**HOMS** ....... Homme et Societe [*A publication*]
**HOMS** ....... Hydrological Operational Multipurpose Subprogramme [*World Meteorological Organization*] [*Information service or system*] (IID)
**HOMSTD** ... Homestead (DLA)
**HOMT** ...... Hydroxyindole O-Methyltransferase [*Also, HIOMT*] [*An enzyme*]
**HON** .......... Handbook of the Nations [*A publication*]
**HON** .......... Hold Off Normal
**HON** .......... Honey (DSUE)
**HON** .......... Honeywell Electro-Optics Center Library, Lexington, MA [*OCLC symbol*] (OCLC)
**HON** .......... Honeywell, Inc. [*Formerly, MH, M-H*] [*NYSE symbol*] (SPSG)
**HON** .......... Honiton [*Municipal borough in England*]
**HON** .......... Honolulu [*Hawaii*] [*Seismograph station code, US Geological Survey*] (SEIS)
**HON** .......... Honolulu [*Hawaii*] [*Geomagnetic observatory code*]
**HON** .......... Honorable
**HON** .......... Honorary (MSA)
**Hon** ............ [*Pope*] Honorius [*Authority cited in pre-1607 legal work*] (DSA)
**Hon** ............ Honorius de Kent [*Flourished, 1185-1208*] [*Authority cited in pre-1607 legal work*] (DSA)
**HON** .......... Huron [*South Dakota*] [*Airport symbol*] (OAG)
**HON** .......... Hydroxyoxo-L-norvaline [*Antibiotic*]
**HON** .......... Revue Commerciale [*A publication*]
**HONAA** .... Helvetica Odontologica Acta [*A publication*]
**HON AF** .... Honorary Admiral of the Fleet [*Navy*] [*British*] (ROG)
**Hon ARAM** ... Honorary Associate of the Royal Academy of Music [*British*]
**HonASTA** ... Honorary Associate of the Swimming Teachers' Association [*British*] (DBQ)
**HONBLE** .. Honorable
**HONCAUS** ... Honoris Causa [*For the Sake of Honor, Honorary*] [*Latin*] (ADA)
**HOND** ....... Honduras
**HOND** ....... Honoured (ROG)
**HonDrRCA** ... Honorary Doctorate of the Royal College of Art [*British*] (DBQ)
**HONEST** .. Helicopter Operations in a Night Environment Against a Simulated Target [*Military*] (MCD)
**Honeywell Comput J** ... Honeywell Computer Journal [*A publication*]
**HonFBID** ... Honorary Fellow of the British Institute of Interior Design (DBQ)
**Hon FEIS** .. Honorary Fellow of the Educational Institute of Scotland
**HonFHCIMA** ... Honorary Fellow of the Hotel, Catering, and Institutional Management Association [*British*] (DBQ)
**HonFIGasE** ... Honorary Fellow of the Institution of Gas Engineers [*British*] (DBQ)
**HonFIIM** ... Honorary Fellow of the Institution of Industrial Managers [*British*] (DBQ)
**HonFIMarE** ... Honorary Fellow of the Institute of Marine Engineers [*British*] (DBQ)
**HonFIMechE** ... Honorary Fellow of the Institution of Mechanical Engineers [*British*] (DBQ)
**HonFIMM** ... Honorary Fellow of the Institution of Mining and Metallurgy [*British*] (DBQ)
**HonFInstE** ... Honorary Fellow of the Institute of Energy [*British*] (DBQ)
**HonFInstMC** ... Honorary Fellow of the Institute of Measurement [*British*] (DBQ)
**HonFInstNDT** ... Honorary Fellow of the British Institute of Non-Destructive Testing (DBQ)
**HonFIQA** .. Honorary Fellow of the Institute of Quality Assurance [*British*] (DBQ)
**HonFIRSE** ... Honorary Fellow of the Institution of Railway Signal Engineers [*British*] (DBQ)
**HonFIWHTE** ... Honorary Fellow of the Institution of Works and Highways Technician Engineers [*British*] (DBQ)
**Hon FNDTS** ... Honorary Fellow of the Non-Destructive Testing Society of Great Britain
**HonFPRI** ... Honorary Life Member of the Plastics and Rubber Institute [*British*] (DBQ)
**Hon FRAM** ... Honorary Fellow of the Royal Academy of Music [*British*]
**Hon FRPS** ... Honorary Fellow of the Royal Photographic Society [*British*]
**HonFSCP** .. Honorary Fellow of the Society of Certified Professionals [*British*] (DBQ)
**HonFSE** ..... Honorary Fellow of the Society of Engineers, Inc. [*British*] (DBQ)
**HonFSGT** ... Honorary Fellow of the Society of Glass Technology [*British*] (DBQ)
**HonFSLAET** ... Honorary Fellow of the Society of Licensed Aircraft Engineers and Technologists [*British*] (DBQ)
**HonFWeldI** ... Honorary Fellow of the Welding Institute [*British*] (DBQ)
**Hongik Univ J** ... Hongik University. Journal [*Republic of Korea*] [*A publication*]
**Hong Kong Eng** ... Hong Kong Engineer [*A publication*]
**Hong Kong Engr** ... Hong Kong Engineer [*A publication*]
**Hong Kong LJ** ... Hong Kong Law Journal [*A publication*] (DLA)
**Hong Kong LR** ... Hong Kong Law Reports [*A publication*] (DLA)
**Hong Kong Nurs J** ... Hong Kong Nursing Journal [*A publication*]
**Hong Kong UL Jo** ... Hong Kong University. Law Journal [*A publication*] (DLA)
**Hong Kong Univ Fish J** ... Hong Kong University. Fisheries Journal [*A publication*]
**HonGSM** ... Honorary Member of the Guildhall School of Music and Drama [*British*] (DBQ)
**HONI** ........ Hon Industries, Inc. [*NASDAQ symbol*] (NQ)
**HONKAY** ... Hokkaido National Agricultural Experiment Station. Soil Survey Report [*A publication*]
**HON L** ....... Honorary Lieutenant [*Navy*] [*British*] (ROG)
**HON M** ..... Honorary Member (ROG)

**Hon Magist** ... Honorary Magistrate [*Australia*] (DLA)
**HonMInst NDT** ... Honorary Member of the British Institute of Non-Destructive Testing (DBQ)
**Hon MNDTS** ... Honorary Member of the Non-Destructive Testing Society of Great Britain
**HonMRIN** ... Honorary Member of the Royal Institute of Navigation [*British*] (DBQ)
**HonMWES** ... Honorary Member of the Women's Engineering Society [*British*] (DBQ)
**HONO**....... Honolulu [*Hawaii*] (CINC)
**Honolulu Ad** ... Honolulu Advertiser [*A publication*]
**Hon RAM** ... Honorary Member of the Royal Academy of Music [*British*]
**HonRCM**... Honorary Member of the Royal College of Music [*British*] (DBQ)
**HonRNCM** ... Honorary Member of the Royal Northern College of Music [*British*] (DBQ)
**Hon RSCM** ... Honorary Member of the Royal School of Church Music [*British*]
**HONS**........ Honors
**HON SCH MOD LANG** ... Honour School of Modern Languages [*British*] (ROG)
**HON SEC** ... Honorary Secretary (ROG)
**HON SURG LIEUT COL** ... Honorary Surgeon Lieutenant-Colonel [*Military*] [*British*] (ROG)
**HON VA** ... Honorary Vice-Admiral [*Navy*] [*British*] (ROG)
**HOO**.......... Avila College, Kansas City, MO [*OCLC symbol*] (OCLC)
**HOO**.......... Hanford Operations Office [*Nuclear energy*] (MCD)
**HOO**.......... Hiroo [*Japan*] [*Seismograph station code, US Geological Survey*] (SEIS)
**HOOD**....... Hereditary Osteo-Onychodysplasia [*Medicine*]
**Hood**.......... Neighborhood [*Slang*]
**Hood Ex**..... Hood on Executors [*A publication*] (DLA)
**HOOK**....... Handbook of Occupational Keywords [*For use in employment services*] [*Department of Labor*]
**HOOK**....... Hook Drugs, Inc. [*NASDAQ symbol*] (NQ)
**Hook**.......... Hooker's Reports [*25-62 Connecticut*] [*A publication*] (DLA)
**Hooker**....... Hooker's Reports [*25-62 Connecticut*] [*A publication*] (DLA)
**Hoon**.......... Hoonahan's Sind Reports [*India*] [*A publication*] (DLA)
**Hoonahan**.. Hoonahan's Sind Reports [*India*] [*A publication*] (DLA)
**HOOP**......... Handbook of Operating Procedures
**HOOPS**..... Hierarchical Object-Oriented Picture System [*Data processing*]
**Hoosier Sch Lib** ... Hoosier School Libraries [*A publication*]
**HOOV**....... [*The*] Hoover Co. [*NASDAQ symbol*] (NQ)
**HOP**........... Handoff Point (FAAC)
**HOP**........... HEDL [*Hanford Engineering Development Laboratory*] Overpower [*Nuclear energy*] (NRCH)
**HOP**........... Helicopter Operations (FAAC)
**HOP**........... Helium Oxidizer-Tank Pressure (AAG)
**HOP**........... High-Order Position (AFIT)
**HOP**........... High Oxygen Pressure
**HOP**........... Hope [*Jamaica*] [*Seismograph station code, US Geological Survey*] [*Closed*] (SEIS)
**Hop**............ Hopital [*A publication*]
**HOP**........... Hopkinsville, KY [*Location identifier*] [*FAA*] (FAAL)
**HOP**........... House Operating Tape [*Telecommunications*] (TEL)
**HOP**........... Hybrid Operating Program [*Data processing*] (IEEE)
**HOP**........... Hydrographic Office Publications [*Obsolete*] [*Navy*]
**HOP**........... Hydroxydaunomycin [*Adriamycin*], Oncovin [*Vincristine*], Prednisone [*Antineoplastic drug regimen*]
**HOPA**........ Hopantenate Calcium [*Cerebral activator*]
**Hop Aide Soc Par** ... Hopital et l'Aide Sociale a Paris [*A publication*]
**Hop Aujourd** ... Hopital d'Aujourd'hui [*A publication*]
**Hop Belge**.. Hopital Belge [*A publication*]
**Hop & C**..... Hopwood and Coltman's English Registration Appeal Cases [*A publication*] (DLA)
**HOPC**........ Hydro Optics, Inc. [*NASDAQ symbol*] (NQ)
**Hop & Colt** ... Hopwood and Coltman's English Registration Appeal Cases [*A publication*] (DLA)
**HOPE**........ Halley Optical Probe Experiment
**HOPE**........ Health Opportunity for People Everywhere [*Philanthropic project operating hospital ship*]
**HOPE**........ Health Organization to Preserve the Environment
**HOPE**........ Health-Oriented Physician Education
**HOPE**........ Help Obese People Everywhere
**HOPE**........ Highlights of Personal Experience in Agriculture Department
**HOPE**........ Highly Instrumented Orbiting Primate Experiment
**HOPE**........ Hispanic Organization of Professionals and Executives [*Silver Spring, MD*] (EA)
**HOPE**........ History of Political Economy [*A publication*]
**HOPE**........ Home Ownership and Opportunity for People Everywhere [*Program*] [*HUD*]
**HOPE**........ Homes of Private Enterprise (EA)
**Hope**.......... Hope (of Kerse). Manuscript Decisions, Scotch Court of Session [*A publication*] (DLA)
**HOPE**........ Hospital-Oriented Programmed Environment
**HOPE**........ Housing Our People Economically
**HOPE**........ Humanistic Organization for Personal Expansion
**HOPE**........ Hydrogen-Oxygen Primary Extraterrestrial [*Fuel cell*] [*NASA*]
**HOPEC**..... Hand-Operated Positive Energy Control
**HOPEC**..... Hydrogen Organization for Progress, Education, and Cooperation [*Defunct*] (EA)
**Hope Com Law** ... Hope's Compendium of the Commercial Law of the Pacific [*A publication*] (DLA)
**Hope Dec** ... Hope (of Kerse). Manuscript Decisions, Scotch Court of Session [*A publication*] (DLA)
**Hope Maj Pr** ... Hope's Major Practicks [*Scotland*] [*A publication*] (DLA)
**Hope Min Pr** ... Hope's Minor Practicks [*Scotland*] [*A publication*] (DLA)
**Hope Rep Q** ... Hope Reports Quarterly [*A publication*]
**Hopf Rdsch** ... Hopfen Rundschau [*A publication*]
**HOPG**........ Highly Oriented Pyrolytic Graphite [*Engineering*]
**HOPI**......... Handbook of Operating Instructions [*Navy*] (MCD)
**HOPING**... Helping Other Parents in Normal Grieving (EA)
**Hopk**.......... Hopkins' New York Chancery Reports [*A publication*] (DLA)
**Hopk Adm** ... Hopkinson's Pennsylvania Admiralty Judgments [*A publication*] (DLA)
**Hopk Adm Dec** ... Admiralty Decisions of Hopkinson in Gilpin's Reports [*A publication*] (DLA)
**Hopk Av**..... Hopkins' Average [*4th ed.*] [*1884*] [*A publication*] (DLA)
**Hopk CC**.... Hopkins' New York Chancery Reports [*A publication*] (DLA)
**Hopk Ch**.... Hopkins' New York Chancery Reports [*A publication*] (DLA)
**Hopk Chanc Rep** ... Hopkins' New York Chancery Reports [*A publication*] (DLA)
**Hopkins Q** ... Hopkins Quarterly [*A publication*]
**Hopk Judg** ... Hopkinson's Pennsylvania Admiralty Judgments [*A publication*] (DLA)
**Hopk Mar Ins** ... Hopkins on Marine Insurance [*A publication*] (DLA)
**Hopk Rep**... Hopkins' New York Chancery Reports [*A publication*] (DLA)
**Hopk W**..... Hopkinson's Works [*Pennsylvania*] [*A publication*] (DLA)
**Hopk Wks** ... Hopkinson's Works [*Pennsylvania*] [*A publication*] (DLA)
**Hopk Works (PA)** ... Hopkinson's Works [*Pennsylvania*] [*A publication*] (DLA)
**HOPL**........ History of Programming Languages
**Hop Maj Pr** ... [*Sir T.*] Hope. Major Practicks [*Scotland*] [*A publication*] (DLA)
**Hop Min**.... Hope's Minor Practicks [*Scotland*] [*A publication*] (DLA)
**Hoppe-Seyler's Z Physiol Chem** ... Hoppe-Seyler's Zeitschrift fuer Physiologische Chemie [*A publication*]
**Hoppe-Seylers Zs** ... Hoppe-Seyler's Zeitschrift fuer Physiologische Chemie [*A publication*]
**Hoppe-Seyler's Ztschr Physiol Chem** ... Hoppe-Seyler's Zeitschrift fuer Physiologische Chemie [*A publication*]
**Hop & Ph**... Hopwood and Philbrick's English Registration Appeal Cases [*A publication*] (DLA)
**Hop & Phil** ... Hopwood and Philbrick's English Registration Appeal Cases [*A publication*] (DLA)
**HopQ**......... Hopkins Quarterly [*A publication*]
**Hop R**......... Hopkins Review [*A publication*]
**HOPS**........ Helmet-Mounted Optical Projection System
**HOPS**........ Heterodyne Optical Optimization Communication System with Stops [*NASA*]
**HOPT**........ Handbook of Powder Technology [*Elsevier Book Series*] [*A publication*]
**HOPT**........ Hypoparathyroidism [*Endocrinology*]
**HO Publ**.... Hydrographic Office. Publication [*A publication*]
**HO Purdue Univ Coop Ext Serv** ... HO-Purdue University. Cooperative Extension Service [*A publication*]
**Hop U Stud** ... Johns Hopkins University. Studies in Historical and Political Science [*A publication*]
**Hopw & C**.. Hopwood and Coltman's English Registration Appeal Cases [*A publication*] (DLA)
**Hopw & Colt** ... Hopwood and Coltman's English Registration Appeal Cases [*A publication*] (DLA)
**Hopw & P**... Hopwood and Philbrick's English Registration Appeal Cases [*A publication*] (DLA)
**Hopw & Phil** ... Hopwood and Philbrick's English Registration Appeal Cases [*A publication*] (DLA)
**HOQ**.......... Hansard Oral Questions [*Database*] [*House of Commons*] [*Canada*] [*Information service or system*] (CRD)
**HOQ**.......... Hof [*West Germany*] [*Airport symbol*] (OAG)
**HOQ**.......... Hysteroid-Obsessoid Questionnaire [*Psychology*]
**HOQNO**.... Heptyl(hydroxy)quinoline N-Oxide [*Organic chemistry*]
**HOR**.......... Heliocentric Orbit Rendezvous (MCD)
**HOR**.......... Holder of Record [*Investment term*]
**HOR**.......... Home of Record
**HOR**.......... Hoover-Owens-Rentschler [*Engines*]
**HOR**.......... Horace [*Roman poet, 65-8BC*] [*Classical studies*] (ROG)
**Hor**............ Horayoth (BJA)
**Hor**............ Horizon [*A publication*]
**HOR**.......... Horizon (KSC)
**HOR**.......... Horizontal
**Hor**............ Horizontal Lights [*Navigation signal*]
**HOR**.......... Horn & Hardart Co. [*AMEX symbol*] (SPSG)
**Hor**............ Horologium [*Constellation*]
**HOR**.......... Horology
**HOR**.......... Horta [*Azores*] [*Seismograph station code, US Geological Survey*] (SEIS)
**HOR**.......... Horta [*Faial Island*] [*Azores*] [*Airport symbol*] (OAG)
**Hor**............ Horyzonty [*A publication*]
**HOR**.......... Hot Resources Ltd. [*Vancouver Stock Exchange symbol*]
**HOR**.......... University of Minnesota, the Hormel Institute, Austin, MN [*OCLC symbol*] (OCLC)

**HORACE**.. $H_2O$ Reactor Aldermaston Critical Experiment [*British*] (DEN)
**HORAD**.... Horizontal RADAR Display
**Horat Mand**... Horatius Mandosius [*Deceased, 1594*] [*Authority cited in pre-1607 legal work*] (DSA)
**HORC**........ Horizon Health Corporation [*NASDAQ symbol*] (NQ)
**HOR CL**.... Horizontal Clearance [*Nautical charts*]
**HORD**....... Hordeum [*Barley*] [*Pharmacy*] (ROG)
**HOR DECU**... Hora Decubitus [*At Bedtime*] [*Pharmacy*]
**HOR DECUB**... Hora Decubitus [*At Bedtime*] [*Pharmacy*] (ROG)
**HO-RE-CA**... Federation Internationale des Organisations d'Hoteliers, Restaurateurs, et Cafetiers [*International Organization of Hotel and Restaurant Associations*] (EAIO)
**HORECOM**... International Exhibition for the Hotel and Restaurant Trades Communities (TSPED)
**HOREN**..... Horizontal Enlarger [*Photography*]
**HORI**......... Horizons [*A publication*]
**HOR INTERM**... Horis Intermediis [*In the Intermediate Hours*] [*Pharmacy*]
**HORIZ**...... Horizon (MSA)
**Horiz**.......... Horizons [*A publication*]
**HORIZ**...... Horizontal (AABC)
**HORIZ**...... Horizontal Polarization
**Horiz Biochem Biophys**... Horizons in Biochemistry and Biophysics [*A publication*]
**Horizons Bib Th**... Horizons in Biblical Theology [*A publication*]
**HORL**........ Home Office Reference Laboratory, Inc. [*NASDAQ symbol*] (NQ)
**HORM**...... Hybrid Orbital Rehybridization Method [*Atomic physics*]
**Horm Behav**... Hormones and Behavior [*A publication*]
**Horm Cell Regul**... Hormones and Cell Regulation [*A publication*]
**Hormel Inst Univ Minn Annu Rep**... Hormel Institute. University of Minnesota. Annual Report [*A publication*]
**Horm Metab Res**... Hormone and Metabolic Research [*A publication*]
**Horm Metab Res (Suppl)**... Hormone and Metabolic Research (Supplement) [*A publication*]
**Hormone Beh**... Hormones and Behavior [*A publication*]
**Hormone Met**... Hormone and Metabolic Research [*A publication*]
**Hormone Res**... Hormone Research [*A publication*]
**Horm Res**... Hormone Research [*A publication*]
**Horm Res (Basel)**... Hormone Research (Basel) [*A publication*]
**Horn Afr**..... Horn of Africa [*A publication*]
**Horn Bk**..... Horn Book Magazine [*A publication*]
**Horne Dip**... Horne on Diplomacy [*A publication*] (DLA)
**Horne Mir**... Horne's Mirror of Justice [*A publication*] (DLA)
**Horne MJ**... Horne's Mirror of Justice [*A publication*] (DLA)
**Horner**....... Horner's Reports [*11-23 South Dakota*] [*A publication*] (DLA)
**Horner's Ann St**... Horner's Annotated Revised Statutes [*Indiana*] [*A publication*] (DLA)
**Horner's Rev St**... Horner's Annotated Revised Statutes [*Indiana*] [*A publication*] (DLA)
**HORN GN**... Hornblende Gneisses [*Geology*]
**Horn & H**... Horn and Hurlstone's English Exchequer Reports [*1838-39*] [*A publication*] (DLA)
**Horo**.......... Horologium [*Constellation*]
**HOROL**..... Horology
**Horol J**....... Horological Journal [*A publication*]
**Horr & B Mun Ord**... Horr and Bemis' Treatise on Municipal Police Ordinances [*A publication*] (DLA)
**Horr & T Cas Self-Def**... Horrigan and Thompson's Cases on Self-Defense [*A publication*] (DLA)
**Horr & Th**... Horrigan and Thompson's Cases on Self-Defense [*A publication*] (DLA)
**HORS**........ [*The*] Kentucky Horse Center, Inc. [*NASDAQ symbol*] (NQ)
**HorsAb**...... Horseman's Abstracts [*A publication*]
**HORSE**..... Heavy Operational Repair Squadron Engineer [*Air Force*] (AFM)
**HORSE**..... Hydrofoil-Operated Rocket Submarine (NATG)
**HOR SOM**... Hora Somni [*At Bedtime*] [*Pharmacy*]
**Hort**........... Horticulture [*A publication*]
**HORT**........ Horticulture
**Hort**........... Horticulture News [*A publication*]
**Hort Abstr**... Horticultural Abstracts [*A publication*]
**Hor & Th Cas**... Horrigan and Thompson's Cases on Self-Defense [*A publication*] (DLA)
**HORTI**...... Horticulture [*Freight*]
**HORTIC**... Horticulture
**Hortic Abstr**... Horticultural Abstracts [*A publication*]
**Hortic Adv (Sahranpur)**... Horticultural Advance (Sahranpur) [*A publication*]
**Hortic Bull**... Horticultural Bulletin [*A publication*]
**Hortic Cent Loughgall Annu Rep**... Horticultural Centre Loughgall. Annual Report [*A publication*]
**Hortic Dig Univ Hawaii Coop Ext Serv**... Horticulture Digest. University of Hawaii. Cooperative Extension Service [*A publication*]
**Hortic Fr**.... Horticulture Francaise [*A publication*]
**Hortic Ind**.. Horticulture Industry [*A publication*]
**Hortic News NJ State Hortic Soc**... Horticultural News. New Jersey State Horticultural Society [*A publication*]
**Hortic NZ**.. Horticulture in New Zealand [*A publication*]
**Hortic Res**... Horticultural Research [*A publication*]
**Hortic Res Inst Ont Rep**... Horticultural Research Institute of Ontario. Report [*A publication*]
**Hortic Rev**... Horticultural Reviews [*A publication*]
**Hortic Sci (Calcutta)**... Horticultural Science (Calcutta) [*A publication*]
**Hortic Sci (Stuttg)**... Horticultural Science (Stuttgart) [*A publication*]
**Horticulture Ind**... Horticulture Industry [*A publication*]
**Hortic Vitic Sci (Sofia)**... Horticultural and Viticultural Sciences (Sofia) [*A publication*]
**Hort Mach Leafl**... Horticultural Machinery Leaflet [*A publication*]
**Hort N**........ Horticultural News [*A publication*]
**Hort Pl Breed**... Horticultural Plan Breeding [*A publication*]
**Hort Res**..... Horticultural Research [*A publication*]
**Hort Res (Edinb)**... Horticultural Research (Edinburgh) [*A publication*]
**Hort Res Rec**... Horticultural Research Record. New South Wales Department of Agriculture. Division of Horticulture [*A publication*] (APTA)
**HortSci**...... HortScience [*A publication*]
**HOR UN SPAT**... Horae Unius Spatio [*At the End of an Hour*] [*Pharmacy*]
**HOR UN SPATIO**... Horae Unius Spatio [*At the End of an Hour*] [*Pharmacy*] (ROG)
**Horw YB**.... Horwood's Year Books of Edward I [*A publication*] (DLA)
**HOS**........... [*Krantz*] Health Opinion Survey [*Research test*]
**HOS**........... Heat of Solution
**HOS**........... Heckscher-Ohlin-Samuelson [*Theorem*]
**HOS**........... High-Order Software [*Data processing*] (NASA)
**HOS**........... Holland Shipbuilding [*A publication*]
**HOS**........... Home Orchard Society (EA)
**HOS**........... Hooker Air Services Ltd. [*Gimli, MB*] [*FAA designator*] (FAAC)
**HoS**............ Horse Serum [*Immunology*]
**Hos**............ Hosea [*Old Testament book*]
**Hos**............ Hospitality [*A publication*]
**Hos**............ Hostiensis [*Deceased, 1271*] [*Authority cited in pre-1607 legal work*] (DSA)
**HOS**........... Human Operator Simulator (MCD)
**HOS**........... Human Osteosarcoma [*Medicine*]
**HOS**........... Hydrographic Office Scale [*Obsolete*]
**HOSA**........ Health Occupations Students of America (EA)
**HOSC**........ Hardened Operational Site Concept (AAG)
**HOSC**........ History of Science Cases
**HOSC**........ Huntsville Operations Support Center [*NASA*] (KSC)
**HOSCORP**... New York City Health and Hospitals Corporation (EA)
**Hosea**........ Hosea's Reports [*Ohio*] [*A publication*] (DLA)
**Hosea's Rep**... Cincinnati Superior Court Decisions [*Ohio*] [*A publication*] (DLA)
**Ho Sey Zs**.. Hoppe-Seyler's Zeitschrift fuer Physiologische Chemie [*A publication*]
**Hoshasen Kagaku Append**... Hoshasen Kagaku. Appendix [*Japan*] [*A publication*]
**HOSI**......... Handbook of Service Instructions
**HOSIA**...... Hospitals [*A publication*]
**Hosiery St**... Hosiery Statistics [*A publication*]
**HOSJ**......... Sovereign Hospitaller Order of Saint John (EA)
**Hoskins**...... Hoskins' Reports [*2 North Dakota*] [*A publication*] (DLA)
**HOSP**........ Hospital
**Hosp**........... Hospital [*A publication*]
**Hosp**........... Hospitalia [*A publication*]
**Hosp**........... Hospitalis [*A publication*]
**Hosp**........... Hospitality [*A publication*]
**Hosp**........... Hospitals [*A publication*]
**hosp**........... Hospodarsky [*Economic*] [*Czechoslovakian*]
**HOSP**........ Hosposable Products, Inc. [*Boundbrook, NJ*] [*NASDAQ symbol*] (NQ)
**HOSP**........ Hot Springs National Park
**HospAb**...... Hospital Abstracts [*A publication*]
**Hosp Abstr Serv**... Hospital Abstract Service [*A publication*]
**Hosp Adm Can**... Hospital Administration in Canada [*A publication*]
**Hosp Adm (Chicago)**... Hospital Administration (Chicago) [*A publication*]
**Hosp Admin**... Hospital Administration [*A publication*]
**Hosp Admin Curr**... Hospital Administration Currents [*A publication*]
**Hosp Admitting Mon**... Hospital Admitting Monthly [*A publication*]
**Hosp Adm (New Delhi)**... Hospital Administration (New Delhi) [*A publication*]
**Hosp Assoc J**... Hospitals' Association. Journal [*A publication*] (APTA)
**Hosp Bond Rev**... Hospital Bond Review [*A publication*]
**Hosp Build Bull**... Hospital Building Bulletin [*A publication*]
**Hosp Cap Finance (Chicago)**... Hospital Capital Finance (Chicago) [*A publication*]
**Hosp Care**... Hospital Care [*A publication*]
**Hosp Cent Mil (Lomas De Sotelo Mex) Publ Trimest**... Hospital Central Militar (Lomas De Sotelo, Mexico). Publicacion Trimestral [*A publication*]
**HOSPCO**.. Hospital Company [*Marine Corps*]
**Hosp Comm Psych**... Hospital and Community Psychiatry [*A publication*]
**Hosp Commun**... Hospital and Community Psychiatry [*A publication*]
**Hosp Community Psychiat**... Hospital and Community Psychiatry [*A publication*]
**Hosp Community Psychiatr**... Hospital and Community Psychiatry [*A publication*]
**Hosp Community Psychiatry**... Hospital and Community Psychiatry [*A publication*]
**Hosp Dev**... Hospital Development [*A publication*]
**Hosp Develop**... Hospital Development [*A publication*]

**Hosp Employee Health** ... Hospital Employee Health [*A publication*]
**Hosp Eng** ... Hospital Engineering [*A publication*]
**Hosp Equip Supplies** ... Hospital Equipment and Supplies [*A publication*]
**Hosp Financ Manage** ... Hospital Financial Management [*A publication*]
**Hosp Finan Manage** ... Hospital Financial Management [*A publication*]
**Hosp Fin Mgt** ... Hospital Financial Management [*A publication*]
**Hosp Food Nutr Focus** ... Hospital Food and Nutrition Focus [*A publication*]
**Hosp Formul** ... Hospital Formulary [*A publication*]
**Hosp Formul Manage** ... Hospital Formulary Management [*A publication*]
**Hosp Forum** ... Hospital Forum [*A publication*]
**Hosp Gen (Madr)** ... Hospital General (Madrid) [*A publication*]
**Hosp Gift Shop Manage** ... Hospital Gift Shop Management [*A publication*]
**Hosp and Health** ... Hospital and Health Services Administration [*A publication*]
**Hosp Health Care Newsl** ... Hospital Health Care Newsletter [*A publication*]
**Hosp Health Serv Adm** ... Hospital and Health Services Administration [*A publication*]
**Hosp Health Serv Admin** ... Hospital and Health Services Administration [*A publication*]
**Hosp Health Serv Rev** ... Hospital and Health Services Review [*A publication*]
**Hosp Hlth Care** ... Hospital and Health Care [*A publication*]
**Hosp Hlth Man** ... Hospital and Health Management [*A publication*]
**Hosp Hoje** ... Hospital de Hoje [*A publication*]
**Hosp-Hyg** .. Hospital-Hygiene [*A publication*]
**Hospice J** ... Hospice Journal [*A publication*]
**Hosp Infect Control** ... Hospital Infection Control [*A publication*]
**Hosp Int**..... Hospital International [*A publication*]
**Hospit Abstr** ... Hospital Abstracts [*A publication*]
**Hospital Admin** ... Hospital Administration [*A publication*] (APTA)
**Hospitality Educ** ... Hospitality Educator [*A publication*]
**Hospital Mag** ... Hospital Magazine [*A publication*] (APTA)
**Hospital Mus News** ... Hospital Music Newsletter [*A publication*]
**Hospital (Rio De J)** ... Hospital (Rio De Janeiro) [*A publication*]
**Hospit Lit Index** ... Hospital Literature Index [*A publication*]
**Hospit Manage Rev** ... Hospital Management Review [*A publication*]
**Hosp J**........ Hospice Journal [*A publication*]
**Hosp J**........ Hospital Journal [*A publication*]
**Hosp J Aust** ... Hospital Journal of Australia [*A publication*]
**Hosp Law Newsletter** ... Hospital Law Newsletter [*A publication*]
**Hosp Libr**... Hospital Libraries [*A publication*]
**Hosp Lit Ind** ... Hospital Literature Index [*A publication*]
**Hosp Manag** ... Hospital Management [*A publication*]
**Hosp Manage Commun** ... Hospital Management Communications [*A publication*]
**Hosp Manage Q** ... Hospital Management Quarterly [*A publication*]
**Hosp Manager** ... Hospital Manager [*A publication*]
**Hosp Mater Manage** ... Hospital Materials Management [*A publication*]
**Hosp Mater Manage Q** ... Hospital Materiel Management Quarterly [*A publication*]
**Hosp Med** ... Hospital Medicine [*A publication*]
**Hosp Med Staff** ... Hospital Medical Staff [*A publication*]
**Hosp Med Staff Advocate** ... Hospital Medical Staff Advocate [*A publication*]
**Hospos Zpr** ... Hospodarsky Zpravodaj [*A publication*]
**Hosp Peer Rev** ... Hospital Peer Review [*A publication*]
**Hosp Pharm** ... Hospital Pharmacist [*A publication*]
**Hosp Pharm** ... Hospital Pharmacy [*A publication*]
**Hosp Physician** ... Hospital Physician [*A publication*]
**Hosp Port**... Hospitais Portugueses [*A publication*]
**Hosp Pract** ... Hospital Practice [*A publication*]
**Hosp Practice** ... Hospital Practice [*A publication*]
**Hosp Prog** ... Hospital Progress [*A publication*]
**Hosp Progr** ... Hospital Progress [*A publication*]
**Hosp Purch Manage** ... Hospital Purchasing Management [*A publication*]
**HOSPRATS** ... Hospital Rations [*Navy*]
**Hosp Risk Manage** ... Hospital Risk Management [*A publication*]
**Hosp Secur Saf Manage** ... Hospital Security and Safety Management [*A publication*]
**Hosp Servidores Estado Rev Med** ... Hospital dos Servidores do Estado. Revista Medica [*A publication*]
**Hosp Superv** ... Hospital Supervision [*A publication*]
**Hosp Superv Bull** ... Hospital Supervisors Bulletin [*A publication*]
**Hosp Technol Ser** ... Hospital Technology Series [*A publication*]
**Hosp Top** ... Hospital Topics [*A publication*]
**Hosp Trib** .. Hospital Tribune [*A publication*]
**Hosp Trustee** ... Hospital Trustee [*A publication*]
**Hosp Vina Del Mar Bol Trimest** ... Hospital de Vina Del Mar. Boletin Trimestral [*A publication*]
**Hosp Week** ... Hospital Week [*A publication*]
**HOSS**........ Halo Orbit Space Station [*NASA*]
**HOSS**........ Homing Optical System Study
**HOSS**........ Hornbeck Offshore Services, Inc. [*NASDAQ symbol*] (NQ)
**HOSS**........ Hydrogen/Oxygen Second Stage (MCD)
**HOS-STPL** ... Hospital Operating System - Structured Programming Language [*Data processing*] (CSR)
**HOST**........ Amerihost Properties, Inc. [*NASDAQ symbol*] (NQ)
**HOST**........ Hawaii Ocean Science and Technology Park [*Research center*] (RCD)
**Host**........... Hostiensis [*Deceased, 1271*] [*Authority cited in pre-1607 legal work*] (DSA)
**HOST**........ Hostile
**HOST**........ Hypo-Osmotic Shock Treatment [*Analytical biochemistry*]
**HOSTEX**... Home Study Exchange (EA)
**HOSTF**...... Host Ventures Ltd. [*NASDAQ symbol*] (NQ)
**Hosti**.......... Hostiensis [*Deceased, 1271*] [*Authority cited in pre-1607 legal work*] (DSA)
**HOSTS**...... Hostess (ROG)
**HOSTWOY** ... Home of Selection and Completion of Travel within One Year Is Authorized [*Military*]
**HOT**.......... Hand Over Transmitter
**HOT**.......... HAT [*Hypoxanthine-Aminopterin-Thymidine*] with Ouabain [*Growth medium*] [*Biochemistry*]
**HOT**.......... High-Subsonic Optically Teleguided [*Antitank system*] (INF)
**HOT**.......... Holographic One-Tube [*Goggles*] (MCD)
**HOT**.......... Home on Target [*Military*] (CAAL)
**HOT**.......... Horizontal Output Transformer
**HOT**.......... Horizontal Output Tube
**HOT**.......... Hot Springs [*Arkansas*] [*Airport symbol*] (OAG)
**HOT**.......... Hotel Investors Trust SBI [*NYSE symbol*] (SPSG)
**Hot**............. [*Franciscus*] Hotomannus [*Deceased, 1590*] [*Authority cited in pre-1607 legal work*] (DSA)
**HOT**.......... Human Old Tuberculin
**HOTAC**..... Helicopter Optical Tracking and Control
**HOTAC**..... Hotel Accommodation Service [*British*]
**HOTAS**..... Hands on Throttle and Stick [*Aviation*] (MCD)
**HOTBUN** ... Have Not Yet Begun to Fight [*Simulated war game*]
**HOTCE**..... Hot Critical Experiments [*Nuclear energy*]
**HOTCOG** ... Heart of Texas Council of Governments
**HOTEF**..... Helicopter Operational Test and Evaluation Flight [*Canadian Navy*]
**Hotel Gaz SA** ... Hotel Gazette of South Australia [*A publication*] (APTA)
**Hotel Motel Manage** ... Hotel and Motel Management [*A publication*]
**Hotel & Motel Mgt** ... Hotel and Motel Management [*A publication*]
**Hotel Rest** ... Hotels and Restaurants International [*A publication*]
**HOTLIPS** ... Honorary Order of Trumpeters Living in Possible Sin
**Hoto**........... [*Franciscus*] Hotomannus [*Deceased, 1590*] [*Authority cited in pre-1607 legal work*] (DSA)
**HOTOA**.... Hospital Topics [*A publication*]
**HOTOL**..... Horizontal Takeoff and Landing [*Name of proposed aircraft under development by the British government*]
**Hotom**........ [*Franciscus*] Hotomannus [*Deceased, 1590*] [*Authority cited in pre-1607 legal work*] (DSA)
**Hotom De Verb Feud** ... Hotomannus. De Verbis Feudalibus [*A publication*] (DLA)
**HOTPHOTOREP** ... Hot Photographic Report (MCD)
**HOTRAN** ... Hover and Transition [*Simulator*]
**HOTS**........ Hands-On Training Simulator [*Vehicle*]
**HOTS**........ Higher Order Thinking Skills [*Education*]
**HOT-SHOT** ... Hydrogen-Oxygen Turbine: Super-High Operating Temperatures [*Hydrogen utilization technology*]
**HOTSIT**.... Hot Situation (MCD)
**HOU**.......... Houston [*Texas*] [*Seismograph station code, US Geological Survey*] (SEIS)
**HOU**.......... Houston [*Texas*] [*Airport symbol*]
**HOU**.......... Houston Industries, Inc. [*NYSE symbol*] (SPSG)
**Hou**............ Houston's Delaware Reports [*A publication*] (DLA)
**HOU**.......... United States Department of Housing and Urban Development, Washington, DC [*OCLC symbol*] (OCLC)
**Hou Ang Sax Law** ... Houard's Anglo-Saxon Laws, Etc. [*A publication*] (DLA)
**Houard Ang Sax Laws** ... Houard's Anglo-Saxon Laws [*A publication*] (DLA)
**Houches Ec Ete Phys Theor** ... Houches. Ecole d'Ete de Physique Theoretique [*A publication*]
**Houck Mech Lien** ... Houck on Mechanics' Lien Law [*A publication*] (DLA)
**Houck Riv** ... Houck on the Law of Navigable Rivers [*A publication*] (DLA)
**Hou Dict**.... Houard's Dictionary of the Customs of Normandy [*A publication*] (DLA)
**Hough Am Cons** ... Hough's American Constitutions [*A publication*] (DLA)
**Hough CM** ... Hough's Military Law and Courts-Martial [*A publication*] (DLA)
**Hough C-M Cas** ... Hough's Court-Martial Case Book [*1821*] [*London*] [*A publication*] (DLA)
**Houghton**... Houghton's Reports [*97 Alabama*] [*A publication*] (DLA)
**Hough V-Adm** ... Reports of Cases in Vice-Admiralty of Province of New York [*1715-88*] [*1925 Reprint*] [*A publication*] (DLA)
**Houil Blanc** ... Houille Blanche [*A publication*]
**Houille Bl**... Houille Blanche [*A publication*]
**Hou J Intl L** ... Houston Journal of International Law [*A publication*]
**Hou LR**...... Houston Law Review [*A publication*]
**HO Univ KY Coll Agr Coop Ext Serv** ... HO-University of Kentucky. College of Agriculture. Cooperative Extension Service [*A publication*]
**HOUS**........ Housing
**HOUS**........ Housing Division [*Census*] (OICC)
**Hous**........... Houston's Delaware Reports [*A publication*] (DLA)
**Hous Build Pl** ... Housing, Building, and Planning [*A publication*]
**Hous & Dev Rep** ... Housing and Development Reporter [*Bureau of National Affairs*] [*A publication*] (DLA)
**Hous & Dev Rep BNA** ... Housing and Development Reporter. Bureau of National Affairs [*A publication*]
**House B**..... House Beautiful [*A publication*]

**House Beautiful's Gard Outdoor Living** ... House Beautiful's Gardening and Outdoor Living [*United States*] [*A publication*]
**House Bldr** ... House Builder [*A publication*]
**House & G** ... House and Garden [*A publication*]
**House & Gard** ... House and Garden [*A publication*]
**House Garden Build Guide** ... House and Garden Building Guide [*United States*] [*A publication*]
**Household** ... Household and Personal Products Industry [*A publication*]
**HOUSE-INFO** ... Homeowners Using Savings and Energy Information to Negotiate Fair Offers [*Student legal action organization*] (EA)
**House of L** ... House of Lords Cases [*A publication*] (DLA)
**House Mag** ... House Magazine [*A publication*]
**House Words** ... Household Words [*A publication*]
**HOUSG**..... Housing
**HOUSHD** ... Household [*Marketing*] (ROG)
**Housing 80** ... Housing Industry, 1980-2000 [*A publication*]
**Housing Abs** ... Housing Abstracts [*A publication*]
**Housing Aust** ... Housing Australia [*A publication*]
**Housing & Constr Tech Bull** ... Housing and Construction Technical Bulletin [*A publication*] (APTA)
**Housing & Devel Rep** ... Housing and Development Reporter [*Bureau of National Affairs*] [*A publication*] (DLA)
**Housing Eur** ... Housing Europe [*A publication*]
**Housing Fin R** ... Housing Finance Review [*A publication*]
**Housing Mag** ... Housing Magazine [*A publication*] (APTA)
**Housing Mo** ... Housing Monthly [*A publication*]
**Housing Mthly** ... Housing Monthly [*A publication*]
**Housing and Planning Refs** ... Housing and Planning References [*A publication*]
**Housing Plann Refs** ... Housing and Planning References [*A publication*]
**Housing Plann Rev** ... Housing and Planning Review [*A publication*]
**Housing Rev** ... Housing Review [*A publication*]
**Housing Vic** ... Housing Victoria [*A publication*]
**Housing W Aust** ... Housing Western Australia [*A publication*]
**Hous J Intl L** ... Houston Journal of International Law [*A publication*]
**Hous Law**... Houston Lawyer [*A publication*] (DLA)
**Hous Life Ass** ... Houseman's Life Assurance [*9th ed.*] [*1977*] [*A publication*] (DLA)
**Hous L Rev** ... Houston Law Review [*A publication*]
**HousP**........ Housing and Planning References [*A publication*]
**Hous Pr**...... Housman's Precedents in Conveyancing [*1861*] [*A publication*] (DLA)
**Hous Res Pap** ... Housing Research Papers [*A publication*]
**Houst**......... Houston's Delaware Reports [*A publication*] (DLA)
**Houst Cr**.... Houston's Delaware Criminal Cases [*A publication*] (DLA)
**Houst Cr Cas** ... Houston's Delaware Criminal Cases [*A publication*] (DLA)
**Houst Crim Cas** ... Delaware Criminal Cases [*A publication*] (DLA)
**Houst Crim Cases** ... Delaware Criminal Cases [*A publication*] (DLA)
**Houst Crim (Del)** ... Houston's Delaware Criminal Cases [*A publication*] (DLA)
**Houst Crim Rep** ... Delaware Criminal Cases [*A publication*] (DLA)
**Houst Cr Rep** ... Delaware Criminal Cases [*A publication*] (DLA)
**Houst L Rev** ... Houston Law Review [*A publication*]
**Houstn Chr** ... Houston Chronicle [*A publication*]
**Houstn Mag** ... Houston Magazine [*A publication*]
**Houston** ..... Houston's Delaware Supreme Court Reports [*1855-93*] [*A publication*] (DLA)
**Houston BJ** ... Houston Business Journal [*A publication*]
**Houston Geol Soc Bull** ... Houston Geological Society. Bulletin [*A publication*]
**Houston J Int'l L** ... Houston Journal of International Law [*A publication*]
**Houston J M** ... Houston Journal of Mathematics [*A publication*]
**Houston J Math** ... Houston Journal of Mathematics [*A publication*]
**Houston Law** ... Houston Law Review [*A publication*]
**Houston Law** ... Houston Lawyer [*A publication*] (DLA)
**Houston L Rev** ... Houston Law Review [*A publication*]
**Houston Sym** ... Houston Symphony. Program Notes [*A publication*]
**Houst St Tr** ... Houston's Law of Stoppage in Transitu [*A publication*] (DLA)
**HOV**.......... Heat of Vaporization
**HOV**.......... High Occupancy Vehicle [*Commuter routes*] [*Acronym usually followed by a number indicating the minimum number of people per vehicle*]
**HOV**.......... Homogeneity of Variance [*Statistics*]
**Hov**............ Hovenden on Frauds [*A publication*] (DLA)
**Hov**............ Hovenden's Supplement to Vesey, Jr.'s, English Chancery Reports [*1789-1817*] [*A publication*] (DLA)
**HOV**.......... Hovercraft [*Military*] [*British*]
**HOV**.......... Hovnanian Enterprises, Inc. [*AMEX symbol*] (SPSG)
**HOV**.......... Orsta/Volda [*Norway*] [*Airport symbol*] (OAG)
**HOV**.......... United States Department of Housing and Urban Development, Region I, Boston, MA [*OCLC symbol*] (OCLC)
**HOV**.......... Wichita, KS [*Location identifier*] [*FAA*] (FAAL)
**Hov Ann**..... Hoveden's Annals [*A publication*] (DLA)
**Hov Craft Hydrof** ... Hovering Craft and Hydrofoil [*A publication*]
**HOVE**........ Hovenweep National Monument
**Hoved**......... Hoveden's Chronica [*A publication*] (DLA)
**Hovercr Wld** ... Hovercraft World [*A publication*]
**Hov Fr**......... Hovenden on Frauds [*A publication*] (DLA)
**HOVI**......... Handbook of Overhaul Instructions [*Navy*]
**HOVI**......... Hopewell Village National Historic Site
**HO Voice**... Hartford's Other Voice [*Superseded by Wild Raspberry*] [*A publication*]
**Hov Sup**..... Hovenden's Supplement to Vesey, Jr.'s, English Chancery Reports [*1789-1817*] [*A publication*] (DLA)
**Hov Supp**... Hovenden's Supplement to Vesey, Jr.'s, English Chancery Reports [*1789-1817*] [*A publication*] (DLA)
**HOVVAC** ... Hovering Vehicle Versatile Automatic Control
**HOW**......... Hand over Word
**HOW**......... Handicapped Organized Women [*In association name, HOW, Inc.*] (EA)
**HOW**......... Happiness of Womanhood [*Also known as LOH*] [*Inactive*]
**HOW**......... Healing Our World [*An association*]
**HOW**......... Hercules on Water [*Aircraft*] (MCD)
**HOW**......... Home Owners Warranty [*National Association of Home Builders*]
**How**........... Howard's New York Practice Reports [*A publication*] (DLA)
**How**........... Howard's Reports [*2-8 Mississippi*] [*A publication*] (DLA)
**How**........... Howard's United States Supreme Court Reports [*42-65 United States*] [*A publication*] (DLA)
**HOW**......... Howell Industries, Inc. [*AMEX symbol*] (SPSG)
**How**........... Howell's Reports [*22-26 Nevada*] [*A publication*] (DLA)
**HOW**......... Howitzer (KSC)
**HOW**......... Howrah [*India*] [*Seismograph station code, US Geological Survey*] (SEIS)
**How A Cas** ... Howard's New York Appeal Cases [*A publication*] (DLA)
**How Ann St** ... Howell's Annotated Statutes [*Michigan*] [*A publication*] (DLA)
**How App**.... Howard's New York Appeal Cases [*A publication*] (DLA)
**How App Cas** ... Howard's New York Court of Appeals Cases [*A publication*] (DLA)
**How App Cases** ... Howard's New York Court of Appeals Cases [*A publication*] (DLA)
**Howard**...... Howard's Mississippi Supreme Court Reports [*1834-43*] [*A publication*] (DLA)
**Howard Journal** ... Howard Journal of Penology and Crime Prevention [*A publication*]
**Howard J Penology Crime Prev** ... Howard Journal of Penology and Crime Prevention [*A publication*]
**Howard Law J** ... Howard Law Journal [*A publication*]
**Howard L J** ... Howard Law Journal [*A publication*]
**Howard Pr** ... Howard's New York Practice Reports [*A publication*] (DLA)
**Howard Pr Rep** ... Howard's New York Practice Reports [*A publication*] (DLA)
**Howard Rep** ... Howard's United States Supreme Court Reports [*A publication*] (DLA)
**Howard SC** ... United States Reports [*Vols. 42-65*] [*A publication*] (DLA)
**Howard's Prac Reports** ... Howard's New York Practice Reports [*A publication*] (DLA)
**Howard's Practice** ... Howard's New York Practice Reports [*A publication*] (DLA)
**Howard's Spec Term Rep** ... Howard's New York Practice Reports [*A publication*] (DLA)
**How & Beat** ... Howell and Beatty's Reports [*22 Nevada*] [*A publication*] (DLA)
**How C**........ Howard's Irish Chancery Practice [*A publication*] (DLA)
**How Cas**..... Howard's New York Court of Appeals Cases [*A publication*] (DLA)
**How Cas**..... Howard's Property Cases [*A publication*] (DLA)
**How Ch**...... Howard's Irish Chancery Practice [*A publication*] (DLA)
**How Ch P**... Howard's Irish Chancery Practice [*A publication*] (DLA)
**How Ch Pr** ... Howard's Irish Chancery Practice [*A publication*] (DLA)
**How Cr Tr** ... Howison's Virginia Criminal Trials [*A publication*] (DLA)
**How Ct App Cas** ... Howard's New York Court of Appeals Cases [*A publication*] (DLA)
**How EE**...... Howard's Irish Equity Exchequer Reports [*A publication*] (DLA)
**Howell NP** ... Howell's Nisi Prius Reports [*Michigan*] [*A publication*] (DLA)
**Howell St Tr** ... Howell's English State Trials [*1163-1820*] [*A publication*] (DLA)
**Howe Pr**..... Howe's Practice [*Massachusetts*] [*A publication*] (DLA)
**How Eq Exch** ... Howard's Irish Equity Exchequer Reports [*A publication*] (DLA)
**How Eval Health Programs** ... How to Evaluate Health Programs [*A publication*]
**How & H St** ... Howard and Hutchinson's Mississippi Statutes [*A publication*] (DLA)
**Howitt**........ Howitt's Journal [*A publication*]
**How J**......... Howard Journal [*A publication*] (DLA)
**How J Pen** ... Howard Journal of Penology and Crime Prevention [*A publication*]
**HOWL**........ Help Our Wolves Live
**How Law J** ... Howard Law Journal [*A publication*]
**How LJ**....... Howard Law Journal [*A publication*]
**How L Rev** ... Howard Law Review [*A publication*] (DLA)
**How & N**.... Howell and Norcross' Reports [*23, 24 Nevada*] [*A publication*] (DLA)
**How & Nor** ... Howell and Norcross' Reports [*23, 24 Nevada*] [*A publication*] (DLA)
**How NP (Mich)** ... Howell's Nisi Prius Reports [*Michigan*] [*A publication*] (DLA)

**How NS** ..... Howard's New York Practice Reports, New Series [*A publication*] (DLA)
**How (NY)** .. Howard's New York Practice Reports [*A publication*] (DLA)
**How Pat** ..... Howson on Patents [*A publication*] (DLA)
**How Po Ca** ... Howard's Property Cases [*A publication*] (DLA)
**How Po Cas** ... Howard's Irish Property Cases [*1720-73*] [*A publication*] (DLA)
**How Pr** ....... Howard's New York Practice Reports [*A publication*] (DLA)
**How Prac** ... Howard's New York Practice Reports [*A publication*] (DLA)
**How Prac NS** ... Howard's New York Practice Reports, New Series [*A publication*] (DLA)
**How Prac (NY)** ... Howard's New York Practice Reports [*A publication*] (DLA)
**How Prac Rep** ... Howard's New York Practice Reports [*A publication*] (DLA)
**How Pr NS** ... Howard's New York Practice Reports, New Series [*A publication*] (DLA)
**How Prob Pr** ... Howell's Probate Practice [*Ontario, Canada*] [*A publication*] (DLA)
**How Pr Rep** ... Howard's New York Practice Reports [*A publication*] (DLA)
**How Pr Sup C** ... Howard's New York Practice Reports [*A publication*] (DLA)
**HOWR** ...... However
**Howr** .......... Howitzer [*British military*] (DMA)
**How SC** ...... Howard's United States Supreme Court Reports [*A publication*] (DLA)
**Hows Pat** ... Howson on Patents [*A publication*] (DLA)
**HOWSR** .... Howsoever (ROG)
**Hows Reis Pat** ... Howson on Reissued Patents [*A publication*] (DLA)
**How St** ....... Howell's Annotated Statutes [*Michigan*] [*A publication*] (DLA)
**How State Tr** ... Howell's English State Trials [*1163-1820*] [*A publication*] (DLA)
**How St Tr** .. Howell's English State Trials [*1163-1820*] [*A publication*] (DLA)
**HOWT** ...... Howard Terminal [*Later, HT*] [*AAR code*]
**HOW-TO** .. Housing Operation with Training Opportunity [*Office of Economic Opportunity*]
**How US** ..... Howard's United States Supreme Court Reports [*A publication*] (DLA)
**HOX** .......... New Orleans, LA [*Location identifier*] [*FAA*] (FAAL)
**HOY** .......... Holland Schweiz [*A publication*]
**HOY** .......... Hoy Island [*Scotland*] [*Airport symbol*] [*Obsolete*] (OAG)
**Hoyt Comp L** ... Hoyt's Compiled Laws of Arizona [*A publication*] (DLA)
**HOYU** ....... Hospitality Yukon. Yukon Visitors Association [*A publication*]
**HOZ** .......... Horizontal
**HP** ............. ALAS, SA [*Uruguay*] [*ICAO designator*] (ICDA)
**HP** ............. All India Reporter, Himachal Pradesh [*A publication*] (DLA)
**HP** ............. Half Pay
**HP** ............. Half Plate [*Photography*]
**HP** ............. Half Price (ROG)
**HP** ............. Handicapped Person
**H-P** ............ Handley-Page Ltd.
**HP** ............. Handling Procedure (MCD)
**HP** ............. Handling and Propulsion (AAG)
**HP** ............. Handmade Paper
**Hp** ............. Haptoglobin [*Hematology*]
**HP** ............. Hard Plastic [*Doll collecting*]
**HP** ............. Hard Point
**HP** ............. Hardy Perennial [*Horticulture*] (ROG)
**HP** ............. Harmonic Progression
**Hp** ............. Harp [*Music*]
**HP** ............. Hauptpunkte [*Crystallography*]
**HP** ............. Haustus Purgans [*Purging Draught*] [*Pharmacy*] (ROG)
**HP** ............. Haut Parleur [*Loudspeaker*] [*French*]
**HP** ............. Hawker Siddeley Aviation Ltd. [*Great Britain*] [*ICAO aircraft manufacturer identifier*] (ICAO)
**HP** ............. Hay-Pasturage [*Agriculture*]
**HP** ............. Hazard Prevention [*A publication*] (EAAP)
**HP** ............. Head Postmaster [*British*] (DCTA)
**HP** ............. Headquarters Pamphlet [*Military*] (MCD)
**HP** ............. Health Physics [*Nuclear energy*] (NRCH)
**HP** ............. Healthcare Product
**HP** ............. Heating Plant (NATG)
**HP** ............. Heenan Petroleum Ltd. [*Toronto Stock Exchange symbol*]
**HP** ............. Height of Perigee
**HP** ............. Heir Presumptive
**HP** ............. Helicopter (NATG)
**HP** ............. Heliodor [*Record label*] [*Great Britain*]
**HP** ............. Hellas Planitia [*A filamentary mark on Mars*]
**HP** ............. Helmerich & Payne, Inc. [*NYSE symbol*] (SPSG)
**H/P** ............ Hemipelvectomy [*Medicine*]
**Hp** ............. Hemiplegia [*Medicine*]
**Hp** ............. Heptyl [*Biochemistry*]
**HP** ............. Hesperian Foundation (EA)
**HP** ............. Hewlett-Packard Co.
**HP** ............. High Pass [*Electronics*]
**HP** ............. High Performance
**H/P** ............ High Position (MDG)
**HP** ............. High-Positive (MDG)
**HP** ............. High-Potency [*Pharmacy*]
**HP** ............. High Power
**HP** ............. High Pressure
**HP** ............. High-Pressure Cylinder [*Especially, a locomotive cylinder*]
**HP** ............. High Priest
**HP** ............. High Priority
**HP** ............. High Protein [*Nutrition*]
**H-P** ............ High Purity
**HP** ............. Highest Possible (ROG)
**HP** ............. Highly Purified
**HP** ............. Hippocampal Pyramidal Cell [*Neuroanatomy*]
**HP** ............. Hire Purchase
**H & P** ......... History and Physical [*Examination*] [*Medicine*]
**HP** ............. Hit by Pitcher [*Baseball*]
**HP** ............. Holding Pattern [*Aviation*]
**HP** ............. Holding Pipette
**HP** ............. Holding Potential [*Neurophysiology*]
**HP** ............. Holiday Pay [*Army*] (AABC)
**HP** ............. Holiday Project (EA)
**HP** ............. Hollow Point Bullet
**HP** ............. Homeopathic Pharmacopoeia
**H & P** ......... Hopwood and Philbrick's English Election Cases [*1863-67*] [*A publication*] (DLA)
**HP** ............. Horizontal Parallax [*Navigation*]
**HP** ............. Horizontal Polarization
**HP** ............. Horsepower
**HP** ............. Hospital Participation [*Blood program*] [*Red Cross*]
**HP** ............. Host Processor
**HP** ............. Hot Pack [*or Pad*] [*Physical therapy*]
**HP** ............. Hot Pilot [*An egotistic flying cadet*] [*Slang*] [*Air Force*]
**HP** ............. Hot-Pressed [*Paper*]
**HP** ............. House Painter (ROG)
**HP** ............. House Physician
**HP** ............. Houses of Parliament [*British*]
**HP** ............. Human Plasma [*Hematology*]
**HP** ............. Humanist Party [*Australia*] [*Political party*]
**HP** ............. Humeral Plate [*Entomology*]
**HP** ............. Hundred Pounds
**HP** ............. Hunger Project (EA)
**HP** ............. Hydrogen Purge (MCD)
**HP** ............. Hydrostatic Pressure
**HP** ............. Hydroxyproline [*An amino acid*]
**HP** ............. Hyperparathyroidism [*or Hyperthyroidism*] [*Endocrinology*]
**HP** ............. Hyperphoria
**HP** ............. Hyperpolarization
**HP** ............. Hypersensitivity Pneumonitis [*Medicine*]
**HP** ............. Hypertension and Proteinuria [*Medicine*]
**HP** ............. Hypertransfused Polycythemic [*Medicine*]
**HP** ............. Hysterical Personality
**HP** ............. Panama [*Aircraft nationality and registration mark*] (FAAC)
**HP** ............. Perigee Altitude (NASA)
**HP** ............. Smith & Nephew Pharmaceuticals Ltd. [*Great Britain*] [*Research code symbol*]
**HPA** .......... Head Post Assembly
**HPA** .......... Head Postmen's Association [*A union*] [*British*]
**HPA** .......... Head of a Procuring Activity [*Army*] (AABC)
**HPA** .......... Helvetica Paediatrica Acta [*A publication*]
**HPA** .......... Heteropoly Acid [*Inorganic chemistry*]
**HPA** .......... Heuristic Path Algorithm
**HPA** .......... High-Power Amplifier
**HPA** .......... High-Pressure Air
**HPA** .......... Historical Preservation of America [*Publisher*] (EA)
**HPA** .......... Holding and Positioning Aid (IEEE)
**HPA** .......... Horizontal Planar Array (CAAL)
**HPA** .......... Hospital Physicians Association [*British*]
**HPA** .......... Hurlingham Polo Association [*Midhurst, Sussex, England*] (EAIO)
**HPA** .......... Hybridization Protection Assay [*Analytical biochemistry*]
**HPA** .......... Hydraulic Pneumatic Area (AAG)
**HPA** .......... Hydroxypropyl Acrylate [*Organic chemistry*]
**HPA** .......... Hypothalamic-Pituitary-Adrenocortical [*Endocrinology*]
**HPA** .......... Lifuka [*Tonga Islands*] [*Airport symbol*] (OAG)
**HPAA** ........ High-Pressure Air Accumulator
**HPAA** ........ Hispanic Public Affairs Association (EA)
**HPAAA** ..... Helvetica Paediatrica Acta [*A publication*]
**HPAAS** ...... High-Performance Aerial Attack System (MCD)
**HPA Bull** ... HPA [*Hospital Physicists Association*] Bulletin [*England*] [*A publication*]
**HPAC** ........ Health Policy Advisory Center (EA)
**HPAC** ........ High-Performance Affinity Chromatography
**HPAC** ........ High-Pressure Air Compressor (NVT)
**HPAC** ........ Hydropress Accessory [*Tool*] (AAG)
**HPACA** ..... Helvetica Physica Acta [*A publication*]
**HPAF** ........ Hydraulic Performance Analysis Facility (MCD)
**HPAG** ........ High-Performance Air-to-Ground
**HPAH** ........ Hydroxy Polycyclic Aromatic Hydrocarbon [*Environmental chemistry*]
**HPAL** ........ High Plains Agriculture Laboratory [*University of Nebraska - Lincoln*] [*Research center*] (RCD)
**HPANAJ** ... Handbuch der Pflanzenanatomie [*Encyclopedia of Plant Anatomy*] [*A publication*]

**HPANH** .... Hydroxy Polycyclic Aromatic Nitrogen Heterocycle [*Environmental chemistry*]
**HPAOA** ..... Heating, Piping, and Air Conditioning [*A publication*]
**HPAR** ........ Air-Resistance Horsepower [*Automotive engineering*]
**HPAS** ........ High-Performance Adhesive System
**HPASA** ...... Helvetica Physiologica et Pharmacologica Acta. Supplementum [*A publication*]
**HPASH** ..... Hydroxy Polycyclic Aromatic Sulfur Heterocycle [*Environmental chemistry*]
**HPB** .......... Hand-Printed Books
**HPB** .......... Handmaids of the Precious Blood [*Roman Catholic religious order*]
**HPB** .......... Harbor Patrol Boat
**HPB** .......... Helena Petrovna Blavatsky [*Famous 19th-century occultist*]
**HPB** .......... High-Probability Behavior
**HPB** .......... Hinged Plotting Board
**HPB** .......... Historisch-Politische Blaetter fuer das Katholische Deutschland [*A publication*]
**HPB** .......... Historisch-Politisches Buch [*A publication*]
**HPB** .......... Hooper Bay [*Alaska*] [*Airport symbol*] (OAG)
**HPBC** ........ Home Port Bancorp, Inc. [*NASDAQ symbol*] (CTT)
**HPBC** ........ Hyperpolarizing Bipolar Cell [*In the retina*]
**HPBKD** ..... Historisch-Politische Blaetter fuer das Katholische Deutschland [*A publication*]
**HPBL** ......... Historisch-Politische Blaetter fuer das Katholische Deutschland [*A publication*]
**HPBL** ......... Human Peripheral Blood Leukocyte
**HPBN** ........ Hot-Pressed Boron Nitride [*Materials science and technology*]
**HPBW** ....... Half-Power Beamwidth [*or Bandwidth*] (IEEE)
**HPC** .......... Hale's Pleas of the Crown [*England*] [*A publication*] (DLA)
**HPC** .......... Hawkins' Pleas of the Crown [*England*] [*A publication*] (DLA)
**HPC** .......... Health Physics Center [*Nuclear energy*] (NRCH)
**HPC** .......... Health Policy Council (EA)
**HPC** .......... Helicopter Performance Computer (NG)
**HPC** .......... Helicopter Plane Commander
**HPC** .......... Hematopoietic Progenitor Cell [*Hematology*]
**HPC** .......... Hemipalmitoylcarnitinium [*Biochemistry*]
**HPC** .......... Hemisphere Publishing Company
**HPC** .......... Hercules, Inc. [*Formerly, Hercules Powder Co.*] [*NYSE symbol*] (SPSG)
**HPC** .......... High Point College [*North Carolina*]
**HPC** .......... Hippocampal Pyramidal Cell [*Neuroanatomy*]
**HPC** .......... Hippocampus [*Brain anatomy*]
**HPC** .......... Home Policy Committee of War Cabinet [*British*] [*World War II*]
**HPC** .......... Hope, AR [*Location identifier*] [*FAA*] (FAAL)
**HPC** .......... Hot Pipe Chase [*Nuclear energy*] (NRCH)
**HPC** .......... Howard Payne College [*Texas*]
**HPC** .......... Hydraulic Package Container
**HPC** .......... Hydraulic Piston Corer
**HPC** .......... Hydroxyphenylcinchoninic Acid [*Pharmacology*]
**HPC** .......... Hydroxypropylcellulose [*Organic chemistry*]
**HPCA** ........ High-Performance Communications Adapter
**HPCA** ........ Hiroshima Peace Center Associates [*Defunct*] (EA)
**HPCBR** ...... High-Pressure Chamber
**HPCC** ........ High-Performance Control Center [*Aerospace*] (AAG)
**HPCCEY** ... Handbook of Plant Cell Culture [*A publication*]
**HPCE** ........ High-Performance Capillary Electrophoresis [*Analytical biochemistry*]
**HPCGS** ...... [*Frank-Massy*] Household Purchasing Characteristics Generating System [*Marketing*]
**HPCHD** ..... Harpsichord [*Music*]
**HPCI** ......... High-Pressure Coolant Injection [*Nuclear energy*] (NRCH)
**HPCIS** ....... High-Pressure Coolant Injection System [*Nuclear energy*] (NRCH)
**HPcL** ......... Leeward Community College, Pearl City, HI [*Library symbol*] [*Library of Congress*] (LCLS)
**HPCM** ....... Human Placenta Conditioned Medium
**HPCPC** ...... High-Performance Centrifugal Partition Chromatography
**HPCQA** ..... Human Pathology [*A publication*]
**HPCRB** ...... Hydraulic Power Control Relay Box
**HPCS** ......... High-Pressure Core Spray [*Nuclear energy*] (NRCH)
**HPCUS** ...... Homeopathic Pharmacopoeia Convention of the United States
**HPD** .......... Haloperidol [*Tranquilizer*]
**HPD** .......... Hammerson Properties Investment & Development Corp. PLC [*Toronto Stock Exchange symbol*]
**HPD** .......... Hard Point Defense
**HPD** .......... Harpsichord [*A publication*]
**HPD** .......... Hearing Protection Device
**HPD** .......... Hematoporphyrin Derivative [*Antineoplastic compound*]
**HPD** .......... High-Performance Drone
**HPD** .......... High-Power Density
**HPD** .......... High-Protein Diet
**HPD** .......... Horizontal Polar Diagram
**H-PD** ......... Hough-Powell Digitizer
**HPD** .......... Hourly Precipitation Data [*A publication*]
**HPD** .......... Hydraulic Pump Discharge (AAG)
**HPDC** ........ High Pressure Data Center [*National Institute of Standards and Technology*] [*Information service or system*] (IID)
**HPDF** ........ High-Performance Demonstration Facility
**HPDGF** ..... Human Platelet-Derived Growth Factor [*Biochemistry*]
**HP-DHA** ... High-Purity Dual Hardness Armor (KSC)
**HPDI** ......... Hard Point Defense Interceptor
**HPDLRL** ... High-Power Diffraction Limited Raman LASER
**HPDP** ........ Hispanic Policy Development Project (EA)
**HPDPI** ....... Health Promotion and Disease Prevention Initiative [*Pronounced "hippy dippy"*] [*Department of Health and Human Services*]
**HpD-PT** ..... Hepatoporphyrin Derivative-Phototherapy [*Medicine*]
**HPDS** ........ Hard Point Defense System
**HPDT** ........ Handicapped Persons Discrimination Board [*South Australia*]
**HPE** .......... High-Power Effects [*Radio interference*]
**HPE** .......... History and Physical Examination [*Medicine*]
**HPE** .......... History of Political Economy [*A publication*]
**HPE** .......... Human Proenkephalin [*Biochemistry*]
**HPE** .......... Hydrogenous Polyethylene
**HPE** .......... Inomeni Parataksis Ethnikofronon [*United Front of Nationalists*] [*Political party*] (PPE)
**HPEK** ........ Paul B. Elder Co. [*Research code symbol*]
**HPEN** ........ PEN Hongrois [*A publication*]
**HPEO** ........ Protonous Poly(ethylene oxide) [*Organic chemistry*]
**HPER** ........ Hastings and Prince Edward Regiment [*British military*] (DMA)
**HPER** ........ Health, Physical Education, and Recreation
**HPETE** ...... Hydroxyperoxyeicosatetraenoic Acid [*Biochemistry*]
**HPEW** ....... High-Powered Early Warning (NATG)
**HPF** .......... Hammond, LA [*Location identifier*] [*FAA*] (FAAL)
**HPF** .......... Harbor Patrol Fleet
**HPF** .......... Heat Pipe Furnace
**HPF** .......... High Pass Filter
**HPF** .......... High-Power Field [*Microscopy*]
**HPF** .......... High-Protein Fraction [*Food technology*]
**HPF** .......... Highest Possible [*or Probable*] Frequency [*Electronics*]
**HPF** .......... Historic Preservation Fund [*National Trust for Historic Preservation*]
**HPF** .......... Historic Pullman Foundation (EA)
**HPF** .......... Horizontal Processing Facility [*Operation and Checkout*] [*NASA*] (NASA)
**HPFC** ......... High-Performance Fuel Cell
**HPFH** ........ Hereditary Persistence of Fetal Hemoglobin [*Hematology*]
**HPFL** ......... High-Performance Fuels Laboratory
**HPFL** ......... Highpass Filter (MSA)
**HPFL** ......... Holly Park Field Laboratory [*University of Nevada - Reno*] [*Research center*] (RCD)
**HPFM** ....... Hydropress Form [*Tool*] (AAG)
**HPFP** ......... High-Pressure Fire Protection (NRCH)
**HPFP** ......... High-Pressure Fuel Pump (KSC)
**HPFS** ......... High-Performance File System [*Data processing*]
**HPFT** ......... High-Pressure Fuel Turbopump (MCD)
**HPFTP** ...... High-Pressure Fuel Turbopump (NASA)
**HPG** .......... Harvard Presentation Graphics [*Software Publishing Corp.*] [*Computer software*]
**HPG** .......... High-Power Generator
**HPG** .......... High-Power Group
**HPG** .......... High-Pressure Gas (KSC)
**HPG** .......... Homopolar Generator [*To power high-technology experiments*]
**HPG** .......... Human Pituitary Gonadotrophin [*Endocrinology*]
**HPG** .......... Hydroxypropyl Guar [*Organic chemistry*]
**HPG** .......... Hyperpure Germanium [*Also, HpGe*] [*Chemistry*]
**HPG** .......... Hypothalamic, Pituitary, Gonadal [*Endocrinology*]
**HPGC** ........ Heading per Gyro Compass [*Navigation*]
**HPGC** ........ Hypopressure Gas Chromatography
**HpGe** ......... Hyperpure Germanium [*Also, HPG*] [*Chemistry*]
**HPGF** ........ Hybridoma/Plasmacytome Growth Factor [*Biochemistry*]
**HPGL** ......... Gross Load Horsepower [*Automotive engineering*]
**HPGL** ......... Hewlett-Packard Graphics Language
**HPGPM** .... Hits per Gun per Minute (NVT)
**hpGRF** ...... Human Pancreas Growth Hormone-Releasing Factor [*Immunochemistry*]
**HPGS** ........ High-Pressure Gas System (NASA)
**HPH** .......... Harnischfeger Industries, Inc. [*NYSE symbol*] (SPSG)
**HPH** .......... High-Performance Hoist (MCD)
**HPH** .......... High-Pressure Hose
**HPH** .......... Horsepower-Hour
**HPHAD** ..... Han'guk Pusik Hakhoechi [*A publication*]
**HPHBA** ..... Harvard Public Health Alumni Bulletin [*A publication*]
**HPHD** ....... High-Pressure High-Density
**HP-HR** ...... Horsepower-Hour
**H Phys Pharm A** ... Helvetica Physiologica et Pharmacologica Acta [*A publication*]
**HPI** ............ Cleveland, OH [*Location identifier*] [*FAA*] (FAAL)
**HPI** ............ Handicap Problems Inventory [*Psychology*]
**HPI** ............ Hardwood Plywood Institute [*Later, HPMA*] (EA)
**HPI** ............ Heavy Positive Ion
**HPI** ............ Heifer Project International (EA)
**HPI** ............ Height-Position Indicator (DEN)
**HPI** ............ High-Performance Insulation (MCD)
**HPI** ............ High-Power Illuminator (NATG)
**HPI** ............ High-Pressure Injection [*Nuclear energy*] (NRCH)
**HPI** ............ History of Present Illness
**HPI** ............ Hochschulpolitische Informationen [*A publication*]
**HPI** ............ Holland in South East Asia [*A publication*]

**HPI** ........... Homing Position Indicator (NATG)
**HPI** ........... Howe Peak [*Idaho*] [*Seismograph station code, US Geological Survey*] (SEIS)
**HPI** ........... Hull Product Improvement [*Navy*] (CAAL)
**HPI** ........... Human Productivity Institute (EA)
**HPI** ........... Hydraulic Pressure Indicator
**HPI** ........... Hydrocarbon Processing Industry
**HP-IB** ........ Hewlett-Packard Interface Bus [*Instrumentation*]
**HPIC** ......... Hearing Performance Inventory for Children
**HPIC** ......... High-Performance Immunoaffinity Chromatography
**HPIEC** ....... High-Performance Ion Exchange Chromatography
**HPIEC** ....... High-Pressure Ion Exchange Chromatography
**HPIP** ......... High-Pressure Intensifier Pump
**HPIR** ......... High-Power Illuminator RADAR [*Army*] (AABC)
**HPIR** ......... High-Probability-of-Intercept Receiver [*Telecommunications*] (IEEE)
**HPIS** ......... High-Performance Insulation System
**HPIS** ......... High-Pressure Injection System [*Nuclear energy*] (NRCH)
**HPISS** ....... High-Power Illuminator Signal Source (MCD)
**HPIT** ......... High-Performance Infiltrating Technique [*Materials science*]
**HPJ** ........... High-Power Jammer
**HPJ** ........... High-Pressure Jet
**HPJ** ........... HP [*Heilpraktiker*] Journal [*A publication*]
**HPJ** ........... HP [*Hewlett-Packard*] Journal [*A publication*]
**HPJC** ......... Highland Park Junior College [*Later, Highland Park College*] [*Michigan*]
**HPK** ........... High-Power Klystron
**HPK** ........... Honorary Physician to the King [*British*]
**HPKA** ........ High-Power Klystron Amplifier
**HPKMB** .... Hieratische Papyrus aus den Koeniglichen Museen zu Berlin [*A publication*] (BJA)
**HP Kurier** .. HP [*Heilpraktiker*] Kurier [*A publication*]
**HPKYA** ..... Harbin Gongye Daxue Xuebao [*A publication*]
**HPL** ........... Hamilton Public Library [*UTLAS symbol*]
**HPL** ........... Hartford Public Library, Hartford, CT [*OCLC symbol*] (OCLC)
**HPL** ........... High Polar Latitude [*Geophysics*]
**HPL** ........... High-Power LASER
**HPL** ........... Human Parotid Lysozyme [*An enzyme*]
**HPL** ........... Human Performance Laboratory [*Ball State University*] [*Research center*] (RCD)
**HPL** ........... Human Peripheral Lymphocyte
**HPL** ........... Human Placental Lactogen [*Also, CGP, HCS*] [*Endocrinology*]
**HPL** ........... Hybrid Programming Language [*Data processing*]
**HPL** ........... Nucla, CO [*Location identifier*] [*FAA*] (FAAL)
**HPLAC** ...... High-Performance Liquid Affinity Chromatography
**HPLAP** ...... Human Placental Alkaline Phosphatase [*An enzyme*]
**HPLC** ........ High-Performance [*or High-Pressure*] Liquid Chromatography
**HPLF** ......... High-Pressure Low-Flow
**HPLF** ......... Hydrolyzed Polar Lipid Fraction [*Biochemistry*]
**HPLJ** ......... High-Pressure Liquid Jet
**HP/LP** ....... High-Power/Low-Power
**HPLPC** ...... High-Performance Low-Pressure Chromatography
**HPLR** ......... Hinge Pillar [*Technical drawings*]
**HPLSDO** ... History and Philosophy of the Life Sciences. Pubblicazioni della Stazione Zoologica di Napoli. Section II [*A publication*]
**HPLX** ........ Healthplex, Inc. [*Uniondale, NY*] [*NASDAQ symbol*] (NQ)
**HPM** .......... Head Position Monitor
**HPM** .......... Head Positioning Mechanism
**HPM** .......... Head Postmaster's Manual [*British*] (DCTA)
**HPM** .......... High-Polymer Molecular [*Film*]
**HPM** .......... High-Power Microwave
**HPM** .......... High-Priority Mail (TSSD)
**HPM** .......... Horizontal Panel Mount
**HPM** .......... Human Potential Movement [*Psychotherapy*]
**HPM** .......... Hydraulic Punching Machine
**HPMA** ....... Hardwood Plywood Manufacturers Association [*Reston, VA*] (EA)
**HPMA** ....... High-Power Microwave Assembly (AAG)
**HPMA** ....... Hydroxypropyl Methacrylate [*Organic chemistry*]
**HPMC** ....... Housing Production and Management Credit [*HUD*]
**HPMC** ....... Hydroxypropyl(methyl)cellulose [*Synthetic food gum*] [*Organic chemistry*]
**Hp Mi** ........ Hippias Minor [*of Plato*] [*Classical studies*] (OCD)
**HPMNJ** .... High-Power Microelectronic Noise Jammer
**HPMSK** ..... High-Priority Mission Support Kit [*Military*] (AFIT)
**HPMV** ....... High-Pressure Mercury Vapor
**HPN** .......... Harrison, Purchase, and North Castle [*Airport*]
**HPN** .......... Haustus Purgans Noster [*Purging Draught from the Doctor's Own Prescription*] [*Pharmacy*] (ROG)
**HPN** .......... Health Physics Network [*Nuclear energy*] (NRCH)
**HPN** .......... Heavy Primary Nuclei
**HPN** .......... High Pass Network
**HPN** .......... Horsepower Nominal
**HPN** .......... Hydrogenation of Pyrolysis Naphtha [*Petroleum refining*]
**HPN** .......... Hydroxypropyl Nitrate [*Organic chemistry*]
**HPN** .......... Hypertension [*Medicine*]
**HPN** .......... White Plains [*New York*] [*Airport symbol*] (OAG)
**HPND** ........ Human Pronatriodilatin [*Endocrinology*]
**HPN Hosp Purch News** ... HPN. Hospital Purchasing News [*A publication*]
**HPNJ** ......... High-Power Noise Jammer
**HPNS** ......... High-Pressure Nervous Syndrome [*Deep-sea diving*]
**HPNS** ......... Hunters Point Naval Shipyard
**HPO** ........... Head Post Office
**HPO** ........... High-Pressure Oxygen [*Also, HBO, OHP*]
**HPO** ........... Highway Post Office [*Bus or truck equipped with mail distribution facilities*]
**HPO** ........... Home Port [*Navy*] (NVT)
**HPO** ........... Hourly Postflight (MCD)
**HPO** ........... Hydrogenated Palm Oil
**HPO** ........... Hydroxylamine Phosphate Oxime [*Organic chemistry*]
**HPOC** ........ High Plains Oil Corporation [*Denver, CO*] [*NASDAQ symbol*] (NQ)
**HPOD** ........ Hydroperoxyoctadecadienoic Acid [*Organic chemistry*]
**HPOF** ........ High-Pressure Oil-Filled [*Cable*]
**H Points** ..... High Points [*A publication*]
**HPOP** ........ High-Pressure Oxidizer Pump (NASA)
**HPOQ** ....... Health Policy Quarterly [*A publication*]
**HPOT** ........ Helipotentiometer
**HPOT** ........ High-Pressure Oxidizer Turbopump (MCD)
**HPOT** ........ Hydroperoxyoctadecatrienoic Acid [*Organic chemistry*]
**HPOTP** ..... High-Pressure Oxidizer Turbopump
**HPOX** ........ High-Pressure Oxygen (AFM)
**HPP** ........... Half Page Printer
**HPP** ........... Harvard Project Physics
**HPP** ........... Health Physics Program (NRCH)
**HPP** ........... Hepp [*Alaska*] [*Seismograph station code, US Geological Survey*] (SEIS)
**HPP** ........... Hereditary Pyropoikilocytosis [*Medicine*]
**HPP** ........... Hernieuwde Progressieve Partij [*Renewed Progressive Party*] [*Surinam*] [*Political party*] (PPW)
**HPP** ........... Holding under Promise of Payment
**HPP** ........... Hot Processing Plant [*Nuclear energy*]
**HPP** ........... Human Pancreatic Polypeptide [*Endocrinology*]
**HPP** ........... Hydraulic Pneumatic Panel (AAG)
**HPP** ........... Hydroxyphenyl Pyruvate [*Organic chemistry*]
**HPP** ........... Hydroxypyrazolopyrimidine [*Allopurinol*] [*Antineoplastic drug*]
**HPPA** ........ Hydroxyphenylpyruvic Acid [*Organic chemistry*]
**HPPAA** ..... Helvetica Physiologica et Pharmacologica Acta [*A publication*]
**HPPF** ......... Horizontal Payloads Processing Facility (MCD)
**HPPI** .......... High-Performance Parallel Interface [*Data processing*]
**HPPIDE** ..... Health and Population Perspectives and Issues [*A publication*]
**HPPLC** ...... High-Performance Preparative Liquid Chromatography
**HPPM** ....... High-Performance Propulsion Module (MCD)
**HPPP** ........ High-Priority Production Program [*NATO*] (NATG)
**HPPR** ........ Hydroxypyrazolopyrimidine Ribonucleoside [*Biochemistry*]
**HPPRA** ...... Hydrocarbon Processing and Petroleum Refiner [*Later, Hydrocarbon Processing*] [*A publication*]
**HPPS** ......... Hughes Post Processor, Surveyor
**HPPTS** ...... Hydraulic Package Pressure Test Set
**HPR** ........... Hardware Problem Report (MCD)
**HPR** ........... Harper & Row Publishers, Inc. [*NYSE symbol*] (SPSG)
**HPR** ........... Heart Profile Recorder [*Medicine*]
**HPR** ........... Heat Pipe Reactor
**HPR** ........... Hic Pace Requiescat [*May He Here Rest in Peace*] [*Latin*] (ROG)
**HPR** ........... High-Polymer Rheology
**HPR** ........... High-Powered RADAR (NATG)
**HPR** ........... Highly Protected Risk [*Insurance*]
**HPR** ........... Homiletic and Pastoral Review [*A publication*]
**HPR** ........... Hopper [*Freight*]
**HPR** ........... Horsepower
**HPR** ........... Host-Plant Resistance [*Entomology, phytochemistry*]
**HPR** ........... Housing and Planning References [*A publication*]
**HPR** ........... Howard's New York Practice Reports [*A publication*] (DLA)
**HPr** ........... Howard's New York Practice Reports, New Series [*A publication*] (DLA)
**HPR** ........... Hughes Photoelectric Reader
**HPR** ........... Human Performance Reliability
**HPR** ........... Human Progesterone Receptor [*Endocrinology*]
**HPR** ........... Human Prolactin [*Endocrinology*]
**HPR** ........... Hydrogen Pressure Regulator (MCD)
**HPR** ........... Hydroxyphenylretinamide [*Biochemistry*]
**HPR** ........... Hyperion Resources [*Vancouver Stock Exchange symbol*]
**HPRF** ......... High Pulse Recurrence Frequency (MCD)
**HPRF** ......... Hypersonic Propulsion Research Facility
**HPRL** ........ Human Performance Research Laboratory [*University of Utah*] [*Research center*] (RCD)
**HPRL** ........ Human Prolactin [*Endocrinology*]
**HPRM** ....... Health Promotion Monographs [*A publication*]
**HPRP** ........ High-Performance Reporting Post (NATG)
**HPRP** ........ High-Powered RADAR Post (NATG)
**HPRPC** ...... High-Performance Reversed Phase Chromatography
**HPRR** ........ Health Physics Research Reactor [*Oak Ridge, TN*] [*Oak Ridge National Laboratory*] [*Department of Energy*]
**HPRS** ......... High-Pressure Recirculation System [*Nuclear energy*] (NRCH)
**HPRS** ......... Hopkins Psychiatric Rating Scale [*Personality development test*] [*Psychology*]
**HPRS** ......... Houghton Poultry Research Station [*British*] (ARC)
**HPRT** ........ Hypoxanthine Phosphoribosyltransferase [*Also, HGPRT*] [*An enzyme*]

**HPRV** ........ High-Pressure Relief Valve (KSC)
**HPS** .......... Antisubmarine Helicopter (NATG)
**HPS** .......... Crown Aviation, Inc. [*Texico, NM*] [*FAA designator*] (FAAC)
**HPS** .......... Haitian Philatelic Society (EA)
**HPS** .......... Hamburger Philologische Studien [*A publication*]
**HPS** .......... Handbook of Paper Science [*Elsevier Book Series*] [*A publication*]
**HPS** .......... Hanford Plant Standard [*Formerly, HWS*] [*Nuclear energy*] (NRCH)
**HPS** .......... Hanna Pacific [*Vancouver Stock Exchange symbol*]
**HPS** .......... Hardened Power System
**HPS** .......... Hardy Plant Society (EAIO)
**HPS** .......... Hazardous Polluting Substances [*Shipping*] (DCTA)
**HPS** .......... Health Physics Society (EA)
**HPS** .......... Health Physics Station [*Nuclear energy*] (NRCH)
**HPS** .......... Heat Protection System
**HPS** .......... Helium Pressure Switch (MCD)
**HPS** .......... Hermansky-Pudlak Syndrome [*Medicine*]
**HPS** .......... Hermetic Pivoting Seal
**HPS** .......... Hidden Predictive Saccades [*Ophthalmology*]
**HPS** .......... High-Pressure Separator [*Chemical engineering*]
**HPS** .......... High-Pressure Sintering [*Ceramic technology*]
**HPS** .......... High-Pressure Sodium
**HPS** .......... High-Pressure Steam [*Technical drawings*]
**HPS** .......... High-Protein Supplement [*Nutrition*]
**HPS** .......... Highest Points Scored (ROG)
**HPS** .......... Hospitalization Proneness Scale [*Psychometrics*]
**HPS** .......... Hull Pressure Switch
**HPS** .......... Hybrid Propulsion System
**HPS** .......... Hydraulic Power Section [*Later, HPU*] (AAG)
**HPS** .......... Hydraulic Power Supply
**HPS** .......... Hydraulic Power System (KSC)
**HPS** .......... Hypertrophic Pyloric Stenosis [*Medicine*]
**HPSA** ........ Hellenic Philatelic Society of America (EA)
**HPSA** ........ Honors Program Student Association of the American Sociological Association (EA)
**HPSA** ........ Hydraulic Package Servovalve Actuator
**HPSC** ........ Heading per Standard Compass [*Navigation*]
**HPSC** ........ Health Programs Systems Center
**HPSC** ........ HPSC, Inc. [*NASDAQ symbol*] (NQ)
**HPSC** ........ Hydraulic Package Storage Container
**HPSCI** ....... House Permanent Select Committee on Intelligence (MCD)
**HPSD** ........ High-Power Switching Device
**HPSEC** ...... High-Performance Size Exclusion Chromatography
**HPSEC** ...... High-Pressure Size Exclusion Chromatography
**HPSF** ........ High-Pressure Stopped Flow [*Spectrometry*]
**HPSI** ......... Harpsichord [*Music*]
**HPSI** ......... High-Pressure Safety Injection (NRCH)
**HPSIP** ....... High-Pressure Safety Injection Pump (NRCH)
**HPSIS** ....... High-Pressure Safety Injection System (IEEE)
**HPSK** ........ Hydraulic Power Supply Kit
**HPSL** ......... Health Professions Student Loans
**HPSN** ........ Hot-Pressed Silicon Nitride (RDA)
**HPSO** ........ Historical and Philosophical Society of Ohio. Bulletin [*A publication*]
**HPSP** ......... Health Professions Scholarship Program [*Army*]
**HPSS** ......... Hrvatska Pucka Seljacka Stranka [*Croatian People's Peasant Party*] [*Yugoslavia*] [*Political party*] (PPE)
**HPSSNJ** .... High-Power Self-Screening Noise Jammer [*Military*] (CAAL)
**HPSTGC** ... Heading per Steering Compass [*Navigation*]
**HPSW** ....... High-Pressure Service Water [*Nuclear energy*] (NRCH)
**HPSW** ....... Horizontally Polarized Shear Wave [*Physics*]
**HPSWS** ..... High-Pressure Service Water System [*Nuclear energy*] (NRCH)
**HPSY** ......... Health Psychology [*A publication*]
**HPT** .......... Hampton, IA [*Location identifier*] [*FAA*] (FAAL)
**HPT** .......... Head per Track (BUR)
**HPT** .......... Hexamethylphosphoric Triamide [*Also, HEMPA, HMP, HMPA, HMPT*] [*Organic chemistry*]
**HPT** .......... High-Performance Train (ADA)
**HPT** .......... High Point
**HPT** .......... High-Potential Test [*or Tester*]
**HPT** .......... High-Pressure Tap
**HPT** .......... High-Pressure Test
**HPT** .......... High-Pressure Turbine (NRCH)
**HPT** .......... Home Port [*Navy*] (NVT)
**HPT** .......... Homonuclear Polarization Transfer [*Physics*]
**HPT** .......... Horizontal Plot Table
**HPT** .......... Hormone Pregnancy Test
**HPT** .......... Human Placenta Thyrotrophin [*Endocrinology*]
**HPT** .......... Hydrocylic Pressure Testing
**HPT** .......... Hydropneumatic Trailer (MCD)
**HPT** .......... Hygromycin Phosphotransferase
**HPT** .......... Hyperparathyroidism [*or Hyperthyroidism*] [*Endocrinology*]
**HPTA** ........ High Pressure Technology Association [*British*]
**HPTA** ........ Hinckley Pilot 35 Association (EA)
**HPTB** ........ High-Pressure Turbine [*on a ship*] (DS)
**HPTD** ........ High Point, Thomasville & Denton Railroad Co. [*AAR code*]
**HPTE** ........ Bis(hydroxyphenyl)trichloroethane [*Organic chemistry*]
**HPTE** ........ Heptachlor Epoxide
**HPTE** ........ High-Performance Turbine Engine [*Air Force*]
**HPTF** ......... Hydraulic Power Transmission Fluid (MCD)
**HPTGA** ..... Herpetologica [*A publication*]
**HP Th** ........ Handbuch der Pastoraltheologie [*A publication*]
**HPTLC** ...... High-Performance Thin-Layer Chromatography
**HPTP** ......... Hydraulic Power Transfer Panel
**HPTS** ......... High-Performance Third Stage [*Rocket*] [*Army*] (AABC)
**HPTS** ......... Hydroxypyrenetrisulfonic Acid [*Organic chemistry*]
**HPTW** ....... Hauptwerk [*Masterpiece*] [*German*]
**HPU** .......... Hale Pohaku [*Hawaii*] [*Seismograph station code, US Geological Survey*] (SEIS)
**HPU** .......... Hansard's Publishing Union (ROG)
**HPU** .......... High-Pressure Unit
**HPU** .......... Hydraulic Power Unit (MCD)
**HPU** .......... Hydraulic Pumping Unit (AABC)
**HP(UK)** ..... Hunter Personnel (United Kingdom) Ltd.
**HPUS** ........ Homeopathic Pharmacopoeia of the United States
**HPV** .......... Hauptverband der Papier, Pappe, und Kunststoffe Verarbeitenden Industrie eV [*Paper, Board, and Plastic Industry Association*] [*Federal Republic of Germany*] (EY)
**HPV** .......... Helium Pressure Vessel
**HPV** .......... High-Passage Virus
**HPV** .......... High-Power Veractor
**HPV** .......... High-Powered Vehicle
**HPV** .......... High-Pressure Valve
**HPV** .......... Human Papillomavirus [*or Parvovirus*]
**HPV** .......... Human-Powered Vehicle
**HPV** .......... Hypoxic Pulmonary Vasoconstriction [*Medicine*]
**HPV** .......... Princeville [*Hawaii*] [*Airport symbol*] (OAG)
**HPVD** ........ Hypertensive Pulmonary Vascular Disease [*Medicine*]
**HPV-DE** .... High-Passage Virus [*Grown in*] Duck Embryo [*Cells*]
**HPV-DK** .... High-Passage Virus [*Grown in*] Dog Kidney [*Cells*]
**HPVR** ........ Hypoxic Pulmonary Vascular Response [*Anesthesiology*]
**HPW** ......... High-Purity Water
**HPW** ......... Hopewell, VA [*Location identifier*] [*FAA*] (FAAL)
**HPW** ......... Hot Pressure Welding
**HPWBA** .... Heilpaedagogische Werkblaetter [*A publication*]
**HPWSol** .... High-Protein Wash Solution [*Clinical chemistry*]
**HPX** .......... Homeplex Mortgage Investments [*NYSE symbol*] (SPSG)
**HPY** .......... Baytown, TX [*Location identifier*] [*FAA*] (FAAL)
**HPY** .......... HPY Industry Ltd. [*Vancouver Stock Exchange symbol*]
**$H_4$pyran** ..... Tetrahydropyranyl [*Organic chemistry*]
**HPZ** .......... High-Pressure Zone
**HPZE** ........ High-Performance Zone Electrophoresis
**HQ** ............ British Aerospace PLC [*Great Britain*] [*ICAO designator*] (FAAC)
**H & Q** ........ Hambrecht & Quist [*Investment banking firm*]
**H-Q** ........... Hamstring-Quadriceps [*Anatomy*]
**HQ** ............ Hartford Quarterly [*A publication*]
**HQ** ............ Hawker Siddeley Aviation Ltd. [*Great Britain*] [*ICAO designator*] (ICDA)
**HQ** ............ Headquarters
**HQ** ............ Headquarters Companies [*San Francisco, CA*] (TSSD)
**HQ** ............ High Quality [*Home video systems*]
**HQ** ............ Highly Qualified (AFM)
**HQ** ............ Historical Quotes [*Information retrieval*]
**HQ** ............ Hoc Quaere [*Look For This or See This*] [*Latin*]
**HQ** ............ Hong Qi [*Red Flag*] [*China*]
**HQ** ............ Hoop Quotient [*Basketball*]
**HQ** ............ Hopkins Quarterly [*A publication*]
**HQ** ............ HQ Minerals Ltd. [*Vancouver Stock Exchange symbol*]
**HQ** ............ Hydro-Quebec [*Institut de Recherche d'Hydro-Quebec*] [*Canada*]
**HQ** ............ Hydroquinone [*Organic chemistry*]
**HQ** ............ Hydroxyquinoline [*Organic chemistry*]
**HQ(A)** ........ Headquarters Administration Office [*British police*]
**HQA** .......... Middletown, PA [*Location identifier*] [*FAA*] (FAAL)
**HQAAFV** .. Headquarters, Australian Army Forces, Vietnam
**HQASC** ..... Headquarters, Air Support Command [*NATO*] (NATG)
**HQB** .......... Los Angeles, CA [*Location identifier*] [*FAA*] (FAAL)
**HQBA** ........ Headquarters Base Area
**HQBC** ........ Headquarters, Bomber Command [*Later, HQSTC*] [*British*] (NATG)
**HQBP** ........ High Quality Bonus Point [*Advancement system*] [*Navy*] (NVT)
**HQC** .......... Handling Quality Criteria
**HQC** .......... Headquarters Command [*Air Force*]
**HQC** .......... High "Q" Circuit [*or Coil*]
**HQC** .......... Hydraulic Quick Coupler
**HQC** .......... Hydroxyquinoline Citrate [*Antiseptic*]
**HQC** .......... Hyperquasicenter
**HQ-CAP** .... Headquarters, Civil Air Patrol
**HQCC** ........ Headquarters, Coastal Command [*British*] (NATG)
**HQCMD** .... Headquarters Command [*Military*]
**HQCOM** ... Headquarters Command [*Military*] (KSC)
**HQCOMD** ... Headquarters Command [*Air Force*]
**HQCOMDT** ... Headquarters Commandant (NATG)
**HQCOMDUSAF** ... Headquarters Command, United States Air Force
**HQCS** ........ Heraldic Quality Control System (AABC)
**HQDA** ........ Headquarters, Department of the Army
**HQDM** ....... Headquarters Data Manager (KSC)
**HQDP** ........ Headquarters, Department of the Pacific [*Marine Corps*]

**HQ DSA**..... Headquarters, Defense Supply Agency
**HQDTMS**... Headquarters, Defense Traffic Management Service
**HQE**.......... Hansard Questions Ecrites [*Hansard Written Question - HWQ*] [*Database*] [*House of Commons*] [*French*] [*Information service or system*] (CRD)
**HQEARC**.. Headquarters, Equipment Authorization Review Center [*Army*]
**HQES**........ High-Quality Epitaxial Silicon
**HQFC**........ Headquarters, Fighter Command [*NATO*] (NATG)
**HQG**.......... Hugoton, KS [*Location identifier*] [*FAA*] (FAAL)
**HQH**.......... H & Q Healthcare Investors [*NYSE symbol*] (SPSG)
**HQHRA**.... Half-Quarter Horse Registry of America (EA)
**HQJTF**...... Headquarters, Joint Task Force (MCD)
**HQK**.......... Gulf of Mexico, LA [*Location identifier*] [*FAA*] (FAAL)
**HQL**.......... Cullowhee, NC [*Location identifier*] [*FAA*] (FAAL)
**HQL**.......... High-Quality Life
**HQM**......... High-Quality Matrix [*Electronics*]
**HQM**......... Highland Queen Mines Ltd. [*Vancouver Stock Exchange symbol*]
**HQM**......... Hoquiam, WA [*Location identifier*] [*FAA*] (FAAL)
**HQM**......... Hydro-Quebec, Bibliotheque [*UTLAS symbol*]
**HQMC**...... Headquarters, Marine Corps
**HQMD**...... Headquarters Management Directive [*NASA*]
**HQMME**... Hydroquinone Monomethyl Ether [*Organic chemistry*]
**HQN**.......... Haplequin Lake [*Alaska*] [*Seismograph station code, US Geological Survey*] (SEIS)
**HQNAVMATCOM**... Headquarters, Naval Material Command
**HQNMC**... Headquarters, Naval Material Command (AFIT)
**HQNO**....... Heptyl(hydroxy)quinoline N-Oxide [*Organic chemistry*]
**HQO**.......... Hansard Questions Orale [*Hansard Oral Questions - HOQ*] [*Database*] [*House of Commons*] [*French*] [*Information service or system*] (CRD)
**HQOI**........ HQ Office International, Inc. [*NASDAQ symbol*] (NQ)
**HQOS**........ HQ Office Supplies Warehouse, Inc. [*NASDAQ symbol*] (NQ)
**HQR**.......... Handling Qualities Rating [*Cooper-Harper*]
**HQRS**........ Handling Qualities Rating Scale (MCD)
**HQS**.......... Headquarters
**HQS**.......... Headquarters Staff [*British military*] (DMA)
**HQS**.......... High-Quality Silicon
**HQSA**........ Hydroxyquinolinesulfonic Acid [*Organic chemistry*]
**HQSC**........ Headquarters, Signals Command [*British*] (NATG)
**HQSC**........ Headquarters Support Command [*Australia*]
**HQ & SERV**... Headquarters and Service [*Marine Corps*]
**HQSQ**........ Headquarters Squadron
**HQSQN**..... Headquarters Squadron [*Marine Corps*]
**HQSRN**..... Headquarters Staff of the Royal Navy [*British*]
**HQSTC**..... Headquarters, Strike Command [*Formerly, HQBC*] [*British*] (NATG)
**HQT**.......... Coats, NC [*Location identifier*] [*FAA*] (FAAL)
**HQT**.......... Halogen Quenched Tube
**HQTC**........ Headquarters, Transport Command [*British*] (NATG)
**HQTC**........ High "Q" Tuned Circuit
**HQTR**........ Headquarters (KSC)
**HQ USAF**... Headquarters, United States Air Force (AFM)
**HR**............ Hague Resolutions
**HR**............ Hair Space between Letters [*Proofreader's mark*]
**HR**............ Half-Reversal [*Psychometrics*]
**HR**............ Half-Yearly Review
**HR**............ Hall Wardrobes [*Classified advertising*] (ADA)
**HR**............ Halorhodopsin [*Biochemistry*]
**HR**............ Halton Rifles [*British military*] (DMA)
**HR**............ Hamburger Rundschau [*A publication*]
**HR**............ Hand Receipt (AABC)
**HR**............ Hand Reset
**HR**............ Handling Room
**HR**............ Hard Rolled
**HR**............ Hardware Reliability (MCD)
**H & R**........ Harper & Row Publishers Inc.
**H & R**........ Harrison and Rutherfurd's English Common Pleas Reports [*1865-66*] [*A publication*] (DLA)
**HR**............ Hear (FAAC)
**HR**............ Heart Rate [*Medicine*]
**HR**............ Heart Rhythm [*Cardiology*]
**HR**............ Heat Reflector
**HR**............ Heat Resisting [*Technical drawings*]
**HR**............ Height Range [*RADAR*]
**HR**............ Heir (ROG)
**HR**............ Helicopter Request [*Military*] (NVT)
**HR**............ Helium Rebottled [*System*]
**HR**............ Helium, Refrigerated (AAG)
**HR**............ Hellenic Register [*Greek ship classification society*] (DS)
**HR**............ Hemophilia Research [*An association*] [*Defunct*] (EA)
**HR**............ Hemorrhagic Retinopathy [*Ophthalmology*]
**Hr**.............. Henricus de Baila [*Flourished, 1169-70*] [*Authority cited in pre-1607 legal work*] (DSA)
**HR**............ Henry Russell [*Astronomy*]
**HR**............ Here (FAAC)
**HR**............ Hermes. Messager Scientifique et Populaire de l'Antiquite Classique en Russie [*A publication*]
**HR**............ Hermetic Rite [*Freemasonry*] (ROG)
**HR**............ Heroes of the Reformation [*A publication*]
**HR**............ Herr [*Sir, Mr.*] [*German*]
**H-R**........... Hertzsprung-Russell [*Diagram*] [*Astronomy*]
**HR**............ Hessischer Rundfunk [*Hessian Radio Network*] [*Federal Republic of Germany*]
**HR**............ Heterosexual Relations [*Scale*]
**HR**............ High-Range [*RADAR*] (DEN)
**HR**............ High-Rate Reverse [*Ecology*]
**HR**............ High Resistance
**HR**............ High Resolution (MCD)
**HR**............ High Risk
**HR**............ High Run
**HR**............ Higher (ROG)
**HR**............ Higher Rate
**HR**............ Highhams Railway [*Wales*]
**HR**............ Highland Railway [*Scotland*]
**HR**............ Highland Regiment [*British military*] (DMA)
**hr**............... Hinge Remnant [*Philately*]
**HR**............ Hispanic Review [*A publication*]
**HR**............ Histamine Release [*Immunology*]
**HR**............ Historical Record (NASA)
**HR**............ History of Religions [*A publication*]
**HR**............ Hit Rate (MUGU)
**HR**............ Hit Ratio
**HR**............ Hlas Revoluce [*A publication*]
**HR**............ Hoechst-Roussel Pharmaceuticals, Inc. [*Research code symbol*]
**HR**............ Hoerner [*Horns*] [*Music*]
**HR**............ Hoge Raad [*Dutch Supreme Court*] (DLA)
**HR**............ Hojesteret [*Supreme Court*] [*Netherlands*] (ILCA)
**H & R**........ Holding and Reconsignment [*Military*]
**HR**............ Holding Register
**HR**............ Home Rule
**HR**............ Home Run [*Baseball*]
**HR**............ Homeostatic Regulators [*British*]
**HR**............ Homoreactant [*Medicine*]
**HR**............ Honduras [*Aircraft nationality and registration mark*] (FAAC)
**HR**............ Hook Rail (MSA)
**HR**............ Horizontal Resistance [*Plant pathology*]
**HR**............ Horizontal Retort
**HR**............ Hormone Receptor Complex [*Endocrinology*]
**HR**............ Horology Program [*Association of Independent Colleges and Schools specialization code*]
**HR**............ Hose Rack (AAG)
**HR**............ Hospital Record
**HR**............ Hospital Recruit
**HR**............ Hospitalman Recruit
**HR**............ Hot Rolled (MSA)
**HR**............ Hour (AAG)
**HR**............ House Recedes
**HR**............ House Report
**HR**............ House of Representatives
**HR**............ House of Representatives Bill [*with Number*]
**HR**............ House Resolution
**HR**............ House Roll [*Legal term*] (DLA)
**HR**............ House of Ruth (EA)
**HR**............ Hrvatska Revija [*A publication*]
**H R**........... Hudebni Revue [*A publication*]
**HR**............ Hudson Review [*A publication*]
**HR**............ Human Relations [*A publication*]
**HR**............ Human Reliability
**HR**............ Human Resources
**HR**............ Human Rights Convention [*Council of Europe*] (DLA)
**H & R**........ Humanisme et Renaissance [*A publication*]
**HR**............ Humanisme et Renaissance [*A publication*]
**HR**............ Humanitarian Reassignment [*Military*] (AFM)
**HR**............ Humber Register [*St. Albans, Hertfordshire, England*] (EAIO)
**HR**............ Humidity, Relative
**Hr**.............. Hussar [*British military*] (DMA)
**HR**............ Hydraulics Research Ltd. [*British*] (IRUK)
**HR**............ Hydrogen Recombiner (NRCH)
**HR**............ Hydrogen Relief (NASA)
**HR**............ Hypersensitive Response [*Biology*]
**H & R**........ Hysterectomy and Radiation [*Medicine*]
**HR**............ Robin Avions [*Pierre Robin*] [*France*] [*ICAO aircraft manufacturer identifier*] (ICAO)
**HR**............ Transportes Aereos Rioplatenses [*Argentina*] [*ICAO designator*] (FAAC)
**HRA**.......... [*The*] Harvey Group, Inc. [*AMEX symbol*] (SPSG)
**HRA**.......... Health Resources Administration [*Abolished, 1982, functions transferred to Health Resources and Services Administration*] [*HEW*]
**HRA**.......... Health Risk Appraisal [*or Assessment*] [*Medicine*]
**HRA**.......... Heart Rate Acceleration
**HRA**.......... Heart Rate Audiometry
**HRA**.......... Heavy Replaceable [*or Replacement*] Assembly
**HRA**.......... Hemispherical Reflective Antenna
**HRA**.......... HF [*High-Frequency*] Recovery Antenna
**HRA**.......... Highest Rank Aboard (FAAC)
**HRA**.......... Historical Records of Australia [*A publication*] (APTA)
**HRA**.......... Honorary Royal Academician [*British*]
**HRA**.......... Hour of Revival Association [*British*]
**HRA**.......... Housing Revenue Account [*British*]
**HRA**.......... Human Resource Accounting (ADA)

**HRA**.......... Human Resources Abstracts [*A publication*]
**HRA**.......... Human Resources Administration [*A publication*]
**HRA**.......... Human Rights Advocates (EA)
**HRA**.......... Huna Research Association [*See also HF*] [*Switzerland*] (EAIO)
**HRA**.......... Hydraulic Rotary Actuator
**HRA**.......... Hypersonic Research Airplane [*NASA*]
**HRAA**........ High-Rate Acquisition Assembly (MCD)
**HRAF**........ Human Relations Area Files (EA)
**HRAF/BSR** ... Behavior Science Research. Journal of Comparative Studies. Human Relations Area Files [*A publication*]
**HRAI**......... Heating, Refrigerating, and Air Conditioning Institute of Canada
**HRAI**......... Human Rights Advocates International (EA)
**HRAM**....... Hierarchical Random Access Memory [*Data processing*]
**HRAR**........ Hereafter
**HRART**..... Hampton Roads Army Terminal
**HRAS**........ High-Rate Activated Sludge [*Waste treatment*]
**HRAT**........ Hampton Roads Army Terminal
**HRAT**........ Hereat [*Legal*] [*British*] (ROG)
**HRAV**........ Human Resources Availability (NVT)
**HRB**.......... Block [*H. & R.*], Inc. [*NYSE symbol*] (SPSG)
**HRB**.......... Croatian Revolutionary Brotherhood [*Yugoslavia*] (PD)
**HRB**.......... Harbin [*Manchuria*] [*Airport symbol*] (OAG)
**HRB**.......... Hazard Review Board
**HRB**.......... High-Resolution Bathymetry [*Instrumentation*]
**HRB**.......... Highway Research Board [*Later, TRB*] (EA)
**HRB**.......... Hinged Rotor Blade
**HRB**.......... Hockey Rules Board [*Walton-On-Thames, Surrey, England*] (EAIO)
**HRB**.......... Hopkins Research Bulletin [*A publication*]
**HRB**.......... House of Representatives Bill
**HRB**.......... Hurbanovo [*Czechoslovakia*] [*Geomagnetic observatory code*]
**HRB**.......... Hurbanovo [*Ogyalla, Stara Dala*] [*Czechoslovakia*] [*Seismograph station code, US Geological Survey*] (SEIS)
**HRBA**........ Havana Rabbit Breeders Association (EA)
**HRBA**........ Hoist Rotation Beam Assembly [*Military*] (CAAL)
**H & R Bank** ... Hazlitt and Roche's Bankruptcy Reports [*A publication*] (DLA)
**HRBC**........ Historical Review of Berks County [*A publication*]
**HRBC**........ Horse Red Blood Cells [*Also, HRC*]
**HRBI**......... Hotot Rabbit Breeders International (EA)
**HRC**.......... Haitian Refugee Center (EA)
**HRC**.......... Hardwood Research Council (EA)
**HRC**.......... Harris Ranch [*California*] [*Seismograph station code, US Geological Survey*] [*Closed*] (SEIS)
**HRC**.......... Hasselblad Reflex Camera (MCD)
**HRC**.......... HEALTHSOUTH Rehabilitation Corp. [*NYSE symbol*] (SPSG)
**HRC**.......... HEATH [*Higher Education and the Handicapped*] Resource Center (EA)
**HRC**.......... Helium Research Center
**HRC**.......... Herpes Resource Center (EA)
**HRC**.......... High-Rupturing Capacity
**HRC**.......... Holiday Rambler Corporation
**HRC**.......... Hollycroft Resource Corp. [*Vancouver Stock Exchange symbol*]
**HRC**.......... Holocaust Resource Center (EA)
**HRC**.......... Horeca [*A publication*]
**HRC**.......... Horizontal Redundancy Check (IEEE)
**HRC**.......... Horse Red Blood Cells [*Also, HRBC*]
**HRC**.......... Horticultural Research Center [*University of Massachusetts*] [*Research center*] (RCD)
**HRC**.......... Horticultural Research Center [*Southern Illinois University at Carbondale*] [*Research center*] (RCD)
**HRC**.......... Howard Research Corporation
**HRC**.......... Human Resources Center (EA)
**HRC**.......... Human Rights Commission
**HRC**.......... Hunting Retriever Club (EA)
**HRC**.......... Huntingdon Research Centre Ltd. [*British*] (IRUK)
**HRC**.......... Hybrid Receiver Circuit
**HRC**.......... Hypertension Research Center [*Indiana University*] [*Research center*] (RCD)
**HRC**.......... Hypothetical Reference Circuit [*Telecommunications*] (TEL)
**HRC**.......... Rockwell Hardness (C Scale)
**HRCA**........ Honorary Royal Cambrian Academician [*British*]
**HRCC**........ High-Ratio Compact Chamber [*Automotive engineering*]
**HRCC**........ Humanities Research Council of Canada [*See also CCRH*] [*Later, SSHRCC*]
**HRC CC J High Resolut Chromatogr Chromatogr Commun** ... Journal of High Resolution Chromatography and Chromatography Communications [*West Germany*] [*A publication*]
**HRC/CCPR** ... Human Rights Committee (EA)
**HRCF**........ Human Rights Campaign Fund (EA)
**HRC J High Resolut Chromatogr** ... HRC. Journal of High Resolution Chromatography [*A publication*]
**HR Con Res** ... House of Representatives Concurrent Resolution [*Legal term*] (DLA)
**HRD**.......... Hamburger Romanistische Dissertationen [*A publication*]
**HRD**.......... Hannaford Brothers, Inc. [*NYSE symbol*] (SPSG)
**hrd**............ Hard [*Quality of the bottom*] [*Nautical charts*]
**HRD**.......... Harding Carpets Ltd. [*Toronto Stock Exchange symbol*]
**HRD**.......... Heroin-Related Death [*Epidemiology*]
**HRD**.......... Hertzsprung-Russell Diagram [*Astronomy*]
**HRD**.......... High-Rate Discharge (MCD)
**HRD**.......... High-Rate Dosimeter (MCD)
**HRD**.......... High-Resolution Display
**HRD**.......... Holocaust Remembrance Day (BJA)
**HRD**.......... Human Related Deaths
**HRD**.......... Human Resources Data
**HRD**.......... Human Resources Development
**HRD**.......... Hurricane Research Division [*Miami, FL*] [*National Oceanic and Atmospheric Administration*] (GRD)
**HRD**.......... Hydraulic Rate Damper
**HRD**.......... Kountze/Silsbee, TX [*Location identifier*] [*FAA*] (FAAL)
**HR2D**........ High-Resolution, Two-Dimensional [*Electrophoresis*]
**HRDA**........ High-Rate Data Assembly (MCD)
**HRDG**........ Harding Associates, Inc. [*NASDAQ symbol*] (NQ)
**HRDG**........ Human Resources Development Group [*British*]
**HRDI**......... High-Resolution Doppler Imager (MCD)
**HRDI**......... High-Resolution Dynamic Imaging [*Electrophoresis*]
**HRDI**......... Human Resources Development Institute (EA)
**HRDITS**.... Hereditaments [*Legal*] [*British*] (ROG)
**HRDL**........ Hudson River Day Line [*AAR code*]
**HRDM**....... High-Rate Demultiplexer (MCD)
**HR Doc**...... House of Representatives Document (DLA)
**HRDP**........ Hypothetical Reference Digital Path [*Meteorology*]
**HRDR**........ High-Rate Digital Recorder (MCD)
**HRDS**........ High-Rate Data Section (NASA)
**HRDTY**..... Heredity
**HRE**.......... Harare [*Zimbabwe*] [*Airport symbol*] (OAG)
**HRE**.......... High-Resolution Electrocardiography
**HRE**.......... High-Resolution Electrophoresis [*Analytical biochemistry*]
**HRE**.......... Highridge Exploration Ltd. [*Toronto Stock Exchange symbol*]
**HRE**.......... Holy Roman Emperor [*or Empire*]
**HRE**.......... Homogeneous Reactor Experiments (NRCH)
**HRE**.......... Hormone Regulatory Element [*Endocrinology*]
**HRE**.......... Hormone-Responsive Element [*Endocrinology*]
**HRE**.......... HRE Properties [*Formerly, Hubbard Real Estate Investments*] [*NYSE symbol*] (SPSG)
**HRE**.......... Human Relations Education (MCD)
**HRE**.......... Human Response Element of DNA [*Endocrinology*]
**HRE**.......... Hydrazine Rocket Engine
**HRE**.......... Hydro Reconnaissance Experimental [*British military*] (DMA)
**HRE**.......... Hypersonic Ramjet Engine
**HRE**.......... Hypersonic Research Engine [*NASA*]
**HREBIU**.... Hotel and Restaurant Employees and Bartenders International Union [*Later, HERE*] (EA)
**HREC**........ Health Record
**H Rec A Sc** ... Historical Records of Australian Science [*A publication*]
**HREELS**.... High-Resolution Electron Energy Loss Spectroscopy
**H Rel**......... History of Religions [*A publication*]
**HREM**....... High-Resolution Electron Microscopy
**HRen**......... Humanisme et Renaissance [*A publication*]
**HREOC**..... Human Rights and Equal Opportunity Commission [*Australia*]
**HRept**........ House of Representatives Reports [*A publication*] (DLA)
**HRES**........ High-Resolution Electronic System
**HRES**........ Horizons Research, Inc. [*NASDAQ symbol*] (NQ)
**H Res**......... House Resolution, United States House of Representatives
**HRET**........ Hospital Research and Educational Trust (EA)
**HREU**........ Hotel and Restaurant Employees and Bartenders International Union [*Later, HERE*]
**4-H Rev**...... 4-H Review [*A publication*]
**HRF**.......... Height-Ranger Finder
**HRF**.......... Hemochromatosis Research Foundation (EA)
**HRF**.......... Herb Research Foundation (EA)
**HRF**.......... High Rate of Fire (NATG)
**HRF**.......... High-Resolution Facsimile [*Telecommunications*]
**HRF**.......... Histamine Releasing Factor [*Immunology*]
**HRF**.......... History Record Folder (MCD)
**HRF**.......... Hypersonic Rarefied Flow
**HRFA**........ High-Resolution Frequency Analysis [*of periodic phenomena*]
**HRFA**........ Hungarian Reformed Federation of America (EA)
**HRFADM** ... Annual Research Reviews. Hypothalamic Releasing Factors [*A publication*]
**HRFAX**..... High-Resolution Facsimile [*Telecommunications*] (TEL)
**HRF Bull** ... HRF [*National College for Heating, Ventilating, Refrigeration, and Fan Engineering*] Bulletin [*A publication*]
**HRG**.......... Handwoerterbuch zur Deutschen Rechtsgeschichte [*A publication*]
**HRG**.......... Harrington Public Library, Harrington, DE [*OCLC symbol*] (OCLC)
**HRG**.......... Health Research Group
**HRG**.......... Hearing (ROG)
**HRG**.......... Heritage Roses Group (EA)
**HRG**.......... High River Gold [*Vancouver Stock Exchange symbol*]
**HRG**.......... High River Gold Mines Ltd. [*Toronto Stock Exchange symbol*]
**HRG**.......... Human Rights Group [*Edinburgh, Scotland*] (EAIO)
**HRG**.......... Hurghada [*Egypt*] [*Airport symbol*] (OAG)
**HRGC**........ High-Resolution Gas Chromatography
**HRGM**....... High-Resolution Ground Map
**HRGM**....... Hogg Robinson & Gardner Mountain [*Insurance broker*] [*British*]

**HRGP**........ Hydroxyproline-Rich Glycoprotein [*Biochemistry*]
**HRH**.......... Hand Receipt Holder (MCD)
**HRH**.......... High-Rate Heat
**HRH**.......... His [*or Her*] Royal Highness
**HRH**.......... Howard Robard Hughes [*1905-1976*] [*American businessman*]
**HRH**.......... Hypoplastic Right Heart [*Cardiology*]
**HRH**.......... TextielVisie [*A publication*]
**HRHA**....... Honorary Member of the Royal Hibernian Academy [*British*]
**HRHA**....... Hydronic Radiant Heating Association (EA)
**HRHC**....... Hilb, Rogal & Hamilton Co. [*NASDAQ symbol*] (NQ)
**HRHL**........ Hotelli- ja Ravintolahenkiloekunnan Liitto [*Hotel and Restaurant Workers Union*] [*Finland*] (EY)
**HRHR**....... High-Risk Hearing Register
**HRI**........... Hannah Research Institute [*British*] (ARC)
**HRI**........... Hard Rock International [*Restaurant chain*]
**HRI**........... Hayes Resources, Inc. [*Toronto Stock Exchange symbol*]
**HRI**........... Health Research, Incorporated [*New York State Department of Health*] [*Research center*] (RCD)
**HRI**........... Height-Range Indicator [*Electronics*]
**HRI**........... High-Resolution Image [*or Imager*] [*Astronomy*]
**HRI**........... Holcomb Research Institute [*Butler University*]
**HRI**........... Honorary Member of the Royal Institute of Painters in Water Colours [*British*]
**HRI**........... Horizon Reference Indicator [*Aerospace*] (AAG)
**HRI**........... Horticultural Research Institute (EA)
**HRI**........... Hotel, Restaurant, and Institutional [*Business*]
**H & RI**....... Hotels and Restaurants International [*A publication*]
**HRI**........... [*C. D.*] Howe Research Institute
**HRI**........... Howe Richardson [*AMEX symbol*] (SPSG)
**HRI**........... Human Relations Inventory [*Psychology*]
**HRI**........... Human Resources Institute [*State University of New York at Buffalo*] [*Research center*] (RCD)
**HRI**........... Human Rights International (EA)
**HRI**........... Human Rights Internet (EA)
**HRIAF**...... HRS Industries [*NASDAQ symbol*] (NQ)
**HRIC**........ Hacienda Resorts, Incorporated [*NASDAQ symbol*] (NQ)
**HRIF**........ Histamine-Release Inhibitory Factor [*Antiinflammatory*]
**HRIG**........ Human Rabies Immune Globulin [*Immunology*]
**HR & IH**.... His [*or Her*] Royal and Imperial Highness (ROG)
**HRIN**........ Herein [*Legal*] [*British*] (ROG)
**HRIN**........ Human Resource Information Network [*Executive Telecom System, Inc.*] [*Information service or system*] (IID)
**HRINAR**... Hereinafter [*Legal*] [*British*] (ROG)
**HRINBEFE**... Hereinbefore [*Legal*] [*British*] (ROG)
**HRINBFR**... Hereinbefore [*Legal*] [*British*] (ROG)
**HRIO**........ Height-Range Indicator Operator [*Electronics*]
**HRIO**........ Horticultural Research Institute of Ontario [*Canada*] [*Research center*] (RCD)
**HRIP**........ Hic Requiescit in Pace [*Here Rests in Peace*] [*Latin*]
**HRIP**........ Highway Research in Progress [*British*]
**HRIPA**....... Publications. Hungarian Mining Research Institute [*A publication*]
**HRIR**........ High-Resolution Infrared Radiometer
**HRIRS**....... High-Resolution Infrared Radiation Sounder
**HRIS**......... High-Repetition Illuminator System
**HRIS**......... Highway Research Information Service [*National Academy of Sciences*] [*Washington, DC*]
**HRIS**......... House of Representatives Information System
**HRISAK**.... Food and Nutrition [*A publication*]
**HRIZ**........ Horizon Gold Corp. [*NASDAQ symbol*] (NQ)
**HRJ**.......... High-Range Juno [*Survey meter for radiation*]
**HRJ**.......... Human Rights Journal [*A publication*]
**HRJ Res**.... House of Representatives Joint Resolution [*Legal term*] (DLA)
**HRK**.......... Hard Rock International ADS [*AMEX symbol*] (SPSG)
**HRK**.......... Hardrock Extension, Inc. [*Toronto Stock Exchange symbol*]
**HRK**.......... Kharkov [*USSR*] [*Airport symbol*] (OAG)
**HRK**.......... Racine, WI [*Location identifier*] [*FAA*] (FAAL)
**HR-KMAG**... Historical Report - Korea Military Advisory Group
**HRL**.......... Harlin Resources [*Vancouver Stock Exchange symbol*]
**HRL**.......... Harlingen [*Texas*] [*Airport symbol*] (OAG)
**HRL**.......... Head Rotated Left [*Medicine*]
**HRL**.......... Heat Rejection Loop
**HRL**.......... High Refraction Layer
**HRL**.......... High-Repetition LASER
**HRL**.......... High-Resolution LOFAR [*Military*] (CAAL)
**HRL**.......... Horizontal Reference Line [*Technical drawings*]
**HRL**.......... Hormel [*Geo. A.*] & Co. [*NYSE symbol*] (SPSG)
**HRL**.......... Hughes Research Laboratories [*Hughes Aircraft Co.*]
**HRL**.......... Human Resources Laboratory [*Air Force*] (MCD)
**HRL**.......... Hydraulics Research Laboratory [*British*]
**HRL**.......... Hydrological Research Laboratory [*Silver Spring, MD*] [*National Weather Service*] (GRD)
**HRLC**........ High-Resolution Liquid Chromatography
**HRLD**........ Harold's Stores, Inc. [*NASDAQ symbol*] (NQ)
**HRLI**......... High-Repetition LASER Illuminator
**HRLIS**....... High-Repetition LASER Illuminating System
**HRLM**....... High-Resolution Light Microscopy
**HRLS**........ High-Repetition LASER System
**HRLSD**...... Health and Rehabilitative Library Services Division [*Later, ASCLA*] [*American Library Association*]
**HRLSD J**... HRLSD [*Health and Rehabilitative Library Services Division*] Journal [*A publication*]
**HRLY**........ Herley Industries [*NASDAQ symbol*] (NQ)
**HRM**......... Hardware Read-In Mode
**HRM**......... Hermes Ventures [*Vancouver Stock Exchange symbol*]
**HRM**......... High-Rate Multiplexer (MCD)
**HRM**......... High-Ratio Multiplier (NASA)
**HRM**......... High-Resolution Monitor (MCD)
**HRM**......... His [*or Her*] Royal Majesty [*British*]
**HRM**......... Human Reproductive Medicine [*Elsevier Book Series*] [*A publication*]
**HRM**......... Human Resource Management [*A publication*]
**HRM**......... Human Resources Management
**HRM**......... University of Hartford, West Hartford, CT [*OCLC symbol*] (OCLC)
**HRMC**....... Human Resources Management Center [*Navy*]
**HRMDDHG**... Herr, Regiere Mich durch Deinen Heiligen Geist [*Lord, Rule Me through Thy Holy Spirit*] [*Motto of Eva Christine, Margravine of Brandenburg (1590-1657); Elisabeth, Electress of Brandenburg (1563-1607); Eleonore, daughter of Prince Rudolf of Anhalt-Zerbst (1608-81)*]
**HRMIS**...... Human Resources Management Information System [*Australia*]
**HRMN**...... Harmon Industries, Inc. [*NASDAQ symbol*] (NQ)
**HRMOB**..... Association of Human Resources Management and Organizational Behavior [*Later, AM*] (EA)
**HRMP**....... Harvard Radio Meteor Project
**HRMR**....... Human Read/Machine Read [*Microfilm memory system*]
**HRMR**....... Hunter-Melnor, Inc. [*NASDAQ symbol*] (NQ)
**HRMS**....... High-Resolution Mass Spectrometry
**HRMS**....... Human Resource Management Services, Inc. [*Database producer*] (EISS)
**HRMS**....... Human Resource Management System
**HRMS**....... Human Resources Management Specialist [*Navy*] (NVT)
**HRMSS**..... Human Resources Management Support System [*Navy*] (NVT)
**HRN**.......... Harlyn Products, Inc. [*AMEX symbol*] (SPSG)
**HRN**.......... Harness
**HRN**.......... Harwin Exploration & Development, Inc. [*Vancouver Stock Exchange symbol*]
**HRN**.......... Herrn [*Sirs, Gentlemen*] [*German*] (ROG)
**HRN**.......... Hoerner [*Horns*] [*Music*]
**HRN**.......... Human Research Need (RDA)
**HRN**.......... Human Resources Need (MCD)
**HRN**.......... Human Resources Network [*Information service or system*] (EA)
**HRNA**....... Haflinger Registry of North America (EA)
**hRNA**....... Ribonucleic Acid, Heterogeneous [*Biochemistry, genetics*]
**HRNAR**..... Hereinafter
**HRNB**....... History. Reviews of New Books [*A publication*]
**HRNES**..... Host Remote Node Entry System
**HRNG**....... Hearing
**HRNSW**.... Historical Records of New South Wales [*A publication*] (APTA)
**HRNTWT**... High Reynolds Number Transonic Wind Tunnel
**HRO**.......... Gastvrij [*A publication*]
**HRO**.......... Harrison [*Arkansas*] [*Airport symbol*] (OAG)
**HRO**.......... Hermiston [*Oregon*] [*Seismograph station code, US Geological Survey*] (SEIS)
**HRO**.......... HERO Industries Ltd. [*Toronto Stock Exchange symbol*] [*Vancouver Stock Exchange symbol*]
**HRO**.......... Homes Registration Office
**HRO**.......... Housing Referral Office [*Military*]
**H Ro**......... Hudebni Rozhledy [*A publication*]
**HROB**....... Hi-Tech Robotics Ltd. [*NASDAQ symbol*] (NQ)
**HROI**........ Honorary Member of the Royal Institute of Oil Painters [*British*]
**HROK**....... Home Federal Savings & Loan Association of the Rockies [*NASDAQ symbol*] (NQ)
**HRON**....... Hereon [*Legal*] [*British*] (ROG)
**HRP**.......... Haitian Refugee Project [*Defunct*] (EA)
**HRP**.......... Handbuch der Rechtspraxis [*A publication*]
**HRP**.......... Health & Rehabilitation Properties Trust [*NYSE symbol*] (SPSG)
**HRP**.......... Heat-Resistant Phenolic
**HRP**.......... Heat-Resisting Plastic
**HRP**.......... Highway Regulating Point (AABC)
**HRP**.......... Histidine-Rich Protein [*Biochemistry, immunochemistry*]
**HRP**.......... Historical Review Press [*British*]
**HRP**.......... Holding and Reconsignment Point [*Military*] (AABC)
**H & RP**...... Holding and Reconsignment Point [*Military*]
**HRP**.......... Horizontal Radiation Pattern [*Electronics*] (DEN)
**HRP**.......... Horseradish Peroxidase [*An enzyme*]
**HRP**.......... Human Reliability Program (AFM)
**HRP**.......... Human Resource Planning [*A publication*]
**HRP**.......... Human Rights Party [*Ann Arbor, MI*]
**HRPA**........ Hebrew Religious Protection Association of Greater New York (EA)
**HRPAC**..... Human Rights Political Action Committee (EA)
**HRPC**........ High-Range Pressure Control

**HRPD**........ High-Resolution Powder Diffractometer [*Crystallographic instrument*]
**HRPI**......... High-Resolution Pointable Imager
**H & RPO**... Holding and Reconsignment Point [*Military*]
**HRPO**........ Hot Rolled, Pickled, and Oiled (MSA)
**HRPP**........ Human Rights Protection Party [*Western Samoa*] [*Political party*] (PPW)
**HRPS**......... Hazard Reduction Precedence Sequence (NASA)
**HRPS**......... Human Resource Planning Society [*New York, NY*] (EA)
**HRPS**......... Hydrogen Recombination and Purge System [*Nuclear energy*] (NRCH)
**HRPT**........ High-Resolution Picture Transmission [*Service*]
**HRPV**........ Hermes. Revista del Pais Vasco [*A publication*]
**HRPVD**..... High-Rate Physical Vapor Deposition [*Metal*]
**HRR**.......... Handicapped Rights and Regulations [*A publication*]
**HRR**.......... Hardy-Rand Rittler [*Test for color vision*]
**HRR**.......... Head Rotated Right [*Medicine*]
**HRR**.......... Healy, AK [*Location identifier*] [*FAA*] (FAAL)
**HRR**.......... Heart Rate Range [*Medicine*]
**HRR**.......... Heat Rejection Radiator
**HRR**.......... Heiliges Roemisches Reich [*Holy Roman Empire*] [*German*] (ROG)
**HRR**.......... Heron Resources Ltd. [*Vancouver Stock Exchange symbol*]
**HRR**.......... High-Reliability Relay
**HRR**.......... High-Resolution RADAR
**HRRC**........ Home Recording Rights Coalition (EA)
**HRRC**........ Human Resources Research Center
**HRRC**........ Human Rights Resource Center (EAIO)
**HRRC**........ Walt Disney Hearing Rehabilitation Research Center [*Ear Research Institute*]
**HRRD**........ Human Resources Research Development Program
**HR Rel**....... Historicorum Romanorum Reliquiae [*A publication*] (OCD)
**HR Rep**...... House of Representatives Reports [*A publication*] (DLA)
**HR Rept**..... House of Representatives Reports [*A publication*] (DLA)
**HRRI**......... Human Resources Research Institute
**HRRL**......... Human Resources Research Laboratory [*Air Force*] (MCD)
**hrRNA**....... Ribonucleic Acid, Heavy Ribosomal [*Biochemistry, genetics*]
**HRRO**........ Human Resources Research Office [*NASA*] (AAG)
**HRRVC**..... Holiday Rambler Recreational Vehicle Club (EA)
**HRRWC**.... Hudson River Region Wine Council (EA)
**HRS**.......... Hair Replacement System
**HRS**.......... Hal Roach Studios, Inc.
**HRS**.......... Hard Red Spring [*Wheat*]
**HRS**.......... Harp Renaissance Society [*Defunct*] (EA)
**HRS**.......... Harris Corp. [*NYSE symbol*] (SPSG)
**HRS**.......... Harris, GA [*Location identifier*] [*FAA*] (FAAL)
**HRS**.......... Hawaii Revised Statutes [*A publication*]
**HRS**.......... Hazard Ranking System [*Environmental Protection Agency*]
**HRS**.......... Heading Reference System (AAG)
**HRS**.......... Heat Rejection System
**HRS**.......... Hellenic Register of Shipping (DS)
**HRS**.......... Hepatorenal Syndrome [*Medicine*]
**HRS**.......... High-Rate Station
**HRS**.......... High-Resolution System
**HRS**.......... Historic Record Society [*Record label*]
**HRS**.......... Historical Records and Studies [*A publication*]
**HRS**.......... Historical Records Survey [*A publication*]
**HRS**.......... Home Reunion Society [*British*]
**HRS**.......... Honorary Reserve Section
**HRS**.......... Horizontal Recovery System
**HRS**.......... Hormone Receptor Site [*Endocrinology*]
**HRS**.......... Hospital Reading Society [*Defunct*] (EA)
**HRS**.......... Host Resident Software
**HRS**.......... Hot Rolled Steel
**HRS**.......... Hours (NATG)
**HRS**.......... Housing Referral Service [*Military*] (AABC)
**HRS**.......... Hovering Rocket System [*Army*]
**HRS**.......... Hunza Research Society (EA)
**HRS**.......... Hurricane Research Service [*Information service or system*] (EISS)
**HRS**.......... Hussars [*Military unit*] [*British*]
**HRS**.......... Hydraulics Research Station [*British*]
**HRS**.......... Missionary Sisters of Our Lady of the Holy Rosary [*Roman Catholic religious order*]
**HRSA**........ Health Resources and Services Administration [*Department of Health and Human Services*]
**HRSA**........ Honorary Member of the Royal Scottish Academy
**HRSC**........ Hudson River Sloop Clearwater (EA)
**HRS-D**....... Hamilton Rating Scale for Deafness
**HRSD**........ Hard Rock Silo Development
**HRSD**........ Hazardous Response Support Division [*Environmental Protection Agency*]
**HRSG**........ Heat Recovery Steam Generator [*Industrial engineering*]
**hrsg**........... Herausgegeben [*Edited, Published*] [*German*]
**HRSI**......... High-Temperature Reusable Surface Insulation [*Space shuttle*] [*NASA*]
**HRSNA**..... Histamine Research Society of North America (EA)
**HRSP**......... Association of Human Resource Systems Professionals (EA)
**HRSR**........ Heat Recovery/Seed Recovery [*System*]
**HRSS**......... Host Resident Software System
**HRSS**......... Hrvatska Republikanska Seljacka Stranka [*Croatian Republican Peasant Party*] [*Yugoslavia*] [*Political party*] (PPE)
**HRSSCC**... High-Resolution Spin Scan Cloud Camera (NOAA)
**HRSW**....... Honorary Member of the Royal Scottish Water Colour Society
**HRT**.......... Hartwell Railway Co. [*AAR code*]
**HRT**.......... Heart
**HRT**.......... Helmholtz Reciprocal Theorem [*Physics*]
**HRT**.......... High-Rate Telemetry [*NASA*]
**HRT**.......... High-Resolution Tracker
**HRT**.......... Hillcrest Resources Ltd. [*Toronto Stock Exchange symbol*]
**HRT**.......... Hiring, Retention, and Tenure [*of college professors*]
**HRT**.......... Homogeneous Reactor Test
**HRT**.......... Hormone Replacement Therapy [*Medicine*]
**HRT**.......... Hostage Rescue Team [*Pronounced "hurt"*] [*FBI standardized term*]
**HRT**.......... Hydraulic Retention Time
**HRT**.......... Mary Esther, FL [*Location identifier*] [*FAA*] (FAAL)
**HRTB**........ Heritage Bancorp of California [*NASDAQ symbol*] (NQ)
**HRTC**........ Historic Rehabilitation Tax Credit
**HRTEM**.... High-Resolution Transmission Electron Microscope [*or Microscopy*]
**HRTF**........ High-Resolution Tangential Flow Filtration
**HRTG**........ Heritage. Alberta Department of Culture, Youth, and Recreation [*A publication*]
**HRTG**........ Heritage Bancorporation [*NASDAQ symbol*] (NQ)
**HRTI**......... Hart Industries, Inc. [*Laguna Hills, CA*] [*NASDAQ symbol*] (NQ)
**HRTS**........ High-Rate Telemetry System [*NASA*]
**HRTS**........ High-Resolution Telescope and Spectrograph
**HRTS**........ High-Risk Test Site [*Later, Research Test Site*]
**HRTS**........ Hollywood Radio and Television Society (EA)
**HRU**.......... Harrisburg-Dayton [*Vancouver Stock Exchange symbol*]
**HRU**.......... Herrington, KS [*Location identifier*] [*FAA*] (FAAL)
**HRV**.......... Harvard - Oak Ridge [*Massachusetts*] [*Seismograph station code, US Geological Survey*] (SEIS)
**HRV**.......... Heat Rate Variability
**HRV**.......... Heat Recovery Ventilator
**HRV**.......... High Resolution Visible [*Imager*]
**HRV**.......... Historical Records of Victoria [*A publication*]
**HRV**.......... Human Rhinovirus [*Medicine*]
**HRV**.......... Human Rotaviruses
**HRV**.......... Hydraulic Relief Valve
**HRV**.......... Hypersonic Research Vehicle
**HRV**.......... New Orleans, LA [*Location identifier*] [*FAA*] (FAAL)
**Hrv Geogr Glasn**... Hrvatski Geografski Glasnik [*A publication*]
**Hrv Kolo**.... Hrvatsko Kolo [*A publication*]
**HRVL**........ Human Resources, Veterans, and Labor [*Office of Management and Budget*]
**HRW**......... Hard Red Winter [*Wheat*]
**HRW**......... Holz als Roh- und Werkstoff [*A publication*]
**HRW**......... Human Rights Watch (EA)
**HRW**......... Human Rights for Women (EA)
**HRWS**....... Helicopter Remote Wind Sensor
**HRX**.......... Hereford, TX [*Location identifier*] [*FAA*] (FAAL)
**HRX**.......... Hypothetical Reference Connection [*Meteorology*]
**HRXRS**...... High-Resolution X-Ray Spectroscopy
**HRY**.......... Hallwood Realty Partners LP [*AMEX symbol*] (SPSG)
**HRYG**........ Gisenyi [*Rwanda*] [*ICAO location identifier*] (ICLI)
**HRYI**......... Butare [*Rwanda*] [*ICAO location identifier*] (ICLI)
**HRYO**........ Gabiro [*Rwanda*] [*ICAO location identifier*] (ICLI)
**HRYR**........ Kigali [*Rwanda*] [*ICAO location identifier*] (ICLI)
**HRYU**........ Ruhengeri [*Rwanda*] [*ICAO location identifier*] (ICLI)
**HRZ**.......... High Rainfall Zone
**HRZA**........ Kamembe [*Rwanda*] [*ICAO location identifier*] (ICLI)
**HRZB**........ Horizon Bank, a Savings Bank [*NASDAQ symbol*] (NQ)
**HRZN**........ Horizon (MSA)
**HRZN**........ Horizon Industries, Inc. [*NASDAQ symbol*] (NQ)
**HS**............ Aeronoleggi e Lavoro Aereo (AERAL) [*Italy*] [*ICAO designator*] (ICDA)
**HS**............ Air-Cushion Vehicle built by Hoversport [*US*] [*Usually used in combination with numerals*]
**HS**............ Die Heilige Schrift des Alten Testaments [*Bonn*] [*A publication*] (BJA)
**HS**............ Habitability System [*NASA*] (KSC)
**HS**............ Habituation Stimulus [*to light*]
**HS**............ Hakluyt Society (EA)
**HS**............ Half Strength
**HS**............ Half Subtractor [*Circuitry*]
**HS**............ [*Nathaniel Brassey*] Halked and [*Richard Brinsley*] Sheridan [*Pseudonym*]
**HS**............ Hand-Starter
**HS**............ Hand Surgery [*Medical specialty*] (DHSM)
**HS**............ Hand Switch [*Nuclear energy*] (NRCH)
**HS**............ Handbook of Statistics [*Elsevier Book Series*] [*A publication*]
**HS**............ Handelsschule [*Commercial School*] [*German*]
**HS**............ Handset
**HS**............ Hansard Society [*British*] (ILCA)
**HS**............ Hardened Site
**HS**............ Hardness Surveillance (MSA)
**HS**............ Hardstand

**HS**............. Harmonised System [*Customs commodity coding and description*] [*British*]
**HS**............. Harness or Saddlery
**H & S**......... Harris and Simrall's Reports [*49-52 Mississippi*] [*A publication*] (DLA)
**HS**............. Hartford & Slocomb Railroad Co. [*AAR code*]
**HS**............. Hartman's Solution [*Dentistry*]
**HS**............. Harvey Society (EA)
**HS**............. Hauptsatz [*Leading Theme*] [*Music*]
**HS**............. Hawker Siddeley Aviation Ltd. [*Great Britain*] [*ICAO aircraft manufacturer identifier*] (ICAO)
**HS**............. Haydn Society [*Record label*]
**H & S**......... Head and Shoulders [*Photography*]
**HS**............. Head Sling
**HS**............. Head Suppression (AAG)
**H & S**......... Headquarters and Service [*Battery*] [*Army*]
**HS**............. Headspace [*Above liquids*]
**HS**............. Headspace Sampler [*Instrumentation*]
**H & S**......... Health and Safety [*A publication*]
**H & S**......... Health and Strength [*A publication*]
**HS**............. Heart Sounds [*Medicine*]
**HS**............. Heat Shield [*Aerospace*] (AAG)
**HS**............. Heat Stable
**HS**............. Heather Society (EA)
**HS**............. Heating Surface
**HS**............. Heating System
**HS**............. Heaviside [*Ionosphere*] (AAG)
**HS**............. Hebrew Studies [*Louisville, KY*] [*A publication*]
**HS**............. Heel Strike [*Medicine*]
**HS**............. Height above Spherical Earth
**HS**............. Helicopter Squadron, Antisubmarine (MCD)
**HS**............. Helicopter System
**HS**............. Helmet Shield
**HS**............. Helminthosporium sacchari [*A toxin-producing fungus*]
**H/S**........... Helper/Suppressor [*Cell ratio*]
**HS**............. Hemingway Society (EA)
**Hs**............. Hemisphere [*A publication*]
**HS**............. Hemlock Society (EA)
**HS**............. Hemorrhagic Shock [*Medicine*]
**HS**............. Hemstitched
**HS**............. Henoch-Schoenlein Syndrome [*Medicine*]
**HS**............. Heparin Sulfate [*Biochemistry*]
**HS**............. Hepatic Scintigraphy [*Medicine*]
**HS**............. Hepatosplenic Schistosomiasis [*Medicine*]
**HS**............. Heraldisk Selskab [*An association*] (EAIO)
**HS**............. Heraldry Society (EA)
**HS**............. Hereditary Spherocytosis [*Medicine*]
**HS**............. Herpes Simplex
**HS**............. Hic Sepultus [*Here Is Buried*] [*Latin*]
**HS**............. Hidradenitis Suppurative [*Medicine*]
**HS**............. High School
**HS**............. High Sensitivity
**HS**............. High-Similarity [*Psychology*]
**HS**............. High Speed
**HS**............. High Spontaneous Activity
**HS**............. High Stage (MCD)
**HS**............. High Strength [*Steel*] [*Automotive engineering*]
**HS**............. Highest Score (ADA)
**HS**............. Highly Sensitive System (MCD)
**HS**............. Hindenberg Society (EA)
**HS**............. Hinge Side
**HS**............. Hinged Seat (AAG)
**HS**............. Hispania Sacra [*A publication*]
**HS**............. Histamine Sensitive [*Immunology*]
**HS**............. Historical Studies [*A publication*] (APTA)
**HS**............. Historical Survey
**HS**............. History Section [*Reference and Adult Services Division*] [*American Library Association*]
**HS**............. Hohenzollern Society (EA)
**HS**............. [*The*] Holy See
**HS**............. Home Secretary [*British*]
**HS**............. Home Station [*DoD*]
**HS**............. Home Surgeon [*Medicine*] [*British*]
**HS**............. Homestead (ADA)
**HS**............. Homologous Serum
**HS**............. Honorary Secretary
**HS**............. Hopper Soliday Corp. [*NYSE symbol*] (SPSG)
**HS**............. Hora Somni [*At Bedtime*] [*Pharmacy*]
**HS**............. Horae Soederblomianae (BJA)
**HS**............. Horizon Scanner
**HS**............. Horizon Sensor
**HS**............. Horizontal Shear
**HS**............. Horizontal Stripes [*On buoys, beacons*]
**HS**............. Horizontal Synchronous [*Data processing*]
**HS**............. Horizontal System [*Government arrangement*] (OICC)
**HS**............. Horse Serum [*Immunology*]
**HS**............. Hospital Ship
**HS**............. Hospital Surgeon [*British military*] (DMA)
**HS**............. Hospitals Staff
**HS**............. Hot Shop [*Nuclear energy*] (NRCH)
**HS**............. Hot Spraying
**HS**............. Hot Stuff [*Slang*] [*Bowdlerized version*]
**HS**............. [*Service available during*] Hours of Scheduled Operations
**HS**............. Hours of Sleep [*Medicine*]
**H of S**........ House of Solomon [*Freemasonry*] (ROG)
**HS**............. House Supervisor
**HS**............. House Surgeon
**HS**............. Housing Scheme [*British*]
**HS**............. Housing Statistics
**HS**............. Housman Society (EA)
**HS**............. Humane Society (ROG)
**HS**............. Humanite Society (EA)
**HS**............. Humanities in the South [*A publication*]
**HS**............. Hume Society (EA)
**HS**............. Humic Substances [*Biology*]
**HS**............. Hun-Stoffe [*US Chemical Corp. symbol for mustard gas*] [*Also, HD, HT, M*] [*Later, H*]
**HS**............. Hurler's Syndrome [*Medicine*]
**HS**............. Hybrid Switching [*Telecommunications*]
**HS**............. Hydraulic Supply
**HS**............. Hydraulic System
**HS**............. Hydrazine Sulfate [*Toxic substance*] [*Inorganic chemistry*]
**HS**............. Hydrofoil Ship
**HS**............. Hydrogen Swelling [*Chemistry*]
**HS**............. Hypersonic
**Hs**............. Hypochondriasis [*Psychology*]
**HS**............. Hypothetical Syllogism [*Rule of inference*] [*Logic*]
**H & S**......... Hysterotomy and Sterilization [*Medicine*]
**HS**............. International Journal of Health Services [*A publication*]
**HS**............. Sandoz Pharmaceuticals [*Research code symbol*]
**HS**............. Siglum for Tablets in the Frau Professor Hilprecht Collection of Babylonian Antiquities [*Jena*] (BJA)
**HS**............. Thailand [*Aircraft nationality and registration mark*] (FAAC)
**HSA**........... Haiku Society of America (EA)
**HSA**........... Handicapped SCUBA Association (EA)
**HSA**........... Harvard Student Agencies [*Inc.*]
**HSA**........... Hawaii Surfing Association (EA)
**HSA**........... Hawker Siddeley Aviation Ltd. [*Great Britain*]
**HSA**........... Hawley-Smoot Act [*1930*]
**HSA**........... Headquarters Support Activity
**HSA**........... Health Schools Australia
**HSA**........... Health Service Action [*Later, CNHS*] [*An association*] (EA)
**HSA**........... Health Service Area [*Military*] (AABC)
**HSA**........... Health Services Administration [*Abolished, 1982, functions transferred to Health Resources and Services Administration*]
**HSA**........... Health Services Administration. Publications [*A publication*]
**HSA**........... Health Systems Agency [*New York, NY*]
**HSA**........... Hegel Society of America (EA)
**HSA**........... Hepatic Stimulating Activity [*Physiology*]
**HSA**........... Herb Society of America (EA)
**HSA**........... High Specific Activity [*Radioisotope*]
**HSA**........... High-Strength Adhesive
**HSA**........... Hispanic Society of America (EA)
**HSA**........... Hispanic Surname American
**HSA**........... Hollandse Signaalapparaten
**HSA**........... Holly Society of America (EA)
**HSA**........... Holocaust Survivors of Auschwitz (EA)
**HSA**........... Homo Sapiens [*Human species*]
**HSA**........... Horizon Sensor Assembly
**HSA**........... Horse Serum Albumin [*Immunology*]
**HSA**........... Horsemanship Safety Association (EA)
**HSA**........... Human Serum Albumin
**HSA**........... Hunt Saboteurs Association (EAIO)
**HSA**........... Hydroponic Society of America (EA)
**HSA**........... Hymn Society of America [*Later, HSUSC*] (EA)
**HSA**........... New Hampshire State Library, Processing Center, Concord, NH [*OCLC symbol*] (OCLC)
**HSAA**......... Health Sciences Advancement Award [*National Institutes of Health*]
**HSAAP**...... Holston Army Ammunition Plant (AABC)
**HSAB**......... Hard and Soft Acids and Bases [*Chemistry*]
**HSAB**......... Hydroxy(succinimidyl)azidobenzoate [*Organic chemistry*]
**HSAC**......... Health Security Action Council (EA)
**HSAC**......... Helicopter Safety Advisory Conference (EA)
**HSAC**......... High-Speed Analog Computer (DEN)
**HSAC**......... House Science and Astronautics Committee [*US Congress*] (AAG)
**HSAFOKF**... Help Save America for Our Kids' Future (EA)
**HSAG**......... HEPES-Saline-Albumin-Gelatin [*Medium*] [*Microbiology*]
**HSAK**......... Akobo [*Sudan*] [*ICAO location identifier*] (ICLI)
**HSAM**......... Hierarchical Sequential Access Method [*Data processing*]
**HSan**.......... Helsingin Sanomat [*A publication*]
**HSAP**......... Heat-Stable Alkaline Phosphatase [*An enzyme*]
**HSAP**......... Honeycomb Sandwich Aluminum Panel
**HSARG**...... High-Speed Scintillation Autoradiography
**HSAS**......... Hard Stability Augmentation System
**HSAS**......... Headquarters Support Activity - Saigon [*Obsolete*] [*Military*] (CINC)
**HSAS**......... Hypertrophic Subaortic Stenosis [*Cardiology*]
**HSAT**......... Atbara [*Sudan*] [*ICAO location identifier*] (ICLI)

**HSAT** ........ Die Heilige Schrift des Alten Testaments [*Bonner Bibel*] [*A publication*] (BJA)
**HSATes** ..... Die Heilige Schrift des Alten Testaments [*Bonner Bibel*] [*A publication*] (BJA)
**HSA-UWC** ... Holy Spirit Association for the Unification of World Christianity
**HSAW** ....... Aweil [*Sudan*] [*ICAO location identifier*] (ICLI)
**HSB** .......... Harrisburg, IL [*Location identifier*] [*FAA*] (FAAL)
**HSB** .......... Hartford Steam Boiler Inspection & Insurance Co. [*NYSE symbol*] (SPSG)
**HSB** .......... Heat-Shield Boost [*Aerospace*]
**HSB** .......... Helmet Stowage Bag [*NASA*] (KSC)
**HSB** .......... Hermetically Sealed Bushing
**HSB** .......... High-Speed Buffer
**HSB** .......... High-Speed Bus [*Data processing*]
**HSB** .......... Hobbyists Sourcebook [*A publication*]
**HSB** .......... Hunter-Schreger Bands [*Tooth structure*]
**HSB** .......... Hutterian Brethren [*Acronym is based on former name, Hutterian Society of Brothers*] (EA)
**HSBA** ........ Horizontal Static Balancing Adjustment
**HSBC** ........ Hongkong and Shanghai Banking Corporation
**HSBI** ......... Hyde Stud Bloodstock Investments PLC [*British*]
**HSBK** ........ Hibernia Savings Bank [*NASDAQ symbol*] (NQ)
**HSBP** ........ High-Speed Bench Press
**HSBR** ........ Bor [*Sudan*] [*ICAO location identifier*] (ICLI)
**HSBR** ........ High-Speed Bombing RADAR
**HSBT** ........ Bentu [*Sudan*] [*ICAO location identifier*] (ICLI)
**HS + C** ...... Half-Sample plus Complement [*Statistics*]
**HS-C** ......... Hamilton Standard Carbon Dioxide Absorbent Material (NASA)
**HSC** .......... Hampden-Sydney College [*Virginia*]
**HSC** .......... Hand-Schueller-Christian [*Disease*] [*Medicine*]
**HSC** .......... Hardware-Software Configuration [*Data processing*]
**HSC** .......... Hardware/Software Coordination (NASA)
**HSC** .......... Harsco Corporation [*NYSE symbol*] (SPSG)
**HSC** .......... Hawker Siddeley Canada, Inc. [*Toronto Stock Exchange symbol*] [*Vancouver Stock Exchange symbol*]
**HSC** .......... Health and Safety Commission [*Department of Employment*] [*British*]
**HSC** .......... Health Sciences Consortium (EA)
**HSC** .......... Health Services Centre [*Institute of Organisation and Social Studies, Brunel University*] [*British*] (CB)
**HSC** .......... Health Services Command [*Army*]
**HSC** .......... Heat Sterilization Compound
**HSC** .......... Heavy & Specialized Carriers Tariff Bureau, Washington DC [*STAC*]
**HSC** .......... Hematopoietic Stem Cell [*Hematology*]
**HSC** .......... Henderson State College [*Later, Henderson State University*] [*Arkansas*]
**HSC** .......... Hermetic-Sealed Container (MSA)
**HSC** .......... High School Completion (OICC)
**HSC** .......... High-Speed Carry
**HSC** .......... High-Speed Channel [*Data processing*]
**HSC** .......... High-Speed Concentrator
**HSC** .......... High-Swirl Combustion [*Engine*]
**HSC** .......... Higher School Certificate [*British*]
**HSC** .......... Histoire de la Spiritualite Chretienne [*A publication*]
**HSC** .......... Home Products Safety Council (EA)
**HSC** .......... Home Shopping Club [*of the Home Shopping Network*]
**HSC** .......... Horizon Scanner (MSA)
**HSC** .......... Hospital for Sick Children [*Toronto, ON*] [*Canada*]
**HSC** .......... Hot Stove Club (EA)
**HSC** .......... House Space Committee [*US Congress*] (AAG)
**HS/C** ........ House Spacecraft (KSC)
**HSC** .......... Human SERVE [*Service Employees Registration and Voter Education*] Campaign (EA)
**HSC** .......... Human Skin Collagen
**HSC** .......... Humboldt State College [*Later, Humboldt State University*] [*California*]
**HSC** .......... Humor Stamp Club (EA)
**HSC** .......... Hunting Surveys & Consultants [*Commercial firm*] [*British*]
**HSC** .......... Huntington Society of Canada
**HSCA** ........ Horizontal Sweep Circuit Analyzer
**HSCC** ........ Heavy Specialized Carriers Conference [*Later, SC & RA*]
**HSCC** ........ Hollywood Studio Collectors Club (EA)
**HSCE** ........ Higher School Certificate Examination (ADA)
**HSCF** ........ Health Sciences Computing Facility [*UCLA*]
**HSCG** ........ Erkowit/Carthago [*Sudan*] [*ICAO location identifier*] (ICLI)
**H Sch** ........ High School [*A publication*]
**HSchG** ...... Handelsschutzgesetz [*Trade Protection Law*] [*German*]
**H Sch J** ...... High School Journal [*A publication*]
**H Sch Q** ..... High School Quarterly [*A publication*]
**H Sch Teach** ... High School Teacher [*A publication*]
**HSCI** ......... High School Characteristics Index [*Research test*] [*Psychology*]
**HSCL** ......... Harvard Studies in Comparative Literature [*A publication*]
**HSCL** ......... High-Speed Command Link
**HSCLCS** .... Harpoon Shipboard Command and Launch Control Set [*Missiles*] (NVT)
**HSCLS** ...... Harpoon Shipboard Command and Launch Subsystem [*Missiles*] (MCD)
**HSCO** ........ Hungarian Shipping Co. Ltd. (DS)
**HSCOCS** ... House Select Committee on the Outer Continental Shelf [*US Congress*] [*Marine science*] (MSC)
**HSCOR** ..... House Staff Check on Rounds [*Medicine*]
**HSCP** ........ Harvard Studies in Classical Philology [*A publication*]
**HSCP** ........ Health Science Cluster Program [*University of Connecticut*] [*Research center*] (RCD)
**HSCP** ........ Heat-Shock Cognate Protein [*Biochemistry*]
**HSCP** ........ High-Speed Card Punch [*Data processing*] (AABC)
**HSCPA** ...... Hospital and Community Psychiatry [*A publication*]
**HSCR** ........ High-Speed Card Reader [*Data processing*] (AABC)
**HSCR** ........ High Sub-Chief Ranger [*Ancient Order of Foresters*]
**HSCRA** ...... Hastings Center. Report [*A publication*]
**HSCS** ........ Helicopter Subcontrol Ship [*Navy*] (NVT)
**HSCSBW** .. History of Science Series [*A publication*]
**HSCT** ........ High-Speed Civil Transport [*Supersonic plane*]
**HSCT** ........ High-Speed Compound Terminal [*Data processing*] (MCD)
**HSCT** ........ Hughes Satellite Communications Terminal
**HSCT** ........ Hypersonic Commercial Transport [*Airplane*]
**H & SCTB** ... Heavy & Specialized Carriers Tariff Bureau
**HSCTT** ...... High-Speed Card Teletypewriter Terminal [*Data processing*] (CET)
**HSCU** ........ Helicopter Subcontrol Unit (NVT)
**HSCU** ........ Hydraulic Supply and Checkout Unit (NASA)
**HSCW** ....... Helicopter Sea Control Wing (NVT)
**HSD** .......... Hamilton Standard Division (NASA)
**HSD** .......... Hardsite Defense [*Army*] (AABC)
**HSD** .......... Hawker-Siddeley Dynamics
**HSD** .......... Height Sensing Device
**HSD** .......... Hemisphere Development Corp. [*Vancouver Stock Exchange symbol*]
**HSD** .......... High-Speed Data
**HSD** .......... High-Speed Displacement (IEEE)
**HSD** .......... High-Speed Draft [*Print quality*]
**HSD** .......... Higher Anti-Submarine Detector [*British military*] (DMA)
**HSD** .......... Hit Scoring Device
**HSD** .......... Homer Semana Dia (BJA)
**HSD** .......... Honestly Significant Difference
**HSD** .......... Horizontal Situation Display
**HSD** .......... Hot Shutdown (IEEE)
**HSD** .......... Hot Side
**HSD** .......... Human Services Division [*Air Force*]
**HSD** .......... Human Systems Division [*Brooks Air Force Base, TX*] [*United States Air Force Systems Command*] (GRD)
**HSD** .......... Hydropneumatic Suspension Device
**HSD** .......... Hydroxysteroid Dehydrogenase [*An enzyme*]
**HSD** .......... Hypertonic Saline Dextran [*Medicine*]
**HSDA** ........ High-Speed Data Acquisition [*Data processing*]
**HSDA** ........ High-Speed Data Assembly [*Ground Communications Facility, NASA*]
**HS-DARS** ... High-Speed Data Acquisition and Reduction System
**HSDB** ........ Debba [*Sudan*] [*ICAO location identifier*] (ICLI)
**HSDB** ........ Hastings' Shorter Dictionary of the Bible [*A publication*] (BJA)
**HSDB** ........ Hazardous Substances Data Bank [*National Library of Medicine*] [*Information service or system*] (IID)
**HSDB** ........ High-Speed Data Buffer
**HSDC** ........ Hawaii State Data Center [*Hawaii State Department of Planning and Economic Development*] [*Information service or system*] (IID)
**HSDE** ........ High School Driver Education [*Department of Transportation*]
**HSDF** ........ High-Speed Digital Filter
**HSDG** ........ Hamburg-Sudamerikanische Dampschiffarts-Gesellschaft [*Hamburg-South American Steamship Company*] [*Shipping*] (ROG)
**HSDG** ........ High School Diploma Graduate [*Military*]
**HSDI** ......... High-Speed Data Interface
**HSDL** ........ Dilling [*Sudan*] [*ICAO location identifier*] (ICLI)
**HSDL** ........ High-Speed Data Line [*or Link*]
**HSDM** ....... Dueim [*Sudan*] [*ICAO location identifier*] (ICLI)
**HSDM** ....... Hemisphere Development Corp. [*NASDAQ symbol*] (NQ)
**HSDM** ....... High-Speed Die Mounter
**HSDN** ........ Dongola [*Sudan*] [*ICAO location identifier*] (ICLI)
**HSDP** ........ Hardsite Data Processor [*Army*] (AABC)
**HSDS** ........ Horizontal Situation Display System
**HSDT** ........ High-Speed Distributor Transmitter
**HSDT** ........ Hopper Side Tanks [*on a ship*] (DS)
**HSDZ** ........ Damazin [*Sudan*] [*ICAO location identifier*] (ICLI)
**HsE** ........... Hawker-Siddeley Electronics Ltd., Microform Division, Fairfield, V, Australia [*Library symbol*] [*Library of Congress*] (LCLS)
**HSE** .......... Health and Safety Executive [*Department of Employment*] [*Sheffield, England*]
**HSE** .......... Heat-Shock Element [*Genetics*]
**HSE** .......... Helsinki Stock Exchange [*Finland*]
**HSE** .......... Herpes Simplex Encephalitis [*Medicine*]
**HSE** .......... Hic Sepultus Est [*Here Lies Buried*] [*Latin*]
**HSE** .......... High School Equivalency (OICC)
**HSE** .......... Home Sports Entertainment [*Cable-television system*]
**HSE** .......... Honolulu Stock Exchange [*Hawaii*]
**HSE** .......... House
**HSE** .......... Hungarian Studies in English [*A publication*]
**HSEAD** ..... Historical Society of Early American Decoration (EA)

**Hse Builder** ... House Builder [*A publication*]
**HSEC** ........ Historical Society of the Episcopal Church (EA)
**HSEF** ........ High School Evangelism Fellowship (EA)
**Hse and Garden** ... House and Garden [*A publication*]
**HSEHOLD** ... Household
**HSEKPR** ... Housekeeper (ROG)
**HSEL** ........ High-Speed Selector Channel
**HSELINE** ... Health and Safety Executive Online [*Health and Safety Executive*] [*Bibliographic database*] [*British*]
**HSELL** ...... Hiroshima Studies in English Language and Literature [*A publication*]
**Hse of Lords Select Commit Eur Commun Rep** ... House of Lords. Select Committee on the European Communities. Reports [*A publication*]
**HSEN** ........ Home Sports Entertainment Network [*Cable TV programming service*]
**HSEP** ........ High-Speed Electrostatic Printer
**HSERC** ...... Historical Society of the Evangelical and Reformed Church [*Later, ERHS-UCC*] (EA)
**H/serf** ........ High-Scope Educational Research Foundation (EA)
**HSES** ........ Hughes Satellite Earth Station
**HSES** ........ Hydrostatic Equilibrium System [*For chromatography*]
**HSEUBC** ... Historical Society of the Evangelical United Brethren Church [*Later, General Commission on Archives and History of the United Methodist Church*] (EA)
**HSF** .......... Hartford Seminary Foundation [*Connecticut*]
**HSF** .......... Hawaiian Sea Frontier
**HSF** .......... Heat-Shock Transcription Factor [*Genetics*]
**HSF** .......... Heat-Stable Fraction
**HSF** .......... Hepatocyte Stimulating Factor [*Endocrinology*]
**HSF** .......... High Seas Fleet [*British military*] (DMA)
**HSF** .......... High-Starch Fraction [*Food technology*]
**HSF** .......... Histamine-Induced Suppressor Factor [*Immunology*]
**HSF** .......... Hotel Sundry Fund [*Air Force*]
**HSF** .......... Household Sample File [*Australian Bureau of Statistics*]
**HSF** .......... Human Services Forum (EA)
**HSF** .......... Hyderabad State Force [*British military*] (DMA)
**HSF** .......... Hypergol Servicing Facility [*NASA*] (NASA)
**HSF** .......... Hypersonic Flow
**HSF** .......... Hypothalamic Secretory Factor [*Endocrinology*]
**HSFAE** ...... High-Speed Fuel Air Explosive
**HSFC** ........ Hank Snow Fan Club (EA)
**HSFF** ........ High-Speed Force Feed
**HSFMCV** ... Huguenot Society of the Founders of Manakin in the Colony of Virginia (EA)
**HSFO** ........ High Sulphur Fuel Oil
**HSFPJ** ...... Holocaust Survivors and Friends in Pursuit of Justice (EA)
**HSFS** ........ El Fasher [*Sudan*] [*ICAO location identifier*] (ICLI)
**HSFS** ........ High-Speed Flight Station [*NASA*]
**HSG** .......... Harris Steel Group, Inc. [*Toronto Stock Exchange symbol*]
**HSG** .......... Herpes Simplex Genitalis
**HSG** .......... High School for Girls (ADA)
**HSG** .......... High School Graduate [*Classified advertising*]
**HSG** .......... High Sierra Group [*Nevada-based group proposing CD-ROM standards*]
**HSG** .......... High Sustained G2 Acceleration [*NASA*] (NASA)
**HSG** .......... Holy Shroud Guild (EA)
**HSG** .......... Housing (AABC)
**HSG** .......... Human Standard Globulin [*Medicine*]
**HSG** .......... Hydroshift Gun
**HSG** .......... Hysterosalpingogram [*Gynecology*]
**HS-GC** ...... Headspace Sampling-Gas Chromatography
**HSGF** ........ Gedaref/Azaza [*Sudan*] [*ICAO location identifier*] (ICLI)
**HSGF** ........ Human Skeletal Growth Factor
**HSGG** ........ Dinder/Galegu [*Sudan*] [*ICAO location identifier*] (ICLI)
**HSGM** ........ Honorary Sergeant Major of the Regiment
**HSGMOR** ... Honorary Sergeant Major of the Regiment [*Army*]
**HSGN** ........ Geneina [*Sudan*] [*ICAO location identifier*] (ICLI)
**HSGO** ........ Gogerial [*Sudan*] [*ICAO location identifier*] (ICLI)
**HSGP** ........ High School Geography Project [*Defunct*]
**HSGPC** ...... High-Speed Gel Permeation Chromatography
**HSGT** ........ High-Speed Ground Transportation
**HSGTA** ...... High Speed Ground Transportation Journal [*A publication*]
**HSGTC** ...... High-Speed Ground Test Center [*Later, TTC*] [*Pueblo, CO*]
**HSGTJ** ...... High Speed Ground Transportation Journal [*A publication*]
**HSGZA4** ... Hokkaido Journal of Orthopedic and Traumatic Surgery [*A publication*]
**HSH** .......... Hebrew School Headache (BJA)
**HSH** .......... Heinemann's Scientific Handbooks [*A publication*]
**HSH** .......... His [*or Her*] Serene Highness [*Used for certain Continental European princes or princesses*]
**HSH** .......... Horseshoe (ROG)
**HSHCA** ...... Han'guk Sikmul Poho Hakhoe Chi [*A publication*]
**HSHH** ........ Hill Staffers for the Hungry and Homeless (EA)
**HSHKA** ...... Bulletin. Korean Fisheries Society [*South Korea*] [*A publication*]
**H/SHLD** ... Heat Shield [*Automotive engineering*]
**HSHLD** ...... Household (MSA)
**HSHP** ........ High School for Health Professions
**HSHRA** ...... HSMHA [*Health Services and Mental Health Administration*] Health Report [*A publication*]
**HSHTDS** ... Handbook of Shock Trauma [*A publication*]
**HSI** .......... Handbook of Service Instructions (MCD)
**HSI** .......... Hang Seng Index [*Hong Kong Futures Exchange Index*]
**HSI** .......... Hastings [*Nebraska*] [*Airport symbol*] (OAG)
**HSI** .......... Headquarters Staff Instruction
**HSI** .......... Health Development Services, Incorporated [*Toronto Stock Exchange symbol*]
**HSI** .......... Heat Stress Index
**HSI** .......... Heraldry Society of Ireland (EA)
**HSI** .......... Hi-Shear Industries, Inc. [*NYSE symbol*] (SPSG)
**HSI** .......... High School Equivalency Index
**HSI** .......... High Solar Intensity
**HSI** .......... High-Speed Interferometer [*Measures chemical components of smog*] (KSC)
**HSI** .......... High Strand Intensity
**HSI** .......... Historical Society of Israel (EAIO)
**HSI** .......... Home and School Institute (EA)
**HSI** .......... Horizontal Situation Indicator [*Aviation*]
**HSI** .......... Hoya Society International (EA)
**HSI** .......... Hsinkong [*Republic of China*] [*Also, SGK*] [*Seismograph station code, US Geological Survey*] (SEIS)
**HSI** .......... Hue-Saturation-Intensity [*Video monitor*] (BYTE)
**HSIA** ........ Halogenated Solvents Industry Alliance (EA)
**HSICNI** ..... Honourable Society of the Inns of Court of Northern Ireland
**HSIM** ........ Hill Samuel Investment Management [*British*]
**HSIQ** ........ High School Interest Questionnaire [*Vocational guidance test*]
**H/SIR** ........ Hardware/Software Integration Review (MCD)
**HSIS** ........ Highway Safety Information Service [*National Highway Safety Administration*] (IID)
**HSJ** .......... High School Journal [*A publication*]
**HSJ** .......... Honeycombed Sandwich Joint
**HSJ** .......... Hoshina [*Japan*] [*Seismograph station code, US Geological Survey*] (SEIS)
**HSJ** .......... Housman Society. Journal [*A publication*]
**HSK** .......... Hackensack, MN [*Location identifier*] [*FAA*] (FAAL)
**HSK** .......... Heat Sink Kit
**HSK** .......... Honeysuckle Creek Tracking Station [*NASA*] (KSC)
**HSK** .......... Honorary Surgeon of the King [*British*]
**HSK** .......... Horizontal Sling Kit [*NASA*] (NASA)
**HSK** .......... Hsinking [*Sirkyo, Chang Chun*] [*Republic of China*] [*Seismograph station code, US Geological Survey*] (SEIS)
**HSK** .......... HSK Minerals Ltd. [*Toronto Stock Exchange symbol*]
**HSKA** ........ Kassala [*Sudan*] [*ICAO location identifier*] (ICLI)
**HSKCA** ..... Han'guk Sikp'un Kwahakhoe Chi [*A publication*]
**HSKEA** ...... Hoshasen Seibutsu Kenkyu [*A publication*]
**HSKG** ........ Khashm El Girba [*Sudan*] [*ICAO location identifier*] (ICLI)
**HSKI** ........ Kosti/Rabak [*Sudan*] [*ICAO location identifier*] (ICLI)
**HSKJ** ........ Kago Kaju [*Sudan*] [*ICAO location identifier*] (ICLI)
**HSKP** ........ Kapoeta [*Sudan*] [*ICAO location identifier*] (ICLI)
**HSKPG** ...... Housekeeping (AFM)
**HSL** .......... Hardware Simulation Laboratory (NASA)
**HSL** .......... Hartford Studies in Literature [*A publication*]
**HSL** .......... Health Service Laboratory [*Army*] (AABC)
**HSL** .......... Heenan Senlac Resources Ltd. [*Toronto Stock Exchange symbol*]
**HSL** .......... Helicopter Antisubmarine Squadron Light (NVT)
**HSL** .......... Herpes Simplex Labialis
**HSL** .......... High-Speed Launch [*Navy*]
**HSL** .......... High-Speed Logic
**HSL** .......... Highway Safety Literature Service [*National Academy of Science*] [*Washington, DC*]
**Hsl** ............ Homoserine Lactone [*An amino acid*]
**HSL** .......... Hormone-Sensitive Lipase [*An enzyme*]
**HSL** .......... Hue, Saturation, Lightness [*Color model*] (PCM)
**HSL** .......... Huslia [*Alaska*] [*Airport symbol*] (OAG)
**HSL** .......... Schluesselnummer des Binnenhandels [*Domestic Trade Index*] [*German*]
**HSLA** ........ High-Strength Low-Alloy [*or Light-Alloy*] [*Steel*]
**HSL Abs** .... HSL [*Health and Safety Executive Library*] Abstract [*England*] [*A publication*]
**HSLC** ........ High-Speed Liquid Chromatography
**HSLCG** ..... Health Science Libraries of Central Georgia [*Library network*]
**HSLD** ........ Home Savings & Loan Association, Inc. [*Durham, NC*] [*NASDAQ symbol*] (NQ)
**HSLDA** ..... Home School Legal Defense Association (EA)
**HSLI** ........ Kadugli [*Sudan*] [*ICAO location identifier*] (ICLI)
**HSLIC** ...... Health Science Libraries Information Cooperative [*Library network*]
**HSLLC** ...... High-Speed Liquid-Liquid Chromatography
**HSLP** ........ Haydn Society [*Record label*]
**HSLR** ........ Lirangu [*Sudan*] [*ICAO location identifier*] (ICLI)
**HSLS** ........ Harvard Slavic Studies [*A publication*]
**HSL'S** ...... Hlinkova Slovenska l'Udova Strana [*Hlinka's Slovak People's Party*] [*Also, SL'S*] [*Political party*] (PPE)
**HSLWI** ...... Helical Spring Lock Washer Institute
**HSM** .......... Hand and Shoe Monitor [*Radiation detection*]
**HSM** .......... Handbook of Soil Mechanics [*Elsevier Book Series*] [*A publication*]
**HSM** .......... Handling and Shipping Management [*A publication*]
**HSM** .......... Hard Structure Module
**HSM** .......... Hard Structure Munition

**HSM** .......... Hardened Silo Missile
**HSM** .......... Harvard Semitic Museum (BJA)
**HSM** .......... Health Services and Mental Health Administration [*Later, ADAMHA*] [*Abolished, 1973*] [*HEW*]
**HSM** .......... Health Services and Mental Health Administration. Publications [*A publication*]
**HSM** .......... Hierarchical Storage Manager
**HSM** .......... High-Speed Memory [*Data processing*]
**HSM** .......... His [*or Her*] Serene Majesty
**HSM** .......... Horsham [*Australia*] [*Airport symbol*] [*Obsolete*] (OAG)
**HSM** .......... Horsham Corp. [*Toronto Stock Exchange symbol*] [*NYSE symbol*]
**HSM** .......... Hospital - Surgical - Medical
**HSM** .......... Human Systems Management [*A publication*]
**HSM** .......... Humanitarian Service Medal (MCD)
**HSMA** ....... Hotel Sales Management Association [*Later, HSMAI*] (EA)
**HSMAI** ..... Hotel Sales and Marketing Association International (EA)
**HSMAI-EO** ... Hotel Sales and Marketing Association International - European Office [*Utrecht, Netherlands*] (EAIO)
**HSMCDR** ... High-Speed Multichannel Data Recorder [*Instrumentation*]
**HSMD** ....... Maridi [*Sudan*] [*ICAO location identifier*] (ICLI)
**HSMF** ....... Holocaust Survivors Memorial Foundation (EA)
**HSMGC** .... Heavy Section Machine Gun Corps [*British military*] (DMA)
**H & S Mgmt** ... Handling and Shipping Management [*A publication*]
**HSMHA** .... Health Services and Mental Health Administration [*Later, ADAMHA*] [*Abolished, 1973*] [*HEW*]
**HSMIMP** ... High-Speed Modular Interface Message Processor
**HSMK** ....... Rumbek [*Sudan*] [*ICAO location identifier*] (ICLI)
**HSMPE8** ... Herbs, Spices, and Medicinal Plants [*A publication*]
**HSMR** ....... Merowe [*Sudan*] [*ICAO location identifier*] (ICLI)
**HSMS** ....... High-Speed Microwave Switch
**HSMSR** ..... Hardsite Missile Site RADAR [*Army*] (AABC)
**HSM-WA** ... Hard Structure Munition Weaponization Analysis (MCD)
**HSN** .......... Haglund Industry International [*Vancouver Stock Exchange symbol*]
**HSN** .......... Hawthorne Society. Newsletter [*A publication*]
**HSN** .......... Hereditary Sensory Neuropathies [*Neurology*]
**HSN** .......... Hermaphrodite-Specific Neuron [*Cytology*]
**HSN** .......... Home Shopping Network [*Cable-television system*]
**HSN** .......... Home Shopping Network, Inc. [*NYSE symbol*] (SPSG)
**HSN** .......... Hospital Satellite Network [*Los Angeles, CA*] [*Cable-television system*]
**HSN** .......... Hsinchu [*Republic of China*] [*Seismograph station code, US Geological Survey*] (SEIS)
**HSN** .......... Hughes Sports Network [*Formerly, SNI*]
**HSNA** ....... Nasir [*Sudan*] [*ICAO location identifier*] (ICLI)
**HSND** ....... Shendi [*Sudan*] [*ICAO location identifier*] (ICLI)
**HSNG** ....... Housing
**HSNH** ....... Nahud [*Sudan*] [*ICAO location identifier*] (ICLI)
**H/SNK** ...... Heat Sink [*Automotive engineering*]
**HSNL** ....... Nyala [*Sudan*] [*ICAO location identifier*] (ICLI)
**HSNM** ....... Nimule/Nimule [*Sudan*] [*ICAO location identifier*] (ICLI)
**HSNP** ....... Hawker-Siddeley Nuclear Power Co. Ltd. [*British*]
**HSNP** ....... High-Speed Nonimpact Printer [*Acronym pronounced "hisnip"*] [*Data processing*]
**HSNPL** ..... Harvard Studies and Notes in Philology and Literature [*A publication*]
**HSNR** ....... Sennar [*Sudan*] [*ICAO location identifier*] (ICLI)
**HSNTA** ..... New Testament Apocrypha [*E. Henneke and W. Schneemelcher*] [*A publication*] (BJA)
**HSNW** ....... New Halfa [*Sudan*] [*ICAO location identifier*] (ICLI)
**HSNY** ....... Holland Society of New York (EA)
**HSO** .......... Haifa Symphony Orchestra (BJA)
**HSO** .......... Headquarters Signal Officer (NATG)
**HS & O** ...... Heads of Services and Offices [*Red Cross*]
**HSO** .......... Hershey Oil Corp. [*AMEX symbol*] [*Toronto Stock Exchange symbol*] (SPSG)
**HSO** .......... High Specific Output [*Automotive engineering*]
**HSO** .......... Higher Scientific Officer [*British*]
**HSO** .......... Hydrogen Seal Oil [*System*] (NRCH)
**HSOB** ....... El Obeid [*Sudan*] [*ICAO location identifier*] (ICLI)
**HSOD** ....... Human Superoxide Dismutase [*An enzyme*]
**H SOM** ...... Hora Somni [*At Bedtime*] [*Pharmacy*]
**HSORS** ..... High Seas Oil Recovery System
**HSP** .......... Half-Shade Plate
**HSP** .......... Hardwire Safing Panel
**HSP** .......... Head Start Program [*Education*]
**HSP** .......... Health Stabilization Program [*NASA*] (NASA)
**HSP** .......... Health Systems Plan [*HEW*]
**HSP** .......... Heat Shock Protein [*Physiology*]
**HSP** .......... Heavy, Stressed Platform
**HSP** .......... Heparin Sulfate Proteoglycan [*Biochemistry*]
**HSP** .......... Hereditary Spastic Paraplegia [*Medicine*]
**HSP** .......... High-Speed Printer [*Data processing*]
**HSP** .......... High-Speed Pulse
**HSP** .......... Hospital Service Plan [*British*]
**HSP** .......... Hospitals [*A publication*]
**HSP** .......... Hot Springs, VA [*Location identifier*] [*FAA*] (FAAL)
**HSP** .......... Hot Stamping Press
**HSP** .......... Hrvatska Stranka Prava [*Croatian Party of Rights*] [*Yugoslavia*] [*Political party*] (PPE)
**HSP** .......... Human Sciences Project [*National Science Foundation*]
**HSP** .......... Human Serum Prealbumin
**HSP** .......... Hydrocarbon Solids Process [*Tosco Corp.*] [*Oil shale pyrolysis*]
**HSPA** ....... Hawaiian Sugar Planters' Association (EA)
**HSPA** ....... High-Speed Parallel Adder
**HSPA** ....... Home Savings Association of Pennsylvania [*Tamaqua, PA*] [*NASDAQ symbol*] (NQ)
**HSPA** ....... Human Service Personnel Association [*Defunct*] (EA)
**HSPA** ....... Pachella [*Sudan*] [*ICAO location identifier*] (ICLI)
**HSPC** ....... Heat Sterilizable Potting Compound
**HSPDP** ..... Hill State People's Democratic Party [*India*] [*Political party*] (PPW)
**HSPF** ....... Heating Seasonal Performance Factor
**HSPh** ....... Harvard Studies in Classical Philology [*A publication*]
**HSPhS** ..... Historical Studies in the Physical Sciences [*A publication*]
**HSPI** ......... High-Speed Printer Interface (MCD)
**HSPI** ......... Pibor [*Sudan*] [*ICAO location identifier*] (ICLI)
**HSPL** ........ Harvard Studies and Notes in Philology and Literature [*A publication*]
**HSPLS** ..... Hawaii State Public Library System [*Hawaii State Department of Education*] [*Information service or system*] (IID)
**HSPQ** ....... High School Personality Questionnaire [*Psychology*]
**HSPS** ........ Heat Shock Protein Synthesis
**HSPS** ........ Highway Safety Program Standard [*Department of Transportation*]
**HSPS** ........ Hydrographic Survey Platform System (MCD)
**HSPT** ........ High School Placement Test
**HSPTAL** ... High-Speed Paper Tape Absolute Loader [*Data processing*] (MDG)
**HSPTP** ..... High-Speed Paper Tape Punch [*Data processing*] (AABC)
**HSPTR** ..... High-Speed Paper Tape Reader [*Data processing*] (CET)
**HSQ** .......... Heat-Shield Qualification [*NASA*] (KSC)
**HSQ** .......... Helping Smokers Quit [*American Cancer Society*] (EA)
**HSQ** .......... Home Screening Questionnaire [*Test*] [*Psychology*]
**HSQ** .......... Houston, TX [*Location identifier*] [*FAA*] (FAAL)
**HSQB** ....... Health Standards and Quality Bureau [*HEW*]
**HSQR** ....... High-Strength Quick Release (MCD)
**HSR** .......... Hampshire Swine Registry (EA)
**HSR** .......... Hardware Status Register (MCD)
**HSR** .......... Hart-Scott-Rodino Antitrust Improvements Act [*1976*]
**HSR** .......... Health Service Region [*Army*] (AABC)
**HSR** .......... Health Services Research [*A publication*]
**HSR** .......... High School Percentile Rank
**HSR** .......... High-Speed RADAR (MCD)
**HSR** .......... High-Speed Rail
**HSR** .......... High-Speed Reader [*Data processing*]
**HSR** .......... High-Speed Relay
**HSR** .......... Homestead Resources, Inc. [*Vancouver Stock Exchange symbol*]
**HSR** .......... Homogeneously Staining Region [*Cytology*]
**HSR** .......... Hot Springs, SD [*Location identifier*] [*FAA*] (FAAL)
**HSR** .......... Hungarian Studies Review [*A publication*]
**HSRA** ....... Half Saddlebred Registry of America (EA)
**HSRA** ....... Harvard-Smithsonian Reference Atmosphere
**HSRA** ....... High-Speed Data Regeneration Assembly [*Ground Communications Facility, NASA*]
**HSRA** ....... High Speed Rail Association (EA)
**HSRA** ....... Hollow Shaft Rotary Actuator
**HSRC** ....... Health Services Research Center [*Georgia Institute of Technology*] [*Research center*] (RCD)
**HSRC** ....... High School Red Cross
**HSRD** ....... Health Services Research and Development [*Series*] [*A publication*]
**HSR & D** ... Health Services Research and Development Service [*Washington, DC*] [*Veterans Administration*] (GRD)
**HSRD** ....... Hypertension Secondary to Renal Disease [*Medicine*]
**HSRFO** ..... High-Sulfur Residual Fuel Oil [*Petroleum technology*]
**HSRI** ......... Health Systems Research Institute
**HSRI** ......... Highly Sensitive Refractive Index
**HSRI** ......... Highway Safety Research Institute [*University of Michigan*]
**HSRI (High Saf Res Inst) Res Rev** ... HSRI (Highway Safety Research Institute) Research Review [*A publication*]
**HSRI Rep** .. HSRI [*Highway Safety Research Institute*] Report [*A publication*]
**HSRI Res Rev** ... HSRI [*University of Michigan Highway Safety Research Institute*] Research Review [*A publication*]
**HSRJ** ........ Raga [*Sudan*] [*ICAO location identifier*] (ICLI)
**HSRL** ........ Harvard Studies in Romance Languages [*A publication*]
**HSRN** ....... Renk [*Sudan*] [*ICAO location identifier*] (ICLI)
**HSRO** ....... High-Speed Repetitive Operation
**HSRP** ........ High-Speed Rotary Prism
**HSRPA** ..... Health Services Report [*A publication*]
**HSRS** ........ Hurricane Supersonic Research Site
**HSRTC** ..... Health and Safety Research and Test Center [*Bureau of Mines*]
**HSRTP** ..... Health Services Research and Training Program [*Purdue University*] [*Research center*] (RCD)
**HSRV** ....... Human Spumaretrovirus
**HSS** .......... British Library Catalog: Humanities and Social Sciences [*Information service or system*] (CRD)
**HSS** .......... Habitability Support System (MCD)
**HSS** .......... Hars Systems, Inc. [*Vancouver Stock Exchange symbol*]

**HSS** .......... Harvard Semitic Series [*A publication*]
**HSS** .......... Harvard Slavic Studies [*A publication*]
**HSS** .......... Health Surveillance System [*Shell Oil Co.*]
**HSS** .......... Heeres-Sauerstoffschutzgeraet [*Service Oxygen Breathing Apparatus*] [*German military - World War II*]
**HSS** .......... Helmet Sight Subsystem (RDA)
**HSS** .......... Hepatic Stimulator Substance
**HSS** .......... Heraldry Society of Scotland [*Edinburgh*] (EAIO)
**HSS** .......... Hierarchy Service System [*Toshiba Corp.*]
**HSS** .......... High School Size
**HSS** .......... High-Speed Simultaneous [*Electric trip mechanism*]
**HSS** .......... High-Speed Steel
**HSS** .......... High-Speed Storage [*Data processing*] (IEEE)
**HSS** .......... High-Speed System [*Ground Communications Facility, NASA*]
**HSS** .......... High Spread Shears
**HSS** .......... High-Stress Strain (MCD)
**HSS** .......... Hispano-Suiza Society (EA)
**HSS** .......... Historiae Societatis Socius [*Fellow of the Historical Society*]
**HSS** .......... History of Science Society (EA)
**HSS** .......... Hokkaido University [*Japan*] [*Seismograph station code, US Geological Survey*] (SEIS)
**HSS** .......... Honeycomb-Supported Screen
**HSS** .......... Hospital and Specialist Services [*British*]
**HSS** .......... Hot Springs, NC [*Location identifier*] [*FAA*] (FAAL)
**HSS** .......... Hrvatska Seljacka Stranka [*Croatian Peasant Party*] [*Yugoslavia*] [*Political party*] (PPE)
**HSS** .......... Hull Seal Section
**HSS** .......... Hybrid Simulation System
**HSS** .......... Hydraulic Subsystem Simulator (NASA)
**HSS** .......... Hydropneumatic Suspension System (MCD)
**HSS** .......... Hypertonic Saline Solution
**HSS** .......... Hypertrophic Subaortic Stenosis [*Cardiology*]
**HSSA**.......... Handbag Supply Salesmen's Association (EA)
**HSSA**.......... Health and Safety Science Abstracts [*Cambridge Scientific Abstracts*] [*Information service or system*] (CRD)
**HSSALB** ... Health Service Support Air Land Battle
**HSSC**.......... Heavy SEAL [*Sea-Air-Land*] Support Craft (NVT)
**HSSC**.......... High-Speed Surface Craft, Incorporating Hovering Craft and Hydrofoil [*A publication*]
**HSSC**.......... Historical Society of Southern California. Quarterly [*A publication*]
**HSSCQ**...... Historical Society of Southern California. Quarterly [*A publication*]
**HSSDB**...... High-Speed Serial Data Buffer (MCD)
**HSSDS**...... High-Speed Switched Digital Service [*AT & T*] (TSSD)
**HSSG** ........ Heeres-Sauerstoffschutzgeraet [*Service Oxygen Breathing Apparatus*] [*German military - World War II*]
**HSSG** ........ High-Speed Symbol Generator
**HSSG** ........ Holograph Stress Strain Gauge
**HSSI**.......... Highway Safety Statistical Indicator
**HSSI**.......... Hospital Staffing Services, Incorporated [*NASDAQ symbol*] (NQ)
**HSSJ** ......... Juba [*Sudan*] [*ICAO location identifier*] (ICLI)
**HSSJB**....... Health and Social Services Journal [*A publication*]
**HSSM** ....... Malakal [*Sudan*] [*ICAO location identifier*] (ICLI)
**HSSP**......... Port Sudan [*Sudan*] [*ICAO location identifier*] (ICLI)
**HSSPF**....... Hoehere SS und Polizeifuehrer (BJA)
**HS & SS** .... Headquarters and Service Squadron
**HSSS**......... Khartoum [*Sudan*] [*ICAO location identifier*] (ICLI)
**HSSSR** ...... High School Students for Social Responsibility (EA)
**HSST**......... Heavy Section Steel Technology [*Nuclear Regulatory Commission*]
**HSST**......... High-Speed Surface Transport (MCD)
**HSSTD**...... Historical Sea Surface Temperature Data Project [*WMO*] (MSC)
**HSSW**........ Wadi Halfa/Nuba Lake [*Sudan*] [*ICAO location identifier*] (ICLI)
**HST** .......... [*Virus named for*] Hamazaki, Sato, Takahashi, and Tani, principal investigators [*Medicine*]
**H St**.......... Hamlet Studies [*A publication*]
**HST** .......... Harmonic and Spurious Totalizer
**HST** .......... Harry S Truman [*US president, 1884-1972*]
**HST** .......... Hawaiian Standard Time
**H ST** .......... Head Steward [*Navy*] [*British*] (ROG)
**HST** .......... Heat Shrinkable Tubing
**HSt**.......... Hebrew Studies [*A publication*]
**HST** .......... Helicopter Support Team [*Navy*] (NVT)
**HST** .......... Hexobarbital Sleeping Time [*In experimental animals*]
**HST** .......... High-Speed Technology [*Data processing*] (BYTE)
**HST** .......... High-Speed Telemetry
**HST** .......... High-Speed Train [*British*]
**HST** .......... High-Speed Tunnel [*NASA*]
**HST** .......... Hoist (MSA)
**HST** .......... Holland's Export Magazine. Holland Shipping and Trading [*Rotterdam*] [*A publication*]
**HST** .......... Homestead [*Florida*] [*Airport symbol*] (OAG)
**HST** .......... Homestead, FL [*Location identifier*] [*FAA*] (FAAL)
**HST** .......... Homogenate Survival Time
**HST** .......... Horizontal Seismic Trigger (IEEE)
**HST** .......... Hot Shot Tunnel
**HST** .......... Housing Study Tours [*British*]
**HST** .......... Hubble Space Telescope [*Great Observatory Program*] [*NASA*]
**HST** .......... Hydrostatic Transmission [*Automotive engineering*]
**HST** .......... Hypersonic Transport [*Aircraft*]
**HSTA** ........ High School Teachers' Association [*Australia*]
**HSTA** ........ Honda Sport Touring Association (EA)
**HSTAR**...... Helicopter Surveillance and Target Acquisition RADAR
**HSTC** ........ Henderson State Teachers College [*Later, HSC*] [*Arkansas*]
**HSTCXO**... High-Stability Temperature-Compensated Crystal Oscillator
**H STEPH** ... Henricus Stephanus [*Imprint*] [*Latin*] (ROG)
**HSTF**......... Heat-Shock Transcription Factor [*Genetics*]
**HSTH**........ Hose Thread
**Hst Kreise Olpe** ... Heimatstimmen aus dem Kreise Olpe [*A publication*]
**HSTL**......... Harry S Truman Library
**HSTL**......... High-Speed Telemetry Link
**HSTO** ........ Tong [*Sudan*] [*ICAO location identifier*] (ICLI)
**HSTP**......... Hard Stop (MCD)
**HSTP**......... Heat Sterilization Test Program
**H & STR**.... Headquarters and Service Troop [*Army*]
**HSTR** ........ Torit [*Sudan*] [*ICAO location identifier*] (ICLI)
**HSTRA**...... High-Strength Thermal-Resistant Alloy
**HSTRU** ..... Hydraulic System Test and Repair Unit [*Army*] (RDA)
**HSTS**......... Horizontal Stabilizer Trim Setting
**HSTS**......... Host Software Testing Section [*Social Security Administration*]
**HSTS**......... Hostess (FAAC)
**HSTSF** ...... Harry S Truman Scholarship Foundation (EA)
**HSTT**......... High-Speed Test Track
**HSTTL**...... High-Speed Transistor-Transistor Logic
**HSTU** ........ Tumbura [*Sudan*] [*ICAO location identifier*] (ICLI)
**H Studien**... Hispanistische Studien [*A publication*]
**HSTV** ........ High-Survivability Test Vehicle (MCD)
**HSTVL**...... High Survivability Test Vehicle, Lightweight [*Military*]
**HSTW** ....... Humane Society of Tinplate Workers [*A union*] [*British*]
**HSU**.......... Hardin-Simmons University [*Texas*]
**HSU**.......... Helium Service Unit (MCD)
**HSU**.......... Helium Speech Unscrambler [*Deep sea diving*]
**HSU**.......... Henderson State University [*Arkadelphia, AR*]
**HSU**.......... Humboldt State University [*Los Angeles, CA*]
**HSU**.......... Hydraulic Supply Unit
**HSUG**........ Housing Statistics Users Group (EA)
**HS/UMC** .. Historical Society of the United Methodist Church (EA)
**HSUNA**..... Humanist Student Union of North America
**HSUS** ........ Humane Society of the United States (EA)
**HSUSA**...... Heraldry Society of the United States of America (EA)
**HSUSC**...... Hymn Society in the United States and Canada (EA)
**HSV** .......... Head Small Veins [*Anatomy*]
**HSV** .......... Head Suppression Valve (AAG)
**HSV** .......... Herpes Simplex Virus
**HSV** .......... High-Stage Valve (MCD)
**HSV** .......... Highly Selective Vagotomy [*Medicine*]
**HSV** .......... Hue, Saturation, and Value [*Color model*] (BYTE)
**HSV** .......... Hull Solenoid Valve
**HSV** .......... Huntsville [*Alabama*] [*Airport symbol*]
**HSV** .......... Hydraulic Selector Valve
**HSV** .......... Hydrogen Saturated Vacancy [*Photovoltaic energy systems*]
**HSV** .......... Hydroxyinterlayered Smectite or Vermiculite
**HSVA** ........ Health Systems Vendors Association [*San Francisco, CA*] (EA)
**HSVE** ........ Herpes Simplex Virus Encephalitis [*Medicine*]
**HSVgD**...... Herpes Simplex Virus Glycoprotein D [*Biochemistry*]
**HSVL**......... Highveld Steel & Vanadium Corp. Ltd. [*NASDAQ symbol*] (NQ)
**HSW** .......... Heat Sink Welding [*Nuclear energy*] (NRCH)
**HSW** .......... Helena Southwestern Railroad Co. [*AAR code*]
**HSW** .......... Hot Spot [*Washington*] [*Seismograph station code, US Geological Survey*] [*Closed*] (SEIS)
**HSWA** ....... Hazardous and Solid Waste Amendments [*1984 amendments to RCRA*]
**HSWDC**.... Historical Society of Washington, DC (EA)
**HSWG**....... High-Speed Wire Guidance
**HSWH**....... High-Solid Waste Header [*Nuclear energy*] (NRCH)
**HSWP** ....... Hungarian Socialist Workers' Party [*Political party*] (PPW)
**HSWW**...... Wau [*Sudan*] [*ICAO location identifier*] (ICLI)
**HSY** .......... Health and Society [*A publication*]
**HSY** .......... Hershey Foods Corp. [*NYSE symbol*] (SPSG)
**HSYA** ........ Yambio [*Sudan*] [*ICAO location identifier*] (ICLI)
**HSYE** ........ Yei [*Sudan*] [*ICAO location identifier*] (ICLI)
**HSYL**......... Yirol [*Sudan*] [*ICAO location identifier*] (ICLI)
**HSYNC**..... Horizontal Synchronous [*Data processing*]
**HSYS**......... Hale Systems, Inc. [*NASDAQ symbol*] (NQ)
**HSZA** ........ Zalingei [*Sudan*] [*ICAO location identifier*] (ICLI)
**HSZD** ........ Hermetically Sealed Zener Diode
**H-S Z Physl** ... Hoppe-Seyler's Zeitschrift fuer Physiologische Chemie [*A publication*]
**HT**............. Haavara-Transfer (BJA)
**HT**............. Hadamard-Transform [*Mathematics*]
**HT**............. Haiti [*ANSI two-letter standard code*] (CNC)
**ht** ............... Haiti [*MARC country of publication code*] [*Library of Congress*] (LCCP)
**HT**............. Half-Tilt Containers (DCTA)
**HT**............. Half-Time [*Survey*] [*Shipping*]
**HT**............. Half-Title [*Publishing*]
**HT**............. Half-Tracked [*Vehicle*] (NATG)

H-T ........ Half-Truck [*British*]
HT ........ Halftone [*Photoengraving*]
H & T ........ Hall and Twell's English Chancery Reports [*1849-50*] [*A publication*] (DLA)
HT ........ Halt and Transfer
HT ........ Hand Test [*Psychology*]
HT ........ Hand Translation (MCD)
HT ........ Handling Time
H & T ........ Handling and Transportation (KSC)
HT ........ Hard Top [*Automobile ads*]
H & T ........ Hardened and Tempered [*Steel*]
HT ........ Haustus [*A Drink*] [*Pharmacy*]
HT ........ Hawaiian Territory [*Prior to statehood*]
HT ........ Hawaiian Theater [*Military*]
HT ........ Hawaiian Time
HT ........ Head, Tail [*Coin-tossing probability*]
HT ........ Head-to-Tail [*Polymer structure*]
H/T ........ Head per Track
HT ........ Head Turn [*Industrial engineering*]
HT ........ Headed Type
HT ........ Heart
HT ........ Heart Tones [*Medicine*]
HT ........ Heart Transplantation
HT ........ Heat (AAG)
HT ........ Heat Transfer (NASA)
HT ........ Heat Treat
HT ........ Heavy Tank
HT ........ Heavy Terminal [*AFSCF*] (MCD)
HT ........ Hebrew Text (BJA)
HT ........ Height (AAG)
HT ........ Height of Target
HT ........ Height Technician [*Air Force*]
HT ........ Height Telling [*RADAR*]
HT ........ Helen Thomas [*British author*]
HT ........ Helicopter Training Squadron [*Navy symbol*] (NVT)
HT ........ Herald Tribune [*A publication*]
HT ........ Herd Test
H-T ........ Hesperis-Tamuda [*A publication*]
HT ........ High Technology (MCD)
HT ........ High Temperature
HT ........ High Tension
HT ........ High Tide
HT ........ High Times [*A publication*]
HT ........ High Treason
HT ........ Histologic Transformation [*Medicine*]
HT ........ Historic Towns [*A publication*]
HT ........ Historisk Tidskrift [*A publication*]
H & T ........ History and Theory [*A publication*]
HT ........ History Today [*A publication*]
HT ........ Hittite Texts in the Cuneiform Character from Tablets in the British Museum [*London*] (BJA)
HT ........ Hoc Tempore [*At This Time*] [*Latin*]
HT ........ Hoc Titulo [*In, or Under, This Title*] [*Latin*]
H u T ........ Hoch- und Tiefbau [*A publication*]
HT ........ Hoisting Tool (MCD)
HT ........ Holding Time [*Telecommunications*] (TEL)
HT ........ Hollow Tile [*Technical drawings*]
HT ........ Holy Trinity
HT ........ Home Treatment [*Medicine*]
HT ........ Homing Terrier [*Missile*]
HT ........ Homing Transponders
HT ........ Homing Type (NATG)
HT ........ Horizontal Tabulation [*Data processing*]
HT ........ Horological Times [*A publication*] (EAAP)
HT ........ Horsed Transport [*Military*]
HT ........ Horserace Totalisator [*Set up in 1926 to provide alternative form of betting and to generate income from improvement of racing*] [*British*]
HT ........ Hospital Train
H & T ........ Hospitalization and Treatment
HT ........ Hot Report (NATG)
HT ........ Hot Tin (MSA)
HT ........ House Trailer (AFM)
HT ........ Howard Terminal [*AAR code*]
HT ........ Hubbard Tank [*Medicine*]
HT ........ Hughes Tool Co. [*NYSE symbol*] (SPSG)
HT ........ Huhner Test [*Gynecology*]
HT ........ Human Teratocarcinoma [*A cell line*]
HT ........ Human Thrombin [*Cytochemistry*]
HT ........ Human Toxicology [*A publication*]
HT ........ Human Tumor [*Oncology*]
HT ........ Humboldt-Taschenbuecher [*A publication*]
HT ........ Hunter Transport [*Commercial firm*] [*British*]
HT ........ Hybrid Tea [*Roses*] (ROG)
HT ........ Hydrolyzable Tannin Level
HT ........ Hydrophobic Tail [*Surfactant technology*]
HT ........ Hydrotherapy [*Medicine*]
HT ........ Hydroxytryptamine [*Biochemistry*]
Ht ........ Hypermetropia, Total [*Ophthalmology*]
HT ........ Hypertriglyceridemia [*Medicine*]
HT ........ Hypertropia [*Medicine*]
HT ........ Hypodermic Tablet [*Medicine*]
HT ........ Hypotension [*Medicine*]
HT ........ Hypothalamus [*Neurology*]
HT ........ Mustard Gas [*Also, H, HD, HS, M*] [*Poison gas*] [*US Chemical Corps symbol*]
HT ........ Societe de Transports Aeriens [*Air Tchad*] [*Chad*] [*ICAO designator*] (FAAC)
HTA ........ Handbooks of Theology [*A publication*]
HTA ........ Harness Tracks of America (EA)
Hta ........ Hasta [*Until*] [*Business term*] [*Spanish*]
HTA ........ Heavier than Air
HTA ........ Help the Aged [*Superseded by AAIA*] (EA)
HTA ........ Herb Trade Association (EA)
HTA ........ High-Temperature Adhesive
HTA ........ High-Temperature Alloy
HTA ........ High-Temperature Ashing [*Analytical chemistry*]
HTA ........ Highway Traffic Act
HTA ........ Humanist Teachers' Association [*British*]
HTA ........ Hypophysiotropic Area [*of hypothalamus*] [*Endocrinology*]
HTAC ........ Hexadecyltrimethylammonium Chloride [*Organic chemistry*]
HTACS ........ Human Thyroid Adenyl Cyclase Stimulator [*Endocrinology*]
HTAR ........ Arusha [*Tanzania*] [*ICAO location identifier*] (ICLI)
HTAS ........ Hug-a-Tree and Survive (EA)
HTB ........ Hair Tuning Bar
HTB ........ Heat Treat Block (MCD)
HTB ........ Hexadecimal-to-Binary
H-TB ........ High-Tension Battery
HTB ........ Highway Tariff Bureau [*Later, AMCTB*]
HTB ........ Hoch- und Tiefbau [*A publication*]
HTB ........ Hot Tub Bath [*Medicine*]
HTB ........ Howitzer Test Bed (RDA)
HTB ........ Hypergolic Test Building (KSC)
HTB ........ New York Herald Tribune Books [*A publication*]
HTBA ........ Hood's Texas Brigade Association (EA)
HTBDR ........ High-Temperature Burner-Duct Recuperator System
HTBHA ........ Han'guk T'oyang Bilyo Hakhoe Chi [*A publication*]
HTBK ........ Heritage Bank [*NASDAQ symbol*] (NQ)
HTBU ........ Bukoba [*Tanzania*] [*ICAO location identifier*] (ICLI)
HTC ........ Hand Tool Carrier [*NASA*] (KSC)
HTC ........ Handicapped Travel Club (EA)
HTC ........ Harris Teachers College [*Missouri*]
HTC ........ Harris Transducer Corporation (MCD)
HTC ........ Hartco Enterprises, Inc. [*Toronto Stock Exchange symbol*]
HTC ........ Head to Come [*Publishing*]
HTC ........ Health Care Telecommunications Corporation [*Camp Hill, PA*] (TSSD)
HT & C ........ Heat Transfer and Cryogenics
HTC ........ Heavy Teflon Coating
HTC ........ Heavy Terminal Complex (MCD)
HTC ........ Hebrew Teachers College [*Massachusetts*]
HTC ........ Hebrew Theological College [*Skokie, IL*] (BJA)
HTC ........ Height-to-Time Converter
HTC ........ Height Tracking Console (MCD)
HTC ........ Hepatoma Tissue Culture [*Medicine*]
HTC ........ High-Tar Content [*of cigarettes*]
HTC ........ High-Temperature Carbonization
HTC ........ High-Temperature Catalyst
HTC ........ High-Temperature Coil
HTC ........ High-Temperature Conditioning
HTC ........ Highway Traffic Control
HTC ........ Homozygous Typing Cells [*Immunochemistry*]
HTC ........ Hughes Tool Company
HTC ........ Huston-Tillotson College [*Austin, TX*]
HTC ........ Huston-Tillotson College, Austin, TX [*OCLC symbol*] (OCLC)
HTC ........ Hybrid Technology Computer
HTC ........ Hydraulic Temperature Control (AAG)
HTC ........ Hydraulic Test Chamber (AAG)
HTC ........ Hydrofoil Test Craft
HTCA ........ Human Tumor Clonogenic Assay [*In-vitro testing system*]
HTCH ........ Chunya [*Tanzania*] [*ICAO location identifier*] (ICLI)
HTCH ........ Hutchinson Technology, Inc. [*Hutchinson, MN*] [*NASDAQ symbol*] (NQ)
HTCI ........ High-Tensile Cast Iron
HTCM ........ Master Chief Hull Maintenance Technician [*Formerly, SFCM*] [*Navy rating*]
HTCS ........ Senior Chief Hull Maintenance Technician [*Formerly, SFCS*] [*Navy rating*]
HTD ........ Dansk Historisk Tidskrift [*A publication*]
HTD ........ Hand Target Designator
HTD ........ Hand-Tool Dexterity [*Motor performance test*]
HTD ........ Heated (MSA)
HTD ........ High-Temperature Distillation
HTD ........ High-Torque Drive [*Engineering*]
HTD ........ Higher Telegraphist Detector [*British military*] (DMA)
HTD ........ Horizontal Tactical Display (NG)
HTD ........ Human Therapeutic Dose
HTD ........ Huntingdon International Holdings PLC [*NYSE symbol*] (CTT)
HTDA ........ Dar Es-Salaam/Dar Es-Salaam [*Tanzania*] [*ICAO location identifier*] (ICLI)
HTDC ........ Dar Es-Salaam [*Tanzania*] [*ICAO location identifier*] (ICLI)

**HTDL** ........ High-Temperature Detection Lens
**HTDM** ....... Helicopter Team Defense Missile
**HTDO** ....... Dodoma [*Tanzania*] [*ICAO location identifier*] (ICLI)
**HTDQ** ....... Dar Es-Salaam [*Tanzania*] [*ICAO location identifier*] (ICLI)
**HTDS** ........ Hydrofoil Tactical Data System
**HTDU** ....... Horizontal Tactical Display Unit
**HTE** .......... England AFB (Alexandria), LA [*Location identifier*] [*FAA*] (FAAL)
**HTE** .......... High-Temperature Electrolysis (MCD)
**HTE** .......... Hydraulic Test Equipment
**HTEC** ........ High Technology
**HTEC** ........ Hydrogen Technology Evaluation Center [*Upton, NY*] [*Brookhaven National Laboratory*] [*Department of Energy*] (GRD)
**HTEK** ........ Hytek Microsystems, Inc. [*NASDAQ symbol*] (NQ)
**HTEM** ........ Human Thymic Epithelial Medium [*Endocrinology*]
**HTENY** ...... Hartogen Energy Canada [*NASDAQ symbol*] (NQ)
**HTES** ......... High-Technology Ejection Seat
**HTES** ......... High-Technology Escape System (MCD)
**HTESP** ....... High-Temperature Electrostatic Precipitator [*Anti-smoke pollution device*]
**HTEXCH** .. Heat Exchanger (MCD)
**HTF** .......... Heat Transfer Fluid
**HTF** .......... Heat Treat Fixture (MCD)
**HTF** .......... Height Finding (MSA)
**HTF** .......... Heritage Trails Fund (EA)
**HTF** .......... Highway Trust Fund
**HTF** .......... Historisk Tidskrift foer Finland [*A publication*]
**HTF** .......... How-to-Fight [*Manuals*] [*Military*]
**HTF** .......... Hypersonic Tunnel Facility [*NASA*]
**HTFC** ........ High-Temperature Fuel Cell
**HTFFA** ...... Heat and Fluid Flow [*A publication*]
**HTFFR** ...... High-Temperature Fast-Flow Reactor [*See also HTFS*]
**HTFFS** ...... Heat Transfer and Fluid Flow Service [*Great Britain*]
**HTFFT** ...... Heat Transfer Fluid Flow Thermodynamics (NRCH)
**HTFI** ......... Fort Ikoma [*Tanzania*] [*ICAO location identifier*] (ICLI)
**HTFM** ....... How to Fight Manual [*Military*] (MCD)
**HTFMI** ...... Heat Transfer and Fluid Mechanics Institute (MCD)
**HTFORE** ... Heretofore (ROG)
**HTFS** ........ Heat Transfer and Fluid Flow Service [*Also, HTFFS*] [*Great Britain*]
**HTF/S** ....... How to Fight/How to Support [*Military*] (MCD)
**HTFW** ....... High-Temperature Fluid-Wall [*Incineration process*]
**HTFX** ........ Heat Treat Fixture
**HTG** .......... Handbuch Theologischer Grundbegriffe [*Munich*] [*A publication*] (BJA)
**HTG** .......... Heating (KSC)
**HTG** .......... Heritage Media Corp. [*AMEX symbol*] (CTT)
**HTG** .......... High-Temperature Gas [*Reactor*]
**Htg** ........... Holztechnologie [*A publication*]
**HTG** .......... Hypertriglyceridemia [*Medicine*]
**HTGCR** ..... High-Temperature Gas-Cooled Reactor
**HTGF** ........ Human Transforming Growth Factor [*Biochemistry*]
**HTGL** ........ Hepatic Triglyceride Lipase [*An enzyme*]
**HTGL** ........ High Temperature Gasdynamics Laboratory [*Stanford University*] [*Research center*] (RCD)
**HTGPF** ...... High-Temperature General-Purpose Furnace
**HTGR** ........ High-Temperature Gas-Cooled Reactor
**HTGR-CX** ... High-Temperature Gas-Cooled-Reactor Critical Experiment
**HTGRE** ..... High-Temperature Gas-Cooled-Reactor Experiment
**HTH** .......... Hawthorne [*Nevada*] [*Airport symbol*] [*Obsolete*] (OAG)
**HTH** .......... Heart to Heart Foundation (EA)
**HTH** .......... Helix-Turn-Helix [*Protein structure*]
**HTH** .......... Hexagon Tungsten Honeycomb
**HTH** .......... High-Temperature Heater
**HTH** .......... Home Town Honey [*Slang*]
**HTH** .......... Homeostatic Thymus Hormone [*Immunology*]
**HTHA** ........ Hearing and Tinnitus Help Association [*Later, AEAR*] (EA)
**HtHaN** ....... Northern Montana College, Havre, MT [*Library symbol*] [*Library of Congress*] (LCLS)
**H Th G** ....... Handbuch Theologischer Grundbegriffe [*A publication*]
**H Th K** ....... Herders Theologischer Kommentar zum Neuen Testament [*A publication*]
**HTHM** ....... High Toxic Hazard Material
**HTHPA** ..... High Temperatures - High Pressures [*A publication*]
**HThR** ........ Harvard Theological Review [*A publication*]
**HTHR** ........ Hawthorne Financial Corp. [*NASDAQ symbol*] (NQ)
**HT-HS** ....... High-Temperature, High-Shear Viscometer
**HTHSR** ..... High-Temperature, High-Shear-Rate [*Viscosity measurement*]
**HThSt** ....... Harvard Theological Studies [*Cambridge, MA*] [*A publication*]
**HTI** ........... Haiti [*ANSI three-letter standard code*] (CNC)
**HTI** ........... Hamilton Island [*Australia*] [*Airport symbol*] (OAG)
**HTI** ........... Hand Tools Institute (EA)
**HTI** ........... Hemorrhagic Toxin Inhibitor [*Hematology*]
**HTI** ........... High-Temperature Isotropic
**HTI** ........... Hindu Text Information [*A publication*]
**HTI** ........... Horizontal Tactics Indicator
**HTIG** ......... Hungry Tiger, Inc. [*NASDAQ symbol*] (NQ)
**HTIR** ......... Iringa [*Tanzania*] [*ICAO location identifier*] (ICLI)
**HTIS** ......... Heat Transfer Instrument System (NRCH)
**HT/IT** ........ Homing Terrier/Improved Tartar [*Missile*] (MCD)
**HTJ** ........... H-Plane Tee Junction
**HTJ** ........... Hardware Trade Journal [*A publication*]
**HTJPA** ...... Heat Transfer. Japanese Research [*A publication*]
**HTK** .......... Head to Kum [*Come*] [*Publishing*]
**HTK** .......... Historisk Tidskrift [*A publication*]
**HTK** .......... Howtek, Inc. [*AMEX symbol*] (SPSG)
**HTKA** ........ Kigoma [*Tanzania*] [*ICAO location identifier*] (ICLI)
**HTKI** ......... Kilwa Masoko [*Tanzania*] [*ICAO location identifier*] (ICLI)
**HTKJ** ......... Kilimanjaro [*Tanzania*] [*ICAO location identifier*] (ICLI)
**HTKNT** ..... Herders Theologischer Kommentar zum Neuen Testament [*Freiburg*] [*A publication*] (BJA)
**HTKO** ........ Kongwa [*Tanzania*] [*ICAO location identifier*] (ICLI)
**HTKP** ........ Hard-Target Kill Potential [*Military*] (MCD)
**HTKT** ........ Kilimatinde [*Tanzania*] [*ICAO location identifier*] (ICLI)
**HTL** .......... Hearing Threshold Level
**HTL** .......... Heartland Partners LP Class A [*AMEX symbol*] (SPSG)
**HTL** .......... Heat Transfer Laboratory [*MIT*] (MCD)
**HTL** .......... Heat Transfer Loop (NRCH)
**HTL** .......... Helicopter Transportable Launcher (MUGU)
**HTL** .......... Helper T-Lymphocyte [*Immunology*]
**HTL** .......... High-Temperature Lacquer
**HTL** .......... High Threshold Logic
**HTL** .......... High Turbulence Level
**HTL** .......... Hotel Call, Time, and Charges Mandatory [*Telecommunications*] (TEL)
**HTL** .......... Hotel Revue. Beroepstijdschrift op Managementniveau [*A publication*]
**HTL** .......... Houghton Lake, MI [*Location identifier*] [*FAA*] (FAAL)
**HTLA** ........ High-Titer, Low-Avidity [*Hematology*]
**HTLB** ........ High-Technology Light Brigade [*Army*] (INF)
**HTLD** ........ Heartland Express, Inc. [*Coralville, IA*] [*NASDAQ symbol*] (NQ)
**HTLD** ........ High-Technology Light Division [*DoD*]
**HTLD** ........ Houston Test for Language Development [*Education*]
**HTLI** ......... Lindi [*Tanzania*] [*ICAO location identifier*] (ICLI)
**HTLL** ......... High Test Level Language (NASA)
**HTLM** ....... Lake Manyara [*Tanzania*] [*ICAO location identifier*] (ICLI)
**HTLO** ........ Lobo Wildlife Lodge [*Tanzania*] [*ICAO location identifier*] (ICLI)
**HTLStu** ..... Historia i Teoria Literatury-Studia [*A publication*]
**HTLT** ........ HTL Telemanagement Ltd. [*Burtonsville, MD*] (TSSD)
**HTLT** ........ Hughes Transportable Link Terminal
**HTLTR** ...... High-Temperature Lattice Test Reactor
**HTLV** ........ Human T-Cell Lymphotropic [*formerly, Leukemia*] Virus
**HTLV-III** .. Human T-Cell Lymphotrophic Virus-Type Three
**HTLV-III/LAV** ... Human T-Cell Lymphotropic Virus Type Three/ Lymphadenopathy-Associated Virus
**HTM** .......... Hard Tube Modulator [*Electronics*]
**HTM** .......... Harpoon Trainer Module [*Missiles*] (MCD)
**HTM** .......... Heat Transfer Medium [*Engineering*]
**HTM** .......... Heat Transfer Meter
**HTM** .......... Heat Transfer Module [*Furnace*]
**HTM** .......... High Temperature (IEEE)
**HTM** .......... High-Temperature Materials
**HTM** .......... High-Temperature Metallography
**HTM** .......... High-Trajectory Missiles (NRCH)
**HTM** .......... History Teacher's Magazine [*A publication*]
**HTM** .......... Hypothesis Testing Model (IEEE)
**HTM** .......... Whitman, MA [*Location identifier*] [*FAA*] (FAAL)
**HTMA** ........ Hydraulic Tool Manufacturers Association [*Milwaukee, WI*] (EA)
**HTMA** ........ Mafia [*Tanzania*] [*ICAO location identifier*] (ICLI)
**HTMB** ........ Mbeya [*Tanzania*] [*ICAO location identifier*] (ICLI)
**HTMD** ........ High-Technology Motorized Division
**HTMD** ........ Hold Time Management Display [*NASA*]
**HTMD** ........ Mwadui [*Tanzania*] [*ICAO location identifier*] (ICLI)
**HTM-DB** ... High Temperature Materials Data Bank [*Commission of the European Communities*] [*Information service or system*] (IID)
**HTMG** ........ Morgororo [*Tanzania*] [*ICAO location identifier*] (ICLI)
**HTM Haerterei-Tech Mitt** ... Haerterei-Technische Mitteilungen (HTM) [*West Germany*] [*A publication*]
**HTMI** ......... Masasi [*Tanzania*] [*ICAO location identifier*] (ICLI)
**HTMIAC** .. High Temperature Materials Information Analysis Center [*Formerly, TEPIAC*] [*West Lafayette, IN*] [*DoD*] (GRD)
**HTMK** ........ Mikumi [*Tanzania*] [*ICAO location identifier*] (ICLI)
**HTML** ........ High Temperature Materials Laboratory [*Oak Ridge, TN*] [*Oak Ridge National Laboratory*] [*Department of Energy*] (GRD)
**HTMO** ....... Mombo [*Tanzania*] [*ICAO location identifier*] (ICLI)
**HTMP** ........ High-Temperature Thermomechanical Processing [*Alloy heat resistance*]
**HTMP** ........ High-Temperature Thermomechanical Pulp [*Pulp and paper technology*]
**HTMP** ........ Hydroxy(tetramethyl)piperidineoxyl [*Organic chemistry*]
**HTMP** ........ Mpanda [*Tanzania*] [*ICAO location identifier*] (ICLI)
**HTMR** ........ Msembe-Ruaha National Park [*Tanzania*] [*ICAO location identifier*] (ICLI)
**HTMS** ........ High-Temperature Mass Spectrometry
**HTMS** ........ Moshi [*Tanzania*] [*ICAO location identifier*] (ICLI)
**HTMT** ........ Mtwara [*Tanzania*] [*ICAO location identifier*] (ICLI)

**HTMU**....... Musoma [*Tanzania*] [*ICAO location identifier*] (ICLI)
**HTMW**...... Mwanza [*Tanzania*] [*ICAO location identifier*] (ICLI)
**HTMX**....... Mpwapwa [*Tanzania*] [*ICAO location identifier*] (ICLI)
**HTN** .......... Hantaan [*Virus*]
**HTN** .......... HazTECH News [*A publication*]
**HTN** .......... Heterodyne (FAAC)
**HTN** .......... Hocking Technical College, Nelsonville, OH [*OCLC symbol*] (OCLC)
**HTN** .......... Home Theatre Network [*In network name "HTN Plus"*] [*Cable-television system*]
**HTN** .......... Hotan [*China*] [*Airport symbol*] (OAG)
**HTN** .......... Houghton Mifflin Co. [*NYSE symbol*] (SPSG)
**HTN** .......... HUD [*Department of Housing and Urban Development*] Teleprocessing Network
**HTN** .......... Hughes Television Network [*New York, NY*] [*Cable-television system*]
**HTN** .......... Hypertension [*Medicine*]
**HTN** .......... Miles City, MT [*Location identifier*] [*FAA*] (FAAL)
**HTNA**......... Nachingwea [*Tanzania*] [*ICAO location identifier*] (ICLI)
**HTNG** ....... Ngerengere [*Tanzania*] [*ICAO location identifier*] (ICLI)
**HTNJ** ........ Njombe [*Tanzania*] [*ICAO location identifier*] (ICLI)
**HTNSL**...... High Tensile [*Mechanics*]
**HTO** .......... East Hampton [*New York*] [*Airport symbol*] (OAG)
**HTO** .......... Hereto (ROG)
**HTO** .......... High-Temperature Oxidation (IEEE)
**HTO** .......... Highway Transportation Officer [*Army*]
**HTO** .......... Historisk Tidskrift (Oslo) [*A publication*]
**HTO** .......... Horizontal Takeoff
**HTO** .......... Hospital Transfer Order
**HTOFORE** ... Heretofore
**HTOHL**..... Horizontal Takeoff, Horizontal Landing (KSC)
**HTOT**........ High-Temperature Operating Test (MCD)
**HTP**........... Hardness Test Plan [*Army*] (AABC)
**HTP**........... Harris-Teeter Property [*AMEX symbol*] (SPSG)
**HTP**........... Heat Transfer Printing [*Textile technology*]
**HTP**........... High-Temperature Photochemistry [*Aerochem Research Laboratories, Inc.*] [*Analytical chemistry*]
**HTP**........... High-Temperature Photolysis [*Physics*]
**HTP**........... High-Test Hydrogen-Peroxide
**H-T-P** ........ [*A*] House, a Tree, a Person [*Psychological drawing test*]
**HTP**........... Humidity Test Procedure
**HTP**........... Humor Test of Personality [*Psychology*]
**HTP**........... Hydroxytryptophan [*Biochemistry*]
**HTPB** ........ Hydroxyl-Terminated Polybutadiene [*Organic chemistry*]
**HTPB** ........ Hydroxyl-Terminated Polybutylene [*Organic chemistry*] (NASA)
**HTPE** ........ Pemba [*Tanzania*] [*ICAO location identifier*] (ICLI)
**HTPFP**...... High Technology Professionals for Peace (EA)
**HTPHA**..... Huguenot-Thomas Paine Historical Association (EA)
**HTPM**....... Harvard Total Project Manager [*Computer software*]
**HTPN**....... Home Total Parenteral Nutrition [*Medicine*]
**HTQ** .......... Hsueh Tsung Quarterly [*A publication*]
**HTQ** .......... Revue Francaise de Gestion. Hommes et Techniques [*A publication*]
**HTR**........... Halt and Transfer
**HTR**........... Hanford Test Reactor (NRCH)
**HTR**........... Hard Tissue Replacement [*Dentistry*]
**HTR**........... Harvard Theological Review [*A publication*]
**HTR**........... Hateruma [*Japan*] [*Airport symbol*] (OAG)
**Ht R** .......... Haustechnische Rundschau [*A publication*]
**HTR**........... Heated-Tube Reactor [*Chemical engineering*]
**HTR**........... Heater (AAG)
**HTR**........... Hemolytic Transfusion Reaction [*Medicine*]
**HTR**........... High-Temperature Reactor
**HTR**........... High-Temperature Resistor
**HTR**........... Highway Traffic Regulation (AABC)
**HTR**........... Hitachi Training Reactor [*Japan*]
**HTR**........... Homing Terrier Retrofit [*Missile*] (MCD)
**HTR**........... Homogeneous Thorium Reactor
**HTR**........... Hours to Run (ADA)
**HTR**........... HTR Industries, Inc. [*Vancouver Stock Exchange symbol*]
**HTR**........... Hyperion Total Return Fund [*NYSE symbol*] (SPSG)
**HTRAC** ..... Half-Track [*A type of military vehicle*] (AABC)
**HTRD**........ Heat Transfer Rotating Disc [*Engineering*]
**HTRDA** ..... High-Temperature Reactor Development Associates
**HTRE** ........ Heat Transfer Reactor Experiment
**HTRF** ........ Hollywood Park Enterprises, Inc. [*NASDAQ symbol*] (NQ)
**HTRI** ......... Heat Transfer Research Institute (NRCH)
**HTRI** ......... High Technology Recruitment Index [*A publication*]
**HTRIN** ...... Holy Trinity
**HTRK**........ Half-Track [*A type of military vehicle*]
**HTRMB** .... Heat Treatment of Metals [*A publication*]
**HTRR** ........ Harpoon Transfer Relay Rack [*Missiles*] (MCD)
**HTS** .......... Half-Time Survey [*Shipping*]
**HTS** .......... Hamden Testing Services, Inc.
**HTS** .......... Harness Tracks Security (EA)
**HTS** .......... Harvard Theological Studies [*Cambridge, MA*] [*A publication*]
**HTS** .......... Hawaiian Tracking Station
**HTS** .......... Head, Track, and Selector
**HTS** .......... Heat Transfer Section
**HTS** .......... Heat Transfer System
**HTS** .......... Heat Transport Section [*Apollo*] [*NASA*]
**HTS** .......... Heat Transport System [*NASA*] (NASA)
**HTS** .......... Heat-Treated Steel
**HTS** .......... Height-Telling Surveillance
**HTS** .......... Heights (MCD)
**HTS** .......... Hervormde Teologiese Studies [*A publication*]
**HTS** .......... High-Temperature Steam
**HTS** .......... High-Temperature Superconductor [*Materials science*]
**HTS** .......... High-Tensile Steel
**HTS** .......... High Tensile Strength [*Mechanics*]
**HTS** .......... Historisk Tidskrift (Stockholm) [*A publication*]
**HTS** .......... Home Team Sports [*Cable-television system*]
**HTS** .......... Host-to-Satellite
**HTS** .......... How to Support [*Manuals*] [*Military*] (MCD)
**HTS** .......... Human Thyroid Stimulator [*Endocrinology*]
**HTS** .......... Huntington [*West Virginia*] [*Airport symbol*] (OAG)
**HTS** .......... Hybrid Test Set
**HTS** .......... Hydraulic Test Set [*or Station*]
**HTS** .......... Hydrodynamic Test System
**HTSA** ........ Host-Tenant Support Agreement [*Military*]
**HTSC** ........ High-Temperature Superconductivity [*Materials science*]
**HTSC** ........ High-Temperature Superconductor [*Materials science*]
**HTSC** ........ Highway Traffic Safety Center [*Michigan State University*]
**HTSCA**...... Human Tumor Stem Cell Assay [*Oncology*]
**HTSD** ........ Singida [*Tanzania*] [*ICAO location identifier*] (ICLI)
**HTSE**......... Same [*Tanzania*] [*ICAO location identifier*] (ICLI)
**HTSEC**...... High-Temperature Size-Exclusion Chromatography
**H & T Self-Def** ... Harrigan and Thompson's Cases on the Law of Self-Defense [*A publication*] (DLA)
**HTSF**......... High-Temperature Sodium Facility [*Nuclear energy*] (NRCH)
**HTSF**......... Hydrated Textured Soy Flour
**HTsFi** ........ Historisk Tidskrift foer Finland [*A publication*]
**HTSH** ........ Human Thyroid Stimulating Hormone [*Also, htsh*] [*Endocrinology*]
**HTSH** ........ Mafinga [*Tanzania*] [*ICAO location identifier*] (ICLI)
**HTSHLD** .. Heat Shield
**HTSK** ........ Heat Sink (MSA)
**HTSL**......... Heat Transfer Simulation Loop (IEEE)
**HTSN** ........ Seronera [*Tanzania*] [*ICAO location identifier*] (ICLI)
**HTSO** ........ Songea [*Tanzania*] [*ICAO location identifier*] (ICLI)
**HTSR** ........ High-Temperature Strain Gauge
**HTSS**......... Honeywell Time-Sharing System [*Data processing*] (IEEE)
**HTSt**.......... Hervormde Teologiese Studies [*Pretoria, South Africa*] [*A publication*] (BJA)
**HTST**......... High-Temperature Short-Time [*Pasteurization*] [*Food processing*]
**HTSU** ........ Sumbawanga [*Tanzania*] [*ICAO location identifier*] (ICLI)
**HTSUP**...... Height Supervisor [*RADAR*]
**HTSUS**...... Harmonized Tariff Schedule of the United States
**HTSY** ........ Shinyanga [*Tanzania*] [*ICAO location identifier*] (ICLI)
**HTT**........... Hallett [*Australia*] [*Seismograph station code, US Geological Survey*] (SEIS)
**HTT**........... Heat-Treatment Temperature
**HTT**........... Heavy Tactical Transport
**HTT**........... High-Temperature Thermomechanical Treatment [*Steel forging*]
**HTT**........... High-Temperature Tunnel [*NASA*]
**HTT**........... Hook Tongue Terminal
**HTTB** ........ High-Technology Test Bed [*Army*]
**HTTB** ........ Tabora [*Tanzania*] [*ICAO location identifier*] (ICLI)
**HTTG** ........ Tanga [*Tanzania*] [*ICAO location identifier*] (ICLI)
**HTTL** ........ High-Power Transistor-Transistor Logic (IEEE)
**HTTMT** .... High-Temperature Thermomechanical Treatment [*Steel forging*]
**HTTR** ........ Heat Treat
**HTTS**......... Hydroquench Thrust Termination System [*NASA*] (KSC)
**HTTT** ........ High-Temperature Turbine Technology [*Power generation*]
**HTTU**........ Tunduru [*Tanzania*] [*ICAO location identifier*] (ICLI)
**HTU** .......... Heat Transfer Unit
**HTU** .......... Height of a Transfer Unit [*Distillation*]
**HTU** .......... Horizontal Trail Unit (MCD)
**HTU** .......... Hoyt Peak [*Utah*] [*Seismograph station code, US Geological Survey*] (SEIS)
**HTUR**........ Urambo [*Tanzania*] [*ICAO location identifier*] (ICLI)
**HTV**........... Half Thickness Value (NRCH)
**HTV**........... Harlech Television [*Wales*]
**HTV**........... Herpes-Type Virus
**HTV**........... Hi Tech Ventures, Inc. [*Vancouver Stock Exchange symbol*]
**HTV**........... High-Altitude Test Vehicle (MUGU)
**HTV**........... Home Video Tutorial
**HTV**........... Homing Test Vehicle (NG)
**HTV**........... Hull Test Vehicle [*for submarines*] (MCD)
**HTV**........... Hybrid Test Vehicle [*Gasoline and electric motor*]
**HTV**........... Hydrothermal Vent [*Geology*]
**HTV**........... Hypersonic Test Vehicle [*Air Force*]
**HTW**.......... Chesapeake, OH/Huntington, WV [*Location identifier*] [*FAA*] (FAAL)
**HTW**.......... H2O. Tijdschrift voor Watervoorziening en Afvalwaterbehandeling [*A publication*]
**H & Tw** ...... Hall and Twell's English Chancery Reports [*1849-50*] [*A publication*] (DLA)

**HTW** .......... Haystack [*Washington*] [*Seismograph station code, US Geological Survey*] (SEIS)
**HTW** .......... High-Temperature Water
**HTW** .......... High-Temperature Wire
**HTW** .......... Hoosac Tunnel & Wilmington R. R. [*AAR code*]
**HTWH** ...... Wazo Hill [*Tanzania*] [*ICAO location identifier*] (ICLI)
**HTWK** ....... Ngare Nairobi [*Tanzania*] [*ICAO location identifier*] (ICLI)
**HTWN** ....... Hometown Bancorporation, Inc. [*NASDAQ symbol*] (NQ)
**HTXA** ........ Hitox Corp. of America [*NASDAQ symbol*] (CTT)
**HTXGR** ..... Heat Exchanger (KSC)
**HTXRD** ..... High-Temperature X-Ray Diffraction
**HTY** ........... Hatizyo [*Japan*] [*Geomagnetic observatory code*]
**HTZ** ........... Hato Corozal [*Colombia*] [*Airport symbol*] (OAG)
**HTZA** ........ Zanzibar [*Tanzania*] [*ICAO location identifier*] (ICLI)
**HU** ............. Central Airlines Ltd. [*Nigeria*] [*ICAO designator*] (ICDA)
**hU** ............. Dihydrouridine [*Two-letter symbol; see $H_2$Urd*]
**HU** ............. Haifa University (BJA)
**HU** ............. Hamburger University [*McDonald's Corp.*]
**HU** ............. Hampton Utilities Trust [*AMEX symbol*] (SPSG)
**HU** ............. Hangup [*Telecommunications*] (TEL)
**HU** ............. Harvard University [*Cambridge, MA*]
**H/U** ........... Heatup [*Nuclear energy*] (NRCH)
**HU** ............. Hebrew University [*Jerusalem*] (BJA)
**HU** ............. Hemagglutinating Unit [*Immunochemistry*]
**HU** ............. Hemoglobin Unit [*Of hydrolytic enzyme activity*]
**HU** ............. Hemolytic Unit [*Hematology*]
**HU** ............. High-Usage [*Telecommunications*] (TEL)
**HU** ............. Hubbert Unit [*Petroleum technology*]
**Hu** ............. Hughes' Kentucky Reports [*A publication*] (DLA)
**HU** ............. Hughes Tool Co. [*Aircraft Division*] [*ICAO aircraft manufacturer identifier*] (ICAO)
**Hu** ............. Hughes' United States Circuit Court Reports [*A publication*] (DLA)
**Hu** ............. Hugo de Alberico [*Flourished, 1168-71*] [*Authority cited in pre-1607 legal work*] (DSA)
**Hu** ............. Hugolinus de Presbyteris [*Flourished, 1197-1238*] [*Authority cited in pre-1607 legal work*] (DSA)
**Hu** ............. Huguccio [*Deceased, 1210*] [*Authority cited in pre-1607 legal work*] (DSA)
**HU** ............. Hungary [*ANSI two-letter standard code*] (CNC)
**hu** ............. Hungary [*MARC country of publication code*] [*Library of Congress*] (LCCP)
**HU** ............. Hydroxyurea [*Also, HYD, HYDREA*] [*Antineoplastic drug*]
**HU** ............. Hyperemia Unit
**HU** ............. Trinidad & Tobago Air Services Ltd. [*ICAO designator*] (FAAC)
**HU** ............. University of Hawaii, Honolulu, HI [*Library symbol*] [*Library of Congress*] (LCLS)
**HUA** .......... Hockey Umpires' Association [*British*]
**HUA** .......... Huancayo [*Peru*] [*Geomagnetic observatory code*]
**HUA** .......... Huancayo [*Peru*] [*Seismograph station code, US Geological Survey*] (SEIS)
**HUA** .......... Human Urinary Albumin [*Clinical chemistry*]
**HUA** .......... Huntsville, AL [*Location identifier*] [*FAA*] (FAAL)
**HUAC** ........ House Un-American Activities Committee [*Later, HCIS*] [*US Congress*]
**HUAKA** ..... Hua Hsueh Shih Chieh [*A publication*]
**HUAR** ........ Arua [*Uganda*] [*ICAO location identifier*] (ICLI)
**Hu-Ar** ........ Magyar Orszagos Leveltar, Budapest, Hungary [*Library symbol*] [*Library of Congress*] (LCLS)
**HUB** .......... Handicapped United in Brotherhood
**HUB** .......... Houston, TX [*Location identifier*] [*FAA*] (FAAL)
**HUB** .......... Hub Airlines, Inc. [*Fort Wayne, IN*] [*FAA designator*] (FAAC)
**HUB** .......... Hubbell, Inc. [*AMEX symbol*] (SPSG)
**HUBA** ........ Hudson Bay [*AAR code*]
**Hubb** .......... Hubbard's Reports [*45-51 Maine*] [*A publication*] (DLA)
**Hubbard** ..... Hubbard's Reports [*45-51 Maine*] [*A publication*] (DLA)
**Hubb Succ** ... Hubback's Evidence of Succession [*A publication*] (DLA)
**Hub Ev** ....... Hubback's Evidence of Succession [*A publication*] (DLA)
**HuBG** ......... Allamin Gorkij Konyvtar, Budapest, Hungary [*Library symbol*] [*Library of Congress*] (LCLS)
**HUBIA** ...... Human Biology [*A publication*]
**HuBKPV** ... Human BK Polyomavirus
**Hub Leg Direc** ... Hubbell's Legal Directory [*A publication*] (DLA)
**HuBM** ........ Orszagos Muszaki Konyvtar es Dokumentacios Kozpont, Budapest, Hungary [*Library symbol*] [*Library of Congress*] (LCLS)
**Hub Prael JC** ... Huber's Praelectiones Juris Civilis [*A publication*] (DLA)
**Hub Roz** ..... Hudebni Rozhledy [*A publication*]
**Hub Suc** ..... Hubback's Evidence of Succession [*A publication*] (DLA)
**HUC** .......... Hebrew Union College [*Later, HUC-JIR*]
**HUC** .......... Hebrew Union College, Jewish Institute of Religion, Cincinnati, OH [*OCLC symbol*] (OCLC)
**HUC** .......... Hook Up and Commissioning Conference [*Offshore Conference and Exhibitions Ltd.*] [*British*]
**HUC** .......... Humacao [*Puerto Rico*] [*Airport symbol*] (OAG)
**HUC** .......... Hypouricemia [*Medicine*]
**HUCA** ........ Hebrew Union College. Annual [*A publication*]
**HUCI** ......... Haitian Unity Council, Incorporated [*Defunct*] (EA)
**HUC-JIR** ... Hebrew Union College - Jewish Institute of Religion [*Formerly, HUC*] [*Cincinnati, OH*]
**HUCO** ....... Hughes NADGE [*NATO Air Defense Ground Environment*] Consortium
**HUCR** ........ Harvard University Character Recognizer [*Data processing*]
**HUCR** ........ Highest Useful Compression Ratio [*Aerospace*]
**HUD** .......... Department of Housing and Urban Development
**HUD** .......... Handicapped Users' Database [*CompuServe Information Service*] [*Information service or system*] (CRD)
**HUD** .......... Head-Up Display
**HUD** .......... Hudson Resources Ltd. [*Vancouver Stock Exchange symbol*]
**HUD** .......... Hungarian Digest [*A publication*]
**HUDA** ........ Housing and Urban Development Act
**HUDAC** ..... Housing and Urban Development Association of Canada
**Hud & B** ..... Hudson and Brooke's Irish King's Bench Reports [*1827-31*] [*A publication*] (DLA)
**Hud & Br** ... Hudson and Brooke's Irish King's Bench Reports [*1827-31*] [*A publication*] (DLA)
**Hud & Bro** ... Hudson and Brooke's Irish King's Bench Reports [*1827-31*] [*A publication*] (DLA)
**HUD Chal** ... HUD [*Department of Housing and Urban Development*] Challenge [*A publication*]
**HUDD** ....... Housing and Urban Development Department [*More commonly, HUD*] (KSC)
**HUDDLE** ... Hull Urban Design Development Laboratory Enterprises, Inc.
**HUDE** ....... Head Up Display Electronics (NASA)
**HUDEA** ..... Human Development [*A publication*]
**HuDeAgE** .. Debreceni Agrartudomanyi Egyetem, Debrecen, Hungary [*Library symbol*] [*Library of Congress*] (LCLS)
**Hudelba Res Stn Annu Rep** ... Hudciba Research Station. Annual Report [*A publication*]
**HuDeK** ....... Debreceni Reformatus Kollegium Nagykonyvtara, Debrecen, Hungary [*Library symbol*] [*Library of Congress*] (LCLS)
**HuDeOE** .... Debreceni Orvostudomanyi Egyetem, Debrecen, Hungary [*Library symbol*] [*Library of Congress*] (LCLS)
**Hud Exec** ... Hudson's Executor's Guide [*A publication*] (DLA)
**HUD Intl Bull** ... HUD [*Department of Housing and Urban Development*] International Bulletin [*A publication*]
**HUD Intl Information Series** ... HUD [*Department of Housing and Urban Development*] International Information Series [*A publication*]
**HUDMAP** ... HUD [*Department of Housing and Urban Development*] Mortgage Accounting Project
**Hud Nastroje** ... Hudebni Nastroje [*A publication*]
**HUD News** ... HUD [*Department of Housing and Urban Development*] Newsletter [*A publication*]
**HUDPR** ..... Housing and Urban Development [*Department*] Procurement Regulations
**Hud R** ......... Hudebni Rozhledy [*A publication*]
**Hud R** ......... Hudson Review [*A publication*]
**Hudrobiol Uurim** ... Hudrobioloogilised Uurimused [*A publication*]
**Hud Rozhl** ... Hudebni Rozhledy [*A publication*]
**Hudson** ....... Hudson on Building Contracts [*A publication*] (DLA)
**Hudson** ....... Hudson Review [*A publication*]
**Hudson R** ... Hudson Review [*A publication*]
**Hudson Rev** ... Hudson Review [*A publication*]
**HUDU** ....... Heads-Up Display Unit [*Aviation*]
**Hud Veda** ... Hudebni Veda [*A publication*]
**HUDWAC** ... Heads-Up Display Weapons Aiming Computer (IEEE)
**HUDWAS** ... Heads-Up Display Weapons Aiming System [*Air Force*] (MCD)
**Hud Wills** .. Hudson on Wills [*A publication*] (DLA)
**Hud Zivot** .. Hudobny Zivot [*A publication*]
**HUE** .......... Humera [*Ethiopia*] [*Airport symbol*] (OAG)
**HUE** .......... New Hungarian Exporter [*A publication*]
**HUEC** ........ Entebbe Area Control Center [*Uganda*] [*ICAO location identifier*] (ICLI)
**Huelva A** .... Huelva Arqueologica [*A publication*]
**HUEN** ....... Entebbe/International [*Uganda*] [*ICAO location identifier*] (ICLI)
**Huenefeld Rep** ... Huenefeld Report [*United States*] [*A publication*]
**HUeP** ......... Handelsueblicher Preis [*Market Price*] [*German*]
**huEPO** ....... Human Erythropoietin [*Biochemistry*]
**HUF** ........... Highway Users Federation for Safety and Mobility [*Later, ASF*] (EA)
**HUF** ........... Huffy Corp. [*NYSE symbol*] (SPSG)
**HUF** ........... Hungarian Foreign Trade [*A publication*]
**HUF** ........... Terre Haute [*Indiana*] [*Airport symbol*] (OAG)
**HUFAA** ..... Human Factors [*A publication*]
**HUFB** ........ Hungarofilm Bulletin [*A publication*]
**HUFK** ........ Huffman Koos, Inc. [*River Edge, NJ*] [*NASDAQ symbol*] (NQ)
**HUFP** ........ Fort Portal [*Uganda*] [*ICAO location identifier*] (ICLI)
**HUFSM** .... Highway Users Federation for Safety and Mobility
**HUG** .......... Hastech Users Group (EA)
**HUG** .......... Head of Units Group [*American Library Association*]
**HUG** .......... Help Us Grow [*Australia*]
**HUG** .......... Hiram Ulysses Grant [*US general and president, 1822-1885*]
**HUG** .......... Honeywell Users Group
**HUG** .......... Hug-Laf-Luv (EA)
**HUG** .......... Hughes Supply, Inc. [*NYSE symbol*] (SPSG)
**Hug** ........... Hugo de Alberico [*Flourished, 12th century*] [*Authority cited in pre-1607 legal work*] (DSA)

**Hug**........... Hugolinus de Presbyteris [*Flourished, 1197-1238*] [*Authority cited in pre-1607 legal work*] (DSA)
**Hug**........... Huguccio [*Deceased, 1210*] [*Authority cited in pre-1607 legal work*] (DSA)
**HUG**.......... Hungarian Economy [*A publication*]
**HUG**.......... Lonely, AK [*Location identifier*] [*FAA*] (FAAL)
**HUG's**....... Home User Groups [*Data processing*]
**HUGE**........ Humagen, Inc. [*NASDAQ symbol*] (NQ)
**Hugh**.......... Hughes' Circuit Court Reports [*A publication*] (DLA)
**Hugh**.......... Hughes' Kentucky Reports [*A publication*] (DLA)
**Hugh Abr**... Hughes' Abridgment [*1663-65*] [*England*] [*A publication*] (DLA)
**Hugh Con**... Hughes' Precedents in Conveyancing [*2nd ed.*] [*1855-57*] [*A publication*] (DLA)
**Hugh Conv**... Hughes' Precedents in Conveyancing [*2nd ed.*] [*1855-57*] [*A publication*] (DLA)
**Hugh Ent**... Hughes' Entries [*1659*] [*A publication*] (DLA)
**Hugh Eq D**... Hughes' Edition of Van Heythuysen's Equity Draftsman [*A publication*] (DLA)
**Hughes**....... Hughes' Kentucky Supreme Court Reports [*1785-1801*] [*A publication*] (DLA)
**Hughes**....... Hughes' United States Circuit Court Reports [*A publication*] (DLA)
**Hughes Fed Prac**... Hughes' Federal Practice [*A publication*] (DLA)
**Hughes (US)**... Hughes' Circuit Court Reports [*United States*] [*A publication*] (DLA)
**Hugh Ins**.... Hughes on Insurance [*A publication*] (DLA)
**Hugh Prec**... Hughes' Precedents in Conveyancing [*2nd ed.*] [*1855-57*] [*A publication*] (DLA)
**Hugh Wills**... Hughes on Wills [*A publication*] (DLA)
**Hugh Wr**.... Hughes on Writs [*A publication*] (DLA)
**HUGO**....... Highly Unusual Geophysical Operation [*A meteorological research vehicle*]
**Hugo**.......... Hugolinus [*Authority cited in pre-1607 legal work*] (DSA)
**HUGO**....... Human Genome Organization [*Genetics*]
**Hugo Hist du Droit Rom**... Hugo's Histoire du Droit Romain [*A publication*] (DLA)
**Hugo Hist Dr Rom**... Hugo's Histoire du Droit Romain [*A publication*] (DLA)
**Hugol**......... Hugolinus de Presbyteris [*Flourished, 1197-1238*] [*Authority cited in pre-1607 legal work*] (DSA)
**HUG-SMS**... Honeywell Users Group - Small and Medium Systems [*Later, NAHU*]
**HUGU**....... Gulu [*Uganda*] [*ICAO location identifier*] (ICLI)
**Hugu**.......... Huguccio [*Deceased, 1210*] [*Authority cited in pre-1607 legal work*] (DSA)
**Huguenot Soc S Afr Bull**... Huguenot Society of South Africa. Bulletin [*A publication*]
**HUH**.......... Huahine [*French Polynesia*] [*Airport symbol*] (OAG)
**HUH**.......... Hualalai [*Hawaii*] [*Seismograph station code, US Geological Survey*] (SEIS)
**HUH**.......... University of Hawaii, Hamilton Library, Honolulu, HI [*OCLC symbol*] (OCLC)
**HUHEA**.... Human Heredity [*A publication*]
**HUHO**....... Hughes Homes, Inc. [*NASDAQ symbol*] (NQ)
**HuIFN**....... Human Interferon [*Biochemistry*]
**Huisarts Wet**... Huisarts en Wetenschap [*A publication*]
**HUJ**........... Hebrew University [*Jerusalem*] (BJA)
**HuJCPV**.... Human JC Polyomavirus
**HUJI**......... Jinja [*Uganda*] [*ICAO location identifier*] (ICLI)
**HUK**.......... Hunter-Killer [*Operations against submarines*] [*Navy*]
**HUKASWEX**... Hunter-Killer Antisubmarine Warfare Exercise [*Navy*] (NVT)
**HUKB**........ Kabale [*Uganda*] [*ICAO location identifier*] (ICLI)
**HuKeAgE**.. Agrartudomanyi Egyetem, Keszthely, Hungary [*Library symbol*] [*Library of Congress*] (LCLS)
**HUKF**........ Kabalega Falls [*Uganda*] [*ICAO location identifier*] (ICLI)
**HUKFOR**.. Hunter-Killer Forces [*Navy*]
**HUKFORLANT**... Hunter-Killer Forces, Atlantic [*Navy*]
**HUKFORPAC**... Hunter-Killer Forces, Pacific [*Navy*]
**HUKP**........ Hostile, Unknown, Faker, and Pending [*Used in SAGE to designate certain tracks and raids*]
**HUKS**........ Hukbong Mapagpalaya ng Bayan [*People's Liberation Army, Philippines*] (CINC)
**HUKS**........ Hunter-Killer Submarine [*Navy*]
**HUKS**........ Kasese [*Uganda*] [*ICAO location identifier*] (ICLI)
**HUL**........... Hardware Utilization List (NASA)
**HUL**........... Harvard University, Cambridge, MA [*OCLC symbol*] (OCLC)
**HUL**........... Home University Library [*A publication*]
**HUL**........... Houlton [*Maine*] [*Airport symbol*] (OAG)
**HUL**........... Houlton, ME [*Location identifier*] [*FAA*] (FAAL)
**HUL**........... Houston Law Review [*A publication*]
**Hul**............ Hullin (BJA)
**HULA**........ Lake George [*Uganda*] [*ICAO location identifier*] (ICLI)
**Hule Mex Plast**... Hule Mexicano y Plasticos [*A publication*]
**HULI**......... Lira [*Uganda*] [*ICAO location identifier*] (ICLI)
**Hull Costs**... Hullock on Costs [*A publication*] (DLA)
**Hull Univ Occas Pap Geogr**... Hull University. Occasional Papers in Geography [*A publication*]
**Hult Conv**.. Hulton's Convictions [*1835*] [*A publication*] (DLA)
**HULTEC**... Hull-to-Emitter Correlation [*Navy*] (CAAL)
**HUM**......... Houma [*Louisiana*] [*Airport symbol*] (OAG)
**HUM**......... Human (ROG)
**HUM**......... Human Systems Management [*A publication*]
**HUM**......... Humana, Inc. [*NYSE symbol*] (SPSG)
**Hum**........... Humanidades [*A publication*]
**Hum**........... Humanist [*A publication*]
**HUM**......... Humanitarian (ROG)
**Hum**........... Humanitas [*A publication*]
**HUM**......... Humanities
**HUM**......... Humble (ROG)
**HUM**......... Humidity (NASA)
**HUM**......... Humorous (ADA)
**Hum**........... Humphrey's Tennessee Supreme Court Reports [*1839-51*] [*A publication*] (DLA)
**Hum**........... Humus [*A publication*]
**HU-M**........ University of Hawaii, Leahi Hospital, Hastings H. Walker Medical Library, Honolulu, HI [*Library symbol*] [*Library of Congress*] (LCLS)
**HUMA**...... Mbarara/Obote [*Uganda*] [*ICAO location identifier*] (ICLI)
**HUMAN**... Help Us Make a Nation (EA)
**Human Biol**... Human Biology [*A publication*]
**Human Chr**... Humanites Chretiennes [*A publication*]
**Human Comm Res**... Human Communications Research [*A publication*]
**Human Cont**... Human Context [*A publication*]
**Human Dev**... Human Development [*A publication*]
**Human Ecol**... Human Ecology [*A publication*]
**Human et Entr**... Humanisme et Entreprise [*A publication*]
**Humane R**... Humane Review [*A publication*]
**Human Fact**... Human Factors [*A publication*]
**Humangenet**... Humangenetik [*A publication*]
**Human Hered**... Human Heredity [*A publication*]
**Humanidades Ser 4 Logica Mat**... Humanidades. Serie 4. Logica Matematica [*A publication*]
**Humanit Index**... Humanities Index [*A publication*]
**Human Life R**... Human Life Review [*A publication*]
**Human Org**... Human Organization [*A publication*]
**Human Organ**... Human Organization [*A publication*]
**Human Path**... Human Pathology [*A publication*]
**Human Pracy**... Humanizacja Pracy [*A publication*]
**Human Rel**... Human Relations [*A publication*]
**Human Relat**... Human Relations [*A publication*]
**Human Reprod Med**... Human Reproductive Medicine [*A publication*]
**Human Reproduction & L Rep**... Reporter on Human Reproduction and the Law [*A publication*]
**Human Resour Abstr**... Human Resources Abstracts [*A publication*]
**Human Resource Dev**... Human Resource Development [*A publication*]
**Human Resource Mgt**... Human Resource Management [*A publication*]
**Human Rights J**... Human Rights Journal [*A publication*]
**Human Rights Q**... Human Rights Quarterly [*A publication*]
**Human Rights Rev**... Human Rights Review [*A publication*]
**Human Rts J**... Human Rights Journal [*A publication*] (DLA)
**Human Rts Rev**... Human Rights Review [*A publication*] (DLA)
**Human S**.... Human Studies [*A publication*]
**Human Ser 4 Logica Mat**... Humanidades. Serie 4. Logica Matematica [*Havana*] [*A publication*]
**Human Soc**... Humanities in Society [*A publication*]
**HUMARIS**... Human Materials Resources Information System (DIT)
**Hum Ass Bull**... Humanities Association of Canada. Bulletin [*A publication*]
**Hum Assoc R**... Humanities Association. Review/Revue. Association des Humanites [*A publication*]
**HumB**........ Humanitas (Brescia) [*A publication*]
**Hum(BA)**... Humanidades (Buenos Aires) [*A publication*]
**Hum Behav**... Human Behavior [*A publication*]
**Humber de Bou**... Humbertus de Bouen [*Authority cited in pre-1607 legal work*] (DSA)
**Hum Biol**... Human Biology [*A publication*]
**Hum Biol Oceania**... Human Biology in Oceania [*A publication*]
**Hum (Br)**.... Humanitas (Brescia) [*A publication*]
**HUMCAT**... Humanoid Catalog [*Mutual Unidentified Flying Object Network*]
**Hum Chrom Newsl**... Human Chromosome Newsletter [*A publication*]
**Hum Commun**... Human Communications [*A publication*]
**Hum Contemp**... Humanisme Contemporain [*A publication*]
**Hum Context**... Human Context [*A publication*]
**Hum Dev**.... Human Development [*A publication*]
**Hume**......... Hume's Court of Session Decisions [*1781-1822*] [*Scotland*] [*A publication*] (DLA)
**Hum Ecol**... Human Ecology [*A publication*]
**Hum Ecol Forum**... Human Ecology Forum [*A publication*]
**Hume Com**... Hume's Commentaries on Crimes [*Scotland*] [*A publication*] (DLA)
**Hume Hist Eng**... Hume's History of England [*A publication*] (DLA)
**Hum Environ Swed**... Human Environment in Sweden [*United States*] [*A publication*]
**Hume Stud**... Hume Studies [*A publication*]
**Hum Ev**....... Human Events [*A publication*]
**HUMEVAC**... Humanitarian Emergency Evacuation [*Military*] (NVT)
**Hum Fact**... Human Factors [*A publication*]
**Hum Factors**... Human Factors [*A publication*]
**Hum Fertil**... Human Fertility [*A publication*]
**Hum Genet**... Human Genetics [*A publication*]

**Hum Genet Suppl** ... Human Genetics. Supplement [*A publication*]
**Hum Hered** ... Human Heredity [*A publication*]
**HUMI**........ Masindi [*Uganda*] [*ICAO location identifier*] (ICLI)
**HUMID**..... Hughes Unit Malfunction Isolation Detector
**Hum Immunol** ... Human Immunology [*A publication*]
**Hum Ind**..... Humanities Index [*A publication*]
**HUMINT** ... Human Intelligence [*Spies, double agents, etc.*] [*CIA*] (AFM)
**Hum Lov**.... Humanistica Lovaniensia [*A publication*]
**Hum Mov Sci** ... Human Movement Science [*A publication*]
**Hum Needs** ... Human Needs [*A publication*]
**Hum Neurob** ... Human Neurobiology [*A publication*]
**Hum Neurobiol** ... Human Neurobiology [*A publication*]
**HumNL** ..... Humanitas (Nuevo Leon) [*A publication*]
**Hum(NRH)** ... Humanitas: La Nouvelle Revue des Humanites [*A publication*]
**Hum Nutr Appl Nutr** ... Human Nutrition. Applied Nutrition [*A publication*]
**Hum Nutr Cl** ... Human Nutrition. Clinical Nutrition [*A publication*]
**Hum Nutr Clin Nutr** ... Human Nutrition. Clinical Nutrition [*A publication*]
**Hum Nutr Compr Treatise** ... Human Nutrition. A Comprehensive Treatise [*A publication*]
**HUMO**...... Moroto [*Uganda*] [*ICAO location identifier*] (ICLI)
**Hum Org**.... Human Organization [*A publication*]
**Hum Organ** ... Human Organization [*A publication*]
**Hu Move Sci** ... Human Movement Science [*A publication*]
**Hum Path** .. Human Pathology [*A publication*]
**Hum Pathol** ... Human Pathology [*A publication*]
**Humph**....... Humphrey's Tennessee Reports [*20-30 Tennessee*] [*A publication*] (DLA)
**Humph Dist Reg** ... Humphreys. District Registry Practice and Procedure [*1977*] [*A publication*] (ILCA)
**Humph Prec** ... Humphry's Common Precedents in Conveyancing [*2nd ed.*] [*1882*] [*A publication*] (DLA)
**Hum Physiol** ... Human Physiology [*A publication*]
**Hum Physiol (Engl Transl Fiziol Chel)** ... Human Physiology (English Translation of Fiziologiya Cheloveka) [*A publication*]
**Hum Potential** ... Human Potential [*A publication*]
**Humpty D** ... Humpty Dumpty's Magazine [*A publication*]
**Hum (Q)**..... Humanitas. Boletin Ecuatoriano de Antropologia (Quito) [*A publication*]
**Hum Rel**..... Human Relations [*A publication*]
**Hum Relat** ... Human Relations [*A publication*]
**Hum Relations** ... Human Relations [*A publication*]
**Hum Reprod (Oxford)** ... Human Reproduction (Oxford) [*A publication*]
**Hum (RES)** ... Humanites. Revue d'Enseignement Secondaire et d'Education [*A publication*]
**Hum Resour Abstr** ... Human Resources Abstracts [*A publication*]
**Hum Resource Mgt** ... Human Resource Management [*A publication*]
**Hum Resour Forum** ... Human Resources Forum [*United States*] [*A publication*]
**Hum Resour Manage** ... Human Resource Management [*A publication*]
**Hum Resour Manage (Aust)** ... Human Resource Management (Australia) [*A publication*] (APTA)
**Hum Resour Plann** ... Human Resource Planning [*A publication*]
**Hum Rev**.... Humanities Review [*A publication*]
**Hum Rights** ... Human Rights [*A publication*]
**Hum Rights J** ... Human Rights Journal [*A publication*]
**Hum Rights Rev** ... Human Rights Review [*A publication*]
**Hum (RIPh)** ... Humanitas. Revue Internationale de Philologie Classique et Humanites [*A publication*]
**HumRRO** .. Human Resources Research Organization (EA)
**Hum Rts LJ** ... Human Rights Law Journal [*A publication*] (DLA)
**Hum Rts Q** ... Human Rights Quarterly [*A publication*] (DLA)
**Hum Rts USSR** ... Human Rights in the Union of Soviet Socialist Republics [*A publication*] (DLA)
**HUMS**....... Humanitarian Reasons
**Hum Sci**..... Human Science [*Inkan Kwahak*] [*Republic of Korea*] [*A publication*]
**Hum Settlements** ... Human Settlements [*A publication*]
**Hum Soc**.... Humanities in Society [*A publication*]
**Hum Stud**... Humana Studia [*A publication*]
**Hum Syst Manage** ... Human Systems Management [*A publication*]
**HumT** ........ Humanitas (Tucuman, Argentina) [*A publication*]
**Hum Toxicol** ... Human Toxicology [*A publication*]
**Hum Vetensk Samf i Lund Arsberatt** ... Humanistiska Vetenskaps-Samfundet i Lund Arsberattelse [*A publication*]
**Hum Wld** ... Human World [*A publication*]
**HUN**.......... Hualien [*Taiwan*] [*Airport symbol*] (OAG)
**HUN**.......... Hundersingen [*Federal Republic of Germany*] [*Seismograph station code, US Geological Survey*] (SEIS)
**HUN**.......... Hundred (MUGU)
**hun**............ Hungarian [*MARC language code*] [*Library of Congress*] (LCCP)
**HUN**.......... Hungaropress [*A publication*]
**HUN**.......... Hungary [*ANSI three-letter standard code*] (CNC)
**Hun**........... Hun's New York Appellate Division Supreme Court Reports [*A publication*] (DLA)
**HUN**.......... Hunt Manufacturing Co. [*NYSE symbol*] (SPSG)
**HUN**.......... Huntington Resources, Inc. [*Vancouver Stock Exchange symbol*]
**Hun**........... New York Supreme Court Reports [*A publication*] (DLA)
**HUNA**....... Namulonge Agrometeorology Station [*Uganda*] [*ICAO location identifier*] (ICLI)
**HUND**....... Hundred
**HUNDREDSB** ... Hundredsbarrow [*England*]
**HUNEDR** ... Human Neurobiology [*A publication*]
**HUNG**....... Hungary
**Hung A Biol** ... Hungarica Acta Biologica [*A publication*]
**Hung A Chim** ... Hungarica Acta Chimica [*A publication*]
**Hung Acta Phys** ... Hungarica Acta Physica [*A publication*]
**Hung Agric Rev** ... Hungarian Agricultural Review [*A publication*]
**Hung Agr Rev** ... Hungarian Agricultural Review [*A publication*]
**Hung A Math** ... Hungarica Acta Mathematica [*A publication*]
**Hung A Med** ... Hungarica Acta Medica [*A publication*]
**Hung Annu Meet Biochem Proc** ... Hungarian Annual Meeting for Biochemistry. Proceedings [*A publication*]
**Hung A Phys** ... Hungarica Acta Physica [*A publication*]
**Hung A Physiol** ... Hungarica Acta Physiologica [*A publication*]
**Hungarian J Indust Chem Vesprem** ... Hungarian Journal of Industrial Chemistry Vesprem [*A publication*]
**Hungarofilm Bull** ... Hungarofilm Bulletin [*Budapest*] [*A publication*]
**Hung Econ** ... Hungarian Economy [*A publication*]
**HUNGF**..... Hungerford [*England*]
**Hung Foeldt Intez Evk** ... Hungary. Foeldtani Intezet. Evkoenyve [*A publication*]
**Hung For Sci Rev** ... Hungarian Forest Scientifical Review [*A publication*]
**Hung Heavy Ind** ... Hungarian Heavy Industries [*A publication*]
**Hung J Chem** ... Hungarian Journal of Chemistry [*A publication*]
**Hung J Ind Chem** ... Hungarian Journal of Industrial Chemistry [*A publication*]
**Hung J Indus Chem** ... Hungarian Journal of Industrial Chemistry [*A publication*]
**Hung L Rev** ... Hungarian Law Review [*A publication*]
**Hung Mach** ... Hungarian Machinery [*A publication*]
**Hung Magy Allami Foeldt Intez Evk** ... Hungary. Magyar Allami Foeldtani Intezet. Evkoenyve [*A publication*]
**Hung Med Biblio** ... Hungarian Medical Bibliography [*A publication*]
**HUNGN**.... Hungarian
**Hung Notes World Hung Educ Serv** ... Hunger Notes. World Hunger Education Service [*A publication*]
**Hung Press** ... Hungaropress [*A publication*]
**Hung R**....... Hungarian Review [*A publication*]
**Hung S**....... Hungarian Survey [*A publication*]
**Hung Sci Instrum** ... Hungarian Scientific Instruments [*A publication*]
**Hung St Engl** ... Hungarian Studies in English [*A publication*]
**Hung Tech Abstr** ... Hungarian Technical Abstracts [*A publication*]
**Hung Vet J** ... Hungarian Veterinary Journal [*A publication*]
**HunQ**......... Hungarian Quarterly [*New York*] [*A publication*]
**HUN/RU**... Revista de la Universidad. Universidad Nacional Autonoma de Honduras [*Tegucigalpa*] [*A publication*]
**HUNT** ....... Hunterdon Pharmaceuticals [*NASDAQ symbol*] (NQ)
**Hunt**........... Hunter's Torrens Cases [*Canada*] [*A publication*] (DLA)
**Hunt**........... Hunt's Annuity Cases [*England*] [*A publication*] (DLA)
**Hunt**........... Hunt's Merchants' Magazine [*A publication*]
**Hunt Ann Cas** ... Hunt's Annuity Cases [*England*] [*A publication*] (DLA)
**Hunt Bound** ... Hunt's Law of Boundaries and Fences [*A publication*] (DLA)
**Hunt Cas**.... Hunt's Annuity Cases [*England*] [*A publication*] (DLA)
**Hunt Eq**..... Hunt's Suit in Equity [*A publication*] (DLA)
**Hunter Nat Hist** ... Hunter Natural History [*A publication*]
**Hunter Res Found J** ... Hunter Valley Research Foundation. Journal [*A publication*] (APTA)
**Hunter Rom Law** ... Hunter on Roman Law [*A publication*] (DLA)
**Hunter Suit Eq** ... Hunter's Proceeding in a Suit in Equity [*A publication*] (DLA)
**Hunter Valley Res Fdn Monograph** ... Hunter Valley Research Foundation. Monograph [*A publication*] (APTA)
**Hunter Valley Res Found Spec Rep** ... Hunter Valley Research Foundation. Special Report [*A publication*] (APTA)
**HUNTEST** ... Hunting and Testing [*Apollo*] [*NASA*]
**Hunt Fr Conv** ... Hunt's Fraudulent Conveyances [*2nd ed.*] [*1897*] [*A publication*] (DLA)
**Hunt Gr Rev** ... Hunting Group Review [*A publication*]
**Hunting Group Rev** ... Hunting Group Review [*A publication*]
**Huntington Libr Q** ... Huntington Library. Quarterly [*A publication*]
**Hunt Lib Bull** ... Huntington Library. Bulletin [*A publication*]
**Hunt Lib Q** ... Huntington Library. Quarterly [*A publication*]
**Hunt Libr Q** ... Huntington Library. Quarterly [*A publication*]
**Hunt L & T** ... Hunter's Landlord and Tenant [*Scotland*] [*A publication*] (DLA)
**Hunt Mer Mag** ... Hunt's Merchants' Magazine [*A publication*] (DLA)
**Hunt Rom L** ... Hunter on Roman Law [*A publication*] (DLA)
**HUNTS**..... Huntingdonshire [*County in England*]
**Hunt's AC** ... Hunt's Annuity Cases [*England*] [*A publication*] (DLA)
**Hunt Suit** ... Hunter's Proceeding in a Suit in Equity [*A publication*] (DLA)
**Hunt Torrens** ... Hunter's Torrens Cases [*Canada*] [*A publication*] (DLA)
**Hunt Tr**...... Huntingdon's Trial [*A publication*] (DLA)
**HUO**.......... Huguenot, NY [*Location identifier*] [*FAA*] (FAAL)
**HUORAY** ... Human Organization [*A publication*]
**HuOSzK**.... Orszagos Szechenyi Konyvtar [*National Szechenyi Library*], Budapest, Hungary [*Library symbol*] [*Library of Congress*] (LCLS)
**HUP**........... Hangup

**HUP**.......... Helicopter Utility (Piasecki)
**HUP**.......... Homogenous Uniparental Embryo [*Embryology*]
**HUP**.......... Hospital of the University of Pennsylvania
**HUP**.......... Hospital Utilization Project [*Western Pennsylvania*]
**HUP**.......... Hudspeth, TX [*Location identifier*] [*FAA*] (FAAL)
**hup**............ Hupa [*MARC language code*] [*Library of Congress*] (LCCP)
**HUP**.......... Hydrogen Uranyl Phosphate [*Inorganic chemistry*]
**HuPaB**....... Pannonhalmi Szent Benedek Rend Kozponti Konyvtara, Pannonhalma, Hungary [*Library symbol*] [*Library of Congress*] (LCLS)
**HUPATS**... Heuristic Paper Trimming System (BUR)
**HuPE**......... Pecsi Tudomanyegyetem, Pecs, Hungary [*Library symbol*] [*Library of Congress*] (LCLS)
**HUPH**....... Humphrey, Inc. [*NASDAQ symbol*] (NQ)
**HUPHD**.... Human Physiology [*English Translation*] [*A publication*]
**HUPL**........ Helicopter Utilities Proprietary Ltd. [*Australia*]
**HUPPAE**... Harvard University. Papers of the Peabody Museum of Archaeology and Ethnology [*A publication*]
**HUQ**.......... Houn [*Libya*] [*Airport symbol*] (OAG)
**HUR**.......... Hardware Usage Report (MCD)
**HUR**.......... Heat Up Rate (IEEE)
**HuR**.......... Hudson Review [*A publication*]
**HUR**.......... Human Relations [*A publication*]
**HuR**.......... Humanisme et Renaissance [*A publication*]
**HUR**.......... Hurricane [*Alaska*] [*Seismograph station code, US Geological Survey*] (SEIS)
**HURA**........ Health Underserved Rural Areas
**HURC**........ Hurco Companies, Inc. [*NASDAQ symbol*] (NQ)
**HURCN**..... Hurricane
**$H_2$Urd**........ Dihydrouridine [*Also, D, hU*] [*A nucleoside*]
**Hurd F & B**... Hurd on the Laws of Freedom and Bondage in the United States [*A publication*] (DLA)
**Hurd Hab Cor**... Hurd on the Writ of Habeas Corpus [*A publication*] (DLA)
**Hurd Pers Lib**... Hurd on Personal Liberty [*A publication*] (DLA)
**Hurd's Rev St**... Hurd's Illinois Revised Statutes [*A publication*] (DLA)
**Hurd St**....... Hurd's Illinois Statutes [*A publication*] (DLA)
**HUREEE**.. Human Reproduction [*Oxford*] [*A publication*]
**HUREP**..... Hurricane Report
**HUREVAC**... Hurricane Evacuation (NVT)
**HURI**......... Harvard Ukrainian Research Institute
**HURIDOCS**... Human Rights Information and Documentation System (EA)
**HURIDOCS**... Human Rights International Documentation System (EA)
**HURL**........ Hawaii Undersea Research Laboratory [*University of Hawaii*] [*Research center*] (RCD)
**Hurl Bonds**... Hurlstone on Bonds [*A publication*] (DLA)
**Hurl & C**.... Hurlstone and Coltman's English Exchequer Reports [*A publication*] (DLA)
**Hurl & Colt**... Hurlstone and Coltman's English Exchequer Reports [*A publication*] (DLA)
**Hurl Colt**.... Hurlstone and Coltman's English Exchequer Reports [*A publication*] (DLA)
**Hurl & G**.... Hurlstone and Gordon's English Exchequer Reports [*A publication*] (DLA)
**Hurl & Gord**... Hurlstone and Gordon's English Exchequer Reports [*A publication*] (DLA)
**Hurl & N**.... Hurlstone and Norman's English Exchequer Reports [*156, 158 English Reprint*] [*A publication*] (DLA)
**Hurl & Nor**... Hurlstone and Norman's English Exchequer Reports [*156, 158 English Reprint*] [*A publication*] (DLA)
**Hurlst & C**... Hurlstone and Coltman's English Exchequer Reports [*A publication*] (DLA)
**Hurlst & C (Eng)**... Hurlstone and Coltman's English Exchequer Reports [*A publication*] (DLA)
**Hurlst & G**... Hurlstone and Gordon's English Exchequer Reports [*A publication*] (DLA)
**Hurlst & N (Eng)**... Hurlstone and Norman's English Exchequer Reports [*156, 158 English Reprint*] [*A publication*] (DLA)
**Hurlst & W**... Hurlstone and Walmsley's English Exchequer Reports [*1840-41*] [*A publication*] (DLA)
**Hurls & W (Eng)**... Hurlstone and Walmsley's English Exchequer Reports [*1840-41*] [*A publication*] (DLA)
**Hurl & W**... Hurlstone and Walmsley's English Exchequer Reports [*1840-41*] [*A publication*] (DLA)
**Hurl & Walm**... Hurlstone and Walmsley's English Exchequer Reports [*1840-41*] [*A publication*] (DLA)
**Huron Hist N**... Huron Historical Notes [*A publication*]
**Hurr**........... Hurrian (BJA)
**HURRA**..... Housing and Urban-Rural Recovery Act of 1983
**HURRAH**... Help Us Reach and Rehabilitate America's Handicapped [*State-Federal rehabilitation program*]
**HURRAN**... Hurricane Analog
**HUS**........... Harvard Ukrainian Studies [*A publication*]
**HUS**........... Helicopter Utility Squadron
**HUS**........... Hemolytic-Uremic Syndrome [*Nephrology*]
**HUS**........... Heussler Air Service Corp. [*Buffalo, NY*] [*FAA designator*] (FAAC)
**HUS**........... Hughes [*Alaska*] [*Airport symbol*] (OAG)
**HUSAFICPA**... Headquarters, United States Army Forces, Central Pacific Area
**HUSAFMIDPAC**... Headquarters, United States Army Forces, Middle Pacific [*World War II*]
**HUSAT**..... Human Sciences and Advanced Technology Research Centre [*University of Technology*] [*British*] (CB)
**HUSB**........ Home Unity Savings & Loan Association [*Lafayette Hill, PA*] [*NASDAQ symbol*] (NQ)
**husb**........... Husband
**HUSB**........ Husbandry
**HUSBD**..... Husband (ROG)
**Husb For Med**... Husband's Forensic Medicine [*A publication*] (DLA)
**Husb Mar Wom**... Husband on Married Women [*A publication*] (DLA)
**HUSBN**..... Husbandman
**HUSB & W**... Husband and Wife (DLA)
**HUSHA**..... Hua Hsueh [*Taiwan*] [*A publication*]
**Hushall Sallsk Tidskr**... Hushallnings Sallskapens Tidskrift [*A publication*]
**HUSIA**...... Hungarian Scientific Instruments [*A publication*]
**HUSICON**... Humanities, Science, and Conservation [*Environment*]
**HUSL**........ Hebrew University. Studies in Literature [*A publication*]
**HUSO**........ Soroti [*Uganda*] [*ICAO location identifier*] (ICLI)
**HuSpK**....... Sarospataki Reformatus Kollegium Nagykonyvtara, Sarospatak, Hungary [*Library symbol*] [*Library of Congress*] (LCLS)
**HUSRA**..... Science Reports. Hirosaki University [*A publication*]
**HUSS**........ Hussars [*Military unit*] [*British*] (ROG)
**HussR**........ Husson Review [*Bangor, ME*] [*A publication*]
**Hust**........... Hustings Court [*As in Virginia*] [*Legal term*] (DLA)
**HUSTLE**... Helium Underwater Speech Translating Equipment
**Hust L Tit**... Huston on Land Titles in Pennsylvania [*A publication*] (DLA)
**HuSzOE**.... Szegedi Orvostudomanyi Egyetem, Szeged, Hungary [*Library symbol*] [*Library of Congress*] (LCLS)
**HUT**.......... Hard Upper Torso (MCD)
**HUT**.......... HEDL [*Hanford Engineering Development Laboratory*] Up Transient [*Nuclear energy*] (NRCH)
**HUT**.......... Hold Up Tank (IEEE)
**HUT**.......... Hopkins Ultraviolet Telescope
**HUT**.......... Households Using Television [*Television ratings*]
**HUT**.......... Humboldt Energy [*Vancouver Stock Exchange symbol*]
**HUT**.......... Hutchinson [*Kansas*] [*Airport symbol*] (OAG)
**Hut**............ Hutton's English Common Pleas Reports [*1612-39*] [*A publication*] (DLA)
**Hutch**......... Hutcheson's Reports [*81-84 Alabama*] [*A publication*] (DLA)
**Hutch Car**.. Hutchinson on Carriers [*A publication*] (DLA)
**Hutch Carr**... Hutchinson on Carriers [*A publication*] (DLA)
**Hutch Code**... Hutchinson's Code [*Mississippi*] [*A publication*] (DLA)
**Hutch JP**.... Hutcheson's Justice of the Peace [*A publication*] (DLA)
**Hut Ct Req**... Hutton's Courts of Requests [*A publication*] (DLA)
**HUTMA**..... Houtim [*A publication*]
**Hutn Aktual**... Hutnicke Aktuality [*Czechoslovakia*] [*A publication*]
**Hutn (Katowice)**... Hutnik (Katowice) [*A publication*]
**Hutn Listy**... Hutnicke Listy [*A publication*]
**HUTO**....... Tororo [*Uganda*] [*ICAO location identifier*] (ICLI)
**HUTR**........ Hubbell Trading Post National Historic Site
**HUTRON**... Helicopter Utility Squadron
**Hutt**........... Hutton's English Common Pleas Reports [*1612-39*] [*A publication*] (DLA)
**Hutt Ct Req**... Hutton's Courts of Requests [*A publication*] (DLA)
**Hutton**........ Hutton's English Common Pleas Reports [*1612-39*] [*A publication*] (DLA)
**Hutton (Eng)**... Hutton's English Common Pleas Reports [*1612-39*] [*A publication*] (DLA)
**HUU**.......... Detroit, MI [*Location identifier*] [*FAA*] (FAAL)
**HUU**.......... Huanuco [*Peru*] [*Airport symbol*] (OAG)
**HuV**.......... Handel und Versorgung [*Trade and Supply*] [*German*]
**HUV**.......... Hudiksvall [*Sweden*] [*Airport symbol*] (OAG)
**HUVE**........ Human Umbilical Vein Endothelial
**HUVEC**..... Human Umbilical Vein Endothelial Cell [*Cytology*]
**HUX**.......... Harvard University [*Cambridge, MA*]
**HUX**.......... Sacramento, CA [*Location identifier*] [*FAA*] (FAAL)
**Hux Judg**.... Huxley's Second Book of Judgments [*1675*] [*England*] [*A publication*] (DLA)
**HUY**.......... Humberside [*England*] [*Airport symbol*] (OAG)
**Huyck Felt Bull**... Huyck Felt Bulletin [*A publication*]
**HUZ**.......... Huaraz [*Peru*] [*Seismograph station code, US Geological Survey*] (SEIS)
**HUZ**.......... Mesquite, TX [*Location identifier*] [*FAA*] (FAAL)
**HUzT**......... Hermeneutische Untersuchungen zur Theologie [*Tuebingen*] [*A publication*] (BJA)
**HV**............ Air-Cushion Vehicle built by Hover Vehicles [*New Zealand*] [*Usually used in combination with numerals*]
**HV**............ Boeing-Vertol Division [*The Boeing Co.*] [*ICAO aircraft manufacturer identifier*] (ICAO)
**HV**............ Hand Valve [*Nuclear energy*] (NRCH)
**HV**............ Hard Valve (DEN)
**HV**............ Hardware Virtualizer [*Data processing*] (IEEE)
**HV**............ Haricots Verts [*Green Beans*] [*French*]
**HV**............ Have (FAAC)
**HV**............ Health Visitor
**HV**............ Heat of Vaporization (ROG)
**HV**............ Heater Voltage
**HV**............ Heating and Ventilation (AAG)
**H and V**...... Heating and Ventilation (NATG)
**HV**............ Heavy (AABC)

**H-V** ........... Height-Velocity
**HV** ........... Helminthosporium victoriae [*A toxin-producing fungus*]
**H & V** ........ Hemigastrectomy and Vagotomy [*Medicine*]
**HV** ........... Hepatic Vein [*Anatomy*]
**HV** ........... Herpesvirus
**HV** ........... Hic Verbis [*In These Words*] [*Latin*]
**HV** ........... High Vacuum (ADA)
**HV** ........... High Velocity
**HV** ........... High Visibility (DS)
**HV** ........... High in Volatiles [*Commercial grading*]
**HV** ........... High Voltage
**HV** ........... High Volume
**HV** ........... Highly Variegated Maize
**HV** ........... Historische Vierteljahrschrift [*A publication*]
**HV** ........... Hoc Verbum [*This Word*] [*Latin*]
**HV** ........... Hudebni Veda [*A publication*]
**HV** ........... Hyaline-Vascular [*Oncology*]
**HV** ........... Hydrogen Vent (MCD)
**HV** ........... Hydroxyl Value [*Analytical chemistry*]
**HV** ........... Hypervariable
**HV** ........... Hypervelocity (AABC)
**HV** ........... Hyperventilation
**HV** ........... Transavia Holland BV [*Netherlands*] [*ICAO designator*] (FAAC)
**HV** ........... Vickers Hardness Number [*Also, VH, VHN*]
**HVA** .......... Analalava [*Madagascar*] [*Airport symbol*] (OAG)
**HVA** .......... Health Visitors' Association [*A union*] [*British*] (DCTA)
**HVA** .......... Heeresverwaltungsamt [*Army Administration Office*] [*German military - World War II*]
**HVA** .......... Herpesvirus Ateles
**HVA** .......... High-Voltage-Activated [*Neurochemistry*]
**HVA** .......... Homovanillic Acid [*Biochemistry*]
**HVA** .......... New Haven Airways, Inc. [*New Haven, CT*] [*FAA designator*] (FAAC)
**HVAC** ........ Heating, Ventilating, and Air Conditioning
**HVAC** ........ High Vacuum (IEEE)
**HVAC** ........ High-Voltage Actuator [*Electronics*] (IEEE)
**HVAC** ........ High-Voltage Alternating Current
**HVACC** ..... High-Voltage Apparatus Coordinating Committee [*ANSI*]
**Hvalradets Skr** ... Hvalradets Skrifter [*A publication*]
**HVAP** ........ High-Velocity, Armor-Piercing [*Projectile*]
**HVAPDS** ... High-Velocity, Armor-Piercing, Discarding Sabot [*Projectile*]
**HVAPDSFS** ... High-Velocity, Armor-Piercing, Discarding Sabot, Fin Stabilized [*Projectile*] (MCD)
**HVAPFSDS** ... High-Velocity, Armor-Piercing, Fin Stabilized, Discarding Sabot [*Projectile*] (MCD)
**HVAP-T** .... Hypervelocity, Armor-Piercing - Tracer [*Projectile*] (AABC)
**HVAR** ........ High-Velocity Aircraft Rocket
**HVAT** ........ High-Velocity Antitank [*Projectile*]
**HVB** .......... Hauptverbandplatz [*Clearing Station*] [*German military - World War II*]
**HVB** .......... Hervey Bay [*Australia*] [*Airport symbol*] (OAG)
**HVB** .......... High-Voltage Bias
**HV Bl** ........ Hamburgisches Verordnungsblatt [*A publication*]
**HVC** .......... Hardened Voice Channel [*NASA*] (KSC)
**HVC** .......... Hardened Voice Circuit (CET)
**HVC** .......... Hav-Info Computers, Inc. [*Vancouver Stock Exchange symbol*]
**HVC** .......... Haverford College, Haverford, PA [*OCLC symbol*] (OCLC)
**HVC** .......... Hayden's Viburnum Compound [*Medicine*]
**HVC** .......... Health Visitor's Certificate [*British*]
**HV & C** ...... Heating, Ventilating, and Cooling (AAG)
**HVC** .......... Hernandez Valley [*California*] [*Seismograph station code, US Geological Survey*] (SEIS)
**HVC** .......... High-Voltage Connector
**HVC** .......... High-Voltage Control
**HVC** .......... Hopkinsville, KY [*Location identifier*] [*FAA*] (FAAL)
**HVc** .......... Hyperstriatum Ventralis Pars Caudalis [*Bird brain anatomy*]
**HVc** .......... Ventral Hyperstriatum Caudal Nucleus [*Neuroanatomy*]
**HVCA** ........ Heating and Ventilating Contractors' Association [*British*]
**HVCE** ........ High-Voltage Capillary Electrophoresis
**HVCH** ........ Hardened Voice Channel (MSA)
**HVD** .......... Heaters, Vents, and Drains [*System*] [*Nuclear energy*] (NRCH)
**HVD** .......... Height-Velocity Diagram
**HVD** .......... Hendrik Verwoerd Dam [*South Africa*] [*Seismograph station code, US Geological Survey*] (SEIS)
**HVD** .......... High-Velocity Detonation
**HVD** .......... High-Viscosity Dispenser [*Packaging*]
**HVD** .......... Hypertensive Vascular Disease [*Medicine*]
**HVDC** ........ High-Voltage Direct Current
**HVDCT** ...... High-Voltage Direct-Current Transmission [*Electronics*]
**HVDF** ........ High- and Very-High-Frequency Direction Finding
**HVDGP** ...... Hauptverwaltung Deutsche Grenzpolizei [*Central Administration of the Border Police*] [*Germany*]
**HVDK** ........ Harvard Knitwear, Inc. [*NASDAQ symbol*] (NQ)
**HVDP** ........ Heavy Drop [*Military*] (AABC)
**HVDRR** ...... Hypocalcemic Vitamin D-Resistant Rickets [*Medicine*]
**HVDS** ........ Hypergolic Vapor Detection System [*NASA*] (NASA)
**HVE** .......... Hanksville, UT [*Location identifier*] [*FAA*] (FAAL)
**HVE** .......... High-Vacuum Environment
**HVE** .......... High-Vacuum Evaporator
**HVE** .......... High Voltage Engineering Corp. [*NYSE symbol*] (SPSG)
**HVEC** ........ High Voltage Engineering Corporation
**HVEC** ........ Human Vascular Endothelial Cells
**HVECA** ..... Heating and Ventilating Engineer and Journal of Air Conditioning [*A publication*]
**HVEL** ........ Hypervelocity
**HVEM** ....... High-Voltage Electron Microscopy
**HVES** ........ High-Vacuum Evaporation System
**HVES** ........ High-Voltage Electrical Stimulation [*Meat treatment*]
**HVF** .......... Harmonically Varying Field
**HVF** .......... Haverford College, Haverford, PA [*OCLC symbol*] (OCLC)
**HVF** .......... High-Viscosity Fuel Oil (DCTA)
**HVFB** ........ High-Velocity Fluidized Bed [*Chemical engineering*]
**HVFD** ........ Haverfield Corp. [*NASDAQ symbol*] (NQ)
**HVFS** ........ High-Vacuum Flame Sterilization [*Food technology*]
**HVG** .......... High-Voltage Generator
**HVG** .......... High-Voltage Gradient
**HVG** .......... Honningsvag [*Norway*] [*Airport symbol*] (OAG)
**HVG** .......... Host Versus Graft [*Medicine*]
**HVG** .......... Hypervelocity Gun [*Military*] (SDI)
**HVGLS** ...... High-Velocity Grenade Launcher System [*Projectile*] (MCD)
**HVH** .......... Herpesvirus Hominis
**HVH** .......... Hydrogen Vent Header [*Nuclear energy*] (NRCH)
**HVHA** ........ High-Velocity Hot-Air [*Oven*]
**HVHMD** ... Holographic Visor Helmet-Mounted Display [*Air Force*]
**HVHW** ...... Health Values. Achieving High Level Wellness [*A publication*]
**HVI** ........... Hartman Value Inventory [*Psychology*]
**HVI** ........... Hepatic Volumetric Index
**HVI** ........... High-Value Item (NATG)
**HVI** ........... Home Ventilating Institute [*Later, HVIDAMCA*] (EA)
**HVI** ........... Horizon Village [*Vancouver Stock Exchange symbol*]
**HVIC** ......... High-Voltage Integrated Circuit [*Data processing*]
**HVIDAMCA** ... Home Ventilating Institute Division of the Air Movement Control Association (EA)
**HVIT** ......... High-Volume Information Transfer
**HVJ** ........... Hemagglutinating Virus of Japan [*Medicine*]
**HVJ** ........... Historische Vierteljahrschrift [*A publication*]
**HVJS** ......... Historische Vierteljahrschrift [*A publication*]
**HVK** .......... Holmavik [*Iceland*] [*Airport symbol*] (OAG)
**HVK** .......... Hovik Medical [*Vancouver Stock Exchange symbol*]
**HVL** .......... Half-Value Layer [*Radiology*]
**HVL** .......... Heeresverpflegungslager [*Army Ration Depot*] [*German military - World War II*]
**HVL** .......... High Voltage Laboratory [*MIT*] (MCD)
**HVL** .......... Hypervelocity Launcher [*Military*] (SDI)
**HVLP** ........ High-Volume Low-Pressure [*Spray-painting process*]
**HVLS** ........ Huron Valley Library System [*Library network*]
**HVM** .......... High-Voltage Mode
**HvM** .......... Honar va Mardom [*A publication*]
**HVM** .......... Hydraulic Valve Motor
**HVM** .......... Hypervelocity Missile
**HVM** .......... Hypervelocity Munition
**HVM** .......... Sisters, Home Visitors of Mary [*Roman Catholic religious order*]
**HVMS** ........ Hypervelocity, Medium Support
**HVMVI** ...... High-Voltage Mercury-Vapor Isolator
**HVN** .......... Havana [*Cuba*] [*Geomagnetic observatory code*]
**HVN** .......... Haven (MCD)
**HVN** .......... Home View Network [*Cable-television system*]
**HVN** .......... New Haven [*Connecticut*] [*Airport symbol*] (OAG)
**HVO** .......... Hawaiian Volcano Observatory [*Kilauea*] [*Hawaii*] [*Seismograph station code, US Geological Survey*] (SEIS)
**HVOF** ........ High-Velocity Oxygen/Fuel [*Coating technology*]
**HVOT** ........ Hooper Visual Organization Test [*Psychology*]
**HVP** .......... Half-Value Period
**HVP** .......... Hardware Verification Program (CAAL)
**HVP** .......... Hartman Value Profile [*Personality development test*] [*Psychology*]
**HVP** .......... Hayes Verification Protocol [*Data processing*]
**HVP** .......... Heart Valve Prostheses [*Medicine*]
**HVP** .......... High-Vacuum Pump
**HVP** .......... High-Value Product
**HVP** .......... High Video Pass (NVT)
**HVP** .......... High-Voltage Pump
**HVP** .......... Host Vehicle Pallet
**HVP** .......... Hydrolyzed Vegetable Protein [*Food additive*]
**HVPE** ........ High-Voltage Paper Electrophoresis
**HVPE** ........ Hydride Vapor Phase Epitaxy [*Crystallography*]
**HVPF** ........ Human Vascular Permeability Factor [*Biochemistry*]
**HVPG** ........ Hepatic Venous Pressure Gradient [*Medicine*]
**HVPI** ......... Holland Vocational Preference Inventory [*Psychology*]
**HVPR** ........ High-Voltage Phase Retard
**HVPS** ........ High-Voltage Power Supply
**HVPS** ........ High-Volume Printing System [*Data processing*]
**HVPVE** ..... High-Voltage Photovoltaic Effect [*Physics*]
**HVR** .......... Hardware Vector to Raster
**HVR** .......... Havre [*Montana*] [*Airport symbol*] (OAG)
**HVR** .......... Helicopter Visual Rules
**HVR** .......... High-Resolution Visible Range
**HVR** .......... High-Vacuum Rectifier
**HVR** .......... High-Voltage Rectifier
**HVR** .......... High-Voltage Regulator (MSA)

**HVR** .......... High-Voltage Relay
**HVR** .......... High-Voltage Resistor
**HVR** .......... Highland Valley Resources Ltd. [*Vancouver Stock Exchange symbol*]
**HVR** .......... Highly Variable Regions [*Of chromosomes*] [*Genetics*]
**HVR** .......... Hover (MCD)
**HVR** .......... Hyderabad Volunteer Rifles [*British military*] (DMA)
**HVR** .......... Hypervariable Region [*Genetics*]
**HVR** .......... Hypoxic Ventilatory Response [*Medicine*]
**HVRA** .......... Heating and Ventilating Research Association [*British*]
**HVREA** ..... Heating and Ventilating Review [*A publication*]
**HVRL** .......... High Voltage Research Laboratory [*MIT*] (MCD)
**HVRNG** ..... Hovering
**HVS** .......... Hartsville, SC [*Location identifier*] [*FAA*] (FAAL)
**HVS** .......... Herpesvirus of Saimiri
**HVS** .......... High-Voltage Switch
**HVS** .......... Human Vaginal Swab [*Medicine*]
**HVS** .......... Human Visual System
**HVS** .......... Hypersonic Vehicle Shield
**HVSA** .......... High-Voltage Solar Array
**HVSCR** ...... High-Voltage Selenium Cartridge Rectifier
**HVSE** .......... High-Voltage Solar Experiment
**HVSF** .......... Honeywell Verification Simulation Facility (NASA)
**HVSL** .......... Holidays, Vacation, and Sick Leave (NASA)
**HVSP** .......... High-Voltage Solar Panel
**HVSS** .......... Horizontal Volute Spring Suspension [*Projectile*]
**HVST** .......... High-Voltage Switching Transistor
**HVSU** .......... Heating Ventilating Supply Unit (NRCH)
**HVT** .......... Half-Value Thickness
**HVT** .......... HealthVest SBI [*AMEX symbol*] (SPSG)
**HVT** .......... Hidden Variable Theory [*Physics*]
**HVT** .......... High-Value Target (NVT)
**HVT** .......... High-Voltage Termination
**HVT** .......... High-Voltage Tester
**HVT** .......... High-Voltage Transformer
**HVTP** .......... High-Velocity, Target-Practice [*Projectile*]
**HVTP** .......... Hypervelocity, Target-Practice [*Projectile*]
**HVTPDS** ... High-Velocity, Target-Practice, Discarding Sabot [*Projectile*]
**HVTP-T** .... Hypervelocity, Target-Practice - Tracer [*Projectile*] (AABC)
**HVTS** .......... High-Volume Time Sharing [*Data processing*]
**HVU** .......... Altus, OK [*Location identifier*] [*FAA*] (FAAL)
**HVU** .......... Hansel Valley [*Utah*] [*Seismograph station code, US Geological Survey*] (SEIS)
**HVU** .......... Heating Ventilation Unit (MCD)
**HVU** .......... High-Value Unit [*Torpedo defense system*] (MCD)
**HVV** .......... Hamburger Verkehrsverbund [*Hamburg subway*] [*Federal Republic of Germany*]
**HVV** .......... Helium Vent Valve (MCD)
**HVV** .......... Vrije Volk [*A publication*]
**HVW** .......... High-Voltage Waveform
**HVW** .......... High-Voltage Wire
**HVWP** .......... Hospitalized Veterans Writing Project (EA)
**HVWS** .......... Hebrew Veterans of the War with Spain (EA)
**HVY** .......... Happy Valley, AK [*Location identifier*] [*FAA*] (FAAL)
**HVY** .......... Heavy (AFM)
**HW** .......... Guernsey Airlines Ltd. [*Great Britain*] [*ICAO designator*] (FAAC)
**HW** .......... Hairy Woodpecker [*Ornithology*]
**HW** .......... Half Wave
**HW** .......... Half Word (CET)
**HW** .......... Handset, Wall Model (TEL)
**HW** .......... Handwritten (BJA)
**HW** .......... Hardware [*Data processing*] (NASA)
**HW** .......... Hardwood
**H & W** .......... Harrison and Wollaston's English King's Bench Reports [*A publication*] (DLA)
**HW** .......... Hauptwachtmeister [*First Sergeant*] [*German military - World War II*]
**HW** .......... Hauptwerk [*Masterpiece*] [*German*]
**HW** .......... Haus und Wohnung [*A publication*]
**H u W** .......... Haus und Wohnung [*A publication*]
**H & W** .......... Hazzard and Warburton's Prince Edward Island Reports [*A publication*] (DLA)
**HW** .......... Head Wardmaster [*Navy*] [*British*] (ROG)
**HW** .......... Head Width
**HW** .......... Head Wind [*Navigation*]
**HW** .......... Headwaiter
**HW** .......... Heavy Wall
**HW** .......... Heavy Water
**HW** .......... Heavy Weapons [*British military*] (DMA)
**HW** .......... Herewith [*Enclosures*] [*Navy*]
**HW** .......... Hethitisches Woerterbuch [*Heidelberg*] [*A publication*] (BJA)
**HW** .......... High Water [*Tides and currents*]
**HW** .......... High Wing [*Aviation*] (AIA)
**H/W** .......... Highway
**HW** .......... Hispanic Writers [*A publication*]
**HW** .......... Historical Wyoming [*A publication*]
**HW** .......... Hit Wicket
**Hw** .......... Hochschulwissen in Einzeldarstelungen [*A publication*]
**HW** .......... Hollandsch Weekblad [*A publication*]
**HW** .......... Homing Weapons (NVT)
**HW** .......... Hot Water
**HW** .......... Hot Wire (KSC)
**HW** .......... Hotwell [*Nuclear energy*] (NRCH)
**HW** .......... Housewife
**HW** .......... Howard Aero Manufacturing [*ICAO aircraft manufacturer identifier*] (ICAO)
**HW** .......... Howler [*Communications; electronics*]
**HW** .......... Hunter-Wheel
**H & W** .......... Hurlstone and Walmsley's English Exchequer Reports [*1840-41*] [*A publication*] (DLA)
**HWA** .......... Hallman, W. A., St. Paul MN [*STAC*]
**HWA** .......... Handwritten by Amanuensis (BJA)
**HWA** .......... Hill-Williford Aviation, Inc. [*Atlanta, GA*] [*FAA designator*] (FAAC)
**HWA** .......... Holloway White Allom [*Building contractor*] [*British*]
**HWA** .......... Hot Wire Anemometer
**HWA** .......... Hwalien [*Karenko*] [*Republic of China*] [*Seismograph station code, US Geological Survey*] (SEIS)
**HWAA** .......... Heereswaffenamt [*Army Ordnance Office*] [*German military - World War II*]
**HWAAP** .... Hawthorne Army Ammunition Plant (AABC)
**HWAI** .......... Horseback Writers and Artists, International (EA)
**HWAIFC** ... Hank Williams Appreciation International Fan Club (EA)
**Hware** .......... Hardware Today [*A publication*]
**HWAY** .......... Humble Way [*Exxon Corporation*] [*A publication*]
**HWB** .......... Handwoerterbuch [*Pocket Dictionary*] [*German*]
**HWB** .......... Hot Water Boiler [*on a ship*] (DS)
**hwb** .......... Hot Water Bottle
**Hwb d B** ..... Handwoerterbuch der Betriebswirtschaft [*A publication*]
**HWBC** .......... Hartford Whalers Booster Club (EA)
**Hwb Dt RG** ... Handwoerterbuch zur Deutschen Rechtsgeschichte [*A publication*]
**HWBDU** .... Hot Weather Battle Dress Uniform [*Army*] (INF)
**HWBF** .......... High-Water-Based Fluid [*Hydraulic and cutting fluids*]
**HWBI** .......... Handwoerterbuch des Islam [*Leiden*] [*A publication*] (BJA)
**HWBR** .......... Half-Wave Bridge Rectifier
**Hwb d Sw** ... Handwoerterbuch der Sozialwissenschaften [*A publication*]
**HWC** .......... Health and Welfare Canada
**HWC** .......... Hot Water Circulating [*Technical drawings*]
**HWCA** .......... Housing of Working Classes Act [*British*] (ROG)
**HWCC** .......... Harpoon Weapon Control Console [*Missiles*] (MCD)
**HWCD** .......... HWC Distribution Corp. [*NASDAQ symbol*] (NQ)
**HWCF** .......... High-Water-Content Fluid [*Nonpetroleum lubricant*]
**HWCI** .......... Hardware Configuration Item
**HWCS** .......... Helicopter Wire Cutter System (MCD)
**HWCTR** .... Heavy-Water Components Test Reactor [*Nuclear energy*]
**HWCU** .......... Heated Window Control Unit
**HWD** .......... Hardwood [*Technical drawings*]
**HWD** .......... Hayward, CA [*Location identifier*] [*FAA*] (FAAL)
**HWD** .......... Highwood Resources Ltd. [*Toronto Stock Exchange symbol*]
**HWD** .......... Hill/Wendover/Dugway [*Ranges*] [*Military*] (MCD)
**HWD** .......... Horizontal Weather Depiction
**HWD** .......... Hot Wire Detector [*Analytical instrumentation*]
**HWDMS** ... Hazardous Waste Data [*or Disposal*] Management System [*Environmental Protection Agency*]
**HWDYKY** ... How Well Do You Know Yourself? [*Psychological testing*]
**HWE** .......... East West Center, Honolulu, HI [*OCLC symbol*] (OCLC)
**HWEC** .......... Hallwood Energy Corp. [*NASDAQ symbol*] (NQ)
**HWEP** .......... Hot Wire Emissive Probe
**HWERL** .... Hazardous Waste Engineering Research Laboratory [*Cincinnati, OH*] [*Environmental Protection Agency*] (GRD)
**HWF** .......... Aberdeen/Amory, MS [*Location identifier*] [*FAA*] (FAAL)
**HWF** .......... Hazardous Waste Federation (EA)
**HWF & C** ... High-Water Full and Change [*Tides and currents*]
**HWG** .......... Hallwood Group, Inc. [*NYSE symbol*] (SPSG)
**HWG** .......... House Wednesday Group (EA)
**HWGCR** .... Heavy-Water Moderated Gas-Cooled Reactor [*Nuclear energy*]
**H W Gr** ...... [*H. W.*] Green's New Jersey Equity Reports [*2-4 New Jersey*] [*A publication*] (DLA)
**HWGW** ..... Hiram Walker - Gooderham & Worts [*Canada*]
**HWH** .......... Hot Water Heater (MSA)
**HWI** .......... Hardware Interpreter
**HWI** .......... Hardware Wholesalers, Incorporated
**HWI** .......... Hawk Inlet, AK [*Location identifier*] [*FAA*] (FAAL)
**HWI** .......... Head Width Index
**HWI** .......... Helical Washer Institute [*Defunct*] (EA)
**HWI** .......... Herdiscontering-en Waarborginstituut [*Development bank*] [*Belgium*] (EY)
**HWI** .......... High-Water Interval
**HWI** .......... Howard Winters, Inc. [*Fresno, CA*] [*FAA designator*] (FAAC)
**HWIM** .......... Hear What I Mean [*Speech recognition system*]
**HWIN** .......... Hot Water-Insoluble Nitrogen [*Analytical chemistry*]
**HWIS** .......... Heritage Wisconsin [*NASDAQ symbol*] (NQ)
**HWJFC** ..... Hank Williams Jr. Fan Club (EA)
**HWK** .......... Hawk Resources, Inc. [*Vancouver Stock Exchange symbol*]
**HWK** .......... Hawker [*Australia*] [*Airport symbol*] (OAG)
**HWK** .......... Kaufman [*H. W.*] Financial Group, Inc. [*AMEX symbol*] (SPSG)
**HWKB** .......... Hawkeye Bancorporation [*NASDAQ symbol*] (NQ)
**HWKN** .......... Hawkins Chemical, Inc. [*NASDAQ symbol*] (NQ)
**HWL** .......... Harvey Woods Limited [*Toronto Stock Exchange symbol*]

**HWL**.......... Hauptwiderstandslinie [*Main line of resistance in a delaying action*] [*German military - World War II*]
**HWL**.......... Henry Wadsworth Longfellow [*Initials used as pseudonym*]
**HWL**.......... High-Water Line [*Technical drawings*]
**HWL**.......... Hot Water Line (AAG)
**HWL**.......... Hotwell
**HWL**.......... Howell Corp. [*NYSE symbol*] (SPSG)
**HWLC**....... Hotwell Level Control [*System*] [*Nuclear energy*] (NRCH)
**HWLI**........ High-Water Lunitidal Interval
**HWLS**....... Hostile Weapons Locating System (MCD)
**HWLWR**... Heavy-Water-Moderated, Boiling Light-Water-Cooled Reactor [*Nuclear energy*] (NRCH)
**HWM**........ Hazardous Waste Management
**HWM**........ Helgolaender Wissenschaftliche Meeresuntersuchungen [*A publication*]
**HWM**........ High-Water Mark [*Maps and charts*]
**HWM**........ High Wet Modulus [*Test for rayon*]
**HWM**........ Maui County Free Library, Wailuku, HI [*Library symbol*] [*Library of Congress*] (LCLS)
**HWMC**...... House Ways and Means Committee
**HWMJA**... Hawaii Medical Journal [*A publication*]
**HWN**........ Hazard Warning Network
**HWN**........ High-Water Neaps
**HWN**........ Honolulu, HI [*Location identifier*] [*FAA*] (FAAL)
**HWNA**...... Hosiery Wholesalers National Association (EA)
**HWNC**...... Haywood Savings and Loan Association [*NASDAQ symbol*] (NQ)
**HWO**......... Hollywood, FL [*Location identifier*] [*FAA*] (FAAL)
**HWO**......... Homosexual World Organization
**HWO**......... Hurricane Warning Office [*National Weather Service*]
**HWOCR**.... Heavy-Water Moderated Organic-Cooled Reactor [*Nuclear energy*]
**HWOST**.... High-Water Ordinary Spring Tides [*Maps and charts*]
**HWP**.......... Half-Wave Plate
**HWP**.......... Hardware Work Package (MCD)
**HWP**.......... Heavy-Water Plant [*Nuclear energy*]
**HWP**.......... Hewlett-Packard Co. [*NYSE symbol*] (SPSG)
**HWP**.......... Hours Waiting Parts (MCD)
**HWP**.......... Hungarian Workers' Party [*Political party*] (PPW)
**HWPB**....... Heavy Weather Patrol Boats (CINC)
**HWPC**....... Hollywood Women's Political Committee (EA)
**HWQ**......... Hansard Written Questions [*Database*] [*House of Commons*] [*Canada*] [*Information service or system*] (CRD)
**HWQ**......... Harlowton, MT [*Location identifier*] [*FAA*] (FAAL)
**HWQ**......... High-Water Quadrature
**HWR**.......... Half-Wave Rectifier
**HWR**.......... Heavy-Water Reactor [*Nuclear energy*]
**HWR**.......... Hot Water Return
**HWR**.......... Walker [*Hiram*] Resources Ltd. [*Toronto Stock Exchange symbol*] [*Vancouver Stock Exchange symbol*] (SPSG)
**HWRC**....... Hazardous Waste Research Center [*Louisiana State University*] [*Research center*] (RCD)
**HWRCB**.... Highways and Road Construction [*A publication*]
**HWRD**....... [*The*] Howard Savings Bank [*NASDAQ symbol*] (NQ)
**HWS**.......... Hanford Works Standard [*or Specification*] [*Later, HPS*] [*Nuclear energy*] (NRCH)
**HWS**.......... Harassment Weapon System (MCD)
**HWS**.......... Harpoon Weapons System (NVT)
**HWS**.......... Helicopter Weapons System
**HWS**.......... High Water of Spring Tide
**HWS**.......... Hot Water Soluble
**HWSA**....... Hazardous Waste Services Association [*Defunct*] (EA)
**HWSI**........ HealthWays Systems, Incorporated [*Woodcliff Lake, NJ*] [*NASDAQ symbol*] (NQ)
**HWSNAM**... Hawaiian Shell News [*A publication*]
**HWSSG**.... Heavy Weapons Special Study Group [*Military*] (MCD)
**HW/SW**.... Hardware/Software (MCD)
**HWT**.......... Hot Water Temperature
**HWT**.......... Hypersonic Wind Tunnel
**HWTC**....... Hazardous Waste Treatment Council (EA)
**HWTC**....... Highway Traffic Control
**HWTH**...... Herewith (ROG)
**HWTR**....... Heavy Weapons Testing Range [*Military*] (MCD)
**HWTS**....... Humm-Wadsworth Temperament Scale [*Psychology*]
**HWVE**....... Hot-Wall Vacuum Evaporation [*Photovoltaic energy systems*]
**HWVR**....... However (FAAC)
**HWW**........ H. W. Wilson Co. [*Publisher*]
**HWW**........ Horan, Wall & Walker [*Publisher*] (ADA)
**HWWB**...... Hardwood Weather Board (ADA)
**HWWS**...... Hyperfiltration Wash Water Recovery System [*NASA*] (NASA)
**HWY**.......... Highway
**HWY**.......... Hundred Woman Years [*of exposure*] [*Radiation*]
**HWY**.......... Huntway Partners LP [*NYSE symbol*] (CTT)
**HwyResAb**... Highway Research Abstracts [*A publication*]
**HWZOA**..... Hadassah, The Women's Zionist Organization of America (EA)
**HX**............ Halifax Engineering, Inc. [*AMEX symbol*] (SPSG)
**HX**............ Heat Exchanger (MCD)
**HX**............ Hereodox [*Commercial firm*] [*British*]
**HX**............ Hexagonal [*Technical drawings*]
**Hx**............ Hexode (DEN)
**Hx**............ Hexyl [*Biochemistry*]
**HX**............ High Index [*Aviation*] (FAAC)
**HX**............ Histiocytosis X [*or Histocytosis X*] [*Hematology*]
**Hx**............ History [*Medicine*]
**Hx**............ Hypophysectomized [*Medicine*]
**Hx**............ Hypoxanthine [*Also, Hyp, HYPX*] [*Biochemistry*]
**HX**............ South Pacific Island Airways, Inc. [*Pago Pago, American Samoa*] [*ICAO designator*] (FAAC)
**HX**............ Station Having No Specific Working Hours [*ITU designation*] (CET)
**HXB**.......... Helix Biotech [*Vancouver Stock Exchange symbol*]
**hXBP**........ Human X Box Binding Protein [*Genetics*]
**HXBT**........ Helicopter Expendable Bathythermograph [*Naval Oceanographic Office*]
**HxCDD**..... Hexachlorodibenzo-para-dioxin [*Organic chemistry*]
**HXCL**........ Hexcel
**HXF**.......... Hartford, WI [*Location identifier*] [*FAA*] (FAAL)
**HXIS**......... Hard X-Ray Imaging Spectrometer
**HXK**.......... Berlin, NH [*Location identifier*] [*FAA*] (FAAL)
**HXL**.......... Hexcel Corp. [*NYSE symbol*] (SPSG)
**HXLD**........ Hexcel Corp. [*NASDAQ symbol*] (NQ)
**HXM**......... Hazleton, PA [*Location identifier*] [*FAA*] (FAAL)
**HXM**......... Helicopter Experimental, Medium (MCD)
**HXM**......... Hexamethylmelamine [*Altretamine*] [*Also, HEX, HMM*] [*Antineoplastic drug*]
**HXO**......... Oxford, NC [*Location identifier*] [*FAA*] (FAAL)
**HXQ**......... Hard X-Ray Quanta
**HXRBS**...... Hard X-Ray Burst Spectrometer
**HXW**......... Hopkinsville, KY [*Location identifier*] [*FAA*] (FAAL)
**HXWXL**.... Height by Width by Length (IEEE)
**HXX**.......... Hay [*Australia*] [*Airport symbol*] (OAG)
**Hy**............ All India Reporter, Hyderabad [*A publication*] (DLA)
**HY**............ Heavy (NATG)
**HY**............ Heavy [*Track condition*] [*Thoroughbred racing*]
**HY**............ Hebrew Year [*Freemasonry*] (ROG)
**HY**............ Henry
**HY**............ Hertfordshire Yeomanry [*British military*] (DMA)
**Hy**............ Highway
**H-Y**.......... Histocompatibility Y [*Immunology*]
**Hy**............ History [*Medicine*]
**HY**............ Hundred Yards
**HY**............ Hydrant (ADA)
**HY**............ Hydrocollator [*Hot*] Pack [*Medicine*]
**HY**............ Hydrography
**Hy**............ Hymn [*A publication*]
**Hy**............ Hypermetropia [*Ophthalmology*]
**hy**............ Hypersthene [*CIPW classification*] [*Geology*]
**HY**............ Hypobranchial [*Gland*]
**Hy**............ Hypothenar [*Anatomy*]
**HY**............ Journal of Hydraulic Engineering [*A publication*]
**HY**............ Liberian World Airlines, Inc. [*ICAO designator*] (FAAC)
**HYA**.......... Hyack Air Ltd. [*New Westminster, BC, Canada*] [*FAA designator*] (FAAC)
**HYA**.......... Hyannis [*Massachusetts*] [*Airport symbol*] (OAG)
**Hya**........... Hydrus [*Constellation*]
**Hyacinth Control J**... Hyacinth Control Journal [*A publication*]
**HYACS**...... Hybrid Analog-Switching Attitude Control System for Space Vehicles
**HYAS**........ Hydrogasification [*Gas from coal fuel*]
**Hyatt's PC**... Hyatt's PC News Report [*A publication*]
**HYB**.......... Herzl Year Book [*A publication*]
**HYB**.......... Hybrid (MSA)
**HYB**.......... Hyderabad [*National Geophysics Research Institute*] [*India*] [*Seismograph station code, US Geological Survey*] (SEIS)
**HYB**.......... Hyderabad [*India*] [*Geomagnetic observatory code*]
**HYB**.......... New American High Income Fund [*NYSE symbol*] (SPSG)
**HYBALL**... Hybrid Analog Logic Language (MCD)
**HYBD**........ Hycor Biomedical, Inc. [*NASDAQ symbol*] (NQ)
**HYBENZATE**... o-(4-Hydroxybenzoyl)benzoate [*Organic chemistry*] [*USAN*]
**Hy Bl**......... [*Henry*] Blackstone's English Common Pleas Reports [*1788-96*] [*A publication*] (DLA)
**HYBMED**... Hybrid Microelectronic Device (MSA)
**HYBR**........ Hybritech, Inc. [*NASDAQ symbol*] (NQ)
**HYC**.......... Hampshire Yeomanry Cavalry [*British military*] (DMA)
**HYC**.......... Haney [*British Columbia*] [*Seismograph station code, US Geological Survey*] (SEIS)
**HYC**.......... Hertfordshire Yeomanry Cavalry [*British military*] (DMA)
**HYC**.......... Hydraulic Coupling [*of a ship*] (DS)
**HYCATS**... Hydrofoil Collision Avoidance and Tracking System [*Developed by Sperry*]
**HYCOL**..... Hybrid Computer Link
**HY-COM**.. Highway Communications
**HYCOTRAN**... Hybrid Computer Translator
**HYCYD**..... Haksul Yonguchi - Chungnam Taehakkyo. Chayon Kwahak Yonguso [*A publication*]
**Hyd**........... All India Reporter, Hyderabad [*A publication*] (DLA)
**HYD**.......... Coeur D'Alene, ID [*Location identifier*] [*FAA*] (FAAL)
**HYD**.......... Hyderabad [*India*] [*Seismograph station code, US Geological Survey*] [*Closed*] (SEIS)
**HYD**.......... Hyderabad [*India*] [*Airport symbol*] (OAG)

**HYD** .......... Hydrant (MSA)
**HYD** .......... Hydrargyrum [*Mercury*] [*Pharmacy*]
**HYD** .......... Hydrated
**HYD** .......... Hydraulic (AAG)
**HYD** .......... Hydroelectric Power [*Type of water project*]
**HYD** .......... Hydrogenation [*Chemistry*]
**HYD** .......... Hydrographic
**HYD** .......... Hydrostatics
**HYD** .......... Hydrous
**HYD** .......... Hydroxyurea [*Also, HU, HYDREA*] [*Antineoplastic drug*]
**HYD** .......... International Hydron Corp. [*AMEX symbol*] (SPSG)
**HYDAC**..... Hybrid Digital-Analog Computing [*System*] [*Satellite*]
**HYDAP**..... Hybrid Digital-Analog Pulse Time (MCD)
**HYDAPT** .. Hybrid Digital-Analog Pulse Time
**HYDCA**..... Hydrocarbure [*A publication*]
**HYDE**......... Hyde Athletic Industries, Inc. [*NASDAQ symbol*] (NQ)
**Hyde** .......... Hyde's Bengal Reports [*India*] [*A publication*] (DLA)
**Hyderabad** ... Indian Law Reports, Hyderabad Series [*A publication*] (DLA)
**HYDI**......... Hydromer, Incorporated [*NASDAQ symbol*] (NQ)
**Hydi** .......... Hydrus [*Constellation*]
**HYDIDH**... Scientific Works. Poultry Science. Poultry Research Institute [*A publication*]
**HYDKAK**.. Proceedings. Hoshi College of Pharmacy [*A publication*]
**HYDLAPS** ... Hydrographic Data Logging and Processing Systems [*Australia*]
**HYDM** ...... Hydrometer
**HYD PRO UN** ... Hydraulic Propulsion Units [*on a ship*] (DS)
**HYDR**........ Hydragogue [*Cathartic*] [*Pharmacy*] (ROG)
**HYDR**........ Hydraulic (MSA)
**Hydr**.......... Hydrographer [*British military*] (DMA)
**HYDR**........ Hydrostatics (ROG)
**HYDRA**..... Hydramatic [*Automotive engineering*]
**HYDRA**..... Hydraulic [*or Hydrologic*] Analysis
**HYDRA**..... Hydrographic Digital Positioning and Depth Recording [*System*] [*NOO*]
**Hydra Pneum** ... Hydraulics and Pneumatics [*A publication*]
**HYDRARG** ... Hydrargyrum [*Mercury*] [*Pharmacy*]
**HYDRAUL** ... Hydraulics (ROG)
**Hydraul & Air Engng** ... Hydraulic and Air Engineering [*A publication*]
**Hydraul & Pneum** ... Hydraulics and Pneumatics [*A publication*]
**Hydraul Pneum Mech Power** ... Hydraulic Pneumatic Mechanical Power [*A publication*]
**Hydraul Pneum Power** ... Hydraulic Pneumatic Power [*Later, Hydraulic Pneumatic Mechanical Power*] [*A publication*]
**Hydraul Pneum Pwr** ... Hydraulic Pneumatic Power [*Later, Hydraulic Pneumatic Mechanical Power*] [*A publication*]
**HYDREA** .. Hydroxyurea [*Also, HU, HYD*] [*Antineoplastic drug*]
**HYDRELC** ... Hydroelectric (MSA)
**HYDRO**..... Hydrographic Office [*Terminated, 1963; later, NOO*] [*Navy*]
**HYDRO**..... Hydrography
**HYDRO**..... Hydropathic (ADA)
**HYDRO**..... Hydrostatic (KSC)
**HYDRO**..... Hydrotherapy [*Medicine*]
**Hydrobiol**... Hydrobiologia [*A publication*]
**Hydrobiol Bull** ... Hydrobiological Bulletin [*A publication*]
**Hydrobiol J** ... Hydrobiological Journal [*A publication*]
**Hydrobiol J (Engl Transl Gidrobiol Zh)** ... Hydrobiological Journal (English Translation of Gidrobiologicheskii Zhurnal) [*A publication*]
**Hydrobiol Stud** ... Hydrobiological Studies [*A publication*]
**Hydrocarbn** ... Hydrocarbon Processing [*A publication*]
**Hydrocarbon Process** ... Hydrocarbon Processing [*A publication*]
**Hydrocarbon Process Pet Refiner** ... Hydrocarbon Processing and Petroleum Refiner [*Later, Hydrocarbon Processing*] [*A publication*]
**Hydroc Proc** ... Hydrocarbon Processing [*A publication*]
**HYDRODYN** ... Hydrodynamics
**HYDROELEC** ... Hydroelectric
**Hydro Electr Power** ... Hydro Electric Power [*Japan*] [*A publication*]
**Hydrog**....... Hydrogeography
**Hydrog**....... Hydrographer of the Navy [*British*]
**HYDROG** ... Hydrographic
**Hydrog Bull** ... Hydrographic Bulletin [*A publication*]
**Hydrogen Prog** ... Hydrogen Progress [*United States*] [*A publication*]
**Hydrogeol Inf (Czech)** ... Hydrogeologicke Informace (Czechoslovakia. Ustav Geologickeho Inzenyrstvi) [*A publication*]
**Hydrog Rev** ... Hydrographic Review [*A publication*]
**HYDROL**.. Hydrologic
**Hydro Lab J** ... Hydro-Lab Journal [*A publication*]
**Hydrol Bibl** ... Hydrologische Bibliographie [*A publication*]
**Hydrol Rep St Bur Mines Miner Resour (New Mexico)** ... Hydrologic Reports. State Bureau of Mines and Mineral Resources (New Mexico) [*A publication*]
**Hydrol Sci Bull** ... Hydrological Sciences Bulletin [*England*] [*A publication*]
**Hydrol Sci Bull Int Assoc Hydrol Sci** ... Hydrological Sciences Bulletin. International Association of Hydrological Sciences [*A publication*]
**Hydrol Sci Bull Sci Hydrol** ... Hydrological Sciences. Bulletin des Sciences Hydrologiques [*A publication*]
**Hydrol Ser Aust Water Resour Counc** ... Hydrological Series. Australian Water Resources Council [*A publication*] (APTA)
**Hydrol Ser Aust Wat Resour Coun** ... Hydrological Series. Australian Water Resources Council [*A publication*] (APTA)
**Hydrol Symp Proc (Ottawa)** ... Hydrology Symposium. Proceedings (Ottawa) [*A publication*]
**Hydrol Water Resour Ariz Southwest** ... Hydrology and Water Resources in Arizona and the Southwest [*A publication*]
**Hydromech & Hydraul Engng Abstr** ... Hydromechanics and Hydraulic Engineering Abstracts [*A publication*]
**HYDROPNEU** ... Hydropneumatic [*Freight*]
**Hydro Sci J** ... Hydrological Sciences Journal [*A publication*]
**Hydrotech Constr** ... Hydrotechnical Construction [*A publication*]
**Hydr Pneum** ... Hydraulics and Pneumatics [*A publication*]
**Hydr Pow Transm** ... Hydraulic Power Transmission [*A publication*]
**Hydr Res**.... Hydraulics Research [*A publication*]
**HYDRST**... Hydrostatic (MSA)
**HYDT**........ Hydrant (ADA)
**HYDTD**..... Hydrated (MSA)
**HYDWD**.... Hejubian Yu Dengliziti Wuli [*A publication*]
**HYF**........... Hayfields [*Papua New Guinea*] [*Airport symbol*] (OAG)
**HYF**........... Humbligny [*France*] [*Seismograph station code, US Geological Survey*] (SEIS)
**HyF**............ Hytone Film Lab, Inc., Des Moines, IA [*Library symbol*] [*Library of Congress*] (LCLS)
**HYFAC** ..... Hypersonic Research Facilities [*NASA*]
**HYFES**....... Hypersonic Flight Environmental Simulator
**HYFIX**....... Hyperbolic Fix
**HYG** .......... Hydaburg [*Alaska*] [*Airport symbol*] (OAG)
**Hyg** ............ Hygiene [*A publication*]
**HYG** .......... Hygiene
**HYG** .......... Hygroscopic
**HYGA**........ Hygeia Sciences, Inc. [*Newton, MA*] [*NASDAQ symbol*] (NQ)
**HYGAS** ..... Hydrogen Gasification
**HYGL**........ Hypergolic (KSC)
**Hyg Med**.... Hygiene und Medizin [*A publication*]
**Hyg Ment** .. Hygiene Mentale [*A publication*]
**Hyg Ment Suppl Encephale** ... Hygiene Mentale. Supplement de l'Encephale [*A publication*]
**HYGNA**..... Hyogo-Ken Gan Senta Nenpo [*A publication*]
**HYGNST** .. Hygienist
**Hyg Rundschau** ... Hygienische Rundschau [*A publication*]
**Hyg Sanit**... Hygiene and Sanitation [*A publication*]
**HYGST** ..... Hygienist (AABC)
**Hyg Viande Lait** ... Hygiene de la Viande et du Lait [*A publication*]
**HYHN**........ Hsin-Ya Shu-Yuan Hsueh-Shy Nien-K'an [*A publication*]
**HY/HS** ....... High Yield/High Stereospecificity Technology [*for polypropylene*] [*Himont Corp.*]
**HYI**............ High Yield Income Fund [*NYSE symbol*] (SPSG)
**HYJMUA** ... Mysore University. Half Yearly Journal. Series A. Arts [*A publication*]
**HYKMA**.... Hyogo-Kenritsu Nogyo Shikenjo Kenkyu Hokoku [*A publication*]
**HYKOE3**... Han Guk Journal of Genetic Engineering [*A publication*]
**HYL**........... Hollis, AK [*Location identifier*] [*FAA*] (FAAL)
**HYL**........... Hoyle Resources Limited [*Vancouver Stock Exchange symbol*]
**Hyl** ............ Hydroxylysine [*Also, Hylys*] [*An amino acid*]
**HYLA** ........ Hybrid Language Assembler
**HYLO**........ Hybrid LORAN
**Hylys**.......... Hydroxylysine [*or (OH)Lys*] [*Also, Hyl*] [*An amino acid*]
**HYM** .......... Hyman, TX [*Location identifier*] [*FAA*] (FAAL)
**Hym** ........... Hymenoptera [*Entomology*]
**HYMA**....... Hebrew Young Men's Association
**HYMEA** .... Hygiene Mentale [*A publication*]
**HYMNB**.... Hyomen [*A publication*]
**Hymn Hom Ap** ... Hymnus Homericus ad Apollinem [*Classical studies*] (OCD)
**Hymn Hom Bacch** ... Hymnus Homericus ad Bacchum [*Classical studies*] (OCD)
**Hymn Hom Cer** ... Hymnus Homericus ad Cererem [*Classical studies*] (OCD)
**Hymn Hom Mart** ... Hymnus Homericus ad Martem [*Classical studies*] (OCD)
**Hymn Hom Merc** ... Hymnus Homericus ad Mercurium [*Classical studies*] (OCD)
**Hymn Hom Pan** ... Hymnus Homericus ad Panem [*Classical studies*] (OCD)
**Hymn Hom Ven** ... Hymnus Homericus ad Venerem [*Classical studies*] (OCD)
**Hymn M** .... Hymnologiske Meddelelser. Vaerkstedsblad om Salmer [*A publication*]
**HYMNS**.... Hydrogen MASER for Navigation Satellite (MCD)
**HYN** .......... Halcyon Resources Ltd. [*Vancouver Stock Exchange symbol*]
**HYO** .......... Husky Oil Ltd. [*AMEX symbol*] (SPSG)
**HYOSCYAM** ... Hyoscyamus [*Henbane*] [*Pharmacology*] (ROG)
**HYP**........... Harvard, Yale, and Princeton Universities
**HYP**........... High Yield Plus Fund [*NYSE symbol*] (SPSG)
**HYP**........... Hydroxybenzylpindolol [*Neuropharmacology*]
**Hyp** ............ Hydroxyproline [*Also, Hypro*] [*An amino acid*]
**HYP**........... Hypergolic
**HYP**........... Hyperresonance
**HYP**........... Hypertrophy
**HYP**........... Hyphen Character [*Data processing*]
**HYP**........... Hypnosis
**HYP**........... Hypodermic (ROG)
**HYP**........... Hypotenuse [*Mathematics*]
**HYP**........... Hypothalamus [*Neuroanatomy*]

**hyp** ............ Hypotheque [*Mortgage*] [*French*]
**HYP** ............ Hypothesis
**Hyp** ............ Hypoxanthine [*Also, Hx, HYPX*] [*Biochemistry*]
**HYPACE**... Hybrid Programmable Attitude Control Electronics [*NASA*]
**HYPER**...... Hydrographic Personnel [*Navy*]
**HYPER**...... Hyperhydrated, Hyperventilating with Hyperpyrexia, Hyperexcitability, and Hyperrigidity [*Characteristics of drowning*]
**HYPERB**... Hyperbola [*Mathematics*]
**HYPERDOP** ... Hyperbolic Doppler
**Hyperfine Interact** ... Hyperfine Interactions [*Netherlands*] [*A publication*]
**HYPERIGN** ... Hypergolic Ignition (KSC)
**Hypertens Suppl** ... Hypertension Supplement [*A publication*]
**HYPH**........ Hydrophone
**HYPN**........ Hypertension
**HYPNO**..... Hypnosis
**HYPNOT**.. Hypnotism
**HYPO**........ High Power [*Water boiler atomic reactor*] [*Dismantled*]
**HYPO**........ Hypochondria (DSUE)
**hypo** ........... Hypochromasia [*Hematology*]
**HYPO**........ Hypodermic
**HYPO**........ Hyposulfite of Sodium [*Photography*] (ROG)
**HYPOCON** ... Hypochondria (DSUE)
**HYPOT** ..... Hypotenuse [*Mathematics*] (ROG)
**hypoth**........ Hypotheque [*Mortgage*] [*French*]
**HYPOTH** ... Hypothesis (ADA)
**HYPOTH** ... Hypothetical (MSA)
**HYPOX**..... Hypophysectomy [*Medicine*]
**HYPREM** ... Hyperresponse Electric Motor
**Hypro**......... Hydroxyproline [*or (OH)Pro*] [*Also, Hyp*] [*An amino acid*]
**Hyps**........... Hypsipyle [*of Euripides*] [*Classical studies*] (OCD)
**HYPSES**.... Hydrographic Precision Scanning Echo Sounder
**HYPUB** ..... Hypanthium Pubescence [*Botany*]
**HYPX** ........ Hyponex Corp. [*NASDAQ symbol*] (NQ)
**HYPX** ........ Hypoxanthine [*Also, Hx, Hyp*] [*Biochemistry*]
**HYR**........... Hayward [*Wisconsin*] [*Airport symbol*] (OAG)
**HYR**........... Hycroft Resources & Development Corp. [*Vancouver Stock Exchange symbol*]
**HYS** ........... Hays [*Kansas*] [*Airport symbol*] (OAG)
**HYS** ........... Hysteria
**HYSAA** ..... Hygiene and Sanitation [*A publication*]
**HYSAS**...... Hydrofluidic Stability Augmentation System
**HYST** ........ Hyster Co. [*NASDAQ symbol*] (NQ)
**hyst** ............ Hysterectomy [*Medicine*]
**HYSTAD**... Hydrofoil Stabilization Device
**HYSTERO** ... Hysterosalpingogram [*Gynecology*] (DHSM)
**HYSTRU**... Hydraulic System Test and Repair Unit [*Army*] (MCD)
**HYSURCH** ... Hydrographic Surveying and Charting [*System*] [*NOO*]
**HYT**........... High Year of Tenure
**HYTAC** ..... Hydraulic Tachometer
**HYTEC** ..... Hydrogen Thermal Electrochemical Converter
**HYTK**........ Hytek International Corp. [*NASDAQ symbol*] (NQ)
**HYTREC**... Hydrospace Target Recognition, Evaluation, and Control
**HYTRESS** ... High-Test Recorder and Simulator System (IEEE)
**HYTROSS** ... High-Test Recorder and Simulator System
**HYU** .......... Chesterfield, VA [*Location identifier*] [*FAA*] (FAAL)
**HYU** .......... Lilly Contingent Payment Units [*AMEX symbol*] (SPSG)
**HYV**........... High Yielding Variety [*Agriculture*]
**HYVIA** ...... Hypervelocity Interceptor Armament
**HYW**.......... Conway, SC [*Location identifier*] [*FAA*] (FAAL)
**HYWAYS** ... Hybrid with Advanced Yield for Surveillance [*Strategic Defense Initiative*]
**HYWN** ...... Hypersonic Wedge Nozzle (MCD)
**HYX**........... Hydra Explorations Ltd. [*Toronto Stock Exchange symbol*]
**HYZ**........... Thief River Falls, MN [*Location identifier*] [*FAA*] (FAAL)
**HZ**.............. Dust Haze [*Aviation*]
**HZ**.............. Herpes Zoster [*Medicine*]
**Hz**............... Hertz [*Symbol*] [*SI unit of frequency*] (AABC)
**HZ**.............. Historische Zeitschrift [*A publication*]
**HZ**.............. Hospodarska Zmluva [*Economic Contract*] [*Czechoslovakian*]
**HZ**.............. Hurtownia Zbytu [*Wholesale Outlets*] [*Polish*]
**HZ**.............. Hydralazine [*Antihypertensive agent*]
**HZ**.............. Saudi Arabia [*Aircraft nationality and registration mark*] (FAAC)
**HZ**.............. Thurston Aviation Ltd. [*Great Britain*] [*ICAO designator*] (FAAC)
**HZA**........... Hauptzollamt [*Chief Customs Office*] [*German*] (DLA)
**HZA**........... Herut Zionists of America (EA)
**HZB**........... Horizon Bancorp. [*NYSE symbol*] (SPSG)
**HZBBA** ..... Horizons in Biochemistry and Biophysics [*A publication*]
**HZBL** ........ Holzblaeser [*Woodwind Instrument*] [*Music*]
**HZE**........... High Z and E [*Particles in outer space*]
**Hzea**........... Heliothis Zea [*Corn ear worm*]
**HZG**........... Hanzhong [*China*] [*Airport symbol*] (OAG)
**HZI**............ Hy & Zel's, Inc. [*Toronto Stock Exchange symbol*]
**HZIR** ......... Horizon Air Industries, Inc. [*Seattle, WA*] [*NASDAQ symbol*] (NQ)
**HZK**........... Atlanta, GA [*Location identifier*] [*FAA*] (FAAL)
**HZK**........... Husavik [*Iceland*] [*Airport symbol*] (OAG)
**HZKLA** ..... Herz Kreislauf [*A publication*]
**HZKP**........ Hermes. Zeitschrift fuer Klassische Philologie [*A publication*]
**HZL**........... Hazleton [*Pennsylvania*] [*Airport symbol*] [*Obsolete*] (OAG)
**HZM**.......... Handelingen. Zuidnederlandse Maatschappij voor Taal-En Letterkunde en Geschiedenis [*A publication*]
**HZMP**....... Horizontal Impulse (IEEE)
**HZMTLG** ... Handelingen. Zuidnederlandse Maatschappij voor Taal-En Letterkunde en Geschiedenis [*A publication*]
**HZN** .......... Hazen, NV [*Location identifier*] [*FAA*] (FAAL)
**HZN** .......... Horizon Corp. [*NYSE symbol*] (SPSG)
**HZnMTL**.. Handelingen. Zuidnederlandse Maatschappij voor Taal-En Letterkunde en Geschiedenis [*A publication*]
**HZNT**........ Handbuch zum Neuen Testament [*Lietzmann*] [*A publication*] (BJA)
**HZO** .......... Herpes Zoster Ophthalmicus [*Ophthalmology*]
**HZONP**..... Horizons Bancorp Pfd [*NASDAQ symbol*] (NQ)
**HZOO** ....... Hunick Zoo. Monthly Publication of Tanana Chiefs Conference [*A publication*]
**HZP**........... Hot Zero Power [*Nuclear energy*] (NRCH)
**HZP**........... Zionsville, IN [*Location identifier*] [*FAA*] (FAAL)
**HZR**........... New Roads, LA [*Location identifier*] [*FAA*] (FAAL)
**HZRN**........ Horizontal Reaction
**HZV**........... Herpes Zoster Virus
**HZW**.......... Wichita, KS [*Location identifier*] [*FAA*] (FAAL)
**HZYC**........ Hadassah Zionist Youth Commission (EA)
**HZYO**........ Hashomer Hatzair Zionist Youth Organization [*Later, HHSZYM*] (EA)

# I

I.......... Air Force Training Category [*No training*]
I.......... Angle of Incidence
I.......... Carlo Erba [*Italy*] [*Research code symbol*]
i.......... Class Interval [*Statistics*]
I.......... Electric Current [*Symbol*] [*IUPAC*]
I.......... Fighter [*Russian aircraft symbol*]
I.......... First Interstate Bancorp. [*NYSE symbol*] (SPSG)
I.......... I-Beam [*Structural metal shape*]
I.......... Ibuprofen [*A drug*]
I.......... Id [*That*] [*Latin*] (GPO)
I.......... Idaho
I.......... Identification
I.......... Idler [*A publication*]
I.......... Idus [*The Ides*] [*Latin*]
I.......... Ihr [*Your*] [*German*]
I.......... Illinois State Library, Springfield, IL [*Library symbol*] [*Library of Congress*] (LCLS)
I.......... Illite [*A mineral*]
I.......... Imperator [*or Imperatrix*] [*Emperor or Empress*] [*Latin*]
I.......... Imperial
I.......... Implicit
i.......... Inactive [*Chemistry*]
I.......... Inboard (DS)
I.......... Incendiary [*Bomb*]
i.......... Incisor (Deciduous) [*Dentistry*]
I.......... Incisor (Permanent) [*Dentistry*]
I.......... Inclination
I.......... Income
I.......... Incompatible
I.......... Incomplete
I.......... Incontinent [*Medicine*]
I.......... Incumbent (ROG)
I.......... Independent
i.......... Independent Pump [*Liquid gas carriers*]
I.......... Independent School [*British*]
I.......... Index
I.......... India [*Phonetic alphabet*] [*International*] (DSUE)
i-----.......... Indian Ocean [*MARC geographic area code*] [*Library of Congress*] (LCCP)
I.......... Indicated [*or Indicative*]
I.......... Indicated Horsepower
I.......... Indicated Main Engine
I.......... Indicator
I.......... Induction
I.......... Industrial
I.......... Industrial Premises [*Public-performance tariff*] [*British*]
I.......... Industrial Training School [*British*] (ROG)
I.......... Inertia (AAG)
I.......... Infantry
I.......... Infield
I.......... Information [*Data processing*]
I.......... Inhibitory
I.......... Initial
I.......... Initial Approach [*Aviation*] (FAAC)
I.......... Ink [*Phonetic alphabet*] [*Royal Navy*] [*World War I*] [*Pre-World War II*] (DSUE)
I.......... Inlet [*Rotary piston meter*]
I.......... Inner
I.......... Inosine [*One-letter symbol; see Ino*]
I.......... Input
I.......... Inside
I.......... Inside Edge [*Skating*]
I.......... Insoluble
I.......... Inspector
I.......... Instantaneous
I.......... Institute [*or Institution*]
I.......... Instruction
I.......... Instrument Correction
I.......... Instrumental [*or Instrumentation*]
I.......... Insulated (DS)
I.......... Insulated Tank [*Liquid gas carriers*]
I.......... Intelligence
I.......... Intensity
I.......... Interbank [*Credit cards*]
I.......... Intercept-Aerial [*Missile mission symbol*]
I.......... Interceptor
I.......... Interchangeability (AAG)
I.......... Intercooled [*Automotive engineering*]
I.......... Interest [*Economics*]
I.......... Interference [*Broadcasting*]
I.......... Interlocked Metallic Armor [*Technical drawings*]
I.......... Intermediate [*Car size*]
I.......... Intermediate [*Vessel load line mark*]
I.......... Intermediate
I.......... Intermediate Slope [*Skiing*]
I.......... Intermittent Operation during the Time Indicated [*Broadcasting*]
I.......... Intern
I.......... Internal
I.......... International
I.......... Internist [*Medicine*]
I.......... Interpreter
I.......... Interrupt [*Data processing*] [*Telecommunications*]
I.......... Interstate [*Highways*]
I.......... Intestine
I.......... Intransitive
I.......... Intrinsic-Type, Semiconductor Material
I.......... Introduced [*Ecology*]
I.......... Invasive
I.......... Inventory
I.......... Inverted Sentence [*Used in correcting manuscripts, etc.*]
I.......... Inverter
I.......... Investment
I.......... Iodine [*Chemical element*]
I.......... Ionic Strength
I.......... Iraqi
I.......... Ireland
I.......... Irnerius [*Flourished, 1113-18*] [*Authority cited in pre-1607 legal work*] (DSA)
I.......... Iron [*Chemical element*] [*Symbol is Fe*] (ROG)
I.......... Irradiated (NASA)
I.......... Irregular (ROG)
I.......... Irrigation [*Medicine*]
I.......... Isis [*A publication*]
I.......... Island [*Maps and charts*]
I.......... Isle
I.......... Isoflurane [*An anesthetic*]
I.......... Isoleucine [*One-letter symbol; see Ile*] [*An amino acid*]
I.......... Isometric [*Botany*]
i.......... Isopentenyl [*As substituent on nucleoside*] [*Biochemistry*]
I.......... Isoproterenol [*An adrenergic*]
I.......... Israeli
I.......... Issue (ROG)
I.......... Italica [*A publication*]
I.......... Italy [*Aircraft nationality and registration mark*] (FAAC)
I.......... Italy [*IYRU nationality code*]
I.......... Item [*Phonetic alphabet*] [*World War II*] (DSUE)
I.......... Luminous Intensity [*Symbol*] [*IUPAC*]
I.......... Moment of Inertia [*Symbol*] [*IUPAC*]
I.......... Officer Who Has Passed for Interpreter [*Navy*] [*British*] (ROG)
I.......... One [*Roman numeral*]
I.......... Qualified for Instruction of Artillery [*Military*] [*British*] (ROG)
I.......... Radiant Intensity [*Symbol*] [*IUPAC*]
I.......... Registro Italiano [*Shipping*] (ROG)
I.......... Requires a Doctor [*Search and rescue symbol that can be stamped in sand or snow*]
i.......... Tourist Information [*Traffic sign*] [*British*]
0I.......... Zero Inventory [*Industrial engineering*]
I2.......... Image Intensification
I2.......... International Interchangeability
3-I.......... Indiana, Illinois, Iowa [*Old baseball league*]

**3I** ... Investors in Industry International BV
**I (Bank)** ... Instruction Bank [*Data processing*]
**IA** ... Comando de Material - Fabrica Militar de Aviones [*Argentina*] [*ICAO aircraft manufacturer identifier*] (ICAO)
**IA** ... IATA [*International Air Transport Association*] Containers [*Shipping*] (DCTA)
**IA** ... Ibsen-Aarboken [*A publication*]
**IA** ... Ice Age
**IA** ... Ileostomy Association of Great Britain and Ireland
**IA** ... Im Auftrage [*By Order Of*] [*German*]
**IA** ... Image Acquisition [*Computer graphics*]
**IA** ... Imagery Analyst (MCD)
**IA** ... Immediate Action [*Military*]
**IA** ... Immediate Annuity
**IA** ... Immediately Available
**IA** ... Immune Adherence [*Immunology*]
**Ia** ... Immune Region Associated Antigen [*Immunology*]
**IA** ... Impedance Angle
**IA** ... Imperial Airways Ltd. [*British*] (ADA)
**IA** ... Implementing Agency (KSC)
**IA** ... Impotents Anonymous (EA)
**IA** ... In Absentia [*In Absence*] [*Latin*]
**IA** ... Inactive Account [*Banking*]
**IA** ... Inactive Aerospace Vehicle [*or Aircraft*]
**IA** ... Incidental Appendectomy [*Medicine*]
**IA** ... Incorporated Accountant
**IA** ... Incremental Analysis [*Statistics*]
**IA** ... Independent Action (EA)
**IA** ... Independent Americans (EA)
**IA** ... Indian Affairs (DLA)
**IA** ... Indian Army
**IA** ... Indian Artillery [*British military*] (DMA)
**IA** ... Indiana [*Obsolete*] (ROG)
**IA** ... Indicated Altitude [*Navigation*]
**IA** ... Indicator of Authoritativeness [*Library symbol*]
**IA** ... Indirect Addressing
**IA** ... Indo-Aryan [*Linguistics*]
**IA** ... Indulin Agar [*Microbiology*]
**IA** ... Industrial Arts (OICC)
**IA** ... Infected Area
**IA** ... Inferior Angle [*Anatomy*]
**I & A** ... Information and Action (MUGU)
**IA** ... Information Agency
**IA** ... Information America [*Information service or system*] (EISS)
**IA** ... Infra-Audible [*Sound*]
**IA** ... Initial Appearance [*RADAR*]
**IA** ... Initial Authorization
**IA** ... Initiative America (EA)
**I/A** ... Innovative/Alternative [*Recycling technologies*]
**IA** ... Input Acknowledge (MCD)
**IA** ... Input Axis (KSC)
**IA** ... Insel-Almanach [*A publication*]
**IA** ... Insertion Approval (NRCH)
**IA** ... Inspection Administration [*Navy*]
**I/A** ... Installment Agreement
**IA** ... Institut de l'Amiante [*Asbestos Institute - AI*] (EA)
**IA** ... Institute of Actuaries [*British*]
**IA** ... Instruction Address [*Data processing*]
**IA** ... Instructional Allowance [*British military*] (DMA)
**I of A** ... Instructor of Artillery [*British*]
**IA** ... Instrument Abstracts
**IA** ... Instrument Air [*System*] [*Nuclear energy*] (NRCH)
**IA** ... Instrumentation Amplifier (IEEE)
**IA** ... Insulin Antibody [*Immunology*]
**IA** ... Insurance Adjustment
**IA** ... Insurance Advocate [*A publication*]
**IA** ... Insurance Asia [*Manila*] [*A publication*]
**I/A** ... Insurance Auditor
**IA** ... Intangible Asset [*i.e., Patented rights*]
**IA** ... Integrated Adapter
**IA** ... Intelligence Analysis
**IA** ... Intelligent Assistant [*Data processing*]
**IA** ... Intelligenzalter [*Mental Age*] [*Psychology*]
**IA** ... Intemperate to Alcohol [*An alcoholic*] [*Slang*]
**IA** ... Inter-Action (MCD)
**IA** ... Inter Alia [*Among Other Things*] [*Latin*]
**IA** ... Intercept Arm (MUGU)
**IA** ... Intercessors for America (EA)
**IA** ... Interchangeable Alternate
**IA** ... Interciencia Association [*Caracas, Venezuela*] (EAIO)
**IA** ... Intercity Airways [*Australia*]
**IA** ... Intercoiffure America (EA)
**IA** ... Intercultural Awareness
**I/A** ... Interface Adapter (NASA)
**IA** ... Interface Amplifier
**IA** ... Intermediaire Agree [*Accredited Intermediary*] [*French*]
**IA** ... Intermediate Amplifier
**IA** ... Internal Audit
**IA** ... Internal Auditory (Ear)
**IA** ... International Affairs [*A publication*]
**IA** ... International Affiliation of Independent Accounting Firms [*Later, Independent Accountants International*] (EA)
**IA** ... International Alert (EA)
**IA** ... International Alliance of Theatrical Stage Employees and Moving Picture Machine Operators of the United States and Canada
**IA** ... International Alphabet
**IA** ... International Angstrom
**IA** ... Interval Availability
**IA** ... Intra-Arterial [*Cardiology*]
**IA** ... Intra-Articular [*Medicine*]
**IA** ... Intra-Atrial [*Cardiology*]
**IA** ... Inverter Assembly
**IA** ... Iowa [*Postal code*]
**IA** ... Iowa Reports [*A publication*] (DLA)
**Ia** ... Iowa State Library Commission, Des Moines, IA [*Library symbol*] [*Library of Congress*] (LCLS)
**IA** ... Iphigenia Aulidensis [*of Euripides*] [*Classical studies*] (OCD)
**IA** ... Iranica Antiqua [*A publication*]
**IA** ... Iraqi Airways [*ICAO designator*]
**IA** ... Iron Age
**IA** ... Irrigation Area (ADA)
**IA** ... Irrigation Association (EA)
**I/A** ... Isle Of Angelsey [*Wales*] (ROG)
**IA** ... Isle Of Aran
**IA** ... Isolation Amplifier
**IA** ... Isophthalic Acid [*Organic chemistry*]
**IA** ... Issuing Agency (AFM)
**IA** ... Italia Antichissima [*A publication*]
**IA** ... Italian Army (NATG)
**I/A** ... Item Accounting (MCD)
**IA** ... Law Reports, Privy Council, Indian Appeals [*India*] [*A publication*] (DLA)
**IA** ... Telegraph and Public Address [*JETDS nomenclature*]
**IaA** ... Ames, Public Library, Ames IA [*Library symbol*] [*Library of Congress*] (LCLS)
**IAA** ... Chicago State University, Chicago, IL [*OCLC symbol*] (OCLC)
**IAA** ... Ibero-Amerikanisches Archiv [*A publication*]
**IAA** ... Ibero-Armorican Arc [*A geological area of western Europe*]
**IAA** ... Imidazoleacetic Acid [*Also, I-AC, IMAA*] [*Biochemistry*]
**IAA** ... Immediate Action Authority (AAG)
**IAA** ... In Amguel [*Issek Toufreg*] [*Algeria*] [*Seismograph station code, US Geological Survey*] [*Closed*] (SEIS)
**IAA** ... Inactive Aerospace Vehicle [*or Aircraft*] Authorization
**IAA** ... Incorporated Accountants and Auditors [*British*] (DAS)
**IAA** ... Independent Airlines Association (EA)
**IAA** ... Indian Army Act [*British military*] (DMA)
**IAA** ... Indian Association of America (EA)
**IAA** ... Indoleacetic Acid [*Plant growth promoter*]
**IAA** ... Inpatient Ambulatory Activity Questionnaire [*Medicine*]
**IAA** ... Institute of Administrative Accountants [*Sevenoaks, Kent, England*] (EAIO)
**IAA** ... Institute for Alternative Agriculture (EA)
**IAA** ... Institute of Archeology and Anthropology [*University of South Carolina at Columbia*] [*Research center*] (RCD)
**IAA** ... Institute for Arthritis and Autoimmunity [*Nile Research Center*] [*West Haven, CT*]
**IAA** ... Instrumental Activation Analysis
**IAA** ... Insulin Autoantibody [*Immunology*]
**IAA** ... Insurance Accountants Association [*Later, SIA*]
**IAA** ... Intelligence Analysts Associates [*Air Force*]
**IAA** ... Inter-American Economic Affairs [*Washington*] [*A publication*]
**IAA** ... Interamerican Accounting Association [*Mexico City, Mexico*] (EA)
**IAA** ... Interim Access Authorization
**IAA** ... Interment Association of America [*Later, PIAA*] (EA)
**IAA** ... International Academy of Astronautics [*Paris, France*] (EA)
**IAA** ... International Acetylene Association [*Later, CGA*]
**IAA** ... International Actuarial Association [*See also AAI*] (EAIO)
**IAA** ... International Advertising Association [*Later, AAF*] (EA)
**IAA** ... International Aerosol Association [*Zurich, Switzerland*] (EAIO)
**IAA** ... International Aerospace Abstracts [*American Institute of Aeronautics and Astronautics*] [*Information service or system*] [*A publication*]
**IAA** ... International Apple Association [*Later, IAI*] (EA)
**IAA** ... International Arthroscopy Association (EA)
**IAA** ... International Association of Allergology [*Later, IAACI*]
**IAA** ... International Association of Art [*See also AIAP*] (EA)
**IAA** ... International Association of Astacology (EA)
**IAA** ... International Astrological Association
**IAA** ... International Aviation Affairs [*FAA*] (MCD)
**IAA** ... Intimate Apparel Associates (EA)
**IAA** ... Inventors Association of America (EA)
**IAA** ... Investment Advisers Act [*1940*]
**IAA** ... Iododacetic Acid [*Organic chemistry*]
**IAA** ... Irish Astronomical Association (EAIO)
**IAA** ... Irrigation Association of Australia
**IAAA** ... Integrated Advance Avionics for Aircraft
**IAAA** ... Intermarket Association of Advertising Agencies [*Dayton, OH*] (EA)

**IAAA** ........ International Academy of Aquatic Art (EA)
**IAAA** ........ International Airforwarders and Agents Association (EA)
**IAAAA**....... Intercollegiate Association of Amateur Athletes of America (EA)
**IAAAM**... International Archives of Allergy and Applied Immunology [*A publication*]
**IAAABBP** ... International Association of African and American Black Business People [*Detroit, MI*] (EA)
**IAAAM** ..... International Association for Aquatic Animal Medicine (EA)
**IaAAR**........ United States Department of Agriculture, Agricultural Research Service, National Animal Disease Laboratory, Ames, IA [*Library symbol*] [*Library of Congress*] (LCLS)
**IAAATDC** ... International Association for Advancement of Appropriate Technology for Developing Countries (EA)
**IAAB**.......... Inter-American Association of Broadcasters [*Later, IAB-AIR*]
**IAABB**....... International Association of Amateur Boat Builders (EA)
**IAABO** ...... International Association of Approved Basketball Officials (EA)
**IaAc** .......... Ackley Public Library, Ackley, IA [*Library symbol*] [*Library of Congress*] (LCLS)
**IAAC**.......... International Agricultural Aviation Centre [*Defunct*] (EA)
**IAAC**.......... International Association of Art Critics [*See also AICA*] (EA)
**IAACC**....... Ibero-American Association of Chambers of Commerce [*See also AICO*] [*Bogota, Colombia*] (EAIO)
**IAACC**....... Inter-Allied Aeronautical Commission of Control
**IAACI**........ International Association of Allergology and Clinical Immunology (EA)
**IaAcW**........ World Journal, Ackley, IA [*Library symbol*] [*Library of Congress*] (LCLS)
**IaAdeCoC**.. Dallas County Courthouse, Adel, IA [*Library symbol*] [*Library of Congress*] (LCLS)
**IaAdeN** ...... Dallas County News, Adel, IA [*Library symbol*] [*Library of Congress*] (LCLS)
**IAADFS** .... International Association of Airport Duty Free Stores (EA)
**IaAdN** ........ Adair News, Adair, IA [*Library symbol*] [*Library of Congress*] (LCLS)
**IAADS**....... Integrated Antiairborne Defense System
**IAAE**.......... International Association of Agricultural Economists (EA)
**IAAEES**..... International Association for the Advancement of Earth and Environmental Sciences (EA)
**IAAEJ** ....... Institution of Automotive and Aeronautical Engineers, Australia and New Zealand. Journal [*A publication*] (APTA)
**IAAE Journal** ... Institution of Automotive and Aeronautical Engineers, Australia and New Zealand. Journal [*A publication*] (APTA)
**IAAER**....... International Association for the Advancement of Educational Research
**IAAF**.......... International Agricultural Aviation Foundation (EA)
**IAAF**.......... International Amateur Athletic Federation [*See also FIAA*] [*London, England*] (EAIO)
**IAAFA** ....... Inter-American Air Force Academy [*Operated by US Air Force to provide training for Latin American countries*]
**IaAfSE**....... Afton Star-Enterprise, Afton, IA [*Library symbol*] [*Library of Congress*] (LCLS)
**IAAG** ......... Inter-American Association of Gastroenterology (EA)
**IA Ag Exp** ... Iowa State College of Agriculture and Mechanical Arts. Agricultural Experiment Station. Publications [*A publication*]
**IAAH**......... International Action Against Hunger (EAIO)
**IAAH**......... International Association for Adolescent Health [*Australia*]
**IAAHA9**.... Indian Council of Agricultural Research. Animal Husbandry Series [*A publication*]
**IAAHU**...... International Association of Accident and Health Underwriters [*Later, NAHU*]
**IAAI**.......... International Association of Arson Investigators (EA)
**IaAIBI** ....... IBIA News, Ames, IA [*Library symbol*] [*Library of Congress*] (LCLS)
**IAAIP** ........ Inter-American Association of Industrial Property [*See also ASIPA*] [*Buenos Aires, Argentina*] (EAIO)
**IaAIS** ......... Iowa Starter, Iowa State University, Ames, IA [*Library symbol*] [*Library of Congress*] (LCLS)
**IaAkRT**...... Akron Register-Tribune, Akron, IA [*Library symbol*] [*Library of Congress*] (LCLS)
**IAAL**.......... International Association of Applied Linguistics (EA)
**IaAlb** .......... Albia Public Library, Albia, IA [*Library symbol*] [*Library of Congress*] (LCLS)
**IaAlbMHi** ... Monroe County Historical Society, Albia, IA [*Library symbol*] [*Library of Congress*] (LCLS)
**IaAlbN**....... Monroe County News, Albia, IA [*Library symbol*] [*Library of Congress*] (LCLS)
**IaAlbUR**.... Albia Union-Republican, Albia, IA [*Library symbol*] [*Library of Congress*] (LCLS)
**IaAlcAM**.... Appeal and Marathon Republic, Albert City, IA [*Library symbol*] [*Library of Congress*] (LCLS)
**IaAld** .......... Alden Public Library, Alden, IA [*Library symbol*] [*Library of Congress*] (LCLS)
**IAALD**....... International Association of Agricultural Librarians and Documentalists (EA)
**IAALD Q Bull** ... International Association of Agricultural Librarians and Documentalists. Quarterly Bulletin [*A publication*]
**IaAlg**.......... Algona Public Library, Algona, IA [*Library symbol*] [*Library of Congress*] (LCLS)
**IaAlgKA** .... Kossuth County Advance, Algona, IA [*Library symbol*] [*Library of Congress*] (LCLS)
**IaAlgUD**.... Upper Des Moines, Algona, IA [*Library symbol*] [*Library of Congress*] (LCLS)
**IaAll**........... Allerton Public Library, Allerton, IA [*Library symbol*] [*Library of Congress*] (LCLS)
**IaAlnBCo**... Butler County Courthouse, Allison, IA [*Library symbol*] [*Library of Congress*] (LCLS)
**IaAlnTJ** ..... Butler County Tribune-Journal, Allison, IA [*Library symbol*] [*Library of Congress*] (LCLS)
**IaAlta**......... Alta Public Library, Alta, IA [*Library symbol*] [*Library of Congress*] (LCLS)
**IaAltaA**...... Alta Advertiser, Alta, IA [*Library symbol*] [*Library of Congress*] (LCLS)
**IaAltn**......... Alton Public Library, Alton, IA [*Library symbol*] [*Library of Congress*] (LCLS)
**IaAlto**......... Altoona Public Library, Altoona, IA [*Library symbol*] [*Library of Congress*] (LCLS)
**IaAltoH**...... Herald-Mitchellville Index, Altoona, IA [*Library symbol*] [*Library of Congress*] (LCLS)
**IAAM** ........ Incorporated Association of Assistant Masters [*British*]
**IAAM** ........ International Association of Auditorium Managers (EA)
**IAAM** ........ International Association of Automotive Modelers [*Defunct*] (EA)
**IAAM** ........ Irish Anti-Apartheid Movement (EAIO)
**IAAMRH**.. International Association of Agricultural Medicine and Rural Health (EA)
**IaAna** ......... Anamosa Public Library, Anamosa, IA [*Library symbol*] [*Library of Congress*] (LCLS)
**IaAnaE**....... Anamosa Eureka, Anamosa, IA [*Library symbol*] [*Library of Congress*] (LCLS)
**IaAnaJ** ....... Anamosa Journal, Anamosa, IA [*Library symbol*] [*Library of Congress*] (LCLS)
**IAANBS**.... Internationales Archiv fuer Arbeitsmedizin [*A publication*]
**IaAniF**........ Fontanelle Observer, Anita, IA [*Library symbol*] [*Library of Congress*] (LCLS)
**IaAniT** ....... Anita Tribune, Anita, IA [*Library symbol*] [*Library of Congress*] (LCLS)
**IaAnk** ......... Kirkendall Public Library, Ankeny, IA [*Library symbol*] [*Library of Congress*] (LCLS)
**IaAnkD**...... Des Moines Area Community College, Ankeny, IA [*Library symbol*] [*Library of Congress*] (LCLS)
**IaAnkFB**.... Faith Baptist Bible College, Ankeny, IA [*Library symbol*] [*Library of Congress*] (LCLS)
**IaAnkP** ...... Ankeny Press-Citizen, Ankeny, IA [*Library symbol*] [*Library of Congress*] (LCLS)
**IaAnt**.......... Anthon Public Library, Anthon, IA [*Library symbol*] [*Library of Congress*] (LCLS)
**IaAntH**....... Anthon Herald, Anthon, IA [*Library symbol*] [*Library of Congress*] (LCLS)
**IAAO** ......... International Association of Assessing Officers (EA)
**IAAOC** ...... International Association of Addictions and Offender Counseling (EA)
**IaAp** .......... Aplington Legion Memorial Library, Aplington, IA [*Library symbol*] [*Library of Congress*] (LCLS)
**IAAP**.......... International Association of Amusement Parks [*Later, IAAPA*]
**IAAP**.......... International Association for Analytical Psychology (EA)
**IAAP**.......... International Association of Applied Psychology [*Nijmegen, Netherlands*] (EA)
**IAAP**.......... Iowa Army Ammunition Plant (AABC)
**IAAPA**....... International Association of Amusement Parks and Attractions (EA)
**IAAPEA**.... International Association Against Painful Experiments on Animals (EA)
**IAARA5**..... Indian Council of Agricultural Research. Annual Technical Report [*A publication*]
**IAARC**....... International Administrative Aeronautical Radio Conference [*Also known as WARC*]
**IaArl** .......... Arlington Public Library, Arlington, IA [*Library symbol*] [*Library of Congress*] (LCLS)
**IaArmJ** ...... Armstrong Journal, Armstrong, IA [*Library symbol*] [*Library of Congress*] (LCLS)
**IAAROP**.... Institute of Arctic and Alpine Research. Occasional Papers [*A publication*]
**IAAS**.......... International Association of Agricultural Students [*See also AIEA*] [*Uppsala, Sweden*] (EAIO)
**IaAS**........... Iowa State University of Science and Technology, Ames, IA [*Library symbol*] [*Library of Congress*] (LCLS)
**IAASE** ....... Inter-American Association of Sanitary Engineering [*Later, Inter-American Association of Sanitary and Environmental Engineering*] (EA)
**IAASEES**.. Inter-American Association of Sanitary Engineering and Environmental Sciences (EAIO)
**IAASM**...... International Academy of Aviation and Space Medicine (EAIO)
**IAASS** ....... International Association of Applied Social Scientists [*Later, CCI*]

**IaAS-V** ...... Iowa State University of Science and Technology, School of Veterinary Medicine, Ames, IA [*Library symbol*] [*Library of Congress*] (LCLS)
**IaAT** .......... Ames Daily Tribune, Ames, IA [*Library symbol*] [*Library of Congress*] (LCLS)
**IaAt** ........... Atlantic Public Library, Atlantic, IA [*Library symbol*] [*Library of Congress*] (LCLS)
**IAAT** .......... International Association Against Torture (EAIO)
**IAATCD** .... If Authorized by Air Traffic Control, DME [*Distance Measuring Equipment*] May Be Used [*Aviation*] (FAAC)
**IAATI** ........ International Association Auto Theft Investigators (EA)
**IAATM** ...... International Association for Accident and Traffic Medicine (EA)
**IaAtNT** ...... Atlantic News-Telegraph, Atlantic, IA [*Library symbol*] [*Library of Congress*] (LCLS)
**IaAu** ........... Audubon Public Library, Audubon, IA [*Library symbol*] [*Library of Congress*] (LCLS)
**IaAub** ......... Auburn Public Library, Auburn, IA [*Library symbol*] [*Library of Congress*] (LCLS)
**IaAubE** ...... Auburn Enterprise, Auburn, IA [*Library symbol*] [*Library of Congress*] (LCLS)
**IaAuCoC** .... Audubon County Courthouse, Audubon, IA [*Library symbol*] [*Library of Congress*] (LCLS)
**IaAuNA** ..... Audubon News-Advocate, Audubon, IA [*Library symbol*] [*Library of Congress*] (LCLS)
**IaAur** .......... Aurelia Public Library, Aurelia, IA [*Library symbol*] [*Library of Congress*] (LCLS)
**IaAurS** ....... Aurelia Sentinel, Aurelia, IA [*Library symbol*] [*Library of Congress*] (LCLS)
**IAAV** ......... Alliance of Atomic Veterans [*Acronym is based on former name, International Alliance of Atomic Veterans*] (EA)
**IaAv** ........... Avoca Public Library, Avoca, IA [*Library symbol*] [*Library of Congress*] (LCLS)
**IAAV** ......... International Association of Airborne Veterans (EA)
**IaAvJH** ...... Avoca Journal-Herald, Avoca, IA [*Library symbol*] [*Library of Congress*] (LCLS)
**IaAWD** ...... Wildlife Disease Association, Ames, IA [*Library symbol*] [*Library of Congress*] (LCLS)
**IAAWS** ...... Infantry Antiarmor Weapon Systems [*Military*] (INF)
**IaB** ............. Burlington Free Public Library, Burlington, IA [*Library symbol*] [*Library of Congress*] (LCLS)
**IAB** ............ Immigration Appeal Board [*Canada*]
**IAB** ............ Indirect Address Buffer
**IAB** ............ Industrial Accident Board
**IAB** ............ Industrial Advisory Board [*World War II*]
**IAB** ............ Industrial Arbitration Board [*British*]
**IAB** ............ Institut fuer Arbeitsmarkt- und Berufsforschung [*Institute for Employment Research*] [*Federal Employment Institute*] [*Information service or system*] (IID)
**IAB** ............ Institut fuer Auslandsbeziehungen [*A publication*]
**IAB** ............ Institute of Animal Behavior [*Rutgers University*] [*Research center*] (RCD)
**IAB** ............ Institute of Arctic Biology [*Research center*] (RCD)
**IAB** ............ Interagency Board of Examiners [*Civil Service Commission*]
**IAB** ............ Interim Airframe Bulletin (MCD)
**IAB** ............ Interim Armament Bulletin (MCD)
**IAB** ............ International Abstracting Board [*Also, ICSU AB*] [*International Council of Scientific Unions*]
**IAB** ............ International Association of Bibliophiles [*See also AIB*] [*Paris, France*] (EAIO)
**IAB** ............ International Association of Boards of Examiners in Optometry (EA)
**IAB** ............ International Association of Business (EA)
**IAB** ............ Internationale Akademie fuer Bader-, Sport-, und Freizeitheitbau [*International Board for Aquatic, Sports, and Recreation Facilities*] [*Bad Neustadt/Saale, Federal Republic of Germany*] (EAIO)
**IAB** ............ Interrupt Address to Bus [*Data processing*]
**IAB** ............ Intra-Abdominal [*Artery*]
**IAB** ............ Intra-Aortic Balloon [*Cardiology*]
**IAB** ............ Island Arc Basalt [*Geology*]
**IAB** ............ Italian American Business [*American Chamber of Commerce in Italy*] [*A publication*]
**IAB** ............ John Crerar Library, Chicago, IL [*OCLC symbol*] (OCLC)
**IAB** ............ Wichita, KS [*Location identifier*] [*FAA*] (FAAL)
**IABA** .......... Inter-American Bar Association (EA)
**IABA** .......... International Amateur Boxing Association
**IABA** .......... International Association of Aircraft Brokers and Agents [*Norway*] (EAIO)
**IABA** .......... Intra-Aortic Balloon Assist [*Cardiology*]
**IaBag** .......... Bagley Public Library, Bagley, IA [*Library symbol*] [*Library of Congress*] (LCLS)
**IaBagG** ....... Bagley Gazette, Bagley, IA [*Library symbol*] [*Library of Congress*] (LCLS)
**IAB-AIR** .... International Association of Broadcasting - Asociacion Internacional de Radiodifusion [*Formerly, Inter-American Association of Broadcasters*] (EA)
**IaBanR** ....... Bancroft Register, Bancroft, IA [*Library symbol*] [*Library of Congress*] (LCLS)
**IA Bar Rev** ... Iowa Bar Review [*A publication*] (DLA)
**IaBatB** ........ Batavia Beacon, Batavia, IA [*Library symbol*] [*Library of Congress*] (LCLS)
**IaBaxNE** .... Baxter New Era, Baxter, IA [*Library symbol*] [*Library of Congress*] (LCLS)
**IaBaxWC** ... Baxter Women's Club, Baxter, IA [*Library symbol*] [*Library of Congress*] (LCLS)
**IaBay** .......... Bayard Public Library, Bayard, IA [*Library symbol*] [*Library of Congress*] (LCLS)
**IaBayN** ...... Bayard News, Bayard, IA [*Library symbol*] [*Library of Congress*] (LCLS)
**IABBE** ....... International Association for Better Basic Education (EA)
**IABBE** ....... International Association of Black Business Educators (EA)
**IABBS** ....... International Amateur Boat Building Society [*Defunct*]
**IABC** .......... International Association of Building Companions [*See also IBO*] [*Marche-En-Famenne, Belgium*] (EAIO)
**IABC** .......... International Association of Business Communicators (EA)
**IABC** .......... Intra-Aortic Balloon Counterpulsation [*Cardiology*]
**IaBcIHi** ...... Ida County Historical Society, Battle Creek, IA [*Library symbol*] [*Library of Congress*] (LCLS)
**IaBcT** ......... Battle Creek Times, Battle Creek, IA [*Library symbol*] [*Library of Congress*] (LCLS)
**IaBDHi** ...... Des Moines County Historical Society, Burlington, IA [*Library symbol*] [*Library of Congress*] (LCLS)
**IABE** .......... Ibero-American Bureau of Education [*See also OEI*] [*Madrid, Spain*] (EAIO)
**IaBedTP** .... Bedford Times-Press, Bedford, IA [*Library symbol*] [*Library of Congress*] (LCLS)
**IaBelm** ....... Belmond Public Library, Belmond, IA [*Library symbol*] [*Library of Congress*] (LCLS)
**IaBelmI** ...... Belmond Independent, Belmond, IA [*Library symbol*] [*Library of Congress*] (LCLS)
**IaBepU** ...... Belle Plaine Union, Belle Plaine, IA [*Library symbol*] [*Library of Congress*] (LCLS)
**IaBetN** ....... Bettendorf News, Bettendorf, IA [*Library symbol*] [*Library of Congress*] (LCLS)
**IaBev** .......... Bellevue Public Library, Bellevue, IA [*Library symbol*] [*Library of Congress*] (LCLS)
**IaBevHL** .... Bellevue Herald-Leader, Bellevue, IA [*Library symbol*] [*Library of Congress*] (LCLS)
**IABF** .......... Inter-American Bar Foundation (EA)
**IABF** .......... International Association of Business Forecasting (EA)
**IABG** .......... International Association of Botanic Gardens [*Australia*] (EA)
**IABG** .......... International Association of Buying Groups [*See also IVE*] (EAIO)
**IABK** .......... International Association of Book-Keepers [*Sevenoaks, Kent, England*] (EA)
**IaBl** ............ Bloomfield Public Library, Bloomfield, IA [*Library symbol*] [*Library of Congress*] (LCLS)
**IABL** .......... Independent Association of Builders' Labourers [*A union*] [*British*]
**IABLA** ....... Izvestiya Akademii Nauk Azerbaidzhanskoi SSR Seriya Biologicheskikh Nauk [*A publication*]
**IaBlak** ........ Blakesburg Public Library, Blakesburg, IA [*Library symbol*] [*Library of Congress*] (LCLS)
**IaBlaSP** ..... South Benton Star Press, Blairstown, IA [*Library symbol*] [*Library of Congress*] (LCLS)
**IaBlD** ........ Bloomfield Democrat, Bloomfield, IA [*Library symbol*] [*Library of Congress*] (LCLS)
**IaBlDR** ...... Davis County Republican, Bloomfield, IA [*Library symbol*] [*Library of Congress*] (LCLS)
**IaBlGen** ..... Davis County Genealogical Society, Bloomfield, IA [*Library symbol*] [*Library of Congress*] (LCLS)
**IABM** ......... International Academy of Biological Medicine [*Defunct*] (EA)
**IABM** ......... International Association of Broadcast Monitors (EA)
**IABM** ......... International Association of Broadcasting Manufacturers [*Hayes, Middlesex, England*] (EAIO)
**IABNA** ...... Izvestiya Akademii Nauk Armyanskoi SSR Biologicheskie Nauki [*A publication*]
**IaBo** ........... Ericson Public Library, Boone, IA [*Library symbol*] [*Library of Congress*] (LCLS)
**IABO** ......... Internacia Asocio de Bibliistoj kaj Orientalistoj [*International Association of Biblicists and Orientalists - IABO*] (EA)
**IABO** ......... International Association for Biological Oceanography [*Aberdeen, Scotland*] (EAIO)
**IaBoCoC** .... Boone County Courthouse, Boone, IA [*Library symbol*] [*Library of Congress*] (LCLS)
**IaBonR** ....... Bonaparte Record-Republican, Bonaparte, IA [*Library symbol*] [*Library of Congress*] (LCLS)
**IaBoNR** ...... Boone News-Republican, Boone, IA [*Library symbol*] [*Library of Congress*] (LCLS)
**IABP** .......... International Association of Businessmen and Professionals (EA)
**IABP** .......... Intra-Aortic Balloon Pump [*Cardiology*]
**IABPAI** ...... International Association of Blue Print and Allied Industries [*Later, IRGBA, IRA*] (EA)
**IABPBD** .... International Alliance of Bill Posters, Billers, and Distributors of US and Canada [*Defunct*]
**IABPC** ....... International Association of Book Publishing Consultants [*Inactive*] (EA)
**IABPFF** ..... International Association of Black Professional Fire Fighters (EA)

**IABR**......... Index to Australian Book Reviews [*A publication*]
**IaBreN**....... Breda News, Breda, IA [*Library symbol*] [*Library of Congress*] (LCLS)
**IaBrEN**...... Brighton Enterprise-News, Brighton, IA [*Library symbol*] [*Library of Congress*] (LCLS)
**IA B Rev**.... Iowa Bar Review [*A publication*] (DLA)
**IaBriNT**..... Britt News-Tribune, Britt, IA [*Library symbol*] [*Library of Congress*] (LCLS)
**IABRM**...... International Association for Bear Research and Management (EA)
**IaBroC**....... Brooklyn Chronicle, Brooklyn, IA [*Library symbol*] [*Library of Congress*] (LCLS)
**IABS**.......... Installation Automated Budget System [*Army*]
**IABS**.......... International Abstracts of Biological Sciences [*A publication*]
**IABS**.......... International Alban Berg Society (EA)
**IABS**.......... International Association of Biological Standardization [*See also AISB*] [*ICSU*] [*Geneva, Switzerland*] (EAIO)
**IABS**.......... International Association of Buddhist Studies (EA)
**IABS**.......... International Association for Byzantine Studies [*See also AIEB*] [*Thessaloniki, Greece*] (EAIO)
**IABSE**....... International Association for Bridge and Structural Engineering [*Research center*] [*ICSU*] [*Zurich, Switzerland*] (EA)
**IABSOIW**... International Association of Bridge, Structural, and Ornamental Iron Workers (EA)
**IABTI**........ International Association of Bomb Technicians and Investigators (EA)
**IaBucCT**.... Buffalo Center Tribune, Buffalo Center, IA [*Library symbol*] [*Library of Congress*] (LCLS)
**IABWMT**... International Association of Black and White Men Together [*Later, NABWMT*] (EA)
**IAC**........... Chicago, IL [*Location identifier*] [*FAA*] (FAAL)
**IAC**........... De Paul University, Chicago, IL [*OCLC symbol*] (OCLC)
**IAC**........... Iceberg Athletic Club (EA)
**IAC**........... Identification Accuracy [*Rate*] (MCD)
**IAC**........... Idle Air Control [*Automotive engineering*]
**IAC**........... Immigration Appeal Cases [*Canada*] [*A publication*] (DLA)
**IAC**........... Improved Anode Catalyst
**IAC**........... Indian Airlines Corporation [*India*]
**IAC**........... Indian Army Circular [*British military*] (DMA)
**IAC**........... Indo-Asian Culture [*A publication*]
**IAC**........... Industrial Accident Commission Decisions [*A publication*] (DLA)
**IAC**........... Industry Advisory Committee [*World War II*]
**IAC**........... Industry Advisory Conference [*Underwriters Laboratories*] [*Telecommunications*]
**IAC**........... Industry Advisory Council [*Formerly, DIAC*]
**IAC**........... Information Access Company [*Information service or system*] (IID)
**IAC**........... Information Analysis Center [*DoD*]
**IAC**........... Information and Communication
**IAC**........... Inheritance of Acquired Characteristics
**IAC**........... Initial Approach Course [*Aviation*]
**IAC**........... Inner Approach Channel
**IAC**........... Inspection and Agency Corporation [*Burma*] (DS)
**IAC**........... Institute for Advanced Concepts [*In 1980 film "Simon"*]
**IAC**........... Institute for Antiquity and Christianity [*Claremont University*] [*Research center*] (RCD)
**IAC**........... Institute of Applied Clicheology
**IAC**........... Instrument Approach Chart (AAG)
**IAC**........... Instrument Array Cable
**IAC**........... Insurance Advertising Conference [*Later, IMCA*] (EA)
**IAC**........... Integrating Assembly Contractor
**IAC**........... Integrating Associate Contractor
**IAC**........... Integration, Assembly, and Checkout
**IAC**........... Intelligence Analysis Center [*Marine Corps*] (MCD)
**IAC**........... Interactive Array Computer
**IAC**........... Interagency Committee for Outdoor Recreation [*Department of the Interior*]
**IAC**........... Interagency Conference (MCD)
**IAC**........... Interapplication Communication [*Apple Computer, Inc.*]
**IAC**........... Interarray Communications (NVT)
**IAC**........... Interdepartmental Advisory Committee [*World War II*]
**IAC**........... Interface Assurance Contractor
**IAC**........... Interim Acceptance Criteria (NRCH)
**IAC**........... Interim Action Committee [*British*]
**IAC**........... Intermediate Air Command [*Air Force*] (AFM)
**IAC**........... Intermittent Abdominal Compression
**IAC**........... Internal Auditory Canal [*Anatomy*]
**IAC**........... International Academy of Ceramics [*See also AIC*] [*Geneva, Switzerland*] (EAIO)
**IAC**........... International Academy of Cytology [*Quebec, PQ*] (EA)
**IAC**........... International Activities Committee [*American Chemical Society*]
**IAC**........... International Advisory Committee [*ANSI*]
**IAC**........... International Advisory Council for Homosexual Men and Women in Alcoholics Anonymous (EA)
**IAC**........... International Aerobatic Club (EA)
**IAC**........... International Agricultural Club (EA)
**IAC**........... International Air Convention
**IAC**........... International Algebraic Compiler
**IAC**........... International Analysis Code [*Meteorology*]
**IAC**........... International Anti-Counterfeiting Coalition (EA)
**IAC**........... International Artists' Cooperation (EAIO)
**IAC**........... International Association of Charities [*See also AIC*] (EAIO)
**IAC**........... International Association for Cybernetics [*See also AIC*] [*Namur, Belgium*] (EAIO)
**IAC**........... International Astronautical Congress
**IAC**........... International Aviation Corporation [*Minneapolis, MN*] [*FAA designator*] (FAAC)
**IAC**........... Interview-after-Combat
**IAC**........... Intra-Arterial Chemotherapy [*Medicine*]
**IAC**........... Inventory of Anger Communication [*Personality development test*] [*Psychology*]
**IAC**........... Ipsilateral Associational-Commissural [*Anatomy*]
**IAC**........... Israel Aliyah Center (EA)
**IaCa**.......... Duncan Memorial Library, Casey, IA [*Library symbol*] [*Library of Congress*] (LCLS)
**IACA**......... Independent Air Carriers Association [*Defunct*] (EA)
**IACA**......... Indian Arts and Crafts Association (EA)
**IACA**......... Inter-American College Association (EA)
**IACA**......... Inter-American Cultural Association (EA)
**IACA**......... International Air Carrier Association [*Zaventhem, Belgium*] (EAIO)
**IACA**......... International Association for Classical Archaeology [*See also AIAC*] [*Rome, Italy*] (EAIO)
**IACA**......... Irish American Cultural Association (EA)
**IACAAC**.... International Artists' Cooperation Audio Art Center (EA)
**I-ACAC**..... Inter-American Commercial Arbitration Commission (EA)
**IACAC**...... International Association of Civil Aviation Chaplains (EA)
**IAC/ADP**.. Interagency Committee on Automatic Data Processing [*Office of Management and Budget*]
**IACAPAP**... International Association for Child and Adolescent Psychiatry and Allied Professions [*Copenhagen, Denmark*] (EA)
**IaCar**......... Carroll Public Library, Carroll, IA [*Library symbol*] [*Library of Congress*] (LCLS)
**IaCarCH**.... Carroll County Historical Society Museum, Carroll, IA [*Library symbol*] [*Library of Congress*] (LCLS)
**IaCarl**........ Carlisle Public Library, Carlisle, IA [*Library symbol*] [*Library of Congress*] (LCLS)
**IaCarlC**...... Carlisle Citizen, Carlisle, IA [*Library symbol*] [*Library of Congress*] (LCLS)
**IaCarsT**...... Carson Times, Carson, IA [*Library symbol*] [*Library of Congress*] (LCLS)
**IaCarTH**.... Daily Times-Herald, Carroll, IA [*Library symbol*] [*Library of Congress*] (LCLS)
**IaCasPA**.... Cascade Pioneer-Advertiser, Cascade, IA [*Library symbol*] [*Library of Congress*] (LCLS)
**IaCb**.......... Council Bluffs Free Public Library, Council Bluffs, IA [*Library symbol*] [*Library of Congress*] (LCLS)
**IACB**......... Indian Arts and Crafts Board [*Department of the Interior*]
**IACB**......... Inter-Agency Consultative Board (EY)
**IACB**......... International Association of Convention Bureaus [*Later, IACVB*] (EA)
**IACBD**...... International Academy for Child Brain Development (EA)
**IaCbN**....... Nonpareil, Council Bluffs, IA [*Library symbol*] [*Library of Congress*] (LCLS)
**IACC**......... India-America Chamber of Commerce (EA)
**IACC**......... Industrial Analysis and Control Council
**IACC**......... Integrating Assembly and Checkout Contractor
**IACC**......... Inter-Agency Air Cartographic Committee
**IACC**......... Inter-American Cultural Council (EA)
**IACC**......... Interamerican Confederation of Cattlemen (EA)
**IACC**......... International Alliance of Catholic Churches (EA)
**IACC**......... International Anticounterfeiting Coalition (EA)
**IACC**......... International Art Cinemas Confederation (EAIO)
**IACC**......... International Association of Conference Centers (EA)
**IACC**......... Iran American Chamber of Commerce (EA)
**IACC**......... Italian-American Chamber of Commerce (EA)
**IACC**......... Italy-America Chamber of Commerce (EA)
**IaCc**.......... John E. Clegg Library, Central City, IA [*Library symbol*] [*Library of Congress*] (LCLS)
**IAC of Cal**... Decisions of the Industrial Accident Commission of California [*A publication*] (DLA)
**IACCE**....... Inter-American Confederation for Catholic Education [*Bogota, Colombia*] (EAIO)
**IACCI**........ International Association of Computer Crime Investigators (EA)
**IACCI**........ International Association of Credit Card Investigators (EA)
**IaCcL**........ Linn News-Letter, Central City, IA [*Library symbol*] [*Library of Congress*] (LCLS)
**IACCP**....... Inter-American Council of Commerce and Production
**IACCP**....... International Association for Cross-Cultural Psychology [*Canada*] (EA)
**IAC-CPR**... Interposed Abdominal Compression - Cardiopulmonary Resuscitation
**IACD**........ International Association of Clothing Designers (EA)
**IAC Dec**..... Decisions of the Industrial Accident Commission of California [*A publication*] (DLA)
**IACDLA**.... International Advisory Committee on Documentation, Libraries, and Archives [*UNESCO*] (DIT)
**IACDT**....... International Association of Certified Duncan Teachers (EA)
**IACE**......... International Air Cadet Exchange

**IACE**........ International Association for Computing in Education [*Also, an information service or system*] (EA)
**IACEAA**.... Indian Council of Agricultural Research. Cereal Crop Series [*A publication*]
**IACED**....... Inter-African Advisory Committee on Epizootic Diseases
**IaCenv**........ Drake Public Library, Centerville, IA [*Library symbol*] [*Library of Congress*] (LCLS)
**IaCenvI**...... Iowegian & Citizen, Centerville, IA [*Library symbol*] [*Library of Congress*] (LCLS)
**IACET**....... International Association for Continuing Education and Training (EA)
**IaCf**........... Cedar Falls Public Library, Cedar Falls, IA [*Library symbol*] [*Library of Congress*] (LCLS)
**IACF**.......... International Amateur Cycling Federation (EA)
**IACF**.......... International Association for Cultural Freedom [*Defunct*] (EA)
**IaCfE**......... Eastern Area Library Cooperative, Cedar Falls, IA [*Library symbol*] [*Library of Congress*] (LCLS)
**IACFHG**.... Inter Action Council of Former Heads of Government (EA)
**IaCfHi**........ Cedar Falls Historical Society, Cedar Falls, IA [*Library symbol*] [*Library of Congress*] (LCLS)
**IACFM**...... International Association of Concert and Festival Managers [*Later, ISPAA*] (EA)
**IaCfNI**....... Northern Iowan, Cedar Falls, IA [*Library symbol*] [*Library of Congress*] (LCLS)
**IaCfR**......... Cedar Falls Record, Cedar Falls, IA [*Library symbol*] [*Library of Congress*] (LCLS)
**IaCfT**......... University of Northern Iowa, Cedar Falls, IA [*Library symbol*] [*Library of Congress*] (LCLS)
**IACG**......... Institute for American Church Growth (EA)
**IaCh**........... Free Public Library, Chariton, IA [*Library symbol*] [*Library of Congress*] (LCLS)
**IACH**......... Inter-Association Committee on Health
**IACHA**...... Iowa Automated Clearing House Association
**IaChc**......... Charles City Public Library, Charles City, IA [*Library symbol*] [*Library of Congress*] (LCLS)
**IaChcP**....... Charles City Press, Charles City, IA [*Library symbol*] [*Library of Congress*] (LCLS)
**IaChe**......... Cherokee Public Library, Cherokee, IA [*Library symbol*] [*Library of Congress*] (LCLS)
**IACHE**...... International Association of Cylindrical Hydraulic Engineers (EA)
**IaCheCHi**.. Cherokee County Historical Society, Cherokee, IA [*Library symbol*] [*Library of Congress*] (LCLS)
**IaCheCoC**.. Cherokee County Courthouse, Cherokee, IA [*Library symbol*] [*Library of Congress*] (LCLS)
**IaChHP**..... Chariton Herald-Patriot, Chariton, IA [*Library symbol*] [*Library of Congress*] (LCLS)
**IaChL**......... Chariton Leader, Chariton, IA [*Library symbol*] [*Library of Congress*] (LCLS)
**IaChoT**....... Charter Oak Times, Charter Oak, IA [*Library symbol*] [*Library of Congress*] (LCLS)
**IACHR**...... Inter-American Commission on Human Rights (EA)
**IaChu**......... Churdan City Library, Churdan, IA [*Library symbol*] [*Library of Congress*] (LCLS)
**IACI**........... Industrial Acoustics Company, Incorporated [*NASDAQ symbol*] (NQ)
**IACI**........... Inter-American Children's Institute [*Research center*] [*Uruguay*] (IRC)
**IACI**........... Iran Aircraft Industries (MCD)
**IACI**........... Irish American Cultural Institute (EA)
**IACIA**........ Interagency Committee for International Athletics [*Defunct*]
**IACID**........ Inter-American Center for Integral Development [*OAS*]
**IACITC**..... International Advisory Committee of the International Teletraffic Congress (EAIO)
**IACJ**........... Inter-American Council of Jurists [*Organization of American States*] [*Washington, DC*]
**IaCjGS**....... Columbus Gazette & Columbus Safeguard, Columbus Junction, IA [*Library symbol*] [*Library of Congress*] (LCLS)
**IaCkvS**....... Clarksville Star, Clarksville, IA [*Library symbol*] [*Library of Congress*] (LCLS)
**IACL**.......... International Aeradio Caribbean Limited
**IACL**.......... International Association of Constitutional Law [*See also AIDC*] [*Belgrade, Yugoslavia*] (EAIO)
**IaCla**......... Clarion Public Library, Clarion, IA [*Library symbol*] [*Library of Congress*] (LCLS)
**IACLA**....... International Association of Clinical Laser Acupuncturists (EA)
**IaClad**........ Clarinda Public Library, Clarinda, IA [*Library symbol*] [*Library of Congress*] (LCLS)
**IaCladHJ**... Clarinda Herald-Journal, Clarinda, IA [*Library symbol*] [*Library of Congress*] (LCLS)
**IaClaM**...... Wright County Monitor, Clarion, IA [*Library symbol*] [*Library of Congress*] (LCLS)
**IaClar**......... Edna Zybell Memorial Library, Clarence, IA [*Library symbol*] [*Library of Congress*] (LCLS)
**IaClarCHi**... Cedar County Historical Society, Clarence, IA [*Library symbol*] [*Library of Congress*] (LCLS)
**IACLAV**.... International Anesthesiology Clinics [*A publication*]
**IACLEA**.... International Association of Campus Law Enforcement Administrators (EA)
**IaClfC**........ Clearfield Chronicle, Clearfield, IA [*Library symbol*] [*Library of Congress*] (LCLS)
**IaCli**.......... Clinton Public Library, Clinton, IA [*Library symbol*] [*Library of Congress*] (LCLS)
**IaCliC**........ Clinton Corn Processing Co., Clinton, IA [*Library symbol*] [*Library of Congress*] (LCLS)
**IaCliCC**...... Clinton Community College, Clinton, IA [*Library symbol*] [*Library of Congress*] (LCLS)
**IaCliCHi**.... Clinton County Historical Society, Clinton, IA [*Library symbol*] [*Library of Congress*] (LCLS)
**IaCliH**........ Clinton Herald, Clinton, IA [*Library symbol*] [*Library of Congress*] (LCLS)
**IaCliM**....... Mount Saint Clare College, Clinton, IA [*Library symbol*] [*Library of Congress*] (LCLS)
**IaCll**........... Clear Lake Public Library, Clear Lake, IA [*Library symbol*] [*Library of Congress*] (LCLS)
**IaClvS**........ Clarksville Star, Clarksville, IA [*Library symbol*] [*Library of Congress*] (LCLS)
**IACM**........ International Association of Circulation Managers
**IACM**........ International Association of Concert Managers [*Later, ISPAA*] (EA)
**IACME**...... International Association of Coroners and Medical Examiners (EA)
**IACME**...... International Association of Crafts and Small and Medium-Sized Enterprises [*Berne, Switzerland*]
**IACO**......... Conservative Orthopedics International Association (EA)
**IACO**......... Inter-African Coffee Organization (EAIO)
**IACO**......... International Association of Correctional Officers (EA)
**IACOA**...... Independent Armored Car Operators Association (EA)
**IACOCCA**... I Am Chairman of Chrysler Corporation of America [*Acronym formed from name of Chrysler chairman Lee Iacocca*]
**IaCogM**...... Coggan Monitor, Coggan, IA [*Library symbol*] [*Library of Congress*] (LCLS)
**IaCol**.......... Colfax Free Public Library, Colfax, IA [*Library symbol*] [*Library of Congress*] (LCLS)
**IaColJ**........ Jasper County Tribune, Colfax, IA [*Library symbol*] [*Library of Congress*] (LCLS)
**IaColn**........ Collins Public Library, Collins, IA [*Library symbol*] [*Library of Congress*] (LCLS)
**IACOMS**... International Advisory Committee on Marine Sciences [*United Nations*]
**IaConR**....... Conrad Record, Conrad, IA [*Library symbol*] [*Library of Congress*] (LCLS)
**IaCoon**....... Coon Rapids Enterprise, Coon Rapids, IA [*Library symbol*] [*Library of Congress*] (LCLS)
**IACOP**....... International Armaments Cooperative Opportunities Plan
**IaCorn**........ Corning Free Public Library, Corning, IA [*Library symbol*] [*Library of Congress*] (LCLS)
**IaCornFP**... Adams County Free Press, Corning, IA [*Library symbol*] [*Library of Congress*] (LCLS)
**IaCorrN**..... Correctionville News, Correctionville, IA [*Library symbol*] [*Library of Congress*] (LCLS)
**IaCorv**........ Coralville Public Library, Coralville, IA [*Library symbol*] [*Library of Congress*] (LCLS)
**IaCorvC**..... Coralville Courier, Coralville, IA [*Library symbol*] [*Library of Congress*] (LCLS)
**IaCorwH**.... Corwith Herald, Corwith, IA [*Library symbol*] [*Library of Congress*] (LCLS)
**IaCoryTR**... Corydon Times-Republican, Corydon, IA [*Library symbol*] [*Library of Congress*] (LCLS)
**IaCoryWCoC**... Wayne County Courthouse, Corydon, IA [*Library symbol*] [*Library of Congress*] (LCLS)
**IACP**.......... International Association of Chiefs of Police (EA)
**IACP**.......... International Association for Child Psychiatry and Allied Professions [*Later, IACAPAP*]
**IACP**.......... International Association of Computer Programmers
**IACP**.......... International Association of Cooking Professionals (EA)
**IACPA**....... Proceedings. International Astronautical Congress [*A publication*]
**IACPAP**.... International Association for Child Psychiatry and Allied Professions [*Later, IACAPAP*]
**IACPP**....... International Association of Crime Prevention Practitioners (EA)
**IACPS**....... Inter-American Committee on Peaceful Settlement (EA)
**IACPS**....... International Academy of Chest Physicians and Surgeons (EA)
**IACPWR**... Inter-Allied Committee on Post-War Requirements [*World War II*]
**IaCr**........... Cedar Rapids Public Library, Cedar Rapids, IA [*Library symbol*] [*Library of Congress*] (LCLS)
**IACR**.......... Institue of Arable Crop Research [*British*]
**IACR**.......... Inter-American Congress of Radiology
**IACR**.......... International Association of Cancer Registries [*Lyon, France*] (EAIO)
**IACR**.......... International Association for Cryptologic Research (EA)
**IaCrC**......... Coe College, Cedar Rapids, IA [*Library symbol*] [*Library of Congress*] (LCLS)
**IACRD**....... Inter-American Center for Regional Development (EAIO)
**IACRDP**.... International Association of Cross-Reference Directory Publishers (EA)

**IACRDVT** ... Inter-American Centre for Research and Documentation on Vocational Training [*See also CINTERFOR*] [*Montevideo, Uruguay*] (EAIO)
**IACREE** ..... International Association of Corporate Real Estate Executives (EA)
**IACREOT** ... International Association of Clerks, Recorders, Election Officials, and Treasurers (EA)
**IaCres** ........ Matilda J. Gibson Memorial Library, Creston, IA [*Library symbol*] [*Library of Congress*] (LCLS)
**IaCresco**..... Cresco Public Library, Cresco, IA [*Library symbol*] [*Library of Congress*] (LCLS)
**IaCrescoCoC** ... Howard County Courthouse, Cresco, IA [*Library symbol*] [*Library of Congress*] (LCLS)
**IaCrescoTP** ... Cresco Times-Plain Dealer, Cresco, IA [*Library symbol*] [*Library of Congress*] (LCLS)
**IaCresNA** .. Creston News-Advertiser, Creston, IA [*Library symbol*] [*Library of Congress*] (LCLS)
**IaCrG**......... Cedar Rapids Gazette, Cedar Rapids, IA [*Library symbol*] [*Library of Congress*] (LCLS)
**IaCrK** ......... Kirkwood Community College, Cedar Rapids, IA [*Library symbol*] [*Library of Congress*] (LCLS)
**IACRL** ........ Italian-American Civil Rights League
**IaCrL** ......... Linn County Heritage Society, Cedar Rapids, IA [*Library symbol*] [*Library of Congress*] (LCLS)
**IACRLRD** ... International Association for Comparative Research on Leukemia and Related Diseases (EA)
**IaCrM**........ Iowa Masonic Library, Cedar Rapids, IA [*Library symbol*] [*Library of Congress*] (LCLS)
**IaCrMM**.... Mount Mercy College, Cedar Rapids, IA [*Library symbol*] [*Library of Congress*] (LCLS)
**IaCrMT** ..... Micro-Technology, Inc., Cedar Rapids, IA [*Library symbol*] [*Library of Congress*] (LCLS)
**IACRP** ....... International Association for the Child's Right to Play (EAIO)
**IACRS** ....... International Association of Concrete Repair Specialists (EA)
**IACS** .......... IAL Consultancy Services [*Southall, England*] [*Telecommunications*] (TSSD)
**IACS** .......... Inertial Attitude Control System [*Aerospace*]
**IACS** .......... Integrated Acoustic Communication System [*Military*] (NVT)
**IACS** .......... Integrated Armament Control System (MCD)
**IACS** .......... Integrated Avionics Control System (RDA)
**IACS** .......... Interactive Computer System [*Information science*]
**IACS** .......... International Academy of Cosmetic Surgery [*Rome, Italy*] (EA)
**IACS** .......... International Annealed Copper Standard
**IACS** .......... International Arms-Control Symposium
**IACS** .......... International Association of Classification Societies (EAIO)
**IACS** .......... International Association of Cooking Schools (EA)
**IACS** .......... International Association of Counseling Services (EA)
**IACS** .......... Italian-American Cultural Society (EA)
**IACSE** ....... Interagency Advisory Committee on Security Equipment
**IACSS**........ Inter-American Conference on Social Security [*See also CISS*] [*Mexico City, Mexico*] (EAIO)
**IACSS**........ International Association for Computer Systems Security (EA)
**IACST** ....... International Association for Commodity Science and Technology (EAIO)
**IACSW** ...... Interstate Association of Commissions on the Status of Women
**IACT**.......... Inter-Association Commission on Tsunami [*Brussels, Belgium*] (EAIO)
**IACT**.......... International Association for Clear Thinking (EA)
**IACT**.......... International Association to Combat Terrorism [*Defunct*] (EA)
**IACUC**....... Institutional Animal Care and Use Committee [*Department of Agriculture*]
**IACUG** ...... International Association of Computer Users Groups (EA)
**IACVB** ....... International Association of Convention and Visitor Bureaus (EA)
**IACVF** ....... International Association of Cancer Victors and Friends (EA)
**I/ACVIA**.... Interaction/American Council for Voluntary International Action (EA)
**IACW** ........ Inter-American Commission of Women [*Organization of American States*] [*Washington, DC*]
**IACW** ........ International Association of Crime Writers (EAIO)
**IAD**............ Eastern Illinois University, Charleston, IL [*OCLC symbol*] (OCLC)
**IAD**............ Immediate Action Directive
**IAD**............ Index of Axis Deficiency [*Embryology*]
**IAD**............ Information and Documentation [*British Film Institute*]
**IAD**............ Initial Address Designator
**IAD**............ Initiation Area Discriminator [*RADAR*]
**IAD**............ Inland Steel Industries, Inc. [*NYSE symbol*] (SPSG)
**IAD**............ Installation, Assembly or Detail (AAG)
**IAD**............ Institute for American Democracy (EA)
**IAD**............ Integrated Airbase Defense
**IAD**............ Integrated Automatic Documentation [*System*]
**IAD**............ Interface Agreement Document (KSC)
**IAD**............ Interface Analysis Document (KSC)
**IAD**............ Internal Absorbed Dose
**IAD**............ International Association of Documentalists and Information Officers [*France*] (EY)
**IAD**............ International Astrophysical Decade
**IAD**............ International Automotive Design
**IAD**............ Internationale Arbeitsgemeinschaft Donauforschung [*International Working Association for Danube Research*] (EAIO)
**IAD**............ Inventory Adjustment Document
**IAD**............ Inventory Available Date (TEL)
**IAD**............ Ion-Assisted Deposition [*Coating technology*]
**IAD**............ Ion Beam Activated Deposition [*Coating technology*]
**IAD**............ Washington [*District of Columbia*] Dulles Airport [*Airport symbol*]
**IaDa** ........... Davenport Public Library, Davenport, IA [*Library symbol*] [*Library of Congress*] (LCLS)
**IADA** ......... Independent Aeronautical Dealers Association [*Defunct*] (EA)
**IADA** ......... Independent Automotive Damage Appraisers Association [*Milwaukee, WI*] (EA)
**IADA** ......... International Atomic-Development Authority [*Proposed by Bernard M. Baruch, 1946, but never created*]
**IADA** ......... Internationale Arbeitsgemeinschaft der Archiv-, Bibliotheks-, und Graphikrestauratoren [*International Association for Conservation of Books, Paper, and Archival Material*] [*Federal Republic of Germany*] (EAIO)
**IADA** ......... Interstate Agreement on Detainers Act [*1970*]
**IaDaCM** .... Catholic Messenger, Davenport, IA [*Library symbol*] [*Library of Congress*] (LCLS)
**IaDaCoC**.... Scott County Courthouse, Davenport, IA [*Library symbol*] [*Library of Congress*] (LCLS)
**IaDaGL**...... Grant Law Library, Davenport, IA [*Library symbol*] [*Library of Congress*] (LCLS)
**IaDaM** ....... Davenport Public Museum, Davenport, IA [*Library symbol*] [*Library of Congress*] (LCLS)
**IaDaMC** .... Marycrest College, Davenport, IA [*Library symbol*] [*Library of Congress*] (LCLS)
**IaDaP**......... Palmer College of Chiropractic, Davenport, IA [*Library symbol*] [*Library of Congress*] (LCLS)
**IaDaPM**..... Putnam Museum, Davenport, IA [*Library symbol*] [*Library of Congress*] (LCLS)
**IaDaSA**...... Saint Ambrose College, Davenport, IA [*Library symbol*] [*Library of Congress*] (LCLS)
**IaDayR** ...... Dayton Review, Dayton, IA [*Library symbol*] [*Library of Congress*] (LCLS)
**IADB** ......... Inter-American Defense Board (EA)
**IADB** ......... Inter-American Development Bank [*Also, IDB*]
**IADBWA**... Inter-American Development Bank's Wives Association (EA)
**IaDc** ........... Dallas Center Public Library, Dallas Center, IA [*Library symbol*] [*Library of Congress*] (LCLS)
**IADC** ......... Inter-American Defense College [*Washington, DC*]
**IADC** ......... Inter-American Development Commission
**IADC** ......... International Alliance for Distribution by Cable [*Formerly, International Alliance for Distribution by Wire*] (EA)
**IADC** ......... International Association of Defense Counsel (EA)
**IADC** ......... International Association of Dentistry for Children [*London, England*] (EAIO)
**IADC** ......... International Association of Dredging Companies [*The Hague, Netherlands*] (EA)
**IADC** ......... International Association of Drilling Contractors (EA)
**IaDCC**........ College Chips, Luther College, Decorah, IA [*Library symbol*] [*Library of Congress*] (LCLS)
**IADD** ......... Index to American Doctoral Dissertations [*A publication*]
**IAdEM** ...... Internacia Asocio de Esperantistaj Matematikistoj [*International Association of Esperantist Mathematicians*] (EAIO)
**IaDen** ......... Denison Carnegie Library, Denison, IA [*Library symbol*] [*Library of Congress*] (LCLS)
**IaDenB**....... Denison Bulletin, Denison, IA [*Library symbol*] [*Library of Congress*] (LCLS)
**IaDenR** ...... Denison Review, Denison, IA [*Library symbol*] [*Library of Congress*] (LCLS)
**IaDewO**...... Observer, De Witt, IA [*Library symbol*] [*Library of Congress*] (LCLS)
**IaDexM** ..... Dexter Museum, Dexter, IA [*Library symbol*] [*Library of Congress*] (LCLS)
**IADF**.......... Icelandic Air Defense Force (MUGU)
**IADF**.......... Inter-American Association for Democracy and Freedom (EA)
**IADF**.......... Irish American Defense Fund (EA)
**IADH**......... International Association of Dentistry for the Handicapped [*Toronto, ON*] (EAIO)
**IADHS** ...... Inappropriate Antidiuretic Hormone Syndrome [*Endocrinology*]
**IaDiaR** ....... Diagonal Reporter, Diagonal, IA [*Library symbol*] [*Library of Congress*] (LCLS)
**IADIC**........ Integration Analog-to-Digital Converter (IEEE)
**IADIWU**.... International Association for the Development of International and World Universities [*See also AIDUIM*] [*Aulnay-Sous-Bois, France*] (EAIO)
**IaDJ** ........... Decorah Journal, Decorah, IA [*Library symbol*] [*Library of Congress*] (LCLS)
**IADL**.......... International Association of Democratic Lawyers [*Brussels, Belgium*] (EA)
**IaDL** .......... Luther College, Decorah, IA [*Library symbol*] [*Library of Congress*] (LCLS)
**IaDm**.......... Des Moines Public Library, Des Moines, IA [*Library symbol*] [*Library of Congress*] (LCLS)

**IaDmB** ....... Iowa Commission for the Blind, Des Moines, IA [*Library symbol*] [*Library of Congress*] (LCLS)
**IaDmC** ....... Iowa State Commerce Commission, Records and Information Center, Des Moines, IA [*Library symbol*] [*Library of Congress*] (LCLS)
**IaDmD** ....... Drake University, Des Moines, IA [*Library symbol*] [*Library of Congress*] (LCLS)
**IaDmDC** .... Dowling College, Des Moines, IA [*Library symbol*] [*Library of Congress*] (LCLS)
**IaDmD-L** ... Drake University, Law School, Des Moines, IA [*Library symbol*] [*Library of Congress*] (LCLS)
**IaDmE** ....... Iowa State Education Association, Des Moines, IA [*Library symbol*] [*Library of Congress*] (LCLS)
**IADMFR** ... International Association of Dento-Maxillo-Facial Radiology (EAIO)
**IaDmG** ....... Grand View College, Des Moines, IA [*Library symbol*] [*Library of Congress*] (LCLS)
**IaDmHN** .... Highland Park News, Des Moines, IA [*Library symbol*] [*Library of Congress*] (LCLS)
**IaDmL** ....... Iowa Legionnaire, Des Moines, IA [*Library symbol*] [*Library of Congress*] (LCLS)
**IaDmLN** .... Lee Town News, Des Moines, IA [*Library symbol*] [*Library of Congress*] (LCLS)
**IaDmMet** ... Des Moines Metropolitan Service Area Library Cooperative, Des Moines, IA [*Library symbol*] [*Library of Congress*] (LCLS)
**IaDmOF** .... Odd Fellows Temple, Des Moines, IA [*Library symbol*] [*Library of Congress*] (LCLS)
**IaDmPH** .... Pioneer Hi-Bred International, Inc., Des Moines, IA [*Library symbol*] [*Library of Congress*] (LCLS)
**IaDmR** ....... Daily Record, Des Moines, IA [*Library symbol*] [*Library of Congress*] (LCLS)
**IaDmRT** ..... Des Moines Register-Tribune, Des Moines, IA [*Library symbol*] [*Library of Congress*] (LCLS)
**IaDmS** ........ College of Osteopathic Medicine and Surgery, Des Moines, IA [*Library symbol*] [*Library of Congress*] (LCLS)
**IaDmV** ....... United States Veterans Administration Hospital, Des Moines, IA [*Library symbol*] [*Library of Congress*] (LCLS)
**IaDN** .......... Norwegian-American Historical Museum and Library, Decorah, IA [*Library symbol*] [*Library of Congress*] (LCLS)
**IaDo** .......... Dows Community Library, Dows, IA [*Library symbol*] [*Library of Congress*] (LCLS)
**IaDon** ......... Donnellson Public Library, Donnellson, IA [*Library symbol*] [*Library of Congress*] (LCLS)
**IaDonS** ....... Donnellson Star, Donnellson, IA [*Library symbol*] [*Library of Congress*] (LCLS)
**IaDooP** ....... Press, Doon, IA [*Library symbol*] [*Library of Congress*] (LCLS)
**IADP** .......... INTELSAT Assistance and Development Program
**IADP** .......... Inter-American Driving Permit
**IADP** .......... International Association of Dollbaby Parents [*Defunct*] (EA)
**IADPC** ....... Interagency Data Processing Committee
**IADPG** ....... Intelligence Automatic Data Processing Group (CINC)
**IaDPO** ....... Decorah Public Opinion, Decorah, IA [*Library symbol*] [*Library of Congress*] (LCLS)
**IaDQT** ....... Quad City Times, Davenport, IA [*Library symbol*] [*Library of Congress*] (LCLS)
**IADR** ......... Institute for Animal Disease Research [*United Kingdom*] [*Research center*] (IRC)
**IADR** ......... International Association for Dental Research (EA)
**IADRS** ........ International Association of Dive Rescue Specialists (EA)
**IADS** .......... Integrated Air Defense System (MCD)
**IADS** .......... International Agricultural Development Service [*Later, WIIAD*] [*Department of Agriculture*]
**IADS** .......... International Association of Dental Students [*British*]
**IADS** .......... International Association of Department Stores [*See also AIGM*] (EAIO)
**IADS Newsl** ... International Association of Dental Students. Newsletter [*A publication*]
**IADT** ......... Initial Active Duty for Training [*Military*] (AABC)
**IADT** ......... Integrated Automatic Detection and Tracking [*Military*] (CAAL)
**IaDu** .......... Carnegie-Stout Free Public Library, Dubuque, IA [*Library symbol*] [*Library of Congress*] (LCLS)
**IaDuA** ........ Aquinas Institute, Dubuque, IA [*Library symbol*] [*Library of Congress*] (LCLS)
**IaDuAn** ...... Antique Trade Weekly, Dubuque, IA [*Library symbol*] [*Library of Congress*] (LCLS)
**IaDuCl** ....... Clarke College, Dubuque, IA [*Library symbol*] [*Library of Congress*] (LCLS)
**IaDuCo** ...... Clarke Courier, Dubuque, IA [*Library symbol*] [*Library of Congress*] (LCLS)
**IaDuL** ........ Loras College, Dubuque, IA [*Library symbol*] [*Library of Congress*] (LCLS)
**IaDuLe** ....... Dubuque Leader, Dubuque, IA [*Library symbol*] [*Library of Congress*] (LCLS)
**IaDuN** ........ New Melleray Abbey, Dubuque, IA [*Library symbol*] [*Library of Congress*] (LCLS)
**IaDunR** ...... Dunlap Reporter, Dunlap, IA [*Library symbol*] [*Library of Congress*] (LCLS)
**IaDuT** ........ Schools of Theology in Dubuque, Dubuque, IA [*Library symbol*] [*Library of Congress*] (LCLS)
**IaDuU** ........ University of Dubuque, Dubuque, IA [*Library symbol*] [*Library of Congress*] (LCLS)
**IaDuU-S** .... University of Dubuque, Theological Seminary, Dubuque, IA [*Library symbol*] [*Library of Congress*] (LCLS)
**IaDuW** ....... Wartburg Theological Seminary, Dubuque, IA [*Library symbol*] [*Library of Congress*] (LCLS)
**IaDuWi** ...... Dubuque Witness, Dubuque, IA [*Library symbol*] [*Library of Congress*] (LCLS)
**IaDv** ........... Denver Public Library, Denver, IA [*Library symbol*] [*Library of Congress*] (LCLS)
**IaDvF** ......... Forum, Denver, IA [*Library symbol*] [*Library of Congress*] (LCLS)
**IADWS** ...... Interim Air Defense Weapon System [*Army*]
**IaDy** .......... Matthias M. Hoffman Public Library, Dyersville, IA [*Library symbol*] [*Library of Congress*] (LCLS)
**IaDyC** ........ Dyersville Commercial, Dyersville, IA [*Library symbol*] [*Library of Congress*] (LCLS)
**IaDysR** ....... Dysart Reporter, Dysart, IA [*Library symbol*] [*Library of Congress*] (LCLS)
**IaE** ............. Eagle Grove Public Library, Eagle Grove, IA [*Library symbol*] [*Library of Congress*] (LCLS)
**IAE** ............ Felician College, Chicago, IL [*OCLC symbol*] (OCLC)
**IAE** ............ India Economic Bulletin [*A publication*]
**IAE** ............ Infrared Auroral Emission
**IAE** ............ Institut d'Administration des Entreprises [*Institute of Company Management*] [*Information service or system*] (IID)
**IAE** ............ Institute for the Advancement of Engineering (EA)
**IAE** ............ Institute of Atomic Energy [*Academy of Sciences, USSR*]
**IAE** ............ Institute of Automobile Engineers
**IAE** ............ Integral of Absolute Error
**IAE** ............ Inter-Asia Equities [*Vancouver Stock Exchange symbol*]
**IAE** ............ International Association of Ethicists (EA)
**IAE** ............ Internationales Archiv fuer Ethnographie [*A publication*]
**IAE** ............ Iscrizioni Antico-Ebraici Palestinesi (BJA)
**IAE** ............ Iskra Associated Enterprise [*Yugoslavia*] [*Telecommunications*]
**IAEA** .......... Inter-American Education Association (EA)
**IAEA** .......... International Agricultural Exchange Association [*Edinburgh, Scotland*] (EA)
**IAEA** .......... International Association for Educational Assessment (EA)
**IAEA** .......... International Association of Empirical Aesthetics [*Paris, France*] (EAIO)
**IAEA** .......... International Atomic Energy Agency [*United Nations*] [*Austria*] [*Database originator and operator*]
**IAEA Bibliogr Ser** ... International Atomic Energy Agency. Bibliographical Series [*A publication*]
**IAEA Bull** ... International Atomic Energy Agency. Bulletin [*A publication*]
**IAEAC** ....... International Association of Environmental Analytical Chemistry [*Therwil, Switzerland*] (EAIO)
**IAEACPD** ... Inter-American Emergency Advisory Committee for Political Defense
**IAEA Proc Ser** ... International Atomic Energy Agency. Proceedings Series [*A publication*]
**IaEarE** ....... Earlham Echo, Earlham, IA [*Library symbol*] [*Library of Congress*] (LCLS)
**IaEarv** ........ Ruth Suckhow Memorial Library, Earlville, IA [*Library symbol*] [*Library of Congress*] (LCLS)
**IaEaryN** ..... Early News, Early, IA [*Library symbol*] [*Library of Congress*] (LCLS)
**IAEA Saf Ser** ... International Atomic Energy Agency. Safety Series [*A publication*]
**IAEA Tech Rep Ser** ... International Atomic Energy Agency. Technical Report Series [*A publication*]
**IAEC** .......... International Association of Electrical Contractors [*See also AIE*] (EAIO)
**IAEC** .......... International Association of Environmental Coordinators [*Belgium*] (DCTA)
**IAEC** .......... International Atomic Energy Committee
**IAECOSOC** ... Inter-American Economic and Social Council [*United Nations*]
**IAED** ......... International Association of Exchange Dealers [*London, England*] (EA)
**IaEdd** ......... Eddyville Public Library, Eddyville, IA [*Library symbol*] [*Library of Congress*] (LCLS)
**IaEddT** ....... Eddyville Tribune, Eddyville, IA [*Library symbol*] [*Library of Congress*] (LCLS)
**IaEdgR** ....... Edgewood Reminder, Edgewood, IA [*Library symbol*] [*Library of Congress*] (LCLS)
**IAEDP** ....... International Association of Eating Disorders Professionals (EA)
**IaEE** ........... Eagle, Eagle Grove, IA [*Library symbol*] [*Library of Congress*] (LCLS)
**IAeE** ........... Institute of Aeronautical Engineers
**IAEE** .......... International Association for Earthquake Engineering [*ICSU*] [*Tokyo, Japan*] (EAIO)
**IAEE** .......... International Association of Energy Economists (EA)
**IAEG** ......... International Association of Engineering Geology [*International Union of Geological Sciences*] [*ICSU*] [*Paris, France*] (EA)
**IAEHD** ...... International Archives of Occupational and Environmental Health [*A publication*]

**IAEHDW** .. International Archives of Occupational and Environmental Health [*A publication*]
**IAEI** .......... International Association of Electrical Inspectors (EA)
**IAEJ** .......... Interfaith Action for Economic Justice (EA)
**IAEL** .......... Initial Allowance Equipage List [*Military*] (CAAL)
**IAEL** .......... International Association of Electrical Leagues [*Later, ILEA*] (EA)
**IAEL** .......... International Association of Entertainment Lawyers [*Amsterdam, Netherlands*] (EAIO)
**IAEL** .......... International Association for Esperanto in Libraries [*See also TEBA*] (EAIO)
**IaElbTHi** ... Tama County Historical Society, Elberon, IA [*Library symbol*] [*Library of Congress*] (LCLS)
**IaEld** .......... Eldon Carnegie Library, Eldon, IA [*Library symbol*] [*Library of Congress*] (LCLS)
**IaEldF** ........ Eldon Forum, Eldon, IA [*Library symbol*] [*Library of Congress*] (LCLS)
**IaEldoHHi** ... Hardin County Historical Society, Eldora, IA [*Library symbol*] [*Library of Congress*] (LCLS)
**IaEldoHL** .. Herald-Ledger, Eldora, IA [*Library symbol*] [*Library of Congress*] (LCLS)
**IaEldoI** ....... Hardin County Index, Eldora, IA [*Library symbol*] [*Library of Congress*] (LCLS)
**IaEldr** ......... Scott County Library, Eldridge, IA [*Library symbol*] [*Library of Congress*] (LCLS)
**IaEldrN** ...... North Scott Press, Eldridge, IA [*Library symbol*] [*Library of Congress*] (LCLS)
**IaElgE** ........ Elgin Echo, Elgin, IA [*Library symbol*] [*Library of Congress*] (LCLS)
**IaElk** .......... Elkader Public Library, Elkader, IA [*Library symbol*] [*Library of Congress*] (LCLS)
**IaElkCR** ..... Clayton County Register, Elkader, IA [*Library symbol*] [*Library of Congress*] (LCLS)
**IaElkHi** ...... Elkader Historical Society, Elkader, IA [*Library symbol*] [*Library of Congress*] (LCLS)
**IaElkhR** ..... Elk Horn-Kimballton Review, Elk Horn, IA [*Library symbol*] [*Library of Congress*] (LCLS)
**IaEll** ........... Elliott Public Library, Elliott, IA [*Library symbol*] [*Library of Congress*] (LCLS)
**IaElmR** ...... Elma Reminder, Elma, IA [*Library symbol*] [*Library of Congress*] (LCLS)
**IaEls** .......... Ellsworth Public Library, Ellsworth, IA [*Library symbol*] [*Library of Congress*] (LCLS)
**IaEm** .......... Emmetsburg Public Library, Emmetsburg, IA [*Library symbol*] [*Library of Congress*] (LCLS)
**IAEMAA** ... Indian Council of Agricultural Research. Entomological Monographs [*A publication*]
**IAEMS** ...... International Association of Environmental Mutagen Societies [*Helsinki, Finland*] (EAIO)
**IAEN** ......... Department of Indian and Northern Affairs. Education Section. Northern Services Division. Newsletter [*A publication*]
**IAEP** .......... International Academy of Eclectic Psychotherapists [*St. Ives, NSW, Australia*] (EAIO)
**IaEpD** ........ Divine Word College, Epworth, IA [*Library symbol*] [*Library of Congress*] (LCLS)
**IAEPO** ....... International Association of Educational Peace Officers (EA)
**IAER** .......... Institute of Applied Economic Research [*Concordia University*] [*Canada*] [*Research center*] (RCD)
**IaEs** ............ Estherville Public Library, Estherville, IA [*Library symbol*] [*Library of Congress*] (LCLS)
**IAES** .......... Institute of Aerospace [*formerly, Aeronautical*] Sciences
**IAES** .......... International Association of Electrotypers and Stereotypers [*Later, Printing Platemakers Association*]
**IAESC** ....... Inter-American Economic and Social Council [*United Nations*]
**IAESC** ....... International Association of Evening Student Councils [*Later, USAES*] (EA)
**IaEsN** ......... Estherville Daily News, Estherville, IA [*Library symbol*] [*Library of Congress*] (LCLS)
**IAESR** ....... Institute of Applied Economic and Social Research [*Australia*]
**IAESTE** ..... International Association for the Exchange of Students for Technical Experience [*Lisbon, Portugal*] (EAIO)
**IAESTE/US** ... International Association for the Exchange of Students for Technical Experience - United States [*Later, AIPT*]
**IaEsxFN** .... First National Bank, Essex, IA [*Library symbol*] [*Library of Congress*] (LCLS)
**IaEsxI** ........ Essex Independent, Essex, IA [*Library symbol*] [*Library of Congress*] (LCLS)
**IAET** .......... In-Flight Aeromedical Evacuation Team
**IAET** .......... International Association for Enterostomal Therapy (EA)
**IAETF** ....... International Anti-Euthanasia Task Force (EA)
**IAETL** ....... International Association of Environmental Testing Laboratories (EA)
**IaEveN** ....... Everly News, Everly, IA [*Library symbol*] [*Library of Congress*] (LCLS)
**IAEVG** ....... International Association for Educational and Vocational Guidance [*See also AIOSP*] [*Belfast, Northern Ireland*] (EAIO)
**IAEVI** ........ International Association for Educational and Vocational Information [*See also AIISUP*] [*Paris, France*] (EAIO)
**IaEvS** ......... Black Hawk County Sun, Evansdale, IA [*Library symbol*] [*Library of Congress*] (LCLS)
**IAEWP** ...... International Association of Educators for World Peace (EA)
**IaExJ** ......... Audubon County Journal, Exira, IA [*Library symbol*] [*Library of Congress*] (LCLS)
**IAF** ............ First Australia Fund, Inc. [*AMEX symbol*] (SPSG)
**IAF** ............ Governors State University, Park Forest South, IL [*OCLC symbol*] (OCLC)
**IAF** ............ Independent Air Force [*British military*] (DMA)
**IAF** ............ Indian Air Force
**IAF** ............ Indian Army Form [*British military*] (DMA)
**IAF** ............ Indian Auxiliary Force [*British*]
**IAF** ............ Indium Arsenide Filter
**IAF** ............ Indonesian Air Force
**IAF** ............ Industrial Areas Foundation (EA)
**IAF** ............ Information and Forwarding (MUGU)
**IAF** ............ Initial Approach Fix [*Aviation*] (AFM)
**IAF** ............ Initiative America Foundation (EA)
**IAF** ............ Institut Armand-Frappier [*University of Quebec*] [*Formerly, Institute of Microbiology and Hygiene of Montreal*] [*Research center*] (RCD)
**IAF** ............ Institute for Alternative Futures [*Defunct*] (EA)
**IAF** ............ Institute on American Freedoms [*Defunct*]
**IAF** ............ Instrument Air Filter
**IAF** ............ Instrument Approach Fix
**IAF** ............ Inter-American Foundation (MCD)
**IAF** ............ Interactive Facility [*Control Data Corp.*]
**IAF** ............ Interallied Force [*NATO*] (NATG)
**IAF** ............ International Abolitionist Federation [*India*]
**IAF** ............ International Activities Fund [*Canadian Labour Congress*] [*See also FAI*]
**IAF** ............ International Aeronautical Federation
**IAF** ............ International Aikido Federation [*Tokyo, Japan*] (EAIO)
**IAF** ............ International Apparel Federation [*Berlin, Federal Republic of Germany*] (EAIO)
**IAF** ............ International Aquaculture Foundation (EA)
**IAF** ............ International Arab Federation
**IAF** ............ International Archery Federation (EA)
**IAF** ............ International Association for Falconry and Conservation of Birds of Prey (EAIO)
**IAF** ............ International Astronautical Federation [*France*]
**IAF** ............ International Athletic Footwear and Apparel Manufacturers Association [*Zurich, Switzerland*] (EAIO)
**IAF** ............ International Autumn Fair [*British*] (ITD)
**IAF** ............ Internationales Afrikaforum [*A publication*]
**IAF** ............ Intra-Alaska Facsimile [*National Weather Service*]
**IAF** ............ Israel Air Force (BJA)
**IAF** ............ Italian Air Force (NATG)
**IAF** ............ Italian American Forum (EA)
**IAF** ............ Office of Information for the Armed Forces (AABC)
**IAFA** .......... Inter-American Foundation for the Arts [*Defunct*]
**IAFA** .......... International Association for the Fantastic in the Arts (EA)
**IAFA** .......... International Aviation Facilities Act [*1948*]
**IAFAE** ....... Inter-American Federation for Adult Education
**IaFair** ......... Fairfield Public Library, Fairfield, IA [*Library symbol*] [*Library of Congress*] (LCLS)
**IaFairL** ....... Fairfield Daily Ledger, Fairfield, IA [*Library symbol*] [*Library of Congress*] (LCLS)
**IaFairM** ..... Maharishi International University, Fairfield, IA [*Library symbol*] [*Library of Congress*] (LCLS)
**IaFarmL** ..... Van Buren County Leader, Farmington, IA [*Library symbol*] [*Library of Congress*] (LCLS)
**IaFay** .......... Fayette Community Library, Fayette, IA [*Library symbol*] [*Library of Congress*] (LCLS)
**IaFayHHi** .. Fayette County Helpers Club and Historical Society, Fayette, IA [*Library symbol*] [*Library of Congress*] (LCLS)
**IaFayL** ....... Fayette Leader, Fayette, IA [*Library symbol*] [*Library of Congress*] (LCLS)
**IaFayU** ....... Upper Iowa University, Fayette, IA [*Library symbol*] [*Library of Congress*] (LCLS)
**IAFB** .......... Interim Airframe Bulletin
**IAFBAG** .... International Commission for the Northwest Atlantic Fisheries. Research Bulletin [*A publication*]
**IAFC** .......... Instantaneous Automatic Frequency Control
**IAFC** .......... Inter-American Freight Conference - Section C (EA)
**IAFC** .......... Interim Airframe Change (NG)
**IAFC** .......... International Association of Fire Chiefs (EA)
**IAFC** .......... Irwin Allen Fan Club [*Defunct*] (EA)
**IAFCF** ........ International Association of Fire Chiefs Foundation (EA)
**IAFCI** ........ Inter-American Federation of the Construction Industry [*See also FIIC*] [*Mexico City, Mexico*] (EAIO)
**IaFcS** .......... Forest City Summit, Forest City, IA [*Library symbol*] [*Library of Congress*] (LCLS)
**IAFCT** ....... International Association of French-Speaking Congress Towns [*See also AIVFC*] [*Angers, France*] (EAIO)
**IaFcW** ........ Waldorf College, Forest City, IA [*Library symbol*] [*Library of Congress*] (LCLS)
**IaFd** ............ Fort Dodge Public Library, Fort Dodge, IA [*Library symbol*] [*Library of Congress*] (LCLS)
**IAFD** .......... International Association on Food Distribution
**IaFdIC** ....... Iowa Central Community College, Fort Dodge, IA [*Library symbol*] [*Library of Congress*] (LCLS)

**IaFdM**........ Fort Dodge Messenger, Fort Dodge, IA [*Library symbol*] [*Library of Congress*] (LCLS)
**IAFE**.......... International Association of Fairs and Expositions (EA)
**IAFE**.......... International Association of Fish Ethologists [*Normal, IL*] (ASF)
**IAFES**........ International Association for the Economics of Self-Management [*Belgrade, Yugoslavia*] (EAIO)
**IAFF**.......... International Air Freight Forwarder (AABC)
**IAFF**.......... International Association of Fire Fighters (EA)
**IAFI**........... Infantile Amaurotic Family Idiocy [*Medicine*]
**IAFLUP**..... International Association of French-Language University Presses (EA)
**IaFm**........... Cattermole Memorial Library, Fort Madison, IA [*Library symbol*] [*Library of Congress*] (LCLS)
**IaFmD**........ Fort Madison Democrat, Fort Madison, IA [*Library symbol*] [*Library of Congress*] (LCLS)
**IaFmLHi**.... North Lee County Historical Society, Fort Madison, IA [*Library symbol*] [*Library of Congress*] (LCLS)
**IAFMM**..... International Association of Fish Meal Manufacturers [*Potters Bar, Hertfordshire, England*] (EAIO)
**IaFon**.......... Fonda Public Library, Fonda, IA [*Library symbol*] [*Library of Congress*] (LCLS)
**IaFonT**....... Fonda Times, Fonda, IA [*Library symbol*] [*Library of Congress*] (LCLS)
**IaFontO**..... Fontanelle Observer, Fontanelle, IA [*Library symbol*] [*Library of Congress*] (LCLS)
**IAFP**.......... Intergovernmental Affairs Fellowship Program (RDA)
**IAFP**.......... International Alliance of Film Producers [*Later, IAIP*] (EA)
**IAFP**.......... International Association of Filipino Patriots (EA)
**IAFP**.......... International Association for Financial Planning (EA)
**IAFPAO**.... International Commission for the Northwest Atlantic Fisheries. Special Publication [*A publication*]
**IAFPE**........ Indian American Forum for Political Education (EA)
**IaFre**.......... Upham Memorial Library, Fredericksburg, IA [*Library symbol*] [*Library of Congress*] (LCLS)
**IaFremG**.... Fremont Gazette, Fremont, IA [*Library symbol*] [*Library of Congress*] (LCLS)
**IaFreN**....... Fredericksburg News, Fredericksburg, IA [*Library symbol*] [*Library of Congress*] (LCLS)
**IAFS**.......... International Animated Film Society (EA)
**IAFS**.......... International Association of Family Sociology (EA)
**IAFS**.......... International Association for Food Self-Sufficiency (EA)
**IAFS**.......... International Association of Forensic Sciences (EA)
**IAFSA**....... International Association of French-Speaking Aircrews (EAIO)
**IAFSDEI**... International Association of French-Speaking Directors of Educational Institutions (EAIO)
**IAFU**.......... Improved Assault Fire Units [*Military*] (MCD)
**IAFV**.......... Infantry Armored Fighting Vehicle (NATG)
**IAFVH**....... Indian Advanced Field Veterinary Hospital [*British military*] (DMA)
**IAFWA**...... International Association of Fish and Wildlife Agencies (EA)
**IAFWNO**.. Inter-American Federation of Working Newspapermen's Organizations
**IAG**............ Greenville College, Greenville, IL [*OCLC symbol*] (OCLC)
**IAG**............ Industry Advisory Group [*Underwriters Laboratories*] [*Telecommunications*]
**IAG**............ Informatique et Gestion [*France*] [*A publication*]
**IAG**............ Intelligence Analysis Group [*Military*]
**IAG**............ Inter-Association Group
**IAG**............ Interagency Advisory Group [*Civil Service Commission*]
**IAG**............ Interagency Agreement
**IAG**............ International Academy of Gnathology - American Section (EA)
**IAG**............ International Applications Group [*IFIP*]
**IAG**............ International Art Guild (EA)
**IAG**............ International Association of Geodesy [*ICSU*] [*Paris, France*] (EAIO)
**IAG**............ International Association of Gerontology (EA)
**IAG**............ International Auditing Guideline
**IAG**............ Investitionsauftraggeber [*Capital Investment Contractor*] [*German*]
**IAG**............ Niagara Falls, NY [*Location identifier*] [*FAA*] (FAAL)
**IaG**............ Stewart Public Library, Grinnell, IA [*Library symbol*] [*Library of Congress*] (LCLS)
**IAGA**......... International Association of Geomagnetism and Aeronomy [*Scotland*]
**IAGA**......... International Association of Golf Administrators (EA)
**IAGAE**....... International Association for Gerda Alexander Eutony [*See also AIEGA*] [*Switzerland*] (EAIO)
**IAGAL**....... Industry Advisory Group for Air Logistics
**IaGar**.......... Garner Public Library, Garner, IA [*Library symbol*] [*Library of Congress*] (LCLS)
**IaGarL**....... Garner Leader and Signal and Herald, Garner, IA [*Library symbol*] [*Library of Congress*] (LCLS)
**IaGavoHi**... Garnavillo Historical Society, Garnavillo, IA [*Library symbol*] [*Library of Congress*] (LCLS)
**IaGavoT**..... Granavillo Tribune, Granavillo, IA [*Library symbol*] [*Library of Congress*] (LCLS)
**IaGc**........... Gilmore City Public Library, Gilmore City, IA [*Library symbol*] [*Library of Congress*] (LCLS)
**IAGC**......... Instantaneous Automatic Gain Control [*or Circuit*] [*RADAR*]
**IAGC**......... International Association of Geochemistry and Cosmochemistry [*Edmonton, AB*] (EA)
**IAGC**......... International Association of Geophysical Contractors (EA)
**IAGCBP**.... Contributi. Istituto di Ricerche Agrarie Milano [*A publication*]
**IAGCW**..... International Association of Greeting Card Workers
**IaGen**......... Iowa State Genealogical Society, Genealogical Library, Des Moines, IA [*Library symbol*] [*Library of Congress*] (LCLS)
**IaGeoN**...... Lyon County News, George, IA [*Library symbol*] [*Library of Congress*] (LCLS)
**IAGFA**....... International Association of Governmental Fair Agencies (EA)
**IAGFA**....... Izvestiya Akademii Nauk SSSR Seriya Geofizicheskaya [*A publication*]
**IAGFCC**.... International Association of Game, Fish, and Conservation Commissioners [*Later, IAFWA*] (EA)
**IaGG**.......... Grinnell College, Grinnell, IA [*Library symbol*] [*Library of Congress*] (LCLS)
**IAGGA**...... Izvestiya Akademii Nauk Armyanskoi SSR Geologicheskie i Geograficheskie Nauki [*A publication*]
**IaGHR**....... Herald-Register, Grinnell, IA [*Library symbol*] [*Library of Congress*] (LCLS)
**IAG J**......... IAG [*International Federation for Information Processing. Administrative Data Processing Group*] Journal [*A publication*]
**IaGjG**......... Globe Free Press, Grand Junction, IA [*Library symbol*] [*Library of Congress*] (LCLS)
**IAGL**.......... Interactive Applicon Graphics Language [*Automotive engineering*]
**IaGleOT**.... Opinion-Tribune, Glenwood, IA [*Library symbol*] [*Library of Congress*] (LCLS)
**IaGliG**........ Glidden Graphic, Glidden, IA [*Library symbol*] [*Library of Congress*] (LCLS)
**IAG Lit Auto**... IAG [*International Federation for Information Processing. Administrative Data Processing Group*] Literature on Automation [*A publication*]
**IAGLL**....... International Association of Germanic Languages and Literatures [*See also IVG*] (EAIO)
**IAGLO**...... International Association of Governmental Labor Officials [*Later, NAGLO*] (EA)
**IAGLP**....... International Association of Great Lakes Ports (EA)
**IAGLR**....... International Association for Great Lakes Research (EA)
**IAGM**........ International Association of Garment Manufacturers [*Absorbed by NOSA*] (EA)
**IAGMA**..... Illuminating and Allied Glassware Manufacturers Association [*Defunct*] (EA)
**IAGOD**...... International Association of the Genesis of Ore Deposits [*ICSU*] [*Prague, Czechoslovakia*] (EAIO)
**IaGow**........ Gowrie News, Gowrie, IA [*Library symbol*] [*Library of Congress*] (LCLS)
**IAGP**.......... International Antarctic Glaciological Project (EA)
**IAGP**.......... International Association of Group Psychotherapy (EA)
**IAGPBU**.... Investigaciones Agropecuarias [*Lima, Peru*] [*A publication*]
**IaGra**.......... Graettinger Public Library, Graettinger, IA [*Library symbol*] [*Library of Congress*] (LCLS)
**IaGraT**....... Graettinger Times, Graettinger, IA [*Library symbol*] [*Library of Congress*] (LCLS)
**IaGrc**.......... Grundy Center Public Library, Grundy Center, IA [*Library symbol*] [*Library of Congress*] (LCLS)
**IaGrcI**........ Iowa Farm Bureau Spokesman, Grundy Center, IA [*Library symbol*] [*Library of Congress*] (LCLS)
**IaGrcR**....... Grundy Center Register, Grundy Center, IA [*Library symbol*] [*Library of Congress*] (LCLS)
**IAGRD4**.... Investigacion Agricola [*Santiago*] [*A publication*]
**IaGre**.......... Greene Public Library, Greene, IA [*Library symbol*] [*Library of Congress*] (LCLS)
**IAgrE**......... Institution of Agricultural Engineers (EAIO)
**IaGrefFP**.... Adair County Free Press, Greenfield, IA [*Library symbol*] [*Library of Congress*] (LCLS)
**IaGreR**....... Greene Recorder, Greene, IA [*Library symbol*] [*Library of Congress*] (LCLS)
**IaGrisA**...... Griswold American, Griswold, IA [*Library symbol*] [*Library of Congress*] (LCLS)
**IAGS**.......... Inter-American Geodetic Survey
**IAGS**.......... International Association for Germanic Studies (EAIO)
**IaGucG**...... Guthrian, Guthrie Center, IA [*Library symbol*] [*Library of Congress*] (LCLS)
**IaGucT**....... Guthrie Center Times, Guthrie Center, IA [*Library symbol*] [*Library of Congress*] (LCLS)
**IaGut**.......... Guttenberg Public Library, Guttenberg, IA [*Library symbol*] [*Library of Congress*] (LCLS)
**IaGutP**....... Guttenberg Press, Guttenberg, IA [*Library symbol*] [*Library of Congress*] (LCLS)
**IAGYA**....... Izvestiya Akademii Nauk SSSR Seriya Geograficheskaya i Geofizicheskaya [*A publication*]
**IAH**............ Houston [*Texas*] Intercontinental [*Airport symbol*] (OAG)
**IAH**............ Idiopathic Adrenal Hyperplasia [*Medicine*]
**IAH**............ Illinois Institute of Technology, Chicago, IL [*OCLC symbol*] (OCLC)
**IAH**............ Implantable Artificial Heart
**IAH**............ Institute for the Advancement of Health (EA)

**IAH**........... International Association of Hydrogeologists [*Arnhem, Netherlands*] (EA)
**IAH**........... International Association of Hydrology
**IAH**........... Internationales Arbeiter-Hilfswerk [*International Workers Aid*] [*Bonn, Federal Republic of Germany*] (EAIO)
**IAH**........... Island Airlines Hawaii [*Honolulu, HI*] [*FAA designator*] (FAAC)
**IAHA**......... Immune Adherence Hemagglutination [*Immunochemistry*]
**IAHA**......... Inter-American Hospital Association [*Defunct*]
**IAHA**......... Inter-American Hotel Association
**IAHA**......... International Arabian Horse Association (EA)
**IAHA**......... International Association of Historians of Asia [*Quezon City, Philippines*] (EA)
**IAHA**......... International Association of Hospitality Accountants [*Austin, TX*] (EA)
**Ia-HA**......... Iowa State Department of History and Archives, Des Moines, IA [*Library symbol*] [*Library of Congress*] (LCLS)
**IAHAIO**.... International Association of Human-Animal Interaction Organizations (EA)
**IaHamb**...... Hamburg Public Library, Hamburg, IA [*Library symbol*] [*Library of Congress*] (LCLS)
**IaHambR**... Hamburg Reporter, Hamburg, IA [*Library symbol*] [*Library of Congress*] (LCLS)
**IaHampC**... Hampton Chronicle, Hampton, IA [*Library symbol*] [*Library of Congress*] (LCLS)
**IaHampCoC**... Franklin County Courthouse, Hampton, IA [*Library symbol*] [*Library of Congress*] (LCLS)
**IaHampFN**... US Farm News, Hampton, IA [*Library symbol*] [*Library of Congress*] (LCLS)
**IaHampHi**... Franklin County Historical Society, Hampton, IA [*Library symbol*] [*Library of Congress*] (LCLS)
**IaHampJ**... Dumont Journal, Hampton, IA [*Library symbol*] [*Library of Congress*] (LCLS)
**IaHampT**... Hampton Times, Hampton, IA [*Library symbol*] [*Library of Congress*] (LCLS)
**IaHar**......... Harlan Public Library, Harlan, IA [*Library symbol*] [*Library of Congress*] (LCLS)
**IaHarNA**... Harlan News-Advertiser, Harlan, IA [*Library symbol*] [*Library of Congress*] (LCLS)
**IaHarS**....... Shelby County Museum, Harlan, IA [*Library symbol*] [*Library of Congress*] (LCLS)
**IaHarT**....... Harlan Tribune, Harlan, IA [*Library symbol*] [*Library of Congress*] (LCLS)
**IaHart**........ Hartley Public Library, Hartley, IA [*Library symbol*] [*Library of Congress*] (LCLS)
**IaHartS**...... Hartley Sentinel, Hartley, IA [*Library symbol*] [*Library of Congress*] (LCLS)
**IaHaw**........ Hawarden Public Library, Hawarden, IA [*Library symbol*] [*Library of Congress*] (LCLS)
**IAHB**......... Institute for the Advancement of Human Behavior (EA)
**IAHB**......... International Association of Human Biologists [*ICSU*] [*Newcastle-Upon-Tyne, England*] (EAIO)
**IAHCP**....... International Academy of Health Care Professionals (EA)
**IAHCSM**... International Association of Healthcare Central Service Materials Management (EA)
**IAHD**......... International Association of Hillel Directors (EA)
**IAHE**......... International Association for Hydrogen Energy (EA)
**IAHEES**.... Iowa Agriculture and Home Economics Experiment Station [*Iowa State University*] [*Research center*] (RCD)
**IaHeJ**......... Hedrick Journal, Hedrick, IA [*Library symbol*] [*Library of Congress*] (LCLS)
**IAHES**....... Implantable Artificial Heart Energy System
**IAHFIAW**... International Association of Heat and Frost Insulators and Asbestos Workers
**IAHHP**...... International Association of Holistic Health Practitioners (EA)
**IAHI**.......... International Archives of the History of Ideas [*A publication*]
**IAHI**.......... International Association of Hail Insurers (EA)
**IAHI**.......... International Association of Holiday Inns (EA)
**IaHi**............ State Historical Society of Iowa, Iowa City, IA [*Library symbol*] [*Library of Congress*] (LCLS)
**IAHIC**........ International Association of Home Improvement Councils [*Defunct*] (EA)
**IAHM**........ Incorporated Association of Head Masters [*British*]
**IAHM**........ International Academy of the History of Medicine (EA)
**IAHMS**..... International Association of Hotel Management Schools (EA)
**IaHoDHi**... Delaware County Historical Society, Hopkinton, IA [*Library symbol*] [*Library of Congress*] (LCLS)
**IaHoDL**..... Delaware County Leader, Hopkinton, IA [*Library symbol*] [*Library of Congress*] (LCLS)
**IaHoL**........ Lenox College, Hopkinton, IA [*Library symbol*] [*Library of Congress*] (LCLS)
**IaHol**.......... Stubbs Public Library, Holstein, IA [*Library symbol*] [*Library of Congress*] (LCLS)
**IaHolA**....... Holstein Advance, Holstein, IA [*Library symbol*] [*Library of Congress*] (LCLS)
**IAHP**......... Institutes for the Achievement of Human Potential (EA)
**IAHP**......... International Association of Heart Patients [*Formerly, IAPP*] (EA)
**IAHP**......... International Association of Horticultural Producers
**IAHR**......... International Association for the History of Religions [*Marburg, Federal Republic of Germany*] (EAIO)
**IAHR**......... International Association for Hydraulic Research [*ICSU*] [*Delft, Netherlands*] (EA)
**IAHRC**...... Inter-American Human Rights Commission
**IAHS**......... International Academy of the History of Science [*Paris, France*] (EA)
**IAHS**......... International Association for Hospital Security [*Later, IAHSS*] (EA)
**IAHS**......... International Association for Housing Science (EA)
**IAHS**......... International Automotive Hall of Shame (EA)
**IAHSS**....... International Association for Healthcare Security and Safety (EA)
**IAHU**......... International Association of Health Underwriters [*Later, NAHU*] (EA)
**IaHubS**...... South Hardin Signal-Review, Hubbard, IA [*Library symbol*] [*Library of Congress*] (LCLS)
**IaHud**......... Hudson Public Library, Hudson, IA [*Library symbol*] [*Library of Congress*] (LCLS)
**IaHudH**..... Hudson Herald, Hudson, IA [*Library symbol*] [*Library of Congress*] (LCLS)
**IaHuI**......... Sioux County Index, Hull, IA [*Library symbol*] [*Library of Congress*] (LCLS)
**IaHuIR**...... Sioux County Index-Reporter, Hull, IA [*Library symbol*] [*Library of Congress*] (LCLS)
**IaHum**........ Humbolt Public LIbrary, Humbolt, IA [*Library symbol*] [*Library of Congress*] (LCLS)
**IaHume**...... Humeston Public Library, Humeston, IA [*Library symbol*] [*Library of Congress*] (LCLS)
**IaHumeN**... Humeston New Era, Humeston, IA [*Library symbol*] [*Library of Congress*] (LCLS)
**IaHumHi**... Humbolt County Historical Association, Humbolt, IA [*Library symbol*] [*Library of Congress*] (LCLS)
**IaHumI**...... Humbolt Independent, Humbolt, IA [*Library symbol*] [*Library of Congress*] (LCLS)
**IaHumR**..... Humbolt Republican, Humbolt, IA [*Library symbol*] [*Library of Congress*] (LCLS)
**IaHweye**..... Hawkeye Public Library, Hawkeye, IA [*Library symbol*] [*Library of Congress*] (LCLS)
**IAI**............. Hayner Public Library, Alton, IL [*Library symbol*] [*Library of Congress*] (LCLS)
**IAI**............. Illinois State University, Normal, IL [*OCLC symbol*] (OCLC)
**IAI**............. Inactive Aerospace Vehicle [*or Aircraft*] Inventory
**IAI**............. Infertility Associates International [*Commercial firm*] (EA)
**IAI**............. Information Associates of Ithaca [*Information service or system*] (IID)
**IAI**............. Informational Acquisition and Interpretation
**IAI**............. Initial Address Information [*Telecommunications*] (TEL)
**IAI**............. Integrated Aircraft Instrumentation
**IAI**............. International African Institute [*London, England*]
**IAI**............. International Apple Institute (EA)
**IAI**............. International Association for Identification (EA)
**IAI**............. International Association of Incubators (EA)
**IAI**............. Ion Atom Interaction
**IAI**............. Isethionyl Acetimidate [*Biochemistry*]
**IAI**............. Israel Aircraft Industries Ltd.
**IAI**............. Istituto Affairi Internazionali [*Institute for International Affairs*] [*Italy*]
**IAI**............. Izvestija na Bulgarskija Archeologiceski Institut [*A publication*]
**IAIA**.......... Institute of American Indian and Alaska Native Culture and Arts Development (EA)
**IAIA**.......... International Association for Impact Assessment (EA)
**IaIa**............ Iowa City Public Library, Iowa City, IA [*Library symbol*] [*Library of Congress*] (LCLS)
**IAIAA**........ International Association for Iranian Art and Archaeology (EA)
**IAIABC**..... International Association of Industrial Accident Boards and Commissions (EA)
**IAIAD**........ International Acronyms, Initialisms, and Abbreviations Dictionary [*A publication*]
**IAIAF**........ International Affiliation of Independent Accounting Firms (EA)
**IaIaI**........... Daily Iowan, Iowa City, IA [*Library symbol*] [*Library of Congress*] (LCLS)
**IAIALAR**... Ibero-American Institute of Agrarian Law and Agrarian Reform [*See also IIDARA*] [*Mexida, Venezuela*] (EAIO)
**IaIaP**.......... Iowa City Press-Citizen, Iowa City, IA [*Library symbol*] [*Library of Congress*] (LCLS)
**IAIAS**........ Inter-American Institute of Agricultural Sciences [*Later, IICA*] [*OAS*]
**IaIaS**.......... Seven Rivers Library Cooperative, Iowa City, IA [*Library symbol*] [*Library of Congress*] (LCLS)
**IAIB**.......... International Association of Islamic Banks
**IAIC**.......... International Association of Insurance Counsel [*Later, IADC*] (EA)
**IAICM**....... International Association of Ice Cream Manufacturers [*Later, IICA*] (EA)
**IAICU**........ International Association of Independent Colleges and Universities (EA)
**IAID**.......... Indium Arsenide Infrared Detector
**IaIdgIHi**..... Ida County Historical Society, Ida Grove, IA [*Library symbol*] [*Library of Congress*] (LCLS)

**IaIdgPR** ..... Ida County Pioneer-Record, Ida Grove, IA [*Library symbol*] [*Library of Congress*] (LCLS)
**IAIDPA** ..... International Association for Information and Documentation in Public Administration (EAIO)
**IAIE** .......... Inter-American Institute of Ecology [*Ecological Society of America*]
**IAIE** .......... International Association for Integrative Education [*Versoix, Switzerland*] (EAIO)
**IAIES** ......... Institute for Advanced Interdisciplinary Engineering Studies [*Purdue University*] (MCD)
**IAIES** ......... International Association of Intermodal Equipment Surveyors (EA)
**IaIf** ............ Carnegie Ellsworth Public Library, Iowa Falls, IA [*Library symbol*] [*Library of Congress*] (LCLS)
**IaIfC** .......... Iowa Falls Citizen, Iowa Falls, Iowa [*Library symbol*] [*Library of Congress*] (LCLS)
**IaIfE** ........... Ellsworth Commumity College, Iowa Falls, IA [*Library symbol*] [*Library of Congress*] (LCLS)
**IaIfT** ........... Hardin County Times, Iowa Falls, IA [*Library symbol*] [*Library of Congress*] (LCLS)
**IAI/I** .......... Indiana. Beitraege zur Voelker- und Sprachenkunde, Archaeologie, und Anthropologie des Indianischen Amerika. Ibero-Amerikanisches Institut [*A publication*]
**IAII** ............ Inter-American Indian Institute [*OAS*] [*Mexico City, Mexico*] (EA)
**IAIMS** ....... Integrated Academic Information Management System [*Georgetown University Medical Center*]
**IAIN** .......... International Association of Institutes of Navigation [*London, England*] (EAIO)
**IaIndianR** .. Record-Herald and Tribune, Indianola, IA [*Library symbol*] [*Library of Congress*] (LCLS)
**IaIndianS** ... Simpson College, Indianola, IA [*Library symbol*] [*Library of Congress*] (LCLS)
**IaIndpC** ...... Independence Conservative, Independence, IA [*Library symbol*] [*Library of Congress*] (LCLS)
**IaIndpCoC** ... Buchanan County Courthouse, Independence, IA [*Library symbol*] [*Library of Congress*] (LCLS)
**IaInwH** ...... West Lyon Herald, Inwood, IA [*Library symbol*] [*Library of Congress*] (LCLS)
**IaIonCHi** ... Chickasaw County Historical Society, Ionia, IA [*Library symbol*] [*Library of Congress*] (LCLS)
**IAIP** ........... Inorganic Ablative Insulative Plastic
**IAIP** ........... International Association of Independent Producers (EA)
**IAIP** ........... International Association of Individual Psychology (EA)
**IAIPS** .......... Integrated Automated Intelligence Processing System (MCD)
**IAIR** ........... Independent Air Holdings, Inc. [*Hapeville, GA*] [*NASDAQ symbol*] (NQ)
**IAIRI** ......... International Association of Insurance and Reinsurance Intermediaries [*See also BIPAR*] [*Paris, France*] (EAIO)
**IAIRS** ........ Installation Aircraft Inventory Reporting System [*Army*]
**IAIS** ........... Indian and Inuit Supporter. A Newsletter of the Indian and Inuit Support Group of Newfoundland and Labrador [*A publication*]
**IAIS** ........... Industrial Aerodynamics Information Service [*British*] (IID)
**IAIS** ........... International Association of Independent Scholars (EA)
**IAIU** ........... Insurance Agents International Union
**IAJ** ............. Institute for Administrative Justice [*University of the Pacific*] [*Research center*] (RCD)
**IAJ** ............. International Association of Judges [*Rome, Italy*] (EAIO)
**IA J** ............ Iowa Journal of History and Politics [*A publication*]
**IaJ** .............. Jefferson Public Library, Jefferson, IA [*Library symbol*] [*Library of Congress*] (LCLS)
**IAJAM** ...... Industrial Association of Juvenile Apparel Manufacturers (EA)
**IAJAP** ........ International Association of Jai Alai Players (EA)
**IaJB** ........... Jefferson Bee, Jefferson, IA [*Library symbol*] [*Library of Congress*] (LCLS)
**IAJBBSC** ... International Association of Jim Beam Bottle and Specialties Clubs (EA)
**IAJC** .......... Inter-American Juridical Committee
**IAJE** .......... Internacia Socio de Juristoj-Esperantistoj [*International Association of Esperantist Lawyers*]
**IAJE** .......... International Association of Jazz Educators (EA)
**IaJesC** ........ Jesup Citizen Herald, Jesup, IA [*Library symbol*] [*Library of Congress*] (LCLS)
**IaJew** ......... Montgomery Memorial Library, Jewell, IA [*Library symbol*] [*Library of Congress*] (LCLS)
**IaJewR** ....... South Hamilton Record-News, Jewell, IA [*Library symbol*] [*Library of Congress*] (LCLS)
**IAJFCM** .... International Association of Juvenile and Family Court Magistrates [*Paris, France*] (EA)
**IaJGCoC** .... Greene County Courthouse, Jefferson IA [*Library symbol*] [*Library of Congress*] (LCLS)
**IaJH** ........... Jefferson Herald, Jefferson, IA [*Library symbol*] [*Library of Congress*] (LCLS)
**IaJoN** ......... Northern Polk County News, Johnston, IA [*Library symbol*] [*Library of Congress*] (LCLS)
**IAJRC** ....... IAJRC [*International Association of Jazz Record Collectors*] Journal [*A publication*]
**IAJRC** ....... International Association of Jazz Record Collectors (EA)
**IAJS** ........... Index of Articles on Jewish Studies [*A publication*]
**IAJS** ........... International Al Jolson Society (EA)
**IAJV** .......... International Association of Justice Volunteerism (EA)
**IAK** ............ Information Economique Africaine [*A publication*]
**IAK** ............ Internationales Auschwitz-Komitee [*International Auschwitz Committee*] [*Warsaw, Poland*] (EAIO)
**IaK** ............. Keokuk Public Library, Keokuk, IA [*Library symbol*] [*Library of Congress*] (LCLS)
**IAK** ............ Lake Forest College, Lake Forest, IL [*OCLC symbol*] (OCLC)
**IaKalN** ....... Kalona News, Kalona, IA [*Library symbol*] [*Library of Congress*] (LCLS)
**IaKan** ......... Kanawha Public Library, Kanawha, IA [*Library symbol*] [*Library of Congress*] (LCLS)
**IaKanR** ...... Kanawha Reporter, Kanawha, IA [*Library symbol*] [*Library of Congress*] (LCLS)
**IaKanRL** .... Rural Life, Kanawha, IA [*Library symbol*] [*Library of Congress*] (LCLS)
**IAKE** .......... International Association of Knowledge Engineers (EA)
**IaKe** ........... Keosauqua Public Library, Keosauqua, IA [*Library symbol*] [*Library of Congress*] (LCLS)
**IaKen** ......... Kensett Public Library, Kensett, IA [*Library symbol*] [*Library of Congress*] (LCLS)
**IaKeoE** ....... Keota Eagle, Keota, IA [*Library symbol*] [*Library of Congress*] (LCLS)
**IaKeVR** ...... Van Buren County Register, Keosauqua, IA [*Library symbol*] [*Library of Congress*] (LCLS)
**IaKey** .......... Keystone Public Library, Keystone, IA [*Library symbol*] [*Library of Congress*] (LCLS)
**IAKF** .......... International Amateur Karate Federation (EA)
**IAKFA** ....... Izvestiya Akademii Nauk Kazakhskoi SSR Seriya Fiziko-Matematicheskikh Nauk [*A publication*]
**IaKG** .......... Keokuk Gate City, Keokuk, IA [*Library symbol*] [*Library of Congress*] (LCLS)
**IaKiN** ......... Kingsley News-Tribune, Kingsley, IA [*Library symbol*] [*Library of Congress*] (LCLS)
**IaKK** .......... Keosippi Library Cooperative, Keokuk, IA [*Library symbol*] [*Library of Congress*] (LCLS)
**IaKn** ........... Knoxville Public Library, Knoxville, IA [*Library symbol*] [*Library of Congress*] (LCLS)
**IaKnE** ......... Knoxville Express, Knoxville, IA [*Library symbol*] [*Library of Congress*] (LCLS)
**IaKnJ** ......... Knoxville Journal, Knoxville, IA [*Library symbol*] [*Library of Congress*] (LCLS)
**IaKnV** ........ United States Veterans Administration Hospital, Knoxville, IA [*Library symbol*] [*Library of Congress*] (LCLS)
**IAKS** .......... Internationaler Arbeitskreis Sport- und Freizeiteninrichtungen [*International Working Group for the Construction of Sports and Leisure Facilities*] (EAIO)
**IAKSA** ....... Izvestiya Akademii Nauk SSSR [*A publication*]
**IAL** ............. Immediate Action Letter (NASA)
**IAL** ............. Imperial Airways Limited [*British*]
**IAL** ............. Industries Alimentaires et Agricoles [*A publication*]
**IAL** ............. Infrared Aiming Light [*Military*] (INF)
**IAL** ............. Inland Airlines
**IAL** ............. Instrument Approach and Landing Chart [*Aviation*]
**IAL** ............. Interlaminar Adhesive Layer
**IAL** ............. International Aeradio Ltd. [*United Kingdom*]
**IAL** ............. International Affairs (London) [*A publication*]
**IAL** ............. International Algebraic Language [*Programming language*] [*Replaced by ALGOL*]
**IAL** ............. International Algorithmic Language [*Data processing*] (BUR)
**IAL** ............. International Aluminum Corp. [*NYSE symbol*] (SPSG)
**IAL** ............. International Association of Laryngectomees (EA)
**IAL** ............. International Association of Linguistics (DIT)
**IAL** ............. International Association of Theoretical and Applied Limnology [*ICSU*] (EA)
**IAL** ............. Investment Analysis Language [*Data processing*] (BUR)
**Ia-L** ............ Iowa State Law Library, Des Moines, IA [*Library symbol*] [*Library of Congress*] (LCLS)
**IaL** .............. Lamoni Public Library, Lamoni, IA [*Library symbol*] [*Library of Congress*] (LCLS)
**IAL** ............. Loyola University, Chicago, IL [*OCLC symbol*] (OCLC)
**IALA** .......... International African Law Association
**IALA** .......... International Association of Lighthouse Authorities [*Paris, France*] (EA)
**IALA** .......... International Auxiliary Language Association [*Later, UMI*]
**IALA** .......... Islamic Alliance for the Liberation of Afghanistan (PD)
**IALAA** ........ Industries Alimentaires et Agricoles [*A publication*]
**IALAB** ........ Lucrari Stiintifice. Institutul Agronomic "Dr. Petru Groza" (Cluj). Seria Agricultura [*A publication*]
**IALACS** ..... International Association of Latin American and Caribbean Studies (EAIO)
**IaLamtL** ..... Lamont Leader, Lamont, IA [*Library symbol*] [*Library of Congress*] (LCLS)
**IaLanJ** ....... Allamakee Journal, Lansing, IA [*Library symbol*] [*Library of Congress*] (LCLS)
**IaLau** .......... Laurens Public Library, Laurens, IA [*Library symbol*] [*Library of Congress*] (LCLS)
**IaLauS** ....... Laurens Sun, Laurens, IA [*Library symbol*] [*Library of Congress*] (LCLS)
**IA Law Rev** ... Iowa Law Review [*A publication*]
**IAlb** ............ Albion Public Library, Albion, IL [*Library symbol*] [*Library of Congress*] (LCLS)

**IAL Bol Inst Adolfo Lutz** ... IAL Boletim. Instituto Adolfo Lutz [*A publication*]
**IALBull**...... Institut Archeologique Liegeois. Bulletin [*A publication*]
**IA L Bull**.... Iowa Law Bulletin [*A publication*] (DLA)
**IALC**.......... Indonesia Australia English Language Centre [*Australia*]
**IALC**.......... Institute of Allegheny Life and Culture (EA)
**IALC**.......... Instrument Approach and Landing Chart [*Aviation*]
**IALC**.......... International Association of Lions Clubs
**IALC**.......... International Association of Lyceum Clubs
**IALC**.......... Irish-American Labor Coalition [*Later, ALCHRNI*] (EA)
**IALC**.......... Italian American Librarians Caucus (EA)
**IaLC**.......... Lamoni Chronicle, Lamoni, IA [*Library symbol*] [*Library of Congress*] (LCLS)
**IaLcG**......... Lake City Graphic, Lake City, IA [*Library symbol*] [*Library of Congress*] (LCLS)
**IALCO**....... International Aircraft Leasing Company
**IAlCU**........ Alton Community Unit 11, Alton, IL [*Library symbol*] [*Library of Congress*] (LCLS)
**IALD**.......... International Association of Lighting Designers (EA)
**IAlE**........... East Alton Elementary 13, Alton, IL [*Library symbol*] [*Library of Congress*] (LCLS)
**IALE**.......... Instrumented Architectural Level Emulation
**IALEFI**...... International Association of Law Enforcement Firearms Instructors (EA)
**IALEIA**...... International Association of Law Enforcement Intelligence Analysts (EA)
**IaLem**......... Le Mars Public Library, Le Mars, IA [*Library symbol*] [*Library of Congress*] (LCLS)
**IaLemS**...... Daily Sentinel, Le Mars, IA [*Library symbol*] [*Library of Congress*] (LCLS)
**IaLemW**..... Westmar College, Le Mars, IA [*Library symbol*] [*Library of Congress*] (LCLS)
**IaLeo**.......... Leon Public Library, Leon, IA [*Library symbol*] [*Library of Congress*] (LCLS)
**IaLeoJR**..... Leon Journal-Reporter, Leon, IA [*Library symbol*] [*Library of Congress*] (LCLS)
**IaLew**......... Lewis Public Library, Lewis, IA [*Library symbol*] [*Library of Congress*] (LCLS)
**IALF**.......... Inter-American Literacy Foundation (EA)
**IALF**.......... International Association of Law Firms (EA)
**IaLG**........... Graceland College, Lamoni, IA [*Library symbol*] [*Library of Congress*] (LCLS)
**IAlH**........... Alton Memorial Hospital, Alton, IL [*Library symbol*] [*Library of Congress*] (LCLS)
**IALHI**........ International Association of Labour History Institutions [*Zurich, Switzerland*] (EAIO)
**IALL**.......... International Association of Law Libraries (EAIO)
**IALL**.......... International Association for Learning Laboratories (EA)
**IALL Bull**.. Bulletin. International Association of Law Libraries [*A publication*] (DLA)
**IALM**......... Integrated Anchor Leg Mooring [*Naval engineering*]
**IALMAB**... Institutul Agronomic "Dr. Petru Groza" (Cluj). Lucrari Stiintifice. Seria Medicina Veterinara si Zootehnie [*A publication*]
**IALMC**...... International Association of Lighting Maintenance Contractors [*Later, NALMCO*] (EA)
**IaLmG**....... Lake Mills Graphic, Lake Mills, IA [*Library symbol*] [*Library of Congress*] (LCLS)
**IAlMH**....... Alton Mental Health Center, Development and Training Center, Staff Library, Alton, IL [*Library symbol*] [*Library of Congress*] (LCLS)
**IaLnP**......... Lost Nation Press, Lost Nation, IA [*Library symbol*] [*Library of Congress*] (LCLS)
**IaLoH**........ Logan Herald-Observer, Logan, IA [*Library symbol*] [*Library of Congress*] (LCLS)
**IaLoHi**....... Harrison County Historical Society, Logan, IA [*Library symbol*] [*Library of Congress*] (LCLS)
**IaLohr**........ J. J. Hands Library, Lohrville, IA [*Library symbol*] [*Library of Congress*] (LCLS)
**IaLowS**....... Sun News, Lowden, IA [*Library symbol*] [*Library of Congress*] (LCLS)
**IALP**.......... International Association of Logopedics and Phoniatrics [*Dublin, Republic of Ireland*] (EA)
**IaLpcPR**.... La Porte City Progress-Review, La Porte City, IA [*Library symbol*] [*Library of Congress*] (LCLS)
**IaLpN**......... Lake Park News, Lake Park, IA [*Library symbol*] [*Library of Congress*] (LCLS)
**IALR**.......... International Anthropological and Linguistic Review [*A publication*]
**IA LR**......... Iowa Law Review [*A publication*]
**IALRB**....... Indian Journal of Animal Research [*A publication*]
**IALRBR**.... Indian Journal of Animal Research [*A publication*]
**IA L Rev**..... Iowa Law Review [*A publication*]
**IALRW**...... International Association of Liberal Religious Women (EA)
**IALS**.......... International Association of Legal Science [*See also AISJ*] [*Paris, France*] (EAIO)
**IAlsA**......... Alsip-Merrionette Park Library District, Alsip, IL [*Library symbol*] [*Library of Congress*] (LCLS)
**IaLsH**......... Lime Springs Herald, Lime Springs, IA [*Library symbol*] [*Library of Congress*] (LCLS)
**IALSSA**..... International Air Line Stewards and Stewardesses Association
**IAlStA**....... Saint Anthony's Hospital, Medical Library, Alton, IL [*Library symbol*] [*Library of Congress*] (LCLS)
**IAlStJ**........ Saint Joseph's Hospital, Medical Information Services, Alton, IL [*Library symbol*] [*Library of Congress*] (LCLS)
**IAlta**.......... Altamont Public Library, Altamont, IL [*Library symbol*] [*Library of Congress*] (LCLS)
**IaLtR**......... Lone Tree Reporter, Lone Tree, IA [*Library symbol*] [*Library of Congress*] (LCLS)
**IaLuHi**....... Lucas County Historical Society, Lucas, IA [*Library symbol*] [*Library of Congress*] (LCLS)
**IaLv**........... Lake View Public Library, Lake View, IA [*Library symbol*] [*Library of Congress*] (LCLS)
**IaLvR**......... Lake View Resort, Lake View, IA [*Library symbol*] [*Library of Congress*] (LCLS)
**IAM**........... Anderson Public Library, Anderson, IN [*OCLC symbol*] (OCLC)
**IAM**........... ILA [*Instruction Look Ahead*] Associative Memory [*Data processing*]
**IAM**........... Immobilized Artificial Membranes [*Chemistry*]
**IAM**........... In Amenas [*Algeria*] [*Airport symbol*] (OAG)
**IAM**........... Incidental Amplitude Modulation
**IAM**........... Indefinite Admittance Matrix [*Network analysis*] (IEEE)
**IAM**........... Initial Address Message (TEL)
**IAM**........... Inscriptions Antiques du Maroc (BJA)
**IAM**........... Institute of Administrative Management [*British*] (DCTA)
**IAM**........... Institute of Advanced Motorists [*British*]
**IAM**........... Institute of the American Musical (EA)
**IAM**........... Institute of Appliance Manufacturers [*Later, GAMA*] (EA)
**IAM**........... Institute of Applied Mathematics [*University of British Columbia*] [*Canada*] [*Research center*] (RCD)
**IAM**........... Institute of Aviation Medicine [*RAF*] [*British*]
**IAM**........... Interactive Algebraic Manipulation [*Data processing*]
**IAM**........... Internal Auditory Meatus [*Anatomy*]
**IAM**........... International Academy of Management [*Knoxville, TN*] (EA)
**IAM**........... International Academy of Metabology (EA)
**IAM**........... International Academy of Myodontics (EA)
**IAM**........... International Academy of Myodontics, Oceanic Chapter [*Sydney, NSW, Australia*] (EAIO)
**IAM**........... International Affairs (Moscow) [*A publication*]
**IAM**........... International Afro-American Museum [*Later, AAM*] (EA)
**IAM**........... International Amco Corp. [*Toronto Stock Exchange symbol*]
**IAM**........... International Association of Machinists and Aerospace Workers (EA)
**IAM**........... International Association of Metaphysicians
**Ia-M**........... Iowa State Medical Library, Des Moines, IA [*Library symbol*] [*Library of Congress*] (LCLS)
**IAM**........... Istanbul Asariatika Muzeleri Nesriyati [*A publication*]
**IAMA**........ Informed Americans Monitor (EA)
**IAMA**........ International Abstaining Motorists' Association [*Hagersten, Sweden*] (EAIO)
**IAMA**........ International Academy of Myodontics, Asian Chapter [*Tokyo, Japan*] (EAIO)
**IAMA**........ International Arts Medicine Association [*Philadelphia, PA*]
**IAMA**........ Intimate Apparel Manufacturers Association (EA)
**IaMa**.......... Marshalltown Public Library, Marshalltown, IA [*Library symbol*] [*Library of Congress*] (LCLS)
**IAMACS**... International Association for Mathematics and Computers in Simulation
**IaMall**........ Mallard Public Library, Mallard, IA [*Library symbol*] [*Library of Congress*] (LCLS)
**IaMalv**....... Malvern Public Library, Malvern, IA [*Library symbol*] [*Library of Congress*] (LCLS)
**IaMalvL**..... Malvern Leader, Malvern, IA [*Library symbol*] [*Library of Congress*] (LCLS)
**IAMAM**.... International Association of Museums of Arms and Military History [*Ingolstadt, Federal Republic of Germany*] (EA)
**IaMancP**.... Manchester Press, Manchester, IA [*Library symbol*] [*Library of Congress*] (LCLS)
**IAMANEH** ... International Association for Maternal and Neonatal Health [*Zurich, Switzerland*] (EAIO)
**IaMannM**.. Manning Monitor, Manning, IA [*Library symbol*] [*Library of Congress*] (LCLS)
**IaManS**...... Marion Sentinel, Marion, IA [*Library symbol*] [*Library of Congress*] (LCLS)
**IaMansJ**.... Manson Journal, Manson, IA [*Library symbol*] [*Library of Congress*] (LCLS)
**IaManT**..... Manilla Times, Manilla, IA [*Library symbol*] [*Library of Congress*] (LCLS)
**IaManyS**.... Manly Signal, Manly, IA [*Library symbol*] [*Library of Congress*] (LCLS)
**IAMAP**...... International Association of Meteorology and Atmospheric Physics (EA)
**IaMap**........ Mapleton Public Library, Mapleton, IA [*Library symbol*] [*Library of Congress*] (LCLS)
**IaMapP**...... Mapleton Press, Mapleton, IA [*Library symbol*] [*Library of Congress*] (LCLS)
**IaMaq**........ Maquoketa Free Public Library, Maquoketa, IA [*Library symbol*] [*Library of Congress*] (LCLS)
**IaMaqHi**.... Jackson County Historical Society, Maquoketa, IA [*Library symbol*] [*Library of Congress*] (LCLS)

**IaMaqP**...... Maquoketa Community Press, Maquoketa, IA [*Library symbol*] [*Library of Congress*] (LCLS)
**IaMaqS**...... Jackson Sentinel, Maquoketa, IA [*Library symbol*] [*Library of Congress*] (LCLS)
**IaMara**....... Marathon Public Library, Marathon, IA [*Library symbol*] [*Library of Congress*] (LCLS)
**IaMarc**....... Marcus Public Library, Marcus, IA [*Library symbol*] [*Library of Congress*] (LCLS)
**IaMare**....... Marengo Public Library, Marengo, IA [*Library symbol*] [*Library of Congress*] (LCLS)
**IaMarePR** ... Marengo Pioneer-Republican, Marengo, IA [*Library symbol*] [*Library of Congress*] (LCLS)
**IaMari** ....... Marion Carnegie Library, Marion, IA [*Library symbol*] [*Library of Congress*] (LCLS)
**IAMAT**...... International Association for Medical Assistance to Travellers (EA)
**IaMaTR**..... Marshalltown Times-Republican, Marshalltown, IA [*Library symbol*] [*Library of Congress*] (LCLS)
**IaMaxHi**.... Community Historical Society, Maxwell, IA [*Library symbol*] [*Library of Congress*] (LCLS)
**IaMay** ........ Maynard Community Library, Maynard, IA [*Library symbol*] [*Library of Congress*] (LCLS)
**IaMayr**....... Mount Ayr Public Library, Mount Ayr, IA [*Library symbol*] [*Library of Congress*] (LCLS)
**IaMayrHi** .. Ringgold County Historical Society, Mount Ayr, IA [*Library symbol*] [*Library of Congress*] (LCLS)
**IaMayrR**.... Record-News, Mount Ayr, IA [*Library symbol*] [*Library of Congress*] (LCLS)
**IAMB** ........ International Association for the Protection of Monuments and Restoration of Buildings (EAIO)
**IAMBE**...... International Association of Medicine and Biology of Environment [*See also AIMBE*] [*Paris, France*] (EAIO)
**IAMBI**....... Iambic Verse (DSUE)
**IaMbr** ........ Marble Rock Public Library, Marble Rock, IA [*Library symbol*] [*Library of Congress*] (LCLS)
**IAMC** ........ Indian Army Medical Corps
**IAMC** ........ Institute for Advancement of Medical Communication [*Defunct*] (EA)
**IAMC** ........ Institute of Association Management Companies (EA)
**IAMC** ........ Inter-American Markets Corporation [*Latin America*]
**IAMC** ........ Inter-American Music Council (EAIO)
**IAMC** ........ International Association for Mobilization of Creativity
**IaMc** .......... Mason City Public Library, Mason City, IA [*Library symbol*] [*Library of Congress*] (LCLS)
**IAMCA**...... International Association of Milk Control Agencies (EA)
**IaMcG** ....... Mason City Globe-Gazette, Mason City, IA [*Library symbol*] [*Library of Congress*] (LCLS)
**IaMcg** ........ McGregor Public Library, McGregor, IA [*Library symbol*] [*Library of Congress*] (LCLS)
**IaMcgHi**.... McGregor Historical Society, McGregor, IA [*Library symbol*] [*Library of Congress*] (LCLS)
**IaMcgN** ..... North Iowa Times, McGregor, IA [*Library symbol*] [*Library of Congress*] (LCLS)
**IaMcN** ....... North Iowa Cooperative Library Extension, Mason City, IA [*Library symbol*] [*Library of Congress*] (LCLS)
**IaMcNC**..... North Iowa Area Community College, Mason City, IA [*Library symbol*] [*Library of Congress*] (LCLS)
**IAMCR**...... International Association for Mass Communication Research [*Leicester, England*]
**IAMCS**...... International Alliance of Messianic Congregations and Synagogues (EA)
**IAME** ........ International Association of Medical Esperantists (EA)
**IAME** ........ International Association for Modular Exhibitry (EA)
**IAMEA**...... Inter-American Economic Affairs [*A publication*]
**IaMedi** ....... Mediapolis Public Library, Mediapolis, IA [*Library symbol*] [*Library of Congress*] (LCLS)
**IaMediN** .... New Era, Mediapolis, IA [*Library symbol*] [*Library of Congress*] (LCLS)
**IaMel** ......... Melvin Public Library, Melvin, IA [*Library symbol*] [*Library of Congress*] (LCLS)
**IaMelbR** .... Melbourne Record, Melbourne, IA [*Library symbol*] [*Library of Congress*] (LCLS)
**IaMer**......... Merrill Public Library, Merrill, IA [*Library symbol*] [*Library of Congress*] (LCLS)
**IAMFC** ...... International Association for Marriage and Family Counselors (EA)
**IAMFE** ...... International Association on Mechanization of Field Experiments [*Aas, Norway*] (EA)
**IAMFES**.... International Association of Milk, Food, and Environmental Sanitarians (EA)
**IAMFPA** ... International Association of Mouth and Foot Painting Artists (EA)
**IAMFS** ...... International Association for Maxillo-Facial Surgery (EA)
**IAMG**........ International Association for Mathematical Geology (EA)
**IAMHIST** ... International Association of Audio-Visual Media in Historical Research and Education [*Bologna, Italy*] (EAIO)
**IAMI**.......... Iron Age Metalworking International [*Later, Chilton's IAMI Iron Age Metalworking International*] [*A publication*]
**IAMIC**....... International Association of Mutual Insurance Companies [*See also AISAM*] (EAIO)
**IaMil**.......... Milo Public Library, Milo, IA [*Library symbol*] [*Library of Congress*] (LCLS)
**IaMilf**......... Milford Memorial Library, Milford, IA [*Library symbol*] [*Library of Congress*] (LCLS)
**IaMilfM**..... Milford Mail, Milford, IA [*Library symbol*] [*Library of Congress*] (LCLS)
**IaMilfN** ..... Milford News, Milford, IA [*Library symbol*] [*Library of Congress*] (LCLS)
**IaMisv** ....... Missouri Valley Public Library, Missouri Valley, IA [*Library symbol*] [*Library of Congress*] (LCLS)
**IaMisvTN** ... Missouri Valley Times-News, Missouri Valley, IA [*Library symbol*] [*Library of Congress*] (LCLS)
**IAML**......... International Association of Music Libraries, Archives, and Documentation Centers (EAIO)
**IAMLADP** ... Inter-Agency Meeting on Language Arrangements, Documentation, and Publications [*United Nations*]
**IAMLO** ..... International African Migratory Locust Organization [*See also OICMA*] (EA)
**IAMLT**...... International Association of Medical Laboratory Technologists [*Bootle, Merseyside, England*] (EA)
**IAMM** ....... International Association of Medical Museums [*Later, IAP*]
**IAMM & D** ... Institute for Advanced Materials, Mechanics, and Design [*Army Materiel Command*]
**IAMMM** ... International Association of Margaret Morris Method [*Glasgow, Scotland*] (EAIO)
**IAMN**........ Istanbul Asariatica Muzeleri Nesriyati (BJA)
**IAMNA** ..... Izvestiya Akademii Nauk Armyanskoi SSR Seriya Fiziko-Matematicheskikh Nauk [*A publication*]
**IAMOAM** ... Indian Council of Agricultural Research. Monograph [*A publication*]
**IaMonM** .... Monroe Mirror, Monroe, IA [*Library symbol*] [*Library of Congress*] (LCLS)
**IaMono** ...... Murphy Memorial Library, Monona, IA [*Library symbol*] [*Library of Congress*] (LCLS)
**IaMonoB**.... Monona Billboard, Monona, IA [*Library symbol*] [*Library of Congress*] (LCLS)
**IaMonoHi** ... Monona Historical Society, Monona, IA [*Library symbol*] [*Library of Congress*] (LCLS)
**IaMont**....... Monticello Public Library, Monticello, IA [*Library symbol*] [*Library of Congress*] (LCLS)
**IaMontE** .... Monticello Express, Monticello, IA [*Library symbol*] [*Library of Congress*] (LCLS)
**IaMonteR** .. Montezuma Republican, Montezuma, IA [*Library symbol*] [*Library of Congress*] (LCLS)
**IaMontJHi** ... Jones County Historical Society, Monticello, IA [*Library symbol*] [*Library of Congress*] (LCLS)
**IaMoraU**.... Moravia Union, Moravia, IA [*Library symbol*] [*Library of Congress*] (LCLS)
**IaMorn**....... Mellinger Memorial Library, Morning Sun, IA [*Library symbol*] [*Library of Congress*] (LCLS)
**IaMornN** ... Morning Sun News-Herald, Morning Sun, IA [*Library symbol*] [*Library of Congress*] (LCLS)
**IaMou** ........ Garrett Memorial Library, Moulton, IA [*Library symbol*] [*Library of Congress*] (LCLS)
**IaMouT**...... Moulton Weekly Tribune, Moulton, IA [*Library symbol*] [*Library of Congress*] (LCLS)
**IAMP**......... Imagery Acquisition and Management Plan
**IAMP**......... Innovative Agricultural Marketing Program [*Australia*]
**IAMP**......... International Academy of Medicine and Psychology [*Australia*] (EA)
**IAMP**......... International Association of Mathematical Physics (EA)
**IAMP**......... International Association of Meat Processors (EA)
**IAMP**......... International Association of Mercury Producers [*Spain, Italy, Turkey, Yugoslavia, Peru, Algeria*]
**IaMp**.......... Mount Pleasant Public Library, Mount Pleasant, IA [*Library symbol*] [*Library of Congress*] (LCLS)
**IaMpI** ........ Iowa Wesleyan College, Mount Pleasant, IA [*Library symbol*] [*Library of Congress*] (LCLS)
**IaMpN** ....... Mount Pleasant News, Mount Pleasant, IA [*Library symbol*] [*Library of Congress*] (LCLS)
**IAMPTH**... International Association of Master Penmen and Teachers of Handwriting (EA)
**IAMR** ........ Institute of Arctic Mineral Resources [*University of Alaska*]
**IAMR** ........ International Association for Medical Research and Cultural Exchange
**IAMS**......... Individual Aerial Mobility System [*Military*] (MCD)
**IAMS**......... Initial Attack Management System [*Weather system*]
**IAMS**......... Instantaneous Audience Measurement System
**IAMS**......... Institute of Advanced Marketing Studies - American Marketing Association (EA)
**IAMS**......... Institute of Applied Mathematics and Statistics [*University of British Columbia*] [*Research center*] (RCD)
**IAMS**......... Institute for Archaeo-Metallurgical Studies [*British*] (IRUK)
**IAMS**......... International Advanced Microlithography Society (EA)
**IAMS**......... International Association of Microbiological Societies [*ICSU*] [*Later, IUMS*]
**IAMS**......... International Association for Mission Studies [*Hamburg, Federal Republic of Germany*] (EAIO)
**IAMS**......... International Association of Municipal Statisticians [*Later, IARUS*]

**IAMSLIC** ... International Association of Marine Science Libraries and Information Centers (EA)
**IAMSO** ...... Inter-African and Malagasy States Organization (NATG)
**IAMTACT** ... Institute of Advanced Machine Tool and Control Technology [*British*]
**IaMu** .......... P. M. Musser Public Library, Muscatine, IA [*Library symbol*] [*Library of Congress*] (LCLS)
**IaMuJ** ........ Muscatine Journal, Muscatine, IA [*Library symbol*] [*Library of Congress*] (LCLS)
**IAMUS** ...... Installation Automated Manpower Utilization System [*Army*]
**IaMvC** ........ Cornell College, Mount Vernon, IA [*Library symbol*] [*Library of Congress*] (LCLS)
**IaMvCor** .... Cornellian, Mount Vernon, IA [*Library symbol*] [*Library of Congress*] (LCLS)
**IaMvH** ....... Hawkeye and Libson Herald, Mount Vernon, IA [*Library symbol*] [*Library of Congress*] (LCLS)
**IaMvS** ........ Sun Hawkeye Record, Mount Vernon, IA [*Library symbol*] [*Library of Congress*] (LCLS)
**IAMW** ....... Improved Antimateriel Warhead
**IAMWH** .... Improved Antimateriel Warhead
**IAMWMW** ... International Association of Ministers' Wives and Ministers' Widows (EAIO)
**IAN** ............ Illustrated Australian News [*A publication*]
**IAN** ............ Imagery Analysis Notice (MCD)
**IAN** ............ International Artist Network (EA)
**IAN** ............ Internationale des Amis de la Nature [*International Federation of Friends of Nature*]
**IAN** ............ Izvestiya Akademii Nauk SSSR Seriya Literatury i Jazyka [*Moscow*] [*A publication*]
**IAN** ............ Kennedy-King College of the City College of Chicago, Chicago, IL [*OCLC symbol*] (OCLC)
**IAN** ............ Kiana [*Alaska*] [*Airport symbol*] (OAG)
**IANA** ......... International Alliance of Nutrimedical Associations (EA)
**IANAB** ...... Izvestiya Akademii Nauk Azerbaidzhanskoi SSR [*A publication*]
**IANAP** ....... Interagency Noise Abatement Program
**IaNas** ......... Nashua Public Library, Nashua, IA [*Library symbol*] [*Library of Congress*] (LCLS)
**IaNasPN** .... Plainfield News, Nashua, IA [*Library symbol*] [*Library of Congress*] (LCLS)
**IaNasR** ....... Nashua Reporter, Nashua, IA [*Library symbol*] [*Library of Congress*] (LCLS)
**IANC** ......... International Academy of Nutritional Consultants [*Absorbed by AANC*] (EA)
**IANC** ......... International Air Navigation Convention
**IANC** ......... International Airline Navigators Council [*Defunct*]
**IANC** ......... International Anatomical Nomenclature Committee [*London, England*] (EAIO)
**IANC** ......... Invest-in-America National Council [*Later, RA*] (EA)
**IANCA** ...... Interamerican Naval Coordinating Authority (CINC)
**IANDS** ....... International Association for Near-Death Studies [*See also AEEPM*] (EA)
**IANEC** ....... Inter-American Nuclear Energy Commission [*Organization of American States*] (NRCH)
**IaNeoG** ...... Gazette Reporter and Minden-Shelby News, Neloa, IA [*Library symbol*] [*Library of Congress*] (LCLS)
**IaNev** ......... Nevada Public Library, Nevada, IA [*Library symbol*] [*Library of Congress*] (LCLS)
**IaNevJ** ....... Nevada Evening Journal, Nevada, IA [*Library symbol*] [*Library of Congress*] (LCLS)
**IaNewM** ..... Newell Mirror, Newell, IA [*Library symbol*] [*Library of Congress*] (LCLS)
**IaNewt** ....... Newton Public Library, Newton, IA [*Library symbol*] [*Library of Congress*] (LCLS)
**IaNewtCoC** ... Jasper County Courthouse, Newton, IA [*Library symbol*] [*Library of Congress*] (LCLS)
**IaNewtHi** ... Newton Historical Society, Newton, IA [*Library symbol*] [*Library of Congress*] (LCLS)
**IaNewtN** .... Newton Daily News, Newton, IA [*Library symbol*] [*Library of Congress*] (LCLS)
**IANF** .......... Individual Account Number File [*IRS*]
**IANF** .......... Inter-Allied Nuclear Force (AABC)
**IANFA** ....... Izvestiya Akademii Nauk Seriya Fizicheskaya [*A publication*]
**IaNhE** ........ New Hampton Economist, New Hampton, IA [*Library symbol*] [*Library of Congress*] (LCLS)
**IaNl** ............ H. J. Nugen Public Library, New London, IA [*Library symbol*] [*Library of Congress*] (LCLS)
**IaNlJ** .......... New London Journal, New London, IA [*Library symbol*] [*Library of Congress*] (LCLS)
**IANLS** ....... International Association for Neo-Latin Studies [*St. Andrews, Scotland*] (EAIO)
**IaNm** .......... New Market Public Library, New Market, IA [*Library symbol*] [*Library of Congress*] (LCLS)
**IANMA** ..... Izvestiya Akademii Nauk SSSR Otdelenie Tekhnicheskikh Nauk Metallurgiya i Toplivo [*A publication*]
**IaNmM** ...... New Market Monitor, New Market, IA [*Library symbol*] [*Library of Congress*] (LCLS)
**IaNoengR** ... North English Record, North English, IA [*Library symbol*] [*Library of Congress*] (LCLS)
**IAN-OGN** ... Izvestiya Akademii Nauk SSSR Otdeleniya Gumanitarnykh Nauk [*A publication*]
**IAN-OLJa** ... Izvestiya Akademii Nauk SSSR Otdeleniya Literatury i Jazyka [*A publication*]
**IAN OON** ... Izvestiya Akademii Nauk SSSR Otdeleniya Obscestvennykh Nauk [*A publication*]
**IAN ORJaSL** ... Izvestiya Akademii Nauk SSSR Otdeleniya Russkogo Jazyka i Slavesnosti Akademii Nauk [*A publication*]
**IaNosA** ...... Nora Springs Advertiser, Nora Springs, IA [*Library symbol*] [*Library of Congress*] (LCLS)
**IaNowdA** .... Northwood Anchor, Northwood, IA [*Library symbol*] [*Library of Congress*] (LCLS)
**IaNowdCoC** ... Worth County Courthouse, Northwood, IA [*Library symbol*] [*Library of Congress*] (LCLS)
**IaNowkN** ... North Warren Town and County News, Norwalk, IA [*Library symbol*] [*Library of Congress*] (LCLS)
**IANPE** ....... Institute for the Advancement of Notary Public Education (EA)
**IANPM** ..... International Academy of Nutrition and Preventive Medicine (EA)
**IANR (Inst Agric Nat Resour) Q** ... IANR (Institute of Agriculture and Natural Resources) Quarterly [*A publication*]
**IANRP** ....... International Association of Natural Resource Pilots (EA)
**IANS** .......... Institute of Applied Natural Science (EA)
**IANSA** ....... Izvestiya Akademii Nauk SSSR Otdelenie Tekhnicheskikh Nauk Mekhanika i Mashinostroenie [*A publication*]
**IAN SSS Bio** ... Izvestiya Akademii Nauk SSSR Seriya Biologicheskaya [*A publication*]
**IAN SSS FAO** ... Izvestiya Akademii Nauk SSSR Seriya Fizika Atmosfery i Okeana [*A publication*]
**IAN SSS Fiz** ... Izvestiya Akademii Nauk SSSR Seriya Fizicheskaya [*A publication*]
**IANTA** ...... Izvestiya Akademii Nauk SSSR Otdelenie Tekhnicheskikh Nauk [*A publication*]
**IANTN** ...... Inter-American Naval Telecommunications Network (MCD)
**IANU** ......... Italo American National Union (EA)
**IANUz** ....... Izvestiya Akademii Nauk Uzbekistanskoj SSSR [*A publication*]
**IaNv** ........... New Virginia Public Library, New Virginia, IA [*Library symbol*] [*Library of Congress*] (LCLS)
**IaNvN** ........ New Virginian, New Virginia, IA [*Library symbol*] [*Library of Congress*] (LCLS)
**IANVS** ....... International Association for Non-Violent Sport [*See also AICVS*] [*Monte Carlo, Monaco*] (EAIO)
**IANZA** ...... Industrie-Anzeiger [*A publication*]
**IAO** ............ Immediately after Onset [*Medicine*]
**IAO** ............ In and Out [*of clouds*] [*Aviation*] (FAAC)
**IAO** ............ Incorporated Association of Organists [*British*]
**IAO** ............ Independent Aviation Operators
**IAO** ............ Information Activities Office [*or Officer*]
**IAO** ............ Institute of Apostolic Oblates (EA)
**IAO** ............ Insurers' Advisory Organization of Canada
**IAO** ............ Intermittent Aortic Occlusion [*Cardiology*]
**IAO** ............ Internal Automation Operation
**IAO** ............ International Association of Orthodontics (EA)
**IAO** ............ Northeastern Illinois University, Chicago, IL [*OCLC symbol*] (OCLC)
**IAOAD** ...... International Association of Original Art Diffusors (EAIO)
**IaOak** ......... Eckels Memorial Library, Oakland, IA [*Library symbol*] [*Library of Congress*] (LCLS)
**IaOakA** ...... Oakland Acorn, Oakland, IA [*Library symbol*] [*Library of Congress*] (LCLS)
**IAOC** ......... Indian Army Ordnance Control [*British*]
**IAOC** ......... Irish Amateur Open Championship [*Golf*] (ROG)
**IaOcD** ........ Democrat, Orange City, IA [*Library symbol*] [*Library of Congress*] (LCLS)
**IaOch** ......... Ocheyedan Public Library, Ocheyedan, IA [*Library symbol*] [*Library of Congress*] (LCLS)
**IaOchMH** ... Melvin News, Ocheyedan, IA [*Library symbol*] [*Library of Congress*] (LCLS)
**IaOchP** ...... Ocheyedan Press, Ocheyedan, IA [*Library symbol*] [*Library of Congress*] (LCLS)
**IaOcN** ........ Northwestern College, Orange City, IA [*Library symbol*] [*Library of Congress*] (LCLS)
**IaOcSC** ...... Sioux County Capital, Orange City, IA [*Library symbol*] [*Library of Congress*] (LCLS)
**IAOD** ......... In Addition to Other Duties [*Military*]
**IAOD** ......... International Academy of Optimum Dentistry (EA)
**IAOD** ......... International Association of Opera Directors (EAIO)
**IaOdC** ........ Odebolt Chronicle, Odebolt, IA [*Library symbol*] [*Library of Congress*] (LCLS)
**IAOE** ......... International Association of Optometric Executives (EA)
**IaOe** ........... Oelwein Public Library, Oelwein, IA [*Library symbol*] [*Library of Congress*] (LCLS)
**IaOeR** ........ Daily Register, Oelwein, IA [*Library symbol*] [*Library of Congress*] (LCLS)
**IaOgd** ......... Ogden Public Library, Ogden, IA [*Library symbol*] [*Library of Congress*] (LCLS)
**IaOgdR** ...... Ogden Reporter, Ogden, IA [*Library symbol*] [*Library of Congress*] (LCLS)
**IAOH** ......... In Appreciation of the Hollies (EA)
**IAOHD** ...... International Archives of Allergy and Applied Immunology [*A publication*]

**IAOHRA**... International Association of Official Human Rights Agencies (EA)
**IAOL** ......... International Association of Orientalist Librarians (EA)
**IAOMO**..... International Association of Olympic Medical Officers [*Rugby, Warwickshire, England*] (EAIO)
**IAOMS**...... International Association of Oral and Maxillofacial Surgeons (EA)
**IaOn**........... Onawa Public Library, Onawa, IA [*Library symbol*] [*Library of Congress*] (LCLS)
**IaOnCoC** ... Monona County Courthouse, Onawa, IA [*Library symbol*] [*Library of Congress*] (LCLS)
**IaOnD**........ Onawa Democrat, Onawa, IA [*Library symbol*] [*Library of Congress*] (LCLS)
**IaOnS** ........ Onawa Sentinel, Onawa IA [*Library symbol*] [*Library of Congress*] (LCLS)
**IAOP** ......... International Association of Oral Pathologists (EA)
**IAOPA**....... International Council of Aircraft Owner and Pilot Associations (EA)
**IAOR** ......... International Abstracts in Operations Research [*A publication*]
**IaOrM** ....... Mid-American Reformed Seminary, Orange City, IA [*Library symbol*] [*Library of Congress*] (LCLS)
**IAOS**.......... International Association of Ocular Surgeons (EA)
**IAOS**.......... International Association for Official Statistics [*International Statistical Institute*] [*Voorburg, Netherlands*] (EAIO)
**IAOS**.......... International Association of Oral Surgeons (EAIO)
**IaOsa** ......... Sage Library, Osage, IA [*Library symbol*] [*Library of Congress*] (LCLS)
**IaOsaCoC** ... Mitchell County Courthouse, Osage, IA [*Library symbol*] [*Library of Congress*] (LCLS)
**IaOsaP**....... Mitchell County Press-News, Osage, IA [*Library symbol*] [*Library of Congress*] (LCLS)
**IaOsc**.......... Osceola Public Library, Osceola, IA [*Library symbol*] [*Library of Congress*] (LCLS)
**IaOscS** ....... Osceola Sentinel, Osceola, IA [*Library symbol*] [*Library of Congress*] (LCLS)
**IaOsk** ......... Oskaloosa Public Library, Oskaloosa, IA [*Library symbol*] [*Library of Congress*] (LCLS)
**IaOskH**...... Oskaloosa Daily Herald, Oskaloosa, IA [*Library symbol*] [*Library of Congress*] (LCLS)
**IaOskMHi** ... Mahaska County Historical Society, Oskaloosa, IA [*Library symbol*] [*Library of Congress*] (LCLS)
**IaOskW** ..... William Penn College, Oskaloosa, IA [*Library symbol*] [*Library of Congress*] (LCLS)
**IaOss**.......... Ossian Public Library, Ossian, IA [*Library symbol*] [*Library of Congress*] (LCLS)
**IaOssB**....... Ossian Bee, Ossian, IA [*Library symbol*] [*Library of Congress*] (LCLS)
**IAOT** ......... International Association of Organ Teachers USA [*Later, KTA*] (EA)
**IaOt**............ Ottumwa Public Library, Ottumwa, IA [*Library symbol*] [*Library of Congress*] (LCLS)
**IaOtC** ......... Ottumwa Heights College, Ottumwa, IA [*Library symbol*] [*Library of Congress*] (LCLS)
**IaOtCo** ....... Ottumwa Courier, Ottumwa, IA [*Library symbol*] [*Library of Congress*] (LCLS)
**IaOtS** ......... Southern Iowa Library Cooperative, Ottumwa, IA [*Library symbol*] [*Library of Congress*] (LCLS)
**IaOxj**.......... Wreigie Memorial Library, Oxford Junction, IA [*Library symbol*] [*Library of Congress*] (LCLS)
**IAP**............. Image Array Processor
**IAP**............. Improved Accuracy Program (MCD)
**IAP**............. Incentive Awards Program [*of the federal government, administered by CSC*]
**IAP**............. Indonesian Acquisition Project [*Australia*]
**IAP**............. Indoor Air Pollution
**IAP**............. Industry Applications Programs [*Data processing*] (IBMDP)
**IAP**............. Initial Aiming Point [*Gunnery*]
**IAP**............. Initial Approach [*Aviation*]
**IAP**............. Initial Approved Program
**IAP**............. Inlet Absolute Pressure
**IAP**............. Inorganic Ablative Plastic
**IAP**............. Institute of Animal Physiology [*British*]
**IAP**............. Institute of Atmospheric Physics [*University of Arizona*] [*Research center*]
**IAP**............. Instrument Approach Procedure [*Aviation*] (AFM)
**IAP**............. Insurance Accounting Principles
**IAP**............. Integrated Aeronautic Program [*Military*] (AFIT)
**IAP**............. Interactive Programming [*Data processing*]
**IAP**............. Interarray Processor (NVT)
**IAP**............. Interceptor Aim Points
**IAP**............. Intermittent Acute Porphyria [*Medicine*]
**IAP**............. Internal Air Portability
**IAP**............. Internal Array Processor [*Data General Corp.*]
**IAP**............. International Academy of Pathology (EA)
**IAP**............. International Academy of Proctology (EA)
**IAP**............. International Activities Program [*US Army Western Command*]
**IAP**............. International Aero Press
**IAP**............. International Airport
**IAP**............. International Association of Parapsychologists (EA)
**IAP**............. International Association of Photoplatemakers (EA)
**IAP**............. International Association of Planetology [*Brussels, Belgium*] (EA)
**IAP**............. Interport Corp. [*Portland, ME*] [*FAA designator*] (FAAC)
**IAP**............. Intra-Abdominal Pressure
**IAP**............. Intra-Arterial Pressure
**IAP**............. Intracisternal A-Particle [*Biochemistry*]
**IAP**............. Iodoantipyrine [*Biochemistry*]
**IAP**............. Iona Appliances, Inc. [*Toronto Stock Exchange symbol*]
**IAP**............. Iranian Aircraft Program [*Military*] (MCD)
**IAP**............. Islet-Activating Protein [*Biochemistry*]
**IAP**............. Isopropylantipyrine [*Biochemistry*]
**IAP**............. Oakton Community College, Morton Grove, IL [*OCLC symbol*] (OCLC)
**IAP**............. Portland, OR [*Location identifier*] [*FAA*] (FAAL)
**IAPA**.......... Inter-American Police Academy (AABC)
**IAPA**.......... Inter-American Press Association (EA)
**IAPA**.......... International Airline Passengers Association (EA)
**IAPA**.......... International Association of Physicians in Audiology (EAIO)
**IaPal** .......... Palmer Public Library, Palmer, IA [*Library symbol*] [*Library of Congress*] (LCLS)
**IaPanV**....... Guthrie County Vedette, Panora, IA [*Library symbol*] [*Library of Congress*] (LCLS)
**IaParE** ....... Eclipse-News-Review, Parkersburg, IA [*Library symbol*] [*Library of Congress*] (LCLS)
**IAPAR (Fund Inst Agron Parana) Circ** ... IAPAR (Fundacao Instituto Agronomico do Parana) Circular [*A publication*]
**IaParnHi**.... Iowa County Historical Society, Parnell, IA [*Library symbol*] [*Library of Congress*] (LCLS)
**IaPau**.......... Paullina Free Public Library, Paullina, IA [*Library symbol*] [*Library of Congress*] (LCLS)
**IaPauT**....... Paullina Times, Paullina, IA [*Library symbol*] [*Library of Congress*] (LCLS)
**IAPB**.......... Inter-Allied Personnel Board [*World War II*]
**IAPB**.......... International Agency for the Prevention of Blindness (EA)
**IAPB**.......... International Association for the Prevention of Blindness [*Later, International Agency for the Prevention of Blindness*] (EA)
**IAPBPPV**.. International Association of Plant Breeders for the Protection of Plant Varieties (EAIO)
**IAPBT** ....... International Association of Piano Builders and Technicians (EA)
**IAPC**.......... Institute for the Advancement of Philosophy for Children (EA)
**IAPC**.......... Instrument Approach Procedure Chart [*Aviation*] (NOAA)
**IAPC**.......... Inter-American Peace Committee [*Later, Inter-American Committee on Peaceful Settlement*] [*OAS*]
**IAPC**.......... International Association of Pet Cemeteries (EA)
**IAPC**.......... International Association of Political Consultants (EA)
**IAPC**.......... International Association for Pollution Control [*Defunct*] (EA)
**IaPcN**......... Prairie City News, Prairie City, IA [*Library symbol*] [*Library of Congress*] (LCLS)
**IAPCO**....... International Association of Professional Congress Organizers [*Brussels, Belgium*] (EAIO)
**IAPD**.......... International Association of Parents of the Deaf [*Later, ASDC*] (EA)
**IAPE**.......... Independent Association of Publishers' Employees (EA)
**IaPe**........... Pella Public Library, Pella, IA [*Library symbol*] [*Library of Congress*] (LCLS)
**IaPeC** ......... Central College, Pella, IA [*Library symbol*] [*Library of Congress*] (LCLS)
**IaPeCh**....... Pella Chronicle, Pella, IA [*Library symbol*] [*Library of Congress*] (LCLS)
**IaPeCR** ...... Central Ray, Pella, IA [*Library symbol*] [*Library of Congress*] (LCLS)
**IaPerC**........ Chief, Perry, IA [*Library symbol*] [*Library of Congress*] (LCLS)
**IaPersHi**.... Harrison County Historical Society, Persia, IA [*Library symbol*] [*Library of Congress*] (LCLS)
**IAPES**........ International Association of Personnel in Employment Security (EA)
**IAPESGW** ... International Association of Physical Education and Sport for Girls and Women (EA)
**IaPet** .......... Kirchner-French Memorial Library, Peterson, IA [*Library symbol*] [*Library of Congress*] (LCLS)
**IaPetP**........ Peterson Patriot, Peterson, IA [*Library symbol*] [*Library of Congress*] (LCLS)
**IAPF** .......... Inter-American Peacekeeping Force
**IAPG**.......... Iberian Atlantic Planning Guidance (NATG)
**IAPG**.......... Interagency Advanced Power Group
**IAPG**.......... International Association of Psychoanalytic Gerontology [*Paris, France*] (EAIO)
**IAPGPD**.... Inter-American Parliamentary Group on Population and Development (EA)
**IAPGR**....... Institute of Animal Physiology and Genetics Research [*United Kingdom*] [*Research center*] (IRC)
**IAPH** ......... International Association of Ports and Harbors [*Japan*]
**IAPHC**....... International Association of Printing House Craftsmen (EA)
**IAPI**........... Institute of American Poultry Industries [*Later, PEIA*] (EA)
**IaPierP**....... Pierson Press, Pierson, IA [*Library symbol*] [*Library of Congress*] (LCLS)
**IAPIP** ........ International Association for the Protection of Industrial Property
**IAPL**........... Initial Allowance Parts List [*Military*] (CAAL)

**IAPL**.......... International Association of Penal Law [*Freiburg, Federal Republic of Germany*] (EAIO)
**IAPL**.......... International Association for Philosophy and Literature (EA)
**IaPlaBHi**... Bremer County Historical Society, Plainsfield, IA [*Library symbol*] [*Library of Congress*] (LCLS)
**IaPleN**....... Marion County News, Pleasantville, IA [*Library symbol*] [*Library of Congress*] (LCLS)
**IAPLLT**..... Interamerican Program for Linguistics and Language Teaching (EA)
**IAPLSP**..... International Association for Philosophy of Law and Social Philosophy [*See also AIPDPS*]
**IAPM**......... Institute of Applied Physiology and Medicine [*Formerly, Institute of Environmental Medicine and Physiology*] [*Research center*] (RCD)
**IAPM**......... International Academy of Preventive Medicine (EA)
**IAPMA**...... International Association of Hand Papermakers and Paper Artists (EAIO)
**IAPMA**...... Monographs in Pathology [*A publication*]
**IAPMAV**... International Academy of Pathology. Monograph [*A publication*]
**IAPMO**..... International Association of Plumbing and Mechanical Officials (EA)
**IAPN**......... International Association of Professional Numismatists [*See also AINP*] [*Zurich, Switzerland*] (EAIO)
**IAPNH**...... International Association of Professional Natural Hygienists (EA)
**IAPO**......... Industrial Accountable Property Officer [*Air Force*]
**IAPO**......... Interchangeable at Attachment Point Only (AAG)
**IAPO**......... International Association of Physical Oceanography [*Later, IAPSO*]
**IaPocR**....... Pocahontas Record Democrat, Pocahontas, IA [*Library symbol*] [*Library of Congress*] (LCLS)
**IaPolc**......... Polk City Community Library, Polk City, IA [*Library symbol*] [*Library of Congress*] (LCLS)
**IaPolcN**...... Big Creek News, Polk City, IA [*Library symbol*] [*Library of Congress*] (LCLS)
**IaPom**......... Pomeroy Public Library, Pomeroy, IA [*Library symbol*] [*Library of Congress*] (LCLS)
**IaPomH**..... Pomeroy Herald, Pomeroy, IA [*Library symbol*] [*Library of Congress*] (LCLS)
**IaPos**.......... Postville Public Library, Postville, IA [*Library symbol*] [*Library of Congress*] (LCLS)
**IaPosH**....... Postville Herald, Postville, IA [*Library symbol*] [*Library of Congress*] (LCLS)
**IAPP**.......... International Association of Pacemaker Patients [*Later, IAHP*] (EA)
**IAPP**.......... International Association for Plant Physiology [*Australia*] (EAIO)
**IAPP**.......... International Association of Police Professors [*Later, ACJS*]
**IAPP**.......... Ion Acoustic Plasma Pulse
**IAPP**.......... Islet Amyloid Polypeptide [*Biochemistry*]
**I App**.......... Law Reports, Privy Council, Indian Appeals [*A publication*]
**IAP/P**......... Pesquisas. Anuario do Instituto Anchietano de Pesquisas [*A publication*]
**IAPPHAP**... International Association for Past and Present History of the Art of Printing (EA)
**IAPPI**......... International Association of Public Pawnbroking Institutions [*Milan, Italy*] (EA)
**IAPPP**........ International Amateur-Professional Photoelectric Photometry
**IAPPW**....... International Association of Pupil Personnel Workers (EA)
**IAPR**.......... Institute of Advanced Philosophic Research (EA)
**IAPR**.......... International Association for Pattern Recognition [*London, England*] (EA)
**IAPR**.......... International Association for Psychotronic Research [*Prague, Czechoslovakia*] (EA)
**IaPreT**....... Preston Times, Preston, IA [*Library symbol*] [*Library of Congress*] (LCLS)
**IaPreWHi**... Wayne County Historical Society, Promise City, IA [*Library symbol*] [*Library of Congress*] (LCLS)
**IaPri**........... Primghar Public Library, Primghar, IA [*Library symbol*] [*Library of Congress*] (LCLS)
**IaPriB**........ O'Brien County Bell, Primghar, IA [*Library symbol*] [*Library of Congress*] (LCLS)
**IAPS**.......... Incorporated Association of Preparatory Schools [*British*] (DCTA)
**IAPS**.......... Independent Association of Preparatory Schools
**IAPS**.......... Inductosyn Angle Position Simulator
**IAPS**.......... Institute for Advanced Pastoral Studies (EA)
**IAPS**.......... Interim Antenna Pointing Subsystem [*Deep Space Instrumentation Facility, NASA*]
**IAPS**.......... International Association for the Properties of Steam [*Later, IAPWS*] (EA)
**IAPS**.......... Ion Auxiliary Propulsion System [*for satellites*]
**IAPSAC**..... International Association of Parents and Professionals for Safe Alternatives in Childbirth (EA)
**IAPSB**........ Antennas and Propagation Society. International Symposium [*A publication*]
**IAPSC**....... Inter-African Phytosanitary Commission
**IAPSC**....... International Association of Pipe Smokers Clubs (EA)
**IAPSC**....... International Association of Professional Security Consultants (EA)
**IAPSO**....... International Association for the Physical Sciences of the Ocean (EA)
**IAPSP**........ Inter-American Program for Social Progress [*AID*]
**IAPSRS**...... International Association of Psycho-Social Rehabilitation Services (EA)
**IAPT**.......... International Association for Plant Taxonomy [*Utrecht, Netherlands*] (EA)
**IA/PT**........ Item Acquisition/Production Trade-Off Model
**IAPTA**....... International Allied Printing Trades Association (EA)
**IAPUP**....... International Association on the Political Use of Psychiatry [*Amsterdam, Netherlands*] (EAIO)
**IAPV**.......... Institute Against Prejudice and Violence (EA)
**IAPVA**....... Industria Alimentara. Produse Vegetale [*A publication*]
**IAPW**......... International Association for Personnel Women (EA)
**IAPWA**...... International Journal of Air and Water Pollution [*A publication*]
**IaPwdC**...... Packwood Clarion, Packwood, IA [*Library symbol*] [*Library of Congress*] (LCLS)
**IAPWS**...... International Association for the Properties of Water and Steam (EA)
**IAQ**............ Independent Activities Questionnaire [*Psychology*]
**I Aq**............ Indian Antiquary [*A publication*]
**IAQ**............ Indoor Air Quality
**IAQ**............ International Academy for Quality [*Grobenzell, Federal Republic of Germany*] (EAIO)
**IAQ**............ Internationales Asienforum [*A publication*]
**IAQ**............ Parkland College, Champaign, IL [*OCLC symbol*] (OCLC)
**IAQC**......... International Association of Quality Circles (EA)
**IAQDE**...... Independent Association of Questioned Document Examiners (EA)
**IAQSB**....... Industries Atomiques et Spatiales [*A publication*]
**IAR**............ Iliamna Air Taxi, Inc. [*Iliamna, AK*] [*FAA designator*] (FAAC)
**I-Ar**........... Illinois State Library, Archives Division, Springfield, IL [*Library symbol*] [*Library of Congress*] (LCLS)
**IAR**............ Imagery Analysis Report (MCD)
**IAR**............ Inactive Air Reserve
**IAR**............ Indian Affairs Record [*A publication*]
**IAR**............ Indirect Address Register
**IAR**............ Individual Action Report
**IAR**............ Institute for Aerobics Research (EA)
**IAR**............ Institute of American Relations (EA)
**IAR**............ Institute of Andean Research (EA)
**IAR**............ Instruction Address Register [*Data processing*] (MDG)
**IAR**............ Instrument Air Receiver (AAG)
**IAR**............ Integrity and Reliability [*Military*] (AFIT)
**IAR**............ Interagency Rate (AFM)
**IAR**............ Interavia Aerospace Review [*Interavia Publications*] [*Information service or system*] (CRD)
**IAR**............ Interment Is Authorized for the Remains Of [*Military*]
**IAR**............ International Art Register
**IAR**............ International Association of Radiopharmacology (EA)
**IAR**............ International Automotive Review [*A publication*]
**IAR**............ Interrupt Address Register
**IAR**............ Intersection of Air Routes [*Aviation*]
**IAR**............ Inventory Adjustment Rate
**IAR**............ Inventory Adjustment Report [*Military*]
**IAR**............ Isobaric Analog Resonance [*Nuclear structure*]
**IAR**............ Ivor's Art Review [*A publication*] (APTA)
**IAR**............ Roosevelt University, Chicago, IL [*OCLC symbol*] (OCLC)
**IARA**......... Inter-Allied Reparations Agency [*Brussels*]
**IARA**......... International Animal Rights Alliance (EA)
**IARA**......... International Association of Rebekah Assemblies, IOOF [*Independent Order of Odd Fellows*] (EA)
**IaRa**........... Rake Public Library, Rake, IA [*Library symbol*] [*Library of Congress*] (LCLS)
**IARASM**... Institute for Advanced Research in Asian Science and Medicine (EA)
**IARB**.......... Inspection Analysis Review Board (MCD)
**IARB**.......... Inter-American Review of Bibliography [*A publication*]
**IArc**........... Arcola Public Library, Arcola, IL [*Library symbol*] [*Library of Congress*] (LCLS)
**IARC**.......... Independent Assessment and Research Centre [*British*] (CB)
**IARC**.......... International Action for the Rights of the Child [*See also AIDE*] [*Paris, France*] (EAIO)
**IARC**.......... International Agency for Research on Cancer [*World Health Organization*] [*Research center*] [*Lyon, France*] (EAIO)
**IARC**.......... International Agricultural Research Center
**IAR/C**........ Interviewing, Assessment, and Referral or Counseling (ADA)
**IaRcA**......... Rockwell City Advocate, Rockwell City, IA [*Library symbol*] [*Library of Congress*] (LCLS)
**IARCC**....... IARC [*International Agency for Research on Cancer*] Scientific Publications [*A publication*]
**IARCC**....... Interagency Arctic Research Coordinating Committee [*National Science Foundation*] [*Terminated, 1978*]
**IaRcCHi**.... Calhoun County Historical Society, Rockwell City, IA [*Library symbol*] [*Library of Congress*] (LCLS)
**IaRcfR**........ Rockford Register, Rockford, IA [*Library symbol*] [*Library of Congress*] (LCLS)
**IARC (Int Agency Res Cancer) Publ**... IARC (International Agency for Research on Cancer) Publications [*A publication*]

**IARC Monogr** ... IARC [*International Agency for Research on Cancer*] Monographs [*A publication*]
**IARC Monogr Eval Carcinog Risk Chem Hum** ... IARC [*International Agency for Research on Cancer*] Monographs. Evaluation of the Carcinogenic Risk of Chemicals to Humans [*A publication*]
**IARC Monogr Eval Carcinog Risk Chem Hum Suppl** ... IARC [*International Agency for Research on Cancer*] Monographs. Evaluation of the Carcinogenic Risk of Chemicals to Humans. Supplement [*A publication*]
**IARC Sci Publ** ... IARC [*International Agency for Research on Cancer*] Scientific Publications [*A publication*]
**IARE** .......... Improved Amphibious Reconnaissance Equipment [*Military*] (MCD)
**IARE** .......... Institute of Animal Resource Ecology [*University of British Columbia*] [*Research center*] (RCD)
**IARE** .......... International Association of Railway Employees (EA)
**IAREC** ....... Irrigated Agriculture Research and Extension Center [*Washington State University*] [*Research center*] (RCD)
**IaRedf** ........ Redfield Public Library, Redfield, IA [*Library symbol*] [*Library of Congress*] (LCLS)
**IaRedfRS** ... Dexfield Review Sentinel, Redfield, IA [*Library symbol*] [*Library of Congress*] (LCLS)
**IaRedo** ........ Red Oak Public Library, Red Oak, IA [*Library symbol*] [*Library of Congress*] (LCLS)
**IaRedoE** ..... Red Oak Express, Red Oak, IA [*Library symbol*] [*Library of Congress*] (LCLS)
**IaReiC** ........ Reinbeck Courier, Reinbeck, IA [*Library symbol*] [*Library of Congress*] (LCLS)
**IaRemBE** ... Remsen Bell-Enterprise, Remsen, IA [*Library symbol*] [*Library of Congress*] (LCLS)
**IaRen** ......... Renwick Public Library, Renwick, IA [*Library symbol*] [*Library of Congress*] (LCLS)
**IARF** .......... International Amateur Racquetball Federation (EA)
**IARF** .......... International Association for Religious Freedom (EA)
**IARFA** ....... Independent Aluminum Residential Fabricators Association (EA)
**IARFP** ....... International Association of Registered Financial Planners (EA)
**IArg** ........... Argonne National Laboratory, Argonne, IL [*Library symbol*] [*Library of Congress*] (LCLS)
**IArgoC** ....... CPC International, Inc., Argo, IL [*Library symbol*] [*Library of Congress*] (LCLS)
**IARI** ........... Indian Agricultural Research Institute
**IARI** ........... Industrial Advertising Research Institute [*Later, CMC*] (EA)
**IaRicP** ........ Richland Plainsman, Richland, IA [*Library symbol*] [*Library of Congress*] (LCLS)
**IARIGAI** ... International Association of Research Institutes for the Graphic Arts Industry [*St. Gallen, Switzerland*]
**IaRinD** ....... Ringsted Dispatch, Ringsted, IA [*Library symbol*] [*Library of Congress*] (LCLS)
**IaRiR** ......... Riceville Record, Riceville, IA [*Library symbol*] [*Library of Congress*] (LCLS)
**IARIW** ....... International Association for Research in Income and Wealth (EA)
**IARKA** ....... Izvestiya Akademii Nauk Armyanskoi SSR Khimicheskie Nauki [*A publication*]
**IARLD** ....... International Association for Research in Learning Disabilities
**IArlh** .......... Arlington Heights Public Library, Arlington Heights, IL [*Library symbol*] [*Library of Congress*] (LCLS)
**IARM** ........ Interim Antiradiation Missile (MCD)
**IARMCLRS** ... International Agreement Regarding the Maintenance of Certain Lights in the Red Sea (EA)
**IARMI** ....... International Association of Rattan Manufacturers and Importers [*Defunct*] (EA)
**IARO** ......... Indian Army Reserve of Officers
**IaRol** .......... Rolfe Public Library, Rolfe, IA [*Library symbol*] [*Library of Congress*] (LCLS)
**IaRolA** ........ Rolfe Arrow, Rolfe, IA [*Library symbol*] [*Library of Congress*] (LCLS)
**IAROO** ...... International Association of Railway Operating Officers (EA)
**IARP** .......... International Association for Religion and Parapsychology [*Tokyo, Japan*] (EA)
**IARP** .......... International Association of Retired Persons [*Superseded by IFA*] (EA)
**IARR** .......... International Association for Radiation Research [*Rijswijk, Netherlands*] (EAIO)
**IaRrLCoC** ... Lyon County Courthouse, Rock Rapids, IA [*Library symbol*] [*Library of Congress*] (LCLS)
**IaRrLR** ...... Lyon County Reporter, Rock Rapids, IA [*Library symbol*] [*Library of Congress*] (LCLS)
**IARS** .......... Improved Aerial Refueling System Program
**IARS** .......... Independent Air Revitalization System (NASA)
**IARS** .......... Institute for Advanced Russian Studies [*Smithsonian Institution*]
**IARS** .......... International Anesthesia Research Society (EA)
**IARSB** ....... International Association of Rolling Stock Builders [*See also AICMR*] (EAIO)
**IARSC** ....... International Association of Religious Science Churches [*Later, RSI*] (EA)
**IARSL** ....... Institute of Agriculture Remote Sensing Laboratory [*University of Minnesota*]
**IArt** ........... Arthur Public Library, Arthur, IL [*Library symbol*] [*Library of Congress*] (LCLS)
**IARTAS** .... Indian Council of Agricultural Research. Report Series [*A publication*]
**IARU** ......... International Amateur Radio Union (EA)
**IaRu** .......... Ruthven Public Library, Ruthven, IA [*Library symbol*] [*Library of Congress*] (LCLS)
**IARUS** ....... International Association for Regional and Urban Statistics [*Voorburg, Netherlands*] (EA)
**IaRuZ** ......... Ruthven Zipcode, Ruthven, IA [*Library symbol*] [*Library of Congress*] (LCLS)
**IaRvB** ......... Rock Valley Bee, Rock Valley, IA [*Library symbol*] [*Library of Congress*] (LCLS)
**IARW** ........ International Association of Refrigerated Warehouses (EA)
**IAS** ............. Iasi [*Romania*] [*Seismograph station code, US Geological Survey*] (SEIS)
**IAS** ............. Iasi [*Romania*] [*Airport symbol*] (OAG)
**IAS** ............. Ideal Adsorbed Solution [*Physical chemistry*]
**IAS** ............. IEEE Industry Applications Society (EA)
**IAS** ............. Immediate Access Storage (AFM)
**IAS** ............. Impact Assessment Sheet (NASA)
**IAS** ............. India-America Society
**IAS** ............. Indian Administrative Service [*British*]
**IAS** ............. Indian Astronautical Society
**IAS** ............. Indicated Air Speed
**IAS** ............. Industrial Arbitration Service [*A publication*] (APTA)
**IAS** ............. Information Acquisition System (MCD)
**IAS** ............. Inspector of Army Schools [*British military*] (DMA)
**IAS** ............. Institute for Advanced Studies [*Army*]
**IAS** ............. Institute for the Advancement of Sailing [*Commercial firm*] (EA)
**IAS** ............. Institute of Aerospace [*formerly, Aeronautical*] Sciences [*Later, AIAA*]
**IAS** ............. Institute for American Strategy [*Later, ASCF*]
**IAS** ............. Institute of Andean Studies (EA)
**IAS** ............. Institute of Animal Sciences (ASF)
**IAS** ............. Institute of Asian Studies (EA)
**IAS** ............. Institute for Atmospheric Sciences [*South Dakota School of Mines*] [*Research center*] [*Environmental Science Services Administration*]
**IAS** ............. Instructor Aid System (MCD)
**IAS** ............. Instrument Air System [*Nuclear energy*] (NRCH)
**IAS** ............. Instrument Approach System
**IAS** ............. Integrated Automation Systems
**IAS** ............. Integrated Avionics System (MCD)
**IAS** ............. Interactive Analysis System [*Data processing*] (PCM)
**IAS** ............. Interactive Applications Supervisor
**IAS** ............. Interest Assessment Scales
**IAS** ............. Internal Alignment Sensor (MCD)
**IAS** ............. International Academy of Sciences (EAIO)
**IAS** ............. International Accountants Society
**IAS** ............. International AIDS Society (EAIO)
**IAS** ............. International Air Service Co. [*Napa, CA*] [*FAA designator*] (FAAC)
**IAS** ............. International Army Staff (MCD)
**IAS** ............. International Army Staff Talks Program
**IAS** ............. International Aroid Society (EA)
**IAS** ............. International Association of Sedimentologists [*Liege, Belgium*] (EA)
**IAS** ............. International Association of Siderographers (EA)
**IAS** ............. International Atherosclerosis Society (EA)
**IAS** ............. International Audiovisual Society (EA)
**IAS** ............. International Aviation Service [*FAA*]
**IAS** ............. International Review of Administrative Sciences [*A publication*]
**IAS** ............. Intra-Amniotic Saline [*Infusion*] [*Medicine*]
**IAS** ............. Intra-Articular Steroid [*Physiology*]
**IAS** ............. Intrusion Alarm System
**IAS** ............. Isobaric Analog State
**IAS** ............. Israeli Air Services (MCD)
**IAS** ............. Los Angeles, CA [*Location identifier*] [*FAA*] (FAAL)
**IAS** ............. Sangamon State University, Springfield, IL [*OCLC symbol*] (OCLC)
**IASA** .......... Independent Automotive Service Association (EA)
**IASA** .......... Indo-American Sports Association [*Later, FIA-USC*]
**IASA** .......... Institute for Atomic Sciences in Agriculture
**IASA** .......... Insurance Accounting and Statistical Association [*Later, Insurance Accounting and Systems Association*] (EA)
**IASA** .......... Insurance Accounting and Systems Association [*Durham, NC*] (EA)
**IASA** .......... Integrated Assessment of Security Assistance [*Military*]
**IASA** .......... Integrated AUTODIN System Architecture (MCD)
**IASA** .......... International Air Safety Association (EA)
**IASA** .......... International Alliance for Sustainable Agriculture (EA)
**IASA** .......... International Association of Schools in Advertising
**IASA** .......... International Association of Sound Archives [*Milton, Keynes, England*] (EAIO)
**IASAA** ....... International Agricultural Students Association of the Americas (EA)
**IaSab** .......... Sabula Public Library, Sabula, IA [*Library symbol*] [*Library of Congress*] (LCLS)

**IaSacLS**..... Lytton Star, Sac City, IA [*Library symbol*] [*Library of Congress*] (LCLS)
**IaSacS**........ Sac Sun, Sac City, IA [*Library symbol*] [*Library of Congress*] (LCLS)
**IASAIL**...... International Association for the Study of Anglo-Irish Literature [*Maynooth, Republic of Ireland*] (EAIO)
**IASAJ**........ International Association of Supreme Administration Jurisdictions [*See also AIHJA*] (EAIO)
**IaSal**........... Crew Public Library, Salem, IA [*Library symbol*] [*Library of Congress*] (LCLS)
**IaSan**.......... Sanborn Public Library, Sanborn, IA [*Library symbol*] [*Library of Congress*] (LCLS)
**IAS Annu Meet Conf Rec** ... Industry Applications Society. Annual Meeting. Conference Record [*United States*] [*A publication*]
**IaSanP**....... Sanborn Pioneer, Sanborn, IA [*Library symbol*] [*Library of Congress*] (LCLS)
**IASAP**....... Intercollegiate Association for Study of the Alcohol Problem (EA)
**IASB**.......... Indian Art Sketch Book [*A publication*]
**IASB**.......... Installation Aviation Standardization Board (MCD)
**IASB**.......... International Academy at Santa Barbara (EA)
**IASBFLC**.. Institute for the Advanced Study of Black Family Life and Culture (EA)
**IASC**.......... Indexing and Abstracting Society of Canada [*Toronto, ON*]
**IASC**.......... Indian Army Service Corps [*British military*] (DMA)
**IASC**.......... Inter-American Safety Council (EA)
**IASC**.......... Inter-American Scout Committee [*See also CIE*] [*San Jose, Costa Rica*] (EAIO)
**IASC**.......... International Accounting Standards Committee [*of the International Federation of Accountants*] [*London, England*] (EAIO)
**IASC**.......... International Afroid Science Conference (MCD)
**IASC**.......... International Aloe Science Council (EA)
**IASC**.......... International Association of Seed Crushers [*London, England*] (EAIO)
**IASC**.......... International Association for Statistical Computing (EA)
**IASC**.......... Intimate Apparel Square Club (EA)
**IASC**.......... Italian American Stamp Club (EA)
**IaSc**........... Sioux City Public Library, Sioux City, IA [*Library symbol*] [*Library of Congress*] (LCLS)
**IASCA**....... International Auto Sound Challenge Association (EA)
**IaScB**......... Briar Cliff College, Sioux City, IA [*Library symbol*] [*Library of Congress*] (LCLS)
**IASCB**....... Ibero-American Society for Cell Biology [*See also SIABC*] (EAIO)
**IASCB**....... International Association of Sand Castle Builders (EA)
**IASCE**....... International Association for the Study of Cooperation in Education (EA)
**IaSce**.......... Sioux Center Public Library, Sioux Center, IA [*Library symbol*] [*Library of Congress*] (LCLS)
**IaSceD**....... Dordt College, Sioux Center, IA [*Library symbol*] [*Library of Congress*] (LCLS)
**IaSchH**...... Schaller Herald, Schaller, IA [*Library symbol*] [*Library of Congress*] (LCLS)
**IaSchlL**...... Schleswig Leader, Schleswig, IA [*Library symbol*] [*Library of Congress*] (LCLS)
**IaScM**........ Morningside College, Sioux City, IA [*Library symbol*] [*Library of Congress*] (LCLS)
**IaScNR**...... Northwest Regional Library System, Sioux City, IA [*Library symbol*] [*Library of Congress*] (LCLS)
**IASCO**....... International Association of Service Companies [*Absorbed by NACSA*] (EA)
**IASCP**....... Institute for Advanced Study of the Communication Processes [*University of Florida*] [*Research center*] (RCD)
**IASCS**........ International Association for Shopping Center Security (EA)
**IaScS**.......... Siouxland Libraries Cooperative, Sioux City, IA [*Library symbol*] [*Library of Congress*] (LCLS)
**IaScT**......... Trinity College, Sioux City, IA [*Library symbol*] [*Library of Congress*] [*Obsolete*] (LCLS)
**IAS Current Review** ... Industrial Arbitration Service. Current Review [*A publication*] (APTA)
**IaScWI**...... West Iowa Technical Community College, Sioux City, IA [*Library symbol*] [*Library of Congress*] (LCLS)
**IASD**.......... Interatrial Septal Defect [*Cardiology*]
**IASDI**......... Inter-American Social Development Institute [*Later, IAF*]
**IASEES**..... International Association of South-East European Studies [*See also AIESEE*] [*Bucharest, Romania*] (EAIO)
**IaSeyH**...... Seymour Herald, Seymour, IA [*Library symbol*] [*Library of Congress*] (LCLS)
**IASF**.......... Instrumentation in Aerospace Simulation Facilities
**IASF**.......... International Amateur Surfing Federation (EA)
**IASF**.......... International Amateur Swimming Federation (EA)
**IASF**.......... International Atlantic Salmon Foundation [*Canada*] (EA)
**IASF**.......... Irish American Sports Foundation (EA)
**IASF**.......... Isaac Asimov's Science Fiction Magazine [*A publication*]
**IASFAP**..... International Atlantic Salmon Foundation. Special Publication Series [*A publication*]
**IASH**......... International Association of Scientific Hydrology [*Later, International Association of Hydrological Sciences*] [*of International Union of Geodesy and Geophysics*]
**IASH**......... Israeli Academy of Sciences and Humanities
**IaSh**........... Shenandoah Public Library, Shenandoah, IA [*Library symbol*] [*Library of Congress*] (LCLS)
**IaShe**.......... Sheldon Public Library, Sheldon, IA [*Library symbol*] [*Library of Congress*] (LCLS)
**IaShefP**...... Sheffield Press, Sheffield, IA [*Library symbol*] [*Library of Congress*] (LCLS)
**IaSheHi**..... Sheldon County Historical Society, Sheldon, IA [*Library symbol*] [*Library of Congress*] (LCLS)
**IaSheM**...... Sheldon Mail, Sheldon, IA [*Library symbol*] [*Library of Congress*] (LCLS)
**IaSheS**....... Sheldon Sun, Sheldon, IA [*Library symbol*] [*Library of Congress*] (LCLS)
**IaShr**.......... Shell Rock Public Library, Shell Rock, IA [*Library symbol*] [*Library of Congress*] (LCLS)
**IASI**........... Inter-American Statistical Institute (EA)
**IASI**........... International Association for Sports Information [*The Hague, Netherlands*] (EA)
**IASILL**...... International Association for the Study of the Italian Language and Literature [*See also AISLLI*] [*Padua, Italy*] (EAIO)
**Iasi Univ An Stiint Sect 2 B Ser Noua** ... Iasi Universitatea. Analele Stiintifice. Sectiunea 2-B. Geologie. Serie Noua [*A publication*]
**IASL**.......... International Association of School Librarianship (EA)
**IASL**.......... International Association for the Study of the Liver [*Gottingen, Federal Republic of Germany*] (EAIO)
**IASL**.......... Internationales Archiv fuer Sozialgeschichte der Deutschen Literatur [*A publication*]
**IaSl**............ Storm Lake Public Library, Storm Lake, IA [*Library symbol*] [*Library of Congress*] (LCLS)
**IaSla**.......... Slater Public Library, Slater, IA [*Library symbol*] [*Library of Congress*] (LCLS)
**IaSlB**.......... Buena Vista College, Storm Lake, IA [*Library symbol*] [*Library of Congress*] (LCLS)
**IASLC**....... International Association for the Study of Lung Cancer (EA)
**IASLIC**...... Indian Association of Special Libraries and Information Centres (EAIO)
**IASLIC Bull** ... IASLIC [*Indian Association of Special Libraries and Information Centres*] Bulletin [*A publication*]
**IASM**......... Independent Association of Stocking Manufacturers [*Defunct*]
**IASM**......... Institute of Aerospace Safety and Management [*University of Southern California*]
**IASM**......... International Association for Seminar Management (EA)
**IASM**......... International Association of Structural Movers (EA)
**IASM**......... Istituto per l'Assistenza allo Sviluppo del Mezzogiorno [*Italy*] (EY)
**IASMHF**... International Association of Sports Museums and Halls of Fame (EA)
**IASMIRT**... International Association for Structural Mechanics in Reactor Technology (EAIO)
**IASOC**....... International Association for the Study of Organized Crime (EA)
**IASODL**.... International Advances in Surgical Oncology [*A publication*]
**IASOP**....... Institute of African Studies. Occasional Publications [*A publication*]
**IASOR**....... Ice and Snow on Runway [*Aviation*]
**IASOS**....... Institute of Antarctic and Southern Ocean Studies [*University of Tasmania*] [*Australia*]
**IASP**.......... Integrated Attack Sensor Package
**IASP**.......... International Arts and Sciences Press
**IASP**.......... International Association of Scholarly Publishers [*Norway*]
**IASP**.......... International Association for Social Progress
**IASP**.......... International Association of Space Philatelists (EA)
**IASP**.......... International Association of Sports Physicians (EA)
**IASP**.......... International Association for the Study of Pain (EA)
**IASP**.......... International Association of Sublimation Printers (EA)
**IASP**.......... International Association for Suicide Prevention (EA)
**IASPA**....... International Auto Show Producers Association (EA)
**IASPC**....... International Association of Strategic Planning Consultants [*Defunct*] (EA)
**IASPEI**...... International Association of Seismology and Physics of the Earth's Interior [*ICSU*] [*Newbury, Berkshire, England*] (EAIO)
**IASPHA**.... International American Saddlebred Pleasure Horse Association (EA)
**IASPM**...... International Association for the Study of Popular Music [*Berlin, German Democratic Republic*] (EAIO)
**IaSpr**.......... Springville Public Library, Springville, IA [*Library symbol*] [*Library of Congress*] (LCLS)
**IASPS**........ International Association for Statistics in Physical Sciences
**IASR**.......... Intermediate Altitude Sounding Rocket (MUGU)
**IASRA**....... International Arthur Schnitzler Research Association (EA)
**IASRR**....... Institute of African Studies. Research Review [*A publication*]
**IASS**.......... International Air Safety Seminar
**IASS**.......... International Association of Sanskrit Studies (EA)
**IASS**.......... International Association for Scandinavian Studies [*Norwich, England*] (EAIO)
**IASS**.......... International Association of Security Service (EA)
**IASS**.......... International Association of Semiotic Studies [*Palermo, Italy*] (EA)
**IASS**.......... International Association for Shell and Spatial Structures [*Madrid, Spain*] (EA)
**IASS**.......... International Association of Soil Science

**IASS** ......... International Association of Survey Statisticians [*See also AISE*] [*France*] (EA)
**IASSD** ....... International Association of School Security Directors [*Later, NASSD*] (EA)
**IASSIST** .... International Association for Social Science Information Service and Technology (EA)
**IASSMD** ... International Association for the Scientific Study of Mental Deficiency [*Dublin, Republic of Ireland*] (EA)
**IASSW** ...... International Association of Schools of Social Work [*Austria*]
**IAST** ......... Integrated Avionic System Trainer [*Military*] (CAAL)
**IASTA** ....... Institute for Advanced Studies in the Theatre Arts (EA)
**IaStaE** ........ Saint Ansgar Enterprise, St. Ansgar, IA [*Library symbol*] [*Library of Congress*] (LCLS)
**IaStan** ........ Stanton Community Library, Stanton, IA [*Library symbol*] [*Library of Congress*] (LCLS)
**IaStc** ........... Gutenkunst Public Library, State Center, IA [*Library symbol*] [*Library of Congress*] (LCLS)
**IASTED** .... International Association of Science and Technology for Development [*Calgary, AB*] (EAIO)
**IaStoc** ......... Story City Public Library, Story City, IA [*Library symbol*] [*Library of Congress*] (LCLS)
**IaStrp** ......... Strawberry Point Public Library, Strawberry Point, IA [*Library symbol*] [*Library of Congress*] (LCLS)
**IaStrpP** ...... Strawberry Point Press-Journal, Strawberry Point, IA [*Library symbol*] [*Library of Congress*] (LCLS)
**IASTV** ....... Incorporated Association of Secondary Teachers of Victoria [*Australia*]
**IASTWL** .... International Association for Social Tourism and Workers' Leisure (EAIO)
**IaSu** ........... General N. B. Baker Library, Sutherland, IA [*Library symbol*] [*Library of Congress*] (LCLS)
**IASU** .......... International Association of Satellite Users [*Later, IASUS*] (EA)
**IASUAB** .... Institute of Agricultural Sciences. University of Alaska. Bulletin [*A publication*]
**IA Sup Vol** ... English Law Reports, Indian Appeals, Supplementary Volume [*A publication*] (DLA)
**IASURR** .... Institute of Agricultural Sciences. University of Alaska. Research Reports [*A publication*]
**IASUS** ....... International Association of Satellite Users and Suppliers (EA)
**IASV** .......... Internationale Arbeitsgemeinschaft von Sortimentsbuchhaendler Vereinigungen [*International Community of Booksellers' Associations*]
**IaSwc** ......... Swea City Public Library, Swea City, IA [*Library symbol*] [*Library of Congress*] (LCLS)
**IASWR** ...... Institute for Advanced Studies of World Religions (EA)
**IAsy** ........... Ashley Public Library, Ashley, IL [*Library symbol*] [*Library of Congress*] (LCLS)
**IASY** .......... International Active Sun Years
**IAsyCD** ...... Ashley Community Consolidated District 15, Ashley, IL [*Library symbol*] [*Library of Congress*] (LCLS)
**IAT** ............ Image Auto Tracker
**IAT** ............ Immunoaugmentative Therapy [*Oncology*]
**IAT** ............ Indicated Air Temperature (AFM)
**IAT** ............ Indirect Antiglobulin Test [*Clinical chemistry*]
**IAT** ............ Individual Acceptance Tests
**IAT** ............ Information Assessment Team (NRCH)
**IAT** ............ Inside Air Temperature
**IAT** ............ Inspection Apply Template (MCD)
**IAT** ............ Institute for Advanced Technology [*Control Data Corp.*] [*Bloomington, MN*] [*Telecommunications*]
**IAT** ............ Institute of Animal Technology [*London*]
**IAT** ............ Institute for Applied Technology [*Superseded by NEL*] [*National Institute of Standards and Technology*]
**IAT** ............ Institute of Asphalt Technology [*British*]
**IAT** ............ Integrated Avionics Test (MCD)
**IAT** ............ Integration Acceptance Test [*Military*] (CAAL)
**IAT** ............ Interactive Audio Teletraining System [*Valencia Community College*] [*Orlando, FL*] (TSSD)
**IAT** ............ Interionic Attraction Theory
**IAT** ............ Internal Air Transportability (MCD)
**IAT** ............ International Air Tours [*Australia*]
**IAT** ............ International Association of Trichologists (EA)
**IAT** ............ International Atomic Time
**IAT** ............ International Automatic Time
**IAT** ............ Intraoperative Autologous Transfusion [*Medicine*]
**IAT** ............ Invasive Activity Test [*Oncology*]
**IAT** ............ Inventory of Affective Tolerance [*Psychology*]
**IAT** ............ Iodine Azide Test [*Medicine*]
**IAT** ............ Iowa Terminal Railroad Co. [*AAR code*]
**IAT** ............ Island Air Transfer Ltd. [*Honolulu, HI*] [*FAA designator*] (FAAC)
**IAT** ............ Izvestiya Akademii Nauk Turkmenskoi SSSR Seriya Obshchestvennych Nauk [*A publication*]
**IAT** ............ Southern Illinois University, Edwardsville Campus, Edwardsville, IL [*OCLC symbol*] (OCLC)
**IATA** .......... International Air Transport [*formerly, Traffic*] Association [*Canada*]
**IATA** .......... International Amateur Theatre Association [*Denmark*]
**IATA** .......... International Appropriate Technology Association [*Inactive*] (EA)
**IATA** .......... Is Amended to Add
**IATADS** .... Initial Airborne Target Acquisition Designation System (MCD)
**IATAL** ....... International Association of Theoretical and Applied Limnology [*See also SILTA*] (EA)
**IATB** .......... International Aviation Theft Bureau [*Superseded by ACPI*] (EA)
**IATC** .......... India America Trade Council
**IATC** .......... Inter-American Travel Congresses
**IATC** .......... International Air Traffic Communications
**IATC** .......... International Association of Tool Craftsmen (EA)
**IATC** .......... International Association of Torch Clubs (EA)
**IATC** .......... International Association of Triathlon Clubs (EA)
**IATCA** ....... International Air Transportation Competition Act of 1979
**IATCB** ....... Interdepartmental Air Traffic Control Board
**IATCL** ....... International Association for Textile Care Labelling (EA)
**IATCR** ....... International Air Traffic Communications Receiver Station
**IATCS** ....... International Air Traffic Communications Station
**IATCS** ....... International Air Traffic Communications System (MCD)
**IATCT** ....... International Air Traffic Communications Transmitter Station
**IATD** ......... Is Amended to Delete
**IATDP** ....... International Association of Textile Dyers and Printers [*See also AITIT*] (EAIO)
**IATE** .......... International Accounting and Traffic Analysis Equipment [*Telecommunications*] (TEL)
**IATE** .......... International Association for Television Editors
**IATE** .......... International Association for Temperance Education [*Later, IVES*] (EA)
**IATE** .......... International Association of Trade Exchanges [*Later, IRTA*] (EA)
**IATE** .......... International Association of Travel Exhibitors (EA)
**IATEFL** ..... International Association of Teachers of English as a Foreign Language [*Whitstable, Kent, England*] (EAIO)
**IATF** .......... Interagency Task Force [*for Indochina*] [*South Vietnam refugee relief*]
**IATFAI** ...... Inter-Association Task Force on Alcohol Issues (EA)
**IATG** .......... International Association of Teachers of German [*See also IDV*] [*Copenhagen, Denmark*] (EAIO)
**IATHA** ...... Informations Aerauliques et Thermiques [*A publication*]
**IaTip** ......... Tipron Public Library, Tipron, IA [*Library symbol*] [*Library of Congress*] (LCLS)
**IaTit** .......... Titonka Public Library, Titonka, IA [*Library symbol*] [*Library of Congress*] (LCLS)
**IATJ** .......... International Association of Travel Journalists (EA)
**IATL** .......... International Academy of Trial Lawyers (EA)
**IATL** .......... International Association of Theological Libraries
**IATM** ........ International Association for Testing Materials (IEEE)
**IATM** ........ International Association of Transport Museums [*See also AIMT*] [*Berne, Switzerland*] (EAIO)
**IATM-NAR** ... International Association of Tour Managers - North American Region (EA)
**IATN** ......... International Association of Telecomputer Networks (EA)
**IaTo** .......... Toledo Public Library, Toledo, IA [*Library symbol*] [*Library of Congress*] (LCLS)
**IATOD** ...... In Addition to Other Duties [*Military*]
**IATP** .......... Individual Aircraft Tracking Program (MCD)
**IATP** .......... International Association of Tungsten Producers
**IATR** .......... Is Amended to Read
**IATRA** ....... International Academy of Toxicological Risk Assessment (EA)
**Iatr Ath** ...... Iatrikai Athenai [*A publication*]
**IATROS** .... Organisation Mondiale des Medicins Independants [*International Organization of Private and Independent Doctors*] (EAIO)
**IATS** .......... Individual Accession and Training System (MCD)
**IATSC** ....... International Aeronautical Telecommunications Switching Center
**IATSE** ....... International Alliance of Theatrical Stage Employees and Moving Picture Machine Operators of the US and Canada (EA)
**IATSS** ........ International Association of Traffic and Safety Sciences [*Tokyo, Japan*] (EAIO)
**IATT** .......... International Academy of Twirling Teachers (EA)
**IATTC** ....... Inter-American Tropical Tuna Commission (EA)
**IATU** .......... Inter-American Telecommunications Union [*US*]
**IATUL** ....... International Association of Technological University Libraries [*Goteborg, Sweden*]
**IATUL Proc** ... International Association of Technological University Libraries. Proceedings [*A publication*]
**IATV** .......... Interactive Alphanumeric Television
**IAU** ........... Austin College, Sherman, TX [*OCLC symbol*] (OCLC)
**IAU** ........... Infrastructure Account Unit (NATG)
**IAU** ........... Institute for American Universities (EA)
**IAU** ........... Interface Adapter Unit [*Data processing*] (MCD)
**IAU** ........... Internal Auditor [*A publication*]
**IAU** ........... International Academic Union (EA)
**IAU** ........... International Association of Universities [*France*]
**IAU** ........... International Astronomical Union (EAIO)
**IAU** ........... Internationale Armbrustschutzen Union [*International Crossbow Shooting Union*] (EAIO)
**iau** ............. Iowa [*MARC country of publication code*] [*Library of Congress*] (LCCP)
**IAU** ........... Italian Actors Union (EA)

**IaU** ........ University of Iowa, Iowa City, IA [*Library symbol*] [*Library of Congress*] (LCLS)
**IAub** ........ Auburn Public Library, Auburn, IL [*Library symbol*] [*Library of Congress*] (LCLS)
**IaU-B** ........ University of Iowa, Botany-Chemistry Library, Iowa City, IA [*Library symbol*] [*Library of Congress*] (LCLS)
**IAUC** ........ Irish American Unity Conference (EA)
**IAU Circ** .... International Astronomical Union. Circular [*A publication*]
**IAUD** ........ International Association for a Union of Democracies (EA)
**IAUF** ........ Interamerican Underwater Festival
**IAug** ........ Tri-County Public Library District, Augusta, IL [*Library symbol*] [*Library of Congress*] (LCLS)
**IaU-L** ........ University of Iowa, College of Law, Iowa City, IA [*Library symbol*] [*Library of Congress*] (LCLS)
**IaU-M** ........ University of Iowa, Health Sciences Library, Iowa City, IA [*Library symbol*] [*Library of Congress*] (LCLS)
**IAUMS** ...... Installation, Administrative Use, and Command Design Motor Vehicle Management System [*Army*]
**IAUP** ........ International Association of University Presidents [*Bangkok, Thailand*]
**IAUPE** ...... International Association of University Professors of English [*British*]
**IAUPL** ...... International Association of University Professors and Lecturers (EAIO)
**IaUpV** ........ Vennard College, University Park, IA [*Library symbol*] [*Library of Congress*] (LCLS)
**IAur** ........ Aurora Public Library, Aurora, IL [*Library symbol*] [*Library of Congress*] (LCLS)
**IAUR** ........ Institute for Art and Urban Resources (EA)
**IaUr** ........ Urbandale Public Library, Urbandale, IA [*Library symbol*] [*Library of Congress*] (LCLS)
**IAurC** ........ Aurora College, Aurora, IL [*Library symbol*] [*Library of Congress*] (LCLS)
**IAUSA** ...... International Astronomical Union. Symposium [*A publication*]
**IAUTA** ...... Ingenieurs de l'Automobile [*A publication*]
**IaUte** ........ Ute Public Library, Ute, IA [*Library symbol*] [*Library of Congress*] (LCLS)
**IAV** ........ Indium Antimode Varactor
**IAV** ........ Innotech Aviation Enterprises Ltd. [*Toronto Stock Exchange symbol*]
**IAV** ........ Institute for American Values (EA)
**IAV** ........ Intra-Arterial Vasopressin [*Endocrinology*]
**IAV** ........ Intransit Asset Visibility (MCD)
**IAV** ........ Inventory Adjustment Voucher [*Military*] (AFM)
**IAV** ........ Island-Arc Volcanic [*Geology*]
**IAV** ........ Southern Illinois University, School of Medicine, Springfield, IL [*OCLC symbol*] (OCLC)
**IAV** ........ VIDION/International Association of Video (EA)
**IAVA** ........ Industrial Audio-Visual Association [*Later, AVMA*] (EA)
**IAVC** ........ Indian Army Veterinary Corps [*British military*] (DMA)
**IAVC** ........ Instantaneous Automatic Video Control (IEEE)
**IAVC** ........ Instantaneous Automatic Volume Control [*Electronics*]
**IAVCEI** ..... International Association of Volcanology and Chemistry of the Earth's Interior [*Federal Republic of Germany*]
**IAVCM** ...... International Association of Visual Communications Management [*Formerly, SRE*]
**IAVD** ........ Interactive Videodisc [*Army*] (INF)
**IAVE** ........ International Association for Volunteer Education (EA)
**IAVE** ........ International Association of Volunteer Effort (EA)
**IAveECl** ..... Institute of Automotive Engineers Council [*Australia*]
**IAVFH** ...... International Association of Veterinary Food Hygienists
**IAVG** ........ International Association for Vocational Guidance
**IAVI** ........ International Association of Voice Identification [*Later, IAI*] (EA)
**IaVin** ........ Vinton Public Library, Vinton, IA [*Library symbol*] [*Library of Congress*] (LCLS)
**IaVol** ........ Volga Public Library, Volga, IA [*Library symbol*] [*Library of Congress*] (LCLS)
**IAVS** ........ International Association for Vegetation Science [*See also IVV*] [*Gottingen, Federal Republic of Germany*] (EAIO)
**IAVSD** ...... International Association for Vehicle Systems Dynamics [*ICSU*] [*Delft, Netherlands*] (EAIO)
**IAVTC** ...... International Audio-Visual Technical Centre [*Netherlands*] (DIT)
**IAW** ........ Improved Antimateriel Warhead
**IAW** ........ In Accordance With
**IAW** ........ Institute of the American West [*Later, INAW*] (EA)
**IAW** ........ International Alliance of Women [*See also AIF*] [*Valetta, Malta*] (EAIO)
**IAW** ........ International Association of Wholesalers [*Defunct*]
**IAW** ........ Isotopic Atomic Weight
**IAW** ........ Triton College, River Grove, IL [*OCLC symbol*] (OCLC)
**IaW** ........ Waterloo Public Library, Waterloo, IA [*Library symbol*] [*Library of Congress*] (LCLS)
**IAWA** ........ Independent American Whiskey Association [*Later, ABAA*] (EA)
**IAWA** ........ International Association of Wood Anatomists [*Utrecht, Netherlands*] (EA)
**IaWa** ........ Washington Public Library, Washington, IA [*Library symbol*] [*Library of Congress*] (LCLS)
**IAWA Bull** ... IAWA [*International Association of Wood Anatomists*] Bulletin [*A publication*]
**IAWABV** ... International Association of Wood Anatomists. Bulletin [*A publication*]
**IaWaJ** ........ Washington Evening Journal, Washington, IA [*Library symbol*] [*Library of Congress*] (LCLS)
**IaWal** ........ Walnut Public Library, Walnut, IA [*Library symbol*] [*Library of Congress*] (LCLS)
**IaWall** ........ Wall Lake Public Library, Wall Lake, IA [*Library symbol*] [*Library of Congress*] (LCLS)
**IaWap** ........ Wapello Public Library (Keck Memorial Library), Wapello, IA [*Library symbol*] [*Library of Congress*] (LCLS)
**IaWas** ........ Washta Library, Washta, IA [*Library symbol*] [*Library of Congress*] (LCLS)
**IaWauE** ...... Jerico Community Echo, Waucoma, IA [*Library symbol*] [*Library of Congress*] (LCLS)
**IaWaukCoC** ... Allamakee County Courthouse, Waukon, IA [*Library symbol*] [*Library of Congress*] (LCLS)
**IaWaukD** ... Waukon Democrat, Waukon, IA [*Library symbol*] [*Library of Congress*] (LCLS)
**IaWauke** .... Waukee Public Library, Waukee, IA [*Library symbol*] [*Library of Congress*] (LCLS)
**IaWaukR** ... Waukon Republican-Standard, Waukon, IA [*Library symbol*] [*Library of Congress*] (LCLS)
**IaWavBHi** ... Bremer County Historical Society, Waverly, IA [*Library symbol*] [*Library of Congress*] (LCLS)
**IaWavCoC** ... Bremer County Courthouse, Waverly, IA [*Library symbol*] [*Library of Congress*] (LCLS)
**IaWavD** ..... Waverly Democrat, Waverly, IA [*Library symbol*] [*Library of Congress*] (LCLS)
**IaWavH** ..... Waverly House, Waverly, IA [*Library symbol*] [*Library of Congress*] (LCLS)
**IaWavI** ....... Bremer County Independent, Waverly, IA [*Library symbol*] [*Library of Congress*] (LCLS)
**IaWavW** .... Wartburg College, Waverly, IA [*Library symbol*] [*Library of Congress*] (LCLS)
**IaWayN** ..... Wayland News, Wayland, IA [*Library symbol*] [*Library of Congress*] (LCLS)
**IaWb** ........ Enlow Public Library, West Branch, IA [*Library symbol*] [*Library of Congress*] (LCLS)
**IaWbe** ........ West Bend Public Library, West Bend, IA [*Library symbol*] [*Library of Congress*] (LCLS)
**IaWbeJ** ...... West Bend Journal, West Bend, IA [*Library symbol*] [*Library of Congress*] (LCLS)
**IaWbH** ....... Herbert Hoover Presidential Library, West Branch, IA [*Library symbol*] [*Library of Congress*] (LCLS)
**IaWbT** ....... West Branch Times, West Branch, IA [*Library symbol*] [*Library of Congress*] (LCLS)
**IaWbuN** ..... Des Moines County News, West Burlington, IA [*Library symbol*] [*Library of Congress*] (LCLS)
**IaWC** ........ Daily Courier, Waterloo, IA [*Library symbol*] [*Library of Congress*] (LCLS)
**IAWCC** ...... International Association of Wall and Ceiling Contractors [*Later, AWCI*] (EA)
**IAWCC/GD** ... International Association of Wall and Ceiling Contractors - Gypsum Drywall Contractors International [*Later, AWCI*] (EA)
**IAWCM** .... International Association of Wiping Cloth Manufacturers (EA)
**IaWdmB** .... New Iowa Bystander, West Des Moines, IA [*Library symbol*] [*Library of Congress*] (LCLS)
**IaWdmGS** ... Church of Jesus Christ of Latter-Day Saints, Genealogical Society Library, Des Moines Branch, West Des Moines, IA [*Library symbol*] [*Library of Congress*] (LCLS)
**IaWdmNB** ... New Iowa Bystander, West Des Moines, IA [*Library symbol*] [*Library of Congress*] (LCLS)
**IAWE** ........ International Association for Wind Engineering [*Aachen, Federal Republic of Germany*] (EAIO)
**IaWec** ........ Kendall Young Library, Webster City, IA [*Library symbol*] [*Library of Congress*] (LCLS)
**IaWecAJ** .... Aberdeen-Angus Journal, Webster City, IA [*Library symbol*] [*Library of Congress*] (LCLS)
**IaWecF** ...... Freeman-Journal, Webster City, IA [*Library symbol*] [*Library of Congress*] (LCLS)
**IaWelmA** ... Wellman Advance, Wellman, IA [*Library symbol*] [*Library of Congress*] (LCLS)
**IaWels** ........ Wellsburg Public Library, Wellsburg, IA [*Library symbol*] [*Library of Congress*] (LCLS)
**IaWG** ........ Henry W. Grout Museum of History and Science, Waterlook, IA [*Library symbol*] [*Library of Congress*] (LCLS)
**IAWG** ........ Inter-American War Game (MCD)
**IAWG** ........ Interagency Working Group (MCD)
**IAWGSA** ... Inter-Agency Working Group on Southern Africa [*Canadian Council for International Cooperation*]
**IaWH** ........ Hawkeye Institute of Technology, Area VII, Waterloo, IA [*Library symbol*] [*Library of Congress*] (LCLS)
**IAWH** ........ Improved Antimateriel Warhead
**IaWhaP** ..... What Cheer Patriot-Chronicle, What Cheer, IA [*Library symbol*] [*Library of Congress*] (LCLS)
**IaWhitC** ..... Whittmore Champion, Whittmore, IA [*Library symbol*] [*Library of Congress*] (LCLS)

**IAWHPJ** ... International Association of Women and Home Page Journalists (EA)
**IaWij** .......... Wilton Public Library, Wilton Junction, IA [*Library symbol*] [*Library of Congress*] (LCLS)
**IaWijS** ........ S-R Advocate News, Wilton Junction, IA [*Library symbol*] [*Library of Congress*] (LCLS)
**IaWinfB** ..... Beacon and Wayland News, Winfield, IA [*Library symbol*] [*Library of Congress*] (LCLS)
**IaWinN** ...... Winthrop News, Winthrop, IA [*Library symbol*] [*Library of Congress*] (LCLS)
**IaWint** ........ Winterset Public Library, Winterset, IA [*Library symbol*] [*Library of Congress*] (LCLS)
**IaWintM** .... Winterset Madisonian, Winterset, IA [*Library symbol*] [*Library of Congress*] (LCLS)
**IAWISP** ..... International Accidental War Information Sharing Project [*Nuclear Age Peace Foundation*] (EA)
**IaWl** ........... Free Public Library, West Liberty, IA [*Library symbol*] [*Library of Congress*] (LCLS)
**IAWL** .......... International Association for Water Law [*See also AIDA*] [*Rome, Italy*] (EAIO)
**IaWlI** ......... West Liberty Index, West Liberty, IA [*Library symbol*] [*Library of Congress*] (LCLS)
**IAWM** ....... International Association of Women Ministers (EA)
**IaWmbgI** ... Iowa County Farmer, Williamsburg, IA [*Library symbol*] [*Library of Congress*] (LCLS)
**IaWmbgJT** ... Williamsburg Jounal-Tribune, Williamsburg, IA [*Library symbol*] [*Library of Congress*] (LCLS)
**IAWMC** .... International Association of Workers for Troubled Children and Youth [*See also AIEJI*] (EAIO)
**IaWob** ........ Woodbine Public Library, Woodbine, IA [*Library symbol*] [*Library of Congress*] (LCLS)
**IaWobT** ...... Woodbine Twiner, Woodbine, IA [*Library symbol*] [*Library of Congress*] (LCLS)
**IaWow** ........ Woodward Public Library, Woodward, IA [*Library symbol*] [*Library of Congress*] (LCLS)
**IaWowN** .... Northeast Dallas County Record, Woodward, IA [*Library symbol*] [*Library of Congress*] (LCLS)
**IAWP** ......... Inter-National Association for Widowed People (EA)
**IAWP** ......... International Association of Women Philosophers [*Zurich, Switzerland*] (EAIO)
**IAWP** ......... International Association of Women Police (EA)
**IaWp** .......... West Point Public Library, West Point, IA [*Library symbol*] [*Library of Congress*] (LCLS)
**IaWpB** ....... West Point Bee, West Point, IA [*Library symbol*] [*Library of Congress*] (LCLS)
**IAWPR** ...... International Association on Water Pollution Research [*Later, IAWPRC*]
**IAWPR** ...... International Association of Water Polo Referees (EA)
**IAWPRC** ... International Association on Water Pollution Research and Control [*London, England*] (EA)
**IAWR** ........ Institute of Air Weapons Research [*Air Force*]
**IAWR** ........ Internationale Arbeitsgemeinschaft der Wasserwerke im Rheineinzugsgebiet [*International Association of Waterworks in the Rhine Basin Area - IAWRBA*] (EAIO)
**IAWRBA** ... International Association of Waterworks in the Rhine Basin Area (EAIO)
**IAWTC** ...... Integrated Air Warfare Training Complex [*Military*] (CAAL)
**IaWu** .......... Heiseman Memorial Library, West Union, IA [*Library symbol*] [*Library of Congress*] (LCLS)
**IaWuCoC** ... Fayette County Courthouse, West Union, IA [*Library symbol*] [*Library of Congress*] (LCLS)
**IaWuU** ....... Fayette County Union, West Union, IA [*Library symbol*] [*Library of Congress*] (LCLS)
**IAWWE** ..... International Association of Workshop Way Educators (EA)
**IaWyo** ........ Roche Memorial Library, Wyoming, IA [*Library symbol*] [*Library of Congress*] (LCLS)
**IAX** ........... University of Illinois at the Medical Center, Chicago, IL [*OCLC symbol*] (OCLC)
**IAY** ........... International Atomic Energy Agency. Bulletin [*A publication*]
**IAY** ........... Island Canyon Mines, Inc. [*Vancouver Stock Exchange symbol*]
**IAY** ........... University of Illinois at Chicago Circle, Chicago, IL [*OCLC symbol*] (OCLC)
**IAYC** ......... Interim Accessory Change (MCD)
**IAYM** ........ International Association of Youth Magistrates [*Later, IAJFCM*]
**IAYMC** ...... International Association of Y's Men's Clubs [*Geneva, Switzerland*] (EA)
**IAZ** ........... Industrie-Anzeiger [*A publication*]
**IAZ** ........... Inner Artillery Zone
**IAZ** ........... Western Illinois University, Macomb, IL [*OCLC symbol*] (OCLC)
**IaZN** .......... Tri-County News, Zearing, IA [*Library symbol*] [*Library of Congress*] (LCLS)
**Ib** ............... Ibero-Romania [*A publication*]
**IB** ............... Ibidem [*In the Same Place*] [*Latin*]
**Ib** ............... Ibis [*of Ovid*] [*Classical studies*] (OCD)
**IB** ............... Identifier Block
**IB** ............... Immune Body
**I & B** .......... Improvement and Betterments [*Real estate*]
**IB** ............... In Bond [*Wines and Spirits*]
**IB** ............... Inboard (NASA)
**IB** ............... Inbound
**IB** ............... Incendiary Bomb
**IB** ............... Inclusion Body [*Cytology*]
**IB** ............... Index of Body Build [*Anatomy*]
**IB** ............... India-Burma [*World War II*]
**IB** ............... Individual Bias
**IB** ............... Indogermanische Bibliothek [*A publication*]
**IB** ............... Induction Balance (ADA)
**IB** ............... Induction Brazing
**IB** ............... Industrial Board [*Australia*]
**IB** ............... Industrial Business [*Insurance term*] [*British*]
**I d B** ........... Industries du Bois en Europe [*A publication*]
**IB** ............... Inert Building [*NASA*] (KSC)
**IB** ............... Infantry Battalion [*Army*]
**IB** ............... Infantry Brigade [*British military*] (DMA)
**IB** ............... Infectious Bronchitis [*Veterinary medicine*]
**IB** ............... Information Bulletin
**IB** ............... Information Bureau [*Telecommunications*] (TEL)
**IB** ............... Inner Bottom [*Technical drawings*]
**IB** ............... Input Buffer [*Telecommunications*] (TEL)
**IB** ............... Input Bus [*Data processing*]
**IB** ............... Inspection Bulletin
**IB** ............... Institute of Biology [*British*]
**IB** ............... Institute of Brewing [*Also, IOB*] [*British*]
**IB** ............... Institute of Building [*British*]
**IB** ............... Instruction Bank [*Data processing*]
**IB** ............... Instruction Book
**IB** ............... Instruction Bus [*Data processing*]
**IB** ............... Intelligence Branch
**IB** ............... Interface Bus [*Data processing*]
**IB** ............... Internal Bond [*Pulp and paper technology*]
**IB** ............... Internal Bus [*Data processing*]
**IB** ............... International Bank for Reconstruction and Development [*Also known as World Bank*]
**IB** ............... International Bibliography [*A publication*]
**IB** ............... International Broadcasting
**IB** ............... International Butec Industry [*Vancouver Stock Exchange symbol*]
**IB** ............... Interpreter's Bible
**IB** ............... Investigation Branch [*Great Britain*] [*Australia*] (DCTA)
**IB** ............... Invoice Book [*Business term*]
**IB** ............... Irish Baron (ROG)
**IB** ............... Irish Book [*Bibliographical Society of Ireland*] [*A publication*]
**IB** ............... Iron Bolts
**IB** ............... Ironing Board (MSA)
**IB** ............... Issue Book [*DoD*]
**IB** ............... Lineas Aereas du Espanalos [*Iberia*] [*Spain*] [*ICAO designator*]
**IB** ............... RAB [*Radio Advertising Bureau*] Instant Background [*A publication*]
**IBA** ............ Bradley University, Peoria, IL [*OCLC symbol*] (OCLC)
**IBA** ............ Ibadan [*Nigeria*] [*Airport symbol*] (OAG)
**IBA** ............ Igniter Booster Assembly [*Aerospace*]
**IBA** ............ Ignorant Bloody Aircrafthand [*British Royal Air Force slang*]
**IBA** ............ Independent Bakers Association (EA)
**IBA** ............ Independent Banker [*A publication*]
**IBA** ............ Independent Bar Association (EA)
**IBA** ............ Independent Board Authority [*Board granting franchises to new companies*] [*British*]
**IBA** ............ Independent Broadcasting Authority [*Formerly, ITA*] [*British*]
**IBA** ............ Indolebutyric Acid [*Plant growth regulator*]
**IBA** ............ Indonesian-British Association (DS)
**IBA** ............ Industrial Biotechnology Association (EA)
**IBA** ............ Inflatable Boat Association (EA)
**IBA** ............ Inner Blanket Assembly [*Nuclear energy*] (NRCH)
**IBA** ............ Inspection by Attribute
**IBA** ............ Institute for Bioenergetic Analysis [*Later, IIBA*] (EA)
**IBA** ............ Institute for Briquetting and Agglomeration (EA)
**IBA** ............ Institute of British Architects
**IBA** ............ Institute of Business Appraisers (EA)
**IBA** ............ Institution of Business Agents [*British*]
**IBA** ............ International Backgammon Association (EA)
**IBA** ............ International Backpackers Association [*Later, AHS*] (EA)
**IBA** ............ International Banana Association (EA)
**IBA** ............ International Banker Association (EA)
**IBA** ............ International Banking Act [*1978*]
**IBA** ............ International Bar Association [*London, England*] (EA)
**IBA** ............ International Bartenders Association [*Paris, France*] (EAIO)
**IBA** ............ International Baseball Association (EA)
**IBA** ............ International Basketball Association (EA)
**IBA** ............ International Bauxite Association [*Kingston, Jamaica*]
**IBA** ............ International Biliary Association [*Later, IHBPA*] (EAIO)
**IBA** ............ International Biometric Association (EA)
**IBA** ............ International Board of Auditors (NATG)
**IBA** ............ International Bocce Association (EA)
**IBA** ............ International Braford Association (EA)
**IBA** ............ International Bridge Academy [*The Hague, Netherlands*] (EA)
**IBA** ............ International Bryozoology Association [*See also AIB*] [*Paris, France*] (EAIO)
**IBA** ............ Investing Builders Association
**IBA** ............ Investment Bankers Association of America [*Later, SIA*] (EA)
**IBA** ............ Iodosobenzoic Acid [*Organic chemistry*] (RDA)

**IBA** ........... Isobutylamine [*Organic chemistry*]
**IBAA**........... Independent Bankers Association of America (EA)
**IBA of A**..... Investment Bankers Association of America. Bulletin [*A publication*]
**IBAA**........... Italian Baptist Association of America [*Later, AEIM*] (EA)
**IBAC**........... Information Bulletin of Australian Criminology [*A publication*]
**IBAC**........... International Business Aviation Council (EA)
**IBAC**........... Ivan [*the Terrible*], Borgia [*the Poisoner*], Attila [*the Hun*], Caligula [*the Emperor*] [*Initials that form the name of the villain in "Captain Marvel" comic strip and also indicate the sources of his powers*]
**Ibadan**........ Ibadan Review [*A publication*]
**Ibadan Univ Dep For Bull** ... Ibadan University. Department of Forestry. Bulletin [*A publication*]
**IBAG** ........ Ich Bau auf Gott [*I Build on God*] [*German*] [*Motto of Heinrich Posthumus, Count Reuss (1572-1635)*]
**IBAHP**....... Inter-African Bureau for Animal Health and Protection
**IBAHRS**.... Inflatable Body and Head Restraint System [*Aviation*] (RDA)
**IBAN** ........ Imperial Bancorp [*NASDAQ symbol*] (NQ)
**IBAP**......... Intervention Board for Agricultural Products [*Government body*] [*British*]
**I Bar**.......... I Baruch [*Apocrypha*] (BJA)
**IBAR**.......... Inter-African Bureau of Animal Resources [*Kenya*]
**IBarA**......... American Can Co., Barrington, IL [*Library symbol*] [*Library of Congress*] (LCLS)
**IBarQ**......... Quaker Oats Co., Research Library, Barrington, IL [*Library symbol*] [*Library of Congress*] (LCLS)
**IBart**.......... Alpha Park Public Library, Bartonville, IL [*Library symbol*] [*Library of Congress*] (LCLS)
**IBartL**........ Limestone Community High School, Bartonville, IL [*Library symbol*] [*Library of Congress*] (LCLS)
**IBAS**.......... Instructional-Based Appraisal System [*Education*]
**IBAS**.......... Intelligent Body Assembly System [*Robotics*] [*Nissan Motor Co. Ltd.*]
**IBASB** ....... Izvestiya na Sektsiyata po Astronomiya. Bulgarska Akademiya na Naukite [*A publication*]
**IBASF**........ Intervals between Aircraft in Stream Type Formation (FAAC)
**IBA Tech Rev** ... IBA [*Independent Broadcasting Authority*] Technical Review [*A publication*]
**IBatF**.......... FERMILAB, Batavia, IL [*Library symbol*] [*Library of Congress*] (LCLS)
**IBAZA**....... Proceedings of the Convention. Institute of Brewing (Australia and New Zealand Section) [*A publication*]
**IBB**............ Chicago Transit Authority, Chicago, IL [*OCLC symbol*] (OCLC)
**IBB**............ Intentional Bases on Balls [*Baseball*]
**IBB**............ International Book Bank (EA)
**IBB**............ International Bottler and Packer [*A publication*]
**IBB**............ International Bowling Board (EA)
**IBB**............ International Brotherhood of Bookbinders [*Later, Graphic Arts International Union*]
**IBB**............ Invest in Britain Bureau
**IBB**............ Isobutylbenzene [*Organic chemistry*]
**IBBA**.......... Inland Bird Banding Association (EA)
**IBBA**.......... International Brangus Breeders Association (EA)
**IBBA**.......... International Business Brokers Association (EA)
**IBBBA**....... International Bundle Branch Block Association (EA)
**IBBD Bol Inf** ... IBBD [*Instituto Brasileiro de Bibliografia e Documentacao*] Boletim Informativo [*A publication*]
**IBBD Not Diversas** ... IBBD [*Instituto Brasileiro de Bibliografia e Documentacao*] Noticias Diversas [*A publication*]
**IBBFIC**...... International B & B [*Bed and Breakfast*] Fly-Inn Club (EA)
**IBBH** ......... Internationaler Bund der Bau-Haolzarbeiter [*International Federation of Building and Woodworkers*]
**IBBIT** ........ Internal Bean Bacterial Infusion Test [*Plant pathology*]
**IBBL**.......... Islamic Bank of Bangladesh [*Commercial bank*] (EY)
**IBBM**......... Ion-Binding/Ion-Bouncing Model [*Physical chemistry*]
**IBBM**......... Iron Body Bronze-Mounted
**IBBNA5**..... International Bulletin of Bacteriological Nomenclature and Taxonomy [*A publication*]
**IBBR**.......... International Beefalo Breeders' Registry (EA)
**IBBRIS**...... International Biodeterioration Bulletin. Reference Index [*A publication*]
**IBBTPS**..... Ivory and Bone Brushmakers' Trade Protection Society [*A union*] [*British*]
**IBBY**.......... International Board on Books for Young People [*Basel, Switzerland*] (EA)
**IBC**............ De Paul University, Law Library, Chicago, IL [*OCLC symbol*] (OCLC)
**IBC**............ Iceland Base Command [*Army*] [*World War II*]
**IBC**............ Imperial Bushmen Contingent [*British military*] (DMA)
**IBC**............ Independent Bakers' Cooperative [*W. E. Long Co.*] (EA)
**IBC**............ Information-Based Complexity [*Mathematics*]
**IBC**............ Input Bias Current
**IBC**............ Inside Back Cover
**IBC**............ Institute for Biomedical Communication [*South African Medical Research Council*] [*Information service or system*] (IID)
**IBC**............ Institutional Biosafety Committee [*National Institutes of Health*]
**IBC**............ Instrument Bus Computer
**IBC**............ Insurance Bureau of Canada
**IBC**............ Intelligent Buildings Corporation [*Broomfield, CO*] [*Telecommunications service*] (TSSD)
**IBC**............ Interboard Committee for Christian Work in Japan [*Later, JNAC*] (EA)
**IBC**............ Intermediate Bulk Containers [*Shipping*]
**IBC**............ International Ballet Competition
**IBC**............ International Banana Club (EA)
**IBC**............ International Banking Centre [*British*]
**IBC**............ International Betta Congress (EA)
**IBC**............ International Biographical Centre [*British*] (CB)
**IBC**............ International Biophysical Center
**IBC**............ International Biotoxicological Center [*World Life Research Institute*] [*US*] (ASF)
**IBC**............ International Board of Cytopathology [*International Academy of Cytology*] [*Quebec, PQ*] (EAIO)
**IBC**............ International Borzoi Council (EA)
**IBC**............ International Brightness Coefficient
**IBC**............ International Broadcasting Convention [*Legal term*] (DLA)
**IBC**............ International Broadcasting Corp. [*Vancouver Stock Exchange symbol*]
**IBC**............ International Bus Collectors Club (EA)
**IBC**............ International Business Centre [*Australia*]
**IBC**............ International Business Communications [*Commercial firm*] [*British*]
**IBC**............ International Business Contacts
**IBC**............ International Business Corporation
**IBC**............ International Business Council (EA)
**IBC**............ International Federation of the Blue Cross [*Formerly, International Federation of the Temperance Blue Cross Societies*] (EA)
**IBC**............ Interstate Bakeries Corporation [*Formerly, Interstate Brands Corporation*] [*NYSE symbol*] (SPSG)
**IBC**............ Inverted Bowl Centrifuge
**IBC**............ Iodine Binding Capacity [*of starch*]
**IBC**............ Iron-Binding Capacity [*Clinical chemistry*]
**IBC**............ Isobaric Cooling [*Geology*]
**IBC**............ World Institute of Buddhist Culture
**IBCA**.......... Department of the Interior Board of Contract Appeals
**IBCA**.......... Industry Bar Code Alliance (EA)
**IBCA**.......... Institute of Burial and Cremation Administration [*British*]
**IBCA**.......... Interior Board of Contract Appeals (in United States Interior Decisions) [*A publication*] (DLA)
**IBCA**.......... International Braille Chess Association [*Abcoude, Netherlands*] (EA)
**IBCA**.......... International Brick Collectors' Association (EA)
**IBCA**.......... International Broadcasting Corp. [*NASDAQ symbol*] (NQ)
**IBCA**.......... Isobutyl Cyanoacrylate [*Organic chemistry*]
**IBCASA**..... International Banking Campaign Against South Africa [*Later, ICABA*] (EAIO)
**IBCC**.......... Intelligent Business Communications Corporation [*Hauppauge, NY*] [*NASDAQ symbol*] (NQ)
**IBCC**.......... International Building Classification Committee [*Netherlands*]
**IBCC**.......... International Business Contact Club
**IBCC**.......... Intra-Bureau Change Committee
**IBCFP**........ International Board of Standards and Practices for Certified Financial Planners (EA)
**IBCL**.......... Instrument Bus Control Language [*National Instruments Corp.*] [*Austin, TX*]
**IBCL**.......... Interface Bus Control Language [*Data processing*]
**IBCM**......... Integrated Battlefield Casualty Manikin [*Medical training*] [*Navy*]
**IBCM**......... International Business Council Midamerica (EA)
**IBCN** ......... Integrated Broadband Communication Network [*Telecommunications*]
**IBCO** ......... International Barrier Corp. [*NASDAQ symbol*] (NQ)
**IBCOEH**.... Indian Botanical Contactor [*A publication*]
**IBCP**.......... Imperial British Conservative Party [*Political party*] (ADA)
**IBCP**.......... Independent Bank Corporation [*Ionia, MI*] [*NASDAQ symbol*] (NQ)
**IBCPAG** .... Atti. Istituto Botanico e Laboratorio Crittogamico. Universita di Pavia [*A publication*]
**IBCS**.......... Inflight Blood Collection System [*On space flights*]
**IBCS**.......... Integrated Battlefield Control System [*Army*]
**IBCSVP**..... International Breeding Consortium for St. Vincent Parrot (EAIO)
**IBD** ............ Baylor College of Dentistry, Dallas, TX [*OCLC symbol*] (OCLC)
**IBD** ............ Ibadan [*Nigeria*] [*Geomagnetic observatory code*]
**IBD** ............ Incomplete Block Design (MCD)
**IBD** ............ Infant Behavior and Development [*A publication*]
**IBD** ............ Infectious Bursal Disease [*Avian pathology*]
**IBD** ............ Inflammatory Bowel Disease [*Medicine*]
**IBD** ............ Inhabited Building Distance [*Army*] (AABC)
**IBD** ............ Institute of Business Designers (EA)
**IBD** ............ Interest Bearing Deposit [*Banking*] (ADA)
**IBD** ............ Interior Ballistic Division [*Ballistic Research Laboratory*] [*Army*] (RDA)
**IBD** ............ Internationaal Opereren [*A publication*]
**IBD** ............ International Business Database [*Information service or system*] (IID)

**IBD**........... International Business Development Program [*Northwestern University*] [*Research center*] (RCD)
**IBD**........... Internationale Bildungs- und Informations- Datenbank [*International Education and Information Data Bank*] [*Thiede & Thiede Mittelstandische Systemberatung GmbH*] [*Information service or system*] (IID)
**IBD**........... Ion Beam Deposition [*Coating technology*]
**IBD**........... Sandoz Pharmaceuticals [*Research code symbol*]
**IBDA**......... Indirect Bomb-Damage Assessment
**IBDA**......... International Balance Disorder Association [*Defunct*] (EA)
**IBDB**......... Internationaal Belasting Documentatie Bureau [*International Bureau of Fiscal Documentation*] (EAIO)
**IBDB**......... International Battery Data Base [*Robert Morey Associates*] [*Information service or system*] (IID)
**IBDBAD**.... International Biodeterioration Bulletin [*A publication*]
**IBDCC**....... International Barbie Doll Collectors Club (EA)
**IBDEDP**.... Infant Behavior and Development [*A publication*]
**IBDM**......... Interim Bomber Defense Missile
**IBDPW**...... International Brotherhood of Du Pont Workers (EA)
**IBDS**.......... Improved Biological Detection System [*Military*] (MCD)
**IBDT**.......... Insulation Breakdown Tester
**IBDU**......... Isobutylidenediurea [*Organic chemistry*]
**IBDV**......... Infectious Bursal Disease Virus
**IBDVS**....... Indian Base Depot Veterinary Stores [*British military*] (DMA)
**IBE**............ Ibague [*Colombia*] [*Airport symbol*] (OAG)
**IBE**............ Inner Back End (MSA)
**IBE**............ Institute of British Engineers (DAS)
**IBE**............ International Beverage Co. [*Vancouver Stock Exchange symbol*]
**IBE**............ International Bureau of Education [*See also BIE*] [*UNESCO*] (EAIO)
**IBE**............ International Bureau for Epilepsy [*Alderley Edge, Cheshire, England*] (EAIO)
**IBE**............ Rosary College, River Forest, IL [*OCLC symbol*] (OCLC)
**IBea**........... Beardstown Public Library, Beardstown, IL [*Library symbol*] [*Library of Congress*] (LCLS)
**IBEA**.......... Industrial Base Engineering Activity (RDA)
**IBEAR**....... International Business Education and Research Program [*University of Southern California*] [*Research center*] (RCD)
**IBEA Reports**... Illinois Business Education Association. Reports [*A publication*]
**IBEC**.......... International Bank for Economic Cooperation [*Moscow, USSR*] (EY)
**IBEC**.......... International Basic Economic Cooperation [*Investment term*] (DS)
**IBECO**....... Inboard Booster Engine Cutoff (MCD)
**IBEC Res Inst Bull**... IBEC Research Institute. Bulletin [*A publication*]
**IBED**.......... Inter-African Bureau for Epizootic Diseases [*Later, IBAR*]
**IBEE**.......... Illustrated Broadcast Equipment Encyclopedia [*A publication*]
**IBEE**.......... International Builders Exchange Executives (EA)
**IBEF**.......... International Bio-Environmental Foundation (EA)
**IBEG**.......... International Book Export Group
**IBEJA8**...... Indian Bee Journal [*A publication*]
**IBel**........... Belleville Public Library, Belleville, IL [*Library symbol*] [*Library of Congress*] (LCLS)
**IBEL**.......... Interest-Bearing Eligible Liabilities
**IBelC**......... Belleville Area College, Belleville, IL [*Library symbol*] [*Library of Congress*] (LCLS)
**IBelHS**....... Altoff High School, Belleville, IL [*Library symbol*] [*Library of Congress*] (LCLS)
**IBelHSD**.... Harmony-Emge-Ellis School District 175, Belleville, IL [*Library symbol*] [*Library of Congress*] (LCLS)
**IBelS**......... Saint Henry's Seminary, Belleville, IL [*Library symbol*] [*Library of Congress*] (LCLS)
**IBelSCM**... Saint Clair County Mental Health Board, Belleville, IL [*Library symbol*] [*Library of Congress*] (LCLS)
**IBelSD**....... Belleville Public Schools District 118, Belleville, IL [*Library symbol*] [*Library of Congress*] (LCLS)
**IBelSH**....... Saint Elizabeth's Hospital, Belleville, IL [*Library symbol*] [*Library of Congress*] (LCLS)
**IBelTSD**.... Belleville Township High School District 201, Belleville, IL [*Library symbol*] [*Library of Congress*] (LCLS)
**IBelv**......... Ida Public Library, Belvidere, IL [*Library symbol*] [*Library of Congress*] (LCLS)
**IBelVS**....... Belle Valley School, Belleville, IL [*Library symbol*] [*Library of Congress*] (LCLS)
**IBelw**......... Bellwood Public Library, Bellwood, IL [*Library symbol*] [*Library of Congress*] (LCLS)
**IBem**.......... Bement Township Library, Bement, IL [*Library symbol*] [*Library of Congress*] (LCLS)
**IBEM**......... International Board of Environmental Medicine (EA)
**IBEN**.......... Incendiary Bomb with Explosive Nose
**IBer**........... Berwyn Public Library, Berwyn, IL [*Library symbol*] [*Library of Congress*] (LCLS)
**IBER**.......... Institute for Biomedical Engineering Research [*University of Akron*] [*Research center*] (RCD)
**IBerk**......... Berkeley Public Library, Berkeley, IL [*Library symbol*] [*Library of Congress*] (LCLS)
**IBERLANT**... Iberian Atlantic Area [*NATO*] (NATG)
**IBerMH**..... MacNeal Memorial Hospital, Berwyn, IL [*Library symbol*] [*Library of Congress*] (LCLS)
**Ibero**.......... Ibero-Romania [*A publication*]
**IBerO**......... Olympic Savings & Loan Association, Berwyn, IL [*Library symbol*] [*Library of Congress*] (LCLS)
**Ibero Am**.... Ibero-Americana [*A publication*]
**IBES**.......... Institutional Brokers Estimate System [*Lynch, Jones & Ryan*] [*New York, NY*] [*Database*] [*Information service or system*] (IID)
**IBES**.......... International Bronchoesophagological Society (EA)
**IBES**.......... International Business Earth Stations [*Communications Satellite Corp.*]
**IBeth**......... Bethalto Public Library, Bethalto, IL [*Library symbol*] [*Library of Congress*] (LCLS)
**IBethCU**.... Bethalto Community Unit 8, Bethalto, IL [*Library symbol*] [*Library of Congress*] (LCLS)
**IBEU**.......... Independent Bakery Employees Union (EA)
**IBEW**......... International Brotherhood of Electrical Workers (EA)
**IBEX**.......... International Building Exposition (TSPED)
**IBF**............ Chicago Municipal Reference Library, Chicago, IL [*OCLC symbol*] (OCLC)
**IBF**............ First Iberian Fund [*AMEX symbol*] (SPSG)
**IBF**............ Immature Brown-Fat [*Cells*]
**IBF**............ Internally Blown Flap [*Aviation*]
**IBF**............ International Badminton Federation [*Cheltenham, Gloustershire, England*] (EAIO)
**IBF**............ International Balint Federation [*Brussels, Belgium*] (EAIO)
**IBF**............ International Balut Federation [*Bangkok, Thailand*] (EAIO)
**IBF**............ International Bandy Federation [*Lulea, Sweden*] (EAIO)
**IBF**............ International Banking Facility
**IBF**............ International Bar Fly [*Sign in Harry's New York Bar, Paris*]
**IBF**............ International Bicycle Fund (EA)
**IBF**............ International Bobsled Federation
**IBF**............ International Booksellers Federation [*Formerly, ICBA*] (EA)
**IBF**............ International Boxing Federation (EA)
**IBFAN**....... International Baby Food Action Network (EA)
**IBFC**.......... Iron Butterfly Fan Club [*Later, IBIN*] (EA)
**IBFCC**........ International Border Fancy Canary Club (EA)
**IBFD**.......... International Bureau of Fiscal Documentation (EAIO)
**IBFEG**....... Internationaler Bund Freier Evangelischer Gemeinden [*International Federation of Free Evangelical Churches - IFFEC*] (EA)
**IBFF**.......... Impulse Base Flow Facility [*NASA*]
**IBFG**.......... Internationaler Bund Freier Gewerkschaften [*International Confederation of Free Trade Unions*]
**IBFI**........... International Business Forms Industries (EA)
**IBFM**......... Institute of Broadcasting Financial Management [*Later, BCFMA*]
**IBFMP**...... International Bureau of the Federations of Master Printers
**IBFN**.......... Integrated Broadband Fiber Optic Network [*Telecommunications*]
**IBFO**.......... International Brotherhood of Firemen and Oilers (EA)
**IBFRBTWB**... International Book Fair of Radical Black and Third World Books
**IBFS**.......... International Benjamin Franklin Society [*Defunct*] (EA)
**IBG**............ CNA Financial Corp., Library, Chicago, IL [*OCLC symbol*] [*Inactive*] (OCLC)
**IBG**............ Incorporated Brewers' Guild [*London, England*] (EAIO)
**IBG**............ Institute for Behavioral Genetics [*University of Colorado - Boulder*] [*Research center*] (RCD)
**IBG**............ Inter Block Gap
**IBG**............ Intermediate BTU [*British Thermal Unit*] Gas
**IBG**............ International Beverage News [*A publication*]
**IBG**............ International Boxing Guild
**IBG**............ Internationale Brecht Gesellschaft [*International Brecht Society*] (EAIO)
**IBG**............ Internationale Bruckner Gesellschaft [*Vienna, Austria*] (EAIO)
**IBG**............ Internationales Buro fuer Gebirgsmechanik [*International Bureau of Strato-Mechanics - IBSM*] (EAIO)
**IBGE/R**..... Revista Brasileira de Geografia. Conselho Nacional de Geografia. Instituto Brasileiro de Geografia e Estatistica [*A publication*]
**IBGE/RBE**... Revista Brasileira de Estatistica. Ministerio do Planejamento e Coordenacao Geral. Instituto Brasileiro de Geografia e Estatistica [*A publication*]
**IBGI**.......... Independent Bankgroup, Incorporated [*NASDAQ symbol*] (NQ)
**IBG/T**........ Transactions. Institute of British Geographers [*A publication*]
**IBH**............ Initial Beachhead [*Military*]
**IBHA**......... International Buckskin Horse Association (EA)
**IBHD**......... Initial Beachhead [*Military*]
**IBHF**.......... International Boxing Hall of Fame (EA)
**IBHI**.......... Independent Bureau for Humanitarian Issues (EAIO)
**IBHR**......... International Bibliography of the History of Religions [*A publication*] (BJA)
**IBHS**.......... International Bibliography of Historical Sciences [*A publication*]
**IBi**............. Blue Island Public Library, Blue Island, IL [*Library symbol*] [*Library of Congress*] (LCLS)
**i-bi---**.......... British Indian Ocean Territory [*MARC geographic area code*] [*Library of Congress*] (LCCP)

**IBI**.............. College of Du Page, Glen Ellyn, IL [*OCLC symbol*] (OCLC)
**IBi**.............. Illustrazione Biellese [*A publication*]
**IBI**.............. Independent Broadcast Institute [*British*]
**IBI**.............. Insulation Board Institute [*Later, ABPA*] (EA)
**IBI**.............. Intelligent Buildings Institute (EA)
**IBI**.............. Interburst Interval [*Electrophysiology*]
**IBI**.............. Intergovernmental Bureau for Informatics [*Telecommunications*] (EA)
**IBI**.............. Interim Ballistic Instrumentation
**IBI**.............. Intermittent Bladder Irrigation [*Medicine*]
**IBI**.............. International Bankers, Incorporated
**IBI**.............. International Biomass Institute (EA)
**IBI**.............. International Biotechnologies, Inc.
**IBI**.............. International Boat Industry [*A publication*]
**IBI**.............. International Brace Resources [*Vancouver Stock Exchange symbol*]
**IBI**.............. International Broadcast Institute [*Later, IIC*]
**IBI**.............. International Bureau for Informatics (CSR)
**iBi**.............. International Business Intelligence [*A publication*]
**IBI**.............. Internationales Burgen-Institut [*International Castles Institute*] [*Rozendaal, Netherlands*] (EA)
**IBI**.............. Interpersonal Behavior Inventory [*Veterans Administration*]
**IBI**.............. Interview-Oriented Background Investigation (MCD)
**IBI**.............. Invoice Book Inward [*Business term*]
**IBI**.............. Islamic Bank International
**IBI**.............. Istituto Bancario Italiano SpA [*Italy*] (EY)
**IBIA**............ Institute of British Industrial Art
**IBIA**............ Interior Board of Indian Affairs (in United States Interior Decisions) [*A publication*] (DLA)
**IBIB**............ Isobutyl Isobutyrate [*Organic chemistry*]
**IBIC**............ Interface Bus Interactive Control [*Data processing*]
**IBICT**.......... Instituto Brasileiro de Informacao em Ciencia e Tecnologia [*Brazilian Institute for Information in Science and Technology*] [*Information service or system*] [*National Council of Scientific and Technological Development*] (IID)
**IBID**............ Ibidem [*In the Same Place*] [*Latin*]
**IBID**............ International Bibliographical Description
**IBID**............ International Bibliography, Information, and Documentation [*A publication*]
**IBID**............ Izvestija na Balgarskoto Istoricesko Druzestvo [*A publication*]
**IBIFAG**...... Instituto Nacional de Pesca [*Ecuador*]. Boletin Informativo [*A publication*]
**IBIGB**......... Information Bulletin on Isotopic Generators [*A publication*]
**IBI-ICC**...... Intergovernmental Bureau for Informatics - International Computation Center (CSR)
**IBIN**............ Iron Butterfly Information Network (EA)
**IBIO**............ International Biotechnologies, Inc. [*New Haven, CT*] [*NASDAQ symbol*] (NQ)
**IBIODC**...... Specialist Periodical Reports. Inorganic Biochemistry [*A publication*]
**IBIP**............ International Books in Print [*A publication*]
**IBIRDL**...... Irish Birds [*A publication*]
**IBIS**............ IBI Security Service, Inc. [*Long Island City, NY*] [*NASDAQ symbol*] (NQ)
**IBIS**............ ICAO [*International Civil Aviation Organization*] Bird Strike Information System [*Information service or system*] (IID)
**IBIS**............ Infrared Background Imaging Seeker (MCD)
**IBIS**............ Intense Bunched Ion Source (IEEE)
**IBIS**............ Intensive Biometric Intertidal Survey [*Botany*]
**IBIS**............ International Bank Information System
**IBIS**............ International Book Information Service
**IBIS**............ Inventaire Bibliographique des Isiaca (BJA)
**IBIS**............ Issue-Based Information System [*Data processing*]
**IBiS**............ Saint Francis Hospital, Blue Island, IL [*Library symbol*] [*Library of Congress*] (LCLS)
**IBIT**............ ICBM [*Intercontinental Ballistic Missile*] Blast Interference Test (MCD)
**IBIT**............ Issue by Issue Tally
**IBJ**.............. Illinois Bar Journal [*A publication*]
**IBJ**.............. Industrial Bank of Japan
**IBJ**.............. Instrument Bearing Jewel
**IBJ**.............. Loop College, Chicago, IL [*OCLC symbol*] (OCLC)
**IBJCA**......... International Blue Jay Class Association (EA)
**IBJM**.......... International Board of Jewish Missions (EA)
**IBK**.............. Illinois Banker [*A publication*]
**IBk**.............. Index to Book Reviews in the Humanities [*A publication*]
**IBK**.............. [*The*] Industrial Bank of Kuwait
**IBK**.............. Infectious Bovine Keratoconjunctivitis [*Veterinary medicine*]
**IBK**.............. Innsbruck [*Austria*] [*Seismograph station code, US Geological Survey*] (SEIS)
**IBK**.............. Innsbrucker Beitraege zur Kulturwissenschaft [*A publication*]
**IBK**.............. Institute of Bookkeepers [*British*] (DAS)
**IBK**.............. International Banknote Co. [*AMEX symbol*] (SPSG)
**IBK**.............. Knox College, Galesburg, IL [*OCLC symbol*] (OCLC)
**IBKA**.......... Ikatan Buruh Kereta Api [*Railroad Workers' Union*] [*Indonesia*]
**IBKB**.......... Ikatan Buruh Kendaaran Bermotor [*Motor Transport Workers' Union*] [*Indonesia*]
**I BKR**......... Ice Breaker [*Freight*]
**IBKT**.......... Industrial Valley Bank [*NASDAQ symbol*] (NQ)
**IBKW**......... International Bank [*NASDAQ symbol*] (NQ)
**IBL**.............. Boehringer Mannheim Corp., Indianapolis, IN [*OCLC symbol*] (OCLC)
**IBL**.............. Instytut Badan Literackick Polskiej Akademii Nauk [*A publication*]
**IBL**.............. Interest-Bearing Liability
**IBL**.............. Interior Ballistics Laboratory [*Aberdeen, MD*] [*Army*]
**IBL**.............. International Brotherhood of Longshoremen
**IBL**.............. Iroquois Brands Limited [*AMEX symbol*] (SPSG)
**IBLA**.......... Institut Belles-Lettres Arabes. Revue [*Tunis*] [*A publication*]
**IBLA**.......... Inter-American Bibliographical and Library Association (EA)
**IBLC**.......... International B-24 Liberator Club (EA)
**IBLE**.......... International Brotherhood of Locomotive Engineers (EA)
**IBLM**......... International Bureau of Legal Metrology
**IBlo**............ Withers Public Library, Bloomington, IL [*Library symbol*] [*Library of Congress*] (LCLS)
**IBloA**......... Illinois Agricultural Association, Bloomington, IL [*Library symbol*] [*Library of Congress*] (LCLS)
**IBloC**.......... Corn Belt Library System, Bloomington, IL [*Library symbol*] [*Library of Congress*] (LCLS)
**IBloHi**........ McLean County Historical Society, Bloomington, IL [*Library symbol*] [*Library of Congress*] (LCLS)
**IBloMH**..... Mennonite Hospital Association, Medical-Nursing Library, Bloomington, IL [*Library symbol*] [*Library of Congress*] (LCLS)
**IBloStJ**...... Saint Joseph's Hospital, Bloomington, IL [*Library symbol*] [*Library of Congress*] (LCLS)
**IBloW**........ Illinois Wesleyan University, Bloomington, IL [*Library symbol*] [*Library of Congress*] (LCLS)
**IBLS**.......... International Brotherhood of Live Steamers (EA)
**IBM**............ I Built a Macintosh [*Humorous translation of the letters in IBM Corp., referring to improved graphics capabilities of IBM computers*]
**IBM**............ I Buy Money [*Humorous translation of the letters in IBM Corp., referring to the appeal of investing in its stocks*]
**IBM**............ Instant Big Mouth [*Martini*] [*Slang*]
**IBM**............ Interacting Boson Model [*Of nuclear structure*]
**IBM**............ Intercontinental Ballistic Missile
**IBM**............ International Brotherhood of Magicians (EA)
**IBM**............ International Business Machines Corp. [*White Plains, NY*] [*Computer manufacturer*] [*NYSE symbol*] [*Toronto Stock Exchange symbol*] (SPSG)
**IBM**............ Kimball, NE [*Location identifier*] [*FAA*] (FAAL)
**IBM**............ Kirkland & Ellis, Chicago, IL [*OCLC symbol*] (OCLC)
**IBMA**......... Independent Battery Manufacturers Association (EA)
**IBMA**......... Interior Board of Mine Operations Appeals (in United States Interior Decisions) [*A publication*] (DLA)
**IBMA**......... International Bluegrass Music Association (EA)
**IBMA**......... Isobutoxymethyl Acrylamide [*Organic chemistry*]
**IBMC**......... International Brotherhood of Motorcycle Campers (EA)
**IBMC**......... International Buddhist Meditation Center (EA)
**IBME**......... Institute of Biomedical Engineering [*University of Toronto*] [*Research center*] (RCD)
**IBM J**........ IBM [*International Business Machines Corp.*] Journal of Research and Development [*A publication*]
**IBM J R D**... IBM [*International Business Machines Corp.*] Journal of Research and Development [*A publication*]
**IBM J Res**... IBM [*International Business Machines Corp.*] Journal of Research and Development [*A publication*]
**IBM J Res and Dev**... IBM [*International Business Machines Corp.*] Journal of Research and Development [*A publication*]
**IBM J Res Dev**... IBM [*International Business Machines Corp.*] Journal of Research and Development [*A publication*]
**IBM J Res Develop**... IBM [*International Business Machines Corp.*] Journal of Research and Development [*A publication*]
**IBM Jrl**...... IBM [*International Business Machines Corp.*] Journal of Research and Development [*A publication*]
**IBMK**......... Isobutyl Methyl Ketone [*Organic chemistry*]
**IBMM**........ Integrated Book Manufacturing Machine
**IBM Nachr**... IBM [*International Business Machines Corp.*] Nachrichten [*A publication*]
**IBMOC**...... Intercontinental Ballistic Missile Operational Capability (AAG)
**IBMOEX**... International Bioscience Monographs [*A publication*]
**IBMP**......... International Board of Medicine and Psychology [*Later, IAMP*] (EA)
**IBMP**......... Isobutyl(methoxy)pyrazine [*Organic chemistry*]
**IBMS**......... Ion Beam Mass Spectrometer
**IBM Systems J**... IBM [*International Business Machines Corp.*] Systems Journal [*A publication*]
**IBM Syst J**... IBM [*International Business Machines Corp.*] Systems Journal [*A publication*]
**IBM Tech Discl Bull**... IBM [*International Business Machines Corp.*] Technical Disclosure Bulletin [*A publication*]
**IBM Tech Disclosure Bull**... IBM [*International Business Machines Corp.*] Technical Disclosure Bulletin [*A publication*]
**IBM TSS**... International Business Machine's Timesharing System (TEL)
**IBM User**.. IBM [*International Business Machines Corp.*] System User [*A publication*]
**IBMX**......... Isobutylmethylxanthine [*Also, MIX*] [*Biochemistry*]
**IBN**............ Blackburn College, Carlinville, IL [*OCLC symbol*] (OCLC)

**IBN** ........... Identification Beacon
**IBN** ........... Institut Belge de Normalisation [*Belgian Institute for Standardization*] [*Information service or system*] (IID)
**IBN** ........... International Biosciences Network
**IBND** ........ Inbound (FAAC)
**IBNR** ........ Incurred but Not Reported [*Insurance*]
**IBNS** ......... International Bank Note Society (EA)
**IBNS** ......... International Bank Note Society. Quarterly Magazine [*A publication*]
**IbNY** ......... Iberica (New York) [*A publication*]
**IBO** ........... Ibotenic Acid [*Organic acid*]
**IBO** ........... Idabel, OK [*Location identifier*] [*FAA*] (FAAL)
**IBO** ........... Instruction by Objective
**IBO** ........... International Baccalaureate Office [*See also OBI*] [*Later, International Baccalaureate Organization*] [*Grand-Saconnex, Switzerland*] (EAIO)
**IBO** ........... International Broadcasting Organization
**IBO** ........... Internationale Bouworde [*International Association of Building Companions - IABC*] [*Marche-En-Famenne, Belgium*] (EAIO)
**IBO** ........... Invoice Book Outbound [*Business term*]
**IBO** ........... Lutheran General Hospital, Park Ridge, IL [*OCLC symbol*] (OCLC)
**IBOB** ......... International Brotherhood of Old Bastards (EA)
**IBOC** ......... Iso and Bizzarrini Owners Club (EA)
**IBOC** ......... Isobutoxycarbonylation [*Organic chemistry*]
**IBOJ** ......... Informacni Bulletin pro Otazky Jazykovedne [*A publication*]
**IBOL** ......... Interactive Business-Oriented Language
**IBOLB** ....... Informatore Botanico Italiano [*A publication*]
**IBOND** ...... IGOSS [*Integrated Global Ocean Station System*] Basic Observation Network Design [*Marine science*] (MSC)
**IBOP** ......... Institute of British Oil Paintings
**IBOP** ......... International Balance of Payments Reporting System
**IBOP** ......... International Brotherhood of Operative Potters [*Later, IBPAW*] (EA)
**IBOT** ......... In-Branch Operator Training [*British*] (DCTA)
**IBOT** ......... Introduction to the Books of the Old Testament [*A publication*] (BJA)
**IBoT** ......... Istanbul Arkeoloji Muzelerinde Bulunan Bogazkoy Tableteri I and II [*Istanbul*] [*A publication*] (BJA)
**IBP** ........... IBP, Inc. [*NYSE symbol*] (SPSG)
**IBP** ........... Industrial Base Program
**IBP** ........... Informed Birth and Parenting [*Later, IH/IBP*] (EA)
**IBP** ........... Initial Boiling Point (MCD)
**IBP** ........... Inner [*Edge of*] Basal Piece
**IBP** ........... Institute for Better Packaging [*Later, PPC*] (EA)
**IBP** ........... Institute for Business Planning
**IBP** ........... Insulated Binding Post
**IBP** ........... Integrated Basic Research [*of ASRA*] [*National Science Foundation*]
**IBP** ........... International Balance of Payments (AFM)
**IBP** ........... International Biological Program [*Concluded, 1974*] [*National Academy of Sciences*]
**IBP** ........... International Book Project (EA)
**IBP** ........... Intraspecific Brood Parasitism [*Biology*]
**IBP** ........... Ion Beam Projector
**IBP** ........... Iron-Binding Protein
**IBP** ........... Italian Books and Periodicals [*A publication*]
**IBP** ........... Principia College, Elsah, IL [*OCLC symbol*] (OCLC)
**IBPA** ......... Iminobispropylamine [*Organic chemistry*]
**IBPA** ......... International Book Printers Association [*Later, NABM*] (EA)
**IBPA** ......... International Bridge Press Association (EA)
**IBPAT** ....... International Brotherhood of Painters and Allied Trades (EA)
**IBPAW** ...... International Brotherhood of Pottery and Allied Workers [*Formerly, IBOP*] (EA)
**IBpB** ......... Bedford Park Public Library District, Bedford Park, IL [*Library symbol*] [*Library of Congress*] (LCLS)
**IBPCA** ....... International Bureau of the Permanent Court of Arbitration (EAIO)
**IBP/CT** ...... International Biological Programme/Conservation of Terrestrial Biological Communities [*London, England*]
**IBPCT** ....... International Customs Tariffs Bureau [*Acronym is based on former name, International Bureau for the Publication of Customs Tariffs*] (EAIO)
**IBPF** ......... International Black Peoples' Foundation (EA)
**IBPFM** ...... Independent Board for Presbyterian Foreign Missions (EA)
**IBPG** ......... Icon-Based Program Generators [*Software*] [*Data processing*]
**IBPGR** ....... International Board for Plant Genetic Resources [*FAO*] [*Italy*]
**IBP (Int Biol Programme) Handb** ... IBP (International Biological Programme) Handbook [*A publication*]
**IBP (Int Biol Programme) Norden** ... IBP (International Biological Programme) i Norden [*A publication*]
**IBPM** ......... International Brotherhood of Papermakers [*Later, United Paperworkers International Union*]
**IBPMS** ....... Indirect Blood Pressure Measuring System
**IBPO** ......... International Brotherhood of Police Officers (EA)
**IBPOEW** ... Improved Benevolent Protective Order of Elks of the World (EA)
**IBPRDM** ... International Biological Programme Series [*A publication*]
**IBQ** ........... Institutional Bond Quote Service [*Database*] [*Chase Econometrics Interactive Data*] [*Information service or system*] (CRD)
**IBQ** ........... International Baron Resources [*Vancouver Stock Exchange symbol*]
**IBQ** ........... Quincy College, Quincy, IL [*OCLC symbol*] (OCLC)
**IBR** ........... Iberia Air Lines of Spain (MCD)
**IBR** ........... Infectious Bovine Rhinotracheitis [*Also, IBRV*] [*Virus*]
**IBR** ........... Information Bearing Radiation
**IBR** ........... Infrablack Region
**IBR** ........... Institute for Basic Research [*National Institute of Standards and Technology*]
**IBR** ........... Institute for Behavioral Research [*York University*] [*Canada*] [*Research center*] (IID)
**IBR** ........... Institute for Biblical Research (EA)
**IBR** ........... Institute for Biotechnology Research [*University of Waterloo*] [*Research center*] (RCD)
**IBR** ........... Institute of Boiler and Radiator Manufacturers [*Later, Hydronics Institute*] (EA)
**IBR** ........... Institutes for Behavior Resources (EA)
**IBR** ........... Integral Boiling Reactor
**IBR** ........... Integrated Bridge Rectifier (IEEE)
**IBR** ........... International Business Reply [*Post Office*] [*British*]
**IBR** ........... Irish Broadcasting Revenue
**IBR** ........... Issues in Bank Regulation [*Bank Administration Institute*] [*A publication*]
**IBR** ........... Rockford College, Rockford, IL [*OCLC symbol*] (OCLC)
**IBra** .......... Bradford Public Library, Bradford, IL [*Library symbol*] [*Library of Congress*] (LCLS)
**IBRA** ......... International Bee Research Association [*Cardiff, Wales*] (EA)
**IBRA** ......... International Bible Reading Association [*Redhill, Surrey, England*] (EAIO)
**IBRAPE** ..... Industria Brasileira de Produtos Eletronicos e Electricos, SA
**IBRC** ......... Indiana Business Research Center [*Indiana University*] [*Bloomington, IN*] [*Information service or system*] (IID)
**IBRD** ......... International Bank for Reconstruction and Development [*Also known as World Bank*]
**IBre** .......... Breese Public Library, Breese, IL [*Library symbol*] [*Library of Congress*] (LCLS)
**IBreD** ........ Breese Elementary District 12, Breese, IL [*Library symbol*] [*Library of Congress*] (LCLS)
**IBREDR** .... Indian Botanical Reporter [*A publication*]
**IBreMHS** .. Mater Dei High School, Breese, IL [*Library symbol*] [*Library of Congress*] (LCLS)
**IBreSJH** .... Saint Joseph's Hospital, Breese, IL [*Library symbol*] [*Library of Congress*] (LCLS)
**IBRG** ......... International Biodeterioration Research Group (EA)
**IBri** .......... Brighton Memorial Library, Brighton, IL [*Library symbol*] [*Library of Congress*] (LCLS)
**IBRI** ......... Interdisciplinary Biblical Research Institute (EA)
**IBRIC** ........ Institute for Behavioral Research in Creativity [*Research center*] (RCD)
**IBritishE** .... Institute of British Engineers
**IBRL** ......... Initial Bomb Release Line
**IBRM** ........ Institute of Baths and Recreation Management [*British*]
**IBRM** ........ Institute of Boiler and Radiator Manufacturers [*Later, Hydronics Institute*]
**IBRM** ........ International Basic Resources, Inc. [*NASDAQ symbol*] (NQ)
**IBRMA** ...... Institute for Biophysical Research and Macromolecular Assemblies [*Johns Hopkins University*]
**IBRMR** ...... Institute for Basic Research on Mental Retardation
**IBro** .......... Brookfield Free Public Library, Brookfield, IL [*Library symbol*] [*Library of Congress*] (LCLS)
**IBRO** ......... International Brain Research Organization [*Paris, France*] (EA)
**IBRO Bull** ... International Brain Research Organization. Bulletin [*A publication*]
**IBRO Handb Ser** ... IBRO Handbook Series [*A publication*]
**IBRO (Int Brain Res Org) Handb Ser Methods Neurosci** ... IBRO (International Brain Research Organisation) Handbook Series. Methods in the Neurosciences [*A publication*]
**IBrov** .......... Broadview Public Library, Broadview, IL [*Library symbol*] [*Library of Congress*] (LCLS)
**IBrowSD** .... Brownstown Community School District No. 201, Brownstown, IL [*Library symbol*] [*Library of Congress*] (LCLS)
**IBRRC** ....... International Bird Rescue Research Center (EA)
**IBRS** ......... Index to Book Reviews in the Sciences [*A publication*]
**IBrS** .......... Suburban Library System, Burr Ridge, IL [*Library symbol*] [*Library of Congress*] (LCLS)
**IBRSDZ** ..... International Brain Research Organization. Monograph Series [*A publication*]
**IBrus** ......... South County Public Library District of Calhoun County, Brussels, IL [*Library symbol*] [*Library of Congress*] (LCLS)
**IBrusRSD** .. Brussels-Richwood Community Consolidated School District 41, Brussels, IL [*Library symbol*] [*Library of Congress*] (LCLS)
**IBrusSD** ..... Brussels Community High School District 37, Brussels, IL [*Library symbol*] [*Library of Congress*] (LCLS)
**IBrv** .......... Bridgeview Public Library, Bridgeview, IL [*Library symbol*] [*Library of Congress*] (LCLS)

**IBRV**.......... Infectious Bovine Rhinotracheitis Virus [*Also, IBR*]
**IBS**............ Ball State University, Muncie, IN [*OCLC symbol*] (OCLC)
**IBS**............ Imidazole Buffered Saline [*Clinical chemistry*]
**IBS**............ Immediate Business Systems [*Commercial firm*] [*British*]
**IBS**............ Impulse Balance System
**IBS**............ Incentive Bonus Scheme [*British*]
**IBS**............ Incorporated Bronte Society [*Keighley, West Yorkshire, England*] (EAIO)
**IBS**............ Inflatable Boat, Small (NVT)
**IBS**............ Informacion Comercial Espanola [*A publication*]
**IBS**............ Innsbrucker Beitraege zur Sprachwissenschaft [*A publication*]
**IBS**............ Institute for Basic Standards [*Later, NSL*] [*National Institute of Standards and Technology*]
**IBS**............ Institute of Behavioral Science [*University of Colorado - Boulder*] [*Research center*] (RCD)
**IBS**............ Institute for Biotechnological Studies [*University of Kent*] [*British*] (IRUK)
**IBS**............ Institute of Black Studies (EA)
**IBS**............ Integrated Bridge System (MCD)
**IBS**............ INTELSAT Business Service [*MCI Communications Corp.*]
**IBS**............ Intercollegiate Broadcasting System (EA)
**IBS**............ Interference Blanker Set
**IBS**............ International Bach Society [*Defunct*] (EA)
**IBS**............ International Benchrest Shooters (EA)
**IBS**............ International Benevolent Society (EA)
**IBS**............ International Bentham Society [*London, England*] (EAIO)
**IBS**............ International Bible Society (EA)
**IBS**............ International Bibliography of the Social Sciences, Economics, and Sociology [*International Committee for Social Science Information and Documentation*] [*Information service or system*] (CRD)
**IBS**............ International Book Service, Inc.
**IBS**............ International Boundary Study [*A publication*]
**IBS**............ International Brancusi Society (EA)
**IBS**............ International Brecht Society [*See also IBG*] (EA)
**IBS**............ International Bronchoesophagological Society (EA)
**IBS**............ International Business Services [*Telecommunications*] (TSSD)
**IBS**............ Interpersonal Behavior Survey [*Psychology*]
**IBS**............ Ion Beam Scanning
**IBS**............ Irritable Bowel Syndrome [*Medicine*]
**IBS**............ Island Base Section [*Navy*]
**IBSA**.......... Immunoreactive Bovine Serum Albumin [*Immunochemistry*]
**IBSA**.......... Indian Behavioural Science Abstracts [*A publication*]
**IBSA**.......... International Barber Schools Association (EA)
**IBSA**.......... International Bible Students Association (EA)
**IBSA**.......... International Blind Sports Association [*See also AISA*] [*Farsta, Sweden*] (EAIO)
**IBSAC**....... Industrialized Building Systems and Components (IEEE)
**IBSC**.......... International Bankcard Services Corp. [*NASDAQ symbol*] (NQ)
**IBSCA**....... International Bibliography of Social and Cultural Anthropology [*A publication*]
**IBSEDEX**... International Building Services Index [*Database*] [*BSRIA*] [*Information service or system*] (CRD)
**Ibsen Yearb**... Ibsen Yearbook [*A publication*]
**IBSFC**........ International Baltic Sea Fishery Commission (EAIO)
**IBSH**.......... Institute of the Brothers of the Sacred Heart [*See also IFSC*] [*Rome, Italy*] (EAIO)
**IBSHR**....... Integral Boiling and Superheat Reactor
**IBSI**........... Independent Bankshares, Incorporated [*NASDAQ symbol*] (NQ)
**IBSJBB**..... Instituut voor Biologisch en Scheikundig Onderzoek van Landbouwgewassen (Wageningen). Jaarverslag [*A publication*]
**IBSL**.......... International Broadcast Systems, Inc. [*NASDAQ symbol*] (NQ)
**IBSM**......... International Bureau of Strata Mechanics [*See also IBG*] (EAIO)
**IBSMA**...... Interior Board of Surface Mine Appeals (in United States Interior Decisions) [*A publication*] (DLA)
**IBSN**.......... Infantile Bilateral Striatal Necrosis [*Ophthalmology*]
**IBSRAM**... International Board for Soil Research and Management [*Thailand*] (ECON)
**IBSS**........... Infrared Background Signature Survey [*Military*] (SDI)
**IBSS**........... Insect Balanced Salt Solution [*Cytology*]
**IBSS**........... International Bibliography of the Social Sciences [*A publication*]
**IBS/SPS**.... Inflatable Boat, Small/Silent Propulsion System (MCD)
**IBSSU**....... Internal Bearing Stabilized Sighting Unit (MCD)
**IBST**.......... IBS Technologies Ltd. [*Houston, TX*] [*NASDAQ symbol*] (NQ)
**IBST**.......... International Bureau of Social Tourism [*See also BITS*] [*Brussels, Belgium*] (EAIO)
**IBST**.......... International Bureau of Software Test
**IBSWU**...... International Boot and Shoe Workers' Union
**IBSYS**........ International Business Machines System
**IBT**............ Field Museum of Natural History, Chicago, IL [*OCLC symbol*] (OCLC)
**IBT**............ IBS Technologies Ltd. [*Vancouver Stock Exchange symbol*]
**IBT**............ Immunoblastic T-Cell [*Lymphadenopathy*]
**IBT**............ Implantable Beacon Transmitter [*Oceanography*]
**IBT**............ Inclined Bottom Tank [*Fermenter*]
**I-BT**........... India-Burma Theater [*World War II*]
**IBT**............ Indianapolis Ballet Theatre
**IBT**............ Industrial Bio-Test Laboratories, Inc.
**IBT**............ Initial Boiling-Point Temperature
**IBT**............ Instrumented Bend Test
**IBT**............ Insulation Breakdown Tester
**IBT**............ [*The*] International Bridge & Terminal Co. [*AAR code*]
**IBT**............ International Broadcasting Trust [*British*]
**IBT**............ International Brotherhood of Teamsters, Chauffeurs, Warehousemen, and Helpers of America (EA)
**IBT**............ Ion Beam Technology
**IBT**............ Ion-Implanted Base Transistor
**IBT**............ Irrational Beliefs Test [*Psychology*]
**IBT**............ Isatin-beta-thiosemicarbazone [*Organic chemistry*]
**IBTA**.......... International Baton Twirling Association of America and Abroad (EA)
**IBTC**.......... International Brands and Their Companies [*Formerly, ITND*] [*A publication*]
**IB of TCWHA**... International Brotherhood of Teamsters, Chauffeurs, Warehousemen, and Helpers of America
**IBTEN**....... Instituto Boliviano de Ciencia y Tecnologia Nuclear [*Bolivian Institute of Nuclear Science and Technology*] (EY)
**IBTF**.......... Investment Bank for Trade and Finance [*United Arab Emirates*]
**IBTMA**...... International Black Toy Manufacturers Association (EA)
**IBTOM**...... Iranian B'nei Torah Movement (EA)
**IBTS**.......... International Beer Tasting Society (EA)
**IBTS**.......... International Bicycle Touring Society (EA)
**IBTTA**....... International Bridge, Tunnel, and Turnpike Association (EA)
**IBTU**.......... Instructors Basic Training Unit
**IBU**............ Eureka College, Eureka, IL [*OCLC symbol*] (OCLC)
**IBU**............ Ibukiyama [*Ibukisan*] [*Japan*] [*Seismograph station code, US Geological Survey*] [*Closed*] (SEIS)
**IBU**............ Ikatan Buruh Umum [*General Workers' Union*] [*Indonesia*]
**IBU**............ Independent Business Unit
**IBU**............ Interference Blanking Unit
**IBU**............ International Benzoate Unit [*Pharmacology*]
**IBU**............ International Burgers Now Ltd. [*Vancouver Stock Exchange symbol*]
**IBU**............ International Business Unit [*British*] [*Information service or system*] (IID)
**IBud**.......... Mason Memorial Public Library, Buda, IL [*Library symbol*] [*Library of Congress*] (LCLS)
**IBun**.......... Bunker Hill Public Library, Bunker Hill, IL [*Library symbol*] [*Library of Congress*] (LCLS)
**IBunMCD**... Macoupin Community District 8, Bunker Hill, IL [*Library symbol*] [*Library of Congress*] (LCLS)
**IBur**........... South Stickney District Library, Burbank, IL [*Library symbol*] [*Library of Congress*] (LCLS)
**IBure**......... Leepertown Township Library, Bureau, IL [*Library symbol*] [*Library of Congress*] (LCLS)
**IBureLSD**.. Leepertown Consolidated Community School District 175, Bureau, IL [*Library symbol*] [*Library of Congress*] (LCLS)
**IBV**............ Independent Booksellers of Victoria [*Australia*]
**IBV**............ Infectious Bronchitis Virus [*Avian*]
**IBV**............ Inspection by Variables
**IBV**............ International Bellevue Ventures Ltd. [*Vancouver Stock Exchange symbol*]
**IBV**............ Internationale Buchhandler-Vereinigung [*International Booksellers Federation - IBF*] (EAIO)
**IBV**............ Newberry Library, Chicago, IL [*OCLC symbol*] (OCLC)
**IBVE**.......... Isobutyl Vinyl Ether [*Organic chemistry*]
**IBVM**......... Institute of the Blessed Virgin Mary [*Sisters of Loretto*] [*Roman Catholic religious order*]
**IBW**........... Borg-Warner Corp., Des Plaines, IL [*OCLC symbol*] (OCLC)
**IBW**........... Ideal Body Weight [*Medicine*]
**IBW**........... Impulse Bandwidth (MCD)
**IBW**........... In Black and White [*A publication*]
**IBW**........... Institute of the Black World (EA)
**IBW**........... Intelligence Bandwidth
**IBW**........... International Black Writers (EA)
**IBW**........... Ion Beam Weapon
**IBW**........... Irrotationally Bound Water [*Biophysics*]
**IBW**........... Israel Book World [*A publication*]
**IBWA**......... International Bank for West Africa Ltd.
**IBWA**......... International Black Writers and Artists (EA)
**IBWA**......... International Bottled Water Association (EA)
**IBWA**......... International Boxing Writers Association (EA)
**IBWC**......... International Black Women's Congress (EA)
**IBWC**......... International Black Writers Conference [*Later, IBW*] (EA)
**IBWC**......... International Boundary and Water Commission
**IBWCA**...... International Barbed Wire Collectors Association (EA)
**IBWM**....... International Bureau of Weights and Measures
**IBWZ**......... Internationale Bank fuer Wirtschaftliche Zusammenarbeit [*International Bank for Economic Cooperation*] [*German*]
**IBX**............ Integrated Business Exchange (MCD)
**IBX**............ Schiff, Hardin & Waite, Chicago, IL [*OCLC symbol*] (OCLC)
**IBY**............ International Bank of Yemen
**IBY**............ International Biological Year
**IBY**............ International Book Year [*1972*] [*UNESCO*]

**Ibyc** ........... Ibycus [*Sixth century BC*] [*Classical studies*] (OCD)
**IBYC** ......... Institute in Basic Youth Conflicts (EA)
**IBZ** ............ Columbia College, Chicago, IL [*OCLC symbol*] [*Inactive*] (OCLC)
**IBZ** ............ Ibiza [*Spain*] [*Airport symbol*] (OAG)
**IBZ** ............ Inner Border Zone
**IBZ** ............ Internationale Bibliographie der Zeitschriftenliteratur [*International Index to Periodicals*] [*A publication*]
**IC** .............. Chicago Public Library, Chicago, IL [*Library symbol*] [*Library of Congress*] (LCLS)
**IC** .............. Ice Chest
**IC** .............. Ice Crystals
**IC** .............. Iceland [*NATO*]
**ic** ............... Iceland [*MARC country of publication code*] [*Library of Congress*] (LCCP)
**IC** .............. Icelandic Canadian [*A publication*]
**IC** .............. Icon [*Plate engraving*]
**IC** .............. Iconclass [*Elsevier Book Series*] [*A publication*]
**IC** .............. Identification Code
**I and C** ....... Ideology and Consciousness [*A publication*]
**IC** .............. Iesus Christus [*Jesus Christ*] [*Latin*]
**IC** .............. Illinois Central [*Illinois Central Gulf Railroad Co.*] [*AAR code*]
**IC** .............. Illinois Central Transportation Co. [*NYSE symbol*] (CTT)
**IC** .............. Image Communications [*Computer graphics*]
**IC** .............. Imagination, Cognition, and Personality [*A publication*]
**IC** .............. Immediate Constituent
**IC** .............. Immune Complex [*Immunology*]
**I & C** .......... Impact and Capabilities [*Study*] [*DoD*]
**IC** .............. Implementation of Change
**IC** .............. Implementation and Conversion (MCD)
**IC** .............. Impoverished Conditions
**IC** .............. Impulse Conductor (MSA)
**IC** .............. In Charge Of
**IC** .............. In Command (ADA)
**IC** .............. In-Commission (MCD)
**IC** .............. Incense Cedar [*Botany*]
**IC** .............. Incentive Compensation (MCD)
**I/C** ............. Incoming [*Telecommunications*] (TEL)
**IC** .............. Incremental Cost (KSC)
**IC** .............. Incurved Cactus [*Horticulture*]
**IC** .............. Independent Contractor
**IC** .............. Independent Telephone Company [*Telecommunications*]
**IC** .............. Index Catalogue
**I on C** ........ Index on Censorship [*A publication*]
**IC** .............. Index Chemicus [*See also ICRS*]
**I/C** ............. Index Concordance [*International Serials Catalogue*] [*A publication*]
**IC** .............. Index Correction [*on a sextant*] [*Navigation*]
**IC** .............. Indian Airlines Corporation [*India*] [*ICAO designator*] (FAAC)
**IC** .............. Indian Cases [*India*] [*A publication*] (DLA)
**IC** .............. Indian Culture [*A publication*]
**IC** .............. Indicating Controller (NRCH)
**IC** .............. Indicator and Control
**IC** .............. Indifference Curve [*Economics*]
**IC** .............. Individual/Collective (MCD)
**IC** .............. Indochina
**IC** .............. Inductance-Capacitance
**IC** .............. Inductive Coupling
**IC** .............. Industrial Arbitration Cases [*Western Australia*] [*A publication*] (APTA)
**I/C** ............. Industrial/Commercial
**IC** .............. Industrial Court (DLA)
**IC** .............. Industry Competitive (AFIT)
**IC** .............. Inertial Component
**IC** .............. Inferior Colliculus [*Also, ICC*] [*Brain anatomy*]
**IC** .............. Infinite Capitalism [*Book title*]
**IC** .............. Informal Communication
**IC** .............. Information Center
**IC** .............. Information Circular
**IC** .............. Information Content (DEN)
**I & C** .......... Information and Coordination (ADA)
**IC** .............. Infrastructure Committee of the North Atlantic Council [*NATO*] (NATG)
**IC** .............. Ingenieur Constructeur [*Academic degree*]
**IC** .............. Inhibition Concentration [*Biochemistry*]
**IC** .............. Initial Conditions
**IC** .............. Initial Course [*Navigation*]
**IC** .............. Initiation of Contraction
**IC** .............. Inland Container [*Shipping*] (DCTA)
**IC** .............. Inlet Contact
**IC** .............. Inner Cabin
**IC** .............. Inner Circle [*Numismatics*]
**IC** .............. Inner Circle [*An association*] (EA)
**IC** .............. Inner Core [*Geology*]
**IC** .............. Innocent Civilian [*Military*]
**IC** .............. Inorganic Carbon
**IC** .............. Input Circuit
**IC** .............. Input Current
**IC** .............. Inside Cloud Lightning [*Meteorology*]
**IC** .............. Inspected and Condemned [*Military*]
**I & C** .......... Inspected and Condemned [*Military*] (AAG)
**IC** .............. Inspecting Commander [*Military*] [*British*] (ROG)
**IC** .............. Inspection Card
**IC** .............. Inspection Chamber
**IC** .............. Inspection Committee
**IC** .............. Inspiratory Capacity [*Physiology*]
**IC** .............. Inspiratory Center [*Physiology*]
**I & C** .......... Installation and Checkout [*Military*] (AFM)
**I & C** .......... Installation and Construction [*Military*]
**IC** .............. Installed Capacity [*Electronics*] (IEEE)
**IC** .............. Institute of Ceramics [*Stoke-On-Trent, Staffordshire, England*] (EAIO)
**IC** .............. Institute of Charity [*Rosminians*] [*Roman Catholic religious order*]
**IC** .............. Institute of Chemistry [*British*]
**IC** .............. Institute for Congress
**IC** .............. Institutional Care [*British*]
**IC** .............. Instituto Coimbra [*A publication*]
**IC** .............. Instruction Card (MSA)
**IC** .............. Instruction Cell
**IC** .............. Instruction Code (AAG)
**IC** .............. Instruction Counter [*Data processing*]
**IC** .............. Instructor in Cookery [*Navy*] [*British*] (ROG)
**IC** .............. Instrument Correction
**I & C** .......... Instrumentation and Communications [*Cable system*] (KSC)
**I & C** .......... Instrumentation and Control [*Aerospace*] (AAG)
**IC** .............. Instrumentation Controller (KSC)
**IC** .............. Insulated Conductors (MCD)
**IC** .............. Intake Closes [*Valve position*]
**IC** .............. Integrated Chromatography
**IC** .............. Integrated Circuit [*Electronics*]
**IC** .............. Integrating Contractor (AAG)
**I & C** .......... Integration and Checkout (KSC)
**IC** .............. Integration Control (MCD)
**IC** .............. Intelligence Center (CAAL)
**IC** .............. Intelligence Collator [*British police term*]
**IC** .............. Intelligence Committee [*NATO*] (NATG)
**IC** .............. Intelligence Community [*Military*] (MCD)
**IC** .............. Intelligence Corps [*Military unit*] [*British*]
**IC** .............. Intensive Care [*Medicine*]
**IC** .............. Inter Cibos [*Between Meals*] [*Pharmacy*]
**IC** .............. Intercept Controller
**IC** .............. Interceptor Command
**I/C** ............. Interchange
**IC** .............. Interchange Center
**I/C** ............. Intercom (KSC)
**IC** .............. Intercommunications
**IC** .............. Intercomputer (MCD)
**IC** .............. Intercomputer Channel (KSC)
**IC** .............. Interconnect Carrier [*Telecommunications*]
**IC** .............. Intercostal [*Between the ribs*] [*Medicine*]
**IC** .............. Intercrystalline Corrosion [*Metallurgy*]
**IC** .............. Interexchange Carrier [*Telecommunications*]
**IC** .............. Interface Control [*or Controller*]
**IC** .............. Interface Coordinator (MCD)
**IC** .............. Interfaces in Computing [*Later, Computer Standards and Interfaces*] [*A publication*]
**IC** .............. Interfacial Communications (MCD)
**IC** .............. Interim Change (AFM)
**IC** .............. Interim Commission
**IC** .............. Interim Committee
**IC** .............. Interior Communication
**IC** .............. Interior Communications Electrician [*Navy rating*]
**IC** .............. Intermediate Care [*Medicine*]
**IC** .............. Intermediate Command
**IC** .............. Internal Capsule [*Neuroanatomy*]
**IC** .............. Internal Combustion
**IC** .............. Internal Communications (CAAL)
**IC** .............. Internal Connection [*Electronics*]
**IC** .............. International Conference
**IC** .............. International Control
**IC** .............. International Cooperation
**IC** .............. International Corporation [*Generic term*]
**IC** .............. International Curator Resources [*Vancouver Stock Exchange symbol*]
**IC** .............. Internment Camp
**IC** .............. Internuclear Company
**IC** .............. Interpretation Canada [*Federal agency*]
**IC** .............. Interspecies Communication [*An association*] (EA)
**IC** .............. Interstate Club (EA)
**IC** .............. Interstate Commerce Reports [*A publication*] (DLA)
**IC** .............. Interstitial Cells [*Histology*]
**IC** .............. Interstitial Cyst [*Pulmonary medicine*]
**IC** .............. Interstitial Cystitis [*Nephrology*]
**IC** .............. Intervalve Coupling (DEN)
**IC** .............. Intracardiac [*Medicine*]
**IC** .............. Intracavitary [*Medicine*]
**IC** .............. Intracellular
**IC** .............. Intracerebral [*Medicine*]
**ic** ............... Intracerebroventricular [*Also, ICTV, ICV*] [*Brain anatomy*]
**IC** .............. Intracloud [*Climatology*]
**IC** .............. Intracoronary [*Cardiology*]

**IC** Intracranial
**IC** Intracutaneous [*Medicine*]
**IC** Inverse Check
**IC** Investment Company
**IC** Investment Tax Credit
**IC** Investors Chronicle [*A publication*]
**IC** Ion Chamber [*Nucleonics*]
**IC** Ion Chromatography
**IC** Ionization Chamber
**IC** Irish Constitution (ADA)
**IC** Iron City [*Pittsburgh, PA*]
**IC** Irregular Cavalry [*British military*] (DMA)
**IC** Irritable Colon [*Medicine*]
**IC** Ischemic Cardiomyopathy [*Cardiology*]
**IC** Ischemic Contracture [*Hematology*]
**IC** Islamic Congress
**IC** Islamic Culture [*A publication*]
**IC** Island of Calleja [*Neuroanatomy*]
**IC** Islet Cells [*of the pancreas*] [*Endocrinology*]
**IC** Isolation Condenser (NRCH)
**IC** Istoriski Casopis [*A publication*]
**IC** Jesus [*First and third letters of His name in Greek*]
**IC1** Interior Communications Electrician, First Class [*Navy rating*]
**IC2** Interior Communications Electrician, Second Class [*Navy rating*]
**2IC** Second in Command
**IC3** Interior Communications Electrician, Third Class [*Navy rating*]
**IC50** Inhibition of Protein Content, 50% [*Biochemistry*]
**ICA** Art Institute of Chicago, Chicago, IL [*Library symbol*] [*Library of Congress*] (LCLS)
**ICA** Aurora College, Aurora, IL [*OCLC symbol*] (OCLC)
**ICa** Cairo Public Library, Cairo, IL [*Library symbol*] [*Library of Congress*] (LCLS)
**ICA** Ica [*Peru*] [*Seismograph station code, US Geological Survey*] (SEIS)
**ICA** Icabaru [*Venezuela*] [*Airport symbol*] (OAG)
**ICA** Immediate Constituent Analyzer [*Data processing*] (DIT)
**ICA** Immunocytochemical Analysis
**ICA** Immunological Chromatographic Analysis
**ICA** Imperial Corporation of America [*NYSE symbol*] (SPSG)
**ICA** Independent Cost Assessment (MCD)
**ICA** Indian Community Action
**ICA** Individual Combat Actions [*Army*]
**ICA** Industrial Catering Association [*British*]
**ICA** Industrial Cooperative Association (EA)
**ICA** Initial Cruise Altitude
**ICA** Inner Circle of Advocates [*Tucson, AZ*] (EA)
**ICA** Institut Canadien des Actuaires [*Canadian Institute of Actuaries*]
**ICA** Institut Canadien d'Acupuncture [*Canadian Acupuncture Institute*]
**ICA** Institut Culturel Africain [*African Cultural Institute*] (EAIO)
**ICA** Institute for Cell Analysis [*University of Miami*] [*Research center*] (RCD)
**ICA** Institute of Chartered Accountants [*Australia*]
**ICA** Institute of Clinical Analysis
**ICA** Institute of Company Accountants [*British*] (DAS)
**ICA** Institute of Contemporary Arts [*British*]
**ICA** Institute of Cost Analysis [*Later, SCEA*] (EA)
**ICA** Institute of Cultural Affairs (EA)
**ICA** Instrument Compressed Air (AAG)
**ICA** Instrument Control and Automation
**ICA** Instrumentation Control and Automation [*Water industry*] [*British*]
**ICA** Integrated Circuit Array
**ICA** Integrated Communications Adapter (MCD)
**ICA** Integrated Conformal Array
**ICA** Integrated Cost Accounting
**ICA** Integration Change Allowance (MCD)
**ICA** Intelligence Collection Area [*Military*] (NATG)
**ICA** Inter City Airlines [*Great Britain*]
**ICA** Inter-Coastal Airways, Inc. [*Punta Gorda, FL*] [*FAA designator*] (FAAC)
**ICA** Interbank Card Association [*Mastercard International*] (EA)
**ICA** Intercomputer Adapter
**ICA** Intergovernmental Council for ADP [*Automatic Data Processing*]
**ICA** Interlochen Center for the Arts (EA)
**ICA** Intermuseum Conservation Association (EA)
**ICA** Internal Carotid Artery [*Anatomy*]
**ICA** International Cartographic Association [*Australia*] (EA)
**ICA** International Carwash Association (EA)
**ICA** International Caterers Association (EA)
**ICA** International Catholic Auxiliaries (EA)
**ICA** International Center for Aquaculture [*Auburn University*] [*Research center*] (RCD)
**ICA** International Ceramic Association (EA)
**ICA** International Chefs' Association (EA)
**ICA** International Chianina Association (EAIO)
**ICA** International Chiropractors Association (EA)
**ICA** International Claim Association [*Rock Island, IL*] (EA)
**ICA** International Co-Operative Alliance [*Grand-Saconnex, Switzerland*] (EA)
**ICA** International Coffee Agreement [*Signed September, 1962*]
**ICA** International College of Angiology (EA)
**ICA** International Commission on Acoustics [*Aachen, Federal Republic of Germany*] (EAIO)
**ICA** International Commodity Agreement
**ICA** International Communication Agency [*Also, USICA*] [*Formerly called BECA and USIA, it later became known again as USIA*]
**ICA** International Communication Association (EA)
**ICA** International Communications Association (EA)
**ICA** International Confederation of Accordionists [*Vienna, Austria*] (EA)
**ICA** International Conference of Administrators of Residential Centers for Youth (EA)
**ICA** International Congress of Acarology
**ICA** International Congress of African Studies (EAIO)
**ICA** International Congress of Africanists [*Lagos, Nigeria*] (EAIO)
**ICA** International Congress of Americanists [*Manchester, England*] (EA)
**ICA** International Cooperation Administration [*Later, Agency for International Development*]
**ICA** International Council on Archives [*UNESCO*] (EA)
**ICA** International Credit Association [*St. Louis, MO*] (EA)
**ICA** Interstate Commerce Act [*1887*]
**ICA** Interstitial Cystitis Association (EA)
**ICA** Intracranial Aneurysm [*Medicine*]
**ICA** Invalid Care Allowance [*British*]
**ICA** Inventors Clubs of America (EA)
**ICA** Investigative and Corrective Action (KSC)
**ICA** Investment Canada Act
**ICA** Investment Company Act [*1940*]
**ICA** Ionized Calcium Analyzer
**ICA** Iowa Code, Annotated [*A publication*] (DLA)
**ICA** Iron Caulkers' Association [*A union*] [*British*]
**ICA** Islet Cell Antibody [*Immunology*]
**ICA** Italian Charities of America (EA)
**ICA** Item Change Analysis (KSC)
**ICA** Item Control Area (NRCH)
**IC4A** Intercollegiate Association of Amateur Athletes of America [*Also, IAAAA, ICAAAA*]
**ICAA** Australian Accounting Database [*Institute of Chartered Accountants in Australia*] [*Information service or system*] (IID)
**ICAA** Institut Canadien des Affaires Africaines [*Canadian Institute of African Affairs*]
**ICAA** Institute of Chartered Accountants in Australia (ADA)
**ICAA** Insulation Contractors Association of America (EA)
**ICAA** Integrated Cost Accounting Application
**ICAA** International Civil Airports Association [*Orly, France*] (EAIO)
**ICAA** International Committee on Arctic Arboviruses
**ICAA** International Council on Alcohol and Addictions [*Switzerland*]
**ICAA** Invalid Children's Aid Association [*London*]
**ICAA** Investment Counsel Association of America (EA)
**ICAAAA** Intercollegiate Association of Amateur Athletes of America [*Also, IAAAA, IC4A*] (EA)
**ICAAC** Interscience Conference on Antimicrobial Agents and Chemotherapy
**ICAB** International Cargo Advisory Bureau
**ICAB** International Council Against Bullfighting (EA)
**ICABA** International Campaign Against Banking on Apartheid (EAIO)
**ICABF** American Bar Foundation, Chicago, IL [*Library symbol*] [*Library of Congress*] (LCLS)
**ICAC** American College of Surgeons, Chicago, IL [*Library symbol*] [*Library of Congress*] (LCLS)
**ICAC** Independent College Assistance Center (EA)
**ICAC** Independent Commission Against Corruption [*Australia*]
**ICAC** International Committee for Accounting Co-Operation
**ICAC** International Cotton Advisory Committee (EA)
**ICACCP** International Commission Against Concentration Camp Practices [*Brussels, Belgium*] (EAIO)
**ICACM** Associated Colleges of the Midwest, Periodical Bank, Chicago, IL [*Library symbol*] [*Library of Congress*] (LCLS)
**ICACMu** American Conservatory of Music, Chicago, IL [*Library symbol*] [*Library of Congress*] (LCLS)
**ICAD** Integrated Control and Display
**ICAD** International Committee for Automobile Documentation
**ICADA** American Dental Association, Chicago, IL [*Library symbol*] [*Library of Congress*] (LCLS)
**ICADE** Interactive Computer-Aided Design Evaluation
**ICADIS** Instituto Centroamericano de Documentacion y Investigacion Social (EA)
**ICADS** Integrated Cover and Deception Systems [*Military*] (MCD)
**ICADTS** International Committee on Alcohol, Drugs, and Traffic Safety [*Linkoping, Sweden*] (EA)
**ICAE** Integrated Communications Adapter Extended (BUR)
**ICAE** International Centre for Art Education (EAIO)
**ICAE** International Commission of Agricultural Engineering
**ICAE** International Commission on Atmospheric Electricity (EA)

**ICAE**.......... International Conference of Agricultural Economists [*Later, IAAE*]
**ICAE**.......... International Council for Adult Education [*Toronto, ON*] (EAIO)
**ICAE**.......... United States Army, Corps of Engineers, Chicago, IL [*Library symbol*] [*Library of Congress*] (LCLS)
**ICAEC**....... International Confederation of Associations of Experts and Consultants [*Paris, France*] (EA)
**ICAEO**....... International Center for Athletic and Educational Opportunities (EA)
**ICAEW**...... Institute of Chartered Accountants in England and Wales
**ICAF**.......... [*The*] Industrial College of the Armed Forces [*Later, UND*]
**ICAF**.......... International Committee on Aeronautical Fatigue [*Delft University of Technology*] [*Netherlands*] (EAIO)
**ICAF**.......... International Contemporary Art Fair [*London, England*]
**ICAFFH**.... International Committee for the Anthropology of Food and Food Habits [*Defunct*] (EA)
**ICAH**......... American Hospital Association, Chicago, IL [*Library symbol*] [*Library of Congress*] (LCLS)
**ICah**........... Cahokia Public Library, Cahokia, IL [*Library symbol*] [*Library of Congress*] (LCLS)
**ICahSD**...... Cahokia Community Unit School District 187, Cahokia, IL [*Library symbol*] [*Library of Congress*] (LCLS)
**ICAI**........... American Institute of Baking, Chicago, IL [*Library symbol*] [*Library of Congress*] (LCLS)
**ICAI**........... Institut Canadien des Affaires Internationales [*Canadian Institute of International Affairs*]
**ICAI**........... Institute of Cultural Affairs International (EA)
**ICAI**........... Intelligent Computer-Assisted Instruction
**ICAI**........... International Commission for Agricultural Industries
**ICAIE**........ International Committee Against Involuntary Exile (EA)
**ICA Inf**....... ICA [*Instituto Colombiano Agropecuario*] Informa [*A publication*]
**ICA Informa Inst Colomb Agropecu** ... ICA Informa. Instituto Colombiano Agropecuario [*A publication*]
**ICA (Inst Colomb Agropecu) Bol Tec** ... ICA (Instituto Colombiano Agropecuario) Boletin Tecnico [*A publication*]
**ICAITI**....... Instituto Centroamericano de Investigacion y Tecnologia Industrial [*Central American Institute of Research and Industrial Technology*] [*Research center*] [*Guatemalan*] (IRC)
**ICALA**....... American Library Association, Chicago, IL [*Library symbol*] [*Library of Congress*] (LCLS)
**ICALEO**.... International Congress on Applications of Lasers and Electro-Optics [*Laser Institute of America*] (TSPED)
**ICALU**....... International Confederation of Arab Labour Unions
**ICAM**........ American Medical Association, Chicago, IL [*Library symbol*] [*Library of Congress*] (LCLS)
**ICAM**........ Improved Cobra Agility and Maneuverability [*Military*] (MCD)
**ICAM**........ Integrated Communications Access Method [*Data processing*]
**ICAM**........ Integrated Computer-Aided Manufacturing (IEEE)
**ICAM**........ Intercellular Adhesion Molecule [*Biochemistry*]
**ICAM**........ International Confederation of Architectural Museums [*Montreal, PQ*] (EAIO)
**ICAMA**...... Industria della Carta [*A publication*]
**ICAMC**...... International Conference on Automatic Control of Mines and Collieries
**ICAME**...... International Center for the Advancement of Management Education [*Stanford University*]
**ICAMI**....... International Committee Against Mental Illness (EA)
**ICAM J**..... Institute of Corn and Agricultural Merchants. Journal [*A publication*]
**ICAMP**...... Integrated Conventional Ammunition Maintenance Plan [*DoD*] (RDA)
**ICAMQ**..... International Committee of Automation of Mines and Quarries [*Budapest, Hungary*] (EAIO)
**ICAMR**...... Interagency [*or Interdepartmental*] Committee for Applied Meteorological Research
**ICAMRS**... International Civil Aviation Message Routing System
**ICAMT**...... International Centre of Ancient and Modern Tapestry
**ICAN**......... Individual Circuit Analysis [*Telecommunications*] (TEL)
**ICAN**......... Integrated Circuit Analysis [*Data processing*]
**ICAN**......... International College of Applied Nutrition (EA)
**ICAN**......... International Commission for Air Navigation
**ICAN**......... Iowa Computer-Assisted Network [*Iowa State Library*] [*Des Moines*] [*Information service or system*] (IID)
**ICan**........... Parlin-Ingersoll Public Library, Canton, IL [*Library symbol*] [*Library of Congress*] (LCLS)
**ICA/NCC**.. International Carwash Association/National Carwash Council [*Later, ICA*] (EA)
**ICanS**......... Spoon River College, Canton, IL [*Library symbol*] [*Library of Congress*] (LCLS)
**ICAO**......... American Osteopathic Association, Chicago, IL [*Library symbol*] [*Library of Congress*] (LCLS)
**ICAO**......... International Civil Aviation Organization [*Montreal, PQ*]
**ICAO Bull**... ICAO [*International Civil Aviation Organization*] Bulletin [*Canada*] [*A publication*]
**ICAP**.......... Improved Capability [*for aircraft*] (MCD)
**ICAP**.......... Improved Cobra Armament Program [*Military*] (MCD)
**ICAP**.......... Independent Cinema Artists and Producers (EA)
**ICAP**.......... Indian Community Action Program (OICC)
**ICAP**.......... Inductively Coupled Argon Plasma [*Spectrometry*]
**ICAP**.......... Instituto Centroamericano de Administracion Publica [*Central American Institute of Public Administration*] [*Costa Rica*]
**ICAP**.......... Integrated Correction Action Plan [*Military*] (MCD)
**ICAP**.......... Integrated Criminal Apprehension Program
**ICAP**.......... Inter-American Committee for the Alliance for Progress [*Superseded by Permanent Executive Committee of the Inter-American Economic and Social Council*]
**ICAP**.......... International Centre for the Application of Pesticides [*British*] (IRUK)
**ICAP**.......... International College Art Program [*Red Cross Youth*]
**ICAP**.......... International Committee of Architectural Photogrammetry
**ICAPDG**.... Indian Journal of Comparative Animal Physiology [*A publication*]
**ICAPP**....... Integrated Conventional Ammunition Procurement Plan
**ICAPR**....... Interdepartmental Committee on Air Pollution Research [*British*]
**ICAPS**....... Integral Carrier ASW [*Antisubmarine Warfare*] Prediction System [*Marine science*] (MSC)
**ICAPS**....... Integrated Carrier Acoustic Prediction System [*Navy*] (NVT)
**ICAPS**....... Integrated Command ASW [*Antisubmarine Warfare*] Prediction System [*Navy*] (CAAL)
**ICAR**.......... ICAR [*Interstate Cinderellans and Revenuers*] Educational Club (EA)
**ICAR**.......... Indian Council for Agricultural Research
**ICAR**.......... Inner Circle of American Revenuers (EA)
**ICAR**.......... Integrated Command Accounting and Reporting
**I-CAR**........ Inter-Industry Conference on Auto Collision Repair (EA)
**ICAR**.......... Intercargo Corp. [*NASDAQ symbol*] (NQ)
**ICAR**.......... Interface Control Action Request (NRCH)
**ICAR**.......... Inventory of Canadian Agri-Food Research [*Canandian Agricultural Research Council*] [*Information service or system*]
**ICAR**.......... Investigation and Corrective Action Report (KSC)
**ICARA**....... International Child Abduction Remedies Act [*1988*]
**ICARA**....... International Conference on Assistance for Refugees in Africa [*See also CIARA*] [*United Nations*] [*Geneva, Switzerland*] (EAIO)
**ICARAJ**..... Indian Council of Agricultural Research. Miscellaneous Bulletin [*A publication*]
**IC Arb Q**.... Indian Council of Arbitration. Quarterly [*A publication*] (DLA)
**ICarbS**....... Southern Illinois University, Carbondale, IL [*Library symbol*] [*Library of Congress*] (LCLS)
**ICARDA**.... International Center for Agricultural Research in Dry Areas [*Syria*]
**ICARDS**.... Integrated Carrier [*or Command*] ASW Prediction System
**ICARES**..... Institut International Catholique de Recherches Socio-Ecclesiales [*International Catholic Institute for Socio-Religious Research*] [*Later, FERES*]
**ICarl**.......... Carlinville Public Library, Carlinville, IL [*Library symbol*] [*Library of Congress*] (LCLS)
**ICarlB**........ Blackburn College, Carlinville, IL [*Library symbol*] [*Library of Congress*] (LCLS)
**ICarlMCD**... Macoupin Community District 1, Carlinville, IL [*Library symbol*] [*Library of Congress*] (LCLS)
**ICarly**......... Case-Halstead Library, Carlyle, IL [*Library symbol*] [*Library of Congress*] (LCLS)
**ICarlyS**...... Carlyle School, Carlyle, IL [*Library symbol*] [*Library of Congress*] (LCLS)
**ICARMO**... International Council of the Architects of Historical Monuments
**ICArmour**.. Armour & Co., Chicago, IL [*Library symbol*] [*Library of Congress*] [*Obsolete*] (LCLS)
**ICarr**.......... Carrollton Public Library, Carrollton, IL [*Library symbol*] [*Library of Congress*] (LCLS)
**ICarrCD**..... Carrollton Community Unit, District 1, Carrollton, IL [*Library symbol*] [*Library of Congress*] (LCLS)
**ICart**........... Carthage Public Library, Carthage, IL [*Library symbol*] [*Library of Congress*] (LCLS)
**ICARUS**.... Index of Conservation and Analytical Records: Unified System [*Data processing*]
**ICARUS**.... Inter-Continental Aerospacecraft-Range Unlimited System
**ICARVS**.... Interplanetary Craft for Advanced Research in Vicinity of Sun
**ICAS**.......... Acme Steel Co., Chicago, IL [*Library symbol*] [*Library of Congress*] (LCLS)
**ICas**............ Casey Township Library, Casey, IL [*Library symbol*] [*Library of Congress*] (LCLS)
**ICAS**.......... Improved Cobra Armament System [*Military*] (MCD)
**ICAS**.......... Independent Collision Avoidance System
**ICAS**.......... Instant Computer Arbitration Search [*Database*] [*Labor Relations Press*] [*Information service or system*] (CRD)
**ICAS**.......... Institute of Combined Arms and Support [*Fort Leavenworth, KS*] [*Army*]
**ICAS**.......... Intel Communications Amplifications Specification [*Interface*]
**ICAS**.......... Interdepartmental Committee for Atmospheric Sciences [*Terminated, 1976*]
**ICAS**.......... Intermittent Commercial and Amateur Service [*Radio*]
**ICAS**.......... International Council of the Aeronautical Sciences
**ICAS**.......... International Council of Air Shows (EA)

**ICAS** ........ International Council of Associations of Surfing (EA)
**ICA-S** ........ School of the Art Institute of Chicago, Chicago, IL [*Library symbol*] [*Library of Congress*] (LCLS)
**ICASALS** .. International Center for Arid and Semi-Arid Land Studies [*Texas Technological University*]
**ICASC** ....... International Contraception, Abortion, and Sterilization Campaign [*Later, WGNRR*] (EAIO)
**ICASE** ....... Institute for Computer Applications in Science and Engineering [*Universities Space Research Association*] [*Research center*] (RCD)
**ICASE** ....... International Council of Associations for Science Education [*See also FIAPS*] (EAIO)
**ICASIS** ...... International Conference of African States on Insurance Supervision [*See also CICA*] [*Gabon*] (EAIO)
**ICASSP** ..... International Conference on Acoustics, Speech, and Signal Processing (MCD)
**ICasv** ......... Caseyville Public Library, Caseyville, IL [*Library symbol*] [*Library of Congress*] (LCLS)
**ICat** ........... Catlin Public Library, Catlin, IL [*Library symbol*] [*Library of Congress*] (LCLS)
**ICAT** .......... International Committee for the Coordination of Clinical Application and Teaching of Autogenic Therapy [*North Vancouver, BC*] (EAIO)
**ICATAP** .... Indian Council of Agricultural Research. Technical Bulletin [*A publication*]
**ICATL** ....... International Council of Associations of Theological Libraries (EA)
**ICATS** ....... Intermediate Capacity Automated Telecommunications System [*Air Force*] (CET)
**ICATU** ....... International Confederation of Arab Trade Unions
**ICATVT** .... International Centre for Advanced Technical and Vocational Training [*British*]
**ICAV** ......... American Veterinary Medical Association, Chicago, IL [*Library symbol*] [*Library of Congress*] (LCLS)
**ICAV** ......... Intracavity [*Dentistry*]
**ICAVE** ....... International Coalition Against Violent Entertainment (EA)
**ICAVS** ....... United States Army, Medical Department, Veterinary School, Chicago, IL [*Library symbol*] [*Library of Congress*] (LCLS)
**ICB** ............ Barat College of the Sacred Heart, Lake Forest, IL [*OCLC symbol*] (OCLC)
**ICB** ............ ICP [*International Computer Programs, Inc.*] Business Software Review [*A publication*]
**ICB** ............ Image Capture Board [*Video monitor*] [*AT & T*] (BYTE)
**ICB** ............ Incoming Call Barred [*Telecommunications*] (TEL)
**ICB** ............ Individual Case Basis (TEL)
**ICB** ............ Industrial & Commercial Bank [*China*] (ECON)
**ICB** ............ Inertia Compensated Balance
**ICB** ............ Inner-Core Boundary [*Geology*]
**ICB** ............ Institut Royal Colonial Belge. Compte Rendu des Seances [*A publication*]
**ICB** ............ Institute of Collective Bargaining and Group Relations (EA)
**ICB** ............ Integration Change Board [*NASA*]
**ICB** ............ Intercapital Income Securities, Inc. [*NYSE symbol*] (SPSG)
**ICB** ............ Interface Control Board (NRCH)
**ICB** ............ Interim Change Bulletin (NASA)
**ICB** ............ Interior Control Board
**ICB** ............ Internal Common Bus [*Data processing*]
**ICB** ............ International Christian Broadcasters [*Defunct*] (EA)
**ICB** ............ International Co-operative Bulletin [*A publication*]
**ICB** ............ International Competitive Bid (NATG)
**ICB** ............ International Computer Bibliography [*A publication of National Computing Center*]
**ICB** ............ International Container Bureau [*Paris*]
**ICB** ............ Interrupt Control Block (NASA)
**ICB** ............ Ivory Coast Basin [*Geology*]
**ICBA** .......... International Community of Booksellers' Associations [*Later, IBF*]
**ICBAH** ...... Booz, Allen & Hamilton, Inc., Chicago, IL [*Library symbol*] [*Library of Congress*] (LCLS)
**ICBB** .......... Ind Coope Burton Brewery [*British*]
**ICBB** .......... International Commission for Bee Botany [*Later, ICPBR*] (EA)
**ICBBA** ....... International Cornish Bantam Breeders' Association (EA)
**ICBC** .......... Blue Cross Association, Chicago, IL [*Library symbol*] [*Library of Congress*] (LCLS)
**ICBC** .......... Inclined Cleated Belt Conveyor
**ICBC** .......... Institute of Certified Business Counselors (EA)
**ICBC** .......... Interagency Committee on Back Contamination [*Aerospace*]
**ICBC** .......... International Center for Biological Control [*University of California, Berkeley and Riverside*]
**ICBC** .......... International Commercial Bank of China [*Taiwan*]
**ICBCBE** ..... International Congress of Biochemistry. Abstracts [*A publication*]
**ICBCG** ....... Boston Consulting Group, Chicago, IL [*Library symbol*] [*Library of Congress*] (LCLS)
**ICBD** .......... International Children's Book Day [*Australia*]
**ICBD** .......... International Council of Ballroom Dancing [*London, England*] (EAIO)
**ICBD** .......... Ionized Cluster Beam Deposition [*Coating technology*]
**ICBEA** ....... Industrie Chimique Belge [*A publication*]
**ICBF** .......... Beatrice Foods Co., Chicago, IL [*Library symbol*] [*Library of Congress*] (LCLS)
**ICBI** ........... International Consumer Brands, Incorporated [*New York, NY*] [*NASDAQ symbol*] (NQ)
**ICBIF** ......... Inner City Business Improvement Forum
**ICBLB** ....... International Committee for Breaking the Language Barrier
**ICBM** ......... Bank Marketing Association, Chicago, IL [*Library symbol*] [*Library of Congress*] (LCLS)
**ICBM** ......... Intercontinental Ballistic Missile
**ICBMS** ...... Intercontinental Ballistic Missile System
**ICBN** .......... International Code of Botanical Nomenclature
**ICBO** .......... International Conference of Building Officials (EA)
**ICBO** .......... Interracial Council for Business Opportunity [*New York, NY*] (EA)
**ICBOSS** ..... Interactive Computer-Based Office Support System [*Military*] (MCD)
**ICBP** .......... International Council for Bird Preservation [*Cambridge, England*] (EAIO)
**ICBP** .......... Intracellular-Binding Proteins [*Medicine*]
**ICBPA** ....... Insurance Company and Bank Purchasing Agents Association
**IC-BPH** ..... Illinois Regional Library for the Blind and Physically Handicapped, Chicago Public Library, Chicago, IL [*Library symbol*] [*Library of Congress*] (LCLS)
**ICBR** .......... Ice-Cuber
**ICBR** .......... Iceberg Research. Scott Polar Research Institute [*A publication*]
**ICBR** .......... Institute for Child Behavior Research (IID)
**ICBRAO** .... India. Coffee Board. Annual Report [*A publication*]
**ICBRSD** .... International Council for Building Research, Studies, and Documentation (DIT)
**ICBS** .......... Incorporated Church Building Society [*British*]
**ICBS** .......... Interconnected Business System
**ICBS** .......... International Cigar Band Society [*Defunct*] (EA)
**ICBS** .......... National Association of Blue Shield Plans [*Later, BSA*], Chicago, IL [*Library symbol*] [*Library of Congress*] (LCLS)
**ICBT** .......... Intercontinental Ballistic Transport
**ICBWR** ...... Improved-Cycle Boiling-Water Reactor [*Nuclear energy*]
**ICC** ............ Article 19 - International Centre on Censorship (EAIO)
**ICC** ............ Association Internationale de Chimie Cerealiere [*International Association for Cereal Chemistry*] [*Also, AICC*]
**ICc** ............ Calumet City Public Library, Calumet City, IL [*Library symbol*] [*Library of Congress*] (LCLS)
**ICC** ............ Calumet College, Whiting, IN [*OCLC symbol*] (OCLC)
**ICC** ............ Ice Crystal Cloud
**ICC** ............ Illinois Cancer Council Comprehensive Cancer Center [*Research center*] (RCD)
**ICC** ............ Image Converter Camera
**ICC** ............ Immunocytochemistry [*Immunology*]
**ICC** ............ Imperial Camel Corps [*British military*] (DMA)
**ICC** ............ Imperial Communications [*World War II*]
**ICC** ............ Inadequate Core Cooling [*Nuclear energy*] (NRCH)
**ICC** ............ Income Capital Certificate
**ICC** ............ Independent Community Consultants (EA)
**ICC** ............ Indian Claims Commission [*Terminated, 1976*]
**ICC** ............ Indian Cultural Center [*Defunct*] (EA)
**ICC** ............ Individual Concealment Cover
**ICC** ............ Industrial Capacity Committee of the Production Council [*British*] [*World War II*]
**ICC** ............ Industrial and Commercial Company
**ICC** ............ Industrial Communication Council
**ICC** ............ Inferior Colliculus [*Also, IC*] [*Brain anatomy*]
**ICC** ............ Infinity Color-Corrected System [*Optics*]
**ICC** ............ Information Center Complex [*ORNL*] (GRD)
**ICC** ............ Information Coordination Control [*Computer*] (MCD)
**ICC** ............ Information des Cours Complementaires [*A publication*]
**ICC** ............ Initial Communications Connectivity [*DoD*]
**ICC** ............ Initial Contingency Capability (MCD)
**IC & C** ....... Installation Calibration and Checkout (KSC)
**ICC** ............ Installation Calibration and Checkout (KSC)
**ICC** ............ Institut Canadien de Conservation [*Canadian Conservation Institute - CCI*]
**ICC** ............ Institute of Chinese Culture (EA)
**ICC** ............ Instituto Caro y Cuervo [*A publication*]
**ICC** ............ Instrument Control Center (KSC)
**ICC** ............ Instrument Control Computer
**ICC** ............ Instrumentation Checkout Complex (MCD)
**ICC** ............ Instrumentation Control Center (AAG)
**ICC** ............ Integrated Chip Circuit
**ICC** ............ Integrated Communications Control (MCD)
**ICC** ............ Intensive Coronary Care [*Medicine*]
**ICC** ............ Inter-Company Correspondence
**ICC** ............ Interchangeable Cycle Check (MCD)
**ICC** ............ Interchannel Communicator (MCD)
**ICC** ............ Intercomputer Channel (NASA)
**ICC** ............ Intercomputer Communication (MCD)
**ICC** ............ Interface Control Chart (NASA)
**ICC** ............ Interior Communications Electrician, Chief [*Navy rating*]
**ICC** ............ Intermediaire des Chercheurs et des Curieux [*A publication*]
**I d CC** ........ Intermediaire des Chercheurs et des Curieux [*A publication*]
**ICC** ............ Internal Conversion Coefficient [*Radiology*]
**ICC** ............ International Association for Cereal Chemistry (EAIO)

**ICC**............ International Association for Cereal Science and Technology [*Formerly, International Association of Cereal Chemists*] [*Acronym represents association's former name*] [*Austria*]
**ICC**............ International Cablecasting Technologies [*Vancouver Stock Exchange symbol*]
**ICC**............ International Camaro Club (EA)
**ICC**............ International Cello Centre [*Duns, Scotland*] (EAIO)
**ICC**............ International Chamber of Commerce [*See also CCI*] [*Paris, France*] (EAIO)
**ICC**............ International Chessology Club (EA)
**ICC**............ International Children's Centre [*Paris, France*]
**ICC**............ International Clergy Council (EA)
**ICC**............ International College of Chiropractors (EA)
**ICC**............ International College in Copenhagen [*Denmark*]
**ICC**............ International Committee of ICOM [*International Council of Museums*] for Conservation [*Later, ICOM-CC*] (EAIO)
**ICC**............ International Communications Corporation [*Miami, FL*] (CSR)
**ICC**............ International Computaprint Corporation [*Fort Washington, PA*]
**ICC**............ International Computation Center [*Sponsored by UNESCO*] [*Rome, Italy*]
**ICC**............ International Computer Casting [*Information service or system*] (IID)
**ICC**............ International Conference on Communications [*IEEE*]
**ICC**............ International Congregational Council
**ICC**............ International Control Commission [*Composed of representatives of Canada, India, and Poland, and charged with supervising the cease-fire in Laos established at Geneva Conference of 1962*]
**ICC**............ International Controls Corporation
**ICC**............ International Cooperation Council [*Later, UDC*]
**ICC**............ International Coordinating Committee for the Presentation of Science and the Development of Out-of-School Scientific Activities [*See also CIC*] (EAIO)
**ICC**............ International Corrosion Council [*Orsay, France*] (EAIO)
**ICC**............ International Counseling Center (EA)
**ICC**............ International Cricket Conference (EA)
**ICC**............ [*The*] International Critical Commentary on the Holy Scriptures of the Old and New Testament [*Edinburgh*] [*A publication*] (BJA)
**ICC**............ Interprocessor Communication and Control Routine (MCD)
**ICC**............ Interstate Carriers Conference (EA)
**ICC**............ Interstate Commerce Commission [*Independent government agency*]
**ICC**............ Interventional Cardiac Catheterization [*Medicine*]
**ICC**............ Intra-Class Correlation Coefficient
**ICC**............ Intracompany Correspondence (AAG)
**ICC**............ Inuit Circumpolar Conference [*Godthaab, Greenland, Denmark*] (EAIO)
**ICC**............ Invasive Cancer of the Cervix [*Oncology*]
**ICC**............ Inventory Control Center [*of Field Army Support Command*]
**ICC**............ Inventory Control Company
**ICC**............ Invitational Computer Conference
**IC & C**........ Invoice Cost and Charges [*Business term*]
**ICC**............ Irish Council of Churches
**ICC**............ Islanders Coordinating Council [*Australia*]
**ICC**............ Italian Chamber of Commerce (EA)
**ICC**............ Italian Culture Council (EA)
**ICC**............ Item Characteristic Curve [*Statistics*]
**ICCA**.......... Independent Computer Consultants Association (EA)
**ICCA**.......... Infants' and Children's Coat Association [*Later, ICGSCA*] (EA)
**ICCA**.......... Initial Cash Clothing Allowance [*Military*]
**ICCA**.......... Institut Canadien des Comptables Agrees [*Canadian Institute of Chartered Accountants*]
**ICCA**.......... Institut Canadien de la Construction en Acier [*Canadian Institute of Steel Construction*]
**ICCA**.......... Interagency Coordinating Committee for Astronomy [*Federal Council for Science and Technology*] [*Terminated, 1976*]
**ICCA**.......... International Computer Chess Association
**ICCA**.......... International Conference on Computer Applications [*in developing countries*] [*1977*]
**ICCA**.......... International Congress and Convention Association [*Amsterdam, Netherlands*] (EA)
**ICCA**.......... International Consumer Credit Association [*Later, ICA*] (EA)
**ICCA**.......... International Correspondence of Corkscrew Addicts (EA)
**ICCA**.......... International Corrugated Case Association [*Paris, France*] (EAIO)
**ICCA**.......... International Council for Commercial Arbitration [*Vienna, Austria*] (EAIO)
**ICCAC**....... Interagency Clean Car Advisory Committee [*HEW*] [*Terminated*] (EGAO)
**ICCAIA**..... International Coordinating Council of Aerospace Industries Associations (EA)
**ICCAM**...... International Committee of Children's and Adolescents' Movements
**ICCAP**....... International Coordination Committee for the Accounting Profession
**ICCAS**....... Chicago Academy of Sciences, Matthew Laflin Memorial Library, Chicago, IL [*Library symbol*] [*Library of Congress*] (LCLS)
**ICCAS**....... International Center for Communication Arts and Sciences
**ICCAT**....... International Commission for the Conservation of Atlantic Tunas [*Spain*]
**ICCATCI**... International Committee to Coordinate Activities of Technical Groups in Coatings Industry [*Paris, France*] (EAIO)
**ICCB**.......... Integrated Change Control Board [*NASA*] (NASA)
**ICCB**.......... Intermediate Change Control Board
**ICCB**.......... Intermediate Configuration Control Board [*Western Electric*] (AABC)
**ICCB**.......... International Catholic Child Bureau [*Geneva, Switzerland*]
**IC-CBPH**... Chicago Library Services for the Blind and Physically Handicapped (Subregional), Chicago Public Library, Chicago, IL [*Library symbol*] [*Library of Congress*] (LCLS)
**ICCC**.......... Columbia College, Chicago, IL [*Library symbol*] [*Library of Congress*] (LCLS)
**ICCC**.......... Ice Cream Connoisseurs Club [*Defunct*] (EA)
**ICCC**.......... ImmuCell Corp. [*NASDAQ symbol*] (NQ)
**ICCC**.......... Information Center on Children's Cultures [*Defunct*] (EA)
**ICCC**.......... International Center for Comparative Criminology (EA)
**ICCC**.......... International Color Computer Club (EA)
**ICCC**.......... International Concentration Camp Committee [*Vienna, Austria*] (EAIO)
**ICCC**.......... International Concerns Committee for Children (EA)
**ICCC**.......... International Conference of Catholic Charities
**ICCC**.......... International Conference on Circuits and Computers (MCD)
**ICCC**.......... International Conference of Coordination Chemistry
**ICCC**.......... International Council of Christian Churches (EA)
**ICCC**.......... International Council of Community Churches (EA)
**ICCC**.......... International Council for Computer Communication (EA)
**ICCCA**........ International C Class Catamaran Association of America (EA)
**ICCD**.......... Information Center on Crime and Delinquency [*National Council on Crime and Delinquency*] (IID)
**ICCD**.......... Internal Coordination Control Drawing
**ICCE**.......... Iceland Communications and Control Enhancement
**ICCE**.......... International Congress on Combustion Engines
**ICCE**.......... International Council of Commerce Employers
**ICCE**.......... International Council for Computers in Education (EA)
**ICCE**.......... International Council for Correspondence Education [*Later, ICDE*]
**ICCE**.......... Intracapsular Cataract Extraction [*Ophthalmology*]
**ICCEA**....... International Committee for the Study and Conservation of Earthen Architecture (EAIO)
**ICCEC**....... India Chemists and Chemical Engineers Club (EA)
**ICCEcPI**.... Intracapsular Cataract Extraction with Peripheral Iridectomy [*Ophthalmology*]
**ICCERSP**.. Interagency Coordinating Committee for Earth Resource Survey Programs [*National Aeronautics and Space Council*]
**ICCert**........ Intensive Care Certificate [*Australia*]
**ICCET**....... Imperial College of Science and Technology Centre for Environmental Technology [*British*] (IRUK)
**ICCF**.......... Interactive Computing and Control Facility [*IBM Corp. program product*]
**ICCF**.......... Interexchange Carrier and Carrier Forum [*Exchange Carriers Standards Association*] [*Telecommunications*]
**ICCF**.......... International Correspondence Chess Federation
**ICC-FF**...... [*Designation used on tariffs filed with*] Interstate Commerce Commission by Freight Forwarders
**ICCFM**...... International Confederation of Christian Family Movements (EAIO)
**ICCFS**........ Imperial College of Science and Technology Centre for Fusion Studies [*British*] (IRUK)
**ICCFTI**...... International Center for Companies of the Food Trade and Industry (EA)
**ICCG**.......... Intercommunication-Communication Control Group [*Navy*] (NVT)
**ICCGB**....... Indian Chamber of Commerce in Great Britain (DS)
**ICCGB**....... Italian Chamber of Commerce in Great Britain (DS)
**ICCH**......... Cook County Hospital, Dr. Frederick Tice Memorial Library, Chicago, IL [*Library symbol*] [*Library of Congress*] (LCLS)
**ICch**........... Country Club Hills Public Library District, Country Club Hills, IL [*Library symbol*] [*Library of Congress*] (LCLS)
**ICCH**......... International Catholic Confederation of Hospitals [*Later, IHF*] (EA)
**ICCH**......... International Commodities Clearing House [*British*] [*Business term*]
**ICCH**......... International Conference on Computers and the Humanities
**ICChH**....... Children's Memorial Hospital, Joseph Brennemann Medical Library, Chicago, IL [*Library symbol*] [*Library of Congress*] (LCLS)
**ICC of H & HH**... International Club for Collectors of Hatpins and Hatpin Holders (EA)
**ICCHS**....... Intercampus Committee for Handicapped Students (EA)
**ICCICA**..... Interim Co-ordinating Committee for International Commodity Arrangements

**ICCICE**...... Islamic Chamber of Commerce, Industry and Commodity Exchange [*See also CICIEM*] [*Karachi, Pakistan*] (EAIO)
**ICCILMB** ... Interim Committee for Coordination of Investigations of the Lower Mekong Basin (EA)
**ICCIR** ........ International Coordination Committee for Immunology of Reproduction [*Research center*] [*Bulgaria*] (IRC)
**ICCJ** .......... International Committee for the Cooperation of Journalists (NATG)
**ICCJ** .......... International Council of Christians and Jews [*Heppenheim, Federal Republic of Germany*] (EAIO)
**ICCK**.......... Chadwell, Kayser, Ruggles, McGee & Hasting, Chicago, IL [*Library symbol*] [*Library of Congress*] (LCLS)
**ICCL**.......... Cook County Law Library, Chicago, IL [*Library symbol*] [*Library of Congress*] (LCLS)
**ICCL**.......... Interface Control Configuration List
**ICCL**.......... International Committee for the Centennial of Light
**ICCL**.......... Irish Council for Civil Liberties (EAIO)
**ICCLY**....... International Council to Combat Lethal Yellowing
**ICCM**......... Idiopathic Congestive Cardiomyopathy [*Medicine*]
**ICCM**......... Institute of Critical Care Medicine [*University of Southern California*] [*Research center*] (RCD)
**ICCM**......... International Christian Classic Motorcyclists (EA)
**ICCM**......... International Committee for the Conservation of Mosaics [*Hungerford, Berkshire, England*] (EAIO)
**ICCM**......... International Council of Catholic Men [*See also FIHC*] [*Vatican City, Vatican City State*] (EAIO)
**ICCM**......... Interstitial Cell-Conditioned Medium [*Clinical chemistry*]
**ICCM**......... Master Chief Interior Communications Electrician [*Navy rating*]
**ICCM**......... University of Health Sciences - Chicago Medical School, Chicago, IL [*Library symbol*] [*Library of Congress*] (LCLS)
**ICCMB**...... International Committee for the Conservation of Mud-Brick (EAIO)
**ICCMG**...... Clausen, Miller, Gorman, Caffrey & Witous, Chicago, IL [*Library symbol*] [*Library of Congress*] (LCLS)
**ICCN** ......... Cook County School of Nursing, Chicago, IL [*Library symbol*] [*Library of Congress*] (LCLS)
**ICCN** ......... International Committee of Catholic Nurses [*See also CICIAMS*] [*Vatican City, Vatican City State*] (EAIO)
**ICCNA**....... CNA Financial Corp., Chicago, IL [*Library symbol*] [*Library of Congress*] (LCLS)
**ICCNA**....... International Center for Control of Nutritional Anemia [*University of Kansas*] [*Research center*] (RCD)
**ICCO** ......... Chicago College of Osteopathic Medicine, Chicago, IL [*Library symbol*] [*Library of Congress*] (LCLS)
**ICCO** ......... International Carpet Classification Organization [*Brussels, Belgium*] (EAIO)
**ICCO** ......... International Cocoa Organization [*London, England*] (EAIO)
**ICCO** ......... International Council of Containership Operators [*London*] (DCTA)
**ICComE**..... Commonwealth Edison Co., Chicago, IL [*Library symbol*] [*Library of Congress*] (LCLS)
**ICCon**......... Continental Group Co., Inc., Chicago, IL [*Library symbol*] [*Library of Congress*] (LCLS)
**ICCP**.......... Impressed Current Corrosion Protection
**ICCP**.......... Institute for Certification of Computer Professionals (EA)
**ICCP**.......... Integrated Communication Control Panel (MCD)
**ICCP**.......... Intelligence Civilian Career Program [*Army*] (AABC)
**ICCP**.......... Interface Coordination and Control Procedure (NASA)
**ICCP**.......... International Camp Counselor Program (EA)
**ICCP**.......... International Committee for Coal Petrology [*Liege, Belgium*] (EAIO)
**ICCP**.......... International Conference on Cataloging Principles
**ICCP**.......... International Council for Children's Play [*Groningen, Netherlands*] (EAIO)
**ICCPBS**..... International Chemical Congress of Pacific Basin Societies (EA)
**ICCPC** ....... International Computing Center's Preparatory Committee
**ICCPDQ**.... International Journal of Cancer Control and Prevention [*A publication*]
**ICC Prac J** ... ICC [*Interstate Commerce Commission*] Practitioners' Journal [*A publication*]
**ICC Pract J** ... ICC [*Interstate Commerce Commission*] Practitioners' Journal [*A publication*]
**ICCR**.......... Interactive Cash and Credit Register [*Datacap Systems, Inc.*]
**ICCR**.......... Interfaith Center on Corporate Responsibility (EA)
**ICCR**.......... International Committee for Coal Research [*Brussels, Belgium*] (EAIO)
**ICCR**.......... International Committee for Contraceptive Research
**ICCR**.......... Interstate Commerce Commission Reports [*A publication*] (DLA)
**ICCra** ......... Crane Co., Chicago, IL [*Library symbol*] [*Library of Congress*] (LCLS)
**ICC Rep**..... Interstate Commerce Commission Reports [*A publication*] (DLA)
**ICCRI** ........ Istituto di Credito delle Casse di Risparmio Italiane [*Italy*] (ECON)
**ICCROM**... International Centre for the Study of the Preservation and the Restoration of Cultural Property [*Rome, Italy*] (EAIO)
**ICCS** .......... Integrated Catapult Control Station (MCD)
**ICCS** .......... Integrated Communications Collection System [*Military*] (MCD)
**ICCS** .......... Intercomputer Communication System
**ICCS** .......... Interdisciplinary Center for Creative Studies [*State University College at Buffalo*] [*Research center*] (RCD)
**ICCS** .......... Interim Command and Control System (MCD)
**ICCS** .......... International Centre for Chemical Studies [*See also CIEC*] (EAIO)
**ICCS** .......... International Commission on Civil Status [*See also CIEC*] [*Strasbourg, France*] (EAIO)
**ICCS** .......... International Commission of Control and Supervision [*Composed of representatives of Canada, Hungary, Indonesia, and Poland, and charged with supervising the ceasefire in Vietnam, 1973*]
**ICCS** .......... International Committee on Clinical Sociology [*See also CISC*] [*Later, International Group on Clinical Sociology*] (EAIO)
**ICCS** .......... International Committee of Creole Studies [*Aix-En-Provence, France*] (EAIO)
**ICCS** .......... International Conference on Composite Structures [*Paisley, Scotland*] (EAIO)
**ICCS** .......... International Convention on the Continental Shelf (NOAA)
**ICCS** .......... International Cork Cutters' Society [*A union*]
**ICCS** .......... International Council for Canadian Studies [*See also CIEC*]
**ICCS** .......... International Group on Clinical Sociology [*Formerly, International Committee on Clinical Sociology*] (EA)
**ICCS** .......... Senior Chief Interior Communications Electrician [*Navy rating*]
**ICCSASW** ... International Commission for the Co-ordination of Solidarity among Sugar Workers [*Canada*]
**ICCSHE** .... Interagency Committee for Computer Support of Handicapped Employees [*General Services Administration*] (EGAO)
**ICCSP**........ Chicago School of Professional Psychology, Chicago, IL [*Library symbol*] [*Library of Congress*] (LCLS)
**ICCSR** ....... Interagency Committee on Climate Services and Research
**ICCSSSAR** ... International Coordinating Committee on Solid State Sensors and Actuators Research (EA)
**ICCSTR**..... International Coordinating Committee on Solid State Transducers Research (EA)
**ICCT**.......... Consoer, Townsend & Associates, Chicago, IL [*Library symbol*] [*Library of Congress*] (LCLS)
**ICCT**.......... Initial Contact Control Time [*Aerospace*] (AAG)
**ICCT**.......... International College of Career Training [*Australia*]
**ICCT**.......... Iowa Community College Telenetwork [*Marshalltown*] (TSSD)
**ICCTA**........ International Consultative Council of Travel Agents
**ICC-TM**..... Interstate Commerce Commission Transport Mobilization [*Federal emergency order*]
**ICCTR**....... Intelligence Case Control and Time Reporting System [*IRS*]
**ICCU** ......... Intensive Coronary Care Unit [*of a hospital*]
**ICCU** ......... Inter-Channel Comparison Unit [*Nuclear energy*] (NRCH)
**ICCU** ......... Intercomputer Compatibility Unit [*Data processing*]
**ICCU** ......... Intermediate Coronary Care Unit [*Medicine*]
**ICCU** ......... International Cross-Country Union (EA)
**ICCUS**....... International Claims Commission of the United States [*Abolished, 1954*] [*Department of State*]
**ICCUSA** .... Interagency Coordinating Committee on US-Soviet Affairs [*Department of State*]
**ICCUSA** .... International Child Care (USA) (EA)
**ICC Valuation Rep** ... Interstate Commerce Commission Valuation Reports [*A publication*] (DLA)
**ICCW**......... In-Containment Chilled Water [*Nuclear energy*] (NRCH)
**IC & CY**..... Inns of Court and City Yeomanry [*Military unit*] [*British*]
**ICCY**.......... International Cultural Centers for Youth (EA)
**ICCYM**...... Central YMCA Community College, Chicago, IL [*Library symbol*] [*Library of Congress*] (LCLS)
**ICD** ............ College of Saint Francis, Joliet, IL [*OCLC symbol*] (OCLC)
**ICD** ............ De Paul University, Chicago, IL [*Library symbol*] [*Library of Congress*] (LCLS)
**ICD** ............ Iesu Christo Duce [*With Jesus Christ as Leader*] [*Latin*]
**ICD** ............ Imitative Communication Deception [*Military*]
**ICD** ............ Immune Complex Disease
**ICD** ............ Industrial Cooperation Division [*Navy*]
**ICD** ............ Inland Clearance Depot [*Shipping*]
**ICD** ............ Installation Completion Date (CET)
**ICD** ............ Installation Control Drawing [*DoD*]
**ICD** ............ Institute of Civil Defence [*London, England*] (EAIO)
**ICD** ............ Instrumentation Control Document (KSC)
**ICD** ............ Inter Canadian Development [*Vancouver Stock Exchange symbol*]
**ICD** ............ Intercanthal Distance [*Anatomy*]
**ICD** ............ Interface Control Diagram (NRCH)
**ICD** ............ Interface Control Document [*Apollo*] [*NASA*]
**ICD** ............ Interface Control Drawings (NRCH)
**ICD** ............ Interim Checkout Device
**ICD** ............ International Candle
**ICD** ............ International Center for the Disabled (EA)
**ICD** ............ International Circulation Distributors, Inc.
**ICD** ............ International Classification of Diseases [*A publication*]
**ICD** ............ International Climatic Decades
**ICD** ............ International College of Dentists (EA)
**ICD** ............ International Congress for Data Processing
**ICD** ............ Intrauterine Contraceptive Device [*Medicine*]

**ICD**........... Ischemic Coronary Disease [*Medicine*]
**ICD**........... Isocitrate Dehydrogenase [*Also, ICDH, IDH*] [*An enzyme*]
**ICD-9**......... International Classification of Diseases. 9th Revision [*A publication*] (DHSM)
**ICDA**......... Industrial Compressor Distributors Association (EA)
**ICDA**......... Infantry Combat Developments Agency [*Pronounced "ick-da"*] [*Army*]
**ICDA**......... Institute for Community Design Analysis (EA)
**ICDA**......... International Catholic Deaf Association (EA)
**ICDA**......... International Cheese and Deli Association [*Later, IDDA*] (EA)
**ICDA**......... International Classification of Diseases, Adopted for Use in the United States
**ICDA**......... International Coalition for Development Action [*See also CIAD*] (EAIO)
**ICDA**......... International Congress of Dealers Associations (EA)
**ICDA**......... International Cooperative Development Association [*Later, ACDI*]
**ICDA-8**...... International Classification of Diseases, Adopted for Use in the United States. 8th Revision [*A publication*] (DHSM)
**ICDB**.......... Integrated Corporate Database
**ICDBL**....... International Committee for the Defense of the Breton Language [*See also CISLB*] [*Brussels, Belgium*] (EAIO)
**ICDC**.......... Industrial and Commercial Development Corporation [*Kenya*]
**ICDC**.......... National Dairy Council, Chicago, IL [*Library symbol*] [*Library of Congress*] (LCLS)
**ICD-9-CM** ... International Classification of Diseases. 9th Revision. Clinical Modification [*A publication*] (DHSM)
**ICDD**......... International Center for Dynamics of Development (EA)
**ICDDB**....... Internal Control Description Database
**ICDE**.......... International Council for Distance Education [*Australia*] (EAIO)
**ICDF**.......... International Christian Dance Fellowship (EAIO)
**ICDFS**....... Increased Capacity Drum Feed System (MCD)
**ICDH**......... Isocitrate Dehydrogenase [*Also, ICD, IDH*] [*An enzyme*]
**ICDI**.......... Imperial Court, Daughters of Isis (EA)
**ICD-L**........ De Paul University, Law Library, Chicago, IL [*Library symbol*] [*Library of Congress*] (LCLS)
**ICDL**.......... Integrated Circuit Description Language
**ICDL**.......... Inter-Center Data Link (MCD)
**ICDL**.......... Interface Control Documentation Log (KSC)
**ICDL**.......... Internal Control Description Language
**ICDM**......... Industrial Civil Defense Management
**ICDM**......... Institut Canadien pour la Deficience Mentale [*Canadian Institute on Mental Retardation*] [*Canada*]
**ICDMA**..... Independent Carbon-Dioxide Manufacturers Association (EA)
**ICDO**......... International Civil Defence Organization [*Switzerland*]
**ICDP**.......... Intelligence Career Development Program (AFM)
**ICDP**.......... International Center for Development Policy (EA)
**ICDP**.......... International Confederation for Disarmament and Peace [*London, England*]
**ICDR**......... Incremental Critical Design Review (NASA)
**ICDR**......... International Council for Dispute Resolution (EA)
**ICDR**......... Inward Call Detail Recording [*Telecommunications*] (TEL)
**ICDR**......... Ion Cyclotron Double Resonance
**IC DRUM**... Intercommunication Drum (MSA)
**ICDS**.......... Integrated Control and Display System (MCD)
**ICDS**.......... Interim Contractor Depot Support [*DoD*]
**ICD Sci Educ J**... ICD [*International College of Dentists*] Scientific and Educational Journal [*A publication*]
**ICDSD6**..... Indian Journal of Chest Diseases and Allied Sciences [*A publication*]
**ICDSRHP**... International Committee for the Defense of Salman Rushdie and His Publishers (EAIO)
**ICDT**.......... Chicago Daily Tribune, Chicago, IL [*Library symbol*] [*Library of Congress*] (LCLS)
**ICDT**.......... Incident (AABC)
**ICDT**.......... Islamic Centre for Development of Trade [*See also CIDC*] [*Casablanca, Morocco*] (EAIO)
**ICDU**......... Inertial Coupling Data Unit (NASA)
**ICDU**......... Inertial Coupling Display Unit (KSC)
**ICDV**......... Import Certificate Delivery Verification [*Military*]
**ICDY**......... Intercontinental Dynamics [*NASDAQ symbol*] (NQ)
**ICE**............ Arctic Alaska Fisheries [*NYSE symbol*] (SPSG)
**ICE**............ Concordia Teachers College, River Forest, IL [*OCLC symbol*] (OCLC)
**ICE**............ Economist Newspapers, Chicago, IL [*Library symbol*] [*Library of Congress*] (LCLS)
**ICE**............ Ice Station Resources [*Vancouver Stock Exchange symbol*]
**ICE**............ Iceland
**ice**.............. Icelandic [*MARC language code*] [*Library of Congress*] (LCCP)
**ICE**............ Illness-Correctional Environments
**ICE**............ Implicit Continuous-Fluid Eulerian
**ICE**............ Improved Cost Estimate (RDA)
**ICE**............ Improving Career Education (OICC)
**ICE**............ In-Circuit Emulator [*A trademark*]
**ICE**............ Increased Combat Effectiveness (AFM)
**ICE**............ Independent Cost Estimate
**ICE**............ Index of Combat Effectiveness (CINC)
**ICE**............ Individual Career Exploration [*Vocational guidance test*]
**ICE**............ Individual Commitment to Excellence [*DoD*]
**ICE**............ Induction Certificate Examination [*British Institute of Innkeeping*]
**ICE**............ Industrial Cost Exclusion [*Amendment to Federal Clean Water Act which limits use of federal money*]
**ICE**............ Informacion Comercial Espanola [*A publication*]
**ICE**............ Information Center on Education [*New York State Education Department*] [*Albany*] [*Information service or system*] (IID)
**ICE**............ Information Collection and Exchange [*Peace Corps*]
**ICE**............ Infrared Countermeasures Equipment [*Military*] [*Electronics*] (CAAL)
**ICE**............ Initial Combat Employment [*of new munitions*]
**ICE**............ Initial Cooling Experiment [*Nuclear physics research*]
**ICE**............ Inner City Enterprises [*British*]
**ICE**............ Input-Checking Equipment
**ICE**............ Input Control Element (MCD)
**ICE**............ Institute for Chemical Education (EA)
**ICE**............ Institute for Community Economics (EA)
**ICE**............ Institute for Consumer Ergonomics [*British*] (IRUK)
**ICE**............ Institution of Chemical Engineers [*British*] (EAIO)
**ICE**............ Institution of Civil Engineers [*British*]
**ICE**............ Instrument Checkout Equipment [*NASA*] (KSC)
**ICE**............ Instrument Communication
**ICE**............ Instrumentation Communication Equipment (NASA)
**ICE**............ Integrated Circuits Engineering Corp.
**ICE**............ Integrated Conceptual Environment [*Data processing*]
**ICE**............ Integrated Cooling for Electronics
**ICE**............ Integration with Controlled Error (MCD)
**ICE**............ Intelligence and Counterespionage [*Fictitious organization in the Matt Helm series of books and movies*]
**ICE**............ Intercity Experimental [*Electric train*] [*Federal Republic of Germany*]
**ICE**............ Interfaith Coalition on Energy (EA)
**ICE**............ Interference Cancellation Equipment [*Telecommunications*]
**ICE**............ Intermediate Cable Equalizers (IEEE)
**ICE**............ Internal Combustion Engine
**ICE**............ International Center for the Environment
**ICE**............ International Centre for Economics [*British*]
**ICE**............ International Cirrus Experiment [*Funded by West Germany, Britain, France, Sweden, and the European Communities Commission*] [*Climatology*]
**ICE**............ International Cometary Explorer [*Formerly, International Sun-Earth Explorer*] [*NASA*]
**ICE**............ International Commercial Exchange [*Defunct*] (EA)
**ICE**............ International Computer Component Exchange
**ICE**............ International Congress of Entomology [*Later, CICE*] (EA)
**ICE**............ International Construction Equipment Exhibition (ITD)
**ICE**............ International Council on Electrocardiology [*Glasgow, Scotland*] (EAIO)
**ICE**............ International Cultural Exchange
**ICE**............ Interstate Cost Estimate [*Federal Highway Administration*]
**ICE**............ Intreprinderea de Comert Exterior [*Foreign Trade Enterprise*] [*Romanian*]
**ICE**............ Ion Chromatography Exclusion
**ICE**............ Ion Convection Electrodynamics (MCD)
**ICE**............ Islamic Council of Europe
**ICE**............ Isothermal Controlled Electrophoresis
**ICE**............ Italian Cultural Exchange in the United States (EA)
**ICE**............ It's Close Enough
**ICEA**.......... Institut Canadien d'Education des Adultes [*Canadian Institute of Adult Education*]
**ICEA**.......... Instrument Contracting and Engineering Association (EA)
**ICEA**.......... Insulated Cable Engineers Association (EA)
**ICEA**.......... International Childbirth Education Association (EA)
**ICEA**.......... International Christian Education Association (EA)
**ICEA**.......... International Christian Esperanto Association (EA)
**ICEA**.......... International Community Education Association [*Australia*]
**Ice Abs**....... Ice Abstracts [*A publication*]
**ICEAM**...... Institute of Computer Aided Engineering and Management [*University of Dundee*] [*United Kingdom*] (IRUK)
**ICEAM**...... International Committee on Economic and Applied Microbiology [*ICSU*] (EAIO)
**ICEATT**.... Index of Continuing Education Attitudes
**ICEBAC**.... International Council of Employers of Bricklayers and Allied Craftsmen (EA)
**ICEC**.......... Interagency Career Education Committee (OICC)
**ICEC**.......... Intercontinental Energy Corporation [*NASDAQ symbol*] (NQ)
**ICEC**.......... International Committee of Enamelling Creators (EAIO)
**ICEC**.......... International Conference on Education in Chemistry
**ICEC**.......... International Cost Engineering Council (EA)
**ICEC**.......... International Council for Exceptional Children [*Later, CEC*]
**ICEC**.......... International Cryogenic Engineering Committee (EAIO)
**ICEC**.......... Interuniversity Consortium for Educational Computing [*Database*]
**ICECAN**.... Iceland-Canada Submarine Cable System [*Telecommunications*] (TEL)
**ICECON**.... Control of Sea Ice Information (NATG)
**Ice Cream Field Ice Cream Trade J**... Ice Cream Field and Ice Cream Trade Journal [*A publication*]
**Ice Cream R**... Ice Cream Review [*A publication*]
**Ice Cream Rev**... Ice Cream Review [*A publication*]

**Ice Cream Trade J** ... Ice Cream Trade Journal [*A publication*]
**ICED**......... Industrial and Construction Equipment Division (EA)
**ICED**......... Institute for Community Education Development [*Ball State University*] [*Research center*] (RCD)
**ICED**......... Interface Control Envelope Drawings (KSC)
**ICED**......... International Council for Educational Development (EA)
**ICED**......... Interprofessional Council on Environmental Design (EA)
**ICEDEFOR** ... Iceland Defense Force
**ICEdit**........ EDITEC, Chicago, IL [*Library symbol*] [*Library of Congress*] (LCLS)
**ICEDS**....... Insurance Company Education Directors Society (EA)
**ICEEC**....... International Congress of Electrical and Electronic Communications
**ICEED**....... International Research Center for Energy and Economic Development [*University of Colorado*] [*Research center*]
**ICEF**.......... Institute for the Community as Extended Family (EA)
**ICEF**.......... Interactive Composition and Editing Facility [*IBM Corp.*]
**ICEF**.......... International Children's Emergency Fund [*United Nations*] (DLA)
**ICEF**.......... International Committee for Research and Study on Environmental Factors
**ICEF**.......... International Council for Educational Films [*Later, ICEM*]
**ICEF**.......... International Federation of Chemical, Energy, and General Workers' Unions [*Belgium*] (DCTA)
**ICEI**........... Independent Cold Extruders Institute
**ICEI**........... Indonesian Cultural and Educational Institute
**ICEI**........... Internal Combustion Engine Institute [*Later, EMA*] (EA)
**ICEL**.......... Ice (London) [*A publication*]
**ICEL**.......... Icelandic
**ICEL**.......... International Committee on English in the Liturgy (EA)
**ICEL**.......... International Committee for Ethnic Liberty [*See also IKEL*] (EAIO)
**ICEL**.......... International Council of Environmental Law [*Bonn, Federal Republic of Germany*] (EA)
**Icel Fish Lab Annu Rep** ... Icelandic Fisheries Laboratories. Annual Report [*A publication*]
**ICEM**......... Incremental Cost Effectiveness Model
**ICEM**......... Independent Cluster Emission Model [*Atomic physics*]
**ICEM**......... Induced Contamination Experimental Monitor (MCD)
**ICEM**......... Intergovernmental Committee for European Migration [*Later, ICM*]
**ICEM**......... International Confederation for Electroacoustic Music (EA)
**ICEM**......... International Council for Educational Media [*Formerly, ICEF*]
**ICEM**......... Inverted Coaxial Magnetron (MCD)
**ICEM**......... Irish Council European Movement
**ICen**.......... Centralia Public Library, Centralia, IL [*Library symbol*] [*Library of Congress*] (LCLS)
**ICEN**......... Ice News. Artec, Inc. [*A publication*]
**ICEN**......... ICEA [*International Childbirth Education Association*] News [*A publication*]
**ICEN**......... [*The*] Israel Commercial Economic Newsletter [*A publication*] [*Also, an information service or system*] (IID)
**ICenC**......... Centralia Correctional Center, Centralia, IL [*Library symbol*] [*Library of Congress*] (LCLS)
**ICenHS**...... Centralia District High School, District 200, Centralia, IL [*Library symbol*] [*Library of Congress*] (LCLS)
**ICEOB**........ Sea Ice Observation Code [*Marine science*] (MSC)
**ICEP**.......... Institute for Cultural Exchange thru Photography (EA)
**ICEP**.......... Instituto do Comercio Externo (Lisbon, Portugal) [*Institute of Commercial Exports*] (EY)
**ICEPART** ... Index of Continuing Education Participation
**ICEPAT**..... Iceland Patrol [*Navy*]
**ICEPAX**.... International Congress of Entomology. Proceedings [*A publication*]
**ICEPF**........ International Commission for the Eriksson Prize Fund (EAIO)
**ICEPM**...... Internal Combustion Engine Powered Material (MCD)
**ICER**.......... ICEA [*International Childbirth Education Association*] Review [*A publication*]
**ICER**.......... Information Centre of the European Railways
**ICER**.......... Infrared Cell, Electronically Refrigerated
**ICER**.......... Institute for Central European Research (EA)
**ICER**.......... Interdepartmental Committee of External Relations [*Canada*]
**Ice Refrig**... Ice and Refrigeration [*A publication*]
**ICEROCC**... Iceland Regional Operational Control Center [*Aircraft surveillance*]
**ICERR**....... Interstate Congress for Equal Rights and Responsibilities (EA)
**ICES**.......... Import Cargo Electronic System
**ICES**.......... Institution of Surveyors in Civil Engineering [*British*]
**ICES**.......... Integrated Civil Engineering System [*Programming language*] [*Data processing*]
**IC/ES**......... Intercommunications/Emergency Station (MCD)
**ICES**.......... International Centre for Ethnic Studies (EA)
**ICES**.......... International Council for the Exploration of the Sea [*Denmark*]
**ICES**.......... International Cultural Exchange Service
**ICES**.......... National Easter Seal Society for Crippled Children and Adults, Chicago, IL [*Library symbol*] [*Library of Congress*] (LCLS)
**ICESA**....... International Conference on Environmental Sensing and Assessment
**ICESA**....... Interstate Conference of Employment Security Agencies (EA)
**ICESC**........ Industry Crew Escape Systems Committee
**ICESC**........ International Committee for European Security and Co-Operation [*See also CISCE*] (EAIO)
**ICESSP**..... International Council for Elementary and Secondary School Philosophy (EA)
**ICET**.......... Forty-Eight Item Counseling Evaluation Test [*Psychology*]
**ICET**.......... Institute for the Certification of Engineering Technicians [*Later, National Institute for Certification in Engineering Technologies*]
**ICET**.......... Institute for Comparative and Environmental Toxicology [*Cornell University*] [*Research center*] (RCD)
**ICET**.......... Interagency Committee on Excavation Technology [*Federal Council for Science and Technology*] [*Terminated, 1976*]
**ICET**.......... International Centre for Earth Tides [*See also CIMT*] [*Belgium*] (EAIO)
**ICET**.......... International Council on Education for Teaching (EA)
**ICETK**....... International Committee of Electrochemical Thermodynamics and Kinetics (IEEE)
**ICETT**....... Industrial Council for Educational Training Technology [*United Kingdom*] (DS)
**ICEUM**...... International Conference on Energy Use Management
**ICEV**.......... Initial Condition Evaluation [*Orbit identification*]
**ICEVH**....... International Council for Education of the Visually Handicapped [*Bensheim, Federal Republic of Germany*] (EAIO)
**ICEX**.......... Intelligence Coordination and Exploitation [*Joint CIA-MACV program*]
**ICEXBO**.... International Council for the Exploration of the Sea. Cooperative Research Report [*A publication*]
**ICEY**.......... International Capital Equipment Ltd. [*NASDAQ symbol*] (NQ)
**ICF**............ Field Museum of Natural History, Chicago, IL [*Library symbol*] [*Library of Congress*] (LCLS)
**ICF**............ George Williams College, Downers Grove, IL [*OCLC symbol*] (OCLC)
**ICF**............ Indirect Centrifugal Flotation
**ICF**............ Indoor Cricket Federation [*Australia*]
**ICF**............ Inertial Confinement Fusion [*Nuclear physics*]
**ICF**............ Inspection Check Fixture (MSA)
**ICF**............ Installation Confinement Facility [*Army*] (AABC)
**ICF**............ Institut Canadien du Film [*Canadian Film Institute - CFI*]
**ICF**............ Institute for Canadian Futures
**ICF**............ Integrated Control Facility [*Sperry UNIVAC*]
**ICF**............ Intelligence Contingency Funds (CINC)
**ICF**............ Intensive Care Facility [*Medicine*]
**ICF**............ Inter-Bureau Citation of Funds [*Navy*]
**ICF**............ Interacting Correlated Fragment [*Physical chemistry*]
**ICF**............ Interactive Communications Feature [*IBM Corp.*]
**ICF**............ Intercommunication Flip-Flop [*Data processing*]
**ICF**............ Interconnect Facility
**ICF**............ Interface Control Function (MCD)
**ICF**............ Intermediate Care Facility [*Medicine*]
**ICF**............ International Canoe Federation [*See also FIC*] [*Florence, Italy*] (EAIO)
**ICF**............ International Cardiology Foundation (EA)
**ICF**............ International Carpet Fair (TSPED)
**ICF**............ International Casting Federation (EAIO)
**ICF**............ International Cheerleading Foundation (EA)
**ICF**............ International Congregational Fellowship (EA)
**ICF**............ International Congress on Fracture [*ICSU*] [*Sendai, Japan*] (EAIO)
**ICF**............ International Consultants Foundation (EA)
**ICF**............ International Crane Foundation (EA)
**ICF**............ International Craniofacial Foundations (EA)
**ICF**............ International Cremation Federation (EAIO)
**ICF**............ International Curling Federation (EAIO)
**ICF**............ International Federation of Chemical and General Workers Union
**ICF**............ Intracellular Fluid [*Physiology*]
**ICF**............ Intravascular Coagulation and Fibrinolysis Syndrome [*Medicine*]
**ICF**............ Intrinsic Coercive Force
**ICF**............ Iota-Cam Fiberscope [*Also, ICFS*]
**ICF**............ Italian Catholic Federation Central Council (EA)
**ICF-A**......... Field Museum of Natural History, Edward E. Ayer Ornithological Library, Chicago, IL [*Library symbol*] [*Library of Congress*] (LCLS)
**ICFA**.......... Fireman Apprentice, Interior Communications Electrician, Striker [*Navy rating*]
**ICFA**.......... Independent College Funds of America [*Later, FIHE*] (EA)
**ICFA**.......... Inland Commercial Fisheries Association (EA)
**ICFA**.......... Institute of Chartered Financial Analysts [*Later, AIMR*] (EA)
**ICFA**.......... International Committee on Future Accelerators [*International Union of Pure and Applied Physics*]
**ICFAD**....... International Council of Fine Arts Deans (EA)
**ICFAR**....... Federal Archives and Records Center, General Services Administration, Chicago, IL [*Library symbol*] [*Library of Congress*] (LCLS)
**ICFAR**....... Indianapolis Center for Advanced Research [*Indiana University - Purdue University at Indianapolis*] [*Research center*] (RCD)
**ICFATCM**... Individual Cleared for Access to Classified Material (AAG)

**ICFATCMUTAI** ... Individual Cleared for Access to Classified Material Up to and Including
**ICFB** .......... Integrative Control Functions of the Brain [*Elsevier Book Series*] [*A publication*]
**ICFC** .......... Felician College, Chicago, IL [*Library symbol*] [*Library of Congress*] (LCLS)
**ICFC** .......... Industrial and Commercial Finance Corporation [*British*]
**ICFC** .......... International Centre of Films for Children
**ICFC** .......... International Council of Fan Clubs [*Defunct*] (EA)
**IC & FCD**... Interior Communication and Fire Control Distribution (MSA)
**ICFCM** ...... International Convention of Faith, Churches, and Ministers (EA)
**ICFCYP**..... International Centre of Films for Children and Young People [*France*] (EY)
**ICFE** .......... Independent Colleges of Further Education [*British*]
**ICFE** .......... Institute for Consumer Financial Education (EA)
**ICFE** .......... International Contract Flooring Exhibition [*Great Britain*] (ITD)
**ICFF** .......... International Contemporary Furniture Fair (ITD)
**ICFFO** ....... International Council of Folklore Festival Organizations and Folk Art (EA)
**ICFI** ........... International Cooperative Fracture Institute
**ICFI** ........... Iota-Cam Fiberscope Instrument
**ICFK** .......... Friedman and Koven, Library, Chicago, IL [*Library symbol*] [*Library of Congress*] (LCLS)
**ICFL** .......... International Council of the French Language [*See also CILF*] [*Paris, France*] (EAIO)
**ICFLC**........ International Curling Federation - Ladies Committee [*Defunct*] (EA)
**ICFLPRMFS** ... Items Not Available through Cannibalization, Fabrication, or Local Procurement or Replacement from Maintenance Float Stock
**ICFM**......... International Convention of Faith Ministries (EA)
**ICFMA**...... International Cystic Fibrosis Mucoviscidosis Association (EA)
**ICFMC**...... FMC Corp., Chicago, IL [*Library symbol*] [*Library of Congress*] (LCLS)
**ICFMH**...... International Committee on Food Microbiology and Hygiene [*ICSU*] [*Frederiksberg, Denmark*] (EAIO)
**ICFMR**...... Intermediate Care Facility for the Mentally Retarded
**ICF-MR/DD** ... Intermediate Care Facility for the Mentally Retarded/ Developmentally Disabled
**ICFN**.......... Fireman, Interior Communications Electrician, Striker [*Navy rating*]
**ICFNB**....... First National Bank of Chicago, Chicago, IL [*Library symbol*] [*Library of Congress*] (LCLS)
**ICFP** .......... Institute of Certified Financial Planners (EA)
**ICFPW** ...... International Confederation of Former Prisoners of War
**ICFR**.......... Intercollegiate Conference of Faculty Representatives (EA)
**ICFRB** ....... Federal Reserve Bank of Chicago, Chicago, IL [*Library symbol*] [*Library of Congress*] (LCLS)
**ICFRU**....... Idaho Cooperative Fishery Research Unit [*University of Idaho*] [*Research center*] (RCD)
**ICFS** .......... Industry Coalition for Fire Safety [*Defunct*] (EA)
**ICFS** .......... Installation CONUS FORSTAT System [*Military*]
**ICFS** .......... Iota-Cam Fiberscope [*Also, ICF*]
**ICFSHG** .... International Committee of French-Speaking Historians and Geographers (EAIO)
**ICFSRT**..... International Council of French-Speaking Radio and Television (EAIO)
**ICFTU**....... International Confederation of Free Trade Unions [*Belgium*]
**ICFTUE** .... International Center of Free Trade Unionists in Exile [*France*]
**ICFTU Econ & Social Bul** ... ICFTU [*International Confederation of Free Trade Unions*] Economic and Social Bulletin [*A publication*]
**ICFU**.......... International Council on the Future of the University [*Defunct*]
**ICG** ............ Icing [*Meteorology*] (FAAC)
**ICG** ............ Illinois Benedictine College, Lisle, IL [*OCLC symbol*] (OCLC)
**ICG** ............ Illinois Central Gulf Railroad Co. [*AAR code*]
**ICG** ............ In-Flight Coverall Garment [*Apollo*] [*NASA*]
**ICG** ............ Indochina Curriculum Group (EA)
**ICG** ............ Indocyanine Green [*Liver function test*] [*Medicine*]
**ICG** ............ Integrated Combat Group [*Air Force*]
**ICG** ............ Inter-City Gas Corp. [*AMEX symbol*] [*Toronto Stock Exchange symbol*] (SPSG)
**ICG** ............ Interactive Computer Graphics
**ICG** ............ International Commission on Glass [*See also CIV*] [*Prague, Czechoslovakia*] (EAIO)
**ICG** ............ International Conference Group [*Commercial firm*] (EA)
**ICG** ............ International Congress of Genetics
**ICG** ............ Interviewer's Classification Guide
**ICGA** ......... International Carnival Glass Association (EA)
**ICGAD** ...... IEEE. Computer Graphics and Applications [*A publication*]
**ICGB**.......... International Cargo Gear Bureau (EA)
**ICGCD**....... Gardner, Carton, and Douglas, Chicago, IL [*Library symbol*] [*Library of Congress*] (LCLS)
**ICGE**.......... International Center of Genetic Epistemology [*Geneva, Switzerland*]
**ICGEB**....... International Centre for Genetic Engineering and Biotechnology (EAIO)
**ICGEC**....... Interagency Collaborative Group on Environmental Carcinogenesis [*National Institutes of Health*] [*Bethesda, MD*] (EGAO)
**ICGGI**........ Internationale Coronelli-Gesellschaft fuer Globen- und Instrumentkunde [*International Coronelli Society - ICS*] (EAIO)
**ICGH**......... Greeley & Hansen Engineering Library, Chicago, IL [*Library symbol*] [*Library of Congress*] (LCLS)
**ICGH**......... International Confederation of Genealogy and Heraldry [*See also CIGH*] [*Paris, France*] (EAIO)
**ICGI**........... Integrated Computer Graphics, Incorporated [*Atlanta, GA*] [*NASDAQ symbol*] (NQ)
**ICGI**........... International Council of Goodwill Industries (EA)
**ICGIC**........ Icing in Clouds [*Meteorology*] (FAAC)
**ICGICIP**.... Icing in Clouds and in Precipitation [*Meteorology*] (FAAC)
**ICGIP**........ Icing in Precipitation [*Meteorology*] (FAAC)
**ICGM**........ Intercontinental Glide [*or Guided*] Missile (KSC)
**ICGM**........ International Colloquium about Gas Marketing (EA)
**ICGN**......... ICC Technologies, Inc. [*NASDAQ symbol*] (NQ)
**ICGR**.......... Ivory Coast - Ghana Ridge [*Geology*]
**ICGRAF**.... Indian Cotton Growing Review [*A publication*]
**ICGRC**....... International Connoisseurs of Green and Red Chile (EA)
**ICGS**.......... International Catholic Girls' Society
**ICGS**.......... Interreligious Committee of General Secretaries (EA)
**ICGSCA** .... Infants', Children's, and Girls' Sportswear and Coat Association (EA)
**ICh**............ Chicago Heights Free Public Library, Chicago Heights, IL [*Library symbol*] [*Library of Congress*] (LCLS)
**ICH**............ ICH Corp. [*AMEX symbol*] (SPSG)
**ICH**............ Ichthyology
**ICH**............ Illinois College, Jacksonville, IL [*OCLC symbol*] (OCLC)
**ICH**............ Incumbent Come Home [*Political humor*] [*Pronounced "itch"*]
**ICH**............ Induction-Conduction Heating
**ICH**............ Infectious Canine Hepatitis [*Veterinary medicine*]
**ICH**............ Information Clearing House, Inc.
**ICH**............ Inhalation Cycle Histogram [*Biometrics*]
**ICH**............ Instructor Contact Hours (MCD)
**ICH**............ Interchanger (NASA)
**ICH**............ Intracerebral Hemorrhage [*Medicine*]
**ICH**............ Intracranial Hemorrhage [*Medicine*]
**ICHAA** ...... Inorganica Chimica Acta [*A publication*]
**ICham**........ Champaign Public Library, Champaign, IL [*Library symbol*] [*Library of Congress*] (LCLS)
**IChamBH**.. Burnham City Hospital, Champaign, IL [*Library symbol*] [*Library of Congress*] (LCLS)
**IChamCE**... United States Army Construction Engineering Research Laboratory, Champaign, IL [*Library symbol*] [*Library of Congress*] (LCLS)
**IChamGS**... Church of Jesus Christ of Latter-Day Saints, Genealogical Society Library, Champaign Stake Branch, Champaign, IL [*Library symbol*] [*Library of Congress*] (LCLS)
**IChamL**...... Lincoln Trail Libraries, Champaign, IL [*Library symbol*] [*Library of Congress*] (LCLS)
**IChamMH** ... Illinois Department of Mental Health and Developmental Disabilities, Herman M. Adler Center Library, Champaign, IL [*Library symbol*] [*Library of Congress*] (LCLS)
**IChamP**...... Parkland College, Champaign, IL [*Library symbol*] [*Library of Congress*] (LCLS)
**ICHAP**....... Improved Chaparral [*Military*] (MCD)
**IChar**.......... Charleston Carnegie Public Library, Charleston, IL [*Library symbol*] [*Library of Congress*] (LCLS)
**ICharE**....... Eastern Illinois University, Charleston, IL [*Library symbol*] [*Library of Congress*] (LCLS)
**ICharH** ...... Charleston Community Memorial Hospital, Charleston, IL [*Library symbol*] [*Library of Congress*] (LCLS)
**ICHC** ......... International Committee for Horticultural Congresses
**ICHC** ......... International Congress of Heterocyclic Chemistry
**ICHCA** ...... International Cargo Handling Coordination Association [*London, England*] (EA)
**ICHCA J** ... ICHCA [*International Cargo Handling Coordination Association*] Journal [*A publication*]
**ICHCA Mon J** ... ICHCA [*International Cargo Handling Coordination Association*] Monthly Journal [*A publication*]
**ICHD**......... Inter-Society Commission for Heart Disease Resources (EA)
**ICHDA**...... International Cooperative Housing Development Association
**ICHDR**...... Intersociety Commission for Heart Disease Resources [*Absorbed by American Heart Association - AHA*]
**I Ch E**......... Institution of Chemical Engineers [*British*]
**ICHE**......... International Commission on Human Ecology (EA)
**ICHE**......... International Councils on Higher Education [*Defunct*]
**I Chem E**.... Institution of Chemical Engineers [*British*]
**ICherSD** .... Cherry School District 92, Cherry, IL [*Library symbol*] [*Library of Congress*] (LCLS)
**ICHF**.......... International Child Health Foundation (EA)
**ICHFC**....... Household Finance Corporation, Chicago, IL [*Library symbol*] [*Library of Congress*] (LCLS)
**ICHG**......... International Conference on the Holocaust and Genocide (EAIO)
**IChGS**........ Church of Jesus Christ of Latter-Day Saints, Genealogical Society Library, Chicago Heights Branch, Chicago Heights, IL [*Library symbol*] [*Library of Congress*] (LCLS)

**ICHi**.......... Chicago Historical Society, Chicago, IL [*Library symbol*] [*Library of Congress*] (LCLS)
**ICHIA**........ Ingegneria Chimica [*A publication*]
**ICHID**....... Harrington Institute of Interior Design, Chicago, IL [*Library symbol*] [*Library of Congress*] (LCLS)
**IChil**.......... Chillicothe Township Free Public Library, Chillicothe, IL [*Library symbol*] [*Library of Congress*] (LCLS)
**IChildMag**... Subject Index to Children's Magazines [*A publication*]
**ICHLM**..... International Conference of Historians of the Labour Movement [*Vienna, Austria*] (EAIO)
**ICHMH**..... Interstate Clearing House on Mental Health [*Defunct*]
**ICHMT**..... International Centre for Heat and Mass Transfer (EAIO)
**ICHOHYP**... International Committee of Hard of Hearing Young People [*Frederiksberg, Denmark*] (EAIO)
**ICHP**......... International Commission of Health Professionals for Health and Human Rights (EA)
**ICHP**......... Investors Chronicle/Hillier Parker [*British*] [*A publication*]
**IChP**.......... Prairie State College, Learning Center, Chicago Heights, IL [*Library symbol*] [*Library of Congress*] (LCLS)
**ICHPCG**.... Acta Genetica Sinica [*A publication*]
**ICHP/CINPROS**... International Commission of Health Professionals for Health and Human Rights/Commission Internationale des Professionals de la Sante (EAIO)
**ICHPER**.... International Council for Health, Physical Education, and Recreation (EA)
**IChr**........... Chrisman Public Library, Chrisman, IL [*Library symbol*] [*Library of Congress*] (LCLS)
**ICHR**......... Illinois Catholic Historical Review [*A publication*]
**ICHR**......... Indian Council of Historical Research
**ICHR**......... Inter-American Commission on Human Rights [*OAS*] (PD)
**ICHR**......... Interfaith Council for Human Rights (EA)
**I Ch R**......... Irish Chancery Reports [*A publication*] (DLA)
**ICHRI**........ Islamic Committee for Human Rights in Iraq [*Later, IODHRI*] (EA)
**ICHRPI**..... International Commission for the History of Representative and Parliamentary Institutions [*Rome, Italy*] (EAIO)
**ICHRT**....... International Committee for Human Rights in Taiwan (EA)
**ICHS**.......... Inter-African Committee for Hydraulic Studies [*See also CIEH*] [*Ouagadougou, Burkina Faso*] (EAIO)
**ICHS**.......... International Center for Holocaust Studies (EA)
**ICHS**.......... International Committee for Historical Sciences [*Paris, France*] (EA)
**ICHS**.......... International Council of Homehelp Services [*See also CISAF*] [*Driebergen-Rijsenburg, Netherlands*] (EAIO)
**ICHSMSS**... International Commission for the History of Social Movements and Social Structures [*Paris, France*] (EAIO)
**ICHSPP**..... International Congress on High-Speed Photography and Photonics (EA)
**ICHSWW**... International Committee for the History of the Second World War (EAIO)
**ICHT**......... Harris Trust and Savings Bank, Chicago, IL [*Library symbol*] [*Library of Congress*] (LCLS)
**ICHTH**...... Ichthyology
**Ichthyol Aquarium J**... Ichthyologica: The Aquarium Journal [*A publication*]
**Ichthyol Bull JLB Smith Inst Ichthyol**... Ichthyological Bulletin. J. L. B. Smith Institute of Ichthyology [*A publication*]
**Ichthyol Ser Dep Biol Coll Sci Tunghai Univ**... Ichthyological Series. Department of Biology. College of Science. Tunghai University [*A publication*]
**ICHTHYS**... Jesous Christos, Theou Uios Soter [*Jesus Christ, Son of God, Savior*]
**I Ch'uan Hsueh Pao Acta Genet Sin**... I Ch'uan Hsueh Pao. Acta Genetica Sinica [*A publication*]
**ICHY**......... International Council of Hindoo Youth (EAIO)
**ICI**............. Cicia [*Fiji*] [*Airport symbol*] (OAG)
**ICI**............. Ice Condenser Instrumentation [*Nuclear energy*] (NRCH)
**ICI**............. ICI Pharmaceuticals [*Great Britain*] [*Research code symbol*]
**ICI**............. Illinois Institute of Technology, Chicago, IL [*Library symbol*] [*Library of Congress*] (LCLS)
**ICI**............. Imperial Chemical Industries Ltd. [*NYSE symbol*] (SPSG)
**ICI**............. Imperial Chemical Industries PLC [*Information service or system*] (IID)
**ICI**............. Incoming Call Identification [*Telecommunications*]
**ICI**............. Independent Curators, Incorporated (EA)
**ICI**............. Index to Current Information [*A publication*] (APTA)
**ICI**............. Individual/Collective Integration
**ICI**............. Information Centre International [*Telecommunications service*] (TSSD)
**ICI**............. Information Concepts, Incorporated
**ICI**............. Information Consultants, Incorporated [*Information service or system*] (IID)
**ICI**............. Informations Catholiques Internationales [*A publication*]
**ICI**............. Initial Capabilities Inspection [*Military*] (AFM)
**ICI**............. Institut Canadien des Ingenieurs [*Engineering Institute of Canada*]
**ICI**............. Insurance Corporation of Ireland [*Export credit agency*]
**ICI**............. Intelligent Communications Interface (IEEE)
**ICI**............. Inter-American Children's Institute [*OAS*]
**ICI**............. Inter-American Cooperative Institute
**ICI**............. Interagency Committee on Intelligence
**ICI**............. Interagency Cooperative Issuances (OICC)
**ICI**............. Interclick Interval [*Entomology*]
**ICI**............. Interim Cargo Integrator (MCD)
**ICI**............. Internal Change Identifier (MCD)
**ICI**............. International Castles Institute (EA)
**ICI**............. International Commission on Illumination [*Since 1951, has been known exclusively as CIE, which see*]
**ICI**............. Interpersonal Communication Inventory [*Interpersonal skills and attitudes test*]
**ICI**............. Inuit Cultural Institute [*Canada*]
**ICI**............. Investment Casting Institute (EA)
**ICI**............. Investment Company Institute (EA)
**ICI**............. Ion Composition Instrument [*Cometary physics*]
**ICI**............. Istituto Chemioterapico Italiano [*Italy*] [*Research code symbol*]
**ICI**............. Italian Cultural Institute (EA)
**ICI**............. MacMurray College, Jacksonville, IL [*OCLC symbol*] (OCLC)
**ICI-A**.......... Illinois Institute of Technology, Armour Research Foundation, Chicago, IL [*Library symbol*] [*Library of Congress*] (LCLS)
**ICIA**........... Institute of Cultural Affairs International [*Information service or system*] (IID)
**ICIA**........... International Center of Information on Antibiotics (EAIO)
**ICIA**........... International Communications Industries Association (EA)
**ICIA**........... International Conference Industry Association [*Defunct*] (EA)
**ICIA**........... International Credit Insurance Association [*Zurich, Switzerland*] (EAIO)
**ICIA**........... International Crop Improvement Association [*Later, AOSCA*] (EA)
**ICIA Inf Bull**... ICIA [*International Center of Information on Antibiotics*] Information Bulletin [*A publication*]
**ICIANZ**..... Imperial Chemical Industries of Australia and New Zealand Ltd.
**ICIAP**........ Interagency Committee on International Aviation Policy [*Department of State*] (AFM)
**ICIASF**...... International Congress on Instrumentation in Aerospace Simulation Facilities
**ICic**............ Cicero Public Library, Cicero, IL [*Library symbol*] [*Library of Congress*] (LCLS)
**ICIC**........... Interagency Committee on Intermodal Cargo
**ICIC**........... Interdisciplinary Committee on Institutes and Conferences
**ICIC**........... International Cancer Information Center [*Public Health Service*] [*Information service or system*] (IID)
**ICICI**......... Industrial Credit & Investment Corporation of India Ltd.
**ICICLE**...... Integrated Cryogenic Isotope Cooling Equipment
**ICicM**........ Morton College, Cicero, IL [*Library symbol*] [*Library of Congress*] (LCLS)
**ICICO**........ Illinois College of Optometry, Chicago, IL [*Library symbol*] [*Library of Congress*] (LCLS)
**ICICS**......... International College of Surgeons, Chicago, IL [*Library symbol*] [*Library of Congress*] (LCLS)
**ICI-D**......... Illinois Institute of Technology, Institute of Design, Chicago, IL [*Library symbol*] [*Library of Congress*] (LCLS)
**ICID**........... Information Center for Individuals with Disabilities (EA)
**ICID**........... International Commission on Irrigation and Drainage [*See also CIID*] [*ICSU*] [*New Delhi, India*] (EAIO)
**ICID Bull**... ICID [*International Commission on Irrigation and Drainage*] Bulletin [*A publication*]
**ICID Bull Int Comm Irrig Drain**... ICID Bulletin. International Commission on Irrigation and Drainage [*A publication*]
**ICIDCA Bol**... ICIDCA [*Instituto Cubano de Investigaciones de los Derivados de la Cana de Azucar*] Boletin [*A publication*]
**ICIDH**....... International Classification of Impairments, Disabilities, and Handicaps [*Occupational therapy*]
**ICIDI**......... Independent Commission on International Development Issues [*Also known as the Brandt Commission*] [*Studies problems arising from the inequity between more developed Northern nations and less developed Southern countries*]
**ICIDR**........ International Collaboration in Infectious Diseases Research [*Tulane University*] [*Research center*] (RCD)
**ICIE**........... Infogrow Communications Information Exchange [*Information service or system*] (IID)
**ICIE**........... Information Center for Internal Exposure [*Department of Energy*] [*Defunct*] (IID)
**ICIE**........... International Center for Industry and the Environment (DCTA)
**ICIE**........... International Council of Industrial Editors [*Later, IABC*]
**ICIE**........... International Council of Industrial Engineers
**ICI Engng Plast**... ICI [*Imperial Chemical Industries Ltd.*] Engineering Plastics [*A publication*]
**ICIEQ**........ Illinois Institute for Environmental Quality, Chicago, IL [*Library symbol*] [*Library of Congress*] (LCLS)
**ICIF**........... International Cooperative Insurance Federation [*Manchester, England*] (EAIO)
**ICIFI**.......... International Council of Infant Food Industries
**ICI-G**......... Illinois Institute of Technology, Institute of Gas Technology, Chicago, IL [*Library symbol*] [*Library of Congress*] (LCLS)
**ICIg**............ Intracytoplasmic Immunoglobulin
**ICII**............ International Controlled Investments, Inc. [*NASDAQ symbol*] (NQ)

**ICIJ** .......... Institute for Juvenile Research, Chicago, IL [*Library symbol*] [*Library of Congress*] (LCLS)
**ICI-K**.......... Illinois Institute of Technology, Chicago-Kent College of Law, Chicago, IL [*Library symbol*] [*Library of Congress*] (LCLS)
**ICIL** .......... IFIP [*International Federation for Information Processing*] Committee for International Liaison
**ICIM**.......... Institute for Computer Integrated Manufacturing [*Strathclyde University*] [*British*]
**ICI Mag**..... ICI [*Imperial Chemical Industries*] Magazine [*A publication*]
**ICIN**.......... Independent Curriculum Information Network [*Australia*]
**ICINR**........ Institute of Natural Resources, Chicago, IL [*Library symbol*] [*Library of Congress*] (LCLS)
**ICIntR**........ Library of International Relations, Chicago, IL [*Library symbol*] [*Library of Congress*] (LCLS)
**ICIO**.......... Interim Cargo Integration Operations (MCD)
**ICIP** .......... Indirect Component Improvement Program
**ICIP** .......... Institute for Psychoanalysis, Chicago, IL [*Library symbol*] [*Library of Congress*] (LCLS)
**ICIP** .......... International Conference on Information Processing [*Paris, 1959*]
**ICIPE**......... International Centre of Insect Physiology and Ecology [*ICSU*] [*Nairobi, Kenya*] (EAIO)
**ICIR**.......... In Commission, In Reserve [*Vessel status*] [*Navy*]
**ICIREPAT** ... International Cooperation in Information Retrieval among Examining Patent Offices
**ICI Rev**....... Imperial Chemical Industries Review [*A publication*]
**ICIRO**........ Interim Commission of the International Refugee Organization
**ICIS** .......... Independent Chemical Information Services Ltd. [*Information service or system*] (IID)
**ICIS** .......... Integrated Chemical Information System [*Information Consultants, Inc.*] [*Information service or system*] (IID)
**ICIS** .......... Interdepartmental Committee on Internal Security [*Washington, DC*]
**ICIS** .......... International Centre for Industrial Studies [*United Nations*]
**ICIS** .......... International Council for Infant Survival [*Later, NCGIS*] (EA)
**ICIS** .......... IUD Claims Information Source (EA)
**ICis** .......... Willow Branch Library, Cisco, IL [*Library symbol*] [*Library of Congress*] (LCLS)
**ICISI**.......... International Center for Interdisciplinary Studies of Immunology at Georgetown [*Georgetown University*] [*Research center*] (RCD)
**ICIST**......... Institut Canadien de l'Information Scientifique et Technique [*Canadian Institute for Scientific and Technical Information - CISTI*]
**ICIT** .......... Information Center on Instructional Technology
**ICITA** ........ Instituto Cubano de Investigaciones Tecnologicas. Serie de Estudios sobre Trabajos de Investigacion [*A publication*]
**ICITA** ........ International Chain of Industrial and Technical Advertising Agencies (EA)
**ICITA** ........ International Cooperative Investigations of the Tropical Atlantic [*Navy*]
**ICITO**........ Interim Commission for the International Trade Organization
**ICIU**.......... University of Illinois at Chicago Circle, Chicago, IL [*Library symbol*] [*Library of Congress*] (LCLS)
**ICIU-PM**... University of Illinois at Chicago Circle, Peoria School of Medicine, Peoria, IL [*Library symbol*] [*Library of Congress*] (LCLS)
**ICIU-RM**... University of Illinois at Chicago Circle, Rockford School of Medicine, Rockford, IL [*Library symbol*] [*Library of Congress*] (LCLS)
**ICIU-S**...... University of Illinois at Chicago Circle, Science Library, Chicago, IL [*Library symbol*] [*Library of Congress*] (LCLS)
**ICIWWW** ... International Congress of Industrial Waste Water and Wastes
**ICJ** .......... Incoming Junction [*Telecommunications*] (TEL)
**ICJ** .......... Insurance Counsel Journal [*A publication*]
**ICJ** .......... International Commission of Jurists [*Switzerland*]
**ICJ** .......... International Court of Justice [*United Nations*]
**ICJ** .......... International Court of Justice Reports [*United Nations*] [*A publication*] (DLA)
**ICJ** .......... John Crerar Library, Chicago, IL [*Library symbol*] [*Library of Congress*] (LCLS)
**ICJ** .......... McKendree College, Lebanon, IL [*OCLC symbol*] (OCLC)
**ICJA** .......... Intelligence and Criminal Justice Academy (EA)
**ICJA** .......... International Criminal Justice Association (EA)
**ICJB** .......... Jenner and Block, Chicago, IL [*Library symbol*] [*Library of Congress*] (LCLS)
**ICJC** .......... Immaculate Conception Junior College [*New Jersey*]
**ICJC** .......... International Council of Jews from Czechoslovakia [*London, England*] (EAIO)
**ICJC** .......... International Criminal Justice Clearinghouse [*Law Enforcement Assistance Administration*] [*Information service or system*]
**ICJCS**........ International Conference of Jewish Communal Service [*Later, WCJCS*] (EA)
**ICJKM** ...... Jesuit-Krauss-McCormick Library, Chicago, IL [*Library symbol*] [*Library of Congress*] (LCLS)
**ICJL**.......... Institute for Computers in Jewish Life (EA)
**ICJM** ......... John Marshall Law School, Chicago, IL [*Library symbol*] [*Library of Congress*] (LCLS)
**ICJP**.......... Irish Commission for Justice and Peace [*An association*] (EAIO)
**ICJR** .......... Institute for Criminal Justice, University of Richmond (DLA)
**ICJRAU** .... Indian Central Jute Committee. Annual Report of the Jute Agricultural Research Institute [*A publication*]
**ICJ Rev**...... Review. International Commission of Jurists [*A publication*]
**ICJS**.......... Independent Carpenters' and Joiners' Society [*A union*] [*British*]
**ICJS**.......... Spertus College of Judaica, Chicago, IL [*Library symbol*] [*Library of Congress*] (LCLS)
**ICJSh** ........ John G. Shedd Aquarium, Chicago, IL [*Library symbol*] [*Library of Congress*] (LCLS)
**ICJST** ........ Jesuit School of Theology in Chicago, Chicago, IL [*Library symbol*] [*Library of Congress*] (LCLS)
**ICJUB** ....... Intercontinental Jet Unmanned Bomber
**ICJV** .......... Jewish Vocational Service Library, Chicago, IL [*Library symbol*] [*Library of Congress*] (LCLS)
**ICJW** ......... International Council of Jewish Women (EA)
**ICJYB**........ International Court of Justice. Yearbook [*A publication*]
**ICK** .......... Inscriptions Cuneiformes du Kultepe (BJA)
**ICK** .......... International Cherokee [*Vancouver Stock Exchange symbol*]
**ICK** .......... Metlakatla, AK [*Location identifier*] [*FAA*] (FAAL)
**ICK** .......... Millikin University, Decatur, IL [*OCLC symbol*] (OCLC)
**ICK** .......... Nieuw Nickerie [*Surinam*] [*Airport symbol*] (OAG)
**ICKCMX**... Integrated Circuit Keyset Central Multiplexer (CAAL)
**ICKE**.......... Kirkland & Ellis, Chicago, IL [*Library symbol*] [*Library of Congress*] (LCLS)
**ICKK**.......... Kennedy-King College of the City College of Chicago, Chicago, IL [*Library symbol*] [*Library of Congress*] (LCLS)
**ICKL**.......... International Council of Kinetography Laban (EA)
**ICKMC**...... Keck, Mahin, and Cate, Chicago, IL [*Library symbol*] [*Library of Congress*] (LCLS)
**ICL**............ Clarinda, IA [*Location identifier*] [*FAA*] (FAAL)
**ICL**............ Income Contingent Loan
**ICL**............ Incoming Correspondence Log (AAG)
**ICL**............ Incoming Line
**ICL**............ Indal Limited [*Toronto Stock Exchange symbol*]
**ICL**............ Inflight Calibration Lamp [*Instrumentation*]
**ICL**............ Inserted Connection Loss [*Telecommunications*]
**ICL**............ Instructional Center Library
**ICL**............ Instrument Calibration Laboratory
**ICL**............ Instrument Control Language [*Data processing*]
**ICL**............ Integrated Circuit Logic
**ICL**............ Integrated Configuration List (NG)
**ICL**............ Intellicall, Inc. [*NYSE symbol*] (SPSG)
**ICL**............ Interagency Checklist [*United States Employment Service*] (OICC)
**ICL**............ Intercommunication Logic
**ICL**............ Interdepartmental Committee on Land [*Canada*]
**ICL**............ Interest Checklist [*US Employment Service*] [*Department of Labor*]
**ICL**............ Internal Control Loop [*Chemical engineering*]
**ICL**............ International Cancer League (EA)
**ICL**............ International Catholic Library [*A publication*]
**ICL**............ International Christian Leadership (EA)
**ICL**............ International Clinical Laboratories, Inc.
**ICL**............ International Communications Limited [*Fayville, MA*] [*Telecommunications service*] (TSSD)
**ICL**............ International Computers Limited [*Great Britain*] [*Computer manufacturer*]
**ICL**............ International Congress of Linguists. Proceedings [*A publication*]
**ICL**............ International Cooperative Logistics (AFIT)
**ICL**............ International Council for Christian Leadership (EA)
**ICL**............ Interpersonal Check List [*Psychology*]
**ICL**............ Interpretive Coding Language
**ICL**............ Loyola University, Chicago, IL [*Library symbol*] [*Library of Congress*] (LCLS)
**ICL**............ Monmouth College, Monmouth, IL [*OCLC symbol*] (OCLC)
**ICl** ............ Vespasian Warner Public Library, Clinton, IL [*Library symbol*] [*Library of Congress*] (LCLS)
**ICLA** .......... International Committee on Laboratory Animals
**ICLA** .......... International Comparative Literature Association (EA)
**ICLAE** ....... International Council of Library Association Executives (EA)
**ICLAM**...... International Committee for Life Assurance Medicine [*Zurich, Switzerland*] (EAIO)
**ICLARM** ... International Center for Living Aquatic Resources Management [*Makati, Metro Manila, Philippines*] (EAIO)
**ICLAS** ....... Intracavity LASER Absorption Spectroscopy
**IClaw** ........ Chicago Law Institute, Chicago, IL [*Library symbol*] [*Library of Congress*] (LCLS)
**ICLB** .......... International Clinical Laboratories, Inc. [*NASDAQ symbol*] (NQ)
**ICL-B**......... Loyola University, Julia Deal Lewis Library, Chicago, IL [*Library symbol*] [*Library of Congress*] (LCLS)
**IcLc**........... Identity Correct, Location Correct [*Psychology*]
**ICLC** .......... International Centre for Local Credit [*The Hague, Netherlands*] (EAIO)
**ICLC** .......... International Criminal Law Commission (EA)
**ICLCP** ....... International Conference on Large Chemical Plants [*Antwerp, Belgium*] (EAIO)

**ICLD**.......... International Center for Law in Development (EA)
**ICL-D**........ Loyola University, Dental School, Chicago, IL [*Library symbol*] [*Library of Congress*] (LCLS)
**ICLE**.......... Institute of Continuing Legal Education [*Research center*] (RCD)
**ICLES**........ International Common Law Exchange Society (EA)
**ICLES**........ International Conference on Large Electrical Systems
**IClh**........... Clarendon Hills Public Library, Clarendon Hills, IL [*Library symbol*] [*Library of Congress*] (LCLS)
**IClH**.......... John Warner Hospital, Clinton, IL [*Library symbol*] [*Library of Congress*] (LCLS)
**IcLi**............ Identity Correct, Location Incorrect [*Psychology*]
**ICLIAD**..... Investigacion Clinica [*Maracaibo*] [*A publication*]
**ICLM**......... Index to Commonwealth Little Magazines [*A publication*]
**ICLM**......... Inter-California Line in Mexico R. R. [*AAR code*]
**ICLM**......... International Christian Leprosy Mission (EA)
**ICL-M**....... Loyola University, School of Medicine, Maywood, IL [*Library symbol*] [*Library of Congress*] (LCLS)
**ICLMC**...... Intersociety Council on Laboratory Medicine of Canada
**ICLoop**....... Loop College, Chicago, IL [*Library symbol*] [*Library of Congress*] (LCLS)
**ICLP**.......... Internal Connectionless Protocol [*Telecommunications*]
**ICL Publ**.... ICL [*International Combustion Limited*] Publications [*A publication*]
**I & CLQ**..... International and Comparative Law Quarterly [*A publication*]
**ICLQ**.......... International and Comparative Law Quarterly [*A publication*]
**ICLR**.......... Interdepartmental Committee on Labour Requirements [*British*] [*World War II*]
**ICLR**.......... International Committee for Lift Regulations [*See also CIRA*] [*Saint-Yvelines, France*] (EAIO)
**ICLR**.......... Irish Common Law Reports [*A publication*] (DLA)
**ICLR Can**.. Index to Current Legal Research in Canada [*A publication*] (DLA)
**ICLREW**... Incorporated Council of Law Reporting for England and Wales [*Established in 1866*]
**ICLRN**....... Interagency Council on Library Resources for Nursing (EA)
**ICLS**.......... Inequality Constrained Least-Squares [*Statistics*]
**ICLS**.......... Integrated Carrier Landing System [*Military*] (MCD)
**ICLS**.......... International Courtly Literature Society (EA)
**ICLSA**....... United States League of Savings Associations, Chicago, IL [*Library symbol*] [*Library of Congress*] (LCLS)
**ICLT**.......... Lutheran School of Theology, Chicago, IL [*Library symbol*] [*Library of Congress*] (LCLS)
**ICL Tech J**... ICL [*International Computers Limited*] Technical Journal [*A publication*]
**ICM**........... ICM Property Investors, Inc. [*NYSE symbol*] (SPSG)
**ICM**........... Imperial and Colonial Magazine [*A publication*]
**ICM**........... Imposto sobre a Circulacao de Mercadorias [*Tax on Movement of Merchandise*] [*Portuguese*]
**ICM**........... Improved Capability Missile [*Air Force*]
**ICM**........... Improved Conventional Munitions
**ICM**........... Incoming Message [*Telecommunications*]
**ICM**........... Independent Citizens' Movement [*US Virgin Islands*] (PPW)
**ICM**........... Indian Campaign Medal
**ICM**........... Individual Clutch Modulation [*Automotive engineering*]
**ICM**........... Initiator Command Module
**ICM**........... Inner Cell Mass [*Embryology*]
**ICM**........... Instantaneous Center of Motion
**ICM**........... Institut Canadien de la Mediterranee [*Canadian Mediterranean Institute*]
**ICM**........... Institut Canadien des Mines et de la Metallurgie [*Canadian Institute of Mining and Metallurgy*] (EAIO)
**ICM**........... Institute of Caster Manufacturers (EA)
**ICM**........... Institute for Complementary Medicine [*An association*] (EAIO)
**ICM**........... Institute for Composite Materials [*Defunct*] (EA)
**ICM**........... Institute of Construction Management [*British*]
**ICM**........... Institute for Court Management of the National Center for State Courts (EA)
**ICM**........... Institute of Credit Management [*British*]
**ICM**........... Instruction Control Memory
**ICM**........... Instrumentation and Communications Monitor
**ICM**........... Integrated Circuit Mask
**ICM**........... Integrated Controller Module [*Automotive engineering*]
**ICM**........... Integrated Crop Management [*Agriculture*]
**ICM**........... Interchangeable Control Media (MCD)
**ICM**........... Intercommunication (MSA)
**ICM**........... Intercostal Margin [*Anatomy*]
**ICM**........... Interface Coordination Memorandum (MCD)
**ICM**........... Interference Control Monitor (AAG)
**ICM**........... Interim Catalog Module [*MEDLARS*]
**ICM**........... International Chaplain's Ministry (EA)
**ICM**........... International Colour Management [*Commercial firm*] [*British*]
**ICM**........... International Confederation of Midwives [*London, England*] (EAIO)
**ICM**........... International Congress of Mathematicians
**ICM**........... International Congress on Mechanical Behaviour of Materials (EAIO)
**ICM**........... International Creative Management [*Commercial firm*]
**ICM**........... Inventory Control Manager (MCD)
**ICM**........... Investment Casting Mold (MCD)
**ICM**........... Ion Chromatography Module
**ICM**........... Ion Conductance Modulator [*Cytochemistry*]
**ICM**........... Irish Church Missions
**ICM**........... Isolation, Control, and Monitoring [*Pollution control*]
**ICM**........... Mundelein College, Chicago, IL [*OCLC symbol*] (OCLC)
**ICM**........... Soeurs Missionnaires du Coeur Immacule de Marie [*Missionary Sisters of the Immaculate Heart of Mary*] [*Italy*] (EAIO)
**ICMA**........ Chartered Institute of Management Accountants (EAIO)
**ICMA**........ Imino(cyanomorpholinyl)deaminoadriamycin [*Antineoplastic drug*]
**ICMA**........ Independent Cabinet Makers' Association [*A union*] [*British*]
**ICMA**........ Initial Clothing Monetary Allowance [*Military*]
**ICMA**........ Institute of Certified Management Accountants [*Montvale, NJ*] (EA)
**ICMA**........ Institute for Computational Mathematics and Applications [*University of Pittsburgh*] [*Research center*] (RCD)
**ICMA**........ Institute of Cost and Management Accountants [*British*]
**ICMA**........ International Center of Medieval Art (EA)
**ICMA**........ International Christian Maritime Association [*Felixstone, Suffolk, England*] (EAIO)
**ICMA**........ International Cigarette Makers' Association [*A union*]
**ICMA**........ International Circulation Managers Association (EA)
**ICMA**........ International City Management Association [*Later, ICMA-The Professional Local Government Management Association*] (EA)
**ICMAD**..... Independent Cosmetic Manufacturers and Distributors (EA)
**ICMARD**... International Center for Marine Resources Development (ASF)
**ICMASA**... Intersociety Committee on Methods for Air Sampling and Analysis (EA)
**ICMay**....... Mayfair College, Chicago, IL [*Library symbol*] [*Library of Congress*] (LCLS)
**ICMB**......... Moody Bible Institute, Chicago, IL [*Library symbol*] [*Library of Congress*] (LCLS)
**ICMBP**...... Mayer, Brown & Platt Law Library, Chicago, IL [*Library symbol*] [*Library of Congress*] (LCLS)
**ICMC**......... International Catholic Migration Commission [*See also CICM*] [*Geneva, Switzerland*] (EAIO)
**ICMC**......... International Christian Media Commission (EA)
**ICMC**......... International Cryogenic Materials Conference (EA)
**ICMcC**....... McCormick Theological Seminary, Chicago, IL [*Library symbol*] [*Library of Congress*] (LCLS)
**ICMC Ne**... ICMC [*International Catholic Migration Commission*] News [*A publication*]
**ICME**......... International Code of Medical Ethics
**ICME**......... International Conference on Medical Electronics
**ICME**......... International Contemporary Music Exchange (EA)
**ICMe**.......... Meadville Theological School, Chicago, IL [*Library symbol*] [*Library of Congress*] (LCLS)
**ICMEDC**... International Council of Masonry Engineering for Developing Countries [*Formerly, International Symposium on Reinforced and Prestressed Masonry*] (EA)
**ICMen**....... Chicago Mercantile Exchange, Chicago, IL [*Library symbol*] [*Library of Congress*] (LCLS)
**ICMer**........ Charles E. Merriam Center for Public Administration, Merriam Center Library, Chicago, IL [*Library symbol*] [*Library of Congress*] (LCLS)
**ICMFA**...... Indian Chemical Manufacturer [*A publication*]
**ICMH**........ Institut Canadien de Microreproductions Historiques [*Canadian Institute for Historical Microreproductions - CIHM*]
**ICMH**........ International Commission of Military History
**ICMH**........ Mercy Hospital and Medical Center, Chicago, IL [*Library symbol*] [*Library of Congress*] (LCLS)
**ICMI**.......... International Commission on Mathematical Instruction [*British*]
**ICMICA**.... Pax Romana, International Catholic Movement for Intellectual and Cultural Affairs [*See also MIIC*] [*Geneva, Switzerland*] (EAIO)
**ICMJD**...... International Cast Metals Journal [*A publication*]
**ICML**......... International Center for Medicine and Law (EA)
**ICMLT**...... International Congress of Medical Laboratory Technologists
**ICMM**....... Illinois Masonic Medical Center, Chicago, IL [*Library symbol*] [*Library of Congress*] (LCLS)
**ICMM**....... International Congress of Maritime Museums (EA)
**ICMMB**..... International Conference on Mechanics in Medicine and Biology (EA)
**ICMMP**..... International Committee of Military Medicine and Pharmacy [*Belgium*]
**ICMO**........ Integrated Configuration Management Office [*NASA*] (NASA)
**ICMP**......... Interchannel Master Pulse
**ICMP**......... International Conference on Marine Pollution (ILCA)
**ICMPH**...... International Center of Medical and Psychological Hypnosis [*Milan, Italy*] (EA)
**ICMPS**...... Induction Compass
**ICMR**......... Chicago Municipal Reference Library, Chicago, IL [*Library symbol*] [*Library of Congress*] (LCLS)
**ICMR**......... Instrument Calibration and Maintenance Record (MCD)
**ICMRD**...... International Center for Marine Resources Development [*University of Rhode Island*]
**ICMREF**... Interagency Committee on Marine Science, Research, Engineering, and Facilities

**ICMR (Int Cent Med Res) Ann** ... ICMR (International Center for Medical Research) Annals [*A publication*]
**ICMS**......... Indirect Cost Management System (NASA)
**ICMS**......... Instrument Calibration and Maintenance Schedule
**ICMS**......... Integrated Circuit and Message Switch
**ICMS**......... Interdepartmental Committee for Meteorological Services [*National Weather Service*]
**ICMS**......... International Commission on Mushroom Science [*Later, ISMS*] (EA)
**ICMSE**...... Interagency Committee on Marine Science and Engineering [*Federal Council for Science and Technology*]
**ICMSF**...... International Commission on Microbiological Specifications for Foods (EA)
**ICMST**...... International Conference on Machine Searching and Translation
**ICMT**......... Intercontract Material Transfer
**ICMU**......... Isolation Configuration and Monitor Unit (MCD)
**ICMUA**...... International Commission on the Meteorology of the Upper Atmosphere
**ICMund**..... Mundelein College, Chicago, IL [*Library symbol*] [*Library of Congress*] (LCLS)
**ICMW**....... Inherent Corrective Maintenance Workload
**ICMX**......... Malcolm X College of the City College of Chicago, Chicago, IL [*Library symbol*] [*Library of Congress*] (LCLS)
**ICN**........... ICN Pharmaceuticals, Inc. [*Formerly, International Chemical & Nuclear Corp.*] [*NYSE symbol*] [*Also research code symbol*] (SPSG)
**ICN**........... In Christi Nomine [*In the Name of Christ*] [*Latin*]
**ICN**........... Inclusion Conjunctivitis Neonate [*Ophthalmology*]
**ICN**........... Index of Community Noise
**ICN**........... Indonesian Commercial Newsletter [*A publication*]
**ICN**........... Inocan Technologies Ltd. [*Vancouver Stock Exchange symbol*]
**ICN**........... Instrumentation and Calibration Network (AAG)
**ICN**........... Integrated Computer Network
**ICN**........... Intensive Care Nursery [*Medicine*]
**ICN**........... Interface Change Notice (MCD)
**ICN**........... Interim Change Notice (AFM)
**ICN**........... International Communes Network (EAIO)
**ICN**........... International Council of Nurses [*Geneva, Switzerland*]
**ICN**........... Intromogenous Computer Network
**ICN**........... Newberry Library, Chicago, IL [*Library symbol*] [*Library of Congress*] (LCLS)
**ICN**........... North Central College, Naperville, IL [*OCLC symbol*] (OCLC)
**ICNA**......... Infants' and Children's Novelties Association (EA)
**ICNABY**.... International Commission for the Northwest Atlantic Fisheries. Statistical Bulletin [*A publication*]
**ICNAF**....... International Commission for the Northwest Atlantic Fisheries [*Superseded by NAFO*]
**ICNAF**....... International Commission for the Northwest Atlantic Fisheries. Research Bulletin [*A publication*]
**ICNAFSP**... International Commission for the Northwest Atlantic Fisheries. Special Publication [*A publication*]
**IC/NATAS**... International Council - National Academy of Television Arts and Sciences (EA)
**IC/NATVAS**... International Council of the National Academy of Television Arts and Sciences (EA)
**ICNCP**....... International Commission for the Nomenclature of Cultivated Plants [*Wageningen, Netherlands*] (EA)
**ICNE**......... Northeastern Illinois University, Chicago, IL [*Library symbol*] [*Library of Congress*] (LCLS)
**ICNEM**...... Internacia Centro de la Neutrala Esperanto-Movado [*International Center of the Neutral Esperanto Movement*] (EAIO)
**ICNEM**...... International Center of the Neutral Esperanto Movement (EA)
**ICNEP**....... Initiative Committee for National Economic Planning
**ICNF**......... Irredundant Conjunctive Normal Formula
**ICNFAE**.... International Commission for the Northwest Atlantic Fisheries. Annual Proceedings [*A publication*]
**ICNI**.......... Integrated Communication, Navigation, Identification [*System*]
**ICNIA**........ Integrated Communication, Navigation, and Identification Avionics [*Air Force*]
**ICNICP**..... Integrated Communication/Navigation/Identification Control Panel (MCD)
**ICNICS**..... Integrated Communication/Navigation/Identification Control Set (MCD)
**ICNND**...... Interdepartmental Committee on Nutrition for National Defense
**ICNP**.......... ICN Pharmaceuticals, Inc. [*NASDAQ symbol*] (NQ)
**ICNP**.......... International Commission on National Parks [*Later, CNPAA*] (EA)
**ICNPT**....... North Park College and Theological Seminary, Chicago, IL [*Library symbol*] [*Library of Congress*] (LCLS)
**ICNS**.......... Ice Cap News. American Society of Polar Philatelists [*A publication*]
**ICNS**.......... Information Center on Nuclear Standards [*American Nuclear Society*] [*Information service or system*]
**ICNS**.......... Integrated Communications and Navigation System
**ICNS**.......... National Safety Council, Chicago, IL [*Library symbol*] [*Library of Congress*] (LCLS)
**ICNSAJ**..... Iowa Conservationist [*A publication*]
**ICNT**......... INCOMNET, Inc. [*Formerly, Intelligent Commercial Net*] [*NASDAQ symbol*] (NQ)
**ICNT**......... Informal Composite Negotiating Text [*United Nations Conference on the Law of the Sea*]
**ICNT**......... Northern Trust Co., Chicago, IL [*Library symbol*] [*Library of Congress*] (LCLS)
**ICNTG**....... Intracoronary Nitroglycerine [*Pharmacology*]
**ICNU**......... National College of Education, Urban Campus, Chicago, IL [*Library symbol*] [*Library of Congress*] (LCLS)
**ICN-UCLA Symp Mol Cell Biol** ... ICN-UCLA [*International Chemical and Nuclear Corp. - University of California at Los Angeles*] Symposia on Molecular and Cellular Biology [*A publication*]
**ICNV**......... International Committee on Nomenclature of Viruses [*Later, ICTV*]
**ICNWAV**... International Commission for the Northwest Atlantic Fisheries. Redbook. Part III [*A publication*]
**ICNY**......... International Center in New York (EA)
**ICNY**......... Islamic Center of New York (EA)
**ICO**........... Illinois College of Optometry [*Chicago*]
**ICO**........... Illinois Wesleyan University, Bloomington, IL [*OCLC symbol*] (OCLC)
**ICO**........... Immediate Commanding Officer
**ICO**........... In Case Of
**ICO**........... Indian Commissioned Officer [*British military*] (DMA)
**ICO**........... Information for the Contracting Officer (MCD)
**ICO**........... Input Current Offset [*Data processing*]
**ICO**........... Inspecting Chief Officer [*Military*] [*British*] (ROG)
**I & C/O**...... Installation and Checkout (NASA)
**ICO**........... Institute of Careers Officers [*British*]
**ICO**........... Institute of Chemists-Opticians [*British*] (DAS)
**ICO**........... Instrumentation Control Officer (AAG)
**ICO**........... Integrated Checkout (NASA)
**ICO**........... Integrator Cutoff
**ICO**........... Interagency Committee on Oceanography [*Later, ICMSE*]
**ICO**........... Intercristo [*An association*] (EA)
**ICO**........... International Carbohydrate Organization [*Aberdeen, Scotland*] (EAIO)
**ICO**........... International Cardero Resources [*Vancouver Stock Exchange symbol*]
**ICO**........... International Coffee Organization (EAIO)
**ICO**........... International College of Officers [*Salvation Army*]
**ICO**........... International Commission for Optics [*See also CIO*] [*ICSU*] [*Delft, Netherlands*] (EAIO)
**ICO**........... International Computer Orphanage (EA)
**ICO**........... International Council of Ophthalmology (EA)
**ICO**........... Inventory Control Officer
**ICO**........... Le Iscrizioni Fenicie e Puniche delle Colonie in Occidente (BJA)
**ICOA**......... International Castor Oil Association (EA)
**ICOA**......... International CBX Owners Association (EA)
**ICOAB5**..... India. Coffee Board. Research Department. Annual Detailed Technical Report [*A publication*]
**ICOBA**....... International Confederation of Book Actors (EA)
**ICOC**......... ICO, Inc. [*NASDAQ symbol*] (NQ)
**ICOC**......... Instructions for Commodores of Convoys [*Navy*] [*Obsolete*]
**ICOC**......... International Commission for Orders of Chivalry (EA)
**ICOCS**....... Interim Circuit Order Control System [*Bell System*]
**ICOD**......... Intelligence Cutoff Date [*Military*] (MCD)
**ICOD**......... International Centre for Ocean Development [*Canada*] [*See also CIEO*]
**ICOD**......... International Council on Disability (EA)
**ICODS**....... Interagency Committee on Dam Safety [*Federal Emergency Management Agency*] [*Washington, DC*] (EGAO)
**ICOEES**.... Interagency Committee on Ocean Exploration and Environmental Services [*Terminated, 1971*] (NOAA)
**ICOEI**........ Integral Components of End Items (MCD)
**ICOF**.......... Industrial Common Ownership Finance [*An association*] [*British*]
**ICOFAJ**..... Indian Coffee [*A publication*]
**I-COFT**...... Institutional Conduct of Fire Trainer [*Army*]
**ICOGRADA**... International Council of Graphic Design Associations [*London, England*] (EA)
**ICOH**......... International Commission of Occupational Health (EA)
**ICOHEPANS**... International Conference on High Energy Physics and Nuclear Structure
**ICOHH**..... International Concatenated Order of Hoo-Hoo [*Later, International Order of Hoo-Hoo*] (EA)
**ICOHTEC**... International Committee for the History of Technology (EA)
**ICOI**.......... International Congress of Oral Implantologists (EA)
**ICOJ**......... ICO [*Institute of Chemist-Opticians*] Journal [*A publication*]
**ICOJAV**.... Indian Coconut Journal [*A publication*]
**ICol**........... Collinsville Public Library, Collinsville, IL [*Library symbol*] [*Library of Congress*] (LCLS)
**IColCU**...... Collinsville Community Unit 10, Collinsville, IL [*Library symbol*] [*Library of Congress*] (LCLS)
**ICOLD**....... International Commission on Large Dams [*See also CIGB*] [*ICSU*] [*Paris, France*] (EAIO)
**IColu**......... Columbia Public Library, Columbia, IL [*Library symbol*] [*Library of Congress*] (LCLS)

**IColuD** ....... Columbia Unit District 4, Columbia, IL [*Library symbol*] [*Library of Congress*] (LCLS)
**ICOM** ........ Improved Conventional Mine System [*Military*] (MCD)
**ICOM** ........ Industrial Common Ownership Movement [*British*]
**ICOM** ........ Institute of Computational Mechanics [*University of Cincinnati*] [*Research center*] (RCD)
**ICOM** ........ Intercommunications (NASA)
**ICOM** ........ International Council of Museums [*France*]
**ICOMC** ..... International Conference on Organometallic Chemistry
**ICOM-CC** ... ICOM [*International Council of Museums*] Committee for Conservation (EAIO)
**ICOME** ..... International Committee on Microbial Ecology [*ICSU*] (EAIO)
**ICOMIA**.... International Council of Marine Industry Associations [*Weybridge, Surrey, England*] (EA)
**ICOMOS**... International Council of Monuments and Sites (EA)
**ICOMP**...... Iceland Ocean Meeting Point [*Navy*]
**ICOMP**...... International Council on Management of Population Programmes [*Kuala Lumpur, Malaysia*] (EAIO)
**ICON** ......... [*A*] programming language [*1977*] (CSR)
**ICON** ......... Iconoclasm (ADA)
**ICON** ......... Iconography
**ICON** ......... Indexed Currency Option Note [*Student Loan Marketing Association*]
**ICON** ......... Integrated Control
**ICON** ......... Inter-Institutional Committee on Nutrition
**ICON** ......... International Communication of Orthodox Nations
**ICONDA** ... International Construction Database [*Information Centre for Regional Planning and Building Construction of the Fraunhofer-Society*] [*Database*]
**ICONDC** ... Annual Research Reviews. Intrauterine Contraception [*A publication*]
**Icon Fau Fl Medit** ... Iconographie de la Faune et de la Flore Mediterraneennes [*A publication*]
**Icon Med Prat** ... Iconographie Medicale du Praticien [*A publication*]
**ICONMIG** ... International Conference on Numerical Methods in Geomechanics
**Icon Pl Afr** ... Icones Plantarum Africanarum [*A publication*]
**Icon Pl As Or** ... Iconographia Plantarum Asiae Orientalis [*A publication*]
**ICONS**....... Information Center on Nuclear Standards [*American Nuclear Society*] [*La Grange Park, IL*] [*Information service or system*]
**ICONS**....... Isotopes of Carbon, Oxygen, Nitrogen, and Sulfur [*AEC project*]
**ICOP**.......... Imported Crude Oil Processing
**ICOP**.......... Intelligence Collect Program
**ICOP**.......... Interagency Contingency Options Plan [*Military*]
**ICOP**.......... Inventory Control Point
**ICOPA**....... Industria Conserve [*A publication*]
**ICOPAF** .... Industria Conserve [*Parma*] [*A publication*]
**ICOPS** ....... Institute for the Comparative Study of Political Systems
**ICOR** ......... Incremental Capital Output Ratio
**ICOR** ......... Intergovernmental Conference on Oceanic Research
**ICOR** ......... Meicor, Inc. [*NASDAQ symbol*] (NQ)
**ICORS** ....... International Conference of Raman Spectroscopy
**ICOS**.......... Improved Crew Optical Sight (NASA)
**ICOS**.......... Integrated Checkout System (KSC)
**ICOS**.......... Interactive COBOL Operating System
**ICOS**.......... International Committee of Onomastic Sciences [*Belgium*]
**ICOS**.......... Interpretation Canada. Ontario Section [*A publication*]
**ICOSA** ....... International Council of Seamen's Agencies (EA)
**ICOSI** ........ International Committee on Smoking Issues [*Brussels, Belgium*] (EAIO)
**ICOSO**....... International Committee for Outer Space Onomastics
**ICOT** ......... ICOT Corp. [*NASDAQ symbol*] (NQ)
**ICOT** ......... Institute of Coastal Oceanography and Tides [*British*]
**ICOT** ......... Institute of New Generation Computer Technology [*Japan*]
**ICOTA**....... International Review of Connective Tissue Research [*A publication*]
**ICOTAS** .... International Committee on the Organisation of Traffic at Sea [*British*] (DS)
**ICOTS** ....... Interagency Committee on Transportation Security [*Department of Transportation*]
**ICOTS** ....... International Conference on Teaching Statistics
**ICOTT**....... Industry Coalition on Technology Transfer (EA)
**ICOU** ......... International Consommateurs Organization des Unions [*International Organization of Consumers Unions*]
**ICP**............ Ignition Control Programmer (MCD)
**ICP**............ Incentive Compensation Plan (MCD)
**ICP**............ INCOLSA [*Indiana Cooperative Library Services Authority*] Processing Center, Indianapolis, IN [*OCLC symbol*] (OCLC)
**ICP**............ Incoming [*Message*] Process [*Telecommunications*] (TEL)
**ICP**............ Index to Chinese Periodicals [*A publication*]
**ICP**............ Indian Communications Project
**ICP**............ Indicator Control Panel
**ICP**............ Inductively Coupled Plasma [*Spectrometry*]
**ICP**............ Industrial Control Products (MCD)
**ICP**............ Industrial Coupling Program [*Refers to university-industry interaction*]
**ICP**............ Industry Cooperative Program [*United Nations*]
**ICP**............ Infection-Control Practitioner [*Medicine*]
**ICP**............ Infectious Cell Protein [*Genetics*]
**ICP**............ Informacao Cultural Portugues [*A publication*]
**ICP**............ Initial Connection Protocol
**ICP**............ Inner City Partnership [*EEC and British program to regenerate blighted areas*]
**ICP**............ Insecticidal Crystal Protein [*Agrochemistry*]
**ICP**............ Installation Input Change Package (MCD)
**ICP**............ Instant Control Point [*British police*]
**ICP**............ Institute for Circadian Physiology [*Boston, MA*]
**ICP**............ Institute for Comprehensive Planning (EA)
**ICP**............ Instructor Control Panel
**ICP**............ Instrument Calibration Procedure
**ICP**............ Insurance Conference Planners (EA)
**ICP**............ Integral Circuit Package
**ICP**............ Intelligence Collection Plan [*Military*] (AFM)
**ICP**............ Intelligent Communications Processor
**IC-P** .......... Intelligent Copier-Printer [*Electrophotography*]
**ICP**............ Inter-University Case Program
**ICP**............ Interdisciplinary Communications Program
**ICP**............ Interface Control Panel (MCD)
**ICP**............ Internal Combustion Powered (ADA)
**ICP**............ Internal Connection Protocol [*Telecommunications*]
**ICP**............ International Center of Photography (EA)
**ICP**............ International Computer Programs, Inc. [*Indianapolis, IN*] [*Information service or system*]
**ICP**............ International Congress of Publishers (DIT)
**ICP**............ International Control Plan (MCD)
**ICP**............ International Council of Psychologists (EA)
**ICP**............ International Currency Review [*A publication*]
**ICP**............ Interoceanic Canal Project [*National Oceanic and Atmospheric Administration*] (NOAA)
**ICP**............ Intracranial Pressure [*Medicine*]
**ICP**............ Intracuff Pressure [*In mechanical ventilation*] [*Medicine*]
**ICP**............ Intrinsically Conductive Plastic [*Organic chemistry*]
**ICP**............ Inventory Control Point
**ICP**............ Ion Coupled Plasma [*Oil analysis*]
**ICP**............ Iraqi Communist Party [*Political party*] (PPW)
**ICP**............ Irish Company Profiles [*Institute of Industrial Research and Standards - IIRS*] [*Dublin, Ireland*] [*Information service or system*] (IID)
**ICP**............ Ischemic Cardiac Pain [*Cardiology*]
**ICP**............ Islands of Cartilage Pattern [*Anatomy*]
**ICP**............ Italian Communist Party
**ICP**............ Item Control Point (AFM)
**ICPA** .......... Information Centre for Polish Affairs (EAIO)
**ICPA** .......... International Commission for the Prevention of Alcoholism [*Later, International Commission for the Prevention of Alcoholism and Drug Dependency*]
**ICPA** .......... International Conference of Police Associations [*Defunct*]
**ICPA** .......... International Cooperative Petroleum Association (EA)
**ICPA** .......... International Cruise Passengers Association (EA)
**ICPA** .......... Public Administration Service, Joint Reference Library, Chicago, IL [*Library symbol*] [*Library of Congress*] (LCLS)
**ICPAC** ....... Instantaneous Compressor Performance Analysis Computer
**ICPADC**.... Investigative and Cell Pathology [*A publication*]
**ICPADD**.... International Commission for the Prevention of Alcoholism and Drug Dependency (EA)
**ICP Admin** ... ICP [*International Computer Programs, Inc.*] Interface Administrative and Accounting [*A publication*]
**ICP-AES**.... Inductively Coupled Plasma - Atomic Emission Spectrometry [*See also ICPES*]
**ICPAM** ...... International Centre for Pure and Applied Mathematics [*United Nations*] (EA)
**ICPas** ......... Passionist Academic Institute, Chicago, IL [*Library symbol*] [*Library of Congress*] (LCLS)
**ICPB** .......... Inert Components Parts Building
**ICP Bank Indus** ... ICP [*International Computer Programs, Inc.*] Interface Banking Industry [*A publication*]
**ICPBC** ....... Institute of Certified Professional Business Consultants [*Chicago, IL*] (EA)
**ICPBR** ....... International Commission for Plant-Bee Relationships (EAIO)
**ICPC** .......... International Cable Protection Committee [*London, England*] (EAIO)
**ICPC** .......... International Commission of Catholic Prison Chaplains (EA)
**ICPC** .......... International Confederation of Popular Credit [*See also CICP*] [*Paris, France*] (EAIO)
**ICPC** .......... International Conference of Police Chaplains (EA)
**ICPC** .......... International Criminal Police Commission [*Later, INTERPOL*]
**ICPC** .......... Interrange Communications Planning Committee
**ICPCC** ....... International Council for Pastoral Care and Counselling (EAIO)
**ICPDATA** ... Commodity Production Statistics [*United Nations Statistical Office*] [*Information service or system*] (CRD)
**ICPDES**..... International Cancer Patient Data Exchange System
**ICP DP Mgmt** ... ICP [*International Computer Programs, Inc.*] Interface Data Processing Management [*A publication*]
**ICPE** .......... International Center for Public Enterprises in Developing Countries [*Ljubljana, Yugoslavia*] (EAIO)
**ICPE** .......... International Commission on Physics Education [*See also CIEP*] (EA)
**ICPE** .......... Inventory Control Point Europe

**ICPEAC**..... International Conference on the Physics of Electronic and Atomic Collisions
**ICPEMC** ... International Commission for Protection Against Environmental Mutagens and Carcinogens [*Rijswljk, Netherlands*] (EAIO)
**ICPERS**..... Instant Computer Public Employment Relations Search [*Database*] [*Labor Relations Press*] [*Information service or system*] (CRD)
**ICPES**........ Inductively Coupled Plasma Emission Spectrometry [*See also ICP-AES*]
**ICPES**........ Intergovernmental Committee for Physical Education and Sport [*United Nations*] [*France*] (EY)
**ICPFF**........ Incentive Cost plus Fixed Fee [*Contracts*]
**ICPFR**........ International Council for Physical Fitness Research [*Research center*] [*Canada*] (IRC)
**ICPG**.......... People Gas Light Co., Chicago, IL [*Library symbol*] [*Library of Congress*] (LCLS)
**ICPHS**....... International Council for Philosophy and Humanistic Studies [*Paris, France*]
**ICPHS/D** .. Diogenes. International Council for Philosophy and Humanistic Studies [*A publication*]
**ICPI**........... Insurance Crime Prevention Institute [*Westport, CT*] (EA)
**ICPI**........... Interagency Committee on Product Information (EA)
**ICPI**........... Intersociety Committee on Pathology Information (EA)
**ICPICH**..... International Commission for the Preservation of Islamic Cultural Heritage (EA)
**ICPIGP**...... Internationale Chretienne Professionelle pour les Industries Graphiques et Papetieres [*International Federation of Christian Trade Unions of Graphical and Paper Industries*]
**ICPIWC**..... International Council for Philosophical Inquiry with Children (EA)
**ICP J Inf Prod and Serv** ... ICP [*International Computer Programs, Inc.*] Journal of Information Products and Services [*A publication*]
**ICP J Software Prod and Serv** ... ICP [*International Computer Programs, Inc.*] Journal of Software Products and Services [*A publication*]
**ICpKSD**..... J. F. Kennedy Consolidated Community School District 129, Cedar Point, IL [*Library symbol*] [*Library of Congress*] (LCLS)
**ICPL**.......... International Committee of Passenger Lines
**ICPL**.......... Iowa City Public Library [*Iowa*]
**ICPLS**........ International College of Podiatric Laser Surgery (EA)
**ICPM**......... Illinois College of Podiatric Medicine, Chicago, IL [*Library symbol*] [*Library of Congress*] (LCLS)
**ICPM**......... Institute of Certified Professional Managers [*Harrisonburg, VA*] (EA)
**ICPME**...... International Center for Peace in the Middle East (EA)
**ICPMM**..... Incisors, Canines, Premolars, Molars [*Dentistry*]
**ICPMM**..... Peat, Marwick, and Mitchell, Chicago, IL [*Library symbol*] [*Library of Congress*] (LCLS)
**ICPMP**...... International Commission for the Protection of the Moselle Against Pollution (EA)
**ICP-MS**..... Inductively Coupled Plasma - Mass Spectrometry
**ICPMS**...... International Council of Prison Medical Services [*Vancouver, BC*] (EAIO)
**ICPN**.......... International Committee of Plant Nutrition (EA)
**ICPO**.......... Institute for Certified Park Operators (EA)
**ICPO**.......... International Criminal Police Organization [*France*]
**ICPO**.......... Investment Co-Operative Programme Office [*UNIDO*]
**ICPOA**....... Intelligence Center, Pacific Ocean Areas [*Obsolete*]
**ICP-OES**... Inductively Coupled Plasma - Optical Emission Spectrometry
**ICPP**.......... Idaho Chemical Processing Plant [*AEC*]
**ICPP**.......... Interactive Computer Presentation Panel [*To display computer-generated information for military use*]
**ICPP**.......... International Comparative Political Parties Project [*Northwestern University*] [*Inactive*] (IID)
**ICPR**.......... Incoming Capital Property Record
**ICPR**.......... Industrial Cost and Performance Report (NG)
**ICPR**.......... Integrated Circuit Parameter Retrieval [*Information Handling Services*] [*Database*]
**ICPR**.......... Inter-University Consortium for Political Research [*Later, ICPSR*] (EA)
**ICPR**.......... International Clinical Products Review [*A publication*]
**ICP/R**........ Revista. Instituto de Cultura Puertorriquena [*A publication*]
**ICPRAP**..... International Commission for the Protection of the Rhine Against Pollution [*See also ICPRP, IKSR*] [*Koblenz, Federal Republic of Germany*] (EAIO)
**ICPRB**....... Interstate Commission on the Potomac River Basin
**ICPRCPCO** ... Intergovernmental Committee for Promoting the Return of Cultural Property to Its Countries of Origin or Its Restitution in Case of Illicit Appropriation (EA)
**ICPRCU**.... Polish Roman Catholic Union of America, Chicago, IL [*Library symbol*] [*Library of Congress*] (LCLS)
**ICPRS**........ Petersen, Ross, Schloerb & Seidel, Library, Chicago, IL [*Library symbol*] [*Library of Congress*] (LCLS)
**ICPS**.......... Industrial and Commercial Power Systems (MCD)
**ICPS**.......... Interamerican College of Physicians and Surgeons (EA)
**ICPS**.......... International Carnivorous Plant Society (EA)
**ICPS**.......... International Cerebral Palsy Society [*London, England*] (EAIO)
**ICPS**.......... International Conference on the Properties of Steam
**ICPS**.......... International Congress of Photographic Science
**ICPS**.......... International Council of Perfusion Societies [*Defunct*] (EA)
**ICP Soft Bus Rev** ... ICP [*International Computer Programs, Inc.*] Software Business Review [*A publication*]
**ICP Software J** ... ICP [*International Computer Programs, Inc.*] Software Journal [*A publication*]
**ICPSR**........ Inter-University Consortium for Political and Social Research (EA)
**ICPTO**....... International China Painting Teachers Organization [*Later, International Porcelain Artist Teachers*]
**ICPTUR**.... International Conference for Promoting Technical Uniformity on Railways [*Berne, Switzerland*] (EAIO)
**ICPU**.......... International Catholic Press Union [*Later, UCIP*]
**ICPUAE**.... International Conference on the Peaceful Uses of Atomic Energy
**IC Publ**....... IC [*International Combustion Products Limited*] Publications [*A publication*]
**ICPV**.......... International Committee on Polar Viruses
**ICPVT**....... International Council for Pressure Vessel Technology (EA)
**ICPY**.......... Institute of Clinical Pharmacology PLC [*Dublin, Ireland*] [*NASDAQ symbol*] (NQ)
**i-cq---**.......... Comoro Islands [*MARC geographic area code*] [*Library of Congress*] (LCCP)
**ICQ**........... Internal Control Questionnaire (ADA)
**ICQ**........... International Capri Resources [*Vancouver Stock Exchange symbol*]
**ICQA**......... International Columbian Quincentenary Alliance (EA)
**ICr**............. Chicago Ridge Public Library, Chicago Ridge, IL [*Library symbol*] [*Library of Congress*] (LCLS)
**ICR**........... Corona Corp. [*AMEX symbol*] [*Toronto Stock Exchange symbol*] (SPSG)
**ICR**........... Identification and Compliance Record (MCD)
**ICR**........... Iliac Crest [*Anatomy*]
**ICR**........... Illinois Central Railroad
**ICR**........... Immunodeficiency Cancer Registry
**ICR**........... In-Commission Rate
**ICR**........... Independent Component Release [*Data processing*] (IBMDP)
**ICR**........... Indirect Control Register [*Data processing*]
**ICR**........... Inductance-Capacitance-Resistance
**ICR**........... Industrial Cases Reports [*Law reports*] [*British*] (DCTA)
**ICR**........... Industrial Cost Recovery [*Environmental Protection Agency*]
**ICR**........... Industrial Court Reports [*England*] [*A publication*] (DLA)
**ICR**........... Input and Compare Register
**ICR**........... Input Control Register [*Data processing*]
**ICr**............. Inscriptiones Creticae [*A publication*]
**ICR**........... Instantaneous Center of Rotation
**ICR**........... Institute for Cancer Research (EA)
**ICR**........... Institute for Communications Research [*Texas Tech University*] [*Research center*] (RCD)
**ICR**........... Institute for Computer Research [*University of Waterloo*] [*Canada*] [*Research center*] (RCD)
**ICR**........... Institute for Cooperative Research
**ICR**........... Institute for Creation Research (EA)
**ICR**........... Institute for Cultural Research [*Research center*] [*British*] (IRC)
**ICR**........... Instruction Change Request (NASA)
**ICR**........... Instrumentation Control Racks (AAG)
**ICR**........... Insulated Core Reactor
**ICR**........... Integral Cesium Reservoir
**ICR**........... Integrated Color Removal [*Printing technology*]
**ICR**........... Intelligence Collection Requirement [*Army*] (RDA)
**ICR**........... Intelligent Character Recognition [*Data processing*]
**ICR**........... Intercolonial Railway [*1858-1923*] [*Canada*]
**ICR**........... Interface Compatibility Record (NASA)
**ICR**........... Internal Control Region [*Genetics*]
**ICR**........... Internal Control Review [*DoD*]
**ICR**........... International Committee on Refugees [*World War II*]
**ICR**........... International Computer Resources, Inc. [*Information service or system*] (IID)
**ICR**........... International Congress of Radiology
**ICR**........... International Consumer Reports [*Consumers' Association*] [*Great Britain*] [*Information service or system*] (IID)
**ICR**........... International Corona Resources Ltd. [*Vancouver Stock Exchange symbol*]
**ICR**........... International Council for Reprography
**IC/R**.......... International Cruiser/Race Class [*Yachting*]
**ICR**........... International Currency Report [*A publication*]
**ICR**........... Interrupt Control Register [*Data processing*]
**ICR**........... Intracranial Reinforcement
**ICR**........... Inventory Change Report
**ICR**........... Ion Cyclotron Radiation
**ICR**........... Ion Cyclotron Resonance [*Spectrometry*]
**ICR**........... Irish Chancery Reports [*A publication*] (DLA)
**ICR**........... Irish Circuit Reports [*1841-43*] [*A publication*] (DLA)
**ICR**........... Iron-Core Reactor (MSA)
**ICR**........... Item Change Request (AFIT)
**ICR**........... Nicaro [*Cuba*] [*Airport symbol*] [*Obsolete*] (OAG)
**ICRA**......... Indian Civil Rights Act [*1968*]

**ICRA**.......... Industrial Chemical Research Association (EA)
**ICRA**.......... Interagency Committee on Radiological Assistance
**ICRA**.......... International Catholic Rural Association
**ICRA**.......... International Centre for Research in Accounting [*University of Lancaster*] [*British*] (CB)
**ICRA**.......... Islamic Correctional Reunion Association (EA)
**ICRAEE**.... International Commission on Rules for the Approval of Electrical Equipment [*Later, CEE*]
**ICRAF**....... Institut Canadien de Recherches pour l'Avancement de la Femme [*Canadian Research Institute for the Advancement of Women*]
**ICRAF**....... International Council for Research in Agroforestry [*See also ICRAF*] [*Kenya*] (EAIO)
**ICRaH**....... Ravenswood Hospital Medical Center, Chicago, IL [*Library symbol*] [*Library of Congress*] (LCLS)
**ICRand**...... Rand McNally & Co., Chicago, IL [*Library symbol*] [*Library of Congress*] (LCLS)
**ICRAR**....... Interfaith Center to Reverse the Arms Race (EA)
**ICRAS**....... International Committee for the Release of Anatoly Scharansky [*Defunct*] (EA)
**ICRB**.......... International Center for Research on Bilingualism [*Universite Laval*] [*Canada*]
**ICRB**.......... International Co-Operative Reinsurance Bureau [*Manchester, England*] (EAIO)
**I & CRB**..... Investigation and Censure Review Branch [*BUPERS*]
**ICRC**.......... Interagency Classification Review Committee [*Abolished, 1978*] [*DoD*]
**ICRC**.......... International Committee to the Red Cross [*Geneva, Switzerland*] (EAIO)
**ICRC**.......... Roosevelt University, Chicago, IL [*Library symbol*] [*Library of Congress*] (LCLS)
**ICRC-N**..... Roosevelt University, North Campus, Arlington Heights, IL [*Library symbol*] [*Library of Congress*] (LCLS)
**ICRD**.......... Index of Codes for Research Drugs [*A publication*]
**ICRD**.......... Input Collection Reports Data [*IRS*]
**ICRD**.......... Institute for Community Resource Development [*Australia*]
**ICRD**.......... Intellicard International, Inc. [*Colorado Springs, CO*] [*NASDAQ symbol*] (NQ)
**ICRD**.......... Interior Committee on Research and Development
**ICRDA**....... Independent Cash Register Dealers Association (EA)
**ICRDB**....... International Cancer Research Data Bank [*National Cancer Institute*] [*Database producer*] (IID)
**ICre**........... Crete Public Library, Crete, IL [*Library symbol*] [*Library of Congress*] (LCLS)
**ICRE**.......... Iceland Review [*A publication*]
**ICREB**....... International Champlain-Richelieu Engineering Board [*Canada*]
**ICREF**....... International Corona Resources Ltd. [*NASDAQ symbol*] (NQ)
**IC Rep**........ Interstate Commerce Commission Reports [*A publication*] (DLA)
**ICRETT**..... International Cancer Research Technology Transfer [*Program*]
**ICREW**...... International Cancer Research Workshop
**ICRF**.......... Imperial Cancer Research Fund [*British*]
**ICRF**.......... Ion Cyclotron Resonance Frequency [*Nuclear energy*]
**ICRF 159**... Imperial Cancer Research Fund 159 [*Razoxane*] [*Antineoplastic drug*]
**IC & RFS**... Indoor Citrus and Rare Fruit Society (EA)
**ICRFSDD**... Independent Citizens Research Foundation for the Study of Degenerative Diseases (EA)
**ICRGR**....... International Consultative Research Group on Rape [*See also GCIRC*] (EAIO)
**ICRH**.......... Information Center - Recreation for the Handicapped
**ICRH**.......... Institute for Computer Research in the Humanities [*New York University*]
**ICRH**.......... Ion Cyclotron Resonance Heating (MCD)
**ICRH**.......... Michael Reese Hospital and Medical Center, Lillian W. Florsheim Memorial Library, Chicago, IL [*Library symbol*] [*Library of Congress*] (LCLS)
**ICRHO**...... Ross, Hardies, O'Keefe, Babcock, and Parsons, Chicago, IL [*Library symbol*] [*Library of Congress*] (LCLS)
**ICRI**........... International Child Resource Institute (EA)
**ICRI**........... International Coma Recovery Institute (EA)
**ICRI**........... Iron Casting Research Institute (EA)
**ICRICE**...... International Centre of Research and Information on Collective Economy
**ICRIP**........ International Circle for Research in Philosophy [*Research center*] (RCD)
**ICRISAT**... International Crops Research Institute for the Semi-Arid Tropics [*India*]
**ICRISAT Annu Rep**... ICRISAT [*International Crops Research Institute for the Semi-Arid Tropics*] Annual Report [*A publication*]
**ICRISAT (Int Crops Res Inst Semi-Arid Trop) Res Bull**... ICRISAT (International Crops Research Institute for the Semi-Arid Tropics) Research Bulletin [*A publication*]
**ICRL**.......... Center for Research Libraries, Chicago, IL [*Library symbol*] [*Library of Congress*] (LCLS)
**ICRL**.......... Individual Component Repair List [*DoD*]
**ICRL**.......... Injury Control Research Laboratory [*HEW*]
**ICRL(ARL)**... Foreign Newspaper Microfilm Project, Association of Research Libraries, Center for Research Libraries, Chicago, IL [*Library symbol*] [*Library of Congress*] (LCLS)
**ICRL(CAMP)**... Cooperative Africana Microform Project, Archives-Libraries Committee, African Studies Association, Center for Research Libraries, Chicago, IL [*Library symbol*] [*Library of Congress*] (LCLS)
**ICRL-RR**... Injury Control Research Laboratory Research Report [*HEW*]
**ICRL(SAMP)**... South Asian Microform Project, South Asian Microform and Library Committee, Association for Asian Studies, Center for Research Libraries, Chicago, IL [*Library symbol*] [*Library of Congress*] (LCLS)
**I CRM**........ Ice Cream [*Freight*]
**ICRM**......... Institute of Certified Records Managers (EA)
**ICRM**......... International Carpet and Rug Market (ITD)
**ICRM**......... International Cliff Richard Movement (EAIO)
**ICRM**......... Rush Medical College, Chicago, IL [*Library symbol*] [*Library of Congress*] (LCLS)
**ICRO**......... Interallied Confederation of Reserve Officers [*See also CIOR*] (EAIO)
**ICRO**......... International Cell Research Organization [*ICSU*] [*Paris, France*] (EAIO)
**ICROSS**..... International Community for the Relief of Starvation and Suffering (EA)
**ICRP**.......... International Climatic Research Program
**ICRP**.......... International Commission on Radiological Protection [*International Society of Radiology*] [*London, England*]
**ICRPDS**.... Ion Cyclotron Resonance Photodissociation [*Spectrometry*]
**ICRPG**....... Interagency Chemical Rocket Propulsion Group
**ICRPMA**... International Committee for Recording the Productivity of Milk Animals [*See also CICPLB*] [*Rome, Italy*] (EAIO)
**ICRP Publ**... ICRP [*International Commission on Radiological Protection*] Publication [*A publication*]
**IC & RR**..... Inventory Control and Requirements Review Board [*CNO*]
**ICRRA2**..... Indian Council of Agricultural Research. Research Series [*A publication*]
**ICRS**.......... Index Chemicus Registry System [*Information service or system*] [*A publication*]
**ICRS**.......... Institute of Contemporary Russian Studies [*Fordham University*]
**ICRS**.......... Instrument Calibration and Recall System [*Nuclear energy*] (NRCH)
**ICRS**.......... Integrated Chemical Retrieval System [*Pergamon InfoLine*] [*Data processing*]
**ICRS**.......... Intelligence Collection Reporting System [*Military*] (MCD)
**ICRSC**....... International Council for Research in the Sociology of Co-operation
**ICRS Med Rep Monogr Sov Med Sci**... ICRS [*Institute of Contemporary Russian Studies*] Medical Reports. Monographs in Soviet Medical Science [*A publication*]
**ICRT**.......... Individual Criterion-Referenced Test [*Education*]
**ICRU**......... International Commission on Radiation Units and Measurements (EA)
**IcRU**......... University of Icelands (Haskoli Islands), Reykjavik, Iceland [*Library symbol*] [*Library of Congress*] (LCLS)
**ICRUM**..... International Commission on Radiation Units and Measurements
**ICRU Rep**... ICRU [*International Commission on Radiological Units*] Report [*A publication*]
**ICRV**.......... Inns of Court Rifle Volunteers [*Military*] [*British*] (ROG)
**ICRW**......... International Center for Research on Women (EA)
**ICRW**......... International Convention for the Regulation of Whaling (ASF)
**ICS**............ Illinois Classical Studies [*A publication*]
**ICS**............ Immunochemistry System [*Medicine*]
**ICS**............ Imperial College of Science [*British*]
**ICS**............ Impulse Conducting System [*Physiology*]
**ICS**............ In-Can System [*Device that improves quality of beer and ale*] [*British*]
**ICS**............ Incident Command System [*Regional emergency response system*] (DHSM)
**ICS**............ Indian Civil Service [*British*]
**ICS**............ Induction Communications System
**ICS**............ Industrial Control System
**ICS**............ Infinity Color-Corrected System [*Optics*]
**ICS**............ Information Calling Services [*Telecommunications*]
**ICS**............ Information Centers Service [*United States Information Agency*] (IID)
**ICS**............ Information Control System [*Military*]
**ICS**............ Infrared Calibration System
**ICS**............ Infrared Camera System
**ICS**............ Infrared Communications System
**ICS**............ Infrared Countermeasures System [*Military*] [*Electronics*]
**ICS**............ Inland Computer Service (IEEE)
**ICS**............ Innes Clan Society (EA)
**ICS**............ Input Contactor Switch
**ICS**............ Input Control Subsystem
**ICS**............ Insert Card Section
**ICS**............ Institute of Chartered Shipbrokers [*British*]
**ICS**............ Institute of Child Study [*University of Toronto*] [*Research center*] (RCD)
**ICS**............ Institute for Christian Studies
**ICS**............ Institute for Cognitive Science [*University of California, San Diego*] [*Research center*] (RCD)

**ICS** ............ Institute of Cognitive Science [*University of Colorado - Boulder*] [*Research center*] (RCD)
**ICS** ............ Institute of Commonwealth Studies [*British*]
**ICS** ............ Institute of Complementary Sciences [*Defunct*] (EA)
**ICS** ............ Institute for Contemporary Studies (EA)
**ICS** ............ Institute of Cornish Studies [*British*]
**ICS** ............ Institute for Cultural Studies (EA)
**ICS** ............ Institution of Computer Sciences [*British*] (DIT)
**ICS** ............ Instructional Communications Systems [*University of Wisconsin*] [*Telecommunications service*] (TSSD)
**ICS** ............ Instrumentation Checkout Station (AAG)
**ICS** ............ Instrumentation and Communication Subsystem [*NASA*] (KSC)
**I & C(S)** ...... Instrumentation and Communication (System)
**ICS** ............ Instrumentation and Control Subsystem
**ICS** ............ Insurance Communication Service [*IBM Information Network*] [*Tampa, FL*] [*Telecommunications*] (TSSD)
**ICS** ............ Integrated Checkout System (KSC)
**ICS** ............ Integrated Circuit System (IMH)
**ICS** ............ Integrated Combat Ship
**ICS** ............ Integrated Combat System
**ICS** ............ Integrated Command System
**ICS** ............ Integrated Communication Systems, Inc. [*Roswell, GA*] [*Telecommunications*] (IEEE)
**ICS** ............ Integrated Computer Systems [*Culver City, CA*] [*Telecommunications service*] (TSSD)
**ICS** ............ Integrated Configuration Summary (AAG)
**ICS** ............ Integrated Control Storage [*Data processing*]
**ICS** ............ Integrated Control System (NRCH)
**ICS** ............ Intelligence Center and School [*Army*] (RDA)
**ICS** ............ Intelligence Community Staff [*Military*] (MCD)
**ICS** ............ Intensive Care Society [*London, England*] (EAIO)
**ICS** ............ Intensive Care, Surgical [*Medicine*]
**ICS** ............ Inter-Celtic Society (EAIO)
**ICS** ............ Interactive Communications Software
**ICS** ............ Interagency Communications System [*Military*]
**ICS** ............ Intercommunication Control Station (KSC)
**ICS** ............ Intercommunications System
**ICS** ............ Intercostal Space [*Medicine*]
**ICS** ............ Interface Control Specification (MCD)
**ICS** ............ Interference Check Sample [*Spectroscopy*]
**ICS** ............ Interim Contractor Support (MCD)
**ICS** ............ Interior Contractor Support
**ICS** ............ Interlinked Computerized Storage and Processing System of Food and Agricultural Data [*United Nations*] [*Databank*] [*Information service or system*] (IID)
**ICS** ............ Intermittent Control System [*Environmental Protection Agency*]
**ICS** ............ Internal Chemical Shift
**ICS** ............ Internal Communication System [*Space Flight Operations Facility, NASA*]
**ICS** ............ Internal Countermeasures Set (MCD)
**ICS** ............ International Camellia Society [*Worcester, England*] (EAIO)
**ICS** ............ International Cardiovascular Society
**ICS** ............ International Catacomb Society (EA)
**ICS** ............ International Chamber of Shipping [*London, England*] (EAIO)
**ICS** ............ International Chemical Society [*Proposed*]
**ICS** ............ International Chemometrics Society [*Brussels, Belgium*] (EAIO)
**ICS** ............ International Chili Society (EA)
**ICS** ............ International Churchill Society (EA)
**ICS** ............ International Clarinet Society [*Later, ICS/CI*] (EA)
**ICS** ............ International Cogeneration Society (EA)
**ICS** ............ International Cold Storage
**ICS** ............ International College of Scientists [*See also ISK*] [*International Academy of Sciences*] [*Paderborn, Federal Republic of Germany*] (EAIO)
**ICS** ............ International College of Surgeons (EA)
**ICS** ............ International Committee on Sarcoidosis [*London, England*] (EAIO)
**ICS** ............ International Committee of Slavists [*Sofia, Bulgaria*] (EAIO)
**ICS** ............ International Communications Sciences
**ICS** ............ International Communications System
**ICS** ............ International Congress Series [*Elsevier Book Series*] [*A publication*]
**ICS** ............ International Conrad Society (EA)
**ICS** ............ International Controlled Industry [*Vancouver Stock Exchange symbol*]
**ICS** ............ International Coronelli Society [*See also ICGGI*] (EAIO)
**ICS** ............ International Correspondence School
**ICS** ............ International Craniopathic Society [*Absorbed by SORSI*] (EA)
**ICS** ............ International Crocodilian Society [*Defunct*] (EA)
**ICS** ............ Interphone Control Station
**ICS** ............ Interphone Control System
**ICS** ............ Interpretive Computer Simulator
**ICS** ............ Intracapillary Space [*In bioreactor*]
**ICS** ............ Intracommunication System
**ICS** ............ Intracranial Self-Stimulation [*Also, ICSS*] [*Neurophysiology*]
**ICS** ............ Intracranial Stimulation [*Neurophysiology*]
**ICS** ............ Inventory Control System [*Data processing*]
**ICS** ............ Iron Castings Society (EA)
**ICS** ............ Isolation Containment Spray [*Nuclear energy*] (IEEE)
**ICS** ............ Issued Capital Stock
**ICS** ............ Italia Che Scrive [*A publication*]
**ICS** ............ Saint Xavier College, Chicago, IL [*OCLC symbol*] (OCLC)
**ICS** ............ Society of Inter-Celtic Arts and Culture (EA)
**ICS2** .......... Intelligent Communication Subsystem Two Board [*Controls input from computer terminals to mainframe*] [*Prime Computer, Inc.*]
**ICSA** .......... In-Core Shim Assembly [*Nuclear energy*] (NRCH)
**ICSA** .......... Indian Council of South America [*See also CISA*] [*Lima, Peru*] (EAIO)
**ICSA** .......... Institute of Chartered Secretaries and Administrators [*Australia*]
**ICSA** .......... International Cemetery Supply Association (EA)
**ICSA** .......... International Chain Salon Association (EA)
**ICSA** .......... International Christian Studies Association (EA)
**ICSA** .......... International Claims Settlement Act of 1949
**ICSA** .......... International Committee Against Apartheid, Racism, and Colonialism in Southern Africa [*London, England*] (EAIO)
**ICSA** .......... International Correspondence Society of Allergists (EA)
**ICSA** .......... International Customer Service Association [*Chicago, IL*] (EA)
**ICSA** .......... Intracranial Self-Administration [*Neurophysiology*]
**ICSA** .......... Islet Cell Surface Antibody [*Immunology*]
**ICSA** .......... Sidley and Austin Library, Chicago, IL [*Library symbol*] [*Library of Congress*] (LCLS)
**ICSAB** ....... International Civil Service Advisory Board
**ICSAC** ....... International Confederation of Societies of Authors and Composers
**ICSAF** ........ International Commission for the Southeast Atlantic Fisheries [*See also CIPASE*] (EAIO)
**ICSAL** ....... Integrated Communications System, Alaska [*Air Force, FAA*]
**ICSB** .......... Interim Command Switchboard [*Navy*] (NVT)
**ICSB** .......... International Committee on Systematic Bacteriology [*London, ON*] (EA)
**ICSB** .......... International Council for Small Business (EA)
**ICSBC** ........ Interstate Council of State Boards of Cosmetology [*Later, NIC*]
**ICSBS** ........ International Chinese Snuff Bottle Society (EA)
**ICSC** .......... Institute for Cardiovascular Studies [*University of Houston*] [*Research center*] (RCD)
**ICSC** .......... Integrated Command Support Center [*Military*] (MCD)
**ICSC** .......... Interim Communications Satellite Committee
**ICSC** .......... International Civil Service Commission (EA)
**ICSC** .......... International Communications Satellite Consortium (MCD)
**ICSC** .......... International Council of Shopping Centers (EA)
**ICSC** .......... Irish Christian Study Centre [*New University of Ulster*] [*United Kingdom*] (CB)
**ICSC** .......... Italy and Colonies Study Circle (EA)
**ICSC** .......... Swift & Company, Research Laboratory Library, Chicago, IL [*Library symbol*] [*Library of Congress*] (LCLS)
**ICSCA** ....... Institute for Computing Science and Computer Applications [*University of Texas at Austin*] [*Research center*] (RCD)
**ICS/CI** ....... International Clarinet Society/Clarinetwork International (EA)
**I & C in Scot** ... Instrumentation and Control in Scotland [*A publication*]
**ICSD** .......... Inorganic Crystal Structure Database [*University of Bonn*] [*Federal Republic of Germany*]
**ICSD** .......... Ionization Chamber Smoke Detector [*Nuclear energy*] (NRCH)
**ICSD** .......... Metropolitan Sanitary District of Greater Chicago, Chicago, IL [*Library symbol*] [*Library of Congress*] (LCLS)
**ICS/DMC** ... Institute for Continuing Studies in Design, Management and Communication [*University of Cincinnati*] [*Research center*] (RCD)
**ICSDW** ...... International Council of Social Democratic Women [*Later, SIW*] (EA)
**ICSE** .......... Intermediate Current Stability Experiment (DEN)
**ICSEAF** ..... International Commission for the Southeast Atlantic Fisheries
**ICSears** ...... Sears, Roebuck & Co., Chicago, IL [*Library symbol*] [*Library of Congress*] (LCLS)
**ICSEES** ..... International Committee for Soviet and East European Studies (EAIO)
**ICSEM** ...... International Center of Studies on Early Music
**ICSEM** ...... International Commission for the Scientific Exploration of the Mediterranean Sea (EAIO)
**ICSEMS** .... International Commission for the Scientific Exploration of the Mediterranean Sea (NOAA)
**ICSEP** ........ International Center for the Solution of Environmental Problems (EA)
**ICSEP** ........ International Council of Sex Education and Parenthood (EA)
**ICSey** ......... Seyfarth, Shaw, Fairweather & Geraldson, Chicago, IL [*Library symbol*] [*Library of Congress*] (LCLS)
**ICSF** .......... International Collegiate Sports Foundation (EA)
**ICSG** .......... International Center for Social Gerontology [*Later, TCSG*] (EA)
**ICSH** .......... International Committee for Standardization in Haematology [*Louvain, Belgium*] [*Research center*] (EAIO)
**ICSH** .......... Interstitial Cell Stimulating Hormone [*Also, LH, LSH*] [*Endocrinology*]
**ICSHB** ....... International Committee for Standardization in Human Biology
**ICSI** .......... Institut Canadien de la Sante Infantile [*Canadian Institute of Child Health*]
**ICSI** .......... International Commission on Snow and Ice

**ICSI** .......... International Conference on Scientific Information
**ICSI** .......... International Container Systems, Incorporated [*Tampa, FL*] [*NASDAQ symbol*] (NQ)
**ICSID** ........ International Centre for Settlement of Investment Disputes (EA)
**ICSID** ........ International Council of Societies of Industrial Design [*Helsinki, Finland*] (EA)
**ICSISP** ...... International Center for Science Information Services in Phytovirology
**ICS/JCCP** ... Journal of Commonwealth and Comparative Politics. University of London. Institute of Commonwealth Studies [*A publication*]
**ICSK** .......... International Cultural Society of Korea [*Seoul, Republic of Korea*] (EAIO)
**ICSK** .......... Intracoronary Streptokinase [*An enzyme*]
**ICSL** .......... Inner-City Simulation Laboratory [*Teacher training game*]
**ICSL** .......... Presbyterian Saint Luke's Hospital, Chicago, IL [*Library symbol*] [*Library of Congress*] (LCLS)
**ICSM** ......... Instant Corn-Soya-Milk
**ICSM** ......... International Confederation of Societies of Music (EA)
**ICSMAQ** ... International Clearinghouse on Science and Mathematics. Curricular Developments Report [*A publication*]
**ICSMM** ..... International Conference on Superlattices, Microstructures, and Microdevices
**ICSMP** ...... Interactive Continuous Systems Modeling Program
**ICSN** .......... Chicago Sun-Times and Chicago Daily News, Chicago, IL [*Library symbol*] [*Library of Congress*] (LCLS)
**ICSOG** ....... International Correspondence Society of Obstetricians and Gynecologists (EA)
**ICSOM** ...... International Conference of Symphony and Opera Musicians (EA)
**ICSon** ......... Sonicraft, Inc., Chicago, IL [*Library symbol*] [*Library of Congress*] (LCLS)
**ICSP** .......... Illinois State Psychiatric Institute, Chicago, IL [*Library symbol*] [*Library of Congress*] (LCLS)
**ICSP** .......... International Council of Societies of Pathology (EA)
**ICSP** .......... Issues in Canadian Science Policy [*A publication*]
**ICSPD4** ..... Immunologia Clinica e Sperimentale [*A publication*]
**ICSPE** ........ International Council of Sport and Physical Education
**ICSPFT** ..... International Committee on the Standardization of Physical Fitness Tests
**ICSPRDC** ... International Committee on Social Psychological Research in Developing Countries (EA)
**ICSPRO** .... Inter-Secretariat Committee on Scientific Problems Relating to Oceanography [*United Nations*]
**ICSR** .......... Intercontinental Services Corp. [*NASDAQ symbol*] (NQ)
**ICSR** .......... International Conference of Sociology of Religion [*Paris, France*] (EA)
**ICSR** .......... Interuniversity Centre for the Study of Religion [*Canada*]
**ICSR** .......... Scottish Rite of Freemasonry Library, Chicago, IL [*Library symbol*] [*Library of Congress*] (LCLS)
**ICSRE** ....... International Centre for Studies in Religious Education [*Brussels, Belgium*] (EAIO)
**ICSRI** ......... Intelligent Computer Systems Research Institute [*University of Miami*] [*Research center*] (RCD)
**ICSRI** ......... Interfaith Committee on Social Responsibility in Investments [*Later, ICCR*] (EA)
**ICSS** .......... Inter-University Committee on the Superior Student [*Defunct*] (EA)
**ICSS** .......... International Commission on Signs and Symbols
**ICSS** .......... International Committee for the Sociology of Sport
**ICSS** .......... International Council for the Social Studies (DIT)
**ICSS** .......... Intracranial Self-Stimulation [*Also, ICS*] [*Neurophysiology*]
**ICSSD** ....... International Committee for Social Science Information and Documentation [*Information service or system*] (IID)
**ICSSID** ...... International Committee for Social Science Information and Documentation [*Paris, France*] [*Information service or system*] (IID)
**ICSSPE** ..... International Council of Sport Science and Physical Education (EA)
**ICSSR** ........ Indian Council of Social Science Research [*New Delhi, India*]
**ICSSR Res Abstr Q** ... ICSSR [*Indian Council of Social Science Research*] Research Abstracts Quarterly [*A publication*]
**ICSST** ........ Institute of Child Study Security Test [*Psychology*]
**ICSST** ........ International Conference on Solid State Transducers (EA)
**ICSSVM** .... International Commission for Small Scale Vegetation Maps [*Pondicherry, India*] (EAIO)
**ICST** .......... Institute for Chemical Science and Technology [*Canada*]
**ICST** .......... Institute [*formerly, Center*] for Computer Sciences and Technology [*Gaithersburg, MD*] [*NIST*]
**ICST** .......... Integrated Combined System Test
**ICST** .......... International Concept Study Team [*for bridges*] [*US, Great Britain, Germany*] (RDA)
**ICSTF** ........ Integrated Combat Systems Test Facility (NVT)
**ICSTI** ......... International Center for Scientific and Technical Information [*Moscow, USSR*] (EAIO)
**ICSTI** ......... International Council for Scientific and Technical Information [*Information service or system*] (IID)
**ICSTK** ....... Intracoronary Streptokinase [*An enzyme*]
**ICSTO** ....... International Civil Service Training Organization
**ICSU** .......... Chicago State University, Chicago, IL [*Library symbol*] [*Library of Congress*] (LCLS)
**ICSU** .......... Independent Canadian Steelworkers' Union
**ICSU** .......... International Council of Scientific Unions [*Research center*] [*France*]
**ICSU AB** ... International Council of Scientific Unions Abstracting Board [*Also, IAB*] [*Later, ICSTI*] (EA)
**ICSU-CTS** ... Committee on the Teaching of Science of the International Council of Scientific Unions [*York, England*] (EAIO)
**ICSU Rev**... International Council of Scientific Unions. Review [*A publication*]
**ICSU Rev World Sci** ... ICSU [*International Council of Scientific Unions*] Review of World Science [*A publication*]
**ICSU Short Rep** ... ICSU [*International Council of Scientific Unions*] Short Reports [*A publication*]
**ICSW** ......... Interdepartmental Committee on the Status of Women [*Terminated, 1978*]
**ICSW** ......... International Committee on Seafarer's Welfare Office (EAIO)
**ICSW** ......... International Conference of Social Work
**ICSW** ......... International Council on Social Welfare (EA)
**ICSW** ......... Sherwin Williams Chemicals, Chicago, IL [*Library symbol*] [*Library of Congress*] (LCLS)
**ICSWBD** ... Interior Communications Switchboard
**ICSWSA**.... International Chain Saw Wood Sculptors Association (EA)
**ICSX** .......... Saint Xavier College, Chicago, IL [*Library symbol*] [*Library of Congress*] (LCLS)
**ICT** ............ Chicago Theological Seminary, Chicago, IL [*Library symbol*] [*Library of Congress*] (LCLS)
**ICT** ............ Icterus [*Jaundice*] [*Medicine*]
**ICT** ............ Iesu Christo Tutore [*With Jesus Christ as Protector*] [*Latin*]
**ICT** ............ Image Converter Tube
**ICT** ............ Immunoreactive Calcitonin [*Endocrinology*]
**ICT** ............ Incoming Trunk [*Telecommunications*] (BUR)
**ICT** ............ Indirect Coombs' Test [*Immunochemistry*]
**ICT** ............ Indirect Coulometric Titration [*Analytical chemistry*]
**ICT** ............ Individual Collective Training [*Army*]
**ICT** ............ Industrial and Commercial Training [*A publication*]
**ICT** ............ Inflammation of Connective Tissue [*Medicine*]
**ICT** ............ Influence Coefficient Tests (MCD)
**ICT** ............ Information and Communication Technology
**ICT** ............ Insect Carrier Toxicant
**ICT** ............ Inspection Check Template (MSA)
**ICT** ............ Institute of Circuit Technology [*Oxford, England*] (EAIO)
**ICT** ............ Institute of Clay Technology [*British*]
**ICT** ............ Institute of Computer Technology
**ICT** ............ Institute of Concrete Technology [*British*]
**ICT** ............ Insulated [*or Insulating*] Core Transformer
**ICT** ............ Insulin Coma Therapy [*Medicine*]
**ICT** ............ Integrated Circuit Tester
**ICT** ............ Integrated Computer Telemetry
**ICT** ............ Intelligence Cycle Time (MCD)
**ICT** ............ Inter Cable Communications, Inc. [*Toronto Stock Exchange symbol*]
**ICT** ............ Interactive Command Test [*Data processing*]
**ICT** ............ Interchangeability Control Tool (MCD)
**ICT** ............ Interface Control Tooling (NASA)
**ICT** ............ International Call for Tenders (NATG)
**ICT** ............ International CMOS Technology [*Data processing*]
**ICT** ............ International Coal Trade [*Bureau of Mines*] [*A publication*]
**ICT** ............ International Commission on Trichinellosis (EA)
**ICT** ............ International Computers and Tabulators Ltd. [*Later, ICL*]
**ICT** ............ International Council of Tanners [*See also CIT*] [*Lewes, East Sussex, England*] (EAIO)
**ICT** ............ International Critical Tables
**ICT** ............ Intradermal Cancer Test [*Oncology*]
**ICT** ............ Irrigated, Conventionally Tilled [*Agriculture*]
**ICT** ............ Trinity College, Deerfield, IL [*OCLC symbol*] (OCLC)
**ICT** ............ Wichita [*Kansas*] [*Airport symbol*] (OAG)
**ICTA** .......... Chicago Transit Authority, Chicago, IL [*Library symbol*] [*Library of Congress*] (LCLS)
**ICTA** .......... Industry Council for Tangible Assets [*Washington, DC*] (EA)
**ICTA** .......... Institute of Certified Travel Agents (EA)
**ICTA** .......... International Center for the Typographic Arts
**ICTA** .......... International Confederation for Thermal Analysis [*Jerusalem, Israel*] (EA)
**ICTAB** ....... Institut Canadien de Tole d'Acier en Batiment [*Canadian Sheet Steel Building Institute*]
**ICTASD** .... International Convention on Transistors and Semiconductor Devices
**ICTB** .......... International Companies and Their Brands [*A publication*]
**ICTB** .......... International Customs Tariffs Bureau (DLA)
**ICTBA** ....... Infants', Children's, and Teens' Wear Buyers Association (EA)
**ICTC** .......... Inertial Components Temperature Controller (KSC)
**ICTC** .......... International Capital & Technology Corporation [*NASDAQ symbol*] (NQ)
**ICTC** .......... International Cooperative Training Center
**ICTCD** ....... Insecticide (MSA)
**ICTD** .......... Individual and Collective Training Development (MCD)
**ICTD** .......... Inter-Channel Time Displacement
**ICTD Pr**..... ICT [*International Computers and Tabulators Limited*] Data Processing Journal [*A publication*]

**ICTE**........ Inertial Component Test Equipment
**ICTED**....... International Cooperation in the Field of Transport Economics Documentation [*European Conference of Ministers of Transport*] [*Information service or system*] (IID)
**ICTF**......... International Cocoa Trades Federation [*British*]
**ICTF**......... International Commission on the Taxonomy of Fungi
**ICTH**......... International Commission for the Teaching of History [*Brussels, Belgium*] (EA)
**ICTH**......... International Committee on Thrombosis and Hemostasis
**ICTI**.......... International Committee of Toy Industries (EA)
**ICTI**.......... Interstate Cellular Telecommunications, Incorporated [*Plainview, NY*] [*NASDAQ symbol*] (NQ)
**ICTL**......... Image Control Table (MCD)
**ICTM**........ Integrated Circuits, Inc. [*NASDAQ symbol*] (NQ)
**ICTM**........ International Council for Traditional Music (EA)
**ICTMM**..... International Congresses on Tropical Medicine and Malaria
**ICTN**......... Industry Center for Trade Negotiations [*Defunct*]
**ICTOC**....... Independent Corps Tactical Operations Center
**ICTP**......... Individual/Collective Training Plan [*Army*]
**ICTP**......... Institute for Certification of Tax Professionals (EA)
**ICTP**......... Intensified Combat Training Program
**ICTP**......... International Center for Theoretical Physics [*Trieste, Italy*] (EA)
**ICTPDC**.... Imperial College Thermophysical Properties Data Centre [*British*] (CB)
**ICTPDF**..... Isozymes. Current Topics in Biological and Medical Research [*A publication*]
**ICTR**......... International Center of Theatre Research (EA)
**ICTr**.......... Truman College, Chicago, IL [*Library symbol*] [*Library of Congress*] (LCLS)
**ICTRA**....... Iron and Coal Trades Review [*A publication*]
**ICTRM**...... Interagency Committee on the Transportation of Radioactive Materials
**ICTS**.......... Integrated Circuit Test Set
**ICTS**.......... Integrated Computerized Test Set
**ICTS**.......... Intermediate Capacity Transit System
**ICTS**.......... International Catholic Truth Society (EA)
**ICTS**.......... International Center for Transportation Studies (EAIO)
**ICTS**.......... International Congress of the Transplantation Society
**ICTSDI**...... IMLS [*Institute of Medical Laboratory Sciences*] Current Topics in Medical Laboratory Sciences [*A publication*]
**ICTT**.......... Intensified Confirmatory Troop Test (AABC)
**ICTU**......... Catholic Theological Union, Chicago, IL [*Library symbol*] [*Library of Congress*] (LCLS)
**ICTU**......... Independent Canadian Transit Union
**ICTU**......... Iraqi Confederation of Trade Unions
**ICTU**......... Irish Congress of Trade Unions
**ICTV**......... Interactive Cable Television
**ICTV**......... International Committee on Taxonomy of Viruses [*ICSU*] [*Rennes, France*] (EAIO)
**ICTV**......... Intracerebroventricular [*Also, ic, ICV*] [*Brain anatomy*]
**ICtvS**......... Shawnee Library System, Carterville, IL [*Library symbol*] [*Library of Congress*] (LCLS)
**ICTX**......... Interference Control Technologies, Inc. [*Gainesville, VA*] [*NASDAQ symbol*] (NQ)
**ICTZ**......... I Corps Tactical Zone [*Vietnamese designation for both a military zone and a political region*]
**ICU**........... Hebdomadaire de la Production a la Distribution [*Paris*] [*A publication*]
**ICU**........... ICG Utility Investments Ltd. [*Toronto Stock Exchange symbol*]
**ICU**........... Implementation Co-Ordination Unit [*Malaysia*] (DS)
**ICU**........... Indicator Control Unit
**ICU**........... Industrial Consulting Unit [*Australia*]
**ICU**........... Informatie en Communicatie Unie [*Information and Communication United*] [*Dutch publishing house*]
**ICU**........... Infrared Command Unit
**ICU**........... Institut d'Urbanisme du Canada [*Town Planning Institute of Canada*]
**ICU**........... Instruction Control Unit
**ICU**........... Integrated Control Unit
**ICU**........... Intelligent Connector Unit [*Telecommunications*] (TSSD)
**ICU**........... Intensive-Care Unit [*of a hospital*]
**ICU**........... Intensive Caring Unlimited [*An association*] (EA)
**ICU**........... Interactive Chart Utility [*IBM Corp.*]
**ICU**........... Interconnection Unit [*Data processing*]
**ICU**........... Interface Control Unit [*Army*]
**ICU**........... Intermediate Care Unit [*of a hospital*]
**ICU**........... International Christian University [*Tokyo*]
**ICU**........... International Christian University Library [*UTLAS symbol*]
**ICU**........... International [*or Internal*] Communication Unit [*Telecommunications*] (TEL)
**ICU**........... International Cycling Union (EA)
**ICU**........... Texas Christian University, Fort Worth, TX [*OCLC symbol*] (OCLC)
**ICU**........... United Capital Corp. [*AMEX symbol*] (SPSG)
**ICU**........... University of Chicago, Chicago, IL [*Library symbol*] [*Library of Congress*] (LCLS)
**ICUA**......... Institute for College and University Administrators [*Later, CPAA*] (EA)
**ICUA**......... Interdenominational Church Ushers Association
**ICUAE**....... International Congress of University Adult Education [*Fredericton, NB*] (EAIO)
**ICUAER**.... International Committee on Urgent Anthropological and Ethnological Research [*Vienna, Austria*] (EAIO)
**ICUAER/B**... Bulletin. International Committee on Urgent Anthropological and Ethnological Research [*A publication*]
**ICUC**......... Union Carbide Corp., Film-Packaging Division, Chicago, IL [*Library symbol*] [*Library of Congress*] (LCLS)
**ICU-D**........ University of Chicago, Divinity School, Chicago, IL [*Library symbol*] [*Library of Congress*] (LCLS)
**ICUE**......... International Committee on the University Emergency (EA)
**ICUEPR**.... International Conference on University Education for Public Relations
**ICU-FE**...... University of Chicago, Far Eastern Library, Chicago, IL [*Library symbol*] [*Library of Congress*] (LCLS)
**ICUFON**... Intercontinental UFO Galactic Spacecraft Research and Analytic Network (EA)
**ICUFR**....... International Council on United Fund Raising (EA)
**ICUGA**...... International Computer Users Groups Association (EA)
**ICU-H**........ University of Chicago, Center for Health Administration Studies, Chicago, IL [*Library symbol*] [*Library of Congress*] (LCLS)
**ICUIS**........ Institute on the Church in Urban-Industrial Society
**ICUIS Abstr Service**... ICUIS [*Institute on the Church in Urban-Industrial Society*] Abstract Service [*A publication*]
**ICUIS Bibliog**... Institute on the Church in Urban-Industrial Society. Bibliography Series [*A publication*]
**ICUIS Occasional Paper**... Institute on the Church in Urban-Industrial Society. Occasional Papers [*A publication*]
**ICUIS Occ Paper**... Institute on the Church in Urban-Industrial Society. Occasional Papers [*A publication*]
**ICU-L**........ University of Chicago, Law Library, Chicago, IL [*Library symbol*] [*Library of Congress*] (LCLS)
**ICU-LS**...... University of Chicago, Graduate Library School, Chicago, IL [*Library symbol*] [*Library of Congress*] (LCLS)
**ICU-M**....... University of Chicago, Bio-Medical Libraries, Chicago, IL [*Library symbol*] [*Library of Congress*] (LCLS)
**ICUMSA**... International Commission for Uniform Methods of Sugar Analysis [*Mackay, QLD, Australia*] (EAIO)
**ICUNA5**.... Improving College and University Teaching [*A publication*]
**ICUnC**....... University Club of Chicago, Chicago, IL [*Library symbol*] [*Library of Congress*] (LCLS)
**ICUnW**...... United Way of Metropolitan Chicago, Chicago, IL [*Library symbol*] [*Library of Congress*] (LCLS)
**ICUP**.......... Individual Circuit Usage and Peg Count [*Telecommunications*] (TEL)
**ICUP**.......... International Catholic Union of the Press (EA)
**ICURR**....... Intergovernmental Committee on Urban and Regional Research [*Canada*]
**ICUS**.......... Inside Continental United States [*Military*]
**ICUS**.......... International Committee on Urgent Surgery [*Milan, Italy*] (EAIO)
**ICUS**.......... International Conference on the Unity of the Sciences
**ICUSA**....... International Christians for Unity in Social Action (EA)
**ICUSQ**....... United States Quartermaster Corps, Food and Container Institute [*for the Armed Forces*], Chicago, IL [*Library symbol*] [*Library of Congress*] (LCLS)
**ICUT**.......... Improving College and University Teaching [*A publication*]
**ICU-Y**........ University of Chicago, Yerkes Observatory, Williams Bay, WI [*Library symbol*] [*Library of Congress*] (LCLS)
**ICV**........... Elmhurst College, Elmhurst, IL [*OCLC symbol*] (OCLC)
**ICV**........... Ice-Cream Van [*Slang*] [*British*]
**ICV**........... Improved Capital Value [*Business term*] (ADA)
**ICV**........... Indice do Custo de Vida [*Cost of Living Index*] [*Portuguese*]
**ICV**........... Infantry Combat Vehicle (MCD)
**ICV**........... Initial Calibration Verification
**ICV**........... Initial Chaining Value [*Data processing*]
**ICV**........... Inter-Center Vector (MCD)
**ICV**........... Internal Correction Voltage
**ICV**........... Interphase Chromosome Volume
**ICV**........... Intracerebroventricular [*Also, ic, ICTV*] [*Brain anatomy*]
**ICV**........... United States Veterans Administration, West Side Hospital, Chicago, IL [*Library symbol*] [*Library of Congress*] (LCLS)
**ICVA**......... International Council of Voluntary Agencies (EA)
**ICVAN**...... International Committee on Veterinary Anatomical Nomenclature [*See also CINAV*] [*Zurich, Switzerland*] (EAIO)
**ICVC**......... VanderCook College of Music, Chicago, IL [*Library symbol*] [*Library of Congress*] (LCLS)
**ICVD**......... Inns of Court Volunteer Decoration [*Military*] [*British*] (ROG)
**ICVF**......... Inner-City Ventures Fund [*National Trust for Historical Preservation*]
**ICVGAN**.... International Committee on Veterinary Gross Anatomical Nomenclature [*Cornell University*] [*Ithaca, NY*] (EY)
**ICVNA**...... Visiting Nurses Association, Chicago, IL [*Library symbol*] [*Library of Congress*] (LCLS)
**ICvR**.......... River Bend Library System, Coal Valley, IL [*Library symbol*] [*Library of Congress*] (LCLS)
**ICVS**.......... International Cardiovascular Society (EA)
**ICVS**.......... International Society for Cardiovascular Surgery (EA)

**ICw**............ Crestwood Library District, Crestwood, IL [*Library symbol*] [*Library of Congress*] (LCLS)
**ICW**........... In Compliance With (MUGU)
**ICW**........... In Connection With
**ICW**........... India-China Wing [*World War II*]
**ICW**........... Initial Condition Word [*Data processing*]
**ICW**........... Input Command Word
**ICW**........... Input Control Word [*Data processing*] (MCD)
**ICW**........... Intake Cooling Water (IEEE)
**ICW**........... Inter-American Commission of Women [*OAS*]
**ICW**........... Interactive Courseware [*Air Force*]
**ICW**........... Intercoastal Waterway
**ICW**........... Interface Control Word [*Data processing*]
**ICW**........... International Chemical Workers Union
**ICW**........... International Council of Women [*France*]
**ICW**........... Interrupted Continuous Waves [*Electronics*]
**ICW**........... Intracellular Water [*Physiology*]
**ICW**........... Western Society of Engineers, Chicago, IL [*Library symbol*] [*Library of Congress*] (LCLS)
**ICW**........... Wheaton College, Wheaton, IL [*OCLC symbol*] (OCLC)
**ICWA**........ Indian Child Welfare Act [*1978*]
**ICWA**........ Institute of Current World Affairs (EA)
**ICWA**........ International Coil Winding Association (EA)
**ICWA**........ Italian Culture and Welfare Association [*Australia*]
**ICWAR**...... Improved Continuous-Wave Acquisition RADAR [*Army*] (AABC)
**ICWB**......... World Book-Childcraft International, Inc., Chicago, IL [*Library symbol*] [*Library of Congress*] (LCLS)
**ICWC**......... Wilbur Wright Community College, Chicago, IL [*Library symbol*] [*Library of Congress*] (LCLS)
**ICWD**........ Interface Control/Weapon Delivery
**ICWDP**....... International Committee for World Day of Prayer (EA)
**ICWeH**...... Louis A. Weiss Memorial Hospital, Chicago, IL [*Library symbol*] [*Library of Congress*] (LCLS)
**ICWES**...... International Conference of Women Engineers and Scientists
**ICWG**........ Interface Control Working Group [*NASA*] (KSC)
**ICWG**........ International Clubroot Working Group (EAIO)
**ICWG**........ International Co-operative Women's Guild
**ICWGA**..... Interface Control Working Group Action [*NASA*] (KSC)
**ICWI**.......... International Car Wash Institute (EA)
**ICWL**......... International Creative Writers League (EA)
**ICWM**....... Interdepartmental Committee on Weather Modification [*Military*]
**ICWM**....... International Committee on Weights and Measures
**ICWM**....... International Congress on Women in Music (EA)
**ICWMA**.... International Country and Western Music Association (EA)
**ICWO**........ Indications Center Watch Officer [*Military*] (MCD)
**ICWO**........ Intercomponent Work Order
**ICWORR**... International Conference on Waste Oil Recovery and Reuse
**ICWP**......... International Council of Women Psychologists [*Later, ICP*]
**ICWP**......... Interstate Conference on Water Policy (EA)
**ICWR**......... Interagency Committee on Water Resources
**ICWRBS**.... International Commission on Whaling. Report [*A publication*]
**ICWS**......... Improved Commander's Weapon Station
**ICWS**......... Institute of Civil War Studies (EA)
**ICWS**......... Winston & Strawn, Chicago, IL [*Library symbol*] [*Library of Congress*] (LCLS)
**ICWSG**...... Infants' and Children's Wear Salesmen's Guild (EA)
**ICWT**......... Inter-Component Work Transmitted (MCD)
**ICWU**........ International Chemical Workers Union (EA)
**ICWWP**..... Interagency Committee for World Weather Programs [*Department of Commerce*] (NOAA)
**ICX**........... International Cultural Exchange
**ICX**........... Lewis University, Lockport, IL [*OCLC symbol*] (OCLC)
**ICY**........... Augustana College, Rock Island, IL [*OCLC symbol*] (OCLC)
**ICY**........... ICEE USA [*AMEX symbol*] (SPSG)
**ICY**........... International Christian Youth (EA)
**ICY**........... International Commission on Yeasts and Yeast-Like Microorganisms [*ICSU*] [*France*] (EAIO)
**ICY**........... International Cooperation Year [*1965*] [*20th anniversary of UN*]
**ICYE**.......... International Christian Youth Exchange (EA)
**ICYF**.......... International Catholic Youth Federation [*Later, WFCY*]
**ICYP**.......... Iodocyanopindolol [*Biochemistry*]
**ICYRA**....... Inter-Collegiate Yacht Racing Association [*of North America*] [*Later, ICYRA/NA*]
**ICYRA/NA**... Inter-Collegiate Yacht Racing Association of North America (EA)
**ICYSB**....... International Review of Cytology. Supplement [*A publication*]
**ICYT**.......... Instituto de Informacion y Documentacion en Ciencia y Tecnologia [*Institute for Information and Documentation in Science and Technology*] [*Database originator and host*] [*Information service or system*] [*Spain*] (IID)
**ICZ**............ International Climate Zone
**ICZ**............ Intertropical Convergence Zone [*Trade winds*] [*Meteorology*]
**ICZ**............ Isthmian Canal Zone
**ICZ**............ North Park College and Theological Seminary, Chicago, IL [*OCLC symbol*] (OCLC)
**ICZN**......... International Commission on Zoological Nomenclature [*London, England*] (EAIO)
**ID**.............. Atlantic Deutsche Luftverkehrs AG [*West Germany*] [*ICAO designator*] (FAAC)
**ID**.............. Idaho [*Postal code*]
**ID**.............. Idaho Operations Office [*Energy Research and Development Administration*]
**ID**.............. Idaho Reports [*A publication*] (DLA)
**Id**............... Idaho State Library, Boise, ID [*Library symbol*] [*Library of Congress*] (LCLS)
**ID**.............. Iddin-Dagan (BJA)
**ID**.............. Idea [*Slang*]
**ID**.............. Idem [*The Same*] [*Latin*]
**ID**.............. Identification [*Data processing*]
**ID**.............. Identification Data
**ID**.............. Identification Date
**ID**.............. Identification Dissector (MCD)
**ID**.............. Identifier [*Online database field identifier*]
**ID**.............. [*The*] Ides
**Id**............... Idylls [*of Theocritus*] [*Classical studies*] (OCD)
**ID**.............. Image Digitizer [*Data processing*]
**ID**.............. Image Dissector (KSC)
**ID**.............. Immediate Delivery [*Shipping*]
**ID**.............. Immunodeficiency [*Immunology*]
**ID**.............. Immunodiffusion [*Immunology*]
**ID**.............. Immunological Distance [*in primate phylogeny*]
**ID**.............. Import Duty [*Customs*] (DS)
**ID**.............. Inanna's Descent (BJA)
**ID**.............. Inaugural Dissertation (BJA)
**I & D**......... Incision and Drainage [*Medicine*]
**ID**.............. Inclusion Disease [*Medicine*]
**ID**.............. Income Debenture [*Type of bond*] [*Investment term*]
**ID**.............. Indefinite Delivery [*Shipping*]
**ID**.............. Independence Dogs [*An association*] (EA)
**ID**.............. Independent Distributor
**ID**.............. Index of Discrimination
**ID**.............. Index of Dissimilarity
**ID**.............. Indicating Device
**ID**.............. Indicator Driver (MSA)
**ID**.............. Indirect Damage [*Insurance*]
**I/D**............ Indirect Labor (AAG)
**ID**.............. Individual Development
**ID**.............. Individual Dose [*Radioactivity calculations*]
**ID**.............. Indonesia [*ANSI two-letter standard code*] (CNC)
**ID**.............. Induced Draft
**ID**.............. Industrial Democracy
**ID**.............. Industrial Development
**ID**.............. Industrial Dynamics [*Management analysis*]
**ID**.............. Infantry Division
**ID**.............. Infectious Disease [*Medicine*]
**ID**.............. Infective Dose
**ID**.............. Informal Decorative [*Horticulture*]
**ID**.............. Information Distributor
**ID**.............. Information and Documentation [*Royal Tropical Institute*] [*Information service or system*] (IID)
**ID**.............. Inhibitory Dose [*Medicine*]
**ID**.............. Initial Distribution
**I & D**......... Initiation and Development
**ID**.............. Injected Dose
**ID**.............. Inner Diameter
**ID**.............. Inniskilling Dragoons [*Military*] [*British*]
**ID**.............. Innovator's Digest [*The Infoteam, Inc.*] [*Information service or system*] (IID)
**ID**.............. Inoculum Density
**ID**.............. Inside Diameter
**ID**.............. Inside Dimensions
**I & D**......... Install and Dismantle [*Expositions and exhibitions*]
**ID**.............. Installation Data
**ID**.............. Institute of Distribution [*Defunct*] (EA)
**ID**.............. Institutional Distribution [*A publication*]
**I/D**............ Instruction/Data (IEEE)
**ID**.............. Instructional Developer (MCD)
**ID**.............. Instrumentation Directorate [*White Sands Missile Range*] [*Army*]
**ID**.............. Insulation Displacement
**I & D**......... Integrate and Dump Detection [*Telecommunications*] (TEL)
**ID**.............. Intellectual Digest [*A publication*]
**ID**.............. Intelligence Department [*Army*] (MCD)
**ID**.............. Intelligence Division [*NATO*] (NATG)
**ID**.............. Intelligence Duties
**ID**.............. Intelligent Digitizer
**I-D**............ Intensity Duration (Curve)
**ID**.............. Interactive Debugging (IEEE)
**ID**.............. Intercommunication Devices (MCD)
**ID**.............. Interconnection Device (MCD)
**ID**.............. Interdigital [*Telecommunications*] (IEEE)
**ID**.............. Interdisciplinary
**ID**.............. Interest Deductible [*Banking*] (ADA)
**ID**.............. Interface Document (NASA)
**ID**.............. Interferometer and Doppler
**ID**.............. Interim Dividend [*Investment term*]
**ID**.............. Interior Department

**ID**.............. Interior Department Decisions [*United States*] [*A publication*] (DLA)
**ID**.............. Interlocking Directorate [*Business term*]
**ID**.............. Intermediate Description (IEEE)
**ID**.............. Intermodulation Distortion
**ID**.............. Internal Diameter (MSA)
**ID**.............. International Daleco Technology [*Vancouver Stock Exchange symbol*]
**ID**.............. International Division [*Army Service Forces*] [*World War II*]
**ID**.............. Interrectal Spike Discharge [*Neurophysiology*]
**ID**.............. Intestinal Distress
**ID**.............. Intradermal [*Medicine*]
**ID**.............. Intraductal [*Anatomy*]
**ID**.............. Inventory Difference [*Formerly, MUF*] [*NRC/ERDA*]
**ID**.............. Invoice Distribution
**ID**.............. Ionospheric Data [*A publication*]
**ID**.............. Iraqi Dinar [*Monetary unit*] (BJA)
**ID**.............. Iris Diaphragm [*Photography*]
**ID**.............. Irish Digest [*A publication*]
**ID**.............. Irish Duke (ROG)
**ID**.............. Islamic Dinar [*Monetary unit*] (EY)
**ID**.............. Island (ADA)
**ID**.............. Isotope Dilution
**ID**.............. Issue Date
**ID**.............. Italia Dialettale [*A publication*]
**ID**.............. Item Description
**ID**.............. Item Documentation (IEEE)
**ID**.............. Izquierda Democratica [*Democratic Left*] [*Ecuador*] [*Political party*] (PPW)
**ID**.............. Noncathode Ray Tube Indicators [*JETDS nomenclature*] [*Military*] (CET)
**ID**.............. Sumitomo Chemical Co. [*Japan*] [*Research code symbol*]
**$ID_{50}$**.............. Infective Dose, Median
**ID-86**.......... Infantry Division - 1986
**IDA**............ Dallas Baptist College, Dallas, TX [*OCLC symbol*] (OCLC)
**IDA**............ Idaho
**IDA**............ Idaho Array [*Idaho*] [*Seismograph station code, US Geological Survey*] [*Closed*] (SEIS)
**IDA**............ Idaho Falls [*Idaho*] [*Airport symbol*] (OAG)
**IDA**............ Idaho Power Co. [*NYSE symbol*] (SPSG)
**Ida**............ Idaho Reports [*A publication*] (DLA)
**IDA**............ Iminodiacetic Acid [*Organic chemistry*]
**IDA**............ Immediate Damage Assessment
**IDA**............ Immortalis Dei Auspicio [*With the Help of God*] [*Latin*]
**IDA**............ Import Duty Act [*British*] (DS)
**IDA**............ In Defense of Animals (EA)
**IDA**............ Indicator Digest Average [*Stock exchange term*] (SPSG)
**IDA**............ Industrial Design Award
**IDA**............ Industrial Development Abstracts [*Database*] [*UNIDO*] [*Information service or system*] (CRD)
**IDA**............ Industrial Development Authority [*Ireland*]
**IDA**............ Industrial Diamond Association of America (EA)
**IDA**............ Information, Decision, Action
**IDA**............ Infrared Detection Array
**IDA**............ Initial Denial Authority (AABC)
**IDA**............ Input Data Assembler
**IDA**............ Inspekteur der Artillerie [*Inspector of Artillery*] [*German military - World War II*]
**IDA**............ Institute for Defense Analyses (EA)
**IDA**............ Institute for Development Anthropology (EA)
**IDA**............ Integrated Digital Access [*Telecommunications*]
**IDA**............ Integrated Digital Avionics (MCD)
**IDA**............ Integrated Disbursing and Accounting (MCD)
**IDA**............ Integrated Disk Adapter [*Sperry UNIVAC*]
**IDA**............ Integro-Differential Analyzer
**IDA**............ Intelligent Data Access
**IDA**............ Intelligent Database Assistant
**IDA**............ Intelligent Drive Array [*COMPAQ Computer Corp.*] [*Data processing*]
**IDA**............ Inter-Divisional Agreement
**IDA**............ Interactive Debugging Aid
**IDA**............ Interactive Differential Analyzer
**IDA**............ Intercollegiate Dramatic Association [*Defunct*] (EA)
**IDA**............ Interdigitated Array [*Electronics*]
**IDA**............ Interface Display Assembly [*NASA*] (NASA)
**IDA**............ International Dance Alliance (EA)
**IDA**............ International Data and Analysis [*Bureau of Mines*]
**IDA**............ International Database Association [*Defunct*] (EA)
**IDA**............ International Defenders of Animals (EA)
**IDA**............ International Deployment of Accelerometers [*Project*] [*Seismography*]
**IDA**............ International Desalination Association (EA)
**IDA**............ International Development Association (EA)
**IDA**............ International Discotheque Association [*Defunct*] (EA)
**IDA**............ International Dispensary Association [*Acronym is used as association name*] (EAIO)
**IDA**............ International Documentary Association (EA)
**IDA**............ International Doll Association [*Defunct*] (EA)
**IDA**............ International Downtown Association (EA)
**IDA**............ International Drapery Association (EA)
**IDA**............ International Dredging Association
**IDA**............ Intrusion Detection Alarm (CINC)
**IDA**............ Investment Dealers Association of Canada
**IDA**............ Ionospheric Dispersion Analysis [*Air Force*]
**IDA**............ Iron Deficiency Anemia [*Medicine*]
**IDA**............ Islamic Democratic Alliance [*Pakistan*] [*Political party*]
**IDA**............ Isotope Dilution Analysis
**IDA**............ Isotopic Dilution Analysis
**IDAA**.......... Industrial Diamond Association of America
**IDAA**.......... International Doctors in Alcoholics Anonymous (EA)
**IDAADC**..... Infectious Diseases and Antimicrobial Agents [*A publication*]
**IDAAS**....... International Directory of Astronomical Associations and Societies [*A publication*]
**IDAB**.......... Industrial Development Advisory Board [*British*]
**IDABA**....... Annual Bulletin. International Dairy Federation [*A publication*]
**IDABAC**.... International Dairy Federation. Annual Bulletin [*A publication*]
**ID AC**......... Idem Ac [*The Same As*] [*Latin*]
**IDAC**.......... Instant Data Access Control [*National Design Center, Inc.*] [*Information service or system*] (IID)
**IDAC**.......... Integrated Data Acquisition and Control [*Jet Propulsion Laboratory, NASA*]
**IDAC**.......... Integrated Digital-Analog Converter (MCD)
**IDAC**.......... Interconnecting Digital-Analog Converter (NG)
**IDAC**.......... Interim Digital-Analog Converter
**IDAC**.......... International Decorative Accessories Center (EA)
**IDACE**....... Association des Industries des Aliments Dietetiques de la CEE [*Association of Dietetic Foods Industries of the European Economic Community*]
**ID-ACK**..... Identification-Acknowledge (MCD)
**IDACON**... Iterative Differential Analyzer Control
**IDA-CRD**.. Institute for Defense Analysis-Communications Research Division
**IDACS**....... Integrated Detection and Classification Station
**IDAD**.......... Internal Defense and Development [*Army*] (AABC)
**IDADS**....... Interactive Drafting and Digitizing System (MCD)
**IDAF**.......... International Defence and Aid Fund for Southern Africa [*London, England*] (EAIO)
**IDAF**.......... International Defense and Aid Fund for Southern Africa, US Committee (EA)
**IDAGAM**.. Institute for Defense Analysis Gaming Model (MCD)
**IDA-HEAL-NET**... Idaho Health Libraries Network [*Library network*]
**Idaho**.......... Idaho Reports [*A publication*]
**Idaho**.......... Idaho Supreme Court Reports [*A publication*] (DLA)
**Idaho Ag Exp**... Idaho. Agricultural Experiment Station. Publications [*A publication*]
**Idaho Agric Exp Stn Res Bull**... Idaho. Agricultural Experiment Station. Research Bulletin [*A publication*]
**Idaho Agr Res Progr Rep**... Idaho Agricultural Research Progress Report. University of Idaho. College of Agriculture [*A publication*]
**Idaho Agr Sci**... Idaho Agricultural Science. University of Idaho. College of Agriculture [*A publication*]
**Idaho Bur Mines Geol Bull**... Idaho. Bureau of Mines and Geology. Bulletin [*A publication*]
**Idaho Bur Mines Geol County Rep**... Idaho. Bureau of Mines and Geology. County Report [*A publication*]
**Idaho Bur Mines Geol Inf Circ**... Idaho. Bureau of Mines and Geology. Information Circular [*A publication*]
**Idaho Bur Mines Geol Miner Resour Rep**... Idaho. Bureau of Mines and Geology. Mineral Resources Report [*A publication*]
**Idaho Bur Mines and Geology Earth Sci Ser**... Idaho. Bureau of Mines and Geology. Earth Sciences Series [*A publication*]
**Idaho Bur Mines Geol Pam**... Idaho. Bureau of Mines and Geology. Pamphlet [*A publication*]
**Idaho Dep Fish Game Wildl Bull**... Idaho. Department of Fish and Game. Wildlife Bulletin [*A publication*]
**Idaho Dep Reclam Water Inf Bull**... Idaho. Department of Reclamation. Water Information Bulletin [*A publication*]
**Idaho Dept Reclamation Water Inf Bull**... Idaho. Department of Reclamation. Water Information Bulletin [*A publication*]
**Idaho Dep Water Adm Water Inf Bull**... Idaho. Department of Water Administration. Water Information Bulletin [*A publication*]
**Idaho Dep Water Resour Basic Data Release**... Idaho. Department of Water Resources. Basic Data Release [*A publication*]
**Idaho Dep Water Resour Water Inf Bull**... Idaho. Department of Water Resources. Water Information Bulletin [*A publication*]
**Idaho Div Environ Dep Health Welfare Water Qual Ser**... Idaho. Division of Environment. Department of Health and Welfare. Water Quality Series [*A publication*]
**Idaho For Wildl Range Exp Stn Bull**... Idaho. Forest, Wildlife, and Range Experiment Station. Bulletin [*A publication*]
**Idaho For Wildl Range Exp Stn Inf Ser**... Idaho. Forest, Wildlife, and Range Experiment Station. Information Series [*A publication*]
**Idaho For Wildl Range Exp Stn Note**... Idaho. Forest, Wildlife, and Range Experiment Station. Note [*A publication*]
**Idaho For Wildl Range Exp Stn Pap**... Idaho. Forest, Wildlife, and Range Experiment Station. Paper [*A publication*]
**Idaho For Wildl Range Exp Stn Stn Note**... Idaho. Forest, Wildlife, and Range Experiment Station. Station Note [*A publication*]
**Idaho For Wildl Range Exp Stn Tech Rep**... Idaho. Forest, Wildlife, and Range Experiment Station. Technical Report [*A publication*]

**Idaho Libn** ... Idaho Librarian [*A publication*]
**Idaho Librn** ... Idaho Librarian [*A publication*]
**Idaho LJ** .... Idaho Law Journal [*A publication*] (DLA)
**Idaho L Rev** ... Idaho Law Review [*A publication*]
**Idaho Min Industry Ann Rept** ... Idaho Mining Industry. Annual Report [*A publication*]
**Idaho NS**.... Idaho Reports, New Series [*A publication*] (DLA)
**Idaho Power Co Bull** ... Idaho Power Company. Bulletin [*A publication*]
**Idaho Sess Laws** ... Session Laws of Idaho [*A publication*] (DLA)
**Idaho Stat**.. Idaho Statesman [*A publication*]
**Idaho State Hortic Assoc Proc Annu Conv** ... Idaho. State Horticultural Association. Proceedings of the Annual Convention [*A publication*]
**Idaho Univ Agric Exp Stn Curr Inf Ser** ... Idaho University. Agricultural Experiment Station. Current Information Series [*A publication*]
**Idaho Univ Curr Inf Ser** ... Idaho University. Current Information Series [*A publication*]
**Idaho Univ Eng Exp Sta Bull** ... Idaho University. Engineering Experiment Station. Bulletin [*A publication*]
**Idaho Univ For Range Wildl Exp Stn Res Note** ... Idaho University. Forest, Range, and Wildlife Experiment Station. Research Note [*A publication*]
**Idaho Univ Water Resour Res Inst Res Tech Completion Rep** ... Idaho University. Water Resources Research Institute. Research Technical Completion Report [*A publication*]
**Idaho Yest** ... Idaho Yesterdays [*A publication*]
**Ida IAB** ...... Idaho Industrial Accident Board Reports [*A publication*] (DLA)
**IdAlN**......... Albion State Normal School, Albion, ID [*Library symbol*] [*Library of Congress*] (LCLS)
**Ida LR**........ Idaho Law Review [*A publication*]
**IdAlS**.......... Southern Idaho College of Education, Albion, ID [*Library symbol*] [*Library of Congress*] [*Obsolete*] (LCLS)
**IDAM**........ Indexed Direct Access Method
**IDAMIS**.... Integrated Drug Abuse Management Information Systems
**IDAMS**...... Image Display and Manipulation System [*NASA*]
**IDAMS**...... Isotope Dilution Analysis Mass Spectrometry
**IDAMST**... Integrated Digital Avionics for Medium STOL Transport (MCD)
**IDAN**......... Idan Software Industries ISI Ltd. [*NASDAQ symbol*] (NQ)
**IDanvi**........ Danville Public Library, Danville, IL [*Library symbol*] [*Library of Congress*] (LCLS)
**IDanviC**..... Danville Junior College, Danville, IL [*Library symbol*] [*Library of Congress*] (LCLS)
**IDanviL**...... Lake View Memorial Hospital, Doctor's Library, Danville, IL [*Library symbol*] [*Library of Congress*] (LCLS)
**IDanviStE** ... Saint Elizabeth Hospital, Danville, IL [*Library symbol*] [*Library of Congress*] (LCLS)
**IDanviVA** .. United States Veterans Administration Hospital, Danville, IL [*Library symbol*] [*Library of Congress*] (LCLS)
**IDAP**.......... Industrial Design Assistance Program [*National Design Council, Canada*]
**IDAP**.......... Internal Development and Assistance Program (AFM)
**IDAP**.......... International Development and Assistance Program (KSC)
**IDAP**.......... Isomorphously Doped Ammonium Perchlorate
**IDAP**.......... Iterative Differential Analyzer Pinboard
**IDAPS**....... Image Data Processing System
**IDARP**....... Integrated Drug Abuse Reporting Process [*National Institutes of Health*]
**IDAS**.......... Information Displays Automatic Drafting System (IEEE)
**IDAS**.......... Instrument Data Acquisition System
**IDAS**.......... Integrated Data Acquisition System (MCD)
**IDAS**.......... Integrated Design Automation System (MCD)
**IDAS**.......... International Database Access Service [*Bahrain Telecommunications Co.*] [*Information service or system*] (IID)
**IDAS**.......... Intrusion Detection Alarm System
**IDAS**.......... Iterative Differential Analyzer Slave
**IDAST**....... Interpolated Data and Speech Transmission [*Data processing*]
**Ida Supp**..... Idaho Supplement [*A publication*] (DLA)
**IDAT**......... Interfacility Data [*FAA*] (FAAC)
**IDATU**...... Irish Distributive and Administrative Trade Union (EAIO)
**IDA (USA)** ... Indian Dental Association (USA) (EA)
**IDAV**......... Immune Deficiency Associated Virus
**IdB**............ Boise Public Library, Boise, ID [*Library symbol*] [*Library of Congress*] (LCLS)
**IDB**............ Illicit Diamond Buyer [*or Buying*]
**IDB**............ Illinois Central College, East Peoria, IL [*OCLC symbol*] (OCLC)
**IDB**............ In-Suit Drink Bag [*Aerospace*] (MCD)
**IDB**............ Inductance Decade Box
**IDB**............ Industrial Data Bank Department [*Gulf Organization for Industrial Consulting*] [*Information service or system*] (IID)
**IDB**............ Industrial Development Bank
**IDB**............ Industrial Development Bond
**IDB**............ Inertial Data Box (KSC)
**IDB**............ Infared Diving Binoculors (MCD)
**IDB**............ INPADOC [*International Patent Documentation Center*] Data Base [*Information service or system*] (CRD)
**IDB**............ Input Data Buffer
**IDB**............ Inspection Data Bulletin
**IDB**............ Insurance Development Bureau [*Guelph, ON*] (EAIO)
**IDB**............ Integrated Data Base [*Data processing*]
**IDB**............ Inter-American Defense Board (EA)
**IDB**............ Inter-American Development Bank [*Also, IADB*]
**IDB**............ Inter-Dealer Broker [*British*]
**IDB**............ Inter-Dynamic Balance
**IDB**............ Interaction Database
**IDB**............ Intercept During Boost [*Aerospace*]
**IDB**............ International Data Base [*Bureau of Census*] [*Database*]
**IDB**............ Interpreter's Dictionary of the Bible
**IDB**............ Inverni & Della Beffa [*Italy*] [*Research code symbol*]
**IDB**............ Islamic Development Bank [*Saudi Arabia*]
**IDBA**......... International Deli-Bakery Association (EA)
**IdBB**.......... Boise State College, Boise, ID [*Library symbol*] [*Library of Congress*] (LCLS)
**IDBB**.......... IDB Bankholding Corp. Ltd. [*NASDAQ symbol*] (NQ)
**IdBfGS**....... Church of Jesus Christ of Latter-Day Saints, Genealogical Society Library, Blackfoot West Branch, Stake Center, Blackfoot, ID [*Library symbol*] [*Library of Congress*] (LCLS)
**IdBLM-B**... Bureau of Land Management, Boise, ID [*Library symbol*] [*Library of Congress*] (LCLS)
**IDBMA**..... International Data Base Management Association (EA)
**IdBMK**....... Morrison-Krudsen Co., Inc., Records and Micrographics Center, Boise, ID [*Library symbol*] [*Library of Congress*] (LCLS)
**IDBMS**...... Integrated Database Management System
**IDBN**......... Integrated Digital Backbone Network [*Telecommunications*]
**Id-BPH**...... Idaho State Library, Blind and Physically Handicapped Services, Boise, ID [*Library symbol*] [*Library of Congress*] (LCLS)
**IDBRA**....... International Drivers' Behaviour Research Association [*Paris, France*] (EAIO)
**IdBurGS**.... Church of Jesus Christ of Latter-Day Saints, Genealogical Society Library, Burley Branch, Burley, ID [*Library symbol*] [*Library of Congress*] (LCLS)
**IDBX**.......... IDB Communications Group, Inc. [*Culver City, CA*] [*NASDAQ symbol*] (NQ)
**IdC**............ Coeur D'Alene Public Library, Coeur D'Alene, ID [*Library symbol*] [*Library of Congress*] (LCLS)
**IDC**............ Idiopathic Dilated Cardiomyopathy [*Cardiology*]
**IDC**............ Image Dissector Camera
**IDC**............ IMBLMS [*Integrated Medical Behavioral Measurement System*] Digital Computer (MCD)
**IDC**............ Imperial Defence College [*British*]
**IDC**............ Indirect Costs
**IDC**............ Individual Defense Counsel
**IDC**............ Industrial Design Certificate [*British*]
**IDC**............ Industrial Development Certificate [*Department of Industry*] [*British*]
**IDC**............ Industrial Development Corporation
**IDC**............ Information Design Change (NG)
**IDC**............ Information and Direction Center
**IDC**............ Information and Documentation Center [*Royal Institute of Technology Library*] [*Information service or system*] (IID)
**IDC**............ Information Dynamics Corporation
**IDC**............ Infrared Detector Cryostat
**IDC**............ Input Display Console [*Data processing*]
**IDC**............ Inspection Data Card (MCD)
**I/D & C**...... Instrumentation/Displays and Controls [*Subsystem*] (MCD)
**IDC**............ Intangible Drilling Costs [*Petroleum industry*]
**IDC**............ Integrated Device Controller
**IDC**............ Integrated Disk Control [*NCR Corp.*]
**IDC**............ Integrated Displays and Controls (MCD)
**IDC**............ Inter Documentation Company AG, Zug, Switzerland [*Library symbol*] [*Library of Congress*] (LCLS)
**IDC**............ Interactive Data Class [*Telecommunications*]
**IDC**............ Interceptor Distance Computer
**IDC**............ Interdepartmental Committee
**IDC**............ Interdepartmental Communication
**IDC**............ Interest During Construction
**IDC**............ Interface Document Control (MCD)
**IDC**............ Interior Designers of Canada [*See also DIC*]
**IDC**............ Internal Data Channel
**IDC**............ Internal Document Control
**IDC**............ International Dairy Committee
**IDC**............ International Dance Council [*See also CIDD*] (EAIO)
**IDC**............ International Data Corporation [*Information service or system*] (IID)
**IDC**............ International Development Conference (EA)
**IDC**............ International Development Corporation [*Proposed corporation to combine Alliance for Progress and Agency for International Development*]
**IDC**............ International Diamond Council [*Antwerp, Belgium*] (EAIO)
**IDC**............ International Diastema Club (EA)
**IDC**............ International Display Corporation [*Vancouver Stock Exchange symbol*]
**IDC**............ International Documentation Center

**IDC** ........... International Documentation in Chemistry (DIT)
**IDC** ........... International Drycleaners Congress (EA)
**IDC** ........... Internationale Dokumentationsgesellschaft fuer Chemie [*International Company for Documentation in Chemistry*] [*Frankfurt, West Germany*]
**IDC** ........... Intraductal Carcinoma [*Oncology*]
**IDC** ........... Intransit Data Card (AFM)
**IDC** ........... Inventor's Desktop Companion [*A publication*]
**IDC** ........... Iodine Dextrin Color
**IDC** ........... Iranian Democratic Committee (EA)
**IDC** ........... Irrigated, Double Cropped [*Agriculture*]
**IDC** ........... Item Design Change
**IDC** ........... Item Detail Card [*Military*] (AABC)
**IDC** ........... Peoples Gas, Light & Coke Co., Chicago, IL [*OCLC symbol*] (OCLC)
**IdCa** ........... Caldwell Public Library, Caldwell, ID [*Library symbol*] [*Library of Congress*] (LCLS)
**ID(C)A** ....... Indecent Displays (Control) Act [*British*]
**IDCA** ......... Indian Diamond and Colorstone Association (EA)
**IDCA** ......... International Design Conference in Aspen (EA)
**IDCA** ......... International Development Cooperation Act of 1979
**IDCA** ......... [*US*] International Development Cooperation Agency [*Independent government agency*]
**IDCA** ......... International Dragon Class Association (EAIO)
**ID & CA** ..... Inverter Distribution and Control Assembly (MCD)
**IdCaC** ......... College of Idaho, Caldwell, ID [*Library symbol*] [*Library of Congress*] (LCLS)
**IDCAS** ....... Industrial Development Center for Arab States [*Later, AIDO*]
**IDCC** .......... Integrated Data Communications Controller
**IDCC** .......... INTEK Diversified Corporation [*NASDAQ symbol*] (NQ)
**IDCC** .......... Interactive Display and Control Component (MCD)
**IDCCC** ....... Interim Data Communications Collection Center
**IDCCC** ....... International Dredging Conference Coordinating Committee (EAIO)
**IDCDA** ...... Independent Dealer Committee Dedicated to Action (EA)
**IDCFC** ....... International David Cassidy Fan Club (EAIO)
**IDCIDC** ...... International Development Research Centre. Publication IDRC [*A publication*]
**IDCL** .......... Information Design Change List (MCD)
**IDCMA** ..... Independent Data Communications Manufacturers Association (EA)
**IDCN** ......... Interchangeability Document Change Notice (KSC)
**IdCN** .......... North Idaho College, Coeur d'Alene, ID [*Library symbol*] [*Library of Congress*] (LCLS)
**IDCNA** ...... Insulation Distributor Contractors National Association [*Later, NICA*] (EA)
**IDCNY** ...... International Design Center, New York
**IDCOR** ...... Industry Degraded Core Rulemaking Program [*Nuclear industry sponsored group*]
**IDCP** .......... International Data Collecting Platform (TEL)
**IDCQA** ...... Industrie Ceramique [*A publication*]
**IDCR** ......... Interchangeability Document Change Request (MCD)
**IDCR** ......... International Decade of Cetacean Research
**IDCS** .......... IDC Services, Inc. [*Chicago, IL*] [*NASDAQ symbol*] (NQ)
**IDCS** .......... Image Dissector Camera System
**IDCS** .......... Initial Defense Communications Satellite (MCD)
**IDCS** .......... Instrumentation/Data Collection System
**IDCS** .......... Integrated Data Coding System (NG)
**IDCS** .......... International Digital Channel Service [*Federal Trade Commission*]
**IDCSP** ....... Initial Defense Communications Satellite Program [*or Project*]
**IDCSP** ....... Interim Defense Communications Satellite Program [*DoD*]
**IDCSP-A** ... Initial Defense Communications Satellite Program-Augmented (CET)
**IDCSS** ....... Initial Defense Communications Satellite System (NATG)
**IDCT** .......... Integrated Daily Cycle Test (MCD)
**IDCTR** ....... Inductor (MSA)
**IDD** ........... Detroit Diesel Allison Division, General Motors Corp., Indianapolis, IN [*OCLC symbol*] (OCLC)
**IDD** ........... Illicit Diamond Dealing (ROG)
**IDD** ........... Image Definition Device
**IDD** ........... Indirect by Direct (MCD)
**IDD** ........... Industrial Development Division [*Vietnam*]
**IDD** ........... Infant Development Distress Syndrome [*Medicine*] (ADA)
**IDD** ........... Insulin-Dependent Diabetes
**IDD** ........... Integrated Data Dictionary
**IDD** ........... Inter-Director Designation (NG)
**IDD** ........... Interface Definition Document (MCD)
**IDD** ........... Interface Designation Drawing
**IDD** ........... Interim Drydocking [*Navy*] (NVT)
**IDD** ........... International Direct Dialing [*Telecommunications*]
**IDD** ........... International Dorado Resources [*Vancouver Stock Exchange symbol*]
**IDD** ........... Inventory to Diagnose Depression [*Psychology*]
**IDD** ........... Iowa State University of Science and Technology. Doctoral Dissertations. Abstracts and References [*A publication*]
**IDDA** ......... International Dairy-Deli Association (EA)
**IDDC** ......... International Demographic Data Center [*Bureau of the Census*] [*Database*] [*Information service or system*] (IID)
**IDDC** ......... International Development Data Center [*Georgia Institute of Technology*]
**IDDD** ......... International Demographic Data Directory [*Agency for International Development*] (IID)
**IDDD** ......... International Direct Distance Dialing [*AT & T*]
**IDDF** .......... Intermediate Digital Distribution Frame [*Telecommunications*] (TEL)
**Iddings DRB** ... Iddings' Dayton Term Reports [*Ohio*] [*A publication*] (DLA)
**Iddings TRD** ... Iddings' Dayton Term Reports [*Ohio*] [*A publication*] (DLA)
**IDDIS** ........ IDD Information Services, Inc. (EISS)
**IDDJ** .......... Interim Decisions of the Department of Justice
**IDDM** ........ Insulin-Dependent Diabetes Mellitus
**IDDP** ......... Interface Design Definition Paper [*Military*] (CAAL)
**IDDP** ......... International Dairy Development Programme [*Formed by a merger of FAO/DANIDA Dairy Development Programme and International Scheme for the Coordination of Dairy Development*] [*United Nations*] (EAIO)
**IDDP** ......... Isodecyl Diphenyl Phosphate [*Organic chemistry*]
**IDDRG** ...... International Deep Drawing Research Group [*British*]
**IdDrGS** ...... Church of Jesus Christ of Latter-Day Saints, Genealogical Society Library, Driggs Branch, Driggs, ID [*Library symbol*] [*Library of Congress*] (LCLS)
**IDDS** .......... Improved Data Display System
**IDDS** .......... Instrumentation Data Distribution System (MUGU)
**IDDS** .......... Integrated Data Display System
**IDDS** .......... International Dairy Development Scheme
**IDDS** .......... International Digital Data Service [*Western Union Corp.*] [*Data transmission service*]
**IDD TR** ...... Iddings' Dayton Term Reports [*Ohio*] [*A publication*] (DLA)
**IDE** ............ Idea. The Journal of Law and Technology [*A publication*]
**IDE** ............ Industry-Developed Equipment (AAG)
**IDE** ............ Infrared Decoy Evaluator
**IDE** ............ Initial Design Evaluation (MCD)
**IDE** ............ Institute for Democratic Education [*Absorbed by Anti-Defamation League of B'nai B'rith*] (EA)
**IDE** ............ Institute of Developing Economics, Tokyo [*UTLAS symbol*]
**IDE** ............ Insulin-Degrading Enzyme [*Biochemistry*]
**IDE** ............ Integrated Development Environment
**IDE** ............ Integrated Device Electronics
**IDE** ............ Intelligent Drive Electronics
**IDE** ............ Interactive Data Entry
**IDE** ............ Interim Data Element [*Army*] (AABC)
**IDE** ............ Intrusion Detection Equipment
**IDE** ............ Investigational Device Exemption [*Food and Drug Administration*]
**IDE** ............ Isla Desecheo [*Puerto Rico*] [*Seismograph station code, US Geological Survey*] (SEIS)
**Idea** ........... Idea. The Journal of Law and Technology [*A publication*]
**IDEA** ......... Ideas/Idees. Department of Indian and Northern Affairs [*A publication*]
**IDEA** ......... IDEAssociates, Inc. [*Telecommunications*] (TSSD)
**IDEA** ......... Identification, Distribution, and Exchange for Action [*Project*]
**IDEA** ......... Improved Data Effectiveness and Availability
**IDEA** ......... Index for Design Engineering Applications [*Data retrieval service*] [*Product engineering*]
**IDEA** ......... Inductive Data Exploration and Analysis [*Data processing*]
**I/D/E/A** .... Institute for Development of Educational Activities (EA)
**IDEA** ......... Interactive Data Entry Access [*Data General Corp.*]
**IDEA** ......... Interface and Display Electronics Assembly
**IDEA** ......... International Dalkon Shield Victims Education Association (EA)
**IDEA** ......... International Dance-Exercise Association (EA)
**IDEA** ......... International Desalination and Environmental Association [*Later, IDA*] (EA)
**IDEA** ......... International Downtown Executives Association [*Later, IDA*] (EA)
**IDEA** ......... Invention, Design, Engineering Associates, Inc. [*NASDAQ symbol*] (NQ)
**IDEA** ......... Isolation of Dimensions and Elimination of Alternatives
**Idea** ........... Patent, Trademark, and Copyright Journal of Research and Education [*A publication*] (DLA)
**IDEALS** ..... Ideal Design of Effective and Logical Systems
**IDEALS** ..... Institute for the Development of Emotional and Life Skills (EA)
**Ideal Stud** ... Idealistic Studies [*A publication*]
**IDEAS** ....... Institutional Development and Economic Affairs Service (EA)
**IDEAS** ....... Integrated Design Analysis System [*Space shuttle*] [*NASA*]
**IDEAS** ....... Integrated Design and Engineering Automated System (IEEE)
**IDEAS** ....... Intelligence Data Element Authorization Standards [*Military*] (MCD)
**IDEAS** ....... Interest Determination and Assessment System [*Vocational guidance test*]
**IDEAS** ....... International Development - Economics Awareness System
**Ideas Manage** ... Ideas for Management [*A publication*]
**Ideas for Mgmt** ... Ideas for Management [*A publication*]
**IDec** ........... Decatur Public Library, Decatur, IL [*Library symbol*] [*Library of Congress*] (LCLS)
**IDEC** .......... Interior Design Educators Council (EA)
**IDEC** .......... International Drug Enforcement Conference
**IDecH** ........ Decatur Memorial Hospital, Medical Staff and Nursing School Library, Decatur, IL [*Library symbol*] [*Library of Congress*] (LCLS)

**IDecJ** ......... James Millikin University, Decatur, IL [*Library symbol*] [*Library of Congress*] (LCLS)
**IDecM**........ Adolph Meyer Mental Health Center, Decatur, IL [*Library symbol*] [*Library of Congress*] (LCLS)
**IDecR**......... Rolling Prairie Libraries, Decatur, IL [*Library symbol*] [*Library of Congress*] (LCLS)
**IDECS** ....... Image Discrimination, Enhancement, and Combination System [*Electronic optical system*]
**IDecStM**.... Saint Mary's Hospital, Medical Staff and Nursing Library, Decatur, IL [*Library symbol*] [*Library of Congress*] (LCLS)
**IDEDS** ....... International Development Education Documentation Service [*University of Pittsburgh*] (IID)
**IDEEA**....... Information and Data Exchange Experimental Activities
**IDEEA**....... International Defense Equipment Exhibitors Association (EA)
**IDEF**.......... Institut International de Droit d'Expression Francaise [*International Institute of Law of the French Speaking Countries - IILFSC*] [*Paris, France*] (EAIO)
**IDEF**.......... Integrated System Definition Language [*Data processing*] (IEEE)
**Ideggyogy Sz** ... Ideggyogyaszati Szemle [*A publication*]
**Ideggyogy Szle** ... Ideggyogyaszati Szemle [*A publication*]
**IDeKN** ....... Northern Illinois University, De Kalb, IL [*Library symbol*] [*Library of Congress*] (LCLS)
**IDeKN-LS** ... Northern Illinois University, Department of Library Sciences, De Kalb, IL [*Library symbol*] [*Library of Congress*] (LCLS)
**IDEL**.......... Ideal School Supply Corp. [*Oak Lawn, IL*] [*NASDAQ symbol*] (NQ)
**IDelan**........ Goose Creek Township Carnegie Library, De Land, IL [*Library symbol*] [*Library of Congress*] (LCLS)
**IDelanSD**... Bond County Community Unit, School District 2, De Land, IL [*Library symbol*] [*Library of Congress*] (LCLS)
**IDelav** ........ Ayer Public Library, Delavan, IL [*Library symbol*] [*Library of Congress*] (LCLS)
**Idemitsu Pet J** ... Idemitsu Petroleum Journal [*Japan*] [*A publication*]
**Idengaku Zasshi Suppl** ... Idengaku Zasshi. Supplement [*Japan*] [*A publication*]
**IDENT**....... Identical (MSA)
**IDENT**....... Identification (AFM)
**IDENTIFD** ... Identified (ROG)
**Ideo** ........... Ideological
**IDep** .......... DePue Public Library, DePue, IL [*Library symbol*] [*Library of Congress*] (LCLS)
**IDEP**.......... Industry Data Exchange Program
**IDEP**.......... Institut Africain de Developpement Economique et de Planification [*African Institute for Economic Development and Planning*] (EAIO)
**IDEP**.......... Inter-Department Data Exchange Program [*Air Force*] (AFM)
**IDEP**.......... Interagency Data Exchange Program [*Later, GIDEP*] (RDA)
**IDEP**.......... Interservice Data Exchange Program (AFIT)
**IDEP**.......... Ion Density Electronics Package
**IDepSD**...... DePue Unit, School District 103, DePue, IL [*Library symbol*] [*Library of Congress*] (LCLS)
**IDERA**....... International Development Education Resources Association
**IDES**.......... Image Dissector Echelle Spectrograph [*Instrumentation*]
**IDES**.......... Institute for Demographic and Economic Studies [*Research center*] (RCD)
**IDES**.......... Integrated Defense System
**IDES**.......... Interactive Drawing Editing Station (MCD)
**IDesA**......... American Foundrymen's Society, Des Plaines, IL [*Library symbol*] [*Library of Congress*] (LCLS)
**IDesB** ......... Borg-Warner Corp., Ingersoll Research Center, Des Plaines, IL [*Library symbol*] [*Library of Congress*] (LCLS)
**IDesD**......... De Soto, Inc., Des Plaines, IL [*Library symbol*] [*Library of Congress*] (LCLS)
**IDES/DE**... Desarrollo Economico. Instituto de Desarrollo Economico y Social [*A publication*]
**IDesN** ........ National Association of Independent Insurers, Des Plaines, IL [*Library symbol*] [*Library of Congress*] (LCLS)
**IDesU** ........ Universal Oil Products Co., Des Plaines, IL [*Library symbol*] [*Library of Congress*] (LCLS)
**IDEX**.......... Initial Defense Experiment (IEEE)
**IDF**............ Belleville Area College, Belleville, IL [*OCLC symbol*] (OCLC)
**IDf**............. Deerfield Public Library, Deerfield, IL [*Library symbol*] [*Library of Congress*] (LCLS)
**IDF**............ Image Description File
**IDF**............ Immune Deficiency Foundation (EA)
**IDF**............ In-Flight Diverted Force (CINC)
**IDF**............ Innovative Design Fund, Inc. (EA)
**IDF**............ Instantaneous Direction Finding (MCD)
**IDF**............ Integrated Data File
**IDF**............ Interactive Dialogue Facility [*Programming language*] (CSR)
**IDF**............ Interceptor Day Fighter (NATG)
**IDF**............ Intermediate Distributing Frame [*Telecommunications*]
**IDF**............ Internal Delay Factor [*Data processing*]
**IDF**............ International Dairy Federation [*See also FIL*] [*Brussels, Belgium*] (EAIO)
**IDF**............ International Democratic Fellowship
**IDF**............ International Dental Federation [*British*]
**IDF**............ International Development Foundation (EA)
**IDF**............ International Diabetes Federation [*See also FID*] (EA)
**IDF**............ International Distress Frequency (MUGU)
**IDF**............ International Domesticated Furs Ltd. [*Vancouver Stock Exchange symbol*]
**IDF**............ International Drilling Federation (EA)
**IDF**............ Isotropic Distribution Function
**IDF**............ Israeli Defense Forces
**IDF**............ Item Data File (MCD)
**IDFB**.......... Internationales Daunen- und Federn-Bureau [*International Down and Feather Bure au*] (EAIO)
**IDFF** .......... Internationale Demokratische Frauenfoederation [*Women's International Democratic Federation*]
**IDFM**......... Induced Directional FM
**IDFN** ......... In Domino Fiducia Nostra [*In the Lord Is Our Trust*] [*Latin*] [*Motto of August, Prince of Anhalt-Plotzkau (1575-1653)*]
**IDFOR**....... Idle Waiting Convoy Forward [*Vessel status*] [*Navy*]
**IDFR**.......... Identified Friendly [*Military*]
**IDFS**.......... Interferometer Direction Finding System [*Military*] (CAAL)
**IDFSS**........ Infantry Direct-Fire Simulation System (MCD)
**IDFT**.......... Inverse Discrete Fourier Transform [*Electronics*] (IEEE)
**IDfT** .......... Trinity Evangelical Divinity School, Deerfield, IL [*Library symbol*] [*Library of Congress*] (LCLS)
**IDFTA**....... International Dwarf Fruit Trees Association (EA)
**IDfTD**........ Trinity Evangelical Divinity School, Deerfield, IL [*Library symbol*] [*Library of Congress*] (LCLS)
**IDFUN** ...... International Dull Folks Unlimited (EA)
**IDFV**.......... In Deo Faciemus Virtutem [*Through God We Shall Do Valiantly*] [*Latin*] [*(Ps., IX. 12) Motto of August, Prince of Anhalt-Plotzkau (1575-1653)*]
**IDFW**......... Institute for a Drug-Free Workplace (EA)
**IDG**............ Chicago Theological Seminary, Chicago, IL [*OCLC symbol*] (OCLC)
**IDG**............ Ida Grove, IA [*Location identifier*] [*FAA*] (FAAL)
**IDG**............ Indigo Technologies, Inc. [*Vancouver Stock Exchange symbol*]
**IDG**............ Individual Drop Glider
**IDG**............ Industrial Development Group (MCD)
**IDG**............ Inniskilling Dragoon Guards [*British military*] (DMA)
**IDG**............ Inspector of Degaussing [*Navy*]
**IDG**............ Integrated Drive Generator (MCD)
**IDG**............ Internal Drive Generator
**IDG**............ International Data Group [*Publisher of computer magazines*] [*Framingham, MA*]
**IDG**............ Irish Distillers Group (ECON)
**Idg B** .......... Indogermanische Bibliothek [*A publication*]
**IDG/CMG** ... IDG Conference Management Group [*Framingham, MA*] (TSSD)
**IDGEAH** ... Industrial Gerontology [*A publication*]
**Idg Forsch** ... Indogermanische Forschungen [*A publication*]
**IDGI** .......... International Design Group, Inc. [*NASDAQ symbol*] (NQ)
**IDGIT**........ Integrated Data Generation Implementation Technique
**IDH**........... Isocitrate Dehydrogenase [*Also, ICD, ICDH*] [*An enzyme*]
**IDH**........... Meadville Theological School, Chicago, IL [*OCLC symbol*] (OCLC)
**IDHA**......... International District Heating Association [*Later, IDHCA*] (EA)
**IDHAA**....... Industrie und Handel [*A publication*]
**IDHCA**...... International District Heating and Cooling Association (EA)
**IDHEC** ...... Institut des Hautes Etudes Cinematographiques [*French institute for the study of the motion picture*]
**IDHF** ......... International Dental Health Foundation (EA)
**IDHHB**...... Institute for the Development of the Harmonious Human Being (EA)
**IdHi** ........... Idaho State Historical Society, Boise, ID [*Library symbol*] [*Library of Congress*] (LCLS)
**IDHIDH**.... In dem Herrn Ist das Heil [*In the Lord Is Salvation*] [*German*] [*Motto of Dorothee, Princess of Anhalt (1580-1618)*]
**IdHi-G** ....... Idaho Genealogical Society, Boise, ID [*Library symbol*] [*Library of Congress*] (LCLS)
**IDHLA9** .... International Digest of Health Legislation [*A publication*]
**IDHOA**...... Proceedings. International District Heating Association [*A publication*]
**IDHS** ......... Information Data Handling System
**IDHS** ......... Integrated Data Handling System
**IDHS** ......... Intelligence Data Handling System (AFM)
**IDHSC**....... Intelligence Data Handling System Communications (MCD)
**IDI** ............ Bethany and Northern Baptist Theological Seminaries Library, Oak Brook, IL [*OCLC symbol*] (OCLC)
**IDI** ............ Improved Data Interchange
**IDI** ............ Indiana, PA [*Location identifier*] [*FAA*] (FAAL)
**IDI** ............ Indirect Injection Engine [*Engineering*]
**IDI** ............ Induction-Delivery Interval [*Medicine*]
**IDI** ............ Industrial Designers' Institute [*Later, IDSA*] (EA)
**IDI** ............ Industrial Development Institute [*France*]
**IDI** ............ Information Dimensions, Incorporated [*Information service or system*] (IID)
**IDI** ............ Inspection Departmental Instruction (AAG)
**IDI** ............ Institut de Droit International [*Institute of International Law*]
**IDI** ............ Instrumentation Data Items (NASA)
**IDI** ............ Integrated Design Inspection (NRCH)
**IDI** ............ Intelligent Dual Interface

**IDI** ............ Intercomp Design, Incorporated [*Neshanic Station, NJ*] [*Telecommunications*] (TSSD)
**IDI** ............ Interdivision Invoice (AAG)
**IDI** ............ International Defense Intelligence [*A publication*]
**IDI** ............ International Development Institute [*Agency for International Development program*]
**IDI** ............ International Dialect Institute
**IDI** ............ Intractable Diarrhea of Infancy [*Pediatrics*]
**IDI** ............ Ion Dipole Interaction
**IDI** ............ Management Today [*A publication*]
**IDIA** .......... Industrial Disputes Investigation Act [*Canada*]
**IDIA** .......... Informativo de Investigaciones Agricolas [*A publication*]
**IDIA Supl** .. IDIA [*Informativo de Investigaciones Agricolas*]. Suplemento [*A publication*]
**IDIC** .......... Institut de Developpement International et de Cooperation [*Institute for International Development and Cooperation - IIDC*] [*University of Ottawa*] [*Canada*]
**IDIC** .......... Intelligence Division Indications Center [*Military*] (MCD)
**IDIC** .......... Internal Dose Information Center [*ORNL*]
**IDID** .......... Industrial Documentation and Information Department [*Industrial Development Center for Arab States*] [*Information service or system*] (IID)
**IdIf** ............ Idaho Falls Public Library, Idaho Falls, ID [*Library symbol*] [*Library of Congress*] (LCLS)
**IdIfA** .......... Aerojet Nuclear Co., Idaho Falls, ID [*Library symbol*] [*Library of Congress*] (LCLS)
**IdIfGS** ........ Church of Jesus Christ of Latter-Day Saints, Genealogical Society Library, Idaho Falls Branch, Idaho Falls, ID [*Library symbol*] [*Library of Congress*] (LCLS)
**IDIIOM** ..... Information Displays, Incorporated, Input-Output Machine
**IDIMS** ....... Interactive Digital Image Manipulation System [*Minicomputer*]
**Idings TRD** ... Iddings' Dayton Term Reports [*Ohio*] [*A publication*] (DLA)
**IDIOT** ........ Instrumentation Digital On-Line Transcriber [*Data processing*]
**IDIP** ........... Intelligence Data Input Package (MCD)
**IDIP** ........... Intensified Drug Inspection Program [*FDA*]
**IDIP** ........... International Directories in Print [*A publication*]
**IDIS** ........... Idaho Drug Information Service [*Information service or system*] (IID)
**IDIS** ........... Institut fuer Dokumentation und Information ueber Sozialmedizin und Oeffentliches Gesundheitswesen [*Institute for Documentation and Information in Social Medicine and Public Health*] [*Information retrieval*] [*Federal Republic of Germany*]
**IDIS** ........... Institut fuer Dokumentation, Information, und Statistik [*Institute for Documentation, Information, and Statistics*] [*Information service or system*] (IID)
**IDIS** ........... Iowa Drug Information Service [*University of Iowa*] [*Information service or system*] (IID)
**IDIU** ........... Interdivisional Information Unit [*Department of Justice intelligence unit*]
**IDJ** ............. Catholic Theological Union, Chicago, IL [*OCLC symbol*] (OCLC)
**IDJ** ............. I Dance Jazz [*Jazz music group*] (ECON)
**idJ** .............. In Diesem Jahr [*In This Year*] [*German*] [*Correspondence*]
**IDJC** ........... India Docks Joint Committee (ROG)
**IDJOAS** .... International Dental Journal [*A publication*]
**IDK** ............ Internal Derangement of Knee Joint
**IDK** ............ Jesuit-Krauss-McCormick Library, Chicago, IL [*OCLC symbol*] (OCLC)
**IDKKB** ....... Iwate Daigaku Kyoikugakubu Kenkyu Nenpo [*A publication*]
**IDKKBM** ... Annual Report. Faculty of Education. University of Iwate [*A publication*]
**IDKSA** ....... Ibaraki Daigaku Kogakubu Kenkyu Shuho [*A publication*]
**Id-L** ............ Idaho Supreme Court, Idaho State Law Library, Boise, ID [*Library symbol*] [*Library of Congress*] (LCLS)
**IDL** ............ Ideal Basic Industries, Inc. [*NYSE symbol*] (SPSG)
**IDL** ............ Ideal Group of Companies, Inc. [*Toronto Stock Exchange symbol*]
**IDL** ............ Idler
**IDL** ............ Indentured Drawing List
**IDL** ............ Index to Dental Literature [*A publication*]
**IDL** ............ Indianola, MS [*Location identifier*] [*FAA*] (FAAL)
**ID(L)** .......... Infantry Division (Light) [*Army*] (INF)
**IDL** ............ Information Description Language
**IDL** ............ Instruction Definition Language
**IDL** ............ Instructional Development Laboratory [*University of Minnesota of Minneapolis Saint Paul*] [*Research center*] (RCD)
**IDL** ............ Instrument Development Laboratories
**IDL** ............ Interdisciplinary Materials Laboratory [*Various universities*]
**IDL** ............ Intermediate Density Lipoprotein [*Biochemistry*]
**IDL** ............ International Date Line (MCD)
**IDL** ............ Isotope Development Limited
**IDL** ............ Rush University, Chicago, IL [*OCLC symbol*] (OCLC)
**IDLC** .......... Integrated Digital Logic Circuit
**IDLE** .......... Idle Wild Foods, Inc. [*NASDAQ symbol*] (NQ)
**IDLEB** ....... Industrial Engineering [*A publication*]
**IdLGS** ........ Church of Jesus Christ of Latter-Day Saints, Genealogical Society Library, Lewiston Branch, Stake Center, Lewiston, ID [*Library symbol*] [*Library of Congress*] (LCLS)
**IDLH** ......... Immediately Dangerous to Life and Health
**IDLIS** ........ International Desert Locust Information Service
**ID LJ** ......... Idaho Law Journal [*A publication*] (DLA)
**IdLN** .......... Lewis-Clark State College, Lewiston, ID [*Library symbol*] [*Library of Congress*] (LCLS)
**IdLNP** ........ Nez Perce County Free Library District, Lewiston, ID [*Library symbol*] [*Library of Congress*] (LCLS)
**IDLOD** ...... Idle Waiting to Load [*Shipping*]
**ID LR** ......... Idaho Law Review [*A publication*]
**IDLR** .......... Instrumentation Development Laboratory Report (MCD)
**IDL & RS** ... International Data Library and Reference Service
**IDLS** .......... Integrated Decoy Launching System [*Navy*] (CAAL)
**IDLT** .......... Identification Light
**IDLT** .......... Increment-Decrement Life Table [*Statistics*]
**IDM** ........... Ignition Diagnostic Monitor [*Automotive engineering*]
**IDM** ........... Illinois Valley Library System, Pekin, IL [*OCLC symbol*] (OCLC)
**IDM** ........... Indirect Method
**IDM** ........... Induced Dipole Moment
**IDM** ........... Infant of Diabetic Mother [*Medicine*]
**IDM** ........... Information Document Matching Program [*IRS*]
**IDM** ........... Integrative Decision Making (MCD)
**IDM** ........... Intelligent Database Machine [*Data processing*]
**IDM** ........... Interdiction Mission [*Air Force*]
**IDM** ........... International Direct Mail [*British*]
**IDM** ........... Interpolating Delta Modulator
**IDM** ........... Ion Drift Meter [*Instrumentation*]
**IDM** ........... Issue Definition Memorandum [*Jimmy Carter Administration*]
**IDMA** ........ International Destination Management Association (EAIO)
**IDMA** ........ International Doll Makers Association (EA)
**IDMA Bull** ... IDMA [*Indian Drug Manufacturers' Association*] Bulletin [*A publication*]
**IdMaGS** ..... Church of Jesus Christ of Latter-Day Saints, Genealogical Society Library, Malad Stake Branch, Malad City, ID [*Library symbol*] [*Library of Congress*] (LCLS)
**IDMAS** ...... Interactive Database Manipulator and Summarizer
**IDMB** ........ International Dictionary of Medicine and Biology [*A publication*]
**IDMC** ........ Interdigestive Motility Complex [*Gastroenterology*]
**IDMC** ........ International Dull Men's Club (EA)
**IDMGB** ..... Industrial Management [*A publication*]
**IDMH** ........ Input Destination Message Handler
**IDMI** ......... International Dun's Market Identifiers [*Dun & Bradstreet International*] [*Information service or system*] (IID)
**IDMM** ....... Intermediate and Depot Maintenance Manual (NASA)
**IdMoGS** ..... Church of Jesus Christ of Latter-Day Saints, Genealogical Society Library, Moore Branch, Lost River Stake Center, Moore, ID [*Library symbol*] [*Library of Congress*] (LCLS)
**IdMonGS** ... Church of Jesus Christ of Latter-Day Saints, Genealogical Society Library, Bear Lake Branch, Montpelier, ID [*Library symbol*] [*Library of Congress*] (LCLS)
**IDMP** ........ Intraductal Mammary Pressure
**IDMS** ......... Improved Deep Moored Sweep [*Military*] (MCD)
**IDMS** ......... Information for Decision-Makers System (MCD)
**IDMS** ......... Integrated Database Management System
**IDMS** ......... Integrated Disposal Management System [*DoD*]
**IDMS** ......... Isotope Dilution Mass Spectrometry
**IDN** ............ Chicago, IL [*Location identifier*] [*FAA*] (FAAL)
**IDN** ............ In Dei Nomine [*In God's Name*] [*Latin*]
**IDN** ............ Inanna's Descent to the Netherworld (BJA)
**IDN** ............ Indagen [*Papua New Guinea*] [*Airport symbol*] (OAG)
**IDN** ............ Indonesia [*ANSI three-letter standard code*] (CNC)
**IDN** ............ Inspection Due Notice [*Military*]
**IDN** ............ Integrated Digital Network [*Telecommunications*]
**IDN** ............ Intelligent Data Network
**IDN** ............ International Destron Technologies, Inc. [*Vancouver Stock Exchange symbol*]
**IDN** ............ United Way of Metropolitan Chicago, Chicago, IL [*OCLC symbol*] (OCLC)
**IDNE** ......... Indictione [*In the Indiction*] [*Latin*] (ROG)
**IDNF** ......... Irredundant Disjunctive Normal Formula
**IDNGA** ...... Ibaraki Daigaku Nogakubu Gakujutsu Hokoku [*A publication*]
**IDNHA** ...... Iwate Daigaku Nogakubu Hokoku [*A publication*]
**IDNIYRA** ... International DN [*Detroit News*] Ice Yacht Racing Association (EA)
**IdNN** .......... Northwest Nazarene College, Nampa, ID [*Library symbol*] [*Library of Congress*] (LCLS)
**IDNSS** ....... International Directory of Non-Official Statistical Sources [*A publication*]
**IdNTS** ........ National Reactor Testing Station, Technical Library, Phillips Petroleum Co., Idaho Falls, ID [*Library symbol*] [*Library of Congress*] (LCLS)
**IDO** ............ Idaho Operations Office [*Energy Research and Development Administration*] (MCD)
**IDO** ............ Identification Officer [*Military*]
**IDO** ............ Industrial Development Organization [*United Nations*]
**IDO** ............ Industrial Diesel Oil (ADA)
**IDO** ............ Infrared Drying Oven
**IDO** ............ Inspekteur der Ordnungspolizei [*Inspector of Uniformed Police*] [*German military - World War II*]
**IDO** ............ Intelligence Duty Officer
**IDO** ............ Interdivisional Operations [*NASA*] (NASA)

**IDO**........... Interdivisional Order
**IDO**........... Interim Development Order (ADA)
**IDO**........... International Disarmament Organization
**IDO**........... International District Office
**IdO**........... Osburn Public Library, Osburn, ID [*Library symbol*] [*Library of Congress*] (LCLS)
**IDO**........... Santa Isabel Do Morro [*Brazil*] [*Airport symbol*] (OAG)
**IDOC**......... Inside Diameter of Outer Conductor
**IDOC**......... International Documentation on the Contemporary Church [*Later, International Documentation and Communication Center*] (EA)
**IDOC Bul**.. IDOC [*International Documentation*] Bulletin [*A publication*]
**IDOCO**...... Internationale des Organisations Culturelles Ouvrieres [*Wimpassing, Austria*] (EAIO)
**IDOCS**....... Intrusion Detection Optical Communications System [*Computer system security*]
**IDOD**......... International Directory of Directories [*A publication*]
**IDOE**......... International Decade of Ocean Exploration [*1970's*]
**IDOFOR**... Improving the Definition of the Objective Force [*Military*]
**Idoj**........... Idojaras [*A publication*]
**IDOJA**....... Idojaras [*A publication*]
**IDol**........... Dolton Public Library District, Dolton, IL [*Library symbol*] [*Library of Congress*] (LCLS)
**IDON**......... Idongus [*Proper*] [*Pharmacy*] (ROG)
**IDON VEHIC**... Idoneo-Vehiculo [*In a Suitable Vehicle*] [*Pharmacy*]
**IDOS**......... Interactive Disk Operating System [*Computer Associates, Inc.*]
**IDOS**......... Interrupt Disk Operating System
**IDoV**.......... United States Veterans Administration Hospital, Downey, IL [*Library symbol*] [*Library of Congress*] (LCLS)
**IDow**.......... Downers Grove Public Library, Downers Grove, IL [*Library symbol*] [*Library of Congress*] (LCLS)
**IDowG**....... George Williams College, Downers Grove, IL [*Library symbol*] [*Library of Congress*] (LCLS)
**IDP**........... Image Data Processor
**IDP**........... Immunodiffusion Procedure [*Immunochemistry*]
**IDP**........... Improvement Data Plan (MCD)
**IDP**........... Incremental Dividend Preferred [*Share*] [*Investment term*]
**IDP**........... Indenture Part List (KSC)
**IDP**........... Independence, KS [*Location identifier*] [*FAA*] (FAAL)
**IDP**........... Independence Petroleums [*Vancouver Stock Exchange symbol*]
**IDP**........... Independent Democratic Party [*Gibraltar*] [*Political party*]
**IDP**........... Individual Development Plan (RDA)
**IDP**........... Individual Development Program [*Civil Service Commission*]
**IDP**........... Industrial Data Processing
**IDP**........... Information and Data Base Publishing Report [*A publication*]
**IDP**........... Information Data Processing
**IDP**........... Initial Delay Position [*Military*] (AABC)
**IDP**........... Inosine Diphosphate [*Biochemistry*]
**IDP**........... Input Data Processor (CET)
**IDP**........... Institute of Data Processing [*Later, IDPM*]
**IDP**........... Instructor Display Panel
**IDP**........... Instrumentation Development Plan (MCD)
**IDP**........... Integrated Data Presentation (MCD)
**IDP**........... Integrated Data Processing
**IDP**........... Interactive Display Panel (MCD)
**IDP**........... Intercept Deployment Plan [*National Security Agency*]
**IDP**........... Interdigit Pause [*Telecommunications*] (TEL)
**IDP**........... Interface Design Plan [*Air Force*]
**IDP**........... Intermodulation Distortion Percentage
**IDP**........... Internal Defense Plans (CINC)
**IDP**........... Internal Development and Production Program
**IDP**........... Internal Distribution Publication [*Navy*] (MCD)
**IDP**........... International Driving Permit
**IDP**........... Interpersonal Diagnosis of Personality [*Psychology*]
**IDP**........... Interplanetary Dust Particle
**IDP**........... Investment Dollar Premium (ADA)
**IDP**........... Isotope Development Program [*AEC*] (MCD)
**IDPA**.......... Inland Daily Press Association
**IDPAI**........ International Directory of Professional Astronomical Institutions [*A publication*]
**IDPC**.......... Integrated Data Processing Center
**IdPf**........... Post Falls Public Library, Post Falls, ID [*Library symbol*] [*Library of Congress*] (LCLS)
**IDPGA**....... Industrial and Commercial Photography [*A publication*]
**IdPGS**........ Church of Jesus Christ of Latter-Day Saints, Genealogical Society Library, Pocatello Branch, Pocatello, ID [*Library symbol*] [*Library of Congress*] (LCLS)
**IDPH**......... Idiopathic Pulmonary Hemosiderosis [*Medicine*]
**IdPI**........... Idaho State University, Pocatello, ID [*Library symbol*] [*Library of Congress*] (LCLS)
**IDPI**........... International Data Processing Institute (MCD)
**IDPM**........ Industry Direct Purchase Manufacturer (AFIT)
**IDPM**........ Initial Draft Presidential Memorandum
**IDPM**........ Institute of Data Processing Management [*Formed by a merger of DPMA and Institute of Data Processing - IDP*] (EAIO)
**IDPM**........ Institute for Development Policy and Management [*University of Manchester*] [*British*] (ECON)
**IDPN**......... Iminodipropionitrile [*Biochemistry*]
**IDP Rep**..... IDP [*Information and Data Base Publishing*] Report [*United States*] [*A publication*]
**IDPS**.......... Improvement Data Plan Sheet (MCD)
**IDPS**.......... Incremental Differential Pressure System (AAG)
**IDPS**.......... Instrument Data Processing System
**IDPS**.......... Integrated Data Processing System
**IDPS**.......... Interactive Direct Processing System [*NCR Corp.*]
**IDPS**.......... Interface Digital Processor (MCD)
**IDPSS**........ IGOSS [*Integrated Global Ocean Station System*] Data Processing and Services System (MSC)
**IDPT**.......... Image Dissector Photomultiplier Tube
**IDPT**.......... International Donkey Protection Trust (EAIO)
**IDPTF**....... Indirect Productive Time Factors (MCD)
**IDPY**.......... Information Displays [*NASDAQ symbol*] (NQ)
**IDQ**........... Industrial Development Quotient
**IDQ**........... International Delta Resources [*Vancouver Stock Exchange symbol*]
**IDQ**........... Quincy Public Library, Quincy, IL [*OCLC symbol*] (OCLC)
**IDQA**......... Individual Documented Quality Assurance
**IDR**........... Greeley & Hansen, Chicago, IL [*OCLC symbol*] (OCLC)
**IDR**........... Identification Record [*Data processing*] (MCD)
**IDR**........... Im Deutschen Reich. Zeitschrift des Central-Vereins Deutscher Staatsbuerger Juedischen Glaubens [*Berlin*] [*A publication*] (BJA)
**IDR**........... Iminodaunorubicin [*Antineoplastic drug*]
**IDR**........... Implementation Delay Report [*Social Security Administration*]
**IDR**........... Incremental Digital Recorder
**IDR**........... Independent Design Review (NRCH)
**IDR**........... Indian Defense Rules
**IDR**........... Indore [*India*] [*Airport symbol*] (OAG)
**IDR**........... Industrial Damage Reports [*Formerly, ITR*] [*British*] [*World War II*]
**IDR**........... Industrial Data Reduction (MUGU)
**IDR**........... Industrial Development Revenue Bond [*Investment term*]
**IDR**........... Industrial Relations [*A publication*]
**IDR**........... Industrie Diamanten Rundschau [*A publication*]
**IDR**........... Infantry Drill Regulations
**IDR**........... Information Dissemination and Retrieval [*System*] [*Reuters Ltd.*]
**IDR**........... Initial Design Review
**IDR**........... Input Data Request
**IDR**........... Inspection Discrepancy Report (MCD)
**IDR**........... Installation Data Record
**IDR**........... Institute for Delphinid Research (EA)
**IDR**........... Instrumentation Development Request (MCD)
**IDR**........... Interface Data Report (NRCH)
**IDR**........... Interim Depot Repair
**IDR**........... Interim Development Report
**IDR**........... Interim Discrepancy Report
**IDR**........... Intermediate Design Review (NASA)
**IDR**........... Intermittent-Duty Rating
**IDR**........... Internal Development Report
**IDR**........... International Damascus Resources [*Vancouver Stock Exchange symbol*]
**IDR**........... International Defense Review [*Interavia Publications*] [*Information service or system*] [*A publication*] (CRD)
**IDR**........... International Depositary Receipt [*Investment term*]
**IDR**........... Invoice Discrepancy Report [*Business term*]
**IDR**........... Japan Letter [*A publication*]
**IDR**........... Winder, GA [*Location identifier*] [*FAA*] (FAAL)
**IDRA**......... Insanity Defense Reform Act of 1984
**IDRA**......... Intercultural Development Research Association (EA)
**IDRA**......... International Desert Racing Association [*Automobile racing*]
**IDRB**.......... Industrial-Development Revenue Bond [*Issued by a state or local government to finance construction by a private company, which then becomes responsible for repaying the debt*] [*Investment term*]
**IDRC**......... Industrial Development Research Council (EA)
**IDRC**......... International Development Research Centre [*ICSU*] [*Research center*] [*Canada*]
**IDRCE2**..... International Development Research Centre. Technical Studies IDRC-TS [*A publication*]
**IDRC (Int Dev Res Cent) TS**... IDRC (International Development Research Centre) TS [*A publication*]
**IDRC Rep**.. IDRC [*International Development Research Centre*] Reports [*A publication*]
**IDRD**......... Information Definition Requirements Document (NASA)
**IDRD**......... Internal Data Requirement Description (MCD)
**IDR & DS**.. International Directory of Research and Development Scientists [*A publication*]
**IDREA**....... Idle Other Reasons [*Vessel status*] [*Navy*]
**IdRR**.......... Ricks College, Rexburg, ID [*Library symbol*] [*Library of Congress*] (LCLS)
**IDRS**.......... Integrated Data Retrieval System [*Department of the Treasury*]
**IDRS**.......... International Double Reed Society (EA)
**IDRSA**........ Industrial Research [*A publication*]
**IDRTY**........ Indirectly
**IDRV**......... Ionic Drive
**IDS**............ Identification Section
**IDS**............ Identification Supervisor [*Military*]
**IDS**............ Image Display System
**IDS**............ Image Dissector Scanner [*Instrumentation*]
**IDS**............ Immune Deficiency State
**IDS**............ Improvement Data System (MCD)

**IDS**............ Impulse Duplexer Study
**IDS**............ Inadvertent Destruct [*Aerospace*] (AAG)
**IDS**............ Income Data Service [*Research firm*] [*British*]
**IDS**............ India Development Service (EA)
**IDS**............ Indicator Drive Screw
**IDS**............ Industrial Development [*A publication*]
**IDS**............ Industry Data Sources [*Information Access Co.*] [*Information service or system*] (CRD)
**IDS**............ Inertial Data System
**IDS**............ Inertial Doppler System
**IDS**............ Information Data Search, Inc. [*Information service or system*] (IID)
**IDS**............ Information Delivery Service [*Telecommunications*]
**IDS**............ Information Display System
**IDS**............ Information Dissemination System (OICC)
**IDS**............ Infrared Detection Set
**IDS**............ Infrared Discrimination System
**IDS**............ Inhibitor of DNA Synthesis [*Immunochemistry*]
**IDS**............ Input Data Strobe
**IDS**............ Institut fuer Deutsche Sprache [*Institute for German Language*] [*Information service or system*] (IID)
**IDS**............ Institute for Democratic Socialism (EA)
**IDS**............ Instrument Data System
**IDS**............ Instrument Development Section
**IDS**............ Instrument Development Set
**IDS**............ Integrated Data Store [*or System*] [*Honeywell, Inc.*] [*Data processing*]
**IDS**............ Integrated Defensive System
**IDS**............ Integrated Display Set
**IDS**............ Integrated Display Situation
**IDS**............ Intelligence Data System
**IDS**............ Intelligent Display System [*Data processing*]
**IDS**............ Interactive Data System [*Data processing*]
**IDS**............ Interactive Display System
**IDS**............ Interagency Dialing System [*Telephones*]
**IDS**............ Interdepartmental Dial Service [*or System*] [*Telephones*]
**IDS**............ Interdictor Strike
**IDS**............ Interface Data Sheet (NASA)
**IDS**............ Interface Design Specification (CAAL)
**IDS**............ Interim Decay Storage [*Nuclear energy*] (NRCH)
**IDS**............ Interior Design Society (EA)
**IDS**............ Interlibrary Delivery Service of Pennsylvania [*Library network*]
**IDS**............ Intermediate Decay Storage [*Nuclear energy*] (NRCH)
**IDS**............ Intermediate Direct Support [*DoD*]
**IDS**............ Intermediate Drum Storage (CET)
**IDS**............ Internal Distribution System [*Television*]
**IDS**............ International Data Services Corp. [*Vancouver Stock Exchange symbol*]
**IDS**............ International Development Services
**IDS**............ International Development Strategy [*United Nations*]
**IDS**............ International Doctor's Society (EA)
**IDS**............ International Documents Service [*Defunct*] (EA)
**IDS**............ International Dostoevsky Society (EA)
**IDS**............ International Dove Society (EA)
**IDS**............ Intrusion Detection System (MCD)
**IDS**............ Investors Diversified Services, Inc. [*Mutual funds*]
**IDS**............ Ion Drift Semiconductor
**IDS**............ Isotope Detection System [*Nuclear energy*] (NRCH)
**IDS**............ Item Description Sheet (NASA)
**IDS**............ Izvestiya na Druzestovoto na Filolozite-Slavisti v Balgarija (Sofija) [*A publication*]
**Id-S**............ Office of the Secretary of State, Boise, ID [*Library symbol*] [*Library of Congress*] (LCLS)
**IDS**............ Spoon River College, Canton, IL [*OCLC symbol*] (OCLC)
**IDSA**.......... Industrial Designers' Society of America (EA)
**IDSA**.......... Infectious Diseases Society of America (EA)
**IDSA**.......... International Dark-Sky Association (EA)
**IDSA**.......... International Diving Schools Association (EA)
**IDSA J**........ IDSA [*Institute for Defense Studies and Analyses*] Journal [*India*] [*A publication*]
**IDSB**.......... Independent Double Sideband
**IDSB**.......... International Dostoevsky Society. Bulletin [*A publication*]
**IDS Bulletin** ... IDS [*Institute of Development Studies*] Bulletin [*A publication*]
**IDSC**.......... International Die Sinkers' Conference (EA)
**IDSCM**...... Initial Defense Satellite Communication (KSC)
**IDSCP**....... Initial Defense Satellite Communications Project [*Telecommunications*] (TEL)
**IDSCS**....... Initial Defense Satellite Communication System (KSC)
**IDSD**.......... Institutional Data System Division [*Johnson Space Center*] [*NASA*] (NASA)
**IDSEG**....... International Development Studies Group
**IDSF**.......... Intelligence Defector Source File [*Military*] (MCD)
**IDSF**.......... Inter-Agency Data Systems Facility [*General Services Administration*] (MCD)
**IDSF**.......... Interim Data Switching Facility (ADA)
**IDSFA**....... Institute for Defence Studies and Analyses. Journal [*India*] [*A publication*]
**IDSI**........... Interactive Data Services, Incorporated [*Database producer*] [*Information service or system*] (IID)
**IDSIA**........ Immune Deficiency Syndrome "Innocently" Acquired (ADA)
**IDS/IGS**.... Intermediate Direct Support/Intermediate General Support [*Army*]
**IDSL**.......... Intrusion Detection and Sensor Laboratory [*Army*] (RDA)
**IDSM**......... Indian Distinguished Service Medal [*British*]
**IDSM**......... Inertial Dampened Servomotor
**IDSM**......... Integrated Direct Support Maintenance (MCD)
**IDSM**......... Intermediate Direct Support Maintenance (MCD)
**IDSO**......... Interdivisional Sales Order [*NASA*] (NASA)
**IDSOT**....... Interim Daily System Operational Test [*Navy*] (NG)
**IDS Report** ... Incomes Data Services Ltd. International Report [*A publication*]
**IDSRS**....... Ionization-Detected Stimulated Raman Spectroscopy
**IDSS**.......... ICAM [*Integrated Computer-Aided Manufacturing*] Decision Support System (IEEE)
**IDSS**.......... Image Data System Simulation [*NASA*]
**IDSSA**....... Infectious Diseases Society of Southern Africa (EAIO)
**IDSTO**....... Idle Used for Storage [*Shipping*]
**IdSulGS**..... Church of Jesus Christ of Latter-Day Saints, Genealogical Society Library, Salmon Branch, Salmon River Stake Center, Salmon, ID [*Library symbol*] [*Library of Congress*] (LCLS)
**IDT**............ I-Load Data Tape (NASA)
**IDT**............ Image Dissector Tube
**IDT**............ Implantation Doping Technique
**IDT**............ Inactive Duty Training [*Military*] (AABC)
**IDT**............ Industrial Disputers Tribunal [*British*]
**IDT**............ Information Display Technology, Inc. [*AMEX symbol*] (SPSG)
**IDT**............ Inspection Discrepancy Tag (KSC)
**IDT**............ Instrument Definition Team
**IDT**............ Integracion Latinoamericana [*A publication*]
**IDT**............ Integrated Dynamic Tester
**IDT**............ Intelligent Data Terminal
**IDT**............ Interactive Display Terminal (MCD)
**IDT**............ Interdigital Transducer [*Physics*]
**IDT**............ Interdisciplinary Team [*Education*]
**IDT**............ Interdivision Time [*Cytology*]
**IDT**............ Interdivision Transfer (AAG)
**IDT**............ International Diagnostic Technology [*Medicine*]
**IDT**............ Interrupt-Descriptor Table [*Data processing*]
**IDT**............ Ion Doping Technique
**IDT**............ Isodensitracer
**IDT**............ Peoria Heights Public Library, Peoria Heights, IL [*OCLC symbol*] (OCLC)
**IDTA**.......... Interdivisional Technical Agreement [*NASA*] (NASA)
**IDTA**.......... International Differential Treatment Association
**IDTAA**....... Industrie Agrarie [*A publication*]
**IDTC**.......... Indefinite Delivery Type Contract [*DoD*]
**ID TER**...... Idaho Territory
**IDTF**.......... International Documents Task Force [*Government Documents Round Table*] [*American Library Association*]
**IdTf**............ Twin Falls Public Library, Twin Falls, ID [*Library symbol*] [*Library of Congress*] (LCLS)
**IdTfGS**....... Church of Jesus Christ of Latter-Day Saints, Genealogical Society Library, Twin Falls Branch, Twin Falls, ID [*Library symbol*] [*Library of Congress*] (LCLS)
**IDTI**........... Integrated Device Technology, Incorporated [*Santa Clara, CA*] [*NASDAQ symbol*] (NQ)
**IDTKA**....... Industriell Teknik [*A publication*]
**IDTM**......... Integrated Development Test Matrix [*Army*]
**IDTOC**....... Independent Division Tactical Operations Center [*Army*] (AABC)
**IDTP**.......... Integrated Data Transmittal Package
**IDTS**.......... Improved Doppler Tracking System
**IDTS**.......... Instrumentation Data Test Station
**IDTS**.......... Instrumentation Data Transmission System
**IDTS**.......... Iron Dressers Trade Society [*A union*] [*British*]
**IDTSC**....... Instrumentation Data Transmission System Controller
**IDTV**.......... Improved Definition Television
**IDTW**......... International Union of Doll and Toy Workers of the US and Canada [*Later, IUANPW*] (EA)
**IDTY**.......... Intermittent Duty (MSA)
**IDU**............ De Pauw University, Greencastle, IN [*OCLC symbol*] (OCLC)
**idu**............. Idaho [*MARC country of publication code*] [*Library of Congress*] (LCCP)
**IDU**............ Idoxuridine [*or Iododeoxyuridine*] [*Also, IDUR*] [*Pharmacology*]
**IDU**............ Immunological Distance Unit [*Genetics*]
**IDU**............ Industrial Development Unit (IEEE)
**IDU**............ Industry, TX [*Location identifier*] [*FAA*] (FAAL)
**IDU**............ Infrared Detection Unit
**IDU**............ Interface Demonstration Unit (NASA)
**IDU**............ Intermittent Drive Unit
**IDU**............ International Democrat Union (EA)
**IDU**............ International Dendrology Union
**IdU**............ University of Idaho, Moscow, ID [*Library symbol*] [*Library of Congress*] (LCLS)
**IdUA**.......... Iduronic Acid
**IDUD**......... Independent Deployable Unit Detachment (MCD)
**IdU-L**......... University of Idaho, Law Library, Moscow, ID [*Library symbol*] [*Library of Congress*] (LCLS)

**IDun** .......... Dunlap Public Library District, Dunlap, IL [*Library symbol*] [*Library of Congress*] (LCLS)
**IDup** .......... A. C. Dougherty Memorial Township Library, Dupo, IL [*Library symbol*] [*Library of Congress*] (LCLS)
**IDUPA** ...... Issledovaniya po Uprugosti i Plastichnosti [*A publication*]
**IDupHS** ..... Dupo Junior-Senior High School, Dupo, IL [*Library symbol*] [*Library of Congress*] (LCLS)
**IDUR** ......... Idoxuridine [*or Iododeoxyuridine*] [*Also, IDU, IdUrd*] [*Pharmacology*]
**IdUrd** ......... Iododeoxyuridine [*Pharmacology*]
**IDV** ........... Dunlap Public Library District, Dunlap, IL [*OCLC symbol*] (OCLC)
**IDV** ........... Initial Development Ltd. [*Vancouver Stock Exchange symbol*]
**IDV** ........... Integrating Digital Voltmeter
**IDV** ........... Intermittent Demand Ventilation [*Medicine*]
**IDV** ........... International Distillers & Vintners [*British*]
**IDV** ........... International Trade Documentation [*A publication*]
**IDV** ........... Internationaler Deutschlehrerverband [*International Association of Teachers of German - IATG*] [*Copenhagen, Denmark*] (EAIO)
**IDVC** ......... Import and Delivery Verification Certificate [*Singapore*]
**IDVC** ......... Indwelling Venous Catheter [*Medicine*]
**IDVM** ........ Integrating Digital Voltmeter
**IDVP** .......... Independent Design Verification Program (NRCH)
**IDW** .......... Industriemagazin. Management, Marketing, Technologie [*A publication*]
**IDW** .......... Industry Week [*A publication*]
**IDW** .......... Input Data Word
**IDW** .......... Institut fuer Dokumentationswesen [*Federal Republic of Germany*]
**IDW** .......... Washington Township Library, Washington, IL [*OCLC symbol*] (OCLC)
**IDWA** ........ Interdivisional Work Authorization
**IDWD** ........ Input Data Word (MCD)
**IDWF** ......... Individual Drinking Water Flavors [*Developed by Natick Research and Development Center to encourage soldiers to drink more fluids to prevent dehydration*] (INF)
**IDWI** ......... Imperial Direct West India Mail Service Co. (ROG)
**IDWO** ........ Inter-Division Work Order
**IDX** ........... Caterpillar Tractor Co., Peoria, IL [*OCLC symbol*] (OCLC)
**IDX** ........... Index (MSA)
**IDXX** ......... Identix, Inc. [*NASDAQ symbol*] (NQ)
**IDY** ........... Fondulac Public Library District, East Peoria, IL [*OCLC symbol*] (OCLC)
**IDYN** ......... Interdyne Co. [*NASDAQ symbol*] (NQ)
**IDZ** ........... Bank Marketing Association, Chicago, IL [*OCLC symbol*] (OCLC)
**IDZ** ........... Inner Defense Zone
**IE** .............. Evanston Public Library, Evanston, IL [*Library symbol*] [*Library of Congress*] (LCLS)
**IE** .............. Id Est [*That Is*] [*Latin*]
**IE** .............. Idees pour l'Europe [*Paris, France*] (EAIO)
**IE** .............. Illuminating Engineering [*A publication*]
**IE** .............. Imbedded Error [*Factor analysis*]
**IE** .............. Immediate-Early [*Genetics*]
**IE** .............. Immobilized Enzyme [*Physiology*]
**IE** .............. Immunitaetseinheit [*Immunizing Unit*] [*Medicine*]
**IE** .............. Immunoelectrophoresis [*Analytical biochemistry*]
**IE** .............. Import Executive [*British*]
**IE** .............. In Excess
**IE** .............. Independent Estimate [*Army*]
**IE** .............. Independent Evaluation (MCD)
**IE** .............. Index of Enrichment
**IE** .............. Index Error [*Navigation*]
**IE** .............. [*Order of the*] Indian Empire
**IE** .............. Indo-European
**IE** .............. Industrial Electronics (MCD)
**IE** .............. Industrial Engineer [*or Engineering*]
**I & E** .......... Industrial and Entertainment Funds [*Correctional institutions*]
**IE** .............. Infection Efficiency [*Pathology*]
**IE** .............. Infective Endocarditis [*Cardiology*]
**I & E** .......... Information and Editorial [*Career program*]
**I & E** .......... Information and Education [*Military*]
**IE** .............. Information Enterprises [*Chesterfield, MO*] [*Telecommunications service*] (TSSD)
**IE** .............. Information Express [*Australia*]
**IE** .............. Informations Economiques [*A publication*]
**IE** .............. Infrared Emission
**I/E** ............. Ingress/Egress
**IE** .............. Initial Equipment [*Navy aircraft*]
**IE** .............. Initial Establishment [*British military*] (DMA)
**IE** .............. Initiating Event (NRCH)
**IE** .............. Insert Exon [*Genetics*]
**IE** .............. Inside Edge
**IE** .............. Inspection and Enforcement (NRCH)
**IE** .............. Inspection Equipment
**IE** .............. Inspection Error (KSC)
**I/E** ............. Inspiratory-Expiratory (Ratio) [*Physiology*]
**IE** .............. Installation Equipment [*Army*] (AABC)
**IE** .............. Institute of Energy [*An association*] (EAIO)
**IE** .............. Institute of Engineers and Technicians [*London, England*]
**IE** .............. Institute of Expertology (EA)
**IE** .............. Institute of Export [*British*]
**IE** .............. Instrument Engineering
**I & E** .......... Intake and Exhaust [*Automotive engineering*]
**IE** .............. Intake (of a Unit of Food) Energy [*Nutrition*]
**IE** .............. Interconnection Equipment
**IE** .............. Interdisciplinary Essays [*A publication*]
**IE** .............. Intermediate Early [*Genetics*]
**IE** .............. Intermediate Erection
**IE** .............. Internal Elastica [*Artery anatomy*]
**IE** .............. Internal Environment
**I & E** .......... Internally and Externally (NRCH)
**IE** .............. International Exhibition (IMH)
**IE** .............. Interrupt Enable [*Data processing*]
**IE** .............. Ionization Energy [*Chemistry*]
**IE** .............. Ionospheric Explorer [*NASA/National Bureau of Standards*]
**ie** ............... Ireland [*MARC country of publication code*] [*Library of Congress*] (LCCP)
**IE** .............. Ireland [*ANSI two-letter standard code*] (CNC)
**IE** .............. Irish Earl (ROG)
**IE** .............. Irradiation Effects (NRCH)
**IE** .............. Isoetharine [*Medicine*]
**IE** .............. Solomon Islands Airways Ltd. [*ICAO designator*] (FAAC)
**IE** .............. US International Transportation Exposition [*FAA*] (FAAC)
**IEA** ........... American Hospital Supply Corp., Evanston, IL [*Library symbol*] [*Library of Congress*] (LCLS)
**IEa** ............ East Alton Public Library, East Alton, IL [*Library symbol*] [*Library of Congress*] (LCLS)
**IEA** ........... East Texas State University, Commerce, TX [*OCLC symbol*] (OCLC)
**IEA** ........... Immunoelectroadsorption [*Analytical biochemistry*]
**IEA** ........... Import Entitlement Agreement [*United Arab Republic*]
**IEA** ........... Index of Economic Activity (ADA)
**IEA** ........... Indian-Eskimo Association of Canada [*Later, CASNP*] (EA)
**IEA** ........... Indian Evidence Act (ROG)
**IEA** ........... Indolecthanol [*Organic chemistry*]
**IEA** ........... Industrial Editors Association
**IEA** ........... Institute of Economic Affairs [*British*]
**IEA** ........... Institute for Economic Analysis (EA)
**IEA** ........... Institute for Educational Affairs (EA)
**IEA** ........... Institute of Environmental Action (EA)
**IEA** ........... Institute for Environmental Awareness (EA)
**IEA** ........... Institute for Expressive Analysis (EA)
**IEA** ........... Instruments, Electronics, and Automation [*Exhibit*]
**IEA** ........... Integrated Electronic Assembly [*NASA*]
**IEA** ........... Inter Echanges Assistance [*Inter Exchanges Assistance*] [*Maltot, France*] (EAIO)
**IEA** ........... Interment Exchange of America
**IEA** ........... International Association for the Evaluation of Educational Achievement [*See also AIERS*] [*University of Stockholm*] [*Sweden*] (EAIO)
**IEA** ........... International Economic Association [*See also AISE*] [*Paris, France*] (EAIO)
**IEA** ........... International Education Act
**IEA** ........... International Education Assembly [*World War II*]
**IEA** ........... International Education Association
**IEA** ........... International Emergency Action [*See also AUI*] [*Paris, France*] (EAIO)
**IEA** ........... International Energy Agency [*OECD*] [*Research center*] [*France*] (IRC)
**IEA** ........... International Entrepreneurs Association [*Later, AEA*] (EA)
**IEA** ........... International Epidemiological Association (EA)
**IEA** ........... International Ergonomics Association (EA)
**IEA** ........... International Exchange Association (EA)
**IEA** ........... International Executives Association (EA)
**IEA** ........... International Exhibitors Association (EA)
**IEA** ........... Intravascular Erythrocyte Aggregation [*Hematology*]
**IEAB** .......... Internacia Esperanto-Asocio de Bibliotekistoj [*International Association of Esperanto-Speaking Librarians*] [*Later, IAEL*] (EA)
**IEACS** ....... Institut Europeen des Armes de Chasse et de Sport [*European Institute of Hunting and Sporting Weapons - EIHSW*] (EAIO)
**IEAF** .......... Imperial Ethiopian Air Force
**IEAHC** ...... Institute of Early American History and Culture (EA)
**IEAJ** .......... Internacia Esperanto - Asocio de Juristoj [*International Esperanto - Association of Jurists*] [*Graz, Austria*] (EAIO)
**IEAP** .......... Institut Europeen d'Administration Publique [*European Institute of Public Administration - EIPA*] (EAIO)
**IEar** ........... Earl Township Public Library, Earlville, IL [*Library symbol*] [*Library of Congress*] (LCLS)
**IEAR** .......... Internacia Esperanto-Amikaro de Rotarianoj [*International Esperanto Fellowship of Rotarians - IEFR*] (EAIO)
**IEarFSD** .... Freedom Community Unit, School District 245, Earlville, IL [*Library symbol*] [*Library of Congress*] (LCLS)
**IEarSD** ...... Earlville Community Unit, School District 9, Earlville, IL [*Library symbol*] [*Library of Congress*] (LCLS)
**IEAS** .......... Institute of East Asian Studies [*University of California, Berkeley*] [*Research center*] (RCD)

**IEAS**......... International Economic Appraisal Service [*The Economist Publications Ltd.*] [*Great Britain*] [*Information service or system*]
**IEAS/R**...... Revista de Estudios Agro-Sociales. Instituto de Estudios Agro-Sociales [*A publication*]
**IEAust**........ Institution of Engineers of Australia
**IEB**............ Elkhart Public Library, Elkhart, IN [*OCLC symbol*] (OCLC)
**IEB**............ Industrial Evaluation Board [*BDSA*]
**IEB**............ Infanterie-Ersatzbataillon [*Infantry Replacement Training Battalion*] [*German military - World War II*]
**IEB**............ Institute of Economic Botany [*New York Botanical Garden*]
**IEB**............ Interdiction Executive Board (MCD)
**IEB**............ International Energy Bank Ltd. [*Great Britain*]
**IEB**............ International Environmental Bureau for the Non-Ferrous Metals Industry
**IEB**............ International Executive Board [*UAW*]
**IEB**............ International Exhibitions Bureau
**IEB**............ Irish Export Board
**IEB**............ Office of Inspection and Enforcement. Bulletin [*A publication*] (NRCH)
**IEBEA**....... IEEE. Transactions on Biomedical Engineering [*A publication*]
**IEBM**......... Institute of Epidemiology and Behavioral Medicine [*Medical Research Institute of San Francisco*] [*Research center*] (RCD)
**IEBR**.......... Institute for Economic and Business Research [*University of Kansas*] [*Research center*] (RCD)
**IEBY**.......... Iowa English Bulletin. Yearbook [*A publication*]
**IEC**............ Earlham College, Richmond, IN [*OCLC symbol*] (OCLC)
**IEC**............ Independent Electrical Contractors (EA)
**IEc**............ Index of Economic Articles [*A publication*]
**IEC**............ Industrial Electrification Council [*Later, TEC*] (EA)
**I & EC**........ Industrial and Engineering Chemistry [*A publication*]
**IEC**............ Industrial and Engineering Chemistry [*A publication*]
**IEC**............ Information Exchange Center
**IEC**............ Infused Emitter Coupling
**IEC**............ Inherent Explosion Clause [*Insurance*]
**IEC**............ Injection Electrode Catheter
**IEC**............ Institut d'Estudis Catalans [*A publication*]
**IEC**............ Institut d'Etudes Congolaises [*Congolese Institute of Studies*]
**IEC**............ Institut Europeen de la Communication [*European Institute for the Media - EIM*] (EAIO)
**IEC**............ Institute of Educational Cinematography [*British*]
**IEC**............ Institute of Employment Consultants Ltd. [*British*]
**IEC**............ Institute of Engineers of Chile
**IEC**............ Integrated Electronic Components (BUR)
**IEC**............ Integrated Electronic Control
**IEC**............ Integrated Engine Control
**IEC**............ Integrated Environmental Control (AAG)
**IEC**............ Integrated Equipment Component
**IEC**............ Intelligence Evaluation Committee [*Department of Justice*]
**IEC**............ Intensive English Centre [*Australia*]
**IEC**............ Interexchange Carrier [*Telecommunications*]
**IEC**............ International Economic Review [*A publication*]
**IEC**............ International Edsel Club (EA)
**IEC**............ International Educational and Cultural Exchange
**IEC**............ International Egg Commission [*London, England*] (EAIO)
**IEC**............ International Electronics Corporation (MUGU)
**IEC**............ International Electrotechnical Commission [*See also CEI*] [*Standards body*] [*Geneva, Switzerland*] (EAIO)
**IEC**............ Interstate Electronics Corporation (MCD)
**IEC**............ Intraepithelial Carcinoma [*Medicine*]
**IEC**............ Inverse Electrode Current
**IEC**............ Ion Exchange Chromatography
**IEC**............ Iris Epithelium Cell [*Cytology*]
**IEC**............ Iso-Echo Contour
**IEC**............ Israel Economic Conference
**IEC**............ Item Entry Control (AFM)
**IEC**............ Office of Inspection and Enforcement. Circular [*A publication*] (NRCH)
**IEC**............ PEC Israel Economic Corporation [*AMEX symbol*] (SPSG)
**IECA**.......... Independent Educational Consultants Association (EA)
**IECA**.......... Industry, Education Councils of America (OICC)
**IECA**.......... International Erosion Control Association (EA)
**IEC Bull**..... IEC [*International Electrotechnical Commission*] Bulletin [*A publication*]
**IECC**.......... International Economic Conversion Campaign (EA)
**IECD**.......... Institute of Early Childhood Development [*Melbourne College of Advanced Education*] [*Australia*]
**IECE**.......... IEC Electronics Corp. [*Newark, NY*] [*NASDAQ symbol*] (NQ)
**IECE**.......... Institute on East Central Europe [*Columbia University*] [*Research center*] (RCD)
**IECE**.......... International Educational and Cultural Exchange [*Washington, DC*] [*A publication*]
**IECEC**....... Intersociety Energy Conversion Engineering Conference
**IECEE**....... International Electrotechnical Commission System for Conformity Testing to Standards for Safety of Electrical Equipment (EA)
**IECEJ**........ Institute of Electronic Communications Engineers of Japan
**IECEJ**........ Interreligious Emergency Campaign for Economic Justice (EA)
**IECFA**....... Industrial and Engineering Chemistry. Fundamentals [*A publication*]
**IECG**.......... Independent Energy Consultants Group [*British*]
**IECG**.......... Interagency Emergency Coordinating Group [*Federal disaster planning*]
**IECHA**...... Industrial and Engineering Chemistry [*A publication*]
**IECI**........... Industrial Electronics and Control Instrumentation (MCD)
**IECI**........... Institute for Esperanto in Commerce and Industry (EA)
**IECI Annu Conf Proc**... IECI [*Industrial Electronics and Control Instrumentation Group*] Annual Conference Proceedings [*United States*] [*A publication*]
**IECL**.......... International Esperantist Chess League [*See also ESLI*] (EAIO)
**IECLB**....... Igreia Evangelica de Confissao Luterana do Brasil [*Protestant church*] [*Brazil*] (EY)
**IECM**......... Induced Environmental Contamination Monitor (MCD)
**IECM**......... Internal Electronic Countermeasure
**IECMB**...... IEEE. Transactions on Communications [*A publication*]
**IECMS**...... Inflight Engine Condition Monitoring System [*Military*] (CAAL)
**IECO**......... Inboard Engine Cutoff
**IECOK**....... International Economic Consultative Organization for Korea [*Ten-nation consortium*]
**I Econ J**...... Indian Economic Journal [*A publication*]
**IECP**.......... Injected Electric Current Perturbation
**IECP**.......... Interface Engineering Change Procedure
**IEC Process Des Dev**... Industrial and Engineering Chemistry. Process Design and Development [*A publication*]
**IEC Prod Res Dev**... Industrial and Engineering Chemistry. Product Research and Development [*A publication*]
**IECPS**........ International Electronic Packaging Symposium (MCD)
**IECS**.......... Igloo Environment Control Subsystem (MCD)
**IECS**.......... Intelligence Evaluation Center [*Obsolete*] [*Saigon*] (CINC)
**IEd**............ Edwardsville Free Public Library, Edwardsville, IL [*Library symbol*] [*Library of Congress*] (LCLS)
**IED**............ Impact Energy Density
**IED**............ Improved Explosive Device
**IED**............ Improvised Explosive Device
**IED**............ Income Equalization Deposit (ADA)
**IED**............ Independent Exploratory Development [*Navy*] (NG)
**IED**............ Individual Effective Dose (IEEE)
**IED**............ Initial Engine Development [*Air Force*]
**IED**............ Institute for Educational Development [*Defunct*]
**IED**............ Instrumental Engineering Division [*National Weather Service*]
**IED**............ Interacting Equipment Documents (MCD)
**IED**............ International Electronic Devices [*Conference*] (MCD)
**IED**............ Ion Exchange Desalination
**IED**............ Ionospheric Electron Density
**IED**............ Suburban Library System, Burr Ridge, IL [*OCLC symbol*] (OCLC)
**IeDL**.......... Lembaga Ilmu Pengetahuan Indonesia, Pusat Dokumentasi Ilmiah Nasional, Jakarta, Indonesia [*Library symbol*] [*Library of Congress*] (LCLS)
**IEdL**.......... Lewis and Clark Library System, Edwardsville, IL [*Library symbol*] [*Library of Congress*] (LCLS)
**IEdL-A**....... Lewis and Clark Library System, Alhambra, Alhambra, IL [*Library symbol*] [*Library of Congress*] (LCLS)
**IEdL-C**....... Lewis and Clark Library System, Chesterfield, Chesterfield, IL [*Library symbol*] [*Library of Congress*] (LCLS)
**IEdL-H**...... Lewis and Clark Library System, Hamel, Hamel, IL [*Library symbol*] [*Library of Congress*] (LCLS)
**IEdL-HP**.... Lewis and Clark Library System, Hillsboro Prison, Edwardsville, IL [*Library symbol*] [*Library of Congress*] (LCLS)
**IEdL-L**....... Lewis and Clark Library System, Livingston, Livingston, IL [*Library symbol*] [*Library of Congress*] (LCLS)
**IEdL-M**..... Lewis and Clark Library System, Marine, Marine, IL [*Library symbol*] [*Library of Congress*] (LCLS)
**IEdL-Mg**.... Lewis and Clark Library System, Mulberry Grove, Mulberry Grove, IL [*Library symbol*] [*Library of Congress*] (LCLS)
**IEdL-P**....... Lewis and Clark Library System, Palmyra, Palmyra, IL [*Library symbol*] [*Library of Congress*] (LCLS)
**IEdL-Sh**..... Lewis and Clark Library System, Shipman, Shipman, IL [*Library symbol*] [*Library of Congress*] (LCLS)
**IEdL-StJ**.... Lewis and Clark Library System, St. Jacob, St. Jacob, IL [*Library symbol*] [*Library of Congress*] (LCLS)
**IeDP**.......... Perpustakaan Museum Pusat, Jakarta, Indonesia [*Library symbol*] [*Library of Congress*] (LCLS)
**IEdS**.......... Southern Illinois University, Edwardsville Campus, Edwardsville, IL [*Library symbol*] [*Library of Congress*] (LCLS)
**IEdSD**........ Edwardsville Community Unit, School District 7, Edwardsville, IL [*Library symbol*] [*Library of Congress*] (LCLS)
**IEdS-D**....... Southern Illinois University, School of Dental Medicine, Biomedical Library, Edwardsville, IL [*Library symbol*] [*Library of Congress*] (LCLS)
**IEE**............ Indian Economic Journal [*A publication*]
**IEE**............ Induced Electrical Effect
**IEE**............ Induced Electron Emission
**IEE**............ Inner Enamel Epithelium [*Dentistry*]
**IEE**............ Institute for Earth Education (EA)
**IEE**............ Institute of Electrical Engineering [*Hitchin, Herts., England*] (NATG)
**IEE**............ Institute of Electrology Educators (EA)

**IEE**............ Institute for Environmental Education (EA)
**IEE**............ Institute of Environmental Engineers [*Later, IES*]
**IEE**............ Institution of Electrical Engineers [*London, England*] [*Database producer*]
**IEE**............ Interim Expendable Emitter (NVT)
**IEE**............ National College of Education, Evanston, IL [*Library symbol*] [*Library of Congress*] (LCLS)
**IEE**............ North Suburban Library System, Wheeling, IL [*OCLC symbol*] (OCLC)
**IEECA**....... IEEE. Transactions on Electronic Computers [*A publication*]
**IEE Conf Publ (Lond)** ... IEE [*Institution of Electrical Engineers*] Conference Publication (London) [*A publication*]
**IEE Control Engrg Ser** ... IEE [*Institution of Electrical Engineers*] Control Engineering Series [*A publication*]
**IEEE**.......... Institute of Electrical and Electronics Engineers (EA)
**IEEE Acoust** ... IEEE. Transactions on Acoustics, Speech, and Signal Processing [*A publication*]
**IEEE Aer El** ... IEEE. Transactions on Aerospace and Electronic Systems [*A publication*]
**IEEE Annu Text Ind Tech Conf** ... IEEE. Annual Textile Industry Technical Conference [*A publication*]
**IEEE Annu Text Ind Tech Conf Proc** ... IEEE. Annual Textile Industry Technical Conference. Proceedings [*United States*] [*A publication*]
**IEEE Antenn** ... IEEE. Transactions on Antennas and Propagation [*A publication*]
**IEEE Auto C** ... IEEE. Transactions on Automatic Control [*A publication*]
**IEEE Biomed** ... IEEE. Transactions on Biomedical Engineering [*A publication*]
**IEEE Broadc** ... IEEE. Transactions on Broadcasting [*A publication*]
**IEEE Cem Ind Tech Conf Pap** ... IEEE. Cement Industry Technical Conference Paper [*A publication*]
**IEEE Circ S** ... IEEE. Transactions on Circuits and Systems [*A publication*]
**IEEE Circuits Syst Mag** ... IEEE. Circuits and Systems Magazine [*United States*] [*A publication*]
**IEEE Commun** ... IEEE. Transactions on Communications [*A publication*]
**IEEE Commun Mag** ... IEEE. Communications Magazine [*A publication*]
**IEEE Commun Soc Mag** ... IEEE. Communications Society. Magazine [*Later, IEEE. Communications Magazine*] [*A publication*]
**IEEE Comput** ... IEEE. Transactions on Computers [*A publication*]
**IEEE Comput Graphics and Appl** ... IEEE. Computer Graphics and Applications [*A publication*]
**IEEE Comput Group News** ... IEEE. Computer Group News [*A publication*]
**IEEE Conf Rec Annu Conf Electr Eng Probl Rubber Plast Ind** ... IEEE. Conference Record. Annual Conference of Electrical Engineering Problems in the Rubber and Plastics Industries [*A publication*]
**IEEE Conf Rec Ind Commer Power Syst Tech Conf** ... IEEE. Conference Record. Industrial and Commercial Power Systems. Technical Conference [*A publication*]
**IEEE Conf Rec Thermion Convers Spec Conf** ... IEEE. Conference Records. Thermionic Conversion Specialist Conference [*A publication*]
**IEEE Cons E** ... IEEE. Transactions on Consumer Electronics [*A publication*]
**IEEE Control Syst Mag** ... IEEE. Control Systems Magazine [*A publication*]
**IEEE-CS**.... Institute of Electrical and Electronics Engineers - Computer Society
**IEEE Device** ... IEEE. Transactions on Electron Devices [*A publication*]
**IEEE Educat** ... IEEE. Transactions on Education [*A publication*]
**IEEE Electromagn Compat Symp** ... IEEE. Electromagnetic Compatibility Symposium. Record [*A publication*]
**IEEE Electron Aerosp Syst Conv Rec** ... IEEE. Electronics and Aerospace Systems. Convention Record [*United States*] [*A publication*]
**IEEE Electron Device Lett** ... IEEE. Electron Device Letters [*United States*] [*A publication*]
**IEEE El Ins** ... IEEE. Transactions on Electrical Insulation [*A publication*]
**IEEE Elmagn** ... IEEE. Transactions on Electromagnetic Compatibility [*A publication*]
**IEEE Eng Manage Rev** ... IEEE. Engineering Management Review [*A publication*]
**IEEE Eng Med and Biol Mag** ... IEEE. Engineering in Medicine and Biology Magazine [*A publication*]
**IEEE Geosci** ... IEEE. Transactions on Geoscience Electronics [*A publication*]
**IEEE Ind Ap** ... IEEE. Transactions on Industry Applications [*A publication*]
**IEEE Ind El** ... IEEE. Transactions on Industrial Electronics and Control Instrumentation [*Later, IEEE. Transactions on Industrial Electronics*] [*A publication*]
**IEEE Info T** ... IEEE. Transactions on Information Theory [*A publication*]
**IEEE Instr** ... IEEE. Transactions on Instrumentation and Measurement [*A publication*]
**IEEE Int Conv Dig** ... IEEE. International Convention. Digest [*A publication*]
**IEEE Int Conv Rec** ... IEEE. International Convention. Record [*A publication*]
**IEEE Intercon Tech Pap** ... IEEE. Intercon Technical Papers [*A publication*]
**IEEE J Ocean Eng** ... IEEE. Journal of Oceanic Engineering [*A publication*]
**IEEE J Oceanic Eng** ... IEEE. Journal of Oceanic Engineering [*A publication*]
**IEEE Journal of Oceanic Engineering** ... IEEE. Journal of Oceanic Engineering [*A publication*]
**IEEE J Q El** ... IEEE. Journal of Quantum Electronics [*A publication*]
**IEEE J Quantum Electron** ... IEEE. Journal of Quantum Electronics [*A publication*]
**IEEE J Sel** ... IEEE. Journal on Selected Areas in Communications [*A publication*]
**IEEE J Sel Areas Commun** ... IEEE. Journal on Selected Areas in Communications [*A publication*]
**IEEE J Soli** ... IEEE. Journal of Solid-State Circuits [*A publication*]
**IEEE J Solid-State Circuits** ... IEEE. Journal of Solid-State Circuits [*A publication*]
**IEE Electromagn Waves Ser** ... IEE [*Institution of Electrical Engineers*] Electromagnetic Waves Series [*A publication*]
**IEEE Magnet** ... IEEE. Transactions on Magnetics [*A publication*]
**IEEE Manage** ... IEEE. Transactions on Engineering Management [*A publication*]
**IEEE Med Im** ... IEEE. Transactions on Medical Imaging [*A publication*]
**IEEE Micr T** ... IEEE. Transactions on Microwave Theory and Techniques [*A publication*]
**IEEE Nucl S** ... IEEE. Transactions on Nuclear Science [*A publication*]
**IEEE Parts** ... IEEE. Transactions on Parts, Hybrids, and Packaging [*A publication*]
**IEEE/PES** ... Power Engineering Society of the Institute of Electrical and Electronic Engineers (ITD)
**IEEE Photovoltaic Spec Conf Conf Rec** ... IEEE. Photovoltaic Specialists Conference. Conference Record [*United States*] [*A publication*]
**IEEE Plas S** ... IEEE. Transactions on Plasma Science [*A publication*]
**IEEE Power** ... IEEE. Transactions on Power Apparatus and Systems [*A publication*]
**IEEE Power Eng Rev** ... IEEE. Power Engineering Review [*A publication*]
**IEEE Proc** ... IEEE. Proceedings [*A publication*]
**IEEE Proc Annu Symp Rel** ... IEEE. Proceedings. Annual Symposium on Reliability [*A publication*]
**IEEE Proc Conf Elec Appl Text Ind** ... IEEE. Proceedings. Conference on Electrical Applications for the Textile Industry [*A publication*]
**IEEE Proc Conf Eng Med Biol** ... IEEE. Proceedings. Conference on Engineering in Medicine and Biology [*A publication*]
**IEEE Proc Electron Components Conf** ... IEEE. Proceedings. Electronic Components Conference [*A publication*]
**IEEE Proc Intermag Conf** ... IEEE. International Conference on Magnetics. Proceedings of the Intermag Conference [*A publication*]
**IEEE Proc Nat Aerosp Electron Conf** ... IEEE. Proceedings. National Aerospace and Electronics Conference [*A publication*]
**IEEE Proc Natl Aerosp Electron Conf** ... IEEE. Proceedings. National Aerospace and Electronics Conference [*A publication*]
**IEEE Prof C** ... IEEE. Transactions on Professional Communications [*A publication*]
**IEEE Reg Six (West USA) Conf Rec** ... IEEE. Region Six (Western USA). Conference Record [*A publication*]
**IEEE Reliab** ... IEEE. Transactions on Reliability [*A publication*]
**IEEE S**...... IEEE. Spectrum [*A publication*]
**IEEE Son Ul** ... IEEE. Transactions on Sonics and Ultrasonics [*A publication*]
**IEEE Spectr** ... IEEE. Spectrum [*A publication*]
**IEEE Spectrum** ... IEEE. Spectrum [*A publication*]
**IEEE Stand Publ** ... IEEE. Standards Publications [*A publication*]
**IEEE Stud Pap** ... IEEE. Student Papers [*A publication*]
**IEEE Syst M** ... IEEE. Transactions on Systems, Man, and Cybernetics [*A publication*]
**IEEE Tech Act Guide** ... IEEE. Technical Activities Guide [*United States*] [*A publication*]
**IEEE T El Dev** ... IEEE. Transactions on Electron Devices [*A publication*]
**IEEE T Nucl Sci** ... IEEE. Transactions on Nuclear Science [*A publication*]
**IEEE T Pl Sci** ... IEEE. Transactions on Plasma Science [*A publication*]
**IEEE Trans** ... IEEE. Transactions on Computers [*A publication*]
**IEEE Trans Acoust Speech Signal Process** ... IEEE. Transactions on Acoustics, Speech, and Signal Processing [*A publication*]
**IEEE Trans Aerosp** ... IEEE. Transactions on Aerospace [*Later, IEEE. Transactions on Aerospace and Electronic Systems*] [*A publication*]
**IEEE Trans Aerospace Electron Systems** ... IEEE. Transactions on Aerospace and Electronic Systems [*A publication*]
**IEEE Trans Aerospace and Electron Systems** ... IEEE. Transactions on Aerospace and Electronic Systems [*A publication*]
**IEEE Trans Aerosp Electron Syst** ... IEEE. Transactions on Aerospace and Electronic Systems [*A publication*]
**IEEE Trans Aerosp and Electron Syst** ... IEEE. Transactions on Aerospace and Electronic Systems [*A publication*]
**IEEE Trans Aerosp Navig Electron** ... IEEE. Transactions on Aerospace and Navigational Electronics [*A publication*]
**IEEE Trans Antennas Propag** ... IEEE. Transactions on Antennas and Propagation [*A publication*]
**IEEE Trans Antennas Propagat** ... IEEE. Transactions on Antennas and Propagation [*A publication*]
**IEEE Trans Antennas and Propagation** ... IEEE. Transactions on Antennas and Propagation [*A publication*]
**IEEE Trans Applic Ind** ... IEEE. Transactions on Applications and Industry [*A publication*]
**IEEE Trans Appl Ind** ... IEEE. Transactions on Applications and Industry [*A publication*]
**IEEE Trans ASSP** ... IEEE. Transactions on Acoustics, Speech, and Signal Processing [*A publication*]

**IEEE Trans Audio** ... IEEE. Transactions on Audio [*A publication*]
**IEEE Trans Audio and Electroacoust** ... IEEE. Transactions on Audio and Electroacoustics [*A publication*]
**IEEE Trans Audio Electroacoust** ... IEEE. Transactions on Audio and Electroacoustics [*A publication*]
**IEEE Trans Automat Contr** ... IEEE. Transactions on Automatic Control [*A publication*]
**IEEE Trans Automat Control** ... IEEE. Transactions on Automatic Control [*A publication*]
**IEEE Trans Automatic Control** ... IEEE. Transactions on Automatic Control [*A publication*]
**IEEE Trans Autom Control** ... IEEE. Transactions on Automatic Control [*A publication*]
**IEEE Trans Bio Med Electron** ... IEEE. Transactions on Bio-Medical Electronics [*A publication*]
**IEEE Trans Biomed Eng** ... IEEE. Transactions on Biomedical Engineering [*A publication*]
**IEEE Trans Broadcast** ... IEEE. Transactions on Broadcasting [*A publication*]
**IEEE Trans Broadcast Telev Receivers** ... IEEE. Transactions on Broadcast and Television Receivers [*A publication*]
**IEEE Trans Broadcast and Telev Receivers** ... IEEE. Transactions on Broadcast and Television Receivers [*A publication*]
**IEEE Trans Cable Telev** ... IEEE. Transactions on Cable Television [*A publication*]
**IEEE Trans CAS** ... IEEE. Transactions on Circuits and Systems [*A publication*]
**IEEE Trans CATV** ... IEEE. Transactions on Cable Television [*A publication*]
**IEEE Trans CE** ... IEEE. Transactions on Consumer Electronics [*A publication*]
**IEEE Trans Circuits and Syst** ... IEEE. Transactions on Circuits and Systems [*A publication*]
**IEEE Trans Circuits Syst** ... IEEE. Transactions on Circuits and Systems [*A publication*]
**IEEE Trans Circuits and Systems** ... IEEE. Transactions on Circuits and Systems [*A publication*]
**IEEE Trans Circuit Theory** ... IEEE. Transactions on Circuit Theory [*A publication*]
**IEEE Trans Com** ... IEEE. Transactions on Communications [*A publication*]
**IEEE Trans Comm** ... IEEE. Transactions on Communications [*A publication*]
**IEEE Trans Commun** ... IEEE. Transactions on Communications [*A publication*]
**IEEE Trans Commun Electron** ... IEEE. Transactions on Communication and Electronics [*A publication*]
**IEEE Trans Commun Syst** ... IEEE. Transactions on Communications Systems [*A publication*]
**IEEE Trans Commun Technol** ... IEEE. Transactions on Communication Technology [*Later, IEEE. Transactions on Communications*] [*A publication*]
**IEEE Trans Component Parts** ... IEEE. Transactions on Component Parts [*A publication*]
**IEEE Trans Components Hybrids and Manuf Technol** ... IEEE. Transactions on Components, Hybrids, and Manufacturing Technology [*A publication*]
**IEEE Trans Components Hybrids Manuf Technol** ... IEEE. Transactions on Components, Hybrids, and Manufacturing Technology [*A publication*]
**IEEE Trans Comput** ... IEEE. Transactions on Computers [*A publication*]
**IEEE Trans Comput-Aided Des Integrated Circuits and Syst** ... IEEE. Transactions on Computer-Aided Design of Integrated Circuits and Systems [*A publication*]
**IEEE Trans Computers** ... IEEE. Transactions on Computers [*A publication*]
**IEEE Trans Com Tech** ... IEEE. Transactions on Communication Technology [*Later, IEEE. Transactions on Communications*] [*A publication*]
**IEEE Trans Consum Electron** ... IEEE. Transactions on Consumer Electronics [*A publication*]
**IEEE Trans Educ** ... IEEE. Transactions on Education [*A publication*]
**IEEE Trans Elec Insul** ... IEEE. Transactions on Electrical Insulation [*A publication*]
**IEEE Trans Electr Insul** ... IEEE. Transactions on Electrical Insulation [*A publication*]
**IEEE Trans Electromagn Compat** ... IEEE. Transactions on Electromagnetic Compatibility [*A publication*]
**IEEE Trans Electron Comput** ... IEEE. Transactions on Electronic Computers [*United States*] [*A publication*]
**IEEE Trans Electron Devices** ... IEEE. Transactions on Electron Devices [*A publication*]
**IEEE Trans Eng Manag** ... IEEE. Transactions on Engineering Management [*A publication*]
**IEEE Trans Eng Manage** ... IEEE. Transactions on Engineering Management [*A publication*]
**IEEE Trans Engng Man** ... IEEE. Engineering Management [*A publication*]
**IEEE Trans Engng Wrtg Speech** ... IEEE. Transactions on Engineering Writing and Speech [*A publication*]
**IEEE Trans Eng Writing Speech** ... IEEE. Transactions on Engineering Writing and Speech [*A publication*]
**IEEE Trans Eng Writ and Speech** ... IEEE. Transactions on Engineering Writing and Speech [*A publication*]
**IEEE Trans Geosci Electron** ... IEEE. Transactions on Geoscience Electronics [*A publication*]
**IEEE Trans Geosci Electronics** ... IEEE. Transactions on Geoscience Electronics [*A publication*]
**IEEE Trans Geosci Remote Sens** ... IEEE. Transactions on Geoscience and Remote Sensing [*United States*] [*A publication*]
**IEEE Trans Geosci and Remote Sensing** ... IEEE. Transactions on Geoscience and Remote Sensing [*A publication*]
**IEEE Trans Geosci Remote Sensing** ... IEEE. Transactions on Geoscience and Remote Sensing [*A publication*]
**IEEE Trans Hum Factors Electron** ... IEEE. Transactions on Human Factors in Electronics [*United States*] [*A publication*]
**IEEE Trans Ind Appl** ... IEEE. Transactions on Industry Applications [*A publication*]
**IEEE Trans Ind Electron** ... IEEE. Transactions on Industrial Electronics [*A publication*]
**IEEE Trans Ind Electron Control Instrum** ... IEEE. Transactions on Industrial Electronics and Control Instrumentation [*Later, IEEE. Transactions on Industrial Electronics*] [*A publication*]
**IEEE Trans Ind Electron and Control Instrum** ... IEEE. Transactions on Industrial Electronics and Control Instrumentation [*Later, IEEE. Transactions on Industrial Electronics*] [*A publication*]
**IEEE Trans Ind Gen Appl** ... IEEE. Transactions on Industry and General Applications [*Later, IEEE. Transactions on Industry Applications*] [*A publication*]
**IEEE Trans Ind and Gen Appl** ... IEEE. Transactions on Industry and General Applications [*Later, IEEE. Transactions on Industry Applications*] [*A publication*]
**IEEE Trans Information Theory** ... IEEE. Transactions on Information Theory [*A publication*]
**IEEE Trans Inform Theory** ... IEEE. Transactions on Information Theory [*A publication*]
**IEEE Trans Inf Theory** ... IEEE. Transactions on Information Theory [*A publication*]
**IEEE Trans Instrum and Meas** ... IEEE. Transactions on Instrumentation and Measurement [*A publication*]
**IEEE Trans Instrum Meas** ... IEEE. Transactions on Instrumentation and Measurement [*A publication*]
**IEEE Trans Magn** ... IEEE. Transactions on Magnetics [*A publication*]
**IEEE Trans Man-Mach Syst** ... IEEE. Transactions on Man-Machine Systems [*A publication*]
**IEEE Trans Manuf Technol** ... IEEE. Transactions on Manufacturing Technology [*A publication*]
**IEEE Trans Med Imaging** ... IEEE. Transactions on Medical Imaging [*A publication*]
**IEEE Trans Microwave Theory and Tech** ... IEEE. Transactions on Microwave Theory and Techniques [*A publication*]
**IEEE Trans Microwave Theory Tech** ... IEEE. Transactions on Microwave Theory and Techniques [*A publication*]
**IEEE Trans Mil Electron** ... IEEE. Transactions on Military Electronics [*A publication*]
**IEEE Trans Nucl Sci** ... IEEE. Transactions on Nuclear Science [*A publication*]
**IEEE Trans Parts Hybrids Packag** ... IEEE. Transactions on Parts, Hybrids, and Packaging [*A publication*]
**IEEE Trans Parts Hybrids and Packag** ... IEEE. Transactions on Parts, Hybrids, and Packaging [*A publication*]
**IEEE Trans Parts Mater and Packag** ... IEEE. Transactions on Parts, Materials, and Packaging [*A publication*]
**IEEE Trans Parts Mater Packag** ... IEEE. Transactions on Parts, Materials, and Packaging [*A publication*]
**IEEE Trans Pattern Anal and Mach Intell** ... IEEE. Transactions on Pattern Analysis and Machine Intelligence [*A publication*]
**IEEE Trans Plasma Sci** ... IEEE. Transactions on Plasma Science [*A publication*]
**IEEE Trans Power Appar and Syst** ... IEEE. Transactions on Power Apparatus and Systems [*A publication*]
**IEEE Trans Power App Syst** ... IEEE. Transactions on Power Apparatus and Systems [*A publication*]
**IEEE Trans Prod Eng Prod** ... IEEE. Transactions on Product Engineering and Production [*A publication*]
**IEEE Trans Prof Commun** ... IEEE. Transactions on Professional Communications [*A publication*]
**IEEE Trans PS** ... IEEE. Transactions on Plasma Science [*A publication*]
**IEEE Trans Rel** ... IEEE. Transactions on Reliability [*A publication*]
**IEEE Trans Reliab** ... IEEE. Transactions on Reliability [*A publication*]
**IEEE Trans Reliability** ... IEEE. Transactions on Reliability [*A publication*]
**IEEE Trans SE** ... IEEE. Transactions on Software Engineering [*A publication*]
**IEEE Trans Software Eng** ... IEEE. Transactions on Software Engineering [*A publication*]
**IEEE Trans Software Engrg** ... IEEE. Transactions on Software Engineering [*A publication*]
**IEEE Trans Sonics Ultrason** ... IEEE. Transactions on Sonics and Ultrasonics [*A publication*]
**IEEE Trans Sonics & Ultrason** ... IEEE. Transactions on Sonics and Ultrasonics [*A publication*]
**IEEE Trans Space Electron Telem** ... IEEE. Transactions on Space Electronics and Telemetry [*A publication*]
**IEEE Trans System** ... IEEE. Transactions on Systems, Man, and Cybernetics [*A publication*]

**IEEE Trans Systems Man Cybernet** ... IEEE. Transactions on Systems, Man, and Cybernetics [*A publication*]
**IEEE Trans Syst Man and Cybern** ... IEEE. Transactions on Systems, Man, and Cybernetics [*A publication*]
**IEEE Trans Syst Man Cybern** ... IEEE. Transactions on Systems, Man, and Cybernetics [*A publication*]
**IEEE Trans Syst Sci and Cybern** ... IEEE. Transactions on Systems, Science, and Cybernetics [*A publication*]
**IEEE Trans Syst Sci Cybern** ... IEEE. Transactions on Systems, Science, and Cybernetics [*A publication*]
**IEEE Trans Ultrason Eng** ... IEEE. Transactions on Ultrasonics Engineering [*A publication*]
**IEEE Trans Ultrasonics Eng** ... IEEE. Transactions on Ultrasonics Engineering [*A publication*]
**IEEE Trans Veh Commun** ... IEEE. Transactions on Vehicular Communications [*A publication*]
**IEEE Trans Veh Technol** ... IEEE. Transactions on Vehicular Technology [*A publication*]
**IEEE Veh T** ... IEEE. Transactions on Vehicular Technology [*A publication*]
**IEEE Wescon Conven Rec** ... IEEE. Wescon Convention Record [*A publication*]
**IEEE Wescon Tech Pap** ... IEEE. Wescon Technical Papers [*A publication*]
**IEEI** .......... International Electronics Engineering, Incorporated (AAG)
**IEEI** .......... University of Illinois Hospital Eye and Ear Infirmary [*University of Illnois at Chicago*] [*Research center*] (RCD)
**IEEIE** ........ Institution of Electrical and Electronics Incorporated Engineers (DS)
**IEE-IERE Proc (India)** ... IEE-IERE [*Institution of Electrical Engineers-Institution of Electronic and Radio Engineers*] Proceedings (India) [*A publication*]
**IEE J Comput and Digital Tech** ... IEE [*Institution of Electrical Engineers*] Journal on Computers and Digital Techniques [*A publication*]
**IEE J Comput Digital Tech** ... IEE [*Institution of Electrical Engineers*] Journal on Computers and Digital Techniques [*A publication*]
**IEE J Electron Circuits Syst** ... IEE [*Institution of Electrical Engineers*] Journal on Electronic Circuits and Systems [*A publication*]
**IEE J Electron Circuits and Syst** ... IEE [*Institution of Electrical Engineers*] Journal on Electronic Circuits and Systems [*A publication*]
**IEE J Electr Power Appl** ... IEE [*Institution of Electrical Engineers*] Journal on Electric Power Applications [*A publication*]
**IEE J Microwaves Opt Acoust** ... IEE [*Institution of Electrical Engineers*] Journal on Microwaves, Optics, and Acoustics [*A publication*]
**IEE J Solid-State Electron Devices** ... IEE [*Institution of Electrical Engineers*] Journal on Solid-State and Electron Devices [*A publication*]
**IEE J Solid-State and Electron Devices** ... IEE [*Institution of Electrical Engineers*] Journal on Solid-State and Electron Devices [*A publication*]
**IEELG** ....... International Education Exchange Liaison Group (EA)
**IEE Monogr Ser** ... IEE [*Institution of Electrical Engineers*] Monograph Series [*A publication*]
**IEEP** .......... Incapacitated Emergency Egress Practice [*NASA*] (KSC)
**IEEP** .......... Institute for European Environmental Policy (EAIO)
**IEEP** .......... Interagency Energy/Environment Program [*Environmental Protection Agency*]
**IEEPA** ....... International Emergency Economic Powers Act [*1977*]
**IEE Proc A** ... IEE [*Institution of Electrical Engineers*] Proceedings. Part A [*A publication*]
**IEE Proc B Elect Pwr Applics** ... IEE [*Institution of Electrical Engineers*] Proceedings. Part B. Electric Power Applications [*A publication*]
**IEE Proc B Electr Power Appl** ... IEE [*Institution of Electrical Engineers*] Proceedings. Part B. Electric Power Applications [*A publication*]
**IEE Proc C** ... IEE [*Institution of Electrical Engineers*] Proceedings. Part C. Generation, Transmission, and Distribution [*A publication*]
**IEE Proc C Gener Transm Distrib** ... IEE [*Institution of Electrical Engineers*] Proceedings. Part C. Generation, Transmission, and Distribution [*A publication*]
**IEE Proc D** ... IEE [*Institution of Electrical Engineers*] Proceedings. Part D. Control Theory and Applications [*A publication*]
**IEE Proc D Control Theory Applics** ... IEE [*Institution of Electrical Engineers*] Proceedings. Part D. Control Theory and Applications [*A publication*]
**IEE Proc E** ... IEE [*Institution of Electrical Engineers*] Proceedings. Part E. Computers and Digital Techniques [*A publication*]
**IEE Proc E Comput Digit Tech** ... IEE [*Institution of Electrical Engineers*] Proceedings. Part E. Computers and Digital Techniques [*A publication*]
**IEE Proc E Computers Digit Techniques** ... IEE [*Institution of Electrical Engineers*] Proceedings. Part E. Computers and Diigital Techniques [*A publication*]
**IEE Proc F** ... IEE [*Institution of Electrical Engineers*] Proceedings. Part F. Communications, Radar, and Signal Processing [*A publication*]
**IEE Proc F Commun Radar Signal Process** ... IEE [*Institution of Electrical Engineers*] Proceedings. Part F. Communications, Radar, and Signal Processing [*A publication*]
**IEE Proc G** ... IEE [*Institution of Electrical Engineers*] Proceedings. Part G. Electronic Circuits and Systems [*A publication*]
**IEE Proc G Electron Circuits Syst** ... IEE [*Institution of Electrical Engineers*] Proceedings. Part G. Electronic Circuits and Systems [*A publication*]
**IEE Proc Generation Transm Distrib** ... IEE [*Institution of Electrical Engineers*] Proceedings. Part C. Generation, Transmission, and Distribution [*A publication*]
**IEE Proc H** ... IEE [*Institution of Electrical Engineers*] Proceedings. Part H. Microwaves, Optics, and Antennas [*A publication*]
**IEE Proc H Microwaves Opt Antennas** ... IEE [*Institution of Electrical Engineers*] Proceedings. Part H. Microwaves, Optics, and Antennas [*A publication*]
**IEE Proc I** ... IEE [*Institution of Electrical Engineers*] Proceedings. Part I. Solid-State and Electron Devices [*A publication*]
**IEE Proc I Solid-State Electron Devices** ... IEE [*Institution of Electrical Engineers*] Proceedings. Part I. Solid-State and Electron Devices [*A publication*]
**IEE Proc Part C** ... IEE [*Institution of Electrical Engineers*] Proceedings. Part C. Generation, Transmission, and Distribution [*England*] [*A publication*]
**IEE Proc Part D** ... IEE [*Institution of Electrical Engineers*] Proceedings. Part D. Control Theory and Applications [*England*] [*A publication*]
**IEE Proc Part E** ... IEE [*Institution of Electrical Engineers*] Proceedings. Part E. Computers and Digital Techniques [*England*] [*A publication*]
**IEE Proc Part F** ... IEE [*Institution of Electrical Engineers*] Proceedings. Part F. Communications, Radar, and Signal Processing [*England*] [*A publication*]
**IEE Proc Part G** ... IEE [*Institution of Electrical Engineers*] Proceedings. Part G. Electronic Circuits and Systems [*England*] [*A publication*]
**IEE Proc Part H** ... IEE [*Institution of Electrical Engineers*] Proceedings. Part H. Microwaves, Optics, and Antennas [*England*] [*A publication*]
**IEE Proc Part I** ... IEE [*Institution of Electrical Engineers*] Proceedings. Part I. Solid-State and Electron Devices [*England*] [*A publication*]
**IEER** .......... Institute of Energy and Earth Resources [*CSIRO*]
**IEE Rev** ...... IEE [*Institution of Electrical Engineers*] Reviews [*A publication*]
**IEES** .......... International Education Exchange Service [*Department of State*]
**IEETE** ....... Institution of Electrical and Electronics Technician Engineers (MCD)
**IEEUA** ....... IEEE. Transactions on Audio [*A publication*]
**IE-Ex** ......... Evanston Public Library, Extension (Bookmobile), Evanston, IL [*Library symbol*] [*Library of Congress*] (LCLS)
**IEF** ............ Indian Expeditionary Force [*British military*] (DMA)
**IEF** ............ INTACT [*Infants Need to Avoid Circumcision Trauma*] Educational Foundation [*Later, NO-CIRC*] (EA)
**IEF** ............ International Equestrian Federation (EAIO)
**IEF** ............ International Exhibitions Foundation (EA)
**IEF** ............ International Eye Foundation (EA)
**IEF** ............ Isoelectric Focusing [*Analytical chemistry*]
**IEF** ............ Israel Education Fund
**IEF** ............ Italian Expeditionary Force
**IEF** ............ Starved Rock Library System, Ottawa, IL [*OCLC symbol*] (OCLC)
**IEFC** .......... International Emergency Food Council [*Post-World War II*]
**IEFFA** ........ Industrie-Elektronik in Forschung und Fertigung [*A publication*]
**IEFP** .......... International Exposition for Food Processors (ITD)
**IEFR** .......... International Esperanto Fellowship of Rotarians [*See also IEAR*] (EAIO)
**IEFUA** ....... International Electronic Facsimile Users Association (EA)
**IEG** ............ Garrett-Evangelical Theological Seminary, Evanston, IL [*Library symbol*] [*Library of Congress*] (LCLS)
**IEG** ............ Harry S Truman College, Chicago, IL [*OCLC symbol*] (OCLC)
**IEG** ............ Immediately Early Gene [*Genetics*]
**IEG** ............ Imperial Ethiopian Government (CINC)
**IEG** ............ Independent Evaluation Group (SDI)
**IEG** ............ Industrial Electronics Group [*of General Motors Corp.*]
**IEG** ............ Information Exchange Group [*National Institutes of Health*]
**IEG** ............ Zielona Gora [*Poland*] [*Airport symbol*] (OAG)
**IEGNA** ...... Environmental Geology Notes. Illinois State Geological Survey [*A publication*]
**IEGP** .......... Interagency Economic Growth Project [*Department of Transportation*]
**IEGRBU** .... Imperial Ethiopian Government Institute of Agricultural Research. Report [*A publication*]
**IEH** ............ American Library Association, Chicago, IL [*OCLC symbol*] (OCLC)
**IEHA** ......... International Economic History Association [*Paris, France*] (EA)
**IEHC** ......... IEH Corporation [*NASDAQ symbol*] (NQ)
**IEHD** ......... Institute for the Editing of Historical Documents

**IEHFA**....... IEEE. Transactions on Human Factors in Electronics [*A publication*]
**IEHIURM**... Institute for Encyclopedia of Human Ideas on Ultimate Reality and Meaning (EA)
**IEHO**......... Institute of Environmental Health Officers [*British*]
**IEI**............. Immunocytochemistry, ELISA [*Enzyme-Linked Immunosorbent Assay*], and Immunoblotting
**IEI**............. Indeterminate Engineering Items
**IEI**............. Indiana Energy, Incorporated [*NYSE symbol*] (SPSG)
**IEI**............. Industrial Education Institute
**IEI**............. Industrial Engineering Institute
**IEI**............. Institute for Educational Innovation [*Later, Education Development Center*]
**IEI**............. Internacia Esperanto Instituto [*International Esperanto Institute*] (EAIO)
**IEI**............. International Educator's Institute (EA)
**IEI**............. International Enamellers Institute [*Derby, England*] (EAIO)
**IEI**............. International Epitek, Inc. [*Toronto Stock Exchange symbol*]
**IEI**............. International Esperanto Institute [*The Hague, Netherlands*] (EAIO)
**IEI**............. International Evaluations, Incorporated
**IEI**............. Investment Education Institute (EA)
**IEI**............. Iran Electronics Industries
**IEIAS**......... Institut Europeen Interuniversitaire de l'Action Sociale [*Inter-University European Institute on Social Welfare - IEISW*] (EAIO)
**IEIB**........... International Electronics, Inc. [*NASDAQ symbol*] (NQ)
**IE & ID**...... Interiors Engineering and Industrial Design (MCD)
**IEIDATA**.. International Economic Indicators Database [*Columbia Business School*] [*Information service or system*] (CRD)
**IEIM**.......... Izvestiya na Etnografskija Institut Muzej [*A publication*]
**IE Ind Eng**... IE. Industrial Engineering [*A publication*]
**IEIP**........... Institut Europeen des Industries de la Pectine [*European Institute of the Pectin Industries*]
**IEIS**........... Integrated Engine Instrument System (MCD)
**IEISW**....... Inter-University European Institute on Social Welfare (EA)
**IEJ**............. Deere & Co., Moline, IL [*OCLC symbol*] (OCLC)
**IEJ**............. Indian Economic Journal [*A publication*]
**IEJ**............. Indiana English Journal [*A publication*]
**IEJ**............. Institut Europeen du Jouet [*European Toy Institute - ETI*] (EAIO)
**IEJ**............. Israel Exploration Journal [*A publication*]
**IEJ**............. Nieuws uit Japan [*A publication*]
**IEKA**.......... Internacia Esperanto Klubo Automobilista [*International Automobile Esperanto Club*] (EAIO)
**IEKKK**....... Invisible Empire Knights of the Ku Klux Klan (EA)
**IEKNA**....... Izvestiya Energeticheskogo Instituta Akademiya Nauk SSSR [*A publication*]
**IEKU**......... Institut foer Eskimologi. Kobenhavns Universitet [*A publication*]
**IEKV**.......... Internationale Eisenbahn-Kongress-Vereinigung [*International Railway Congress Association*]
**IEL**............. IE Industries, Inc. [*NYSE symbol*] (SPSG)
**IEL**............. Industrial Equity Limited [*Australia*]
**IEL**............. Information Exchange List [*Military*] (AABC)
**IEL**............. Institute for Educational Leadership (EA)
**IEL**............. Intraepithelial Lymphocyte [*Hematology*]
**IEL**............. Iota Exploration Ltd. [*Vancouver Stock Exchange symbol*]
**IEL**............. Parlin Public Library, Canton, IL [*OCLC symbol*] (OCLC)
**IELA**.......... International Exhibition Logistics Associates [*Geneva, Switzerland*] (EAIO)
**IElg**............ Gail Borden Public Library, Elgin, IL [*Library symbol*] [*Library of Congress*] (LCLS)
**IELG**.......... International Esperantist League for Go (EA)
**IElgB**.......... Brethren Historical Library and Archives, Elgin, IL [*Library symbol*] [*Library of Congress*] (LCLS)
**IElgC**.......... Elgin Community College, Elgin, IL [*Library symbol*] [*Library of Congress*] (LCLS)
**IElm**........... Elmhurst Public Library, Elmhurst, IL [*Library symbol*] [*Library of Congress*] (LCLS)
**IElmC**........ Elmhurst College, Elmhurst, IL [*Library symbol*] [*Library of Congress*] (LCLS)
**IELS**........... Isotope Exciter Light Source
**IElsP**.......... Principia College, Elsah, IL [*Library symbol*] [*Library of Congress*] (LCLS)
**IElw**........... Morrison and Mary Wiley Public Library, Elmwood, IL [*Library symbol*] [*Library of Congress*] (LCLS)
**IElwp**......... Elmwood Park Public Library, Elmwood Park, IL [*Library symbol*] [*Library of Congress*] (LCLS)
**IEM**........... East Texas State University, Metroplex Center, Commerce, TX [*OCLC symbol*] (OCLC)
**IEM**........... Ideal Effort Multiplier
**IEM**........... Immune Electron Microscopy
**IEM**........... Inborn Error of Metabolism [*Medicine*]
**IEM**........... Individual Engagement Model (MCD)
**IEM**........... Industrial Engineer for Management
**IEM**........... Infrared Projector Energy Monitor (MCD)
**IEM**........... Installation Equipment Management System (MCD)
**IEM**........... Institute of Experimental Meteorology [*USSR*]
**IEM**........... Interim Examination and Maintenance [*Nuclear energy*] (NRCH)
**IEM**........... Internal Environment Monitoring
**IEM**........... Intromission and Ejaculatory Mechanism [*Physiology*]
**IEM**........... Ion Exchange Membrane
**IEMA**......... Immunoenzymometric Assay [*Clinical chemistry*]
**IEMA**......... Independent Electrical Manufacturers Association (EA)
**IEMATS**... Improved Emergency Message Automatic Transmission System (MCD)
**IEMC**......... Independent Electronic Music Center [*Defunct*]
**IEMC**......... Industrial Equipment Manufacturers Council [*Later, ICED*] (EA)
**IEMC**......... International Electronics Manufacturing Company (AAG)
**IEMCAP**... Intrasystem Electromagnetic Compatibility Analysis Program [*Data processing*] [*Air Force*]
**IEME**......... Corps of Indian Electrical and Mechanical Engineers [*British military*] (DMA)
**IEMG**......... Integrated Electromyogram [*Medicine*]
**IEMO**......... Installation Equipment Management Office [*Military*] (AFIT)
**IEMP**......... Induced Electromagnetic Pulse (RDA)
**IEMP**......... Institute of Environmental Medicine and Physiology
**IEMP**......... Interior Electromagnetic Pulse (MCD)
**IEMS**......... IEM SA de CV [*NASDAQ symbol*] (NQ)
**IEMS**......... Installation Equipment Management System
**I/EMS**....... Intergraph Corp./Engineering Modeling System
**IEMS**......... Interim Electronic Maintenance Support (AFIT)
**IEMSA**....... Izoliatsiya Elektricheskikh Mashin. Sbornik Sostavlen po Materialam Konferentsii Sozvannoi Leningradskim Otdelenium Nauchno-Tekhnicheskogo Obshchestva Energetekii [*A publication*]
**IEMT**......... Intermediate Emergency Medical Technician [*Also, EMT-I*] (DHSM)
**IEMTF**...... Interim Examination and Maintenance Training Facility [*Nuclear energy*] (NRCH)
**IEMVT**...... Institut d'Elevage et de Medecine Veterinaire des Pays Tropicaux [*Institute of Stockraising and Veterinary Medicine in Tropical Countries*] [*France*]
**IEN**............ Die Israelitischen Eigennamen [*A publication*] (BJA)
**IE-N**.......... Evanston Public Library, North Branch, Evanston, IL [*Library symbol*] [*Library of Congress*] (LCLS)
**IEN**............ Industrial Engineering [*A publication*]
**IEN**............ Industrial Equipment News [*A publication*]
**IEN**............ Interpenetrating Elastomeric Networks [*Organic chemistry*]
**IEN**............ Northwestern University, Evanston, IL [*Library symbol*] [*Library of Congress*] (LCLS)
**IEN-C**........ Northwestern University, Joseph Schaffner Library of Commerce, Chicago, IL [*Library symbol*] [*Library of Congress*] (LCLS)
**IEN-D**........ Northwestern University, Dental School, Chicago, IL [*Library symbol*] [*Library of Congress*] (LCLS)
**IEN-L**........ Northwestern University, Law Library, Chicago, IL [*Library symbol*] [*Library of Congress*] (LCLS)
**IEN-M**....... Northwestern University, Medical School, Chicago, IL [*Library symbol*] [*Library of Congress*] (LCLS)
**IEN-T**........ Northwestern University, Technological Institute, Evanston, IL [*Library symbol*] [*Library of Congress*] (LCLS)
**IEN-Tr**....... Northwestern University, Transportation Library, Evanston, IL [*Library symbol*] [*Library of Congress*] (LCLS)
**IEO**........... Incoherent Electronic Oscillator
**IEO**........... Interim Engineering Order (AAG)
**IEO**........... International Education Office [*World War II*]
**IEO**........... International Exchange Office (AFM)
**IEOCS**....... Interim Equipment Order Control System [*Bell System*]
**IEON**......... International Esperantist Organization of Naturists [*See also INOE*] [*Frankfurt, Federal Republic of Germany*] (EAIO)
**IEOP**.......... Immunoelectroosmophoresis [*Analytical biochemistry*]
**IEOTSG**.... Integral Economizer Once-Through Steam Generator (NRCH)
**IEP**............ Evansville Public Library and Vanderburgh County Public Library, Evansville, IN [*OCLC symbol*] (OCLC)
**IEp**............ Fondulac District Library, East Peoria, IL [*Library symbol*] [*Library of Congress*] (LCLS)
**IEP**............ Immunoelectrophoresis [*Analytical biochemistry*]
**IEP**............ Independent Evaluation Plan
**IEP**............ Independent Exchange Plan
**IEP**............ Indicateur Electronique de Pilotage [*Electronic Pilotage Indicator*] [*Aviation*]
**IEP**............ Individual Evaluation Plan [*Army*]
**IEP**............ Individualized Education Program [*For the education of a handicapped person*]
**IEP**............ Industrial Equity Pacific Ltd. [*Hong Kong*] (ECON)
**IEP**............ Information Economics and Policy [*A publication*]
**IEP**............ Information Exchange Program [*or Project*] [*Military*]
**IEP**............ Informe Economico [*A publication*]
**IEP**............ Ingestion Exposure Pathway [*Nuclear emergency planning*]
**IEP**............ Institut fuer Europaeische Politik [*Institute of European Politics*] (EAIO)
**IEP**............ Institut Europeen pour la Promotion des Entreprises
**IEP**............ Institute for Ecological Policies [*Defunct*] (EA)
**IEP**............ Institute of European Politics (EA)
**IEP**............ Institute for Experimental Psychiatry
**IEP**............ Instrument for Evaluation of Photographs
**IEP**............ Integrated Engineering Program
**IEP**............ Internal Economic Problems [*British*]

**IEP**............ International Economic Policy
**IEP**............ International Energy Program
**IEP**............ International Express Post [*Australia*]
**IEP**............ International Potential [*Vancouver Stock Exchange symbol*]
**IEP**............ Intext Educational Publishers
**IEP**............ Inverted Energy Population
**IEP**............ Isoelectric Point [*Also, IP*] [*Chemistry*]
**IEPA**.......... Independent Electron Pair Approximation [*Physics*]
**IEPA**.......... International Economic Policy Act of 1972
**IEPA**.......... International Economic Policy Association (EA)
**IEPA**.......... International Environment Protection Act of 1983
**IEPA**.......... Intra-European Payments Agreement
**IEPB**.......... Interagency Emergency Planning Board [*Federal disaster planning*]
**IEPC**.......... Instantaneous Effective Photocathodes (MCD)
**IEPC**.......... Interagency Emergency Planning Committee
**IEPDA**....... Industrial and Engineering Chemistry. Process Design and Development [*A publication*]
**IEpE**.......... East Peoria Elementary School District, East Peoria, IL [*Library symbol*] [*Library of Congress*] (LCLS)
**IEPFCHK** ... International Elvis Presley Fan Club, Hong Kong (EAIO)
**IEPG**.......... Independent European Program Group [*NATO*]
**IEpI**........... Illinois Central College, East Peoria, IL [*Library symbol*] [*Library of Congress*] (LCLS)
**IEPP**.......... Institute of Earth and Planetary Physics [*University of Alberta*] [*Research center*] (RCD)
**IEPPL**........ Integrated Engineering Planning Parts List
**IEPRA**....... Industrial and Engineering Chemistry. Product Research and Development [*A publication*]
**IEPRC**....... International Electronic Publishing Research Centre [*Research center*] [*British*] (IRC)
**IEPS**.......... International Electronics Packaging Society (EA)
**IEPT**.......... International Encyclopedia of Pharmacology and Therapeutics [*A publication*]
**IEQ**............ Illinois Prairie District Public Library, Metamora, IL [*OCLC symbol*] (OCLC)
**I Eq R**......... Irish Equity Reports [*A publication*] (DLA)
**IER**............ Independent Evaluation Report
**IER**............ Indian Economic Review [*A publication*]
**IER**............ Individual Education Record
**IER**............ Individual Evaluation Report
**IER**............ Industrial Equipment Reserve
**IER**............ Infanterie-Ersatzregiment [*Infantry Replacement Training Regiment*] [*German military - World War II*]
**IER**............ Inherent Equipment Reliability
**IER**............ Initial Engagement Range (MCD)
**IER**............ Installation Enhancement Release [*Data processing*]
**IER**............ Institute for Econometric Research (EA)
**IER**............ Institute for Ecumenical Research (EAIO)
**IER**............ Institute of Educational Research (EA)
**IER**............ Institute of Engineering Research [*United Kingdom*] [*Research center*] (IRC)
**IER**............ Institute of Engineering Research [*University of California*] (MCD)
**IER**............ Institute for Environmental Research [*Environmental Science Services Administration*]
**IER**............ Institute of Exploratory Research [*Army*]
**IER**............ Interface Evaluation Report (KSC)
**IER**............ Interim Engineering Report
**IER**............ Internal Economic Rate of Return
**IER**............ International Economic Review [*A publication*]
**IER**............ Inventory Equipment Requirement
**IER**............ Ion Exchange Resin
**IER**............ Irish Ecclesiastical Record [*A publication*]
**IER**............ Irish Ecclesiastical Review [*A publication*]
**IER**............ Irish Equity Reports [*A publication*] (DLA)
**IER**............ Mackinaw Township Library, Mackinaw, IL [*OCLC symbol*] (OCLC)
**IER**............ Natchitoches, LA [*Location identifier*] [*FAA*] (FAAL)
**IER**............ Organization for International Economic Relations [*Vienna, Austria*] (EAIO)
**IERBA2**..... Iowa. Agricultural Experiment Station. Research Bulletin [*A publication*]
**IERC**.......... International Electronic Research Corporation (MCD)
**IERD**.......... Industry Energy Research and Development Program [*Canada*]
**IERE**.......... Institute of Electronics and Radio Engineers [*London, England*] (TEL)
**IERE Conf Proc (Lond)**... IERE [*Institution of Electronic and Radio Engineers*] Conference Proceedings (London) [*A publication*]
**IERESM**.... Institut Europeen de Recherches et d'Etudes Superieures en Management [*European Institute for Advanced Studies in Management - EIASM*] [*Brussels, Belgium*] (EA)
**IERF**.......... International Education Research Foundation (EA)
**IERI**........... Illuminating Engineering Research Institute (EA)
**IERL**.......... Industrial Environmental Research Laboratory [*Environmental Protection Agency*]
**IERM**......... Individual Employment Rights Manual [*A publication*]
**IERO**......... Institute for Engineering Research in the Oceans [*Marine science*] (MSC)
**IERS**.......... Inventory Equipment Requirement Specification
**IERTM**...... Institute for Environmental Research Technical Memorandum
**IERW**......... Initial Entry Rotary Wing [*Student*] (MCD)
**IERWA**...... IEE [*Institution of Electrical Engineers*] Reviews [*A publication*]
**IEs**............. East St. Louis Public Library, East St. Louis, IL [*Library symbol*] [*Library of Congress*] (LCLS)
**IES**............ Eli Lilly & Co., Indianapolis, IN [*OCLC symbol*] (OCLC)
**IE-S**........... Evanston Public Library, South Branch, Evanston, IL [*Library symbol*] [*Library of Congress*] (LCLS)
**IES**............ Id, Ego, Superego [*Test*] [*Psychology*]
**IES**............ IEEE Industrial Electronics Society (EA)
**IES**............ Illuminating Engineering Society
**IES**............ Incoming Echo Suppressor [*Telecommunications*] (TEL)
**IES**............ Independent Educational Services (EA)
**IES**............ Indian Educational Service [*British*]
**IES**............ Inductive Energy Storage
**IES**............ Industrial Electronic System
**IES**............ Industrial Engineering Services
**IES**............ Industrial Engineering Standard (MCD)
**IES**............ Institute for Earth Sciences [*Environmental Science Services Administration*]
**IES**............ Institute of Ecosystem Studies
**IES**............ Institute of Environmental Sciences (EA)
**IES**............ Institute for Environmental Studies [*University of Toronto*] [*Research center*] (RCD)
**IES**............ Institute for Environmental Studies [*University of Wisconsin, Madison*] [*Research center*] (RCD)
**IES**............ Institute for Environmental Studies [*University of Washington*] [*Research center*] (RCD)
**IES**............ Institute of European Studies (EA)
**IES**............ Institution of Environmental Sciences (EAIO)
**IES**............ Integral Error Squared (IEEE)
**IES**............ Integrated Electronic System
**IES**............ Intelligence Evaluation Staff
**IES**............ Intensive Employability Services [*Work Incentive Program*]
**IES**............ Internal Environment Simulator
**IES**............ International Ecology Society (EA)
**IES**............ International Education Series [*A publication*]
**IES**............ International Exchange Service [*For publications*] [*Smithsonian Institution*]
**IES**............ International Explorers Society
**IES**............ Intrinsic Electric Strength (IEEE)
**IES**............ Inventory Equipment Sheet
**IES**............ Inverness Petroleum Ltd. [*Toronto Stock Exchange symbol*]
**IES**............ Inverted Echo Sounder
**IES**............ Ion Energy Selector
**IES**............ Ion Engine Simulator
**IES**............ Ion Engine System
**IES**............ Irish Emigrant Society (EA)
**IES**............ Irradiation Effects Simulation (NRCH)
**IESA**.......... Instituto de Estudios Superiores de Administracion [*Institute of Higher Studies of Administration*] [*Venezuela*]
**IESA**.......... Insurance Economics Society of America [*Inactive*] (EA)
**IEsAHS**..... Assumption High School, East St. Louis, IL [*Library symbol*] [*Library of Congress*] (LCLS)
**IESB**.......... Bulletin of Indonesian Economic Studies [*Canberra*] [*A publication*]
**IESC**.......... International Executive Service Corps [*Stamford, CT*] (EA)
**IESCDD**.... Irish Journal of Environmental Science [*A publication*]
**IEsCH**........ Christian Welfare Hospital, East St. Louis, IL [*Library symbol*] [*Library of Congress*] (LCLS)
**IEsCTH**..... Centreville Township Hospital, East St. Louis, IL [*Library symbol*] [*Library of Congress*] (LCLS)
**IESD**.......... Instrumentation and Electronic Systems Division [*NASA*] (MCD)
**IES-DC**...... IES [*Information Exchange System*] Data Collections [*Commission of the European Communities*] [*Information service or system*] (CRD)
**IESEB**........ Ion Exchange and Solvent Extraction [*A publication*]
**IESH**.......... Indian Economic and Social History Review [*A publication*]
**IES Lighting Rev**... IES [*Illuminating Engineering Societies of Australia*] Lighting Review [*A publication*] (APTA)
**IES Light Rev**... IES [*Illuminating Engineering Societies of Australia*] Lighting Review [*A publication*] (APTA)
**IES Ltg Rev**... IES [*Illuminating Engineering Societies of Australia*] Lighting Review [*A publication*] (APTA)
**IESM**......... Inductive Energy Storage Modulator
**IES Mon**.... IES [*Illuminating Engineering Society*] Monograph [*A publication*]
**IESNA**........ Illuminating Engineering Society of North America (EA)
**IESP**.......... Integrated Electronic Signal Processor
**IEsP**........... Parks College of Aeronautical Technology, East St. Louis, IL [*Library symbol*] [*Library of Congress*] (LCLS)
**IESPA**........ Proceedings. Institute of Environmental Sciences [*A publication*]
**IESPAF**..... Institute of Environmental Sciences. Proceedings [*A publication*]
**IEsPC**........ Project Choice, East St. Louis, IL [*Library symbol*] [*Library of Congress*] (LCLS)
**IESq**.......... Intelligence Exploitation Squadron [*Air Force*]
**IESR**.......... International English Shepherd Registry (EA)

**IESS**.......... International Encyclopedia of the Social Sciences [*A publication*]
**IESS**.......... Ion Engine System Section
**IESSC**........ Irish El Salvador Support Committee (EAIO)
**IEsSC**......... State Community College of East St. Louis, Learning Resources Center, East St. Louis, IL [*Library symbol*] [*Library of Congress*] (LCLS)
**IEsSD**........ East Saint Louis Public School District 189, East St. Louis, IL [*Library symbol*] [*Library of Congress*] (LCLS)
**IEsSMH**.... Saint Mary's Hospital, East St. Louis, IL [*Library symbol*] [*Library of Congress*] (LCLS)
**IESV**.......... Institute for Epidemiologic Studies of Violence (EA)
**IET**............ East Texas State University, Texarkana, Texarkana, TX [*OCLC symbol*] (OCLC)
**IET**............ Impact Excited Transmitter
**IET**............ Implanted Electrode Technique
**IET**............ Independent Evaluation Teams [*Army Systems Acquisitions Review Council*] (MCD)
**IET**............ Initial Engine Test
**IET**............ Initial Entry Training
**IET**............ Institute of Educational Technology [*British*]
**IET**............ Institute of Engineers and Technicians [*London, England*] (EAIO)
**IET**............ Instrument and Electrical Technician (MCD)
**IET**............ Integrated Equipment Test [*Nuclear energy*]
**IET**............ Interest Equalization Tax
**IET**............ Interval Embossed Tube
**IET**............ Israel Economist [*A publication*]
**IETA**.......... International Electrical Testing Association (EAIO)
**IETAB**....... IEEE. Transactions on Acoustics, Speech, and Signal Processing [*A publication*]
**IETAS**....... Interim Escort Towed Array System (MCD)
**IETC**.......... Interagency Emergency Transportation Committee
**IETCA**....... International E-22 Class Association (EA)
**IETE**.......... Institution of Electronics and Telecommunications Engineers [*Information service or system*] (TSSD)
**IETF**.......... Initial Engine Test Facility
**IETF**.......... Integrated Equipment Test Facility [*Department of Energy*]
**IETMB**...... IEEE. Transactions on Manufacturing Technology [*A publication*]
**IETP**.......... Individualized Education and Training Plan (OICC)
**IETS**.......... Inelastic Electron Tunneling Spectroscopy
**IETS**.......... Intermediate Examiner Training School [*Federal Home Loan Bank Board*]
**IETS**.......... International Embryo Transfer Society (EA)
**IET Z Elektr Inf Energietech**... IET: Zeitschrift fuer Elektrische Informations- und Energietechnik [*A publication*]
**IEU**........... Forum International: International Ecosystems University (EA)
**IEU**........... Input Expansion Unit
**IEU**........... Integrated Electronics Unit (MCD)
**IEU**........... Interface Electronics Unit [*NASA*]
**IEU**........... Intermediate Education Unit
**IEU**........... Ion Exchange Unit
**IEU**........... Lewis and Clark Library System, Edwardsville, IL [*OCLC symbol*] (OCLC)
**IEuC**.......... Eureka College, Eureka, IL [*Library symbol*] [*Library of Congress*] (LCLS)
**IEUP**.......... Institut fuer Europaeische Umweltpolitik [*Institute for European Environmental Policy - IEEP*] (EAIO)
**IEV**............ International Electrotechnical Vocabulary (IEEE)
**IEV**............ Kewanee Public Library, Kewanee, IL [*OCLC symbol*] (OCLC)
**IEV**............ Kiev [*USSR*] [*Airport symbol*] (OAG)
**IEVCA**....... IEEE. Transactions on Vehicular Communications [*A publication*]
**IEVD**.......... Integrated Electronic Vertical Display
**IEvp**........... Evergreen Park Public Library, Evergreen Park, IL [*Library symbol*] [*Library of Congress*] (LCLS)
**IE-W**.......... Evanston Public Library, West Branch, Evanston, IL [*Library symbol*] [*Library of Congress*] (LCLS)
**IEW**........... Indogermanisches Etymologisches Woerterbuch [*A publication*]
**IEW**........... Intelligence and Electronic Warfare [*System*] [*Military*] (RDA)
**IEW**........... Pekin Public Library, Pekin, IL [*OCLC symbol*] (OCLC)
**IEW**........... Winters, TX [*Location identifier*] [*FAA*] (FAAL)
**I/EW FOSS**... Intelligence/Electronic Warfare Family of Systems Study [*Military*] (MCD)
**IEWNI**....... Washington National Insurance Co., Evanston, IL [*Library symbol*] [*Library of Congress*] (LCLS)
**IEWS**......... Integrated Electronic Warfare System
**IEWT**......... National Woman's Christian Temperance Union, Evanston, IL [*Library symbol*] [*Library of Congress*] (LCLS)
**IEW-UAV**... Intelligence/Electronic Warfare Unmanned Aerial Vehicle [*Army*]
**IEX**............ Harrington Institute of Interior Design, Design Library, Chicago, IL [*OCLC symbol*] (OCLC)
**IEX**............ IDEX Corp. [*NYSE symbol*] (SPSG)
**IEX**............ Ion Exchanger
**IEX**............ Issue Exception Code [*Air Force*] (AFIT)
**IEX**............ Journal of Energy and Development [*A publication*]
**IEXMBW**.. Ion Exchange and Membranes [*A publication*]
**IEXS**.......... Integrated Expert System [*Data processing*]
**IEY**............ Barrow, AK [*Location identifier*] [*FAA*] (FAAL)
**IEY**............ Chicago Board of Trade, Chicago, IL [*OCLC symbol*] (OCLC)
**IEY**............ International Education Year [*UN designation*]
**IEY**............ Iowa English Yearbook [*A publication*]
**IEZ**............ Cumberland Trail Library System, Flora, IL [*OCLC symbol*] (OCLC)
**IEZ**............ Institut Europeen du Zinc [*European Zinc Institute - EZI*] (EA)
**IF**............... Ice Fog
**IF**............... Ideational Fluency [*Research test*]
**I/F**............ Image-to-Frame Ratio (MUGU)
**IF**............... Immersion Fixation [*Microbiology*]
**IF**............... Immunofluorescence [*Immunochemistry*]
**IF**............... Importance Factor [*Statistics*]
**IF**............... Imprest Fund (MCD)
**IF**............... In-Flight (AAG)
**IF**............... In Full
**IF**............... Independent Force [*British military*] (DMA)
**IF**............... Independent Foundation
**IF**............... Indian Financial Questions [*British*]
**IF**............... Indirect Fluorescent
**IF**............... Indogermanische Forschungen [*A publication*]
**IF**............... Indonesia Fund [*NYSE symbol*] (SPSG)
**IF**............... Industrial Appointment Full Time [*Chiropody*] [*British*]
**IF**............... Industrial Fund (AFM)
**IF**............... Industrialization Forum [*Canada*] [*A publication*]
**IF**............... Infielder [*Position in baseball*]
**IF**............... Information Feedback
**IF**............... Infrared (MCD)
**IF**............... Infrared Filter
**IF**............... Inhibiting Factor
**IF**............... Initiation Factor [*Protein biosynthesis*]
**IF**............... Inside Frosted
**IF**............... Installation Fixtures (MCD)
**IF**............... Institute of Fuel [*British*]
**IF**............... Instruction Field
**IF**............... Instruction Folder (MSA)
**IF**............... Insufficient Funds
**IF**............... Insular Force
**IF**............... Insurance Forum [*A publication*]
**IF**............... Integration Facility (MCD)
**IF**............... Intellectual Framework
**IF**............... Intellectual Freedom
**I/F**............ Interface [*Data processing*] (KSC)
**IF**............... Interference Filter
**IF**............... Interferon [*Also, IFN*] [*Biochemistry*]
**IF**............... Interferon Foundation (EA)
**IF**............... Interflug, Gesellschaft fuer Internationalen Flugverkehr mbH [*Germany*] [*ICAO designator*] (FAAC)
**IF**............... Interfuture (EA)
**IF**............... Intermediate Filament [*Anatomy*]
**IF**............... Intermediate Fix (FAAC)
**IF**............... Intermediate Frequency [*Electronics*]
**IF**............... Internally Flawless [*Diamond clarity grade*]
**IF**............... International Federation of American Homing Pigeon Fanciers (EA)
**IF**............... International Forum (EA)
**IF**............... Interrupt Flag [*Data processing*]
**IF**............... Interstitial Fluid [*Physiology*]
**IF**............... Intrinsic Factor [*Biochemistry*]
**IF**............... Inventrepreneurs' Forum (EA)
**IF**............... Ipse Fecit [*He Did It Himself*] [*Latin*]
**IF**............... Ipso Facto [*By the Fact Itself*] [*Latin*]
**IF**............... Ireland Fund (EA)
**IF**............... Irish Fusiliers [*British military*] (DMA)
**IF**............... Irregular Force [*Military*] (CINC)
**IF**............... Israel Forum [*A publication*]
**IFA**............ Association Internationale de l'Industrie des Engrais [*International Fertilizer Industry Association - IFA*] (EAIO)
**IFA**............ Fort Worth Public Library, Fort Worth, TX [*OCLC symbol*] (OCLC)
**IFA**............ Igniter-Fuel Assembly
**IFA**............ Imero Fiorentino Associates, Inc. [*New York, NY*] [*Telecommunications*] (TSSD)
**IFA**............ Immunofluorescence [*or Immunofluorometric*] Assay [*Also, IFMA*] [*Analytical biochemistry*]
**IFA**............ Immunofluorescent Antibody [*Immunochemistry*]
**IFA**............ In-Flight Abort (MCD)
**IFA**............ In-Flight Analysis
**IFA**............ Incomplete Freund's Adjuvant
**IFA**............ Independent Fee Appraiser, Member [*Designation awarded by National Association of Independent Fee Appraisers, Inc.*]
**IFA**............ Independent Financial Adviser [*British*] (ECON)
**IFA**............ Independent Financial Analysis (ADA)
**IFA**............ Indirect Fluorescent Antibody [*Immunochemistry*]
**IFA**............ Industrial Forestry Association [*Later, NFA*] (EA)
**IFA**............ Inslee Family Association (EA)
**IFA**............ Institute of Financial Accountants (EAIO)
**IFA**............ Insulation Fabricators Association [*Defunct*] (EA)
**IFA**............ Integrated Feed Antenna
**IFA**............ Integrated File Adapter [*Data processing*] (BUR)

**IFA** ........ Inter-Financial Association (EA)
**IFA** ........ Intercessors for America (EA)
**IFA** ........ Intercollegiate Fencing Association (EA)
**IFA** ........ Interface Functional Analysis (NASA)
**IFA** ........ Interim Functional Alternate
**IFA** ........ Intermediate Frequency Amplifier [*or Attenuator*]
**IFA** ........ International Federation of Accountants (ADA)
**IFA** ........ International Federation of Actors
**IFA** ........ International Federation on Ageing [*Formerly, IARP*] (EA)
**IFA** ........ International Federation of Airworthiness [*Middlesex, England*] (EAIO)
**IFA** ........ International Ferret Association (EA)
**IFA** ........ International Fertility Association [*Defunct*]
**IFA** ........ International Fertilizer Industry Association [*Paris, France*] (EAIO)
**IFA** ........ International Festivals Association (EA)
**IFA** ........ International Fiction Association (EAIO)
**IFA** ........ International Fighter Aircraft
**IFA** ........ International Filariasis Association (EA)
**IFA** ........ International Finance Alert [*Financial Times Business Information*] [*Great Britain*] [*Information service or system*] (CRD)
**IFA** ........ International Finn Association [*Madrid, Spain*] (EAIO)
**IFA** ........ International Fiscal Association [*Rotterdam, Netherlands*] (EAIO)
**IFA** ........ International Florists Association [*Later, National Florists Association*] (EA)
**IFA** ........ International Footprint Association (EA)
**IFA** ........ International Footwear Association (EA)
**IFA** ........ International Franchise Association (EA)
**IFA** ........ International Frisbee Association [*Later, IFDA*]
**IFA** ........ Interracial Family Alliance (EA)
**IFA** ........ Ionization Front Accelerator [*Physics*]
**IFA** ........ Iowa Falls, IA [*Location identifier*] [*FAA*] (FAAL)
**IFA** ........ Irish Features Agency [*News agency*]
**IFA** ........ Israel Folktale Archive (BJA)
**IFA** ........ Istituto di Fisica dell'Atmosfera [*Institute of Atmospheric Physics*] [*Italy*]
**IFA** ........ Majma'a al-Fiqh al-Islami [*Islamic Jurisprudence Academy - IJA*] (EAIO)
**IFAA** ........ International Federation of Advertising Agencies [*Sarasota, FL*] (EA)
**IFAA** ........ International Federation of Associations of Anatomists (EA)
**IFAA** ........ International Flight Attendants Association (EA)
**IFAA** ........ International Flow Aids Association (EA)
**IFAA** ........ International Furniture and Accessory Association (EA)
**IFAB** ........ Integrated Fire Direction System for the Artillery Battery [*German*]
**IFABA** ........ Izvestiya na Fizicheskiya Instituta ANEB. Bulgarska Akademiya na Naukite [*A publication*]
**IFABC** ........ International Federation of Audit Bureaux of Circulations (EAIO)
**IFAC** ........ Independent Fee Appraiser/Counselor [*Designation awarded by National Association of Independent Fee Appraisers, Inc.*]
**IFAC** ........ International Federation of Accountants [*New York, NY*] (EA)
**IFAC** ........ International Federation of Automatic Control (EAIO)
**IFAC** ........ International Food Additives Council (EA)
**IFAD** ........ Interactive Finite Element Analysis and Design [*Software*] [*Automotive engineering*]
**IFAD** ........ International Foundation for Agricultural Development (EA)
**IFAD** ........ International Fund for Agricultural Development [*United Nations*]
**I Fa De** ........ Ilahiyat Fakueltesi Dergisi [*Ankara*] [*A publication*]
**IFAE** ........ International Farmers Association for Education [*Defunct*] (EA)
**IFaf** ........ Fairfield Public Library, Fairfield, IL [*Library symbol*] [*Library of Congress*] (LCLS)
**IFAFA** ........ Italian Folk Art Federation of America (EA)
**IFAHPF** ........ International Federation of American Homing Pigeon Fanciers (EA)
**IFAI** ........ Industrial Fabrics Association International (EA)
**IFAI** ........ International Fire Administration Institute
**IFALPA** ........ International Federation of Air Line Pilots Associations [*Egham, England*] (EAIO)
**IFAM** ........ Initial-Final Address Message [*Telecommunications*] (TEL)
**IFAM** ........ Inverted File Access Method
**IFA Monogr Ser** ... IFA [*Institutul de Fizica Atomica*] Monograph Series [*A publication*]
**IFAMP** ........ If Approach Missed Proceed [*Aviation*] (FAAC)
**IFAMS** ........ Integrated Force Administration System [*Bell System*]
**IFAN** ........ Institut Francais d'Afrique Noire [*French Institute of Black Africa*]
**IFAN** ........ Internationale Foderation der Ausschusse Normenpraxis [*International Federation for the Application of Standards*] (EAIO)
**IFANC** ........ International Free Academy of New Cosmology (EA)
**IFA News** ... IFA (International Fiscal Association) News [*A publication*]
**IFAOA** ........ Izvestiya Akademii Nauk SSSR Fizika Atmosfery i Okeana [*A publication*]
**IFAOBE** ........ Institut Francais d'Archeologie Orientale. Bibliotheque d'Etude [*A publication*]
**IFAO Bibl d'Et** ... Institut Francais d'Archeologie Orientale du Caire. Bibliotheque d'Etude [*A publication*] (BJA)
**IFAP** ........ International Federation of Agricultural Producers (EA)
**IFAPA** ........ International Foundation of Airline Passengers Associations (EAIO)
**IFAPAO** ........ International Federation of Asian and Pacific Associations of Optometrists [*Australia*] (EAIO)
**IFAP Ne** ... International Federation of Agricultural Producers. News [*A publication*]
**IFAPWE** ........ Institute of Ferro-Alloy Producers in Western Europe (EA)
**IFAR** ........ International Foundation for Art Research (EA)
**IFARD** ........ International Federation of Agricultural Research Systems for Development [*Netherlands*]
**IFarE** ........ Farmington East Unit District No. 324, Farmington, IL [*Library symbol*] [*Library of Congress*] (LCLS)
**IFARS** ........ Individual Flight Activity Reporting System [*Navy*]
**IFAS** ........ Independent Fee Appraiser, Senior [*Designation awarded by National Association of Independent Fee Appraisers, Inc.*]
**IFAS** ........ International Federation of Aquarium Societies
**IFASC** ........ Integrated Functions Assessment Steering Committee [*NASA*] (NASA)
**IFaSD** ........ Farina-LaGrove Community Unit, School District 206, Farina, IL [*Library symbol*] [*Library of Congress*] (LCLS)
**IFAST** ........ Integrated Facility for Avionics System Test [*Air Force*]
**IFAT** ........ Indirect Fluorescent Antibody Test [*Immunology*]
**IFAT** ........ Indirect Immunofluorescent Antibody Test [*Clinical chemistry*]
**IFATCA** ........ International Federation of Air Traffic Controllers' Associations [*Dublin, Republic of Ireland*] (EAIO)
**IFATCC** ........ International Federation of Associations of Textile Chemists and Colourists [*Pratteln, Switzerland*]
**IFATE** ........ International Federation of Airworthiness Technology and Engineering [*Later, IFA*]
**IFATSEA** .. International Federation of Air Traffic Safety Electronic Associations [*London, England*] (EAIO)
**IFAVWU** ... International Federation of Audio-Visual Workers Unions [*See also FISTA*] (EAIO)
**IFAW** ........ International Fund for Animal Welfare (EA)
**IFAWPCA** ... International Federation of Asian and Western Pacific Contractors' Associations [*Pasig, Metro Manila, Philippines*] (EAIO)
**IFAX** ........ International Facsimile Service [*Telecommunications*] (TEL)
**IFAXA** ........ International Facsimile Association (EA)
**IFB** ........ Fort Wayne Bible College, Fort Wayne, IN [*OCLC symbol*] (OCLC)
**IFB** ........ Incendiary Fragmentation Bomb
**IFB** ........ Independent Forward Bloc [*Mauritian political party*]
**IFB** ........ Industry of Free China [*A publication*]
**IFB** ........ Initiation for Bid
**IFB** ........ Institute of Foreign Bankers [*New York, NY*] (EA)
**IFB** ........ International Feather Bureau (EAIO)
**IFB** ........ International Federation of the Blind [*Later, WBU*]
**IFB** ........ Internationales Federn-Bureau [*International Feather Bureau - IFB*] (EAIO)
**IFB** ........ Invitation for Bid
**IFBA** ........ International Fire Buff Associates (EA)
**IFBB** ........ International Federation of Bodybuilders [*Montreal, PQ*] (EA)
**IFBC** ........ International Federation of the Blue Cross (EA)
**IFBDO** ........ International Federation of Blood Donor Organizations [*See also FIODS*] [*Dole, France*] (EAIO)
**IFBM** ........ Improved Fleet Ballistic Missile
**IFBPW** ........ International Federation of Business and Professional Women (EA)
**IFBQA8** ........ Industria Farmaceutica y Bioquimica [*A publication*]
**IFBS** ........ International Fashion and Boutique Show (ITD)
**IFBSO** ........ International Federation of Boat Show Organisers (EA)
**IFBSS** ........ Individual Flexible Barrier Shelter Systems (MCD)
**IFBTBI** ........ Boletim Tecnico. Instituto Florestal [*A publication*]
**IFBWW** ........ International Federation of Building and Wood Workers [*Sweden*]
**IFC** ........ Franklin College of Indiana, Franklin, IN [*OCLC symbol*] (OCLC)
**IFC** ........ If Clause
**IFC** ........ Imasco Financial Corp. [*Vancouver Stock Exchange symbol*] [*Toronto Stock Exchange symbol*]
**IFC** ........ Improved Flotation Chamber
**IFC** ........ In-Flight Calibration (KSC)
**IFC** ........ Incremental Frequency Control
**IFC** ........ Independent Fire Control [*Area*] (NATG)
**IFC** ........ Industrial Frequency Changer
**IFC** ........ Industry of Free China [*Taipei*] [*A publication*]
**IFC** ........ Infant Formula Council (EA)
**IFC** ........ Infrared Fire Control
**IFC** ........ Initial Floristic Composition [*Theory of plant succession*]
**IFC** ........ Instantaneous Frequency Correlation
**IFC** ........ Instrument Flight Center [*Air Force*]
**IFC** ........ Integrated Fire Control [*RADAR*]
**IFC** ........ Intellectual Freedom Committee [*American Library Association*]
**IFC** ........ Inter-Faith Compassionists (EA)
**IFC** ........ Interfirm Comparison (ADA)
**IFC** ........ InterFirst Corporation [*NYSE symbol*] (SPSG)

IFC............ Interfruitlet Corking [*of pineapple*]
IFC............ International Federation of Master-Craftsmen [*See also IFH*] (EAIO)
IFC............ International Film Completion Corp.
IFC............ International Finance Corporation [*Affiliate of International Bank for Reconstruction and Development*]
IFC............ International Fisheries Commission [*Later, IPHC*] [*US and Canada*]
IFC............ Interstate and Foreign Commerce (DLA)
IFC............ Intrinsic Factor Concentrate [*Biochemistry*]
IFCA.......... Independent Fundamental Churches of America (EA)
IFCA.......... Instrumentation to Follow the Course of an Accident [*Nuclear energy*] (NRCH)
IFCA.......... International Fan Club Association [*Formerly, FCA*] (EA)
IFCA.......... International Federation of Catholic Alumnae (EA)
IFCAA....... International Fire Chiefs' Association of Asia (EAIO)
IFCAS........ Indirect Fire Casualty Assessment/Suppression System [*Military*] (MCD)
IFCATI...... International Federation of Cotton and Allied Textile Industries [*Later, ITMF*]
IFCB.......... International Federation of Cell Biology [*Toronto, ON*] (EAIO)
IFCB.......... International Friendly Circle of the Blind (EA)
IFCbl.......... Intrinsic Factor Cobalamin (Complex) [*Biochemistry*]
IFCC.......... Iconized Flowchart Compilers [*Software*] [*Data processing*]
IFCC.......... Initial Fleet Command Center [*Navy*] (CAAL)
IFCC.......... Interim Fleet Command Center [*Navy*] (MCD)
IFCC.......... International Federation of Camping and Caravanning
IFCC.......... International Federation of Children's Communities [*Later, FICE*]
IFCC.......... International Federation of Clinical Chemistry [*Vienna, Austria*] (EA)
IFCCA....... International Federation of Community Centre Associations
IFCCTE..... International Federation of Commercial, Clerical, and Technical Employees
IFCE.......... Integral Fire Control Equipment (AAG)
IFCF.......... Integrated Fuel Cycle Facilities [*Nuclear energy*] (NRCH)
IFCF.......... Intermediate Frequency Crystal Filter
IFCF.......... International Frederic Chopin Foundation (EAIO)
IFCJ.......... International Federation of Catholic Journalists
IFCM.......... International Federation for Choral Music (EA)
IFCM.......... International Federation of Christian Metalworkers Unions
IFCMI....... International Federation of Children of Mary Immaculate [*Paris, France*] (EAIO)
IFCMU...... International Federation of Christian Miners' Unions
IFCN.......... Interfacility Communication Network
IFCNA....... Information and Control [*A publication*]
IFCND7..... FAO [*Food and Agriculture Organization of the United Nations*] Indo-Pacific Fishery Commission. Proceedings [*A publication*]
IFCO.......... International Fan Club Organization (EA)
IFCO.......... Interreligious Foundation for Community Organization (EA)
IFCO.......... Interstate Financial Corporation [*NASDAQ symbol*] (NQ)
IFCP.......... Institute for Financial Crime Prevention [*Later, NACFE*] (EA)
IFCP.......... International Federation of Catholic Pharmacists
IFCP.......... International Federation of the Cinematographic Press [*See also FIPRESCI*] (EAIO)
IFCP.......... International Fund for Concerned Photography [*Later, ICP*]
IFCPC........ International Federation of Cervical Pathology and Colposcopy [*Dundee, Scotland*] (EAIO)
IFCPD....... International Foundry Congress. Congress Papers [*A publication*]
IFCR.......... International Foundation for Cancer Research (EA)
IFCRM....... International Federation of Catholic Rural Movements (EAIO)
IFCS.......... Improved Fire Control System [*Military*] (MCD)
IFCS.......... In-Flight Checkout System (IEEE)
IFCS.......... Infrared Fire Control System
IFCS.......... Institute for Family and Child Study [*Michigan State University*] [*Research center*] (RCD)
IFCS.......... Integrated Flight Control System
IFCS.......... International Federation of Computer Sciences
IFCSS........ Independent Federation of Chinese Students and Scholars (EA)
IFCTIO..... International Federation of Commercial Travelers Insurance Organizations [*Later, CTIF*] (EA)
IFCTU....... International Federation of Christian Trade Unions [*Often uses initialism CISC, based on name in French, to avoid confusion with ICFTU*]
IFCTUBWW ... International Federation of Christian Trade Unions of Building and Wood Workers
IFCTUGP ... International Federation of Christian Trade Unions of Graphical and Paper Industries
IFCU.......... International Federation of Catholic Universities [*See also FIUC*] [*Paris, France*] (EAIO)
IFCUAW... International Federation of Christian Unions of Agricultural Workers
IFCWU...... International Federation of Chemical Workers' Unions
IFD............ Idealization to Frustration to Demoralization
IFD............ Image File Directory [*Data processing*]
IFD............ In Flagrante Delicto [*Caught in the Act*] [*Latin*]
IFD............ In-Flight Deployment
IFD............ In-Line Filter Degasser
IFD............ Incipient Fire Detection
IFD............ Infrared Detector
IFD............ Initial Fill Date [*Army*] (AABC)
IFD............ Instantaneous Frequency Discriminator (IEEE)
IFD............ Integrated Flight Director [*Aviation*]
IFD............ Inter-Fighter Director
IFD............ Interfiber Distance
IFD............ International Federation for Documentation [*Also, FID*] [*Later, IFID*]
IFD............ International Foundation Directory [*A publication*]
IFD............ Internationale Foderation des Dachdeckerhandwerks [*International Federation of Roofing Contractors*] (EAIO)
IFDA.......... Independent Film Distributors' Association [*British*]
IFDA.......... Institutional Food Distributors of America [*Later, NAWGA*] (EA)
IFDA.......... International Foodservice Distributors Association (EA)
IFDA.......... International Foundation for Development Alternatives [*See also FIPAD*] [*Nyon, Switzerland*] (EAIO)
IFDA.......... International Franchised Dealers Association [*Later, SFDA*] (EA)
IFDA.......... International Frisbee Disc Association [*Formerly, IFA*] (EA)
IFDA.......... International Furnishings and Design Association (EA)
IFDAI........ Istanbuler Forschungen. Deutsches Archaeologisches Institut [*A publication*]
IFDAPS..... Integrated Flight Data Processing System [*Air Force*]
IFDAS....... International Federation of Dental Anesthesiology Societies [*London, England*] (EAIO)
IFDC.......... Industrial Funding Corp. [*NASDAQ symbol*] (NQ)
IFDC.......... International Fertilizer Development Center (EA)
IFDC.......... Intraductal and Infiltrating Duct Carcinoma [*Oncology*]
IFDCAUS ... International Flying Dutchman Class Association of the US (EA)
IFDCO....... International Flying Dutchmen Class Organization [*Berlin, Federal Republic of Germany*] (EAIO)
IFDI.......... Israel Folk Dance Institute (EA)
IFDM.......... International Foundation of Doll Makers (EA)
IFDO.......... International Federation of Dalit Organizations (EA)
IFDO.......... International Federation of Data Organizations for the Social Sciences [*Amsterdam, Netherlands*] (EAIO)
IFDP.......... Institute for Food and Development Policy (EA)
IFDS.......... Inertial Flight Data System (KSC)
IFDS.......... Integrated Flagship Data System [*Navy*] (NG)
IFDVS....... Indian Field Depot Veterinary Stores [*British military*] (DMA)
IFE............ Image Feature Extraction [*Air Force*]
IFE............ Immunofixation Electrophoresis [*Clinical chemistry*]
IFE............ In-Flight Emergency (MCD)
IFE............ Inner Front End (MSA)
IFE............ Institut Francais de l'Energie [*French Institute of Energy*] [*Paris*] [*Information service or system*] (IID)
IFE............ Institute of Financial Education [*Chicago, IL*] (EA)
IFE............ Institute of Fire Engineers
IFE............ Institute for Fluitronics Education (EA)
IFE............ Internal Field Emission
IFE............ International Fasteners Exposition (ITD)
IFE............ International Food and Drink Exhibition [*Great Britain*] (ITD)
Ife Afr Stud ... Ife African Studies [*A publication*]
IFEAT........ International Federation of Essential Oils and Aroma Trades [*London, England*] (EAIO)
IFEBP........ International Foundation of Employee Benefit Plans (EA)
IFEC.......... International Foodservice Editorial Council (EA)
IFED.......... Inter Federal Savings Bank [*NASDAQ symbol*] (NQ)
IFEEX........ International Fishing Equipment Exposition [*Canada*] (ITD)
IFEF.......... Internacia Fervojista Esperanto Federacio [*International Federation of Esperantist Railwaymen*] (EAIO)
IFEH.......... International Federation of Europe Houses [*See also FIME*] (EAIO)
IFEI........... Imagine Films Entertainment, Inc. [*NASDAQ symbol*] (NQ)
IFEL.......... Inverse Free Electron LASER [*Plasma physics*]
IFEM.......... Institute of Fireplace Equipment Manufacturers (EA)
IFEMA...... Industrial Finishing Equipment Manufacturers Association (EA)
IFEMS....... International Federation of Electron Microscope Societies
IFEP.......... In-Flight Experiments Panel
IFEP.......... Inflation from an Energy Perspective [*Economic theory*]
IFEPFC..... International Federation of Elvis Presley Fan Clubs (EA)
IFER.......... International Federation of Engine Reconditioners [*See also FIRM*] [*Paris, France*] (EAIO)
IFER.......... International Foundation for Ethical Research (EA)
IFER.......... Internationale Foederation der Eisenbahn-Reklame-Gesellschaften [*International Federation of Railway Advertising Companies*] [*London, England*] (EA)
IFERS........ International Flat Earth Research Society (EA)
IFES.......... Image Feature Extraction System [*Air Force*]
IFES.......... International Fellowship of Evangelical Students (EA)
IFES.......... International Foundation for Electoral Systems (EA)
IFESLG..... International Fellowship of Evangelical Students Link Group (EA)
IFeT.......... Intestinal Iron (Ferrum) Transport [*Physiology*]
IFEW.......... Inter-American Federation of Entertainment Workers
IFEX.......... IFEX, Inc. [*New York, NY*] [*NASDAQ symbol*] (NQ)
IFf............ Frankfort Public Library District, Frankfort, IL [*Library symbol*] [*Library of Congress*] (LCLS)

**IFF** ............ Identification, Friend or Foe [*Military*]
**IFF** ............ If and Only If (IEEE)
**IFF** ............ Iffley [*Australia*] [*Airport symbol*] [*Obsolete*] (OAG)
**IFF** ............ Individual Freedom Federation (EA)
**IFF** ............ Induced Fluid Flow
**IFF** ............ Inert Fluid Fill (AAG)
**IFF** ............ Institute of Freight Forwarders [*British*]
**IFF** ............ Institute for the Future
**IFF** ............ Institute of Natural Resources, Springfield, IL [*OCLC symbol*] (OCLC)
**IFF** ............ Intensity Fluctuation Factor [*Telecommunications*] (TEL)
**IFF** ............ Interchange File Format [*Data processing*]
**IF & F**........ Intermediate Flush and Fill (AAG)
**IFF** ............ International Federal Film [*Fictitious organization of agents in TV series "Scarecrow and Mrs. King"*]
**IFF** ............ International Federation of Falerists (EA)
**IFF** ............ International Fencing Federation [*Paris, France*] (EA)
**IFF** ............ International Film Foundation
**IFF** ............ International Flavors & Fragrances, Inc. [*NYSE symbol*] (SPSG)
**IFF** ............ International Flying Farmers (EA)
**IFF** ............ International Forum Foundation
**IFF** ............ International Freedom Foundation (EA)
**IFF** ............ Ionized Flow Field
**IFF** ............ Iran Freedom Foundation (EA)
**IFF** ............ Isoelectric Focusing Facility
**IFF** ............ Item Intelligence File [*DoD*]
**IFFA** .......... Independent Federation of Flight Attendants (EA)
**IFFA** .......... Interactive Flash Flood Analyzer
**IFFA** .......... International Federation of Film Archives
**IFFA** .......... International Frozen Food Association (EA)
**IFF/ATCRBS** ... Identification Friend or Foe/Air-Traffic Control RADAR Beacon System [*Military*]
**IFFBB**........ IFF [*Institut fuer Festkoerperforschung*] Bulletin [*A publication*]
**IFF Bull** ..... IFF [*Institut fuer Festkoerperforschung*] Bulletin [*A publication*]
**IFFC** .......... Integrated Flight and Fire Control
**IFFCO** ....... Indian Farmers Fertiliser Cooperative Ltd. [*Gujarat, India*]
**IFFCS** ....... International Fancy Food and Confection Show (ITD)
**IFFEC**........ International Federation of Free Evangelical Churches (EA)
**IFFEX**........ International Frozen Food Exhibition and Congress (TSPED)
**IFFF**.......... Internationale Frauenliga fuer Frieden und Freiheit [*Women's International League for Peace and Freedom*]
**IFFH**.......... International Federation for Family Health [*Bandung, Indonesia*] (EA)
**IFFJ** .......... International Federation of Free Journalists [*Great Britain*]
**IFFJP** ........ International Federation of Fruit Juice Producers [*See also FIJU*] [*Paris, France*] (EAIO)
**IFFLP**........ International Federation for Family Life Promotion (EA)
**IFFN**.......... Identification, Friend or Foe or Neutral (MCD)
**IFFPA**........ International Federation of Film Producers' Associations
**IFFPAP** ..... Indian Forest Records. Forest Pathology [*A publication*]
**IFFS**.......... Identification, Friend or Foe, Switching Circuit [*Military*] (MSA)
**IFFS**.......... International Federation of Fertility Societies (EAIO)
**IFFS**.......... International Federation of Film Societies
**IFFSA**........ Inflight Food Service Association (EA)
**IFFSH** ....... Instrument Formation Flight System for Helicopters
**IFF/SIF** ..... Identification, Friend or Foe/Selective Identification Feature [*Military*]
**IFFTU** ....... International Federation of Free Teachers' Unions [*See also SPIE*] [*Amsterdam, Netherlands*] (EAIO)
**IFF-UK**...... International Freedom Foundation - United Kingdom Branch (EAIO)
**IFG**............ Institute for Research on Educational Finance and Governance [*Department of Education*] (GRD)
**IFG**............ Instream Flow Service Group [*United States Fish and Wildlife Service*]
**IFG**............ Inter-Regional Financial Group, Inc. [*NYSE symbol*] (SPSG)
**IFG**............ International Fashion Group [*Later, Fashion Group International*] (EA)
**IFG**............ Kaskaskia Library System, Smithton, IL [*OCLC symbol*] (OCLC)
**IFGA**.......... International Fancy Guppy Association (EA)
**IFGA**.......... International Federation of Grocers' Associations [*See also IVLD*] [*Bern, Switzerland*] (EAIO)
**IFGB**.......... Institute of Chartered Foresters [*British*]
**IFGE**.......... International Foundation for Gender Education (EA)
**IFGL**.......... Initial File Generation Language
**IFGMA**...... International Federation of Grocery Manufacturers Associations (EA)
**IFGN** ......... [*The*] InferGene Co. [*Benicia, CA*] [*NASDAQ symbol*] (NQ)
**IFGO** ......... International Federation of Gynecology and Obstetrics
**IFGS**.......... International Fantasy Gaming Society (EA)
**IFGVP** ....... International Federation of Gastronomical and Vinicultural Press
**IFH** ............ In-Flight Helium
**IFH** ............ International Foundation for Homeopathy (EA)
**IFH** ............ Internationale Foderation des Handwerks [*International Federation of Master-Craftsmen - IFMC*] [*Vienna, Austria*] (EAIO)
**IFH** ............ Judson College Library, Elgin, IL [*OCLC symbol*] (OCLC)
**IFH/C**........ Conjonction. Institut Francais d'Haiti [*A publication*]
**IFHE**.......... International Federation for Home Economics [*See also FIEF*] [*Paris, France*] (EAIO)
**IFHG** ......... Illawarra Family History Group [*Australia*]
**IFHG** ......... Institute of Family History and Genealogy (EA)
**IFhGS**........ Grant-Illini School 110, Fairview Heights, IL [*Library symbol*] [*Library of Congress*] (LCLS)
**IFhGSD**..... Grant Community Consolidated School District 110, Fairview Heights, IL [*Library symbol*] [*Library of Congress*] (LCLS)
**IFHOH**...... International Federation of the Hard of Hearing [*Kampen, Netherlands*] (EAIO)
**IFHOL**....... If Holding [*Aviation*] (FAAC)
**IFHP**.......... International Federation of Health Professionals (EA)
**IFHP**.......... International Federation for Housing and Planning [*Netherlands*]
**IFHPM**...... International Federation of Hydraulic Platform Manufacturers [*Later, IPAF*] (EAIO)
**IFHPMSM** ... International Federation for Hygiene, Preventive Medicine, and Social Medicine [*Nancy, France*] (EA)
**IFhPSD** ..... Pontiac-William Holliday School District 105, Fairview Heights, IL [*Library symbol*] [*Library of Congress*] (LCLS)
**IFHPSM** ... International Federation for Hygiene, Preventive, and Social Medicine (EAIO)
**IFHRO** ...... International Federation of Health Records Organizations [*Munich, Federal Republic of Germany*] (EAIO)
**IFHS**.......... Irish Family History Society (EA)
**IFHTP** ....... International Federation for Housing and Town Planning
**IFI**............. In-Flight Insertion (NG)
**IFI**............. Industrial Fasteners Institute (EA)
**IFI**............. Infisy Systems, Incorporated [*Vancouver Stock Exchange symbol*]
**IFI**............. International Fabricare Institute (EA)
**IFI**............. International Federation of Interior Architects/Interior Designers [*Amsterdam, Netherlands*] (EAIO)
**IFI**............. International Feedstuffs Institute [*Utah State University*] [*Research center*] [*Defunct*] (RCD)
**IFI**............. International Film Institute
**IFI**............. International Financial Institution
**IFI**............. International Foundation for Independence (EA)
**IFI**............. International Fund for Ireland [*United States, Canada, and New Zealand*]
**IFI**............. Istituto Finanziaro Industriale SpA [*Italian*]
**IFI**............. Kingfisher, OK [*Location identifier*] [*FAA*] (FAAL)
**IFI**............. Sidley & Austin, Chicago, IL [*OCLC symbol*] (OCLC)
**IFIA** .......... Intermountain Forest Industry Association (EA)
**IFIA** .......... International Federation of Inventors' Associations [*Stockholm, Sweden*] (EAIO)
**IFIA** .......... International Federation of Ironmongers and Iron Merchants Associations [*See also FIDAQ*] [*Zurich, Switzerland*] (EAIO)
**IFIA** .......... International Fence Industry Association (EA)
**IFIA** .......... International Financial Institutions Act [*1977*]
**IFIAS**......... International Federation of Institutes for Advanced Study [*ICSU*] [*Toronto, ON*] (EAIO)
**IFIAT** ........ International Federation of Independent Air Transport
**IFIC** .......... International Ferrocement Information Center [*Asian Institute of Technology*] (IID)
**IFIC** .......... International Food Information Council (EA)
**IFICO** ........ Industrial Finance and Investment Corp. [*Great Britain*]
**IFID** .......... International Federation for Information and Documentation [*See also FIID*] (EAIO)
**IFIDA** ........ Independent Film Importers and Distributors of America [*Defunct*] (EA)
**IFIEA7** ...... Anales. Instituto Forestal de Investigaciones y Experiencias [*Madrid*] [*A publication*]
**IFIEC**......... International Federation of Industrial Energy Consumers [*Geneva, Switzerland*] (EA)
**IFIF**............ International Federation of Industrial Organizations and General Workers' Unions
**IFIF**............ International Federation for Internal Freedom [*Later, Castalia Foundation*] (EA)
**IFIFAA**...... Irish Fisheries Investigations. Series A. Freshwater [*A publication*]
**IFIFR**......... International Federation of International Furniture Removers [*See also FIDI*] [*Brussels, Belgium*] (EAIO)
**IFII** ............ Indiana Financial Investors, Incorporated [*NASDAQ symbol*] (NQ)
**IFIIA**.......... Industrial Finishing (Wheaton, Illinois) [*A publication*]
**IFIJG**......... International Federation of Infantile and Juvenile Gynecology [*See also FIGIJ*] [*Sierre, Switzerland*] (EAIO)
**IFIM** .......... International Flight Information Manual
**IFIMAV** .... Irish Fisheries Investigations. Series B. Marine [*A publication*]
**IFINS** ......... If Instrument Conditions Encountered [*Aviation*] (FAAC)
**IFIO**........... Information for Industry Office [*Air Force*] (MCD)

**IFIP** .......... International Federation for Information Processing [*Formerly, IFIPS*] (EA)
**IFIPC** .......... IFIP [*International Federation for Information Processing*] Congress Series [*Elsevier Book Series*] [*A publication*]
**IFIP (Int Fed Inf Process) Med Inf Monogr Ser** ... IFIP (International Federation for Information Processing) Medical Informatics Monograph Series [*A publication*]
**IFIP (Int Fed Inf Process) World Conf Ser Med Inf** ... IFIP (International Federation for Information Processing) World Conference Series on Medical Informatics [*A publication*]
**IFIP Med Inf Monogr Ser** ... IFIP [*International Federation for Information Processing*] Medical Informatics Monograph Series [*A publication*]
**IFIPS** .......... International Federation of Information Processing Societies [*Later, IFIP*]
**IFIPW** .......... IFIP [*International Federation for Information Processing*] World Conference Series on Medical Informatics [*Elsevier Book Series*] [*A publication*]
**IFIS** .......... Industry File Index System [*Chemical Information Systems, Inc.*] [*Information service or system*] (CRD)
**IFIS** .......... Instrument Flight Instructors School [*Navy*]
**IFiS** .......... Instytut Filozofii i Socjologii Pan [*A publication*]
**IFIS** .......... Integrated Flight Instrument System
**IFIS** .......... International Food Information Service [*Database producer*] [*Frankfurt, West Germany*]
**IFISRR** .......... International Federation of Institutes for Socio-Religious Research [*Louvain, Belgium*] (EA)
**IFIWA** .......... International Federation of Importers and Wholesale Grocers Associations [*The Hague, Netherlands*] (EAIO)
**IFJ** .......... Franklin-Johnson County Public Library, Franklin, IN [*OCLC symbol*] (OCLC)
**IFJ** .......... International Federation of Journalists [*See also FIJ*] [*Brussels, Belgium*] (EAIO)
**IFJ** .......... Isafjordur [*Iceland*] [*Airport symbol*] (OAG)
**IFJ** .......... Winnfield, LA [*Location identifier*] [*FAA*] (FAAL)
**IFJOD** .......... IFLA [*International Federation of Library Associations and Institutions*] Journal [*A publication*]
**IFK** .......... Installations Fragenkommission [*Later, International Commission on Rules for the Approval of Electrical Equipment*] [*CEE*]
**IFK** .......... River Bend Library System, Coal Valley, IL [*OCLC symbol*] (OCLC)
**IFKC** .......... International Federation of Kennel Clubs (EA)
**IFKKA** .......... Izvestiya Sektora Fiziko-Khimicheskogo Analiza Institut Obshchei i Neorganicheskoi Khimii Imeni N. S. Kurnakova Akademiya Nauk SSSR [*A publication*]
**IFKM** .......... Internationale Foederation fuer Kurzschrift und Maschinenschreiben [*International Federation of Shorthand and Typewriting*]
**IFKT** .......... International Federation of Knitting Technologists [*See also FITB*] [*Frauenfeld, Switzerland*] (EAIO)
**IFL** .......... Flora Carnegie Library, Flora, IL [*Library symbol*] [*Library of Congress*] (LCLS)
**IFL** .......... Icelandic Federation of Labor
**IFL** .......... IMC Fertilizer Group [*NYSE symbol*] (SPSG)
**IFL** .......... Imperial Fascist League [*British*]
**IFL** .......... Inflatable (MSA)
**IFL** .......... Initial Flight Level
**IFL** .......... Innisfail [*Australia*] [*Airport symbol*]
**IFL** .......... Intelligent Fault Locator [*McDonnell Douglas Helicopter Co.*] [*Army*]
**IFL** .......... International Financial Law Review [*A publication*]
**IFL** .......... International Frequency List (NATG)
**IFL** .......... International Friendship League [*Defunct*] (EA)
**IFLA** .......... International Federation of Landscape Architects [*Versailles, France*] (EAIO)
**IFLA** .......... International Federation of Library Associations and Institutions
**IFLA News** ... International Federation of Library Associations. News [*A publication*]
**IFLASC** .......... International Federation of Latin American Study Centers [*Mexico City, Mexico*] (EAIO)
**IFLB** .......... Iowa Foreign Language Bulletin [*A publication*]
**IFLB** .......... Islamic Front for the Liberation of Bahrain [*Political party*] (PD)
**IFLBP** .......... International Federation of the Little Brothers of the Poor [*See also FIPFP*] (EAIO)
**IFLC** .......... International Frequency List Committee
**IFlCL** .......... Cumberland Trail Library System, Flora, IL [*Library symbol*] [*Library of Congress*] (LCLS)
**IFL-DFL** .......... Inflating-Deflating
**IFLG** .......... International Federation of Leather Guilds (EA)
**IfL Mitt** .......... IfL [*Institut fuer Leichtbau und Oekonomische Verwendung von Werkstoffen*] Mitteilung [*East Germany*] [*A publication*]
**IFLN** .......... Interstate Freeze Lobbying Network (EA)
**IFlo** .......... Flossmoor Public Library, Flossmoor, IL [*Library symbol*] [*Library of Congress*] (LCLS)
**IFLOT** .......... Intermediate Focal Length Optical Tracker
**IFLOWS** .......... Integrated Flood Observing and Warning System [*National Oceanic and Atmospheric Administration*]
**IFLP** .......... Index to Foreign Legal Periodicals [*A publication*]
**IFL Rev** .......... International Financial Law Review [*A publication*] (DLA)
**IFLRY** .......... International Federation of Liberal and Radical Youth (EAIO)
**IFLS** .......... International Federation of Law Students (DLA)
**IFLS** .......... International Federation of Little Singers (EAIO)
**IFLTT** .......... Intermediate Focal Length Tracking Telescope (MUGU)
**IFM** .......... Improved Frequency Modulation (MCD)
**IFM** .......... In-Flight Maintenance
**IFM** .......... Information and Management [*Netherlands*] [*A publication*]
**IFM** .......... Instantaneous Frequency Measurement
**IFM** .......... Institute of Fisheries Management [*British*]
**IFM** .......... Instrument Flag Motor
**IFM** .......... Integrating Fluctuation Meter
**IFM** .......... Interactive File Manager [*Data processing*]
**IFM** .......... Intermediate Frame Memory [*Data processing*]
**IFM** .......... International Falcon Movement
**IFM** .......... International Finance Managers Study [*Database*] [*Research Services Ltd.*] [*Information service or system*] (CRD)
**IFM** .......... International Financial Markets Trading Ltd.
**IFM** .......... International Fund for Monuments
**IFM** .......... Intrafusal Muscle [*Anatomy*]
**IFM** .......... Iowa Farm-to-Market Carriers Tariff Bureau, Ottumwa IA [*STAC*]
**IFM** .......... Tifton, GA [*Location identifier*] [*FAA*] (FAAL)
**IFMA** .......... Immunofluorescence [*or Immunofluorometric*] Assay [*Also, IFA*] [*Analytical biochemistry*]
**IFMA** .......... Immunofluorometric Assay [*Analytical biochemistry*]
**IFMA** .......... Interdenominational Foreign Mission Association of North America (EA)
**IFMA** .......... International Facility Management Association (EA)
**IFMA** .......... International Farm Management Association [*Reading, Berkshire, England*] (EAIO)
**IFMA** .......... International Federation of Margarine Associations [*Brussels, Belgium*] (EAIO)
**IFMA** .......... International Foodservice Manufacturers Association (EA)
**IFMAA** .......... Istanbul Universitesi Fen Fakultesi Mecmuasi. Seri A. Matematik-Fizik-Kimya [*A publication*]
**IFMBA** .......... Istanbul Universitesi Fen Fakultesi Mecmuasi. Seri B [*A publication*]
**IFMBE** .......... International Federation for Medical and Biological Engineering [*ICSU*] [*Ottawa, ON*] (EA)
**IFMC** .......... International Federation of Master-Craftsmen (EA)
**IFMC** .......... International Folk Music Council [*Later, ICTM*]
**IFMCA** .......... Istanbul Universitesi Fen Fakultesi Mecmuasi. Seri C. Astronomi-Fizik-Kimya [*A publication*]
**IFMCJ** .......... International Folk Music Council. Journal [*A publication*]
**IFMCY** .......... International Folk Music Council. Yearbook [*A publication*]
**IFME** .......... International Federation for Medical Electronics
**IFME** .......... International Federation of Municipal Engineers [*See also FIIM*] [*London, England*] (EAIO)
**IF/MF** .......... Intermediate Frequency/Medium Frequency (NATG)
**IFMIS** .......... Implementation Field Microfilm/Micrographics Information System
**IFMIS** .......... Industrial Facilities and Material Information System
**IFMIS** .......... Integrated Facilities Management Information System
**IFML** .......... International Film Management Limited [*Australia*]
**IFMLL** .......... International Federation for Modern Languages and Literatures [*A publication*]
**IFMM** .......... International Federation of Manual Medicine (EA)
**IFMO** .......... Imperial and Foreign Money Orders
**IFMP** .......... International Federation of Maritime Philately [*Livorno, Italy*] (EAIO)
**IFMP** .......... International Federation of Married Priests (EAIO)
**IFMP** .......... International Federation for Medical Psychotherapy [*See also IGAP*] [*Oslo, Norway*] (EAIO)
**IFMS** .......... Impact Force Measuring System
**IFMS** .......... In-Flight Management System
**IFMS** .......... Integrated Farm Management System
**IFMS** .......... Integrated Financial Management System (AABC)
**IFMS** .......... International Federation of Magical Societies [*See also FISM*] (EAIO)
**IFMSA** .......... International Federation of Medical Students Associations [*See also FIAEM*] [*Vienna, Austria*] (EAIO)
**IFM-SEI** .......... International Falcon Movement - Socialist Educational International
**IFMSS** .......... International Federation of Multiple Sclerosis Societies [*London, England*] (EAIO)
**IFMX** .......... Informix Corp. [*Menlo Park, CA*] [*NASDAQ symbol*] (NQ)
**IFN** .......... Information [*Data processing*] (MDG)
**IFN** .......... Interferon [*Also, IF*] [*Biochemistry*]
**IFN** .......... International Friends of Nature [*See also NFI*] [*Zurich, Switzerland*] (EAIO)
**IFN** .......... Isfahan [*Iran*] [*Airport symbol*] (OAG)
**IFNA** .......... International Federation of Netball Associations [*Glasgow, Scotland*] (EAIO)
**IFNA** .......... International FidoNet Association (EA)
**IFNA** .......... International Flying Nurses Association (EA)
**IFND** .......... Interfund Corp. [*Cannon Falls, MN*] [*NASDAQ symbol*] (NQ)
**IFNE** .......... International Federation for Narcotic Education
**IFNS** .......... International Financial News Survey [*A publication*]
**IFNS** .......... Irish Family Names Society (EA)

**IFO** ............ Identified Flying Object [*Air Force*]
**Ifo**............. Ifo-Schnelldienst [*A publication*]
**IFO** ............ Improved Fiber Optics
**IFO** ............ Info-Stop Communications [*Vancouver Stock Exchange symbol*]
**IFO** ............ Information Systems Office [*NASA*] (NASA)
**IFO** ............ International Field Office [*FAA*] (FAAC)
**IFO** ............ Interphone (FAAC)
**IFOA**.......... Isotta Fraschini Owner's Association (EA)
**IFOAM**...... International Federation of Organic Agriculture Movements [*Witzenhausen, Federal Republic of Germany*] (EA)
**IFOB**.......... Improved Fiber Optics Bundle
**IFOBAS**..... Indian Forest Bulletin [*A publication*]
**IFOBRL** .... In-Flight Operable Bomb Rack Lock (MCD)
**IFOC**.......... Intermountain Field Operations Center [*Bureau of Mines*] [*Denver, CO*] (GRD)
**IFOC**.......... International Fiber Optics and Communications [*A publication*]
**IFOC Int Fiber Opt** ... IFOC. International Fiber Optics and Communications [*A publication*]
**IFOFSAG** ... International Fellowship of Former Scouts and Guides [*Brussels, Belgium*]
**IFOMA**...... Independent Fuel Oil Marketers of America [*Defunct*] (EA)
**IFOMA**...... Instructions for Mailers [*A publication*]
**IFop**........... Forest Park Public Library, Forest Park, IL [*Library symbol*] [*Library of Congress*] (LCLS)
**IFOP**.......... Institut Francais d'Opinion Publique [*French Institute of Public Opinion*]
**IFOR**.......... Internal Format Object Report (MCD)
**IFOR**.......... International Fellowship of Reconciliation [*Alkmaar, Netherlands*] (EA)
**IFORA8**..... Indian Forester [*A publication*]
**IFORD**....... Institut de Formation et de Recherche Demographiques [*Institute for Training and Demographic Research - ITDR*] (EAIO)
**IFORS** ....... International Federation of Operational Research Societies [*ICSU*] [*Lyngby, Denmark*] (EAIO)
**IFORVU**.... International Federation of Recreational Vehicle Users [*Later, FOR*] (EA)
**IFOS** .......... International Federation of Ophthalmological Societies [*Nijmegen, Netherlands*] (EA)
**IFOS** .......... International Federation of Oto-Rhino-Laryngological Societies [*Berchem, Belgium*] (EAIO)
**IFOS** .......... Ion Formation from Organic Solids [*International conference*]
**IFOSS**........ Intelligence Family of Systems Study [*Military*] (MCD)
**IFOT**.......... In-Flight Operations and Training (MCD)
**IFOTES**..... International Federation of Telephonic Emergency Services [*Jorn, Sweden*] (EA)
**IFOV**.......... Individual Field of View
**IFOV**.......... Instantaneous Field of View
**IFOV**.......... Instrument Field of View
**IFP**............. Illinois Functional Programming Language [*Data processing*]
**IFP**............. In-Flight Performance
**IFP**............. In Forma Pauperis [*As a Pauper*] [*Latin*]
**IFP**............. Independent Feature Project (EA)
**IFP**............. Index to Free Periodicals [*A publication*]
**IFP**............. Indexes of Firepower Potential
**IFP**............. Inflammatory Fibroid Polyp [*Gastroenterology*]
**IFP**............. Institut Francais du Petroles [*French Institute of Petroleum*] [*Paris*]
**IFP**............. Institute of Fluid Power
**IFP**............. Institute of Physical Problems [*USSR*] (MCD)
**IFP**............. Integrated File Processor
**IFP**............. International Federation of Pedestrians (EA)
**IFP**............. International Federation of Purchasing
**IFP**............. International Fixed Public
**IFP**............. International Forest Products Ltd. [*Toronto Stock Exchange symbol*] [*Vancouver Stock Exchange symbol*]
**IFP**............. Interns for Peace (EA)
**IFP**............. Invitation for Proposal (NOAA)
**IFPA**.......... Independent Fluorspar Producers Association (EA)
**IFPA**.......... Independent Free Papers of America (EA)
**IFPA**.......... Industrial Fire Protection Association of Great Britain
**IFPA**.......... Information Film Producers of America [*Later, Association of Visual Communicators*] (EA)
**IFPA**.......... Institute for Foreign Policy Analysis, Inc. [*Tufts University*] [*Research center*] (RCD)
**IFPA**.......... International Federation of Photographic Art
**IFPA**.......... International Federation of Psoriasis Associations [*Stockholm, Sweden*] (EAIO)
**IFPA**.......... International Fire Photographers Association (EA)
**IFPA**.......... Isoelectric Focusing in Polyacrylamide [*Gel*] [*Analytical chemistry*]
**IFPAAU** .... Indian Food Packer [*A publication*]
**IFPAAW** ... International Federation of Plantation, Agricultural, and Allied Workers [*Switzerland*]
**IFPC**.......... Integrated Flight and Propulsion Control (MCD)
**IFPCA** ....... International Federation of Press Cutting Agencies (EA)
**IFPCS**........ International Federation of Unions of Employees in Public and Civil Services
**IFPCW** ...... International Federation of Petroleum and Chemical Workers (EA)
**IFPD**.......... International Federation of Postcard Dealers (EA)
**IFPE** .......... Institute of Fiscal and Political Education (EA)
**IFPE** .......... International Federation for Parent Education [*See also FIEP*] [*Sevres, France*] (EAIO)
**IFPEC**........ Independent Film Producers Export Corporation [*Defunct*]
**IFPFP**........ Individual Flight Plans from This Point (FAAC)
**IFPI** ........... International Federation of the Phonographic Industry (EAIO)
**IFPI** ........... International Federation of the Photographic Industry
**IFPITB** ...... Inorganic Feed Phosphates International Technical Bureau (EAIO)
**IFPLA**........ Information Processing Letters [*A publication*]
**IFPM**.......... In-Flight Performance Monitor
**IFPM**.......... International Federation of Physical Medicine
**IFPMA** ...... International Federation of Pharmaceutical Manufacturers Associations [*See also FIIM*] [*Geneva, Switzerland*] (EAIO)
**IFPMM**..... International Federation of Purchasing and Materials Management [*Aarau, Switzerland*] (EAIO)
**IFPMO**...... International Federation of Psychological-Medical Organizations [*See also FIOPM*] [*Lausanne, Switzerland*] (EAIO)
**IFPMR** ...... International Federation of Physical Medicine and Rehabilitation (EA)
**IFPNT** ....... International Federation of Practitioners of Natural Therapeutics [*British*]
**IFPO**.......... International Foundation for Protection Officers (EA)
**IFPP** .......... Industrial Facilities Protection Program [*DoD*]
**IFPP** .......... Irradiated Fuel Processing Plant (DEN)
**IFPRA** ....... Interamerican Federation of Public Relations Associations
**IFPRA** ....... International Family Planning Research Association [*Later, ISRM*] (EA)
**IFPRA** ....... International Federation of Park and Recreation Administration [*Reading, England*] (EAIO)
**IFPRI**......... International Food Policy Research Institute (EA)
**IFPS**........... [*A*] programming language [*1979*] (CSR)
**IFPS**........... International Federation of Palynological Societies (EAIO)
**IFPS**........... International Federation of Philosophical Societies [*See also FISP*] [*Fribourg, Switzerland*] (EAIO)
**IFPS**........... International Federation of Popular Sports [*See also IVV*] (EAIO)
**IFPS**........... International Federation of Psychoanalytic Societies (EA)
**IFPSM**....... International Federation for Preventive and Social Medicine (EAIO)
**IFPTE**........ International Federation of Professional and Technical Engineers (EA)
**IFPTO** ....... International Federation of Popular Travel Organisations [*Paris, France*] (EAIO)
**IFPTS**........ Intertype Fototronic Photographic System (DIT)
**IFPV**.......... International Federation of Pelota Vasca (EA)
**IFPVP**........ International Federation of Phonogram and Videogram Producers (EA)
**IFPW**......... International Federation of Petroleum Workers
**IFPWA** ...... International Federation of Protestant Workers' Associations
**IFPWA** ...... International Federation of Public Warehousing Associations (EAIO)
**IFPWKA** ... International Federation of Public Warehouse Keepers Associations [*Later, IFPWA*] (EAIO)
**IFQ** ........... Invitation for Quote (MCD)
**IFQAA**....... Informacion de Quimica Analitica [*A publication*]
**IFR**............ Ifrane [*Morocco*] [*Seismograph station code, US Geological Survey*] (SEIS)
**IFR**............ Image-to-Frame Ratio
**IFR**............ Imported Food Regulations [*British*]
**IFR**............ Impulse Fast Reactor [*USSR*]
**IFR**............ In-Flight Refueling
**IFR**............ Increasing Failure Rate
**IFR**............ Incremental Financial Rate of Return
**IFR**............ Independent Funds Research [*Australia*]
**IFR**............ Indian Foodgrain Requirements [*British*]
**I & FR** ........ Indian and Foreign Review [*A publication*]
**IFR**............ Infrared
**IFR**............ Infrared Filter Radiometer
**IFR**............ Inspiratory Flow Rate [*Physiology*]
**IFR**............ Instantaneous Frequency [*Indicating*] Receivers (IEEE)
**IFR**............ Institute of Fisheries Research [*University of North Carolina*]
**IFR**............ Instrument Flight Recovery [*NASA*]
**IFR**............ Instrument Flight Rules [*Aviation*]
**IFR**............ Integral Fast Reactor [*Nuclear energy*]
**IFR**............ Interface Register
**IFR**............ Intermediate Frequency Range (MCD)
**IFR**............ Internal Function Register
**IFR**............ International Fiction Review [*A publication*]
**IFR**............ International Fighter RADAR
**IFR**............ International Film Representatives [*Division of International Film Completion Corp.*]
**IFR**............ International Financing Review [*A publication*]
**IFR**............ International Flyer Resources Ltd. [*Vancouver Stock Exchange symbol*]
**IFR**............ Internationaler Frauenrat [*International Council of Women*]

**IFR**............ Isolated Flow Responder [*Physiology*]
**IFr**............ Italia Francescana [*A publication*]
**IFRA**.......... INCA [*International Newspaper Color Association*]-FIEJ [*Federation Internationale des Editeurs de Journaux*] Research Association [*Research center*] [*Federal Republic of Germany*] (IRC)
**IFRA**.......... Increasing Failure Rate Average [*Statistics*]
**IFRA**.......... Independent Fabric Retailers Association [*Defunct*] (EA)
**IFRA**.......... Infrasonics, Inc. [*San Diego, CA*] [*NASDAQ symbol*] (NQ)
**IFRA**.......... International Family Recreation Association (EA)
**IFRA**.......... International Foundation for Research in the Field of Advertising
**IFRA**.......... International Fragrance Association [*Geneva, Switzerland*] (EAIO)
**IFRA**.......... International Fund-Raising Association (EA)
**IFRAA**....... Interfaith Forum on Religion, Art, and Architecture (EA)
**IFRAA6**..... Indian Forest Records. Wood Anatomy [*A publication*]
**IFRAC**....... International Federation of Railway Advertising Companies [*London, England*] (EA)
**IFRB**.......... International Frequency Registration Board [*ITU*] [*United Nations*]
**IFRBA9**..... Indian Forest Records. Botany [*A publication*]
**IFRC**.......... Inland Forest Resource Council (EA)
**IFRC**.......... Instantaneous Frequency Correlation (NG)
**IFRC**.......... International Federation of Roofing Contractors [*See also IFD*] (EAIO)
**IFRC**.......... International Ford Retractable Club (EA)
**IFRCC**....... International Fight'n Rooster Cutlery Club (EA)
**IFRD**.......... International Federation of Retail Distributors (EAIO)
**IFRE**.......... Institute for Family Research and Education (EA)
**IFREAI**...... Indian Forest Records. Entomology [*A publication*]
**IFREDL**..... Indian Forest Records. Forest Management and Mensuration [*A publication*]
**IFREMER**... Institut Francais de Recherche pour l'Exploitation de la Mer [*French Research Institute for Ocean Utilization*] [*Information service or system*] (IID)
**IFRF**.......... International Federation of Resistance Fighters (BJA)
**IFRF**.......... International Flame Research Foundation [*Research center*] [*Netherlands*]
**IFRGA**....... Industriefeuerung [*A publication*]
**IFrHS**........ Freeburg Community High School 77, Freeburg, IL [*Library symbol*] [*Library of Congress*] (LCLS)
**IFRI**........... International Fund-Raising Institute [*Later, IFRA*]
**IFRIS**......... Intelligence Finished Reports Information Subsystem [*Data processing*]
**IFRM**......... International Federation of Resistance Movements [*Vienna, Austria*] (EA)
**IFRM**......... International Federation of the Rights of Man (EA)
**IFRMA8**.... Indian Forest Records. Mycology [*A publication*]
**IFRO**.......... Internal Feed Rate Override
**IFRP**.......... International Fertility Research Program [*Later, FHI*]
**IFRPA**....... Izvestiya na Instituta po Fiziologiya na Rasteniyata. Bulgarska Akademiya na Naukite [*A publication*]
**IFRS**.......... IFR Systems, Inc. [*Wichita, KS*] [*NASDAQ symbol*] (NQ)
**IFRS**.......... Individuals for a Rational Society [*Defunct*] (EA)
**IFRSAQ**.... Indian Forest Records. Silviculture [*A publication*]
**IFRSBR**.... Indian Forest Records. Statistical [*A publication*]
**IFRSDT**.... Indian Forest Records. Silvics [*A publication*]
**IFRT**.......... Intellectual Freedom Round Table [*American Library Association*]
**IFRTA**....... International Federation of Railwaymen's Travel Associations (EA)
**IFRTAT**..... Indian Forest Records. Timber Mechanics [*A publication*]
**IFRU**.......... In-Flight Replaceable Unit (KSC)
**IFRU**.......... Interference Frequency Rejection Unit [*Military*]
**i-fs---**.......... French Southern and Antarctic Lands [*MARC geographic area code*] [*Library of Congress*] (LCCP)
**IFS**............ Identification, Friend or Foe, Switching Circuit [*Military*]
**IFS**............ In-Flight Safety
**IFS**............ Inactivated Fetal-Calf Serum [*Immunology*]
**IFS**............ Independent Front Suspension [*Automotive engineering*]
**IFS**............ Indian Forest Service [*British*]
**IFS**............ Information Flow Standards (KSC)
**IFS**............ Information Strategy. The Executive's Journal [*A publication*]
**IFS**............ Infrared Frequency Synthesis
**IFS**............ Inshore Fire Support Ship [*Later, LFR*]
**IFS**............ Institute for Fiscal Studies [*British*]
**IFS**............ Institute of Flight Structures [*Columbia University*]
**IFS**............ Instructions for Service
**IFS**............ Instrument Flight Simulator (MCD)
**IFS**............ Integrated Facilities System [*Army*]
**IFS**............ Integrated Flight System
**IFS**............ Interactive File Sharing
**IFS**............ Interactive Flow Simulator (TEL)
**IFS**............ Interchange File Separator [*Data processing*] (BUR)
**IFS**............ Interface Specification
**IFS**............ Intermediate Frequency Strip
**IFS**............ International Federation of Settlements and Neighbourhood Centers (EAIO)
**IFS**............ International Federation of Surveyors [*See also FIG*] (EAIO)
**IFS**............ International Film Seminars (EA)
**IFS**............ International Financial Statistics [*International Monetary Fund*] [*Information service or system*] [*A publication*]
**IFS**............ International Focus Resources, Inc. [*Vancouver Stock Exchange symbol*]
**IFS**............ International Foundation for Science [*See also FIS*] [*ICSU*] [*Stockholm, Sweden*] (EAIO)
**IFS**............ International Foundation for Stutterers (EA)
**IFS**............ International Frankenstein Society (EA)
**IFS**............ Interrelated Flow Simulation
**IFS**............ Investment Feasibility Studies (TEL)
**IFS**............ Ionospheric Forward Scatter (TEL)
**IFS**............ Irish Free State [*Later, Republic of Ireland*]
**IFS**............ Iron Fortified Common Salt [*Nutrition*]
**IFS**............ Iterated Function System [*Data processing*] (BYTE)
**IFSA**.......... International Federation of Scoliosis Associations (EA)
**IFSA**.......... International Federation of Sports Acrobatics [*Sofia, Bulgaria*] (EAIO)
**IFSA**.......... International Fuzzy Systems Association (EA)
**IFSAL**........ Integral Frequency Scan Approach and Landing
**IFSAT**........ International Financial Services and Technology Exhibition [*British*]
**IFSB**.......... Independence Federal Savings Bank [*Washington, DC*] [*NASDAQ symbol*] (NQ)
**IFSB**.......... International Flying Saucer Bureau [*Defunct*]
**IFSBAC**..... Institute for Folklore Studies in Britain and Canada
**IFSC**.......... Institut des Freres du Sacre-Coeur [*Institute of the Brothers of the Sacred Heart - IBSH*] [*Rome, Italy*] (EAIO)
**IFSC**.......... Interferon Sciences, Inc. [*NASDAQ symbol*] (NQ)
**IFSC**.......... International Federation of Surgical Colleges [*Dublin, Republic of Ireland*] (EAIO)
**IFSC**.......... Introduction to the Federal Supply Catalog System
**IFSCC**........ International Federation of Societies of Cosmetic Chemists [*Luton, England*] (EAIO)
**IFSCS**........ International Federation of the Societies of Classical Studies (EA)
**IFSD**.......... Inflight Shutdown (MCD)
**IFSDA**....... International Federation of Stamp Dealers' Associations (EA)
**IFSDP**........ International Federation of the Socialist and Democratic Press [*Milan, Italy*] (EAIO)
**IFSEA**........ International Federation of Scientific Editors' Associations (EA)
**IFSEA**........ International Food Service Executive's Association (EA)
**IFSEC**........ International Fire and Security Exhibition and Conference [*British*] (ITD)
**IFSECN**..... International Federation of Societies for Electroencephalography and Clinical Neurophysiology [*Amsterdam, Netherlands*] (EA)
**IFSED**........ Initial Full-Scale Engineering Development
**IFSEM**....... International Federation of Societies for Electron Microscopy (EA)
**IFSF**........... Irradiated Fuels Storage Facility [*National Reactor Testing Station*]
**IFSH**.......... International Federation of Sound Hunters (EA)
**IFSHC**....... International Federation of Societies for Histochemistry and Cytochemistry [*London, England*] (EAIO)
**IFSHJ**........ International Federation for Secular Humanistic Judaism (EA)
**IFSI**............ Interface, Inc. [*NASDAQ symbol*] (NQ)
**IFSIS**......... Iterated Function System-Image Synthesizer [*Data processing*] (BYTE)
**IFSIT**......... In-Flight Safety Inhibit Test
**IFSL**........... Indiana Federal Corp. [*NASDAQ symbol*] (NQ)
**IFSL**........... Industrial Fire Safety Library [*National Fire Protection Association*]
**IFSM**......... International Federation of Sports Medicine (EA)
**IFSMA**...... International Federation of Shipmasters Associations [*See also FIAPN*] (EAIO)
**IFSMTF**.... International Fusion Superconducting Magnet Test Facility [*Oak Ridge National Laboratory*]
**IFSNC**....... International Federation of Settlements and Neighbourhood Centres [*Defunct*]
**IFSO**.......... International Federation of Sanitarians Organizations [*Defunct*] (EA)
**IFSOT**....... Irradiated Fused Silica Open Tubular [*Column for chromatography*]
**IFSP**........... International Federation of Societies of Philosophy
**IFSPO**....... International Federation of Senior Police Officers (EA)
**IFSPS**........ International Federation of Students in Political Sciences
**IFSR**.......... International Federation for Systems Research (EAIO)
**IFSR**.......... International Flight Service Receiver Site (FAAC)
**IFSRA**........ Information Storage and Retrieval [*A publication*]
**IFSRC**........ Independent Family Schools Resource Center (EA)
**IFSRD**....... IF. Industrialization Forum [*A publication*]
**IFSS**........... If Signal Source (MCD)
**IFSS**........... Index of Federal Specifications and Standards
**IFSS**........... Instrument Flight Safety System (MUGU)
**IFSS**........... International Federation of Sleddog Sports (EA)
**IFSS**........... International Fertilizer Supply Scheme [*FAO*] [*United Nations*]
**IFSS**........... International Flight Service Station [*FAA*]
**IFSSH**....... International Federation of Societies for Surgery of the Hand (EA)

**IFSSO**........ International Federation of Social Science Organizations [*See also FIOSS*] [*Copenhagen, Denmark*] (EAIO)
**IFSSykt**..... Istoriko-Filologiceskij Sbornik Syktyvbar [*A publication*]
**IFST**........... Institute of Food Science and Technology of the United Kingdom
**IFST**........... International Federation of Shorthand and Typewriting
**IFST**........... International Flight Service Transmitter Site (FAAC)
**IFSTA**........ International Fire Service Training Association (EA)
**IFSTAD**..... Islamic Foundation for Science, Technology, and Development (EA)
**IFSTD**........ Irish Journal of Food Science and Technology [*A publication*]
**IFSTD3**...... Irish Journal of Food Science and Technology [*A publication*]
**IFSTM**....... International Federation of Sewing Thread Manufacturers (EA)
**IFSW**......... International Federation of Social Workers [*Switzerland*]
**IFSWA**...... International Figure Skating Writers Association [*Defunct*]
**IFT**............ Immunofluorescence Test [*Immunology*]
**IFT**............ In-Flight Test [*Air Force*]
**IFT**............ Informations Economiques (Tunis) [*A publication*]
**IFT**............ Input Frequency Tolerance [*Data processing*]
**IFT**............ Instantaneous Fourier Transform [*Data processing*]
**IFT**............ Institute of Food Technologists (EA)
**IFT**............ Instructor-Flown Advisory Target
**IFT**............ Interface Tool (MCD)
**IFT**............ Interfacial Tension [*Physical chemistry*]
**IFT**............ Interfacial Test
**IFT**............ Intermediate Frequency Transformer
**IFT**............ International Federation of Translators [*See also FIT*] [*Ghent, Belgium*] (EAIO)
**IFT**............ International Foundation for Telemetering (EA)
**IFT**............ International Foundation for Timesharing (EA)
**IFT**............ International Frequency Tables
**IFT**............ Io Flux Tube [*Cosmology*]
**IFT**............ Ion Focusing Technique
**IFTA**.......... In-Flight Thrust Augmentation
**IFTA**.......... In-Flight Training Aid
**IFTA**.......... International Federation of Teachers' Associations [*Later, WCOTP*] (EAIO)
**IFTA**.......... International Federation of Television Archives [*See also FIAT*] [*Madrid, Spain*] (EAIO)
**IFTA**.......... International Federation of Thanatologists Associations [*Saint-Ouen, France*] (EA)
**IFTA**.......... International Free Trade Area
**IFTAC**........ Inter-American Federation of Touring and Automobile Clubs [*See also FITAC*] (EAIO)
**IF TACCAR**... Intermediate Frequency Time Averaged Clutter Coherent Airborne RADAR (NG)
**IFTAD**....... Initial and Final Terminal Arrival Date [*Army*] (AABC)
**IFTA Res Pap**... IFTA [*Institut Francais de Transport Aerien*] Research Papers [*A publication*]
**IFTBCS**..... International Federation of the Temperance Blue Cross Societies [*Later, IBC*] (EA)
**IFTC**.......... International Federation of Thermalism and Climatism [*Bad Ragaz, Switzerland*] (EA)
**IFTC**.......... International Film and Television Council [*Rome, Italy*]
**IFTC**.......... International Fox-Tango Club (EA)
**IFTDO**....... International Federation of Training and Development Organizations (EA)
**IFTE**.......... Intermediate Forward Test Equipment
**IFTEX**........ International Flower Trades Exhibition [*British*] (ITD)
**IFTF**.......... Institute for the Future [*Research center*] [*Telecommunications*] (RCD)
**IFTF**.......... Inter-Faith Task Force (EA)
**IFTF**.......... International Federation of Teachers of French [*See also FIPF*] [*Sevres, France*] (EAIO)
**IFTF**.......... International Fur Trade Federation [*London, England*] (EAIO)
**IFTL**.......... Institute for Friendship through Learning (EA)
**IFTM**......... In-Flight Test and Maintenance (KSC)
**IFTM**......... Inverse Fourier Transform Module [*An enzyme*] (MCD)
**IFTN**......... Information for the Nation [*Program*] [*Australia*]
**IFTO**.......... International Federation of Tour Operators [*Lewes, East Sussex, England*] (EAIO)
**IFTOA**....... Independent Fuel Terminal Operators' Association
**IFToMM**... International Federation for the Theory of Machines and Mechanisms [*Warsaw, Poland*] (EAIO)
**IFTPNDC**... Institute on the Federal Theatre Project and New Deal Culture [*George Mason University*] [*Research center*] (RCD)
**IFTPP**........ International Federation of the Technical and Periodical Press (DIT)
**IFTR**.......... International Federation of Teachers of Rhythmics (EA)
**IFTR**.......... International Foundation for Theatrical Research (EA)
**IFTS**........... In-Flight Test System
**IFTS**........... International Federation of Teratology Societies (EA)
**IFTS**........... Irradiated Fuel Transfer System [*Nuclear energy*] (NRCH)
**IFTU**.......... International Federation of Teachers' Unions
**IFTU**.......... International Federation of Trade Unions
**IFTU**.......... Iraq Federation of Trade Unions
**IFTUTW**... International Federation of Trade Unions of Transport Workers [*See also FIOST*] [*Brussels, Belgium*] (EAIO)
**IFTW**......... International Federation of Tobacco Workers
**IFTWA**....... International Federation of Textile Workers' Associations
**IFTwA**....... International Federation of Tiddlywinks Associations (EA)
**IFU**............ IMF [*International Monetary Fund*] Survey [*A publication*]
**IFU**............ Infusion-Forming Units [*Medicine*]
**IFU**............ Instruction Fetch Unit [*Data processing*]
**IFU**............ Integrated Fluorescence Unit [*Image formation*]
**IFU**............ Intelligence Field Unit [*Navy*]
**IFU**............ Inter-Democracy Federal Union [*Australia*]
**I/FU**.......... Interface Unit [*Data processing*] (NASA)
**IFUN**......... If Unable [*Aviation*] (FAAC)
**IF/USA**...... Interfurnishings USA (TSPED)
**IFUW**........ International Federation of University Women (EA)
**IFV**............ Igniter-Fuel Valve (KSC)
**IFV**............ Infantry Fighting Vehicle
**IFV**............ Informatie Bulletin [*A publication*]
**IFV**............ Internationaler Faustball-Verband (EAIO)
**IFV**............ Intracellular Fluid Volume [*Physiology*]
**IFVA**.......... Independent Film and Video Makers' Association [*British*]
**IFVC**.......... International Federation for Victory over Communism
**IF-VCA**...... Immunofluorescence-Viral Capsid Antigen [*Clinical chemistry*]
**IFVH**......... Indian Field Veterinary Hospital [*British military*] (DMA)
**IFVHSF**..... Federation of Health Funds - International [*Acronym is based on former name, International Federation of Voluntary Health Service Funds*] (EAIO)
**IFVLS**........ If Flight Visibility Becomes Less Than [*Aviation*] (FAAC)
**IFVM**......... Intermediate Frequency Video Microwave (MCD)
**IFVME**...... Inspectorate of Fighting Vehicles and Mechanical Equipment [*Military*]
**IFVR**.......... If Visibility Remains [*Aviation*] (FAAC)
**IFVTCC**..... Internationale Foderation der Vereine der Textilchemiker und Coloristen [*International Federation of Associations of Textile Chemists and Colorists*] (EAIO)
**IFW**........... International Federation of Wargaming [*Defunct*] (EA)
**IFWA**......... International Federation for Weeks of Art
**IFWEA**...... International Federation of Workers' Educational Associations [*See also IVB*] [*Tel Aviv, Israel*] (EAIO)
**IFWHA**..... International Federation of Women's Hockey Associations
**IFWJ**......... Indian Federation of Working Journalists
**IFWL**......... International Federation of Women Lawyers (EA)
**IFWRI**....... Institute of the Furniture Warehousing and Removing Industry (EAIO)
**IFWS**......... International Federation of Wines and Spirits [*See also FIVS*] (EAIO)
**IFWSTI**..... International Federation of Wines and Spirits, Trade, and Industry (EA)
**IFWTO**...... International Federation of Women's Travel Organizations (EA)
**IFX**............ Immunofixation [*Clinical chemistry*]
**IFY**............ Independent Fission Yield
**IFYC**.......... International Federation of Young Cooperators
**IFYGL**....... International Field Year for the Great Lakes
**IFYGL Bull**... International Field Year for the Great Lakes. Bulletin [*A publication*]
**IFZ**............ Istoriko-Filologiceskij Zurnal [*A publication*]
**IG**.............. ALISARDA SpA [*Italy*] [*ICAO designator*] (ICDA)
**IG**.............. Galesburg Public Library, Galesburg, IL [*Library symbol*] [*Library of Congress*] (LCLS)
**IG**.............. IGI, Inc. [*AMEX symbol*] (SPSG)
**IG**.............. Igloo [*Spacelab Pallet Missions*]
**IG**.............. Ignitor [*Electron device*] (MSA)
**IG**.............. Illustrators Guild [*Later, GA*] (EA)
**IG**.............. Image Generator (MCD)
**IG**.............. Immune Globulin
**Ig**.............. Immunoglobulin [*Immunology*]
**IG**.............. Immunology [*Medical specialty*] (DHSM)
**IG**.............. Imperial Gallon
**IG**.............. In-Ground (ADA)
**IG**.............. Indicator Group (MCD)
**IG**.............. Indische Gids [*A publication*]
**IG**.............. Indo-Germanic [*Language, etc.*]
**IG**.............. Industriegewerkschaft [*Industrial Trade Union*] [*Federal Republic of Germany*]
**IG**.............. Inertial Guidance
**IG**.............. Inner Gimbal
**IG**.............. Inner Guard [*Freemasonry*]
**IG**.............. Inscriptiones Graecae [*Epigraphic notation*]
**IG**.............. Inscriptiones Graecae [*A publication*]
**IG**.............. Inside Guardian [*Freemasonry*] (ROG)
**IG**.............. Inspection Gauge (MCD)
**IG**.............. Inspector General [*Air Force, Army, Marine Corps*]
**IG**.............. Institute of Geophysics [*Later, IGPP*] [*University of California*] (MCD)
**IG**.............. Institute of Groundsmanship (EA)
**IG**.............. Institution of Geologists (EAIO)
**IG**.............. Instruction [*or Instructor*] Guide
**IG**.............. Instructor in Gunnery [*Military*] [*British*]
**IG**.............. Instrument Ground (NASA)
**IG**.............. Instrumentation Group
**IG**.............. Insulated Gate (DEN)
**IG**.............. Integrated Genetics
**IG**.............. Intelligence Generator
**IG**.............. Intendant-General
**IG**.............. Inter-Gas System

**IG** ........ Inter-Granular (MCD)
**IG** ........ Interagency Group [*Federal government*]
**IG** ........ Interconnect Group (CAAL)
**IG** ........ Interdepartmental Group [*DoD*]
**IG** ........ Interest Group
**IG** ........ Intergranular [*Metallurgy*]
**IG** ........ Intermediaire des Genealogistes [*A publication*]
**IG** ........ Internal Guidance (NASA)
**IG** ........ International General (EA)
**IG** ........ International Graphics [*Formerly, IGI*] (EA)
**IG** ........ Internationale Kunstgilde [*International Art Guild - IAG*] (EAIO)
**IG** ........ Intestinal Groove
**IG** ........ Intragastric
**IG** ........ Inverse Gain (NVT)
**IG** ........ Inverse Gaussian [*Statistics*]
**IG** ........ Investment Grant [*British*]
**IG** ........ Irish Guards [*Military unit*]
**IG** ........ Irvine Group [*An association*] (EA)
**IG** ........ Isotope Geoscience [*A publication*]
**IG** ........ Istorijski Glasnik [*A publication*]
**IG** ........ Izmenyaemaya Geometriya [*Variable Geometry*] [*Suffix letters on Soviet combat aircraft*]
**IGA** ........ Dallas Public Library, Dallas, TX [*OCLC symbol*] (OCLC)
**IgA** ........ Immunoglobulin A [*Immunology*]
**IGA** ........ Inagua [*Bahamas*] [*Airport symbol*] (OAG)
**IGA** ........ Independent Grocers Alliance Distributing Co. [*Facetious translation: "I Get Attention"*] (EA)
**IGA** ........ Industry and General Applications (MCD)
**IGA** ........ Inhaled Gas Analyzer
**IGA** ........ Inner Gimbal Angle (NASA)
**IGA** ........ Inner Gimbal Assembly
**IGA** ........ Inner Gimbal Axis
**IGA** ........ Inscriptiones Graecae Antiquissimae (BJA)
**IGA** ........ Integrated Grant Administration
**IGA** ........ Integrating Gyro Accelerometer
**IGA** ........ Intergranular Attack [*Nuclear energy*] (NRCH)
**IGA** ........ International Galdos Association (EA)
**IGA** ........ International Gamers Association (EA)
**IGA** ........ International Gay Association - International Association of Lesbians/Gay Women and Gay Men (EAIO)
**IGA** ........ International General Aviation
**IGA** ........ International Geneva Association (EA)
**IGA** ........ International Geographical Association [*Esperantist*]
**IGA** ........ International Golf Association (EA)
**IGA** ........ International Graduate Achievement [*Defunct*] (EA)
**IGA** ........ International Grains Arrangement
**IGA** ........ International Green Alliance (EA)
**IGA** ........ International Journal of Government Auditing [*A publication*]
**IGA** ........ Interstate Gambling Activities
**IGA** ........ Ion Gun Assembly
**IGA** ........ Ipoh Garden Australia Ltd.
**IGAAS** ........ Integrated Ground/Airborne Avionics System (MCD)
**IGAB** ........ International Group of Agents and Bureaus (EA)
**IGACS** ........ Integrated Guidance and Control System [*Aerospace*]
**IGaDC** ........ Illinois State Department of Conservation, Division of Parks and Memorials, Galena, IL [*Library symbol*] [*Library of Congress*] (LCLS)
**IGADD** ........ Intergovernmental Authority on Drought and Development [*Djibouti*] (EY)
**IGAEA** ........ International Graphic Arts Education Association (EA)
**IGAeM** ........ Internationale Gesellschaft fuer Aerosole in der Medizin [*International Society for Aerosols in Medicine - ISAeM*] (EAIO)
**IgAIC** ........ Immunoglobulin A Immune Complex [*Immunochemistry*]
**IGal** ........ Galva Township Library, Galva, IL [*Library symbol*] [*Library of Congress*] (LCLS)
**IGAM** ........ Internationale Gesellschaft fuer Allgemeinmedizin [*International Society of General Medicine*]
**IgAN** ........ Immunoglobulin A Nephropathy [*Nephrology*]
**IGAP** ........ Institute for Grassland and Animal Production [*United Kingdom*] [*Research center*] (IRC)
**IGAP** ........ Internationale Gesellschaft fuer Arztliche Psychotherapie [*International Federation for Medical Psychotherapy - IFMP*] [*Oslo, Norway*] (EAIO)
**IGAS** ........ International General Assembly of Spiritualists [*Later, LDTF*] (EA)
**IGAS** ........ International Graphic Arts Society (EA)
**IGAS** ........ International Graphoanalysis Society (EA)
**IGAX** ........ Inner Gimbal Axis (NASA)
**IGAYA** ........ Igaku No Ayumi [*Japan*] [*A publication*]
**IGB** ........ Columbus, MS [*Location identifier*] [*FAA*] (FAAL)
**IGB** ........ Illicit Gold Buyer [*or Buying*]
**IGB** ........ Inlet Gear Box (MCD)
**IGB** ........ Inter-German Border (MCD)
**IGB** ........ Intercontinental Glide Bomber [*Unmanned*]
**IGB** ........ Interference Guard Bands
**IGB** ........ International Gravimetric Bureau [*Toulouse, France*] (EAIO)
**IGB** ........ International Trade Forum [*A publication*]
**IGB** ........ Internationaler Genossenschaftsbund [*International Cooperative Alliance*]
**IGB** ........ Internationales Gewerkschafts Buro [*International Trades Union Office*]
**IGB** ........ Israelitisches Gemeindeblatt [*Muelheim/Koeln*] [*A publication*] (BJA)
**IGB** ........ National College of Education, Evanston, IL [*OCLC symbol*] (OCLC)
**IGBC** ........ Interagency Grizzly Bear Committee [*Forest Service*] [*Missoula, MT*] (EGAO)
**IGBD** ........ Impotent Grain Boundary Dislocation
**IGBE** ........ International Gold Bullion Exchange [*Bankrupt investment firm*]
**IGBLBZ** ........ Immergruene Blaetter [*A publication*]
**IGBMA** ........ Izvestiya na Geofizichniya Institut. Bulgarska Akademiya na Naukite [*A publication*]
**IGBP** ........ International Geosphere-Biosphere Program [*ICSU*] [*Proposed for 1992*]
**IGBST** ........ Interagency Grizzly Bear Study Team [*Montana State University*] [*Bozeman, MT*] (EGAO)
**IGC** ........ Atlantica and Iceland Review [*A publication*]
**IGC** ........ Goshen College, Goshen, IN [*OCLC symbol*] (OCLC)
**IGC** ........ Inspector-General of Communications [*British military*] (DMA)
**IGC** ........ Institute for Graphic Communication (EA)
**IGC** ........ Intellectually Gifted Children
**IGC** ........ Intelligence Graphics Controller [*Data processing*]
**IGC** ........ Inter-Governmental Conferences [*European Community*] (ECON)
**IGC** ........ Inter-Union Geodynamics Commission [*Also, ICG*] (MSC)
**IGC** ........ Intergovernmental Committee on Refugees [*Post-World War II*] (DLA)
**IGC** ........ Intergovernmental Copyright Committee [*See also CIDA*] [*Paris, France*] (EAIO)
**IGC** ........ Intermagnetics General Corporation
**IGC** ........ International Garden Club (EA)
**IGC** ........ International Geological Congress
**IGC** ........ International Geophysical Committee [*Also, CIG*]
**IGC** ........ International Geophysical Cooperation [*World Meteorological Organization*]
**IGC** ........ International Glaucoma Congress (EA)
**IGC** ........ International Grassland Congress
**IGC** ........ International Guides' Club (EAIO)
**IGC** ........ Interstate General LP [*AMEX symbol*] (SPSG)
**IGC** ........ Inverse Gas Chromatography
**IGC** ........ Ion Gun Collector
**IGC** ........ Isothermal Gas Chromatography
**IGCA** ........ International Guild of Candle Artisans (EA)
**IGCA** ........ Italian Greyhound Club of America (EA)
**IGCBT** ........ Interagency Group for Computer-Based Training [*Later, IGITT*] (EA)
**IGCC** ........ Institute on Global Conflict and Cooperation [*University of California, Berkeley*]
**IGCC** ........ Insulating Glass Certification Council (EA)
**IGCC** ........ Integrated Gasification-Combined Cycle [*Chemical engineering*]
**IGCC** ........ Interagency Geothermal Coordinating Council
**IGCC** ........ Intergovernmental Copyright Committee [*See also CIDA*]
**IGCC** ........ Intergovernmental Panel on Climate Change [*World Meteorological Organization*]
**IGCE** ........ Independent Government Cost Estimate [*Army*]
**IGCG** ........ Inertial Guidance and Calibration Group [*Air Force*]
**IGCI** ........ Industrial Gas Cleaning Institute (EA)
**IGCJAP** ........ International Guild of Craft Journalists, Authors, and Photographers [*Inactive*] (EA)
**IGCO** ........ International Genealogy Consumer Organization (EA)
**IGCP** ........ Intelligence Guidance for COMINT Programming (MCD)
**IGCP** ........ International Geological Correlation Programme [*See also PICG*] [*ICSU*] [*Paris, France*] (EAIO)
**IGCPK** ........ Industrie Gewerkschaft Chemie, Papier, und Keramik [*West German union*]
**IGCR** ........ Intergovernmental Committee on Refugees [*Post-World War II*]
**IGCS** ........ Imperial Glass Collectors Society (EA)
**IGCS** ........ Integrated Guidance and Control System [*Aerospace*] (AAG)
**IGCS** ........ International Guide to Classical Studies [*A publication*]
**IGD** ........ Illicit Gold Dealer
**IgD** ........ Immunoglobulin D [*Immunology*]
**IGD** ........ Indian Gold Resources Ltd. [*Vancouver Stock Exchange symbol*]
**IGD** ........ Inspector General's Department
**IGD** ........ Institute of Grocery Distribution Ltd. [*British*]
**IGD** ........ Interaction Graphics Display
**IGD** ........ Interactive Grafics Digitizer [*Data processing*]
**IGDGA** ........ Ingenieur-Digest [*A publication*]
**IGDM** ........ Infant of Gestational Diabetic Mother [*Obstetrics*]
**IGDMR** ........ Initial Gross Depot Maintenance Requirement [*Military*]
**IGDO** ........ International Guild of Opticians [*Acronym is based on former name, International Guild of Dispensing Opticians*] (EAIO)
**IGDR** ........ Interim Geophysical Data Record [*From spacecraft data*]
**IGDS** ........ Interactive Graphics Design System (MCD)

**IGDS**.......... Interactive Graphics Display Systems [*Computer monitor*] [*Military*]
**IGDS**.......... Iodine Generating and Dispensing System (NASA)
**IGE**............ Iguela [*Gabon*] [*Airport symbol*] [*Obsolete*] (OAG)
**IgE**............ Immunoglobulin E [*Immunology*]
**IGE**............ Imposta Generale sull'Entrata [*Income Tax*] [*Italian*]
**IGE**............ In-Ground Effect [*Aviation*] (NG)
**IGE**............ Independent Government Estimate (MCD)
**IGE**............ Individually Guided Education [*for upgrading students' skills*]
**IGE**............ Institution of Gas Engineers [*British*] (DAS)
**IGE**............ Instrumentation Ground Equipment (MCD)
**IGE**............ International Geographics [*Vancouver Stock Exchange symbol*]
**IGE**............ International Geophysical Extension
**IGE**............ International Guiding Eyes (EA)
**IGECB**........ Institution of Gas Engineers. Communications [*A publication*]
**IGEI**.......... International Genetic Engineering, Incorporated [*Santa Monica, CA*] [*NASDAQ symbol*] (NQ)
**IGEIEPSI**... International Group for the Exchange of Information and Experience Among Postal Savings Institutions [*Geneva, Switzerland*] (EAIO)
**IGEM**........ Intergem, Inc. [*NASDAQ symbol*] (NQ)
**IGEN**......... Current Source (MSA)
**IGenD**........ DuPage Library System, Geneva, IL [*Library symbol*] [*Library of Congress*] (LCLS)
**IGeo**.......... Georgetown Public Library, Georgetown, IL [*Library symbol*] [*Library of Congress*] (LCLS)
**IGES**.......... Initial Graphics Exchange Specification [*or System*] [*National Standards Institute*]
**IGES/PDES**... Initial Graphics Exchange Specification/Product Definition Exchange Specification
**IGESUCO**... International Ground Environment Subcommittee [*NATO*]
**IGF**............ Fondation Internationale pour la Sauvegarde du Gibier [*International Foundation for the Conservation of Game*] (EAIO)
**IGF**............ IGF Metals, Inc. [*Vancouver Stock Exchange symbol*]
**IGF**............ Image Generation Facility (MCD)
**IGF**............ India Growth Fund, Inc. [*NYSE symbol*] (CTT)
**Ig F**............ Indogermanische Forschungen [*A publication*]
**IGF**............ Inspector-General of Fortifications [*British*]
**IGF**............ Insulin Gene Family
**IGF**............ Insulin-Like Growth Factor
**IGF**............ International Genetics Federation [*See also FIG*] [*England*] (EA)
**IGF**............ International Graphical Federation [*See also FGI*] [*Berne, Switzerland*] (EAIO)
**IGF**............ International Gymnastic Federation [*See also FIG*] (EAIO)
**IGF**............ Irish Genealogical Foundation (EA)
**IGFA**.......... Inspector General, Foreign Assistance [*Department of State*]
**IGFA**.......... Interessen Gemeinschaft der Farbenindustrie Aktiengesellschaft [*A dye trust*] [*Germany*]
**IGFA**.......... International Game Fish Association (EA)
**IGFA**.......... Isaac Garrison Family Association (EA)
**IGFES**........ Interactive Graphics Finite Element System (RDA)
**IGFET**........ Insulated-Gate Field-Effect Transistor [*Electronics*]
**IGFET**........ Isolated-Gate Field-Effect Transistor [*Electronics*]
**IGFM**.......... Internal Gamma Flux Monitor
**IGFM**.......... Internationale Gesellschaft fuer Menschenrechte [*International Society for Human Rights - ISHR*] (EA)
**IGFO**.......... Inspector General Field Office [*Military*]
**IGForsch**.... Indogermanische Forschungen [*A publication*]
**IGFOV**........ Instantaneous Geometric Field of View
**IGFPIL**........ International Grotius Foundation for the Propagation of International Law
**IGFR**.......... International Genealogical Fellowship of Rotarians (EA)
**IGFS**.......... International Gem Finders Society
**IGFVP**........ Interservice Group for Flight Vehicle Power [*Military*]
**IGG**............ IGG [*Instituto Geografico e Geologico de Sao Paulo*] Revista [*A publication*]
**IGG**............ Igiugig [*Alaska*] [*Airport symbol*] (OAG)
**IgG**............ Immunoglobulin G [*Immunology*]
**IGG**............ Inert Gas Generator
**IGG**............ Internationale Gesellschaft fuer Geschichtsdidaktik [*International Society for History Didactics*] (EAIO)
**IG & GA**..... International Grooving and Grinding Association (EA)
**IGGDA**........ International G. G. Drayton Association (EA)
**IGGEA**........ Ingegneria [*A publication*]
**IGGI**.......... Inter-Governmental Group for Indonesia
**IgGIC**.......... Immunoglobulin G Immune Complex [*Immunochemistry*]
**IGGMA**........ Izvestiya na Geologicheskiya Institut. Bulgarska Akademiya na Naukite. Seriya Geokhimiya, Mineralogiya, i Petrografiya [*A publication*]
**IgH**............ Immunoglobulin Heavy Chain [*Biochemistry*]
**IGH**............ Ingham [*Australia*] [*Airport symbol*]
**IGH**............ International Guild of Hypnotists (EA)
**IGHIA**........ International Garden Horticultural Industry Association (EA)
**IGI**............ Industrial Graphics International [*Later, IG*] [*An association*] (EA)
**IGI**............ Industrial Guest Investigator [*NASA*]
**IGI**............ Information Gatekeepers, Incorporated [*Telecommunications*] [*Information service or system*] (IID)
**IGI**............ Information General, Incorporated [*Information service or system*] (IID)
**IGI**............ Inner Grid Injection
**IGI**............ Institutional Goals Inventory [*Test*]
**IGI**............ Interlocked Grain Index [*Botany*]
**IGI**............ International Gallery Invitational (ITD)
**IGI**............ International Genealogical Index
**IGI**............ International Graphics, Incorporated [*Defunct*] (EA)
**IGI**............ Investors Group, Inc. [*Toronto Stock Exchange symbol*]
**IGIA**.......... Interagency Group on International Aviation
**IGib**.......... Moyer Library, Gibson City, IL [*Library symbol*] [*Library of Congress*] (LCLS)
**IGibH**........ Gibson Community Hospital, Gibson City, IL [*Library symbol*] [*Library of Congress*] (LCLS)
**IGIC**.......... International Gay Information Center (EA)
**IGII**.......... Intermark Gaming International, Incorporated [*Scottsdale, AZ*] [*NASDAQ symbol*] (NQ)
**IGil**............ Douglas Township Library, Gilman, IL [*Library symbol*] [*Library of Congress*] (LCLS)
**IGill**.......... Gillespie Public Library, Gillespie, IL [*Library symbol*] [*Library of Congress*] (LCLS)
**IGillMCD**... Macoupin Community District 7, Gillespie, IL [*Library symbol*] [*Library of Congress*] (LCLS)
**IGINA**........ Ingenieria e Industria (Argentina) [*A publication*]
**IG Inf Ser**... IG [*Industrial Group, United Kingdom Atomic Energy Authority*] Information Series [*A publication*]
**IGIP**.......... Internationale Gesellschaft fuer Ingenieurpaedagogik [*International Society for Engineering Education*] (EAIO)
**IGIPAS**........ Interagency Group on International Programs in Atmospheric Science
**IGir**.......... Girard Township Library, Girard, IL [*Library symbol*] [*Library of Congress*] (LCLS)
**IGirMCD**... Macoupin Community District 3, Girard, IL [*Library symbol*] [*Library of Congress*] (LCLS)
**IGIS**.......... Intelligent Geographic System [*Data processing*]
**IGIS**.......... International Group of Users of Information Systems (IID)
**IGITT**........ Interagency Group for Interactive Training Technologies (EA)
**IGIW**.......... Indices of General Industrial Worth
**IGJ**............ Indian Geographical Journal [*Madras*] [*A publication*]
**IGK**............ Infanteriegeschuetz - Kompanie [*Infantry Howitzer Company*] [*German military - World War II*]
**IGK**............ Knox College, Galesburg, IL [*Library symbol*] [*Library of Congress*] (LCLS)
**IGKB**.......... Internationale Gewasserschutz Kommission fur den Bodensee [*International Commission for the Protection of Lake Constance*] (EA)
**IGKG**.......... Internationale Gesellschaft fuer Kiefer- und Gesichtschirurgie [*International Association for Maxillo-Facial Surgery*] (EAIO)
**IGL**............ Ideal Gas Law
**IGL**............ Igloolik [*Northwest Territories*] [*Seismograph station code, US Geological Survey*] (SEIS)
**IGL**............ Information Grouping Logic [*Data processing*]
**IGL**............ Infrared Gunfire Locator
**IGL**............ Interactive Graphics Language
**IGL**............ Intergeniculate Leaflet [*Anatomy*]
**IGL**............ Internationale Gesellschaft fuer Lymphologie [*International Society of Lymphology*] (EAIO)
**IGL**............ Ionized Gas LASER
**IGL**............ Izmir [*Turkey*] Cigli Airport [*Airport symbol*] (OAG)
**IGlc**.......... Glencoe Public Library, Glencoe, IL [*Library symbol*] [*Library of Congress*] (LCLS)
**IGlca**.......... Glen Carbon Library, Glen Carbon, IL [*Library symbol*] [*Library of Congress*] (LCLS)
**IGLD**.......... International Great Lakes Datum
**IGle**............ Glen Ellyn Public Library, Glen Ellyn, IL [*Library symbol*] [*Library of Congress*] (LCLS)
**IGleD**.......... College of Du Page, Glen Ellyn, IL [*Library symbol*] [*Library of Congress*] (LCLS)
**IGleM**........ Maryknoll Seminary, Glen Ellyn, IL [*Library symbol*] [*Library of Congress*] (LCLS)
**IGLM**.......... Limnos [*Greece*] [*ICAO location identifier*] (ICLI)
**IGlN**.......... United States Naval Training Center, Great Lakes, IL [*Library symbol*] [*Library of Congress*] (LCLS)
**IGLOSS**..... Integrated Global Ocean Station System [*Surrey, England*] [*See also IGOSS*] [*UNESCO*]
**IGLQ**.......... Igalaaq. Nortext [*Ottawa*] [*A publication*]
**IGLS**.......... Inscriptions Grecques et Latines de la Syrie [*A publication*]
**IGLS**.......... Insituform Group Ltd. [*NASDAQ symbol*] (NQ)
**IGLSyr**........ Inscriptions Grecques et Latines de la Syrie [*A publication*]
**IGlvK**.......... Kraftco Corp., Research and Development Library, Glenview, IL [*Library symbol*] [*Library of Congress*] (LCLS)
**IGlw**.......... Glenwood Public Library District, Glenwood, IL [*Library symbol*] [*Library of Congress*] (LCLS)
**IGM**............ I Got Mine [*Slang describing attitude of some nouveaux riches*]
**IgM**............ Immunoglobulin Macro [*Also known as RF*] [*Immunology*]
**IGM**............ Inertial Guidance Mode
**IGM**............ Instituto Geografico Militar [*Ecuador*]
**IGM**............ Interactive Guidance Mode (NASA)
**IGM**............ Intergalactic Medium
**IGM**............ International Grail Movement (EA)

**IGM** .......... Internationale Gesellschaft fuer Menschenrechte [*International Society for Human Rights - ISHR*] (EAIO)
**IGM** .......... Internationale Gesellschaft fuer Moorforschung [*International Society for Research on Moors*]
**IGM** .......... ISDN [*Integrated Services Digital Network*] Gateway Module [*Telecommunications*]
**IGM** .......... Iterative Guidance Mode [*NASA*]
**IGM** .......... Kingman [*Arizona*] [*Airport symbol*] (OAG)
**IGMA** ........ International Guild of Miniature Artisans (EA)
**IGMC** ........ Independent Gasoline Marketers Council [*Inactive*] (EA)
**IGMCA** ..... Imperial German Military Collector's Association (EA)
**IGMEA**...... Ingegneria Meccanica [*A publication*]
**IGME/RG** ... Revista Geografica. Instituto Geografico Militar del Ecuador. Departamento Geografico [*A publication*]
**IGMG** ........ Institute of Geriatric Medicine and Gerontology [*British*]
**IGMG** ........ Internationale Gustav Mahler Gesellschaft [*International Gustav Mahler Society*] (EA)
**IgMIC**........ Immunoglobulin M Immune Complex [*Immunochemistry*]
**Ig Microb Epidem** ... Igiena, Microbiologie, si Epidemiologie [*A publication*]
**Ig Microbiol Epidemiol** ... Igiena, Microbiologie, si Epidemiologie [*A publication*]
**Ig Mod** ....... Igiene Moderna [*A publication*]
**IgM-RF**...... Immunoglobulin M - Rheumatoid Factor [*Medicine*]
**IGMS**........ International Guide to Medieval Studies [*A publication*]
**IGMT** ........ Impingement [*Engineering*]
**IGN**............ Ignition (KSC)
**IGN**............ Ignitron [*Electronics*]
**IGN**............ Ignorant
**IGN**............ Ignotus [*Unknown*] [*Latin*]
**IGN**............ Iligan [*Philippines*] [*Airport symbol*] (OAG)
**IGN**............ International-Great Northern [*AAR code*]
**IGN**............ Kingston, NY [*Location identifier*] [*FAA*] (FAAL)
**IGNC**......... International Good Neighbor Council [*See also CIBV*] [*Monterrey, Mexico*] (EAIO)
**IgND**.......... Immunoglobulin ND [*Immunology, provisional class*]
**IGNDET**.... Ignition Detector
**IGNE** ......... IGENE Biotechnology, Inc. [*Columbia, MD*] [*NASDAQ symbol*] (NQ)
**IGNKB** ...... Ispol'zovanie Gaza v Narodnom Khozyaistve [*A publication*]
**IGNR**......... Igniter
**IGNS** ......... Interactive Graphics Network System (MCD)
**IGNTA** ...... Ingenieurs et Techniciens [*A publication*]
**IGNTB**...... Ingenioer-Nytt [*A publication*]
**IGNTR** ...... Igniter (MSA)
**IGNVB** ...... Izvestiya na Geologicheskiya Institut. Bulgarska Akademiya na Naukite. Seriya Neftena i Vuglishtna Geologiya [*Bulgaria*] [*A publication*]
**IGO**........... Chigorodo [*Colombia*] [*Airport symbol*] (OAG)
**IGO**........... Inspector General's Office [*Air Force*]
**IGO**........... Intergovernmental Organization [*Generic term*]
**IGO**........... Investment Grant Office [*British*]
**IGOA**......... Independent Garage Owners of America [*Later, Automotive Service Councils*] (EA)
**IGoL**.......... Lewis and Clark Community College, Godfrey, IL [*Library symbol*] [*Library of Congress*] (LCLS)
**IGoM**......... Monticello College, Godfrey, IL [*Library symbol*] [*Library of Congress*] (LCLS)
**IGOPA** ...... Izvestiya Glavnoi Astronomicheskoi Observatorii v Pulkove [*A publication*]
**IGOR**......... Instrument Ground Optical Recording
**IGOR**......... Intercept Ground Optical Recorder [*NASA*]
**IGORTT**.... Intercept Ground Optical Recorder Tracking Telescope [*NASA*]
**IGOSS**....... Integrated Global Ocean Station System [*Great Britain*] [*See also IGLOSS*] [*UNESCO*]
**IGOSS**....... International Group on Soil Sampling
**IGP** ........... Gary Public Library, Gary, IN [*OCLC symbol*] (OCLC)
**IGP** ........... Imidazole Glycerol Phosphate [*Biochemistry*]
**IGP** ........... Inertial Guidance Package
**IGP** ........... Inertial Guidance Platform
**IGP** ........... Inspection Gauges Production (MCD)
**IGP** ........... Institute of the Great Plains (EA)
**IGP** ........... Intelligent Gateway Processor [*Data processing*]
**IGP** ........... International Geodynamics Project
**IGP** ........... International Green Party - Ecologism USA (EA)
**IGP** ........... International Guild of Prestidigitators [*Defunct*] (EA)
**IGP** ........... Investment Guaranty Program [*AID*]
**IGP** ........... Ion-Getter-Pumping [*Electron microscopy*]
**IGPA**.......... Igor-Patrick Air Force Base (KSC)
**IGPC**.......... Inter-Governmental Philatelic Corporation (EA)
**IGPD** ......... Imidazoleglycerol-phosphate Dehydratase [*An enzyme*]
**IGPE**.......... International Guild of Professional Electrologists (EA)
**IGPIA**........ Public Information Circular. Iowa Geological Survey [*A publication*]
**IGPM** ........ Imperial Gallons per Minute
**IGPP**.......... Institute of Geophysics and Planetary Physics [*Livermore, CA*] [*Department of Energy*] (MCD)
**IGPP**.......... Interactive Graphics Packaging Program [*Data processing*]
**IGR**............ Grace College, Winona Lake, IN [*OCLC symbol*] (OCLC)
**IGR**............ Igitur [*Therefore*] [*Latin*] (ADA)
**IGR**............ Iguazu [*Argentina*] [*Airport symbol*] (OAG)
**IGR**............ Improved Ground Rents (ROG)
**IGR**............ Increased Growth Response [*Botany*]
**IGR**............ Infanteriegranate [*Infantry Howitzer Shell*] [*German military - World War II*]
**IGR**............ Inscriptiones Graecae ad Res Romanas Pertinentes [*A publication*] (BJA)
**IGR**............ Insect Growth Regulator
**IGR**............ Institute of Geomantic Research (EAIO)
**IGR**............ Inter-Globe Resources Ltd. [*Vancouver Stock Exchange symbol*]
**IGR**............ Intergovernmental Review System (OICC)
**IGrac**.......... Granite City Public Library, Granite City, IL [*Library symbol*] [*Library of Congress*] (LCLS)
**IGracCU**.... Granite City Community Unit 12, Granite City, IL [*Library symbol*] [*Library of Congress*] (LCLS)
**IGRAF**....... Inspector-General of the Royal Air Force [*British*]
**IGrafPM**.... Pere Marquette Residential Center, Grafton, IL [*Library symbol*] [*Library of Congress*] (LCLS)
**IGralC**........ College of Lake County, Grayslake, IL [*Library symbol*] [*Library of Congress*] (LCLS)
**IGranHS**.... Hopkins Elementary School, Granville, IL [*Library symbol*] [*Library of Congress*] (LCLS)
**IGranPSD** ... Putnam County Community Unit, School District 535, Granville, IL [*Library symbol*] [*Library of Congress*] (LCLS)
**IGRE**.......... Improved Ground Reconnaissance Equipment [*Military*] (MCD)
**IGREB**....... Report. Institute of Geological Sciences [*A publication*]
**IGref** .......... Greenfield Public Library, Greenfield, IL [*Library symbol*] [*Library of Congress*] (LCLS)
**IGrefCU**..... Greenfield Community Unit, District 10, Greenfield, IL [*Library symbol*] [*Library of Congress*] (LCLS)
**IGrevi**......... Greenville Public Library, Greenville, IL [*Library symbol*] [*Library of Congress*] (LCLS)
**IGreviC** ...... Greenville College, Greenville, IL [*Library symbol*] [*Library of Congress*] (LCLS)
**IGRF**.......... International Geomagnetic Reference Field
**IGRL**.......... Inter-Globe Resources Limited [*Vancouver, BC*] [*NASDAQ symbol*] (NQ)
**IG Rom** ...... Inscriptiones Graecae ad Res Romanas Pertinentes [*A publication*] (OCD)
**IGR & P**..... Inert Gas Receiving and Processing (NRCH)
**IGRP**.......... International Genetic Resources Programme [*Later, RAFI-USA*] (EA)
**IGRPS** ....... Inert Gas Receiving and Processing System (NRCH)
**IGRR** ......... Inscriptiones Graecae ad Res Romanas Pertinentes [*A publication*]
**IGrSD**........ Grand Ridge Consolidated Community School District 95, Grand Ridge, IL [*Library symbol*] [*Library of Congress*] (LCLS)
**IGS**............ Carl Sandburg Birthplace Association, Galesburg, IL [*Library symbol*] [*Library of Congress*] (LCLS)
**IGS**............ Gary Community School Corp., Gary, IN [*OCLC symbol*] (OCLC)
**IGS**............ Immigrant Genealogical Society (EA)
**IGS**............ Immunogold Stain [*Cytochemistry*]
**IGS**............ Imperial General Staff
**IGS**............ Improved Gray Scale
**IGS**............ Inappropriate Gonadotrophin Secretion [*Endocrinology*]
**IGS**............ Indicator Group Speed
**IGS**............ Inert Gas Storage
**IGS**............ Inert Gas System [*Engineering*]
**IGS**............ Inertial Guidance System [*NASA*]
**IGS**............ Information Group Separator
**IGS**............ Inner Glide Slope [*Aviation*] (NASA)
**IGS**............ Institute of General Semantics (EA)
**IGS**............ Institute of Geological Sciences [*British*]
**IGS**............ Institute of Government Studies [*University of California at Berkeley*]
**IGS**............ Instrumentation Ground System
**IGS**............ Integrated Graphics System [*Data processing*] (BUR)
**IGS**............ Interactive Graphics System [*Data processing*]
**IGS**............ Interchange Group Separator [*Data processing*] (BUR)
**IGS**............ Intermediate General Support [*Army*]
**IGS**............ Internal Guide Sequence [*Genetics*]
**IGS**............ International Geranium Society (EA)
**IGS**............ International Glaciological Society [*Cambridge, England*]
**IGS**............ International Graphological Society (EA)
**IGS**............ Irish Genealogical Society (EA)
**IGS**............ Irish Georgian Society (EA)
**IGS**............ Isla Grande Flying School [*Hato Rey, PR*] [*FAA designator*] (FAAC)
**IGSA**.......... Indoor Gardening Society of America (EA)
**IGSA**.......... International Golf Sponsors' Association [*Later, AGS*]
**Ig Sanita Pubblica** ... Igiene e Sanita Pubblica [*A publication*]
**Ig San Pubbl** ... Igiene e Sanita Pubblica [*A publication*]
**IGSBDO**.... Proceedings. Academy of Sciences of the Georgian SSR. Biological Series [*A publication*]
**IGSC**.......... Carl Sandburg College, Galesburg, IL [*Library symbol*] [*Library of Congress*] (LCLS)
**IGSC**.......... Inspector General, Supply Corps
**IGSCC** ....... Intergranular Stress-Corrosion Cracking [*Plant engineering*]

**IGSE**.......... In-Space Ground Support Equipment [*NASA*] (NASA)
**IGSE**.......... Instrument Ground Support Equipment (MCD)
**IGSHPA**.... International Ground Source Heat Pump Association (EA)
**IGSI**........... Insituform Gulf South, Incorporated [*Pasadena, TX*] [*NASDAQ symbol*] (NQ)
**IGSKD**....... Izvestiya Akademii Nauk Gruzinskoi SSR Seriya Khimicheskaya [*A publication*]
**IGSM**......... Indian General Service Medal [*British*]
**IGSMA**...... Inertial Guidance System Maintenance Area [*Aerospace*] (AAG)
**IGSOBM**... International Guild of Symphony, Opera, and Ballet Musicians (EA)
**IGSP**.......... Institute for Gravitational Strain Pathology (EA)
**IGSP**.......... Internationale Gesellschaft der Schriftpsychologie [*International Society for the Psychology of Writing*]
**IGSPS**........ International Gold and Silver Plate Society (EA)
**IGSS**.......... Immunogold Silver Staining [*Cytochemistry*]
**IGSSA**....... Illinois State Geological Survey. Guidebook Series [*A publication*]
**IGSU**.......... Improved Gunner's Sight Unit [*Military*] (MCD)
**IGT**............ Impaired Glucose Tolerance [*Physiology*]
**IGT**............ Ingot (MSA)
**IGT**............ Ingot Resources Ltd. [*Vancouver Stock Exchange symbol*]
**IGT**............ Inspector-General to the Forces for Training [*British military*]
**IGT**............ Inspector-General of Transportation [*British military*] (DMA)
**IGT**............ Institute of Gas Technology (EA)
**IGT**............ Instrument Guide Tube [*Nuclear energy*] (NRCH)
**IGT**............ Integrated Ground Test
**IGT**............ Interactive Graphics Terminal [*Data processing*]
**IGT**............ International Game Technology [*NYSE symbol*] (SPSG)
**IGT**............ Intragastric Titration [*Gastroenterology*]
**IGT**............ Ionization Gauge Tube
**IGT**............ Nightmute, AK [*Location identifier*] [*FAA*] (FAAL)
**IGTA**.......... International Gay Travel Association (EA)
**IGTAAN**.... Institutul de Cercetari pentru Cereale si Plante Tehnice Fundulea Probleme de Genetica Teoretica si Aplicata [*A publication*]
**IGTC**.......... International Glutamate Technical Committee (EA)
**IGTI**........... International Gas Turbine Institute [*Later, ASMEIGTI*] (EA)
**IGTJA**........ Indian Geotechnical Journal [*A publication*]
**IGT Nie**...... IGT [*Instituut voor Grafische Techniek*] Nieuws [*A publication*]
**IGTT**.......... Intravenous Glucose Tolerance Test [*Clinical medicine*]
**IGTYF**........ International Good Templar Youth Federation [*Oslo, Norway*] (EAIO)
**IGU**............ Iguassu Falls [*Brazil*] [*Airport symbol*] (OAG)
**IGU**............ International Gas Union [*See also UIIG*] (EAIO)
**IGU**............ International Geographical Union [*ICSU*] [*Edmonton, AB*] (EA)
**IGU**............ International Geophysical Union
**IGU**............ Internationale Gewerbeunion [*International Association of Crafts and Small and Medium Sized Enterprises - IACME*] [*Berne, Switzerland*] (EAIO)
**IGUA**.......... International Guards Union of America (EA)
**IGUC**.......... Information Gained per Unit Cost [*Data processing*]
**IGU Newsl**... IGU [*International Geographical Union*] Newsletter [*A publication*]
**IGUTP**........ Instituti Geographici Universitatis Turkuensis. Publications [*A publication*]
**IGV**............ Incremental Growth Vehicle (MCD)
**IGV**............ Inlet Guide Valve (MCD)
**IGV**............ Inlet Guide Vane
**IGV**............ International Gravis Computer Technology, Inc. [*Formerly, Gravis Computer Peripherals, Inc.*] [*Vancouver Stock Exchange symbol*]
**IGVP**.......... International Guild of Vatican Philatelists (EA)
**IGW**........... Image West Entertainment Corp. [*Vancouver Stock Exchange symbol*]
**IGW**........... Internal Gravity Wave [*in the atmosphere*]
**IGW**........... Internationales Gewerbearchiv der Kleinbetrieb und Mittelbetrieb in der Modernen Wirtschaft [*A publication*]
**IGWAP**...... CPA [*Canadian Psychological Association*] Interest Group on Women and Psychology
**IGWF**......... International Garment Workers' Federation
**IGW Inf**..... IGW [*Institut fuer Gesellschaft und Wissenschaft*] Informationen zur Wissenschaftsentwicklung [*A publication*]
**IGWIS**........ Integrated Ground Water Information System
**IGWMC**.... International Ground Water Modeling Center [*Butler University*]
**IGWP**......... International Group of Women Pilots (EA)
**IGWT**......... Internationale Gesellschaft fuer Warenkunde und Technologie [*International Association for Commodity Science and Technology*] (EA)
**IGWU**........ International Glove Workers' Union of America [*Later, ACTWU*]
**IGY**............ International Geophysical Year [*1958-1959*] [*ICSU*]
**IGY Bull**.... IGY [*International Geophysical Year*] Bulletin [*A publication*]
**IGY Gen Rep Ser**... IGY [*International Geophysical Year*] General Report Series [*A publication*]
**IGY Oc Rep**... IGY [*International Geophysical Year*] Oceanography Report [*A publication*]
**IGY Sat Rep Ser**... IGY [*International Geophysical Year*] Satellite Report Series [*A publication*]
**IGY-WDC**... International Geophysical Year, World Data Center
**IGY World Data Center A Gen Rept Ser**... International Geophysical Year. World Data Center. A. General Report Series [*A publication*]
**IGY World Data Center A Glaciolog Rept Ser**... International Geophysical Year. World Data Center. A. Glaciological Report Series [*A publication*]
**IH**.............. Algesa Aerolineas Guineacuatorial [*Equatorial Guinea*] [*ICAO designator*] (FAAC)
**IH**.............. Hinsdale Public Library, Hinsdale, IL [*Library symbol*] [*Library of Congress*] (LCLS)
**IH**.............. Iacet Hic [*Here Lies*] [*Latin*]
**IH**.............. Ice Haulage
**IH**.............. Idiopathic Hemachromatosis [*Medicine*]
**IH**.............. Idiopathic Hypercalciuria [*Medicine*]
**IH**.............. Immediate Hypersensitivity [*Immunology*]
**IH**.............. Impact on Hunger (EA)
**IH**.............. In Home [*Men's lacrosse position*]
**IH**.............. In-House
**IH**.............. Incipient Heavies [*Slang for rising young bureaucrats in the foreign policy field*]
**IH**.............. Index of Homogeneity [*Botany*]
**IH**.............. Indirectly Heated (DEN)
**IH**.............. Indo-Hittite (BJA)
**I/H**............ Industria del Hierro [*Part of a large Mexican industrial complex*]
**IH**.............. Industrial House (ROG)
**IH**.............. Industrial Hygienist [*Occupational Safety and Health Administration*]
**IH**.............. Infectious Hepatitis [*Medicine*]
**I & H**.......... Information and Historical [*Military*]
**IH**.............. Information Historique [*A publication*]
**IH**.............. Information Hotline [*A publication*]
**IH**.............. Informed Homebirth [*Later, IH/IBP*] (EA)
**IH**.............. Inhibit
**IH**.............. Inhibiting Hormone
**IH**.............. Initial Heading
**IH**.............. Innateness Hypothesis [*Linguistics*]
**IH**.............. Inpatient, Hospital
**IH**.............. Inside Height
**IH**.............. Inside Home [*Baseball*]
**IH**.............. Inspector-General of Hospitals and Fleets [*Navy*] [*British*] (ROG)
**IH**.............. Inspired Humidity [*Anesthesiology*]
**IH**.............. Installation Handbook
**IH**.............. Institute of Housing [*British*]
**IH**.............. Institute of Hydrology [*British*]
**IH**.............. Instrument Head
**IH**.............. International Harvester Co.
**IH**.............. International Humanism Magazine [*Netherlands*] [*A publication*]
**IH**.............. Internationale Horngesellschaft [*International Horn Society*] (EAIO)
**IH**.............. Internationaler Holzmarkt [*A publication*]
**IH**.............. Irish Horse [*British military*] (DMA)
**IH**.............. Iron Hematoxylin [*A dye*]
**IH**.............. Isme-Dagan Hymn (BJA)
**IH**.............. Israel's Herald [*A publication*] (BJA)
**IH**.............. Ita Humanidades [*A publication*]
**IHa**............ Harvey Public Library, Harvey, IL [*Library symbol*] [*Library of Congress*] (LCLS)
**IHA**............ Idiopathic Hyperplastic Aldosteronism [*Endocrinology*]
**IHA**............ Immune Hemolytic Anemia [*Medicine*]
**IHA**............ Indirect Hemagglutination [*Clinical chemistry*]
**IHA**............ Individual Housing Account
**IHA**............ Industrie Hoteliere [*A publication*]
**IHA**............ Information d'Histoire de l'Art [*A publication*]
**IHA**............ Infusion Hepatic Angiography [*Medicine*]
**IHA**............ Interfaith Hunger Appeal (EA)
**IHA**............ Interim Housing Allowance [*Military*] (AFM)
**IHA**............ International Hahnemannian Association [*Defunct*]
**IHA**............ International Hopkins Association
**IHA**............ International Hotel Association [*Paris, France*] (EA)
**IHA**............ International House Association [*Defunct*]
**IHA**............ Islam d'Hier et Aujourd'hui [*A publication*]
**IHA**............ Reese Hospital and Medical Center, Chicago, IL [*OCLC symbol*] (OCLC)
**IHAB**.......... International Horticultural Advisory Board
**IHAC**.......... Industrial Health Advisory Council [*British*]
**IHAD**.......... I Have a Dream Foundation (EA)
**IHADSS**..... Integrated Helmet and Display Sight System
**IHAF**.......... Institut d'Histoire de l'Amerique Francaise [*Institute of French America History*] [*Canada*]
**IHAH**.......... Illustrated Handbooks of Art History [*A publication*]
**IHaI**............ Ingalls Memorial Hospital, Harvey, IL [*Library symbol*] [*Library of Congress*] (LCLS)
**IHAI**........... Institute of Heating and Air-Conditioning Industries

**IH-ANES** .. Inhalation Anesthesia
**IHAP** ......... International Human Assistance Programs (EA)
**IHardCSD** ... Calhoun Community Unit, School District 40, Hardin, IL [*Library symbol*] [*Library of Congress*] (LCLS)
**IHardR** ...... Hardin Reading Center, Hardin, IL [*Library symbol*] [*Library of Congress*] (LCLS)
**IHart** .......... Hartford Public Library, Hartford, IL [*Library symbol*] [*Library of Congress*] (LCLS)
**IHAS** ......... Integrated Helicopter Avionics System [*Navy*] (NG)
**IHASFC** .... International Hearts Air Supply Fan Club (EA)
**IHATIS** ..... International Hide and Allied Trades Improvement Society
**IHAWK** ..... Improved Homing All the Way Killer [*Missile*]
**IHB** ........... Barnes, Hickam, Pantzer & Boyd, Indianapolis, IN [*OCLC symbol*] (OCLC)
**IHB** ........... Indiana Harbor Belt Railroad Co. [*AAR code*]
**IHB** ........... Indiana History Bulletin [*A publication*]
**IHB** ........... International Hydrographic Bureau [*Later, IHO*] [*Monaco*]
**IHB** ........... International Journal of Social Economics (Bradford) [*A publication*]
**IHB** ........... Internationale Hoptrenbaubuero [*International Hop Growers Convention*]
**IHBCA** ...... International H Boat Class Association (EA)
**IHBI** .......... Indian Head Banks, Incorporated [*NASDAQ symbol*] (NQ)
**IHBPA** ........ International Hepato-Biliary-Pancreatic Association (EA)
**IHBS** .......... International Hajji Baba Society (EA)
**IHBT** ......... Incompatible Hemolytic Blood Transfusion
**IHC** ........... Hanover College, Hanover, IN [*OCLC symbol*] (OCLC)
**IHC** ........... Idiopathic Hypercalcemia [*Medicine*]
**IHC** ........... Immaculate Heart College [*California*]
**IHC** ........... Indian Hospital Corps [*British military*] (DMA)
**IHC** ........... Indirectly Heated Cathode
**IHC** ........... Infant Hypercalcemia [*Medicine*]
**IHC** ........... Inner Hair Cells [*of cochlea*] [*Anatomy*]
**IHC** ........... International Harvester Company
**IHC** ........... International Health Consultants (EA)
**IHC** ........... International Health Council (EA)
**IHC** ........... International Help for Children
**IHC** ........... International Hug Center (EA)
**IHC** ........... Ionic Heated Cathode
**IHCA** ......... In Hands of Civil Authorities [*Military*]
**IHCA** ......... International Hebrew Christian Alliance [*Ramsgate, Kent, England*] (EA)
**IHCA** ......... International Hobie Class Association (EA)
**IHCC** ......... International Harvester Credit Corporation (ADA)
**IHCOS** ...... Isotope-Heated Catalytic Oxidizer System (KSC)
**IHCP** ......... Institute on Hospital and Community Psychiatry (EA)
**IHCPV** ....... Initial Hydrocarbon Pore Volume [*Petroleum technology*]
**IHCSERS** ... International Health Centre of Socio-Economics Researches and Studies [*See also CIERSES*] [*Lailly En Val, France*] (EAIO)
**IHCTA2** .... International Histological Classification of Tumors [*A publication*]
**IHD** ........... American Hospital Association Library, Chicago, IL [*OCLC symbol*] (OCLC)
**IHD** ........... Indian Head, PA [*Location identifier*] [*FAA*] (FAAL)
**IHD** ........... Institut Henry-Dunant [*Henry Dunant Institute*] [*Geneva, Switzerland*] (EAIO)
**IHD** ........... Institute of Human Development [*University of California, Berkeley*] [*Research center*] (RCD)
**IHD** ........... International Hard Suits [*Vancouver Stock Exchange symbol*]
**IHD** ........... International Hydrological Decade [*UNESCO*] [*Later, IHP*]
**IHD** ........... Ischemic Heart Disease
**IHDI** .......... International Hearing Dog, Incorporated (EA)
**IHDRT** ...... Interim High-Data Rate Terminal (CAAL)
**IHDS** ......... Institute for Higher Defense Studies [*National Defense University*]
**IHDS** ......... Integrated Helmet Display System
**IHE** ........... Evanston Public Library, Evanston, IL [*OCLC symbol*] (OCLC)
**IHE** ........... Indice Historico Espanol [*A publication*]
**IHE** ........... Insensitive High Explosive (MCD)
**IHE** ........... Institute of Health Education [*British*]
**IHE** ........... Institute of Higher Education
**IHE** ........... Institute of Highway Engineers [*British*]
**IHE** ........... Institute of Home Economics [*of ARS, Department of Agriculture*]
**IHE** ........... Institute of Hospital Engineering (EAIO)
**IHE** ........... Institute of Hospital Engineers [*Australia*]
**IHE** ........... Institute for the Human Environment (EA)
**IHE** ........... Intergranular Hydrogen Embrittlement [*Metallurgy*]
**IHE** ........... Interhome Energy, Inc. [*Toronto Stock Exchange symbol*]
**IHE** ........... Intermediate Heat Exchanger [*Nuclear energy*]
**IHE** ........... International Historic Enterprises
**IHE** ........... International Hospital Equipment [*A publication*]
**IHE** ........... Interservice Home Exchange [*Commercial firm*] (EA)
**IHEA** ......... Industrial Heating Equipment Association (EA)
**IHEA** ......... International Health Evaluation Association (EA)
**IHEI** .......... Interhome Energy, Inc. [*NASDAQ symbol*] (NQ)
**IHEJAG** .... Indian Heart Journal [*A publication*]
**IHEMI** ...... International Health Economics and Management Institute (EA)
**IHen** .......... Henry Public Library, Henry, IL [*Library symbol*] [*Library of Congress*] (LCLS)
**IHenn** ......... Putnam County Library, Hennepin, IL [*Library symbol*] [*Library of Congress*] (LCLS)
**IHennC** ...... Hennepin Attendance Center, Hennepin, IL [*Library symbol*] [*Library of Congress*] (LCLS)
**IHenn-G** .... Putnam County Library, Granville Branch, Granville, IL [*Library symbol*] [*Library of Congress*] (LCLS)
**IHenn-H** .... Putnam County Library, Hennepin Branch, Hennepin, IL [*Library symbol*] [*Library of Congress*] (LCLS)
**IHenn-M** ... Putnam County Library, Magnolia Branch, Magnolia, IL [*Library symbol*] [*Library of Congress*] (LCLS)
**IHenn-Mc** ... Putnam County Library, McNabb Branch, McNabb, IL [*Library symbol*] [*Library of Congress*] (LCLS)
**IHenn-P** ..... Putnam County Library, Condit Branch, Putnam, IL [*Library symbol*] [*Library of Congress*] (LCLS)
**IHenn-S** ..... Putnam County Library, Standard Branch, Standard, IL [*Library symbol*] [*Library of Congress*] (LCLS)
**IHEP** ......... Insensitive High Explosives and Propellants [*DoD/DOE program*] (RDA)
**IHEP** ......... Institute of High Energy Physics [*USSR*]
**IHERC** ....... Inter-Hemispheric Education Resource Center (EA)
**Iheringia Ser Antropol** ... Iheringia. Serie Antropologia [*A publication*]
**Iheringia Ser Bot** ... Iheringia. Serie Botanica [*A publication*]
**Iheringia Ser Divulg** ... Iheringia. Serie Divulgacao [*A publication*]
**Iheringia Ser Geol** ... Iheringia. Serie Geologia [*A publication*]
**Iheringia Ser Zool** ... Iheringia. Serie Zoologia [*A publication*]
**IHERS** ....... Institute of Higher Education Research and Services [*University of Alabama*] [*Research center*] (RCD)
**IHETS** ....... Indiana Higher Education Telecommunication System [*Indianapolis*] [*Telecommunications*] (TSSD)
**IHEU** ......... International Humanist and Ethical Union [*Utrecht, Netherlands*] (EA)
**IHF** ........... Industrial Health Foundation (EA)
**IHF** ........... Industrial Hygiene Foundation of America
**IHF** ........... Inhibit Halt Flip-Flop [*Data processing*]
**IHF** ........... Institute of Gas Technology, Chicago, IL [*OCLC symbol*] (OCLC)
**IHF** ........... Institute of High Fidelity [*Formerly, IHFM*] [*Later, EIA*] (EA)
**IHF** ........... Integrated Hazard Function
**IHF** ........... Integration Host Factor [*Genetics*]
**IHF** ........... International Handball Federation [*Basel, Switzerland*] (EA)
**IHF** ........... International Health Foundation [*Brussels, Belgium*] (EAIO)
**IHF** ........... International Helicopter Foundation [*Later, HFI*] (EA)
**IHF** ........... International Hospital Federation (EA)
**IHF** ........... International Lawn Hockey Federation
**IHF** ........... Internazionale Holding Fiat SA [*Italy*]
**IHF** ........... Inverse Hyperbolic Function
**IHF** ........... Irish Heritage Foundation (EA)
**IHF** ........... Irish Hotels Federation (EAIO)
**IHF** ........... Isothermal Heating Furnace
**IHF** ........... Israel Histadrut Foundation (EA)
**IHFAS** ....... Integrated High-Frequency Antenna System
**IHFF** .......... Inhibit Halt Flip-Flop [*Data processing*] (MSA)
**IHFHR** ....... International Helsinki Federation for Human Rights (EA)
**IHFLBS** ..... Institutt foer Husdyrernaering og Foringslaere Norges Landbrukshogskole Beretning [*A publication*]
**IHFM** ........ Institute of High Fidelity Manufacturers [*Later, IHF*]
**IHFMA** ..... International Home Furnishings Marketing Association (EA)
**IHFRA** ....... International Home Furnishings Representatives Association (EA)
**IHG** ........... Internationale Hegel Gesellschaft (EA)
**IHG** ........... Investitionshilfegesetz [*A publication*]
**IHG** ........... Irish Banking Review [*A publication*]
**IHG** ........... Skokie Public Library, Skokie, IL [*OCLC symbol*] (OCLC)
**IHGC** ......... International Hop Growers Convention [*See also CICH*] [*Zalec, Yugoslavia*] (EAIO)
**IHGMA** ..... International Herb Growers and Marketers Association (EA)
**IHGS** ......... Institute of Heraldic and Genealogical Studies [*British*]
**IHh** ........... Eisenhower Public Library District, Harwood Heights, IL [*Library symbol*] [*Library of Congress*] (LCLS)
**IHH** ........... Huntington College, Huntington, IN [*OCLC symbol*] (OCLC)
**IHH** ........... Idiopathic Hypogonadotropic Hypogonadism [*Endocrinology*]
**IHHA** ........ International Halfway House Association (EA)
**IHHI** ......... In Home Health, Incorporated [*NASDAQ symbol*] (NQ)
**IHHO** ........ Institute of Home Help Organisers [*British*]
**IH & HU** .... Industrial Health and Hazards Update [*Merton Allen Associates*] [*Information service or system*] (CRD)
**IHi** ............ Illinois State Historical Library, Springfield, IL [*Library symbol*] [*Library of Congress*] (LCLS)
**IHI** ............ Improved Holographic Image
**IHI** ............ Integrated Hit Indicator
**IHI** ............ Ishikawajima-Harima Heavy Industries Co. Ltd. [*Japan*]
**IHI** ............ Lincoln Trail Libraries System, Champaign, IL [*OCLC symbol*] (OCLC)
**IHIA** .......... Include This Headquarters Information Addressee [*Army*] (AABC)
**IHIA** .......... International Health Industries Association (EA)
**IH/IBP** ...... Informed Homebirth/Informed Birth and Parenting (EA)
**IHI Eng Rev** ... IHI [*Ishikawajima-Harima Heavy Industries*] Engineering Review [*A publication*]

**IHig**.......... Louis Latzer Memorial Library, Highland, IL [*Library symbol*] [*Library of Congress*] (LCLS)
**IHigp**.......... Highland Park Public Library, Highland Park, IL [*Library symbol*] [*Library of Congress*] (LCLS)
**IHigSD**...... Highland Community Unit, School District 5, Highland, IL [*Library symbol*] [*Library of Congress*] (LCLS)
**IHII**.......... Independent Health Insurance Institute [*Inactive*] (EA)
**IHil**.......... Hillside Public Library, Hillside, IL [*Library symbol*] [*Library of Congress*] (LCLS)
**IHilb**.......... Hillsboro Public Library, Hillsboro, IL [*Library symbol*] [*Library of Congress*] (LCLS)
**IHilbSD**..... Hillsboro Community Unit, School District 3, Hillsboro, IL [*Library symbol*] [*Library of Congress*] (LCLS)
**IHineJ**........ John J. Madden Mental Health Center, Training Staff Development Library, Hines, IL [*Library symbol*] [*Library of Congress*] (LCLS)
**IHineV**....... United States Veterans Administration Hospital, Hines, IL [*Library symbol*] [*Library of Congress*] (LCLS)
**IHIPIR**...... Improved High-Power Illuminator RADAR [*IHAWK Missile*] (MCD)
**IHIR**.......... International HRS Industries, Inc. [*Toronto, ON*] [*NASDAQ symbol*] (NQ)
**IHIS**.......... Integrated Hit Indicator System
**I Hist**.......... Indian Historian [*A publication*]
**IHJ**.......... Institute of the Heart of Jesus [*See also GEM*] [*Paris, France*] (EAIO)
**IHJ**.......... International Heroines of Jericho [*Later, General Conference of Grand Courts Heroines of Jericho, Prince Hall Affiliation, USA*] (EA)
**IHK**.......... Imperial Holly Corp. [*AMEX symbol*] (SPSG)
**IHK**.......... Industrie und Handelskammer [*A publication*]
**IHK**.......... International Homestock Resources Ltd. [*Vancouver Stock Exchange symbol*]
**IHK**.......... Ionic Heated Kathode
**IHL**.......... Illinois Health Libraries Consortium [*Library network*]
**IHL**.......... Imperial Light Horse [*Military*] [*British*] (ROG)
**IHL**.......... International Hockey League (EA)
**IHL**.......... International Homeopathic League
**IHLCADS**... Interim High-Level Container Airdrop System
**IHLS**.......... International Herring Larvae Survey
**IHLZY**....... Ichud Habonim Labor Zionist Youth (EA)
**IHM**.......... Daughters of the Immaculate Heart of Mary [*Roman Catholic religious order*]
**i-hm---**........ Heard and McDonald Islands [*MARC geographic area code*] [*Library of Congress*] (LCCP)
**IHM**.......... Mansfield, MA [*Location identifier*] [*FAA*] (FAAL)
**IHM**.......... Sisters of the Immaculate Heart of Mary [*California Institute of the Most Holy and Immaculate Heart of the BVM*] [*Roman Catholic religious order*]
**IHM**.......... Sisters, Servants of the Immaculate Heart of Mary [*Roman Catholic religious order*]
**IHMA**........ Industrialized Housing Manufacturer's Association (EA)
**IHMA**........ International House Members Association [*University of Sydney*] [*Australia*]
**IHMB**........ Industrie des Huiles Minerales de Belgique [*Industry of Mineral Oils of Belgium*] (EY)
**IH & MEE**... International Hotel and Motel Educational Exposition [*Later, IHM & RS*] (EA)
**IHMI**.......... Institute for Housing Management Innovations (EA)
**IHML**.......... International Henry Miller Letter [*A publication*]
**IHM & RS**... International Hotel/Motel and Restaurant Show (EA)
**IHMSA**..... International Handgun Metallic Silhouette Association (EA)
**IHN**.......... In His Name
**IHN**.......... Infectious Hematopoietic Necrosis [*Fish pathology*]
**IHN**.......... International Handicappers' Net (EA)
**IHN**.......... Iron Horse Resources, Inc. [*Vancouver Stock Exchange symbol*]
**IHo**.......... Hoopestown Public Library, Hoopestown, IL [*Library symbol*] [*Library of Congress*] (LCLS)
**IHO**.......... Idiopathic Hypertrophic Osteoarthropathy [*Medicine*]
**IHO**.......... Impartial Hearing Officer
**IHO**.......... Impeded Harmonic Operation
**IHO**.......... In Honor Of
**IHO**.......... Inorganic Halogen Oxidizer
**IHO**.......... Institute of Human Origins (EA)
**IHO**.......... International Hydrographic Organization [*See also BHI*] [*Monaco*]
**IHod**.......... Hodgkins Public Library District, Hodgkins, IL [*Library symbol*] [*Library of Congress*] (LCLS)
**IHoH**.......... Hoopestown Community Memorial Hospital, Hoopestown, IL [*Library symbol*] [*Library of Congress*] (LCLS)
**IHom**.......... Homer Community Library, Homer, IL [*Library symbol*] [*Library of Congress*] (LCLS)
**IHOP**.......... International House of Pancakes [*Restaurant chain*] [*Pronounced "eye-hop"*]
**I Horizons**... Indian Horizons [*A publication*]
**IHot**.......... Hometown Public Library, Hometown, IL [*Library symbol*] [*Library of Congress*] (LCLS)
**IHOU**.......... Institute of Home Office Underwriters [*Louisville, KY*] (EA)
**IHow**.......... Homewood Public Library, Homewood, IL [*Library symbol*] [*Library of Congress*] (LCLS)
**IHP**.......... Hammond Public Library, Hammond, IN [*OCLC symbol*] (OCLC)
**IHP**.......... Idiopathic Hypoparathyroidism [*Medicine*]
**IHP**.......... Indicated Horsepower
**IHP**.......... Individualized Habilitation Plan
**IHP**.......... Information Handling Project (DIT)
**IHP**.......... Inositol Hexaphosphate [*Biochemistry*]
**IHP**.......... Institute for Human Progress [*Defunct*]
**IHP**.......... Instrumentation Habitability Power (MCD)
**IHP**.......... Intergovernmental Council for the International Hydrological Programme (EA)
**IHP**.......... International Hydrographic Program
**IHP**.......... International Hydrological Program [*UNESCO*] [*France*]
**IHP**.......... Inverted Hand Position [*Neuropsychology*]
**IHPA**.......... International Hardwood Products Association (EA)
**IH3PA**....... International Home and Private Poker Players Association (EA)
**IHPAB**....... Health Physics Research Abstracts [*A publication*]
**IHPC**.......... International Hydrolyzed Protein Council (EA)
**IHPD**.......... International Health Physics Data Base [*Creative Information Systems, Inc.*] [*Information service or system*] (CRD)
**IHPH**.......... Indicated Horsepower-Hour
**IHP-HR**..... Indicated Horsepower-Hour
**IHPI**.......... IHS [*Information Handling Services*] Product/Subject Index [*Information service or system*] (CRD)
**IHPI**.......... Improved High-Power Illuminator (CAAL)
**IHPI**.......... Independent Health Plan [*NASDAQ symbol*] (NQ)
**IHPO**.......... International Health Program Office [*Atlanta, GA*] [*Department of Health and Human Services*] (GRD)
**IHPP**.......... Intergovernmental Health Policy Project (EA)
**IHPRS**....... International Husserl and Phenomenological Research Society (EA)
**IHPTET**.... Integrated High-Performance Turbine Engine Technology Initiative [*NASA and DOD*]
**IHPVA**...... International Human Powered Vehicle Association (EA)
**IHQ**.......... Indian Historical Quarterly [*A publication*]
**IHQ**.......... Rolling Prairie Libraries, Decatur, IL [*OCLC symbol*] (OCLC)
**IH/QAS**..... Indian Head [*Maryland*] - Quality Assurance Department [*Naval ordnance station*]
**IHR**.......... Carl Sandburg College, LRC, Galesburg, IL [*OCLC symbol*] (OCLC)
**IHR**.......... Cocoa, FL [*Location identifier*] [*FAA*] (FAAL)
**IHR**.......... Increased Hazard Rate
**IHR**.......... Infrared Heterodyne Radiometer
**IHR**.......... Institute for Historical Review (EA)
**IHR**.......... Institute of Horticultural Research [*United Kingdom*] [*Research center*] (IRC)
**IHR**.......... International Hotel Review [*A publication*]
**IHR**.......... Intrinsic Heart Rate [*Cardiology*]
**IHR**.......... Ishihara [*Japan*] [*Seismograph station code, US Geological Survey*] [*Closed*] (SEIS)
**IHRA**.......... Increasing Hazard Rate Average
**IHRA**.......... International Hot Rod Association (EA)
**IHRB**.......... Industrial Health Research Board [*British*]
**IHRB**.......... Institute of Historical Research. Bulletin [*A publication*]
**IHRBLR**.... International Human Resources, Business, and Legal Research Association (EA)
**IHRC**.......... Immigration History Research Center [*University of Minnesota*] [*Research center*] (RCD)
**IHRC**.......... In-Home Respite Care
**IHRC**.......... Proceedings. Indian Historical Records Commission [*A publication*]
**IH Rev**........ IH Review [*New Zealand Society for the Intellectually Handicapped*] [*A publication*]
**IHRG**.......... Interdisciplinary Health Research Group [*See also GRIS*] [*Universite de Montreal*] [*Canada*] [*Research center*]
**IHRLG**...... International Human Rights Law Group (EA)
**IHRR**.......... Institute for Human Rights Research (EA)
**IHS**.......... Fort Carson, CO [*Location identifier*] [*FAA*] (FAAL)
**IHS**.......... Iesous Hemeteros Soter [*Jesus, Our Savior*] [*Greek*]
**IHS**.......... Iesus Heiland Seligmacher [*Jesus, Savior, Sanctifier*] [*German*]
**IHS**.......... Iesus Hominum Salvator [*Jesus, Savior of Mankind*] [*Latin*] (ADA)
**IHS**.......... Immigration History Society (EA)
**IHS**.......... Improved HAWK Simulator [*Military*]
**IHS**.......... In Hoc Signo (Vinces) [*In This Sign (You Will Conquer)*] [*Latin*]
**IHS**.......... Inactivated Horse Serum [*Immunology*]
**IHS**.......... Indescor Hydrodynamics, Inc. [*Vancouver Stock Exchange symbol*]
**IHS**.......... Indian Health Service
**IHS**.......... Information Handling Services [*Englewood, CO*]
**IHS**.......... Infrared Homing System (AAG)
**IHS**.......... Infrared Horizon Sensor
**IHS**.......... Institute for Humane Studies, Inc. [*Research center*] (RCD)
**IHS**.......... Institute for Hydrogen Systems [*UTLAS symbol*]
**IHS**.......... Institute of Hypertension Studies - Institute of Hypertension School of Research [*Later, NIHS*] (EA)
**IHS**.......... International Health Society (EA)
**IHS**.......... International Heritage Site [*UNESCO*]
**IHS**.......... International Hibernation Society (EA)

**IHS** ........... International Horn Society (EA)
**IHS** ........... International Hydrofoil Society (EAIO)
**IHS** ........... Intrahepatic Arteriovenous Shunt [*Medicine*]
**IHS** ........... Irish Historical Studies [*A publication*]
**IHS** ........... Isotope Heat Source
**IHS** ........... Italian Historical Society of America (EA)
**IHS** ........... Jesus, Heavenly Savior
**IHS** ........... Suburban Library System, Hinsdale, IL [*Library symbol*] [*Library of Congress*] (LCLS)
**IHS** ........... University of Texas, Health Science Center at Dallas, Dallas, TX [*OCLC symbol*] (OCLC)
**IHSA** ......... Intercollegiate Horse Show Association (EA)
**IHSA** ......... International Headquarters of the Salvation Army (EA)
**IHSA** ......... Iodinated Human Serum Albumin
**IHSB** .......... In-Flight Helmet Stowage Bag (KSC)
**IHSBR** ....... Improved High-Speed Bombing RADAR
**IHSD** ......... In-House Systems Developer [*Personal computer*] (PCM)
**IHSD** ......... Inertial Height Sensing Device
**IHSDC** ....... Irish Health Services Development Corporation
**IHSG** ......... Internationale Heinrich Schutz-Gesellschaft [*International Heinrich Schutz Society*] (EAIO)
**IHSP** .......... Indiana Historical Society. Publications [*A publication*]
**IHSPCB** .... International Healthcare Safety Professional Certification Board (EA)
**IHSPRS** ..... Indiana Historical Society. Prehistory Research Series [*A publication*]
**IHSR** .......... Institute for Health Services Research [*Tulane University*] [*Research center*] (RCD)
**IH/SR** ........ Integration Hardware and Software Review (MCD)
**IHSS** .......... Idiopathic Hypertrophic Subaortic Stenosis [*Medicine*]
**IHSS** .......... Institute of Human Science and Services [*University of Rhode Island*] [*Research center*] (RCD)
**IHSS** .......... International Heinrich Schutz Society [*See also IHSG*] [*Federal Republic of Germany*] (EA)
**IHT** ........... Icelandic Horse Trekkers (EA)
**IHT** ........... Impact Hand Tool
**IHT** ........... Inheritance Tax [*British*]
**IHT** ........... Inspection Hold Tag
**IHT** ........... Institute of Heat Technology
**IHT** ........... International Herald Tribune [*A publication*]
**IHT** ........... Trinity Evangelical Divinity School, Rolfing Memorial Library, Deerfield, IL [*OCLC symbol*] (OCLC)
**IHTA** ......... International Health and Temperance Association (EA)
**IH-TAS** ..... Improved HAWK-Tracking Adjunct System [*Military*] (MCD)
**IHTD** ......... Improved HAWK Training Detachment
**IHTS** .......... Intermediate Heat Transport System [*Nuclear energy*] (NRCH)
**IHTTA** ....... International High-Technology Training Association (EA)
**IHTU** ......... Interservice Hovercraft Trials Unit [*Military*]
**IHTV** ......... Interim Hypersonics Test Vehicle [*NASA*] (NASA)
**IHU** ........... Chicago Mercantile Exchange, Chicago, IL [*OCLC symbol*] (OCLC)
**IHU** ........... Ihu [*Papua New Guinea*] [*Airport symbol*] (OAG)
**IHU** ........... Interservice Hovercraft Unit [*Military*]
**IHUOA9** .... Institut de Recherches pour les Huiles et Oleagineux [*IRHO*]. Rapport Annuel [*A publication*]
**IHuSD** ....... Hutsonville Community Unit, School District 1, Hutsonville, IL [*Library symbol*] [*Library of Congress*] (LCLS)
**IHV** ........... Highland Park Public Library, Highland Park, IL [*OCLC symbol*] (OCLC)
**IHV** ........... Institute of Human Values [*Canada*] [*See also IMH*]
**IHV** ........... Internationale Hegel-Vereinigung [*Munich, Federal Republic of Germany*] (EAIO)
**IHVC** ......... IHV Corporation [*Torrance, CA*] [*NASDAQ symbol*] (NQ)
**IHVE** ......... Institution of Heating and Ventilating Engineers [*Later, CIBSE*]
**IHVE J** ...... IHVE [*Institution of Heating and Ventilating Engineers*] Journal [*A publication*]
**IHW** .......... International Halley Watch (EA)
**IHW** .......... Internationale Hefte der Widerstandsbewegung [*A publication*]
**IHW** .......... John G. Shedd Aquarium, Chicago, IL [*OCLC symbol*] (OCLC)
**IHW Ber** .... IHW [*Institut fuer Handwerkswirtschaft*] Berichte [*A publication*]
**IHWG** ........ Internationale Hugo Wolf Gesellschaft [*Vienna, Austria*] (EAIO)
**IHWU** ........ Independent Hospital Workers Union (EA)
**IHX** ........... Interloop Heat Exchanger [*NASA*] (NASA)
**IHX** ........... Intermediate Heat Exchanger [*Nuclear energy*]
**IHX** ........... Western Illinois Library System, Monmouth, IL [*OCLC symbol*] (OCLC)
**IHXGV** ...... Intermediate Heat Exchanger Guard Vessel [*Nuclear energy*] (NRCH)
**IHY** ........... Ela Area Public Library District, Lake Zurich, IL [*OCLC symbol*] (OCLC)
**IHYHA** ...... Industrial Hygiene Highlights [*A publication*]
**IHYP** ......... Iodohydroxybenzylpindolol [*Organic chemistry*]
**IHYRB** ....... Industrial Hygiene Review [*A publication*]
**IHZ** ........... Warren-Newport Public Library District, Gurnee, IL [*OCLC symbol*] (OCLC)
**II** ............... Aer Arann Teoranta [*Ireland*] [*ICAO designator*] (ICDA)
**I/I** .............. Current to Current [*Converter*] (NRCH)
**II** ............... Evex Fluggesellschaft mbH und Co. KG, Dusseldorf [*West Germany*] [*ICAO designator*] (FAAC)
**II** ............... Igniter Initiator
**II** ............... Ikebana International [*Japan*]
**I-I** .............. Illegal Immigrant
**II** ............... Illustrazione Italiana [*A publication*]
**II** ............... Image Intensifier
**II** ............... Imagery Interpretation
**II** ............... Immigrant Inspector [*Immigration and Naturalization Service*]
**II** ............... Imperial Institute [*British*] (DAS)
**II** ............... Implementation Instructions (MCD)
**II** ............... Incarcerated Innocent
**ii** ................ India [*MARC country of publication code*] [*Library of Congress*] (LCCP)
**II** ............... Individualized Instruction
**II** ............... Indochina Institute (EA)
**I/I** .............. Indorsement Irregular [*Banking*]
**I & I** ........... Industrial and Institutional [*Business term*]
**II** ............... Information Index [*LIMRA*]
**II** ............... Ingot Iron
**II** ............... Initial Issue
**II** ............... Innovators International (EA)
**II** ............... Input Impedance
**II** ............... Inscriptiones Italiae [*A publication*]
**II** ............... Insol International (EA)
**I-I** .............. Inspector-Instructor [*Marine Corps*]
**II** ............... Installation Instruction
**II** ............... Institutional Investor [*A publication*]
**II** ............... Institutional Investor [*Business term*]
**II** ............... Instituto Interamericano (EA)
**II** ............... Interlingua Institute (EA)
**II** ............... Interrupt Inhibit
**II** ............... Interval International (EA)
**I & I** ........... Intoxication and Intercourse
**II** ............... Intransit Inventory (AFM)
**II** ............... Inventory and Inspection Report [*Army*]
**II** ............... Irish Independent [*A publication*]
**II** ............... Irish Institute (EA)
**II** ............... Italia Intellettuale [*A publication*]
**II** ............... Item Identification (MSA)
**II** ............... Requires Medical Supplies [*Search and rescue symbol that can be stamped in sand or snow*]
**IIA** ............. Carnegie Public Library, Angola, IN [*OCLC symbol*] (OCLC)
**IIA** ............. If Incorrect Advise [*Aviation*]
**IIA** ............. ILA [*Instruction Look Ahead*] Interrupt Address [*Data processing*]
**IIA** ............. Image Intensifier Assembly
**IIA** ............. Impotence Institute of America (EA)
**IIA** ............. Incinerator Institute of America [*Later, NSWMA*] (EA)
**IIA** ............. Independent Innkeepers Association (EA)
**IIA** ............. Inertial Instrument Assembly
**IIA** ............. Information Industry Association (EA)
**IIA** ............. Institut International d'Anthropologie [*International Institute of Anthropology*] (EAIO)
**IIA** ............. Institute of Inter-American Affairs [*Washington, DC*]
**IIA** ............. Institute of Internal Affairs
**IIA** ............. Institute of Internal Auditors [*Altamonte Springs, FL*] (EA)
**IIA** ............. Institute of International Affairs
**IIA** ............. Insurance Institute of America (EA)
**IIA** ............. Intelligence Industries Association (EA)
**I & IA** ........ Interior and Insular Affairs
**IIA** ............. International Illawarra Association [*Defunct*] (EA)
**IIA** ............. International Imagery Association (EA)
**IIA** ............. International Information Administration [*Transferred to USIS, 1953*] [*Department of State*]
**IIA** ............. International Institute of Agriculture
**IIA** ............. International Institute of Andragogy [*See also INSTIA*] (EAIO)
**IIA** ............. International Institute of Anthropology (EA)
**IIA** ............. International Inventor's Association (EA)
**IIA** ............. International Investors Association (EA)
**IIA** ............. Invention Industry Association of America
**IIAA** ........... Independent Insurance Agents of America [*New York, NY*] (EA)
**IIAA** ........... Institute of Inter-American Affairs [*United Nations*]
**IIAAR** ........ International Institute for Arab-American Relations (EA)
**IIAC** ........... Impulse International Auto Club (EA)
**IIAC** ........... Industrial Injuries Advisory Council [*British*] (DCTA)
**IIAC** ........... Infrared Information and Analysis Center [*University of Michigan*] (MCD)
**IIAC** ........... International Insurance Advisory Council [*Later, IIC*] (EA)
**IIAF** ........... Imperial Iranian Air Force
**IIAFC** ......... International Irwin Allen Fan Club (EA)
**IIAI** ............ International Institute of American Ideals (EA)
**IIAILS** ........ Interim Integrated Aircraft Instrumentation and Letdown System
**IIAL** ........... International Institute of Arts and Letters
**IIALM** ........ International Institute for Adult Literacy Methods [*Tehran, Iran*] (EAIO)
**IIAP** ........... Institut International d'Aluminium Primaire [*International Primary Aluminum Institute*] (EAIO)
**IIAP** ........... Insurance Institute for Asia and the Pacific (DS)

**IIAR**.......... Incurably Ill for Animal Research (EA)
**IIAR**.......... International Institute of Ammonia Refrigeration (EA)
**IIAS**.......... Institute of Interamerican Studies [*University of Miami*] [*Research center*] (RCD)
**IIAS**.......... International Institute of Administrative Sciences [*Brussels, Belgium*]
**IIAS**.......... International Institute for Advanced Studies (EA)
**IIASA**........ International Institute for Applied Systems Analysis [*Laxenburg, Austria*]
**IIASA Collab Publ** ... International Institute for Applied Systems Analysis. Collaborative Publications [*A publication*]
**IIASA (Int Inst Appl Syst Anal) Collab Proc Ser** ... IIASA (International Institute for Applied Systems Analysis) Collaborative Proceedings Series [*A publication*]
**IIASA (Int Inst Appl Syst Anal) Exec Rep** ... IIASA (International Institute for Applied Systems Analysis) Executive Report [*A publication*]
**IIASA Proc Ser** ... IIASA [*International Institute for Applied Systems Analysis*] Proceedings Series [*A publication*]
**IIASA Prof Pap** ... International Institute for Applied Systems Analysis. Professional Paper [*A publication*]
**IIASA Rep** ... IIASA [*International Institute for Applied Systems Analysis*] Reports [*A publication*]
**IIASA Research Reports** ... International Institute for Applied Systems Analysis. Research Reports [*A publication*]
**IIASA Res Memo** ... International Institute for Applied Systems Analysis. Research Memorandum [*A publication*]
**IIASA Res Rep** ... International Institute for Applied Systems Analysis. Research Reports [*A publication*]
**IIAS/IRAS** ... International Review of Administrative Sciences. International Institute of Administrative Sciences [*A publication*]
**IIB**.......... Butler University, Indianapolis, IN [*OCLC symbol*] (OCLC)
**IIB**.......... Illinois Intrastate Motor Carrier Rate & Tariff Bureau, Springfield IL [*STAC*]
**IIB**.......... Independence, IA [*Location identifier*] [*FAA*] (FAAL)
**IIB**.......... Independent Infantry Battalion
**IIB**.......... Industrial Information Bulletin [*A publication*]
**IIB**.......... Information Industry Bulletin [*Digital Information Group*] [*Information service or system*] (IID)
**IIB**.......... Institut International de Bibliographie
**IIB**.......... Institut International des Brevets [*International Patent Institute*]
**IIB**.......... Intense Ion Beam
**IIB**.......... International Investment Bank [*Moscow, USSR*]
**IIB**.......... Internordic Investment Bank [*Scandinavia*]
**IIB**.......... Irish Intercontinental Bank Ltd.
**IIB**.......... Italian International Bank
**IIBA**.......... International Institute for Bioenergetic Analysis (EA)
**IIBA**.......... International Intelligent Buildings Association [*Washington, DC*] (EA)
**II Bar**.......... II Baruch [*Pseudepigrapha*] (BJA)
**IIBD**.......... Incorporated Institute of British Decorators (DAS)
**IIBDA**.......... Izvestiya Vuzov Mashinostroenie [*A publication*]
**IIBE**.......... Izvestiya na Instituta za Belgarski Ezik [*A publication*]
**IIBH**.......... International Institute of Biological Husbandry [*Ipswich, Suffolk, England*] (EAIO)
**IIBL**.......... Izvestiya na Instituta za Belgarska Literatura [*A publication*]
**IIBS**.......... Interactive International Banking System [*NCR Corp.*]
**IIBT**.......... International Institute of Business and Technology [*Australia*]
**IIC**.......... AMIGOS [*Access Method for Indexed Data Generalized for Operating System*] Bibliographic Council, Dallas, TX [*OCLC symbol*] (OCLC)
**IIC**.......... Igniter Initiator Cartridge [*or Container*]
**IIC**.......... Image Interpretation Cell
**IIC**.......... Impact Isolation Class [*Noise rating of insulation*]
**IIC**.......... Independent Insurance Conference
**IIC**.......... Independent Investment Company [*British*]
**IIC**.......... Industrial Intelligence Centre [*British*] [*World War II*]
**IIC**.......... Information Industries Committee [*Information service or system*] (EISS)
**IIC**.......... Institut International des Communications [*International Institute of Communications*] (EA)
**IIC**.......... Intelligence Information Center [*Military*] (MCD)
**IIC**.......... Interceptor Identification Capability
**IIC**.......... Interdepartmental Intelligence Conference [*Interagency conference of the National Security Council*] (EGAO)
**IIC**.......... International Ice Patrol [*Coast Guard*]
**IIC**.......... International Institute of Communications [*Formerly, IBI*] (EA)
**IIC**.......... International Institute for Conservation of Historic and Artistic Works [*London, England*]
**IIC**.......... International Institute for the Conservation of Museum Objects
**IIC**.......... International Institute for Cotton [*Belgium*] (FEA)
**IIC**.......... International Insurance Council (EA)
**IIC**.......... International Ionarc, Inc. [*Vancouver Stock Exchange symbol*]
**IIC**.......... International Review of Industrial Property and Copyright Law [*A publication*]
**IIC**.......... Ion-Ion Collision
**IIC**.......... Iron Information Center [*Battelle Memorial Institute*] [*Information service or system*] (IID)
**IIC**.......... Isotopes Information Center [*ORNL*]
**IIC**.......... Item Identification Code
**IIC**.......... Rita Coyotepec [*Mexico*] [*Seismograph station code, US Geological Survey*] (SEIS)
**IICA**.......... Indians into Communications Association (EA)
**IICA**.......... Instituto Interamericano de Cooperacion para la Agricultura [*Inter-American Institute for Cooperation on Agriculture*] [*Information service or system*] (IID)
**IICA**.......... Instituto Internacional de Ciencias Administrativas [*International Institute of Administrative Sciences*]
**IICA**.......... Interamerican Institute for Cooperation on Agriculture [*Formerly, IAIAS*] (EA)
**IICA**.......... International Ice Cream Association (EA)
**IIC Abstr** ... IIC [*International Institute for the Conservation of Museum Objects*] Abstracts [*A publication*]
**IICA (Inst Interam Cienc Agric) Ser Publ Misc** ... IICA (Instituto Interamericano de Ciencias Agricolas) Serie Publicaciones Miscelaneas [*A publication*]
**IICATS**...... Integrated Instrumentation, Control, Automation, and Telemetry System [*Australia*]
**IICBM**....... Intermediate Intercontinental Ballistic Missile
**IICC**.......... Institut International d'Etude et de Documentation en Matiere de Concurrence Commerciale [*International Institute for Commercial Competition*] [*Belgium*] (EA)
**IICC**.......... International Institute for Study and Research in the Field of Commercial Competition
**IICC**.......... Inuit. Inuit Circumpolar Conference [*Greenland*] [*A publication*]
**IICE**.......... Institut International des Caisses d'Epargne [*International Savings Banks Institute - ISBI*] [*Geneva, Switzerland*] (EAIO)
**IICE**.......... Institute for Internal Combustion Engines (MCD)
**IICEA**.......... Industria Italiana del Cemento [*A publication*]
**IICEW**....... Industria Italiana del Cemento [*A publication*]
**IICG**.......... ICSU [*International Council of Scientific Unions*] Inter-Union Commission for Geodynamics [*Marine science*] (MSC)
**IICHAW**.... International Institute for Conservation of Historic and Artistic Works
**IICL**.......... Institute of International Container Lessors (EA)
**IICLRR**...... International Institute for Children's Literature and Reading Research [*Vienna, Austria*] (EA)
**IICMSD**.... International Institute for Comparative Music Studies and Documentation [*Berlin, Federal Republic of Germany*] (EA)
**IiCN**.......... National Library of India, Calcutta, India [*Library symbol*] [*Library of Congress*] (LCLS)
**IICNTR**..... International Institute of Children's Nature and Their Rights (EA)
**IICODV**.... Infection Control [*Thorofare*] [*A publication*]
**IICP**.......... International Intersociety Committee on Pathology
**IICR**.......... Inspection Item Change Request (MCD)
**IICR**.......... Israel Investors Corporation [*NASDAQ symbol*] (NQ)
**IICS**.......... International Interactive Communications Society [*San Francisco, CA*] [*Telecommunications service*] (TSSD)
**IICU**.......... Infant Intensive Care Unit [*of a hospital*]
**IICU**.......... Intermediate Intensive Care Unit [*Medicine*]
**IICUC**....... International Institute of Carpet and Upholstery Certification (EA)
**IICY**.......... International Independent Christian Youth [*See also JICI*] [*Paris, France*] (EAIO)
**IICY**.......... International Investment Corporation for Yugoslavia (IMH)
**IID**.......... Iida [*Japan*] [*Seismograph station code, US Geological Survey*] (SEIS)
**IID**.......... Image Intensifier Device
**IID**.......... Impact Ionization Diode
**IID**.......... Independent Identically Distributed [*Statistics*] (IEEE)
**IID**.......... Information Industry Directory [*A publication*]
**IID**.......... Infrared Intrusion Detection (NVT)
**IID**.......... Institute for Integral Development (EA)
**IID**.......... Insurgent Incident Data
**IID**.......... Integrated Information Display (MCD)
**IID**.......... Integrated Instrument Development
**IID**.......... Interaural Intensity Disparity [*Audiology*]
**IID**.......... Intrinsic Infrared Detector
**IID**.......... Investment in Default [*Business term*]
**IID**.......... Ion Implantation Doping
**IID**.......... Ionospheric Ion Density
**IID**.......... Izvestiya na Istoriceskoto Druzestvo [*A publication*]
**IIDA**.......... Instituto Interamericano de Direito de Autor [*Interamerican Copyright Institute*] (EAIO)
**IIDARA**..... Instituto Iberoamericano de Derecho Agrario y Reforma Agraria [*Ibero-American Institute of Agrarian Law and Agrarian Reform - IAIALAR*] (EAIO)
**IiDaU**.......... University of North Bengal, Darjeeling District, West Bengal, India [*Library symbol*] [*Library of Congress*] (LCLS)
**IIDB**.......... Illawarra Industry Development Board [*Australia*]
**IIDC**.......... Institute for International Development and Cooperation [*University of Ottawa*] [*Canada*] [*See also IDIC*]
**IIDC/C**...... Civilizations. International Institute of Differing Civilizations [*A publication*]
**IID Comm** ... IID [*Institut International de Documentation*] Communications [*A publication*]

**IIDH** ........ Institut International de Droit Humanitaire [*International Institute of Humanitarian Law - IIHL*] (EAIO)
**IIDH** ........ Instituto Interamericano de Derechos Humanos [*Inter-American Institute of Human Rights - IIHR*] (EA)
**IIDLC** ........ Institut International de Droit Linguistique Compare [*International Institute of Comparative Linguistic Law*] (EAIO)
**IIDP** ........ Integrated Instrument Development Program
**IIDP** ........ Integrated Intelligence Development Plan (MCD)
**IIDS** ........ Integrated Information Display System (MCD)
**IIDS** ........ Izvestija na Istoriceskoto Druzestvo [*A publication*]
**IIDT** ........ Ion Implantation Doping Technique
**IIDWA** ........ Informatik [*A publication*]
**IIE** ........ Imperial Institute of Entomology [*British*]
**IIE** ........ Initial Ion Event
**IIE** ........ Installation Identification Element (MCD)
**IIE** ........ Institut International de l'Epargne
**IIE** ........ Institute for Independent Education (EA)
**IIE** ........ Institute of Industrial Engineers (EA)
**IIE** ........ Institute for International Economics
**IIE** ........ Institute of International Education (EA)
**IIE** ........ Instituto Interamericano de Estadistica [*Inter-American Statistical Institute - IASI*] [*Washington, DC*]
**IIE** ........ Instituto do Investimento Estrangeiro [*Overseas Investment Institute*] [*Lisbon, Portugal*] (GEA)
**IIE** ........ Inter-American Institute of Ecology [*Ecological Society of America*]
**IIE** ........ International Institute of Embryology [*Later, ISDB*]
**IIE/A** ........ Anales. Instituto de Investigaciones Esteticas [*A publication*]
**IIEA** ........ Immediate Identifiable Emergency Action [*Red Cross*]
**IIEA** ........ International Institute for Environmental Affairs [*Later, IIED*]
**IIEBB** ........ Izvestiya na Instituta po Elektronika. Bulgarska Akademiya na Naukite [*A publication*]
**IIEC** ........ Inter-Industry Emission Control [*Program*] (EA)
**IIED** ........ International Institute for Environment and Development [*Research center*] [*Great Britain*] (IRC)
**IIEE** ........ Institut International d'Etudes sur l'Education [*International Institute for Education Studies*]
**IIEG** ........ Interest Inventory for Elementary Grades [*Psychology*]
**IIEH** ........ Institut Indochinois pour l'Etude de l'Homme. Bulletin et Travaux [*A publication*]
**IIEL** ........ Institut International d'Etudes Ligures [*International Institute for Ligurian Studies - IILS*] (EAIO)
**IIENB** ........ Institute of International Education. News Bulletin [*A publication*]
**IIEP** ........ International Institute for Educational Planning [*Paris, France*] [*United Nations*] (EA)
**IIER** ........ International Institute for Economic Research (EA)
**IIES** ........ Institut International d'Etudes Sociales (EAIO)
**IIES** ........ Institute of Immigration and Ethnic Studies [*La Trobe University*] [*Australia*]
**IIES** ........ International Institute for Environmental Studies (ASF)
**IIE Trans** ... IIE [*Institute of Industrial Engineers, Inc.*] Transactions [*A publication*]
**IIF** ........ IBM [*International Business Machines Corp.*] IGES [*Initial Graphics Exchange Specification*] Format
**IIF** ........ Immune Interferon [*Cell biology*]
**IIF** ........ Imprint Immuno-Fixation [*Immunochemistry*]
**IIF** ........ Independent Investors Forum [*Information service or system*] (IID)
**IIF** ........ Indirect Immunofluorescence [*Immunochemistry*]
**IIF** ........ Institut International du Froid [*International Institute of Refrigeration*]
**IIF** ........ Institute of International Finance [*Washington, DC*] (EA)
**IIF** ........ Intense Irregular Field
**IIF** ........ Internals Indexing Fixture (NRCH)
**IIF** ........ International Institute of Forecasters [*See also IIM*] (EA)
**IIFA** ........ International Institute of Films on Art
**IIFAR** ........ Incurably Ill for Animal Research (EA)
**IIFAS** ........ Integration of Intelligence from All Sources (MCD)
**IIFET** ........ International Institute of Fisheries Economics and Trade (EA)
**IIFFL** ........ International Institute of Foods and Family Living (EA)
**IIFP** ........ Institut International de Finances Publiques [*International Institute of Public Finance*] (EAIO)
**IIFP** ........ International Index to Film Periodicals [*A publication*]
**IIFPAC** ........ Publicacion Especial. Instituto Nacional de Investigaciones Forestales [*Mexico*] [*A publication*]
**I/IFR** ........ Intermittent Instruments [*Aviation*] (FAAC)
**IIFSO** ........ International Islamic Federation of Student Organizations [*Salimiyan, Kuwait*] (EAIO)
**IIFSP** ........ Integrated Individual Fighting System Program [*Army*] (INF)
**IIFT** ........ Indirect Immunofluorescence Technique [*Immunochemistry*]
**IIFV** ........ Interim Infantry Fighting Vehicle [*Military*] (MCD)
**IIG** ........ Illuminated Internal Graticule
**IIG** ........ Imagery Intelligence Group [*Military*] (MCD)
**IIGC** ........ IGC, Incorporated [*NASDAQ symbol*] (NQ)
**IIGF** ........ Imperial Iranian Ground Forces
**IIH** ........ Isoimmune Hydrops [*Medicine*]
**IIHA** ........ Intercollegiate Ice Hockey Association [*Later, ECHA*] (EA)
**IIHC** ........ Investors Insurance Holding [*NASDAQ symbol*] (NQ)
**IIHD** ........ Institute for International Health and Development (EA)
**IIHF** ........ International Ice Hockey Federation (EA)
**IIHL** ........ International Institute for Home Literature [*See also MIKK*] [*Belgrade, Yugoslavia*] (EAIO)
**IIHL** ........ International Institute of Humanitarian Law [*See also IIDH*] [*San Remo, Italy*] (EAIO)
**IIHR** ........ Inter-American Institute of Human Rights [*See also IIDS*] [*San Jose, Costa Rica*] (EAIO)
**IIHR** ........ International Institute of Human Rights (EA)
**IIHR** ........ Iowa Institute of Hydraulic Research [*University of Iowa*] [*Research center*] (MCD)
**IIHR Rep** ... IIHR [*Iowa Institute of Hydraulic Research*] Report [*A publication*]
**IIHR Report** ... Iowa Institute of Hydraulic Research. Report [*A publication*]
**IIHS** ........ Insurance Institute for Highway Safety (EA)
**IIHSC** ........ Inter-Industry Highway Safety Committee [*Later, DSMC*] (EA)
**III** ........ Idealist International, Inc. (EA)
**III** ........ Illumination Industries, Incorporated
**III** ........ Indiana Central University, Indianapolis, IN [*OCLC symbol*] (OCLC)
**III** ........ Industrial Marketing Digest [*A publication*]
**III** ........ Information Intelligence, Incorporated [*Information service or system*] (IID)
**III** ........ Information International, Incorporated [*Phoenix, AZ*] [*Information broker*] (MCD)
**III** ........ Innovative Interfaces, Incorporated [*Information service or system*] (IID)
**III** ........ Insteel Industries [*AMEX symbol*] (SPSG)
**III** ........ Institute for Information Industry [*Information service or system*] (IID)
**III** ........ Institute of the Ironworking Industry (EA)
**III** ........ Institutional Investor. International Edition [*A publication*]
**III** ........ Instituto Indigenista Interamericano [*Inter-American Indian Institute*] (EAIO)
**III** ........ Insurance Information Institute [*New York, NY*] (EA)
**III** ........ Inter-American Indian Institute [*OAS*]
**III** ........ International Industrial Information Ltd. [*Information service or system*] (IID)
**III** ........ International Insurance Intelligence
**III** ........ International Intertrade Index [*Information service or system*] [*No longer available online*] (IID)
**III** ........ Interstate Identification Index [*NCIC*]
**III** ........ Investors in Industry [*British*]
**III** ........ Sturgeon Bay, WI [*Location identifier*] [*FAA*] (FAAL)
**III/AI** ........ America Indigena. Instituto Indigenista Interamericano [*A publication*]
**III Bar** ........ III Baruch [*Pseudepigrapha*] (BJA)
**IIIC** ........ Inovex Industries, Inc. [*NASDAQ symbol*] (NQ)
**IIIC** ........ International Irrigation Information Center (IID)
**IIIC (LN)** ... International Institute of Intellectual Cooperation of the League of Nations [*Obsolete*]
**IIIHS** ........ International Institute of Integral Human Sciences [*See also IISHI*] (EAIO)
**IIIIP** ........ Imperial Industries, Incorporated Pfd [*NASDAQ symbol*] (NQ)
**IIIL** ........ International Institute of Iberoamerican Literature (EA)
**IIIMB** ........ International Institute of Investment and Merchant Banking [*Washington, DC*] (EA)
**IIIR** ........ Integrated Instructional Information Resource [*Educational Products Information Exchange Institute*] [*Information service or system*] (CRD)
**IIIS** ........ Interim International Information Service [*World War II*]
**IIIT** ........ International Institute of Instructional Technology [*British*]
**IIIT** ........ International Institute of Islamic Thought (EA)
**IIJ** ........ Indo-Iranian Journal [*A publication*]
**IIJM** ........ Institut International Jacques Maritain [*International Jacques Maritain Institute - IJMI*] (EAIO)
**IIK** ........ Imagery Interpretation Key
**IIK** ........ Kipnuk, AK [*Location identifier*] [*FAA*] (FAAL)
**IIKMA** ........ Izvestiya na Instituta po Khidrologiya i Meteorologiya. Bulgarska Akademiya na Naukite [*A publication*]
**IIL** ........ Indianapolis Law Catalog Consortium, Indiana University School of Law Library, Indianapolis, IN [*OCLC symbol*] (OCLC)
**IIL** ........ Induction Ion LASER
**IIL** ........ Institute of Industrial Launderers (EA)
**IIL** ........ Institute of International Law [*Geneva, Switzerland*] (EA)
**IIL** ........ Integrated Injection Logic [*Microprocessing*] (BUR)
**IILA** ........ Instituto Italo Latino Americano [*Italo-Latin American Institute*] (EAIO)
**IiLc** ........ Identity Incorrect, Location Correct [*Psychology*]
**IILFSC** ........ International Institute of Law of the French Speaking Countries [*See also IDEF*] [*Paris, France*] (EAIO)
**IiLi** ........ Identity Incorrect, Location Incorrect [*Psychology*]
**IILI** ........ Instituto Internacional de Literatura Iberoamericana [*International Institute of Iberoamerican Literature*] (EA)
**IILP** ........ Index to Indian Legal Periodicals [*A publication*] (DLA)
**IILP** ........ Institute of International Licensing Practitioners (EAIO)
**IILP** ........ International Institute for Lath and Plaster (EA)
**IILR** ........ Institute of International Labor Research (EA)
**IILS** ........ International Institute for Labor Studies [*Switzerland*] (IEEE)

**IILS** ........... International Institute for Ligurian Studies (EA)
**IILSAH** ..... Investigations of Indiana Lakes and Streams [*A publication*]
**IIM** ........... Children's Museum of Indianapolis, Indianapolis, IN [*OCLC symbol*] (OCLC)
**IIM** ........... Institut International des Meteorologists [*International Institute of Forecasters*] (EAIO)
**IIM** ........... Institute for Information Management (EA)
**IIM** ........... Institution of Industrial Managers [*British*]
**IIM** ........... Interagency Intelligence Memorandum (MCD)
**IIM** ........... International Insurance Monitor [*A publication*]
**IIM** ........... International Investment Monitor [*Global Analysis Systems*] [*Information service or system*] (CRD)
**IIM** ........... Inventory in Motion
**IIM** ........... Item Intelligence Maintenance [*DoD*]
**IIM** ........... Izvestiya na Instituta za Muzika [*A publication*]
**IIMA**.......... Insurance Industry Meetings Association [*St. Louis, MO*] (EA)
**IIMC**.......... International Industrial Marketing Club [*Formerly, MMEC*] [*Defunct*] (EA)
**IIMC**.......... International Institute of Maritime Culture (EA)
**IIMC**.......... International Institute of Municipal Clerks (EA)
**IIME**.......... Institute of International Medical Education
**IIMI**........... International Irrigation Management Institute [*Research center*] [*Sri Lanka*] (IRC)
**IIMMI**....... International Index to Multi-Media Information [*A publication*]
**I-IMP**......... I-Labeled Iodoamphetamine
**IIMP**.......... Information Industry Market Place [*A publication*]
**IIMS**.......... Intensive Item Management System (AABC)
**IIMS**.......... Ion Implantation Manufacturing System
**IIMT**.......... International Institute for the Management of Technology [*Defunct*] (EA)
**IIn** ............ Index India [*A publication*]
**IIN** ............ Institutional Investor [*A publication*]
**IIN** ............ Instituto Interamericano del Nino [*Inter-American Children's Institute*] [*Uruguay*] (EA)
**IIN** ............ INX Insearch Group of Companies Ltd. [*Vancouver Stock Exchange symbol*]
**IIN** ............ Item Identification Number (AFM)
**IINA** .......... International Islamic News Agency [*Jeddah, Saudi Arabia*] (EAIO)
**IiNaU**......... University of Nagpur, Nagpur, India [*Library symbol*] [*Library of Congress*] (LCLS)
**IINC**........... Initials +, Incorporated [*San Francisco, CA*] [*NASDAQ symbol*] (NQ)
**IINCEH**..... Intercellular and Intracellular Communication [*A publication*]
**I Inf Sc**....... Institute of Information Scientists [*British*] (DLA)
**IiNI** ........... Indian National Scientific Documentation Centre, New Delhi, India [*Library symbol*] [*Library of Congress*]
**IiNN**.......... Nehru Memorial Museum and Library, New Delhi, India [*Library symbol*] [*Library of Congress*] (LCLS)
**IINS**........... Image Intensifier Night Sight
**I/Ins**........... Inactive Insurance (DLA)
**IINS**........... Incoherent Inelastic Neutron Scattering [*Physics*]
**IINS**........... Integrated Inertial Navigation System (MCD)
**IINS**........... Investors Insurance Corp. [*NASDAQ symbol*] (NQ)
**IINSE**......... International Institute of Nuclear Science and Engineering
**IINT**........... Information International, Inc. [*NASDAQ symbol*] (NQ)
**IINTE**........ Instytut Informacji Naukowej, Technicznej, i Ekonomicznej [*Institute of Scientific, Technical, and Economic Information*] [*Information service or system*] (IID)
**IIO** ............ Image Intensifier Orthicon
**IIO** ............ Information Item Only
**IIO** ............ Institute for International Order [*Later, IWO*]
**IIO** ............ Inter-Allied Insurance Organization [*NATO*] (NATG)
**IIODRFES** ... International Information Office of the Democratic Revolutionary Front of El Salvador [*See also OIIFDRES*] [*San Jose, Costa Rica*] (EAIO)
**IIOE**.......... International Indian Ocean Expedition [*Navy*]
**IIOIC**......... International Intra-Ocular Implant Club (EAIO)
**IIOOD**....... IO Management-Zeitschrift [*A publication*]
**IIOP**.......... Integrated Input/Output Processor
**IIP**............. El Pinto [*Mexico*] [*Seismograph station code, US Geological Survey*] (SEIS)
**IIP**............. Implementation/Installation Plan [*Telecommunications*] (TEL)
**IIP**............. Inadvertent Ignition Panel
**IIP**............. Increasing Intracranial Pressure [*Medicine*]
**IIP**............. Index of Industrial Production
**IIP**............. Individual Implementation Plan [*For the education of a handicapped person*]
**IIP**............. Industrial and Intellectual Property in Australia [*A publication*]
**IIP**............. Inorganic Insulative Plastic
**IIP**............. Instantaneous Impact Points (KSC)
**IIP**............. Instantaneous Impact Predictor
**IIP**............. Institut International de Philosophie [*International Institute of Philosophy*] (EAIO)
**IIP**............. Institut International de la Potasse [*International Potash Institute*] (EAIO)
**IIP**............. Institut International de la Presse [*International Press Institute*]
**IIP**............. Institute of Incorporated Photographers [*British*]
**IIP**............. Interceptor Improvement Program
**IIP**............. Intergovernmental Informatics Programme [*UNESCO*]
**IIP**............. Interim Impact Predictor (AAG)
**IIP**............. International Ice Patrol [*Coast Guard*]
**IIP**............. International Income Property, Inc. [*AMEX symbol*] (SPSG)
**IIP**............. International Institute for Peace [*Vienna, Austria*] (EA)
**IIP**............. Irish Independence Party [*Political party*] (PPW)
**IIPA**.......... Industrial and Intellectual Property in Australia [*A publication*] (APTA)
**IIPA**.......... International Icelandic Pony Association (EA)
**IIPA**.......... International Intellectual Property Association
**IIPACS**...... Integrated Information Presentation and Control System [*Aviation*]
**IIPC**.......... Image Intensifier Plumbicon Camera
**IIPE**.......... Institut International de Planification de l'Education [*International Institute for Educational Planning*]
**IIPEC**......... Institute for Interconnecting and Packaging Electronic Circuits (EA)
**IIPER**........ International Institute for Production Engineering Research (EAIO)
**IIPF**.......... International Institute of Public Finance [*Saarbrucken, Federal Republic of Germany*] (EAIO)
**IIPG**.......... International Institute of Practical Geomancy [*Formerly, Society for Symbolic Studies*] (EA)
**IIPL**.......... Independent Investor Protective League (EA)
**IIPM**......... Irish International Peace Movement (EAIO)
**IIPO**.......... Illinois Inventory of Parent Opinion
**IIPP**.......... International Institute for Promotion and Prestige [*Geneva, Switzerland*] (EAIO)
**IIPR**.......... Installation Inspection Procedure Report
**IIPTA**........ Izvestiya Nauchno-Issledovatel'skogo Instituta Postoyannogo Toka [*A publication*]
**IIQ**............ Initial Issue Quantities [*Military*]
**IIR**............. Image Interpreter Response
**IIR**............. Imaging Infrared [*Air Force*] (MCD)
**IIR**............. Infinite-Duration Impulse-Response (IEEE)
**IIR**............. Infinite Impulse Response [*Electronics*]
**IIR**............. Institute of Industrial Relations [*Loyola University of Chicago*] [*Research center*] (RCD)
**IIR**............. Institute of Intermodal Repairers (EA)
**IIR**............. Institute for International Research [*Australia*]
**IIR**............. Integrated Instrumentation RADAR
**IIR**............. Intelligence Information Report (NVT)
**IIR**............. Intercom Information Resources, Inc. [*Information service or system*] (IID)
**IIR**............. Intermediate Infrared
**IIR**............. International Impala Resources [*Vancouver Stock Exchange symbol*]
**IIR**............. International Institute of Refrigeration [*Paris, France*] (EA)
**IIR**............. International Institute of Rehabilitation [*Defunct*] (EA)
**IIR**............. International Institute for Robotics (EA)
**IIR**............. Inventory and Inspection Report [*Army*] (MUGU)
**IIR**............. Isobutene-Isoprene Rubber
**IIRA**.......... International Industrial Relations Association [*Geneva, Switzerland*] (EA)
**IIRB**.......... Institut International de Recherches Betteravieres [*International Institute for Sugar Beet Research*] [*Brussels, Belgium*] (EA)
**IIRB Rev Inst Int Rech Better** ... IIRB. Revue de l'Institut International de Recherches Betteravieres [*A publication*]
**IIRC**.......... Inactive Item Review Card [*Military*] (AFIT)
**IIRC**.......... Incident Investigation Review Committee [*Nuclear Regulatory Commission*] (NRCH)
**IIRC**.......... Indiana Interstate Railroad Company, Inc. [*AAR code*]
**IIRD**.......... International Interdependent Research and Development (AABC)
**IIRE**.......... International Institute for Resource Economics (EA)
**IIRG**.......... Institut International de Recherches Graphologiques
**IIRM**......... Improved Infrared Missile
**IIRM**......... Irish Immigration Reform Movement (EA)
**IIRMS**....... Industrial Information's Record Management System [*Data processing*]
**IIRP**.......... Integrated Installation Requirement Plan (MCD)
**IIRR**.......... Institute of Industrial Race Relations
**IIRR**.......... International Institute of Rural Reconstruction (EA)
**IIRS**.......... Institute of Industrial Research and Standards [*Ireland*] [*Database producer*] (IID)
**IIRS**.......... Instrumentation Inertial Reference Set [*Aviation*]
**IIRV**.......... Improved Inter-Range Vector (MCD)
**IIS**............. Image Intensified System
**IIS**............. Imagery Interpretation System (MCD)
**IIS**............. Improved Infrared Source
**IIS**............. INA Investment Securities, Inc. [*NYSE symbol*] (SPSG)
**IIS**............. Indirect Identification System [*Military*] (MCD)
**IIS**............. Industrial Information Services [*Southern Methodist University*] [*Dallas, TX*]
**IIS**............. Inflationary Impact Statement [*Economics*]
**IIS**............. Information Industries Strategy
**IIS**............. Infrared Imaging System
**IIS**............. Infrared Instrumentation System
**IIS**............. Inspection Instruction Sheet
**IIS**............. Inspection Item Sheet (MCD)

**IIS** ............. Inspections and Investigations Staff [*Vietnam*]
**IIS** ............. Institut International de la Soudure [*International Institute of Welding - IIW*] (EAIO)
**IIS** ............. Institut International de Statistique [*International Statistical Institute*]
**IIS** ............. Institute of Information Scientists [*London, England*] (EAIO)
**IIS** ............. Institute for Information Studies [*Research center*] [*Inactive*] (RCD)
**IIS** ............. Institute for Intercultural Studies (EA)
**IIS** ............. Institute of International Studies (EA)
**IIS** ............. Integrated Information System
**IIS** ............. Integrated Instrument Sheet (MCD)
**IIS** ............. Integrated Instruments System
**IIS** ............. Integrated Insulation System
**IIS** ............. Interactive Instructional System [*IBM Corp.*]
**IIS** ............. International Information Service Ltd. [*Information service or system*] (IID)
**IIS** ............. International Institute of Seismology and Earthquake Engineering [*Japan*] [*Seismograph station code, US Geological Survey*] (SEIS)
**IIS** ............. International Institute of Sociology
**IIS** ............. International Institute of Stress (EA)
**IIS** ............. International Institutional Services (EA)
**IIS** ............. International Insurance Seminars [*University, AL*] (EA)
**IIS** ............. International Insurance Society (EAIO)
**IIS** ............. International Isotope Society (EA)
**IIS** ............. International Medical Imagery [*Vancouver Stock Exchange symbol*]
**IIS** ............. Internationales Institut der Sparkassen [*International Savings Banks Institute*]
**IIS** ............. Ion Implantation Study
**IIS** ............. Nissan Island [*Papua New Guinea*] [*Airport symbol*] (OAG)
**IISA** ........... Institut International des Sciences Administratives [*International Institute for Administrative Sciences*]
**IISA** ........... Interservice/Interagency Support Agreement (MCD)
**IISBR** ......... International Institute for Sugar Beet Research (EA)
**IISD** ........... If Incorrect Service Direct [*Aviation*] (FAAC)
**IISD** ........... International Institute for the Study of Death (EA)
**IISDI** ......... International Institute for the Study of Death and Immortality [*Later, IISD*] (EA)
**IISE** ........... International Institute of Social Economics [*Hull, England*] (EAIO)
**IISG** ........... Internationaal Instituut voor Sociale Geschiedenis [*International Institute for Social History*] (EA)
**IISHI** ......... Institut International des Sciences Humaines Integrales [*International Institute of Integral Human Sciences - IIIHS*] (EAIO)
**IISI** ........... International Iron and Steel Institute [*Research center*] [*Brussels, Belgium*] (EA)
**IISJ** ........... Institute for Independent Social Journalism (EA)
**IISL** ........... IIS [*Intelligent Information Systems*] Limited [*Haifa, Israel*] [*NASDAQ symbol*] (NQ)
**IISL** ........... International Institute of Space Law [*Baarn, Netherlands*] (EAIO)
**IISL** ........... Istituto Internazionale di Studi Liguri [*International Institute for Ligurian Studies*]
**IISO** ........... If Incorrect Service Originator [*Aviation*] (FAAC)
**IISP** ........... International Institute of Site Planning (EA)
**IISRP** ......... International Institute of Synthetic Rubber Producers (EA)
**IISS** ........... Integrated Information Support System [*Data processing*]
**IISS** ........... Intelligence Information Subsystem [*Military*] (MCD)
**IISS** ........... International Institute for the Science of Sintering [*Belgrade, Yugoslavia*] (EAIO)
**IISS** ........... International Institute for Strategic Studies (EA)
**IISSA** ......... Ionosfernye Issledovaniya [*A publication*]
**IISSM** ......... Istituto Internazionale Suore di Santa Marcellina [*Milan, Italy*] (EAIO)
**IIST** ........... Institute for Information Storage Technology [*University of Santa Clara*] [*Research center*] (RCD)
**IIST** ........... Intense Islet Stimulation Test [*Endocrinology*]
**IIST** ........... International Institute for Safety in Transportation [*Formerly, IST*] (EA)
**I Ist Kul't Narod Uzbek** ... Iz Istorii Kul'tury Narodov Uzbekistana [*A publication*]
**IIT** ............. Illinois Institute of Technology (IID)
**IIT** ............. Image Intensifier Tube
**IIT** ............. Inclinable Indexing Table
**IIT** ............. Indian Institute of Technology (NRCH)
**IIT** ............. Individual Inclusive Tour [*Air fare plan*]
**IIT** ............. Information der Internationalen Treuhand AG [*A publication*]
**IIT** ............. Institut des Ingenieurs des Transports [*Institute of Transportation Engineers*] [*Canada*]
**IIT** ............. Institut Interafricain du Travail
**IIT** ............. Institut Internationale du Theatre [*International Theatre Institute - ITI*] (EAIO)
**IIT** ............. International Investment Trust
**IIT** ............. Israel Institute of Technology (KSC)
**IITA** ........... Inland International Trade Association [*Sacramento, CA*] (EA)
**IITA** ........... International Institute of Tropical Agriculture [*Ibadan, Nigeria*] [*Research center*] (EAIO)
**IITC** ........... International Indian Treaty Council (EA)
**IITCS** ......... Igloo Internal Thermal Control Section [*Aerospace*] (MCD)
**IITD** ........... Institute of International Trade and Development (EA)
**I/ITEC** ....... Interservice/Industry Training Equipment Conference [*Military*]
**IITF** ........... Information Industries Training Foundation [*Australia*]
**IITRAN** ...... [*A*] programming language (CSR)
**IITRI** ......... Illinois Institute of Technology Research Institute [*Information service or system*] (IID)
**IITS** ........... Igniter Initiator Test Set
**IITS** ........... Intratheater Imagery Transmission System [*Air Force*]
**I/ITSC** ....... Interservice/Industry Training Systems Conference [*Military*]
**IITT-IITW** ... Institut International du Travail Temporaire - International Institute for Temporary Work (EAIO)
**IITYWYBMAD** ... If I Tell You, Will You Buy Me a Drink? [*Tavern sign*]
**IIU** ............. Input Interface Unit [*Data processing*]
**IIU** ............. Instruction Input Unit
**IIV** ............. Image Intensifier Viewer
**IIV** ............. International Institute of Valuers (EA)
**IIVD** ........... Image Intensifier Viewing Device
**IIVI** ........... II-VI, Inc. [*NASDAQ symbol*] (NQ)
**IIVI 0-7** ...... International Institute for Visually Impaired, Zero-7 (EA)
**IIVS** ........... Intransit Item Visibility System (MCD)
**IIVT** ........... Intensive Intravenous Treatment [*Medicine*]
**IIVW** ........... Internationales Institut fuer Verwaltungswissenschaften [*International Institute of Administrative Sciences*]
**II & W** ........ Intelligence Interface and Warning [*Military*] (MCD)
**IIW** ............ International Institute of Welding [*See also IIS*] [*London, England*] (EAIO)
**IIWG** .......... International Industry Working Group [*of the Air Transport Association of America*] (EAIO)
**IIWI** ........... Interior Insulating Window Institute (EA)
**IIWPA** ........ International Information/Word Processing Association [*Formerly, IWPA*] [*Later, IWP*] (EA)
**IIWPL** ........ International Institute for Women's Political Leadership (EA)
**IIYA** ........... Institute for International Youth Affairs
**IJ** ............... Im Jahre [*In the Year*] [*German*]
**IJ** ............... Indian Jurist, Old Series [*A publication*] (DLA)
**IJ** ............... Indogermanische Jahrbuch [*A publication*]
**IJ** ............... Instructor's Journal [*Air Force*]
**IJ** ............... Internal Jugular [*Anatomy*]
**IJ** ............... International Journal [*A publication*]
**IJ** ............... Irish Jurist [*A publication*]
**IJ** ............... Jacksonville Public Library, Jacksonville, IL [*Library symbol*] [*Library of Congress*] (LCLS)
**IJ** ............... Sisters of the Holy Infant Jesus [*Roman Catholic religious order*]
**IJ** ............... Touraine Air Transport [*France*] [*ICAO designator*] (FAAC)
**IJA** ............. Imperial Japanese Army [*World War II*]
**IJA** ............. Institute of Jewish Affairs (EA)
**IJA** ............. Institute of Judicial Administration (EA)
**IJA** ............. International Journal of Advertising [*A publication*]
**IJA** ............. International Journal of Andrology [*A publication*]
**IJA** ............. International Jugglers Association (EA)
**IJA** ............. Inventory of Job Attitudes [*LIMRA*]
**IJA** ............. Irving Independent School District, Irving, TX [*OCLC symbol*] (OCLC)
**IJA** ............. Islamic Jurisprudence Academy [*See also IFA*] (EAIO)
**IJAB** ........... Internationaler Jugendaustausch und Besucherdienst der Bundesrepublik Deutschland [*International Youth Exchange and Visitor Service of the Federal Republic of Germany*]
**IJACB** ......... Indian Journal of Agricultural Chemistry [*A publication*]
**IJACBO** ..... Indian Journal of Agricultural Chemistry [*A publication*]
**IJACDQ** ..... Indian Journal of Acarology [*A publication*]
**I Ja DS** ....... Institut Jazykoznanija. Doklady i Soobscenija [*A publication*]
**IJAE** ........... Indian Journal of Agricultural Economics [*A publication*]
**IJAGAZ** ..... Indian Journal of Agronomy [*A publication*]
**IJAGC3** ...... Iranian Journal of Agricultural Research [*A publication*]
**I J Agr Sci** ... Indian Journal of Agricultural Science [*A publication*]
**IJAHA4** ...... Indian Journal of Animal Health [*A publication*]
**IJAHE8** ...... International Journal of Adolescent Medicine and Health [*A publication*]
**I Jahrb** ....... Indogermanische Jahrbuch [*A publication*]
**IJAHS** ......... International Journal of African Historical Studies [*A publication*]
**IJAIDA** ...... International Journal. Academy of Ichthyology [*A publication*]
**IJAJ** ........... Intentional Jitter Antijam [*Military*]
**IJAL** ........... International Journal of American Linguistics [*A publication*]
**IJALAG** ...... Irish Journal of Agricultural Research [*A publication*]
**IJANBN** ..... Indian Journal of Anaesthesia [*A publication*]
**IJANDP** ..... International Journal of Andrology [*A publication*]
**IJAOD** ........ International Journal of Artificial Organs [*A publication*]
**IJAODS** ..... International Journal of Artificial Organs [*A publication*]
**IJAPA** ......... International Journal of Air Pollution [*A publication*]
**IJAPBT** ...... Indian Journal of Applied Psychology [*A publication*]
**IJAR** ........... Israel Journal of Agricultural Research [*A publication*]
**IJARAY** ..... International Journal of Applied Radiation and Isotopes [*A publication*]
**IJARC** ......... Indian Journal of Agricultural Research [*A publication*]
**IJARC2** ...... Indian Journal of Agricultural Research [*A publication*]
**IJAS** ........... Indian Journal of American Studies [*A publication*]

**IJaS** ........... Inostrannye Jazyki v Skole [*A publication*]
**IJASA3** ...... Indian Journal of Agricultural Science [*A publication*]
**IJb** ............ Indogermanische Jahrbuch [*A publication*]
**IJB** ............ International Journal of Bank Marketing [*A publication*]
**IJB** ............ Internationale Jugendbibliothek [*International Youth Library - IYL*] [*Munich, Federal Republic of Germany*] (EAIO)
**IJB** ............ Interstate Job Bank
**IJB** ............ Israel Journal of Botany [*A publication*]
**IJBBA** ........ International Junior Brangus Breeders Association (EA)
**IJBCAS** ..... Indian Journal of Biochemistry [*Later, Indian Journal of Biochemistry and Biophysics*] [*A publication*]
**IJBCB** ........ International Journal of Biomedical Computing [*A publication*]
**IJBCBT** ..... International Journal of Bio-Medical Computing [*A publication*]
**IJBDDY** .... International Journal of Behavioral Development [*A publication*]
**IJBEAY** ..... International Journal of Biomedical Engineering [*A publication*]
**IJBF** .......... International Jacques Brel Foundation (EA)
**I J Bioch B** ... Indian Journal of Biochemistry and Biophysics [*A publication*]
**IJBMAO** ... International Journal of Biometeorology [*A publication*]
**IJBMDR** ... International Journal of Biological Macromolecules [*A publication*]
**IJBOAU** .... Israel Journal of Botany [*A publication*]
**IJBOBV** .... International Journal of Biochemistry [*A publication*]
**IJBODX** .... Indian Journal of Botany [*A publication*]
**IJBPD2** ...... International Journal of Biological Research in Pregnancy [*A publication*]
**I Jb Pol** ...... Internationales Jahrbuch der Politik [*A publication*]
**IJBS** .......... Integrated Joint Broadband System [*Army*] (AABC)
**IJC** ............ Indian Journal of Commerce [*Chandigarh*] [*A publication*]
**IJC** ............ International Joint Commission (EA)
**IJC** ............ International Journal of Computer and Information Sciences [*A publication*]
**IJC** ............ Irvine's Justiciary Cases [*England*] [*A publication*] (DLA)
**IJC** ............ Irving Public Library System, Irving, TX [*OCLC symbol*] (OCLC)
**IJC** ............ Itasca Junior College [*Later, Itasca Community College*] [*Minnesota*]
**IJC** ............ Itawamba Junior College [*Fulton, MS*]
**IJCAAR** ..... Indian Journal of Cancer [*A publication*]
**IJCADU** .... Indian Journal of Chemistry. Section A. Inorganic, Physical, Theoretical, and Analytical [*A publication*]
**IJCAI** ......... International Joint Conference on Artificial Intelligence
**IJ Cas** ......... Irvine's Justiciary Cases [*England*] [*A publication*] (DLA)
**IJCBA** ........ International Journal of Chronobiology [*A publication*]
**IJCBAU** .... International Journal of Chronobiology [*A publication*]
**IJCBD** ....... International Journal of Clinical Pharmacology and Biopharmacy [*A publication*]
**IJCBDX** .... International Journal of Clinical Pharmacology and Biopharmacy [*A publication*]
**IJCCE3** ...... International Journal of Cell Cloning [*A publication*]
**IJCDA2** ..... Indian Journal of Chest Diseases [*Later, Indian Journal of Chest Diseases and Allied Sciences*] [*A publication*]
**IJCDD5** ..... International Journal of Cardiology [*A publication*]
**IJCEA** ........ Indian Journal of Chemical Education [*A publication*]
**IJCGD** ....... International Journal of Coal Geology [*A publication*]
**IJCHA** ....... Indian Journal of Child Health [*A publication*]
**I J Chem** .... Indian Journal of Chemistry [*A publication*]
**IJCIC** ......... International Jewish Committee on Interreligious Consultations (EA)
**IJCIS** ......... International Journal of Computer and Information Sciences [*A publication*]
**IJCKBO** .... International Journal of Chemical Kinetics [*A publication*]
**IJCMDW** .. International Journal of Cosmetic Science [*A publication*]
**IJCNAW** ... International Journal of Cancer [*A publication*]
**IJCNF2** ...... International Journal of Clinical Neuropsychology [*A publication*]
**IJCNN** ....... International Joint Conference on Neural Networks
**IJCPB5** ...... International Journal of Clinical Pharmacology, Therapy, and Toxicology [*A publication*]
**IJCR** .......... Institute for Jewish-Christian Relations (EA)
**IJCRD** ....... Indian Journal of Cryogenics [*A publication*]
**IJCREE** ..... International Journal of Crude Drug Research [*A publication*]
**IJCS** .......... Integrated Joint Communication System [*Military*] (AABC)
**IJCSEH** ..... Indonesian Journal of Crop Science [*A publication*]
**IJCS-PAC** ... Integrated Joint Communication System - Pacific [*Military*]
**IJD** ............ Institutum Judaicum Delitzschianum (BJA)
**IJDA** .......... International Joseph Diseases Association (EA)
**IJDEAA** .... Indian Journal of Dermatology [*Later, Indian Journal of Dermatology, Venereology, and Leprology*] [*A publication*]
**IJDEBB** ..... International Journal of Dermatology [*A publication*]
**IJDF** .......... International Joseph Diseases Foundation (EA)
**IJDL** .......... International Journal of Dravidian Linguistics [*A publication*]
**IJDLDY** .... Indian Journal of Dermatology, Venereology, and Leprology [*A publication*]
**IJDMAY** ... Israel Journal of Dental Medicine [*A publication*]
**IJDN** .......... International Journal of Developmental Neuroscience [*A publication*]
**IJDND6** ..... International Journal of Developmental Neuroscience [*A publication*]
**IJDSAI** ...... Indian Journal of Dairy Science [*A publication*]
**IJDVAR** .... Indian Journal of Dermatology and Venereology [*Later, Indian Journal of Dermatology, Venereology, and Leprology*] [*A publication*]
**IJDW** ......... Im Jahre der Welt [*In the Year of the World*] [*German*]
**IJE** ............ Indian Journal of Economics [*A publication*]
**IJE** ............ International Journal of Ethics [*A publication*]
**IJE** ............ Inverse Joule Effect
**IJe** ............ Jerseyville Free Library, Jerseyville, IL [*Library symbol*] [*Library of Congress*] (LCLS)
**IJEAA3** ..... International Journal of Environmental Analytical Chemistry [*A publication*]
**IJEAB** ........ Indian Journal of Earth Sciences [*A publication*]
**IJEAB4** ...... Indian Journal of Earth Sciences [*A publication*]
**IJEAD** ....... Electric Power Applications. IEE Journal [*A publication*]
**IJEBA6** ...... Indian Journal of Experimental Biology [*A publication*]
**IJECDC** ..... Indian Journal of Ecology [*A publication*]
**IJeH** .......... Jersey Community Hospital, Jerseyville, IL [*Library symbol*] [*Library of Congress*] (LCLS)
**IJEHA** ....... International Journal of Clinical and Experimental Hypnosis [*A publication*]
**IJEHAO** .... International Journal of Clinical and Experimental Hypnosis [*A publication*]
**IJEHB** ....... Indian Journal of Environmental Health [*A publication*]
**IJEHBP** .... Indian Journal of Environmental Health [*A publication*]
**IJEMA5** .... Israel Journal of Experimental Medicine [*A publication*]
**IJENA8** .... Indian Journal of Entomology [*A publication*]
**IJENB9** .... Israel Journal of Entomology [*A publication*]
**IJENEC** .... International Journal of Entomology [*A publication*]
**IJEPAE** .... Indian Journal of Experimental Psychology [*A publication*]
**IJEPBF** .... International Journal of Epidemiology [*A publication*]
**IJERAK** .... Israel Journal of Earth-Sciences [*A publication*]
**IJERD** ....... International Journal of Energy Research [*A publication*]
**IJES** .......... Indian Journal of English Studies [*Calcutta*] [*A publication*]
**IJES** .......... International Journal of Environmental Studies [*A publication*]
**IJES** .......... Israel Journal of Earth-Sciences [*A publication*]
**IJeSD** ........ Jersey Community Unit, School District 100, Jerseyville, IL [*Library symbol*] [*Library of Congress*] (LCLS)
**IJESDQ** .... International Journal of Ecology and Environmental Sciences [*A publication*]
**IJEVAW** .... International Journal of Environmental Studies [*A publication*]
**IJewAr** ....... Index of Articles on Jewish Studies [*A publication*]
**IJewPer** ...... Index to Jewish Periodicals [*A publication*]
**I J Ex Biol** ... Indian Journal of Experimental Biology [*A publication*]
**IJF** ............ International Jazz Federation (EA)
**IJF** ............ Internationale Judo Foederation [*International Judo Federation*] [*German Democratic Republic*] (EA)
**IJF** ............ Robinson Crusoe Island [*Juan Fernandez Archipelago*] [*Seismograph station code, US Geological Survey*] (SEIS)
**IJFIAW** .... Indian Journal of Fisheries [*A publication*]
**IJFMDD** ... International Journal of Food Microbiology [*A publication*]
**IJFODJ** .... Indian Journal of Forestry [*A publication*]
**IJFPDM** .... International Journal of Family Psychiatry [*A publication*]
**IJFSBT** .... Indian Journal of Farm Sciences [*A publication*]
**IJGBAG** .... Indian Journal of Genetics and Plant Breeding [*A publication*]
**I J Genet P** ... Indian Journal of Genetics and Plant Breeding [*A publication*]
**IJGOAL** .... International Journal of Gynaecology and Obstetrics [*A publication*]
**IJGPA** ....... International Journal of Group Psychotherapy [*A publication*]
**IJGPAO** .... International Journal of Group Psychotherapy [*A publication*]
**IJGPDR** .... International Journal of Gynecological Pathology [*A publication*]
**IJGSAX** .... International Journal of General Systems [*A publication*]
**IJGU** .......... Internationales Jahrbuch fuer Geschichtsunterricht [*A publication*]
**IJH** ............ Iowa Journal of History [*A publication*]
**IJHE** .......... International Journal of Health Education [*A publication*]
**IJHEAU** .... Indian Journal of Helminthology [*A publication*]
**IJHM** ......... Indian Journal of the History of Medicine [*A publication*]
**IJHMA** ...... International Journal of Heat and Mass Transfer [*A publication*]
**IJHOAQ** ... Indian Journal of Horticulture [*A publication*]
**IJHP** .......... Iowa Journal of History and Politics [*A publication*]
**IJHPBU** .... Indian Journal of Hospital Pharmacy [*A publication*]
**IJHYEQ** .... International Journal of Hyperthermia [*A publication*]
**IJI** ............ Illinois College, Jacksonville, IL [*Library symbol*] [*Library of Congress*] (LCLS)
**IJI** ............ International Journal of Industrial Organization [*A publication*]
**IJI** ............ International Juridical Institute (ILCA)
**IJI** ............ Islamic Jamhoori Ittedad [*Islamic Democratic Alliance*] [*Pakistan*] [*Political party*]
**IJIAA** ........ Indian Journal of Science and Industry. Section A. Agricultural Sciences [*Later, Indian Journal of Agricultural Research*] [*A publication*]
**IJIDAW** .... Indian Journal of Industrial Medicine [*A publication*]
**IJIDE2** ....... International Journal of Invertebrate Reproduction and Development [*A publication*]
**IJIL** ........... Indian Journal of International Law [*A publication*]

**IJIMBQ**..... International Journal of Insect Morphology and Embryology [*A publication*]
**IJIMDS**..... International Journal of Immunopharmacology [*A publication*]
**IJIMET**..... International Journal of Immunotherapy [*A publication*]
**I J Ind Rel** ... Indian Journal of Industrial Relations [*A publication*]
**IJIR** ........... International Journal of Intercultural Relations [*A publication*]
**IJIRD9** ...... International Journal of Invertebrate Reproduction [*A publication*]
**IJ/JJ**.......... Jamaica Journal. Institute of Jamaica [*A publication*]
**IJJU** .......... Intentional Jitter Jamming Unit [*Military*]
**IJK**............ Internationale Juristen-Kommission [*International Commission of Jurists*]
**IJL** ............. Indian Journal of Linguistics/Praci-Bhasha-Vijnan [*A publication*]
**IJL** ............. Institute of Jewish Life Media Project [*Later, JMS*]
**IJLAA4**...... Indian Journal of Animal Sciences [*A publication*]
**IJLB**........... International Jewish Labor Bund (EA)
**IJLEAG**..... International Journal of Leprosy [*Later, International Journal of Leprosy and Other Mycobacterial Diseases*] [*A publication*]
**IJLL**........... International Journal of Law Libraries [*A publication*]
**IJM**............ International Journal of Manpower [*A publication*]
**IJMA**.......... Infant and Juvenile Manufacturers Association (EA)
**IJMAA9**.... Indian Journal of Malariology [*A publication*]
**IJMac** ........ MacMurray College, Jacksonville, IL [*Library symbol*] [*Library of Congress*] (LCLS)
**IJMBA** ...... Indian Journal of Microbiology [*A publication*]
**IJMCEJ** .... International Journal of Clinical Monitoring and Computing [*A publication*]
**IJMDAI** .... Israel Journal of Medical Sciences [*A publication*]
**I J Med Res** ... Indian Journal of Medical Research [*A publication*]
**IJMEEP**.... Italian Journal of Medicine [*A publication*]
**IJMES**....... International Journal of Middle East Studies [*A publication*]
**IJMI** .......... International Jacques Maritain Institute [*See also IIJM*] (EAIO)
**IJMLEC**.... International Journal of Mycology and Lichenology [*A publication*]
**IJMNB**...... Indian Journal of Marine Sciences [*A publication*]
**IJMS** ......... Israel Journal of Medical Sciences [*A publication*]
**IJMSAT**.... Irish Journal of Medical Science [*A publication*]
**IJMVT** ...... International Journal of Micrographics and Video Technology [*A publication*]
**IJN**............ Imperial Japanese Navy [*World War II*]
**IJN**............ International Journal of Neuroscience [*A publication*]
**IJN**............ International Justice Network (EA)
**IJNA**.......... International Journal of Nautical Archaeology and Underwater Exploration [*A publication*]
**IJNGD**....... International Journal for Numerical and Analytical Methods in Geomechanics [*A publication*]
**IJNMC**...... International Journal of Nuclear Medicine and Biology [*A publication*]
**IJNSD3** ..... Italian Journal of Neurological Sciences [*A publication*]
**IJNUB**....... International Journal of Neuroscience [*A publication*]
**I J Nutr D** .. Indian Journal of Nutrition and Dietetics [*A publication*]
**IJO**............ Independent Jewelers Organization (EA)
**IJO**............ Individual Job Order
**IJO**............ International Journal of Operations and Production Management [*A publication*]
**IJO**............ International Juridical Organization [*Later, IJOED*] (EAIO)
**IJO**............ International Jute Organization (EAIO)
**IJO**............ Inventory of Job Openings [*State Employee Security Agency*] (OICC)
**IJOA**.......... International Journal of the Addictions [*A publication*]
**IJOA**.......... International Juvenile Officers' Association (EA)
**IJOAAJ**..... Israel Journal of Agricultural Research [*A publication*]
**IJOADM**... International Journal of Acarology [*A publication*]
**IJOAR**....... International Journal of Opinion and Attitude Research [*A publication*]
**IJOCAP**..... Indian Journal of Chemistry [*A publication*]
**IJOED**....... International Juridical Organization for Environment and Development (EAIO)
**IJOH** ......... International Journal of Oral History [*Canada*] [*A publication*]
**IJol**............ Joliet Public Library, Joliet, IL [*Library symbol*] [*Library of Congress*] (LCLS)
**IJolStF**....... College of Saint Francis, Joliet, IL [*Library symbol*] [*Library of Congress*] (LCLS)
**IJOPM** ...... International Journal of Operations and Production Management [*A publication*]
**IJP** ............ Inhibitory Junction Potential [*Neurophysiology*]
**IJP** ............ Ink Jet Printing
**IJP** ............ International Journal of Parapsychology [*A publication*]
**IJP** ............ International Journal of Physical Distribution and Materials Management [*A publication*]
**IJP** ............ International Journal of Psychiatry [*A publication*]
**IJP** ............ International Journal of Public Administration [*A publication*]
**IJP** ............ International Juvenile Publications
**IJP** ............ Israel Jewish Press (BJA)
**IJPA** .......... Indian Journal of Public Administration [*A publication*]
**IJPA** .......... International Jelly and Preserve Association (EA)
**I J PA Phys** ... Indian Journal of Pure and Applied Physics [*A publication*]
**IJPDMM** .. International Journal of Physical Distribution and Materials Management [*A publication*]
**IJPE**........... International Journal of Political Education [*A publication*]
**IJPHC** ....... Iran Journal of Public Health [*A publication*]
**IJPHCD** .... Iranian Journal of Public Health [*A publication*]
**I J Physics** ... Indian Journal of Physics [*A publication*]
**IJPLBO**..... Iranian Journal of Plant Pathology [*A publication*]
**IJPP**........... Interpretation. A Journal of Political Philosophy [*A publication*]
**IJPPC**........ International Journal of Peptide and Protein Research [*A publication*]
**IJPPR**........ Institute for Jewish Policy Planning and Research (EA)
**IJPR** .......... International Journal of Production Research [*A publication*]
**IJPR** .......... Israel Journal of Psychiatry and Related Sciences [*A publication*]
**IJPS**........... Indian Journal of Political Science [*A publication*]
**IJPsa**.......... International Journal of Psychoanalysis [*A publication*]
**IJPSMHI** .. Industrial Jacks Product Section of the Material Handling Institute (EA)
**I J Psychol** ... Indian Journal of Psychology [*A publication*]
**IJR**............ Institute for Justice Research [*American University*] [*Research center*] (RCD)
**IJR**............ Institute for Juvenile Research [*Illinois Department of Mental Health-University of Illinois at Chicago*] [*Research center*] (RCD)
**IJR**............ International Journal of Research in Marketing [*A publication*]
**IJRCS**........ International Joint Rules Committee on Softball [*Later, ASA*] (EA)
**IJRE** .......... International Journal of Religious Education [*A publication*]
**IJRED** ....... International Journal of Radiation Engineering [*A publication*]
**IJ Rel Soz** .. Internationales Jahrbuch fuer Religionssoziologie [*A publication*]
**IJRR** .......... [*The*] International Journal of Robotics Research [*A publication*]
**IJRRDK** .... Internationale Zeitschrift fuer Rehabilitationsforschung [*A publication*]
**IJRS**........... International Journal of Rumanian Studies [*A publication*]
**IJRSA**........ Indian Journal of Radio and Space Physics [*A publication*]
**IJRSD**........ International Journal of Radiation Sterilization [*A publication*]
**IJS** ............ Inostrannye Jazyki v Skole [*A publication*]
**IJS** ............ Institute of Jazz Studies [*Rutgers University, University of New Jersey*] [*Research center*] (EA)
**IJS** ............ Interactive Job Submission [*Data processing*]
**IJS** ............ International Journal of Sexology [*A publication*]
**IJS** ............ International Journal of Social Economics [*A publication*]
**IJS** ............ Interrupt Jet Sensor
**IJS** ............ Rutgers-[*The*] State University, Institute of Jazz Studies, Newark, NJ [*OCLC symbol*] (OCLC)
**IJSBA**........ International Jet Ski Boating Association (EA)
**IJSBDB**..... Indian Journal of Chemistry. Section B. Organic Chemistry, Including Medicinal Chemistry [*A publication*]
**IJSCC**........ International Journal of Sulfur Chemistry [*A publication*]
**IJSCDE**..... Islamabad Journal of Sciences [*A publication*]
**IJSE**........... International Journal of Social Economics [*A publication*]
**IJSEA**........ Indian Journal of Sericulture [*A publication*]
**IJSL**........... International Journal of the Sociology of Language [*A publication*]
**IJSLP** ........ International Journal of Slavic Linguistics and Poetics [*A publication*]
**I J Soc Res** ... Indian Journal of Social Research [*A publication*]
**IJSPA**........ International Journal of Social Psychiatry [*A publication*]
**IJSPDJ**....... International Journal of Andrology. Supplement [*A publication*]
**IJS Rep R** .. IJS [*Institut "Jozef Stefan"*] Report R [*A publication*]
**IJSS**........... International John Steinbeck Society (EA)
**IJSSET**...... Italian Journal of Surgical Sciences [*A publication*]
**IJSTBT** ..... Iranian Journal of Science and Technology [*A publication*]
**IJSTDV**..... Italian Journal of Sports Traumatology [*A publication*]
**IJSW** ......... Indian Journal of Social Work [*A publication*]
**IJSym** ........ International Journal of Symbology [*A publication*]
**IJT**............ Indian Journal of Theology [*A publication*]
**IJT**............ International Journal of Transport Economics [*A publication*]
**IJTBAD**..... Indian Journal of Tuberculosis [*A publication*]
**I J Techn**.... Indian Journal of Technology [*A publication*]
**IJTEDP**..... Tissue Reactions [*A publication*]
**I J Theor P** ... Indian Journal of Theoretical Physics [*A publication*]
**IJU**............ Ijui [*Brazil*] [*Airport symbol*] (OAG)
**I Jug Os I K** ... Izvestija Jugo-Osetinskogo Instituta Kraevedenija [*A publication*]
**IJUSC3**...... International Journal of Health Services [*A publication*]
**IJV**............ Jeffersonville Township Public Library, Jeffersonville, IN [*OCLC symbol*] (OCLC)
**IJVEAW**.... Indian Journal of Agricultural and Veterinary Education [*A publication*]
**IJVIEE**...... Indian Journal of Virology [*A publication*]
**IJVMDP** ... Indian Journal of Veterinary Medicine [*A publication*]
**IJVMEQ** ... Israel Journal of Veterinary Medicine [*A publication*]
**IJVSD9**...... Indian Journal of Veterinary Surgery [*A publication*]
**IJWS** ......... International Journal of Women's Studies [*A publication*]
**IJWU**......... International Jewelry Workers Union [*Later, Service Employees International Union*] (EA)
**IJX**............ Jacksonville, IL [*Location identifier*] [*FAA*] (FAAL)

**IJZ** ............ Israel Journal of Zoology [*A publication*]
**IJZ** ............ Summersville, WV [*Location identifier*] [*FAA*] (FAAL)
**IJZOAE** .... Israel Journal of Zoology [*A publication*]
**IK** .............. Ihud ha-Kibbutsim (BJA)
**Ik** ............... Ikon [*A publication*]
**IK** .............. Immobilized Knee [*Orthopedics*]
**IK** .............. Immunekoerper [*Immune Bodies*] [*Medicine*]
**IK** .............. Indeks Kupovne Snage [*Purchasing Power Index*] [*Yugoslavian*]
**IK** .............. Indicator Kit
**IK** .............. Infanteriekolonne [*Infantry Supply Column*] [*German military - World War II*]
**IK** .............. Infusoria Killing [*Unit*] [*Medicine*]
**IK** .............. Inner Keel
**I/K** ............ Inspector/Killer
**IK** .............. Interbank (ADA)
**IK** .............. Intercollegiate Knights [*An association*] (EA)
**IK** .............. Interkinase Domain [*Genetics*]
**IK** .............. [*The*] Interlake Corp. [*NYSE symbol*] (SPSG)
**IK** .............. Interstitial Keratitis [*Ophthalmology*]
**IK** .............. Inukshuk. Frobisher Bay [*A publication*]
**IK** .............. Irodalomtorteneti Kozlemenyek [*A publication*]
**IK** .............. Iskusstvo Kino [*A publication*]
**IK** .............. Tradewinds Airways Ltd. [*Great Britain*] [*ICAO designator*] (FAAC)
**IKA** ........... International Kitefliers Association (EA)
**IKampR** ..... Kampsville Reading Center, Kampsville, IL [*Library symbol*] [*Library of Congress*] (LCLS)
**IKan** .......... Kansas Community Memorial Library, Kansas, IL [*Library symbol*] [*Library of Congress*] (LCLS)
**IKAOA** ...... Izvestiya Krymskoi Astrofizicheskoi Observatorii [*A publication*]
**IKAR** .......... Internationale Kommission fuer Alpines Rettungswesen [*International Commission for Alpine Rescue*] [*Birchwil, Switzerland*] (EAIO)
**IKAT** .......... Interactive Keyboard and Terminal [*Data processing*] (MCD)
**IKB** ............ International Klein Blue [*Color named after French painter Yves Klein*]
**IKB** ............ Internationale Kommunistenbond [*International Communist League*] [*Netherlands*] (PPW)
**IKB** ............ Wilkesboro, NC [*Location identifier*] [*FAA*] (FAAL)
**IKBD** .......... Intelligent Keyboard Device
**IKBKA** ....... Izvestiya na Khimicheskiya Institut. Bulgarska Akademiya na Naukite [*A publication*]
**IKBS** .......... Intelligent Knowledge-Based System [*Artificial intelligence*]
**IKC** ............ International Kennel Club of Chicago (EA)
**IKC** ............ Kankakee Community College, Kankakee, IL [*Library symbol*] [*Library of Congress*] (LCLS)
**IKE** ............ Iberiul-K'avk'asiuri Enatmecniereba [*A publication*]
**IKE** ............ Ion Kinetic Energy
**IKe** ............ Kewanee Public Library, Kewanee, IL [*Library symbol*] [*Library of Congress*] (LCLS)
**IKEA** .......... Ingvar Kamprad, Elmtaryd, Agunnaryd [*Initialism is company name derived from the names of its founder, the farm on which he grew up, and a Swedish village*]
**IKeB** .......... Black Hawk College, East Campus, Kewanee, IL [*Library symbol*] [*Library of Congress*] (LCLS)
**IKEL** .......... Ike Lovelady, Inc. [*NASDAQ symbol*] (NQ)
**IKEL** .......... Internacia Komitato por Etnaj Liberecoj [*International Committee for Ethnic Liberty - ICEL*] [*Eschweiler, Federal Republic of Germany*] (EAIO)
**IKEND** ...... Iwate-Ken Eisei Kenkyusho Nenpo [*A publication*]
**IKES** .......... Ion Kinetic Energy Spectrometry
**IKET** .......... Individual Knowledge Evaluation Test (AFM)
**IKF** ............ Institut fuer Kernphysik der Johann-Wolfgang-Goethe-Universitaet (Frankfurt) [*A publication*]
**IKF** ............ International Kart Federation (EA)
**IKF** ............ International Korfball Federation (EA)
**IKF** ............ International Kraft Federation (EA)
**IKFC** .......... International Knife and Fork Clubs (EA)
**IKFS** .......... International Kids Fashion Show (ITD)
**IKG** ............ Champaign Public Library, Champaign, IL [*OCLC symbol*] (OCLC)
**IKG** ............ Internationale Kommission fuer Glas [*International Commission on Glass*]
**IKG** ............ Israelitische Kultusgemeinde [*Vienna*] [*A publication*] (BJA)
**IKH** ............ Ihre Koenigliche Hoheit [*His (or Her) Royal Highness*] [*German*]
**IKHS** .......... International Kodak Historical Society (EA)
**IKI** ............. Iki [*Japan*] [*Airport symbol*] (OAG)
**IKI** ............. Institute of Space Research [*USSR*] [*Acronym is based on foreign phrase*]
**IKIF** .......... Individual Name and Address Key Index File [*IRS*]
**IKJ** ............ Ikusaka [*Japan*] [*Seismograph station code, US Geological Survey*] (SEIS)
**IKJ** ............ Internationales Kuratorium fuer das Jugendbuch [*International Board on Books for Young People*]
**IKK** ............ Internationale Kamer van Koophandel [*A publication*]
**IKK** ............ Kankakee, IL [*Location identifier*] [*FAA*] (FAAL)
**IKKF** .......... Izvestija Karel'skogo i Kol'skogo Filialov Akademii Nauk [*A publication*]
**IKL** ............ Isaenmaallinen Kansanliike [*Patriotic People's Movement*] [*Finland*] [*Political party*] (PPE)
**IKM** ........... In Kind Matching (OICC)
**IKM** ........... Texas State Library and Historical Commission, Austin, TX [*OCLC symbol*] (OCLC)
**IKMB** ......... Internationale Katholische Mittelstandsbewegung [*International Catholic Union of the Middle Class*]
**IKMK** ........ Istvan Kiraly Muzeum Koezlemenyei [*A publication*]
**IKMLA** ...... Ikonomicheska Mis'l [*A publication*]
**IKN** ............ Delco Electronics Division, General Motors Corp., Technical Library, Kokomo, IN [*OCLC symbol*] (OCLC)
**IKN** ............ Internationale Kommission fuer Numismatik [*International Numismatic Commission*]
**IKNG** ......... International King's Table, Inc. [*NASDAQ symbol*] (NQ)
**IKO** ............ Nikolski [*Alaska*] [*Airport symbol*] (OAG)
**IKO Inn Kolonisation Land Gemeinde** ... IKO. Innere Kolonisation Land und Gemeinde [*A publication*]
**ikon** ........... Economic [*Bulgarian*]
**IKON** ......... Olivet Nazarene College, Kankakee, IL [*Library symbol*] [*Library of Congress*] (LCLS)
**Ikon Mekh Selsk Stop** ... Ikonomika i Mekhanizatsiya na Selskoto Stopanstvo [*A publication*]
**Ikon Selskoto Stop Rural Econ** ... Ikonomika na Selskoto Stopanstvo. Rural Economics [*A publication*]
**IKOR** ......... Immediate Knowledge of Results
**I & KP** ....... Initial and Key Personnel
**IKP** ............ Inkopah [*California*] [*Seismograph station code, US Geological Survey*] (SEIS)
**IKP** ............ Instructor and Key Personnel
**IKP** ............ Kokomo Public Library, Kokomo, IN [*OCLC symbol*] (OCLC)
**IKPO** ......... Internationale Kriminalpolizeiliche Organisation [*International Criminal Police Organization*]
**IKPT** .......... Instructor and Key Personnel Training
**IKRA** .......... International Kirlian Research Association (EA)
**IKRD** ......... Inverse Kinetics Rod Drop [*Nuclear energy*] (NRCH)
**IKRK** .......... Internationales Komitee vom Roten Kreuz [*International Committee of the Red Cross*]
**IKS** ............ Integrated Key Set [*Data processing*]
**IKS** ............ International Kodaly Society (EAIO)
**IKS** ............ International Kolping Society [*See also IKW*] [*Cologne, Federal Republic of Germany*] (EAIO)
**IKS** ............ Inverse Kinetics Simulator
**IKSIA2** ...... Trudy Samarskogo Sel'skokhozyaistvennogo Instituta [*A publication*]
**IKSR** .......... Internationale Kommission zum Schutze des Rheins Gegen Verunreinigung [*International Commission for the Protection of the Rhine Against Pollution - ICPRAP*] (EAIO)
**Ikt** ............. Iktisadi [*Economy, Economic*] [*Turkish*]
**IKT** ............ Irkutsk [*USSR*] [*Airport symbol*] (OAG)
**IKTS** .......... International Klaus Tennstedt Society (EA)
**IKU** ............ Interface Keying Unit [*Data processing*] (KSC)
**IKUE** .......... Internacia Katolica Unuigo Esperantista [*International Catholic Esperanto Association*] (EA)
**Ikushugaku Zasshi/Jap J Breed** ... Ikushugaku Zasshi/Japanese Journal of Breeding [*A publication*]
**IKV** ............ International Kongress der Volkserzaehlungsforscher [*A publication*]
**IKV** ............ Internationaler Kranckenhausverbaund [*International Hospital Federation*]
**IKVSA** ....... Internationale Katholische Vereinigung fuer Soziale Arbeit [*Catholic International Union for Social Service*]
**IKW** ........... Indicated Kilowatts per Hour [*Engine emissions testing*]
**IKw** ............ Inmun Kwahak [*A publication*]
**IKW** ........... Internationales Kolpingwerk [*International Kolping Society - IKS*] [*Cologne, Federal Republic of Germany*] (EAIO)
**IKX** ............ Windsor Locks, CT [*Location identifier*] [*FAA*] (FAAL)
**IKZ** ............ Internationale Kirchliche Zeitschrift [*A publication*]
**IKZKA** ....... Itogi Nauki i Tekhniki Korroziya i Zashchita ot Korrozii [*A publication*]
**IL** .............. Bomber [*Russian aircraft symbol*]
**I & L** .......... Iazyk i Literatura [*A publication*]
**IL** .............. Iceland [*IYRU nationality code*]
**IL** .............. Identification List
**I & L** .......... Ideologies and Literature [*A publication*]
**IL** .............. Idle (BUR)
**Il** ............... Iliad [*of Homer*] [*Classical studies*] (OCD)
**IL** .............. Illinois [*Postal code*]
**IL** .............. Illinois Music Educator [*A publication*]
**IL** .............. Illinois Supreme Court Reports [*A publication*] (DLA)
**IL** .............. Illite [*A mineral*]
**il** ............... Illustrated [*or Illustrator*]
**IL** .............. Illustration
**il** ............... Ilmenite [*Also, ILM*] [*CIPW classification*] [*Geology*]
**IL** .............. Ilyushin [*USSR aircraft type*] [*World War II*]
**IL** .............. Ilyushin [*USSR*] [*ICAO aircraft manufacturer identifier*] (ICAO)
**IL** .............. I'm Leavin' Elvis Photos, Exclusive (EA)
**IL** .............. Imperial Life Assurance Co. of Canada [*Toronto Stock Exchange symbol*]
**I/L** ............ Import License

**IL** ... In Ladestreifen [*Loaded in Clips*] [*German military - World War II*]

**I-L** ... In-Law

**IL** ... In-Lock

**IL** ... Incisolingual [*Dentistry*]

**IL** ... Inclined Ladder (AAG)

**IL** ... Including Loading

**IL** ... Incoming Letter

**IL** ... Independent Living (EA)

**IL** ... Index Library [*A publication*]

**IL** ... Index Linked [*Government bonds*] [*British*]

**IL** ... Index Lists [*DoD*]

**IL** ... Indian Linguistics [*A publication*]

**IL** ... Indicating Light

**IL** ... Individualized Learning (OICC)

**IL** ... Inertial Laboratory [*NASA*] (KSC)

**IL** ... Information Labeling

**IL** ... Information Litteraire [*A publication*]

**IL** ... Insertion Loss

**IL** ... Inside Layer [*Technical drawings*]

**IL** ... Inside Left [*Soccer position*]

**IL** ... Inside Leg (ADA)

**IL** ... Inside Length [*Technical drawings*]

**I & L** ... Installations and Logistics

**IL** ... Instruction Leaflet (MSA)

**IL** ... Instruction List

**IL** ... Instructor-Lieutenant [*Navy*] [*British*]

**IL** ... Instrumentation Laboratory (MCD)

**IL** ... Insulators [*JETDS nomenclature*] [*Military*] (CET)

**IL** ... Intelligence Liaison [*Program*] [*Department of State*]

**IL** ... InterContinental Airways, Inc. [*ICAO designator*] (FAAC)

**IL** ... Intereact Limited [*British*]

**IL** ... Interior Length

**IL** ... Interleukin [*Biochemistry*]

**IL** ... Interline

**IL** ... Intermediary Letter

**IL** ... Intermediate Language [*Data processing*] (BUR)

**IL** ... Intermediate Level (MCD)

**IL** ... Intermediate Loop

**IL** ... International League [*Baseball*]

**IL** ... International Library [*A publication*]

**IL** ... International List

**IL** ... International Literature [*USSR*] [*A publication*]

**IL** ... International Logistics (AABC)

**IL** ... Interpolated Learning [*Psychology*]

**IL** ... Irish Land Reports (Fitzgibbon) [*A publication*] (DLA)

**IL** ... Israel [*ANSI two-letter standard code*] (CNC)

**IL** ... Israel Lira (BJA)

**IL** ... Italian Lira [*Monetary unit*]

**IL** ... Item List (AFIT)

**IL** ... [*The*] Item Requested Is a Special Distribution Item and Is Not Available for General Distribution [*Advice of supply action code*] [*Army*]

**IL** ... Ives Laboratories [*Research code symbol*]

**IL** ... Ivy League (EA)

**IL** ... L'Internationale Liberale

**IL** ... Lisle Library District, Lisle, IL [*Library symbol*] [*Library of Congress*] (LCLS)

**I$^2$L** ... Integrated Injection Logic [*Microprocessing*]

**IL-2** ... Interleukin-2 [*Immunology*]

**I$^3$L** ... Isoplanar Integrated Injection Logic

**ILA** ... Ilan [*Giran*] [*Republic of China*] [*Seismograph station code, US Geological Survey*] (SEIS)

**ILA** ... Illaga [*Indonesia*] [*Airport symbol*] (OAG)

**IL A** ... Illinois Appellate Court Reports [*A publication*] (DLA)

**ILa** ... Incisolabial [*Dentistry*]

**ILA** ... Independent Label Association (EA)

**ILA** ... Indian Limitation Act [*British*] (ROG)

**ILA** ... Institute of Landscape Architects [*British*]

**ILA** ... Instruction Look-Ahead [*Unit*] [*Data processing*]

**ILA** ... Instrument Landing Aid

**ILA** ... Instrument Landing Approach

**ILA** ... Instrument Low Approach [*Aircraft landing method*]

**ILA** ... Insulin-Like Activity

**ILA** ... Integrated Laboratory Automation

**ILA** ... Intelligent Line Adapter

**ILA** ... International Language for Aviation

**ILA** ... International Laundry Association

**ILA** ... International Law Association [*London, England*] (EA)

**ILA** ... International Leprosy Association [*India*]

**ILA** ... International Listening Association (EA)

**ILA** ... International Literary Annual [*London*] [*A publication*]

**ILA** ... International Llama Association (EA)

**ILA** ... International Longshoremen's Association (EA)

**ILA** ... Iterative Logic Array (MCD)

**ILA** ... Lafayette School Corp., Lafayette, IN [*OCLC symbol*] (OCLC)

**ILa** ... Lansing Public Library, Lansing, IL [*Library symbol*] [*Library of Congress*] (LCLS)

**ILA** ... Williams, CA [*Location identifier*] [*FAA*] (FAAL)

**ILAA** ... Independent Literary Agents Association (EA)

**ILAA** ... International Lawyers in Alcoholics Anonymous (EA)

**ILAA** ... International Legal Aid Association [*Defunct*]

**ILAADS** ... Interim Low-Altitude Air Defense System

**ILAAS** ... Integrated Light Attack Aircraft [*or Attack Avionics*] System

**ILAAT** ... Interlaboratory Air-to-Air Missile Technology (MCD)

**ILAB** ... Bureau of International Labor Affairs [*Department of Labor*]

**ILAB** ... International League of Antiquarian Booksellers [*See also LILA*] [*Bonn, Federal Republic of Germany*] (EAIO)

**ILABAY** ... Instruments et Laboratoires [*A publication*]

**ILAC** ... International Laboratory Accreditation Conference [*Gaithersburg, MD*] [*National Institute of Standards and Technology*] (EGAO)

**ILACD** ... Ibero Latin American College of Dermatology (EA)

**ILACDE** ... Instituto Latinoamericano de Cooperacion y Desarrollo [*Latin American Institute for Cooperation and Development*] (EAIO)

**ILACO** ... International Land Development Consultants Ltd.

**ILad** ... Ladd Public Library, Ladd, IL [*Library symbol*] [*Library of Congress*] (LCLS)

**IL A 2d** ... Illinois Appellate Court Reports, Second Series [*A publication*] (DLA)

**IL A 3d** ... Illinois Appellate Court Reports, Third Series [*A publication*] (DLA)

**ILadSD** ... Ladd Consolidated Community School District 94, Ladd, IL [*Library symbol*] [*Library of Congress*] (LCLS)

**ILADT** ... Instituto Latinoamericano de Derecho Tributario [*Latin American Tax Law Institute*] (EAIO)

**ILAE** ... International League Against Epilepsy (EA)

**ILAF** ... Identical Location of Accelerometer and Force [*NASA*]

**ILAFA** ... Instituto Latinoamericano del Fierro y el Acero [*Latin American Iron and Steel Institute*] (EAIO)

**ILAG** ... Abbreviation of German phrase meaning "prison camp for civilians"

**ILAG** ... INLOGOV [*Institute of Local Government*] Local Authority Game

**ILag** ... La Grange Public Library, La Grange, IL [*Library symbol*] [*Library of Congress*] (LCLS)

**ILagp** ... La Grange Park Library District, La Grange Park, IL [*Library symbol*] [*Library of Congress*] (LCLS)

**ILagpS** ... Suburban Audio-Visual Service, La Grange Park, IL (LCLS)

**ILAI** ... Italo-Latin American Institute (EA)

**ILAIS** ... Institute for Latin American and Iberian Studies [*Columbia University*] [*Research center*] (RCD)

**ILAM** ... Institute of Leisure and Amenity Management (EAIO)

**ILam** ... LaMoille-Clarion District Library, LaMoille, IL [*Library symbol*] [*Library of Congress*] (LCLS)

**ILAMS** ... Infrared LASER Atmospheric Monitoring System

**ILamSD** ... LaMoille Community Unit, School District 303, LaMoille, IL [*Library symbol*] [*Library of Congress*] (LCLS)

**ILANET** ... Information and Libraries Access Network [*Australia*]

**ILANUD** ... Instituto Latinoamericano de Naciones Unidas para la Prevencion del Delito y Tratamiento del Delincuente [*United Nations Latin American Institute for Crime Prevention and Treatment of Offenders*] [*Information service or system*] (IID)

**ILAR** ... Institute of Laboratory Animal Resources (EA)

**ILAR** ... International League Against Rheumatism (EA)

**ILAR** ... International League for Animal Rights (EA)

**ILA Rec** ... Illinois Library Association. Record [*A publication*]

**ILAS** ... Instrument Low-Approach System [*Aircraft landing method*]

**ILAS** ... International Laser Acupuncture Society (EA)

**ILAS** ... Interrelated Logic Accumulating Scanner

**ILas** ... LaSalle Public Library, LaSalle, IL [*Library symbol*] [*Library of Congress*] (LCLS)

**I$^2$L$^2$AS** ... Infantry Issues and Lessons Learned Analysis System [*Software*] (INF)

**ILasC** ... Carus Chemical Co., Inc., LaSalle, IL [*Library symbol*] [*Library of Congress*] (LCLS)

**ILASE** ... Internacia Ligo de Agrikulturaj Specialistoj-Esperantistoj [*International League of Agricultural Specialists-Esperantists - ILASE*] (EAIO)

**ILasH** ... Hygiene Institute, Medical Library, LaSalle, IL [*Library symbol*] [*Library of Congress*] (LCLS)

**ILasJ** ... Jefferson Elementary School, LaSalle, IL [*Library symbol*] [*Library of Congress*] (LCLS)

**ILasL** ... Lincoln Junior High School, LaSalle, IL [*Library symbol*] [*Library of Congress*] (LCLS)

**ILasN** ... Northwest Elementary School, LaSalle, IL [*Library symbol*] [*Library of Congress*] (LCLS)

**ILASS** ... Integrated Light Attack Avionics System [*Navy*] (NVT)

**ILASS** ... Intermediate Level Avionics Support System (MCD)

**ILasSD** ... LaSalle-Peru Township High School, LaSalle, IL [*Library symbol*] [*Library of Congress*] (LCLS)

**IlATos** ... Ilmij Asarlari. V. I. Lenin Monidagi Toskent Davlat Universiteti [*A publication*]

**I-LAW** ... Improved Light Antiarmor [*or Antitank*] Weapon (RDA)

**ILaw** ... Lawrence Township Library, Lawrenceville, IL [*Library symbol*] [*Library of Congress*] (LCLS)

**ILB** ... Eli Lilly & Co., Business Library, Indianapolis, IN [*OCLC symbol*] (OCLC)

**ILB** ... Illinois Business Review [*A publication*]

**ILB** ... Initial Load Block

**ILB** ........ Inner Lead Bond [*Integrated circuit technology*]
**ILB** ........ Insurance Law Bulletin [*Australia*] [*A publication*]
**ILB** ........ Involvement Limited to Bone [*Oncology*]
**ILBA** ........ International League for Bolivarian Action (EA)
**ILBB** ........ Improved Life Blower Bearing
**ILBC** ........ International Livestock Brand Conference (EA)
**ILBE** ........ International League of Blind Esperantists [*See also LIBE*] [*Belgrade, Yugoslavia*] (EAIO)
**ILBEA** ........ Industrie Lackier-Betrieb [*A publication*]
**ILBFRLP** ... International Lelio Basso Foundation for the Rights and Liberation of Peoples (EA)
**ILBTC** ........ International Livestock Brand and Theft Conference (EA)
**ILBW** ........ Infant, Low Birth Weight
**ILC** ........ Idle Load Compensator [*Automotive engineering*]
**ILC** ........ Incipient Lethal Concentration
**ILC** ........ Independent Labor Congress [*Nigeria*]
**ILC** ........ Independent Living Centres [*Australia*]
**ILC** ........ Industrial Liaison Centre [*British*]
**ILC** ........ Industry-Labor Council (EA)
**ILC** ........ Initial Launch Capability [*Aerospace*]
**ILC** ........ Insearch Language Centre [*Australia*]
**ILC** ........ Institute of Land Combat [*Army*]
**ILC** ........ Institute for Liberty and Community (EA)
**ILC** ........ Instruction Length Code [*Data processing*] (BUR)
**ILC** ........ Instruction Location Counter
**ILC** ........ Instructor Lieutenant-Commander [*Navy*] [*British*]
**ILC** ........ Integrated Launch Complex (MCD)
**ILC** ........ Integrated Logic Circuit
**ILC** ........ Intermediate-Level Cell [*Nuclear energy*] (NRCH)
**ILC** ........ Internal Locus of Control [*Psychology*]
**ILC** ........ International Labelling Centre [*Defunct*] (EA)
**ILC** ........ International Labor Conference [*A section of the International Labor Organization*] [*United Nations*]
**ILC** ........ International Latex Corporation
**ILC** ........ International Law Commission [*United Nations*]
**ILC** ........ International Leadership Center (EA)
**ILC** ........ International Legal Center [*Formerly, SAILER*] [*Later, International Center for Law and Development*] (EA)
**ILC** ........ International Licensed Carrier [*Telecommunications*]
**ILC** ........ International Logistics Center [*Army*]
**ILC** ........ Irrevocable Letter of Credit [*Business term*]
**ILC** ........ ISDN [*Integrated Services Digital Network*] Link Controller [*Telecommunications*]
**ILC** ........ Lake County Public Library, Merrillville, IN [*OCLC symbol*] (OCLC)
**ILC** ........ Wilson Creek, NV [*Location identifier*] [*FAA*] (FAAL)
**ILCA** ........ Belgique Judiciaire [*A publication*] (ILCA)
**ILCA** ........ Indian Land Consolidation Act [*1983*]
**ILCA** ........ Insurance Loss Control Association [*Indianapolis, IN*] (EA)
**ILCA** ........ International Labor Communications Association (EA)
**ILCA** ........ International Lactation Consultant Association (EA)
**ILCA** ........ International Lightning Class Association (EA)
**ILCA** ........ International Livestock Centre for Africa [*Addis Ababa, Ethiopia*]
**ILCA** ........ Inverter Light Control Assembly (MCD)
**ILCA (Int Livest Centr Afr) Res Rep** ... ILCA (International Livestock Centre for Africa) Research Report [*A publication*]
**ILCC** ........ Initial Launch Capability Complex [*Aerospace*]
**ILCC** ........ Integrated Launch Control and Checkout (KSC)
**ILCCG** ........ International Laity and Christian Community Group [*See also LAEEC*] [*Sion, Switzerland*] (EAIO)
**Ill C Cl** ........ Illinois Court of Claims Reports [*A publication*] (DLA)
**ILCCS** ........ Integrated Launch Control and Checkout System
**ILCCTC** ........ International Liaison Committee on Co-Operative Thrift and Credit [*Paris, France*] (EA)
**ILCEP** ........ Inter-Laboratory Committee on Editing and Publishing [*Navy*] (MCD)
**ILCF** ........ Inter-Laboratory Committee on Facilities [*Navy*] (MCD)
**ILCK** ........ Inductosyn Linearity Checkout Kit
**ILCM** ........ Individual Level Cost Method [*Insurance*]
**ILC Newl** ... International Legal Center. Newsletter [*A publication*] (DLA)
**ILCO** ........ Infrastructural, Logistics, Council Operations [*NATO*]
**ILCO** ........ Instantaneous Launch Control Officer [*Aerospace*] (AAG)
**ILCO** ........ Intercontinental Life Corporation [*NASDAQ symbol*] (NQ)
**ILCO** ........ International Logistics Control Office
**Il Cons Mar** ... Il Consolato del Mare [*A publication*] (DLA)
**ILCOP** ........ International Liaison Committee of Organizations for Peace
**ILCORK** ........ International Liaison Committee for Research on Korea
**ILCS** ........ Induction Loop Communications System
**ILCT** ........ ILC Technology, Inc. [*NASDAQ symbol*] (NQ)
**ILCTA** ........ International League of Commercial Travelers and Agents (EA)
**ILC (UN)** ... International Law Commission of the United Nations
**ILCV** ........ Inscriptiones Latinae Christianae Veteres
**ILD** ........ Eli Lilly & Co., Agricultural Library, Greenfield, IN [*OCLC symbol*] (OCLC)
**ILD** ........ In-Lock Detector
**ILD** ........ Indent Load Deflection [*Measure of hardness*]
**ILD** ........ Information Lead Distance
**ILD** ........ Injection LASER Diode (TEL)
**ILD** ........ Injection Luminescence Device
**ILD** ........ Inland Recovery Group [*Vancouver Stock Exchange symbol*]
**ILD** ........ International Labor Defense [*An association*]
**ILD** ........ International Labour Documentation [*A publication*]
**ILD** ........ Interstitial Lung Disease
**ILD** ........ Ischemic Leg Disease [*Medicine*]
**ILD** ........ Ischemic Limb Disease [*Medicine*]
**IL 2d** ........ Illinois Supreme Court Reports, Second Series [*A publication*] (DLA)
**ILDA** ........ Industrial Lighting Distributors of America (EA)
**ILDA** ........ International Lutheran Deaf Association (EA)
**ILDC** ........ International Legal Defense Counsel (EA)
**ILDCF** ........ Interlake Development [*NASDAQ symbol*] (NQ)
**ILDCSI** ........ Individual Learning Disabilities Classroom Screening Instruments
**ILDIS** ........ International Legume Database and Information Service
**ILDP** ........ Interlook Dormant Period (NVT)
**ILDR** ........ Index of Limited Distribution Reports [*A publication*]
**ILDS** ........ Integrated Logistics Data System
**ILDS** ........ International League of Dermatological Societies [*Vancouver, BC*] (EAIO)
**ILDT** ........ Item Logistics Data Transmittal
**ILDTF** ........ Item Logistics Data Transmittal Form (NATG)
**Ile** ........ Ilerda [*A publication*]
**ILE** ........ Ileum [*Anatomy*]
**ILE** ........ Indiana Law Encyclopedia [*A publication*] (DLA)
**ILE** ........ Inel Resources Ltd. [*Vancouver Stock Exchange symbol*]
**ILE** ........ Institution of Lighting Engineers (EAIO)
**ILE** ........ Intelligent Life Elsewhere
**ILE** ........ Interface Latching Element
**ILE** ........ International Logo Exchange [*A publication*]
**Ile** ........ Isoleucine [*or iLeu, Ileu*] [*Also, I*] [*An amino acid*]
**ILE** ........ Killeen [*Texas*] [*Airport symbol*] (OAG)
**ILE** ........ Killeen, TX [*Location identifier*] [*FAA*] (FAAL)
**ILE** ........ Lincolnwood Public Library District, Lincolnwood, IL [*OCLC symbol*] (OCLC)
**ILEA** ........ Inner London Education Authority [*British*]
**ILEA** ........ International League of Electrical Associations (EA)
**ILeb** ........ Lebanon Public Library, Lebanon, IL [*Library symbol*] [*Library of Congress*] (LCLS)
**ILebHS** ........ Lebanon High School, Lebanon, IL [*Library symbol*] [*Library of Congress*] (LCLS)
**ILebM** ........ McKendree College, Lebanon, IL [*Library symbol*] [*Library of Congress*] (LCLS)
**ILeD** ........ De Andreis Seminary, Lemont, IL [*Library symbol*] [*Library of Congress*] (LCLS)
**ILEF** ........ Internacia Ligo de Esperantistaj Foto-Kino-Magnetofon-Amatoroj [*International League of Esperantist Amateur Photographers, Cinephotographers, and Tape-Recording*] (EAIO)
**ILEI** ........ Internacia Ligo de Esperantistaj Instruistoj [*International League of Esperantist Teachers*] (EAIO)
**ILelSD** ........ Leland Community Unit, School District 1, Leland, IL [*Library symbol*] [*Library of Congress*] (LCLS)
**ILENDP** .... Industrial Engineering [*A publication*]
**ILEOA** ........ International Law Enforcement Officers Association (EA)
**ILEP** ........ Federation Internationale des Associations Contre la Lepre [*International Federation of Anti-Leprosy Associations - ILEP*] (EAIO)
**ILERA** ........ International League of Esperantist Radio Amateurs (EA)
**ILERT** ........ Independent Librarians Exchange Round Table [*American Library Association*]
**ILESA** ........ International Law Enforcement Stress Association (EA)
**ILET** ........ Instituto Latinoamericano de Estudios Transnacionales [*Latin American Institute for Transnational Studies - LAITS*] (EAIO)
**Ileu** ........ Isoleucine [*or iLeu, Ile*] [*Also, I*] [*An amino acid*]
**ILEUA** ........ Izvestiya Leningradskogo Elektrotekhnicheskogo Instituta [*A publication*]
**ILEX** ........ International Leisure Enterprises, Inc. [*NASDAQ symbol*] (NQ)
**ILF** ........ Idaho Laboratory Facility [*Later, IRC*] [*Idaho Falls, ID*] [*Department of Energy*] (GRD)
**ILF** ........ Immigrants in the Labour Force [*British*]
**ILF** ........ Indian Local Forces [*Military*] [*British*]
**ILF** ........ Inductive Loss Factor (IEEE)
**ILF** ........ Infra Low-Frequency [*Telecommunications*] (TEL)
**ILF** ........ Institut de la Langue Francaise [*France*]
**ILF** ........ Integral Lift Fan [*Aviation*]
**ILF** ........ Integrity Loss Factor
**ILF** ........ International Falcon Resources Ltd. [*Vancouver Stock Exchange symbol*]
**ILF** ........ International Lacrosse Federation (EA)
**ILF** ........ International Landworkers' Federation [*Later, IFPAAW*]
**ILF** ........ International Liaison Forum of Peace Forces [*See also FILFP*] [*Moscow, USSR*] (EAIO)
**ILF** ........ International Lifeboat Federation [*England*] (EAIO)
**ILF** ........ International Luge Federation [*Austria*]
**ILf** ........ Lake Forest Library, Lake Forest, IL [*Library symbol*] [*Library of Congress*] (LCLS)
**ILF** ........ Studii si Cercetari de Istorie Literara si Folclor [*A publication*]

**ILfB**........... Barat College of the Sacred Heart, Lake Forest, IL [*Library symbol*] [*Library of Congress*] (LCLS)
**ILFC**.......... International Lease Finance Corporation [*NASDAQ symbol*] (NQ)
**ILfC**........... Lake Forest College, Lake Forest, IL [*Library symbol*] [*Library of Congress*] (LCLS)
**ILFCG**....... International Logistics Functional Coordinating Group (MCD)
**ILFI**........... International Labour Film Institute [*Defunct*]
**IL & FM**.... Assistant Secretary of the Army for Installations, Logistics, and Financial Management (MCD)
**ILFO**.......... International Logistics Field Office [*Army*] (AABC)
**ILFP**.......... Forum International de Liaison des Forces de la Paix [*International Liaison Forum of Peace Forces - ILF*] (EA)
**ILFZ**.......... Ivanhoe Lake Fault Zone [*Canada*] [*Geology*]
**ILG**............ Consolidated Inland Recovery [*Vancouver Stock Exchange symbol*]
**ILG**............ Indian Labour Gazette [*A publication*]
**ILG**............ Inge Lehmann [*Greenland*] [*Seismograph station code, US Geological Survey*] [*Closed*] (SEIS)
**ILG**............ Instrument Landing Guidance
**ILG**............ International Leisure Group [*Commercial firm*] [*British*]
**ILG**............ Irish Linen Guild [*Defunct*] (EA)
**ILG**............ University of Illinois, Graduate School of Library Science, Urbana, IL [*OCLC symbol*] (OCLC)
**ILG**............ Wilmington [*Delaware*] [*Airport symbol*] (OAG)
**ILGA**.......... Institute of Local Government Administration [*British*]
**ILGA**.......... International Lesbian and Gay Association [*Formerly, International Gay Association*] (EA)
**I L de Gaule**... Inscriptions Latines des Trois Gaules [*A publication*] (OCD)
**ILGB**.......... International Laboratory of Genetics and Biophysics
**ILGCA**........ Illinois State Geological Survey. Circular [*A publication*]
**ILGF**.......... Insulin-Like Growth Factor
**ILGIA**........ Report of Investigations. Illinois State Geological Survey [*A publication*]
**ILGPA**....... Illinois State Geological Survey. Illinois Petroleum [*A publication*]
**ILGPNWU**... International Leather Goods, Plastic, and Novelty Workers' Union (EA)
**ILGSA**....... Indoor Light Gardening Society of America (EA)
**ILGU**......... Izvestiya Leningradskogo Gosudarstvennogo Universiteta [*A publication*]
**ILGWU**..... International Ladies' Garment Workers' Union (EA)
**ILH**............ Del Rio, TX [*Location identifier*] [*FAA*] (FAAL)
**ILH**............ Imperial Light Horse [*Military*] [*British*] (ROG)
**ILH**............ Jus Liberorum Habens [*Possessing the Right of Children*] [*Latin*]
**ILH**............ Northern Illinois University, Department of Library Science, De Kalb, IL [*OCLC symbol*] (OCLC)
**ILHL**.......... International Leisure Hosts Limited [*NASDAQ symbol*] (NQ)
**ILHP**.......... Illinois Journal of Health, Physical Education, and Recreation [*A publication*]
**ILHR**......... International League for Human Rights (EA)
**ILI**.............. Ili [*USSR*] [*Seismograph station code, US Geological Survey*] [*Closed*] (SEIS)
**ILI**.............. Iliamna [*Alaska*] [*Airport symbol*] (OAG)
**ILI**.............. Iliamna, AK [*Location identifier*] [*FAA*] (FAAL)
**ILI**.............. Indiana Limestone Institute of America (EA)
**ILI**.............. Indiana University, School of Law Library, Indianapolis, IN [*OCLC symbol*] (OCLC)
**ILI**.............. Injection LASER Illuminator
**ILI**.............. Instant Lunar Ionosphere
**ILI**.............. Institute for Land Information [*Research center*] [*Information service or system*] (RCD)
**ILI**.............. Institute of Life Insurance [*Later, ACLI*] (EA)
**ILI**.............. Inter-African Labour Institute
**ILI**.............. Interamerican Labour Institute
**ILI**.............. Intercan Leasing, Inc. [*Toronto Stock Exchange symbol*]
**ILI**.............. International Law Institute (EA)
**ILIA**........... Indiana Limestone Institute of America
**ILIA**........... International Livestock Investigators Association (EA)
**ILib**............ Cook Memorial Public Library District, Libertyville, IL [*Library symbol*] [*Library of Congress*] (LCLS)
**I Lib**........... Indian Librarian [*A publication*]
**ILIC**........... In-Line Integrated Circuit
**ILIC**........... International Library Information Center (EA)
**IL-IC-IM**... It's Life, I Can't, I Must [*Element of psychotherapist Joseph Bird's self-help theory*]
**I L Ideol L**... I and L. Ideologies and Literature [*A publication*]
**I-LIDS**........ Indian Legal Information Development Service (EA)
**ILIF**........... International Logistics Information File (MCD)
**Iliff R**.......... Iliff Review [*A publication*]
**ILIMA**....... International Licensing Industry and Merchandisers' Association (EA)
**ILing**.......... Incontri Linguistici [*A publication*]
**I Ling**......... Initiation a la Linguistique [*A publication*]
**ILinL**.......... Lincoln Christian College, Lincoln, IL [*Library symbol*] [*Library of Congress*] (LCLS)
**ILinw**.......... Lincolnwood Public Library, Lincolnwood, IL [*Library symbol*] [*Library of Congress*] (LCLS)
**ILIO**........... Ilio, Inc. [*NASDAQ symbol*] (NQ)
**ILIOS**........ In-Line Infinity Optical System
**ILIP**........... In-Line Instrument Package [*Nuclear energy*] (NRCH)
**ILIR**........... In-House Laboratories Independent Research Program [*Army*] (RDA)
**ILIR**........... Institute of Labor and Industrial Relations [*University of Illinois*] [*Research center*] (RCD)
**ILIR**........... Institute of Labor and Industrial Relations [*University of Michigan*] [*Research center*] (RCD)
**I Lit**............ Iasul Literar [*A publication*]
**I Lit**............ Indian Literature [*A publication*]
**ILit**............. Litchfield Carnegie Public Library, Litchfield, IL [*Library symbol*] [*Library of Congress*] (LCLS)
**I-LITE**....... Iowa Library Information Teletype Exchange [*Des Moines, IA*] [*Telecommunications*] [*Library network*]
**ILitSD**........ Litchfield Community Unit, School District 12, Litchfield, IL [*Library symbol*] [*Library of Congress*] (LCLS)
**ILivSD**....... Livingston Community Consolidated School District, Livingston, IL [*Library symbol*] [*Library of Congress*] (LCLS)
**ILJ**............. Indiana Law Journal [*A publication*]
**ILJ**............. Insurance Law Journal [*A publication*]
**ILJ**............. Springfield, MO [*Location identifier*] [*FAA*] (FAAL)
**ILJM**......... Illinois Journal of Mathematics [*A publication*]
**ILK**............ IIT Chicago-Kent College of Law, Chicago, IL [*OCLC symbol*] (OCLC)
**ILK**............ Interlock [*Technical drawings*]
**ILKE**.......... Internacia Libro-Klubo Esperantista (EA)
**ILL**............. Air Illinois, Inc. [*Carbondale, IL*] [*FAA designator*] (FAAC)
**ILL**............. Illinois (AFM)
**Ill**............... Illinois Reports [*A publication*] (DLA)
**Ill**............... Illiterati [*A publication*]
**ILL**............. Illuminating [*Ammunition*] (NATG)
**ILL**............. Illusion
**ill**............... Illustrated (BJA)
**ILL**............. Illustration
**ILL**............. Illustration [*A publication*]
**ill**............... Illustrator [*MARC relator code*] [*Library of Congress*] (LCCP)
**ILL**............. Illustrissimus [*Most Illustrious*] [*Latin*]
**ILL**............. Impact Limit Lines (MUGU)
**ILL**............. Individual Learning Laboratory (OICC)
**ILL**............. Input Logic Level
**ILL**............. Institut Laue-Langevin [*French*] (IRUK)
**ILL**............. Institute of Languages and Linguistics (DIT)
**ILL**............. Institute of Lifetime Learning (EA)
**ILL**............. Interlibrary Loan
**ILL**............. Intermediate Lymphocytic Lymphoma [*Medicine*]
**ILL**............. International Labour Documentation [*A publication*]
**ILL**............. International Larder Minerals, Inc. [*Toronto Stock Exchange symbol*]
**ILL**............. Interstate Loan Library [*Council of State Governments*] (IID)
**ILL**............. Irving Langmuir Laboratory [*New Mexico Institute of Mining and Technology*] [*Research center*] (RCD)
**ILL**............. Ontario Library Service - Escarpment, Hamilton [*UTLAS symbol*]
**ILL**............. Willmar, MN [*Location identifier*] [*FAA*] (FAAL)
**Ill A**............ Illinois Appellate Court Reports [*A publication*] (DLA)
**Ill Admin Code**... Illinois Administrative Code [*A publication*]
**Ill Admin Reg**... Illinois Register [*A publication*] (DLA)
**Ill Ag Exp**.. Illinois. Agricultural Experiment Station. Publications [*A publication*]
**Ill Agr Econ**... Illinois Agricultural Economics [*A publication*]
**Ill Agric Econ**... Illinois Agricultural Economics [*A publication*]
**Ill Agric Econ Dep Agric Econ Ill Univ Agric Exp Stn**... Illinois Agricultural Economics. Department of Agricultural Economics. Illinois University. Agricultural Experiment Station [*A publication*]
**Ill Agric Exp Stn Bull**... Illinois. Agricultural Experiment Station. Bulletin [*A publication*]
**Ill Agric Exp Stn Circ**... Illinois. Agricultural Experiment Station. Circular [*A publication*]
**Ill Agric Exp Stn Dep For For Res Rep**... Illinois. Agricultural Experiment Station. Department of Forestry. Forestry Research Report [*A publication*]
**Ill Agric Exp Stn For Note**... Illinois. Agricultural Experiment Station. Forestry Note [*A publication*]
**Ill Ann Stat**... Smith-Hurd's Illinois Annotated Statutes [*A publication*] (DLA)
**Ill Ann Stat (Smith-Hurd)**... Smith-Hurd's Illinois Annotated Statutes [*A publication*]
**Ill Ap**.......... Illinois Appellate Court Reports [*A publication*] (DLA)
**Ill App**........ Illinois Appellate Court Reports [*A publication*] (DLA)
**Ill App Ct Rep**... Illinois Appellate Court Reports [*A publication*] (DLA)
**Ill App 2d**... Illinois Appellate Court Reports, Second Series [*A publication*] (DLA)
**Ill App 3d**... Illinois Appellate Court Reports, Third Series [*A publication*] (DLA)
**Ill Apps**...... Illinois Appellate Court Reports [*A publication*] (DLA)
**Illawarra Hist Soc Newsletter**... Illawarra Historical Society. Newsletter [*A publication*] (APTA)
**Illaw Hist Soc M Notice**... Illawarra Historical Society. Monthly Notice [*A publication*] (APTA)
**ILLB**.......... Insurance and Liability Law Bulletin [*A publication*]

**Ill BA Bull** ... Illinois State Bar Association. Quarterly Bulletin [*A publication*] (DLA)
**Ill Bar J**...... Illinois Bar Journal [*A publication*]
**Ill Biol Mon** ... Illinois Biological Monographs [*A publication*]
**Ill Biol Monogr** ... Illinois Biological Monographs [*A publication*]
**Ill B J**......... Illinois Bar Journal [*A publication*]
**Ill Bus R**..... Illinois Business Review [*A publication*]
**Ill Cath His R** ... Illinois Catholic Historical Review [*A publication*]
**Ill CC**......... Illinois Commerce Commission Opinions and Orders [*A publication*] (DLA)
**Ill CC**......... Matthew and Bangs' Illinois Circuit Court Reports [*A publication*] (DLA)
**Ill Cir**......... Illinois Circuit Court (DLA)
**Ill Cir Ct**..... Illinois Circuit Court Reports [*A publication*] (DLA)
**Ill Classic Stud** ... Illinois Classical Studies [*A publication*]
**Ill Class Stud** ... Illinois Classical Studies [*A publication*]
**Ill CLE**....... Illinois Continuing Legal Education [*A publication*]
**Ill Coal M Investigations B** ... Illinois Coal Mining Investigations. Cooperative Agreement. Bulletin [*A publication*]
**Ill Cont L Ed** ... Illinois Continuing Legal Education [*A publication*] (DLA)
**Ill Cont Legal Ed** ... Illinois Continuing Legal Education [*A publication*]
**Ill Ct Cl**...... Illinois Court of Claims Reports [*A publication*]
**ILLD**......... Illustrated (ROG)
**Ill 2d**.......... Illinois Reports, Second Series [*A publication*] (DLA)
**Ill Dec**........ Illinois Decisions [*A publication*] (DLA)
**Ill Dent J**.... Illinois Dental Journal [*A publication*]
**Ill Dep Conserv Tech Bull** ... Illinois. Department of Conservation. Technical Bulletin [*A publication*]
**Ill Div Fish Spec Fish Rep** ... Illinois. Division of Fisheries. Special Fisheries Report [*A publication*]
**Ill Div Indus Plan and Devel Atlas Ill Res** ... Illinois. Division of Industrial Planning and Development. Atlas of Illinois Resources [*A publication*]
**Ill Educ**...... Illinois Education [*A publication*]
**Ill Energy Notes** ... Illinois Energy Notes [*A publication*]
**Ill Eng**........ Illuminating Engineering [*Later, Illuminating Engineering Society. Journal*] [*A publication*]
**IL LF**.......... Illinois Law Forum (DLA)
**Ill Geogr Soc Bull** ... Illinois Geographical Society. Bulletin [*A publication*]
**Ill Geol Surv Guide Leafl** ... Illinois State Geological Survey. Guide Leaflet [*A publication*]
**Ill Geol Surv Oil Gas Drill Ill Mon Rep** ... Illinois. Geological Survey. Oil and Gas Drilling in Illinois. Monthly Report [*A publication*]
**Ill Geol Surv Rev Act** ... Illinois State Geological Survey. Review of Activities [*A publication*]
**Ill G S B**..... Illinois State Geological Survey. Bulletin [*A publication*]
**Ill His Col**.. Illinois State Historical Library. Collections [*A publication*]
**Ill His J**...... Illinois State Historical Society. Journal [*A publication*]
**Ill His L**..... Illinois State Historical Library. Publications [*A publication*]
**Ill His S Trans** ... Illinois State Historical Society. Transactions [*A publication*]
**Ill Hist Coll** ... Illinois State Historical Library. Collections [*A publication*]
**Ill His Trans** ... Illinois State Historical Society. Transactions [*A publication*]
**Ill Hlth Ne** ... Illinois Health News [*A publication*]
**Ill Horiz**..... Illinois Horizons [*A publication*]
**ILLIAC**...... Illinois Institute for Advanced Computing
**ILLIAC**...... Illinois Integrator and Automatic Computer [*University of Illinois*] (BUR)
**ILLIC LAG OBTURAT** ... Illico Lagena Obturatur [*Stopper the Bottle at Once*] [*Pharmacy*]
**ILLIN**........ Illinantur [*Anoint*] [*Pharmacy*] (ROG)
**ILLINEND** ... Illinendus [*To Be Smeared*] [*Pharmacy*]
**ILLINET**... Illinois Library and Information Network [*Library network*]
**Illinois Acad Sci Trans** ... Illinois State Academy of Science. Transactions [*A publication*]
**Illinois F**..... Illinois Farmer [*A publication*]
**Illinois Geol Survey Circ** ... Illinois State Geological Survey. Circular [*A publication*]
**Illinois J Math** ... Illinois Journal of Mathematics [*A publication*]
**Illinois Med J** ... Illinois Medical Journal [*A publication*]
**Illinois Miner Notes** ... Illinois Mineral Notes [*A publication*]
**Illinois MJ** ... Illinois Medical Journal [*A publication*]
**Illinois Rep** ... Illinois Reports [*A publication*] (DLA)
**Illinois Water Survey Rept Inv** ... Illinois State Water Survey. Reports of Investigations [*A publication*]
**Ill Issues**.... Illinois Issues [*A publication*]
**ILLIT**......... Illiterate
**Ill J Math**.. Illinois Journal of Mathematics [*A publication*]
**ILLL**.......... International Lutheran Laymen's League (EA)
**Ill Law Rev** ... Illinois Law Review [*A publication*]
**Ill Laws**...... Laws of Illinois [*A publication*] (DLA)
**Ill LB**.......... Illinois Law Bulletin [*A publication*] (DLA)
**Ill Legis Serv** ... Illinois Legislative Service (West) [*A publication*] (DLA)
**Ill Legis Serv (West)** ... Illinois Legislative Service (West) [*A publication*]
**Ill Leg N**..... Illustrated Legal News [*India*] [*A publication*] (DLA)
**Ill Lib**......... Illinois Libraries [*A publication*]
**Ill Libr**....... Illinois Libraries [*A publication*]
**Ill LQ**......... Illinois Law Quarterly [*A publication*] (DLA)
**Ill L Rec**..... Illinois Law Record [*A publication*] (DLA)
**Ill L Rev**..... Illinois Law Review [*A publication*]
**ILLLTV**..... Integrated Low-Light-Level Television
**ILLM**......... Illinois Marine Bancorp, Inc. [*Elmhurst, IL*] [*NASDAQ symbol*] (NQ)
**Ill Med Bull** ... Illinois Medical Bulletin [*A publication*]
**Ill Med J**.... Illinois Medical Journal [*A publication*]
**Ill Mo**......... Illinois Monthly Magazine [*A publication*]
**ILLMO**...... Illustrissimo [*Most Illustrious*] [*Latin*]
**Ill Monogr Med Sci** ... Illinois Monographs in Medical Sciences [*A publication*]
**Ill Nat Hist Surv Biol Notes** ... Illinois Natural History Survey. Biological Notes [*A publication*]
**Ill Nat Hist Surv Bull** ... Illinois Natural History Survey. Bulletin [*A publication*]
**Ill Nat Hist Surv Circ** ... Illinois Natural History Survey. Circular [*A publication*]
**Illne Scient** ... Illustrazione Scientifica [*A publication*]
**Ill N H Soc Tr** ... Illinois Natural History Society. Transactions [*A publication*]
**Ill Op Att'y Gen** ... Illinois Attorney General's Opinion [*A publication*] (DLA)
**Ill Pet**......... Illinois Petroleum [*A publication*]
**Ill PUC Ops** ... Illinois Public Utilities Commission Opinions and Orders [*A publication*] (DLA)
**Ill Q**........... Illinois Quarterly [*A publication*]
**Ill R**........... Illinois Reports [*A publication*] (DLA)
**Ill Reg**........ Illinois Register [*A publication*]
**Ill Rep**........ Illinois Reports [*A publication*] (DLA)
**Ill Res**......... Illinois Research [*A publication*]
**Ill Res Agric Exp Stn** ... Illinois Research. Illinois Agricultural Experiment Station [*A publication*]
**Ill Rev Stat** ... Illinois Revised Statutes [*A publication*] (DLA)
**ILLRI**......... Industrial Lift and Loading Ramp Institute [*Defunct*] (EA)
**ILLRP**........ Inscriptiones Latinae Liberae Rei Publicae [*A publication*] (OCD)
**Ill R & WC** ... Illinois Railroad and Warehouse Commission Reports [*A publication*] (DLA)
**Ill R & WCD** ... Illinois Railroad and Warehouse Commission Decisions [*A publication*] (DLA)
**ILLS**.......... Illinois (ROG)
**Ills**............. Illinois Reports [*A publication*] (DLA)
**Ills App**...... Illinois Appellate Court Reports [*A publication*] (DLA)
**Ill SBA**....... Illinois State Bar Association. Reports [*A publication*] (DLA)
**Ill SBAQB** ... Illinois State Bar Association. Quarterly Bulletin [*A publication*] (DLA)
**Ill Sch J**..... Illinois Schools Journal [*A publication*]
**Ill Soc Eng** ... Illinois Society of Engineers and Surveyors [*A publication*]
**Ills R**.......... Illinois Reports [*A publication*] (DLA)
**Ills Rep**....... Illinois Reports [*A publication*] (DLA)
**Ill St Ac Sc Tr** ... Illinois State Academy of Science. Transactions [*A publication*]
**Ill State Acad Sci Trans** ... Illinois State Academy of Science. Transactions [*A publication*]
**Ill State Florists Assoc Bull** ... Illinois State Florists Association. Bulletin [*A publication*]
**Ill State Geol Surv Bull** ... Illinois State Geological Survey. Bulletin [*A publication*]
**Ill State Geol Surv Circ** ... Illinois State Geological Survey. Circular [*A publication*]
**Ill State Geol Surv Guideb Ser** ... Illinois State Geological Survey. Guidebook Series [*A publication*]
**Ill State Geol Surv Ill Miner Note** ... Illinois State Geological Survey. Illinois Minerals Note [*A publication*]
**Ill State Geol Surv Ill Petrol** ... Illinois State Geological Survey. Illinois Petroleum [*A publication*]
**Ill State Geol Surv Ind Miner Notes** ... Illinois State Geological Survey. Industrial Minerals Notes [*A publication*]
**Ill State Hist Soc Jour** ... Illinois State Historical Society. Journal [*A publication*]
**Ill State Hort Soc N L** ... Illinois State Horticultural Society. Newsletter [*A publication*]
**Ill State Mus Pop Sci Ser Sci Paper Story Ill Ser** ... Illinois State Museum. Popular Science Series. Scientific Papers. Story of Illinois Series [*A publication*]
**Ill State Mus Rep Invest** ... Illinois State Museum. Reports of Investigations [*A publication*]
**Ill State Univ Jour** ... Illinois State University. Journal [*A publication*]
**Ill State Water Surv Bull** ... Illinois State Water Survey. Bulletin [*A publication*]
**Ill State Water Surv Circ** ... Illinois State Water Survey. Circular [*A publication*]
**Ill State Water Survey Cooperative Ground-Water Rept** ... Illinois State Water Survey. Cooperative Ground-Water Report [*A publication*]
**Ill State Water Survey Div Bull Circ Rept Inv** ... Illinois State Water Survey. Division Bulletin. Circular. Reports of Investigations [*A publication*]
**Ill State Water Surv Rep Invest** ... Illinois State Water Survey. Reports of Investigations [*A publication*]
**Ill State Water Surv State Geol Surv Coop Resour Rep** ... Illinois State Water Survey and State Geological Survey. Cooperative Resources Report [*A publication*]
**Ill St Lab N H B** ... Illinois State Laboratory of Natural History. Bulletin [*A publication*]

**Ill St Mus N H B** ... Illinois State Museum of Natural History. Bulletin [*A publication*]
**ILLSTN**..... Illustration
**Ill Stud Anthropol** ... Illinois Studies in Anthropology [*A publication*]
**ILLT** .......... Illinois Terminal Railroad Co.
**Ill Teach**..... Illinois Teacher [*A publication*]
**Ill Teach Home Econ** ... Illinois Teacher of Home Economics [*A publication*]
**Ill U Eng Exp Sta Bul** ... Illinois University. Engineering Experiment Station. Bulletin [*A publication*]
**Ill U Eng Exp Sta Circ** ... Illinois University. Engineering Experiment Station. Circular [*A publication*]
**ILLUM**...... Illuminate (KSC)
**Illum Eng**... Illuminating Engineering [*Later, Illuminating Engineering Society. Journal*] [*A publication*]
**Illum Eng (London)** ... Illuminating Engineer (London) [*A publication*]
**Illum Eng Soc J** ... Illuminating Engineering Society. Journal [*A publication*]
**Illum Eng Soc Trans** ... Illuminating Engineering Society. Transactions [*A publication*]
**Ill Univ B Univ Studies** ... Illinois University. Bulletin. University Studies [*A publication*]
**Ill Univ (Chicago Circle) Dep Geol Sci Tech Rep** ... Illinois University (Chicago Circle). Department of Geological Sciences. Technical Report [*A publication*]
**Ill Univ Civ Eng Stud Constr Res Ser** ... Illinois University. Civil Engineering Studies. Construction Research Series [*A publication*]
**Ill Univ Civ Eng Stud Hydraul Eng Ser** ... Illinois University. Civil Engineering Studies. Hydraulic Engineering Series [*A publication*]
**Ill Univ Civ Eng Stud Soil Mech Ser** ... Illinois University. Civil Engineering Studies. Soil Mechnanics Series [*A publication*]
**Ill Univ Civ Eng Stud Struct Res Ser** ... Illinois University. Civil Engineering Studies. Structural Research Series [*A publication*]
**Ill Univ Coop Ext Serv Circ** ... Illinois University. Cooperative Extension Service. Circular [*A publication*]
**Ill Univ Dep Civ Eng Struct Res Ser** ... Illinois University. Department of Civil Engineering. Structural Research Series [*A publication*]
**Ill Univ Dep Electr Eng Aeron Lab Aeron Rep** ... Illinois University. Department of Electrical Engineering. Aeronomy Laboratory. Aeronomy Report [*A publication*]
**Ill Univ Dep Theor Appl Mech TAM Rep** ... Illinois University. Department of Theoretical and Applied Mechanics. TAM Report [*A publication*]
**Ill Univ Eng Exp Sta Bull** ... Illinois University. Engineering Experiment Station. Bulletin [*A publication*]
**Ill Univ Eng Exp Stn Tech Rep** ... Illinois University. Engineering Experiment Station. Technical Report [*A publication*]
**Ill Univ Eng Expt Sta Bull Circ** ... Illinois University. Engineering Experiment Station. Bulletin. Circulars [*A publication*]
**Ill Univ Proc Sanit Eng Conf** ... Illinois University. Proceedings of the Sanitary Engineering Conference [*A publication*]
**Ill Univ TAM Rep** ... Illinois University. Department of Theoretical and Applied Mechanics. TAM Report [*A publication*]
**Ill Univ Water Resour Cent Res Rep** ... Illinois University. Water Resources Center. Research Report [*A publication*]
**ILLUS** ....... Illustrate [*or Illustration*] (AABC)
**Illus Archaeol** ... Illustrated Archaeologist [*A publication*]
**Illus Landwirtsch Ztg** ... Illustrierte Landwirtschaftlichte Zeitung [*A publication*]
**Illus Lond N** ... Illustrated London News [*A publication*]
**Illus London News** ... Illustrated London News [*A publication*]
**ILLUSTN** ... Illustration
**ILLUSTR**.. Illustrator (ROG)
**Illus W Ind** ... Illustrated Weekly of India [*A publication*]
**Illus W Ind A** ... Illustrated Weekly of India. Annual [*A publication*]
**Ill Vet**......... Illinois Veterinarian [*A publication*]
**Ill WCC** ..... Illinois Workmen's Compensation Cases [*A publication*] (DLA)
**IL & M**....... Ichthyological Laboratory and Museum [*University of Miami*]
**ILM** ........... Iliamna [*Alaska*] [*Seismograph station code, US Geological Survey*] (SEIS)
**ILM** ........... Ilmenite [*Also, il*] [*Geology*]
**ILM** ........... Immobilized-Liquid Membrane [*Chemical engineering*]
**ILM** ........... Independent Landing Monitor [*RADAR-TV landing guidance*] [*NASA*]
**ILM** ........... Industrial Minerals [*A publication*]
**ILM** ........... Information Logic Machine (IEEE)
**ILM** ........... Institute of Labour Management
**ILM** ........... Insulin-Like Material
**ILM** ........... Intermediate Language Machine [*Data processing*]
**ILM** ........... International Legal Materials [*A publication*]
**ILM** ........... Lincoln Library, Springfield, IL [*OCLC symbol*] (OCLC)
**ILM** ........... Wilmington [*North Carolina*] [*Airport symbol*] (OAG)
**ILM** ........... Wilmington, NC [*Location identifier*] [*FAA*] (FAAL)
**ILMA**......... Immunochemiluminometric Assay [*Analytical biochemistry*]
**ILMA**......... Incandescent Lamp Manufacturers Association [*Defunct*] (EA)
**ILMA**......... Independent Lubricant Manufacturers Association (EA)
**ILMA**......... International Licensing and Merchandisers' Association [*Later, ILIMA*] (EA)
**ILMA**......... Intraocular Lens Manufacturers Association (EA)
**ILMA**......... Morton Arboretum, Lisle, IL [*Library symbol*] [*Library of Congress*] (LCLS)
**ILMD** ........ Item Logistics Management Data [*DoD*]
**Ilmenau Tech Hochsch Wiss Z** ... Ilmenau, Technische Hochschule, Wissenschaftliche Zeitschrift [*A publication*]
**ILMH** ........ Institute for Labor and Mental Health (EA)
**ILML**......... Istituto Lombardo. Accademia di Scienze e Lettere. Memorie della Classe di Lettere [*A publication*]
**ILMN** ........ Il Mondo [*A publication*]
**ILMP**......... Integrated Logistic Management Program (NG)
**ILMT**......... Integrated Logistics Management Team
**ILMT**......... Intermediate-Level Maintenance Training
**ILMWSC** .. International Lifesaving Museum and Water Safety Center (EA)
**ILN** ........... East Peoria Elementary Schools, East Peoria, IL [*OCLC symbol*] (OCLC)
**ILN** ........... Idle Line Network
**ILN** ........... Illustrated London News [*A publication*]
**ILN** ........... Indonesia Letter [*A publication*]
**ILN** ........... International Law News [*A publication*]
**ILN** ........... International Logistics Negotiations [*Military export sales*]
**ILN** ........... Island Lagoon [*Australia*] [*Seismograph station code, US Geological Survey*] [*Closed*] (SEIS)
**ILN** ........... Wilmington, OH [*Location identifier*] [*FAA*] (FAAL)
**ILNY**......... International League of New York
**ilo** .............. Ilocano [*MARC language code*] [*Library of Congress*] (LCCP)
**ILO** ........... Iloilo [*Philippines*] [*Airport symbol*] (OAG)
**ILO** ........... Iloilo [*Philippines*] [*Seismograph station code, US Geological Survey*] [*Closed*] (SEIS)
**ILO** ........... In Lieu Of
**ILO** ........... Individual Load Operation
**ILO** ........... Industrial Liaison Organization [*MIT*]
**ILO** ........... Injection-Locked Oscillator (IEEE)
**ILO** ........... Internally Linked Operation
**ILO** ........... International Labor Office [*A section of the International Labor Organization*] [*United Nations*]
**ILO** ........... International Labour Organisation [*Geneva, Switzerland*] [*United Nations*] (EA)
**ILO** ........... Interservice Liaison Office [*Military*] (CAAL)
**ILo**............. Iodine Lotion [*Medicine*]
**ILO** ........... School of the Art Institute of Chicago Library, Chicago, IL [*OCLC symbol*] (OCLC)
**ILOAD** ...... Initialization Load (MCD)
**ILOC**.......... Irrevocable Letter of Credit [*Business term*] (DS)
**ILoc**........... Lockport Township Public Library, Lockport, IL [*Library symbol*] [*Library of Congress*] (LCLS)
**ILoC**........... National College of Chiropractic, Lombard, IL [*Library symbol*] [*Library of Congress*] (LCLS)
**ILocL** ......... Lewis University, Lockport, IL [*Library symbol*] [*Library of Congress*] (LCLS)
**ILocL-L**...... Lewis University, College of Law, Glen Ellyn, IL [*Library symbol*] [*Library of Congress*] (LCLS)
**Ilocos R** ...... Ilocos Review [*A publication*]
**ILod** .......... Loda Public Library, Loda, IL [*Library symbol*] [*Library of Congress*] (LCLS)
**ILoE**........... National College of Education, Lombard, IL [*Library symbol*] [*Library of Congress*] (LCLS)
**ILOP**.......... Initial Light Off Procedure (MCD)
**ILos**........... Lostant Community Library, Lostant, IL [*Library symbol*] [*Library of Congress*] (LCLS)
**ILosHSD** ... Lostant Consolidated High School District 400, Lostant, IL [*Library symbol*] [*Library of Congress*] (LCLS)
**ILOSS**........ Integrated LASER Optical Sight Set
**ILosSD** ...... Lostant Consolidated Community School District 25, Lostant, IL [*Library symbol*] [*Library of Congress*] (LCLS)
**ILOST** ....... International Liaison Center of Schools of Cinema and Television
**ILOSU**....... International Labor Organization Staff Union [*Geneva, Switzerland*] (EAIO)
**ILOUE**........ In Lieu of Until Exhausted [*Military*]
**ILovjD**........ Lovejoy Unit, District 188, Lovejoy, IL [*Library symbol*] [*Library of Congress*] (LCLS)
**ILO Yb**........ ILO [*International Labour Organisation*] Yearbook [*A publication*]
**ILP**............ Clausen, Miller, Gorman, Caffrey & Witous, Chicago, IL [*OCLC symbol*] (OCLC)
**ILP**............ Il Ponte [*A publication*]
**ILP**............ Ile Des Pins [*New Caledonia*] [*Airport symbol*] (OAG)
**ILP**............ Illinois Law and Practice [*A publication*] (DLA)
**ILP**............ In-Line Printer
**ILP**............ Independent Labour Party [*British*]
**ILP**............ Independent Liberal Party [*Israel*] [*Political party*] (BJA)
**ILP**............ Index to Legal Periodicals [*A publication*]
**ILP**............ Individual Learning Package (OICC)
**ILP**............ Industrial Liaison Program [*Refers to university-industry interaction*]
**ILP**............ Integer Linear Programming Model [*Statistics*]
**ILP**............ Integrated Logistics Panel (NASA)
**ILP**............ Intermediate Language Processor [*Data processing*] (BUR)
**ILP**............ Intermediate Language Program [*Data processing*]
**ILP**............ International Logistics Program

**ILP**............ Irish Labour Party [*Political party*] (ROG)
**ILP**............ Islamic Liberation Party [*Political party*] [*Tunisia*] (MENA)
**ILP**............ Israel Labor Party [*Political party*]
**ILPA**.......... International Labor Press Association (EA)
**ILPBC**........ International League of Professional Baseball Clubs (EA)
**ILPC**.......... International Linen Promotion Commission (EA)
**ILPEAG**.... Agricultural Science [*Jogjakarta*] [*A publication*]
**ILPES**........ Instituto Latinoamericano de Planificacion Economica y Social [*Latin American Institute for Economic and Social Planning*] [*Santiago, Chile*] [*United Nations*]
**ILPF**.......... Ideal Low Pass Filter
**ILPL**.......... Index to Legal Periodical Literature [*1887-1937*] [*A publication*] (DLA)
**ILPO**.......... Il Polo. Istituto Geografico Polare [*A publication*]
**ILPPSM**.... International Library of Philosophy, Psychology, and Scientific Method [*Book publishing*] [*British*]
**ILQ**............ Chadwell, Kayser, Ruggles, McGee & Hastings, Chicago, IL [*OCLC symbol*] (OCLC)
**ILQ**............ Indian Law Quarterly [*A publication*] (DLA)
**ILQ**............ International Law Quarterly [*A publication*]
**ILQR**.......... Indian Law Quarterly Review [*A publication*] (DLA)
**ILR**............ Burns, OR [*Location identifier*] [*FAA*] (FAAL)
**ILR**............ Ilorin [*Nigeria*] [*Airport symbol*] (OAG)
**ILR**............ In-Line Reciprocator
**ILR**............ Incurred Loss Ratio [*Insurance*]
**ILR**............ Independent Local Radio [*British*]
**ILR**............ Indian Law Reports [*A publication*] (DLA)
**ILR**............ Indian Law Review [*A publication*]
**ILR**............ Indicating Light Relay
**ILR**............ Industrial and Labor Relations
**ILR**............ Industrial and Labor Relations Review [*A publication*]
**ILR**............ Industrial Law Review [*A publication*] (ILCA)
**ILR**............ Infanterie-Lehrregiment [*Infantry Demonstration Regiment*] [*German military - World War II*]
**ILR**............ Institute of Library Research [*University of California*] (DIT)
**ILR**............ Institute of Logistics Research [*Army*] (RDA)
**ILR**............ Insurance Law Reporter [*A publication*] (DLA)
**ILR**............ International Labour Review [*A publication*]
**ILR**............ International Laco Resources [*Vancouver Stock Exchange symbol*]
**ILR**............ International Language Reporter [*A publication*]
**ILR**............ International Law Reports
**ILR**............ International Luggage Registry [*Computer system for recovery of airline luggage*]
**ILR**............ Iowa Law Review [*A publication*]
**ILR**............ Irish Law Reports [*A publication*] (DLA)
**ILR**............ Israel Business and Investors' Report [*A publication*]
**ILR**............ Israel Law Review [*A publication*]
**ILRA**.......... Inbred Livestock Registry Association (EA)
**ILRA**.......... International Log Rolling Association
**ILRAD**....... International Laboratory for Research on Animal Diseases [*Nairobi, Kenya*]
**ILR All**....... Indian Law Reports, Allahabad Series [*A publication*] (DLA)
**ILR And**..... Indian Law Reports, Andhra Series [*A publication*] (DLA)
**ILR Assam**... Indian Law Reports, Assam Series [*A publication*] (DLA)
**ILRBBI**...... Istituto Lombardo. Accademia di Scienze e Lettere. Rendiconti. B. Scienze Biologiche e Mediche [*A publication*]
**ILR Bom**.... Indian Law Reports, Bombay Series [*A publication*] (DLA)
**ILRC**.......... Indian Law Reports, Calcutta Series [*A publication*] (DLA)
**ILRC**.......... Indian Law Resource Center (EA)
**ILR Cal**...... Indian Law Reports, Calcutta Series [*A publication*] (DLA)
**ILR Calc**.... Indian Law Reports, Calcutta Series [*A publication*] (DLA)
**ILR Cut**...... Indian Law Reports, Orissa Series [*A publication*] (DLA)
**ILRERF**...... International Labor Rights Education and Research Fund (EA)
**ILR Hyderabad**... Indian Law Reports, Hyderabad Series [*A publication*] (DLA)
**ILRI**........... International Institute for Land Reclamation and Improvement [*Netherlands*]
**ILRIS**......... Intermediate Long-Range Interceptor System
**ILR Kar**...... Indian Law Reports, Karachi Series [*A publication*] (DLA)
**ILR Ker**...... Indian Law Reports, Kerala Series [*A publication*] (DLA)
**ILRL**.......... Istituto Lombardo. Accademia di Scienze e Lettere. Rendiconti. Classe de Lettere [*A publication*]
**ILR Lah**..... Indian Law Reports, Lahore Series [*A publication*] (DLA)
**ILRLP**........ International League for the Rights and Liberation of Peoples [*Rome, Italy*] (EAIO)
**ILR Luck**... Indian Law Reports, Lucknow Series [*A publication*] (DLA)
**ILRM**......... International League for the Rights of Man [*Later, ILHR*]
**ILRM**......... Irish Law Reports Monthly [*A publication*]
**ILR Mad**.... Indian Law Reports, Madras Series [*A publication*] (DLA)
**ILR Madhya Bharat**... Indian Law Reports, Madhya Bharat Series [*A publication*] (DLA)
**ILR Mysore**... Indian Law Reports, Mysore Series [*A publication*] (DLA)
**ILR Nag**..... Indian Law Reports, Nagpur Series [*A publication*] (DLA)
**ILRO**.......... Industrial Labor Relations Office [*DoD*]
**ILR Or**....... Indian Law Reports, Orissa Series [*A publication*] (DLA)
**ILRP**.......... Indian Law Reports, Patna Series [*A publication*] (DLA)
**ILR Pat**...... Indian Law Reports, Patna Series [*A publication*] (DLA)
**ILR Patiala**... Indian Law Reports, Patiala Series [*A publication*] (DLA)
**ILR Pun**..... Indian Law Reports, Punjab Series [*A publication*] (DLA)
**ILRR**.......... Industrial and Labor Relations Review [*A publication*]
**ILR Rajasthan**... Indian Law Reports, Rajasthan Series [*A publication*] (DLA)
**ILR Ran**..... Indian Law Reports, Rangoon Series [*A publication*] (DLA)
**ILR Rev**..... Industrial and Labor Relations Review [*A publication*] (DLA)
**ILRRJ**........ International League for the Repatriation of Russian Jews (EA)
**ILRS**.......... Interlibrary Resource Sharing Section [*National Library of Australia*]
**ILRS**.......... International League of Religious Socialists [*Aerdenhout, Netherlands*] (EAIO)
**ILRSS**........ International Labour Review. Statistical Supplement [*A publication*]
**ILRT**.......... Integrated Leak Rate Test [*Nuclear energy*] (NRCH)
**ILRT**.......... Intermediate Level Reactor Test (IEEE)
**ILR Trav-Cochin**... Indian Law Reports, Kerala Series [*A publication*] (DLA)
**ILRV**.......... In-Line Relief Valve
**ILRV**.......... Integral [*or Integrated*] Launch and Recovery [*or Reentry*] Vehicle [*NASA*]
**ILRVS**........ Integral [*or Integrated*] Launch and Recovery [*or Reentry*] Vehicle System [*NASA*]
**ILRWG**...... International Labor Rights Working Group (EA)
**ILS**............ Ideal Liquidus Structures (IEEE)
**ILS**............ Identification List
**ILS**............ Illinois Benedictine College, Lisle, IL [*Library symbol*] [*Library of Congress*] (LCLS)
**ILS**............ Incorporated Law Society [*British*]
**ILS**............ Increase in Life-Span
**ILS**............ Independent Living Skills [*Needed by the handicapped*]
**ILS**............ Indiana Union List of Serials, Indianapolis, IN [*OCLC symbol*] (OCLC)
**ILS**............ Industrial Locomotive Society [*British*]
**ILS**............ Information & Library Services [*Information service or system*] (IID)
**ILS**............ Inland Library System [*Library network*]
**ILS**............ Inscriptiones Latinae Selectae [*A publication*]
**ILS**............ Inspection Lot Size
**ILS**............ Institute of Lithuanian Studies (EA)
**ILS**............ Instrument Landing System [*Aviation*]
**ILS**............ Integrated Laboratory Sequence [*A system of teaching chemistry devised by Mary L. Good at Louisiana State University in New Orleans*]
**ILS**............ Integrated LASER System [*Salford Engineering*]
**ILS**............ Integrated LASER Systems [*Software*] [*British*]
**ILS**............ Integrated Library System [*National Library of Medicine*] [*Information service or system*] (IID)
**ILS**............ Integrated Logistics Support [*DoD*]
**ILS**............ Integrated Logistics System
**ILS**............ Interferometric LASER Source
**ILS**............ International Latitude Service
**ILS**............ International Laughter Society [*Commercial firm*] (EA)
**ILS**............ International Learning Systems
**ILS**............ International Lilac Society (EA)
**ILS**............ International Limnological Society [*See also SIL*] (ASF)
**ILS**............ International Line Selector
**ILS**............ International Lunar Society (EA)
**ILS**............ Interrupt Level Subroutine (CMD)
**ILS**............ Interstate Land Sales [*HUD*]
**ILS**............ Inventory Locator Service [*Database*] [*Inventory Locator Service, Inc.*] [*Information service or system*] (CRD)
**ILSA**.......... Insured Locksmiths and Safemen of America [*Defunct*] (EA)
**ILSA**.......... Integrated Logistic Support Analysis Paper (MCD)
**ILSA**.......... Inter-American Legal Services Association (EA)
**ILSA**.......... International Law Students Association (EAIO)
**ILSA**.......... International Lending Supervision Act of 1983
**ILSAA**........ Improved Lighting System for Army Aircraft (RDA)
**ILSAP**........ Instrument Landing System Approach [*Aviation*]
**ILSC**.......... Integrated Logistics Support Cadre (AFIT)
**ILSCM**....... Integrated Logistics Support Control Manual (MCD)
**ILSCM**....... Integrated Logistics Support Coordination Meeting (MCD)
**ILSDF**........ Integrated Logistics Support Data File
**ILSDP**........ International Logistics Supply Delivery Plan (MCD)
**ILS-DS**...... Integrated Logistic Support - Detail Specification
**ILSE**.......... Interagency Life Sciences Supporting Space Research and Technology Exchange
**ILSF**.......... Incandescent Liquid Spheroidal Formation [*Combustion technology*]
**ILSF**.......... Intermediate Level Sample Flow (IEEE)
**ILSG**.......... Integrated Logistics Subgroup [*Military*] (MCD)
**ILSG**.......... Interim Logistics Support Guide (NVT)
**ILSGB**........ International Language Society of Great Britain
**ILSI**........... International Life Sciences Institute [*Later, ILSI-NF*] (EA)
**ILSI**........... International Life Services, Incorporated (EA)
**ILSI-NF**..... International Life Sciences Institute - Nutrition Foundation (EA)
**ILS/IS/D**... Integrated Logistics Support/Information System/Dictionary
**ILS/LAR**... Integrated Logistics System and Logistics Assessment Review (MCD)
**ILSM**......... Integrated Logistics Support Manager [*Military*] (MCD)
**ILSM**......... Integrated Logistics Support Model [*Military*] (MCD)
**ILSMH**....... International League of Societies for Persons with Mental Handicap [*Brussels, Belgium*] (EA)

**ILSMP**....... Integrated Logistic Support Maintenance [*or Management*] Plan (MCD)
**ILSMRS**.... Integrated Logistics Support Milestone Reporting System [*Military*] (MCD)
**ILSMRT**.... Integrated Logistic Support Management Review Team
**ILSMT**...... Integrated Logistic Support Management Team
**ILSNI**........ Incorporated Land Society of Northern Ireland
**ILSO**.......... Incremental Life Support Operations
**ILSO**.......... Integrated Logistic Support Office [*DoD*]
**ILSP**........... Instrument Landing System - Partial [*Aviation*] (FAAC)
**ILSP**........... Integrated Logistic Support Plan [*or Program*]
**ILSP**........... International Library of Sports and Pastimes [*A publication*]
**ILSPER**..... Integrated Logistics Support Performance Evaluation Report [*Military*] (MCD)
**ILSPIP**...... International Logistics Supply Performance Improvement Program (NG)
**ILSR**.......... Institute for Local Self-Reliance (EA)
**ILSR**.......... Integrated Logistics Support Review [*Military*] (MCD)
**ILSS**........... Integrated Life Support System [*NASA*]
**ILSSA-VIOLA**... Industria Lamiere Speciali Soc. Az.-Carlo Viola [*Italian*]
**ILSSE**......... Integrated Life Science Shuttle Experiments (MCD)
**ILSTAC**...... Instrument Landing System and TACAN
**ILSUS**........ Integrated Library System Users Society (EA)
**ILSW**......... Interrupt Level Status Word
**ILT**............ Albuquerque, NM [*Location identifier*] [*FAA*] (FAAL)
**ILT**............ Il Tesaur [*A publication*]
**ILT**............ In Lieu Thereof [*Military*]
**ILT**............ Infantry Liaison Team (INF)
**ILT**............ Infectious Laryngo-Tracheitis [*Medicine*] (ADA)
**ILT**............ Inferolateral Trunk [*Neuroanatomy*]
**ILT**............ Installation Lead Time
**ILT**............ Intermediate Lay-Up Tool [*Plastics technology*]
**ILT**............ International Logistics Training
**ILT**............ Irish Law Times [*A publication*]
**ILT**............ Iultin [*USSR*] [*Seismograph station code, US Geological Survey*] (SEIS)
**ILT**............ Keck, Mahin & Cate, Chicago, IL [*OCLC symbol*] (OCLC)
**ILTA**.......... Independent Liquid Terminals Association (EA)
**ILTF**.......... International Lawn Tennis Federation [*Later, ITF*]
**ILT Jo**........ Irish Law Times Journal [*A publication*] (DLA)
**ILTMS**...... International Leased Telegraph Message Switching Service [*British Telecom*] [*Telecommunications*] (TEL)
**ILTR**.......... Irish Law Times Reports [*A publication*] (DLA)
**ILTS**.......... Industrial Language Training Service [*British*]
**ILTS**.......... Integration Level Test Series [*Psychology*]
**ILTS**.......... Intermediate Level Test Station (MCD)
**ILTSJ**........ Institute of Low Temperature Science. Contributions (Japan) [*A publication*]
**ILT & SJ**.... Irish Law Times and Solicitors' Journal [*A publication*]
**ILTTA**....... International Light Tackle Tournament Association (EA)
**ilu**.............. Illinois [*MARC country of publication code*] [*Library of Congress*] (LCCP)
**ILU**............ Illinois University (IEEE)
**ilu**.............. Illuminator [*MARC relator code*] [*Library of Congress*] (LCCP)
**ILU**............ Texas Tech University, Lubbock, TX [*OCLC symbol*] (OCLC)
**ILUMS**...... Innovations in Land Use Management Symposium
**ILUVM**...... I Love You Very Much [*Correspondence*] (DSUE)
**ILV**............ Industrial Launch Vehicle
**ILV**............ International Laser Tech, Inc. [*Vancouver Stock Exchange symbol*]
**ILv**............. Lake Villa District Library, Lake Villa, IL [*Library symbol*] [*Library of Congress*] (LCLS)
**ILV**............ Sonnenschein, Carlin, Nath & Rosenthal, Chicago, IL [*OCLC symbol*] (OCLC)
**ILVBIDT**... In Liebe Vereint bis in dem Tod [*United in Love until Death*] [*German*]
**ILVSI**......... Instant Lead Vertical Speed Indicator (MCD)
**ILW**........... Intermediate-Level Wastes (IEEE)
**ILW**........... International Association of Assessing Officers, Chicago, IL [*OCLC symbol*] (OCLC)
**ILW**........... International Low Water
**ILW**........... Investment Laws of the World [*A publication*] (DLA)
**ILWAS**...... Integrated Lake-Watershed Acidification Study
**ILWC**......... Intermediate-Level Waste Concentrate [*Nuclear energy*] (NRCH)
**ILWC**......... International League of Women Composers (EA)
**ILWCHSG**... International Labor and Working Class History Study Group (EA)
**ILWD**........ Intermediate-Level Waste Distillate [*Nuclear energy*] (NRCH)
**ILWF**......... Intermediate-Level Waste Feed [*Nuclear energy*] (NRCH)
**ILWML**..... International Lutheran Women's Missionary League (EA)
**ILWU**........ International Longshoremen's and Warehousemen's Union (EA)
**ILX**............ Visiting Nurse Association of Chicago, Chicago, IL [*OCLC symbol*] (OCLC)
**ILY**............ Islay [*Scotland*] [*Airport symbol*] (OAG)
**ILy**............. Lyons Public Library, Lyons, IL [*Library symbol*] [*Library of Congress*] (LCLS)
**ILY**............ Northern Illinois University, Law Library, Glen Ellyn, IL [*OCLC symbol*] (OCLC)
**ILYA**.......... Inland Lake Yachting Association (EA)
**I-LYA**........ Inter-Lake Yachting Association (EA)
**ILz**............. Ela Area Public Library, Lake Zurich, IL [*Library symbol*] [*Library of Congress*] (LCLS)
**ILZ**............ Isham, Lincoln & Beale, Chicago, IL [*OCLC symbol*] (OCLC)
**ILZ**............ Newport, RI [*Location identifier*] [*FAA*] (FAAL)
**ILZRO**....... International Lead Zinc Research Organization (EA)
**ILZSG**....... International Lead and Zinc Study Group [*London, England*] (EA)
**Im**.............. Illuminare [*A publication*]
**IM**............. Im Mittel [*On an Average*] [*German*]
**Im**.............. Imaginary [*Mathematics*]
**Im**.............. Imagination [*A publication*]
**Im**.............. Imago [*A publication*]
**IM**............. Imago Mundi [*A publication*]
**IM**............. Immature
**IM**............. Immuno-Suppression Method [*For increasing fertility*]
**IM**............. Impact Memorandum (MCD)
**IM**............. Imperial Measure
**I & M**........ Improvement and Modernization (AABC)
**IM**............. Impulse Modulation
**IM**............. In Maintenance
**IM**............. In-Use Maintenance Test
**IM**............. Income Maintenance (OICC)
**IM**............. Incontri Musicali [*A publication*]
**IM**............. Index Medicus [*A publication*]
**IM**............. Individual Medley [*Swimming*]
**IM**............. Indomethacin [*An analgesic*]
**IM**............. Induced Magnetization
**IM**............. Industrial Magistrate [*Australia*]
**IM**............. Industrial Management [*A publication*]
**IM**............. Industrial Manager
**IM**............. Industrial Minerals [*A publication*]
**IM**............. Industry Motion Picture [*FCC*] (MCD)
**IM**............. Infant Mortality (ROG)
**IM**............. Infantile Myofibromatosus [*Medicine*]
**IM**............. Infectious Mononucleosis [*Medicine*]
**IM**............. Informal Memorandum (MCD)
**IM**............. Information Manager
**IM**............. Information Manager [*A publication*]
**IM**............. Information Market [*Commission of the European Communities*] [*Information service or system*] (IID)
**IM**............. Information Memory (MCD)
**IM**............. Informes y Memorias de la Comisaria General de Excavaciones Arqueologicas [*A publication*]
**IM**............. Ingot Metallurgy
**IM**............. Initial Mass [*Agronomy*]
**IM**............. Injection Mold (MCD)
**IM**............. Inland Marine [*Insurance*]
**IM**............. Inner Marker [*Part of an instrument landing system*] [*Aviation*]
**I/M**........... Inside of Metal (MSA)
**I & M**........ Inspection and Maintenance
**IM**............. Inspection Manual (MCD)
**IM**............. Inspection Memorandum
**IM**............. Inspector of Machinery
**I & M**........ Installation and Maintenance
**IM**............. Institute of Marketing (EAIO)
**IM**............. Institute of Medicine [*National Academy of Sciences*]
**IM**............. Institution of Metallurgists [*British*]
**IM**............. Instruction Manual
**IM**............. Instruction Memory
**I of M**........ Instructor of Musketry [*British*]
**IM**............. Instrumentation (MDG)
**IM**............. Instrumentation Manager [*NASA*] (KSC)
**IM**............. Instrumentation and Measurement (MCD)
**IM**............. Instrumentman [*Navy rating*]
**IM**............. Insurance Magazine [*A publication*]
**IM**............. Integrated Master (NRCH)
**IM**............. Integrated MODEM
**IM**............. Integration Modified
**IM**............. Intelligence Memorandum
**IM**............. Intensity Measuring Devices [*JETDS nomenclature*] [*Military*] (CET)
**IM**............. Intensity Modulation
**IM**............. Inter Mirifica [*Decree on the Instruments of Social Communication*] [*Vatican II document*]
**IM**............. Interact Ministries [*An association*] (EA)
**IM**............. Interceptor Missile
**IM**............. Interdepartmental Memorandum (AAG)
**IM**............. Interface Module (MCD)
**IM**............. Interfaith Movement (EA)
**IM**............. Interim Memorandum
**IM**............. Intermediate Maintenance (MCD)
**IM**............. Intermediate Missile (MSA)
**IM**............. Intermediate Modulation
**IM**............. Intermediate Moisture (KSC)
**IM**............. Intermodulation
**IM**............. Internal Medicine
**IM**............. Internal Memorandum
**IM**............. International Journal of Instructional Media [*A publication*]
**IM**............. International Management [*A publication*]

**IM** ............ International Missions [*An association*] (EA)
**IM** ............ International Musician [*A publication*]
**IM** ............ Interrupt Mask
**IM** ............ Intestinal Metaplasia [*Medicine*]
**IM** ............ Intramedullary [*Medicine*]
**IM** ............ Intramural
**IM** ............ Intramuscular [*Injection*] [*Medicine*]
**IM** ............ Invasive Mole
**I/M** ........... Inventory Management [*Business term*]
**IM** ............ Inventory Manager [*Military*]
**IM** ............ Inverted Microscope [*Instrumentation*]
**IM** ............ Invicta International Airlines Ltd. [*Great Britain*] [*ICAO designator*] (FAAC)
**IM** ............ Invisible Ministry (EA)
**IM** ............ Iowa Mountaineers (EA)
**IM** ............ Iraq Museum (BJA)
**IM** ............ Irish Marquis (ROG)
**I of M** ........ Isle Of Man [*England*]
**IM** ............ Isle Of Man [*England*]
**IM** ............ Israel Museum (BJA)
**IM** ............ Istanbuler Mitteilungen [*A publication*] (BJA)
**IM** ............ Item Management
**IM** ............ Item Mark (BUR)
**IM1** ........... Instrumentman, First Class [*Navy rating*]
**IM2** ........... Instrumentman, Second Class [*Navy rating*]
**IM3** ........... Instrumentman, Third Class [*Navy rating*]
**IMA** ........... Iamalele [*Papua New Guinea*] [*Airport symbol*] (OAG)
**IMA** ........... IMCERA Group [*NYSE symbol*] (SPSG)
**IMA** ........... Immobilized Metal Affinity [*Protein chromatography*]
**IMA** ........... Impedance Matching Attenuator
**IMA** ........... Independent Manufacturing Assessment (MCD)
**IMA** ........... Indian Military Academy
**IMA** ........... Indian Mountain [*Alaska*] [*Seismograph station code, US Geological Survey*] (SEIS)
**IMA** ........... Individual Mobilization Augmentation [*DoD*]
**IMA** ........... Industrial Marketing Associates (EA)
**IMA** ........... Industrial Medical Association [*Later, AOMA*] (EA)
**IMA** ........... Inferior Mesenteric Artery [*Anatomy*]
**IMA** ........... Information Medicale Automatisee [*Automated Medical Information*] [*INSERM*] [*Information service or system*] (IID)
**IMA** ........... Information Mission Area
**IMA** ........... Initial Military Assistance (CINC)
**IMA** ........... Input Message Acknowledgment [*Data processing*]
**IMA** ........... Installation Maintenance Activity (MCD)
**IMA** ........... Institute of Management Accounting (EA)
**IMA** ........... Institute for Mathematics and Its Applications [*University of Minnesota*] [*Research center*] (RCD)
**IMA** ........... Institute of Mathematics and Its Applications [*South-End-On-Sea, England*] (CSR)
**IMA** ........... Institute for Media Analysis (EA)
**IMA** ........... Institute for Mediterranean Affairs (EA)
**IMA** ........... Institute of Mercantile Agents [*Australia*]
**IMA** ........... Institute for Military Assistance [*Army*]
**IMA** ........... Instituto Magdelena Aulina [*Magdalena Aulina Institute*] [*Barcelona, Spain*] (EAIO)
**IMA** ........... Instituts Mitteilungen [*A publication*]
**IMA** ........... Inter-Mountain Airways [*Boulder, CO*] [*FAA designator*] (FAAC)
**IMA** ........... Interbank Merchants Association [*Pigeon Forge, TN*] (EA)
**IMA** ........... Interchurch Medical Assistance (EA)
**IMA** ........... Interface Management Agent (MCD)
**IMA** ........... Intermediate Maintenance Activity
**IMA** ........... Internal Mammary Artery (Implant) [*Medicine*]
**IMA** ........... International Magnesium Association (EA)
**IMA** ........... International Maintenance Agency
**IMA** ........... International Management Association [*Later, AMA/I*] (EA)
**IMA** ........... International Medical Assistance [*Society*]
**IMA** ........... International Message Centre [*Vancouver Stock Exchange symbol*]
**IMA** ........... International Metaphysical Association (EA)
**IMA** ........... International MIDI [*Musical Instrument Digital Interface*] Association (EA)
**IMA** ........... International Military Archives (EA)
**IMA** ........... International Milling Association [*See also AIM*] [*Brussels, Belgium*] (EAIO)
**IMA** ........... International Mineralogical Association [*ICSU*] [*Marburg, Federal Republic of Germany*] (EA)
**IMA** ........... International Minilab Association (EA)
**IMA** ........... International Mobjack Association (EA)
**IMA** ........... International Mohair Association (EAIO)
**IMA** ........... International Music Association
**IMA** ........... International Mycological Association [*See also AIM*] [*England*] (EAIO)
**IMA** ........... International Mycophagist Association (EA)
**IMA** ........... Invalid Memory Address [*Data processing*]
**I & MA** ....... Inventory and Management Analysis (AFM)
**IMA** ........... Ion Microprobe Analyzer
**IMA** ........... Irish Medical Association
**IMA** ........... Islamic Medical Association (EA)
**IMA** ........... Islamic Mission of America (EA)
**IMA** ........... Issues Management Association (EA)
**IMAA** ......... Imidazoleacetic Acid [*Biochemistry*]
**IMAA** ......... Industrial Medical Administrators' Association [*Later, OMAA*] (EA)
**IMAA** ......... Institute for Mediterranean Art and Archaeology [*Defunct*] (EA)
**IMAA** ......... Intelligence Mission Area Analysis [*Military*] (MCD)
**IMAA** ......... International Marketing Audit Association (EA)
**IMAAWS** ... Infantry Manportable Antiarmor Weapon System
**IMAC** ......... Integrated Microwave Amplifier Converter
**IMAC** ......... International Marine and Air Catering [*A publication*]
**IMAC** ......... International Movement of Apostolate of Children [*Paris, France*] (EA)
**IMACA** ...... International Mobile Air Conditioning Association (EA)
**IMACE** ...... Association des Industries Margarinieres des Pays de la CEE [*Association of Margarine Industries of the EEC Countries*] [*Belgium*]
**IMacoW** ..... Western Illinois University, Macomb, IL [*Library symbol*] [*Library of Congress*] (LCLS)
**IMACS** ...... International Association for Mathematics and Computers in Simulation (EA)
**IMAD** ........ Integrated Multisensor Airborne Display
**IMad** .......... Madison Public Library, Madison, IL [*Library symbol*] [*Library of Congress*] (LCLS)
**IMadCU** .... Madison Community, Unit 12, Madison, IL [*Library symbol*] [*Library of Congress*] (LCLS)
**IMAF** ......... International Martial Arts Federation (EAIO)
**IMAG** ........ Image Retailing Group, Inc. [*NASDAQ symbol*] (NQ)
**IMAG** ........ Imaginary (MSA)
**Imag** .......... Imagines [*of Philostratus*] [*Classical studies*] (OCD)
**IMAG** ........ Instituut voor Mechanisatie, Arbeid en Gebouwen [*Institute of Agricultural Engineering*] [*Information service or system*] (IID)
**IMAGE** ...... Institute for Molecular and Agricultural Genetic Engineering [*University of Idaho*] [*Research center*]
**IMAGE** ...... Instruction in Motivation Achievement and General Education [*YMCA program*]
**IMAGE** ...... Intruder Monitoring and Guidance Equipment (MCD)
**Image Dyn Sci Med** ... Image Dynamics in Science and Medicine [*A publication*]
**Image J Nurs Sch** ... Image. Journal of Nursing Scholarship [*A publication*]
**Image & S** .. Image et Son [*A publication*]
**IMAGES** ... Instructional Material Adequacy Guide and Evaluation Standard (RDA)
**IMAGES** ... Instrumental Manual Adequacy Guide and Evaluation Standard
**IMAGES** ... Interactive Modal Analysis and Gain Estimation for Eigensystem [*NASA digital computer program*]
**Images Marquette Univ Dent Reflections** ... Images. Marquette University Dental Reflections [*A publication*]
**Image Technol** ... Image Technology [*A publication*]
**Image Vis C** ... Image and Vision Computing [*A publication*]
**IMah** .......... Mahomet Township Public Library, Mahomet, IL [*Library symbol*] [*Library of Congress*] (LCLS)
**IMA (Inst Math Appl) J Math Appl Med Biol** ... IMA (Institute of Mathematics and Its Applications) Journal of Mathematics Applied in Medicine and Biology [*A publication*]
**IMAJ** ......... Initiative d'Un Mouvement d'Animation Jeunesse pour l'Annee Internationale de la Jeunesse en 1985 [*Canada*]
**IMA J Appl Math** ... IMA [*Institute of Mathematics and Its Applications*] Journal of Applied Mathematics [*A publication*]
**IMA J Numer Anal** ... IMA [*Institute of Mathematics and Its Applications*] Journal of Numerical Analysis [*London*] [*A publication*]
**IMan** .......... Blue Ridge Township Public Library, Mansfield, IL [*Library symbol*] [*Library of Congress*] (LCLS)
**IMAN** ........ International Mail Art Network (EA)
**IMANCO** .. Image Analysing Computers, Inc.
**IMANF** ...... Institute of Manufacturing [*Royal Leamington Spa, Warwickshire, England*] (EAIO)
**IMAO** ........ International Military Assistance Office
**IMAP** ......... Immediately after Passing [*Aviation*] (FAAC)
**IMAPPA** ... International Martial Arts Pen Pal Association (EA)
**IMAR** ........ Imark Industries, Inc. [*NASDAQ symbol*] (NQ)
**IMar** .......... Markham Public Library, Markham, IL [*Library symbol*] [*Library of Congress*] (LCLS)
**IMARD** ..... Industrial Marketing [*Later, Business Marketing*] [*A publication*]
**IMarE** ........ Institute of Marine Engineers [*British*] [*Database producer*]
**IMars** ......... Marshall Public Library, Marshall, IL [*Library symbol*] [*Library of Congress*] (LCLS)
**IMarse** ....... Marseilles Public Library, Marseilles, IL [*Library symbol*] [*Library of Congress*] (LCLS)
**IMarseHS** ... Marseilles High School, Marseilles, IL [*Library symbol*] [*Library of Congress*] (LCLS)
**IMarseMSD** ... Miller Township Consolidated Community, School District 210, Marseilles, IL [*Library symbol*] [*Library of Congress*] (LCLS)
**IMART** ...... International Medical Association for Radio and Television [*Brussels, Belgium*] (EAIO)
**IMart** ......... Martinsville Township Library, Martinsville, IL [*Library symbol*] [*Library of Congress*] (LCLS)

**IMaryR**...... Maryville Reading Center, Maryville, IL [*Library symbol*] [*Library of Congress*] (LCLS)
**IMAS**......... Impurity Monitoring and Analysis System [*Nuclear energy*] (NRCH)
**IMAS**......... Industrial Management Assistance Survey [*Air Force*]
**IMAS**......... International Marine and Shipping Conference (NOAA)
**IMas**.......... Mascoutah Public Library, Mascoutah, IL [*Library symbol*] [*Library of Congress*] (LCLS)
**IMASDR**... Mississippi. Agricultural and Forestry Experiment Station. Information Sheet [*A publication*]
**IMasHS**..... Mascoutah High School, Mascoutah, IL [*Library symbol*] [*Library of Congress*] (LCLS)
**IMA Spec Rep**... International Management Association. Special Report [*A publication*]
**IMAT**........ Imatron, Inc. [*NASDAQ symbol*] (NQ)
**IMAT**........ Integrated, Modification and Trial
**IMAT**........ Interim Maintenance Assistance Team (MCD)
**IMAT**........ International Mechanism for Appropriate Technology
**IMATA**...... Independent Military Air Transport Association [*Later, Independent Airlines Association*]
**IMatH**....... Memorial Hospital District Library, Mattoon, IL [*Library symbol*] [*Library of Congress*] (LCLS)
**IMatL**........ Sara Bush Lincoln Health Center, Mattoon, IL [*Library symbol*] [*Library of Congress*] (LCLS)
**ImatLC**...... Lake Land College, Mattoon, IL [*Library symbol*] [*Library of Congress*] (LCLS)
**IMatt**.......... Matteson Public Library, Matteson, IL [*Library symbol*] [*Library of Congress*] (LCLS)
**IMAU**........ International Movement for Atlantic Union (EA)
**IMAV**........ Intermediate Maintenance Availability
**IMAW**........ International Molders' and Allied Workers' Union [*AFL-CIO*]
**IM & AWU**... International Molders' and Allied Workers' Union [*AFL-CIO*] (EA)
**IMAX**........ Image-Maximum [*Photography*]
**IMay**.......... Maywood Public Library, Maywood, IL [*Library symbol*] [*Library of Congress*] (LCLS)
**IMB**........... Imbaimadai [*Guyana*] [*Airport symbol*] (OAG)
**IMB**........... Independent Mixed Brigade [*Military*]
**IMB**........... Independent Mortar Battery [*British military*] (DMA)
**IMB**........... Indian Mountain Battery [*British military*] (DMA)
**IMB**........... Input Memory Buffer [*Data processing*]
**IMB**........... Institute for Marine Biochemistry [*British*]
**IMB**........... Institute of Microbiology
**IMB**........... Institute of Molecular Biophysics [*Florida State University*] [*Research center*] (RCD)
**IMB**........... Instrument Material Bulletin (MCD)
**IMB**........... Intercontinental Medical Book Corp.
**IMB**........... Intermenstrual Bleeding [*Medicine*]
**IMB**........... Intermountain Tariff Bureau, Inc., Salt Lake City UT [*STAC*]
**IMB**........... International Maritime Bureau [*Research center*] [*Great Britain*] (IRC)
**IMB**........... International Medieval Bibliography [*A publication*]
**IMB**........... International Merchant Bank Ltd. [*Nigerian*]
**IMB**........... International Mission Board (EA)
**IMB**........... Internationaler Metalarbeiterbund [*International Metalworkers' Federation*]
**IMB**........... Irvine/Michigan/Brookhaven [*Experiment on proton decay*]
**IMB**........... Kimberly, OR [*Location identifier*] [*FAA*] (FAAL)
**IMBA**........ International Media Buyers Association [*Defunct*] (EA)
**IMBA**........ International Morab Breeders Association (EA)
**IMBA**........ International Mountain Bicycling Association (EA)
**IMBB**......... Institute of Molecular Biology and Biochemistry [*Simon Fraser University*] [*Canada*]
**IMBC**......... Indirect Maximum Breathing Capacity [*Medicine*]
**IMBE**......... Institute for Minority Business Education [*Defunct*] (EA)
**IMBEX**...... International Men's and Boys' Wear Exhibition
**IMBI**.......... Institute of Medical and Biological Illustration [*British*]
**IMBLMS**.. Integrated Medical and Behavioral Laboratory Measurement System
**IMBM**....... Institute of Municipal Building Management [*British*]
**IMBMA**..... Izvestiya na Instituta po Morfologiya. Bulgarska Akademiya na Naukite [*A publication*]
**IMBO**........ Indian and Metis Brotherhood Organization
**IMBR**......... Institute of Marine Biomedical Research [*University of North Carolina at Wilmington*] [*Research center*] (RCD)
**IMBS**......... Individual Motor Behavior Survey [*Test*]
**IMBT**......... Iron Masters Board of Trade
**IMC**........... Chief Instrumentman [*Navy rating*]
**IMC**........... Image Motion Compensation [*or Compensator*]
**IMC**........... Image Motion Configuration
**IMC**........... Imco Resources Ltd. [*Vancouver Stock Exchange symbol*]
**IMC**........... Incident Management Center [*Nuclear Regulatory Commission*] (NRCH)
**IMC**........... Industrial Metal Containers Section of the Material Handling Institute (EA)
**ImC**........... Industrial Microfilm Company, Detroit, MI [*Library symbol*] [*Library of Congress*] (LCLS)
**IMC**........... Information Management Consultants [*Database producer*] (IID)
**IMC**........... Initial Marks [*Held*] Constant [*Psychology*]
**IMC**........... Inspection Method Control
**IMC**........... Institute of Management Consultants [*New York, NY*] (EA)
**IMC**........... Institute of Measurement and Control [*British*]
**IMC**........... Instructional Materials Center
**IMC**........... Instrument [*Flight*] Meteorological Conditions [*Aviation*]
**IMC**........... Integrated Maintenance Chart [*or Concept*]
**IMC**........... Integrated Microelectronic Circuitry (AAG)
**IMC**........... Integrated Microwave Circuit
**IMC**........... Integrated Monolithic Circuit
**IMC**........... Integrated Multiplexer Channel
**IMC**........... Intelligent Matrix Control [*T-Bar, Inc.*]
**IMC**........... Interactive Module Controller
**IMC**........... Intercollegiate Men's Chorus, a National Association of Male Choruses (EA)
**IMC**........... Interdigestive Myoelectric Complex [*Gastroenterology*]
**IMC**........... Interim Message Change
**IMC**........... INTERMARC [*International Machine-Readable Cataloging*] [*French National Library*] [*Source file*] [*UTLAS symbol*]
**IMC**........... Intermetallic Matrix Composite [*Materials science*]
**IMC**........... Internal Model Control [*Chemical engineering*] [*Data processing*]
**IMC**........... International Conference Management, Inc. [*Telecommunications service*] (TSSD)
**IMC**........... International Information Management Congress (EA)
**IMC**........... International Magazine Collection [*JA Micropublishing, Inc.*] [*Eastchester, NY*] [*Information service or system*] (IID)
**IMC**........... International Mailbag Club (EA)
**IMC**........... International Maintenance Control [*Telecommunications*]
**IMC**........... International Management Communications, Inc. [*Database producer*]
**IMC**........... International Management Council (EA)
**IMC**........... International Maritime Committee
**IMC**........... International Marketing Commission [*See also CIM*] [*Brixham, Devonshire, England*] (EAIO)
**IMC**........... International Materials Conference (DCTA)
**IMC**........... International Medical Centers
**IMC**........... International Medical Corps (EA)
**IMC**........... International Meteorological Committee
**IMC**........... International Micrographic Congress (EA)
**IMC**........... International Minerals & Chemical Corp.
**IMC**........... International Missionary Council [*Later, CWME*]
**IMC**........... International Monetary Conference (ECON)
**IMC**........... International Multifoods Corporation [*NYSE symbol*] (SPSG)
**IMC**........... International Music Council [*Paris, France*] (EA)
**IMC**........... Intestinal Mast Cells [*Anatomy*]
**IMC**........... Inventory Management Center (MCD)
**IMC**........... Item Management Coding [*Military*] (AABC)
**IMC**........... Item Management Concept
**IMC**........... Item Master Card [*Military*] (AABC)
**IMC**........... Marion College, Marion, IN [*OCLC symbol*] (OCLC)
**IMC**........... Preparatory Committee for the International Medical Commission for Health and Human Rights (EAIO)
**IMCA**........ Indian Major Crimes Act [*1909*]
**IMCA**........ Indian Motorcycle Club of America (EA)
**IMCA**........ Information Management and Consulting Association [*Information service or system*] (IID)
**IMCA**........ Insurance Marketing Communications Association (EA)
**IMCA**........ International Motor Contest Association (EA)
**IMCA**........ Investment Management Consultants Association (EA)
**IMCAB**...... Internal Mammary Coronary Artery Bypass [*Cardiology*]
**IMCAR**...... International Movement of Catholic Agricultural and Rural Youth [*See also MIJARC*]
**IMCARY**... International Movement of Catholic Agricultural and Rural Youth [*See also MIJARC*] [*Louvain, Belgium*] (EAIO)
**IMCAS**...... Interactive Man/Computer Augmentation System
**IMCAST**... Instructor Model Characteristics for Automated Speech Technology (MCD)
**IMCA-US**... International Moth Class Association - US (EA)
**IMCC**......... Image Motion Compensation and Calibration
**IMCC**......... Integrated Mission Control Center [*NASA*]
**IMCC**......... Interstate Mining Compact Commission (EA)
**IMCC**......... Item Management Control Code (AABC)
**IMcc**........... McCook Public Library District, McCook, IL [*Library symbol*] [*Library of Congress*] (LCLS)
**IMccA**........ Armak Co., McCook, IL [*Library symbol*] [*Library of Congress*] (LCLS)
**IMCCSRA**... International MC Class Sailboat Racing Association (EA)
**IMCD**........ Inner Medullary Collecting Ducts [*Kidney anatomy*]
**IMCD**........ Input Marginal Checking and Distribution
**IMCE**......... Institute for Molecular and Cellular Evolution [*University of Miami*] [*Research center*] (RCD)
**IMCE**......... Instituto Mexicano de Comercio Exterior [*Mexican Foreign Trade Institute*]
**IMCE**......... International Meeting of Cataloging Experts
**IMCEA**....... International Military Club Executives Association (EA)
**IMCHAZ**.. Immunochemistry [*A publication*]
**IMCI**.......... Individual and Marriage Counseling Inventory [*Psychology*]
**IMC J**........ IMC [*International Micrographic Congress*] Journal [*A publication*]
**IMCJ**......... International Movement of Catholic Jurists (EAIO)
**IMC Jrnl**... IMC [*International Information Management Congress*] Journal [*A publication*]

**IMCM**....... In Medio Currere Metuo [*I Fear to Go in the Middle*] [*Latin*] [*Motto of Julius, Duke of Braunschweig-Wolfenbuttel (1529-89)*]
**IMCM**....... Master Chief Instrumentman [*Navy rating*]
**IMCO**........ Improved Combustion
**IMCO**........ Intergovernmental Maritime Consultative Organization [*Later, IMO*]
**IMCO**........ International Maritime Consultive Organization
**IMCO**........ International Metered Communications
**IMCO**........ Interwest Medical Corporation [*Fort Worth, TX*] [*NASDAQ symbol*] (NQ)
**IMCoS**....... International Map Collectors' Society (EAIO)
**IMCP**......... Integrated Monitor and Control Panel (MCD)
**IMCP**......... Item Management Coding Program [*Military*] (AFM)
**IMCR**......... Institute for Mediation and Conflict Resolution (EA)
**IMC/RMC**... Instructional Materials Centers/Regional Media Centers
**IMCS**......... Pax Romana, International Movement of Catholic Students [*See also MIEC*] [*Fribourg, Switzerland*] [*Paris, France*] (EAIO)
**IMCS**......... Senior Chief Instrumentman [*Navy rating*]
**IMCSAC**... International Movement of Catholic Students - African Secretariat [*An association*] (EAIO)
**IMcSC**....... John Swaney Attendance Center, McNabb, IL [*Library symbol*] [*Library of Congress*] (LCLS)
**IMCSMHI**... Industrial Metal Containers Section of the Material Handling Institute (EA)
**IMCSRS**.... Installation Materiel Condition Status Reporting System [*Army*]
**IMCVA9**.... Investigaciones Marinas. Universidad Catolica de Valparaiso [*A publication*]
**IMCWR**..... International Movement of Conscientious War Resisters [*Tel Aviv, Israel*] (EAIO)
**IM & D**...... Image Mapping and Display (NOAA)
**IMD**.......... Immunologically Mediated Disease [*Medicine*]
**IMD**.......... Imo Industries, Inc. [*NYSE symbol*] (SPSG)
**IMD**.......... Imonda [*Papua New Guinea*] [*Airport symbol*] (OAG)
**IMD**.......... Indian Medical Department [*British military*] (DMA)
**IMD**.......... Indianapolis-Marion County Public Library, Indianapolis, IN [*OCLC symbol*] (OCLC)
**IMD**.......... Industrial Marketing Management [*A publication*]
**IMD**.......... Inertia-Measuring Device [*Mechanical engineering*]
**IMD**.......... Inhibit Momentum Dump
**IMD**.......... Institute for Muscle Disease [*Defunct*] (EA)
**IMD**.......... Intercept Monitoring Display
**IMD**.......... Intermediate (NASA)
**IMD**.......... Intermittent Motion Driver
**IMD**.......... Intermodulation Distortion (MSA)
**IMD**.......... International Market Development Program [*Department of Energy*]
**IMD**.......... International MTM [*Methods-Time-Measurement*] Directorate (EA)
**IMD**.......... Ion Mobility Detector [*Instrumentation*]
**IMD**.......... Isove's Modified Dulbrecco's Medium [*Oncology*]
**IMDA**........ Independent Medical Distributors Association (EA)
**IMDA**........ Indian Mineral Development Act of 1982
**IMDA**........ International Magic Dealers Association (EA)
**IMDA**........ International Mail Dealers Association (EA)
**IMDA**........ International Map Dealers Association (EA)
**IMDB**........ Integrated Maintenance Database (MCD)
**IMDC**........ Inamed Corp. [*NASDAQ symbol*] (NQ)
**IMDC**........ Instructional Media Distribution Center [*University of Wisconsin - Madison*] [*Research center*] (RCD)
**IMDC**........ Interceptor Missile Direction Center
**IMDC**........ Internal Message Distribution Center (NATG)
**IMDD**........ Idiopathic Midline Destructive Disease [*Dentistry*]
**IMDEG**..... Insurance Management Decision Game
**IMDES**...... Item Management Data Element Standardization [*or System*] [*Military*]
**IMDG**........ International Maritime Dangerous Goods
**IMDGC**..... International Maritime Dangerous Goods Code (MCD)
**IMDI**......... International Management and Development Institute
**IMDJBD**... Irish Medical Journal [*A publication*]
**IMDM**....... Iscove's Modified Dulbecco's Medium [*For nematode culture*]
**IMDO**........ Installation and Materiel District Office [*FAA*]
**IMDO**........ Intelligence Material Development Office [*Military*] (MCD)
**IMDQ**........ Injected Minimum Detectable Quantity [*Analytical chemistry*]
**IMDS**......... International Meat Development Scheme [*United Nations*] (EAIO)
**IMDSO**..... Intelligence Materiel Development and Support Office [*Army*] (RDA)
**IMD Spec Rep Ser**... IMD [*Institute of Metal Division. American Institute of Mining, Metallurgical, and Petroleum Engineers*] Special Report Series [*A publication*]
**IMDT**........ Immediate (FAAC)
**IMDT**........ International Institute for Music, Dance, and Theatre in the Audio-Visual Media [*Later, Mediacult International Institute for Audio-Visual Communication and Cultural Development*]
**IMDur**....... Inscriptiones Mithriacae Duranae (BJA)
**IME**........... Incendiary Munitions Evaluation
**IME**........... Independent Medical Examination [*British*]
**IME**........... Indirect Manufacturing Expense
**IME**........... Information Management & Engineering Ltd. [*Information service or system*] (IID)
**IME**........... Institute of Makers of Explosives (EA)
**IME**........... Institute of Marine Engineers [*British*]
**IME**........... Institute of Mechanical Engineers [*British*]
**IME**........... Institute on the Military and the Economy (EA)
**IME**........... Institute of Mining Engineers [*British*]
**IME**........... Institute for Municipal Engineering
**IME**........... Insurance, Mathematics, and Economics [*A publication*]
**IME**........... International Magnetospheric Explorer [*NASA/ESRO*]
**IME**........... International Materiel Evaluation Program [*Army*] (RDA)
**IME**........... International Medical Exchange [*Defunct*] (EA)
**IME**........... International Microcomputer Exposition
**IME**........... International Mirtone, Inc. [*Toronto Stock Exchange symbol*]
**IME**........... Interplanetary Meteoroid Experiment [*NASA*]
**IME**........... Iparmueveszeti Muzeum Evkoenyvei [*A publication*]
**IME**........... Mennonite Biblical Seminary Library, Elkhart, IN [*OCLC symbol*] (OCLC)
**IMEA**........ International Middle East Association (EA)
**IMEAC**...... Northeast Interagency Motor Equipment Advisory Committee [*Terminated, 1981*] [*General Services Administration*] (EGAO)
**IMEB**......... International Movement of Esperantist Bicyclists [*See also BEMI*] [*The Hague, Netherlands*] (EAIO)
**IMEC**......... Institut Mondial d'Ecologie et de Cancerologie [*World Institute of Ecology and Cancer - WIEC*] (EAIO)
**IMEC**......... Interstate Migrant Education Council (EA)
**I Mech E**.... Institution of Mechanical Engineers [*British*]
**IMECO**..... Intreprinderea de Comert Exterior [*Foreign Trade Enterprise*] [*Romanian*]
**IMed**.......... Index Medicus [*A publication*]
**IMEG**........ International Management and Engineering Group [*British*]
**IMEIDH**... Investigacion Medica Internacional [*A publication*]
**IMEKO**..... Internationale Messtechnische Konfoderation [*International Measurement Confederation*] [*ICSU*] [*Budapest, Hungary*] (EAIO)
**IMel**........... Melvin Public Library, Melvin, IL [*Library symbol*] [*Library of Congress*] (LCLS)
**IMelp**......... Melrose Park Public Library, Melrose Park, IL [*Library symbol*] [*Library of Congress*] (LCLS)
**IMelpA**...... Alberto-Culver Co., Melrose Park, IL [*Library symbol*] [*Library of Congress*] (LCLS)
**IMEM**....... Improved Minimum Essential Medium [*Microbiology*]
**IMEM**....... International Mass Education Movement (EA)
**IMEMME**... Institution of Mining Electrical and Mining Mechanical Engineers (EAIO)
**IMen**.......... Graves Public Library, Mendota, IL [*Library symbol*] [*Library of Congress*] (LCLS)
**IMenHS**.... Mendota High School, Mendota, IL [*Library symbol*] [*Library of Congress*] (LCLS)
**IMenN**....... Northbrook Elementary School, Mendota, IL [*Library symbol*] [*Library of Congress*] (LCLS)
**IMEO**........ Initial Mass in Earth Orbit [*NASA*]
**IMEO**........ Interim Maintenance Engineering Order (AAG)
**IMEP**......... Indicated Mean Effective Pressure [*Aerospace*]
**IMEP**......... International Materiel Evaluation Program [*Army*] (RDA)
**IMER**......... Immobilized-Enzyme Reactor
**IMER**......... Institute for Marine Environmental Research [*British*] (ARC)
**IMerD**........ Meredosia-Chambersburg River Valley Public Library District, Meredosia, IL [*Library symbol*] [*Library of Congress*] (LCLS)
**IMES**......... Integrated Missile Electronics Set
**IMET**......... Intermetrics, Inc. [*NASDAQ symbol*] (NQ)
**IMET**......... International Military Education and Training [*Program of grant military training in the United States for foreign military and civilian personnel*]
**IMETP**...... International Military Education and Training Program [*DoD*]
**IMEX**......... Imex Medical Systems, Inc. [*NASDAQ symbol*] (NQ)
**IMEX**......... Integrated Manufacturing Exposition [*Penton/IPC*] (TSPED)
**IMF**............ Allen County Public Library, Fort Wayne, IN [*OCLC symbol*] (OCLC)
**IMF**............ Immunofixation [*Analytical biochemistry*]
**IMF**............ Immunofluorescent [*Immunology*]
**IMF**............ Impact Mechanical Fuse (MCD)
**IMF**............ Imphal [*India*] [*Airport symbol*] (OAG)
**IMF**............ Impossible Mission Force [*Fictitious group of undercover agents in TV series, "Mission: Impossible"*]
**IMF**............ Individual Master File
**IMF**............ [*The*] Inefficient-Market Fund [*AMEX symbol*] (SPSG)
**IMF**............ Informatienieuws [*A publication*]
**IMF**............ Initial Mass Function [*Galactic science*]
**IMF**............ Installation Master File (MCD)
**IMF**............ [*The*] Institute of Metal Finishing [*British*]
**IMF**............ Institute for Metal Forming [*Lehigh University*] [*Research center*] (RCD)
**IMF**............ Integrated Maintenance Facility
**IMF**............ Intense Magnetic Field
**IMF**............ Intermediate Maintenance Facility
**IMF**............ Intermediate Moisture Food
**IMF**............ Internal Magnetic Focus

**IMF**........... International Marketing Federation [*Paris, France*] (EAIO)
**IMF**........... International Metalworkers Federation [*See also FIOM*] [*Geneva, Switzerland*] (EAIO)
**IMF**........... International Ministerial Federation [*Defunct*] (EA)
**IMF**........... International Monetary Fund (EA)
**IMF**........... International Monetary Fund. Staff Papers [*A publication*]
**IMF**........... International Myomassethics Federation (EA)
**IMF**........... Interplanetary Magnetic Field
**IMF**........... Interrogation Sign [*Question mark*] [*Aviation code*] (FAAC)
**IMF**........... Inventory Master File (NASA)
**IMF**........... Israel Music Foundation (EA)
**IMF**........... Iuliu Maniu American Romanian Relief Foundation (EA)
**i-mf---**......... Mauritius [*MARC geographic area code*] [*Library of Congress*] (LCCP)
**IMFC**......... Immaculate Mary Fan Club (EA)
**IMFC**......... Iron Maiden Fan Club [*London, England*] (EAIO)
**IMF F & D**... International Monetary Fund. Finance and Development [*A publication*]
**IMF/IBRD**... International Monetary Fund and International Bank for Reconstruction and Development
**IMFK**......... Integrated Multifunction Keyboard (MCD)
**IMFL**......... Inventory of Marriage and Family Literature [*Sage Publications, Inc.*] (IID)
**IMFP**......... Inelastic Mean Free [*or Face*] Path [*Surface analysis*]
**IMFP**......... Interaction Mean Free Path [*Astrophysics*]
**IMFR**......... Institute of Marriage and Family Relations (EA)
**IMFRAD**... Integrated Multifrequency RADAR (MCD)
**IMFS**......... Interstate Motor Freight System [*NASDAQ symbol*] (NQ)
**IMF/SP**..... Staff Papers. International Monetary Fund [*A publication*]
**IMFSS**....... Integrated Missile Flight Safety System
**IMF Staff Pa**... International Monetary Fund. Staff Papers [*A publication*]
**IMF Svy**..... IMF [*International Monetary Fund*] Survey [*A publication*]
**IMF Symp Publ**... IMF [*Institute of Metal Finishing*] Symposium. Publication [*A publication*]
**IMFU**........ Imperial Military Foul-Up [*Bowdlerized version*] (DSUE)
**IMFWUNA**... International Molders' and Foundry Workers' Union of North America [*Later, IM & AWU*]
**IMG**........... Image
**IMG**........... Immigration
**ImG**........... Immunogenetics
**IMG**........... Indian Medical Gazette [*A publication*]
**IMG**........... Inertial Measurement Group (KSC)
**IMG**........... Inferior Mesenteric Ganglia [*Anatomy*]
**IMG**........... Informational Media Guaranty
**IMG**........... Installation and Maintenance Guide
**IMG**........... International Management [*A publication*]
**IMG**........... International Management Group
**IMG**........... International Marxist Group [*British*] (PPW)
**IMG**........... International Music Guide [*A publication*]
**IMG**........... Mead Johnson & Co., Research Library, Evansville, IN [*OCLC symbol*] (OCLC)
**IMg**........... Morton Grove Public Library, Morton Grove, IL [*Library symbol*] [*Library of Congress*] (LCLS)
**IMG**........... Musicland Group [*NYSE symbol*] (SPSG)
**IMGCN**..... Integrated Missile Ground Control Network
**IMGCSA**... Islamic Missionaries Guild of the Caribbean and South America (EAIO)
**IMGE**........ IMNET, Inc. [*NASDAQ symbol*] (NQ)
**IMGI**......... Improved Maintenance Guidance Information
**IMGIA**....... Itogi Nauki i Tekhniki Mestorozhdeniya Goryuchikh Poleznykh Iskopaemykh [*A publication*]
**IMGN**........ ImmunoGen, Inc. [*NASDAQ symbol*] (NQ)
**IMgO**......... Oakton Community College, Morton Grove, IL [*Library symbol*] [*Library of Congress*] (LCLS)
**IMgO-Dp**... Oakton Community Colleges, Learning Resources Center, Des Plaines, IL [*Library symbol*] [*Library of Congress*] (LCLS)
**IMGR**........ International Movie Group, Inc. [*NASDAQ symbol*] (NQ)
**IMGT**........ Interim Missile Guidance Test (MCD)
**IMgT**......... Travenol Laboratories, Morton Grove, IL [*Library symbol*] [*Library of Congress*] (LCLS)
**IMGTechE**... Institution of Mechanical General Technician Engineers [*British*]
**IMH**........... Idiopathic Myocardial Hypertrophy [*Cardiology*]
**IMH**........... Indiana Magazine of History [*A publication*]
**IMH**........... Inlet Manhole [*Technical drawings*]
**IMH**........... Institut des Moeurs Humaines [*Institute of Human Values - IHV*] [*Canada*]
**IMH**........... International Majestic Holdings Ltd. [*Formerly, Majestic Resources Corp.*] [*Vancouver Stock Exchange symbol*]
**IMH**........... International Marketing Handbook [*A publication*]
**IMH**........... Itim Mizrah News Agency Hadashot. Current Comment [*A publication*]
**IMH**........... Mennonite Historical Library, Goshen College, Goshen, IN [*OCLC symbol*] (OCLC)
**IMHE**........ Industrial Materials Handling Equipment
**IMHEP**...... Ideal Man Helicopter Engineering Project
**IMHEPFC**... Idol of My Heart Elvis Presley Fan Club (EA)
**IMHP**........ Isopropyl Methyl Pyrimidinone [*Organic chemistry*]
**IMHQ**........ International Military Headquarters (CINC)
**IMHR**........ International Miniature Horse Registry (EA)
**IMHV**........ Intermediate and Medial Part of the Hyperstriatum Ventrale [*Bird brain anatomy*]
**IMI**........... ICAN Minerals Ltd. [*Toronto Stock Exchange symbol*]
**IMI**........... Ignition Manufacturers Institute [*Later, TMI*] (EA)
**ImI**........... IMI of Philadelphia, Camp Hill, PA [*Library symbol*] [*Library of Congress*] (LCLS)
**IMI**........... Imipramine [*Antidepressant*]
**IMI**........... Imperial Metal Industries Ltd. [*British*]
**IMI**........... Implantable Micro-Identification Device [*for laboratory animals*]
**IMI**........... Improved Manned Interceptor [*Proposed plane*] [*Air Force*]
**IMI**........... Incentives Management Index [*Test*]
**IMI**........... Ine [*Marshall Islands*] [*Airport symbol*] (OAG)
**IMI**........... Inferior Myocardial Infarction [*Cardiology*]
**IMI**........... Information Marketing International [*Information service or system*] (IID)
**IMI**........... Infrared Measurement Instrument
**IMI**........... Installation and Maintenance Instruction
**IMI**........... Institute for Marine Information (EA)
**IMI**........... Institute on Money and Inflation (EA)
**IMI**........... Integrally Molded Insulation
**IMI**........... Intensive Management Items (MCD)
**IMI**........... Intermark, Incorporated [*AMEX symbol*] (SPSG)
**IMI**........... Intermediate Machine Instruction
**IMI**........... Intermediate Manned Interceptor (MUGU)
**IMI**........... International Maintenance Institute (EA)
**IMI**........... International Management Information [*A publication*]
**IMI**........... International Management Institute [*Switzerland*]
**IMI**........... International Maple Institute
**IMI**........... International Marketing Institute (EA)
**IMI**........... International Masonry Institute (EA)
**IMI**........... International Ministries to Israel (EA)
**IMI**........... International Missions (EA)
**IMI**........... Interrogation Sign [*Question mark*] [*Communications*] (FAAC)
**IMI**........... Intraoperative Myocardial Ischemia [*Cardiology*]
**IMI**........... Invention Marketing, Incorporated [*Information service or system*] (IID)
**IMI**........... Invention Marketing Institute (EA)
**IMI**........... Investment Management Institute [*Information service or system*] (IID)
**IMI**........... Ion Microwelding Instrument
**IMI**........... Israeli Military Industry
**IMI**........... Marian College, Indianapolis, IN [*OCLC symbol*] (OCLC)
**IMIA**.......... Institute of Mathematics and Its Applications [*South-End-On-Sea, England*]
**IMIA**.......... International Machinery Insurers Association [*Munich, Federal Republic of Germany*] (EAIO)
**IMIA**.......... International Medical Informatics Association [*IFIP special interest group*] [*Richmond Hill, ON*] (EAIO)
**IMIAT**....... International Masonry Institute Apprenticeship and Training (EA)
**IMIB**.......... Inland Marine Insurance Bureau [*Later, ISO*] (EA)
**IMIC**.......... Independent Medical Insurance Consultants Ltd. [*British*]
**IMIC**.......... International Medical Information Center, Inc. [*Tokyo, Japan*]
**IMIC**.......... International Music Industry Conference
**IMID**.......... Inadvertent Missile Ignition Detection
**IMid**.......... Midlothian Public Library, Midlothian, IL [*Library symbol*] [*Library of Congress*] (LCLS)
**IMIDB**....... Instrumentation in the Mining and Metallurgy Industries [*A publication*]
**IMIDCA**.... Interim Motorized Infantry Division Capability Analysis [*Military*]
**IMIE**.......... Institution of Mining Engineers [*British*]
**IMIF**.......... International Maritime Industries Forum [*London, England*] (EAIO)
**IMil**........... Milford Township Public Library, Milford, IL [*Library symbol*] [*Library of Congress*] (LCLS)
**IMilsSD**..... Millstadt Community Consolidated School District 160, Millstadt, IL [*Library symbol*] [*Library of Congress*] (LCLS)
**IMiM**......... Inner Mitochondrial Membrane [*Cytology*]
**IMIMI**....... Industrial Mineral Insulation Manufacturers Institute [*Later, TIMA*]
**IMIND**...... Immunitaet und Infektion [*A publication*]
**IMINDI**..... Immunitaet und Infektion [*A publication*]
**IMinE**........ Institution of Mining Engineers [*British*]
**IMINEJ**.... Immunological Investigations [*A publication*]
**IMINICO**... Iranian Marine International Oil Company
**IMINT**....... Imaging Intelligence [*RADAR, photos, etc.*]
**IMIP**.......... Industrial Management Improvement Program (NG)
**IMIP**.......... Industrial Modernization Incentive Program [*DoD*]
**IMIR**.......... Interceptor Missile Interrogation RADAR
**IMIS**.......... Installation Management Information System [*Army*]
**IMIS**.......... Integrated Management Information System [*Air Force*]
**IMIS**.......... Integrated Motorists' Information System [*Computerized guidance system to speed traffic and avoid tie-ups*]
**IMIS**.......... Intelligence Management Information System [*Military*] (MCD)
**IMIT**.......... Imitation (MSA)
**IMIT**.......... IMT, Inc. [*New York, NY*] [*NASDAQ symbol*] (NQ)

**IM-IT** ........ Insured Municipals-Income Trust [*Investment term*]
**IMIT** ......... Izraelita Magyar Irodalmi Tarsulat Evkonyv [*A publication*]
**IMITAC** .... Image Input to Automatic Computers
**I Mitt** ......... Istanbuler Mitteilungen [*A publication*]
**IMIX** ......... Imaging Workstation in X-Ray Microanalysis
**IMJ** ........... Illinois Medical Journal [*A publication*]
**IMJ** ........... Illustrierte Monatshefte fuer die Gesammten Interessen des Judentums [*A publication*]
**IMJ** ........... Infrared Miniaturized Jammer
**IMJ** ........... RCA [*Radio Corp. of America*] Consumer Electronics Library, Indianapolis, IN [*OCLC symbol*] (OCLC)
**IMK** ........... Incentive Marketing [*A publication*]
**IMK** ........... Income Monitoring Kit
**IMK** ........... Increased Maneuverability Kit
**IMK** ........... Industrial Marketing [*Later, Business Marketing*] [*A publication*]
**IMK** ........... Injection Molding Kit
**IMK** ........... Instrument Marking Kit
**IMK** ........... International Makaoo [*Vancouver Stock Exchange symbol*]
**IMK** ........... Simikot [*Nepal*] [*Airport symbol*] (OAG)
**IMK** ........... Union Carbide Corp., Library, Indianapolis, IN [*OCLC symbol*] (OCLC)
**IMKR** ........ Inner Marker [*Part of an instrument landing system*] [*Aviation*]
**IMKRA3**..... Imkerfreund [*A publication*]
**IMKT**......... Ingles Markets, Inc. [*NASDAQ symbol*] (NQ)
**IML** ........... Imperial, NE [*Location identifier*] [*FAA*] (FAAL)
**IML** ........... Incoming Matching Loss [*Telecommunications*] (TEL)
**IML** ........... Indusmin Limited [*Toronto Stock Exchange symbol*]
**IML** ........... Information [*A publication*]
**IML** ........... Information Manipulation Language
**IML** ........... Initial Machine Load [*Data processing*] (IBMDP)
**IML** ........... Initial Measurement List (KSC)
**IML** ........... Initial Microprogram Load [*Also, IMPL*] [*Data processing*] (IBMDP)
**IML** ........... Inside Mold Line [*Technical drawings*]
**IML** ........... Institute for Medical Literature [*South African Medical Research Council*] [*Information service or system*] (IID)
**IML** ........... Institute of Modern Languages
**IML** ........... Instructional Media Laboratory
**IML** ........... Intermediate Language [*Data processing*] (TEL)
**IML** ........... Intermediate Maintenance Level
**IML** ........... Internal Medullary Lamina [*Neuroanatomy*]
**IML** ........... International Microgravity Laboratory
**ImL** ........... Irish Microforms Ltd., Dublin, Ireland [*Library symbol*] [*Library of Congress*] (LCLS)
**IML** ........... Irradiated Materials Laboratory
**IML** ........... Miles Laboratories, Inc., Library Resources and Services, Elkhart, IN [*OCLC symbol*] (OCLC)
**IMLB**......... Intermountain Laboratories [*NASDAQ symbol*] (NQ)
**IMLCA**...... Immunological Communications [*A publication*]
**IMLCAV**... Immunological Communications [*A publication*]
**IMLED**...... Immunology Letters [*A publication*]
**IMLED6**.... Immunology Letters [*A publication*]
**IMLS**......... Institute of Medical Laboratory Sciences [*British*]
**IMLSG**...... Interim Mobile Logistic Support Group [*Military*] (CAAL)
**IMLS Gaz** ... Institute of Medical Laboratory Sciences. Gazette [*A publication*]
**IMLS (Inst Med Lab Sci) Curr Top Med Lab Sci** ... IMLS (Institute of Medical Laboratory Sciences) Current Topics in Medical Laboratory Sciences [*A publication*]
**IMLSS**....... Integrated Maneuvering and Life Support System [*NASA*]
**IMM**.......... Immaculata College, Immaculata, PA [*OCLC symbol*] (OCLC)
**IMM**.......... Immediate
**IMM**.......... Immokalee, FL [*Location identifier*] [*FAA*] (FAAL)
**IMM**.......... Immune [*or Immunization*] (AFM)
**IMM**.......... Independent Manned Manipulator [*NASA*] (KSC)
**IMM**.......... Industrial Marketing Management [*A publication*]
**IMM**.......... Inhibitor-Containing Minimal Medium [*Microbiology*]
**IMM**.......... Inner Mitochondrial Membrane [*Cytology*]
**IMM**.......... Institute for Manpower Management (EA)
**IMM**.......... Institute of Municipal Management [*Australia*]
**IMM**.......... Institution of Mining and Metallurgy [*London, England*]
**IMM**.......... Integrated Maintenance Management
**IMM**.......... Integrated Maintenance Manual
**IMM**.......... Integrated Materiel Management [*or Manager*]
**IMM**.......... Intelligent Memory Manager [*Data processing*]
**IMM**.......... Intermediate Maintenance Manual [*Military*] (CAAL)
**IMM**.......... International Maggie Mines Ltd. [*Vancouver Stock Exchange symbol*]
**IMM**.......... International Mobile Machines Corp.
**IMM**.......... International Monetary Market [*Chicago Mercantile Exchange*]
**IMM**.......... International Money Management [*Business term*]
**IMMA**....... Institute of Metals and Minerals Australasia
**IMMA**....... Institute of Muslim Minority Affairs (EAIO)
**IMMA**....... International Model Managers Association (EA)
**IMMA**....... International Motorcycle Manufacturers Association (EAIO)
**IMMA**....... Ion Microprobe Mass Analyzer
**IMM Abstr** ... IMM [*Institute of Mining and Metallurgy*] Abstracts [*A publication*]
**IMMAC** .... Immaculate
**Imm AR** ..... Immigration Appeal Reports [*A publication*] (DLA)
**IMMAT**..... Immaterial (AABC)
**IMMAT**..... Immature
**IMMC** ....... International Mobile Machines Corporation [*NASDAQ symbol*] (NQ)
**IMME** ....... IMM Energy Service & Technology [*NASDAQ symbol*] (NQ)
**IMME** ....... Isobaric Multiplet Mass Equation
**IMMED** .... Immediate (AFM)
**Immergrune Bl** ... Immergruene Blaetter [*A publication*]
**IMMH**....... Indirect Maintenance Man-Hour
**IMMI** ........ International Mass Media Institute (EA)
**IMMIG** ..... Immigration
**Immig B Bull** ... Immigration Bar Bulletin [*A publication*] (DLA)
**Immig & Naturalization Serv Mo Rev** ... United States Immigration and Naturalization Service, Monthly Review [*A publication*] (DLA)
**Immig Newsl** ... Immigration Newsletter [*A publication*] (DLA)
**IMMIRS** ... Integrated Maintenance Management Information Retrieval System [*DoD*]
**Imm J**......... Immigration Journal [*A publication*]
**IMMLC**..... Industrie Minerale. Serie Mineralurgie [*A publication*]
**IMMLDW** ... Immunologiya [*A publication*]
**IMMLEP** .. Immunization Against Leprosy Program [*World Health Organization*]
**IMMLS**..... Interim Military Microwave Landing System (RDA)
**IMMNB** .... Industrie Minerale. Serie Mine [*A publication*]
**IMMND4** ... Immunobiology [*A publication*]
**IMMOB** .... Immobilize [*Medicine*]
**IMMP** ....... Information Management Master Plan [*DoD*]
**IMMP** ....... Information Mission Management Plan
**IMMP** ....... Integrated Maintenance Management Plan
**IMMR** ....... Installation, Modification, Maintenance, and Repair (AAG)
**IMMR** ....... Institute for Mining and Mineral Research [*University of Kentucky*] [*Research center*] (RCD)
**IMMRRI**... Idaho Mining and Minerals Resources Research Institute [*University of Idaho*] [*Research center*] (RCD)
**IMMS**........ Indore Mill Mazdoor Sangh [*Indore Textile Labour Association*] [*India*]
**IMMS**........ Installation Maintenance Management System (MCD)
**IMMS**........ Integrated Maintenance Management System [*Army*]
**IMMS**........ Interactive Multimedia System (MCD)
**IMMS**........ Interim Manpower Maintenance System
**IMMS**........ International Material Management Society (EA)
**IMMT** ....... Integrated Maintenance Management Team
**IMMTS**..... Indian Mercantile Marine Training Ship [*British*]
**IMMU**....... Immunomedics, Inc. [*NASDAQ symbol*] (NQ)
**IMMU**....... Independent Munitions Maintenance Unit
**IMMUAM** ... Immunology [*A publication*]
**IMMUDP** ... Immunopharmacology [*A publication*]
**IMMUN**.... Immunity
**IMMUN**.... Immunology (ADA)
**Immun**........ Immunology [*A publication*]
**Immun Bull** ... Immunity Bulletin [*A publication*]
**Immun Commun** ... Immunological Communications [*A publication*]
**IMMUNHMTLGY** ... Immunohematology
**Immun Infekt** ... Immunitaet und Infektion [*A publication*]
**Immunoassay Technol** ... Immunoassay Technology [*A publication*]
**Immunochem** ... Immunochemistry [*A publication*]
**Immunogenet** ... Immunogenetics [*A publication*]
**IMMUNOL** ... Immunology
**Immunol Clin Sper** ... Immunologia Clinica e Sperimentale [*A publication*]
**Immunol Com** ... Immunological Communications [*A publication*]
**Immunol Commun** ... Immunological Communications [*A publication*]
**Immunol Invest** ... Immunological Investigations [*A publication*]
**Immunol Lett** ... Immunology Letters [*A publication*]
**Immunology Ser** ... Immunology Series [*A publication*]
**Immunol Pol** ... Immunologia Polska [*A publication*]
**Immunol Res** ... Immunologic Research [*A publication*]
**Immunol Rev** ... Immunological Reviews [*A publication*]
**Immut**......... Quod Deus Sit Immutabilis [*Philo*] (BJA)
**IMMV** ....... Iris Mild Mosaic Virus
**IMMY** ....... Immediately
**IMMY** ....... Information Marketing Achievement Award [*Information Industry Association*]
**IMN**........... Idiopathic Membranous Nephropathy [*Nephrology*]
**IMN**........... Indicated Mach Number (AFM)
**IMN**........... Internal-Mix Nozzle
**IMN**........... Irisleabhar Mha Nuad [*A publication*]
**IMN**........... Manchester College, North Manchester, IN [*OCLC symbol*] (OCLC)
**IMNB** ........ Isopropyl(methyl)nitrobenzene [*Organic chemistry*]
**IMNET**...... International MarketNet [*System of broker work stations created by IBM Corp. and Merrill Lynch & Co.*] [*New York, NY*]
**IMNGA**..... Immunologiya [*A publication*]
**IMNGBK** .. Immunogenetics [*A publication*]
**IMNH**........ Idaho Museum of Natural History [*Idaho State University*] [*Research center*] (RCD)
**IMNO**........ ImmunoTherapeutics, Inc. [*NASDAQ symbol*] (NQ)
**IMNS** ........ Imperial Military Nursing Service [*British*]
**IMNSA**...... Izvestiya na Mikrobiologicheskiya Institut. Bulgarska Akademiya na Naukite [*A publication*]

**IMNX**........ Immunex Corp. [*NASDAQ symbol*] (NQ)
**IMO**.......... Asheville, NC [*Location identifier*] [*FAA*] (FAAL)
**IMO**.......... Immobilized (NVT)
**Imo**............ [*Johannes de*] Imola [*Deceased, 1436*] [*Authority cited in pre-1607 legal work*] (DSA)
**IMO**.......... Imperial Oil Ltd. [*AMEX symbol*] [*Toronto Stock Exchange symbol*] [*Vancouver Stock Exchange symbol*] (SPSG)
**IMO**.......... Improper Order
**IMO**.......... Indianapolis Museum of Art, Indianapolis, IN [*OCLC symbol*] (OCLC)
**IMO**.......... Installation Maintenance Officer [*Military*] (AABC)
**IMO**.......... Institute of Market Officers [*British*]
**IMO**.......... Inter-American Municipal Organization
**IMO**.......... Interband Magneto-Optic [*Effect*] (DEN)
**IMO**.......... Interface Management Office
**IMO**.......... International Insurance Monitor [*A publication*]
**IMO**.......... International Maritime Organization [*See also OMI*] [*ICSU*] [*London, England*] (EAIO)
**IMO**.......... International Materials Organization (NATG)
**IMO**.......... International Mathematical Olympiad (RDA)
**IMO**.......... International Messianic Outreach (EA)
**IMO**.......... International Meteorological Organization [*Later, World Meteorological Organization*]
**IMO**.......... International Money Order [*Business term*] (DS)
**IMO**.......... Isla Mona [*Puerto Rico*] [*Seismograph station code, US Geological Survey*] (SEIS)
**IMO**.......... Itim Mizrah News Agency. Bulletin on Palestinian Organizations [*A publication*]
**IMOG**........ Interagency Mechanical Operations Group [*Lawrence Livermore Laboratory*]
**IMoH**......... John and Mary Kirby Hospital, Monticello, IL [*Library symbol*] [*Library of Congress*] (LCLS)
**Imol**............ [*Johannes de*] Imola [*Deceased, 1436*] [*Authority cited in pre-1607 legal work*] (DSA)
**IMol**........... Moline Public Library, Moline, IL [*Library symbol*] [*Library of Congress*] (LCLS)
**IMolB**........ Black Hawk College, Moline, IL [*Library symbol*] [*Library of Congress*] (LCLS)
**IMolD**........ Deere & Co., Moline, IL [*Library symbol*] [*Library of Congress*] (LCLS)
**IMonC**....... Monmouth College, Monmouth, IL [*Library symbol*] [*Library of Congress*] (LCLS)
**Imono J Japan Foundrymen's Soc**... Imono. Journal of the Japan Foundrymen's Society [*A publication*]
**IMont**......... Allerton Public Library, Monticello, IL [*Library symbol*] [*Library of Congress*] (LCLS)
**IMonW**...... Western Illinois Library System, Monmouth, IL [*Library symbol*] [*Library of Congress*] (LCLS)
**IMOP**........ Infantry Mortar Program (MCD)
**IMOR**........ Imperial Oil Review [*A publication*]
**IMort**......... Morton Public Library, Morton, IL [*Library symbol*] [*Library of Congress*] (LCLS)
**IMOS**........ Inadvertent Modification of the Stratosphere [*Interagency government task force*]
**IMOS**........ Interactive Multiprogramming Operating System [*NCR Corp.*]
**IMOS**........ Ion-Implanted Metal-Oxide Semiconductor
**IMOT**........ Installed Maximum Operating Time
**IMOT**........ Interim Maximum Operating Time
**IMP**........... Cargo Information Message Procedures [*IATA*] (DS)
**IMP**........... Illustrated Melbourne Post [*A publication*]
**IMP**........... Image Processing Program [*Computer program*]
**IMP**........... Immunoperoxidase [*An enzyme*]
**IMP**........... Impact (KSC)
**Imp**............ Impact [*A publication*]
**IMP**........... Impact Predictor [*NASA*] (MUGU)
**IMP**........... Impaired
**imp**............ Impaye [*Unpaid*] [*French*]
**IMP**........... Impedance (KSC)
**IMP**........... Impeller
**IMP**........... Imperative
**IMP**........... Imperator [*or Imperatrix*] [*Emperor or Empress*] [*Latin*]
**IMP**........... Imperatriz [*Brazil*] [*Airport symbol*] (OAG)
**IMP**........... Imperfect
**IMP**........... Imperial (AFM)
**Imp**............ Imperial [*Record label*] [*Germany, etc.*]
**IMP**........... Imperial Airlines [*Imperial, CA*] [*FAA designator*] (FAAC)
**IMP**........... Imperious [*Grammar*] (ROG)
**IMP**........... Imperium [*Empire*] [*Latin*]
**IMP**........... Impersonal
**IMP**........... Impersonating [*FBI standardized term*]
**Imp**............ Impetus [*A publication*]
**IMP**........... Implement (AFM)
**IMP**........... Implementation Language [*Edinburgh multiaccess system*] (CSR)
**IMP**........... Important
**IMP**........... Imported
**IMP**........... Impracticable (FAAC)
**IMP**........... Impression
**IMP**........... Imprimatur [*Let It Be Printed*] [*Latin*]
**Imp**............ Imprime [*Printed*] [*French*] (ILCA)
**Imp**............ Imprimeur [*Printer*] [*French*] (ILCA)
**IMP**........... Imprint
**IMP**........... Impropriator (ROG)
**IMP**........... Improved
**IMP**........... Improved Maintenance Program [*Air Force*] (AFM)
**IMP**........... Improved Mobility Package [*Wheelchair system*]
**IMP**........... Improvement [*Real estate*]
**IMP**........... Improvement Maintenance Program (MCD)
**Imp**............ Impulse [*A publication*]
**IMP**........... Impulse (KSC)
**IMP**........... Impulse Generator
**IMP**........... Independent Motion Picture Co.
**IMP**........... Indeterminate Mass Particle
**IMP**........... Index to Maritime Publications [*A publication*]
**IMP**........... Individual Merit Promotion
**IMP**........... Industrial Management Program
**IMP**........... Industrial Membrane Processing [*Chemical engineering*]
**IMP**........... Industrial Mobilization Planning
**IMP**........... Industrial Models and Patterns [*A publication*] (EAAP)
**IMP**........... Infantry Mortar Plan (MCD)
**IMP**........... Inflatable Micrometeoroid Paraglide
**IMP**........... Information Management Plan [*DoD*]
**IMP**........... Information Management Program [*Army*]
**IMP**........... Initial Memory Protection (MCD)
**IMP**........... Initial Military Program (NATG)
**IMP**........... Injection Microwave Plasma [*Oak Ridge National Laboratory*]
**IMP**........... Inosine Monophosphate [*Biochemistry*]
**IMP**........... Inpatient Multidimensional Psychiatric Scale
**IMP**........... Input Message Processor
**IMP**........... Insoluble Metaphosphate [*Inorganic chemistry*]
**IMP**........... Installation Master Planning [*Military*]
**IMP**........... Institute of Modern Procedures [*Defunct*] (EA)
**IMP**........... Instrument Maintenance Procedure [*Nuclear energy*] (NRCH)
**IMP**........... Instrumented Monkey Pod
**IMP**........... Integral Membrane Protein [*Cytology*]
**IMP**........... Integrated Maintenance Plan [*or Procedure*]
**IMP**........... Integrated Memory Processor
**IMP**........... Integrated Microprocessor [*National Semiconductor*]
**IMP**........... Integrated Microwave Products (IEEE)
**IMP**........... Integrated MIDI [*Musical Instrument Digital Interface*] Processor
**IMP**........... Integrated Monitoring Panel
**IMP**........... Integrating Motor Pneumotachograph
**IMP**........... Interactive Microprogrammable Control (MCD)
**IMP**........... Interagency Integrated Pest Management Coordinating Committee [*Terminated, 1980*] [*Council on Environmental Quality*] (EGAO)
**IMP**........... Interface Management Plan [*Air Force*]
**IMP**........... Interface Message Processor [*Data processing*]
**IMP**........... Interim Monitoring Program
**IMP**........... Intermodulation Product
**IMP**........... International Maple Leaf Resource Corp. [*Vancouver Stock Exchange symbol*]
**IMP**........... International Match Point [*Game of bridge*]
**IMP**........... International Micro-Print Preservation, Inc.
**IMP**........... International Mimes and Pantomimists [*Defunct*]
**IMP**........... Interplanetary Magnetometer Probe
**IMP**........... Interplanetary Measurement Probe
**IMP**........... Interplanetary Monitoring Platform [*A spacecraft*]
**IMP**........... Interplanetary Monitoring Probe [*A spacecraft*]
**IMP**........... Intra-Industry Management Program [*Small Business Administration*]
**IMP**........... Intramembranous Particle [*Cytology*]
**IMP**........... Intrinsic Multiprocessing (IEEE)
**IMP**........... Inventory Management Plan [*Military*] (AFIT)
**IMP**........... Ion Microprobe [*Surface analysis*]
**IMP**........... Ion Moderated Partition [*Chromatography*]
**IMP**........... Marathon, TX [*Location identifier*] [*FAA*] (FAAL)
**IMP**........... Mishawaka Public Library, Mishawaka, IN [*OCLC symbol*] (OCLC)
**IMPA**......... Incisal Mandibular Plane Angle [*Dentistry*]
**IMPA**......... Independent Media Producers Association [*Later, IMPC*] (EA)
**IMPA**......... Information Management and Processing Association (EA)
**IMPA**......... International Maritime Pilots Association [*London, England*] (EAIO)
**IMPA**......... International Master Printers Association [*Brussels, Belgium*]
**IMPA**......... International Meat Processors Association (EA)
**IMPA**......... International Motor Press Association (EA)
**IMPA**......... International Museum Photographers Association (EA)
**IMPA**......... International Myopia Prevention Association (EA)
**IMPAC**...... Immediate Psychiatric Aid and Referral Center
**IMPAC**...... Interagency Map and Publications Acquisitions Committee [*Department of State*] [*Washington, DC*]
**IMPAC**...... International Microfiche Parts Access Catalogue [*Auto parts*] [*A publication*]
**IMPACS**.... International Packet-Switching Service [*MCI International, Inc.*] [*Rye Brook, NY*] [*Telecommunications*] (TSSD)
**IMPACT**... Image Processing and Color Transmission [*Time, Inc. photograph transmission center*]
**IMPACT**... Implanted Advanced Composed Technology [*Texas Instruments, Inc.*]

**IMPACT** ... Implementation Planning and Control Technique [*Data processing*]
**IMPACT** ... Improved Management Procurement and Contracting Technique (AABC)
**IMPACT** ... Improved Manpower Production and Controller Technique [*Navy*]
**IMPACT** ... Improved Modern Pricing and Costing Techniques [*Air Force*] (MCD)
**IMPACT** ... Integrated Management Planning and Control Technique [*British*]
**IMPACT** ... Integrated Managerial Programming Analysis Control Technique [*Air Force*]
**IMPACT** ... Integrated Materials Handling Production and Control Technology
**IMPACT** ... Interdisciplinary Model Programs in the Arts for Children and Teachers
**IMPACT** ... International Marketing Program for Agricultural Commodities and Trade Center [*Washington State University*] [*Research center*] (RCD)
**IMPACT** ... Intervention Moves Parents and Children Together [*Drug abuse treatment program sponsored by Phoenix House Foundation*]
**IMPACT** ... Inventory Management Program and Control Technique [*IBM Corp.*] [*Data processing*]
**Impact Agric Res Tex Annu Rep** ... Impact. Agricultural Research in Texas. Annual Report [*A publication*]
**Impacts Aust Econ** ... Impacts on the Australian Economy [*A publication*]
**Impact Sci** ... Impact of Science on Society [*A publication*]
**Impact Sci Soc** ... Impact of Science on Society [*A publication*]
**Impact Sci Soc (Engl Ed)** ... Impact of Science on Society (English Edition) [*A publication*]
**IMPALA** ... International Motion Picture and Lecturers Association (EA)
**IMPATT** ... Impact Ionization Avalanche Transit Time [*Solid state diodes*] [*Transistor technology*]
**IMPBA** ...... International Model Power Boat Association (EA)
**IMPC** ......... Independent Media Producers Council (EA)
**IMPC** ......... Infantry Mortar Platoon Course (INF)
**IMPC** ......... Institutional and Municipal Parking Congress (EA)
**IMPCA** ...... International Methanol Producers and Consumers Association [*British*]
**IMPCE** ...... Importance
**IMPCM** ..... Improved Capability Missile [*Air Force*] (MCD)
**Imp Coll Sci Technol Appl Geochem Res Group Tech Commun** ... Imperial College of Science and Technology. Applied Geochemistry Research Group. Technical Communication [*A publication*]
**Imp Coll Sci Technol Geochem Prospect Res Cent Tech Commun** ... Imperial College of Science and Technology. Geochemical Prospecting Research Centre. Technical Communication [*A publication*]
**Imp Coll Sci Technol Rock Mech Res Rep** ... Imperial College of Science and Technology. Rock Mechanics Research Report [*A publication*]
**Imp Coll Trop Agric (Trinidad) Circ** ... Imperial College of Tropical Agriculture (Trinidad). Circular [*A publication*]
**Imp Coll Trop Agric (Trinidad) Low Temp Res Stn Mem** ... Imperial College of Tropical Agriculture (Trinidad). Low Temperature Research Station. Memoirs [*A publication*]
**Imp Coll Trop Agric (Trinidad) Mem Mycol Ser** ... Imperial College of Tropical Agriculture (Trinidad). Memoirs. Mycological Series [*A publication*]
**IMPD** ........ Impedance [*Electricity*]
**IMPD** ........ Improved [*Real estate*] (ROG)
**IMPDAA** ... Independent Motion Picture Distributors Association of America
**IMPDH** ..... Inosine Monophosphate Dehydrogenase [*An enzyme*]
**IMP DICT** ... Imperial Dictionary [*A publication*] (ROG)
**IMPE** ......... Impetus. Magazine Supplement of the Financial Post [*A publication*]
**Imp Earthquake Investigation Com B** ... Imperial Earthquake Investigation Committee. Bulletin [*A publication*]
**IMPEND** ... Improved Effectiveness Nuclear Depth Bomb
**IMPER** ...... Imperative
**IMPER** ...... Imperfect
**IMPER** ...... Impersonal (ROG)
**IMPERF** .... Imperfect
**IMPERF** .... Imperforate [*Philately*]
**Imperial Oil R** ... Imperial Oil Review [*A publication*]
**IMPERS** .... Impersonal
**IMPES** ...... Implicit Pressure, Explicit Saturation [*Petroleum reservoir simulation*]
**Imp Ethiop Gov Inst Agric Res Rep** ... Imperial Ethiopian Government Institute of Agricultural Research. Report [*A publication*]
**Imp Exp** ..... Import/Export News [*A publication*]
**IMPF** ......... Imperfect (MSA)
**IMPFT** ....... Imperfect (ADA)
**IMPG** ........ Imperial Group Ltd.
**IMPG** ........ Impregnate (KSC)
**IMPGAC** ... Improved Guidance and Control (MCD)
**IMPHOS** ... Institut Mondial du Phosphate [*World Phosphate Institute*] [*Morocco*]
**IMPI** .......... International Microwave Power Institute (EA)
**IMPID** ....... Impianti [*A publication*]
**Imp Inst Agric Res (Pusa) Bull** ... Imperial Institute of Agricultural Research (Pusa). Bulletin [*A publication*]
**IMPIS** ........ Indirect Material Purchasing Information Standards
**IMPIS** ........ Integrated Management Planning Information Systems [*Data processing*]
**IMPL** ......... Illustrated Maintenance Parts List
**IMPL** ......... Impell Corp. [*NASDAQ symbol*] (NQ)
**Impl** ............ Imperial [*British military*] (DMA)
**IMPL** ......... Implement (AABC)
**IMPL** ......... Impulse (FAAC)
**IMPL** ......... Initial Microprogram Load [*Also, IML*] [*Data processing*]
**IMPLR** ...... Impeller [*Mechanical engineering*]
**IMPLS** ....... Impulse (MSA)
**Imp Man** .... Impey's Law and Practice of Mandamus [*1826*] [*A publication*] (DLA)
**IMPO** ........ Imposition (DSUE)
**IMPODM** ... Immunologia Polska [*A publication*]
**Imp Oil R** ... Imperial Oil Review [*A publication*]
**IMPOP** ...... Integrated Maintenance Program Operation (MCD)
**IMPOSN** ... Imposition (ROG)
**IMPOSS** .... Impossible (ADA)
**IMPOT** ...... Imposition (DSUE)
**IMPP** ......... Industrial Mobilization Production Planning [*DoD*]
**IMPPA** ...... Independent Motion Picture Producers Association (EA)
**Imp Pl** ........ Impey's Modern Pleader [*2nd ed.*] [*1814*] [*A publication*] (DLA)
**Imp Pr CP** ... Impey's Practice, Common Pleas [*A publication*] (DLA)
**Imp Pr KB** ... Impey's Practice, King's Bench [*A publication*] (DLA)
**IMPR** ......... Impedor
**IMPR** ......... Impractical (AABC)
**IMPR** ......... Impression (ROG)
**IMPR** ......... Imprint [*Online database field identifier*]
**IMPR** ......... Improved
**IMPRAC** ... Impracticable (DSUE)
**ImprAr** ....... Imperial Aramaic (BJA)
**IMPREG** ... Impregnable (ADA)
**IMPREG** ... Impregnated (TEL)
**IMPRESS** ... Interdisciplinary Machine Processing for Research and Education in Social Sciences [*Dartmouth College, Hanover, NH*] [*Data processing system*]
**Imp Rev** ...... Imperial Review [*A publication*] (APTA)
**IMPRG** ...... Impregnate (AABC)
**Impr Hum P** ... Improving Human Performance [*A publication*]
**Imprim Ind Graphiques** ... Imprimerie et Industries Graphiques [*A publication*]
**IMPRINT** ... Imbricated Program for Information Transfer [*Data processing*]
**IMPRINT** ... Improved Medical Programs and Readiness Immediately, Not Tomorrow [*TROA*]
**IMPRL** ...... Imperial (MSA)
**Impr Med** ... Imprensa Medica [*A publication*]
**IMPROME** ... Impuesto Minimo a la Produccion Media [*Minimum Tax on Average Production*] [*Spanish*]
**IMPROME** ... Impuesto a la Produccion Minima de las Explotaciones Agro [*Tax on Minimum Crop Yields*] [*Spanish*]
**IMPROP** ... Improper (ADA)
**IMPROV** ... Improvement (MSA)
**Improv Coll Univ Teach** ... Improving College and University Teaching [*A publication*]
**Improv Coll & Univ Teach** ... Improving College and University Teaching [*A publication*]
**Improving Coll & Univ Teach** ... Improving College and University Teaching [*A publication*]
**Impr Pubbl** ... Impresa Pubblica [*A publication*]
**IMPRSN** ... Impression (MSA)
**IMPRV** ..... Improvement (AABC)
**IMPRVMT** ... Improvement
**IMPS** ......... Imperial Tobacco Company Shares [*Stock exchange term*] [*British*] (DSUE)
**IMPS** ......... Impose (MSA)
**IMPS** ......... Individual Multipurpose Shelter [*Army*] (INF)
**IMPS** ......... Industry Media Publishing System [*Omni Industry Corp.*] [*Information service or system*] (IID)
**IMPS** ......... Inpatient Multidimensional Psychiatric Scale
**IMPS** ......... Institutional Meat Purchase Specification [*Department of Agriculture*]
**IMPS** ......... Integrated Mail Preparation System
**IMPS** ......... Integrated Master Programming and Scheduling
**IMPS** ......... Integrated Modular Panel System
**IMPS** ......... International M [*formerly, Mensa*] Philatelists Society (EA)
**IMPS** ......... International Medical Placement Services [*Australia*]
**IMPS** ......... International Microprogrammers' Society
**Imp Sci Soc** ... Impact of Science on Society [*A publication*]
**Imp Sh** ....... Impey's Office of Sheriff [*6th ed.*] [*1835*] [*A publication*] (DLA)
**IMPT** ......... Impact Energy, Inc. [*NASDAQ symbol*] (NQ)
**IMPT** ......... Important (FAAC)
**Impt** ........... Imprisonment [*British military*] (DMA)
**IMPT** ......... Improvement [*Real estate*] (ROG)
**IMPTR** ...... Importer (ADA)

**Imp & Trac RB** ... Implement and Tractor Red Book [*A publication*]
**Imp & Tractr** ... Implement and Tractor [*A publication*]
**IMPTS** ...... Improved Programmer Test Station (IEEE)
**Impul'snaya Fotom** ... Impul'snaya Fotometriya [*A publication*]
**Impulstech** ... Impulstechniken [*A publication*]
**Imp Univ Tokyo Fac Sci J** ... Tokyo. Imperial University. Faculty of Science. Journal [*A publication*]
**IMPV**......... Imperative
**IMPVD**...... Improved [*Real estate*] (ROG)
**IMPVE**...... Improve [*Real estate*] (ROG)
**IMPX**......... Impaction [*Dentistry*]
**IMPX**......... Imperatrix [*Empress*] [*Latin*]
**IMPX**......... International Microelectronic Products, Inc. [*NASDAQ symbol*] (NQ)
**Imp Zootech Exp Stn Bull** ... Imperial Zootechnical Experiment Station. Bulletin [*A publication*]
**IMQ**.......... La Porte County Library, La Porte, IN [*OCLC symbol*] (OCLC)
**IMR**.......... Impala Resources [*Vancouver Stock Exchange symbol*]
**IMR**.......... Imperial Military Railways [*British military*] (DMA)
**IMR**.......... Independent Modification Review [*Military*] (AFIT)
**IMR**.......... Individual Medical Record
**IMR**.......... Infant Mortality Rate
**IMR**.......... Informal Memorandum Report
**IMR**.......... Initial Missile Report (CINC)
**IMR**.......... Inner Metropolitan Region (ADA)
**IMR**.......... Institute of Man and Resources
**IMR**.......... Institute of Marine Resources [*University of California*] [*Research center*] (RCD)
**IMR**.......... Institute of Masonry Research [*Defunct*] (EA)
**IMR**.......... Institute for Materials Research [*Later, NSL*] [*National Institute of Standards and Technology*]
**IMR**.......... Institute for Medical Research [*Camden, New Jersey*]
**IMR**.......... Institute of Metal Repair (EA)
**IMR**.......... Institution for Mentally Retarded [*Generic term*] (DHSM)
**IMR**.......... Internal Mold Release [*Plastics technology*]
**IMR**.......... International Medical Research
**IMR**.......... Internationale Maschinenrundschau [*A publication*]
**IMR**.......... Interrupt-Mask Register [*Data processing*]
**IMR**.......... Inventory Management Record [*Military*] (AFM)
**IMR**.......... Inventory Modified Round
**IMR**.......... Isla Mona [*Puerto Rico*] [*Seismograph station code, US Geological Survey*] [*Closed*] (SEIS)
**IMR**.......... Monroe County Public Library, Bloomington, IN [*OCLC symbol*] (OCLC)
**IMRA**........ Incentive Manufacturers Representatives Association [*Naperville, IL*] (EA)
**IMRA**........ Independent Motorcycle Retailers of America (EA)
**IMRA**........ Industrial Marketing Research Association [*British*]
**IMRA**........ Infrared Monochromatic Radiation
**IMRA**........ Insurance Market Risk Assessment
**IMRA**........ International Manufacturers Representatives Association [*Tulsa, OK*] (EA)
**IMRA**........ International Military Recreation Association (EA)
**IMRA**........ International Mission Radio Association (EA)
**IMRAD**..... Introduction, Methods, Results, and Discussion [*Scientific writing*]
**IMRADS**... Information Management, Retrieval, and Dissemination System (DIT)
**IMRAN**..... International Marine Radio Aids to Navigation
**IMRB**........ Improved Main Rotor Blade (RDA)
**IMRC**........ Instructional Materials Reference Center [*Absorbed by American Printing House for the Blind - APH*] (EA)
**IMRC**........ International Management & Research Corporation [*Philadelphia, PA*] [*NASDAQ symbol*] (NQ)
**IMRC**........ Inventory [*or Item*] Management Responsibility Code
**IMRE**........ Imre Corp. [*NASDAQ symbol*] (NQ)
**IMRE**........ Institute for Medical Record Economics (EA)
**IMREC**...... Interior Ministerial Real Estate Committee [*Vietnam*]
**IMRED2**.... Immunological Reviews [*A publication*]
**IMREP**...... Immediately Report
**IMRETES** ... Immunization Readiness Training Exercises [*Army*]
**IMRF**........ Independent Manufacturers Representatives Forum (EA)
**IMRF**........ International Medical and Research Foundation [*Later, AMREF*] (EA)
**IMRG**........ Imreg, Inc. [*New Orleans, LA*] [*NASDAQ symbol*] (NQ)
**IMRHS**...... Inactive Materiel Request History and Status File [*Army*]
**IMRI**......... IMCO Recycling, Inc. [*NASDAQ symbol*] (NQ)
**IMR Ind Manage Rev** ... IMR. Industrial Management Review [*A publication*]
**IMRL**......... Immediate Material Requirement List
**IMRL**......... Individual Maintenance Readiness List
**IMRL**......... Individual Material Readiness List [*DoD*]
**IMRL**......... Intermediate Maintenance Repair Level (MCD)
**IMRL**......... Intermediate Maintenance Requirements List
**IMRO**........ Internal Macedonian Revolutionary Organization [*Bulgaria*] [*Political party*] (PPE)
**IMRO**........ Interplant Material Requisition Order
**IMRO**........ Investment Managers Regulatory Organisation [*British*] (ECON)
**IMRP**......... International Meeting on Radiation Processing (EA)
**IMRRS**...... Installation Materiel Readiness Reporting System [*Army*]
**IMRRS**...... Institute of Market and Reward Regional Surveys [*British*]
**IMRS**......... Immersion (MSA)
**IMRS**......... Industrial Market Research Service [*Thailand*] (DS)
**IMRSB8**.... Indian Council of Medical Research. Technical Report Series [*A publication*]
**IMRSEB**.... Immunologic Research [*A publication*]
**IM-RSI**...... International Military Rationalization, Standardization, and Interoperability (RDA)
**IMRU**........ Institute of Microbiology, Rutgers University [*New Jersey*]
**IMRVB**...... International Metallurgical Reviews [*A publication*]
**IMS**........... Idle Matrix Search [*Data processing*]
**IMS**........... IEEE Instrumentation and Measurement Society (EA)
**IMS**........... Image Motion Simulator
**IMS**........... Imasco Ltd. [*Toronto Stock Exchange symbol*] [*Vancouver Stock Exchange symbol*]
**ImS**........... Immune Serum [*Also, IS*]
**IMS**........... Impact of Science on Society [*A publication*]
**IMS**........... In-Core Monitoring System [*Nuclear energy*] (NRCH)
**IMS**........... In-Flight Management System
**IMS**........... Indian Medical Service [*British*]
**IMS**........... Indirect Measuring System
**IMS**........... Individualized Mathematics System [*Education*]
**IMS**........... Industrial Management Society (EA)
**IMS**........... Industrial Mathematics Society (EA)
**IMS**........... Industrial Medicine and Surgery [*A publication*]
**IMS**........... Industrial Methylated Spirit
**IMS**........... Inertial Measuring Set [*or System*] (NVT)
**IMS**........... Information Management Specialists, Inc. [*Denver, CO*] [*Information service or system*] (IID)
**IMS**........... Information Management System [*IBM Corp.*] [*Data processing*]
**IMS**........... Infrared Measuring System
**IMS**........... Initial Measurement System [*Nuclear missiles*]
**IMS**........... Inshore Minesweeper [*Navy*] [*British*]
**IMS**........... Institute on Man and Science [*Formerly, Council on World Tensions*]
**IMS**........... [*The*] Institute of Management Sciences
**IMS**........... Institute of Management Services [*British*]
**IMS**........... Institute of Management Specialists [*Royal Leamington Spa, Warwickshire, England*] (EAIO)
**IMS**........... Institute of Manpower Studies [*Department of Employment*] [*British*]
**IMS**........... Institute of Marine Science [*University of Alaska*] [*Research center*]
**IMS**........... Institute of Materials Science (KSC)
**IMS**........... Institute of Mathematical Statistics (EA)
**IMS**........... Institute of Mental Subnormality [*British*]
**IMS**........... Institute for Mesoamerican Studies [*State University of New York, Albany*] [*Research center*] (RCD)
**IMS**........... Institute of Museum Services [*National Foundation of the Arts and the Humanities*] (GRD)
**IMS**........... Instructional Management System (IEEE)
**IMS**........... Instrumented Measuring System
**IMS**........... Integrated Maintenance Schedule
**IMS**........... Integrated Maintenance System
**IMS**........... Integrated Mapping System
**IMS**........... Integrated Medical Services
**IMS**........... Integrated Meteorological System [*Army*] (IEEE)
**IMS**........... Integrated Microcomputer Systems, Inc.
**IMS**........... Intensive Manpower Services (OICC)
**IMS**........... Interactive Market Systems [*New York, NY*] [*Information service or system*] (IID)
**IMS**........... Interactive Media Systems [*Information service or system*] (IID)
**IMS**........... Interim Meteorological Satellite
**IMS**........... Intermediate Maintenance Squadron (MCD)
**IMS**........... Internal Management System [*Military*] (AFIT)
**IMS**........... International Magnetospheric Study [*1976-78*] [*National Science Foundation*]
**IMS**........... International Maledicta Society (EA)
**IMS**........... International Management Services, Inc. [*Framingham, MA*] [*Information service or system*] (IID)
**IMS**........... International Marine Science [*IOC*] [*A publication*]
**IMS**........... International Marketing Services
**IMS**........... International Measurement System [*Sailing*]
**IMS**........... International Meditation Society
**IMS**........... International Metallographic Society (EA)
**IMS**........... International Metric System
**IMS**........... International Military Services Ltd. [*Ministry of Defence*] [*British*]
**IMS**........... International Military Staff [*NATO*]
**IMS**........... International Mountain Society (EA)
**IMS**........... International Multihull Society [*Formerly, International Hydrofoil and Multihull Society*] (EA)
**IMS**........... International Musicological Society [*Basel, Switzerland*] (EA)
**IMS**........... International Musicological Society. Report of the Congress [*A publication*]
**IMS**........... Internationale Monatsschrift [*A publication*]
**IMS**........... Interplanetary Mission Support
**IMS**........... Inventory Management and Simulator
**IMS**........... Inventory Management System (NASA)

IMS........... Ion Mass Spectrometer
IMS........... Ion Mobility Spectrometry
IMS........... Ionization and Momentum Sensor
IMS........... Irradiance Measuring System
IMS........... Island Missionary Society (EA)
IMS........... Madison, IN [*Location identifier*] [*FAA*] (FAAL)
IMS........... St. Mary-Of-The-Woods College, Library, St. Mary-Of-The-Woods, IN [*OCLC symbol*] (OCLC)
IMSA......... Illinois Mathematics and Science Academy
IMSA......... International Management Systems Association [*Later, Internet-International Management Systems Association*] (EA)
IMSA......... International Motor Sports Association (EA)
IMSA......... International Municipal Signal Association (EA)
IMSA......... Seaman Apprentice, Instrumentman, Striker [*Navy rating*]
IMSAM..... Interceptor Missile, Surface-to-Air-Missile (MCD)
IMSC......... Industry Missile and Space Conference
IMSC & D ... Inventory Manager Stock Control and Distribution [*Military*] (AFM)
IMSC & DS ... Inventory Manager Stock Control and Distribution System [*Military*]
IMSCE2 .... IRCS [*International Research Communications System*] Medical Science [*A publication*]
IMS Clin Proc ... IMS [*Industrial Management Society*] Clinical Proceedings [*A publication*]
IMSCOM ... International Military Staff Communication [*NATO*] (NATG)
IMSE......... Integrated Mean Square Error [*Statistics*]
IMSE......... Interagency Materials Sciences Exchange
IMSED7 .... Immunology Series [*A publication*]
IMSF......... Institut fuer Marxistische Studien und Forschungen [*A publication*]
IMSF......... International Microcomputer Software, Inc. [*NASDAQ symbol*] (NQ)
IMSG......... Imperial Merchant Service Guild [*A union*] [*British*]
IMSI.......... IMS International, Inc. [*NASDAQ symbol*] (NQ)
IMSI.......... Information Management System Interface
IMSI.......... International Maple Syrup Institute (EA)
IMSI.......... International Microcomputer Software, Inc. (BYTE)
IMSIM...... Information Management Simulation (KSC)
IMS INC ... International Management Services, Incorporated [*Franklyn, MA*] (TSSD)
IMS/INQ .. Information Management System Inquiry
IMSL......... International Mathematical and Statistical Libraries, Inc.
IMSM........ International Military Staff Memorandum [*NATO*] (NATG)
IMSN ........ Institute of Marine Science. Notes. University of Alaska [*A publication*]
IMSN ........ Internal-Mix Spray Nozzle
IMSN ........ Seaman, Instrumentman, Striker [*Navy rating*]
IMSO ........ Initial Materiel Support Office [*Army*] (AABC)
IMSOC....... Interceptor Missile Squadron Operations Center [*Air Force*]
IMSP......... Integrated Mass Storage Processor
IMSR......... Image Management Systems, Inc. [*Providence, RI*] [*NASDAQ symbol*] (NQ)
IMSR......... Interplanetary Mission Support Requirements
IMSS......... In-Flight Medical Support System [*Skylab*] [*NASA*]
IMSS......... Item Management Statistical Series
IMSSCE.... Interceptor Missile Squadron and Supervisory Control Equipment
IMSSS....... Institute for Mathematical Studies in the Social Sciences [*Stanford University*] [*Research center*] (RCD)
IMSSS....... Interceptor Missile Squadron Supervisory Station
IMST......... Institute of Marine Sciences and Technology
IMST......... International Mushroom Society for the Tropics (EAIO)
IMSUA....... Industrial Medicine and Surgery [*A publication*]
IMSUAI .... Industrial Medicine and Surgery [*A publication*]
IMSUM..... International Military Staff Summary [*NATO*] (NATG)
IMS/VS...... Information Management System/Virtual Storage (MCD)
IMSWE..... Investigations of Marine Shallow Water Ecosystems (NOAA)
IMSWM..... International Military Staff Working Memorandum [*NATO*] (NATG)
IMSX......... International Medical Systems, Inc. [*NASDAQ symbol*] (NQ)
IMT........... Idaho Motor Tariff Bureau, Boise ID [*STAC*]
IMT........... Immediate
IMT........... Immediate Money Transfer (DCTA)
IMT........... Induced Muscular Tension [*Physiology*]
IMT........... Industrial Management [*Canada*] [*A publication*]
IMT........... Intelligent Microimage Terminal [*Kodak*]
IMT........... Intermachine Trunk [*Telecommunications*] (TEL)
IMT........... Intermediate Tape [*Telecommunications*] (TEL)
IMT........... International Markatech [*Vancouver Stock Exchange symbol*]
IMT........... International Military Tribunal [*Post-World War II*]
IMT........... Iron Mountain [*Michigan*] [*Airport symbol*] (OAG)
IMT........... Iron Mountain/Kingsford, MI [*Location identifier*] [*FAA*] (FAAL)
IMT........... Morton Grove Public Library, Morton Grove, IL [*OCLC symbol*] (OCLC)
IMTA ........ Institut de la Medecine du Travail et des Ambiances [*Institute of Occupational and Environmental Health*] [*Canada*]
IMTA ........ Institute of Municipal Treasurers and Accountants [*Later, CIPFA*] [*British*]
IMTA ........ International Marine Transit Association (EA)
IMTA ........ International Mass Transit Association (EA)
IMTB......... Isle Of Man Tourist Board (DCTA)
IMTC......... Imtec, Inc. [*Bellows Falls, VT*] [*NASDAQ symbol*] (NQ)
IMTC......... Infantry Moving Target Carrier [*Army*]
IMtca......... Mount Carmel Public Library, Mt. Carmel, IL [*Library symbol*] [*Library of Congress*] (LCLS)
IMtcaSD.... Mount Carmel Community Unit School District No. 348, Mt. Carmel, IL [*Library symbol*] [*Library of Congress*] (LCLS)
IMTCE7 .... Immunoassay Technology [*A publication*]
IMTE......... Institut de la Medecine du Travail et de l'Environnement [*Institute of Occupational and Environmental Health*] [*Canada*]
IMTE......... International Military Tribunal for Europe [*Post-World War II*]
IMTEC...... IMTEC - The International Learning Cooperative (EAIO)
IMTEC...... Institute of Marine and Terrestrial Ecology [*Research center*] (RCD)
IMTEC...... International Marine Trades Exhibit and Convention [*National Marine Manufacturers Association*] (TSPED)
IMTEC...... International Movements toward Educational Change [*Later, IMTEC-The International Learning Cooperative*] (EAIO)
IMTFJ....... International Military Tribunal for Japan [*Post-World War II*]
IMTG ........ Internationale Moor und Torf-Gesellschaft [*International Peat Society - IPS*] (EAIO)
IMTI.......... International Mirtone, Inc. [*NASDAQ symbol*] (NQ)
IMTK......... Information Management Technologies Corp. [*NASDAQ symbol*] (NQ)
IMTNE...... International Meteorological Teletype Network Europe (NATG)
IMto........... Mount Olive Public Library, Mount Olive, IL [*Library symbol*] [*Library of Congress*] (LCLS)
IMTOA ..... Itogi Nauki i Tekhniki Metallovedenie i Termicheskaya Obrabotka [*A publication*]
IMTOD8 ... Immunology Today [*A publication*]
IMtoMCD ... Macoupin Community, District 5, Mount Olive, IL [*Library symbol*] [*Library of Congress*] (LCLS)
IMTP......... Industrial Mobilization Training Program
IMTP......... Integrated Maintenance Test Plan
IMTP......... Itim Mizrah News Agency. Teleprinter Service (BJA)
IMTRO ..... Integrated Maintenance Test Requirement Outline
IMTS......... Improved Mobile Telephone Service [*Telecommunications*]
IMTS......... Individualized Manpower Training System (OICC)
IMTS......... International Machine Tool Show (ITD)
IMtv........... Mount Vernon Public Library, Mt. Vernon, IL [*Library symbol*] [*Library of Congress*] (LCLS)
IMtvSD...... Summersville School District 79, Mount Vernon, IL [*Library symbol*] [*Library of Congress*] (LCLS)
IMTX......... Interactive Media Technologies, Inc. (NQ)
IMU........... Immudyne, Inc. [*Vancouver Stock Exchange symbol*]
IMU........... Impedance Matching Unit (MCD)
IMU........... Income Maintenance Unit [*Work Incentive Program*] [*Department of Labor*]
IMU........... Increment Memory Unit
IMU........... Inertial Measurement Unit
IMU........... Instruction Memory Unit
IMU........... Internal Measurement Unit (NASA)
IMU........... International Mailers Union [*Later, International Typographical Union*] (EA)
IMU........... International Mathematical Union [*See also UMI*] [*ICSU*] [*Helsinki, Finland*] (EAIO)
IMU........... International Milliunit
IMU........... Internationale Metall Union [*International Metal Union*] (EA)
IMU........... Irish Missionary Union (EAIO)
IMU........... Italia Medioevale e Umanistica [*A publication*]
IMU........... Muncie Public Library, Muncie, IN [*OCLC symbol*] (OCLC)
IMUA......... Inland Marine Underwriters Association [*New York, NY*] (EA)
IMUA......... Interservice Materiel Utilization Agency [*Military*] (AABC)
IMUDS...... Illustration Makeup Data Sheet
IMulgSD.... Mulberry Grove Community Unit, School District 1, Mulberry Grove, IL [*Library symbol*] [*Library of Congress*] (LCLS)
IMunE ....... Institution of Municipal Engineers [*British*]
IMunS........ Saint Mary of the Lake Seminary, Mundelein, IL [*Library symbol*] [*Library of Congress*] (LCLS)
IMUR......... Interactive Multiple Regression System (MCD)
IMUS......... Internal Measuring Unit System (MCD)
IMUS......... Inventario Musical [*Database*] [*Ministerio de Cultura*] [*Spanish*] [*Information service or system*] (CRD)
IMV........... Cornell College, Mount Vernon, IA [*OCLC symbol*] (OCLC)
IMV........... Industrija Motornih Vozil [*Yugoslav automaker*]
IMV........... Inferior Mesenteric Vein [*Anatomy*]
IMV........... Intermittent Mandatory Ventilation [*Respiratory therapy*] [*Medicine*]
IMV........... Internal Motor Vehicle [*Type of tugboat*] (DS)
IMV........... International Movie Group [*Vancouver Stock Exchange symbol*]
IMV........... Internationaler Metzgermeisterverband [*International Federation of Meat Traders' Associations*] (EAIO)
IMV........... Internationaler Milchwirtschaftverband [*International Dairy Federation*]

**IMVCi** ....... Indole, Methyl-Red, Voges-Proskauer, Citrate Test [*Bacteriology*]
**IMVH** ........ Indian Military Veterinary Hospital [*British military*] (DMA)
**IMVP** ........ International Motor Vehicle Program [*MIT*]
**IMVS** ........ Indian Mobile Veterinary Stores [*British military*] (DMA)
**IMW** .......... International Map of the World
**IMW** .......... Knox County Public Library, Vincennes, IN [*OCLC symbol*] (OCLC)
**IMW** .......... Sloan Management Review [*A publication*]
**IMWA** ....... International Mine Water Association [*Madrid, Spain*] (EAIO)
**IMWA** ....... International Ministers' and Widows' Association (EA)
**IMX** ........... Indiana Institute of Technology, McMillen Library, Fort Wayne, IN [*OCLC symbol*] (OCLC)
**IMX** ........... Inquiry Message Exchange
**IMX** ........... Island Mining [*Vancouver Stock Exchange symbol*]
**IMY** ........... Ida-May Resources Ltd. [*Vancouver Stock Exchange symbol*]
**IMY** ........... International Mahogany Corp. [*Toronto Stock Exchange symbol*] [*Vancouver Stock Exchange symbol*]
**IMY** ........... Michigan City Public Library, Michigan City, IN [*OCLC symbol*] (OCLC)
**IMZ** ........... Binghamton, NY [*Location identifier*] [*FAA*] (FAAL)
**IMZ** ........... Internationales Musikzentrum [*International Music Center*] [*Vienna, Austria*] (EAIO)
**IMZ Bul**..... IMZ [*Internationales Musikzentrum*] Bulletin [*A publication*]
**IN**.............. Aerlinte Eireann Teoranta [*Irish Air Lines*] [*ICAO designator*] (FAAC)
**IN**.............. Ice (Deposition) Nuclei [*Atmospheric science*]
**IN**.............. Icterus Neonatorum [*Medicine*]
**IN**.............. Idaho Nuclear (MCD)
**IN**.............. Ilioinguinal Nerve [*Anatomy*]
**IN**.............. Illinois Northern Railway [*AAR code*]
**I & N** .......... Immigration and Nationality Laws Administrative Decisions [*Department of Justice*] [*A publication*] (DLA)
**I & N** .......... Immigration and Naturalization [*Service*] [*Department of Justice*]
**IN**.............. Inch (EY)
**In**.............. Income
**IN**.............. India [*ANSI two-letter standard code*] (CNC)
**IN**.............. Indian Navy
**In**.............. Indian Reports [*A publication*] (DLA)
**IN**.............. Indiana [*Postal code*]
**IN**.............. Indiana Musicator [*A publication*]
**IN**.............. Indiana Names [*Indiana State University*] [*A publication*]
**In**.............. Indiana State Library, Indianapolis, IN [*Library symbol*] [*Library of Congress*] (LCLS)
**In**.............. Indium [*Chemical element*]
**IN**.............. Industrial Marketing [*Later, Business Marketing*] [*A publication*]
**IN**.............. Inertial (MCD)
**IN**.............. Infantry [*Army*]
**IN**.............. Information Systems Directorate [*Kennedy Space Center*] [*NASA*] (NASA)
**IN**.............. Initial Dose [*Medicine*]
**IN**.............. Inlet [*Maps and charts*]
**In**.............. [*Pope*] Innocent IV [*Deceased, 1254*] [*Authority cited in pre-1607 legal work*] (DSA)
**IN**.............. Input (MDG)
**IN**.............. INS Insurance [*Vancouver Stock Exchange symbol*]
**IN**.............. Institute of Navigation [*US and British*]
**IN**.............. Institution [*Online database field identifier*]
**In**.............. Instructor [*Navy*] [*British*]
**IN**.............. Instructor Navigator (AFM)
**IN**.............. Instrument Note
**IN**.............. Instrumentalist [*A publication*]
**IN**.............. Instrumentation Notice (AAG)
**In**.............. Insula [*A publication*]
**IN**.............. Insulated [*Shipping*] (DCTA)
**In**.............. Insulin
**IN**.............. Insurance
**IN**.............. Intake
**IN**.............. Intelligence
**IN**.............. Intelligence Corps [*Army*] (RDA)
**IN**.............. Intelligent Network [*Telecommunications*]
**IN**.............. Intensity
**IN**.............. Interception [*Football*]
**IN**.............. Interest [*Finance, Law*] (ADA)
**IN**.............. Interference-to-Noise Ratio (IEEE)
**IN**.............. Intermittent Noise
**IN**.............. Internal Note
**IN**.............. International House - World Trade Center [*Later, WTC*] (EA)
**IN**.............. International NOTAMS [*Notices to Airmen*] [*A publication*]
**In**.............. Interpretation [*A publication*]
**IN**.............. Interpreter [*A publication*]
**IN**.............. Intertechnique
**IN**.............. Intraductal [*Medicine*]
**IN**.............. Intranasal
**IN**.............. Inventory Nonrecurring (MCD)
**IN**.............. Investigator
**IN**.............. Irish Nationalist (ROG)
**IN**.............. Italia Numismatica [*A publication*]
**IN**.............. Italian Navy (NATG)
**IN**.............. Item Name [*Military*]
**IN**.............. Neisler Laboratories, Inc. [*Research code symbol*]
**IN**.............. Office of Inspection and Enforcement Information Notice [*Nuclear energy*] (NRCH)
**IN²** ............ Square Inch
**IN³** ............ Cubic Inch
**INA** ........... Anderson College, Anderson, IN [*OCLC symbol*] (OCLC)
**INA** ........... Department of Indian and Northern Affairs Library [*UTLAS symbol*]
**INA** ........... Ice Nucleating Activity [*Biology*] [*Physics*]
**INA** ........... Iinan [*Japan*] [*Seismograph station code, US Geological Survey*] (SEIS)
**INA** ........... Immunonephelometric Assay [*Clinical chemistry*]
**INA** ........... Inactivator Accelerator [*Immunology*]
**INA** ........... Independent Newsletter Association
**INA** ........... Indian National Airways
**INA** ........... Indian National Army [*World War II*]
**INA** ........... Indian and Northern Affairs Department [*Canada*]
**INA** ........... Indiana Airways, Inc. [*Indiana, PA*] [*FAA designator*] (FAAC)
**InA** ........... Indiana Appellate Court Reports [*A publication*] (DLA)
**INA** ........... Individual Nonrecurrence Action (KSC)
**INA** ........... Industrija Nafta [*State-owned company*] [*Yugoslavia*]
**INA** ........... Information Not Available (OICC)
**INA** ........... Initial Approach [*Aviation*] (FAAC)
**INA** ........... Innopac, Inc. [*Toronto Stock Exchange symbol*]
**In A** ........... Insel-Almanach [*A publication*]
**INA** ........... Inspector of Naval Aircraft
**INA** ........... Institute for Anthropology [*State University of New York at Albany*] [*Research center*] (RCD)
**INA** ........... Institute of Nautical Archaeology (EA)
**INA** ........... Institute for New Antibiotics [*USSR*]
**INA** ........... Institution of Naval Architects [*British*]
**INA** ........... Insurance Co. of North America
**INA** ........... Integrated Network Architecture
**INA** ........... Interface Age/Computing for Business [*A publication*]
**INA** ........... International Affairs [*A publication*]
**INA** ........... International Nannoplankton Association. Newsletter [*A publication*]
**INA** ........... International Nanny Association (EA)
**INA** ........... International Naturopathic Association [*Later, IAHHP*] (EA)
**INA** ........... International Newsreel and News Film Association [*Later, INANEWS*] (EAIO)
**INA** ........... International Normal Atmosphere
**INA** ........... Iodonaphthyl Azide [*Organic chemistry*]
**INA** ........... Iraqi News Agency
**INA** ........... Irish Northern Aid
**INA** ........... Iron Nickel Alloy
**INA** ........... Isonicotinic Acid [*Organic chemistry*]
**INA** ........... Israel News Agency
**INAA** ......... Instrumental Neutron Activation Analysis
**INAAP**....... Indiana Army Ammunition Plant (AABC)
**INAB** ......... Indian and Northern Affairs Backgrounder [*A publication*]
**INABU** ...... Imprimerie Nationale du Burundi [*Government publishing house*] [*Burundi*] (EY)
**INAC** ......... Inacomp Computer Centers, Inc. [*Troy, MI*] [*NASDAQ symbol*] (NQ)
**inac**............ Inactive
**INAC** ......... Indian and Northern Affairs Communique [*A publication*]
**InAcdC-T**... Anderson College, Graduate School of Theology, Anderson, IN [*Library symbol*] [*Library of Congress*] (LCLS)
**INACDUTRA** ... Inactive Duty Training [*Air Force*] (AFM)
**INACT**....... Inactive (AABC)
**INACTFLTPAC** ... Inactive Fleet, Pacific Fleet
**INACTLANT** ... Inactive Fleet, Atlantic Fleet
**INACTPAC** ... Inactive Fleet, Pacific Fleet
**INACTSHIPFAC** ... Inactive Ship Maintenance Facility [*Navy*]
**INACTV**.... Inactivate [*or Inactive*] (MSA) (MSA)
**INAD**......... Inadequate (AFM)
**INAD**......... Inadvertent
**INADES**.... Institut Africain pour le Developpement Economique et Social (EAIO)
**INAE** ......... International Newspaper Advertising Executives [*Later, INAME*] (EA)
**INAETP**.... Indian and Native American Employment and Training Program [*Department of Labor*]
**InAF**.......... Indian Air Force
**INAF**......... Individual Name and Address File [*IRS*]
**INAFBO**.... International Association for Business Organizations [*Baltimore, MD*] (EA)
**INAGAT**.... Indian Agriculturist [*A publication*]
**INAH**......... Isonicotinic Acid Hydrazide [*See also INH, ISONIAZID*] [*Antituberculous agent*]
**INAI** .......... IntelliCorp, Incorporated [*NASDAQ symbol*] (NQ)
**INAI** .......... Iowa Natural Areas Inventory [*Iowa State Conservation Commission*] [*Des Moines*] [*Information service or system*] (IID)
**INA/IC**...... Inactive - In Commission, In Reserve [*Vessel status*] [*Navy*]
**INA/IS** ...... Inactive - In Service, In Reserve [*Vessel status*] [*Navy*]
**INAJA4**..... Irish Naturalists' Journal [*A publication*]
**InAk**........... Akron Carnegie Public Library, Akron, IN [*Library symbol*] [*Library of Congress*] (LCLS)

**INALA**....... Industria Alimentara [*A publication*]
**INALB**....... Industrie Alimentari [*A publication*]
**InAlb**......... Noble County Public Library, Albion, IN [*Library symbol*] [*Library of Congress*] (LCLS)
**InAle**.......... Alexandria Public Library, Alexandria, IN [*Library symbol*] [*Library of Congress*] (LCLS)
**InAleN**....... Alexandria News, Alexandria, IN [*Library symbol*] [*Library of Congress*] (LCLS)
**InAleTT**..... Alexandria Times-Tribune, Alexandria, IN [*Library symbol*] [*Library of Congress*] (LCLS)
**INAM**........ Indian America [*A publication*]
**INAME**..... International Newspaper Advertising and Marketing Executives (EA)
**InAnd**......... Anderson Carnegie Public Library, Anderson, IN [*Library symbol*] [*Library of Congress*] (LCLS)
**InAndB**...... Anderson Daily Bulletin, Anderson, IN [*Library symbol*] [*Library of Congress*] (LCLS)
**InAndC**...... Anderson College, Anderson, IN [*Library symbol*] [*Library of Congress*] (LCLS)
**InAndH**...... Anderson Herald, Anderson, IN [*Library symbol*] [*Library of Congress*] (LCLS)
**INANEWS**... International Newsreel Association (EAIO)
**InAng**......... Carnegie Public Library, Angola, IN [*Library symbol*] [*Library of Congress*] (LCLS)
**InAngT**...... Tri-State University, Angola, IN [*Library symbol*] [*Library of Congress*] (LCLS)
**InAnw**........ Andrews-Dallas Township Public Library, Andrews, IN [*Library symbol*] [*Library of Congress*] (LCLS)
**INAO**......... Institut National des Appellations d'Origine [*Semigovernmental organization that fixes the appellations on all French wines*]
**INA/OC**.... Inactive - Out of Commission, In Reserve [*Vessel status*] [*Navy*]
**INA/OS**..... Inactive - Out of Service, In Reserve [*Vessel status*] [*Navy*]
**INAP**......... Integrated Neutron Activation Prediction [*Code system*]
**INap**.......... Nichols Library, Naperville, IL [*Library symbol*] [*Library of Congress*] (LCLS)
**INapC**........ College & Seminary Library, Inc., Naperville, IL [*Library symbol*] [*Library of Congress*] [*Obsolete*] (LCLS)
**INAPEN**.... International AIDS Prospective Epidemiology Network (EA)
**INapGS**..... Church of Jesus Christ of Latter-Day Saints, Genealogical Society Library, Naperville Branch, Naperville, IL [*Library symbol*] [*Library of Congress*] (LCLS)
**INapN**........ North Central College, Naperville, IL [*Library symbol*] [*Library of Congress*] (LCLS)
**INapS**........ Standard Oil Research Center, Naperville, IL [*Library symbol*] [*Library of Congress*] (LCLS)
**InAr**........... Argos Public Library, Argos, IN [*Library symbol*] [*Library of Congress*] (LCLS)
**INARA**...... Ingenieur-Archiv. Gesellschaft fuer Angewandte Mathematik und Mechanik [*A publication*]
**IN ARCH**.. Inland Architect [*A publication*] (ROG)
**InArcT**....... Tri Town Topics, Arcadia, IN [*Library symbol*] [*Library of Congress*] (LCLS)
**InArT**......... Argos Tribune, Argos, IN [*Library symbol*] [*Library of Congress*] (LCLS)
**INAS**.......... Indexing and Abstracting Services
**INAS**.......... Industrial Naval Air Stations (NG)
**INAS**.......... Inertial Navigation and Attack System (MCD)
**INAS**.......... Interbank National Authorization System
**INas**........... Nashville Public Library, Nashville, IL [*Library symbol*] [*Library of Congress*] (LCLS)
**INasHS**...... Nashville High School, Nashville, IL [*Library symbol*] [*Library of Congress*] (LCLS)
**INasSD**...... Nashville Community High School District 99, Nashville, IL [*Library symbol*] [*Library of Congress*] (LCLS)
**INAT**......... Indiana National Corp. [*NASDAQ symbol*] (NQ)
**INat**........... New Athens Public Library, New Athens, IL [*Library symbol*] [*Library of Congress*] (LCLS)
**INATA**...... Industries Atomiques [*A publication*]
**INATAPROBU**... International Association of Professional Bureaucrats (EA)
**INatCD**...... New Athens Community Consolidated District 60, New Athens, IL [*Library symbol*] [*Library of Congress*] (LCLS)
**INATS**....... Interruption of Air Traffic Service (FAAC)
**InAtt**.......... Attica Public Library, Attica, IN [*Library symbol*] [*Library of Congress*] (LCLS)
**InAttCF**..... Covington Friend, Attica, IN [*Library symbol*] [*Library of Congress*] (LCLS)
**InAttFO**..... Attica Friendly Oracle, Attica, IN [*Library symbol*] [*Library of Congress*] (LCLS)
**InAttLT**..... Attica Daily Ledger Tribune, Attica, IN [*Library symbol*] [*Library of Congress*] (LCLS)
**INAUA**...... Instrumentenbau Musik International [*A publication*]
**INAUA3**.... Instruments and Automation [*A publication*]
**InAub**........ Eckhart Public Library, Auburn, IN [*Library symbol*] [*Library of Congress*] (LCLS)
**InAubS**....... Auburn Evening Star, Auburn, IN [*Library symbol*] [*Library of Congress*] (LCLS)
**INAUG**...... Inaugurated (ADA)
**InAur**......... Aurora Public Library, Aurora, IN [*Library symbol*] [*Library of Congress*] (LCLS)
**IN AUR**..... In Auri [*To the Ear*] [*Pharmacy*]
**InAurHi**..... Hillforest Historical Foundation, Inc., Aurora, IN [*Library symbol*] [*Library of Congress*] (LCLS)
**InAusN**...... Austin-Crothersville News, Austin, IN [*Library symbol*] [*Library of Congress*] (LCLS)
**INAW**........ Institute of the Northamerican West (EA)
**INAZ**......... Interference Accommodation Zone [*Geology*]
**INB**........... Bartholomew County Library, Columbus, IN [*OCLC symbol*] (OCLC)
**InB**............ Bedford Public Library, Bedford, IN [*Library symbol*] [*Library of Congress*] (LCLS)
**IN B**........... In Bonis [*In the Goods Of*] [*Latin*] (ADA)
**INB**........... In Bono [*In Good Order*]
**INB**........... In Business [*A publication*]
**INB**........... Independence [*Belize*] [*Airport symbol*] (OAG)
**INB**........... Indiana Motor Rate and Tariff Bureau Inc., Indianapolis IN [*STAC*]
**INB**........... Interbev Packaging Corp. [*Vancouver Stock Exchange symbol*]
**InB**............ International Bulletin of Missionary Research [*A publication*]
**INB**........... Israel Numismatic Bulletin [*A publication*]
**INb**............ Northbrook Public Library, Northbrook, IL [*Library symbol*] [*Library of Congress*] (LCLS)
**INB**........... Oakland, CA [*Location identifier*] [*FAA*] (FAAL)
**INBA**......... InBancshares [*NASDAQ symbol*] (NQ)
**INBA**......... International Nubian Breeders Association (EA)
**INBACS**.... Infantry Battalion as a Combat System [*Study*] (MCD)
**InBaHT**..... Batesville Herald Tribune, Batesville, IN [*Library symbol*] [*Library of Congress*] (LCLS)
**INBC**......... Independence Bancorp, Inc. [*NASDAQ symbol*] (NQ)
**INBC**......... Interlibrary Network of Baltimore County [*Library network*]
**InBCR**........ Lawrence County Recorder's Office, Bedford, IN [*Library symbol*] [*Library of Congress*] (LCLS)
**INBD**......... Inboard (KSC)
**INBD**......... Inbound
**InBer**.......... Berne Public Library, Berne, IN [*Library symbol*] [*Library of Congress*] (LCLS)
**INBF**.......... INB Financial Corp. [*NASDAQ symbol*] (NQ)
**INBH**......... Brokaw Hospital Medical Center, Normal, IL [*Library symbol*] [*Library of Congress*] (LCLS)
**INBID9**...... Indian Biologist [*A publication*]
**INBIEA**..... International Biodeterioration Bulletin [*A publication*]
**InBiKN**...... Knox County Daily News, Bicknell, IN [*Library symbol*] [*Library of Congress*] (LCLS)
**INBIS**........ INBIS [*Industrial and Business Information Services*] Australia
**INBIT**........ Input BIT [*Binary Digit*] [*Data processing*] (NASA)
**INBK**......... Indiana Bancshares, Inc. [*NASDAQ symbol*] (NQ)
**InBl**............ Bloomfield Public Library, Bloomfield, IN [*Library symbol*] [*Library of Congress*] (LCLS)
**INBLA**....... Ingenieursblad [*A publication*]
**InBlCR**....... Greene County Recorder's Office, Bloomfield, IN [*Library symbol*] [*Library of Congress*] (LCLS)
**InBLHi**...... Lawrence County Historical Society, Bedford, IN [*Library symbol*] [*Library of Congress*] (LCLS)
**InBlo**.......... Monroe County Public Library, Bloomington, IN [*Library symbol*] [*Library of Congress*] (LCLS)
**InBloHT**.... Bloomington Herald-Telephone, Bloomington, IN [*Library symbol*] [*Library of Congress*] (LCLS)
**InBloKi**...... Alfred C. Kinsey Institute for Sex Research, Bloomington, IN [*Library symbol*] [*Library of Congress*] (LCLS)
**InBlu**.......... Bluffton-Wells County Public Library, Bluffton, IN [*Library symbol*] [*Library of Congress*] (LCLS)
**InBlWN**..... Bloomfield Evening World and News, Bloomfield, IN [*Library symbol*] [*Library of Congress*] (LCLS)
**InBoM**....... Borden Museum, Borden, IN [*Library symbol*] [*Library of Congress*] [*Obsolete*] (LCLS)
**InBoo**......... Boonville Warrick County Public Library, Boonville, IN [*Library symbol*] [*Library of Congress*] (LCLS)
**InBooE**....... Warrick Enquirer, Boonville, IN [*Library symbol*] [*Library of Congress*] (LCLS)
**InBooS**....... Boonville Standard, Boonville, IN [*Library symbol*] [*Library of Congress*] (LCLS)
**InBosE**....... Boswell Enterprise, Boswell, IN [*Library symbol*] [*Library of Congress*] (LCLS)
**InBou**......... Bourbon Public Library, Bourbon, IN [*Library symbol*] [*Library of Congress*] (LCLS)
**In-BPH**...... Indiana State Library, Blind and Physically Handicapped Division, Indianapolis, IN [*Library symbol*] [*Library of Congress*] (LCLS)
**InBra**.......... Brazil Public Library, Brazil, IN [*Library symbol*] [*Library of Congress*] (LCLS)
**InBraCHi**... Clay County Historical Society, Brazil, IN [*Library symbol*] [*Library of Congress*] (LCLS)
**InBraT**....... Brazil Times, Brazil, IN [*Library symbol*] [*Library of Congress*] (LCLS)
**InBrb**.......... Brownsburg Public Library, Brownsburg, IN [*Library symbol*] [*Library of Congress*] (LCLS)
**InBrbG**...... Brownsburg Guide, Brownsburg, IN [*Library symbol*] [*Library of Congress*] (LCLS)
**INBRD**...... Inboard (ADA)

**InBre**.......... W. E. Walter Memorial Library (Bremen Public Library), Bremen, IN [*Library symbol*] [*Library of Congress*] (LCLS)
**InBreE**....... Bremen Enquirer, Bremen, IN [*Library symbol*] [*Library of Congress*] (LCLS)
**InBri**........... Bristol-Washington Township Public Library (Bristol Public Library), Bristol, IN [*Library symbol*] [*Library of Congress*] (LCLS)
**InBriEHi**.... Elkhart County Historical Society, Bristol, IN [*Library symbol*] [*Library of Congress*] (LCLS)
**InBrkvA**..... Brookville American, Brookville, IN [*Library symbol*] [*Library of Congress*] (LCLS)
**InBrkvCR**.. Franklin County Recorder's Office, Brookville, IN [*Library symbol*] [*Library of Congress*] (LCLS)
**InBrkvD**..... Brookville Democrat, Brookville, IN [*Library symbol*] [*Library of Congress*] (LCLS)
**InBro**.......... Brook-Iroquois Public Library, Brook, IN [*Library symbol*] [*Library of Congress*] (LCLS)
**InBroA**....... George Ade Hazeldon Home, Brook, IN [*Library symbol*] [*Library of Congress*] (LCLS)
**InBrt**.......... Brownstown Public Library, Brownstown, IN [*Library symbol*] [*Library of Congress*] (LCLS)
**InBrtB**........ Brownstown Banner, Brownstown, IN [*Library symbol*] [*Library of Congress*] (LCLS)
**InBrtHi**...... Jackson County Historical Society, Brownstown, IN [*Library symbol*] [*Library of Congress*] (LCLS)
**INBS**.......... Iowa National Bankshares Corp. [*NASDAQ symbol*] (NQ)
**INBSV**....... Interim Narrow-Band Secure Voice (NVT)
**InBTM**....... Bedford Times-Mail, Bedford, IN [*Library symbol*] [*Library of Congress*] (LCLS)
**InBu**........... Butler Carnegie Library, Butler, IN [*Library symbol*] [*Library of Congress*] (LCLS)
**InBuB**......... Butler Bulletin, Butler, IN [*Library symbol*] [*Library of Congress*] (LCLS)
**In Bus**......... In Business [*A publication*]
**INbW**......... Wiss, Janney, Elstner, & Associates, Northbrook, IL [*Library symbol*] [*Library of Congress*] (LCLS)
**InC**............. Crawfordsville District Public Library, Crawfordsville, IN [*Library symbol*] [*Library of Congress*] (LCLS)
**INC**............ Ice Navigation Center [*Marine science*] (MSC)
**INC**............ Idaho Nuclear Corporation
**INC**............ Iglesia Ni Cristo [*Religious organization*]
**INC**............ Igniter Nozzle Closure
**INC**............ In Cloud [*Aviation*] (FAAC)
**INC**............ In Nomine Christi [*In the Name of Christ*] [*Latin*]
**INC**............ Incendiary
**INC**............ Inchon [*Tyosen, Zinsen*] [*South Korea*] [*Seismograph station code, US Geological Survey*] [*Closed*] (SEIS)
**INC**............ Incidit [*Engraved*] [*Latin*] (ROG)
**INC**............ Incinerator
**inc**.............. Incision
**INC**............ Incisus [*Being Cut*] [*Pharmacy*] (ROG)
**INC**............ Inclosure
**INC**............ Including
**INC**............ Inclusive
**INC**............ Income (ROG)
**INC**............ Incoming [*Telecommunications*] (KSC)
**INC**............ Incoming Trunk [*Telecommunications*] (TEL)
**INC**............ Incomplete
**INC**............ Inconclusive
**INC**............ Incontinent [*Medicine*]
**INC**............ Incorporated (EY)
**INC**............ Increase (AABC)
**INC**............ Increment
**INC**............ Incumbent (ROG)
**inc**.............. Incurred
**INC**............ Indian National Congress
**INC**............ Indian Numismatic Chronicle [*A publication*]
**INC**............ Indiana Cooperative Library Services Authority, Indianapolis, IN [*OCLC symbol*] (OCLC)
**inc**.............. Indic [*MARC language code*] [*Library of Congress*] (LCCP)
**INC**............ Inertial Navigation Computer (MCD)
**INC**............ Information and Censorship [*Allied Forces*] [*World War II*]
**INC**............ Input Control System [*Military*]
**INC**............ Insectivorous Cyprinids [*Pisciculture*]
**INC**............ Insertable Nuclear Components (MCD)
**INC**............ Installation Notice Card (KSC)
**INC**............ Installation Notification Certification (MCD)
**INC**............ Intelligence Coordination [*Program*] [*Department of State*]
**INC**............ International Controls Corp. [*AMEX symbol*] (SPSG)
**INC**............ International Numismatic Commission
**INC**............ International Nut Council (EAIO)
**INC**............ Invermay Resources [*Vancouver Stock Exchange symbol*]
**INC**............ Irish National Caucus (EA)
**INC**............ Item Name Code [*Military*] (AFM)
**INC**............ Yinchuan [*China*] [*Airport symbol*] (OAG)
**INcA**.......... Abbott Laboratories, North Chicago, IL [*Library symbol*] [*Library of Congress*] (LCLS)
**InCa**........... Carlisle Public Library, Carlisle, IN [*Library symbol*] [*Library of Congress*] (LCLS)
**INCA**......... Idaho Nuclear Code Automation [*AEC*]
**INCA**......... In-Core Analysis [*Nuclear energy*] (NRCH)
**INCA**......... Information Council of the Americas (EA)
**INCA**......... Institute for Numerical Computation and Analysis (MCD)
**INCA**......... Integrated Catalog Algorithm (MCD)
**INCA**......... Integrated Communications Agency [*Air Force*]
**INCA**......... Integrated Navigation and Communications, Automatic
**INCA**......... Integrated Nuclear and Chemical Analysis
**INCA**......... Integrated Nuclear Communications Assessment
**INCA**......... Integrated Numerical Control Approach
**INCA**......... Intelligence Communications Architecture
**INCA**......... International Narcotics Control Act
**INCA**......... International Newspaper and Colour Association [*Later, IFRA*] (EA)
**INCAD**...... Incapacitated Passengers' Handling Advice [*British*]
**INCAE**....... Instituto Centroamericano de Administracion de Empresas [*Central American Institute of Business Administration*] [*Nicaragua*]
**INCAIR**..... Including Air
**Incalz**......... Incalzando [*Music*]
**InCam**........ Camden-Jackson Township Public Library, Camden, IN [*Library symbol*] [*Library of Congress*] (LCLS)
**InCan**......... Cannelton Public Library, Cannelton, IN [*Library symbol*] [*Library of Congress*] (LCLS)
**InCanCR**.... Perry County Recorder's Office, Cannelton, IN [*Library symbol*] [*Library of Congress*] (LCLS)
**INCAND**... Incandescent (MSA)
**INCAP**....... Instituto de Nutricion de Centro America y Panama [*Institute of Nutrition of Central America and Panama*] [*Guatemala, Guatemala*] (EAIO)
**InCar**.......... Carmel Public Library, Carmel, IN [*Library symbol*] [*Library of Congress*] (LCLS)
**INCAR**....... International Committee Against Racism (EA)
**InCarNJ**.... Carmel News Journal, Carmel, IN [*Library symbol*] [*Library of Congress*] (LCLS)
**Inc Aust Insurance Inst J**... Incorporated Australian Insurance Institute. Journal [*A publication*] (APTA)
**InCayHN**... Cayuga Herald News, Cayuga, IN [*Library symbol*] [*Library of Congress*] (LCLS)
**IncB**............ Inclusion Body [*Cytology*]
**INCB**......... International Narcotics Control Board [*See also OICS*] (EA)
**INCB**......... International Nuclear Credit Bank (NRCH)
**INCBE**....... Israel National Committee on the Biosphere and Environment
**INCBR**....... Incubator (MSA)
**InCc**........... Cambridge City Public Library, Cambridge City, IN [*Library symbol*] [*Library of Congress*] (LCLS)
**INCC**......... Institut National du Cancer du Canada [*National Cancer Institute of Canada*] (EAIO)
**INCC**......... Interim National Coordinating Committee [*Ghana*] (PPW)
**INCC**......... International Network Controlling Center [*Telecommunications*] (TEL)
**INCC**......... International Newspaper Collector's Club (EA)
**INCC**......... International Nippon Collectors Club (EA)
**InCcNR**...... National Road Traveler, Cambridge City, IN [*Library symbol*] [*Library of Congress*] (LCLS)
**INCD**......... Incandescent
**INCD**......... Incendiary (AABC)
**INCD**......... Incorporated [*Legal term*] (EY)
**INCDT**...... Incident (MSA)
**InCe**........... Centerville and Center Township Library, Centerville, IN [*Library symbol*] [*Library of Congress*] (LCLS)
**INCE**......... Institute of Noise Control Engineering (EA)
**INCE**......... Insurance
**INCEI**........ Instituto Nacional de Comercio Exterior e Interior [*National Institute of Foreign and Domestic Trade*] [*Nicaraguan*]
**INCEP**....... Interceptor
**INCEPT**.... Inception (ROG)
**INCERFA**... Message Relates to Uncertainty Phase [*Aviation code*] (FAAC)
**IncFB**......... Increase Feedback
**INCFO**....... Institute of Newspaper Controllers and Finance Officers [*Later, INFE*] (EA)
**INCH**......... Integrated Chopper
**INCH**......... Interim Charging [*Electric vehicle technology*]
**INCH**......... International Center for High Quality Scrap [*Scrap salvage*]
**InCha**......... Charlestown Township Public Library, Charlestown, IN [*Library symbol*] [*Library of Congress*] (LCLS)
**InChe**......... Westchester Public Library, Chesterton, IN [*Library symbol*] [*Library of Congress*] (LCLS)
**InCheT**....... Chesterton Tribune, Chesterton, IN [*Library symbol*] [*Library of Congress*] (LCLS)
**INCHO**...... Inchoate (ADA)
**IN CH Q**.... Indian Church Quarterly Review [*A publication*] (ROG)
**INCIBC**..... Instituto de Nutricion de Centro America y Panama. Informe Anual [*A publication*]
**INCID**........ Incide [*Cut*] [*Pharmacy*]
**INCIDI**...... Institut International des Civilisations Differentes [*International Institute of Differing Civilizations*]
**INCIN**........ Incinerator (MSA)
**INCINC**..... International Copyright Information Center (EA)
**INCIS**........ Incisus [*Being Cut*] [*Pharmacy*] (ROG)
**INCJHS**.... International Network of Children of Jewish Holocaust Survivors (EA)

**InCJR**........ Crawfordsville Journal and Review, Crawfordsville, IN [*Library symbol*] [*Library of Congress*] (LCLS)
**INCL**.......... Inclination [*Angular distance from equator in degrees*]
**INCL**.......... Inclosure (AFM)
**INCL**.......... Including (EY)
**INCL**.......... Inclusive
**INCL**.......... Inconclusive
**IncL**........... Incorporated Linguist [*London*] [*A publication*]
**InClcN**....... Clay City News, Clay City, IN [*Library symbol*] [*Library of Congress*] (LCLS)
**INCLD**....... Including [*Freight*]
**INCLD**....... International Classification [*A publication*]
**InCli**........... Clinton Public Library, Clinton, IN [*Library symbol*] [*Library of Congress*] (LCLS)
**InCliC**........ Daily Clintonian, Clinton, IN [*Library symbol*] [*Library of Congress*] (LCLS)
**Inc Linguist**... Incorporated Linguist [*A publication*]
**INCLN**...... Inclined (MSA)
**INCLN**...... Inclusion
**INCLR**....... Intercooler
**INCLS**....... Inclosure (MSA)
**INCLU**....... Inclusive (ROG)
**INCLV**....... Inclusive (FAAC)
**InCLW**....... General Lew Wallace Studio, Crawfordsville, IN [*Library symbol*] [*Library of Congress*] (LCLS)
**INCM**........ Incoming (MSA)
**INCM**........ InteCom, Inc. [*NASDAQ symbol*] (NQ)
**INCMG**..... Incoming
**INCND**...... Incendiary (MSA)
**Incntv Mkt**... Incentive Marketing [*A publication*]
**InCo**........... Connersville Public Library, Connersville, IN [*Library symbol*] [*Library of Congress*] (LCLS)
**INCO**......... Installation and Checkout [*Military*] (CAAL)
**INCO**......... Instrumentation and Communications Officer [*NASA*]
**INCO**......... International Chamber of Commerce (IEEE)
**INCO**......... International Nickel Company
**InCoa**......... Coatesville Public Library, Coatesville, IN [*Library symbol*] [*Library of Congress*] (LCLS)
**InCODA**.... International Congress of Dealers Associations (EA)
**INCODEL**... Interstate Commission on the Delaware River Basin
**incog**........... Incognito [*Unknown*] [*Latin*]
**INCOG**...... Indian Nations Council of Governments
**INCOH**...... Incoherent (MSA)
**InColc**........ Peabody Library, Columbia City, IN [*Library symbol*] [*Library of Congress*] (LCLS)
**InColcCR**... Whitley County Recorder's Office, Columbia City, IN [*Library symbol*] [*Library of Congress*] (LCLS)
**InColo**........ Bartholomew County Library, Columbus, IN [*Library symbol*] [*Library of Congress*] (LCLS)
**INCOLR**.... Intercooler
**INCOLSA**... Indiana Cooperative Library Services Authority [*Indianapolis, IN*] [*Library network*]
**InColu**........ Bartholomew County Library, Columbus, IN [*Library symbol*] [*Library of Congress*] (LCLS)
**InColuHi**.... Bartholomew County Historical Society, Columbus, IN [*Library symbol*] [*Library of Congress*] (LCLS)
**INCOM**..... Incomplete (AABC)
**Income Tax Rep**... Income Tax Reporter [*A publication*]
**INCOMEX**... Instituto Mexicano de Comercio Exterior [*Mexican Foreign Trade Institute*]
**INCOMEX**... International Computer Exhibition
**INCOMINDIOS**... International Committee for the Indians of the Americas [*Kaiseraugst, Switzerland*] (EAIO)
**INCOMP**.. Incomplete (MSA)
**INCOMPAT**... Incompatible [*Medicine*]
**Incompat Newsl**... Incompatibility Newsletter [*A publication*]
**INCOMPL**... Incomplete
**InCon**......... Converse Jackson Township Public Library, Converse, IN [*Library symbol*] [*Library of Congress*] (LCLS)
**INCON**...... Installation Console (MCD)
**INCONCRYO-ISC**... International Conference on Cryogenics - International Steering Committee (EAIO)
**InCoNE**...... Connersville News-Examiner, Connersville, IN [*Library symbol*] [*Library of Congress*] (LCLS)
**InCor**.......... Corydon Public Library, Corydon, IN [*Library symbol*] [*Library of Congress*] (LCLS)
**INCOR**...... Incorporated [*Legal term*]
**INCOR**...... Incorrect (MSA)
**INCOR**...... Intergovernmental Conference on Oceanographic Research (MCD)
**InCorCP**..... Harrison County Press, Corydon, IN [*Library symbol*] [*Library of Congress*] (LCLS)
**InCorCR**.... Harrison County Recorder's Office, Corydon, IN [*Library symbol*] [*Library of Congress*] (LCLS)
**InCorD**....... Corydon Democrat, Corydon, IN [*Library symbol*] [*Library of Congress*] (LCLS)
**INCORP**.... Incorporated [*Legal term*] (EY)
**Incorp Bus**... Incorporating Your Business [*A publication*]
**Incorp Ling**... Incorporated Linguist [*A publication*]
**INCORPN**... Incorporation [*Legal term*] (ROG)
**INCORR**... Incorrect (ADA)
**INCOS**....... Integrated Control System [*Navy*] (NVT)
**INCOT**...... In-Core Test Facility [*Nuclear energy*] (NRCH)
**INCOTEC**... International Committee for Training and Education of Co-Operators (EAIO)
**INCOTERM**... International Commerce Term [*International Chamber of Commerce*]
**InCov**......... Covington Public Library, Covington, IN [*Library symbol*] [*Library of Congress*] (LCLS)
**InCovFS**..... Fountain County Star, Covington, IN [*Library symbol*] [*Library of Congress*] (LCLS)
**INCPA**....... Instrumentation in the Chemical and Petroleum Industries [*A publication*]
**INCPD ACCT**... Incorporated Accountant [*British*] (ROG)
**INCPT**....... Intercept
**INCR**......... Inca Resources, Inc. [*NASDAQ symbol*] (NQ)
**INCR**......... Increase (AFM)
**INCR**......... Increment (AFM)
**INCR**......... Interrupt Control Register [*Data processing*] (MSA)
**INCRA**....... International Copper Research Association [*Research center*] [*Great Britain*] (IRC)
**INCRA Res Rep**... INCRA [*International Copper Research Association, Inc.*] Research Report [*A publication*]
**INCRE**....... Increment
**INCREM**... Incremental
**Incremental Motion Control Syst Devices Newsl**... Incremental Motion Control Systems and Devices. Newsletter [*A publication*]
**INCREP**.... Incident Report [*Military*] (CINC)
**InCrp**.......... Crown Point Center Public Library, Crown Point, IN [*Library symbol*] [*Library of Congress*] (LCLS)
**InCrpCS**.... Crown Point Community Schools, Crown Point, IN [*Library symbol*] [*Library of Congress*] (LCLS)
**InCrpLS**..... Lake County Star, Crown Point, IN [*Library symbol*] [*Library of Congress*] (LCLS)
**INCS**.......... Integrated Battlefield Control System (MCD)
**INCS**.......... International Netsuke Collectors Society [*Commercial firm*] (EA)
**INCSEA**.... Incident at Sea [*Navy*] (NVT)
**inc sed**........ Incertae Sedis [*Uncertain Position*] [*Biology, taxonomy*]
**INCSR**....... International Narcotics Control Strategy Report [*Department of State*]
**INCT**......... Incumbent (ROG)
**Inc Tax Cas**... Reports of Cases Relating to Income Tax [*A publication*] (DLA)
**Inc Tax LJ**... Income Tax Law Journal [*India*] [*A publication*] (DLA)
**Inc Tax R**... Income Tax Reports [*India*] [*A publication*] (DLA)
**InCu**.......... Culver Public Library, Culver, IN [*Library symbol*] [*Library of Congress*] (LCLS)
**INCUMB**.. Incumbent
**INCUMBCE**... Incumbrance (ROG)
**INCUMBD**... Incumbered (ROG)
**INCUN**...... Incunabula (ADA)
**INCUR**...... Incurable [*Medicine*]
**INCV**......... Inclusive (MSA)
**InCW**......... Wabash College, Crawfordsville, IN [*Library symbol*] [*Library of Congress*] (LCLS)
**INCWF**...... Indian National Cement Workers' Federation
**INCY**......... Incendiary Bomb (DSUE)
**InCyA**........ Cynthiana Argus, Cynthiana, IN [*Library symbol*] [*Library of Congress*] (LCLS)
**Ind**.............. Adversus Indoctum [*of Lucian*] [*Classical studies*] (OCD)
**IND**........... Improvised Nuclear Device
**IN D**........... In Dies [*Daily*] [*Pharmacy*]
**IND**........... In Nomine Dei [*In the Name of God*] [*Latin*]
**IND**........... Indecent [*FBI standardized term*]
**IND**........... Independent
**IND**........... Independent [*A publication*]
**Ind**.............. Independents [*Political party*] [*Pakistan*]
**IND**........... Index
**IND**........... India [*ANSI three-letter standard code*] [*IYRU nationality code*] (CNC)
**IND**........... Indian (AABC)
**IND**........... Indiana
**Ind**.............. Indiana Reports [*A publication*]
**Ind**.............. Indiana Supreme Court Reports [*A publication*] (DLA)
**IND**........... Indianapolis [*Indiana*] [*Airport symbol*] (OAG)
**IND**........... Indicate [*or Indicator*] (KSC)
**IND**........... Indicative (ROG)
**Ind**.............. Indice de Arte y Letras [*A publication*]
**IND**........... Indies
**IND**........... Indigo
**IND**........... Indirect
**IND**........... Indomethacin [*An analgesic*]
**ind**.............. Indonesian [*MARC language code*] [*Library of Congress*] (LCCP)
**IND**........... Indoors (ROG)
**IND**........... Indorse [*Legal term*] (AABC)
**IND**........... Induced Nuclear Disintegration
**IND**........... Inductance
**IND**........... Induction (MSA)
**Ind**.............. Indus [*Constellation*]
**IND**........... Industrial

**IND**........... Industrial Distribution [*A publication*]
**Ind**............. Industrie [*A publication*]
**IND**........... Industry (AFM)
**IND**........... Industry Division [*Census*] (OICC)
**IND**........... Inter Mountain Development, Inc. [*Vancouver Stock Exchange symbol*]
**IND**........... Intercept Director [*Military*]
**IND**........... International Number Dialing [*Telecommunications*] (TEL)
**IND**........... Investigational New Drug [*Application*] [*FDA*]
**IND**........... University of Notre Dame, Notre Dame, IN [*OCLC symbol*] (OCLC)
**Ind 2000**..... Industry 2000. New Perspectives [*A publication*]
**INDA**......... INDA, Association of the Nonwoven Fabrics Industry [*Formerly, International Nonwovens and Disposables Association*]
**IndA**........... Independent Agent [*A publication*]
**Ind Acad Sci Proc** ... Indiana Academy of Science. Proceedings [*A publication*]
**Ind Acc Com** ... Decisions of the Industrial Accident Commission of California [*A publication*] (DLA)
**Ind Acts**...... Acts of Indiana [*A publication*] (DLA)
**Ind A Dig**... United States Indian Affairs Office, Digest of Decisions [*A publication*] (DLA)
**Ind Admin Code** ... Indiana Administrative Code [*A publication*]
**Ind Admin R** ... Burns' Indiana Administrative Rules and Regulations [*A publication*] (DLA)
**Ind Adv**...... Indian Advocate [*A publication*]
**Ind Advocate** ... Indian Advocate [*A publication*] (DLA)
**Ind Aeron**... Index Aeronauticus [*A publication*]
**Ind Ag Exp** ... Purdue University. Indiana Agricultural Experiment Station. Publications [*A publication*]
**Indag Math** ... Indagationes Mathematicae [*A publication*]
**Ind Agr**....... Industrie Agrarie [*Italy*] [*A publication*]
**Ind Agr**....... Revue Internationale des Industries Agricoles [*A publication*]
**Ind Agri Am Lat Caribe** ... Indice Agricole de America Latina y el Caribe [*A publication*]
**Ind A Ind**.... Industrial Arts Index [*A publication*]
**INDAIR**..... Identification of Aircraft
**Ind Aliment** ... Industria Alimentaria [*A publication*]
**Ind Aliment Agr** ... Industries Alimentaires et Agricoles [*A publication*]
**Ind Aliment Agric (Paris)** ... Industries Alimentaires et Agricoles (Paris) [*A publication*]
**Ind Aliment Anim** ... Industries de l'Alimentation Animale [*A publication*]
**Ind Aliment (Bucharest)** ... Industria Alimentara (Bucharest) [*A publication*]
**Ind Aliment (Havana)** ... Industria Alimenticia (Havana) [*A publication*]
**Ind Aliment (Mexico City)** ... Industrias de la Alimentacion (Mexico City) [*A publication*]
**Ind Aliment (Pinerolo Italy)** ... Industrie Alimentari (Pinerolo, Italy) [*A publication*]
**Ind Aliment Prod Anim** ... Industria Alimentara. Produse Animale [*A publication*]
**Ind Aliment Prod Veg** ... Industria Alimentara. Produse Vegetale [*Romania*] [*A publication*]
**Ind Aliment Veget** ... Industria Alimentara. Produse Vegetale [*A publication*]
**Ind Amer Per Verse** ... Index of American Periodical Verse [*A publication*]
**InDaN**........ Dale News, Dale, IN [*Library symbol*] [*Library of Congress*] (LCLS)
**InDan**......... Danville Public Library, Danville, IN [*Library symbol*] [*Library of Congress*] (LCLS)
**Ind Analyt Canc** ... Index Analyticus Cancerologiae [*A publication*]
**InDanCR** ... Hendricks County Recorder's Office, Danville, IN [*Library symbol*] [*Library of Congress*] (LCLS)
**InDanN**...... Central Normal College, Danville, IN [*Library symbol*] [*Library of Congress*] [*Obsolete*] (LCLS)
**InDanR**...... Danville Republican, Danville, IN [*Library symbol*] [*Library of Congress*] (LCLS)
**Ind Ant**....... Indian Antiquary [*A publication*]
**Ind Anthro** ... Indian Anthropologist [*A publication*]
**Ind-Anz**...... Industrie-Anzeiger [*A publication*]
**Ind App**...... Indiana Court of Appeals Reports [*A publication*] (DLA)
**Ind App**...... Law Reports, Indian Appeals [*A publication*] (DLA)
**Ind App Ct** ... Indiana Appellate Court Reports [*A publication*] (DLA)
**Ind App Supp** ... Supplemental Indian Appeals, Law Reports [*A publication*] (DLA)
**InDar** ......... Darlington Public Library, Darlington, IN [*Library symbol*] [*Library of Congress*] (LCLS)
**Ind Arch**..... Industrial Architecture [*A publication*]
**Ind Archaeol** ... Industrial Archaeology [*A publication*]
**Ind Archaeol Rev** ... Industrial Archaeology Review [*A publication*]
**Ind Arts Index** ... Industrial Arts Index [*A publication*]
**Ind-Arts M** ... Industrial-Arts Magazine [*A publication*]
**Ind Arts & Voc Ed** ... Industrial Arts and Vocational Education/Technical Education [*A publication*]
**INDASAT** ... Indian Scientific Satellite
**Ind As Cult** ... Indo-Asian Culture [*A publication*]
**INDAT** ...... Incoming Data (MCD)
**Ind At**....... Industries Atomiques [*A publication*]
**Ind At & Spat** ... Industries Atomiques et Spatiales [*A publication*]
**Ind At Spatiales** ... Industries Atomiques et Spatiales [*A publication*]
**Ind Aurel**.... Index Aureliensis [*A publication*]
**Ind Aust & Min Standard** ... Industrial Australian and Mining Standard [*A publication*] (APTA)
**Ind Austr Min Stand** ... Industrial Australian and Mining Standard [*A publication*]
**Ind Awards** ... Industrial Awards Recommendations [*New Zealand*] [*A publication*] (DLA)
**Ind Azucar** ... Industria Azucarera [*A publication*]
**INDB**......... Independent Bank Corp. [*Rockland, MA*] [*NASDAQ symbol*] (NQ)
**Ind Bcasting** ... Independent Broadcasting [*United Kingdom*] [*A publication*]
**Ind Bevande** ... Industrie delle Bevande [*A publication*]
**Ind Bibl**...... Index Bibliographicus [*A publication*]
**Ind Bl**......... Industrieblatt [*A publication*]
**Ind Bldg**..... Industrialised Building [*A publication*]
**Ind Buk Kenk** ... Indogaku Bukkyogaku Kenkyu [*A publication*]
**Ind Bull**...... Industrial Bulletin [*A publication*]
**Ind Bull Arthur D Little Inc** ... Industrial Bulletin of Arthur D. Little, Incorporated [*A publication*]
**Ind Bull NY State Dep Labor** ... Industrial Bulletin. New York State Department of Labor [*A publication*]
**INDC**......... Indicate (FAAC)
**INDC**......... International Nuclear Data Committee [*of International Atomic Energy Agency*]
**INDCA**...... Industrial Chemist [*A publication*]
**Ind Can**...... Industrial Canada [*A publication*]
**Ind Can L P Lit** ... Index to Canadian Legal Periodical Literature [*A publication*] (DLA)
**Ind Carta**.... Industria della Carta [*A publication*]
**Ind Carta Arti Grafiche** ... Industria della Carta e delle Arti Grafiche [*A publication*]
**Ind Cas**....... Indian Cases [*India*] [*A publication*] (DLA)
**Ind C Aw**.... Industrial Court Awards [*England*] [*A publication*] (DLA)
**Ind Ceram** ... Industrie Ceramique [*A publication*]
**Ind Ceram Silicat** ... Industria della Ceramica e Silicati [*A publication*]
**Ind Chem**.... Industrial Chemist [*A publication*]
**Ind Chem Bull** ... Industrial Chemistry Bulletin [*A publication*]
**Ind Chem N** ... Industrial Chemical News [*A publication*]
**Ind Ch HR** ... Indian Church History Review [*A publication*]
**Ind Child Mag** ... Subject Index to Children's Magazines [*A publication*]
**Ind Chim**.... Industrie Chimique [*A publication*]
**Ind Chim Belge** ... Industrie Chimique Belge [*A publication*]
**Ind Chim Min Metall** ... Industria Chimica, Mineraria, e Metallurgica [*A publication*]
**Ind Chim (Paris)** ... Industrie Chimique (Paris) [*A publication*]
**Ind Chim Phosph** ... Industrie Chimique, le Phosphate [*A publication*]
**Ind Chim (Rome)** ... Industria Chimica (Rome) [*A publication*]
**Ind Chur Hist R** ... Indian Church History Review [*A publication*]
**Ind Code**..... Indiana Code [*A publication*]
**Ind Code Ann** ... Burns' Indiana Statutes, Annotated Code Edition [*A publication*] (DLA)
**Ind Code Ann (Burns)** ... Burns' Indiana Statutes, Annotated Code Edition [*A publication*]
**Ind Code Ann (West)** ... West's Annotated Indiana Code [*A publication*]
**Ind Com Law** ... Indermaur and Thwaites' Principles of the Common Law [*12th ed.*] [*1914*] [*A publication*] (DLA)
**Ind & Coml Training** ... Industrial and Commercial Training [*A publication*]
**Ind Comm Dev** ... Industry, Commerce, Development [*A publication*]
**Ind Commercial Photographer** ... Industrial and Commercial Photographer [*A publication*]
**Ind Commerc Train** ... Industrial and Commercial Training [*A publication*]
**Ind Commer Photogr** ... Industrial and Commercial Photographer [*A publication*]
**Ind Comm Gas** ... Industrial and Commercial Gas [*A publication*]
**Ind Conserve** ... Industria Conserve [*A publication*]
**Ind Conserve (Parma)** ... Industria Conserve (Parma) [*A publication*]
**Ind Constr Mater Constr** ... Industria Constructiilor si a Materialelor de Constructii [*A publication*]
**Ind Coop R** ... Indian Cooperative Review [*A publication*]
**Ind Corps Gras** ... Industries des Corps Gras [*A publication*]
**Ind Cott Grow Rev** ... Indian Cotton Growing Review [*A publication*]
**Ind Cott Text Ind** ... Indian Cotton Textile Industry [*A publication*]
**Ind Court Aw** ... Industrial Court Awards [*England*] [*A publication*] (DLA)
**Ind Ct Awards** ... Industrial Court Awards [*England*] [*A publication*] (DLA)
**INDCTR**.... Indicator
**Ind Cult**...... Indian Culture [*A publication*]
**Ind Cult Esp** ... Indice Cultural Espanol [*A publication*]
**Ind Cult Q** ... India Cultures Quarterly [*A publication*]
**Ind Curr Urb Doc** ... Index to Current Urban Documents [*A publication*]
**Ind Datatek** ... Industriell Datateknik [*A publication*]
**Ind Dec**....... Indiana Decisions [*A publication*] (DLA)
**Ind Dec**....... Indiana Decisions and Law Reporter [*A publication*] (DLA)
**Ind Dent J** ... Indian Dental Journal [*A publication*]
**Ind Dent Rev** ... Indian Dental Review [*A publication*]
**Ind Des**....... Industrial Design [*A publication*]
**Ind Design** ... Industrial Design [*A publication*]
**Ind Dev** ...... Industrial Development [*A publication*]
**Ind Dev** ...... Industrial Development and Manufacturers Record [*Later, Industrial Development*] [*A publication*]
**Ind Dev Abstr** ... Industrial Development Abstracts [*A publication*]
**Ind Devel**.... Industrial Development [*A publication*]
**Ind Develop Abstr** ... Industrial Development Abstracts [*A publication*]

**Ind Development of WA** ... Industrial Development of Western Australia [*A publication*] (APTA)
**Ind Dev Manuf Rec** ... Industrial Development and Manufacturers Record [*Later, Industrial Development*] [*A publication*]
**Ind Dev Officers** ... Industrial Development Officers [*A publication*]
**Ind Diamanten Rundsch** ... Industrie Diamanten Rundschau [*A publication*]
**Ind Diam Dev** ... Industrial Diamond Development [*A publication*]
**Ind Diamond Abstr** ... Industrial Diamond Abstracts [*A publication*]
**Ind Diamond Rev** ... Industrial Diamond Review [*A publication*]
**Ind Diam Re** ... Industrial Diamond Review [*A publication*]
**Ind Diam Rev** ... Industrial Diamond Review [*A publication*]
**Ind Dig**....... All India Reporter, Indian Digest [*1946-52*] [*A publication*] (DLA)
**Ind Distr** .... Industrial Distribution [*A publication*]
**Ind Distrib** ... Industrial Distribution [*A publication*]
**Ind Div**....... Inderwick's Divorce and Matrimonial Causes Acts [*1862*] [*A publication*] (DLA)
**Ind Div Water Res Bull** ... Indiana. Division of Water Resources. Bulletin [*A publication*]
**INDE**......... Independence National Historical Park
**Ind E**.......... Industrial Engineer
**INDEA** ...... Information Dentaire [*A publication*]
**Ind East Eng** ... Indian and Eastern Engineer [*A publication*]
**Indebt**......... Indebtedness [*Legal term*] (DLA)
**InDec** ......... Decatur Public Library, Decatur, IN [*Library symbol*] [*Library of Congress*] (LCLS)
**I & N Dec**... Immigration and Nationality Laws Administrative Decisions [*A publication*] (DLA)
**indec**........... Indeclinable (BJA)
**INDEC** ....... Interdepartmental Committee
**Ind Eccl St** ... Indian Ecclesiastical Studies [*A publication*]
**INDECL**.... Indeclinable [*Grammar*]
**Ind Econ J** ... Index of Economic Journals [*A publication*]
**Ind Econ J** ... Indian Economic Journal [*A publication*]
**Ind Econ R** ... Indian Economic Review [*A publication*]
**Ind Econ Soc Hist R** ... Indian Economic and Social History Review [*A publication*]
**Ind Ec Rev** ... Industrial Economics Review [*A publication*]
**IndEcSt**...... Indian Ecclesiastical Studies [*Belgium*] [*A publication*]
**Ind Ed M** ... Industrial Education Magazine [*A publication*]
**Ind Ed News** ... Industrial Education Council. Newsletter [*A publication*]
**Ind Educ**..... Industrial Education Magazine [*A publication*]
**Ind Educ M** ... Industrial Education Magazine [*A publication*]
**Ind Educ R** ... Indian Educational Review [*A publication*]
**INDEF**....... Indefinite (AABC)
**INDEFOPS** ... Indefinite Operations (NVT)
**Ind EJ** ........ Indian Economic Journal [*A publication*]
**InDel**......... Delphi Public Library, Delphi, IN [*Library symbol*] [*Library of Congress*] (LCLS)
**InDelCC**..... Carroll County Comet, Delphi, IN [*Library symbol*] [*Library of Congress*] (LCLS)
**InDelCHi**... Carroll County Historical Museum, Delphi, IN [*Library symbol*] [*Library of Congress*] (LCLS)
**InDelCR**..... Carroll County Recorder's Office, Delphi, IN [*Library symbol*] [*Library of Congress*] (LCLS)
**Ind Elect**..... Industrial Electronics [*A publication*]
**Ind Electr Electron** ... Industries Electriques et Electroniques [*A publication*]
**Ind Electron** ... Industrial Electronics [*England*] [*A publication*]
**Ind Electron** ... Industries Electroniques [*A publication*]
**Ind Electr (Osaka)** ... Industry and Electricity (Osaka) [*Japan*] [*A publication*]
**Ind-Elektr Elektron** ... Industrie-Elektrik und Elektronik [*A publication*]
**Ind-Elektron Forsch Fertigung** ... Industrie-Elektronik in Forschung und Fertigung [*West Germany*] [*A publication*]
**INDELISA** ... Indirect Enzyme-Linked Immunosorbent Assay
**INDELSEC** ... Industrial Electronic Security (AABC)
**Indem**......... Indemnity [*Legal term*] (DLA)
**INDEMY** .. Indemnity (ROG)
**Ind Eng** ...... Industrial Engineer [*A publication*]
**Ind Eng** ...... Industrial Engineering [*A publication*]
**Ind & Eng Chem** ... Industrial and Engineering Chemistry [*A publication*]
**Ind Eng Chem** ... Industrial and Engineering Chemistry [*A publication*]
**Ind Eng Chem Anal Ed** ... Industrial and Engineering Chemistry. Analytical Edition [*United States*] [*A publication*]
**Ind Eng Chem Analyt Ed** ... Industrial and Engineering Chemistry. Analytical Edition [*A publication*]
**Ind Eng Chem Fundam** ... Industrial and Engineering Chemistry. Fundamentals [*A publication*]
**Ind Eng Chem Fundamentals** ... Industrial and Engineering Chemistry. Fundamentals [*A publication*]
**Ind & Eng Chem Fundamentals** ... Industrial and Engineering Chemistry. Fundamentals [*A publication*]
**Ind Eng Chem News Ed** ... Industrial and Engineering Chemistry. News Edition [*United States*] [*A publication*]
**Ind and Eng Chem Process Des and Dev** ... Industrial and Engineering Chemistry. Process Design and Development [*A publication*]
**Ind & Eng Chem Process Design** ... Industrial and Engineering Chemistry. Process Design and Development [*A publication*]
**Ind Eng Chem Process Design Develop** ... Industrial and Engineering Chemistry. Process Design and Development [*A publication*]
**Ind Eng Chem Prod Res Dev** ... Industrial and Engineering Chemistry. Product Research and Development [*A publication*]
**Ind and Eng Chem Prod Res and Dev** ... Industrial and Engineering Chemistry. Product Research and Development [*A publication*]
**Ind Eng F**... Industrial and Engineering Chemistry. Fundamentals [*A publication*]
**Ind Engng** .. Industrial Engineering [*A publication*]
**Ind Engng Chem Analyt Edn** ... Industrial and Engineering Chemistry. Analytical Edition [*A publication*]
**Ind & Engng Chem Fundam** ... Industrial and Engineering Chemistry. Fundamentals [*A publication*]
**Ind & Engng Chem Process Des & Dev** ... Industrial and Engineering Chemistry. Process Design and Development [*A publication*]
**Ind Eng 1922-1931 (NY)** ... Industrial Engineering 1922-1931 (New York) [*A publication*]
**Ind Eng PDD** ... Industrial and Engineering Chemistry. Process Design and Development [*A publication*]
**Ind Eng PRD** ... Industrial and Engineering Chemistry. Product Research and Development [*A publication*]
**INDENT** ... Indenture (ROG)
**Indent Engl** ... Indent. Journal of International Dentistry. English Edition [*A publication*]
**Ind Environ** ... Industry and Environment [*Japan*] [*A publication*]
**Ind Environ Res Lab (Research Triangle Park) Annu Rep** ... Industrial Environmental Research Laboratory (Research Triangle Park). Annual Report [*A publication*]
**INDEP**....... Independent [*A publication*]
**INDEP**....... Independent (AFM)
**Indep Broadcast** ... Independent Broadcasting [*A publication*]
**Indep Coal Oper** ... Independent Coal Operator [*United States*] [*A publication*]
**INDEP CONTR** ... Independent Contractor (DLA)
**Indep Ed** ..... Independent Education [*A publication*]
**Indep Educ** ... Independent Education [*A publication*] (APTA)
**Independent Petroleum Assoc America Monthly** ... Independent Petroleum Association of America. Monthly [*A publication*]
**Independ J Phil** ... Independent Journal of Philosophy [*A publication*]
**Indep F J**.... Independent Film Journal [*A publication*]
**Indep J Philos** ... Independent Journal of Philosophy [*A publication*]
**Indep Pet Assoc Am Mon** ... Independent Petroleum Association of America. Monthly [*A publication*]
**INDEP R**... Independent Review [*London*] [*A publication*] (ROG)
**INDEPTY** ... Independently (ROG)
**Ind Equip Mater & Serv** ... Industrial Equipment Materials and Services [*A publication*]
**Ind Equip News** ... Industrial Equipment News [*A publication*]
**Inde Rest**.... Independent Restaurants [*A publication*]
**Ind E St**...... Indian Ecclesiastical Studies [*A publication*]
**INDET**....... Indeterminate (MSA)
**indeterm**..... Indeterminative (BJA)
**Ind Ethn**..... Index Ethnographicus [*A publication*]
**Ind-Eur** ...... Indo-European
**IN-DEV-IL** ... Institute for the Development of Indian Law (EA)
**INDEX** ...... Index on Censorship. Writers and Scholars International [*A publication*]
**INDEX** ...... Indian Ocean Experiment
**INDEX** ...... Indiana Exchange, Inc.
**INDEX** ...... Inter-NASA Data Exchange (IEEE)
**Index Am Period Verse** ... Index of American Periodical Verse [*A publication*]
**Index Anal Cancerol** ... Index Analyticus Cancerologiae [*A publication*]
**Index Book Rev Humanit** ... Index to Book Reviews in the Humanities [*A publication*]
**Index Can Leg Period Lit** ... Index to Canadian Legal Periodical Literature [*A publication*]
**Index Cat Med Vet Zool** ... Index Catalog of Medical and Veterinary Zoology [*A publication*]
**Index Censor** ... Index on Censorship [*A publication*]
**Index Commonw Leg Period** ... Index to Commonwealth Legal Periodicals [*A publication*]
**Index Conf Proc Received by BLLD** ... Index of Conference Proceedings Received by the British Library Lending Division [*A publication*]
**Index Current Urban Docs** ... Index to Current Urban Documents [*A publication*]
**Index Curr Urban Doc** ... Index to Current Urban Documents [*A publication*]
**Index Dent Lit** ... Index to Dental Literature [*A publication*]
**Index Econ Artic J Collect Vols** ... Index of Economic Articles in Journals and Collective Volumes [*A publication*]
**Index Econ J** ... Index of Economic Journals [*A publication*]
**Index Fed Tax Artic Supp** ... Index to Federal Tax Articles. Supplement [*A publication*]
**Index Foreign Leg Per** ... Index to Foreign Legal Periodicals [*A publication*]
**Index Foreign Leg Per Collect Essays** ... Index to Foreign Legal Periodicals and Collections of Essays [*A publication*]
**Index Free Period** ... Index to Free Periodicals [*A publication*]
**Index Gov Orders** ... Index to Government Orders [*A publication*]
**Index IEEE Publ** ... Index to IEEE [*Institute of Electrical and Electronic Engineers*] Publications [*A publication*]
**Index Indian Period Lit** ... Index to Indian Periodical Literature [*A publication*]

**Index Jew Period** ... Index to Jewish Periodicals [*A publication*]
**Index JSMPE** ... Index of Transactions and Journal. Society of Motion Picture Engineers [*A publication*]
**Index JSMPTE** ... Index to the Journal of the Society of Motion Picture and Television Engineers [*A publication*]
**Index Legal Period** ... Index to Legal Periodicals [*United States*] [*A publication*]
**Index Leg Period** ... Index to Legal Periodicals [*A publication*]
**Index Lit Am Indian** ... Index to Literature on the American Indian [*A publication*]
**Index Lit Food Invest** ... Index to the Literature of Food Investigation [*A publication*]
**Index Math Pap** ... Index of Mathematical Papers [*A publication*]
**Index Med** ... Index Medicus [*A publication*]
**Index New Engl Period** ... Index to New England Periodicals [*A publication*]
**Index New Z Period** ... Index to New Zealand Periodicals [*A publication*]
**Index Park Pract** ... Index to Park Practice [*A publication*]
**Index Park Pract Prog** ... Index. Park Practice Program [*A publication*]
**Index Period Artic Blacks** ... Index to Periodical Articles by and about Blacks [*A publication*]
**Index Period Artic Negroes** ... Index to Periodical Articles by and about Negroes [*A publication*]
**Index Period Artic Relat Law** ... Index to Periodical Articles Related to Law [*A publication*]
**Index Philip Period** ... Index to Philippine Periodicals [*A publication*]
**Ind Explos** ... Industrial Explosives [*Japan*] [*A publication*]
**Index Publ Am Soc Mech Eng** ... Index to Publications. American Society of Mechanical Engineers [*A publication*]
**Index Quad** ... Index Quaderni Camerti di Studi Romanistici [*A publication*]
**Index to Relig Period Lit** ... Index to Religious Periodical Literature [*A publication*]
**Index Sci Rev** ... Index to Scientific Reviews [*A publication*]
**Index Soc Sci Humanit Proc** ... Index to Social Sciences and Humanities Proceedings [*A publication*]
**Index South Afr Period** ... Index to South African Periodicals [*A publication*]
**Index Specif Stand** ... Index Specifications and Standards [*A publication*]
**Index US Gov Period** ... Index to US Government Periodicals [*A publication*]
**Ind F** .......... Indian Farming [*A publication*]
**IndF** .......... Indiana Folklore [*A publication*]
**Ind Farm** .... Indian Farming [*A publication*]
**Ind Farm Bioquim** ... Industria Farmaceutica y Bioquimica [*A publication*]
**Ind Fin** ....... Industrial Finishing [*A publication*]
**Ind Finish** .. Industrial Finishing [*A publication*]
**Ind Finish Surf Coat** ... Industrial Finishing and Surface Coatings [*A publication*]
**Ind Finish & Surf Coatings** ... Industrial Finishing and Surface Coatings [*A publication*]
**Ind Finish (Wheaton Ill)** ... Industrial Finishing (Wheaton, Illinois) [*A publication*]
**Ind Finish Yearb** ... Industrial Finishing Yearbook [*A publication*]
**Ind For** ....... Indian Forester [*A publication*]
**Ind For Leafl** ... Indian Forest Leaflets [*A publication*]
**Ind For Rec** ... Indian Forest Records [*A publication*]
**Ind Fr Equip** ... Industries Francaises d'Equipement [*France*] [*A publication*]
**Ind Gas** ...... Industrial Gas [*A publication*]
**Ind Gas Acquedotti** ... Industria del Gas e degli Acquedotti [*A publication*]
**Ind Gas (Duluth)** ... Industrial Gas (Duluth) [*A publication*]
**Ind Gas Energy** ... Industrial Gas and Energy [*United States*] [*A publication*]
**Ind Geog J** ... Indian Geographical Journal [*A publication*]
**Ind Geogr** ... Indian Geographer [*A publication*]
**Ind Geogr J** ... Indian Geographical Journal [*A publication*]
**Ind Geront** ... Industrial Gerontology [*A publication*]
**Ind Gerontol** ... Industrial Gerontology [*A publication*]
**Ind d Gomma** ... Industria della Gomma [*Italy*] [*A publication*]
**Ind Gomma** ... Industria della Gomma. Minsiledi Economia e Tenica Degil Elastomeri [*A publication*]
**INDH** ......... Independent Insurance Group, Inc. [*NASDAQ symbol*] (NQ)
**INDH** ......... Indirect Hire [*Military*]
**Ind Handel** ... Industrie und Handel [*A publication*]
**Ind Health** ... Industrial Health [*A publication*]
**Ind Health Care** ... Industry and Health Care [*A publication*]
**Ind Health Care (Cambridge MA)** ... Industry and Health Care (Cambridge, Massachusetts) [*A publication*]
**Ind Health (Kawasaki)** ... Industrial Health (Kawasaki) [*A publication*]
**Ind Health Rev** ... Industrial Health Review [*A publication*]
**Ind Heart J** ... Indian Heart Journal [*A publication*]
**Ind Heat** ..... Industrial Heating [*A publication*]
**Ind Heat Eng** ... Industrial Heating Engineer [*A publication*]
**Ind Heat (Pittsburg)** ... Industrial Heating (Pittsburg) [*A publication*]
**Ind Heat (Tokyo)** ... Industrial Heating (Tokyo) [*A publication*]
**Ind His Col** ... Indiana Historical Commission. Collections [*A publication*]
**Ind His S** .... Indiana Historical Society. Publications [*A publication*]
**Ind Hist Bull** ... Indiana History Bulletin [*A publication*]
**Ind Hist Esp** ... Indice Historico Espanol [*A publication*]
**Ind Hist Q** ... Indian Historical Quarterly [*A publication*]
**Ind Hist Soc Publ** ... Indiana Historical Society. Publications [*A publication*]
**Ind Hom Rev** ... Indian Homoeopathic Review [*A publication*]
**Ind Hor** ...... Indian Horizons [*A publication*]
**Ind Horizons** ... Indian Horizons [*A publication*]
**Ind Hyg Bull** ... Industrial Hygiene Bulletin [*A publication*]
**Ind Hyg Dig** ... Industrial Hygiene Digest [*A publication*]
**Ind Hyg Found Am Leg Ser Bull** ... Industrial Hygiene Foundation of America. Legal Series. Bulletin [*A publication*]
**Ind Hyg Found Am Med Ser Bull** ... Industrial Hygiene Foundation of America. Medical Series. Bulletin [*A publication*]
**Ind Hyg Found Am Trans Bull** ... Industrial Hygiene Foundation of America. Transactions. Bulletin [*A publication*]
**Ind Hyg Highlights** ... Industrial Hygiene Highlights [*United States*] [*A publication*]
**Ind Hygiene** ... Industrial Hygiene [*Japan*] [*A publication*]
**Ind Hyg Ne** ... Industrial Hygiene News [*A publication*]
**Ind Hyg Rev** ... Industrial Hygiene Review [*United States*] [*A publication*]
**INDI** .......... Indepth Data, Inc. [*NASDAQ symbol*] (NQ)
**INDI** .......... Indiana
**INDI** .......... Indicate
**Indi** ............ Indus [*Constellation*]
**India AEC Bhabha At Res Cent Rep** ... India. Atomic Energy Commission. Bhabha Atomic Research Centre. Report [*A publication*]
**India AIR Manual** ... AIR [*All India Law Reporter*] Manual: Unrepealed Central Acts [*2nd ed.*] [*India*] [*A publication*] (DLA)
**India Cen Acts** ... Central Acts, India [*A publication*] (DLA)
**India Code Civ P** ... Code of Civil Procedure [*India*] [*A publication*] (DLA)
**(India) Code Civ Proc** ... Code of Civil Procedure (India) [*A publication*]
**India Code Crim P** ... Code of Criminal Procedure [*India*] [*A publication*] (DLA)
**(India) Code Crim Proc** ... Code of Criminal Procedure (India) [*A publication*]
**India Coffee Bd Res Dep Annu Detailed Tech Rep** ... India. Coffee Board. Research Department. Annual Detailed Technical Report [*A publication*]
**India Coffee Board Annu Rep** ... India. Coffee Board. Annual Report [*A publication*]
**India Coffee Board Res Dep Annu Detailed Tech Rep** ... India. Coffee Board. Research Department. Annual Detailed Technical Report [*A publication*]
**India Coffee Board Res Dep Annu Rep** ... India. Coffee Board. Research Department. Annual Report [*A publication*]
**India Coffee Board Res Dep Bull** ... India. Coffee Board. Research Department. Bulletin [*A publication*]
**India Crim LJR** ... Criminal Law Journal Reports [*India*] [*A publication*] (DLA)
**India CSIR Zool Mem** ... India. CSIR [*Council of Scientific and Industrial Research*] Zoological Memoir [*A publication*]
**(India) Curr Cen Leg** ... Current Central Legislation (India) [*A publication*]
**India Dir Plant Prot Quar Storage Plant Prot Bull** ... India. Directorate of Plant Protection, Quarantine, and Storage. Plant Protection Bulletin [*A publication*]
**India Econ Soc Hist R** ... Indian Economic and Social History Review [*A publication*]
**India Gen R & O** ... General Rules and Orders, India [*A publication*] (DLA)
**India Geol Surv Bull Ser A** ... India. Geological Survey. Bulletins. Series A. Economic Geology [*A publication*]
**India Geol Surv Bull Ser B** ... India. Geological Survey. Bulletins. Series B. Engineering Geology and Ground-Water [*A publication*]
**India Geol Surv Mem** ... India. Geological Survey. Memoirs [*A publication*]
**India Geol Surv Mem Palaeontol Indica New Ser** ... India. Geological Survey. Memoirs. Palaeontologia Indica. New Series [*A publication*]
**India Geol Surv Misc Publ** ... India. Geological Survey. Miscellaneous Publication [*A publication*]
**India Geol Surv News** ... India. Geological Survey. News [*A publication*]
**India J Pol Sci** ... Indian Journal of Political Science [*A publication*]
**India LC** ..... Law Commission of India (DLA)
**Indiana** ....... Indiana Reports [*A publication*] (DLA)
**Indiana Acad Sci Monogr** ... Indiana Academy of Science. Monograph [*A publication*]
**Indiana Agric Exp Stn Insp Rep** ... Indiana. Agricultural Experiment Station. Inspection Report [*A publication*]
**Indiana Agric Exp Stn Res Prog Rep** ... Indiana. Agricultural Experiment Station. Research Progress Report [*A publication*]
**Indiana Bs** ... Indiana Business [*A publication*]
**Indiana Busin R** ... Indiana Business Review [*A publication*]
**Indiana Bus R** ... Indiana Business Review [*A publication*]
**Indian Acad Geosci J** ... Indian Academy of Geoscience. Journal [*A publication*]
**Indian Acad Med Sci Ann** ... Indian Academy of Medical Sciences. Annual [*A publication*]
**Indian Acad Sci Pro** ... Indian Academy of Sciences. Proceedings [*A publication*]
**Indian Acad Sci Proc Sect A** ... Indian Academy of Sciences. Proceedings. Section A [*A publication*]
**Indian Acad Sci Proc Sect B** ... Indian Academy of Sciences. Proceedings. Section B [*A publication*]
**Indiana Div Water Bull** ... Indiana. Division of Water. Bulletin [*A publication*]
**Indiana Geol Surv Bull** ... Indiana. Geological Survey. Bulletin [*A publication*]
**Indiana Geol Survey Mineral Economics Ser** ... Indiana. Geological Survey. Mineral Economics Series [*A publication*]
**Indiana Geol Surv Mineral Econ Ser** ... Indiana. Geological Survey. Mineral Economics Series [*A publication*]
**Indiana Geol Surv Miner Econ Ser** ... Indiana. Geological Survey. Mineral Economics Series [*A publication*]

**Indiana Geol Surv Misc Map** ... Indiana. Geological Survey. Miscellaneous Map [*A publication*]
**Indiana Geol Surv Occas Pap** ... Indiana. Geological Survey. Occasional Paper [*A publication*]
**Indiana Geol Surv Rep Prog** ... Indiana. Geological Survey. Report of Progress [*A publication*]
**Indiana Geol Surv Spec Rep** ... Indiana. Geological Survey. Special Report [*A publication*]
**Indian Agr** ... Indian Agriculturist [*A publication*]
**Indian Agric** ... Indian Agriculturist [*A publication*]
**Indian Agric Res Inst (New Delhi) Annu Rep** ... Indian Agricultural Research Institute (New Delhi). Annual Report [*A publication*]
**Indian Agric Res Inst (New Delhi) Annu Sci Rep** ... Indian Agricultural Research Institute (New Delhi). Annual Scientific Report [*A publication*]
**Indiana Law** ... Indiana Law Journal [*A publication*]
**Indiana Leg Forum** ... Indiana Legal Forum [*A publication*]
**Indiana LJ** ... Indiana Law Journal [*A publication*]
**Indiana L Rev** ... Indiana Law Review [*A publication*]
**Indiana Mag Hist** ... Indiana Magazine of History [*A publication*]
**Indiana Med** ... Indiana Medicine [*A publication*]
**Indian Ant** ... Indian Antiquary [*A publication*]
**Indian App** ... Law Reports, Privy Council, Indian Appeals [*India*] [*A publication*] (DLA)
**Indian Archt** ... Indian Architect [*A publication*]
**Indian Assoc Cultiv Sci Proc** ... Indian Association for the Cultivation of Science. Proceedings [*A publication*]
**Indiana State Univ Dep Geogr Geol Prof Pap** ... Indiana State University. Department of Geography and Geology. Professional Paper [*A publication*]
**Indiana Sup Ct Rep** ... Indiana Reports [*A publication*] (DLA)
**Indiana Theory R** ... Indiana Theory Review [*A publication*]
**India Natl Acad Sci Proc Sect B** ... India. National Academy of Science. Proceedings. Section B [*A publication*]
**Indiana Univ Ed Bul** ... Indiana University. School of Education. Bulletin [*A publication*]
**Indiana Univ Math J** ... Indiana University. Mathematics Journal [*A publication*]
**Indian Bee J** ... Indian Bee Journal [*A publication*]
**Indian Behav Sci Abstr** ... Indian Behavioural Sciences Abstracts [*A publication*]
**Indian Biol** ... Indian Biologist [*A publication*]
**Indian Bot Contactor** ... Indian Botanical Contactor [*A publication*]
**Indian Bot Rep** ... Indian Botanical Reporter [*A publication*]
**Indian Bur Mines Miner Econ Div Mark Surv Ser** ... Indian Bureau of Mines. Mineral Economics Division. Market Survey Series [*A publication*]
**Indian Cas** ... Indian Cases [*A publication*]
**Indian Cas** ... Indiana Cases [*A publication*] (DLA)
**Indian Cent Jute Comm Annu Rep Jute Agric Res Inst** ... Indian Central Jute Committee. Annual Report of the Jute Agricultural Research Institute [*A publication*]
**Indian Ceram** ... Indian Ceramics [*India*] [*A publication*]
**Indian Ceramic Soc Trans** ... Indian Ceramic Society. Transactions [*A publication*]
**Indian Ceram Soc Trans** ... Indian Ceramic Society. Transactions [*A publication*]
**Indian Chem Engr** ... Indian Chemical Engineer [*A publication*]
**Indian Chem J** ... Indian Chemical Journal [*A publication*]
**Indian Chem J Ann Number** ... Indian Chemical Journal. Annual Number [*India*] [*A publication*]
**Indian Chem Manuf** ... Indian Chemical Manufacturer [*A publication*]
**Indian Church Hist R** ... Indian Church History Review [*A publication*]
**Indian Coconut J** ... Indian Coconut Journal [*A publication*]
**Indian Cof** ... Indian Coffee [*A publication*]
**Indian Concr J** ... Indian Concrete Journal [*A publication*]
**Indian Cott Grow Rev** ... Indian Cotton Growing Review [*A publication*]
**Indian Cott J** ... Indian Cotton Journal [*A publication*]
**Indian Cotton Grow Rev** ... Indian Cotton Growing Review [*A publication*]
**Indian Counc Agric Res Anim Husb Ser** ... Indian Council of Agricultural Research. Animal Husbandry Series [*A publication*]
**Indian Counc Agric Res Annu Tech Rep** ... Indian Council of Agricultural Research. Annual Technical Report [*A publication*]
**Indian Counc Agric Res Cereal Crop Ser** ... Indian Council of Agricultural Research. Cereal Crop Series [*A publication*]
**Indian Counc Agric Res Entomol Monogr** ... Indian Council of Agricultural Research. Entomological Monographs [*A publication*]
**Indian Counc Agric Res Misc Bull** ... Indian Council of Agricultural Research. Miscellaneous Bulletin [*A publication*]
**Indian Counc Agric Res Monogr** ... Indian Council of Agricultural Research. Monograph [*A publication*]
**Indian Counc Agric Res Rep Ser** ... Indian Council of Agricultural Research. Report Series [*A publication*]
**Indian Counc Agric Res Res Ser** ... Indian Council of Agricultural Research. Research Series [*A publication*]
**Indian Counc Agric Res Rev Ser** ... Indian Council of Agricultural Research. Review Series [*A publication*]
**Indian Counc Agric Res Tech Bull** ... Indian Council of Agricultural Research. Technical Bulletin [*A publication*]
**Indian Counc Med Res Annu Rep** ... Indian Council of Medical Research. Annual Report [*A publication*]
**Indian Counc Med Res Tech Rep Ser** ... Indian Council of Medical Research. Technical Report Series [*A publication*]
**Indian East Eng** ... Indian and Eastern Engineer [*A publication*]
**Indian Ecol** ... Indian Ecologist [*A publication*]
**Indian Econ R** ... Indian Economic Review [*A publication*]
**Indian Econ Soc Hist Rev** ... Indian Economic and Social History Review [*A publication*]
**Indian Eng** ... Indian Engineer [*A publication*]
**Indian Export Trade J** ... Indian Export Trade Journal [*A publication*]
**Indian Farm Mech** ... Indian Farm Mechanization [*A publication*]
**Indian Fmg** ... Indian Farming [*A publication*]
**Indian Food Pack** ... Indian Food Packer [*A publication*]
**Indian For**.. Indian Forester [*A publication*]
**Indian For Bull** ... Indian Forest Bulletin [*A publication*]
**Indian For Bull For Res Inst (Dehra)** ... Indian Forest Bulletin. Entomology. Forest Research Institute (Dehra) [*A publication*]
**Indian For Leafl** ... Indian Forest Leaflet [*A publication*]
**Indian For Rec** ... Indian Forest Records [*A publication*]
**Indian For Rec Bot** ... Indian Forest Records. Botany [*A publication*]
**Indian For Rec Entomol** ... Indian Forest Records. Entomology [*A publication*]
**Indian For Rec For Manage & Mensuration** ... Indian Forest Records. Forest Management and Mensuration [*A publication*]
**Indian For Rec For Pathol** ... Indian Forest Records. Forest Pathology [*A publication*]
**Indian For Rec Mycol** ... Indian Forest Records. Mycology [*A publication*]
**Indian For Rec Silvic** ... Indian Forest Records. Silviculture [*A publication*]
**Indian For Rec Silvics** ... Indian Forest Records. Silvics [*A publication*]
**Indian For Rec Stat** ... Indian Forest Records. Statistical [*A publication*]
**Indian For Rec Timber Mech** ... Indian Forest Records. Timber Mechanics [*A publication*]
**Indian For Rec Wild Life Recreat** ... Indian Forest Records. Wild Life and Recreation [*A publication*]
**Indian For Rec Wild Life Recreation** ... Indian Forest Records. Wild Life and Recreation [*A publication*]
**Indian For Rec Wood Anat** ... Indian Forest Records. Wood Anatomy [*A publication*]
**Indian For Rec Wood Preserv** ... Indian Forest Records. Wood Preservation [*A publication*]
**Indian For Rec Wood Seas** ... Indian Forest Records. Wood Seasoning [*A publication*]
**Indian For Rec Wood Technol** ... Indian Forest Records. Wood Technology [*A publication*]
**Indian Foundry J** ... Indian Foundry Journal [*A publication*]
**Indian Geohydrol** ... Indian Geohydrology [*A publication*]
**Indian Geol Assoc Bull** ... Indian Geologists Association. Bulletin [*A publication*]
**Indian Geol Index** ... Indian Geological Index [*A publication*]
**Indian Geotech J** ... Indian Geotechnical Journal [*A publication*]
**Indian Heart J** ... Indian Heart Journal [*A publication*]
**Indian Heart J Teach Ser** ... Indian Heart Journal. Teaching Series [*A publication*]
**Indian Highw** ... Indian Highways [*A publication*]
**Indian Hist** ... Indian Historian [*A publication*]
**Indian Hist Q** ... Indian Historical Quarterly [*A publication*]
**Indian Hort** ... Indian Horticulture [*A publication*]
**Indian Hortic** ... Indian Horticulture [*A publication*]
**Indian Ind**.. Indian Industries [*A publication*]
**Indian Inst of Archts Jnl** ... Indian Institute of Architects. Journal [*A publication*]
**Indian Inst Bankers J** ... Journal. Indian Institute of Bankers [*A publication*]
**Indian J Acarol** ... Indian Journal of Acarology [*A publication*]
**Indian J Agr Econ** ... Indian Journal of Agricultural Economics [*A publication*]
**Indian J Agric Chem** ... Indian Journal of Agricultural Chemistry [*A publication*]
**Indian J Agric Econ** ... Indian Journal of Agricultural Economics [*A publication*]
**Indian J Agric Res** ... Indian Journal of Agricultural Research [*A publication*]
**Indian J Agric Sci** ... Indian Journal of Agricultural Science [*A publication*]
**Indian J Agric Vet Educ** ... Indian Journal of Agricultural and Veterinary Education [*A publication*]
**Indian J Agron** ... Indian Journal of Agronomy [*A publication*]
**Indian J Agr Sci** ... Indian Journal of Agricultural Science [*A publication*]
**Indian J Air Pollut Control** ... Indian Journal of Air Pollution Control [*India*] [*A publication*]
**Indian J Anaesth** ... Indian Journal of Anaesthesia [*A publication*]
**Indian J Animal Health** ... Indian Journal of Animal Health [*A publication*]
**Indian J Anim Health** ... Indian Journal of Animal Health [*A publication*]
**Indian J Anim Res** ... Indian Journal of Animal Research [*A publication*]
**Indian J Anim Sci** ... Indian Journal of Animal Sciences [*A publication*]
**Indian J Appl Chem** ... Indian Journal of Applied Chemistry [*A publication*]
**Indian J Appl Psychol** ... Indian Journal of Applied Psychology [*A publication*]
**Indian J Biochem** ... Indian Journal of Biochemistry [*Later, Indian Journal of Biochemistry and Biophysics*] [*A publication*]
**Indian J Biochem Biophys** ... Indian Journal of Biochemistry and Biophysics [*A publication*]
**Indian J Bot** ... Indian Journal of Botany [*India*] [*A publication*]
**Indian J Cancer** ... Indian Journal of Cancer [*A publication*]

**Indian J Cancer Chemother** ... Indian Journal of Cancer Chemotherapy [*A publication*]
**Indian J Chem** ... Indian Journal of Chemistry [*A publication*]
**Indian J Chem A** ... Indian Journal of Chemistry. Section A. Inorganic, Physical, Theoretical, and Analytical [*A publication*]
**Indian J Chem B** ... Indian Journal of Chemistry. Section B. Organic Chemistry, Including Medicinal Chemistry [*A publication*]
**Indian J Chem Educ** ... Indian Journal of Chemical Education [*A publication*]
**Indian J Chem Sect A** ... Indian Journal of Chemistry. Section A. Inorganic, Physical, Theoretical, and Analytical [*A publication*]
**Indian J Chem Sect A Inorg Phys Theor Anal** ... Indian Journal of Chemistry. Section A. Inorganic, Physical, Theoretical, and Analytical [*A publication*]
**Indian J Chem Sect B** ... Indian Journal of Chemistry. Section B [*A publication*]
**Indian J Chem Sect B Org Chem Incl Med Chem** ... Indian Journal of Chemistry. Section B. Organic Chemistry, Including Medicinal Chemistry [*A publication*]
**Indian J Chest Dis** ... Indian Journal of Chest Diseases [*Later, Indian Journal of Chest Diseases and Allied Sciences*] [*A publication*]
**Indian J Chest Dis Allied Sci** ... Indian Journal of Chest Diseases and Allied Sciences [*A publication*]
**Indian J Child Health** ... Indian Journal of Child Health [*India*] [*A publication*]
**Indian J Comp Anim Physiol** ... Indian Journal of Comparative Animal Physiology [*A publication*]
**Indian J Criminol** ... Indian Journal of Criminology [*A publication*]
**Indian J Cryog** ... Indian Journal of Cryogenics [*A publication*]
**Indian J Dairy Sci** ... Indian Journal of Dairy Science [*A publication*]
**Indian J Dermatol** ... Indian Journal of Dermatology [*Later, Indian Journal of Dermatology, Venereology, and Leprology*] [*A publication*]
**Indian J Dermatol Venereol** ... Indian Journal of Dermatology and Venereology [*Later, Indian Journal of Dermatology, Venereology, and Leprology*] [*A publication*]
**Indian J Dermatol Venereol Leprol** ... Indian Journal of Dermatology, Venereology, and Leprology [*A publication*]
**Indian J Earth Sci** ... Indian Journal of Earth Sciences [*A publication*]
**Indian J Ecol** ... Indian Journal of Ecology [*A publication*]
**Indian J Engrg Math** ... Indian Journal of Engineering Mathematics [*A publication*]
**Indian J Ent** ... Indian Journal of Entomology [*A publication*]
**Indian J Entomol** ... Indian Journal of Entomology [*A publication*]
**Indian J Environ Health** ... Indian Journal of Environmental Health [*A publication*]
**Indian J Environ Prot** ... Indian Journal of Environmental Protection [*India*] [*A publication*]
**Indian J Exp Biol** ... Indian Journal of Experimental Biology [*A publication*]
**Indian J Expl Biol** ... Indian Journal of Experimental Biology [*A publication*]
**Indian J Exp Psychol** ... Indian Journal of Experimental Psychology [*A publication*]
**Indian J Ext Educ** ... Indian Journal of Extension Education [*A publication*]
**Indian J Farm Chem** ... Indian Journal of Farm Chemicals [*A publication*]
**Indian J Farm Sci** ... Indian Journal of Farm Sciences [*A publication*]
**Indian J Fish** ... Indian Journal of Fisheries [*A publication*]
**Indian J For** ... Indian Journal of Forestry [*A publication*]
**Indian J Gastroenterol** ... Indian Journal of Gastroenterology [*A publication*]
**Indian J Genet Plant Breed** ... Indian Journal of Genetics and Plant Breeding [*A publication*]
**Indian J Genet Pl Breed** ... Indian Journal of Genetics and Plant Breeding [*A publication*]
**Indian J Helminthol** ... Indian Journal of Helminthology [*A publication*]
**Indian J Hered** ... Indian Journal of Heredity [*A publication*]
**Indian J History Sci** ... Indian Journal of History of Science. National Institute of Sciences of India [*New Delhi*] [*A publication*]
**Indian J Hist Sci** ... Indian Journal of History of Science [*A publication*]
**Indian J Hort** ... Indian Journal of Horticulture [*A publication*]
**Indian J Hortic** ... Indian Journal of Horticulture [*A publication*]
**Indian J Hosp Pharm** ... Indian Journal of Hospital Pharmacy [*A publication*]
**Indian J Ind Med** ... Indian Journal of Industrial Medicine [*A publication*]
**Indian J Ind Rel** ... Indian Journal of Industrial Relations [*A publication*]
**Indian J of Internat L** ... Indian Journal of International Law [*A publication*]
**Indian J Int Law** ... Indian Journal of International Law [*A publication*]
**Indian J Int'l L** ... Indian Journal of International Law [*A publication*]
**Indian J Lepr** ... Indian Journal of Leprosy [*A publication*]
**Indian J Malariol** ... Indian Journal of Malariology [*A publication*]
**Indian J Mar Sci** ... Indian Journal of Marine Sciences [*A publication*]
**Indian J Math** ... Indian Journal of Mathematics [*A publication*]
**Indian J Mech Math** ... Indian Journal of Mechanics and Mathematics [*A publication*]
**Indian J Med Res** ... Indian Journal of Medical Research [*A publication*]
**Indian J Med Research** ... Indian Journal of Medical Research [*A publication*]
**Indian J Med Res Sect A** ... Indian Journal of Medical Research. Section A [*A publication*]
**Indian J Med Res Sect B** ... Indian Journal of Medical Research. Section B [*A publication*]
**Indian J Med Sci** ... Indian Journal of Medical Sciences [*A publication*]
**Indian J Med Surg** ... Indian Journal of Medicine and Surgery [*A publication*]
**Indian J Meteorol and Geophys** ... Indian Journal of Meteorology and Geophysics [*Later, Mausam*] [*A publication*]
**Indian J Meteorol Geophys** ... Indian Journal of Meteorology and Geophysics [*Later, Mausam*] [*A publication*]
**Indian J Meteorol Hydrol and Geophys** ... Indian Journal of Meteorology, Hydrology, and Geophysics [*Later, Mausam*] [*A publication*]
**Indian J Meteorol Hydrol Geophys** ... Indian Journal of Meteorology, Hydrology, and Geophysics [*Later, Mausam*] [*A publication*]
**Indian J Microbiol** ... Indian Journal of Microbiology [*A publication*]
**Indian J Mycol Plant Pathol** ... Indian Journal of Mycology and Plant Pathology [*A publication*]
**Indian J Mycol Res** ... Indian Journal of Mycological Research [*A publication*]
**Indian J Nat Prod** ... Indian Journal of Natural Products [*A publication*]
**Indian J Nematol** ... Indian Journal of Nematology [*A publication*]
**Indian J Nutr Diet** ... Indian Journal of Nutrition and Dietetics [*A publication*]
**Indian J Occup Health** ... Indian Journal of Occupational Health [*A publication*]
**Indian J Ophthalmol** ... Indian Journal of Ophthalmology [*A publication*]
**Indian J Orthop** ... Indian Journal of Orthopaedics [*India*] [*A publication*]
**Indian J Otolaryngol** ... Indian Journal of Otolaryngology [*A publication*]
**Indian J Pathol Bacteriol** ... Indian Journal of Pathology and Bacteriology [*Later, Indian Journal of Pathology and Microbiology*] [*A publication*]
**Indian J Pathol Microbiol** ... Indian Journal of Pathology and Microbiology [*A publication*]
**Indian J Pediatr** ... Indian Journal of Pediatrics [*A publication*]
**Indian J Pharm** ... Indian Journal of Pharmacy [*A publication*]
**Indian J Pharmacol** ... Indian Journal of Pharmacology [*A publication*]
**Indian J Pharm Educ** ... Indian Journal of Pharmaceutical Education [*A publication*]
**Indian J Pharm Sci** ... Indian Journal of Pharmaceutical Sciences [*A publication*]
**Indian J Phys** ... Indian Journal of Physics [*A publication*]
**Indian J Phys Anthropol Hum Genet** ... Indian Journal of Physical Anthropology and Human Genetics [*A publication*]
**Indian J Physiol Allied Sci** ... Indian Journal of Physiology and Allied Sciences [*A publication*]
**Indian J Physiol Pharmacol** ... Indian Journal of Physiology and Pharmacology [*A publication*]
**Indian J Phys Nat Sci** ... Indian Journal of Physical and Natural Sciences [*A publication*]
**Indian J Phys Part A** ... Indian Journal of Physics. Part A [*A publication*]
**Indian J Phys Part B** ... Indian Journal of Physics. Part B [*A publication*]
**Indian J Plant Pathol** ... Indian Journal of Plant Pathology [*A publication*]
**Indian J Plant Physiol** ... Indian Journal of Plant Physiology [*A publication*]
**Indian J Plant Prot** ... Indian Journal of Plant Protection [*A publication*]
**Indian J Poult Sci** ... Indian Journal of Poultry Science [*A publication*]
**Indian J Power River Val Dev** ... Indian Journal of Power and River Valley Development [*A publication*]
**Indian J Power and River Val Dev** ... Indian Journal of Power and River Valley Development [*A publication*]
**Indian J Power River Val Develop** ... Indian Journal of Power and River Valley Development [*A publication*]
**Indian J Psychiatry** ... Indian Journal of Psychiatry [*A publication*]
**Indian J Psychol** ... Indian Journal of Psychology [*A publication*]
**Indian J Psychol Med** ... Indian Journal of Psychological Medicine [*A publication*]
**Indian J Pub Admin** ... Indian Journal of Public Administration [*A publication*]
**Indian J of Publ Adm** ... Indian Journal of Public Administration [*A publication*]
**Indian J Publ Health** ... Indian Journal of Public Health [*A publication*]
**Indian J Public Health** ... Indian Journal of Public Health [*A publication*]
**Indian J Pure Appl Math** ... Indian Journal of Pure and Applied Mathematics [*A publication*]
**Indian J Pure and Appl Math** ... Indian Journal of Pure and Applied Mathematics [*A publication*]
**Indian J Pure Appl Phys** ... Indian Journal of Pure and Applied Physics [*A publication*]
**Indian J Pure and Appl Phys** ... Indian Journal of Pure and Applied Physics [*A publication*]
**Indian J Pure Appl Sci** ... Indian Journal of Pure and Applied Science [*A publication*]
**Indian J Radiol** ... Indian Journal of Radiology [*A publication*]
**Indian J Radiol Imag** ... Indian Journal of Radiology and Imaging [*A publication*]
**Indian J Radio Space Phys** ... Indian Journal of Radio and Space Physics [*A publication*]
**Indian J Radio and Space Phys** ... Indian Journal of Radio and Space Physics [*A publication*]
**Indian J Reg Sci** ... Indian Journal of Regional Science [*A publication*]
**Indian J Sci Ind** ... Indian Journal of Science and Industry [*A publication*]
**Indian J Sci Ind Sect A** ... Indian Journal of Science and Industry. Section A. Agricultural Sciences [*Later, Indian Journal of Agricultural Research*] [*A publication*]
**Indian J Sci Ind Sect A Agric Anim Sci** ... Indian Journal of Science and Industry. Section A. Agricultural and Animal Sciences [*A publication*]
**Indian J Sci Ind Sect B Anim Sci** ... Indian Journal of Science and Industry. Section B. Animal Sciences [*Later, Indian Journal of Animal Research*] [*A publication*]

**Indian J Seric** ... Indian Journal of Sericulture [*A publication*]
**Indian J Social Work** ... Indian Journal of Social Work [*A publication*]
**Indian J Soil Conser** ... Indian Journal of Soil Conservation [*A publication*]
**Indian J Sugar Cane Res Dev** ... Indian Journal of Sugar Cane Research and Development [*A publication*]
**Indian J Surg** ... Indian Journal of Surgery [*A publication*]
**Indian J Tech** ... Indian Journal of Technology [*A publication*]
**Indian J Technol** ... Indian Journal of Technology [*A publication*]
**Indian J Text Res** ... Indian Journal of Textile Research [*A publication*]
**Indian J Theor Phys** ... Indian Journal of Theoretical Physics [*A publication*]
**Indian J Tuberc** ... Indian Journal of Tuberculosis [*A publication*]
**Indian J Tuberculosis** ... Indian Journal of Tuberculosis [*A publication*]
**Indian J Vet Med** ... Indian Journal of Veterinary Medicine [*A publication*]
**Indian J Vet Pathol** ... Indian Journal of Veterinary Pathology [*A publication*]
**Indian J Vet Sci** ... Indian Journal of Veterinary Science and Animal Husbandry [*A publication*]
**Indian J Vet Sci Anim Husb** ... Indian Journal of Veterinary Science and Animal Husbandry [*A publication*]
**Indian J Vet Surg** ... Indian Journal of Veterinary Surgery [*A publication*]
**Indian J Virol** ... Indian Journal of Virology [*A publication*]
**Indian J Weed Sci** ... Indian Journal of Weed Science [*A publication*]
**Indian J Zool** ... Indian Journal of Zoology [*A publication*]
**Indian J Zootomy** ... Indian Journal of Zootomy [*A publication*]
**Indian Lac Res Inst Annu Rep** ... Indian Lac Research Institute. Annual Report [*A publication*]
**Indian Lac Res Inst Bull** ... Indian Lac Research Institute. Bulletin [*A publication*]
**Indian Lac Res Inst Res Notes** ... Indian Lac Research Institute. Research Notes [*A publication*]
**Indian Lac Res Inst Tech Note** ... Indian Lac Research Institute. Technical Notes [*A publication*]
**Indian Lib Assn J** ... Indian Library Association. Journal [*A publication*]
**Indian Libr Ass Bull** ... Indian Library Association. Bulletin [*A publication*]
**Indian Librn** ... Indian Librarian [*A publication*]
**Indian Libr Sci Abstr** ... Indian Library Science Abstracts [*A publication*]
**Indian Lib Sci Abstr** ... Indian Library Science Abstracts [*A publication*]
**Indian LJ** ... Indian Law Journal [*A publication*] (DLA)
**Indian LR**... Indian Law Reports [*A publication*] (DLA)
**Indian L R Calc** ... Indian Law Reports, Calcutta Series [*A publication*] (DLA)
**Indian L Rep Am Indian Law Training Program** ... Indian Law Reporter. American Indian Lawyers Training Program [*A publication*]
**Indian L Rev** ... Indian Law Review [*A publication*]
**Indian LR Mad** ... Indian Law Reports, Madras Series [*A publication*] (DLA)
**Indian Med Forum** ... Indian Medical Forum [*A publication*]
**Indian Med Gaz** ... Indian Medical Gazette [*A publication*]
**Indian Med J (Calcutta)** ... Indian Medical Journal (Calcutta) [*A publication*]
**Indian Med Res Mem** ... Indian Medical Research Memoirs [*A publication*]
**Indian M Gaz** ... Indian Medical Gazette [*A publication*]
**Indian Min Engng J** ... Indian Mining and Engineering Journal [*A publication*]
**Indian Miner** ... Indian Minerals [*A publication*]
**Indian Mineral** ... Indian Mineralogist [*A publication*]
**Indian Miner Yearb** ... Indian Minerals Yearbook [*A publication*]
**Indian MJ** ... Indian Music Journal [*A publication*]
**Indian M S** ... Indian Musicological Society. Journal [*A publication*]
**Indian Mus Bull** ... Indian Museum. Bulletin [*A publication*]
**Indian Mus Q** ... Indian Music Quarterly [*A publication*]
**Indian Mus Rec** ... Indian Museum. Records [*A publication*]
**Indian Natl Sci Acad Proc Part A** ... Indian National Science Academy. Proceedings. Part A. Physical Sciences [*A publication*]
**Indian Nat Sci Acad Bull** ... Indian National Science Academy. Bulletin [*A publication*]
**Indian Paediatr** ... Indian Paediatrics [*A publication*]
**Indian Pediatr** ... Indian Pediatrics [*A publication*]
**Indian Perfum** ... Indian Perfumer [*A publication*]
**Indian Phil Cult** ... Indian Philosophy and Culture [*A publication*]
**Indian Phil Quart** ... Indian Philosophical Quarterly [*A publication*]
**Indian Phys Math J** ... Indian Physico-Mathematical Journal [*A publication*]
**Indian Phytopathol** ... Indian Phytopathology [*A publication*]
**Indianpl B** ... Indianapolis Business Journal [*A publication*]
**Indianpl S**.. Indianapolis Star [*A publication*]
**Indian Potash J** ... Indian Potash Journal [*A publication*]
**Indian Potato J** ... Indian Potato Journal [*A publication*]
**Indian Poult Gaz** ... Indian Poultry Gazette [*India*] [*A publication*]
**Indian Poult Rev** ... Indian Poultry Review [*A publication*]
**Indian Pract** ... Indian Practitioner [*A publication*]
**Indian Psychol Abstr** ... Indian Psychological Abstracts [*A publication*]
**Indian Psychol R** ... Indian Psychological Review [*A publication*]
**Indian Pulp Pap** ... Indian Pulp and Paper [*A publication*]
**Indian Refract Makers Assoc J** ... Indian Refractory Makers Association. Journal [*A publication*]
**Indian Rul** ... Indian Rulings [*A publication*] (DLA)
**Indian Sci Abstr** ... Indian Science Abstracts [*A publication*]
**Indian Sci Abstracts** ... Indian Science Abstracts [*A publication*]
**Indian Sci Cong Assoc Proc** ... Indian Science Congress Association. Proceedings [*A publication*]
**Indian Sci Congr Assoc Proc** ... Indian Science Congress Association. Proceedings [*A publication*]
**Indian Sci Ind** ... Indian Science Index [*A publication*]
**Indian Sci Index** ... Indian Science Index [*A publication*]
**Indian Soc Desert Technol Univ Cent Desert Stud Trans** ... Indian Society of Desert Technology and University Centre of Desert Studies. Transactions [*A publication*]
**Indian Soc Nuclear Tech Agric Biol Newsl** ... Indian Society for Nuclear Techniques in Agriculture and Biology. Newsletter [*A publication*]
**Indian Soc Nucl Tech Agric Biol Newsl** ... Indian Society for Nuclear Techniques in Agriculture and Biology. Newsletter [*A publication*]
**Indian Soc Soil Sci Bull** ... Indian Society of Soil Science. Bulletin [*A publication*]
**Indian Soc Soil Sci J** ... Indian Society of Soil Science. Journal [*A publication*]
**Indian Sug** ... Indian Sugar [*A publication*]
**Indian Tea Assoc Proc Annu Conf** ... Indian Tea Association. Proceedings of the Annual Conference [*A publication*]
**Indian Tea Assoc Sci Dep Tocklai Exp Stn Annu Rep** ... Indian Tea Association. Scientific Department. Tocklai Experimental Station. Annual Report [*A publication*]
**Indian Tea Assoc Sci Dep Tocklai Exp Stn Memo** ... Indian Tea Association. Scientific Department. Tocklai Experimental Station. Memorandum [*A publication*]
**Indian Tea Assoc Tocklai Exp Stn Annu Rep** ... Indian Tea Association. Tocklai Experimental Station. Annual Report [*A publication*]
**Indian Tea Assoc Tocklai Exp Stn Memo** ... Indian Tea Association. Tocklai Experimental Station. Memorandum [*A publication*]
**Indian Tea Assoc Tocklai Exp Stn Memor** ... Indian Tea Association. Tocklai Experimental Station. Memorandum [*A publication*]
**Indian Terr** ... Indian Territory Reports [*A publication*] (DLA)
**Indian Text J** ... Indian Textile Journal [*A publication*]
**Indian Tob J** ... Indian Tobacco Journal [*A publication*]
**Indian Vet J** ... Indian Veterinary Journal [*A publication*]
**Indian Vet Med J** ... Indian Veterinary Medical Journal [*A publication*]
**Indian Weld J** ... Indian Welding Journal [*A publication*]
**Indian Yb of Internat Aff** ... Indian Yearbook of International Affairs [*A publication*]
**Indian Zool** ... Indian Zoologist [*A publication*]
**Indian Zool Mem** ... Indian Zoological Memoirs [*A publication*]
**India Oil Nat Gas Comm Bull** ... India. Oil and Natural Gas Commission. Bulletin [*A publication*]
**India Pen Code** ... Indian Penal Code [*A publication*] (DLA)
**India Pol Sci R** ... Indian Political Science Review [*A publication*]
**India Q**....... India Quarterly [*A publication*]
**India Quar** ... India Quarterly [*A publication*]
**India Rubb R** ... India Rubber Review [*A publication*]
**India S Ct**... India Supreme Court Reports [*A publication*] (DLA)
**India Soc Stud Q** ... Indian Social Studies Quarterly [*A publication*]
**India Subs Leg** ... Subsidiary Legislation [*India*] [*A publication*] (DLA)
**INDIC**........ Indicate (AABC)
**INDIC**........ Indication Report (MCD)
**INDIC**........ Indicative [*Grammar*]
**Indicadores Econs (Mexico)** ... Indicadores Economicos (Mexico) [*A publication*]
**Indicadores Econs (RS)** ... Indicadores Economicos (Rio Grande Do Sul) [*A publication*]
**Indicateurs Econ Centre** ... Indicateurs de l'Economie du Centre [*A publication*]
**Indic Cartotec** ... Indicatore Cartotecnico [*A publication*]
**Indice Agricola Am Lat Caribe** ... Indice Agricola de America Latina y el Caribe [*A publication*]
**Indice Bibliogr Lepra** ... Indice Bibliografico de Lepra [*A publication*]
**Indice Lit Dent Castellano** ... Indice de la Literatura Dental en Castellano [*A publication*]
**Indice Med Esp** ... Indice Medico Espanol [*A publication*]
**Indice Rev Bibliotecol** ... IREBI. Indices de Revista de Bibliotecologia [*A publication*]
**Indic Grafico** ... Indicatore Grafico [*A publication*]
**INDICN** .... Indication
**INDICOM** ... Indications Communications (MCD)
**INDIDJ** ..... International Journal of Eating Disorders [*A publication*]
**INDIG** ....... Indigenous (AABC)
**INDIGO** .... Intelligence Division Gaming Operations
**Indi Math J** ... Indiana University. Mathematics Journal [*A publication*]
**IND IMP**... Indiae Imperator [*Emperor of India*] [*Latin*]
**Ind India** .... Index India [*A publication*]
**Ind India** .... Industrial India [*A publication*]
**Ind Ind LP** ... Index to Indian Legal Periodicals [*A publication*] (DLA)
**Ind Ind Med Per** ... Index of Indian Medical Periodicals [*A publication*]
**Ind Information Bul** ... Industrial Information Bulletin [*A publication*] (APTA)
**Ind & Intell Prop Aust** ... Industrial and Intellectual Property in Australia [*A publication*] (DLA)
**Ind & Int Prop Aus** ... Industrial and Intellectual Property in Australia [*A publication*]
**INDIPEX**.. India International Philatelic Exhibition
**Indirect**....... Indirections [*Ontario Council of Teachers of English*] [*A publication*]
**INDIRS** ..... Indiana Information Retrieval System [*Library network*]
**INDIS**........ Industrial Information and Advisory Services [*UNIDO*] (IID)
**Ind Islam**.... Index Islamicus [*A publication*]

**Ind Ital Cem** ... Industria Italiana del Cemento [*A publication*]
**Ind Ital Conserve** ... Industria Italiana delle Conserve [*A publication*]
**Ind Ital Conserve Aliment** ... Industria Italiana delle Conserve Alimentari [*A publication*]
**Ind Ital Elettrotec** ... Industria Italiana Elettrotecnica [*Italy*] [*A publication*]
**Ind Ital Elettrotec & Elettron** ... Industria Italiana Elettrotecnica ed Elettronica [*A publication*]
**Ind Ital Freddo** ... Industria Italiana del Freddo [*A publication*]
**Ind Ital Laterizi** ... Industria Italiana dei Laterizi [*A publication*]
**INDIV** ....... Individual (AFM)
**Individ Onsite Wastewater Syst** ... Individual Onsite Wastewater Systems [*A publication*]
**Indiv Inst**.... Individual Instruction [*A publication*]
**INDIVL**..... Individual [*Freight*]
**Indiv Psych** ... Individual Psychologist [*A publication*]
**Ind J Ad Ed** ... Indian Journal of Adult Education [*A publication*]
**Ind J Agr Econ** ... Indian Journal of Agricultural Economics [*A publication*]
**Ind J Agric Econ** ... Indian Journal of Agricultural Economics [*A publication*]
**Ind J Agric Sci** ... Indian Journal of Agricultural Science [*A publication*]
**Ind J Agric Vet Educ** ... Indian Journal of Agricultural and Veterinary Education [*A publication*]
**Ind J Ag Sci** ... Indian Journal of Agricultural Science [*A publication*]
**Ind J Anesth** ... Indian Journal of Anesthesia [*A publication*]
**Ind J Commer** ... Indian Journal of Commerce [*A publication*]
**Ind J Econ** ... Indian Journal of Economics [*A publication*]
**Ind Jew Per** ... Index to Jewish Periodicals [*A publication*]
**Ind J Forest** ... Indian Journal of Forestry [*A publication*]
**Ind J Indus Rel** ... Indian Journal of Industrial Relations [*A publication*]
**Ind J Industr Relat** ... Indian Journal of Industrial Relations [*A publication*]
**Ind J Int L** ... Indian Journal of International Law [*A publication*]
**Ind J Int'l L** ... Indiana Journal of International Law [*A publication*] (DLA)
**Ind J Occup Hlth** ... Indian Journal of Occupational Health [*A publication*]
**Ind J Otol** .. Indian Journal of Otolaryngology [*A publication*]
**Ind J Polit** ... Indian Journal of Politics [*A publication*]
**Ind J Polit Sci** ... Indian Journal of Political Science [*A publication*]
**Ind J Pol Sci** ... Indian Journal of Political Science [*A publication*]
**Ind J Psych** ... Indian Journal of Psychiatry [*A publication*]
**Ind J Publ Adm** ... Indian Journal of Public Administration [*A publication*]
**Ind J Soc Res** ... Indian Journal of Social Research [*A publication*]
**Ind J Soc Wk** ... Indian Journal of Social Work [*A publication*]
**Ind J Stat**... Indian Journal of Statistics [*A publication*]
**IndJT**......... Indian Journal of Theology [*Serampore*] [*A publication*]
**Ind J Th**..... Indian Journal of Theology [*A publication*]
**Ind Jud Pr** ... Indermaur's Practice of the Supreme Court of Judicature [*12th ed.*] [*1919*] [*A publication*] (DLA)
**Ind Jur** ....... Indian Jurist [*Calcutta or Madras*] [*A publication*] (DLA)
**Ind Jur NS** ... Indian Jurist, New Series [*A publication*] (DLA)
**Ind Jur OS** ... Indian Jurist, Old Series [*A publication*] (DLA)
**Ind Jur Pr** .. Indermaur's Practice of the Supreme Court of Judicature [*12th ed.*] [*1919*] [*A publication*] (DLA)
**Ind J Vet Sci** ... Indian Journal of Veterinary Science [*A publication*]
**Ind J Vet Sci An Hus** ... Indian Journal of Veterinary Science and Animal Husbandry [*A publication*]
**Ind L** .......... Indian Literature [*A publication*]
**INDL** ......... Industrial (MSA)
**INDLA** ...... Industrial Laboratory [*English Translation*] [*A publication*]
**Ind Lab** ...... Industrial Laboratories [*Chicago*] [*A publication*]
**Ind Lab J** ... Indian Labour Journal [*A publication*]
**Ind and Labor Relations Forum** ... Industrial and Labor Relations Forum [*A publication*]
**Ind and Labor Relations R** ... Industrial and Labor Relations Review [*A publication*]
**Ind and Labor Relations Rept** ... Industrial and Labor Relations Report [*A publication*]
**Ind Labor Relat Rev** ... Industrial and Labor Relations Review [*A publication*]
**Ind & Labor Rel R** ... Industrial and Labor Relations Review [*A publication*]
**Ind and Labor Rels Rev** ... Industrial and Labor Relations Review [*A publication*]
**Ind Lab Rel** ... Industrial and Labor Relations Review [*A publication*]
**Ind & Lab Rel Rev** ... Industrial and Labor Relations Review [*A publication*]
**Ind Lab (US)** ... Industrial Laboratory (United States) [*A publication*]
**Ind Lab (USSR)** ... Industrial Laboratory (USSR) [*A publication*]
**Ind Lackier-Betr** ... Industrie Lackier-Betrieb [*A publication*]
**Ind Lackier-Betrb** ... Industrie Lackier-Betrieb [*A publication*]
**Ind Latt Zootee** ... Industria Lattiera e Zooteenia [*A publication*]
**Ind Law J** ... Industrial Law Journal [*A publication*]
**Ind Law Jour** ... Indiana Law Journal [*A publication*]
**Ind & Lbr Rel R** ... Industrial and Labor Relations Review [*A publication*]
**Ind LC Com Law** ... Indermaur's Leading Cases in Common Law [*10th ed.*] [*1921*] [*A publication*] (DLA)
**Ind LC Eq** .. Indermaur's Leading Cases in Conveyancing and Equity [*A publication*] (DLA)
**Ind Legal F** ... Indiana Legal Forum [*A publication*]
**Ind Leg Per** ... Index to Legal Periodicals [*A publication*]
**Ind Lemnului** ... Industria Lemnului [*A publication*]
**Ind Lemnului Celul Hirtiei** ... Industria Lemnului Celulozei si Hirtiei [*A publication*]
**Ind LH** ....... Indian Law Herald [*A publication*] (DLA)
**Ind Lib** ....... Indian Librarian [*A publication*]
**Ind Ling** ..... Indian Linguistics [*A publication*]
**Ind Linguist** ... Indian Linguistics [*A publication*]
**IndLit**......... Indian Literature [*A publication*]
**Ind Lit Amer Indian** ... Index to Literature on the American Indian [*A publication*]
**Ind Lit Dent** ... Indice de la Literatura Dental en Castellano [*A publication*]
**Ind Little Mag** ... Index to Little Magazines [*A publication*]
**Ind L J** ....... Indiana Law Journal [*A publication*]
**Ind L Mag** ... Indian Law Magazine [*A publication*] (DLA)
**Ind LQ** ....... Indian Law Quarterly [*A publication*] (DLA)
**Ind LQ Rev** ... Indian Law Quarterly Review [*A publication*] (DLA)
**Ind LR**........ Indian Law Reports (East) [*A publication*] (DLA)
**Ind LR**........ Indian Law Review [*A publication*]
**Ind LR**........ Indiana Law Reporter [*1881*] [*A publication*] (DLA)
**Ind LR**........ Indiana Law Review [*A publication*]
**Ind LR**........ Indiana Legal Register [*A publication*] (DLA)
**Ind LR**........ Industrial Law Review [*A publication*] (ILCA)
**Ind LR All** ... Indian Law Reports, Allahabad Series [*A publication*] (DLA)
**Ind LR Alla** ... Indian Law Reports, Allahabad Series [*A publication*] (DLA)
**Ind LR And** ... Indian Law Reports, Andhra Series [*A publication*] (DLA)
**Ind LR Assam** ... Indian Law Reports, Assam Series [*A publication*] (DLA)
**Ind LR Bomb** ... Indian Law Reports, Bombay Series [*A publication*] (DLA)
**Ind LR Calc** ... Indian Law Reports, Calcutta Series [*A publication*] (DLA)
**Ind L Reg** ... Indiana Legal Register [*A publication*] (DLA)
**Ind & L Rel Rev** ... Industrial and Labor Relations Review [*A publication*]
**Ind L Rep** ... Indian Law Reporter [*A publication*] (DLA)
**Ind L Rep** ... Indiana Law Reporter [*1881*] [*A publication*] (DLA)
**Ind L Rev** ... Indiana Law Review [*A publication*]
**Ind LR Hyderabad** ... Indian Law Reports, Hyderabad Series [*A publication*] (DLA)
**Ind LR Kar** ... Indian Law Reports, Karachi Series [*A publication*] (DLA)
**Ind LR Ker** ... Indian Law Reports, Kerala Series [*A publication*] (DLA)
**Ind LR Lah** ... Indian Law Reports, Lahore Series [*A publication*] (DLA)
**Ind LR Luck** ... Indian Law Reports, Lucknow Series [*A publication*] (DLA)
**Ind LR Mad** ... Indian Law Reports, Madras Series [*A publication*] (DLA)
**Ind LR Madhya Bharat** ... Indian Law Reports, Madhya Bharat Series [*A publication*] (DLA)
**Ind LR Mysore** ... Indian Law Reports, Mysore Series [*A publication*] (DLA)
**Ind LR Nag** ... Indian Law Reports, Nagpur Series [*A publication*] (DLA)
**Ind LR Or** .. Indian Law Reports, Orissa Series [*A publication*] (DLA)
**Ind LR Pat** ... Indian Law Reports, Patna Series [*A publication*] (DLA)
**Ind LR Patiala** ... Indian Law Reports, Patiala Series [*A publication*] (DLA)
**Ind LR Pun** ... Indian Law Reports, Punjab Series [*A publication*] (DLA)
**Ind LR Rajasthan** ... Indian Law Reports, Rajasthan Series [*A publication*] (DLA)
**Ind LR Ran** ... Indian Law Reports, Rangoon Series [*A publication*] (DLA)
**Ind LS**........ Indiana Law Student [*A publication*] (DLA)
**Ind L Stud** ... Indiana Law Student [*A publication*] (DLA)
**Ind LT**........ Indian Law Times [*A publication*] (DLA)
**Ind Lubric**.. Industrial Lubrication [*A publication*]
**Ind Lubric Tribology** ... Industrial Lubrication and Tribology [*A publication*]
**Ind Lubr & Technol** ... Industrial Lubrication and Technology [*A publication*]
**Ind Lubr Tribol** ... Industrial Lubrication and Tribology [*A publication*]
**INDM**........ Indemnity [*Legal term*]
**Ind M**......... Independent Monthly [*A publication*]
**Ind M**......... Indiana Magazine of History [*A publication*]
**INDM**........ Infant of Nondiabetic Mother [*Obstetrics*]
**Ind Mach** ... Industrial Machinery [*Japan*] [*A publication*]
**Ind Mag Hist** ... Indiana Magazine of History [*A publication*]
**INDMAN** ... Industrial Manager
**Ind Manage** ... Industrial Management [*A publication*]
**Ind Manage and Data Syst** ... Industrial Management and Data Systems [*A publication*]
**Ind Management** ... Industrial Management [*New York*] [*A publication*]
**Ind Management (London)** ... Industrial Management (London) [*A publication*]
**Ind Management R** ... Industrial Management Review [*A publication*]
**Ind Mark** ... Industrial Marketing [*Later, Business Marketing*] [*A publication*]
**Ind Market** ... Industrial Marketing [*Later, Business Marketing*] [*A publication*]
**Ind Market Dig** ... Industrial Marketing Digest [*A publication*]
**Ind Mark Manage** ... Industrial Marketing Management [*A publication*]
**Ind Math**.... Industrial Mathematics [*A publication*]
**Ind Med** ..... Index Medicus [*A publication*]
**Ind Med** ..... Industrial Medicine [*A publication*]
**Ind Med** ..... Industrial Medicine and Surgery [*A publication*]
**Ind Med Esp** ... Indice Medico Espanol [*A publication*]
**Ind Med For** ... Indian Medical Forum [*A publication*]
**Ind Med Gaz** ... Indian Medical Gazette [*A publication*]
**Ind Med J** .. Indian Medical Journal [*A publication*]
**Ind Med Rec** ... Indian Medical Record [*A publication*]
**Ind Med Res Mem** ... Indian Medical Research Memoirs [*A publication*]
**Ind Med Serv** ... Indian Medical Service [*A publication*]
**Ind Med Serv N** ... Indian Medical Service News [*A publication*]
**Ind Med & Surg** ... Industrial Medicine and Surgery [*A publication*]
**Ind Med Surg** ... Industrial Medicine and Surgery [*A publication*]
**Ind Med Wld** ... Indian Medical World [*A publication*]
**INDMGR**.. Industrial Manager
**Ind Mgt**...... Industrial Management [*New York*] [*A publication*]
**Ind Mgt & Data Syst** ... Industrial Management and Data Systems [*A publication*]
**Ind Mgt R**.. Industrial Management Review [*A publication*]

**Ind Miljoe** ... Industri og Miljoe [*A publication*]
**Ind Min**...... Industrial Minerals [*A publication*]
**Ind Miner**... Industrial Minerals [*A publication*]
**Ind Miner**... Industrie Minerale [*A publication*]
**Ind Miner (London)** ... Industrial Minerals (London) [*A publication*]
**Ind Miner Mine** ... Industrie Minerale. Mine [*A publication*]
**Ind Miner Mineralurgie** ... Industrie Minerale. Mineralurgie [*A publication*]
**Ind Miner (Paris)** ... Industrie Minerale (Paris) [*A publication*]
**Ind Miner Rocks** ... Industrial Minerals and Rocks [*A publication*]
**Ind Miner Ser Mineralurgie** ... Industrie Minerale. Serie Mineralurgie [*France*] [*Later, Industrie Minerale. Serie Techniques*] [*A publication*]
**Ind Miner Ser Tech** ... Industrie Minerale. Serie Techniques [*St. Etienne, France*] [*A publication*]
**Ind Miner (St Etienne)** ... Industrie Minerale (St. Etienne) [*France*] [*A publication*]
**Ind Miner (St Etienne Fr)** ... Industrie Minerale (St. Etienne, France) [*A publication*]
**Ind Miner Suppl Techniques (St Etienne)** ... Industrie Minerale. Supplement. Les Techniques (St. Etienne) [*France*] [*A publication*]
**Ind Miner Tech** ... Industrie Minerale. Techniques [*A publication*]
**Ind Mining Stand** ... Industrial and Mining Standard [*A publication*]
**Ind Min J**... Indian Mining Journal [*A publication*]
**Ind Min (Madrid)** ... Industria Minera (Madrid) [*A publication*]
**Ind Min Quebec** ... Industrie Miniere du Quebec [*A publication*]
**Ind & Min R** ... Industrial and Mining Review [*A publication*] (APTA)
**Ind Min (Rome)** ... Industria Mineraria (Rome) [*A publication*]
**Ind & Min S** ... Industrial and Mining Standard [*A publication*] (APTA)
**Ind & Min Standard** ... Industrial and Mining Standard [*A publication*] (APTA)
**Ind Mkt**...... Industrial Marketing [*Later, Business Marketing*] [*A publication*]
**Ind Mktg**.... Industrial Marketing [*Later, Business Marketing*] [*A publication*]
**Ind Mkt Man** ... Industrial Marketing Management [*A publication*]
**Ind Mkt Mgt** ... Industrial Marketing Management [*A publication*]
**Ind Mktng** ... Industrial Marketing [*Later, Business Marketing*] [*A publication*]
**Ind Mus Not** ... Indian Museum Notes [*A publication*]
**INDN**......... Indian News [*A publication*]
**INDN**......... Induction
**IndNat**........ Independent Nationalist [*Australia*]
**Ind News**.... Industry News [*A publication*]
**Ind Norte Port** ... Industria do Norte de Portugal [*A publication*]
**Ind NZ Per** ... Index to New Zealand Periodicals [*A publication*]
**IndO**........... Indian Ocean
**INDO**......... Indonesia
**INDO**......... Intermediate Neglect of Differential Overlap [*Quantum mechanics*]
**Indo-As**...... Indo-Asia [*A publication*]
**Ind Obst- Gemueseverwert** ... Industrial Obst- und Gemueseverwertung [*A publication*]
**INDOC**...... Indoctrinate (AABC)
**INDOC**...... Indonesian Documentation and Information Centre [*Leiden, Netherlands*] (EAIO)
**INDOCHEM** ... Indian Ocean GEOSECS Program (MSC)
**Indochina**... Indochina Chronicle [*A publication*]
**Ind Odont**... Index Odontologicus [*A publication*]
**INDO-EUR** ... Indo-European (ROG)
**INDO-GER** ... Indo-Germanic [*Language, etc.*] (ROG)
**Indogerm F** ... Indogermanische Forschungen [*A publication*]
**Indo-Germ Forsch** ... Indogermanische Forschungen [*A publication*] (OCD)
**Indo Iran J** ... Indo-Iranian Journal [*A publication*]
**Indo J Geog** ... Indonesian Journal of Geography [*A publication*]
**Ind Olii Miner Grassi** ... Industria degli Olii Minerali i dei Grassi [*A publication*]
**Indon**.......... Indonesia
**Indones Abstr** ... Indonesian Abstracts [*A publication*]
**Indones Dev News** ... Indonesia Development News [*A publication*]
**Indones Dir Geol Publ Chusus** ... Indonesia. Direktorat Geologi. Publikasi Chusus [*A publication*]
**Indones Dir Geol Publ Tek Ser Geofis** ... Indonesia. Direktorat Geologi. Publikasi Teknik. Seri Geofisika [*A publication*]
**Indones Dir Geol Publ Tek Ser Geol Ekon** ... Indonesia. Direktorat Geologi. Publikasi Teknik. Serie Geologi Ekonomi [*A publication*]
**Indones Dir Geol Publ Tek Ser Paleontol** ... Indonesia. Direktorat Geologi. Publikasi Teknik. Seri Paleontologi [*A publication*]
**Indonesia New** ... Indonesia. News and Views [*A publication*] (APTA)
**Indonesian J G** ... Indonesian Journal of Geography [*A publication*]
**Indones Inst Mar Res Oceanogr Cruise Rep** ... Indonesian Institute of Marine Research. Oceanographical Cruise Report [*A publication*]
**Indones J Crop Sci** ... Indonesian Journal of Crop Science [*A publication*]
**Indones J Geogr** ... Indonesian Journal of Geography [*A publication*]
**Indones Pet Assoc Annu Conv Proc** ... Indonesian Petroleum Association. Annual Convention. Proceedings [*A publication*]
**Indones Quart** ... Indonesian Quarterly [*A publication*]
**Indo-Pac Fish Counc Occas Pap** ... Indo-Pacific Fisheries Council. Occasional Papers [*A publication*]
**Indo-Pac Fish Counc Proc** ... Indo-Pacific Fisheries Council. Proceedings [*A publication*]
**Indo-Pac Fish Counc Reg Stud** ... Indo-Pacific Fisheries Council. Regional Studies [*A publication*]
**Indo-Pac Fish Counc Spec Publ** ... Indo-Pacific Fisheries Council. Special Publications [*A publication*]
**Indo-Pac Mollusca** ... Indo-Pacific Mollusca [*A publication*]
**Indo Q**........ Indonesian Quarterly [*A publication*]
**INDOR**...... Internuclear Double Resonance
**Ind Org**...... Industrielle Organisation [*A publication*]
**Ind Org Hlth** ... Industrial Organisation and Health [*A publication*]
**Ind P** .......... Pharmacopoeia of India [*A publication*]
**Ind Parf**...... Industrie de la Parfumerie [*A publication*]
**Ind Parf Cosm** ... Industries de la Parfumerie et de la Cosmetique [*A publication*]
**Ind Parfum Cosmet** ... Industries de la Parfumerie et de la Cosmetique [*A publication*]
**IND PENS** ... Indian Pension [*Army*] [*British*] (ROG)
**Ind Per Art Relat Law** ... Index to Periodical Articles Related to Law [*A publication*]
**Ind Per Blacks** ... Index to Periodical Articles by and about Blacks [*A publication*]
**Ind Per Lit** ... Indian Periodical Literature [*A publication*]
**Ind Per Negroes** ... Index to Periodical Articles by and about Negroes [*Later, Index to Periodical Articles by and about Blacks*] [*A publication*]
**Ind Pet** ....... Industrie du Petrole [*France*] [*A publication*]
**Ind Pet Eur Gaz Chim** ... Industrie du Petrole en Europe. Gaz-Chimie [*A publication*]
**Ind Pet Gaz Chim** ... Industrie du Petrole. Gaz-Chimie [*A publication*]
**Ind Pet Monde Gaz-Chim** ... Industrie du Petrole dans le Monde. Gaz-Chimie [*France*] [*A publication*]
**Ind Petr**...... Industrie du Petrole [*A publication*]
**Ind Petrol Gaz-Chim** ... Industrie du Petrole. Gaz-Chimie [*A publication*]
**IND PH**..... Indian Pharmacopoeia (ROG)
**Ind Pharm** ... Indian Pharmacist [*A publication*]
**Ind Philippines** ... Industrial Philippines [*A publication*]
**Ind Philo A** ... Indian Philosophical Annual [*A publication*]
**Ind Phot**..... Industrial Photography [*A publication*]
**Ind Photogr** ... Industrial Photography [*A publication*]
**Ind Phyc**..... Indian Physician [*A publication*]
**Ind Phys**..... Indian Physiologist [*A publication*]
**Ind Phys Math J** ... Indian Physico-Mathematical Journal [*A publication*]
**Ind Plann Dev** ... Industrial Planning and Development [*A publication*]
**Ind Plast**.... Industrie des Plastiques [*A publication*]
**Ind Plast Mod** ... Industrie des Plastiques Modernes [*A publication*]
**Ind Plast Mod Elastomeres** ... Industrie des Plastiques Modernes et Elastomeres [*Later, Plastiques Modernes et Elastomeres*] [*A publication*]
**Ind Plast (Paris)** ... Industries des Plastiques (Paris) [*A publication*]
**Ind Polit Sci R** ... Indian Political Science Review [*A publication*]
**Ind Pol J**.... Indian Police Journal [*A publication*]
**Ind Pol Sci R** ... Indian Political Science Review [*A publication*]
**Ind Port**...... Industria Portuguesa [*A publication*]
**Ind Power**... Industry and Power [*United States*] [*A publication*]
**Ind Power Mass Prod** ... Industrial Power and Mass Production [*A publication*]
**Ind Power Steam Heat Light Air Fuel Econ** ... Industrial Power, Steam Heat, Light, and Air and the Fuel Economist [*A publication*]
**Ind Probl**.... Indagini e Problemi [*A publication*]
**Ind Process Heat** ... Industrial and Process Heating [*A publication*]
**Ind Prod Eng** ... Industrial and Production Engineering [*A publication*]
**Ind Prod Mag** ... Industrial Products Magazine [*A publication*]
**Ind Prog Dev** ... Industrial Progress and Development [*A publication*]
**Ind Progress** ... Industrial Progress and Development [*A publication*] (APTA)
**Ind Progress and Development** ... Industrial Progress and Development [*A publication*] (APTA)
**Ind Prop**..... Industrial Property [*Legal term*] (DLA)
**Ind Prop Q** ... Industrial Property Quarterly [*A publication*] (DLA)
**Ind Prop Quart** ... Industrial Property Quarterly [*A publication*]
**Ind Prop Sem** ... Industrial Property Seminar (Monash University, 1972) [*A publication*] (APTA)
**IndProt**....... Independent Protectionist [*Australia*]
**Ind Psych R** ... Indian Psychological Review [*A publication*]
**Ind Publ Hlth Munic J** ... Indian Public Health and Municipal Journal [*A publication*]
**Ind Q**.......... India Quarterly [*A publication*]
**INDQ**......... International Dairy Queen, Inc. [*NASDAQ symbol*] (NQ)
**Ind Quality Control** ... Industrial Quality Control [*A publication*]
**Ind Quart**... India Quarterly [*A publication*]
**Ind Quim (Buenos Aires)** ... Industria y Quimica (Buenos Aires) [*A publication*]
**Ind R**.......... Indiana Reports [*A publication*] (DLA)
**INDR**......... Industrial Resources, Inc. [*NASDAQ symbol*] (NQ)
**INDRA**...... Industrial Diamond Review [*A publication*]
**Ind Radiogr** ... Industrial Radiography and Non-Destructive Testing [*A publication*]
**Ind Radiogr Non Destr Test** ... Industrial Radiography and Non-Destructive Testing [*A publication*]
**Ind Rare Met** ... Industrial Rare Metals [*Japan*] [*A publication*]
**INDRB**...... Inactive Nondisability Retirement Branch [*BUPERS*]
**INDRBA**.... Indian Drugs [*A publication*]
**INDRE**...... Indenture

**Ind Reg**....... Indiana Register [*A publication*]
**INDREG** ... Inductance Regulator (IEEE)
**Ind Rel** ....... Industrial Relations [*A publication*]
**Ind Relat** .... Industrial Relations [*A publication*]
**Ind Relations** ... Industrial Relations [*A publication*]
**Ind Relations (Berkeley)** ... Industrial Relations (Berkeley) [*A publication*]
**Ind Relations (Quebec)** ... Industrial Relations (Quebec) [*A publication*]
**Ind Relat J S Afr** ... Industrial Relations Journal of South Africa [*A publication*]
**Ind Relat Rev Rep** ... Industrial Relations Review and Report [*A publication*]
**Ind Rel Briefing** ... Industrial Relations Briefing [*A publication*]
**Ind Rel J** .... Industrial Relations Journal [*A publication*]
**Ind Rel J Econ & Soc** ... Industrial Relations: Journal of Economy and Society [*A publication*] (DLA)
**Ind Rel Law J** ... Industrial Relations Law Journal [*A publication*]
**Ind Rel LJ** ... Industrial Relations Law Journal [*A publication*]
**Ind Rel News** ... Industrial Relations News [*A publication*]
**Ind Rel Rev Rep** ... Industrial Relations Review and Report [*A publication*]
**Ind Rel Soc Proc** ... Industrial Relations Society. Proceedings of Convention [*A publication*] (APTA)
**Ind Rep** ...... Indiana Reports [*A publication*] (DLA)
**Ind Rept Chemicals** ... Industry Report. Chemicals [*A publication*]
**Ind Rept Containers Pkg** ... Industry Report. Containers and Packaging [*A publication*]
**Ind Rept Pulp Pbd** ... Industry Report. Pulp, Paper, and Board [*A publication*]
**Ind Res**....... Industrial Research [*A publication*]
**Ind Res**....... Industrial Research and Development [*A publication*]
**Ind Res/Dev** ... Industrial Research and Development [*United States*] [*A publication*]
**Ind Res & Devel** ... Industrial Research and Development [*A publication*]
**Ind Res (Lond)** ... Industrial Research (London) [*A publication*]
**Ind Res News** ... Industrial Research News [*Australia*] [*A publication*]
**Ind Res News CSIRO** ... Industrial Research News. Commonwealth Scientific and Industrial Research Organisation [*A publication*] (APTA)
**Ind Review Jap** ... Industrial Review of Japan [*A publication*]
**Ind R & Mining Yrbk** ... Industrial Review and Mining Year Book [*A publication*] (APTA)
**Ind Robot** ... Industrial Robot [*A publication*]
**Ind Rom** ..... Index Romanus [*A publication*]
**Ind Rub J** ... India Rubber Journal [*A publication*]
**Ind Rub Wd** ... India Rubber World [*A publication*]
**INDS** ......... In-Core Nuclear Detection System [*Nuclear energy*] (IEEE)
**IndS** ........... Independent Shavian [*A publication*]
**Ind S**........... Indian Studies: Past and Present [*A publication*]
**Ind Saccarif Ital** ... Industria Saccarifera Italiana [*A publication*]
**Ind Sacc Ital** ... Industria Saccarifera Italiana [*Italy*] [*A publication*]
**Ind Saf** ....... Industrial Safety [*A publication*]
**Ind Saf Chron** ... Industrial Safety Chronicle [*A publication*]
**Ind Saf Data File** ... Industrial Safety Data File [*A publication*]
**Ind Safety** .. Industrial Safety [*A publication*]
**Ind Saf Hlth Bull** ... Industrial Safety and Health Bulletin [*A publication*]
**Ind Saf Surv** ... Industrial Safety Survey [*A publication*]
**Ind SA Per** ... Index to South African Periodicals [*A publication*]
**Ind Sapon Olii Stearin Profum** ... Industria Saponiera e degli Olii. Steariniera. Profumiera [*A publication*]
**Ind SBA** ..... Indiana State Bar Association Reports [*A publication*] (DLA)
**Ind Sch Bull** ... Independent School Bulletin [*A publication*]
**Ind Sci Abstr** ... Indian Science Abstracts [*A publication*]
**Ind Sci Agric** ... Indian Scientific Agriculturist [*A publication*]
**Ind Sci Eng** ... Industrial Science and Engineering [*A publication*]
**Ind Sci Instrum** ... Industrial and Scientific Instruments [*A publication*]
**Ind Sci Rev** ... Index to Scientific Reviews [*Institute for Scientific Information*] [*Information service or system*] [*A publication*]
**Ind Sci Technol** ... Industrial Science and Technology [*Japan*] [*A publication*]
**Ind Secera** ... Industrija Secera [*A publication*]
**Ind Sel Per** ... Index to Selected Periodicals [*A publication*]
**Inds Habillement** ... Industries de l'Habillement [*A publication*]
**Ind Short-Term Trends** ... Industrial Short-Term Trends [*A publication*]
**Ind Sid Eur** ... Industrie Siderurgique en Europe [*A publication*]
**Ind Slav St** ... Indiana Slavic Studies [*A publication*]
**Ind Soap J** ... Indian Soap Journal [*A publication*]
**Ind Soc** ....... Indian Sociologist [*A publication*]
**Ind Soc B**.... Indian Sociological Bulletin [*A publication*]
**Ind Soc Rev** ... Indian Sociological Review [*A publication*]
**Ind Spec** ..... Industrial Specification [*A publication*]
**Ind Stand** ... Industrial Standardization [*A publication*]
**Ind Stand Commer Stand Mon** ... Industrial Standardization and Commercial Standards. Monthly [*A publication*]
**Inds et Trav Outremer** ... Industries et Travaux d'Outre-Mer [*A publication*]
**Ind Stud** ..... Indian Studies [*A publication*]
**Ind Sup**....... Industrial Supervisor [*A publication*]
**Ind Super** ... Wilson's Indiana Superior Court Reports [*A publication*] (DLA)
**INDT** ......... Indent (MSA)
**IND T** ........ Indian Territory (ROG)
**INDTA** ...... Industries et Techniques [*A publication*]
**Ind T Ann St** ... Indian Territory Annotated Statutes [*A publication*] (DLA)
**Ind Tech**..... Industries et Techniques [*A publication*]
**Ind Tek** ...... Industriell Teknik [*Sweden*] [*A publication*]
**IND TER**... Indian Territory
**Ind Ter** ....... Indian Territory Reports [*A publication*] (DLA)
**Ind Terr**....... Indian Territory (DLA)
**Ind Text** ..... Industrie Textile [*A publication*]
**Ind Text Eur** ... Industrie Textile en Europe [*A publication*]
**Ind Textil**... Industrie Textile [*A publication*]
**Ind Therm** ... Industries Thermiques [*A publication*]
**Ind Therm Aerauliques** ... Industries Thermiques et Aerauliques [*A publication*]
**INDTNG**... Individual Training [*Navy*] (NVT)
**Ind Today**... Industry Today [*A publication*] (APTA)
**INDTR** ...... Indicator-Transmitter
**Ind de Transformacao** ... Industrias de Transformacao [*A publication*]
**Ind Trav O-Mer** ... Industries et Travaux d'Outre-Mer [*A publication*]
**Indty**........... Indemnity [*Legal term*] (DLA)
**INDUA**....... Industria [*A publication*]
**IndUAP** ..... Independent United Australia Party [*Political party*] (ADA)
**INDUC** ...... Induction (AABC)
**Ind UCD** .... Indiana Unemployment Compensation Division, Selected Appeal Tribunal Decisions [*A publication*] (DLA)
**Ind Un Art B** ... Indiana University. Art Museum. Bulletin [*A publication*]
**Ind Univ Extension Division Bull** ... Indiana University. Extension Division Bulletin [*A publication*]
**Ind Univ Sch Ed B** ... Indiana University. School of Education. Bulletin [*A publication*]
**Indus** .......... Industrialist
**INDUS** ...... Industry
**Indus Cas R** ... Industrial Cases Reports [*Law reports*] [*British*] (DLA)
**Indus Diamond Rev** ... Industrial Diamond Review [*A publication*]
**Indus Eng**... Industrial Engineering [*A publication*]
**Indus and Eng Chemistry** ... Industrial and Engineering Chemistry [*A publication*]
**Indus Fish Prod Mark Rev & Outl** ... Industrial Fishery Products Market Review and Outlook [*A publication*]
**Indus Free China** ... Industry of Free China [*A publication*]
**Ind US Gov Per** ... Index to United States Government Periodicals [*A publication*]
**Indus & Lab Rel F** ... Industrial and Labor Relations Forum [*A publication*]
**Indus & Lab Rel Rev** ... Industrial and Labor Relations Review [*A publication*]
**Indus LJ**..... Industrial Law Journal [*A publication*]
**Indus L Rev** ... Industrial Law Review [*A publication*] (DLA)
**INDUSMIN** ... Industrial Mineral Service [*Midland, ON*]
**Indus Minerals** ... Industrial Minerals [*A publication*]
**Ind Usoara** ... Industria Usoara [*Romania*] [*A publication*]
**Ind Usoara Piel** ... Industria Usoara Pielarie [*A publication*]
**Indus Rel**.... Industrial Relations [*A publication*]
**Indus Rel Guide** ... Industrial Relations Guide [*A publication*] (DLA)
**Indus Rel Guide P-H** ... Industrial Relations Guide. Prentice-Hall [*A publication*]
**Indus Rel LJ** ... Industrial Relations Law Journal [*A publication*]
**INDUSSIM** ... Total Industry Simulation [*Game*]
**Indus Sit Ind** ... Industrial Situation in India [*A publication*]
**INDUST**.... Industrial [*or Industry*]
**Indust Acc Com** ... Decisions of the Industrial Accident Commission of California [*A publication*] (DLA)
**Indust Bull** ... Industrial Bulletin [*A publication*] (DLA)
**Indust C Aw** ... Industrial Court Awards [*England*] [*A publication*] (DLA)
**Indust Ct Aw** ... Industrial Court Awards [*England*] [*A publication*] (DLA)
**Indust Engineering** ... Industrial Engineering [*A publication*]
**Indust Engr** ... Industrial Engineer [*A publication*] (APTA)
**INDUSTL** ... Industrial
**Indust Law Rev** ... Industrial Law Review [*A publication*] (DLA)
**Indust LJ** ... Industrial Law Journal [*A publication*]
**Indust & L Rel Rev** ... Industrial and Labor Relations Review [*A publication*]
**Indust L Rev** ... Industrial Law Review [*A publication*] (DLA)
**Indust L Rev Q** ... Industrial Law Review Quarterly [*A publication*]
**Indust L Soc Bull** ... Bulletin. Industrial Law Society [*A publication*] (DLA)
**Indust Math** ... Industrial Mathematics [*A publication*]
**Indust Med** ... Industrial Medicine and Surgery [*A publication*]
**Indust Progress** ... Industrial Progress and Development [*A publication*] (APTA)
**Indust Prop** ... Industrial Property [*Legal term*] (DLA)
**Indust Prop Q** ... Industrial Property Quarterly [*A publication*] (DLA)
**Indust Prop'y Yb** ... Industrial Property Yearbook [*A publication*] (DLA)
**INDUSTR** ... Industrial (ROG)
**Indust Rel LJ** ... Industrial Relations Law Journal [*A publication*]
**Industr Engng Chem (Int Ed)** ... Industrial and Engineering Chemistry (International Edition) [*A publication*]
**Industr Franc Coton Fibres Alliees** ... Industrie Francaise du Coton et des Fibres Alliees [*A publication*]
**Industr Gerontol** ... Industrial Gerontology [*A publication*]
**Industrial & Labor Rel Rev** ... Industrial and Labor Relations Review [*A publication*]
**Industrial L Rev Q** ... Industrial Law Review Quarterly [*A publication*]
**Industrial Phot** ... Industrial Photography [*A publication*]
**Industrial et Productiv** ... Industrialisation et Productivite [*A publication*]
**Industrie Agr** ... Industrie Agrarie [*A publication*]
**Industrie Aliment** ... Industrie Alimentari [*A publication*]
**Industr Lab Relat R** ... Industrial and Labor Relations Review [*A publication*]

**Industr Progr** ... Industrial Progress and Development [*A publication*] (APTA)
**Industr Prop'y Q** ... Industrial Property Quarterly [*A publication*] (DLA)
**Industr Relat** ... Industrial Relations [*A publication*]
**Industr Relat J** ... Industrial Relations Journal [*A publication*]
**Industr Res Study Timb Res Developm Ass** ... Industrial Research Study. Timber Research and Development Association [*A publication*]
**Industr Trav O-Mer** ... Industries et Travaux d'Outre-Mer [*A publication*]
**Indus Week** ... Industry Week [*A publication*]
**Ind Util Sugar Mill By-Prod** ... Industrial Utilisation of Sugar and Mill By-Products [*A publication*]
**INDV**......... Individually (MSA)
**Ind Veg Turf Pest Manage** ... Industrial Vegetation Turf and Pest Management [*A publication*]
**Ind Vernice** ... Industria della Vernice [*A publication*]
**Ind Vet**....... Index Veterinarius [*A publication*]
**Ind Vic**....... Industrial Victoria [*A publication*] (APTA)
**Ind W**......... Industry Week [*A publication*]
**Ind Waste Conf Proc** ... Industrial Waste Conference Proceedings [*A publication*]
**Ind Wastes** ... Industrial Wastes [*A publication*]
**Ind Wastes (Chicago)** ... Industrial Wastes (Chicago) [*A publication*]
**Ind Water Eng** ... Industrial Water Engineering [*A publication*]
**Ind Water Wastes** ... Industrial Water and Wastes [*A publication*]
**Ind Week** ... Industry Week [*A publication*]
**Ind Weld**.... Industry and Welding [*A publication*]
**Ind Wills**.... Inderwick on Wills [*1866*] [*A publication*] (DLA)
**Ind Woman** ... Independent Woman [*A publication*]
**Ind Wrkr**.... Industrial Worker [*A publication*]
**INDX**......... Index Technology Corp. [*NASDAQ symbol*] (NQ)
**Ind YBIA**... Indian Yearbook of International Affairs [*A publication*]
**Ind Yb Int Aff** ... Indian Yearbook of International Affairs [*A publication*]
**Ind YB Int'l Aff** ... Indian Yearbook of International Affairs [*A publication*] (DLA)
**INE**........... East Chicago Public Library, East Chicago, IN [*OCLC symbol*] (OCLC)
**InE**............ Evansville Public Library and Vanderburgh County Public Library, Evansville, IN [*Library symbol*] [*Library of Congress*] (LCLS)
**INE**........... Incorrect Negative Expectancy [*Psychometrics*]
**ine**............. Indo-European [*MARC language code*] [*Library of Congress*] (LCCP)
**INE**........... Industrieel Eigendom [*A publication*]
**INE**........... Inertial Navigation Equipment (MCD)
**INE**........... Initiatives for Not-for-Profit Entrepreneurship [*Research center*] (RCD)
**INE**........... International Kenergy Resource Corp. [*Vancouver Stock Exchange symbol*]
**INE**........... Missoula, MT [*Location identifier*] [*FAA*] (FAAL)
**IN & EA**.... International Nuclear and Energy Association (EA)
**INEA**........ Internationaler Elektronik-Arbeitskreis [*International Electronics Association*]
**INEAC**....... Institut National pour l'Etude Agronomique du Congo [*National Institute for the Study of Agronomy in the Congo*]
**InEaP**......... Earl Park Public Library, Earl Park, IN [*Library symbol*] [*Library of Congress*] (LCLS)
**InEc**........... East Chicago Public Library, East Chicago, IN [*Library symbol*] [*Library of Congress*] (LCLS)
**INEC**......... IndTech Corp. [*NASDAQ symbol*] (NQ)
**INEC**......... Institut Europeen d'Ecologie et de Cancerologie [*European Institute of Ecology and Cancer - EIEC*] (EA)
**InEcIP**....... Indiana City Press, Indiana City, IN [*Library symbol*] [*Library of Congress*] (LCLS)
**INED**......... Indian-Ed. University of Alberta [*A publication*]
**INED**......... Inedible
**INED**......... Inedites [*Unpublished*] [*French*] (ROG)
**INED**......... Ineditus [*Not Made Known*] [*Latin*]
**INED**......... Institute for New Enterprise Development (EA)
**INED**......... International Network for Educational Information (EAIO)
**INEFFCY** ... Inefficiency
**INEFFY**..... Inefficiency (AABC)
**INeg**.......... Index to Periodical Articles by and about Negroes [*Later, Index to Periodical Articles by and about Blacks*] [*A publication*]
**INEI**.......... Insituform East, Incorporated [*NASDAQ symbol*] (NQ)
**INEI**.......... International Exhibition of Industrial Electronics (MCD)
**INEL**.......... Idaho National Engineering Laboratory [*Department of Energy*] [*Idaho Falls, ID*]
**INEL**.......... Intelligent Electronics, Inc. [*NASDAQ symbol*] (NQ)
**InElk**......... Elkhart Public Library, Elkhart, IN [*Library symbol*] [*Library of Congress*] (LCLS)
**InElkB**....... Mennonite Biblical Seminary, Elkhart, IN [*Library symbol*] [*Library of Congress*] (LCLS)
**InElkM**...... Miles Laboratories, Inc., Elkhart, IN [*Library symbol*] [*Library of Congress*] (LCLS)
**InElkT**....... Elkhart Truth, Elkhart, IN [*Library symbol*] [*Library of Congress*] (LCLS)
**InEllJ**........ Ellettsville Journal, Ellettsville, IN [*Library symbol*] [*Library of Congress*] (LCLS)
**INELTEC**... Exhibition of Industrial Electronics, Electrical Engineering, and Technical Installation (TSPED)
**InElw**......... Elwood Public Library, Elwood, IN [*Library symbol*] [*Library of Congress*] (LCLS)
**InElwCL**.... Elwood Call-Leader, Elwood, IN [*Library symbol*] [*Library of Congress*] (LCLS)
**InEM**......... Mead Johnson Research Center, Evansville, IN [*Library symbol*] [*Library of Congress*] (LCLS)
**INEN**......... Indian Education Newsletter [*Vancouver, British Columbia*] [*A publication*]
**INENE6**.... Invertebrate Endocrinology [*A publication*]
**InEng**......... Crawford County Public Library, English, IN [*Library symbol*] [*Library of Congress*] (LCLS)
**InEngD**...... Crawford County Democrat, English, IN [*Library symbol*] [*Library of Congress*] (LCLS)
**InENR**....... Northside Reporter, Evansville, IN [*Library symbol*] [*Library of Congress*] (LCLS)
**INEOA**...... International Narcotic Enforcement Officers Association (EA)
**InEP**.......... Evansville Press and Courier, Evansville, IN [*Library symbol*] [*Library of Congress*] (LCLS)
**INEP**.......... Index to New England Periodicals [*A publication*]
**INEP**.......... International Nurse Education Program
**INep**.......... Neponset Public Library, Neponset, IL [*Library symbol*] [*Library of Congress*] (LCLS)
**INEPT**....... Insensitive Nuclei Enhanced by Polarization Transfer [*Spectroscopy*]
**Inequal Educ** ... Inequality in Education [*A publication*]
**INER**......... Inertial (KSC)
**INER**......... International Environment Reporter [*A publication*]
**INERT**....... Index of National Enervation and Related Trends [*Department of Commerce*]
**InES**.......... Indiana State University, Evansville Campus, Evansville, IN [*Library symbol*] [*Library of Congress*] (LCLS)
**InESC**........ Evansville-Vanderburgh School Corp., Library Services Center, Evansville, IN [*Library symbol*] [*Library of Congress*] (LCLS)
**INET**.......... Instinet Corp. [*Formerly, Institutional Networks*] [*NASDAQ symbol*] (NQ)
**INET**.......... Intelligent Network [*Telecom Canada*] [*Database*]
**INET**.......... Interbank Network for Electronic Transfer
**InEU**.......... University of Evansville, Evansville, IN [*Library symbol*] [*Library of Congress*] (LCLS)
**INEUB**...... Izvestiya Nauchno-Issledovatel'skogo Instituta Nefte- i Uglekhimicheskogo Sinteza pri Irkutskom Universitete [*A publication*]
**In Evang Iohan** ... Tractatus in Evangelium Iohannis [*of Augustine*] [*Classical studies*] (OCD)
**INew**.......... Newman Township Library, Newman, IL [*Library symbol*] [*Library of Congress*] (LCLS)
**InEW**......... Willard Library, Evansville, IN [*Library symbol*] [*Library of Congress*] (LCLS)
**INEWF**...... Indian National Electricity Workers' Federation
**INEWS**...... Integrated Electronic Warfare System
**InEWS**....... West Side Story, Evansville, IN [*Library symbol*] [*Library of Congress*] (LCLS)
**INewt**......... Newton Public Library, Newton, IL [*Library symbol*] [*Library of Congress*] (LCLS)
**IN EX**........ In Extenso [*At Full Length*] [*Latin*] (ROG)
**IN F**........... In Fine [*Finally*] [*Latin*]
**INF**........... Infamous [*FBI standardized term*]
**INF**........... Infant
**INF**........... Infantry (AFM)
**INF**........... Infection [*Medicine*]
**INF**........... Inferior
**INF**........... Infinite (MSA)
**INF**........... Infinite Resources, Inc. [*Vancouver Stock Exchange symbol*]
**INF**........... Infinitive
**INF**........... Infinity
**Inf**............ Infinity Science Fiction [*A publication*]
**INF**........... Infirmary
**INF**........... Influenza [*Medicine*]
**INF**........... Informaatiopalvelulaitos [*Information Service*] [*Technical Research Center of Finland*] [*Espoo*] [*Information service or system*] (IID)
**INF**........... Information [*Data processing*]
**INF**........... Information and Management [*A publication*]
**INF**........... Information Services and Use [*A publication*]
**Inf**............ Information ueber Steuer und Wirtschaft [*A publication*]
**INF**........... Informationszentrum und Bibliotheken [*Information retrieval*]
**INF**........... Informed
**Inf**............ Infortiatum [*A publication*] (DSA)
**INF**........... Infra [*Beneath or Below*] [*Latin*]
**INF**........... Infunde [*Pour In*] [*Pharmacy*]
**INF**........... Infusion [*Medicine*]
**INF**........... Infusum [*Infusion*] [*Pharmacy*] (ROG)
**INF**........... Inland Navigation Facility
**InF**........... Inozemna Filologiya [*L'vov*] [*A publication*]
**INF**........... Interceptor Night Fighter (NATG)
**INF**........... Interface (KSC)
**INF**........... Interface. Data Processing Management [*A publication*]
**INF**........... Interference (KSC)

**INF** ........... Intermediate-Range Nuclear Forces
**INF** ........... International Naturist Federation [*Antwerp, Belgium*] (EA)
**INF** ........... International Nuclear Forces (NATG)
**INF** ........... Iranian National Front (PPW)
**INF** ........... Irredundant Normal Formula
**INF** ........... Parke, Davis & Co. [*Great Britain*] [*Research code symbol*]
**infa---** ......... Faroe Islands [*MARC geographic area code*] [*Library of Congress*] (LCCP)
**Inf A** .......... Informacion Arqueologica [*A publication*]
**INFA** .......... International Federation of Aestheticians [*Brussels, Belgium*] (EAIO)
**INFA** .......... International Nuclear Fuel Authority
**INFAA2** ....... Indian Farming [*A publication*]
**INFAC** ....... Interfaces [*A publication*]
**INFACON** ... International Ferro-Alloys Congress
**INFACT** .... Infant Formula Action Coalition (EA)
**Inf Aerauliques Therm** ... Informations Aerauliques et Thermiques [*A publication*]
**Inf Age** ....... Information Age [*A publication*]
**Inf Agric** ..... Informacion Agricola [*A publication*]
**Inf Agric (Paris)** ... Information Agricole (Paris) [*A publication*]
**Inf Agropecu Empresa Pesqui Agropecu Minas Gerais** ... Informe Agropecuario [*Agricultural Report*]. Empresa de Pesquisa Agropecuaria de Minas Gerais [*A publication*]
**InFai** .......... Fairmount Public Library, Fairmount, IN [*Library symbol*] [*Library of Congress*] (LCLS)
**InFaiN** ....... Fairmount News, Fairmount, IN [*Library symbol*] [*Library of Congress*] (LCLS)
**INFANT** .... Interactive Networks Functioning on Adaptive Neural Topographies [*Robot*]
**INFANT** .... Iroquois Night Fighter and Night Tracker (MCD)
**Infant Behav & Dev** ... Infant Behavior and Development [*A publication*]
**Infantry** ...... Infantry Magazine [*A publication*]
**INFANTS** ... Interested Future Attorneys Negotiating for Tot Safety [*Student legal action organization*]
**InFarl** ......... Farmland Public Library, Farmland, IN [*Library symbol*] [*Library of Congress*] (LCLS)
**InFb** ........... Fort Branch Public Library, Fort Branch, IN [*Library symbol*] [*Library of Congress*] (LCLS)
**INFBAT** .... Infantry Battalion [*Army*]
**Inf Battelle Frankfurt** ... Information Battelle Frankfurt [*A publication*]
**Inf Bienenw** ... Information Bienenwirtschaft [*A publication*]
**Inf Bienenzucht** ... Information Bienenzucht [*A publication*]
**Inf Bild Wiss** ... Informationen Bildung Wissenschaft [*A publication*]
**Infbl** .......... Informatieblad van het Economisch en Sociaal Instituut voor de Middenstand [*A publication*]
**InfBl** .......... Informationsblatt fuer die Gemeinden in den Niederdeutschen Lutherischen Landeskirchen [*Hamburg*] [*A publication*]
**Inf Bot Ital** ... Informatore Botanico Italiano [*A publication*]
**InFbT** ......... Fort Branch Times, Fort Branch, IN [*Library symbol*] [*Library of Congress*] (LCLS)
**Inf Bull: Append Provis Nomencl Symb Terminol Conv (IUPAC)** ... Information Bulletin: Appendices on Provisional Nomenclature, Symbols, Terminology, and Conventions (International Union of Pure and Applied Chemistry) [*A publication*]
**Inf Bull Append Provis Nomencl Symb Units Stand (IUPAC)** ... Information Bulletin: Appendices on Provisional Nomenclature, Symbols, Units, and Standards (International Union of Pure and Applied Chemistry) [*A publication*]
**Inf Bull Append Prov Nomencl Symb Terminol Conv (IUPAC)** ... Information Bulletin: Appendices on Provisional Nomenclature, Symbols, Terminology, and Conventions (International Union of Pure and Applied Chemistry) [*A publication*]
**Inf Bull Bitum Coal Res** ... Information Bulletin. Bituminous Coal Research [*A publication*]
**Inf Bull Coop Ext NY St Coll Agric Life Sci** ... Information Bulletin. Cooperative Extension. New York State College of Agriculture and Life Sciences [*A publication*]
**Inf Bull Div Anim Prodn CSIRO** ... Information Bulletin. Division of Animal Production. Commonwealth Scientific and Industrial Research Organisation [*A publication*] (APTA)
**Inf Bull Int Cent Inf Antibiot** ... Information Bulletin. International Center of Information on Antibiotics [*A publication*]
**Inf Bull Int Scient Rad Un** ... Information Bulletin. International Scientific Radio Union [*A publication*]
**Inf Bull Isot Generators** ... Information Bulletin on Isotopic Generators [*France*] [*A publication*]
**Inf Bull ISWA (Int Solid Wastes Public Clean Assoc)** ... Information Bulletin. ISWA (International Solid Wastes Public Cleansing Association) [*A publication*]
**Inf Bull IUPAC Append Provis Nomencl Symb Units Stand** ... Information Bulletin. International Union of Pure and Applied Chemistry. Appendices on Provisional Nomenclature, Symbols, Units, and Standards [*A publication*]
**Inf Bull IUPAC Tech Rep** ... Information Bulletin. International Union of Pure and Applied Chemistry. Technical Reports [*A publication*]
**Inf Bull Libr Autom Syst Inf Exch** ... Information Bulletin. Library Automated Systems Information Exchange [*A publication*]
**Inf Bull NY St Coll Agric** ... Information Bulletin. New York State College of Agriculture [*A publication*]
**Inf Bull Variable Stars** ... Information Bulletin on Variable Stars [*A publication*]
**Inf Byull Inst Geol Arkt** ... Informatsionnyi Byulleten' Instituta Geologii Arktiki [*A publication*]
**Inf Byull Inst Geol Arktiki** ... Informatsionnyi Byulleten' Instituta Geologii Arktiki [*A publication*]
**Inf Byull Mezhved Geofiz Kom Prezidiume Akad Nauk Ukr SSR** ... Informatsionnyi Byulleten' Mezhvedomstvennyi Geofizicheskii Komitet pri Prezidiume Akademii Nauk Ukrainskoi SSR [*A publication*]
**Inf Byull Mikroelem Sib** ... Informatsionnyi Byulleten' Mikroelementy Sibirii [*A publication*]
**Inf Byull Mosk Nauchno Issled Inst Sanit Gig** ... Informatsionnyi Byulleten' Moskovskogo Nauchno Issledovatel'skogo Instituta Sanitarii i Gigieny [*A publication*]
**Inf Byull Nauchn Sov Probl Radiobiol Akad Nauk SSSR** ... Informatsionnyi Byulleten' Nauchnyi Sovet po Problemam Radiobiologii Akademiya Nauk SSSR [*A publication*]
**Inf Byull Sib Inst Fiziol Biokhim Rast** ... Informatsionnyi Byulleten' Sibirskii Institut Fiziologii i Biokhimii Rastenii [*A publication*]
**Inf Byull Sov Antarkt Eksped** ... Informatsionnyi Byulleten' Sovetskoi Antarkticheskoi Ekspeditsii [*A publication*]
**Inf Byull Vses Nauchno Issled Inst Mash Promsti Stroit Mater** ... Informatsionnyi Byulleten' Vsesoyuznyi Nauchno Issledovatel'skii Institut po Mashinam dlya Promyshlennosti Stroitel'nykh Materialov [*A publication*]
**INF-C** ........ Influenza-C [*Medicine*]
**Inf C** ........... Information and Control [*A publication*]
**INFCA** ....... Informations-Chimie [*A publication*]
**Inf Cath Int** ... Informations Catholiques Internationales [*A publication*]
**INFCE** ........ Influence (ROG)
**INFCE** ....... International Nuclear Fuel Cycle Evaluation
**Inf Cent Chem Ind Bull** ... Information Centre on the Chemical Industry. Bulletin [*A publication*]
**Inf Chil Nitrate Agric Serv** ... Information. Chilean Nitrate Agricultural Service [*A publication*]
**Inf-Chim** .... Informations-Chimie [*A publication*]
**Inf Cient** ..... Informaciones Cientificas [*A publication*]
**Inf Circ Arkans Geol Comm** ... Information Circular. Arkansas Geological Commission [*A publication*]
**Inf Circ BHP Central Res Lab** ... Information Circular. BHP [*Broken Hill Proprietary Ltd.*] Central Research Laboratories [*A publication*] (APTA)
**Inf Circ Bur Mines Geosci (Philipp)** ... Information Circular. Bureau of Mines and Geo-Sciences (Philippines) [*A publication*]
**Inf Circ Div Fish Oceanogr CSIRO** ... Information Circular. Division of Fisheries and Oceanography. Commonwealth Scientific and Industrial Research Organisation [*A publication*] (APTA)
**Inf Circ Econ Geol Res Unit Univ Witwaters** ... Information Circular. Economic Geology Research Unit. University of the Witwatersrand [*A publication*]
**Inf Circ GA Geol Water Resour Div** ... Information Circular. Georgia Geologic and Water Resources Division [*A publication*]
**Inf Circ Geol Physiogr Sect Nat Conserv Counc** ... Information Circular. Geology and Physiography Section. Nature Conservancy Council [*A publication*]
**Inf Circ Kentucky Geol Surv** ... Information Circular. Kentucky Geological Survey [*A publication*]
**Inf Circ Newfoundland Labrador Miner Resour Div** ... Information Circular. Newfoundland and Labrador Mineral Resources Division [*A publication*]
**Inf Circ Newfoundland Miner Resour Div** ... Information Circular. Newfoundland Mineral Resources Division [*A publication*]
**Inf Circ Philipp Bur Mines** ... Information Circular. Philippines Bureau of Mines [*A publication*]
**Inf Circ South Pac Comm** ... Information Circular. South Pacific Commission [*A publication*]
**Inf Circ Tenn Div Geol** ... Information Circular. Tennessee Division of Geology [*A publication*]
**Inf Circ US Bur Mines** ... Information Circular. United States Bureau of Mines [*A publication*]
**INFCO** ....... Information Committee [*International Organization for Standardization*] (IEEE)
**Inf Constr** ... Informes de la Construccion [*A publication*]
**Inf Contr** .... Information and Control [*A publication*]
**Inf and Control** ... Information and Control [*A publication*]
**Inf Control** ... Information and Control [*A publication*]
**Inf Cuttings Serv World Min Ind** ... Information Cuttings Service on World Mining Industry [*A publication*]
**INFCY** ....... Infancy (ROG)
**INFD** ......... Infodata Systems, Inc. [*NASDAQ symbol*] (NQ)
**INFD** ......... Informed (ROG)
**Inf Dent** ...... Informacion Dental [*A publication*]
**Inf Dent** ...... Information Dentaire [*A publication*]
**Inf Digest** ... Information Digest [*A publication*] (APTA)
**Inf e Diritto** ... Informatica e Diritto [*A publication*]
**Inf Disp** ...... Information Display [*A publication*]
**Inf Display** ... Information Display [*A publication*]

**Inf & Doc** ... Information et Documentation [*A publication*]
**Inf Doc Sel Teh Nucl** ... Informare si Documentare Selectiva. Tehnica Nucleara [*A publication*]
**INFE** .......... Instituto Nacional de Fomento de la Exportacion [*National Institute of Export Development*] [*Spain*] (EY)
**INFE** .......... International Newspaper Financial Executives (EA)
**INFEA** ....... Ingegneria Ferroviaria [*A publication*]
**Infec Immun** ... Infection and Immunity [*A publication*]
**Inf Econ Inst Econ Agric** ... Informacoes Economicas. Instituto de Economia Agricola [*A publication*]
**Infect Cont** ... Infection Control [*A publication*]
**Infect Control** ... Infection Control [*A publication*]
**Infect Control Dig** ... Infection Control Digest [*A publication*]
**Infect Control Hosp Epidemiol** ... Infection Control and Hospital Epidemiology [*A publication*]
**Infect Control Rounds** ... Infection Control Rounds [*A publication*]
**Infect Control (Thorofare)** ... Infection Control (Thorofare) [*A publication*]
**Infect Control Urol Care** ... Infection Control and Urological Care [*A publication*]
**Infect Dis Antimicrob Agents** ... Infectious Diseases and Antimicrobial Agents [*A publication*]
**Infect Dis Rev** ... Infectious Disease Reviews [*A publication*]
**Infect Dis Ther** ... Infectious Disease and Therapy [*A publication*]
**Infect Immun** ... Infection and Immunity [*A publication*]
**Infect Inflammation & Immun** ... Infection, Inflammation, and Immunity [*A publication*]
**INFEDOP** ... International Federation of Employees in Public Service [*Brussels, Belgium*] (EAIO)
**Infektionskr Ihre Erreger** ... Infektionskrankheiten und Ihre Erreger [*A publication*]
**Infekts Gepatit** ... Infektsionnyi Gepatit [*A publication*]
**Infekts Gepatit Resp Mezhved Sb** ... Infektsionnye Gepatit Respublikanskoi Mezhvedomstvennyi Sbornik [*A publication*]
**Infekts Kult Rast Mold** ... Infektsionnye Zabolevaniya Kul'turnykh Rastenii Moldavii [*A publication*]
**Inf-Elektron** ... Informacio-Elektronika [*A publication*]
**Inf Elettron** ... Informazione Elettronica [*A publication*]
**INFEREX** ... Inference Execution Language
**InFerN** ....... Ferdinand News, Ferdinand, IN [*Library symbol*] [*Library of Congress*] (LCLS)
**Inf Estac Exp Agric La Molina (Lima)** ... Informe. Estacion Experimental Agricola de "La Molina" (Lima) [*A publication*]
**Inf-Fachber** ... Informatik-Fachberichte [*A publication*]
**Inf Fischwirtsch** ... Informationen fuer die Fischwirtschaft [*A publication*]
**Inf Fitopatol** ... Informatore Fitopatologico [*A publication*]
**INFG** ......... Infinite Graphics, Inc. [*Minneapolis, MN*] [*NASDAQ symbol*] (NQ)
**Inf Geogr**.... Information Geographique [*A publication*]
**Inf Geol Sci Terre** ... Informatique Geologique. Sciences de la Terre [*A publication*]
**Inf & Gestion** ... Informatique et Gestion [*A publication*]
**Inf Giovane Entomol** ... Informatore del Giovane Entomologo [*A publication*]
**Inf Grasas Aceites** ... Informaciones sobre Grasas y Aceites [*A publication*]
**InfHA** ........ Influenza Virus Hemagglutinin [*Immunology*]
**Inf Hist** ...... Information Historique [*A publication*]
**Inf Hotline** ... Information Hotline [*United States*] [*A publication*]
**INFIB** ........ Infection and Immunity [*A publication*]
**INFIC** ........ International Network of Feed Information Centers (EA)
**INFID** ........ Information fuer die Fischwirtschaft [*A publication*]
**INFIN** ........ Infinitive [*Grammar*]
**INFINET** .. International Financial Networks
**INF Inf Tec** ... INF [*Inventario Nacional Forestal*] Informacion Tecnica [*A publication*]
**Inf INT** ...... Informativo do INT [*Instituto Nacional de Tecnologia*] [*Brazil*] [*A publication*]
**Inf Intell Online Newsl** ... Information Intelligence Online Newsletter [*A publication*]
**Inf Int Online Newsletter** ... Information Intelligence Online Newsletter [*A publication*]
**INF (Inventario Nac For) Nota** ... INF (Inventario Nacional Forestal) Nota [*A publication*]
**Inf Invest Agric (Mexico)** ... Informe de Investigacion Agricola (Mexico) [*A publication*]
**Inf Invest Cent Invest Tecnol (Pando Urug)** ... Informe de Investigacion. Centro de Investigaciones Tecnologicas (Pando, Uruguay) [*A publication*]
**INFIRM**.... Infirmary
**Infirm Can** ... Infirmiere Canadienne [*A publication*]
**Infirm Fr**.... Infirmiere Francaise [*A publication*]
**Infirm Haiti** ... Infirmiere Haitienne [*A publication*]
**Inf Irradiat Denrees** ... Informations sur l'Irradiation des Denrees [*A publication*]
**Inf Kerntech Normung** ... Informationen Kerntechnische Normung [*A publication*]
**InFl** ........... Flora-Monroe Public Library, Flora, IN [*Library symbol*] [*Library of Congress*] (LCLS)
**INFL**.......... Inflammable
**INFL**.......... Inflated (ADA)
**infl** ............ Inflorescence [*Botany*]
**INFL**.......... Influence
**INFL**.......... Influx
**INFL**.......... Megaphone International, Inc. [*San Francisco, CA*] [*NASDAQ symbol*] (NQ)
**In Flacc** ...... In Flaccum [*of Philo Judaeus*] [*Classical studies*] (OCD)
**INFLAM**... Inflammable
**Inflammatory Dis Ther** ... Inflammatory Disease and Therapy [*A publication*]
**Inf Liaison Bull Ass Afr Geol Surv** ... Information and Liaison Bulletin. Association of African Geological Surveys [*A publication*]
**Inf Litt**........ Information Litteraire [*A publication*]
**INFM** ........ Inform (ROG)
**Inf Manage** ... Information and Management [*A publication*]
**Inf and Manage** ... Information and Management [*A publication*]
**Inf Marmista** ... Informatore del Marmista [*A publication*]
**Inf Med** ...... Informatore Medico [*A publication*]
**Inf Med (Genoa)** ... Informatore Medico (Genoa) [*A publication*]
**Inf Med (Havana)** ... Informaciones Medicas (Havana) [*A publication*]
**Inf Med Roum** ... Information Medicale Roumaine [*A publication*]
**Infme Mens Estac Exp Agric La Molina** ... Informe Mensual. Estacion Experimental Agricola de "La Molina" [*Lima*] [*A publication*]
**Inf Mem Soc Ing Peru** ... Informaciones y Memorias. Sociedad de Ingenieros del Peru [*A publication*]
**Inf Mens Estac Exp Agric La Molina (Lima)** ... Informe Mensual. Estacion Experimental Agricola de "La Molina" [*Lima*] [*A publication*]
**Infmes Cient Tec Univ Nac Cuyo** ... Informes Cientificos y Tecnicos. Universidad Nacional de Cuyo [*A publication*]
**Infme Tec Estac Exp Agropec** ... Informe Tecnico. Estacion Experimental Regional Agropecuaria [*Pergamino*]. Instituto Nacional de Tecnologia Agropecuaria [*A publication*]
**Infme Tec Minst Asuntos Agrarios (Buenos Aires)** ... Informe Tecnico (Provincia de Buenos Aires). Ministerio de Asuntos Agrarios. Direccion de Agricultura [*A publication*]
**Inf MI** ........ Inferior Myocardial Infarction [*Cardiology*]
**INFMRY**... Infirmary
**INFMTL**... Informational
**INFN** ......... Information (ROG)
**INFN** ......... Information North. AINA [*Arctic Institute of North America*] Newsletter [*A publication*]
**INFN** ......... Infotron Systems Corp. [*NASDAQ symbol*] (NQ)
**Inf Nauchno Issled Rab Fil VIN i TI** ... Informatsiya o Nauchno-Issledovatel'skikh Rabotakh Filial Vsesoyuznogo Instituta Nauchnoi i Tekhnicheskoi Informatsii [*A publication*]
**Inf Nauchno Issled Rab Inst Tekh Ekon Inf** ... Informatsiya o Nauchno-Issledovatel'skikh Rabotakh Institut Tekhniko-Ekonomicheskoi Informatsii [*A publication*]
**Inf News**..... Information News [*England*] [*A publication*]
**Inf News & Sources** ... Information News and Sources [*A publication*]
**Inf Nitrate Corp Chile Chil Nitrate Agric Serv** ... Information. Nitrate Corporation of Chile. Chilean Nitrate Agricultural Service [*A publication*]
**Inf Num**...... Information Numismatique [*A publication*]
**InFo**........... Benton County Public Library, Fowler, IN [*Library symbol*] [*Library of Congress*] (LCLS)
**INFO** ......... Info Designs, Inc. [*NASDAQ symbol*] (NQ)
**INFO** ......... Information [*Data processing*] (AFM)
**Info**............. Information [*A publication*]
**INFO** ......... Information Network and File Organization [*Data processing*] (BUR)
**INFO** ......... Information Network for Operations [*Data processing*]
**INFO** ......... Integrated Network Fiber Optics (MCD)
**INFO** ......... International Fortean Organization (EA)
**Info Age** ..... Information Age [*A publication*]
**INFOBANK** ... [*The*] Information Bank [*Computer Sciences of Australia Pty. Ltd.*] [*Information service or system*]
**Infobrief Res Technol** ... Infobrief Research and Technology [*West Germany*] [*A publication*]
**InfoCan** ...... Information Canada
**INFOCEN** ... Information Center (MCD)
**Info Chimie** ... Information Chimie [*A publication*]
**INFOCLIMA** ... World Climate Data Information Referral Service [*World Meteorological Organization*] [*Information service or system*] (IID)
**Info Comer Esp** ... Informacion Comercial Espanola [*A publication*]
**INFOCOMM** ... Information and Communications Technology Exposition (ITD)
**InFoCR** ...... Benton County Recorder's Office, Fowler, IN [*Library symbol*] [*Library of Congress*] (LCLS)
**INFODATA** ... Database Information Science and Practice [*Database*]
**Infodoc** ....... Infodoc Aerospace and Military Equipment [*A publication*]
**INFO/DOC** ... Information/Documentation [*Information service or system*] (IID)
**Info et Docs** ... Informations et Documents [*A publication*]
**Inf Odontostomatol** ... Informatore Odonto-Stomatologico [*A publication*]
**Info Econ**.... Informe Economico [*A publication*]
**Info Econ Afr** ... Information Economique Africaine [*A publication*]
**Info Econ Argentina** ... Informacion Economica de la Argentina [*A publication*]
**INFOES** .... In-Flight Operational Evaluation of a Space System
**INFOEX**.... Information Exchange, Inc. [*Telecommunications service*] (TSSD)
**Info Exec**.... Information Executive [*A publication*]

**INFOHOST** ... Database Guide to German Host Operators [*Database*]
**INFOL**....... Information Oriented Language [*Information retrieval*]
**IN FOL ARG VOLVEND** ... In Folio Argenti Volvendae [*To Be Silvered*] [*Pharmacy*]
**Info Manager** ... Information Manager [*A publication*]
**Info & Mgmt** ... Information and Management [*A publication*]
**Info Mgmt** ... Information Management [*A publication*]
**Info Mgr** .... Information Manager [*A publication*]
**INFONAC** ... Instituto de Fomento Nacional [*Industrial promotion agency*] [*Nicaragua*]
**INFONET** ... Information Network [*British*] [*Telecommunications*] (TEL)
**INFOODS** ... International Network of Food Data Systems [*Massachusets Institute of Technology*] [*Cambridge*] [*Information service or system*] (IID)
**INFO PASS** ... Central Mississippi Library Council [*Library network*]
**INFOR**....... Information (DSUE)
**INFORBW** ... Information on Research in Baden-Wurttemberg [*Fachinformationszentrum Karlsruhe GmbH*] [*Federal Republic of Germany*] [*Information service or system*] (CRD)
**INFOR Canad J Operational Res and Information Processing** ... INFOR. Canadian Journal of Operational Research and Information Processing [*A publication*]
**INFOR Canad J Oper Res Inform Process** ... INFOR. Canadian Journal of Operational Research and Information Processing [*A publication*]
**Info Rec Mgmt** ... Information and Records Management [*A publication*]
**Info and Record Managem** ... Information and Records Management [*A publication*]
**Info and Referral** ... Information and Referral [*A publication*]
**Info Relaciones Mex-Estados Unidos** ... Informe Relaciones Mexico-Estados Unidos [*A publication*]
**INFOREM** ... Inventory Forecasting and Replenishment Modules [*IBM Corp.*]
**INFOREP** ... Information Report (CINC)
**Info Rep EX Can For Serv Policy Anal Program Dev Branch** ... Information Report E-X. Canadian Forestry Service. Policy, Analysis, and Program Development Branch [*A publication*]
**Info Rep M-X Mar For Res Cent** ... Information Report M-X. Maritimes Forest Research Centre. Canadian Forestry Service [*A publication*]
**Info Rep NOR X North For Res Cen Can For Serv** ... Information Report NOR-X. Northern Forest Research Centre. Canadian Forestry Service [*A publication*]
**INFOREQ** ... Information Requested [*or Required*]
**INFOR J** ... INFOR. Canadian Journal of Operational Research and Information Processing [*A publication*]
**INFORM**... Information
**INFORM**... Information Network for Freight Overhead Billing, Rating, and Message Switching
**INFORM**... Information for Optimum Resource Management (MCD)
**INFORM**... International Reference Organization in Forensic Medicine and Sciences (EA)
**Informac-Elektron** ... Informacio-Elektronika [*A publication*]
**Informac Quim Analit** ... Informacion de Quimica Analitica [*A publication*]
**Inform Agr** ... Informatore Agrario [*A publication*]
**INFORMAL** ... Information for Avionics Laboratory
**Inform Apic** ... Informador Apicola [*A publication*]
**Informat et Gestion** ... Informatique et Gestion [*A publication*]
**Informatik-Ber (Bonn)** ... Informatik-Berichte (Bonn) [*A publication*]
**Informatik-Fachber** ... Informatik-Fachberichte [*A publication*]
**Information Bulletin IGCP Project No 61 Sealevel** ... Information Bulletin. International Geological Correlation Programme. Project Number 61. Sealevel [*A publication*]
**Information Commun Europ** ... Information. Commission des Communautes Europeennes [*A publication*]
**Information Processing Lett** ... Information Processing Letters [*A publication*]
**Information Sci** ... Information Sciences [*A publication*]
**Informationsdienst Arbeitsgem Pharm Verfahrenstech** ... Informationsdienst. Arbeitsgemeinschaft fuer Pharmazeutische Verfahrenstechnik [*A publication*]
**Information Syst** ... Information Systems [*A publication*]
**Inform Bull Timb Res Developm Ass** ... Information Bulletin. Timber Research and Development Association [*A publication*]
**Inform Card Clemson Agr Coll Ext Serv** ... Information Card. Clemson Agricultural College. Extension Service [*A publication*]
**Inform Cathol Int** ... Informations Catholiques Internationales [*A publication*]
**Inform Com Esp** ... Informacion Comercial Espanola [*A publication*]
**Inform Constit Parl** ... Informations Constitutionnelles et Parlementaires [*A publication*]
**Inform Contr** ... Information and Control [*A publication*]
**Inform and Control** ... Information and Control [*A publication*]
**Inform Coop** ... Informations Cooperatives [*A publication*]
**Inform et Doc** ... Informations et Documents [*A publication*]
**Inform Doc Agr** ... Informations et Documentation Agricoles [*A publication*]
**Informe Anu Labores Costa Rica Min Agr Ganad** ... Informe Anual de Labores. Costa Rica. Ministerio de Agricultura y Ganaderia [*A publication*]
**Inform-Elektron** ... Informacio-Elektronika [*A publication*]
**Informe Mens Estac Exp Agr "La Molina" (Lima)** ... Informe Mensual. Estacion Experimental Agricola de "La Molina" (Lima) [*A publication*]
**Informes PMV Am Lat** ... Informes de Pro Mundi Vita America Latina [*A publication*]
**Informe Tec** ... Informe Tecnico. Instituto Forestal [*Chile*] [*A publication*]
**Informe Tec Estac Exp Agropecuar (Pergamino)** ... Informe Tecnico. Estacion Experimental Agropecuaria (Pergamino) [*A publication*]
**Inform Fitopatol** ... Informatore Fitopatologico [*A publication*]
**Inform Geogr** ... Information Geographique [*A publication*]
**Inform Grasas Aceites** ... Informaciones sobre Grasas y Aceites [*A publication*]
**Inform Kybernet Rechentech** ... Informatik - Kybernetik - Rechentechnik [*A publication*]
**INFORMN** ... Information
**Inform Process Japan** ... Information Processing in Japan [*A publication*]
**Inform Process Lett** ... Information Processing Letters [*A publication*]
**Inform Process Mach** ... Information Processing Machines [*A publication*]
**Inform Raumentwicklung** ... Informationen zur Raumentwicklung [*A publication*]
**Inform Rep For Fire Res Inst (Ottawa)** ... Information Report. Forest Fire Research Institute (Ottawa) [*A publication*]
**Inform Rep For Mgmt Inst (Ottawa)** ... Information Report. Forest Management Institute (Ottawa) [*A publication*]
**Inform Rep For Prod Lab (Vancouver)** ... Information Report. Forest Products Laboratory (Vancouver) [*A publication*]
**Inform Rep For Res Lab (Calgary)** ... Information Report. Forest Research Laboratory (Calgary) [*A publication*]
**Inform Rep For Res Lab (Quebec)** ... Information Report. Forest Research Laboratory (Quebec) [*A publication*]
**Inform Rep For Res Lab (Victoria BC)** ... Information Report. Forest Research Laboratory (Victoria, British Columbia) [*A publication*]
**Inform Sci**.. Information Science Abstracts [*A publication*]
**Inform Sci**.. Information Sciences [*A publication*]
**Inform Sci Humaines** ... Informatique et Sciences Humaines [*A publication*]
**Inform Ser Agr Econ Univ Calif Agr Ext Serv** ... Information Series in Agricultural Economics. University of California. Agricultural Extension Service [*A publication*]
**Inform Ser NZ For Serv** ... Information Series. New Zealand Forest Service [*A publication*]
**Inform Sheet Miss Agr Exp Sta** ... Information Sheet. Mississippi Agricultural Experiment Station [*A publication*]
**Inform Soc (Paris)** ... Informations Sociales (Paris) [*A publication*]
**Inform Stor Retrieval** ... Information Storage and Retrieval [*A publication*]
**Inform (Swed)** ... Information (Swedish Pulp and Paper Association) [*A publication*]
**Inform Tech Ser** ... Information Technology Series [*A publication*]
**Inform Univ Profes Int** ... Informations Universitaires et Professionnelles Internationales [*A publication*]
**Inform Yugoslav** ... Informatologia Yugoslavica [*A publication*]
**Inform Zootec** ... Informatore Zootecnico [*A publication*]
**Inf Orthod Kieferorthop** ... Informationen aus Orthodontie und Kieferorthopaedie mit Beitraegen aus der Internationalen Literatur [*A publication*]
**Inf Ortoflorofruttic** ... Informatore di Ortoflorofrutticoltura [*A publication*]
**Infort Traum Lav** ... Infortunistica e Traumatologia del Lavoro [*A publication*]
**INFOS**....... Information Network for Official Statistics [*Department of Statistics*] [*Information service or system*] (IID)
**InfoS** .......... Information Sciences [*A publication*]
**INFOS**....... Informationszentrum fuer Schnittwerte [*Cutting Data Information Center*] [*Federal Republic of Germany*] [*Information service or system*] (IID)
**Info Serv Leafl Div Mech Eng CSIRO** ... Information Service Leaflet. Division of Mechanical Engineering. Commonwealth Scientific and Industrial Research Organisation [*A publication*] (APTA)
**Info Soc**...... Informacao Social [*A publication*]
**INFOSOR** ... Information Sources [*Information service or system*] (IID)
**Infospecs**.... Information Specialists Ltd. [*Information service or system*] (IID)
**Info Stud Vivaldiani** ... Informazioni e Studi Vivaldiani [*A publication*]
**Infosys** ....... Infosystems [*Wheaton, IL*] [*A publication*]
**Info Sys New** ... Information Systems News [*A publication*]
**Info Systems** ... Information Systems [*Elmsford, NY*] [*A publication*]
**Info Tech**.... Information Technology and Libraries [*A publication*]
**Info Technol** ... Information Technology [*A publication*]
**INFOTERM** ... International Information Centre for Terminology [*UNESCO*] (IID)
**INFOTERRA** ... International Referral System for Sources of Environmental Information [*Formerly, IRS*] [*United Nations Environment Program*] (ASF)
**INFOTEX** ... Information via Telex [*Telecommunications*] (TEL)
**Info Times** ... Information Times [*A publication*]
**Info Wash** .. Information Washington [*A publication*]
**Info Wld Rv** ... InfoWorld in Review. Special Report from InfoWorld [*A publication*]
**InfP**........... Information Processing Journal [*A publication*]
**INFPA**....... Infrared Physics [*A publication*]
**Inf Pap Aust AEC** ... Information Paper. Australian Atomic Energy Commission [*A publication*]

**Inf Privacy** ... Information Privacy [*A publication*]
**Inf Pr Man** ... Information Processing and Management [*A publication*]
**Inf Processing & Mgt** ... Information Processing and Management [*A publication*]
**Inf Process Lett** ... Information Processing Letters [*A publication*]
**Inf Process Mach** ... Information Processing Machines [*A publication*]
**Inf Process and Manage** ... Information Processing and Management [*A publication*]
**Inf Process Manage** ... Information Processing and Management [*A publication*]
**Inf Process Soc Jpn (Joho Shori)** ... Information Processing Society of Japan (Joho Shori) [*A publication*]
**Inf Proc Man** ... Information Processing and Management [*A publication*]
**Inf Prov Buenos Aires Com Invest Cient** ... Informes. Provincia de Buenos Aires. Comision de Investigaciones Cientificas [*A publication*]
**Inf Psiquiat** ... Informaciones Psiquiatricas [*A publication*]
**Inf Psychiat** ... Information Psychiatrique [*A publication*]
**Inf Psychiatr** ... Information Psychiatrique [*A publication*]
**Inf: Pt 1** ...... Information: Part 1: News/Sources/Profiles [*A publication*]
**Inf: Pt 2** ...... Information: Part 2: Reports/Bibliographies [*A publication*]
**Inf Publ Stredisko Tech Inf Potravin Prum** ... Informacni Publikace. Stredisko Technickych Informacni Potravinarskeho Prumyslu [*A publication*]
**Inf Quim Anal** ... Informacion de Quimica Analitica [*A publication*]
**Inf Quim Anal (Madrid)** ... Informacion de Quimica Analitica (Madrid) [*A publication*]
**Inf Quim Anal Pura Apl Ind** ... Informacion de Quimica Analitica, Pura, y Aplicada a la Industria [*A publication*]
**INFR**.......... Inferior (ROG)
**INFR**.......... Infrared Industries, Inc. [*NASDAQ symbol*] (NQ)
**INFRA**....... Information Research Analysts [*Database producer*] (IID)
**Inf Rade Koncar** ... Informacije Rade Koncar [*A publication*]
**INFRA DIG** ... Infra Dignitatem [*Undignified*] [*Latin*]
**INFRAL**.... Information Retrieval Automatic Language [*Data processing*]
**INFRAPTUM** ... Infrascriptum [*Written Below*] [*Latin*] (ROG)
**Infrared Phys** ... Infrared Physics [*A publication*]
**Infrar Phys** ... Infrared Physics [*A publication*]
**Inf Raumentwickl** ... Informationen zur Raumentwicklung [*A publication*]
**Inf and Referral J Alliance Inf Referral Syst** ... Information and Referral. Journal of the Alliance of Information and Referral Systems [*A publication*]
**In Freight**... International Freighting Weekly [*A publication*]
**InFrem**....... Fremont Public Library, Fremont, IN [*Library symbol*] [*Library of Congress*] (LCLS)
**InFren**........ Melton Public Library, French Lick, IN [*Library symbol*] [*Library of Congress*] (LCLS)
**InFrenSH**.. Springs Valley Herald, French Lick, IN [*Library symbol*] [*Library of Congress*] (LCLS)
**Inf Rep Bibliogr** ... Information Reports and Bibliographies [*A publication*]
**Inf Rep Chem Control Res Inst (Can)** ... Information Report. Chemical Control Research Institute (Canada) [*A publication*]
**Inf Rep Chem Control Res Inst Envir Can For Serv** ... Information Report. Chemical Control Research Institute. Environment Canada Forestry Service [*A publication*]
**Inf Rep FMR-X For Manage Inst** ... Information Report FMR-X. Forest Management Institute [*A publication*]
**Inf Rep FPM-X For Pest Manage Inst** ... Information Report FPM-X. Forest Pest Management Institute [*A publication*]
**Inf Rep NOR-X North For Res Cent** ... Information Report NOR-X. Northern Forest Research Centre [*A publication*]
**Inf Rep Ser Fish** ... Information Report Series. Fisheries [*A publication*]
**Inf Rept Bibliog** ... Information Reports and Bibliographies [*A publication*]
**Inf Rep Washington Res** ... Information Report. Washington Researches [*United States*] [*A publication*]
**Inf Retr Libr Automn** ... Information Retrieval and Library Automation Letter [*A publication*]
**InFrf**.......... Frankfort Community Public Library, Frankfort, IL [*Library symbol*] [*Library of Congress*] (LCLS)
**INF RHEI** ... Infusum Rhei [*Infusion of Rhubarb*] [*Pharmacy*] (ROG)
**INFRIC** ..... Infricetur [*Let It Be Rubbed In*] [*Pharmacy*]
**InFrl**.......... Franklin Public Library, Franklin, IN [*Library symbol*] [*Library of Congress*] (LCLS)
**InFrlC**........ Franklin College of Indiana, Franklin, IN [*Library symbol*] [*Library of Congress*] (LCLS)
**InFrlCR**..... Johnson County Recorder's Office, Franklin, IN [*Library symbol*] [*Library of Congress*] (LCLS)
**InFrlJ**......... Franklin Daily Journal, Franklin, IN [*Library symbol*] [*Library of Congress*] (LCLS)
**InFrlJM**..... Johnson County Museum, Franklin, IN [*Library symbol*] [*Library of Congress*] (LCLS)
**INFRN**....... Inference (MSA)
**INFROSS** ... Information Requirements of the Social Sciences [*British*] (DIT)
**InFrv**.......... Francesville-Salem Township Public Library, Francesville, IN [*Library symbol*] [*Library of Congress*] (LCLS)
**InFrvT**........ Francesville Tribune, Francesville, IN [*Library symbol*] [*Library of Congress*] (LCLS)
**Inf Sb Inst Zemnoi Kory Sib Otd Akad Nauk SSSR** ... Informatsionnyi Sbornik Institut Zemnoi Kory Sibirskoe Otdelenie Akademiya Nauk SSSR [*A publication*]
**Inf Sb Tr Vychisl Tsentra Irkutsk Gos Univ** ... Informatsionnyi Sbornik Trudov Vychislitel'nogo Tsentra Irkutskii Gosudarstvennyi Universitet [*A publication*]
**Inf Sb Vses Nauchno Issled Geol Inst** ... Informatsionnyi Sbornik Vsesoyuznyi Nauchno-Issledovatel'skii Geologicheskii Institut [*A publication*]
**Inf Sci**......... Information Sciences [*A publication*]
**Inf Sci**......... Informations Scientifiques [*A publication*]
**InfSciAb**..... Information Science Abstracts [*A publication*]
**Inf Sciences** ... Information Sciences [*A publication*]
**Inf Scient**.... Information Scientist [*A publication*]
**Inf Scientist** ... Information Scientist [*A publication*]
**Inf Ser Colorado Geol Surv** ... Information Series. Colorado Geological Survey [*A publication*]
**Inf Ser Dep Scient Ind Res (NZ)** ... Information Series. New Zealand Department of Scientific and Industrial Research [*A publication*]
**Inf Ser NZ Dep Sci Ind Res** ... Information Series. New Zealand Department of Scientific and Industrial Research [*A publication*]
**Inf Ser NZ For Serv** ... Information Series. New Zealand Forest Service [*A publication*]
**Inf Serv** ...... National Council of Churches of Christ in the USA. Information Service [*A publication*]
**Inf Serv Leafl CILES CSIRO** ... Information Service Leaflet. Central Information, Library, and Editorial Section. Commonwealth Scientific and Industrial Research Organisation [*A publication*] (APTA)
**Inf Serv Sheet Div Build Res CSIRO** ... Information Service Sheet. Division of Building Research. Commonwealth Scientific and Industrial Research Organisation [*A publication*] (APTA)
**Inf Serv Sheet Div Mech Eng CSIRO** ... Information Service Sheet. Division of Mechanical Engineering. Commonwealth Scientific and Industrial Research Organisation [*A publication*] (APTA)
**Inf Serv Use** ... Information Services and Use [*Netherlands*] [*A publication*]
**Inf Sheet Miss State Univ Coop Ext Serv** ... Information Sheet. Mississippi State University. Cooperative Extension Service [*A publication*]
**Inf Sh Miss Agric Exp Stn** ... Information Sheet. Agricultural Experiment Station. Mississippi State University [*A publication*]
**Inf So** ......... Informazioni Soimet [*A publication*]
**Inf Soc**........ Information Society [*A publication*]
**Inf Soc**........ Informations Sociales [*Paris*] [*A publication*]
**Inf Soc Franc Photogr** ... Informations. Societe Francaise de Photographie [*A publication*]
**Inf Soc (L)** ... Informaciones Sociales (Lima) [*A publication*]
**Inf Soc (P)** ... Informations Sociales (Paris) [*A publication*]
**Inf-Spektrum** ... Informatik-Spektrum [*A publication*]
**Infs Tech Serv Vet** ... Informations Techniques des Services Veterinaires [*A publication*]
**Inf Storage** ... Information Storage and Retrieval [*A publication*]
**Inf Storage Retr** ... Information Storage and Retrieval [*A publication*]
**Inf Storage & Retr** ... Information Storage and Retrieval [*A publication*]
**Inf Stor Retr** ... Information Storage and Retrieval [*A publication*]
**Inf Syst**....... Information Systems [*A publication*]
**INFT**.......... Infant (ROG)
**INFT**.......... Infinity Broadcasting Corp. [*New York, NY*] [*NASDAQ symbol*] (NQ)
**INFT**.......... Informal Training (NASA)
**InFtbhP** ..... United States Army, Post Library, Fort Benjamin Harrison, IN [*Library symbol*] [*Library of Congress*] (LCLS)
**INFTD**....... Informant [*A publication*]
**Inf Tec Argent Repub Estac Exp Agropecu Manfredi** ... Informacion Tecnica. Argentine Republic. Estacion Experimental Agropecuaria Manfredi [*A publication*]
**Inf Tec Estac Exp Reg Agropecu (Pergamino)** ... Informe Tecnico. Estacion Experimental Regional Agropecuaria (Pergamino) [*A publication*]
**Inf Tech Cent Tech Interprof Ol Metrop** ... Informations Techniques. Centre Technique Interprofessionnel des Oleagineux Metropolitains [*A publication*]
**Inf Techn CETIOM** ... Informations Techniques. Centre Technique Interprofessionnel des Oleagineux Metropolitains [*A publication*]
**Inf Technol and Libr** ... Information Technology and Libraries [*A publication*]
**Inf Technol Libr** ... Information Technology and Libraries [*A publication*]
**Inf Technol Res and Dev** ... Information Technology. Research and Development [*A publication*]
**Inf Tech People** ... Information Technology and People [*A publication*]
**Inf Tec ICAITI** ... Informe Tecnico. Instituto Centroamericano de Investigacion y Tecnologia Industrial [*A publication*]
**Inf Tec Inst Centroam Invest Tecnol Ind** ... Informe Tecnico. Instituto Centroamericano de Investigacion y Tecnologia Industrial [*A publication*]
**Inf Tec Inst For (Santiago Chile)** ... Informe Tecnico. Instituto Forestal (Santiago, Chile) [*A publication*]
**INFTET**..... Infectologia [*Mexico*] [*A publication*]
**Inftore Agr** ... Informatore Agrario [*A publication*]
**Inftore Fitopatol** ... Informatore Fitopatologico [*A publication*]
**InFtv** .......... Carnegie Public Library District, Fortville, IN [*Library symbol*] [*Library of Congress*] (LCLS)

**InFtvT**........ Fortville Tribune, Fortville, IN [*Library symbol*] [*Library of Congress*] (LCLS)
**Infty**........... Infantry [*British military*] (DMA)
**InFu**........... Phyllis Meyer Library, Fulton, IN [*Library symbol*] [*Library of Congress*] (LCLS)
**INFUND**... Infunde [*Pour In*] [*Pharmacy*]
**INFUS**....... Infusum [*Infusion*] [*Pharmacy*] (ROG)
**Infusionsther Klin Ernaehr**... Infusionstherapie und Klinische Ernaehrung [*A publication*]
**Infusionsther Klin Ernaehr Sonderh**... Infusionstherapie und Klinische Ernaehrung. Sonderheft [*A publication*]
**Infusionsther Klin Ernaer Forsch Prax**... Infusionstherapie und Klinische Ernaehrung. Forschung und Praxis [*A publication*]
**InFw**........... Public Library of Fort Wayne and Allen County, Fort Wayne, IN [*Library symbol*] [*Library of Congress*] (LCLS)
**InFwAHi**.... Allen County-Fort Wayne Historical Society Library, Fort Wayne, IN [*Library symbol*] [*Library of Congress*] (LCLS)
**InFwB**........ Fort Wayne Bible College, Fort Wayne, IN [*Library symbol*] [*Library of Congress*] (LCLS)
**InFwC**........ Concordia Senior College, Fort Wayne, IN [*Library symbol*] [*Library of Congress*] (LCLS)
**InFwCT**...... Concordia Theological Seminary, Fort Wayne, IN [*Library symbol*] [*Library of Congress*] (LCLS)
**InFwGS**...... Church of Jesus Christ of Latter-Day Saints, Genealogical Society Library, Fort Wayne Branch, Fort Wayne, IN [*Library symbol*] [*Library of Congress*] (LCLS)
**InFwI**......... Indiana Institute of Technology, Fort Wayne, IN [*Library symbol*] [*Library of Congress*] (LCLS)
**InFwIP**....... Indiana-Purdue University, Fort Wayne, IN [*Library symbol*] [*Library of Congress*] (LCLS)
**InFwJG**...... Fort Wayne Journal-Gazette, Fort Wayne, IN [*Library symbol*] [*Library of Congress*] (LCLS)
**InFwL**........ Lincoln National Life Foundation, Fort Wayne, IN [*Library symbol*] [*Library of Congress*] (LCLS)
**InFWl-F**..... National Life Insurance Co., Lincoln National Life Foundation, Louis A. Warren Lincoln Library and Museum, Fort Wayne, IN [*Library symbol*] [*Library of Congress*] (LCLS)
**InFwM**....... Magnavox Co., Fort Wayne, IN [*Library symbol*] [*Library of Congress*] (LCLS)
**Inf World (Abingdon)**... Information World (Abingdon) [*England*] [*A publication*]
**Inf World Rev**... Information World Review [*A publication*]
**Inf World (Washington DC)**... Information World (Washington, DC) [*A publication*]
**InFwSF**...... Saint Francis College, Fort Wayne, IN [*Library symbol*] [*Library of Congress*] (LCLS)
**INFX**.......... Inspection Fixture
**Infy**............ Infantry [*British military*] (DMA)
**Inf Zootec**... Informatore Zootecnico [*A publication*]
**Inf Zp VLIS**... Informacni Zpravodaj VLIS [*Vojenska Lekarska Informacni Sluzba*] [*A publication*]
**Inf Zukunfts-Friedensforsch**... Information Zukunfts- und Friedensforschung [*A publication*]
**ING**........... Ambler, PA [*Location identifier*] [*FAA*] (FAAL)
**InG**........... Gary Public Library, Gary, IN [*Library symbol*] [*Library of Congress*] (LCLS)
**ING**........... Inactive National Guard
**ING**........... Inertial Navigation and Guidance [*Aerospace*] (AAG)
**ING**........... Inertial Navigation Gyro
**Ing**........... Ingenieur [*A publication*]
**ING**........... Ingenieur [*Engineer*] [*French*] (EY)
**ING**........... Inglis Ltd. [*Toronto Stock Exchange symbol*]
**ING**........... Ingram Ranch [*California*] [*Seismograph station code, US Geological Survey*] (SEIS)
**ING**........... Inguinal [*Anatomy*]
**ING**........... Inside Nazi Germany [*A publication*]
**ING**........... Integrated News Gathering
**ING**........... Intense Neutron Generator
**ING**........... International Newspaper Group (EA)
**ING**........... Lago Argentino [*Argentina*] [*Airport symbol*] (OAG)
**INGA**......... Indium Gallium Arsenide
**INGA**......... Inspection Gauge
**INGA**......... Interactive Graphics Analysis
**INGAA**...... Interstate Natural Gas Association of America (EA)
**InGaAs APD**... Indium Gallium Arsenide Avalanche Photodiode
**INGAB8**.... Ingenieria Agronomica [*Caracas*] [*A publication*]
**Ing Aeronaut Astronaut**... Ingenieria Aeronautica y Astronautica [*Spain*] [*A publication*]
**Ing Agron**... Ingenieria Agronomica [*A publication*]
**Ing Agron (Caracas)**... Ingenieria Agronomica (Caracas) [*A publication*]
**Ing Ambientale**... Ingegneria Ambientale [*Italy*] [*A publication*]
**InGar**......... Garrett Public Library, Garrett, IN [*Library symbol*] [*Library of Congress*] (LCLS)
**InGarC**....... Garrett Clipper, Garrett, IN [*Library symbol*] [*Library of Congress*] (LCLS)
**Ing-Arch**.... Ingenieur-Archiv. Gesellschaft fuer Angewandte Mathematik und Mechanik [*West Germany*] [*A publication*]
**Ing Arquit**.. Ingenieria y Arquitectura [*A publication*]
**Ing Arts Metiers**... Ingenieurs. Arts et Metiers [*A publication*]
**INGAT**...... Ingatestone [*Village in England*]
**Ing Auto**..... Ingenieurs de l'Automobile [*A publication*]
**Ing B**.......... Ingenium Baccalaureus [*Bachelor of Engineering*]
**Ing Bygningsvaes**... Ingenioer- og Bygningsvaesen [*Denmark*] [*A publication*]
**Ing Bygningsv Ugeovers**... Ingenioer- og Bygningsvaesen Ugeoversigt [*Denmark*] [*A publication*]
**InGc**........... Gas City-Mill Township Public Library, Gas City, IN [*Library symbol*] [*Library of Congress*] (LCLS)
**INGC**......... International Nutrition and Genetics Corp. [*NASDAQ symbol*] (NQ)
**Ing Chim (Brussels)**... Ingenieur Chimiste (Brussels) [*A publication*]
**Ing Chim It**... Quaderni dell'Ingegnere Chimico Italiano [*A publication*]
**Ing Chim (Milan)**... Ingegneria Chimica (Milan) [*A publication*]
**Ing Civ (Havana)**... Ingenieria Civil (Havana) [*A publication*]
**Ing Civil**..... Ingenieria Civil [*A publication*]
**Ing Comp**... Ingram's Compensation for Interest in Lands [*2nd ed.*] [*1869*] [*A publication*] (DLA)
**Ing D**.......... Ingenium Doctor [*Doctor of Engineering*]
**Ing-Dig**....... Ingenieur-Digest [*A publication*]
**Ing Dig**....... Ingersoll's Digest of the Laws of the United States [*A publication*] (DLA)
**Ing Dt Bu Po**... Ingenieur der Deutschen Bundespost [*A publication*]
**InGe**........... Geneva Public Library, Geneva, IN [*Library symbol*] [*Library of Congress*] (LCLS)
**INGEA**...... Ingenioeren (1892-1966) [*A publication*]
**Ing Ec Super Phys Chim Ind**... Ingenieurs de l'Ecole Superieure de Physique et de Chimie Industrielles [*A publication*]
**InGeL**......... Limberlost State Memorial, Geneva, IN [*Library symbol*] [*Library of Congress*] (LCLS)
**Ing Electr & Mec**... Ingenieria Electrica y Mecanica [*A publication*]
**Ingen For**... Ingenieria Forestal [*A publication*]
**Ingenieria Hidraul Mex**... Ingenieria Hidraulica en Mexico [*A publication*]
**INGENINST**... Office of the Inspector General Instructions [*Navy*]
**Ingenioersvetenskapsakad Handl**... Ingenioersvetenskapsakademien. Handlingar [*A publication*]
**Ingenioervidensk Skr**... Ingenioervidenskabelige Skrifter [*A publication*]
**Ingenioervidensk Skr Ser A**... Ingenioervidenskabelige Skrifter. Series A [*A publication*]
**Ingenioervidensk Skr Ser B**... Ingenioervidenskabelige Skrifter. Series B [*A publication*]
**Ingen Villes France**... Ingenieurs des Villes de France [*A publication*]
**Ing EPCI**.... Ingenieurs de l'Ecole Superieure de Physique et de Chimie Industrielles [*A publication*]
**InGerar**...... In Gerardagum [*A publication*]
**Ing Ferrov**.. Ingegneria Ferroviaria [*A publication*]
**Ing-Forsk**... Ingenioeren-Forskning [*Denmark*] [*A publication*]
**Ing Hab Corp**... Ingersoll on Habeas Corpus [*A publication*] (DLA)
**InGHi**........ Gary Historical and Cultural Society, Gary, IN [*Library symbol*] [*Library of Congress*] (LCLS)
**Ing Hidraul Mexico**... Ingenieria Hidraulica en Mexico [*A publication*]
**INGIFPI**.... Irish National Group of International Federation of the Phonographic Industry (EAIO)
**Ing Insolv**... Ingraham on Insolvency [*Pennsylvania*] [*A publication*] (DLA)
**Ing M**......... Ingenium Magister [*Master of Engineering*]
**Ing-Mag**..... Ingenioer-Magasinet [*Denmark*] [*A publication*]
**Ing Mecc**..... Ingegneria Meccanica [*A publication*]
**Ing Mec y Electr**... Ingenieria Mecanica y Electrica [*A publication*]
**INGN**......... Integrated Genetics [*NASDAQ symbol*] (NQ)
**INGNA**...... Industrial Gas [*A publication*]
**Ing Nav (Madrid)**... Ingenieria Naval (Madrid) [*A publication*]
**Ing Ned Indie**... Ingenieur in Nederlandsch Indie [*A publication*]
**Ing Nucl**..... Ingegneria Nucleare [*A publication*]
**InGo**........... Goshen College, Goshen, IN [*Library symbol*] [*Library of Congress*] (LCLS)
**INGO**......... International Non-Governmental Organization
**InGoM**....... Mennonite Historical Library, Goshen College, Goshen, IN [*Library symbol*] [*Library of Congress*] (LCLS)
**InGoN**........ Goshen News, Goshen, IN [*Library symbol*] [*Library of Congress*] (LCLS)
**InGoo**......... Goodland Public Library (Mitten Memorial Library), Goodland, IN [*Library symbol*] [*Library of Congress*] (LCLS)
**InGoP**........ Goshen Public Library, Goshen, IN [*Library symbol*] [*Library of Congress*] (LCLS)
**InGP**.......... Indol Glycerophosphate [*Biochemistry*]
**Ing Pet**........ Ingenieria Petrolera [*Mexico*] [*A publication*]
**InGPS**........ Indoleglycerolphosphate Synthase [*Biochemistry*]
**InGPT**........ Gary Post-Tribune, Gary, IN [*Library symbol*] [*Library of Congress*] (LCLS)
**Ing Quim Ind**... Ingenieria Quimica e Industrias [*A publication*]
**Ing Quim (Medellin Colombia)**... Ingenieria Quimica (Medellin, Colombia) [*A publication*]
**Ing Quim (Mexico City)**... Ingenieria Quimica (Mexico City) [*A publication*]
**InGr**........... Greencastle-Putnam County Library, Greencastle, IN [*Library symbol*] [*Library of Congress*] (LCLS)
**INGR**......... Intergraph Corp. [*NASDAQ symbol*] (NQ)
**INGRA**...... Ingenieur [*A publication*]
**InGrBG**...... Greencastle Banner-Graphic, Greencastle, IN [*Library symbol*] [*Library of Congress*] (LCLS)
**InGrD**........ De Pauw University, Greencastle, IN [*Library symbol*] [*Library of Congress*] (LCLS)

**INGRD**...... Ingredient
**InGrD-Ar**... De Pauw University, Archives, Greencastle, IN [*Library symbol*] [*Library of Congress*] (LCLS)
**InGreb**........ Greensburg Public Library, Greensburg, IN [*Library symbol*] [*Library of Congress*] (LCLS)
**InGrebCR**.. Decatur County Recorder's Office, Greensburg, IN [*Library symbol*] [*Library of Congress*] (LCLS)
**InGrebDHi** ... Decatur County Historical Society, Greensburg, IN [*Library symbol*] [*Library of Congress*] (LCLS)
**InGref**........ Greenfield Public Library, Greenfield, IN [*Library symbol*] [*Library of Congress*] (LCLS)
**InGrefL**...... Eli Lilly & Co., Library Agricultural Services, Greenfield, IN [*Library symbol*] [*Library of Congress*] (LCLS)
**INGRES**.... Interactive Graphic and Retrieval System
**InGretN**..... Howard County News, Greentown, IN [*Library symbol*] [*Library of Congress*] (LCLS)
**InGrew**....... Greenwood Public Library, Greenwood, IN [*Library symbol*] [*Library of Congress*] (LCLS)
**Ing Roc**....... Ingersoll's Edition of Roccus' Maritime Law [*A publication*] (DLA)
**InGS**.......... Gary School System, Gary, IN [*Library symbol*] [*Library of Congress*] (LCLS)
**INGS**......... Inland Gold and Silver Corp. [*NASDAQ symbol*] (NQ)
**Ing Sanit**.... Ingegneria Sanitaria [*A publication*]
**INGSOC**.... English Socialism [*From George Orwell's novel, "1984"*]
**Ing & Tech** ... Ingenieurs et Techniciens [*A publication*]
**Ing Text (Barcelona)** ... Ingenieria Textil (Barcelona) [*A publication*]
**Ing Ugebl**... Ingenioerens Ugeblad [*A publication*]
**Ing Ves**....... Vesey, Junior's, English Chancery Reports, Edited by Ingraham [*A publication*] (ILCA)
**Ing Vetenskaps Akad Medd** ... Ingeniors Vetenskaps Akademien. Meddelande [*A publication*]
**INH**........... Improved Nike Hercules [*Missile*]
**IN/H**.......... Inches per Hour
**INH**........... Inhalation
**INH**........... Inhibit (NASA)
**INH**........... Isangel [*New Hebrides*] [*Seismograph station code, US Geological Survey*] (SEIS)
**INH**........... Isonicotinic Acid Hydrazide [*or Isonicotinylhydrazine*] [*See also INAH, ISONIAZID*] [*Antituberculous agent*]
**INHAB**...... Inhabitant
**INHABD**... Inhabited (ROG)
**InHag**......... Hagerstown Public Library, Hagerstown, IN [*Library symbol*] [*Library of Congress*] (LCLS)
**InHagE**...... Hagerstown Exponent, Hagerstown, IN [*Library symbol*] [*Library of Congress*] (LCLS)
**INHAL**...... Inhalatio [*Inhalation*] [*Pharmacy*]
**Inhaled Part** ... Inhaled Particles [*A publication*]
**Inhal Ther** ... Inhalation Therapy [*A publication*]
**InHam**........ Hammond Public Library, Hammond, IN [*Library symbol*] [*Library of Congress*] (LCLS)
**InHamP**..... Purdue University, Calumet Campus, Hammond, IN [*Library symbol*] [*Library of Congress*] (LCLS)
**InHamT**..... Hammond Times, Hammond, IN [*Library symbol*] [*Library of Congress*] (LCLS)
**InHan**........ Hanover College, Hanover, IN [*Library symbol*] [*Library of Congress*] (LCLS)
**InHar**......... Hartford City Public Library, Hartford City, IN [*Library symbol*] [*Library of Congress*] (LCLS)
**InHarBHi**.. Blackford County Historical Society, Hartford City, IN [*Library symbol*] [*Library of Congress*] (LCLS)
**Inha Univ IIR** ... Inha University IIR [*A publication*]
**InHazN**...... White River News, Hazelton, IN [*Library symbol*] [*Library of Congress*] (LCLS)
**INHB**......... Inhibit (MSA)
**INHBA**...... Bulletin. Illinois Natural History Survey [*A publication*]
**INHBD**...... Inhibited
**INHCE**...... Inheritance [*Legal term*] (ROG)
**INHEA**...... Industrial Health [*A publication*]
**INHEAO**... Industrial Health [*A publication*]
**InHeb**......... Hebron Public Library, Hebron, IN [*Library symbol*] [*Library of Congress*] (LCLS)
**InHebPH**... Porter County Herald, Hebron, IN [*Library symbol*] [*Library of Congress*] (LCLS)
**INHEES**.... Index Hepaticarum [*A publication*]
**Inher**.......... Inheritance [*Legal term*] (DLA)
**Inher Est & Gift Tax Rep (CCH)** ... Inheritance, Estate, and Gift Tax Reports (Commerce Clearing House) [*A publication*] (DLA)
**InHhW**...... Workingmen's Institute, New Harmony, IN [*Library symbol*] [*Library of Congress*] (LCLS)
**InHi**........... Indiana Historical Society, Indianapolis, IN [*Library symbol*] [*Library of Congress*] (LCLS)
**INHIB**....... Inhibition
**INHIGEO** ... International Commission on the History of the Geological Sciences [*ICSU*] [*Paris, France*] (EAIO)
**INHO**........ Independence Holding Co. [*NASDAQ symbol*] (NQ)
**INHOAK**... Indian Horticulture [*A publication*]
**InHoG**........ Hobart Gazette, Hobart, IN [*Library symbol*] [*Library of Congress*] (LCLS)
**InHoHi**...... Pleak Memorial Library/Hobart Historical Society, Hobart, IN [*Library symbol*] [*Library of Congress*] (LCLS)
**INHP**......... Indiana Journal. Indiana Association for Health, Physical Education, and Recreation [*A publication*]
**INHS**......... Illinois Natural History Survey [*Illinois Institute of Natural Resources*] [*Research center*] (RCD)
**INHS**......... Irish National Hunt Steeplechase (ROG)
**INHTA**...... Industrial Heating [*A publication*]
**InHu**........... Huntington Public Library, Huntington, IN [*Library symbol*] [*Library of Congress*] (LCLS)
**InHub**......... Huntingburg Public Library, Huntingburg, IN [*Library symbol*] [*Library of Congress*] (LCLS)
**InHuH**....... Huntington College, Huntington, IN [*Library symbol*] [*Library of Congress*] (LCLS)
**InHuHi**...... Huntington County Historical Society, Huntington, IN [*Library symbol*] [*Library of Congress*] (LCLS)
**InHuHP**..... Huntington Herald-Press, Huntington, IN [*Library symbol*] [*Library of Congress*] (LCLS)
**INI**............ In Nomine Iesu [*In the Name of Jesus*] [*Latin*]
**INI**............ Incipient Nonequilibrium Index
**InI**............. Indianapolis-Marion County Public Library, Indianapolis, IN [*Library symbol*] [*Library of Congress*] (LCLS)
**INI**............ Industrial Networking, Inc. [*Joint venture of Ungermann-Bass, Inc. and General Electric Corp.*]
**INI**............ Inner Integument [*Botany*]
**INI**............ Instituto Nacional de Industria [*National Institute for Industry*] [*Spain*]
**INI**............ Interface Noise Inverter
**INI**............ International Nursing Index [*A publication*]
**INI**............ Intervideo Network, Incorporated [*Beverly Hills, CA*] [*Telecommunications*] (TSSD)
**INI**............ Intranuclear Inclusion
**InIA**........... Indiana Academy of Science, Indianapolis, IN [*Library symbol*] [*Library of Congress*] (LCLS)
**InIAL**......... American Legion, National Headquarters Library, Indianapolis, IN [*Library symbol*] [*Library of Congress*] (LCLS)
**InIB**........... Butler University, Indianapolis, IN [*Library symbol*] [*Library of Congress*] (LCLS)
**InIBHM**.... President Benjamin Harrison Memorial Home, Indianapolis, IN [*Library symbol*] [*Library of Congress*] (LCLS)
**InIBHP**...... Barnes, Hickam, Pantzer & Boyd, Law Library, Indianapolis, IN [*Library symbol*] [*Library of Congress*] (LCLS)
**InIBio**......... Bio-Dynamics, Inc., BMC Library, Indianapolis, IN [*Library symbol*] [*Library of Congress*] (LCLS)
**InIB-P**........ Butler University, College of Pharmacy, Indianapolis, IN [*Library symbol*] [*Library of Congress*] (LCLS)
**INIC**.......... Ideal Current Negative Immittance Converter
**InIC**........... Indianapolis Commercial, Indianapolis, IN [*Library symbol*] [*Library of Congress*] (LCLS)
**InICC**......... Indiana Central University, Indianapolis, IN [*Library symbol*] [*Library of Congress*] (LCLS)
**InICM**........ Children's Museum of Indianapolis, Indianapolis, IN [*Library symbol*] [*Library of Congress*] (LCLS)
**INICR**........ Institute for Childhood Resources (EA)
**InID**........... General Motors Corp., Detroit Diesel Allison Division, Plant 8 Library, Indianapolis, IN [*Library symbol*] [*Library of Congress*] (LCLS)
**INID**.......... Institutul National de Informare si Documentare [*National Institute for Information and Documentation*] [*National Council for Science and Technology*] [*Information service or system*] (IID)
**InIFHi**....... Franklin Township Historical Society, Indianapolis, IN [*Library symbol*] [*Library of Congress*] (LCLS)
**INIG**.......... International Nutritional Immunology Group (EA)
**InIGS**......... Church of Jesus Christ of Latter-Day Saints, Genealogical Society Library, Indianapolis Branch, Indianapolis, IN [*Library symbol*] [*Library of Congress*] (LCLS)
**InII**............ Indiana Cooperative Library Service Authority (INCOLSA), Indianapolis, IN [*Library symbol*] [*Library of Congress*] (LCLS)
**InIJ**............ Herron School of Art, Indianapolis, IN [*Library symbol*] [*Library of Congress*] (LCLS)
**InIL**............ Eli Lilly & Co., Scientific Library, Indianapolis, IN [*Library symbol*] [*Library of Congress*] (LCLS)
**InILB**......... Eli Lilly & Co., Business Library, Indianapolis, IN [*Library symbol*] [*Library of Congress*] (LCLS)
**InILS**......... Indianapolis Law School, Indianapolis, IN [*Library symbol*] [*Library of Congress*] (LCLS)
**InIM**.......... Marian College, Indianapolis, IN [*Library symbol*] [*Library of Congress*] (LCLS)
**InIMu**........ Indianapolis Museum of Art, Reference Library, Indianapolis, IN [*Library symbol*] [*Library of Congress*] (LCLS)
**ININA**....... Industrial India [*A publication*]
**IN INIT**..... In Initio [*In the Beginning*] [*Latin*]
**INIP**.......... Institute of Non-Numerical Information Processing [*Switzerland*] [*Information service or system*] (IID)
**InIPE**......... Indiana University - Purdue University at Indianapolis, School of Physical Education, Indianapolis, IN [*Library symbol*] [*Library of Congress*] (LCLS)
**InIR**........... James Whitcomb Riley Home, Indianapolis, IN [*Library symbol*] [*Library of Congress*] (LCLS)

**InIRCA**...... RCA, Selectavision Video Disc Operations Library, Indianapolis, IN [*Library symbol*] [*Library of Congress*] (LCLS)
**INIREB**..... Instituto Nacional de Investigaciones sobre Recursos Bioticos [*National Institute for Research on Biological Resources*] [*Information service or system*] (IID)
**INIREB Informa Inst Invest Recur Bioticos** ... INIREB Informa. Instituto de Investigaciones sobre Recursos Bioticos [*A publication*]
**INIS**.......... INIS [*International Nuclear Information System*] Atomindex [*A publication*]
**INIS**.......... International Nuclear Information System [*International Atomic Energy Agency*] (IID)
**INIS ATOMINDEX** ... International Nuclear Information System [*International Atomic Energy Agency*] [*Vienna, Austria*] [*Bibliographic database*]
**INIST**........ Institute de l'Information Scientifique et Technique [*Institute of Scientific and Technical Information*] [*Information service or system*] (EISS)
**INISWF**..... Indian National Iron and Steel Workers' Federation
**InIT**........... Christian Theological Seminary, Indianapolis, IN [*Library symbol*] [*Library of Congress*] (LCLS)
**INIT**.......... Initial (AFM)
**INIT**.......... Initialization (KSC)
**INIT**.......... Initiate (NASA)
**INIT**.......... Initiation (MSA)
**INIT**.......... Initio [*In the Beginning*] [*Latin*] (ROG)
**INITB**........ Installatore Italiano [*A publication*]
**Initiative**..... Industrial Arts Initiative [*A publication*]
**Initiatives Popul** ... Inititatives in Population [*A publication*]
**INIT & REF** ... Initiative and Referendum [*Legal term*] (DLA)
**INITUNIFALW** ... Initial Uniform Allowance [*Military*]
**InIU**.......... Indiana University - Purdue University at Indianapolis, Downtown Campus, Indianapolis, IN [*Library symbol*] [*Library of Congress*] (LCLS)
**InIU-L**....... Indiana University - Purdue University at Indianapolis, School of Law, Indianapolis, IN [*Library symbol*] [*Library of Congress*] (LCLS)
**InIWis**........ Wishard Memorial Hospital, Indianapolis, IN [*Library symbol*] [*Library of Congress*] (LCLS)
**Iniz**............ Iniziative [*A publication*]
**INJ**............ In Nomine Jesu [*In the Name of Jesus*] [*Latin*]
**INJ**............ Inject
**INJ**............ Injectio [*An Injection*] [*Pharmacy*]
**INJ**............ Injector (KSC)
**Inj**............. Injunction [*Legal term*]
**INJ**............ Injure (AABC)
**INJ**............ International North American Resources, Inc. [*Vancouver Stock Exchange symbol*]
**INJ**............ Internationales Verkehrswesen; Fachzeitschrift fuer Information und Kommunikation in Verkehr [*A publication*]
**INJ**............ Israel Numismatic Journal [*A publication*]
**InJ**............. Jasper Public Library, Jasper, IN [*Library symbol*] [*Library of Congress*] (LCLS)
**INJABN**.... International Journal of the Addictions [*A publication*]
**InJaL**......... Jasonville Leader, Jasonville, IN [*Library symbol*] [*Library of Congress*] (LCLS)
**InJamP**...... Jamestown Press, Jamestown, IN [*Library symbol*] [*Library of Congress*] (LCLS)
**INJCT**....... Injunction [*Legal term*]
**InJDHi**...... Dubois County Historical Society, Jasper, IN [*Library symbol*] [*Library of Congress*] (LCLS)
**InJe**........... Jeffersonville Township Public Library, Jeffersonville, IN [*Library symbol*] [*Library of Congress*] (LCLS)
**INJECT**..... Injection [*Medicine*]
**Injectable Contraceptives Newsl** ... Injectable Contraceptives Newsletter [*A publication*]
**INJ ENEM** ... Injiciatur Enema [*Let an Enema Be Injected*] [*Pharmacy*]
**INJFA3**..... International Journal of Fertility [*A publication*]
**InJH**.......... Jasper Herald, Jasper, IN [*Library symbol*] [*Library of Congress*] (LCLS)
**INJHA**...... Indian Journal of Heredity [*A publication*]
**INJHA9**.... Indian Journal of Heredity [*A publication*]
**INJ HYP**... Injectio Hypodermica [*Hypodermic Injection*] [*Pharmacy*]
**INJIC**....... Injiciatur [*Let It Be Given*] [*Pharmacy*] (ROG)
**INJICIAT** ... Injiciatur [*Let It Be Given*] [*Pharmacy*] (ROG)
**INJN**.......... Injunction [*Legal term*] (ROG)
**InJo**........... Jonesboro Public Library, Jonesboro, IN [*Library symbol*] [*Library of Congress*] (LCLS)
**INJON**...... Injunction [*Legal term*] (ROG)
**INJPA**....... Indian Journal of Psychology [*A publication*]
**INJR**.......... International North American Resources, Inc. [*Vancouver, BC*] [*NASDAQ symbol*] (NQ)
**INK**........... International Coast Minerals Corp. [*Vancouver Stock Exchange symbol*]
**INK**........... Inuvik [*Northwest Territories*] [*Seismograph station code, US Geological Survey*] (SEIS)
**INK**........... Wink, TX [*Location identifier*] [*FAA*] (FAAL)
**INKA**......... Informationssystem Karlsruhe [*Karlsruhe Information System*] [*Information service or system*] [*Federal Republic of Germany*]
**INKA-CONF** ... Informationssystem Karlsruhe - Conference [*Database*]
**INKA-CORP** ... Informationssystem Karlsruhe - Corporates in Energy [*Database*] [*Defunct*]
**INKA-DATACOMP** ... Informationssystem Karlsruhe - Data Compilations in Energy and Physics [*Database*]
**INKA-MATH** ... Informationssystem Karlsruhe - Mathematics [*Database*]
**INKA-MATHDI** ... Informationssystem Karlsruhe - Mathematical Education [*Database*]
**INKA-NUCLEAR PART INIS** ... Informationssystem Karlsruhe - Nuclear Database Part: International Nuclear Information System [*Database*]
**INKA-NUCLEAR PART KKK** ... Informationssystem Karlsruhe - Nuclear Database Part: Conference Papers: Nuclear Research, Nuclear Technology [*Database*]
**INKA-NUCLEAR PART NSA** ... Informationssystem Karlsruhe - Nuclear Database Part: Nuclear Science Abstracts [*Database*]
**INKA-PHYS** ... Informationssystem Karlsruhe - Physics [*Database*]
**InKend**....... Kendallville Public Library, Kendallville, IN [*Library symbol*] [*Library of Congress*] (LCLS)
**InKendNS** ... Kendallville News-Sun, Kendallville, IN [*Library symbol*] [*Library of Congress*] (LCLS)
**InKent**........ Kentland Public Library, Kentland, IN [*Library symbol*] [*Library of Congress*] (LCLS)
**InKentCR**... Newton County Recorder's Office, Kentland, IN [*Library symbol*] [*Library of Congress*] (LCLS)
**InKentE**..... Newton County Enterprise, Kentland, IN [*Library symbol*] [*Library of Congress*] (LCLS)
**InKew**......... Kewanna Public Library, Kewanna, IN [*Library symbol*] [*Library of Congress*] (LCLS)
**InKewO**...... Kewanna Observer, Kewanna, IN [*Library symbol*] [*Library of Congress*] (LCLS)
**InKir**.......... Kirklin Public Library, Kirklin, IN [*Library symbol*] [*Library of Congress*] (LCLS)
**InKni**.......... Knightstown Public Library, Knightstown, IN [*Library symbol*] [*Library of Congress*] (LCLS)
**InKniB**....... Knightstown Banner, Knightstown, IN [*Library symbol*] [*Library of Congress*] (LCLS)
**InKno**......... Henry F. Schricker Library, Knox, IN [*Library symbol*] [*Library of Congress*] (LCLS)
**InKnoCHi**.. Starke County Historical Museum, Knox, IN [*Library symbol*] [*Library of Congress*] (LCLS)
**InKnoCR**.... Starke County Recorder's Office, Knox, IN [*Library symbol*] [*Library of Congress*] (LCLS)
**InKo**........... Kokomo Public Library, Kokomo, IN [*Library symbol*] [*Library of Congress*] (LCLS)
**InKoC**........ Cabot Corporation, Stellite Division, Kokomo, IN [*Library symbol*] [*Library of Congress*] (LCLS)
**InKoT**......... Kokomo Tribune, Kokomo, IN [*Library symbol*] [*Library of Congress*] (LCLS)
**InKouT**....... Kouts Times, Kouts, IN [*Library symbol*] [*Library of Congress*] (LCLS)
**INKYD**...... Rihaknonjip. Research Institute of Applied Science. Kon-Kuk University [*A publication*]
**InL**............. Indian Literature [*A publication*]
**INL**............ Inland Natural Gas Co. Ltd. [*Toronto Stock Exchange symbol*] [*Vancouver Stock Exchange symbol*]
**INL**............ Inlet (KSC)
**INL**............ Inner Nuclear Layer
**InL**............. Inostrannaya Literatura [*Moscow*] [*A publication*]
**INL**............ Internal Noise Level (IEEE)
**INL**............ International Falls [*Minnesota*] [*Airport symbol*] (OAG)
**INL**............ International Falls, MN [*Location identifier*] [*FAA*] (FAAL)
**InL**............. Wells Memorial Library, Lafayette, IN [*Library symbol*] [*Library of Congress*] (LCLS)
**INLA**......... International Nuclear Law Association [*See also AIDN*] [*Brussels, Belgium*] (EAIO)
**INLA**......... Irish National Liberation Army
**InLacN**....... Lacrosse Regional News, La Crosse, IN [*Library symbol*] [*Library of Congress*] (LCLS)
**InLad**......... Ladoga-Clark Township Public Library, Ladoga, IN [*Library symbol*] [*Library of Congress*] (LCLS)
**InLag**......... LaGrange County Library, LaGrange, IN [*Library symbol*] [*Library of Congress*] (LCLS)
**InLagHi**..... LaGrange County Historical Society, LaGrange, IN [*Library symbol*] [*Library of Congress*] (LCLS)
**INLAN**...... Instant Language [*Trademark*] [*Data processing*]
**Inland Archt** ... Inland Architect [*A publication*]
**Inland P**..... Inland Printer/American Lithographer [*A publication*]
**Inland Printer Am Lithogr** ... Inland Printer/American Lithographer [*A publication*]
**Inland Ptr**... Inland Printer [*A publication*]
**InLap**......... La Porte Public Library, La Porte, IN [*Library symbol*] [*Library of Congress*] (LCLS)
**InLapHA**.... LaPorte Herald-Argus, LaPorte, IN [*Library symbol*] [*Library of Congress*] (LCLS)
**InLapHi**..... LaPorte County Historical Society, LaPorte, IN [*Library symbol*] [*Library of Congress*] (LCLS)
**InLaR**......... Lapel Review, Lapel, IN [*Library symbol*] [*Library of Congress*] (LCLS)
**InLasH**...... Hygiene Institute, La Salle, IN [*Library symbol*] [*Library of Congress*] (LCLS)

**INLAW**...... Infantry LASER Weapon (MCD)
**InLaw**........ Lawrenceburg Public Library, Lawrenceburg, IN [*Library symbol*] [*Library of Congress*] (LCLS)
**InLawCR**... Dearborn County Recorder's Office, Lawrenceburg, IN [*Library symbol*] [*Library of Congress*] (LCLS)
**IN-LB**........ Inch-Pound
**In-LB**......... Indiana Legislative Council, State House, Indianapolis, IN [*Library symbol*] [*Library of Congress*] (LCLS)
**Inl Bird-Banding News**... Inland Bird-Banding News [*A publication*]
**INLC**.......... Initial Launch Capability (IEEE)
**InLcLM**..... Lincoln Boyhood National Memorial, Lincoln City, IN [*Library symbol*] [*Library of Congress*] (LCLS)
**INLD**......... Inland (FAAC)
**INLE**.......... Instituto Nacional del Libro Espanol
**InLeb**.......... Lebanon Public Library, Lebanon, IN [*Library symbol*] [*Library of Congress*] (LCLS)
**InLebCR**.... Boone County Recorder's Office, Lebanon, IN [*Library symbol*] [*Library of Congress*] (LCLS)
**InLebR**....... Lebanon Reporter, Lebanon, IN [*Library symbol*] [*Library of Congress*] (LCLS)
**IN LF**......... Indiana Legal Forum [*A publication*]
**INLF**.......... Investors Heritage Life Insurance Co. [*NASDAQ symbol*] (NQ)
**InLi**............ Incontri Linguistici [*A publication*]
**InLib**.......... Union County Public Library, Liberty, IN [*Library symbol*] [*Library of Congress*] (LCLS)
**InLibCN**.... College Corner News, Liberty, IN [*Library symbol*] [*Library of Congress*] (LCLS)
**InLibH**....... Liberty Herald, Liberty, IN [*Library symbol*] [*Library of Congress*] (LCLS)
**Inlichitingsblad CCMB**... Inlichitingsblad van de Christelijke Centrale der Metaalbewerkers van Belgie [*A publication*]
**InLigAL**..... Ligonier Advance-Leader, Ligonier, IN [*Library symbol*] [*Library of Congress*] (LCLS)
**IN LIM**...... In Limine [*At the Outset*] [*Latin*]
**InLind**........ Linden Public Library, Linden, IN [*Library symbol*] [*Library of Congress*] (LCLS)
**INLINON**... Interlineation (ROG)
**InLint**......... Linton Public Library, Linton, IN [*Library symbol*] [*Library of Congress*] (LCLS)
**InLintC**...... Linton Daily Citizen, Linton, IN [*Library symbol*] [*Library of Congress*] (LCLS)
**IN LITT**..... In Litteris [*In Correspondence*] [*Latin*]
**IN LJ**......... Indiana Law Journal [*A publication*]
**InLJC**........ Lafayette Journal and Courier, Lafayette, IN [*Library symbol*] [*Library of Congress*] (LCLS)
**INLND6**.... Informationen zu Naturschutz und Landschaftspflege in Nordwestdeutschland [*A publication*]
**INLO**......... In Lieu Of
**IN LOC**...... In Loco [*In the Place Of*] [*Latin*]
**IN LOC CIT**... In Loco Citato [*In the Place Mentioned*] [*Latin*] (ROG)
**InLog**.......... Logansport-Cass County Public Library, Logansport, IN [*Library symbol*] [*Library of Congress*] (LCLS)
**InLogCHi**.. Cass County Historical Society Museum Library, Logansport, IN [*Library symbol*] [*Library of Congress*] (LCLS)
**INLOGOV**... Institute of Local Government Studies [*British*]
**InLogPT**.... Pharos-Tribune, Logansport, IN [*Library symbol*] [*Library of Congress*] (LCLS)
**InLoo**.......... Frances L. Folks Memorial Library (Loogootee Public Library), Loogootee, IN [*Library symbol*] [*Library of Congress*] (LCLS)
**InLooT**....... Loogootee Tribune, Loogootee, IN [*Library symbol*] [*Library of Congress*] (LCLS)
**InLow**........ Lowell Public Library, Lowell, IN [*Library symbol*] [*Library of Congress*] (LCLS)
**InLowT**...... Lowell Tribune, Lowell, IN [*Library symbol*] [*Library of Congress*] (LCLS)
**InLP**........... Purdue University, Lafayette, IN [*Library symbol*] [*Library of Congress*] (LCLS)
**InLP-Ham**... Purdue University, Calumet Campus, Hammond, IN [*Library symbol*] [*Library of Congress*] [*Obsolete*] (LCLS)
**IN LR**......... Indiana Law Review [*A publication*]
**INLR**.......... Item No Longer Required
**INLR-A**..... International Labour Review [*A publication*]
**InLS**........... Lafayette Schools System, Lafayette, IN [*Library symbol*] [*Library of Congress*] (LCLS)
**INLT**.......... Inlet [*Board on Geographic Names*] (MCD)
**InLTHi**...... Tippecanoe County Historical Association, Lafayette, IN [*Library symbol*] [*Library of Congress*] (LCLS)
**InLv**............ Lake Village Library, Lake Village, IN [*Library symbol*] [*Library of Congress*] (LCLS)
**InLy**........... Washington Township Public Library, Lynn, IN [*Library symbol*] [*Library of Congress*] (LCLS)
**INM**........... Imbokodvo National Movement [*Swaziland*] [*Political party*] (PPW)
**INM**........... Industrial Management [*A publication*]
**INM**........... Industrie Textile. Revue Mensuelle Internationale Technique et Economique Textile [*A publication*]
**INM**........... Inspector of Naval Machinery
**INM**........... Inspector of Naval Material
**INM**........... Institute of Naval Medicine [*British*] (DMA)
**INM**........... Interception Mission [*Air Force*]
**INM**........... International Narcotics Matters [*Department of State*]
**INM**........... International Nautical Mile
**INMA**........ Intermagnetics General Corp. [*NASDAQ symbol*] (NQ)
**INMA**........ International Newspaper Marketing Association (EA)
**INMAD**..... Invention Management [*A publication*]
**InMad**........ Madison-Jefferson County Public Library, Madison, IN [*Library symbol*] [*Library of Congress*] (LCLS)
**InMadC**..... Madison Daily Courier, Madison, IN [*Library symbol*] [*Library of Congress*] (LCLS)
**InMar**........ Marion Public Library, Marion, IN [*Library symbol*] [*Library of Congress*] (LCLS)
**InMarC**...... Marion College, Marion, IN [*Library symbol*] [*Library of Congress*] (LCLS)
**InMarCT**... Marion Chronicle Tribune, Marion, IN [*Library symbol*] [*Library of Congress*] (LCLS)
**InMarGHi**... Grant County Historical Society, Marion, IN [*Library symbol*] [*Library of Congress*] (LCLS)
**INMARSAT**... International Maritime Satellite Organization (TSSD)
**InMart**....... Morgan County Public Library, Martinsville, IN [*Library symbol*] [*Library of Congress*] (LCLS)
**InMarV**...... United States Veterans Administration Hospital, Marion, IN [*Library symbol*] [*Library of Congress*] (LCLS)
**InMat**......... Matthews Public Library, Matthews, IN [*Library symbol*] [*Library of Congress*] (LCLS)
**INMC**......... Inmac Corp. [*Santa Clara, CA*] [*NASDAQ symbol*] (NQ)
**INMC**......... International Network Management Center [*Telecommunications*] (TEL)
**INMD**........ Inmedica Development Corp. [*Salt Lake City, UT*] [*NASDAQ symbol*] (NQ)
**InMe**.......... Bell Memorial Public Library, Mentone, IN [*Library symbol*] [*Library of Congress*] (LCLS)
**INMED**..... Indians into Medicine (EA)
**InMelRP**.... Richland Press, Mellott, IN [*Library symbol*] [*Library of Congress*] (LCLS)
**IN MEM**... In Memoriam [*In Memory Of*] [*Latin*] (ROG)
**InMerL**...... Lake County Public Library, Merrillville, IN [*Library symbol*] [*Library of Congress*] (LCLS)
**Inmersion Cienc**... Inmersion y Ciencia [*A publication*]
**INMETRO**... Instituto Nacional de Metrologia, Normalizacao e Qualidade Industrial [*Government advisory body*] [*Brazil*] (EY)
**INMHC**..... International Network for Mutual Help Centers (EA)
**INMI**......... Institute of Microbiology (of the Academy of Sciences, USSR)
**INMI**......... International Migration [*A publication*]
**InMic**......... Michigan City Public Library, Michigan City, IN [*Library symbol*] [*Library of Congress*] (LCLS)
**InMicLM**... Old Lighthouse Museum, Michigan City, IN [*Library symbol*] [*Library of Congress*] (LCLS)
**InMicND**... Michigan City News-Dispatch, Michigan City, IN [*Library symbol*] [*Library of Congress*] (LCLS)
**INMID**...... Industria Minera [*A publication*]
**InMidb**....... Middlebury Public Library, Middlebury, IN [*Library symbol*] [*Library of Congress*] (LCLS)
**InMidbI**..... Middlebury Independent, Middlebury, IN [*Library symbol*] [*Library of Congress*] (LCLS)
**InMidN**...... Middletown News, Middletown, IN [*Library symbol*] [*Library of Congress*] (LCLS)
**InMil**.......... Milford Public Library, Milford, IN [*Library symbol*] [*Library of Congress*] (LCLS)
**InMilMJ**... Milford Mail-Journal, Millford, IN [*Library symbol*] [*Library of Congress*] (LCLS)
**InMis**.......... Mishawaka Public Library, Mishawaka, IN [*Library symbol*] [*Library of Congress*] (LCLS)
**InMisB**...... Bethel College, Mishawaka, IN [*Library symbol*] [*Library of Congress*] (LCLS)
**InMisER**.... Mishawaka Enterprise-Record, Mishawaka, IN [*Library symbol*] [*Library of Congress*] (LCLS)
**InMit**.......... Mitchell Community Public Library, Mitchell, IN [*Library symbol*] [*Library of Congress*] (LCLS)
**INMM**....... Institute of Nuclear Materials Management (EA)
**INMOA**..... Ingenieur (Montreal) [*A publication*]
**InMon**........ Monon Town and Township Library, Monon, IN [*Library symbol*] [*Library of Congress*] (LCLS)
**InMonN**..... Monon News, Monon, IN [*Library symbol*] [*Library of Congress*] (LCLS)
**InMont**....... Monterrey-Tippecanoe Township Public Library Monterrey, IN [*Library symbol*] [*Library of Congress*] (LCLS)
**InMop**........ Montpelier Public Library, Montpelier, IN [*Library symbol*] [*Library of Congress*] (LCLS)
**InMopH**..... Montpelier Herald, Montpelier, IN [*Library symbol*] [*Library of Congress*] (LCLS)
**InMotc**....... Monticello Union Township Public Library, Monticello, IN [*Library symbol*] [*Library of Congress*] (LCLS)
**InMotz**....... Montezuma Public Library, Montezuma, IN [*Library symbol*] [*Library of Congress*] (LCLS)
**INMR**........ Insider Network Market Report [*Information service or system*] (EISS)
**INMR**........ Instrumentarium Corp. [*NASDAQ symbol*] (NQ)
**INMRA**..... Industria Mineraria [*A publication*]
**INMT**........ Intermet Corp. [*NASDAQ symbol*] (NQ)

**InMtv**......... Alexandrian Free Public Library, Mount Vernon, IN [*Library symbol*] [*Library of Congress*] (LCLS)
**InMu**.......... Muncie Public Library, Muncie, IN [*Library symbol*] [*Library of Congress*] (LCLS)
**InMuB**....... Ball State University, Muncie, IN [*Library symbol*] [*Library of Congress*] (LCLS)
**InMuP**....... Muncie Evening Press, Muncie, IN [*Library symbol*] [*Library of Congress*] (LCLS)
**InMuSP**..... Muncie Morning Star-Evening Press, Muncie, IN [*Library symbol*] [*Library of Congress*] (LCLS)
**INMWF**..... Indian National Mine Workers' Federation
**INN**........... Independent Network News [*Television*]
**INN**........... Innsbruck [*Austria*] [*Seismograph station code, US Geological Survey*] [*Closed*] (SEIS)
**INN**........... Innsbruck [*Austria*] [*Airport symbol*] (OAG)
**INN**........... International Nonproprietary Names [*World Health Organization*]
**INN**........... Minneapolis, MN [*Location identifier*] [*FAA*] (FAAL)
**INN**........... New Albany-Floyd County Public Library, New Albany, IN [*OCLC symbol*] (OCLC)
**InNap**......... Nappanee Public Library, Nappanee, IN [*Library symbol*] [*Library of Congress*] (LCLS)
**InNapAN**... Nappanee Advance News, Nappanee, IN [*Library symbol*] [*Library of Congress*] (LCLS)
**InNas**......... Brown County Public Library, Nashville, IN [*Library symbol*] [*Library of Congress*] (LCLS)
**InNasBHi**.. Brown County Historical Society, Nashville, IN [*Library symbol*] [*Library of Congress*] (LCLS)
**InNasCR**.... Brown County Recorder's Office, Nashville, IN [*Library symbol*] [*Library of Congress*] (LCLS)
**InNasD**...... Brown County Democrat, Nashville, IN [*Library symbol*] [*Library of Congress*] (LCLS)
**InNcar**........ New Carlisle and Olive Township Public Library, New Carlisle, IN [*Library symbol*] [*Library of Congress*] (LCLS)
**InNcas**....... New Castle - Henry County Public Library, New Castle, IN [*Library symbol*] [*Library of Congress*] (LCLS)
**InNcasCT**.. New Castle Courier Times, New Castle, IN [*Library symbol*] [*Library of Congress*] (LCLS)
**InNcasHi**... Henry County Historical Society, Reference Room, New Castle, IN [*Library symbol*] [*Library of Congress*] (LCLS)
**InNcasNR**... Henry County News-Republican, New Castle, IN [*Library symbol*] [*Library of Congress*] (LCLS)
**InNd**.......... University of Notre Dame, Notre Dame, IN [*Library symbol*] [*Library of Congress*] (LCLS)
**INNDDK**... Investigational New Drugs [*A publication*]
**InNd-L**....... University of Notre Dame, Law School, Notre Dame, IN [*Library symbol*] [*Library of Congress*] (LCLS)
**InNd-LS**..... University of Notre Dame, Life Sciences Research Library, Notre Dame, IN [*Library symbol*] [*Library of Congress*] (LCLS)
**InNdS**........ Saint Mary's College, Notre Dame, IN [*Library symbol*] [*Library of Congress*] (LCLS)
**InNea**.......... New Albany-Floyd County Public Library, New Albany, IN [*Library symbol*] [*Library of Congress*] (LCLS)
**Inn Eas**....... Innes on Easements [*8th ed.*] [*1911*] [*A publication*] (DLA)
**Inn Ease**..... Innes on Easements [*8th ed.*] [*1911*] [*A publication*] (DLA)
**InNeaTL**.... New Albany Tribune and Ledger-Tribune, New Albany, IN [*Library symbol*] [*Library of Congress*] (LCLS)
**InNeb**......... Newburgh-Ohio Township Public Library, Newburgh, IN [*Library symbol*] [*Library of Congress*] (LCLS)
**InNep**......... Newport-Vermillion County Library, Newport, IN [*Library symbol*] [*Library of Congress*] (LCLS)
**Innere Med** ... Innere Medizin [*A publication*]
**INNERV**.... Innervation [*Medicine*]
**Innes**.......... Innes' Registration of Title [*A publication*] (ILCA)
**Innes Rev** ... Innes Review [*A publication*]
**InNhvAT** ... Allen County Times, New Haven, IN [*Library symbol*] [*Library of Congress*] (LCLS)
**Innisfail Canegr** ... Innisfail Canegrower [*A publication*]
**INNL**......... Improved Nonnuclear LANCE
**INNLA**....... INIS [*International Nuclear Information System*] Newsletter [*A publication*]
**Inno**........... [*Pope*] Innocent IV [*Deceased, 1254*] [*Authority cited in pre-1607 legal work*] (DSA)
**INNO**......... Innocente [*Innocently*] [*Music*] (ROG)
**INNO**......... Innotron Diagnostics [*NASDAQ symbol*] (NQ)
**Inno**........... Innovations [*Record label*]
**INNO**......... Inter-Nord [*A publication*]
**InNob**......... Noblesville Public Library, Noblesville, IN [*Library symbol*] [*Library of Congress*] (LCLS)
**InNobL**...... Noblesville Daily Ledger, Noblesville, IN [*Library symbol*] [*Library of Congress*] (LCLS)
**INNO-BM** ... SA Innovation-Bon Marche NV [*Belgium*]
**InNoj**.......... North Judson-Wayne Township Public Library, North Judson, IN [*Library symbol*] [*Library of Congress*] (LCLS)
**InNoman**.... North Manchester Public Library, North Manchester, IN [*Library symbol*] [*Library of Congress*] (LCLS)
**InNomanC** ... Manchester College, North Manchester, IN [*Library symbol*] [*Library of Congress*] (LCLS)
**InNomanNJ** ... North Manchester News-Journal, North Manchester, IN [*Library symbol*] [*Library of Congress*] (LCLS)
**INNOTECH** ... Regional Center for Educational Innovation and Technology [*SEAMEO*] [*Research center*] [*Philippines*] (IRC)
**Innov High Educ** ... Innovative Higher Education [*A publication*]
**InNovJ**....... Jennings County Public Library, North Vernon, IN [*Library symbol*] [*Library of Congress*] (LCLS)
**INNS**......... International Nuclear News Service [*A publication*] (APTA)
**INNS**......... Krisch American Inns, Inc. [*Roanoke, VA*] [*NASDAQ symbol*] (NQ)
**Inn Sc Leg Ant** ... Innes' Scotch Legal Antiquities [*A publication*] (DLA)
**INNUA**....... Ingegneria Nucleare [*A publication*]
**INO**............ Indonesia [*A publication*]
**Ino**.............. [*Pope*] Innocent IV [*Deceased, 1254*] [*Authority cited in pre-1607 legal work*] (DSA)
**INO**............ Inongo [*Zaire*] [*Airport symbol*] (OAG)
**Ino**.............. Inosine [*Also, I*] [*A nucleoside*]
**INO**............ Inspector of Naval Ordnance [*British*]
**INO**............ Institute for Naval Oceanography [*Bay St. Louis, MS*] [*Navy*]
**INO**............ Inter-Oceanic Resources Ltd. [*Formerly, Inter-Oceanic Oil & Gas*] [*Vancouver Stock Exchange symbol*]
**INO**............ Internuclear Ophthalmoplegia
**INO**............ Issue Necessary Orders
**INO**............ Item Number
**INO**............ Iterative Natural Orbital [*Atomic physics*]
**INO**............ Northbrook Public Library, Northbrook, IL [*OCLC symbol*] (OCLC)
**INOA**......... International Norton Owners' Association (EA)
**INOAVNOT** ... If Not Available Notify This Office at Once
**INOC**......... Inoculation (AABC)
**INOC**......... Iraqi National Oil Company [*Government company*]
**INOCA**...... Inorganic Chemistry [*A publication*]
**InOcC**........ Oakland City College, Oakland City, IN [*Library symbol*] [*Library of Congress*] (LCLS)
**Inoc III**....... [*Pope*] Innocent III [*Deceased, 1216*] [*Authority cited in pre-1607 legal work*] (DSA)
**InOd**........... Odon Winkelpeck Memorial Library, Odon, IN [*Library symbol*] [*Library of Congress*] (LCLS)
**INODC**...... Indian National Oceanographic Data Centre [*Information service or system*] (IID)
**INODEP**.... Institut Oecumenique pour le Developpement des Peuples [*Ecumenical Institute for the Development of Peoples*] [*Paris, France*] (EAIO)
**InOdJ**........ Odon Journal, Odon, IN [*Library symbol*] [*Library of Congress*] (LCLS)
**INOE**......... Internacia Naturista Organizo Esperantista [*International Esperantist Organization of Naturists - IEON*] (EAIO)
**IN OEDIB** ... In Oedibus [*In the House Of*] [*Latin*] (ROG)
**INOGA**...... Industrielle Obst- und Gemueseverwertung [*A publication*]
**INOGAV**... Industrielle Obst- und Gemueseverwertung [*A publication*]
**INOK**......... Inuit Okakheet. Kitikmeot Inuit Association [*A publication*]
**INok**........... Nokomis Public Library, Nokomis, IL [*Library symbol*] [*Library of Congress*] (LCLS)
**INokSD**..... Nokomis Community Unit, School District 22, Nokomis, IL [*Library symbol*] [*Library of Congress*] (LCLS)
**INol**............ Northlake Public Library District, Northlake, IL [*Library symbol*] [*Library of Congress*] (LCLS)
**INOMA**..... Inorganic Materials [*English Translation*] [*A publication*]
**INOP**......... Inoperative
**INOPA**...... Investigations in Ophthalmology and Visual Science [*A publication*]
**INOPAO**... Investigative Ophthalmology [*Later, Investigative Ophthalmology and Visual Science*] [*A publication*]
**INOPD**...... International Ophthalmology [*A publication*]
**InOr**........... Orleans Public Library, Orleans, IN [*Library symbol*] [*Library of Congress*] (LCLS)
**INORG**...... Inorganic
**Inorg Chem** ... Inorganic Chemistry [*A publication*]
**Inorg Chem Main Group Elem** ... Inorganic Chemistry of the Main Group Elements [*A publication*]
**Inorg Chem Transition Elem** ... Inorganic Chemistry of the Transition Elements [*A publication*]
**Inorg Chim** ... Inorganica Chimica Acta [*A publication*]
**Inorg Chim Acta** ... Inorganica Chimica Acta [*A publication*]
**Inorg Chim Acta Rev** ... Inorganica Chimica Acta. Reviews [*A publication*]
**Inorg Macromol Rev** ... Inorganic Macromolecules Reviews [*A publication*]
**Inorg Mater** ... Inorganic Materials [*A publication*]
**Inorg Mater (USSR)** ... Inorganic Materials (USSR) [*A publication*]
**Inorg Nucl** ... Inorganic and Nuclear Chemistry Letters [*A publication*]
**Inorg Nucl Chem Lett** ... Inorganic and Nuclear Chemistry Letters [*A publication*]
**Inorg and Nucl Chem Lett** ... Inorganic and Nuclear Chemistry Letters [*A publication*]
**Inorg Perspect Biol Med** ... Inorganic Perspectives in Biology and Medicine [*A publication*]
**Inorg React Mech** ... Inorganic Reaction Mechanisms [*A publication*]
**InOrPE**...... Orleans Progress-Examiner, Orleans, IN [*Library symbol*] [*Library of Congress*] (LCLS)
**InOsJ**......... Osgood Journal, Osgood, IN [*Library symbol*] [*Library of Congress*] (LCLS)
**InOssJ**....... Ossian Journal, Ossian, IN [*Library symbol*] [*Library of Congress*] (LCLS)
**InostrJazyki** ... Inostrannye Jazyki v Skole [*A publication*]

**INOV**......... Association Internationale du Nouvel Objet Visuel [*International Association for New Visual Objects*] [*Paris, France*] (EAIO)
**InOw**......... Owensville Public Library, Owensville, IN [*Library symbol*] [*Library of Congress*] (LCLS)
**InOwSE**..... Owensville Star-Echo, Owensville, IN [*Library symbol*] [*Library of Congress*] (LCLS)
**InOx**......... Oxford Public Library, Oxford, IN [*Library symbol*] [*Library of Congress*] (LCLS)
**InOxG**........ Oxford Gazette, Oxford, IN [*Library symbol*] [*Library of Congress*] (LCLS)
**InozF**......... Inozemna Filolohiji [*A publication*]
**INP**............ If Not Possible [*Aviation*] (FAAC)
**INP**............ In Pace [*In Peace*] [*Latin*]
**INP**............ Indiana, PA [*Location identifier*] [*FAA*] (FAAL)
**INP**............ Inert Nitrogen Protection (IEEE)
**INP**............ Information-Need-Product [*Sales technique*]
**INP**............ Initial Program Load [*Data processing*]
**INP**............ Input (MSA)
**INP**............ Integrated Network Processor
**INP**............ Intelligent Network Processor
**INP**............ Intelligent Systems Corp. [*AMEX symbol*] (SPSG)
**INP**............ Inter-Net Predicts (MCD)
**INP**............ International News Photo
**INPA**......... International Newspaper Promotion Association (EA)
**InPa**.......... Paoli Public Library, Paoli, IN [*Library symbol*] [*Library of Congress*] (LCLS)
**INPAA**....... Instrument Practice [*A publication*]
**INPADOC**... International Patent Documentation Center [*Information service or system*] (IID)
**InPaN**........ Paoli News, Paoli, IN [*Library symbol*] [*Library of Congress*] (LCLS)
**InPaR**......... Paoli Republican, Paoli, IN [*Library symbol*] [*Library of Congress*] (LCLS)
**INPBM**...... Information Not Provided by Manufacturer
**INPC**.......... Irish National Petroleum Corp.
**INPC**.......... Isopropyl Phenylcarbamate [*Also, IPC, IPPC*] [*Herbicide*]
**InPEN**........ Indian PEN [*A publication*]
**InPen**.......... Pendleton and Fall Creek Township Public Library, Pendleton, IN [*Library symbol*] [*Library of Congress*] (LCLS)
**InPenT**....... Pendleton Times, Pendleton, IN [*Library symbol*] [*Library of Congress*] (LCLS)
**InPer**.......... Peru and Miami County Public Library, Peru, IN [*Library symbol*] [*Library of Congress*] (LCLS)
**InPerM**...... Miami County Historical Museum, Peru, IN [*Library symbol*] [*Library of Congress*] (LCLS)
**InPerT**....... Peru Tribune, Peru, IN [*Library symbol*] [*Library of Congress*] (LCLS)
**InPet**.......... Barrett Memorial Library, Petersburg, IN [*Library symbol*] [*Library of Congress*] (LCLS)
**InPetPD**..... Petersburg Press-Dispatch, Petersburg, IN [*Library symbol*] [*Library of Congress*] (LCLS)
**INPEX**....... International Postage Stamp Exhibition
**INPFC**....... International North Pacific Fisheries Commission (EA)
**INPFCB**..... International North Pacific Fisheries Commission. Bulletin [*A publication*]
**INPFC-US**... International North Pacific Fisheries Commission, United States Section
**IN PH**........ Indian Pharmacopoeia [*A publication*] (ROG)
**INPH**......... Interphase Corp. [*Dallas, TX*] [*NASDAQ symbol*] (NQ)
**INPH**......... Interphone
**INPH**......... Iproniazid Phosphate [*Organic chemistry*]
**INPHA**...... Industrial Photography [*A publication*]
**InPHO**....... International Photographic Historical Organization (EA)
**INPI**.......... Information Pipeline. Norman Wells Project Review [*A publication*]
**INPI**.......... Institut National de la Propriete Industrielle [*National Institute for Industrial Property*] [*France*] [*Information service or system*] (IID)
**InPi**............ Pierceton and Washington Township Library, Pierceton, IN [*Library symbol*] [*Library of Congress*] (LCLS)
**InPla**.......... Plainfield Public Library, Plainfield, IN [*Library symbol*] [*Library of Congress*] (LCLS)
**InPla-Hi**..... Plainfield Public Library, Guilford Township and Hendricks County Historical Collection, Plainfield, IN [*Library symbol*] [*Library of Congress*] (LCLS)
**In-Plant Reprod**... In-Plant Reproductions [*United States*] [*A publication*]
**InPly**.......... Plymouth Public Library, Plymouth, IN [*Library symbol*] [*Library of Congress*] (LCLS)
**InPlyHi**...... Marshall County Historical Society Library, Plymouth, IN [*Library symbol*] [*Library of Congress*] (LCLS)
**INPO**......... Institute for Nonprofit Organizations
**INPO**......... Institute of Nuclear Power Operations (EA)
**INPO Impact**... INPO [*Institute of Nuclear Power Operations*] Impact [*United States*] [*A publication*]
**INPOLSE**... International Police Services
**INPO Rev**.. INPO [*Institute of Nuclear Power Operations*] Review [*United States*] [*A publication*]
**InPorP**....... Portage Press, Portage, IN [*Library symbol*] [*Library of Congress*] (LCLS)
**InPorS**........ Portage Township Schools, Portage, IN [*Library symbol*] [*Library of Congress*] (LCLS)
**InPosN**....... Posey County News, Poseyville, IN [*Library symbol*] [*Library of Congress*] (LCLS)
**INPOWER**... Independent Power Generation Conference and Exhibition [*British*] (ITD)
**IN PR**......... In Principio [*In the Beginning*] [*Latin*] (ROG)
**INPR**.......... In Progress
**INPR**.......... Institute for Natural Products Research [*University of Georgia*] [*Research center*] (RCD)
**InPr**............ Princeton Public Library, Princeton, IN [*Library symbol*] [*Library of Congress*] (LCLS)
**INPRA**....... International Public Relations Association
**In Pract**...... In Practice [*A publication*]
**INPRC**....... Item Name Policy Review Committee [*DoD*] [*Washington, DC*] (EGAO)
**InPrC**......... Princeton Daily Clarion, Princeton, IN [*Library symbol*] [*Library of Congress*] (LCLS)
**INPRODE**... Instituto Profesional para el Desarrollo [*Professional Development Institute*] [*Colombia*]
**INPRONS**... Information Processing in the Central Nervous System
**INPS**.......... Individual Psychology [*A publication*]
**INPT**.......... In Port [*Navy*] (NVT)
**InPtlC**........ Jay County Commercial Review, Portland, IN [*Library symbol*] [*Library of Congress*] (LCLS)
**InPtlCR**..... Jay County Recorder's Office, Portland, IN [*Library symbol*] [*Library of Congress*] (LCLS)
**IN PULM**... In Pulmento [*In Gruel*] [*Pharmacy*]
**INPV**.......... Intermittent Negative-Pressure Ventilation [*Medicine*]
**INPXAJ**..... Internistische Praxis [*A publication*]
**INQ**............ Index of Nutritional Quality
**INQ**............ Innovatie Informatiebulletin ter Bevordering van de Industriele Vernieuwing in Ons Land [*A publication*]
**Inq**.............. Inquiry [*A publication*]
**INQ**............ Inquiry (AFM)
**INQ**............ Intercontinental Venture [*Vancouver Stock Exchange symbol*]
**INQB**......... Information North Quebec. Bulletin de Liaison des Centres de Recherches Nordique de Quebec [*A publication*]
**INQD**......... Inquired (ROG)
**INQ PM**.... Inquisitio Post-Mortem [*Latin*] (ROG)
**INQT**......... Inquest (ROG)
**INQU**......... Indians of Quebec. Confederation of Indians of Quebec [*A publication*]
**INQUA**...... International Union for Quaternary Research [*Research center*] [*France*] (IRC)
**Inqueritos Nac de Precos (Capitais)**... Inqueritos Nacional de Precos (Capitais) [*A publication*]
**Inqueritos Nac de Precos (Unidades da Federacao)**... Inqueritos Nacional de Precos (Unidades da Federacao) [*A publication*]
**Inquiry Mag**... Inquiry Magazine [*A publication*]
**INQY**......... Inquiry (ROG)
**INQYA**...... Inquiry [*A publication*]
**INR**............ Bureau of Intelligence and Research [*Department of State*]
**INR**............ Impact Noise Rating [*of insulation*]
**INR**............ Industrial Relations [*Canada*] [*A publication*]
**INR**............ Inertial Reference (MCD)
**INR**............ Informatie [*Netherlands*] [*A publication*]
**INR**............ Inner (MSA)
**INR**............ Insilco Corp. [*Formerly, International Silver Co.*] [*NYSE symbol*] (SPSG)
**INR**............ Institut National de Radiodiffusion [*Belgium*]
**INR**............ Institute of Natural Resources [*University of Georgia*] [*Research center*] (RCD)
**INR**............ Institute of Natural Resources [*Montana State University*] [*Research center*] (RCD)
**INR**............ Institute of Nuclear Research [*Poland*]
**INR**............ Interaction Resources Ltd. [*Toronto Stock Exchange symbol*]
**INR**............ Interference-to-Noise Ratio
**INR**............ International Normalized Ratio [*Hematology*]
**INR**............ Morrisson-Reeves Public Library, Richmond, IN [*OCLC symbol*] (OCLC)
**INRA**......... Inland Navigational Rules Act of 1980
**INRA**......... Institut National de la Recherche Agronomique [*National Institute of Agronomic Research*] [*Information service or system*] (IID)
**INRA**......... International Natural Rubber Agreement
**INRA**......... International Network for Religion and Animals (EA)
**INRA**......... International Research Associates [*Thailand*] (DS)
**INRAD**...... Interactive Real-Time Advanced Display
**INRC**......... Indian Nation Restoration Committee
**InRCS**........ Richmond Community School, Richmond, IN [*Library symbol*] [*Library of Congress*] (LCLS)
**INRD**......... INRAD, Inc. [*NASDAQ symbol*] (NQ)
**InRE**.......... Earlham College, Richmond, IN [*Library symbol*] [*Library of Congress*] (LCLS)
**IN RE**......... In Regard To
**INRE**.......... Indian Record [*A publication*]
**IN REF**...... In Reference To
**INREM**..... Internal REM [*Roentgen-Equivalent-Man*] [*Radiation dose*]
**InRem**........ Remington Carpenter Township Public Library, Remington, IN [*Library symbol*] [*Library of Congress*] (LCLS)

**InRen** ........ Jasper County Public Library, Rensselaer, IN [*Library symbol*] [*Library of Congress*] (LCLS)
**InRenS** ....... Saint Joseph's College, Rensselaer, IN [*Library symbol*] [*Library of Congress*] (LCLS)
**INREP** ....... Installation Damage Report [*Air Force*]
**INREP** ....... Replenishment conducted between two ships while in port [*Navy symbol*] (NVT)
**INREPL** .... Incoming Replacement [*Army*] (AABC)
**INREQ** ...... Information on Request (MCD)
**INREQ** ...... Information Requested
**INREQS** .... Information Requests [*Army*] (AABC)
**INRES** ....... Independent Reservation System [*Hotels and motels*]
**INRES/TCDC** ... Information Referral System for Technical Cooperation among Developing Countries [*United Nations*] [*Information service or system*] (IID)
**In Rev** ......... In Review. Canadian Books for Young People [*A publication*]
**INRF** .......... International Nutrition Research Foundation (EA)
**INRFDC** .... Interferon [*A publication*]
**INRH** ......... Institut National de Recherches en Hydrologie [*National Hydrology Research Institute*] [*Canada*]
**INRI** .......... Iesus Nazarenus Rex Iudaeorum [*Jesus of Nazareth, King of the Jews*] [*Latin*]
**INRI** .......... Imperator Napoleon Rex Italiae [*Emperor Napoleon, King of Italy*] [*Latin*]
**INRIA** ........ Institut National de Recherche en Informatique et en Automatique [*National Institute for Research in Informatics and Automation*] [*France*] [*Research center and database originator*] [*Information service or system*] (IID)
**InRid** .......... Ridgeville Public Library, Ridgeville, IN [*Library symbol*] [*Library of Congress*] (LCLS)
**InRis** .......... Ohio County Public Library, Rising Sun, IN [*Library symbol*] [*Library of Congress*] (LCLS)
**InRisCN** ..... Ohio County News, Rising Sun, IN [*Library symbol*] [*Library of Congress*] (LCLS)
**InRisCR** ..... Ohio County Recorder's Office, Rising Sun, IN [*Library symbol*] [*Library of Congress*] (LCLS)
**InRisHi** ...... Ohio County Historical Society, Rising Sun, IN [*Library symbol*] [*Library of Congress*] (LCLS)
**InRisR** ........ Rising Sun Recorder, Rising Sun, IN [*Library symbol*] [*Library of Congress*] (LCLS)
**INRLF** ....... Interaction Resources [*NASDAQ symbol*] (NQ)
**InRM** ......... Morrison-Reeves Public Library, Richmond, IN [*Library symbol*] [*Library of Congress*] (LCLS)
**INRO** ......... International Natural Rubber Organization [*Kuala Lumpur, Malaysia*] (EAIO)
**INRO** ......... International Naval Research Organization (EA)
**InRo** ........... Roachdale Public Library, Roachdale, IN [*Library symbol*] [*Library of Congress*] (LCLS)
**InRoa** ......... Roanoke Public Library, Roanoke, IN [*Library symbol*] [*Library of Congress*] (LCLS)
**INROADS** ... Information on Roads [*Australian Road Research Board*] [*Information service or system*] (IID)
**InRoc** .......... Fulton County Public Library, Rochester, IN [*Library symbol*] [*Library of Congress*] (LCLS)
**InRocCR** .... Fulton County Recorder's Office, Rochester, IN [*Library symbol*] [*Library of Congress*] (LCLS)
**InRocFHi** ... Fulton County Historical Society, Rochester, IN [*Library symbol*] [*Library of Congress*] (LCLS)
**InRocS** ....... Rochester Sentinel, Rochester, IN [*Library symbol*] [*Library of Congress*] (LCLS)
**InRomS** ...... Gene Stratton-Porter Memorial, Rome City, IN [*Library symbol*] [*Library of Congress*] (LCLS)
**InRoyR** ....... Royal Center Record, Royal Center, IN [*Library symbol*] [*Library of Congress*] (LCLS)
**InRPI** ......... Richmond Palladium-Item, Richmond, IN [*Library symbol*] [*Library of Congress*] (LCLS)
**InRpt** .......... Rockport-Ohio Township Public Library, Rockport, IN [*Library symbol*] [*Library of Congress*] (LCLS)
**InRptD** ....... Rockport Democrat, Rockport, IN [*Library symbol*] [*Library of Congress*] (LCLS)
**InRptJ** ........ Rockport Journal, Rockport, IN [*Library symbol*] [*Library of Congress*] (LCLS)
**INRS** .......... Institut National de la Recherche Scientifique [*National Institute for Scientific Research*] [*Canada*] [*Research center*]
**INRSDH** ... International Goat and Sheep Research [*A publication*]
**INRT** ......... Inertia (KSC)
**INRTFLR** ... Inert Filler
**INRTG** ...... Inert Gas
**INRTL** ....... Inertial (MSA)
**INRTLVEL** ... Inertial Velocity (MCD)
**InRusCR** .... Rush County Recorder's Office, Rushville, IN [*Library symbol*] [*Library of Congress*] (LCLS)
**InRusR** ....... Rushville Republican, Rushville, IN [*Library symbol*] [*Library of Congress*] (LCLS)
**InRv** ........... Rockville Public Library, Rockville, IN [*Library symbol*] [*Library of Congress*] (LCLS)
**InRvCR** ...... Parke County Recorder's Office, Rockville, IN [*Library symbol*] [*Library of Congress*] (LCLS)
**INS** ............ Idiopathic Nephrotic Syndrome
**INS** ............ Illinois State University, Normal, IL [*Library symbol*] [*Library of Congress*] (LCLS)
**INS** ............ Immigration and Naturalization Service [*Department of Justice*]
**INS** ............ Improved Navigational Satellite
**INS** ............ Improved Night Sight
**INS** ............ In Situ [*In Place*] [*Latin*] (ADA)
**INS** ............ Inches (EY)
**IN/S** .......... Inches per Second
**INS** ............ Independent News Service [*In TV series "The Night Stalker"*]
**INS** ............ Indian Springs, NV [*Location identifier*] [*FAA*] (FAAL)
**INS** ............ Industrial Society [*A publication*]
**INS** ............ Inertial Navigation System [*Aviation*]
**INS** ............ Information Network System [*Japan*]
**INS** ............ Information Systems (KSC)
**INS** ............ Initial Navigation System (AABC)
**InS** ............ Inland Seas [*A publication*]
**INS** ............ Inlet Resources Ltd. [*Vancouver Stock Exchange symbol*]
**Ins** ............ Inositol [*Biochemistry*]
**INS** ............ Insane (ROG)
**INS** ............ Inscribed
**ins** ............ Inscriber [*MARC relator code*] [*Library of Congress*] (LCCP)
**INS** ............ Inscription (ADA)
**INS** ............ Insect
**INS** ............ Insert (NVT)
**INS** ............ Insertion Burn [*Orbital Maneuvering Subsystem 1*] [*NASA*] (NASA)
**INS** ............ Insertion Mutation [*Genetics*]
**INS** ............ Inside (MSA)
**INS** ............ Insight [*A publication*]
**Ins** ............ Insolvency [*Legal term*] (DLA)
**INS** ............ Inspection Division [*Coast Guard*]
**INS** ............ Inspector
**INS** ............ Institute for Naval Studies
**INS** ............ Institute of Neurological Science [*University of Pennsylvania*]
**INS** ............ Institute of Nuclear Studies [*Oak Ridge, TN*]
**INS** ............ Institute for Nuclear Study [*Japan*]
**Ins** ............ Instrumentalist [*A publication*]
**Ins** ............ Insula [*A publication*]
**INS** ............ Insular
**INS** ............ Insulate
**INS** ............ Insurance [*A publication*]
**INS** ............ Insurance (AFM)
**INS** ............ Insure
**INS** ............ Integrated Navigation System
**INS** ............ Integrated Network Systems, Inc.
**I-NS** .......... Inter-Nation Simulation [*Simulation of international relations*]
**INS** ............ Interchangeable-Substitute Items (AAG)
**INS** ............ Internal Navigation System
**INS** ............ International Navigation System
**INS** ............ International Network for Self-Reliance (EA)
**INS** ............ International News Service [*Later, UPI*]
**INS** ............ International Numismatic Society (EAIO)
**INS** ............ Interstation Noise Suppression
**INS** ............ Intravenous Nurses Society (EA)
**INS** ............ Ion-Neutralization Spectroscopy
**INS** ............ Iron Nickel System
**INS** ............ Iron Soldering
**INS** ............ Israel Naval Ship (BJA)
**INS** ............ Israel News Service (BJA)
**INS** ............ Northern Illinois Library System, Rockford, IL [*OCLC symbol*] (OCLC)
**InS** ............ South Bend Public Library, South Bend, IN [*Library symbol*] [*Library of Congress*] (LCLS)
**INSA** .......... Institut National de Systematique Appliquee [*Canada*]
**INSA** .......... International Naples Sabot Association (EA)
**INSA** .......... International Shipowners' Association [*See also MAS*] [*Gdynia, Poland*] (EAIO)
**InSa** ........... Salem Public Library, Salem, IN [*Library symbol*] [*Library of Congress*] (LCLS)
**INSAA** ....... Ingegneria Sanitaria [*A publication*]
**INSAB** ....... International Numismatic Society Authentication Bureau (EA)
**INSA Bull** ... Indian National Science Academy. Bulletin [*A publication*]
**InSaCR** ...... Washington County Recorder's Office, Salem, IN [*Library symbol*] [*Library of Congress*] (LCLS)
**INSACS** ..... Information Network in Social and Community Services [*Australia*]
**INSACS** ..... Interstate Airways Communications Station
**INSAFI** ...... Instituto Salvadoreno de Fomento Industrial [*Industrial promotion agency*] [*El Salvador*]
**INSAIR** ..... Inspector of Naval Aircraft
**InSaLD** ...... Salem Leader/Democrat, Salem, IN [*Library symbol*] [*Library of Congress*] (LCLS)
**INSAR** ....... Instruction Address Register [*Data processing*]
**INSAT** ....... Indian National Satellite System [*Bangalore, India*] [*Telecommunications*]
**INSATRAC** ... Interception with Satellite Tracking
**INSAV** ....... Interim Shipboard Availability (MCD)
**InSaWHi** ... Washington County Historical Society, Salem, IN [*Library symbol*] [*Library of Congress*] (LCLS)
**INSB** .......... Intelligence and Security Board [*Army*] (RDA)

**In-SC** ......... Indiana State Supreme Court, Law Library, Indianapolis, IN [*Library symbol*] [*Library of Congress*] (LCLS)
**INSC**.......... Inscribed [*or Inscription*] (MSA)
**INSC**.......... Insulating Concrete [*Technical drawings*]
**Ins C**........... Insurance Code [*A publication*] (DLA)
**INSC**.......... Internal Shape Components (CINC)
**InSc**............ Scott County Public Library, Scottsburg, IN [*Library symbol*] [*Library of Congress*] (LCLS)
**INSCA**....... International Natural Sausage Casing Association (EA)
**INSCAIRS** ... Instrumentation Calibration Incident Repair Service
**INSCE**....... Insurance
**Inschr**......... Inschrift (BJA)
**INSCI**........ Information Science, Incorporated [*Information service or system*] (IID)
**INSCOM**... Intelligence and Security Command [*Army*] (RDA)
**Ins Coun J** ... Insurance Counsel Journal [*A publication*]
**Ins Counsel J** ... Insurance Counsel Journal [*A publication*]
**Ins Couns J** ... Insurance Counsel Journal [*A publication*] (DLA)
**INSCR**....... Inscription
**INSCRUIT** ... Inspector of Navy Recruiting and Naval Officer Procurement
**INSD** ......... Insured
**INSDC**....... Indian National Scientific Documentation Centre [*New Delhi*]
**INSDEN**.... Inspector of Dental Activities
**INSDOC**.... Indian National Scientific Documentation Centre [*Council of Scientific and Industrial Research*] [*New Delhi, India*]
**INSEA**....... International Society for Education through Art [*Corsham, England*]
**In Search**.... In Search/En Quete [*Canada*] [*A publication*]
**INSEC**....... Internal Security
**Insecta Matsum** ... Insecta Matsumurana [*A publication*]
**Insecta Matsumurana Suppl** ... Insecta Matsumurana. Supplement [*A publication*]
**Insect Answers Coop Ext Serv Wash St Univ** ... Insect Answers. Cooperative Extension Service. Washington State University [*A publication*]
**Insect Bioc** ... Insect Biochemistry [*A publication*]
**Insect Biochem** ... Insect Biochemistry [*A publication*]
**Insect Dis Rep US For Serv North Reg** ... Insect Disease Report. United States Forest Service. Northern Region [*A publication*]
**Insect Ecol** ... Insect Ecology [*A publication*]
**Insectes Soc** ... Insectes Sociaux [*A publication*]
**INSECTI**... Insecticide(s) [*Freight*]
**Insectic Acaricide Tests** ... Insecticide and Acaricide Tests [*A publication*]
**Insect Sci Appl** ... Insect Science and Its Application [*A publication*]
**Insect Sci Its Applica** ... Insect Science and Its Application [*A publication*]
**Insects Micronesia** ... Insects of Micronesia [*A publication*]
**Insect Soc**... Insectes Sociaux [*Social Insects*] [*A publication*]
**Insects Soc Soc Insects** ... Insectes Sociaux/Social Insects [*A publication*]
**Insect Wld Dig** ... Insect World Digest [*A publication*]
**INSEE**....... Institut National de la Statistique et des Etudes Economiques [*National Institute of Statistics and Economic Research*] [*Paris, France*]
**InSelS**........ Sellersburg Star, Sellersburg, IN [*Library symbol*] [*Library of Congress*] (LCLS)
**INSEM**...... Insemination
**INSENG**.... Inspector of Naval Engineering
**INSEP**....... Inseparable (MSA)
**INSERM**... Institut National de la Sante et de la Recherche Medicale [*National Institute for Health and Medical Research*] [*France*] [*Information service or system*] (IID)
**INSERM Colloq** ... INSERM [*Institut National de la Sante et de la Recherche Medicale*] Colloque [*A publication*]
**INSERM Symp** ... INSERM [*Institut National de la Sante et de la Recherche Medicale*] Symposia [*A publication*]
**INSERV**.... In Service [*Military*] (CAAL)
**InSey**.......... Seymour Public Library, Seymour, IN [*Library symbol*] [*Library of Congress*] (LCLS)
**InSeyT**....... Seymour Daily Tribune, Seymour, IN [*Library symbol*] [*Library of Congress*] (LCLS)
**INSF**.......... Insulating Fill [*Technical drawings*]
**Ins Field (Fire Ed)** ... Insurance Field (Fire and Casualty Edition) [*A publication*]
**Ins Field (Life Ed)** ... Insurance Field (Life Edition) [*A publication*]
**INSGCY**.... Insurgency (AABC)
**INSGEN**.... Inspector General [*Navy*]
**INSGENLANTFLT** ... Inspector General, Atlantic Fleet [*Navy*]
**INSGENPAC** ... Inspector General, Pacific Fleet and Pacific Ocean Areas [*Navy*]
**Ins Geog Geol Estado Sao Paulo Bol** ... Instituto Geografico e Geologico. Estado de Sao Paulo. Boletim [*A publication*]
**INSH**......... Inspection Shell
**INSH**......... International Shipholding Corp. [*NASDAQ symbol*] (NQ)
**InShe**.......... Shelbyville-Shelby County Public Library, Shelbyville, IN [*Library symbol*] [*Library of Congress*] (LCLS)
**InSheCR**.... Shelby County Recorder's Office, Shelbyville, IN [*Library symbol*] [*Library of Congress*] (LCLS)
**InSheN** ...... Shelbyville News, Shelbyville, IN [*Library symbol*] [*Library of Congress*] (LCLS)
**InSherN**..... Sheridan News, Sheridan, IN [*Library symbol*] [*Library of Congress*] (LCLS)
**InSho**......... Shoals Public Library, Shoals, IN [*Library symbol*] [*Library of Congress*] (LCLS)
**InShoD** ...... Martin County Democrat, Shoals, IN [*Library symbol*] [*Library of Congress*] (LCLS)
**InShoHi**..... Martin County Historical Society, Shoals, IN [*Library symbol*] [*Library of Congress*] (LCLS)
**InShoN** ...... Shoals News, Shoals, IN [*Library symbol*] [*Library of Congress*] (LCLS)
**INSHOREPAT** ... Inshore Patrol
**INSHORUNSEAWARGRU** ... Inshore Undersea Warfare Group [*Navy*]
**INSI**........... Information Science, Inc. [*NASDAQ symbol*] (NQ)
**INSI**........... Insight [*A publication*]
**INSIA**......... Industria Saccarifera Italiana [*A publication*]
**Inside Canb** ... Inside Canberra [*A publication*] (APTA)
**Inside Educ** ... Inside Education [*A publication*]
**Inside Prt**... Inside Print. The Voice of Print Advertising [*A publication*]
**Insiders' Chr** ... Insiders' Chronicle [*A publication*]
**INSILCO**... International Silver Company [*Acronym now used as firm's name*]
**INSINSTR** ... Inspector-Instructor, Naval Reserve
**INSIS**......... Inter-Institutional Integrated Services Information System
**INSITE**...... Institutional Space Inventory Technique [*Data processing*]
**INSITE**...... Integrated Sensor Interpretation Techniques
**In Situ Oil Coal Shale Miner** ... In Situ. Oil-Coal-Shale-Minerals [*A publication*]
**INSL**.......... Insulate
**INSLAW**... Institute for Law and Social Research (IID)
**Ins Law J**... Insurance Law Journal [*A publication*]
**Ins Liability Rep** ... Insurance Liability Reports [*A publication*] (DLA)
**Ins L J**........ Insurance Law Journal [*A publication*]
**Ins LR**........ Insurance Law Reporter [*A publication*] (DLA)
**Ins LR**........ Insurance Litigation Reporter [*A publication*]
**Ins L Rep**... Insurance Law Reporter [*A publication*] (DLA)
**Ins L Rep CCH** ... Insurance Law Reports. Commerce Clearing House [*A publication*]
**INSM**........ Insituform Mid-America, Inc. [*NASDAQ symbol*] (NQ)
**INSMACH** ... Inspector of Naval Machinery
**INSMAT**... Inspector of Naval Material
**INSMAT PET** ... Inspector of Naval Material, Petroleum
**INSMD4**... Intersectum [*A publication*]
**Ins Mon**..... Insurance Monitor [*A publication*] (DLA)
**INSNA**...... International Network for Social Network Analysis [*University of Toronto*] [*Toronto, ON*] (EAIO)
**INSNAVMAT** ... Inspector of Navigational Material
**InSNHi**...... Northern Indiana State Historical Society, South Bend, IN [*Library symbol*] [*Library of Congress*] (LCLS)
**INSO**......... Innovative Software, Inc. [*NASDAQ symbol*] (NQ)
**INSOA7**.... Insectes Sociaux [*Social Insects*] [*A publication*]
**INSOL**...... Insoluble (MSA)
**INSOLT**.... I've Never Seen One Like That [*Antiques market*]
**Insolv**......... Insolvency [*Legal term*] (DLA)
**INSOLV**.... Insolvent [*Legal term*] (ADA)
**INSOLVT**... Insolvent (ROG)
**INSORD**.... Inspector of Ordnance
**INSORDINC** ... Inspector of Ordnance in Charge
**InSow**......... South Whitley Cleveland Township Public Library, South Whitley, IN [*Library symbol*] [*Library of Congress*] (LCLS)
**InSowTN**... South Whitley Tribune-News, South Whitley, IN [*Library symbol*] [*Library of Congress*] (LCLS)
**INSP**.......... Inspect [*or Inspector*] (AFM)
**INSP**.......... InSpeech, Inc. [*Norristown, PA*] [*NASDAQ symbol*] (NQ)
**INSP**.......... Inspiration
**InSp**........... Speedway Public Library, Speedway, IN [*Library symbol*] [*Library of Congress*] (LCLS)
**Insp Adv**..... Inspection and Advice [*A publication*]
**INSPAT**.... Inshore Patrol
**InSpe**.......... Spencer Public-Owen County Contractual Library, Spencer, IN [*Library symbol*] [*Library of Congress*] (LCLS)
**INSPEC**..... Information Services in Physics, Electronics, and Computers [*Information service or system*]
**INSPEC**..... Initial Specialty [*Military*] (INF)
**INSPEC**..... Inspection
**INSPEC**..... International Information Services for the Physics and Engineering Communities
**INSPECT** ... Integrated Nationwide System for Processing Entries from Customs Terminals [*Australia*]
**INSPEL**..... INSPEL. International Journal of Special Libraries [*A publication*]
**INSPEL**..... International Newsletter of Special Libraries [*A publication*]
**INSPEL**..... International Newsletter of Special Libraries. IFLA [*International Federation of Library Associations*] [*A publication*]
**INSPETRES** ... Inspector of Petroleum Reserves
**InSpeW**...... Spencer Evening World, Spencer, IN [*Library symbol*] [*Library of Congress*] (LCLS)
**INSPEX**..... International Measurement and Inspection Technology Exposition (TSPED)
**INSP-INSTR** ... Inspector-Instruction [*Marine Corps*]
**INSPIR**...... Inspiretur [*Let It Be Inspired*] [*Pharmacy*]

**INSPIRE**... Institute for Public Interest Representation [*Later, CCCIPR*] [*Georgetown University*]
**INSP L**........ Inspection Laws (DLA)
**INSPON**.... Inspection (ROG)
**INSPR**....... Inspector
**INSPR**....... Intelligence Systems Program Review [*Military*] (MCD)
**INSP W & M**... Inspector of Weights and Measures [*British*] (ROG)
**INSR**.......... Insert (MSA)
**INSRADMAT**... Inspector of Radio Material
**INSRAG**.... Instrumentation [*A publication*]
**INSRE**....... Institut National de la Statistique et de la Recherche Economique [*National Institute of Statistics and Economic Research*] [*Ministry of Finance and Economy*] [*Information service or system*] (IID)
**Ins Rep**....... Insurance Reporter [*A publication*] (DLA)
**Insrg Soc**.... Insurgent Sociologist [*A publication*]
**INSRP**....... Inter-Agency Network Safety Review Panel [*NASA*] (NASA)
**INSRP**....... Interagency Nuclear Safety Review Panel
**INSSCC**..... Interim National Space Surveillance Control Center
**Inst**............ Coke's Institutes [*England*] [*A publication*] (DLA)
**INST**.......... In Nomine Sanctae Trinitatis [*In the Name of the Holy Trinity*] [*Latin*]
**INST**.......... Insert Screw Thread
**INST**.......... Installed
**INST**.......... Installment [*Business term*]
**INST**.......... Instans [*The Current Month*] [*Latin*]
**INST**.......... Instant
**INST**.......... Instantaneous (MSA)
**INST**.......... Institute [*or Institution*] (AFM)
**Inst**............ Institutes of England, in Two Parts, or A Commentary upon Littleton by Sir Edward Coke [*A publication*] (DLA)
**Inst**............ Institutio Oratoria [*of Quintilian*] [*Classical studies*] (OCD)
**Inst**............ Institutions [*A publication*]
**INST**.......... Instruction [*or Instructor*] (AFM)
**Inst**............ Instructor [*A publication*]
**INST**.......... Instrument (AAG)
**INST**.......... International Numbering System for Tides (MSC)
**Inst**............ Justinian's Institutes [*A publication*] (DLA)
**INST**.......... Revenue Canada - Customs and Excise Institutions List [*Revenue Canada - Customs and Excise*] [*Information service or system*] (CRD)
**InST**........... South Bend Tribune, South Bend, IN [*Library symbol*] [*Library of Congress*] (LCLS)
**INSTA**....... Instruments Authorized [*Aviation*] (FAAC)
**INSTA**....... Inter-Nordic Standardization
**INSTA**....... Interstate (FAAC)
**INSTAAR**... Institute of Arctic and Alpine Research [*University of Colorado*]
**INSTAB**.... Information Service on Toxicity and Biodegradability [*Water Pollution Research Laboratory*] [*British*] (IID)
**InstAct**....... Institute of Actuaries [*British*]
**Inst Actuaries J**... Journal. Institute of Actuaries [*A publication*]
**INSTAD**.... Institute for Training and Development
**Inst Ad Legal Stud Ann**... Institute of Advanced Legal Studies. Annals [*A publication*] (DLA)
**Inst Aeronaut Sci Sherman M. Fairchild Publ Fund Prepr**... Institute of the Aeronautical Sciences. Sherman M. Fairchild Publication Fund. Preprint [*A publication*]
**Inst Afr Stud**... Institute of African Studies [*A publication*]
**Inst Agric Res Annu Rep (Addis Ababa)**... Institute of Agricultural Research. Annual Report (Addis Ababa) [*A publication*]
**Inst Agric Res Annu Res Semin Proc (Addis Ababa)**... Institute of Agricultural Research. Annual Research Seminar. Proceedings (Addis Ababa) [*A publication*]
**Inst Agric Res Prog Rep (Addis Ababa)**... Institute of Agricultural Research. Progress Report (Addis Ababa) [*A publication*]
**Inst Agric Res Samaru Annu Rep**... Institute of Agricultural Research. Samaru. Annual Report [*A publication*]
**Inst Agron Dr Petru Groza (Cluj) Lucr Stiint Ser Agric**... Institutul Agronomic "Dr. Petru Groza" (Cluj). Lucrari Stiintifice. Seria Agricultura [*A publication*]
**Inst Agron Dr Petru Groza (Cluj) Lucr Stiint Ser Med Vet**... Institutul Agronomic "Dr. Petru Groza" (Cluj). Lucrari Stiintifice. Seria Medicina Veterinara [*A publication*]
**Inst Agron Dr Petru Groza (Cluj) Lucr Stiint Ser Zooteh**... Institutul Agronomic "Dr. Petru Groza" (Cluj). Lucrari Stiintifice. Seria Zootehnie [*A publication*]
**Inst Agron Ion Ionescu de la Brad (Iasi) Lucr Stiint**... Institutul Agronomic "Ion Ionescu de la Brad" (Iasi). Lucrari Stiintifice [*A publication*]
**Inst Agron Timisoara Lucr Stiint Ser Agron**... Institutul Agronomic Timisoara Lucrari Stiintifice. Seria Agronomie [*A publication*]
**Inst Agron Timisoara Lucr Stiint Ser Med Vet**... Institutul Agronomic Timisoara Lucrari Stiintifice. Seria Medicina Veterinara [*A publication*]
**Inst Agron Timisoara Lucr Stiint Ser Zooteh**... Institutul Agronomic Timisoara Lucrari Stiintifice. Seria Zootehnie [*A publication*]
**INSTAL**.... Installation
**Inst Alatne Masine Alate Monogr**... Institut za Alatne Masine i Alate. Monografije [*A publication*]
**Inst Alatne Masine Alate Saopstenja**... Institut za Alatne Masine i Alate. Saopstenja [*A publication*]
**Installatore Ital**... Installatore Italiano [*A publication*]
**Install Ital**... Installatore Italiano [*Italy*] [*A publication*]
**INSTALLN**... Installation
**Inst Anim Physiol Rep**... Institute of Animal Physiology. Report [*A publication*]
**Inst Antart Argent Contrib**... Instituto Antartico Argentino. Contribuciones [*A publication*]
**Inst Antart Chileno Bol**... Instituto Antartico Chileno. Boletin [*A publication*]
**Instant Res**... Instant Research on Peace and Violence [*A publication*]
**Instant Res Peace Violence**... Instant Research on Peace and Violence [*A publication*]
**Inst Appl Res Nat Resour (Abu Ghraib Iraq) Tech Rep**... Institute for Applied Research on Natural Resources (Abu-Ghraib, Iraq). Technical Report [*A publication*]
**Inst Appl Res Nat Resour Tech Rep (Bull)**... Institute for Applied Research on Natural Resources. Technical Report (Bulletin) [*A publication*]
**INSTAR**.... Inertialess Scanning, Tracking, and Ranging
**Inst Arch Ethnog**... Internationales Archiv fuer Ethnographie [*A publication*]
**Inst Arct Alp Res Univ Colo Occas Pap**... Institute of Arctic and Alpine Research. University of Colorado. Occasional Paper [*A publication*]
**INSTARS**... Information Storage and Retrieval System [*Data processing*]
**Inst At Energ I V Kurchatova Rap IAE**... Institut Atomnoi Energii Imeni I. V. Kurchatova. Raport IAE [*A publication*]
**Inst Aust Foundrymen Annu Proc**... Institute of Australian Foundrymen. Annual Proceedings [*A publication*]
**Inst Bankers J**... Institute of Bankers. Journal [*A publication*]
**Inst Bauwissenschaftliche Forsch Publ**... Institut fuer Bauwissenschaftliche Forschung. Publikation [*A publication*]
**Inst Bauwissensch Forsch Publ**... Institut fuer Bauwissenschaftliche Forschung. Publikation [*Switzerland*] [*A publication*]
**Inst BE**....... Institution of British Engineers
**Inst Belge Amelior Betterave Publ**... Institut Belge pour l'Amelioration de la Betterave. Publication [*A publication*]
**Inst Belge Amelior Betterave Publ Trimest**... Institut Belge pour l'Amelioration de la Betterave. Publication Trimestrielle [*A publication*]
**Inst Biol Apl Publ (Barcelona)**... Instituto de Biologia Aplicada. Publicaciones (Barcelona) [*A publication*]
**Inst Biol Bahia Bol**... Instituto Biologico da Bahia. Boletim [*A publication*]
**Inst Biol J**.. Institute of Biology [*London*]. Journal [*A publication*]
**Inst Biol (Lond) Symp**... Institute of Biology (London). Symposium [*A publication*]
**Inst Biol Mar (Mar Del Plata) Contrib**... Instituto de Biologia Marina (Mar Del Plata). Contribucion [*A publication*]
**Inst Biol Mar (Mar Del Plata) Mem Anu**... Instituto de Biologia Marina (Mar Del Plata). Memoria Anual [*A publication*]
**Inst Biol Mar (Mar Del Plata) Ser Contrib**... Instituto de Biologia Marina (Mar Del Plata). Serie Contribuciones [*A publication*]
**Inst Biol Pesqui Tecnol (Curitiba) Bol**... Instituto de Biologia e Pesquisas Tecnologicas (Curitiba). Boletim [*A publication*]
**Inst Biol Scheikd Onderz Landbouwgewassen (Wageningen) Jaarb**... Instituut voor Biologisch en Scheikundig Onderzoek van Landbouwgewassen (Wageningen). Jaarboek [*A publication*]
**Inst Biol Scheikd Onderz Landbouwgewassen (Wageningen) Meded**... Instituut voor Biologisch en Scheikundig Onderzoek van Landbouwgewassen (Wageningen). Mededeling [*A publication*]
**Inst Biol Stud Biol**... Institute of Biology's Studies in Biology [*A publication*]
**Inst Biol Symp (Lond)**... Institute of Biology. Symposia (London) [*A publication*]
**Inst Bodemvruchtbaarheid Haren-Gr Jaarversl**... Instituut voor Bodemvruchtbaarheid Haren-Groningen. Jaarverslag [*A publication*]
**Inst Bodemvruchtbaarheid Haren-Gr Rapp**... Instituut voor Bodemvruchtbaarheid Haren-Groningen. Rapport [*A publication*]
**Inst Bodemvruchtbaarheid Jaarversl**... Instituut voor Bodemvruchtbaarheid. Jaarverslag [*A publication*]
**Inst Bodemvruchtbaarheid Rapp**... Instituut voor Bodemvruchtbaarheid. Rapport [*A publication*]
**Inst Bot Acad Sin Monogr Ser**... Institute of Botany. Academia Sinica Monograph Series [*A publication*]
**Inst Bot "Dr Goncalo Sampaio" Fac Cien Univ Porto Publ**... Instituto de Botanica "Dr. Goncalo Sampaio." Faculdade de Ciencias. Universidade do Porto. Publicacoes [*A publication*]
**Inst Brew (Aust NZ Sect) Proc Conv**... Institute of Brewing (Australia and New Zealand Section). Proceedings of the Convention [*A publication*]
**Inst Br Geographers Trans**... Institute of British Geographers. Transactions [*A publication*]
**Inst Br Geogr Trans**... Institute of British Geographers. Transactions [*A publication*]
**INSTBY**.... Instability (FAAC)

**Inst Cancer Res (Phila) Sci Rep** ... Institute for Cancer Research (Philadelphia). Scientific Report [*A publication*]
**Inst Cercet Ind Chim Aliment Lucr Cercet** ... Institutul de Cercetari pentru Industrie si Chimie Alimentara. Lucrari de Cercetare [*A publication*]
**Inst Certif Mech Electr Eng S Afr Arthur Hallet Mem Lect** ... Institution of Certificated Mechanical and Electrical Engineers. South Africa. Arthur Hallet Memorial Lectures [*A publication*]
**Inst Chem Eng Q Bull** ... Institution of Chemical Engineers. Quarterly Bulletin [*A publication*]
**Inst Chem Eng Symp Ser** ... Institution of Chemical Engineers. Symposium Series [*A publication*]
**Inst Chem Eng Trans** ... Institution of Chemical Engineers. Transactions [*A publication*]
**Inst Chem Irel J** ... Institute of Chemistry of Ireland. Journal [*A publication*]
**Inst Chim Aliment Lucr Cercet** ... Institutul de Chimie Alimentara. Lucrari de Cercetare [*A publication*]
**Inst Ciencias Socs R** ... Revista. Instituto de Ciencias Sociales [*A publication*]
**Inst Cienc Nat Mat Univ El Salvador Comun** ... Instituto de Ciencias Naturales y Matematicas. Universidad de El Salvador. Comunicaciones [*A publication*]
**Inst Civ Engr Proc** ... Institution of Civil Engineers. Proceedings [*A publication*]
**Inst Civ Engrs Proc Part 1** ... Institution of Civil Engineers. Proceedings. Part 1. Design and Construction [*A publication*]
**Inst Civ Engrs Proc Part 2** ... Institution of Civil Engineers. Proceedings. Part 2. Research and Theory [*A publication*]
**Inst Cler**..... Instructor Clericalis (DLA)
**Inst of Clerks of Works Jnl** ... Institute of Clerks of Works. Journal [*A publication*]
**Inst Colomb Agropecu Bol Tec** ... Instituto Colombiano Agropecuario. Boletin Tecnico [*A publication*]
**Inst Com Com** ... Interstate Commerce Commission Reports [*A publication*] (DLA)
**INST/COMM** ... Instrumentation and Communication (MCD)
**Inst Control Engrg** ... Technical University of Poznan. Institute of Control Engineering [*A publication*]
**Inst Cubano Invest Tecnol Ser Estud Trab Invest** ... Instituto Cubano de Investigaciones Tecnologicas. Serie de Estudios sobre Trabajos de Investigacion [*Cuba*] [*A publication*]
**INSTD**....... Instead (ROG)
**InstD**.......... Institute of Directors [*British*]
**Inst Def Anal Pap** ... Institute for Defense Analyses. Paper [*A publication*]
**Inst Def Stud Anal J** ... Institute for Defence Studies and Analyses. Journal [*A publication*]
**Inst Dent Res Bienn Rep (Syd)** ... Institute of Dental Research. Biennial Report (Sydney) [*A publication*]
**Inst Dent Res United Dent Hosp Sydney Annu Rep** ... Institute of Dental Research. United Dental Hospital of Sydney. Annual Report [*A publication*]
**Inst Dev Stud Bull** ... Institute of Development Studies. Bulletin [*England*] [*A publication*]
**InstDokAB** ... Institutionendokumentation zur Arbeitsmarkt- und Berufsforschung [*Database*] [*Institut fuer Arbeitsmarkt- und Berufsforschung der Bundesanstalt fuer Arbeit*] [*German*] [*Information service or system*] (CRD)
**Inst E B**...... Instituto de Estudos Brasileiros [*A publication*]
**Inst Econ Prod Ganad Ebro Comun** ... Instituto de Economia y Producciones Ganaderas del Ebro. Comunicaciones [*A publication*]
**Inst Ecuat Cienc Nat Contrib** ... Instituto Ecuatoriano de Ciencias Naturales. Contribucion [*A publication*]
**Inst E E J**... Institution of Electrical Engineers. Journal [*A publication*]
**Inst E E Proc** ... Institution of Electrical Engineers. Proceedings [*A publication*]
**Inst d'Egypte Bull** ... Institut d'Egypte Bulletin [*A publication*]
**Inst Elec Eng Conf Publ** ... Institution of Electrical Engineers. Conference Publication [*A publication*]
**Inst Elec Eng J** ... Institution of Electrical Engineers. Journal [*A publication*]
**Inst Elect & Electronics Eng Proc** ... Institute of Electrical and Electronics Engineers. Proceedings [*A publication*]
**Inst Elect & Electronics Eng Trans IA** ... Institute of Electrical and Electronics Engineers. Transactions on Industry Application [*A publication*]
**Inst Elect & Electronics Eng Trans PAS** ... Institute of Electrical and Electronics Engineers. Transactions on Power Apparatus and Systems [*A publication*]
**Inst Electron Radio Eng Conf Proc** ... Institution of Electronic and Radio Engineers. Conference Proceedings [*A publication*]
**Inst Electron Telecommun Eng J** ... Institution of Electronics and Telecommunication Engineers. Journal [*A publication*]
**Inst Elie Cartan** ... Institut Elie Cartan [*A publication*]
**Inst Energ Biul** ... Instytut Energetyki. Biuletyn [*A publication*]
**Inst Eng Aust Chem Eng Aust** ... Institution of Engineers of Australia. Chemical Engineering in Australia [*A publication*] (APTA)
**Inst Eng Aust Chem Eng Trans** ... Institution of Engineers of Australia. Chemical Engineering Transactions [*A publication*] (APTA)
**Inst Eng Aust Civ Eng Trans** ... Institution of Engineers of Australia. Civil Engineering Transactions [*A publication*] (APTA)
**Inst Eng (Aust) Elec Eng Trans** ... Institution of Engineers of Australia. Electrical Engineering Transactions [*A publication*]
**Inst Eng Aust Electr Eng Trans** ... Institution of Engineers of Australia. Electrical Engineering Transactions [*A publication*] (APTA)
**Inst Eng (Aust) Gen Eng Trans** ... Institution of Engineers of Australia. General Engineering Transactions [*A publication*]
**Inst Eng Aust J** ... Institution of Engineers of Australia. Journal [*A publication*] (APTA)
**Inst Eng (Aust) Mech Chem Eng Trans** ... Institution of Engineers of Australia. Mechanical and Chemical Engineering Transactions [*A publication*]
**Inst Eng Aust Mech and Chem Eng Trans** ... Institution of Engineers of Australia. Mechanical and Chemical Engineering Transactions [*A publication*]
**Inst Eng Aust Mech & Chem Trans** ... Institution of Engineers of Australia. Mechanical and Chemical Engineering Transactions [*A publication*] (APTA)
**Inst Eng (Aust) Mech Eng Trans** ... Institution of Engineers of Australia. Mechanical Engineering Transactions [*A publication*]
**Inst Eng Aust Queensland Div Tech Pap** ... Institution of Engineers of Australia. Queensland Division. Technical Papers [*A publication*] (APTA)
**Inst Eng Aust South Aust Div Bull** ... Institution of Engineers of Australia. South Australia Division. Bulletin [*A publication*] (APTA)
**Inst Eng (Ceylon) Trans** ... Institution of Engineers (Ceylon). Transactions [*A publication*]
**Inst Engineers Aust J** ... Institution of Engineers of Australia. Journal [*A publication*] (APTA)
**Inst Engrs Tas Bul** ... Institution of Engineers of Australia. Tasmania Division. Bulletin [*A publication*] (APTA)
**Inst Environ Sci Annu Tech Meet Proc** ... Institute of Environmental Sciences. Annual Technical Meeting. Proceedings [*A publication*]
**Inst Environ Sci Proc** ... Institute of Environmental Sciences. Proceedings [*A publication*]
**Inst Environ Sci Tech Meet Proc** ... Institute of Environmental Sciences. Technical Meeting. Proceedings [*A publication*]
**INSTEP**..... Indian Steel Training and Education Program [*India*]
**Inst Epil**..... Epilogue to (a Designated Part or Volume of) Coke's Institutes [*A publication*] (DLA)
**Inst Ernaehrungsforsch (Rueschlikon-Zuerich) Schriftenr** ... Institut fuer Ernaehrungsforschung (Rueschlikon-Zuerich). Schriftenreihe [*A publication*]
**Inst Esp Oceanogr Notas Resumenes** ... Instituto Espanol de Oceanografia. Notas y Resumenes [*A publication*]
**Inst Estate Plan** ... Institute on Estate Planning [*A publication*]
**Inst Ethmus Sel Repts** ... Institute of Ethnomusicology. Selected Reports [*A publication*]
**Inst Exp Invest Fom Agric Ganad (St Fe) Publ Tec** ... Instituto Experimental de Investigacion y Fomento Agricola-Ganadero (Santa Fe). Publicacion Tecnica [*A publication*]
**InstF**........... Institute of Fuel [*British*]
**Inst Farb Lakierow Biul Inf** ... Instytut Farb i Lakierow. Biuletyn Informacyjny [*A publication*]
**Inst Fed Rech For Mem** ... Institut Federal de Recherches Forestieres. Memoires [*A publication*]
**Inst Fed Tax** ... Institute on Federal Taxation (DLA)
**Inst Ferment Res Commun (Osaka)** ... Institute for Fermentation Research Communications (Osaka) [*A publication*]
**Inst Fire Eng Q** ... Institution of Fire Engineers. Quarterly [*A publication*]
**Inst Fisico-Geog Nac Costa Rica An** ... Instituto Fisico-Geografico Nacional de Costa Rica. Anales [*A publication*]
**Inst Fiz At Rep (Rom)** ... Institutul de Fizica Atomica. Report (Romania) [*A publication*]
**Inst Fiz Ing Nucl Rep (Rom)** ... Institutul de Fizica si Inginerie Nucleara. Report (Romania) [*A publication*]
**Inst Florest Bol Tec (Sao Paulo)** ... Instituto Florestal. Boletim Tecnico (Sao Paulo) [*A publication*]
**Inst Florest Publ (Sao Paulo)** ... Instituto Florestal. Publicacao (Sao Paulo) [*A publication*]
**INSTFLTNG** ... Instrument Flight Training (NVT)
**Inst Folk** .... Boletin. Instituto de Folklore [*A publication*]
**Inst Fom Algod (Bogota)** ... Instituto de Fomento Algodonero (Bogota) [*A publication*]
**Inst Fom Pesq Bol Cient** ... Instituto de Fomento Pesquero. Boletin Cientifico [*A publication*]
**Inst Fom Pesq Publ** ... Instituto de Fomento Pesquero. Publicacion [*A publication*]
**Inst Fondam Afr Noire Bull Ser A** ... Institut Fondamental d'Afrique Noire. Bulletin. Serie A. Sciences Naturelles [*Dakar*] [*A publication*]
**Inst For Aust Newslett** ... Institute of Foresters of Australia. Newsletter [*A publication*] (APTA)
**Inst Foresters Aust Newsl** ... Institute of Foresters of Australia. Newsletter [*A publication*] (APTA)
**Inst Foresters Aust Newslett** ... Institute of Foresters of Australia. Newsletter [*A publication*] (APTA)
**Inst For Invest Exp Comun** ... Instituto Forestal de Investigaciones y Experiencias (Madrid). Comunicacion [*A publication*]
**Inst For Invest Exper (Madrid) An** ... Instituto Forestal de Investigaciones y Experiencias (Madrid). Anales [*A publication*]
**Inst For Invest Exper (Madrid) Bol** ... Instituto Forestal de Investigaciones y Experiencias (Madrid). Boletin [*A publication*]

**Inst For Invest Exper (Madrid) Comun** ... Instituto Forestal de Investigaciones y Experiencias (Madrid). Comunicacion [*A publication*]
**Inst For Invest Exper (Madrid) Trab** ... Instituto Forestal de Investigaciones y Experiencias (Madrid). Trabajos [*A publication*]
**Inst For Nac Foll Tec For** ... Instituto Forestal Nacional. Folleto Tecnico Forestal [*A publication*]
**Inst For Prod Colleg For Resour Univ Wash Contrib** ... Institute of Forest Products. College of Forest Resources. University of Washington. Contribution [*A publication*]
**Inst Forum** ... Institute Forum [*A publication*]
**Inst For Zool Res Notes** ... Institute of Forest Zoology. Research Notes [*A publication*]
**Inst Francais d'Haiti Mem** ... Institut Francais d'Haiti. Memoires [*A publication*]
**Inst Francais Petrole Rev** ... Institut Francais du Petrole. Revue et Annales des Combustible Liquides [*Later, Institut Francais du Petrole. Revue*] [*A publication*]
**Inst Fr Cafe Cacao Bull** ... Institut Francais du Cafe et du Cacao. Bulletin [*A publication*]
**Inst Freshwater Res (Drottningholm) Rep** ... Institute of Freshwater Research (Drottningholm). Report [*A publication*]
**Inst Freshw Res (Drottningholm) Rep** ... Institute of Freshwater Research (Drottningholm). Report [*A publication*]
**Inst Fr Etud Andines** ... Institut Francais d'Etudes Andines. Bulletin [*A publication*]
**Inst Fr Pet Rev** ... Institut Francais du Petrole. Revue et Annales des Combustible Liquides [*Later, Institut Francais du Petrole. Revue*] [*A publication*]
**Inst Fuel (London) Bull** ... Institute of Fuel (London). Bulletin [*A publication*]
**Inst Fuel (London) Wartime Bull** ... Institute of Fuel (London). Wartime Bulletin [*A publication*]
**Inst Fuel Symp Ser (London)** ... Institute of Fuel. Symposium Series (London) [*A publication*]
**Inst Gas Eng** ... Institution of Gas Engineers. Communications [*Finland*] [*A publication*]
**Inst Gas Eng Commun** ... Institution of Gas Engineers. Communications [*A publication*]
**Inst Gas Eng J** ... Institution of Gas Engineers. Journal [*A publication*]
**Inst Gas Technol** ... Institute of Gas Technology [*A publication*]
**Inst Gas Technol (Chicago) Res Bull** ... Institute of Gas Technology (Chicago). Research Bulletin [*A publication*]
**Inst Gas Technol (Chicago) Tech Rep** ... Institute of Gas Technology (Chicago). Technical Report [*A publication*]
**Inst Gemol Esp Bol** ... Instituto Gemologico Espanol. Boletin [*A publication*]
**Inst Geofis Andes Colomb Publ Ser A** ... Instituto Geofisico de los Andes Colombianos. Publicacion. Serie A. Sismologia [*A publication*]
**Inst Geog Nac Bol Geol (Guatemala)** ... Instituto Geografico Nacional. Boletin Geologico (Guatemala) [*A publication*]
**Inst Geogr Geol Estado Sao Paulo Bol** ... Instituto Geografico e Geologico. Estado de Sao Paulo. Boletim [*A publication*]
**Inst Geogr Na (Guatem) Bol Geol** ... Instituto Geografico Nacional (Guatemala). Boletin Geologico [*A publication*]
**Inst Geol Bassin Aquitaine Bull** ... Institut de Geologie du Bassin d'Aquitaine. Bulletin [*A publication*]
**Inst Geol Bassin Aquitaine Mem** ... Institut de Geologie du Bassin d'Aquitaine. Memoires [*A publication*]
**Inst Geol Geofiz Stud Teh Econ Ser E** ... Institutul de Geologie si Geofizica. Studii Tehnice si Economice. Seria E. Hidrogeologie [*A publication*]
**Inst Geol Geofiz Stud Teh Econ Ser I** ... Institutul de Geologie si Geofizica. Studii Tehnice si Economice. Seria I. Mineralogie-Petrografie [*A publication*]
**Inst Geol Min Esp Mapa Geol Esp** ... Instituto Geologico y Minero de Espana. Mapa Geologico de Espana [*A publication*]
**Inst Geol Min Rev Univ Nac Tucuman** ... Instituto de Geologia y Mineria. Revista. Universidad Nacional de Tucuman [*A publication*]
**Inst Geol Sci Charles Univ Rep Res** ... Institute of Geological Science. Charles University. Report on Research [*A publication*]
**Inst Geol Sci (London) Rep** ... Institute of Geological Sciences (London). Report [*A publication*]
**Inst Geol Sci Overseas Mem** ... Institute of Geological Sciences. Overseas Memoir [*A publication*]
**Inst Geol Sci Rep** ... Institute of Geological Sciences. Report [*England*] [*A publication*]
**Inst Geol Stud Teh Econ Ser E** ... Institutul Geologic. Studii Tehnice si Economice. Seria E. Hidrogeologie [*A publication*]
**Inst Geol Stud Teh Econ Ser I** ... Institutul Geologic. Studii Tehnice si Economice. Seria I. Mineralogie-Petrografie [*A publication*]
**Inst Geol Urug Bol** ... Instituto Geologico del Uruguay. Boletin [*A publication*]
**Inst Geol (Warsaw) Pr** ... Instytut Geolgiczny (Warsaw). Prace [*A publication*]
**Inst Gerontol Ser** ... Institute of Gerontology Series [*A publication*]
**Inst Gezondheidstech TNO Rapp** ... Instituut voor Gezondheidstechniek TNO [*Toegepast-Natuurwetenschappelijk Onderzoek*]. Rapport [*A publication*]
**Inst Goryuch Iskop Tr** ... Institut Goryuchikh Iskopaemykh Trudy [*A publication*]
**Inst Grand Ducal Luxemb Sect Sci Nat Phys Math Arch** ... Institut Grand-Ducal de Luxembourg. Section des Sciences Naturelles. Physiques et Mathematiques. Archives [*A publication*]
**Inst Hautes Etudes Sci Publ Math** ... Institut des Hautes Etudes Scientifiques. Publications Mathematiques [*A publication*]
**Inst Hierro Acero (Madrid) Publ** ... Instituto del Hierro y del Acero (Madrid). Publicaciones [*A publication*]
**Inst Highw Engrs J** ... Institution of Highway Engineers. Journal [*A publication*]
**Inst Husdyrernaer Foringslaere Nor Landbrukshogsk Beret** ... Institutt foer Husdyrernaering og Foringslaere Norges Landbrukshogskole Beretning [*A publication*]
**Inst Husdyrernaering Foringslaere Nor Landbrukshogsk Beret** ... Institutt foer Husdyrernaering og Foringslaere Norges Landbrukshogskole Beretning [*A publication*]
**Inst Hutn Pr** ... Instytutow Hutniczych. Prace [*A publication*]
**Inst Hydromech Wasserwirtsch Eidg Tech Hochsch Zuerich** ... Institut fuer Hydromechanik und Wasserwirtschaft. Eidgenoessische Technische Hochschule Zuerich [*A publication*]
**Insti**........... Institutes of Justinian [*Roman law*] [*A publication*] (DSA)
**INSTIA** ..... Instituto Internacional de Andragogia [*International Institute of Andragogy - IIA*] (EAIO)
**INSTILL** ... Instillandus [*To Be Dropped In*] [*Pharmacy*]
**INSTINET** ... Institutional Networks Corp.
**Inst Int Educ N Bul** ... Institute of International Education. News Bulletin [*A publication*]
**Inst Interam Nino Bol** ... Instituto Interamericano del Nino. Boletin [*A publication*]
**Inst Internat Admin Publique Bul** ... Bulletin. Institut International d'Administration Publique [*A publication*]
**Inst Interuniv Sci Nucl Monogr** ... Institut Interuniversitaire des Sciences Nucleaires. Monographie [*A publication*]
**Inst Interuniv Sci Nucl Rapp Annu** ... Institut Interuniversitaire des Sciences Nucleaires. Rapport Annuel [*A publication*]
**Inst Int Rech Better Congr Hiver CR** ... Institut International de Recherches Betteravieres. Congres d'Hiver. Compte Rendu [*A publication*]
**Inst Int Rech Better CR Definitif Assem** ... Institut International de Recherches Betteravieres. Compte Rendu Definitif de l'Assemblee [*A publication*]
**Inst Int Rech Better Rev** ... Institut International de Recherches Betteravieres. Revue [*A publication*]
**Inst Int Rel Proc** ... Institute of International Relations. Proceedings [*A publication*]
**Inst Int Stat R** ... Institut International de Statistique. Revue [*A publication*]
**Inst Invest** ... Institutional Investor [*A publication*]
**Inst Invest Agron (Angola) Ser Cient** ... Instituto de Investigacao Agronomica (Angola). Serie Cientifica [*A publication*]
**Inst Invest Agron (Angola) Ser Tec** ... Instituto de Investigacao Agronomica (Angola). Serie Tecnica [*A publication*]
**Inst Invest Agron (Mocambique) Ser Mem** ... Instituto de Investigacao Agronomica (Mocambique). Serie Memorias [*A publication*]
**Inst Invest Biomed Univ Nac Auton Mex Inf** ... Instituto de Investigaciones Biomedicas. Universidad Nacional Autonoma de Mexico. Informe [*A publication*]
**Inst Invest Cient (Angola) Relat Comun** ... Instituto de Investigacao Cientifica (Angola). Relatorios e Comunicacoes [*A publication*]
**Inst Investor** ... Institutional Investor [*A publication*]
**Inst Invest Recur Mar (Callao) Inf** ... Instituto de Investigacion de los Recursos Marinos (Callao). Informe [*A publication*]
**Inst Invst**.... Institutional Investor [*A publication*]
**Institutes**.... Institutes of Justinian [*Roman law*] [*A publication*] (DLA)
**Institutiones Math** ... Institutiones Mathematicae [*A publication*]
**Inst Iust**...... Institutiones Iustiniani [*Classical studies*] (OCD)
**InStjN**........ Saint Joe News, Saint Joe, IN [*Library symbol*] [*Library of Congress*] (LCLS)
**Inst Jozef Stefan IJS Porocilo** ... Institut Jozef Stefan. IJS Porocilo [*A publication*]
**Inst Jozef Stefan IJS Rep** ... Institut Jozef Stefan. IJS Report [*A publication*]
**Inst Jur Angl** ... Institutiones Juris Anglicani, by Cowell [*A publication*] (DLA)
**Inst Kerntech Tech Univ (Berlin) Ber** ... Institut fuer Kerntechnik der Technischen Universitaet (Berlin). Bericht [*A publication*]
**Inst Khim Akad Nauk Tadzh SSR Tr** ... Institut Khimii Akademiya Nauk Tadzhikskoi SSR Trudy [*A publication*]
**INSTL**....... Installation (AFM)
**Inst Lab Rel Bull** ... Institute for Labor Relations. Bulletin [*A publication*] (DLA)
**Inst Lake Super Geol Tech Sess Abstr Field Guides** ... Institute on Lake Superior Geology. Technical Sessions, Abstracts, and Field Guides [*A publication*]
**INSTL & C/O** ... Installation and Checkout (NASA)
**Inst Lekow Biul Inf** ... Instytut Lekow. Biuletyn Informacyjny [*A publication*]
**INSTLN**.... Installation
**Inst Locomotive Eng J** ... Institution of Locomotive Engineers. Journal [*A publication*]
**INSTLR**..... Installer
**INSTM**...... Instrumentation (MSA)
**Inst Mar Eng Annu Rep** ... Institute of Marine Engineers. Annual Report [*A publication*]

**Inst Mar Eng Annu Vol** ... Institute of Marine Engineers. Annual Volume [*A publication*]
**Inst Mar Eng Trans** ... Institute of Marine Engineers. Transactions [*A publication*]
**Inst Mar Eng Trans Ser C** ... Institute of Marine Engineers. Transactions. Series C [*A publication*]
**Inst Mar Environ Res Rep** ... Institute for Marine Environmental Research. Report [*A publication*]
**Inst Marine Sci Pub** ... Institute of Marine Science. Publications [*A publication*]
**Inst Mar Peru (Callao) Inf** ... Instituto del Mar del Peru (Callao). Informe [*A publication*]
**Inst Mar Res Lysekil Ser Biol Rep** ... Institute of Marine Research. Lysekil Series Biology Report [*A publication*]
**Inst Mar Sci Rep Univ Alaska** ... Institute of Marine Science. Report. University of Alaska [*A publication*]
**InStmaS**..... St. Mary-Of-The-Woods College, St. Mary-Of-The-Woods, IN [*Library symbol*] [*Library of Congress*] (LCLS)
**Inst Mater Modelos Estruct Bol Tec Univ Cent Venez** ... Instituto de Materiales y Modelos Estructurales. Boletin Tecnico. Universidad Central de Venezuela [*A publication*]
**Inst Mater Ogniotrwalych Biul Inf** ... Instytut Materialow Ogniotrwalych. Biuletyn Informacyjny [*A publication*]
**Inst Math Its Appl Bull** ... Institute of Mathematics and Its Applications. Bulletin [*A publication*]
**Inst Math Statist Bull** ... Institute of Mathematical Statistics. Bulletin [*A publication*]
**Inst Maurice Thorez Cah Hist** ... Cahiers d'Histoire. Institut Maurice Thorez [*A publication*]
**Inst Maurice Thorez Confs** ... Conferences. Institut Maurice Thorez [*A publication*]
**INSTMC**... Institute of Measurement and Control [*London, England*] (EAIO)
**Inst M E**..... Institute of Media Executives [*British*]
**InStme** ....... St. Meinrad College and Seminary, St. Meinrad, IN [*Library symbol*] [*Library of Congress*] (LCLS)
**Inst Mech Eng J & Proc** ... Institution of Mechanical Engineers. Journal and Proceedings [*A publication*]
**Inst Mech Eng (Lond) Proc** ... Institution of Mechanical Engineers (London). Proceedings [*A publication*]
**Inst Mech Eng Proc** ... Institution of Mechanical Engineers. Proceedings [*A publication*]
**Inst Mech Eng Ry Div J** ... Institution of Mechanical Engineers. Railway Division. Journal [*London*] [*A publication*]
**Inst Mech Eng War Emerg Proc** ... Institution of Mechanical Engineers. War Emergency Proceedings [*A publication*]
**Inst Meh Moskov Gos Univ Naucn Trudy** ... Institut Mehaniki Moskovskogo Gosudarstvennogo Universiteta Naucnye Trudy [*A publication*]
**Inst M Eng Tr** ... Institution of Mining Engineers. Transactions [*A publication*]
**InstMet**...... Institute of Metals [*British*]
**Inst Metall Autumn Rev Course Ser 3 (London)** ... Institution of Metallurgists. Autumn Review Course. Series 3 (London) [*A publication*]
**Inst Metall Course Vol Ser 3 (London)** ... Institution of Metallurgists. Course Volume. Series 3 (London) [*A publication*]
**Inst Metall Ser 3 (London)** ... Institution of Metallurgists. Series 3 (London) [*A publication*]
**Inst Metall Spring Resid Course Ser 3 (London)** ... Institution of Metallurgists. Spring Residential Course. Series 3 (London) [*A publication*]
**Inst Metall Tech Conf Pap (London)** ... Institute of Metallurgical Technicians. Conference Papers (London) [*A publication*]
**Inst Metals J** ... Institute of Metals. Journal [*A publication*]
**Inst Metal Zelaza Pr** ... Instytut Metalurgii Zelaza. Prace [*A publication*]
**Inst Meteorol Hidrol Culegere Lucr Meteorol** ... Institutul de Meteorologie si Hidrologie. Culegere de Lucrari de Meteorologie [*A publication*]
**Inst Meteorol Hidrol Stud Cercet Partea 1** ... Institutul de Meteorologie si Hidrologie. Studii si Cercetari. Partea 1. Meteorologie [*A publication*]
**Inst Meteorol Hidrol Stud Cercet Partea 2** ... Institutul de Meteorologie si Hidrologie. Studii si Cercetari. Partea 2. Hidrologie [*A publication*]
**Inst Met Monogr Rep Ser** ... Institute of Metals. Monograph and Report Series [*A publication*]
**Inst Met Niezelazn Biul** ... Instytut Metali Niezelaznych. Biuletyn [*A publication*]
**Inst Mex Minas Met Inf** ... Instituto Mexicano de Minas y Metalurgia. Informes y Memorias [*A publication*]
**Inst Mex Pet Publ** ... Instituto Mexicano del Petroleo. Publicacion [*A publication*]
**Inst Mex Petrol Rev** ... Institute Mexicano del Petroleo. Revista [*A publication*]
**Inst Mex Recur Nat Renov Ser Mesas Redondas** ... Instituto Mexicano de Recursos Naturales Renovables. Serie de Mesas Redondas [*A publication*]
**Inst Microbiol Rutgers Univ Annu Rep** ... Institute of Microbiology. Rutgers University. Annual Report [*A publication*]
**Inst Mine Petrosani Lucr Stiint** ... Institutul de Mine Petrosani. Lucrarile Stiintifice [*A publication*]
**Inst Mining Met Trans Sect B** ... Institution of Mining and Metallurgy. Transactions. Section B. Applied Earth Science [*A publication*]
**Inst Min L** ... Institute on Mineral Law [*A publication*]
**Inst Min Metall Bull** ... Institution of Mining and Metallurgy. Bulletin [*A publication*]
**Inst Min Metall Trans Sect A** ... Institution of Mining and Metallurgy. Transactions. Section A. Mining Industry [*A publication*]
**Inst Min Metall Trans Sect A Min Ind** ... Institution of Mining and Metallurgy. Transactions. Section A. Mining Industry [*A publication*]
**Inst Min Metall Trans Sect B** ... Institution of Mining and Metallurgy. Transactions. Section B. Applied Earth Science [*A publication*]
**Inst Min Metall Trans Sect C** ... Institution of Mining and Metallurgy. Transactions. Section C. Mineral Processing and Extractive Metallurgy [*A publication*]
**Inst Min & Met Trans** ... Institution of Mining and Metallurgy. Transactions [*A publication*]
**Inst Min Miner Res Univ K Tech Rep** ... Institute for Mining and Mineral Research. University of Kentucky. Technical Report [*A publication*]
**INSTMN**... Instrumentation
**Inst Munic Cienc Nat Misc Zool** ... Instituto Municipal de Ciencias Naturales Miscelanea. Zoologica [*A publication*]
**Inst Munic Engrs J** ... Institution of Municipal Engineers. Journal [*A publication*]
**Inst Munic Eng S Afr Dist Annu J** ... Institution of Municipal Engineers. South African District. Annual Journal [*A publication*]
**INSTN**....... Institution
**INSTN**....... Instruction [*Data processing*] (TEL)
**INSTN**....... Instrumentation (MUGU)
**InSTN**........ Tri-County News, South Bend, IN [*Library symbol*] [*Library of Congress*] (LCLS)
**Inst Nac Carbon (Oviedo Spain) Bol Inf** ... Instituto Nacional del Carbon (Oviedo, Spain). Boletin Informativo [*A publication*]
**Inst Nac Carbon Sus Deriv "Francisco Pintado Fe" Publ INCAR** ... Instituto Nacional del Carbon y Sus Derivados "Francisco Pintado Fe." Publicacion INCAR [*A publication*]
**Inst Nac Conserv Nat Estac Cent Ecol Bol (Spain)** ... Instituto Nacional para la Conservacion de la Natureleza. Estacion Central de Ecologia. Boletin (Spain) [*A publication*]
**Inst Nac Conserv Nat Nat Hisp** ... Instituto Nacional para la Conservacion de la Naturaleza. Naturalia Hispanica [*A publication*]
**Inst Nac Invest Agrar Comun Ser Prot Veg (Spain)** ... Instituto Nacional de Investigaciones Agrarias. Comunicaciones. Serie: Protcccion Vegetal (Spain) [*A publication*]
**Inst Nac Invest Agric SAG (Mex) Foll Tec** ... Instituto Nacional de Investigaciones Agricolas. Secretaria de Agricultura y Ganaderia (Mexico). Folleto Tecnico [*A publication*]
**Inst Nac Invest Agric Secr Agric Ganad (Mex) Foll Tec** ... Instituto Nacional de Investigaciones Agricolas. Secretaria de Agricultura y Ganaderia (Mexico). Folleto Tecnico [*A publication*]
**Inst Nac Invest Agron Bol** ... Instituto Nacional de Investigaciones Agronomicas. Boletin [*Spain*] [*A publication*]
**Inst Nac Invest Agron (Madr) Conf** ... Instituto Nacional de Investigaciones Agronomicas (Madrid). Conferencias [*A publication*]
**Inst Nac Invest Agron (Spain) Cuad** ... Instituto Nacional de Investigaciones Agronomicas (Spain). Cuaderno [*A publication*]
**Inst Nac Invest Fom Min (Peru) Ser Memo** ... Instituto Nacional de Investigacion y Fomento Mineros (Peru). Serie Memorandum [*A publication*]
**Inst Nac Med Leg Colomb Rev** ... Instituto Nacional de Medicina Legal de Colombia. Revista [*A publication*]
**Inst Nac Nutr Caracas Publ** ... Instituto Nacional de Nutricion. Caracas. Publicacion [*A publication*]
**Inst Nac Pesca Bol Cient Tec** ... Instituto Nacional de Pesca. Boletin Cientifico y Tecnico [*A publication*]
**Inst Nac Pesca (Cuba) Cent Invest Pesq Bol Divulg Tec** ... Instituto Nacional de la Pesca (Cuba). Centro de Investigaciones Pesqueras. Boletin de Divulgacion Tecnica [*A publication*]
**Inst Nac Pesca (Cuba) Cent Invest Pesq Contrib** ... Instituto Nacional de la Pesca (Cuba). Centro de Investigaciones Pesqueras. Contribucion [*A publication*]
**Inst Nac Pesca (Ecuador) Bol Inf** ... Instituto Nacional de Pesca (Ecuador). Boletin Informativo [*A publication*]
**Inst Nac Pesca Inf Espec** ... Instituto Nacional de Pesca. Informativo Especial [*A publication*]
**Inst Nac Pesqui Amazonia Publ Quim** ... Instituto Nacional de Pesqui Amazonia. Publicacao Quimica [*A publication*]
**Inst Nac Tecnol Agropecu Bol Inf** ... Instituto Nacional de Tecnologia Agropecuaria. Boletin Informativo [*A publication*]
**Inst Nac Tecnol Agropecu Suelos Publ** ... Instituto Nacional de Tecnologia Agropecuaria. Suelos Publicacion [*A publication*]
**Inst Nac Tecnol Ind Bol Tec (Argentina)** ... Instituto Nacional de Tecnologia Industrial. Boletin Tecnico (Argentina) [*A publication*]
**Inst Napoleon R** ... Institut Napoleon. Revue [*A publication*]
**Inst Nat Amelior Conserves Legumes Bull Trimest (Belg)** ... Institut National pour l'Amelioration des Conserves de Legumes. Bulletin Trimestriel (Belgium) [*A publication*]

**Inst Nat Ind Charbonniere Bull Tech-Mines** ... Institut National de l'Industrie Charbonniere. Bulletin Technique - Mines [*A publication*]
**Inst Nat Ind Extr Bull Tech-Mines Carrieres** ... Institut National des Industries Extractives. Bulletin Technique. Mines et Carrieres [*Liege*] [*A publication*]
**Inst Natl Amelior Conserves Legumes Bull Bimest (Belg)** ... Institut National pour l'Amelioration des Conserves de Legumes. Bulletin Bimestriel (Belgium) [*A publication*]
**Inst Nat Lang Lect Ser** ... Institute of National Language. Lecture Series [*A publication*]
**Inst Natl Genevois Bull** ... Institut National Genevois. Bulletin [*A publication*]
**Inst Natl Genevois Bull NS** ... Institut National Genevois. Bulletin. New Series [*A publication*]
**Inst Natl Ind Extr (Liege) Bull Tech Mines Carrieres** ... Institut National des Industries Extractives (Liege). Bulletin Technique. Mines et Carrieres [*A publication*]
**Inst Natl Radioelem (Belg) Rapp** ... Institut National des Radioelements (Belgium). Rapport [*A publication*]
**Inst Natl Rech Agron Serv Ind Agric Aliment** ... Institut National de la Recherche Agronomique au Service des Industries Agricoles et Alimentaires [*A publication*]
**Inst Natl Rech Agron Tunisie Doc Tech** ... Institut National de la Recherche Agronomique de Tunisie. Documents Techniques [*A publication*]
**Inst Natl Rech Agron Tunisie Lab Arboric Fruit Rapp Act** ... Institut National de la Recherche Agronomique de Tunisie. Laboratoire d'Arboriculture Fruitiere. Rapport d'Activite [*A publication*]
**Inst Natl Rech Agron Tunis Lab Aboriculture Fruit Rapp Act** ... Institut National de la Recherche Agronomique de Tunisie. Laboratoire d'Arboriculture Fruitiere. Rapport d'Activite [*A publication*]
**Inst Nat Rech Agron (Paris)** ... Institut National de la Recherche Agronomique (Paris) [*A publication*]
**Inst Nat Rech Agron Tunisie** ... Institut National de la Recherche Agronomique de Tunisie [*A publication*]
**Inst Nat Sci Nanyang Univ Tech Rep** ... Institute of Natural Sciences. Nanyang University. Technical Report [*A publication*]
**Inst Neorg Khim Elektrokhim Akad Nauk Gruz SSR Sb** ... Institut Neorganicheskoi Khimii i Elektrokhimii Akademiya Nauk Gruzinskoi SSR Sbornik [*A publication*]
**Inst Nisk Temp Badan Strukt PAN Pr Ser Pr Kom Krystalogr** ... Instytut Niskich Temperatur i Badan Strukturalnych PAN Prace. Seria. Prace Komitetu Krystalografii [*A publication*]
**INSTNL** .... Institutional
**Inst N L** ...... Instituto Nacional do Livro [*A publication*]
**Inst Nomads Pet Expo Symp** ... Institute of Nomads. Petroleum Exposition Symposium [*A publication*]
**INSTNS** .... Institutions (ROG)
**INSTNS** .... Instructions
**Inst Nucl Phys (Cracow) Rep** ... Institute of Nuclear Physics (Cracow). Report [*A publication*]
**Inst Nucl Res (Warsaw) Rep** ... Institute of Nuclear Research (Warsaw). Report [*A publication*]
**Inst Nucl Study Univ Tokyo Rep** ... Institute for Nuclear Study. University of Tokyo. Reports [*A publication*]
**Inst Oceanogr Ann** ... Institut Oceanographique. Annales [*A publication*]
**Inst Oceanogr Nha Trang** ... Institut Oceanographique de Nha Trang [*A publication*]
**Inst Oceanogr Ribar Split Biljeske** ... Institut za Oceanografiju i Ribarstvo Split Biljeske [*A publication*]
**Inst Oceanogr Sci Annu Rep** ... Institute of Oceanographic Sciences. Annual Report [*A publication*]
**Inst Oil & Gas L & Taxation** ... Institute on Oil and Gas Law and Taxation [*A publication*]
**INSTOP** .... Instrument or on-Top-of-Clouds Authorized
**Inst Orientac Asist Tec Oeste Anu** ... Instituto de Orientacion y Asistencia Tecnica del Oeste. Anuario [*A publication*]
**Inst Parcs Nationaux Congo Belge Explor Parc Natl Albert** ... Institut des Parcs Nationaux du Congo Belge. Exploration du Parc National Albert [*A publication*]
**Inst Parcs Nationaux Congo Explor Parc Natl Albert** ... Institut des Parcs Nationaux du Congo Belge. Exploration du Parc National Albert [*A publication*]
**Inst Pasteur Bangui Rapp Annu** ... Institut Pasteur Bangui. Rapport Annuel [*A publication*]
**Inst Pasteur Repub Unie Cameroun Rapp Fonct Tech** ... Institut Pasteur de la Republique Unie du Cameroun. Rapport sur le Fonctionnement Technique [*A publication*]
**Inst Pathol Ig Anim Colect Indrumari (Buchar)** ... Institutul de Pathologie si Igiena Animala. Colectia Indrumari (Bucharest) [*A publication*]
**Inst Pathol Ig Anim Probl Epizootol Vet (Buchar)** ... Institutul de Pathologie si Igiena Animala. Probleme de Epizootologie Veterinara (Bucharest) [*A publication*]
**Inst Peches Marit Rev Trav** ... Institut des Peches Maritimes. Revue des Travaux [*A publication*]
**Inst Personnel Mgmt Dig** ... Institute of Personnel Management. Digest [*A publication*]
**Inst Pesqui Agron Pernambuco Bol Tec** ... Instituto de Pesquisas Agronomicas de Pernambuco. Boletim Tecnico [*A publication*]
**Inst Pesqui Agron Pernambuco Circ** ... Instituto de Pesquisas Agronomicas de Pernambuco. Circular [*A publication*]
**Inst Pesqui Agron Pernambuco Publ** ... Instituto de Pesquisas Agronomicas de Pernambuco. Publicacao [*A publication*]
**Inst Pesqui Agron (Recife) Bol Tec** ... Instituto de Pesquisas Agronimicas (Recife). Boletim Tecnico [*A publication*]
**Inst Pesqui Agropecu Norte Bol Tec** ... Instituto de Pesquisas Agropecuarias do Norte. Boletim Tecnico [*A publication*]
**Inst Pesqui Agropecu Norte (IPEAN) Bol Tec** ... Instituto de Pesquisa Agropecuaria do Norte (IPEAN). Boletim Tecnico [*A publication*]
**Inst Pesqui Agropecu Norte (IPEAN) Ser Fitotec** ... Instituto de Pesquisas e Experimentacao Agropecuarias do Norte (IPEAN). Serie Fitotecnia [*A publication*]
**Inst Pesqui Agropecu Sul Bol Tec** ... Instituto de Pesquisas Agropecuarias do Sul. Boletim Tecnico [*A publication*]
**Inst Pesqui Exp Agropecu Norte (Belem) Bol Tec** ... Instituto de Pesquisas e Experimentacao Agropecuarias do Norte (Belem). Boletim Tecnico [*A publication*]
**Inst Pesqui Exp Agropecu Norte (IPEAN) (Belem) Bol Tec** ... Instituto de Pesquisas e Experimentacao Agropecuarias do Norte (IPEAN) (Belem). Boletim Tecnico [*A publication*]
**Inst Pesqui Exp Agropecu Norte (IPEAN) Ser Bot Fisiol Veg** ... Instituto de Pesquisas e Experimentacao Agropecuarias do Norte (IPEAN). Serie Botanica e Fisiologia Vegetal [*A publication*]
**Inst Pesqui Exp Agropecu Norte (IPEAN) Ser Cult Amazonia** ... Instituto de Pesquisas e Experimentacao Agropecuarias do Norte (IPEAN). Serie Culturas da Amazonia [*A publication*]
**Inst Pesqui Exp Agropecu Norte (IPEAN) Ser Estud Bovinos** ... Instituto de Pesquisas e Experimentacao Agropecuarias do Norte (IPEAN). Serie Estudos sobre Bovinos [*A publication*]
**Inst Pesqui Exp Agropecu Norte (IPEAN) Ser Estud Bubalinos** ... Instituto de Pesquisas e Experimentacao Agropecuarias do Norte (IPEAN). Serie Estudos sobre Bubalinos [*A publication*]
**Inst Pesqui Exp Agropecu Norte (IPEAN) Ser Estud Ens** ... Instituto de Pesquisas e Experimentacao Agropecuarias do Norte (IPEAN). Serie Estudos e Ensaios [*A publication*]
**Inst Pesqui Exp Agropecu Norte (IPEAN) Ser Estud Ensaios** ... Instituto de Pesquisas e Experimentacao Agropecuarias do Norte (IPEAN). Serie Estudos e Ensaios [*A publication*]
**Inst Pesqui Exp Agropecu Norte (IPEAN) Ser Fertil Solos** ... Instituto de Pesquisas e Experimentacao Agropecuarias do Norte (IPEAN). Serie Fertilidade de Solos [*A publication*]
**Inst Pesqui Exp Agropecu Norte (IPEAN) Ser Fitotec** ... Instituto de Pesquisas e Experimentacao Agropecuarias do Norte (IPEAN). Serie Fitotecnia [*A publication*]
**Inst Pesqui Exp Agropecu Norte (IPEAN) Ser Quim Solos** ... Instituto de Pesquisas e Experimentacao Agropecuarias do Norte (IPEAN). Serie Quimica de Solos [*A publication*]
**Inst Pesqui Exp Agropecu Norte (IPEAN) Ser Solos Amazonia** ... Instituto de Pesquisas e Experimentacao Agropecuarias do Norte (IPEAN). Serie Solos da Amazonia [*A publication*]
**Inst Pesqui Exp Agropecu Norte (IPEAN) Ser Tecnol** ... Instituto de Pesquisas e Experimentacao Agropecuarias do Norte (IPEAN). Serie Tecnologia [*A publication*]
**Inst Pesqui Exp Agropecu Norte Ser Bot Fisiol Veg** ... Instituto de Pesquisas e Experimentacao Agropecuarias do Norte (IPEAN). Serie Botanica e Fisiologia Vegetal [*A publication*]
**Inst Pesqui Exp Agropecu Norte Ser Cult Amazonia** ... Instituto de Pesquisas e Experimentacao Agropecuarias do Norte (IPEAN). Serie Culturas da Amazonia [*A publication*]
**Inst Pesqui Exp Agropecu Norte Ser Estud Bovinos** ... Instituto de Pesquisas e Experimentacao Agropecuarias do Norte (IPEAN). Serie Estudos sobre Bovinos [*A publication*]
**Inst Pesqui Exp Agropecu Norte Ser Estud Bubalinos** ... Instituto de Pesquisas e Experimentacao Agropecuarias do Norte (IPEAN). Serie Estudos sobre Bubalinos [*A publication*]
**Inst Pesqui Exp Agropecu Norte Ser Estud Ens** ... Instituto de Pesquisas e Experimentacao Agropecuarias do Norte (IPEAN). Serie Estudos e Ensaios [*A publication*]
**Inst Pesqui Exp Agropecu Norte Ser Fertil Solos** ... Instituto de Pesquisas e Experimentacao Agropecuarias do Norte (IPEAN). Serie Fertilidade do Solos [*A publication*]
**Inst Pesqui Exp Agropecu Norte Ser Fitotec** ... Instituto de Pesquisas e Experimentacao Agropecuarias do Norte (IPEAN). Serie Fitotecnia [*A publication*]
**Inst Pesqui Exp Agropecu Norte Ser Quim Solos** ... Instituto de Pesquisas e Experimentacao Agropecuarias do Norte (IPEAN). Serie Quimica de Solos [*A publication*]
**Inst Pesqui Exp Agropecu Norte Ser Solos Amazonia** ... Instituto de Pesquisas e Experimentacao Agropecuarias do Norte (IPEAN). Serie Solos da Amazonia [*A publication*]
**Inst Pesqui Exp Agropecu Norte Ser Tecnol** ... Instituto de Pesquisas e Experimentacao Agropecuarias do Norte (IPEAN). Serie Tecnologia [*A publication*]
**Inst Pesqui Exp Agropecu Sul Circ** ... Instituto de Pesquisas e Experimentacao Agropecuarias do Sul. Circular [*A publication*]

**Inst Pesqui Tecnol (Sao Paulo) Boletim** ... Instituto de Pesquisas Tecnologicas (Sao Paulo). Boletim [*A publication*]
**Inst Pesqui Tecnol (Sao Paulo) Publ** ... Instituto de Pesquisas Tecnologicas (Sao Paulo). Publicacao [*A publication*]
**Inst Pet Abstr** ... Institute of Petroleum. Abstracts [*A publication*]
**Inst Pet Gaze Bucuresti Stud** ... Institutul de Petrol si Gaze din Bucuresti. Studii [*A publication*]
**Inst Pet J** ... Institute of Petroleum. Journal [*A publication*]
**Inst Pet (Lond) Pap** ... Institute of Petroleum (London). Papers [*A publication*]
**Inst Petroleum Rev** ... Institute of Petroleum. Review [*A publication*]
**Inst Petroleum Tech J** ... Institution of Petroleum Technologists. Journal [*A publication*]
**Inst Petrol Tech Pap** ... Institute of Petroleum. Technical Papers [*A publication*]
**Inst Pet Tech Pap IP** ... Institute of Petroleum. Technical Paper IP [*A publication*]
**Inst Phonet Rep** ... Institute of Phonetics. Report [*A publication*]
**Inst Phys Chem Res Rikagaku Kenkyusho Sci Pap** ... Institute of Physical and Chemical Research. Rikagaku Kenkyusho. Scientific Papers [*A publication*]
**Inst Phys Conf Dig** ... Institute of Physics. Conference Digest [*A publication*]
**Inst Phys Conf Ser** ... Institute of Physics. Conference Series [*A publication*]
**Inst Phys Nucl Eng Rep (Rom)** ... Institute for Physics and Nuclear Engineering Report (Romania) [*A publication*]
**Inst Phytopathol Res Annu Rep** ... Institute of Phytopathology Research. Annual Report [*A publication*]
**Inst Plant Eng J** ... Institution of Plant Engineers. Journal [*England*] [*A publication*]
**Inst on Plan Zon and Eminent Domain Proc** ... Institute on Planning, Zoning, and Eminent Domain. Proceedings [*A publication*]
**Inst Plan & Zoning** ... Institute on Planning, Zoning, and Eminent Domain. Proceedings [*A publication*] (DLA)
**Inst Plan Zoning & ED** ... Institute on Planning, Zoning, and Eminent Domain. Proceedings [*A publication*] (DLA)
**Inst on Plan Zoning & Eminent Domain** ... Institute on Planning, Zoning, and Eminent Domain. Proceedings [*Southwestern Legal Foundation*] (DLA)
**Inst Pluimveeonderz "Het Spelderholt" Jaarversl** ... Instituut voor Pluimveeonderzoek "Het Spelderholt." Jaarverslag [*A publication*]
**Inst Pluimveeonderz "Het Spelderholt" Meded** ... Instituut voor Pluimveeonderzoek "Het Spelderholt." Mededeling [*A publication*]
**Inst Pluimveeteelt "Het Spelderholt" Meded** ... Instituut voor de Pluimveeteelt "Het Spelderholt." Mededeling [*A publication*]
**INSTPN** .... Instrument Panel
**Inst Politeh Gheorghe Gheorghiu Dej Bucuresti Bul Ser Chim** ... Institutul Politehnic "Gheorghe Gheorghiu-Dej" Bucuresti. Buletinul. Seria Chimie [*A publication*]
**Inst Politeh Gheorghe Gheorghiu Dej Bucuresti Bul Ser Mec** ... Institutul Politehnic "Gheorghe Gheorghiu-Dej" Bucuresti. Buletinul. Seria Mecanica [*A publication*]
**Inst Politeh Iasi Bul Sect 1** ... Institutul Politehnic din Iasi. Buletinul. Sectia 1. Matematica, Mecanica Teoretica, Fizica [*Romania*] [*A publication*]
**Inst Politeh Iasi Bul Sect 5** ... Institutul Politehnic din Iasi. Buletinul. Sectia 5. Constructii-Arhitectura [*A publication*]
**Inst Politeh Traian Vuia Semin Mat Fiz Lucr** ... Institutul Politehnic "Traian Vuia." Seminarul di Matematica si Fizica. Lucrarile [*A publication*]
**Inst Post Office Elec Eng Paper** ... Institution of Post Office Electrical Engineers. Paper [*A publication*]
**Inst Printed Circuits Tech Rep** ... Institute of Printed Circuits. Technical Report [*A publication*]
**Inst Private Investments** ... Institute on Private Investments Abroad and Foreign Trade [*A publication*]
**Inst on Priv Invest and Investors Abroad Proc** ... Institute on Private Investments and Investors Abroad. Proceedings [*A publication*]
**Inst on Priv Inv & Inv Abroad** ... Institute on Private Investments and Investors Abroad. Proceedings [*A publication*] (DLA)
**Inst Proem** ... Proeme [*Introduction to Coke's Institutes*] [*A publication*] (DLA)
**Inst Prof Librn Ont Newsl** ... Institute of Professional Librarians of Ontario. Newsletter [*A publication*]
**Inst Prov Agropecuar (Mendoza) Bol Tec** ... Instituto Provincial Agropecuario (Mendoza). Boletin Tecnica [*A publication*]
**Inst Prov Paleontol Sabadell Bol Inf** ... Instituto Provincial de Paleontologia de Sabadell. Boletin Informativo [*A publication*]
**Inst Przem Org Pr** ... Instytut Przemyslu Organicznego. Prace [*A publication*]
**Inst Przem Tworzyw Farb Biul Inf** ... Instytut Przemyslu Tworzyw i Farb. Biuletyn Informacyjny [*A publication*]
**Inst Przem Wiazacych Mater Budow Krakow Biul Inf** ... Instytut Przemyslu Wiazacych Materialow Budowlanych. Krakow. Biuletyn Informacyjny [*A publication*]
**InstPS** ........ Institute of Purchasing and Supply [*British*]
**Inst Psychiatry Maudsley Monogr** ... Institute of Psychiatry. Maudsley Monographs [*A publication*]
**Inst Public Serv Vocat Train Bull** ... Institute for Public Service and Vocational Training. Bulletin [*A publication*]
**Inst Quim Agric (Rio De Janeiro) Mem** ... Instituto de Quimica Agricola (Rio De Janeiro). Memoria [*A publication*]
**Inst Quim Apl Farm (Lima) Bol Inf** ... Instituto de Quimica Aplicada a la Farmacia (Lima). Boletim Informativo [*A publication*]
**INSTR** ....... Instruct [*or Instructor*] (AABC)
**INSTR** ....... Instruction
**Instr** ........... Instructor [*A publication*]
**INSTR** ....... Instrument
**Inst Radio Electron Eng (Aust) Proc** ... Institution of Radio and Electronics Engineers of Australia. Proceedings [*A publication*]
**Inst Radio & Electron Engrs Aust Proc** ... Institution of Radio and Electronics Engineers of Australia. Proceedings [*A publication*] (APTA)
**Inst Radio Eng Proc** ... Institute of Radio Engineers. Proceedings [*A publication*]
**INSTRAT** ... Investment Strategy [*Game*]
**Instr & Autom** ... Instruments and Automation [*A publication*]
**INSTRAW** ... International Research and Training Institute for the Advancement of Women [*United Nations*] [*Research center*] [*Dominican Republic*] (IRC)
**Instr Cler** ... Instructor Clericalis (DLA)
**Inst R Colon Belge Bull Seances** ... Institut Royal Colonial Belge. Bulletin des Seances [*A publication*]
**Inst R Colon Belge Sect Sci Nat Med Mem Collect 4o** ... Institut Royal Colonial Belge. Section des Sciences Naturelles et Medicales. Memoires. Collection in Quarto [*A publication*]
**Instr Contr** ... Instruments and Control Systems [*A publication*]
**Instr Course Lect** ... Instructional Course Lectures [*A publication*]
**INSTRD** .... Instructed (ROG)
**Inst Rech Caoutch Viet Nam Arch** ... Institut des Recherches sur le Caoutchouc au Viet-Nam. Archive [*A publication*]
**Inst Rech Caoutch Viet Nam Laikhe Rapp Annu** ... Institut des Recherches sur le Caoutchouc au Viet-Nam Laikhe. Rapports Annuels [*A publication*]
**Inst Rech Entomol Phytopathol Evine Dep Bot** ... Institut de Recherches Entomologiques et Phytopathologiques d'Evine. Departement de Botanique [*A publication*]
**Inst Rech Huiles Oleagineux (IRHO) Rapp Annu** ... Institut de Recherches pour les Huiles et Oleagineux (IRHO). Rapport Annuel [*A publication*]
**Inst Rech Huiles Ol Rapp Annu** ... Institut de Recherches pour les Huiles et Oleagineux [*IRHO*]. Rapport Annuel [*A publication*]
**Inst Rech Ressour Hydraul (Budapest) Commun Lang Etrang** ... Institut de Recherches des Ressources Hydrauliques (Budapest). Communications en Langues Etrangeres [*A publication*]
**Inst Res Ment Retard Monogr (Oxford)** ... Institute for Research into Mental Retardation. Monograph (Oxford) [*A publication*]
**Inst Res Ment Retard (Oxford) Symp** ... Institute for Research into Mental Retardation (Oxford). Symposium [*A publication*]
**Instr Exp Techn** ... Instruments and Experimental Techniques [*A publication*]
**Inst Ribni Resur (Varna) Izv** ... Institut po Ribni Resursi (Varna). Izvestiya [*A publication*]
**INSTRIMPEX** ... China National Instruments Import & Export Corp. [*People's Republic of China*] (IMH)
**Instr Innov** ... Instructional Innovator [*A publication*]
**Instr Innovator** ... Instructional Innovator [*A publication*]
**INSTRL**..... Instructional
**INSTRM** ... Instrumented
**Inst R Meteorol Belg Bull Trimest Obs Ozone** ... Institut Royal Meteorologique de Belgique. Bulletin Trimestriel. Observations d'Ozone [*A publication*]
**INSTRMT** ... Instrument
**INSTRN** .... Instruction
**Instr Naut** .. Instructions Nautiques [*A publication*]
**INSTRNL** ... Instructional
**Instrn Technol** ... Instrumentation Technology [*A publication*]
**INSTRONS** ... Instructions (ROG)
**Inst Roy Sci Natur Belgique Bul** ... Institut Royal des Sciences Naturelles de Belgique. Bulletin [*A publication*]
**INSTRPI** ... Instrument Pilot Instructor [*Air Force*]
**INSTRPIT** ... Instructor Pilot [*Air Force*]
**Instr Sci** ..... Instructional Science [*A publication*]
**Inst R Sci Nat Belg Bull** ... Institut Royal des Sciences Naturelles de Belgique. Bulletin [*A publication*]
**Inst R Sci Nat Belg Bull Sci Terre** ... Institut Royal des Sciences Naturelles de Belgique. Bulletin. Sciences de la Terre [*A publication*]
**Inst R Sci Nat Belg Doc Trav** ... Institut Royal des Sciences Naturelles de Belgique. Documents de Travail [*A publication*]
**Inst R Sci Nat Belg Mem** ... Institut Royal des Sciences Naturelles de Belgique. Memoires [*A publication*]
**Inst R Sci Nat Belg Mem Deuxieme Ser** ... Institut Royal des Sciences Naturelles de Belgique. Memoires. Deuxieme Serie [*A publication*]
**Instr Sh Cent Exp Fm (Ottawa)** ... Instruction Sheet. Central Experimental Farm (Ottawa) [*A publication*]
**Instr Teach** ... Instructor and Teacher [*A publication*]
**Instr Tech** .. Instrumentation Technology [*A publication*]
**INSTRU** .... Instrumentation
**INSTRUC** ... Instruction

**INSTRUCTA** ... Intelligent Naval Structures Assistant
**INSTRUM** ... Instrumentation Subsystem [*NASA*] (NASA)
**Instrum Abstr** ... Instrument Abstracts [*A publication*]
**Instrum Aerosp Ind** ... Instrumentation in the Aerospace Industry [*A publication*]
**Instrum Autom** ... Instrumentation and Automation [*A publication*]
**Instrum Automat** ... Instruments and Automation [*A publication*]
**Instrum Bull** ... Instrumentation Bulletin [*A publication*]
**Instrum Chem Pet Ind** ... Instrumentation in the Chemical and Petroleum Industries [*A publication*]
**Instrum Constr (USSR)** ... Instrument Construction (USSR) [*A publication*]
**Instrum Control Engng** ... Instrument and Control Engineering [*A publication*]
**Instrum Control Syst** ... Instruments and Control Systems [*A publication*]
**Instrum and Control Syst** ... Instruments and Control Systems [*A publication*]
**Instrum Contr Syst** ... Instruments and Control Systems [*A publication*]
**Instrum Cryog Ind** ... Instrumentation in the Cryogenic Industry [*A publication*]
**Instrum Electr Dev** ... Instruments and Electronics Developments [*A publication*]
**Instrum Eng** ... Instrument Engineer [*A publication*]
**Instrument** ... Instrumentalist [*A publication*]
**Instrumentation Tech** ... Instrumentation Technology [*A publication*]
**Instrumentenbau Z** ... Instrumentenbau-Zeitschrift [*A publication*]
**Instrum and Exp Tech** ... Instruments and Experimental Techniques [*A publication*]
**Instrum Exp Tech** ... Instruments and Experimental Techniques [*A publication*]
**Instrum Food Beverage Ind** ... Instrumentation in the Food and Beverage Industry [*A publication*]
**Instrum Forsch** ... Instrument und Forschung [*A publication*]
**Instrum India** ... Instruments India [*A publication*]
**Instrum Iron Steel Ind** ... Instrumentation in the Iron and Steel Industry [*A publication*]
**Instrum Lab** ... Instruments et Laboratoires [*A publication*]
**Instrum Maint Manage** ... Instrument Maintenance Management [*A publication*]
**Instrum Maker** ... Instrument Maker [*A publication*]
**Instrum Manuf** ... Instrument Manufacturing [*A publication*]
**Instrum Med** ... Instrumentation in Medicine [*England*] [*A publication*]
**Instrum Met Ind** ... Instrumentation in the Metals Industries [*A publication*]
**Instrum Min Metall Ind** ... Instrumentation in the Mining and Metallurgy Industries [*A publication*]
**Instrum News** ... Instrument News [*A publication*]
**Instrum Nucl** ... Instrumentation Nucleaire [*France*] [*A publication*]
**Instrum Power Ind** ... Instrumentation in the Power Industry [*A publication*]
**Instrum Pract** ... Instrument Practice [*A publication*]
**Instrum Pulp Pap Ind** ... Instrumentation in the Pulp and Paper Industry [*United States*] [*A publication*]
**Instrum Rev** ... Instrument Review [*England*] [*A publication*]
**Instrum Rev (Leiden)** ... Instrument Revue (Leiden) [*A publication*]
**Instrum Soc Amer Conf Preprint** ... Instrument Society of America. Conference Preprint [*A publication*]
**Instrum Soc Am Instrum Index** ... Instrument Society of America. Instrumentation Index [*A publication*]
**Instrum Soc India J** ... Instrument Society of India. Journal [*A publication*]
**Instrum Tech** ... Instrumentation Technology [*A publication*]
**Instrum Technol** ... Instrumentation Technology [*A publication*]
**Instrum Test Rep Bur Meteor** ... Instrumentation Test Report. Bureau of Meteorology [*A publication*] (APTA)
**Inst Sci Agron Burundi (ISABU) Rapp Annu Notes Annexes** ... Institut des Sciences Agronomiques du Burundi (ISABU). Rapport Annuel et Notes Annexes [*A publication*]
**Inst Sci Cherifien Trav Ser Gen** ... Institut Scientifique Cherifien. Travaux. Serie Generale [*A publication*]
**Inst Sci Cherifien Trav Ser Sci Phys** ... Institut Scientifique Cherifien. Travaux. Serie Sciences Physiques [*A publication*]
**Inst Sci Mag** ... Institute of Science Magazine [*A publication*]
**Inst Sec Reg** ... Institute on Securities Regulation [*A publication*] (DLA)
**Inst on Sec Reg** ... Institute on Securities Regulation [*A publication*]
**Inst Securities Reg** ... Institute on Securities Regulation [*A publication*]
**Inst Sewage Purif J Proc** ... Institute of Sewage Purification. Journal and Proceedings [*A publication*]
**Inst Skoglig Mat Stat Rapp Uppsatser** ... Institutionen foer Skoglig Matematisk Statistik Rapporter och Uppsatser [*A publication*]
**Inst Skogsforyngring Rapp Uppsatser** ... Institutionen foer Skogsforyngring Rapporter och Uppsatser [*A publication*]
**Inst Skogszool Rapp Uppsatser** ... Institutionen foer Skogszoologi Rapporter och Uppsatser [*A publication*]
**Inst SMM** ... Institute of Sales and Marketing Management [*British*]
**Inst Social Science (Tokyo) Annals** ... Annals. Institute of Social Sciences (Tokyo) [*A publication*]
**Inst Socioeconomic Studies J** ... Institute for Socioeconomic Studies. Journal [*A publication*]
**Inst Sociol R** ... Revue. Institut de Sociologie [*A publication*]
**Inst Soil Sci Acad Sin Soil Res Rep** ... Institute of Soil Science. Academia Sinica. Soil Research Report [*A publication*]
**Inst Sound Vib** ... Institute of Sound and Vibration [*A publication*]
**Inst Space Aeronaut Sci Univ Tokyo Rep** ... Institute of Space and Aeronautical Science. University of Tokyo. Report [*A publication*]
**Inst Stud Proiect Energ Bul** ... Institutul de Studii si Proiectari Energetice. Buletinul [*Romania*] [*A publication*]
**Inst Suisse Rech For Mem** ... Institut Suisse de Recherches Forestieres. Memoires [*A publication*]
**INSTSYS** .. Instrumentation System (MCD)
**Inst Tech**.... Instrumentation Technology [*A publication*]
**Inst Tech Batim Trav Pub Ann** ... Institut Technique du Batiment et des Travaux Publics. Annales [*A publication*]
**Inst Technol Mater Elektron Pr** ... Instytut Technologii Materialow Elektronicznych. Prace [*A publication*]
**Inst Tec Monterrey Div Cienc Agropecu Marit Inf Invest** ... Instituto Tecnologico de Monterrey. Division de Ciencias Agropecuarias y Maritimas. Informe de Investigacion [*A publication*]
**Inst Tecnol Estud Super Monterrey Dep Quim Bol** ... Instituto Tecnologico y de Estudios Superiores de Monterrey. Departamento de Quimica. Boletin [*A publication*]
**Inst Tecnol Ind Estado Minas Gerais Avulso** ... Instituto de Tecnologia Industrial. Estado de Minas Gerais. Avulso [*A publication*]
**Inst Tecnol Ind Estado Minas Gerais Boletim** ... Instituto de Tecnologia Industrial. Estado de Minas Gerais. Boletim [*A publication*]
**Inst Tecnol Monterrey Div Cien Agropecu Marit Inf Invest** ... Instituto Tecnologico de Monterrey. Division de Ciencias Agropecuarias y Maritimas. Informe de Investigacion [*A publication*]
**Inst Tecnol Rio Grande Sul Bol** ... Instituto Tecnologico do Rio Grande Do Sul. Boletim [*A publication*]
**Inst Text Faserforsch Stuttgart Ber** ... Institut fuer Textil- und Faserforschung. Stuttgart. Berichte [*A publication*]
**Inst Text Fr Nord Bull Inf** ... Institut Textile de France-Nord. Bulletin d'Information [*A publication*]
**Inst Toegepast Biol Onderzoek Meded** ... Instituut voor Toegepast Biologisch Onderzoek in de Natuur [*Institute for Biological Field Research*]. Mededeling [*A publication*]
**Inst Tsvetna Metal (Plovdiv) God** ... Institut po Tsvetna Metalurgiya (Plovdiv). Godishnik [*A publication*]
**Inst Univ Pedagog Caracas Monogr Cient Augusto Pi Suner** ... Instituto Universitario Pedagogico de Caracas. Monografias Cientificas Augusto Pi Suner [*A publication*]
**Inst Verkstadstek Forsk IVF Resultat** ... Institutet fuer Verkstadsteknisk Forskning. IVF Resultat [*A publication*]
**Inst Vitreous Enamellers Bull** ... Institute of Vitreous Enamellers. Bulletin [*A publication*]
**Inst Vol Feed** ... Institutions/Volume Feeding [*A publication*]
**Inst/Vol Feeding Mgt** ... Institutions/Volume Feeding Management [*Later, Institutions/Volume Feeding*] [*A publication*]
**Inst Water Eng J** ... Institution of Water Engineers. Journal [*Later, Institution of Water Engineers and Scientists. Journal*] [*A publication*]
**Inst Water Eng Sci J** ... Institution of Water Engineers and Scientists. Journal [*A publication*]
**Inst World Affairs Proc** ... Institute of World Affairs. Proceedings [*A publication*]
**Inst Zast Bilja Posebna Izd** ... Institut za Zastitu Bilja. Posebna Izdanja [*A publication*]
**Inst Zool Parazitol Akad Nauk Tadzh SSR Tr** ... Institut Zoologii i Parazitologii Akademiya Nauk Tadzhikskoi SSR Trudy [*A publication*]
**Inst Zootech Biul Inf** ... Instytut Zootechniki. Biuletyn Informacyjny [*A publication*]
**Inst Zootech Pol Wyniki Oceny Wartosci Hodowlanej Buhajow** ... Instytut Zootechniki w Polsce Wyniki Oceny Wartosci Hodowlanej Buhajow [*A publication*]
**Inst Zootec (Sao Paulo) Bol Tec** ... Instituto de Zootecnia (Sao Paulo). Boletim Tecnico [*A publication*]
**InSU** .......... Indiana University at South Bend, South Bend, IN [*Library symbol*] [*Library of Congress*] (LCLS)
**INSU** ......... Insituform of North America, Inc. [*NASDAQ symbol*] (NQ)
**InSu** ........... Sullivan County Public Library, Sullivan, IN [*Library symbol*] [*Library of Congress*] (LCLS)
**InSuCR** ...... Sullivan County Recorder's Office, Sullivan, IN [*Library symbol*] [*Library of Congress*] (LCLS)
**INSUF** ....... Insufficient (AABC)
**INSUFF**..... Insufflatio [*An Insufflation*] [*Pharmacy*]
**InSuHi** ....... Sullivan County Historical Society, Sullivan, IN [*Library symbol*] [*Library of Congress*] (LCLS)
**Insul** ........... Insulana [*A publication*]
**INSUL** ....... Insulated [*or Insulation*]
**Insul** ........... Insulation [*A publication*]
**Insulation J** ... Insulation Journal [*A publication*]
**Insulatn**...... Insulation [*A publication*]
**Insulatn**...... Insulation Journal [*A publication*]
**Insul/Circuits** ... Insulation/Circuits [*A publication*]
**INSULR** .... Insulator
**INSUPGENCRUIT** ... Inspect, Supervise, Generally Superintend Recruitment Methods
**Insur**.......... Insurance
**Insurance D** ... Insurance Decisions [*A publication*]

**Insurance F** ... Insurance Facts [*A publication*]
**Insurance Math Econom** ... Insurance, Mathematics, and Economics [*A publication*]
**Insur Couns J** ... Insurance Counsel Journal [*A publication*]
**INSURE**.... Industry Network for Social, Urban, and Rural Efforts
**Insurg Soc** ... Insurgent Sociologist [*A publication*]
**Insur Law J** ... Insurance Law Journal [*A publication*]
**Insur Lines** ... Insurance Lines [*A publication*] (APTA)
**Insur LJ** ..... Insurance Law Journal [*A publication*]
**Insur L Rep** ... Insurance Law Reporter [*A publication*] (DLA)
**INSURR**.... Insurrection (DLA)
**Insur Rec Aust NZ** ... Insurance Record of Australia and New Zealand [*A publication*]
**INSURV**.... Board of Inspection and Survey [*Navy*]
**INSURVINST** ... Board of Inspection and Survey, Instructions [*Navy*]
**InSuT**......... Sullivan Daily Times, Sullivan, IN [*Library symbol*] [*Library of Congress*] (LCLS)
**INSUWG** .. Inshore Undersea Warfare Group [*Navy*]
**InSw**........... Swayzee Public Library, Swayzee, IN [*Library symbol*] [*Library of Congress*] (LCLS)
**Ins Wkr**...... Insurance Worker [*A publication*]
**INSY**.......... Interim Systems Corp. [*NASDAQ symbol*] (NQ)
**InSy**........... Syracuse Public Library, Syracuse, IN [*Library symbol*] [*Library of Congress*] (LCLS)
**INT** ........... Ad Interim Specification [*Navy*]
**Int**.............. De Interpretatione [*of Aristotle*] [*Classical studies*] (OCD)
**INT** ........... Greensboro/High Point/West Salem [*North Carolina*] Reynolds [*Airport symbol*] (OAG)
**INT** ........... Induction Neutralizing Transformer [*Data processing*]
**INT** ........... Infrared Nondestructive Testing [*Electrical technique*]
**INT** ........... Intake
**INT** ........... Integer
**INT** ........... Integral (MSA)
**INT** ........... Integrase [*Biochemistry*]
**INT** ........... Integrated (MCD)
**INT** ........... Integrated Test (NASA)
**INT** ........... Integrated Testing (NASA)
**INT** ........... Integrator [*Aviation*] (FAAC)
**INT** ........... Intelligence
**INT** ........... Intelligence and Law Enforcement Division [*Coast Guard*]
**int** .............. Intense [*Philately*]
**INT** ........... Intensifier [*Linguistics*]
**INT** ........... Intensity
**INT** ........... Intent [*FBI standardized term*]
**INT** ........... Intercept [*or Interceptor*] (CINC)
**INT** ........... Interchange
**Int**.............. Interchange: Papers on Biblical and Current Questions [*A publication*] (APTA)
**Int**.............. Interessi [*Interest*] [*Italian*] [*Business term*]
**INT** ........... Interest [*Finance, Law*] (AFM)
**INT** ........... Interface
**INT** ........... Interfaces [*A publication*]
**INT** ........... Interim (MSA)
**INT** ........... Interior (KSC)
**INT** ........... Interjection
**int** .............. Interlingua [*MARC language code*] [*Library of Congress*] (LCCP)
**INT** ........... INTERMARC [*International Machine-Readable Cataloging*] [*French National Library*] [*UTLAS symbol*]
**INT** ........... Intermediate (MCD)
**INT** ........... Intermetco Ltd. [*Toronto Stock Exchange symbol*]
**INT** ........... Intermittent
**INT** ........... Internal (AAG)
**INT** ........... International (EY)
**INT** ........... International Recovery Corp. [*NYSE symbol*] (SPSG)
**INT** ........... International Science Fiction [*A publication*]
**INT** ........... International Textiles [*A publication*]
**INT** ........... Interne [*Medicine*] [*British*]
**INT** ........... Interned (AABC)
**INT** ........... Internist [*Medicine*]
**INT** ........... Interphone (MDG)
**INT** ........... Interpoint Corp. [*NASDAQ symbol*] (NQ)
**Int**.............. Interpretation. A Journal of Bible and Theology [*Richmond, VA*] [*A publication*]
**INT** ........... Interpreter
**Int**.............. Interpreter [*A publication*]
**INT** ........... Interrogate (MDG)
**INT** ........... Interrogation [*British naval signaling*]
**INT** ........... Interrupt
**INT** ........... Interrupter (MSA)
**INT** ........... Intersection (FAAC)
**INT** ........... Interstate Airlines, Inc. [*Ypsilanti, MI*] [*FAA designator*] (FAAC)
**INT** ........... Interstate Railroad Co. [*AAR code*]
**INT** ........... Interval
**INT** ........... Interview
**int** .............. Interviewer
**INT** ........... Intransitive
**Int**.............. Introduction (DLA)
**INT** ........... Introit
**INT** ........... Iodonitrotetrazolium Violet
**INT** ........... Irrigated, No Tillage [*Agriculture*]
**INT** ........... Isaac Newton Optical Telescope
**INT** ........... North Texas State University, Denton, TX [*OCLC symbol*] (OCLC)
**INT** ........... Winston-Salem, NC [*Location identifier*] [*FAA*] (FAAL)
**INTA** ......... Interaction [*A publication*]
**INTA** ......... International Association for the Development and Management of Existing and New Towns (EAIO)
**INTA** ......... International New Thought Alliance (EA)
**INTA** ......... International New Towns Association [*See also AIVN*] (EAIO)
**INTA** ......... Interrupt Acknowledge [*Data processing*]
**Int A Aller** ... International Archives of Allergy and Applied Immunology [*A publication*]
**INTAAS**.... Integrated Aircraft Armament System (MCD)
**Int Abstr Biol Sci** ... International Abstracts of Biological Sciences [*A publication*]
**Int Abstr Oper Res** ... International Abstracts in Operations Research [*A publication*]
**Int Abstr Surg** ... International Abstracts of Surgery [*A publication*]
**INTAC**...... Intercept Tracking and Control Group
**Int Acad Pathol Monogr** ... International Academy of Pathology. Monograph [*A publication*]
**INTA/CONIE Inf Aeroesp** ... INTA/CONIE [*Instituto Nacional de Tecnica Aeroespacial/Comision Nacional de Investigacion del Espacio*] Informacion Aeroespacial [*Spain*] [*A publication*]
**INTACS**.... Integrated Tactical Communications Study [*or System*] [*Army*] (AABC)
**Int Advertiser** ... International Advertiser [*A publication*]
**Int Adv Nondestr Test** ... International Advances in Nondestructive Testing [*A publication*]
**Int Adv Surg Oncol** ... International Advances in Surgical Oncology [*A publication*]
**IntAe**.......... International Aerospace Abstracts [*A publication*]
**Int Aerosp Abstr** ... International Aerospace Abstracts [*A publication*]
**INTA Estac Exp Manfredi Inf Tec** ... INTA [*Instituto Nacional de Tecnologia Agropecuaria*]. Estacion Experimental Manfredi. Informacion Tecnica [*A publication*]
**INTA Estac Exp Reg Agropecu (Parana) Ser Tec** ... INTA [*Instituto Nacional de Tecnologia Agropecuaria*]. Estacion Experimental Regional Agropecuaria (Parana). Serie Tecnica [*A publication*]
**INTA Estac Exp Reg Agropecu Pergamino Inf Tec** ... INTA [*Instituto Nacional de Tecnologia Agropecuaria*]. Estacion Experimental Regional Agropecuaria (Pergamino). Informe Tecnico [*A publication*]
**INTA Estac Exp Reg Agropecu Pergamino Publ Tec** ... INTA [*Instituto Nacional de Tecnologia Agropecuaria*]. Estacion Experimental Regional Agropecuaria (Pergamino). Publicacion Tecnica [*A publication*]
**Int Aff** ........ International Affairs [*A publication*]
**Int Affairs** .. International Affairs [*England*] [*A publication*]
**Int Aff Bull** ... International Affairs. Bulletin [*A publication*]
**Int Aff (London)** ... International Affairs (London) [*A publication*]
**Int Aff Stud** ... International Affairs. Studies [*A publication*]
**Int Afr Bibliogr** ... International African Bibliography [*A publication*]
**Int Afr Forum** ... Internationales Afrikaforum [*A publication*]
**INTAG** ...... Intaglio [*Engraving*] (ROG)
**INTAGCY** ... Interagency
**Int Agency Res Cancer Monogr Eval Carcinog Risk Chem Man** ... International Agency for Research on Cancer. Monographs on the Evaluation of Carcinogenic Risk of Chemicals to Man [*A publication*]
**INTA (Inst Nac Tecnol Agropecu) Colecc Cient** ... INTA (Instituto Nacional de Tecnologia Agropecuaria) Coleccion Cientifica [*A publication*]
**INTA (Inst Nac Tecnol Agropecu) Man Agropecu** ... INTA (Instituto Nacional de Tecnologia Agropecuaria) Manual Agropecuario [*A publication*]
**INTA (Inst Nac Tecnol Agropecu) Ser Tec** ... INTA (Instituto Nacional de Tecnologia Agropecuaria). Serie Tecnia [*A publication*]
**INTAL**....... Instituto para la Integracion de America Latina [*Institute for Latin American Integration*] (EAIO)
**INT AL**...... Inter Alia [*Among Other Things*] [*Latin*]
**INTAMEL** ... International Association of Metropolitan City Libraries [*The Hague, Netherlands*] (EA)
**INTAMIC** ... International Microcircuit Card Association [*Paris, France*] (EAIO)
**Intam Inst Mus Res** ... Inter-American Institute for Musical Research. Yearbook [*A publication*]
**Int-Am L Rev** ... Inter-American Law Review [*A publication*]
**Intam Mus B** ... Boletin Interamericano de Musica/Inter-American Music Bulletin [*A publication*]
**Intam Mus B (Eng Ed)** ... Inter-American Music Bulletin (English Edition) [*A publication*]
**Intam Mus R** ... Inter-American Music Review [*A publication*]
**Intam Mus Res Yrbk** ... Inter-American Musical Research. Yearbook [*A publication*]
**Int Anal**...... International Analyst [*A publication*]
**Int Anesthesiol Clin** ... International Anesthesiology Clinics [*A publication*]
**Int Angiol**... International Angiology [*A publication*]

**Int A Occup** ... International Archives of Occupational and Environmental Health [*A publication*]
**INTAPUC** ... International Association of Public Cleansing [*Later, ISWA*]
**INTAR**....... International Arts Relations
**Int Arb J** .... International Arbitration Journal [*A publication*] (DLA)
**Int Arch Allergy Appl Immunol** ... International Archives of Allergy and Applied Immunology [*A publication*]
**Int Arch Arbeitsmed** ... Internationales Archiv fuer Arbeitsmedizin [*A publication*]
**Int Arch Arbeits-Umweltmed** ... Internationales Archiv fuer Arbeits- und Umweltmedizin [*A publication*]
**Int Arch Gewerbepathol Gewerbehyg** ... Internationales Archiv fuer Gewerbepathologie und Gewerbehygiene [*A publication*]
**Int Archit** ... International Architect [*A publication*]
**Int Archiv Ethnog** ... Internationales Archiv fuer Ethnographie [*A publication*]
**Int Arch Occup Environ Health** ... International Archives of Occupational and Environmental Health [*A publication*]
**Int Arch Occup Health** ... International Archives of Occupational Health [*Later, International Archives of Occupational and Environmental Health*] [*A publication*]
**Int Arch Photogramm** ... International Archives of Photogrammetry [*A publication*]
**Int Archs Allergy Appl Immun** ... International Archives of Allergy and Applied Immunology [*A publication*]
**INTASAFCON** ... International Tanker Safety Conference (DS)
**INTASAT** ... Instituto Nacional de Tecnica Aeroespacial Satellite [*Spain*] (NASA)
**Int As For**... Internationales Asienforum [*A publication*]
**INTASGRO** ... Interallied Tactical Study Group [*NATO*] (NATG)
**Int Asienf**... Internationales Asienforum [*A publication*]
**Int Asien Forum** ... Internationales Asienforum [*A publication*]
**Int Ass**........ International Association [*A publication*]
**Int Ass Bridge Struct Eng Publ** ... International Association for Bridge and Structural Engineering. Publications [*A publication*]
**Int Assoc/Assoc Int** ... International Associations/Associations Internationales [*A publication*]
**Int Assoc Dairy Milk Insp Annu Rep** ... International Association of Dairy and Milk Inspectors. Annual Report [*A publication*]
**Int Assoc Dent Child J** ... International Association of Dentistry for Children. Journal [*A publication*]
**Int Assoc Eng Geol Bull** ... International Association of Engineering Geology. Bulletin [*A publication*]
**Int Assoc Engng Geol Bull** ... International Association of Engineering Geology. Bulletin [*A publication*]
**Int Assoc Hydraul Res Congr Proc** ... International Association for Hydraulic Research. Congress. Proceedings [*A publication*]
**Int Assoc Hydrogeol Mem** ... International Association of Hydrogeologists. Memoirs [*A publication*]
**Int Assoc Hydrol Sci Assoc Int Sci Hydrol Publ** ... International Association of Hydrological Sciences - Association Internationale des Sciences Hydrologiques. Publication [*A publication*]
**Int Assoc Hydrol Sci Hydrol Sci Bull** ... International Association of Hydrological Sciences. Hydrological Sciences Bulletin [*A publication*]
**Int Assoc Hydrol Sci Publ** ... International Association of Hydrological Sciences. Publication [*A publication*]
**Int Assoc Math Geol J** ... International Association for Mathematical Geology. Journal [*A publication*]
**Int Assoc Sci Hydrol Bull** ... International Association of Scientific Hydrology. Bulletin [*A publication*]
**Int Assoc Theor Appl Limnol Commun** ... International Association of Theoretical and Applied Limnology. Communication [*West Germany*] [*A publication*]
**Int Assoc Theor Appl Limnol Proc** ... International Association of Theoretical and Applied Limnology. Proceedings [*A publication*]
**Int Assoc Volcanol Chem Earth's Inter Spe Ser** ... International Association of Volcanology and Chemistry of the Earth's Interior. Special Series [*A publication*]
**Int Assoc Wood Anat Bull** ... International Association of Wood Anatomists. Bulletin [*A publication*]
**Int Astronaut Congr Proc** ... International Astronautical Congress. Proceedings [*A publication*]
**Int Astron Union Symp** ... International Astronomical Union. Symposium [*A publication*]
**Int At Energy Ag Bibliogr Ser** ... International Atomic Energy Agency. Bibliographical Series [*A publication*]
**Int At Energy Agency Bull** ... International Atomic Energy Agency. Bulletin [*A publication*]
**Int At Energy Agency Saf Ser** ... International Atomic Energy Agency. Safety Series [*A publication*]
**Int At Energy Agency Tech Rep Ser** ... International Atomic Energy Agency. Technical Report Series [*A publication*]
**Int At Energy Ag Proc Ser** ... International Atomic Energy Agency. Proceedings Series [*A publication*]
**Int Atl Salmon Found Spec Publ Ser** ... International Atlantic Salmon Foundation. Special Publication Series [*A publication*]
**Int Aud**....... Internal Auditor [*A publication*]
**Int Auditor** ... Internal Auditor [*A publication*]
**INTAVA**.... International Aviation Association
**Int Bar J**..... International Bar Journal [*A publication*] (DLA)
**Int Bauxite Assoc Q Rev** ... International Bauxite Association. Quarterly Review [*A publication*]
**INTBEB**.... Interferon y Biotecnologia [*A publication*]
**Int Beekeep Congr Prelim Sci Meet** ... International Beekeeping Congress. Preliminary Scientific Meeting [*A publication*]
**Int Beekeep Congr Summ** ... International Beekeeping Congress. Summaries of Papers [*A publication*]
**Int Beekeep Congr Summ Suppl** ... International Beekeeping Congress. Summaries Supplement [*A publication*]
**Int Behav Scientist** ... International Behavioural Scientist [*A publication*]
**Int Bergwirtsch Bergtech** ... Internationale Bergwirtschaft und Bergtechnik [*A publication*]
**Int Bibliogr** ... International Bibliography [*A publication*]
**Int Bibliogr Book Rev** ... International Bibliography of Book Reviews [*A publication*]
**Int Bibliogr Book Rev Schol Lit** ... International Bibliography of Book Reviews of Scholarly Literature [*A publication*]
**Int Bibliogr Hist Relig** ... International Bibliography of the History of Religions [*A publication*]
**Int Bibliogr Period Lit** ... International Bibliography of Periodical Literature [*A publication*]
**Int Bibliogr Zeitschriftenliteratur Allen Gebieten Wissens** ... Internationale Bibliographie der Zeitschriftenliteratur aus Allen Gebieten des Wissens [*A publication*]
**Int Bibl Soc Sci** ... International Bibliography of the Social Sciences [*A publication*]
**Int Biod B**... International Biodeterioration Bulletin [*A publication*]
**Int Biodeterior** ... International Biodeterioration Bulletin [*A publication*]
**Int Biodeterior Bull** ... International Biodeterioration Bulletin [*A publication*]
**Int Biol Programme** ... International Biological Programme Series [*A publication*]
**Int Biol Programme Handb** ... International Biological Programme. Handbook [*A publication*]
**Int Biosci Monogr** ... International Bioscience Monographs [*A publication*]
**Int B Miss R** ... International Bulletin of Missionary Research [*A publication*]
**Int Bot Congr** ... International Botanical Congress. Papers [*A publication*]
**Int Bot Congr Recent Advan Bot** ... International Botanical Congress. Recent Advances in Botany [*A publication*]
**Int Brain Res Organ Monogr Ser** ... International Brain Research Organization. Monograph Series [*A publication*]
**Int Broadcast Eng** ... International Broadcast Engineer [*A publication*]
**Int Broadcast Syst and Oper** ... International Broadcasting Systems and Operation [*A publication*]
**Int Broadc Engr** ... International Broadcast Engineer [*A publication*]
**Int Build Serv Abstr** ... International Building Services Abstracts [*A publication*]
**INTBUL**.... Intelligence Bulletin (CINC)
**Int Bull Bacteriol Nomencl Taxon** ... International Bulletin of Bacteriological Nomenclature and Taxonomy [*A publication*]
**Int Bull Bibliogr Educ** ... International Bulletin of Bibliography on Education [*A publication*]
**Int Bull Indust Prop** ... International Bulletin of Industrial Property [*A publication*] (DLA)
**Int Bull Inf Refrig** ... International Bulletin on Information on Refrigeration [*A publication*]
**Int Bull Res E Eur** ... International Bulletin for Research on Law in Eastern Europe [*A publication*]
**Int Bul Miss R** ... International Bulletin of Missionary Research [*A publication*]
**Int Bur Ed B** ... International Bureau of Education. Bulletin [*A publication*]
**Int Bus Equip** ... International Business Equipment [*A publication*]
**Int Bus Lawy** ... International Business Lawyer [*A publication*] (DLA)
**Int Bus Res Ser** ... International Business Research Series [*A publication*]
**INTC** ......... Intel Corporation [*NASDAQ symbol*] (NQ)
**INTC** ......... Intelligence Corps [*Army*]
**INTC** ......... International Nick Tate Club (EAIO)
**InTc**............ Tell City-Perry County Public Library, Tell City, IN [*Library symbol*] [*Library of Congress*] (LCLS)
**Int Cancer Congr Abstr** ... International Cancer Congress. Abstracts [*A publication*]
**Int Cancer Res Found Rep Act** ... International Cancer Research Foundation. Report of Activities [*A publication*]
**Int Cas** ....... Rowe's Interesting Cases [*England and Ireland*] [*A publication*] (DLA)
**Int Case**...... Rowe's Interesting Cases [*England and Ireland*] [*A publication*] (DLA)
**Int Cast Met J** ... International Cast Metals Journal [*A publication*]
**Int Cataloguing** ... International Cataloguing [*A publication*]
**Int Cent Arid Semi-Arid Land Stud Publ** ... International Center for Arid and Semi-Arid Land Studies. Publication [*A publication*]
**Int Cent Mech Sci Courses Lect** ... International Centre for Mechanical Sciences. Courses and Lectures [*A publication*]
**Int Cent Med Res Semin Proc** ... International Center for Medical Research. Seminar Proceedings [*A publication*]
**Int Chem En** ... International Chemical Engineering [*A publication*]
**Int Chem Eng** ... International Chemical Engineering [*A publication*]
**Int Chem Engng** ... International Chemical Engineering [*A publication*]
**Int Chem Eng Process Ind** ... International Chemical Engineering and Processing Industries [*A publication*]
**Int Chem Export Ind** ... International Chemical and Export Industry [*A publication*]

**INTCHG** ... Interchangeable (MSA)
**INTCHGR** ... Interchanger (NASA)
**INT CIB** .... Inter Cibos [*Between Meals*] [*Pharmacy*]
**Int Civ Eng Mon** ... International Civil Engineering Monthly [*A publication*]
**Int Classif** .. International Classification [*A publication*]
**Int Classification** ... International Classification [*A publication*]
**Int Clgh Sci Math Curricular Dev Rep** ... International Clearinghouse on Science and Mathematics. Curricular Developments Report [*A publication*]
**InTcN** ........ Tell City News, Tell City, IN [*Library symbol*] [*Library of Congress*] (LCLS)
**INTCNTL** ... Intercontinental
**INTC/O**..... Integrated Checkout (NASA)
**INTCO** ...... International Code of Signals
**Int Coal Rep** ... International Coal Report [*England*] [*A publication*]
**INTCOL**.... Intelligence Collection [*Military*] (NVT)
**Int Com Com** ... Interstate Commerce Commission. Reports [*A publication*] (DLA)
**Int Com Commn** ... Interstate Commerce Commission [*Independent government agency*] (DLA)
**Int Comet Q** ... International Comet Quarterly [*A publication*]
**Int Comm**... International Commerce [*A publication*]
**Int Comm Bird Preserv Pan Am Sect Res Rep** ... International Committee for Bird Preservation. Pan American Section. Research Report [*A publication*]
**Int Commer** ... International Commerce [*A publication*]
**Int Comm Hist Geol Sci Newsl** ... International Committee on the History of Geological Sciences. Newsletter [*A publication*]
**Int Comm Illum Proc** ... International Commission on Illumination. Proceedings [*A publication*]
**Int Comm Northwest Atl Fish Annu Proc** ... International Commission for the Northwest Atlantic Fisheries. Annual Proceedings [*A publication*]
**Int Comm Northwest Atl Fish Annu Rep** ... International Commission for the Northwest Atlantic Fisheries. Annual Report [*A publication*]
**Int Comm Northwest Atl Fish Redb Part III** ... International Commission for the Northwest Atlantic Fisheries. Redbook. Part III [*A publication*]
**Int Comm Northwest Atl Fish Res Bull** ... International Commission for the Northwest Atlantic Fisheries. Research Bulletin [*A publication*]
**Int Comm Northwest Atl Fish Sel Pap** ... International Commission for the Northwest Atlantic Fisheries. Selected Papers [*A publication*]
**Int Comm Northwest Atl Fish Spec Publ** ... International Commission for the Northwest Atlantic Fisheries. Special Publication [*A publication*]
**Int Comm Northwest Atl Fish Stat Bull** ... International Commission for the Northwest Atlantic Fisheries. Statistical Bulletin [*A publication*]
**Int Comm Radiol Prot Ann** ... International Commission on Radiological Protection. Annals [*A publication*]
**Int Comm Radiol Prot Publ** ... International Commission on Radiological Protection. Publication [*A publication*]
**Int Commun Heat and Mass Transfer** ... International Communications in Heat and Mass Transfer [*A publication*]
**Int Comm Whaling Rep** ... International Commission on Whaling. Report [*A publication*]
**Int Comp**.... Interactive Computing [*A publication*]
**Int & Comp** ... International and Comparative Law Quarterly [*A publication*]
**Int Comp Law Q** ... International and Comparative Law Quarterly [*A publication*]
**Int Comp Law Quart** ... International and Comparative Law Quarterly [*A publication*]
**Int & Comp L Q** ... International and Comparative Law Quarterly [*A publication*]
**Int Comp Pub Pol** ... International and Comparative Public Policy [*A publication*]
**Int Com Rep** ... Interstate Commerce Commission Reports [*A publication*] (DLA)
**INTCON**... Interconnection (MSA)
**Int Concil**... International Conciliation [*A publication*]
**Int Conf Cent High Energy Form Proc** ... International Conference. Center for High Energy Forming. Proceedings [*A publication*]
**Int Conf Dev Power Syst Prot** ... International Conference on Developments in Power System Protection [*A publication*]
**Int Conf Fire Saf Proc** ... International Conference on Fire Safety. Proceedings [*A publication*]
**Int Conf Fluid Sealing Proc** ... International Conference on Fluid Sealing. Proceedings [*A publication*]
**Int Conf Food Sci Refrig Air Cond** ... International Conference on Food Science. Refrigeration and Air Conditioning [*A publication*] (APTA)
**Int Conf Freq Control Synth** ... International Conference on Frequency Control and Synthesis [*A publication*]
**Int Conf Genet** ... International Conference on Genetics [*A publication*]
**Int Conf Heavy Crude Tar Sands** ... International Conference on Heavy Crude and Tar Sands [*A publication*]
**Int Conf High Energy Phys Proc** ... International Conference on High Energy Physics. Proceedings [*A publication*]
**Int Conf High Energy Rate Fabr Proc** ... International Conference on High Energy Rate Fabrication. Proceedings [*A publication*]
**Int Conf Hyperbaric Med Proc** ... International Conference on Hyperbaric Medicine. Proceedings [*A publication*]
**Int Conf Insect Path Biol Control** ... International Conference on Insect Pathology and Biological Control [*A publication*]
**Int Conf Large Electr Syst Proc** ... International Conference on Large Electric Systems. Proceedings [*France*] [*A publication*]
**Int Conf Nat Glasses** ... International Conference on Natural Glasses [*A publication*]
**Int Conf Noise Control Eng Proc** ... International Conference on Noise Control Engineering. Proceedings [*A publication*]
**Int Conf Org Coat Sci Technol Proc (Technomic Publ)** ... International Conference in Organic Coatings Science and Technology. Proceedings (Technomic Publication) [*A publication*]
**Int Conf Quar Plant Prot Pests Dis Rep Soviet Deleg** ... International Conference on Quarantine and Plant Protection Against Pests and Diseases. Report of the Soviet Delegation [*A publication*]
**Int Conf Soil Mech Found Eng Proc** ... International Conference on Soil Mechanics and Foundation Engineering. Proceedings [*A publication*]
**Int Conf Therm Anal Proc** ... International Conference on Thermal Analysis. Proceedings [*A publication*]
**Int Conf Transfer Water Resour Knowl Proc** ... International Conference on Transfer of Water Resources Knowledge. Proceedings [*A publication*]
**Int Conf Water Pollut Res** ... International Conference on Water Pollution Research. Proceedings [*A publication*]
**Int Cong Chem Cem Proc** ... International Congress on the Chemistry of Cement. Proceedings [*A publication*]
**Int Congr Anim Reprod Artif Insemin** ... International Congress on Animal Reproduction and Artificial Insemination [*A publication*]
**Int Congr Appl Lasers Electro-Opt Proc** ... International Congress of Applications of Lasers and Electro-Optics. Proceedings [*A publication*]
**Int Congr Astronaut Proc** ... International Congress on Astronautics. Proceedings [*A publication*]
**Int Congr Biochem Abstr** ... International Congress of Biochemistry. Abstracts [*A publication*]
**Int Congr Biogenet** ... International Congress of Biogenetics [*A publication*]
**Int Congr Catal Prepr** ... International Congress on Catalysis. Preprints [*A publication*]
**Int Congr Electron Micros Proc** ... International Congress on Electron Microscopy. Proceedings [*A publication*]
**Int Congr Entomol Proc** ... International Congress of Entomology. Proceedings [*A publication*]
**Int Congr Hematol Lect** ... International Congress of Hematology. Lectures [*A publication*]
**Int Congr Industr Chem** ... International Congress of Industrial Chemistry [*A publication*]
**Int Congr Large Dams** ... International Congress on Large Dams [*A publication*]
**Int Congr Microbiol Symp** ... International Congress for Microbiology. Symposia [*A publication*]
**Int Congr Ophthalmol** ... International Congress of Ophthalmology [*A publication*]
**Int Congr Pl Prot** ... International Congress of Plant Protection [*A publication*]
**Int Congr Pteridines Handb** ... International Congress on Pteridines. Handbook [*A publication*]
**Int Congr Sedimentology** ... International Congress on Sedimentology [*A publication*]
**Int Congr Ser Excerpta Med** ... International Congress Series. Excerpta Medica [*Netherlands*] [*A publication*]
**Int Congr Soc Advanc Breed Res Asia Oceania** ... International Congress. Society for the Advancement of Breeding Researches in Asia and Oceania [*A publication*] (APTA)
**Int Congr Speleol Abh** ... International Congress of Speleology. Abhandlungen [*A publication*]
**Int Cong Zool Pr** ... International Congress of Zoology. Proceedings [*A publication*]
**Int Constr**... International Construction [*A publication*]
**Int Copper Inf Bull** ... International Copper Information Bulletin [*A publication*]
**Int Counc Explor Sea Coop Res Rep** ... International Council for the Exploration of the Sea. Cooperative Research Report [*A publication*]
**Int Counc Explor Sea Coop Res Rep Ser A** ... International Council for the Exploration of the Sea. Cooperative Research Report. Series A [*A publication*]
**Int Counc Explor Sea Coop Res Rep Ser B** ... International Council for the Exploration of the Sea. Cooperative Research Report. Series B [*A publication*]
**Int Counc Sci Unions Inter-Union Comm Geodynamics Rep** ... International Council of Scientific Unions. Inter-Union Commission on Geodynamics. Report [*A publication*]
**INTCP**....... Intercept (AFM)
**Int Crim Police Rev** ... International Criminal Police Review [*A publication*]
**Int Cryog Eng Conf** ... International Cryogenic Engineering Conferences [*A publication*]

**InTCS**........ Commercial Solvents Corp., Terre Haute, IN [*Library symbol*] [*Library of Congress*] [*Obsolete*] (LCLS)
**Int Currency R** ... International Currency Review [*A publication*]
**Int Curr Meter Group Rep** ... International Current Meter Group. Report [*A publication*]
**Int Curr Rev** ... International Currency Review [*A publication*]
**INTCYL**.... Intercylinder
**InTD**.......... Eugene V. Debs Foundation, Terre Haute, IN [*Library symbol*] [*Library of Congress*] (LCLS)
**INTD**......... Institut National des Techniques de la Documentation [*National Institute for Information Science*] [*France*] [*Information service or system*] (IID)
**Int Dairy Fed Annu Bull** ... International Dairy Federation. Annual Bulletin [*A publication*]
**INTDD**...... Intended
**Int Demogr** ... International Demographics [*A publication*]
**Int Dent J**... International Dental Journal [*A publication*]
**INTDEPT** ... Interdepartmental
**Int Des**....... Interior Design [*A publication*]
**Int Dev Abstr** ... International Development Abstracts [*A publication*]
**Int Develop R** ... International Development Review [*A publication*]
**Int Dev Res Cent Publ IDRC** ... International Development Research Centre. Publication IDRC [*A publication*]
**Int Dev Res Cent Tech Stud IDRC-TS** ... International Development Research Centre. Technical Studies IDRC-TS [*A publication*]
**Int Dev Rev** ... International Development Review [*A publication*]
**Int Dialog Z** ... Internationale Dialog Zeitschrift [*A publication*]
**Int Dig**........ International Digest [*A publication*]
**Int Dig Health Legis** ... International Digest of Health Legislation [*A publication*]
**INTDISP**... Interdisciplinary
**Int Dist Heat Assoc Off Proc** ... International District Heating Association. Official Proceedings [*A publication*]
**Int Dredg Abstr** ... International Dredging Abstracts [*A publication*]
**Int Dredging Rev** ... International Dredging Review [*A publication*]
**Int Drug Regul Monit** ... International Drug Regulatory Monitor [*A publication*]
**Int Dyer**...... International Dyer, Textile Printer, Bleacher, and Finisher [*A publication*]
**Int Dyer Text Printer Bleacher Finish** ... International Dyer, Textile Printer, Bleacher, and Finisher [*A publication*]
**INTE**.......... Intech, Inc. [*NASDAQ symbol*] (NQ)
**INTE**.......... Interrupt Enable [*Data processing*]
**INTEAG**.... Internist [*A publication*]
**INTEC**....... Interference [*Telecommunications*] (MDG)
**INTECH**.... Integrated Information Technology Conference and Exposition [*National Trade Productions*] (TSPED)
**InTech (Instrum Technol)** ... InTech (Instrumentation Technology) [*A publication*]
**INTECOL** ... International Association for Ecology [*University of Georgia*] [*Athens, GA*] (EAIO)
**INTECOM** ... International Council for Technical Communication [*Wokingham, Berkshire, England*]
**Int Econ R** ... International Economic Review [*A publication*]
**Int Ec R**...... International Economic Review [*A publication*]
**Int Ed & Cul Exch** ... International Educational and Cultural Exchange [*A publication*]
**INTEG**....... Integrate [*or Integrating*] (MSA)
**Integ Ed**..... Integrated Education: Race and Schools [*A publication*]
**Integ Educ** ... Integrated Education [*A publication*]
**INTEGR**.... Integrate [*or Integration*] (NASA)
**Integrated Circuits Int** ... Integrated Circuits International [*A publication*]
**Integrated Educ** ... Integrated Education [*A publication*]
**Integr Ind**... Integral Industrial [*Colombia*] [*A publication*]
**INTEL**....... Integrated Electronics
**INTEL**....... Intelligence (AABC)
**INTELCEN** ... Intelligence Center
**INTELCENPAC** ... Intelligence Center, Pacific Ocean Areas [*Obsolete*]
**INTELCOM** ... Worldwide Intelligence Communication (MCD)
**Int El Dep Conf** ... International Electrodeposition Conference [*A publication*]
**Int Electrotech Comm Publ** ... International Electrotechnical Commission. Publications [*A publication*]
**Int Elektr** ... Internationale Elektronische Rundschau [*A publication*]
**Int Elektron Rundsch** ... Internationale Elektronische Rundschau [*A publication*]
**INTELEVENT** ... International Televent (EA)
**INTELL**..... Intelligence (ROG)
**Intell Dig**.... Intelligence Digest [*A publication*]
**Intellectual Property L Rev** ... Intellectual Property Law Review [*A publication*] (DLA)
**INTELLIVISION** ... Intelligent Television [*Home video game*] [*Mattel, Inc.*]
**Intell Prop L Rev** ... Intellectual Property Law Review [*A publication*]
**INTELO**.... Intelligence Officer [*Military*]
**Intel Obs**.... Intellectual Observer [*A publication*]
**INTELPOST** ... International Electronic Post [*Postal Service*]
**INTELSAT** ... International Telecommunications Satellite Organization (EA)
**INTELTNG** ... Intelligence Training [*Military*] (NVT)
**INTEN** ...... Intensity (MSA)
**Inten Agric** ... Intensive Agriculture [*A publication*]
**Int Enc Comp Law** ... International Encyclopedia of Comparative Law [*A publication*] (DLA)
**Int Endod J** ... International Endodontic Journal [*A publication*]
**Int Energie Forum** ... Internationales Energie-Forum [*A publication*]
**INTENS**.... Intensive
**Intensive Agr** ... Intensive Agriculture [*A publication*]
**Intensive Care Med** ... Intensive Care Medicine [*A publication*]
**Intensive Care Nurs** ... Intensive Care Nursing [*A publication*]
**Intensivmed Diagn** ... Intensivmedizin und Diagnostik [*A publication*]
**Intensivmed Notfallmed** ... Intensivmedizin und Notfallmedizin [*A publication*]
**Intensivmed Notfallmed Anaesthesiol** ... Intensivmedizin, Notfallmedizin, Anaesthesiologie [*A publication*]
**Intensivmed Prax** ... Intensivmedizinische Praxis [*A publication*]
**INTENTN** ... Intention (ROG)
**Int Environ Saf** ... International Environment and Safety [*A publication*]
**Int Env Saf** ... International Environment and Safety [*A publication*]
**INTER**....... Interception [*Football*]
**Inter**........... Interiors [*A publication*]
**INTER**....... Intermediate (AAG)
**INTER**....... Intermittent
**INTER**....... Internal (KSC)
**IntER**......... International Economic Review [*A publication*]
**INTER**....... Interphone (MCD)
**INTER**....... Interrogation (ADA)
**INTER**....... Interrogative
**INTER**....... Interrupt
**INTERACT** ... Integrated Research Aircraft Control Technology (MCD)
**INTERACT** ... Interactive Television Network [*Dartmouth-Hitchcock Medical Center*] [*Hanover, NH*] [*Telecommunications*] (TSSD)
**INTERALIS** ... International Advanced Life Information System (BUR)
**INTERALP** ... Intercultural Action Learning Program
**Inter-Am**.... Inter-American [*A publication*]
**Inter-Am Econ Affairs** ... Inter-American Economic Affairs [*A publication*]
**Inter-Amer Econ Aff** ... Inter-American Economic Affairs [*A publication*]
**Inter Amer M Bul** ... Inter-American Music Bulletin [*A publication*]
**Inter-Amer M R** ... Inter-American Music Review [*A publication*]
**Interam J P** ... Interamerican Journal of Psychology [*A publication*]
**Inter-Am L Rev** ... Inter-American Law Review [*A publication*]
**Inter Am M** ... Inter-American Music Review [*A publication*]
**Inter-Am Q** ... Inter-American Quarterly [*A publication*]
**Interam Rev Bibliogr** ... Inter-American Review of Bibliography [*A publication*]
**Inter-Am Trop Tuna Comm Bull** ... Inter-American Tropical Tuna Commission. Bulletin [*A publication*]
**Inter-Am Trop Tuna Comm Spec Rep** ... Inter-American Tropical Tuna Commission. Special Report [*A publication*]
**INTER ARTS** ... Intermediate of Arts [*British*] (ROG)
**INTERASMA** ... International Association of Asthmology [*Lisbon, Portugal*] (EAIO)
**INTERATOM** ... Internationale Atomreactorbau [*German*]
**Interavia (Engl Ed)** ... Interavia (English Edition) [*A publication*]
**INTER BA** ... Intermediate Bachelor of Arts [*British*] (ROG)
**Inter B C** ... Interracial Books for Children. Bulletin [*A publication*]
**INTERBEV** ... International Beverage Industry Exhibition and Congress [*National Soft Drink Association*] (TSPED)
**INTERBOR** ... Union Internationale des Techniciens Orthopedistes [*International Association of Orthotists and Prosthetists*] (EA)
**INTERBRABANT** ... Union Intercommunale des Centrales Electriques du Brabant SA [*Belgium*]
**INTERBRIGHT** ... International Literary and Information Centre in Science Extension (IID)
**INTERCARGO** ... International Association of Dry Cargo Shipowners (EAIO)
**INTERCEDE** ... International Coalition to End Domestics' Exploitation
**Intercell Intracell Commun** ... Intercellular and Intracellular Communication [*A publication*]
**INTERCENTRE** ... International Centre for the Terminology of the Social Sciences [*Grand-Saconnex, Switzerland*] (EA)
**Interchurch N** ... Interchurch News [*A publication*]
**INTERCO** ... International Council on Jewish Social and Welfare Services [*Geneva, Switzerland*] (EAIO)
**INTERCODE** ... International CODEN Service [*Chemical Abstracts Service*] [*Information service or system*] (IID)
**INTERCOL** ... Intercolonial (ADA)
**Intercolon Med J Australas** ... Intercolonial Medical Journal of Australasia [*A publication*]
**INTERCOM** ... Intercommunication System
**INTERCOM** ... Intertribal Christian Communications
**INTERCOM** ... Societe Intercommunale Belge de Gaz et d'Electricite SA [*Belgium*]
**INTERCON** ... Interconnection (KSC)
**INTERCON** ... Intermediate-Size Cargo Container
**INTERCON** ... International Convention
**Intercont**.... Intercontinental Press [*A publication*]
**Intercontinental Pr** ... Intercontinental Press [*A publication*]
**INTERCOOP** ... International Organization for Consumer Co-Operative Distributive Trade (EAIO)

**INTERCOSMOS** ... Council on International Cooperation in the Study and Utilization of Outer Space
**INTERDACO** ... Intercontinental Data Control Corp. Ltd. [*Ottawa, ON*] [*Telecommunications*] (TSSD)
**Interdep Comm Atmos Sci Rep US** ... Interdepartmental Committee for Atmospheric Sciences. Report. United States [*A publication*]
**Inter Depend** ... Inter Dependent [*A publication*]
**INTERDEPT** ... Interdepartmental (KSC)
**Inter Des**.... Interior Design [*A publication*]
**INTERDICT** ... Interference Detection and Interdiction Countermeasures Team [*Electromagnetic compatibility programs*]
**Interdisciplinary Math** ... Interdisciplinary Mathematics [*A publication*]
**Interdisciplinary Sci Rev** ... Interdisciplinary Science Reviews [*A publication*]
**Interdisciplinary Systems Res** ... Interdisciplinary Systems Research [*A publication*]
**Interdiscip Sci Rev** ... Interdisciplinary Science Reviews [*A publication*]
**Interdiscip Top Gerontol** ... Interdisciplinary Topics in Gerontology [*A publication*]
**INTERDOK** ... International Documentation and Information Centre
**Interecon**.... Intereconomics [*A publication*]
**Inter Econ Indic & Comp Tr** ... International Economic Indicators and Competitive Trends [*A publication*]
**Inter Ed & Cul Ex** ... International Educational and Cultural Exchange [*A publication*]
**INTEREG** ... Internationales Institut fuer Nationalitatenrecht und Regionalismus [*International Institute for Ethnic Group Rights and Regionalism*] (EA)
**INTEREGEN** ... Internal Regenerative (KSC)
**Inter Electron** ... Inter Electronique [*France*] [*A publication*]
**INTEREX** ... International Exchangors Association (EA)
**INTERF**.... Interferometer
**Interface Comput Educ Q** ... Interface. The Computer Education Quarterly [*A publication*]
**Interfaces Comput** ... Interfaces in Computing [*Later, Computer Standards and Interfaces*] [*A publication*]
**INTERFER** ... Interference
**Interferon Biotecnol** ... Interferon y Biotecnologia [*A publication*]
**INTERFILM** ... International Inter-Church Film Center [*Hilversum, Netherlands*] (EAIO)
**INTERFOOD** ... International Exhibition of Foodstuffs, Fast Food, and Traditional and Mass Catering (TSPED)
**INTERFRIGO** ... International Railway-Owned Company for Refrigerated Transport (EAIO)
**INTERGALVA** ... International Galvanizing Conference (MCD)
**Intergov Oceanogr Comm Tech Ser** ... Intergovernmental Oceanographic Commission. Technical Series [*A publication*]
**Intergov Oceanogr Comm Workshop Rep** ... Intergovernmental Oceanographic Commission. Workshop Report [*A publication*]
**Intergov Persp** ... Intergovernmental Perspective [*A publication*]
**INTERGOVT** ... Intergovernmental
**INTERGU** ... Internationale Gesellschaft fuer Urheberrecht [*International Copyright Society*] (EAIO)
**INTERHYBRID** ... Association Intercontinentale du Mais Hybride
**Interior Dec** ... Decisions of the Department of the Interior [*A publication*] (DLA)
**Interior Des** ... Interior Design [*A publication*]
**Interior Landscape Intl** ... Interior Landscape International [*A publication*]
**INTERJ**..... Interjection
**INTERLAINE** ... Comite des Industries Lainieres de la CEE [*Committee of the Wool Textile Industry in the EEC*] (EAIO)
**Interlend and Doc Supply** ... Interlending and Document Supply [*A publication*]
**Interlending Rev** ... Interlending Review [*A publication*]
**INTERLISP** ... [*A*] programming language [*1974*] (CSR)
**Inter M**....... International Monthly [*A publication*]
**INTERMAC** ... International Association of Merger and Acquisition Consultants (EA)
**INTERMAG** ... International Conference on Magnetics (MCD)
**INTERMAMA** ... International Congress for Measurement and Automation (IEEE)
**INTERMARC** ... International Machine Readable Catalogue
**INTERMED** ... Intermediate (ADA)
**Intermed Sci Curric Study Newsl** ... Intermediate Science Curriculum Study. Newsletter [*A publication*]
**INTERMET** ... International Association for Metropolitan Research and Development
**Intermex**.... International Mexican Bank Ltd. [*London, England*] (EY)
**INTERMILPOL** ... International Military Police [*NATO*]
**INTERMORGEO** ... International Organization for Marine Geology [*Council for Mutual Economic Assistance*] [*Riga, Union of Soviet Socialist Republics*] (EAIO)
**Intermountain Econ R** ... Intermountain Economic Review [*A publication*]
**INTERMSTA** ... Intermediate Station
**Intermt Assoc Geol Annu Field Conf Guideb** ... Intermountain Association of Geologists. Annual Field Conference. Guidebook [*A publication*]
**Intermt Assoc Pet Geol Annu Field Conf Guideb** ... Intermountain Association of Petroleum Geologists. Annual Field Conference. Guidebook [*A publication*]
**Intermt Econ Rev** ... Intermountain Economic Review [*A publication*]
**INTERMTRA** ... Intermediate Training [*Naval Air*]
**INTERN**.... Internal
**INTERN**.... International
**Interna LN** ... International Law Notes [*London*] [*A publication*] (DLA)
**Internasjonal Polit** ... Internasjonal Politikk [*Norway*] [*A publication*]
**INTERNAT** ... International
**Internat**...... International Quarterly [*A publication*]
**Internat Abstr Surg** ... International Abstracts of Surgery [*A publication*]
**Internat Affairs (London)** ... International Affairs (London) [*A publication*]
**Internat Affairs (Moscow)** ... International Affairs (Moscow) [*A publication*]
**Internat Afrikaforum** ... Internationales Afrikaforum [*A publication*]
**Internat Anesth Clin** ... International Anesthesiology Clinics [*A publication*]
**Internat Annals Criminology** ... International Annals of Criminology [*A publication*]
**Internat Arch Allergy** ... International Archives of Allergy and Applied Immunology [*A publication*]
**Internat Archiv f Ethno** ... Internationales Archiv fuer Ethnologie [*A publication*]
**Internat Asienforum** ... Internationales Asienforum [*A publication*]
**Internat Ass Med Mus Bull** ... International Association of Medical Museums. Bulletin and Journal of Technical Methods [*A publication*]
**Internat Assoc Sci Hydrology Bull** ... International Association of Scientific Hydrology. Bulletin [*A publication*]
**Internat Assoc Sci Hydrology Bull Pub** ... International Association of Scientific Hydrology. Bulletin. Publication [*A publication*]
**Internat Assoc Sci Hydrology Pub** ... International Association of Scientific Hydrology. Publications [*A publication*]
**Internat Bar Assoc** ... International Bar Association (DLA)
**Internat Betriebswirt Zeitschriftenreport** ... Internationaler Betriebswirtschaftlicher Zeitschriftenreport [*A publication*]
**Internat Bus** ... International Business [*A publication*]
**Internat Chem Engng** ... International Chemical Engineering [*A publication*]
**Internat Clin** ... International Clinics [*A publication*]
**Internat Comm Coal Petrology Proc** ... International Committee for Coal Petrology. Proceedings [*A publication*]
**Internat Commer Bank China Econ R** ... International Commercial Bank of China. Economic Review [*A publication*]
**Internat Comm Jurists R** ... International Commission of Jurists. Review [*A publication*]
**Internat and Comparative Law Q 4th Ser** ... International and Comparative Law Quarterly. Fourth Series [*A publication*]
**Internat Comp LQ** ... International and Comparative Law Quarterly [*A publication*]
**Internat Contract** ... International Contract [*A publication*]
**Internat Correspondence Schools Serial** ... International Correspondence Schools. Serial [*A publication*]
**Internat Currency R** ... International Currency Review [*A publication*]
**Internat Development R** ... International Development Review [*A publication*]
**Internat Econ Indicators** ... International Economic Indicators [*A publication*]
**Internat Econom Rev** ... International Economic Review [*A publication*]
**Internat Econ R** ... International Economic Review [*A publication*]
**Internat Entwicklung** ... Internationale Entwicklung [*A publication*]
**Internat Family Planning Perspectives** ... International Family Planning Perspectives [*A publication*]
**Internat Family Planning Perspectives and Dig** ... International Family Planning Perspectives and Digest [*A publication*]
**Internat Fin Chase** ... International Finance. Chase Manhattan Bank [*A publication*]
**Internat Geology Rev** ... International Geology Review [*A publication*]
**International R Ed** ... International Review of Education [*A publication*]
**Internat J Accounting** ... International Journal of Accounting [*A publication*]
**Internat J Bio-Med Comput** ... International Journal of Bio-Medical Computing [*A publication*]
**Internat J Circuit Theory Appl** ... International Journal of Circuit Theory and Applications [*A publication*]
**Internat J Comput and Fluids** ... International Journal. Computers and Fluids [*A publication*]
**Internat J Comput Information Sci** ... International Journal of Computer and Information Sciences [*A publication*]
**Internat J Comput Inform Sci** ... International Journal of Computer and Information Sciences [*A publication*]
**Internat J Comput Math** ... International Journal of Computer Mathematics. Section A [*A publication*]
**Internat J Control** ... International Journal of Control [*A publication*]
**Internat J Electron** ... International Journal of Electronics [*A publication*]
**Internat J Engng Science** ... International Journal of Engineering Science [*A publication*]
**Internat J Engrg Sci** ... International Journal of Engineering Science [*A publication*]
**Internat J Environmental Studies** ... International Journal of Environmental Studies [*A publication*]
**Internat J Fertil** ... International Journal of Fertility [*A publication*]
**Internat J Fracture** ... International Journal of Fracture [*A publication*]
**Internat J Game Theory** ... International Journal of Game Theory [*A publication*]
**Internat J Gen Syst** ... International Journal of General Systems [*A publication*]
**Internat J Gen Systems** ... International Journal of General Systems [*A publication*]

**Internat J Heat Fluid Flow** ... International Journal of Heat and Fluid Flow [*A publication*]
**Internat J Heat Mass Transfer** ... International Journal of Heat and Mass Transfer [*A publication*]
**Internat J of Leg Res** ... International Journal of Legal Research [*A publication*] (DLA)
**Internat J Leprosy** ... International Journal of Leprosy [*A publication*]
**Internat J Man-Machine Studies** ... International Journal of Man-Machine Studies [*A publication*]
**Internat J Man-Mach Stud** ... International Journal of Man-Machine Studies [*A publication*]
**Internat J Math Ed Sci Tech** ... International Journal of Mathematical Education in Science and Technology [*A publication*]
**Internat J Math Math Sci** ... International Journal of Mathematics and Mathematical Sciences [*A publication*]
**Internat J Mental Health** ... International Journal of Mental Health [*A publication*]
**Internat J Middle East Studies** ... International Journal of Middle East Studies [*A publication*]
**Internat J Mineral Proc** ... International Journal of Mineral Processing [*A publication*]
**Internat J Multiphase Flow** ... International Journal of Multiphase Flow [*A publication*]
**Internat J Neuropsychiat** ... International Journal of Neuropsychiatry [*A publication*]
**Internat J Non-Linear Mech** ... International Journal of Non-Linear Mechanics [*A publication*]
**Internat J Numer Analyt Methods Geomech** ... International Journal for Numerical and Analytical Methods in Geomechanics [*A publication*]
**Internat J Numer Methods Engrg** ... International Journal for Numerical Methods in Engineering [*A publication*]
**Internat J Numer Methods Fluids** ... International Journal for Numerical Methods in Fluids [*A publication*]
**Internat Jour Rock Mechanics and Mining Sci** ... International Journal of Rock Mechanics and Mining Sciences [*Later, International Journal of Rock Mechanics and Mining Sciences and Geomechanics Abstracts*] [*A publication*]
**Internat J Physical Distribution and Materials Mgt** ... International Journal of Physical Distribution and Materials Management [*A publication*]
**Internat J Policy Anal Inform Systems** ... International Journal of Policy Analysis and Information Systems [*A publication*]
**Internat J Social Econ** ... International Journal of Social Economics [*A publication*]
**Internat J Sociol** ... International Journal of Sociology [*A publication*]
**Internat J Solids and Structures** ... International Journal of Solids and Structures [*A publication*]
**Internat J Systems Sci** ... International Journal of Systems Science [*A publication*]
**Internat J Theoret Phys** ... International Journal of Theoretical Physics [*A publication*]
**Internat J Urban and Regional Research** ... International Journal of Urban and Regional Research [*A publication*]
**INTERNATL** ... International
**Internat Labour R** ... International Labour Review [*A publication*]
**Internat Lawyer** ... International Lawyer. Quarterly Publication of the Section of International and Comparative Law of the American Bar Association [*A publication*]
**Internatl Cong Hist Sci Proc** ... International Congress of Historical Sciences. Proceedings [*A publication*]
**Internat Legal Materials** ... International Legal Materials [*A publication*]
**Internatl Goat Sheep Res** ... International Goat and Sheep Research [*A publication*]
**Internatl Jour** ... International Journal [*A publication*]
**Internat LN** ... International Law Notes [*A publication*] (DLA)
**Internat Logic Rev** ... International Logic Review [*A publication*]
**Internatl Organ** ... International Organization [*A publication*]
**Internat LQ** ... International Law Quarterly [*A publication*]
**Internat M** ... International Magazine [*A publication*]
**Internat Math News** ... International Mathematical News [*A publication*]
**Internat Mgt** ... International Management [*A publication*]
**Internat Migration** ... International Migration [*A publication*]
**Internat Migration R** ... International Migration Review [*A publication*]
**Internat Mo** ... International Monthly [*A publication*]
**Internat Monetary Fund Staff Pas** ... International Monetary Fund. Staff Papers [*A publication*]
**Internat Oceanog Found Bull** ... International Oceanographic Foundation. Bulletin [*A publication*]
**Internat Org** ... International Organization [*A publication*]
**Internat Perspectives (Can)** ... International Perspectives (Canada) [*A publication*]
**Internat Problems** ... International Problems [*A publication*]
**Internat Problems (Tel Aviv)** ... International Problems (Tel Aviv) [*A publication*]
**Internat R** .. International Review [*A publication*]
**Internat R Admin Science (Brussels)** ... International Review of Administrative Sciences (Brussels) [*A publication*]
**Internat R Admin Sciences** ... International Review of Administrative Sciences [*A publication*]
**Internat R Criminal Policy** ... International Review of Criminal Policy [*A publication*]
**Internat Recht und Diplomatie** ... Internationales Recht und Diplomatie [*A publication*]
**Internat Rec Med** ... International Record of Medicine [*A publication*]
**Internat Relations** ... Relations Internationales/International Relations [*A publication*]
**Internat Rev Trop Med** ... International Review of Tropical Medicine [*A publication*]
**Internat Schriftenreihe Numer Math** ... Internationale Schriftenreihe zur Numerischen Mathematik [*A publication*]
**Internat Security** ... International Security [*A publication*]
**Internat Security R** ... International Security Review [*A publication*]
**Internat Ser Appl Systems Anal** ... International Series on Applied Systems Analysis [*A publication*]
**Internat Ser Mod Appl Math Comput Sci** ... International Series in Modern Applied Mathematics and Computer Science [*A publication*]
**Internat Ser Monographs in Natural Philos** ... International Series of Monographs in Natural Philosophy [*A publication*]
**Internat Ser Monographs Pure Appl Math** ... International Series of Monographs in Pure and Applied Mathematics [*A publication*]
**Internat Ser Natural Philos** ... International Series in Natural Philosophy [*A publication*]
**Internat Ser Nonlinear Math Theory Methods Appl** ... International Series in Nonlinear Mathematics. Theory, Methods, and Application [*A publication*]
**Internat Ser Numer Math** ... International Series of Numerical Mathematics [*A publication*]
**Internat Ser Pure Appl Math** ... International Series in Pure and Applied Mathematics [*A publication*]
**Internat Social Science J** ... International Social Science Journal [*A publication*]
**Internat Spectator** ... Internationale Spectator [*A publication*]
**Internat Statist Rev** ... International Statistical Review [*A publication*]
**Internat Studies (New Delhi)** ... International Studies (New Delhi) [*A publication*]
**Internat Tax J** ... International Tax Journal [*A publication*]
**Internat Trade Forum** ... International Trade Forum [*A publication*]
**Internat Trade Law and Practice** ... International Trade Law and Practice [*A publication*]
**Internat Z Landw** ... Internationale Zeitschrift der Landwirtschaft [*A publication*]
**Intern Audit** ... Internal Auditor [*A publication*]
**Intern Biodet Bull** ... International Biodeterioration Bulletin. Reference Index [*A publication*]
**Intern Combust Eng** ... Internal Combustion Engine [*Japan*] [*A publication*]
**INTERNET** ... INTERNET - International Project Management Association [*Formerly, International Management Systems Association*] [*Zurich, Switzerland*] (EA)
**Internist Prax** ... Internistische Praxis [*A publication*]
**Internist Welt** ... Internistische Welt [*A publication*]
**Intern J System Bacteriol** ... International Journal of Systematic Bacteriology [*A publication*]
**Internl Photogr** ... International Photographer [*A publication*]
**Intern Med** ... Internal Medicine [*A publication*]
**Intern Med News** ... Internal Medicine News [*A publication*]
**Intern Med (Tokyo)** ... Internal Medicine (Tokyo) [*A publication*]
**INTER NOCT** ... Inter Noctem [*During the Night*] [*Pharmacy*]
**Intern Pbd Ind** ... International Paper Board Industry [*European Edition*] [*A publication*]
**Intern Phot** ... International Photography [*A publication*]
**Intern Phot Tech** ... International Photography Techniques [*A publication*]
**Intern Rep Miner Policy Sector Dep Energy Mines Resour (Can)** ... Internal Report. Mineral Policy Sector. Department of Energy, Mines, and Resources (Canada) [*A publication*]
**Intern Sci Technol** ... International Science and Technology [*A publication*]
**Interntl F G** ... International Film Guide [*A publication*]
**INTEROG** ... Interrogate (NASA)
**INTEROP** ... Interoperability
**Interp** ......... Interpretation [*A publication*]
**INTERP** .... Interpreter
**Inter-Parliamentary Bul** ... Inter-Parliamentary Bulletin [*A publication*]
**Interpers D** ... Interpersonal Development [*A publication*]
**INTERPET** ... International Petroleum Co.
**INTERPEX** ... International Philatelic Exhibition [*American Stamp Dealers Association*] (TSPED)
**INTERPHES** ... International Pharmaceutical Cosmetics, Toiletry, and Allied Industries Exhibition [*England*]
**INTERPHIL** ... International Standing Conference on Philanthropy [*Yalding, Kent, England*] (EAIO)
**INTERPLAN** ... International Group for Studies in National Planning
**INTERPLAS** ... International Plastics and Rubber Exhibition [*British Plastics Federation*] (TSPED)
**INTERPOL** ... International Criminal Police Organization
**Interp Op** ... Interpretative Opinion [*Legal term*] (DLA)
**Interpr** ........ Interpretation. A Journal of Bible and Theology [*Richmond, VA*] [*A publication*]
**Interpretat** ... Interpretation [*A publication*]
**INTERPRO** ... International Probation Organization (EA)

**INTERPRON** ... Photointerpretation Squadron [*Military*]
**interr** .......... Interrogative (BJA)
**INTERR** .... Interrogator [*Aviation*] (FAAC)
**Interracial Bks Child Bull** ... Interracial Books for Children. Bulletin [*A publication*]
**Interracial Rev** ... Interracial Review [*A publication*]
**Inter Reg** .... Inter Regions [*A publication*]
**Inter Rev for Bus Ed** ... International Review for Business Education [*A publication*]
**INTERROG** ... Interrogation
**INTERROGS** ... Interrogatories (ROG)
**INTERROGY** ... Interrogatory (ROG)
**Intersch Ath Adm** ... Interscholastic Athletic Administration [*A publication*]
**Intersch Athl Adm** ... Interscholastic Athletic Administration [*A publication*]
**Intersci Conf Antimicrob Agents Chemother Proc** ... Interscience Conference on Antimicrobial Agents and Chemotherapy. Proceedings [*A publication*]
**Interscience Libr Chem Eng Process** ... Interscience Library of Chemical Engineering and Processing [*A publication*]
**Intersci Monogr Texts Phys Astron** ... Interscience Monographs and Texts in Physics and Astronomy [*A publication*]
**Inter Sci Techn** ... International Science and Technology [*A publication*]
**Inters Com Rep** ... Interstate Commerce Commission Reports [*A publication*] (DLA)
**INTERSEC** ... Intermediate Section
**INTERSECT** ... International Security Technics [*Organization in TV series "The Gemini Man"*]
**Inter Ser Monogr Chem** ... International Series of Monographs on Chemistry [*A publication*]
**Intersoc Energy Convers Eng Conf Proc** ... Intersociety Energy Conversion Engineering Conference. Proceedings [*A publication*]
**INTERSPUTNIK** ... International Organization of Space Communications [*Moscow, USSR*] (EAIO)
**Interstate** ... Forecast. First Interstate Bank. Annual Report [*A publication*]
**Interstate Com R** ... Interstate Commerce Reports [*A publication*] (DLA)
**Interstate Conf of Headmistresses** ... Interstate Conference of Headmistresses of Australian Girls' Schools. Report [*A publication*] (APTA)
**Interstate Oil Compact Comm Comm Bull** ... Interstate Oil Compact Commission. Committee Bulletin [*A publication*]
**Interstate Oil Compact Quart Bull** ... Interstate Oil Compact. Quarterly Bulletin [*A publication*]
**Interst Com R** ... Interstate Commerce Commission Reports [*A publication*] (DLA)
**INTERSTENO** ... Federation Internationale de Stenographie et de Dactylographie [*International Federation of Shorthand and Typewriting*] [*Bonn, Federal Republic of Germany*] (EAIO)
**INTERSTOL** ... Inter-City Short Takeoff and Landing [*Aviation*]
**INTERTANKO** ... International Association of Independent Tanker Owners [*Oslo, Norway*] (EAIO)
**INTERTEL** ... International Intelligence, Inc.
**INTERTEL** ... International Legion of Intelligence [*Acronym is used as official name of association*] (EA)
**INTERTEX** ... International Textile and Fabrics Trade Fair (TSPED)
**Inter-Union Comm Geodyn Sci Rep** ... Inter-Union Commission on Geodynamics. Scientific Report [*A publication*]
**Inter-Univ Electron Ser** ... Inter-University Electronics Series [*A publication*]
**Interuniv Fac Work Conf** ... Inter-University Faculty Work Conference [*A publication*]
**INTERV** .... Interval
**Interv** .......... Interview [*A publication*]
**INTERV** .... Interview
**Intervirolo** .. Intervirology [*A publication*]
**INTERWOOLABS** ... International Association of Wool and Textile Laboratories (EAIO)
**INTEST** ..... Intestinal
**INTEX** ....... International Fallout Warning Exercise (NATG)
**Int Exec** ...... International Executive [*A publication*]
**Int Export Chem** ... International Export Chemist [*A publication*]
**INTEXT** .... International Textbook Co.
**INTF** .......... Interface (NASA)
**INTF** .......... Interface Systems, Inc. [*NASDAQ symbol*] (NQ)
**Int Fam Plann Dig** ... International Family Planning Digest [*A publication*]
**Int Fam Plann Perspect** ... International Family Planning Perspectives [*A publication*]
**INTFC** ....... Interface (MSA)
**INTFC** ....... Interference (FAAC)
**INTFER** .... Interference (AABC)
**Int Fict R** .... International Fiction Review [*A publication*]
**Int Field Year Great Lakes Tech Man Ser** ... International Field Year for the Great Lakes. Technical Manual Series [*A publication*]
**Int Fire Fighter** ... International Fire Fighter [*A publication*]
**Int Folk Bibliogr** ... International Folklore Bibliography [*A publication*]
**Int Folk Mus Council Jl** ... International Folk Music Council. Journal [*A publication*]
**Int Forum Inf and Doc** ... International Forum on Information and Documentation [*A publication*]
**Int Forum Inf Docum** ... International Forum on Information and Documentation [*A publication*]
**Int Forum Logotherapy** ... International Forum for Logotherapy [*A publication*]
**Int Foundry Cong Congr Pap** ... International Foundry Congress. Congress Papers [*Switzerland*] [*A publication*]
**INTFR** ....... Interference (KSC)
**Int Freight** ... International Freighting Weekly [*A publication*]
**Int Fruchtsaftunion Wiss-Tech Komm Ber** ... Internationale Fruchtsaftunion. Wissenschaftlich-Technische Kommission. Berichte [*A publication*]
**Int Fruit World** ... International Fruit World [*A publication*]
**INTFU** ....... Interface Unit [*Data processing*]
**Int Fund Res Symp** ... International Fundamental Research Symposium [*A publication*]
**INTG** ......... Integration (NASA)
**INTG** ......... [*The*] Intergroup Corp. [*Los Angeles, CA*] [*NASDAQ symbol*] (NQ)
**INTG** ......... Interrogate (AABC)
**INTGA** ...... In Theory Only [*A publication*]
**Int Gas Technol Highlights** ... International Gas Technology Highlights [*A publication*]
**Int G Class Stud** ... International Guide to Classical Studies [*A publication*]
**INTGEN** ... Interpreter Generator
**Int Geochem Explor Symp Proc** ... International Geochemical Exploration Symposium. Proceedings [*A publication*]
**Int Geog Cong Rp Verh** ... International Geographical Congress. Report. Verhandlungen [*A publication*]
**Int Geogr Congr** ... International Geographical Congress [*A publication*]
**Int Geogr Congr Pap - Congr Int Geogr Commun** ... International Geographical Congress. Papers - Congres International de Geographie. Communications [*A publication*]
**Int Geol Congr** ... International Geological Congress [*A publication*]
**Int Geol Congr Abstr Congr Geol Int Resumes** ... International Geological Congress. Abstracts. Congres Geologique International. Resumes [*A publication*]
**Int Geol Rev** ... International Geology Review [*A publication*]
**Int Geophys Ser** ... International Geophysics Series: A Series of Monographs [*A publication*]
**INTGL** ....... Integral (KSC)
**Int Glaciospeleological Surv Bull** ... International Glaciospeleological Survey. Bulletin [*A publication*]
**Int Goat Sheep Res** ... International Goat and Sheep Research [*A publication*]
**INTGR** ...... Integrate (AABC)
**INTGRD** ... Integrated
**Int Gstaad Symp Proc** ... International Gstaad Symposium. Proceedings [*A publication*]
**IntGuC** ....... International Guide to Classical Studies [*A publication*]
**Int Guide Classical Stud** ... International Guide to Classical Studies [*A publication*]
**Int Gym** ...... International Gymnast [*A publication*]
**INTH** ......... Intrathecal [*Medicine*]
**Int Health News** ... International Health News [*A publication*]
**Int Histol Classif Tumors** ... International Histological Classification of Tumors [*A publication*]
**Int Hist R** ... International History Review [*A publication*]
**InTho** ......... Thorntown Public Library, Thorntown, IN [*Library symbol*] [*Library of Congress*] (LCLS)
**Int Holzmarkt** ... Internationaler Holzmarkt [*A publication*]
**Int Hort Congr** ... International Horticulture Congress [*A publication*]
**Int Hyd Rev** ... International Hydrographic Review [*A publication*]
**Int Hydrocarbon Process** ... International Hydrocarbon Processing [*A publication*]
**Int Hydrogr Conf** ... International Hydrographic Conference [*A publication*]
**Int Hydrogr Rev** ... International Hydrographic Review [*A publication*]
**Int Hydrol Decade Newsl** ... International Hydrological Decade. Newsletter [*A publication*]
**InTI** ............ Indiana State University, Terre Haute, IN [*Library symbol*] [*Library of Congress*] (LCLS)
**InTi** ............ Tipton County Public Library, Tipton, IN [*Library symbol*] [*Library of Congress*] (LCLS)
**INTIB** ........ Industrial and Technological Information Bank [*UNIDO*] (IID)
**INTIM** ....... Interrupt and Timing [*Telecommunications*] (TEL)
**InTIMC** ..... IMC Chemical Group, Inc., Technical Library, Terre Haute, IN [*Library symbol*] [*Library of Congress*] (LCLS)
**Intime** ......... Information on Technology in Manufacturing Engineering [*Society of Manufacturing Engineers*] [*Dearborn, MI*]
**Int Ind** ........ International Index [*A publication*]
**Int Ind** ........ International Industry [*A publication*]
**Int Index** .... International Index [*A publication*]
**Int Index Annu Cumu** ... International Index. Annual Cumulation [*A publication*]
**Int Index Film Period** ... International Index to Film Periodicals [*A publication*]
**Int Index Multi Media Inf** ... International Index to Multi-Media Information [*A publication*]
**Int Index Period** ... International Index to Periodicals [*A publication*]
**Int Ind Film** ... International Index to Film Periodicals [*A publication*]
**Int Inst Appl Syst Anal Collab Proc Ser** ... International Institute for Applied Systems Analysis. Collaborative Proceedings Series [*A publication*]

**Int Inst Appl Syst Anal Res Mem** ... International Institute for Applied Systems Analysis. Research Memorandum [*A publication*]
**Int Inst Land Reclam Impr (Netherlands) Bibliogr** ... International Institute for Land Reclamation and Improvement (Netherlands). Bibliography [*A publication*]
**Int Inst Land Reclam Impr (Netherlands) Bull** ... International Institute for Land Reclamation and Improvement (Netherlands). Bulletin [*A publication*]
**Int Inst Land Reclam Impr (Netherlands) Publ** ... International Institute for Land Reclamation and Improvement (Netherlands). Publication [*A publication*]
**Int Inst Land Reclam Improv Annu Rep** ... International Institute for Land Reclamation and Improvement. Annual Report [*A publication*]
**Int Inst Land Reclam Improv Bull** ... International Institute for Land Reclamation and Improvement. Bulletin [*A publication*]
**Int Inst Land Reclam Improv (Neth) Pub** ... International Institute for Land Reclamation and Improvement (Netherlands). Publication [*A publication*]
**Int Inst Land Reclam Improv Publ** ... International Institute for Land Reclamation and Improvement. Publication [*A publication*]
**Int Inst Ld Reclam Improv** ... International Institute for Land Reclamation and Improvement. Publication [*A publication*]
**Int Inst Ph** ... International Institute of Philosophy. Symposia [*A publication*]
**Int Inst Seismol Earthquake Eng Bull** ... International Institute of Seismology and Earthquake Engineering. Bulletin [*A publication*]
**Int Inst Seismol Earthquake Eng Individ Stud** ... International Institute of Seismology and Earthquake Engineering. Individual Studies by Participants [*A publication*]
**Int Inst Sugar Beet Res J** ... International Institute for Sugar Beet Research. Journal [*A publication*]
**INTIP**........ Integrated Information Processing
**INTIPS**...... Integrated Information Processing System [*Air Development Center, Rome, NY*]
**Int J**............ International Journal [*A publication*]
**Int J A Aff** ... International Journal of Agrarian Affairs [*A publication*]
**Int J Acad Ichthyol** ... International Journal. Academy of Ichthyology [*A publication*]
**Int J Acarol** ... International Journal of Acarology [*A publication*]
**Int J Addic** ... International Journal of the Addictions [*A publication*]
**Int J Addict** ... International Journal of the Addictions [*A publication*]
**Int J Adhes Adhes** ... International Journal of Adhesion and Adhesives [*England*] [*A publication*]
**Int J Adhesion & Adhesives** ... International Journal of Adhesion and Adhesives [*A publication*]
**Int J Adolesc Med Health** ... International Journal of Adolescent Medicine and Health [*A publication*]
**Int J Adult Orthodon Orthognath Surg** ... International Journal of Adult Orthodontics and Orthognathic Surgery [*A publication*]
**Int J Adult Youth Ed** ... International Journal of Adult and Youth Education [*A publication*]
**Int J Adv Couns** ... International Journal for the Advancement of Counselling [*A publication*]
**Int J Afr H** ... International Journal of African Historical Studies [*A publication*]
**Int J Afric Hist Stud** ... International Journal of African Historical Studies [*A publication*]
**Int J Afr Stud** ... International Journal of African Historical Studies [*A publication*]
**Int J Ag Affairs** ... International Journal of Agrarian Affairs [*A publication*]
**Int J Aging** ... International Journal of Aging and Human Development [*A publication*]
**Int J Aging Hum Dev** ... International Journal of Aging and Human Development [*A publication*]
**Int J Agr Aff** ... International Journal of Agrarian Affairs [*A publication*]
**Int J Air Pollut** ... International Journal of Air Pollution [*A publication*]
**Int J Air Water Pollut** ... International Journal of Air and Water Pollution [*England*] [*A publication*]
**Int J Amb Energy** ... International Journal of Ambient Energy [*A publication*]
**Int J Ambient Energy** ... International Journal of Ambient Energy [*England*] [*A publication*]
**Int J Amer** ... International Journal of American Linguistics [*A publication*]
**Int J Am Ling** ... International Journal of American Linguistics [*A publication*]
**Int J Androl** ... International Journal of Andrology [*A publication*]
**Int J Andrology** ... International Journal of Andrology [*A publication*]
**Int J Androl Suppl** ... International Journal of Andrology. Supplement [*A publication*]
**Int J Anesth** ... International Journal of Anesthesia [*A publication*]
**Int J Appl Radiat** ... International Journal of Applied Radiation and Isotopes [*A publication*]
**Int J Appl Radiat and Isot** ... International Journal of Applied Radiation and Isotopes [*A publication*]
**Int J Appl Radiat Isot** ... International Journal of Applied Radiation and Isotopes [*A publication*]
**Int J Appl Radiat Isotopes** ... International Journal of Applied Radiation and Isotopes [*A publication*]
**Int J A Rad** ... International Journal of Applied Radiation and Isotopes [*A publication*]
**Int J Artif Organs** ... International Journal of Artificial Organs [*A publication*]
**Int J Behav Dev** ... International Journal of Behavioral Development [*A publication*]
**Int J Behav Geriatrics** ... International Journal of Behavioral Geriatrics [*A publication*]
**Int J Bioch** ... International Journal of Biochemistry [*A publication*]
**Int J Biochem** ... International Journal of Biochemistry [*A publication*]
**Int J Bioclim** ... International Journal of Bioclimatology and Biometeorology [*A publication*]
**Int J Bioclimatol Biometeorol** ... International Journal of Bioclimatology and Biometeorology [*A publication*]
**Int J Bioclim Biomet** ... International Journal of Bioclimatology and Biometeorology [*A publication*]
**Int J Biol Macromol** ... International Journal of Biological Macromolecules [*A publication*]
**Int J Biol Res Pregnancy** ... International Journal of Biological Research in Pregnancy [*A publication*]
**Int J Bio-M** ... International Journal of Bio-Medical Computing [*A publication*]
**Int J Biom** ... International Journal of Biometeorology [*A publication*]
**Int J Biomed Comp** ... International Journal of Biomedical Computing [*A publication*]
**Int J Bio-Med Comput** ... International Journal of Bio-Medical Computing [*A publication*]
**Int J Biomed Eng** ... International Journal of Biomedical Engineering [*A publication*]
**Int J Biometeorol** ... International Journal of Biometeorology [*A publication*]
**Int Jb Pol** ... Internationales Jahrbuch der Politik [*A publication*]
**Int Jb Relig Soziol** ... Internationales Jahrbuch fuer Religionssoziologie [*A publication*]
**Int J Canc** .. International Journal of Cancer [*A publication*]
**Int J Cancer** ... International Journal of Cancer [*A publication*]
**Int J Cancer Control Prev** ... International Journal of Cancer Control and Prevention [*A publication*]
**Int J Cardiol** ... International Journal of Cardiology [*A publication*]
**Int J C E Hy** ... International Journal of Clinical and Experimental Hypnosis [*A publication*]
**Int J Cell Cloning** ... International Journal of Cell Cloning [*A publication*]
**Int J Cement Composites** ... International Journal of Cement Composites [*A publication*]
**Int J Chem Kinet** ... International Journal of Chemical Kinetics [*A publication*]
**Int J Child** ... International Journal of Child Psychotherapy [*A publication*]
**Int J Ch K** .. International Journal of Chemical Kinetics [*A publication*]
**Int J Chronobiol** ... International Journal of Chronobiology [*A publication*]
**Int J C Inf** .. International Journal of Computer and Information Sciences [*A publication*]
**Int J Circuit Theory and Appl** ... International Journal of Circuit Theory and Applications [*A publication*]
**Int J Circuit Theory Appl** ... International Journal of Circuit Theory and Applications [*A publication*]
**Int J Clin**.... International Journal of Clinical Pharmacology and Biopharmacy [*A publication*]
**Int J Clin Exp Hypn** ... International Journal of Clinical and Experimental Hypnosis [*A publication*]
**Int J Clin Exp Hypnos** ... International Journal of Clinical and Experimental Hypnosis [*A publication*]
**Int J Clin & Exp Hypnosis** ... International Journal of Clinical and Experimental Hypnosis [*A publication*]
**Int J Clin Monit Comput** ... International Journal of Clinical Monitoring and Computing [*A publication*]
**Int J Clin Neuropsychol** ... International Journal of Clinical Neuropsychology [*A publication*]
**Int J Clin Pharm** ... International Journal of Clinical Pharmacology, Therapy, and Toxicology [*A publication*]
**Int J Clin Pharmacol Biopharm** ... International Journal of Clinical Pharmacology and Biopharmacy [*A publication*]
**Int J Clin Pharmacol Res** ... International Journal of Clinical Pharmacology Research [*A publication*]
**Int J Clin Pharmacol Ther Toxicol** ... International Journal of Clinical Pharmacology, Therapy, and Toxicology [*A publication*]
**Int J Clin Pharm Res** ... International Journal of Clinical Pharmacology Research [*A publication*]
**Int J Coal Geol** ... International Journal of Coal Geology [*Netherlands*] [*A publication*]
**Int J Com M** ... International Journal of Computer Mathematics [*A publication*]
**Int J Com P** ... International Journal of Community Psychiatry and Experimental Psychotherapy [*A publication*]
**Int J Comp** ... International Journal of Comparative Sociology [*A publication*]
**Int J Compar Sociol** ... International Journal of Comparative Sociology [*A publication*]
**Int J Comp Soc** ... International Journal of Comparative Sociology [*A publication*]
**Int J Comp Sociol** ... International Journal of Comparative Sociology [*A publication*]
**Int J Comput & Inf Sci** ... International Journal of Computer and Information Sciences [*A publication*]
**Int J Comput Math** ... International Journal of Computer Mathematics [*A publication*]

**Int J Comput Math Sect A** ... International Journal of Computer Mathematics. Section A. Programming Languages. Theory and Methods [*A publication*]
**Int J Comput Math Sect B** ... International Journal of Computer Mathematics. Section B. Computational Methods [*A publication*]
**Int J Con S** ... International Journal of Contemporary Sociology [*A publication*]
**Int J Contemp Sociol** ... International Journal of Contemporary Sociology [*A publication*]
**Int J Contr** ... International Journal of Control [*A publication*]
**Int J Control** ... International Journal of Control [*A publication*]
**Int J Cosmet Sci** ... International Journal of Cosmetic Science [*A publication*]
**Int J Criminol** ... International Journal of Criminology and Penology [*A publication*] (DLA)
**Int J Crude Drug Res** ... International Journal of Crude Drug Research [*A publication*]
**Int J Dermatol** ... International Journal of Dermatology [*A publication*]
**Int J Dev Biol** ... International Journal of Developmental Biology [*A publication*]
**Int J Dev Neurosci** ... International Journal of Developmental Neuroscience [*A publication*]
**Int J Dravid Ling** ... International Journal of Dravidian Linguistics [*A publication*]
**Int J Earthquake Eng Struct Dyn** ... International Journal of Earthquake Engineering and Structural Dynamics [*A publication*]
**Int J Eating Disord** ... International Journal of Eating Disorders [*A publication*]
**Int J Ecol Environ Sci** ... International Journal of Ecology and Environmental Sciences [*A publication*]
**Int J Elec Eng Educ** ... International Journal of Electrical Engineering Education [*A publication*]
**Int J Elec Engng Educ** ... International Journal of Electrical Engineering Education [*A publication*]
**Int J Elect** .. International Journal of Electronics [*A publication*]
**Int J Electr Eng Educ** ... International Journal of Electrical Engineering Education [*A publication*]
**Int J Electron** ... International Journal of Electronics [*A publication*]
**Int J Electr Power Energy Syst** ... International Journal of Electrical Power Amp Energy Systems [*England*] [*A publication*]
**Int J El En** ... International Journal of Electrical Engineering Education [*A publication*]
**Int J Energy Res** ... International Journal of Energy Research [*A publication*]
**Int J Engng Sci** ... International Journal of Engineering Science [*A publication*]
**Int J Eng S** ... International Journal of Engineering Science [*A publication*]
**Int J Eng Sci** ... International Journal of Engineering Science [*A publication*]
**Int J Entomol** ... International Journal of Entomology [*A publication*]
**Int J Environ Anal Chem** ... International Journal of Environmental Analytical Chemistry [*A publication*]
**Int J Environ Stud** ... International Journal of Environmental Studies [*A publication*]
**Int J Environ Studies** ... International Journal of Environmental Studies [*A publication*]
**Int J Env S** ... International Journal of Environmental Studies [*A publication*]
**Int J Epid**... International Journal of Epidemiology [*A publication*]
**Int J Epidemiol** ... International Journal of Epidemiology [*A publication*]
**Int J Equilib Res** ... International Journal of Equilibrium Research [*A publication*]
**Int J Ethics** ... International Journal of Ethics [*A publication*]
**Int J Fam Psychiatry** ... International Journal of Family Psychiatry [*A publication*]
**Int J Fatigue** ... International Journal of Fatigue [*A publication*]
**Int J Fert**.... International Journal of Fertility [*A publication*]
**Int J Fertil** ... International Journal of Fertility [*A publication*]
**Int J F Mic** ... International Journal of Food Microbiology [*A publication*]
**Int J Food Microbiol** ... International Journal of Food Microbiology [*A publication*]
**Int J Forensic Dent** ... International Journal of Forensic Dentistry [*A publication*]
**Int J Fract** ... International Journal of Fracture [*A publication*]
**Int J Fract Mech** ... International Journal of Fracture Mechanics [*A publication*]
**Int J Fusion Energy** ... International Journal of Fusion Energy [*A publication*]
**Int J Game Theory** ... International Journal of Game Theory [*A publication*]
**Int J Gen S** ... International Journal of General Systems [*A publication*]
**Int J Gen Syst** ... International Journal of General Systems [*A publication*]
**Int J Group Psychother** ... International Journal of Group Psychotherapy [*A publication*]
**Int J Group Tensions** ... International Journal of Group Tensions [*A publication*]
**Int J Grp P** ... International Journal of Group Psychotherapy [*A publication*]
**Int J Grp T** ... International Journal of Group Tensions [*A publication*]
**Int J Gynaecol Obstet** ... International Journal of Gynaecology and Obstetrics [*A publication*]
**Int J Gynecol Pathol** ... International Journal of Gynecological Pathology [*A publication*]
**Int J Healt** ... International Journal of Health Education [*A publication*]
**Int J Health Educ** ... International Journal of Health Education [*A publication*]
**Int J Health Plann Manage** ... International Journal of Health Planning and Management [*A publication*]
**Int J Health Serv** ... International Journal of Health Services [*A publication*]
**Int J Heat** .. International Journal of Heat and Mass Transfer [*A publication*]
**Int J Heat Fluid Flow** ... International Journal of Heat and Fluid Flow [*England*] [*A publication*]
**Int J Heat Mass Transfer** ... International Journal of Heat and Mass Transfer [*A publication*]
**Int J Heat & Mass Transfer** ... International Journal of Heat and Mass Transfer [*A publication*]
**Int J He Se** ... International Journal of Health Services [*A publication*]
**Int J Hosp Manage** ... International Journal of Hospitality Management [*A publication*]
**Int J Housing Sc Applications** ... International Journal for Housing Science and Its Applications [*A publication*]
**Int J Hous Sci Appl** ... International Journal for Housing Science and Its Applications [*A publication*]
**Int J Hybrid Microelectron** ... International Journal for Hybrid Microelectronics [*A publication*]
**Int J Hydrogen Energy** ... International Journal of Hydrogen Energy [*A publication*]
**Int J Hyg Environ Med** ... International Journal of Hygiene and Environmental Medicine [*A publication*]
**Int J Hyperthermia** ... International Journal of Hyperthermia [*A publication*]
**Int J Immunochem** ... International Journal of Immunochemistry [*England*] [*A publication*]
**Int J Immunopharmacol** ... International Journal of Immunopharmacology [*A publication*]
**Int J Immunother** ... International Journal of Immunotherapy [*A publication*]
**Int J Infrared Millim Waves** ... International Journal of Infrared and Millimeter Waves [*United States*] [*A publication*]
**Int J Insect Morph Embryol** ... International Journal of Insect Morphology and Embryology [*A publication*]
**Int J Insect Morphol Embryol** ... International Journal of Insect Morphology and Embryology [*A publication*]
**Int J Inst Mangt in Higher Educ** ... International Journal of Institutional Management in Higher Education [*A publication*]
**Int J Instr Media** ... International Journal of Instructional Media [*A publication*]
**Int J Invertebr Reprod** ... International Journal of Invertebrate Reproduction [*A publication*]
**Int J Invertebr Reprod Dev** ... International Journal of Invertebrate Reproduction and Development [*A publication*]
**Int J Law Lib** ... International Journal of Law Libraries [*A publication*]
**Int J Law Libr** ... International Journal of Law Libraries [*A publication*]
**Int J Law Psychiatry** ... International Journal of Law and Psychiatry [*A publication*]
**Int J Law Sci** ... International Journal of Law and Science [*A publication*]
**Int J Lepr**... International Journal of Leprosy [*Later, International Journal of Leprosy and Other Mycobacterial Diseases*] [*A publication*]
**Int J Lepr Other Mycobact Dis** ... International Journal of Leprosy and Other Mycobacterial Diseases [*A publication*]
**Int J Life Educ** ... International Journal of Lifelong Education [*A publication*]
**Int J Mach** ... International Journal of Machine Tool Design and Research [*A publication*]
**Int J Mach Tool Des Res** ... International Journal of Machine Tool Design and Research [*A publication*]
**Int J Magn** ... International Journal of Magnetism [*A publication*]
**Int J Mamm Biol** ... International Journal of Mammalian Biology [*A publication*]
**Int J Man-M** ... International Journal of Man-Machine Studies [*A publication*]
**Int J Man-Mach Stud** ... International Journal of Man-Machine Studies [*A publication*]
**Int J Manpower** ... International Journal of Manpower [*A publication*]
**Int J Masonry Constr** ... International Journal of Masonry Construction [*A publication*]
**Int J Mass** ... International Journal of Mass Spectrometry and Ion Physics [*Later, International Journal of Mass Spectrometry and Ion Processes*] [*A publication*]
**Int J Mass Spectrom and Ion Phys** ... International Journal of Mass Spectrometry and Ion Physics [*Later, International Journal of Mass Spectrometry and Ion Processes*] [*A publication*]
**Int J Mass Spectrom Ion Phys** ... International Journal of Mass Spectrometry and Ion Physics [*Later, International Journal of Mass Spectrometry and Ion Processes*] [*A publication*]
**Int J Mass Spectrom Ion Processes** ... International Journal of Mass Spectrometry and Ion Processes [*A publication*]
**Int J Mater Eng Appl** ... International Journal of Materials in Engineering Applications [*A publication*]
**Int J Mater Eng Res** ... International Journal of Materials Engineering Research [*A publication*]
**Int J Math Educ Sci Technol** ... International Journal of Mathematical Education in Science and Technology [*A publication*]
**Int J Math Educ Sci and Technol** ... International Journal of Mathematical Education in Science and Technology [*A publication*]
**Int J Mech** ... International Journal of Mechanical Sciences [*A publication*]
**Int J Mech Engng Educ** ... International Journal of Mechanical Engineering Education [*A publication*]
**Int J Mech Sci** ... International Journal of Mechanical Sciences [*A publication*]

**Int J Med Microbiol** ... International Journal of Medical Microbiology [*A publication*]
**Int J Ment** ... International Journal of Mental Health [*A publication*]
**Int J Ment Health** ... International Journal of Mental Health [*A publication*]
**Int J M E St** ... International Journal of Middle East Studies [*A publication*]
**Int J Microbiol Hyg Ser A** ... International Journal of Microbiology and Hygiene. Series A. Medical Microbiology, Infectious Diseases, Virology, Parasitology [*A publication*]
**Int J Microcirc Clin Exp** ... International Journal of Microcirculation. Clinical and Experimental [*A publication*]
**Int J Micrgr and Video Technol** ... International Journal of Micrographics and Video Technology [*A publication*]
**Int J Middle East Stud** ... International Journal of Middle East Studies [*A publication*]
**Int J Mid East Stud** ... International Journal of Middle East Studies [*A publication*]
**Int J Mid E Stud** ... International Journal of Middle East Studies [*A publication*]
**Int J Min Eng** ... International Journal of Mining Engineering [*A publication*]
**Int J Miner Process** ... International Journal of Mineral Processing [*A publication*]
**Int J Mine Water** ... International Journal of Mine Water [*A publication*]
**Int J Mini and Microcomput** ... International Journal of Mini and Microcomputers [*A publication*]
**Int J Multiphase Flow** ... International Journal of Multiphase Flow [*A publication*]
**Int J Multiph Flow** ... International Journal of Multiphase Flow [*A publication*]
**Int J Mycol Lichenol** ... International Journal of Mycology and Lichenology [*A publication*]
**Int J Naut** .. International Journal of Nautical Archaeology and Underwater Exploration [*A publication*]
**Int J Naut Archaeol Underwater Explor** ... International Journal of Nautical Archaeology and Underwater Exploration [*A publication*]
**Int J Nephrol Urol Androl** ... International Journal of Nephrology, Urology, Andrology [*A publication*]
**Int J Neuro** ... International Journal of Neurology [*A publication*]
**Int J Neurol** ... International Journal of Neurology [*A publication*]
**Int J Neuropharmacol** ... International Journal of Neuropharmacology [*A publication*]
**Int J Neuropsychiatr** ... International Journal of Neuropsychiatry [*A publication*]
**Int J Neuropsychiatry** ... International Journal of Neuropsychiatry [*A publication*]
**Int J Neuropsychiatry Suppl** ... International Journal of Neuropsychiatry. Supplement [*A publication*]
**Int J Neurosci** ... International Journal of Neuroscience [*A publication*]
**Int J Neurs** ... International Journal of Neuroscience [*A publication*]
**Int Jnl Adv** ... International Journal of Advertising [*A publication*]
**Int J Nondestr Test** ... International Journal of Nondestructive Testing [*A publication*]
**Int J Nondestruct Test** ... International Journal of Nondestructive Testing [*A publication*]
**Int J Non-Linear Mech** ... International Journal of Non-Linear Mechanics [*A publication*]
**Int J Nucl Med & Biol** ... International Journal of Nuclear Medicine and Biology [*A publication*]
**Int J Nucl Med Biol** ... International Journal of Nuclear Medicine and Biology [*A publication*]
**Int J Nuc M** ... International Journal of Nuclear Medicine and Biology [*A publication*]
**Int J Num Anal Meth Geomech** ... International Journal for Numerical and Analytical Methods in Geomechanics [*A publication*]
**Int J Numer and Anal Methods Geomech** ... International Journal for Numerical and Analytical Methods in Geomechanics [*A publication*]
**Int J Numer Anal Methods Geomech** ... International Journal for Numerical and Analytical Methods in Geomechanics [*A publication*]
**Int J Numer Methods Eng** ... International Journal for Numerical Methods in Engineering [*A publication*]
**Int J Numer Methods Engng** ... International Journal for Numerical Methods in Engineering [*A publication*]
**Int J Numer Methods Fluids** ... International Journal for Numerical Methods in Fluids [*A publication*]
**Int J Num Meth Eng** ... International Journal for Numerical Methods in Engineering [*A publication*]
**Int J Num Meth Engng** ... International Journal for Numerical Methods in Engineering [*A publication*]
**Int J Nurs** .. International Journal of Nursing Studies [*A publication*]
**Int J Nurs Stud** ... International Journal of Nursing Studies [*A publication*]
**Int J Obes** .. International Journal of Obesity [*A publication*]
**Int J Occ H** ... International Journal of Occupational Health and Safety [*A publication*]
**Int J Occup Health Saf** ... International Journal of Occupational Health and Safety [*A publication*]
**Int J Occup Health and Saf** ... International Journal of Occupational Health and Safety [*A publication*]
**Int J Oceanol Limnol** ... International Journal of Oceanology and Limnology [*A publication*]
**Int J Offen** ... International Journal of Offender Therapy [*Later, International Journal of Offender Therapy and Comparative Criminology*] [*A publication*]
**Int J Offend Therapy** ... International Journal of Offender Therapy and Comparative Criminology [*A publication*]
**Int J Oper and Prod Manage** ... International Journal of Operations and Production Management [*A publication*]
**Int J Oral** ... International Journal of Oral History [*A publication*]
**Int J Oral Maxillofac Implants** ... International Journal of Oral and Maxillofacial Implants [*A publication*]
**Int J Oral Maxillofac Surg** ... International Journal of Oral and Maxillofacial Surgery [*A publication*]
**Int J Oral Myol** ... International Journal of Oral Myology [*A publication*]
**Int J Oral Surg** ... International Journal of Oral Surgery [*A publication*]
**Int J Orofacial Myology** ... International Journal of Orofacial Myology [*A publication*]
**Int J Or Su** ... International Journal of Oral Surgery [*A publication*]
**Int J Orthod** ... International Journal of Orthodontics [*A publication*]
**Int J Orthod Dent Child** ... International Journal of Orthodontia and Dentistry for Children [*A publication*]
**Int J Orthodont** ... International Journal of Orthodontics [*A publication*]
**Int J Paras** ... International Journal for Parasitology [*A publication*]
**Int J Parasitol** ... International Journal for Parasitology [*A publication*]
**Int J Partial Hosp** ... International Journal of Partial Hospitalization [*A publication*]
**Int J PE**...... International Journal of Physical Education [*A publication*]
**Int J Pediatr Nephrol** ... International Journal of Pediatric Nephrology [*A publication*]
**Int J Pediatr Otorhinolaryngol** ... International Journal of Pediatric Otorhinolaryngology [*A publication*]
**Int J Pept** ... International Journal of Peptide and Protein Research [*A publication*]
**Int J Peptide Protein Res** ... International Journal of Peptide and Protein Research [*A publication*]
**Int J Peptide Prot Res** ... International Journal of Peptide and Protein Research [*A publication*]
**Int J Pept Protein Res** ... International Journal of Peptide and Protein Research [*A publication*]
**Int J Periodontics Restorative Dent** ... International Journal of Periodontics and Restorative Dentistry [*A publication*]
**Int J Pharm** ... International Journal of Pharmaceutics [*A publication*]
**Int J Pharm (Amst)** ... International Journal of Pharmaceutics (Amsterdam) [*A publication*]
**Int J Pharm Technol Prod Manuf** ... International Journal of Pharmaceutical Technology and Product Manufacture [*A publication*]
**Int J Phil**.... International Journal for Philosophy of Religion [*A publication*]
**Int J Philos Relig** ... International Journal for Philosophy of Religion [*A publication*]
**IntJPhilRel** ... International Journal for Philosophy of Religion [*The Hague*] [*A publication*]
**Int J Phil Relig** ... International Journal for Philosophy of Religion [*A publication*]
**Int J Ph Rel** ... International Journal for Philosophy of Religion [*A publication*]
**Int J Phys Distrib J Ser** ... International Journal of Physical Distribution [*Later, International Journal of Physical Distribution and Materials Management*]. Journal Series [*A publication*]
**Int J Phys Distrib Monogr Ser** ... International Journal of Physical Distribution [*Later, International Journal of Physical Distribution and Materials Management*]. Monograph Series [*A publication*]
**Int J Phys Educ** ... International Journal of Physical Education [*A publication*]
**Int J Plant Physiol** ... International Journal of Plant Physiology [*A publication*]
**Int J Plant Physiol (Stuttgart)** ... International Journal of Plant Physiology (Stuttgart) [*A publication*]
**Int J Pol**..... International Journal of Politics [*A publication*] (DLA)
**Int J Policy Anal Inf Syst** ... International Journal of Policy Analysis and Information Systems [*United States*] [*A publication*]
**Int J Policy and Inf** ... International Journal on Policy and Information [*A publication*]
**Int J Polit**... International Journal of Politics [*A publication*]
**Int J Polym Mat** ... International Journal of Polymeric Materials [*A publication*]
**Int J Polym Mater** ... International Journal of Polymeric Materials [*A publication*]
**Int J Powd** ... International Journal of Powder Metallurgy [*A publication*]
**Int J Powder Metall** ... International Journal of Powder Metallurgy [*A publication*]
**Int J Powder Metall & Powder Tech** ... International Journal of Powder Metallurgy and Powder Technology [*A publication*]
**Int J Powder Metall Powder Technol** ... International Journal of Powder Metallurgy and Powder Technology [*A publication*]
**Int J Powder Metall Technol** ... International Journal of Powder Metallurgy and Powder Technology [*A publication*]
**Int J Pressure Vessels Piping** ... International Journal of Pressure Vessels and Piping [*A publication*]
**Int J Primatol** ... International Journal of Primatology [*A publication*]
**Int J Prod Res** ... International Journal of Production Research [*A publication*]

**Int J Prophyl Med Sozialhyg** ... Internationales Journal fuer Prophylaktische Medizin und Sozialhygiene [*A publication*]
**Int J Prosthod** ... International Journal of Prosthodontics [*A publication*]
**Int J Protein Res** ... International Journal of Protein Research [*A publication*]
**Int J Ps Ps** ... International Journal of Psychoanalytic Psychotherapy [*A publication*]
**Int J Psych** ... International Journal of Psychoanalysis [*A publication*]
**Int J Psychiat** ... International Journal of Psychiatry [*A publication*]
**Int J Psychiatry** ... International Journal of Psychiatry [*A publication*]
**Int J Psychiatry Med** ... International Journal of Psychiatry in Medicine [*A publication*]
**Int J Psychoanal** ... International Journal of Psychoanalysis [*A publication*]
**Int J Psychoanal Psychother** ... International Journal of Psychoanalytic Psychotherapy [*A publication*]
**Int J Psychobiol** ... International Journal of Psychobiology [*A publication*]
**Int J Psychol** ... International Journal of Psychology [*A publication*]
**Int J Psychophysiol** ... International Journal of Psychophysiology [*A publication*]
**Int J Psychosom** ... International Journal of Psychosomatics [*A publication*]
**Int J Psyci** ... International Journal of Psychiatry [*A publication*]
**Int J Psyco** ... International Journal of Psychology [*A publication*]
**Int J Psy M** ... International Journal of Psychiatry in Medicine [*A publication*]
**Int J Publ Hlth** ... International Journal of Public Health [*A publication*]
**Int J Quant** ... International Journal of Quantum Chemistry [*A publication*]
**Int J Quant Chem** ... International Journal of Quantum Chemistry [*A publication*]
**Int J Quant Chem Quant Biol Symp** ... International Journal of Quantum Chemistry. Quantum Biology Symposium [*United States*] [*A publication*]
**Int J Quant Chem Symp** ... International Journal of Quantum Chemistry. Symposium [*A publication*]
**Int J Quantum Chem** ... International Journal of Quantum Chemistry [*A publication*]
**Int J Quantum Chem Quantum Biol Symp** ... International Journal of Quantum Chemistry. Quantum Biology Symposium [*A publication*]
**Int J Quantum Chem Quantum Chem Symp** ... International Journal of Quantum Chemistry. Quantum Chemistry Symposia [*A publication*]
**Int J Quantum Chem Sym** ... International Journal of Quantum Chemistry. Symposium [*A publication*]
**Int J Quantum Chem Symp** ... International Journal of Quantum Chemistry. Symposium [*A publication*]
**Int J Rad Appl Instrum A** ... International Journal of Radiation Applications and Instrumentation. Part A. Applied Radiation and Isotopes [*A publication*]
**Int J Rad Appl Instrum B** ... International Journal of Radiation Applications and Instrumentation. Part B. Nuclear Medicine and Biology [*A publication*]
**Int J Rad B** ... International Journal of Radiation Biology [*A publication*]
**Int J Radiat Biol** ... International Journal of Radiation Biology and Related Studies in Physics, Chemistry, and Medicine [*A publication*]
**Int J Radiat Biol Relat Stud Phys Chem Med** ... International Journal of Radiation Biology and Related Studies in Physics, Chemistry, and Medicine [*A publication*]
**Int J Radiat Eng** ... International Journal of Radiation Engineering [*Israel*] [*A publication*]
**Int J Radiat Oncol-Biol-Phys** ... International Journal of Radiation: Oncology-Biology-Physics [*A publication*]
**Int J Radiat Oncology Biol Phys** ... International Journal of Radiation: Oncology-Biology-Physics [*A publication*]
**Int J Radiat Phys and Chem** ... International Journal for Radiation Physics and Chemistry [*Later, Radiation Physics and Chemistry*] [*A publication*]
**Int J Radiat Phys Chem** ... International Journal for Radiation Physics and Chemistry [*Later, Radiation Physics and Chemistry*] [*A publication*]
**Int J Radiat Steril** ... International Journal of Radiation Sterilization [*Israel*] [*A publication*]
**Int J Rad O** ... International Journal of Radiation: Oncology-Biology-Physics [*A publication*]
**Int J Rad P** ... International Journal for Radiation Physics and Chemistry [*Later, Radiation Physics and Chemistry*] [*A publication*]
**Int J Rap S** ... International Journal of Rapid Solidification [*A publication*]
**Int J Refract Hard Met** ... International Journal of Refractory and Hard Metals [*A publication*]
**Int J Refract and Hard Met** ... International Journal of Refractory and Hard Metals [*A publication*]
**Int J Refrig** ... International Journal of Refrigeration [*A publication*]
**Int J Rehabil Res** ... International Journal of Rehabilitation Research [*A publication*]
**Int J Relig Ed** ... International Journal of Religious Education [*A publication*]
**Int J Remot** ... International Journal of Remote Sensing [*A publication*]
**Int J Remote Sens** ... International Journal of Remote Sensing [*A publication*]
**Int J Res Manage** ... International Journal of Research Management [*United States*] [*A publication*]
**Int J Rock** .. International Journal of Rock Mechanics [*A publication*]
**Int J Rock Mech Mining Sci** ... International Journal of Rock Mechanics and Mining Sciences [*Later, International Journal of Rock Mechanics and Mining Sciences and Geomechanics Abstracts*] [*A publication*]
**Int J Rock Mech Mining Sci Geomech Abstr** ... International Journal of Rock Mechanics and Mining Sciences and Geomechanics Abstracts [*A publication*]
**Int J Rock Mech Min Sci** ... International Journal of Rock Mechanics and Mining Sciences [*Later, International Journal of Rock Mechanics and Mining Sciences and Geomechanics Abstracts*] [*A publication*]
**Int J Rock Mech and Min Sci and Geomech Abstr** ... International Journal of Rock Mechanics and Mining Sciences and Geomechanics Abstracts [*A publication*]
**Int J Rock Mech Min Sci Geomech Abstr** ... International Journal of Rock Mechanics and Mining Sciences and Geomechanics Abstracts [*A publication*]
**Int J Sex** .... International Journal of Sexology [*A publication*]
**Int J Soc Econ** ... International Journal of Social Economics [*A publication*]
**Int J Soc F** ... International Journal of Sociology of the Family [*A publication*]
**Int J Social Psychiat** ... International Journal of Social Psychiatry [*A publication*]
**Int J Sociol** ... International Journal of Sociology [*A publication*]
**Int J Sociol Family** ... International Journal of Sociology of the Family [*A publication*]
**Int J Sociol Lang** ... International Journal of the Sociology of Language [*A publication*]
**Int J Sociol Law** ... International Journal of the Sociology of Law [*A publication*]
**Int J Sociol Soc Policy** ... International Journal of Sociology and Social Policy [*A publication*]
**Int J Soc L** ... International Journal of the Sociology of Language [*A publication*]
**Int J Soc Lang** ... International Journal of the Sociology of Language [*A publication*]
**Int J Soc P** ... International Journal of Social Psychiatry [*A publication*]
**Int J Soc Psych** ... International Journal of Social Psychiatry [*A publication*]
**Int J Soc Psychiatr** ... International Journal of Social Psychiatry [*A publication*]
**Int J Soc Psychiatry** ... International Journal of Social Psychiatry [*A publication*]
**Int J Soil Dyn and Earthquake Eng** ... International Journal of Soil Dynamics and Earthquake Engineering [*A publication*]
**Int J Solar Energy** ... International Journal of Solar Energy [*A publication*]
**Int J Sol Energy** ... International Journal of Solar Energy [*A publication*]
**Int J Solids and Struct** ... International Journal of Solids and Structures [*A publication*]
**Int J Solids Struct** ... International Journal of Solids and Structures [*A publication*]
**Int J Speleol** ... International Journal of Speleology [*A publication*]
**Int J Sport Psy** ... International Journal of Sport Psychology [*A publication*]
**Int J Sport Psychol** ... International Journal of Sport Psychology [*A publication*]
**Int J Sports Med** ... International Journal of Sports Medicine [*A publication*]
**Int J Sp Ps** ... International Journal of Sport Psychology [*A publication*]
**Int J Study Anim Probl** ... International Journal for the Study of Animal Problems [*A publication*]
**Int J Sulfur Chem** ... International Journal of Sulfur Chemistry [*A publication*]
**Int J Sulfur Chem Part A** ... International Journal of Sulfur Chemistry. Part A. Original Experimental [*A publication*]
**Int J Sulfur Chem Part B** ... International Journal of Sulfur Chemistry. Part B. Quarterly Reports on Sulfur Chemistry [*A publication*]
**Int J Sulfur Chem Part C** ... International Journal of Sulfur Chemistry. Part C. Mechanisms of Reactions of Sulfur Compounds [*A publication*]
**Int J Sy B**... International Journal of Systematic Bacteriology [*A publication*]
**Int J Symb** ... International Journal of Symbology [*A publication*]
**Int J Syst** ... International Journal of Systems Science [*A publication*]
**Int J Syst Bacteriol** ... International Journal of Systematic Bacteriology [*A publication*]
**Int J Syst Sci** ... International Journal of Systems Science [*A publication*]
**Int J Technol Assess Health Care** ... International Journal of Technology Assessment in Health Care [*A publication*]
**Int J Theor** ... International Journal of Theoretical Physics [*A publication*]
**Int J Theor Phys** ... International Journal of Theoretical Physics [*A publication*]
**Int J Therm** ... International Journal of Thermophysics [*A publication*]
**Int J Thermophys** ... International Journal of Thermophysics [*A publication*]
**Int J Tissue React** ... International Journal on Tissue Reactions [*A publication*]
**Int J Transp Econ** ... International Journal of Transport Economics [*A publication*]
**Int J Trop Agric** ... International Journal of Tropical Agriculture [*A publication*]
**Int J Trop Plant Dis** ... International Journal of Tropical Plant Diseases [*A publication*]
**Int J Urban Reg Res** ... International Journal of Urban and Regional Research [*A publication*]

**Int Jurid Assn Bull** ... International Juridical Association. Bulletin [*A publication*] (DLA)
**Int J Veh Des** ... International Journal of Vehicle Design [*A publication*]
**Int J Vitam Nutr Res** ... International Journal for Vitamin and Nutrition Research [*A publication*]
**Int J Vit N** ... International Journal for Vitamin and Nutrition Research [*A publication*]
**Int J Womens Stud** ... International Journal of Women's Studies [*A publication*]
**Int J Wood Preserv** ... International Journal of Wood Preservation [*A publication*]
**Int J Zoonoses** ... International Journal of Zoonoses [*A publication*]
**INTK** ......... Intake (MSA)
**INTK** ......... Intertank (KSC)
**Int Kath Z** .. Internationale Katholische Zeitschrift [*A publication*]
**IntKiZ** ........ Internationale Kirchliche Zeitschrift [*Bern*] [*A publication*]
**Int Kongr Tier Fortpflanz Kuenstliche Besamung** ... Internationaler Kongress ueber die Tierische Fortpflanzung und die Kuenstliche Besamung [*A publication*]
**INTL**.......... Inter-Tel, Inc. [*NASDAQ symbol*] (NQ)
**INTL**.......... Internal
**INTL**.......... International (AFM)
**Int Lab** ....... International Laboratory [*A publication*]
**Int Labmate** ... International Labmate [*A publication*]
**Int Labor Organ Occup Saf Health Ser** ... International Labor Organization. Occupational Safety and Health Series [*A publication*]
**Int Labor W** ... International Labor and Working Class History [*A publication*]
**Int Labour Doc** ... International Labour Documentation [*A publication*]
**Int Labour Off Occup Saf Health Ser** ... International Labour Office. Occupational Safety and Health Series [*A publication*]
**Int Labour R** ... International Labour Review [*A publication*]
**Int Labour Rev** ... International Labour Review [*A publication*]
**Int Labour R Stat Sup** ... International Labour Review. Statistical Supplement [*A publication*]
**Int Lab R**.... International Labour Review [*A publication*]
**Int Lab Rev** ... International Labour Review [*A publication*]
**Int'l Arb Awards** ... Reports of International Arbitral Awards [*A publication*] (DLA)
**Int'l Arb J** .. International Arbitration Journal [*A publication*] (DLA)
**Intl Archt**... International Architect [*A publication*]
**Intl Asbestos Cement Review** ... International Asbestos-Cement Review [*A publication*]
**Int'l Assoc L Lib Bull** ... International Association of Law Libraries. Bulletin [*A publication*] (DLA)
**Int Law**....... International Lawyer [*A publication*]
**Int Law Tr** ... International Law Tracts [*A publication*] (DLA)
**Int Lawyer** ... International Lawyer [*A publication*]
**Int'l BA Bull** ... International Bar Association. Bulletin [*A publication*] (DLA)
**Int'l Bar J** .. International Bar Journal [*A publication*] (DLA)
**Int'l BJ**....... International Bar Journal [*A publication*] (DLA)
**Int Lbr R**.... International Labour Review [*A publication*]
**Int L Bull** ... International Law Bulletin [*A publication*] (DLA)
**Int'l Bull Research E Eur** ... International Bulletin for Research on Law in Eastern Europe [*A publication*]
**Intl Bus Law** ... International Business Lawyer [*A publication*]
**Int'l Bus Lawyer** ... International Business Lawyer [*London, England*] [*A publication*] (DLA)
**Int'l Bus Ser** ... International Business Series [*A publication*] (DLA)
**INTL COMB** ... Internal Combustion [*Freight*]
**Intl Comm Jurists Rev** ... International Commission of Jurists. Review [*A publication*]
**Int'l & Comp L Bull** ... International and Comparative Law Bulletin [*A publication*] (DLA)
**Int'l & Comp LQ** ... International and Comparative Law Quarterly [*A publication*]
**Intl Comp Symp** ... International Computer Symposium Proceedings [*A publication*]
**Int'l Crim Pol Rev** ... International Criminal Police Review [*A publication*] (DLA)
**Int'l Dig**...... International Digest [*A publication*]
**Int'l Dig Health Leg** ... International Digest of Health Legislation [*A publication*] (DLA)
**Int Legal Materials** ... International Legal Materials [*A publication*] (DLA)
**Int'l Encycl Comp L** ... International Encyclopedia of Comparative Law [*A publication*] (DLA)
**Int'l Fin L Rev** ... International Financial Law Review [*A publication*] (DLA)
**Int Lib**......... Intrationum Liber [*A publication*] (DSA)
**Int Lib Ph** .. International Library of Philosophy [*A publication*]
**Int Lib R** .... International Library Review [*A publication*]
**Int Libr Re** ... International Library Review [*A publication*]
**Int Libr Rev** ... International Library Review [*A publication*]
**Int Lighting Rev** ... International Lighting Review [*A publication*]
**INTLINE** .. International Online Data Base [*The WEFA Group*] [*Information service or system*]
**Int'l J** ......... International Journal [*A publication*]
**Intl J Comp and App Crim Just** ... International Journal of Comparative and Applied Criminal Justice [*A publication*]
**Int'l J Crimin & Penol** ... International Journal of Criminology and Penology [*A publication*] (DLA)
**Int'l J Crim & Pen** ... International Journal of Criminology and Penology [*A publication*] (DLA)
**Int'l J Envir Stud** ... International Journal of Environmental Studies [*A publication*]
**Intl J Legal Info** ... International Journal of Legal Information [*A publication*]
**Int'l J Legal Infor** ... International Journal of Legal Information [*A publication*]
**Int'l J Legal Res** ... International Journal of Legal Research [*A publication*] (DLA)
**Intl JL Lib** ... International Journal of Law Libraries [*A publication*]
**Intl J L and Psych** ... International Journal of Law and Psychiatry [*A publication*]
**Intl Jnl of Ambient Energy** ... International Journal of Ambient Energy [*A publication*]
**Intl Jnl Rel Ed** ... International Journal of Religious Education [*A publication*]
**Intl J Offend Ther and Comp Criminology** ... International Journal of Offender Therapy and Comparative Criminology [*A publication*]
**Int'l J Off Ther & Comp Crim** ... International Journal of Offender Therapy and Comparative Criminology [*A publication*] (DLA)
**Int'l J Pol**... International Journal of Politics [*A publication*]
**Int'l J of PRD** ... International Journal of Periodontics and Restorative Dentistry [*A publication*]
**Intl J Soc L** ... International Journal of the Sociology of Law [*A publication*]
**Int'l Jurid Ass'n Bull** ... International Juridical Association. Bulletin [*A publication*] (DLA)
**INTLK**....... Interlock (MSA)
**Int'l Lab Off Leg S** ... International Labour Office. Legislative Series [*London, England*] [*A publication*]
**Int'l Lab Reports** ... International Labour Reports [*A publication*] (DLA)
**Int'l Lab Rev** ... International Labour Review [*A publication*]
**Int'l L Ass'n** ... Reports of the International Law Association [*A publication*] (DLA)
**Int'l L Ass'n Bull** ... Bulletin. International Law Association [*1936-38*] [*A publication*] (DLA)
**Int'l Law**..... International Law [*A publication*] (DLA)
**Intl Law**...... International Lawyer [*A publication*]
**Int'l Lawyer** ... International Lawyer [*A publication*]
**Int'l L Comm'n** ... International Law Commission [*United Nations*] (DLA)
**Int'l L Doc** ... International Law Documents [*A publication*] (DLA)
**Int'l Legal Ed Newsl** ... International Legal Education Newsletter [*A publication*] (DLA)
**Intl Legal Mat** ... International Legal Materials [*A publication*]
**Int'l Legal Materials** ... International Legal Materials [*A publication*]
**Intl Lighting Review** ... International Lighting Review [*A publication*]
**Int'l LLL**.... International Lutheran Laymen's League (EA)
**Int'l L News** ... International Law News [*A publication*]
**Int'l L Persp** ... International Law Perspective [*A publication*] (DLA)
**Int'l LQ**...... International Law Quarterly [*A publication*]
**Int'l LR**...... International Law Reports [*A publication*]
**Int'l L Rep** ... International Law Reports [*A publication*] (DLA)
**Int'l L Stud** ... International Law Studies [*Naval War College*] [*A publication*] (DLA)
**Int LN**........ International Law Notes [*A publication*] (DLA)
**Int L News** ... International Law News [*A publication*]
**Int L Notes** ... International Law Notes [*England*] [*A publication*] (DLA)
**Int Log Rev** ... International Logic Review [*A publication*]
**Intl Org**...... International Organization [*A publication*]
**Int'l Prop Inv J** ... International Property Investment Journal [*A publication*] (DLA)
**Int LQ**........ International Law Quarterly [*A publication*]
**Int LR**........ International Labour Review [*A publication*]
**Int'l Rev Ad Sci** ... International Review of Administrative Sciences [*A publication*] (DLA)
**Int'l Rev Crim Policy** ... International Review of Criminal Policy [*United Nations*] (DLA)
**Int'l Rev Ind Prop & C'right L** ... International Review of Industrial Property and Copyright Law [*A publication*]
**Int'l Rev Ind Prop'y & Copyr** ... International Review of Industrial Property and Copyright Law [*A publication*]
**Intl Rev L and Econ** ... International Review of Law and Economics [*A publication*]
**Int'l Soc'y of Barr Q** ... International Society of Barristers. Quarterly [*A publication*] (DLA)
**Int'l Surv LDLL** ... International Survey of Legal Decisions on Labour Law [*1925-38*] [*A publication*] (DLA)
**Int'l Sym Comp L** ... International Symposium on Comparative Law [*A publication*] (DLA)
**Int'l Tax & Bus Law** ... International Tax and Business Lawyer [*A publication*] (DLA)
**Intl Tax J**... International Tax Journal [*A publication*]
**Int Ltg Rev** ... International Lighting Review [*A publication*]
**Intl Trade LJ** ... International Trade Law Journal [*A publication*]
**Int'l Trade L & Prac** ... International Trade Law and Practice [*A publication*]
**Intl Trade Rep BNA** ... International Trade Reporter. Bureau of National Affairs [*A publication*]
**INTLVR**.... Interleaver (MCD)
**Int'l Woman Law** ... International Woman Lawyer [*A publication*] (DLA)
**INTM**........ Intermediate (KSC)
**INTM**........ Intermountain Exploration Co. [*NASDAQ symbol*] (NQ)

**INTMA** ..... International Mail [*A publication*]
**Int Manag** ... International Management [*A publication*]
**Int Manage** ... International Management [*A publication*]
**Int Man Dig** ... International Management Digest [*A publication*]
**Int Man Inf** ... International Management Information [*A publication*]
**Int Man Ser** ... International Management Series [*A publication*]
**INTMD** ..... Intermediate (MSA)
**INTMED**... Intermediate (AFM)
**INTMED**... Internal Medicine (AABC)
**Int Med Abstr Rev** ... International Medical Abstracts and Reviews [*A publication*]
**Int Med Dig** ... International Medical Digest [*A publication*]
**Int Medieval Bibliogr** ... International Medieval Bibliography [*A publication*]
**Int Med Mag** ... International Medical Magazine [*A publication*]
**Int Med Surg Surv** ... International Medical and Surgical Survey [*A publication*]
**Int Metall Rev** ... International Metallurgical Reviews [*A publication*]
**Int Metall Revs** ... International Metallurgical Reviews [*A publication*]
**Int Met Rev** ... International Metals Reviews [*A publication*]
**Int Mgmt**.... International Management [*A publication*]
**Int Mgt**....... International Management [*A publication*]
**Int Microelectron Symp Proc** ... International Microelectronic Symposium. Proceedings [*A publication*]
**Int Migration R** ... International Migration Review [*A publication*]
**Int Migr Re** ... International Migration Review [*A publication*]
**Int Min**....... International Mining [*A publication*]
**Int Min Equip** ... International Mining Equipment [*A publication*]
**Int Miner Scene** ... International Minerals Scene [*A publication*]
**Int Mitt Bodenkd** ... Internationale Mitteilungen fuer Bodenkunde [*A publication*]
**IntMJ** ........ International Microfilm Journal of Legal Medicine, New York, NY [*Library symbol*] [*Library of Congress*] (LCLS)
**Int Mod Foundry** ... International Modern Foundry [*A publication*]
**Int Monetar** ... International Monetary Fund. Staff Papers [*A publication*]
**Int Monetary Fund Staff Pa** ... International Monetary Fund. Staff Papers [*A publication*]
**Int Monet Fund Staff Pap** ... International Monetary Fund. Staff Papers [*A publication*]
**IntMP** ........ International Micro-Print Preservation, Inc., New York, NY [*Library symbol*] [*Library of Congress*] (LCLS)
**INTMS**...... Internal Messenger Service [*Hotels*]
**INTMT**...... Intermittent (MSA)
**Int Mus** ...... International Musician [*A publication*]
**Int Mus Ed** ... International Music Educator [*A publication*]
**INTN** ......... Intention
**INTN** ......... Inuit Today Newsletter. Inuit Ublumi Tusagatsangit [*A publication*]
**INTNEW**... International News [*Database*] (IT)
**Int Newsl Chem Educ** ... International Newsletter on Chemical Education [*A publication*]
**Int Nickel**... International Nickel [*A publication*]
**INTN'L**...... International
**Intnl Advt**... International Advertiser [*A publication*]
**Intnl Def R** ... International Defense Review [*A publication*]
**Intnl Demo** ... International Demographics [*A publication*]
**Intnl Info**.... International Info [*A publication*]
**Intnl Sec**..... International Security [*A publication*]
**INT NOCT** ... Inter Noctem [*During the Night*] [*Pharmacy*]
**Int North Pac Fish Comm Annu Rep** ... International North Pacific Fisheries Commission. Annual Report [*A publication*]
**Int North Pac Fish Comm Bull** ... International North Pacific Fisheries Commission. Bulletin [*A publication*]
**INTNS**....... In Transit
**IntNurI** ...... International Nursing Index [*A publication*]
**Int Nurs Index** ... International Nursing Index [*A publication*]
**Int Nurs Re** ... International Nursing Review [*A publication*]
**Int Nurs Rev** ... International Nursing Review [*A publication*]
**Int Nutr Policy Ser** ... International Nutrition Policy Series [*A publication*]
**INTO** ......... Industrial Training Opportunities Exhibition (ITD)
**INTO** ......... Inhibited Nitrogen Tetroxide
**INTO** ......... Initio, Inc. [*NASDAQ symbol*] (NQ)
**INTO** ......... Intelligence Officer [*Army*]
**INTO** ......... Intuitive Network Total Office [*Benchmark Associates*] [*Data processing*]
**INTO** ......... Iran National Tourist Organization
**INTO** ......... Irish National Teachers' Organisation
**Int Off Cocoa Choc Period Bull** ... International Office of Cocoa and Chocolate. Periodic Bulletin [*A publication*]
**Int Oil Scouts Assoc Yearb** ... International Oil Scouts Association. Yearbook [*A publication*]
**INTOP**....... International Operations Simulation (IEEE)
**Int Ophthalmol** ... International Ophthalmology [*A publication*]
**Int Ophthalmol Clin** ... International Ophthalmology Clinics [*A publication*]
**INTOPS**.... Interdiction Operations [*Navy*] (NVT)
**INTOR** ...... International TOKAMAK Reactor [*Thermonuclear-fusion system*]
**Int Org** ....... International Organization [*A publication*]
**Int Organ** ... International Organization [*A publication*]
**Int Orthop** ... International Orthopaedics [*A publication*]
**INTOSAI** .. International Organization of Supreme Audit Institutions [*Vienna, Austria*] (EA)
**INTOX** ...... Intoxication
**INTOX L**... Intoxicating Liquor [*Legal term*] (DLA)
**Int P** ........... International Pharmacopoeia [*A publication*]
**Int Pac Halibut Comm Annu Rep** ... International Pacific Halibut Commission. Annual Report [*A publication*]
**Int Pac Halibut Comm Sci Rep** ... International Pacific Halibut Commission. Scientific Report [*A publication*]
**Int Pac Halibut Comm Tech Rep** ... International Pacific Halibut Commission. Technical Report [*A publication*]
**Int Packag Abs** ... International Packaging Abstracts [*A publication*]
**Int Packag Abstr** ... International Packaging Abstracts [*A publication*]
**Int Pac Salmon Fish Comm Annu Rep** ... International Pacific Salmon Fisheries Commission. Annual Report [*A publication*]
**Int Pac Salmon Fish Comm Bull** ... International Pacific Salmon Fisheries Commission. Bulletin [*A publication*]
**Int Pac Salmon Fish Comm Prog Rep** ... International Pacific Salmon Fisheries Commission. Progress Report [*A publication*]
**Int Peat Congr Proc** ... International Peat Congress. Proceedings [*A publication*]
**Int Peat Soc Bull** ... International Peat Society. Bulletin [*A publication*]
**Int Perspect** ... International Perspectives [*A publication*]
**Int Perspect Urol** ... International Perspectives in Urology [*A publication*]
**Int Pest Contr** ... International Pest Control [*A publication*]
**Int Pest Control** ... International Pest Control [*A publication*]
**Int Pet Abstr** ... International Petroleum Abstracts [*A publication*]
**Int Petrol Annu** ... International Petroleum Annual [*A publication*]
**Int Petrol Times** ... International Petroleum Times [*A publication*]
**Int Petr Tms** ... International Petroleum Times [*A publication*]
**Int Pet Technol** ... International Petroleum Technology [*A publication*]
**Int Pet Times** ... International Petroleum Times [*A publication*]
**INTPH** ...... Interphone
**Int Pharm Abstr** ... International Pharmaceutical Abstracts [*A publication*]
**Int Pharmac** ... International Pharmacopsychiatry [*A publication*]
**Int Pharmacopsychiatry** ... International Pharmacopsychiatry [*A publication*]
**INTPHIBRFT** ... Interim Amphibious Refresher Training [*Navy*] (NVT)
**Int Philo Q** ... International Philosophical Quarterly [*A publication*]
**Int Philos Q** ... International Philosophical Quarterly [*A publication*]
**Int Phil Q**... International Philosophical Quarterly [*A publication*]
**Int Phil Quart** ... International Philosophical Quarterly [*A publication*]
**Int Photobiol Congr** ... International Photobiological Congress [*A publication*]
**Int Photogr** ... International Photographer [*A publication*]
**Int Photo Tech** ... International Photo-Technik [*A publication*]
**INTPHTR** ... Interphase Transformer [*Electronics*]
**Int Phys Workshop Ser** ... International Physics Workshop Series [*A publication*]
**Int Pipe Ln** ... International Pipe Line Industry [*A publication*]
**Int Pipes Pipelines** ... International Pipes and Pipelines [*A publication*]
**Int Plann Parent Fed Med Bull** ... International Planned Parenthood Federation. Medical Bulletin [*A publication*]
**INTPLDR** ... Interpleader [*Legal*] [*British*] (ROG)
**INTPN**....... Interpretation (AFM)
**INTPO**....... Interpole [*Electromagnetics*]
**Int Polit (Bergen)** ... Internasjonal Politikk (Bergen) [*A publication*]
**Int Polit (O)** ... Internasjonal Politikk (Oslo) [*A publication*]
**Int Polit Sci Abstr** ... International Political Science Abstracts [*A publication*]
**IntPolSc**..... International Political Science Abstracts [*A publication*]
**Int Polym Sci & Technol** ... International Polymer Science and Technology [*A publication*]
**Int Potash Inst Bull** ... International Potash Institute. Bulletin [*A publication*]
**Int Potash Inst Colloq Proc** ... International Potash Institute. Colloquium. Proceedings [*A publication*]
**Int Potash Inst Res Top** ... International Potash Institute. Research Topics [*A publication*]
**Int Power Generation** ... International Power Generation [*England*] [*A publication*]
**INTPR**....... Interpret (AFM)
**Intpr** ........... Interpretation. A Journal of Bible and Theology [*A publication*]
**Int Presidents Bul** ... International President's Bulletin [*A publication*]
**Int Private Law** ... Private International Law [*A publication*] (DLA)
**Int Probl (Belgrade)** ... International Problems (Belgrade) [*A publication*]
**Int Probl (Tel-Aviv)** ... International Problems (Tel-Aviv) [*A publication*]
**Int Prog Urethanes** ... International Progress in Urethanes [*A publication*]
**Int Proj**....... International Projectionist [*United States*] [*A publication*]
**Int Psychiatry Clin** ... International Psychiatry Clinics [*A publication*]
**Int Psycho-Anal Assoc Monogr Ser** ... International Psycho-Analytical Association. Monograph Series [*A publication*]
**Int Q**.......... International Quarterly [*A publication*]
**INTQ**.......... International Tourism Quarterly [*A publication*]
**Int Q Entomol** ... International Quarterly of Entomology [*A publication*]
**Int Qk** ........ Interrupted Quick [*Flashing*] Light [*Navigation signal*]
**INTQKFL** ... Interrupted Quick Flashing Light [*Navigation signal*]
**INTR** ......... Interior (KSC)
**INTR** ......... Intermec Corp. [*NASDAQ symbol*] (NQ)
**INTR** ......... Intermittent (AFM)
**INTR** ......... Internal (KSC)
**Int (R)** ........ Interpretation (Richmond) [*A publication*]
**INTR** ......... Interpreter [*A publication*]
**INTR** ......... Interrupt [*Data processing*] [*Telecommunications*]
**INTR** ......... Intransitive
**INTR** ......... Introduction
**INTR** ......... Intruder

**InTR** .......... Rose Polytechnic Institute, Terre Haute, IN [*Library symbol*] [*Library of Congress*] (LCLS)
**Intra** ........... Intramural (DLA)
**Int R Admin Sci** ... International Review of Administrative Sciences [*A publication*]
**Int R Adm Sci** ... International Review of Administrative Sciences [*A publication*]
**Int R Aesthetics Sociology M** ... International Review of the Aesthetics and Sociology of Music [*A publication*]
**Int R Aesthetics & Soc** ... International Review of the Aesthetics and Sociology of Music [*A publication*]
**Int R Aesthetics & Soc Mus** ... International Review of the Aesthetics and Sociology of Music [*A publication*]
**INTRAFAX** ... Facsimile System [*Western Union trade name*]
**INTRAFILM** ... International Travel-Adventure Film Guild (EA)
**Int R Ag** ...... International Review of Agriculture [*A publication*]
**Int R Ag Econ** ... International Review of Agricultural Economics [*A publication*]
**Int Railw Gaz** ... International Railway Gazette [*A publication*]
**Int Railw J** ... International Railway Journal [*A publication*]
**Intra L Rev (Am U)** ... Intramural Law Review of American University [*A publication*]
**Intra L Rev (NYU)** ... Intramural Law Review of New York University [*A publication*]
**Intra L Rev (St LU)** ... Intramural Law Review (St. Louis University) [*A publication*] (DLA)
**Intra L Rev (UCLA)** ... Intramural Law Review of University of California at Los Angeles [*A publication*]
**Intramural LJ** ... Intramural Law Journal [*A publication*] (DLA)
**Intramural L Rev** ... Intramural Law Review [*A publication*] (DLA)
**INTRAN** ... Infrared Transmitting
**INTRAN** ... Input Translator [*IBM Corp.*] [*Data processing*]
**IN TRANS** ... In Transitu [*In Transit*] [*Latin*] (ROG)
**INTRANS** ... Intransitive (ROG)
**Intra-Sci Chem Rep** ... Intra-Science Chemistry Reports [*A publication*]
**INTRC**....... Intricate (MSA)
**Int R Com Dev** ... International Review of Community Development [*A publication*]
**Int R Comm Dev** ... International Review of Community Development [*A publication*]
**Int R Community Develop** ... International Review of Community Development [*A publication*]
**Int Read Assn Conf Pa** ... International Reading Association Conference. Papers [*A publication*]
**Int Read Assn Conv Pa** ... International Reading Association Convention. Papers [*A publication*]
**Int Recht u Diplom** ... Internationales Recht und Diplomatie [*A publication*]
**Int Rec Med** ... International Record of Medicine [*A publication*]
**Int Rec Med Gen Pract Clin** ... International Record. Medicine and General Practice Clinics [*A publication*]
**Int R Ed** ..... International Review of Education [*A publication*]
**Int R Ed Cinemat** ... International Review of Educational Cinematography [*A publication*]
**INTREDIS** ... International Tree Disease Register System for Literature Retrieval in Forest Pathology [*National Agricultural Library*]
**Int R Educ** ... International Review of Education [*A publication*]
**Int Reg Sci Rev** ... International Regional Science Review [*United States*] [*A publication*]
**Int Rehabil Med** ... International Rehabilitation Medicine [*A publication*]
**Int Rehab Rev** ... International Rehabilitation Review [*A publication*]
**Int Rel**........ International Relations [*A publication*]
**Int Relat (London)** ... International Relations (London) [*A publication*]
**Int Relat (Prague)** ... International Relations (Prague) [*A publication*]
**Int Relat (Teheran)** ... International Relations (Teheran) [*A publication*]
**INTREP**.... Intelligence Report (NATG)
**Int Rep Div Mech Eng CSIRO** ... Internal Report. Division of Mechanical Engineering. Commonwealth Scientific and Industrial Research Organisation [*A publication*] (APTA)
**INTREPT** ... Intelligence Report
**Int Res Commun Syst Med Sci Libr Compend** ... International Research Communications System Medical Science. Library Compendium [*A publication*]
**Int Rescuer** ... International Rescuer [*A publication*]
**Int Res Group Refuse Disposal Inf Bull** ... International Research Group on Refuse Disposal Information. Bulletin [*A publication*]
**INT REV**... Internal Revenue (ROG)
**Int Rev Aerosol Phys Chem** ... International Reviews in Aerosol Physics and Chemistry [*A publication*]
**Int Rev Aes** ... International Review of the Aesthetics and Sociology of Music [*A publication*]
**Int Rev Army Navy Air Force Med Serv** ... International Review of the Army, Navy, and Air Force Medical Services [*A publication*]
**Int Rev Biochem** ... International Review of Biochemistry [*A publication*]
**Int Rev Bull** ... Internal Revenue Bulletin [*A publication*] (DLA)
**Int Rev Chiro** ... International Review of Chiropractic [*A publication*]
**Int Rev Connect Tissue Res** ... International Review of Connective Tissue Research [*A publication*]
**Int Rev Crim Pol** ... International Review of Criminal Policy [*United Nations*] (DLA)
**Int Rev Cyt** ... International Review of Cytology [*A publication*]
**Int Rev Cytol** ... International Review of Cytology [*A publication*]
**Int Rev Cytol Suppl** ... International Review of Cytology. Supplement [*A publication*]
**Int Rev Edu** ... International Review of Education [*A publication*]
**Int Rev Educ** ... International Review of Education [*A publication*]
**Int Rev Exp Pathol** ... International Review of Experimental Pathology [*A publication*]
**Int Rev For Res** ... International Review of Forestry Research [*A publication*]
**Int Rev Gen Exp Zool** ... International Review of General and Experimental Zoology [*A publication*]
**Int Rev Gesamten Hydrobiol** ... Internationale Revue der Gesamten Hydrobiologie [*A publication*]
**Int Rev Gesamten Hydrobiol Hydrogr** ... Internationale Revue der Gesamten Hydrobiologie und Hydrographie [*A publication*]
**Int Rev Gesamten Hydrobiol Syst Beih** ... Internationale Revue der Gesamten Hydrobiologie. Systematische Beihefte [*A publication*]
**Int Rev His** ... International Review of History and Political Science [*A publication*]
**Int Rev Med Surg** ... International Review of Medicine and Surgery [*A publication*]
**Int Rev Mod** ... International Review of Modern Sociology [*A publication*]
**Int Rev Neurobiol** ... International Review of Neurobiology [*A publication*]
**Int Rev Neurobiol Suppl** ... International Review of Neurobiology. Supplement [*A publication*]
**Int Rev Phys Chem** ... International Reviews in Physical Chemistry [*England*] [*A publication*]
**Int Rev Physiol** ... International Review of Physiology [*A publication*]
**Int Rev Poult Sci** ... International Review of Poultry Science [*A publication*]
**Int Rev Serv** ... International Review Service [*United States*] [*A publication*]
**Int Rev S H** ... International Review of Social History [*A publication*]
**Int Rev Soc Hist** ... International Review of Social History [*A publication*]
**Int Rev Sport Soc** ... International Review of Sport Sociology [*A publication*]
**Int Rev Trach** ... International Review of Trachoma [*A publication*]
**Int Rev Trop Med** ... International Review of Tropical Medicine [*A publication*]
**INTREX**.... Information Transfer Exchange [*Library science*]
**INTREX**.... Information Transfer Experiment [*Massachusetts Institute of Technology*] (DIT)
**INTRF**....... Interference [*Telecommunications*] (MSA)
**INTRFT** .... Interim Refresher Training [*Navy*]
**INTRG** ...... Integrate (AFIT)
**INTRG** ...... Interrogate (MSA)
**Int R Hist Polit Sci** ... International Review of History and Political Science [*A publication*]
**Int R Hist Pol Sci** ... International Review of History and Political Science [*A publication*]
**Int Rice Comm Newsl** ... International Rice Commission. Newsletter [*A publication*]
**Int Rice Res Inst (Los Banos) Annu Rep** ... International Rice Research Institute (Los Banos). Annual Report [*A publication*]
**Int Rice Res Inst (Los Banos) Tech Bull** ... International Rice Research Institute (Los Banos). Technical Bulletin [*A publication*]
**Int Rice Res Inst Res Pap Ser** ... International Rice Research Institute. Research Paper Series [*A publication*]
**Int Rice Res Newsl** ... International Rice Research Newsletter [*A publication*]
**INTRLCD** ... Interlaced
**INTRLKD** ... Interlocked
**INTRLVR** ... Interleaver (NASA)
**Int R Miss** ... International Review of Missions [*A publication*]
**Int R Missions** ... International Review of Missions [*A publication*]
**Int R Mod Sociol** ... International Review of Modern Sociology [*A publication*]
**INTRMT**... Interment (AABC)
**INTRMTRGN** ... Intermountain Region [*Aviation*] (FAAC)
**INTRN** ...... Intravenous [*Medicine*]
**INTRO** ...... Introduction (MSA)
**INTROD** ... Introduction
**INTROD** ... Introduzione [*Introductory Movement*] [*Music*] (ROG)
**Introd Aklim Rosl Ukr** ... Introduktsiya ta Aklimatizatsiya Roslin na Ukraini [*A publication*]
**Introd Eksp Ekol Rosl** ... Introduktsiya ta Eksperimental'na Ekologiya Roslin [*A publication*]
**Int Roehrenind** ... Internationale Roehrenindustrie [*A publication*]
**Int Ropeway Rev** ... International Ropeway Review [*A publication*]
**INTROPTA** ... Introscripta [*Written Within*] [*Latin*] (ROG)
**INTRP**....... Interrupt
**INTRPL** .... Interpolation (MSA)
**INTRPLRY** ... Interpupillary
**INTRPT** .... Interrupt (MSA)
**Intrpub NR** ... Interpublic Group of Companies, Incorporated. News Release [*A publication*]
**Int R Sci & Prac Ag** ... International Review of the Science and Practice of Agriculture [*A publication*]
**Int R Scl Hist** ... International Review of Social History [*A publication*]
**Int R Soc Hist** ... International Review of Social History [*A publication*]
**Int R Sport Sociol** ... International Review of Sport Sociology [*A publication*]
**INTRSTG** ... Interstage (KSC)
**Int Rubb Dig** ... International Rubber Digest [*A publication*]
**Int Rv**......... International Review [*A publication*]
**INTS**.......... Intense

**InTS**........... Terre Haute Spectator, Terre Haute, IN [*Library symbol*] [*Library of Congress*] (LCLS)
**Int Salzburg Conf** ... International Salzburg Conference [*A publication*]
**Int Sci**......... International Science [*A publication*]
**Int Sci Counc Trypanosomiasis Res Control Publ** ... International Scientific Council for Trypanosomiasis Research and Control. Publication [*A publication*]
**Int Sci Counc Trypanosomiasis Res Publ** ... International Scientific Council for Trypanosomiasis. Research Publication [*A publication*]
**Int Sci Res News** ... International Science Research News [*A publication*]
**Int Sci Rev Ser** ... International Science Review Series [*A publication*]
**Int Sci Technol** ... International Science and Technology [*A publication*]
**INTSCT** .... Intersect (MSA)
**Int Sec**........ International Security [*A publication*]
**Int Secur** .... International Security [*A publication*]
**Int Secur Rev** ... International Security Review [*A publication*]
**Int Seismol Cent Bull** ... International Seismological Centre. Bulletin [*A publication*]
**Int Semin Reprod Physiol Sex Endocrinol** ... International Seminar on Reproductive Physiology and Sexual Endocrinology [*A publication*]
**Int Ser Biomech** ... International Series on Biomechanics [*A publication*]
**Int Ser Exp Psychol** ... International Series in Experimental Psychology [*A publication*]
**Int Ser Mater Sci Technol** ... International Series on Materials Science and Technology [*A publication*]
**Int Ser Monogr Anal Chem** ... International Series of Monographs in Analytical Chemistry [*A publication*]
**Int Ser Monogr Exp Psychol** ... International Series of Monographs in Experimental Psychology [*A publication*]
**Int Ser Monogr Nat Philos** ... International Series of Monographs in Natural Philosophy [*A publication*]
**Int Ser Monogr Nucl Energy** ... International Series of Monographs on Nuclear Energy [*A publication*]
**Int Ser Monogr Nucl Energy Div 7** ... International Series of Monographs on Nuclear Energy. Division 7. Reactor Engineering [*A publication*]
**Int Ser Monogr Oral Biol** ... International Series of Monographs in Oral Biology [*A publication*]
**Int Ser Monogr Pure Appl Biol Div Biochem** ... International Series of Monographs on Pure and Applied Biology. Division Biochemistry [*A publication*]
**Int Ser Monogr Pure Appl Biol Div Bot** ... International Series of Monographs on Pure and Applied Biology. Division Botany [*A publication*]
**Int Ser Monogr Pure Appl Biol Mod Trends Physiol Sci** ... International Series of Monographs on Pure and Applied Biology. Modern Trends in Physiological Sciences [*A publication*]
**Int Ser Monogr Sci Solid State** ... International Series of Monographs in the Science of the Solid State [*A publication*]
**Int Ser Pure Appl Biol Zool Div** ... International Series of Monographs on Pure and Applied Biology. Zoology Division [*A publication*]
**Int Ser Sci Solid State** ... International Series of Monographs in the Science of the Solid State [*A publication*]
**Int Ser Sport Sci** ... International Series on Sport Sciences [*A publication*]
**INTSF** ....... Intensify
**INTSFY**..... Intensify [*Meteorology*] (FAAC)
**Int Shade Tree Conf Proc** ... International Shade Tree Conference. Proceedings [*A publication*]
**Int Shipbldg Progr** ... International Shipbuilding Progress [*A publication*]
**Int Shipbuild Prog** ... International Shipbuilding Progress [*A publication*]
**Int Shipbuild Progress** ... International Shipbuilding Progress [*A publication*]
**Int Ship Painting Corros Conf Proc** ... International Ship Painting and Corrosion Conference. Proceedings [*A publication*]
**INTSHP**.... Intership
**Int Soc Dev** ... International Social Development Review [*A publication*]
**Int Social R** ... International Socialist Review [*A publication*]
**Int Social Sci J** ... International Social Science Journal [*UNESCO*] [*A publication*]
**Int Soc Rock Mech Congr Proc** ... International Society for Rock Mechanics. Congress Proceedings [*A publication*]
**Int Soc Sci** ... International Social Science Journal [*UNESCO*] [*A publication*]
**Int Soc Sci J** ... International Social Science Journal [*UNESCO*] [*A publication*]
**Int Soc Secur R** ... International Social Security Review [*A publication*]
**Int Soc Secur Rev** ... International Social Security Review [*A publication*]
**Int Soc Work** ... International Social Work [*A publication*]
**Int Sol Energy Soc Am Sect Proc Annu Meet** ... International Solar Energy Society. American Section. Proceedings of the Annual Meeting [*A publication*]
**Int Solid Wastes Public Clean Assoc Inf Bull** ... International Solid Wastes and Public Cleansing Association. Information Bulletin [*A publication*]
**INTSORMIL** ... International Sorghum and Millet Research
**Int Sourceb Corros Mar Environ** ... International Sourcebook. Corrosion in Marine Environment [*A publication*]
**INTSOY**.... International Soybean Program
**Int Spect**..... Internationale Spectator [*A publication*]
**Int Spectator** ... International Spectator [*A publication*]
**INTST** ....... Intensity
**INTST** ....... Interest [*Finance, Law*] (ROG)
**Int Stat R**... International Statistical Review [*A publication*]
**Int Stat Rev** ... International Statistical Review [*A publication*]
**INTSTDTHD** ... International Standard Thread (MCD)
**Int St E As** ... International Studies. East Asian Series Research Publication [*A publication*]
**INTSTG** .... Interstage
**Int St Rvw** .. International Statistical Review [*A publication*]
**Int Stud** ...... International Studies [*New Delhi*] [*A publication*]
**Int Studio** ... International Studio [*A publication*]
**Int Stud Manage Org** ... International Studies of Management and Organization [*A publication*]
**Int Stud (New Delhi)** ... International Studies (New Delhi) [*A publication*]
**Int Stud Phil** ... International Studies in Philosophy [*A publication*]
**Int Stud Q** .. International Studies Quarterly [*A publication*]
**Int Stud Quart** ... International Studies Quarterly [*A publication*]
**Int Stud Sparrows** ... International Studies on Sparrows [*A publication*]
**Int Stud (Stockholm)** ... Internationelle Studier (Stockholm) [*A publication*]
**Int Sugar Confect Manuf Assoc Period Bull** ... International Sugar Confectionery Manufacturers' Association. Periodic Bulletin [*A publication*]
**Int Sugar J** ... International Sugar Journal [*A publication*]
**Int Sug J** .... International Sugar Journal [*A publication*]
**INTSUM**... Intelligence Summary
**Int Surg**...... International Surgery [*A publication*]
**Int Symp Adjuvants Agrochem** ... International Symposium on Adjuvants for Agrochemicals [*A publication*]
**Int Symp Adv Struct Mat** ... International Symposium on Advanced Structural Materials [*A publication*]
**Int Symp Can Soc Immunol** ... International Symposium. Canadian Society for Immunology [*A publication*]
**Int Symp Carotenoids Other than Vitam A Abstr Commun** ... International Symposium on Carotenoids Other than Vitamin A. Abstracts of Communications [*A publication*]
**Int Symp Chemother** ... International Symposium on Chemotherapy [*A publication*]
**Int Symp Combust Pap** ... International Symposium on Combustion. Papers [*A publication*]
**Int Symp Corals Coral Reefs Proc** ... International Symposium on Corals and Coral Reefs. Proceedings [*A publication*]
**Int Symp Crop Prot Pap** ... International Symposium on Crop Protection. Papers [*A publication*]
**Int Symp Flammability Fire Retard Proc** ... International Symposium on Flammability and Fire Retardants. Proceedings [*A publication*]
**Int Symp Forest Hydrol (Pennsylvania)** ... International Symposium on Forest Hydrology (Pennsylvania) [*A publication*]
**Int Symp Fresh Water Sea Proc** ... International Symposium on Fresh Water from the Sea. Proceedings [*A publication*]
**Int Symp Heterog Catal Proc** ... International Symposium on Heterogeneous Catalysis. Proceedings [*A publication*]
**Int Symp Humidity and Moisture** ... International Symposium on Humidity and Moisture [*A publication*]
**Int Symp Landslide Control Proc** ... International Symposium on Landslide Control. Proceedings [*A publication*]
**Int Symp Microb Drug Resist** ... International Symposium on Microbial Drug Resistance [*A publication*]
**Int Symp Princess Takamatsu Cancer Res Fund** ... International Symposium. Princess Takamatsu Cancer Research Fund [*A publication*]
**Int Symp Radiosensitizers Radioprot Drugs** ... International Symposium on Radiosensitizers and Radioprotective Drugs [*A publication*]
**Int Symp Remote Sensing Environ Proc** ... International Symposium on Remote Sensing of Environment. Proceedings [*A publication*]
**INTT**.......... Interest [*Finance, Law*] (ROG)
**Int Tax J**.... International Tax Journal [*A publication*]
**Int Tax Jour** ... International Tax Journal [*A publication*] (DLA)
**Int Teach**.... Intermediate Teacher [*A publication*]
**Int Teamster** ... International Teamster [*A publication*]
**Int Telem Conf Proc** ... International Telemetering Conference. Proceedings [*A publication*]
**Int Telemetering Conf (Proc)** ... International Telemetering Conference (Proceedings) [*United States*] [*A publication*]
**Int Text Bull Dyeing Print Finish** ... International Textile Bulletin. Dyeing/Printing/Finishing [*World Edition*] [*A publication*]
**Int Text Mach** ... International Textile Machinery [*A publication*]
**Int Text Rev** ... International Textile Review [*A publication*]
**Int Thyroid Conf Proc** ... International Thyroid Conference. Proceedings [*A publication*]
**Int Tijdschr Brouw Mout** ... Internationaal Tijdschrift voor Brouwertj en Mouterij [*A publication*]
**Int Tin Res Counc Rep** ... International Tin Research Council. Reports [*A publication*]
**Int Tracts Comput Sci Technol Their Appl** ... International Tracts in Computer Science and Technology and Their Application [*A publication*]
**Int Trade Forum** ... International Trade Forum [*A publication*]
**Int Trade LJ** ... International Trade Law Journal [*A publication*] (DLA)
**Int Tree Crops J** ... International Tree Crops Journal [*A publication*]

**InTTS** ........ Terre Haute Tribune-Star, Terre Haute, IN [*Library symbol*] [*Library of Congress*] (LCLS)
**Int Tug Conv (Proc)** ... International Tug Convention (Proceedings) [*A publication*]
**Int Turtle Tortoise Soc J** ... International Turtle and Tortoise Society. Journal [*A publication*]
**INTU** ......... Indian Truth [*A publication*]
**INTUC** ...... Indian National Trades Union Congress
**INTUG** ...... International Telecommunications Users Group [*Telecommunications*] [*Information service or system*] (IID)
**Int Union Air Pollut Prev Assoc Int Clean Air Congr Pap** ... International Union of Air Pollution Prevention Associations. International Clean Air Congress. Papers [*A publication*]
**Int Union Biol Sci Ser B** ... International Union of Biological Sciences. Series B [*A publication*]
**Int Union Biol Sci Ser D Newsl** ... International Union of Biological Sciences. Series D. Newsletter [*A publication*]
**Int Union Cancer Monogr Ser** ... International Union Against Cancer. Monograph Series [*A publication*]
**Int Union Cancer Tech Rep Ser** ... International Union Against Cancer. Technical Report Series [*A publication*]
**Int Union Conserv Nat Nat Resour Annu Rep** ... International Union for Conservation of Nature and Natural Resources. Annual Report [*A publication*]
**Int Union Crystallogr Comm Crystallogr Appar Bibliogr** ... International Union of Crystallography. Commission on Crystallographic Apparatus. Bibliography [*A publication*]
**Int Union Geol Sci Int Subcomm Stratigr Cl Circ** ... International Union of Geological Sciences. International Subcommission on Stratigraphic Classification. Circular [*A publication*]
**Int Union Geol Sci Ser A** ... International Union of Geological Sciences. Series A [*A publication*]
**Int Urol Nephrol** ... International Urology and Nephrology [*A publication*]
**INTV** ......... Association of Independent Television Stations (EA)
**INTV** ......... Instrumentation Television (AFM)
**INTV** ......... Interview (CINC)
**INTV** ......... InterVoice, Inc. [*Richardson, TX*] [*NASDAQ symbol*] (NQ)
**InTV** .......... Vigo County Public Library, Terre Haute, IN [*Library symbol*] [*Library of Congress*] (LCLS)
**Int Ver Theor Angew Limnol Mitt** ... International Vereinigung fuer Theoretische und Angewandte Limnologie. Mitteilungen [*West Germany*] [*A publication*]
**Int Ver Theor Angew Limnol Verh** ... Internationale Vereinigung fuer Theoretische und Angewandte Limnologie und Verhandlungen [*A publication*]
**Int Vet Bull** ... International Veterinary Bulletin [*A publication*]
**Int Vet News** ... International Veterinary News [*A publication*]
**Int Virol** ..... International Virology [*A publication*]
**INTVL** ....... Interval (MSA)
**INTVLM** ... Intervalometer [*Military ordnance*]
**InTVS** ........ Vigo County School Corp., Instructional Materials Center, Terre Haute, IN [*Library symbol*] [*Library of Congress*] (LCLS)
**INTVW** ..... Interview (AFM)
**INTW** ........ IntraWest Financial Corp. [*NASDAQ symbol*] (NQ)
**Int Water Pollut Res Conf Pap** ... International Water Pollution Research Conference. Papers [*A publication*]
**Int Water Power Dam** ... International Water Power and Dam Construction [*A publication*]
**Int Water Power & Dam Constr** ... International Water Power and Dam Construction [*A publication*]
**Int Water Supply Assoc Congr** ... International Water Supply Association. Congress [*A publication*]
**INTWF** ...... Indian National Textile Workers' Federation
**Int Whaling Comm Rep** ... International Whaling Commission. Reports [*A publication*]
**Int Whaling Comm Rep Comm** ... International Whaling Commission. Report of the Commission [*A publication*]
**InTWHi** ..... Wabash Valley Historical Society, Terre Haute, IN [*Library symbol*] [*Library of Congress*] (LCLS)
**Int Wildl** .... International Wildlife [*A publication*]
**Int Wildlife** ... International Wildlife [*A publication*]
**Int Wire Cable Symp Proc** ... International Wire and Cable Symposium. Proceedings [*A publication*]
**Int Wiss Kolloq Tech Hochsch Ilmenau** ... Internationales Wissenschaftliches Kolloquium. Technische Hochschule Ilmenau [*A publication*]
**Int Wiss Korresp Gesch Dtsch Arb-Bew** ... Internazionale Wissenschaftliche Korrespondenz zur Geschichte der Deutschen Arbeiterbewegung [*A publication*]
**Int Woman L** ... International Woman Lawyer [*A publication*] (DLA)
**Int Woodworker** ... International Woodworker [*A publication*]
**Int Workshop Nude Mice Proc** ... International Workshop on Nude Mice. Proceedings [*A publication*]
**INTWORLSA** ... International Third World Legal Studies Association (EA)
**INTXN** ...... Intersection (FAAC)
**INTY** ......... [*The*] Integrity Financial Group, Inc. [*NASDAQ symbol*] (NQ)
**INTY** ......... Intestacy [*Legal*] (ROG)
**Int Yearbook Ag Leg** ... International Yearbook of Agricultural Legislation [*A publication*]
**Int Yearbook of Ed** ... International Yearbook of Education [*A publication*]
**Int Yrbk Ed** ... International Yearbook of Education [*A publication*]
**Int Z Angew Phsyiol Einschl Arbeitsphysiol** ... Internationale Zeitschrift fuer Angewandte Physiologie Einschliesslich Arbeitsphysiologie [*A publication*]
**Int Z Angew Physiol** ... Internationale Zeitschrift fuer Angewandte Physiologie Einschliesslich Arbeitsphysiologie [*West Germany*] [*A publication*]
**Int Z Bibelwiss** ... Internationale Zeitschriftenschau fuer Bibelwissenschaft und Grenzgebiete [*A publication*]
**Int Z Bohrtech Erdoelbergbau Geol** ... Internationale Zeitschrift fuer Bohrtechnik, Erdoelbergbau, und Geologie [*A publication*]
**Int Zeitschriftenschau Bibelwissenschaft Grenzgeb** ... Internationale Zeitschriftenschau fuer Bibelwissenschaft und Grenzgebiete [*A publication*]
**Int Z Elektrowaerme** ... Internationale Zeitschrift fuer Elektrowaerme [*A publication*]
**Int Z Erzieh** ... Internationale Zeitschrift fuer Erziehungswissenschaft [*A publication*]
**Int Z Klin Pharmakol Ther Toxicol** ... Internationale Zeitschrift fuer Klinische Pharmakologie Therapie und Toxicologie [*A publication*]
**Int Z Landwirtsch** ... Internationale Zeitschrift der Landwirtschaft [*A publication*]
**Int Z Metallogr** ... Internationale Zeitschrift fuer Metallographie [*A publication*]
**Int Zool Cong** ... International Zoological Congress [*A publication*]
**Int Zoo Yearb** ... International Zoo Yearbook [*A publication*]
**Int Z Phys Chem Biol** ... Internationale Zeitschrift fuer Physikalisch Chemische Biologie [*A publication*]
**Int Z Theor Angew Genet** ... Internationale Zeitschrift fuer Theoretische und Angewandte Genetik [*A publication*]
**Int Z Vitam-Ernaehrungsforsch** ... Internationale Zeitschrift fuer Vitamin und Ernaehrungsforschung [*A publication*]
**Int Z Vitamforsch** ... Internationale Zeitschrift fuer Vitaminforschung [*A publication*]
**Int Z Vitaminforsch** ... Internationale Zeitschrift fuer Vitaminforschung [*A publication*]
**Int Z Vitaminforsch Beih** ... Internationale Zeitschrift fuer Vitaminforschung. Beiheft [*A publication*]
**inu** ............. Indiana [*MARC country of publication code*] [*Library of Congress*] (LCCP)
**InU** ............ Indiana University, Bloomington, IN [*Library symbol*] [*Library of Congress*] (LCLS)
**INU** ........... Inertial Navigation Unit
**INU** ........... Integration Unit
**INU** ........... International Nutrition & Genetics Corp. [*Vancouver Stock Exchange symbol*]
**INU** ........... Inuyama [*Japan*] [*Seismograph station code, US Geological Survey*] (SEIS)
**INU** ........... Nauru [*Nauru*] [*Airport symbol*] (OAG)
**InU-A** ......... Indiana University, Anatomy-Physiology Laboratory, Bloomington, IN [*Library symbol*] [*Library of Congress*] (LCLS)
**InU-B** ......... Indiana University, Biology Library, Bloomington, IN [*Library symbol*] [*Library of Congress*] (LCLS)
**InU-BA** ...... Indiana University, School of Business Administration, Bloomington, IN [*Library symbol*] [*Library of Congress*] (LCLS)
**InUc** .......... Union City Public Library, Union City, IN [*Library symbol*] [*Library of Congress*] (LCLS)
**INUCA** ...... Inorganic and Nuclear Chemistry Letters [*A publication*]
**INucE** ......... Institution of Nuclear Engineers [*British*]
**InU-D** ........ Indiana University, School of Dentistry, Indianapolis, IN [*Library symbol*] [*Library of Congress*] (LCLS)
**InU-Fw** ...... Indiana University, Fort Wayne Regional Campus, Fort Wayne, IN [*Library symbol*] [*Library of Congress*] (LCLS)
**InU-I** .......... Indiana University, Indianapolis Regional Campus, Indianapolis, IN [*Library symbol*] [*Library of Congress*] (LCLS)
**INUI** .......... Inuit Today [*A publication*]
**InU-ISR** ..... Indiana University, Institute for Sex Research, Bloomington, IN [*Library symbol*] [*Library of Congress*] (LCLS)
**InU-K** ......... Indiana University, Kokomo Regional Campus, Kokomo, IN [*Library symbol*] [*Library of Congress*] (LCLS)
**InU-L** ......... Indiana University, Law Library, Indianapolis, IN [*Library symbol*] [*Library of Congress*] (LCLS)
**INUL** ......... Inulirijut. Department of Indian and Northern Affairs. Education Section. Social Development Division [*Canada*] [*A publication*]
**InU-Li** ........ Indiana University, Lilly Library, Bloomington, IN [*Library symbol*] [*Library of Congress*] (LCLS)
**InU-M** ........ Indiana University, School of Medicine, Indianapolis, IN [*Library symbol*] [*Library of Congress*] (LCLS)
**INUM** ........ Inummarit [*A publication*]
**INUMRC** .. Northwest Indiana Health Science Library Consortium [*Library network*]
**InU-N** ........ Indiana University, Northwest Regional Campus, Gary, IN [*Library symbol*] [*Library of Congress*] (LCLS)
**INUN** ......... Inuit North [*Nortext, Ottawa*] [*A publication*]

**InU-Nea**..... Indiana University Southeast, New Albany, IN [*Library symbol*] [*Library of Congress*] (LCLS)
**In Univ Fol** ... Indiana University. Folklore Institute. Monograph Series [*A publication*]
**InU-O** ........ Indiana University, Optometry Library, Bloomington, IN [*Library symbol*] [*Library of Congress*] (LCLS)
**InUpT** ........ Taylor University, Upland, IN [*Library symbol*] [*Library of Congress*] (LCLS)
**InU-R** ......... Indiana University at Bloomington, Lilly Rare Books, Bloomington, IN [*Library symbol*] [*Library of Congress*] (LCLS)
**INURAQ** ... Investigative Urology [*A publication*]
**INUS** ......... Inside the United States
**INUSA** ....... Industria Usoara [*A publication*]
**InU-Sb** ....... Indiana University, South Bend Regional Campus, South Bend, IN [*Library symbol*] [*Library of Congress*] (LCLS)
**InU-Se** ....... Indiana University, Southeastern Regional Campus, Jeffersonville, IN [*Library symbol*] [*Library of Congress*] (LCLS)
**INUT** ......... Inuttitut [*A publication*]
**INUV** ......... Inuvialuit [*A publication*]
**INV** ........... In-Line Needle Valve
**INV** ........... Inductive Null Voltage
**INV** ........... Invasion
**INV** ........... Invective
**INV** ........... Invenit [*He, or She, Designed It*] [*Latin*]
**INV** ........... Invent (AABC)
**Inv** ........... Inventario [*A publication*]
**INV** ........... Inventory (AFM)
**INV** ........... Inveralochy [*Australia*] [*Seismograph station code, US Geological Survey*] (SEIS)
**INV** ........... Inverness [*Scotland*] [*Airport symbol*] (OAG)
**INV** ........... Inverse [*or Invert*]
**INV** ........... Inverter (KSC)
**INV** ........... Investigation
**INV** ........... Investment
**INV** ........... Investment Review [*A publication*]
**INV** ........... Invitation
**INV** ........... Invitational Race [*Harness racing*]
**INV** ........... Invoice [*Billing*] (AFM)
**INV** ........... Involuntary
**INVAC** ...... Investment Account [*Postal Service*] [*British*]
**INVADJ** .... Inventory Adjustment (MCD)
**InVal** ......... Valparaiso-Porter County Public Library System, Valparaiso, IN [*Library symbol*] [*Library of Congress*] (LCLS)
**InValCR**..... Porter County Recorder's Office, Valparaiso, IN [*Library symbol*] [*Library of Congress*] (LCLS)
**InValHi**...... Historical Society of Porter County, Valparaiso, IN [*Library symbol*] [*Library of Congress*] (LCLS)
**InValU** ....... Valparaiso University, Valparaiso, IN [*Library symbol*] [*Library of Congress*] (LCLS)
**InValVM** ... Valparaiso Vidette-Messenger, Valparaiso, IN [*Library symbol*] [*Library of Congress*] (LCLS)
**INVAR** ...... Invariant
**InVb** .......... Van Buren Public Library, Van Buren, IN [*Library symbol*] [*Library of Congress*] (LCLS)
**Inv Banking** ... Investment Banking [*A publication*]
**INVCE**....... Invoice [*Billing*] (ROG)
**Inv Chron**... Investors Chronicle and Stock Exchange Gazette [*A publication*]
**Inv DD** ....... Investment Dealers' Digest [*A publication*]
**INV DOC ATTACH** ... Invoice with Documents Attached [*Billing*] (ROG)
**InVe** .......... Switzerland County Public Library, Vevay, IN [*Library symbol*] [*Library of Congress*] (LCLS)
**InVeCR**...... Switzerland County Recorder's Office, Vevay, IN [*Library symbol*] [*Library of Congress*] (LCLS)
**INVENT**.... Institute for Ventures in New Technology
**Inventaire Mal Plantes Can** ... Inventaire des Maladies des Plantes au Canada [*A publication*]
**Inventaire Mineral Fr** ... Inventaire Mineralogique de la France [*A publication*]
**Invent Intell** ... Invention Intelligence [*India*] [*A publication*]
**Invention**.... Invention Intelligence [*A publication*]
**Invent Manage** ... Invention Management [*United States*] [*A publication*]
**Invent Math** ... Inventiones Mathematicae [*A publication*]
**InVeRE**...... Vevay Reville-Enterprise, Vevay, IN [*Library symbol*] [*Library of Congress*] (LCLS)
**INVERN**.... Inverness [*County in Scotland*]
**InVerR** ....... Versailles Republican, Versailles, IN [*Library symbol*] [*Library of Congress*] (LCLS)
**InVerRHi**... Ripley County Historical Society, Versailles, IN [*Library symbol*] [*Library of Congress*] (LCLS)
**Inverse Pr**... Inverse Problems [*A publication*]
**INVERTEB** ... Invertebrate
**Invertebr Endocrinol** ... Invertebrate Endocrinology [*A publication*]
**Invertebr Reprod Dev** ... Invertebrate Reproduction and Development [*A publication*]
**INVES** ....... Investigate [*or Investigation*] (AFM)
**InVeSD**...... Switzerland Democrat, Vevay, IN [*Library symbol*] [*Library of Congress*] (LCLS)
**INVEST** .... Investigation
**INVEST** .... Investment
**Invest Agric (Santiago)** ... Investigacion Agricola (Santiago) [*A publication*]
**Invest Agropecu (Lima)** ... Investigaciones Agropecuarias (Lima, Peru) [*A publication*]
**Invest Agropecu (Peru)** ... Investigaciones Agropecuarias (Lima, Peru) [*A publication*]
**Invest Anal J** ... Investment Analysts Journal [*A publication*]
**Invest Cell Pathol** ... Investigative and Cell Pathology [*A publication*]
**Invest Cetacea** ... Investigations on Cetacea [*A publication*]
**Invest Clin Lab** ... Investigacion en la Clinica y en el Laboratorio [*A publication*]
**Invest Clin (Maracaibo)** ... Investigacion Clinica (Maracaibo) [*A publication*]
**Invest Econ** ... Investigacion Economica [*A publication*]
**Invest Fish Control** ... Investigations in Fish Control [*A publication*]
**Invest For**... Investment Forum [*A publication*]
**Invest Geotherm Potential UK Br Geol Surv** ... Investigation of the Geothermal Potential of the UK. British Geological Survey [*A publication*]
**Invest Geotherm Potential UK Inst Geol Sci** ... Investigation of the Geothermal Potential of the UK. Institute of Geological Sciences [*A publication*]
**INVESTIG** ... Investigation
**Investigacion Agric** ... Investigacion Agricola [*A publication*]
**Investigacion Econ** ... Investigacion Economica [*A publication*]
**Investigacion Oper** ... Investigacion Operacional [*Havana*] [*A publication*]
**Investigacion Pesq** ... Investigacion Pesquera [*A publication*]
**Investigation Air Pollut-Deposit Gauge Lead Diox Candle** ... Investigation of Air Pollution - Deposit Gauge and Lead Dioxide Candle [*A publication*]
**Investigation Air Pollut Smoke Sulph Diox Surv** ... Investigation of Air Pollution - Smoke and Sulphur Dioxide Survey [*A publication*]
**Investigation Report-CSIRO Institute of Earth Resources** ... Investigation Report. Commonwealth Scientific and Industrial Research Organization. Institute of Earth Resources [*A publication*]
**Invest Indiana Lakes Streams** ... Investigations of Indiana Lakes and Streams [*A publication*]
**Invest Inf Text** ... Investigacion e Informacion Textil [*A publication*]
**Invest Inf Text Tens** ... Investigacion e Informacion Textil y de Tensioactivos [*A publication*]
**Invest Lab Quim Biol Univ Nac Cordoba** ... Investigaciones. Laboratorio de Quimica Biologica. Universidad Nacional de Cordoba [*A publication*]
**Invest Mar Univ Catol Valparaiso** ... Investigaciones Marinas. Universidad Catolica de Valparaiso [*A publication*]
**Invest Med Int** ... Investigacion Medica Internacional [*A publication*]
**Investment Dealers Dig** ... Investment Dealers' Digest [*A publication*]
**Invest Microtech Med Biol** ... Investigative Microtechniques in Medicine and Biology [*A publication*]
**Invest New Drugs** ... Investigational New Drugs [*A publication*]
**Invest Ophth** ... Investigative Ophthalmology [*A publication*]
**Invest Ophthalmol** ... Investigative Ophthalmology [*Later, Investigative Ophthalmology and Visual Science*] [*A publication*]
**Invest Ophthalmol Vis Sci** ... Investigative Ophthalmology and Visual Science [*A publication*]
**Invest Ophthalmol Visual Sci** ... Investigative Ophthalmology and Visual Science [*A publication*]
**Invest Ophthal Visual Sci** ... Investigative Ophthalmology and Visual Science [*A publication*]
**Investor Owned Hosp Rev** ... Investor-Owned Hospital Review [*A publication*]
**Investors Chron** ... Investors Chronicle [*A publication*]
**Investors Chronicle** ... Investors Chronicle and Financial World [*A publication*]
**Invest Pediatr** ... Investigacion Pediatrica [*A publication*]
**Invest Pesq** ... Investigacion Pesquera [*A publication*]
**Invest Prog Agric** ... Investigacion y Progreso Agricola [*A publication*]
**Invest Radiol** ... Investigative Radiology [*A publication*]
**Invest Rep CSIRO (Aust)** ... Investigation Reports. Commonwealth Scientific and Industrial Research Organisation (Australia) [*A publication*]
**Invest Rep CSIRO Inst Earth Resour** ... CSIRO [*Commonwealth Scientific and Industrial Research Organisation*] Institute of Earth Resources. Investigation Report [*A publication*] (APTA)
**Invest Rep CSIRO Miner Res Lab** ... CSIRO [*Commonwealth Scientific and Industrial Research Organisation*] Minerals Research Laboratories. Investigation Report [*A publication*] (APTA)
**Invest Rep Div Miner Chem CSIRO** ... Investigation Report. Division of Mineral Chemistry. Commonwealth Scientific and Industrial Research Organisation [*A publication*] (APTA)
**Invest Rep Div Miner CSIRO** ... Investigation Report. Division of Mineralogy. Commonwealth Scientific and Industrial Research Organisation [*A publication*] (APTA)
**Invest Rep Div Miner Phys CSIRO** ... Investigation Report. Division of Mineral Physics. Commonwealth Scientific and Industrial Research Organisation [*A publication*] (APTA)
**Invest Rep Miner Res Lab CSIRO** ... Investigation Report. Minerals Research Laboratories. Commonwealth Scientific and Industrial Research Organisation [*A publication*] (APTA)
**Invest Tec Papel** ... Investigacion y Tecnica del Papel [*A publication*]
**Invest Urol** ... Investigative Urology [*A publication*]

**Invest Zool Chil** ... Investigaciones Zoologicas Chilenas [*A publication*]
**INVEX** ....... International Exhibition of Inventions and Novel Features (TSPED)
**INVF** .......... Investors Financial Corp. [*NASDAQ symbol*] (NQ)
**INVG** ......... INVG Mortgage Securities Corp. [*Formerly, Investors GNMA Trust*] [*NASDAQ symbol*] (NQ)
**InVi** ............ Vincennes and Knox County Public Libraries, Vincennes, IN [*Library symbol*] [*Library of Congress*] (LCLS)
**Inv Ind Lakes and Streams** ... Investigations of Indiana Lakes and Streams [*A publication*]
**InViSC** ....... Vincennes Sun Commercial, Vincennes, IN [*Library symbol*] [*Library of Congress*] (LCLS)
**INVIT** ......... Invitation (KSC)
**In Vitro Cell Dev Biol** ... In Vitro Cellular and Developmental Biology [*A publication*]
**In Vitro J Tissue Cult Assoc** ... In Vitro. Journal of the Tissue Culture Association [*A publication*]
**In Vitro Monogr** ... In Vitro Monograph [*A publication*]
**InViU** ......... Vincennes University, Vincennes, IN [*Library symbol*] [*Library of Congress*] (LCLS)
**InViU-Hi** ... Vincennes University, Byron R. Lewis Historical Collections Library, Vincennes, IN [*Library symbol*] [*Library of Congress*] (LCLS)
**INVL** .......... Inuvialuit [*A publication*]
**INVLT** ....... Involute
**INVMDJ** ... Invasion and Metastasis [*A publication*]
**INVN** ......... Inventory (MSA)
**INVN** ......... Invitron Corp. [*NASDAQ symbol*] (NQ)
**InVnCR** ...... Jennings County Recorder's Office, Vernon, IN [*Library symbol*] [*Library of Congress*] (LCLS)
**INVO** ......... Indian Voice [*A publication*]
**INVOF** ...... In the Vicinity Of (FAAC)
**INVOL** ....... Involuntary
**INVOLEX** ... Involuntary Extension
**INVOLV** .... Involve [*Coat*] [*Pharmacy*]
**Inv Ophth** .. Investigative Ophthalmology [*Later, Investigative Ophthalmology and Visual Science*] [*A publication*]
**Inv Pesq** ..... Investigacion Pesquera [*A publication*]
**Inv Radiol** .. Investigative Radiology [*A publication*]
**INVRAV** .... Investigative Radiology [*A publication*]
**Inv Reg Cas** ... Notes of Decisions of Appeal Court of Registration at Inverness [*1835-53*] [*Scotland*] [*A publication*] (DLA)
**Inv Rhet** ..... De Inventione Rhetorica [*of Cicero*] [*Classical studies*] (OCD)
**INVRN** ...... Inversion (FAAC)
**INVS** .......... Inverse (MSA)
**INVS** .......... Investors Savings Corp. [*Minnetonka, MN*] [*NASDAQ symbol*] (NQ)
**INVSTAR** ... Investigate and Report (FAAC)
**INVT** ......... Incorp, Inc. [*NASDAQ symbol*] (NQ)
**INVT** ......... Invenit [*He, or She, Designed It*] [*Latin*] (ROG)
**INVT** ......... Inventory (AABC)
**INVT** ......... Invert (MSA)
**INVT** ......... Investext [*Business Research Corp.*]
**INVTR** ....... Inverter
**Inv Urol** ...... Investigative Urology [*A publication*]
**INVX** ......... Innovex, Inc. [*NASDAQ symbol*] (NQ)
**INVY** ......... Inventory (ROG)
**Inv Zool Chilenas** ... Investigaciones Zoologicas Chilenas [*A publication*]
**INW** ........... Winslow [*Arizona*] [*Airport symbol*] (OAG)
**INW** ........... Winslow, AZ [*Location identifier*] [*FAA*] (FAAL)
**INWAB** ....... Industrial Wastes [*A publication*]
**InWab** ........ Wabash Carnegie Public Library, Wabash, IN [*Library symbol*] [*Library of Congress*] (LCLS)
**InWabHi** .... Wabash County Historical Museum, Wabash, IN [*Library symbol*] [*Library of Congress*] (LCLS)
**InWabPD** .. Wabash Plain Dealer, Wabash, IN [*Library symbol*] [*Library of Congress*] (LCLS)
**InWak** ........ Wakarusa Public Library, Wakarusa, IN [*Library symbol*] [*Library of Congress*] (LCLS)
**InWal** ......... Walkerton-Lincoln Township Public Library, Walkerton, IN [*Library symbol*] [*Library of Congress*] (LCLS)
**InWalIN** .... Walkerton Independent-News, Walkerton, IN [*Library symbol*] [*Library of Congress*] (LCLS)
**InWan** ........ Wanatah Public Library, Wanatah, IN [*Library symbol*] [*Library of Congress*] (LCLS)
**InWars** ....... Warsaw Public Library, Warsaw, IN [*Library symbol*] [*Library of Congress*] (LCLS)
**InWarsR** .... Kosciusko County Recorder's Office, Warsaw, IN [*Library symbol*] [*Library of Congress*] (LCLS)
**InWarsTU** ... Warsaw Times-Union, Warsaw, IN [*Library symbol*] [*Library of Congress*] (LCLS)
**InWas** ........ Carnegie Public Library, Washington, IN [*Library symbol*] [*Library of Congress*] (LCLS)
**INWAS** ....... Inertial Navigation and Weapons Attack System (MCD)
**InWasTH** .. Washington Times-Herald, Washington, IN [*Library symbol*] [*Library of Congress*] (LCLS)
**InWat** ......... Waterloo-Grant Township Public Library, Waterloo, IN [*Library symbol*] [*Library of Congress*] (LCLS)
**INWATS** ... Inward Wide Area Telephone Service [*Bell System*]
**InWav** ........ Waveland Public Library, Waveland, IN [*Library symbol*] [*Library of Congress*] (LCLS)
**INWD** ........ Inward (MSA)
**InWebaC** .... West Baden College, West Baden Springs, IN [*Library symbol*] [*Library of Congress*] (LCLS)
**InWele** ....... West Lebanon Pike Township Public Library, West Lebanon, IN [*Library symbol*] [*Library of Congress*] (LCLS)
**Inwest i Budown** ... Inwestycje i Budownictwo [*A publication*]
**InWevP** ...... Purdue University, North Central Campus, Westville, IN [*Library symbol*] [*Library of Congress*] (LCLS)
**INWG** ........ International Network Working Group [*International Federation for Information Processing*]
**InWh** .......... Whiting Public Library, Whiting, IN [*Library symbol*] [*Library of Congress*] (LCLS)
**InWhC** ....... Calumet College, Whiting, IN [*Library symbol*] [*Library of Congress*] (LCLS)
**InWhHi** ..... Whiting-Robertsdale Historical Society, Whiting, IN [*Library symbol*] [*Library of Congress*] (LCLS)
**INWI** ......... International Wildlife [*A publication*]
**InWil** .......... Williamsport-Washington Township Public Library, Williamsport, IN [*Library symbol*] [*Library of Congress*] (LCLS)
**InWilCR** .... Warren County Recorder's Office, Williamsport, IN [*Library symbol*] [*Library of Congress*] (LCLS)
**InWilR** ....... Williamsport Review-Republican, Williamsport, IN [*Library symbol*] [*Library of Congress*] (LCLS)
**InWina** ....... Pulaski County Public Library, Winamac, IN [*Library symbol*] [*Library of Congress*] (LCLS)
**InWincCR** ... Randolph County Recorder's Office, Winchester, IN [*Library symbol*] [*Library of Congress*] (LCLS)
**InWinFM** .. Free Methodist Historical Center, Winona Lake, IN [*Library symbol*] [*Library of Congress*] (LCLS)
**InWinG** ...... Grace College, Winona Lake, IN [*Library symbol*] [*Library of Congress*] (LCLS)
**INWL** ........ International Network of Women Liberals (EAIO)
**INWN** ........ International Systems & Technology, Inc. [*NASDAQ symbol*] (NQ)
**INWO** ........ Indian World [*A publication*]
**InWo** .......... Worthington Jefferson Township Public Library, Worthington, IN [*Library symbol*] [*Library of Congress*] (LCLS)
**InWol** ......... Wolcott Public Library, Wolcott, IN [*Library symbol*] [*Library of Congress*] (LCLS)
**InWolE** ...... New Wolcott Enterprise, Wolcott, IN [*Library symbol*] [*Library of Congress*] (LCLS)
**InWoT** ....... Worthington Times, Worthington, IN [*Library symbol*] [*Library of Congress*] (LCLS)
**INWWAH** ... Industrial Water and Wastes [*A publication*]
**INX** ........... Eigen Vervoer. Magazine voor Eigen Vervoerders en Verladers [*A publication*]
**INX** ........... Index Character [*Data processing*]
**INX** ........... Inexco Oil Co. [*Toronto Stock Exchange symbol*]
**INX** ........... Ion Exchange (NRCH)
**INXLTR** .... Input Translator [*IBM Corp.*] [*Data processing*] (MSA)
**INXS** .......... Australian rock band [*Pronounced "in excess"*]
**INY** ........... Batesville, AR [*Location identifier*] [*FAA*] (FAAL)
**INY** ........... Ithaca [*New York*] [*Seismograph station code, US Geological Survey*] (SEIS)
**INZ** ........... In Salah [*Algeria*] [*Airport symbol*] (OAG)
**INZAA** ...... Insatsu Zasshi [*A publication*]
**Inz Apar Chem** ... Inzynieria i Aparatura Chemiczna [*Poland*] [*A publication*]
**Inz Budownictwo** ... Inzynieria i Budownictwo [*A publication*]
**Inz Chem** .... Inzynieria Chemiczna [*A publication*]
**Inz Chem i Proc** ... Inzynieria Chemiczny i Procesowa [*A publication*]
**Inz-Fiz Z** .... Inzenerno-Fiziceskii Zurnal [*A publication*]
**Inzhenerno Fizicheskii Zh** ... Inzhenerno Fizicheskii Zhurnal [*A publication*]
**Inzh-Fiz Zh** ... Inzhenerno-Fizicheskii Zhurnal [*A publication*]
**Inzh-Fiz Zh Akad Nauk Belorus SSR** ... Inzhenerno-Fizicheskii Zhurnal Akademiya Nauk Beloruskoi SSR [*A publication*]
**Inzh Sb** ....... Inzhenernyi Sbornik [*USSR*] [*A publication*]
**Inzh Zh** ...... Inzhenernyi Zhurnal [*USSR*] [*A publication*]
**Inzh Zh Mekh Tverd Tela** ... Inzhenernyi Zhurnal, Mekhanika Tverdogo Tela [*A publication*]
**Inz Materialowa** ... Inzynieria Materialowa [*A publication*]
**INZSA** ....... Inzhenernyi Sbornik [*A publication*]
**InZSM** ....... Sullivan Museum, Zionsville, IN [*Library symbol*] [*Library of Congress*] (LCLS)
**Inz Stavby** .. Inzenyrske Stavby [*A publication*]
**Inz-Stroitel Inst Kuibysev Sb Trudov** ... Moskovskii Ordena Trudovogo Krasnogo Znameni Inzenerno-Stroitel'nyi Institut Imeni V. V. Kuibyseva Sbornik Trudov [*A publication*]
**Inz Z Meh Tverd Tela** ... Inzenernyi Zurnal Mehanika Tverdogo Tela [*A publication*]
**IO** .............. British Indian Ocean Territory [*ANSI two-letter standard code*] (CNC)
**IO** .............. Image Orthicon
**IO** .............. In Order
**I/O** ............ Inboard-Outboard [*Boating*]
**IO** .............. Incoming Orders
**IO** .............. India Office [*British*]
**IO** .............. Indian Ocean
**io** ............... Indonesia [*pt (Portuguese Timor) used in records cataloged before January 1978*] [*MARC country of publication code*] [*Library of Congress*] (LCCP)

**IO**.............. Industrial Operations (MCD)
**I/O**............ Industry/Occupation (OICC)
**IO**.............. Infant Orphan [*British*] (ROG)
**IO**.............. Infantry Officer [*British military*] (DMA)
**IO**.............. Inferior Oblique [*Muscle*] [*Anatomy*]
**IO**.............. Inferior Olive [*Neuroanatomy*]
**IO**.............. Information Officer
**IO**.............. Information Overload
**IO**.............. Initial Only (AFM)
**IO**.............. Injector Orifice
**I & O**......... Inlet and Outlet (MSA)
**I/O**............ Input/Output [*Data processing*]
**IO**.............. Inspection Opening (ADA)
**IO**.............. Inspection Order (NATG)
**IO**.............. Inspection Outline
**IO**.............. Institute for Oceanography [*Environmental Science Services Administration*]
**I/O**............ Instructor/Operator
**IO**.............. Intake Opens [*Valve position*]
**I & O**......... Intake and Output [*Medicine*]
**IO**.............. Intelligence Office [*or Officer*]
**IO**.............. Intercept Officer
**IO**.............. Interest Only Strip [*Mortgage security*]
**IO**.............. Intermediary Organization [*Physiology*]
**IO**.............. International Organizations [*A publication*]
**IO**.............. Interpreter Officer [*Military*] [*British*]
**IO**.............. Interpretive Operation
**IO**.............. Intestinal Obstruction [*Medicine*]
**IO**.............. Intraocular
**IO**.............. Inventory Objective
**IO**.............. Investigating Officer
**io**............... Iodo [*As substituent on nucleoside*] [*Biochemistry*]
**IO**.............. Ion Engine (AAG)
**Io**............... Ionium [*$Th^{230}$, radioactive isotope of thorium*]
**IO**.............. Iowa
**IO**.............. Iowa Music Educator [*A publication*]
**IO**.............. Irish Office
**I & O**......... Issues & Observations [*A publication*] (EAAP)
**IO**.............. Issuing Office
**IO**.............. Iterative Operation
**IO**.............. Touraine Air Transport Export [*France*] [*ICAO designator*] (FAAC)
**IOA**........... Impact Office Automation [*Australia*]
**IOA**........... Indian Ocean Area (MCD)
**IOA**........... Indian Overseas Airways
**IOA**........... Inflammatory Osteoarthritis [*Medicine*]
**IOA**........... Initial Outfitting Allowance [*Navy*]
**IOA**........... Input-Output Adapter [*Data processing*] (NASA)
**IOA**........... Input-Output Address [*Data processing*] (KSC)
**IOA**........... Input-Output Analysis [*Economics*]
**IOA**........... Input-Output Assembly [*Data processing*] (MCD)
**IOA**........... Institute on Aging [*University of Wisconsin - Madison*] [*Research center*] (RCD)
**IOA**........... Institute on Aging [*Portland State University*] [*Research center*] (RCD)
**IOA**........... Institute of Outdoor Advertising [*New York, NY*] (EA)
**IOA**........... Instrument Operating Assembly
**IOA**........... Instrumentation Operating Area
**IOA**........... International Office for Audiophonology (EA)
**IOA**........... International Olympic Academy
**IOA**........... International Omega Association (EA)
**IOA**........... International Order of the Armadillo (EA)
**IOA**........... International Orthoptic Association [*London, England*] (EAIO)
**IOA**........... International Osteopathic Association (EA)
**IOA**........... International Ozone Association (EA)
**IOA**........... Interocular Asynchrony [*Ophthalmology*]
**IOA**........... Intraoperative Autotransfusion [*Medicine*]
**IOA**........... Ioannina [*Greece*] [*Airport symbol*] (OAG)
**IOA**........... Iona Industries, Inc. [*Vancouver Stock Exchange symbol*]
**IOa**............ Oak Park Public Library, Oak Park, IL [*Library symbol*] [*Library of Congress*] (LCLS)
**IOAC**......... Infantry Officer Advanced Course [*Army*] (INF)
**IOAC/RC**.. Infantry Officer Advanced Correspondence Course/Reserve Component (INF)
**IOa-D**........ Oak Park Public Library, Dole Branch, Oak Park, IL [*Library symbol*] [*Library of Congress*] (LCLS)
**IOaHS**....... Oak Park-River Forest High School, Oak Park, IL [*Library symbol*] [*Library of Congress*] (LCLS)
**IOa-M**........ Oak Park Public Library, Maze Branch, Oak Park, IL [*Library symbol*] [*Library of Congress*] (LCLS)
**IOAT**......... International Organization Against Trachoma [*Creteil, France*] (EA)
**IOAU**......... Input/Output Access Unit [*Data processing*]
**IOAVF**....... Iona Industries, Inc. [*NASDAQ symbol*] (NQ)
**IOaWH**...... West Suburban Hospital, Oak Park, IL [*Library symbol*] [*Library of Congress*] (LCLS)
**IOB**........... Briar Cliff College, Sioux City, IA [*OCLC symbol*] (OCLC)
**IOB**........... Industrial Order of Battle (MCD)
**IOB**........... Input/Output Block [*Data processing*] (CMD)
**IOB**........... Input-Output Box [*Data processing*] (MCD)
**IOB**........... Input-Output Buffer [*Data processing*]
**I/OB**......... Input/Output Bus [*Data processing*] (NASA)
**IOB**........... Installation Operation Budget (AABC)
**IOB**........... Institute of Bankers [*Later, CIB*] (EAIO)
**IOB**........... Institute of Brewing [*Also, IB*] [*British*]
**IOB**........... Institute of Building [*or Builders*] [*British*]
**IOB**........... Intelligence Oversight Board [*Federal government*]
**IOB**........... Inter-Organization Board for Information Systems [*United Nations*] (IID)
**IOB**........... Internal Operating Budget
**IOBB**......... Independent Order of B'nai B'rith [*Later, BBI*]
**IObC**......... Chicago Bridge & Iron Co., Oak Brook, IL [*Library symbol*] [*Library of Congress*] (LCLS)
**IOBC**......... Infantry Officer Basic Course [*Army*]
**IOBC**......... International Organization for Biological Control of Noxious Animals and Plants [*See also OILB*] [*ICSU*] [*Research center*] [*Montpellier, France*] (EAIO)
**IOBKA**....... Izvestiya na Instituta po Obshta i Neorganichna Khimiya. Bulgarska Akademiya na Naukite [*A publication*]
**IOBLAM**... Iowa Bird Life [*A publication*]
**IOBPS**....... Input-Output Box and Peripheral Simulator [*Data processing*] (MCD)
**IOBS**......... Input/Output Buffering System [*Data processing*]
**IObT**......... Bethany and Northern Baptist Theological Seminaries Library, Oak Brook, IL [*Library symbol*] [*Library of Congress*] (LCLS)
**IOC**........... Clarke College, Dubuque, IA [*OCLC symbol*] (OCLC)
**IOC**........... Image Orthicon Camera
**IOC**........... Image Orthicon Control
**IOC**........... Immediate-or-Cancel Order [*Stock exchange term*]
**IOC**........... Imperial Owners Club, International (EA)
**IOC**........... In Our Culture
**IOC**........... In-Out Converter
**IOC**........... Indian Ocean Commission [*Port Louis, Mauritius*] (EAIO)
**IOC**........... Indirect Operating Costs
**IOC**........... Initial Operating Capability
**IOC**........... Initial Operational Capability [*Military*]
**IOC**........... Initial Order Condition (MCD)
**IOC**........... Input Offset Current
**IOC**........... Input-Output Channel [*Data processing*] (DIT)
**IOC**........... Input-Output Comparator [*Data processing*]
**I/OC**......... Input/Output Console [*Data processing*] (CAAL)
**IOC**........... Input-Output Controller [*Data processing*]
**IOC**........... Input-Output Converter [*Data processing*]
**IOC**........... Installation and Operational Checkout
**IOC**........... Institute of Chemistry [*British*] (DAS)
**IOC**........... Institutes for Oceanography [*Marine science*] (MSC)
**IOC**........... Integrated Optical Circuit [*or Component*]
**IOC**........... Integrated Optimization Control [*Engineering*]
**IOC**........... Integrated Optoelectronic Circuit
**IOC**........... INTELSAT Operations Center
**IOC**........... Inter-Office Channel [*Telecommunications*] (TSSD)
**IOC**........... Intergovernmental Oceanographic Commission [*See also COI*] [*ICSU*] [*Paris, France*] (EAIO)
**IOC**........... Interim Operational Capability
**IOC**........... Internationaal Ontmoetings Centrum [*International Network for Self-Reliance - INS*] (EA)
**IOC**........... International Oceanographic Commission [*NASA*]
**IOC**........... International Olympic Committee [*Switzerland*]
**IOC**........... International Ornithological Congress [*New Zealand*]
**IOC**........... International Ozone Commission [*IAMAP*] (NOAA)
**IOC**........... Interoffice Correspondence
**IOC**........... Interstate Oil Compact
**IOC**........... Iron Ore Company of Canada Ltd.
**IOC**........... Isotopes in Organic Chemistry [*Elsevier Book Series*] [*A publication*]
**IOC**........... Iterative Orbit Calculator
**IOC**........... Kiowa, CO [*Location identifier*] [*FAA*] (FAAL)
**IOCA**......... Independent Oil Compounders Association [*Later, ILMA*] (EA)
**IOCA**......... Intercollegiate Outing Club Association (EA)
**IOC/B & CC**... Intergovernmental Oceanographic Commission - Bureau and Consultative Council [*UNESCO*]
**IOCC**......... Infantry Officer Career Course [*Army*]
**IOCC**......... Input-Output Control Center [*or Command*] [*Data processing*]
**I/OCC**....... Input/Output Control Console [*Data processing*] (CAAL)
**IOCC**......... International Office of Cocoa and Chocolate [*Later, IOCCSC*] (EAIO)
**IOCC**......... Interstate Oil Compact Commission (EA)
**IOCC Bull**... Interstate Oil Compact Commission. Bulletin [*A publication*] (DLA)
**IOCCSC**.... International Office of Cocoa, Chocolate, and Sugar Confectionary [*Formed by a merger of IOCC and International Sugar Confectionary Manufacturers Association*] (EAIO)
**IOCD**......... Initial Operation Capability Date [*Military*] (AABC)
**IOCD**......... International Organization for Chemical Sciences in Development [*Brussels, Belgium*] (EA)
**IOCEB7**..... Specialist Periodical Reports. Inorganic Chemistry of the Transition Elements [*A publication*]
**IOC/EC**..... Intergovernmental Oceanographic Commission/Executive Council (MSC)

**IOCF**.......... International Oil Compensation Fund
**IOC-FDTE** ... Initial Operational Capability - Force Development Testing and Experimentation
**IOCG**.......... Industrial Oil Consumers Group (EA)
**IOCHC**....... International Organization for Cooperation in Health Care [*See also MMI*] [*Nijmegen, Netherlands*] (EAIO)
**IOCHS**....... International Organization for Cultivating Human Spirit [*Later, OISCA*]
**IOCI**........... Imperial Order of the Crown of India [*British*] (ROG)
**IOCI**........... Interstate Organized Crime Index [*Computer databank*]
**IOC/M**....... Memorias. Instituto Oswaldo Cruz [*A publication*]
**IOCP**.......... Indian Overseas Communication Project
**IOCP**.......... Input/Output Control Processor [*Data processing*]
**IOCP**.......... Input/Output Control Program [*Data processing*]
**IOCS**.......... Input-Output Control System [*Data processing*]
**IOCS**.......... Instant Ocean Culture System
**IOCS**.......... Interoffice Comment Sheet (NATG)
**IOCTAH** ... Intergovernmental Oceanographic Commission. Technical Series [*A publication*]
**IOCTL**........ Indian Ocean Conventional Target List (MCD)
**IOCU**.......... Input-Output Control Unit [*Data processing*]
**IOCU**.......... International Organization of Consumers Unions [*The Hague, Netherlands*] (EA)
**IOCV**.......... International Organization of Citrus Virologists (EA)
**IOC/VAP**.. Intergovernmental Oceanographic Commission/Voluntary Assistance Program (MSC)
**IOD**............ Drake University, Des Moines, IA [*OCLC symbol*] (OCLC)
**IOD**............ Identified Outward Dialing [*Telecommunications*] (TEL)
**IOD**............ Immediate Oxygen Demand [*Marine science*] (MSC)
**IOD**............ Imperial Order of the Dragon (EA)
**IOD**............ Information on Demand, Inc. [*Information service or system*] (IID)
**IOD**............ Injured on Duty
**IOD**............ Input/Output Device [*Telecommunications*] (TEL)
**IOD**............ Institute of Directors [*British*] (DCTA)
**IOD**............ Institute of Diving (EA)
**IOD**............ Institute of Outdoor Drama (EA)
**IOD**............ Integrated Observation Device (MCD)
**IOD**............ Integrated Optical Density [*Instrumentation*]
**IOD**............ Iron Overload Diseases Association (EA)
**IODA**.......... Iron Overload Diseases Association (EA)
**IODC**.......... Input-Output Data Channel [*Data processing*]
**IODC**.......... Input-Output Delay Counter [*Data processing*]
**IODD**.......... Input-Output Data Document [*Data processing*] (MCD)
**IODE**.......... Imperial Order of Daughters of the Empire [*Canada*]
**IODE**.......... International Oceanographic Data Exchange
**IODHRI**.... International Organization for the Defense of Human Rights in Iraq (EA)
**IODMM**.... International Office of Documentation on Military Medicine (EA)
**IODS**.......... International Ocean Disposal Symposium (EA)
**IOE**............ Buena Vista College, Storm Lake, IA [*OCLC symbol*] (OCLC)
**IOE**............ Industry and Development [*A publication*]
**IOE**............ Input-Output Error Log Table [*Data processing*] (MCD)
**IOE**............ Institute of Ecology [*Research center*] (RCD)
**IOE**............ Institute for the Officialization of Esperanto
**IOE**............ Institute of Offshore Engineering [*Heriot-Watt University*] [*Information service or system*] (IID)
**IOE**............ Instrumentation Operations Engineer (MCD)
**IOE**............ Intensity of Operational Employment [*Army*] (RDA)
**IOE**............ International Office of Epizootics
**IOE**............ International Organization of Employers [*Geneva, Switzerland*]
**IOE**............ International Organization of Experts (EAIO)
**IOEH**.......... Institute of Occupational and Environmental Health [*See also IMTA, IMTE*]
**IOEHI**........ International Organization for the Education of the Hearing Impaired (EA)
**IOEMTFS**... Independent Order of Engineers and Machinists Trade and Friendly Society [*A union*] [*British*]
**IOf**.............. Acorn Library District, Oak Forest, IL [*Library symbol*] [*Library of Congress*] (LCLS)
**IOF**............ Graceland College, Lamoni, IA [*OCLC symbol*] (OCLC)
**IOF**............ Independent Order of Foresters [*Buffalo, NY*] (EA)
**IOF**............ Infrared Optical Film
**IOF**............ Initial Operational Flight (MCD)
**IOF**............ Input/Output Front End [*Data processing*]
**IOF**............ Interactive Operations Facility [*Honeywell, Inc.*]
**IOF**............ International Oceanographic Foundation (EA)
**IOF**............ International Orienteering Federation (EA)
**IOF**............ Internationale Orientierungslauf Foderation [*International Orienteering Federation*] (EA)
**IOfa**........... O'Fallon Public Library, O'Fallon, IL [*Library symbol*] [*Library of Congress*] (LCLS)
**IOfaCD**...... O'Fallon Community Consolidated District 90, O'Fallon, IL [*Library symbol*] [*Library of Congress*] (LCLS)
**IOfaSD**...... O'Fallon Township High School District 203, O'Fallon, IL [*Library symbol*] [*Library of Congress*] (LCLS)
**IOFB**.......... Intraocular Foreign Body [*Medicine*]
**IOFC**.......... Indian Ocean Fishery Commission [*FAO*] [*Italy*] [*United Nations*]
**IOfH**.......... Oak Forest Hospital, Oak Forest, IL [*Library symbol*] [*Library of Congress*] (LCLS)
**IOFI**........... International Organization of the Flavor Industry [*Geneva, Switzerland*] (EAIO)
**IOFOS**....... International Organization for Forensic Odonto-Stomatology [*Formerly, International Society of Forensic Odonto-Stomatology*] (EA)
**IOFS**.......... International Organ Festival Society (EA)
**IOFSG**....... International Orienteering Federation, Scientific Group [*See also IOFWA*] (EAIO)
**IOFSI**........ Independent Order of the Free Sons of Israel [*Freemasonry*] (ROG)
**IOFT**.......... Institution on Farm Training
**IOFWA**...... Internationale Orientierungslauf Foderation, Wissenschaftliche Arbeitsgruppe [*International Orienteering Federation, Scientific Group - IOFSG*] (EAIO)
**IOG**............ Grinnell College, Grinnell, IA [*OCLC symbol*] (OCLC)
**IOG**............ Input-Output Gate [*Data processing*]
**IOG**............ Institute of Groundsmanship [*British*] (ITD)
**IOG**............ Intercollegiate Opera Group [*Defunct*] (EA)
**IOG**............ International Organization [*A publication*]
**IOg**............. Oglesby Public Library, Oglesby, IL [*Library symbol*] [*Library of Congress*] (LCLS)
**IOGA**.......... Industry-Organized Government-Approved
**IOgd**........... Rose Library, Ogden, IL [*Library symbol*] [*Library of Congress*] (LCLS)
**IOGE**.......... Integrated Operational Ground Equipment
**IOGEN**....... Input-Output Generation [*Data processing*]
**IOgIV**......... Illinois Valley Community College, Oglesby, IL [*Library symbol*] [*Library of Congress*] (LCLS)
**IOGP**.......... International Outboard Grand Prix
**IOgPS**........ Oglesby Public Schools, Oglesby, IL [*Library symbol*] [*Library of Congress*] (LCLS)
**IOGR**.......... International Order of the Golden Rule [*Springfield, IL*] (EA)
**IOGT**.......... International Organization of Good Templars [*Oslo, Norway*] (EAIO)
**IOH**............ Idiopathic Orthostatic Hypotension [*Medicine*]
**IOH**............ Indication of Hostilities [*Military*]
**I & OH**....... Inlet and Outlet Head (MSA)
**IOH**............ Inside-Out Helmholtz
**IOH**............ [*The*] Institute of Heraldry [*Military*]
**IOH**............ Inventory on Hand
**IOH**............ Item [*or Items*] on Hand
**IOH**............ Luther College, Decorah, IA [*OCLC symbol*] (OCLC)
**IOh**............. Ohio Township Library, Ohio, IL [*Library symbol*] [*Library of Congress*] (LCLS)
**IOHE**.......... Inter-American Organization for Higher Education [*See also OUI*]
**IOHE**.......... International Organization for Human Ecology (EAIO)
**IOHFI**........ International Organization for Housing Finance Institutions (EA)
**IOHH**......... International Order of Hoo-Hoo (EA)
**IOHS**.......... Integrated Operational Hydrological System [*Marine science*] (MSC)
**IOHSA**....... International Journal of Occupational Health and Safety [*A publication*]
**IOI**............. Interest on Investment (AFIT)
**IOI**............. Interim Operating Instructions
**IOI**............. Internal Operating Instruction
**IOI**............. International Ocean Institute [*Valetta, Malta*] (EAIO)
**IOI**............. International Ombudsman Institute [*University of Alberta*] [*Research center*] [*Edmonton, AB*] (EAIO)
**IOI**............. International Orphans, Incorporated (EA)
**IOI**............. International Ozone Institute [*Later, IOA*] (EA)
**IOI**............. Iori Enterprises, Incorporated [*Vancouver Stock Exchange symbol*]
**IOI**............. Iowa Wesleyan College, Mount Pleasant, IA [*OCLC symbol*] (OCLC)
**IOIC**........... Integrated Operational Intelligence Center
**IOIH**........... Input/Output Interrupt Handler [*Data processing*]
**IOIRS**......... International Online Information Retrieval Service [*Institute of Scientific and Technical Information of China*] [*Beijing*] [*Information service or system*] (IID)
**IOIS**........... Integrated Operational Intelligence System (MCD)
**IOITBAG**.. International Oil Industry TBA Group (EA)
**IOJ**............. Institute of Journalists [*British*]
**IOJ**............. International Organization of Journalists [*See also OIJ*] [*Prague, Czechoslovakia*] (EAIO)
**IOJ**............. St. Ambrose College, Davenport, IA [*OCLC symbol*] (OCLC)
**IOJD**.......... International Order of Job's Daughters (EA)
**IOJD**.......... International Organization for Justice and Development (EAIO)
**IOK**............ International Order of Kabbalists (EA)
**IOK**............ Iokea [*Papua New Guinea*] [*Airport symbol*] (OAG)
**IOK**............ Simpson College, Indianola, IA [*OCLC symbol*] (OCLC)
**IOkCD**....... West Washington County Community District 10, Okawville, IL [*Library symbol*] [*Library of Congress*] (LCLS)
**IOKDS**....... International Order of the King's Daughters and Sons (EA)
**IOKKA**...... Izvestiya na Instituta po Organichna Khimiya. Bulgarska Akademiya na Naukite [*Bulgaria*] [*A publication*]

**IOKNA**...... Izvestiya na Otdelenieto za Khimicheski Nauki. Bulgarska Akademiya na Naukite [*A publication*]
**IOL**........... India Office Library and Records [*British*]
**IOL**........... Initial Outfitting List [*for advanced naval bases*]
**IOL**........... Instantaneous Overload
**IOL**........... Intermediate Objective Lens
**IOL**........... International Old Lacers (EA)
**IOL**........... Intraocular Lens [*Ophthalmology*]
**IOL**........... Loras College, Dubuque, IA [*OCLC symbol*] (OCLC)
**IOl**........... Oak Lawn Public Library, Oak Lawn, IL [*Library symbol*] [*Library of Congress*] (LCLS)
**IOLA**......... Input/Output Link Adapter [*Data processing*]
**IOlC**.......... Christ Hospital, Oak Lawn, IL [*Library symbol*] [*Library of Congress*] (LCLS)
**IOLC**......... Input/Output Link Control [*Data processing*]
**IOlE**.......... Evangelical School of Nursing, Oak Lawn, IL [*Library symbol*] [*Library of Congress*] (LCLS)
**IOLI**.......... International Old Lacers, Incorporated (EA)
**IOLIM**....... International Online Information Meeting
**IOLM**........ International Organization for Legal Metrology
**IOln**.......... Olney Carnegie Public Library, Olney, IL [*Library symbol*] [*Library of Congress*] (LCLS)
**IOLRAM**... Israel Oceanographic and Limnological Research. Annual Report [*A publication*]
**IOLS**......... Integrated Online Library Systems
**IOLS**......... Iterated Ordinary Least Squares [*Statistics*]
**IOLS**......... Vision Technologies International, Inc. [*NASDAQ symbol*] (NQ)
**IOLTA**....... Interest on Lawyers' Trust Accounts
**IOLV**......... Independent Order Ladies of Vikings (EA)
**IOM**.......... Index Octane Moteur [*French*]
**IOM**.......... Indian Order of Merit
**IOM**.......... Inert Operational Missile (NG)
**IOM**.......... Inferior Orbitomeatal Line [*Brain anatomy*]
**IOM**.......... Innovator of the Month
**IOM**.......... Input-Output Module [*Data processing*] (MCD)
**I/OM**........ Input-Output Multiplexer [*Data processing*]
**IOM**.......... Insoluble Organic Material [*or Matter*] [*Analytical chemistry*]
**IOM**.......... Inspector of Ordnance Machinery [*British military*] (DMA)
**IOM**.......... Institute of Medicine [*National Academy of Sciences*] (EA)
**IOM**.......... Institute of Metals [*Formed by a merger of Institution of Metallurgists - IM and Metals Society - MS*] (EAIO)
**IOM**.......... Institute of Occupational Medicine [*United Kingdom*] (IRUK)
**I & OM**..... Intermediate and Organizational Maintenance (MCD)
**IOM**.......... International Options Market [*Australian Options Market, European Options Exchange in Amsterdam, Montreal Exchange, and Vancouver Stock Exchange*]
**IOM**.......... International Organization for Migration (EAIO)
**IOM**.......... International Organization for Mycoplasmology (EA)
**IOM**.......... Interoffice Memorandum
**IOM**.......... Isle Of Man [*England*] [*Airport symbol*] (OAG)
**IOM**.......... Isle Of Man [*England*]
**IOM**.......... Morningside College, Sioux City, IA [*OCLC symbol*] (OCLC)
**IOMA**....... International Oxygen Manufacturers Association (EA)
**IOMC**....... International Organization for Medical Cooperation
**IOME**....... Irgun Olej Merkas Europa (BJA)
**IOMG**....... Iomega Corp. [*NASDAQ symbol*] (NQ)
**I/OMI**....... Integration/Operations and Maintenance Instruction [*NASA*] (NASA)
**IOMMP**.... International Organization of Masters, Mates, and Pilots
**IOMO**....... Invitation of Member Only
**IOMP**....... International Organization for Medical Physics (EA)
**IOMR**....... Isle Of Man Railways [*British*] (ROG)
**IOMS**....... Interim Operation Meteorological System
**IOMS**....... International Organization for Masoretic Studies
**IOMSPCo**... Isle Of Man Steam Packet Company [*British*] (ROG)
**IOMT**....... Isomet Corp. [*NASDAQ symbol*] (NQ)
**IOMTR**..... International Organization for Motor Trades and Repairs [*Rijswljk, Netherlands*] (EAIO)
**IOMVM**.... International Organization of Motor Vehicle Manufacturers (EAIO)
**ION**........... Bionaire, Inc. [*Toronto Stock Exchange symbol*]
**ION**........... Biotech Electronics Ltd. [*Toronto Stock Exchange symbol*]
**ION**........... Coe College, Cedar Rapids, IA [*OCLC symbol*] (OCLC)
**ION**........... Impfondo [*Congo*] [*Airport symbol*] (OAG)
**ION**........... Inferior Olivary Nucleus [*Neuroanatomy*]
**ION**........... Institute of Navigation (EA)
**ION**........... Institute of Neuroscience [*University of Oregon*] [*Research center*] (RCD)
**ION**........... Institute of Neurotoxicology [*Yeshiva University*] [*Research center*] (RCD)
**ION**........... Institute for Optimum Nutrition [*British*]
**ION**........... International Organization of Nerds (EA)
**ION**........... Ione, WA [*Location identifier*] [*FAA*] (FAAL)
**ION**........... Ionic
**ION**........... Ionics, Inc. [*NYSE symbol*] (SPSG)
**ION**........... Ionosphere and Aural Phenomena Advisory Committee [*European Space Research Organization*] (IEEE)
**ION**........... Ischemic Optic Neuropathy [*Medicine*]
**ION**........... Isthmo-Optic Nucleus [*or Nuclei*] [*In midbrain of chick*]
**Iona**........... De Iona [*Philo*] (BJA)
**IOna**.......... Onarga Public Library, Onarga, IL [*Library symbol*] [*Library of Congress*] (LCLS)
**IONDS**...... Initial Operational Nuclear Detection System
**IONDS**...... Integrated Operational Nuclear Detonation Detection System
**Ion Exch**..... Ion Exchange and Membranes [*A publication*]
**Ion Exch Membr**... Ion Exchange and Membranes [*A publication*]
**Ion Exch and Membranes**... Ion Exchange and Membranes [*A publication*]
**Ion Exch Prog**... Ion Exchange Progress [*A publication*]
**Ion Exch Solvent Extr**... Ion Exchange and Solvent Extraction [*A publication*]
**IONO**........ Ionosphere (MSA)
**Ionos Issled**... Ionosfernye Issledovaniya [*USSR*] [*A publication*]
**IONS**........ Institute of Noetic Sciences (EA)
**IONS**........ Intraoperative Neurosonography [*Radiology*]
**Ion-Selective Electrode Rev**... Ion-Selective Electrode Reviews [*A publication*]
**Ion-Sel Electrode Rev**... Ion-Selective Electrode Reviews [*A publication*]
**IOO**........... ICOR Oil & Gas Co. Ltd. [*Toronto Stock Exchange symbol*]
**IOO**........... Idaho Operations Office [*Energy Research and Development Administration*]
**IOO**........... Inspecting Ordnance Officer
**IOO**........... Northwestern College, Orange City, IA [*OCLC symbol*] (OCLC)
**IOOC**........ Integrated Optics and Optical Fiber Communications (MCD)
**IOOC**........ International Olive Oil Council [*See also COI*] [*Madrid, Spain*] (EAIO)
**IOOC**........ Iranian Oil Operating Companies
**IOOF**........ Independent Order of Odd Fellows (EA)
**IOOL**........ International Optometric and Optical League [*London, England*] (EAIO)
**IOOP**........ Input/Output Operation [*Data processing*]
**IOOSF**...... Integrated Orbital Operations Simulation Facility
**IOOTS**...... International Organization of Old Testament Scholars
**IOOW**....... In Our Own Way (EA)
**IOP**........... Central College, Pella, IA [*OCLC symbol*] (OCLC)
**IOP**........... Ibero-American Organization of Pilots [*See also OIP*] [*Mexico City, Mexico*] (EAIO)
**IOP**........... In-Orbit Plane (KSC)
**I & OP**....... In and Out Processing [*Data processing*] (AFM)
**I/OP**......... Inboard/Outboard Profile (NASA)
**IOP**........... Initial Operating Production (MCD)
**IOP**........... Input-Output Package [*IBM Corp.*] [*Data processing*]
**IOP**........... Input-Output Port [*Data processing*] (MCD)
**IOP**........... Input-Output Processor [*Data processing*]
**IOP**........... Input-Output Pulse [*Data processing*]
**IOP**........... Inspection Operation Procedure (MCD)
**IOP**........... Installation Operating Program (AABC)
**IOP**........... Institute of Painters in Oil Colours [*British*]
**IOP**........... Institute of Plumbing (EAIO)
**IOP**........... Institute of Printing [*British*]
**IOP**........... Institute of Pyramidology [*Harpenden, Hertfordshire, England*] (EA)
**IOP**........... Integrated Obstacle Plan [*Military*]
**IOP**........... Integrated Operation Plan [*NASA*] (NASA)
**IOP**........... Integrated Ordnance Package (MCD)
**IOP**........... Interim Operating Procedure (NVT)
**IOP**........... Internal Operating Procedure
**IOP**........... International Journal of Operations and Production Management [*A publication*]
**IOP**........... International Organization of Palaeobotany [*Great Britain*]
**IOP**........... International Organization of Psychophysiology [*See also IPO*] [*Montreal, PQ*] (EAIO)
**IOP**........... International Potter Distilling Corp. [*Toronto Stock Exchange symbol*] [*Vancouver Stock Exchange symbol*]
**IOP**........... Intraocular Pressure [*Ophthalmology*]
**IOP**........... Ioma [*Papua New Guinea*] [*Airport symbol*] (OAG)
**IOP**........... Iranian Oil Participants Ltd.
**IOp**........... Orland Park Public Library, Orland Park, IL [*Library symbol*] [*Library of Congress*] (LCLS)
**IOPA**........ International Organizations Procurement Act of 1947
**IOPAB**...... International Organization for Pure and Applied Biophysics
**IOPB**........ International Organization of Plant Biosystematists [*St. Anne De Bellevue, PQ*] (EA)
**IOPC**........ Institute of Paper Conservation (EA)
**IOPC**........ Interagency Oil Policy Committee
**IOPC**........ International Oil Pollution Compensation [*In association name IOPC Fund*] [*See also FIPOL*]
**IOPCA**...... International Ophthalmology Clinics [*A publication*]
**IO/PG**....... Indian Ocean/Persian Gulf
**IOPIA**....... Itogi Nauki i Tekhniki Obogashchenie Poleznykh Iskopaemykh [*A publication*]
**IOPKG**...... Input/Output Package [*IBM Corp.*] [*Data processing*]
**IOPL**........ I/O [*Input/Output*] Privilege Level [*Data processing*]
**IOPL**........ Integrated Open Problem List (NASA)
**IOPO**........ Interest-Only/Principal-Only [*Stock exchange term*]
**IoPP**......... Institute of Packaging Professionals (EA)
**IOPS**........ Input-Output Programming System [*Data processing*]
**IOQ**........... Input-Output Queue [*Data processing*] (IBMDP)
**IOQ**........... Institute of Quarrying [*British*]
**IOQ**........... Iowa State Historical Society, Iowa City, IA [*OCLC symbol*] (OCLC)
**IOQE**........ Input-Output Queue Element [*Data processing*] (MCD)

**IOR** ........... Independent Order of Rechabites
**IOR** ........... Index Octane Recherche [*French*]
**IOR** ........... Index of Refraction (MCD)
**IOR** ........... Indian Ocean Region [*INTELSAT*]
**IOR** ........... Indian Other Rank [*British military*] (DMA)
**IOR** ........... Input-Output Register [*SAGE*]
**IOR** ........... Instituto per le Opere di Religione [*Institute for Religious Works*] [*The Vatican bank*]
**IOR** ........... International Offshore Rule [*Yachting*]
**IOR** ........... International Order of Runeberg (EA)
**IOR** ........... Iowa Resources, Inc. [*NYSE symbol*] (SPSG)
**IOR** ........... Issue on Request [*or Requisition*]
**IOR** ........... Management Zeitschrift [*A publication*]
**IOR** ........... Marycrest College, Davenport, IA [*OCLC symbol*] (OCLC)
**IORB** ......... Input/Output Record Block [*Data processing*]
**IORD** ......... International Organization for Rural Development
**IOREQ** ...... Input/Output Request [*Data processing*]
**IORM** ........ Improved Order of Red Men
**IORMA3** ... Specialist Periodical Reports. Inorganic Reaction Mechanisms [*A publication*]
**IORR** ......... It's Only Rock 'n' Roll: Rolling Stones Fan Club (EAIO)
**IORS** ......... Inflatable Occupant Restraint System
**IORT** ......... Intraoperative Radiation Therapy [*Medicine*]
**IORV** ......... Inadvertent Opening of a Safety Relief Valve [*Nuclear energy*] (NRCH)
**IOS** ........... Davenport Public Library, Davenport, IA [*OCLC symbol*] (OCLC)
**Ios** ............. De Iosepho [*Philo*] (BJA)
**IOS** ........... IGOSS [*Integrated Global Ocean Station System*] Observing System [*Marine science*] (MSC)
**IOS** ........... Ilheus [*Brazil*] [*Airport symbol*] (OAG)
**IOS** ........... Image Optical Scanner
**IOS** ........... Image Orthicon System
**IOS** ........... Independent Order of Svithiod (EA)
**IOS** ........... Indian Ocean Ship
**IOS** ........... Indian Ocean Station (MCD)
**IOS** ........... Input-Output Selector [*Data processing*] (IEEE)
**IOS** ........... Input-Output Sense [*Data processing*] (KSC)
**IOS** ........... Input-Output Skip [*Data processing*]
**IOS** ........... Input-Output Supervision [*Data processing*] (NASA)
**IOS** ........... Input-Output Switch [*Data processing*]
**IOS** ........... Input/Output System [*General Automation*] [*Data processing*]
**IOS** ........... Inspection Operation Sheet (AAG)
**IOS** ........... Inspection Operation System (AAG)
**IOS** ........... Inspector of Schools [*British*] (DAS)
**IOS** ........... Institute of Ocean Sciences [*Canadian Department of Fisheries and Oceans*] [*Research center*] (RCD)
**IOS** ........... Institute of Oceanographic Sciences [*United Kingdom*] [*Research center*] (IRC)
**IOS** ........... Institute of Optimization and Systems Theory [*Stockholm*]
**IOS** ........... Instructor Operation Station [*Army*] (NASA)
**IOS** ........... Instrument Operating System
**IOS** ........... Instrumentation Operation Station
**IOS** ........... Integrated Operator System [*Telecommunications*]
**IOS** ........... Intelligence Operations Specialist [*Military*] (MCD)
**IOS** ........... Interactive Operating System [*Data processing*]
**IOS** ........... Interim Operational System
**IOS** ........... International Oleander Society (EA)
**IOS** ........... International Organization for Standardization [*Official initialism is ISO*]
**IOS** ........... International Orthokeratology Society (EA)
**IOS** ........... Internationale Organisation fuer Sukkulentenforschung [*International Organization for Succulent Plant Study - IOS*] (EAIO)
**IOS** ........... Investors Overseas Services Ltd. [*Firm which sells mutual funds in foreign countries*]
**IOs** ............ Oswego Township Library, Oswego, IL [*Library symbol*] [*Library of Congress*] (LCLS)
**IOSA** .......... Input/Output Systems Association [*Defunct*] (EA)
**IOSA** .......... Integrated Optical Spectrum Analyzer (CAAL)
**IOSA** .......... International Oil Scouts Association (EA)
**IOSC** .......... Integrated Operations Support Center [*NASA*] (NASA)
**IOSCR** ....... Institute of Ocean Sciences. Patricia Bay. Contractor Report [*A publication*]
**IOSCS** ....... International Organization for Septuagint and Cognate Studies (EA)
**IOSD** ......... Information and Office Systems Division [*Exxon Research and Engineering Company*] [*Information service or system*] (EISS)
**IOS Data Report** ... Institute of Oceanographic Sciences. Data Report [*A publication*]
**IOSEWR** ... International Organization for the Study of the Endurance of Wire Ropes [*Paris, France*] (EAIO)
**IOSGT** ....... International Organization for the Study of Group Tensions (EA)
**IOSH** ......... Independent Order Sons of Hermann
**IOSHD** ...... International Organization for the Study of Human Development (EA)
**IOSI** .......... International Oculoplastic Society, Incorporated (EA)
**IOSL** .......... Independent Order of St. Luke [*Richmond, VA*] (EA)
**IOSM** ........ Independent Order of Sons of Malta
**IOSN** ......... Indian Ocean Standard Net
**IOS/OSI**.... International Organization for Standardization Open Systems Interconnection Model
**IOSOT** ....... International Organization for the Study of the Old Testament [*Great Britain*]
**IOS Report** ... Institute of Oceanographic Sciences. Report [*A publication*]
**IOSS** .......... Indian Ocean Station Support
**IOSS** .......... Input/Output Subsystem [*NCR Corp.*]
**IOSS** .......... Integrated Ocean Surveillance System [*Navy*] (NG)
**IOSS** .......... Integrated Operational Support Study (MCD)
**IOSS** .......... Intelligence Organization Stationing Study [*Army*] (MCD)
**IOSS** .......... Intraoperative Spinal Sonography [*Radiology*]
**IOSTA** ....... Comission Internationale de l'Organisation Scientifique du Travail [*International Committee of Work Study and Labour Management in Agriculture*] (EAIO)
**IOT** ........... British Indian Ocean Territory [*ANSI three-letter standard code*] (CNC)
**IOT** ........... Dordt College, Sioux Center, IA [*OCLC symbol*] (OCLC)
**IOT** ........... Income Opportunity Realty [*AMEX symbol*] (SPSG)
**IOT** ........... Individual Operation Test
**IOT** ........... Induction Output Tube
**IOT** ........... Initial Operational Test [*Army*]
**IOT** ........... Initial Orbit Time [*Aerospace*]
**IOT** ........... Input-Output Termination [*Data processing*]
**I/OT** .......... Input/Output Test [*Data processing*] (NASA)
**IOT** ........... Input-Output Transfer [*Data processing*]
**IOT** ........... Inspection Operation Tag
**IOT** ........... Institute of Operating Theatre Technicians [*British*]
**IOT** ........... International Optical Telecommunications, Inc. [*Information service or system*] (IID)
**IOT** ........... Interocular Transfer [*Ophthalmology*]
**IOT** ........... Ipsilateral Optic Tectum [*Medicine*]
**IOt**............. Reddick's Library, Ottawa, IL [*Library symbol*] [*Library of Congress*] (LCLS)
**IOTA** ......... Inbound/Outbound Traffic Analysis [*Military*] (AABC)
**IOTA** ......... Information Overload Testing Aid [*or Apparatus*]
**IOTA** ......... Institute of Theoretical Astronomy [*University of Cambridge*]
**IOTA** ......... Institute of Transport Administration [*Great Britain*] (DCTA)
**IOTA** ......... Integrated On-Line Text Arrangement
**IOTA** ......... Interest on Trust Accounts Program
**IOTA** ......... International Occultation Timing Association (EA)
**IOtBD** ........ LaSalle County Board for Developmentally Disabled, Ottawa, IL [*Library symbol*] [*Library of Congress*] (LCLS)
**IOTC** ......... Infantry Officers Training Camp
**IOTC** ......... International Originating Toll Center [*Bell System*]
**IOtCE** ........ LaSalle County Cooperative Extension, Ottawa, IL [*Library symbol*] [*Library of Congress*] (LCLS)
**IOTCG** ...... International Organization for Technical Cooperation in Geology (EAIO)
**IOtCH**........ Community Hospital of Ottawa, Ottawa, IL [*Library symbol*] [*Library of Congress*] (LCLS)
**IOtDSD** ..... Deer Park Consolidated Community School District 82, Ottawa, IL [*Library symbol*] [*Library of Congress*] (LCLS)
**IOTE**.......... Individual Operator Training Equipment (MCD)
**IOT & E** .... Initial Operating Test and Evaluation (MCD)
**IOTE**.......... Initial Outfitting Technical Evaluation (MCD)
**IOTEP**....... Initial Operating Test and Evaluation Period [*Navy*]
**IOtES**........ LaSalle County Educational Service Region, Ottawa, IL [*Library symbol*] [*Library of Congress*] (LCLS)
**IOtF** .......... Friendship Facilities, Ottawa, IL [*Library symbol*] [*Library of Congress*] (LCLS)
**IOTG** ......... Input/Output Task Group [*CODASYL*]
**IOTG** ......... Isooctyl Thioglycolate [*Organic chemistry*]
**IOtGH** ....... Ottawa General Hospital, Ottawa, IL [*Library symbol*] [*Library of Congress*] (LCLS)
**IOtHS**........ Ottawa Township High School District 140, Ottawa, IL [*Library symbol*] [*Library of Congress*] (LCLS)
**IOtM**.......... Marquette High School, Ottawa, IL [*Library symbol*] [*Library of Congress*] (LCLS)
**IOTR** ......... Intratrabecular Osteoclastic Tunneling Resorption [*Medicine*]
**IOTR** ......... Item Operation Trouble Report (AAG)
**IOtRP** ........ LaSalle County Regional Planning Commission, Ottawa, IL [*Library symbol*] [*Library of Congress*] (LCLS)
**IOtRSD** ..... Rutland Consolidated Community School District 230, Ottawa, IL [*Library symbol*] [*Library of Congress*] (LCLS)
**IOtS** .......... Starved Rock Library System, Ottawa, IL [*Library symbol*] [*Library of Congress*] (LCLS)
**IOTT & E** .. Improved Operational Test, Training, and Evaluation [*Military*]
**IOtWSD** .... Wallace Consolidated Community School District 195, Ottawa, IL [*Library symbol*] [*Library of Congress*] (LCLS)
**IOU**........... I Owe You [*Slang*]
**IOU**........... Immediate Operation Use
**IOU**........... Input-Output Unit [*Computer chip*]
**IOU**........... Input-Output Utility [*Data processing*]
**IOU**........... Public Library of Des Moines, Des Moines, IA [*OCLC symbol*] (OCLC)
**IOUBC** ...... Institute of Oceanography, University of British Columbia
**IOV**........... Independent Order of Vikings [*Des Plaines, IL*] (EA)
**IOV**........... Input Offset Voltage
**IOV**........... Inside-Out Vesicle [*Biochemistry*]

**IOV**........... Institute of Virology [*British*] (ARC)
**IOV**........... University of Dubuque, Dubuque, IA [*OCLC symbol*] (OCLC)
**IOVC**......... In the Overcast [*Aviation*]
**IOVSDA**.... Investigative Ophthalmology and Visual Science [*A publication*]
**IOVST**....... International Organization for Vacuum Science and Technology
**IOW**........... In Other Words
**IOW**........... Inert Ordnance Warehouse
**IOW**........... Iowa City, IA [*Location identifier*] [*FAA*] (FAAL)
**Iow**............ Iowa Reports [*A publication*] (DLA)
**IOW**........... Isle Of Wight
**IOW**........... Wartburg College, Waverly, IA [*OCLC symbol*] (OCLC)
**IOWA**........ Interorganizational Work Authorization (KSC)
**Iowa**........... Iowa Reports [*A publication*]
**Iowa**........... Iowa Supreme Court Reports [*A publication*] (DLA)
**Iowa Acad Sci Proc** ... Iowa Academy of Science. Proceedings [*A publication*]
**Iowa Ac Sc Pr** ... Iowa Academy of Science. Proceedings [*A publication*]
**Iowa Acts** ... Acts and Joint Resolutions of the State of Iowa [*A publication*] (DLA)
**Iowa Admin Bull** ... Iowa Administrative Bulletin [*A publication*] (DLA)
**Iowa Admin Code** ... Iowa Administrative Code [*A publication*] (DLA)
**Iowa Agric Exp Stn Res Bull** ... Iowa. Agricultural Experiment Station. Research Bulletin [*A publication*]
**Iowa Agric Home Econ Exp Stn Res Bull** ... Iowa. Agriculture and Home Economics Experiment Station. Research Bulletin [*A publication*]
**Iowa Agric Home Econ Exp Stn Soil Surv Rep** ... Iowa. Agriculture and Home Economics Experiment Station. Soil Survey Reports [*A publication*]
**Iowa Agric Home Econ Exp Stn Spec Rep** ... Iowa. Agriculture and Home Economics Experiment Station. Special Report [*A publication*]
**Iowa Bar Rev** ... Iowa Bar Review [*A publication*] (DLA)
**Iowa B Rev** ... Iowa Bar Review [*A publication*] (DLA)
**Iowa Code Ann (West)** ... Iowa Code, Annotated (West) [*A publication*]
**Iowa Conserv** ... Iowa Conservationist [*A publication*]
**Iowa Dent Bull** ... Iowa Dental Bulletin [*A publication*]
**Iowa Dent J** ... Iowa Dental Journal [*A publication*]
**Iowa Drug Inf Serv** ... Iowa Drug Information Service [*A publication*]
**Iowa Farm Sci** ... Iowa Farm Science [*A publication*]
**Iowa Geol Survey Water Atlas** ... Iowa. Geological Survey. Water Atlas [*A publication*]
**Iowa Geol Survey Water-Supply Bull** ... Iowa. Geological Survey. Water-Supply Bulletin [*A publication*]
**Iowa Geol Surv Rep Invest** ... Iowa. Geological Survey. Report of Investigations [*A publication*]
**Iowa Geol Surv Tech Pap** ... Iowa. Geological Survey. Technical Paper [*A publication*]
**Iowa Hist Rec** ... Iowa Historical Record [*A publication*]
**Iowa Institutions B** ... Iowa State Institutions. Bulletin [*A publication*]
**Iowa Jour Hist and Pol** ... Iowa Journal of History and Politics [*A publication*]
**Iowa Law R** ... Iowa Law Review [*A publication*]
**Iowa LB**...... Iowa Law Bulletin [*A publication*] (DLA)
**Iowa L Bull** ... Iowa Law Bulletin [*A publication*] (DLA)
**Iowa Legis Serv** ... Iowa Legislative Service (West) [*A publication*] (DLA)
**Iowa Legis Serv (West)** ... Iowa Legislative Service (West) [*A publication*]
**Iowa Lib Q** ... Iowa Library Quarterly [*A publication*]
**Iowa L Rev** ... Iowa Law Review [*A publication*]
**Iowa Med**... Iowa Medicine [*A publication*]
**Iowa Med J** ... Iowa Medical Journal [*A publication*]
**Iowa Nat**.... Iowa Naturalist [*A publication*]
**IowaR**......... Iowa Review [*A publication*]
**Iowa RC**..... Iowa Railroad Commissioners Reports [*A publication*] (DLA)
**Iowa SBA**... Iowa State Bar Association. Proceedings [*A publication*] (DLA)
**Iowa State Coll Agric Mech Arts Eng Exp Stn Bull** ... Iowa State College of Agriculture and Mechanical Arts. Engineering Experiment Station. Bulletin [*A publication*]
**Iowa State Coll Agric Mech Arts Eng Exp Stn Eng Rep** ... Iowa State College of Agriculture and Mechanical Arts. Engineering Experiment Station. Engineering Report [*A publication*]
**Iowa State Coll Eng Expt Sta Eng Rept Proj** ... Iowa State College. Engineering Experiment Station. Engineering Report. Project [*A publication*]
**Iowa State Coll J Sci** ... Iowa State College. Journal of Science [*A publication*]
**Iowa State Coll Vet** ... Iowa State College Veterinarian [*A publication*]
**Iowa State J Res** ... Iowa State Journal of Research [*A publication*]
**Iowa State J Sci** ... Iowa State Journal of Science [*A publication*]
**Iowa State Univ (Ames) Eng Res Inst Rep** ... Iowa State University (Ames). Engineering Research Institute. Report [*A publication*]
**Iowa State Univ Dept Earth Sci Pub** ... Iowa State University. Department of Earth Sciences. Publication [*A publication*]
**Iowa State Univ Eng Exp Sta Bull** ... Iowa State University of Science and Technology. Engineering Experiment Station. Bulletin [*Ames, IA*] [*A publication*]
**Iowa State Univ Sci Technol Eng Exp Stn Bull** ... Iowa State University of Science and Technology. Engineering Experiment Station. Bulletin [*A publication*]
**Iowa State Univ Sci Technol Eng Exp Stn Eng Rep** ... Iowa State University of Science and Technology. Engineering Experiment Station. Engineering Report [*A publication*]
**Iowa State Univ Sci and Technology Eng Expt Sta Bull** ... Iowa State University of Science and Technology. Engineering Experiment Station. Bulletin [*A publication*]
**Iowa State Univ Stat Lab Annu Rep** ... Iowa State University. Statistical Laboratory. Annual Report [*A publication*]
**Iowa State Univ Vet** ... Iowa State University Veterinarian [*A publication*]
**Iowa State Water Resour Res Inst Annu Rep** ... Iowa State Water Resources Research Institute. Annual Report [*A publication*]
**Iowa St BA News Bull** ... Iowa State Bar Association. News Bulletin [*A publication*]
**Iowa St BAQ** ... Iowa State Bar Association. Quarterly [*A publication*] (DLA)
**Iowa St J Sci** ... Iowa State Journal of Science [*A publication*]
**Iowa Univ Lab N H B** ... Iowa State University. Laboratories of Natural History. Bulletin [*A publication*]
**Iowa Univ L Bull** ... Iowa University. Law Bulletin [*A publication*] (DLA)
**IOWE**........ International Organization of Women Executives [*Defunct*] (EA)
**IOWIT**....... International Organization of Women in Telecommunications [*Defunct*] (TSSD)
**IOWMC**.... International Organization of Wooden Money Collectors (EA)
**IOWT**........ International Organization of Women in Telecommunications [*Defunct*] (EA)
**IOX**........... William Penn College, Oskaloosa, IA [*OCLC symbol*] (OCLC)
**IOY**........... Upper Iowa University, Fayette, IA [*OCLC symbol*] (OCLC)
**IOZ**........... State Library Commission of Iowa, Des Moines, IA [*OCLC symbol*] (OCLC)
**IOZP**.......... Indian Ocean Zone of Peace
**IP**.............. Cathode-Ray Tube Indicators [*JETDS nomenclature*] [*Military*] (CET)
**I/P**............. Current/Pneumatic [*Nuclear energy*] (NRCH)
**IP**.............. Empresa AVIAIMPORT [*Cuba*] [*ICAO designator*] (ICDA)
**IP**.............. Ice Pellets [*Meteorology*] (FAAC)
**IP**.............. Ice Point
**IP**.............. Icterus Precox [*Medicine*]
**IP**.............. Identification Peculiarity
**IP**.............. Identification Point
**IP**.............. Identification of Position
**IP**.............. Identity Preserved [*Wheat*] [*Department of Agriculture*]
**IP**.............. Igloo Pallet [*Spacelab*] [*NASA*] (NASA)
**IP**.............. Iles de Paix [*Islands of Peace*] (EAIO)
**IP**.............. Image Process
**IP**.............. Imaginary Part [*of a complex number*] (DEN)
**IP**.............. Immediate Permanent Incapacitation [*Radiation casualty criterion*] [*Army*]
**IP**.............. Immune Precipitate [*Immunology*]
**IP**.............. Immunoperoxidase (Technique) [*Clinical chemistry*]
**IP**.............. Impact Point (AFM)
**IP**.............. Impact Predictor [*NASA*]
**IP**.............. Impact Printer [*Data processing*]
**IP**.............. Impact Prognosticator [*Aerospace*] (AAG)
**IP**.............. Impedance Probe
**IP**.............. Imperial Preference (ADA)
**IP**.............. Impingement Point
**IP**.............. Implementation Period
**IP**.............. Implementation of Plan (NG)
**IP**.............. Impostor Phenomenon [*Subject of book "If I'm So Successful, Why Do I Feel Like a Fake? - The Impostor Phenomenon" by Joan C. Harvey*] [*Psychology*]
**IP**.............. Improvement Program (AFM)
**IP**.............. Improvement Purchase (ADA)
**iP**.............. Impulse P Wave [*Earthquakes*] [*Exclamation point signifies a very sharp earthquake*]
**IP**.............. In-Phase [*Gynecology*]
**IP**.............. In Place [*Dancing*]
**IP**.............. In Process
**I/P**............. In Progress (MCD)
**IP**.............. Incentive Pay
**IP**.............. Incisoproximal [*Dentistry*]
**IP**.............. Incisopulpal [*Dentistry*]
**IP**.............. Incubation Period [*Medicine*]
**IP**.............. Index of Performance
**I & P**.......... Indexed and Paged
**IP**.............. India Paper
**IP**.............. Indian Pattern [*British military*] (DMA)
**IP**.............. Indian Preference [*Civil Service*]
**IP**.............. Indicator Panel
**IP**.............. Indirect Proof [*Method in logic*]
**IP**.............. Indochina Project [*An association*] (EA)
**IP**.............. Induced Polarization [*Geophysical prospecting*]
**IP**.............. Induction Period [*Medicine*]
**IP**.............. Industrial Participation [*Civil Defense*]
**IP**.............. Industrial Planning
**IP**.............. Industrial Police
**IP**.............. Industrial Policy
**IP**.............. Industrial Production
**IP**.............. Inertial Platform
**IP**.............. Inertial Processing (MCD)
**I & P**.......... Inerting and Preheating [*Nuclear energy*] (NRCH)
**IP**.............. Infection Prevention
**IP**.............. Information Processing (BUR)
**IP**.............. Information Provider

IP ............... Information Publication [*HUD*]
IP ............... Information Publications [*Singapore, Hong Kong, Australia*]
IP ............... Information Publishing
IP ............... Inhaled Particles [*or Particulates*] [*Environmental chemistry*]
IP ............... Initial Phase (IEEE)
IP ............... Initial Point [*Military*]
IP ............... Initial Position
IP ............... Initial Post [*Military*]
IP ............... Initial Production
IP ............... Initial Provisioning (MCD)
IP ............... Innings Pitched [*Baseball*]
IP ............... Inpatient [*Medicine*]
I/P............... Input [*Data processing*]
IP ............... Input Power [*Data processing*]
IP ............... Input Processor [*Data processing*]
IP ............... Insolated Platform
IP ............... Inspection Pit [*Motor garage*] (ROG)
IP ............... Inspection Procedure [*Nuclear energy*] (NRCH)
IP ............... Installation Procedure
IP ............... Installment Paid [*Business term*]
IP ............... Institute of Petroleum [*British*]
IP ............... Institute of Physics [*London, England*] (EAIO)
IP ............... Institute of Printing [*British*]
IP ............... Institute for Psychohistory (EA)
IP ............... Instruction Pamphlet
IP ............... Instruction Plate (MSA)
IP ............... Instruction Pointer [*Data processing*]
IP ............... Instruction Processor [*Data processing*]
IP ............... Instruction Pulse (MSA)
IP ............... Instructional Psychologist (MCD)
IP ............... Instructor-Patient [*Medicine*]
IP ............... Instructor Pilot [*Air Force*] (AFM)
IP ............... Instrumentation Papers [*Air Force*] (MCD)
IP ............... Instrumentation Payload (NASA)
IP ............... Instrumentation Plan (MUGU)
IP ............... Instrumentation Power (MCD)
IP ............... Insulated Platform (MCD)
IP ............... Insurance Patient [*Medicine*]
IP ............... Integrated Processor [*Data processing*]
IP ............... Intellectual Property (MCD)
IP ............... Intelligence Publications (MCD)
IP ............... Intercept Point [*Air Force*]
IP ............... Interchangeable Solid and Screen Panels [*Technical drawings*]
IP ............... Interdigital Pause [*Telecommunications*] (TEL)
IP ............... Interface Processor [*Data processing*]
IP ............... Interference Pattern (CAAL)
IP ............... Intermediate Pallet (NASA)
IP ............... Intermediate Pressure
IP ............... Internal Phloem [*Botany*]
IP ............... International Paper Co. [*NYSE symbol*] (SPSG)
IP ............... International Pharmacopoeia
IP ............... Internet Protocol [*Facilitates data communications among networks*]
IP ............... Interphalangeal [*Anatomy*]
IP ............... Interplanetary
IP ............... Interscience Publishers
IP ............... Intraperitoneal [*Medicine*]
IP ............... Inuit Nipingat. Baker Lane. Northwest Territory [*A publication*]
IP ............... Investigacion y Progreso [*A publication*]
IP ............... Ionization Potential
IP ............... Ipatropium [*Pharmacology*]
IP ............... Irate Parent (ADA)
IP ............... Irish Party (ROG)
IP ............... Iron Pipe
I/P............... Irregular Input Process [*Telecommunications*] (TEL)
IP ............... Isidis Planitia [*A filamentary mark on Mars*]
IP ............... Isoelectric Point [*Also, IEP*] [*Chemistry*]
IP ............... Isolation Pulse
IP ............... Isoproterenol [*An adrenergic*]
IP ............... Israel Philatelist [*A publication*]
IP ............... Israeli Pound (BJA)
IP ............... Issue Paper
IP ............... Issue Price [*Business term*]
IP ............... Issuing Point
IP ............... Item Processing
IP ............... Office of International Programs [*Nuclear energy*] [*National Science Foundation*] (NRCH)
IP ............... Peer of Ireland (ROG)
IP ............... Peoria Public Library, Peoria, IL [*Library symbol*] [*Library of Congress*] (LCLS)
IP's............. Issue Priority Designators (AFIT)
IPA............. Allied Agencies Center, Peoria, IL [*Library symbol*] [*Library of Congress*] (LCLS)
IPA............. Idrocarburi Policiclici Aromatici [*Italian*]
IPA............. Image Processing Applications [*Computer graphics*]
IPA............. Immunoperoxidase Antibody Assay [*Clinical chemistry*]
IPA............. Imperial Pale Ale
IPA............. Including Particular Average [*Insurance*]
IPA............. Incorporeal Personal Agency [*Parapsychology*]
IPA............. Independent-Practice Association [*Medical insurance*]
IPA............. Independent Public Accountant
IPA............. Independent Publishers' Association [*Canada*]
IPA............. India Pale Ale
IPA............. India Press Agency
IPA............. Indicated Pressure Altitude
IPA............. Individual Practice Association [*Medicine*]
IPA............. Industrial Participation Association [*British*]
IPA............. Industrial Perforators Association (EA)
IPA............. Industrial Property Administration
IPA............. Industrial Publicity Association (EA)
IPA............. Information Process Analysis (BUR)
IPA............. Information Processing Association [*Israel*]
IPA............. Information for Public Affairs, Inc. [*Information service or system*] (IID)
IPA............. Institute of Patent Attorneys [*Australia*]
IPA............. Institute for Physics of the Atmosphere
IPA............. Institute for Polyacrylate Absorbents (EA)
IPA............. Institute of Practitioners in Advertising
IPA............. Institute of Public Administration (EA)
IPA............. Institute of Public Affairs [*Dalhousie University*] [*Canada*] [*Research center*]
IPA............. Institute of Public Affairs. Review [*A publication*]
IPA............. Institutional Patent Agreements [*General Services Administration*]
IPA............. Instrument Performance Assessment
IPA............. Integrated Peripheral Adapter
IPA............. Integrated Photodetection Assemblies (IEEE)
IPA............. Integrated Plan of Action (MCD)
IPA............. Integrated Printer Adapter
IPA............. Intelligence Production Activity [*Military*] (MCD)
IPA............. Inter-Pacific Resource Corp. [*Vancouver Stock Exchange symbol*]
IPA............. Interamerican Press Association
IPA............. Intergovernmental Personnel Act [*1970*]
IPA............. Interior Plantscape Association [*Later, ALCA/IPD*] (EA)
IPA............. Intermediate Power Amplifier [*Electronics*]
IPA............. International Association for the Child's Right to Play [*Acronym is based on former name, International Playground Association*] (EA)
IPA............. International Journal of Public Administration [*A publication*]
IPA............. International Paddleball Association [*Later, AARA*] (EA)
IPA............. International Palaeontological Association (EA)
IPA............. International Patent Agreement (IEEE)
IPA............. International Peace Academy (EA)
IPA............. International Pediatric Association [*See also AIP*] [*Paris, France*] (EAIO)
IPA............. International Petroleum Annual [*Department of Energy*] [*Database*]
IPA............. International Pharmaceutical Abstracts [*American Society of Hospital Pharmacists*] [*Bibliographic database*] [*A publication*]
IPA............. International Phonetic Alphabet
IPA............. International Phonetic Association [*University College*] [*Leeds, England*] (EA)
IPA............. International Phototherapy Association (EA)
IPA............. International Pietenpol Association (EA)
IPA............. International Pinball Association (EA)
IPA............. International Pipe Association [*Later, TPF*] (EA)
IPA............. International Platform Association (EA)
IPA............. International Police Academy [*Formerly, Inter-American Police Academy*]
IPA............. International Police Association [*Maidstone, Kent, England*] (EAIO)
IPA............. International Polka Association (EA)
IPA............. International Porcelain Artist (EA)
IPA............. International Prepress Association (EA)
IPA............. International Press Association [*Defunct*] (EA)
IPA............. International Psycho-Analytical Association [*London, England*] (EAIO)
IPA............. International Psychohistorical Association (EA)
IPA............. International Publishers Association [*See also UIE*] [*Geneva, Switzerland*] (EAIO)
IPA............. International Pumpkin Association (EA)
IPA............. Investment Partnership Association (EA)
IPA............. Ipota [*Vanuatu*] [*Airport symbol*] (OAG)
IPA............. Isopentenyladenosine [*Biochemistry*]
IPA............. Isophthalic Acid [*Organic chemistry*]
IPA............. Isopropanc [*Organic chemistry*]
IPA............. Isopropyl Alcohol [*Organic chemistry*]
IPA............. Issue-Position-Argument [*Data processing*] (BYTE)
IPAA........... Independent Petroleum Association of America (EA)
IPAA........... Industrial Photographers Association of America [*Later, Industrial Photographers of New Jersey*] (EA)
IPAA........... Instrumental Photon Activation Analysis [*National Institute of Standards and Technology*]
IPAA........... International Pesticide Applicators Association (EA)
IPAA........... International Prisoners Aid Association (EA)
IPAA........... Inventario del Patrimonio Arquitectonico [*Database*] [*Ministerio de Cultura*] [*Spanish*] [*Information service or system*] (CRD)
IPAC........... Independent Petroleum Association of Canada

**IPAC**.......... Information Processing and Control [*Systems Laboratory*] [*Northwestern University*]
**IPAC**.......... Institute of Public Administration of Canada
**IPAC**.......... Intelligence Center, Pacific [*Military*] (MCD)
**IPAC**.......... Intelligence, PACOM (MCD)
**IPACE**....... Interprovincial Advisory Council on Energy [*Canada*]
**IPACS**....... Integrated Power and Attitude-Control System [*NASA*]
**IPAD**.......... Incoming Procurement Authorization Document [*Air Force*] (AFM)
**IPAD**.......... Integrated Program Aircraft Design
**IPAD**.......... Integrated Programs for Aerospace-Vehicle Design
**IPAD**.......... International Plastics Association Directors
**IPADAE**.... Integrated Passive Action Detection Acquisition Equipment
**IPADD**....... Intra-Governmental Professional Advisory Council on Drugs and Devices [*Inactive*] [*FDA*] (EGAO)
**IPADS**....... Interactive Processing and Display System (MCD)
**IPAE**.......... (Isopropylamino)ethanol [*Organic chemistry*]
**IPAF**.......... International Powered Access Federation (EAIO)
**IPAFUG**.... International PAF User's Group (EA)
**IPAGBA**.... Investigacion y Progreso Agricola [*A publication*]
**IPAHGEIS**... Inter-Professional Ad Hoc Group for Environmental Information Sharing
**IPAI**........... International Primary Aluminium Institute [*London, England*] (EAIO)
**IPAJ**.......... International Phonetic Association Journal [*A publication*]
**IPAL**.......... Index to Periodical Articles Related to Law [*A publication*] (DLA)
**IPal**............ Palatine Public Library District, Palatine, IL [*Library symbol*] [*Library of Congress*] (LCLS)
**IPale**........... La Motte Township Library, Palestine, IL [*Library symbol*] [*Library of Congress*] (LCLS)
**IPalH**......... William Rainey Harper College, Palatine, IL [*Library symbol*] [*Library of Congress*] (LCLS)
**IPalmSD**.... Northwestern Community Unit, School District 2, Palmyra, IL [*Library symbol*] [*Library of Congress*] (LCLS)
**IPANA**....... Indian People's Association in North America (EA)
**IPANY**....... Individual Psychology Association of New York
**IPAP**.......... Iodophenyl(piperidinoacetyl)piperazine [*Biochemistry*]
**IPAR**.......... Improved Pulse Acquisition RADAR (AABC)
**IPAR**.......... Innovative Photovoltaics Applications for Residences
**IPAR**.......... Institute of Personality Assessment and Research [*University of California*] [*Research center*]
**IPAR**.......... Intercepted Photosynthetically Active Radiation [*Photosynthesis*]
**IPAR**.......... IPA [*Institute of Public Affairs*] Review [*A publication*] (APTA)
**IPar**............ Paris Carnegie Public Library, Paris, IL [*Library symbol*] [*Library of Congress*] (LCLS)
**IPAR**.......... United States Department of Agriculture, Agricultural Research Service, Northern Research Center Library, Peoria, IL [*Library symbol*] [*Library of Congress*] (LCLS)
**IPARA**....... International Publishers Advertising Representatives Association
**IPARC**....... International Pesticide Application Research Centre [*Imperial College at Silwood Park*] [*British*] (CB)
**IPARCOM**... Interim Paris Commission [*British*]
**IPA Rev**..... IPA [*Institute of Public Affairs*] Review [*A publication*] (APTA)
**IPA Rev**..... IPA [*International Pharmaceutical Abstracts*] Review [*A publication*]
**Ipargazd Szle**... Ipargazdasagi Szemle [*A publication*]
**IParH**......... Paris Community Hospital, Paris, IL [*Library symbol*] [*Library of Congress*] (LCLS)
**Ipari Energiagazd**... Ipari Energiagazdalkodas [*A publication*]
**IParkA**....... American Society of Anesthesiologists, Park Ridge, IL [*Library symbol*] [*Library of Congress*] (LCLS)
**IParkD**....... Dames and Moore Chicago Branch Library, Park Ridge, IL [*Library symbol*] [*Library of Congress*] (LCLS)
**IParkL**....... Lutheran General Hospital, Park Ridge, IL [*Library symbol*] [*Library of Congress*] (LCLS)
**IPARL**....... Index to Periodical Articles Related to Law [*A publication*]
**Iparmuveszeti Muz Ev**... Iparmueveszeti Muzeum Evkoenyvei [*A publication*]
**IPARS**....... International Passenger Airline Reservations System
**IPAS**.......... Independants et Paysans d'Action Sociale [*Independents and Peasants of Social Action*] [*French*] (PPE)
**IPAS**.......... Integrated Pneumatic Air System (MCD)
**IPAS**.......... Interplatform Alignment System (MCD)
**IPASS**....... Interactive Policy Analysis Simulation System [*Department of Agriculture*]
**IPAT**.......... Institute for Personality and Ability Testing [*Champaign, IL*]
**IPAT**.......... International Porcelain Art Teachers [*Later, IPA*] (EA)
**IPAT**.......... Inventario del Patrimonio Historico Artistico Espanol [*Ministerio de Cultura*] [*Spain*] [*Information service or system*] (CRD)
**IPat**............ Patoka Public Library, Patoka, IL [*Library symbol*] [*Library of Congress*] (LCLS)
**IPATA**....... Independent Pet and Animal Transportation Association (EA)
**IPA (VIC) R**... Institute of Public Affairs (Victoria). Review [*A publication*] (APTA)
**IPAVS**....... International Project of the Association for Voluntary Sterilization
**IPax**........... Paxton Carnegie Library, Paxton, IL [*Library symbol*] [*Library of Congress*] (LCLS)
**IPaxH**........ Paxton Community Hospital, Paxton, IL [*Library symbol*] [*Library of Congress*] (LCLS)
**IPB**............. Bradley University, Peoria, IL [*Library symbol*] [*Library of Congress*] (LCLS)
**IPB**............. Illuminated Push Button (NASA)
**IPB**............. Illustrated Parts Breakdown (AFIT)
**IPB**............. Inert Processing Building
**IPB**............. Information Parts Breakdown (MCD)
**IPB**............. Installation Property Book [*Military*] (AABC)
**IPB**............. Institute of Professional Businesswomen (EA)
**IPB**............. Integrated Processor Board
**IPB**............. Intelligence Preparation of the Battlefield [*Army*] (RDA)
**IPB**............. Intercept Priorities Board [*Armed Forces Security Agency*]
**IPB**............. International Pathfinder, Inc. [*Toronto Stock Exchange symbol*]
**IPB**............. International Peace Bureau [*Geneva, Switzerland*] (EA)
**IPB**............. Interprocessor Buffer
**IPB**............. Jenner & Block, Chicago, IL [*OCLC symbol*] (OCLC)
**IPBC**.......... India Pakistan Bangladesh Conference (DS)
**IPBC**.......... Iodopropynyl Butyl Carbamate [*Wood preservative*]
**IP & BE**...... Initial Program and Budget Estimate [*Army*]
**IPBKA**....... Izvestiya Sektora Platiny i Drugikh Blagorodnykh Metallov Institut Obshchei i Neorganicheskoi Khimii Akademiya Nauk SSSR [*A publication*]
**IPBM**......... Integrated Program, Budget, Manpower [*System*] [*Defense Supply Agency*]
**IPBM**......... Interplanetary Ballistic Missile [*Air Force*]
**IPBNet**....... International Plant Biotech Network (EA)
**IPBS**.......... Israel Plate Block Society (EA)
**IPC**............. Easter Island [*Airport symbol*] (OAG)
**IPC**............. Idaho Potato Commission (EA)
**IPC**............. Illinois Power Company [*NYSE symbol*] (SPSG)
**IPC**............. Illustrated Parts Catalog (AAG)
**IPC**............. Image Processing Center [*Drexel University*] [*Research center*] (RCD)
**IPC**............. Image Products Company
**IPC**............. Imaging Proportional Counter [*Astronomy*]
**IPC**............. Indian Philosophy and Culture. Quarterly [*A publication*]
**IPC**............. Indirect Photometric Chromatography
**IPC**............. Indirect Pulp Capping [*Dentistry*]
**IPC**............. Individual Plan of Care
**IPC**............. Industrial Planning Committee [*NATO*] (NATG)
**IPC**............. Industrial Policy Council [*Washington, DC*] (EA)
**IPC**............. Industrial Process Control [*by computers*]
**IPC**............. Industrial Property Committee [*US Military Government, Germany*]
**IPC**............. Industrial Publishing Company
**IPC**............. Industry Planning Council (EA)
**IPC**............. Information Processing Center [*of General Motors Corp.*]
**IPC**............. Information Processing Code (DIT)
**IPC**............. Information Publishing Corp. [*Telecommunications service*] (TSSD)
**IPC**............. Initial Planning Conference [*Military*] (INF)
**IPC**............. Institute for Interconnecting and Packaging Electronic Circuits [*Formerly, Institute of Printed Circuits*] (EA)
**IPC**............. Institute of Paper Chemistry [*Lawrence University*] [*Research center*] (EA)
**IPC**............. Institute of Paper Conservation [*Formerly, International Institute for Conservation of Historic and Artistic Works Paper Group*] (EA)
**IPC**............. Institute of Pastoral Care (EA)
**IPC**............. Institute for Personal Computing (EA)
**IPC**............. Institute of Production Control [*British*]
**IPC**............. Instrumentation Package Container
**IP & C**........ Instrumentation Program and Component (KSC)
**IPC**............. Integral Plate Chamber
**IPC**............. Integrated Peripheral Channel
**IPC**............. Integrated Peripheral Controller [*Computer chip*]
**IPC**............. Integrated Pest Control
**IPC**............. Integrated Pollution Control
**IPC**............. Integrated Procedures Control
**IPC**............. Integrated Programme for Commodities [*UNCTAD*] (EY)
**IPC**............. Intelligence Priorities Committee [*British*] [*World War II*]
**IPC**............. Intelligent Peripheral Controller [*Data processing*]
**IPC**............. Inter-African Phytosanitary Commission
**IPC**............. Intercalated Polymer-Derived Carbon [*Chemistry*]
**IPC**............. Interconnections Packaging Circuitry (MCD)
**IPC**............. Intermediate Processing Centers
**IPC**............. Intermittent Positive Control [*Aviation*]
**IPC**............. International Pacific Cypress Minerals Ltd. [*Vancouver Stock Exchange symbol*]
**IPC**............. International Patent Classification
**IPC**............. International PBX [*Private Branch Exchange*]/Telecommunicators (EA)
**IPC**............. International Peace Campaign
**IPC**............. International Penpal Club (EAIO)
**IPC**............. International Pepper Community [*Research center*] [*Indonesia*] (IRC)

**IPC**............ International Petroleum Cartel
**IPC**............ International Photosynthesis Committee [*Stockholm, Sweden*] (EAIO)
**IPC**............ International Planning Corporation
**IPC**............ International Plasma Corporation
**IPC**............ International Poliomyelitis Congress
**IPC**............ International Poplar Commission [*FAO*] [*Rome, Italy*] [*United Nations*] (EA)
**IPC**............ International Publishing Corporation [*England*]
**IPC**............ Interplanetary Communications (AAG)
**IPC**............ Interprocess Controller
**IPC**............ Interprocessor Communication (BUR)
**IPC**............ Interstate Processing Center [*Department of Labor*]
**IPC**............ Investors Planning Corporation
**IPC**............ Ion-Pair Comonomers [*Organic chemistry*]
**IPC**............ Iraqi Petroleum Company
**IPC**............ Irish Peace Council (EAIO)
**IPC**............ Irish Presbyterian Church (ROG)
**IPC**............ Iron Phosphate Coating
**IPC**............ Isolation-Physiological Characterization [*Microbiology*]
**IPC**............ Isopropyl Carbanilate [*Also, INPC, IPPC*] [*Herbicide*]
**IPC**............ Item Processing Card
**IPC**............ Purdue University, Calumet Campus, Hammond, IN [*OCLC symbol*] (OCLC)
**IPCA**.......... Independent Parametric Cost Analysis (MCD)
**IPCA**.......... Independent Police Complaints Authority [*British*]
**IPCA**.......... International Plate Collectors Association (EA)
**IPCA**.......... International Postcard Collectors Association (EA)
**IPCBA**....... Bibliographic Series. Institute of Paper Chemistry [*A publication*]
**IPCC**.......... Infantry Precommand Course [*Army*] (INF)
**IPCC**.......... Information Processing in Command and Control [*Air Force*]
**IPCC**.......... Intergovernmental Panel on Climate Change [*World Meteorological Organization*]
**IPCC**.......... International Pin Collectors Club (EA)
**IPCCB**....... Inter-Parliamentary Consultative Council of Benelux (EA)
**IPCCC**....... International Peace, Communication, and Coordination Center [*The Hague, Netherlands*] (EAIO)
**IPCCIOS**... Indo-Pacific Council of the International Committee of Scientific Management
**IPCCS**........ Information Processing in Command and Control Systems [*Air Force*]
**IPCDA**....... International Penguin Class Dinghy Association (EA)
**IPCE**.......... Independent Parametric Cost Estimate (AABC)
**IPCEA**....... Insulated Power Cable Engineers Association [*Later, ICEA*] (EA)
**IPCF**.......... Interprocess Communication Facility [*Digital Equipment Corp.*]
**IPCF**.......... Interprogram Communication Facility [*Prime Computer, Inc.*]
**IPCG**.......... International Plate Collectors Guild (EA)
**IPCh**........... Israel Philatelist (Chur) [*A publication*]
**IPCL**.......... Central Illinois Light Co., Resource Center, Peoria, IL [*Library symbol*] [*Library of Congress*] (LCLS)
**IPCL**.......... Instrumentation Program and Component List (NASA)
**IPCL**.......... International Postal Collectors League [*Commercial firm*] (EA)
**IPC Mg**...... IPC [*Institute of Philippine Culture*] Monographs [*A publication*]
**IPCO**.......... Idaho Power Company
**IPCOG**....... Informal Policy Committee for Germany
**IPCOG**....... Interdepartmental Planning Committee on Germany [*US*]
**IPC Pap**..... IPC [*Institute of Philippine Culture*] Papers [*A publication*]
**IPCPP**........ International Physicians Commission for the Protection of Prisoners (EA)
**IPCRESS**... Induction of Psychoneuroses by Conditioned Reflex under Stress [*In book and film "The Ipcress File"*]
**IPCS**.......... Image Photon Counting System [*Instrumentation*]
**IPCS**.......... Infrapatellar Contracture Syndrome [*Sports medicine*]
**IPCS**.......... Institute of Professional Civil Servants [*British*]
**IPCS**.......... Integrated Propulsion Control System [*Air Force*]
**IPCS**.......... Interactive Problem-Control System [*IBM Corp.*]
**IPCS**.......... International Petula Clark Society (EAIO)
**IPCS**.......... International Playing-Card Society (EA)
**IPCS**.......... International Programme on Chemical Safety (EA)
**IPCS**.......... Intrauterine Progesterone Contraceptive System [*Gynecology*]
**IPCT**.......... Caterpillar Tractor Co., Business Library, Peoria, IL [*Library symbol*] [*Library of Congress*] (LCLS)
**IPCTAO**.... Impact. Agricultural Research in Texas. Annual Report [*A publication*]
**IPCT-T**...... Caterpillar Tractor Co., Technical Information Center, Peoria, IL [*Library symbol*] [*Library of Congress*] (LCLS)
**IPD**............ Illustrated Provisioning Document (MCD)
**IPD**............ Impact Prediction Data (AFM)
**IPD**............ Implicit Price Deflator
**IPD**............ Improved Point Defense
**IPD**............ In Praesentia Dominorum [*In the Presence of the Lords of Session*] [*Latin*]
**IPD**............ Individual Package Delivery [*Shipping*]
**IPD**............ Industrial Planning Department [*Burma*] (DS)
**IPD**............ Information Processing Division [*NASA*] (NASA)
**IPD**............ Initial Performance Data
**IPD**............ Insertion Phase Delay
**IPD**............ Inspection Planning Document [*Military*] (MCD)
**IPD**............ Institute of Professional Designers
**IPD**............ Institute for Professional Development (EA)
**IPD**............ Instructional Program Development (NVT)
**IPD**............ Integrated Pin Diode
**IPD**............ Integrated Process Demonstration [*Nuclear energy*]
**IPD**............ Intelligence Planning Document [*Military*] (MCD)
**IPD**............ Intelligent Protection Device [*American Solenoid Co.*] [*Somerset, NJ*]
**IPD**............ Inter-Provincial Diversified Holding Ltd. [*Toronto Stock Exchange symbol*]
**IPD**............ Intermittent Peritoneal Dialysis [*Medicine*]
**IPD**............ International Journal of Physical Distribution and Materials Management [*A publication*]
**IPD**............ International Police Dogs (EA)
**IPD**............ Interpupillary Distance
**IPD**............ Inventory of Psychosocial Development
**IPD**............ Investment Property Databank [*London, England*]
**IPD**............ Isophorone Diamine [*Organic chemistry*]
**IPD**............ Isotope-Powered Device
**IPD**............ Issue Priority Designator
**IPD**............ Iterated Prisoner's Dilemma [*Psychology*]
**IPDA**.......... International Periodical Distributors Association (EA)
**IPDA**.......... Intrapulse Demodulation Analysis
**IPDB**.......... Intelligence Production Database [*Military*] (MCD)
**IPDC**.......... International Program for the Development of Communications [*UNESCO*]
**IPDD**.......... Initial Project Design Description (NRCH)
**IPDH**.......... In-Service Planned Derated Hours [*Electronics*] (IEEE)
**IPDI**........... Isophorone Diisocyanate [*Organic chemistry*]
**IPDL**.......... Isotopes Process Development Laboratory [*AEC*]
**IPDM**......... Institute of Physical Distribution Management [*British*]
**IPDMS**....... Integrated Point Defense Missile System [*Military*] (CAAL)
**IPDN**.......... International Paleoclimatic Data Network
**IPDP**.......... Intervals of Pulsations of Diminishing Period
**IPDP**.......... Isopropylphenyl(diphenyl)phosphate [*Fire-resistant hydraulic fluid*]
**IPDR**.......... Incremental Preliminary Design Review (MCD)
**IPDS**.......... Intelligent Printer Data Systems
**IPDSMS**.... Improved Point Defense Surface Missile System
**IPDU**.......... Instantaneous Panoramic Display Unit
**IPE**............ Incentive PERT [*Program Evaluation and Review Technique*] Events
**IPE**............ Industrial Plant [*or Production*] Equipment
**IPE**............ Information Processing Equipment
**IPE**............ Initial Portable Equipment
**IPE**............ Inscriptiones Orae Septentrionalis Ponti Euxini [*A publication*] (OCD)
**IPE**............ Institute of Production Engineers [*British*]
**IPE**............ Institution of Plant Engineers [*British*]
**IPE**............ Inter-Pacific Equity [*Australia*]
**IPE**............ International Paper Board Industry. Corrugated Manufacture and Conversion [*A publication*]
**IPE**............ International Petroleum Exchange [*London, England*]
**IPE**............ International Prism Exploration Ltd. [*Vancouver Stock Exchange symbol*]
**IPE**............ Interpret Parity Error
**IPE**............ Inverse Photoelectric Effect
**IPE**............ Investimentos e Participacoes do Estado, SARL [*Nationalized industry*] [*Portugal*] (EY)
**IPE**............ Isopropyl Ether [*Organic chemistry*]
**IPe**............. Peotone Township Library, Peotone, IL [*Library symbol*] [*Library of Congress*] (LCLS)
**IPEA**.......... Independent Poster Exchanges of America (EA)
**IPEC**.......... International Police Exhibition and Conference [*British*] (ITD)
**IPEC**.......... International Power and Engineering Consultants
**IPECAC**..... Ipecacuanha [*Pharmacy*] (ROG)
**IPECS**........ Integrated Power and Environmental Control System (MCD)
**IPEDS**....... Integrated Postsecondary Education Data System [*National Center for Education Statistics*] (OICC)
**IPEE**.......... Inclination of a Plane to the Plane of the Earth's Equator [*Aerospace*]
**IPEE**.......... International Peace, Economy, and Ecology (EA)
**IPE/EE**...... Estudos Economicos. Universidad de Sao Paulo. Instituto de Pesquisas Economicas [*A publication*]
**IPEF Inst Pesqui Estud Florestais** ... IPEF. Instituto de Pesquisas e Estudos Florestais [*A publication*]
**IPEF Publ Semest** ... IPEF [*Instituto de Pesquisas e Estudos Florestais*] Publicacao Semestral [*A publication*]
**IPEH**.......... Intravascular Papillary Endothelial Hyperplasia [*Medicine*]
**IPE Ind Prod Eng** ... IPE. Industrial and Production Engineering [*A publication*]
**IPE Int Ind Prod Eng** ... IPE International Industrial and Production Engineering [*A publication*]
**IPek**........... Pekin Public Library, Pekin, IL [*Library symbol*] [*Library of Congress*] (LCLS)
**IPekC**......... Pekin Community High School District No. 30, Pekin, IL [*Library symbol*] [*Library of Congress*] (LCLS)
**IPekH**......... Pekin Memorial Hospital, Pekin, IL [*Library symbol*] [*Library of Congress*] (LCLS)

**IPEME**...... International Program in Environmental Management Education
**IPEN**.......... Indian PEN [*A publication*]
**IPEN**.......... Pan American Institute of Naval Engineering (EAIO)
**IPENI**......... International PEN - Ireland (EAIO)
**IPENS**........ International PEN - Scotland (EAIO)
**IPENUS**.... International PEN - United States [*Later, PCUSAW*] (EA)
**IPENY**....... International PEN - Yiddish (EA)
**IPEPO**....... Instituto para la Propaganda Espanola de los Productos del Olivar [*Industrial association*] [*Spain*] (EY)
**IPER**.......... Industrial Production Equipment Reserve (NG)
**IPer**........... Peru Public Library, Peru, IL [*Library symbol*] [*Library of Congress*] (LCLS)
**IPERAS**..... Indian Perfumer [*A publication*]
**IPerIH**....... Illinois Valley Community Hospital, Peru, IL [*Library symbol*] [*Library of Congress*] (LCLS)
**IPERS**........ Industrial Plant Equipment Reutilization System [*DoD*]
**IPerSD**....... Peru Consolidated Community School District 124, Peru, IL [*Library symbol*] [*Library of Congress*] (LCLS)
**IPerStB**...... Saint Bede Academy, Peru, IL [*Library symbol*] [*Library of Congress*] (LCLS)
**IPES**.......... Inverse Photoemission Spectroscopy
**IPESAV**..... Investigacion Pesquera [*A publication*]
**I Pest Cntrl**... International Pest Control [*A publication*]
**IPET**.......... Independent Professional Electronic Technicians
**IPETA**....... Industrie du Petrole [*A publication*]
**IPETAC**..... Interim Police Education and Training Advisory Council [*New South Wales, Australia*]
**IPetM**........ Edgar Lee Masters Memorial Museum, Petersburg, IL [*Library symbol*] [*Library of Congress*] (LCLS)
**IPEU**.......... International Photo-Engravers Union [*Later, GAIU*] (EA)
**IPEUB**....... Industrie du Petrole en Europe. Gaz-Chimie [*A publication*]
**IPEX**.......... Instant Purchase Excursion Fares [*Aviation*]
**IPEX**.......... International Printing Exhibition
**IPF**............ Idiopathic Pulmonary Fibrosis [*Medicine*]
**IPF**............ In-Process Factor
**IPF**............ Indicative Planning Figure
**IPF**............ Initial Production Facilities (AABC)
**IPF**............ Initial Protective Force
**IPF**............ Institute of Public Finance [*British*] (ECON)
**IPF**............ Intaken Piled Fathom [*Shipping*] (DS)
**IPF**............ Intellectual Property Forum [*A publication*]
**IPF**............ International Pain Foundation (EA)
**IPF**............ International Pigeon Federation [*See also FCI*] (EAIO)
**IPF**............ International Podrabinek Fund (EA)
**IPF**............ International Poetry Forum (EA)
**IPF**............ International Powerlifting Federation [*Hagersten, Sweden*] (EAIO)
**IPF**............ International Prayer Fellowship (EA)
**IPF**............ Isotope Production Facility
**IPF**............ IUS Processing Facility [*NASA*] (NASA)
**IPF**............ Japan Pulp and Paper [*A publication*]
**IPf**............. Park Forest Public Library, Park Forest, IL [*Library symbol*] [*Library of Congress*] (LCLS)
**IPFA**.......... Institute for Psychiatry and Foreign Affairs [*Inactive*] (EA)
**IPFA**.......... Insurance Premium Finance Association (EA)
**IPFA**.......... International Physical Fitness Association (EA)
**IPFA**.......... Member of the Chartered Institute of Public Finance and Accountancy [*British*]
**IPFAA**....... International Police and Fire Athletic Association [*Defunct*] (EA)
**IPFABH**.... Instituto de Pesquisas e Experimentacao Agropecuarias do Norte (IPEAN). Serie Estudos sobre Forrageiras na Amazonia [*A publication*]
**iPFC**........... Indirect Plaque-Forming Cell [*Immunology*]
**IPFC**.......... Indo-Pacific Fishery Commission (EAIO)
**IPFEO**....... Institut des Producteurs de Ferro-Alliages d'Europe Occidentale [*Institute of Ferro-Alloy Producers in Western Europe - IFAPWE*] (EA)
**IPFM**......... Integral Pulse Frequency Modulation (IEEE)
**IPFP**.......... Institut Professionnel de la Fonction Publique du Canada [*Professional Institute of the Public Service of Canada - PIPS*]
**IPFP**.......... Iterated Proportional Fitting Procedure [*Statistics*]
**IPFR**.......... Institute of Plasma and Fusion Research [*University of California, Los Angeles*] [*Research center*] (RCD)
**IPFS**.......... Integrated Polygenerator Fertilizer System
**IPFS**.......... International Pen Friend Service (EA)
**IPfs**........... Park Forest South Public Library, Park Forest South, IL [*Library symbol*] [*Library of Congress*] (LCLS)
**IPfsG**......... Governors State University, Park Forest South, IL [*Library symbol*] [*Library of Congress*] (LCLS)
**IPfsI**.......... Inolex Pharmaceutical Co., Park Forest South, IL [*Library symbol*] [*Library of Congress*] (LCLS)
**IPFW**......... Indiana University - Purdue University at Fort Wayne
**IPG**........... Immediate Participation Guarantee Plan [*Insurance*]
**IPG**........... Immobilized pH Gradients [*Chemistry*]
**IPG**........... Impedance Plethysmography [*Medicine*]
**IPG**........... Independent Publishers Group
**IPG**........... Independent Publishers' Guild [*Great Britain*]
**IPG**........... Induction Plasma Gun
**IPG**........... Industrial Performance Group [*Australia*]
**IPG**........... Industrial Physics Group [*University of Essex*] [*British*] (IRUK)
**IPG**........... Information Publishing Group [*The Thomson Corp.*]
**IPG**........... Inositol-Phosphoglycan [*Biochemistry*]
**IPG**........... Institut de Physique du Globe [*France*] (NOAA)
**IPG**........... Interactive Presentation Graphics [*IBM Corp.*]
**IPG**........... International Pagurian Corp. Ltd. [*Toronto Stock Exchange symbol*] [*Vancouver Stock Exchange symbol*]
**IPG**........... International Parliamentary Group for Human Rights in the Soviet Union (EA)
**IPG**........... International Payments Group (NATG)
**IPG**........... International Piano Guild (EA)
**IPG**........... International Planning Glossaries [*Elsevier Book Series*] [*A publication*]
**IPG**........... International Planning Group [*Belgium, Germany, Netherlands*] (AABC)
**IPG**........... International Portrait Gallery
**IPG**........... Interproject Group
**IPG**........... [*The*] Interpublic Group of Companies, Inc. [*NYSE symbol*] (SPSG)
**IPG**........... Isopropylidene Glycerol [*Biochemistry*]
**IPG**........... Isopropylthiogalactoside [*Also, IPTG*] [*Organic chemistry*]
**IPG**........... Isotope Power Generator
**IPG**........... Issue Priority Group [*Army*]
**IPGA**......... Island Park Geothermal Area
**IPGCU**...... International Printing and Graphic Communications Union
**iPGE**......... Prostaglandin E, immunoreactive [*Biochemistry*]
**IPGF**......... Immobilized pH Gradient Isoelectric Focusing [*Analytical biochemistry*]
**IPGI**.......... Institute on Pluralism and Group Identity (EA)
**IPGP**......... Illegal Possession of Government Property
**IPGS**......... Intercollegiate Program of Graduate Studies
**IPGS**......... International Percy Grainger Society (EA)
**IPGS**......... Internationale Paracelsus-Gesellschaft zu Salzburg (EAIO)
**IPH**........... Idiopathic Portal Hypertension [*Medicine*]
**IPH**........... Idiopathic Pulmonary Hemosiderosis [*Medicine*]
**IPH**........... Impressions per Hour [*Printing*]
**IPH**........... Inches per Hour (TEL)
**IPH**........... Industrial and Pastoral Holdings (ADA)
**IPH**........... Industrial Process Heat
**IPH**........... Inflammatory Papillary Hyperplasia [*Dentistry*]
**IPH**........... Interdisciplinary Programs in Health [*Harvard University*]
**IPH**........... International Association of Paper Historians (EA)
**IPH**........... International Pharmadyne Ltd. [*Vancouver Stock Exchange symbol*]
**IPH**........... Interphalangeal [*Anatomy*]
**IPH**........... Intraparenchymal Hemorrhage [*Medicine*]
**IPH**........... Ipoh [*Malaysia*] [*Airport symbol*] (OAG)
**IPh**............ Peoria Heights Public Library, Peoria Heights, IL [*Library symbol*] [*Library of Congress*] (LCLS)
**IPHA**......... Interior Plantscaping and Hire Association [*Australia*]
**IPHC**......... International Pacific Halibut Commission (EA)
**IPHCSR**.... International Pacific Halibut Commission. Scientific Report [*A publication*]
**IPHCTR**.... International Pacific Halibut Commission. Technical Report [*A publication*]
**IPHE**......... Individual Personal Hygiene Equipment (KSC)
**IPHE**......... Institute of Public Health Engineers [*British*]
**IPhe**.......... Palos Heights Public Library, Palos Heights, IL [*Library symbol*] [*Library of Congress*] (LCLS)
**IP/HHCL**... Initial Point/H-Hour Control Line [*Aviation*]
**IPhi**........... Green Hills Public Library District, Palos Hills, IL [*Library symbol*] [*Library of Congress*] (LCLS)
**IPHi**.......... Peoria Historical Society, Peoria, IL [*Library symbol*] [*Library of Congress*] (LCLS)
**IPhil**.......... Philo Township Public Library, Philo, IL [*Library symbol*] [*Library of Congress*] (LCLS)
**IPhiM**........ Moraine Valley Community College, Palos Hills, IL [*Library symbol*] [*Library of Congress*] (LCLS)
**IPHJAJ**..... Israel Pharmaceutical Journal [*A publication*]
**IPHM**........ Individual Personal Hygiene Module (KSC)
**IP-HPLC**... Ion-Pair High-Performance Liquid Chromatography [*Medicine*]
**IPHRD**...... International Program for Human Resource Development (EA)
**IPHSA**....... Institute of Physics. Conference Series [*A publication*]
**IPHYA**....... Indian Phytopathology [*A publication*]
**IPI**............ Identified Friendly Prior to Interception [*Military*]
**IPI**............ Image Processing Interface [*Data processing*] (PCM)
**IPI**............ Immigration Patrol Inspector [*Immigration and Naturalization Service*]
**IPI**............ In Partibus Infidelium [*In the Countries, Lands, or Regions of Unbelievers*] [*Latin*]
**IPI**............ Index of Production Industries [*Department of Employment*] [*British*]
**IPI**............ Individually Planned [*or Prescribed*] Instruction [*Education*]
**IPI**............ Information Publications International [*Publisher*] [*British*]
**IPI**............ Initial Product Inspection
**IPI**............ Institute of Patentees and Inventors [*British*] (ILCA)
**IPI**............ Institute of Physical Medicine and Rehabilitation, Peoria, IL [*Library symbol*] [*Library of Congress*] (LCLS)

**IPI**............. Institute of Poultry Industries
**IPI**............. Institute for Practical Idealism (EA)
**IPI**............. Institute of Professional Investigators (EA)
**IPI**............. Institute for Public Information
**IPI**............. Insurance Periodicals Index [*Nils Publishing Co.*] [*Chatsworth, CA*] [*Information service or system*] (IID)
**IPI**............. Integrated Position Indicator
**IPI**............. Intelligence Publications Index [*Published January, 1953, through February, 1968, by the Defense Intelligence Agency*]
**IPI**............. Intelligent Peripheral Interface [*Data processing*]
**IPI**............. Intelligent Printer Interface
**IPI**............. Intense Product Inspection
**IPI**............. Interchemical Printing Inks
**IPI**............. International Patent Institute [*Later, EPO*] (DIT)
**IPI**............. International Pesticide Institute
**IPI**............. International Phototherapy Institute [*Defunct*] (EA)
**IPI**............. International Population Institute [*Defunct*] (EA)
**IPI**............. International Potash Institute [*See also IIP*] (EAIO)
**IPI**............. International Press Institute [*London, England*]
**IPI**............. International Press Institute, American Committee (EA)
**IPI**............. International Psychosomatics Institute (EA)
**IPI**............. Interpulse Interval
**IPI**............. Intrapair Interval
**IPI**............. Inventory, Print, and Index [*System*]
**IPI**............. Investment Publications Information Services Pty. Ltd. [*Australia*]
**IPI**............. Ipiales [*Colombia*] [*Airport symbol*] (OAG)
**IPiaMCD**... Macoupin Community Unit, District 9, Piasa, IL [*Library symbol*] [*Library of Congress*] (LCLS)
**IPiaSD**....... Southwestern Community Unit, School District 9, Piasa, IL [*Library symbol*] [*Library of Congress*] (LCLS)
**IPIBD3**...... IPI [*International Potash Institute*] Bulletin [*A publication*]
**IPI Bull**...... IPI [*International Potash Institute*] Bulletin [*A publication*]
**IPIC**........... Institute of Personal Image Consultants (EA)
**IPIECA**...... International Petroleum Industry Environmental Conservation Association [*London, England*] (EAIO)
**IPIF**........... Institute of Pacific Islands Forestry [*Department of Agriculture*] [*Honolulu, HI*] (GRD)
**IPI/MIS**.... Individually Planned Instruction/Management and Information System
**IPIN**........... Instituto Panamericano de Ingenieria Naval [*Pan American Institute of Naval Engineering*] (EAIO)
**IPIP**........... Implantable Programmable Infusion Pump [*Medicine*]
**IPIP**........... Information Processing Improvement Program
**IPIP**........... Interprovincial Pipe Line Ltd. [*NASDAQ symbol*] (NQ)
**IPip**........... Piper City Public Library, Piper City, IL [*Library symbol*] [*Library of Congress*] (LCLS)
**IPIPS**......... Interactive Planetary Image Processing System
**IPIR**........... Immediate Photograph Intelligence Report [*Military*] (AFM)
**IPIR**........... Initial Photographic Interpretation Report [*Air Force*]
**IPIR**........... Institute for Public Interest Representation [*Later, CCCIPR*] [*Georgetown University*]
**IPIR**........... Integrated Personnel Information Report (AAG)
**IPI Res Top**... IPI [*International Potash Institute*] Research Topics [*A publication*]
**IPIS**........... Individually Prescribed Instructional Systems (OICC)
**IPIS**........... Institute for Peace and International Security (EA)
**IPIS**........... Instrument Pilot Instructor School [*Air Force*]
**IPISD**......... Interservice Procedures for Instructional Systems Development
**IPit**............. Pittsfield Public Library, Pittsfield, IL [*Library symbol*] [*Library of Congress*] (LCLS)
**IPIV**........... Illinois Valley Library System, Peoria, IL [*Library symbol*] [*Library of Congress*] (LCLS)
**IPJ**............. Institute for Peace and Justice (EA)
**IPJ**............. Intellectual Property Journal [*A publication*]
**IPJ**............. International Pursuit Corp. [*Toronto Stock Exchange symbol*]
**IPJP**........... Interpost Junction Panel
**IPK**............. International Prototype Kilogram
**IPK**............. Painter Creek, AK [*Location identifier*] [*FAA*] (FAAL)
**IPK**............. Peoria Kindergarten Primary Training School, Peoria, IL [*Library symbol*] [*Library of Congress*] (LCLS)
**IPK**............. Petroleum Economist [*A publication*]
**IPKC**........... International Pot and Kettle Clubs (EA)
**IPKO**........... International Information on Peace-Keeping Operations
**IPL**............. El Centro/Imperial [*California*] [*Airport symbol*] (OAG)
**IPL**............. Identified Parts List
**IPL**............. Illustrated Parts List (NATG)
**IPL**............. Illustrated Pocket Library [*A publication*]
**IPL**............. Image Processing Laboratory [*University of Houston*] [*Research center*] (RCD)
**IPL**............. Imperial, CA [*Location identifier*] [*FAA*] (FAAL)
**IPL**............. Indentured Parts List
**IPL**............. Independent Publishers League [*Commercial firm*] (EA)
**IPL**............. Individual Protection Laboratory [*Natick, MA*] [*Army*] (RDA)
**IPL**............. Inferior Parietal Lobule [*Anatomy*]
**IPL**............. Information Processing Language [*Data processing*]
**IPL**............. Initial Program Load [*Data processing*]
**IPL**............. Inner Plexiform Layer [*Retina*]
**IPL**............. Installation Parts List (AAG)
**IPL**............. Institute of Professional Librarians [*Canada*]
**IPL**............. Instrument Panel Lighting (MCD)
**IPL**............. Instrumentation Program List
**IPL**............. Integrated Payload [*NASA*]
**IPL**............. Integrated Perceived Level [*Acoustics*]
**IPL**............. Integrated Priority List [*DoD*]
**IPL**............. Interconnected Porosity Level
**IPL**............. Interim Parts List [*Navy*]
**IPL**............. Interprovincial Pipe Line Ltd. [*Toronto Stock Exchange symbol*]
**IPL**............. Interrupt Priority Level
**IPL**............. Intrapleural
**IPL**............. IPALCO Enterprises, Inc. [*NYSE symbol*] (SPSG)
**IPL**............. Purdue University, Lafayette, IN [*OCLC symbol*] (OCLC)
**IPLA**........... Instituto Pastoral Latinoamericano
**IPLA**........... Interstate Producers Livestock Association (EA)
**IPLAN**....... Joint IOC/WMO Planning Group for IGOSS [*Marine science*] (MSC)
**IPLCA**....... International Pipe Line Contractors Association [*Later, IPOCA*] (EA)
**IPLE**........... Instutution of Public Lighting Engineers [*British*]
**IPLGY**....... Institute for the Protection of Lesbian and Gay Youth (EA)
**IPLL**........... Illinois Publications in Language and Literature [*A publication*]
**IPLL**........... InterPharm Laboratories Limited [*NASDAQ symbol*] (NQ)
**IPLMAE**... Instituut voor de Pluimveeteelt "Het Spelderholt." Mededeling [*A publication*]
**IPLO Q**...... IPLO [*Institute of Professional Librarians of Ontario*] Quarterly [*A publication*]
**IPLRB**........ Revue. Institut Pasteur de Lyon [*A publication*]
**IPLS**........... IPL Systems, Inc. [*NASDAQ symbol*] (NQ)
**IPLV**........... Information Processing Language Five
**IPLV**........... Intermediate Payload Launch Vehicle
**IPlx**............. International Plant Index [*A publication*]
**IPM**............ Illumination per Minute
**IPM**............ Immediate Past Master [*Freemasonry*]
**IPM**............ Imperial Metals Corp. [*Toronto Stock Exchange symbol*] [*Vancouver Stock Exchange symbol*]
**IPM**............ Impulses per Minute [*Telecommunications*]
**IPM**............ Inches per Minute
**IPM**............ Incident Power Monitor [*Military*] (CAAL)
**IPM**............ Incidental Phase [*or Pulse*] Modulation
**IPM**............ Indomethacin-Treated Platelet Microsomes
**IPM**............ Industrial Preparedness Measures
**IPM**............ Industrial Products Magazine [*A publication*]
**IPM**............ Information Processing and Management [*A publication*]
**IPM**............ Inner Peace Movement (EA)
**IPM**............ Insect Populations Management Research Unit [*Department of Agriculture*] (GRD)
**IPM**............ Institute of Personnel Management [*British*] (DCTA)
**IPM**............ Institute of Practical Mathematics [*Germany*]
**IPM**............ Institute of Printing Management [*British*]
**IPM**............ Integrated Pest Management [*Agronomy*]
**IPM**............ Intelligent Power Management [*Laptop computers*] (BYTE)
**IPM**............ Inter-Processor/Multiplexer (MCD)
**IPM**............ Interference Prediction Model
**IPM**............ Internal Polarization Modulation (IEEE)
**IPM**............ International Prison Ministry (EA)
**IPM**............ International Prototype Meter
**IPM**............ Interpersonal Perception Method [*Psychology*]
**IPM**............ Interruptions per Minute
**IPM**............ IPM Technology, Inc. [*Later, MAX*] [*AMEX symbol*] (SPSG)
**IPM**............ Isopropyl Myristate [*Pharmacology*]
**IPM**............ Morrison and Mary Wiley Public Library, Elmwood, IL [*OCLC symbol*] (OCLC)
**IPM**............ Peoria Masonic Temple, Peoria, IL [*Library symbol*] [*Library of Congress*] (LCLS)
**IPMA**......... In-Plant Management Association (EA)
**IPMA**......... In-Plant Printing Management Association
**IPMA**......... Interlocking Paving Manufacturers Association [*Defunct*] (EA)
**IPMA**......... International Personnel Management Association (EA)
**IPMA**......... International Planned Music Association (EA)
**IPMA**......... International Primary Market Association (EAIO)
**IPMANA**... Interstate Postgraduate Medical Association of North America (EA)
**IPMCD**...... Industrie du Petrole dans le Monde. Gaz-Chimie [*A publication*]
**IPMH**........ Methodist Hospital of Central Illinois, Peoria, IL [*Library symbol*] [*Library of Congress*] (LCLS)
**IPMH-M**... Methodist Medical Center of Illinois, Medical Library, Peoria, IL [*Library symbol*] [*Library of Congress*] (LCLS)
**IPMI**.......... International Precious Metals Institute (EA)
**IPMP**......... Industrial Plant Modernization Program [*Air Force*]
**IPMP**......... Isopropyl(methoxy)pyrazine [*Organic chemistry*]
**IPMPC**...... International Journal of Powder Metallurgy and Powder Technology [*A publication*]
**IPMS**......... Impact Predictor Monitor Set [*NASA*] (AAG)
**IPMS**......... Infinite Periodic Minimal Surface
**IPMS**......... Integrated Program Management System [*Navy*]
**IPMS**......... International Polar Motion Service
**IPMS**......... International Primitive Money Society (EA)
**IPM/S**....... Interruptions per Minute/Second (DEN)
**IPMS**......... Investment Performance Monitoring Service [*British*]

**IPMS/USA** ... International Plastic Modelers Society/US Branch (EA)
**IPN** ... Impulse Noise
**IPN** ... Indigenous People's Network (EA)
**IPN** ... Infectious Pancreatic Necrosis [*Medicine*]
**IPN** ... Information Processing Network
**IPN** ... Inspection Progress Notification
**IPN** ... Instant Private Network
**IPN** ... Instrumentation Plan Number (MUGU)
**IPN** ... Intellectual Property Network, Ltd. [*Information service or system*] (IID)
**IPN** ... International Platinum Corp. [*Toronto Stock Exchange symbol*]
**IPN** ... International Polio Network (EA)
**IPN** ... Interpenetrating Polymer Network [*Organic chemistry*]
**IPN** ... Ipatinga [*Brazil*] [*Airport symbol*] (OAG)
**IPN** ... Isophthalonitrile [*Organic chemistry*]
**IPN** ... Purdue University, North Central Campus, Westville, IN [*OCLC symbol*] (OCLC)
**IPNA** ... Instituto Peruano-Norte Americano [*A publication*]
**IPNA** ... International Pediatric Nephrology (EA)
**IPNA** ... Isopropylnoradrenaline
**IPNC** ... Independence Plan for Neighborhood Councils (EA)
**IPNFC** ... International Peter Noone Fan Club (EA)
**IPNJ** ... Industrial Photographers of New Jersey (EA)
**I/PNL** ... Instrument Panel [*Automotive engineering*]
**IPNL** ... Integrated Perceived Noise Level [*Acoustics*]
**IPNS** ... Intense Pulsed Neutron Source
**IPNS** ... Interpenetrating Networks of Samples [*Statistics*]
**IPNV** ... Infectious Pancreatic Necrosis Virus
**IPO** ... Crown Point Community Schools, Crown Point, IN [*OCLC symbol*] (OCLC)
**IPO** ... Indophenol Oxidase [*An enzyme*]
**IPO** ... Initial Public Offering [*Business term*]
**IPO** ... Inspection Planning Order
**IPO** ... Installation Planning Order
**IPO** ... Installation Production Order
**IPO** ... Installation Productivity Option [*IBM Corp.*]
**IPO** ... Instantaneous Power Output
**IPO** ... Intellectual Property Owners (EA)
**IPO** ... International Pact Organization
**IPO** ... International Parents' Organization [*Later, PS*] (EA)
**IPO** ... International Payment Order (DCTA)
**IPO** ... International Progress Organization [*Vienna, Austria*] (EAIO)
**IPOC** ... Iberian Peninsula Operating Committee [*World War II*]
**IPOCA** ... International Pipe Line and Offshore Contractors Association (EAIO)
**IPOD** ... International Program of Ocean Drilling [*Formerly, DSDP*] [*National Science Foundation*]
**IPO/E** ... Installation Productivity Option/Extended [*IBM Corp.*]
**IPOEE** ... Institute of Post Office Electrical Engineers [*British*]
**IPOFA** ... Integrated Programmed Operational and Functional Appraisals
**IPOFAC** ... International Project on Family and Community [*Australia*]
**IPOGA** ... Indian Musician [*A publication*]
**IPoH** ... Saint James Hospital, Pontiac, IL [*Library symbol*] [*Library of Congress*] (LCLS)
**IPOL** ... Institute of Polarology [*British*]
**I Polit Sci** ... Indian Political Science Review [*A publication*]
**IPOM** ... Intelligent Plant Operating Manual [*Combustion Engineering Simcon, Inc.*]
**IPOMS** ... International Polar-Orbiting Meteorological Satellite
**IPOP** ... Installer Point of Purchase
**IPOR** ... International Population Research Center [*University of California*] [*Defunct*]
**IPOSA** ... International Photo Optical Show Association (EA)
**IPOT** ... Inductive Potentiometer (MDG)
**IPot** ... Potomac Public Library, Potomac, IL [*Library symbol*] [*Library of Congress*] (LCLS)
**IPOTA** ... Izobreteniya Promyshlennye Obraztsy Tovarnye Znaki [*A publication*]
**IPP** ... British Institute of Practical Psychology
**IPP** ... Imaging Polarimeter [*or Photopolarimetry*] [*NASA*]
**IPP** ... Immediate Past President (ADA)
**IPP** ... Impact Prediction Point [*NASA*]
**IPP** ... Impaired Physician Program (EA)
**IPP** ... Import Parity Pricing (ADA)
**IPP** ... In Propria Persona [*In Person*] [*Latin*] [*Legal term*] (DLA)
**IPP** ... Inanities per Page [*Facetious criterion for determining insignificance of Supreme Court Justices*] [*Proposed by University of Chicago professor David P. Currie*]
**IPP** ... Independent Power Producer
**IPP** ... Index of Prices Paid [*Economics*]
**IPP** ... India Paper Proofs
**IPP** ... Indianapolis Public Schools, Indianapolis, IN [*OCLC symbol*] (OCLC)
**IPP** ... Individual Parameter Perturbation
**IPP** ... Individual Program Plan
**IPP** ... Industrial Preparedness Planning [*DoD*]
**IPP** ... Information Processing Professional
**IPP** ... Infrared Pointer Package
**IPP** ... Input Processor Programs [*Data processing*]
**IPP** ... Inspired Partial Pressure [*Physiology*]
**IPP** ... Integrated Plotting Package (NRCH)
**IPP** ... Interface Program Plan (MCD)
**IPP** ... Intermittent Positive Pressure [*Medicine*]
**IPP** ... Internal Packet Protocol [*Telecommunications*]
**IPP** ... International Partners in Prayer (EA)
**IPP** ... International Phototelegraph Position [*Telecommunications*] (TEL)
**IPP** ... International Priority Paid (ADA)
**IPP** ... Internationally Protected Person (ADA)
**IPP** ... Interprocessor Process [*Telecommunications*] (TEL)
**IPP** ... Intrapleural Pressure [*Biology*]
**IPP** ... Inverse Polarity Protection
**IPP** ... Ionospheric Propagation Path
**IPP** ... Ipplepen [*England*]
**IPP** ... Isopentenyl Pyrophosphate [*Organic chemistry*]
**IPP** ... Isopropyl Percarbonate [*or Diisopropyl Peroxydicarbonate*] [*Organic chemistry*]
**IPP** ... Isothermal Pressure Profile
**IPp** ... Paw Paw Public Library, Paw Paw, IL [*Library symbol*] [*Library of Congress*] (LCLS)
**IPPA** ... Independent Programme Producers' Association [*British*]
**IPPA** ... Indo-Pacific Prehistory Association [*Australia*] (EA)
**IPPA** ... Inspection, Palpation, Percussion, Auscultation [*Medicine*]
**IPPA** ... Instant Potato Products Association [*Defunct*] (EA)
**IPPA** ... Institute for Public Policy and Administration [*Later, CPPUI*] (EA)
**IPPA** ... Intercontinental Press Publishing Association (EA)
**IPPA** ... International Paintball Players Association (EA)
**IPPA** ... International Pentecostal Press Association (EA)
**IPPA** ... International Printing Pressmen and Assistants' Union of North America [*Later, IPGCU*]
**IPPA** ... International Program for Population Analysis
**IPPA** ... Isopropylphenyl Acetate [*Organic chemistry*]
**IPpa** ... Palos Park Public Library, Palos Park, IL [*Library symbol*] [*Library of Congress*] (LCLS)
**IPPAU** ... International Printing Pressmen and Assistants' Union of North America [*Later, IPGCU*] (EA)
**IPPB** ... Intermittent Positive Pressure Breathing [*Medicine*]
**IPPB/I** ... Intermittent Positive Pressure Breathing/Inspiratory
**IPPBS** ... Integrated Personnel Planning and Budgeting System
**IPPC** ... Infrastructure Payments and Progress Committee [*NATO*] (NATG)
**IPPC** ... International Penal and Penitentiary Commission [*Later, IPPF*]
**IPPC** ... International Philatelic Press Club (EA)
**IPPC** ... International Plant Protection Center [*Oregon State University*] [*Research center*] (RCD)
**IPPC** ... International Plant Protection Convention
**IPPC** ... Isopropyl N-phenylcarbamate [*Also, INPC, IPC*] [*Herbicide*]
**IPPCA** ... Independent Professional Painting Contractors Association of America (EA)
**IPPD** ... Isopropyl(phenyl)para-phenylene Diamine [*Organic chemistry*]
**IPPDSEU** ... International Plate Printers, Die Stampers, and Engravers' Union of North America (EA)
**IPPF** ... Instruction Preprocessing Function
**IPPF** ... International Penal and Penitentiary Foundation [*See also FIPP*] [*Bonn, Federal Republic of Germany*] (EAIO)
**IPPF** ... International Planned Parenthood Federation (EA)
**IPPF Med Bull** ... IPPF [*International Planned Parenthood Federation*] Medical Bulletin [*A publication*]
**IPPF/WHR** ... International Planned Parenthood Federation, Western Hemisphere Region (EA)
**IPPH** ... Proctor Community Hospital, Peoria, IL [*Library symbol*] [*Library of Congress*] (LCLS)
**IPPHA** ... International Peruvian Paso Horse Association (EA)
**IPPI** ... Instructional Procedures Preference Inventory
**IPPI** ... International Public Policy Institute
**IPPI** ... Interruption of Pregnancy for Psychiatric Indication
**IPPIC** ... Instrumentation in the Pulp and Paper Industry [*A publication*]
**IPPJ** ... Institute of Plasma Physics, Japan
**IPPL** ... Indentured Parts Price List (MCD)
**IPPL** ... Industrial Preparedness Planning List
**IPPL** ... Integrated Planning Parts List (MCD)
**IPPL** ... International Primate Protection League (EA)
**IPPMA** ... In-Plant Powder Metallurgy Association (EA)
**IPPMA** ... In-Plant Printing Management Association
**IPPMHN** ... International Post-Partum Mental Health Network (EA)
**IPPNO** ... International Philosophers for the Prevention of Nuclear Omnicide (EA)
**IPPNW** ... International Physicians for the Prevention of Nuclear War (EA)
**IPPO** ... Intermittent Positive Pressure with Oxygen [*Medicine*]
**IPPP** ... Industrial Property Policy Program [*Insurance*]
**IPPP** ... Institute for Philosophy and Public Policy (EA)
**IPP Presseinf** ... IPP [*Max Planck Institut fuer Plasmaphysik*] Presseinformationen [*A publication*]
**IPPR** ... Industrial Production Performance Reporting
**IPPR** ... Institute for Public Policy Research [*British*] (ECON)
**IPPR** ... Intermittent Positive Pressure Respiration
**IPPS** ... Improved Processing System (MCD)
**IPPS** ... International Plant Propagators Society, Eastern Region (EA)
**IPpS** ... Paw Paw School System, Paw Paw, IL [*Library symbol*] [*Library of Congress*] (LCLS)

**IPPSA** ........ Israel-Palestine Philatelic Society of America [*Later, SIP*]
**IPPT** .......... Inter-Person Perception Test [*Personality development test*] [*Psychology*]
**IPPTA** ....... Indian Pulp and Paper Technical Association. Journal [*A publication*]
**IPPUAD** .... Immediate Postprandial Upper Abdominal Distress
**IPPV** .......... Intermittent Positive Pressure Ventilation
**IPQ** ............ International Petroleum Quarterly [*A publication*]
**IPQ** ............ International Philosophical Quarterly [*A publication*]
**IPQ** ............ International Praxis Resources [*Vancouver Stock Exchange symbol*]
**IPQ** ............ Intimacy Potential Quotient
**IPQC** ......... In-Process Quality Control
**IPQI** .......... Intermediate Personality Questionnaire for Indian Pupils [*Personality development test*] [*Psychology*]
**IPR** ............. In-Place Repair
**IPR** ............. In-Process Report
**IPR** ............. In-Process Review
**IPR** ............. In Pulse to Register [*Telecommunications*] (TEL)
**IPR** ............. Inches per Revolution
**IPR** ............. Independent Professional Review [*Medicaid*] (DHSM)
**IPR** ............. Index of Prices Received [*Economics*]
**IPR** ............. Individual Pay Record [*Military*]
**IPR** ............. Indochina Postwar Reconstruction
**IPR** ............. Industry Planning Representative [*DoD*]
**IPR** ............. Informal Progress Report
**IPR** ............. Initial Pressure Regulator [*Nuclear energy*] (NRCH)
**IPR** ............. Institute of Pacific Relations
**IPR** ............. Institute for Policy Research [*University of Cincinnati*] [*Research center*] (RCD)
**IPR** ............. Institute for Policy Research [*University of Wyoming*] [*Research center*] (RCD)
**IPR** ............. Institute of Population Registration [*British*]
**IPR** ............. Institute of Psychophysical Research [*British*]
**IPR** ............. Institute of Public Relations [*Great Britain*]
**IPR** ............. Institute for Puerto Rican Policy, Inc. [*Research center*] (RCD)
**IPR** ............. Intellectual Property Reports [*Australia*] [*A publication*]
**IPR** ............. Intellectual Property Right
**IPR** ............. Intelligence Production Requests
**IPR** ............. Intelligence Production Requirement (AFIT)
**IPR** ............. Inter-City Products Corp. [*AMEX symbol*] (SPSG)
**IPR** ............. Interdepartmental Procurement Request
**IPR** ............. Interdepartmental Purchase Request [*DoD*] (AFIT)
**IPR** ............. Interim Problem Report (NASA)
**IPR** ............. Interim Progress Report
**IPR** ............. Interior Procurement Regulations [*Department of the Interior*]
**IPR** ............. Internacia Pedagogia Recuo [*A publication*]
**IPR** ............. Internal Progress Report
**IPR** ............. International Public Relations (ADA)
**IPR** ............. Internationales Privatrecht [*Private International Law*] [*German*] (ILCA)
**IPR** ............. Interpersonal Process Recall [*Psychology*]
**IPR** ............. Inward Processing Relief (DCTA)
**IPR** ............. Ion Production Rate
**IPR** ............. Isoproterenol [*An adrenergic*]
**IPRA** .......... In-Place Repairable Assembly (MCD)
**IPRA** .......... International Paddle Racket Association [*Later, AARA*]
**IPRA** .......... International Peace Research Association (EA)
**IPRA** .......... International Professional Rodeo Association (EA)
**IPRA** .......... International Public Relations Association, US Section (EA)
**IPRAA** ....... Indian Practitioner [*A publication*]
**IPRADB** .... Intensivmedizinische Praxis [*A publication*]
**IPRB** .......... Installations Planning and Review Board [*DoD*]
**IPRB** .......... Inter-Allied Postwar Requirements Bureau [*World War II*]
**IPRCDH** .... In Practice [*A publication*]
**IPRDA** ....... Israeli Annals of Psychiatry [*A publication*]
**IPRDAH** .... Israel Annals of Psychiatry and Related Disciplines [*A publication*]
**IPRE** .......... International Professional Association for Environmental Affairs (EA)
**IPREA** ....... Institute of Petroleum. Review [*A publication*]
**IPRHA** ....... Industrial and Process Heating [*A publication*]
**IPri** ............ Matson Public Library, Princeton, IL [*Library symbol*] [*Library of Congress*] (LCLS)
**IPriBSD** ..... Bureau Township Consolidated School District 250, Princeton, IL [*Library symbol*] [*Library of Congress*] (LCLS)
**I-PRIDE** .... Interracial-Intercultural Pride (EA)
**IPriDS** ....... Douglas Elementary School, Princeton, IL [*Library symbol*] [*Library of Congress*] (LCLS)
**IPriHi** ........ Bureau County Historical Society, Princeton, IL [*Library symbol*] [*Library of Congress*] (LCLS)
**IPriJS** ........ Jefferson Elementary School, Princeton, IL [*Library symbol*] [*Library of Congress*] (LCLS)
**IPriLH** ....... Logan Junior High School, Princeton, IL [*Library symbol*] [*Library of Congress*] (LCLS)
**IPriPH** ....... Perry Memorial Hospital, Princeton, IL [*Library symbol*] [*Library of Congress*] (LCLS)
**IPriv** .......... Lillie M. Evans Memorial Library, Princeville, IL [*Library symbol*] [*Library of Congress*] (LCLS)
**IPriWS** ...... Washington Middle School, Princeton, IL [*Library symbol*] [*Library of Congress*] (LCLS)
**IPRO** ......... Eye Care Centers of America, Inc. [*San Antonio, TX*] [*NASDAQ symbol*] (NQ)
**I-PRO** ........ Independent Professional Representatives Organization (EA)
**IProD** ......... Prospect Heights Public Library District, Prospect Heights, IL [*Library symbol*] [*Library of Congress*] (LCLS)
**I Prod E** ...... Institution of Production Engineers [*British*]
**IP-RPLC** .... Ion-Pair-Reversed-Phase Liquid Chromatography
**IPRR** .......... Integrated Personnel Requirement Report (AAG)
**IPRS** .......... International Confederation for Plastic and Reconstructive Surgery [*Montreal, PQ*] (EAIO)
**IPRSDV** ..... Israel Journal of Psychiatry and Related Sciences [*A publication*]
**IPS** ............ American Income Properties LP [*AMEX symbol*] (SPSG)
**IPS** ............ Ibero-American Philosophical Society [*Madrid, Spain*] (EAIO)
**IPS** ............ Illustrative Planning Scenario [*DoD*]
**IPS** ............ Image Processing System (MCD)
**IPS** ............ Impact Predictor System [*NASA*]
**IPS** ............ Imperial Parliament Series [*A publication*]
**IPS** ............ Improved Processing System
**IPS** ............ Impulses per Second [*Telecommunications*] (TEL)
**IPS** ............ In Pulse to Sender [*Telecommunications*] (TEL)
**IPS** ............ Inches per Second
**IPS** ............ Index Preparation System [*Foxon-Maddocks Associates*] [*Information service or system*] (IID)
**IPS** ............ Indian Point Station [*Nuclear energy*] (NRCH)
**IPS** ............ Indian Police Service [*British*]
**IPS** ............ Indian Political Service [*British*]
**IPS** ............ Industrial Planning Specification
**IPS** ............ Industrial Program Services [*Australia*]
**IPS** ............ Information Processing System
**IPS** ............ Inner Polar Site [*Cytology*]
**IPS** ............ Installation Performance Specification [*Data processing*] (IBMDP)
**IPS** ............ Institute for Palestine Studies (EA)
**IPS** ............ Institute for Planetary Synthesis [*See also ISP*] [*Geneva, Switzerland*] (EAIO)
**IPS** ............ Institute of Polar Studies [*Ohio State University*] [*Later, BPRC*]
**IPS** ............ Institute for Policy Studies (EA)
**IPS** ............ Institute of Purchasing and Supply [*British*]
**IPS** ............ Instructions per Second [*Data processing*]
**IPS** ............ Instrument Pointing System (MCD)
**IPS** ............ Instrumentation Power Supply
**IPS** ............ Instrumentation Power System [*or Subsystem*] [*NASA*] (NASA)
**IPS** ............ Integrated Power System
**IPS** ............ Integrated Procurement System [*Army*]
**IPS** ............ Integrated Program Study (MCD)
**IPS** ............ Integrated Program Summary [*Military*] (CAAL)
**IPS** ............ Intelligent Power Management System [*Laptop computers*] (BYTE)
**IPS** ............ Intelligent Printing System [*Dataroyal, Inc.*]
**IPS** ............ Inter/Press Service - Third World News Agency (EA)
**IPS** ............ Interactive Pictures Systems [*In IPS Dance, a computer program for choreographers*]
**IPS** ............ Interceptor Pilot Simulator [*SSTM*]
**IPS** ............ Interface Problem Sheet (NASA)
**IPS** ............ Interim Policy Statement (NRCH)
**IPS** ............ Interim POMSEE [*Performance, Operating, and Maintenance Standards for Electronic Equipment*] Sheet
**IPS** ............ Interlink Press Service (EA)
**IPS** ............ International Confederation for Plastic Surgery
**IPS** ............ International Palm Society (EA)
**IPS** ............ International Paracelsus Society [*Salzburg, Austria*] (EA)
**IPS** ............ International Peat Society [*See also IMTG*] [*Helsinki, Finland*] (EAIO)
**IPS** ............ International Perimetric Society (EA)
**IPS** ............ International Phenomenological Society (EA)
**IPS** ............ International Phycological Society (EA)
**IPS** ............ International Pipe Standard
**IPS** ............ International Planetarium Society (EA)
**IPS** ............ International Plastics Selector, Inc. [*Information service or system*] (IID)
**IPS** ............ International Polaris Energy Corp. [*Toronto Stock Exchange symbol*]
**IPS** ............ International Preview Society (EA)
**IPS** ............ International Primatological Society (EA)
**IPS** ............ International Processes Simulation [*Game*]
**IPS** ............ International Publishing Service [*Australia*]
**IPS** ............ Internationale Paracelsus-Gesellschaft zu Salzburg [*International Paracelsus Society*] (EA)
**IPS** ............ Interplanetary Scintillation
**IPS** ............ Interpretive Programming System
**IPS** ............ Interruptions per Second
**IPS** ............ Intractable Pain Society of Great Britain and Ireland
**IPS** ............ Intraperitoneal Shock [*Psychology*]
**IPS** ............ Introductory Physical Science [*Project*] [*Education*]
**IPS** ............ Inventing and Patenting Sourcebook [*A publication*]
**IPS** ............ Inventory of Perceptual Skills [*Visual and auditory test*]
**IPS** ............ Inverse Photoemission Spectroscopy
**IPS** ............ Inverter Power Supply (NASA)
**IPS** ............ Investors Protection Scheme (DCTA)

**IPS** ............ Ion Plating Supply
**IPS** ............ Ionospheric Prediction Service [*Telecommunications*] (TEL)
**IPS** ............ Item Processing System (BUR)
**IPS** ............ Office of Information Programmes and Services [*UNESCO*] (IID)
**IPSA** .......... Incremental Microwave Power Spectrum Analyzer [*Air Force*]
**IPSA** .......... Independent Postal System of America [*Alternative to US Postal Service*]
**IPSA** .......... Institute for Psychological Study of the Arts [*University of Florida*] [*Research center*] (RCD)
**IPSA** .......... International Passenger Ship Association [*Defunct*] [*Merger of Atlantic Passenger Steamship Conference, Trans-Atlantic Passenger Steamship Conference, Caribbean Cruise Association*]
**IPSA** .......... International Political Science Association (EA)
**IPSA** .......... International Professional Security Association [*Paignton, Devonshire, England*] (EAIO)
**IPSA** .......... International Professional Surrogates Association (EA)
**IPSAM** ...... International Presort Airmail [*US Postal Service*]
**IPSANET** ... Sharp [*I. P.*] Communications Network [*I.P. Sharp Associates Ltd.*] [*Toronto, ON*] (TSSD)
**IPSAR** ....... Integrated Plant Safety Assessment Report [*Nuclear energy*] (NRCH)
**IPSB** .......... Interprocessor Signal Bus
**IPSC** .......... Information Processing Standards for Computers
**IPSC** .......... Information Processing Supplies Council (EA)
**IPSC** .......... Inhibitory Postsynaptic Current [*Neurophysiology*]
**IPSC** .......... Interagency Primate Steering Committee [*National Institutes of Health*]
**IPSE** .......... Integrated Programming Support Environment [*BIS Applied Systems*] [*British*]
**IPSEP** ........ International Project for Soft Energy Paths (EA)
**IPSF** .......... Intermediate Postsurgical Fitting [*Medicine*]
**IPSF** .......... International Pharmaceutical Students' Federation [*Jerusalem, Israel*] (EAIO)
**IPSFC** ........ International Pacific Salmon Fisheries Commission [*Canada*] (EA)
**IPSFCPR**... International Pacific Salmon Fisheries Commission. Progress Reports [*A publication*]
**IPSG** .......... International Programs Steering Group [*DoD*]
**IPSICM** ..... International PSI Committee of Magicians [*See also CIEPP*] (EAIO)
**IPSJ** ........... Information Processing Society of Japan [*Information service or system*] (IID)
**IPSL** ........... Interface Problem Status Log (NASA)
**IPSO** .......... International Programs and Studies Office [*Later, DIA*] (EA)
**IPSOC** ....... Information Processing Society of Canada
**IPSOCS** ..... Institute of Polar Studies (Ohio). Contribution Series [*A publication*]
**IPSP** .......... Inhibitory Postsynaptic Potential [*Neurophysiology*]
**IPSP** .......... Intelligence Priorities for Strategic Planning [*Military*]
**IPSR** .......... Institute of Plant Science Research [*United Kingdom*] [*Research center*] (IRC)
**IPSRA** ....... International Professional Ski Racers Association (EA)
**IPSS** .......... Institute of Planetary and Space Science (MCD)
**IPSS** .......... Interactive Population Statistical System [*Data processing*]
**IPSS** .......... International Packet Switch Stream [*Data processing*]
**IPSS** .......... International Packet Switching Service [*British Telecom International, Inc.*] [*Telecommunications service*] (TSSD)
**IPSS** .......... International Pilot Study of Schizophrenia [*WHO*]
**IPSS** .......... Interprocessor Signaling System [*Telecommunications*] (TEL)
**IPSSB** ........ Information Processing Systems Standards Board [*Later, Board of Standards Review of ANSI*] [*American Standards Association*]
**IPSSG** ........ International Printers Supply Salesmen's Guild (EA)
**IPST** .......... In-Process Self Test (MCD)
**IPST** .......... Institute for Physical Science and Technology [*University of Maryland*] [*Research center*] (RCD)
**IPST** .......... Israel Program for Scientific Translations [*An agency of the Government of Israel*]
**IPStF** ......... Saint Francis Hospital, Peoria, IL [*Library symbol*] [*Library of Congress*] (LCLS)
**IPS/UIS** .... [*Office of*] International Programmes and Services/UNESCO Information Services (IID)
**IPSW** ......... Ipswich [*City in England*] (ROG)
**IPSYA** ....... Individual Psychologist [*A publication*]
**I Psychol R** ... Indian Psychological Review [*A publication*]
**IPT** ............ Icelandic Pony Trekkers [*Later, IHT*] (EA)
**IPT** ............ Image Processing Technology [*Computer graphics*]
**IPT** ............ Immunoprecipitation Technique [*Clinical chemistry*]
**IPT** ............ Improved Programming Technologies (BUR)
**IPT** ............ In-Plant Test (KSC)
**IPT** ............ In-Plant Training
**IPT** ............ In-Plant Transporter (MCD)
**IPT** ............ In Port [*Navy*] (NVT)
**IPT** ............ Incremental Proof Testing
**IPT** ............ Indexed, Paged, and Titled (ADA)
**IPT** ............ Induction Plasma Torch
**IPT** ............ Industrial Power Tube
**IPT** ............ Information Processing Technology
**IPT** ............ Infrared Plume Target
**IPT** ............ Initial Production Test [*Army*] (AABC)
**IPT** ............ Installation Preflight Test
**IPT** ............ Institute for Paralegal Training [*Later, Philadelphia Institute*] [*Commercial firm*] (EA)
**IPT** ............ Institute of Petroleum Technologists
**IPT** ............ Institute of Property Taxation (EA)
**IPT** ............ Internal Pipe Thread
**IPT** ............ International Pipe Thread (NASA)
**IPT** ............ International Planning Team [*NATO*] (NATG)
**IPT** ............ Interpersonal Therapy [*Mental health treatment technique*]
**IPT** ............ Interplanetary Travel (AAG)
**IPT** ............ IP Timberlands Ltd. [*NYSE symbol*] (SPSG)
**IPT** ............ Iron Pipe Thread (MSA)
**IPT** ............ MAP International, Wheaton, IL [*OCLC symbol*] (OCLC)
**IPT** ............ Williamsport [*Pennsylvania*] [*Airport symbol*] (OAG)
**IPT** ............ Williamsport, PA [*Location identifier*] [*FAA*] (FAAL)
**IPTA** .......... International Patent and Trademark Association [*Later, IIPA*] (EA)
**IPTA** .......... International Piano Teachers Association [*Defunct*]
**IPTAAS** ..... Isolated Patients Travel and Accommodation Assistance Scheme [*Australia*]
**IPTAR** ....... Institute for Psychoanalytic Training and Research
**IPTC** .......... International Polar Transportation Conference
**IPTC** .......... International Press Telecommunications Council [*See also CIPT*] [*Telecommunications*] [*An association*] (EA)
**IPTCB** ....... Collection. Colloques et Seminaires. Institut Francais du Petrole [*A publication*]
**IPTCS** ........ Igloo Passive Thermal Control Section [*Aerospace*] (MCD)
**IPTEA** ....... Internacia Postista kaj Telekomunikista Esperanto-Asocio [*International Esperanto Association of Post and Telecommunication Workers*] (EAIO)
**IPTF** .......... Indo-Pacific Theosophical Federation (EAIO)
**IPTG** .......... Isopropylthiogalactoside [*Also, IPG*] [*Organic chemistry*]
**IPTH** .......... Immunoreactive Parathyroid Hormone [*Endocrinology*]
**IPTHA5** ..... International Congress on Pteridines. Handbook [*A publication*]
**IPTLF** ........ International Phasor Telecom [*NASDAQ symbol*] (NQ)
**IPTM** ......... Interval Pulse Time Modulation
**IPTN** .......... Independent Professional Typists Network (EA)
**IPTO** .......... International Pet Trade Organization (EAIO)
**IPTS** .......... International Practical Temperature Scale [*National Institute of Standards and Technology*]
**IPTT** .......... Internationale du Personnel des Postes, Telegraphes, et Telephones [*Postal, Telegraph, and Telephone International - PTTI*] [*Geneva, Switzerland*] (EAIO)
**IPU** ............ Eastern New Mexico University, Portales, NM [*OCLC symbol*] (OCLC)
**IPU** ............ Information Processing Utility
**IPU** ............ Inpatient Unit [*Medicine*]
**IPU** ............ Institute for Public Understanding (EA)
**IPU** ............ Institute of Public Utilities (EA)
**IPU** ............ Instruction Processing Unit (BUR)
**IPU** ............ Integrated Physiological Unit
**IPU** ............ Inter-Parliamentary Union [*See also UI*] [*Switzerland*]
**IPU** ............ Interface and Priority Unit
**IPU** ............ International Paleontological Union
**IPU** ............ International Peasant Union
**IPU** ............ Interphase Unit
**IPU** ............ Interprocessor Unit
**IPU** ............ Irish Postal Union
**IPU** ............ Isotope Power Unit
**IPUR** .......... Innova/Pure Water, Inc. [*Clearwater, FL*] [*NASDAQ symbol*] (NQ)
**IPV** ............ Improve (FAAC)
**IPV** ............ In-Plant Verification (AFIT)
**IPV** ............ Inaccessible Pore Volume [*Petroleum technology*]
**IPV** ............ Inactivated Poliovirus Vaccine
**IPV** ............ Infectious Pustular Vaginitis [*Medicine*]
**IPV** ............ Infectious Pustular Vulvovaginitis [*Veterinary medicine*]
**IPV** ............ Inner Pilot Valve
**IPV** ............ Internal Podalic Version [*Obstetrics*]
**IPV** ............ International Prime Tech [*Vancouver Stock Exchange symbol*]
**IPV** ............ Intrinsic Payload Value
**IPV** ............ Isopycnic Potential Vorticity [*Oceanography*]
**IPV** ............ Italian Polydor Variable Microgroove [*Record label*]
**IPVG** .......... Isopycnic Potential Vorticity Gradient [*Oceanography*]
**IPVRA** ....... International Professional Vinyl Repair Association (EA)
**IPVS** .......... International Pig Veterinary Society [*Amer, Spain*] (EAIO)
**IPVS** .......... Ion Pump Vacuum System
**IPW** ........... International Powertech Systems, Inc. [*Vancouver Stock Exchange symbol*]
**IPW** ........... Interrogation Prisoner of War
**IPW** ........... Interstate Power Co. [*NYSE symbol*] (SPSG)
**IPW Ber** ..... IPW [*Institut fuer Internationale Politik und Wirtschaft der Deutschen Demokratischen Republik*] Berichte [*A publication*]
**IPW Forsch-H** ... IPW [*Institut fuer Internationale Politik und Wirtschaft der Deutschen Demokratischen Republik*] Forschungshefte [*A publication*]

**IPW Forschungshefte** ... IPW (Institut fuer Internationale Politik und Wirtschaft der Deutschen Demokratischen Republik) Forschungshefte [*A publication*]
**IPWI** ......... Infrared Proximity Warning Indicator
**IPWIA** ......... Instrumentation in the Power Industry [*A publication*]
**IPWO** ......... Interplant Work Order (MCD)
**IPWS** ......... Iron Plate Workers' Society [*A union*] [*British*]
**IPX** ......... International Phasor Telecom [*Vancouver Stock Exchange symbol*]
**IPX** ......... Internetwork Packet Exchange
**IPXI** ......... Intrinsic Peroxidase Inhibition Solution [*Clinical chemistry*]
**IPY** ......... Inches per Year
**IPY** ......... International Phoenix Energy [*Vancouver Stock Exchange symbol*]
**IPY** ......... International Polar Year
**IPY** ......... Ion Pair Yield
**IPZ** ......... George A. Zeller Zone Center, Professional Library, Peoria, IL [*Library symbol*] [*Library of Congress*] (LCLS)
**IPZ** ......... Investment Promotion Zone
**IPZ** ......... IPC International Prospector [*Vancouver Stock Exchange symbol*]
**IPZ** ......... World Book - Childcraft International, Inc., Research Library, Chicago, IL [*OCLC symbol*] (OCLC)
**IPZP** ......... Iranian Peace Zebra Program [*Military*] (MCD)
**IQ** ......... Caribbean Airways [*Barbados*] [*ICAO designator*] (FAAC)
**IQ** ......... I Quit [*Smoking*]
**IQ** ......... Ideal Quota [*Vitamin supplement*] [*British*]
**IQ** ......... Idem Quod [*The Same As*] [*Latin*]
**IQ** ......... Import Quota System [*Japan*] (IMH)
**I/Q** ......... In Phase/Quadrature (MCD)
**IQ** ......... Indefinite Quantity (AFM)
**IQ** ......... India Quarterly [*A publication*]
**IQ** ......... Inflation Quotient
**IQ** ......... Inquix Consulting Ltd. [*Information service or system*] (EISS)
**IQ** ......... Institute of Quarrying [*British*]
**IQ** ......... Intelligence Quotient [*Psychological and educational testing*]
**IQ** ......... Internal Quality
**IQ** ......... International Quarterly of Community Health Education [*A publication*]
**IQ** ......... International Quorum of Film and Video Producers (EA)
**IQ** ......... Interrupted Quick [*Flashing*] Light [*Navigation signal*]
**IQ** ......... Investment Quality Trends [*A publication*]
**IQ** ......... Investment Quotient
**IQ** ......... Iowa Quality [*of pigs*]
**iq** ......... Iraq [*MARC country of publication code*] [*Library of Congress*] (LCCP)
**IQ** ......... Iraq [*ANSI two-letter standard code*] (CNC)
**IQ** ......... Islamic Quarterly [*A publication*]
**IQ** ......... Italian Quarterly [*A publication*]
**IQ** ......... Quincy Free Public Library, Quincy, IL [*Library symbol*] [*Library of Congress*] (LCLS)
**IQA** ......... Inertial Quality Attitude
**IQA** ......... Inspection Quality Assurance
**IQA** ......... Institute of Quality Assurance [*British*]
**IQA** ......... International Quality Award [*LIMRA*]
**IqAF** ......... Iraqi Air Force
**IQAPA** ......... Informacion de Quimica Analitica, Pura, y Aplicada a la Industria [*A publication*]
**Iqbal R** ......... Iqbal Review [*A publication*]
**IQC** ......... Industrial Quality Control
**IQC** ......... International Quality Centre
**IQC** ......... Quincy College, Quincy, IL [*Library symbol*] [*Library of Congress*] (LCLS)
**IQCH** ......... International Quarterly of Community Health Education [*A publication*]
**IQE** ......... Israel Quarterly of Economics [*A publication*]
**IQED** ......... Id Quod Erat Demonstrandum [*That Which Was to Be Proved*] [*Latin*]
**IQF** ......... Individually Quick-Frozen [*Food technology*]
**IQF** ......... Interactive Query Facility [*Data processing*]
**IQF** ......... International Quail Foundation (EA)
**IQG** ......... Great River Library System, Quincy, IL [*Library symbol*] [*Library of Congress*] (LCLS)
**IQHE** ......... Integral Quantum Hall Effect [*Solid-state physics*]
**IQI** ......... Image Quality Indicator
**IQI** ......... Instructional Quality Inventory
**IQISA** ......... Interest Questionnaire for Indian South Africans [*Vocational guidance test*]
**I Qk** ......... Interrupted Quick [*Flashing*] Light [*Navigation signal*]
**I Qk Fl** ......... Interrupted Quick Flashing Light [*Navigation signal*]
**IQL** ......... Interactive Query Language [*Digital Equipment Corp.*] [*Data processing*]
**IQL** ......... Intermediate Query Language [*Data processing*]
**IQM** ......... Qiemo [*China*] [*Airport symbol*] (OAG)
**IQMF** ......... Image Quality Merit Function [*Color image*]
**IQMH** ......... Input Queue Message Handler [*Data processing*]
**IQN** ......... Inner Quantum Number
**IQN** ......... Qingyang [*China*] [*Airport symbol*] (OAG)
**IQO** ......... Initial Quantity Order (NG)
**IQPF** ......... International Quick Printing Foundation (EA)
**IQQ** ......... Iquique [*Chile*] [*Seismograph station code, US Geological Survey*] (SEIS)
**IQQ** ......... Iquique [*Chile*] [*Airport symbol*] (OAG)
**IQR** ......... Interquartile Range
**IqR** ......... Iqbal Review [*A publication*]
**IQRC** ......... Institut Quebecois de la Recherche sur la Culture [*Database producer*]
**IQRP** ......... Interactive Query and Report Processor [*IBM Corp.*] [*Data processing*]
**IQS** ......... Institute of Quantity Surveyors [*Later, RICS*]
**IQS** ......... International "Q" Signal
**IQ & S** ......... Iron, Quinine, and Strychnine [*Elixir*]
**IQSY** ......... International Quiet Sun Year [*1964-65*] [*Also, IYQS*]
**IQT** ......... Initial Qualification Training
**IQT** ......... International Tourism Quarterly [*A publication*]
**IQT** ......... Interquest Resources Corp. [*Toronto Stock Exchange symbol*]
**IQT** ......... Iquitos [*Peru*] [*Airport symbol*] (OAG)
**IQU** ......... University of New Mexico, Albuquerque, NM [*OCLC symbol*] (OCLC)
**IQV** ......... Pekin Community High School, Pekin, IL [*OCLC symbol*] (OCLC)
**IQW** ......... Individuelle Quantitative Wert [*Mean Total Ridge Count*] [*Anatomy*]
**IQW** ......... John Wood Community College, Quincy, IL [*Library symbol*] [*Library of Congress*] (LCLS)
**IQW** ......... Western New Mexico University, Silver City, NM [*OCLC symbol*] (OCLC)
**IQX** ......... Bradford Public Library, Bradford, IL [*OCLC symbol*] (OCLC)
**IQY** ......... Inquiry [*A publication*]
**IQY** ......... Limestone High School, Bartonville, IL [*OCLC symbol*] (OCLC)
**IQZ** ......... Farmington East High School, Farmington, IL [*OCLC symbol*] (OCLC)
**IR** ......... Ice Rinks [*Public-performance tariff class*] [*British*]
**IR** ......... Ice on Runway [*Aviation*] (FAAC)
**IR** ......... IFR [*Instrument Flight Rules*] Military Training Route (FAAC)
**IR** ......... Iliff Review [*A publication*]
**IR** ......... Illumination Rate (CAAL)
**IR** ......... Illuminator RADAR (NATG)
**IR** ......... Illustration Request
**IR** ......... Image Readout [*Computer graphics*]
**IR** ......... Image Rejection
**IR** ......... Immediate Reserve [*Air Force*] [*British*]
**IR** ......... Immune Response [*Also, Ir*] [*Genetics*]
**IR** ......... Immunization Rate (AFM)
**IR** ......... Immunoreactive
**IR** ......... Improved Retrofit (CAAL)
**IR** ......... Impurity Removal Subsystem (MCD)
**IR** ......... Incident Report
**IR** ......... Inclination of the Ascending Return [*Aviation*] (NASA)
**IR** ......... Independent Research (NG)
**IR** ......... India-Rubber (DEN)
**IR** ......... Indian Rulings [*A publication*] (DLA)
**IR** ......... Indiana Railroad System
**IR** ......... Individual Recorder [*Sports*]
**IR** ......... Individual Referral (OICC)
**IR** ......... Industrial Relations
**IR** ......... Industrial Relations [*A publication*]
**IR** ......... Industrial Relations Review and Report [*A publication*]
**IR** ......... Industrial Reports [*Australia*] [*A publication*]
**I-R** ......... Industrial Research
**IR** ......... Inferior Rectus [*Muscle*] [*Anatomy*]
**IR** ......... Informal Report
**I & R** ......... Information and Referral [*Services*] [*Used to assist the handicapped*]
**IR** ......... Information Release (DLA)
**IR** ......... Information Report
**IR** ......... Information Request (AAG)
**IR** ......... Information Requirement [*Military intelligence*] (INF)
**IR** ......... Information Retrieval [*Data processing*]
**IR** ......... Infrared
**IR** ......... Infrared Radiation
**IR** ......... Infrared Radiometer
**Ir** ......... Ingenieur [*Engineer*] [*French*]
**IR** ......... Ingersoll-Rand Co. [*NYSE symbol*] (SPSG)
**IR** ......... Ingram-Rude Information Researchers [*Information service or system*] (IID)
**IR** ......... Initial Reactive Results
**IR** ......... Initial Release (MCD)
**IR** ......... Initial Reserve
**I & R** ......... Initiative and Referendum
**IR** ......... Ink Receptivity
**IR** ......... Inland Revenue [*British*]
**IR** ......... Inner Roll Gimbal (NASA)
**IR** ......... Innere Reich [*A publication*]
**IR** ......... Inside Radius [*Technical drawings*]
**IR** ......... Inside Right [*Soccer position*]
**IR** ......... Insoluble Residue
**IR** ......... Inspection Record (MCD)
**IR** ......... Inspection Rejection

**IR** ... Inspection Release
**IR** ... Inspection [*or Inspector's*] Report
**IR** ... Installation Report
**IR** ... Installation Restoration (MCD)
**IR** ... Instantaneous Relay
**IR** ... Institute of Refrigeration [*British*]
**IR** ... Instruction Register [*Data processing*]
**I/R** ... Instrument Rating [*Aviation*] (AIA)
**IR** ... Instrument Reading (AFM)
**IR** ... Instrumentation Report
**IR** ... Instrumentation Requirements (MUGU)
**IR** ... Insulation Resistance
**I & R** ... Integrity and Reliability [*Military*] (AFIT)
**IR** ... Intelligence Ratio
**I & R** ... Intelligence and Reconnaissance
**IR** ... Intelligence Report
**IR** ... Intelligence Requirement [*Military*] (INF)
**IR** ... Intelligence Review
**IR** ... Interaction Resistance [*Plant pathology*]
**I & R** ... Interchangeability and Replaceability [*or Replacement*] (AAG)
**IR** ... Intergovernmental Relations (OICC)
**IR** ... Interim Report
**IR** ... Intermediate Range (MCD)
**IR** ... Intermediate Review (NATG)
**IR** ... Internal Reliability
**IR** ... Internal Repeat [*Genetics*]
**IR** ... Internal Report
**IR** ... Internal Resistance
**IR** ... Internal Revenue
**IR** ... Internal Revenue Decisions [*Department of the Treasury*] [*A publication*] (DLA)
**IR** ... Internal Review [*Army*] (AABC)
**IR** ... Internal Rotation [*Myology*]
**IR** ... International Randonneurs [*An association*] (EA)
**IR** ... International Relations [*A publication*]
**IR** ... International Rendezvous (MCD)
**IR** ... Internationale de la Resistance [*Resistance International - RI*] (EAIO)
**IR** ... Interpretation Report
**IR** ... InterRent [*Car rental group*]
**IR** ... Interrogation Report
**IR** ... Interrogator-Responder
**IR** ... Interval Rate [*Army*] (AABC)
**IR** ... Invention Report
**IR** ... Inversion Recovery [*NMR imaging*]
**IR** ... Inverted Repeat [*Genetics*]
**IR** ... Investigation Record
**IR** ... Investment Recurring (MCD)
**IR** ... Investor Relations
**IR** ... Iowa Journal of Research in Music Education [*A publication*]
**ir** ... Iran [*MARC country of publication code*] [*Library of Congress*] (LCCP)
**IR** ... Iran [*ANSI two-letter standard code*] (CNC)
**IR** ... Iran National Airlines Corp. [*ICAO designator*] (FAAC)
**Ir** ... Iredell's North Carolina Equity Reports [*A publication*] (DLA)
**Ir** ... Iredell's North Carolina Law Reports [*A publication*] (DLA)
**IR** ... Ireland [*IYRU nationality code*] (ROG)
**Ir** ... Iridium [*Chemical element*]
**IR** ... Irish
**IR** ... Irish Law Reports [*A publication*] (DLA)
**IR** ... Irish Reports [*A publication*]
**Ir** ... Irnerius [*Flourished, 1113-18*] [*Authority cited in pre-1607 legal work*] (DSA)
**ir** ... Iron [*CIPW classification*] [*Geology*]
**IR** ... Irrelevancy [*Used in correcting manuscripts, etc.*]
**IR** ... Isoprene Rubber
**IR** ... Isotope Reactor [*USSR*]
**IR** ... Israelitische Rundschau [*Berlin*] [*A publication*]
**IR** ... Item Record (AFIT)
**I-R** ... Ito-Reenstierna [*Reaction*] [*Medicine*]
**IR** ... Iton Rishmi [*Official Gazette*] [*A publication*]
**IR** ... Izquierda Republicana [*Republican Left*] [*Spain*] [*Political party*] (PPE)
**IR** ... Journal of Irrigation and Drainage [*A publication*]
**IR** ... Rock Island Public Library, Rock Island, IL [*Library symbol*] [*Library of Congress*] (LCLS)
**IR** ... South Australian Industrial Reports [*A publication*] (APTA)
**IR1** ... Iran Long-Period Array [*Iran*] [*Seismograph station code, US Geological Survey*] (SEIS)
**I²R** ... Imaging Infrared [*Pronounced "eye-squared ar"*]
**IR2** ... Iran Long-Period Array [*Iran*] [*Seismograph station code, US Geological Survey*] (SEIS)
**IR3** ... Iran Long-Period Array [*Iran*] [*Seismograph station code, US Geological Survey*] (SEIS)
**IR4** ... Iran Long-Period Array [*Iran*] [*Seismograph station code, US Geological Survey*] (SEIS)
**IR5** ... Iran Long-Period Array [*Iran*] [*Seismograph station code, US Geological Survey*] (SEIS)
**IR6** ... Iran Long-Period Array [*Iran*] [*Seismograph station code, US Geological Survey*] (SEIS)
**IR7** ... Iran Long-Period Array [*Iran*] [*Seismograph station code, US Geological Survey*] (SEIS)
**IRA** ... Augustana College, Rock Island, IL [*Library symbol*] [*Library of Congress*] (LCLS)
**IRA** ... Ileorectal Anastomosis [*Medicine*]
**IRA** ... Immunoregulatory alpha-Globulin [*Immunology*]
**IRA** ... Independent Regulatory Agency [*US Government*]
**IRA** ... Indian Registration Act [*British*] (ROG)
**IRA** ... Indian Reorganization Act (OICC)
**IRA** ... Indian Rights Association (EA)
**IRA** ... Individual Retirement Account
**IRA** ... Individual Retirement Annuity [*Insurance*]
**IRA** ... Industrial Relations Act [*1971*] [*British*] (DCTA)
**IR & A** ... Information Research and Analysis [*Oak Ridge National Laboratory*] [*Oak Ridge, TN*] [*Department of Energy*] (GRD)
**IRA** ... Information Resource Administration
**IRA** ... Input Reference Axis (IEEE)
**IRA** ... Inspector of the Royal Artillery [*British*]
**IRA** ... Inspector's Report Addendum (AAG)
**IRA** ... Institute of Registered Architects [*British*]
**IRA** ... Integrated RADOME [*RADAR Dome*] Antenna
**IRA** ... Intelligence Related Activities [*Military*] (MCD)
**IRA** ... Intercollegiate Rowing Association (EA)
**IRA** ... Internal Revenue Act
**IRA** ... International Racquetball Association [*Later, AARA*] (EA)
**IRA** ... International Reading Association (EA)
**IRA** ... International Recreation Association [*Later, WLRA*]
**IRA** ... International Reprographics Association (EA)
**IRA** ... International Review of Administrative Sciences [*A publication*]
**IRA** ... International Rodeo Association (EA)
**IRA** ... International Roleo Association [*Later, International Log Rolling Association*] (EA)
**IRA** ... International Rubber Association [*Kuala Lumpur, Malaysia*] (EAIO)
**IRA** ... Internationale Rundschau der Arbeit [*A publication*]
**IRA** ... Investment Recovery Association (EA)
**ira** ... Iranian [*MARC language code*] [*Library of Congress*] (LCCP)
**IRA** ... Iranian Airways Co.
**IRA** ... Irish Republican Army
**IRA** ... Iron Age [*A publication*]
**IRA** ... Ithaca Railroad Association [*Defunct*] (EA)
**IRA** ... Kira Kira [*Solomon Islands*] [*Airport symbol*] (OAG)
**IRA** ... Rutland, VT [*Location identifier*] [*FAA*] (FAAL)
**IRAA** ... Independent Refiners Association of America [*Later, AIRA*] (EA)
**IRAA & A** .. Increase and Replacement of Armor, Armament, and Ammunition [*Naval budget appropriation title*]
**IRAAM** ... Improved Remote-Area Armor Mine (MCD)
**IRAB** ... Index to Reviews of Australian Books [*A publication*]
**IRAC** ... Indochina Resource Action Center (EA)
**IRAC** ... Information Resources Administration Councils [*General Services Administration*] [*Washington, DC*] (EGAO)
**IRAC** ... Infrared Advisory Center
**IRAC** ... Infrared Array Camera
**IRAC** ... Intelligence Resources Advisory Committee [*To supervise US intelligence budget*]
**IRAC** ... Interdepartment Radio Advisory Committee [*Department of Commerce*] (EGAO)
**IRAC** ... Interfraternity Research and Advisory Council [*Defunct*] (EA)
**IRAC** ... Interim Rapid Action Change (MCD)
**IR & AC** ... Internal Review and Audit Compliance [*Army*]
**IRACOR** ... Infrared Acquisition RADAR (MSA)
**IRACQ** ... Infrared Acquisition RADAR
**IRACQ** ... Instrumentation RADAR and Acquisition
**IRACQ** ... Instrumented Range Acquisition (KSC)
**IRACT** ... Incident Response Action Coordination Team [*Nuclear energy*] (NRCH)
**IRAD** ... Inbound Radial [*Aviation*] (FAAC)
**IRAD** ... Independent Research and Development
**IRAD** ... Infrared Ambush Device
**IRAD** ... Institute for Research on Animal Diseases [*British*]
**IRAD** ... Institutional Research and Development Office [*Kirksville College of Osteopathic Medicine*] [*Research center*] (RCD)
**IRADDS** ... Infrared Air Defense Detection System
**IRAF** ... Individual Retirement Account File [*IRS*]
**Ir Age Int** ... Iron Age Metalworking International [*Later, Chilton's IAMI Iron Age Metalworking International*] [*A publication*]
**IRAH** ... Infrared Active Homing (MCD)
**IRAH** ... Infrared Alternate Head
**IRAL** ... International Review of Applied Linguistics in Language Teaching [*A publication*]
**IR All** ... Indian Rulings, Allahabad Series [*A publication*] (DLA)
**IRAM** ... Improved Reliability and Maintainability
**IRAM** ... Institut de Recherches et d'Applications des Methodes de Developpement [*Institute of Research and Application of Development Methods - IRAM*] (EAIO)
**IRAM** ... Integrated Random-Access Memory [*Data processing*]

**IRAMD** ..... International Review of the Aesthetics and Sociology of Music [*A publication*]
**IRAN** ......... Inspect and Repair as Necessary [*Aviation*]
**Iran** ........... Iran Journal. British Institute of Persian Studies [*A publication*]
**IRAN** ......... Iranian [*Language, etc.*] (ROG)
**IRAN** ......... Izvestiia Rossiiskoi Akademii Nauk [*A publication*]
**Iran Antiq** .. Iranica Antiqua [*A publication*]
**IRanASD**... Allen Township Consolidated Community School District 65, Ransom, IL [*Library symbol*] [*Library of Congress*] (LCLS)
**Iran Dep Bot Minist Agric Dev Rural** ... Iran. Departement de Botanique. Ministere de l'Agriculture et du Developpement Rural [*A publication*]
**IRANDOC** ... Iranian Documentation Centre [*Ministry of Culture and Higher Education*] [*Tehran*]
**IRANF**....... Immunoreactive Atrial Natriuretic Factor
**Iran Geol Surv Rep** ... Iran Geological Survey. Report [*A publication*]
**Iranian R Internat Relations** ... Iranian Review of International Relations [*A publication*]
**Iranica Ant** ... Iranica Antiqua [*A publication*]
**Iran J Agric Res** ... Iranian Journal of Agricultural Research [*A publication*]
**Iran J Agric Sci** ... Iranian Journal of Agricultural Sciences [*A publication*]
**Iran J Plant Pathol** ... Iranian Journal of Plant Pathology [*A publication*]
**Iran J Public Health** ... Iranian Journal of Public Health [*A publication*]
**Iran J Sci and Technol** ... Iranian Journal of Science and Technology [*A publication*]
**Iran J Sci Technol** ... Iranian Journal of Science and Technology [*A publication*]
**Iran Plant Pests Dis Res Inst Dep Bot Publ** ... Iran Plant Pests and Diseases Research Institute. Department of Botany. Publication [*A publication*]
**Iran R Int Relat** ... Iranian Review of International Relations [*A publication*]
**IranS**.......... Iranian Studies [*A publication*]
**IRANSAT** ... Iranian Government Communications Satellite [*NASA*] (NASA)
**Iran Stud**.... Iranian Studies [*A publication*]
**IrAnt**.......... Iranica Antiqua [*Leiden*] [*A publication*]
**IRant**.......... Rantoul Public Library, Rantoul, IL [*Library symbol*] [*Library of Congress*] (LCLS)
**IRAP**.......... Industrial Research Assistance Program [*Canada*]
**IRAP**.......... Interagency Radiological Assistance Program [*Nuclear Regulatory Commission*] (NRCH)
**Iraqi Chem Soc J** ... Iraqi Chemical Society. Journal [*A publication*]
**Iraqi Dent J** ... Iraqi Dental Journal [*A publication*]
**Iraqi Geogr J** ... Iraqi Geographical Journal [*A publication*]
**Iraqi J Sci** .. Iraqi Journal of Science [*A publication*]
**Iraq Nat Hist Mus Publ** ... Iraq Natural History Museum. Publication [*A publication*]
**Iraq Nat Hist Mus Rep** ... Iraq Natural History Museum. Report [*A publication*]
**IRAR**.......... Impulse Response Area Ratio
**IRAR**.......... Individual Retirement Account Register [*IRS*]
**IRAR**.......... Infrared Augmentation Reliability (MCD)
**Ir Archaeol Res Forum** ... Irish Archaeological Research Forum [*A publication*]
**IRAS**.......... Infrared Astronomical Satellite [*NASA*] (MCD)
**IRAS**.......... Infrared Attack System
**IRAS**.......... Infrared Reflection Absorption Spectroscopy [*Also, IRRAS, RAIR, RAIRS, RAIS*]
**IRAS**.......... Institute on Religion in an Age of Science (EA)
**IRAS**.......... Integrated RADOME [*RADAR Dome*] Antenna Structure
**IRAS**.......... Iranica Antiqua. Supplements [*A publication*]
**IRASA**....... International Radio Air Safety Association
**IRASER**...... Infrared Amplification by Stimulated Emission of Radiation
**IRASER**...... Infrared MASER (CET)
**IRASI**........ Internal Review and System Improvement [*Army*]
**IRASM**...... International Review of the Aesthetics and Sociology of Music [*A publication*]
**Ira Stud**...... Iranian Studies [*A publication*]
**IRAT**.......... Institut de Recherche Appliquee sur le Travail [*Canada*]
**IRAT**.......... Institut de Recherches Agronomiques Tropicales et des Cultures Vivrieres [*Food and agricultural research foundation supported by France and several African states*]
**IRATE**....... Intelligence Review and Assessment Task Element [*Study of the effectiveness of the air war in Southeast Asia*]
**IRATE**....... Interim Remote Area Terminal Equipment [*Air Force*]
**IRAWS**...... Infrared Attack Weapon System
**IRayL**......... Lincolnwood Community Reading Center, Raymond, IL [*Library symbol*] [*Library of Congress*] (LCLS)
**IRaySD**...... Panhandle Community Unit, School District 2, Raymond IL [*Library symbol*] [*Library of Congress*] (LCLS)
**IRB**............. Improved Rotor Blade [*Rotorcraft*]
**IRB**............. Impulse Resistance Bridge
**IRB**............. Individual Records Brief [*Military*] (AABC)
**IRB**............. Inducto-Ratio Bridge
**IRB**............. Industrial Readjustment Branch
**IRB**............. Industrial Relations Board [*Navy*]
**IRB**............. Industrial Relations Bulletin [*A publication*] (AAG)
**IRB**............. Industrial Revenue Bond
**IRB**............. Inflatable Rescue Boat
**IRB**............. Informationszentrum Raum und Bau [*Information Center for Regional Planning and Building Construction*] [*Federal Republic of Germany*] [*Information service or system*] (IID)
**IRB**............. Infrared Brazing
**IRB**............. Inner Radiation Belt
**IRB**............. Inside Reactor Building (NRCH)
**IRB**............. Inspection Review Board (KSC)
**IRB**............. Institutional Review Board
**IRB**............. Insurance Rating Board [*Later, ISO*]
**IRB**............. Internal Revenue Bulletin
**IRB**............. International Resources Bank
**IRB**............. International Rice Bran Industries Ltd. [*Vancouver Stock Exchange symbol*]
**IRB**............. International Rugby Board
**IRB**............. Interrupt Request Block (CMD)
**IRB**............. Irish Republican Brotherhood
**IRB**............. Iron Rotating Band
**IRB**............. Irregular Route Motor Carriers Bureau, Oklahoma City OK [*STAC*]
**IRb**............. Red Bud Public Library, Red Bud, IL [*Library symbol*] [*Library of Congress*] (LCLS)
**IRBA**.......... International Rhythm and Blues Association (EA)
**IRBAA**....... Bulletin. Institut International du Froid. Annexe [*A publication*]
**IRBB**.......... Institut Royal Colonial Belge. Bulletin des Seances [*A publication*]
**IRBBB**....... Incomplete Right Bundle Branch Block [*Cardiology*]
**IRBEL**....... Indexed References to Biomedical Engineering Literature [*A publication*] (IID)
**Ir Birds**....... Irish Birds [*A publication*]
**IRBM**......... Intermediate-Range Ballistic Missile
**IRBO**.......... Infrared Homing Bomb (IEEE)
**IR Bom**....... Indian Rulings, Bombay Series [*A publication*] (DLA)
**IRBP**.......... Interstitial Retinol-Binding Protein [*Biochemistry*]
**IRbSCH**..... Saint Clement Hospital, Red Bud, IL [*Library symbol*] [*Library of Congress*] (LCLS)
**IRC**............ Circle [*Alaska*] [*Airport symbol*] (OAG)
**IRC**............ Incident Response Center [*Nuclear Regulatory Commission*] (NRCH)
**IRC**............ Independent Record Charts (EA)
**IRC**............ Indications Review Committee [*Military*] (CINC)
**IRC**............ Industrial Relations Center [*University of Minnesota*] [*Research center*] (RCD)
**IRC**............ Industrial Relations Commission [*Australia*]
**IRC**............ Industrial Relations Council for the Plumbing and Pipe Fitting Industry [*Chicago, IL*] (EA)
**IRC**............ Industrial Relations Counselors [*New York, NY*] (EA)
**IRC**............ INEL [*Idaho National Engineering Laboratory*] Research Center [*Idaho Falls, ID*] [*Department of Energy*] (GRD)
**IRC**............ Information Recovery Capsule
**IRC**............ Information Research Center (DIT)
**IRC**............ Information Resource Consultants [*Information service or system*] (IID)
**IRC**............ Information Resources Center [*of Mental Health Materials Center*]
**IRC**............ Information Retrieval Center [*BBDO International*] [*Information service or system*] (IID)
**IRC**............ Infrared Countermeasures [*Military electronics*]
**IRC**............ Initiative Resource Center (EA)
**IRC**............ Inland Revenue Commissioners [*British*]
**IRC**............ Inspection Record Card [*Navy*] (NG)
**IRC**............ Inspiration Resources Corp. [*NYSE symbol*] [*Toronto Stock Exchange symbol*] (SPSG)
**IRC**............ Institute for Research in Construction [*National Research Council of Canada*] [*Database producer*] (IID)
**IRC**............ Institutional Research Council [*Defunct*] (EA)
**IRC**............ Institutional Review Committee [*Generic term*]
**IRC**............ Insurance Research Council (EA)
**IRC**............ Integrated Radio Control (NVT)
**IRC**............ Inter-Regional Capital Account [*Inter-American Development Bank*]
**IRC**............ Interchange Resource Center (EA)
**IRC**............ Interdisciplinary Research Centre [*British*]
**IRC**............ Intergovernmental Refugee Committee [*London*] [*World War II*]
**IRC**............ Internal Revenue Code
**IRC**............ International Radiation Commission [*of the International Association of Meteorology and Atmospheric Physics*] (EAIO)
**IRC**............ International Rainwear Council
**IRC**............ International Rating Class [*Yachting*]
**IRC**............ International Record Carrier [*Telecommunication companies providing international service*] (TSSD)
**IRC**............ International Record Carrier, Inc. [*Telecommunications*]
**IRC**............ International Red Cross and Red Crescent Movement (EAIO)
**IRC**............ International Relations Committee [*American Library Association*]
**IRC**............ International Reply Coupon
**IRC**............ International Rescue Committee (EA)
**IRC**............ International Research Council [*Later, ICSU*]

**IRC** ........... International Resistance Company (AAG)
**IRC** ........... International Resistor Center
**IRC** ........... International Rice Commission [*See also CIR*] (EAIO)
**IRC** ........... Ion Recombination Chamber
**IRC** ........... Ionosphere Research Committee (MCD)
**IRC** ........... Iraqi Communist Party [*Political party*] [*Also, ICP*] (MENA)
**IRC** ........... IRC International Water and Sanitation Centre [*Acronym is based on former name, International Reference Centre for Community Water Supply and Sanitation*] (EAIO)
**IRC** ........... Iron Canyon [*California*] [*Seismograph station code, US Geological Survey*] (SEIS)
**IRC** ........... Ironclad
**IRC** ........... Irregular Route Carrier
**IRC** ........... Item Responsibility Code
**IRC** ........... Steel Times (Redhill) [*A publication*]
**IRCA**.......... Immigration Reform and Control Act of 1986
**IRCA**.......... International Radio Club of America (EA)
**IRCA**.......... International Ragdoll Cat Association (EA)
**IRCA**.......... International Railway Congress Association [*Belgium*]
**IRCA**.......... International Remodeling Contractors Association (EA)
**IR Cal**......... Indian Rulings, Calcutta Series [*A publication*] (DLA)
**IRCAR**....... International Reference Center for Abortion Research (IID)
**IRCAS** ....... Information Requirements Control Automated System [*Defense Supply Service/Pentagon*] (AABC)
**IRCAT** ....... Infrared Radiometer Clear Air Turbulence [*Instrument*]
**IRC Bull**..... IRC [*Indian Roads Congress*] Bulletin [*A publication*]
**IRCC**.......... Instruction and Research Computer Center [*Ohio State University*] [*Research center*] (RCD)
**IRCC**.......... International Radio Consultative Committee
**IRCC**.......... International Record Collectors' Club [*Record label*]
**IRCC**.......... International Red Cross Committee [*World War II*]
**IRCCD**........ Infrared Charge-Coupled Device
**IRCCM**...... Infrared Counter-Countermeasures [*Military electronics*]
**IRCCOPR** ... Inter-Research Council Committee on Pollution Research [*British*]
**IRCD** ......... Information Retrieval Center on the Disadvantaged [*ERIC*]
**IRCD** ......... International Research Centers Directory [*A publication*]
**IRCD-A** ..... International Review of Community Development [*A publication*]
**IRCD Bul**... Yeshiva University. Information Retrieval Center on the Disadvantaged. Bulletin [*A publication*]
**IRCDP**....... International Research Career Development Program [*Public Health Service*]
**Ir Ch**........... Irish Chancery Reports [*A publication*] (DLA)
**Ir Ch Rep** ... Irish Chancery Reports [*A publication*] (DLA)
**IRCICA** ..... Research Centre for Islamic History, Art, and Culture [*of the Organization of the Islamic Conference*] (EAIO)
**IRCIHE**..... International Referral Center for Information Handling Equipment [*Yugoslavia*] [*UNESCO*] (IID)
**Ir Cir** .......... Irish Circuit Reports [*1841-43*] [*A publication*] (DLA)
**Ir Cir Cas**... Crawford and Dix's Irish Circuit Court Cases [*A publication*] (DLA)
**Ir Circ Cas** ... Irish Circuit Cases [*A publication*] (DLA)
**Ir Circ Rep** ... Irish Circuit Reports [*1841-43*] [*A publication*] (DLA)
**Ir Cir Rep**... Reports of Irish Circuit Cases [*A publication*] (DLA)
**IRCL**.......... International Research Centre on Lindane [*See also CIEL*] [*Brussels, Belgium*] (EAIO)
**Ir CL** .......... Irish Common Law Reports [*A publication*] (DLA)
**IRCL**.......... Irish Reports, Common Law Series [*A publication*] (DLA)
**IRCM**......... Impot sur les Revenues de Capitaux Mobilier [*French*] (IMH)
**IRC & M**.... Increase and Replacement of Construction and Machinery [*Naval budget appropriation title*]
**IRCM**......... Infrared Countermeasures [*Military electronics*] (NVT)
**IRCM**......... Integrated Relay Controller Module [*Ford Motor Co.*] [*Automotive engineering*]
**IRCM**......... Intermediate Range Cruise Missile [*Military*] (CAAL)
**IRCN** ......... Interagency Report Control Number
**IRCND** ...... International Research Council of Neuromuscular Disorders (EA)
**IRCO** ......... International Rubber Conference Organization [*London, England*] (EAIO)
**IRCOBI** ..... International Research Committee on the Biokinetics of Impacts [*Later, International Research Council on the Biokinetics of Impacts*] (EAIO)
**Ir Com Law Rep** ... Irish Common Law Reports [*A publication*] (DLA)
**Ir Com L Rep** ... Irish Common Law Reports [*A publication*] (DLA)
**Ir Comput**... Irish Computer [*A publication*]
**IR Comrs** ... Inland Revenue Commissioners [*England*] (DLA)
**IRCOPPS** ... Interprofessional Research Commission on Pupil Personnel Services [*Defunct*]
**IRCP**.......... Intermediate Range Construction Program [*Military*]
**IRCPA** ....... IRE [*Institute of Radio Engineers*] Transactions on Component Parts [*A publication*]
**IRCPAL**..... International Research Council on Pure and Applied Linguistics (EA)
**IRCPPFI** ... Industrial Relations Council for the Plumbing and Pipe Fitting Industry (EA)
**IRCPUBS** ... Publications of the Institute for Research in Construction [*National Research Council of Canada*] [*Information service or system*] (IID)
**IRCS** .......... Inertial Reference and Control System [*Aerospace*] (AAG)
**IRCS**.......... Infrared Communications System
**IRCS**.......... International Radio Call Sign
**IRCS**.......... International Research Communications System [*Electronic journal publisher*] [*British*]
**IRCS**.......... Intersite Radio Communications System (MCD)
**IRCS**.......... Italian Red Cross Society
**IRCSA** ....... International Reference Collection of Soybean Arthropods [*INTSOY*]
**IRCSI**......... International Rabbinic Committee for the Safety of Israel (EA)
**IRCS (Int Res Commun Syst) Med Sci** ... IRCS (International Research Communications System) Medical Science [*A publication*]
**IRCS Med Sci-Libr Compend** ... IRCS [*International Research Communications System*] Medical Science. Library Compendium [*A publication*]
**IRCT**.......... Institut de Recherches du Coton et des Textiles Exotiques [*Institute for Research in Cotton and Exotic Textiles*] [*International Cooperation Center of Agricultural Research for Development*] [*Information service or system*] (IID)
**IRCT**.......... International Research on Communist Techniques
**IRCTD**....... IRCS [*International Research Communications System*] Research on Clinical Pharmacology and Therapeutics [*A publication*]
**IRCYA**....... International Review of Cytology [*A publication*]
**IRD** ........... Ice-Rafted Debris [*Oceanography*]
**IRD** ........... Immune Renal Disease [*Medicine*]
**IRD** ........... Income in Respect of a Decedent [*Banking*]
**IR & D**........ Independent Research and Development
**IR & D**........ Industrial Research and Development
**IRD** ........... Information Requirements Description [*or Document*] (KSC)
**IRD** ........... Infrared Detector
**IRD** ........... Infrared Display
**IRD** ........... Initiating Reference Document (MCD)
**IRD** ........... Inland Rail Depot (DCTA)
**IRD** ........... Institute on Religion and Democracy (EA)
**I/RD**.......... Institutes and Research Divisions [*National Institutes of Health*]
**IRD** ........... Interface Requirements Document
**IRD** ........... Internal Revenue Department
**IRD** ........... International Research and Development
**IRD** ........... International Research & Development Co. Ltd. [*British*] (IRUK)
**IRD** ........... International Resource Development, Inc. [*Norwalk, CT*] [*Telecommunications*] [*Information service or system*] (IID)
**IRD** ........... Iron Lady Resources [*Vancouver Stock Exchange symbol*]
**IRD** ........... Ishurdi [*Bangladesh*] [*Airport symbol*] (OAG)
**IRD** ........... Isotopes and Radiation Division [*American Nuclear Society*]
**IRD** ........... Itinerant Recruiting Detail
**IRDA** ......... Infrared Detection Array
**IRDA** ......... Interactive Route Development and Analysis (CAAL)
**IRDB**.......... Information Retrieval Databank (IEEE)
**IR & D/B & P** ... Independent Research and Development/Bid and Proposal
**IRDC** ......... Intelligence Research and Development Council (MCD)
**IRDC** ......... International Road Documentation Center
**IRDC** ......... International Rubber Development Committee
**Ir Dent J** .... Irish Dental Journal [*A publication*]
**IRDF**.......... Interactive Report Definition Facility (MCD)
**IRDG** ......... Inter-Range Documentation Group [*White Sands Missile Range*]
**IRDHS**....... Imagery Related Data Handling System (MCD)
**IRDL**.......... Information Retrieval and Display Language [*Data processing*] (AABC)
**IRDLO**....... Infantry Research and Development Liaison Office [*Army*] (RDA)
**IRDM** ........ International Rendezvous and Docking Mission [*Aerospace*]
**IRDN** ......... Illinois Resource and Dissemination Network [*Illinois State Board of Education*] [*Information service or system*] [*No longer in operation*] (IID)
**IRDN**......... Important Risk Data Notice [*Insurance*]
**IRDN**......... Industrial Research and Development News [*A publication*]
**IRD News**.. News from International Resource Development, Incorporated [*A publication*]
**IRDO** ......... Infrared Drying Oven
**IRDO** ......... Intermediate Retention of Differential Overlap [*Physics*]
**IRDOE** ...... Institute for Research and Development in Occupational Education [*City University of New York*] [*Research center*] (RCD)
**IRDP**.......... Icelandic Research Drilling Project
**IRDP**.......... Industrial Regional Development Program [*Canada*]
**IRDS**.......... Idiopathic Respiratory Distress Syndrome [*Pediatrics*]
**IRDS**.......... Infant Respiratory Distress Syndrome [*Medicine*]
**IRDS**.......... Infrared Detecting Set [*or System*] (MCD)
**IRDS**.......... Integrated Reliability Data System (AAG)
**IRD & S** ..... International Research, Development, and Standardization [*Division*] [*Army*] (RDA)
**IRDU** ......... Infrared Detection Unit
**IRDV** ......... International Research & Development Corp. [*NASDAQ symbol*] (NQ)
**IRE**............ IFF Reply Evaluator
**IRE**............ Immediate Ready Element [*Military*] (AABC)
**IRE**............ Infrared Emission

**IRE**............ Institute of Radio Engineers [*Later, IEEE*]
**IRE**............ Institute for Responsive Education (EA)
**IRE**............ Integrated Resources, Inc. [*NYSE symbol*] (SPSG)
**IRE**............ Intelligence Resources [*Program*] [*Department of State*]
**IRE**............ Interferon Regulatory Element [*Biochemistry*]
**IRE**............ Internal Reflection Element [*Spectroscopy*]
**IRE**............ International Association of Railway Employees
**IRE**............ International Research and Evaluation [*Research Center*] [*Also, an information service or system*] (IID)
**IRE**............ International Retail Systems, Inc. [*Toronto Stock Exchange symbol*] [*Vancouver Stock Exchange symbol*]
**IRE**............ International Royal Enterprises (EA)
**IRE**............ Investigative Reporters and Editors (EA)
**IRE**............ Ireland
**IRE**............ Iron Replacement Element [*Biosynthesis*]
**IRE**............ Iron-Responsive Element [*Genetics*]
**i-re---**.......... Reunion [*MARC geographic area code*] [*Library of Congress*] (LCCP)
**IREB**.......... Intense Relativistic Electron Beams [*Physics*]
**IREBI**........ Indices de Revista de Bibliotecologia [*A publication*]
**IRE-BP**...... Iron-Responsive Element - Binding Protein
**IREC**.......... Increase and Replacement of Emergency Construction [*Ships*] [*Naval budget appropriation title*]
**IREC**.......... International Registry of Early Corvettes (EA)
**IREC**.......... International Rotary Engine Club [*Later, RX-7 Club of America*] (EA)
**IRECA**....... International Rescue and Emergency Care Association (EA)
**Ir Eccl**........ Irish Ecclesiastical Reports, by Milward [*1819-43*] [*A publication*] (DLA)
**IrEccRec**.... Irish Ecclesiastical Record [*A publication*]
**Ir Econ Soc Hist**... Irish Economic and Social History [*A publication*]
**IRECUS**.... Sherbrooke University Institut de Recherche et d'Enseignement pour les Cooperatives [*Canada*] [*Research center*] (RCD)
**IRED**.......... Infrared-Emitting Diode (IEEE)
**IRED**.......... Innovations et Reseaux pour le Developpement [*Development Innovations and Networks*] [*Geneva, Switzerland*] (EAIO)
**Ired**............ Iredell's North Carolina Equity Reports [*36-43 North Carolina*] [*A publication*] (DLA)
**Ired Dig**...... Iredell's North Carolina Digest [*A publication*] (DLA)
**Ired Eq**....... Iredell's North Carolina Equity Reports [*36-43 North Carolina*] [*A publication*] (DLA)
**Ired Eq (NC)**... Iredell's North Carolina Equity Reports [*36-43 North Carolina*] [*A publication*] (DLA)
**Ired L**......... Iredell's North Carolina Equity Reports [*36-43 North Carolina*] [*A publication*] (DLA)
**Ired L (NC)**... Iredell's North Carolina Law Reports [*A publication*] (DLA)
**IreDNL**...... National Library of Ireland, Dublin, Ireland [*Library symbol*] [*Library of Congress*] (LCLS)
**IreDR**......... Royal Dublin Society, Ballsbridge, Dublin, Ireland [*Library symbol*] [*Library of Congress*] (LCLS)
**IreDT**......... Trinity College, University of Dublin, Dublin, Ireland [*Library symbol*] [*Library of Congress*] (LCLS)
**IREE**.......... Institut de Recherches et d'Etudes Europeennes [*Institute of European Research and Studies*] (EAIO)
**IREF**.......... International Real Estate Federation
**IREG**.......... Irregular (FAAC)
**IREH**......... Institute for Rural Environmental Health [*Colorado State University*] [*Research center*] (RCD)
**IREHR**....... Institute for Research and Education on Human Rights (EA)
**IREI**........... International Real Estate Institute (EA)
**IRE Int Conv Rec**... IRE [*Institute of Radio Engineers*] International Convention Record [*A publication*]
**IRE-ITTD**... International Research and Evaluation - Information and Technology Transfer Database [*International Research and Evaluation*] [*Information service or system*] (CRD)
**IREL**.......... Australian Industrial Relations Database [*Brisbane College of Advanced Education*] [*Information service or system*] (IID)
**Irel Dep Fish For Trade Inf Sect Fish Leafl**... Ireland. Department of Fisheries and Forestry. Trade and Information Section. Fishery Leaflet [*A publication*]
**Ireld Yrbk**.. Ireland Administration. Yearbook and Diary [*A publication*]
**Irel Geol Surv Bull**... Ireland. Geological Survey. Bulletin [*A publication*]
**Irel Natl Soil Surv Soil Surv Bull**... Ireland National Soil Survey. Soil Survey Bulletin [*A publication*]
**IREM**......... Incorporation of Readiness into Effectivenss Modeling (MCD)
**IREM**......... Institut de Recherche en Exploration Minerale [*Mineral Exploration Research Institute*] [*Canada*] [*Research center*] (RCD)
**IREM**......... Institute of Real Estate Management [*Chicago, IL*] (EA)
**IREM**......... Integrated Regional Environmental Management Project (EA)
**IREMAM**... Institut de Recherches et d'Etudes sur le Monde Arabe et Musulman [*Institute for Research and Studies on the Arab and Muslim World*] [*France*] [*Information service or system*] (IID)
**Iren**............ Irenikon [*A publication*]
**IREP**.......... Integrated Reliability Evaluation Program [*Nuclear energy*] (NRCH)
**IREP**.......... Interdisciplinary Research Equipment Program
**IREP**.......... Interim Reliability Evaluation Program [*Nuclear energy*]
**IREPS**........ Integrated Refractive Effects Prediction System [*Military*] (CAAL)
**IREQ**......... Institut de Recherche d'Hydro-Quebec [*Canada*]
**IR Eq**......... Irish Reports, Equity Series [*A publication*] (DLA)
**Ir Eq Rep**... Irish Equity Reports [*A publication*] (DLA)
**IRER**......... Infrared Extra Rapid (ADA)
**IrERec**........ Irish Ecclesiastical Record [*Dublin*] [*A publication*]
**IRES**.......... Institute for Resource and Environmental Studies [*Dalhousie University*] [*Canada*] [*Research center*] (RCD)
**IRES**.......... IOC [*Intergovernmental Oceanographic Commission*] Group of Experts on Oceanographic Research as It Relates to IGOSS [*Marine science*] (MSC)
**IRET**.......... Institute for Rational-Emotive Therapy (EA)
**IRET**.......... Institute for Research on the Economics of Taxation [*Research center*] (RCD)
**IRETIJ**...... Institut de Recherches et d'Etudes pour le Traitement de l'Information Juridique [*Institute of Research and Study for the Treatment of Legal Information*] [*University of Montpellier*] [*Information service or system*] (IID)
**IRE Trans Aeronaut Navig Electron**... IRE [*Institute of Radio Engineers*] Transactions on Aeronautical and Navigational Electronics [*A publication*]
**IRE Trans Aerosp Navig Electron**... IRE [*Institute of Radio Engineers*] Transactions on Aerospace and Navigational Electronics [*A publication*]
**IRE Trans Audio**... IRE [*Institute of Radio Engineers*] Transactions on Audio [*A publication*]
**IRE Trans Autom Control**... IRE [*Institute of Radio Engineers*] Transactions on Automatic Control [*A publication*]
**IRE Trans Bio Med Electron**... IRE [*Institute of Radio Engineers*] Transactions on Bio-Medical Electronics [*A publication*]
**IRE Trans Broadcast**... IRE [*Institute of Radio Engineers*] Transactions on Broadcasting [*A publication*]
**IRE Trans Broadcast Telev Receivers**... IRE [*Institute of Radio Engineers*] Transactions on Broadcast and Television Receivers [*A publication*]
**IRE Trans Broadcast Transm Syst**... IRE [*Institute of Radio Engineers*] Transactions on Broadcast Transmission Systems [*A publication*]
**IRE Trans Circuit Theory**... IRE [*Institute of Radio Engineers*] Transactions on Circuit Theory [*A publication*]
**IRE Trans Commun Syst**... IRE [*Institute of Radio Engineers*] Transactions on Communications Systems [*A publication*]
**IRE Trans Component Parts**... IRE [*Institute of Radio Engineers*] Transactions on Component Parts [*A publication*]
**IRE Trans Electron Comput**... IRE [*Institute of Radio Engineers*] Transactions on Electronic Computers [*A publication*]
**IRE Trans Inform Theory**... Institute of Radio Engineers. Transactions on Information Theory [*A publication*]
**IRE Trans Instrum**... IRE [*Institute of Radio Engineers*] Transactions on Instrumentation [*A publication*]
**IRE Trans Microwave Theory Tech**... IRE [*Institute of Radio Engineers*] Transactions on Microwave Theory and Techniques [*A publication*]
**IRE Trans Mil Electron**... IRE [*Institute of Radio Engineers*] Transactions on Military Electronics [*A publication*]
**IRE Trans Nucl Sci**... IRE [*Institute of Radio Engineers*] Transactions on Nuclear Science [*A publication*]
**IRE Trans Prod Tech**... IRE [*Institute of Radio Engineers*] Transactions on Production Techniques [*A publication*]
**IRE Trans Reliab Qual Control**... IRE [*Institute of Radio Engineers*] Transactions on Reliability and Quality Control [*A publication*]
**IRE Trans Telem Remote Control**... IRE [*Institute of Radio Engineers*] Transactions on Telemetry and Remote Control [*A publication*]
**IRE Trans Ultrason Eng**... IRE [*Institute of Radio Engineers*] Transactions on Ultrasonics Engineering [*A publication*]
**IRE Trans Veh Commun**... IRE [*Institute of Radio Engineers*] Transactions on Vehicular Communications [*A publication*]
**IRETS**......... Infantry Remote Targeting System [*Army*] (RDA)
**IREW**......... Infrared Electronic Warfare
**IRE WESCON Conv Rec**... IRE [*Institute of Radio Engineers*] WESCON [*Western Electronics Show and Convention*] Convention Record [*A publication*]
**IREWS**...... Infrared Early Warning System
**IREX**.......... Ideas, Resources, Exchange [*Computer*] [*British*]
**IREX**.......... International Research and Exchanges Board (EA)
**IRF**............ Immediate Reaction Force [*Military*] (AABC)
**IRF**............ Induced Radiation Flux
**IRF**............ Inducing Resistance Factor [*Plant pathology*]
**IRF**............ Input Register Full
**IRF**............ Instrument Response Function
**IRF**............ Intermittent Reinforcement [*Psychology*]
**IRF**............ International Rectifier Corp. [*NYSE symbol*] (SPSG)
**IRF**............ International Reform Federation (EA)
**IRF**............ International Religious Fellowship (EA)
**IRF**............ International Road Federation (EA)
**IRF**............ International Rowing Federation
**IRF**............ Interrogation Repetition Frequency [*RADAR beacon*]
**IRF**............ Island Resources Foundation (EA)

**IRF**............ Islands Research Foundation [*Inactive*] (EA)
**IRFA**.......... Institut de Recherches sur les Fruits et Agrumes [*Institute of Research on Fruits and Citrus Fruits*] [*International Cooperation Center of Agricultural Research for Development*] [*Database producer*]
**IRFAA**....... International Rescue and First Aid Association [*Later, IRECA*] (EA)
**IRFAP**....... International Religious Fine Art Program (EA)
**IRFB**......... International Radio Frequency Board
**IR Fed Ct**... Indian Rulings, Federal Court [*A publication*] (DLA)
**Ir Fish Invest Ser A Freshwater**... Irish Fisheries Investigations. Series A. Freshwater [*A publication*]
**Ir Fish Invest Ser B Mar**... Irish Fisheries Investigations. Series B. Marine [*A publication*]
**IRFITS**...... Infrared Fault Isolation Test System
**IRFM**......... Integral Reactor Flow Model [*Nuclear energy*] (NRCH)
**IRFNA**........ Inhibited Red Fuming Nitric Acid [*Rocket fuel*]
**IRFN/UDMH**... Inhibited Red Fuming Nitric Acid and Unsymmetrical Dimethylhydrazine [*Rocket fuel*]
**IRFOA4**..... Irish Forestry [*A publication*]
**Ir For**......... Irish Forestry [*A publication*]
**IRFP**.......... International Relations and Foreign Policy [*Army*] [*British*]
**IRFRH**....... Institut de Recherche et de Formation aux Relations Humaines [*Institute for Research and Training in Human Relations*] [*Research center*] [*France*] (IRC)
**IRFT**.......... Interim Refresher Training [*Navy*] (NVT)
**IRG**............ Immunoreactive Glucagon [*Immunochemistry*]
**IRG**............ Inertial Rate Gyro (KSC)
**IRG**............ Information Resource Group [*Information service or system*] (IID)
**IRG**............ Infrared Generator
**IRG**............ Initial Review Group [*National Institutes of Health*]
**IRG**............ Inner Roll Gimbal (MCD)
**IRG**............ Institut de Reescompte et de Garantie [*Development bank*] [*Belgium*] (EY)
**IRG**............ Inter-Record Gap [*Data processing*] [*Telecommunications*] (MCD)
**IRG**............ Interagency Regulatory Group
**IRG**............ Interagency Review Group [*Nuclear Regulatory Commission*] (NRCH)
**IRG**............ Interdepartmental Regional Group [*Army*] (AABC)
**IRG**............ International Research Group on Wood Preservation [*Stockholm, Sweden*] (EAIO)
**IRG**............ Internationale des Resistants a la Guerre [*War Resisters International - WRI*] [*London, England*] (EA)
**IRG**............ Issues in Bank Regulation [*A publication*]
**IRG**............ Lockhart Rivers [*Australia*] [*Airport symbol*] (OAG)
**IRGA**.......... Infrared Gas Analyzer
**IRgA**.......... International Reprographics Association (EA)
**IRGAR**........ Infrared Gas Radiation
**IRGBA**....... International Repro Graphic Blueprint Association [*Later, IRA*] (EA)
**IRGCVD**.... International Research Group on Colour Vision Deficiencies [*Ghent, Belgium*] (EAIO)
**Ir Geogr B**... Irish Geographical Bulletin [*A publication*]
**IRGGA**...... Internationales Archiv fuer Gewerbepathologie und Gewerbehygiene [*A publication*]
**IRGGAJ**.... Internationales Archiv fuer Gewerbepathologie und Gewerbehygiene [*A publication*]
**IRGH**......... Immunoreactive Growth Hormone [*Immunology*]
**IR-GIP**....... Immunoreactive Gastric Inhibitory Peptide [*Biochemistry*]
**IRGl**........... Immunoreactive Glucagon [*Immunochemistry*]
**IRGL**.......... Infrared Gunfire Locator
**IRGP**.......... Infrared Guided Projectile (MCD)
**IRGPG**....... Inter-Range and Global Planning Group [*White Sands Missile Range*] (MUGU)
**IRGRD**...... International Research Group on Refuse Disposal [*Later, ISWA*]
**IRH**............ Inductive Recording Head
**IRH**............ Infrared Heater
**IRH**............ Inspection Requirements Handbook [*Navy*] (NG)
**IRH**............ Institute for Reproductive Health (EA)
**IRH**............ Institute for Research in History
**IRH**............ Institute for Research in Hypnosis [*Later, IRHP*] (EA)
**IRH**............ Institutes of Religion and Health (EA)
**IRH**............ International Rhodes Resources [*Vancouver Stock Exchange symbol*]
**IRHA**......... Injured as Result of Hostile Action [*Military*] (NVT)
**IRHA**......... Interchurch Response for the Horn of Africa (EA)
**IRHC**......... Isolated Rat Hepatocyte Complex
**IRHD**......... International Rubber Hardness Degree
**IRHD**......... Internationaler Rat der Hauspflegedienste [*International Council of Home-Help Services*]
**IRHF**......... Integral Radiative Heat Flux
**Ir Hist St**... Irish Historical Studies [*A publication*]
**Ir Hist Stud**... Irish Historical Studies [*A publication*]
**IRHP**......... Institute for Research in Hypnosis and Psychotherapy (EA)
**IRHR**......... Institute for Research in Human Relations (MCD)
**IRHS**.......... Intraoral Recurrent Herpes Simplex [*Medicine*]
**IRI**............. Image Resources, Incorporated [*Winter Park, FL*] [*Telecommunications*] (TSSD)
**IRI**............. Immunobiology Research Institute [*Annandale, NJ*]
**IRI**............. Immunoreactive Insulin
**IRI**............. Inca Resources, Inc. [*Toronto Stock Exchange symbol*] [*Vancouver Stock Exchange symbol*]
**IRI**............. Industrial Research Institute [*Canada*] [*Research center*] (RCD)
**IRI**............. Industrial Risk Insurers (EA)
**IRI**............. Informal Reading Inventory [*Education*]
**IRI**............. Information Researchers, Incorporated [*Information service or system*] (IID)
**IRI**............. Information Resources, Incorporated [*Information service or system*] (IID)
**IRI**............. Information Retrieval, Incorporated
**IRI**............. Infrared Imagery
**IRI**............. Infrared Instrumentation
**IRI**............. Innovative Resources, Incorporated
**IRI**............. Institution of the Rubber Industry [*British*]
**IRI**............. Insulin Radioimmunoassay
**IRI**............. Integrated Range Instrumentation
**IRI**............. International Industrial Relations Institute
**IRI**............. International Reference Ionosphere
**IRI**............. International Relay, Incorporated [*New York, NY*] [*Telecommunications*] (TSSD)
**IRI**............. Intravehicular Referenced Information [*NASA*]
**IRI**............. Inveresk Research International Ltd. [*United Kingdom*] (IRUK)
**IRI**............. Iringa [*Tanzania*] [*Airport symbol*] (OAG)
**iri**............... Irish [*MARC language code*] [*Library of Congress*] (LCCP)
**IRI**............. Istituto per la Ricostruzione Industriale [*Institute for Industrial Reconstruction*] [*Government holding company*] [*Italy*]
**IRIA**........... Infrared Information and Analysis Center [*DoD*] [*Ann Arbor, MI*] [*DoD*]
**IRIA**........... Institut de Recherche d'Informatique et d'Automatique [*French*] [*Research center*]
**IRIABC**..... Indian Agricultural Research Institute [*New Delhi*]. Annual Report [*A publication*]
**IRIAC**........ Infrared Information and Analysis Center [*University of Michigan*]
**IRIC**........... Information Resources, Incorporated [*NASDAQ symbol*] (NQ)
**IRIC**........... Infrared Image Converter
**IRIC**........... Inter-Regional Insurance Conference [*Later, ISO*]
**IRICBM**.... Intermediate-Range Intercontinental Ballistic Missile
**IRICON**..... Infrared Vidicon Tube
**IRICON**..... International Information Service via a Computer-Oriented Network (TSSD)
**IRicv**.......... Richview Township Public Library, Richview, IL [*Library symbol*] [*Library of Congress*] (LCLS)
**IRid**........... Elwood Township Carnegie Library, Ridge Farm, IL [*Library symbol*] [*Library of Congress*] (LCLS)
**IRIE**........... Infrared Information Exchange
**IR/IED**...... Independent Research/Independent Exploratory Development
**IRIG**........... Inertial Rate Integrating Gyro (NASA)
**IRIG**........... Inertial Reference Integrating Gyro [*NASA*] (NASA)
**IRIG**........... Inter-Range Instrumentation Group [*White Sands Missile Range*]
**IRIG-MWG**... Inter-Range Instrumentation Group - Meteorological Working Group [*White Sands Missile Range*]
**IRIN**........... International Robomation/Intelligence [*NASDAQ symbol*] (NQ)
**IRIP**........... Indonesian Resources and Information Programme [*Australia*]
**IRIRC**........ International Refugee Integration Resource Centre [*Later, CDR*] (EAIO)
**IRIS**........... IBM [*International Business Machines Corp.*] Recruitment Information System
**IRIS**........... Incorporated Research Institutions for Seismology
**IRIS**........... Increased Readiness Information System
**IRIS**........... Industrial Relations Information Service [*Labour Canada*]
**IRIS**........... Inertial Reactor with Internal Separation [*Coal furnace*] [*Tecogen, Inc.*]
**IRIS**........... Information Relayed Instantly from the Source [*Project*]
**IRIS**........... Information Resources Information System [*Library of Congress*]
**IRIS**........... Infrared Image Scanner
**IRIS**........... Infrared Imaging Seeker
**IRIS**........... Infrared Imaging System
**IRIS**........... Infrared Information System [*Sadtler Research Laboratories, Inc.*] [*Philadelphia, PA*] [*Database*]
**IRIS**........... Infrared Interferometer Spectrometer
**IRIS**........... Infrared Intruder System
**IRIS**........... Infrared Research Information Symposium (AAG)
**IRIS**........... Instant Response Information System (IEEE)
**IRIS**........... Institute for Regional and International Studies (EA)
**IRIS**........... Institute for Research in Information and Scholarship [*Brown University*] [*Research center*] (RCD)
**IRIS**........... Institute for Research on Interactive Systems [*Research center*] (TSSD)
**IRIS**........... Instruction and Research Information Systems [*Data processing*]
**IRIS**........... Instructional Resources Information System [*Ohio State University*] [*Information service or system*]

**IRIS** .......... Insurance Regulatory Information System [*National Association of Insurance Commissioners*]
**IRIS** .......... Integrated Radio and Intercommunications System [*Canada*]
**IRIS** .......... Integrated Reconnaissance Intelligence System (IEEE)
**IRIS** .......... Integrated Risk Information System [*Environmental Protection Agency*]
**IRIS** .......... Intelligence Reports Information Subsystem [*Data processing*]
**IRIS** .......... Intelligent Remote Input Stand [*Data processing*]
**IRIS** .......... Interactive Real-Time Information System [*Marine science*] (MSC)
**IRIS** .......... Interactive Recorded Information Service [*British*] [*Telecommunications*] (TEL)
**IRIS** .......... International Radiation Investigation Satellite [*NASA*]
**IRIS** .......... International Radio Interferometric Surveying [*International Association of Geodesy*]
**IRIS** .......... International Relations Information System [*Forschungsinstitut fuer Internationale Politik und Sicherheit*] [*Federal Republic of Germany*] (IID)
**IRIS** .......... International Remote Imaging Systems, Inc. [*NASDAQ symbol*] (NQ)
**IRIS** .......... International Reporting and Information Services [*International Private Intelligence Service*] [*Terminated, 1983*]
**IRIS** .......... International Reporting Information Systems
**IRIS** .......... International Research Information Service [*American Foundation for the Blind*]
**IRIS** .......... International REST [*Restricted Environmental Stimulation Techniques*] Investigators Society (EA)
**IRIS** .......... International Rights Information Service
**IRIS** .......... Interrogation Requirements Information System [*DoD*] (AFIT)
**IRIS** .......... Italian Research Interim Stage (NASA)
**IRISAV**...... Indian Agricultural Research Institute [*New Delhi*]. Annual Scientific Report [*A publication*]
**IRISH**........ Infrared Imaging Seeker Head (MCD)
**Irish Agr Creamery Rev** ... Irish Agricultural and Creamery Review [*A publication*]
**Irish Astr** ... Irish Astronomical Journal [*A publication*]
**Irish Astron J** ... Irish Astronomical Journal [*A publication*]
**Irish Banking R** ... Irish Banking Review [*A publication*]
**Irish Bcasting R** ... Irish Broadcasting Review [*Republic of Ireland*] [*A publication*]
**Irish Beekpr** ... Irish Beekeeper [*A publication*]
**Irish Bldr & Engineer** ... Irish Builder and Engineer [*A publication*]
**Irish Bus** .... Business and Finance (Ireland) [*A publication*]
**Irish Econ** .. Irish Economist [*A publication*]
**Irish Folk M Stud** ... Irish Folk Music Studies [*A publication*]
**Irish For**..... Irish Forestry [*A publication*]
**Irish Georgian Soc Bull** ... Irish Georgian Society. Bulletin [*A publication*]
**Irish Georgian Soc Qly Bull** ... Irish Georgian Society. Quarterly Bulletin [*A publication*]
**Irish Hist** ... Irish Historical Studies [*A publication*]
**Irish Hist Stud** ... Irish Historical Studies [*A publication*]
**Irish J Agr** ... Irish Journal of Agricultural Research [*A publication*]
**Irish J Agric Econ and Rural Sociol** ... Irish Journal of Agricultural Economics and Rural Sociology [*A publication*]
**Irish J Agr Res** ... Irish Journal of Agricultural Research [*A publication*]
**Irish J Ed** ... Irish Journal of Education [*A publication*]
**Irish J Food Sci Technol** ... Irish Journal of Food Science and Technology [*A publication*]
**Irish J Med** ... Irish Journal of Medical Science [*A publication*]
**Irish J Psy** ... Irish Journal of Psychology [*A publication*]
**Irish Jur**..... Irish Jurist [*A publication*]
**Irish Lib Bul** ... Irish Library Bulletin [*A publication*]
**Irish Lit S** .. Irish Literary Studies [*A publication*]
**Irish LT** ..... Irish Law Times [*A publication*]
**Irish Med J** ... Irish Medical Journal [*A publication*]
**Irish Med Times** ... Irish Medical Times [*A publication*]
**Irish Mo**..... Irish Monthly [*A publication*]
**Irish Num** .. Irish Numismatics [*A publication*]
**Irish Q**........ Irish Quarterly Review [*A publication*]
**Irish S**........ Irish Sword [*A publication*]
**Irish Stat**.... Irish Statistical Bulletin [*A publication*]
**Irish Statis Bul** ... Irish Statistical Bulletin [*A publication*]
**IrishThQ**.... Irish Theological Quarterly [*Maynooth*] [*A publication*]
**Irish U Rev** ... Irish University Review [*A publication*]
**Irish Wildfowl Comm Publ** ... Irish Wildfowl Committee. Publication [*Ireland*] [*A publication*]
**IRIS-M**...... Infrared Interferometer Spectrometer - Michelson
**IRivd** .......... Riverdale Library District, Riverdale, IL [*Library symbol*] [*Library of Congress*] (LCLS)
**IRivf**.......... River Forest Public Library, River Forest, IL [*Library symbol*] [*Library of Congress*] (LCLS)
**IRivfR** ........ Rosary College, River Forest, IL [*Library symbol*] [*Library of Congress*] (LCLS)
**IRivfT** ........ Concordia Teachers College, River Forest, IL [*Library symbol*] [*Library of Congress*] (LCLS)
**IRivg** .......... River Grove Public Library, River Grove, IL [*Library symbol*] [*Library of Congress*] (LCLS)
**IRivgT**........ Triton College, River Grove, IL [*Library symbol*] [*Library of Congress*] (LCLS)
**IRivs**.......... Riverside Public Library, Riverside, IL [*Library symbol*] [*Library of Congress*] (LCLS)
**IRJ** ............ European Rubber Journal [*A publication*]
**IRJ** ............ Industrial Relations Journal [*A publication*]
**IRJ** ............ Industrial Relations Law Journal [*A publication*]
**IRJ** ............ Infrared Jammer
**IRJ** ............ La Rioja [*Argentina*] [*Airport symbol*] (OAG)
**IRJADJ**..... Iranian Journal of Agricultural Sciences [*A publication*]
**Ir J Agric Res** ... Irish Journal of Agricultural Research [*A publication*]
**Ir J Agr Res** ... Irish Journal of Agricultural Research [*A publication*]
**IRJaSI**........ Institut Russkogo Jazyka i Slovesnosti pri Akademii Nauk SSSR [*A publication*]
**IRJE** .......... Infrared Jammer Equipment
**IRJE** .......... Interactive Remote Job Entry
**Ir J Environ Sci** ... Irish Journal of Environmental Science [*A publication*]
**Ir J Food Sci Technol** ... Irish Journal of Food Science and Technology [*A publication*]
**Ir J Med Sci** ... Irish Journal of Medical Science [*A publication*]
**IR Jour**........ Indian Rulings, Journal Section [*A publication*] (DLA)
**IRJPAR**..... Irish Journal of Psychology [*A publication*]
**IRJPDU** .... Irish Journal of Psychotherapy [*A publication*]
**Ir J Psychol** ... Irish Journal of Psychology [*A publication*]
**Ir J Psychol Med** ... Irish Journal of Psychological Medicine [*A publication*]
**Ir J Psychother** ... Irish Journal of Psychotherapy [*A publication*]
**Ir J Psychother Psychosom Med** ... Irish Journal of Psychotherapy and Psychosomatic Medicine [*A publication*]
**IRJSD5**...... Iraqi Journal of Science [*A publication*]
**Ir Jur**.......... Irish Jurist [*A publication*]
**Ir Jur**.......... Irish Jurist Reports [*1849-66*] [*A publication*] (DLA)
**Ir Jur NS** ... Irish Jurist. New Series [*1856-67*] [*A publication*]
**Ir Jur R**...... Irish Jurist Reports [*A publication*]
**Ir Jur Rep** .. Irish Jurist Reports [*1849-66*] [*A publication*] (DLA)
**IRK** ............ Infrared Kit
**IRK** ............ Insulin Receptor Kinase [*An enzyme*]
**IRK** ............ Interlake Development [*Vancouver Stock Exchange symbol*]
**IRK** ............ Irkutsk [*USSR*] [*Seismograph station code, US Geological Survey*] (SEIS)
**IRK** ............ Kirksville [*Missouri*] [*Airport symbol*] (OAG)
**IRK** ............ Kirksville, MO [*Location identifier*] [*FAA*] (FAAL)
**Irkutsk Politehn Inst Trudy** ... Irkutskii Politehniceskii Institut Trudy [*A publication*]
**IRL**............ Industrial Reactor Laboratories [*New Jersey*]
**IRL**............ Industrial Relations Law Journal [*A publication*]
**IRL**............ Industrial Research Laboratories [*A publication*]
**IRL**............ Information Requirements List (KSC)
**IRL**............ Information Research Limited [*Information service or system*] (IID)
**IRL**............ Information Retrieval Language [*Data processing*]
**IRL**............ Information Retrieval Limited [*Database originator*] [*British*] [*Information service or system*]
**IRL**............ Infrared Lamp [*or Light*]
**IRL**............ Infrared Lens
**IRL**............ Initiating Reference Letter (MCD)
**IRL**............ Institute for Rational Living [*Absorbed by IRET*]
**IRL**............ Institute on Religious Life (EA)
**IRL**............ Interactive Reader Language [*Data processing*]
**IRL**............ Interface Requirement List (NASA)
**IRL**............ International Meridian Resources [*Vancouver Stock Exchange symbol*]
**IRL**............ Internationaler Ring fuer Landarbeit [*International Committee of Scientific Management in Agriculture*]
**IRL**............ Interrogation and Locating
**IRL**............ Intersection of Range Legs
**IRL**............ Ireland [*ANSI three-letter standard code*] (CNC)
**IrL**............ Irish Law Reports [*A publication*] (DLA)
**IRLA**.......... Independent Research Libraries Association (EA)
**IRLA**.......... Information Retrieval and Library Automation [*A publication*]
**IRLA**.......... International Religious Liberty Association (EA)
**IR Lah**........ Indian Rulings, Lahore Series [*A publication*] (DLA)
**IRLAS**........ Infrared LASER
**Ir Law & Ch** ... Irish Common Law and Chancery Reports, New Series [*1850-53*] [*A publication*] (DLA)
**Ir Law & Eq** ... Irish Law and Equity Reports [*1838-50*] [*A publication*] (DLA)
**Ir Law Rec** ... Irish Law Recorder [*1827-38*] [*A publication*] (DLA)
**Ir Law Rec NS** ... Irish Law Recorder, New Series [*1833-38*] [*A publication*] (DLA)
**Ir Law Rep** ... Irish Law Reports [*A publication*] (DLA)
**Ir Law Rep NS** ... Irish Common Law Reports, New Series [*A publication*] (DLA)
**Ir Law T**..... Irish Law Times [*A publication*]
**IRLC**.......... Illinois Regional Library Council [*Library network*]
**IRLCAW**... IRCS [*International Research Communications System*] Medical Science. Library Compendium [*A publication*]
**IRLCD**....... IRCS [*International Research Communications System*] Medical Science. Library Compendium [*A publication*]
**IRLCO-CSA** ... International Red Locust Control Organization for Central and Southern Africa (EAIO)
**IRLCS**........ International Red Locust Control Service
**IRLD**.......... Institute for Research on Learning Disabilities [*University of Minnesota*] [*Research center*] (RCD)

**IRLDA**....... Independent Retail Lumber Dealers Association
**IrL & Eq**..... Irish Law and Equity Reports [*1838-50*] [*A publication*] (DLA)
**IRLG**.......... Interagency Regulatory Liaison Group [*Comprising several federal agencies*] [*Terminated, 1981*]
**IRLI**........... Italianistica. Revista di Letteratura Italiana [*A publication*]
**IRLIB**......... Industrial Relations Legal Information Bulletin [*A publication*]
**Ir LJ**........... Irish Law Journal [*1895-1902*] [*A publication*] (DLA)
**Ir L NS**....... Irish Common Law Reports, New Series [*A publication*] (DLA)
**IRLR**.......... Industrial Relations Law Reports [*British*] (DCTA)
**IRLR**.......... Infrared LASER Ranger (MCD)
**Ir LR**.......... Irish Law Reports [*A publication*] (DLA)
**Ir L Rec**...... Irish Law Recorder, First Series [*1827-31*] [*A publication*] (DLA)
**Ir L Rec NS** ... Law Recorder, New Series [*Ireland*] [*A publication*] (DLA)
**Ir L Rec 1st Ser** ... Law Recorder, First Series [*Ireland*] [*A publication*] (DLA)
**IRLS**........... Infrared LASER Spectrometer
**IRLS**........... Infrared Line Scanner (MCD)
**IRLS**........... Interrogation, Recording, and Locating System [*Naval Oceanographic Office*]
**IRLSC**........ Industrial Relations and Labor Studies Center [*University of Maryland*] [*Research center*] (RCD)
**Ir L T**.......... Irish Law Times [*A publication*]
**Ir L Times and Solicitors' J** ... Irish Law Times and Solicitors' Journal. A Weekly Gazette of Legal News and Information [*A publication*]
**Ir LTJ**......... Irish Law Times Journal [*A publication*] (DLA)
**Ir LTJ**......... Irish Law Times and Solicitors' Journal [*A publication*]
**Ir LT Jour** ... Irish Law Times Journal [*A publication*] (DLA)
**Ir LT Journal** ... Irish Law Times and Solicitors' Journal [*A publication*]
**Ir LTR**........ Irish Law Times Reports [*A publication*] (DLA)
**Ir LT Rep**... Irish Law Times Reports [*A publication*] (DLA)
**IRM**........... Illinois Railway Museum (EA)
**IRM**........... Improved Risk Mutuals (EA)
**IRM**........... Induced Remanent Magnetization
**IRM**........... Information Management [*A publication*]
**IRM**........... Information and Records Management [*A publication*]
**IRM**........... Information and Records Management
**IRM**........... Information Resource Management [*Data processing*]
**IRM**........... Infrared Mapper
**IRM**........... Infrared Measurement
**IRM**........... Inherited Releasing Mechanism [*Psychiatry*]
**IRM**........... Initial Release Memorandum
**IRM**........... Innate Release Mechanism [*Endocrinology*]
**IRM**........... Inspection Requirements Manual (AAG)
**IRM**........... Institute for Resource Management (EA)
**IRM**........... Institute of Risk Management (EAIO)
**IRM**........... Integrated Range Missile (MCD)
**IRM**........... Integrated Range Mission [*Military*]
**IRM**........... Interim Research Memo
**IRM**........... Intermediate Range Monitor (NRCH)
**IRM**........... Intermediate Restorative Material [*Dentistry*]
**IRM**........... International Review of Missions [*A publication*]
**IRM**........... International Royalon Minerals, Inc. [*Vancouver Stock Exchange symbol*]
**IRM**........... Iodine Radiation Monitor (IEEE)
**IRM**........... Ion Release Module [*Spacecraft*] [*Germany*]
**IrM**............ Irish Monthly [*A publication*]
**IRM**........... Isothermal Remanent Magnetization
**IRMA**......... Immissionsratenmessapparatur [*Immission Rate Measuring Apparatus*] [*Analytical chemistry*] [*German*]
**IRMA**......... Immunoradiometric Assay [*Immunology*]
**IRMA**......... Individual Retirement Mortgage Account
**IRMA**......... Individual Reverse Mortgage Account [*American Homestead, Inc.*]
**IRMA**......... Information Referral Manual
**IRMA**......... Information Revision and Manuscript Assembly
**IRMA**......... Infrared Miss-Distance Approximator
**IRMA**......... International Rehabilitation Medicine Association (EA)
**IRMA**......... International Rock 'n' Roll Music Association (EA)
**IRMA**......... Intraretinal Microangiopathy [*Ophthalmology*]
**IRMA**......... Intraretinal Microvascular Abnormality [*Ophthalmology*]
**IRMA**......... Inverted Roof Membrane Assembly [*Construction*]
**IR Mad**...... Indian Rulings, Madras Series [*A publication*] (DLA)
**IRMA J**...... IRMA [*Indian Refractory Makers Association*] Journal [*A publication*]
**IRMAS**...... International Review of Music Aesthetics and Sociology [*Later, International Review of the Aesthetics and Sociology of Music*] [*A publication*]
**IRMC**......... Information Resource Management Council [*DoD*]
**IRMC**......... Institute of Risk Management Consultants [*Later, SRMC*] (EA)
**IRME**......... Initiator Resistance Measuring Equipment (NASA)
**Ir Med J**..... Irish Medical Journal [*A publication*]
**IRMFSG** ... Inter-Range Missile Flight Safety Group [*White Sands Missile Range*]
**I & R Mgmt** ... Information and Records Management [*A publication*]
**IRMGSG**... Inter-Range Missile Ground Safety Group [*White Sands Missile Range*] (KSC)
**IRMI**.......... International Risk Management Institute [*Dallas, TX*] (EA)
**IR-MIM** .... Published Internal Revenue Mimeograph [*A publication*] (DLA)
**IRMJ**......... Infrared Miniaturized Jammer
**IRMLA**...... IRE [*Institute of Radio Engineers*] Transactions on Military Electronics [*A publication*]
**IRMMD2**.. IRMMH [*Institute for Research into Mental and Multiple Handicap*] Monograph [*A publication*]
**IRMMH**.... Institute for Research into Mental and Multiple Handicap [*British*]
**IRMMH Monogr** ... IRMMH [*Institute for Research into Mental and Multiple Handicap*] Monograph [*A publication*]
**IRMNA2**... Institute for Research into Mental Retardation. Monograph [*Oxford*] [*A publication*]
**IRMO**........ Information Resources Management Office [*Army Corps of Engineers*]
**IRMP**......... Industrial Readiness and Mobilization Production Planning [*Military*]
**IRMP**......... Infrared Measurement Program
**IRMP**......... Infrared Multiple-Photon [*Physics*]
**IRMP**......... Interservice Radiation Measurement Program
**IRMPC**...... Industrial Raw Materials Planning Committee [*NATO*] (NATG)
**IRMPD**...... Infrared Multiple-Photon Dissociation [*Physics*]
**IRMR**........ Institute for Research into Mental Retardation
**IRMRA**...... Infrared Monochromatic Radiation (MSA)
**IR/MRBM** ... Intermediate-Range/Medium-Range Ballistic Missile (NG)
**IRMS**......... Information Resource Management Service [*Veterans Administration Medical Center*] [*Information service or system*] (IID)
**IRMS**......... Infrared Mapping System
**IRMS**......... Integrated Radio Management System (MCD)
**IRMS**......... International Robert Musil Society [*See also SIRM*] [*Saarbrucken, Federal Republic of Germany*] (EAIO)
**IRMS**......... Isotope Ratio Mass Spectrometry
**IRMT**......... International Register of Manipulative Therapists
**Ir Mthl**....... Irish Monthly [*A publication*]
**IRN**........... Illinois Resource Network [*University of Illinois*] [*Urbana*] [*Information service or system*] (IID)
**IRN**........... Import Release Note (DS)
**IRN**........... Interface Revision Notice [*NASA*] (KSC)
**IRN**........... Internal Reference Number
**IRN**........... Internal Routing Network
**IRN**........... International Rivers Network (EA)
**IRN**........... Invoice Register Number [*Business term*] (MCD)
**IRN**........... Iran [*ANSI three-letter standard code*] (CNC)
**IRN**........... Iron River Resources [*Vancouver Stock Exchange symbol*]
**IRN**........... Iron or Steel [*Freight*]
**IRN**........... [*The*] Ironton Railroad Co. [*Absorbed into Consolidated Rail Corp.*] [*AAR code*]
**IRN**........... Item Removal Notice [*Nuclear energy*] (NRCH)
**IRNA**......... Iranian [*or Islamic Republic*] News Agency
**I-RNA**........ Ribonucleic Acid, Immune [*Biochemistry, genetics*]
**IR Nag**....... Indian Rulings, Nagpur Series [*A publication*] (DLA)
**Ir Nat J**....... Irish Naturalists' Journal [*A publication*]
**IRND**......... Interand Corp. [*NASDAQ symbol*] (NQ)
**IRNDT**...... Infrared Nondestructive Testing [*Electrical technique*]
**IRNES**....... Institut de Recherches et de Normalisation Economiques en Scientifiques [*Canada*]
**IRNGA**...... Itogi Nauki i Tekhniki Razrabotka Neftyanykh i Gazovykh Mestorozhdenii [*A publication*]
**IRNRAJ**.... Iraq Natural History Museum. Report [*A publication*]
**IRNSA**....... IRE [*Institute of Radio Engineers*] Transactions on Nuclear Science [*A publication*]
**IRNU**......... Institut de Recherche des Nations Unies pour le Developpement Social [*United Nations Research Institute for Social Development*]
**Ir Nurse J**.. Irish Nurses Journal [*A publication*]
**Ir Nurs Hosp W** ... Irish Nursing and Hospital World [*A publication*]
**Ir Nurs Hosp World** ... Irish Nursing and Hospital World [*A publication*]
**Ir Nurs News** ... Irish Nursing News [*A publication*]
**IRNV**......... Increase and Replacement of Naval Vessels [*Naval budget appropriation title*]
**IRO**........... Independent Retailer Organisation (EAIO)
**IRO**........... Industrial Relations Office [*Army*]
**IRO**........... Inflight Refueling Operator
**IRO**........... Infrared Oven
**IRO**........... Inland Revenue Office [*or Officer*] [*British*]
**IRO**........... Interim Range Operations (MUGU)
**IRO**........... Internal Revenue Office [*or Officer*]
**IRO**........... International Reception Operators [*Defunct*] (EA)
**IRO**........... International Refugee Organization [*Later, UNHCR*]
**IRO**........... International Relations Office [*American Library Association*]
**IRO**........... International Relief Organization [*Post-World War II*]
**IRO**........... Inventory Research Office [*Army*]
**iro**............ Iroquoian [*MARC language code*] [*Library of Congress*] (LCCP)
**IRo**............ Rockford Public Library, Rockford, IL [*Library symbol*] [*Library of Congress*] (LCLS)
**IROA**......... Independent Rabbinate of America
**IROAN**...... Inspect and Repair Only as Necessary [*or Needed*] [*Military*]

**IRob** .......... Robinson Public Library, Robinson, IL [*Library symbol*] [*Library of Congress*] (LCLS)
**IRobb** ........ Robbins Public Library District, Robbins, IL [*Library symbol*] [*Library of Congress*] (LCLS)
**IRobSD**...... Robinson Community School District 2, Robinson, IL [*Library symbol*] [*Library of Congress*] (LCLS)
**IROC** ......... International Race of Champions [*Auto racing*]
**IROC** ......... International Rose O'Neill Club (EA)
**IROC** ......... International Royalty & Oil Company [*NASDAQ symbol*] (NQ)
**IRoC**.......... Rockford College, Rockford, IL [*Library symbol*] [*Library of Congress*] (LCLS)
**IRockt** ........ Talcott Free Public Library, Rockton, IL [*Library symbol*] [*Library of Congress*] (LCLS)
**IROD** ......... Instantaneous Readout Detector [*Satellite instrument*]
**Irodal F** ...... Irodalomtorteneti Fuzetek [*A publication*]
**IRODP**....... International Registry of Organization Development Professionals (EA)
**IRODS**....... Inertial Rate of Descent Sensor (MCD)
**Irod Szle**..... Irodalmi Szemle [*A publication*]
**IROF**.......... Imagery Requirement Objectives File (MCD)
**Ir Offshore Rev** ... Irish Offshore Review [*A publication*]
**IRO-FIET** ... Interamerican Regional Organization of the International Federation of Commercial, Clerical, Professional, and Technical Employees [*Willemstad, Netherlands Antilles*] (EAIO)
**IROL**.......... Imagery Requirements Objectives List (MCD)
**IRoMH**...... Rockford Memorial Hospital, Rockford, IL [*Library symbol*] [*Library of Congress*] (LCLS)
**Iron** ............ Ironical (ROG)
**IRON**......... Ironstone Group, Inc. [*NASDAQ symbol*] (NQ)
**Iron** ............ Ironwood [*A publication*]
**IRoN**.......... Northern Illinois Library for Mental Health, Rockford, IL [*Library symbol*] [*Library of Congress*] (LCLS)
**Iron Age** ..... Iron Age. Metal Producing Management Edition [*A publication*]
**Iron Age Metalwork Int** ... Iron Age Metalworking International [*Later, Chilton's IAMI Iron Age Metalworking International*] [*A publication*]
**Iron Coal Trades Rev** ... Iron and Coal Trades Review [*England*] [*A publication*]
**IRoNL**........ Rockford Northern Illinois Library System, Rockford, IL [*Library symbol*] [*Library of Congress*] (LCLS)
**Ironmaking Conf Proc** ... Ironmaking Conference Proceedings [*A publication*]
**Ironmaking Proc AIME** ... Ironmaking Proceedings. Metallurgical Society of AIME. Iron and Steel Division [*A publication*]
**Ironmkg Steelmkg** ... Ironmaking and Steelmaking [*A publication*]
**Irons Pol Law** ... Irons on Police Law [*A publication*] (DLA)
**Irons Pub H** ... Irons on Public Houses [*A publication*] (DLA)
**Iron St**........ Iron and Steel [*A publication*]
**Iron Steel** ... Iron and Steel [*A publication*]
**Iron Steel Eng** ... Iron and Steel Engineer [*A publication*]
**Iron and Steel Eng** ... Iron and Steel Engineer [*A publication*]
**Iron Steel Inst Carnegie Scholarship Mem** ... Iron and Steel Institute. Carnegie Scholarship Memoirs [*A publication*]
**Iron Steel Inst (London) Bibliogr Ser** ... Iron and Steel Institute (London). Bibliographical Series [*A publication*]
**Iron Steel Inst (London) Publ** ... Iron and Steel Institute (London). Publication [*A publication*]
**Iron Steel Inst (London) Spec Rep** ... Iron and Steel Institute (London). Special Report [*A publication*]
**Iron Steel Int** ... Iron and Steel International [*A publication*]
**Iron and Steel Int** ... Iron and Steel International [*A publication*]
**Iron St Int**.. Iron and Steel International [*A publication*]
**Iron Tr R**.... Iron Trade Review [*A publication*]
**IRoo** ........... Roodhouse Public Library, Roodhouse, IL [*Library symbol*] [*Library of Congress*] (LCLS)
**IROP**.......... Imagery Requirements Objectives Plan (MCD)
**IROPG**....... Inter-Range Operations Planning Group [*White Sands Missile Range*]
**IROR** ......... Improved Range-Only RADAR (MCD)
**IROR** ......... Inspection, Repair, Overhaul, and Rebuild
**IROR** ......... Interest Rate of Return [*Finance*]
**IROR** ......... Internal Rate of Return [*Telecommunications*] (TEL)
**IRoR**.......... Rockford Newspapers, Inc., Rockford, IL [*Library symbol*] [*Library of Congress*] (LCLS)
**IROS**.......... Increase Reliability of Operational Systems (AFM)
**IROS**.......... Infrared Operational Satellite (NOAA)
**IROS**.......... Instant Response Ordering System [*Teleordering system*] [*Information service or system*] (IID)
**IROS**.......... Ipsilateral Routing of Signal
**IRoSA** ........ Sundstrand Aviation, Engineering Library, Rockford, IL [*Library symbol*] [*Library of Congress*] (LCLS)
**IROSB**........ Inactive Reserve Officer Status Branch [*BUPERS*]
**IRoSH**........ Swedish-American Hospital, Rockford, IL [*Library symbol*] [*Library of Congress*] (LCLS)
**IRoStA**....... Saint Anthony Hospital, Rockford, IL [*Library symbol*] [*Library of Congress*] (LCLS)
**IRoStT** ....... Saint Thomas High School, Rockford, IL [*Library symbol*] [*Library of Congress*] (LCLS)
**IROT** ......... Infrared on Target
**IR Oudh**..... Indian Rulings, Oudh Series [*A publication*] (DLA)
**IRoWM** ..... Winnebago County Medical Society, Rockford, IL [*Library symbol*] [*Library of Congress*] (LCLS)
**IRox** ........... Roxana Public Library, Roxana, IL [*Library symbol*] [*Library of Congress*] (LCLS)
**IRoxCU** ..... Roxana Community Unit 1, Roxana, IL [*Library symbol*] [*Library of Congress*] (LCLS)
**IRP**............. Ice on Runway - Patchy [*Aviation*]
**IRP**............. Immunoglobulin Reference Preparation [*Clinical chemistry*]
**IRP**............. Immunoreactive Proinsulin [*Immunochemistry*]
**IRP**............. Improved Replenishment-at-Sea Program (MCD)
**IRP**............. Individual Responsibility Program [*Medicine*] (DHSM)
**IRP**............. Individualized Reading Program [*Education*]
**IRP**............. Industrial Readiness Planning [*Military*] (NG)
**IRP**............. Industry Recognition Program (MCD)
**IRP**............. Inertial Reference Package (MCD)
**IRP**............. Information Resources Press [*Washington, DC*]
**IRP**............. Information Return Program [*IRS*]
**IRP**............. Information Returns Processing [*Data processing*]
**IRP**............. Infrared Preamplifier
**IRP**............. Infrared Projector (MCD)
**IRP**............. Infrared Radiation Profile
**IRP**............. Infrared Responsive Phosphor
**IRP**............. Initial Receiving Point
**IRP**............. Institute for Research on Poverty [*University of Wisconsin - Madison*] [*Research center*] (RCD)
**IRP**............. Institute for Retired Professionals (EA)
**IRP**............. Institutional Revolutionary Party [*Mexico*] [*Political party*]
**IRP**............. Intelligence Report Plan (NATG)
**IRP**............. Interference Reporting Point (NATG)
**IRP**............. Intermediate Related Power
**IRP**............. Intermediate Rotating Plug (NRCH)
**IRP**............. Internal Reflection Plate
**IRP**............. International Petroleum Corp. [*Vancouver Stock Exchange symbol*] [*Toronto Stock Exchange symbol*]
**IRP**............. International Reference Preparation [*World Health Organization*]
**IRP**............. International Rostrum of Young Performers [*See also TIJE*] (EAIO)
**IRP**............. International Routing Plan [*Telecommunications*] (TEL)
**IRP**............. Isiro [*Zaire*] [*Airport symbol*] (OAG)
**IRP**............. Islahat Refah Partisi [*Reformation and Welfare Party*] [*Turkish Cypriot*] (PPE)
**IRP**............. Islamic Republican Party [*Iran*] [*Political party*] (PPW)
**IRp** ............. Richton Park Library District, Richton Park, IL [*Library symbol*] [*Library of Congress*] (LCLS)
**IRPA**.......... Institut de Recherche sur le Profil d'Apprentissage [*Canada*]
**IRPA**.......... International Radiation Protection Association [*Vienna, Austria*] (EAIO)
**IR Pat**......... Indian Rulings, Patna Series [*A publication*] (DLA)
**IRPC**.......... Indian Rulings, Privy Council [*1929-47*] [*A publication*] (DLA)
**IRPC**.......... Indirect Reading Pocket Chamber
**IRPC**.......... Industrial Relations Policy Committee [*General Council of British Shipping*] (DS)
**IRPD**.......... Industrial Relations and Personnel Development [*A publication*]
**IRPEG**....... Tax on Legal Entities [*Italian*] (IMH)
**IR Pesh** ...... Indian Rulings, Peshawar Series [*1933-47*] [*A publication*] (DLA)
**IR Peshawar** ... Indian Rulings, Peshawar Series [*1933-47*] [*A publication*] (DLA)
**Ir Pet SJ**..... Irish Petty Sessions Journal [*A publication*] (DLA)
**IRPFC**........ International Ray Price Fan Club (EA)
**IRPG**......... Iranian Research and Publication Group
**IRPHD** ....... International Review of Physiology [*A publication*]
**IRPI** .......... Individual Rod Position Indicator [*Nuclear energy*] (NRCH)
**IRPIA** ........ Intelligence Information Report Photo Index [*Military*] (MCD)
**IRPL**.......... Index to Religious Periodical Literature [*Database*]
**IRPL**.......... Interim Repair Parts List
**IRPL**.......... Interservice Radio Propagation Laboratory (MCD)
**IRPM**......... Individual Risk Premium Modification [*Insurance*]
**IRPM**......... Infrared Physical Measurement
**IRPOD**....... Individual Repair Parts Ordering Data [*Program*] [*DoD*]
**IRPOS**....... Interdisciplinary Research Relevant to Problems of Our Society [*Later, RANN*] [*National Science Foundation*]
**IRPP**.......... Industrial Readiness Planning Program
**IRPP**.......... Infrared Pointer Package
**IRPP**.......... Institute for Research on Public Policy [*Canada*]
**IR Pr C**....... Indian Rulings, Privy Council [*1929-47*] [*A publication*] (DLA)
**IRPRD**....... In-Plant Reproductions [*A publication*]
**IRPRL** ....... Initial Repair Parts Requirements List (MCD)
**IRPS** .......... Individual Resource Protection Sensor
**IRPS** .......... Institute of Reconstructive Plastic Surgery [*New York University*] [*Research center*] (RCD)
**IRPS** .......... Institute for Research in Public Safety [*Indiana University*] [*Research center*] (RCD)
**IRPS** .......... International Review of Publications in Sociology [*Sociological Abstracts, Inc.*] [*Information service or system*] (CRD)

**IRPSDZ**..... IRRI [*International Rice Research Institute*] Research [*A publication*]
**IRPT**......... Inland Rivers Ports and Terminals (EA)
**IRPTC**....... International Register of Potentially Toxic Chemicals [*United Nations Environment Program*] [*Geneva, Switzerland*]
**IRPWA**...... Irrigation and Power [*A publication*]
**IRQ**........... Interpersonal Relations Questionnaire [*Personality development test*] [*Psychology*]
**IRQ**........... Interrupt Request [*Data processing*]
**IRQ**........... Intimate Relationship Questionnaire
**IRQ**........... Iraq [*ANSI three-letter standard code*] (CNC)
**IRQ**........... Rose-Hulman Institute of Technology Library, Terre Haute, IN [*OCLC symbol*] (OCLC)
**IRQC**......... Infrared Quantum Counter
**IRQR**......... Information Requirement [*Military*]
**IRR**........... Immediate Ready Reserve [*Army*]
**IRR**........... Improved Rearming Rates [*Military*] (NG)
**IRR**........... Indian River Resources, Inc. [*Vancouver Stock Exchange symbol*]
**IRR**........... Individual Ready Reserve [*Army*]
**IRR**........... Individual Retirement Record [*Air Force*] (AFM)
**IRR**........... Industrial Relations Research Association. Proceedings [*A publication*]
**IRR**........... Industrial Retaining Ring Co.
**IRR**........... Information Reduction Research [*Information service or system*] (IID)
**IRR**........... Infrared Radiometer
**IRR**........... Infrared Receiver
**IRR**........... Initial Rate of Return [*Finance*] (MCD)
**IRR**........... Inspection Rejection Report [*NASA*] (KSC)
**IRR**........... Installation and Removal Record [*NASA*] (KSC)
**IRR**........... Institute of Race Relations [*London, England*] (EAIO)
**IRR**........... Institute for Reactor Research [*Switzerland*]
**IRR**........... Institute for Rehabilitation and Research [*Baylor College of Medicine*] [*Research center*] (RCD)
**IRR**........... Institute for Risk Research [*University of Waterloo*] [*Canada*] [*Research center*] (RCD)
**IRR**........... Institute of Rubber Research (MCD)
**IRR**........... Integral Rocket Ramjet [*Navy*]
**IRR**........... Integrated Radio Room (MCD)
**IRR**........... Intelligence RADAR Reporting
**IRR**........... Interim Release Request (MCD)
**IRR**........... Internal Rate of Return [*Finance*]
**IRR**........... Internal Revenue Looseleaf Regulations System
**IRR**........... International Rate of Return [*Finance*]
**IRR**........... International Revenue Record [*New York City*] [*A publication*] (DLA)
**IRR**........... Interrupt Return Register
**Ir R**............ Irish Law Reports [*A publication*] (DLA)
**Ir R**............ Irish Review [*A publication*]
**IRR**........... Irish Royal Rifles [*Military*] [*British*] (ROG)
**IRR**........... Iron Range Research Center, Chisholm, MN [*OCLC symbol*] (OCLC)
**irr**.............. Irradiation
**IRR**........... Irredeemable [*Banking*]
**IRR**........... Irrigation [*Type of water project*]
**IRR**........... Irritant
**IRR**........... Israeli Research Reactor
**IRRA**......... Industrial Relations Research Association (EA)
**IRRA**......... Industrial Relations Research Association. Proceedings [*A publication*]
**IRRAD**....... Infrared Range and Detection
**Irradiat Aliments** ... Irradiation des Aliments [*A publication*]
**Irradiat Aliments (Engl Ed)** ... Irradiation des Aliments (English Edition) [*A publication*]
**IRRADN** ... Irradiation
**Irr Age**........ Irrigation Age [*A publication*]
**IR Ran**........ Indian Rulings, Rangoon Series [*A publication*] (DLA)
**IRRAPST**.. Individual Ready Reserve - Alternative Preassignment System Test (MCD)
**IRRAS**....... Infrared Reflection Absorption Spectroscopy [*Also, IRAS, RAIR, RAIRS, RAIS*]
**IRRB**......... International Rubber Research Board
**IRRC**......... International Relief and Rescue Committee [*Post-World War II*]
**IRRC**......... International Rubber Regulation Committee [*World War II*]
**IRRC**......... Investor Responsibility Research Center (EA)
**Ir R Ch**....... Irish Chancery Reports [*A publication*] (DLA)
**Ir RCL**....... Irish Reports, Common Law Series [*A publication*] (DLA)
**IRRCS**....... Institute for Regional, Rural, and Community Studies [*Western Illinois University*] [*Research center*] (RCD)
**IRRD**......... Institute for Research of Rheumatic Diseases (EA)
**IRRD**......... International Road Research Documentation [*OECD*] [*Information service or system*]
**IRRDB**....... International Rubber Research and Development Board [*Brickendonbury, Hertford, England*] (EAIO)
**IRRED**....... Irredeemable (ROG)
**IRREG**....... Irregular (KSC)
**Irreg**........... Irregular Light [*Navigation signal*]
**IR Rep**....... Reports of Inland Revenue Commissioners [*A publication*] (DLA)
**Ir Rep Ch**... Irish Chancery Reports [*A publication*] (DLA)
**Ir Rep CL**... Irish Reports, Common Law Series [*A publication*] (DLA)
**Ir Rep Eq**... Irish Reports, Equity Series [*A publication*] (DLA)
**Ir Rep NS**... Irish Common Law Reports, New Series [*A publication*] (DLA)
**Ir Rep VR**... Irish Reports, Verbatim Reprint [*A publication*] (DLA)
**Ir R Eq**....... Irish Reports, Equity Series [*A publication*] (DLA)
**IR Research Repts** ... IR Research Reports [*A publication*]
**IRREV**....... Irrevocable
**IRRF**......... Institut pour la Repression des Ravageurs Forestiers [*Forest Pest Management Institute*] [*Canada*]
**IRRG**......... Irrigation
**IRRI**.......... Industrial Relations Research Institute [*University of Wisconsin - Madison*] [*Research center*] (RCD)
**IRRI**.......... Interagency Rehabilitation Research Information System [*National Institute on Disability and Rehabilitation Research*] [*Washington, DC*] [*Information service or system*] (IID)
**IRRI**.......... International Rice Research Institute [*Philippines*]
**IRRICAB**... Current Annotated Bibliography of Irrigation [*Bet Dagan, Israel*] [*A publication*]
**IRRIG**........ Irrigate
**Irrig Age**.... Irrigation Age [*A publication*]
**Irrig Drain Pap** ... Irrigation and Drainage Paper [*A publication*]
**Irrig Drain Pap (FAO)** ... Irrigation and Drainage Paper (Food and Agriculture Organization of the United Nations) [*A publication*]
**Irrig Eng Maint** ... Irrigation Engineering and Maintenance [*A publication*]
**Irrig Farmer** ... Irrigation Farmer [*A publication*] (APTA)
**Irrig Fmr**.... Irrigation Farmer [*A publication*] (APTA)
**Irrig J**......... Irrigation Journal [*A publication*]
**Irrig Power** ... Irrigation and Power [*A publication*]
**Irrig & Power Abstr** ... Irrigation and Power Abstracts [*A publication*]
**Irrig Sci**...... Irrigation Science [*A publication*]
**Irrig Winter Wheat Tech Publ** ... Irrigated Winter Wheat. Technical Publication [*A publication*]
**IRRI Res Pap Ser** ... IRRI [*International Rice Research Institute*] Research Paper Series [*A publication*]
**IRRI Res Pap Ser Int Rice Res Inst** ... IRRI Research Paper Series. International Rice Research Institute [*A publication*]
**IRRIS**......... International Rehabilitation Research Information System [*National Institute of Handicapped Research*] [*Database*]
**IRRL**.......... Information Retrieval Research Laboratory [*University of Illinois*] [*Urbana*] [*Information service or system*] (IID)
**IRR & L**..... Irish Reports, Registry and Land Cases [*A publication*] (DLA)
**IRRM**........ Information Requested in Above Referenced Message [*Army*] (AABC)
**IRRMP**...... Infrared RADAR Measurement Program
**IRRN**......... Illinois Research and Reference Center Libraries
**Irr N**.......... Tasmanian Irregular Notes [*A publication*]
**IRR Newsl**... Individual Rights and Responsibilities Newsletter [*A publication*] (DLA)
**IRRP**.......... Icefield Ranges Research Project
**IRRP**.......... Improved Rearming Rate Program [*Military*] (NVT)
**IRRPOS**.... Interdisciplinary Research Relevant to Problems of Our Society [*Later, RANN*] [*National Science Foundation*]
**IRRR**.......... Industrial Relations Review and Report [*A publication*]
**Ir R Reg App**... Irish Reports, Registration Appeals [*1868-76*] [*A publication*] (DLA)
**Ir R Reg & L**... Irish Reports, Registry and Land Cases [*A publication*] (DLA)
**IRRS**.......... Individual Ready Reserve System [*Military*]
**IRRS**.......... Infrared Reconnaissance System (MCD)
**IRRS**.......... Infrared Reflection Spectroscopy
**IRRS**.......... Irish Railway Record Society
**IRRSA8**..... Indian Council of Agricultural Research. Review Series [*A publication*]
**IRRSAM**... Integral Rocket Ramjet Surface-to-Air Missile (MCD)
**IRRSSM**.... Integral Rocket Ramjet Surface-to-Surface Missile (MCD)
**IRRT**.......... International Relations Round Table [*American Library Association*]
**IRRTS**....... Infrared Resolution Target System (MCD)
**IRRTTM**... Integral Rocket Ramjet Torpedo Tube Missile (MCD)
**IRRV**.......... Institute of Revenues, Rating, and Valuation [*British*]
**IRS**............ Immunoreactive Secretin [*Endocrinology*]
**IRS**............ Immunoreactive Somatostatin [*Endocrinology*]
**IRS**............ Inactive Reserve Section [*Military*]
**IRS**............ Inboard Rotating Shield
**IRS**............ Incremental Range Summary
**IRS**............ Independent Rear Suspension [*Automotive engineering*]
**IRS**............ Independent Research Service [*Defunct*]
**IRS**............ Indian Register of Shipping (DS)
**IRS**............ Indian Remote-Sensing Satellite
**IRS**............ Indirect Representative Supplement [*British*]
**IRS**............ Induction and Recruiting Station [*Marine Corps*]
**IRS**............ Industrial Rehabilitation Service [*Australia*]
**IRS**............ Industrial Relations Section [*Princeton University*] [*Research center*] (RCD)
**IRS**............ Ineligible Reserve Section
**IRS**............ Inertial Reference System (KSC)
**IRS**............ Infant Rating Scale [*Child development test*]

**IRS**............ Informal Routing Slip
**IRS**............ Information Recovery [*or Retrieval*] System [*or Subsystem*]
**IRS**............ Information Research Services [*Information service or system*] (IID)
**IRS**............ Information Resources Specialists [*Information service or system*] (IID)
**IRS**............ Information Retrieval Service [*Memphis State University Libraries*] (OLDSS)
**IRS**............ Information Retrieval Service [*European Space Agency*] [*Host*] (IID)
**IRS**............ Information Retrieval System (OICC)
**IRS**............ Infrared RADAR Suppressor (MCD)
**IRS**............ Infrared Reconnaissance Set (MCD)
**IRS**............ Infrared Reflective Spectra
**IRS**............ Infrared Soldering
**IRS**............ Infrared Source
**IRS**............ Infrared Spectrometer [*or Spectroscopy*]
**IRS**............ Inorganic Resin System [*Fire-resistant cement*]
**IRS**............ Input Read Submodule
**IRS**............ Inquiry and Reporting System
**IRS**............ Inspection Record Sheet
**IRS**............ Installation Readiness System [*Army*]
**IRS**............ Instructional Review System
**IRS**............ Instrumentation RADAR Set
**I & RS**........ Instrumentation and Range Safety [*NASA*] (KSC)
**IRS**............ Insurance Sales [*A publication*]
**IRS**............ Integrated Rate System
**IRS**............ Integrated Record System (KSC)
**IRS**............ Integration Review Section [*Social Security Administration*]
**IRS**............ Intelligence Research Specialist [*Military*] (MCD)
**IRS**............ Interchange Record Separator [*Data processing*] (BUR)
**IRS**............ Interface Requirements Document [*DoD*]
**IRS**............ Interferon Response Sequence [*Genetics*]
**IRS**............ Intergroup Rhabdomyosarcoma Study [*Oncology*]
**IRS**............ Intermediate Reference Structure
**IRS**............ Internal Reflection Spectroscopy
**IRS**............ Internal Revenue Service [*Department of the Treasury*] [*Washington, DC*]
**IRS**............ Internal Revenue Service Library, Washington, DC [*OCLC symbol*] (OCLC)
**IRS**............ International Radio Silence
**IRS**............ International Records Syndicate, Inc.
**IRS**............ International Referral System [*United Nations Environment Programme*]
**IRS**............ International Repeater Station [*Telecommunications*] (TEL)
**IRS**............ International Rhinologic Society (EA)
**IRS**............ International Rorschach Society [*Strasbourg, France*] (EA)
**IRS**............ Inverse Raman Scattering [*Spectroscopy*]
**IRS**............ Iodine Removal System [*Nuclear energy*] (NRCH)
**IRS**............ Ionospheric Radio Signal
**IRS**............ Iran Service [*A publication*]
**IRS**............ Isoleucyl-tRNA Synthetase [*An enzyme*]
**IRS**............ Isotope Radiography System
**IRS**............ Isotope Removal Service (IEEE)
**IRS**............ Item Reduction Studies (MSA)
**IRS**............ Sturgis, MI [*Location identifier*] [*FAA*] (FAAL)
**IRSA**.......... Improved Radiator Standards Association (EA)
**IRSA**.......... International Racquet Sports Association [*Later, IRSAAQC*] (EA)
**IRSA**.......... International Rett Syndrome Association (EA)
**IRSA**.......... International Rural Sociology Association (EA)
**IRSAAQC**... IRSA [*International Racquet Sports Association*], the Association of Quality Clubs (EA)
**IRSAC**....... Institut pour la Recherche Scientifique en Afrique Centrale [*Brussels*]
**IRS Alcohl**... Alcohol, Tobacco, and Firearms Summary Statistics. US Internal Revenue Service [*A publication*]
**IRSB**.......... Institute for Research in Social Behavior [*Research center*] (RCD)
**IRSC**.......... Institut de Recherches Scientifiques au Congo
**IRSC**.......... Internal Revenue Service Centers
**IRSCAN**.... Infrared Scanner
**IRSCD2**..... Irrigation Science [*A publication*]
**IRSCL**........ International Research Society for Children's Literature [*Cadaujac, France*] (EA)
**IRSCOT**.... Infrared Structural Correlation Tables [*A publication*]
**IRSE**.......... Infrared Systems Engineering
**IRSE**.......... Institution of Railway Signal Engineers [*British*]
**IRSF**.......... Inland Revenue Staff Federation [*A union*] [*British*] (DCTA)
**IRSF**.......... International Roller Skating Federation (EA)
**IRSFC**........ International Rayon and Synthetic Fibres Committee [*See also CIRFS*] [*Paris, France*] (EAIO)
**IRSG**.......... International Rubber Study Group [*London, England*] (EAIO)
**IRSG**.......... Internationale Richard Strauss Gesellschaft [*An association*] (EAIO)
**IRSGHL**.... Infrared Systems and Guidance Heads Laboratory
**IRSH**.......... International Review of Social History [*A publication*]
**IRSI**........... Industrial Research and Service Institute
**IRSI**........... International Remote Sensing Institute (MCD)
**IR Sind**....... Indian Rulings, Sind Series [*A publication*] (DLA)
**IRSIO**........ International Rationalization, Standardization, and Interoperability Office (MCD)
**IRS Kurz-Inf Reihe A**... IRS [*Institut fuer Reaktorischerheit der Technischen Ueberwachungs-Vereine*] Kurz-Information. Reihe A [*West Germany*] [*A publication*]
**IRS Kurz-Inf Reihe B**... IRS [*Institut fuer Reaktorischerheit der Technischen Ueberwachungs-Vereine*] Kurz-Information. Reihe B [*West Germany*] [*A publication*]
**IRS Kurz-Inf Reihe C**... IRS [*Institut fuer Reaktorischerheit der Technischen Ueberwachungs-Vereine*] Kurz-Information. Reihe C [*West Germany*] [*A publication*]
**IRS Kurz-Inf Reihe D**... IRS [*Institut fuer Reaktorischerheit der Technischen Ueberwachungs-Vereine*] Kurz-Information. Reihe D [*West Germany*] [*A publication*]
**IRSL**.......... International Review of Slavic Linguistics [*A publication*]
**IRSLL**......... Image Recording System, Low Light
**IRSM**......... Immunoreactive Somatomedin [*Endocrinology*]
**IRSM**......... Infrared Systems Manufacturing
**IRS Mitt**.... IRS [*Institut fuer Reaktorischerheit der Technischen Ueberwachungs-Vereine*] Mitteilungen [*West Germany*] [*A publication*]
**IRSN**.......... Irvine Sensors Corp. [*NASDAQ symbol*] (NQ)
**IRSNAW**... Koninklijk Belgisch Instituut voor Natuurwetenschappen. Studiedocumenten [*A publication*]
**IRSO**.......... Infrared Solder Oven
**IRSO**.......... Institute of Road Safety Officers [*British*]
**IRSP**.......... Infrared Spectrometer [*or Spectroscopy*]
**IRSP**.......... Irish Republican Socialist Party [*Pairti Poblachtach Soisialach na h-Eireann*] (PPW)
**IRSPECT**.. Infrared Spectrometer [*or Spectroscopy*] (MCD)
**Ir Spelaeol**... Irish Spelaeology [*A publication*]
**IRSR**.......... Immediate Replacement Support Requirement (MCD)
**IRSS**.......... Inertial Reference Stabilization System
**IRSS**.......... Infrared Search Set
**IRSS**.......... Infrared Search System [*Institut za Nuklearne Nauke Boris Kidric*] [*Yugoslavia*] [*Information service or system*] (CRD)
**IRSS**.......... Infrared Search System [*Database*] [*Environmental Protection Agency*] [*Information service or system*] (CRD)
**IRSS**.......... Infrared Sensor System
**IRSS**.......... Infrared Smoke Simulator (MCD)
**IRSS**.......... Infrared Surveillance Subsystem
**IRSS**.......... Institute for Religious and Social Studies (EA)
**IRSS**.......... Institute for Research in Social Science [*University of North Carolina at Chapel Hill*] [*Research center*] (RCD)
**IRSS**.......... Institute for Resource and Security Studies (EA)
**IRSS**.......... Instrumentation and Range Safety System [*NASA*] (KSC)
**IRSSO**....... Infrared Search Set Operator
**IRST**.......... Infrared Search and Track
**Ir Stat**......... Irish Statutes [*A publication*] (DLA)
**IRSTS**......... Infrared Search and Track System
**Ir St Tr**....... Irish State Trials (Ridgeway's) [*A publication*] (DLA)
**IRSU**.......... International Radio Scientific Union (DEN)
**IRSU**.......... International Religious Studies Unit [*American Topical Association*] (EA)
**IRSU**.......... ISDN [*Integrated Services Digital Network*] Remote Subscriber Unit [*Telecommunications*]
**Ir Sword**..... Irish Sword [*A publication*]
**IRT**............. Icing Research Tunnel [*Built at Lewis Research Center in 1944 by the National Advisory Committee for Aeronautics*]
**IRT**............. Image Rejection Technology [*RADAR detection*]
**IRT**............. Immunoreactive Trypsin
**IRT**............. In-Reactor Thimble (IEEE)
**IRT**............. In Reference To (NVT)
**IRT**............. In Regard To (MCD)
**IRT**............. In Reply To (NVT)
**IRT**............. In Response To (NVT)
**IRT**............. Index Return Character [*Data processing*]
**IRT**............. Indicating Round Technique [*British*]
**IRT**............. Individual Reliability Test
**IRT**............. Industrial Reading Test
**IRT**............. Infinite-Resolution Trimmer
**IRT**............. Information Retrieval Technique (AAG)
**IRT**............. Infrared Radiation Thermometer (NOAA)
**IRT**............. Infrared Telescope
**IRT**............. Infrared Temperature
**IRT**............. Infrared Thermography
**IRT**............. Infrared Thermometer
**IRT**............. Infrared Tracker
**IRT**............. Infrared Tube
**IRT**............. Initialize Reset Tape
**IRT**............. Input Revision Typewriter
**IRT**............. [*The*] Inscriptions of Roman Tripolitania (BJA)
**IRT**............. Institute for Radiological Technologists
**IRT**............. Institute for Rapid Transit [*Later, APTA*] (EA)
**IRT**............. Institute for Reality Therapy (EA)
**IRT**............. Institute of Reprographic Technology
**IRT**............. Institute for Research on Teaching [*East Lansing, MI*] [*Department of Education*] (GRD)
**IRT**............. Integrated Readiness Testing
**IRT**............. Interboro Rapid Transit [*A New York City subway line*]

**IRT**............ Interim Remote Terminals (MCD)
**IRT**............ Intermediate-Range Technology
**IRT**............ Intermediate Rated Thrust [*Military*] (CAAL)
**IRT**............ Internal Reflection Technique
**IRT**............ International Research and Technology, Inc.
**IRT**............ Interresponse Time [*Psychometrics*]
**IRT**............ Interrogator-Responder-Transducer
**IRT**............ Interrupted Ring Tone [*Telecommunications*] (TEL)
**IRT**............ Inverse Reflex Tetrode [*Physics*]
**IRT**............ Irish Times [*A publication*]
**IRT**............ IRT Property Co. [*Formerly, Investors Realty Trust*] [*NYSE symbol*] (SPSG)
**IRT**............ Richmond Community Schools, Richmond, IN [*OCLC symbol*] (OCLC)
**IRTA**.......... Independent Retail Tobacconists Association of America [*Defunct*] (EA)
**IRTA**.......... International Reciprocal Trade Association (EA)
**IRTA**.......... Intramural Research Training Award [*National Institutes of Health*]
**IRTAC**....... International Round Table for the Advancement of Counseling [*Great Britain*]
**IRTAFS**..... International Ready-to-Assemble Furniture Show (ITD)
**IRTC**......... Infantry Replacement Training Center
**IRTCA4**..... Instrumentation Technology [*A publication*]
**IRTCM**...... Integrated Real-Time Contamination Monitor [*Module*]
**IRTD**.......... Infantry Reinforcement Training Depot [*British military*] (DMA)
**IRTD**.......... Infrared Target Detector
**IrTD**........... Iranian Documentation Centre, Tehran, Iran [*Library symbol*] [*Library of Congress*] (LCLS)
**IRTE**.......... Institut de Radio-Telediffusion pour Enfants [*Children's Broadcast Institute*] [*Canada*]
**IRTE**.......... Institute of Road Transport Engineers (EAIO)
**Ir Term Rep** ... Irish Term Reports, by Ridgeway, Lapp, and Schoales [*A publication*] (DLA)
**Ir Text J**..... Irish Textile Journal [*A publication*]
**IRTF**.......... Infrared Telescope Facility
**IRTF**.......... Inter-Religious Task Force on Central America (EA)
**IRTF**.......... Intermediate-Range Task Force
**IRTM**......... Infrared Thermal Mapper [*NASA*]
**IRT Nucl J** ... IR and T Nuclear Journal [*United States*] [*A publication*]
**IRTOD9** .... IPI [*International Potash Institute*] Research Topics [*A publication*]
**IRTP**.......... Initial Recruiting and Training Plan [*Military*]
**IRTP**.......... Integrated Reliability Test Program
**IrTQ**........... Irish Theological Quarterly [*Maynooth*] [*A publication*]
**Ir TR**.......... Irish Term Reports, by Ridgeway, Lapp, and Schoales [*A publication*] (DLA)
**IRTR**.......... IRT Realty Services, Inc. [*NASDAQ symbol*] (NQ)
**IRTRAN**.... Infrared Transmitting
**IRTRN**...... Infrared Transmission
**IRTS**.......... Infrared Target Seeker (MSA)
**IRTS**.......... Interim Recovery Technical Specification (IEEE)
**IRTS**.......... International Radio and Television Society (EA)
**IRTU**.......... Integrating Regulatory Transcription Units [*Genetics*]
**IRTU**.......... Intelligent Remote Terminal Unit
**IRTU**.......... International Railway Temperance Union
**IRTWG**...... Interrange Telemetry Working Group
**IRTWS**...... Infrared Tail Warning Set (MCD)
**IRU**............ Indefeasible Right of User [*Telecommunications*] (TEL)
**IRU**............ Industrial Rehabilitation Units [*British*]
**IRU**............ Inertial Reference Unit
**IRU**............ Information Resources Unit [*CSIRO*] [*Australia*] [*Information service or system*] (IID)
**IRU**............ Interferon Reference Unit
**IRU**............ International Radium Unit
**IRU**............ International Raiffeisen Union (EA)
**IRU**............ International Relief Union
**IRU**............ International Road Transport Union [*Geneva, Switzerland*] (EAIO)
**IRU**............ Internationale Raiffeisen-Union [*International Raiffeisen Union*] (EAIO)
**IRU**............ Irvine Research Unit [*University of California, Irvine*]
**IRU**............ New Mexico State University, Las Cruces, NM [*OCLC symbol*] (OCLC)
**IRUC**.......... Information and Research Utilization Center in Physical Education and Recreation for the Handicapped [*American Association for Health, Physical Education, and Recreation*]
**IRUS**.......... Infantry Rifle Unit Study [*Army*]
**IRut**........... Rutland Community Library, Rutland, IL [*Library symbol*] [*Library of Congress*] (LCLS)
**IRV**............ Inglewood [*Forest*] Rifle Volunteers [*British military*] (DMA)
**IRV**............ Inspiratory Reserve Volume [*Physiology*]
**IRV**............ Inter-Range Vector [*NASA*] (KSC)
**IRV**............ International Rex Ventures, Inc. [*Vancouver Stock Exchange symbol*]
**IRV**............ Internationale Rat fuer Vogelschutz [*International Council for Bird Preservation*]
**IRV**............ Interrupt Request Vector
**IRV**............ Inversed Ratio of Ventilation
**Irv**.............. Irvine's Scotch Justiciary Reports [*1851-68*] [*A publication*] (DLA)
**IRV**............ Isotope Reentry Vehicle [*NASA*] (NASA)
**IRV**............ Istituto Tecnico Statale Commerciale e per Geometri Roberto Valturio [*Rimini*] [*A publication*]
**IRVC**.......... Indian Remount and Veterinary Corps [*British military*] (DMA)
**Irv Civ Law** ... Irving's Civil Law [*A publication*] (DLA)
**Ir Vet J**....... Irish Veterinary Journal [*A publication*]
**IRVH**.......... Integrated Reactor Vessel Head [*Nuclear energy*] (NRCH)
**Irvine Just Cas** ... Irvine's Justiciary Cases [*England*] [*A publication*] (DLA)
**Irving Civ Law** ... Irving's Civil Law [*A publication*] (DLA)
**Irving View** ... Irving Trust Company. Economic View from One Wall Street [*A publication*]
**Irv Just**....... Irvine's Justiciary Cases [*England*] [*A publication*] (DLA)
**IRVSS**........ Infrared Vertical Sounding System [*Oceanography*] (MSC)
**IRW**............ Index of Relative Worth (MCD)
**IRW**............ Indirect Reference Word (BUR)
**IRW**............ Infrared Window
**IRW**............ Institute for Rural Water (EA)
**IRW**............ International Rehabilitation Week [*Trade show*]
**IRW**............ International Rocket Week
**IRW**............ Rubber World [*A publication*]
**IRWA**.......... International Right of Way Association (EA)
**IRWA**.......... International Rodeo Writers Association [*Later, RMA*] (EA)
**IRWC**.......... International Registry of World Citizens
**Ir WCC**....... Irish Workmen's Compensation Cases [*A publication*] (DLA)
**IRWEP**....... International Register for the White Eared Pheasant (EAIO)
**Irwin's Code** ... Clark, Cobb, and Irwin's Code [*Georgia*] [*A publication*] (DLA)
**IRWJF**........ Irwin Toy Ltd. Vtg [*NASDAQ symbol*] (NQ)
**IRWKF**....... Irwin Toy Ltd. Non Vtg [*NASDAQ symbol*] (NQ)
**Ir WLR**....... Irish Weekly Law Reports [*1895-1902*] [*A publication*] (DLA)
**IRWN**......... Irwin Magnetic Systems, Inc. [*Ann Arbor, MI*] [*NASDAQ symbol*] (NQ)
**IRWR**......... Infrared Warning Receiver [*Aviation*] (MCD)
**IRX**............ Interactive Resource Executive [*NCR Corp.*]
**IRY**............ Iron Bay Trust [*Toronto Stock Exchange symbol*]
**IRYDA**........ Instituto Nacional de Reforma y Desarrollo Agrario [*National Institute for Agrarian Reform and Development*] [*Spain*] (EY)
**IRZ**............ Inner Radiation Zone
**IRZ**............ International Reference Zero [*Level for pure-tone audiometers*]
**IS**............... Air Survey Co. of India Ltd. [*ICAO designator*] [*Obsolete*] (FAAC)
**IS**............... Ibbi-Sin (BJA)
**IS**............... Ice Screamers (EA)
**IS**............... Iceland [*ANSI two-letter standard code*] (CNC)
**IS**............... Ideological Survey [*Psychology*]
**IS**............... IDS Aircraft Ltd. [*United Kingdom*] [*ICAO designator*] (ICDA)
**IS**............... Immortalist Society (EA)
**IS**............... Immune Serum [*Also, ImS*]
**IS**............... Immunological Similarity
**IS**............... Immunosuppressive [*Immunochemistry*]
**IS**............... Improved Suspension (MCD)
**IS**............... In Service [*Telecommunications*] (TEL)
**IS**............... In Shop (MCD)
**IS**............... In Situ [*In Place*] [*Latin*]
**IS**............... Including Sheeting
**IS**............... Income Statement [*Business term*]
**IS**............... Incomplete Sequence (MSA)
**IS**............... Independent Sector (EA)
**IS**............... Independent Shoemen of America [*Defunct*] (EA)
**IS**............... Independent Spherical Aluminum Tank [*on a ship*] (DS)
**IS**............... Indexed Sequential [*Data processing*]
**IS**............... Indexing in Source
**IS**............... Indicating Switch (NRCH)
**IS**............... Induction Soldering
**IS**............... Industrial School [*British*] (ROG)
**IS**............... Industrial Service [*Equipment specifications*]
**IS**............... Industrial Society [*A publication*]
**IS**............... Industrial Specialist
**IS**............... Industrial Systems (DS)
**IS**............... Inertial Systems (AFIT)
**IS**............... [*The*] Infantry School [*Army*] (MCD)
**IS**............... Infection Structure [*Plant pathology*]
**IS**............... Information Science (IEEE)
**IS**............... Information Seekers
**IS**............... Information Separator [*Control character*] [*Data processing*]
**IS**............... Information Service
**IS**............... Information System
**IS**............... Information Systems [*Ori, Inc.*] [*Information service or system*] (IID)
**IS**............... Infrasonic
**IS**............... Inglish Speling 3soesiaesh3n [*An organization to reform spelling*] [*See also IS3*] (EA)
**IS**............... Initial Shortage (AFM)
**IS**............... Initiation Supervisor
**IS**............... Inner Sheath [*Botany*]
**IS**............... Input Secondary [*Electronics*]

**IS**............... Input Simulator
**IS**............... Insect Screen (AAG)
**IS**............... INSERM [*Institut National de la Sante et de la Recherche Medicale*] Symposia [*Elsevier Book Series*] [*A publication*]
**IS**............... Insertion Sequence [*Genetics*]
**I/S**............... Inside [*Automotive engineering*]
**IS**............... Inside Sentinel [*Freemasonry*]
**I & S**.......... Inspection and Security
**IS**............... Inspection Services, Inc. (EA)
**I & S**.......... [*Board of*] Inspection and Survey [*Military*]
**I & S**.......... Installation and Services
**IS**............... Installation Start [*Telecommunications*] (TEL)
**IS**............... Installation Support (KSC)
**IS**............... Institute of Statisticians [*Great Britain*]
**IS**............... Instruction Sheet
**IS**............... Instructions to Ship (AAG)
**IS**............... Instrumentation Ships Project [*Navy*]
**IS**............... Instrumentation Summary (MUGU)
**IS**............... Instrumentation System (KSC)
**IS**............... Insufficiently Stamped [*Post office*] [*British*] (ROG)
**IS**............... Insulating Sleeve
**IS**............... Insurance Salesman [*A publication*]
**IS**............... Integrally Stiffened
**IS**............... Integrated Satellite [*Military spacecraft*]
**IS**............... Integrating Support
**IS**............... Intelligence in the Sky [*An extraterrestrial intelligence with whom Dr. Andrija Puharich and psychic Uri Geller claim to have communicated*]
**IS**............... Intelligence Specialist [*Navy*]
**IS**............... Intelligence Support [*Program*] [*Department of State*]
**IS**............... Intelligence Systems [*Military*] (MCD)
**I & S**.......... Interchangeability and Substitutability (AFM)
**IS**............... Interconnecting Station (MCD)
**IS**............... Intercostal Space [*Medicine*]
**IS**............... Interference Suppressor (IEEE)
**IS**............... Interior Surface
**IS**............... Intermediate School
**IS**............... Intermediate Suppression (MCD)
**IS**............... Internal Security [*Military*] [*British*]
**IS**............... Internal Shield [*Electronics*]
**IS**............... Internal Standard [*Chemistry*]
**IS**............... Internal Surface (AAG)
**IS**............... International Services [*Red Cross*]
**IS**............... International Socialist [*A publication*]
**IS**............... International Socialists
**IS**............... International Society of Sculptors, Painters, and Gravers
**IS**............... International Staff (NATG)
**IS**............... International Standard
**IS**............... International Stock [*Business term*]
**IS**............... International Studies [*A publication*]
**IS**............... Internationale Schutzenunion [*International Shooting Union*] (EAIO)
**IS**............... Internationaler Suchdienst [*International Tracing Service*] (EAIO)
**IS**............... Intersegmental
**IS**............... Interservice
**IS**............... Intership [*Freight forwarding company*] [*British*]
**IS**............... Interspace
**I/S**............... Interstage
**IS**............... Interstate
**IS**............... Interstate/Johnson Lane [*Formerly, Interstate Securities, Inc.*] [*NYSE symbol*] (SPSG)
**IS**............... Interval Signal
**IS**............... Intraspinal [*Injection*]
**IS**............... Invalided from Service [*Medicine*] [*Navy*]
**I/S**............... Inventory to Sales Ratio [*Business term*]
**IS**............... Inventory Schedule
**I & S**.......... Investigation and Suspension
**I-S**............... Investment-Savings Curve [*Economics*]
**IS**............... Ion Source [*Spectroscopy*]
**IS**............... Irish Society
**IS**............... Irish Statesman [*A publication*]
**I & S**.......... Iron and Steel
**Is**............... Isaiah [*Old Testament book*]
**Is**............... Isidore [*Authority cited in pre-1607 legal work*] (DSA)
**Is**............... Isis [*A publication*]
**Is**............... Islam (BJA)
**Is**............... Islands [*Maps and charts*]
**IS**............... Isle (EY)
**I/S**............... Isle Of Skye [*Scotland*] (ROG)
**IS**............... Isolated Step
**IS**............... Isolation
**IS**............... Isotopic Separation [*Subsystem*] (MCD)
**is**............... Israel [*MARC country of publication code*] [*Library of Congress*] (LCCP)
**Is**............... Israel [*IYRU nationality code*] (BJA)
**IS**............... ISSN [*International Standard Serial Number*] [*Online database field identifier*]
**IS**............... Issue Code [*Online database field identifier*]
**IS**............... Istituto Superiore di Sanita [*Italy*] [*Research code symbol*]
**IS**............... Italian Studies [*A publication*]
**IS**............... Italienische Studien [*A publication*]
**IS**............... Staatsblad van Indonesie [*A publication*]
**I2S**............... Imagerie, Industrie, Systeme [*Machine vision manufacturer*] [*France*]
**I2S**............... Integrated Information System [*Marine Corps*]
**IS3**............... Ingglish Speling 3soesiaesh3n [*English Spelling Association*] (EA)
**4IS**............... Four-Wheel Independent Suspension [*Automotive engineering*]
**I-10/S**......... Invert Sugar [*10%*] in Saline [*Medicine*]
**I2S2**............... Intelligence Information Subsystem [*Military*]
**ISA**............... Ibsen Society of America (EA)
**ISA**............... Idle Speed Actuator [*Automotive engineering*]
**ISA**............... Ignition and Separation Assembly
**ISA**............... Illinois Studies in Anthropology [*A publication*]
**ISA**............... Independent Scholars of Asia (EA)
**ISA**............... Independent Shoemen of America [*Defunct*]
**ISA**............... Independent Signcrafters of America (EA)
**ISA**............... Individual Savings Account [*Proposed*]
**ISA**............... Indonesian Sawmill Association (DS)
**ISA**............... Inductee Special Assignment
**ISA**............... Industrie Siderurgiche Associate [*Associated Iron and Steel Industries*] [*Italy*] (EY)
**ISA**............... Inertial Sensor Assembly [*Military*] (CAAL)
**ISA**............... Infantry Sailing Association [*British*]
**ISA**............... Information Science Abstracts [*A publication*]
**ISA**............... Information Systems Architecture [*AT & T*]
**ISA**............... Information Systems Association (EA)
**ISA**............... Innkeepers Society of America [*Defunct*] (EA)
**ISA**............... Inorganic Sampling and Analysis
**ISA**............... Insecta Research [*Vancouver Stock Exchange symbol*]
**ISA**............... Installation Supply Accounting
**ISA**............... Installation Supply Activity
**ISA**............... Installations and Services Agency [*Army Materiel Command*]
**ISA**............... Institute for Scientific Analysis (EA)
**ISA**............... Institute of Systems Analysis [*Army*]
**ISA**............... Instruction Set Architecture [*Data processing*] [*Army*] (RDA)
**ISA**............... Instructional Systems Association (EA)
**ISA**............... Instrument Society of America (EA)
**ISA**............... Instrument Subassembly (IEEE)
**ISA**............... Insulating Siding Association [*Defunct*] (EA)
**ISA**............... Insurance Service Associates [*Later, Assurex International*]
**ISA**............... Integrated Support Area (NVT)
**ISA**............... Intelligence Support Activity [*Military*]
**ISA**............... Intercoastal Steamship Freight Association, New York NY [*STAC*]
**ISA**............... Interconexion Electrica, Sociedad Anonima
**ISA**............... Interface Switching Assembly
**ISA**............... Intergalactic SYSOP [*System Operator*] Alliance (EA)
**ISA**............... Interim Stowage Assembly
**ISA**............... Intermediate Specific Activity [*Radioisotope*]
**ISA**............... Internal Storage Area [*Data processing*] (BYTE)
**ISA**............... International Safety Academy
**ISA**............... International Schools Association [*Geneva, Switzerland*] (EA)
**ISA**............... International Seabed Authority
**ISA**............... International Security Affairs [*DoD*]
**ISA**............... International Security Agency
**ISA**............... International Service Agencies
**ISA**............... International Shakespeare Association (EA)
**ISA**............... International Shipmasters Association of the Great Lakes (EA)
**ISA**............... International Shuffleboard Association (EA)
**ISA**............... International Sign Association [*Absorbed by NESA*] (EA)
**ISA**............... International Silk Association - USA (EA)
**ISA**............... International Silo Association (EA)
**ISA**............... International Skateboard Association (EA)
**ISA**............... International Skeeter Association
**ISA**............... International Society of Appraisers [*Hoffman Estates, IL*] (EA)
**ISA**............... International Society of Arboriculture (EA)
**ISA**............... International Society of Women Airline Pilots (EA)
**ISA**............... International Sociological Association [*Research center*] [*Spain*] (IRC)
**ISA**............... International Soling Association [*Bordon, Hampshire, England*] (EAIO)
**ISA**............... International Songwriters' Association (EAIO)
**ISA**............... International Standard Atmosphere
**ISA**............... International Standards Association
**ISA**............... International Stiltwalkers Association (EA)
**ISA**............... International Strabismological Association (EAIO)
**ISA**............... International Studies Association (EA)
**ISA**............... International Subscription Agencies Pty. Ltd. [*Australia*]
**ISA**............... International Sugar Agreement [*1958*]
**ISA**............... International Surfing Association [*Swansea, England*] (EAIO)
**ISA**............... International Swift Association (EA)
**ISA**............... Interplant Shipping Authority
**ISA**............... Interrupt Storage Area
**ISA**............... Intersecting Storage Accelerator [*In name of atomic reactor, Isabelle*]
**ISA**............... Interservice Support Agreement [*Military*]
**ISA**............... Intrinsic Sympathomimetic Activity [*Biochemistry*]
**ISA**............... Investment Savings Account (ADA)
**ISA**............... Iodinated Serum Albumin [*Medicine*]

**ISA**.......... Ion Scattering Analysis
**ISA**.......... Iron and Steel Authority [*Philippines*] (DS)
**ISA**.......... Irregular Serials and Annuals [*A publication*]
**ISA**.......... Irregular Spiking Activity [*Electrophysiology*]
**ISA**.......... Isabella [*California*] [*Seismograph station code, US Geological Survey*] (SEIS)
**Isa**.......... Isaiah [*Old Testament book*]
**ISA**.......... Isaias [*Old Testament book*] [*Douay version*]
**ISA**.......... Mount Isa [*Australia*] [*Airport symbol*] (OAG)
**ISA**.......... Pacific Island Airways [*Agana, GU*] [*FAA designator*] (FAAC)
**ISA**.......... UNRWA [*United Nations Relief and Works Agency*] International Staff Association (EAIO)
**ISA + 21**... International Social Affiliation of Women Airline Pilots [*Later, ISWAP*] (EA)
**ISAA**.......... Insurance Service Association of America [*Later, Assurex International*] (EA)
**ISAA**.......... Intercollegiate Soccer Association of America (EA)
**ISAAC**....... Information System for Advanced Academic Computing (EISS)
**ISAAC**....... Integrated System for Automated Acquisition and Control
**ISAAC**....... International Society for Alternative and Augmentative Communication (EA)
**IS/A AMPE**... Inter-Service Agency Automated Message Processing Exchange
**ISAARE**.... Information System for Adaptive, Assistive, and Rehabilitation Equipment [*For the handicapped*]
**ISABC**....... International Society Against Breast Cancer (EAIO)
**ISABEL**..... ISO [*International Organization for Standardization*] Status Accumulating Binaries [*Using*] Extraordinary Logic
**ISABPS**..... Integrated Submarine Automated Broadcasting Processing System (MCD)
**ISABR**....... International Society for Animal Blood Group Research [*Australia*] (EAIO)
**ISABS**........ Integrated Submarine Automated Broadcast Processing System [*Navy*] (CAAL)
**ISAC**.......... Industrial Safety Advisory Council [*British*]
**ISAC**.......... Industrial Security Association of Canada
**ISAC**.......... Industry Sector Advisory Committee [*Established by Trade Reform Act for industry-to-government advice*]
**ISAC**.......... Instrumentation System Assessment Center (MCD)
**ISAC**.......... International Security Affairs Committee
**ISAC**.......... International Society for Autistic Children (EA)
**ISAC**.......... Interuniversity Southeast Asia Committee [*of the Association for Asia*]
**ISAC**.......... Issues and Commentary [*Alaska*] [*A publication*]
**ISACCC**...... Initial Satellite Communications Control Center (MCD)
**ISACMETU**... International Secretariat of Arts, Communications Media, and Entertainment Trade Unions (EAIO)
**ISAD**.......... Information Science and Automation Division [*Later, LITA*] [*American Library Association*]
**ISADC**....... Interim Standard Airborne Digital Computer (MCD)
**ISADPM**... International Society for the Abolition of Data Processing Machines (EA)
**ISADS**....... Innovative Strategic Aircraft Design Studies (IEEE)
**ISAE**.......... Internacia Scienca Asocio Esperantista [*International Association of Esperanto-Speaking Scientists*] [*Oslo, Norway*] (EA)
**Isae**.......... Isaeus [*Fourth century BC*] [*Classical studies*] (OCD)
**ISAeM**....... International Society for Aerosols in Medicine [*See also IGAeM*] (EAIO)
**ISAF**.......... Intermediate Super-Abrasion Furnace
**ISAF**.......... Isotopic Source Adjustable Fissometer [*Nuclear energy*] (NRCH)
**IsAF**.......... Israeli Air Force
**ISAFA**....... Industrial Safety [*A publication*]
**ISAG**.......... Office of the Auditor General, Springfield, IL [*Library symbol*] [*Library of Congress*] (LCLS)
**ISAGA**....... International Simulation and Gaming Association (EA)
**ISAGE**....... International Symposium on Antarctic Glaciological Exploration
**ISAGEX**.... International Satellite Geodesy Experiment
**ISAGL**....... International Shipmasters Association of the Great Lakes
**ISAGUG**.... International Software AG Users Group (EA)
**ISAI**.......... Independent Schools Association [*British*]
**ISA J**.......... ISA [*Instrument Society of America*] Journal [*A publication*]
**ISAJA**........ ISA [*Instrument Society of America*] Journal [*A publication*]
**ISal**.......... Bryan-Bennett Public Library, Salem, IL [*Library symbol*] [*Library of Congress*] (LCLS)
**ISAL**.......... Information System Access Lines [*Data processing*]
**ISALC**....... International Society of Animal License Collectors (EA)
**ISalCD**....... Selmaville Community Consolidated District 10, Salem, IL [*Library symbol*] [*Library of Congress*] (LCLS)
**ISALPA**..... Incorporated Society of Auctioneers and Landed Property Agents [*British*] (ILCA)
**ISAM**......... Indexed Sequential Access Method [*Pronounced "i-sam"*] [*Data processing*]
**ISAM**......... Institute for Studies in American Music (EA)
**ISAM**......... Integrated Switching and Multiplexing [*IBM Corp.*]
**ISAM**......... International Society for Aerosols in Medicine (EAIO)
**ISAM**......... Israeli Society for the Application of Mathematics (MCD)
**ISAMS**...... Improved Stratospheric and Mesospheric Sounder (MCD)
**ISan**.......... Sandwich Township Public Library, Sandwich, IL [*Library symbol*] [*Library of Congress*] (LCLS)
**ISanCH**...... Sandwich Community Hospital, Sandwich, IL [*Library symbol*] [*Library of Congress*] (LCLS)
**ISandSD**.... Sandoval Community Unit School District 501, Sandoval, IL [*Library symbol*] [*Library of Congress*] (LCLS)
**ISanH**........ Lynn G. Haskin School, Sandwich, IL [*Library symbol*] [*Library of Congress*] (LCLS)
**ISanHS**...... Sandwich Community High School, Sandwich, IL [*Library symbol*] [*Library of Congress*] (LCLS)
**ISanJS**....... Sandwich Junior High School, Sandwich, IL [*Library symbol*] [*Library of Congress*] (LCLS)
**ISanP**......... Prairie View School, Sandwich, IL [*Library symbol*] [*Library of Congress*] (LCLS)
**I-SANTA**... Industrial Stapling and Nailing Technical Association (EA)
**ISANTA**.... International Staple, Nail, and Tool Association (EA)
**ISanW**........ W. W. Woodbury School, Sandwich, IL [*Library symbol*] [*Library of Congress*] (LCLS)
**ISAO**.......... International Society for Artificial Organs (EA)
**ISAP**.......... Individual System Automation Plans [*Military*]
**ISAP**.......... Information Sort and Predict
**ISAP**.......... Institute for the Study of Animal Problems [*Defunct*] (EA)
**ISAP**.......... Instituto Sudamericano del Petroleo [*South American Petroleum Institute*]
**ISAP**.......... Integrated Safety Assessment Program [*Nuclear energy*] (NRCH)
**ISAP**.......... International School Art Program [*Defunct*]
**ISAP**.......... International Society of Art and Psychopathology [*Paris, France*] (EA)
**ISAPA**....... International Screen Advertising Producer's Association [*Defunct*] (EA)
**ISA Prepr**.. ISA [*Instrument Society of America*] Conference Preprint [*A publication*]
**ISA Proc Int Power Instrum Symp**... ISA [*Instrument Society of America*] Proceedings. International Power Instrumentation Symposium [*A publication*]
**ISA Proc Natl Aerosp Instrum Symp**... ISA [*Instrument Society of America*] Proceedings. National Aerospace Instrumentation Symposium [*United States*] [*A publication*]
**ISA Proc Natl Power Instrum Symp**... ISA [*Instrument Society of America*] Proceedings. National Power Instrumentation Symposium [*United States*] [*A publication*]
**ISAR**.......... Information Storage and Retrieval [*Data processing*] (DIT)
**ISAR**.......... Institute for Soviet-American Relations (EA)
**ISAR**.......... Inter-Seamount Acoustic Range
**ISAR**.......... International Society for Animal Rights (EA)
**ISAR**.......... International Society for Astrological Research (EA)
**ISARC**....... Installation Shipping and Receiving Capability [*Army*] (AABC)
**ISAS**.......... Infrared Small Astronomical Spacecraft
**ISAS**.......... Institute of Space and Aeronautical Science [*Japan*]
**ISAS**.......... Integrated Smart Artillery Synthesis (RDA)
**ISAS**.......... International Society of African Scientists (EA)
**ISAS**.......... Isotopic Source Assay System
**ISAS**.......... Iterative Single Wavelength Anomalous Scattering [*Crystallography*]
**ISASC**....... International Society of Antique Scale Collectors (EA)
**ISASI**........ International Society of Air Safety Investigators (EA)
**ISASNP**..... International Symposium on Aerospace Nuclear Propulsion (MCD)
**ISAST**....... International Society for the Arts, Sciences, and Technology (EA)
**ISAT**.......... Initial Surface Absorption Test
**ISAT**.......... International Society of Analytical Trilogy [*See also SITA*] [*Sao Paulo, Brazil*] (EAIO)
**ISAT**.......... Invite, Show, and Test [*Military*] (SDI)
**ISATA**....... ISA [*Instrument Society of America*] Transactions [*A publication*]
**ISATAZ**..... ISA [*Instrument Society of America*] Transactions [*A publication*]
**ISA Trans**.. ISA [*Instrument Society of America*] Transactions [*A publication*]
**ISAUS**....... Indonesian Students Association in the United States (EA)
**ISAUS**....... Iranian Students Association in the United States
**ISAV**.......... Institute of Sound and Vibration (MCD)
**ISAV**.......... Instituto de Sistemas Audio-Visuales [*Institute of Audio-Visual Media*] [*Colombia*]
**ISAW**......... International Society of Aviation Writers
**ISAZ**.......... Isolation Accommodation Zone [*Geology*]
**ISB**............ Illinois Baptist Historical Library, Springfield, IL [*Library symbol*] [*Library of Congress*] (LCLS)
**ISB**............ Independent School Bulletin [*A publication*]
**ISB**............ Independent Sideband
**ISB**............ Independent Society of Bricklayers [*A union*] [*British*]
**ISB**............ Industry Service Bureaus
**ISB**............ Information Services Branch [*Chalk River Nuclear Laboratories*] [*Atomic Energy of Canada Ltd.*] [*Information service or system*] (IID)
**ISB**............ Information Systems Branch [*National Institutes of Health*] (IID)
**ISB**............ Institute of Scientific Business [*British*]
**ISB**............ Institute of Small Business [*British*]

**ISB**............ Intelligence and Security Board [*Military*] (MCD)
**ISB**............ Interchange Financial Services Corp. [*Formerly, Interchange State Bank*] [*AMEX symbol*] (SPSG)
**ISB**............ Interchangeability Survey Board
**ISB**............ Intermediate Sideband (NATG)
**ISB**............ Intermediate Staging Base
**ISB**............ Intermediate Support Base [*Military*] (NVT)
**ISB**............ International Sinabarb [*Vancouver Stock Exchange symbol*]
**ISB**............ International Society of Bassists (EA)
**ISB**............ International Society of Bassists. Newsletter [*A publication*]
**ISB**............ International Society of Biometeorology [*See also SIB*] [*Zurich, Switzerland*] (EAIO)
**ISB**............ International Society of Biorheology (EA)
**ISB**............ International Symposium on Biomembranes
**ISB**............ Internationale Spectator [*A publication*]
**ISB**............ Internationaler Studentenbund [*International Union of Students*]
**ISB**............ Interstate Tariff Bureau, Inc., Lakewood OH [*STAC*]
**ISB**............ Investors Service Bureau [*Investment term*]
**ISB**............ Islamabad/Rawalpindi [*Pakistan*] [*Airport symbol*] (OAG)
**ISB**............ Southern Methodist University, Bridwell Library, Dallas, TX [*OCLC symbol*] (OCLC)
**ISBA**.......... Incorporated Society of British Advertisers [*British*]
**ISBA**.......... Independent Safety Board Act of 1974
**ISBA**.......... Independent Schools Bursars' Association [*British*]
**ISBA**.......... International Ships-in-Bottles Association (EA)
**ISBB**.......... International Society of Bioclimatology and Biometeorology (IEEE)
**ISBC**.......... Infantry Squad Battle Course [*Army*]
**ISBC**.......... Institute of Certified Business Counselors (EA)
**ISBC**.......... Interdepartmental Savings Bond Committee [*Military*] (AABC)
**ISBC**.......... International Society of Bible Collectors (EA)
**ISBD**.......... International Soap Box Derby, Inc. (EA)
**ISBD**.......... International Standard Bibliographic Description [*Library of Congress*]
**ISBD(A)**.... International Standard Bibliographic Description - Antiquarian
**ISBD(CM)**... International Standard Bibliographic Description for Cartographic Materials [*Library of Congress*]
**ISBD(CP)**.. International Standard Bibliographic Description (Component Parts) (ADA)
**ISBD(G)**.... International Standard Bibliographic Description - General
**ISBD(M)**... International Standard Bibliographic Description for Monographs [*Library of Congress*]
**ISBD(NBM)**... International Standard Bibliographic Description for Non-Book Materials
**ISBD(PM)**... International Standard Bibliographic Description for Printed Music
**ISBD(S)**..... International Standard Bibliographic Description for Serials [*Library of Congress*]
**ISBE**.......... Independent Small Business Employers of America (EA)
**ISBE**.......... International Society for Boundary Elements (EAIO)
**ISBE**.......... International Society for Business Education, US Chapter [*Reston, VA*] (EA)
**ISBE**.......... International Standard Bible Encyclopaedia [*A publication*] (BJA)
**ISBEA**....... Independent Small Business Employers of America [*Later, ISBE*] (EA)
**ISBF**.......... Interactive Search of Bibliographic Files
**ISBGFH**.... International Society for British Genealogy and Family History (EA)
**ISBI**........... International Savings Banks Institute [*See also IICE*] [*Geneva, Switzerland*] (EAIO)
**ISBI**........... International Society for Burn Injuries (EA)
**ISBIC**......... Interservice Balkan Intelligence Committee [*World War II*]
**ISBL**.......... Information System Base Language
**ISBL**.......... Inside Battery Limits [*Chemical engineering*]
**ISBM**......... International Society of Biophysical Medicine [*British*] (IRUK)
**ISBN**......... International Standard Book Number [*Library of Congress*]
**ISBO**.......... Islamic States Broadcasting Organization [*Jeddah, Saudi Arabia*] (EAIO)
**ISBP**.......... International Society for Biochemical Pharmacology
**ISBRA**....... International Society Biomedical Research on Alcoholism (EAIO)
**ISBS**.......... International Specialized Books Services [*Book distributor*]
**ISBT**.......... International Society of Blood Transfusion (EA)
**ISC**............ Concordia Theological Seminary, Springfield, IL [*Library symbol*] [*Library of Congress*] [*Obsolete*] (LCLS)
**ISC**............ Duneland School Corp., Chesterton, IN [*OCLC symbol*] (OCLC)
**ISc**............ Iconic Store, Central [*Psychophysiology*]
**ISC**............ Idle Speed Control [*Automotive engineering*]
**I-SC**.......... Illinois Supreme Court, Springfield, IL [*Library symbol*] [*Library of Congress*] (LCLS)
**ISC**............ Immune Spleen Cell
**ISC**............ Imperial Service College [*British*]
**ISC**............ In Situ Combustion [*Engineering*]
**ISC**............ Incorporated Staff Sight-Singing College [*London*]
**ISC**............ Independent Search Consultants (EA)
**ISC**............ Index of Status Characteristics
**ISC**............ Indian Staff Corps [*British*] (ROG)
**ISC**............ Indirect Strike Control
**ISC**............ Indoor Sports Club (EA)
**ISC**............ Industrial Support Contractor (KSC)
**ISC**............ Inertial Start Command
**ISC**............ Infiltration Surveillance Center (CINC)
**ISC**............ Information Science Center (MCD)
**ISC**............ Information Services Control Branch [*Control Commission for Germany*] [*World War II*]
**ISC**............ Information Services of Cranston [*Information service or system*] (IID)
**ISC**............ Information Society of Canada (MCD)
**ISC**............ Information Systems Command [*DoD*]
**ISC**............ Infrared Sightline Control
**ISC**............ Infrastructure Special Committee [*NATO*] (NATG)
**ISC**............ Initial Software Configuration Map (MCD)
**ISC**............ Initial Student Characteristics
**ISC**............ Insoluble Collagen [*Biochemistry*]
**ISC**............ Institute for the Study of Conflict [*British*]
**ISC**............ Instruction Staticizing Control (IEEE)
**ISC**............ Instrumentation System Corporation (MCD)
**ISC**............ Instrumentation Systems Center [*University of Wisconsin - Madison*] [*Research center*] (RCD)
**ISC**............ Insurance and Superannuation Commission [*Australia*]
**ISC**............ Integrated Storage Control
**ISC**............ Intelligence Subject Code
**ISC**............ Intelligence Support Center
**ISC**............ Intelligent Systems Corporation
**ISC**............ Inter-American Society of Cardiology [*Mexico City, Mexico*] (EAIO)
**ISC**............ Inter-Service Communication [*British*] [*World War II*]
**ISC**............ Inter-Service Sports Council [*Military*]
**ISC**............ Inter-State Commission [*Australia*]
**ISC**............ Interactive Sciences Corporation [*Information service or system*] (IID)
**ISC**............ Interagency Staff Committee on Public Law 480 [*Department of Agriculture*] (EGAO)
**ISC**............ Intercompany Services Coordination [*Telecommunications*] (TEL)
**ISC**............ Intercomponent Subcontractor (MCD)
**ISC**............ Interdisciplinary Scientific Commission [*COSPAR*]
**ISC**............ Interface Signal Chart
**ISC**............ International Cruiseships [*Vancouver Stock Exchange symbol*]
**ISC**............ International Salmonella Center
**ISC**............ International Salon of Cartoons (EA)
**ISC**............ International Scientific Publications [*Tel Aviv, Israel*]
**ISC**............ International Security Conference and Exposition (ITD)
**ISC**............ International Security Council (EA)
**ISC**............ International Seismological Centre [*ICSU*] [*Newbury, Berkshire, England*] (EAIO)
**ISC**............ International Serials Catalogue [*A publication*]
**ISC**............ International Sericultural Commission [*See also CSI*] [*La Mulatiere, France*] (EAIO)
**ISC**............ International Society of Cardiology [*Later, ISFC*]
**ISC**............ International Society of Chemotherapy [*Bad Heilbrunn, Federal Republic of Germany*] (EAIO)
**ISC**............ International Society for Chronobiology (EA)
**ISC**............ International Society of Citriculture (EA)
**ISC**............ International Society of Cryosurgery [*Turin, Italy*] (EAIO)
**ISC**............ International Society of Cryptozoology (EA)
**ISC**............ International Softball Congress (EA)
**ISC**............ International Space Congress
**ISC**............ International Space Corporation
**ISC**............ International Statistical Classification
**ISC**............ International Student Conference
**ISC**............ International Sugar Council [*London*] [*Later, ISO*]
**ISC**............ International Supply Committee [*World War II*]
**ISC**............ International Supreme Council of World Masons (EA)
**ISC**............ International Switching Center [*Communications*]
**ISC**............ International Symposium on Chemiluminescence
**ISC**............ Interservice Support Code [*Military*]
**ISC**............ Intersociety Committee on Methods for Air Sampling and Analysis
**ISC**............ Interstage Section Container
**ISC**............ Interstate Commerce
**ISC**............ Interstellar Communications (AAG)
**ISC**............ Interstitial Cells [*Histology*]
**ISC**............ Intersystem Crossing
**ISC**............ Interval Selection Circuit
**ISC**............ Interview Schedule for Children
**ISC**............ Intrasite Cabling (CET)
**ISC**............ Invention Submission Corporation [*Information service or system*] (IID)
**ISC**............ Iowa State College of Agriculture and Mechanic Arts [*Later, Iowa State University*] (MCD)
**ISC**............ Irreversibly Sickled Cell [*Hematology*]
**ISC**............ Isles Of Scilly [*England*] [*Airport symbol*] (OAG)
**ISC**............ Israeli Shippers Council (DS)
**ISC**............ Italian Shippers Council (DS)
**ISC**............ Italian Space Commission
**ISC**............ Item Status Code (NATG)
**ISCA**.......... Idle Speed Control Actuator [*Automotive engineering*]
**ISCA**.......... Industrial Specialty Chemical Association (EA)

**ISCA**.......... Interlake Sailing Class Association (EA)
**ISCA**.......... International Sailing Craft Association [*Exeter, Devonshire, England*] (EAIO)
**ISCA**.......... International Senior Citizens Association (EA)
**ISCA**.......... International Shooting Coaches Association (EA)
**ISCA**.......... International Show Car Association (EA)
**ISCA**.......... International Society of Copier Artists (EA)
**ISCA**.......... International Sunfish Class Association (EA)
**ISCA**.......... Irish Setter Club of America (EA)
**IScAF**.......... United States Air Force, Base Library, Scott AFB, IL [*Library symbol*] [*Library of Congress*] (LCLS)
**IScAF-A**.... United States Air Force, Airlift Operations School, Scott Air Force Base, IL [*Library symbol*] [*Library of Congress*] (LCLS)
**IScAF-E**..... United States Air Force, Environmental Technical Applications Center, Air Weather Service Technical Library, Scott Air Force Base, IL [*Library symbol*] [*Library of Congress*] (LCLS)
**ISCAMPME**... Iodosuccinyl CAMP Tyrosine Methyl Ester [*Biochemistry*]
**ISCAMS**.... Installation Standard Command Automated Data Processing Management System [*Army*]
**ISCAN**....... Inertialess Steerable Communications Antenna
**ISCAN**....... International Sanitary Convention for Air Navigation
**ISCAS**........ Integrated Submarine Communications Antenna System [*Navy*] (CAAL)
**ISCAS**........ International Symposium on Circuits and Systems [*IEEE*] (MCD)
**ISCAY**....... International Solidarity Committee with Algerian Youth
**ISCB**.......... Interallied Staff Communications Board [*World War II*]
**ISCB**.......... International Society for Cell Biology [*Later, IFCB*] (ASF)
**ISCB**.......... International Society for Classical Bibliography [*Paris, France*] (EAIO)
**ISCB**.......... International Society for Clinical Biostatistics (EAIO)
**ISCBA**....... Insulating Siding Core Board Association [*Defunct*] (EA)
**ISCBMC**.... International Single Comb Black Minorca Club (EA)
**ISCC**.......... Inter-Society Color Council (EA)
**ISCC**.......... Inter-Society Cytology Council [*Later, American Society of Cytology - ASC*]
**ISCC**.......... International Service Coordination Center [*Communications*]
**ISCC**.......... International Standard Commodity Classification of All Goods and Services
**ISCC**.......... Interstate Solar Coordination Council (EA)
**ISCC**.......... Iranian Students Counseling Center (EA)
**ISCC Newsl**... Inter-Society Color Council Newsletter [*A publication*]
**ISCCP**........ International Satellite Cloud Climatology Project
**ISCD**.......... Interface Specification Control Document (KSC)
**ISCD**.......... International Society for Community Development (EA)
**ISCDD**....... International Scheme for the Coordination of Dairy Development (EAIO)
**ISCDP**....... International Standing Committee on Distribution Problems [*International Water Supply Association*]
**ISCDS**....... International Stop Continental Drift Society (EA)
**ISCE**.......... Institute for the Study of Conscious Evolution (EA)
**ISCE**.......... International Society of Chemical Ecology (EA)
**ISCE**.......... International Society of Christian Endeavor (EA)
**ISCE**.......... International Society for Clinical Enzymology [*Hanover, Federal Republic of Germany*] (EAIO)
**ISCE**.......... International Society for a Complete Earth (EA)
**ISCE**.......... Interstate Substitute Cost Estimate [*Federal Highway Administration*]
**ISCEBS**..... International Society of Certified Employee Benefit Specialists [*Brookfield, WI*] (EA)
**ISCED**....... International Society of Continuing Education in Dentistry [*See also SIECD*] [*Brussels, Belgium*] (EAIO)
**ISCED**....... International Standard Classification of Education (MCD)
**ISCEH**....... International Society for Clinical and Experimental Hypnosis [*Charles University*] (EA)
**ISCERG**..... International Society for Clinical Electroretinography
**ISCET**........ International Society of Certified Electronics Technicians (EA)
**ISCF**.......... Industrial Sentence Completion Form [*Psychology*]
**ISCF**.......... Inter-School Christian Fellowship [*Australia*]
**ISch**........... Steger-South Chicago Heights Library District, South Chicago Heights, IL [*Library symbol*] [*Library of Congress*] (LCLS)
**ISCHDR**.... Inter-Society Commission for Heart Disease Resources
**ISCI**........... Information Systems Consultants, Incorporated [*Information service or system*] (IID)
**ISCII**.......... International Standard Code for Information Interchange (NATG)
**ISCJ**........... International Ski Club of Journalists (EAIO)
**ISCLC**........ International Symposium on Column Liquid Chromatography [*1986*] [*San Francisco, CA*]
**ISCLT**........ International Society for Clinical Laboratory Technology (EA)
**ISCM**......... International Society for Contemporary Music (EA)
**ISCM**......... International Society of Cybernetic Medicine (EA)
**ISCME**....... International Society for Computational Methods in Engineering (EAIO)
**ISCO**.......... Independent Schools Careers Organisation [*British*]
**ISCO**.......... Initial Systems Checkout
**ISCO**.......... Instrumentation Specialties Company
**ISCO**.......... Interactive Systems Corporation [*NASDAQ symbol*] (NQ)
**ISCO**.......... Istituto Nazionale per lo Studio della Congiuntura [*Data Resources, Inc.*] [*Database*]
**ISCOM**...... Island Commander
**ISCOMADEIRA**... Island Commander Madeira (AABC)
**ISCOMAZORES**... Island Commander Azores
**ISCOMBERMUDA**... Island Commander Bermuda
**ISCOMFAROES**... Island Commander Faroes
**ISCOMGREENLAND**... Island Commander Greenland
**ISCOMICELAND**... Island Commander Iceland
**ISCOR**....... South African Iron & Steel Corporation
**ISCORE**.... Intelligence Score (MCD)
**ISCOS**....... Institute for Security and Cooperation in Outer Space (EA)
**ISCOSS**..... International Symposium on the Chemistry of the Organic Solid State
**ISCP**.......... India Study Circle for Philately (EA)
**ISCP**.......... Installation Spill Contingency Plan [*DoD*] (AFIT)
**ISCP**.......... Intermediate Sodium Characterization Package [*Nuclear energy*] (NRCH)
**ISCP**.......... International Society for Chinese Philosophy (EA)
**ISCP**.......... International Society of Clinical Pathology [*Later, WASP*]
**ISCP**.......... International Society for Comparative Psychology (EA)
**ISCP**.......... Inventory Stock Cataloging Program
**ISCPET**..... Illinois Statewide Curriculum Study Center in the Preparation of Secondary School English Teachers
**ISCRE**....... International Symposium on Chemical Reaction Engineering
**ISCRO**....... Industrial Security Clearance Review Office [*DoD*]
**ISCRP**........ International Society of City and Regional Planners [*See also AIU*]
**ISCS**.......... Information Service Computer System (DIT)
**ISCS**.......... Integrated Submarine Communications System (MCD)
**ISCS**.......... Interim Sea Control Ship (MCD)
**ISCS**.......... Intermediate Science Curriculum Study
**ISCS**.......... International Sand Collectors Society (EA)
**ISCS**.......... International Society of Communications Specialists (EA)
**ISCS**.......... International Stamp Collectors Society (EA)
**ISCS**.......... Interservice/Cross Service [*Support*]
**ISCS**.......... ISC Systems Corp. [*NASDAQ symbol*] (NQ)
**ISCSC**........ International Society for the Comparative Study of Civilizations (EA)
**ISCSH**....... Independent Scientific Committee on Smoking and Health [*British*]
**ISCSS**........ Illawarra & South Coast Steam Ship Co. [*Australia*]
**ISCT**.......... Inner Seal Collar Tool [*Nuclear energy*] (NRCH)
**ISCT**.......... Ito System Color Television [*Japan*]
**ISCTF**........ Interservice Committee on Technical Facilities [*Aerospace*] (AAG)
**ISCTP**........ International Study Commission for Traffic Police
**ISC/USO**... Intercompany Services Coordination/Universal Service Order [*Telecommunications*] (TEL)
**ISCVS**........ International Society of Cardiovascular Surgeons
**ISCWFD**.... Intergovernmental Steering Committee on World Food Day (EA)
**ISCWQT**... International Standing Committee on Water Quality and Treatment [*International Water Supply Association*]
**ISCX**.......... Integrated Software Systems Corporation [*NASDAQ symbol*] (NQ)
**ISCYRA**..... International Star Class Yacht Racing Association (EA)
**ISD**............. Cabot Corp., Stellite Division, Kokomo, IN [*OCLC symbol*] (OCLC)
**ISD**............. Indian Stores Depot [*British military*] (DMA)
**ISD**............. Induction System Deposit
**ISD**............. Information Services Department [*Ohio State University Libraries*] [*Columbus*] [*Information service or system*] (IID)
**ISD**............. Information Services Division [*Mississippi State Research and Development Center*] [*Jackson*] [*Information service or system*] (IID)
**ISD**............. Information Structure Design
**ISD**............. Information System Development [*Telecommunications*] (TEL)
**ISD**............. Information Systems Department [*Franklin Research Center, Inc.*] [*Information service or system*] (IID)
**ISD**............. Information Systems Division [*Ori, Inc.*] [*Bethesda, MD*]
**ISD**............. Infrared Suppression Device
**ISD**............. Inhibited Sexual Desire [*Sex therapy*]
**ISD**............. Initial Search Depth
**ISD**............. Initial Selection Done
**ISD**............. Initial Ship Design
**ISD**............. Insert Subcaliber Device [*Weaponry*] (INF)
**ISD**............. Installation Specification Drawing (MCD)
**ISD**............. Installation Start Date (CET)
**ISD**............. Installation Supply Division [*Military*] (AABC)
**ISD**............. Institute for Security Design (EA)
**ISD**............. Institute of Surplus Dealers (EA)
**ISD**............. Instructional System Design Model
**ISD**............. Instructional Systems Development (AFM)
**ISD**............. Integrated Symbolic Debugger [*Data processing*] (IID)
**ISD**............. Integrated Systems Demonstrator (MCD)
**ISD**............. Intensity, Severity, and Discharge [*Medicine*] (DHSM)
**ISD**............. Intermediate Storage Device

**ISD**............ Internal Security Division [*Abolished 1973; functions transferred to Criminal Division*] [*Department of Justice*]
**ISD**............ International Society of Dermatology: Tropical, Geographic, and Ecologic (EA)
**ISD**............ International Society of Differentiation (EA)
**ISD**............ International Society of Dramatists (EA)
**ISD**............ International Subscriber Dialing [*Later, IDD*] [*Telecommunications*]
**ISD**............ Intersystem Designation (CAAL)
**ISD**............ Investors Services and Discounts (Australia) Proprietary Ltd.
**ISD**............ Invoice Shipping Documentation [*Business term*]
**ISD**............ Isosorbide Dinitrite [*Coronary vasodilator*]
**ISD**............ MENU - the International Software Database [*Menu the International Software Database Corp.*] [*Information service or system*] (CRD)
**ISD**............ Winner, SD [*Location identifier*] [*FAA*] (FAAL)
**ISDA**.......... Indian Self-Determination Act [*1975*]
**ISDA**.......... Institute for the Study of Drug Addiction [*Later, ISDM*] (EA)
**ISDA**.......... International Sculpteurs et Designers Associes [*Paris, France*] (EAIO)
**ISDA**.......... International Security and Detective Alliance (EA)
**ISDA**.......... International Swap Dealers' Association
**ISDAIC**..... International Staff Disaster Assistance Information Coordinator [*NATO*] (NATG)
**ISDB**.......... Initial Subordinate Dominates Bystander [*Sociology*]
**ISDB**.......... International Society of Development Biologists [*Formerly, IIE*] [*Nogent-Sur-Marne, France*]
**ISDC**.......... Indiana State Data Center [*Indiana State Library*] [*Indianapolis*] [*Information service or system*] (IID)
**ISDC**.......... Intense Sample Data Collection System (MCD)
**ISDCC**....... Illinois State Data Center Cooperative [*Illinois State Bureau of the Budget*] [*Springfield*] [*Information service or system*] (IID)
**ISDCI**........ International Society of Developmental and Comparative Immunology (EA)
**ISDD**.......... Institute for the Study of Drug Dependence [*London*]
**ISDE**.......... International Six Days Enduro [*Motorcycle racing*]
**ISDE**.......... International Society for Diseases of the Esophagus [*Tokyo, Japan*] (EAIO)
**ISDF**.......... Impact Short Delay Fuze (MCD)
**ISDF**.......... Intermediate Sodium Disposal Facility [*Nuclear energy*] (NRCH)
**ISDF**.......... International Shooter Development Fund [*National Rifle Association*]
**ISDI**........... International Social Development Institute
**ISDI**........... International Society of Dietetic Including All Infant and Young Children Food Industries (EAIO)
**ISDIN**........ Isosorbide Dinitrate [*Also, ISDN*] [*Coronary vasodilator*]
**ISDM**......... Institute for the Study of Drug Misuse [*Formerly, ISDA*] (EA)
**ISDM**......... International Society for Disaster Medicine (EA)
**ISDN**......... Information Service Data Network [*Telecommunications*]
**ISDN**......... Institute for the Study of Developing Nations (EA)
**ISDN**......... Integrated Services Digital Network [*Telecommunications*]
**ISDN**......... International Society for Developmental Neuroscience (EA)
**ISDN**......... Isosorbide Dinitrate [*Also, ISDIN*] [*Coronary vasodilator*]
**ISDNA**....... Inverse Standard Deviation of Nucleolar Area [*Oncology*]
**ISDO**......... Institute for Systems Design and Optimization
**ISDO**......... International Staff Duty Officer [*NATO*] (NATG)
**ISDOS**....... Information Systems Design Optimization System
**ISDP**......... International Society for Developmental Psychobiology (EA)
**ISDRA**....... International Sled Dog Racing Association (EA)
**ISDS**.......... Inadvertent Separation and Destruct System [*Aerospace*]
**ISDS**.......... Institute for Social Dance Studies (EA)
**ISDS**.......... Institute for the Study of Defects in Solids [*State University of New York at Albany*] [*Research center*] (RCD)
**ISDS**.......... Integrated Ship Design System (IEEE)
**ISDS**.......... Integrated Software Development System
**ISDS**.......... Integrated Switched Data Service [*Telecommunications*] (TEL)
**ISDS**.......... Intelligence Support Display System [*Military*] (MCD)
**ISDS**.......... International Serials Data System [*Database*] (EA)
**ISDS**.......... International Sheep Dog Society [*Bedford, England*] (EAIO)
**ISDS**.......... International Society of Dermatologic Surgery (EA)
**ISDSI**......... Insulated Steel Door Systems Institute (EA)
**ISDT**.......... Instructional Systems Development Team [*Air Force*]
**ISDT**.......... International Six Days Trial [*Motorcycling*]
**ISDTS**........ Iron and Steel Dressers Trade Society [*A union*] [*British*]
**ISDX**.......... Integrated Services Digital Exchange [*British*]
**ISE**............ Ibadan Studies in English [*A publication*]
**ISE**............ In-Service Education (ADA)
**ISE**............ In-Service Engineering [*Navy*]
**ISE**............ Independent Scheduled Exercises
**ISE**............ Independent Ship Exercise [*Navy*]
**ISE**............ Indian Service of Engineers [*British*]
**ISE**............ Indiana State University, Evansville, Evansville, IN [*OCLC symbol*] (OCLC)
**ISE**............ Individual Ship Exercises [*Navy*]
**ISE**............ Induced Surface Effect
**ISE**............ Information in Science Extension [*INTERBRIGHT database*] [*Budapest, Hungary*] [*Information service or system*] (IID)
**ISE**............ Information Services to Education [*American Society for Information Science*]
**ISE**............ Initial Support Element (MCD)
**I & SE**........ Installation and Service Engineering (IEEE)
**ISE**............ Installation Support and Evaluation (AAG)
**ISE**............ Institute of Sanitary Engineers [*British*] (DAS)
**ISE**............ Institute of Social Ethics (EA)
**ISE**............ Institute for Software Engineering (EA)
**ISE**............ Institution of Structural Engineers [*London, England*] (EAIO)
**ISE**............ Instrumentation Suitability Evaluation (MCD)
**ISE**............ Integral Squared Error
**ISE**............ Integrated Safeguards Experiment
**ISE**............ Integrated Storage Element [*Data processing*]
**ISE**............ Intelligence Support Element [*Military*] (MCD)
**ISE**............ Intercept System Environment [*Army*] (AABC)
**ISE**............ Intermountain Stock Exchange [*Salt Lake City, UT*]
**ISE**............ International Journal of Social Economics [*A publication*]
**ISE**............ International Semi-Tech Microelectronics, Inc. [*Toronto Stock Exchange symbol*]
**ISE**............ International Society of Electrochemistry [*Graz, Austria*] (EA)
**ISE**............ International Society for Electrostimulation (EA)
**ISE**............ International Society of Endocrinology (EA)
**ISE**............ International Society of Endoscopy
**ISE**............ International Sports Exchange (EA)
**ISE**............ International Stock Exchange
**ISE**............ Interpret Sign Error
**ISE**............ Interrupt System Enable
**ISE**............ Ion-Selective Electrode [*Instrumentation*]
**ISE**............ Irish School of Ecumenics
**ISE**............ Ise [*Japan*] [*Seismograph station code, US Geological Survey*] (SEIS)
**i-se---**.......... Seychelles [*MARC geographic area code*] [*Library of Congress*] (LCCP)
**ISEA**.......... Industrial Safety Equipment Association [*Arlington, VA*] (EA)
**ISEA**.......... Inservice Engineering Agent [*Military*] (CAAL)
**ISEA**.......... International Stamp Exchange Association
**ISEAS**........ Institute of Southeast Asian Studies
**ISEBD4**..... International Series on Biomechanics [*A publication*]
**ISEC**.......... Information System Electronic Command [*Army*]
**ISEC**.......... Institute for Social Economic Change
**ISEC**.......... International Solvent Extraction Conference [*Toronto, ON, 1977*] [*Canada*]
**ISEC**.......... International Standard Electric Corporation (NATG)
**ISEC**.......... International Statistical Education Centre [*India*]
**ISECS**........ International Society for Eighteenth-Century Studies [*See also SIEDS*] [*Oxford, England*] (EAIO)
**ISED**.......... Institute for Social Evaluation and Design
**ISEE**.......... Incident-Shock Equilibrium Expansion
**ISEE**.......... Initial System Evaluation Experiment [*Photovoltaic energy systems*]
**ISEE**.......... International Sun-Earth Explorer [*NASA/ESRO satellite*]
**ISEEP**........ Infrared Sensitive Element Evaluation Program
**ISEF**.......... International Science and Engineering Fair
**ISEG**.......... Independent Safety Engineering Group [*Nuclear energy*] (NRCH)
**ISEGR**....... Institute of Social, Economic, and Governmental Research [*Later, ISER*] [*University of Alaska*]
**ISEGRN**.... Institute of Social, Economic, and Government Research. University of Alaska. Research Notes [*A publication*]
**ISEGROP**... Institute of Social, Economic, and Government Research. University of Alaska. Occasional Papers [*A publication*]
**ISEGRR**.... Institute of Social, Economic, and Government Research. University of Alaska. Report [*A publication*]
**ISEGRS**..... Institute of Social, Economic, and Government Research. University of Alaska. Research Summary [*A publication*]
**ISEI**........... International Standard Engineering, Incorporated (NATG)
**ISEK**.......... International Society of Electromyographic Kinesiology (EA)
**ISEK**.......... International Society of Electrophysiological Kinesiology [*Montreal, PQ*] (EA)
**ISEL**.......... Institute of Shipping Economics and Logistics [*See also ISL*] [*Bremen, Federal Republic of Germany*] (EAIO)
**ISELS**........ Institute of Society, Ethics, and Life Sciences [*Later, HC*] (EA)
**ISEM**......... Immunosorbent Electron Microscopy
**ISEM**......... Institute for the Study of Earth and Man [*Southern Methodist University*] [*Research center*] (RCD)
**ISEM**......... Integrated Simulation Evaluation Model
**ISEM**......... International Society for Ecological Modelling [*Vaerloese, Denmark*] (EAIO)
**ISEMS**....... International Society of Emergency Medical Services (EA)
**ISEN**.......... Interactive Satellite Education Network [*IBM Corp.*] [*New York, NY*] (TSSD)
**ISen**............ Seneca Public Library, Seneca, IL [*Library symbol*] [*Library of Congress*] (LCLS)
**ISEO**.......... Institute of Shortening and Edible Oils (EA)
**ISEP**.......... Instructional Scientific Equipment Program [*National Science Foundation*]
**ISEP**.......... International Society for Educational Planning (EA)
**ISEP**.......... International Society of Esperantist-Philologists [*See also IUEFI*] (EAIO)
**ISEP**.......... International Society for Evolutionary Protistology (EA)

**ISEP** .......... International Student Exchange Program [*United States Information Agency*]
**ISEP** .......... Interservice Experiments Program
**ISEPDC**..... International Series in Experimental Psychology [*A publication*]
**ISEPS**........ International Sun-Earth Physics Satellite
**ISER**.......... Institute of Social and Economic Research [*Formerly, ISEGR*] [*University of Alaska*]
**ISER**.......... Institute of Social and Economic Research [*Memorial University of Newfoundland*] [*Research center*] [*Canada*] (RCD)
**ISER**.......... Integral Systems Experimental Requirements (NRCH)
**ISerSD**....... Serena Consolidated High School District 390, Serena, IL [*Library symbol*] [*Library of Congress*] (LCLS)
**ISES**........... In Silentio et Spe [*In Silence and in Hope*] [*Latin*] [*Motto of Bernhard, Prince of Anhalt (1572-96)*]
**ISES**........... Institute for Socioeconomic Studies (EA)
**ISES**........... International Ship Electric Service Association [*London, England*] (EAIO)
**ISES**........... International Society of Explosives Specialists (EA)
**ISES**........... International Solar Energy Society [*Australia*] (EAIO)
**ISES**........... International Special Events Society (EA)
**ISES**........... Iron Safe Engineers' Society [*A union*] [*British*]
**ISETAP**..... Intergovernmental Science, Engineering, and Technology Advisory Panel [*National Science Foundation*]
**ISETC**........ International Society for Environmental Toxicology and Cancer (EAIO)
**ISETU**....... International Secretariat of Entertainment Trade Unions [*Geneva, Switzerland*]
**ISEU**.......... International Stereotypers and Electrotypers Union [*Later, IPGCU*]
**ISEW**......... Intelligence, Security, and Electronic Warfare [*DoD*]
**ISF**............. Alpha Park Public Library District, Pekin, IL [*OCLC symbol*] (OCLC)
**ISF**............. Imagination Science Fiction [*A publication*]
**ISF**............. Imperial Smelting Furnace [*Zinc and lead*]
**ISF**............. Incremental Stretch Forming
**ISF**............. Indian States Force [*British military*] (DMA)
**ISF**............. Individual Store and Forward
**ISF**............. Industrial Space Facility [*Space Industries, Inc.*]
**ISF**............. Infant Soy Formula
**ISF**............. Infrasonic Frequency
**ISF**............. Integrated Subject File
**ISF**............. Interdistrict Settlement Fund [*Banking*]
**ISF**............. Intermediate Scale Facility [*Department of Energy*]
**ISF**............. International School Sport Federation (EAIO)
**ISF**............. International Science Foundation (EA)
**ISF**............. International Scleroderma Federation [*Later, SF*] (EA)
**ISF**............. International Shipping Federation [*London, England*] (EAIO)
**ISF**............. International Ski Federation
**ISF**............. International Snowshoe Federation (EA)
**ISF**............. International Society for Fat Research
**ISF**............. International Society of Financiers (EA)
**ISF**............. International Softball Federation (EA)
**ISF**............. International Spiritualist Federation [*Great Britain*]
**ISF**............. International Spring Fair [*Great Britain*] (ITD)
**ISF**............. Internationale Schulsport Foderation [*International School Sport Federation*] (EAIO)
**ISF**............. Interstitial Fluid [*Physiology*]
**ISF**............. Ionizer, Slab Fabrication
**ISF**............. Isfjord [*Norway*] [*Seismograph station code, US Geological Survey*] [*Closed*] (SEIS)
**ISF**............. Isotope Separation Factor (MCD)
**ISFA**.......... Intercoastal Steamship Freight Association (EA)
**ISFA**.......... International Scientific Film Association
**ISFA**.......... Isaac Garrison Family Association (EA)
**ISFAA**........ Intercollegiate Soccer-Football Association of America [*Later, ISAA*] (EA)
**ISFAA**........ International Society of Fine Arts Appraisers (EA)
**IS-FACT**.... Irwin Stone Foundation for Ascorbate Capability and Therapy
**ISFAHSIG** ... International Society for the Advancement of Humanistic Studies in Gynecology (EA)
**ISFAM**...... Israelitisches Familienblatt [*Hamburg*] [*A publication*]
**ISFC**.......... Indicated Specific Fuel Consumption
**ISFC**.......... International Short Film Conference (EAIO)
**ISFC**.......... International Society and Federation of Cardiology [*Formed by a merger of International Cardiology Federation and International Society of Cardiology - ISC*] (EAIO)
**ISFD**.......... Integrated Software Functional Design
**ISFE**........... Incident-Shock Frozen Expansion
**ISFE**........... Integrated Site Facilities and Equipment (MCD)
**ISFE**........... International Society of Flying Engineers (EA)
**ISFET**........ Ion-Selective Field Effect Transistor
**ISFFSR**...... Institute for the Study of Fatigue Fracture and Structural Reliability [*George Washington University*]
**ISFGW**...... International Society of Friendship and Good Will (EA)
**ISFHC**....... International Society of Folk Harpers and Craftsmen (EA)
**I2S(FIN)**.... Integrated Information System (Financial) [*Marine Corps*]
**ISFIS**......... Selective Fisheries Information Service (IID)
**ISFL**........... International Scientific Film Library
**ISFL**........... International Society of Family Law [*Cambridge, England*] (EAIO)
**ISFM**......... Indexed Sequential File Manager [*Data processing*]
**ISFMS**....... Indexed Sequential File Management System [*Data processing*] (BUR)
**ISFNR**....... International Society for Folk-Narrative Research [*Turku, Finland*] (EA)
**ISFR**.......... International Society for Fluoride Research (EA)
**ISFSC**........ International Society of Food Service Consultants [*Later, FCSI*] (EA)
**ISFSC**........ International Society of Free Space Colonizers [*Superseded by Political Action Caucus*] (EA)
**ISFSF**........ Independent Spent Fuel Storage Facility [*Nuclear energy*] [*Department of Energy*]
**ISFSI**......... Independent Spent Fuel Storage Installation [*Nuclear energy*] (NRCH)
**ISFSI**......... International Society of Fire Service Instructors (EA)
**ISG**............ Ayer Public Library, Delavan, IL [*OCLC symbol*] (OCLC)
**ISG**............ Immune Serum Globulin
**ISG**............ Imperial Standard Gallon
**ISG**............ Inland Shipping Group [*British*]
**ISG**............ Institute for the Study of Genocide (EA)
**ISG**............ Interchangeable and Substitute Group [*Military*] (AFIT)
**ISG**............ Interconnected Systems Group
**ISG**............ Interfacial Surface Generation [*Instrumentation*]
**ISG**............ Internal Shutter Grid
**ISG**............ Interservice Group [*Military*]
**ISG**............ Intersubblock Gap
**ISG**............ Ishigaki [*Japan*] [*Airport symbol*] (OAG)
**ISGA**.......... International Stained Glass Association (EA)
**ISGA**.......... International Study Group for Aerogrammes
**ISGBBC**..... Israel. Geological Survey. Bulletin [*A publication*]
**ISGC**.......... International Society of Guatemala Collectors (EA)
**ISGC**.......... International Steel Guitar Convention (EA)
**ISGD**.......... International Study Group of Diabetes in Children and Adolescents [*Linkoping, Sweden*] (EAIO)
**ISGE**.......... International Society of Gastroenterology
**ISGE**.......... International Society for Geothermal Engineering (EA)
**ISGEA**....... Issledovaniya po Genetike [*A publication*]
**Is Geol Univ Milano Pubbl Ser G** ... Istituto di Geologia. Universita di Milano. Pubblicazione. Serie G [*A publication*]
**ISGE Trans Geotherm J** ... ISGE [*International Society for Geothermal Engineering*] Transactions and the Geothermal Journal [*United States*] [*A publication*]
**ISGE Trans Geotherm World J** ... ISGE [*International Society for Geothermal Engineering*] Transactions and Geothermal World Journal [*United States*] [*A publication*]
**ISGI**........... International Sheep and Goat Institute [*Utah State University*] [*Research center*] (RCD)
**ISGML**...... International Study Group for Mathematics Learning [*British*]
**ISGN**......... Insignia (MSA)
**ISGO**......... International Society of Geographic Ophthalmology [*Montreal, PQ*] (EAIO)
**ISGOTT**.... International Safety Guide for Oil Tankers and Terminals (DS)
**ISGP**.......... International Society of Geographical Pathology [*Australia*] (EY)
**ISGS**.......... Illinois State Geological Survey [*Champaign*] [*Information service or system*] (IID)
**ISGS**.......... International Society for General Semantics (EA)
**ISGSH**....... International Study Group for Steroid Hormones [*Rome, Italy*] (EAIO)
**ISgW**.......... Waubonsee Community College, Sugar Grove, IL [*Library symbol*] [*Library of Congress*] (LCLS)
**ISGWRCA** ... International Study Group for Waterworks in the Rhine Catchment Area [*See also IAWR*] (EAIO)
**ISH**............ Caterpillar Tractor Co., Technical Information Center, Peoria, IL [*OCLC symbol*] (OCLC)
**ISH**............ Icteric Serum Hepatitis [*Medicine*]
**ISH**............ In Situ Hybridization [*Biology*]
**I Sh**............ Independent Shavian [*A publication*]
**ISH**............ Institute for Scientific Humanism [*Later, WISH*]
**ISH**............ Interim Scout Helicopter (MCD)
**ISH**............ International Society of Hematology (EA)
**ISH**............ International Society of Hypertension (EA)
**ISH**............ International Sterling [*Vancouver Stock Exchange symbol*]
**ISH**............ Ishtion [*USSR*] [*Seismograph station code, US Geological Survey*] (SEIS)
**ISHAE**....... International Society of Hotel Association Executives (EA)
**ISHAM**..... International Society for Human and Animal Mycology [*London School of Hygiene and Tropical Medicine*] [*Great Britain*]
**I Shaw**........ Independent Shavian [*A publication*]
**ISHC**.......... International Siberian Husky Club
**ISHC**.......... International Symposium on Homogeneous Catalysis
**IShCoH**..... Shelby County Memorial Hospital, Shelbyville, IL [*Library symbol*] [*Library of Congress*] (LCLS)
**ISHE**.......... International Safety and Health Exhibition [*Great Britain*] (ITD)
**ISHE**.......... International Society of Healthcare Executives (EA)
**ISHE**.......... International Society for Human Ethology (EA)
**IShe**........... Sheldon Township Public Library, Sheldon, IL [*Library symbol*] [*Library of Congress*] (LCLS)

**ISherESD** .. Sheridan Elementary School District 272, Sheridan, IL [*Library symbol*] [*Library of Congress*] (LCLS)
**ISHGA** ...... Ishikawajima-Harima Giho [*A publication*]
**ISHI** .......... Institute for the Study of Human Issues (EA)
**ISHI** .......... International Society for the History of Ideas (EA)
**Ishikawajima-Harima Eng Rev** ... Ishikawajima-Harima Engineering Review [*A publication*]
**ISHK** ......... Institute for the Study of Human Knowledge (EA)
**ISHL** .......... International Society for Historical Linguistics (EAIO)
**ISHM** ........ International Society for Hybrid Microelectronics (EA)
**ISHM J** ..... ISHM [*International Society for Hybrid Microelectronics*] Journal [*A publication*]
**ISHM Proc** ... ISHM [*International Society for Hybrid Microelectronics*] Proceedings [*A publication*]
**ISho** ........... South Holland Public Library, South Holland, IL [*Library symbol*] [*Library of Congress*] (LCLS)
**ISHOF** ....... International Swimming Hall of Fame (EA)
**IShoSHi** ..... South Suburban Genealogical and Historical Society, South Holland, IL [*Library symbol*] [*Library of Congress*] (LCLS)
**IShoT** ......... Thornton Community College, South Holland, IL [*Library symbol*] [*Library of Congress*] (LCLS)
**ISHOW** ..... Information System for Hazardous Organics in Water [*Database*] [*Environmental Protection Agency*] [*Information service or system*] (CRD)
**(I)SHP** ....... (Intermediate) Shaft Horsepower
**ISHR** .......... Intermediate Scale Homogeneous Reactor
**ISHR** .......... International Society for Heart Research [*Winnipeg, MB*] (EA)
**ISHR** .......... International Society for the History of Rhetoric (EA)
**ISHR** .......... International Society for Human Rights [*See also IGM*] [*Frankfurt, Federal Republic of Germany*] (EAIO)
**ISHRA** ....... Iron and Steel Holdings and Realisation Agency [*British*]
**ISHS** .......... Illinois State Historical Society. Journal [*A publication*]
**ISHS** .......... Improved Spartan Homing Sensor [*Missiles*]
**ISHS** .......... International Society for Horticultural Science [*See also SISH*] [*ICSU*] [*Wageningen, Netherlands*] (EAIO)
**ISHS** .......... International Society for Humor Studies (EA)
**ISHSJ** ........ Illinois State Historical Society. Journal [*A publication*]
**ISHT** .......... International Society for Heart Transplantation (EA)
**ISHTCP** .... Inventory of Sources for History of Twentieth Century Physics [*University of California, Berkeley*] [*Information service or system*] (IID)
**ISHVBS** .... International Society for Hildegard Von Bingen Studies (EA)
**ISI** ............. Chillicothe Township Free Public Library, Chillicothe, IL [*OCLC symbol*] (OCLC)
**ISI** ............. In-Service Inspection (NRCH)
**ISI** ............. In-Service Institute [*National Science Foundation*]
**ISI** ............. Indian Standards Institution
**ISI** ............. Indian Statistical Institute
**ISI** ............. Induced Spatial Incoherence [*Physics*]
**ISI** ............. Industrial Static Inverter
**ISI** ............. Industry Standard Item (AAG)
**ISI** ............. Infarct Size Index [*Cardiology*]
**ISI** ............. Infodata Systems, Incorporated [*Information service or system*] (IID)
**ISI** ............. Informal Spelling Inventory [*Education*]
**ISI** ............. Information Service of India
**ISI** ............. Information Services, Incorporated [*Information service or system*] (IID)
**ISI** ............. Information Services International [*Information service or system*] (IID)
**ISI** ............. Information Storage, Incorporated
**ISI** ............. Inhibited Sporozoite Invasion [*Immunology*]
**ISI** ............. Initial Shipping Instructions (MCD)
**ISI** ............. Initial Support Increments [*Army*] (AABC)
**ISI** ............. Initial Support Item
**ISI** ............. Initial Systems Installation (NASA)
**ISI** ............. Injury Severity Index (MCD)
**ISI** ............. Institute for Scientific Information [*Philadelphia, PA*] [*Database producer*]
**ISI** ............. Institute for Social Inquiry [*University of Connecticut*] [*Storrs*] [*Information service or system*] (IID)
**ISI** ............. Instrumentation Support Instruction (KSC)
**ISI** ............. Integra Systems, Inc. [*Toronto Stock Exchange symbol*] [*Vancouver Stock Exchange symbol*]
**ISI** ............. Inter-Services Intelligence [*Pakistan*] (ECON)
**ISI** ............. Intercollegiate Studies Institute (EA)
**ISI** ............. Interim Support Item (MCD)
**ISI** ............. Internally Specified Index
**ISI** ............. International Safety Institute [*Defunct*] (EA)
**ISI** ............. International Satellite, Inc. [*Telecommunications*]
**ISI** ............. International Satellite for Ionospheric Studies [*NASA-Canada*] (NOAA)
**ISI** ............. International Sensitivity Index [*Hematology*]
**ISI** ............. International Statistical Institute [*ICSU*] [*Voorburg, Netherlands*] (EA)
**ISI** ............. International Students, Incorporated (EA)
**ISI** ............. Interpersonal Style Inventory [*Personality development test*] [*Psychology*]
**ISI** ............. Interspike Interval [*Neurophysiology*]
**ISI** ............. Interstimulus Interval
**ISI** ............. Intersymbol Interference
**ISI** ............. Ion Source Injector
**ISI** ............. Ishigakijima [*Ryukyu Islands*] [*Seismograph station code, US Geological Survey*] (SEIS)
**ISI** ............. Isisford [*Australia*] [*Airport symbol*] (OAG)
**ISI** ............. ISS-International Service System, Incorporated [*AMEX symbol*] (SPSG)
**ISI** ............. Item Station and Indenture (AAG)
**ISIA** ........... Ice Skating Institute of America (EA)
**ISIA** ........... International Snowmobile Industry Association (EA)
**ISIA** ........... Italo Svevo International Association (EA)
**ISIADL** ...... Insect Science and Its Application [*A publication*]
**ISIAL** ......... Incorporated Society of Irish/American Lawyers (EA)
**ISIB** ........... Inter-Service Ionosphere Bureau [*Military*]
**ISI Bull** ...... ISI [*Indian Standards Institution*] Bulletin [*A publication*]
**ISIC** ........... Immediate Superior in Command [*Military*]
**ISIC** ........... Intelligence Support and Indications Center [*Military*] (MCD)
**ISIC** ........... International Standard Industrial Classification (EY)
**ISIC** ........... Intersymbol Interference Corrector
**ISICCE** ...... International Society of India Chemists and Chemical Engineers (EA)
**ISID** ........... International Society of Interior Designers (EA)
**ISid** ............ Sidell District Library, Sidell, IL [*Library symbol*] [*Library of Congress*] (LCLS)
**ISIDB** ........ Instruments India [*A publication*]
**ISIDHI** ...... International Society on Infectious Diseases and Human Infertility (EA)
**ISidn** .......... Sidney Community Library, Sidney, IL [*Library symbol*] [*Library of Congress*] (LCLS)
**ISIFM** ........ International Society of Industrial Fabric Manufacturers (EA)
**ISIG** ........... Irish Special Interest Group of American Mensa (EA)
**ISII** ............ Integra Systems, Incorporated [*NASDAQ symbol*] (NQ)
**ISI/IST** ...... In-Service Inspections and In-Service Testing
**ISI/ISTP & B** ... ISI/Index to Scientific and Technical Proceedings and Books [*Institute for Scientific Information*] [*Philadelphia, PA*] [*Bibliographic database*]
**ISIJ** ............ Iron and Steel Institute of Japan
**ISIL** ........... Interim Support Items List (NASA)
**ISIM** .......... International Society of Internal Medicine [*Langenthal, Switzerland*] (EA)
**ISIMC** ....... International Study Institution of the Middle Classes [*Brussels, Belgium*] (EAIO)
**ISIMM** ...... International Society for the Interaction of Mechanics and Mathematics (EA)
**ISINC** ........ Immediate Superior in Command [*Military*]
**ISIP** ........... Indexed Security Investment Plan [*Canada*]
**ISIP** ........... Iron and Steel Industry Profiles [*A publication*]
**ISIR** ........... In Service, In Reserve [*Vessel status*] [*Navy*]
**ISIR** ........... Interactive Single Isomorphous Replacement [*Crystallographic procedure*]
**ISIR** ........... International Society for the Immunology of Reproduction (EA)
**ISIR** ........... International Society of Invertebrate Reproduction (EA)
**ISIR** ........... Iterative Single Isomorphous Replacement [*Crystallography*]
**ISIRC** ......... International Statistical Institute Research Center [*Research center*] [*Netherlands*] (IRC)
**ISIRS** ......... International Sorption Information Retrieval System [*Nuclear Energy Agency*] (EY)
**ISIRTA** ...... I'm Sorry, I'll Read That Again [*BBC radio comedy program*]
**ISIS** ............ Independence Square Income Securities, Inc. [*NASDAQ symbol*] (NQ)
**ISIS** ............ Independent Schools Information Service [*British*]
**ISIS** ............ Indian School of International Studies [*Delhi*]
**ISIS** ............ Individualized Science Instructional System [*National Science Foundation project*]
**ISIS** ............ Information System Indexing System [*Federal Judicial Center*] [*Database*]
**ISIS** ............ Institute of Scrap Iron and Steel [*Later, ISRI*] (EA)
**ISIS** ............ Institute for the Study of Inquiring Systems
**ISIS** ............ Institutional Sector Investment Services [*Chase Manhattan Securities*] [*British*]
**ISIS** ............ Integral Spar Inspection System
**ISIS** ............ Integrated Safeguard Information System (NRCH)
**ISIS** ............ Integrated Scientific Information System
**ISIS** ............ Integrated Strike and Interceptor System
**ISIS** ............ Integrated System for Improved Separations [*Membrane filtration*]
**ISIS** ............ Integriertes Statistisches Informationssystem [*Integrated Statistical Information System*] [*Central Statistical Office*] [*Vienna, Austria*] [*Information service or system*] (IID)
**ISIS** ............ Interchangeability and Substitutability Item Subgroup (MCD)
**ISIS** ............ Internally Switched Interface System [*Tymnet, Inc.*]
**ISIS** ............ International Satellite for Ionospheric Studies [*NASA-Canada*]
**ISIS** ............ International Science Information Services [*Earth sciences data center*] [*Dallas, TX*]
**ISIS** ............ International Shipping Information Service (DS)
**ISIS** ............ International Society of Introduction Services (EA)
**ISIS** ............ International Species Information System (EISS)
**ISIS** ............ International Species Inventory System [*Data processing for animal mating*] [*Minnesota Zoological Gardens*] [*Apple Valley, MN*]

**ISIS**............ International Student Information Service
**ISIS**............ International Study of Infarct Survival [*Medicine*]
**ISIS**............ Internationally Syndicated Information Services [*Information service or system*] [*Defunct*] (IID)
**ISIS**............ Interstate Settlement Information System [*AT & T*]
**ISIS**............ Investigative Support Information System [*Federal Bureau of Investigation*]
**ISIS**............ Item Standardization Information System [*DoD*]
**ISISA**......... Individual Scale for Indian South Africans [*Intelligence test*]
**ISISSAPORCI** ... International Section of ISSA [*International Social Security Association*] on the Prevention of Occupational Risks in the Construction Industry [*Boulogne-Billancourt, France*] (EAIO)
**ISIS-WICCE** ... ISIS [*Women's International Information Communication Service*] - Women's International Cross-Cultural Exchange (EAIO)
**ISIT**........... Intensified Silicon Intensifier Target (MCD)
**ISIYM**....... International Society of Industrial Yarn Manufacturers [*Later, ISIFM*] (EA)
**ISJ**............ Institute for Social Justice (EA)
**ISJ**............ Israel Export and Trade Journal [*A publication*]
**ISJ**............ Saint Joseph's College, Rensselaer, IN [*OCLC symbol*] (OCLC)
**ISJC**.......... Independent Schools Joint Council [*British*]
**ISJCAT**..... Israel Journal of Chemistry [*A publication*]
**IsJJNL**...... Jewish National and University Library, Hebrew University, Jerusalem, Israel [*Library symbol*] [*Library of Congress*] (LCLS)
**ISJL**.......... International Society of Jewish Librarians (EA)
**ISJM**......... Israeli Journal of Mathematics [*A publication*]
**ISJP**.......... International Society for Japanese Philately (EA)
**ISJR**.......... Iowa State Journal of Research [*A publication*]
**ISJRA**........ Iowa State Journal of Research [*A publication*]
**ISJRA6**...... Iowa State Journal of Research [*A publication*]
**ISJSA9**...... Iowa State Journal of Science [*A publication*]
**ISJTA**........ Intensive Student Jet Training Area
**ISJTAC**..... Israel Journal of Technology [*A publication*]
**ISK**............ Galva Township Public Library, Galva, IL [*OCLC symbol*] (OCLC)
**ISK**............ Insert Storage Key (IEEE)
**ISK**............ Instruction Space Key
**ISK**............ Internacia Scienca Kolegio [*International College of Scientists - ICS*] [*Paderborn, Federal Republic of Germany*] (EAIO)
**ISK**............ International Society of the Knee (EA)
**ISK**............ Internationale Seidenbau Kommission [*International Sericultural Commission*]
**ISK**............ Ion Source Kit
**ISK**............ Iskut Gold Corp. [*Vancouver Stock Exchange symbol*]
**ISK**............ Istanbul-Kandilli [*Turkey*] [*Geomagnetic observatory code*]
**ISK**............ Istanbul-Kandilli [*Turkey*] [*Seismograph station code, US Geological Survey*] (SEIS)
**ISK**............ Nasik [*India*] [*Airport symbol*] (OAG)
**ISk**............ Skokie Public Library, Skokie, IL [*Library symbol*] [*Library of Congress*] (LCLS)
**ISKA**.......... International Saw and Knife Association (EA)
**ISKCON**.... International Society for Krishna Consciousness (EA)
**ISKDC**....... International Study of Kidney Disease in Children
**ISkH**.......... Hebrew Theological College, Skokie, IL [*Library symbol*] [*Library of Congress*] (LCLS)
**ISKHDI**..... Ishikawa-Ken Nogyo Shikenjo Kenkyu Hokoku [*A publication*]
**ISKI**........... International Secretariat of the Knitting Industries [*Paris, France*] (EAIO)
**ISKO**.......... Isco, Inc. [*Lincoln, NE*] [*NASDAQ symbol*] (NQ)
**ISkS**........... G. D. Searle & Co., Inc., Skokie, IL [*Library symbol*] [*Library of Congress*] (LCLS)
**ISkT**........... Triodyne, Skokie, IL [*Library symbol*] [*Library of Congress*] (LCLS)
**Iskus K**....... Iskusstvo Kino [*A publication*]
**Iskusstvo K** ... Iskusstvo Kino [*A publication*]
**Iskusstv Sputniki Zemli** ... Iskusstvennye Sputniki Zemli [*A publication*]
**Iskusstv Sputniki Zemli Akad Nauk SSSR** ... Iskusstvennye Sputniki Zemli Akademiya Nauk SSSR [*USSR*] [*A publication*]
**Iskusstv Volokno** ... Iskusstvennoe Volokno [*A publication*]
**ISL**............ Iceland [*ANSI three-letter standard code*] (CNC)
**ISL**............ Inactive Status List (MUGU)
**ISL**............ Indiana State Library, Indianapolis, IN [*OCLC symbol*] (OCLC)
**ISL**............ Industrial Security Letter [*DoD*]
**ISL**............ Industrie Lackier-Betrieb. Zentralblatt fuer Lackiertechnik und Beschichtungstechnik [*A publication*]
**ISL**............ Informatics Services [*Oakville, ON*] [*Telecommunications service*] (TSSD)
**ISL**............ Information Search Language
**ISL**............ Information Services Limited [*Publisher*] [*British*]
**ISL**............ Information System Language [*Data processing*] (IEEE)
**ISL**............ Initial Stocks List
**ISL**............ Initial System Loading
**ISL**............ Institut fuer Seeverkehrwirtschaft und Logistik [*Institute of Shipping Economics and Logistics - ISEL*] [*Bremen, Federal Republic of Germany*] (EAIO)
**ISL**............ Institute of Space Law
**ISL**............ Instructional Systems Language [*Data processing*] (IEEE)
**ISL**............ Instrument Standards Laboratory [*Space Flight Operations Facility, NASA*]
**ISL**............ Instrumental Services Laboratory [*Australia*]
**ISL**............ Integrated Schottky Logic (IEEE)
**ISL**............ Integrated Stock Listing
**ISL**............ Integrated Synthesis Logic [*Data processing*]
**ISL**............ Interactive Simulation Language [*Data processing*] (IEEE)
**ISL**............ Internal Standard Line
**ISL**............ International Soccer League
**ISL**............ International Society of Literature [*Ilkley, Yorkshire, England*] (EAIO)
**ISL**............ International Society of Lymphology (EA)
**ISL**............ International Subcommittee on Lactobacilli and Closely Related Organisms
**ISL**............ Intersatellite Link
**ISL**............ Intersystem Link
**ISL**............ Island [*Board on Geographic Names*]
**ISL**............ Isle
**ISL**............ Islington (ROG)
**ISL**............ Item Selection List
**ISL**............ Item Study Listings
**ISL**............ Lincoln Library, Springfield, IL [*Library symbol*] [*Library of Congress*] (LCLS)
**ISLA**.......... International Survey Library Association (EA)
**ISLADE**..... Interactive Structural Layout and Design [*Module*]
**Islam**.......... Der Islam. Zeitschrift fuer Geschichte und Kultur des Islamischen Orients [*A publication*]
**Islamabad J Sci** ... Islamabad Journal of Sciences. Journal of Mathematics and Sciences [*A publication*]
**Islam Cult**.. Islamic Culture [*A publication*]
**Islam Mod Age** ... Islam and the Modern Age [*A publication*]
**Islam Stud** ... Islamic Studies [*A publication*]
**IS of LANG** ... Islets of Langerhans [*Anatomy*]
**ISLC**.......... International Sporting and Leisure Club
**ISLC**.......... Lincoln Land Community College, Springfield, IL [*Library symbol*] [*Library of Congress*] (LCLS)
**ISLCBS**..... International Seal, Label, and Cigar Band Society (EA)
**ISLD**.......... Inter-Services Liaison Department [*World War II*]
**ISLE**.......... Isle Resources, Inc. [*NASDAQ symbol*] (NQ)
**ISLEC**........ Institute for the Study of Labor and Economic Crisis (EA)
**ISLF**........... Improved Saturn Launch Facility
**ISLFD**........ Incorporated Society of London Fashion Designers
**ISLH**.......... International Holding Capital Corp. [*Formerly, International Savings & Loan Association Ltd.*] [*NASDAQ symbol*] (NQ)
**ISLIC**......... Israel Society of Special Libraries and Information Centers
**ISLIC Bull** ... Israel Society of Special Libraries and Information Centers. Bulletin [*A publication*]
**Is Lit**.......... Islamic Literature [*A publication*]
**ISLL**........... Illinois Studies in Language and Literature [*A publication*]
**ISLL**........... International Survey of Legal Decisions on Labour Law [*1925-38*] [*A publication*] (DLA)
**Isl Landbunadarrannsoknir** ... Islenzkar Landbunadarrannsoknir [*Journal of Agricultural Research in Iceland*] [*A publication*]
**ISLLSL**...... International Society for Labor Law and Social Legislation [*Later, International Society for Labor Law and Social Security United States National Branch*] (EA)
**ISLLSS**...... International Society for Labor Law and Social Security [*Formed by a merger of International Congresses of Labour Law and International Society for Social Law*] (EAIO)
**ISLM**......... Integration Shop/Laboratory Manager (MCD)
**Islm Wld D** ... Islamic World Defence [*A publication*]
**ISLN**.......... Isolation (MSA)
**I2S(LOG)**.. Integrated Information System (Logistics) [*Marine Corps*]
**IslQ**............ Islamic Quarterly [*London*] [*A publication*]
**ISLR**.......... Integrated Side-Lobe Ratio
**ISLR**.......... Isolator (MSA)
**Is LR**.......... Israel Law Review [*A publication*]
**ISLRBH**.... Islenzkar Landbunadarrannsoknir [*Journal of Agricultural Research in Iceland*] [*A publication*]
**ISLRS**........ Inactive Status List Reserve Section
**ISLS**.......... Information System Language Studies [*A publication*]
**ISLS**.......... Interrogation Side-Lobe Suppression
**ISLS**.......... Islands [*Board on Geographic Names*]
**ISLSCP**..... International Satellite Land Surface Climatology Project [*Federal government*]
**Isl St**.......... Islamic Studies [*A publication*]
**ISLW**......... Indian Spring Low Water [*Tides and currents*]
**ISLWF**....... International Shoe and Leather Workers' Federation
**ISLWG**...... Working Group on International Shipping Legislation [*UNCTAD*] (DS)
**ISLY**.......... Isaly Co., Inc. [*NASDAQ symbol*] (NQ)
**ISM**........... Iesus Salvator Mundi [*Jesus, Savior of the World*] [*Latin*]
**ISM**........... Imperial Service Medal [*British*]
**ISM**........... Improved Sensing Munitions (RDA)
**ISM**........... Incorporated Society of Musicians [*British*]
**ISM**........... Indian Supply Mission [*World War II*]
**ISM**........... Industrial Security Manual (MCD)
**ISM**........... Information System Manager (NATG)
**ISM**........... Information Systems for Management (IEEE)

**ISM**........... Information Systems Marketing, Inc. [*Information service or system*] (IID)
**ISM**........... Infrared Systems Manufacturing
**ISM**........... Initial Segment Membrane
**ISM**........... Institute of Sanitation Management [*Later, EMA*] (EA)
**ISM**........... Institute of Sports Medicine [*British*]
**ISM**........... Institute for the Study of Man (EA)
**ISM**........... Institute of Supervisory Management [*British*]
**ISM**........... Integrated Sander Machine [*Disk controller*] [*Apple Computer, Inc.*] (BYTE)
**ISM**........... Integrated Skills Method [*Education*]
**ISM**........... Interavia Space Markets [*Interavia Publications*] [*Information service or system*] (CRD)
**ISM**........... International Camero Resources [*Vancouver Stock Exchange symbol*]
**ISM**........... International Society for Metaphysics (EA)
**ISM**........... International Soil Museum
**ISM**........... International Studies of Management and Organization [*A publication*]
**ISM**........... International Sweets Market [*Trade fair*] [*Cologne, West Germany*] [*1982*]
**ISM**........... International Symposium on Microtechniques
**ISM**........... International Systems Meeting [*Data processing*]
**ISM**........... Interpretive Structural Modeling [*A computer-assisted learning process for structuring information*]
**ISM**........... Interstellar Medium [*Planetary science*]
**ISM**........... Ion Selective Microelectrodes [*Instrumentation*]
**ISM**........... Irish School of Music (ROG)
**I & SM**....... Iron & Steelmaker [*A publication*] (EAAP)
**ISM**........... ISDN [*Integrated Services Digital Network*] Subscriber Module [*Telecommunications*]
**ISM**........... Istituto Internazionale Suore di Santa Marcellina [*An association*] (EAIO)
**ISM**........... Kissimmee, FL [*Location identifier*] [*FAA*] (FAAL)
**ISM**........... Mitteilungen. Internationale Stiftung Mozarteum [*A publication*]
**ISM**........... Southern Methodist University, Central Library, Dallas, TX [*OCLC symbol*] (OCLC)
**ISMA**......... Industrial Silencer Manufacturers Association (EA)
**ISMA**......... International Security Management Association [*Boston, MA*] (EA)
**ISMA**......... International Shipmasters Association (EA)
**ISMA**......... International Superphosphate Manufacturers' Association [*Later, IFA*]
**Is Mag**........ Island Magazine [*A publication*]
**ISMB**......... Information System Management Board [*NATO*] (NATG)
**ISMB**......... International Society of Mathematical Biology [*See also SIBM*] [*Antony, France*] (EAIO)
**ISMC**......... Independent Schools Microelectronics Centre [*British*]
**ISMC**......... International Switching Maintenance Center [*Communications*]
**ISMCEE**.... International Series of Monographs on Chemistry [*A publication*]
**ISMD**......... Indian Subordinate Medical Department [*British military*] (DMA)
**ISMDA**...... Independent Sewing Machine Dealers Association (EA)
**ISMDKTS** ... Iron, Steel, Metal Dressers, and Kindred Trades Society [*A union*] [*British*]
**ISME**......... Institute of Sheet Metal Engineering [*British*]
**ISME**......... International Society for Music Education [*London, England*] (EA)
**ISMEC** ...... Information Service in Mechanical Engineering [*Cambridge Scientific Abstracts*] [*Great Britain*] [*Information service or system*] (IID)
**ISMEC Bull** ... ISMEC [*Information Service in Mechanical Engineering*] Bulletin [*A publication*]
**ISMED**....... International Society on Metabolic Eye Disease (EA)
**ISMES**....... Experimental Institute for Models and Structures [*Italy*]
**ISMET** ...... Inter-Service Metallurgical Research Council [*British*] (MCD)
**ISME Yb** ... ISME [*International Society for Music Education*] Yearbook [*A publication*]
**ISMF** ......... Inactive Ship Maintenance Facility
**ISMF** ......... International Sports Massage Federation (EA)
**ISMG**......... International Scientific Management Group [*GARP*] (NOAA)
**ISMGF** ...... International Stoke Mandeville Games Federation [*Aylesbury, Buckinghamshire, England*] (EA)
**ISMGR**....... Island Manager [*Aviation*] (FAAC)
**ISMH** ........ Input Source Message Handler
**ISMH** ........ International Society of Medical Hydrology and Climatology
**ISMHC**....... International Society of Medical Hydrology and Climatology (EA)
**ISMIS**........ Interservice Depot Maintenance Interrogation Systems
**ISMJAV**.... Israel Medical Journal [*A publication*]
**ISmK**.......... Kaskaska Library System, Smithton, IL [*Library symbol*] [*Library of Congress*] (LCLS)
**ISML**......... Institute for the Study of Matrimonial Laws (EA)
**ISML**......... Intermediate System Mock-Up Loop (IEEE)
**ISMLS**....... Interim Standard Microwave Landing System [*Aviation*]
**ISMM**........ International Society of Mini- and Micro-Computers [*Calgary, AB*] (EAIO)
**ISMMRRI** ... Iowa State Mining and Mineral Resources Research Institute [*Iowa State University*] [*Research center*] (RCD)
**ISMMS**..... Integrated Stores Monitor and Management System [*Later, Armament Control Panel*] (MCD)
**ISMO** ........ Ion-Sieve-Type Manganese Oxide [*Inorganic chemistry*]
**ISMPH**...... International Society for Medical and Psychological Hypnosis (EA)
**I2S(MPR)** ... Integrated Information System (Manpower) [*Marine Corps*]
**I2S(MPR/MMS)** ... Integrated Information System (Manpower and Functional Area Manpower Management System) [*Marine Corps*]
**ISMR**......... Independent Snowmobile Medical Research [*An association*] (EA)
**ISMRC**...... Inter-Services Metallurgical Research Council [*British*]
**ISMS** ......... Image Store Management System
**ISMS** ......... Industrial Standards and Military Specifications [*Information Handling Services*] [*Information service or system*] (CRD)
**ISMS** ......... Information Systems and Media Services [*Eastern Illinois University*] [*Information service or system*] (IID)
**ISMS** ......... Infrared Spectral Measurement System (MCD)
**ISMS** ......... Integrated Software Maintenance System
**ISMS** ......... International Society for Mushroom Science [*Braunschweig, Federal Republic of Germany*] (EA)
**ISMSD** ...... Istituto delle Suore Maestre di Santa Dorotea [*Rome, Italy*] (EAIO)
**ISmSD** ....... Smithton Community Consolidated School District 130, Smithton, IL [*Library symbol*] [*Library of Congress*] (LCLS)
**ISMTB** ...... Instrumentalist [*A publication*]
**ISMUN** ..... International Youth and Student Movement for the United Nations [*Geneva, Switzerland*] (EA)
**ISMV**......... Iris Severe Mosaic Virus
**ISMX**......... Integrated Subrate Data Multiplexer (TEL)
**ISMX**......... Isomedix, Inc. [*NASDAQ symbol*] (NQ)
**ISN** ........... Information Systems Network [*AT & T*] [*Telecommunications*]
**ISN** ........... Instron Corp. [*AMEX symbol*] (SPSG)
**ISN** ........... International Society of Nephrology
**ISN** ........... International Society for Neurochemistry [*Kjeller, Norway*] (EA)
**ISN** ........... International Suneva Resources [*Vancouver Stock Exchange symbol*]
**ISN** ........... Internment Serial Number
**ISN** ........... Interplant Shipping Notice
**ISN** ........... Ishinomaki [*Japan*] [*Seismograph station code, US Geological Survey*] (SEIS)
**ISN** ........... Item Sequence Number (MCD)
**ISN** ........... Saint Mary's College, Notre Dame, IN [*OCLC symbol*] (OCLC)
**ISN** ........... Williston [*North Dakota*] [*Airport symbol*] (OAG)
**ISN** ........... Williston, ND [*Location identifier*] [*FAA*] (FAAL)
**ISNA**.......... International Society for New Atlantis (EA)
**ISNA**.......... International Space: 1999 Alliance (EA)
**ISNA**.......... International Symposium on Novel Aromatic Compounds
**ISNAC**....... Inactive Ships Navy Custody (NVT)
**ISNAR**....... International Service for National Agricultural Research [*The Hague, Netherlands*]
**ISNP**.......... Independent Scholarship National Program (EA)
**ISNP**.......... International Society of Naturopathic Physicians
**ISNR**.......... State of Illinois, Institute of Natural Resources, Energy Information Library, Springfield, IL [*Library symbol*] [*Library of Congress*] (LCLS)
**ISNR-E**...... State of Illinois, Institute of Natural Resources, Division of Environmental Management, Chicago, IL [*Library symbol*] [*Library of Congress*] (LCLS)
**ISNS** .......... International Society for Neoplatonic Studies (EA)
**ISNSL**........ Incremental Stock Number Sequence List [*Military*] (CAAL)
**ISNT**.......... Informal Single Negotiating Text [*Marine science*] (MSC)
**ISNTAW**... Indian Society for Nuclear Techniques in Agriculture and Biology. Newsletter [*A publication*]
**ISNU** ......... Illinois State Normal University
**ISNV**.......... Institute for the Study of Nonviolence [*Defunct*] (EA)
**ISNY**.......... Insurance Society of New York [*New York, NY*] (EA)
**ISO** ........... I'm So Optimistic [*Dance company*]
**ISO** ........... Imaging Spectrometric Observatory (MCD)
**ISO** ........... Imperial Service Order [*British*]
**ISO** ........... Incentive Stock Option
**ISO** ........... Individual System Operation
**ISO** ........... Information Services Officer
**ISO** ........... Information Systems Office [*Library of Congress*]
**ISO** ........... Infrared Space Observatory
**ISO** ........... Installation Supply Officer [*Military*]
**ISO** ........... Insurance Services Office [*An association*] (EA)
**IS(O)**.......... Intelligence Section, Operations [*Control Commission for Germany*] [*World War II*]
**ISO** ........... Internal Standard Organization Code (CMD)
**ISO** ........... International Organization for Standardization [*United Nations*] [*Geneva, Switzerland*]
**ISO** ........... International Science Organization
**ISO** ........... International Self-Service Organization
**ISO** ........... International Shopfitting Organization [*Zurich, Switzerland*] (EAIO)

**ISO** ........... International Sikh Organization (EA)
**ISO** ........... International Socialist Organization (EA)
**ISO** ........... International Society of Organbuilders [*Levallois-Perret, France*] (EAIO)
**ISO** ........... International Sugar Organization [*See also OIA*] [*London, England*] (EAIO)
**ISO** ........... Interplant Shipping Order
**ISO** ........... ISG Technologies, Inc. [*Toronto Stock Exchange symbol*]
**ISO** ........... Isochromatic (ROG)
**ISO** ........... Isoflurane [*An anesthetic*]
**ISO** ........... Isola [*France*] [*Seismograph station code, US Geological Survey*] (SEIS)
**ISO** ........... Isolation
**ISO** ........... Isometric (MSA)
**Iso** ........... Isophase
**ISO** ........... Isoproterenol [*An adrenergic*]
**ISO** ........... Isotope
**ISO** ........... Isotropic (KSC)
**ISO** ........... Israel Students Organization
**ISO** ........... Kinston [*North Carolina*] [*Airport symbol*] (OAG)
**ISO** ........... Kinston, NC [*Location identifier*] [*FAA*] (FAAL)
**ISO** ........... Oxford Bulletin of Economics and Statistics [*A publication*]
**ISO** ........... South Bend Public Library, South Bend, IN [*OCLC symbol*] (OCLC)
**ISO-ALPHABET** ... International Standards Organization-Authorized Alphabetic Characters (MCD)
**ISOB** .......... International Society of Barristers (EA)
**ISOBA** ....... Izotopy v SSSR [*A publication*]
**Isoc** ........... De Isocrate [*of Dionysius Halicarnassensis*] [*Classical studies*] (OCD)
**ISOC** .......... Instituto de Informacion y Documentacion en Ciencias Sociales y Humanidades [*Institute for Information and Documentation in the Social Sciences and Humanities*] [*Higher Council for Scientific Research*] [*Information service or system*] (IID)
**Isoc** ........... Isocrates [*436-338BC*] [*Classical studies*] (OCD)
**ISoCaRP** .... International Society of City and Regional Planners [*See also AIU*] [*The Hague, Netherlands*] (EAIO)
**ISO-CMOS** ... Isolated Fully Recessed Complementary Metal-Oxide Semiconductor (TEL)
**ISOD** ......... International Society for Orbital Disorders (EAIO)
**ISOD** ......... International Sports Organization for the Disabled [*Farstn, Sweden*] (EA)
**ISODARCO** ... International School of Disarmament and Research on Conflicts
**ISODATA** ... Iterative Self-Organizing Data Analysis Technique A [*Data processing*]
**ISODOC** .... International Information Centre for Standards in Information and Documentation (ADA)
**ISOE** .......... ISOETEC Communications, Inc. [*NASDAQ symbol*] (NQ)
**ISOF** .......... International Society for Ocular Fluorophotometry (EAIO)
**ISOHP** ....... International Society for Organ History and Preservation (EA)
**ISOKD** ....... Izvestiya Sibirskogo Otdeleniya Geologicheskogo Komiteta [*A publication*]
**ISOL** .......... Information Solutions, Inc. [*NASDAQ symbol*] (NQ)
**ISOL** .......... Isolation (KSC)
**ISOLD** ....... Isolated (FAAC)
**ISOLN** ....... Isolation
**ISOLR** ....... Isolationer
**ISOM** ........ International Standard Orthopaedic Measurements [*Medicine*]
**ISOM** ........ Isometric (KSC)
**ISom** .......... Somonauk Public Library, Somonauk, IL [*Library symbol*] [*Library of Congress*] (LCLS)
**ISOMATA** ... Idyllwild School of Music and the Arts [*California*]
**ISomSD** ..... Somonauk Community Unit, School District 432, Somonauk, IL [*Library symbol*] [*Library of Congress*] (LCLS)
**ISONET** .... ISO [*International Organization for Standardization*] Information Network [*Information service or system*] (IID)
**ISONIAZID** ... Isonicotinic Acid Hydrazide [*See also INAH, INH*] [*Antituberculous agent*]
**ISOO** ......... Information Security Oversight Office [*National Archives and Records Service*]
**ISOOA** ...... Izvestiya Sibirskogo Otdeleniya Akademii Nauk SSSR Seriya Obshchestvennykh Nauk [*A publication*]
**ISO/OSI** .... International Standards Organization/Open System Interface [*Motorola, Inc.*]
**ISOP** .......... Integrated Spacecraft Operations Plan [*NASA*]
**ISOP** .......... Internal Standard Operating Procedure [*Military*] (MCD)
**ISOPAR** .... Improved Symbolic Optimizing Assembly Routine
**ISOPEP** .... Isometric Piping Efficiency Program
**ISOPGU** .... International Security Officer's Police and Guard Union (EA)
**IS(Ops)** ...... Intelligence Section, Operations [*Joint Intelligence Subcommittee of Chiefs of Staff*] [*World War II*]
**I2S(OPS)** ... Integrated Information System (Operational) [*Marine Corps*]
**ISORID** ..... International Information System on Research in Documentation [*International Federation for Documentation*] [*UNESCO*] (IID)
**ISORT** ....... Interdisciplinary Student-Originated Research Training [*National Science Foundation*]
**ISOS** .......... International Southern Ocean Study [*National Science Foundation*]
**ISOS** .......... Interplanetare Sonnensonde
**ISOS** .......... Isosceles [*Triangle*]
**ISOSC** ....... International Society for Soilless Culture [*Wageningen, Netherlands*] (EAIO)
**ISOSJ** ........ Institute of Social Order of the Society of Jesus [*Later, JCSS*] (EA)
**ISOSS** ........ Immobile Suspension Feeders on Soft Substrata [*Oceanography*]
**ISOT** .......... International Symposium on Olfaction and Taste
**ISOTAP** .... Interservice Occupational Task Analysis Program [*Military*] (NVT)
**ISOTEC** .... Isotope Thermoelectric Converter
**Isot Generator Inf Cent (Gif Sur Yvette) Newsl** ... Isotopic Generator Information Centre (Gif-Sur-Yvette). Newsletter [*A publication*]
**Isot Geosci** ... Isotope Geoscience [*A publication*]
**ISOTH** ...... Isothermal (KSC)
**Isot Ind Landwirtsch** ... Isotope in Industrie und Landwirtschaft [*A publication*]
**Isot News** ... Isotope News [*Japan*] [*A publication*]
**Isotopenprax** ... Isotopenpraxis [*A publication*]
**Isotopes Radiat** ... Isotopes Radiation [*A publication*]
**Isotop Radiat Technol** ... Isotopes and Radiation Technology [*A publication*]
**Isot Radiat** ... Isotopes and Radiation [*Japan*] [*A publication*]
**Isot Radiat Res** ... Isotope and Radiation Research [*Egypt*] [*A publication*]
**Isot Radiat Res Anim Dis Vec** ... Isotope and Radiation Research on Animal Diseases and Their Vectors. Proceedings [*A publication*]
**Isot Radiat Technol** ... Isotopes and Radiation Technology [*A publication*]
**ISOU** .......... International Society for Ophthalmic Ultrasound (EA)
**ISOW** ......... Iceland-Scotland Overflow Water [*Oceanography*]
**Isozymes Curr Top Biol Med Res** ... Isozymes. Current Topics in Biological and Medical Research [*A publication*]
**ISP** ............ Henry Public Library, Henry, IL [*OCLC symbol*] (OCLC)
**ISp** ............ Iconic Store, Peripheral [*Psychophysiology*]
**ISP** ............ Image Stabilization Program [*Photography*]
**ISP** ............ Image Store Processor [*Data processing*]
**ISP** ............ Immunoreactive Substance P [*Immunology*]
**ISP** ............ Imperial Smelting Process
**ISP** ............ Implementation Support Package [*Army*]
**ISP** ............ Impulse, Specific (KSC)
**ISP** ............ In-Store Promotions [*Marketing events for US goods held by retail establishments in foreign countries*] [*Department of Commerce*]
**ISP** ............ Independent Service Provider [*Telecommunications*]
**ISP** ............ Independent Studies Project [*Navy*]
**ISP** ............ Independent Study Program [*IBM Corp.*]
**ISP** ............ Indexed Sequential Processor
**ISP** ............ Individual Service Plan
**ISP** ............ Industrial Security Plan [*Nuclear energy*] (NRCH)
**ISP** ............ Industrial Security Program [*Air Force, Army*]
**ISP** ............ Industry Service Package
**ISP** ............ Information Search and Processing [*Database search service*] (OLDSS)
**ISP** ............ Information System Plan (MCD)
**ISP** ............ Information Systems Program [*University of Oklahoma*] [*Norman, OK*]
**ISP** ............ Infrared Spectrophotometer
**ISP** ............ Initial Specific Impulse (MCD)
**ISP** ............ Instantaneous Sound Pressure
**ISP** ............ Institut pour une Synthese Planetaire [*Institute for Planetary Synthesis - IPS*] [*Geneva, Switzerland*] (EAIO)
**ISP** ............ Institute of Sales Promotion [*British*] [*ICSU*]
**ISP** ............ Institute of Store Planners (EA)
**ISP** ............ Institute for Studies in Pragmaticism [*Texas Tech University*] [*Research center*] (RCD)
**ISP** ............ Instituto de Seguros de Portugal [*Insurance regulatory agency*] [*Portugal*] (EY)
**ISP** ............ Instruction Set Processor [*1971*] [*Data processing*]
**ISP** ............ Instructional System Package (MCD)
**ISP** ............ Instrumentation Support Plan (MCD)
**ISP** ............ Integrated Shear Plate
**ISP** ............ Integrated Support Plan (MCD)
**ISP** ............ Integrated System Peripheral [*Data processing*]
**ISP** ............ Integrated Systems Planning, Inc. [*Baltimore, MD*] (TSSD)
**ISP** ............ Interamerican Society of Psychology (EA)
**ISP** ............ Intergovernmental Science Programs
**ISP** ............ Interim Support Period
**ISP** ............ Interim Support Plan (MCD)
**ISP** ............ Internal Security Plan (CINC)
**ISP** ............ Internally Stored Program (AAG)
**ISP** ............ International Shadow Project (EA)
**ISP** ............ International Society for Photogrammetry [*Later, ISPRS*]
**ISP** ............ International Society of Postmasters [*Montreal, PQ*] (EAIO)
**ISP** ............ International Solar Polar [*Mission*] [*NASA*]
**ISP** ............ International Streptomyces Project
**ISP** ............ International Student Pugwash [*Formerly, USSPC*] [*Later, Student Pugwash (USA)*] (EA)
**ISP** ............ Internationale des Services Publics [*Public Service International - PSI*] [*Ferney Voltaire, France*] (EAIO)

**ISP** ............ Intraspinal
**ISP** ............ Inverse Sampling Procedure
**ISP** ............ Ipsco, Inc. [*Toronto Stock Exchange symbol*]
**ISP** ............ Islip, NY [*Location identifier*] [*FAA*] (FAAL)
**ISP** ............ Isolated Safflower Protein [*Food technology*]
**ISP** ............ Isolated Soy Protein [*Food technology*]
**ISP** ............ Isotope Separation Power
**ISP** ............ Italian Society of Physics
**ISP** ............ Long Island [*New York*] MacArthur [*Airport symbol*] (OAG)
**ISp** ............ Schiller Park Public Library, Schiller Park, IL [*Library symbol*] [*Library of Congress*] (LCLS)
**ISP** ............ Specific Impulse (MCD)
**ISPA** .......... International Screen Publicity Association
**ISPA** .......... International Society of Parametric Analysts (EA)
**ISPA** .......... International Society for the Protection of Animals [*Later, WSPA*] [*British*] (EA)
**ISPA** .......... International Sporting Press Association
**ISPA** .......... International Squash Players Association [*Cardiff, Wales*] (EAIO)
**ISPAA** ....... International Society of Performing Arts Administrators (EA)
**ISPAA** ....... International Society of Plastic and Audio-Visual Art
**ISPBA**........ Buletinul. Institutului de Studii si Projectari Energetice [*A publication*]
**ISPC** .......... International Sound Programming Center [*Telecommunications*]
**ISPC** .......... International Spotted Pony Club (EA)
**ISPC** .......... International Statistical Programs Center [*Department of Commerce*] (IID)
**ISPC** .......... Interspec, Inc. [*NASDAQ symbol*] (NQ)
**ISPCAN** .... International Society for Prevention of Child Abuse and Neglect (EA)
**ISPD** .......... International Society for Peritoneal Dialysis (EA)
**ISPE** .......... Improved SONAR Processing Equipment [*Military*] (CAAL)
**ISPE** .......... International Society of Pharmaceutical Engineers (EA)
**ISPE** .......... International Society for Philosophical Enquiry (EA)
**ISPEC**........ Insulation Specification (MSA)
**ISPF**........... Interactive System Productivity Facility [*Data processing*]
**ISPF**........... International Save the Pun Foundation (EA)
**ISPF**........... International Science Policy Foundation (EAIO)
**ISPF/PDF** ... Interactive System Productivity Facility/Program Development Facility [*Data processing*]
**ISPG**.......... Institute of Sedimentary and Petroleum Geology [*Geological Survey of Canada*] [*Research center*] (RCD)
**ISPG**.......... Institutional Support Planning Group [*NASA*] (NASA)
**ISPH**.......... International Society for Professional Hypnosis (EA)
**ISPH**.......... International Society of Psychology of Handwriting [*Milan, Italy*] (EA)
**ISPHS** ....... International Society for Phenomenology and Human Sciences (EA)
**ISPhS** ........ International Society of Phonetic Sciences (EA)
**ISPI** .......... Illinois State Psychiatric Institute
**ISPK**.......... Isolated Spontaneous Psychokinesis [*Parapsychology*]
**ISPL**........... Incremental System Programming Language [*Data processing*]
**ISPL**........... Instruction Set Processor Language [*Data processing*]
**ISPL**........... Interim Spare Parts List (AAG)
**ISPL**........... International Society for Phenomenology and Literature (EA)
**ISPM** ......... International Society of Plant Morphologists [*Delhi, India*] (EAIO)
**ISPM** ......... International Solar Polar Mission [*NASA*]
**ISPM** ......... International Staff Planners Message [*NATO*] (NATG)
**ISPMB** ...... International Society of Plant Molecular Biology (EA)
**ISPMB** ...... International Society for the Protection of Mustangs and Burros (EA)
**ISPMEMO** ... International Staff Planners Memo [*NATO*] (NATG)
**ISPMM** ..... International Symposium on Purine Metabolism in Man
**ISPN**.......... International Society for Pediatric Neurosurgery (EA)
**ISPN**.......... International Standard Program Number [*Numbering system for software*]
**ISPN**.......... International Students Peace Network (EA)
**ISPO**.......... Industrial Staffing Plan Occupations (MCD)
**ISPO**.......... Instrumentation Ships Project Office [*Navy*]
**ISPO**.......... International Society for Preventive Oncology (EA)
**ISPO**.......... International Society for Prosthetics and Orthotics - US National Member Society (EA)
**ISPO**.......... International Sports Equipment Fair [*Federal Republic of Germany*] (TSPED)
**ISPO**.......... International Statistical Programs Office [*Department of Commerce*] (IEEE)
**Ispol'z Gaza Nar Khoz** ... Ispol'zovanie Gaza v Narodnom Khozyaistve [*USSR*] [*A publication*]
**Ispolz Mikroorg Nar Khoz** ... Ispol'zovanie Mikroorganizmov v Narodnom Khozyaistve [*A publication*]
**Ispol'z Neorg Resur Okeanicheskoi Vody** ... Ispol'zovanie Neorganicheskikh Resursov Okeanicheskoi Vody [*A publication*]
**Ispol'z Tverd Topl Sernistykh Mazutov Gaza** ... Ispol'zovanie Tverdykh Topliv Sernistykh Mazutov i Gaza [*USSR*] [*A publication*]
**ISPOR**....... Institute of Polar Studies (Ohio). Reports [*A publication*]
**ISPOUSC** ... International Society for Prosthetics and Orthotics - US Committee [*Later, ISPO*] (EA)
**ISPP**........... International Society for Plant Pathology (EAIO)
**ISPP**........... International Society of Political Psychology (EA)
**ISPP**........... International Society for Portuguese Philately (EA)
**ISPP**........... International Society of Prenatal and Perinatal Psychology and Medicine (EAIO)
**ISPP**........... International Society for Retirement Planning [*Later, ISRP*] (EA)
**ISPP**........... International Society for the Study of Prenatal Psychology (EAIO)
**ISPP**........... Internationale Studiengemeinschaft fuer Pranatale Psychologie [*International Society for the Study of Prenatal Psychology - ISPP*] (EAIO)
**ISPPP** ........ International Symposium on HPLC of Proteins, Peptides, and Polynucleotides
**ISPPS** ........ Item Support Plan Policies Statement (AFIT)
**ISPR** .......... Infantry Systems Program Review [*Army*] (AABC)
**ISPR** .......... Information Security Program Regulation (MCD)
**ISPR** .......... Integrated Support Parts Requirement (KSC)
**ISPR** .......... International Special Commission on Radio Interference (MCD)
**ISPRS**........ International Society for Photogrammetry and Remote Sensing [*Royal Institute of Technology*] [*Research center*] [*Sweden*] (IRC)
**ISprv** .......... Spring Valley Public Library, Spring Valley, IL [*Library symbol*] [*Library of Congress*] (LCLS)
**ISprvHSD** ... Hall Township High School District 502, Spring Valley, IL [*Library symbol*] [*Library of Congress*] (LCLS)
**ISprvSD**..... Spring Valley Consolidated Community School District 99, Spring Valley, IL [*Library symbol*] [*Library of Congress*] (LCLS)
**ISPS**........... Instruction Set Processor Specification [*1977*] [*Data processing*] (CSR)
**ISPS**........... International Society of Phonetic Sciences (EA)
**ISPS**........... International Standard Paper Sizes
**ISPT** .......... Initial Satisfactory Performance Test (AAG)
**ISPT** .......... Institute for Studies in Psychological Testing
**ISPT** .......... Intergovernmental Science and Public Technology [*of ASRA*] [*National Science Foundation*]
**ISPW** ......... International Society for the Psychology of Writing (EA)
**ISPWP**....... International Society for the Prevention of Water Pollution [*Alton, Hampshire, England*] (EAIO)
**ISPX** .......... Secular Institute of Pius X (EA)
**ISQ** ............ In Status Quo
**ISQ** ............ Informatie. Maandblad voor Informatieverwerking [*A publication*]
**ISQ** ............ Information Standards Quarterly [*A publication*]
**IsQ** ............ Islamic Quarterly [*A publication*]
**ISQ** ............ Lillie M. Evans Memorial Library, Princeville, IL [*OCLC symbol*] (OCLC)
**ISQ** ............ Manistique, MI [*Location identifier*] [*FAA*] (FAAL)
**ISQD** ......... Identification System for Questioned Documents [*Book title*]
**ISR**............. Identification Safety Range [*Military*] (NVT)
**ISR**............. Image Storage Retrieval
**ISR**............. Impulse Sequencing Relay
**ISR**............. In-Service Recruiter [*Army*]
**ISR**............. Incstar Corp. [*AMEX symbol*] (SPSG)
**ISR**............. Index to Scientific Reviews [*Institute for Scientific Information*] [*Information service or system*] [*A publication*]
**ISR**............. Indian State Railway (ROG)
**ISR**............. Individual Soldier's Report
**ISR**............. Industrial Security Regulations [*DoD*]
**ISR**............. Information Processing and Management [*A publication*]
**ISR**............. Information Service Representative [*Veterans Administration*]
**ISR**............. Information Storage and Retrieval [*Data processing*]
**IS & R** ........ Information Storage and Retrieval [*Data processing*]
**ISR**............. Infrared Scanning Radiometer (KSC)
**ISR**............. Initial System Release (MCD)
**ISR**............. Institute of Seaweed Research [*British*]
**ISR**............. Institute of Semiconductor Research [*USSR*]
**ISR**............. Institute for Sex Research, Inc. [*National Institute of Mental Health*] (IID)
**ISR**............. Institute for Social Research [*York University*] [*Information service or system*] (IID)
**ISR**............. Institute for Social Research [*University of Michigan*] (EA)
**ISR**............. Institute of Social Research [*Indiana University*] [*Information service or system*] (IID)
**ISR**............. Institute for Storm Research (MCD)
**ISR**............. Institute for Study of Regulation [*Defunct*] (EA)
**ISR**............. Institute of Surgical Research [*San Antonio, TX*] [*Army*]
**ISR**............. Instructional System Review
**ISR**............. Instrumentation Status Report (MUGU)
**ISR**............. Integral Superheat Reactor
**ISR**............. Integrated Support Requirements (AAG)
**ISR**............. Interagency Source Register [*Intelligence*] (MCD)
**ISR**............. Interdisciplinary Science Reviews [*A publication*]
**ISR**............. Interim Scientific Report
**ISR**............. Intermediate Sodium Removal [*Nuclear energy*] (NRCH)
**ISR**............. Internal Scientific Report
**ISR**............. International Sacred Recordings, Christian Artists' Record Corp. [*Record label*]
**ISR**............. International Sanitary Regulations [*World Health Organization*]

**ISR**............ International Shasta Resources [*Vancouver Stock Exchange symbol*]
**ISR**............ International Society of Radiology [*Berne, Switzerland*] (EA)
**ISR**............ International Sourdough Reunion (EA)
**ISR**............ International Star Registry
**ISR**............ International Student Relief [*Later, WUS*]
**ISR**............ International Survey Research [*London consultancy firm*]
**ISR**............ International Synthetic Rubber Co. [*United Kingdom*]
**ISR**............ Interrupt Service Routine (IEEE)
**ISR**............ Intersecting Storage Ring [*High-energy physics*]
**ISR**............ Inventory Status Report
**ISR**............ Israel [*ANSI three-letter standard code*] (CNC)
**ISR**............ Methodist Medical Center of Illinois, Peoria, IL [*OCLC symbol*] (OCLC)
**ISRA**.......... Installment Sales Revision Act of 1980
**ISRA**.......... International Seabed Research Authority
**ISRA**.......... International Ski Racers Association [*Later, WPS-RA*]
**ISRA**.......... International Society for Research on Aggression (EA)
**ISRAC**....... ITT [*International Telephone & Telegraph Corp.*] Secure Ranging and Communications System
**ISRAD**....... Institute for Social Research and Development [*University of New Mexico*]
**ISRAD**....... Integrated Software Research and Development Program (MCD)
**Isr AEC IA Rep** ... Israel. Atomic Energy Commission. IA Report [*A publication*]
**Isr AEC LS Rep** ... Israel. Atomic Energy Commission. LS Report [*A publication*]
**Israel Ann Psychiat** ... Israel Annals of Psychiatry [*A publication*]
**Israel Bus**... Israel Business [*A publication*]
**Israel E** ...... Israel Economist [*A publication*]
**Israel Inv**.... Israel Business and Investors' Report [*A publication*]
**Israel J Agric Res** ... Israel Journal of Agricultural Research [*A publication*]
**Israel J Agr Res** ... Israel Journal of Agricultural Research [*A publication*]
**Israel J Bot** ... Israel Journal of Botany [*A publication*]
**Israel J Chem** ... Israel Journal of Chemistry [*A publication*]
**Israel J Earth Sci** ... Israel Journal of Earth-Sciences [*A publication*]
**Israel J Ent** ... Israel Journal of Entomology [*A publication*]
**Israel J Math** ... Israel Journal of Mathematics [*A publication*]
**Israel J Med Sc** ... Israel Journal of Medical Sciences [*A publication*]
**Israel J Tech** ... Israel Journal of Technology [*A publication*]
**Israel J Technol** ... Israel Journal of Technology [*A publication*]
**Israel J Zool** ... Israel Journal of Zoology [*A publication*]
**Israel Law R** ... Israel Law Review [*A publication*]
**Israel L Rev** ... Israel Law Review [*A publication*]
**Israel Stud Criminol** ... Israel Studies in Criminology [*Jerusalem, Israel*] [*A publication*] (DLA)
**Israel Yb on Human Rights** ... Israel Yearbook on Human Rights [*A publication*]
**Isr Agric Res Organ Spec Publ** ... Israel. Agricultural Research Organization. Special Publication [*A publication*]
**Isr Agric Res Org Div For Trienn Rep Res** ... Israel. Agricultural Research Organization. Division of Forestry. Triennial Report of Research [*A publication*]
**Isr Ann Psy** ... Israel Annals of Psychiatry and Related Disciplines [*A publication*]
**Isr Ann Psychiatry** ... Israel Annals of Psychiatry and Related Disciplines [*A publication*]
**Isr Ann Psychiatry Relat Discip** ... Israel Annals of Psychiatry and Related Disciplines [*A publication*]
**Isr Aquacult Bamidgeh** ... Israeli Journal of Aquaculture Bamidgeh [*A publication*]
**ISRB**.......... Inter-Service Research Bureau [*British*]
**ISRC**.......... International Society of Radiology Congress
**ISRD**.......... International Society for Rehabilitation of the Disabled [*Later, Rehabilitation International*]
**ISRDS**....... Istituto di Studi sulla Ricerca e Documentazione Scientifica [*Institute for Study of Scientific Research and Documentation*] [*National Research Council*] [*Information service or system*] (IID)
**IsrEJ**.......... Israel Exploration Journal [*Jerusalem*] [*A publication*]
**I S Revw**..... International Socialist Review [*A publication*]
**Isr Ex J**...... Israel Exploration Journal [*A publication*]
**Isr Expl J**... Israel Exploration Journal [*A publication*]
**ISRF**.......... International Squash Rackets Federation [*Cardiff, Wales*] (EAIO)
**ISRF**.......... International Sugar Research Foundation [*Later, WSRO*] (EA)
**ISRG**.......... Independent Space Research Group (EA)
**Isr Geol Soc Annu Meet** ... Israel Geological Society. Annual Meeting [*A publication*]
**Isr Geol Surv Bull** ... Israel. Geological Survey. Bulletin [*A publication*]
**Isr Geol Surv Geol Data Process Unit Rep** ... Israel. Geological Survey. Geological Data Processing Unit. Report [*A publication*]
**Isr Geol Surv Rep** ... Israel. Geological Survey. Report [*A publication*]
**ISRGLU**.... Independent Ship, Riverside, and General Labourers' Union [*British*]
**ISRHAI**..... International Secretariat for Research on the History of Agricultural Implements [*Lyngby, Denmark*] (EAIO)
**Isr Hydrol Serv Rep** ... Israel. Hydrological Service. Report [*A publication*]
**ISRIC**......... International Soil Reference and Information Centre [*Research center*] [*Netherlands*] (IRC)
**Isr Inst Agric Eng Sci Act** ... Israel. Institute of Agricultural Engineering. Scientific Activities [*A publication*]
**Isr Inst Anim Sci Sci Act** ... Israel. Institute of Animal Science. Scientific Activities [*A publication*]
**Isr Inst Field Gard Crops Sci Act** ... Israel. Institute of Field and Garden Crops. Scientific Activities [*A publication*]
**Isr Inst Hortic Sci Act** ... Israel. Institute of Horticulture. Scientific Activities [*A publication*]
**Isr Inst Plant Prot Sci Act** ... Israel. Institute of Plant Protection. Scientific Activities [*A publication*]
**Isr Inst Soils Water Sci Act** ... Israel. Institute of Soils and Water. Scientific Activities [*A publication*]
**Isr Inst Technol Storage Agric Prod Sci Act** ... Israel. Institute for Technology and Storage of Agricultural Products. Scientific Activities [*A publication*]
**Isr J Agric Res** ... Israel Journal of Agricultural Research [*A publication*]
**Isr J Bot**..... Israel Journal of Botany [*A publication*]
**Isr J Chem** ... Israel Journal of Chemistry [*A publication*]
**Isr J Dent Med** ... Israel Journal of Dental Medicine [*A publication*]
**Isr J Earth** ... Israel Journal of Earth-Sciences [*A publication*]
**Isr J Earth-Sci** ... Israel Journal of Earth-Sciences [*A publication*]
**Isr J Entomol** ... Israel Journal of Entomology [*A publication*]
**Isr J Exp Med** ... Israel Journal of Experimental Medicine [*A publication*]
**Isr J Math** ... Israel Journal of Mathematics [*A publication*]
**Isr J Med S** ... Israel Journal of Medical Sciences [*A publication*]
**Isr J Med Sci** ... Israel Journal of Medical Sciences [*A publication*]
**Isr J Psychiatr Relat Sci** ... Israel Journal of Psychiatry and Related Sciences [*A publication*]
**Isr J Psychiatry Relat Sci** ... Israel Journal of Psychiatry and Related Sciences [*A publication*]
**Isr J Tech**... Israel Journal of Technology [*A publication*]
**Isr J Technol** ... Israel Journal of Technology [*A publication*]
**Isr J Vet Med** ... Israel Journal of Veterinary Medicine [*A publication*]
**Isr J Zool** ... Israel Journal of Zoology [*A publication*]
**ISRL**.......... Isramco, Inc. [*NASDAQ symbol*] (NQ)
**Isr Law Rev** ... Israel Law Review [*A publication*]
**IsrLLetters** ... Israel Life and Letters [*New York*] [*A publication*]
**ISRM**......... Index of Stability of Relative Magnitudes [*Statistics*]
**ISRM**......... Information Systems Resource Manager
**ISRM**......... Inter-Service Radio Measurements [*British*] [*World War II*]
**ISRM**......... International Society for Range Management (EA)
**ISRM**......... International Society of Reproductive Medicine (EA)
**ISRM**......... International Society for Rock Mechanics [*Lisbon, Portugal*] (EA)
**Isr Med J** ... Israel Medical Journal [*A publication*]
**Isr Min Agr Water Comm Hydrol Serv Hydrol Paper** ... Israel. Ministry of Agriculture. Water Commission. Hydrological Service. Hydrological Paper [*A publication*]
**Isr Mus N** .. Israel Museum News [*A publication*]
**ISRN**.......... Incorporated Society of Registered Naturopaths [*British*]
**Isr Natl Counc Res Dev Rep** ... Israel. National Council for Research and Development. Report [*A publication*]
**Isr Natl Counc Res Dev Rep NCRD** ... Israel. National Council for Research and Development. Report NCRD [*A publication*]
**ISRNI**........ Incest Survivors Resource Network, International (EA)
**Isr Num J**... Israel Numismatic Journal [*A publication*]
**ISRO**.......... International Securities Regulatory Organisation [*London, England*] [*Business term*]
**ISRO**.......... Isle Royale National Park
**Isr Oceanogr Limnol Res Annu Rep** ... Israel Oceanographic and Limnological Research. Annual Report [*A publication*]
**Isr Orient Stud** ... Israel Oriental Studies [*A publication*]
**ISRP**.......... Initial Spares and Repair Parts
**ISRP**.......... Internal Surface Reverse Phase [*Chromatography column*]
**ISRP**.......... International Society for Respiratory Protection (EA)
**ISRP**.......... International Society for Retirement Planning (EA)
**Isr Pharm J** ... Israel Pharmaceutical Journal [*A publication*]
**ISRR**.......... International Soundex Reunion Registry (EA)
**ISRREC**..... Institute for Sex Research Library Records [*Database*] [*Kinsey Institute for Research in Sex, Gender, and Reproduction*] [*Information service or system*] (CRD)
**ISRRT**....... International Society of Radiographers and Radiological Technicians [*Don Mills, ON*] (EA)
**ISRRT Newsl** ... ISRRT [*International Society of Radiographers and Radiological Technicians*] Newsletter [*England*] [*A publication*]
**ISRS**.......... Impulsive Stimulated Raman Scattering [*Physics*]
**ISRS**.......... Information Search and Recording System [*of UMREL*]
**ISRS**.......... Integrated Status Reporting System (MCD)
**ISRSM**...... International Symposium on Rocket and Satellite Meteorology
**Isr Soc Spec Libr Inf Cent Bull** ... Israel Society of Special Libraries and Information Centers. Bulletin [*A publication*]
**ISRT**.......... International Spinal Research Trust [*Great Britain*]
**ISRT**.......... Iowa Silent Reading Tests [*Education*]
**ISRT**.......... Isotopes and Radiation Technology [*A publication*]
**ISRTAI**...... Isotopes and Radiation Technology [*A publication*]
**ISRU**.......... Intergovernmental Science and Research Utilization [*National Science Foundation*]
**ISRU**.......... international Scientific Radio Union [*Also, URSI*]
**IsRW**.......... Weizmann Institute of Science, Rehovot, Israel [*Library symbol*] [*Library of Congress*] (LCLS)

**ISS** ............ Ideal Solidus Structures (IEEE)
**ISS** ............ Ignition Shielding System
**ISS** ............ Image Sensor System
**ISS** ............ Imperfect Single Stamp [*Philately*]
**ISS** ............ Imperial Service Sappers [*British military*] (DMA)
**ISS** ............ Independent Sweep System
**ISS** ............ Index of Specifications and Standards (MCD)
**ISS** ............ Indiana Slavic Studies [*A publication*]
**ISS** ............ Inductive Storage Switch
**ISS** ............ Industrial Security Section [*NATO*] (NATG)
**ISS** ............ Industry Sole Source (AFIT)
**ISS** ............ Industry Standard Specifications (AAG)
**ISS** ............ Inertial Sensor System (KSC)
**ISS** ............ Inertial Subsystem (MCD)
**ISS** ............ Information Science Section [*Australia*]
**ISS** ............ Information Storage System (IEEE)
**ISS** ............ Information Support System [*Nondestructive Testing Information Analysis Center - NTIAC*] [*Southwest Research Institute*] [*Information service or system*] (CRD)
**ISS** ............ Information Systems [*Subdivision*] (MCD)
**ISS** ............ Information Systems Section [*Battelle Memorial Institute*] [*Information service or system*] (IID)
**ISS** ............ Information Systems Security
**ISS** ............ Information Systems Services [*Brigham Young University*] [*Research center*] (RCD)
**ISS** ............ Infrared Sensor System
**ISS** ............ Infrared Surveillance Set
**ISS** ............ Inhibit/Override Summary Snapshot Display (NASA)
**ISS** ............ Initial Space Station (KSC)
**ISS** ............ Input Subsystem
**ISS** ............ Inside Skin (MCD)
**ISS** ............ Inside Surface (MCD)
**ISS** ............ Installation Site Survey (MCD)
**ISS** ............ Installation Support School [*Army*]
**ISS** ............ Installation Support Services (NASA)
**ISS** ............ Institute of Salesian Studies
**ISS** ............ Institute of Social Studies [*The Hague*] (ECON)
**ISS** ............ Institute for Socioeconomic Studies (EA)
**ISS** ............ Institute for Southern Studies (EA)
**ISS** ............ Institute for Space Studies [*NASA*]
**ISS** ............ Institute of Special Studies [*Army*]
**ISS** ............ Institute for Strategic Studies [*Obsolete*] [*Later, IISS*]
**ISS** ............ Instruction Summary Sheet (NASA)
**ISS** ............ Instrument Servo System
**ISS** ............ Instrumentation Support Service
**ISS** ............ Integrated Satellite System
**ISS** ............ Integrated Sealift Study [*Army*] (AABC)
**ISS** ............ Integrated Separation Systems [*Electrophoresis*]
**ISS** ............ Integrated Start System (AAG)
**ISS** ............ Integrated System Schematic (NASA)
**ISS** ............ Integration Support Service
**ISS** ............ Intelligence Support System
**ISS** ............ Intelligent Support System
**ISS** ............ INTERCO, Inc. [*Formerly, International Shoe Co.*] [*NYSE symbol*] (SPSG)
**ISS** ............ Intercommunication Service System Inc. [*Information service or system*] (IID)
**ISS** ............ Interface Simulation System (CAAL)
**ISS** ............ Interim Standard Set
**ISS** ............ Interim Stowage Shelf (KSC)
**ISS** ............ Intermediate Service School [*Military*] (AFM)
**ISS** ............ Internal Switching System
**ISS** ............ International Savant Society (EA)
**ISS** ............ International School of Sailing
**ISS** ............ International Schools Services (EA)
**ISS** ............ International Scientific Series [*A publication*]
**ISS** ............ International Scotist Society [*See also SIS*] [*Rome, Italy*] (EAIO)
**ISS** ............ International Seaweed Association (EAIO)
**ISS** ............ International Self-Service Organization [*Cologne, Federal Republic of Germany*] (EAIO)
**ISS** ............ International Sinatra Society (EA)
**ISS** ............ International Skeletal Society (EA)
**ISS** ............ International Social Service [*See also SSI*] [*Geneva, Switzerland*] (EAIO)
**ISS** ............ International Society of Shropshires (EA)
**ISS** ............ International Society for Stereology (EA)
**ISS** ............ International Society of Surgery (EA)
**ISS** ............ International Softbill Society (EA)
**ISS** ............ International Steamboat Society (EA)
**ISS** ............ International Students Society [*Defunct*] (EA)
**ISS** ............ International Sunshine Society (EA)
**ISS** ............ Internationale Gesellschaft fuer Stereologie [*International Society for Stereology*] (EAIO)
**ISS** ............ Interrupt Service Subroutine (CMD)
**ISS** ............ Interservice Supply Support [*Military*] (AABC)
**ISS** ............ Interstage Section Shell
**ISS** ............ Interstellar Scattering [*of radio waves in the galaxy*]
**ISS** ............ Interstellar [*Phase*] Scintillation [*Galactic science*]
**ISS** ............ Inventory Service System (AFIT)
**ISS** ............ Involuntary Servitude and Slavery
**ISS** ............ Ion-Scattering Spectrometer [*or Spectrometry*]
**ISS** ............ Ionospheric Sounding Satellite [*Japan*]
**ISS** ............ Iron and Steel Society - of AIME (EA)
**ISS** ............ Issue (AABC)
**ISS** ............ Issy-Les Moulineaux Airport [*France*]
**ISS** ............ St. Meinrad College, St. Meinrad, IN [*OCLC symbol*] (OCLC)
**ISS** ............ Sangamon State University, Springfield, IL [*Library symbol*] [*Library of Congress*] (LCLS)
**ISS** ............ Wiscasset, ME [*Location identifier*] [*FAA*] (FAAL)
**ISS** ............ YMCA [*Young Men's Christian Association*] International Student Service (EA)
**ISSA** .......... Information Systems Security Association (EA)
**ISSA** .......... Institute of Social Services Alternatives (EA)
**ISSA** .......... Institute for the Study of Sexual Assault (EA)
**ISSA** .......... International Sailing Schools Association (EA)
**ISSA** .......... International Sanitary Supply Association (EA)
**ISSA** .......... International Ship Suppliers Association [*Wimbledon, England*] (EA)
**ISSA** .......... International Slurry Seal Association (EA)
**ISSA** .......... International Social Security Association [*Geneva, Switzerland*] (EA)
**ISSA** .......... International Society of Stress Analysts (EA)
**ISSA** .......... International Strategic Studies Association (EA)
**ISSA** .......... Interservice Supply Support Agreements [*Military*]
**ISS/AB** ...... International Social Service, American Branch (EA)
**ISSAC** ........ Integrated Surface Search and Attack Coordinate
**ISSAS** ........ Interactive Structural Sizing and Analysis System [*Data processing*]
**ISSB** .......... Information Systems Standards Board [*American National Standards Institute*] [*Telecommunications*]
**ISSB** .......... Interservice Security Board [*World War II*]
**ISSBD** ........ International Society for the Study of Behavioural Development [*Nijmegen, Netherlands*] (EAIO)
**ISSC** .......... International Ship Structures Congress (NOAA)
**ISSC** .......... International Smart Shoppers Club (EA)
**ISSC** .......... International Snowshoe Council (EA)
**ISSC** .......... International Social Science Council [*See also CISS*] [*Paris, France*] [*Research center*] (EAIO)
**ISSC** .......... Interservice Sports Council [*Later, ISC*]
**ISSC** .......... Interservice Supply Support Committee [*or Coordinator*] [*Military*] (AABC)
**ISSC** .......... ISSC Industries Solid State [*NASDAQ symbol*] (NQ)
**ISSCAAP** .. International Standard Statistical Classification of Aquatic Animals and Plants
**ISSCB** ........ International Society for Sandwich Construction and Bonding
**ISSCC** ........ International Solid State Circuits Conference (MCD)
**ISSCM** ....... International Society for the Study of Church Monuments [*Later, CMS*] (EA)
**ISSCO** ....... Integrated Software Systems Corporation
**ISSCT** ........ International Society of Sugar Cane Technologists [*Piracicaoa, Brazil*] (EA)
**ISSCT (Int Soc Sugarcane Technol) Entomol Newsl** ... ISSCT (International Society of Sugarcane Technologists) Entomology Newsletter [*A publication*]
**ISSD** .......... Information Systems and Services Division [*Department of Commerce*] (IID)
**ISSD** .......... International Society for Social Defence [*See also SIDS*] [*Paris, France*] (EAIO)
**ISSDN** ....... Integrated Services Satellite Digital Network (MCD)
**ISSE** .......... International Sight and Sound Exposition
**ISSE** .......... International Society for the Study of Expressionism [*Formerly, ETMS*] (EA)
**ISSE-ETMS** ... International Society for the Study of Expressionism - Ernst Toller Memorial Society (EA)
**ISSEL** ........ University of Illinois Solid State Electronics Laboratory [*Research center*] (RCD)
**ISSEP** ........ Integrated System Safety Engineering Plan
**ISSET** ........ International Symposium on Space Electronics (MCD)
**ISSF** .......... Izvestija na Seminara po Slavjanska Filologija [*A publication*]
**I & SSFR** ... Investigation and Security Service Field Representative [*Veterans Administration*]
**ISSG** .......... Illustrated Shipboard Shopping Guide [*Navy*]
**ISSHCAB** ... International Society for the Study of the Human-Companion Animal Bond [*Later, IAHAIO*] (EA)
**ISSI** ........... International Social Science Institute [*Later, International Academy at Santa Barbara*] (EA)
**ISSID** ......... International Society for the Study of Individual Differences (EAIO)
**ISSJ** .......... International Social Science Journal [*UNESCO*] [*A publication*]
**ISSK** .......... International Society for the Sociology of Knowledge [*St. John's, NF*] (EAIO)
**ISSL** ........... Initial Spares Support List (AFM)
**Issled Betonu Zhelezobetonu** ... Issledovaniya po Betonu i Zhelezobetonu [*A publication*]
**Issled Bionike** ... Issledovaniya po Bionike [*A publication*]
**Issled Dalnevost Morei SSSR** ... Issledovaniya Dal'nevostochnykh Morei SSSR [*A publication*]

**Issled Elektrokhim Magnetokhim Elektrokhim Metodam Anal** ... Issledovaniya po Elektrokhimii Magnetokhimii i Elektrokhimicheskim Metodam Analiza [*A publication*]
**Issled Fauny Morei** ... Issledovaniya Fauny Morei [*A publication*]
**Issled Fiz Atmos Akad Nauk Est SSR** ... Issledovaniya po Fizike Atmosfery Akademiya Nauk Estonskoi SSR [*Estonian SSR*] [*A publication*]
**Issled Fiz Kipeniya** ... Issledovaniya po Fizike Kipeniya [*USSR*] [*A publication*]
**Issled Genet** ... Issledovaniya po Genetike [*A publication*]
**Issled Geomagn Aeron Fiz Solntsa** ... Issledovaniya po Geomagnetizmii, Aeronomii, i Fizike Solntsa [*A publication*]
**Issled Ispolz Soln Energ** ... Issledovaniya po Ispol'zovaniyu Solnechnoi Energii [*A publication*]
**Issled Kosm Prostranstva** ... Issledovanie Kosmicheskogo Prostranstva [*A publication*]
**Issled Mikrobiol** ... Issledovaniya po Mikrobiologii [*A publication*]
**Issled Nekotoryh Voprosov Mat Kibernet** ... Issledovanija Nekotoryh Voprosov Matematiceskoi Kibernetiki [*A publication*]
**Issled Obl Fiz Khim Kauch Rezin** ... Issledovaniya v Oblasti Fiziki i Khimii Kauchukov i Rezin [*A publication*]
**Issled Obl Fiz Tverd Tela** ... Issledovaniya v Oblasti Fiziki Tverdogo Tela [*A publication*]
**Issled Obl Khim Tekhnol Prod Pererab Goryuch Iskop** ... Issledovaniya v Oblasti Khimii i Tekhnologii Produktov Pererabotki Goryuchikh Iskopaemykh [*A publication*]
**Issled Obl Kinet Model Optim Khim Protsessov** ... Issledovaniya v Oblasti Kinetiki Modelirovaniya i Optimizatsii Khimicheskikh Protsessov [*A publication*]
**Issled Obl Kompleksn Ispol'z Topl** ... Issledovaniya v Oblasti Kompleksnogo Ispol'zovaniya Topliv [*USSR*] [*A publication*]
**Issled Obl Plast Obrab Met Davleniem** ... Issledovaniya v Oblasti Plastichnosti i Obrabotki Metallov Davleniem [*A publication*]
**Issled Operacii i Statist** ... Issledovanie Operacii i Statisticeskoe Modelirovanie [*A publication*]
**Issled Plazmennykh Sgustkov** ... Issledovanie Plazmennykh Sgustkov [*A publication*]
**Issled Prikl Mat** ... Kazanskii Universitet Issledovanija po Prikladnoi Matematike [*A publication*]
**Issled Protsessov Obrab Met Davleniem** ... Issledovanie Protsessov Obrabotki Metallov Davleniem [*A publication*]
**Issled Sist** .. Issledovanie Sistem [*A publication*]
**Issled Splavov Tsvetn Met** ... Issledovanie Splavov Tsvetnykh Metallov [*A publication*]
**Issled Stroit** ... Issledovaniya po Stroitel'stvu [*Estonian SSR*] [*A publication*]
**Issled Strukt Sostoyaniya Neorg Veshchestv** ... Issledovaniya Strukturnogo Sostoyaniya Neorganicheskikh Veshchestv [*A publication*]
**Issled Tekhnol Stroit Mater** ... Issledovaniia po Tekhnologii Stroitel'nykh Materialov [*A publication*]
**Issled Teor Plastin Obolochek** ... Issledovaniya po Teorii Plastin i Obolochek [*A publication*]
**Issled Teor Plastin i Obolochek** ... Kazanskii Universitet Issledovaniya po Teorii Plastin i Obolochek [*A publication*]
**Issled Tsentr Am Morei** ... Issledovaniya Tsentral'no-Amerikanskikh Morei [*A publication*]
**Issled Uprug Plast** ... Issledovaniya po Uprugosti i Plastichnosti [*A publication*]
**Issled Vodopodgot** ... Issledovaniya po Vodopodgotovke [*A publication*]
**Issled Vyazhushchikh Veshchestv Izdelii Ikh Osn** ... Issledovaniya Vyazhushchikh Veshchestv i Izdelii na Ikh Osnove [*A publication*]
**Issled Zharoproch Splavam** ... Issledovaniya po Zharoprochnym Splavam [*USSR*] [*A publication*]
**ISSLS** ........ International Symposium on Subscribers' Loops and Services [*Telecommunications*] (TEL)
**ISSM** ......... Independent Society of Stick Makers [*A union*] [*British*]
**ISSM** ......... Interim Surface-to-Surface Missile [*Military*] (CAAL)
**ISSM** ......... Sangamon County Medical Society, Springfield, IL [*Library symbol*] [*Library of Congress*] (LCLS)
**ISSMB** ........ Information Systems Standards Management Board
**ISSMC** ........ Interim Surface-to-Surface Missile Capability [*Military*] (CAAL)
**ISSMFE** .... International Society for Soil Mechanics and Foundation Engineering [*See also SIMSTF*] (EA)
**ISSMIS** ..... Integrated Support Services Management Information System (AABC)
**ISSMPD** .... International Society for the Study of Multiple Personality and Dissociation (EA)
**ISSMS** ....... Interim Surface-to-Surface Missile System [*Military*] (NVT)
**ISSN** ......... International Standard Serial Number [*Library of Congress*]
**ISSO** .......... Institute of Strategic and Stability Operations [*Army*]
**ISSO** .......... International Side-Saddle Organization (EA)
**ISSOA8** ..... Impact of Science on Society [*English Edition*] [*A publication*]
**ISSOL** ......... International Society for the Study of the Origin of Life (EA)
**ISSOT** ........ Inactive Ship Supply Overhaul Team
**ISSP** .......... International Society of Sports Psychology (EA)
**ISSP** .......... Interservice Supply Support Program [*Military*] (AABC)
**ISSPA** ........ International Sport Show Producers Association (EA)
**ISSPP** ........ Integrated System Safety Program Plan [*DoD*]
**ISSR** .......... Information Storage, Selection, and Retrieval [*Data processing*]
**ISSR** .......... Institute for Social Science Research [*Research center*] (RCD)
**ISSRO** ........ Interservice Supply Support Records Office [*Military*] (AABC)
**ISSRU** ........ Information Science and Scientometrics Research Unit [*Hungarian Academy of Sciences Library*] [*Budapest*] [*Information service or system*] (IID)
**ISSS** ........... Installation Service Supply Support
**ISSS** ........... Institute for Space and Security Studies (EA)
**ISSS** ........... Institute for the Study of Sport and Society
**ISSS** ........... International Seebeck Study Society (EA)
**ISSS** ........... International Society for Socialist Studies
**ISSS** ........... International Society of Soil Science [*See also AISS*] [*ICSU*] [*Wageningen, Netherlands*] (EAIO)
**ISSS** ........... International Society of Sport Sponsors (EA)
**ISSS** ........... International Society for the Study of Symbols
**ISSSA** ........ International Society for Strategic Studies (Africa) [*Formerly, Africa Society for Strategic Studies*] (EA)
**ISSSC** ........ Interservice Supply Support Subcommittee [*Military*] (CINC)
**ISSSE** ........ International Society of Statistical Science in Economics (EA)
**ISSSP** ........ International Sacerdotal Society Saint Pius X (EA)
**ISSST** ........ Integrated Submarine SONAR System Technician
**Iss Stud** ...... Issues and Studies [*A publication*]
**ISST** ........... Infrared Surveillance of Surface Targets [*Military*] (CAAL)
**ISST** ........... International Society for the Study of Time (EA)
**ISST** ........... Involuntary Second SEA [*Southeast Asia*] Tour [*Air Force*]
**ISSTA** ........ Israel Student Tourist Association
**ISSTDR** ..... International Society for STD [*Sexually Transmitted Diseases*] Research (EA)
**ISSU** .......... Inter-Services Signals Unit [*British military*] (DMA)
**ISSUE** ....... Information System Software Update Environment
**Issue Briefing Pap USDA Off Gov Pub Aff** ... Issue Briefing Paper. United States Department of Agriculture. Office of Governmental and Public Affairs [*A publication*]
**Issues Account Educ** ... Issues in Accounting Education [*A publication*]
**Issues Bank Regul** ... Issues in Bank Regulation [*A publication*]
**Issues Compr Pediatr Nurs** ... Issues in Comprehensive Pediatric Nursing [*A publication*]
**Issues Crim** ... Issues in Criminology [*A publication*]
**Issues Eng** ... Issues in Engineering [*United States*] [*A publication*]
**Issues Engng J Prof Activities Proc ASCE** ... Issues in Engineering. Journal of Professional Activities. Proceedings of the American Society of Civil Engineers [*A publication*]
**Issues Health Care Women** ... Issues in Health Care of Women [*A publication*]
**Issues Law Med** ... Issues in Law and Medicine [*A publication*]
**Issues Ment Health Nurs** ... Issues in Mental Health Nursing [*A publication*]
**Issues Policy Summ** ... Issues and Policy Summaries [*United States*] [*A publication*]
**Issues Stud** ... Issues and Studies [*A publication*]
**Issues and Stud** ... Issues and Studies [*A publication*]
**IST** ............ Incremental System Test
**IST** ............ Indexing Slide Table
**IST** ............ Individual Sales Transaction
**IST** ............ Industrielle-Services Techniques Inc. [*Industrial Life-Technical Services Inc.*] [*Information service or system*] (IID)
**IST** ............ Information Science and Technology (BUR)
**IST** ............ Initial Service Test (AABC)
**IST** ............ Initial Support Team [*Military*] (AFM)
**IST** ............ Innovative Science and Technology [*DoD*]
**ISt** ............ Insemnari Stiintifice [*A publication*]
**IST** ............ Instantaneous Spatial Transference
**IST** ............ Institute of Science and Technology [*University of Michigan*] [*Research center*] (RCD)
**IST** ............ Institute for Simulation and Training [*University of Central Florida*] [*Research center*] (RCD)
**IST** ............ Institutional Skill Training (OICC)
**IST** ............ Instrumentation Support Team (KSC)
**IST** ............ Insulin Sensitivity Test
**IST** ............ Insulin Shock Therapy [*Psychiatry*]
**IST** ............ Integral Simulation Test [*Nuclear energy*] (NRCH)
**IST** ............ Integrated Switching and Transmission [*Telecommunications*] (TEL)
**IST** ............ Integrated System Trainer (MCD)
**IST** ............ Integrated System Transformer (IEEE)
**IST** ............ Integrated Systems Test [*NASA*] (KSC)
**IST** ............ International Institute for Safety in Transportation [*Later, IIST*] (EA)
**IST** ............ International Society on Toxinology (EA)
**IST** ............ International Standard [*Vancouver Stock Exchange symbol*]
**IST** ............ International Standard Thread (MSA)
**IST** ............ Interstation Transmission (KSC)
**IST** ............ Interstellar Travel (AAG)
**IST** ............ Iron, Steel and Heavy Transporters Association, Cleveland OH [*STAC*]
**IST** ............ Isothermal Storage Test [*For hazardous chemicals*]
**IST** ............ Istanbul [*Turkey*] [*Seismograph station code, US Geological Survey*] (SEIS)
**IST** ............ Istanbul [*Turkey*] [*Airport symbol*] (OAG)
**ISt** ............ Italian Studies [*A publication*]
**IST** ............ Missouri Airlines, Inc. [*Kansas City, MO*] [*FAA designator*] (FAAC)
**IST** ............ Morton Public Library, Morton, IL [*OCLC symbol*] (OCLC)

**ISt** .......... Stickney-Forest View Library District, Stickney, IL [*Library symbol*] [*Library of Congress*] (LCLS)
**ISTA** .......... Independent Secretarial Training Association [*British*]
**ISTA** .......... Intelligence, Surveillance, and Target Acquisition [*Military*]
**ISTA** .......... International Seed Testing Association [*Switzerland*]
**ISTA** .......... International Sightseeing and Tours Association [*Defunct*] (EA)
**ISTA** .......... International Special Tooling Association [*Frankfurt, Federal Republic of Germany*] (EA)
**ISTA** .......... Intertank Structural Test Assembly [*NASA*] (NASA)
**ISTAC** ....... International Skilled Trades Advisory Committee [*UAW*]
**ISTAIA**...... Institute for the Study of Traditional American Indian Arts (EA)
**Istanbul Ark Muz Yilligi** ... Istanbul Arkeologi Muzeleri Yilligi [*A publication*]
**Istanbul Contrib Clin Sci** ... Istanbul Contribution to Clinical Science [*A publication*]
**Istanbuler Beitr Klin Wiss** ... Istanbuler Beitrage zur Klinischen Wissenschaft [*A publication*]
**Istanbul Med Fac Med Bull Istanbul Univ** ... Istanbul Medical Faculty Medical Bulletin. Istanbul University [*A publication*]
**Istanbul Tek Univ Bul** ... Istanbul Teknik Universitesi Bulteni [*A publication*]
**Istanbul Tek Univ Derg** ... Istanbul Teknik Universitesi Dergisi [*A publication*]
**Istanbul Tek Univ Nukl Enerji Enst Bul** ... Istanbul Teknik Universitesi Nukleer Enerji Enstitusu. Bulten [*A publication*]
**Istanbul Tip Fak Mecm** ... Istanbul Tip Fakultesi Mecmuasi [*A publication*]
**Istanbul Univ Dishekim Fak Derg** ... Istanbul Universitesi Dishekimligi Fakultesi Dergisi [*A publication*]
**Istanbul Univ Eczacilik Fak Mecm** ... Istanbul Universitesi Eczacilik Fakultesi Mecmuasi [*A publication*]
**Istanbul Univ Edebiyat Fak Turk ve Edebiyat Dergisi** ... Istanbul Universitesi Edebiyat Fakultesi Turk ve Edebiyat Dergisi [*A publication*]
**Istanbul Univ Fen Fak Hidrobiol Arastirma Enst Yayin** ... Istanbul Universitesi Fen Fakultesi Hidrobiologi Arastirma Enstitusu Yayinlari [*A publication*]
**Istanbul Univ Fen Fak Mecm** ... Istanbul Universitesi Fen Fakultesi Mecmuasi [*A publication*]
**Istanbul Univ Fen Fak Mecm Ser A** ... Istanbul Universitesi Fen Fakultesi Mecmuasi. Seri A. Sirfi ve Tatbiki Matematik [*A publication*]
**Istanbul Univ Fen Fak Mecm Ser B** ... Istanbul Universitesi Fen Fakultesi Mecmuasi. Seri B. Tabii Ilimler [*A publication*]
**Istanbul Univ Fen Fak Mecm Ser C** ... Istanbul Universitesi Fen Fakultesi Mecmuasi. Seri C. Astronomi-Fizik-Kimya [*A publication*]
**Istanbul Univ Fen Fak Mecm Seri B Tabii Ilimler** ... Istanbul Universitesi Fen Fakultesi Mecmuasi. Seri B. Tabii Ilimler [*A publication*]
**Istanbul Univ Med Bull** ... Istanbul University. Medical Bulletin [*A publication*]
**Istanbul Univ Med Fac Med Bull** ... Istanbul University. Medical Faculty. Medical Bulletin [*A publication*]
**Istanbul Univ Obs Yazilari** ... Istanbul Universitesi Observatuari Yazilari [*A publication*]
**Istanbul Univ Orman Fak Derg Seri A** ... Istanbul Universitesi Orman Fakultesi Dergisi. Seri A [*A publication*]
**Istanbul Univ Rev Geog Inst Internat Ed** ... Istanbul University. Review of the Geographical Institute. International Edition [*A publication*]
**Istanbul Univ Tip Fak Mecm** ... Istanbul Universitesi Tip Fakultesi Mecmuasi [*A publication*]
**Istanbul Univ Vet Fak Derg** ... Istanbul Universitesi Veteriner Fakultesi Dergisi [*A publication*]
**Istanbul Univ Vet Fak Derg J Fac Vet Med Univ Istanbul** ... Istanbul Universitesi Veteriner Fakultesi Dergisi/Journal of the Faculty of Veterinary Medicine. University of Istanbul [*A publication*]
**Istanbul Univ Yay (Orm Fak)** ... Istanbul Universitesi Yaymlam (Orman Fakultesi) [*A publication*]
**Istanb Univ fen Fak Mecm** ... Istanbul Universitesi fen Fakueltesi Mecmuasi [*A publication*]
**Istanb Univ Orman Fak Derg** ... Istanbul Universitesi Orman Fakultesi Dergisi [*A publication*]
**ISTAR** ....... Image Storage Translation and Reproduction
**ISTAR** ....... Information Science Technology Assessment for Research [*Army*]
**Ist Ark Etnog Sred Azii** ... Istoriia, Arkheologiia, i Etnografiia Srednei Azii [*A publication*]
**ISTAT** ....... International Society of Transport Aircraft Trading (EA)
**IStau** .......... Staunton Public Library, Staunton, IL [*Library symbol*] [*Library of Congress*] (LCLS)
**IStauMCD** ... Macoupin Community District 6, Staunton, IL [*Library symbol*] [*Library of Congress*] (LCLS)
**Ist Autom Univ Roma Not** ... Istituto di Automatica. Universita di Roma Notiziario [*A publication*]
**ISTB** .......... Integrated Subsystem Test Bed (NASA)
**ISTB** .......... Interstate Tariff Bureau, Inc.
**ISTB** .......... Introductory Science Text-Books [*A publication*]
**Ist Bologna R Ac Sc Cl Sc Fis Mem** ... Istituto de Bologna. Reale Accademia delle Scienze. Classe di Scienze Fisiche. Memorie [*A publication*]
**ISTC** .......... Incunable Short Title Catalogue [*British Library*] [*Information service or system*] (IID)
**ISTC** .......... Institute of Scientific and Technical Communicators [*British*]
**ISTC** .......... Instructivision, Inc. [*Livingston, NJ*] [*NASDAQ symbol*] (NQ)
**ISTC** .......... Interdepartmental Screw Thread Committee [*Departments of Commerce and Defense*]
**ISTC** .......... International Shade Tree Conference [*Later, ISA*] (EA)
**ISTC** .......... International Society for Training and Culture
**ISTC** .......... International Spa and Tub Council (EA)
**ISTC** .......... International Stress and Tension Control Association (EA)
**ISTC** .......... International Student Travel Confederation [*Switzerland*] (EAIO)
**ISTC** .......... International Switching and Testing Center [*Communications*]
**ISTC** .......... Iron and Steel Trades Confederation [*British*]
**IStc**............ Saint Charles Public Library District, Saint Charles, IL [*Library symbol*] [*Library of Congress*] (LCLS)
**Ist Chim Agrar Sper Gorizia Nuovi Ann Pubbl** ... Istituto Chimico Agrario Sperimentale de Gorizia. Nuovi Annali. Pubblicazione [*A publication*]
**ISTD**.......... Imperial Society of Teachers of Dancing
**ISTD**.......... Institute for the Study and Treatment of Delinquency [*British*]
**ISTD**.......... Inter-Service Topographical Department [*British*]
**ISTD**.......... International Society of Tropical Dermatology [*Later, International Society of Dermatology: Tropical, Geographic, and Ecologic - ISD*]
**ISTDA** ....... Institutional and Service Textile Distributors Association (EA)
**Ist Dzerela Vykorystannja** ... Istorycni Dzerela ta ich Vykorystannja [*A publication*]
**ISTE** .......... International Society for Tropical Ecology (EA)
**ISTE** .......... Istec Industries and Technologies Ltd. [*NASDAQ symbol*] (NQ)
**ISte**............ Saint Elmo Public Library, St. Elmo, IL [*Library symbol*] [*Library of Congress*] (LCLS)
**ISTEA** ....... Initial Screening Training Effectiveness Analysis
**ISTEC**....... International Superconductivity Technology Center [*Japan*]
**ISteSD** ....... Saint Elmo Community Unit, School District 202, Saint Elmo, IL [*Library symbol*] [*Library of Congress*] (LCLS)
**ISTES TEMP** ... Istesso Tempo [*Same Time*] [*Music*] (ROG)
**ISTF**.......... Integrated Servicing and Test Facilities [*Canada*]
**ISTF**.......... Integrated System Test Flow (NASA)
**ISTF**.......... International Social Travel Federation [*See also FITS*] [*Brussels, Belgium*] (EAIO)
**ISTF**.......... International Society of Tropical Foresters [*See also SIIFT*] (EA)
**ISTFA**........ International Society for Testing and Failure Analysis (MCD)
**Ist Fed Ric For Mem** ... Istituto Federale di Ricerche Forestali. Memorie [*A publication*]
**Ist-Filol Z** .. Istoriko-Filologiceskij Zurnal [*A publication*]
**Ist Filol Zh** ... Istoriko-Filologicheskii Zhurnal [*A publication*]
**Ist Fil Zhur A N Armian** ... Istoriko-Filologicheskii Zhurnal. Akademia Nauk Armianskoi [*A publication*]
**Ist Geof (Trieste) Pubbl** ... Istituto Geofisico (Trieste). Pubblicazione [*A publication*]
**ISTH**.......... International Society on Thrombosis and Hemostasis (EA)
**ISTH**.......... Isthmus [*Board on Geographic Names*]
**ISTHM**...... Isthmian (ROG)
**Isthm**.......... Isthmian Odes [*of Pindar*] [*Classical studies*] (OCD)
**ISTI** .......... International Spa and Tub Institute (EA)
**ISTIC**......... Institute of Scientific and Technical Information of China [*INFOTERM*] [*Beijing*]
**ISTIM** ....... Interchange of Scientific and Technical Information in Machine Language [*Office of Science and Technology*]
**ISTIS**......... International Scientific and Technical Information System (EAIO)
**Istit Lombardo Accad Sci Lett Rend A** ... Istituto Lombardo. Accademia di Scienze e Lettere. Rendiconti. A. Scienze Matematiche, Fisiche, Chimiche, e Geologiche [*A publication*]
**Istit Veneto Sci Lett Arti Atti Cl Sci Mat Natur** ... Istituto Veneto di Scienze, Lettere, ed Arti. Venezia. Atti. Classe di Scienze Matematiche e Naturali [*A publication*]
**IStjo** ........... Saint Joseph Township Library (Swearingen Memorial Library), St. Joseph, IL [*Library symbol*] [*Library of Congress*] (LCLS)
**IStJSD**....... Tiraid Community Unit, School District 2, St. Jacob, IL [*Library symbol*] [*Library of Congress*] (LCLS)
**ISTL** .......... Inner Sydney Transport Link [*Australia*]
**Ist Lomb Accad Sci Lett Rend A Sci Mat Fis Chim Geol** ... Istituto Lombardo. Accademia di Scienze e Lettere. Rendiconti. A. Scienze Matematiche, Fisiche, Chimiche, e Geologiche [*A publication*]
**Ist Lombardo Accad Sci e Lettere Rend** ... Istituto Lombardo. Accademia di Scienze e Lettere. Rendiconti [*A publication*]
**Ist Lombardo Accad Sci Lett Rend A** ... Istituto Lombardo. Accademia di Scienze e Lettere. Rendiconti. Scienze Matematiche, Fisiche, Chimiche, e Geologiche. A [*A publication*]
**Ist Lombardo Accad Sci Lett Rend Sci Biol Med B** ... Istituto Lombardo. Accademia di Scienze e Lettere. Rendiconti. Scienze Biologiche e Mediche. B [*A publication*]
**ISTM** .......... International Society for Testing Materials

**Ist Mat Kul't Uzbek** ... Istoriia Material-noj Kul'tury Uzbekistana [*A publication*]
**ISTMH**...... Indefinite Substitute Temporary Mail Handler [*US Postal Service employee classification*]
**Ist Mit**........ Istanbuler Mitteilungen [*A publication*]
**Ist Mitt**....... Istanbuler Mitteilungen [*A publication*]
**Ist Mitt**....... Mitteilungen. Deutsches Archaeologische Institut. Abteilung Istanbul [*A publication*]
**Ist Mitt Bh** ... Istanbuler Mitteilungen. Beiheft [*A publication*]
**ISTN**.......... Integrated Switching and Transmission Network [*Telecommunications*] (TEL)
**Ist Naz Genet Cerealicolt Nazareno Strampelli** ... Istituto Nazionale di Genetica per la Cerealicoltura Nazareno Strampelli [*A publication*]
**ISTO**.......... Information Science and Technology Office [*DoD*] [*Arlington, VA*] (TSSD)
**Istochniki Rudn Veshchestva Endog Mestorozhd** ... Istochniki Rudnogo Veshchestva Endogonnykh Mestorozhdenii [*A publication*]
**Istor-Astronom Issled** ... Istoriko-Astronomiceskie Issledovanija [*A publication*]
**Istor Estestvoznan Tehn Armen** ... Akademija Nauk Armjanskoi SSR. Istorija Estest'voznanija i Tehniki v Armenii [*A publication*]
**Istoria Artei** ... Studii si Cercetari de Istoria Artei [*A publication*]
**Istor-Mat Issled** ... Istoriko-Matematiceskie Issledovanija [*A publication*]
**Istor Metodol Estestv Nauk** ... Istoriya i Metodologiya Estestvennykh Nauk [*A publication*]
**Istor SSSR** ... Istorija SSSR [*A publication*]
**IS & TP**...... Index to Scientific and Technical Proceedings [*A publication*]
**ISTP** .......... International Solar Terrestrial Physics [*Proposed NASA mission*]
**ISTP** .......... International Stretch Products, Inc. [*NASDAQ symbol*] (NQ)
**Ist Patologia Libro Boll** ... Istituto di Patologia del Libro. Bollettino [*A publication*]
**ISTP & B** ... Index to Scientific and Technical Proceedings and Books [*Institute for Scientific Information*] [*Database*]
**ISTPW** ...... Impact Signature Training Practice Warhead [*Army*]
**ISTR** .......... Indexed Sequential Table Retrieval
**ISTR** .......... International Standard Resources Ltd. [*NASDAQ symbol*] (NQ)
**IStr**............ Streator Public Library, Streator, IL [*Library symbol*] [*Library of Congress*] (LCLS)
**ISTRA** ....... Interplanetary Space Travel Research Association
**ISTRACON** ... Interstation Supersonic Track Conferences (MCD)
**IStrESD**..... Eagle Elementary Consolidated School District 43, Streator, IL [*Library symbol*] [*Library of Congress*] (LCLS)
**IStrHSD** .... Streator Township High School District 40, Streator, IL [*Library symbol*] [*Library of Congress*] (LCLS)
**ISTRO** ....... International Soil Tillage Research Organization [*Netherlands*] (EAIO)
**IStrOSD** .... Otter Creek Elementary School District 56, Streator, IL [*Library symbol*] [*Library of Congress*] (LCLS)
**IStrSD** ....... Streator Elementary School District 45, Streator, IL [*Library symbol*] [*Library of Congress*] (LCLS)
**IStrSMH** ... Saint Mary's Hospital, Henegen Medical Library, Streator, IL [*Library symbol*] [*Library of Congress*] (LCLS)
**ISTRUCTE** ... Institution of Structural Engineers [*British*]
**ISTS**........... Institute for Space and Terrestrial Science [*Research center*] [*Canada*] (RCD)
**ISTS**........... International Simultaneous Translation Service
**ISTS**........... International Society for Twin Studies [*Rome, Italy*] (EA)
**ISTS**........... International Symposium on Space Technology and Science (MCD)
**ISTS**........... Intersite Transmission Subsystem [*Ground Communications Facility, NASA*]
**ISTS**........... Intradermal Skin Test Score [*Immunology*]
**Ist Sb Inst Ist Arheol Etnogr** ... Istoriceskij Sbornik Instituta Istorii, Arheologii, i Etnografii [*A publication*]
**ISTSP**........ Independent Schools Talent Search Program [*Later, A Better Chance*] (EA)
**Ist Sper Met Leggeri Mem Rapp** ... Istituto Sperimentale dei Metalli Leggeri. Memorie e Rapport [*A publication*]
**Ist Sper Talassogr (Trieste) Pubbl** ... Istituto Sperimentale Talassografico (Trieste). Pubblicazione [*A publication*]
**Ist SSSR**.... Istorija SSSR [*A publication*]
**Ist Super Sanita Lab Fis Rapp** ... Istituto Superiore di Sanita. Laboritori di Fisica. Rapporti [*A publication*]
**Ist Svizz Ric For Mem** ... Istituto Svizzero di Ricerche Forestali. Memorie [*A publication*]
**ISTT** .......... In-Service Training of Teachers [*Scottish National Committee*]
**ISTT** .......... Intersegmental Travel Time [*Zoology*]
**Ist Tec Agr Stat (Macerata)** ... Istituto Tecnico Agrario Statale (Macerata) [*A publication*]
**IsTU**........... Tel Aviv University, Tel Aviv, Israel [*Library symbol*] [*Library of Congress*] (LCLS)
**Ist Univ Nav (Napoli) Ann** ... Istituto Universitario Navale (Napoli). Annali [*A publication*]
**Ist Veneto Sci Lett Arti Atti Cl Sci Mat Natur** ... Istituto Veneto di Scienze, Lettere, ed Arti. Venezia. Atti. Classe di Scienze Matematiche e Naturali [*A publication*]
**ISTVS**........ International Society for Terrain-Vehicle Systems (EA)
**IstZap** ........ Istoriceskii Zapiski [*A publication*]
**ISU** ............ In-Arm Suspension Unit [*Tank Technology*]
**ISU** ............ Independent Signal Unit [*Telecommunications*] (TEL)
**ISU** ............ Indiana State University [*Terre Haute*]
**ISU** ............ Indiana State University, Terre Haute, IN [*OCLC symbol*] (OCLC)
**ISU** ............ Inertial Sensing Unit
**ISU** ............ Information Service Unit [*International Potato Center*] [*Information service or system*] (IID)
**ISU** ............ Information Services and Use [*A publication*]
**ISU** ............ Initial Signal Unit [*Telecommunications*] (TEL)
**ISU** ............ Instruction Storage Unit
**ISU** ............ Integrated Sight Unit [*Weaponry*] (INF)
**ISU** ............ Interface Sharing Unit
**ISU** ............ Interface Switching Unit (BUR)
**ISU** ............ International Scientific Union
**ISU** ............ International Seaman's Union
**ISU** ............ International Shooting Union
**ISU** ............ International Sigma Security, Inc. [*Vancouver Stock Exchange symbol*]
**ISU** ............ International Skating Union [*See also UIP*] [*Davos-Platz, Switzerland*] (EAIO)
**ISU** ............ International Society of Urology [*See also SIU*] [*Paris, France*] (EAIO)
**ISU** ............ International Sugar Journal [*A publication*]
**ISU** ............ International System of Units
**ISU** ............ Iowa Southern Utilities [*Southern Industrial Railroad, Inc.*] [*AAR code*]
**ISU** ............ Iowa State University [*Ames*]
**ISU** ............ Italian Service Unit [*Italian prisoners of war who became volunteers in the Allied war effort*]
**ISu**.............. Summit-Argo Public Library, Summit, IL [*Library symbol*] [*Library of Congress*] (LCLS)
**ISUDO** ...... International Symposium on Ultrasonic Diagnostics in Ophthalmology [*Later, ISOU*] (EA)
**ISUDS** ....... Iterative Scheme Using a Direct Solution
**ISUDX**....... Information Services and Use [*A publication*]
**ISUH** ......... Institute for the Study of Universal History through Arts and Artifacts [*Defunct*] (EA)
**ISUM**......... Intelligence Summary
**ISUM**......... Southern Illinois University, School of Medicine, Springfield, IL [*Library symbol*] [*Library of Congress*] (LCLS)
**ISU Mitt**.... Interdisziplinarer Sonderbereich Umweltschutz. Mitteilungen [*A publication*]
**ISumSD** ..... Red Hill Community Unit, School District 10, Sumner, IL [*Library symbol*] [*Library of Congress*] (LCLS)
**ISUP**.......... ISDN [*Integrated Services Digital Network*] User Part [*Telecommunications*]
**ISUPTTS** .. International Sports Union of Post, Telephone, and Telecommunications Service (EA)
**ISURSL**..... Indiana State University Remote Sensing Laboratory [*Research center*] (RCD)
**ISUSAIC**... Intelligence School, United States Army Intelligence Center
**ISUSE** ....... International Secretariat for the University Study of Education
**ISV**............ Independent Software Vendor [*Data processing*]
**ISV**............ Informations-Chimie [*A publication*]
**ISV**............ Input Signal Voltage
**ISV**............ Instantaneous Speed Variation [*Tape recorders*]
**ISV**............ International Scientific Vocabulary
**ISV**............ International Society of Videographers (EA)
**ISV**............ Interorbital Space Vehicle
**ISV**............ Interval Service Value (BUR)
**ISV**............ Irradiated Silicon Vidicon
**ISV**............ Iso Ventures, Inc. [*Vancouver Stock Exchange symbol*]
**ISV**............ Neponset Public Library, Neponset, IL [*OCLC symbol*] (OCLC)
**ISv**............. Sauk Village Library District, Sauk Village, IL [*Library symbol*] [*Library of Congress*] (LCLS)
**ISVA**.......... Incorporated Society of Valuers and Auctioneers (EAIO)
**ISVA**.......... International Satellite Verification Agency
**ISVBM** ...... International Society of Violin and Bow Makers [*Mittenwald, Federal Republic of Germany*] (EAIO)
**ISVCS**........ Improved Secure Voice Conferencing System [*Military*] (MCD)
**ISVD**.......... Information System for Vocational Decisions Program
**ISVE** .......... Istituto di Studi per lo Sviluppo Economico [*Institute for the Study of Economic Development*] [*Italy*]
**ISVESTA** .. Individual Survival Vest for Aircrew [*Army*] (RDA)
**ISVL**.......... Vachel Lindsay Association, Springfield, IL [*Library symbol*] [*Library of Congress*] (LCLS)
**ISVP** .......... International Society for Vehicle Preservation (EA)
**ISVR**.......... Institute of Sound and Vibration Research [*Southampton University, England*]
**ISVS** .......... Integrated Secure Voice System
**ISVS** .......... International Secretariat for Volunteer Service [*Defunct*]
**ISVSK**........ Internationaler Staendiger Verband fuer Schiffahrt-Kongresse [*Permanent International Association of Navigation Congresses*]
**ISW**............ Ice Shelf Water [*Oceanography*]
**ISW**............ Information Services of Warwick [*Rhode Island*] [*Information retrieval*] (IID)
**ISW**............ Institute for Solid Wastes

**ISW**........... Intermediate Scale Warfare
**ISW**........... Interstitial Water [*Physiology*]
**ISW**........... Toulon Public Library, Toulon, IL [*OCLC symbol*] (OCLC)
**ISW**........... Wisconsin Rapids [*Wisconsin*] [*Airport symbol*] (OAG)
**ISW**........... Wisconsin Rapids, WI [*Location identifier*] [*FAA*] (FAAL)
**ISWA**......... Insect Screening Weavers Association (EA)
**ISWA**......... International Science Writers Association
**ISWA**......... International Ski Writers Association [*Riehen, Switzerland*] (EA)
**ISWA**......... International Solid Wastes and Public Cleansing Association [*Formed by a merger of INTAPUC and IRGRD*] (EAIO)
**ISWA Inf Bull** ... ISWA [*International Solid Wastes and Public Cleansing Association*] Information Bulletin [*A publication*]
**ISWAP**...... International Society of Women Airline Pilots (EA)
**ISWBBHA** ... Iron, Steel, and Wood Barge Builders' and Helpers' Association [*A union*] [*British*]
**ISWC**......... Industrial Social Welfare Center [*Columbia University*] [*Research center*] (RCD)
**ISWC**......... International Society for the Welfare of Cripples [*Later, Rehabilitation International*]
**ISWG**......... Imperial Standard Wire Gauge
**ISWG**......... Integrated Support Working Group (SDI)
**ISWG**......... Item Selection Working Group [*NATO*] (NATG)
**ISWL**......... Isolated Single Wheel Load (AIA)
**ISWM**........ Institute of Solid Waste Management [*British*] (DCTA)
**ISWM**........ International Society of Weighing and Measurement (EA)
**ISWNE**...... International Society of Weekly Newspaper Editors (EA)
**ISWOS**...... Israelitische Wochenschrift [*Breslau/Magdeburg*] [*A publication*]
**ISWRRI**..... Iowa State Water Resources Research Institute [*Department of the Interior*] [*Iowa State University*] [*Research center*] (RCD)
**ISWS**......... Illinois State Water Survey [*Illinois Department of Energy and Natural Resources*] [*Research center*] (RCD)
**ISWS Bull Ill Water Surv** ... ISWS Bulletin. Illinois Water Survey [*A publication*]
**ISWSC**....... International Society of Worldwide Stamp Collectors [*Formerly, Worldwide Collectors' Club - WCC*]
**ISWT**......... International Society of Wine Tasters (EA)
**ISWU**......... International Society of Wang Users (EA)
**ISWU**......... Iron and Steel Workers' Union [*India*]
**ISX**............ Impurity Study Experiment [*Oak Ridge National Laboratory*]
**ISX**............ Wyoming Public Library, Wyoming, IL [*OCLC symbol*] (OCLC)
**ISY**............ Black Hawk College, East Campus, Gustav E. Lundberg Learning Center, Kewanee, IL [*OCLC symbol*] (OCLC)
**ISY**............ IBM [*International Business Machines Corp.*] Systems Journal [*A publication*]
**ISY**............ Instrument Systems Corp. [*AMEX symbol*] (SPSG)
**ISY**............ International Space Year [*1992*]
**ISY**............ Intrasynovial [*Medicine*]
**ISy**............ Sycamore Public Library, Sycamore, IL [*Library symbol*] [*Library of Congress*] (LCLS)
**IsYAEC**..... Israel Atomic Energy Commission, Soreq Nuclear Research Centre, Yavne, Israel [*Library symbol*] [*Library of Congress*] (LCLS)
**ISYN**.......... Inductosyn
**ISYVO**....... International Sivananda Yoga Vedanta Organization [*Val Morin, PQ*] (EAIO)
**ISZ**............ Increment and Skip on Zero [*Data processing*]
**I Sz**............ Irodalmi Szemle [*A publication*]
**ISZ**............ Iskustvennyi Sputnik Zemil [*USSR*]
**IT**.............. Air Inter, Societe [*France*] [*ICAO designator*] (ICDA)
**It**.............. Biblioteca Nazionale Centrale, Rome, Italy [*Library symbol*] [*Library of Congress*] (LCLS)
**IT**.............. Idaho Territory [*Obsolete*] (ROG)
**IT**.............. Identification Transponder (MCD)
**IT**.............. Illusion Theater (EA)
**IT**.............. Immediate Transient Incapacitation [*Radiation casualty criterion*] [*Army*]
**IT**.............. Immediate Transportation
**IT**.............. Immunity Test
**IT**.............. Immunoreactive Tag [*Clinical chemistry*]
**IT**.............. Immunotherapy [*Medicine*]
**IT**.............. Immunotoxin
**IT**.............. Immunoturbidimetry [*Analytical biochemistry*]
**IT**.............. Implosive Therapy [*Type of behavior therapy*]
**IT**.............. Improved Tartar
**IT**.............. In Transitu [*In Transit*] [*Latin*]
**IT**.............. Incentive Travel [*Travel industry*]
**IT**.............. Income Tax
**IT**.............. Income Tax Unit Rulings [*US Internal Revenue Service*]
**IT**.............. Incomplete Translation [*Telecommunications*] (TEL)
**IT**.............. Indeks Troskova Zivota [*Cost of Living Index*] [*Yugoslavian*]
**IT**.............. Indent Tab Character [*Data processing*]
**IT**.............. Independent Tank (DS)
**IT**.............. Index Term [*Data processing*]
**IT**.............. Index Translationum [*UNESCO*]
**IT**.............. Indian Territory [*in United States*]
**IT**.............. Indisch Tijdschrift van het Recht [*A publication*]
**IT**.............. Individual Therapy
**IT**.............. Individual Training [*Army*]
**IT**.............. Industrial Technology
**IT**.............. Industrial Training
**IT**.............. Industrial Tribunal [*British*] (DCTA)
**IT**.............. Industry Telephone Maintenance [*FCC*] (IEEE)
**IT**.............. Infection Type [*Pathology*]
**IT**.............. Inferior Temporal [*Anatomy*]
**IT**.............. Information Technology
**IT**.............. Information Theory (MCD)
**IT**.............. Information Today [*A publication*]
**IT**.............. Information Transform [*Information service or system*] (IID)
**IT**.............. Inhalation Therapy [*Medicine*]
**I/T**............. Initial Track (MCD)
**IT**.............. Inner Temple
**IT**.............. Innovative Test
**IT**.............. Input Terminal
**IT**.............. Input Translator [*IBM Corp.*] [*Data processing*]
**IT**.............. Inspection Tag
**I & T**.......... Inspection and Test (NRCH)
**IT**.............. Installation Test (NASA)
**I & T**.......... Installation and Test [*Army*] (AABC)
**IT**.............. Institut du Textile [*Textile Institute*] (EAIO)
**IT**.............. Institute of Technology [*Air Force*]
**IT**.............. Institute of Trichologists (EAIO)
**IT**.............. Institutional Training (OICC)
**IT**.............. Instruction Tag (MSA)
**IT**.............. Instructional Technology
**IT**.............. Instructor Trainer [*Red Cross*]
**IT**.............. Instrument Technician
**IT**.............. Instrument Test [*or Tree*] [*Nuclear energy*] (NRCH)
**IT**.............. Instrument Transformer
**IT**.............. Instrumented Laboratory Training
**IT**.............. Insulated Tank Container [*Shipping*] (DCTA)
**IT**.............. Insulating Transformer (KSC)
**I & T**.......... Integration and Test
**IT**.............. Integrity Team [*Australia*]
**IT**.............. Intelligent Terminal [*Data processing*]
**IT**.............. Intelogic Trace, Inc. [*NYSE symbol*] (SPSG)
**IT**.............. Interceptor Trap
**IT**.............. Intermediate Technology [*An association*] (EA)
**IT**.............. Intermediate Treatment [*Special provision of British law for juvenile offenders*]
**IT**.............. Internal Thread
**IT**.............. Internal Translator [*Carnegie Institute*] [*IBM Corp.*]
**IT**.............. International Technology Corp.
**IT**.............. International Tolerance
**IT**.............. International Traders Association (EA)
**IT**.............. International Travellers [*YWCA*]
**IT**.............. International Trumpet Guild. Newsletter [*A publication*]
**IT**.............. Interrogator-Transponder (KSC)
**IT**.............. Interstate Theft
**I/T**............. Intertank (NASA)
**IT**.............. Intertoll [*Trunk*] [*Telecommunications*] (TEL)
**IT**.............. Intertuberous [*Diameter*] [*Medicine*]
**IT**.............. Interval Timer [*Data processing*]
**IT**.............. Interval Training [*Physical fitness program*]
**IT**.............. Intestinal Type [*of epithelium*]
**IT**.............. Intrathecal [*Medicine*]
**IT**.............. Intrathoracic [*Medicine*]
**IT**.............. Intratracheal [*Medicine*]
**IT**.............. Intratracheal Tube [*Medicine*]
**IT**.............. Inventory Transfer
**IT**.............. Ion Trap [*Instrumentation*]
**IT**.............. Iphigenia Taurica [*of Euripides*] [*Classical studies*] (OCD)
**IT**.............. Iraq Times [*A publication*]
**IT**.............. Irrelevant Talk [*Slang*]
**IT**.............. Ischial Tuberosity [*Medicine*]
**IT**.............. Island Telephone Co. Ltd. [*Toronto Stock Exchange symbol*]
**IT**.............. Islenzk Tunga [*A publication*]
**It**.............. Islet [*Maps and charts*]
**IT**.............. Isomeric Transition [*Radioactivity*]
**IT**.............. Isothermal Transformation [*Metallurgy*]
**IT**.............. Isotocin [*Endocrinology*]
**It**.............. Italia Che Scrive [*A publication*]
**IT**.............. Italian
**It**.............. Italica [*A publication*]
**IT**.............. Italy [*ANSI two-letter standard code*] (CNC)
**it**.............. Italy [*MARC country of publication code*] [*Library of Congress*] (LCCP)
**IT**.............. Item (MCD)
**IT**.............. Item Transfer
**IT**.............. National Organization of Industrial Trade Unions
**IT**.............. Societe Air Inter [*France*] [*ICAO designator*] (FAAC)
**IT**.............. Tour-Based Fare [*Airline fare code*]
**it**.............. Vetus Itala (BJA)
**I2T2**.......... Intelligence Interactive Test Terminal
**ITA**............ Great River Library System, Quincy, IL [*OCLC symbol*] (OCLC)
**ITA**............ Illinois Motor Truck Operators Association, Chicago IL [*STAC*]
**IT-A**........... Immunotoxin with A-Chain

**ITA** ........... Income Tax Act Regulations [*Commerce Clearing House Canadian Ltd.*] [*Information service or system*] (CRD)
**ITA** ........... Independent Telecommunications Analysts [*Boulder, CO*] (TSSD)
**ITA** ........... Independent Television Authority [*Later, IBA*] [*British*]
**ITA** ........... Individual Task Authorization
**ITA** ........... Indoor Tennis Association [*Later, NTA*] (EA)
**ITA** ........... Industrial Technological Associates, Inc. [*Information service or system*]
**ITA** ........... Industrial Truck Association [*Washington, DC*] (EA)
**ITA** ........... Industry and Trade Administration [*Later, International Trade Administration*] [*Department of Commerce*]
**ITA** ........... Inferior Tympanic Artery [*Anatomy*]
**i/t/a** ........... Initial Teaching Alphabet [*A 44-symbol alphabet planned to simplify beginning reading by representing sounds more precisely*]
**ITA** ........... Inner Transport Area
**ITA** ........... Institut du Transport Aerien [*Institute of Air Transport*] [*Research center*] [*France*] (IRC)
**ITA** ........... Institute for Telecommunications and Aeronomy [*ESSA*] (MCD)
**ITA** ........... Institute of Theoretical Astronomy [*Leningrad, USSR*]
**ITA** ........... Institute of Traffic Administration [*British*]
**ITA** ........... Institute of Transport Administration [*Later, IoTA*] (EAIO)
**ITA** ........... Institute of Transport Aviation (KSC)
**ITA** ........... Instrument Time (Actual)
**ITA** ........... Instrumentation Technology Associates, Inc.
**ITA** ........... Integrated Test Area (MCD)
**ITA** ........... Integrated Thruster Assembly (KSC)
**ITA** ........... Inter-Air, Inc. [*Denver, CO*] [*FAA designator*] (FAAC)
**ITA** ........... Interavia. Revue Internationale Aeronautique, Astronautique, Electronique [*A publication*]
**ITA** ........... Interface Test Adapters (MCD)
**ITA** ........... Intermediate Teachers Association
**ITA** ........... Intermediate Thrust Arc
**ITA** ........... Intermodal Transportation Association (EA)
**ITA** ........... International 210 Association (EA)
**ITA** ........... International Tape/Disc Association (EA)
**ITA** ........... International Taxicab Association (EA)
**ITA** ........... International Telegraph Alphabet (NATG)
**ITA** ........... International Television Almanac [*A publication*]
**ITA** ........... International Temperance Association [*Later, IHTA*] (EA)
**ITA** ........... International Texcan Tech [*Vancouver Stock Exchange symbol*]
**ITA** ........... International Thermographers Association (EA)
**ITA** ........... International Tin Agreement
**ITA** ........... International Tire Association (EA)
**ITA** ........... International Tornado Association [*Sudbury, England*] (EAIO)
**ITA** ........... International Touring Alliance
**ITA** ........... International Track Association [*Defunct*]
**ITA** ........... International Trade Administration [*Washington, DC*] [*Department of Commerce*]
**ITA** ........... International Trade Administration Report [*A publication*]
**ITA** ........... International Trombone Association (EA)
**ITA** ........... International Tube Association [*Leamington Spa, Warwickshire, England*] (EAIO)
**ITA** ........... International Tunnelling Association (EA)
**ITA** ........... International Turquoise Association (EA)
**ITA** ........... International Twins Association (EA)
**ITA** ........... International Typographic Association (MCD)
**ITA** ........... Interstate Towing Auxiliary (EA)
**ITA** ........... Ionization Test Apparatus
**ITA** ........... Itaconic Acid [*Organic chemistry*]
**ita** ........... Italian [*MARC language code*] [*Library of Congress*] (LCCP)
**ITA** ........... Italy [*ANSI three-letter standard code*] (CNC)
**ITA** ........... Italy Fund, Inc. [*NYSE symbol*] (SPSG)
**ITA#2** ........ Internationality Alphabet #2 (MCD)
**ITAA** .......... Income Tax Assessment Act [*Australia*] (ADA)
**ITAA** .......... International Theatrical Agencies Association (EA)
**ITAA** .......... International Transactional Analysis Association (EA)
**ITAADS** .... Installation the Army Authorization Document System
**ITAADS** .... Interim Target Acquisition and Designation System
**ITAC** .......... Intelligence and Threat Analysis Center
**ITAC** .......... Interagency Textile Administrative Committee
**ITAC** .......... International Target Audience Code [*International Federation of Library Associations*]
**ITAC** .......... Intestinal Type Adenocarcinoma [*Oncology*]
**ITACC** ....... Incremental Tactical Communications Capability Study [*Military*] (MCD)
**ITACS** ....... Integrated Tactical Air Control System
**ITAD** ......... Individual Training Analysis and Design (MCD)
**ITAD** ......... Intelligence Threat Analysis Detachment [*Army*] (RDA)
**ITAE** ......... Integrated Time and Absolute Error
**It Agr** ......... Italia Agricola [*A publication*]
**ITA J** ......... International Trombone Association. Journal [*A publication*]
**ITAK** .......... Illankai Tamil Arasu Kadchi [*Federal Party*] [*Sri Lanka*] [*Political party*] (PPW)
**ITAL** .......... Information Technology and Libraries [*A publication*]
**ITAL** .......... Initial Task Assignment List
**ITAL** .......... Introductory Trials Allowance List [*Military*] (AFIT)
**ITAL** .......... Inventory Trial Allowance List
**ITAL** .......... Italian
**Ital** ............. Italianistica. Revista di Letteratura Italiana [*A publication*]
**ITAL** .......... Italic [*or Italics*]
**Ital** ............. Italica [*A publication*]
**Ital A** .......... Italian Americana [*A publication*]
**Ital Agr** ...... Italia Agricola [*A publication*]
**Ital Agric** .... Italia Agricola [*A publication*]
**Ital Am** ....... Italian Americana [*A publication*]
**Italamer** ..... Italamerican [*A publication*]
**Ital Aust Bul Commerce** ... Italian-Australian Bulletin of Commerce [*A publication*] (APTA)
**Ital Cereali** ... Italia e i Cereali [*A publication*]
**Ital Dial** ...... Italic Dialects [*A publication*] (OCD)
**Ital Exped Karakorum Hindu Kush Sci Rep** ... Italian Expeditions to the Karakorum [*$K^2$ A publication*]
**Ital For Mont** ... Italia Forestale e Montana [*A publication*]
**Ital Gen Rev Derm** ... Italian General Review of Dermatology [*A publication*]
**Ital Gen Rev Dermatol** ... Italian General Review of Dermatology [*A publication*]
**Ital Gen Rev Oto-Rhino-Laryng** ... Italian General Review of Oto-Rhino-Laryngology [*A publication*]
**Italia Agric** ... Italia Agricola [*A publication*]
**Italian Am Bus** ... Italian American Business [*A publication*]
**Italian Yb of Int'l L** ... Italian Yearbook of International Law [*A publication*] (DLA)
**Italia R Comitato G B** ... Italia Real Comitato Geologico. Bollettino [*A publication*]
**Ital J Bioc** .. Italian Journal of Biochemistry [*A publication*]
**Ital J Biochem** ... Italian Journal of Biochemistry [*A publication*]
**Ital J Biochem (Engl Ed)** ... Italian Journal of Biochemistry (English Edition) [*A publication*]
**Ital J Chest Dis** ... Italian Journal of Chest Diseases [*A publication*]
**Ital J Gastroenterol** ... Italian Journal of Gastroenterology [*A publication*]
**Ital J Med** ... Italian Journal of Medicine [*A publication*]
**Ital J Neurol Sci** ... Italian Journal of Neurological Sciences [*A publication*]
**Ital J Orthop Traumatol** ... Italian Journal of Orthopaedics and Traumatology [*A publication*]
**Ital J Orthop Traumatol Suppl** ... Italian Journal of Orthopaedics and Traumatology. Supplementum [*A publication*]
**Ital J Sports Traumatol** ... Italian Journal of Sports Traumatology [*A publication*]
**Ital J Surg Sci** ... Italian Journal of Surgical Sciences [*A publication*]
**Ital J Zool** .. Italian Journal of Zoology [*A publication*]
**Ital L** .......... Italian Linguistics [*A publication*]
**Ital Med** ..... Italia Medica [*A publication*]
**Ital Q** .......... Italian Quarterly [*A publication*]
**Ital Quart** ... Italian Quarterly [*A publication*]
**Ital Rev Orthop Traumatol** ... Italian Review of Orthopaedics and Traumatology [*A publication*]
**Ital Vinic Agrar** ... Italia Vinicola ed Agraria [*A publication*]
**ITALY** ....... I Trust and Love You [*Correspondence*] (DSUE)
**Italy Ann** .... Annuario Statistico Italiano [*A publication*]
**Italy Doc Notes** ... Italy. Documents and Notes [*A publication*]
**Italy Docs and Notes** ... Italy. Documents and Notes [*A publication*]
**Italy Ist Super Poste Telecomun Note Recens Not** ... Italy. Istituto Superiore delle Poste e delle Telecomunicazioni. Note Recensioni e Notizie [*A publication*]
**Italy Minist Agric For Collana Verde** ... Italy. Ministero dell'Agricoltura e delle Foreste Collana Verde [*A publication*]
**Italy Serv Geol Boll** ... Italy. Servizio Geologico. Bollettino [*A publication*]
**Italy Serv Geol Mem** ... Italy. Servizio Geologico. Memorie per Servire alla Descrizione della Carta Geologica d'Italia [*A publication*]
**ITAM** ........ Integrated Training Area Management [*Military*] (INF)
**ITAMA** ...... Information Technology Acquisition and Marketing Association (EA)
**ITAM VETS** ... Italian American War Veterans of the United States (EA)
**ITA N** ........ International Trombone Association. Newsletter [*A publication*]
**ITAP** .......... Information Technology Advisory Panel [*British*]
**IT & AP** ..... Inspection Test and Analysis Plan (NRCH)
**ITAP** .......... Integrated Technical Assessment Panel [*NASA*] (NASA)
**ITAR** .......... International Trade and Arms Regulations
**ITAR** .......... International Traffic in Arms Regulation [*US*]
**ITAR** .......... Interstate Transportation in Aid of Racketeering
**ITAS** .......... Improved Tactical Attack System
**ITAS** .......... Indicated True Air Speed [*Aviation*] (AFM)
**ITAS** .......... Integrated Tactical Attack System (MCD)
**ITAS** .......... Integrated Test and Alignment System
**ITAS** .......... Inter-American Travel Agents Society (EA)
**ITAS** .......... Interamerican Travel Agents Society (EA)
**ITASS** ........ Interim Towed Array Surveillance System [*Military*] (NVT)
**ITAV** .......... Individual Tactical Air Vehicle
**ITAVS** ....... Integrated Testing, Analysis, and Verification System
**ITAWDS** ... Integrated Tactical Amphibious Warfare Data System [*Navy*] (NVT)
**ITAX** .......... Intermountain Aviation, Inc. [*Air carrier designation symbol*]
**ITAX** .......... Italics
**ITB** ............ Abbott Laboratories, North Chicago, IL [*OCLC symbol*] (OCLC)
**ITB** ............ Iliotibial Band [*Anatomy*]
**ITB** ............ In the Business [*Refers to television and film industries*]
**ITB** ............ Individual Tour Basing [*Fares*]

**ITB**............ Industrial Training Board [*British*]
**ITB**............ Institut Technique du Batiment [*Technical Institute for Building*] [*France*] [*Information service or system*] (IID)
**ITB**............ Integral Terminal Block
**ITB**............ Integrated Test Block
**ITB**............ Integrated Training Brigade [*Navy*]
**ITB**............ Integrated Tug Barge (DS)
**ITB**............ Intermediate Text Block
**ITB**............ Intermediate Transmission Block [*Data processing*] (BUR)
**ITB**............ Intermountain Tariff Bureau, Inc.
**ITB**............ Internal Transfer Bus
**ITB**............ International Terminal Building [*Australia*]
**ITB**............ International Thomson Books
**ITB**............ International Thoroughbred Breeders, Inc. [*AMEX symbol*] (SPSG)
**ITB**............ International Time Bureau
**ITB**............ International Training Branch [*Office of Education*]
**ITB**............ Internationaler Turnerbund [*International Gymnastic Federation*]
**ITB**............ Invitation to Bid
**ITB**............ Ion Thruster Beam
**ITB**............ Irish Tourist Board (EA)
**ITB**............ Island Tug & Barge [*AAR code*]
**ItB**............ It Beaken [*A publication*]
**ItBa**............ Biblioteca Comunale "Angelillo", Servizio Prestito, Bari, Italy [*Library symbol*] [*Library of Congress*] (LCLS)
**ITBA**.......... International Toy Buff's Association (EA)
**ItBar**.......... Biblioteca Comunale di Barletta, Barletta, Italy [*Library symbol*] [*Library of Congress*] (LCLS)
**ItBaU**.......... Universita degli Studi di Bari, Bari, Italy [*Library symbol*] [*Library of Congress*] (LCLS)
**ITB-ID**....... International Thomson Books - International Division
**ITBL**.......... Incompressible Turbulent Boundary Layer
**ITBP**.......... International Thomson Business Press, Inc. [*Publisher*]
**ITBS**.......... Iowa Tests of Basic Skills
**ITBTP**........ Institut Technique du Batiment et des Travaux Publics [*Technical Institute for Building and Public Works*] [*Information service or system*] (IID)
**ITC**............ Concordia Theological Seminary, Fort Wayne, IN [*OCLC symbol*] (OCLC)
**ITC**............ Igloo Thermal Control [*Aerospace*] (MCD)
**ITC**............ Illinois Terminal Railroad Company [*AAR code*]
**ITC**............ Imperial Tobacco Company [*of Great Britain and Ireland*] Ltd.
**ITC**............ In-Track Contiguous
**ITC**............ Inclusive Tour Charter
**ITC**............ Independent Tank Center [*of a ship*] (DS)
**ITC**............ Independent Television Commission [*British*] (ECON)
**ITC**............ Industrial Technology Centre [*Manitoba Research Council*] [*Canada*] [*Research center*] (RCD)
**ITC**............ Industrial Technology Centre [*Australia*]
**ITC**............ Industrial Training Council
**ITC**............ Infantry Training Center [*Army*]
**ITC**............ Ingredient Technology Corporation [*NYSE symbol*] (SPSG)
**ITC**............ Inland Transport Committee [*United Nations*]
**ITC**............ Institute of Tax Consultants (EA)
**ITC**............ Instructional Telecommunications Consortium (EA)
**ITC**............ Instructor Training Course
**ITC**............ Instrumentation Tracking Controller
**ITC**............ Integrated Telemetry Complex
**ITC**............ Integrated Trajectory Computations
**ITC**............ Inter-American Travel Congresses
**ITC**............ Interagency Testing Committee [*Toxicology*]
**ITC**............ Intercept [*Telecommunications*] (TEL)
**ITC**............ Interchurch Transportation Council [*Defunct*] (EA)
**ITC**............ Intercontinental Trailsea Corporation
**ITC**............ Interdata Transaction Controller [*Perkin-Elmer*]
**ITC**............ Intermediate Toll Center [*Telecommunications*] (TEL)
**ITC**............ Intern Training Center [*DARCOM*]
**ITC**............ International Chemalloy Corp. [*Toronto Stock Exchange symbol*]
**ITC**............ International Institute for Aerial Survey and Earth Sciences [*Later, International Institute for Aerospace Survey and Earth Sciences*] [*Netherlands*]
**ITC**............ International Institute for Aerospace Survey and Earth Sciences (EAIO)
**ITC**............ International Tar Conference [*See also CIG*] [*Paris, France*] (EAIO)
**ITC**............ International Tea Committee (EAIO)
**ITC**............ International Technology Council [*Defunct*] (EA)
**ITC**............ International Telemetering Conference
**ITC**............ International Teletraffic Congress [*Telecommunications*]
**ITC**............ International Television Center [*Communications*]
**ITC**............ International Tin Council [*See also CIE*] [*London, England*] (EAIO)
**ITC**............ International Toastmistress Clubs (EA)
**ITC**............ International Trade Centre [*Switzerland*] [*United Nations*] (MCD)
**ITC**............ International Trade Club of Chicago [*Later, IBCM*] (EA)
**ITC**............ International Trade Commission [*Databank originator*]
**ITC**............ International Trade Council (EA)
**ITC**............ International Traders Club (EA)
**ITC**............ International Trading Certificate (DS)
**ITC**............ International Trading Company [*Thailand*] (IMH)
**ITC**............ International Training College [*Salvation Army*]
**ITC**............ International Training in Communication (EA)
**ITC**............ International Trans Asia [*Vancouver Stock Exchange symbol*]
**ITC**............ International Translations Centre [*Formerly, ETC*] (EA)
**ITC**............ International Travel Catering [*A publication*]
**ITC**............ International Tuberculosis Campaign
**ITC**............ International Typeface Corporation
**ITC**............ Intertropical Convergence [*Trade winds*] [*Meteorology*]
**ITC**............ Investment Tax Credit
**ITC**............ Ionic Thermoconductivity [*or Thermocurrent*]
**ITC**............ Israel Trade Commission
**ItC**............ Italian Culture [*A publication*]
**ITC**............ Italian Tile Center (EA)
**ITC**............ Italian Trade Commission (EA)
**ITC**............ Spinivasan's Reports of Income Tax Cases [*India*] [*A publication*] (DLA)
**ITC**............ Srinivasan's Reports of Income Tax Cases [*India*] [*1886-*] [*A publication*] (ILCA)
**ITCA**.......... Independent Television Companies Association [*British*]
**ITCA**.......... Indian Transcontinental Airways
**ITCA**.......... Inspector of Training Corps and Cadets [*Military*] [*British*]
**ITCA**.......... Instituto Tecnologico Centroamericano [*El Salvador*]
**ITCA**.......... Inter-American Technical Council on Archives (DIT)
**ITCA**.......... Intercollegiate Tennis Coaches Association (EA)
**ITCA**.......... International Technical Caramel Association (EA)
**IT/CA**........ International Tele/Conferencing Association (EA)
**ITCA**.......... International Thunderbird Class Association (EA)
**ITCA**.......... International Typographic Composition Association [*Later, TIA*] (EA)
**ITCA**.......... Invest to Compete Alliance [*Washington, DC*] (EA)
**ITCA**.......... Irish Terrier Club of America (EA)
**ITCABIC**... Inter-Territorial Catholic Bishops' Conference (EAIO)
**ITCAL**........ International Table Calorie
**ITCAN**........ Inspect, Test, and Correct as Necessary (MCD)
**ItCaU**......... Universita di Cagliari, Sardinia, Italy [*Library symbol*] [*Library of Congress*] (LCLS)
**ITCC**.......... Industrial Training Corporation [*Herndon, VA*] [*NASDAQ symbol*] (NQ)
**ITCC**.......... International Technical Communications Conference [*Society for Technical Communication*]
**ITCC**.......... Interstate Truckload Carriers Conference
**ITCCC**........ ITCC [*International Technical Cooperation Centre*] Review [*A publication*]
**ITCC Rev**... ITCC [*International Technical Cooperation Centre*] Review [*Israel*] [*A publication*]
**ITCG**.......... Information Technology Co-Ordinating Group [*International Electrotechnical Commission*] [*ISO*] (DS)
**ITCH**.......... Infotechnology, Inc. [*NASDAQ symbol*] (NQ)
**ITCI**........... International CMOS Technology, Inc. [*NASDAQ symbol*] (NQ)
**ITCI**........... International Tree Crops Institute USA (EA)
**ITCM**.......... Integrated Tactical Countermeasures [*Army*]
**ITCM**.......... INTERCIM Corp. [*NASDAQ symbol*] (NQ)
**ITCP**.......... Integrated Test and Checkout Procedures (MCD)
**ItCr**........... Biblioteca Statale di Cremona, Cremona, Italy [*Library symbol*] [*Library of Congress*] (LCLS)
**ITCRA**........ International Textile Care and Rental Association [*Netherlands*] (EY)
**ITCS**.......... Installation Training/Coordination Section [*Social Security Administration*]
**ITCS**.......... Institute for 21st Century Studies (EA)
**ITCS**.......... Integrated Target Central System [*Military*] (CAAL)
**ITCSA**........ In Vitro. Journal of the Tissue Culture Association [*A publication*]
**ITCSA**........ Institute of Technical Communicators of Southern Africa (EAIO)
**ITCSAF**..... In Vitro [*Rockville*] [*A publication*]
**ITCTLA**..... ITC [*International Trade Commission*] Trial Lawyers Association (EA)
**ITCUA**........ International Telephone Credit Union Association (EA)
**ITCZ**.......... Intertropical Convergence Zone [*Trade winds*] [*Meteorology*]
**ITD**............ Inception-to-Date
**ITD**............ Individual'naya Trudovaya Deyatel'nost' [*Individual Labor Activity*] [*Government program designed to foster private enterprise*] [*Russian*]
**ITD**............ Information Technology Development [*Project*] [*DoD*] (RDA)
**ITD**............ Information Technology Division [*Naval Research Laboratory*]
**ITD**............ Infrared Target Detector
**ITD**............ Institute of Training and Development (EAIO)
**ITD**............ Integral Trap Door [*Technical drawings*]
**ITD**............ Integrated Technology Demonstration
**ITD**............ Integrated Test Document (MCD)
**ITD**............ Integration Test and Demonstration (SDI)
**ITD**............ Interaural Time Difference [*Andiology*]
**ITD**............ Interchannel Time Displacement [*Magnetic recording*]
**ITD**............ Intercontinental Data [*Vancouver Stock Exchange symbol*]
**ITD**............ Interface Timing Diagram
**ITD**............ Internal Test Directive (KSC)
**ITD**............ Intertropical Discontinuity [*Meteorology*]

**ITD** ........ Ion Trap Detector [*Spectroscopy*]
**ITD** ........ University of Texas at Dallas, Richardson, TX [*OCLC symbol*] (OCLC)
**ITDA** ........ Income Tax Decisions of Australasia [*A publication*] (APTA)
**ITDA** ........ Independent Truckers and Drivers Association (EA)
**ITDA** ........ Indirect Target Damage Assessment (AAG)
**ITDA** ........ Integrated Tunnel Diode Amplifier
**ITDC** ........ International Trade Development Centre [*Australia*]
**ITDE** ........ Interchannel Time Displacement Error [*Magnetic recording*]
**ITDG** ........ Intermediate Technology Development Group [*Rugby, Warwickshire, England*] (EAIO)
**ITDG/NA** ... Intermediate Technology Development Group of North America (EA)
**ITDM** ........ Intelligent Time-Division Multiplexer
**ITDP** ........ Institute for Transportation and Development Policy (EA)
**ITDR** ........ Institute for Training and Demographic Research (EA)
**ITDT** ........ Integrated Technical Documentation and Training
**ITDU** ........ Infantry Trials and Development Unit [*British military*] (DMA)
**ITDU** ........ Infrared Tracking Display Unit
**ITE** ........ In the Ear [*Hearing aid*]
**ITE** ........ Individual Training Evaluation (MCD)
**ITE** ........ Input Test Equipment
**ITE** ........ Institute of Telecommunications Engineers
**ITE** ........ Institute of Terrestrial Ecology [*Research center*] [*British*] (IRC)
**ITE** ........ Institute of Traffic Engineers (EA)
**ITE** ........ Institute of Transportation Engineers (EA)
**ITE** ........ Instrumentation Test Equipment (KSC)
**ITE** ........ Integration Test Equipment (MCD)
**ITE** ........ International Telephone Exchange [*Telecommunications*] (TEL)
**ITE** ........ Intersite Transportation Equipment [*NASA*] (NASA)
**ITE** ........ Interstrat Resources, Inc. [*Vancouver Stock Exchange symbol*]
**ITE** ........ Inverse Time Element (MUGU)
**ITEA** ........ Infraestructura Teatral [*Ministerio de Cultura*] [*Spain*] [*Information service or system*] (CRD)
**ITEA** ........ International Technology Education Association (EA)
**ITEA** ........ International Test and Evaluation Association (EA)
**ITEAA5** ..... INTA [*Instituto Nacional de Tecnologia Agropecuaria*]. Estacion Experimental Regional Agropecuaria [*Parana*]. Serie Tecnica [*A publication*]
**ITeC** ........ Information Technology Centre [*Australia*]
**ITEC** ........ Information Technology Electronics and Computers [*A publication*]
**ITEC** ........ International Thoroughbred Exposition and Conference [*Kentucky Thoroughbred Association, Inc.*] (TSPED)
**ITEC** ........ International Transport Exhibition (TSPED)
**ITECH** ....... Joint IOC/WMO Group of Experts on IGOSS Technical Systems Design and Development and Service Requirements [*Marine science*] (MSC)
**ITED** ........ Integrated Trajectory Error Display [*Aviation*]
**ITED** ........ Iowa Tests of Educational Development
**ITEF** ........ Integrated Test Equipment Facility (MCD)
**ITEF** ........ International Trade Exhibitions in France (EA)
**ITEG** ........ Individual Training Evaluation Group (MCD)
**ITE J** ........ ITE [*Institute of Transportation Engineers*] Journal [*United States*] [*A publication*]
**ITEL** ........ Joint WMO/IOC Group of Experts on Telecommunications (MSC)
**ITEM** ........ Intelligence Threat Evaluation Model [*Military*] (MCD)
**ITEM** ........ Interference Technology Engineer's Master (IEEE)
**ITEME** ...... Institution of Technician Engineers in Mechanical Engineering [*British*]
**ITEMS** ...... In-Service Inspection, Testing, Evaluation, and Monitoring Service
**ITEMS** ...... INCOTERM [*International Commerce Term*] Transaction Entry Management System
**ITEP** ........ Individual Training and Evaluation Program [*Army*] (INF)
**ITEP** ........ Integrated Test/Evaluation Program (AABC)
**ITEP** ........ Interim Tactical ELINT [*Electronic Intelligence*] Processor
**ITER** ........ International Thermonuclear Experimental Reactor
**ITER** ........ Interstrat Resources, Inc. [*NASDAQ symbol*] (NQ)
**ITEST** ....... Institute for Theological Encounter with Science and Technology (EA)
**ITeuS** ........ Saint Joseph Seminary, Teutopolis, IL [*Library symbol*] [*Library of Congress*] (LCLS)
**ITeuSD** ...... Teutopolis Community Unit, School District 50, Teutopolis, IL [*Library symbol*] [*Library of Congress*] (LCLS)
**ITEWS** ...... Integrated Tactical Electronic Warfare System
**ITEX** ........ Information Technology Exchange Exhibition [*British*] (ITD)
**ITEX** ........ Internal Tide Experiment [*Marine science*] (MSC)
**ITF** ........ Impulse Transfer Function (KSC)
**ITF** ........ In Trust For [*Banking*]
**ITF** ........ Independent Teachers Federation [*Australia*]
**ITF** ........ Indian Territorial Force [*British military*] (DMA)
**ITF** ........ Industrial Technology Fund [*British*]
**ITF** ........ Industrial and Trade Fairs Ltd. [*Solihull, West Midlands, England*] (TSSD)
**ITF** ........ Instant Transference
**ITF** ........ Institut Textile de France [*French Textile Institute*] [*Boulogne-Billancourt*] [*Information service or system*] (IID)
**ITF** ........ Institute of Tropical Forestry [*Rio Piedras, PR*] [*Department of Agriculture*] [*Research center*]
**ITF** ........ Integrated Test Facility [*Data processing*]
**ITF** ........ Integrated Thermal Flux (AAG)
**ITF** ........ Intelligence Terminal Family [*Military*] (MCD)
**ITF** ........ Interactive Terminal Facility
**ITF** ........ Interim [*Contact*] File (MCD)
**ITF** ........ Intermediate Test Facility (MCD)
**ITF** ........ International Tennis Federation [*Formerly, ILTF*] (EA)
**ITF** ........ International Trade Fair [*New Zealand*]
**ITF** ........ International Trade Forum [*A publication*]
**ITF** ........ International Transport Workers' Federation [*London, England*] (EAIO)
**ITF** ........ Interstate Transportation of Fireworks
**ITF** ........ Interstitial Transfer Facility [*Nuclear energy*] (NRCH)
**ITF** ........ Inverse Trigonometric Function
**ITF** ........ Islamic Thought Foundation (EAIO)
**ITF** ........ Italfarmaco [*Italy*] [*Research code symbol*]
**ITF** ........ Italy. Documents and Notes [*A publication*]
**ItF** ........ Italyan Filolojisi [*A publication*]
**ItFB** ........ Biblioteca Berenson, Florence, Italy [*Library symbol*] [*Library of Congress*] (LCLS)
**ItFBM** ....... Biblioteca Marucelliana di Firenze, Servizio Prestito, Florence, Italy [*Library symbol*] [*Library of Congress*] (LCLS)
**ITFCA** ....... International Track and Field Coaches Association [*Athens, Greece*] (EAIO)
**ITFCC** ....... Initial [*or Interim*] Tactical Flag Command Center (MCD)
**ITFCS** ....... Institute for Twenty-First Century Studies (EA)
**ITFMC** ...... Indian Territorial Force Medical Corps [*British military*] (DMA)
**ITFO** ........ International Trade Fairs Office [*Department of Commerce*]
**It For Montan** ... Italia Forestale e Montana [*A publication*]
**ITFS** ........ Instructional Television Fixed Service [*Educational TV*]
**ITFS** ........ International Tropical Fern Society [*Defunct*] (EA)
**ITFTRIA** ... Instrument Tree Flow and Temperature Removal Instrument Assembly [*Nuclear energy*] (NRCH)
**ITG** ........ Australian Income Tax Guide [*A publication*]
**ITG** ........ Industrial Tachometer Generator
**ITG** ........ Industry Technology Group [*Air Force*] (MCD)
**ITG** ........ Industry Test Group [*Air Force*]
**ITG** ........ Information and Telecommunications Technologies Group [*Electronic Industries Association*] [*Washington, DC*] (TSSD)
**ITG** ........ Innovationstechnik GmbH & Co. [*Database producer*] (IID)
**ITG** ........ Institute Technical Group
**ITG** ........ Integra-A Hotel/Restaurant [*NYSE symbol*] (SPSG)
**ITG** ........ Integrated Terminal Guidance
**ITG** ........ Inter-Continental Energy [*Vancouver Stock Exchange symbol*]
**ITG** ........ Interdiction Target Graphic (MCD)
**ITG** ........ International Trumpet Guild (EA)
**ITG** ........ International Trumpet Guild. Journal [*A publication*]
**ITGA** ........ Isothermogravimetric Analysis
**ITGB** ........ Institute of Transport of Great Britain
**ITGBL** ....... International through Government Bill of Lading
**ITGD** ........ Interstate Transportation of Gambling Devices
**ITGEA** ....... Interdisciplinary Topics in Gerontology [*A publication*]
**ITGEAR** .... Interdisciplinary Topics in Gerontology [*A publication*]
**ITG J** ........ International Trumpet Guild. Journal [*A publication*]
**ITGLWF** ... International Textile, Garment, and Leather Workers' Federation [*See also FITTHC*] [*Brussels, Belgium*] (EAIO)
**ITGN** ........ Integon Corp. [*NASDAQ symbol*] (NQ)
**ITG N** ........ International Trumpet Guild. Newsletter [*A publication*]
**ITGR** ........ Integra Financial Corp. [*NASDAQ symbol*] (NQ)
**ITGWF** ...... International Textile and Garment Workers' Federation [*Later, ITGLWF*]
**ITGWU** ..... Irish Transport and General Workers' Union (DCTA)
**ITH** ........ Internationaler Holzmarkt [*A publication*]
**ITh** ........ Interthecal [*Anesthesiology*]
**ITh** ........ Intrathoracic [*Anatomy*]
**ITH** ........ Island Technologies Corp. [*Vancouver Stock Exchange symbol*]
**ITH** ........ Ithaca [*New York*] [*Seismograph station code, US Geological Survey*] [*Closed*] (SEIS)
**ITH** ........ Ithaca [*New York*] [*Airport symbol*] (OAG)
**ITH** ........ Ithaca, NY [*Location identifier*] [*FAA*] (FAAL)
**ITh** ........ Thornton Public Library, Thornton, IL [*Library symbol*] [*Library of Congress*] (LCLS)
**ITHI** ........ International Thomson Holdings, Incorporated
**ITHI** ........ International Travelers Health Institute (EA)
**ITHL** ........ Internal Triangular Hinge Ligament [*of scallops*]
**ITHM** ........ Intertherm, Inc. [*NASDAQ symbol*] (NQ)
**ITHOF** ...... International Tennis Hall of Fame (EA)
**ITHP** ........ Increased Take-Home Pay
**I Th Q** ........ Irish Theological Quarterly [*A publication*]
**ITI** ........ Immediate Transient Incapacitation [*Radiation casualty criterion*] [*Army*] (AABC)
**ITI** ........ Industrial Technology Institute [*Research center*] (RCD)
**ITI** ........ Infaunal Trophic Index [*Marine pollution*]

**ITI**............ Information Transform, Incorporated [*Information service or system*] (IID)
**ITI**............ Initial Task Index (AAG)
**ITI**............ Inspection and Test Instruction (NASA)
**ITI**............ Institut TNO voor Toegepaste Informatica [*TNO Institute of Applied Computer Science*] [*Information service or system*] (IID)
**ITI**............ Insurance Testing Institute [*Malvern, PA*] (EA)
**ITI**............ Integrated Task Index (AAG)
**ITI**............ Interactive Terminal Interface [*Data processing*] (IEEE)
**ITI**............ Intermediair. Informatie voor Leidinggevende Functionarissen [*A publication*]
**ITI**............ Intermittent Trouble Indication [*Telecommunications*] (TEL)
**ITI**............ International Tax Institute (EA)
**ITI**............ International Technical Institute of Flight Engineers
**ITI**............ International Technology Institute (EA)
**ITI**............ International Telecharge, Incorporated [*AMEX symbol*] (SPSG)
**ITI**............ International Telesis Industries Corp. [*Vancouver Stock Exchange symbol*]
**ITI**............ International Theatre Institute [*Paris, France*] (EAIO)
**ITI**............ International Thrift Institute
**ITI**............ Intertrial Interval [*Psychology*]
**ITIA**.......... International Trade and Investment Act [*1984*]
**ITIA**.......... International Tungsten Industry Association (EAIO)
**ITIAL**........ Items Troop Installed or Authorized List (MCD)
**ITIC**.......... Inter-Tribal Indian Ceremonial Association (EA)
**ITIC**.......... International Tsunami Information Center (EA)
**ITIC**.......... Investors Title Company [*Chapel Hill, NC*] [*NASDAQ symbol*] (NQ)
**ITIES**........ Interservice Technical Information Exchange System [*Military*] (AFIT)
**ITIF**.......... Individual Taxpayer Information File [*IRS*]
**ITII**.......... Internal-to-Internal Interface (MCD)
**ITII**.......... International Thomson Information, Inc. [*Later, ITLS*]
**ITIM**.......... Itonut Yisrael Meugedet [*ITIM News Agency of the Associated Israel Press Ltd.*]
**ITIN**.......... Investors Trust, Incorporated [*Indianapolis, IN*] [*NASDAQ symbol*] (NQ)
**Itin**............ Itinerari [*A publication*]
**ITIN**.......... Itinerary (AFM)
**ITIN**.......... Itinerating (ROG)
**IT Info**....... Income Tax Information Release (DLA)
**ITIP**.......... Improved Transtage Injector Program (MCD)
**ITIP**.......... International Thomson Industrial Press
**ITIPAT**...... Institute for the Technology and Industrialization of Tropical Agricultural Products [*Ivory Coast*]
**ITIPD5**...... Informes Tecnicos. Instituto de Investigaciones Pesqueras [*A publication*]
**ITIPI**......... Interim Tactical Information Processing and Interpretation
**ITIRC**........ IBM Technical Information Retrieval Center [*International Business Machines Corp.*] [*Armonk, NY*]
**ITIS**.......... Industrial Technical Information Service [*Singapore*] (IID)
**ITIS**.......... Integrated Tank Insulation System
**ITIS**.......... Integrated Technical Information System [*Department of Energy*] [*Information service or system*] (IID)
**IT-IS**......... Intermediate Technology Industrial Services [*ITDG*] [*British*]
**ITIS**.......... Internal Translation Information Subsystem [*Data processing*]
**ITIS**.......... International Trade Information Service
**ITIS**.......... Italians in Service of the US [*World War II*]
**ITis**........... Tiskilwa Township Library, Tiskilwa, IL [*Library symbol*] [*Library of Congress*] (LCLS)
**ITisP**......... Plow Creek Commune Library, Tiskilwa, IL [*Library symbol*] [*Library of Congress*] (LCLS)
**ITISS**......... Integrated Tactical Intelligence Support System (MCD)
**ITisSD**....... Tiskilwa Community Unit, School District 300, Tiskilwa, IL [*Library symbol*] [*Library of Congress*] (LCLS)
**ITIU**.......... Inventory Temporarily in Use [*Army*] (AABC)
**ITI/US**....... International Theatre Institute of the United States (EA)
**ITJ**............ Indian Tax Journal [*A publication*] (DLA)
**ITJ**............ International Tax Journal [*A publication*]
**ITJ**............ International Trojan Development Corp. [*Vancouver Stock Exchange symbol*]
**ITK**............ Itokama [*Papua New Guinea*] [*Airport symbol*] (OAG)
**ITKBA**....... Izvestiya na Tsentralnata Khelmintologichna Laboratoriya. Bulgarska Akademiya na Naukite [*A publication*]
**ITKF**.......... International Traditional Karate Federation (EA)
**ITKSA**....... Instituut vir Tegniese Kommunikators van Suidelike Afrika [*Institute of Technical Communicators of Southern Africa*] (EAIO)
**ITL**............ American Inter-Island, Inc. [*Virgin Islands*] [*FAA designator*] (FAAC)
**ITL**............ Ignition Transmission Line
**ITL**............ Incoming Transaction Listing (AFM)
**ITL**............ Incomplete Task Log (AAG)
**ITL**............ Industrial Test Laboratory [*Philadelphia Navy Yard*] [*Navy*]
**ITL**............ Instrumented Team Learning (ADA)
**ITL**............ Integrate-Transfer-Launch [*Complex*] [*NASA*]
**ITL**............ Intent to Launch (NG)
**ITL**............ Interactive Technology Laboratory [*New York Institute of Technology*] [*Research center*] (RCD)
**ITL**............ Intermediate Transfer Language
**ITL**............ International Theological Library [*A publication*]
**ITL**............ Inverse Taper Lens
**ITL**............ Inverse Time Limit (MSA)
**ITL**............ Isomeric Transition Level [*Radioactivity*]
**ITL**............ ITEL Corp. [*NYSE symbol*] (SPSG)
**ITL**............ ITL Industries Ltd. [*Toronto Stock Exchange symbol*]
**ITLBV**....... Individual Tactical Load Bearing Vest [*Army*] (INF)
**ITLC**.......... Instant Thin-Layer Chromatography
**ITLGSWF**... Interamerican Textile, Leather, Garment, and Shoe Workers Federation (EA)
**ITLJ**.......... Income Tax Law Journal [*India*] [*A publication*] (DLA)
**ITLMCF**.... Instrument Technicians Labor-Management Cooperation Fund (EA)
**ITLS**.......... International Thomson Library Services
**ITLSA**........ Integrated Torso Limb Suit Assembly [*NASA*] (KSC)
**ITLT**.......... Interstate Transportation of Lottery Tickets
**ITM**........... Inch Trim Moment [*Nautical*]
**ITM**........... Indirect Tag Memory
**ITM**........... Induction Tube Modulation
**ITM**........... Infantry Target Mechanism [*Army*]
**ITM**........... Inspector of Torpedoes and Mines [*Navy*]
**ITM**........... Institute of Thread Machiners [*Defunct*]
**ITM**........... Interceptor Tactical Missile [*Air Force*]
**ITM**........... Interim Technical Memorandum
**ITM**........... Intermedics, Inc. [*NYSE symbol*] (SPSG)
**ITM**........... Internal Technical Memorandum
**ITM**........... Internal Tympaniform Membrane [*Zoology*]
**ITM**........... Investment Trust Funds under Management
**ITM**........... ISDN [*Integrated Services Digital Network*] Trunk Module [*Telecommunications*]
**ITM**........... Item [*Online database field identifier*]
**ITM**........... Ithomi [*Greece*] [*Seismograph station code, US Geological Survey*] (SEIS)
**ITMA**........ Institute for Training in Municipal Administration (EA)
**ITMA**........ International Tanning Manufacturers Association (EA)
**ITMA**........ Investigation on Teaching Using Microcomputers as an Aid
**ITMA**........ Irradiation Test Management Activity (NRCH)
**ITMA**........ It's That Man Again [*Long-running English radio comedy, 1939-1949*]
**ITMC**......... International Transmission Maintenance Center [*Communications*]
**IT & ME**.... Incentive Travel and Meeting Executives Show [*Trade show*]
**IT/ME**....... Incentive Travel and Meeting Executives Show [*Trade show*] (ITD)
**ITMF**......... International Textile Manufacturers Federation [*Zurich, Switzerland*] (EA)
**ITMG**........ Integrated Thermal Micrometeoroid Garment [*Spacesuit*]
**ItMGM**...... Italian MGM [*Record label*]
**ITMIB2**..... Instituto Tecnologico de Monterrey. Division de Ciencias Agropecuarias y Maritimas. Informe de Investigacion [*A publication*]
**ITMID**....... Item Identification File
**ITMIS**....... Integrated Transportation Management Information System [*Army*]
**ITMRC**...... International Travel Market Research Council
**ITMS**......... In-Core Temperature Monitoring System [*Nuclear energy*] (NRCH)
**ITMS**......... Ingestible Thermal Monitoring System
**ITMS**......... Integrated Training Management System [*DoD*]
**ITMS**......... International Tax Management System [*Price Waterhouse & Co.*]
**ITMZBJ**.... Intensivmedizin [*A publication*]
**ITN**........... In Touch Networks (EA)
**ITN**........... Independent Television News [*British*]
**ITN**........... Institute for TransPacific Networking [*Oakland, CA*] [*Telecommunications service*] (TSSD)
**ITN**........... Integrated Teleprocessing Network
**ITN**........... Interim Technical Note
**ITN**........... International Television News [*A publication*] (EAAP)
**ITN**........... International Turbine Tech [*Vancouver Stock Exchange symbol*]
**ITN**........... InterTan, Inc. [*NYSE symbol*] (CTT)
**ITN**........... Itabuna [*Brazil*] [*Airport symbol*] (OAG)
**ITNA**......... Independent Television News Association [*News service*]
**ITNC**......... In-Track Noncontiguous
**ITND**......... International Trade Names Dictionary [*Later, IBTC*] [*A publication*]
**ITNFSA**..... International Tanker Nominal Freight Scale Association
**ITNOTGAOTU**... In the Name of the Great Architect of the Universe [*Freemasonry*] (ROG)
**ITNRNT**.... Itinerant (FAAC)
**ITNS**......... Integrated Tactical Navigation System [*Navy*]
**ITNS/D-AHRS**... Integrated Tactical Navigation System/Doppler - Altitude Heading Reference System
**ItNU**.......... Universita di Napoli, Naples, Italy [*Library symbol*] [*Library of Congress*] (LCLS)
**ItNU-IC**..... Universita di Napoli, Istituto Chimico, Naples, Italy [*Library symbol*] [*Library of Congress*] (LCLS)
**ITO**........... Hilo [*Hawaii*] [*Airport symbol*] (OAG)
**ITO**........... Hilo, HI [*Location identifier*] [*FAA*] (FAAL)

**ITO**........... Impulse Transfer Orbit
**ITO**........... In Theory Only [*A publication*]
**ITO**........... Income Tax Office (DAS)
**ITO**........... Indium Tin Oxide
**ITO**........... Individual Travel Order [*Military*] (CINC)
**ITO**........... Industrial Therapy Organisation [*British*]
**ITO**........... Inspecting Torpedo Officer [*Navy*]
**ITO**........... Installation Transportation Office [*or Officer*] [*Air Force*] (AFM)
**ITO**........... Institution of Training Officers [*British*]
**ITO**........... Instrument Takeoff
**ITO**........... Integration and Test Order (MCD)
**ITO**........... Interim Technical Order (AFM)
**ITO**........... Intermediate Training Objective [*Army*] (INF)
**ITO**........... International Thomson Organisation [*Later, The Thomson Corp.*]
**ITO**........... International Trade Organization
**ITO**........... International Travel Orders
**ITO**........... Invitational Travel Order [*Army*] (AABC)
**ITO**........... Ito [*Japan*] [*Seismograph station code, US Geological Survey*] [*Closed*] (SEIS)
**ITOA**......... Independent Tanker Owners Association (DS)
**ITOA**......... Independent Terminal Operators Association (EA)
**ITOBAO**.... Akhboroti Akademiyai Fankhoi RSS Tochikiston Shu-Bai Fankhoi Biologi [*A publication*]
**ITOF**.......... Ion Time of Flight
**ITOFCN**.... Interim Technical Order Field Change Notice [*Air Force*] (MCD)
**Itogi Eksp Rab Molodykh Issled Vopr Sel'sk Khoz** ... Itogi Eksperimental'nykh Rabot Molodykh Issledovatelei po Voprosam Sel'skogo Khozyaistva [*A publication*]
**Itogi Nauki Astron** ... Itogi Nauki Astronomiya [*A publication*]
**Itogi Nauki Biol Khim** ... Itogi Nauki Biologicheskaya Khimiya [*A publication*]
**Itogi Nauki Biol Nauki** ... Itogi Nauki Biologicheskie Nauki [*A publication*]
**Itogi Nauki Biol Osn Rastenievod** ... Itogi Nauki Biologicheski Osnovy Rastenievodstva [*A publication*]
**Itogi Nauki Biol Ultrastrukt** ... Itogi Nauki Biologicheskie Ul'trastruktury [*A publication*]
**Itogi Nauki Elektrokhim** ... Itogi Nauki Elektrokhimiya [*A publication*]
**Itogi Nauki Embriol** ... Itogi Nauki Embriologiya [*A publication*]
**Itogi Nauki Farmakol Khimioter Sredstva** ... Itogi Nauki Farmakologiya. Khimioterapevticheskie Sredstva [*A publication*]
**Itogi Nauki Farmakol Toksikol** ... Itogi Nauki Farmakologiya. Toksikologiya [*A publication*]
**Itogi Nauki Fiziol Chel Zhivotn** ... Itogi Nauki Fiziologiya, Cheloveka, i Zhivotnykh [*A publication*]
**Itogi Nauki Fiz Khim** ... Itogi Nauki Fizicheskaya Khimiya [*A publication*]
**Itogi Nauki Fiz Mat Nauki** ... Itogi Nauki Fiziko-Matematicheskie Nauki [*A publication*]
**Itogi Nauki Geofiz** ... Itogi Nauki Geofizika [*A publication*]
**Itogi Nauki Geokhim Mineral Petrogr** ... Itogi Nauki Geokhimiya Mineralogiya Petrografiya [*A publication*]
**Itogi Nauki Khim Nauki** ... Itogi Nauki Khimicheskie Nauki [*A publication*]
**Itogi Nauki Khim Tekhnol Vysokomol Soedin** ... Itogi Nauki Khimiya i Tekhnologiya Vysokomolekulyarnykh Soedinenii [*A publication*]
**Itogi Nauki Korroz Zashch Korroz** ... Itogi Nauki Korroziya i Zashchita ot Korrozii [*A publication*]
**Itogi Nauki Kristallokhim** ... Itogi Nauki Kristallokhimiya [*A publication*]
**Itogi Nauki Nemet Posezn Iskop** ... Itogi Nauki Nemetallicheskie Poseznye Iskopaemye [*A publication*]
**Itogi Nauki Neorg Khim** ... Itogi Nauki Neorganicheskaya Khimiya [*A publication*]
**Itogi Nauki Obshch Genet** ... Itogi Nauki Obshchaya Genetika [*A publication*]
**Itogi Nauki Obshch Vopr Patol** ... Itogi Nauki Obshchie Voprosy Patologii [*A publication*]
**Itogi Nauki Onkol** ... Itogi Nauki Onkologiya [*A publication*]
**Itogi Nauki Rudn Mestorozhd** ... Itogi Nauki Rudnye Mestorozhdeniya [*A publication*]
**Itogi Nauki Tekh At Energ** ... Itogi Nauki i Tekhniki Atomnaya Energetika [*A publication*]
**Itogi Nauki Tekh Biofiz** ... Itogi Nauki Tekhniki Biofizika [*A publication*]
**Itogi Nauki Tekh Elektrokhim** ... Itogi Nauki i Tekhniki Elektrokhimiya [*A publication*]
**Itogi Nauki Tekh Farmakol Khimioter Sredstva Toksikol** ... Itogi Nauki i Tekhniki Farmakologiya Khimioterapevticheski Sredstva Toksikolog iya [*A publication*]
**Itogi Nauki Tekh Fiziol Chel Zhivotn** ... Itogi Nauki i Tekhniki Fiziologiya Cheloveka i Zhivotnykh [*A publication*]
**Itogi Nauki Tekh Fiziol Rast** ... Itogi Nauki i Tekhniki Fiziologiya Rastenii [*A publication*]
**Itogi Nauki Tekh Fiz Khim Kinet** ... Itogi Nauki i Tekhniki Fizicheskaya Khimiya Kinetika [*A publication*]
**Itogi Nauki Tekh Genet Chel** ... Itogi Nauki i Tekhniki Genetika Cheloveka [*A publication*]
**Itogi Nauki Tekh Geokhim Mineral Petrogr** ... Itogi Nauki i Tekhniki Geokhimiya Mineralogiya Petrografiya [*A publication*]
**Itogi Nauki Tekh Gidrogeol Inzh Geol** ... Itogi Nauki i Tekhniki Gidrogeologiya, Inzhenernaya Geologiya [*A publication*]
**Itogi Nauki Tekh Gorn Delo** ... Itogi Nauki i Tekhniki Gornoe Delo [*A publication*]
**Itogi Nauki Tekh Issled Kosm Prostranstva** ... Itogi Nauki i Tekhniki Issledovanie Kosmicheskogo Prostranstva [*A publication*]
**Itogi Nauki Tekh Khim Tekhn Vysokimol Soedin** ... Itogi Nauki i Tekhniki Khimiya i Tekhnologiya Vysokimolekulyarnykh Soedininii [*A publication*]
**Itogi Nauki Tekh Khim Termodin Ravnovesiya** ... Itogi Nauki i Tekhniki Khimicheskaya Termodinamika i Ravnovesiya [*A publication*]
**Itogi Nauki Tekh Korroz Zashch Korroz** ... Itogi Nauki i Tekhniki Korroziya i Zashchita ot Korrozii [*USSR*] [*A publication*]
**Itogi Nauki Tekh Kristallokhim** ... Itogi Nauki i Tekhniki Kristallokhimiya [*A publication*]
**Itogi Nauki Tekh Mestorozhd Goryuch Polezn Iskop** ... Itogi Nauki i Tekhniki Mestorozhdeniya Goryuchikh Poleznykh Iskopaemykh [*USSR*] [*A publication*]
**Itogi Nauki Tekh Metalloved Term Obrab** ... Itogi Nauki i Tekhniki Metallovedenie i Termicheskaya Obrabotka [*A publication*]
**Itogi Nauki Tekh Metall Tsvetn Redk Met** ... Itogi Nauki i Tekhniki Metallurgiya Tsvetnykh i Redkikh Metallov [*A publication*]
**Itogi Nauki Tekh Mikrobiol** ... Itogi Nauki i Tekhniki Mikrobiologiya [*A publication*]
**Itogi Nauki Tekh Mol Biol** ... Itogi Nauki i Tekhniki Molekulyarnaya Biologiya [*A publication*]
**Itogi Nauki Tekh Nauki** ... Itogi Nauki Tekhnicheskie Nauki [*A publication*]
**Itogi Nauki Tekh Nemet Polezn Iskop** ... Itogi Nauki i Tekhniki Nemetallicheskie Poleznye Iskopaemye [*A publication*]
**Itogi Nauki Tekh Neorg Khim** ... Itogi Nauki i Tekhniki Neorganicheskaya Khimiya [*A publication*]
**Itogi Nauki Tekhnol Org Veshchestv** ... Itogi Nauki Tekhnologiya Organicheskikh Veshchestv [*A publication*]
**Itogi Nauki Tekh Obogashch Polezn Iskop** ... Itogi Nauki i Tekhniki Obogashchenie Poleznykh Iskopaemykh [*A publication*]
**Itogi Nauki Tekh Obshch Ekol Biotsenol** ... Itogi Nauki i Tekhniki Obshchaya Ekologiya, Biotsenologiya [*A publication*]
**Itogi Nauki Tekh Obshch Geol** ... Itogi Nauki i Tekhniki Obshchaya Geologiya [*A publication*]
**Itogi Nauki Tekh Onkol** ... Itogi Nauki i Tekhniki Onkologiya [*A publication*]
**Itogi Nauki Tekh Pozharnaya Okhr** ... Itogi Nauki i Tekhniki Pozharnaya Okhrana [*A publication*]
**Itogi Nauki Tekh Proizvod Chuguna Stali** ... Itogi Nauki i Tekhniki Proizvodstvo Chuguna i Stali [*A publication*]
**Itogi Nauki Tekh Rudn Mestorozhd** ... Itogi Nauki i Tekhniki Rudnye Mestorozhdeniya [*A publication*]
**Itogi Nauki Tekh Ser Biotekhnol** ... Itogi Nauki i Tekhniki Seriya Biotekhnologiya [*A publication*]
**Itogi Nauki Tekh Ser Tekhnol Mashinostr** ... Itogi Nauki i Tekhniki Seriya Tekhnologiya Mashinostroeniya [*A publication*]
**Itogi Nauki Tekh Svarka** ... Itogi Nauki i Tekhniki Svarka [*A publication*]
**Itogi Nauki Tekh Svetotekh Infrakrasnaya Tekh** ... Itogi Nauki i Tekhniki Svetotekhnika i Infrakrasnaya Tekhniki [*A publication*]
**Itogi Nauki Tekh Tekhnol Mashinostr** ... Itogi Nauki i Tekhniki Tekhnologiya Mashinostroeniya [*A publication*]
**Itogi Nauki Tekh Teor Metall Protsessov** ... Itogi Nauki i Tekhniki Teoriya Metallurgicheskikh Protsessov [*A publication*]
**Itogi Nauki Tekh Toksikol** ... Itogi Nauki i Tekhniki Toksikologiya [*A publication*]
**Itogi Nauki Tekh Virusol** ... Itogi Nauki i Tekhniki Virusologiya [*A publication*]
**Itogi Nauki Tekh Zhivotnovod Vet** ... Itogi Nauki i Tekhniki Zhivotnovodstvo i Veterinariya [*A publication*]
**Itogi Nauki Tsitol Obshch Genet Genet Chel** ... Itogi Nauki Tsitologiya Obshchaya Genetika. Genetika Cheloveka [*A publication*]
**Itogi Nauki Vet** ... Itogi Nauki Veterinariya [*A publication*]
**Itogi Nauki Virusol Mikrobiol** ... Itogi Nauki Virusologiya i Mikrobiologiya [*A publication*]
**Itogi Nauki Vysokomol Soedin** ... Itogi Nauki Vysokomolekulyarnye Soedineniya [*A publication*]
**Itogi Nauki Zashch Rast** ... Itogi Nauki Zashchita Rastenii [*A publication*]
**Itogi Nauk & Tekh Ser Issled Kosm Prostranstva** ... Itogi Nauki i Tekhniki Seriya Issledovanie Kosmicheskogo Prostranstva [*A publication*]
**Itogi Polev Rabot Inst Etnogr** ... Itogi Polevyh Rabot Instituta Etnografii [*A publication*]
**ITOI**........... International Thomson Organisation, Incorporated
**ITOIAE**..... Izvestija Tavreiceskogo Obscestva Istorii, Archeologii, Etnografii [*A publication*]
**ITOL**.......... International Thomson Organisation Ltd. [*Later, TTC*]
**ITol**............ Toluca City Library, Toluca, IL [*Library symbol*] [*Library of Congress*] (LCLS)
**ITolo**.......... Tolono Township Library, Tolono, IL [*Library symbol*] [*Library of Congress*] (LCLS)
**ITolSD**....... Toluca Community Unit, School District 2306, Toluca, IL [*Library symbol*] [*Library of Congress*] (LCLS)
**ITOM**......... Interstate Transportation of Obscene Matter
**ITOMA**..... Industries et Travaux d'Outre-Mer [*A publication*]
**ITONA**...... Iveco Trucks of North America, Inc.

**ITonSD** ...... Tonica Consolidated Community School District 79 and Consolidated High School District 360, Tonica, IL [*Library symbol*] [*Library of Congress*] (LCLS)
**I-TOO** ........ Independent Truck Owner/Operator Association (EA)
**ITOP** .......... Integrated Test Operate Panel
**ITOP** .......... International Test Operations Procedure [*DoD*]
**ITOPF** ........ International Tanker Owners Pollution Federation
**ITOPLC** .... International Thomson Organisation Public Limited Company
**ITOR** ......... Intercept Target Optical Reader
**ITORGO** ... Izvestija Turkestanskogo Otdela Russkogo Geograficeskogo Obscestva [*A publication*]
**ITOS** .......... Improved TIROS [*Television Infrared Observation Satellite*] Operational Satellite [*or System*] [*National Oceanic and Atmospheric Administration*]
**ITOS** .......... Iterative Time Optimal System
**ITOSS** ....... Integrated Toolkit for Operating System Security [*Computer security system*]
**ITou** ........... Toulon Public Library, Toulon, IL [*Library symbol*] [*Library of Congress*] (LCLS)
**ITOW** ........ Improved Tube-Launched, Optically Tracked, Wire-Guided [*Weapon*] (RDA)
**ITP** ............ Idiopathic Thrombocytopenic Purpura [*Medicine*]
**ITP** ............ Immune Thrombocytopenic Purpura [*Medicine*]
**ITP** ............ Income Tax Professional (ADA)
**ITP** ............ Independent Television Publications [*British*] (ECON)
**ITP** ............ Individual Training Plan [*Army*]
**ITP** ............ Individual Training Program (MCD)
**ITP** ............ Individual Treatment Plan [*For the medical care and the education of a handicapped person*]
**ITP** ............ Inferior Thalamic Peduncle [*Anatomy*]
**ITP** ............ Initial Trial Phase (NG)
**ITP** ............ Inosine Triphosphate [*Biochemistry*]
**ITP** ............ Input Translator Program [*Data processing*]
**I & T(P)** ...... Inspection and Test (Planning) (MCD)
**ITP** ............ Inspection Test Procedure
**ITP** ............ Installation Test Program
**ITP** ............ Instruction to Proceed (NATG)
**ITP** ............ Integrated Test Package (CAAL)
**ITP** ............ Integrated Test Program
**ITP** ............ Interactive Terminal Protocol [*Data processing*]
**ITP** ............ Intercon Petroleum, Inc. [*Vancouver Stock Exchange symbol*]
**ITP** ............ Interim Test Procedure (MCD)
**ITP** ............ Interim Training Program [*Army*] (INF)
**ITP** ............ International Thomson Publishing [*Also, ITPI*]
**ITP** ............ Interrupted Task Paradigm [*Psychometrics*]
**ITP** ............ Intrathoracic Pressure [*Medicine*]
**ITP** ............ Isotachophoresis [*Analytical biochemistry*]
**It P** ............ Italian Pharmacopoeia [*A publication*]
**ITp** ............ Tinley Park Public Library, Tinley Park, IL [*Library symbol*] [*Library of Congress*] (LCLS)
**ITPA** .......... Illinois Test of Psycholinguistic Abilities
**ITPA** .......... Independent Telephone Pioneer Association (EA)
**ITPA** .......... International Tea Promotion Association [*Rotterdam, Netherlands*] (EAIO)
**ITPA** .......... International Trotting and Pacing Association (EA)
**ITPA** .......... International Truck Parts Association (EA)
**ITPAIS** ...... Image Technology Patent Information System [*Printing technology*] [*Rochester Institute of Technology*] [*Rochester, NY*]
**ItPavU** ....... Universita degli Studi, Pavia, Italy [*Library symbol*] [*Library of Congress*] (LCLS)
**ITPB** .......... Integrated Test Program Board
**ITPC** .......... International Television Program Center [*Telecommunications*] (TEL)
**ITPFF** ........ Interstate Transportation of Prize Fight Films
**ITPI** ........... International Thomson Publishing, Incorporated [*Also, ITP*]
**ITPI** ........... International Transfer Printing Institute (EA)
**ITP-ID** ....... International Thomson Publishing - International Division
**ITpM** ......... Tinley Park Mental Health Center, Tinley Park, IL [*Library symbol*] [*Library of Congress*] (LCLS)
**ITPMG** ...... Interstate Transportation of Prison-Made Goods
**ITPO** .......... International TOGA [*Tropical Ocean Global Atmosphere*] Project Office [*Geneva, Switzerland*] (EAIO)
**ITPP** .......... Individual Training Plan Proposal [*Army*]
**ITPP** .......... International Thomson Professional Publishing
**ITPR** .......... Infrared Temperature Profile Radiometer
**ITPR** .......... Inuit Tapirisat of Canada. Press Release [*A publication*]
**ITPRL** ........ Individual Training and Performance Research Laboratory [*Army*] (RDA)
**ITPS** .......... Institute for Theological and Philosophical Studies (EA)
**ITPS** .......... Integrated Teleprocessing System (IEEE)
**ITPS** .......... Internal Teleprocessing System (CMD)
**ITPS** .......... International Thomson Publishing Services
**ITPSB** ........ IEEE. Transactions on Plasma Science [*A publication*]
**ITPTBG** ..... Interpretation [*A publication*]
**ITPX** .......... Inteleplex Corp. [*NASDAQ symbol*] (NQ)
**ITQ** ............ Infant Temperament Questionnaire
**ITQ** ............ International Thesaurus of Quotations [*A publication*]
**ITQ** ............ Invitation to Quote (MCD)
**ITQ** ............ Irish Theological Quarterly [*A publication*]
**ItQ** ............ Italian Quarterly [*A publication*]
**ITR** ............ Australian Income Tax Reports [*A publication*] (DLA)
**ITR** ............ Ignition Test Reactor (MCD)
**IT-R** .......... Immunotoxin with Ricin
**ITR** ............ Improved Tartar Retrofit [*Missile*] (MCD)
**ITR** ............ In-Core Thermionic Reactor [*Nuclear energy*]
**ITR** ............ In-Transit Rendezvous
**ITR** ............ Income Tax Reports [*India*] [*A publication*] (DLA)
**ITR** ............ Incremental Tape Recorder
**ITR** ............ Indian Tax Reports [*A publication*] (ILCA)
**ITR** ............ Industrial Target Report [*Later, IDR*] [*British*] [*World War II*]
**ITR** ............ Industrial Tribunal Reports (DCTA)
**ITR** ............ Infantry Training Regiment [*Marine Corps*]
**ITR** ............ Infantry Training Replacement
**ITR** ............ Information Technology Research [*Waltham, MA*] [*Telecommunications*] (TSSD)
**ITR** ............ Initial Training Requirement
**ITR** ............ Inlet Temperature Rise
**ITR** ............ Inspection Test Report
**ITR** ............ Instrument Test Rig [*Liquid Metal Engineering Center*] [*Energy Research and Development Administration*] (IEEE)
**ITR** ............ Instrumentation Tape Recorder
**ITR** ............ Instrumented Test Range [*Fort Huachuca, AZ*] [*United States Army Electronic Proving Ground*] (GRD)
**ITR** ............ Integrated Technology Rotor
**ITR** ............ Integrated Telephone Recorder [*Telecommunications*] (TEL)
**ITR** ............ Integrated Test Requirements
**ITR** ............ Intense Thermal Radiation
**ITR** ............ Interim Technical Report
**ITR** ............ Interim Test Report
**ITR** ............ Internal Technical Report
**ITR** ............ International Trade Reporter [*A publication*]
**ITR** ............ Intraocular Tension Recorder
**ITR** ............ Intratracheal [*Medicine*]
**IT/R** .......... Inventory Transfer Receipt
**ITR** ............ Inverse Time Relay (KSC)
**ITR** ............ Inverted Terminal Repeat [*Genetics*]
**ITR** ............ Invitation to Register (ADA)
**ITR** ............ Irish Term Reports, by Ridgeway, Lapp, and Schoales [*A publication*] (DLA)
**ITR** ............ ITR Airlines, Inc. D/B/A Frontier Commuter [*Denver, CO*] [*FAA designator*] (FAAC)
**ITRA** .......... Integrated Test Requirements Analysis (CAAL)
**ITRA** .......... International Truck Restorers Association (EA)
**ITRB** .......... Interservice Training Review Board (MCD)
**ItRC** ........... Consiglio Nazionale delle Ricerche, Rome, Italy [*Library symbol*] [*Library of Congress*] (LCLS)
**ITRC** .......... International Technology Resources, Inc. [*NASDAQ symbol*] (NQ)
**ITRC** .......... International Tin Research Council [*Middlesex, England*] (EAIO)
**ITRCDB** .... Interciencia [*A publication*]
**ITRD** .......... Integrated Test Requirements Documents (MCD)
**ITRDB** ........ International Tree-Ring Data Bank [*University of Arizona*] (IID)
**ITRDS** ........ Integrated Test Requirements Documents (MCD)
**ITRE** .......... Institute for Transportation Research and Education [*University of North Carolina*] [*Research center*] (RCD)
**ITre** ............ Trenton Public Library, Trenton, IL [*Library symbol*] [*Library of Congress*] (LCLS)
**ITreWHS** .. Weslin Junior-Senior High School, Trenton, IL [*Library symbol*] [*Library of Congress*] (LCLS)
**ITRI** ........... Inhalation Toxicology Research Institute [*Albuquerque, NM*] [*Department of Energy*]
**ITRI** ........... International Tin Research Institute (EAIO)
**ITRIA** ........ Instrument Tree Removable Instrument Assembly [*Nuclear energy*] (NRCH)
**ITRID** ........ Itogi Nauki i Tekhniki Razrabotka Mestorozhdenii Tverdykh Poleznykh Iskopaemykh [*A publication*]
**ITRIS** ......... International Trade and Resource Information System [*University of Alaska at Anchorage*] [*Information service or system*] (CRD)
**ITRJDW** ... International Tree Crops Journal [*A publication*]
**ITRL** .......... Instrument Test Repair Laboratory (AAG)
**ITRM** ......... Inverse Thermoremanent Magnetization
**ITRMB5** ..... Conseil Scientifique International de Recherches sur les Trypanosomiases [*A publication*]
**ITRN** ......... Intertrans Corp. [*NASDAQ symbol*] (NQ)
**ITRO** ......... Installation Test Requirements Outline (MCD)
**ITRO** ......... Integrated Test Requirements Outline
**ITRO** ......... Interservice Training Review Organization [*Military*] (NVT)
**ITro** .......... Tri-Township Library, Troy, IL [*Library symbol*] [*Library of Congress*] (LCLS)
**ITRP** .......... Institute of Transportation and Regional Planning (EA)
**ITRPF** ........ International Tyre, Rubber, and Plastic Federation (EAIO)
**ItRU** .......... Universita degli Studi, Biblioteca Alessandrina, Rome, Italy [*Library symbol*] [*Library of Congress*] (LCLS)
**IT Rulings** ... Income Tax Rulings [*A publication*]
**ITRY** .......... Itinerary (FAAC)
**ITS** ............ Idaho Test Station [*Nuclear energy*] (NRCH)
**ITS** ............ Idle Tracking Switch [*Automotive engineering*]
**ITS** ............ IEEE Information Theory Society (EA)

**ITS**............ Ignition Test Simulator
**ITS**............ Imaginary Transition Structure [*Organic chemistry*]
**ITS**............ Improved Third Stage [*of Minuteman rocket*]
**ITS**............ In-Tank Solidification
**ITS**............ Incident Tracking System
**ITS**............ Inclusive Tour Service (ADA)
**ITS**............ Independent Triggering System
**ITS**............ Indus Tsangpo Suture [*Paleogeography*]
**ITS**............ Industrial Technology Securities [*Investment firm*] [*British*]
**ITS**............ Industrial Television Society [*Later, ITVA*] (EA)
**ITS**............ Infinite Time Span
**ITS**............ Information Technology Services [*California State University, Long Beach*] [*Research center*] (RCD)
**ITS**............ Information Technology Services [*National Library of Canada*] (TSSD)
**ITS**............ Information Technology Services [*Stanford University*] [*California*] [*Information service or system*] (IID)
**ITS**............ Information Technology Systems
**ITS**............ Information Transfer Satellite (KSC)
**ITS**............ Information Transfer [*or Transmission*] System
**ITS**............ Infrared Tracking System
**ITS**............ Initial Training School [*British military*] (DMA)
**ITS**............ Insertion Test Signal [*Telecommunications*] (TEL)
**ITS**............ Institute for Telecommunication Sciences [*Formerly, ITSA*] [*Boulder, CO*] [*Department of Commerce*]
**ITS**............ Institute of Telecommunications Services (MSC)
**ITS**............ Institute of Temporary Services [*Later, National Association of Temporary Services*] (EA)
**ITS**............ Institute of Theoretical Science [*University of Oregon*] [*Research center*] (RCD)
**ITS**............ Institute of Transportation Studies [*University of California*] [*Research center*] (RCD)
**ITS**............ Institute for Transportation Studies [*University of Calgary*] [*Canada*] [*Research center*] (RCD)
**ITS**............ Institute of Turkish Studies (EA)
**ITS**............ Instrument Time (Simulated)
**ITS**............ Instrumentation Telemetry Station [*NASA*] (NASA)
**ITS**............ Insulation Test Specification (MSA)
**ITS**............ Integrated Target System
**ITS**............ Integrated Test Schedule [*Army*]
**ITS**............ Integrated Test Software (CAAL)
**ITS**............ Integrated Tracking System [*Obsolete*] [*ARTRAC*] (MCD)
**ITS**............ Integrated Trajectory System
**ITS**............ Intelligent Terminal System [*IBM Corp.*]
**ITS**............ Interactive Terminal Support [*Data processing*]
**ITS**............ Interim Teleprinter System
**ITS**............ Intermarket Trading System (IEEE)
**ITS**............ Intermediate Tape Store (CET)
**ITS**............ International Technogeographical Society
**ITS**............ International Telecom Systems, Inc. [*Madison, WI*] [*Telecommunications*] (TSSD)
**ITS**............ International Teleproduction Society (EA)
**ITS**............ International Television Service [*Turner Teleport, Inc.*] [*Atlanta, GA*] [*Telecommunications service*] (TSSD)
**ITS**............ International Temperature Scale (MUGU)
**ITS**............ International Tesla Society (EA)
**ITS**............ International Thespian Society (EA)
**ITS**............ International Tracing Service [*Arolsen, Federal Republic of Germany*] (EAIO)
**ITS**............ International Trade Secretariats [*ICFTU*]
**ITS**............ International Training School
**ITS**............ International Travel Show (ITD)
**ITS**............ International Trucking Show (ITD)
**ITS**............ International Turfgrass Society (EA)
**ITS**............ International Twin Study [*University of Southern California*] [*Research center*] (RCD)
**ITS**............ Intersectional Transportation Service
**ITS**............ Interstate Energy [*Vancouver Stock Exchange symbol*]
**ITS**............ Intertime Switch [*Connection or Call*] [*Telecommunications*] (TEL)
**ITS**............ Invitation to Send [*Western Union*] [*Data communications*]
**ITS**............ Ion Thrust System
**ITS**............ Ion Trap System
**ITS**............ Iowa Transfer System
**ITS**............ Irish Texts Society (EAIO)
**ITS**............ Tri-State University, Angola, IN [*OCLC symbol*] (OCLC)
**ITSA**.......... Insider Trading Sanctions Act of 1984
**ITSA**.......... Installation and Test Support Associate Contractor [*Air Force*]
**ITSA**.......... Institute for Telecommunication Sciences and Aeronomy [*Later, ITS*] [*National Oceanic and Atmospheric Administration*]
**ITSA**.......... Institute of Trading Standards Administration [*British*]
**ITSA**.......... Interstate Transportation of Stolen Aircraft
**ITSAADCOTFOIK**... International Twelve-Star Admiral and Deputy Custodian of the Fountain of Inexhaustible Knowledge [*Rank in Junior Woodchucks organization mentioned in Donald Duck comic by Carl Barks*]
**ITSB**.......... Interstate Transportation of Strikebreakers
**ITSC**.......... Industrial Training Systems Corporation [*Marlton, NJ*] [*NASDAQ symbol*] (NQ)
**ITSC**.......... Information Technology Steering Committee [*Australia*]
**ITSC**.......... International Telecommunications Satellite Consortium [*Superseded by International Telecommunications Satellite Organization*]
**ITSC**.......... International Telephone Services Center [*Telecommunications*] (TEL)
**ITSC**.......... Interstate Transportation of Stolen Cattle
**ITSC**.......... It Scale for Children [*Psychology*]
**ITSDC**....... Interagency Toxic Substances Data Committee [*Washington, DC*] [*Environmental Protection Agency*] (EGAO)
**ITSI**.......... International Totalizator Systems, Incorporated [*NASDAQ symbol*] (NQ)
**ITSL**.......... Integrated Two-Step Liquefaction [*Chemical engineering*]
**ITSMA**...... Ispol'zovanie Tverdykh Topliv Sernistykh Mazutov i Gaza [*A publication*]
**ITSMV**...... Interstate Transportation of Stolen Motor Vehicle
**ITSO**.......... Instrument Technician Service Organization
**ITSOD**....... Itogi Nauki i Tekhniki Seriya Okeanologiya [*A publication*]
**IT/SP**......... Instrument Tree/Spool Piece [*Nuclear energy*] (NRCH)
**ITSP**.......... Integrated Training System Plan [*Army*]
**ITSP**.......... Interstate Transportation of Stolen Property
**ITSS**.......... Integrated Tactical Surveillance System
**ITSS**.......... Investment Trust Savings Scheme [*British*]
**ITSYLF**..... Interactive Synthesizer of Letterforms
**ITT**............ Federal Reserve Bank of Chicago Library, Chicago, IL [*OCLC symbol*] (OCLC)
**I & TT**........ Ike and Tina Turner [*Singers*]
**ITT**............ Image Intensification Tube (MCD)
**ITT**............ In These Times [*A publication*]
**ITT**............ Incoming Teletype
**ITT**............ Indicator Time Test [*Chemistry*]
**ITT**............ Individual Technical Training [*Military*]
**ITT**............ Inside Trim Template (MSA)
**ITT**............ Institute of Textile Technology (EA)
**ITT**............ Insulin Tolerance Test [*Physiology*]
**ITT**............ Inter-Theater Transfer [*Army*] (AABC)
**ITT**............ Inter-Turbine Temperature (ADA)
**IT and T**..... International Telephone & Telegraph Corp. [*New York, NY*]
**ITT**............ International Trade in Textiles [*Textile trade agreement*]
**ITT**............ Interrogation-Translation Team [*Military*] (CINC)
**ITT**............ Intertoll Trunk [*Telecommunications*]
**ITT**............ Intertype Training [*Navy*] (NVT)
**ITT**............ Inventaire des Tablettes de Tello. Mission Française en Chaldée [*Paris*] [*A publication*] (BJA)
**ITT**............ ITT Canada Ltd. [*Toronto Stock Exchange symbol*]
**ITT**............ ITT Corp. [*Formerly, International Telephone & Telegraph Corp.*] [*NYSE symbol*] [*Wall Street slang name: "It Girl," the sobriquet for early movie star Clara Bow*] (SPSG)
**ITTAC**....... International Telegraph and Telephonic Advisory Committee (AABC)
**ITTC**.......... Inter-American Tropical Tuna Commission [*Scripps Institution of Oceanography*]
**ITTC**.......... International Travel and Trailer Club (EA)
**ITTCCS**..... ITT Corporate Communications Services, Inc.
**ITTCOM**... International Telephone & Telegraph World Communications, Inc.
**ITTCS**........ International Telephone and Telegraph Communication System
**ITTD**.......... Information and Technology Transfer Database [*International Research and Evaluation*]
**ITTE**.......... Institute for the Transfer of Technology to Education (EA)
**ITTE**.......... Institute of Transportation and Traffic Engineering [*UCLA*]
**ITTE**.......... Interim Terminal Test Environment [*FAA*]
**ITTETS**..... ITT Employment & Training Systems, Inc. [*Telecommunications service*] (TSSD)
**ITTF**.......... International Table Tennis Federation [*Great Britain*]
**ITTF**.......... International Telephone and Telegraph Federal Laboratories
**ITTFA**....... Iterative Target Transformation Factor Analysis [*Data processing*]
**ITTFL**........ International Telephone and Telegraph Federal Laboratories
**ITTL**.......... International Table Tennis League (EA)
**ITTO**.......... International Tropical Timber Organization [*Yokohama, Japan*] [*United Nations*]
**IT & TS**...... International Turtle and Tortoise Society (EA)
**ITTT**.......... Individual Tactical Technical Training [*Military*] (MCD)
**ITTT**.......... Institute of Transportation, Travel, and Tourism
**ITTTA**....... International Technical Tropical Timber Association
**ItTU**.......... Biblioteca Nazional Universitaria di Torino, Servizio Prestito, Turin, Italy [*Library symbol*] [*Library of Congress*] (LCLS)
**ITT-USTS**... ITT United States Transmission Systems, Inc. [*Telecommunications service*] (TSSD)
**ITU**............ Income Tax Unit
**ITU**............ International Taurus Resources [*Vancouver Stock Exchange symbol*]
**ITU**............ International Telecommunication Union [*Formerly, International Telegraphic Union*] [*A specialized agency of the United Nations*] [*Switzerland*] [*Research center*]
**ITU**............ International Temperance Union
**ITU**............ International Typographical Union (EA)
**ITU**............ Inventory Temporarily in Use [*Army*] (AFIT)
**ITU**............ Investment Trust Unit [*British*]
**ITU**............ Taylor University, Upland, IN [*OCLC symbol*] (OCLC)

**ITu** ............ Tuscola Public Library, Tuscola, IL [*Library symbol*] [*Library of Congress*] (LCLS)
**ITUA** ......... Independent Trade Union Association [*Turkey*]
**ITUC**.......... Irish Trade Union Congress
**ITuCoH** ..... Douglas County Jarman Memorial Hospital, Tuscola, IL [*Library symbol*] [*Library of Congress*] (LCLS)
**ITUCSTL**.. International Trade Unions Committee of Social Tourism and Leisure [*See also CSITSL*] [*Prague, Czechoslovakia*] (EAIO)
**ITUFA** ....... Izvestiya Akademii Nauk Turkmenskoi SSR Seriya Fiziko-Tekhnicheskikh, Khimicheskikh, i Geologicheskikh Nauk [*A publication*]
**ITUG** ......... Information Technology Users Group [*Exxon Corp.*]
**ITUG** ......... International Tandem Users' Group (EA)
**ITUR** ......... Interstate Transportation of Unsafe Refrigerators
**ITURM**...... International Typographical Union Ruling Machine
**ITUS**.......... Institute of Totally Useless Skills [*An association*] (EA)
**ITUSA**........ Information Technology Users' Standards Association
**ITUSAF**..... Institute of Technology, United States Air Force [*Wright-Patterson Air Force Base, Dayton, OH*] (AAG)
**ITUSFP**..... Interreligious Taskforce on US Food Policy (EA)
**ITV**............ Improved TOW [*Tube-Launched, Optically Tracked, Wire-Guided (Weapon)*] Vehicle
**ITV**............ Independent Television
**ITV**............ Industrial Television
**ITV**............ Instructional Television
**ITV**............ Instrumental Test Vehicle
**ITV**............ Integrated Technology Validation
**ITV**............ Intermediate Test Vessel (NRCH)
**ITV**............ Israel Television (BJA)
**ItV**............ Italian RCA [*Victor*] [*Record label*]
**ITVA**......... International Television Association (EA)
**ITVAC**....... Industrial Transistor Value Automatic Computer
**ITVB**.......... International Television Broadcasting
**ITVETS**..... Improved TOW [*Tube-Launched, Optically Tracked, Wire-Guided (Weapon)*] Vehicle Evasive Target Simulator [*Military*] (MCD)
**ITvhR**......... Indisch Tijdschrift van het Recht [*A publication*]
**ItVox**.......... Italian Vox [*Record label*]
**ITVSDA**.... Independent Television Service Dealers' Association
**ITVTP**....... Internationale Tieraerztliche Vereinigung fuer Tierproduktion [*International Veterinary Association for Animal Production*]
**ITW**........... Illinois Tool Works, Inc. [*NYSE symbol*] (SPSG)
**ITW**........... Independent Tank Wing [*of a ship*] (DS)
**ITW**........... Independent True Whig Party [*Political party*] [*Liberia*]
**ITW**........... Initial Training Wing [*British military*] (DMA)
**ITW**........... Introducing the World [*An association*] [*Canada*]
**ITWA**......... International Tug-of-War Association (EA)
**ITWC**......... Inland Transport War Council [*World War II*]
**ITWF**......... International Transport Workers' Federation
**ITWG**......... Interface Technical Working Group
**ITWI**.......... Interstate Transmission of Wagering Information
**ITWP**......... Interstate Transportation of Wagering Paraphernalia
**ITX**............ Inclusive Tour Excursion [*Airline fare*]
**ITX**............ Independent Tank Common [*of a ship*] (DS)
**ITX**............ International Technology Corp. [*NYSE symbol*] (SPSG)
**ITX**............ International Tillex Enterprises Ltd. [*Vancouver Stock Exchange symbol*]
**ITXI**........... Interactive Technologies, Incorporated [*North St. Paul, MN*] [*NASDAQ symbol*] (NQ)
**ITXPA9**..... Estacion Experimental Agropecuaria Pergamino. Publicacion Tecnico [*A publication*]
**ITXPA9**..... INTA [*Instituto Nacional de Tecnologia Agropecuaria*]. Estacion Experimental Regional Agropecuaria [*Pergamino*]. Publicacion Tecnica [*A publication*]
**ITY**............ Fort Riley, KS [*Location identifier*] [*FAA*] (FAAL)
**ITY**............ Information Technology Year [*1982*]
**ITY**............ Intensity Resources Ltd. [*Toronto Stock Exchange symbol*]
**Ity**............. Interchangeability
**ITY**............ International Tourist Year
**ITZ**............ Inter-Tropical Convergence Zone
**IU**.............. Identification Unit (MSA)
**IU**.............. Immunizing Unit [*Medicine*]
**IU**.............. Impedance Unit (MCD)
**IU**.............. In Utero [*Gynecology*]
**IU**.............. Indiana University
**IU**.............. Indianapolis Union [*AAR code*]
**IU**.............. Infectious Unit
**IU**.............. Information Unit
**IU**.............. Information Unlimited [*Information service or system*] (IID)
**IU**.............. Input Unit
**IU**.............. Instant Update [*Professional Farmers of America*] [*Information service or system*] (TSSD)
**IU**.............. Instruction Unit [*Data processing*]
**IU**.............. Instrument Unit [*NASA*]
**IU**.............. Integer Unit [*Data processing*]
**IU**.............. Interface Unit [*Data processing*] (MCD)
**IU**.............. Interference Unit [*Military*]
**IU**.............. Interlingue Union
**IU**.............. International Caribbean Tourist, Inc. [*Netherlands*] [*ICAO designator*] (FAAC)
**IU**.............. International Unit
**IU**.............. Interval of Uncertainty [*Psychology*]
**IU**.............. Intrauterine [*Medicine*]
**iu**............... Israel-Syria Demilitarized Zones [*is (Israel) used in records cataloged after January 1978*] [*MARC country of publication code*] [*Library of Congress*] (LCCP)
**IU**.............. IU International Corp. [*NYSE symbol*] [*Toronto Stock Exchange symbol*] [*Vancouver Stock Exchange symbol*] (SPSG)
**IU**.............. Izquierda Unida [*United Left*] [*Peru*] [*Political party*]
**IU**.............. University of Illinois, Urbana, IL [*Library symbol*] [*Library of Congress*] (LCLS)
**IUA**........... Individual Unit Action Model
**IUA**........... Inertial Unit Assembly
**IUA**........... Inter-American University Association
**IUA**........... Interface Unit Adapter [*Data processing*] (MCD)
**IUA**........... Interlibrary Users Association [*University of Maryland*] [*College Park, MD*] [*Library network*]
**IUA**........... International Union of Academies (EA)
**IUA**........... International Union of Architects
**IUA**........... IOMEC Users Association [*Formerly, DUA*] [*Defunct*] (EA)
**IUA**........... University of Texas at Arlington, Arlington, TX [*OCLC symbol*] (OCLC)
**IUAA**......... International Union of Advertisers Associations [*Later, WFA*] (EAIO)
**IUAA**......... International Union of Alpine Associations
**IUACE**....... Indian University Association for Continuing Education
**IUADM**..... International Union of Associations of Doctor-Motorists
**IUAES**....... International Union of Anthropological and Ethnological Sciences [*See also UISAE*] [*ICSU*] [*Gwynedd, Wales*] (EAIO)
**IUAI**.......... International Union of Aviation Insurers [*London, England*] (EAIO)
**IUAJ**.......... International Union of Agricultural Journalists
**IU/AL**........ Anthropological Linguistics; a Publication of the Archives of the Languages of the World. Indiana University. Anthropology Department [*A publication*]
**IUAM**........ Islamic Unity of Afghan Mujahadeen [*Political party*] [*Afghanistan*]
**IUANPW**.. International Union of Allied Novelty and Production Workers (EA)
**IUAO**......... Internationalen Union fuer Angewandte Ornithologie [*International Union for Applied Ornithology*] (EAIO)
**IUAPPA**.... International Union of Air Pollution Prevention Associations [*See also UIAPPA*] [*England*] (EAIO)
**IUAR**......... Institute for Urban Affairs and Research [*Howard University*] [*Research center*] (RCD)
**IU-Ar**......... University of Illinois, Archives, Urbana, IL [*Library symbol*] [*Library of Congress*] (LCLS)
**IUAT**......... International Union Against Tuberculosis [*Later, IUATLD*] (EAIO)
**IUATLD**.... International Union Against Tuberculosis and Lung Disease [*See also UICTMR*] (EAIO)
**IUB**........... Baltimore, MD [*Location identifier*] [*FAA*] (FAAL)
**IUB**........... Indiana University Bookman [*A publication*]
**IUB**........... Indiana University, School of Law Library, Bloomington, IN [*OCLC symbol*] (OCLC)
**IUB**........... International Union of Biochemistry (EA)
**IUB**........... International Universities Bureau
**IU-B**.......... University of Illinois, Biology Library, Urbana, IL [*Library symbol*] [*Library of Congress*] (LCLS)
**IUB (Int Union Biochem) Symp Ser** ... IUB (International Union of Biochemistry) Symposium Series [*A publication*]
**IUBS**.......... International Union of Biological Sciences [*Paris, France*]
**IUBSSA**..... International Union of Building Societies and Savings Associations [*Chicago, IL*] [*Later, IOHFI*] (EA)
**IUC**........... Association for Higher Education, Dallas, TX [*OCLC symbol*] (OCLC)
**IUC**........... Idiopathic Ulcerative Colitis [*Medicine*]
**IUC**........... Immediate Unit Commander [*Navy*] (NVT)
**IUC**........... Instructor Utilization Course (MCD)
**IUC**........... Inter-University Committee for Debate on Foreign Policy [*Defunct*]
**IUC**........... Inter-University Council
**IUC**........... International Underwater Contractors, Inc.
**IUC**........... International Union of Crystallography
**IUC**........... International University of Communication [*Washington, DC*]
**IUC**........... International University Consortium for Telecommunications in Learning [*Later, IUC*] (EA)
**IUC**........... International University Contact for Management Education
**IUCADC**.... Inter-Union Commission of Advice to Developing Countries [*of the International Union of Geodesy and Geophysics*] [*Mississauga, ON*] (EAIO)
**IUCAF**....... Inter-Union Commission on Frequency Allocations for Radio Astronomy and Space Science (EA)
**IUCC Bull** ... IUCC [*Inter-University Committee on Computing*] Bulletin [*A publication*]
**IUCC Newsl** ... IUCC [*Inter-University Committee on Computing*] Newsletter [*A publication*]

**IUCD**......... Intrauterine Contraceptive Device [*Medicine*]
**IUCED**....... Inter-Union Commission of European Dehydrators [*See also CIDE*] [*Paris, France*] (EAIO)
**IUCESD**.... Inter-American University Council for Economic and Social Development (EA)
**IUCF**.......... Indiana University Cyclotron Facility [*Research center*] (RCD)
**IUCFA**....... Inter-Union Commission on Frequency Allocations for Radio Astronomy and Space Science (EA)
**IUCI**........... Inter-University Committee on Israel [*Later, America-Israel Cultural Foundation*] (EA)
**IUCME**...... International University Contact for Management Education
**IUCN**......... International Union for Conservation of Nature and Natural Resources (EA)
**IUCN**......... International Union for Conservation of Nature and Natural Resources. Technical Meeting [*A publication*]
**IUCN Bull** ... IUCN [*International Union for Conservation of Nature and Natural Resources*] Bulletin [*A publication*]
**IUCNNR** ... International Union for Conservation of Nature and Natural Resources [*Research center*] [*ICSU*] [*Switzerland*]
**IUCNPSG** ... International Union for the Conservation of Nature's Primate Specialist Group (EA)
**IUCN Publ New Ser** ... IUCN [*International Union for Conservation of Nature and Natural Resources*] Publications. New Series [*A publication*]
**IUCN Yearb** ... IUCN [*International Union for Conservation of Nature and Natural Resources*] Yearbook [*A publication*]
**IUCO**......... Irwin Union Corporation [*Columbus, IN*] [*NASDAQ symbol*] (NQ)
**IU Cr**.......... International Union of Crystallography [*See also UIC*] (EA)
**IUCRC**....... Industry/University Cooperation Research Center [*National Science Foundation*]
**IUCRCB**.... Inter-University Committee for Research on Consumer Behavior (EA)
**IUCS**......... Instrumentation Unit Update Command System [*NASA*] (NASA)
**IUCSTP**..... Inter-Union Commission on Solar-Terrestrial Physics (MCD)
**IUCTG**....... Inter-University Committee on Travel Grants
**IUCW**........ International Union for Child Welfare [*Geneva, Switzerland*]
**IUD**........... Indiana University, School of Dentistry, Indianapolis, IN [*OCLC symbol*] (OCLC)
**IUD**........... Industrial Union Department [*of AFL-CIO*] (EA)
**IUD**........... Institute for Urban Design (EA)
**IUD**........... Institute for Urban Development
**IUD**........... Intrauterine Death [*Medicine*]
**IUD**........... Intrauterine Device [*A contraceptive*] [*Medicine*]
**IUDH**......... In-Service Unplanned Derated Hours [*Electronics*] (IEEE)
**IUdR**.......... Iodouracildeoxyriboside [*Biochemistry*]
**IUDZG**...... International Union of Directors of Zoological Gardens (EAIO)
**IUE**........... Interface Unit Error Count Table (MCD)
**IUE**........... International Thunderwood Explorations Ltd. [*Vancouver Stock Exchange symbol*] [*Toronto Stock Exchange symbol*]
**IUE**........... International Ultraviolet Explorer [*NASA*]
**IUE**........... International Union of Electrical, Radio, and Machine Workers
**IUE**........... International Union for Electroheat [*Also, IUE-H*]
**IUE**........... International Union of Electronic, Electrical, Technical, Salaried, Machine, and Furniture Workers (EA)
**IUE**........... Niue Island [*Niue*] [*Airport symbol*] (OAG)
**IUE**........... University of Evansville, Evansville, IN [*OCLC symbol*] (OCLC)
**IUEC**......... International Union of Elevator Constructors (EA)
**IUEF**......... Internacia Unuigo de la Esperantistoj-Filologoj [*International Union of Esperantist-Philologists - IUEP*] [*Sofia, Bulgaria*] (EAIO)
**IUEFI**........ Internacia Unuigo de la Esperantistoj-Filologoj [*International Union of Esperantist-Philologists - IUEP*] (EA)
**IUEGS**....... International Union of European Guides and Scouts [*See also UIGSE*] [*Chateau Landon, France*] (EAIO)
**IUE-H**........ International Union for Electroheat [*Also, IUE*]
**IUEP**......... International Union of Esperantist-Philologists (EAIO)
**IUEW**........ International Union of Electrical Workers
**IUF**........... Interamerican Underwater Festival
**IUF**........... International Unicycling Federation (EA)
**IUF**........... International Union of Food and Allied Workers' Associations [*See also IUL*] [*Petit-Lancy, Switzerland*] (EAIO)
**IUF**........... International University Foundation (EA)
**IUF**........... Southern Methodist University, Law Library, Dallas, TX [*OCLC symbol*] (OCLC)
**IUFB**......... Intrauterine Foreign Body [*Gynecology*]
**IUFDT**....... International Union of Food, Drink, and Tobacco Workers' Associations
**IUFLJP**..... International Union of French-Language Journalists and Press [*See also UIJPLF*] [*Paris, France*] (EAIO)
**IUFO**......... International Union of Family Organizations [*Paris, France*]
**IUFoST**...... International Union of Food Science and Technology [*ICSU*] [*Australia*] (EAIO)
**IUFRO**....... International Union of Forestry Research Organizations [*Research center*] [*Vienna, Austria*] (EAIO)
**IUFS**......... Indiana University. Folklore Series [*A publication*]
**Iug**........... Bellum Iugurthinum [*of Sallust*] [*Classical studies*] (OCD)
**IUG**........... ICES [*Integrated Civil Engineering System*] Users Group (EA)
**IUG**........... Intercomm Users' Group (EA)
**IUGB**......... International Union of Game Biologists [*Krakow, Poland*] (EAIO)
**IUGG**......... International Union of Geodesy and Geophysics [*Brussels, Belgium*]
**IUGG Chron** ... IUGG [*International Union of Geodesy and Geophysics*] Chronicle [*A publication*]
**IUGG Newsl** ... International Union of Geodesy and Geophysics. Newsletter [*A publication*]
**IUGM**........ International Union of Gospel Missions (EA)
**Iugosl Physiol Pharmacol Acta** ... Iugoslavica Physiologica Pharmacologica Acta [*A publication*]
**IUGR**......... Intrauterine Growth Retardation [*Medicine*]
**IUGRI**........ International Union of Graphic Reproduction Industries [*Later, IUI*] (EAIO)
**IUGS**......... International Union of Geological Sciences [*ICSU*] [*Trondheim, Norway*] (EA)
**IU-GS**........ University of Illinois, Illinois State Geological Survey, Urbana, IL [*Library symbol*] [*Library of Congress*] (LCLS)
**IUH**........... In Touch with the Dutch [*A publication*]
**IUH**........... Indiana University, School of Medicine, Health Library Cooperative, Indianapolis, IN [*OCLC symbol*] (OCLC)
**IUH**........... Instantaneous Unit Hydrograph
**IU-H**......... University of Illinois, School of Basic Medical Sciences, Library of Public Health Sciences, Urbana, IL [*Library symbol*] [*Library of Congress*] (LCLS)
**IUHE**......... International Union of Health Education [*See also UIES*] [*Paris, France*] (EAIO)
**IUHPS**....... International Union of the History and Philosophy of Science [*ICSU*] (EAIO)
**IUHR**......... International Union of Hotel, Restaurant, and Bar Workers
**IU-HS**........ Illinois Historical Survey, University of Illinois, Urbana, IL [*Library symbol*] [*Library of Congress*] (LCLS)
**IUHS**......... Indiana University. Humanities Series [*A publication*]
**IUI**............ Interim Use Item (MCD)
**IUI**............ Shawnee Library System, Carterville, IL [*OCLC symbol*] (OCLC)
**IUIN**......... International Union for Inland Navigation [*Strasbourg, France*] (EA)
**IUIS**.......... International Union of Immunological Societies (EA)
**IUJ**........... John Marshall Law School, Chicago, IL [*OCLC symbol*] (OCLC)
**IUJCD**....... Internationale Union Junger Christlicher Demokraten [*International Union of Young Christian Democrats*]
**IUJHUSC** ... International Union of Journeymen Horseshoers of the United States and Canada (EA)
**Iul**............ Divus Iulius [*of Suetonius*] [*Classical studies*] (OCD)
**IUL**........... Indian Unattached List [*British military*] (DMA)
**IUL**........... Indiana University, Bloomington, IN [*OCLC symbol*] (OCLC)
**IUL**........... Institute of Urban Life (EA)
**IU/L**.......... International Units per Liter
**IUL**........... Internationale Union der Lebens- und Genussmittelarbeiter-Gewerkschaften [*International Union of Food and Allied Workers Associations - IUF*] [*Petit-Lancy, Switzerland*] (EAIO)
**IU-L**.......... University of Illinois, Lincoln Room, Urbana, IL [*Library symbol*] [*Library of Congress*] (LCLS)
**IULA**......... International Union of Local Authorities [*The Hague, Netherlands*] (EA)
**IULC**......... Committee on Instruction in the Use of Libraries [*Later, CUILL*] (EA)
**IULC**......... Independent United Labor Congress [*Nigeria*]
**IULC-RAILS** ... Interuniversity Library Council: Reference and Interlibrary Loan Service [*Library network*]
**IULCS**....... International Union of Leather Chemists Societies
**IULCW**...... International Union of Liberal Christian Women
**IULD**......... International Union of Lorry Drivers [*See also UICR*] (EAIO)
**IULEC**....... Inter-University Labor Education Committee
**IULIA**........ International Union of Life Insurance Agents [*Milwaukee, WI*] (EA)
**IULS**......... Indiana Union List of Serials
**IU-LS**........ University of Illinois, Graduate School of Library Science, Urbana, IL [*Library symbol*] [*Library of Congress*] (LCLS)
**IULVTFT** ... International Union for Land Value Taxation and Free Trade [*London, England*] (EAIO)
**IUM**........... Honolulu, HI [*Location identifier*] [*FAA*] (FAAL)
**IUM**........... Indiana University, School of Medicine, Indianapolis, IN [*OCLC symbol*] (OCLC)
**IUM**........... Interim Use Material (MCD)
**IU-M**......... University of Illinois at the Medical Center, Chicago, IL [*Library symbol*] [*Library of Congress*] (LCLS)
**IUMA**........ Interim Use Material Authorization (MCD)
**IUMI**......... International Union of Marine Insurance [*Basel, Switzerland*]
**IUMMSW** ... International Union of Mine, Mill, and Smelter Workers [*Later, USWA*]
**IUMP**........ International Union of Master Painters [*See also UNIEP*] [*Brussels, Belgium*] (EAIO)
**IUMP**........ International Union of the Medical Press (DIT)
**IUMS**......... International Union of Microbiological Societies [*University of Newcastle*] (EA)

**IUMS**......... International Union for Moral and Social Action
**IUMSBD**... IUMS [*International Union of Microbiological Societies*] Bacteriology Division [*Beckenham, Kent, England*] (EAIO)
**IUMSWA** ... Industrial Union of Marine and Shipbuilding Workers of America (EA)
**IU-Mu**........ University of Illinois, Music Library, Urbana, IL [*Library symbol*] [*Library of Congress*] (LCLS)
**IUNA**......... Irish United Nations Association (EAIO)
**IUNDH** ..... In-Service Unit Derated Hours [*Electronics*] (IEEE)
**IU-Ne**......... University of Illinois at Urbana-Champaign, University of Illinois Newspaper Library, Urbana-Champaign, IL [*Library symbol*] [*Library of Congress*] (LCLS)
**IU-NH** ....... University of Illinois, Illinois Natural History Survey, Urbana, IL [*Library symbol*] [*Library of Congress*] (LCLS)
**IUNS** ......... International Union of Nutritional Sciences [*Wageningen, Netherlands*]
**IUNT** ......... Interservice Undergraduate Navigator Training
**IUO**........... ICG Utilities (Ontario) Ltd. [*Toronto Stock Exchange symbol*]
**IUOE**......... International Union of Operating Engineers (EA)
**IUOMWH** ... Independent United Order of Mechanics - Western Hemisphere (EA)
**IUOTO**...... International Union of Official Travel Organisations [*Later, WTO*]
**IUP** ............ Indiana University of Pennsylvania
**IUP** ............ Indiana University Press
**IUP** ............ Indiana University - Purdue University at Indianapolis, Indianapolis, IN [*OCLC symbol*] (OCLC)
**IUP** ............ Industrial Union Party (EA)
**IUP** ............ Installed User Program [*Data processing*]
**IUP** ............ International Union of Phlebology [*Paris, France*] (EA)
**IUP** ............ Intrauterine Pressure [*Gynecology*]
**IUP** ............ Irish University Press
**IUP** ............ Israel Universities Press
**IUPA** ......... International Union of Police Associations (EA)
**IUPA** ......... International Union of Practitioners in Advertising
**IUPAB**....... International Union of Pure and Applied Biophysics [*Research center*] [*ICSU*] [*Pecs, Hungary*] (EA)
**IUPAC**....... International Union of Pure and Applied Chemistry [*Research center*] [*ICSU*] [*Oxford, England*] (IRC)
**IUPAC Inf Bull** ... International Union of Pure and Applied Chemistry. Information Bulletin [*A publication*]
**IUPAC Inf Bull Append Provis Nomencl Symb Terminol Conv** ... International Union of Pure and Applied Chemistry. Information Bulletin. Appendices on Provisional Nomenclature, Symbols, Terminology, and Conventions [*A publication*]
**IUPAC Inf Bull Append Tentative Nomencl Symb Units Stand** ... International Union of Pure and Applied Chemistry. Information Bulletin. Appendices on Tentative Nomenclature, Symbols, Units, and Standards [*A publication*]
**IUPAL**....... Indiana University Publications. Anthropology and Linguistics [*A publication*]
**IUPAP**....... International Union of Pure and Applied Physics [*ICSU*] [*Goteborg, Sweden*] (EA)
**IUPESM** ... International Union for Physical and Engineering Sciences in Medicine [*ICSU*] [*Ottawa, ON*] (EAIO)
**IUPFS**........ Indiana University Publications. Folklore Series [*A publication*]
**IUPHAR** ... International Union of Pharmacology [*ICSU*] [*Buckingham, England*] (MSC)
**IUPHS**....... Indiana University Publications. Humanistic Series [*A publication*]
**IUPIW**....... International Union of Petroleum and Industrial Workers (EA)
**IUPLAW**... International Union for the Protection of Literary and Artistic Works
**IUPLSM** ... Indiana University Publications. Language Science Monographs [*A publication*]
**IUPM** ........ International Union for Protecting Public Morality [*Later, International Union for Moral and Social Action*]
**IUPN** ......... International Union for the Protection of Nature [*Later, IUCN*]
**IUPPE**....... Independent Union of Plant Protection Employees (EA)
**IUPPR**....... Institute for Urban and Public Policy Research [*University of Colorado - Denver*] [*Research center*] (RCD)
**IUPPS** ....... International Union of Prehistoric and Protohistoric Sciences [*Ghent, Belgium*] (EAIO)
**Iupp Trag**... Iuppiter Tragoedus [*of Lucian*] [*Classical studies*] (OCD)
**IUPS**.......... International Union of Psychological Science (EA)
**IUPSEES**.. Indiana University Publications. Slavic and East European Series [*A publication*]
**IUPsyS** ...... International Union of Psychological Science (EA)
**IUPT**.......... International Union of Public Transportation
**IUPUAS**.... Indiana University Publications. Uralic and Altaic Series [*A publication*]
**IUPUI**........ Indiana University - Purdue University at Indianapolis
**IUPW** ........ International Union of Petroleum Workers [*Later, IUPIW*] (EA)
**IUQ**............ Interrupted Ultraquick [*Flashing*] Light [*Navigation signal*]
**IUQ**............ Quaker Oats Co., Research Library, Barrington, IL [*OCLC symbol*] (OCLC)
**IUR** ............ Insured Unemployment Rate (OICC)
**IUR** ............ Inter-User Reliability
**IUR** ............ International UFO Reporter [*Center for Unidentified Flying Object Studies*] [*A publication*]
**IUR** ............ International Union of Radioecologists (EA)
**IUR** ............ International Union of Railways [*Paris*]
**IUR** ............ International Union Resources, Inc. [*Vancouver Stock Exchange symbol*]
**IUR** ............ Irish University Review [*A publication*]
**IU-R**........... University of Illinois, Rare Book Room, Urbana, IL [*Library symbol*] [*Library of Congress*] (LCLS)
**IUr** ............. Urbana Free Library, Urbana, IL [*Library symbol*] [*Library of Congress*] (LCLS)
**IURC** ......... International Underwater Research Corporation
**IURC** ......... International Union for Research of Communication [*Berne, Switzerland*] (EAIO)
**IURCAFL** ... Indiana University. Research Center in Anthropology, Folklore, and Linguistics [*A publication*]
**IUrCH** ....... Carle Foundation Hospital, Urbana, IL [*Library symbol*] [*Library of Congress*] (LCLS)
**IUrE-E**....... Educational Resources Information Center, Elementary and Early Childhood Education (ERIC/ECE), Urbana, IL [*Library symbol*] [*Library of Congress*] (LCLS)
**IUrE-NC**.... Educational Resources Information Center, National Council of Teachers of English, Urbana, IL [*Library symbol*] [*Library of Congress*] (LCLS)
**IURES**....... International Union of Reticuloendothelial Societies (EA)
**IUrG** .......... Illinois State Geological Survey, Urbana, IL [*Library symbol*] [*Library of Congress*] (LCLS)
**IURGRQR** ... Item Urgently Required [*Army*] (AFIT)
**IUrH** .......... Mercy Hospital, Urbana, IL [*Library symbol*] [*Library of Congress*] (LCLS)
**IURMS**...... International Union of Railway Medical Services (EA)
**IURP**.......... Integrated Unit Record Processor
**IURP**.......... International Union of Roofing and Plumbing (EAIO)
**IURS**.......... Institute of Urban and Regional Studies [*Washington University*] [*Research center*] (RCD)
**IURS**.......... International Union of Radio Science (MSC)
**IUrW** ......... Illinois State Water Survey, Urbana, IL [*Library symbol*] [*Library of Congress*] (LCLS)
**IUS** ............ Industrie [*A publication*]
**IUS** ............ Inertial [*formerly, Interim*] Upper Stage [*Air Force*]
**IUS** ............ Information Unit Separator [*Data processing*]
**IUS** ............ Initial Upper Stage [*NASA*]
**IUS** ............ Initial Upper State (IEEE)
**IUS** ............ Institute of Urban Studies, University of Winnipeg [*UTLAS symbol*]
**IUS** ............ Inter-University Seminar on Armed Forces and Society (EA)
**IUS** ............ Interchange Unit Separator [*Data processing*] (BUR)
**IUS** ............ Interim Upper Stage [*Missile*]
**IUS** ............ Interim Use Sheet (NASA)
**IUS** ............ Interior Upper Stage (NASA)
**IUS** ............ International Union of Speleology [*See also UIS*] [*Vienna, Austria*] (EAIO)
**IUS** ............ International Union of Students [*See also UIE*] [*Prague, Czechoslovakia*] (EAIO)
**IUSA**.......... International Underwater Spearfishing Association (EA)
**IUSA**.......... Interserve/USA [*An association*] (EA)
**IUSAMH** .. International Union of Societies for the Aid of Mental Health [*Bordeaux, France*] (EAIO)
**IUSB**.......... Indiana University at South Bend
**IUSB**.......... International Universities' Sports Board [*Defunct*] (EA)
**IUSDT**....... International Union of Socialist Democratic Teachers (EAIO)
**IUSF** .......... India-US Foundation (EA)
**IUSF** .......... International Union of Societies of Foresters [*See also UISIF*] [*Ottawa, ON*] (EAIO)
**IUSF** .......... International Union for Surface Finishing (EAIO)
**IUSHTL**.... Indiana University Studies in the History and Theory of Linguistics [*A publication*]
**IUSO** ......... International Union of Security Officers (EA)
**IUSRAV**.... Iowa State University. Statistical Laboratory. Annual Report [*A publication*]
**IUSS**.......... Integrated Undersea Surveillance System (MCD)
**IUSSI**......... International Union for the Study of Social Insects [*Utrecht, Netherlands*]
**IUSSP**........ International Union for the Scientific Study of Population [*Liege, Belgium*]
**IUSTFI**...... Institute on United States Taxation of Foreign Income [*Later, ITI*] (EA)
**IUSTOC**.... Independent US Tanker Owners Committee [*Inactive*] (EA)
**IUSUHM**.. International Union of School and University Health and Medicine [*See also UIHMSU*] [*Brussels, Belgium*] (EAIO)
**IUSY**.......... International Union of Socialist Youth
**IUT** ............ Industrial Unit of Tribology [*An association*] (EA)
**IUT** ............ Instructor Under Training [*Navy*] (NVT)
**IUT** ............ International Union of Tenants [*Stockholm, Sweden*] (EAIO)
**IUT** ............ Intrauterine Transfusion [*Gynecology*]
**IUt**............. Utica Public Library, Utica, IL [*Library symbol*] [*Library of Congress*] (LCLS)
**IUTAM** ..... International Union of Theoretical and Applied Mechanics [*Stuttgart, Federal Republic of Germany*]

**IUTCA**....... International Union of Technical Cinematograph Associations [*See also UNIATEC*] [*Paris, France*] (EAIO)
**IUTDM**..... International Union of Tool, Die, and Mold Makers (EA)
**IUTDMM**... International Union of Tool, Die, and Mold Makers (EA)
**IUTFAY**.... Istanbul Universitesi Tip Fakultesi Mecmuasi [*A publication*]
**IUTL**.......... Iowa Southern, Inc. [*Formerly, Iowa Southern Utilities*] [*NASDAQ symbol*] (NQ)
**IUUU**......... Industrial Unit, University of Ulster [*United Kingdom*] (IRUK)
**IUUW**........ International Union, United Welders [*Later, IUOE*]
**IUV**........... IATA [*International Air Transport Association*] Unit of Value [*International airline currency*]
**IU-V**........... University of Illinois, Veterinary Medicine Library, Urbana, IL [*Library symbol*] [*Library of Congress*] (LCLS)
**IUVDT**...... International Union Against Venereal Diseases and Treponematoses (EAIO)
**IUVSTA**.... International Union for Vacuum Science, Technique, and Applications [*See also UISTAV*] (EAIO)
**IUW**........... Inshore Undersea Warfare [*Navy*]
**IUWA**........ International Union of Women Architects [*See also UIFA*] [*Paris, France*] (EAIO)
**IUWC**........ Inshore Undersea Warfare Craft [*Navy*]
**IUWCC**...... Inshore Undersea Warfare Control Center [*Navy*] (NVT)
**IUWDS**...... International URSI [*Union Radio Scientifique Internationale*]-gram and World Day Service
**IUWG**........ Inshore Undersea Warfare Group [*Navy*]
**IU-WS**....... University of Illinois, Illinois State Water Survey, Champaign, IL [*Library symbol*] [*Library of Congrcss*] (LCLS)
**IUYCD**...... International Union of Young Christian Democrats [*Rome, Italy*]
**IV**.............. Der Israelitische Volkslehrer [*A publication*]
**IV**.............. Evans Public Library, Vandalia, IL [*Library symbol*] [*Library of Congress*] (LCLS)
**IV**.............. Iceland Veterans (EA)
**I & V**.......... Ideas y Valores [*A publication*]
**IV**.............. Illustrazione Vaticana [*A publication*]
**IV**.............. Improved Value (ADA)
**IV**.............. In Vapour (ROG)
**IV**.............. In Verbo [*Under the Word*] [*Latin*]
**IV**.............. In View
**IV**.............. Increased Value
**IV**.............. Induct Vent
**IV**.............. Initial Value
**IV**.............. Initial Velocity [*Ballistics*]
**I/V**............. Inlet Valve (MCD)
**IV**.............. Input Voltage
**IV**.............. Integrated Vehicle (MCD)
**IV**.............. Intensifier Vidicon
**IV**.............. Interface Volume (MCD)
**IV**.............. Intermediate Voltage (MSA)
**IV**.............. Interventricular [*Medicine*]
**IV**.............. Intervertebral [*or Intravertebral*] [*Medicine*]
**IV**.............. Intravascular [*Medicine*]
**IV**.............. Intravehicular (MCD)
**IV**.............. Intravenous [*Medicine*]
**IV**.............. Intraventricular [*Cardiology*]
**IV**.............. Inverted Vertical [*Aircraft engine*]
**IV**.............. Inverter
**IV**.............. Invoice Value [*Business term*]
**IV**.............. Iodine Value [*Analytical biochemistry*]
**IV**.............. Irish Viscount (ROG)
**IV**.............. Irish Volunteers [*British military*] (DMA)
**IV**.............. Istoritcheskii Viestnik [*A publication*]
**IV**.............. [*The*] Item You Requested Is Frozen for Inventory. It Will Be Processed and Shipped to You When the Inventory Is Completed [*Advice of supply action code*] [*Army*]
**iv**................ Ivory Coast [*MARC country of publication code*] [*Library of Congress*] (LCCP)
**IV**.............. Lineas Aereas Guinea Ecuatorial [*ICAO designator*] (FAAC)
**IV**.............. Mark IV Industries, Inc. [*NYSE symbol*] (SPSG)
**IVA**........... Ambanja [*Madagascar*] [*Airport symbol*] (OAG)
**IVA**........... Evansville-Vanderburgh School Corp., Evansville, IN [*OCLC symbol*] (OCLC)
**IVA**........... Imposta sul Valore Aggiunto [*Value-Added Tax*] [*Italian*]
**IVA**........... Impuesto al Valor Agregado [*Value-Added Tax*] [*Spanish*]
**IVA**........... Impuesto sobre el Valor Anadido [*Value-Added Tax*] [*Spanish*]
**IVA**........... Independent Voters Association [*Political organization in North Dakota, 1918-1932*]
**IVA**........... Industrial Veterinarians' Association [*Later, AAIV*] (EA)
**IVA**........... Inlet Vane Actuator
**IVA**........... Inspection Visual Aid (AAG)
**IVA**........... Integrated Vulnerability Assessment [*Military*]
**IVA**........... Interactive Video Association (EA)
**IVA**........... Intermediate Volitility Agents (MCD)
**IVA**........... International Volleyball Association [*Defunct*] (EA)
**IVA**........... International Voyage Alliance (EA)
**IVA**........... Internationale Vereinigung der Anschlussgeleise-Benuetzer [*International Association of Users of Private Sidings*]
**IVA**........... Internationaler Verband fuer Arbeiterbildung [*International Federation of Workers' Educational Associations - IFWEA*] (EAIO)
**IVA**........... Intravehicular Activity
**IVA**........... Inventory Valuation Adjustment [*Business term*]
**IVA**........... IVA [*Ingenjoersvetenskapsakademien*] och des Laboratorien [*A publication*]
**IVA**........... IVA [*Ingenjoersvetenskapsakademien*] Tidskrift foer Teknisk-Vetenskaplig Forskning [*A publication*]
**IVA**........... Ivac [*Intravenous monitor*] [*Medicine*] (DHSM)
**IVA**........... Ivaco, Inc. [*Toronto Stock Exchange symbol*]
**IVA**........... Jugobanka. Economic News [*A publication*]
**IVAAA**....... IVA [*Ingenjoersvetenskapsakademien*] Tidskrift foer Teknisk-Vetenskaplig Forskning [*A publication*]
**IVAAP**....... International Veterinary Association for Animal Production [*See also AIVPA*] [*Brussels, Belgium*] [*Research center*] (EAIO)
**IVAC**.......... Inland Vacuum Industries, Inc. [*Upper Saddle River, NJ*] [*NASDAQ symbol*] (NQ)
**IVAC**.......... International Video and Communications Exhibition [*Great Britain*] (ITD)
**IVACG**....... International Vitamin A Consultative Group (EA)
**IVAD**......... Izvestija na Varnenskoto Archeologicesko Druzestvo [*A publication*]
**IVAG**......... Institutionenverzeichnis Auslaendischer Gesellschaften [*NOMOS Database*] [*Information service or system*]
**IVA (Ingenjoersvetenskapsakad) Medd**... IVA (Ingenjoersvetenskapsakademien) Meddelande [*A publication*]
**IVAK**.......... Igloo Vertical Access Kit [*Aerospace*] (NASA)
**IVALA**....... Integrated Visual Approach and Landing Aid [*System*] [*RADAR*]
**IValSD**....... Valmeyer Community Unit School District 3, Valmeyer, IL [*Library symbol*] [*Library of Congress*] (LCLS)
**IVAM**........ Interorbital Vehicle Assembly Mode
**IV-ANES**... Intravenous Anesthetic [*Medicine*]
**Ivano Frankivs'kii Derzh Med Inst Nauk Zap**... Ivano-Frankivs'kii Derzhavnii Medichnii Institut Naukovi Zapiski [*A publication*]
**Ivanov Gos Ped Inst Ucen Zap**... Ivanovskii Gosudarstvennyi Pedagogiceskii Institut Imeni D. A. Furmanova Ivanovskoe Matematiceskoe Obscestvo Ucenye Zapiski [*A publication*]
**Ivanov Gos Univ Ucen Zap**... Ivanovskii Gosudarstvennyi Universitet Ucenye Zapiski [*A publication*]
**IVANS**....... Insurance Value-Added Network Services [*Insurance Institute for Research*] (TSSD)
**IVAR**......... Insertion Velocity Adjust Routine [*NASA*]
**IVAR**......... Internal Variable (NASA)
**IVAR**......... International Voluntary Action and Voluntary Association Research Organization [*Defunct*] (EA)
**IVAS**......... International Veterinary Acupuncture Society (EA)
**IVat**.......... Illustrazione Vaticana [*A publication*]
**IVA Tidskr Tek-Vetenskaplig Forsk**... IVA [*Ingenjoersvetenskapsakademien*] Tidskrift foer Teknisk-Vetenskaplig Forskning [*A publication*]
**IVA Tidskr Tek Vetensk Forsk**... IVA [*Ingenjoersvetenskapsakademien*] Tidskrift foer Teknisk-Vetenskaplig Forskning [*Sweden*] [*A publication*]
**IvB**............ Innenstadt von Babylon [*A publication*] (BJA)
**IVB**............ Intermediate Vector Boson [*Physics*]
**IVB**............ Internationaler Verband fuer Arbeiterbildung [*International Federation of Workers' Educational Associations - IFWEA*] (EAIO)
**IVB**............ Mason Memorial Public Library, Buda, IL [*OCLC symbol*] (OCLC)
**IVBA**.......... International Veteran Boxers Association (EA)
**IVBA**.......... International Volleyball Association [*Defunct*]
**IVBAT**....... Intravascular Bronchoalveolar Tumor [*Oncology*]
**IVBC**.......... Integrated Vehicle Baseline Configuration (MCD)
**IVBF**.......... International Volleyball Federation (EA)
**IVBH**......... Internationale Vereinigung fuer Brueckenbau und Hochbau [*International Association for Bridge and Structural Engineering*]
**IVC**........... Imperial Valley College [*California*]
**IVC**........... Independent Viewing Console
**IVC**........... Individual Viable Cells [*Metabolic studies*]
**IVC**........... Industrial View Camera
**IVC**........... Inferior Vena Cava [*Anatomy*]
**IVC**........... Integrated Vacuum Circuit
**IVC**........... Interactive Videodisc Consortium (EA)
**IVC**........... Intervehicular Communication (KSC)
**IVC**........... Intravenous Cholangiography [*Medicine*]
**IVC**........... Intraventricular Cannula [*Medicine*]
**IVC**........... Invercargill [*New Zealand*] [*Airport symbol*] (OAG)
**IVC**........... Permanent Committee for the International Veterinary Congresses
**IVC**........... Vandalia Correctional Center, Vandalia, IL [*Library symbol*] [*Library of Congress*] (LCLS)
**IVC**........... Vigo County Public Library, Terre Haute, IN [*OCLC symbol*] (OCLC)
**IVCAP**....... International Video Contest for Amateurs and Professionals [*British*]
**IVCC**.......... Intravascular Consumption Coagulopathy [*Medicine*]

**IVCD** ......... Indian Veterinary Convalescent Depot [*British military*] (DMA)
**IVCD** ......... Intraventricular Conduction Defect [*Pathology*]
**IVCF** .......... Inter-Varsity Christian Fellowship of the United States of America (EA)
**IVCI** ........... International Venture Capital Institute (EA)
**IVCI** ........... IVCI Corp. [*NASDAQ symbol*] (NQ)
**IVCP** .......... Inferior Vena Cava Pressure [*Medicine*]
**IVCR** .......... Invacare Corp. [*Elyria, OH*] [*NASDAQ symbol*] (NQ)
**IVCS** .......... Integrated Vehicular Communication System (MCD)
**IVCS** .......... Integrated [*or Interior*] Voice Communications System (MCD)
**Iv Cst** .......... Ivory Coast
**IVCV** .......... Inferior Venacavography [*Medicine*]
**IVD** ............ Image Velocity Detector
**IVD** ............ In Vitro Diagnostics [*Clinical chemistry*]
**IVD** ............ Indirect Video Display (MCD)
**IVD** ............ Information Viewing Device
**IVD** ............ Interactive Videodisc (INF)
**IVD** ............ International Vending Technologies Corp. [*Vancouver Stock Exchange symbol*]
**IVD** ............ Intervertebral Disc [*Medicine*]
**IVD** ............ Ion Vapor Deposition [*Coating technology*]
**IVD** ............ University of Dallas, Irving, TX [*OCLC symbol*] (OCLC)
**IVDA** .......... Intravenous Drug Abuser
**IVDA** .......... Investors Daily [*JA Micropublishing, Inc.*]
**IVDBA** ........ Imperial Valley Dune Buggy Association
**iv Dei** .......... Institut Voluntas Dei (EA)
**IVDS** .......... Independent Variable Depth SONAR
**IVDSA** ........ Intravenous Digital Subtraction Angiography
**IVDT** .......... Integrated [*or Interactive*] Voice Data Terminal [*Telecommunications*]
**IVDU** .......... Intravenous Drug User
**IVE** ............ Image of Vocational Education [*ERIC*]
**IVE** ............ Institute of Vitreous Enamellers [*British*]
**IVE** ............ Interface Verification Equipment (NASA)
**IVE** ............ International Video Entertainment
**IVE** ............ Internationale Vereinigung von Einkaufsverbanden [*International Association of Buying Groups - IABG*] (EAIO)
**IVE** ............ Internationale Vereinigung der Eisenwaren- und Eisenhaendlerverbaende [*International Federation of Ironmongers and Iron Merchants Association*]
**IVE** ............ Investment Equipment (MCD)
**IVE** ............ Isobutyl Vinyl Ether [*Organic chemistry*]
**IVE** ............ University of Chicago, Graduate Library School, Chicago, IL [*OCLC symbol*] (OCLC)
**IVen** ........... Venice Public Library, Venice, IL [*Library symbol*] [*Library of Congress*] (LCLS)
**IVenCU** ....... Venice Community Unit 3, Venice, IL [*Library symbol*] [*Library of Congress*] (LCLS)
**Iv Ersk** ........ Ivory. Notes on Erskine's Institutes [*A publication*] (ILCA)
**IVES** .......... Internationaler Verband fuer Erziehung zu Suchtmittelfreiem Leben [*International Association for Education to a Life without Drugs*] (EAIO)
**IVES** .......... Investment Technologies, Inc. [*Edison, NJ*] [*NASDAQ symbol*] (NQ)
**Ives Mil Law** ... Ives on Military Law [*A publication*] (DLA)
**IVET** .......... InnoVet, Inc. [*NASDAQ symbol*] (NQ)
**IVETA** ........ International Vocational Education and Training Association (EA)
**IVF** ............ In Vitro Fertilization [*Gynecology*]
**IVF** ............ Internationale Viola Forschunggesellschaft [*International Viola Society*] (EAIO)
**IVF** ............ Intravascular Fluid [*Medicine*]
**IVF** ............ Triodyne, Inc., Information Center, Skokie, IL [*OCLC symbol*] (OCLC)
**IVFGR** ........ Internationale Vereinigung fuer Gewerblichen Rechtsschultz [*International Association for the Protection of Industrial Property*]
**IVF J In Vitro Fert Embryo Transfer** ... IVF. Journal of In Vitro Fertilization and Embryo Transfer [*A publication*]
**IVFRC** ........ In Visual Flight Rules Conditions (FAAC)
**IVFZ** .......... International Veterinary Federation of Zootechnics [*Later, IVAAP*]
**IVg** ............ Camargo Township Library, Villa Grove, IL [*Library symbol*] [*Library of Congress*] (LCLS)
**IVG** ............ Internationale Vereinigung fuer Germanische Sprach - und Literaturwissenschaft [*International Association of Germanic Studies - IAGS*] [*Tokyo, Japan*] (EAIO)
**IVG** ............ Interrupt Vector Generator
**IVGGD** ....... Internationale Vereinigung fuer Geschichte und Gegenwart der Druckkunst [*International Association for Past and Present History of the Art of Printing*] (EAIO)
**IVGMA** ...... International Violin and Guitar Makers Association (EA)
**IVGO** ......... Izvestija Vsesojuznogo Geograficeskogo Obscestva [*A publication*]
**IVGOA** ...... Izvestiya Vsesoyuznogo Geograficheskogo Obshchestva [*A publication*]
**IVGPI** ........ Izvestiya Voronezhskogo Gosudarstvennogo Pedagogiceskogo Instituta [*A publication*]
**IVGTT** ....... Intravenous Glucose Tolerance Test [*Clinical medicine*]
**IVGWP** ....... Internationaler Verband der Gastronomie- und Weinbuau-Presse [*International Federation of Gastronomical and Vinicultural Press*]
**IVH** ............ Independent Variable Hull [*Statistics*]
**IVH** ............ Indian Veterinary Hospital [*British military*] (DMA)
**IVH** ............ Intravenous Hyperalimentation [*Medicine*]
**IVH** ............ Intraventricular Hemorrhage [*Cardiology*]
**IVH** ............ Ivishak, AK [*Location identifier*] [*FAA*] (FAAL)
**IVHM** ......... In-Vessel Handling Machine [*Nuclear energy*] (NRCH)
**IVHM-EM** ... In-Vessel Handling Machine-Engineering Model [*Nuclear energy*] (NRCH)
**IVHW** ......... Internationaler Verband fuer Hauswirtschaft [*International Federation for Home Economics*]
**IVHX** ......... In-Vessel Heat Exchanger [*Nuclear energy*] (NRCH)
**IVI** ............. American Conservatory of Music, Chicago, IL [*OCLC symbol*] (OCLC)
**IVI** ............. Ikuska. Instituto Vasco de Investigaciones [*A publication*]
**IVI** ............. Incremental Velocity Indicator [*NASA*]
**IVI** ............. Initial Ventricular Impulse
**IVI** ............. Initial Voluntary Indefinite [*Status*] [*Army*] (INF)
**IVI** ............. Instant Visual Index
**IVI** ............. Internal Vibration Isolator
**IVI** ............. International Verifact, Inc. [*Toronto Stock Exchange symbol*]
**IVI** ............. Inventory Index (MCD)
**IVI** ............. Ivigtut [*Greenland*] [*Seismograph station code, US Geological Survey*] [*Closed*] (SEIS)
**IVI** ............. Tucson, AZ [*Location identifier*] [*FAA*] (FAAL)
**IVIA** ........... Interactive Video Industry Association (EA)
**IVIA** ........... International Videotex Industry Association
**IVIE** ........... Independent Visually Impaired Enterprisers (EA)
**IVING** ......... Ivinghoe [*England*]
**IVIP** ........... Internationale Vereinigung fuer Individualpsychologie [*International Association of Individual Psychology*]
**IVIPA** ......... International Videotex Information Providers' Association [*British*] [*Information service or system*] (IID)
**IVird** .......... Virden Public Library, Virden, IL [*Library symbol*] [*Library of Congress*] (LCLS)
**IVirdMCD** ... Macoupin Community District 4, Virden, IL [*Library symbol*] [*Library of Congress*] (LCLS)
**IVIS** ........... International Visitors Information Service (EA)
**IVIZ** ........... Institutionenverzeichnis fuer Internationale Zusammenarbeit [*Institutions for International Cooperation*] [*NOMOS Datapool*] [*Database*] (IID)
**IVJ** ............ Oak Lawn Public Library, Oak Lawn, IL [*OCLC symbol*] (OCLC)
**IVJC** .......... Intervertebral Joint Complex [*Medicine*]
**IVJH** .......... Internationale Vereinigung fuer Jugendhilfe [*International Union for Child Welfare*]
**IVJS** ........... International Jewish Vegetarian Society [*Formerly, Jewish Vegetarian Society*] (EA)
**IVKMH** ...... Internationale Vereinigung der Klein- und Mittelbetriebe des Handels [*International Federation of Small and Medium-Sized Commercial Enterprises*]
**IVL** ............ Internationale Vereinigung der Lehrerverbaende [*International Federation of Teachers' Associations*]
**IVL** ............ Internationale Vereinigung fuer Theoretische und Angewandte Limnologie [*International Association of Theoretical and Applied Limnology*]
**IVL** ............ Internationale Wirtschaft mit den Mitteilungen der Bundeswirtschaftskammer [*A publication*]
**IVL** ............ Intervalometer (KSC)
**IVL** ............ Invader Resources Limited [*Vancouver Stock Exchange symbol*]
**IVL** ............ Inventory Validation Listing [*Data processing*]
**IVL** ............ Ivalo [*Finland*] [*Airport symbol*] (OAG)
**IVLA** .......... International Visual Literacy Association (EA)
**IVL Bull** ..... IVL [*Instituet foer Vatten och Luftvardsforskning*] Bulletin [*A publication*]
**IVLD** .......... Internationale Vereinigung der Organisationen von Lebensmittel-Detail-Listen [*International Federation of Grocers' Associations - IFGA*] (EAIO)
**IVLS** .......... Illinois Valley Library System [*Library network*]
**IVM** ........... Improved Visible Marker
**IVM** ........... Incentive Marketing [*A publication*]
**IVM** ........... Initial Virtual Memory
**IVM** ........... Institute of Value Management [*British*]
**IVM** ........... Integrated Vector Management [*Insect control*]
**IVM** ........... Interface Virtual Machine [*Data processing*]
**IVM** ........... Inventory Verification Manual
**IVMA** ......... Industrial Vegetation Management Association (EA)
**IVMA** ......... Intermountain Veterinary Medical Association (EA)
**IVMA** ......... Iodovinylmethoprenol Analog [*Organic chemistry*]
**IVMB** ......... Internationale Vereinigung der Musikbibliotheken, Musikarchive, und Dokumentationszentren [*International Association of Music Libraries, Archives, and Documentation Centers*] (EAIO)
**IVMF** ......... Inter-Varsity Missions Fellowship (EA)
**IVMI** .......... Ivy Medical, Incorporated [*Minneapolis, MN*] [*NASDAQ symbol*] (NQ)
**IVMJDL** ... Indian Veterinary Medical Journal [*A publication*]
**IVMOD2** ... In Vitro Monograph [*A publication*]

**IVMP**......... Intravenous Methylprednisolone [*Medicine*]
**IVMS**......... Instrumented Vibration Measuring System
**IVMS**......... Integrated Voice Messaging System [*Commterm, Inc.*] [*Atlanta, GA*] (TSSD)
**IVMU**........ Inertial Velocity Measurement Unit (IEEE)
**IVN**............ Internationale Vereniging voor Neerlandistiek [*International Association of Dutch Studies*] (EAIO)
**IVN**............ Intravenous Nutrition [*Medicine*]
**IVNAA**...... In Vivo Neutron Activation Analysis [*Analytical chemistry*]
**IVNCDN**... Investigations on Cetacea [*A publication*]
**IVO**............ Improved Virtual Orbitals [*Atomic physics*]
**IVO**............ Inova Optics, Inc. [*Vancouver Stock Exchange symbol*]
**IVO**............ Input Voltage Offset
**Ivor's Art R**... Ivor's Art Review [*A publication*] (APTA)
**Ivory Coast Dir Mines Geol Bull**... Ivory Coast. Direction des Mines et de la Geologie. Bulletin [*A publication*]
**IVOX**......... Intravascular Oxygenator [*Artificial lung*] [*Medicine*]
**IVP**............ Initial Vapor Pressure
**IVP**............ Inspected Variety Purity [*Agriculture*]
**IVP**............ Installation Verification Procedure (MCD)
**IVP**............ Inter-Varsity Press [*British*]
**IVP**............ Intravenous Push [*Medicine*]
**IVP**............ Intravenous Pyelogram [*Radiology*]
**IVP**............ Ion Vacuum Pump
**IVPA**.......... Independent Video Programmers Association (EA)
**IVPB**.......... Intravenous Piggyback [*Medicine*]
**IVPC**.......... Internationaler Verband der Petroleum- und Chemiearbeiter [*International Federation of Petroleum and Chemical Workers*]
**IVPD**.......... In Vitro Protein Digestibility [*Nutrition*]
**IVPO**.......... Inside Vapor Phase Oxidation [*Glass technology*]
**IVPT**.......... Inter-Vehicle Power Transfer (MCD)
**IVQ**............ Interrupted Very Quick [*Flashing*] Light [*Navigation signal*]
**IVR**............ Inner Vertical Resonance [*Physics*]
**IVR**............ Integrated Voltage Regulator (IEEE)
**IVR**............ Interactive Voice Response
**IVR**............ Internal Visual Reference [*Motion sickness*]
**IVR**............ International Association for the Rhine Vessels Register [*Netherlands*] (EY)
**IVR**............ International Journal of Physical Distribution and Materials Management [*A publication*]
**IVR**............ Internationale Vereinigung fuer Rechts- und Sozialphilosophie [*International Association for Philosophy of Law and Social Philosophy*] (EAIO)
**IVR**............ Intramolecular Vibrational Redistribution [*Chemistry*]
**IVR**............ Inverell [*Australia*] [*Airport symbol*] (OAG)
**IVR**............ Irvco Resources [*Vancouver Stock Exchange symbol*]
**IVR**............ Isolated Volume Responders [*Physiology*]
**IVRD**.......... In Vitro Rumen Digestibility [*Nutrition*]
**IVRG**.......... International Verticillium Research Group (EAIO)
**IVRYA**........ Intervirology [*A publication*]
**IVRYAK**.... Intervirology [*A publication*]
**IVS**............ In-Vessel Storage [*Nuclear energy*] (NRCH)
**IVS**............ Independent Vertical System
**IVS**............ Index of Veterinary Specialities [*A publication*] (APTA)
**IVS**............ Infrared Viewing Set
**IVS**............ Input Voltage Supply
**IVS**............ Insect Visual System
**IVS**............ Intact Ventricular System [*Cardiology*]
**IVS**............ International Vestor Resources [*Vancouver Stock Exchange symbol*]
**IVS**............ International Voluntary Services (EA)
**IVS**............ Intervening Sequence [*Genetics*]
**IVS**............ Interventricular Septum [*Cardiology*]
**IVS**............ Vigo County School Corp., Terre Haute, IN [*OCLC symbol*] (OCLC)
**IVSA**.......... International Veterinary Students Association [*Utrecht, Netherlands*] (EAIO)
**IVSD**.......... Interventricular Septal Defect [*Cardiology*]
**IVSD**.......... Vandalia Community Unit, School District 203, Vandalia, IL [*Library symbol*] [*Library of Congress*] (LCLS)
**IVSI**............ Instantaneous Vertical Speed Indicator [*NASA*]
**IVSK**.......... Intravenous Streptokinase [*An enzyme*]
**IVSM**.......... In-Vessel Storage Module [*Nuclear energy*] (NRCH)
**IVSN**.......... Initial Voice Switched Network [*NATO integrated communications system*] (NATG)
**IVSOIRGO**... Izvestija Vostocno-Sibirskogo Otdela Imperatorskogo Russkogo Geograficeskogo Obscestva [*A publication*]
**IVSORGO**... Izvestija Vostocno-Sibirskogo Otdela Russkogo Geograficeskogo Obscestva [*A publication*]
**IVSS**.......... Internationale Vereinigung fuer Soziale Sicherheit [*International Social Security Association*]
**IVSU**.......... International Veterinary Students Union [*Later, IVSA*]
**IVT**............ Index of Vertical Transmission [*Cultural evolution*]
**IVT**............ Inferential Value Testing (KSC)
**IVT**............ Inspection Verification Tag
**IVT**............ Integrated Video Terminal
**IVT**............ Interactive Video Technology [*Database*] [*Heartland Communications*] [*Information service or system*] (CRD)
**IVT**............ Internationale Vereinigung der Textileinkaufsverbande [*International Association of Textile Purchasing Societies*]
**IVT**............ Intervehicular Transfer (KSC)
**IVT**............ Intravenous Transfusion [*Medicine*]
**IVT**............ Intraventricular [*Cardiology*]
**IVT**............ Iventronics Ltd. [*Toronto Stock Exchange symbol*]
**IVT**............ Iverson Technology Corp. [*AMEX symbol*] (SPSG)
**IVTD**.......... Integrated Visual Testing Device
**IVT Jaarversl**... IVT [*Instituut voor de Veredeling van Tuinbouwgewassen*] Jaarverslag [*A publication*]
**IVTLAP**..... International Association of Theoretical and Applied Limnology. Proceedings [*A publication*]
**IVTM**.......... In-Vessel Transfer Machine [*Nuclear energy*] (NRCH)
**IVTMAS**... Communications. International Association of Theoretical and Applied Limnology [*A publication*]
**IVT Mededel**... IVT [*Instituut voor de Veredeling van Tuinbouwgewassen*] Mededeling [*A publication*]
**IVTRBA**.... In Vitro v CSSR [*A publication*]
**IVU**............ International Vegetarian Union [*Stockport, Cheshire, England*]
**IVU**............ Intravehicular Umbilical [*NASA*] (KSC)
**IVU**............ Intravenous Urogram [*or Urography*] [*Medicine*]
**IVU**............ Valparaiso University, Valparaiso, IN [*OCLC symbol*] (OCLC)
**IVUAA**...... Izvestiya Vysshikh Uchebnykh Zavedenii Aviatsionnaya Tekhnika [*A publication*]
**IVUGA**...... Izvestiya Vysshikh Uchebnykh Zavedenii Geologiya i Razvedka [*A publication*]
**IVUKA**...... Izvestiya Vysshikh Uchebnykh Zavedenii Khimiya i Khimicheskaya Tekhnologiya [*A publication*]
**IVUMA**..... Izvestiya Vysshikh Uchebnykh Zavedenii Chernaya Metallurgiya [*A publication*]
**IVUNA**...... Izvestiya Vysshikh Uchebnykh Zavedenii Neft' i Gaz [*A publication*]
**IVUPA**....... Izvestiya Vysshikh Uchebnykh Zavedenii Pishchevaya Tekhnologiya [*A publication*]
**IVUPA8**..... Izvestiya Vysshikh Uchebnykh Zavedenii Pishchevaya Tekhnologiya [*A publication*]
**IVUZ Fiz**... Izvestiya Vysshikh Uchebnykh Zavedenii Fizika [*A publication*]
**IV & V**........ Independent Validation and Verification (CAAL)
**IVV**............ Instantaneous Vertical Velocity
**IVV**............ Internationale Vereinigung fuer Vegetationskunde [*International Association for Vegetation Science - IAVS*] (EAIO)
**IVV**............ Internationaler Volkssportverband [*International Federation of Popular Sports - IFPS*] (EAIO)
**IVV**............ Intravenous Vasopressin [*Endocrinology*]
**IVV**............ Lebanon, NH [*Location identifier*] [*FAA*] (FAAL)
**IVV**............ Vincennes University, Vincennes, IN [*OCLC symbol*] (OCLC)
**IVVI**.......... Instantaneous Vertical Velocity Indicator
**IVVS**.......... Instantaneous Vertical Velocity Sensor (NATG)
**IVWO**........ International Vine and Wine Office
**IVWSR**...... Internationaler Verband fuer Wohnungswesen, Staedtebau und Raumordnung [*International Federation for Housing and Planning*]
**IVX**............ Columbus, OH [*Location identifier*] [*FAA*] (FAAL)
**IVX**............ Imperial Valley College, Imperial, CA [*OCLC symbol*] (OCLC)
**IVX**............ IVAX Corp. [*AMEX symbol*] (SPSG)
**IVY**............ Ivory Oil & Minerals [*Vancouver Stock Exchange symbol*]
**IVYBR**........ Ivybridge [*England*]
**IVZ**............ Valparaiso University, Law Library, Valparaiso, IN [*OCLC symbol*] (OCLC)
**IVZEA**....... Izvestiya Vysshikh Uchebnykh Zavedenii Energetika [*A publication*]
**IW**.............. Index Word [*Online database field identifier*]
**IW**.............. Indications and Warning [*Subsystems*] [*Military*] (MCD)
**IW**.............. Indirect Waste
**IW**.............. Individual Weapon (MCD)
**IW**.............. Induction Welding
**IW**.............. Information World [*A publication*]
**IW**.............. Inland Waterways [*Organization that administered British canals during World War II. Since most of the barge crews were women, the initials were sometimes sardonically interpreted to mean "Idle Women"*]
**IW**.............. Inside Width
**IW**.............. Inside Wire [*Telecommunications*] (TEL)
**IW**.............. Inspector of Works
**I/W**............ Interchangeable With (AAG)
**IW**.............. International Air Bahama [*ICAO designator*] (FAAC)
**IW**.............. International Wattier [*Process*] [*A method of making transparencies for rotogravure plates*]
**I of W**......... Isle Of Wight
**IW**.............. Isle Of Wight
**IW**.............. Isotopic Weight
**iw**.............. Israel-Jordan Demilitarized Zones [*is (Israel) used in records cataloged after January 1978*] [*MARC country of publication code*] [*Library of Congress*] (LCCP)
**IW**.............. Israelitisches Wochenblatt [*A publication*]
**IW**.............. Wheaton Public Library, Wheaton, IL [*Library symbol*] [*Library of Congress*] (LCLS)
**I5/W**.......... Invert Sugar [*5%*] in Water [*Medicine*]
**IWA**.......... Independent Watchmen's Association (EA)
**IWA**.......... Inland Waterways Association [*British*] (DCTA)
**IWA**.......... Institute of World Affairs [*Later, UFSI-IWA*] (EA)

**IWA**.......... International Waterproofing Association [*See also AIE*] [*Brussels, Belgium*] (EAIO)
**IWA**.......... International Wheat Agreement [*London*]
**IWA**.......... International Women's Auxiliary to the Veterinary Profession
**IWA**.......... International Woodworkers of America (EA)
**IWA**.......... Iowa State University of Science and Technology, Ames, IA [*OCLC symbol*] (OCLC)
**IWAAC**...... Inland Waterways Amenity Advisory Council [*British*] (DCTA)
**I/WAC**....... Interface/Weapon Aiming Computer (MCD)
**IWAC**........ International Women's Anthropology Conference (EA)
**IWAHMA**... Industrial Warm Air Heater Manufacturers
**IWAK**........ Improved Water Analysis Kit
**IWal**.......... Walnut Township Library, Walnut, IL [*Library symbol*] [*Library of Congress*] (LCLS)
**IWalHSD**.. Walnut Consolidated High School District 508, Walnut, IL [*Library symbol*] [*Library of Congress*] (LCLS)
**IWalSD**...... Walnut Consolidated Community School District 285, Walnut, IL [*Library symbol*] [*Library of Congress*] (LCLS)
**IWaltSD**.... Waltonville Community Unit, School District 1, Waltonville, IL [*Library symbol*] [*Library of Congress*] (LCLS)
**IWARDS**... Iowa Water Resources Data System [*Iowa State Geological Survey*] [*Iowa City*] [*Information service or system*] (IID)
**IWARS**...... Installation Worldwide Ammunition Reporting System [*Army*]
**IWas**.......... Washington Township Library, Washington, IL [*Library symbol*] [*Library of Congress*] (LCLS)
**IWas-Su**..... Washington Township Library, Sunnyland Branch, Sunnyland, IL [*Library symbol*] [*Library of Congress*] (LCLS)
**IWat**.......... Watseka Public Library, Watseka, IL [*Library symbol*] [*Library of Congress*] (LCLS)
**Iwata Tob Shikenjo Hokoku Bull Iwata Tob Exp Stn**... Iwata Tob Shikenjo Hokoku/Bulletin. Iwata Tobacco Experimental Station [*A publication*]
**Iwate Univ Technol Rep**... Iwate University. Faculty of Engineering. Technology Reports [*A publication*]
**IWatH**........ Iroquois Memorial Hospital, Watseka, IL [*Library symbol*] [*Library of Congress*] (LCLS)
**IWatl**.......... Morrison-Talbott Library, Waterloo, IL [*Library symbol*] [*Library of Congress*] (LCLS)
**IWatlGHS**... Gibault High School, Waterloo, IL [*Library symbol*] [*Library of Congress*] (LCLS)
**IWatlSD**.... Waterloo Community School District 3, Waterloo, IL [*Library symbol*] [*Library of Congress*] (LCLS)
**IWau**.......... Waukegan Public Library, Waukegan, IL [*Library symbol*] [*Library of Congress*] (LCLS)
**IWayc**........ Wayne City Public Library, Wayne City, IL [*Library symbol*] [*Library of Congress*] (LCLS)
**IWaycCD**... Wayne City Community Unit, District 100, Wayne City, IL [*Library symbol*] [*Library of Congress*] (LCLS)
**IWB**........... Council Bluffs Free Public Library, Council Bluffs, IA [*OCLC symbol*] (OCLC)
**IWB**........... Israelitisches Wochenblatt (Berlin) [*A publication*]
**IWB**........... Literatuurinformatie Wetenschapsbeleid [*A publication*]
**IWBC**......... Interim Wideband Communications (MCD)
**IWBP**......... Integration with Britain Party [*Gibraltar*] (PPE)
**IWBS**......... Congregation of the Incarnate Word and the Blessed Sacrament [*Roman Catholic women's religious order*]
**IWBS**......... Importwarenbegleitschein [*Import Bill of Lading*] [*Legal term*] [*German*]
**IWBS**......... Indirect Work Breakdown Structure (NASA)
**IWBS**......... Integral Weight and Balance System [*Aviation*]
**IWC**........... Ice Water Content
**IWC**........... Imperial War Cabinet [*British military*] (DMA)
**IWC**........... Incarnate Word College [*Texas*]
**IWC**........... Individual Weapons Captured
**IWC**........... Infant Welfare Certificate [*Australia*]
**IWC**........... Inland Waterways Corporation [*Later, Federal Barge Lines, Inc.; liquidated, 1963*]
**IWC**........... Institute for Workers' Control
**IWC**........... International Whaling Commission [*Cambridge, England*]
**IWC**........... International Wheat Council [*See also CIB*] [*London, England*] (EAIO)
**IWC**........... International Wildcat Resources [*Vancouver Stock Exchange symbol*]
**IWC**........... International Wildlife Coalition (EA)
**IWC**........... Interwest Corporation [*AMEX symbol*] (SPSG)
**IWC**........... Iowa Wesleyan College
**IWC**........... Wabash College, Crawfordsville, IN [*OCLC symbol*] (OCLC)
**IWCA**........ Inside Wiring Cable [*Telecommunications*] (TEL)
**IWCA**........ International Windsurfer Class Association (EA)
**IWCA**........ International World Calendar Association (EA)
**IWCA**........ Irish Wolfhound Club of America (EA)
**IWCC**......... International Women's Cricket Council [*Australia*] (EAIO)
**IWCC**......... International Wrought Copper Council [*London, England*] (EAIO)
**IWCCA**...... Inland Waterways Common Carriers Association [*Defunct*] (EA)
**IWCI**......... Industrial Water Conditioning Institute (EA)
**IWCI**......... Industrial Wire Cloth Institute [*Later, AWCI*] (EA)
**IWCR**......... International Whaling Commission. Reports [*A publication*]
**IWCR**......... IWC Resources Corp. [*Indianapolis, IN*] [*NASDAQ symbol*] (NQ)
**IWCRSI**..... International Whaling Commission. Reports. Special Issue [*A publication*]
**IWCS**......... Integrated Weapons Control System
**IWCS**......... Integrated Wideband Communications System [*Military*]
**IWCS**......... Interceptor Weapon Control System
**IWCS**......... International Wood Collectors Society (EA)
**IWCS/SEA**... Integrated Wideband Communications System/Southeast Asia (IEEE)
**IWCT**......... International War Crimes Tribunal
**IWCTF**...... Interdepartmental Workers' Compensation Task Force [*Department of Labor*] [*Terminated, 1976*] (EGAO)
**IWD**........... Drake University, Law Library, Des Moines, IA [*OCLC symbol*] (OCLC)
**IWD**........... Inland Waters Directorate [*Canada*]
**IWD**........... Intermediate Water Depth (MCD)
**IWD**........... International Women's Day
**IWD**........... International Women's Decade
**IWD**........... Iron or Wood [*Freight*]
**IWD**........... Ironwood [*Michigan*] [*Airport symbol*] (OAG)
**IWD**........... Ironwood, MI [*Location identifier*] [*FAA*] (FAAL)
**IWDA**......... Independent Wire Drawers Association [*Later, AWPA*]
**IWDM**........ Intermediate Water Depth Mine (MCD)
**IWDS**......... International World Day Service
**IWE**........... Camden, AL [*Location identifier*] [*FAA*] (FAAL)
**IWE**........... Illustrated World Encyclopedia [*A publication*]
**IWE**........... Institute of Water Engineers [*British*]
**IWE**........... Institute for Wholistic Education [*Later, SCIWE*] (EA)
**IWe**........... Westchester Public Library, Westchester, IL [*Library symbol*] [*Library of Congress*] (LCLS)
**IWE**........... Winnetka Public Library, Winnetka, IL [*OCLC symbol*] (OCLC)
**IWedSD**..... Wedron Consolidated Community School District 201, Wedron, IL [*Library symbol*] [*Library of Congress*] (LCLS)
**IWEEA**...... Industry Week [*A publication*]
**IWEGA**...... Industrial Water Engineering [*A publication*]
**IWEGAA**... Industrial Water Engineering [*A publication*]
**IWEM**........ Institution of Water and Environmental Management (EAIO)
**IWem**......... Westmont Public Library, Westmont, IL [*Library symbol*] [*Library of Congress*] (LCLS)
**IWen**.......... Bond Public Library, Wenona, IL [*Library symbol*] [*Library of Congress*] (LCLS)
**IWenSD**..... Wenona Community Unit, School District 1, Wenona, IL [*Library symbol*] [*Library of Congress*] (LCLS)
**IWERC**...... Industrial Waste Elimination Research Center [*Illinois Institute of Technology*] [*Research center*] (RCD)
**IWERRI**.... Idaho Water and Energy Resources Research Institute [*University of Idaho*] [*Research center*] (RCD)
**IWes**.......... West Salem Public Library, West Salem, IL [*Library symbol*] [*Library of Congress*] (LCLS)
**IWesp**......... Thomas Ford Memorial Library, Western Springs, IL [*Library symbol*] [*Library of Congress*] (LCLS)
**IWev**.......... Westville Public Library, Westville, IL [*Library symbol*] [*Library of Congress*] (LCLS)
**IWEWSULOTATDTO**... I Wish Everyone Would Stop Using Letters of the Alphabet to Designate Their Organizations [*Originated by Bea von Boeselager in "Line o' Type," Chicago Tribune*]
**IWEX**......... Internal Wave Experiment (NOAA)
**IWF**........... International Weightlifting Federation [*See also FHI*] [*Budapest, Hungary*] (EAIO)
**IWF**........... International Woodworking Machinery and Furniture Supply Fair (ITD)
**IWFA**......... Intercollegiate Women's Fencing Association [*Later, NIWFA*]
**IWFA**......... International Women's Fishing Association (EA)
**IWFAI**....... International Watch Fob Association, Incorporated (EA)
**IWFI**.......... Italian Wine and Food Institute (EA)
**IWFP**......... International Women's Film Project (EA)
**IWFS**......... Industrial Waste Filter System (IEEE)
**IWFS**......... International Wine and Food Society [*London, England*] (EAIO)
**IWG**........... Grand View College, Des Moines, IA [*OCLC symbol*] (OCLC)
**IWG**........... Imperial Wire Gauge (ROG)
**IWG**........... Implementation Work Group on Justice Information and Statistics [*See also GMO*] [*Canada*]
**IWG**........... Intelligence Working Group [*Military*] (CINC)
**IWG**........... Interface Working Group [*NASA*] (NASA)
**IWG**........... Intergovernmental Working Group [*United Nations*]
**IWG**........... International Working Group [*NATO*] (NATG)
**IWG**........... International Writers Guild
**IWG**........... Investigator's Working Group [*Spacelab mission*]
**IWG**........... Iowa-Illinois Gas & Electric Co. [*NYSE symbol*] (SPSG)
**IWG**........... Iron Wire Gauge
**IWGA**........ International Wheat Gluten Association (EA)
**IWGA**........ International World Games Association (EA)
**IWGC**........ Imperial War Graves Commission [*British*]
**IWGCSFIPERM**... Inter-Service Working Group for Cooperation and Standardization of Foto Interpretation Procedures, Equipment, and Related Matters
**IWGFR**...... International Working Group on Fast Reactors (NRCH)

**IWGGDM** ... International Working Group on Graminaceous Downy Mildews (EAIO)
**IWGIA** ........ International Work Group for Indigenous Affairs [*Copenhagen, Denmark*] (EAIO)
**IWGIAD** .... IWGIA [*International Work Group for Indigenous Affairs*] Document [*A publication*]
**IWGIAN** .... IWGIA [*International Work Group for Indigenous Affairs*] Newsletter [*A publication*]
**IWGM** ....... Intergovernmental Working Group on Monitoring or Surveillance [*United Nations*] (ASF)
**IWGMP** ..... Intergovernmental Working Group on Marine Pollution [*Inter-Governmental Maritime Consultative Organization*]
**IWGMS** ..... Intergovernmental Working Group on Monitoring or Surveillance [*United Nations*] (MSC)
**IWH** ........... Wabash, IN [*Location identifier*] [*FAA*] (FAAL)
**IWHC** ........ International Women's Health Coalition (EA)
**IWhh** .......... White Hall Township Library, White Hall, IL [*Library symbol*] [*Library of Congress*] (LCLS)
**IWhhB** ....... Beecham Laboratories, White Hall, IL [*Library symbol*] [*Library of Congress*] (LCLS)
**IWhhSD** .... North Greene Community Unit, School District 3, White Hall, IL [*Library symbol*] [*Library of Congress*] (LCLS)
**IWhI** .......... Indian Trails Public Library District, Wheeling, IL [*Library symbol*] [*Library of Congress*] (LCLS)
**IWhN** ......... North Suburban Library System, Wheeling, IL [*Library symbol*] [*Library of Congress*] (LCLS)
**IWHS** ........ Institute of Works and Highways Superintendents [*British*]
**IWHSD** ..... Irish War Hospital Supply Depot [*British military*] (DMA)
**IWI** ............ International Werner Tech [*Vancouver Stock Exchange symbol*]
**IWI** ............ Inventors' Workshop International [*Later, IWIEF*] (EA)
**IWI** ............ Irreversible Warmup Indicator [*To detect whether frozen foods have risen above an acceptable temperature level*] [*Pronounced "ee-wee"*]
**IWI** ............ Wishard Memorial Hospital, Indianapolis, IN [*OCLC symbol*] (OCLC)
**IWi** ............ Witt Memorial Library, Witt, IL [*Library symbol*] [*Library of Congress*] (LCLS)
**IWIEF** ....... Inventors Workshop International Education Foundation (EA)
**IWilGS** ...... Church of Jesus Christ of Latter-Day Saints, Genealogical Society Library, Wilmette Branch, Wilmette, IL [*Library symbol*] [*Library of Congress*] (LCLS)
**IWin** .......... Winnetka Public Library, Winnetka, IL [*Library symbol*] [*Library of Congress*] (LCLS)
**IWin-N** ...... Winnetka Public Library District, Northfield Branch, Northfield, IL [*Library symbol*] [*Library of Congress*] (LCLS)
**IWIS** .......... Interceptor Weapons Instructor School [*Air Force*]
**IWiSD** ........ Witt Community Unit, School District 66, Witt, IL [*Library symbol*] [*Library of Congress*] (LCLS)
**IWISTK** ..... Issue While in Stock
**IWIU** ......... Insurance Workers International Union
**IWK** .......... Internationale Wissenschaftliche Korrespondenz zur Geschichte der Deutschen Arbeiterbewegung [*A publication*]
**IWK** .......... Israelitische Wochenschrift (Klausner) [*A publication*]
**IWL** .......... Insensible Water Loss [*Medicine*]
**IWL** .......... Institute Warranty Limits [*Shipping*] (DS)
**IWL** .......... International Walther League (EA)
**IWL** .......... Italian Welfare League (EA)
**IWL** .......... Willard Library, Evansville, IN [*OCLC symbol*] (OCLC)
**IWLA** ......... Izaak Walton League of America (EA)
**IWLAE** ...... Izaak Walton League of America Endowment (EA)
**IWLE** ......... Individual Whole of Life and Endowment [*Insurance*] (ADA)
**IWLRAA** ... Indian Forest Records. Wild Life and Recreation [*A publication*]
**IWLS** ......... Iterative Weighted Least Squares [*Statistics*]
**IWM** .......... Bluffton-Wells County Public Library, Bluffton, IN [*OCLC symbol*] (OCLC)
**IWM** .......... Imperial War Museum [*England*]
**IWM** .......... Industrial Waste Management (MCD)
**IWM** .......... Institute of Wastes Management [*British*]
**IWM** .......... Institution of Works Managers [*British*]
**IWM** .......... Integrated Woz Machine [*Apple Computer, Inc.*]
**IWM** .......... MAP International, Wheaton, IL [*Library symbol*] [*Library of Congress*] (LCLS)
**IWMA** ....... Institute of Weights and Measures Administration [*Wales*]
**IWMA** ....... International Wire and Machinery Association [*Leamington Spa, Warwickshire, England*] (EAIO)
**IWMI** ........ Inferior Wall Myocardial Infarction [*Cardiology*]
**IWMP** ........ International Women's Media Project (EA)
**IWMS** ........ Integrated Weed Management System [*Agriculture*]
**IWN** .......... North Iowa Area Community College, Mason City, IA [*OCLC symbol*] (OCLC)
**IWO** .......... Informationsdienst West-Ost [*A publication*]
**IWO** .......... Institute for World Order (EA)
**IWO** .......... Intelligence Watch Officer [*Military*] (MCD)
**IWo** ........... Worth Public Library District, Worth, IL [*Library symbol*] [*Library of Congress*] (LCLS)
**IWOC** ........ International Wizard of Oz Club (EA)
**IWor** .......... Wood River Public Library, Wood River, IL [*Library symbol*] [*Library of Congress*] (LCLS)
**IWordR** ...... Worden Reading Center, Worden, IL [*Library symbol*] [*Library of Congress*] (LCLS)
**IWordSD** ... Worden Community Unit, School District 16, Worden, IL [*Library symbol*] [*Library of Congress*] (LCLS)
**IWorH** ....... Wood River Township Hospital, Medical Library, Wood River, IL [*Library symbol*] [*Library of Congress*] (LCLS)
**IWorHS** ..... East Alton-Wood River Community High School 14, Wood River, IL [*Library symbol*] [*Library of Congress*] (LCLS)
**IWori** ........ Woodridge Public Library, Woodridge, IL [*Library symbol*] [*Library of Congress*] (LCLS)
**IWOSC** ...... International Working-Group of Soilless Culture
**IWP** .......... Idaho White Pine [*Lumber*]
**IWP** .......... Illawarra Workers Party [*Australia*]
**IWP** .......... Indicative World Plan for Agricultural Development [*United Nations*]
**IWP** .......... Indo-West Pacific [*Biogeographic region*]
**IWP** .......... Internal Working Paper
**IWP** .......... International Information/Word Processing Association [*Formerly, IWPA*] (EA)
**IWP** .......... International Working Party
**IWP** .......... Internationale Weltfriedens Partei [*International World Peace Party*] [*Federal Republic of Germany*] [*Political party*] (PPW)
**IWP** .......... Irish Workers' Party [*Political party*] (PPW)
**IWP** .......... Sioux City Public Library, Sioux City, IA [*OCLC symbol*] (OCLC)
**IWPA** ........ Independent Wire Producers Association [*Later, AWPA*] (EA)
**IWPA** ........ International Word Processing Association [*Later, IIWPA, IWP*]
**IWPC** ........ Institute of Water Pollution Control [*Later, IWEM*] (EAIO)
**IWPCD** ..... International Water Power and Dam Construction [*A publication*]
**IWR** .......... Cedar Rapids Public Library, Cedar Rapids, IA [*OCLC symbol*] (OCLC)
**IWR** .......... Connecticut Institute of Water Resources [*Storrs, CT*] [*Department of the Interior*] (GRD)
**IWR** .......... Improved Weather Reconnaissance
**IWR** .......... Information World Review [*A publication*] [*Information service or system*] (IID)
**IWR** .......... Institute for Water Resources [*Army*] [*Fort Belvoir, VA*] (MSC)
**IWR** .......... Institute for Wildlife Research (EA)
**IWR** .......... Islamic World Review [*A publication*]
**IWR** .......... Isle Of Wight Railway [*British*]
**IWR** .......... Isle Of Wight Rifles [*British military*] (DMA)
**IWR** .......... Isolated Word Recognition (MCD)
**IWRA** ........ International Water Resources Association (EA)
**IWRA** ........ International Wild Rice Association (EA)
**IWRB** ........ International Waterfowl and Wetlands Research Bureau (EAIO)
**IWRBBR** ... Iowa. Agriculture and Home Economics Experiment Station. Research Bulletin [*A publication*]
**IWRC** ........ Independent Wire Rope Center [*or Core*]
**IWRC** ........ International Wildlife Rehabilitation Council (EA)
**IWRC** ........ Iron Wire Rope Core [*Nuclear energy*] (NRCH)
**IWRM** ....... Integrated Warfare Requirements Methodology
**IWRMA** .... Independent Wire Rope Manufacturers Association (EA)
**IWRO** ........ Interdepartmental Work Release Order
**IWRP** ........ Individualized Written Rehabilitation Program [*Department of Education*]
**IWRRC** ...... International Wheelchair Road Racers Club (EA)
**IWRUAR** ... Institute for Water Resources. University of Alaska. Report [*A publication*]
**IWS** ........... Impact Warning System
**IWS** ........... Industrial Water Supply
**IWS** ........... Industrial Water System (KSC)
**IWS** ........... Industrial Welfare Society [*British*] (ILCA)
**IWS** ........... Inland Waterway Service
**IWS** ........... Integrated Weapon System
**IWS** ........... Integrated Work Statement (MCD)
**IWS** ........... International Wildrose Resources, Inc. [*Vancouver Stock Exchange symbol*]
**IWS** ........... International Wine Society (EA)
**IWS** ........... International Wool Secretariat [*London, England*]
**IWS** ........... Western Iowa Technical Community College, Sioux City, IA [*OCLC symbol*] (OCLC)
**IWSA** ........ International Water Supply Association [*London, England*] (EAIO)
**IWSA** ........ International Workers Sport Association
**IWSAW** ..... Institute for Women's Studies in the Arab World [*Beirut, Lebanon*] (EAIO)
**IWSB** ........ Insect Wire Screening Bureau [*Later, Insect Screening Weavers Association*] (EA)
**IWSc** ......... Institute of Wood Science Ltd. [*British*]
**IWSCA** ...... Irish Water Spaniel Club of America (EA)
**IWSG** ........ International Wool Study Group [*London, England*] (EAIO)
**IWS/IT** ...... Integrated Work Sequence/Inspection Traveler (NRCH)
**IWSM** ........ Integrated Weapon Support Management (AFM)
**IWSO** ........ Instructor Weapons System Officer [*Military*]
**IWSOE** ...... International Weddell Sea Oceanographic Expedition
**IWSP** ......... Integrated Weapon Secret Panel (MCD)

**IWSR**.......... Integrated Weapon System Representative [*or Review*] (MCD)
**IWSR**.......... International Wine and Spirit Record
**IWSRBC**.... Iowa. Agriculture and Home Economics Experiment Station. Special Report [*A publication*]
**IWSS**.......... International Weed Science Society (EA)
**IWSSA**...... Interservice Warehousing Support Services Agreement
**IWST**.......... Integrated Weapon System Training [*Air Force*]
**IWT**.......... I Was There
**IWT**.......... Indian Writing Today [*A publication*]
**IWT**.......... Indiana Writing Today [*A publication*]
**IWT**.......... Industrial Waste Treatment Management (MCD)
**IWT**.......... Inland Water Transport [*British*]
**IWT**.......... Institute of Women Today (EA)
**IWT**.......... Integrated Waste Water Treatment
**IWT**.......... International Working Team [*NATO*] (NATG)
**IWT**.......... Irwin Toy Ltd. [*Toronto Stock Exchange symbol*]
**IWT**.......... Schools of Theology in Dubuque, Dubuque, IA [*OCLC symbol*] (OCLC)
**IWTC**.......... Inland Water Transport Corporation [*Burma*] (DS)
**IWTC**.......... International Women's Tribune Centre (EA)
**IWTO**.......... International Wool Textile Organization [*See also FLI*] [*Brussels, Belgium*] (EAIO)
**IWTR**.......... Indianapolis Water [*NASDAQ symbol*] (NQ)
**IWTS**.......... Indications and Warning Training System [*Military*] (MCD)
**IWTS**.......... Individual Weapon Thermal Sight [*Army*] (INF)
**IWTS**.......... Industrial Waste Treatment System (NRCH)
**IWU**.......... Illegal Wearing of Uniform
**IWU**.......... Illinois Wesleyan University [*Bloomington*]
**IWU**.......... Isolation Working Unit [*Telecommunications*] (TEL)
**IWU**.......... Texas Woman's University, Denton, TX [*OCLC symbol*] (OCLC)
**IWV**.......... Internationale Warenhaus-Vereinigung [*International Association of Department Stores*]
**IWV**.......... Waterloo Public Library, Waterloo, IA [*OCLC symbol*] (OCLC)
**IWVA**.......... International War Veterans' Alliance (EA)
**IWVMTS**.. Interim Water Velocity Meter Test Set
**IWW**.......... Industrial Workers of the World (EA)
**IWW**.......... Inland Waterway (AABC)
**IWW**.......... International Westward Development Corp. [*Vancouver Stock Exchange symbol*]
**IWW**.......... International Who's Who [*A publication*]
**IWW**.......... Intracoastal Waterway
**IWW**.......... Kenai, AK [*Location identifier*] [*FAA*] (FAAL)
**IWW**.......... Westmar College, Le Mars, IA [*OCLC symbol*] (OCLC)
**IWW**.......... Wheaton College, Wheaton, IL [*Library symbol*] [*Library of Congress*] (LCLS)
**IWWA**.......... International Wild Waterfowl Association (EA)
**IWWCS**..... International Who's Who in Community Service [*A publication*]
**IWWDD**.... Information World [*A publication*]
**IWWDF**..... International Westward Development Corp. [*NASDAQ symbol*] (NQ)
**IWWG**.......... International Women's Writing Guild (EA)
**IWWM**...... International Who's Who in Music and Musicians Directory [*A publication*]
**IWWP**.......... International Who's Who in Poetry [*A publication*]
**IWWRB**..... International Waterfowl and Wetlands Research Bureau (EAIO)
**IWX**.......... Aspekten van Internationale Samenwerking [*A publication*]
**IWY**.......... International Women's Year [*1975*]
**IWY**.......... New York, NY [*Location identifier*] [*FAA*] (FAAL)
**IWya**.......... Raymond A. Sapp Memorial Library, Wyanet, IL [*Library symbol*] [*Library of Congress*] (LCLS)
**IWyaSD**..... Wyanet Consolidated High School District 510, Wyanet, IL [*Library symbol*] [*Library of Congress*] (LCLS)
**IWyo**.......... Wymoning Public Library, Wymoning, IL [*Library symbol*] [*Library of Congress*] (LCLS)
**IX**.......... Iesus Christus [*Jesus Christ*] [*Latin*]
**IX**.......... In Christo [*In Christ*] [*Latin*]
**IX**.......... Index [*Data processing*] (BUR)
**IX**.......... Industry Manufacturers [*FCC*] (MCD)
**IX**.......... Internacional de Aviacion SA [*Panama*] [*ICAO designator*] (FAAC)
**IX**.......... Ion Exchanger (NRCH)
**IX**.......... IRT Corp. [*AMEX symbol*] (SPSG)
**IX**.......... Unclassified Miscellaneous [*Navy ship symbol*]
**IXA**.......... Agartala [*India*] [*Airport symbol*] (OAG)
**i-xa---**.......... Christmas Island [*Indian Ocean*] [*MARC geographic area code*] [*Library of Congress*] (LCCP)
**IXA**.......... Ion-Excited X-Ray Analysis
**IXA**.......... University of Texas at Austin, Austin, TX [*OCLC symbol*] (OCLC)
**IXAE**.......... International X-Ray Astrophysics Explorer
**IXB**.......... Bagdogra [*India*] [*Airport symbol*] (OAG)
**i-xb---**.......... Cocos [*Keeling*] Islands [*MARC geographic area code*] [*Library of Congress*] (LCCP)
**IXC**.......... Chandigarh [*India*] [*Airport symbol*] (OAG)
**IXC**.......... Interexchange Channel [*Telecommunications*]
**IXC**.......... Interexchange Circuit [*Telecommunications*] (TSSD)
**IXC**.......... Interexchange Mileage (CET)
**IXC**.......... Ixora Communications System [*Vancouver Stock Exchange symbol*]
**i-xc---**.......... Maldives [*MARC geographic area code*] [*Library of Congress*] (LCCP)
**IXD**.......... Allahabad [*India*] [*Airport symbol*] (OAG)
**IXD**.......... Olathe, KS [*Location identifier*] [*FAA*] (FAAL)
**IXE**.......... Mangalore [*India*] [*Airport symbol*] (OAG)
**IXEE**.......... International X-Ray and Extreme Ultraviolet Explorer
**IXF**.......... Industrial X-Ray Film
**IXG**.......... Belgaum [*India*] [*Airport symbol*] (OAG)
**IXI**.......... Lilabari [*India*] [*Airport symbol*] (OAG)
**IXJ**.......... Jammu [*India*] [*Airport symbol*] (OAG)
**IXK**.......... Keshod [*India*] [*Airport symbol*] (OAG)
**IXL**.......... Leh [*India*] [*Airport symbol*] (OAG)
**IXM**.......... Madurai [*India*] [*Airport symbol*] (OAG)
**IXO**.......... Inlet and Outlet
**i-xo---**.......... Socotra Island [*MARC geographic area code*] [*Library of Congress*] (LCCP)
**IXOH**.......... Inlet and Outlet Head
**IXR**.......... Integrated X-Ray Reflection
**IXR**.......... Intersection of Runways [*Aviation*]
**IXR**.......... Ranchi [*India*] [*Airport symbol*] (OAG)
**IXRALM**... Imaging Soft X-Ray LASER Microscope
**IXS**.......... Information Exchange System [*or Subsystem*] [*Military*] (CAAL)
**IXS**.......... International Social Science Journal [*A publication*]
**IXS**.......... Silchar [*India*] [*Airport symbol*] (OAG)
**IXSAAZ**.... International Council for the Exploration of the Sea. Cooperative Research Report. Series A [*A publication*]
**IXSBB5**...... International Council for the Exploration of the Sea. Cooperative Research Report. Series B [*A publication*]
**IXSS**.......... Unclassified Miscellaneous Submarine [*Navy symbol*] (NVT)
**IXT**.......... Christian Theological Seminary, Indianapolis, IN [*OCLC symbol*] (OCLC)
**IXT**.......... Interaction Cross Talk [*Telecommunications*] (TEL)
**IXT**.......... Ixtapalapa [*Mexico*] [*Seismograph station code, US Geological Survey*] [*Closed*] (SEIS)
**IXTR**.......... Intelligible Crosstalk Ratio
**IXU**.......... Aurangabad [*India*] [*Airport symbol*] (OAG)
**IXZ**.......... Port Blair [*Andaman Islands*] [*Airport symbol*] (OAG)
**IY**.......... Idaho Yesterdays [*A publication*]
**IY**.......... Imperial Yeomanry [*British*]
**IY**.......... Ionized Yeast
**iy**.......... Iraq-Saudi Arabia Neutral Zone [*MARC country of publication code*] [*Library of Congress*] (LCCP)
**IY**.......... Yemen Airlines [*ICAO designator*] (FAAC)
**IYA**.......... Indian Youth of America (EA)
**IYaSh**.......... Inostrannye Jazyki v Skole [*A publication*]
**IYB**.......... Imperial Yeomanry Bearer Corps [*British military*] (DMA)
**IYB**.......... [*The*] Israel Year Book [*A publication*]
**IYC**.......... Individual Yield Coverage Program [*Department of Agriculture*]
**IYC**.......... International Year of the Child [*1979*] [*United Nations*]
**IYC**.......... International Youth Congress
**IYC**.......... International Youth Council (EA)
**IYCM**.......... International Year of Canadian Music [*1986*]
**IYCO**.......... Ito-Yokado Company Ltd. [*NASDAQ symbol*] (NQ)
**IYCW**.......... International Young Christian Workers [*See also JOCI*] (EAIO)
**IYDP**.......... International Year of the Disabled Person [*1981*]
**IYDU**.......... International Young Democratic Union (EAIO)
**IYEP**.......... International Youth Exchange Program [*Australia*]
**IYF**.......... International Youth Federation for Environmental Studies and Conservation (EAIO)
**IYFS**.......... International Young Fish Survey [*Denmark, Great Britain, Norway, West Germany*] [*1987-88*] [*Oceanography*]
**IY'H**.......... Im Yirtseh Hashem (BJA)
**IYH**.......... Imperial Yeomanry Hospitals [*Military*] [*British*] (ROG)
**IYH**.......... Israel Youth Horizon [*Jerusalem*] [*A publication*]
**IYHF**.......... International Youth Hostel Federation [*See also FAIJ*] [*Welwyn Garden City, Hertfordshire, England*] (EAIO)
**IYHR**.......... Israel Yearbook on Human Rights [*A publication*]
**IYIA**.......... Indian Yearbook of International Affairs [*A publication*]
**IYJGDH**.... Italian Journal of Gastroenterology [*A publication*]
**IYK**.......... Inyokern [*California*] [*Airport symbol*] (OAG)
**IYK**.......... Inyokern, CA [*Location identifier*] [*FAA*] (FAAL)
**IYL**.......... International Youth Library [*See also IJB*] [*Munich, Federal Republic of Germany*] (EAIO)
**IYP**.......... Instant Yellow Pages [*Information service or system*]
**IYPD**.......... International Year for the Preparation of Disarmament [*Pugwash Conference*]
**IYQS**.......... International Year of the Quiet Sun [*1964-65*] [*Also, IQSY*] (KSC)
**IYRU**.......... International Yacht Racing Union [*London, England*]
**IYS**.......... Inverted Y-Suspensor [*Medicine*]
**IYSH**.......... International Year of Shelter for the Homeless [*1987*]
**IYTA**.......... International Yoga Teachers Association (ADA)
**IYU**.......... Baylor University, Waco, TX [*OCLC symbol*] (OCLC)
**IYY**.......... International Youth Year [*1985*] [*United Nations*]
**IYYC**.......... International Youth Year Commission (EA)
**IYYYA8**..... Immok Yukchong Yonku-So Yongu Pogo [*A publication*]
**IZ**.......... Arkia Israel Inland Airlines [*ICAO designator*] (FAAC)

**IZ** .............. Informationszentrum Sozialwissenschaften [*Social Sciences Information Center*] [*Information service or system*] (IID)
**IZ** .............. Inspection Zone
**IZ** .............. Instrumentenbau-Zeitschrift [*A publication*]
**IZ** .............. Interfacial Zone
**IZ** .............. Intermediate Zone
**IZ** .............. Isolation Zone [*Nuclear energy*] (NRCH)
**IZ** .............. Istoriceskii Zapiski Akademii Nauk SSSR [*A publication*]
**IZ** .............. Istoriceskij Zurnal [*A publication*]
**Iz** .............. Izvestiya [*Moscow*] [*A publication*]
**IZ** .............. Spofa Ltd. [*Czechoslovakia*] [*Research code symbol*]
**IZ** .............. Zion-Benton Public Library District, Zion, IL [*Library symbol*] [*Library of Congress*] (LCLS)
**IZA** ........... International Zen Association [*Formerly, European Zen Association*] (EA)
**IZAA**.......... Independent Zinc Alloyers Association (EA)
**IZAA**.......... Isotope-Shift, Zeeman-Effect Atomic Absorption
**IZAPA**....... Internationale Zeitschrift fuer Angewandte Physiologie [*A publication*]
**IZBA**.......... International Zebu Breeders Association (EA)
**Iz Balg Muz** ... Izvestiia na Balgarskite Muzei [*A publication*]
**IZBB**.......... Interagency Zero-Based Budgeting [*Federal government*]
**IZBG**.......... Internationale Zeitschriftenschau fuer Bibelwissenschaft und Grenzgebiete [*Stuttgart/Duesseldorf*] [*A publication*]
**IzBID**......... Izvestiia na B'lgarskoto Istorichesko Druzestvo [*A publication*]
**IZBTBM** ... Instituto de Zootecnia [*Sao Paulo*]. Boletim Tecnico [*A publication*]
**IZC**............ International Zetcentrum [*International Typesetting Center, The Netherlands*]
**IZCA**.......... International Zuma Class Association (EA)
**IZD**............ Implanted Zener Diode (MCD)
**IZD**............ Internationaler Zivildienst [*International Voluntary Service*]
**Izd Zavod Hidroteh Gradevinskog Fak Sarajevu** ... Izdanja Zavod za Hidrotehniku Gradevinskog Fakulteta u Sarajevu [*A publication*]
**IZE**............ Elizabeth City, NC [*Location identifier*] [*FAA*] (FAAL)
**IZE**............ International Association of Zoo Educators (EA)
**IZFMB**....... Izvestiya Akademii Nauk Moldavskoi SSR Seriya Fiziko-Tekhnicheskikh i Matematicheskikh Nauk [*A publication*]
**Izhevsk Med Inst Tr** ... Izhevskii Meditsinskii Institut Trudy [*A publication*]
**Iz Istor Biol** ... Iz Istorii Biologii [*A publication*]
**IZK** ............ Iizuka [*Japan*] [*Seismograph station code, US Geological Survey*] [*Closed*] (SEIS)
**Izk** ............ Izkustvo [*A publication*]
**IZK** ............ Wilkes-Barre/Scranton, PA [*Location identifier*] [*FAA*] (FAAL)
**IZKPAK**.... Internationale Zeitschrift fuer Klinische Pharmakologie, Therapie, und Toxikologie [*A publication*]
**IZL**............ Irgun Zeva'i Le'umi (BJA)
**IZM** ........... Izmir [*Turkey*] [*Airport symbol*] (OAG)
**IZM** ........... Izmir [*Turkey*] [*Seismograph station code, US Geological Survey*] (SEIS)
**Izmen Pochv Okyl't Klassif Diagnostika "Kolos"** ... Izmenenie Pochvy pri Okyl'turivanii Ikh Klassifikatsiya i Diagnostika "Kolos" [*A publication*]
**Izmer Techn** ... Izmerital'naja Technika [*A publication*]
**Izmer Tekh** ... Izmeritel'naya Tekhnika [*A publication*]
**Izmer Tekh Proverochn Delo** ... Izmeritel'naya Tekhnika i Proverochnoe Delo [*A publication*]
**IZN** ........... Izone International Ltd. [*Vancouver Stock Exchange symbol*]
**Iz Narod Muz (Rousse)** ... Izvestiia na Narodniia Muzei (Rousse) [*A publication*]
**Iz Narod Muz Sumen** ... Izvestiia Narodni Muzefa Sumen Bulgaria [*A publication*]
**Iz Narod Muz (Varna)** ... Izvestiia na Narodniia Muzei (Varna) [*A publication*]
**Iznos Zashch Konstr Prom Zdanii** ... Iznos i Zashchita Konstruktsu Promyshlennykh Zdanii [*A publication*]
**IZO** ........... Izumo [*Japan*] [*Airport symbol*] (OAG)
**Izobret Prom Obraztsy Tovarnye Znaki** ... Izobreteniya Promyshlennye Obraztsy Tovarnye Znaki [*A publication*]
**Izobret Ratsion** ... Izobretatel i Ratsionalizator [*USSR*] [*A publication*]
**IZOCAZ**.... Investigaciones Zoologicas Chilenas [*A publication*]
**Izol Elektr Mash** ... Izolyatsiya Elektricheskikh Mashin [*A publication*]
**IZR**............ San Antonio, TX [*Location identifier*] [*FAA*] (FAAL)
**IZS**............ Insulin Zinc Suspension
**IZSch**......... Internationale Zeitschriftenschau fuer Bibelwissenschaft und Grenzgebiete [*Stuttgart/Duesseldorf*] [*A publication*]
**IZSEA** ....... Izvestiya Akademii Nauk SSSR Seriya Ekonomicheskaia [*A publication*]
**IZSORGO** ... Izvestija Zapadno-Sibirskogo Otdela Russkogo Geograficeskogo Obscestva [*A publication*]
**IZTO** ......... Interzonal Trade Office [*NATO*] (NATG)
**IZU** ........... Izuhara [*Japan*] [*Seismograph station code, US Geological Survey*] (SEIS)
**Izv Abhaz Inst Jaz Lit Ist** ... Izvestija Abhazskogo Instituta Jazyka, Literatury, i Istorii [*A publication*]
**Izv Acad Sci USSR Atmos and Oceanic Phys** ... Izvestiya. Academy of Sciences USSR. Atmospheric and Oceanic Physics [*A publication*]
**Izv Acad Sci USSR Atmos Oceanic Phys** ... Izvestiya. Academy of Sciences USSR. Atmospheric and Oceanic Physics [*A publication*]
**Izv Acad Sci USSR Atmospher Ocean Phys** ... Izvestiya. Academy of Sciences USSR. Atmospheric and Oceanic Physics [*A publication*]
**Izv Acad Sci USSR Geol Ser** ... Izvestiya. Academy of Sciences USSR. Geologic Series [*A publication*]
**Izv Acad Sci USSR Phys Solid Earth** ... Izvestiya. Academy of Sciences USSR. Physics of the Solid Earth [*A publication*]
**Izv Akad Krupnogo Sots Selsk Khoz** ... Izvestiya Akademii Krupnogo Sotsialisticheskogo Sel'skogo Khozyaistva [*A publication*]
**Izv Akad Latv SSR Ser Fiz Tekh Nauk** ... Izvestiya Akademii Latviiskoi SSR Seriya Fizicheskikh i Tekhnicheskikh Nauk [*Latvian SSR*] [*A publication*]
**Izv Akad Nauk** ... Izvestiya Akademii Nauk [*A publication*]
**Izv Akad Nauk Armjan SSR Ser Fiz** ... Izvestija Akademii Nauk Armjanskoi SSR Serija Fizika [*A publication*]
**Izv Akad Nauk Armjan SSR Ser Mat** ... Izvestija Akademii Nauk Armjanskoi SSR Serija Matematika [*A publication*]
**Izv Akad Nauk Armjan SSR Ser Meh** ... Izvestija Akademii Nauk Armjanskoi SSR Serija Mehanika [*A publication*]
**Izv Akad Nauk Armjan SSR Ser Tehn Nauk** ... Izvestija Akademii Nauk Armjanskoi SSR Serija Tehniceskih Nauk [*A publication*]
**Izv Akad Nauk Arm SSR** ... Izvestiya Akademii Nauk Armyanskoi SSR [*A publication*]
**Izv Akad Nauk Arm SSR Biol Nauki** ... Izvestiya Akademii Nauk Armyanskoi SSR Biologicheskie Nauki [*A publication*]
**Izv Akad Nauk Arm SSR Biol S-Kh Nauki** ... Izvestiya Akademii Nauk Armyanskoi SSR Biologicheskie i Sel'skokhozyaistvennye Nauki [*A publication*]
**Izv Akad Nauk Arm SSR Estestv Nauki** ... Izvestiya Akademii Nauk Armyanskoi SSR Estestvennye Nauki [*A publication*]
**Izv Akad Nauk Arm SSR Fiz** ... Izvestiya Akademia Nauk Armyanskoi SSR Fizika [*A publication*]
**Izv Akad Nauk Arm SSR Fiz Mat Estest Tekh Nauki** ... Izvestiya Akademii Nauk Armyanskoi SSR Fiziko Matematicheskie Estestvennye i T ekhnicheskie Nauki [*A publication*]
**Izv Akad Nauk Arm SSR Geol Geogr Nauki** ... Izvestiya Akademii Nauk Armyanskoi SSR Geologicheskie i Geograficheskie Nauki [*Armenian SSR*] [*A publication*]
**Izv Akad Nauk Arm SSR Khim Nauki** ... Izvestiya Akademii Nauk Armyanskoi SSR Khimicheskie Nauki [*Armenian SSR*] [*A publication*]
**Izv Akad Nauk Arm SSR Med Nauki** ... Izvestiya Akademii Nauk Armyanskoi SSR Meditsinskie Nauki [*A publication*]
**Izv Akad Nauk Arm SSR Mekh** ... Izvestiya Akademii Nauk Armyanskoi SSR Mekhanika [*A publication*]
**Izv Akad Nauk Arm SSR Nauki Zemle** ... Izvestiya Akademii Nauk Armyanskoi SSR Nauki po Zemle [*Armenian SSR*] [*A publication*]
**Izv Akad Nauk Arm SSR Ser Fiz-Mat Nauk** ... Izvestiya Akademii Nauk Armyanskoi SSR Seriya Fiziko-Matematicheskikh Nauk [*Armenian SSR*] [*A publication*]
**Izv Akad Nauk Arm SSR Ser Mat** ... Izvestiya Akademii Nauk Armyanskoi SSR Seriya Matematika [*Armenian SSR*] [*A publication*]
**Izv Akad Nauk Arm SSR Ser Mekh** ... Izvestiya Akademii Nauk Armyanskoi SSR Seriya Mekhanika [*Armenian SSR*] [*A publication*]
**Izv Akad Nauk Arm SSR Ser Tekh Nauk** ... Izvestiya Akademii Nauk Armyanskoi SSR Seriya Tekhnicheskikh Nauk [*Armenian SSR*] [*A publication*]
**Izv Akad Nauk Armyan SSR Biol Nauk** ... Izvestiya Akademiya Nauk Armyanskoi SSR Biologicheskie Nauk [*A publication*]
**Izv Akad Nauk Armyan SSR Ser Mekh** ... Izvestiya Akademii Nauk Armyanskoi SSR Seriya Mekhanika [*A publication*]
**Izv Akad Nauk Armyan SSR Ser Tekhn Nauk** ... Izvestiya Akademii Nauk Armyanskoi SSR Seriya Tekhnicheskikh Nauk [*A publication*]
**Izv Akad Nauk Azerbaidzan SSR Ser Fiz Tehn Mat Nauk** ... Izvestija Akademii Nauk Azerbaidzanskoi SSR Serija Fiziko-Tehniceskih i Matematiceskih Nauk [*A publication*]
**Izv Akad Nauk Azerb SSR** ... Izvestiya Akademii Nauk Azerbaidzhanskoi SSR [*A publication*]
**Izv Akad Nauk Azerb SSR Ser Biol Nauk** ... Izvestiya Akademii Nauk Azerbaidzhanskoi SSR Seriya Biologicheskikh Nauk [*A publication*]
**Izv Akad Nauk Azerb SSR Ser Lit Jaz Isk** ... Izvestija Akademii Nauk Azerbajdzanskogo SSR Serija Literatury, Jazyka, i Iskusstva [*A publication*]
**Izv Akad Nauk Azerb SSR Ser Nauk Zemle** ... Izvestiya Akademii Nauk Azerbajdzhanskoj SSR Seriya Nauk i Zemle [*A publication*]
**Izv Akad Nauk Az SSR** ... Izvestiya Akademii Nauk Azerbaidzhanskoi SSR [*A publication*]
**Izv Akad Nauk Az SSR Ser Biol Med Nauk** ... Izvestiya Akademii Nauk Azerbaidzhanskoi SSR Seriya Biologicheskikh i Meditsinskikh Nauk [*A publication*]
**Izv Akad Nauk Az SSR Ser Biol Nauk** ... Izvestiya. Akademii Nauk Azerbaidzhanskoi SSR Seriya Biologicheskikh Nauk [*A publication*]
**Izv Akad Nauk Az SSR Ser Fiz-Tekh i Mat Nauk** ... Izvestiya Akademii Nauk Azerbaidzhanskoi SSR Seriya Fiziko-Tekhnicheskikh i Matematicheskikh Nauk [*A publication*]

**Izv Akad Nauk Az SSR Ser Fiz-Tekh Mat Nauk** ... Izvestiya Akademii Nauk Azerbaidzhanskoi SSR Seriya Fiziko-Tekhnicheskikh i Matematicheskikh Nauk [*Azerbaidzhan SSR*] [*A publication*]
**Izv Akad Nauk Beloruss SSR Ser Biol Nauk** ... Izvestiya Akademii Nauk Belorusskoi SSR. Seriya Biologicheskikh Nauk [*A publication*]
**Izv Akad Nauk B SSR** ... Izvestiya Akademii Nauk Belorusskoi SSR [*A publication*]
**Izv Akad Nauk B SSR Ser Biol Nauk** ... Izvestiya Akademii Nauk Belorusskoi SSR Seriya Biologicheskikh Nauk [*A publication*]
**Izv Akad Nauk BSSR Ser Fiz-Mat Nauk** ... Izvestiya Akademii Nauk BSSR Seriya Fiziko-Matematicheskikh Nauk [*Belorussian S SR*] [*A publication*]
**Izv Akad Nauk B SSR Ser S Kh Nauk** ... Izvestiya Akademii Nauk Belorusskoi SSR Seriya Sel'skokhozyaistvennykh Nauk [*A publication*]
**Izv Akad Nauk BSSR Ser S-Kh Navuk** ... Izvestiia Akademii Nauk BSSR. Seriia Selskokhoziaistvennykh Navuk [*A publication*]
**Izv Akad Nauk Ehst SSR Geol** ... Izvestiya Akademii Nauk Ehstonskoj SSR Geologiya [*A publication*]
**Izv Akad Nauk Ehst SSR Khim Geol** ... Izvestiya Akademii Nauk Ehstonskoj SSR Khimiya i Geologiya [*A publication*]
**Izv Akad Nauk Estonskoi SSR Fiz Mat** ... Izvestiya Akademii Nauk Estonskoi SSR Seriya Fizichesko. Matematicheskaya [*A publication*]
**Izv Akad Nauk Estonskoi SSR Khim** ... Izvestiya Akademii Nauk Estonskoi SSR Seriya Khimicheskaya [*A publication*]
**Izv Akad Nauk Eston SSR Obsc Nauki** ... Izvestija Akademii Nauk Estonskoj SSR Obscestvennye Nauki [*A publication*]
**Izv Akad Nauk Eston SSR Ser Biol** ... Izvestiya Akademii Nauk Estonskoi SSR Seriya Biologicheskaya [*A publication*]
**Izv Akad Nauk Est SSR Biol** ... Izvestiia Akademii Nauk Estonskoi SSR. Biologiia [*A publication*]
**Izv Akad Nauk Est SSR Fiz Mat** ... Izvestiya Akademii Nauk Estonskoi SSR Fizika Matematika [*Estonian SSR*] [*A publication*]
**Izv Akad Nauk Est SSR Khim Eesti NSV Tead Akad Toim Keem** ... Izvestiia Akademii Nauk Estonskoi SSR Khimiia Eesti NSV Teaduste Akadeemia Toimetised Keemia [*A publication*]
**Izv Akad Nauk Est SSR Ser Biol** ... Izvestiya Akademii Nauk Estonskoi SSR Seriya Biologicheskaya [*A publication*]
**Izv Akad Nauk Est SSR Ser Fiz Mat Tekh Nauk** ... Izvestiia Akademii Nauk Estonskoi SSR Seriia Fiziko-Matematicheskikh i Tekhnicheskikh Nauk [*Estonian SSR*] [*A publication*]
**Izv Akad Nauk Gruz SSR Ser Biol** ... Izvestiya Akademii Nauk Gruzinskoi SSR Seriya Biologicheskaya [*Georgian SSR*] [*A publication*]
**Izv Akad Nauk Gruz SSR Ser Khim** ... Izvestiya Akademii Nauk Gruzinskoi SSR Seriya Khimicheskaya [*A publication*]
**Izv Akad Nauk Kazah SSR Ser Fiz-Mat** ... Izvestija Akademii Nauk Kazahskoj SSR Serija Fiziko-Matematiceskaja [*A publication*]
**Izv Akad Nauk Kazah SSR Ser Obsc Nauk** ... Izvestija Akademii Nauk Kazahskoj SSR Serija Obscestvennyh Nauk [*A publication*]
**Izv Akad Nauk Kazakh SSR** ... Izvestiya Akademii Nauk Kazakhskoi SSR [*A publication*]
**Izv Akad Nauk Kazakh SSR Ser Biol** ... Izvestiya Akademii Nauk Kazakhskoi SSR Seriya Biologicheskaya [*A publication*]
**Izv Akad Nauk Kazakh SSR Ser Bot Pochvoved** ... Izvestiya Akademii Nauk Kazakhskoi SSR Seriya Botaniki i Pochvovedeniya [*A publication*]
**Izv Akad Nauk Kaz SSR Ser Astron Fiz** ... Izvestiya Akademii Nauk Kazakhskoi SSR Seriya Astronomicheskaya i Fizicheskaya [*A publication*]
**Izv Akad Nauk Kaz SSR Ser Astron Fiz Mat Mekh** ... Izvestiya Akademii Nauk Kazakhskoi SSR Seriya Astronomii, Fiziki, Matematiki , Mekhaniki [*A publication*]
**Izv Akad Nauk Kaz SSR Ser Biol** ... Izvestiya Akademii Nauk Kazakhskoi SSR Seriya Biologicheskaya [*A publication*]
**Izv Akad Nauk Kaz SSR Ser Biol Nauk** ... Izvestiya Akademii Nauk Kazakhskoi SSR Seriya Biologicheskikh Nauk [*A publication*]
**Izv Akad Nauk Kaz SSR Ser Bot Pochvoved** ... Izvestiya Akademii Nauk Kazakhskoi SSR Seriya Botaniki i Pochvovedeniya [*A publication*]
**Izv Akad Nauk Kaz SSR Ser Energ** ... Izvestiya Akademii Nauk Kazakhskoi SSR Seriya Energeticheskaya [*A publication*]
**Izv Akad Nauk Kaz SSR Ser Fiziol** ... Izvestiya Akademii Nauk Kazakhskoi SSR Seriya Fiziologicheskaya [*A publication*]
**Izv Akad Nauk Kaz SSR Ser Fiziol Biokhim Rast** ... Izvestiya Akademii Nauk Kazakhskoi SSR Seriya Fiziologii i Biokhimii Rastenii [*A publication*]
**Izv Akad Nauk Kaz SSR Ser Fiz-Mat** ... Izvestiya Akademii Nauk Kazakhskoi SSR Seriya Fiziko-Matematicheskaya [*A publication*]
**Izv Akad Nauk Kaz SSR Ser Fiz-Mat Nauk** ... Izvestiya Akademii Nauk Kazakhskoi SSR Seriya Fiziko-Matematicheskikh Nauk [*Kazakh SSR*] [*A publication*]
**Izv Akad Nauk Kaz SSR Ser Geol** ... Izvestiya Akademii Nauk Kazakhskoi SSR Seriya Geologicheskaya [*A publication*]
**Izv Akad Nauk Kaz SSR Ser Gorn Dela** ... Izvestiya Akademii Nauk Kazakhskoi SSR Seriya Gornogo Dela [*A publication*]
**Izv Akad Nauk Kaz SSR Ser Gorn Dela Metall Stroit Stroimat** ... Izvestiya Akademii Nauk Kazakhskoi SSR Seriya Gornogo Dela Metallurgii Stroitel'stva i Stroimaterialov [*A publication*]
**Izv Akad Nauk Kaz SSR Ser Khim** ... Izvestiya Akademii Nauk Kazakhskoi SSR Seriya Khimicheskaya [*A publication*]
**Izv Akad Nauk Kaz SSR Ser Mat Mekh** ... Izvestiya Akademii Nauk Kazakhskoi SSR Seriya Matematiki i Mekhaniki [*A publication*]
**Izv Akad Nauk Kaz SSR Ser Med Fiziol** ... Izvestiya Akademii Nauk Kazakhskoi SSR Seriya Meditsiny i Fiziologii [*A publication*]
**Izv Akad Nauk Kaz SSR Ser Med Nauk** ... Izvestiya Akademii Nauk Kazakhskoi SSR Seriya Meditsinskikh Nauk [*A publication*]
**Izv Akad Nauk Kaz SSR Ser Metall Obogashch Ogneuporov** ... Izvestiya Akademii Nauk Kazakhskoi SSR Seriya Metallurgii. Obogashcheniya i Ogneuporov [*A publication*]
**Izv Akad Nauk Kaz SSR Ser Mikrobiol** ... Izvestiya Akademii Nauk Kazakhskoi SSR Seriya Mikrobiologicheskaya [*A publication*]
**Izv Akad Nauk Kaz SSR Ser Tekh Khim Nauk** ... Izvestiya Akademii Nauk Kazakhskoi SSR Seriya Tekhnicheskikh Khimicheskikh Nauk [*A publication*]
**Izv Akad Nauk Kaz SSR Ser Zool** ... Izvestiya Akademii Nauk Kazakhskoi SSR Seriya Zoologicheskaya [*A publication*]
**Izv Akad Nauk Kirgiz SSR** ... Izvestija Akademija Nauk Kirgizskoi SSR [*A publication*]
**Izv Akad Nauk Kirgiz SSR Ser Biol Nauk** ... Izvestiya Akademii Nauk Kirgizskoi SSR Seriya Biologicheskikh Nauk [*A publication*]
**Izv Akad Nauk Kirg SSR** ... Izvestiya Akademii Nauk Kirgizskoi SSR [*A publication*]
**Izv Akad Nauk Kirg SSR Ser Biol Nauk** ... Izvestiya Akademii Nauk Kirgizskoi SSR Seriya Biologicheskikh Nauk [*A publication*]
**Izv Akad Nauk Kirg SSR Ser Estestv Tekh Nauk** ... Izvestiya Akademii Nauk Kirgizskoi SSR Seriya Estestvennykh i Tekhnicheskikh Nauk [*Kirgiz SSR*] [*A publication*]
**Izv Akad Nauk Latvii SSR** ... Izvestiya Akademii Nauk Latviiskoi SSR [*A publication*]
**Izv Akad Nauk Latv SSR** ... Izvestiya Akademii Nauk Latviiskoi SSR [*A publication*]
**Izv Akad Nauk Latv SSR Khim** ... Izvestiya Akademii Nauk Latviiskoi SSR Seriya Khimicheskikh Nauk [*A publication*]
**Izv Akad Nauk Latv SSR Ser Fiz Tekh Nauk** ... Izvestiya Akademii Nauk Latviiskoi SSR Seriya Fizicheskikh i Tekhnicheskikh Nauk [*A publication*]
**Izv Akad Nauk Latv SSR Ser Khim** ... Izvestiya Akademii Nauk Latviiskoi SSR Seriya Khimicheskaya [*A publication*]
**Izv Akad Nauk Moldav SSR** ... Izvestiya Akademii Nauk Moldavskoi SSR [*A publication*]
**Izv Akad Nauk Moldav SSR Ser Fiz-Tehn Mat Nauk** ... Izvestija Akademii Nauk Moldavskoj SSR Serija Fiziko-Tehniceskih i Matematiceskih Nauk [*A publication*]
**Izv Akad Nauk Mold SSR** ... Izvestiya Akademii Nauk Moldavskoi SSR [*A publication*]
**Izv Akad Nauk Mold SSR Ser Biol** ... Izvestiya Akademii Nauk Moldavskoi SSR Seriya Biologicheskaya [*A publication*]
**Izv Akad Nauk Mold SSR Ser Biol Khim Nauk** ... Izvestiya Akademii Nauk Moldavskoi SSR Seriya Biologicheskikh i Khimicheskikh Nauk [*A publication*]
**Izv Akad Nauk Mold SSR Ser Biol S-Kh Nauk** ... Izvestiya Akademii Nauk Moldavskoi SSR Seriya Biologicheskikh i Sel'skokhozyaistvennykh Nauk [*A publication*]
**Izv Akad Nauk Mold SSR Ser Fiz-Tekh Mat Nauk** ... Izvestiya Akademii Nauk Moldavskoi SSR Seriya Fiziko-Tekhnicheskikh i Matematicheskikh Nauk [*A publication*]
**Izv Akad Nauk Mold SSR Ser Obsc Nauk** ... Izvestija Akademii Nauk Moldavskoj SSR Serija Obscestvennyh Nauk [*A publication*]
**Izv Akad Nauk SSR Mekh Zhidk Gaza** ... Izvestiya Akademii Nauk SSSR Mekhanika Zhidkosti i Gaza [*A publication*]
**Izv Akad Nauk SSSR** ... Izvestiya Akademii Nauk SSSR [*A publication*]
**Izv Akad Nauk SSSR Biol** ... Izvestiya Akademii Nauk SSSR Seriya Biologicheskaya [*A publication*]
**Izv Akad Nauk SSSR Energ Transp** ... Izvestiya Akademii Nauk SSSR Energetika i Transport [*A publication*]
**Izv Akad Nauk SSSR Fiz** ... Izvestiya Akademii Nauk SSSR Seriya Fizicheskaya [*A publication*]
**Izv Akad Nauk SSSR Fiz Atmos i Okeana** ... Izvestiya Akademii Nauk SSSR Fizika Atmosfery i Okeana [*A publication*]
**Izv Akad Nauk SSSR Fiz Atmos Okeana** ... Izvestiya Akademii Nauk SSSR Fizika Atmosfery i Okeana [*A publication*]
**Izv Akad Nauk SSSR Fiz Zemli** ... Izvestiya Akademii Nauk SSSR Fizika Zemli [*A publication*]
**Izv Akad Nauk SSSR Khim** ... Izvestiya Akademii Nauk SSSR Seriya Khimicheskaya [*A publication*]
**Izv Akad Nauk SSSR Meh Tverd Tela** ... Izvestija Akademii Nauk SSSR Mehanika Tverdogo Tela [*A publication*]
**Izv Akad Nauk SSSR Meh Zidk Gaza** ... Izvestija Akademii Nauk SSSR Mehanika Zidkosti i Gaza [*A publication*]

**Izv Akad Nauk SSSR Mekh** ... Izvestiya Akademii Nauk SSSR Mekhanika [*A publication*]
**Izv Akad Nauk SSSR Mekh Mashinostr** ... Izvestiya Akademii Nauk SSSR Mekhanika i Mashinostroenie [*A publication*]
**Izv Akad Nauk SSSR Mekh Tverd Tela** ... Izvestiya Akademii Nauk SSSR Mekhanika Tverdogo Tela [*A publication*]
**Izv Akad Nauk SSSR Mekh Zhidk i Gaza** ... Izvestiya Akademii Nauk SSSR Mekhanika Zhidkosti i Gaza [*A publication*]
**Izv Akad Nauk SSSR Mekh Zhidk Gaza** ... Izvestiya Akademii Nauk SSSR Mekhanika Zhidkosti i Gaza [*A publication*]
**Izv Akad Nauk SSSR Mekh Zhidkosti Gaza** ... Izvestiya Akademii Nauk SSSR Mekhanika Zhidkosti i Gaza [*A publication*]
**Izv Akad Nauk SSSR Met** ... Izvestiya Akademii Nauk SSSR Metally [*A publication*]
**Izv Akad Nauk SSSR Metall Gorn Delo** ... Izvestiya Akademii Nauk SSSR Metallurgiya i Gornoe Delo [*A publication*]
**Izv Akad Nauk SSSR Metally** ... Izvestiya Akademii Nauk SSSR Metally [*A publication*]
**Izv Akad Nauk SSSR Neorg Mater** ... Izvestiya Akademii Nauk SSSR Neorganicheskie Materialy [*A publication*]
**Izv Akad Nauk SSSR Otd Mat Estestv Nauk** ... Izvestiya Akademii Nauk SSSR Otdelenie Matematicheskikh i Estestvennykh Nauk [*A publication*]
**Izv Akad Nauk SSSR Otd Tekh Nauk** ... Izvestiya Akademii Nauk SSSR Otdelenie Tekhnicheskikh Nauk [*USSR*] [*A publication*]
**Izv Akad Nauk SSSR Otd Tekh Nauk Energ Avtom** ... Izvestiya Akademii Nauk SSSR Otdelenie Tekhnicheskikh Nauk Energetika i Avtomatika [*USSR*] [*A publication*]
**Izv Akad Nauk SSSR Otd Tekh Nauk Energ Transp** ... Izvestiya Akademii Nauk SSSR Otdelenie Tekhnicheskikh Nauk Energetika i Transport [*A publication*]
**Izv Akad Nauk SSSR Otd Tekh Nauk Mekh Mashinstr** ... Izvestiya Akademii Nauk SSSR Otdelenie Tekhnicheskikh Nauk Mekhanika i Mashinostroenie [*USSR*] [*A publication*]
**Izv Akad Nauk SSSR Otd Tekh Nauk Mekh Masinostr** ... Izvestiya Akademii Nauk SSSR Otdelenie Tekhnicheskikh Nauk Mekhanika i Mashinostroenie [*A publication*]
**Izv Akad Nauk SSSR Otd Tekh Nauk Metall Topl** ... Izvestiya Akademii Nauk SSSR Otdelenie Tekhnicheskikh Nauk Metallurgiya i Toplivo [*USSR*] [*A publication*]
**Izv Akad Nauk SSSR Ser Biol** ... Izvestiya Akademii Nauk SSSR Seriya Biologicheskaya [*A publication*]
**Izv Akad Nauk SSSR Ser Ekon** ... Izvestija Akademii Nauk SSSR Serija Ekonomiceskaja [*A publication*]
**Izv Akad Nauk SSSR Ser Fiz** ... Izvestiya Akademii Nauk SSSR Seriya Fizicheskaya [*A publication*]
**Izv Akad Nauk SSSR Ser Fiz Atmosfer i Okeana** ... Izvestija Akademii Nauk SSSR Serija Fizika Atmosfery i Okeana [*A publication*]
**Izv Akad Nauk SSSR Ser Fiz Zemli** ... Izvestija Akademii Nauk SSSR Serija Fizika Zemli [*A publication*]
**Izv Akad Nauk SSSR Ser Geofiz** ... Izvestiya Akademii Nauk SSSR Seriya Geofizicheskaya [*USSR*] [*A publication*]
**Izv Akad Nauk SSSR Ser Geogr** ... Izvestiya Akademii Nauk SSSR Seriya Geograficheskaya [*A publication*]
**Izv Akad Nauk SSSR Ser Geogr Geofiz** ... Izvestiya Akademii Nauk SSSR Seriya Geograficheskaya i Geofizicheskaya [*A publication*]
**Izv Akad Nauk SSSR Ser Geol** ... Izvestiya Akademii Nauk SSSR Seriya Geologicheskaya [*A publication*]
**Izv Akad Nauk SSSR Ser Geol (Transl Abstr)** ... Izvestiya Akademii Nauk SSSR Seriya Geologicheskaya (Translated Abstracts) [*A publication*]
**Izv Akad Nauk SSSR Ser Khim** ... Izvestiya Akademii Nauk SSSR Seriya Khimicheskaya [*A publication*]
**Izv Akad Nauk SSSR Ser Mat** ... Izvestiya Akademii Nauk SSSR Seriya Matematicheskaya [*A publication*]
**Izv Akad Nauk SSSR Tehn Kibernet** ... Izvestija Akademii Nauk SSSR Tekhniceskaja Kibernetika [*A publication*]
**Izv Akad Nauk SSSR Tekh Kibern** ... Izvestiya Akademii Nauk SSSR Tekhnicheskaya Kibernetika [*A publication*]
**Izv Akad Nauk SSSR Tekhn Kibernet** ... Izvestiya Akademii Nauk SSSR Tekhnicheskaya Kibernetika [*A publication*]
**Izv Akad Nauk Tadzhik SSR Otd Biol Nauk** ... Izvestiya Akademii Nauk Tadzhikskoi SSR Otdelenie Biologicheskikh Nauk [*A publication*]
**Izv Akad Nauk Tadzhik SSR Otdel Fiz-Mat Khim i Geol Nauk** ... Izvestiya Akademii Nauk Tadzhikskoi SSR Otdelenie Fiziko-Matematicheskikh, Khimicheskikh, i Geologicheskikh Nauk [*A publication*]
**Izv Akad Nauk Tadzhik SSR Otd Fiz-Tekh Khim Nauk** ... Izvestiya Akademii Nauk Tadzhikskoi SSR Otdelenie Fizichesko-Tekhnicheskikh Kh imicheskikh Nauk [*A publication*]
**Izv Akad Nauk Tadzh SSR Otd Biol Nauk** ... Izvestiya Akademii Nauk Tadzhikskoi SSR Otdelenie Biologicheskikh Nauk [*A publication*]
**Izv Akad Nauk Tadzh SSR Otd Estestv Nauk** ... Izvestiya Akademii Nauk Tadzhikskoi SSR Otdelenie Estestvennykh Nauk [*A publication*]
**Izv Akad Nauk Tadzh SSR Otd Fiz-Mat Geol-Khim Nauk** ... Izvestiya Akademii Nauk Tadzhikskoi SSR Otdelenie Fiziko-Matematicheskikh i Geologo-Khimicheskikh Nauk [*Later, Izvestiya Akademi Nauk Tadzhikskoi SSR Otdelenie Fiziko-Matematicheskikh, Khimicheskikh, i Geologicheskikh Nauk*] [*A publication*]
**Izv Akad Nauk Tadzh SSR Otd Fiz Mat Khim Geol Nauk** ... Izvestiya Akademii Nauk Tadzhikskoi SSR Otdelenie Fiziko-Matematicheskikh, Khimicheskikh, i Geologicheskikh Nauk [*A publication*]
**Izv Akad Nauk Tadzh SSR Otd Fiz-Tekh Khim Nauk** ... Izvestiya Akademii Nauk Tadzhikskoi SSR Otdelenie Fiziko-Tekhnicheskikh i Khimicheskikh Nauk [*Tadzhik SSR*] [*A publication*]
**Izv Akad Nauk Tadzh SSR Otd S-Kh Biol Nauk** ... Izvestiya Akademii Nauk Tadzhikskoi SSR Otdelenie Sel'skokhozyaistvennykh i Biologicheskikh Nauk [*A publication*]
**Izv Akad Nauk Tadzik SSR Otdel Fiz-Mat i Geolog-Him Nauk** ... Izvestija Akademii Nauk Tadzikskoi SSR Otdelenie Fiziko-Matematiceskih i Geologo-Himiceskih Nauk [*A publication*]
**Izv Akad Nauk Tadz SSR Otdelenie Obsc Nauk** ... Izvestija Akademii Nauk Tadzikiskoj SSR Otdelenie Obscestvennyh Nauk [*A publication*]
**Izv Akad Nauk Turkmen SSR Ser Biol Nauk** ... Izvestiya Akademii Nauk Turkmenskoi SSR Seriya Biologicheskikh Nauk [*A publication*]
**Izv Akad Nauk Turkmen SSR Ser Fiz-Tehn Him Geol Nauk** ... Izvestija Akademii Nauk Turkmenskoi SSR Serija Fiziko-Tehniceskih Himiceskih i Geologiceskih Nauk [*A publication*]
**Izv Akad Nauk Turkm SSR** ... Izvestiya Akademii Nauk Turkmenskoi SSR [*A publication*]
**Izv Akad Nauk Turkm SSR Ser Biol Nauk** ... Izvestiya Akademii Nauk Turkmenskoi SSR Seriya Biologicheskikh Nauk [*A publication*]
**Izv Akad Nauk Turkm SSR Ser Fiz-Tekh Khim Geol Nauk** ... Izvestiya Akademii Nauk Turkmenskoi SSR Seriya Fiziko-Tekhnicheskikh, Khimicheskikh, i Geologicheskikh Nauk [*A publication*]
**Izv Akad Nauk Turkm SSR Ser Obsc Nauk** ... Izvestija Akademii Nauk Turkmenskoj SSR Serija Obscestvennyh Nauk [*A publication*]
**Izv Akad Nauk Turkm SSSR Ser Obshchestv Nauk** ... Izvestiya Akademii Nauk Turkmenskoi SSSR Seriya Obshchestvennykh Nauk [*A publication*]
**Izv Akad Nauk Uzb SSR** ... Izvestiya Akademii Nauk Uzbekskoi SSR [*A publication*]
**Izv Akad Nauk Uzb SSR Ser Biol** ... Izvestiya Akademii Nauk Uzbekskoi SSR Seriya Biologicheskaya [*A publication*]
**Izv Akad Nauk Uzb SSR Ser Fiz-Mat Nauk** ... Izvestiya Akademii Nauk Uzbekskoi SSR Seriya Fiziko-Matematicheskikh Nauk [*A publication*]
**Izv Akad Nauk Uzb SSR Ser Geol** ... Izvestiya Akademii Nauk Uzbekskoi SSR Seriya Geologicheskaya [*A publication*]
**Izv Akad Nauk Uzb SSR Ser Khim Nauk** ... Izvestiya Akademii Nauk Uzbekskoi SSR Seriya Khimicheskikh Nauk [*A publication*]
**Izv Akad Nauk Uzb SSR Ser Med** ... Izvestiya Akademii Nauk Uzbekskoi SSR Seriya Meditsinskaya [*A publication*]
**Izv Akad Nauk Uzb SSR Ser Tekh Nauk** ... Izvestiya Akademii Nauk Uzbekskoi SSR Seriya Tekhnicheskikh Nauk [*A publication*]
**Izv Akad Nauk UzSSR Ser Fiz-Mat Nauk** ... Izvestija Akademii Nauk UzSSR. Serija Fiziko-Matematiceskih Nauk [*A publication*]
**Izv Akad Nauk UzSSR Ser Tekh Nauk** ... Izvestiya Akademii Nauk Uzbekskoi SSR Seriya Tekhnicheskikh Nauk [*A publication*]
**Izv Akad Pedagog Nauk RSFSR** ... Izvestiya Akademii Pedagogicheskikh Nauk RSFSR [*A publication*]
**Izv Akad Uzb SSR** ... Izvestiya Akademii Nauk Uzbekskoi SSR [*A publication*]
**Izv Akad Uzb SSR Fiz-Mat** ... Izvestiya Akademii Nauk Uzbekskoi SSR Seriya Fiziko-Matematicheskikh Nauk [*A publication*]
**Izv Ak N Armj SSR** ... Izvestija Akademii Nauk Armjanskoj SSR [*A publication*]
**Izv Ak N Kaz** ... Izvestija Akademii Nauk Kazahskoj SSR [*A publication*]
**Izv Ak N Mold SSR** ... Izvestija Akademii Nauk Moldavskoj SSR [*A publication*]
**Izv Ak N SSSR** ... Izvestija Akademii Nauk SSSR [*A publication*]
**Izv Ak N SSSR Ser Geogr** ... Izvestija Akademii Nauk SSSR Serija Geograficeskaja I Geofiziceskaja [*A publication*]
**Izv Altai Otd Geogr O-Va SSSR** ... Izvestiya Altaiskogo Otdela Geograficheskogo Obscestva SSSR [*A publication*]
**IzvAN**......... Izvestiya Akademii Nauk SSSR Otdelenie Literatury i Jazyka [*A publication*]
**IzvANArm** ... Izvestiya Akademii Nauk Armjanskoj SSR Obscestvennyh Nauk [*A publication*]
**IzvANAzerb** ... Izvestiya Akademii Nauk Azerbajdzhanskoj SSR Seriya Obscestvennych Nauk [*A publication*]

**IzvANKaz**.. Izvestiya Akademii Nauk Kazakhshkoi SSR Seriya Filologii i Iskusstvovedeniya [*A publication*]
**Izv ANO Ch N** ... Izvestija Akademii Nauk Otdelenie Chimiceskich Nauk [*A publication*]
**Izvanredna Izd Farmakol Inst Zagrebu** ... Izvanredna Izdanja Farmakoloskog Instituta Zagrebu [*A publication*]
**IzvANTadz** ... Izvestiya Akademii Nauk Tadzhikskoi SSR Otdelenie Obscestvennych Nauk [*A publication*]
**IzvANTurkm** ... Izvestiya Akademii Nauk Turkmenskoi SSSR Seriya Obshchestvennych Nauk [*A publication*]
**Izv Arch Inst** ... Izvestija na Archeologiceskija Institut [*A publication*]
**Izv Arm Fil Akad Nauk SSSR** ... Izvestiya Armyanskogo Filiala Akademii Nauk SSSR [*A publication*]
**Izv Arm Fil Akad Nauk SSSR Estestv Nauki** ... Izvestiya Armyanskogo Filiala Akademii Nauk SSSR Estestvennye Nauki [*A publication*]
**IzvArmZPI** ... Izvestiya Armyanskogo Gosudarstvennogo Zaocnogo Pedagogiceskogo Instituta [*A publication*]
**Izv Astrofiz Inst Akad Nauk Kaz SSR** ... Izvestiya Astrofizicheskogo Instituta. Akademiya Nauk Kazakhshkoi SSR [*A publication*]
**IZVBA**....... Internationale Zeitschrift fuer Vitaminforschung. Beiheft [*A publication*]
**IzvBAI** ....... Izvestiya na Balgarskiya Archeologiceski Institut [*A publication*]
**Izv Batum Bot Sada** ... Izvestiya Batumskogo Botanicheskogo Sada [*A publication*]
**Izv Batum Bot Sada Akad Nauk Gruz SSR** ... Izvestiya Batumskogo Botanicheskogo Sada Akademii Nauk Gruzinskoi SSR [*A publication*]
**Izv Biol Geogr Nauchno Issled Inst Irkutsk Gos Univ** ... Izvestiya Biologo-Geograficheskogo Nauchno-Issledovatel'skogo Instituta pri Irkutskom Gosudarstvennom Universitete [*A publication*]
**Izv Biol Nauchno-Issled Inst Biol Stn Permsk Gos Univ** ... Izvestiya Biologicheskogo Nauchno-Issledovatel'skogo Instituta i Biologicheskoi Stantsii pri Permskom Gosudarstvennom Universitete [*A publication*]
**Izv Biol Nauchno Issled Inst Molotov Gos Univ** ... Izvestiya Biologicheskogo Nauchno-Issledovatel'skogo Instituta pri Molotovskom Gosudarstvennom Universitete [*A publication*]
**Izv Bot Inst** ... Izvestija na Botaniceskija Institut [*A publication*]
**Izv Bot Inst B Akad Nauk Otd Biol Nauki** ... Izvestiya na Botanicheskiya Instituta B'lgarska Akademiya Naukite Otdelenie za Biologichni Nauki [*A publication*]
**Izv Bot Inst B'lg Akad Nauk** ... Izvestiya na Botanicheskiya Instituta B'lgarska Akademiya na Naukite [*A publication*]
**Izv Bulg Akad Nauk Otd Fiz Mat Tekh Nauki Ser Fiz** ... Izvestiya na Bulgarskata Akademiya na Naukite. Otdelenie za Fiziko-Matematicheski i Tekhnicheski Nauki Seriya Fizicheska [*A publication*]
**Izv Burgas** ... Izvestija na Narodnija Muzej Burgas [*A publication*]
**Izv Cent Chelmint Lab** ... Izvestija na Centralnata Chelmintologicna Laboratorija [*A publication*]
**IzvCIngNII** ... Izvestiya Ceceno-Ingusskogo Naucno-Issledovatel-Skogo Instituta Istorii, Jazyka, i Literatury [*A publication*]
**Izv Dnepropetr Gorn Inst** ... Izvestiya Dnepropetrovskogo Gornogo Instituta [*A publication*]
**Izv Dobruzhan Selskostop Nauchnoizsled Inst Tolbukhin** ... Izvestiya na Dobrudzhanskiya Selskostopanski Nauchnoizsledovatelski Institut Tolbukhin [*A publication*]
**IzvDS** ......... Izvestiya na Druzestovoto na Filolozite-Slavisti v Balgarija (Sofija) [*A publication*]
**Izv Ekaterinosl Vyssh Gorn Uchil** ... Izvestiya Ekaterinoslavskogo Vysshago Gornago Uchilishcha [*A publication*]
**Izv Energ Inst Akad Nauk SSSR** ... Izvestiya Energeticheskogo Instituta Akademiya Nauk SSSR [*A publication*]
**Izv Estestvennonauchn Inst Permsk Gos Univ** ... Izvestiya Estestvennonauchnogo Instituta pri Permskom Gosudarstvennom Universitet [*USSR*] [*A publication*]
**Izv Estestv Nauchn Inst Im P S Lesgafta** ... Izvestiya Estestvenno-Nauchnogo Instituta Imeni P. S. Lesgafta [*A publication*]
**Izv Estestv-Nauchn Inst Molotov Gos Univ Im M Gor'kogo** ... Izvestiya Estestvenno-Nauchnogo Instituta pri Molotovskom Gosudarstvennom Universiteta Imeni M. Gor'kogo [*A publication*]
**Izvestija Inst MBAN** ... Izvestija na Instituta za Muzyka pri Bulgarskata Akademija na Naukite [*A publication*]
**Izvest Imp Akad Nauk (S Petersburg)** ... Izvestiya Imperatorskoi Akademii Nauk (St. Petersburg) [*A publication*]
**Izvestiya Akad Nauk SSSR** ... Izvestiya Akademii Nauk SSSR Otdelenie Literatury i Jazyka [*A publication*]
**Izvestiya Jugo-Oset Nauc-Issl Inst** ... Izvestiya Jugo-Osetinskogo Naucno-Issledovatel'skogo Instituta Akademii Nauk-Gruzinskoj SSR [*A publication*]
**Izvestiya Kirgiz Filiala Akad Nauk SSSR** ... Izvestiya Kirgizskogo Filiala Akademii Nauk SSSR [*A publication*]
**Izvestiya Turkm Filiala Akad Nauk SSSR** ... Izvestiya Turkmenskogo Filiala Akademii Nauk SSSR [*A publication*]
**Izvestiya Voronezskogo Gos Ped Inst** ... Izvestiya Voronezskogo Gosudarstvennego Pedagogiceskogo Instituta [*A publication*]
**Izvest Ross Akad Nauk** ... Izvestiia Rossiiskoi Akademii Nauk [*A publication*]
**Izv Fak S kh Nauk Moshonmad'yarovar Vengriya** ... Izvestiya Fakul'teta Sel'skokhozyaistvennykh Nauk Moshonmad'yarovar Vengriya [*A publication*]
**Izv Fiz-Khim Nauchno-Issled Inst Irkutsk Gos Univ** ... Izvestiya Fiziko-Khimicheskogo Nauchno-Issledovatel'skogo Instituta pri Irkutskom Gosudarstvennom Universitete [*A publication*]
**Izv Geofiz Inst** ... Izvestiya na Geofizichniya Institut [*A publication*]
**Izv Geofiz Inst Bulg Akad Nauk** ... Izvestiya na Geofizichniya Institut. Bulgarska Akademiya na Naukite [*Bulgaria*] [*A publication*]
**Izv Geol Inst Bulg Akad Nauk** ... Izvestiya na Geologicheskiya Institut. Bulgarska Akademiya na Naukite [*A publication*]
**Izv Geol Inst Bulg Akad Nauk Ser Geokhim Mineral Petrogr** ... Izvestiya na Geologicheskiya Institut. Bulgarska Akademiya na Naukite. Seriya Geokhimiya, Mineralogiya, i Petrografiya [*Bulgaria*] [*A publication*]
**Izv Geol Inst Bulg Akad Nauk Ser Geotekton** ... Izvestiya na Geologicheskiya Institut. Bulgarska Akademiya na Naukite. Seriya Geotektonika [*A publication*]
**Izv Geol Inst Bulg Akad Nauk Ser Geotektonika Stratigr Litol** ... Izvestiya na Geologicheskiya Institut. Bulgarska Akademiya na Naukite. Seriya Geotektonika. Stratigrafiya i Litologiya [*A publication*]
**Izv Geol Inst Bulg Akad Nauk Ser Inzh Geol Khidrogeol** ... Izvestiya na Geologicheskiya Institut. Bulgarska Akademiya na Naukite. Seriya Inzhenerna Geologiya i Khidrogeologiya [*A publication*]
**Izv Geol Inst Bulg Akad Nauk Ser Neftena Vuglishtna Geol** ... Izvestiya na Geologicheskiya Institut. Bulgarska Akademiya na Naukite. Seriya Neftena i Vuglishtna Geologiya [*A publication*]
**Izv Geol Inst Bulg Akad Nauk Ser Paleontol** ... Izvestiya na Geologicheskiya Institut. Bulgarska Akademiya na Naukite. Seriya Paleontologiya [*A publication*]
**Izv Geol Inst Bulg Akad Nauk Ser Prilozhna Geof** ... Izvestiya na Geologicheskiya Institut. Bulgarska Akademiya na Naukite. Seriya Prilozhna Geofizika [*A publication*]
**Izv Geol Inst Bulg Akad Nauk Ser Stratigr Litol** ... Izvestiya na Geologicheskiya Institut. Bulgarska Akademiya na Naukite. Seriya Stratigrafiya i Litologiya [*A publication*]
**Izv Geol Inst Ser Paleontol (Sofia)** ... Izvestiya na Geologicheskiya Institut. Seriya Paleontologiya (Sofia) [*A publication*]
**Izv Geol Inst Ser Prilozh Geofiz** ... Izvestiya na Geologicheskiya Institut. Seriya Prilozhna Geofizika [*A publication*]
**Izv Geol Ova Gruz** ... Izvestiya Geologicheskogo Obshchestva Gruzii [*A publication*]
**Izv Gl Astron Obs Pulkove** ... Izvestiya Glavnoi Astronomicheskoi Observatorii v Pulkove [*A publication*]
**Izv Gorskogo S'kh Inst** ... Izvestiya Gorskogo Sel'skokhozyaistvennogo Instituta [*A publication*]
**Izv Gos Nauchno-Issled Inst Kolloidn Khim** ... Izvestiya Gosudarstvennogo Nauchno-Issledovatel'skogo Instituta Kolloidnoi Khimii [*A publication*]
**Izv Gos Nauchno-Issled Inst Ozern Rechn Rybn Khoz** ... Izvestiya Gosudarstvennogo Nauchno-Issledovatel'skogo Instituta Ozernogo i Rechnogo Rybnogo Khozyaistva [*A publication*]
**IzvIBE**........ Izvestiya na Instituta za Belgarski Ezik [*A publication*]
**Izv Imp Akad Nauk** ... Izvestiya Imperatorskoi Akademii Nauk [*A publication*]
**Izv Inst Biokhim Bulg Akad Nauk** ... Izvestiya na Instituta po Biokhimiya. Bulgarska Akademiya na Naukite [*A publication*]
**Izv Inst Biol Bulg Akad Nauk** ... Izvestiya na Instituta po Biologiya. Bulgarska Akademiya na Naukite [*A publication*]
**Izv Inst Biol "Metod Popov" Bulg Akad Nauk** ... Izvestiya na Instituta po Biologiya "Metodii Popov." Bulgarskoi Akademii Nauk [*A publication*]
**Izv Inst Chist Khim Reakt** ... Izvestiya Instituta Chistykh Khimicheskikh Reaktivov [*A publication*]
**Izv Inst Eksp Med Bulg Akad Nauk** ... Izvestiya na Instituta po Eksperimentalna Meditsina. Bulgarska Akademiya na Naukite [*A publication*]
**Izv Inst Eksp Vet Med Bulg Akad Nauk** ... Izvestiya na Instituta po Eksperimentalna Veterinarna Meditsina. Bulgarska Akademiya na Naukite [*A publication*]
**Izv Inst Elektron** ... Izvestiya na Instituta po Elektronika [*A publication*]
**Izv Inst Elektron Bulg Akad Nauk** ... Izvestiya na Instituta po Elektronika. Bulgarska Akademiya na Naukite [*A publication*]
**Izv Inst Energ Bulg Akad Nauk** ... Izvestiya na Instituta po Energetika. Bulgarska Akademiya na Naukite [*A publication*]
**Izv Inst Fiziol B'lg Akad Nauk** ... Izvestiya na Instituta po Fiziologiya. B'lgarska Akademiya na Naukite [*A publication*]
**Izv Inst Fiziol Rast Bulg Akad Nauk** ... Izvestiya na Instituta po Fiziologiya na Rasteniyata. Bulgarska Akademiya na Naukite [*Bulgaria*] [*A publication*]
**Izv Inst Fiziol Rast "Metodii Popov" Bulg Akad Nauk** ... Izvestiya na Instituta po Fiziologiya na Rasteniyata "Metodii Popov." Bulgarska Akademiya na Naukite [*A publication*]
**Izv Inst Fiziol Rast "Metod Popov" Bulg Akad Nauk** ... Izvestiya na Instituta po Fiziologiya na Rasteniyata "Metodii Popov." Bulgarskoi Akademii Nauk [*A publication*]

**Izv Inst Fiziol (Sofia)** ... Izvestiia na Instituta po Fiziologiia (Sofia) [*A publication*]
**Izv Inst Fiz Khim Anal Akad Nauk SSSR** ... Izvestiya Instituta Fiziko-Khimicheskogo Analiza. Akademiya Nauk SSSR [*A publication*]
**Izv Inst Furazhite Pleven** ... Izvestiya. Institut po Furazhite. Pleven [*A publication*]
**Izv Inst Gorata Akad Selskostop Nauki Bulg** ... Izvestiya na Instituta za Gorata. Akademiya na Selskostopanskite Nauki v Bulgariya [*A publication*]
**Izv Inst Izuch Platin Drugikh Blagorodn Met Akad Nauk SSSR** ... Izvestiya na Instituta po Izucheniya Platiny i Drugikh Blagorodnykh Metallov. Akademiya Nauk SSSR [*A publication*]
**Izv Inst Khidrol Meteor** ... Izvestiya na Instituta po Khidrologiya i Meteorologiya. Bulgarska Akademiya na Naukite [*A publication*]
**Izv Inst Khidrol Meteorol Bulg Akad Nauk** ... Izvestiya na Instituta po Khidrologiya i Meteorologiya. Bulgarska Akademiya na Naukite [*Bulgaria*] [*A publication*]
**Izv Inst Khidrotekh Melior Akad Selskostop Nauki Bulg** ... Izvestiya na Instituta Khidrotekhnika i Melioratsii. Akademiya Selskostopanskite Nauki v Bulgariya [*A publication*]
**Izv Inst Khranene Bulg Akad Nauk** ... Izvestiya na Instituta po Khranene. Bulgarska Akademiya na Naukite [*A publication*]
**Izv Inst Klin Obshchest Med Bulg Akad Nauk** ... Izvestiya na Instituta za Klinichna i Obshchestvena Meditsina. Bulgarska Akademiya na Naukite [*A publication*]
**Izv Inst Lozar Vinar (Pleven) Akad Selskostop Nauki Bulg** ... Izvestiya na Instituta po Lozarstvo i Vinarstvo (Pleven). Akademiya na Selskostopanskite Nauki v Bulgariya [*A publication*]
**Izv Inst Morfol B'lg Akad Nauk Med Nauki** ... Izvestiya na Instituta po Morfologiya. Bulgarska Akademiya na Naukite za Meditsinski Nauki [*A publication*]
**Izv Inst Morfol Bulg Akad Nauk** ... Izvestiya na Instituta po Morfologiya. Bulgarska Akademiya na Naukite [*Bulgaria*] [*A publication*]
**Izv Inst Nauk Iskusstv SSR Arm** ... Izvestiya Instituta Nauk i Iskusstv SSR Armenii [*A publication*]
**Izv Inst Obshcha Sravn Patol B'lg Akad Nauk** ... Izvestiya na Instituta po Obshcha i Sravnitelna Patologiya. Bulgarska Akademiya na Naukite [*A publication*]
**Izv Inst Obshcha Sravn Patol Bulg Akad Nauk** ... Izvestiya na Instituta po Obshcha i Sravnitelna Patologiya. Bulgarska Akademiya na Naukite [*A publication*]
**Izv Inst Obshch Sravn Patol Bulg Akad Nauk** ... Izvestiya na Instituta po Obshcha i Sravnitelna Patologiya. Bulgarska Akademiya na Naukite [*Bulgaria*] [*A publication*]
**Izv Inst Obshta Neorg Khim Bulg Akad Nauk** ... Izvestiya na Instituta po Obshta i Neorganichna Khimiya. Bulgarska Akademiya na Naukite [*A publication*]
**Izv Inst Okeanogr Ribno Stop Bulg Akad Nauk** ... Izvestiya na Instituta po Okeanografiya i Ribno Stopanstvo. Bulgarska Akademiya na Naukite [*A publication*]
**Izv Inst Org Khim Bulg Akad Nauk** ... Izvestiya na Instituta po Organichna Khimiya. Bulgarska Akademiya na Naukite [*A publication*]
**Izv Inst Ovoshcharstvo** ... Izvestiya na Instituta po Ovoshcharstvo. Gara Kostinbrod [*A publication*]
**Izv Inst Pamuka (Chirpan)** ... Izvestiya na Instituta po Pamuka (Chirpan) [*A publication*]
**Izv Inst Pshenitsata Slunchogleda (Tolbukhin)** ... Izvestiya. Institut po Pshenitsata i Slunchogleda (Tolbukhin) [*A publication*]
**Izv Inst Rast Bulg Akad Nauk** ... Izvestiya na Instituta po Rastenievudstvo. Bulgarska Akademiya na Naukite [*A publication*]
**Izv Inst Rastenievud Akad Selskostop Nauki Bulg** ... Izvestiya na Instituta po Rastenievudstvo. Akademiya na Selskostopanskite Nauki v Bulgariya [*A publication*]
**Izv Inst Ribni Resur (Varna)** ... Izvestiya. Institut Ribni Resursov (Varna) [*A publication*]
**Izv Inst Rybn Resur** ... Izvestiya Institut Rybnykh Resursov (Varna) [*A publication*]
**Izv Inst Sravn Patol Zhivotn** ... Izvestiya na Instituta po Sravnitelna Patologiya na Zhivotnite [*A publication*]
**Izv Inst Sravn Patol Zhivotn B'lg Akad Nauk Otd Biol Nauki** ... Izvestiya na Instituta po Sravnitelna Patologiya na Zhivotnite. Bulgarska Akademiya na Naukite Otdelenie za Biologichni Nauki [*A publication*]
**Izv Inst Sravn Patol Zhivotn Bulg Akad Nauk** ... Izvestiya na Instituta po Sravnitelna Patologiya na Zhivotnite. Bulgarska Akademiya na Naukite [*A publication*]
**Izv Inst Srav Patol Zhivotn Bulg Akad Nauk** ... Izvestiya na Instituta po Sravnitelna Patologiya na Zhivotnite. Bulgarska Akademiya na Naukite [*Bulgaria*] [*A publication*]
**Izv Inst Tekh Kibern** ... Izvestiya na Instituta po Tekhnicheska Kibernetika [*A publication*]
**Izv Inst Tekh Mekh Bulg Akad Nauk** ... Izvestiya na Instituta po Tekhnicheska Mekhanika. Bulgarska Akademiya na Naukite [*A publication*]
**Izv Inst Tsarevitsata-Knezha** ... Izvestiya na Instituta po Tsarevitsata-Knezha [*A publication*]
**Izv Inst Tyutyuna (Plovdiv) Akad Selskostop Nauki Bulg** ... Izvestiya na Instituta po Tyutyuna (Plovdiv). Akademiya na Selskostopanskite Nauki v Bulgariya [*A publication*]
**Izv Inst Vodni Probl Bulg Akad Nauk** ... Izvestiya na Instituta po Vodni Problemi. Bulgarska Akademiya na Naukite [*A publication*]
**Izv Inst Vodno Stop Stroit Bulg Akad Nauk** ... Izvestiya na Instituta po Vodno Stopanstvo i Stroitelstvo. Bulgarska Akademiya na Naukite [*A publication*]
**Izv Inst Vodn Probl Bulg Akad Nauk** ... Izvestiya na Instituta po Vodni Problemi. Bulgarska Akademiya na Naukite. Otdelenie za Tekhnicheskij Nauki [*A publication*]
**Izv Inst Zhivotn Bulg Akad Nauk** ... Izvestiia. Institut za Zhivotnovudstvo Bulgarska Akademiia na Naukite [*A publication*]
**Izv Inst Zhivotnovud (Kostinbrod) Akad Selskostop Nauki Bulg** ... Izvestiya na Instituta po Zhivotnovudstvo (Kostinbrod). Akademiya na Selskostopanskite Nauki v Bulgariya [*A publication*]
**IzvIRGruz**.. Izvestiya. Institut Rukopisej Akademii Nauk Gruzinskoj SSR [*A publication*]
**Izv Irkutsk Nauchno-Issled Protivochumn Inst Sib Dal'n Vost** ... Izvestiya Irkutskogo Nauchno-Issledovatel'skogo Protivochumnogo Instituta Sibiri i Dal'nego Vostoka [*A publication*]
**Izv Irkutsk Skh Inst** ... Izvestiya Irkutskogo Sel'skokhozyaistvennogo Instituta [*A publication*]
**Izv Ivanovo Voznesensk Politekh Inst** ... Izvestiya Ivanovo-Voznesenskogo Politekhnicheskogo Instituta [*A publication*]
**Izv Ivanov Skh Inst** ... Izvestiya Ivanovskogo Sel'skokhozyaistvennogo Instituta [*A publication*]
**Izvjesca Inst Oceanogr Ribar Splitu** ... Izvjesca. Institut za Oceanografiju i Ribarstvo u Splitu [*A publication*]
**IzvJOsNII** ... Izvestiya Jugo-Osetinskogo Naucno-Issledovatel'skogo Instituta [*A publication*]
**Izv Jugo Oset Nauc-Issled Inst Akad Nauk Gruz SSR** ... Izvestija Jugo-Osetinskogo Naucno-Issledovatelskogo Instituta Akademii Nauk Gruzinskoj SSR [*A publication*]
**IzvJuOsI**.... Izvestiya Jugo-Osetinskogo Naucno-Issledovatel'skogo Instituta Akademii Nauk-Gruzinskoj SSR [*A publication*]
**Izv Kamarata Nar Kult Ser Biol Zemed Lesovud** ... Izvestiya na Kamarata na Narodnata Kultura. Seriya Biologiya Zemedelie i Lesovudstvo [*A publication*]
**Izv Karel Kolsk Fil Akad Nauk SSSR** ... Izvestiya Karel'skogo i Kol'skogo Filialov Akademii Nauk SSSR [*A publication*]
**Izv Kazan Fil Akad Nauk SSR** ... Izvestiya Kazanskogo Filiala Akademii Nauk SSR [*A publication*]
**Izv Kazan Fil Akad Nauk SSSR Ser Biol Nauk** ... Izvestiya Kazanskogo Filiala Akademii Nauk SSSR Seriya Biologicheskikh Nauk [*A publication*]
**Izv Kazan Fil Akad Nauk SSSR Ser Biol Skh Nauk** ... Izvestiya Kazanskogo Filiala Akademii Nauk SSSR Seriya Biologicheskikh i Sel's kokhozyaistvennykh Nauk [*A publication*]
**Izv Kazan Fil Akad Nauk SSSR Ser Fiz-Mat i Tehn Nauk** ... Izvestija Kazanskogo Filiala Akademii Nauk SSSR Serija Fiziko-Matematiceskih i Tehniceskih Nauk [*A publication*]
**Izv Kazan Fil Akad Nauk SSSR Ser Fiz Mat Tekh Nauk** ... Izvestiya Kazanskogo Filiala Akademii Nauk SSSR Seriya Fiziko-Matematicheskikh i Tekhnicheskikh Nauk [*A publication*]
**Izv Kazan Fil Akad Nauk SSSR Ser Geol Nauk** ... Izvestiya Kazanskogo Filiala Akademii Nauk SSSR Seriya Geologicheskikh Nauk [*A publication*]
**Izv Kazan Fil Akad Nauk SSSR Ser Khim Nauk** ... Izvestiya Kazanskogo Filiala Akademii Nauk SSSR Seriya Khimicheskikh Nauk [*A publication*]
**Izv Kazan Lesotekh Inst** ... Izvestiya Kazanskogo Lesotekhnicheskogo Instituta [*A publication*]
**Izv Khidravl Lab Vissh Inzh Stroit Inst** ... Izvestiya na Khidravlicheskata Laboratoriya Vissh Inzhenerno-Stroitelen Institut [*A publication*]
**Izv Khim** .... Izvestiya po Khimiya [*A publication*]
**Izv Khim Inst Bulg Akad Nauk** ... Izvestiya na Khimicheskiya Institut. Bulgarska Akademiya na Naukite [*Bulgaria*] [*A publication*]
**Izv Khlopchatobum Prom** ... Izvestiya Khlopchatobumazhnoi Promyshlennosti [*A publication*]
**Izv Kiev Politekh Inst** ... Izvestiya Kievskogo Politekhnicheskogo Instituta [*A publication*]
**Izv Kirg Fil Akad Nauk SSSR** ... Izvestiya Kirgizskogo Filiala Akademii Nauk SSSR [*A publication*]
**Izv Kirg Fil Vses Ova Pochvovedov** ... Izvestiya Kirgizskogo Filiala Vsesoyuznogo Obshchestva Pochvovedov [*A publication*]
**Izv Kirg Geogr Ova** ... Izvestiya Kirgizskogo Geograficheskogo Obshchestva [*A publication*]
**Izv Kom Fiz Planet Akad Nauk SSSR** ... Izvestiya Komissii po Fizike Planet Akademiya Nauk SSSR [*A publication*]
**Izv Komi Fil Geogr Obsc SSSR** ... Izvestija Komi Filiala Geograficeskogo Obscestva SSSR [*A publication*]
**Izv Komi Fil Vses Geogr Obshch** ... Izvestiya Komi Filiala Vsesoyuznogo Geograficheskogo Obshchestva [*A publication*]
**Izv Komi Fil Vses Geogr O-Va SSSR** ... Izvestiya Komi Filiala Vsesoyuznogo Geograficheskogo Obshchestva SSSR [*A publication*]

**Izv Kompleks Selskostop Nauchnoizsled Inst (Karnobat)** ... Izvestiya na Kompleksniya Selskostopanski Nauchnoizsledvatelski Institut (Karnobat) [*A publication*]
**Izv Krym Astrofiz Obs** ... Izvestiya Krymskoi Astrofizicheskoi Observatorii [*A publication*]
**Izv Krym Otd Geogr Ova SSSR** ... Izvestiya Krymskogo Otdela Geograficheskogo Obshchestva SSSR [*A publication*]
**Izv Krym Pedagog Inst** ... Izvestiya Krymskogo Pedagogicheskogo Instituta [*A publication*]
**Izv Krymsk Otd Geog Obshch Soyuza SSR** ... Izvestiya Krymskogo Otdela Geograficheskogo Obshchestva SSSR [*A publication*]
**Izv Kuibyshev Inzh Melior Inst** ... Izvestiya Kuibyshevskogo Inzhenerno-Meliorativnogo Instituta [*A publication*]
**Izv Kuibyshev Sel'khoz Inst** ... Izvestiya Kuibyshevskogo Sel'skokhozyaistvennogo Instituta [*A publication*]
**Izv Kuibyshev S-Kh Inst** ... Izvestiya Kuibyshevskogo Sel'skokhozyaistvennogo Instituta [*A publication*]
**Izv Leningr Elektrotekh Inst** ... Izvestiya Leningradskogo Elektrotekhnicheskogo Instituta [*A publication*]
**Izv Lesotekh Akad** ... Izvestiya Lesotekhnicheskoi Akademii [*A publication*]
**Izv Med Inst Bulg Akad Nauk** ... Izvestiya na Meditsinskite Institut. Bulgarska Akademiya na Naukite [*A publication*]
**Izv Mikrobiol Inst Bulg Akad Nauk** ... Izvestiya na Mikrobiologicheskiya Institut. Bulgarska Akademiya na Naukite [*A publication*]
**Izv Mikrobiol Inst Sof** ... Izvestiya na Mikrobiologicheskiya Institut Sofiya [*A publication*]
**Izv Minist Proizvod Zagotovok S-Kh Prod Arm SSR** ... Izvestiya Ministerstvo Proizvodstva i Zagotovok Sel'skokhozyaistvennykh Productov Armyanskoi SSR [*A publication*]
**Izv Minist Selsk Khoz Arm SSR** ... Izvestiya Ministerstvo Sel'skogo Khozyaistva Armyanskoi SSR [*A publication*]
**Izv Minist Sel'sk Khoz Arm SSR S-Kh Nauki** ... Izvestiya Ministerstvo Sel'skogo Khozyaistva Armyanskoi SSR Sel'skokhozyaistvennye Nauki [*A publication*]
**Izv Minist Skh Arm SSR** ... Izvestiya Ministerstvo Sel'skogo Khozyaistva Armyanskoi SSR [*A publication*]
**Izv Mold Fil Akad Nauk SSSR** ... Izvestiya Moldavskogo Filiala Akademii Nauk SSSR [*A publication*]
**Izv Mosk Skh Inst** ... Izvestiya Moskovskogo Selskokhozyaistvennogo Instituta [*A publication*]
**Izv Mosk Tekst Inst** ... Izvestiya Moskovskii Tekstil'nyi Institut [*A publication*]
**Izv Muz Juz Balg** ... Izvestija na Muzeite ot Juzna Balgarija [*Bulletin des Musees de la Bulgarie du Sud*] [*A publication*]
**Izv Nachnoizsled Inst Okeanogr Ribno Stop (Varna)** ... Izvestiya na Nauchnoizsledovatelskiya Institut po Okeanografiya i Ribno Stopanstvo (Varna) [*A publication*]
**Izv Nauchno-Issled Inst Nefte Uglekhim Sint Irkutsk Univ** ... Izvestiya Nauchno-Issledovatel'skogo Instituta Nefte- i Uglekhimicheskogo Sinteza pri Irkutskom Universitete [*A publication*]
**Izv Nauchno Issled Inst Ozern Rechn Rybn Khoz** ... Izvestiya Nauchno-Issledovatel'skogo Instituta Ozernogo i Rechnogo Rybnogo Khozyaistva [*A publication*]
**Izv Nauchno-Issled Inst Postoyan Toka** ... Izvestiya Nauchno-Issledovatel'skogo Instituta Postoyannogo Toka [*USSR*] [*A publication*]
**Izv Nauchnoizsled Geol Inst (Sofia)** ... Izvestiya na Nauchnoizsledovatelskiya Geolozhki Institut (Sofia) [*A publication*]
**Izv Nauchnoizsled Inst Kinematogr Radio** ... Izvestiya na Nauchnoizsledovatelskiya Institut po Kinematografiya i Radio [*A publication*]
**Izv Nauchnoizsled Inst Ribno Stop Okeanogr (Varna)** ... Izvestiya na Nauchnoizsledovatelskiya Institut za Ribno Stopanstvo i Okeanografiya (Varna) [*A publication*]
**Izv Omsk Otd Geogr O-Va SSR** ... Izvestiya Omskogo Otdeleniya Geograficheskogo Obshchestva SSR [*A publication*]
**Izv Otd Biol Med Nauki Bulg Akad Nauk** ... Izvestiya na Otdelenieto za Biologicheski i Meditsinski Nauki. Bulgarska Akademiya na Naukite [*A publication*]
**Izv Otdel Obshchest Nauk A N Tadzh** ... Izvestiia Otdeleniia Obshchestvennykh Nauk Akademiia Nauk Tadzhikskoi SSR [*A publication*]
**Izv Otd Estestv Nauk Akad Nauk Tadzh SSR** ... Izvestiya Otdeleniya Estestvennykh Nauk. Akademiya Nauk Tadzhikskoi SSR [*A publication*]
**Izv Otd Khim Nauki Bulg Akad** ... Izvestiya na Otdelenieto za Khimicheski Nauki. Bulgarska Akademiya na Naukite [*A publication*]
**Izv Otd Khim Nauki Bulg Akad Nauk** ... Izvestiya na Otdelenieto za Khimicheski Nauki. Bulgarska Akademiya na Naukite [*A publication*]
**Izv Permsk Biol Nauchno-Issled Inst** ... Izvestiya Permskogo Biologicheskogo Nauchno-Issledovatel'skogo Instituta [*A publication*]
**Izv Petrovsk Skh Akad** ... Izvestiya Petrovskoi Sel'skokhozyaistvennoi Akademii [*A publication*]
**Izv Petrovsk Zemled Lesn Akad** ... Izvestiya Petrovskoi Zemledel'cheskoi i Lesnoi Akademii [*A publication*]
**Izv Phys Solid Earth** ... Izvestiya. Physics of the Solid Earth [*A publication*]
**Izv Pochv Inst Bulg Akad Nauk** ... Izvestiya na Pochveniya Institut. Bulgarska Akademiya na Naukite [*A publication*]
**Izv Povolzh Lesotekh Inst** ... Izvestiya Povolzhskogo Lesotekhnicheskogo Instituta [*A publication*]
**Izv Ross Inst Prikl Khim** ... Izvestiya Rossiiskogo Instituta Prikladnoi Khimii [*A publication*]
**Izv Rostov Donu Nauchno-Issled Inst Epidemiol Mikrobiol Gig** ... Izvestiya Rostovskogo na Donu Nauchno-Issledovatel'skogo Instituta Epidemiologii Mikrobiologii i Gigieny [*A publication*]
**Izv Sakhalin Otd Geogr Ova SSSR** ... Izvestiya Sakhalinskogo Otdela Geograficheskogo Obshchestva SSSR [*A publication*]
**Izv Samar Skh Inst** ... Izvestiya Samarskogo Sel'skokhozyaistvennogo Instituta [*A publication*]
**Izv Sarat Ova Estestvoispyt** ... Izvestiya Saratovskogo Obshchestva Estestvoispytatelei [*A publication*]
**Izv Sekt Fiz-Khim Anal Inst Obshch Neorg Khim Akad Nauk SSSR** ... Izvestiya Sektora Fiziko-Khimicheskogo Analiza Institut Obshchei i Neorganicheskoi Khimii Akademiya Nauk SSSR [*A publication*]
**Izv Sekt Platiny Drugikh Obshch Neorg Khim Akad Nauk SSSR** ... Izvestiya Sektora Platiny i Drugikh Blagorodnykh Metallov Institut Obshchei i Neorganicheskoi Khimii Akademiya Nauk SSSR [*USSR*] [*A publication*]
**Izv Sekts Astron Bulg Akad Nauk** ... Izvestiya na Sektsiyata po Astronomiya. Bulgarska Akademiya na Naukite [*A publication*]
**Izv Sel'khoz Nauk** ... Izvestiya Sel'skokhozyaistvennykh Nauk [*A publication*]
**Izv Sel'-Khoz Nauki Minist Sel' Khoz Armyan SSR** ... Izvestiya Sel'skokhozyaistvennoi Nauki Ministerstvo Sel'skogo Khozyaistva Armyanskoi SSR [*A publication*]
**Izv Severo-Kavkaz Nauchn Tsentra Vyssh Shkoly Ser Tekhn Nauk** ... Izvestiya Severo-Kavkazskogo Nauchnogo Tsentra Vysshei Shkoly Seriya Tekhnicheskie Nauki [*A publication*]
**Izv Severo-Kavkaz Naucn Centra Vyss Skoly Ser Estestv Nauk** ... Izvestija Severo-Kavkazskogo Naucnogo Centra Vyssei Skoly Serija Estestvennye Nauki [*A publication*]
**Izv Severo-Kavkaz Naucn Centra Vyss Skoly Ser Tehn Nauk** ... Izvestija Severo-Kavkazskogo Naucnogo Centra Vyssei Skoly Serija Tehniceskie Nauki [*A publication*]
**Izv Sev-Kavk Nauc Centra Vyss Skoly Ser Obsc Nauk** ... Izvestija Severo-Kavkazskogo Naucnogo Centra Vyssei Skoly Serija Obscestvennyh Nauk [*A publication*]
**Izv Sev-Kavk Nauchn Tsentra Vyssh Shk Estestv Nauki** ... Izvestiya Severo-Kavkazskogo Nauchnogo Tsentra Vysshei Shkoly Seriya Estestvennye Nauki [*A publication*]
**Izv Sev-Kavk Nauchn Tsentra Vyssh Shk Ser Estestv Nauk** ... Izvestiya Severo-Kavkazskogo Nauchnogo Tsentra Vysshei Shkoly Seriya Estestvennye Nauki [*USSR*] [*A publication*]
**Izv Sibir Otd Akad Nauk SSSR** ... Izvestiya Sibirskogo Otdeleniya Akademii Nauk SSSR [*A publication*]
**Izv Sibir Otd Akad Nauk SSSR Khim** ... Izvestiya Sibirskogo Otdeleniya Akademii Nauk SSSR Seriya Khimicheskikh Nauk [*A publication*]
**Izv Sibir Otd Akad Nauk SSSR Ser Khim Nauk** ... Izvestiya Sibirskogo Otdeleniya Akademii Nauk SSSR Seriya Khimicheskikh Nauk [*A publication*]
**Izv Sibir Otd Akad Nauk SSSR Ser Tekh Nauk** ... Izvestiya Sibirskogo Otdeleniya Akademii Nauk SSSR Seriya Tekhnicheskikh Nauk [*A publication*]
**Izv Sibir Otd Akad Nauk SSSR Tekh** ... Izvestiya Sibirskogo Otdeleniya Akademii Nauk SSSR Seriya Tekhnicheskikh Nauk [*A publication*]
**Izv Sibir Otdel Akad Nauk SSSR Ser Biol Nauk** ... Izvestija Sibirskogo Otdelenija Akademii Nauk SSSR Serija Biologiceskih Nauk [*A publication*]
**Izv Sibirsk Otdel Akad Nauk SSSR** ... Izvestija Sibirskogo Otdelenija Akademija Nauk SSSR [*A publication*]
**Izv Sibirsk Otdel Akad Nauk SSSR Ser Tehn Nauk** ... Izvestija Sibirskogo Otdelenija Akademija Nauk SSSR Serija Tehniceskih Nauk [*A publication*]
**Izv Sib Mekh-Mashinostroit Inst** ... Izvestiya Sibirskogo Mekhaniko-Mashinostroitel'nogo Instituta [*A publication*]
**Izv Sib Otd Akad Nauk SSSR** ... Izvestiya Sibirskogo Otdeleniya Akademii Nauk SSSR [*A publication*]
**Izv Sib Otd Akad Nauk SSSR Geol Geofiz** ... Izvestiya Sibirskogo Otdeleniya Akademii Nauk SSSR Geologiya i Geofizika [*A publication*]
**Izv Sib Otd Akad Nauk SSSR Ser Biol-Med Nauk** ... Izvestiya Sibirskogo Otdeleniya Akademii Nauk SSSR Seriya Biologo-Meditsinskikh Nauk [*A publication*]
**Izv Sib Otd Akad Nauk SSSR Ser Biol Nauk** ... Izvestiya Sibirskogo Otdeleniya Akademii Nauk SSSR Seriya Biologicheskikh Nauk [*A publication*]
**Izv Sib Otd Akad Nauk SSSR Ser Khim Nauk** ... Izvestiya Sibirskogo Otdeleniya Akademii Nauk SSSR Seriya Khimicheskikh Nauk [*A publication*]
**Izv Sib Otd Akad Nauk SSSR Ser Obshchestv Nauk** ... Izvestiya Sibirskogo Otdeleniya Akademii Nauk SSSR Seriya Obshchestvennykh Nauk [*USSR*] [*A publication*]
**Izv Sib Otd Akad Nauk SSSR Ser Tekh Nauk** ... Izvestiya Sibirskogo Otdeleniya Akademii Nauk SSSR Seriya Tekhnicheskikh Nauk [*A publication*]

**Izv Sib Otdel Akad Nauk SSSR Ser Biol-Med Nauk** ... Izvestiya Sibirskogo Otdeleniya Akademii Nauk SSSR Seriya Biologo-Meditsinskikh Nauk [*A publication*]
**Izv Sib Otdel Akad Nauk SSSR Ser Biol Nauk** ... Izvestiya Sibirskogo Otdeleniya Akademii Nauk SSSR Seriya Biologicheskikh Nauk [*A publication*]
**Izv Sib Otdel Akad Nauk SSSR Ser Obsc Nauk** ... Izvestija Sibirskogo Otdelenija Akademii Nauk SSSR Serija Obscestvennyh Nauk [*A publication*]
**Izv Sib Otd Geol Kom** ... Izvestiya Sibirskogo Otdeleniya Geologicheskogo Komiteta [*USSR*] [*A publication*]
**Izv Sib Tekhnol Inst** ... Izvestiya Sibirskogo Tekhnologicheskogo Instituta [*A publication*]
**Izv Skh Akad Im K A Timiryazeva** ... Izvestiya Sel'skokhozyaistvennoi Akademii Imeni K. A. Timiryazeva [*A publication*]
**Izv S-Kh Nauk** ... Izvestiya Sel'skokhozyaistvennykh Nauk [*A publication*]
**IzvSLF** ....... Izvestiya Seminara po Slavjanske Filologija [*A publication*]
**IzvSOsNII** ... Izvestiya Severo-Osetinskogo Naucno-Issledovatel'skogo Instituta [*A publication*]
**IzvTadzikAN** ... Izvestiya Tadzikskogo Filiala Akademii Nauk [*A publication*]
**Izv Tbilis Nauchno Issled Inst Sooruzh Gidroenerg** ... Izvestiya Tbilisskogo Nauchno-Issledovatel'skogo Instituta Sooruzhenii i Gidroenergetiki [*A publication*]
**Izv Tekst Promsti Torg** ... Izvestiya Tekstil'noi Promyshlennosti i Torgovli [*A publication*]
**Izv Tikhookean Nauchno-Issled Inst Rybn Khoz Okeanogr** ... Izvestiya Tikhookeanskogo Nauchno-Issledovatel'skogo Instituta Rybnogo Khozyaistva i Okeanografii [*A publication*]
**Izv Timiryazev Sel'-Khoz Akad** ... Izvestiya Timiryazevskoi Sel'skokhozyaistvennoi Akademii [*A publication*]
**Izv Timiryazev S-Kh Akad** ... Izvestiya Timiryazevskoi Sel'skokhozyaistvennoi Akademii [*A publication*]
**Izv Tomsk Ind Inst** ... Izvestiya Tomskogo Industrial'nogo Instituta [*A publication*]
**Izv Tomsk Otd Vses Bot Ova** ... Izvestiya Tomskogo Otdeleniya Vsesoyuznogo Botanicheskogo Obshchestva [*A publication*]
**Izv Tomsk Politehn Inst** ... Izvestija Tomskogo Ordena Trudovogo Krasnogo Znameni Politehniceskogo Instituta Imeni S. M. Kirova [*A publication*]
**Izv Tomsk Politekh Inst** ... Izvestiya Tomskogo Politekhnicheskogo Instituta Imeni S. M. Kirova [*A publication*]
**Izv Tomsk Politekh Inst Mekh Mashinostr** ... Izvestiya Tomskogo Politekhnicheskogo Instituta Mekhanika i Mashinostroenia [*A publication*]
**Izv Tr Kharb Politekh Inst** ... Izvestiya i Trudy Kharbinskogo Politekhnicheskogo Instituta [*A publication*]
**Izv Tsent Nauchnoizsled Inst Zasht Rast** ... Izvestiya na Tsentralniya Nauchnoizsledovatelski Institut za Zashnita na Rasteniyata [*A publication*]
**Izv Tsent Nauchnoizsled Inst Zhivotnovud "Georgi Dimitrov"** ... Izvestiya na Tsentralniya Nauchnoizsledovatelski Institut po Zhivotnovudstvo "Georgi Dimitrov" [*A publication*]
**Izv Tsentr Khelmintol Lab B'lg Akad Nauk** ... Izvestiya na Tsentralnata Khelmintologichna Laboratoriya. Bulgarska Akademiya na Naukite [*A publication*]
**Izv Tsentr Lab Biokhim Bulg Akad Nauk** ... Izvestiya na Tsentralnata Laboratoriya po Biokhimiya. Bulgarska Akademiya na Naukite [*A publication*]
**Izv Tsentr Lab Energ Bulg Akad Nauk** ... Izvestiya na Tsentralnata Laboratoriya po Energetika. Bulgarska Akademiya na Naukite [*A publication*]
**Izv Tsentr Nauchno Issled Inst Kozh Promsti** ... Izvestiya Tsentral'nogo Nauchno-Issledovatel'skogo Instituta Kozhevennoi Promyshlennosti [*A publication*]
**Izv Turkm Fil Akad Nauk SSR** ... Izvestiya Turkmenskogo Filiala Akademii Nauk SSR [*A publication*]
**Izv Ural Gorn Inst Ekaterinburge** ... Izvestiya Ural'skogo Gornogo Instituta v Ekaterinburge [*A publication*]
**Izv Ural Politekh Inst** ... Izvestiya Ural'skogo Politekhnicheskogo Instituta [*A publication*]
**Izv Uzb Fil Geogr Ova SSSR** ... Izvestiya Uzbekistanskogo Filiala Geograficheskogo Obshchestva SSSR [*A publication*]
**Izv Uzb Geogr Ova** ... Izvestiya Uzbekskogo Geograficheskogo Obshchestva [*A publication*]
**Izv Varna** ... Izvestija na Narodnija Muzej Varna [*A publication*]
**Izv Veng S'kh Nauchno-Issled Inst A** ... Izvestiya Vengerskikh Sel'skokhozyaistvennykh Nauchno-Issledovatel'skikh Institutow A. Rastenievodstvo [*A publication*]
**Izv Veng S kh Nauchno-Issled Inst C** ... Izvestiya Vengerskikh Sel'skokhozyaistvennykh Nauchno-Issledovatel'skikh Institutow C. Sadovodstvo [*A publication*]
**Izv Vet Inst Virusol Akad Selskostop Nauki Bulg** ... Izvestiya na Veterinarniya Institut po Virusologiya. Akademiya na Selskostopanskite Nauki v Bulgaria [*A publication*]
**Izv Vissh Mash-Elektrotekh Inst Lenin** ... Izvestiya na Visshiya Mashinno-Elektrotekhnicheski Institut Lenin [*Bulgaria*] [*A publication*]
**Izv Vmei "Lenin"** ... Izvestiya na Vmei "Lenin" [*A publication*]
**Izv Voronez Gos Ped Inst** ... Izvestija Voronezskogo Gosudarstvennogo Pedagogiceskogo Instituta [*A publication*]
**Izv Voronezh Gos Ped Inst** ... Izvestiya Voronezhskogo Gosudarstvennogo Pedagogicheskogo Instituta [*A publication*]
**Izv Voronez Pedag Inst** ... Izvestija Voronezskogo Pedagogiceskogo Instituta [*A publication*]
**IzvVorPI** .... Izvestiya Voronezskogo Gosudarstvennogo Pedagogiceskogo Instituta [*A publication*]
**Izv Vost Fil Akad Nauk SSSR** ... Izvestiya Vostochnykh Filialov Akademii Nauk SSSR [*A publication*]
**Izv Vost Filial Akad Nauk SSSR** ... Izvestiya Vostochnykh Filialov Akademii Nauk SSSR [*USSR*] [*A publication*]
**Izv Vostochnosib Skh Inst** ... Izvestiya Vostochnosibirskogo Sel'skokhozyaistvennogo Instituta [*A publication*]
**Izv Vost Sib Otd Geogr Ova SSSR** ... Izvestiya Vostochno-Sibirskogo Otdela Geograficheskogo Obshchestva SSSR [*A publication*]
**Izv Vses Geogr Obshch** ... Izvestiya Vsesoyuznogo Geograficheskogo Obshchestva [*A publication*]
**Izv Vses Geogr O-Va** ... Izvestiya Vsesoyuznogo Geograficheskogo Obshchestva [*A publication*]
**Izv Vses Nauchno-Issled Inst Gidrotekh** ... Izvestiya Vsesoyuznogo Nauchno-Issledovatel'skogo Instituta Gidrotekhniki [*USSR*] [*A publication*]
**Izv Vses Nauchno Issled Inst Ozern Rechn Rybn Khoz** ... Izvestiya Vsesoyuznogo Nauchno-Issledovatel'skogo Instituta Ozernogo i Rechnogo Rybnogo Khozyaistva [*A publication*]
**Izv Vsesojuz Geogr Obsc** ... Izvestija Vsesojuznogo Geograficeskogo Obscestva [*A publication*]
**Izv Vses Teplotekh Inst** ... Izvestiya Vsesoyuznogo Teplotekhnicheskogo Instituta [*A publication*]
**Izv VUZ Aviats Tekh** ... Izvestiya Vysshikh Uchebnykh Zavedenii Aviatsionnaya Tekhnika [*A publication*]
**Izv VUZ Chernaya Metall** ... Izvestiya Vysshikh Uchebnykh Zavedenii Chernaya Metallurgiya [*A publication*]
**Izv VUZ Elektromekh** ... Izvestiya Vysshikh Uchebnykh Zavedenii Elektromekhanika [*A publication*]
**Izv VUZ Energ** ... Izvestiya Vysshikh Uchebnykh Zavedenii Energetika [*A publication*]
**Izv VUZ Fiz** ... Izvestiya Vysshikh Uchebnykh Zavedenii Fizika [*A publication*]
**Izv VUZ Gornyi Zh** ... Izvestiya Vysshikh Uchebnykh Zavedenii Gornyi Zhurnal [*A publication*]
**Izv VUZ Khim i Khim Tekhnol** ... Izvestiya Vysshikh Uchebnykh Zavedenii Khimiya i Khimicheskaya Tekhnologiya [*A publication*]
**Izv VUZ Kh i Kh Tekh** ... Izvestiya Vysshikh Uchebnykh Zavedenii Khimiya i Khimicheskaya Tekhnologiya [*A publication*]
**Izv VUZ Lesnoi Zh** ... Izvestiya Vysshikh Uchebnykh Zavedenii Lesnoi Zhurnal [*A publication*]
**Izv VUZ Mashinostr** ... Izvestiya Vysshikh Uchebnykh Zavedenii Mashinostroenie [*A publication*]
**Izv VUZ Mat** ... Izvestiya Vysshikh Uchebnykh Zavedenii Matematika [*A publication*]
**Izv Vuzov Mashinostr** ... Izvestiya Vuzov Mashinostroenie [*USSR*] [*A publication*]
**Izv VUZ Pishch Tekhnol** ... Izvestiya Vysshikh Uchebnykh Zavedenii Pishchevaya Tekhnologiya [*A publication*]
**Izv VUZ Priborostr** ... Izvestiya Vysshikh Uchebnykh Zavedenii Priborostroenie [*A publication*]
**Izv VUZ Radioelektron** ... Izvestiya Vysshikh Uchebnykh Zavedenii Radioelektronika [*A publication*]
**Izv VUZ Radiofiz** ... Izvestiya Vysshikh Uchebnykh Zavedenii Radiofizika [*A publication*]
**Izv VUZ Tekh Leg Prom** ... Izvestiya Vysshikh Uchebnykh Zavedenii Tekhnologiya Legkoi Promyshlennosti [*A publication*]
**Izv VUZ Tekhnol Legkoi Prom-St** ... Izvestiya Vysshikh Uchebnykh Zavedenii Tekhnologiya Legkoi Promyshlennosti [*A publication*]
**Izv VUZ Tekhnol Tekstil Prom** ... Izvestiya Vysshikh Uchebnykh Zavedenii Tekhnologiya Tekstil'noi Promyshlennosti [*A publication*]
**Izv VUZ Tsvetn Metall** ... Izvestiya Vysshikh Uchebnykh Zavedenii Tsvetnaya Metallurgiya [*A publication*]
**Izv Vyssh Uchebn Zaved Aviats Tekh** ... Izvestiya Vysshikh Uchebnykh Zavedenii Aviatsionnaya Tekhnika [*A publication*]
**Izv Vyssh Uchebn Zaved Chern Metall** ... Izvestiya Vysshikh Uchebnykh Zavedenii Chernaya Metallurgiya [*A publication*]
**Izv Vyssh Uchebn Zaved Ehlektromekh** ... Izvestiya Vysshikh Uchebnykh Zavedenii Ehlektromekhanika [*A publication*]
**Izv Vyssh Uchebn Zaved Ehnerg** ... Izvestiya Vysshikh Uchebnykh Zavedenii Ehnergetika [*A publication*]
**Izv Vyssh Uchebn Zaved Fiz** ... Izvestiya Vysshikh Uchebnykh Zavedenij Fizika [*A publication*]
**Izv Vyssh Uchebn Zaved Geod Aerofotos'emka** ... Izvestiya Vysshikh Uchebnykh Zavedenii Geodeziya i Aerofotos'emka [*USSR*] [*A publication*]
**Izv Vyssh Uchebn Zaved Geol Razved** ... Izvestiya Vysshikh Uchebnykh Zavedenii Geologiya i Razvedka [*A publication*]
**Izv Vyssh Uchebn Zaved Gorn Zh** ... Izvestiya Vysshikh Uchebnykh Zavedenij Gornyj Zhurnal [*A publication*]

**Izv Vyssh Uchebn Zaved Khim Khim Tekhnol** ... Izvestiya Vysshikh Uchebnykh Zavedenii Khimiya i Khimicheskaya Tekhnologiya [*A publication*]
**Izv Vyssh Uchebn Zaved Lesn Zh** ... Izvestiya Vysshikh Uchebnykh Zavedenii Lesnoi Zhurnal [*A publication*]
**Izv Vyssh Uchebn Zaved Mashinostr** ... Izvestiya Vysshikh Uchebnykh Zavedenii Mashinostroenie [*A publication*]
**Izv Vyssh Uchebn Zaved Neft' Gaz** ... Izvestiya Vysshikh Uchebnykh Zavedenii Neft' i Gaz [*A publication*]
**Izv Vyssh Uchebn Zaved Pishch Tekhnol** ... Izvestiya Vysshikh Uchebnykh Zavedenii Pishchevaya Tekhnologiya [*A publication*]
**Izv Vyssh Uchebn Zaved Priborostr** ... Izvestiya Vysshikh Uchebnykh Zavedenii Priborostroenie [*A publication*]
**Izv Vyssh Uchebn Zaved Radioelektron** ... Izvestiya Vysshikh Uchebnykh Zavedenii Radioelektronika [*A publication*]
**Izv Vyssh Uchebn Zaved Radiofiz** ... Izvestiya Vysshikh Uchebnykh Zavedenij Radiofizika [*A publication*]
**Izv Vyssh Uchebn Zaved Radiotekh** ... Izvestiya Vysshikh Uchebnykh Zavedenii Radiotekhnika [*A publication*]
**Izv Vyssh Uchebn Zaved Stroit Arkhit** ... Izvestiya Vysshikh Uchebnykh Zavedenii Stroitel'stvo i Arkhitektura [*A publication*]
**Izv Vyssh Uchebn Zaved Tekhnol Legk Promsti** ... Izvestiya Vysshikh Uchebnykh Zavedenii Tekhnologiya Legkoi Promyshlennosti [*A publication*]
**Izv Vyssh Uchebn Zaved Tekhnol Tekst Promsti** ... Izvestiya Vysshikh Uchebnykh Zavedenii Tekhnologiya Tekstil'noi Promyshlennosti [*A publication*]
**Izv Vyssh Uchebn Zaved Tsvetn Metall** ... Izvestiya Vysshikh Uchebnykh Zavedenii Tsvetnaya Metallurgiya [*A publication*]
**Izv Vyssh Ucheb Zaved Chern Met** ... Izvestiya Vysshikh Uchebnykh Zavedenii Chernaya Metallurgiya [*A publication*]
**Izv Vyssh Ucheb Zaved Elektromekh** ... Izvestiya Vysshikh Uchebnykh Zavedenii Elektromekhanika [*A publication*]
**Izv Vyssh Ucheb Zaved Energ** ... Izvestiya Vysshikh Uchebnykh Zavedenii Energetika [*A publication*]
**Izv Vyssh Ucheb Zavedenii Geol Razvedka** ... Izvestiya Vysshikh Uchebnykh Zavedenii Geologiya i Razvedka [*A publication*]
**Izv Vyssh Ucheb Zaved Geol i Razved** ... Izvestiya Vysshikh Uchebnykh Zavedenii Geologiya i Razvedka [*A publication*]
**Izv Vyssh Ucheb Zaved Gorn Zh** ... Izvestiya Vysshikh Uchebnykh Zavedenii Gornyi Zhurnal [*A publication*]
**Izv Vyssh Ucheb Zaved Khim i Khim** ... Izvestiya Vysshikh Uchebnykh Zavedenii Khimiya i Khimicheskaya [*A publication*]
**Izv Vyssh Ucheb Zaved Neft i Gaz** ... Izvestiya Vysshikh Uchebnykh Zavedenii Neft' i Gaz [*A publication*]
**Izv Vyssh Ucheb Zaved Ser Pishch Tekhnol** ... Izvestiya Vysshikh Uchebnykh Zavedenii Seriya Pishchevaya Tekhnologiya [*A publication*]
**Izv Vyssh Ucheb Zaved Tekh Legk** ... Izvestiya Vysshikh Uchebnykh Zavedenii Tekhnologiya Legkoi Promyshlennosti [*A publication*]
**Izv Vyssh Ucheb Zaved Tsvet Met** ... Izvestiya Vysshikh Uchebnykh Zavedenii Tsvetnaya Metallurgiya [*A publication*]
**Izv Vyss Ucebn Zaved Aviacion Tehn** ... Izvestija Vyssih Ucebnyh Zavedenii Aviacionnaja Tehnika [*A publication*]
**Izv Vyss Ucebn Zaved Elektromehanika** ... Izvestija Vyssih Ucebnyh Zavedenii Elektromehanika [*A publication*]
**Izv Vyss Ucebn Zaved Fizika** ... Izvestija Vyssih Ucebnyh Zavedenii Fizika [*A publication*]
**Izv Vyss Ucebn Zaved Geod i Aerofot** ... Izvestija Vyssih Ucebnyh Zavedenii Geodezija i Aerofotos Emka [*A publication*]
**Izv Vyss Ucebn Zaved Matematika** ... Izvestija Vyssih Ucebnyh Zavedenii Matematika [*A publication*]
**Izv Vyss Ucebn Zaved Radiofizika** ... Izvestija Vyssih Ucebnyh Zavedenii Radiofizika [*A publication*]
**Izv Zabaik Fil Geogr O-Va SSSR** ... Izvestiya Zabaikal'skogo Filiala Geograficheskogo Obshchestva SSSR [*USSR*] [*A publication*]
**IZWWAX** ... Instytut Zootechniki w Polsce Wydawnictwa Wlasne [*A publication*]
**IZY**............ Intermediate Zone Yaw
**IZY**............ International Zoo Yearbook [*A publication*]

# J

J ................ Air Force Training Category [*Officer training program*]
J ................ Australian Journalist [*A publication*]
J ................ Business Class [*Also, C*] [*Airline fare code*]
J ................ Cable Jointing [*Section of the British Royal Navy*]
J ................ Clubs [*Public-performance tariff class*] [*British*]
j ................ Dissenting Opinion Citation in Dissenting Opinion [*Used in Shepard's Citations*] [*Legal term*] (DLA)
J ................ Electric Current Density [*Symbol*] [*IUPAC*] (DEN)
J ................ Electromechanical [*JETDS nomenclature*]
J ................ Flux [*Symbol*] [*IUPAC*]
J ................ Institutes of Justinian [*Roman law*] [*A publication*] (DLA)
J ................ Irradiation Correction
J ................ Jack [*In card game*]
J ................ Jack [*Technical drawings*]
J ................ Jackpot Enterprises, Inc. [*NYSE symbol*] (CTT)
J ................ Jacobeian Determinant (ROG)
J ................ Jacobus de Porta Ravennate [*Deceased, 1178*] [*Authority cited in pre-1607 legal work*] (DSA)
J ................ January
J ................ Janvier [*January*] [*French*]
J ................ Japan [*IYRU nationality code*]
J ................ Jargon [*Used in correcting manuscripts, etc.*]
J ................ Jerusalem Talmud (BJA)
J ................ Jesus (ROG)
J ................ Jet [*Aircraft*]
J ................ Jet Fuel
J ................ Jet Route [*Followed by identification*]
J ................ Jeunesse [*A publication*]
J ................ Jewish
J ................ Jewish Chaplain [*Territorial Force*] [*Military*] [*British*] (ROG)
J ................ Jewish School [*British*]
J ................ Jezik [*A publication*]
J ................ Jig [*Phonetic alphabet*] [*World War II*] (DSUE)
J ................ Job (IEEE)
J ................ Jobber [*Merchant middleman*]
J ................ Johannes Galensis [*Flourished, 13th century*] [*Authority cited in pre-1607 legal work*] (DSA)
J ................ Johnnie [*Phonetic alphabet*] [*Royal Navy*] [*World War I*] (DSUE)
J ................ Johnny [*Phonetic alphabet*] [*Pre-World War II*] (DSUE)
J ................ Johnson's New York Reports [*A publication*] (DLA)
J ................ Join
J ................ Joinable Containers [*Shipping*] (DCTA)
J ................ Joiner [*Machinery*]
J ................ Joining [*Also, JNG*] [*Genetics*]
J ................ Joint
J ................ Joint Matriculation Board [*British*]
J ................ Joist [*Technical drawings*]
J ................ Jonckheere Test [*Fisheries*]
J ................ Joshua [*Old Testament book*] [*Freemasonry*]
J ................ Joule [*Symbol*] [*SI unit of energy*] (GPO)
j ................ Jour [*Day*] [*French*]
J ................ Journal
J ................ Journalism
J ................ Judaeo-Persian
J ................ Judean or Yahwistic [*Used in biblical criticism to designate Yahwistic material*]
J ................ Judex [*Judge*] [*Latin*]
J ................ Judgment
J ................ Judiciary [*A publication*]
J ................ Juice
J ................ Juliett [*Phonetic alphabet*] [*International*] (DSUE)
J ................ July
J ................ Junction
J ................ Junction Devices [*JETDS nomenclature*] [*Military*] (CET)
J ................ June
J ................ Junior
J ................ Jupiter
J ................ Juris [*Of Law*] [*Latin*] (ADA)
J ................ Jus [*Law*] [*Latin*]
J ................ Justice [*i.e., a judge; plural is JJ*]
J ................ Justiciary Cases [*Scotland*] [*A publication*] (DLA)
J ................ Juta's South African Reports [*A publication*] (DLA)
J ................ Jute-Asphalted [*Nonmetallic armor*] (AAG)
J ................ Juvenile
J ................ Lower Canada Jurist, Quebec [*1848-91*] [*A publication*] (DLA)
J ................ Massieu Function [*Symbol*] [*IUPAC*]
J ................ Mechanical Equivalent of Heat [*Symbol*]
J ................ Radiant Intensity [*Symbol*]
J ................ Scottish Jurist [*1829-73*] [*A publication*] (DLA)
J ................ Special Test, Temporary [*Aircraft classification letter*]
j ................ Total Angular Momentum Quantum Number of a Single Particle [*Symbol*] [*Spectroscopy*]
J ................ Total Angular Momentum Quantum Number of a System [*Symbol*] [*Spectroscopy*]
J ................ VEB Fahlberg-List [*East Germany*] [*Research code symbol*]
J ................ Yahwist Source [*Biblical scholarship*]
J-1 ............. Jaeger Test Type One [*Ophthalmology*]
J-1 ............. Personnel Section [*of a joint military staff; also, the officer in charge of this section*]
J-2 ............. Intelligence Section [*of a joint military staff; also, the officer in charge of this section*]
J-3 ............. Operations and Training Section [*of a joint military staff; also, the officer in charge of this section*]
J-4 ............. Logistics Section [*of a joint military staff; also, the officer in charge of this section*]
J-5 ............. General Administration Section [*of a joint military staff; also the officer in charge of this section*]
J-6 ............. Communications-Electronics Section [*of a joint military staff; also, the officer in charge of this section*]
9J .............. Zambia [*Aircraft nationality and registration mark*] (FAAC)
J17 ............. Just Seventeen [*A publication*]
3J's............ Jam, Jute, and Journalism [*3 major industries of Dundee, Scotland*]
J (Cars)...... Designation for certain General Motors front-wheel-drive cars
JA .............. Aquair Luftfahrt GmbH und Co. Betriebs KG [*West Germany*] [*ICAO designator*] (FAAC)
JA .............. Jack Adapter
Ja .............. Jacobus de Albenga [*Flourished, 13th century*] [*Authority cited in pre-1607 legal work*] (DSA)
Ja .............. Jacobus Balduini [*Deceased, 1235*] [*Authority cited in pre-1607 legal work*] (DSA)
Ja .............. Jacobus de Ravanis [*Deceased, 1296*] [*Authority cited in pre-1607 legal work*] (DSA)
JA .............. Jahrbuch fuer Amerikastudien [*A publication*]
JA .............. Jama'at Ahmadiyyah [*Ahmadiyya Muslim Association*] (EAIO)
JA .............. Jamaica
JA .............. January [*A publication*]
JA .............. January
ja .............. Japan [*ry (Ryukyu Islands, Southern) used in records cataloged before January 1978*] [*MARC country of publication code*] [*Library of Congress*] (LCCP)
JA .............. Japan [*Aircraft nationality and registration mark*] (FAAC)
JA .............. Japan
JA .............. Japan Architect [*A publication*]
JA .............. Jetevator Assembly
JA .............. Jeune Afrique [*A publication*]
JA .............. Jewelers of America (EA)
JA .............. Jewish Advocate [*Bombay*] [*A publication*]
JA .............. Jewish Affairs [*A publication*]
JA .............. Jewish Art, An Illustrated History [*A publication*] (BJA)
JA .............. Job Aid
JA .............. Job Analysis
JA .............. Jockey's Association [*Defunct*] (EA)
JA .............. John Adams [*US president, 1735-1826*]
JA .............. Joint Account
JA .............. Joint Agent
J A.............. Journal A. Presses Academiques Europeennes [*A publication*]
JA .............. Journal of Advertising [*A publication*]
JA .............. Journal of Aesthetics and Art Criticism [*A publication*]
JA .............. Journal. American Musicological Society [*A publication*]

**JA** .......... Journal of Andrology [*A publication*]
**JA** .......... Journal of Apocrypha [*A publication*]
**JA** .......... Journal Asiatique [*A publication*]
**JA** .......... Judge Advocate
**JA** .......... Judge of Appeal
**JA** .......... Judicature Act (ROG)
**JA** .......... Judicial Authority [*British*]
**JA** .......... Jump Address
**JA** .......... Junior Achievement [*Stamford, CT*] (EA)
**JA** .......... Junior Ambassadors [*Defunct*] (EA)
**JA** .......... Justice of Appeal [*Legal term*] (DLA)
**J & A** .......... Justification and Approval [*Army*]
**JAA** .......... American Dental Association, Chicago, IL [*OCLC symbol*] (OCLC)
**JAA** .......... Jamiat Adduwal Alarabia [*League of Arab States - LAS*] (EAIO)
**JAA** .......... Journal of Accounting Auditing and Finance [*A publication*]
**JAA** .......... Journal of African Administration [*A publication*]
**JAA** .......... Journal of Anthropological Archaeology [*A publication*]
**JAA** .......... Journal of Astrophysics and Astronomy [*A publication*]
**JAA** .......... Journal. British Archaeological Association [*A publication*]
**JAA** .......... Judge Advocates Association (EA)
**JAAA** .......... Jabara Award for Airmanship [*Military decoration*]
**JAAB** .......... Joint Airlift Allocations Board
**JAAC** .......... Joint Airlift Allocations Committee
**JAAC** .......... Journal of Aesthetics and Art Criticism [*A publication*]
**JAACP** .......... Journal. American Chamber of Commerce of the Philippines [*A publication*]
**JAACS** .......... John A. Andrew Clinical Society (EA)
**JAADDB** ... Journal. American Academy of Dermatology [*A publication*]
**JAAF** .......... Japanese Army Air Force
**JAAF** .......... Joint Action Armed Forces
**JAAF** .......... Joint Army-Air Force
**JAAFAR** .... Joint Army-Air Force Adjustment Regulations
**JAAFCTB** ... Joint Army-Air Force Commercial Traffic Bulletin
**JAAFPC** .... Joint Army-Air Force Procurement Circular
**JAAFU** .......... Joint Anglo-American Foul Up [*World War II slang*] [*Bowdlerized version*]
**JAAHBL** ... Journal. American Animal Hospital Association [*A publication*]
**JAAK** .......... Jahrbuch fuer Aesthetik und Allgemeine Kunstwissenschaft [*A publication*]
**JAAMI J Assoc Adv Med Instrum** ... JAAMI. Journal. Association for the Advancement of Medical Instrumentation [*A publication*]
**JAAML** .......... Journal. American Academy of Matrimonial Lawyers [*A publication*] (DLA)
**JAAMRS** ... Joint Air-to-Air Missile Requirement Study (MCD)
**Ja Ann Int Law** ... Japanese Annual of International Law [*A publication*]
**Ja Ann Law Pol** ... Japan Annual of Law and Politics [*A publication*]
**J AANNT** ... Journal. American Association of Nephrology Nurses and Technicians [*A publication*]
**JAAOC** .......... Joint Antiaircraft Operation Center [*NATO*] (NATG)
**JAAP** .......... Joint Airborne Advance Party [*Military*] (AFM)
**JAAP** .......... Joliet Army Ammunition Plant (AABC)
**JAAP** .......... Journal. American Academy of Psychoanalysis [*A publication*]
**JAAPCC** .... Journal. American Academy of Psychoanalysis [*A publication*]
**JAAPD** .......... Journal of Analytical and Applied Pyrolysis [*A publication*]
**JAAPDD** ... Journal of Analytical and Applied Pyrolysis [*A publication*]
**JAAR** .......... Journal. American Academy of Religion [*A publication*]
**Jaarb Ak Amst** ... Jaarboek. Akademie te Amsterdam [*A publication*]
**Jaarb Inst Biol Scheik Onderz LandbGewass** ... Jaarboek. Instituut voor Biologisch en Scheikundig Onderzoek van Landbouwgewassen [*A publication*]
**Jaarb K Acad Overzeese Wet (Brussels)** ... Jaarboek. Koninklijke Academie voor Overzeese Wetenschappen (Brussels) [*A publication*]
**Jaarb Kankeronderz Kankerbestrijding Ned** ... Jaarboek van Kankeronderzoek en Kankerbestrijding in Nederland [*Netherlands*] [*A publication*]
**Jaarb Karakul Breeders Soc S Afr** ... Jaarboek. Karakul Breeders Society of South Africa [*A publication*]
**Jaarbl Bot Ver S-Afr** ... Jaarblad. Botaniese Vereniging van Suid-Afrika [*A publication*]
**Jaarb Ned Natuurk Ver** ... Jaarboek. Nederlandse Natuurkundige Vereniging [*Netherlands*] [*A publication*]
**Jaarboek BZ** ... Jaarboek van het Ministerie van Buitenlandse Zaken [*A publication*]
**Jaarb Proefstat Boomkwekerij Boskoop** ... Jaarboek. Proefstation voor de Boomkwekerij te Boskoop [*A publication*]
**Jaarb Rijksuniv Utrecht** ... Jaarboek. Rijksuniversiteit te Utrecht [*A publication*]
**Jaarb Sticht Fundam Onderz Mater Sticht Inst Kernphys Onderz** ... Jaarboek. Stichting voor Fundamenteel Onderzoek der Materie en Stichting Instituut voor Kernphysisch Onderzoek [*A publication*]
**Jaarb VRG** ... Jaarboek van het Vlaams Rechtsgenootschap [*A publication*]
**Ja Are** .......... Jacobus de Arena [*Deceased, 1297*] [*Authority cited in pre-1607 legal work*] (DSA)
**JAARS** .......... Jungle Aviation & Radio Service, Inc. [*Mission plane service*]
**JAAR Thematic St** ... Journal. American Academy of Religion. Thematic Studies [*A publication*]
**Jaarversl Inst Graan Meel Brood (Wageningen)** ... Jaarverslag. Institut voor Graan, Meel, en Brood (Wageningen) [*A publication*]
**Jaarversl Lab Bloembollenonderz Lisse** ... Jaarverslag. Laboratorium voor Bloembollenonderzoek Lisse [*A publication*]
**Jaarversl TNO** ... Jaarverslag. TNO [*Toegepast Natuurwetenschappelijk Onderzoek*] [*A publication*]
**JAAS** .......... Jewish Academy of Arts and Sciences (EA)
**JAAS** .......... Journal. Aberystwyth Agriculture Society [*A publication*]
**JAAS** .......... Journal of Analytical Atomic Spectrometry [*Formerly, ARAAS*] [*A publication*]
**JAAS** .......... Journal of Asian and African Studies [*A publication*]
**JAASAJ** .... Journal. Alabama Academy of Science [*A publication*]
**JAASD** .......... Journal. American Audiology Society [*A publication*]
**JAAT** .......... Joint Air Attack Team [*Military*] (INF)
**JAATT** .......... Joint Air Attack Team Tactics (MCD)
**JA/ATT** .......... Joint Airborne/Air Transportability Training
**JAB** .......... American Library Association, Booklist, Chicago, IL [*OCLC symbol*] (OCLC)
**JAB** .......... January Assumption Budget [*Budget based on economic forecasts available as of January*]
**JAB** .......... Joint Activity Briefing [*Military*] (AFM)
**JAB** .......... Joint Amphibious Board [*Military*]
**JAB** .......... Journal of Applied Behavioral Science [*A publication*]
**JAB** .......... Journal of Applied Biochemistry [*A publication*]
**JABA** .......... Journal of Applied Behavior Analysis [*A publication*]
**JABAA4** .... Journal of Applied Bacteriology [*A publication*]
**JABAE8** .... Journal of Animal Breeding and Genetics [*A publication*]
**JABCAA** ... Journal of Abnormal Child Psychology [*A publication*]
**J Abdom Surg** ... Journal of Abdominal Surgery [*A publication*]
**JABES** .......... Just Another Break-Even Situation [*Slang*]
**JABGDP** ... Journal. Adelaide Botanic Gardens [*A publication*]
**JABIDV** .... Journal of Applied Biochemistry [*A publication*]
**J Abnorm Child Psychol** ... Journal of Abnormal Child Psychology [*A publication*]
**J Abnorm Psychol** ... Journal of Abnormal Psychology [*A publication*]
**J Abnorm Psychol Monogr** ... Journal of Abnormal Psychology. Monograph [*A publication*]
**J Abnorm Soc Psychol** ... Journal of Abnormal and Social Psychology [*A publication*]
**J Abn Psych** ... Journal of Abnormal Psychology [*A publication*]
**JABOWA** ... Janak-Botkin-Wallis [*Data processing program regarding forest growth; named for three men involved in program*]
**JAbP** .......... Journal of Abnormal Psychology [*A publication*]
**JABPAF** .... Journal of Abnormal Psychology. Monograph [*A publication*]
**JABQC** .......... Job Assembly Breakdown and Quality Control Section [*Social Security Administration*]
**JABS** .......... Journal of Applied Behavioral Science [*A publication*]
**JABSBP** .... Journal of Abdominal Surgery [*A publication*]
**J Abstr Br Ship** ... Journal of Abstracts. British Ship Research Association [*A publication*]
**J Abstr Int Educ** ... Journal of Abstracts in International Education [*A publication*]
**JABUP** .......... Joint Air Base Utilization Plan (MCD)
**JAC** .......... CEGEP [*College d'Enseignement General et Professionnel*] John Abbott College Library [*UTLAS symbol*]
**JAC** .......... Jackson [*Wyoming*] [*Airport symbol*] (OAG)
**JAC** .......... Jackson, WY [*Location identifier*] [*FAA*] (FAAL)
**JAC** .......... Jacksonville [*Florida*] [*Seismograph station code, US Geological Survey*] [*Closed*] (SEIS)
**Jac** .......... Jacob's English Chancery Reports [*1821-22*] [*A publication*] (DLA)
**Jac** .......... Jacob's Law Dictionary [*A publication*] (DLA)
**Jac** .......... Jacobus [*James*] [*King of England*] (DLA)
**Jac** .......... Jacobus Balduini [*Deceased, 1235*] [*Authority cited in pre-1607 legal work*] (DSA)
**JAC** .......... Jahrbuch fuer Antike und Christentum [*A publication*]
**JAC** .......... Jet Age Conference
**JAC** .......... Jet Aircraft Coating
**JAC** .......... Jeunesse Anarchiste Communiste [*French student group*]
**JAC** .......... Joint Action Company [*Marine Corps*]
**JAC** .......... Joint Advisory Committee [*Military*]
**JAC** .......... Joint Aircraft Committee [*World War II*]
**JAC** .......... Joint Apprenticeship Committee
**JAC** .......... Joint Arms Control
**JAC** .......... Journal of Accountancy [*A publication*]
**JAC** .......... Journal of Applied Chemistry [*A publication*]
**J Acad Gen Dent** ... Journal. Academy of General Dentistry [*A publication*]
**J Acad Libnship** ... Journal of Academic Librarianship [*A publication*]
**J Acad Libr** ... Journal of Academic Librarianship [*A publication*]
**J Acad Librarianship** ... Journal of Academic Librarianship [*A publication*]
**J Acad Nat Sci Phila** ... Journal. Academy of Natural Sciences of Philadelphia [*A publication*]
**JACBB** .......... Journal of Applied Chemistry and Biotechnology [*A publication*]
**JACC** .......... Jobless Action Community Campaign [*Australia*]
**JACC** .......... Joint Airborne Communications Center (MCD)
**JACC** .......... Joint Alternate Command Center [*Military*] (CINC)
**JACC** .......... Joint Automatic Control Conference [*IEEE*]
**JACC** .......... Journalism Association of Community Colleges (EA)
**JACCC** .......... Joint Air Control and Coordination Center [*Air Force*] (AFM)
**JACC/CP** .. Joint Airborne Communications Center/Command Post (AFM)
**JACCDI** .... Journal. American College of Cardiology [*A publication*]

**J Accel Sci Technol** ... Journal of Accelerator Science and Technology [*A publication*]
**JACCI** ....... Joint Allocation Committee Civil Intelligence [*of US and Great Britain*] [*World War II*]
**J Accidental Med** ... Journal of Accidental Medicine [*Japan*] [*A publication*]
**JACC J Am Coll Cardiol** ... JACC. Journal. American College of Cardiology [*A publication*]
**J Account** ... Journal of Accountancy [*A publication*]
**J Accountancy** ... Journal of Accountancy [*A publication*]
**J Account Audit Finance** ... Journal of Accounting Auditing and Finance [*A publication*]
**J Accountin** ... Journal of Accounting Research [*A publication*]
**J Accounting Res** ... Journal of Accounting Research [*A publication*]
**J Account Res** ... Journal of Accounting Research [*A publication*]
**J Acct** ......... Journal of Accountancy [*A publication*] (DLA)
**J Acctcy** ..... Journal of Accountancy [*A publication*]
**J Acct Res** ... Journal of Accounting Research [*A publication*]
**J Accy** ........ Journal of Accountancy [*A publication*]
**JACDA** ...... Journal. American College of Dentists [*A publication*]
**Jac Dict** ...... Jacob's Law Dictionary [*A publication*] (DLA)
**JACE** ......... Joint Allied Communications Element (AFM)
**JACE** ......... Joint Alternate Command Element
**JACEB** ...... JACEP. Journal of the American College of Emergency Physicians [*A publication*]
**JACEP** ....... Journal. American College of Emergency Physicians [*A publication*]
**JACEP** ....... Journal. American College of Emergency Physicians and the University Association for Emergency Medical Services [*A publication*]
**Jac Fish Dig** ... Jacob's American Edition of Fisher's English Digest [*A publication*] (DLA)
**JACFU** ...... Joint American-Chinese Foul Up [*World War II slang*] [*Bowdlerized version*]
**JACGUAR** ... Johns and Call Girls United Against Repression (EA)
**JACh** .......... Jahrbuch fuer Antike und Christentum [*A publication*]
**JACH** ......... Journal of American College Health [*A publication*]
**JACHD** ..... Journal of Antimicrobial Chemotherapy [*A publication*]
**JACHDX** ... Journal of Antimicrobial Chemotherapy [*A publication*]
**JACHEY** ... Journal of American College Health [*A publication*]
**Ja Christ Q** ... Japan Christian Quarterly [*A publication*]
**JACHS** ...... Australian Catholic Historical Society. Journal [*A publication*] (APTA)
**JACI** .......... Journal. American Concrete Institute [*A publication*]
**JACIA** ....... Journal. American Concrete Institute [*A publication*]
**JACIBY** ..... Journal of Allergy and Clinical Immunology [*A publication*]
**Jac Int** ........ Jacob's Introduction to the Common, Civil, and Canon Law [*A publication*] (DLA)
**JACK** ......... Jackpot Enterprises, Inc. [*NASDAQ symbol*] (NQ)
**JACK** ......... Junior American Coin Klub (EA)
**JACK** ......... Junior Assistant Cook [*British military*] (DMA)
**Jack Geo Ind** ... Jackson's Index to the Georgia Reports [*A publication*] (DLA)
**Jack & G Landl & Ten** ... Jackson and Gross' Treatise on the Law of Landlord and Tenant in Pennsylvania [*A publication*] (DLA)
**Jack Journl** ... Jackson Journal of Business [*A publication*]
**Jack & L** .... Jackson and Lumpkin's Reports [*59-64 Georgia*] [*A publication*] (DLA)
**JACKPHY** ... Japanese, Arabic, Chinese, Korean, Persian, Hebrew, Yiddish [*Nonroman languages*] [*Library of Congress*]
**Jack Pl** ....... Jackson on Pleadings [*1933*] [*A publication*] (DLA)
**JACKPOT** ... Joint Airborne Communications Center and Command Post
**Jackson** ...... Jackson's Reports [*1-29 Texas Court of Appeals*] [*A publication*] (DLA)
**Jackson** ...... Jackson's Reports [*46-58 Georgia*] [*A publication*] (DLA)
**Jackson & Lumpkin** ... Jackson and Lumpkin's Reports [*59-64 Georgia*] [*A publication*] (DLA)
**Jack Tex App** ... Jackson's Reports [*A publication*] (DLA)
**JACL** ......... Japanese American Citizens League (EA)
**Jac Law Dict** ... Jacob's Law Dictionary [*A publication*] (DLA)
**Jac LD** ....... Jacob's Law Dictionary [*A publication*] (DLA)
**Jac L Dict** .. Jacob's Law Dictionary [*A publication*] (DLA)
**Jac Lex Mer** ... Jacob's Lex Mercatoria [*A publication*] (DLA)
**Jac LG** ....... Jacob's Law Grammar [*A publication*] (DLA)
**JACM** ........ Journal of Alternative and Complementary Medicine [*A publication*]
**JACM** ........ Journal. Association for Computing Machinery [*A publication*]
**JACNE** ...... Joint Advisory Committee on Nutrition Education [*British*]
**JACO** ......... Jaco Electronics, Inc. [*NASDAQ symbol*] (NQ)
**JACO** ......... Joint Actions Control Office (AABC)
**Jacob** .......... Jacob's English Chancery Reports [*1821-22*] [*A publication*] (DLA)
**Jacob** .......... Jacob's Law Dictionary [*A publication*] (DLA)
**Jacob Ardiz** ... Jacobus de Ardizone [*Flourished, 1213-50*] [*Authority cited in pre-1607 legal work*] (DSA)
**JACODK** ... Journal of Altered States of Consciousness [*A publication*]
**J Acoust Emiss** ... Journal of Acoustic Emission [*A publication*]
**J Acoustical Soc Am** ... Journal. Acoustical Society of America [*A publication*]
**J Acoust So** ... Journal. Acoustical Society of America [*A publication*]
**J Acoust Soc Am** ... Journal. Acoustical Society of America [*A publication*]
**J Acoust Soc Amer** ... Journal. Acoustical Society of America [*A publication*]
**J Acoust Soc Am Suppl** ... Journal. Acoustical Society of America. Supplement [*A publication*]
**J Acoust Soc India** ... Journal. Acoustical Society of India [*A publication*]
**J Acoust Soc Jap** ... Journal. Acoustical Society of Japan [*A publication*]
**J Acoust Soc Jpn** ... Journal. Acoustical Society of Japan [*A publication*]
**JACP** ......... Japanese American Curriculum Project (EA)
**JACPA** ...... Journal. American Academy of Child Psychiatry [*A publication*]
**J Acquired Immune Defic Syndr** ... Journal of Acquired Immune Deficiency Syndromes [*A publication*]
**JACRAQ** ... Journal of Apicultural Research [*A publication*]
**JACS** ......... Jet Attitude Control System (KSC)
**JACS** ......... Joint Action in Community Service (EA)
**JAcS** .......... Journal. Acoustical Society of America [*A publication*]
**JACS** ......... Journal. American Chemical Society [*A publication*]
**JACS** ......... Journal of Applied Communication Series [*A publication*]
**JACS** ......... JUMPS Army Coding System (MCD)
**JACSA** ....... Journal. American Chemical Society [*A publication*]
**JACSAT** .... Journal. American Chemical Society [*A publication*]
**Jac Sea Laws** ... Jacobsen's Law of the Sea [*A publication*] (DLA)
**JACSPAC** ... Joint Air Communications of the Pacific
**JACT** ......... [*The*] Joint Association of Classical Teachers [*British*]
**JACT** ......... Journal. American College of Toxicology [*A publication*]
**JACTA** ...... Journal. American Ceramic Society [*A publication*]
**JACTA** ...... Journal. Australasian Commercial Teachers' Association [*A publication*] (APTA)
**JACTDZ** ... Journal. American College of Toxicology [*A publication*]
**Jac & W** ..... Jacob and Walker's English Chancery Reports [*37 English Reprint*] [*A publication*] (DLA)
**Jac & Walk** ... Jacob and Walker's English Chancery Reports [*37 English Reprint*] [*A publication*] (DLA)
**Jac & W (Eng)** ... Jacob and Walker's English Chancery Reports [*37 English Reprint*] [*A publication*] (DLA)
**JAD** ........... Joint Application Design [*Data processing*]
**JAD** ........... Joint Resource Assessment Database
**JAD** ........... Journal of Advertising Research [*A publication*]
**JAD** ........... Wheaton Public Library, Wheaton, IL [*OCLC symbol*] (OCLC)
**JADAA** ...... Journal. American Dietetic Association [*A publication*]
**JADAAE** ... Journal. American Dietetic Association [*A publication*]
**Jadav J Comp Lit** ... Jadavpur Journal of Comparative Literature [*A publication*]
**JADB** ......... Joint Air Defense Board
**JADC** ......... Joint Administrative Committee [*Military*]
**J Addict Res Found** ... Journal. Addiction Research Foundation [*A publication*]
**JADE** ......... Japanese Air Defense Environment
**JADE** ......... Journal of Alcohol and Drug Education [*A publication*]
**JADE** ......... Junior Administrator Development Examination (AFM)
**JADEA** ...... Jaderna Energie [*A publication*]
**J Adelaide Bot Gard** ... Journal. Adelaide Botanic Gardens [*A publication*]
**Jad Energ** ... Jaderna Energie [*A publication*]
**Jadernaja Fiz** ... Jadernaja Fizika [*A publication*]
**JADF** ......... Japan Air Defense Force
**JADF** ......... Joint Air Defense Force (AAG)
**J Adhes** ...... Journal of Adhesion [*A publication*]
**J Adhesion** ... Journal of Adhesion [*A publication*]
**J Adhes Sealant Counc** ... Journal. Adhesive and Sealant Council [*United States*] [*A publication*]
**J Adhes Soc Jpn** ... Journal. Adhesion Society of Japan [*A publication*]
**JADID7** ..... Journal of Affective Disorders [*A publication*]
**JADIS** ........ Joint Air Defense Interoperability Study
**JADITBHKNYC** ... Just a Drop in the Basket Helps Keep New York Clean [*Antilitter campaign*]
**J Admin Overseas** ... Journal of Administration Overseas [*A publication*]
**J Adm Overs** ... Journal of Administration Overseas [*A publication*]
**J Adm Overseas** ... Journal of Administration Overseas [*A publication*]
**JADO** ......... Journal of Administration Overseas [*A publication*]
**JADOC** ....... Joint Air Defense Operation Center
**J Adolesc** ... Journal of Adolescence [*A publication*]
**J Adolescence** ... Journal of Adolescence [*A publication*]
**J Adolesc Health Care** ... Journal of Adolescent Health Care [*A publication*]
**JADOR** ...... Joint Advertising Directors of Recruiting [*Navy*] (NVT)
**JADPDS** .... Journal of Applied Developmental Psychology [*A publication*]
**JADPU** ...... Joint Automatic Data Processing Unit
**JADREP** .... Joint Resource Assessment Data Base Report [*Military*] (AABC)
**Jadr Zbor** ... Jadranski Zbornik. Prolozi za Povijest Istre, Rijeke, i Hrvatskog Primorja [*A publication*]
**JADS** ......... Journal Article Delivery Service [*Carnegie Mellon University*]
**JADSA** ...... Journal. American Dental Association [*A publication*]
**JADSAY** ... Journal. American Dental Association [*A publication*]
**J Adult Ed** ... Journal of Adult Education [*A publication*]
**J Adv** .......... Journal of Advertising [*A publication*]
**J Adv** .......... Judge Advocate [*Legal term*] (DLA)
**J Advanced Transp** ... Journal of Advanced Transportation [*A publication*]
**J Adv Ed** .... Journal of Advanced Education [*A publication*]
**J Adv Educ** ... Journal of Advanced Education [*A publication*] (APTA)
**J Advert** ..... Journal of Advertising [*A publication*]
**J Advertising** ... Journal of Advertising [*A publication*]
**J Advert Res** ... Journal of Advertising Research [*A publication*]
**J Adv Nurs** ... Journal of Advanced Nursing [*A publication*]

**J Adv Res**... Journal of Advertising Research [*A publication*]
**J Adv Transp** ... Journal of Advanced Transportation [*United States*] [*A publication*]
**J Adv Zool** ... Journal of Advanced Zoology [*A publication*]
**JAE**........... Illinois Agricultural Association & Affiliated Co., Bloomington, IL [*OCLC symbol*] (OCLC)
**JAe**............ Jahrbuch fuer Aesthetik und Allgemeine Kunstwissenschaft [*A publication*]
**JAE**........... Japan Aviation Electronics Industry Ltd.
**JAE**........... Jeune Afrique Economie [*A publication*]
**JAE**........... Joint Atomic Exercise [*NATO*] (NATG)
**JAE**........... Journal of Accounting and Economics [*Netherlands*] [*A publication*]
**JAE**........... Journal of Advanced Education [*A publication*] (ADA)
**JAE**........... Journal of Aesthetic Education [*A publication*]
**JAE**........... Journal of Agricultural Economics [*A publication*]
**JAE**........... Training and Development Journal [*A publication*]
**JAEC**......... Japan Atomic Energy Commission
**JAEC**......... Joint Atomic Energy Commission
**JAECAP**.... Journal of Animal Ecology [*A publication*]
**Ja Echo**...... Japan Echo [*A publication*]
**Ja Econ Stud** ... Japanese Economic Studies [*A publication*]
**JAEDB**...... Journal of Aesthetic Education [*A publication*]
**JAEG**......... Jaegdtiger [*Tank-destroyer*] [*German military - World War II*]
**Jaeger Labor Law** ... Jaeger's Cases and Statutes on Labor Law [*A publication*] (DLA)
**Jaehrl**......... Jaehrlich [*Annual*] [*German*] [*Business term*]
**JAEIC**........ Joint Atomic Energy Intelligence Center [*Military*]
**JAEIC**........ Joint Atomic Energy Intelligence Committee (KSC)
**JAEIP**........ Japan Atomic Energy Insurance Pool
**JAEMA**..... Journal. Albert Einstein Medical Center [*A publication*]
**JAEMAL**.. Journal. Albert Einstein Medical Center [*Philadelphia*] [*A publication*]
**JAENES**.... Journal of Agricultural Entomology [*A publication*]
**JAERA2**.... Journal of Agricultural Engineering Research [*A publication*]
**JAERI**........ Japan Atomic Energy Research Institute [*Tokyo*]
**J Aero Med Soc India** ... Journal. Aero Medical Society of India [*A publication*]
**J Aeronaut Soc India** ... Journal. Aeronautical Society of India [*A publication*]
**J Aeronaut Soc S Afr** ... Journal. Aeronautical Society of South Africa [*A publication*]
**J Aero Sci**.. Journal of the Aeronautical Sciences [*A publication*]
**J Aerosol Sci** ... Journal of Aerosol Science [*A publication*]
**J Aerosol Science** ... Journal of Aerosol Science [*A publication*]
**J Aero/Space Sci** ... Journal of the Aero/Space Sciences [*Later, American Institute of Aeronautics and Astronautics. Journal*] [*A publication*]
**J Aerosp Transp Div Am Soc Civ Eng** ... Journal. Aerospace Transport Division. American Society of Civil Engineers [*A publication*]
**JAERT**...... Journal. Association for Education by Radio-Television [*A publication*]
**JAES**......... Journal of African Earth Sciences [*A publication*]
**JAES**......... Journal. Audio Engineering Society [*A publication*]
**J Aes Art C** ... Journal of Aesthetics and Art Criticism [*A publication*]
**J Aes Art Crit** ... Journal of Aesthetics and Art Criticism [*A publication*]
**JAesE**......... Journal of Aesthetic Education [*A publication*]
**J Aes Ed**...... Journal of Aesthetic Education [*A publication*]
**J Aes Educ** ... Journal of Aesthetic Education [*A publication*]
**J Aesth**....... Journal of Aesthetics and Art Criticism [*A publication*]
**J Aesth & Art C** ... Journal of Aesthetics and Art Criticism [*A publication*]
**J Aesth Educ** ... Journal of Aesthetic Education [*A publication*]
**J Aesthet E** ... Journal of Aesthetic Education [*A publication*]
**J Aesthetic Educ** ... Journal of Aesthetic Education [*A publication*]
**J Aesthetics** ... Journal of Aesthetics and Art Criticism [*A publication*]
**JAEW**........ Japanese Airborne Early Warning
**JAF**........... Corn Belt Library System, Normal, IL [*OCLC symbol*] (OCLC)
**JAF**........... James A. Fitzpatrick [*Nuclear power plant*] (NRCH)
**JAF**........... Jamestown Area Furniture Haulers Association, Inc., Buffalo NY [*STAC*]
**JAf**............ Jewish Affairs [*A publication*]
**JAF**........... Job Accounting Facility
**JAF**........... John Augustus Foundation (EA)
**JAF**........... Jordanian Air Force
**JAF**........... Journal of American Folklore [*A publication*]
**JAF**........... Judge Advocate of the Fleet
**JAFC**......... James Allen Fan Club (EA)
**JAFC**......... Jammie Ann Fan Club (EA)
**JAFC**......... Japan Atomic Fuel Corporation
**JAFC**......... John Anderson Fan Club [*Defunct*] (EA)
**JA & FC**..... Journal of Agricultural and Food Chemistry [*A publication*]
**JAFC**......... Junior Acting Field Captain [*Military*] [*British*] (ROG)
**JAFCAU** ... Journal of Agricultural and Food Chemistry [*A publication*]
**JAFE**......... Joint Advanced Fighter Engine
**JAFF**......... Electronic and Chaff Jamming (IEEE)
**JAff**........... Jewish Affairs [*A publication*]
**J Affective Disord** ... Journal of Affective Disorders [*A publication*]
**JAFHRO**... Joint Armed Forces Housing Referral Office (MCD)
**JAFL**......... Journal of American Folklore [*A publication*]
**JAFNA**...... Joint Air Force-NASA
**JAFNC**...... Joint Air Force-Navy Committee
**JAFO**......... Junior Acting Field Officer [*Military*] [*British*] (ROG)
**Ja Found Newsl** ... Japan Foundation Newsletter [*A publication*]
**JAFP**.......... Jewish Agency for Palestine
**JAFPUB**.... Joint Armed Forces Publication
**J Afr Earth Sci** ... Journal of African Earth Sciences [*A publication*]
**J Afr Earth Sci Middle East** ... Journal of African Earth Sciences and the Middle East [*A publication*]
**JAfrH**........ Journal of African History [*A publication*]
**J Afr Hist**... Journal of African History [*A publication*]
**J African Hist** ... Journal of African History [*A publication*]
**J African L** ... Journal of African Law [*A publication*] (DLA)
**J African Law** ... Journal of African Law [*A publication*]
**J African Studies** ... Journal of African Studies [*A publication*]
**J Afric Hist** ... Journal of African History [*A publication*]
**JAfrL**......... Journal of African Languages [*A publication*]
**J Afr L**....... Journal of African Law [*A publication*]
**J Afr Law**... Journal of African Law [*A publication*]
**J Afr S**........ Journal. African Society [*A publication*]
**J Afr Stud**.. Journal of African Studies [*A publication*]
**JAG**........... Indian Trails Public Library District, Wheeling, IL [*OCLC symbol*] (OCLC)
**JAG**........... JAG [*Judge Advocate General, US Air Force*] Bulletin [*A publication*]
**JAG**........... Jaguar [*Automobile*]
**JAG**........... James Abram Garfield [*US president, 1831-1881*]
**JAG**........... Jobs for America's Graduates [*An association*] (EA)
**JAG**........... Journal. Alaska Geological Society [*A publication*]
**JAG**........... Judge Advocate General [*Air Force, Army, Navy*]
**JAGA**......... Military Affairs Division, Office of Judge Advocate General, United States Army (DLA)
**JAGAR**...... Judge Advocate General's Area Representatives
**JAG Bull**.... Judge Advocate General Bulletin [*Air Force*] [*A publication*] (DLA)
**JAGC**......... Judge Advocate General's Corps
**JAG CMR (AF)** ... Judge Advocate General Court-Martial Reports [*Air Force*] [*A publication*] (DLA)
**JAG Comp CMO (Navy)** ... Judge Advocate General Compilation of Court-Martial Orders [*Navy*] [*A publication*] (DLA)
**JAGD**........ Judge Advocate General's Department [*Air Force, Army*]
**JAG Dig Op** ... Judge Advocate General Digest of Opinions [*A publication*] (DLA)
**JAGDR**...... Judge Advocate General's Department Reserve
**J Ag Econ**... Journal of Agricultural Economics [*A publication*]
**J Ag & Food Chem** ... Journal of Agricultural and Food Chemistry [*A publication*]
**JAGGAD**... Journal des Agreges [*A publication*]
**Jagger J**..... Jagger Journal [*A publication*]
**Jagg Torts** ... Jaggard on Torts [*A publication*] (DLA)
**JAGINST** ... Office of the Judge Advocate General Instructions [*Navy*]
**JAGIT**....... Joint Air-Ground Instruction Team
**JAG J**........ JAG [*Judge Advocate General, US Navy*] Journal [*A publication*]
**JAG Journal** ... Judge Advocate General of the Navy. Journal [*US*] [*A publication*]
**JAG L Rev** ... United States. Air Force Judge Advocate General. Law Review [*A publication*] (DLA)
**JAG Man**... Judge Advocate General Manual (Navy) [*A publication*] (DLA)
**J Ag New Zealand** ... New Zealand Journal of Agriculture [*A publication*]
**JAGO**........ Judge Advocate General's Office
**JAGOS**...... Joint Air-Ground Operations System [*Military*]
**J Ag Pratique** ... Journal d'Agriculture Pratique [*A publication*]
**JAGR**......... Jaguar PLC [*Leonia, NJ*] [*NASDAQ symbol*] (NQ)
**JAGRA**...... Journal of Agricultural Research [*A publication*]
**J Agr Ass China** ... Journal. Agricultural Association of China [*A publication*]
**J Agr Che J** ... Journal. Agricultural Chemical Society of Japan [*A publication*]
**J Agr Chem Soc Jap** ... Journal. Agricultural Chemical Society of Japan [*A publication*]
**J Agr Econ** ... Journal of Agricultural Economics [*A publication*]
**J Agr Econ Dev** ... Journal of Agricultural Economics and Development [*A publication*]
**J Agreges**... Journal des Agreges [*A publication*]
**J Agr Eng R** ... Journal of Agricultural Engineering Research [*A publication*]
**J Agr Eng Res** ... Journal of Agricultural Engineering Research [*A publication*]
**J Agr Eng Soc Jap** ... Journal. Agricultural Engineering Society of Japan [*A publication*]
**J Ag Res**..... Journal of Agricultural Research [*A publication*]
**J Agr Exp Sta Chosen** ... Journal. Agricultural Experiment Station of Chosen [*A publication*]
**J Agr Food** ... Journal of Agricultural and Food Chemistry [*A publication*]
**J Agr Food Chem** ... Journal of Agricultural and Food Chemistry [*A publication*]
**J Agric**....... Journal of Agriculture [*A publication*] (APTA)
**J Agric Ass China** ... Journal. Agricultural Association of China [*A publication*]
**J Agric Assoc China New Ser** ... Journal. Agricultural Association of China. New Series [*A publication*]
**J Agric Chem Soc Japan** ... Journal. Agricultural Chemical Society of Japan [*A publication*]

**J Agric Chem Soc Jpn** ... Journal. Agricultural Chemical Society of Japan [*A publication*]
**J Agric Econ** ... Journal of Agricultural Economics [*A publication*]
**J Agric Econ Dev** ... Journal of Agricultural Economics and Development [*A publication*]
**J Agric Eng** ... Journal of Agricultural Engineering [*A publication*]
**J Agric Engin Res** ... Journal of Agricultural Engineering Research [*A publication*]
**J Agric Engng Res** ... Journal of Agricultural Engineering Research [*A publication*]
**J Agric Eng Res** ... Journal of Agricultural Engineering Research [*A publication*]
**J Agric Entomol** ... Journal of Agricultural Entomology [*A publication*]
**J Agric Fd Chem** ... Journal of Agricultural and Food Chemistry [*A publication*]
**J Agric Food Chem** ... Journal of Agricultural and Food Chemistry [*A publication*]
**J Agric For** ... Journal of Agriculture and Forestry [*A publication*]
**J Agric Lab (Chiba)** ... Journal. Agricultural Laboratory (Chiba) [*A publication*]
**J Agric Meteorol** ... Journal of Agricultural Meteorology [*Tokyo*] [*A publication*]
**J Agric Met (Tokyo)** ... Journal of Agricultural Meteorology (Tokyo) [*A publication*]
**J Agric Res** ... Journal of Agricultural Research [*A publication*]
**J Agric Res (Alexandria)** ... Journal of Agricultural Research (Alexandria) [*A publication*]
**J Agric Res China** ... Journal of Agricultural Research of China [*A publication*]
**J Agric Res Icel** ... Journal of Agricultural Research in Iceland [*Islenzkar Landbunadar Rannsoknir*] [*A publication*]
**J Agric (S Aust)** ... Journal of Agriculture (South Australia) [*A publication*]
**J Agric Sci** ... Journal of Agricultural Science [*A publication*]
**J Agric Sci (Camb)** ... Journal of Agricultural Science (Cambridge) [*A publication*]
**J Agric Sci Finl** ... Journal of Agricultural Science in Finland [*A publication*]
**J Agric Sci Res** ... Journal of Agricultural and Scientific Research [*A publication*]
**J Agric Sci Tokyo Nogyo Daigaku** ... Journal of Agricultural Science. Tokyo Nogyo Daigaku [*A publication*]
**J Agric Soc Jpn** ... Journal. Agricultural Society of Japan [*A publication*]
**J Agric Soc Trin** ... Journal. Agricultural Society of Trinidad and Tobago [*A publication*]
**J Agric Soc Trinidad Tobago** ... Journal. Agricultural Society of Trinidad and Tobago [*A publication*]
**J Agric Soc Trin & Tobago** ... Journal. Agricultural Society of Trinidad and Tobago [*A publication*]
**J Agric Soc Univ Coll Wales** ... Journal. Agricultural Society. University College of Wales [*A publication*]
**J Agric Soc Univ Coll Wales (Aberyst)** ... Journal. Agricultural Society. University College of Wales (Aberystwyth) [*A publication*]
**J Agric (South Aust)** ... Journal of Agriculture (South Australia) [*A publication*]
**J Agric Trop** ... Journal d'Agriculture Tropicale [*A publication*]
**J Agric Trop Botan Appl** ... Journal d'Agriculture Tropicale et de Botanique Appliquee [*Later, Journal d'Agriculture Traditionnelle et de Botanique Appliquee*] [*A publication*]
**J Agric Trop Bot Appl** ... Journal d'Agriculture Tropicale et de Botanique Appliquee [*Later, Journal d'Agriculture Traditionnelle et de Botanique Appliquee*] [*A publication*]
**J Agricultural Food Chem** ... Journal of Agricultural and Food Chemistry [*A publication*]
**J Agric Univ PR** ... Journal of Agriculture. University of Puerto Rico [*A publication*]
**J Agric Univ Puerto Rico** ... Journal of Agriculture. University of Puerto Rico [*A publication*]
**J Agric (VIC)** ... Journal of Agriculture (Department of Agriculture. Victoria) [*A publication*] (APTA)
**J Agric (Vict)** ... Journal of Agriculture (Victoria) [*A publication*] (APTA)
**J Agric Vict Dep Agric** ... Journal of Agriculture. Victoria Department of Agriculture [*A publication*]
**J Agric (Victoria)** ... Journal of Agriculture (Victoria) [*A publication*]
**J Agric Water Resour Res** ... Journal of Agriculture and Water Resources Research [*A publication*]
**J Agric W Aust** ... Journal of Agriculture of Western Australia [*A publication*]
**J Agric (West Aust)** ... Journal of Agriculture (Department of Agriculture. Western Australia) [*A publication*] (APTA)
**J Agr Ind SA** ... Journal of Agricultural Industry, South Australia [*A publication*]
**J Agr Lab** ... Journal. Agricultural Laboratory [*A publication*]
**J Agr (Melbourne)** ... Journal of Agriculture (Melbourne) [*A publication*]
**J Agr Meteorol (Japan)** ... Journal of Agricultural Meteorology (Japan) [*A publication*]
**J Agron Crop Sci** ... Journal of Agronomy and Crop Science [*A publication*]
**J Agr Prat** .. Journal d'Agriculture Pratique [*A publication*]
**J Agr Res** ... Journal of Agricultural Research [*A publication*]
**J Agr Res Tokai-Kinki Reg** ... Journal of the Agricultural Research in the Tokai-Kinki Region [*A publication*]
**J Agr (S Aust)** ... Journal of Agriculture (South Australia) [*A publication*]
**J Agr Sci** .... Journal of Agricultural Science [*A publication*]
**J Agr Sci Tokyo Nogyo Daigaku** ... Journal of Agricultural Science. Tokyo Nogyo Daigaku [*A publication*]
**J Agr Soc Trinidad Tobago** ... Journal. Agricultural Society of Trinidad and Tobago [*A publication*]
**J Agr Soc Wales** ... Journal. Agricultural Society. University College of Wales [*A publication*]
**J Agr Tax'n & L** ... Journal of Agricultural Taxation and Law [*A publication*] (DLA)
**J Agr Trad Bot Appl** ... Journal d'Agriculture Traditionnelle et de Botanique Appliquee [*A publication*]
**J Agr Trop Bot Appl** ... Journal d'Agriculture Tropicale et de Botanique Appliquee [*Later, Journal d'Agriculture Traditionnelle et de Botanique Appliquee*] [*A publication*]
**J Agr Univ PR** ... Journal of Agriculture. University of Puerto Rico [*A publication*]
**J Agr W Aust** ... Journal of Agriculture of Western Australia [*A publication*]
**JAGS** ......... Joint Army-Air Force Air-Ground Study
**JAGS** ......... Judge Advocate General's School (DLA)
**J Ag (SA)** ... Journal of Agriculture (South Australia) [*A publication*] (APTA)
**JAGSA** ...... Journal. American Geriatrics Society [*A publication*]
**JAGSAF** .... Journal. American Geriatrics Society [*A publication*]
**JAGT** ......... Procurement Division, Judge Advocate General, United States Army (DLA)
**J Ag T and L** ... Journal of Agricultural Taxation and Law [*A publication*]
**Ja Guara** .... Jacobus Guaraguilia [*Authority cited in pre-1607 legal work*] (DSA)
**J Ag Univ Puerto Rico** ... Journal of Agriculture. University of Puerto Rico [*A publication*]
**JAGVAO** ... Journal of Agriculture [*Victoria*] [*A publication*]
**J Ag (VIC)** ... Journal of Agriculture (Department of Agriculture. Victoria) [*A publication*] (APTA)
**J Ag (WA)** ... Journal of Agriculture (Department of Agriculture. Western Australia) [*A publication*] (APTA)
**JAH** ........... Glencoe Public Library, Glencoe, IL [*OCLC symbol*] (OCLC)
**JAH** ........... Journal of African History [*A publication*]
**JAH** ........... Journal of American History [*A publication*]
**JAHAA** ..... Journal. American College Health Association [*A publication*]
**JAHAAY** ... Journal. American College Health Association [*A publication*]
**JahAs** ......... Jahrbuch fuer Amerikastudien [*A publication*]
**JAHCD9** ... Journal of Adolescent Health Care [*A publication*]
**JAHEDF** ... Journal of Allied Health [*A publication*]
**Jahrb Akad Wiss Gottingen** ... Jahrbuch. Akademie der Wissenschaften in Goettingen [*A publication*]
**Jahrb Akad Wiss Lit (Mainz)** ... Jahrbuch. Akademie der Wissenschaften und der Literatur (Mainz) [*A publication*]
**Jahrb Amerikastud** ... Jahrbuch fuer Amerikastudien [*A publication*]
**Jahrb Arbeitsgemein Futterungsberat** ... Jahrbuch. Arbeitsgemeinschaft fuer Fuetterungsberatung [*A publication*]
**Jahrb Arbeitsgem Fuetterungsberat** ... Jahrbuch. Arbeitsgemeinschaft fuer Fuetterungsberatung [*A publication*]
**Jahrb Bayer Akad Wiss** ... Jahrbuch. Bayerische Akademie der Wissenschaften [*A publication*]
**Jahrb Bergbau Energ Mineraloel Chem** ... Jahrbuch fuer Bergbau Energie Mineraloel und Chemie [*A publication*]
**Jahrb Ber M** ... Jahrbuch. Berliner Museen [*A publication*]
**Jahrb Brandenburg Landesgesch** ... Jahrbuch fuer Brandenburgische Landesgeschichte [*A publication*]
**Jahrb Bundesanst Pflanzebau Samenpruef (Wien)** ... Jahrbuch. Bundesanstalt fuer Pflanzenbau und Samenpruefung (Wien) [*A publication*]
**Jahrb Bundesanst Pflanzenbau Samenpruf** ... Jahrbuch. Bundesanstalt fuer Pflanzenbau und Samenpruefung [*A publication*]
**Jahrb f Cl Phil Suppl** ... Jahrbucher fuer Classische Philologie. Supplementband [*A publication*] (OCD)
**Jahrb Coburg Landesstift** ... Jahrbuch. Coburger Landesstiftung [*A publication*]
**Jahrb Deut Akad Landwirt Wiss (Berlin)** ... Jahrbuch. Deutsche Akademie der Landwirtschaftswissenschaften (Berlin) [*A publication*]
**Jahrb Dtsch Ges Chronom** ... Jahrbuch. Deutsche Gesellschaft fuer Chronometrie [*A publication*]
**Jahrb Eisenbahnwes** ... Jahrbuch des Eisenbahnwesens [*West Germany*] [*A publication*]
**Jahr Berliner Mus** ... Jahrbuch. Berliner Museen [*A publication*]
**Jahrb Geol Bundesanst** ... Jahrbuch. Geologische Bundesanstalt [*A publication*]
**Jahrb Geol Bundesanst Sonderb** ... Jahrbuch. Geologische Bundesanstalt. Sonderband [*A publication*]
**Jahrb Gesch** ... Jahrbuecher fuer Geschichte Osteuropas [*A publication*]
**Jahrb Gesch & Kunst Mittelrheins & Nachbargeb** ... Jahrbuch fuer Geschichte und Kunst des Mittelrheins und Seiner Nachbargebiete [*A publication*]
**Jahrb Gesch Mittel Ostdtschl** ... Jahrbuch fuer die Geschichte Mittel- und Ostdeutschlands [*A publication*]
**Jahrb Gesch Osteur** ... Jahrbuecher fuer Geschichte Osteuropas [*A publication*]
**Jahrb Gesch Osteurop** ... Jahrbuecher fuer Geschichte Osteuropas [*A publication*]
**Jahrb Hafenbautech Ges** ... Jahrbuch. Hafenbautechnische Gesellschaft [*West Germany*] [*A publication*]

**Jahrb Inst Ne-Metall (Plovdiv)** ... Jahrbuch. Institut fuer Ne-Metallurgie (Plovdiv) [*A publication*]
**Jahrb Kinderh** ... Jahrbuch fuer Kinderheilkunde und Physische Erziehung [*A publication*]
**Jahrb Kinderheilkd Phys Erzieh** ... Jahrbuch fuer Kinderheilkunde und Physische Erziehung [*A publication*]
**Jahrb d Kunsthist Samml d Kaiserhauses** ... Jahrbuch. Kunsthistorische Sammlungen des Allerhoechsten Kaiserhauses [*A publication*]
**Jahrb Kunsth Samml Kaiserh** ... Jahrbuch. Kunsthistorische Sammlungen des Allerhoechsten Kaiserhauses [*A publication*]
**Jahrb Lederwirtsch Oesterr** ... Jahrbuch. Lederwirtschaft Oesterreich [*A publication*]
**Jahrb Liturg & Hymnol** ... Jahrbuch fuer Liturgik und Hymnologie [*A publication*]
**Jahrb Nassau Ver Naturkd** ... Jahrbuecher. Nassauischer Verein fuer Naturkunde [*A publication*]
**Jahrb Nordrh Westfal Landesamt Forsch** ... Jahrbuch. Nordrhein Westfalen Landesamt fuer Forschung [*A publication*]
**Jahrb N St** ... Jahrbuecher fuer National-Oekonomie und Statistik [*A publication*]
**Jahrb Oberflaechentech** ... Jahrbuch Oberflaechentechnik [*West Germany*] [*A publication*]
**Jahrb Oberoesterr Musealver** ... Jahrbuch. Oberoesterreichischer Musealverein [*A publication*]
**Jahrb Oesterr Byzantinistik** ... Jahrbuch der Oesterreichischen Byzantinistik [*A publication*]
**Jahrb Opt Feinmech** ... Jahrbuch fuer Optik und Feinmechanik [*A publication*]
**Jahrb Org Chem** ... Jahrbuch der Organischen Chemie [*A publication*]
**Jahrb Philos Fak 2 Univ Bern** ... Jahrbuch der Philosophischen Fakultaet. 2. Universitaet Bern [*A publication*]
**Jahrb Photogr Reproduktionstech** ... Jahrbuch fuer Photographie und Reproduktionstechnik [*A publication*]
**Jahrb Preuss Geol Landesanst** ... Jahrbuch. Preussische Geologische Landesanstalt [*A publication*]
**Jahrb Preuss Kunstsamml** ... Jahrbuch. Preussische Kunstsammlungen [*A publication*]
**Jahrb d Preuss Kunstsamml** ... Jahrbuch. Preussische Kunstsammlungen [*A publication*]
**Jahrb Radioakt Elektron** ... Jahrbuch der Radioaktivitaet und Elektronik [*A publication*]
**Jahrb Reichsstelle Bodenforsch (Ger)** ... Jahrbuch der Reichsstelle fuer Bodenforschung (Germany) [*A publication*]
**Jahrb Schiffbautech Ges** ... Jahrbuch. Schiffbautechnische Gesellschaft [*A publication*]
**Jahrb Schweiz Naturforsch Ges Wiss Teil** ... Jahrbuch der Schweizerischen Naturforschenden Gesellschaft. Wissenschaftlicher Teil [*A publication*]
**Jahrb Sozia** ... Jahrbuch fuer Sozialwissenschaft [*A publication*]
**Jahrb Staatl Mus Mineral Geol Dresden** ... Jahrbuch. Staatliches Museum fuer Mineralogie und Geologie zu Dresden [*A publication*]
**Jahrb Tech Univ Muenchen** ... Jahrbuch. Technische Universitaet Muenchen [*A publication*]
**Jahrbuch Hamburger Kunstsam** ... Jahrbuch. Hamburger Kunstsammlungen [*A publication*]
**Jahrbuch Niederdonau** ... Jahrbuch fuer Landeskunde von Niederdonau [*A publication*]
**Jahrb Ver Schutz Bergwelt** ... Jahrbuch des Vereins zum Schutz der Bergwelt [*A publication*]
**Jahrb Vers Lehranst Brau Berlin** ... Jahrbuch. Versuch und Lehranstalt fuer Brauerei in Berlin [*A publication*]
**Jahrb Volks** ... Jahrbuch fuer Volksliedforschung [*A publication*]
**Jahrb Wiss Bot** ... Jahrbuecher fuer Wissenschaftliche Botanik [*A publication*]
**Jahrb Wiss Forschungsinst Buntmetall (Plovdiv)** ... Jahrbuch. Wissenschaftliches Forschungsinstitut fuer Buntmetallurgie (Plovdiv) [*A publication*]
**Jahr Deutsch Archaeol Inst** ... Jahrbuch. Deutsches Archaeologische Institut [*A publication*]
**Jahresb** ...... Jahresberichte ueber die Fortschritte der Altertumswissenschaft [*1873-*] [*A publication*] (OCD)
**Jahresber Chem Tech Reichsanst** ... Jahresbericht. Chemisch Technische Reichsanstalt [*A publication*]
**Jahresber DFVLR** ... Jahresbericht. Deutsche Forschungs- und Versuchsanstalt fuer Luft- und Raumfahrt [*A publication*]
**Jahresber Dtsch Hydrogr Inst (Hamburg)** ... Jahresbericht. Deutsches Hydrographische Institut (Hamburg) [*A publication*]
**Jahresber Dtsch Pflanzenschutzdienstes** ... Jahresberichte des Deutschen Pflanzenschutzdienstes [*A publication*]
**Jahresber Fortschr Chem Verw Theile Andrer Wiss** ... Jahresbericht ueber die Fortschritte der Chemie und Verwandter Theile Anderer Wissenschaften [*A publication*]
**Jahresber Fortschr Gesamtgeb Agrikulturchem** ... Jahresbericht ueber die Fortschritte auf dem Gesamtgebiete der Agrikulturchemie [*A publication*]
**Jahresber Fortschr Physiol** ... Jahresbericht ueber die Fortschritte der Physiologie [*A publication*]
**Jahresber Fortschr Tierchm** ... Jahresbericht ueber die Fortschritte der Tierchemie [*A publication*]
**Jahresbericht Grabunden** ... Jahresbericht. Historisch-Antiquarische Gesellschaft von Graubuenden [*A publication*]
**Jahresber Inst Strahlenphys Kernphys Univ Bonn** ... Jahresbericht. Institut fuer Strahlen- und Kernphysik. Universitaet Bonn [*A publication*]
**Jahresber Kernforschungsanlage Juelich** ... Jahresbericht. Kernforschungsanlage Juelich [*A publication*]
**Jahresber Kurashiki-Zentralhosp** ... Jahresbericht. Kurashiki-Zentralhospital [*A publication*]
**Jahresber Mitt Oberrheinischen Geol Ver** ... Jahresberichte und Mitteilungen. Oberrheinischer Geologische Verein [*A publication*]
**Jahresber Schweiz Ges Vererbungsforsch** ... Jahresbericht. Schweizerische Gesellschaft fuer Vererbungsforschung [*A publication*]
**Jahresber Univ Wuerzb** ... Jahresbericht. Universitaet Wuerzburg [*A publication*]
**Jahresber Wetterauischen Ges Gesamte Naturkd Hanau** ... Jahresberichte der Wetterauischen Gesellschaft fuer die Gesamte Naturkunde zu Hanau [*A publication*]
**Jahresb Leistung Vet-Med** ... Jahresbericht ueber die Liestungen auf dem Gebiete der Veterinaer-Medizin [*A publication*]
**Jahresb Schles Gesellsch Vaterl Kult** ... Jahresberichte. Schlesische Gesellschaft fuer Vaterlaendische Kultur [*A publication*]
**Jahresb Vet Med** ... Jahresbericht Veterinaer-Medizin [*A publication*]
**Jahresh Geol Landesamtes Baden Wuerttemb** ... Jahresheft. Geologisches Landesamt in Baden Wuerttemberg [*A publication*]
**Jahresh Ges Naturkd Wuerttemb** ... Jahreshefte. Gesellschaft fuer Naturkunde in Wuerttemberg [*A publication*]
**Jahresh Ver Vaterl Naturkd Wuerttemb** ... Jahreshefte. Verein fuer Vaterlaendische Naturkunde in Wuerttemberg [*A publication*]
**Jahreskurse Aerztl Fortbild** ... Jahreskurse fuer Aerztliche Fortbildung [*A publication*]
**Jahr Hamburger Kunstsam** ... Jahrbuch. Hamburger Kunstsammlungen [*A publication*]
**Jahr Kunsthist Sam (Wien)** ... Jahrbuch. Kunsthistorische Sammlungen (Wien) [*A publication*]
**JAHRS** ...... Journal. Andhra Historical Research Society [*A publication*]
**JAHum** ...... Journal of American Humor [*A publication*]
**JAHYA4** .... Journal. American Dental Hygienists' Association [*A publication*]
**JAI** ............ Jahrbuch des Kaiserlichen Archaeologischen Instituts [*A publication*]
**JAI** ............ JAI Press [*Division of Johnson Associates, Inc.*]
**JAI** ............ Jaipur [*India*] [*Geomagnetic observatory code*]
**JAI** ............ Jaipur [*India*] [*Airport symbol*] (OAG)
**JAI** ............ Jami'at Al Islan [*Defunct*] (EA)
**JAI** ............ Japan-America Institute [*Defunct*] (EA)
**JAI** ............ Jewish Agency for Israel [*Absorbed by United Israel Appeal*] (EA)
**JAI** ............ Job Accounting Interface
**Jai** ............ Johnson Associates, Incorporated, Greenwich, CT [*Library symbol*] [*Library of Congress*] (LCLS)
**JAI** ............ Joint Staff Administrative Instruction [*Military*]
**JAI** ............ Journal of Advertising Research [*A publication*]
**JAI** ............ Journal of American Insurance [*A publication*]
**JAI** ............ Journal. Royal Anthropological Institute of Great Britain and Ireland [*A publication*]
**JAI** ............ Journal. Royal Archaeological Institute [*A publication*]
**JAI** ............ Juvenile Amaurotic Idiocy [*Medicine*]
**JAI** ............ Lake Forest Library, Lake Forest, IL [*OCLC symbol*] (OCLC)
**JAIA** .......... Japan Automobile Importers Association
**JAIA** .......... Journal. Archaeological Institute of America [*A publication*]
**JAIA** .......... Journal. Australian Indonesian Association [*A publication*]
**JAIAS** ........ Journal. Australian Institute of Agricultural Science [*A publication*] (APTA)
**JAIB** .......... Journal. Royal Anthropological Institute of Great Britain and Ireland [*A publication*]
**JAIC** .......... Joint Australian Information Council [*Proposed*]
**J Aichi Med Univ Assoc** ... Journal. Aichi Medical University Association [*A publication*]
**JAICI** ......... Japanese Association for International Chemical Information [*Tokyo*]
**JAIEG** ....... Joint Atomic Information Exchange Group [*DoD*]
**JAIF** .......... Japan Atomic Industrial Forum
**JAIH** .......... Journal of Ancient Indian History [*A publication*]
**JAIHA** ....... Journal. American Institute of Homeopathy [*A publication*]
**JAIHAQ** .... Journal. American Institute of Homeopathy [*A publication*]
**JAIL** .......... Adtec, Inc. [*NASDAQ symbol*] (NQ)
**JAIL** .......... Japanese Annual of International Law [*A publication*]
**JaiL** ........... Jazyk i Literatura [*A publication*]
**JAIM** ......... Job Analysis and Interest Measurement
**JAIMS** ....... Japan-American Institute of Management Science
**JAINAA** .... Journal. Anatomical Society of India [*A publication*]
**Jaina Antiq** ... Jaina Antiquary [*A publication*]
**Jain J** ......... Jain Journal [*A publication*]
**Ja Interp** .... Japan Interpreter [*A publication*]
**JAIO** .......... Joint Assessment and Initiatives Office [*Military*]
**Jaipur LJ** ... Jaipur Law Journal [*India*] [*A publication*] (DLA)
**J Aircr** ........ Journal of Aircraft [*A publication*]
**J Aircraft** ... Journal of Aircraft [*A publication*]
**J Air L** ........ Journal of Air Law and Commerce [*A publication*]

**J Air L and Com** ... Journal of Air Law and Commerce [*A publication*]
**J of Air L & Commerce** ... Journal of Air Law and Commerce [*A publication*]
**J Air Pollu** ... Journal. Air Pollution Control Association [*A publication*]
**J Air Pollut Contr A** ... Air Pollution Control Association. Journal [*A publication*]
**J Air Pollut Contr Ass** ... Journal. Air Pollution Control Association [*A publication*]
**J Air Pollut Control Assoc** ... Journal. Air Pollution Control Association [*A publication*]
**J Air Pollution Control Assoc** ... Journal. Air Pollution Control Association [*A publication*]
**J Air Transp Div Am Soc Civ Eng** ... Journal. Air Transport Division. American Society of Civil Engineers [*A publication*]
**JAISDS** ..... Journal. All India Institute of Medical Sciences [*A publication*]
**JAJ** ............ Jewish Affairs (Johannesburg) [*A publication*]
**Ja J** ............ Judge Advocate Journal [*A publication*]
**JAJ** ............ Waubonsee Community College, Sugar Grove, IL [*OCLC symbol*] (OCLC)
**JAJAAA**.... Journal of Antibiotics. Series A [*Tokyo*] [*A publication*]
**JAJC**.......... Journalism Association of Junior Colleges [*Later, JACC*]
**JaJGL**........ Jahrbuecher fuer Juedische Geschichte und Literatur [*A publication*]
**JAJO**......... January, April, July, and October [*Denotes quarterly payments of interest or dividends in these months*] [*Business term*]
**Ja J Rel Stud** ... Japanese Journal of Religious Studies [*A publication*]
**JAK**............ Jahrbuch der Asiatischen Kunst [*A publication*]
**JAk** ............ Jazykovedny Aktuality [*A publication*]
**JAKFORCE** ... Jammu and Kashmir Force [*British military*] (DMA)
**JAKIS**........ Japanese Keyword Indexing Simulator
**JAL**............ Japan Air Lines
**JAL**............ Japan (London) [*A publication*]
**JAL**............ Jet Approach and Landing Chart (FAAC)
**JAL**............ Jewish Affairs (London) [*A publication*]
**JAL**............ Jewish Apocryphal Literature [*A publication*] (BJA)
**JAL**............ Journal of Academic Librarianship [*A publication*]
**JAL**............ Journal of African Languages [*A publication*]
**JAL**............ Journal of African Law [*A publication*]
**JAL**............ Judge Advocate Library, Department of the Navy, Alexandria, VA [*OCLC symbol*] (OCLC)
**JAL**............ Jurisprudence de la Cour d'Appel de Liege [*A publication*]
**J Ala Acad Sci** ... Journal. Alabama Academy of Science [*A publication*]
**J Alab Acad Sci** ... Journal. Alabama Academy of Science [*A publication*]
**Ja Labor B** ... Japan Labor Bulletin [*A publication*]
**J Ala Dent Assoc** ... Journal. Alabama Dental Association [*A publication*]
**JALAP**....... Jalapae [*Jalap*] [*Pharmacology*] (ROG)
**J Alberta Soc Pet Geol** ... Journal. Alberta Society of Petroleum Geologists [*A publication*]
**J Albert Einstein Med Cent** ... Journal. Albert Einstein Medical Center [*A publication*]
**J Albert Einstein Med Cent (Phila)** ... Journal. Albert Einstein Medical Center (Philadelphia) [*A publication*]
**JALC** ......... Jet Approach and Landing Chart (AFM)
**JALC** ......... John Adams Life Corporation [*Los Angeles, CA*] [*NASDAQ symbol*] (NQ)
**J Alc**........... Journal of Alcoholism [*A publication*]
**JALCA** ...... Journal. American Leather Chemists' Association [*A publication*]
**JALCAQ** ... Journal. American Leather Chemists' Association [*A publication*]
**JALCBR**.... Journal of Alcoholism [*A publication*]
**J Alc Drug** ... Journal of Alcohol and Drug Education [*A publication*]
**J Alcohol**.... Journal of Alcoholism [*A publication*]
**J Alcohol & Drug Educ** ... Journal of Alcohol and Drug Education [*A publication*]
**J Algebra** ... Journal of Algebra [*A publication*]
**J Algorithms** ... Journal of Algorithms [*A publication*]
**Ja Lit Today** ... Japanese Literature Today [*A publication*]
**JALL** ......... Journal of African Languages and Linguistics [*A publication*]
**J All** .......... Journal of Allergy [*A publication*]
**J Allerg Cl** ... Journal of Allergy and Clinical Immunology [*A publication*]
**J Allergy** .... Journal of Allergy [*Later, Journal of Allergy and Clinical Immunology*] [*A publication*]
**J Allergy Clin Immun** ... Journal of Allergy and Clinical Immunology [*A publication*]
**J Allergy Clin Immunol** ... Journal of Allergy and Clinical Immunology [*A publication*]
**J Allied Dent Soc** ... Journal. Allied Dental Societies [*A publication*]
**J Allied Health** ... Journal of Allied Health [*A publication*]
**J All India Dent Assoc** ... Journal. All India Dental Association [*A publication*]
**J All India Inst Med Sci** ... Journal. All India Institute of Medical Sciences [*A publication*]
**J All India Inst Ment Health** ... Journal. All India Institute of Mental Health [*A publication*]
**J All India Ophthalmol Soc** ... Journal. All India Ophthalmological Society [*A publication*]
**J All Ind Ophth Soc** ... Journal. All-India Ophthalmological Society [*A publication*]
**J Alloy Phase Diagrams** ... Journal of Alloy Phase Diagrams [*A publication*]
**JALP** ......... Japan Annual of Law and Politics [*A publication*]
**JALPG** ...... Joint Automatic Language Processing Group
**J ALS**......... Journal. American Liszt Society [*A publication*]
**JALT** ......... Journal. Association of Law Teachers [*A publication*] (DLA)
**J Altered States Conscious** ... Journal of Altered States of Consciousness [*A publication*]
**J Alumni Ass Coll Phys and Surg (Baltimore)** ... Journal. Alumni Association. College of Physicians and Surgeons (Baltimore) [*A publication*]
**JaM** ........... J A Micropublishing, Inc., Eastchester, NY [*Library symbol*] [*Library of Congress*] (LCLS)
**JAM** .......... Jail Accounting Microcomputer System
**JAM** .......... Jamaica [*ANSI three-letter standard code*] (CNC)
**JAM** .......... Jamaica Exports. Complimentary Guide to Trade and Investment Opportunities [*A publication*]
**JAM** .......... Jamieson Scotch Dictionary [*A publication*] (ROG)
**JAM** .......... Jamming [*Military*] (NVT)
**JAM** .......... Japanese Association for Microbiology
**JAM** .......... Job Analysis Memorandum
**JAM** .......... Job Assignment Memorandum
**JAM** .......... Journal of American Musicology [*A publication*]
**JAM** .......... Journal. American Planning Association [*A publication*]
**JAM** .......... Journal d'Analyse Mathematique [*Jerusalem*] [*A publication*]
**JAM** .......... Journal of Applied Management [*A publication*]
**JAM** .......... JUMPS Action Memorandum (NVT)
**JAM** .......... Moraine Valley Community College, Palos Hills, IL [*OCLC symbol*] (OCLC)
**JAMA**........ Japan Automobile Manufacturers Association, Washington Office (EA)
**JAMA**........ Journal. American Medical Association [*A publication*]
**JAMA**........ Moslem People's Revolutionary Movement [*Iran*] [*Political party*] (PPW)
**JAMAA**..... Journal. American Medical Association [*A publication*]
**JAMAAP**.. Journal. American Medical Association [*A publication*]
**JAMAC**..... Job Analysis Memorandum Activity Chart
**JAMAC**..... Joint Aeronautical Materials Activity [*Military*] (AABC)
**J Am Acad Appl Nutr** ... Journal. American Academy of Applied Nutrition [*A publication*]
**J Am Acad Child Adolesc Psychiatry** ... Journal. American Academy of Child and Adolescent Psychiatry [*A publication*]
**J Am Acad Child Psych** ... Journal. American Academy of Child Psychiatry [*A publication*]
**J Am Acad Child Psychiatry** ... Journal. American Academy of Child Psychiatry [*A publication*]
**J Am Acad Dermatol** ... Journal. American Academy of Dermatology [*A publication*]
**J Am Academy Child Psychiatry** ... Journal. American Academy of Child Psychiatry [*A publication*]
**J Am Acad Gnathol Orthop** ... Journal. American Academy of Gnathologic Orthopedics [*A publication*]
**J Am Acad Gold Foil Oper** ... Journal. American Academy of Gold Foil Operators [*A publication*]
**J Am Acad P** ... Journal. American Academy of Psychoanalysis [*A publication*]
**J Am Acad Psychoanal** ... Journal. American Academy of Psychoanalysis [*A publication*]
**J Am Acad Rel** ... Journal. American Academy of Religion [*A publication*]
**J Am Acad Relig** ... Journal. American Academy of Religion [*A publication*]
**J Am Acad Religion** ... Journal. American Academy of Religion [*A publication*]
**J Am A Chil** ... Journal. American Academy of Child Psychiatry [*A publication*]
**JAmAcRel** ... Journal. American Academy of Religion [*Brattleboro, VT*] [*A publication*]
**JAMAET** .. Journal. American Mosquito Control Association [*A publication*]
**JAMAG**..... Joint American Military Advisory Group
**Jamaica Ag Soc J** ... Jamaica Agricultural Society. Journal [*A publication*]
**Jamaica Archt** ... Jamaica Architect [*A publication*]
**Jamaica Geol Survey Dept Ann Rept** ... Jamaica. Geological Survey Department. Annual Report [*A publication*]
**Jamaica Geol Survey Dept Bull** ... Jamaica. Geological Survey Department. Bulletin [*A publication*]
**Jamaica Geol Survey Dept Occ Pap** ... Jamaica. Geological Survey Department. Occasional Paper [*A publication*]
**Jamaica Geol Survey Dept Short Pap** ... Jamaica. Geological Survey Department. Short Paper [*A publication*]
**Jamaica Geol Survey Pub** ... Jamaica. Geological Survey Department. Publication [*A publication*]
**Jamaica Handb** ... Jamaica Handbook [*A publication*]
**J Am Analg Soc** ... Journal. American Analgesia Society [*A publication*]
**J Am Anim Hosp Assoc** ... Journal. American Animal Hospital Association [*A publication*]
**J Am A Rel** ... Journal. American Academy of Religion [*A publication*]
**J Am Ass Med Rec Libr** ... Journal. American Association of Medical Record Librarians [*A publication*]
**J Am Assoc** ... Journal. American Association for Hygiene and Baths [*A publication*]
**J Am Assoc Cereal Chem** ... Journal. American Association of Cereal Chemists [*A publication*]
**J Am Assoc Nephrol Nurses Tech** ... Journal. American Association of Nephrology Nurses and Technicians [*A publication*]

**J Am Assoc Nurse Anesth** ... Journal. American Association of Nurse Anesthetists [*A publication*]
**J Am Assoc Promot Hyg Public Baths** ... Journal. American Association for Promoting Hygiene and Public Baths [*A publication*]
**J Am Assoc Teach Educ Agric** ... Journal. American Association of Teacher Educators in Agriculture [*A publication*]
**J Am Assoc Variable Star Obs** ... Journal. American Association of Variable Star Observers [*A publication*]
**J Am Audiol Soc** ... Journal. American Audiology Society [*A publication*]
**J Am Aud Soc** ... Journal. American Auditory Society [*A publication*]
**JAMB**........ Joint Air Movements Board [*Military*]
**J Am Bakers Assoc Am Inst Baking** ... Journal. American Bakers Association and American Institute of Baking [*A publication*]
**J Am Bankers' Assn** ... Journal. American Bankers Association [*A publication*] (DLA)
**J Ambulatory Care Manage** ... Journal of Ambulatory Care Management [*A publication*]
**J Ambul Care Manage** ... Journal of Ambulatory Care Management [*A publication*]
**J Am Ceram** ... Journal. American Ceramic Society [*A publication*]
**J Am Ceram Soc** ... Journal. American Ceramic Society [*A publication*]
**J Am Cer Soc** ... Journal. American Ceramic Society [*A publication*]
**J Am Chem S** ... Journal. American Chemical Society [*A publication*]
**J Am Chem Soc** ... Journal. American Chemical Society [*A publication*]
**J Am Coll Cardiol** ... Journal. American College of Cardiology [*A publication*]
**J Am Coll Dent** ... Journal. American College of Dentists [*A publication*]
**J Am Coll H** ... Journal. American College Health Association [*A publication*]
**J Am Coll Health** ... Journal of American College Health [*A publication*]
**J Am Coll Health Assn** ... Journal. American College Health Association [*A publication*]
**J Am Coll Health Assoc** ... Journal. American College Health Association [*A publication*]
**J Am Coll Nutr** ... Journal. American College of Nutrition [*A publication*]
**J Am Coll Toxicol** ... Journal. American College of Toxicology [*A publication*]
**J Am Concr Inst** ... Journal. American Concrete Institute [*A publication*]
**J Am Cult**... Journal of American Culture [*A publication*]
**JAMDAY** ... Journal. American Medical Technologists [*A publication*]
**J Am Dent A** ... Journal. American Dental Association [*A publication*]
**J Am Dent Assoc** ... Journal. American Dental Association [*A publication*]
**J Am Dent Assoc Dent Cosmos** ... Journal. American Dental Association and the Dental Cosmos [*A publication*]
**J Am Dent Hyg Assoc** ... Journal. American Dental Hygienists' Association [*A publication*]
**J Am Dent Soc Anesthesiol** ... Journal. American Dental Society of Anesthesiology [*A publication*]
**Jam Dep Agric Bull** ... Jamaica. Department of Agriculture. Bulletin [*A publication*]
**J Am Diet A** ... Journal. American Dietetic Association [*A publication*]
**J Am Diet Assoc** ... Journal. American Dietetic Association [*A publication*]
**J Am Dietet A** ... Journal. American Dietetic Association [*A publication*]
**JAME**........ Jamesbury Corp. [*NASDAQ symbol*] (NQ)
**J Amer Ceram Soc** ... Journal. American Ceramic Society [*A publication*]
**J Amer Chem Soc** ... Journal. American Chemical Society [*A publication*]
**J Amer Coll Dent** ... Journal. American College of Dentists [*A publication*]
**J Amer Diet Ass** ... Journal. American Dietetic Association [*A publication*]
**J Amer Inst Planners** ... Journal. American Institute of Planners [*A publication*]
**J Amer Leather Chem Ass** ... Journal. American Leather Chemists' Association [*A publication*]
**J Amer Musicol Soc** ... Journal. American Musicological Society [*A publication*]
**J Amer Oil** ... Journal. American Oil Chemists' Society [*A publication*]
**J Amer Oil Chem Soc** ... Journal. American Oil Chemists' Society [*A publication*]
**J Amer Pharm Ass Sci Ed** ... Journal. American Pharmaceutical Association. Scientific Edition [*A publication*]
**J Amer Plann Assoc** ... Journal. American Planning Association [*A publication*]
**J Amer Soc Agron** ... Journal. American Society of Agronomy [*A publication*]
**J Amer Soc Farm Manage Rural Appraisers** ... Journal. American Society of Farm Managers and Rural Appraisers [*A publication*]
**J Amer Soc Hort Sci** ... Journal. American Society for Horticultural Science [*A publication*]
**J Amer Soc Inform Sci** ... Journal. American Society for Information Science [*A publication*]
**J Amer Soc Safety Eng** ... Journal. American Society of Safety Engineers [*A publication*]
**J Amer Soc Sugar Beet Tech** ... Journal. American Society of Sugar Beet Technologists [*A publication*]
**J Amer Statist Assoc** ... Journal. American Statistical Association [*A publication*]
**J Amer Stud** ... Journal of American Studies [*A publication*]
**J Amer Vet Med Ass** ... Journal. American Veterinary Medical Association [*A publication*]
**J Amer Water Works Ass** ... Journal. American Water Works Association [*A publication*]
**James**........ James' Reports [*2 Nova Scotia*] [*A publication*] (DLA)
**James Arthur Lect Evol Hum Brain** ... James Arthur Lecture on the Evolution of the Human Brain [*A publication*]
**James Bk L** ... James' Bankrupt Law PB (DLA)
**James Const Con** ... Jameson's Constitutional Convention [*A publication*] (DLA)
**James Ct Mar** ... James on Courts-Martial [*A publication*] (DLA)
**James Fr Soc** ... James' Guide to Friendly Societies [*A publication*] (DLA)
**James Joyce Q** ... James Joyce Quarterly [*A publication*]
**James Joy Q** ... James Joyce Quarterly [*A publication*]
**James JS** ... James' Law of Joint Stock Companies [*A publication*] (DLA)
**James Madison J** ... James Madison Journal [*A publication*]
**James & Mont** ... Jameson and Montagu's English Bankruptcy Reports [*Vol. 2 of Glyn and Jameson*] [*1821-28*] [*A publication*] (DLA)
**James (N Sc)** ... James' Reports [*2 Nova Scotia*] [*A publication*] (DLA)
**James Op**... James' Opinions, Charges, Etc. [*A publication*] (DLA)
**James Salv** ... James on Salvage [*1867*] [*A publication*] (DLA)
**James Sel Cas** ... James' Select Cases [*1835-55*] [*Nova Scotia*] [*A publication*] (DLA)
**James Sel Cases** ... James' Select Cases [*1835-55*] [*Nova Scotia*] [*A publication*] (DLA)
**James Sh** ... James' Merchant Shipping [*1866*] [*A publication*] (DLA)
**James Sprunt Hist Publ** ... James Sprunt Historical Publications [*A publication*]
**James Sprunt Hist Stud** ... James Sprunt Historical Studies [*A publication*]
**JAMEX**..... Jamming Exercise [*Military*] (NVT)
**J Am F-Lore** ... Journal of American Folklore [*A publication*]
**J Am Folk** ... Journal of American Folklore [*A publication*]
**J Am Folkl** ... Journal of American Folklore [*A publication*]
**J Am Folklo** ... Journal of American Folklore [*A publication*]
**J Am Folklore** ... Journal of American Folklore [*A publication*]
**JAMG**........ Jamming
**JAMGA**..... Jewellers and Metalsmiths Group of Australia
**Jam Geol Surv Dep Econ Geol Rep** ... Jamaica. Geological Survey Department. Economic Geology Report [*A publication*]
**J Am Geriatrics Soc** ... Journal. American Geriatrics Society [*A publication*]
**J Am Geriatr Soc** ... Journal. American Geriatrics Society [*A publication*]
**J Am Geriat Soc** ... Journal. American Geriatrics Society [*A publication*]
**J Am Ger So** ... Journal. American Geriatrics Society [*A publication*]
**J Am Health Care Assoc** ... Journal. American Health Care Association [*A publication*]
**J Am Helicopter Soc** ... Journal. American Helicopter Society [*A publication*]
**JAMHEP**.. Joint Aircraft Hurricane Plan
**J Am His**.... Journal of American History [*A publication*]
**J Am Hist**.. Journal of American History [*A publication*]
**Jam Hist Rev** ... Jamaican Historical Review [*A publication*]
**J Am Ind Hyg Assoc** ... Journal. American Industrial Hygiene Association [*A publication*]
**J Am Indian Ed** ... Journal of American Indian Education [*A publication*]
**J Am Ins**.... Journal of American Insurance [*A publication*]
**J Am Inst Electr Eng** ... Journal. American Institute of Electrical Engineers [*A publication*]
**J Am Inst Homeop** ... Journal. American Institute of Homeopathy [*A publication*]
**J Am Inst Homeopath** ... Journal. American Institute of Homeopathy [*A publication*]
**J Am Inst Homeopathy** ... Journal. American Institute of Homeopathy [*A publication*]
**J Am Inst P** ... Journal. American Institute of Planners [*A publication*]
**J Am Inst Plann** ... Journal. American Institute of Planners [*A publication*]
**J Am Insur** ... Journal of American Insurance [*A publication*]
**JAMINTEL** ... Jamaica International Telecommunications Ltd. [*Kingston*] [*Telecommunications service*] (TSSD)
**J Am Intraocul Implant Soc** ... Journal. American Intraocular Implant Society [*A publication*]
**Ja Mission B** ... Japan Missionary Bulletin [*A publication*]
**J Am Jud Soc** ... Journal. American Judicature Society [*A publication*]
**J Am Killifish Assoc** ... Journal. American Killifish Association [*A publication*]
**JamKLS**..... Jamaica Library Service, Kingston, Jamaica [*Library symbol*] [*Library of Congress*] (LCLS)
**JamKU** ...... University of the West Indies, Mona, Kingston, Jamaica [*Library symbol*] [*Library of Congress*] (LCLS)
**JAMLD**..... Journal of Applied Metalworking [*A publication*]
**J Am Leath** ... Journal. American Leather Chemists' Association [*A publication*]
**J Am Leath Chem Ass** ... Journal. American Leather Chemists' Association [*A publication*]
**J Am Leather Chem Assoc** ... Journal. American Leather Chemists' Association [*A publication*]
**J Am Leather Chem Assoc Suppl** ... Journal. American Leather Chemists' Association. Supplement [*A publication*]
**Jam LJ**....... Jamaica Law Journal [*A publication*] (DLA)
**JAMM**....... JAMM. Journal for Australian Music and Musicians [*A publication*] (APTA)
**JAMMAT** ... Joint American Military Mission for Aid to Turkey (MUGU)
**JAMMD**.... Journal. Australian Mathematical Society. Series B. Applied Mathematics [*A publication*]
**J Am Med A** ... Journal. American Medical Association [*A publication*]
**J Am Med Ass** ... Journal. American Medical Association [*A publication*]
**J Am Med Assoc** ... Journal. American Medical Association [*A publication*]
**J Am Med Rec Assoc** ... Journal. American Medical Record Association [*A publication*]
**Jam Med Rev** ... Jamaica Medical Review [*A publication*]

**J Am Med Technol** ... Journal. American Medical Technologists [*A publication*]
**J Am Med Wom Ass** ... Journal. American Medical Women's Association [*A publication*]
**J Am Med Wom Assoc** ... Journal. American Medical Women's Association [*A publication*]
**J Am Med Women Assoc** ... Journal. American Medical Women's Association [*A publication*]
**J Am Med Women's Assoc** ... Journal. American Medical Women's Association [*A publication*]
**Jam Mines Geol Div Spec Publ** ... Jamaica. Mines and Geology Division. Special Publication [*A publication*]
**Jam Minist Agric Bull** ... Jamaica. Ministry of Agriculture. Bulletin [*A publication*]
**Jam Minist Agric Fish Bull** ... Jamaica. Ministry of Agriculture and Fisheries. Bulletin [*A publication*]
**Jam Minist Agric Lands Annu Rep** ... Jamaica. Ministry of Agriculture and Lands. Annual Report [*A publication*]
**Jam Minist Agric Lands Bull** ... Jamaica. Ministry of Agriculture and Lands. Bulletin [*A publication*]
**J Am Mosq Control Assoc** ... Journal. American Mosquito Control Association [*A publication*]
**J Am Music** ... Journal. American Musicological Society [*A publication*]
**J Am Mus In** ... Journal. American Musical Instrument Society [*A publication*]
**J Am Oil Ch** ... Journal. American Oil Chemists' Society [*A publication*]
**J Am Oil Chem Soc** ... Journal. American Oil Chemists' Society [*A publication*]
**J Am Optom Assoc** ... Journal. American Optometric Association [*A publication*]
**J Am Orient** ... Journal. American Oriental Society [*A publication*]
**J Am Orient Soc** ... Journal. American Oriental Society [*A publication*]
**J Am Or Soc** ... Journal. American Oriental Society [*A publication*]
**J Am Osteopath A** ... Journal. American Osteopathic Association [*A publication*]
**J Am Osteopath Assoc** ... Journal. American Osteopathic Association [*A publication*]
**JAMOT**..... Julie/Jezebel [*Sonobuoy Systems*] Airborne Maintenance Operator Trainee [*Navy*] (MCD)
**JAMP**........ JINTACCS [*Joint Interoperability of Tactical Command and Control System*] Army Management Plan (MCD)
**JAMPA2**... Journal of Animal Morphology and Physiology [*A publication*]
**JAMPAC** .. Jamming Package [*Air Force*]
**JAMPACK** ... Jamming Package [*Air Force*] (MCD)
**J Am Paraplegia Soc** ... Journal. American Paraplegia Society [*A publication*]
**JAMPB3** ... Journal. American Peanut Research and Education Association [*A publication*]
**J Am Peanut Res Educ Assoc** ... Journal. American Peanut Research and Education Association [*A publication*]
**J Am Peat Soc** ... Journal. American Peat Society [*A publication*]
**J Am Phar** ... Journal. American Pharmaceutical Association. Practical Pharmacy Edition [*A publication*]
**J Am Pharm** ... Journal. American Pharmaceutical Association [*A publication*]
**J Am Pharm Ass** ... Journal. American Pharmaceutical Association [*A publication*]
**J Am Pharm Assoc** ... Journal. American Pharmaceutical Association [*A publication*]
**J Am Pharm Assoc Pract Pharm Ed** ... Journal. American Pharmaceutical Association. Practical Pharmacy Edition [*A publication*]
**J Am Pharm Assoc Sci Ed** ... Journal. American Pharmaceutical Association. Scientific Edition [*A publication*]
**J Am Plann Assoc** ... Journal. American Planning Association [*A publication*]
**JAMPO**..... Joint Allied Military Petroleum Office [*NATO*]
**J Am Podiatr Med Assoc** ... Journal. American Podiatric Medical Association [*A publication*]
**J Am Podiatry Assoc** ... Journal. American Podiatry Association [*A publication*]
**J Am Psycho** ... Journal. American Psychoanalytic Association [*A publication*]
**J Am Psychoanal Ass** ... Journal. American Psychoanalytic Association [*A publication*]
**J Am Psychonal Assoc** ... Journal. American Psychoanalytic Association [*A publication*]
**J Am Real Estate Urban Econ Assoc** ... Journal. American Real Estate and Urban Economics Association [*A publication*]
**JAMREP**... Jamming Report
**J Am Rocket Soc** ... Journal. American Rocket Society [*A publication*]
**JAMS**........ Joint Agency for Municipal Securities Dealers
**JAMS**........ Journal. Academy of Marketing Science [*A publication*]
**JAMS**........ Journal. American Musicological Society [*A publication*]
**JAmS**........ Journal of American Studies [*A publication*]
**JAMSA**...... Journal. Arkansas Medical Society [*A publication*]
**J Am S Hort** ... Journal. American Society for Horticultural Science [*A publication*]
**J Am S Infor** ... Journal. American Society for Information Science [*A publication*]
**J Am Soc Agron** ... Journal. American Society of Agronomy [*A publication*]
**J Am Soc Brew Chem** ... Journal. American Society of Brewing Chemists [*A publication*]
**J Am Soc CLU** ... Journal. American Society of Chartered Life Underwriters [*A publication*]
**J Am Soc Geriatr Dent** ... Journal. American Society for Geriatric Dentistry [*A publication*]
**J Am Soc Heat Vent Eng** ... Journal. American Society of Heating and Ventilating Engineers [*A publication*]
**J Am Soc Hortic Sci** ... Journal. American Society for Horticultural Science [*A publication*]
**J Am Soc Hort Sci** ... Journal. American Society for Horticultural Science [*A publication*]
**J Am Soc Inf Sci** ... Journal. American Society for Information Science [*A publication*]
**J Am Soc Mech Eng** ... Journal. American Society of Mechanical Engineers [*A publication*]
**J Am Soc Nav Eng** ... Journal. American Society of Naval Engineers [*A publication*]
**J Am Soc Prev Dent** ... Journal. American Society for Preventive Dentistry [*A publication*]
**J Am Soc Psychosom Dent** ... Journal. American Society of Psychosomatic Dentistry and Medicine [*A publication*]
**J Am Soc Psychosom Dent Med** ... Journal. American Society of Psychosomatic Dentistry and Medicine [*A publication*]
**J Am Soc Psych Res** ... Journal. American Society for Psychical Research [*A publication*]
**J Am Soc Saf Eng** ... Journal. American Society of Safety Engineers [*A publication*]
**J Am Soc Study Orthod** ... Journal. American Society for the Study of Orthodontics [*A publication*]
**J Am Soc Sugar Beet Technol** ... Journal. American Society of Sugar Beet Technologists [*A publication*]
**J Am Soc Sug Beet Technol** ... Journal. American Society of Sugar Beet Technologists [*A publication*]
**J Am S Psyc** ... Journal. American Society for Psychical Research [*A publication*]
**J Am St**...... Jahrbuch fuer Amerikastudien [*A publication*]
**Jam St**........ Jamaica Statutes [*A publication*] (DLA)
**J Am St**...... Journal of American Studies [*A publication*]
**J Am Stat A** ... Journal. American Statistical Association [*A publication*]
**J Am Stat Assoc** ... Journal. American Statistical Association [*A publication*]
**J Am Steel Treaters' Soc** ... Journal. American Steel Treaters' Society [*A publication*]
**J Am Stud** ... Journal of American Studies [*A publication*]
**J Am Studies** ... Journal of American Studies [*A publication*]
**JAMTD**..... Journal. Canadian Association for Music Therapy [*A publication*]
**JAMTO**..... Joint Airlines Military Traffic Office
**JAMTRAC** ... Jammers Tracked by Azimuth Crossings [*RADAR*]
**J Am Vener Dis Assoc** ... Journal. American Venereal Disease Association [*A publication*]
**J Am Vet Me** ... Journal. American Veterinary Medical Association [*A publication*]
**J Am Vet Med Ass** ... Journal. American Veterinary Medical Association [*A publication*]
**J Am Vet Med Assoc** ... Journal. American Veterinary Medical Association [*A publication*]
**J Am Vet Ra** ... Journal. American Veterinary Radiology Society [*A publication*]
**J Am Vet Radiol Soc** ... Journal. American Veterinary Radiology Society [*A publication*]
**JAMWA**.... Journal. American Medical Women's Association [*A publication*]
**JAMWAN** ... Journal. American Medical Women's Association [*A publication*]
**J Am Water** ... Journal. American Water Works Association [*A publication*]
**J Am Water Works Assoc** ... Journal. American Water Works Association [*A publication*]
**JAMY**........ JAM, Inc. [*Rochester, NY*] [*NASDAQ symbol*] (NQ)
**J Am Zinc Inst** ... Journal. American Zinc Institute [*A publication*]
**JAN** ........... Jackson [*Mississippi*] [*Airport symbol*] (OAG)
**JAN** ........... Jackson, MS [*Location identifier*] [*FAA*] (FAAL)
**JAN** ........... Janina [*Greece*] [*Seismograph station code, US Geological Survey*] (SEIS)
**JAN** ........... Jantar Resources Corp. [*Vancouver Stock Exchange symbol*]
**JAN** ........... January (EY)
**Jan** ............. Janus. Archives Internationales pour l'Histoire de la Medecine [*A publication*]
**JAN** ........... Japan. The Economic and Trade Picture [*London*] [*A publication*]
**JAN** ........... Jet Aircraft Noise
**JAN** ........... Jewish Affairs (New York) [*A publication*]
**JAN** ........... Job Accommodation Network [*President's Committee on Employment of the Handicapped*] [*Information service or system*] (IID)
**JAN** ........... Joint Army and Navy
**JAN** ........... Journal International d'Archeologie Numismatique [*A publication*]
**JAN** ........... Judgment Analysis [*Psychology*]
**JAN** ........... Justification for Authority to Negotiate [*Military*]
**JAN** ........... Lincoln Christian College, Lincoln, IL [*OCLC symbol*] (OCLC)
**JANA** ........ Jamahiriyah News Agency [*Libya*]
**JANAC**...... Joint Army-Navy Assessment Committee [*World War II*]

**JANAF**...... Joint Army-Navy-Air Force
**JANAFPAC** ... Joint Army-Navy-Air Force, Pacific General Message [*Serially numbered*] (CINC)
**JANAIR**.... Joint Army-Navy Aircraft Instrument Research
**J Anal Appl Pyrolysis** ... Journal of Analytical and Applied Pyrolysis [*A publication*]
**J Anal Chem** ... Journal of Analytical Chemistry of the USSR [*A publication*]
**J Anal Math** ... Journal d'Analyse Mathematique [*A publication*]
**JANALP** ... Joint Army-Navy-Air Force Logistics Policy
**JANALP** ... Joint Army-Navy-Air Force Logistics Publication
**J Anal Psych** ... Journal of Analytical Psychology [*A publication*]
**J Anal Psychol** ... Journal of Analytical Psychology [*A publication*]
**J Anal Toxicol** ... Journal of Analytical Toxicology [*A publication*]
**J Analyse Math** ... Journal d'Analyse Mathematique [*Jerusalem*] [*A publication*]
**Jan Angl** .... Jani Anglorum Facies Nova [*1680*] [*A publication*] (DLA)
**JANAP**...... Joint Army-Navy-Air Force Procedure [*NATO*] (NATG)
**JANAP**...... Joint Army-Navy-Air Force Publication
**JANAST** ... Joint Army-Navy-Air Force Sea Transportation Message
**J Anat** ........ Journal of Anatomy [*A publication*]
**J Anat Phys** ... Journal of Anatomy and Physiology [*A publication*]
**J Anat Physiol Norm Pathol Homme Anim** ... Journal de l'Anatomie et de la Physiologie Normales et Pathologiques de l'Homme et des Animaux [*A publication*]
**J Anat Soc Ind** ... Journal. Anatomical Society of India [*A publication*]
**J Anat Soc India** ... Journal. Anatomical Society of India [*A publication*]
**JANBMC**.. Joint Army-Navy Ballistic Missile Committee
**JANC**......... Junior Army and Navy Club [*British*] (DSUE)
**J Anc Ind Hist** ... Journal of Ancient Indian History [*A publication*]
**J Anc Near East Soc** ... Journal. Ancient Near East Society of Columbia University [*A publication*]
**J Anc Near East Soc Columbia Univ** ... Journal. Ancient Near Eastern Society. Columbia University [*A publication*]
**JANCOM** ... Joint Army-Navy Communications
**JANCWR** ... Joint Army and Navy Committee on Welfare and Recreation
**J Andhra Hist Res Soc** ... Journal. Andhra Historical Research Society [*A publication*]
**J Androl**..... Journal of Andrology [*A publication*]
**JANE**......... Joint Air Force-Navy Experiment (MUGU)
**JANES**...... Journal. Ancient Near Eastern Society [*A publication*]
**Janes Def W** ... Jane's Defence Weekly [*A publication*]
**J Anesth**..... Journal of Anesthesia [*A publication*]
**JANET**...... Joint Academic Network [*Proposed supercomputer network*]
**JANET**...... Joint Army-Navy Experimental and Testing Board
**JANET**...... Just Another Network [*University of Waterloo*] [*Canada*]
**JANFU**...... Joint Army-Navy Foul Up [*Military slang*] [*Bowdlerized version*]
**J Ang Chem** ... Journal fuer Angewandte Chemie [*A publication*]
**J Anglo-Mongol Soc** ... Journal. Anglo-Mongolian Society [*A publication*]
**JANGO**..... Junior Army-Navy Guild Organization [*Organization of teenage daughters of military officers, who helped out in war work*] [*World War II*]
**JANGRID** ... Joint Army-Navy Grid System [*NATO*]
**JANIC**....... Joint Army-Navy Information Center
**J Animal Ecol** ... Journal of Animal Ecology [*A publication*]
**J Animal Ecology** ... Journal of Animal Ecology [*A publication*]
**J Animal Sci** ... Journal of Animal Science [*A publication*]
**J Anim Breed Genet** ... Journal of Animal Breeding and Genetics [*A publication*]
**J Anim Ecol** ... Journal of Animal Ecology [*A publication*]
**J Anim Morphol Physiol** ... Journal of Animal Morphology and Physiology [*A publication*]
**J Anim Morph Physiol** ... Journal of Animal Morphology and Physiology [*A publication*]
**J Anim Physiol Anim Nutr** ... Journal of Animal Physiology and Animal Nutrition [*A publication*]
**J Anim Prod Res** ... Journal of Animal Production Research [*A publication*]
**J Anim Prod UAR** ... Journal of Animal Production of the United Arab Republic [*A publication*]
**J Anim Prod Un Arab Repub** ... Journal of Animal Production of the United Arab Republic [*A publication*]
**J Anim Sci** ... Journal of Animal Science [*A publication*]
**J Anim Tech Ass** ... Journal. Animal Technicians Association [*A publication*]
**J Anim Tech Assoc** ... Journal. Animal Technicians Association [*A publication*]
**JANIS**....... Joint Army-Navy Intelligence Studies
**JanL**........... Janua Linguarum [*A publication*]
**JANMA**..... Japanese Nuclear Medicine [*A publication*]
**JANMAT** ... Joint Army-Navy Machine Tools Committee (AAG)
**JANMAT** ... Joint Army-Navy Material
**JANMB**..... Joint Army and Navy Munitions Board [*Terminated, 1947*]
**JANNAF**... Joint-Army-Navy-NASA-Air Force Interagency Propulsion Committee (MCD)
**J Annamalai Univ** ... Journal. Annamalai University [*A publication*]
**J Annamalai Univ Part B** ... Journal. Annamalai University. Part B [*A publication*]
**JANOT**...... Joint Army-Navy Ocean Terminal
**JANP**......... Joint Army-Navy Procedure
**JANP**......... Joint Army-Navy Publication
**JANPA7**.... Journal of Analytical Psychology [*A publication*]
**Jan Pan Evk** ... Janus Pannonius Muzeum Evkoenyve [*A publication*]
**JANPPA** ... Joint Army-Navy Petroleum Purchase Agency
**JANS**......... Jet Aircraft Noise Survey
**JANSA**....... Journal of Animal Science [*A publication*]
**JANSAG**... Journal of Animal Science [*A publication*]
**JANSPEC** ... Joint Army-Navy Specification
**JANSRP**.... Jet Aircraft Noise Survey Research Program
**JANSTD** ... Joint Army-Navy Standard [*NATO*] (NATG)
**JANTAB** ... Joint Army and Navy Technical Aeronautical Board
**JANTAJ**.... Journal of Antibiotics [*Tokyo*] [*A publication*]
**J Anthr**....... Journal of Anthropology [*A publication*]
**JAnthrI**...... Journal. Royal Anthropological Institute of Great Britain and Ireland [*A publication*]
**J Anthropol Res** ... Journal of Anthropological Research [*A publication*]
**J Anthropol Soc Nippon** ... Journal. Anthropological Society of Nippon [*A publication*]
**J Anthropol Soc Oxford** ... Journal. Anthropological Society of Oxford [*A publication*]
**J Anthrop Res** ... Journal of Anthropological Research [*A publication*]
**J Anthrop Soc Bombay** ... Journal. Anthropological Society of Bombay [*A publication*]
**J Anthro Res** ... Journal of Anthropological Research [*A publication*]
**J Anthr Res** ... Journal of Anthropological Research [*A publication*]
**J Anthr S N** ... Journal. Anthropological Society of Nippon [*A publication*]
**J Antibiot**... Journal of Antibiotics [*Tokyo*] [*A publication*]
**J Antibiot Ser B (Japan)** ... Journal of Antibiotics. Series B (Japan) [*A publication*]
**J Antibiot (Tokyo)** ... Journal of Antibiotics (Tokyo) [*A publication*]
**J Antibiot (Tokyo) Ser A** ... Journal of Antibiotics (Tokyo). Series A [*A publication*]
**J Antimicrob Chemother** ... Journal of Antimicrobial Chemotherapy [*A publication*]
**J Ant Ire**..... Journal. Royal Society of Antiquaries of Ireland [*A publication*]
**J Antro Sos** ... Jernal Antropoloji dan Sosioloji [*A publication*]
**JANTX**...... Joint Army-Navy Tested Extra
**JANUS**...... Joint Analog Numeric Understanding System
**JANV**........ Janvier [*January*] [*French*]
**JANWSA**.. Joint Army-Navy War Shipping Administration
**JANY**......... January (ROG)
**JAO** ........... Prospect Heights Public Library District, Prospect Heights, IL [*OCLC symbol*] (OCLC)
**JAOA** ........ Journal. American Osteopathic Association [*A publication*]
**JAOAA**....... Journal. American Osteopathic Association [*A publication*]
**JAOAAZ**... Journal. American Osteopathic Association [*A publication*]
**J AOAC**..... Journal. Association of Official Analytical Chemists [*A publication*]
**JAOC**......... Joint Air Operations Center [*Air Force*]
**JAOCA**...... Journal. American Oil Chemists' Society [*A publication*]
**JAOCA7**.... Journal. American Oil Chemists' Society [*A publication*]
**JAOCS**....... Journal. American Oil Chemists' Society [*A publication*]
**JAOPB**...... Journal. American Optometric Association [*A publication*]
**JAOPBD**... Journal. American Optometric Association [*A publication*]
**JAOS**......... Journal. American Oriental Society [*A publication*]
**J Aoyama Gakuin Woman's Jr Coll** ... Journal. Aoyama Gakuin Woman's Junior College [*A publication*]
**JAp** ............ Against Apion [*Josephus*] (BJA)
**JAP**............ G. D. Searle & Co., Inc., Skokie, IL [*OCLC symbol*] (OCLC)
**JAP**............ Japan (KSC)
**JAP**............ Japanese (ROG)
**JAP**............ Jerusalem Academic Press (BJA)
**JAP**............ Jewish Agency for Palestine
**JAP**............ Jewish-American Princess [*Slang*]
**JAP**............ Joint Acceptance Plan (AAG)
**JAP**............ Joint Apprenticeship Program [*Department of Labor*]
**JAP**............ Journal of Abnormal Psychology [*A publication*]
**JAP**............ Journal of American Photography [*A publication*]
**JAP**............ Journal of Applied Physics [*A publication*]
**JAP**............ Journal of Applied Psychology [*A publication*]
**JAP**............ Judicial Appointments Project (EA)
**JAP**............ Juntas de Accao Patriotica [*Patriotic Action Boards*] [*Portuguese*] [*Political party*] (PPE)
**JAP**............ Jupiter Atmospheric Probe
**JAP**............ Juventudes de Accion Popular [*Spanish*] (PPE)
**JAPA**......... Jane Addams Peace Association (EA)
**JAPA**......... Japan Area
**JAPA**......... Journal. American Planning Association [*A publication*]
**Jap Acad Proc** ... Japan Academy. Proceedings [*A publication*]
**JAPAEA**.... Journal. American Podiatric Medical Association [*A publication*]
**Jap Agric Res Q** ... Japanese Agricultural Research Quarterly [*A publication*]
**Jap Agr Res Q** ... Japan Agricultural Research Quarterly [*A publication*]
**Japan Ann L & Pol** ... Japan Annual of Law and Politics [*A publication*] (DLA)
**Japan Annu Int Law** ... Japanese Annual of International Law [*A publication*]
**Japan Arch** ... Japan Architect [*A publication*]
**Japan Archt** ... Japan Architect [*A publication*]
**Japan A Soc Psychol** ... Japanese Annals of Social Psychology [*A publication*]
**Japan Chem** ... Japan Chemical Week [*A publication*]
**Japan Econ** ... White Paper of Japanese Economy [*English Edition*] [*A publication*]
**Japan Econ Stud** ... Japanese Economic Studies [*A publication*]

**Japanese An Internat Law** ... Japanese Annual of International Law [*A publication*]
**Japanese Econ Studies** ... Japanese Economic Studies [*A publication*]
**Japanese Fin and Industry** ... Japanese Finance and Industry [*A publication*]
**Japanese Jour Geology and Geography** ... Japanese Journal of Geology and Geography [*A publication*]
**Japanese MT** ... Japanese Military Technology. Procedures for Transfers to the United States [*A publication*]
**Japan Inter** ... Japan Interpreter [*A publication*]
**Japan J Geol & Geog** ... Japanese Journal of Geology and Geography [*A publication*]
**Japan J Math** ... Japanese Journal of Mathematics [*A publication*]
**Japan J Math NS** ... Japanese Journal of Mathematics. New Series [*A publication*]
**Japan J Med Sc Pt 4 Pharmacol** ... Japanese Journal of Medical Sciences. Part 4. Pharmacology [*A publication*]
**Japan J Nurs Art** ... Japanese Journal of Nursing Art [*A publication*]
**Japan Lbr Bul** ... Japan Labor Bulletin [*A publication*]
**JAPANMEC** ... Japan International Measuring and Control Industry Show (TSPED)
**Japan Med Gaz** ... Japan Medical Gazette [*A publication*]
**Japan Med World** ... Japan Medical World [*A publication*]
**Jap Ann of Law & Pol** ... Japan Annual of Law and Politics [*A publication*]
**Japan Pestic Inf** ... Japan Pesticide Information [*A publication*]
**Japan Q** ..... Japan Quarterly [*A publication*]
**Japan Quart** ... Japan Quarterly [*A publication*]
**Japan Soc B** ... Japan Society Bulletin [*A publication*]
**Japan Stat** ... Japan Statistical Yearbook [*A publication*]
**Japan Stud** ... Japanese Studies [*A publication*]
**Japan Stud Hist Sci** ... Japanese Studies in the History of Science [*A publication*]
**Jap Arch Int Med** ... Japanese Archives of Internal Medicine [*A publication*]
**JapARE** ..... Japanese Antarctic Research Expedition [*1956-*]
**Jap Assoc Mineral Petrol Econ Geol J** ... Japanese Association of Mineralogists, Petrologists, and Economic Geologists. Journal [*A publication*]
**Jap Assoc Pet Technol J** ... Japanese Association of Petroleum Technologists. Journal [*A publication*]
**JAPATIC** .. Japan Patient Information Center [*Information service or system*] (IID)
**Jap Bee J** ... Japanese Bee Journal [*A publication*]
**J Ap Behav Sci** ... Journal of Applied Behavioral Science [*A publication*]
**JAPC** ......... Joint Air Photo Center [*NATO*] (NATG)
**JAPCA** ...... Journal of Abnormal Psychology [*A publication*]
**JAPCA** ...... Journal. Air Pollution Control Association [*A publication*]
**JAPCAC**.... Journal of Abnormal Psychology [*A publication*]
**Jap Chem Week** ... Japan Chemical Week [*A publication*]
**Jap Chr Q** .. Japan Christian Quarterly [*A publication*]
**Jap Circ J** .. Japanese Circulation Journal [*A publication*]
**JAPCO** ...... Jamestown Paint & Varnish Company
**JAPCO** ...... Japan Atomic Power Company
**J APDSA (Tokyo)** ... Journal. Asian Pacific Dental Student Association (Tokyo) [*A publication*]
**JAPE** ......... Journal of Australian Political Economy [*A publication*] (APTA)
**JAPEAI**..... Journal of Applied Ecology [*A publication*]
**J Ap Ecol** ... Journal of Applied Ecology [*A publication*]
**Jap Econ St** ... Japanese Economic Studies [*A publication*]
**Jap Geol Surv Bull** ... Japan Geological Survey. Bulletin [*A publication*]
**Jap Geol Surv Rep** ... Japan Geological Survey. Report [*A publication*]
**Jap Geotherm Energy Assoc J** ... Japan Geothermal Energy Association. Journal [*A publication*]
**Jap Heart J** ... Japanese Heart Journal [*A publication*]
**JAPIA**........ Japan Auto Parts Industries Association
**JAPIC**........ Japan Pharmaceutical Information Center [*Tokyo*] [*Information service or system*] (IID)
**J Apic Res** ... Journal of Apicultural Research [*A publication*]
**J Apicult R** ... Journal of Apicultural Research [*A publication*]
**Jap Inst Nav J** ... Japan. Institute of Navigation. Journal [*A publication*]
**Jap Inter** .... Japan Interpreter [*A publication*]
**JAPIO** ....... Japan Patent Information Organization [*Database producer*]
**Jap J Allergy** ... Japanese Journal of Allergy [*A publication*]
**Jap J Anaesth** ... Japanese Journal of Anaesthesiology [*A publication*]
**Jap J A Phy** ... Japanese Journal of Applied Physics [*A publication*]
**Jap J Appl Entomol Zool** ... Japanese Journal of Applied Entomology and Zoology [*A publication*]
**Jap J Appl Ent Zool** ... Japanese Journal of Applied Entomology and Zoology [*A publication*]
**Jap J Appl Phys** ... Japanese Journal of Applied Physics [*A publication*]
**Jap J Appl Phys Suppl** ... Japanese Journal of Applied Physics. Supplement [*A publication*]
**Jap J Appl Zool** ... Japanese Journal of Applied Zoology [*A publication*]
**Jap J Astr** .. Japanese Journal of Astronomy [*A publication*]
**Jap J Astr Geophys** ... Japanese Journal of Astronomy and Geophysics [*A publication*]
**Jap J Bot**.... Japanese Journal of Botany [*A publication*]
**Jap J Botan** ... Japanese Journal of Botany [*A publication*]
**Jap J Breed** ... Japanese Journal of Breeding [*A publication*]
**Jap J Canc Res** ... Japanese Journal of Cancer Research [*A publication*]
**Jap J Child** ... Japanese Journal of Child Psychiatry [*A publication*]
**Jap J Clin Med** ... Japanese Journal of Clinical Medicine [*A publication*]
**Jap J Clin Path** ... Japanese Journal of Clinical Pathology [*A publication*]
**Jap J Ecol** .. Japanese Journal of Ecology [*A publication*]
**Jap J Edu P** ... Japanese Journal of Educational Psychology [*A publication*]
**Jap J Exp M** ... Japanese Journal of Experimental Medicine [*A publication*]
**Jap J Exp Med** ... Japanese Journal of Experimental Medicine [*A publication*]
**Jap J Gen**... Japanese Journal of Genetics [*A publication*]
**Jap J Genet** ... Japanese Journal of Genetics [*A publication*]
**Jap J Geol Geogr** ... Japanese Journal of Geology and Geography [*A publication*]
**Jap J Geophys** ... Japanese Journal of Geophysics [*A publication*]
**Jap J Hum G** ... Japanese Journal of Human Genetics [*A publication*]
**Jap J Hum Gen** ... Japanese Journal of Human Genetics [*A publication*]
**Jap J Limnol** ... Japanese Journal of Limnology [*A publication*]
**Jap J Med** ... Japanese Journal of Medicine [*A publication*]
**Jap J Med Electron & Biol Eng** ... Japanese Journal of Medical Electronics and Biological Engineering [*A publication*]
**Jap J Med S** ... Japanese Journal of Medical Science and Biology [*A publication*]
**Jap J Med Sci Biol** ... Japanese Journal of Medical Science and Biology [*A publication*]
**Jap J Micro** ... Japanese Journal of Microbiology [*A publication*]
**Jap J Microb** ... Japanese Journal of Microbiology [*A publication*]
**Jap J Midwife** ... Japanese Journal for the Midwife [*A publication*]
**Jap J Nurs** ... Japanese Journal of Nursing [*A publication*]
**Jap J Nurses Educ** ... Japan Journal of Nurses' Education [*A publication*]
**Jap J Nurs Res** ... Japanese Journal of Nursing Research [*A publication*]
**Jap J Nutr** ... Japanese Journal of Nutrition [*A publication*]
**Jap J Ophthal** ... Japanese Journal of Ophthalmology [*A publication*]
**Jap J Palynol** ... Japanese Journal of Palynology [*A publication*]
**Jap J Parasit** ... Japanese Journal of Parasitology [*A publication*]
**Jap J Pharm** ... Japanese Journal of Pharmacology [*A publication*]
**Jap J Pharmac** ... Japanese Journal of Pharmacology [*A publication*]
**Jap J Pharmacogn** ... Japanese Journal of Pharmacognosy [*A publication*]
**Jap J Phys** ... Japanese Journal of Physiology [*A publication*]
**Jap J Physi** ... Japanese Journal of Physiology [*A publication*]
**Jap J Physiol** ... Japanese Journal of Physiology [*A publication*]
**Jap J Psych** ... Japanese Journal of Psychology [*A publication*]
**Jap J Psychol** ... Japanese Journal of Psychology [*A publication*]
**Jap J Sanit Zool** ... Japanese Journal of Sanitary Zoology [*A publication*]
**Jap J Trop Agr** ... Japanese Journal of Tropical Agriculture [*A publication*]
**Jap J Vet R** ... Japanese Journal of Veterinary Research [*A publication*]
**Jap J Vet Res** ... Japanese Journal of Veterinary Research [*A publication*]
**Jap J Vet S** ... Japanese Journal of Veterinary Science [*A publication*]
**Jap J Vet Sci** ... Japanese Journal of Veterinary Science [*A publication*]
**Jap J Vet Sci Nigon Juigaku Zasshi** ... Japanese Journal of Veterinary Science/Nigon Juigaku Zasshi [*A publication*]
**Jap J Zool** ... Japanese Journal of Zoology [*A publication*]
**Jap J Zootech Sci** ... Japanese Journal of Zootechnical Science [*A publication*]
**JAPLA**....... Journal. Atlantic Provinces Linguistic Association/Revue. Association de Linguistique des Provinces Atlantiques [*A publication*]
**JAPLD** ...... Japanese Journal of Applied Physics. Part 2. Letters [*A publication*]
**JAPMA8**... Journal. American Pharmaceutical Association. Scientific Edition [*A publication*]
**Jap Meteorol Agency Volcanol Bull** ... Japan Meteorological Agency. Volcanological Bulletin [*A publication*]
**J Ap Meterol** ... Journal of Applied Meteorology [*A publication*]
**JAPN**......... Japan Air Lines Co. Ltd. [*NASDAQ symbol*] (NQ)
**Jap Nat Ry Ry Tech Res** ... Japanese National Railways. Railway Technical Research [*A publication*]
**JAPND**...... Japanese Journal of Applied Physics. Part 1. Regular Papers and Short Notes [*A publication*]
**JAPNEF**.... Journal of Animal Physiology and Animal Nutrition [*A publication*]
**J Ap Nutrition** ... Journal of Applied Nutrition [*A publication*]
**JAPO**......... Joint Area Petroleum Office
**JAPOA**...... Journal. American Psychoanalytic Association [*A publication*]
**JAPOAE** ... Journal. American Psychoanalytic Association [*A publication*]
**JAPOS** ...... JAPOS Study Group (EA)
**Jap P**.......... [*The*] Pharmacopoeia of Japan [*A publication*]
**J App Bact** ... Journal of Applied Bacteriology [*A publication*]
**J App Bacteriol** ... Journal of Applied Bacteriology [*A publication*]
**J App Behav Anal** ... Journal of Applied Behavior Analysis [*A publication*]
**J App Behavioral Sci** ... Journal of Applied Behavioral Science [*A publication*]
**J App Behavior Anal** ... Journal of Applied Behavior Analysis [*A publication*]
**J App Behav Sci** ... Journal of Applied Behavioral Science [*A publication*]
**J App Ecol** ... Journal of Applied Ecology [*A publication*]
**Jap Per Ind** ... Japanese Periodicals Index [*A publication*]
**Jap Pestic Inf** ... Japan Pesticide Information [*A publication*]
**Jap Plast Age** ... Japan Plastics Age [*A publication*]
**J Appl Bact** ... Journal of Applied Bacteriology [*A publication*]
**J Appl Bacteriol** ... Journal of Applied Bacteriology [*A publication*]
**J Appl Be A** ... Journal of Applied Behavior Analysis [*A publication*]
**J Appl Beh** ... Journal of Applied Behavioral Science [*A publication*]
**J Appl Behav Anal** ... Journal of Applied Behavior Analysis [*A publication*]
**J Appl Behav Sci** ... Journal of Applied Behavioral Science [*A publication*]
**J Appl Biochem** ... Journal of Applied Biochemistry [*A publication*]
**J Appl Biol** ... Journal of Applied Biology [*A publication*]
**J Appl Ch B** ... Journal of Applied Chemistry and Biotechnology [*A publication*]

**J Appl Chem** ... Journal of Applied Chemistry [*A publication*]
**J Appl Chem** ... Journal of Applied Chemistry of the USSR [*A publication*]
**J Appl Chem Abstr** ... Journal of Applied Chemistry. Abstracts [*A publication*]
**J Appl Chem and Biotechnol** ... Journal of Applied Chemistry and Biotechnology [*A publication*]
**J Appl Chem Biotechnol** ... Journal of Applied Chemistry and Biotechnology [*A publication*]
**J Appl Chem Biotechnol Abstr** ... Journal of Applied Chemistry and Biotechnology. Abstracts [*A publication*]
**J Appl Chem (London)** ... Journal of Applied Chemistry (London) [*A publication*]
**J Appl Chem USSR** ... Journal of Applied Chemistry of the USSR [*A publication*]
**J Appl Cosmetol** ... Journal of Applied Cosmetology [*A publication*]
**J Appl Crys** ... Journal of Applied Crystallography [*A publication*]
**J Appl Crystallogr** ... Journal of Applied Crystallography [*A publication*]
**J Appld Chem USSR** ... Journal of Applied Chemistry of the USSR [*A publication*]
**J Appl Dev Psychol** ... Journal of Applied Developmental Psychology [*A publication*]
**J Appld Math Mech** ... Journal of Applied Mathematics and Mechanics [*A publication*]
**J Appld Mech Tech Physics** ... Journal of Applied Mechanics and Technical Physics [*A publication*]
**J Appld Polymer Science** ... Journal of Applied Polymer Science [*A publication*]
**J Appl Ecol** ... Journal of Applied Ecology [*A publication*]
**J Appl Educ Stud** ... Journal of Applied Educational Studies [*A publication*]
**J Appl Elec** ... Journal of Applied Electrochemistry [*A publication*]
**J Appl Electrochem** ... Journal of Applied Electrochemistry [*A publication*]
**J Appl Entomol** ... Journal of Applied Entomology [*A publication*]
**J Appl Gerontol** ... Journal of Applied Gerontology [*A publication*]
**J Appl Ichthyol** ... Journal of Applied Ichthyology [*A publication*]
**J Applied Ecology** ... Journal of Applied Ecology [*A publication*]
**J Applied Ednl Studies** ... Journal of Applied Educational Studies [*A publication*]
**J Applied Micr (Rochester NY)** ... Journal of Applied Microscopy (Rochester, New York) [*A publication*]
**J Applied Physics** ... Journal of Applied Physics [*A publication*]
**J Appl Manage** ... Journal of Applied Management [*A publication*]
**J Appl Math Mech** ... Journal of Applied Mathematics and Mechanics [*A publication*]
**J Appl Mech** ... Journal of Applied Mechanics. Transactions. ASME [*American Society of Mechanical Engineers*] [*A publication*]
**J Appl Mech Tech Phys** ... Journal of Applied Mechanics and Technical Physics [*A publication*]
**J Appl Mech and Tech Phys** ... Journal of Applied Mechanics and Technical Physics [*A publication*]
**J Appl Mech Trans ASME** ... Journal of Applied Mechanics. Transactions. ASME [*American Society of Mechanical Engineers*] [*A publication*]
**J Appl Med** ... Journal of Applied Medicine [*A publication*]
**J Appl Met** ... Journal of Applied Meteorology [*A publication*]
**J Appl Metalwork** ... Journal of Applied Metalworking [*A publication*]
**J Appl Meteorol** ... Journal of Applied Meteorology [*A publication*]
**J Appl Nutr** ... Journal of Applied Nutrition [*A publication*]
**J Appl Photogr Eng** ... Journal of Applied Photographic Engineering [*A publication*]
**J Appl Phys** ... Journal of Applied Physics [*A publication*]
**J Appl Physiol** ... Journal of Applied Physiology [*Later, Journal of Applied Physiology: Respiratory, Environmental, and Exercise Physiology*] [*A publication*]
**J Appl Physiol Respir Environ Exercise Physiol** ... Journal of Applied Physiology: Respiratory, Environmental, and Exercise Physiology [*A publication*]
**J Appl Physiol Respir Environ Exerc Physiol** ... Journal of Applied Physiology: Respiratory, Environmental, and Exercise Physiology [*A publication*]
**J Appl Pneum** ... Journal of Applied Pneumatics [*A publication*]
**J Appl Poly** ... Journal of Applied Polymer Science [*A publication*]
**J Appl Polym Sci** ... Journal of Applied Polymer Science [*A publication*]
**J Appl Polym Sci Appl Polym Symp** ... Journal of Applied Polymer Science. Applied Polymer Symposium [*A publication*]
**J Appl Probab** ... Journal of Applied Probability [*A publication*]
**J Appl Probability** ... Journal of Applied Probability [*A publication*]
**J Appl Psyc** ... Journal of Applied Psychology [*A publication*]
**J Appl Psychol** ... Journal of Applied Psychology [*A publication*]
**J Appl Sci** .. Journal of Applied Sciences [*A publication*]
**J Appl Sci Eng A** ... Journal of Applied Science and Engineering. Section A. Electrical Power and Information Systems [*A publication*]
**J Appl So P** ... Journal of Applied Social Psychology [*A publication*]
**J Appl Spectrosc** ... Journal of Applied Spectroscopy [*A publication*]
**J Appl Spectrosc (USSR)** ... Journal of Applied Spectroscopy (USSR) [*A publication*]
**J Appl Syst Anal** ... Journal of Applied Systems Analysis [*A publication*]
**J Appl Systems Analysis** ... Journal of Applied Systems Analysis [*A publication*]
**J Appl Toxicol** ... Journal of Applied Toxicology [*A publication*]
**J App Mech** ... Journal of Applied Mechanics [*A publication*]
**J App Meteor** ... Journal of Applied Meteorology [*A publication*]
**J App Nutr** ... Journal of Applied Nutrition [*A publication*]
**Jap Poultry Sci** ... Japanese Poultry Science [*A publication*]
**Jap Poult Sci** ... Japanese Poultry Science [*A publication*]
**J App Physiol** ... Journal of Applied Physiology [*Later, Journal of Applied Physiology: Respiratory, Environmental, and Exercise Physiology*] [*A publication*]
**J App Prob** ... Journal of Applied Probability [*A publication*]
**J App Psy** .. Journal of Applied Psychology [*A publication*]
**J App Psychol** ... Journal of Applied Psychology [*A publication*]
**Jap Prog Climatol** ... Japanese Progress in Climatology [*A publication*]
**J Approximation Theory** ... Journal of Approximation Theory [*A publication*]
**J Approx Th** ... Journal of Approximation Theory [*A publication*]
**J Approx Theory** ... Journal of Approximation Theory [*A publication*]
**J App Soc Psychol** ... Journal of Applied Social Psychology [*A publication*]
**J Ap Psychol** ... Journal of Applied Psychology [*A publication*]
**Jap Psy Res** ... Japanese Psychological Research [*A publication*]
**Jap Public Works Res Inst Rep (Minist Constr)** ... Japan Public Works Research Institute. Report. Ministry of Construction [*A publication*]
**Jap Pulp Pap** ... Japan Pulp and Paper [*A publication*]
**Jap Q** ......... Japan Quarterly [*A publication*]
**Jap Quart**... Japan Quarterly [*A publication*]
**Jap R**.......... Japanese Religions [*A publication*]
**JAPRCP**.... Journal of Anthropological Research [*A publication*]
**JAPRDQ**... Journal of Animal Production Research [*A publication*]
**Jap Rel**....... Japanese Religions [*A publication*]
**JAPS**.......... Japanese American Philatelic Society [*Later, JASP*]
**JAPS**.......... Joint Administrative Planning Section [*Joint Planning Staff*] [*World War II*]
**JAPS**.......... Journal. American Portuguese Society [*A publication*]
**JAPs** .......... Journal of Applied Psychology [*A publication*]
**JAPSA**....... Journal of Applied Psychology [*A publication*]
**Jap Semicond Tech N** ... Japanese Semiconductor Technology News [*A publication*]
**Jap Shipbldg Mar Eng** ... Japan Shipbuilding and Marine Engineering [*A publication*]
**Jap Shipbuild & Mar Engng** ... Japan Shipbuilding and Marine Engineering [*A publication*]
**J Ap Sociol** ... Journal of Applied Sociology [*A publication*]
**Jap Soc Promot Sci Sub-Comm Phys Chem Steelmaking Spec Rep** ... Japan Society for the Promotion of Science. Sub-Committee for Physical Chemistry of Steelmaking. Special Report [*A publication*]
**JAPSS** ....... Joint Automated Planning Support System [*of JOPS*] [*Military*]
**JAPT** ......... Journal of Approximation Theory [*A publication*]
**JAPTB**....... Journal. American Physical Therapy Association [*A publication*]
**Jap Telecom** ... Japan Telecommunications Review [*A publication*]
**Jap Weld Soc Trans** ... Japan Welding Society. Transactions [*A publication*]
**JAPYA** ...... Journal of Applied Physiology [*Later, Journal of Applied Physiology: Respiratory, Environmental, and Exercise Physiology*] [*A publication*]
**JAQ** .......... Jacquinot Bay [*Papua New Guinea*] [*Airport symbol*] (OAG)
**Ja Q** .......... Japan Quarterly [*A publication*]
**JAQ** .......... Job Activities Questionnaire
**JAQ** .......... Journal of Buyouts and Acquisitions [*A publication*]
**JAQ** .......... Passionist Academic Institute, Chicago, IL [*OCLC symbol*] (OCLC)
**J Aquaric** ... Journal of Aquariculture [*A publication*]
**J Aquaric & Aquat Sci** ... Journal of Aquariculture and Aquatic Sciences [*A publication*]
**JA Quart J Automat Control** ... Journal. A Quarterly Journal of Automatic Control [*A publication*]
**J Aquatic Pl Management** ... Journal of Aquatic Plant Management [*A publication*]
**J Aquat Pl** ... Journal of Aquatic Plant Management [*A publication*]
**J Aquat Plant Manage** ... Journal of Aquatic Plant Management [*A publication*]
**JAR**........... J. Arthur Rank [*Motion picture company in England*]
**JAR**........... Jamming Avoidance Response
**JAr**............ Jewish Aramaic (BJA)
**JAR**........... Jews for Animal Rights (EA)
**JAR**........... Joint Airworthiness Requirements (MCD)
**JAR**........... Journal of Accounting Research [*A publication*]
**JAR**........... Journal of Advertising Research [*Advertising Research Foundation*] [*A publication*]
**JAR**........... Journal of Anthropological Research [*A publication*]
**JAR**........... Juedischer Altestenrat [*A publication*]
**JAR**........... Jump Address Register
**JAR**........... Zion-Benton Library District, Zion, IL [*OCLC symbol*] (OCLC)
**J Arab Affairs** ... Journal of Arab Affairs [*A publication*]
**JArabL** ...... Journal of Arabic Literature [*A publication*]
**J Arab Lit** .. Journal of Arabic Literature [*A publication*]
**J Arab Vet Med Assoc** ... Journal. Arab Veterinary Medical Association [*A publication*]
**J Arachnol** ... Journal of Arachnology [*A publication*]
**J Arboric**.... Journal of Arboriculture [*A publication*]
**Jar & By Conv** ... Jarman and Bythewood's Conveyancing [*A publication*] (DLA)

**JARC**......... Jewish Association for Retarded Citizens (EA)
**JARC**......... Joint Air Reconnaissance Center [*NATO*] (NATG)
**JARCA**...... Journal of Aesthetics and Art Criticism [*A publication*]
**JARCC**...... Joint Air Reconnaissance Coordination Center [*Military*] (MCD)
**JARCE**...... Journal. American Research Center in Egypt [*A publication*]
**J Archaeol Chem** ... Journal of Archaeological Chemistry [*A publication*]
**J Archaeol Sci** ... Journal of Archaeological Science [*A publication*]
**J Arch Sci**.. Journal of Archaeological Science [*A publication*]
**Jar Chy Pr** ... Jarman's Chancery Practice [*A publication*] (DLA)
**Jar Cr Tr**.... Jardine's Criminal Trials [*A publication*] (DLA)
**Jard Ind**..... Jardine's Index to Howell's State Trials [*A publication*] (DLA)
**JARE**......... Japanese Antarctic Research Expedition [*1956-*]
**JAREB**...... Japanese Railway Engineering [*A publication*]
**JARED**...... JASCO [*Japan Spectroscopic Company*] Report [*A publication*]
**JARE (Jpn Antarct Res Exped) Data Rep** ... JARE (Japanese Antarctic Research Expedition) Data Reports [*A publication*]
**Ja Rel**......... Japanese Religions [*A publication*]
**JARE Sci Rep Ser E Biol** ... JARE [*Japanese Antarctic Research Expedition*] Scientific Reports. Series E. Biology [*A publication*]
**JARF**......... Journal. Addiction Research Foundation [*A publication*]
**JARG**......... Justice Administration Research Group [*Australia*]
**JARGV**...... Jahrbuch. Arbeitsgemeinschaft der Rheinischen Geschichtsvereine [*A publication*]
**JARI**.......... Journal of Agricultural Research in Iceland [*Islenzkar Landbunadar Rannsoknir*] [*A publication*]
**JARIC**....... Joint Aerial Reconnaissance Interpretation Center (MCD)
**JARIC**....... Joint Air Reconnaissance Intelligence Centre [*British*]
**J Arid Environ** ... Journal of Arid Environments [*A publication*]
**J Ariz Acad Sci** ... Journal. Arizona Academy of Science [*A publication*]
**JArizH**....... Journal of Arizona History [*A publication*]
**J Ariz Hist** ... Journal of Arizona History [*A publication*]
**J Ariz Nev Acad Sci** ... Journal. Arizona-Nevada Academy of Science [*A publication*]
**J Arkansas Med Soc** ... Journal. Arkansas Medical Society [*A publication*]
**J Arms Armour Soc** ... Journal. Arms and Armour Society [*A publication*]
**Jarmuevek Mezoegazd Gepek** ... Jarmuevek, Mezoegazdasagi Gepek [*Hungary*] [*A publication*]
**J Arn Arbor** ... Journal. Arnold Arboretum [*A publication*]
**J Arnold Arbor** ... Journal. Arnold Arboretum. Harvard University [*A publication*]
**J Arnold Arbor Harv Univ** ... Journal. Arnold Arboretum. Harvard University [*A publication*]
**J Arnold Schoenberg Inst** ... Journal. Arnold Schoenberg Institute [*A publication*]
**Jaroslav Gos Ped Inst Dokl Naucn Konfer** ... Jaroslavskii Gosudarstvennyi Pedagogiceskii Institut Doklady na Naucnyh Konferencijah [*A publication*]
**Jaroslav Gos Ped Inst Ucen Zap** ... Jaroslavskii Gosudarstvennyi Pedagogiceskii Institut Imeni K. D. Usinskogo Ucenye Zapiski [*A publication*]
**Jaroslav Tehn Inst Fiz-Mat Nauk Sb Naucn Trudov** ... Jaroslavskii Tehnologiceskii Institut Fiziko-Matematiceskie Nauki Sbornik Naucnyh Trudov [*A publication*]
**Jar Pow Dev** ... Jarman's Edition of Powell on Devises [*A publication*] (DLA)
**JARQ Jap Agric Res Q** ... JARQ. Japan Agricultural Research Quarterly [*A publication*]
**JARQ Jpn Agric Res Q** ... JARQ. Japan Agricultural Research Quarterly [*A publication*]
**JARR**......... Journal of Architectural Research [*A publication*]
**JARRP**...... Japan Association for Radiation Research on Polymers
**JARS**......... Journal. Assam Research Society [*A publication*]
**J Art Mgmt L** ... Journal of Arts Management and Law [*A publication*]
**JARTRAN** ... James A. Ryder Transportation [*Acronym is trade name of truck-rental firm*]
**J Arts Mgt and L** ... Journal of Arts Management and Law [*A publication*]
**Jar Wills**.... Jarman on Wills [*8 eds.*] [*1841-51*] [*A publication*] (DLA)
**JAS**........... Jahrbuch fuer Amerikastudien [*A publication*]
**Jas**............ James [*New Testament book*]
**JAS**........... Jamestown [*California*] [*Seismograph station code, US Geological Survey*] (SEIS)
**JAS**........... Jane Austen Society [*Basingstoke, Hampshire, England*] (EAIO)
**JAS**........... Jasper, TX [*Location identifier*] [*FAA*] (FAAL)
**JAS**........... Jazz Arts Society (EA)
**JAS**........... Jenkins Activity Survey [*Personality development test*] [*Psychology*]
**JAS**........... [*National Fashion*] Jewelry and Accessories Showplace (ITD)
**JAS**........... Jewish Agricultural Society (EA)
**JAS**........... Job Accounting System
**JAS**........... Job Activity Survey
**JAS**........... Job Analysis Schedule [*Department of Labor*]
**JAS**........... Job Analysis System [*Computer program*]
**JAS**........... Job Attitude Scale [*Employment test*]
**JAS**........... Johnny Alfalfa Sprout (EA)
**JAS**........... Joint Administration Services
**JAS**........... Joint Association Survey [*American Petroleum Institute, Independent Petroleum Association of America, and Mid-Continent Oil and Gas Association*]
**JAS**........... Journal Access Service [*Center for Research Libraries*]
**JAS**........... Journal. Acoustical Society of America [*A publication*]
**JAS**........... Journal of Aerospace Science [*A publication*]
**JAS**........... Journal. American Society for Information Science [*A publication*]
**JAS**........... Journal of American Studies [*A publication*]
**JAS**........... Journal of Archaeological Science [*A publication*]
**JAS**........... Journal of Asian Studies [*A publication*]
**JAS**........... Journal. Asiatic Society of Great Britain and Ireland [*A publication*]
**JAs**............ Journal Asiatique [*Paris*] [*A publication*]
**JAS**........... Journal des Associations Patronales [*A publication*]
**JAS**........... Journal of Australian Studies [*A publication*] (APTA)
**JAS**........... Journal of Austronesian Studies [*A publication*]
**JAS**........... Journals Access Service [*Center for Research Libraries*]
**J As**.......... Judicial Assessor [*Ghana*] [*A publication*] (DLA)
**JAS**........... Junior Astronomical Society (EAIO)
**JAS**........... Lake Villa District Library, Lake Villa, IL [*OCLC symbol*] (OCLC)
**JAS-1**........ Japan Amateur Satellite-1
**JASA**......... Jewish Association for Services for the Aged (EA)
**JASA**......... Joint Antisubmarine Action
**JASA**......... Journal. Acoustical Society of America [*A publication*]
**JASA**......... Journal. American Scientific Affiliation [*A publication*]
**JASA**......... Journal. American Statistical Association [*A publication*]
**JASA**......... Junior Assistant Stores Accountant [*British military*] (DMA)
**J As Aff**...... Journal of Asian Affairs [*A publication*]
**J As Afr Stud (T)** ... Journal of Asian and African Studies (Tokyo) [*A publication*]
**J Asahikawa Tech Coll** ... Journal. Asahikawa Technical College [*A publication*]
**J Asahikawa Tech College** ... Journal. Asahikawa Technical College [*A publication*]
**JASAP**....... Julie [*Sonobuoy System*] Automatic Search and Attack Plotter [*Navy*] (MCD)
**JASAR**...... Jittered and Swept Active RADAR
**JASASA**.... Joint Air-Surface Antisubmarine Action
**JASAT**....... Journal. American Studies Association of Texas [*A publication*]
**JASB**......... Joint Advisory Survey Board [*British*]
**JASB**......... Journal. Asiatic Society of Bengal [*A publication*]
**JAS B**........ Journal. Asiatic Society of Bombay [*A publication*]
**JASBA**....... Journal. American Society of Sugar Beet Technologists [*A publication*]
**JASBAO** ... Journal. American Society of Sugar Beet Technologists [*A publication*]
**JASC**......... Japan-America Student Conference (EA)
**JASC**......... Japan Asia Sea Cable
**JASC**......... Journal. Asiatic Society of Calcutta [*A publication*]
**JASC**......... JPL [*Jet Propulsion Laboratory*] Astronautical Star Catalog (KSC)
**JAS Calcutta** ... Journal. Asiatic Society of Calcutta [*A publication*]
**JASCEV**.... Journal of Agronomy and Crop Science [*A publication*]
**J A Schoenb** ... Journal. Arnold Schoenberg Institute [*A publication*]
**J A Scien**.... Journal of Archaeological Science [*A publication*]
**JASCO**...... Joint Assault Signal Company [*Small unit in Pacific amphibious warfare*] [*World War II*]
**JASCO Appl Notes** ... Japan Spectroscopic Company. Application Notes [*A publication*]
**JASCO Rep** ... JASCO [*Japan Spectroscopic Company*] Report [*A publication*]
**J As Cult**.... Journal of Asian Culture [*A publication*]
**JASDA**...... Julie [*Sonobuoy System*] Automatic Sonic Data Analyzer [*Navy*]
**JASDF**....... Japanese Air Self-Defense Force
**JASFE6**..... Journal of Agricultural Science in Finland [*A publication*]
**JASG**......... Joint Advanced Study Group
**JASGP**....... Joint Advanced Study Group
**J As Hist**.... Journal of Asian History [*A publication*]
**JASIAB**..... Journal of Agricultural Science [*A publication*]
**J Asian Afr** ... Journal of Asian and African Studies [*A publication*]
**J Asian & Afric Stud** ... Journal of Asian and African Studies [*A publication*]
**J Asian Afr Stud** ... Journal of Asian and African Studies [*A publication*]
**J Asian His** ... Journal of Asian History [*A publication*]
**J Asian Hist** ... Journal of Asian History [*A publication*]
**J Asian St**.. Journal of Asian Studies [*A publication*]
**J Asian Stud** ... Journal of Asian Studies [*A publication*]
**J Asia Stud** ... Journal of Asian Studies [*A publication*]
**J Asiat**........ Journal Asiatique [*A publication*]
**J Asiat Soc** ... Journal. Asiatic Society [*A publication*]
**J Asiat Soc Bangla** ... Journal. Asiatic Society of Bangladesh [*A publication*]
**J Asiat Soc Bangladesh Sci** ... Journal. Asiatic Society of Bangladesh. Science [*A publication*]
**J Asiat Soc Bengal Lett** ... Journal. Asiatic Society of Bengal. Letters [*A publication*]
**J Asiat Soc Bengal Sci** ... Journal. Asiatic Society of Bengal. Science [*A publication*]
**J Asiat Soc Bombay** ... Journal. Asiatic Society of Bombay [*A publication*]
**J Asiat Soc Sci** ... Journal. Asiatic Society. Science [*A publication*]
**J Asiat Stud** ... Journal of Asiatic Studies [*A publication*]
**JASIN**....... Joint Air Sea Interaction [*National Science Foundation/United Kingdom*]
**JASIS**........ Journal. American Society for Information Science [*A publication*]

**JASL**......... Journal. Asiatic Society. Letters [*A publication*]
**JASLS**....... Japanese American Society for Legal Studies (EA)
**JASMA**..... Journal. Acoustical Society of America [*A publication*]
**JASMAN**.. Journal. Acoustical Society of America [*A publication*]
**JASMU**..... Journal pour l'Avancement des Soins Medicaux d'Urgence [*A publication*]
**JASN**......... Jason, Inc. [*NASDAQ symbol*] (NQ)
**JASNA**...... Jane Austen Society of North America (EA)
**Ja Socialist R** ... Japan Socialist Review [*A publication*]
**Ja Soc Lond B** ... Japan Society of London. Bulletin [*A publication*]
**JASP**.......... Japanese American Society for Philately (EA)
**JASP**.......... Journal of Abnormal and Social Psychology [*A publication*]
**JASP**.......... Journal of Applied Social Psychology [*A publication*]
**JASP**.......... Journal. Asiatic Society of Pakistan [*A publication*]
**JASPA**....... Jesuit Association of Student Personnel Administrators (EA)
**J As Pac World** ... Journal of Asian-Pacific and World Perspectives [*A publication*]
**JASPAW**... Journal of Abnormal and Social Psychology [*A publication*]
**JASPR**....... Jasper [*Gem*] (ROG)
**JASPR**....... Journal. American Society for Psychical Research [*A publication*]
**JASR**......... Jane Austen Society. Report [*A publication*]
**JASR**......... JTPA [*Job Training and Partnership Act*] Annual Status Report (OICC)
**JASRE8**..... Journal of Agricultural and Scientific Research [*A publication*]
**JASS**.......... Joint Anti-Submarine School [*British military*] (DMA)
**JASS**.......... Joint Antisatellite Study
**JASS**.......... JUMPS Automated Support [*or Supplemental*] System [*Military*]
**JASSA**....... JASSA. Journal of the Australian Society of Security Analysts [*A publication*] (APTA)
**JASS-AC**... JUMPS Automated Supplemental System-Active Component [*Military*]
**J Ass Advan Med Instrum** ... Journal. Association for the Advancement of Medical Instrumentation [*A publication*]
**J Assam Res Soc** ... Journal. Assam Research Society [*A publication*]
**J Assam Sci Soc** ... Journal. Assam Science Society [*A publication*]
**JASSC**....... Japan-America Society of Southern California
**J Ass Comput Mach** ... Journal. Association for Computing Machinery [*A publication*]
**JASSM**...... Joint Acoustic Surveillance System Model [*Military*] (CAAL)
**J Ass'n L Teachers** ... Journal. Association of Law Teachers [*A publication*] (DLA)
**J Assoc Adv Med Instrum** ... Journal. Association for the Advancement of Medical Instrumentation [*A publication*]
**J Assoc Am Med Coll** ... Journal. Association of American Medical Colleges [*A publication*]
**J Assoc Can Radiol** ... Journal. Association Canadienne des Radiologistes [*A publication*]
**J Assoc Care Child Health** ... Journal. Association for the Care of Children's Health [*A publication*]
**J Assoc Care Child Hosp** ... Journal. Association for the Care of Children in Hospitals [*A publication*]
**J Assoc Comput Mach** ... Journal. Association for Computing Machinery [*A publication*]
**J Assoc Eng Archit Isr** ... Journal. Association of Engineers and Architects in Israel [*A publication*]
**J Assoc Eng Archit Palest** ... Journal. Association of Engineers and Architects in Palestine [*A publication*]
**J Assoc Eng (Calcutta)** ... Journal. Association of Engineers (Calcutta) [*A publication*]
**J Assoc Eng (India)** ... Journal. Association of Engineers (India) [*A publication*]
**J Assoc Eng Soc** ... Journal. Association of Engineering Societies [*A publication*]
**J Assoc Hosp Med Educ** ... Journal. Association for Hospital Medical Education [*A publication*]
**J Assoc L Teachers** ... Journal. Association of Law Teachers [*A publication*] (DLA)
**J Assoc Lunar and Planet Obs Strolling Astron** ... Journal. Association of Lunar and Planetary Observers. Strolling Astronomer [*A publication*]
**J Assoc Med Can** ... Journal. Association Medicale Canadienne [*A publication*]
**J Assoc Med Illus** ... Journal. Association of Medical Illustrators [*A publication*]
**J Assoc Off Agric Chem** ... Journal. Association of Official Agricultural Chemists [*A publication*]
**J Assoc Off Anal Chem** ... Journal. Association of Official Analytical Chemists [*A publication*]
**J Assoc Offic Anal Chem** ... Journal. Association of Official Analytical Chemists [*A publication*]
**J Assoc Pediatr Oncol Nurses** ... Journal. Association of Pediatric Oncology Nurses [*A publication*]
**J Assoc Pers Comput Chem** ... Journal. Association of Personal Computers for Chemists [*A publication*]
**J Assoc Physicians India** ... Journal. Association of Physicians of India [*A publication*]
**J Assoc Phys Ment Rehabil** ... Journal. Association for Physical and Mental Rehabilitation [*United States*] [*A publication*]
**J Assoc Public Anal** ... Journal. Association of Public Analysts [*A publication*]
**J Assoc Sci Ouest Afr** ... Journal. Association Scientifique de l'Ouest Africain [*A publication*]
**J Assoc Study Percept** ... Journal. Association for the Study of Perception [*A publication*]
**J Ass Off Agric Chem** ... Journal. Association of Official Agricultural Chemists [*A publication*]
**J Ass Off Analyt Chem** ... Journal. Association of Official Analytical Chemists [*A publication*]
**J Ass Offic Anal Chem** ... Journal. Association of Official Analytical Chemists [*A publication*]
**J Asso Teach Ja** ... Journal. Association of Teachers of Japanese [*A publication*]
**J Ass Public Analysts** ... Journal. Association of Public Analysts [*A publication*]
**JASS-RC**... JUMPS Automated Support System - Reserve Corps [*Military*]
**J As Stud P** ... Journal. Association for the Study of Perception [*A publication*]
**JAST**......... Joint Air Support Tactics [*Military*]
**JASt**.......... Journal of Asian Studies [*A publication*]
**JASTAA**.... Journal. Agricultural Society of Trinidad and Tobago [*A publication*]
**JASTD**...... Junior Assistant Steward [*British military*] (DMA)
**J Asthma** ... Journal of Asthma [*A publication*]
**J Asthma Res** ... Journal of Asthma Research [*Later, Journal of Asthma*] [*A publication*]
**JASTOP**.... Jet Assist Stop
**J Astronaut** ... Journal of the Astronautical Sciences [*A publication*]
**J Astronaut Sci** ... Journal of the Astronautical Sciences [*A publication*]
**J Astronomical Soc VIC** ... Journal. Astronomical Society of Victoria [*A publication*] (APTA)
**J Astron (Peiping)** ... Journal of Astronomy (Peiping) [*A publication*]
**J Astrophys Astron** ... Journal of Astrophysics and Astronomy [*A publication*]
**J Astrophys and Astron** ... Journal of Astrophysics and Astronomy [*A publication*]
**JAStud**....... Journal of American Studies [*A publication*]
**Ja Stud Hist Sci** ... Japanese Studies in the History of Science [*A publication*]
**JASU**......... Jet Aircraft Starting Unit (AFM)
**JASW**........ Japan-America Society of Washington (EA)
**JAT**........... Jaarboekje van J. A. Alberdingk-Thym [*A publication*]
**JAT**........... Jabat [*Marshall Islands*] [*Airport symbol*] (OAG)
**JAT**........... Jam Angle Tracking
**JAT**........... Job Accounting Table
**JAT**........... Journal of Accounting and Public Policy [*A publication*]
**JAT**........... Journal of Applied Toxicology [*A publication*]
**JAT**........... Jugoslovenski Aerotransport [*Yugoslav Air Transport*]
**JAT**........... Junior Aptitude Tests [*Educational test*]
**JAT**........... Mennonite Hospital, Health Sciences Library, Bloomington, IL [*OCLC symbol*] (OCLC)
**JATAAQ**... Journal. Animal Technicians Association [*A publication*]
**JATADT**... Journal d'Agriculture Traditionnelle et de Botanique Appliquee. Travaux d'Ethnobotanique et d'Ethnozoologie [*A publication*]
**JATBAT**.... Journal d'Agriculture Tropicale et de Botanique Appliquee [*Later, Journal d'Agriculture Traditionnelle et de Botanique Appliquee*]
**JATC**......... Joint Apprenticeship and Training Committee [*Bureau of Apprenticeship and Training*] [*Department of Labor*]
**JATC**......... Journal of Air Traffic Control [*A publication*]
**JATCC**...... Joint Air Traffic Control Center [*Military*]
**JATCCCP**... Joint Advanced Tactical Command, Control, and Communications Program [*Military*]
**JATCCCS**... Joint Advanced Tactical Command, Control, and Communications System [*Military*] (MCD)
**JATE**......... Joint Air Transport Establishment [*Military*] [*British*]
**J At Energy Comm (Jpn)** ... Journal. Atomic Energy Commission (Japan) [*A publication*]
**J At Energy Soc Jap** ... Journal. Atomic Energy Society of Japan [*A publication*]
**J At Energy Soc Jpn** ... Journal. Atomic Energy Society of Japan [*A publication*]
**JATES**....... Japan Techno-Economics Society (EA)
**JATF**......... Joint Amphibious Task Force (NVT)
**J Atherosclerosis Res** ... Journal of Atherosclerosis Research [*A publication*]
**J Atheroscler Res** ... Journal of Atherosclerosis Research [*A publication*]
**JATI**......... Journal. Association of Teachers of Italian [*A publication*]
**JATJ**......... Journal-Newsletter. Association of Teachers of Japanese [*A publication*]
**JATLA**...... Journal. American Trial Lawyers Association [*A publication*] (DLA)
**JATM**........ Joint Antitactical Missile System (Provisional) [*Army*] (RDA)
**JATMA**..... Japan Automobile Tire Manufacturers Association
**J Atmos Chem** ... Journal of Atmospheric Chemistry [*A publication*]
**J Atmospheric Sci** ... Journal of the Atmospheric Sciences [*A publication*]
**J Atmos Sci** ... Journal of the Atmospheric Sciences [*A publication*]
**J Atmos Terr Phys** ... Journal of Atmospheric and Terrestrial Physics [*A publication*]
**J Atmos and Terr Phys** ... Journal of Atmospheric and Terrestrial Physics [*A publication*]
**J Atm Ter P** ... Journal of Atmospheric and Terrestrial Physics [*A publication*]
**JATO**......... Jet-Assisted Takeoff

**JATOD3**.... Journal of Analytical Toxicology [*A publication*]
**JATP**......... Jazz at the Philharmonic
**JATP**......... Joint Air Training Plan
**JATP**......... Joint Air Transportation Plan (AABC)
**JATS**......... Joint Air Transportation Service
**JATVC**...... Jewellery and Allied Trades Valuers Council [*Australia*]
**JAU**........... American Hospital Supply Corp., Evanston, IL [*OCLC symbol*] (OCLC)
**JAU**........... Jacksboro, TN [*Location identifier*] [*FAA*] (FAAL)
**JAUCB**...... Journal of Autism and Childhood Schizophrenia [*A publication*]
**J Aud Eng S**... Journal. Audio Engineering Society [*A publication*]
**J Aud Eng Soc**... Journal. Audio Engineering Society [*A publication*]
**J Audio Eng Soc**... Journal. Audio Engineering Society [*A publication*]
**J Audiov Media Med**... Journal of Audiovisual Media in Medicine [*A publication*]
**J Aud Res**... Journal of Auditory Research [*A publication*]
**J Aud Res Suppl**... Journal of Auditory Research. Supplement [*A publication*]
**JAUEA**...... Journal of Automotive Engineering [*A publication*]
**JAUK**......... Jahrbuch. Albertus Universitaet zu Koenigsberg [*A publication*]
**JAUMA**..... Journal. Australian Mathematical Society [*A publication*]
**JAUMLA**.. Journal. Australasian Universities Modern Language Association [*A publication*] (APTA)
**JAUN**........ Jaundice [*Medicine*]
**JAUND**..... Jaundice [*Medicine*]
**JAUPA**...... Journal of Agriculture. University of Puerto Rico [*A publication*]
**JAUPA8**.... Journal of Agriculture. University of Puerto Rico [*A publication*]
**JAURA**...... Journal of Auditory Research [*A publication*]
**J Aus I Agr**... Journal. Australian Institute of Agricultural Science [*A publication*]
**J Aus I Met**... Journal. Australian Institute of Metals [*A publication*]
**J Aus Mat A**... Journal. Australian Mathematical Society. Series A. Pure Mathematics and Statistics [*A publication*]
**J Aus Mat B**... Journal. Australian Mathematical Society. Series B. Applied Mathematics [*A publication*]
**J Aust Cath Hist Soc**... Journal. Australian Catholic Historical Society [*A publication*] (APTA)
**J Aust Ceramic Soc**... Journal. Australian Ceramic Society [*A publication*] (APTA)
**J Aust Ceram Soc**... Journal. Australian Ceramic Society [*A publication*]
**J Aust Coll Speech Ther**... Journal. Australian College of Speech Therapists [*A publication*] (APTA)
**J Aust Entomol Soc**... Journal. Australian Entomological Society [*A publication*]
**J Aust Ent Soc**... Journal. Australian Entomological Society [*A publication*]
**J Aust Inst Agric Sci**... Journal. Australian Institute of Agricultural Science [*A publication*]
**J Aust Inst Agr Sci**... Journal. Australian Institute of Agricultural Science [*A publication*]
**J Aust Inst Ag Science**... Journal. Australian Institute of Agricultural Science [*A publication*] (APTA)
**J Aust Inst Hort**... Journal. Australian Institute of Horticulture [*A publication*] (APTA)
**J Aust Inst Hortic**... Journal. Australian Institute of Horticulture [*A publication*]
**J Aust Inst Met**... Journal. Australian Institute of Metals [*A publication*]
**J Aust Inst Metals**... Journal. Australian Institute of Metals [*A publication*] (APTA)
**J Aust Inst Surg Dent Tech**... Journal. Australian Institute of Surgical and Dental Technicians [*A publication*]
**J Aust Math Soc**... Journal. Australian Mathematical Society [*A publication*]
**J Aust Planning Inst**... Journal. Australian Planning Institute [*A publication*] (APTA)
**J Aust Polit Econ**... Journal of Australian Political Economy [*A publication*]
**J Australas Inst Met**... Journal. Australasian Institute of Metals [*A publication*]
**J Australas Inst Metals**... Australasian Institute of Metals. Journal [*A publication*] (APTA)
**J Austral Math Soc Ser A**... Journal. Australian Mathematical Society. Series A [*A publication*]
**J Austral Math Soc Ser B**... Journal. Australian Mathematical Society. Series B [*A publication*]
**J Austronesian Stud**... Journal of Austronesian Studies [*A publication*] (APTA)
**J Aust Stud**... Journal of Australian Studies [*A publication*]
**J Aus War M**... Journal. Australian War Memorial [*A publication*]
**J Autism Ch**... Journal of Autism and Childhood Schizophrenia [*A publication*]
**J Autism & Child Schizo**... Journal of Autism and Childhood Schizophrenia [*A publication*]
**J Autism Child Schizophrenia**... Journal of Autism and Childhood Schizophrenia [*A publication*]
**J Autism Dev Disord**... Journal of Autism and Developmental Disorders [*A publication*]
**J Autism Dev Disorders**... Journal of Autism and Developmental Disorders [*A publication*]
**J Autism & Devel Dis**... Journal of Autism and Developmental Disorders [*A publication*]
**J Autom Chem**... Journal of Automatic Chemistry [*England*] [*A publication*]
**J Automot Eng**... Journal of Automotive Engineering [*A publication*]
**J Auton Nerv Syst**... Journal of the Autonomic Nervous System [*A publication*]
**J Auton Pharmacol**... Journal of Autonomic Pharmacology [*A publication*]
**JAV**........... Chicago, IL [*Location identifier*] [*FAA*] (FAAL)
**JAV**........... Dr. William M. Scholl College of Podiatric Medicine, Chicago, IL [*OCLC symbol*] (OCLC)
**JAV**........... Java
**JAV**........... Javanese
**jav**.............. Javanese [*MARC language code*] [*Library of Congress*] (LCCP)
**Jav**............. Javolenus Priscus [*Flourished, 60-120*] [*Authority cited in pre-1607 legal work*] (DSA)
**JAV**........... Job Analysis Vocabulary (OICC)
**JAVA**......... Jamaica Association of Villas and Apartments [*Later, JRJ*]
**JAVA**......... Jamming Amplitude Versus Azimuth (NVT)
**JAVA**......... Jandel Video Analysis System
**JAVAD5**.... Journal. American Venereal Disease Association [*A publication*]
**JAVI**.......... Javelin International Ltd. [*Montreal, PQ*] [*NASDAQ symbol*] (NQ)
**J Aviat Hist Soc Aust**... Aviation Historical Society of Australia. Journal [*A publication*] (APTA)
**J Aviation Med**... Journal of Aviation Medicine [*A publication*]
**JAVMA**..... Journal. American Veterinary Medical Association [*A publication*]
**JAVMA4**... Journal. American Veterinary Medical Association [*A publication*]
**Javole**......... Javolenus Priscus [*Flourished, 60-120*] [*Authority cited in pre-1607 legal work*] (DSA)
**JAVR**......... Jewish Audio-Visual Review [*A publication*]
**JAVRAJ**.... Journal. American Veterinary Radiology Society [*A publication*]
**JAVS**......... JOVIAL Automated Verification System (MCD)
**JAVTA**...... Journal. South African Veterinary Association [*A publication*]
**JAW**........... Jahresberichte ueber die Fortschritte der Klassischen Altertumswissenschaft [*A publication*]
**JAW**........... Standard Oil Co. (Indiana), Central Research Library, Naperville, IL [*OCLC symbol*] (OCLC)
**JAWAA7**... Journal of Agriculture of Western Australia [*A publication*]
**JAWF**........ Jet Augmented Wing Flap
**JAWPB**..... Joint Atomic Weapons Publications Board (AABC)
**JAWPM**.... Joint Atomic Weapons Planning Manual (AFM)
**JAWPS**...... Joint Atomic Weapons Publication System
**JAWRES**... Journal of Agriculture and Water Resources Research [*A publication*]
**JAWS**........ Jamming and Warning System (MCD)
**JAWS**........ Japan Animal Welfare Society [*London, England*]
**JAWS**........ Joint Airport Weather Studies [*National Center for Atmospheric Research*]
**JAWS**........ Joint Arctic Weather Stations [*Canada-US*]
**JAWS**........ Joint Attack Weapon System [*Military*] (MCD)
**JAWS**........ Josephson AttoWeber Switch [*Data processor circuitry*]
**JAWS**........ Junk Acronyms When Speaking [*Program*]
**JAWTR**..... Junior Assistant Writer [*British military*] (DMA)
**JAWWA**.... Journal. American Water Works Association [*A publication*]
**JAWWA5**.. American Water Works Association. Journal [*A publication*]
**JAWYS**..... Join Airways (FAAC)
**JAX**........... Chicago School of Professional Psychology, Chicago, IL [*OCLC symbol*] (OCLC)
**JAX**........... Jacksonville [*Florida*] [*Airport symbol*] (OAG)
**JAX**........... Mister Jax Fashions, Inc. [*Toronto Stock Exchange symbol*]
**JAY**........... Jayapura [*West Irian*] [*Seismograph station code, US Geological Survey*] (SEIS)
**JAY**........... Journal of Applied Psychology [*A publication*]
**JAY**........... Travenol Laboratories, Morton Grove, IL [*OCLC symbol*] (OCLC)
**JAYA**......... Jayark Corp. [*NASDAQ symbol*] (NQ)
**JAYCEES**... [*United States*] Junior Chamber of Commerce [*Acronym is now used as official name of association*] (EA)
**JAYJ**.......... Jay Jacobs, Inc. [*NASDAQ symbol*] (NQ)
**JAZ**........... Jahrbuch fuer Sozialwissenschaft. Zeitschrift fuer Wirtschaftswissenschaften [*A publication*]
**JazA**........... Jazykovedny Aktuality. Zpravodaj Jazykovedneho Sdruzeni pri Ceskoslovenske Akademii Ved [*A publication*]
**JAZODX**... Journal of Advanced Zoology [*A publication*]
**JazS**........... Jazykovedny Studie [*A publication*]
**JazSb**......... Jazykovedny Sbornik [*A publication*]
**JAZU**......... Jugoslavenske Akademije Znanosti i Umjetnosti [*A publication*]
**Jazz Ed J**... Jazz Educators Journal [*A publication*]
**Jazzf**.......... Jazzforschung [*A publication*]
**Jazz Ieri**..... Jazz di Ieri e di Oggi [*A publication*]
**Jazz J**......... Jazz Journal [*Later, Jazz Journal International*] [*A publication*]
**Jazz J Int**... Jazz Journal International [*A publication*]
**Jazz Jl**........ Jazz Journal [*Later, Jazz Journal International*] [*A publication*]
**Jazz Mag**... Jazz Magazine [*A publication*]
**Jazz Mag (US)**... Jazz Magazine (United States) [*A publication*]
**Jazz Mo**..... Jazz Monthly [*A publication*]
**Jazz R**........ Jazz Review [*A publication*]
**Jazz Rept**... Jazz Report [*A publication*]

**Jazz Res**..... Jazz Research [*A publication*]
**Jazz Rytm**.. Jazz Rytm i Piosenka [*A publication*]
**Jazz T**......... Jazz Times [*A publication*]
**JB**.............. British Caledonian Airways [*Charter*] Ltd. [*Great Britain*] [*ICAO designator*] (FAAC)
**JB**.............. IML Air Services Ltd. [*United Kingdom*] [*ICAO designator*] (ICDA)
**Jb**.............. Jaarboek [*Yearbook*] [*Netherlands*] (BJA)
**JB**.............. Jahrbuch [*Yearbook*] [*German*]
**JB**.............. James Boswell [*Initials used as pseudonym*]
**JB**.............. James Buchanan [*US president, 1791-1868*]
**JB**.............. Jerusalem Bible
**J-B**............ Jet Barrier
**JB**.............. Jet Black [*Derogatory nickname for a black person*]
**JB**.............. Jet Bomb
**JB**.............. Jiffy Bag
**JB**.............. Job (MCD)
**Jb**.............. Job [*Old Testament book*]
**JB**.............. Job Bank (OICC)
**JB**.............. Job Book
**JB**.............. Joggle Blocks (MCD)
**JB**.............. Johannes Baptista [*John the Baptist*] [*Authority cited in pre-1607 legal work*] (DSA)
**JB**.............. John Bull [*The typical Englishman*]
**JB**.............. Johore Bahru [*Refers to Europeans named after Malaysian towns*] (DSUE)
**JB**.............. Joint Army-Navy Board
**JB**.............. Joint Bond
**JB**.............. Journal of Band Research [*A publication*]
**JB**.............. Journal of Broadcasting [*Later, Journal of Broadcasting and Electronic Media*] [*A publication*]
**JB**.............. Journal of Business [*A publication*]
**JB**.............. Judaica Bohemiae [*A publication*]
**JB**.............. Juggle Box
**JB**.............. Jukeboxes [*Public-performance tariff class*] [*British*]
**JB**.............. Junction Box [*Technical drawings*]
**JB**.............. Junior Beadle [*Ancient Order of Foresters*]
**JB**.............. Junior Birdman [*Slang*]
**JB**.............. Junior Bookshelf [*A publication*]
**JB**.............. Juris Baccalaureus [*Bachelor of Laws*]
**J & B**......... Justerini and Brooks [*Scotch*]
**JB**.............. Lakeside Laboratories, Inc. [*Research code symbol*]
**JB**.............. Stetson Hat [*After John Batterson Stetson, 19th-century American hat manufacturer*] [*Slang*]
**JBA**............ Jewel Bearing Assembly
**JBA**............ Jewish Book Annual [*New York*] [*A publication*]
**JBA**............ John Burroughs Association (EA)
**JBA**............ Journal of Banking and Finance [*Netherlands*] [*A publication*]
**JBA**............ Journal. Board of Agriculture [*A publication*]
**JBA**............ Journal of Business Administration [*A publication*]
**JBA**............ Junction Box Assembly
**JBA**............ Junior Bluejackets of America (EA)
**JBAA**......... Journal. British Archaeological Association [*A publication*]
**Jb Absatz und Verbrauchsforsch** ... Jahrbuch der Absatz- und Verbrauchsforschung [*A publication*]
**JbAC**.......... Jahrbuch fuer Antike und Christentum [*A publication*]
**J BAC**........ Journal. International Union of Bricklayers and Allied Craftsmen [*A publication*]
**JbAChr**...... Jahrbuch fuer Antike und Christentum [*A publication*]
**J Bact**......... Journal of Bacteriology [*A publication*]
**J Bacteriol** ... Journal of Bacteriology [*A publication*]
**J BADC**..... Journal. Bar Association of the District of Columbia [*A publication*]
**JBA Dist Colum** ... Journal. Bar Association of the District of Columbia [*A publication*]
**JBAFC**....... Jan Berry and the Alohas Fan Club (EA)
**JBAK**......... Baker [*J.*], Inc. [*NASDAQ symbol*] (NQ)
**J BA Kan** ... Journal. Bar Association of the State of Kansas [*A publication*]
**J Ballist**...... Journal of Ballistics [*A publication*]
**JBalS**......... Journal of Baltic Studies [*A publication*]
**J Bal Stud**.. Journal of Baltic Studies [*A publication*]
**J Baltic St**.. Journal of Baltic Studies [*A publication*]
**J Baltimore Coll Dent Surg** ... Journal. Baltimore College of Dental Surgery [*A publication*]
**JBANC**...... Joint Baltic American National Committee (EA)
**J Band Res** ... Journal of Band Research [*A publication*]
**J Bangladesh Acad Sci** ... Journal. Bangladesh Academy of Sciences [*A publication*]
**J Bankers Inst Australas** ... Bankers' Institute of Australasia. Journal [*A publication*] (APTA)
**J Bank Finance** ... Journal of Banking and Finance [*A publication*]
**J Banking and Fin** ... Journal of Banking and Finance [*A publication*]
**J Bank Res** ... Journal of Bank Research [*A publication*]
**J Bank Research** ... Journal of Bank Research [*A publication*]
**J-BAR**........ Jet Runway Barrier (FAAC)
**Jb AS**......... Jahrbuch fuer Amerikastudien [*A publication*]
**JBASB**....... Journal of Band Research [*A publication*]
**J Basic Eng** ... Journal of Basic Engineering [*A publication*]
**J Basic Eng Trans ASME** ... Journal of Basic Engineering. Transactions. ASME [*American Society of Mechanical Engineers*] [*A publication*]
**J Basic Eng Trans ASME Ser D** ... Journal of Basic Engineering. Transactions. ASME [*American Society of Mechanical Engineers*]. Series D [*A publication*]
**J Basic Microbiol** ... Journal of Basic Microbiology [*A publication*]
**J Basic Sci Hanyang Inst Basic Sci** ... Journal of Basic Sciences. Hanyang Institute of Basic Science [*A publication*]
**J Bas S**....... Journal of Basque Studies [*A publication*]
**JB Assn St Kan** ... Journal. Bar Association of the State of Kansas [*A publication*]
**JBAW**........ Jahrbuch. Bayerische Akademie der Wissenschaften [*A publication*]
**JbAWG**...... Jahrbuch. Akademie der Wissenschaften in Goettingen [*A publication*]
**JbAWL**...... Jahrbuch. Akademie der Wissenschaften und der Literatur [*Mainz*] [*A publication*]
**JbBAW**...... Jahrbuch. Bayerische Akademie der Wissenschaften [*A publication*]
**JBBB**......... JB's Restaurants, Inc. [*NASDAQ symbol*] (NQ)
**Jb Berl Mus** ... Jahrbuch. Berliner Museen [*A publication*]
**JB Bern Hist Mus** ... Jahrbuch. Bernisches Historische Museum [*A publication*]
**JBBF**.......... Judo Black Belt Federation [*Later, USJE*]
**JBBFC**........ James Bond British Fan Club (EAIO)
**Jb Bischof Gymnas Kolleg Petrinum** ... Jahresbericht. Bischoefliches Gymnasium und Dioezesanseminar. Kollegium Petrinum in Urfar [*A publication*]
**JBBMD**..... Journal of Biochemical and Biophysical Methods [*A publication*]
**JBC**............ Jamaica Broadcasting Corporation
**JBC**............ [*The*] Jerome Biblical Commentary [*Englewood Cliffs, NJ*] [*A publication*] (BJA)
**JBC**............ Jewelers' Book Club (EA)
**JBC**............ Jewish Book Council [*of the National Jewish Welfare Board*] [*Later, JWBJBC*] (EA)
**JBC**............ Johnson Bible College [*Tennessee*]
**JBC**............ Joint Blood Council [*Defunct*] (EA)
**JBC**............ Joint Budget Committee (OICC)
**JBC**............ Journal of Business Communication [*A publication*]
**JBC**............ Journal. State Bar of California [*A publication*] (DLA)
**J of Bcasting** ... Journal of Broadcasting [*Later, Journal of Broadcasting and Electronic Media*] [*A publication*]
**Jb Coburg Landesst** ... Jahrbuch. Coburger Landesstiftung [*A publication*]
**JBCS**.......... James Branch Cabell Society (EA)
**JBCSA**....... Journal. British Ceramic Society [*A publication*]
**JBD**............ Becton, Dickinson & Co., Paramus, NJ [*OCLC symbol*] (OCLC)
**JBD**............ Jet Blast Deflector
**JBDAAFES** ... Joint Board of Directors, Army-Air Force Exchange Service (AABC)
**J Bd Ag**...... Journal. Board of Agriculture [*Great Britain*] [*A publication*]
**J Bd Agric (London)** ... Journal. Board of Agriculture (London) [*A publication*]
**JbDAI**........ Jahrbuch. Deutsches Archaeologische Institut [*Berlin*] [*A publication*]
**JbDAI ArAnz** ... Jahrbuch. Deutsches Archaeologische Institut. Archaeologischer Anzeiger [*Berlin*] [*A publication*]
**JbDAW**..... Jahrbuch. Deutsche Akademie der Wissenschaften zu Berlin [*A publication*]
**Jb Deutschen Saengerbundes** ... Jahrbuch des Deutschen Saengerbundes [*A publication*]
**JBDFC**....... James Bond 007 Fan Club (EA)
**JbDG**......... Jahrbuch. Dante Gesellschaft [*A publication*]
**Jb Diplom Akad (Wien)** ... Jahrbuch. Diplomatische Akademie (Wien) [*A publication*]
**JBE**............ Japanese B Encephalitis [*Medicine*]
**JBE**............ Journal of Behavioral Economics [*A publication*]
**JBE**............ Journal of Business Education [*A publication*]
**J Beckett S** ... Journal of Beckett Studies [*A publication*]
**J Beck S**..... Journal of Beckett Studies [*A publication*]
**J Behav Assess** ... Journal of Behavioral Assessment [*A publication*]
**J Behav Exp** ... Journal of Behavior Therapy and Experimental Psychiatry [*A publication*]
**J Behav Med** ... Journal of Behavioral Medicine [*A publication*]
**J Behav Sci** ... Journal of Behavioural Science [*A publication*]
**J Behav Ther Exp Psychiatry** ... Journal of Behavior Therapy and Experimental Psychiatry [*A publication*]
**J Belge Med Phys Rehabil** ... Journal Belge de Medecine Physique et de Rehabilitation [*A publication*]
**J Belge Med Phys Rhumatol** ... Journal Belge de Medecine Physique et de Rhumatologie [*A publication*]
**J Belge Neurol Psychiatr** ... Journal Belge de Neurologie et de Psychiatrie [*A publication*]
**J Belge Radiol** ... Journal Belge de Radiologie [*A publication*]
**J Belgc Radiol Monogr** ... Journal Belge de Radiologie. Monographie [*Belgium*] [*A publication*]
**J Belge Rhumatol Med Phys** ... Journal Belge de Rhumatologie et de Medecine Physique [*A publication*]
**J Belg Rad** ... Journal Belge de Radiologie [*A publication*]
**JbEOL**....... Jaarbericht. Vooraziatische-Egyptisch Genootschap "Ex Oriente Lux" [*A publication*]
**Jber**............ Jahresbericht [*Journal, Annual Report*] [*German*] (BJA)

**Jber Deutsch Math-Verein** ... Jahresbericht. Deutsche Mathematiker-Vereinigung [*A publication*]
**J Bergen Cty Dent Soc** ... Journal. Bergen County Dental Society [*A publication*]
**Jber Hist Ges Graub** ... Jahresbericht. Historisch-Antiquarische Gesellschaft von Graubuenden [*A publication*]
**Jber Inst Vg Frankf** ... Jahresbericht des Instituts fuer Vorgeschichte der Universitaet Frankfurt [*A publication*]
**J Berl M**..... Jahrbuch. Berliner Museen [*A publication*]
**Jber Mus (Han)** ... Jahresbericht Kestner-Museum (Hannover) [*A publication*]
**Jber Naturf Ges Fraubuendens** ... Jahresbericht. Naturforschende Gesellschaft Fraubuendens [*A publication*]
**Jber Naturw Ver Wuppertal** ... Jahresbericht. Naturwissenschaftlicher Verein zu Wuppertal [*A publication*]
**Jber Pro Vindon** ... Jahresbericht. Gesellschaft pro Vindonissa [*A publication*]
**Jb u Ersch Ger Lit** ... Jahresberichte ueber die Erscheinungem auf dem Gebiete der Germanischen Literaturgeschichte [*A publication*]
**Jber (Zuerich)** ... Jahresbericht. Schweizerisches Landesmuseum (Zuerich) [*A publication*]
**JBES**.......... Jodrell Bank Experimental Station [*British*]
**J Bethune Univ Med Sci** ... Journal. Bethune University of Medical Sciences [*A publication*]
**J Beverly Hills Ba** ... Journal. Beverly Hills Bar Association [*A publication*]
**J Bev Hills BA** ... Journal. Beverly Hills Bar Association [*A publication*]
**JBF**............ James Beard Foundation (EA)
**JBF**............ Journal of Business Finance and Accounting [*A publication*]
**JBFC**.......... Jennifer Bassey Fan Club (EA)
**JBFC**.......... Jennifer Burnett Fan Club (EA)
**JBFC**.......... Johnny Bernard Fan Club (EA)
**JBFCI**........ Jon Beryl Fan Club International (EA)
**JbFL**.......... Jahrbuch fuer Fraenkische Landesforschung [*A publication*]
**JBFLP**....... Journal of Banking and Finance Law and Practice [*A publication*]
**Jb Friedens- u Konfliktforsch** ... Jahrbuch fuer Friedens- und Konfliktforschung [*A publication*]
**JBFSAW**... Joint Board on Future Storage of Atomic Weapons
**JBG**............ Brazil Journal [*A publication*]
**JBG**............ Jahrbuch. Barlach-Gesellschaft [*A publication*]
**JBG**............ Jewish Board of Guardians (EA)
**JBG**............ Jinbungaku [*Studies in Humanities*] [*A publication*]
**JBG**............ Journal of Business Logistics [*A publication*]
**Jb Gesch Sozial Land Europas** ... Jahrbuch fuer Geschichte der Sozialistischen Lander Europas [*A publication*]
**Jb Ges Wiener Theater F** ... Jahrbuch. Gesellschaft fuer Wiener Theater-Forschung [*A publication*]
**JBGH**........ Jinbun Gakuho [*Journal of Social Science and Humanities*] [*A publication*]
**JB Goett**..... Jahrbuch. Akademie der Wissenschaften in Goettingen [*A publication*]
**Jb H**........... Jaarboekje van de Vergelijkende van Directeuren van Hypotheekbanken [*A publication*]
**Jb Hamb Ku Samml** ... Jahrbuch. Hamburger Kunstsammlungen [*A publication*]
**JBHCPIUA** ... Journeymen Barbers, Hairdressers, Cosmetologists and Proprietors' International Union of America (EA)
**JBHT**......... Hunt [*J. B.*] Transport Services, Inc. [*NASDAQ symbol*] (NQ)
**JBHVMF**.. Jahresbericht. Historischer Verein fuer Mittelfranken [*A publication*]
**JBI**............ Jacob Blaustein Institute for the Advancement of Human Rights (EA)
**JBI**............ Jewish Braille Institute of America (EA)
**JBIA**.......... Jewish Braille Institute of America (EA)
**J Bib Lit**..... Journal of Biblical Literature [*A publication*]
**J Bibl Lit**.... Journal of Biblical Literature [*A publication*]
**JBIC**.......... Journal of Biocommunication [*A publication*]
**J Bihar Agric Coll** ... Journal. Bihar Agricultural College [*A publication*]
**J Bihar Pur Par** ... Journal. Bihar Puravid Parishad [*A publication*]
**J Bihar RS** ... Journal. Bihar Research Society [*A publication*]
**JBIL**........... Bildner [*J.*] & Sons, Inc. [*Boston, MA*] [*NASDAQ symbol*] (NQ)
**Jb Imkers**... Jahrbuch der Imkers [*A publication*]
**Jb Int R**...... Jahrbuch fuer Internationales und Auslaendisches Oeffentliches Recht [*1948-*] [*A publication*] [*German*] (ILCA)
**Jb Int Recht** ... Jahrbuch fuer Internationales Recht [*A publication*]
**J Biochem**.. Journal of Biochemistry [*A publication*]
**J Biochem and Biophys Methods** ... Journal of Biochemical and Biophysical Methods [*A publication*]
**J Biochem Microbiol Tech Eng** ... Journal of Biochemical and Microbiological Technology and Engineering [*A publication*]
**J Biochem (Tokyo)** ... Journal of Biochemistry (Tokyo) [*A publication*]
**J Biochem Toxicol** ... Journal of Biochemical Toxicology [*A publication*]
**J Biocommun** ... Journal of Biocommunication [*A publication*]
**J Bioelectr** ... Journal of Bioelectricity [*A publication*]
**J Bioenerg** ... Journal of Bioenergetics [*Later, Journal of Bioenergetics and Biomembranes*] [*A publication*]
**J Bioenerg Biomembr** ... Journal of Bioenergetics and Biomembranes [*A publication*]
**J Bioeng**..... Journal of Bioengineering [*A publication*]
**J Bioeth**...... Journal of Bioethics [*A publication*]
**J Biogeogr** ... Journal of Biogeography [*A publication*]
**J Biol Board Can** ... Journal. Biological Board of Canada [*A publication*]
**J Biol (Bronx NY)** ... Journal of Biology (Bronx, NY) [*A publication*]
**J Biol Bucc** ... Journal de Biologie Buccale [*A publication*]
**J Biol Buccale** ... Journal de Biologie Buccale [*A publication*]
**J Biol Chem** ... Journal of Biological Chemistry [*A publication*]
**J Biol Educ** ... Journal of Biological Education [*A publication*]
**J Biological Ed** ... Journal of Biological Education [*A publication*]
**J Biol Osaka City Univ** ... Journal of Biology. Osaka City University [*A publication*]
**J Biol Phot** ... Journal. Biological Photographic Association [*A publication*]
**J Biol Phot Assn** ... Journal. Biological Photographic Association [*A publication*]
**J Biol Photogr** ... Journal of Biological Photography [*A publication*]
**J Biol Photogr Ass** ... Journal. Biological Photographic Association [*A publication*]
**J Biol Photogr Assoc** ... Journal. Biological Photographic Association [*A publication*]
**J Biol Phys** ... Journal of Biological Physics [*A publication*]
**J Biol Psychol** ... Journal of Biological Psychology [*A publication*]
**J Biol Response Mod** ... Journal of Biological Response Modifiers [*A publication*]
**J Biol Response Modif** ... Journal of Biological Response Modifiers [*A publication*]
**J Biol Sci**.... Journal of Biological Sciences [*A publication*]
**J Biol Sci (Baghdad)** ... Journal of Biological Sciences (Baghdad) [*A publication*]
**J Biol Sci (Bombay)** ... Journal of Biological Sciences (Bombay) [*A publication*]
**J Biol Sci Res** ... Journal of Biological Sciences Research [*A publication*]
**J Biol Sci Res Publ** ... Journal of Biological Sciences Research Publication [*A publication*]
**J Biol Stan** ... Journal of Biological Standardization [*A publication*]
**J Biol Stand** ... Journal of Biological Standardization [*A publication*]
**J Biomater Dent** ... Journal de Biomateriaux Dentaires [*A publication*]
**J Biomech**.. Journal of Biomechanics [*A publication*]
**J Biomechan** ... Journal of Biomechanics [*A publication*]
**J Biomech Eng** ... Journal of Biomechanical Engineering [*A publication*]
**J Biomech Eng Trans ASME** ... Journal of Biomechanical Engineering. Transactions. ASME [*American Society of Mechanical Engineers*] [*A publication*]
**J Biomed Eng** ... Journal of Biomedical Engineering [*A publication*]
**J Biomed Mater Res** ... Journal of Biomedical Materials Research [*A publication*]
**J Biomed Mater Res Biomed Mater Symp** ... Journal of Biomedical Materials Research. Biomedical Materials Symposium [*A publication*]
**J Biomed Mat Res** ... Journal of Biomedical Materials Research [*A publication*]
**J Biomed MR** ... Journal of Biomedical Materials Research [*A publication*]
**J Biomed Syst** ... Journal of Biomedical Systems [*A publication*]
**J Biomol Struct Dyn** ... Journal of Biomolecular Structure and Dynamics [*A publication*]
**J Biomol Struct & Dyn** ... Journal of Biomolecular Structure and Dynamics [*A publication*]
**J Biophys Biochem Cytol** ... Journal of Biophysical and Biochemical Cytology [*A publication*]
**J Biophys Biomec** ... Journal de Biophysique et de Biomecanique [*A publication*]
**J Biophys Med Nucl** ... Journal de Biophysique et Medecine Nucleaire [*A publication*]
**J Biophys Soc Jpn** ... Journal. Biophysical Society of Japan [*A publication*]
**J Biophys (Tokyo)** ... Journal of Biophysics (Tokyo) [*A publication*]
**J Biosci**...... Journal of Biosciences [*A publication*]
**J Biosci (Bangalore)** ... Journal of Biosciences (Bangalore) [*A publication*]
**J Biosoc**...... Journal of Biosocial Science [*A publication*]
**J Biosoc Sc** ... Journal of Biosocial Science [*A publication*]
**J Biosoc Sci** ... Journal of Biosocial Science [*A publication*]
**J Biosoc Sci Suppl** ... Journal of Biosocial Science. Supplement [*A publication*]
**J Biotech**.... Journal of Biotechnology [*A publication*]
**J Biotechnol** ... Journal of Biotechnology [*A publication*]
**J Birla Inst Technol Sci** ... Journal. Birla Institute of Technology and Science [*A publication*]
**J Birla Inst Technol and Sci** ... Journal. Birla Institute of Technology and Science [*A publication*]
**J Birla Inst Tech and Sci (Pilani)** ... Journal. Birla Institute of Technology and Science (Pilani) [*A publication*]
**J Birmingham Metall Soc** ... Journal. Birmingham Metallurgical Society [*A publication*]
**JBIRS**........ Journal. Bihar Research Society [*A publication*]
**JBIS**.......... Journal. British Interplanetary Society [*A publication*]
**JBITD4**..... Journal of Biotechnology [*A publication*]
**JBJ**............ Bellum Judaicum [*Josephus*] [*Classical studies*] (BJA)
**JBJ**............ James Bond Journalism [*Term coined by leader Sinnathamby Bajaratman of Singapore and referring to Western journalism*]
**JbJTS**........ Jahresberichte. Juedisch-Theologisches Seminar "Frankelsche Stiftung"
**JBK**............ Berkeley, CA [*Location identifier*] [*FAA*] (FAAL)
**JBK**............ Journal of Banking and Finance [*A publication*]

**JBK**............ Journal. Bar Association of the State of Kansas [*A publication*]
**JbKAF**....... Jahrbuch fuer Kleinasiatische Forschung [*A publication*]
**JBKG**......... Jahrbuch fuer Brandenburgische Kirchengeschichte [*A publication*]
**JBKK**......... Jinbun Kenkyu [*Studies in Humanities*] [*A publication*]
**Jb Kl F**....... Jahrbuch fuer Kleinasiatische Forschung [*A publication*]
**Jb K Mus Schon Kunst Antwerp** ... Jaarboek. Koninklijke Museum voor Schone Kunsten Antwerpen [*A publication*]
**JbKNA**....... Jaarboek. Koninklijke Nederlandsche Academie van Wetenschappen [*A publication*]
**Jb KS (Wien)** ... Jahrbuch. Kunsthistorische Sammlungen (Wien) [*A publication*]
**Jb Kunsthist Samml (Wien)** ... Jahrbuch. Kunsthistorische Sammlungen (Wien) [*A publication*]
**Jb Ku Samml Bad Wuert** ... Jahrbuch. Staatlichen Kunstsammlungen in Baden-Wuerttemberg [*A publication*]
**JbKVA**....... Jaarboek. Koninklijke Vlaamse Academie voor Taal-en Letterkunde [*A publication*]
**JbKVAW**... Jaarboek. Koninklijke Vlaamse Academie voor Wetenschappen [*A publication*]
**JBL**............ James B. Lansing Sound, Inc.
**JBL**............ Jonesboro, LA [*Location identifier*] [*FAA*] (FAAL)
**JBL**............ Journal of Biblical Literature [*A publication*]
**JBL**............ Journal of Business Law [*British*] [*A publication*]
**JBl**............. Juristische Blaetter [*A publication*]
**J Black Poetry** ... Journal of Black Poetry [*A publication*]
**JBlackS** ..... Journal of Black Studies [*A publication*]
**J Black St** .. Journal of Black Studies [*A publication*]
**J Black Stud** ... Journal of Black Studies [*A publication*]
**J of Black Stud** ... Journal of Black Studies [*A publication*]
**J Black Studies** ... Journal of Black Studies [*A publication*]
**Jb Leipzig Bienenztg** ... Jahrbuch. Leipziger Bienenzeitung [*A publication*]
**JBLG**......... Jahresberichte. Berliner Literatur Gesellschaft [*A publication*]
**Jb Liechtenstein** ... Jahrbuch des Historischen Vereins fuer des Fuerstentum Liechtenstein [*A publication*]
**JbLitHymn** ... Jahrbuch fuer Liturgik und Hymnologie [*Kassel*] [*A publication*]
**Jb Liturgik Hymnologie** ... Jahrbuch fuer Liturgik und Hymnologie [*A publication*]
**J/BLK**........ Junction Block [*Automotive engineering*]
**JBLMS**...... Journal of Biblical Literature. Monograph Series [*A publication*]
**JBLS**.......... James Bennett Library Services [*Australia*]
**JBM**........... Jahrbuch. Berliner Museen [*A publication*]
**JBM**........... Jahrbuch. Bernisches Historische Museum [*A publication*]
**JBM**........... Jahrbuch fuer das Bistum (Mainz) [*A publication*]
**JBM**........... Jan Bell Marketing [*AMEX symbol*] (SPSG)
**JBM**........... Journal of Organizational Behavior Management [*A publication*]
**JBMA**........ John Burroughs Memorial Association (EA)
**Jb (Mainz)** ... Jahrbuch. Akademie der Wissenschaften und der Literatur (Mainz) [*A publication*]
**Jb Max Planck Ges Foerd Wiss** ... Jahrbuch. Max-Planck-Gesellschaft zur Foerderung der Wissenschaften [*A publication*]
**JBMI**......... Journalist Biographies Master Index [*A publication*]
**JBM J Bras Med** ... JBM. Jornal Brasileiro de Medicina [*A publication*]
**JBMNA**..... Journal de Biologie et de Medecine Nucleaires [*A publication*]
**JbMNL**...... Jaarboek. Maatschappij der Nederlandsche Letterkunde te Leiden [*A publication*]
**JB Moo**...... [*J. B.*] Moore's English Common Pleas Reports [*A publication*] (DLA)
**J B Moore** ... [*J. B.*] Moore's English Common Pleas Reports [*A publication*] (DLA)
**J B Moore (Eng)** ... [*J. B.*] Moore's English Common Pleas Reports [*A publication*] (DLA)
**Jb M P**....... Jahrbuch der Musikbibliothek Peters [*A publication*]
**JBMTO**..... Joint Bus Military Traffic Office (AABC)
**JbMu**......... Jahrbuch. Marburger Universitaetsbund [*A publication*]
**JB (Muenchen)** ... Jahrbuch. Bayerische Akademie der Wissenschaften (Muenchen) [*A publication*]
**Jb Musik Volks-u Voelkerk** ... Jahrbuch fuer Musikalische Volks- und Voelkerkunde [*A publication*]
**Jb M Volks Volkerkunde** ... Jahrbuch fuer Musikalische Volks- und Voelkerkunde [*A publication*]
**JBN**........... Judaica Book News [*A publication*]
**Jb Nationaloekon und Statis** ... Jahrbuecher fuer Nationaloekonomie und Statistik [*A publication*]
**JBNC**......... Jefferson Bancorp, Inc. [*NASDAQ symbol*] (NQ)
**Jb f Niederdeut Spr** ... Jahrbuch fuer Niederdeutsche Sprachforschung [*A publication*]
**Jb f Niederdt Spr** ... Jahrbuch fuer Niederdeutsche Sprachforschung [*A publication*]
**JBNK**......... Jefferson Bankshares, Inc. [*NASDAQ symbol*] (NQ)
**JbNo**.......... Jahrbuch fuer Landeskunde von Niederoesterreich [*A publication*]
**JBNSA**...... Journal. British Nuclear Energy Society [*A publication*]
**JBO**........... Journal of Buyouts and Acquisitions [*A publication*]
**JBO**........... Journal of Economic Behavior and Organization [*A publication*]
**J Board Agric (GB)** ... Journal. Board of Agriculture (Great Britain) [*A publication*]
**J Board Dir Am Soc Civ Eng** ... Journal. Board of Direction. American Society of Civil Engineers [*A publication*]
**J Board Greenkeeping Res** ... Journal. Board of Greenkeeping Research [*A publication*]
**Jb Oe Byz** .. Jahrbuch der Oesterreichischen Byzantinistik [*A publication*]
**Jb Oeff Rechts** ... Jahrbuch des Oeffentlichen Rechts der Gegenwart [*A publication*]
**Jb Oldenburger Muensterland** ... Jahrbuch fuer das Oldenburger Muensterland [*A publication*]
**J Bombay Nat Hist Soc** ... Journal. Bombay Natural History Society [*A publication*]
**J Bom Natur Hist Soc** ... Journal. Bombay Natural History Society [*A publication*]
**J Bone-Am V** ... Journal of Bone and Joint Surgery (American Volume) [*A publication*]
**J Bone-Br V** ... Journal of Bone and Joint Surgery (British Volume) [*A publication*]
**J Bone Joint Surg** ... Journal of Bone and Joint Surgery [*A publication*]
**J Bone Joint Surg (Am)** ... Journal of Bone and Joint Surgery (American Volume) [*A publication*]
**J Bone Joint Surg (Br)** ... Journal of Bone and Joint Surgery (British Volume) [*A publication*]
**J Bone Jt Surg (Am Vol)** ... Journal of Bone and Joint Surgery (American Volume) [*A publication*]
**J Bone Jt Surg (Br Vol)** ... Journal of Bone and Joint Surgery (British Volume) [*A publication*]
**JBOR**......... Job Bank Operations Review [*Employment and Training Administration*] [*Department of Labor*]
**JBORS**...... Journal. Bihar and Orissa Research Society [*Later, Journal. Bihar Research Society*] [*A publication*]
**JBOS**......... Job Banks Opening Summary [*Department of Labor*]
**Jb Osterreich Kultur Gesch** ... Jahrbuch fuer Oesterreichische Kulturgeschichte [*A publication*]
**J Boston Soc Civ Eng** ... Journal. Boston Society of Civil Engineers [*A publication*]
**J Boston Soc Civ Eng Sect ASCE** ... Journal. Boston Society of Civil Engineers Section. American Society of Civil Engineers [*A publication*]
**Jb Ostrecht** ... Jahrbuch fuer Ostrecht [*A publication*]
**J Bot Br Foreign** ... Journal of Botany. British and Foreign [*A publication*]
**J Bot Soc S Afr** ... Journal. Botanical Society of South Africa [*A publication*]
**J Bot UAR** ... Journal of Botany. United Arab Republic [*A publication*]
**J Bowman Gray Sch Med Wake For Coll** ... Journal. Bowman Gray School of Medicine. Wake Forest College [*A publication*]
**JBP**............ Jettison Booster Package [*NASA*]
**JBPAA**...... Journal. Biological Photographic Association [*A publication*]
**Jb Peters**..... Jahrbuch Peters [*A publication*]
**JBPHB**...... Journal of Biological Physics [*A publication*]
**JBPSA**....... Jornal Brasileiro de Psiquiatria [*A publication*]
**JBR**............ Jonesboro [*Arkansas*] [*Airport symbol*] (OAG)
**JBR**............ Jonesboro, AR [*Location identifier*] [*FAA*] (FAAL)
**JBR**............ Journal of Bank Research [*A publication*]
**JBR**............ Journal of Bible and Religion [*A publication*]
**J Br A Ass** ... Journal. British Archaeological Association [*A publication*]
**J BRANNAM** ... Just Brand Names [*Division of F. W. Woolworth Co.*]
**JBRAS**....... Journal. Bombay Branch. Royal Asiatic Society [*A publication*]
**J Bras Ginecol** ... Jornal Brasileiro de Ginecologia [*A publication*]
**J Bras Med** ... Jornal Brasileiro de Medicina [*A publication*]
**J Bras Neurol** ... Jornal Brasileiro de Neurologia [*A publication*]
**J Bras Psiquiatr** ... Jornal Brasileiro de Psiquiatria [*A publication*]
**J Br Astron Assoc** ... Journal. British Astronomical Association [*A publication*]
**J Bras Urol** ... Jornal Brasileiro de Urologia [*A publication*]
**J Br Boot Shoe Instn** ... Journal. British Boot and Shoe Institution [*A publication*]
**J Br Dent Assoc** ... Journal. British Dental Association [*A publication*]
**Jb Rechnung Hist Mus (Basel)** ... Jahresberichte und Rechnungen. Historisches Museum (Basel) [*Switzerland*] [*A publication*]
**J Br Endod Soc** ... Journal. British Endodontic Society [*A publication*]
**J Brew Soc Jpn** ... Journal. Brewing Society of Japan [*A publication*]
**J Br Fire Serv Assoc** ... Journal. British Fire Services Association [*A publication*]
**J Br Grassl** ... Journal. British Grassland Society [*A publication*]
**J Br Grassld Soc** ... Journal. British Grassland Society [*A publication*]
**J Br Grassl Soc** ... Journal. British Grassland Society [*A publication*]
**J Bridg**....... [*Sir John*] Bridgman's English Common Pleas Reports [*123 English Reprint*] [*A publication*] (DLA)
**J Bridg (Eng)** ... [*Sir John*] Bridgman's English Common Pleas Reports [*123 English Reprint*] [*A publication*] (DLA)
**J Bridgm**..... [*Sir John*] Bridgman's English Common Pleas Reports [*123 English Reprint*] [*A publication*] (DLA)
**J Br Inst Radio Eng** ... Journal. British Institution of Radio Engineers [*A publication*]
**J Brit Archaeol Ass 3 Ser** ... Journal. British Archaeological Association. Series 3 [*A publication*]
**J Brit Ceram Soc** ... Journal. British Ceramic Society [*A publication*]
**J Brit Interplanet Soc** ... Journal. British Interplanetary Society [*A publication*]
**J Brit Nucl Energy Soc** ... Journal. British Nuclear Energy Society [*A publication*]

**J Brit Ship Res Ass** ... Journal. British Ship Research Association [*A publication*]
**J Brit Soc Master Glass Paint** ... Journal. British Society of Master Glass Painters [*A publication*]
**J Brit Soc Phenomenol** ... Journal. British Society for Phenomenology [*A publication*]
**J Brit Stud** ... Journal of British Studies [*A publication*]
**JBRM**........ Journal of Biological Response Modifiers [*A publication*]
**JBRMA**..... Jornal Brasileiro de Medicina [*A publication*]
**JBRNA**...... Jornal Brasileiro de Neurologia [*A publication*]
**Jb'r Nat-Oekon Statist** ... Jahrbuecher fuer National-Oekonomie und Statistik [*A publication*]
**J Br Nucl E** ... Journal. British Nuclear Energy Society [*A publication*]
**J Br Nucl Energy Soc** ... Journal. British Nuclear Energy Society [*A publication*]
**J Broadcast** ... Journal of Broadcasting [*Later, Journal of Broadcasting and Electronic Media*] [*A publication*]
**J Broadcasting** ... Journal of Broadcasting [*Later, Journal of Broadcasting and Electronic Media*] [*A publication*]
**J Broadcst** ... Journal of Broadcasting and Electronic Media [*A publication*]
**J Bromeliad Soc** ... Journal. Bromeliad Society [*A publication*]
**JBRS**.......... Journal. Bihar Research Society [*A publication*]
**JBRS**.......... Journal. Burma Research Society [*A publication*]
**J Br Soc Ph** ... Journal. British Society for Phenomenology [*A publication*]
**J Br Stud**.... Journal of British Studies [*A publication*]
**J Br Waterworks Assoc** ... Journal. British Waterworks Association [*A publication*]
**J Br Wood Preserv Assoc** ... Journal. British Wood Preserving Association [*A publication*]
**J Bryol** ....... Journal of Bryology [*A publication*]
**JBS** ........... Jane Badler Society (EA)
**JBS** ........... Job Search [*Job Training and Partnership Act*] (OICC)
**JBS** ........... John Birch Society (EA)
**JBS** ........... Joly Black Screen
**JBS** ........... Josephine Butler Society (EAIO)
**JBS** ........... Journal of Applied Behavioral Science [*A publication*]
**JBS** ........... Journal of British Studies [*A publication*]
**JBS** ........... Journal of Business Research [*A publication*]
**JBS** ........... Journal of Byelorussian Studies [*A publication*]
**JbSAW** ...... Jahrbuch. Saechsische Akademie der Wissenschaften zu Leipzig [*A publication*]
**Jb Schweiz Ges Ur Fruehgesch** ... Jahrbuch. Schweizerische Gesellschaft fuer Ur- und Fruehgeschichte [*A publication*]
**Jb Schw Ges Urgesch** ... Jahrbuch. Schweizerische Gesellschaft fuer Ur- und Fruehgeschichte [*A publication*]
**JBSDD6**.... Journal of Biomolecular Structure and Dynamics [*A publication*]
**JbShG**........ Jahrbuch. Shakespeare Gesellschaft [*A publication*]
**J Bsns** ........ Journal of Business [*A publication*]
**J Bsns Ed**... Journal of Business Education [*A publication*]
**J Bsns Educ** ... Journal of Business Education [*A publication*]
**Jb Sozialwiss** ... Jahrbuch fuer Sozialwissenschaft [*A publication*]
**Jb Soz -Wiss** ... Jahrbuch fuer Sozialwissenschaft [*A publication*]
**JBSPE9**..... Journal of Biological Sciences Research Publication [*A publication*]
**JBSREF**..... Journal of Biological Sciences Research [*A publication*]
**JBSTB**....... Journal of Biological Standardization [*A publication*]
**Jb Stift Preuss Kul Bes** ... Jahrbuch der Stiftung Preussischer Kulturbesitz [*A publication*]
**Jb St Kunstsamml (Dresden)** ... Jahrbuch. Staatliche Kunstsammlungen (Dresden) [*A publication*]
**JBT**........... Bethel, AK [*Location identifier*] [*FAA*] (FAAL)
**JBT**........... Jewelers Board of Trade (EA)
**JBT**........... Journal of Business Ethics [*A publication*]
**JBU**........... John Brown University [*Siloam Springs, AR*]
**JBU**........... Journal of Business [*A publication*]
**JBU**........... Journal of Business Research [*A publication*]
**JBUA**......... Journal. Bombay University. Arts [*A publication*]
**Jbuch** ......... Jahrbuch ueber die Fortschritte der Mathematik [*A publication*]
**Jbuch Heidelberger Akad Wiss** ... Jahrbuch. Heidelberger Akademie der Wissenschaften [*A publication*]
**J Burn Care Rehabil** ... Journal of Burn Care and Rehabilitation [*A publication*]
**J Bus**......... Journal of Business [*A publication*]
**J Busan Med Coll** ... Journal. Busan Medical College [*A publication*]
**J Bus Commun** ... Journal of Business Communication [*A publication*]
**J Bus Communic** ... Journal of Business Communication [*A publication*]
**JBUSDC**.... Joint Brazil-United States Defense Commission [*Terminated, 1977*]
**J Bus Ed**..... Journal of Business Education [*A publication*]
**J Bus Ethics** ... Journal of Business Ethics [*A publication*]
**J Busin**....... Journal of Business [*A publication*]
**J Bus L**....... Journal of Business Law [*A publication*] [*British*]
**JBUSMC**... Joint Brazil-United States Military Commission
**J Bus Res** ... Journal of Business Research [*A publication*]
**J Bus Research** ... Journal of Business Research [*A publication*]
**J Bus Strategy** ... Journal of Business Strategy [*A publication*]
**JBV**........... Jolt Beverage Co. Ltd. [*Vancouver Stock Exchange symbol*]
**JBV**........... Juedische Buch Vereinigung [*Berlin*] [*A publication*]
**Jb Ver Vgl St R B Nedl** ... Jaarboek. Vereniging voor de Vergelijkende Studie van het Recht van Belgie en Nederland [*A publication*]
**JbVH**......... Jahrbuch fuer Volkskunde der Heimatvertriebenen [*A publication*]
**Jb Volksk Kulturgesch** ... Jahrbuch fuer Volkskunde und Kulturgeschichte [*A publication*]
**Jb Volksliedf** ... Jahrbuch fuer Volksliedforschung [*A publication*]
**Jb Vorarlberg** ... Jahrbuch des Vorarlberger Landesmuseumsvereins [*A publication*]
**Jb Wels**...... Jahrbuch des Musealvereines Wels [*A publication*]
**JbWerkKaTNed** ... Jaarboek. Werkgenootschap van Katholieke Theologen in Nederland [*Hilversum*] [*A publication*]
**Jb Wirtschaftsgesch** ... Jahrbuch fuer Wirtschaftsgeschichte [*A publication*]
**Jb Wirtsch -Gesch** ... Jahrbuch fuer Wirtschaftsgeschichte [*A publication*]
**Jb Wirtsch Osteuropas** ... Jahrbuch der Wirtschaft Osteuropas [*A publication*]
**Jb Wiss Prakt Tierzucht** ... Jahrbuch fuer Wissenschaftliche und Praktische Tierzucht [*A publication*]
**JByelS** ....... Journal of Byelorussian Studies [*A publication*]
**JBZ**........... Mid-Atlantic Journal of Business [*A publication*]
**Jb Z Mus (Mainz)** ... Jahrbuch. Roemisch-Germanisches Zentralmuseum (Mainz) [*A publication*]
**JC**.............. All Seasons Aviation Ltd. [*ICAO designator*] (FAAC)
**JC**.............. J. C. Smith Marketing Corp. [*Vancouver Stock Exchange symbol*]
**JC**.............. Jack Cover
**JC**.............. Janitor Closet (MSA)
**JC**.............. Jazykovedny Casopis [*A publication*]
**JC**.............. Jeanswear Communication (EA)
**JC**.............. Jersey Central Railroad
**JC**.............. Jesus Christ
**JC**.............. Jesus College [*Oxford or Cambridge*] [*England*] (DAS)
**JC**.............. Jewelcor, Inc. [*NYSE symbol*] (SPSG)
**JC**.............. Jewish Chronicle [*London*] [*A publication*]
**JC**.............. [*The*] Jewish Community: Its History and Structure to the American Revolution [*A publication*] (BJA)
**JC**.............. Jimmy Carter [*James Earl Carter, Jr.*] [*US president, 1924-*]
**JC**.............. Job Corps [*Department of Labor*]
**JC**.............. Jockey Club [*Later, TJC*] (EA)
**JC**.............. Johnson's New York Cases [*or Reports*] [*A publication*] (DLA)
**JC**.............. Joint Compound [*Plumbing*]
**J & C**.......... Jones and Cary's Irish Exchequer Reports [*1838-39*] [*A publication*] (DLA)
**JC**.............. Joule Cycle [*Physics*]
**JC**.............. Journal of Chromatography [*A publication*]
**JC**.............. Journal of Church Music [*A publication*]
**JC**.............. Journal Code [*Online database field identifier*]
**JC**.............. Journal of Communication [*A publication*]
**JC**.............. JOVIAL Compiler [*Data processing*]
**JC**.............. Judicial Committee [*Australia*]
**Jc**.............. Juglans cinerea [*Butternut tree*]
**jc**............... Juice
**JC**.............. Julius Caesar [*Shakespearean work*]
**JC**.............. [*Gaius*] Julius Caesar [*Roman soldier, statesman, and writer, 100-44BC*]
**JC**.............. Jump on Condition [*Data processing*] (BUR)
**JC**.............. Junction (ADA)
**JC**.............. Junior College
**JC**.............. Jurisconsult
**JC**.............. Justice Clerk
**JC**.............. Justiciary Cases [*Scotland*] [*A publication*] (DLA)
**JC**.............. Juvenile Court
**JCA**............ Jamming Control Authority (NATG)
**JCA**............ Javelin Class Association (EA)
**JCA**............ Jewelry Crafts Association [*Later, JMA*]
**JCA**............ Jewish Ceremonial Art [*A publication*] (BJA)
**JCA**............ Jewish Colonization Association [*London, England*]
**JCA**............ Jewish Communal Appeal [*Australia*]
**JCA**............ Joint Church Aid [*Biafra relief program in late 1960's*] [*Defunct*]
**JCA**............ Joint Commission on Accreditation of Universities [*Military*]
**JCA**............ Joint Communication Activity
**JCA**............ Joint Communications Agency [*Military*]
**JCA**............ Joint Construction Agency
**JCA**............ Joint Cultural Appeal (EA)
**JCA**............ Joint Custody Association (EA)
**JCA**............ Journal of Color and Appearance [*A publication*]
**JCA**............ Journal of Consumer Affairs [*A publication*]
**JCA**............ Junior Catering Accountant [*British military*] (DMA)
**J-14/CA**..... Jet 14 Class Association (EA)
**JCAB**......... Japan Civil Aviation Bureau (MCD)
**JCAC**......... Joint Civil Affairs Committee
**JCACDM**.. Journal of Carbohydrate Chemistry [*A publication*]
**JCADIS**..... Joint Continental Aerospace Defense Integration Staff [*Military*] (AABC)
**JCAE**......... Joint Committee on Atomic Energy [*of the US Congress*] [*Terminated*]
**JCAEC**...... Joint Congressional Atomic Energy Commission (MUGU)
**JCAH**......... Joint Commission on Accreditation of Hospitals [*Later, JCAHO*] (EA)
**JCAHO**..... Joint Commission on Accreditation of Healthcare Organizations [*An association*]
**JCAHPO**... Joint Commission on Allied Health Personnel in Ophthalmology (EA)

**JCAI**.......... Joint Council of Allergy and Immunology (EA)
**J Caisses Epargne**... Journal des Caisses d'Epargne [*A publication*]
**J Calif Dent Assoc**... Journal. California Dental Association [*A publication*]
**J Calif Hortic Soc**... Journal. California Horticultural Society [*A publication*]
**J Calif State Dent Assoc**... Journal. California State Dental Association [*A publication*]
**JCAM**........ Joint Commission on Atomic Masses
**J Camborne Sch Mines**... Journal. Camborne School of Mines [*A publication*]
**J Camera Club (London)**... Journal. Camera Club (London) [*A publication*]
**J Canad Dent A**... Journal. Canadian Dental Association [*A publication*]
**J Can Art Hist**... Journal of Canadian Art History [*A publication*]
**J Can Assoc Radiol**... Journal. Canadian Association of Radiologists [*A publication*]
**J Can Ath Ther Assoc**... Journal. Canadian Athletic Therapists Association [*A publication*]
**J Can B**...... Juris Canna Baccalaureus [*Bachelor of Canon Law*]
**J Can Ba**.... Journal. Canadian Bar Association [*A publication*]
**J Can B Ass'n**... Journal. Canadian Bar Association [*A publication*]
**J Can Biochim**... Journal Canadien de Biochimie [*A publication*]
**J Can Bot**... Journal Canadien de Botanique [*A publication*]
**J Can Ceram Soc**... Journal. Canadian Ceramic Society [*A publication*]
**J Cancer Cent Niigata Hosp**... Journal. Cancer Center. Niigata Hospital [*Japan*] [*A publication*]
**J Cancer Res**... Journal of Cancer Research [*A publication*]
**J Cancer Res Clin Oncol**... Journal of Cancer Research and Clinical Oncology [*A publication*]
**J Cancer Res Comm Univ Sydney**... Journal. Cancer Research Committee. University of Sydney [*A publication*]
**J Can Ch H**... Journal. Canadian Church Historical Society [*A publication*]
**J Can Chir**... Journal Canadien de Chirurgie [*A publication*]
**J Can Chiro Assoc**... Journal. Canadian Chiropractic Association [*A publication*]
**J Can D**...... Juris Canna Doctor [*Doctor of Canon Law*]
**J Can Dent Assoc**... Journal. Canadian Dental Association [*A publication*]
**J Can Diet Ass**... Journal. Canadian Dietetic Association [*A publication*]
**J Can Diet Assoc**... Journal. Canadian Dietetic Association [*A publication*]
**J Can Fic**.... Journal of Canadian Fiction [*A publication*]
**J Can Fict**.. Journal of Canadian Fiction [*A publication*]
**J Can Genet Cytol**... Journal Canadien de Genetique et de Cytologie [*A publication*]
**J Can Inst Food Sci Technol**... Journal. Canadian Institute of Food Science and Technology [*A publication*]
**J Can M**..... Juris Canna Magister [*Master of Canon Law*]
**J Can Microbiol**... Journal Canadien de Microbiologie [*A publication*]
**J Can Min Inst**... Journal. Canadian Mining Institute [*A publication*]
**J Can Ophtalmol**... Journal Canadien d'Ophtalmologie [*A publication*]
**J Can Otolaryngol**... Journal Canadien d'Otolaryngologie [*A publication*]
**J Can Petrol Technol**... Journal of Canadian Petroleum Technology [*A publication*]
**J Can Pet T**... Journal of Canadian Petroleum Technology [*A publication*]
**J Can Pet Technol**... Journal of Canadian Petroleum Technology [*A publication*]
**J Can Pharm Hosp**... Journal Canadien de la Pharmacie Hospitaliere [*A publication*]
**J Can Physiol Pharmacol**... Journal Canadien de Physiologie et Pharmacologie [*A publication*]
**J Can Rech For**... Journal Canadien de la Recherche Forestiere [*A publication*]
**JCanS**........ Journal of Canadian Studies [*A publication*]
**J Can Sci Appl Sport**... Journal Canadien des Sciences Appliquees au Sport [*A publication*]
**J Can Sci Neurol**... Journal Canadien des Sciences Neurologiques [*A publication*]
**J Can Sci Terre**... Journal Canadien des Sciences de la Terre [*A publication*]
**J Can Soc Forensic Sci**... Journal. Canadian Society of Forensic Science [*A publication*]
**J Can Stud**... Journal of Canadian Studies [*A publication*]
**J Can Studies**... Journal of Canadian Studies [*A publication*]
**J Cant Bot Soc**... Journal. Canterbury Botanical Society [*A publication*]
**J Can Zool**... Journal Canadien de Zoologie [*A publication*]
**JCAP**......... Joint Conventional Ammunition Program [*Army*]
**JCAP-CG**.. Joint Conventional Ammunition Program Coordinating Group [*Army*]
**J Cap Inst Med**... Journal. Capital Institute of Medicine [*A publication*]
**J Cap Mgmt**... Journal of Capacity Management [*A publication*]
**JCAR**......... Joint Commission on Applied Radioactivity
**JCARA**...... Journal. Canadian Association of Radiologists [*A publication*]
**J Carb-Nucl**... Journal of Carbohydrates-Nucleosides-Nucleotides [*A publication*]
**J Carbohyd-Nucl-Nucl**... Journal of Carbohydrates-Nucleosides-Nucleotides [*A publication*]
**J Carbohydr Chem**... Journal of Carbohydrate Chemistry [*A publication*]
**J Carbohydr-Nucleosides-Nucleotides**... Journal of Carbohydrates-Nucleosides-Nucleotides [*A publication*]
**JCARD**...... Joint Committee on Agricultural Research and Development [*Agency for International Development*]
**J Cardiac Rehab**... Journal of Cardiac Rehabilitation [*A publication*]
**J Cardiogr**... Journal of Cardiography [*A publication*]
**J Cardiovasc Med**... Journal of Cardiovascular Medicine [*A publication*]
**J Cardiovasc Pharmacol**... Journal of Cardiovascular Pharmacology [*A publication*]
**J Cardiovasc Surg**... Journal of Cardiovascular Surgery [*A publication*]
**J Cardiovasc Surg (Torino)**... Journal of Cardiovascular Surgery (Torino) [*A publication*]
**J Cardiovasc Ultrason**... Journal of Cardiovascular Ultrasonography [*A publication*]
**J Cardiovas Surg**... Journal of Cardiovascular Surgery [*A publication*]
**J Card Surg**... Journal of Cardiovascular Surgery [*A publication*]
**J Car Ed**..... Journal of Career Education [*A publication*]
**J Catal**....... Journal of Catalysis [*A publication*]
**J Catalysis**... Journal of Catalysis [*A publication*]
**J Cataract Refract Surg**... Journal of Cataract and Refractive Surgery [*A publication*]
**J-CATCH**... Joint Countering Attack Helicopter Exercises (RDA)
**J Cat & Class**... Journal of Cataloging and Classification [*A publication*]
**JCATD**...... Journal of Computer Assisted Tomography [*A publication*]
**J Cathol Med Coll**... Journal. Catholic Medical College [*A publication*]
**J Cathol Nurses Guild Engl Wales**... Journal. Catholic Nurses Guild of England and Wales [*A publication*]
**JCAUD8**.... Journal of Cardiovascular Ultrasonography [*A publication*]
**JCA-USA**.. Joint Church Aid - United States of America [*See also JCA*] [*Defunct*] (EA)
**J CAYC**..... Journal. Canadian Association for Young Children [*A publication*]
**JCB**........... J. C. Bamford Excavators [*British*]
**JCB**........... Japan Convention Bureau (EA)
**JCB**........... Japan Credit Bureau
**JCB**........... Job Control Block [*Data processing*] (BUR)
**JCB**........... Joint Communications Board
**JCB**........... Joint Computer Bureau [*Office of Population Census and Surveys*] [*British*]
**JCB**........... Joint Consultative Board [*NATO*] (NATG)
**JCB**........... Journal of Commercial Bank Lending [*A publication*]
**JCB**........... Journal of Creative Behavior [*A publication*]
**JCB**........... Juris Canonici Baccalaureus [*Bachelor of Canon Law*]
**JCB**........... Juris Civilis Baccalaureus [*Bachelor of Civil Law*]
**JCB**........... Jurisprudence Commerciale de Bruxelles [*A publication*]
**JCB**........... Kansas Judicial Council. Bulletin [*A publication*]
**JCBA**......... Jewish Conciliation Board of America (EA)
**JCBADL**.... Biomedical Applications [*A publication*]
**JCBC**......... Joint Committee on Building Codes [*Later, Model Code Standardization Council*] (EA)
**JCBC**......... Jute Carpet Backing Council (EA)
**JCBF**.......... Journal of Cerebral Blood Flow and Metabolism [*A publication*]
**JCBMDN**... Journal of Cerebral Blood Flow and Metabolism [*A publication*]
**JC Br**.......... Jurisprudence Commerciale de Bruxelles [*Belgium*] [*A publication*] (DLA)
**JCBS**.......... Jacobson Stores, Inc. [*NASDAQ symbol*] (NQ)
**JCBSD7**..... Journal of Cellular Biochemistry. Supplement [*A publication*]
**JCBSF**....... Joint Commission for Black Sea Fisheries
**JCC**........... Jamestown Community College [*New York*]
**JCC**........... Janney Cylinder Company
**JCC**........... Japanese Chamber of Commerce of New York [*Later, JCCINY*] (EA)
**JCC**........... Jarvis Christian College [*Hawkins, TX*]
**JCC**........... Jarvis Christian College, Hawkins, TX [*OCLC symbol*] (OCLC)
**JCC**........... Jesus College, Cambridge [*England*] (ROG)
**JCC**........... Jet Circulation Control
**JCC**........... Jewish Chaplains Council (EA)
**JCC**........... Jewish Community Center
**JCC**........... Jharkhand Coordination Committee [*Jharkhand Samanvaya Samiti*] [*India*] [*Political party*]
**JCC**........... Job Control Card (MCD)
**JCC**........... Job Corps Camp [*Department of Labor*]
**JCC**........... Joint Communications Center (MCD)
**JCC**........... Joint Computer Conference
**JCC**........... Joint Consultative Committee [*of the National Joint Advisory Council*] [*British*] [*World War II*]
**JCC**........... Joint Control Center (MCD)
**JCC**........... Joint Coordination Center (NVT)
**JCC**........... Journal of Carbohydrate Chemistry [*A publication*]
**JCC**........... Journal of Christian Camping [*A publication*]
**JCC**........... Journal of Computational Chemistry [*A publication*]
**JCC**........... Jowett Car Club (EA)
**JC of C**....... Junior Chamber of Commerce
**JCC**........... Junior Chamber of Commerce
**JCC**........... Junior Command Course [*British military*] (DMA)
**JCC**........... San Francisco [*California*] China Bas [*Airport symbol*] (OAG)
**JCCA**......... Japanese Canadian Citizens' Association
**JCCA**......... Japanese Chin Club of America (EA)
**JCCA**......... Joint CONEX [*Container Express*] Control Agency
**JCCANA**... Jewish Community Centers Association of North America (EA)
**JCCBD**...... Journal of Clinical Chemistry and Clinical Biochemistry [*A publication*]
**JCCC**......... Japanese Canadian Citizens' Council
**JCCC**......... Joint Committee on Contemporary China (EA)
**JCCC**......... Joint COMSEC Coordination Center (MCD)

**JCCD**......... Japanese Canadian Committee for Democracy
**JCCDG**...... Joint Command and Control Development Group [*DoD*]
**JCCEP**....... Joint Crisis Communications Exercise Program (MCD)
**JCCFC**....... June Carter Cash Fan Club (EA)
**JCCFE**....... Joint Coordination Center, Far East [*Military*] (CINC)
**JCC-FPM** ... Joint Coordinating Committee on Fundamental Properties of Matter [*US Department of Energy and USSR State Committee on Peaceful Uses of Atomic Energy*]
**JCCIUK** .... Japanese Chamber of Commerce and Industry in the United Kingdom (DS)
**JCCL**.......... Japanese Canadian Citizens' League
**JCCLE**........ Joint Committee on Continuing Legal Education [*Later, ALI-ABA Committee on Continuing Professional Education*] (EA)
**JCCMB**..... Journal of Coordination Chemistry [*A publication*]
**JCCO**......... Joint Container Control Office (MCD)
**JCCOMNET** ... Joint Coordination Center Communications Network
**JCCP**......... Journal of Cross-Cultural Psychology [*A publication*]
**JCCRG**...... Joint Command and Control Requirements Group [*Joint Chiefs of Staff*] [*DoD*]
**JCCS**.......... Jewish Cultural Clubs and Societies (EA)
**JCCS**.......... Journal. Canadian Ceramic Society [*A publication*]
**JCCSA**....... Joint Communications Contingency Station Activity (MCD)
**JCCSA**....... Journal. Canadian Ceramic Society [*A publication*]
**JCCSC**....... Joint Command and Control Standards Committee (AFM)
**JCCSMAS** ... Joint Commission on Competitive Safeguards and the Medical Aspects of Sports [*Later, JCSMS*] (EA)
**JCCTC**....... Joint Customs Consultative Technical Committee [*British*] (DCTA)
**JCD**............ John Chard Decoration [*British military*] (DMA)
**JCD**............ Journal of Community Development [*A publication*]
**JCD**............ Junior College District
**JCD**............ Juris Canonici Doctor [*Doctor of Canon Law*]
**JCD**............ Juris Civilis Doctor [*Doctor of Civil Law*]
**JCDA**......... Junior Catholic Daughters of the Americas [*Defunct*] (EA)
**JCDAA**...... Journal. Canadian Dental Association [*A publication*]
**JCDEA**...... Journal. California State Dental Association [*A publication*]
**JCDIA**...... Journal of Communication Disorders [*A publication*]
**JCDSG**...... Joint Civil Defense Support Group
**JCDSIPS**... Joint Continental Defense Systems Integration Planning Staff [*Air Force*]
**JCDTA**...... Joint Commission on Dance and Theatre Accreditation (EA)
**JCDTBI**..... Journal. Chemical Society. Dalton Transactions [*A publication*]
**JCDVA**...... Journal of Child Development [*A publication*]
**JCE**............ Joint Cadet Executive [*British military*] (DMA)
**jce**............... Jouissance [*Payable Interest*] [*French*] [*Business term*]
**JCE**............ Journal of Christian Education [*A publication*]
**JCEA**......... Joint Committee for European Affairs (EA)
**JCEA**......... Journal of Central European Affairs [*A publication*]
**JCEAG**...... Joint Civilian Employee Advisory Group [*Military*] (CINC)
**JCEB**......... Joint Council on Educational Broadcasting [*Later, JCET*] (EA)
**JCEBD**....... Journal of Cellular Biochemistry [*A publication*]
**JCEC**......... Joint Chapters - Educational Council
**JCEC**......... Joint Communications-Electronics Committee [*Military*]
**JCECPAC** ... Joint Communications-Electronics Committee, Pacific [*Military*] (CINC)
**JC & ED**.... Journal of Chemical and Engineering Data [*A publication*]
**JCEE**......... Joint Council on Economic Education (EA)
**JCEG**......... Joint Communications-Electronics Group [*Military*]
**JCEG**......... Joint Concepts and Evaluation Group [*Military*] (CINC)
**JCEGP**...... Joint Communications-Electronics Group [*Military*]
**J Cell Biochem** ... Journal of Cellular Biochemistry [*A publication*]
**J Cell Biochem Suppl** ... Journal of Cellular Biochemistry. Supplement [*A publication*]
**J Cell Biol**.. Journal of Cell Biology [*A publication*]
**J Cell Comp Physiol** ... Journal of Cellular and Comparative Physiology [*Later, Journal of Cellular Physiology*] [*A publication*]
**J Cell Phys** ... Journal of Cellular Physiology [*A publication*]
**J Cell Physiol** ... Journal of Cellular Physiology [*A publication*]
**J Cell Physiol Suppl** ... Journal of Cellular Physiology. Supplement [*A publication*]
**J Cell Plast** ... Journal of Cellular Plastics [*A publication*]
**J Cell Sci**.... Journal of Cell Science [*A publication*]
**J Cell Sci Suppl** ... Journal of Cell Science. Supplement [*A publication*]
**J Cellular Plastics** ... Journal of Cellular Plastics [*A publication*]
**JCeltS**........ Journal of Celtic Studies [*A publication*]
**JCEM**........ Joint Center for Energy Management [*Research center*] (RCD)
**JCEM**........ Journal of Clinical Endocrinology and Metabolism [*A publication*]
**JCEM**........ Junior Control Electrical Mechanic [*British military*] (DMA)
**JCEN**......... Journal of Continuing Education in Nursing [*A publication*]
**JCEND**...... Journal of Clinical Engineering [*A publication*]
**JCENS**...... Joint Communications-Electronics Nomenclature System [*Military*]
**J Cent Agr Exp Sta** ... Journal. Central Agricultural Experiment Station [*A publication*]
**J Cent Agric Exp Stn** ... Journal. Central Agricultural Experiment Station [*A publication*]
**J Cent Bur Anim Husb Dairy India** ... Journal. Central Bureau for Animal Husbandry and Dairying in India [*A publication*]
**J Cent Eur Aff** ... Journal of Central European Affairs [*A publication*]
**J Cent Eur Affairs** ... Journal of Central European Affairs [*A publication*]
**JCEOI**....... Joint Communications-Electronics Operating Instructions [*Military*] (CET)
**JCEPC**....... Joint United States/Canada Civil Emergency Planning Committee
**J Ceram Soc Jpn** ... Journal. Ceramic Society of Japan [*A publication*]
**J Cereal Sci** ... Journal of Cereal Science [*A publication*]
**J Cereb Blood Flow Metab** ... Journal of Cerebral Blood Flow and Metabolism [*A publication*]
**J Cer Soc Jap** ... Journal. Ceramic Society of Japan [*A publication*]
**JCET**......... Joint Council on Educational Telecommunications [*Defunct*] (EA)
**JCEW**........ Joint Communications Electronic Warfare Simulation
**JCEWG**..... Joint Communications and Electronics Working Group [*NATO*] (NATG)
**JCEWS**...... Joint Command, Control, and Electronic Warfare School
**J Ceylon Br Brit Med Ass** ... Journal. Ceylon Branch. British Medical Association [*A publication*]
**J of Ceylon L** ... Journal of Ceylon Law [*Colombo, Ceylon*] [*A publication*] (DLA)
**J Ceylon Law** ... Journal of Ceylon Law [*A publication*] (ILCA)
**JCF**............ Journal of Canadian Fiction [*A publication*]
**JCFC**......... Jesse Couch Fan Club (EA)
**JCFC**......... John Conlee Fan Club (EA)
**JCFl**........... Jurisprudence Commerciale des Flandres [*A publication*]
**JCFR**......... Junior College of Flat River [*Missouri*]
**JCFRB**....... Journal of Coffee Research [*A publication*]
**JCFS**.......... Jackson County Federal S & L Association [*NASDAQ symbol*] (NQ)
**JCFS**.......... Journal of Comparative Family Studies [*A publication*]
**JCFSBFC**.. Jerry Campbell and Five Star Band Fan Club (EA)
**JCFSO**....... Joint Council of Fire Service Organizations (EA)
**JCG**........... Joint Coordinating Group [*Military*] (AFIT)
**JCG**........... Journal of Commerce. European Edition [*A publication*]
**JCGRO**...... Joint Central Graves Registration Office [*Military*] (CINC)
**JCGS**......... Joint Center for Graduate Study [*Research center*] (RCD)
**J Ch**........... Johnson's New York Chancery Reports [*A publication*] (DLA)
**JCHA**........ Joint Commission on Hospital Accreditation
**J Changchun Geol Inst** ... Journal. Changchun Geological Institute [*A publication*]
**J Charles H. Tweed Int Found** ... Journal. Charles H. Tweed International Foundation [*A publication*]
**J Chart Inst Bld Serv** ... Journal. Chartered Institution of Building Services [*A publication*]
**J Chart Inst Build Serv** ... Journal. Chartered Institution of Building Services [*England*] [*A publication*]
**J Chart Inst Transp** ... Journal. Chartered Institute of Transport [*A publication*]
**JCHAS**...... Journal. Cork Historical and Archaeological Society [*A publication*]
**J Chem An** ... Japan Chemical Annual [*A publication*]
**J Chem Doc** ... Journal of Chemical Documentation [*A publication*]
**J Chem Docum** ... Journal of Chemical Documentation [*A publication*]
**J Chem Ecol** ... Journal of Chemical Ecology [*A publication*]
**J Chem Ed** ... Journal of Chemical Education [*A publication*]
**J Chem Educ** ... Journal of Chemical Education [*A publication*]
**J Chem En D** ... Journal of Chemical and Engineering Data [*A publication*]
**J Chem Eng Data** ... Journal of Chemical and Engineering Data [*A publication*]
**J Chem Eng Educ** ... Journal of Chemical Engineering Education [*A publication*]
**J Chem Eng Jap** ... Journal of Chemical Engineering of Japan [*A publication*]
**J Chem Eng Jpn** ... Journal of Chemical Engineering of Japan [*A publication*]
**J Chem Engng Data** ... Journal of Chemical and Engineering Data [*A publication*]
**J Chem Engng Japan** ... Journal of Chemical Engineering of Japan [*A publication*]
**J Chem Ind Eng** ... Journal of Chemical Industry and Engineering [*A publication*]
**J Chem Inf** ... Journal of Chemical Information and Computer Sciences [*A publication*]
**J Chem Inf Comp Sci** ... Journal of Chemical Information and Computer Sciences [*A publication*]
**J Chem Inf and Comput Sci** ... Journal of Chemical Information and Computer Sciences [*A publication*]
**J Chem Inf Comput Sci** ... Journal of Chemical Information and Computer Sciences [*A publication*]
**J Chem Metall Min Soc S Afr** ... Journal. Chemical, Metallurgical, and Mining Society of South Africa [*A publication*]
**J Chem Metall Soc S Afr** ... Journal. Chemical and Metallurgical Society of South Africa [*A publication*]
**J Chem Neuroanat** ... Journal of Chemical Neuroanatomy [*A publication*]
**J Chemother** ... Journal of Chemotherapy [*A publication*]
**J Chemother Adv Ther** ... Journal of Chemotherapy and Advanced Therapeutics [*A publication*]
**J Chem PET** ... Plant Engineering and Technology. PET Japan. Chemical Week Supplement [*A publication*]
**J Chem Phys** ... Journal of Chemical Physics [*A publication*]
**J Chem Phys** ... Journal fuer Chemie und Physik [*A publication*]
**J Chem Physics** ... Journal of Chemical Physics [*A publication*]
**J Chem Res M** ... Journal of Chemical Research. Part M [*A publication*]

**J Chem Res Part S** ... Journal of Chemical Research. Part S (Synopses) [*A publication*]
**J Chem Res S** ... Journal of Chemical Research. Part S [*A publication*]
**J Chem Res Synop** ... Journal of Chemical Research. Synopses [*England*] [*A publication*]
**J Chem Rev** ... Japan Chemical Review. Japan Chemical Week Supplement [*A publication*]
**J Chem S** ... Japan Chemical Week. Supplement. Where Is Great Change in Chemical Industry's Scope Leading? [*A publication*]
**J Chem S Ch** ... Journal. Chemical Society. Chemical Communications [*A publication*]
**J Chem S Da** ... Journal. Chemical Society. Dalton Transactions [*A publication*]
**J Chem S F I** ... Journal. Chemical Society. Faraday Transactions. I [*A publication*]
**J Chem S F II** ... Journal. Chemical Society. Faraday Transactions. II [*A publication*]
**J Chem Soc** ... Journal. Chemical Society [*A publication*]
**J Chem Soc Abstr** ... Journal. Chemical Society. Abstracts [*A publication*]
**J Chem Soc Chem Commun** ... Journal. Chemical Society. Chemical Communications [*A publication*]
**J Chem Soc Dalton Trans** ... Journal. Chemical Society. Dalton Transactions [*A publication*]
**J Chem Soc D Chem Commun** ... Journal. Chemical Society. D. Chemical Communications [*A publication*]
**J Chem Soc Faraday Trans I** ... Journal. Chemical Society. Faraday Transactions. I [*A publication*]
**J Chem Soc Faraday Trans II** ... Journal. Chemical Society. Faraday Transactions. II [*A publication*]
**J Chem Soc Jap Ind Chem Sect** ... Journal. Chemical Society of Japan. Industrial Chemistry Section [*A publication*]
**J Chem Soc Jpn Chem Ind Chem** ... Journal. Chemical Society of Japan. Chemistry and Industrial Chemistry [*A publication*]
**J Chem Soc Jpn Pure Chem Sect** ... Journal. Chemical Society of Japan. Pure Chemistry Section [*A publication*]
**J Chem Soc (London)** ... Journal. Chemical Society (London) [*A publication*]
**J Chem Soc (London) A Inorg Phys Theor** ... Journal. Chemical Society (London). Section A. Inorganic, Physical, Theoretical [*A publication*]
**J Chem Soc (London) B Phys Org** ... Journal. Chemical Society (London). Section B. Physical, Organic [*A publication*]
**J Chem Soc (London) Chem Commun** ... Journal. Chemical Society (London). Section D. Chemical Communications [*A publication*]
**J Chem Soc (London) C Org** ... Journal. Chemical Society (London). Section C. Organic Chemistry [*A publication*]
**J Chem Soc (London) Dalton Trans** ... Journal. Chemical Society (London). Dalton Transactions [*A publication*]
**J Chem Soc (London) D Chem Commun** ... Journal. Chemical Society (London). Section D. Chemical Communications [*A publication*]
**J Chem Soc (London) Faraday Trans I** ... Journal. Chemical Society (London). Faraday Transactions. I [*A publication*]
**J Chem Soc (London) Faraday Trans II** ... Journal. Chemical Society (London). Faraday Transactions. II [*A publication*]
**J Chem Soc (London) Perkin Trans I** ... Journal. Chemical Society (London). Perkin Transactions. I [*A publication*]
**J Chem Soc (London) Perkin Trans II** ... Journal. Chemical Society (London). Perkin Transactions. II [*A publication*]
**J Chem Soc Perkin Trans** ... Journal. Chemical Society. Perkin Transactions. I [*A publication*]
**J Chem Soc Perkin Trans I** ... Journal. Chemical Society. Perkin Transactions. I [*A publication*]
**J Chem Soc Perkin Trans II** ... Journal. Chemical Society. Perkin Transactions. II [*A publication*]
**J Chem S P I** ... Journal. Chemical Society. Perkin Transactions. I [*A publication*]
**J Chem S P II** ... Journal. Chemical Society. Perkin Transactions. II [*A publication*]
**J Chem Tech Biotech** ... Journal of Chemical Technology and Biotechnology [*A publication*]
**J Chem Tech Biotechnol** ... Journal of Chemical Technology and Biotechnology [*A publication*]
**J Chem Technol Biotechnol** ... Journal of Chemical Technology and Biotechnology [*A publication*]
**J Chem Technol and Biotechnol** ... Journal of Chemical Technology and Biotechnology [*A publication*]
**J Chem Technol Biotechnol A Chem Technol** ... Journal of Chemical Technology and Biotechnology. A. Chemical Technology [*A publication*]
**J Chem Technol Biotechnol B Biotechnology** ... Journal of Chemical Technology and Biotechnology. B. Biotechnology [*A publication*]
**J Chem Ther** ... Journal of Chemical Thermodynamics [*A publication*]
**J Chem Thermodyn** ... Journal of Chemical Thermodynamics [*A publication*]
**J Chem UAR** ... Journal of Chemistry. United Arab Republic [*A publication*]
**J Che Soc Sect C Org Chem** ... Journal. Chemical Society (London). Section C. Organic Chemistry [*A publication*]
**J Chester Archaeol Soc** ... Journal. Chester Archaeological Society [*A publication*]
**J Chester Arch Soc** ... Journal. Chester Archaeological Society [*A publication*]
**J Chiba Med Soc** ... Journal. Chiba Medical Society [*A publication*]
**J Child Contemp Soc** ... Journal of Children in Contemporary Society [*A publication*]
**J Child Lang** ... Journal of Child Language [*A publication*]
**J Child Language** ... Journal of Child Language [*A publication*]
**J Child Neurol** ... Journal of Child Neurology [*A publication*]
**J Child Psy** ... Journal of Child Psychology and Psychiatry [*A publication*]
**J Child Psychol** ... Journal of Child Psychology and Psychiatry [*A publication*]
**J Child Psychol & Psych** ... Journal of Child Psychology and Psychiatry and Allied Disciplines [*Later, Journal of Child Psychology and Psychiatry*] [*A publication*]
**J Child Psychol Psychiat** ... Journal of Child Psychology and Psychiatry [*A publication*]
**J Child Psychol Psychiatry** ... Journal of Child Psychology and Psychiatry and Allied Disciplines [*Later, Journal of Child Psychology and Psychiatry*] [*A publication*]
**J Child Psychol Psychiatry Allied Discipl** ... Journal of Child Psychology and Psychiatry and Allied Disciplines [*Later, Journal of Child Psychology and Psychiatry*] [*A publication*]
**J Child Psychol Psychiatry Book Suppl** ... Journal of Child Psychology and Psychiatry. Book Supplement [*A publication*]
**J Child Psychotherapy** ... Journal of Child Psychotherapy [*A publication*]
**J Child Psych & Psychiatry** ... Journal of Child Psychology and Psychiatry [*A publication*]
**J Chim Med Pharm Toxicol** ... Journal de Chimie Medicale, de Pharmacie, et de Toxicologie [*A publication*]
**J Chim Phys** ... Journal de Chimie Physique [*France*] [*A publication*]
**J Chim Phys** ... Journal de Chimie Physique et de Physico-Chimie Biologique [*A publication*]
**J Chim Phys et Phys-Chim Biol** ... Journal de Chimie Physique et de Physico-Chimie Biologique [*A publication*]
**J Chim Phys Phys-Chim Biol** ... Journal de Chimie Physique et de Physico-Chimie Biologique [*A publication*]
**J Chim Phys Rev Gen Colloides** ... Journal de Chimie Physique et Revue Generale des Colloides [*France*] [*A publication*]
**J China Coal Soc** ... Journal. China Coal Society [*People's Republic of China*] [*A publication*]
**J China Pharm Univ** ... Journal. China Pharmaceutical University [*A publication*]
**J Chin Biochem Soc** ... Journal. Chinese Biochemical Society [*A publication*]
**J Chin Chem** ... Journal. Chinese Chemical Society [*A publication*]
**J Chin Chem Soc** ... Journal. Chinese Chemical Society [*A publication*]
**J Chinese Inst Chem Engrs** ... Journal. Chinese Institute of Chemical Engineers [*A publication*]
**J Chinese Inst Engrs** ... Journal. Chinese Institute of Engineers [*Taipei*] [*A publication*]
**J Chinese Ling** ... Journal of Chinese Linguistics [*A publication*]
**J Chin Foundrymen's Assoc** ... Journal. Chinese Foundrymen's Association [*A publication*]
**J Ching Hua Univ** ... Journal. Ching Hua University [*People's Republic of China*] [*A publication*]
**J Chin Inst Eng** ... Journal. Chinese Institute of Engineers [*A publication*]
**JChinL**....... Journal of Chinese Linguistics [*A publication*]
**J Chin Lang Teach Asso** ... Journal. Chinese Language Teachers Association [*A publication*]
**J Chin Ling** ... Journal of Chinese Linguistics [*A publication*]
**JChinP**....... Journal of Chinese Philosophy [*A publication*]
**J Chin Phil** ... Journal of Chinese Philosophy [*A publication*]
**J Chin Philo** ... Journal of Chinese Philosophy [*A publication*]
**J Chin Rare Earth Soc** ... Journal. Chinese Rare Earth Society [*A publication*]
**J Chin Silicates Soc** ... Journal. Chinese Silicates Society [*A publication*]
**J Chin Soc Vet Sci** ... Journal. Chinese Society of Veterinary Science [*A publication*]
**J Chin U HK** ... Journal. Chinese University of Hong Kong [*A publication*]
**J Chin Univ Hong Kong** ... Journal. Chinese University of Hong Kong [*A publication*]
**J Chir**......... Journal de Chirurgie [*A publication*]
**J Chiro**....... Journal of Chiropractic [*A publication*]
**J Ch L**........ Journal of Child Language [*A publication*]
**JCHOD**..... Journal of Clinical Hematology and Oncology [*A publication*]
**JCHQA**..... Japan Chemical Quarterly [*A publication*]
**JChr**.......... Jewish Chronicle [*London*] [*A publication*]
**J Chr Ed**.... Journal of Christian Education [*A publication*]
**J Christ Educ** ... Journal of Christian Education [*A publication*] (APTA)
**J Christian Ed** ... Journal of Christian Education [*A publication*] (APTA)
**J Christian Educ** ... Journal of Christian Education [*A publication*] (APTA)
**J Christian Juris** ... Journal of Christian Jurisprudence [*A publication*]
**J Christ Juris** ... Journal of Christian Jurisprudence [*A publication*]
**J Christ Med Assoc India** ... Journal. Christian Medical Association of India [*A publication*]
**J Christ Nurs** ... Journal of Christian Nursing [*A publication*]
**J Christ Nurse** ... Journal of Christian Nursing [*A publication*]
**J Chromat** ... Journal of Chromatography [*A publication*]
**J Chromat Biomed Appl** ... Journal of Chromatography. Biomedical Applications [*A publication*]
**J Chromat Chromat Rev** ... Journal of Chromatography. Chromatographic Reviews [*A publication*]
**J Chromatogr** ... Journal of Chromatography [*A publication*]
**J Chromatogr Biomed Appl** ... Journal of Chromatography. Biomedical Applications [*A publication*]
**J Chromatogr Libr** ... Journal of Chromatography Library [*A publication*]
**J Chromatogr Sci** ... Journal of Chromatographic Science [*A publication*]

**J Chromatogr Suppl Vol** ... Journal of Chromatography. Supplementary Volume [*A publication*]
**J Chromat Sci** ... Journal of Chromatographic Science [*A publication*]
**J Chrom Sci** ... Journal of Chromatographic Science [*A publication*]
**J Chron Dis** ... Journal of Chronic Diseases [*A publication*]
**J Chronic Dis** ... Journal of Chronic Diseases [*A publication*]
**J Chr Philos** ... Journal of Christian Philosophy [*A publication*]
**J Ch St**....... Journal of Church and State [*A publication*]
**J Church M** ... Journal of Church Music [*A publication*]
**J Church Mus** ... Journal of Church Music [*A publication*]
**J Church S** ... Journal of Church and State [*A publication*] (DLA)
**J Church St** ... Journal of Church and State [*A publication*]
**J Church & State** ... Journal of Church and State [*A publication*]
**J Church State** ... Journal of Church and State [*A publication*]
**JCI**............ Jaycees International (EA)
**JCI**............ Job Characteristics Inventory
**JCI**............ Johnson Controls, Incorporated [*NYSE symbol*] (SPSG)
**JCI**............ Joint Communications Instruction
**JCI**............ Jute Corporation of India
**JCI**............ Olathe [*Kansas*] [*Airport symbol*] (OAG)
**JCIC**......... Joint Committee on Intersociety Coordination (EA)
**JCICS**........ Journal of Chemical Information and Computer Sciences [*A publication*]
**JCIE/USA** ... Japan Center for International Exchange (EA)
**JCIFC**........ Johnny Comfort International Fan Club (EA)
**JCIHCA**.... Joint Council to Improve Health Care of the Aged [*Defunct*] (EA)
**JCIMD**...... Journal of Clinical Immunology [*A publication*]
**J Cin BA**.... Journal. Cincinnati Bar Association [*A publication*] (DLA)
**JCIRA**....... Japanese Circulation Journal [*English edition*] [*A publication*]
**JCISD**........ Journal of Chemical Information and Computer Sciences [*A publication*]
**JCIT**.......... Joint Committee on Information Technology [*Australia*]
**J City Plann Div Am Soc Civ Eng** ... Journal. City Planning Division. American Society of Civil Engineers [*A publication*]
**J Civ D**....... Journal of Civil Defense [*A publication*]
**J Civ Eng Des** ... Journal of Civil Engineering Design [*United States*] [*A publication*]
**J Civ Eng (Taipei)** ... Journal of Civil Engineering (Taipei) [*A publication*]
**JCIWG**...... Joint Cutover Integrated Working Group [*Military*] (RDA)
**JCJC**.......... Jefferson City Junior College [*Discontinued operation, 1958*] [*Missouri*]
**JCJC**.......... Jones County Junior College [*Ellisville, MS*]
**JCJCCIFC** ... Johnny Cash and June Carter Cash International Fan Club (EA)
**JCK**............ Joint Commission on Korea
**JCK**............ Julia Creek [*Australia*] [*Airport symbol*] (OAG)
**JCL**............ Jackson County Library System, Medford, OR [*OCLC symbol*] (OCLC)
**JCL**............ Job Control Language [*High-level programming language*] [*1979*] [*Data processing*]
**JCL**............ John Crerar Library [*National Translation Center*]
**JCL**............ Johnny Come Lately [*Slang*]
**JCL**............ Journal of Chromatography Library [*Elsevier Book Series*] [*A publication*]
**JCL**............ Journal of Commonwealth Literature [*A publication*]
**JCL**............ Journal of Contract Law [*Australia*] [*A publication*]
**JCL**............ Journal of Corporation Law [*A publication*]
**JCL**............ Journal of Criminal Law [*A publication*]
**JCL**............ Junior Classical League (EA)
**JCL**............ Juris Canonici Lector [*Reader in Canon Law*]
**JCL**............ Juris Canonici Licentiatus [*Licentiate in Canon Law*]
**JCL**............ Juris Civilis Licentiatus [*Licentiate of Civil Law*]
**JCLA**......... Joint Council of Language Associations [*British*]
**JCLA**......... Journal. Canadian Linguistic Association [*Edmonton*] [*A publication*]
**JCLa**.......... Journal of Child Language [*A publication*]
**JCLA**......... Journal of Comparative Literature and Aesthetics [*A publication*]
**J Classif**..... Journal of Classification [*A publication*]
**J Clay Sci Soc Jpn** ... Journal. Clay Science Society of Japan [*A publication*]
**JCLC**......... Joint Committee [*of Congress*] on the Library of Congress
**JCLCPS**.... Journal of Criminal Law, Criminology, and Police Science [*Later, Journal of Criminal Law and Criminology*] [*A publication*]
**JCLE**......... Joint Committee on Library Education
**JCLIA**........ Jornal dos Clinicos [*A publication*]
**JCLIDR**..... Journal of Chromatography Library [*Elsevier Book Series*] [*A publication*]
**JCL & IL** ... Journal of Comparative Legislation and International Law [*A publication*]
**JCLIL**........ Journal of Comparative Legislation and International Law [*A publication*]
**J Clim and Appl Meteorol** ... Journal of Climate and Applied Meteorology [*A publication*]
**J Clim App Meteorol** ... Journal of Climate and Applied Meteorology [*A publication*]
**J Climatol** .. Journal of Climatology [*A publication*]
**J Clin Apheresis** ... Journal of Clinical Apheresis [*A publication*]
**J Clin Chem Clin Biochem** ... Journal of Clinical Chemistry and Clinical Biochemistry [*A publication*]
**J Clin Chil** ... Journal of Clinical Child Psychology [*A publication*]
**J Clin Comput** ... Journal of Clinical Computing [*A publication*]
**J Clin Dent** ... Journal of Clinical Dentistry [*A publication*]
**J Clin Dermatol** ... Journal of Clinical Dermatology [*Japan*] [*A publication*]
**J Clin Dysmorphol** ... Journal of Clinical Dysmorphology [*A publication*]
**J Clin Electron Microsc** ... Journal of Clinical Electron Microscopy [*A publication*]
**J Clin Electron Microsc Soc Jpn** ... Journal. Clinical Electron Microscopy Society of Japan [*A publication*]
**J Clin Endocr** ... Journal of Clinical Endocrinology [*A publication*]
**J Clin Endocrinol** ... Journal of Clinical Endocrinology and Metabolism [*A publication*]
**J Clin Endocrinol Metab** ... Journal of Clinical Endocrinology and Metabolism [*A publication*]
**J Clin Eng** ... Journal of Clinical Engineering [*A publication*]
**J Clin Exp Gerontol** ... Journal of Clinical and Experimental Gerontology [*A publication*]
**J Clin Exp Hypn** ... Journal of Clinical and Experimental Hypnosis [*A publication*]
**J Clin Exp Neuropsychol** ... Journal of Clinical and Experimental Neuropsychology [*A publication*]
**J Clin Exp Psychopathol Q Rev Psychiatry Neurol** ... Journal of Clinical and Experimental Psychopathology and Quarterly Review of Psychiatry and Neurology [*A publication*]
**J Clin Gastroenterol** ... Journal of Clinical Gastroenterology [*A publication*]
**J Clin Hematol Oncol** ... Journal of Clinical Hematology and Oncology [*A publication*]
**J Clin Hosp Pharm** ... Journal of Clinical and Hospital Pharmacy [*A publication*]
**J Clin Hypertens** ... Journal of Clinical Hypertension [*A publication*]
**J Clin Immunoassay** ... Journal of Clinical Immunoassay [*A publication*]
**J Clin Immunol** ... Journal of Clinical Immunology [*A publication*]
**J Clin Inv** ... Journal of Clinical Investigation [*A publication*]
**J Clin Invest** ... Journal of Clinical Investigation [*A publication*]
**J Clin Lab Autom** ... Journal of Clinical Laboratory Automation [*A publication*]
**J Clin Lab Immunol** ... Journal of Clinical and Laboratory Immunology [*A publication*]
**J Clin Med** ... Journal of Clinical Medicine [*A publication*]
**J Clin Micr** ... Journal of Clinical Microbiology [*A publication*]
**J Clin Microbiol** ... Journal of Clinical Microbiology [*A publication*]
**J Clin Monit** ... Journal of Clinical Monitoring [*A publication*]
**J Clin Neuro-Ophthalmol** ... Journal of Clinical Neuro-Ophthalmology [*A publication*]
**J Clin Neurophysiol** ... Journal of Clinical Neurophysiology [*A publication*]
**J Clin Neuropsychol** ... Journal of Clinical Neuropsychology [*A publication*]
**J Clin Nutr** ... Journal of Clinical Nutrition [*A publication*]
**J Clin Oncol** ... Journal of Clinical Oncology [*A publication*]
**J Clin Orthod** ... Journal of Clinical Orthodontics [*A publication*]
**J Clin Path** ... Journal of Clinical Pathology [*London*] [*A publication*]
**J Clin Pathol (Lond)** ... Journal of Clinical Pathology (London) [*A publication*]
**J Clin Pathol (Suppl)** ... Journal of Clinical Pathology (Supplement) [*A publication*]
**J Clin Periodontol** ... Journal of Clinical Periodontology [*A publication*]
**J Clin Phar** ... Journal of Clinical Pharmacology [*A publication*]
**J Clin Pharm** ... Journal of Clinical Pharmacy [*A publication*]
**J Clin Pharmacol** ... Journal of Clinical Pharmacology [*A publication*]
**J Clin Pharmacol** ... Journal of Clinical Pharmacology and the Journal of New Drugs [*A publication*]
**J Clin Pharmacol New Drugs** ... Journal of Clinical Pharmacology and New Drugs [*Later, Journal of Clinical Pharmacology*] [*A publication*]
**J Clin Psyc** ... Journal of Clinical Psychology [*A publication*]
**J Clin Psychiatry** ... Journal of Clinical Psychiatry [*A publication*]
**J Clin Psychol** ... Journal of Clinical Psychology [*A publication*]
**J Clin Psychopharmacol** ... Journal of Clinical Psychopharmacology [*A publication*]
**J Clin Stomatol Conf** ... Journal of Clinical Stomatology Conferences [*A publication*]
**J Clin Surg** ... Journal of Clinical Surgery [*A publication*]
**J Clin Ultrasound** ... Journal of Clinical Ultrasound [*United States*] [*A publication*]
**JCL-OMATIC** ... Job Control Language Automatic Generator [*Data processing*]
**JCLPB**....... Journal of Consulting and Clinical Psychology [*A publication*]
**JCLS**.......... Junior College Libraries Section [*Association of College and Research Libraries*]
**JCLTA**....... Journal. Chinese Language Teachers Association [*A publication*]
**JCLTB**....... Journal of Clinical Ultrasound [*A publication*]
**J Clube Mineral** ... Jornal. Clube de Mineralogia [*A publication*]
**JCM**........... Jacobina [*Brazil*] [*Airport symbol*] (OAG)
**JCM**........... Jettison Control Module
**JCM**........... Jeunesse Chretienne Malgache [*Malagasy Christian Youth*]
**JCM**........... Job Cylinder Map [*Data processing*] (IBMDP)
**JCM**........... Journal of Country Music [*A publication*]
**JCM**........... Juris Civilis Magister [*Master of Civil Law*]
**JCMA**......... Junior Clergy Missionary Association [*British*]
**JCMBS**....... Journeymen Curriers' Mutual Benefit Society [*A union*] [*British*]

**JCMC**........ Joint Crisis Management Capability [*DoD*]
**JCMC**........ Junta Civico-Militar Cubana [*An association*] (EA)
**JCMD**........ Joint Committee on Mobility for the Disabled [*British*]
**JCMEDK**.. Journal of Cardiovascular Medicine [*A publication*]
**JCMHC**..... Joint Commission on Mental Health of Children
**JCMID**...... Journal of Clinical Microbiology [*A publication*]
**JCMIH**...... Joint Commission on Mental Illness and Health [*Defunct*] (EA)
**JCMNA**..... Journal of Communication [*A publication*]
**JCMPO**..... Joint Cruise Missile Program [*or Project*] Office (MCD)
**JCMS**........ Journal of Crystal and Molecular Structure [*A publication*]
**JCMT**........ James Clerk Maxwell Telescope [*Mauna Kea, HI*] [*Operated by the Royal Observatory in Edinburgh, Scotland*]
**JCMVASA**... Journal. Central Mississippi Valley American Studies Association [*A publication*]
**JCN**........... Job Change Notice [*Form*] (AAG)
**JCN**........... Job Control Number
**JCN**........... Joint Control Number
**JCN**........... Journal of Collective Negotiations in the Public Sector [*A publication*]
**JCN**........... Jump on Condition [*Data processing*]
**JCNA**......... Jaguar Clubs of North America (EA)
**JCNEA**...... Journal of Comparative Neurology [*A publication*]
**JCNFC**...... Jimmy C. Newman Fan CLub (EA)
**JCNMT**..... Joint Committee of Nordic Marine Technology [*See also NSTM*] (EAIO)
**JCNMT**..... Joint Committee of Nordic Master Tailors (EA)
**JCNNSRC**... Joint Committee of the Nordic Natural Science Research Councils (EA)
**JCNOD**..... Journal of Clinical Neuro-Ophthalmology [*A publication*]
**JCNPS**....... Journal of Collective Negotiations in the Public Sector [*A publication*]
**JCNRD**...... Journal of Cyclic Nucleotide Research [*A publication*]
**JCO**........... Jesus College, Oxford [*England*] (ROG)
**JCO**........... Justification for Continued Operation [*Nuclear energy*] (NRCH)
**JCOA**......... Jazz Composers Orchestra Association (EA)
**J Coastal Res**... Journal of Coastal Research [*A publication*]
**J Coated Fabr**... Journal of Coated Fabrics [*A publication*]
**J Coated Fabrics**... Journal of Coated Fabrics [*A publication*]
**J Coated Fibrous Mater**... Journal of Coated Fibrous Materials [*A publication*]
**J Coatings Technol**... Journal of Coatings Technology [*A publication*]
**J Coat Technol**... Journal of Coatings Technology [*A publication*]
**JCOC**......... Joint Civilian Orientation Conference [*DoD*]
**JCOC**......... Joint Combat Operations Center [*Navy*] (NVT)
**JCOC**......... Joint Command Operations Center [*NATO*] (NATG)
**JCOCG**...... Joint Cadre Operation Control Group [*Military*]
**J Coconut Ind**... Journal of Coconut Industries [*A publication*]
**J-CODE**..... Justification Code [*NATO*]
**J Coffee Res**... Journal of Coffee Research [*A publication*]
**JCOI**.......... Journal. Cama Oriental Institute [*A publication*]
**J Co Kildare Archaeol Soc**... Journal. County Kildare Archaeological Society [*A publication*]
**J Coll Ag Tokyo**... Journal. College of Agriculture. Tokyo Imperial University [*A publication*]
**J Coll Arts Sci Chiba Univ**... Journal. College of Arts and Sciences. Chiba University [*A publication*]
**J Coll Arts Sci Chiba Univ Nat Sci**... Journal. College of Arts and Sciences. Chiba University. Natural Science [*Japan*] [*A publication*]
**J Coll Dairy Agr**... Journal. College of Dairy Agriculture [*A publication*]
**J Coll Dairy Agric**... Journal. College of Dairy Agriculture [*A publication*]
**J Coll Dairy Agric (Nopporo)**... Journal. College of Dairy Agriculture (Nopporo) [*A publication*]
**J Coll Dairy Agri (Ebetsu Japan)**... Journal. College of Dairy Agriculture (Ebetsu, Japan) [*A publication*]
**J Coll Dairy (Ebetsu Japan)**... Journal. College of Dairying (Ebetsu, Japan) [*A publication*]
**J Coll Dairy Nat Sci (Ebetsu)**... Journal. College of Dairying. Natural Science (Ebetsu) [*A publication*]
**J Coll Dairy (Nopporo)**... Journal. College of Dairying (Nopporo) [*A publication*]
**J Collect Negotiations Public Sect**... Journal of Collective Negotiations in the Public Sector [*A publication*]
**J Coll Educ Seoul Natl Univ**... Journal. College of Education. Seoul National University [*A publication*]
**J College Place**... Journal of College Placement [*A publication*]
**J College Sci Univ Riyadh**... Journal. College of Science. University of Riyadh [*A publication*]
**J Coll Eng Technol Jadavpur Univ**... Journal. College of Engineering and Technology. Jadavpur University [*A publication*]
**J Coll Gen Pract**... Journal. College of General Practitioners [*A publication*]
**J Coll Ind Technol Nihon Univ**... Journal. College of Industrial Technology. Nihon University [*Japan*] [*A publication*]
**J Coll Ind Technol Nihon Univ A**... Journal. College of Industrial Technology. Nihon University. Series A [*A publication*]
**J Coll Ind Technol Nihon Univ B**... Journal. College of Industrial Technology. Nihon University. Series B [*A publication*]
**J Coll I Sc**.. Journal of Colloid and Interface Science [*A publication*]
**J Coll Mar Sci Technol Tokai Univ**... Journal. College of Marine Science and Technology. Tokai University [*A publication*]
**J Colloid and Interface Sci**... Journal of Colloid and Interface Science [*A publication*]
**J Colloid Interface Sci**... Journal of Colloid and Interface Science [*A publication*]
**J Colloid Interface Science**... Journal of Colloid and Interface Science [*A publication*]
**J Colloid Sci**... Journal of Colloid Science [*Later, Journal of Colloid and Interface Science*] [*A publication*]
**J Coll Placement**... Journal of College Placement [*A publication*]
**J Coll Radiol Australas**... Journal. College of Radiologists of Australasia [*A publication*]
**J Coll Radiol Australasia**... Journal. College of Radiologists of Australasia [*A publication*] (APTA)
**J Coll Sci Teach**... Journal of College Science Teaching [*A publication*]
**J Coll Stud**... Journal of College Student Personnel [*A publication*]
**J Coll Student Personnel**... Journal of College Student Personnel [*A publication*]
**J Coll Stud Personnel**... Journal of College Student Personnel [*A publication*]
**J Coll Surgeons Australasia**... Journal. College of Surgeons of Australasia [*A publication*]
**J Coll and U L**... Journal of College and University Law [*A publication*]
**J Coll Univ**... Journal. College and University Personnel Association [*A publication*]
**J Coll & Univ L**... Journal of College and University Law [*A publication*]
**J Coll & Univ Personnel Assn**... Journal. College and University Personnel Association [*A publication*]
**J Col Negot**... Journal of Collective Negotiations in the Public Sector [*A publication*]
**J Colo Dent Assoc**... Journal. Colorado Dental Association [*A publication*]
**J Color**....... Journal of Color and Appearance [*A publication*]
**J Color Appearance**... Journal of Color and Appearance [*A publication*]
**J Colo-Wyo Acad Sci**... Journal. Colorado-Wyoming Academy of Science [*A publication*]
**J Col Placement**... Journal of College Placement [*A publication*]
**J Col Stud Personnel**... Journal of College Student Personnel [*A publication*]
**J Combinatorial Theory Ser A**... Journal of Combinatorial Theory. Series A [*A publication*]
**J Combinatorial Theory Ser B**... Journal of Combinatorial Theory. Series B [*A publication*]
**J Combinatorics Information Syst Sci**... Journal of Combinatorics, Information, and System Sciences [*A publication*]
**J Combin Inform System Sci**... Journal of Combinatorics, Information, and System Sciences [*Delhi*] [*A publication*]
**J Combin Theory Ser A**... Journal of Combinatorial Theory. Series A [*A publication*]
**J Combin Theory Ser B**... Journal of Combinatorial Theory. Series B [*A publication*]
**J Comb Th A**... Journal of Combinatorial Theory. Series A [*A publication*]
**J Comb Th B**... Journal of Combinatorial Theory. Series B [*A publication*]
**J Comb Theory**... Journal of Combinatorial Theory [*A publication*]
**J Comb Theory Ser A**... Journal of Combinatorial Theory. Series A [*A publication*]
**J Comb Theory Ser B**... Journal of Combinatorial Theory. Series B [*A publication*]
**J Combustion Toxicol**... Journal of Combustion Toxicology [*A publication*]
**J Combust Toxic**... Journal of Combustion Toxicology [*A publication*]
**J Combust Toxicol**... Journal of Combustion Toxicology [*A publication*]
**JComLit**..... Journal of Commonwealth Literature [*A publication*]
**J Comm**...... Journal of Communication [*A publication*]
**J Comm Bank Lending**... Journal of Commercial Bank Lending [*A publication*]
**J Comm Dis**... Journal of Communication Disorders [*A publication*]
**J Commer Bank Lending**... Journal of Commercial Bank Lending [*A publication*]
**J Commercio**... Jornal do Commercio [*A publication*]
**J Com Mkt S**... Journal of Common Market Studies [*A publication*]
**J Comm Mkt Stud**... Journal of Common Market Studies [*A publication*]
**J Comm Mt Stud**... Journal of Common Market Studies [*A publication*] (DLA)
**J Common Market Stud**... Journal of Common Market Studies [*A publication*]
**J Common Market Studies**... Journal of Common Market Studies [*A publication*]
**J Common Mark Stud**... Journal of Common Market Studies [*A publication*]
**J Common Mkt Stud**... Journal of Common Market Studies [*A publication*]
**J Commonw Comp Pol**... Journal of Commonwealth and Comparative Politics [*A publication*]
**J Commonwealth Comp Polit**... Journal of Commonwealth and Comparative Politics [*A publication*]
**J Commonwealth Lit**... Journal of Commonwealth Literature [*A publication*]
**J Comm Rural Reconstr China (US Repub China) Plant Ind Ser**... Joint Commission on Rural Reconstruction in China (United States and Republic of China). Plant Industry Series [*A publication*]
**J Commun Dis**... Journal of Communicable Diseases [*A publication*]
**J Commun Disord**... Journal of Communication Disorders [*A publication*]
**J Commun Health**... Journal of Community Health [*A publication*]
**J Communication**... Journal of Communication [*A publication*]
**J Community Action**... Journal of Community Action [*A publication*]
**J Community Educ**... Journal of Community Education [*A publication*]
**J Community Health**... Journal of Community Health [*A publication*]

**J Community Health Nurs** ... Journal of Community Health Nursing [*A publication*]
**J Community Psychol** ... Journal of Community Psychology [*A publication*]
**J Comp Adm** ... Journal of Comparative Administration [*A publication*]
**J Company Master Mar Aust** ... Company of Master Mariners of Australia. Journal [*A publication*] (APTA)
**J Comparative Econ** ... Journal of Comparative Economics [*A publication*]
**J Comp Corp L** ... Journal of Comparative Corporate Law and Securities Regulation [*A publication*] (ILCA)
**J Comp Corp L and Sec** ... Journal of Comparative Corporate Law and Securities Regulation [*A publication*]
**J Comp Corp L and Sec Reg** ... Journal of Comparative Corporate Law and Securities Regulation [*A publication*]
**J Comp Econ** ... Journal of Comparative Economics [*A publication*]
**J Comp Ethol** ... Journal of Comparative Ethology [*A publication*]
**J Comp Family Stud** ... Journal of Comparative Family Studies [*A publication*]
**J Comp Fam Stud** ... Journal of Comparative Family Studies [*A publication*]
**J Com Physl** ... Journal of Comparative and Physiological Psychology [*1947-1982*] [*A publication*]
**J Comp Leg** ... Journal. Society of Comparative Legislation [*A publication*] (DLA)
**J Comp Leg & Int Law** ... Journal of Comparative Legislation and International Law [*A publication*]
**J Comp Legis** ... Journal of Comparative Legislation and International Law [*A publication*]
**J Compliance Health Care** ... Journal of Compliance in Health Care [*A publication*]
**J Comp Med and Vet Arch** ... Journal of Comparative Medicine and Veterinary Archives [*A publication*]
**J Comp Neur** ... Journal of Comparative Neurology [*A publication*]
**J Comp Neurol** ... Journal of Comparative Neurology [*A publication*]
**J Composite Mat** ... Journal of Composite Materials [*A publication*]
**J Compos Ma** ... Journal of Composite Materials [*A publication*]
**J Compos Mater** ... Journal of Composite Materials [*A publication*]
**J Comp Path** ... Journal of Comparative Pathology [*A publication*]
**J Comp Pathol** ... Journal of Comparative Pathology [*A publication*]
**J Comp Pathol Ther** ... Journal of Comparative Pathology and Therapeutics [*A publication*]
**J Comp Path and Therap** ... Journal of Comparative Pathology and Therapeutics [*A publication*]
**J Comp Phys** ... Journal of Comparative Physiology [*A publication*]
**J Comp Physiol** ... Journal of Comparative Physiology [*A publication*]
**J Comp Physiol A** ... Journal of Comparative Physiology. A. Sensory, Neural, and Behavioral Physiology [*A publication*]
**J Comp Physiol A Sens Neural Behav Physiol** ... Journal of Comparative Physiology. A. Sensory, Neural, and Behavioral Physiology [*A publication*]
**J Comp Physiol B** ... Journal of Comparative Physiology. B. Biochemical, Systemic, and Environmental Physiology [*A publication*]
**J Comp Physiol B Biochem Syst Environ Physiol** ... Journal of Comparative Physiology. B. Biochemical, Systemic, and Environmental Physiology [*A publication*]
**J Comp Physiol B Metab Transp Funct** ... Journal of Comparative Physiology. B. Metabolic and Transport Functions [*A publication*]
**J Comp & Physiol Psychol** ... Journal of Comparative and Physiological Psychology [*1947-1982*] [*A publication*]
**J Comp Physiol Psychol** ... Journal of Comparative and Physiological Psychology [*1947-1982*] [*A publication*]
**J Comp Psychol** ... Journal of Comparative Psychology [*A publication*]
**J Comput Appl Math** ... Journal of Computational and Applied Mathematics [*A publication*]
**J Comput Assisted Tomogr** ... Journal of Computer Assisted Tomography [*A publication*]
**J Comput Assist Tomogr** ... Journal of Computer Assisted Tomography [*A publication*]
**J Computational Phys** ... Journal of Computational Physics [*A publication*]
**J Comput Based Instr** ... Journal of Computer-Based Instruction [*A publication*]
**J Comput Chem** ... Journal of Computational Chemistry [*A publication*]
**J Comput Math and Sci Teach** ... Journal of Computers in Mathematics and Science Teaching [*A publication*]
**J Comput Ph** ... Journal of Computational Physics [*A publication*]
**J Comput Phys** ... Journal of Computational Physics [*A publication*]
**J Comput Soc India** ... Journal. Computer Society of India [*A publication*]
**J Comput Sy** ... Journal of Computer and System Sciences [*A publication*]
**J Comput System Sci** ... Journal of Computer and System Sciences [*A publication*]
**J Comput Syst Sci** ... Journal of Computer and System Sciences [*A publication*]
**J Comput and Syst Sci** ... Journal of Computer and System Sciences [*A publication*]
**J Comput Tomogr** ... Journal of Computed Tomography [*A publication*]
**J Con A**...... Journal of Consumer Affairs [*A publication*]
**J Conat Law** ... Journal of Conational Law [*A publication*] (DLA)
**J Conchol**... Journal of Conchology [*A publication*]
**J Conchyl**... Journal de Conchyliologie [*A publication*]
**J Conchyliol** ... Journal de Conchyliologie [*A publication*]
**J Conf Chem Inst Can Am Chem Soc Abstr Pap** ... Joint Conference. Chemical Institute of Canada/American Chemical Society. Abstracts of Papers [*A publication*]
**J Conf CIC/ACS Abstr Pap** ... Joint Conference. Chemical Institute of Canada/American Chemical Society. Abstracts of Papers [*A publication*]
**J Conflict Resol** ... Journal of Conflict Resolution [*A publication*]
**J Conflict Resolu** ... Journal of Conflict Resolution [*A publication*]
**J Conflict Resolution** ... Journal of Conflict Resolution [*A publication*]
**J Confl Res** ... Journal of Conflict Resolution [*A publication*]
**J Conf Res** ... Journal of Conflict Resolution [*A publication*]
**J Conf Workshop** ... Journalism Conference and Workshop [*A publication*]
**J Conn Med Chir** ... Journal des Connaissances Medico-Chirurgicales [*A publication*]
**J Conn State Dent Assoc** ... Journal. Connecticut State Dental Association [*A publication*]
**J Cons Affairs** ... Journal of Consumer Affairs [*A publication*]
**J Cons ASCE** ... Journal. Construction Division. Proceedings of the American Society of Civil Engineers [*A publication*]
**J Cons Clin** ... Journal of Consulting and Clinical Psychology [*A publication*]
**J Cons Cons Int Explor Mer** ... Journal du Conseil. Conseil International pour l'Exploration de la Mer [*A publication*]
**J Conseil**.... Journal du Conseil [*A publication*]
**J Cons Int Explor Mer** ... Journal du Conseil. Conseil International pour l'Exploration de la Mer [*A publication*]
**J Const Div Proc ASCE** ... Journal. Construction Division. Proceedings of the American Society of Civil Engineers [*A publication*]
**J Const Parl Stud** ... Journal of Constitutional and Parliamentary Studies [*A publication*]
**J Constr Div Amer Soc Civil Eng Proc** ... Journal. Construction Division. Proceedings of the American Society of Civil Engineers [*A publication*]
**J Constr Div Am Soc Civ Eng** ... Journal. Construction Division. Proceedings of the American Society of Civil Engineers [*A publication*]
**J Constr Steel Res** ... Journal of Constructional Steel Research [*A publication*]
**J Consult & Clin Psychol** ... Journal of Consulting and Clinical Psychology [*A publication*]
**J Consult Clin Psychol** ... Journal of Consulting and Clinical Psychology [*A publication*]
**J Consulting Psychol** ... Journal of Consulting Psychology [*A publication*]
**J Consult Psychol** ... Journal of Consulting Psychology [*A publication*]
**J Consum Af** ... Journal of Consumer Affairs [*A publication*]
**J Consum Aff** ... Journal of Consumer Affairs [*A publication*]
**J Consumer Aff** ... Journal of Consumer Affairs [*A publication*]
**J Consumer Affairs** ... Journal of Consumer Affairs [*A publication*]
**J Consumer Policy** ... Journal of Consumer Policy [*A publication*]
**J Consumer Prod Flamm** ... Journal of Consumer Product Flammability [*A publication*]
**J Consumer Prod Flammability** ... Journal of Consumer Product Flammability [*A publication*]
**J Consumer Res** ... Journal of Consumer Research [*A publication*]
**J Consumer Studies and Home Econ** ... Journal of Consumer Studies and Home Economics [*A publication*]
**J Consum Prod Flamm** ... Journal of Consumer Product Flammability [*A publication*]
**J Consum Prod Flammability** ... Journal of Consumer Product Flammability [*A publication*]
**J Consum Res** ... Journal of Consumer Research [*A publication*]
**J Cont Bus** ... Journal of Contemporary Business [*A publication*]
**J Cont Ed Nurs** ... Journal of Continuing Education in Nursing [*A publication*]
**J Contemp** ... Journal of Contemporary Asia [*A publication*]
**J Contemp Afr Stud** ... Journal of Contemporary African Studies [*A publication*]
**J Contemp Asia** ... Journal of Contemporary Asia [*A publication*]
**J Contemp Bus** ... Journal of Contemporary Business [*A publication*]
**J Contemp Busin** ... Journal of Contemporary Business [*A publication*]
**J Contemp Hist** ... Journal of Contemporary History [*A publication*]
**J Contemp L** ... Journal of Contemporary Law [*A publication*]
**J Contemporary Bus** ... Journal of Contemporary Business [*A publication*]
**J Contemporary Studies** ... Journal of Contemporary Studies [*A publication*]
**J Contemp RDL** ... Journal of Contemporary Roman-Dutch Law [*A publication*] (DLA)
**J Contemp Stud** ... Journal of Contemporary Studies [*A publication*]
**J Cont Hist** ... Journal of Contemporary History [*A publication*]
**J Contin Educ Nurs** ... Journal of Continuing Education in Nursing [*A publication*]
**J Contin Educ Obstet Gynecol** ... Journal of Continuing Education in Obstetrics and Gynecology [*A publication*]
**J Cont L**..... Journal of Contemporary Law [*A publication*]
**J Cont Psyt** ... Journal of Contemporary Psychotherapy [*A publication*]
**J Controlled Release** ... Journal of Controlled Release [*A publication*]
**J Cooling Tower Inst** ... Journal. Cooling Tower Institute [*A publication*]
**J Coop Educ** ... Journal of Cooperative Education [*A publication*]
**J Coord Ch** ... Journal of Coordination Chemistry [*A publication*]
**J Coord Chem** ... Journal of Coordination Chemistry [*A publication*]
**J Copr Soc'y** ... Journal. Copyright Society of the USA [*A publication*] (DLA)
**J Copyright Entertainment Sports L** ... Journal of Copyright, Entertainment, and Sports Law [*A publication*] (DLA)
**J Copyright Ent & Sports L** ... Journal of Copyright, Entertainment, and Sports Law [*A publication*] (DLA)
**J Copyright Socy USA** ... Journal. Copyright Society of the USA [*A publication*]
**JCOR**........ Jacor Communications, Inc. [*NASDAQ symbol*] (NQ)

**J Cork Hist Archaeol Soc** ... Journal. Cork Historical and Archaeological Society [*A publication*]
**J Corp L**..... Journal of Corporation Law [*A publication*]
**J Corp Law** ... Journal of Corporation Law [*A publication*]
**J Corpn L**... Journal of Corporation Law [*A publication*]
**J Corporate Taxation** ... Journal of Corporate Taxation [*A publication*]
**J Corp Tax** ... Journal of Corporate Taxation [*A publication*]
**J Corp Tax'n** ... Journal of Corporate Taxation [*A publication*] (DLA)
**J Corros Sci Soc Korea** ... Journal. Corrosion Science Society of Korea [*A publication*]
**JCOS**......... Job Corps Opportunity Specialist [*Department of Labor*]
**JCOT**......... Joint Committee on College Teaching
**J Counc Sci Ind Res (Australia)** ... Journal. Council for Scientific and Industrial Research (Australia) [*A publication*]
**J Coun Psyc** ... Journal of Counseling Psychology [*A publication*]
**J Coun Scient Ind Res (Aust)** ... Journal. Council for Scientific and Industrial Research (Australia) [*A publication*]
**J Counsel & Devt** ... Journal of Counseling and Development [*A publication*]
**J Counsel Ply** ... Journal of Counseling Psychology [*A publication*]
**J Counsel Psychol** ... Journal of Counseling Psychology [*A publication*]
**J Couns Psych** ... Journal of Counseling Psychology [*A publication*]
**J Country M** ... Journal of Country Music [*A publication*]
**JCP**........... Japan Communist Party [*Nikon Kyosanto*] [*Political party*] (PPW)
**JCP**........... Jettison Control Panel
**JCP**........... Jewish Communist Party [*Political party*] (BJA)
**JCP**........... Job Content Protection [*UAW*]
**JCP**........... Job Control Program (CMD)
**JCP**........... John Crowe Productions, Inc. [*Houston, TX*] [*Telecommunications*] (TSSD)
**JCP**........... Joint Chiefs of Staff Publications [*Military*]
**JCP**........... Joint [*Congressional*] Committee on Printing
**JCP**........... Jordanian Communist Party [*Political party*] (PD)
**JCP**........... Journal of Clinical Psychology [*A publication*]
**JCP**........... Journal of Comparative Psychology [*A publication*]
**JCP**........... Journal of Counseling Psychology [*A publication*]
**JCP**........... JOVIAL [*Joule's Own Version of the International Algorithmic Language*] Control Program [*Data processing*]
**JCP**........... Jungle Canopy Penetration
**JCP**........... Junior Collegiate Players [*Later, Associate Collegiate Players*] (EA)
**JCP**........... Jurisclasseur Periodique [*A publication*] (DLA)
**JCP**........... Justice of the Common Pleas [*Legal term*] (DLA)
**JCP**........... Penney [*J. C.*] Co., Inc. [*NYSE symbol*] (SPSG)
**JCPC**......... J. C. Penney Communications, Inc. [*J. C. Penney Co., Inc.*] [*Telecommunications service*] (TSSD)
**JCPDS**....... Joint Committee on Powder Diffraction Standards (MCD)
**JCPES**....... Joint Center for Political and Economic Studies (EA)
**JCPFD**....... Journal of Consumer Product Flammability [*A publication*]
**JCPGB**...... Journal of Cross-Cultural Psychology [*A publication*]
**JCPHA**...... Journal of Consulting Psychology [*A publication*]
**JCPOA**...... Joint Council of Post Office Associations [*South Africa*]
**JCPP**.......... Journal of Comparative and Physiological Psychology [*1947-1982*] [*A publication*]
**JCPPA**....... Journal of Comparative and Physiological Psychology [*1947-1982*] [*A publication*]
**JCPPRFNA** ... Joint Commission on Political Prisoners and Refugees in French North Africa [*World War II*]
**JCPQA**...... Journal de Chimie Physique [*A publication*]
**JCPS**.......... Joint Center for Political Studies [*Later, JCPES*] (EA)
**JCPs**.......... Journal of Clinical Psychology [*A publication*]
**JCPS**.......... Journal of Constitutional and Parliamentary Studies [*India*] [*A publication*]
**JCPSA**....... Journal of Chemical Physics [*A publication*]
**JCPSB**....... Journal of Cellular Physiology. Supplement [*A publication*]
**JCPSD**....... Journal of Community Psychology [*A publication*]
**JCPT**......... Journal of Canadian Petroleum Technology [*A publication*]
**JCPX**......... Joint Command Post Exercise [*Military*] (AABC)
**JCPYA**....... Journal of Clinical Psychology [*A publication*]
**JCQ**........... Jacqueline Gold [*Vancouver Stock Exchange symbol*]
**JCQ**........... Japan Christian Quarterly [*A publication*]
**JCQ**........... Jefferson City, MO [*Location identifier*] [*FAA*] (FAAL)
**JCQE**......... Joint Council on Quantum Electronics (MCD)
**JCR**........... Jack Criswell Resources [*Vancouver Stock Exchange symbol*]
**JCR**........... Johnson's New York Chancery Reports [*A publication*] (DLA)
**JCR**........... Joint Council for Repatriation (EA)
**JCR**........... Journal of Christian Reconstruction [*A publication*]
**JCR**........... Journal Citation Reports [*A publication*]
**JCR**........... Journal of Conflict Resolution [*A publication*]
**JCR**........... Journal of Consumer Research [*A publication*]
**JCR**........... Judicial Council Reports [*A publication*] (DLA)
**JCR**........... Junction Current Recovery [*in silicon devices*]
**JCR**........... Junior Common Room [*in British colleges and public schools*]
**JCRA**......... Jewish Committee for Relief Abroad
**J Craniofac Genet Dev Biol Suppl** ... Journal of Craniofacial Genetics and Developmental Biology. Supplement [*A publication*]
**J Craniofacial Genet Dev Biol** ... Journal of Craniofacial Genetics and Developmental Biology [*A publication*]
**J Craniofacial Genet Dev Biol Suppl** ... Journal of Craniofacial Genetics and Developmental Biology. Supplement [*A publication*]
**J Craniomandibular Pract** ... Journal of Cranio-Mandibular Practice [*A publication*]
**JCRAS**....... Journal. Ceylon Branch. Royal Asiatic Society [*A publication*]
**JCRC**......... Joint Casualty Resolution Center (MCD)
**JCRDA**...... Proceedings. Japan Conference on Radioisotopes [*A publication*]
**JCRe**.......... Judentum im Christlichen Religionsunterricht (BJA)
**J Creat Beh** ... Journal of Creative Behavior [*A publication*]
**J Creative Behavior** ... Journal of Creative Behavior [*A publication*]
**JC Rettie**.... Rettie, Crawford, and Melville's Session Cases, Fourth Series [*1873-98*] [*Scotland*] [*A publication*] (DLA)
**JCRFC**....... Jeannie C. Riley Fan Club (EA)
**J Criminal Justice** ... Journal of Criminal Justice [*A publication*]
**J Criminal Law and Criminology** ... Journal of Criminal Law and Criminology [*A publication*]
**J Crim Jus** ... Journal of Criminal Justice [*A publication*]
**J Crim Just** ... Journal of Criminal Justice [*A publication*]
**J Crim L**..... Journal of Criminal Law [*A publication*]
**J Crim L**..... Journal of Criminal Law and Criminology [*A publication*]
**J Crim Law** ... Journal of Criminal Law and Criminology [*A publication*]
**J Crim Law & Criminol** ... Journal of Criminal Law and Criminology [*A publication*]
**J Crim Law Criminol Police Sci** ... Journal of Criminal Law, Criminology, and Police Science [*Later, Journal of Criminal Law and Criminology*] [*A publication*]
**J Crim LC & PS** ... Journal of Criminal Law, Criminology, and Police Science [*Later, Journal of Criminal Law and Criminology*] [*A publication*]
**J Crim L & Crim** ... Journal of Criminal Law and Criminology [*A publication*] (DLA)
**J Crim L and Criminology** ... Journal of Criminal Law and Criminology [*A publication*]
**J Crim L (Eng)** ... Journal of Criminal Law (English) [*A publication*]
**J Crim Sci** ... Journal of Criminal Science [*A publication*] (DLA)
**J Crit Anal** ... Journal of Critical Analysis [*A publication*]
**J Croatian Studies** ... Journal of Croatian Studies [*A publication*]
**J Cross-Cul** ... Journal of Cross-Cultural Psychology [*A publication*]
**J Cross-Cult Psych** ... Journal of Cross-Cultural Psychology [*A publication*]
**J Cross-Cult Psychol** ... Journal of Cross-Cultural Psychology [*A publication*]
**JCRPCC**.... Joint Council on Research in Pastoral Care and Counseling [*Later, COMISS*] (EA)
**JCRR**......... Joint Commission on Rural Reconstruction
**J Crustacean Biol** ... Journal of Crustacean Biology [*A publication*]
**JCRWD**..... Jersey Committee of Resistance Workers and Deportees (EAIO)
**J Cryosurg** ... Journal of Cryosurgery [*A publication*]
**J Crystallogr Soc Jap** ... Journal. Crystallographic Society of Japan [*A publication*]
**J Crystallogr and Spectrosc Res** ... Journal of Crystallographic and Spectroscopal Research [*A publication*]
**J Cryst Gr** ... Journal of Crystal Growth [*A publication*]
**J Cryst Growth** ... Journal of Crystal Growth [*A publication*]
**J Cryst Mol** ... Journal of Crystal and Molecular Structure [*A publication*]
**J Cryst and Mol Struct** ... Journal of Crystal and Molecular Structure [*A publication*]
**J Cryst Mol Struct** ... Journal of Crystal and Molecular Structure [*A publication*]
**JCS**........... Jazz Centre Society [*British*]
**JCS**........... Jewish Chautauqua Society (EA)
**JCS**........... Job Control Statement [*Data processing*]
**JCS**........... Job Creation Scheme [*Department of Employment*] [*British*]
**JCS**........... Joint Chiefs of Staff [*United States*] [*Military*]
**JCS**........... Journal of Celtic Studies [*A publication*]
**JCS**........... Journal of Cereal Science [*A publication*]
**JCS**........... Journal. Chemical Society [*A publication*]
**JCS**........... Journal of Chromatographic Science [*A publication*]
**JCS**........... Journal of Church and State [*A publication*]
**JCS**........... Journal of Classical Studies [*Kyoto University*] [*A publication*]
**JCS**........... Journal of Common Market Studies [*A publication*]
**JCS**........... Journal of Croatian Studies [*A publication*]
**JCS**........... Journal of Cuneiform Studies [*A publication*]
**JCS**........... Journal of Curriculum Studies [*A publication*]
**JCS**........... Journal of Management Consulting [*A publication*]
**JCSA**......... Joseph Conrad Society of America (EA)
**JCSA**......... Journal. Catch Society of America [*A publication*]
**JCSA**......... Journal. Chemical Society. Abstracts [*A publication*]
**JCS-ACA**... Joint Chiefs of Staff Automatic Conference Arranger [*Military*] (CET)
**JCSAN**...... Joint Chiefs of Staff Alerting Network [*Military*]
**JCSAS**....... Joint Chiefs of Staff Alerting System (MCD)
**JCSCA**....... Journal of Colloid Science [*Later, Journal of Colloid and Interface Science*] [*A publication*]
**JCSCDA**.... Journal of Cereal Science [*A publication*]
**JCS Chem Comm** ... Journal. Chemical Society. Chemical Communications [*A publication*]
**JCS Dalton** ... Journal. Chemical Society. Dalton Transactions. Inorganic Chemistry [*A publication*]
**JCSE**.......... Joint Communications Support Element [*DoD*]
**JCSE**.......... Joint Communications Systems Elements (MCD)
**JCS Faraday I** ... Journal. Chemical Society. Faraday Transactions. I. Physical Chemistry [*A publication*]

**JCS Faraday II** ... Journal. Chemical Society. Faraday Transactions. II. Chemical Physics [*A publication*]
**JcSH**.......... Jihocesky Sbornik Historicky [*A publication*]
**JCSI**.......... Joint Combat Systems Integrating
**JCSIdentBad** ... Joint Chiefs of Staff Identification Badge [*Military decoration*] (AABC)
**JCSIDTN** ... Joint Chiefs of Staff Interim Data Transmission Network [*Military*] (CET)
**JCSLHG** ... Joint Center for the Study of Law and Human Genetics
**JCSM** ........ Joint Chiefs of Staff Memorandum [*Military*]
**J/CSM**....... Junior Company Sergeant-Major [*British military*] (DMA)
**JCSMS**...... Joint Commission on Sports Medicine and Science (EA)
**JCSO** ......... Joint Chiefs of Staff Organization [*Military*] (MCD)
**JCSOS**....... Joint and Combined Staff Officer School
**JCS Perkin I** ... Journal. Chemical Society. Perkin Transactions. I. Organic and Bioorganic Chemistry [*A publication*]
**JCS Perkin II** ... Journal. Chemical Society. Perkin Transactions. II. Physical Organic Chemistry [*A publication*]
**JCSPUB**.... Joint Chiefs of Staff Publications [*Military*]
**JCSRE**....... Joint Chiefs of Staff Representative, Europe [*NATO*] (NATG)
**JCSS**.......... Jesuit Center for Social Studies (EA)
**JCSS**.......... Jesus Christ Superstar [*Rock opera*]
**JCSS**.......... Journal of Computer and System Sciences [*A publication*]
**JCSSAB** .... Joint Committee of the States to Study Alcoholic Beverage Laws (EA)
**JCST**.......... Joint Combined System Test (KSC)
**JC St** .......... Journal of Caribbean Studies [*A publication*]
**JCST**.......... Journal of Chemical Society Transactions [*A publication*]
**J C St** ......... Journal of Church and State [*A publication*]
**JCSTC**....... Joint Council for Scientific and Technical Communication [*British*]
**JCSTD**....... Journal of Contemporary Studies [*A publication*]
**JCSTELECON** ... Joint Chiefs of Staff Teletypwriter Conference Network [*Military*] (MCD)
**JCT**............ Jacket (ROG)
**JCT**............ Jewett-Cameron [*Vancouver Stock Exchange symbol*]
**JCT**............ Job Control Table (CMD)
**JCT**............ Joint Committee on Taxation [*US Congress*]
**JCT**............ Jordan Cosmological Theory
**JCT**............ Journal of Common Market Studies [*A publication*]
**JCT**............ Journal of Corporate Taxation [*A publication*]
**JCT**............ Junction [*Texas*] [*Seismograph station code, US Geological Survey*] (SEIS)
**JCT**............ Junction (AFM)
**JCT**............ Junction, TX [*Location identifier*] [*FAA*] (FAAL)
**JCT**............ Jurisconsult (ROG)
**JCTED** ...... Journal of Coatings Technology [*A publication*]
**JCTI** .......... James Crowe Traders International [*Commercial firm*] [*British*]
**JCTI** .......... Jurisconsulti [*Counselors at Law*] [*Latin*] (ROG)
**JCT & M** ... Jordan, Case, Taylor & McGrath [*Advertising agency*]
**JCTN**......... Junction (FAAC)
**JCTOD**...... Journal of Combustion Toxicology [*A publication*]
**J Ctry Mus** ... Journal of Country Music [*A publication*]
**JCTTDW** .. Journal of Chemical Technology and Biotechnology. A. Chemical Technology [*A publication*]
**JCTUS**....... Jurisconsultus [*Counselor at Law*] [*Latin*] (ROG)
**JCU**............ John Carroll University [*University Heights, OH*]
**JCU**............ John Carroll University, Grasselli Library, University Heights, OH [*OCLC symbol*] (OCLC)
**JCU**............ Journal of Clinical Ultrasound [*A publication*]
**JCU J Clin Ultrasound** ... JCU. Journal of Clinical Ultrasound [*A publication*]
**JC and UL** ... Journal of College and University Law [*A publication*]
**JCULS**........ Joint Committee on the Union List of Serials
**J Cuneiform St** ... Journal of Cuneiform Studies [*A publication*]
**J Cuneiform Stud** ... Journal of Cuneiform Studies [*A publication*]
**J Cun S** ...... Journal of Cuneiform Studies [*A publication*]
**J Cun St**..... Journal of Cuneiform Studies [*A publication*]
**J Current Social Issues** ... Journal of Current Social Issues [*A publication*]
**J Curric St** ... Journal of Curriculum Studies [*A publication*]
**J Curr Laser Abstr** ... Journal of Current Laser Abstracts [*A publication*]
**J Curr Soc Issues** ... Journal of Current Social Issues [*United States*] [*A publication*]
**J Curr Stud** ... Journal of Curriculum Studies [*A publication*]
**J Cur Soc Issues** ... Journal of Current Social Issues [*A publication*]
**JCUS**......... Joint Center for Urban Studies of MIT [*Massachusetts Institute of Technology*] and Harvard University [*Research center*] (RCD)
**J Cutaneous Pathol** ... Journal of Cutaneous Pathology [*A publication*]
**J Cutan Pathol** ... Journal of Cutaneous Pathology [*A publication*]
**J Cut Path** ... Journal of Cutaneous Pathology [*A publication*]
**JCV**............ Jentech Ventures Corp. [*Vancouver Stock Exchange symbol*]
**JCV**............ Joule-Clausius Velocity [*Physics*]
**JCV**............ Jurisprudence Commerciale de Verviers [*A publication*]
**JCVS** ......... JOVIAL Compiler Validation System [*Data processing*]
**JCW**........... Japan Chemical Week [*A publication*]
**JCW**........... Jim Creek [*Washington*] [*Seismograph station code, US Geological Survey*] (SEIS)
**JCW**........... Journal of Comparative Business and Capital Market Law [*A publication*]
**JCWG**........ Joint Checklist Working Group [*Military*] (AFIT)
**JCWTS**...... Journal. Civil War Token Society [*A publication*]
**JCY**........... Johnson City, TX [*Location identifier*] [*FAA*] (FAAL)
**J Cyb**.......... Journal of Cybernetics [*A publication*]
**J Cybern** .... Journal of Cybernetics [*A publication*]
**J Cybernet** ... Journal of Cybernetics [*A publication*]
**J Cybern and Inf Sci** ... Journal of Cybernetics and Information Science [*A publication*]
**J Cybern Inf Sci** ... Journal of Cybernetics and Information Science [*A publication*]
**J Cycle Res** ... Journal of Cycle Research [*A publication*]
**J Cyclic Nucleotide Protein Phosphor Res** ... Journal of Cyclic Nucleotide and Protein Phosphorylation Research [*A publication*]
**J Cyclic Nucleotide Protein Phosphorylation Res** ... Journal of Cyclic Nucleotide and Protein Phosphorylation Research [*A publication*]
**J Cyclic Nucleotide Res** ... Journal of Cyclic Nucleotide Research [*A publication*]
**J Cycl Nucl** ... Journal of Cyclic Nucleotide Research [*A publication*]
**JD** ............. Diploma in Journalism (ADA)
**JD** ............. J-Band Detector
**JD** ............. Jet Driver (KSC)
**JD** ............. Jewish Division [*New York Public Library*] (BJA)
**JD** ............. Job Description [*Department of Labor*]
**JD** ............. Job Development (OICC)
**JD** ............. Joggle Die (MCD)
**JD** ............. Joined (AABC)
**JD** ............. Joint Determination (AFM)
**JD** ............. Joint Dictionary [*Dictionary of US Military Terms for Joint Usage*] [*A publication*] (AFM)
**JD** ............. Jordanian Dinar [*Monetary unit*] (BJA)
**JD** ............. Journal of Documentation [*A publication*]
**j/d**.............. Jours de Date [*Days after Date*] [*French*]
**Jd** ............... Jude [*New Testament book*] (BJA)
**JD** ............. Julian Date [*or Day*]
**J & D**.......... June and December [*Denotes semiannual payments of interest or dividends in these months*] [*Business term*]
**JD** ............. Junior Deacon [*Freemasonry*]
**JD** ............. Junior Dean
**JD** ............. Junior Division [*British military*] (DMA)
**JD** ............. Junta Democratica [*Democratic Junta*] [*Spain*] [*Political party*] (PPE)
**JD** ............. Juris Doctor [*A publication*]
**JD** ............. Juris Doctor [*Doctor of Jurisprudence*]
**JD** ............. Jurum Doctor [*Doctor of Laws*]
**JD** ............. Justice Department
**JD** ............. Juvenile Delinquency [*or Delinquent*]
**JD** ............. Toa Domestic Airlines [*Japan*] [*ICAO designator*] (FAAC)
**JDA** ........... Japanese Defense Agency (MCD)
**JDA** ........... Jefferson Davis Association (EA)
**JDA** ........... Joint Defense Appeal [*Defunct*] (EA)
**JDA** ........... Joint Deployment Agency [*DoD*]
**JDA** ........... Joint Development Agency [*DoD*]
**JDA** ........... Journal of Developing Areas [*A publication*]
**JDA** ........... Juvenile Delinquency Act
**JDA** ........... Recueil de Jurisprudence du Droit Administratif et du Conseil d'Etat [*A publication*]
**JDAI**.......... Jahrbuch. Deutsches Archaeologische Institut [*A publication*]
**J Dairy Res** ... Journal of Dairy Research [*A publication*]
**J Dairy Sci** ... Journal of Dairy Science [*A publication*]
**J Dalian Eng Inst** ... Journal. Dalian Engineering Institute [*A publication*]
**J Dalian Inst Technol** ... Journal. Dalian Institute of Technology [*A publication*]
**JdAM** ........ Journal d'Analyse Mathematique [*Jerusalem*] [*A publication*]
**JDASD**...... Jahrbuch. Deutsche Akademie fuer Sprache und Dichtung in Darmstadt [*A publication*]
**J Data Ed**... Journal of Data Education [*A publication*]
**J Data Manage** ... Journal of Data Management [*A publication*]
**J Data Mgt** ... Journal of Data Management [*A publication*]
**JDB**............ Jahrbuch Deutscher Bibliophilen [*A publication*]
**JDB**............ Jewish Daily Bulletin [*A publication*]
**JDBP** ......... Journal of Developmental and Behavioral Pediatrics [*A publication*]
**JDC**............ American Jewish Joint Distribution Committee (EA)
**JDC**............ Deere & Company [*Moline, IL*] [*FAA designator*] (FAAC)
**JDC**............ Japan Airlines Development Company
**JDC**............ Japan Documentation Center [*Columbia University*]
**JDC**............ Jet Deflection Control (AAG)
**JDC**............ Jeunesse Democratique Camerounaise [*Cameroonian Democratic Youth*]
**JDC**............ Jewish Documentation Centre [*See also BJVN*] (EAIO)
**JDC**............ Job Description Card
**JDC**............ Joint Deployment Community [*Military*] (INF)
**JDC**............ Joint Development Community [*DoD*]
**JDC**............ Joslin Diabetes Center (EA)
**JDC**............ Junction Diode Circuit
**J DC Dent Soc** ... Journal. District of Columbia Dental Society [*A publication*]
**JDCE**......... Jeunes Democrates Chretiens Europeens [*European Young Christian Democrats - EYCD*] (EA)
**JDCHA** ..... Journal of Dentistry for Children [*A publication*]

**JDCMC**..... Joint Department of Defense Configuration Management Committee (MCD)
**Jd Co**.......... Journal des Communautes [*A publication*]
**JDCS**......... Joint Deputy Chiefs of Staff [*Military*]
**JDD**........... Journal of Developing Areas [*A publication*]
**JDDD**........ Judicial Discipline and Disability Digest [*American Judicature Society*] [*Information service or system*] (CRD)
**JDE**............ Journal of Development Economics [*A publication*]
**J Debats**..... Journal des Debats [*A publication*]
**JDECU**...... Journal. Department of English. Calcutta University [*A publication*]
**J Dendrol**... Journal of Dendrology [*A publication*]
**JDENL**...... Joined by Enlistment [*Military*]
**J Denning LS** ... Journal. Denning Law Society [*Tanzania*] [*A publication*] (DLA)
**J Denning L Soc'y** ... Journal. Denning Law Society [*Tanzania*] [*A publication*] (DLA)
**J Dent**......... Journal of Dentistry [*A publication*]
**J Dent Assoc S Afr** ... Journal. Dental Association of South Africa [*A publication*]
**J Dent Assoc Thai** ... Journal. Dental Association of Thailand [*A publication*]
**J Dent Aux** ... Journal of the Dental Auxiliaries [*A publication*]
**J Dent Chil** ... Journal of Dentistry for Children [*A publication*]
**J Dent Child** ... Journal of Dentistry for Children [*A publication*]
**J Dent Educ** ... Journal of Dental Education [*A publication*]
**J Dent Eng** ... Journal of Dental Engineering [*A publication*]
**J Dent Guid Counc Handicap** ... Journal. Dental Guidance Council on the Handicapped [*A publication*]
**J Dent Handicap** ... Journal of Dentistry for the Handicapped [*A publication*]
**J Dent Health (Tokyo)** ... Journal of Dental Health (Tokyo) [*A publication*]
**J Dent Med** ... Journal of Dental Medicine [*A publication*]
**J Dent Pract Adm** ... Journal of Dental Practice Administration [*A publication*]
**J Dent Que** ... Journal Dentaire du Quebec [*A publication*]
**J Dent Res** ... Journal of Dental Research [*A publication*]
**J Dent Sch Natl Univ Iran** ... Journal of the Dental School. National University of Iran [*A publication*]
**J Dent Tech** ... Journal of Dental Technics [*A publication*]
**JDEP**......... Juvenile Delinquency Evaluation Project
**J Dep Agric Fish Irel** ... Journal. Department of Agriculture and Fisheries. Republic of Ireland [*A publication*]
**J Dep Agric Repub Irel** ... Journal. Department of Agriculture. Republic of Ireland [*A publication*]
**J Dep Agric S Aust** ... Journal. Department of Agriculture. South Australia [*A publication*] (APTA)
**J Dep Agric Un S Afr** ... Journal. Department of Agriculture. Union of South Africa [*A publication*]
**J Dep Agric Vict** ... Journal. Department of Agriculture. Victoria [*Australia*] [*A publication*]
**J Dep Agric W Aust** ... Journal. Department of Agriculture. Western Australia [*A publication*]
**J Dep Agric West Aust** ... Journal. Department of Agriculture. Western Australia [*A publication*]
**J Dep Geogr Natl Univ Malaysia** ... Journal. Department of Geography. National University of Malaysia [*A publication*]
**J Dept Ag Ireland** ... Journal. Irish Free State Department of Agriculture [*A publication*]
**J Dept Ag Puerto Rico** ... Journal. Department of Agriculture. Puerto Rico [*A publication*]
**J Dept Agr Fish (Dublin)** ... Journal. Department of Agriculture and Fisheries (Dublin) [*A publication*]
**J Dept Agric W Aust** ... Journal. Department of Agriculture. Western Australia [*A publication*] (APTA)
**J Dept Agr S Aust** ... Journal. Department of Agriculture. South Australia [*A publication*]
**J Dept Agr Victoria** ... Journal. Department of Agriculture. Victoria [*A publication*]
**J Dept Agr W Aust** ... Journal. Department of Agriculture. Western Australia [*A publication*]
**J Dept Ag SA** ... Journal. Department of Agriculture. South Australia [*A publication*] (APTA)
**J Dept Ag S Africa** ... Journal. Department of Agriculture. South Africa [*A publication*]
**J Dept Ag S Australia** ... Journal. Department of Agriculture. South Australia [*A publication*] (APTA)
**J Dept Ag VIC** ... Journal. Department of Agriculture. Victoria [*A publication*] (APTA)
**J Dept Ag Victoria** ... Journal. Department of Agriculture. Victoria [*A publication*]
**J Dermatol Surg** ... Journal of Dermatologic Surgery [*A publication*]
**J Dermatol Surg Oncol** ... Journal of Dermatologic Surgery and Oncology [*A publication*]
**J Dermatol (Tokyo)** ... Journal of Dermatology (Tokyo) [*A publication*]
**J Des Autom and Fault-Tolerant Comput** ... Journal of Design Automation and Fault-Tolerant Computing [*A publication*]
**J Des Autom Fault Tolerant Comput** ... Journal of Design Automation and Fault-Tolerant Computing [*A publication*]
**J Design Automat Fault-Tolerant Comput** ... Journal of Design Automation and Fault-Tolerant Computing [*A publication*]
**J Deterg Collect Chem** ... Journal of Detergents and Collective Chemistry [*A publication*]
**J Dev Areas** ... Journal of Developing Areas [*A publication*]
**J Dev Behav Pediatr** ... Journal of Developmental and Behavioral Pediatrics [*A publication*]
**J Devel Areas** ... Journal of Developing Areas [*A publication*]
**J Devel Econ** ... Journal of Development Economics [*A publication*]
**J Develop Areas** ... Journal of Developing Areas [*A publication*]
**J Developing Areas** ... Journal of Developing Areas [*A publication*]
**J Development Econ** ... Journal of Development Economics [*A publication*]
**J Development Planning** ... Journal of Development Planning [*A publication*]
**J Development Studies** ... Journal of Development Studies [*A publication*]
**J Develop Plan** ... Journal of Development Planning [*A publication*]
**J Develop Read** ... Journal of Developmental Reading [*A publication*]
**J Develop Stud** ... Journal of Development Studies [*A publication*]
**J Devel Stud** ... Journal of Development Studies [*A publication*]
**J Devon Trust Nat Conserv** ... Journal. Devon Trust for Nature Conservation [*A publication*]
**J Dev Physiol** ... Journal of Developmental Physiology [*A publication*]
**J Dev Physiol (Oxf)** ... Journal of Developmental Physiology (Oxford) [*A publication*]
**J Dev Planning** ... Journal of Development Planning [*A publication*]
**J Dev Stud** ... Journal of Development Studies [*A publication*]
**J Dev Studies** ... Journal of Development Studies [*A publication*]
**JDEWN**..... John Denver Early Warning Network (EA)
**JDF**........... Jamming Direction Finder [*Military*] (CAAL)
**JDF**........... Jewish Daily Forward [*A publication*]
**JDF**........... Journal Pratique de Droit Fiscal et Financier [*A publication*]
**JDF**........... Juiz De Fora [*Brazil*] [*Airport symbol*] (OAG)
**JDF**........... Juvenile Diabetes Foundation [*Later, JDFI*] (EA)
**JDFC**......... James Darren Fan Club (EA)
**JDFC**......... Jimmie Dale Fan Club (EA)
**JDFC**......... Joanie Dale Fan Club (EA)
**JDFC**......... Joint Danube Fishery Commission [*See also ZKRVD*] [*Zilina, Czechoslovakia*] (EAIO)
**JDFI**.......... Joslin Diabetes Foundation, Incorporated [*Later, JDC*] (EA)
**JDFI**.......... Juvenile Diabetes Foundation International (EA)
**JDFR**......... Joined From [*Military*]
**JDG**.......... Jahrbuch. Droste-Gesellschaft [*A publication*]
**JDH**.......... Jodhpur [*India*] [*Airport symbol*] (OAG)
**J Dharma**... Journal of Dharma [*A publication*]
**JDHE**........ Joint Directory of Higher Education [*A publication*]
**JDHHFC**... John Denver Heart to Heart Fan Club (EA)
**JdI**............ Jahrbuch. Deutsches Archaeologische Institut [*A publication*]
**JDI**............ JDS Investments Ltd. [*Toronto Stock Exchange symbol*]
**JDI**............ Job Description Index
**JDI**............ Joint Declaration of Interest (DS)
**J Diabetic Assoc India** ... Journal. Diabetic Association of India [*A publication*]
**JDIAD**....... Journal of Dialysis [*A publication*]
**J Dial**......... Journal of Dialysis [*A publication*]
**J Diarrhoeal Dis Res** ... Journal of Diarrhoeal Diseases Research [*A publication*]
**JDI-EH**...... Jahrbuch. Deutsches Archaeologische Institut. Ergaenzungsheft [*A publication*]
**J Diet Assoc (Victoria)** ... Journal. Dietetic Association (Victoria) [*A publication*]
**J Diet Home Econ** ... Journal of Dietetics and Home Economics [*South Africa*] [*A publication*]
**J Diff Equa** ... Journal of Differential Equations [*A publication*]
**J Differential Equations** ... Journal of Differential Equations [*A publication*]
**J Differential Geom** ... Journal of Differential Geometry [*A publication*]
**J Differential Geometry** ... Journal of Differential Geometry [*A publication*]
**J Differ Equations** ... Journal of Differential Equations [*A publication*]
**J Digital Syst** ... Journal of Digital Systems [*A publication*]
**J Digital Systems** ... Journal of Digital Systems [*A publication*]
**JDIND**....... Joined by Induction [*Military*]
**JDipMA**.... Joint Diploma in Management Accounting Services [*British*]
**J Dispersion Sci Technol** ... Journal of Dispersion Science and Technology [*A publication*]
**J Distrib**..... Journal of Distribution [*Japan*] [*A publication*]
**JDJ**........... John Donne Journal. Studies in the Age of Donne [*A publication*]
**JDK**........... Joodsch-Democratische Kiespartij [*Political party*] (BJA)
**JDL**........... Jewish Defense League (EA)
**JDL**........... Job Description Language [*Data processing*]
**JDL**........... Job Description Library
**JDL**........... Job Drawing List (MCD)
**JDL**........... Joint Directors of Laboratories [*Military*]
**JdL**........... Jornal de Letras [*A publication*]
**JDL**........... Juneau, AK [*Location identifier*] [*FAA*] (FAAL)
**JDL**........... Lynn-01, AK [*Location identifier*] [*FAA*] (FAAL)
**JDM**.......... Jahrbuch der Musikwelt [*A publication*]
**JDM**.......... Journal of Data Management [*A publication*]
**JDM**.......... Juvenile Diabetes Mellitus [*Medicine*]
**JDMC**........ James Dean Memory Club (EA)
**JDN**.......... Jordan, MT [*Location identifier*] [*FAA*] (FAAL)
**JDN**.......... Jordan Petroleum Ltd. [*Toronto Stock Exchange symbol*]
**JDN**.......... Julian Day Number
**JDNB**........ Jewish Telegraphic Agency. Daily News Bulletin [*A publication*]
**JDO**.......... Jewish Defense Organization (EA)
**JDO**.......... Job Delivery Orders (MCD)
**JDO**.......... Junior Duty Officer (MCD)

**J Doc**.......... Journal of Documentation [*A publication*]
**J Doc Reprod** ... Journal of Documentary Reproduction [*A publication*]
**J Docum**..... Journal of Documentation [*A publication*]
**J Documentation** ... Journal of Documentation [*A publication*]
**JdOI**........... Jahreshefte. Oesterreichisches Archaeologische Institut in Wien [*A publication*]
**JDOP**......... Joint Doppler Operational Project [*For tornado warning*] [*Meteorology*]
**JDOYM**.... Jewish Defense Organization Youth Movement (EA)
**JDP**............ Covington/Cincinnati, OH [*Location identifier*] [*FAA*] (FAAL)
**JDP**............ Job Development Program
**JDP**............ Journal of Development Studies [*A publication*]
**JDP**............ Paris-Moulineaux [*France*] [*Airport symbol*] (OAG)
**JDPA**......... Japan Directory of Professional Associations [*Japan Publications Guide Service*] [*Information service or system*] (CRD)
**JDPA**......... Juvenile Justice Planning Agency (OICC)
**JDPC**......... Joint Defense Production Committee [*Later, Joint War Production Committee*] [*World War II*]
**JDPC**......... Junior Daughters of Peter Claver (EA)
**JDPL**......... Journal des Debats Politiques et Litteraires [*A publication*]
**JDR**............ Journal of Defense Research [*A publication*]
**JDR**............ Juta's Daily Reporter, Cape Provincial Division [*South Africa*] [*A publication*] (DLA)
**JDR3**.......... John D. Rockefeller III [*American philanthropist, 1906-1978*]
**JDREENL** ... Joined by Reenlistment [*Military*]
**J Dr Int**...... Journal du Droit International [*A publication*]
**JDR J Drug Res** ... JDR. Journal of Drug Research [*A publication*]
**JDR J Drugther Res** ... JDR. Journal for Drugtherapy and Research [*A publication*]
**J Droit Afr** ... Journal de Droit Africain [*A publication*]
**J Droit Internat** ... Journal du Droit International [*A publication*]
**J du Droit Int'l** ... Journal du Droit International [*A publication*]
**JDRP**......... Joint Dissemination Review Panels
**J Drug Dev** ... Journal of Drug Development [*A publication*]
**J Drug Educ** ... Journal of Drug Education [*A publication*]
**J Drug Iss** .. Journal of Drug Issues [*A publication*]
**J Drug Issues** ... Journal of Drug Issues [*A publication*]
**J Drug Res (Cairo)** ... Journal of Drug Research (Cairo) [*A publication*]
**J Drug Res JDR** ... Journal for Drug Research. JDR [*A publication*]
**J Drugther Res** ... Journal for Drugtherapy and Research [*A publication*]
**JDS**............ Doctor of Juridical Science
**JDS**............ Jacobean Drama Studies [*A publication*]
**JDS**............ Jaguar Diagnostic System [*Automotive engineering*]
**JDS**............ JDS Capital Ltd. [*Toronto Stock Exchange symbol*]
**JDS**............ Job Data Sheet (IEEE)
**JDS**............ John Dewey Society (EA)
**JDS**............ Joint Defense Staff [*NATO*] (NATG)
**JDS**............ Joint Deployment System
**JDS**............ Joint Disciplinary Scheme [*British*]
**JDS**............ Journal of Development Studies [*A publication*]
**JdS**............ Journal des Savants [*A publication*]
**JDS**............ Jugoslovenska Demokratska Stranka [*Yugoslav Democratic Party*] [*Political party*] (PPE)
**JDS**............ Julian Day of Spring
**JDSEA**...... Jido Seigyo [*A publication*]
**JDSG**......... Jahrbuch. Deutsche Schiller-Gesellschaft [*A publication*]
**JDSh**......... Jahrbuch. Deutsche Shakespeare-Gesellschaft [*A publication*]
**JDSSC**....... Joint Data Systems Support Center [*Military*]
**JDT**............ Jahrbuecher fuer Deutsche Theologie [*Stuttgart/Gotha*] [*A publication*]
**JDT**............ Joint Design Team [*Military*]
**JDT**............ Joint Development Team (MCD)
**JDT**............ Joint Development Testing
**Jdt**............. Judith [*Old Testament book*] [*Roman Catholic canon*]
**JDT**............ Judson Dance Theater
**JDTh**......... Jahrbuecher fuer Deutsche Theologie [*Stuttgart/Gotha*] [*A publication*]
**JDU**........... Journal. Durham University [*A publication*]
**J Durham Sch Agr** ... Journal. Durham School of Agriculture [*A publication*]
**JDY**............ Downey, CA [*Location identifier*] [*FAA*] (FAAL)
**JDYD**......... Juvenile Delinquency and Youth Development Office [*Federal government*]
**J Dyn Syst Meas Control** ... Journal of Dynamic Systems, Measurement, and Control [*A publication*]
**JDZ**............ Jingdezhen [*China*] [*Airport symbol*] (OAG)
**JE**.............. Eurojet SA [*Spain*] [*ICAO designator*] (FAAC)
**JE**.............. Jamin Effect [*Electronics*]
**JE**.............. Jamming Equipment
**JE**.............. Japanese Encephalitis [*Medicine*]
**J & E**......... Jehovistic and Elohistic [*Theology*]
**Je**............... Jeremiah [*Old Testament book*] (BJA)
**JE**.............. Jerseyville & Eastern [*AAR code*]
**JE**.............. Jet Engine
**JE**.............. Jet Exhaust
**Je**............... Jeune [*Junior*] [*French*]
**JE**.............. Jewish Encyclopaedia [*A publication*] (BJA)
**JE**.............. Job Estimate (AAG)
**JE**.............. Joshi Effect [*Physics*]
**JE**.............. Joule Effect [*Physics*]
**J of E**.......... Journal of Education [*A publication*] (ROG)
**JE**.............. Journal of Education [*A publication*]
**JE**.............. Juedisches Echo [*Munich*] [*A publication*]
**JE**.............. June [*A publication*]
**JE**.............. June
**JEA**........... Jesuit Educational Association [*Later split into AJCU and JSEA*] (EA)
**JEA**........... Jewish Educators Assembly (EA)
**JEA**........... Joint Endeavor Agreement
**JEA**........... Joint Engineering Agency
**JEA**........... Joint Export Agent
**JEA**........... Joint Export Association [*Department of Commerce*]
**JEA**........... Journal of Egyptian Archaeology [*A publication*]
**JEA**........... Journal des Etudes Anciennes [*A publication*]
**JEA**........... Journalism Education Association (EA)
**J Ea Afr Nat Hist Soc** ... Journal. East Africa Natural History Society [*A publication*]
**JEAB**......... Journal of the Experimental Analysis of Behavior [*A publication*]
**JEAC**......... Journal of Electroanalytical Chemistry [*A publication*]
**JEADF**...... Joint Eastern Air Defense Force (MUGU)
**Jeaf**............ Jeaffreson's Book about Lawyers [*A publication*] (DLA)
**JEAfrSC**.... Journal. East African Swahili Committee [*A publication*]
**JEAL**......... Junction Emitting Avalanche Light
**Jealott's Hill Bull** ... Jealott's Hill Bulletin [*A publication*]
**JEAN**......... Jean Philippe Fragrances, Inc. [*NASDAQ symbol*] (NQ)
**Jean-Paul-Gesellsch Jahrb** ... Jean-Paul-Gesellschaft. Jahrbuch [*A publication*]
**JE Arch**...... Journal of Egyptian Archaeology [*A publication*]
**JEARD**...... Journal of Eastern African Research and Development [*A publication*]
**J Earth Sci** ... Journal of Earth Sciences [*A publication*]
**J Earth Sci Nagoya Univ** ... Journal of Earth Sciences. Nagoya University [*A publication*]
**J Earth Sci R Dublin Soc** ... Journal of Earth Sciences. Royal Dublin Society [*A publication*]
**J Earth Space Phys (Tehran)** ... Journal of the Earth and Space Physics (Tehran) [*A publication*]
**JEAS**......... Journal of East Asiatic Studies [*A publication*]
**JEASC**....... Journal. East African Swahili Committee [*A publication*]
**J East Afr Nat Hist Soc Natl Mus** ... Journal. East Africa Natural History Society and National Museum [*A publication*]
**J East Afr Res Develop** ... Journal of Eastern African Research and Development [*A publication*]
**J East Asian Affairs** ... Journal of East Asian Affairs [*A publication*]
**J East China Inst Text Sci Technol** ... Journal. East China Institute of Textile Science and Technology [*A publication*]
**J East China Petrol Inst** ... Journal. East China Petroleum Institute [*A publication*]
**J East West Stud** ... Journal of East and West Studies [*A publication*]
**JEAT**......... Joint Emergency Airlift Traffic Management Plan [*DoD*]
**JEB**............ James Ewell Brown Stuart [*American Confederate general known as Jeb Stuart, 1833-1864*]
**JEB**............ Jewish Education Bureau [*British*] (CB)
**JEB**............ Joint Economy Board [*Abolished, 1947*] [*Army-Navy*]
**JEB**............ Joint Electronics Board
**JEB**............ Journal of Economic Behavior [*A publication*]
**JEB**............ Journal of Economic Literature [*Information service or system*] [*A publication*]
**JEB**............ Journal of Economics and Business [*A publication*]
**JEB**............ Journal of Education (Boston University School of Education) [*A publication*]
**JEB**............ Journal of Experimental Botany [*A publication*]
**JEB**............ Junctional Epidermolysis Bullosa [*Medicine*]
**Jebb**............ Jebb's Irish Crown Cases [*1822-40*] [*A publication*] (DLA)
**Jebb & B**.... Jebb and Bourke's Irish Queen's Bench Reports [*1841-42*] [*A publication*] (DLA)
**Jebb & B (Ir)** ... Jebb and Bourke's Irish Queen's Bench Reports [*1841-42*] [*A publication*] (DLA)
**Jebb CC**..... Jebb's Irish Crown Cases [*1822-40*] [*A publication*] (DLA)
**Jebb CC (Ir)** ... Jebb's Irish Crown Cases [*1822-40*] [*A publication*] (DLA)
**Jebb Cr & Pr Cas** ... Jebb's Irish Crown and Presentment Cases [*A publication*] (DLA)
**Jebb & S**..... Jebb and Symes' Irish Queen's Bench Reports [*A publication*] (DLA)
**Jebb & S (Ir)** ... Jebb and Symes' Irish Queen's Bench Reports [*A publication*] (DLA)
**Jebb & Sym** ... Jebb and Symes' Irish Queen's Bench Reports [*A publication*] (DLA)
**JEBH**......... Journal of Economic and Business History [*A publication*]
**JEBM**........ Jet Engine Base Maintenance
**JEC**............ Jacobs Engineering Group, Inc. [*NYSE symbol*] (SPSG)
**JEC**............ Japanese Electrotechnical Committee
**JEC**............ Jersey Electric Company [*British*]
**JEC**............ Jeunesse Etudiante Catholique Internationale [*International Young Catholic Students*] (EAIO)
**Je C**........... Jewish Currents [*A publication*]
**JEC**............ Joint Economic Committee of Congress
**JEC**............ Joint Evaluation Committee [*NSF-UCAR*]
**JEC**............ Journal of Econometrics [*A publication*]
**J Ec**........... Journal des Economistes [*A publication*]

**JECA** ......... Jewel Cave National Monument
**JECAB** ...... Journal of Electrocardiology [*A publication*]
**JECB** ......... Jet Engine Control Bearing
**JECC** ......... Japanese Electronic Computer Company
**JECC** ......... Joint Economic Committee of Congress (MCD)
**JECC** ......... Joint Exercise Control Center (MCD)
**J Ecclesiast Hist** ... Journal of Ecclesiastical History [*A publication*]
**J Eccl H** ..... Journal of Ecclesiastical History [*A publication*]
**J Eccl Hist** ... Journal of Ecclesiastical History [*A publication*]
**JECEA** ...... Journal. Institution of Engineers (India). Chemical Engineering Division [*A publication*]
**J Ec Ent** ..... Journal of Economic Entomology [*A publication*]
**JECFA** ....... Joint Expert Committee on Food Additives [*FDA/WHO*]
**JECI** .......... Jeunesse Etudiante Catholique Internationale [*International Young Catholic Students*]
**Je Ci** ........... Jewish Civilization [*A publication*]
**JECL** ......... JEC Lasers, Inc. [*NASDAQ symbol*] (NQ)
**JECL** ......... Job Entry Control Language
**JECMA** ..... Journal of Electronic Materials [*A publication*]
**JECMB** ..... Joint Executive Committee on Medicine and Biology
**JECMB** ..... Journal of Econometrics [*A publication*]
**JECMOS** .. Joint Electronic Countermeasures Operation Section [*NATO*] (NATG)
**J Ecol** ......... Journal of Ecology [*A publication*]
**J Econ** ........ Journal des Economistes [*A publication*]
**J Econ Abstr** ... Journal of Economic Abstracts [*A publication*]
**J Econ Aff** ... Journal of Economic Affairs [*A publication*]
**J Econ Biol** ... Journal of Economic Biology [*A publication*]
**J Econ and Bus** ... Journal of Economics and Business [*A publication*]
**J Econ Bus** ... Journal of Economics and Business [*A publication*]
**J Econ Bus Hist** ... Journal of Economic and Business History [*A publication*]
**J Econ Dyn and Control** ... Journal of Economic Dynamics and Control [*A publication*]
**J Econ Ed** ... Journal of Economic Education [*A publication*]
**J Econ Educ** ... Journal of Economic Education [*A publication*]
**J Econ Ent** ... Journal of Economic Entomology [*A publication*]
**J Econ Entom** ... Journal of Economic Entomology [*A publication*]
**J Econ Entomol** ... Journal of Economic Entomology [*A publication*]
**J Econ H** .... Journal of Economic History [*A publication*]
**J Econ Hist** ... Journal of Economic History [*A publication*]
**J Econ Iss** .. Journal of Economic Issues [*A publication*]
**J Econ Issues** ... Journal of Economics Issues [*A publication*]
**JEconLit** .... Journal of Economic Literature [*Information service or system*] [*A publication*]
**J Econ Liter** ... Journal of Economic Literature [*Information service or system*] [*A publication*]
**J Econom** ... Journal of Econometrics [*A publication*]
**J Econom Behavior Organization** ... Journal of Economic Behavior and Organization [*A publication*]
**J Econom Dynamics Control** ... Journal of Economic Dynamics and Control [*A publication*]
**J Economet** ... Journal of Econometrics [*A publication*]
**J Econometrics** ... Journal of Econometrics [*A publication*]
**J Economistes** ... Journal des Economistes [*A publication*]
**J Econom Theory** ... Journal of Economic Theory [*A publication*]
**J Econ Soc Hist Or** ... Journal of the Economic and Social History of the Orient [*A publication*]
**J Econ Soc Hist Orient** ... Journal of the Economic and Social History of the Orient [*A publication*]
**J Econ Soc Meas** ... Journal of Economic and Social Measurement [*A publication*]
**J Econ Studies** ... Journal of Economic Studies [*A publication*]
**J Econ Taxon Bot** ... Journal of Economic and Taxonomic Botany [*A publication*]
**J Econ Theo** ... Journal of Economic Theory [*A publication*]
**JECPA** ....... Journal of Experimental Child Psychology [*A publication*]
**J Ec Polytech** ... Journal. Ecole Polytechnique [*A publication*]
**JECS** .......... Job Entry Central Services (MCD)
**J Ec St** ........ Journal of Ecumenical Studies [*A publication*]
**J Ecumen Stud** ... Journal of Ecumenical Studies [*A publication*]
**J Ecum Stud** ... Journal of Ecumenical Studies [*A publication*]
**JECVA** ...... Journal. Institution of Engineers (India). Civil Engineering Division [*A publication*]
**JED** ........... Japan Economic Daily [*Database*] [*Kyodo News International, Inc.*] [*Information service or system*] (CRD)
**JED** ........... Jeddah [*Saudi Arabia*] [*Airport symbol*] (OAG)
**Jed** ............. Jedediah (BJA)
**JED** ........... Jet Engine Duct
**J Ed** ........... Jewish Education [*A publication*]
**JED** ........... Joint Educational Development (EA)
**JED** ........... Journal of Economic Dynamics and Control [*A publication*]
**J Ed** ........... Journal of Education [*A publication*]
**JED** ........... Julian Ephemeris Data (MCD)
**J Ed Admin** ... Journal of Educational Administration [*A publication*] (APTA)
**J Ed Data Process** ... Journal of Educational Data Processing [*A publication*]
**JEDEC** ...... Joint Electron Device Engineering Council (EA)
**JEDI** .......... Jobs for Employable Dependent Individuals Program [*Federal government*]
**JEDI** .......... Joint Electronic Data Interchange [*International trade*]
**J Ed (London)** ... Journal of Education (London) [*A publication*]
**J Ed M** ....... Journal of Educational Measurement [*A publication*]
**J Ednl Admin and History** ... Journal of Educational Administration and History [*A publication*]
**J Ednl Technology** ... Journal of Educational Technology [*A publication*]
**J of Ed (NS)** ... Journal of Education. Department of Education (Nova Scotia) [*A publication*]
**JEDPE** ....... Joint Emergency Defense Plan Europe [*NATO*] (NATG)
**J Ed Psychol** ... Journal of Educational Psychology [*A publication*]
**J Ed Res** ..... Journal of Educational Research [*A publication*]
**JEDS** ......... Japanese Expeditions to the Deep Sea
**JEDS** ......... Jedburgh Teams [*Allied intelligence-gathering units in Europe*] [*World War II*]
**J Ed Soc** ..... Journal of Educational Sociology [*A publication*]
**J Ed Stat** .... Journal of Educational Statisics [*A publication*]
**J Ed Thought** ... Journal of Educational Thought [*A publication*]
**J Educ** ........ Journal of Education [*A publication*]
**J Educ Adm** ... Journal of Educational Administration [*A publication*]
**J Educ Adm Hist** ... Journal of Educational Administration and History [*A publication*]
**J Educ Data Proc** ... Journal of Educational Data Processing [*A publication*]
**J Educ Dept Niigata Univ** ... Journal. Education Department. Niigata University [*A publication*]
**J Educ D P** ... Journal of Educational Data Processing [*A publication*]
**J Educ Fin** ... Journal of Education Finance [*A publication*]
**J Educ Libr** ... Journal of Education for Librarianship [*A publication*]
**J Educ Librarianship** ... Journal of Education for Librarianship [*A publication*]
**J Educ (Lond)** ... Journal of Education (London) [*A publication*]
**J Educ M** ... Journal of Educational Measurement [*A publication*]
**J Educ Media Science** ... Journal of Educational Media Science [*A publication*]
**J Educ Method** ... Journal of Educational Method [*A publication*]
**J Educ Psyc** ... Journal of Educational Psychology [*A publication*]
**J Educ Psych** ... Journal of Education and Psychology [*A publication*]
**J Educ Psychol** ... Journal of Educational Psychology [*A publication*]
**J Educ Res** ... Journal of Educational Research [*A publication*]
**J Educ Soc** ... Journal of Education for Social Work [*A publication*]
**J Educ Soc** ... Journal of Educational Sociology [*A publication*]
**J Educ Social** ... Journal of Educational Sociology [*A publication*]
**J Educ Soc Work** ... Journal of Education for Social Work [*A publication*]
**J Educ for Teach** ... Journal of Education for Teaching [*A publication*]
**J Educ Technol Syst** ... Journal of Educational Technology Systems [*A publication*]
**J Educ Tech Syst** ... Journal of Educational Technology Systems [*A publication*]
**J Educ Th** .. Journal of Educational Thought [*A publication*]
**J Educ Univ Natal** ... Journal of Education. Faculty of Education. University of Natal [*A publication*]
**JEE** ............ Japan Electronic Engineering [*A publication*]
**JEE** ............ Japanese Equine Encephalitis [*Medicine*]
**JEE** ............ JEE. Journal of Electronic Engineering [*A publication*]
**JEE** ............ Jet Engine Exhaust
**JEE** ............ Journal of Engineering Education [*A publication*]
**JEE** ............ Journal of Environmental Economics and Management [*A publication*]
**JEE** ............ Journal of Experimental Education [*A publication*]
**JEEC** ......... Kenneth E. Johnson Environmental and Energy Center [*University of Alabama in Huntsville*] [*Research center*] (RCD)
**JEED** ......... Journal. Environmental Engineering Division. Proceedings of the American Society of Civil Engineers [*A publication*]
**JEEGA** ...... Journal. Environmental Engineering Division. American Society of Civil Engineers [*A publication*]
**JEE J Electron Eng** ... JEE. Journal of Electronic Engineering [*Japan*] [*A publication*]
**JEELA** ....... Journal. Institution of Engineers (India). Electrical Engineering Division [*A publication*]
**JEEMD** ..... Journal of Environmental Economics and Management [*A publication*]
**JEEND** ...... JEE. Journal of Electronic Engineering [*A publication*]
**JEEP** .......... General-Purpose Quarter-Ton Military Utility Vehicle
**JEEP** .......... Joint Effort Evaluation Program [*Military*] (AFM)
**JEEP** .......... Joint Emergency Evacuation Plan [*Military*] (AABC)
**JEEP** .......... Joint Environmental Effects Program [*Military*] (AFM)
**JEEP** .......... Joint Establishment Experimental Pile [*Nuclear reactor*] [*Norway*]
**JEEP** .......... Joint Export Establishment Promotion [*Trade exhibition*] [*Department of Commerce*]
**JEF** ............ Jacobi Elliptic Function [*Mathematics*]
**JEF** ............ Japan Economic Journal [*A publication*]
**JEF** ............ Jefferson City [*Missouri*] [*Airport symbol*] (OAG)
**JEF** ............ Jefferson City, MO [*Location identifier*] [*FAA*] (FAAL)
**JEF** ............ Jefferson Educational Foundation (EA)
**JEF** ............ Jefjen Capital [*Vancouver Stock Exchange symbol*]
**JEF** ............ Jet Engine Fuel
**JEF** ............ Jeunesses Europeennes Federalistes
**JEFDS** ....... Journal. English Folk Dance and Song Society [*A publication*]
**JEFDSS** ..... Journal. English Folk Dance and Song Society [*A publication*]
**JEFF** .......... Jefferson National Corp. [*NASDAQ symbol*] (NQ)
**JEFF** .......... Jefferson National Expansion Memorial National Historic Site

**Jeff**............ Jefferson's Virginia General Court Reports [*A publication*] (DLA)
**JEFF**.......... Judiciously Efficient Fixed Frame [*Data processing*] (MCD)
**Jeff Man**.... Jefferson's Manual of Parliamentary Law [*A publication*] (DLA)
**Jeffrsn B**.... Jefferson Business [*A publication*]
**Jeff (VA)**.... Jefferson's Virginia General Court Reports [*A publication*] (DLA)
**JEFG**......... Jefferies Group, Inc. [*NASDAQ symbol*] (NQ)
**JEFM**........ Jet Engine Field Maintenance
**JEFS**.......... Journal. English Folk Dance and Song Society [*A publication*]
**JEG**........... Joint Exploratory Group [*NATO*] (NATG)
**J Eg Arch**... Journal of Egyptian Archaeology [*A publication*]
**J Eg Or Soc**... Journal. Egyptian and Oriental Society [*A publication*]
**JEGP**......... Journal of English and Germanic Philology [*A publication*]
**JEGPA**...... Journal. Egyptian Public Health Association [*A publication*]
**JEG Ph**...... Journal of English and Germanic Philology [*A publication*]
**JEG Phil**.... Journal of English and Germanic Philology [*A publication*]
**JEGR**......... Jegeroil Corp. [*NASDAQ symbol*] (NQ)
**J Egypt Arch**... Journal of Egyptian Archaeology [*A publication*]
**J Egypt Archaeol**... Journal of Egyptian Archaeology [*A publication*]
**J Egyptian MA**... Journal. Egyptian Medical Association [*A publication*]
**J Egypt Med Ass**... Journal. Egyptian Medical Association [*A publication*]
**J Egypt Med Assoc**... Journal. Egyptian Medical Association [*A publication*]
**J Egypt Med Soc**... Journal. Egyptian Medical Society [*A publication*]
**J Egypt Pharm**... Journal of Egyptian Pharmacy [*A publication*]
**J Egypt Public Health Assoc**... Journal. Egyptian Public Health Association [*A publication*]
**J Egypt Soc Parasitol**... Journal. Egyptian Society of Parasitology [*A publication*]
**J Egypt Vet Med Ass**... Journal. Egyptian Veterinary Medical Association [*A publication*]
**JEH**........... Journal of Ecclesiastical History [*A publication*]
**JEH**........... Journal of Economic History [*A publication*]
**JEHFC**...... Jon-Erik Hexum Fan Club (EA)
**JEHO**........ Jehosaphat [*Biblical*] (ROG)
**JEH/S**....... Journal of Economic History (Supplement) [*A publication*]
**JEHU**........ Joint Experimental Helicopter Unit [*British military*] (DMA)
**JEI**............ Japan Economic Institute of America (EA)
**JEI**............ Japan Electronics Industry [*A publication*]
**JEI**............ Journal of Economic Issues [*A publication*]
**JEI**............ Journal. English Institute [*A publication*]
**JEIA**.......... Japanese Electronic Industries Association
**JEIA**.......... Joint Electronics Information Agency
**JEIA**.......... Joint Export-Import Agency [*Munich*] [*Allied German Occupation Forces*]
**JEIDA**....... Japanese Electronic Industries Development Association
**JEI J Electron Ind**... JEI. Journal of the Electronics Industry [*A publication*]
**JEI Jpn Electron Ind**... JEI. Japan Electronic Industry [*A publication*]
**JEIM**......... Jet Engine Intermediate Maintenance
**JEIND**....... Journal of Endocrinological Investigation [*A publication*]
**JEIPAC**..... JICST [*Japanese Information Center of Science and Technology*] Electronic Information Processing Automatic Computer
**JEIT**.......... Joint Equipment Identification Team [*Military*] (CINC)
**JEJ**............ Japan Economic Journal [*A publication*]
**JEJ**............ Jejunum [*Medicine*]
**JEL**............ Jackson Estuarine Laboratory [*University of New Hampshire*] [*Research center*] (RCD)
**JEL**............ Jealous (DSUE)
**JEL**............ Jeunesses Europeennes Liberales [*Liberal European Youth*]
**JEL**............ Journal of Economic Literature [*Information service or system*] [*A publication*]
**J of EL**....... Journal of Electric Lighting [*A publication*] (ROG)
**JEL**............ Journal of English Linguistics [*A publication*]
**J El Ass J**... Journal. Electrochemical Association of Japan [*A publication*]
**J Elast**........ Journal of Elasticity [*A publication*]
**J Elasticity**... Journal of Elasticity [*A publication*]
**J Elastomers Plast**... Journal of Elastomers and Plastics [*A publication*]
**J Elastoplast**... Journal of Elastoplastics [*Later, Journal of Elastomers and Plastics*] [*A publication*]
**JELC**......... Joint Effort Against Lefthanded Complications
**J Elcardiol**... Journal of Electrocardiology [*San Diego*] [*A publication*]
**J Elchem So**... Journal. Electrochemical Society [*A publication*]
**J El Chem Soc**... Journal. Electrochemical Society [*A publication*]
**J Elec**......... Journal of Electricity [*A publication*]
**J Elec Buy**... Japan Electronics Buyers' Guide [*A publication*]
**J Elec Chem**... Journal of Electroanalytical Chemistry and Interfacial Electrochemistry [*A publication*]
**J Elec Def**.. Journal of Electronic Defense [*A publication*]
**J Elec E**...... Journal of Electronic Engineering [*A publication*]
**J Elec Mat**... Journal of Electronic Materials [*A publication*]
**J Elec Micr**... Journal of Electron Microscopy [*A publication*]
**J Elec Spec**... Journal of Electron Spectroscopy and Related Phenomena [*A publication*]
**J Electr Electron Eng (Aust)**... Journal of Electrical and Electronics Engineering (Australia) [*A publication*]
**J Electr Microsc**... Journal of Electron Microscopy [*A publication*]
**J Electroanal Chem**... Journal of Electroanalytical Chemistry [*Netherlands*] [*A publication*]
**J Electroanal Chem Abstr Sect**... Journal of Electroanalytical Chemistry. Abstract Section [*A publication*]
**J Electroanal Chem Interfacial Electrochem**... Journal of Electroanalytical Chemistry and Interfacial Electrochemistry [*A publication*]
**J Electrocardiol**... Journal of Electrocardiology [*A publication*]
**J Electrocardiol (San Diego)**... Journal of Electrocardiology (San Diego) [*A publication*]
**J Electrochem Soc**... Journal. Electrochemical Society [*A publication*]
**J Electrochem Soc India**... Journal. Electrochemical Society of India [*A publication*]
**J Electrochem Soc Japan**... Journal. Electrochemical Society of Japan [*A publication*]
**J Electron (Beijing)**... Journal of Electronics (Beijing) [*A publication*]
**J Electron Control**... Journal of Electronics and Control [*England*] [*A publication*]
**J Electron Eng**... Journal of Electronic Engineering [*A publication*]
**J Electron Mater**... Journal of Electronic Materials [*A publication*]
**J Electron Microsc**... Journal of Electron Microscopy [*A publication*]
**J Electron Microsc Tech**... Journal of Electron Microscopy Technique [*A publication*]
**J Electron Microsc (Tokyo)**... Journal of Electron Microscopy (Tokyo) [*A publication*]
**J Electron Micry**... Journal of Electron Microscopy [*A publication*]
**J Electron Spectrosc and Relat Phenom**... Journal of Electron Spectroscopy and Related Phenomena [*A publication*]
**J Electron Spectrosc Relat Phenom**... Journal of Electron Spectroscopy and Related Phenomena [*A publication*]
**J Electroph**... Journal of Electrophysiological Techniques [*A publication*]
**J Electrostat**... Journal of Electrostatics [*A publication*]
**J Electr Spectr**... Journal of Electron Spectroscopy and Related Phenomena [*A publication*]
**J Elisha Mitchell Scient Soc**... Journal. Elisha Mitchell Scientific Society [*A publication*]
**J Elisha Mitchell Sci Soc**... Journal. Elisha Mitchell Scientific Society [*A publication*]
**J Elisha Mitch Sci Soc**... Journal. Elisha Mitchell Scientific Society [*A publication*]
**J El Soc**...... Journal. Electrochemical Society [*A publication*]
**JEM**........... Japanese Experiment Module
**JEM**........... Jerusalem and the East Mission
**JEM**........... Jet Engine Modulation (MCD)
**JEM**........... Jewelmasters, Inc. [*AMEX symbol*] (SPSG)
**JEM**........... Joint Endeavor Manager
**JEM**........... Joint Exercise Manual (MCD)
**JEM**........... Journal of Enterprise Management [*A publication*]
**JEM**........... Journal of Environmental Economics and Management [*A publication*]
**JEM**........... Journey's End Motel Corp. [*Toronto Stock Exchange symbol*]
**JEM(A)**..... Junior Electrical Mechanic (Air) [*British military*] (DMA)
**JEMAA**..... Journal. Egyptian Medical Association [*A publication*]
**JEM(AW)**... Junior Electrical Mechanic (Air Weapon) [*British military*] (DMA)
**J Emb Exp M**... Journal of Embryology and Experimental Morphology [*A publication*]
**J Embr Exp Morph**... Journal of Embryology and Experimental Morphology [*A publication*]
**J Embryol Exp Morphol**... Journal of Embryology and Experimental Morphology [*A publication*]
**JEMC**........ Joint Engineering Management Conference
**J Emergency Nurs**... Journal of Emergency Nursing [*A publication*]
**J Emerg Med**... Journal of Emergency Medicine [*A publication*]
**J Emerg Med Serv JEMS**... Journal of Emergency Medical Services. JEMS [*A publication*]
**J Emerg Nurs**... Journal of Emergency Nursing [*A publication*]
**J Emerg Services**... Journal of Emergency Services [*A publication*]
**JEMFA**..... JEMF [*John Edwards Memorial Foundation*] Quarterly [*A publication*]
**JEMFQ**..... JEMF [*John Edwards Memorial Foundation*] Quarterly [*A publication*]
**JEMF Quart**... JEMF [*John Edwards Memorial Foundation*] Quarterly [*A publication*]
**JEMIC Tech Rep**... JEMIC [*Japan Electric Meters Inspection Corporation*] Technical Report [*A publication*]
**Jemna Mech a Opt**... Jemna Mechanika a Optika [*A publication*]
**Jemna Mech Opt**... Jemna Mechanika a Optika [*A publication*]
**J Empl Coun**... Journal of Employment Counseling [*A publication*]
**J Employ Counsel**... Journal of Employment Counseling [*A publication*]
**JEMR**........ Jem Records, Inc. [*South Plainfield, NJ*] [*NASDAQ symbol*] (NQ)
**JEMSA**..... Journal. Elisha Mitchell Scientific Society [*A publication*]
**JEN**............ Japan Economic Newswire [*Kyodo News International, Inc.*] [*Information service or system*] (CRD)
**JEN**............ Jena [*German Democratic Republic*] [*Seismograph station code, US Geological Survey*] [*Closed*] (SEIS)
**JEN**............ Journal of Emergency Nursing [*A publication*]
**J En**............ Journal of English [*A publication*]
**JEN**............ Journal de l'Enregistrement et du Notariat [*A publication*]
**JEN**............ Journal of Enterprise Management [*A publication*]
**JEN**............ Junta de Energia Nuclear [*Spanish nuclear agency*]
**Jenaische Zeitschrift**... Jenaische Zeitschrift fuer Medizin und Naturwissenschaft [*A publication*]

**Jenaische Ztschr Med u Naturw** ... Jenaische Zeitschrift fuer Medizin und Naturwissenschaft [*A publication*]
**Jenaische Ztschr Naturw** ... Jenaische Zeitschrift fuer Naturwissenschaft [*A publication*]
**JENAKAT** ... Jeunesse Nationale Katangaise [*Katangan National Youth*]
**Jena Rev** .... Jena Review [*A publication*]
**Jena Rev Suppl** ... Jena Review. Supplement [*East Germany*] [*A publication*]
**Jena Rundsch** ... Jenaer Rundschau [*A publication*]
**Jena Z Med Naturwiss** ... Jenaische Zeitschrift fuer Medizin und Naturwissenschaft [*East Germany*] [*A publication*]
**Jena Z Naturw** ... Jenaische Zeitschrift fuer Naturwissenschaft [*A publication*]
**Jena Z Naturwiss** ... Jenaische Zeitschrift fuer Naturwissenschaft [*A publication*]
**Jena Zs Med Naturw** ... Jenaische Zeitschrift fuer Medizin und Naturwissenschaft [*A publication*]
**Jenck Bills** ... Jencken's Bills of Exchange [*1880*] [*A publication*] (DLA)
**Jenck Neg S** ... Jencken's Negotiable Securities [*1880*] [*A publication*] (DLA)
**JENDD**...... Journal of Energy and Development [*A publication*]
**J Endocr**..... Journal of Endocrinology [*A publication*]
**J Endocrinol** ... Journal of Endocrinology [*A publication*]
**J Endocrinol Invest** ... Journal of Endocrinological Investigation [*A publication*]
**J Endod**...... Journal of Endodontics [*A publication*]
**J Endodont** ... Journal of Endodontics [*A publication*]
**JENER**...... Joint Establishment for Nuclear Energy Research
**J Energy**..... Journal of Energy [*A publication*]
**J Energy Dev** ... Journal of Energy and Development [*A publication*]
**J Energy & Devel** ... Journal of Energy and Development [*A publication*] (DLA)
**J Energy Develop** ... Journal of Energy and Development [*A publication*]
**J Energy and Development** ... Journal of Energy and Development [*A publication*]
**J Energy Div Am Soc Civ Eng** ... Journal. Energy Division. American Society of Civil Engineers [*A publication*]
**J Energy Div ASCE** ... Journal. Energy Division. American Society of Civil Engineers [*A publication*]
**J Energy Div Proc ASCE** ... Journal. Energy Division. American Society of Civil Engineers. Proceedings [*A publication*]
**J Energy Eng** ... Journal of Energy Engineering [*A publication*]
**J Energy Law and Policy** ... Journal of Energy Law and Policy [*A publication*]
**J Energy L P** ... Journal of Energy Law and Policy [*A publication*]
**J Energy L & Pol'y** ... Journal of Energy Law and Policy [*A publication*]
**J Energy Resources Technol** ... Journal of Energy Resources Technology [*A publication*]
**J Energy Resour Technol** ... Journal of Energy Resources Technology [*A publication*]
**J Energy Resour Technol Trans ASME** ... Journal of Energy Resources Technology. Transactions of the American Society of Mechanical Engineers [*A publication*]
**J Eng Ed**.... Journal of Engineering Education [*A publication*]
**J Eng Educ** ... Journal of Engineering Education [*A publication*]
**J Eng Gas Turbines Power** ... Journal of Engineering for Gas Turbines and Power [*A publication*]
**J Eng and Germ Philol** ... Journal of English and Germanic Philology [*A publication*]
**J Eng Ger Philol** ... Journal of English and Germanic Philology [*A publication*]
**J Eng Ind** ... Journal of Engineering for Industry [*A publication*]
**J Eng Ind Tran ASME** ... Journal of Engineering for Industry. Transactions of the American Society of Mechanical Engineers [*A publication*]
**J Eng Ind Trans ASME** ... Journal of Engineering for Industry. Transactions of the American Society of Mechanical Engineers [*A publication*]
**J Eng L**...... Journal of English Linguistics [*A publication*]
**J Engl Ger** ... Journal of English and Germanic Philology [*A publication*]
**J Engl & Germ Philol** ... Journal of English and Germanic Philology [*A publication*]
**J Engl Place-Name Soc** ... Journal. English Place-Name Society [*A publication*]
**J Eng Mater** ... Journal of Engineering Materials and Technology [*A publication*]
**J Eng Materials & Tech** ... Journal of Engineering Materials and Technology [*A publication*]
**J Eng Mater Technol** ... Journal of Engineering Materials and Technology [*A publication*]
**J Eng Mater Technol Trans ASME** ... Journal of Engineering Materials and Technology. Transactions of the American Society of Mechanical Engineers [*A publication*]
**J Eng Math** ... Journal of Engineering Mathematics [*A publication*]
**J Eng Mat & Tech** ... Journal of Engineering Materials and Technology [*A publication*]
**J Eng Mech** ... Journal of Engineering Mechanics [*A publication*]
**J Eng Mech Div Amer Soc Civil Eng Proc** ... Journal. Engineering Mechanics Division. Proceedings of the American Society of Civil Engineers [*A publication*]
**J Eng Mech Div Am Soc Civ Eng** ... Journal. Engineering Mechanics Division. Proceedings of the American Society of Civil Engineers [*A publication*]
**J Engng Math** ... Journal of Engineering Mathematics [*A publication*]
**J Engng Mech Div Proc ASCE** ... Journal. Engineering Mechanics Division. Proceedings of the American Society of Civil Engineers [*A publication*]
**J Engn Phys** ... Journal of Engineering Physics [*A publication*]
**J Eng Phys** ... Journal of Engineering Physics [*A publication*]
**J Eng Phys (Belgrade)** ... Journal of Engineering Physics (Belgrade) [*A publication*]
**J Eng Phys (Engl Transl)** ... Journal of Engineering Physics (English Translation of Inzhenerno-Fizicheskii Zhurnal) [*Belorussian SSR*] [*A publication*]
**J Eng Power** ... Journal of Engineering for Power [*A publication*]
**J Eng Power Trans ASME** ... Journal of Engineering for Power. Transactions of the American Society of Mechanical Engineers [*A publication*]
**J Eng Psychol** ... Journal of Engineering Psychology [*A publication*]
**J Engrg Math** ... Journal of Engineering Mathematics [*A publication*]
**J Engrg Phys** ... Journal of Engineering Physics [*A publication*]
**J Eng S**....... Journal of English Studies [*A publication*]
**J Eng Sci**.... Journal of Engineering Sciences [*A publication*]
**J Eng Sci (Saudi Arabia)** ... Journal of Engineering Sciences (Saudi Arabia) [*A publication*]
**Jenk** .......... Jenkins' Eight Centuries of Reports, English Exchequer [*145 English Reprint*] [*1220-1623*] [*A publication*] (DLA)
**Jenk Cent**... Jenkins' Eight Centuries of Reports, English Exchequer [*145 English Reprint*] [*1220-1623*] [*A publication*] (DLA)
**Jenk & Formoy** ... Jenkinson and Formoy's Select Cases in the Exchequer of Pleas [*Selden Society Publication, Vol. 48*] [*A publication*] (DLA)
**Jenkins (Eng)** ... Jenkins' Eight Centuries of Reports, English Exchequer [*145 English Reprint*] [*1220-1623*] [*A publication*] (DLA)
**Jenks**.......... Jenks' Reports [*58 New Hampshire*] [*A publication*] (DLA)
**JENN**........ Jennifer Convertibles, Inc. [*NASDAQ symbol*] (NQ)
**Jenn** .......... Jennison's Reports [*14-18 Michigan*] [*A publication*] (DLA)
**Jenn Sug A** ... Jennett's Sugden Acts [*A publication*] (DLA)
**JENS**......... Journal. Eighteen Nineties Society [*A publication*]
**Jen-Sal J**.... Jen-Sal Journal [*A publication*]
**J Ent** .......... Journal of Entomology [*A publication*]
**JENTAC** ... Jentaculum [*Breakfast*] [*Pharmacy*]
**J Enterostom Ther** ... Journal of Enterostomal Therapy [*A publication*]
**J Entomol A** ... Journal of Entomology. Series A. General Entomology [*A publication*]
**J Entomol B** ... Journal of Entomology. Series B. Taxonomy [*A publication*]
**J Entomol Res** ... Journal of Entomological Research [*A publication*]
**J Entomol Res (New Delhi)** ... Journal of Entomological Research (New Delhi) [*A publication*]
**J Entomol Sci** ... Journal of Entomological Science [*A publication*]
**J Entomol Ser A** ... Journal of Entomology. Series A. General Entomology [*A publication*]
**J Entomol Ser A Gen Entomol** ... Journal of Entomology. Series A. General Entomology [*A publication*]
**J Entomol Ser A Physiol Behav** ... Journal of Entomology. Series A. Physiology and Behaviour [*A publication*]
**J Entomol Ser B Taxon** ... Journal of Entomology. Series B. Taxonomy [*A publication*]
**J Entomol Ser B Taxon Syst** ... Journal of Entomology. Series B. Taxonomy and Systematics [*A publication*]
**J Entomol Soc Aust** ... Journal. Entomological Society of Australia [*A publication*]
**J Entomol Soc Aust (NSW)** ... Journal. Entomological Society of Australia (New South Wales) [*A publication*]
**J Entomol Soc BC** ... Journal. Entomological Society of British Columbia [*A publication*]
**J Entomol Soc S Afr** ... Journal. Entomological Society of Southern Africa [*A publication*]
**J Entomol Soc South Afr** ... Journal. Entomological Society of Southern Africa [*A publication*]
**J Entomol Soc Sthn Afr** ... Journal. Entomological Society of Southern Africa [*A publication*]
**J Entomol Zool** ... Journal of Entomology and Zoology [*A publication*]
**J Ent Soc Aust** ... Journal. Entomological Society of Australia [*A publication*]
**J Ent Soc Aust (NSW)** ... Journal. Entomological Society of Australia (New South Wales Branch) [*A publication*] (APTA)
**J Ent Soc BC** ... Journal. Entomological Society of British Columbia [*A publication*]
**J Ent Soc Qd** ... Journal. Entomological Society of Queensland [*A publication*]
**J Ent Soc South Afr** ... Journal. Entomological Society of Southern Africa [*A publication*]
**J Ent Soc Sth Afr** ... Journal. Entomological Society of Southern Africa [*A publication*]
**J Ent Zool** ... Journal of Entomology and Zoology [*A publication*]
**J Env Educ** ... Journal of Environmental Education [*A publication*]
**J Envir Eng** ... Journal. Environmental Engineering Division. American Society of Civil Engineers [*A publication*]
**J Envir Mgm** ... Journal of Environmental Management [*A publication*]
**J Environ Econ Manage** ... Journal of Environmental Economics and Management [*A publication*]
**J Environ Educ** ... Journal of Environmental Education [*A publication*]
**J Environ Eng Div Am Soc Civ Eng** ... Journal. Environmental Engineering Division. American Society of Civil Engineers [*A publication*]

**J Environ Eng Div ASCE** ... Journal. Environmental Engineering Division. American Society of Civil Engineers [*A publication*]
**J Environ Engng Div Proc ASCE** ... Journal. Environmental Engineering Division. Proceedings of the American Society of Civil Engineers [*A publication*]
**J Environ Health** ... Journal of Environmental Health [*A publication*]
**J Environ Hortic** ... Journal of Environmental Horticulture [*A publication*]
**J Environ Manage** ... Journal of Environmental Management [*A publication*]
**J Environmental Econ and Mgt** ... Journal of Environmental Economics and Management [*A publication*]
**J Environ Pathol Toxicol** ... Journal of Environmental Pathology and Toxicology [*A publication*]
**J Environ Pathol Toxicol Oncol** ... Journal of Environmental Pathology, Toxicology, and Oncology [*A publication*]
**J Environ Plann Pollut Control** ... Journal of Environmental Planning and Pollution Control [*A publication*]
**J Environ Pollut Control (Tokyo)** ... Journal of Environmental Pollution Control (Tokyo) [*A publication*]
**J Environ Qual** ... Journal of Environmental Quality [*A publication*]
**J Environ Radioact** ... Journal of Environmental Radioactivity [*A publication*]
**J Environ Sci** ... Journal of Environmental Sciences [*A publication*]
**J Environ Sci Health B** ... Journal of Environmental Science and Health. Part B. Pesticides, Food Contaminants, and Agricultural Wastes [*A publication*]
**J Environ Sci Health (C)** ... Journal of Environmental Science and Health. Part C. Environmental Health Sciences [*A publication*]
**J Environ Sci Health Part A** ... Journal of Environmental Science and Health. Part A. Environmental Science and Engineering [*A publication*]
**J Environ Sci Health Part A Environ Sci Eng** ... Journal of Environmental Science and Health. Part A. Environmental Science and Engineering [*A publication*]
**J Environ Sci Health Part B** ... Journal of Environmental Science and Health. Part B. Pesticides, Food Contaminants, and Agricultural Wastes [*A publication*]
**J Environ Sci Health Part B Pestic Food Contam Agric Wastes** ... Journal of Environmental Science and Health. Part B. Pesticides, Food Contaminants, and Agricultural Wastes [*A publication*]
**J Environ Sci Health Part C** ... Journal of Environmental Science and Health. Part C [*A publication*]
**J Environ Sci Health Part C Environ Carcinog Rev** ... Journal of Environmental Science and Health. Part C. Environmental Carcinogenesis Reviews [*A publication*]
**J Environ Sci Health Part C Environ Health Sci** ... Journal of Environmental Science and Health. Part C. Environmental Health Sciences [*A publication*]
**J Environ Syst** ... Journal of Environmental Systems [*A publication*]
**J Environ Systems** ... Journal of Environmental Systems [*A publication*]
**J Envir Q** ... Journal of Environmental Quality [*A publication*]
**J Envir Qual** ... Journal of Environmental Quality [*A publication*]
**J Envir Quality** ... Journal of Environmental Quality [*A publication*]
**J Envir Sci** ... Journal of Environmental Sciences [*A publication*]
**J Envir Sci Hlth** ... Journal of Environmental Science and Health [*A publication*]
**Jen Zeiss Jb** ... Jenaer Zeiss-Jahrbuch [*A publication*]
**JEOCN**...... Joint European Operations Communications Network
**JEOFD**...... Jeofizik [*A publication*]
**JEOL**......... Jaarbericht. Vooraziatische-Egyptisch Genootschap "Ex Oriente Lux" [*A publication*]
**JEOL (Jpn Electron Opt Lab) News** ... JEOL (Japan Electron Optics Laboratory) News [*A publication*]
**JEP**............ Jepson Corp. [*NYSE symbol*] (SPSG)
**JEP**............ Jet Engine Processor
**JEP**............ Jewish Elite Person
**JEP**............ Journal of Economic Psychology [*A publication*]
**JEP**............ Journal of Educational Psychology [*A publication*]
**JEP**............ Journal of Evolutionary Psychology [*A publication*]
**JEP**............ Journal of General Management [*A publication*]
**JEP**............ Jupiter Entry Probe
**JEPA**......... Job Evaluation Policy Act of 1970
**JEPAP**....... Joint Emergency Personnel Augmentation Plan [*Military*] (CINC)
**JEPI**.......... Junior Eysenck Personality Inventory [*Psychology*]
**JEPIA**........ Japan Electronic Parts Industry Association
**J Epidemiol Community Health** ... Journal of Epidemiology and Community Health [*A publication*]
**JEPLA**....... Journal of Elastomers and Plastics [*A publication*]
**JEPO**......... Joint Engine Project Office (MCD)
**JEPP**.......... Japan English Publications in Print [*Japan Publications Guide Service*] [*Japan*] [*Information service or system*] (CRD)
**JEPS**.......... Job Effectiveness Prediction System [*Test for insurance company employees*]
**JEPS**.......... Job Entry Peripheral Services [*IBM Corp.*] (MCD)
**JEPS**.......... Joint Exercise Planning Staff [*NATO*] (NATG)
**JEPs**.......... Journal of Educational Psychology [*A publication*]
**JEPSA**....... Journal of Experimental Psychology [*A publication*]
**JEPSB**....... Journal Europeen des Steroides [*A publication*]
**JEPSBL**..... European Journal of Steroids [*A publication*]
**JEQ**........... Jequie [*Brazil*] [*Airport symbol*] (OAG)
**Je Q**........... Jerusalem Quarterly [*A publication*]
**J Equine Med Surg** ... Journal of Equine Medicine and Surgery [*A publication*]
**J Equip Electr et Electron** ... Journal de l'Equipement Electrique et Electronique [*A publication*]
**Jer**............. Janvier [*January*] [*French*]
**Jer**............. Jeremiah [*Old Testament book*]
**Jer**............. Jeremias (BJA)
**Jer**............. Jericho (BJA)
**JER**........... Jersey [*Channel Islands*] [*Airport symbol*] (OAG)
**JER**........... Jerusalem [*Israel*] [*Seismograph station code, US Geological Survey*] (SEIS)
**JER**........... Jerusalem
**Jer**............. Jerusalem Talmud (BJA)
**Jer**............. Jerushalmi (BJA)
**JER**........... Journal of Educational Research [*A publication*]
**JERA**......... James E. Rush Associates, Inc. [*Also, an information service or system*] (IID)
**Jerc**........... Junior Executive Research Consultant [*Fictitious position in Commerce Bank of Beverly Hills created for Jethro Bodine on the television show "The Beverly Hillbillies"*]
**Jer Car**....... Jeremy on Carriers [*A publication*] (DLA)
**Jer Dig**........ Jeremy's Digest [*1817-49*] [*A publication*] (DLA)
**Jeremy Eq** ... Jeremy's Equity Jurisdiction [*A publication*] (DLA)
**Jeremy Eq Jur** ... Jeremy's Equity Jurisdiction [*A publication*] (DLA)
**Jer Eq Jur** ... Jeremy's Equity Jurisdiction [*A publication*] (DLA)
**JERI**.......... Journey's End Resorts, Inc. [*NASDAQ symbol*] (NQ)
**JerM**.......... Jersey Microfilming, Clifton, NJ [*Library symbol*] [*Library of Congress*] (LCLS)
**Jernkon Ann** ... Jernkontorets Annaler [*A publication*]
**Jernkontorets Ann** ... Jernkontorets Annaler [*A publication*]
**Jernkontorets Ann Ed A** ... Jernkontorets Annaler. Edition A [*A publication*]
**Jernkontorets Ann Ed B** ... Jernkontorets Annaler. Edition B [*A publication*]
**JerPes**........ Jerusalem Talmud. Pesahim (BJA)
**JERR**......... Jerrico, Inc. [*NASDAQ symbol*] (NQ)
**Jerr Copyr** ... Jerrold on Copyright [*A publication*] (DLA)
**JERS**.......... Japan Earth Remote Sensing Satellite
**JERS**.......... Joint Emergency Relocation Site
**Jersey B**..... Jersey Bulletin and Dairy World [*A publication*]
**Jersey Bul**.. Jersey Bulletin [*A publication*]
**Jersey J**...... Jersey Journal [*A publication*]
**JERTD**...... Journal of Energy Resources Techology [*A publication*]
**JERU**......... Joint Environmental Research Unit (MCD)
**Jerus**.......... Jerusalem (BJA)
**Jerusalem J Int Relat** ... Jerusalem Journal of International Relations [*A publication*]
**Jerusalem Q** ... Jerusalem Quarterly [*A publication*]
**Jerus J Int Rel** ... Jerusalem Journal of International Relations [*A publication*]
**Jerus Symp Quantum Chem Biochem** ... Jerusalem Symposia on Quantum Chemistry and Biochemistry [*A publication*]
**Jerv Cor**..... Jervis. Coroners [*9th ed.*] [*1957*] [*A publication*] (DLA)
**Jerv NR**...... Jervis' New Rules [*A publication*] (DLA)
**JerW**.......... Jerusalemer Warte (BJA)
**JerYeb**........ Jerusalem Talmud. Yebamoth (BJA)
**Jes**............. Analysis and Digest of the Decisions of Sir George Jessel, by A. P Peter [*England*] [*A publication*] (DLA)
**JES**............ Japan Electronics Show
**JES**............ Japan Environmental Systems
**JES**............ Japanese Economic Studies. A Journal of Translations [*A publication*]
**JES**............ Jesuit (DSUE)
**JES**............ Jesup, GA [*Location identifier*] [*FAA*] (FAAL)
**JES**............ Jesus
**JES**............ Jet Ejector System
**JES**............ Job Entry System [*or Subsystem*] [*IBM Corp.*] [*Data processing*]
**JES**............ John Ericsson Society (EA)
**JES**............ Journal of Economic Studies [*A publication*]
**JES**............ Journal of Economics and Sociology [*A publication*]
**JES**............ Journal of Ecumenical Studies [*A publication*]
**JES**............ Journal of English Studies [*A publication*]
**JES**............ Journal of European Studies [*A publication*]
**JESAP**....... Jet Engine Smoke Abatement Program
**JES COLL** ... Jesus College [*Oxford or Cambridge*] [*England*] (ROG)
**JESCOM** .. Jesuits in Communication in the US (EA)
**JESHO**...... Journal of the Economic and Social History of the Orient [*A publication*]
**JESIA**....... Journal. Electrochemical Society of India [*A publication*]
**JESNA**...... Jewish Education Service of North America (EA)
**JESOA**...... Journal. Electrochemical Society [*United States*] [*A publication*]
**JESS**.......... Joint Exercise Simulation System [*DoD*]
**JESS**.......... Joint Exercise Support System [*Military*]
**JESSI**........ Joint European Semiconductor Silicon Initiative
**JESSI**........ Joint European Submicron Silicon [*Project*]
**JESSI**........ Junior Engineers' and Scientists' Summer Institute
**JESt**.......... Journal of Ethiopian Studies [*Addis Ababa/London*] [*A publication*]
**JEST**.......... Jungle Environmental Survival Training [*Military*]
**J Estomat**... Jornal de Estomatologia [*A publication*]
**JET**............ Frankfort, KY [*Location identifier*] [*FAA*] (FAAL)

**JET**........... Jam Exceeds Threshold
**JET**........... Jetronic Industries, Inc. [*AMEX symbol*] (SPSG)
**JET**........... Jettison
**JET**........... Job Element Text (AFM)
**JET**........... Job English Training
**JET**........... Jobs Evaluation and Training
**JET**........... Joint Economic Team
**JET**........... Joint Effort for Talent [*Navy*] (NG)
**JET**........... Joint European TOKAMAK [*Toroidal Kamera Magnetic*] [*or Torus*] [*Nuclear reactor*]
**JET**........... Jointly Endorsed Training [*Union-management*]
**JET**........... Journal of Economic Theory [*A publication*]
**JET**........... Journal of Environmental Systems [*A publication*]
**JET**........... Journal of Real Estate Taxation [*A publication*]
**JET**........... Judicial Education Teleseminar System [*Defunct*] (TSSD)
**Jet**........... Juillet [*July*] [*French*]
**JET**........... Junior Enlisted Travel [*Entitlement*] (MCD)
**JETA**......... Jet America, Inc. [*NASDAQ symbol*] (NQ)
**JETAA**...... Journal. Faculty of Engineering. University of Tokyo. Series A. Annual Report [*A publication*]
**JETAI**........ Journal of Experimental and Theoretical Artificial Intelligence [*A publication*]
**JETBA**....... Journal. Faculty of Engineering. University of Tokyo. Series B [*A publication*]
**JETCA**...... Journal of Ethnic Studies [*A publication*]
**JETD**......... Joint Electronics Type Designator [*Military*] (AABC)
**JETDS**....... Joint Electronics Type Designation System [*Military*] (AFM)
**JETEC**....... Joint Electron Tube Engineering Council [*Later, JEDEC*] (MCD)
**J of Ethiop L**... Journal of Ethiopian Law [*Addis Ababa, Ethiopia*] [*A publication*] (DLA)
**JEthiopSt**... Journal of Ethiopian Studies [*Addis Ababa/London*] [*A publication*]
**J Ethiop Stud**... Journal of Ethiopian Studies [*A publication*]
**J Eth L**....... Journal of Ethiopian Law [*A publication*] (DLA)
**J Ethnic Stud**... Journal of Ethnic Studies [*A publication*]
**J Ethnopharmacol**... Journal of Ethnopharmacology [*A publication*]
**JEthS**......... Journal of Ethiopian Studies [*A publication*]
**J Eth S**....... Journal of Ethnic Studies [*A publication*]
**JETI**.......... JETI. Japan Energy and Technology Intelligence [*A publication*]
**JET J Educ Teach**... JET. Journal of Education for Teaching [*A publication*]
**JETN**......... Jettison
**JETOAS**.... European Journal of Toxicology [*A publication*]
**JETP**.......... Jet-Propelled
**JETP**.......... Journal of Experimental and Theoretical Physics [*A publication*]
**JETPA**....... Jet Propulsion [*A publication*]
**JETP Lett**... JETP Letters [*English Translation of JETP Pis'ma v Redaktsiyu*] [*A publication*]
**Jet Propul**.. Jet Propulsion [*United States*] [*A publication*]
**Jet Propul Lab Tech Memo**... Jet Propulsion Laboratory. Technical Memorandum [*A publication*]
**JETR**......... Japan Engineering Test Reactor
**JETR**......... Jetevator
**JETRO**...... Japan External Trade Organization [*New York, NY*] (EA)
**JETS**.......... Jet Express Ticketing System
**JETS**.......... Jetborne International, Inc. [*NASDAQ symbol*] (NQ)
**JETS**.......... Job Executive and Transport Satellite [*NCR Corp.*]
**JETS**.......... Joint Electronics Type [*Designation*] System [*Military*] (NASA)
**JETS**.......... Joint Enroute Terminal System [*Canada*] (MCD)
**JETS**.......... Journal. Evangelical Theological Society [*A publication*]
**JETS**.......... Junior Engineering Technical Society
**JETT**......... Jettison (KSC)
**JETXA**...... Journal of Existentialism [*A publication*]
**JEU**............ Jeune Afrique [*Paris*] [*A publication*]
**JEU**............ Journal of European Industrial Training [*A publication*]
**JeuneA**....... Jeune Afrique [*A publication*]
**Jeune C**...... Jeune Cinema [*A publication*]
**Jeune Sci**... Jeune Scientifique [*Canada*] [*A publication*]
**Jeunesse**..... Jeunesse et Orgue [*A publication*]
**Jeunes Trav**... Jeunes Travailleurs [*A publication*]
**J Eur Econ Hist**... Journal of European Economic History [*A publication*]
**J Eur Ind Train**... Journal of European Industrial Training [*A publication*]
**J Eur Ind Training**... Journal of European Industrial Training [*A publication*]
**J Europ Training**... Journal of European Training [*A publication*]
**J Eur Pathol For**... Journal Europeen de Pathologie Forestiere [*A publication*]
**J Eur Radiother**... Journal Europeen de Radiotherapie, Oncologie, Radiophysique, Radiobiologie [*A publication*]
**J Eur Steroides**... Journal Europeen des Steroides [*France*] [*A publication*]
**J Eur Stud**... Journal of European Studies [*A publication*]
**J Eur Toxicol**... Journal Europeen de Toxicologie [*A publication*]
**J Eur Toxicol Suppl**... Journal Europeen de Toxicologie. Supplement [*A publication*]
**J Eur Train**... Journal of European Training [*A publication*]
**JEV**............ Japanese Encephalitis Virus [*Medicine*]
**J Evang Th S**... Journal. Evangelical Theological Society [*A publication*]
**Jev Cr Law**... Jevons on Criminal Law [*A publication*] (DLA)
**JEVEB**....... Journal of Environmental Education [*A publication*]
**J Ev Miss**... Jahrbuch Evangelischer Mission [*A publication*]
**J Evol Bioc**... Journal of Evolutionary Biochemistry and Physiology [*A publication*]
**J Evol Biochem Physiol (Engl Transl Zh Evol Biokhim Fiziol)**... Journal of Evolutionary Biochemistry and Physiology (English Translation of Zhurnal Evolyutsionnoi Biokhimii i Fiziologii) [*A publication*]
**J Evol Biochem Physiol (USSR)**... Journal of Evolutionary Biochemistry and Physiology (USSR) [*A publication*]
**J Evolut Biochem Physiol**... Journal of Evolutionary Biochemistry and Physiology [*A publication*]
**JEVQA**...... Journal of Environmental Quality [*A publication*]
**JEVSB**....... Journal of Environmental Systems [*A publication*]
**J Ev Th S**... Journal. Evangelical Theological Society [*A publication*]
**JEVWK**..... Jahrbuch. Evangelischer Verein fuer Westfaelische Kirchengeschichte [*A publication*]
**JEW**........... Jewellery [*British*] (ROG)
**Jew Aff**....... Jewish Affairs [*A publication*]
**JEWC**......... Joint Electronic Warfare Center (MCD)
**JewChron**... Jewish Chronicle [*London*] [*A publication*]
**JEW COLL LOND**... Jewish College, London [*England*] (ROG)
**JEWEL**...... Joint Endeavor for Welfare, Education, and Liberation [*In name of Grenadian political party, the New Jewel Movement, which governed from 1979 until ousted by a coup in 1983. Maurice Bishop, a founder of the party and prime minister under it, was killed during the overthrow*]
**Jew Hist Soc Engl Trans**... Jewish Historical Society of England. Transactions [*A publication*]
**Jewish Cu**.. Jewish Currents [*A publication*]
**Jewish Ed**.. Jewish Education [*A publication*]
**Jewish Educ**... Jewish Education [*A publication*]
**Jewish Hist Soc of England Trans**... Jewish Historical Society of England. Transactions [*A publication*]
**Jewish Soc Stud**... Jewish Social Studies [*A publication*]
**JewJSoc**..... Jewish Journal of Sociology [*London*] [*A publication*]
**Jew J Socio**... Jewish Journal of Sociology [*A publication*]
**JewL**.......... Jewish Life [*New York*] [*A publication*]
**JewQ**.......... Jewish Quarterly Review [*A publication*]
**Jew Q R**..... Jewish Quarterly Review [*A publication*]
**Jew Q Rev**... Jewish Quarterly Review [*A publication*]
**Jew Quart R**... Jewish Quarterly Review [*A publication*]
**JewRev**....... Jewish Review [*London*] [*A publication*]
**JewSocSt**... Jewish Social Studies [*New York*] [*A publication*]
**Jew Soc Stu**... Jewish Social Studies [*A publication*]
**JEWT**........ Jungle Exercise without Trees [*British military*] (DMA)
**Jew YB Int'l L**... Jewish Yearbook of International Law [*A publication*] (DLA)
**JEX**............ Jenks, OK [*Location identifier*] [*FAA*] (FAAL)
**JEX**............ Joint Exercise (NVT)
**J Ex An Beh**... Journal of the Experimental Analysis of Behavior [*A publication*]
**J Excep Child**... Journal of Exceptional Children [*A publication*]
**J Existent**... Journal of Existentialism [*A publication*]
**JExP**.......... Journal of Experimental Psychology [*A publication*]
**J Exp Anal Behav**... Journal of the Experimental Analysis of Behavior [*A publication*]
**J Exp Analysis Behav**... Journal of the Experimental Analysis of Behavior [*A publication*]
**J Exp Anim Sci**... Journal of Experimental Animal Science [*A publication*]
**J Exp Biol**... Journal of Experimental Biology [*A publication*]
**J Exp Bot**... Journal of Experimental Botany [*A publication*]
**J Exp Child Psy**... Journal of Experimental Child Psychology [*A publication*]
**J Exp Child Psychol**... Journal of Experimental Child Psychology [*A publication*]
**J Exp Clin Cancer Res**... Journal of Experimental and Clinical Cancer Research [*A publication*]
**J Exp C Psy**... Journal of Experimental Child Psychology [*A publication*]
**J Exp Ed**.... Journal of Experimental Education [*A publication*]
**J Exp Educ**... Journal of Experimental Education [*A publication*]
**J Exper Anal Behav**... Journal of the Experimental Analysis of Behavior [*A publication*]
**J Exper Biol**... Journal of Experimental Biology [*A publication*]
**J Exper Bot**... Journal of Experimental Botany [*A publication*]
**J Exper Child Psychol**... Journal of Experimental Child Psychology [*A publication*]
**J Exper Educ**... Journal of Experimental Education [*A publication*]
**J Exper Marine Biol & Ecol**... Journal of Experimental Marine Biology and Ecology [*A publication*]
**J Exper Med**... Journal of Experimental Medicine [*A publication*]
**J Exper Psychol Human Learn Mem**... Journal of Experimental Psychology: Human Learning and Memory [*A publication*]
**J Exper Psychol Human Percept & Perf**... Journal of Experimental Psychology: Human Perception and Performance [*A publication*]
**J Exper Social Psychol**... Journal of Experimental Social Psychology [*A publication*]
**J Exper Soc Psychol**... Journal of Experimental Social Psychology [*A publication*]
**J Exper Zool**... Journal of Experimental Zoology [*A publication*]
**J Ex P H P**... Journal of Experimental Psychology: Human Perception and Performance [*A publication*]

**J Ex P L**..... Journal of Experimental Psychology: Human Learning and Memory [*A publication*]
**J Exp M**..... Journal of Experimental Medicine [*A publication*]
**J Exp Mar B** ... Journal of Experimental Marine Biology and Ecology [*A publication*]
**J Exp Mar Biol Ecol** ... Journal of Experimental Marine Biology and Ecology [*A publication*]
**J Exp Med** ... Journal of Experimental Medicine [*A publication*]
**J Exp Med Sci** ... Journal of Experimental Medical Sciences [*A publication*]
**J Exp Pathol** ... Journal of Experimental Pathology [*A publication*]
**J Exp Psy A** ... Journal of Experimental Psychology: Animal Behavior Processes [*A publication*]
**J Exp Psych** ... Journal of Experimental Psychology [*A publication*]
**J Exp Psychol** ... Journal of Experimental Psychology [*A publication*]
**J Exp Psychol (Animal Behav Proc)** ... Journal of Experimental Psychology: Animal Behavior Processes [*A publication*]
**J Exp Psychol Anim Behav Processes** ... Journal of Experimental Psychology. Animal Behavior Processes [*A publication*]
**J Exp Psychol Gen** ... Journal of Experimental Psychology: General [*A publication*]
**J Exp Psychol Hum Learn Mem** ... Journal of Experimental Psychology: Human Learning and Memory [*A publication*]
**J Exp Psychol Hum Percept Perform** ... Journal of Experimental Psychology: Human Perception and Performance [*A publication*]
**J Exp Psychol Hum Perc Perf** ... Journal of Experimental Psychology: Human Perception and Performance [*A publication*]
**J Exp Psychol Learn Mem Cogn** ... Journal of Experimental Psychology. Learning, Memory, and Cognition [*A publication*]
**J Exp Psychol Monogr** ... Journal of Experimental Psychology: Monograph [*A publication*]
**J Exp Psy G** ... Journal of Experimental Psychology: General [*A publication*]
**J Exp Psy H** ... Journal of Experimental Psychology: Human Learning and Memory [*A publication*]
**J Exp Psy P** ... Journal of Experimental Psychology: Human Perception and Performance [*A publication*]
**J Exp Res Pers** ... Journal of Experimental Research in Personality [*A publication*]
**J Exp Soc Psych** ... Journal of Experimental Social Psychology [*A publication*]
**J Exp Soc Psychol** ... Journal of Experimental Social Psychology [*A publication*]
**J Exp S Psy** ... Journal of Experimental Social Psychology [*A publication*]
**J Exp Ther** ... Journal of Experimental Therapeutics [*A publication*]
**J Exp Zool** ... Journal of Experimental Zoology [*A publication*]
**J Ext**.......... Journal of Extension [*A publication*]
**J Extra Corporeal Technol** ... Journal of Extra-Corporeal Technology [*A publication*]
**JEY**........... Journal of Employment Counseling [*A publication*]
**J Eye**.......... Journal of the Eye [*A publication*]
**JEZEX**....... Jezebel [*Sonobuoy*] Exercise [*Navy*] (NVT)
**JF**.............. Crest Aviation [*Great Britain*] [*ICAO designator*] (FAAC)
**JF**.............. Jack Field
**JF**.............. Jackstone Froster Ltd. [*Commercial firm*] [*British*]
**JF**.............. Jamestown Foundation (EA)
**JF**.............. Japan Foundation [*Also, Kokusai Koryu*] (EA)
**JF**.............. Jefferson Foundation (EA)
**JF**.............. Jet Flap
**JF**.............. Jewish Frontier [*A publication*]
**J & F**.......... Job and Function [*Air Force*] (AAG)
**JF**.............. John Flanagan [*Designer's mark, when appearing on US coins*]
**JF**.............. Joint Filler [*Technical drawings*]
**JF**.............. Joint Force [*Military*]
**JF**.............. Jornal de Filologia [*A publication*]
**JF**.............. Journal of Finance [*A publication*]
**JF**.............. Journal Folio (ROG)
**JF**.............. Junction Frequency [*Telecommunications*] (TEL)
**JF**.............. Junctor Frame [*Telecommunications*] (TEL)
**JF**.............. Justice Fellowship (EA)
**JF**.............. Juznoslovenski Filolog [*A publication*]
**JF**.............. Trehaven Aviation Ltd. [*United Kingdom*] [*ICAO designator*] (ICDA)
**JFA**........... Jahresbericht ueber die Fortschritte der Klassischen Altertumswissenschaft [*A publication*]
**JFA**........... Journal of Field Archaeology [*A publication*]
**JFAAD**...... Joint Forward-Area Air Defense (MCD)
**JFAADS**.... Joint Forward-Area Air Defense System
**JfAaK**........ Jahrbuch fuer Aesthetik und Allgemeine Kunstwissenschaft [*A publication*]
**J Fabr Sucre** ... Journal des Fabricants de Sucre [*A publication*]
**J Fac Agric Hokkaido Univ** ... Journal. Faculty of Agriculture. Hokkaido University [*A publication*]
**J Fac Agric Hokkaido Univ Ser Entomol** ... Journal. Faculty of Agriculture. Hokkaido University. Series Entomology [*A publication*]
**J Fac Agric Iwate Univ** ... Journal. Faculty of Agriculture. Iwate University [*A publication*]
**J Fac Agric Kyushu Univ** ... Journal. Faculty of Agriculture. Kyushu University [*A publication*]
**J Fac Agric Shinshu Univ** ... Journal. Faculty of Agriculture. Shinshu University [*A publication*]
**J Fac Agric Tottori Univ** ... Journal. Faculty of Agriculture. Tottori University [*A publication*]
**J Fac Agr Iwate Univ** ... Journal. Faculty of Agriculture. Iwate University [*A publication*]
**J Fac Agr Kyushu Univ** ... Journal. Faculty of Agriculture. Kyushu University [*A publication*]
**J Fac Agr Shinshu Univ** ... Journal. Faculty of Agriculture. Shinshu University [*A publication*]
**J Fac Agr Tottori Univ** ... Journal. Faculty of Agriculture. Tottori University [*A publication*]
**J Fac Appl Biol Sci Hiroshima Univ** ... Journal. Faculty of Applied Biological Science. Hiroshima University [*A publication*]
**J Fac Ed Saga Univ** ... Journal. Faculty of Education. Saga University [*A publication*]
**J Fac Ed Saga Univ Part 1** ... Journal. Faculty of Education. Saga University. Part 1 [*A publication*]
**J Fac Educ Nat Sci Tottori Univ** ... Journal. Faculty of Education. Natural Sciences. Tottori University [*Japan*] [*A publication*]
**J Fac Educ Tottori Univ Nat Sci** ... Journal. Faculty of Education. Tottori University. Natural Science [*A publication*]
**J Fac Eng Chiba Univ** ... Journal. Faculty of Engineering. Chiba University [*A publication*]
**J Fac Eng Ibaraki Univ** ... Journal. Faculty of Engineering. Ibaraki University [*Japan*] [*A publication*]
**J Fac Engng Univ Tokyo** ... Journal. Faculty of Engineering. University of Tokyo [*A publication*]
**J Fac Engrg Chiba Univ** ... Journal. Faculty of Engineering. Chiba University [*A publication*]
**J Fac Engrg Univ Tokyo Ser B** ... Journal. Faculty of Engineering. University of Tokyo. Series B [*A publication*]
**J Fac Eng Shinshu Univ** ... Journal. Faculty of Engineering. Shinshu University [*A publication*]
**J Fac Eng Univ Tokyo** ... Journal. Faculty of Engineering. University of Tokyo [*A publication*]
**J Fac Eng Univ Tokyo Ser A** ... Journal. Faculty of Engineering. University of Tokyo. Series A. Annual Report [*A publication*]
**J Fac Eng Univ Tokyo Ser B** ... Journal. Faculty of Engineering. University of Tokyo. Series B [*A publication*]
**J Fac Fish Anim Husb Hiroshima Univ** ... Journal. Faculty of Fisheries and Animal Husbandry. Hiroshima University [*A publication*]
**J Fac Fish Anim Husb Hir Univ** ... Journal. Faculty of Fisheries and Animal Husbandry. Hiroshima University [*A publication*]
**J Fac Fish Prefect Univ Mie** ... Journal. Faculty of Fisheries. Prefectural University of Mie [*A publication*]
**J Fac Lib Arts Shinshu Univ Part II Nat Sci** ... Journal. Faculty of Liberal Arts. Shinshu University. Part II. Natural Sciences [*A publication*]
**J Fac Liberal Arts Yamaguchi Univ** ... Journal. Faculty of Liberal Arts. Yamaguchi University [*A publication*]
**J Fac Liberal Arts Yamaguchi Univ Natur Sci** ... Journal. Faculty of Liberal Arts. Yamaguchi University. Natural Sciences [*A publication*]
**J Fac Mar Sci Technol Tokai Univ** ... Journal. Faculty of Marine Science and Technology. Tokai University [*A publication*]
**J Fac Med (Baghdad)** ... Journal. Faculty of Medicine (Baghdad) [*A publication*]
**J Fac Med Chulalongkorn Univ (Bangkok)** ... Journal. Faculty of Medicine. Chulalongkorn University (Bangkok) [*A publication*]
**J Fac Med Shin Univ** ... Journal. Faculty of Medicine. Shinshu University [*A publication*]
**J Fac Med Univ Ankara** ... Journal. Faculty of Medicine. University of Ankara [*A publication*]
**J Fac Med Univ Ankara Suppl** ... Journal. Faculty of Medicine. University of Ankara. Supplement [*A publication*]
**J Fac Oceanogr Tokai Univ** ... Journal. Faculty of Oceanography. Tokai University [*A publication*]
**J Fac Pharm Istanbul Univ** ... Journal. Faculty of Pharmacy. Istanbul University [*A publication*]
**J Fac Polit Sci Econ Tokai Univ** ... Journal. Faculty of Political Science and Economics. Tokai University [*A publication*]
**J Fac Rad**... Journal. Faculty of Radiologists [*A publication*]
**J Fac Radiol (Lond)** ... Journal. Faculty of Radiologists (London) [*A publication*]
**J Fac Sci Hokkaido Univ** ... Journal. Faculty of Science. Hokkaido University [*A publication*]
**J Fac Sci Hokkaido Univ Ser IV Geol Mineral** ... Journal. Faculty of Science. Hokkaido University. Series IV. Geology and Mineralogy [*A publication*]
**J Fac Sci Hokkaido Univ Ser V Bot** ... Journal. Faculty of Science. Hokkaido University. Series V. Botany [*A publication*]
**J Fac Sci Hokkaido Univ Ser VII** ... Journal. Faculty of Science. Hokkaido University. Series VII. Geophysics [*A publication*]
**J Fac Sci Hokkaido Univ Ser VI Zool** ... Journal. Faculty of Science. Hokkaido University. Series VI. Zoology [*A publication*]
**J Fac Sci Hokkaido Univ VI** ... Journal. Faculty of Science. Hokkaido University. Series VI. Zoology [*A publication*]
**J Fac Sci Imp Univ Tokyo Sect IV Zool** ... Journal. Faculty of Science. Imperial University of Tokyo. Section IV. Zoology [*A publication*]
**J Fac Sci Niigata Univ Ser II Biol Geol Mineral** ... Journal. Faculty of Science. Niigata University. Series II. Biology, Geology, and Mineralogy [*A publication*]

**J Fac Sci Riyad Univ** ... Riyad University. Faculty of Science. Journal [*A publication*]
**J Fac Sci Shinshu Univ** ... Journal. Faculty of Science. Shinshu University [*A publication*]
**J Fac Sci Tokyo Univ** ... Journal. Faculty of Science. Tokyo University [*A publication*]
**J Fac Sci Univ Tokyo Sect IA** ... Journal. Faculty of Science. University of Tokyo. Section IA. Mathematics [*A publication*]
**J Fac Sci Univ Tokyo Sect IA Math** ... Journal. Faculty of Science. University of Tokyo. Section IA. Mathematics [*A publication*]
**J Fac Sci Univ Tokyo Sect II Geol Mineral Geogr Geophys** ... Journal. Faculty of Science. University of Tokyo. Section II. Geology, Mineralogy, Geography, Geophysics [*A publication*]
**J Fac Sci Univ Tokyo Sect III Bot** ... Journal. Faculty of Science. University of Tokyo. Section III. Botany [*A publication*]
**J Fac Sci Univ Tokyo Sect IV** ... Journal. Faculty of Science. University of Tokyo. Section IV. Zoology [*Japan*] [*A publication*]
**J Fac Sci Univ Tokyo Sect IV Zool** ... Journal. Faculty of Science. University of Tokyo. Section IV. Zoology [*A publication*]
**J Fac Sci Univ Tokyo Sect V** ... Journal. Faculty of Science. University of Tokyo. Section V. Anthropology [*A publication*]
**J Fac Sci Univ Tokyo Sect V Anthropol** ... Journal. Faculty of Science. University of Tokyo. Section V. Anthropology [*A publication*]
**J-FACT** ..... Joint Flight Acceptance Composite Test [*Gemini*] [*NASA*]
**J Fac Text Sci Technol Shinshu Univ Ser A Biol** ... Journal. Faculty of Textile Science and Technology. Shinshu University. Series A. Biology [*A publication*]
**J Fac Text Sci Technol Shinshu Univ Ser B** ... Journal. Faculty of Textile Science and Technology. Shinshu University. Series B. Textile Engineering [*A publication*]
**J Fac Text Sci Technol Shinshu Univ Ser C** ... Journal. Faculty of Textile Science and Technology. Shinshu University. Series C. Chemistry [*A publication*]
**J Fac Text Sci Technol Shinshu Univ Ser D** ... Journal. Faculty of Textile Science and Technology. Shinshu University. Series D. Arts [*A publication*]
**J Fac Text Sci Technol Shinshu Univ Ser E** ... Journal. Faculty of Textile Science and Technology. Shinshu University. Series E. Agriculture and Sericulture [*A publication*]
**J Fac Text Sci Technol Shinshu Univ Ser E Agric Seric** ... Journal. Faculty of Textile Science and Technology. Shinshu University. Series E. Agriculture and Sericulture [*A publication*]
**J Fac Text Seric Shinshu Ser E Seric** ... Journal. Faculty of Textile Science and Sericulture. Shinshu University. Series E. Sericulture [*A publication*]
**J Fac Text Seric Shinshu Univ Ser A** ... Journal. Faculty of Textile Science and Sericulture. Shinshu University. Series A. Biology [*A publication*]
**J Fac Text Seric Shinshu Univ Ser B** ... Journal. Faculty of Textile Science and Sericulture. Shinshu University. Series B. Textile Engineering [*A publication*]
**J Fac Text Seric Shinshu Univ Ser C** ... Journal. Faculty of Textile Science and Sericulture. Shinshu University. Series C. Chemistry [*A publication*]
**J Fac Text Seric Shinshu Univ Ser D** ... Journal. Faculty of Textile Science and Sericulture. Shinshu University. Series D. Arts and Sciences [*A publication*]
**J Fac Text Seric Shinshu Univ Ser E** ... Journal. Faculty of Textile Science and Sericulture. Shinshu University. Series E. Sericulture [*A publication*]
**J Fac Text Sericu Shinshu Univ Ser A Biol** ... Journal. Faculty of Textile Science and Sericulture. Shinshu University. Series A. Biology [*A publication*]
**J Fac Tok I** ... Journal. Faculty of Science. University of Tokyo. Section I. Mathematics, Astronomy, Physics, Chemistry [*A publication*]
**JFACTSU** ... Joint Forward Air Controllers Training and Standards Unit [*British*]
**J Faculty Arts Roy Univ Malta** ... Journal. Faculty of Arts. Royal University of Malta [*A publication*]
**J Fac Vet Med Univ Ankara** ... Journal. Faculty of Veterinary Medicine. University of Ankara [*A publication*]
**JFAI** .......... Joint Formal Acceptance Inspection [*NATO*] (NATG)
**JFAKA** ...... Journal. Faculty of Agriculture. Kyushu University [*A publication*]
**J Fam Couns** ... Journal of Family Counseling [*A publication*]
**J Fam Hist** ... Journal of Family History [*A publication*]
**J Family L** ... Journal of Family Law [*A publication*]
**J Fam L**...... Journal of Family Law [*A publication*]
**J Fam Law** ... Journal of Family Law [*A publication*]
**J Fam Pract** ... Journal of Family Practice [*A publication*]
**J Fam Wel** ... Journal of Family Welfare [*A publication*]
**J Fam Welf** ... Journal of Family Welfare [*A publication*]
**JFAP**.......... Joint Frequency Allocation Panel
**J Farm**........ Jornal dos Farmaceuticos [*A publication*]
**J Farm Econ** ... Journal of Farm Economics [*A publication*]
**J Farmers' Club** ... Journal. Farmers' Club [*A publication*]
**J Farnham Mus Soc** ... Journal. Farnham Museum Society [*A publication*]
**JFBND**...... Journal Francais de Biophysique et Medecine Nucleaire [*A publication*]
**JFC** ........... John Forsyth Co., Inc. [*Toronto Stock Exchange symbol*]
**JFC** ........... Journal of Business Forecasting [*A publication*]
**JFC** ........... LTV Jet Fleet Corporation [*Dallas, TX*] [*FAA designator*] (FAAC)
**JFCB**.......... Job File Control Block [*Data processing*] (BUR)
**JFDA** ......... Jewish Funeral Directors of America (EA)
**JFDH**......... Jahrbuch. Freies Deutsche Hochstift [*A publication*]
**J Fd Hyg Soc Jap** ... Journal. Food Hygienic Society of Japan [*A publication*]
**JFDP** ......... Joint Force Development Process [*or Program*] [*Army*]
**J Fd Sci**...... Journal of Food Science [*A publication*]
**J Fd Sci Technol** ... Journal of Food Science and Technology [*A publication*]
**J Fd Technol** ... Journal of Food Technology [*A publication*]
**JFE** ........... Journal of Farm Economics [*A publication*]
**JFE** ........... Journal of Financial Economics [*A publication*]
**JFE** ........... Journal of Fusion Energy [*A publication*]
**JFEA** ......... Japan Federation of Employers Association
**JFEA** ......... Joint Foreign Exchange Agency [*Berlin*] [*Post-World War II, Germany*]
**JFED** ......... Junction Field-Effect Device
**JFEND** ...... Journal of Fusion Energy [*A publication*]
**JFEO** ......... Japanese Federation of Economic Organizations
**J Ferment Assoc Jpn** ... Journal. Fermentation Association of Japan [*A publication*]
**J Ferment Bioeng** ... Journal of Fermentation and Bioengineering [*A publication*]
**J Ferment Ind** ... Journal of Fermentation Industries [*A publication*]
**J Ferment Techn** ... Journal of Fermentation Technology [*A publication*]
**J Ferment Technol** ... Journal of Fermentation Technology [*A publication*]
**J Ferment Technol (1944-1976)** ... Journal of Fermentation Technology (1944-1976) [*Japan*] [*A publication*]
**J Ferment Technol (Osaka)** ... Journal of Fermentation Technology (Osaka) [*Japan*] [*A publication*]
**J Ferm Tech** ... Journal of Fermentation Technology [*A publication*]
**J Ferrocem** ... Journal of Ferrocement [*A publication*]
**J Ferrocement** ... Journal of Ferrocement [*New Zealand*] [*A publication*]
**J Fert Issues** ... Journal of Fertilizer Issues [*A publication*]
**JFET**.......... Junction Field-Effect Transistor
**JFEW** ........ Jewish Foundation for Education of Women (EA)
**JFF** ............ Aguadilla, PR [*Location identifier*] [*FAA*] (FAAL)
**JFF** ............ Juedische Familien Forschung [*A publication*]
**JFF** ............ Jugend Film Fernsehen [*A publication*]
**JFF** ............ Junior Fashion Fair International [*Great Britain*] (ITD)
**JFFC**.......... Jewish Fighting Force Committee [*British*]
**JFFC**.......... John Fricke Fan Club (EA)
**JFFC**.......... Judy Fields Fan Club (EA)
**JFFJ** .......... Japanese Fantasy Film Journal [*A publication*]
**JFFN** ......... Jefferson Bank [*Haverford, PA*] [*NASDAQ symbol*] (NQ)
**JFG**............ Jahrbuch der Philosophischen Fakultaet. Universitaet zu Goettingen [*A publication*]
**JFG**............ Jumbogroup Frequency Generator [*Bell System*]
**JFH**............ Jam Frequency Hopper
**JFHLA** ...... Federal Home Loan Bank Board. Journal [*A publication*]
**JFHS** ......... Journal. Flintshire Historical Society [*A publication*]
**JFI** ............. James Franck Institute [*University of Chicago*] [*Research center*] (RCD)
**JFI** ............. Japanese Fermentation Institute
**JFI** ............. Jet Flight Information (AFM)
**JFI** ............. John La Farge Institute (EA)
**JFI** ............. Journal of Finance [*A publication*]
**JFI** ............. Journal. Folklore Institute [*A publication*]
**JFI** ............. Journal. Franklin Institute [*A publication*]
**JFI** ............. New Orleans, LA [*Location identifier*] [*FAA*] (FAAL)
**JFIAP**........ Joint Foreign Intelligence Assistance Program (AFM)
**J Field A** .... Journal of Field Archaeology [*A publication*]
**J Field Arch** ... Journal of Field Archaeology [*A publication*]
**J Field Ornithol** ... Journal of Field Ornithology [*A publication*]
**J Fin**........... Journal of Finance [*A publication*]
**JFINA** ....... Journal. Franklin Institute [*A publication*]
**J Finance** ... Journal of Finance [*A publication*]
**J Financ Quant Anal** ... Journal of Financial and Quantitative Analysis [*A publication*]
**J Fin Planning** ... Journal of Financial Planning [*Later, Journal of Financial Planning Today*] [*A publication*]
**J Fin Qu An** ... Journal of Financial and Quantitative Analysis [*A publication*]
**J Fire Flamm** ... Journal of Fire and Flammability [*A publication*]
**J Fire Flammability** ... Journal of Fire and Flammability [*A publication*]
**J Fire Retardant Chem** ... Journal of Fire Retardant Chemistry [*A publication*]
**J Fire Retard Chem** ... Journal of Fire Retardant Chemistry [*A publication*]
**J Fire Sc**..... Journal of Fire Sciences [*A publication*]
**J Fish Biol** ... Journal of Fish Biology [*A publication*]
**J Fish Dis** .. Journal of Fish Diseases [*England*] [*A publication*]
**J Fisheries Res Board Can** ... Journal. Fisheries Research Board of Canada [*A publication*]
**J Fish Res** .. Journal. Fisheries Research Board of Canada [*A publication*]
**J Fish Res Board Can** ... Journal. Fisheries Research Board of Canada [*A publication*]
**J Fiz Malays** ... Jurnal Fizik Malaysia [*A publication*]
**JFJ**............. Jewish Fund for Justice (EA)
**JFJ**............. Jews for Jesus (EA)
**JFK**............ John Fitzgerald Kennedy [*US president, 1917-1963*]

**JFK**........... Kennedy International Airport [*New York*] [*Airport symbol*]
**JFKA**......... Jahresbericht ueber die Fortschritte der Klassischen Altertumswissenschaft [*A publication*]
**JFKAW**..... Jahresberichte ueber die Fortschritte der Klassischen Altertumswissenschaft [*A publication*]
**JFKC**......... John Fitzgerald Kennedy Center for the Performing Arts
**JFKCTRMA**... John F. Kennedy Center for Military Assistance (MCD)
**JFK FDC SU**... John F. Kennedy First Day Cover Study Unit (EA)
**JFKL**.......... John F. Kennedy Library
**JFKPS**....... John F. Kennedy Philatelic Society (EA)
**JFKSC**....... John Fitzgerald Kennedy Spaceflight Center [*Also known as KSC*] [*NASA*]
**JFL**........... Jahrbuch fuer Fraenkische Landesforschung [*A publication*]
**JFL**........... Jewish Family Living [*A publication*]
**JFL**........... Joint Frequency List
**JFL**........... Judy Farquharson Limited [*British*]
**JFLA**.......... Jewish Free Loan Association (EA)
**J Fla Acad Gen Pract**... Journal. Florida Academy of General Practice [*A publication*]
**J Fla Med Ass**... Journal. Florida Medical Association [*A publication*]
**J Fla Med Assoc**... Journal. Florida Medical Association [*A publication*]
**J Fla State Dent Soc**... Journal. Florida State Dental Society [*A publication*]
**J FL Eng Soc**... Journal. Florida Engineering Society [*A publication*]
**JFLF**.......... Jahrbuch fuer Fraenkische Landesforschung [*A publication*]
**J Floresc Miner Soc**... Journal. Fluorescent Mineral Society [*A publication*]
**J Florida MA**... Journal. Florida Medical Association [*A publication*]
**J Flour Anim Feed Milling**... Journal of Flour and Animal Feed Milling [*A publication*]
**J Fluency Dis**... Journal of Fluency Disorders [*A publication*]
**J Fluency Disord**... Journal of Fluency Disorders [*A publication*]
**J Fluid Eng Trans ASME**... Journal of Fluids Engineering. Transactions of the American Society of Mechanical Engineers [*A publication*]
**J Fluid Mec**... Journal of Fluid Mechanics [*A publication*]
**J Fluid Mech**... Journal of Fluid Mechanics [*A publication*]
**J Fluids Eng**... Journal of Fluids Engineering. Transactions of the American Society of Mechanical Engineers [*A publication*]
**J Fluorine**... Journal of Fluorine Chemistry [*A publication*]
**J Fluorine Chem**... Journal of Fluorine Chemistry [*A publication*]
**JFM**........... Jet Flap Model
**JFM**........... Jeunesses Federalistes Mondiales
**JFM**........... Job Function Manual (AAG)
**JFM**........... Joint Force Memorandum [*Military*]
**JFM**........... Journal of Forms Management [*A publication*]
**JFM**........... Journal of Futures Markets [*A publication*]
**JFM**........... Jupiter Flyby Mission [*Aerospace*]
**JFMA**........ Journal. Florida Medical Association [*A publication*]
**JFMIP**....... Joint Financial Management Improvement Program
**JFMO**........ Joint Frequency Management Office (MCD)
**JFN**........... Jefferson, OH [*Location identifier*] [*FAA*] (FAAL)
**JFN**........... Job File Number
**JFNF**......... Jewish Family Name File [*Association for the Study of Jewish Languages*] [*Information service or system*] (CRD)
**JfNG**.......... Jahrbuch fuer Numismatik und Geldgeschichte [*A publication*]
**JFNP**......... Joseph M. Farley Nuclear Plant (NRCH)
**JFNPP**....... James A. FitzPatrick Nuclear Power Plant (NRCH)
**JFOAB**...... Journal Francais d'Oto-Rhino-Laryngologie, Audiophonologie, et Chirurgie Maxillo-Faciale [*A publication*]
**J Foetal Med**... Journal of Foetal Medicine [*A publication*]
**J Folk Inst**... Journal. Folklore Institute [*A publication*]
**J Folkl Inst**... Journal. Folklore Institute [*A publication*]
**J Food Biochem**... Journal of Food Biochemistry [*A publication*]
**J Food Hygienic Soc Jap**... Journal. Food Hygienic Society of Japan [*A publication*]
**J Food Hyg Soc Jap**... Journal. Food Hygienic Society of Japan [*A publication*]
**J Food Hyg Soc Jpn**... Journal. Food Hygienic Society of Japan [*A publication*]
**J Food Nutr (Canberra)**... Journal of Food and Nutrition (Canberra) [*A publication*]
**J Food Process Eng**... Journal of Food Process Engineering [*A publication*]
**J Food Process Preserv**... Journal of Food Processing and Preservation [*A publication*]
**J Food Prot**... Journal of Food Protection [*A publication*]
**J Food Protect**... Journal of Food Protection [*A publication*]
**J Food Qual**... Journal of Food Quality [*A publication*]
**J Food Resour Dev**... Journal of Food Resources Development [*A publication*]
**J Food Saf**... Journal of Food Safety [*A publication*]
**J Food Sci**.. Journal of Food Science [*A publication*]
**J Food Sci Kyoto Women's Univ**... Journal of Food Science. Kyoto Women's University [*A publication*]
**J Food Sci Tech**... Journal of Food Science and Technology [*A publication*]
**J Food Sci Technol**... Journal of Food Science and Technology [*A publication*]
**J Food Sci Technol (Mysore)**... Journal of Food Science and Technology (Mysore) [*A publication*]
**J Food Sci Technol (Tokyo)**... Journal of Food Science and Technology (Tokyo) [*A publication*]
**J Food Serv Syst**... Journal of Food Service Systems [*A publication*]
**J Food Technol**... Journal of Food Technology [*A publication*]
**J Foot Surg**... Journal of Foot Surgery [*A publication*]
**J For**.......... Journal of Forestry [*A publication*]
**J Foraminiferal Res**... Journal of Foraminiferal Research [*A publication*]
**J For Comm**... Journal. Forestry Commission [*A publication*]
**J Forecasting**... Journal of Forecasting [*A publication*]
**J Foren Sci**... Journal of Forensic Sciences [*A publication*]
**J Forensic Med**... Journal of Forensic Medicine [*A publication*]
**J Forensic Odontostomatol**... Journal of Forensic Odonto-Stomatology [*A publication*]
**J Forensic Sci**... Journal of Forensic Sciences [*A publication*]
**J Forensic Sci Soc**... Journal. Forensic Science Society [*A publication*]
**J Forest**...... Journal of Forestry [*A publication*]
**J For Hist**.. Journal of Forest History [*A publication*]
**JFORL**...... Journal Francais d'Oto-Rhino-Laryngologie [*A publication*]
**J For Med**... Journal of Forensic Medicine [*A publication*]
**J Formosan Med Assoc**... Journal. Formosan Medical Association [*A publication*]
**J For Prod Res Soc**... Journal. Forest Products Research Society [*A publication*]
**J For Sci**..... Journal of Forensic Sciences [*A publication*]
**J For Sci Soc**... Journal. Forensic Science Society [*A publication*] (DLA)
**J For Sci Socy**... Journal. Forensic Science Society [*A publication*]
**J For Suisse**... Journal Forestier Suisse [*A publication*]
**J For Suisse Schweiz Z Forstwes**... Journal Forestier Suisse/Schweizerische Zeitschrift fuer Forstwesen [*A publication*]
**J Four Elec**... Journal du Four Electrique [*A publication*]
**JFP**........... Jewish Family Purity (BJA)
**JFP**........... Joint Frequency Panel
**JFP**........... Journal of Financial Planning Today [*A publication*]
**JFPH**......... JUMPS Field Procedures Handbook (NVT)
**JFPRD**....... Journal of Food Protection [*A publication*]
**JFQ**........... Journal of Financial and Quantitative Analysis [*A publication*]
**JFQA**......... Journal of Financial and Quantitative Analysis [*A publication*]
**JFR**........... Jamie Frontier Resources, Inc. [*Toronto Stock Exchange symbol*]
**JFR**........... Jet Flap Rotor
**JFR**........... Joint Fiction Reserve
**JFR**........... Journal of Financial Research [*A publication*]
**JFR**........... Journal of Folklore Research [*A publication*]
**J Fr Agric**... Journal de la France Agricole [*A publication*]
**J Frankl I**... Journal. Franklin Institute [*A publication*]
**J Franklin Inst**... Journal. Franklin Institute [*A publication*]
**JFRB**.......... Journal. Fisheries Research Board of Canada [*A publication*]
**JFRBA**........ Journal. Fisheries Research Board of Canada [*A publication*]
**J Fr Biophys Med Nucl**... Journal Francais de Biophysique et Medecine Nucleaire [*A publication*]
**JFRC**......... James Forrestal Research Center [*Princeton University*] (MCD)
**JFRCD**...... Journal of Fire Retardant Chemistry [*A publication*]
**JFRDD**...... Journal of Food Resources Development [*A publication*]
**J Free Radicals Biol & Med**... Journal of Free Radicals in Biology and Medicine [*A publication*]
**J Free Radic Biol Med**... Journal of Free Radicals in Biology and Medicine [*A publication*]
**J Freshwater**... Journal of Freshwater [*A publication*]
**J Freshwater Ecol**... Journal of Freshwater Ecology [*A publication*]
**J Freshw Ec**... Journal of Freshwater Ecology [*A publication*]
**J Fr Med Chir Thorac**... Journal Francais de Medecine et Chirurgie Thoraciques [*A publication*]
**J Fron**......... Jewish Frontier [*A publication*]
**J Fr Ophtalmol**... Journal Francais d'Ophtalmologie [*A publication*]
**J Fr Oto-Rhino-Laryngol**... Journal Francais d'Oto-Rhino-Laryngologie et Chirurgie Maxillo-Faciale [*Later, Journal Francais d'Oto-Rhino-Laryngologie*] [*A publication*]
**J Fr Oto Rhino Laryngol Audio Phonol Chir Maxillo Fac**... Journal Francais d'Oto-Rhino-Laryngologie, Audio-Phonologie, et Chirurgie Maxillo-Faciale [*A publication*]
**J Fr Oto Rhino Laryngol Chir Maxillo Fac**... Journal Francais d'Oto-Rhino-Laryngologie et Chirurgie Maxillo-Faciale [*Later, Journal Francias d'Oto-Rhino-Laryngologie*] [*A publication*]
**J Frottement Ind**... Journal du Frottement Industriel [*France*] [*A publication*]
**JFRY**......... Jeffrey Martin, Inc. [*NASDAQ symbol*] (NQ)
**JFS**............ Jane's Fighting Ships [*A publication*]
**JFS**............ Jet Fuel Starter
**JFS**............ Jewish Family Service (EA)
**JFS**............ Jewish Friends Society (EA)
**JFS**............ Job Finder System
**JFS**............ Johnston & Frye [*Vancouver Stock Exchange symbol*]
**JFS**............ Joint Foundation Support (EA)
**JFS**............ Jumbogroup Frequency Supply [*Bell System*]
**JFSG**.......... Joint Feasibility Study Group [*Air Force*] (MCD)
**JFSGW**...... Journal. Folklore Society of Greater Washington [*A publication*]
**JFSNY**....... Jewish Folk Schools of New York (EA)
**JFSS**.......... Journal. Folk Song Society [*A publication*]
**JFSUB**....... Journal of Foot Surgery [*A publication*]
**JFT**............ Joint Field Trial (NATG)
**JFTCG**....... Joint Flight Test Control Group (AAG)
**JFTED**....... Journal of Fermentation Technology [*A publication*]
**JFTG**......... Joint Fuze Task Group [*Army*]

**JFTOT** ...... Jet Fuel Thermal Oxidation Test [*or Tester*] [*Analytical chemistry*] [*Air Force*]
**JFTS** .......... Jet Fuel Thermal Stability
**JFTU** ......... Jordan Federation of Trade Unions
**JFTX** .......... Joint Field Training Exercise [*Military*]
**JFU** ........... Journal of Futures Markets [*A publication*]
**JFUB** ......... Joint Facilities Utilization Board [*Military*]
**J Fuel Heat Technol** ... Journal of Fuel and Heat Technology [*A publication*]
**J Fuel Soc Jap** ... Journal. Fuel Society of Japan [*Nenryo Kyokai-Shi*] [*A publication*]
**J Fujian Agric Coll** ... Journal. Fujian Agricultural College [*A publication*]
**J Funct Ana** ... Journal of Functional Analysis [*A publication*]
**J Funct Anal** ... Journal of Functional Analysis [*A publication*]
**J Functional Analysis** ... Journal of Functional Analysis [*A publication*]
**J Fur Higher Educ** ... Journal of Further and Higher Education [*A publication*]
**JFUS** ......... Journal of Forestry (United States) [*A publication*]
**J Fusion Energy** ... Journal of Fusion Energy [*A publication*]
**J Futures Markets** ... Journal of Futures Markets [*A publication*]
**JFuU** .......... Fukui University, Fukui-shi, Japan [*Library symbol*] [*Library of Congress*] (LCLS)
**JFV** ............ Jobs for Veterans National Committee [*Defunct*] (EA)
**JFV** ............ Jupiter Flyby Vehicle [*Aerospace*]
**JFW** ........... Justice for Women (EA)
**JFY** ............ Japanese Fiscal Year (CINC)
**JG** .............. Burnthills Aviation Ltd. [*Great Britain*] [*ICAO designator*] (FAAC)
**JG** .............. Jahrgang [*Year of Publication/Volume*] [*German*]
**JG** .............. Jerusalem und Seine Gelaende [*A publication*] (BJA)
**JG** .............. Jockeys' Guild (EA)
**JG** .............. Journal de Geneve [*A publication*]
**JG** .............. Journal of Geography [*A publication*]
**Jg** ............... Judges [*Old Testament book*] (BJA)
**JG** .............. Juedisches Gemeinde [*A publication*]
**JG** .............. Juedisches Gemeindeblatt fuer die Britische Zone [*A publication*] (BJA)
**JG** .............. Junction Grammar [*Data processing*]
**JG** .............. Junior Grade
**JG** .............. Juxtaglomerular [*Histology*]
**JGA** ............ Jamnagar [*India*] [*Airport symbol*] (OAG)
**J Ga** ............ Jauna Gaita [*A publication*]
**JGA** ............ Jojoba Growers Association (EA)
**JGA** ............ Joseph Guzman & Associates, Inc. [*Palatine, IL*] [*Telecommunications*] [*Defunct*] (TSSD)
**JGA** ............ Juxtaglomerular Apparatus [*Histology*]
**J GA Dent Assoc** ... Journal. Georgia Dental Association [*A publication*]
**J GA Entomol Soc** ... Journal. Georgia Entomological Society [*A publication*]
**J GA Ent Soc** ... Journal. Georgia Entomological Society [*A publication*]
**J Gakugei Tokushima Univ Nat Sci** ... Journal. Gakugei Tokushima University. Natural Science [*A publication*]
**J Galway Archaeol Hist Soc** ... Journal. Galway Archaeological and Historical Society [*A publication*]
**J Gan Jha Kend Sans Vid** ... Journal. Ganganatha Jha Kendriya Sanskrit Vidyapeetha [*A publication*]
**J Garden Hist** ... Journal of Garden History [*A publication*]
**J Gard Hist** ... Journal of Garden History [*A publication*]
**J Gas Chromatogr** ... Journal of Gas Chromatography [*A publication*]
**J Gas Light Water Supply Sanit Improv** ... Journal of Gas Lighting, Water Supply, and Sanitary Improvement [*A publication*]
**JGB** ............ Jewish Guild for the Blind (EA)
**JGC** ............ Grand Canyon [*Arizona*] [*Airport symbol*] (OAG)
**JGC** ............ Jacob Gold Corp. [*Vancouver Stock Exchange symbol*]
**JGC** ............ JGC Corp. [*Formerly, Japan Gasoline Company Ltd.*]
**JG & C** ....... Joint Guidance and Control (KSC)
**JGC** ............ Journal of General Chemistry [*A publication*]
**JGC** ............ Juxtaglomerular Cells [*Histology*]
**JGCC** .......... Juxtaglomerular Cell Count [*Endocrinology*]
**JGCEA** ....... Journal of Geochemical Exploration [*A publication*]
**JGCRA** ....... Journal of Gas Chromatography [*A publication*]
**JGD** ............ Junior Grand Deacon [*Freemasonry*]
**J/Gdsmn** .... Junior Guardsman [*British military*] (DMA)
**JGE** ............ Jaguar Equity, Inc. [*Vancouver Stock Exchange symbol*]
**JGE** ............ Joint Group of Experts [*Marine science*] (MSC)
**JGE** ............ Journal of General Education [*A publication*]
**J Gemmol** ... Journal of Gemmology [*A publication*]
**J Gen A Mic** ... Journal of General and Applied Microbiology [*A publication*]
**J Gen Appl Microbiol** ... Journal of General and Applied Microbiology [*A publication*]
**J Gen Chem USSR** ... Journal of General Chemistry of the USSR [*A publication*]
**J Gen Ed** .... Journal of General Education [*A publication*]
**J Gen Educ** ... Journal of General Education [*A publication*]
**J Genet** ....... Journal of Genetics [*A publication*]
**J Genet & Breed** ... Journal of Genetics and Breeding [*A publication*]
**J Genet Hum** ... Journal de Genetique Humaine [*A publication*]
**J Genet Psy** ... Journal of Genetic Psychology [*A publication*]
**J Genet Psychol** ... Journal of Genetic Psychology [*A publication*]
**J Gen Intern Med** ... Journal of General Internal Medicine [*A publication*]
**J Gen Manag** ... Journal of General Management [*A publication*]
**J Gen Med Chir et Pharm** ... Journal General de Medecine, de Chirurgie, et de Pharmacie [*A publication*]
**J Gen Mgt** ... Journal of General Management [*A publication*]
**J Gen Micro** ... Journal of General Microbiology [*A publication*]
**J Gen Microbiol** ... Journal of General Microbiology [*A publication*]
**J Gen Physiol** ... Journal of General Physiology [*A publication*]
**J Gen Physl** ... Journal of General Physiology [*A publication*]
**J Gen Ps** ..... Journal of Genetic Psychology [*A publication*]
**J Gen Psych** ... Journal of General Psychology [*A publication*]
**J Gen Psychol** ... Journal of General Psychology [*A publication*]
**J Gen Virol** ... Journal of General Virology [*A publication*]
**J Geo** .......... Journal of Geology [*A publication*]
**J Geobot** ..... Journal of Geobotany [*A publication*]
**J Geochem E** ... Journal of Geochemical Exploration [*A publication*]
**J Geochem Explor** ... Journal of Geochemical Exploration [*A publication*]
**J Geochem Soc India** ... Journal. Geochemical Society of India [*A publication*]
**JGEOD** ...... Journal of Geophysics [*A publication*]
**J Geodyn** .... Journal of Geodynamics [*A publication*]
**J Geog** ........ Journal Geographica [*A publication*]
**J Geog** ........ Journal of Geography [*A publication*]
**J Geogr Higher Educ** ... Journal of Geography in Higher Education [*A publication*]
**J Geogr (Tokyo)** ... Journal of Geography (Tokyo) [*A publication*]
**J Geol** ......... Journal of Geology [*A publication*]
**J Geol Educ** ... Journal of Geological Education [*A publication*]
**J Geol S In** ... Journal. Geological Society of India [*A publication*]
**J Geol Soc Aust** ... Journal. Geological Society of Australia [*A publication*]
**J Geol Soc Australia** ... Journal. Geological Society of Australia [*A publication*]
**J Geol Soc India** ... Journal. Geological Society of India [*A publication*]
**J Geol Soc Iraq** ... Journal. Geological Society of Iraq [*A publication*]
**J Geol Soc Jam** ... Journal. Geological Society of Jamaica [*A publication*]
**J Geol Soc Jpn** ... Journal. Geological Society of Japan [*A publication*]
**J Geol Soc London** ... Journal. Geological Society of London [*A publication*]
**J Geol Soc Philipp** ... Journal. Geological Society of the Philippines [*A publication*]
**J Geol Soc (Seoul)** ... Journal. Geological Society (Seoul) [*A publication*]
**J Geol Soc Thailand** ... Journal. Geological Society of Thailand [*A publication*]
**J Geol Soc Tokyo** ... Journal. Geological Society of Tokyo [*A publication*]
**J Geol UAR** ... Journal of Geology. United Arab Republic [*A publication*]
**J Geom** ....... Journal of Geometry [*A publication*]
**J Geomagn G** ... Journal of Geomagnetism and Geoelectricity [*A publication*]
**J Geomagn Geoelec** ... Journal of Geomagnetism and Geoelectricity [*A publication*]
**J Geomagn & Geoelectr** ... Journal of Geomagnetism and Geoelectricity [*A publication*]
**J Geometry** ... Journal of Geometry [*A publication*]
**J Geoph Res** ... Journal of Geophysical Research [*A publication*]
**J Geophys** ... Journal of Geophysics [*A publication*]
**J Geophys Res** ... Journal of Geophysical Research [*A publication*]
**J Geophys Res** ... Journal of Geophysical Research. Atmospheres [*A publication*]
**J Geophys Res B** ... Journal of Geophysical Research. Series B [*A publication*]
**J Geophys Res C Oceans** ... Journal of Geophysical Research. Series C. Oceans [*A publication*]
**J Geophys Res C Oceans Atmos** ... Journal of Geophysical Research. Series C. Oceans and Atmospheres [*A publication*]
**J Geophys Res D Atmos** ... Journal of Geophysical Research. Series D. Atmospheres [*A publication*]
**J Geo R-O A** ... Journal of Geophysical Research. Series C. Oceans and Atmospheres [*A publication*]
**J Geo R-S P** ... Journal of Geophysical Research. Space Physics [*A publication*]
**J Geosci Osaka City Univ** ... Journal of Geosciences. Osaka City University [*A publication*]
**J Geotech Eng Div Amer Soc Civil Eng Proc** ... Journal. Geotechnical Engineering Division. Proceedings of the American Society of Civil Engineers [*A publication*]
**J Geotech Eng Div Am Soc Civ Eng** ... Journal. Geotechnical Engineering Division. Proceedings of the American Society of Civil Engineers [*A publication*]
**J Geotech Engng Div ASCE** ... Journal. Geotechnical Engineering Division. American Society of Civil Engineers [*A publication*]
**J Geotech Engng Div Proc ASCE** ... Journal. Geotechnical Engineering Division. Proceedings of the American Society of Civil Engineers [*A publication*]
**JGEPs** ........ Journal of Genetic Psychology [*A publication*]
**J Geriat Ps** ... Journal of Geriatric Psychiatry [*A publication*]
**J Geriatr Psychiatry** ... Journal of Geriatric Psychiatry [*A publication*]
**J Geront** ..... Journal of Gerontology [*A publication*]
**J Gerontol** ... Journal of Gerontology [*A publication*]
**J Gerontol Nurs** ... Journal of Gerontological Nursing [*A publication*]
**J Gerontology** ... Journal of Gerontology [*A publication*]
**J Gerontol Soc Work** ... Journal of Gerontological Social Work [*A publication*]
**J Gesamte Oberflaechentech** ... Journal of Gesamte Oberflaechentechnik [*A publication*]
**JGF** ............ Jakarta Growth Fund [*NYSE symbol*] (SPSG)
**JGF** ............ Jenaer Germanistische Forschungen [*A publication*]
**JGF** ............ Junctor Grouping Frame [*Telecommunications*] (TEL)
**JGFC** ......... Joe Gallison Fan Club (EA)
**JGFC** ......... John Gilbert Fan Club (EA)

**JGFC**......... John Gill Fan Club (EA)
**JGG**........... Jahrbuch. Goethe-Gesellschaft [*A publication*]
**JGG**........... Jahrbuch. Grillparzer-Gesellschaft [*A publication*]
**JGGAS**...... Journal. Hongkong University. Geographical, Geological, and Archaeological Society [*A publication*]
**JGGJC**...... Jahrbuch. Gesellschaft fuer Geschichte der Juden in der Cechoslovakischen Republik [*Prague*] [*A publication*]
**JGGPO**...... Jahrbuch. Gesellschaft fuer die Geschichte des Protestantismus in Oesterreich [*A publication*]
**JGGPOes**.. Jahrbuch. Gesellschaft fuer die Geschichte des Protestantismus in Oesterreich [*A publication*]
**JGH**........... Jig Grinder Head
**JGI**............ Juxtaglomerular Granulation Index [*Endocrinology*]
**JGI**............ Juxtaglomerular Index [*Endocrinology*]
**JGIFC**........ John Gary International Fan Club (EA)
**JGIN**.......... JG Industries, Inc. [*Chicago, IL*] [*NASDAQ symbol*] (NQ)
**JGJ**............ Jahrbuch fuer die Geschichte der Juden [*A publication*]
**JGJC**.......... Jahrbuch. Gesellschaft fuer Geschichte der Juden in der Cechoslovakischen Republik [*Prague*] [*A publication*]
**JGJJ**.......... Jahrbuch fuer die Geschichte der Juden und des Judentums [*A publication*]
**JGJRI**........ Journal. Ganganatha Jha Research Institute [*A publication*]
**JGL**............ Jahrbuch fuer Juedische Geschichte und Literatur [*A publication*]
**JGL**............ Juedische Gemeinde Luzern [*A publication*]
**J Glaciol**..... Journal of Glaciology [*A publication*]
**J Glass Stud** ... Journal of Glass Studies [*A publication*]
**JGLC**.......... Joint Government Liaison Committee [*Composed of Association of Brass and Bronze Ingot Manufacturers and Brass and Bronze Ingot Institute*] (EA)
**JGLGA**...... Jahrbuch. Gesellschaft fuer Lothringische Geschichte und Altertumskunde [*A publication*]
**JGLGAK**... Jahrbuch. Gesellschaft fuer Lothringische Geschichte und Altertumskunde [*A publication*]
**JGLRD**...... Journal of Great Lakes Research [*A publication*]
**JGLS**.......... Journal. Gypsy Lore Society [*A publication*]
**JGM**........... Jig Grinding Machine
**JGM**........... Journal of General Management [*United Kingdom*] [*A publication*]
**JGMAA**..... Journal of General Management [*A publication*]
**JGMC**........ Judy Garland Memorial Club (EA)
**JGMOD**.... Jahrbuch fuer die Geschichte Mittel- und Ostdeutschlands [*A publication*]
**J GMS OSU** ... Journal. Graduate Music Students. Ohio State University [*A publication*]
**JGN**........... Junction Gate Number
**J Gnathol**... Journal of Gnathology [*A publication*]
**JGNOAC**... Jugoslovenska Ginekologija i Opstetricija [*A publication*]
**JGNSKG**... Jahrbuch. Gesellschaft fuer Niedersaechsische Kirchengeschichte [*A publication*]
**JGO**........... Jahrbuecher fuer Geschichte Osteuropas [*A publication*]
**JGOBA**...... Journal de Gynecologie, Obstetrique, et Biologie de la Reproduction [*Paris*] [*A publication*]
**JGOE**......... Jahrbuecher fuer Geschichte Osteuropas [*A publication*]
**JGOFS**...... Joint Global Ocean Flux Study [*International experiment*]
**JGOLR**...... Jaarboekje voor Geschiedenis en Oudheidkunde van Leiden en Rijnland [*A publication*]
**JGO-US**.... Job Guarantee Office of the United States (OICC)
**JGP**............ Houston [*Texas*] Greenway [*Airport symbol*] (OAG)
**JGP**............ Jem Group Products [*Vancouver Stock Exchange symbol*]
**JGP**............ Journal of General Psychology [*A publication*]
**JGP**............ Journal of Genetic Psychology [*A publication*]
**JGPA**......... Jobbing Grinders' Provident Association [*A union*] [*British*]
**JGPs**......... Journal of General Psychology [*A publication*]
**JGPSA**....... Journal of General Psychology [*A publication*]
**JGPYA**...... Journal of Genetic Psychology [*A publication*]
**JGQ**........... Houston [*Texas*] Guest Quarters [*Airport symbol*] (OAG)
**JGR**............ Journal of Geophysical Research [*A publication*]
**J Grad Res Cent** ... Journal. Graduate Research Center [*A publication*]
**J Grad Res Cent South Methodist Univ** ... Journal. Graduate Research Center. Southern Methodist University [*A publication*]
**J Graph Theory** ... Journal of Graph Theory [*A publication*]
**JGR C**........ Journal of Geophysical Research. Series C. Oceans and Atmospheres [*A publication*]
**J Great Lakes Res** ... Journal of Great Lakes Research [*A publication*]
**JGrG**.......... Jahrbuch. Grillparzer-Gesellschaft [*A publication*]
**JGRI**.......... Journal. Ganganatha Jha Research Institute [*A publication*]
**JGR J Geophys Res C Oceans Atmos** ... JGR. Journal of Geophysical Research. Series C. Oceans and Atmospheres [*A publication*]
**JGR J Geophys Res D Atmos** ... JGR. Journal of Geophysical Research. Series D. Atmospheres [*A publication*]
**J Group Experts Sci Aspects Mar Pollut** ... Joint Group of Experts on the Scientific Aspects of Marine Pollution [*A publication*]
**J Growth**.... Journal of Growth [*A publication*]
**JGRP**......... Jesup Group [*AMEX symbol*] (SPSG)
**JGRP**......... [*The*] Jesup Group, Inc. [*NASDAQ symbol*] (NQ)
**JGRS**......... Journal. Gujarat Research Society [*India*] [*A publication*]
**JGS**............ James Griffiths & Sons [*AAR code*]
**JGS**............ Jewish Genealogical Society (EA)
**JGS**............ Joint General Staff [*Military*] (NATG)
**JGS**............ Journal of Glass Studies [*A publication*]
**Jgs**............. Judges [*Old Testament book*]
**JGSDF**....... Japanese Ground Self-Defense Forces (AABC)
**JGSLA**....... Journal. Geological Society of London [*A publication*]
**JGSTD**...... Journal. Gyeongsang National University. Science and Technology [*A publication*]
**JGSW**........ Journal of Gerontological Social Work [*A publication*]
**JGT**............ Judgment [*Legal term*] (ROG)
**JGT**............ Junction Growth Technique
**JGTC**......... Junior Girls' Training Corps [*British*] [*World War II*]
**JGTL**......... Job Grading System for Trades and Labor Occupations
**JGTOI**....... [*The*] Judge GTO International (EA)
**J Guidance & Control** ... Journal of Guidance and Control [*A publication*]
**J Guidance Control** ... Journal of Guidance and Control [*A publication*]
**J Guid Control** ... Journal of Guidance and Control [*United States*] [*A publication*]
**J Guid and Control** ... Journal of Guidance and Control [*A publication*]
**J Guid Control and Dyn** ... Journal of Guidance, Control, and Dynamics [*A publication*]
**J Gujarat Res Soc** ... Journal. Gujarat Research Society [*India*] [*A publication*]
**J Guj Res Soc** ... Journal. Gujarat Research Society [*India*] [*A publication*]
**JGW**........... Jahresbericht fuer Geschichtswissenschaft [*A publication*]
**JGW**........... Junior Grand Warden [*Freemasonry*]
**JGWT**........ Jahrbuch. Gesellschaft fuer Wiener Theater-Forschung [*A publication*]
**JGWTC**..... Jungle and Guerrilla Warfare Training Center [*Army*]
**J Gyeongsang Natl Univ Nat Sci** ... Journal. Gyeongsang National University. Natural Sciences [*Republic of Korea*] [*A publication*]
**J Gyeongsang Natl Univ Sci Technol** ... Journal. Gyeongsang National University. Science and Technology [*A publication*]
**JGyLS**........ Journal. Gypsy Lore Society [*A publication*]
**J Gynaecol Endocr** ... Journal of Gynaecological Endocrinology [*A publication*]
**J Gynecol Obstet Biol Reprod** ... Journal de Gynecologie, Obstetrique, et Biologie de la Reproduction [*Paris*] [*A publication*]
**J Gynecol Pract** ... Journal of Gynecological Practice [*Japan*] [*A publication*]
**JH**.............. Harland [*John H.*] Co. [*NYSE symbol*] (SPSG)
**JH**.............. Jacob's Horse [*British military*] (DMA)
**J & H**......... Johnson and Hemming's English Vice-Chancellors' Reports [*A publication*] (DLA)
**JH**.............. Journal of History [*A publication*]
**JH**.............. Journal of the House of Representatives [*United States*] [*A publication*] (DLA)
**JH**.............. Juvenile Hormone [*Entomology*]
**JH**.............. Pan Adria [*Yugoslavia*] [*ICAO designator*] (FAAC)
**JHA**........... Japan Hour Association [*Later, JHB*] (EA)
**JHA**........... John Howard Association (EA)
**JHA**........... Juvenile Hormone Analog [*Entomology*]
**J Hand Surg** ... Journal of Hand Surgery [*A publication*]
**J Hanyang Med Coll** ... Journal. Hanyang Medical College [*South Korea*] [*A publication*]
**J Haryana Stud** ... Journal of Haryana Studies [*A publication*]
**J Hattori Bot Lab** ... Journal. Hattori Botanical Laboratory [*A publication*]
**JHAW**....... Jahrbuch. Heidelberger Akademie der Wissenschaften [*A publication*]
**J Hawaii Dent Assoc** ... Journal. Hawaii Dental Association [*A publication*]
**J Hawaii State Dent Assoc** ... Journal. Hawaii State Dental Association [*A publication*]
**J Hazard Mater** ... Journal of Hazardous Materials [*A publication*]
**J Hazard Materials** ... Journal of Hazardous Materials [*A publication*]
**J Hazardous Mat** ... Journal of Hazardous Materials [*A publication*]
**JHB**........... Japan Hour Broadcasting (EA)
**JHB**........... Johore Bahru [*Malaysia*] [*Airport symbol*] (OAG)
**JHBLEM**.. Journal of Human Behavior and Learning [*A publication*]
**JHBP**......... Juvenile Hormone Binding Protein [*Entomology*]
**JHBSA**...... Journal of the History of the Behavioral Sciences [*A publication*]
**JhBW**........ Jahrbuch. Biblische Wissenschaften [*A publication*]
**JHC**........... Garden City [*New York*] [*Airport symbol*] (OAG)
**JHC**........... Johnson Canyon [*California*] [*Seismograph station code, US Geological Survey*] (SEIS)
**J H Clearing House** ... Junior High Clearing House [*A publication*]
**JHCM**....... Journal of Health Care Marketing [*A publication*] (EAAP)
**JHCNHS**... John Henry Cardinal Newman Honorary Society [*Defunct*] (EA)
**JHD**........... Jehuda [*On Hebrew coins of the fourth century*]
**JHD**........... Joint Hypocenter Determination [*Earthquake study*]
**JHD**........... Journal of the Hellenic Diaspora [*A publication*]
**JHDA**........ Journal. Hawaii Dental Association [*A publication*]
**JHDA**........ Junior Hospital Doctors Association [*British*]
**JHe**........... Jewish Heritage [*A publication*] (BJA)
**JHE**........... Johns Hopkins University, Baltimore, MD [*OCLC symbol*] (OCLC)
**JHE**........... Journal of Home Economics [*A publication*]
**J Health Adm Educ** ... Journal of Health Administration Education [*A publication*]
**J Health Care Mark** ... Journal of Health Care Marketing [*A publication*]
**J Health Care Market** ... Journal of Health Care Marketing [*A publication*]
**J Health Care Mkt** ... Journal of Health Care Marketing [*A publication*]
**J Health Care Technol** ... Journal of Health Care Technology [*A publication*]

**J Healthc Educ Train** ... Journal of Healthcare Education and Training [*A publication*]
**J Healthc Mater Manage** ... Journal of Healthcare Materiel Management [*A publication*]
**J Healthc Prot Manage** ... Journal of Healthcare Protection Management [*A publication*]
**J Health Econ** ... Journal of Health Economics [*A publication*]
**J Health Hum Behav** ... Journal of Health and Human Behavior [*A publication*]
**J Health Hum Resour Adm** ... Journal of Health and Human Resources Administration [*A publication*]
**J Health Hum Resources Admin** ... Journal of Health and Human Resources Administration [*A publication*]
**J Health Phys Ed Rec** ... Journal of Health, Physical Education, Recreation [*A publication*]
**J Health Phys Radiat Prot** ... Journal of Health Physics and Radiation Protection [*A publication*]
**J Health Pol** ... Journal of Health Politics, Policy, and Law [*A publication*]
**J Health Polit Policy Law** ... Journal of Health Politics, Policy, and Law [*A publication*]
**J Health Pol Poly and L** ... Journal of Health Politics, Policy, and Law [*A publication*]
**J Health So** ... Journal of Health and Social Behavior [*A publication*]
**J Health & Soc Behav** ... Journal of Health and Social Behavior [*A publication*]
**J Health Soc Behav** ... Journal of Health and Social Behavior [*A publication*]
**J Health & Social Behavior** ... Journal of Health and Social Behavior [*A publication*]
**J Heat Recovery Syst** ... Journal of Heat Recovery Systems [*England*] [*A publication*]
**J Heat Recovery Systems** ... Journal of Heat Recovery Systems [*A publication*]
**J Heat Tran** ... Journal of Heat Transfer. Transactions of the American Society of Mechanical Engineers [*A publication*]
**J Heat Transfer** ... Journal of Heat Transfer. Transactions of the American Society of Mechanical Engineers. Series C [*A publication*]
**J Heat Transfer Trans ASME** ... Journal of Heat Transfer. Transactions of the American Society of Mechanical Engineers [*A publication*]
**J Heat Treat** ... Journal of Heat Treating [*United States*] [*A publication*]
**J Hebd Med** ... Journal Hebdomadaire de Medecine [*A publication*]
**J Hebei Univ Nat Sci Ed** ... Journal. Hebei University. Natural Science Edition [*A publication*]
**JHebrSt**..... Journal of Hebraic Studies [*New York*] [*A publication*]
**JHEL**......... Journal of Hellenic Studies [*A publication*]
**J Hellenic Stud** ... Journal of Hellenic Studies [*A publication*]
**J Hellen St** ... Journal of Hellenic Studies [*A publication*]
**J Hellen Stud** ... Journal of Hellenic Studies [*A publication*]
**J Hell Stud** ... Journal of Hellenic Studies [*A publication*]
**J Helminth** ... Journal of Helminthology [*A publication*]
**J Helminthol** ... Journal of Helminthology [*A publication*]
**J Hel Stud** ... Journal of Hellenic Studies [*A publication*]
**J Hepatol** ... Journal of Hepatology [*A publication*]
**J Hepatol (Amst)** ... Journal of Hepatology (Amsterdam) [*A publication*]
**J Hepatol Suppl** ... Journal of Hepatology. Supplement [*A publication*]
**J Hered**...... Journal of Heredity [*A publication*]
**J Heredity** ... Journal of Heredity [*A publication*]
**J Herpetol** ... Journal of Herpetology [*A publication*]
**J Herpetol Assoc Afr** ... Journal. Herpetological Association of Africa [*A publication*]
**J Hetero Ch** ... Journal of Heterocyclic Chemistry [*A publication*]
**J Heterocycl Chem** ... Journal of Heterocyclic Chemistry [*A publication*]
**JHF**............ Jackson, MS [*Location identifier*] [*FAA*] (FAAL)
**JHFC**......... Jan Howard Friends Club (EA)
**JHG**........... Joule Heat Gradient (IEEE)
**JHGA**........ Jahrbuch. K. K. Heraldische Gesellschaft, "Adler" [*A publication*]
**JHGA**........ Jewish Historical General Archives [*Jerusalem*] (BJA)
**JHGSOWA** ... Joint Household Goods Shipping Office, Washington Area [*Military*] (AABC)
**JHGSW**..... Journal. Heraldic and Genealogical Society of Wales [*A publication*]
**JHH**........... Journal of Health and Human Resources Administration [*A publication*]
**JHHGSO**.. Joint Household Goods Shipping Office [*Military*]
**J & H Hind L** ... Johnson and Houghton's Institutes of Hindoo Law [*A publication*] (DLA)
**JHI**............ John Hancock Investors Trust [*NYSE symbol*] (SPSG)
**JHI**............ Journal of the History of Ideas [*A publication*]
**J Hi E**......... Journal of Higher Education [*A publication*]
**J High Educ** ... Journal of Higher Education [*A publication*]
**J Higher Educ** ... Journal of Higher Education [*A publication*]
**J High Polym (Shanghai)** ... Journal of High Polymers (Shanghai) [*A publication*]
**J High Resolut Chromatogr Chromatogr Commun** ... Journal of High Resolution Chromatography and Chromatography Communications [*West Germany*] [*A publication*]
**J High Temp Soc** ... Journal. High Temperature Society [*Japan*] [*A publication*]
**J High Temp Soc (Jpn)** ... Journal. High Temperature Society (Japan) [*A publication*]
**J Highw Div Am Soc Civ Eng** ... Journal. Highway Division. American Society of Civil Engineers [*A publication*]
**JHINDS**.... Journal of Hospital Infection [*A publication*]
**J Hirnforsch** ... Journal fuer Hirnforschung [*A publication*]
**J Hiroshima Med Assoc** ... Journal. Hiroshima Medical Association [*Japan*] [*A publication*]
**J Hiroshima Univ Dent Soc** ... Journal. Hiroshima University. Dental Society [*A publication*]
**J Hispan Ph** ... Journal of Hispanic Philology [*A publication*]
**J Hist Arabic Sci** ... Journal for the History of Arabic Science [*A publication*]
**J Hist Astron** ... Journal for the History of Astronomy [*A publication*]
**J Hist Astronom** ... Journal for the History of Astronomy [*A publication*]
**J Hist Beh** ... Journal of the History of the Behavioral Sciences [*A publication*]
**J Hist Behav Sci** ... Journal of the History of the Behavioral Sciences [*A publication*]
**J Hist Beh Sci** ... Journal of the History of the Behavioral Sciences [*A publication*]
**J Hist Biol** ... Journal of the History of Biology [*A publication*]
**J Hist Cyto** ... Journal of Histochemistry and Cytochemistry [*A publication*]
**J Hist Firearms Soc S Afr** ... Journal. Historical Firearms Society of South Africa [*A publication*]
**J Hist G**..... Journal of Historical Geography [*A publication*]
**J Hist Geog** ... Journal of Historical Geography [*A publication*]
**J Hist Geogr** ... Journal of Historical Geography [*A publication*]
**J Hist Idea** ... Journal of the History of Ideas [*A publication*]
**J Hist Ideas** ... Journal of the History of Ideas [*A publication*]
**J Hist Med** ... Journal of the History of Medicine and Allied Sciences [*A publication*]
**J Hist Med Allied Sci** ... Journal of the History of Medicine and Allied Sciences [*A publication*]
**J Histochem Cytochem** ... Journal of Histochemistry and Cytochemistry [*A publication*]
**J Histotechnol** ... Journal of Histotechnology [*United States*] [*A publication*]
**J Hist Phil** ... Journal of the History of Philosophy [*A publication*]
**J Hist Philos** ... Journal of the History of Philosophy [*A publication*]
**J Hist Res**.. Journal of Historical Research [*A publication*]
**J Hist Soc Church Wales** ... Journal. Historical Society of the Church in Wales [*A publication*]
**J Hist Sociol** ... Journal of the History of Sociology [*A publication*]
**J Hist Soc Nigeria** ... Journal. Historical Society of Nigeria [*A publication*]
**J Hist Soc QD** ... Historical Society of Queensland. Journal [*A publication*] (APTA)
**J Hist Soc Qld** ... Historical Society of Queensland. Journal [*A publication*] (APTA)
**J Hist Soc SA** ... Journal. Historical Society of South Australia [*A publication*]
**J Hist Stud** ... Journal of Historical Studies [*A publication*]
**J HK Br Roy Asiat Soc** ... Journal. Hong Kong Branch. Royal Asiatic Society [*A publication*]
**JHLB**......... Journal. Federal Home Loan Bank Board [*A publication*]
**JHM**.......... [*Dr.*] J. Howard Mueller [*Virus*] [*Medicine*]
**JHM**.......... JHM Mortgage Securities LP [*NYSE symbol*] (CTT)
**JHM**.......... Journal of the History of Medicine [*A publication*]
**JHM**.......... Juvenile Hormone Mimic [*Entomology*]
**JHMa**......... Johns Hopkins Magazine [*A publication*]
**JHMCO**.... J. H. Morgan Consultants [*Morristown, NJ*] [*Information service or system*] [*Telecommunications*] (TSSD)
**JHMEDL** ... Journal of Holistic Medicine [*A publication*]
**JHMO**....... Junior Hospital Medical Officer
**JHMSDT**.. Journal of Human Movement Studies [*A publication*]
**JHN**........... John Henry Newman [*Initials used as pseudonym*]
**JHN**........... Johnson Air, Inc. [*Batavia, NY*] [*FAA designator*] (FAAC)
**JHN**........... Johnson, KS [*Location identifier*] [*FAA*] (FAAL)
**JHO**........... Journal of Housing [*A publication*]
**JhOAI**........ Jahreshefte. Oesterreichisches Archaeologische Institut in Wien [*A publication*]
**J Ho E**........ Journal of Home Economics [*A publication*]
**J Hokkaido Dent Assoc** ... Journal. Hokkaido Dental Association [*A publication*]
**J Hokkaido Forest Prod Res Inst** ... Journal. Hokkaido Forest Products Research Institute [*A publication*]
**J Hokkaido Gakugei Univ** ... Journal. Hokkaido Gakugei University [*A publication*]
**J Hokkaido Gakugei Univ Sect B** ... Journal. Hokkaido Gakugei University. Section B [*Japan*] [*A publication*]
**J Hokkaido Univ Ed Sect IIA** ... Journal. Hokkaido University of Education. Section II-A [*A publication*]
**J Hokkaido Univ Educ** ... Journal. Hokkaido University of Education [*A publication*]
**J Hokkaido Univ Educ IIB** ... Journal. Hokkaido University of Education. Section II-B [*A publication*]
**J Hokkaido Univ Educ Sect II A** ... Journal. Hokkaido University of Education. Section II-A [*Japan*] [*A publication*]
**J Hokkaido Univ Educ Sect II-B** ... Journal. Hokkaido University of Education. Section II-B [*A publication*]
**J Hokkaido Univ Educ Sect II C** ... Journal. Hokkaido University of Education. Section II-C [*Japan*] [*A publication*]
**J Holistic Med** ... Journal of Holistic Medicine [*A publication*]
**J Holistic Nurs** ... Journal of Holistic Nursing [*A publication*]
**J of Home Ec Ed** ... Journal of Home Economics Education [*A publication*]
**J Home Econ** ... Journal of Home Economics [*A publication*]

**J Homosex** ... Journal of Homosexuality [*A publication*]
**J Homosexuality** ... Journal of Homosexuality [*A publication*]
**J Hong Kong Branch Roy Asiatic Soc** ... Journal. Hong Kong Branch. Royal Asiatic Society [*A publication*]
**J Hopeh Univ Nat Sci** ... Journal. Hopeh University. Natural Science [*People's Republic of China*] [*A publication*]
**J Horol Inst Jpn** ... Journal. Horological Institute of Japan [*A publication*]
**J Hortic Sci** ... Journal of Horticultural Science [*A publication*]
**J Hort Sci** .. Journal of Horticultural Science [*A publication*]
**J Hosp Dent Pract** ... Journal of Hospital Dental Practice [*A publication*]
**J Hosp Infect** ... Journal of Hospital Infection [*A publication*]
**J Hospitality Educ** ... Journal of Hospitality Education [*A publication*]
**J Hosp Supply Process Distrib** ... Journal of Hospital Supply, Processing, and Distribution [*A publication*]
**J Hotel Dieu de Montreal** ... Journal. Hotel Dieu de Montreal [*A publication*]
**J Housing** .. Journal of Housing [*A publication*]
**J Houston Dist Dent Soc** ... Journal. Houston [*Texas*] District Dental Society [*A publication*]
**JHP** .......... Jacketed Hollow-Point [*Ammunition*]
**JHP** .......... Jackson Hole Preserve (EA)
**JHP** .......... Journal of Hispanic Philology [*A publication*]
**JHP** .......... Journal of the History of Philosophy [*A publication*]
**JHP** .......... Peabody Institute of Johns Hopkins University, Conservatory Library, Baltimore, MD [*OCLC symbol*] (OCLC)
**JHPh** ......... Journal of the History of Philosophy [*A publication*]
**JHPLD** ...... Journal of Health Politics, Policy, and Law [*A publication*]
**JHPP** ......... Journal of Health Politics, Policy, and Law [*A publication*]
**JHPS** ......... Judaica Historical Philatelic Society (EA)
**JHPX** ......... Jones/Hosplex Systems [*NASDAQ symbol*] (NQ)
**JHQ** .......... Joint Headquarters [*British military*] (DMA)
**JHQ** .......... Shute Harbour [*Australia*] [*Airport symbol*]
**JHR** .......... Journal of Human Resources [*A publication*]
**JHRP** ......... Joint Highway Research Project [*Purdue University*] [*Research center*] (RCD)
**JHS** .......... Jesus Hominum Salvator [*Jesus, Savior of Men*] (ROG)
**JHS** .......... Jewish History Series [*A publication*]
**JHS** .......... Job Hunter's Sourcebook [*A publication*]
**JHS** .......... John Hancock Income Securities Trust [*NYSE symbol*] (SPSG)
**JHS** .......... Journal of Hellenic Studies [*A publication*]
**JHS** .......... Journal of Historical Studies [*A publication*]
**JHS** .......... Junior High School
**JHS** .......... School of Advanced International Studies, Johns Hopkins University, Washington, DC [*OCLC symbol*] (OCLC)
**JHS-AR** ..... Journal of Hellenic Studies. Archaeological Reports [*A publication*]
**JHSB** ......... Journal of Health and Social Behavior [*A publication*]
**JHSch** ........ Jahresberichte ueber das Hoehre Schulwesen [*A publication*]
**JHSCW** ..... Journal. Historical Society of the Church in Wales [*A publication*]
**JHSE** ......... Jewish Historical Society of England
**JHSEM** ..... Jewish Historical Society of England. Miscellanies [*A publication*]
**JHSET** ...... Jewish Historical Society of England. Transactions [*A publication*]
**JHSL** ......... John Hanson Savings Bank FSB [*Beltsville, MD*] [*NASDAQ symbol*] (NQ)
**JHSN** ......... Johnson Electronics, Inc. [*NASDAQ symbol*] (NQ)
**JHSN** ......... Journal. Historical Society of Nigeria [*A publication*]
**JHSPCW** .. Journal. Historical Society of the Presbyterian Church of Wales [*A publication*]
**JHSRLL** .... Johns Hopkins Studies in Romance Language and Literature [*A publication*]
**JHSS** ......... Journal of History for Senior Students [*A publication*] (APTA)
**JHSSA** ...... Journal. Historical Society of South Australia [*A publication*] (APTA)
**JHStud** ...... Journal of Historical Studies [*A publication*]
**JHSUD** ...... Journal of Hand Surgery [*A publication*]
**JHTR** ......... Japan High Tech Review [*Database*] [*Kyodo News International, Inc.*] [*Information service or system*] (CRD)
**JHU** .......... Johns Hopkins University [*Maryland*]
**J Huazhong Inst Tech** ... Journal. Huazhong Institute of Technology. English Edition [*A publication*]
**J Huazhong Inst Technol** ... Journal. Huazhong Institute of Technology [*People's Republic of China*] [*A publication*]
**J Huazhong Inst Technol Engl Ed** ... Journal. Huazhong Institute of Technology. English Edition [*A publication*]
**J Huazhong Univ Sci Tech** ... Journal. Huazhong [*Central China*] University of Science and Technology. English Edition [*A publication*]
**JHUC** ......... Journal. Hebrew Union College [*Cincinnati*] [*A publication*]
**J Humanistic Psychol** ... Journal of Humanistic Psychology [*A publication*]
**J of Human Rela** ... Journal of Human Relations [*A publication*]
**J Human Resources** ... Journal of Human Resources [*A publication*]
**J Human Stress** ... Journal of Human Stress [*A publication*]
**J Hum Behav Learn** ... Journal of Human Behavior and Learning [*A publication*]
**J Hum Ergol** ... Journal of Human Ergology [*A publication*]
**J Hum Ergol (Tokyo)** ... Journal of Human Ergology (Tokyo) [*A publication*]
**J Hum Evol** ... Journal of Human Evolution [*A publication*]
**J Hum Mov Stud** ... Journal of Human Movement Studies [*A publication*]
**J Hum Nutr** ... Journal of Human Nutrition [*A publication*]
**J Hum Nutr Diet** ... Journal of Human Nutrition and Dietetics [*A publication*]
**J Hu Move Stud** ... Journal of Human Movement Studies [*A publication*]
**J Hum Psy** ... Journal of Humanistic Psychology [*A publication*]
**J Hum Relat** ... Journal of Human Relations [*A publication*]
**J Hum Resources** ... Journal of Human Resources [*A publication*]
**J Hum Stress** ... Journal of Human Stress [*A publication*]
**J Hunan Univ** ... Journal. Hunan University [*A publication*]
**J Hunter Valley Research Foundation** ... Journal. Hunter Valley Research Foundation [*A publication*] (APTA)
**J H U Studies** ... Johns Hopkins University. Studies in Historical and Political Science [*A publication*]
**JHVA** ........ Jehovah (ROG)
**JHVD** ........ Jahrbuch. Historischer Verein Dillingen [*A publication*]
**JHVFB** ...... Jahrbuch. Historischer Verein fuer das Fuerstbistum Bamberg [*A publication*]
**JHVH** ........ Jehovah [*Freemasonry*] (ROG)
**JHW** .......... Jamestown [*New York*] [*Airport symbol*] (OAG)
**JHW** .......... Jamestown, NY [*Location identifier*] [*FAA*] (FAAL)
**JHW** .......... Johns Hopkins University, Welch Medical Library, Baltimore, MD [*OCLC symbol*] (OCLC)
**JHWC** ....... Joint Hurricane Warning Center (CINC)
**JHYDA7** ... Journal of Hydrology [*Amsterdam*] [*A publication*]
**J Hyderabad Geol Surv** ... Journal. Hyderabad Geological Survey [*A publication*]
**J Hydr-ASCE** ... Journal. Hydraulics Division. American Society of Civil Engineers [*A publication*]
**J Hydraul Div Amer Soc Civil Eng Proc** ... Journal. Hydraulics Division. Proceedings of the American Society of Civil Engineers [*A publication*]
**J Hydraul Div Am Soc Civ Eng** ... Journal. Hydraulics Division. American Society of Civil Engineers [*A publication*]
**J Hydraul Div Proc ASCE** ... Journal. Hydraulic Division. Proceedings of the American Society of Civil Engineers [*A publication*]
**J Hydraul Eng (Peking)** ... Journal of Hydraulic Engineering (Peking) [*A publication*]
**J Hydraul Res** ... Journal of Hydraulic Research [*A publication*]
**J Hydraul Res J Rech Hydraul** ... Journal of Hydraulic Research/Journal de Recherches Hydrauliques [*A publication*]
**J Hydrogeol** ... Journal of Hydrogeology [*A publication*]
**J Hydrol** ..... Journal of Hydrology [*New Zealand*] [*A publication*]
**J Hydrol (Amst)** ... Journal of Hydrology (Amsterdam) [*A publication*]
**J Hydrol (Dunedin)** ... Journal of Hydrology (Dunedin) [*A publication*]
**J Hydrol (Neth)** ... Journal of Hydrology (Netherlands) [*A publication*]
**J Hydrol Sci** ... Journal of Hydrological Sciences [*Poland*] [*A publication*]
**J Hydronaut** ... Journal of Hydronautics [*A publication*]
**J Hyg** ......... Journal of Hygiene [*A publication*]
**J Hyg (Camb)** ... Journal of Hygiene (Cambridge) [*A publication*]
**J Hyg Chem** ... Journal of Hygienic Chemistry [*A publication*]
**J Hyg Chem Soc Japan** ... Journal. Hygienic Chemical Society of Japan [*A publication*]
**J Hyg Epidemiol Microbiol Immunol** ... Journal of Hygiene, Epidemiology, Microbiology, and Immunology [*A publication*]
**J Hyg Epidemiol Microbiol Immunol (Prague)** ... Journal of Hygiene, Epidemiology, Microbiology, and Immunology (Prague) [*A publication*]
**J Hyg Ep Mi** ... Journal of Hygiene, Epidemiology, Microbiology, and Immunology [*A publication*]
**J Hygiene** ... Journal of Hygiene [*A publication*]
**J Hyg (Lond)** ... Journal of Hygiene (London) [*A publication*]
**J Hyg (Paris)** ... Journal d'Hygiene Clintologie (Paris) [*A publication*]
**J Hypertens** ... Journal of Hypertension [*A publication*]
**J Hypertens Suppl** ... Journal of Hypertension. Supplement [*A publication*]
**JI** ............... Air Balear [*ICAO designator*] (ICDA)
**JI** ............... Jamaat-i-Islami [*Political party*] [*Pakistan*] (FEA)
**JI** ............... Japan Institute [*Defunct*] (EA)
**JI** ............... Japan Interpreter [*A publication*]
**JI** ............... Jazz Interactions (EA)
**JI** ............... Jazz International
**JI** ............... Jersey Institute
**JI** ............... Jesness Inventory [*Psychology*]
**JI** ............... Jet Interaction (RDA)
**JI** ............... Jetair, Luftfahrt-Verwaltungsgesellschaft, Muenchen [*West Germany*] [*ICAO designator*] (FAAC)
**JI** ............... Jigging Information
**JI** ............... Job Instruction
**JI** ............... Job Insurance [*Job Service*] (OICC)
**ji** ................ Johnston Atoll [*MARC country of publication code*] [*Library of Congress*] (LCCP)
**JI** ............... Journal. American Musical Instrument Society [*A publication*]
**JI** ............... Journal of Insurance [*A publication*]
**JI** ............... Junction Isolation [*Electronics*]
**JI** ............... Jupiter Inlet [*NASA*] (KSC)
**JIA** ............ Joint Interest Audiovisual Requirements (MCD)
**JIA** ............ Journal of Industrial Archaeology [*A publication*]
**JIA** ............ Journal of International Affairs [*A publication*]
**JIAFS** ........ Joint Institute for Acoustics and Flight Sciences (MCD)
**JIAFS** ........ Joint Institute for Advancement of Flight Science [*Research center*] (RCD)
**JIAN** .......... Journal International d'Archeologie Numismatique [*A publication*]

**JIAP** .......... Journal. Indian Academy of Philosophy [*A publication*]
**J IARI Post-Grad Sch** ... Journal. IARI [*Indian Agricultural Research Institute*]. Post-Graduate School [*A publication*]
**JIAS** .......... Journal. Indian Anthropological Society [*A publication*]
**JIAS** .......... Journal of Interamerican Studies [*A publication*]
**JIASRA** ..... Journal. International Arthur Schnitzler Research Association [*A publication*]
**JIAWG** ...... Joint Integrated Avionics Working Group [*DoD*]
**JIB** .......... Djibouti [*Djibouti*] [*Airport symbol*] (OAG)
**JIB** .......... Foodmaker, Inc. [*NYSE symbol*] (SPSG)
**JIB** .......... Jack-in-the-Box Dummy [*CIA*]
**JIB** .......... Jewish Information Bureau (EA)
**JIB** .......... Job Information Block [*Data processing*] (BUR)
**JIB** .......... Jobs Impact Bulletin [*National Committee for Full Employment*] [*A publication*]
**JIB** .......... Joint Information Bureau [*Military*] (MCD)
**JIB** .......... Joint Intelligence Bureau [*British*] (MCD)
**JIB** .......... Jordan Information Bureau (EA)
**JIB** .......... Journal. Institute of Bankers [*A publication*]
**JIB** .......... Journal of International Business Studies [*A publication*]
**JIBEI** ......... Joint Industry Board of the Electrical Industry (EA)
**J I Brewing** ... Journal. Institute of Brewing [*A publication*]
**JIBS** .......... Journal of Indian and Buddhist Studies [*A publication*]
**JIC** .......... Jet-Induced Circulation [*Combustor*]
**JIC** .......... Jewelry Industry Council (EA)
**JIC** .......... Job Information Centre [*Canada*]
**JIC** .......... Joint Ice Center [*Marine science*] (MSC)
**JIC** .......... Joint Industrial Council (EA)
**JIC** .......... Joint Industry Council (EAIO)
**JIC** .......... Joint Insurance Committee [*under the Trading with the Enemy Act*] [*World War II*]
**JIC** .......... Joint Intelligence Center
**JIC** .......... Joint Intelligence Committee
**JIC** .......... Joint Interrogation Center (MCD)
**JIC** .......... Junior International Club (EA)
**JICA** .......... Joint Intelligence Center, Africa
**JICA** .......... Joint Intelligence Collecting Agency
**JICACBI** ... Joint Intelligence Collecting Agency, China, Burma, India [*World War II*]
**JICAME** .... Joint Intelligence Collecting Agency, Middle East [*World War II*]
**JICANA** .... Joint Intelligence Collecting Agency, North Africa [*World War II*]
**JICARC** ..... Joint Intelligence Collecting Agency, Reception Committee [*Navy*]
**JICC** .......... Job Item Cost Code (MCD)
**JICCAR** ..... Joint Industry Committee for Cable Audience Research [*Television*] [*British*]
**JICG** .......... Joint International Coordination Group (MSC)
**JICHS** ....... Joint Industrial Conference on Hydraulic Standards
**J Ichthyol (Engl Trans Vopr Ikhtiol)** ... Journal of Ichthyology (English Translation of Voprosy Ikhtiologii) [*A publication*]
**J Ichthyol (USSR)** ... Journal of Ichthyology (USSR) [*English Translation of Voprosy Ikhtiologii*] [*A publication*]
**JICI** .......... Jeunesse Independante Chretienne Internationale [*International Independent Christian Youth - IICY*] (EA)
**JICJ** .......... Journal. International Commission of Jurists [*A publication*] (DLA)
**Jick Est** ...... Jickling. Legal and Equitable Estates [*1829*] [*A publication*] (DLA)
**JICNARS** ... Joint Industry Committee for National Readership Surveys [*British*]
**JICOA** ....... Japan Information and Communication Association [*Information service or system*] (EISS)
**JICPOA** ..... Joint Intelligence Center, Pacific Ocean Areas
**JICRAR** ..... Joint Industry Committee for Radio Audience Research [*British*]
**JICS** .......... Joint Intelligence Coordination Staff [*Central Intelligence Agency*] (AABC)
**JICST** ........ Japan Information Center of Science and Technology [*Tokyo*] (IID)
**JICTAR** ..... Joint Industry Committee for Television Advertising Research [*Database producer*]
**JICUF** ........ Japan International Christian University Foundation (EA)
**JIDA** .......... Jewelry Industry Distributors Association (EA)
**J Idaho Acad Sci** ... Journal. Idaho Academy of Science [*A publication*]
**JIDS** .......... Job Information Delivery System [*US Employment Service*] [*Department of Labor*]
**JIDSDP** ..... Journal. Idaho Academy of Science [*A publication*]
**JIDXA** ....... Journal. Indiana State Medical Association [*A publication*]
**JIE** .......... Japan Information Exchange [*Comtex Scientific Corp.*] [*Information service or system*] [*Defunct*] (CRD)
**JIE** .......... Jobs in Energy (EA)
**JIE** .......... Journal of Industrial Economics [*A publication*]
**JIE** .......... Journal of International Economics [*A publication*]
**JIE** .......... Junior Institute of Engineers
**JIECA** ........ Journal of Industrial and Engineering Chemistry [*A publication*]
**JIEE** .......... Japanese Institute of Electrical Engineers
**JIEND** ....... Jinetsu Enerugi [*A publication*]
**JIEP** .......... Joint Intelligence Estimate for Planning (AFM)
**JIES** .......... Journal of Indo-European Studies [*A publication*]
**JIF** .......... French Lick, IN [*Location identifier*] [*FAA*] (FAAL)
**JIF** .......... Janus Information Facility [*Later, J2CP Information Services*] (EA)
**JIF** .......... Joint Integrated Firepower [*Task force*] (MCD)
**JIF** .......... Journal of Information Systems Management [*A publication*]
**JIFC** .......... Janis Ian Fan Club (EA)
**JIFC** .......... Journal. International Folk Music Council [*A publication*]
**JIFC** .......... Julio Iglesias Fan Club (EA)
**JIFDATS** .. Joint In-Flight Data Transmission System [*Army*] (MCD)
**JIFE** .......... Junta Internacional de Fiscalizacion de Estupefacientes [*International Narcotics Control Board*]
**JIFFQ** ........ Jiffy Foods Corp. [*NASDAQ symbol*] (NQ)
**JIFM** ......... Journal. International Folk Music Council [*A publication*]
**JIFMC** ....... Journal. International Folk Music Council [*A publication*]
**JIFSA** ........ Journal. Indian Academy of Forensic Sciences [*A publication*]
**JIFTS** ........ Joint In-Flight Transmission System [*Army*] (IEEE)
**JIFUA** ....... Journal. Institute of Fuel [*A publication*]
**J I Fuel** ....... Journal. Institute of Fuel [*A publication*]
**JIFY** .......... Jiffy Industries [*NASDAQ symbol*] (NQ)
**JIG** .......... Jahrbuch fuer Internationale Germanistik [*A publication*]
**JIG** .......... Jinotega [*Nicaragua*] [*Seismograph station code, US Geological Survey*] (SEIS)
**JIG** .......... Joint Industry Group [*An association*] (EA)
**JIG** .......... Joint Intelligence Group [*Military*]
**JIG** .......... Joule Impulse Generator [*Physics*]
**JIG** .......... Journal of Irish Genealogy [*A publication*]
**JIGFET** ..... Junction and Insulated Gate Field Effect Transistor (MCD)
**JIGS** .......... Joule Impulse Generator System [*Physics*]
**JIGTSC** ..... Joint Industry-Government Tall Structures Committee
**JIH** .......... Journal of Indian History [*A publication*]
**JIHS** .......... Journal. Illinois State Historical Society [*A publication*]
**JIHTA** ....... Journal of Industrial Hygiene and Toxicology [*A publication*]
**JIHVE** ....... Journal. Institution of Heating and Ventilating Engineers [*A publication*]
**JII** .......... John Innes Institute [*British*] (ARC)
**JII** .......... Johnston Industries, Incorporated [*NYSE symbol*] (SPSG)
**JIIB** .......... Jewish Immigrants Information Bureau (BJA)
**JIIB** .......... Journal. Indian Institute of Bankers [*A publication*]
**JIIKS** ......... Joint Imagery Interpretation Key Structure (MCD)
**JIIM** .......... Journal of Information and Image Management [*A publication*]
**JIIP** .......... Joint Interface Implementation Program [*Army*] (MCD)
**JIIST** ......... Japan Institute for International Studies and Training
**JIKEA** ....... Jikken Keitaigakushi [*A publication*]
**Jikeikai Med J** ... Jikeikai Medical Journal [*A publication*]
**JIL** .......... George Washington Journal of International Law and Economics [*A publication*]
**JIL** .......... Japan Institute of Labour (DLA)
**JIL** .......... Jet-Induced Lift
**JIL** .......... Journal of Irish Literature [*A publication*]
**JIL** .......... Joy Industries Limited [*Vancouver Stock Exchange symbol*]
**JILA** .......... Joint Institute for Laboratory Astrophysics [*University of Colorado, National Bureau of Standards*] (EA)
**JILA Inf Cent Rep** ... Joint Institute for Laboratory Astrophysics. Information Center. Report [*A publication*]
**JILA Rep** ... Joint Institute for Laboratory Astrophysics. Report [*A publication*]
**JILE** .......... Joint Intelligence Liaison Element (MCD)
**JILEA** ........ Journal. Institution of Locomotive Engineers [*A publication*]
**JILI** .......... Journal. Indian Law Institute [*A publication*]
**J Ill Hist Soc** ... Journal. Illinois State Historical Society [*A publication*]
**JILLHS** ..... Journal. Illinois State Historical Society [*A publication*]
**J Ill State Hist Soc** ... Journal. Illinois State Historical Society [*A publication*]
**J Illum Eng Inst Jap** ... Journal. Illuminating Engineering Institute of Japan [*A publication*]
**J Illum Engng Soc** ... Journal. Illuminating Engineering Society [*A publication*]
**J Illum Eng Soc** ... Journal. Illuminating Engineering Society [*A publication*]
**JILO** .......... Joint Information Liaison Office [*Military*]
**JILTA** ........ Journal. Indian Law Teachers Association [*A publication*] (DLA)
**JIM** .......... Jevreiski Istoriski Muzej (BJA)
**JIM** .......... Jimma [*Ethiopia*] [*Airport symbol*] (OAG)
**JIM** .......... Job Instruction Manual
**JIM** .......... Journal of Industrial Microbiology [*A publication*]
**JIM** .......... Journal of Information Management [*A publication*]
**JIM** .......... Memphis, TN [*Location identifier*] [*FAA*] (FAAL)
**J IMA** ........ Journal. Islamic Medical Association of the United States and Canada [*A publication*]
**J Imaging Technol** ... Journal of Imaging Technology [*A publication*]
**JIMAR** ...... Joint Institute for Marine and Atmospheric Research [*National Oceanic and Atmospheric Administration*] [*Honolulu, HI*] (GRD)
**J I Math Ap** ... Journal. Institute of Mathematics and Its Applications [*A publication*]
**JIMEA** ...... Journal. Institute of Metals [*A publication*]
**JIMGA** ...... Journal of Immunogenetics [*A publication*]
**JIMI** .......... Jimi Hendrix Information Management Institute (EA)
**JIMMA** ..... Journal. Institute of Muslim Minority Affairs [*A publication*]
**J Immun** ..... Journal of Immunology [*A publication*]
**J Immunoassay** ... Journal of Immunoassay [*A publication*]

**J Immunogen** ... Journal of Immunogenetics [*A publication*]
**J Immunogenet** ... Journal of Immunogenetics [*A publication*]
**J Immunogenet (Oxf)** ... Journal of Immunogenetics (Oxford) [*A publication*]
**J Immunol** ... Journal of Immunology [*A publication*]
**J Immunol M** ... Journal of Immunological Methods [*A publication*]
**J Immunol Methods** ... Journal of Immunological Methods [*A publication*]
**J Immunopharmacol** ... Journal of Immunopharmacology [*A publication*]
**J Imp Agr Exp Sta (Tokyo)** ... Journal. Imperial Agricultural Experiment Station (Tokyo) [*A publication*]
**J Imp Coll Chem Eng Soc** ... Journal. Imperial College. Chemical Engineering Society [*A publication*]
**J Imp Coll Chem Soc** ... Journal. Imperial College. Chemical Society [*A publication*]
**J Imp Com H** ... Journal of Imperial and Commonwealth History [*A publication*]
**J Imp Commonw Hist** ... Journal of Imperial and Commonwealth History [*A publication*]
**J Imp Fish Inst (Jpn)** ... Journal. Imperial Fisheries Institute (Japan) [*A publication*]
**JIMS** ......... Journal. Indian Mathematical Society [*A publication*]
**JIMSA**....... Journal. Irish Medical Association [*A publication*]
**JIMSD2** .... Journal of Interdisciplinary Modeling and Simulation [*A publication*]
**JIN**............ Jindabyne [*Australia*] [*Seismograph station code, US Geological Survey*] [*Closed*] (SEIS)
**JIN**............ Journal of International Economics [*A publication*]
**JIN**............ Journal of Israel Numismatics [*A publication*]
**JIN**............ Jump Indirectly [*Data processing*]
**JIN**............ Justice Institute of British Columbia, Instructional Service [*UTLAS symbol*]
**JINBA** ....... Journal. Institute of Brewing [*A publication*]
**J Inc Aust Insurance Inst** ... Journal. Incorporated Australian Insurance Institute [*A publication*] (APTA)
**J Inc Brew Guild** ... Journal. Incorporated Brewers' Guild [*A publication*]
**J Inc Clerks Works Assoc GB** ... Journal. Incorporated Clerks of Works Association of Great Britain [*A publication*]
**J Incl Phen** ... Journal of Inclusion Phenomena [*A publication*]
**J Inclusion Phenom** ... Journal of Inclusion Phenomena [*A publication*]
**J Inclusion Phenom Mol Recognit Chem** ... Journal of Inclusion Phenomena and Molecular Recognition in Chemistry [*A publication*]
**J Ind**.......... Journal of Industry [*A publication*]
**J Ind Acad Philo** ... Journal. Indian Academy of Philosophy [*A publication*]
**J Ind Aero** ... Journal of Industrial Aerodynamics [*A publication*]
**J Ind Aerodyn** ... Journal of Industrial Aerodynamics [*A publication*]
**J Ind Anthropol Soc** ... Journal. Indian Anthropological Society [*A publication*]
**J Ind Arts Ed** ... Journal of Industrial Arts Education [*A publication*]
**J Ind Bot Soc** ... Journal. Indian Botanical Society [*A publication*]
**J Ind Ch S** ... Journal. Indian Chemical Society [*A publication*]
**J Ind Econ** ... Journal of Industrial Economics [*A publication*]
**J Ind Eng** ... Journal of Industrial Engineering [*A publication*]
**J Ind Eng Chem** ... Journal of Industrial and Engineering Chemistry [*United States*] [*A publication*]
**J Ind Engng Chem** ... Journal of Industrial and Engineering Chemistry [*A publication*]
**J Ind Explos Soc (Jap)** ... Journal. Industrial Explosives Society. Explosion and Explosives (Japan) [*A publication*]
**J Ind Fabr** ... Journal of Industrial Fabrics [*A publication*]
**J Ind Gaz** ... Journal des Industries du Gaz [*A publication*]
**J Ind Hist**... Journal of Indian History [*A publication*]
**J Ind Hyg**... Journal of Industrial Hygiene [*A publication*]
**J Ind Hyg**... Journal of Industrial Hygiene and Toxicology [*A publication*]
**J Ind Hyg Toxicol** ... Journal of Industrial Hygiene and Toxicology [*A publication*]
**J Indian Acad Dent** ... Journal. Indian Academy of Dentistry [*A publication*]
**J Indian Acad Forensic Sci** ... Journal. Indian Academy of Forensic Sciences [*A publication*]
**J Indian Acad Geosci** ... Journal. Indian Academy of Geoscience [*A publication*]
**J Indian Acad Phil** ... Journal. Indian Academy of Philosophy [*A publication*]
**J Indian Acad Sci** ... Journal. Indian Academy of Sciences [*A publication*]
**J Indian Acad Wood Sci** ... Journal. Indian Academy of Wood Science [*A publication*]
**J Indiana Dent Assoc** ... Journal. Indiana Dental Association [*A publication*]
**J Indiana MA** ... Journal. Indiana State Medical Association [*A publication*]
**J Indian Anthropol Soc** ... Journal. Indian Anthropological Society [*A publication*]
**J Indianap Dist Dent Soc** ... Journal. Indianapolis District Dental Society [*A publication*]
**J Indian Assoc Commun Dis** ... Journal. Indian Association for Communicable Diseases [*A publication*]
**J Indiana State Dent Assoc** ... Journal. Indiana State Dental Association [*A publication*]
**J Indiana State Med Assoc** ... Journal. Indiana State Medical Association [*A publication*]
**J Indian Bot Soc** ... Journal. Indian Botanical Society [*A publication*]
**J Indian Ceram Soc** ... Journal. Indian Ceramic Society [*A publication*]
**J Indian Chem Soc** ... Journal. Indian Chemical Society [*A publication*]
**J Indian Chem Soc Ind News Ed** ... Journal. Indian Chemical Society. Industrial and News Edition [*India*] [*A publication*]
**J Indian Dent Assoc** ... Journal. Indian Dental Association [*A publication*]
**J Indian Geophys Union** ... Journal. Indian Geophysical Union [*A publication*]
**J Indian Hist** ... Journal of Indian History [*A publication*]
**J Indian I** ... Journal. Indian Institute of Science [*A publication*]
**J Indian Ind Labour** ... Journal of Indian Industries and Labour [*A publication*]
**J Indian Inst Sci** ... Journal. Indian Institute of Science [*A publication*]
**J Indian Inst Sci Sect A** ... Journal. Indian Institute of Science. Section A [*A publication*]
**J Indian Inst Sci Sect B** ... Journal. Indian Institute of Science. Section B [*A publication*]
**J Indian Inst Sci Sect C** ... Journal. Indian Institute of Science. Section C [*A publication*]
**J Indian Inst Sci Sect C Biol Sci** ... Journal. Indian Institute of Science. Section C. Biological Sciences [*A publication*]
**J Indian Leather Technol Assoc** ... Journal. Indian Leather Technologists Association [*A publication*]
**J Indian Math Soc** ... Journal. Indian Mathematical Society [*A publication*]
**J Indian Med A** ... Journal. Indian Medical Association [*A publication*]
**J Indian Med Ass** ... Journal. Indian Medical Association [*A publication*]
**J Indian Med Assoc** ... Journal. Indian Medical Association [*A publication*]
**J Indian Med Prof** ... Journal of the Indian Medical Profession [*A publication*]
**J Indian Musicol Soc** ... Journal. Indian Musicological Society [*A publication*]
**J Indian Nat Soc Soil Mech Found Eng** ... Journal. Indian National Society of Soil Mechanics and Foundation Engineering [*A publication*]
**J Indian P**.. Journal of Indian Philosophy [*A publication*]
**J Indian Pediatr Soc** ... Journal. Indian Pediatric Society [*A publication*]
**J Indian Phil** ... Journal of Indian Philosophy [*A publication*]
**J Indian Potato Assoc** ... Journal. Indian Potato Association [*A publication*]
**J Indian Refract Makers Assoc** ... Journal. Indian Refractory Makers Association [*A publication*]
**J Indian Roads Congr** ... Journal. Indian Roads Congress [*A publication*]
**J Indian Soc Agric Stat** ... Journal. Indian Society of Agricultural Statistics [*A publication*]
**J Indian Soc Agr Statist** ... Journal. Indian Society of Agricultural Statistics [*A publication*]
**J Indian Soc Pedod Prev Dent** ... Journal. Indian Society of Pedodontics and Preventive Dentistry [*A publication*]
**J Indian Soc Soil Sci** ... Journal. Indian Society of Soil Science [*A publication*]
**J Indian Soc Statist Oper Res** ... Journal. Indian Society of Statistics and Operations Research [*A publication*]
**J Indian Statist Assoc** ... Journal. Indian Statistical Association [*A publication*]
**J India Soc Eng** ... Journal. India Society of Engineers [*A publication*]
**J Ind Irradiat Technol** ... Journal of Industrial Irradiation Technology [*A publication*]
**J Individ Psychol** ... Journal of Individual Psychology [*A publication*]
**J Indiv Psy** ... Journal of Individual Psychology [*A publication*]
**J Ind L Inst** ... Journal. Indian Law Institute [*A publication*] (DLA)
**J Ind Microbiol** ... Journal of Industrial Microbiology [*A publication*]
**J Ind Musicol Soc** ... Journal. Indian Musicological Society [*A publication*]
**J Indn Acad Math** ... Indian Academy of Mathematics. Journal [*A publication*]
**J Indn St A** ... Journal. Indian Statistical Association [*A publication*]
**J Indo-Eur** ... Journal of Indo-European Studies [*A publication*]
**J Indo-European Stud** ... Journal of Indo-European Studies [*A publication*]
**J Ind Philo** ... Journal of Indian Philosophy [*A publication*]
**J Ind Pollut Control** ... Journal of Industrial Pollution Control [*A publication*]
**J Ind R** ....... Journal of Industrial Relations [*A publication*]
**J Ind Rel** .... Journal of Industrial Relations [*A publication*]
**J Ind Relations** ... Journal of Industrial Relations [*A publication*] (APTA)
**J Ind Teach Educ** ... Journal of Industrial Teacher Education [*A publication*]
**J Ind Technol** ... Journal of Industrial Technology [*South Korea*] [*A publication*]
**J Ind Technol Myong-Ji Univ** ... Journal of Industrial Technology. Myong-Ji University [*Republic of Korea*] [*A publication*]
**J Ind Trade** ... Journal of Industry and Trade [*A publication*]
**J Indus Rel** ... Journal of Industrial Relations [*A publication*] (APTA)
**J Indust**...... Journal of Industry [*A publication*] (APTA)
**J Indust Hyg** ... Journal of Industrial Hygiene [*A publication*]
**J Indust Hyg Toxicol** ... Journal of Industrial Hygiene and Toxicology [*A publication*]
**J Industr Econ** ... Journal of Industrial Economics [*A publication*]
**J Indust Rel** ... Journal of Industrial Relations [*A publication*]
**J Indust Relations** ... Journal of Industrial Relations [*A publication*] (APTA)
**J Industr Relat** ... Journal of Industrial Relations [*A publication*]
**J Industr Teacher Educ** ... Journal of Industrial Teacher Education [*A publication*]
**J Industry** .. Journal of Industry [*A publication*] (APTA)
**JINEA** ....... Journal. Indian Chemical Society. Industrial and News Edition [*A publication*]
**J Infect**....... Journal of Infection [*A publication*]
**J Infect Dis** ... Journal of Infectious Diseases [*A publication*]
**J Inf Image Manage** ... Journal of Information and Image Management [*A publication*]
**J Info Mgmt** ... Journal of Information Management [*A publication*]
**J Inf and Optimiz Sci** ... Journal of Information and Optimization Sciences [*A publication*]
**J Information Processing** ... Journal of Information Processing [*A publication*]

**J Inform Optim Sci** ... Journal of Information and Optimization Sciences [*A publication*]
**J Inform Process** ... Journal of Information Processing [*A publication*]
**J Info Sci**.... Journal of Information Science. Principles and Practice [*A publication*]
**J Info Sys Mgmt** ... Journal of Information Systems Management [*A publication*]
**J Inf Process Soc Jap** ... Journal. Information Processing Society of Japan [*A publication*]
**J Inf Process Soc Jpn** ... Journal. Information Processing Society of Japan [*A publication*]
**J Inf Sci**...... Journal of Information Science [*Netherlands*] [*A publication*]
**J Inf Sci Princ and Pract** ... Journal of Information Science. Principles and Practice [*A publication*]
**J Inf Tech Ind Fonderie** ... Journal d'Informations Techniques des Industries de la Fonderie [*A publication*]
**J Ing**.......... Journal des Ingenieurs [*A publication*]
**J Inherited Metab Dis** ... Journal of Inherited Metabolic Disease [*A publication*]
**J Inl Fish Soc India** ... Journal. Inland Fisheries Society of India [*A publication*]
**J Inorg Biochem** ... Journal of Inorganic Biochemistry [*A publication*]
**J Inorg Chem (USSR)** ... Journal of Inorganic Chemistry (USSR) [*A publication*]
**J Inorg Nuc** ... Journal of Inorganic and Nuclear Chemistry [*A publication*]
**J Inorg Nucl Chem** ... Journal of Inorganic and Nuclear Chemistry [*A publication*]
**J Inorg and Nucl Chem** ... Journal of Inorganic and Nuclear Chemistry [*A publication*]
**JINR**.......... Joint Institute of Nuclear Research [*Dubna, USSR*]
**J Ins**.......... Journal of Insurance [*A publication*]
**JINS**.......... Juveniles in Need of Supervision [*Classification for delinquent children*]
**JINSA**....... Jewish Institute for National Security Affairs (EA)
**J of Ins of Arbitrators** ... Journal. Institute of Arbitrators [*A publication*] (DLA)
**J Insect Path** ... Journal of Insect Pathology [*A publication*]
**J Insect Pathol** ... Journal of Insect Pathology [*A publication*]
**J Insect Ph** ... Journal of Insect Physiology [*A publication*]
**J Insect Physiol** ... Journal of Insect Physiology [*A publication*]
**Jinsen Med J** ... Jinsen Medical Journal [*A publication*]
**J Insp Sch** ... Journal of Inspectors of Schools of Australia and New Zealand [*A publication*] (APTA)
**J Inst**........ Institutes of Justinian [*Roman law*] [*A publication*]
**J Inst Agric Resour Utiliz Chinju Agric Coll** ... Journal. Institute for Agricultural Resources Utilization. Chinju Agricultural College [*A publication*]
**J Inst Anim Tech** ... Journal. Institute of Animal Technicians [*A publication*]
**J Inst Auto & Aero Engrs** ... Journal. Institution of Automotive and Aeronautical Engineers [*A publication*] (APTA)
**J Inst Automob Eng (London)** ... Journal. Institution of Automobile Engineers (London) [*A publication*]
**J Inst Automot Aeronaut Eng** ... Journal. Institution of Automotive and Aeronautical Engineers [*A publication*]
**J Inst Automotive & Aeronautical Eng** ... Journal. Institution of Automotive and Aeronautical Engineers [*A publication*] (APTA)
**J Inst Automotive & Aeronautical Engrs** ... Journal. Institution of Automotive and Aeronautical Engineers [*A publication*] (APTA)
**J Inst Brew** ... Journal. Institute of Brewing [*A publication*]
**J Inst Br Foundrymen** ... Journal. Institute of British Foundrymen [*A publication*]
**J Inst Can Sci Technol Aliment** ... Journal. Institut Canadien de Science et Technologie Alimentaire [*A publication*]
**J Inst Can Technol Aliment** ... Journal. Institut Canadien de Technologie Alimentaire [*A publication*]
**J Inst Certif Eng (S Afr)** ... Journal. Institution of Certificated Engineers (South Africa) [*A publication*]
**J Inst Chem (India)** ... Journal. Institute of Chemistry (India) [*A publication*]
**J Inst Chem (India)** ... Journal. Institution of Chemists (India) [*A publication*]
**J Inst Civ Eng** ... Journal. Institution of Civil Engineers [*A publication*]
**J Inst Clerks Works GB** ... Journal. Institute of Clerks of Works of Great Britain [*A publication*]
**J Inst Clerks Works G Bt** ... Journal. Institute of Clerks of Works of Great Britain [*A publication*]
**J Inst Comput Sci** ... Journal. Institution of Computer Sciences [*A publication*]
**J Inst Def Stud Anal** ... Journal. Institute for Defence Studies and Analyses [*A publication*]
**J Inst Draftsmen** ... Journal. Institute of Draftsmen [*A publication*]
**JINSTE**..... Junior Institution of Engineers [*British*]
**J Inst Electr Commun Eng Jap** ... Journal. Institute of Electrical Communication Engineers of Japan [*Later, Journal. Institute of Electronics and Communication Engineers of Japan*] [*A publication*]
**J Inst Electr Eng** ... Journal. Institute of Electrical Engineers [*South Korea*] [*A publication*]
**J Inst Electr Eng** ... Journal. Institution of Electrical Engineers [*England*] [*A publication*]
**J Inst Electr Eng (1889-1940)** ... Journal. Institution of Electrical Engineers (1889-1940) [*A publication*]
**J Inst Electr Eng (1949-63)** ... Journal. Institution of Electrical Engineers (1949-63) [*A publication*]
**J Inst Electr Eng Jpn** ... Journal. Institution of Electrical Engineers of Japan [*A publication*]
**J Inst Electr Eng Part 1** ... Journal. Institution of Electrical Engineers. Part 1. General [*A publication*]
**J Inst Electr Eng Part 2** ... Journal. Institution of Electrical Engineers. Part 2. Power Engineering [*A publication*]
**J Inst Electr Eng Part 3** ... Journal. Institution of Electrical Engineers. Part 3. Radio and Communication Engineering [*A publication*]
**J Inst Electron Commun Eng Jap** ... Journal. Institute of Electronics and Communication Engineers of Japan [*A publication*]
**J Inst Electron and Commun Eng Jpn** ... Journal. Institute of Electronics and Communication Engineers of Japan [*A publication*]
**J Inst Electron Telecommun Eng** ... Journal. Institution of Electronics and Telecommunication Engineers [*A publication*]
**J Inst Energy** ... Journal. Institute of Energy [*United Kingdom*] [*A publication*]
**J Inst Eng (Aust)** ... Journal. Institution of Engineers (Australia) [*A publication*]
**J Inst Eng (India)** ... Journal. Institution of Engineers (India) [*A publication*]
**J Inst Eng (India) Chem Eng Div** ... Journal. Institution of Engineers (India). Chemical Engineering Division [*A publication*]
**J Inst Eng (India) Civ Eng Div** ... Journal. Institution of Engineers (India). Civil Engineering Division [*A publication*]
**J Inst Eng (India) Elec Eng Div** ... Journal. Institution of Engineers (India). Electrical Engineering Division [*A publication*]
**J Inst Eng (India) Electron and Telecommun Eng Div** ... Journal. Institution of Engineers (India). Electronics and Telecommunication Engineering Division [*A publication*]
**J Inst Eng (India) Electron Telecommun Eng Div** ... Journal. Institution of Engineers (India). Electronics and Telecommunication Engineering Division [*A publication*]
**J Inst Eng (India) Environ Eng Div** ... Journal. Institution of Engineers (India). Environmental Engineering Division [*A publication*]
**J Inst Eng (India) Gen Eng Div** ... Journal. Institution of Engineers (India). General Engineering Division [*A publication*]
**J Inst Eng (India) Ind Dev Gen Eng Div** ... Journal. Institution of Engineers (India). Industrial Development and General Engineering Division [*A publication*]
**J Inst Eng (India) Interdisciplinary and Gen Eng** ... Journal. Institution of Engineers (India). Interdisciplinary and General Engineering [*A publication*]
**J Inst Eng (India) Mech Eng Div** ... Journal. Institution of Engineers (India). Mechanical Engineering Division [*A publication*]
**J Inst Eng (India) Mining Met Div** ... Journal. Institution of Engineers (India). Mining and Metallurgy Division [*A publication*]
**J Inst Eng (India) Min and Metall Div** ... Journal. Institution of Engineers (India). Mining and Metallurgy Division [*A publication*]
**J Inst Eng (India) Min Metall Div** ... Journal. Institution of Engineers (India). Mining and Metallurgy Division [*A publication*]
**J Inst Eng (India) Part IDGE** ... Journal. Institution of Engineers (India). Part IDGE [*Industrial Development and General Engineering*] [*A publication*]
**J Inst Eng (India) Pub Health Eng Div** ... Journal. Institution of Engineers (India). Public Health Engineering Division [*A publication*]
**J Inst Eng (India) Public Health Eng Div** ... Journal. Institution of Engineers (India). Public Health Engineering Division [*A publication*]
**J Inst Eng (Malaysia)** ... Journal. Institution of Engineers (Malaysia) [*A publication*]
**J Inst Engrs (Aust)** ... Journal. Institution of Engineers (Australia) [*A publication*]
**J Inst Engrs (Australia)** ... Journal. Institution of Engineers (Australia) [*A publication*]
**J Inst Engrs (India)** ... Journal. Institution of Engineers (India) [*A publication*]
**J Inst Engrs (India) Part CI** ... Journal. Institution of Engineers (India). Part CI [*A publication*]
**J Inst Engrs (India) Part ME** ... Journal. Institution of Engineers (India). Part ME [*A publication*]
**J Inst Fuel** ... Journal. Institute of Fuel [*A publication*]
**J Inst Geol Vikram Univ** ... Journal. Institute of Geology. Vikram University [*A publication*]
**J Inst Highw Eng** ... Journal. Institute of Highway Engineers [*A publication*]
**J Inst (India) Electron Telecommun Eng Div** ... Journal. Institution of Engineers (India). Electronics and Telecommunication Engineering Division [*A publication*]
**J Institute Socioecon Stud** ... Journal. Institute for Socioeconomic Studies [*A publication*]
**J Inst Math Appl** ... Journal. Institute of Mathematics and Its Applications [*A publication*]
**J Inst Math and Appl** ... Journal. Institute of Mathematics and Its Applications [*A publication*]
**J Inst Math Applic** ... Journal. Institute of Mathematics and Its Applications [*A publication*]
**J Inst Math Its Appl** ... Journal. Institute of Mathematics and Its Applications [*A publication*]
**J Inst Met (Lond)** ... Journal. Institute of Metals (London) [*A publication*]
**J Inst Mine Surv S Afr** ... Journal. Institute of Mine Surveyors of South Africa [*A publication*]

**J Inst Min Surv S Afr** ... Journal. Institute of Mine Surveyors of South Africa [*A publication*]
**J Inst Munic Eng** ... Journal. Institution of Municipal Engineers [*A publication*]
**J Inst Navig** ... Journal. Institute of Navigation [*A publication*]
**J Instn Engrs (Aust)** ... Journal. Institution of Engineers (Australia) [*A publication*]
**J Instn Gas Engrs** ... Journal. Institution of Gas Engineers [*A publication*]
**J Instn Heat Vent Engrs** ... Journal. Institution of Heating and Ventilating Engineers [*A publication*]
**J Instn Highw Engrs** ... Journal. Institution of Highway Engineers [*A publication*]
**J Instn Loco Engrs** ... Journal. Institution of Locomotive Engineers [*A publication*]
**J Instn Munic Engrs** ... Journal. Institution of Municipal Engineers [*A publication*]
**J Instn Nucl Engrs** ... Journal. Institution of Nuclear Engineers [*A publication*]
**J Instn Rubb Ind** ... Journal. Institution of the Rubber Industry [*A publication*]
**J Inst Nucl Eng** ... Journal. Institution of Nuclear Engineers [*A publication*]
**J Inst Nucl Mater Manage** ... Journal. Institute of Nuclear Materials Management [*A publication*]
**J Instn Wat Engrs** ... Journal. Institution of Water Engineers [*A publication*]
**J Instn Wat Engrs Scientists** ... Journal. Institution of Water Engineers and Scientists [*A publication*]
**J Instn Water Engnrs Sci** ... Journal. Institution of Water Engineers and Scientists [*A publication*]
**J Inst Pet** ... Journal. Institute of Petroleum [*A publication*]
**J Inst Pet Abstr** ... Journal. Institute of Petroleum. Abstracts [*A publication*]
**J Inst Pet Technol** ... Journal. Institution of Petroleum Technologists [*England*] [*A publication*]
**J Inst Polytech Osaka City Univ Ser C** ... Journal. Institute of Polytechnics. Osaka City University. Series C. Chemistry [*A publication*]
**J Inst Polytech Osaka City Univ Ser D** ... Journal. Institute of Polytechnics. Osaka City University. Series D. Biology [*A publication*]
**J Inst Polytech Osaka City Univ Ser E** ... Journal. Institute of Polytechnics. Osaka City University. Series E. Engineering [*A publication*]
**J Inst Polytech Osaka City Univ Ser G** ... Journal. Institute of Polytechnics. Osaka City University. Series G. Geoscience [*A publication*]
**J Inst Polytech Osaka Cy Univ** ... Journal. Institute of Polytechnics. Osaka City University [*A publication*]
**J Inst Prod Eng** ... Journal. Institution of Production Engineers [*A publication*]
**J Inst Public Health Eng** ... Journal. Institution of Public Health Engineers [*A publication*]
**J Instr Psychol** ... Journal of Instructional Psychology [*A publication*]
**J Inst Rubber Ind** ... Journal. Institution of the Rubber Industry [*A publication*]
**J Instrum Soc Am** ... Journal. Instrument Society of America [*A publication*]
**J Instrum Soc India** ... Journal. Instrument Society of India [*A publication*]
**J Inst Saf High Pressure Gas Eng** ... Journal. Institute of Safety of High Pressure Gas Engineering [*Japan*] [*A publication*]
**J Inst Sanit Eng** ... Journal. Institution of Sanitary Engineers [*A publication*]
**J Inst Sci Technol** ... Journal. Institute of Science Technology [*A publication*]
**J Inst Socioecon Stud** ... Journal. Institute for Socioeconomic Studies [*United States*] [*A publication*]
**J Inst Telecommun Eng** ... Journal. Institution of Telecommunication Engineers [*A publication*]
**J Inst Telecommun Eng (New Delhi)** ... Journal. Institution of Telecommunication Engineers (New Delhi) [*A publication*]
**J Inst Telev Eng Jpn** ... Journal. Institute of Television Engineers of Japan [*A publication*]
**J Inst Transp** ... Journal. Institute of Transport [*A publication*]
**J Inst Transport** ... Journal. Institute of Transport (Australian Section) [*A publication*] (APTA)
**J Inst Water Eng** ... Journal. Institution of Water Engineers [*A publication*]
**J Inst Water Engrs & Sci** ... Journal. Institution of Water Engineers and Scientists [*A publication*]
**J Inst Water Eng Sci** ... Journal. Institution of Water Engineers and Scientists [*A publication*]
**J Inst Wood Sci** ... Journal. Institute of Wood Science [*A publication*]
**JINTACCS** ... Joint Interoperability of Tactical Command and Control Systems (MCD)
**J Int Aff** ..... Journal of International Affairs [*A publication*]
**J Int A Mat** ... Journal. International Association for Mathematical Geology [*A publication*]
**J Intam St** .. Journal of Interamerican Studies and World Affairs [*A publication*]
**J Int Ass Math Geol** ... Journal. International Association for Mathematical Geology [*A publication*]
**J Int Assoc Artif Prolongation Hum Specific Lifespan** ... Journal. International Association on the Artificial Prolongation of the Human Specific Lifespan [*A publication*]
**J Int Assoc Dent Child** ... Journal. International Association of Dentistry for Children [*A publication*]
**J Int Assoc Math Geol** ... Journal. International Association for Mathematical Geology [*A publication*]
**J Int Bus Stud** ... Journal of International Business Studies [*A publication*]
**J Int Cancer** ... Journal International du Cancer [*A publication*]
**J Int Coll Dent Jpn** ... Journal. International College of Dentists. Japan Section [*A publication*]
**J Int Coll Surg** ... Journal. International College of Surgeons [*United States*] [*A publication*]
**JINTD** ....... Journal of Industrial Technology. Myong-Ji University [*A publication*]
**J Int Econ** .. Journal of International Economics [*A publication*]
**J Integral Equations** ... Journal of Integral Equations [*A publication*]
**J Interamer Stud** ... Journal of Interamerican Studies and World Affairs [*A publication*]
**J Inter Am Stud** ... Journal of Inter-American Studies and World Affairs [*A publication*]
**J Interam Stud** ... Journal of Interamerican Studies and World Affairs [*A publication*]
**J Interam Stud World Aff** ... Journal of Interamerican Studies and World Affairs [*A publication*]
**J Intercult Stud** ... Journal of Intercultural Studies [*A publication*]
**J Intercultural Stud** ... Journal of Intercultural Studies [*A publication*] (APTA)
**J Interd Cy** ... Journal of Interdisciplinary Cycle Research [*A publication*]
**J Interd H** .. Journal of Interdisciplinary History [*A publication*]
**J Interdiscip Cycle Res** ... Journal of Interdisciplinary Cycle Research [*A publication*]
**J Interdiscip Hist** ... Journal of Interdisciplinary History [*A publication*]
**J Interdiscipl Cycle Res** ... Journal of Interdisciplinary Cycle Research [*A publication*]
**J Interdisciplinary Modeling Simulation** ... Journal of Interdisciplinary Modeling and Simulation [*A publication*]
**J Interdiscip Model Simul** ... Journal of Interdisciplinary Modeling and Simulation [*A publication*]
**J Interdis H** ... Journal of Interdisciplinary History [*A publication*]
**J Interdis Hist** ... Journal of Interdisciplinary History [*A publication*]
**J Interferon Res** ... Journal of Interferon Research [*A publication*]
**J Intergroup Rel** ... Journal of Intergroup Relations [*A publication*]
**J of Intergroup Rela** ... Journal of Intergroup Relations [*A publication*]
**J Internat Affairs** ... Journal of International Affairs [*A publication*]
**J Internat Assoc Mathematical Geol** ... Journal. International Association for Mathematical Geology [*A publication*]
**J Internat Assoc Math Geol** ... Journal. International Association for Mathematical Geology [*A publication*]
**J Internat Bus Studies** ... Journal of International Business Studies [*A publication*]
**J Internat Coll Surgeons** ... Journal. International College of Surgeons [*A publication*]
**J Internat Econ** ... Journal of International Economics [*A publication*]
**J Internat Law and Econ** ... Journal of International Law and Economics [*A publication*]
**J of Internat L and Econ** ... Journal of International Law and Economics [*A publication*]
**J Internat Rel** ... Journal of International Relations [*A publication*]
**J Intern Med** ... Journal of Internal Medicine [*A publication*]
**J Intern Med Suppl** ... Journal of Internal Medicine. Supplement [*A publication*]
**J Intern Rel** ... Journal of International Relations [*A publication*]
**J Int Fed Gynaecol Obstet** ... Journal. International Federation of Gynaecology and Obstetrics [*A publication*]
**J Int Inst Sugar Beet Res** ... Journal. International Institute for Sugar Beet Research [*A publication*]
**J Intl Aff** .... Journal of International Affairs [*A publication*]
**J Int Law E** ... Journal of International Law and Economics [*A publication*]
**J Int Law & Econ** ... Journal of International Law and Economics [*A publication*]
**J Int'l Comm Jur** ... Journal. International Commission of Jurists [*A publication*] (DLA)
**J Int'l & Comp L** ... Journal of International and Comparative Law [*A publication*] (DLA)
**J Int L and Ec** ... Journal of International Law and Economics [*A publication*]
**J Int'l L & Dipl** ... Journal of International Law and Diplomacy [*A publication*] (DLA)
**J Intl L and Econ** ... Journal of International Law and Economics [*A publication*]
**J Int'l L & Pol** ... Journal of International Law and Politics [*A publication*] (DLA)
**J Int Med R** ... Journal of International Medical Research [*A publication*]
**J Int Med Res** ... Journal of International Medical Research [*A publication*]
**J Int Num** .. Journal of International Numismatics [*A publication*]
**J Int Phonetic Assoc** ... Journal. International Phonetic Association [*A publication*]
**J Int Psychol** ... Journal International de Psychologie [*A publication*]
**J Int Relations** ... Journal of International Relations [*A publication*]
**J Int Res Commun** ... Journal of International Research Communications [*A publication*]
**J Int Th C** .. Journal. Interdenominational Theological Center [*A publication*]
**J Int Vitaminol Nutr** ... Journal International de Vitaminologie et de Nutrition [*A publication*]
**J I Nucl En** ... Journal. Institution of Nuclear Engineers [*A publication*]
**J Inver Pat** ... Journal of Invertebrate Pathology [*A publication*]
**J Invertebr Pathol** ... Journal of Invertebrate Pathology [*A publication*]
**J Invert Path** ... Journal of Invertebrate Pathology [*A publication*]

**J Inves Der** ... Journal of Investigative Dermatology [*A publication*]
**J Invest Dermat** ... Journal of Investigative Dermatology [*A publication*]
**J Invest Dermatol** ... Journal of Investigative Dermatology [*A publication*]
**J In Vitro Fert Embryo Transfer** ... Journal of In Vitro Fertilization and Embryo Transfer [*A publication*]
**JIO**............ Joint Information Office [*Military*]
**JIO**............ Journal of Industrial Economics (Oxford) [*A publication*]
**JIO**............ Ontario, CA [*Location identifier*] [*FAA*] (FAAL)
**JIOA**.......... Joint Intelligence Objectives Agency (MCD)
**JIOC**.......... Jensen Interceptor Owners Club (EA)
**JIOS**.......... Journal of Information and Optimization Sciences [*A publication*]
**J Iowa Acad Sci** ... Journal. Iowa Academy of Science [*A publication*]
**J Iowa Med Soc** ... Journal. Iowa Medical Society [*A publication*]
**J Iowa State Med Soc** ... Journal. Iowa State Medical Society [*A publication*]
**JIP**............ Job the Impatient (BJA)
**JIP**............ Job Improvement Plan
**JIP**............ Joint Implementation Plan [*Military*]
**JIP**............ Joint Input
**JIP**............ Joint Input Processing (IEEE)
**JIP**............ Joint Installation Plan (AAG)
**JIP**............ Journal of Indian Philosophy [*A publication*]
**JIPA**.......... Journal. Indian Potato Association [*A publication*]
**JIPA**.......... Journal. International Phonetic Association [*A publication*]
**JIP/AMD** ... JIP/Areal Marketing Database [*Toyo Keizai Shinposha Co. Ltd.*] [*Japan*] [*Information service or system*] (CRD)
**JIPC**.......... Jordan Is Palestine Committee (EA)
**JIPEA**........ Journal. Institute of Petroleum [*A publication*]
**JIPHA**........ Journal of Insect Physiology [*A publication*]
**JIPMER**.... Jawahrlal Institute of Postgraduate Medical Education and Research [*India*]
**J f IR**.......... Jahrbuch fuer Internationales und Auslaendisches Oeffentliches Recht [*A publication*]
**JIR**............ Jewish Institute of Religion
**JIR**............ Jiri [*Nepal*] [*Airport symbol*] (OAG)
**JIR**............ Job Improvement Request
**JIR**............ Journal of Industrial Relations [*A publication*]
**J Iraqi Chem Soc** ... Journal. Iraqi Chemical Society [*A publication*]
**J Iraqi Med Prof** ... Journal of the Iraqi Medical Professions [*A publication*]
**J Ir Coll Physicians Surg** ... Journal. Irish Colleges of Physicians and Surgeons [*A publication*]
**JIRCSM**.... Joint Industry Research Committee for Standardization of Miniature Precision Coaxial Connectors
**J Ir Dent Assoc** ... Journal. Irish Dental Association [*A publication*]
**JIREDJ**..... Journal of Interferon Research [*A publication*]
**JIRIA**......... Jibi To Rinsho [*A publication*]
**J Irish C P** ... Journal. Irish Colleges of Physicians and Surgeons [*A publication*]
**J Irish Lit**... Journal of Irish Literature [*A publication*]
**J Irish MA** ... Journal. Irish Medical Association [*A publication*]
**J Ir Med Assoc** ... Journal. Irish Medical Association [*A publication*]
**J Iron & Steel Eng** ... Journal of Iron and Steel Engineering [*A publication*]
**J Iron Steel Inst Jpn** ... Journal. Iron and Steel Institute of Japan [*A publication*]
**J Iron Steel Inst (London)** ... Journal. Iron and Steel Institute (London) [*A publication*]
**J Iron St Inst** ... Journal. Iron and Steel Institute [*A publication*]
**JIRP**.......... Juneau Icefield Research Project [*University of Idaho*] [*Research center*]
**J Irrig Drain Div Am Soc Civ Eng** ... Journal. Irrigation and Drainage Division. Proceedings of the American Society of Civil Engineers [*A publication*]
**J Irrig Drain Div ASCE** ... Journal. Irrigation and Drainage Division. Proceedings of the American Society of Engineers [*A publication*]
**J Irrig & Drain Div Proc ASCE** ... Journal. Irrigation and Drainage Division. Proceedings of the American Society of Civil Engineers [*A publication*]
**JIRS**.......... Jewish Information and Referral Service Directory [*A publication*] (EAAP)
**JIRS**.......... Joint Information and Retrieval System [*DoD*] (MCD)
**JIS**............ Japan Investment Service [*Reuters Holdings PLC*] [*Great Britain*] [*Information service or system*] (CRD)
**JIS**............ Japanese Industrial Standards
**JIS**............ Jet Inlet System
**JIS**............ Jet Interaction Steering
**JIS**............ Jewish Information Society of America (EA)
**JiS**............ Jezik in Slovstvo [*A publication*]
**JIS**............ Job Information Service [*Department of Labor*]
**JIS**............ Joint Integrated Simulation (NASA)
**JIS**............ Joint Intelligence Staff
**JIS**............ Joint Operations Interim Software (MCD)
**JIS**............ Journal. Institute for Socioeconomic Studies [*A publication*]
**JIS**............ Journal of Insurance [*A publication*]
**JIS**............ Justice Information System [*Australia*]
**JISAO**....... Joint Institute for Study of the Atmosphere and Ocean [*Seattle, WA*] [*University of Washington, NOAA*] (GRD)
**JISC**.......... Japanese Industrial Standards Committee [*Agency of Industrial Science and Technology, Ministry of International Trade and Industry*]
**JISCD**........ Journal of Information Science [*A publication*]
**JISETA**..... Joint Investigation of the Southeastern Tropical Atlantic [*Angola, US*] (MSC)
**JISGA**........ Journal. Institution of Engineers (Australia) [*A publication*]
**JISHS**........ Journal. Illinois State Historical Society [*A publication*]
**J Islam & Comp L** ... Journal of Islamic and Comparative Law [*Nigeria*] [*A publication*] (DLA)
**J'ism Quart** ... Journalism Quarterly [*A publication*]
**JISO**.......... Japanese International Satellite Organization [*Cable-television system*]
**JISPB**........ Joint Intelligence Studies Publishing Board
**JISR**.......... Joint Information Search Unit Retrieval System (MCD)
**J Isr Med Assoc** ... Journal. Israel Medical Association [*A publication*]
**JISS**.......... Journal. Indian Sociological Society [*A publication*]
**JISSD**........ Journal. Institute for Socioeconomic Studies [*A publication*]
**JIT**............ Frozen Food Express Industries, Inc. [*AMEX symbol*] (SPSG)
**JIT**............ Jamiat-i-Talaba [*Pakistan*] [*Political party*] (PD)
**JIT**............ Job Information Test [*Military*] (AFM)
**JIT**............ Job Instruction Training
**JIT**............ Joint Interest Test [*Navy*] (NG)
**JIT**............ Just in Time
**JITA**.......... Japanese Industrial Technology Association
**JITA**.......... Jet Interaction Test Apparatus (MCD)
**JITC**.......... Jewelry Industry Tax Committee [*Defunct*] (EA)
**JITE**.......... Journal. Institution of Telecommunication Engineers [*A publication*]
**JITEBR**..... Oto-Rhino-Laryngology [*Tokyo*] [*A publication*]
**JITF**.......... Joint Interface Test Facility [*Army*] (RDA)
**JITF**.......... Joint Interface Test Force [*Military*] (RDA)
**JITF**.......... Joint Interservice Task Force (MCD)
**JITH**.......... Journal of Indian Textile History [*A publication*]
**JITHA**........ Journal of Ichthyology [*English Translation of Voprosy Ikhtiologii*] [*A publication*]
**JITUD**........ Journal of Industrial Technology. Daegu University [*A publication*]
**JIU**............ Joint Inspection Unit [*United Nations*]
**JIUEAV**.... Junta de Investigacoes do Ultramar. Estudos, Ensaios, e Documentos [*A publication*]
**JIVPAZ**..... Journal of Invertebrate Pathology [*A publication*]
**JIW**............ J. Inglis Wright [*Advertising agency*] [*New Zealand*]
**JIW**............ Jiwani [*Pakistan*] [*Airport symbol*] (OAG)
**J Iwate Daigaku Nogaku** ... Journal. Iwate Daigaku Nogaku-Bu [*A publication*]
**J Iwate Med Assoc** ... Journal. Iwate Medical Association [*A publication*]
**JIWE**.......... Journal of Indian Writing in English [*A publication*]
**J I Wood Sc** ... Journal. Institute of Wood Science [*A publication*]
**JIWSA**....... Journal. Institute of Wood Science [*A publication*]
**JIX**............ [*Sir William*] Joynson-Hicks [*British Home Secretary whose actions caused journalists to use his name as a synonym for "prudish interference"*]
**JIZAAA**..... Journal. Anthropological Society of Nippon [*A publication*]
**JJ**.............. Aviogenex [*Yugoslavia*] [*ICAO designator*] (FAAC)
**J & J**.......... January and July [*Denotes semiannual payments of interest or dividends in these months*] [*Business term*]
**JJ**.............. Jaw Jerk [*Medicine*]
**JJ**.............. Jennifer Jo [*In TV series "The Governor and JJ"*]
**JJ**.............. Jews for Jews (EA)
**JJ**.............. Journal of Jazz Studies [*A publication*]
**JJ**.............. Judges [*Old Testament book*]
**JJ**.............. Junior Judge [*Legal term*] (DLA)
**JJ**.............. Justices
**JJA**............ Jack and Jill of America (EA)
**JJA**............ Judges of Appeal [*Legal term*]
**JJA**............ Justices of Appeal [*Legal term*] (DLA)
**JJAF**.......... Jack and Jill of America Foundation (EA)
**J Jamaica Bauxite Inst** ... Journal. Jamaica Bauxite Institute [*A publication*]
**J Japanese Trade and Industry** ... Journal of Japanese Trade and Industry [*A publication*]
**J Japan Hydraul & Pneum Soc** ... Journal. Japan Hydraulic and Pneumatic Society [*A publication*]
**J Japan Soc Lubr Engrs** ... Journal. Japan Society of Lubrication Engineers [*A publication*]
**J Japan Soc Lubr Enrs Int Edn** ... Journal. Japan Society of Lubrication Engineers. International Edition [*A publication*]
**J Japan Soc Precis Engng** ... Journal. Japan Society of Precision Engineering [*A publication*]
**J Japan Soc Vet Sc** ... Journal. Japanese Society of Veterinary Science [*A publication*]
**J Japan Statist Soc** ... Journal. Japan Statistical Society [*A publication*]
**J Japan Wood Res Soc** ... Journal. Japan Wood Research Society [*A publication*]
**J Jap Ass Mineral Petrol Econ Geol** ... Journal. Japanese Association of Mineralogists, Petrologists, and Economic Geologists [*A publication*]
**J Jap Assoc Autom Control Eng** ... Journal. Japan Association of Automatic Control Engineers [*A publication*]
**J Jap Assoc Infect Dis** ... Journal. Japanese Association for Infectious Diseases [*A publication*]
**J Jap Assoc Philos Sci** ... Journal. Japan Association for Philosophy of Science [*A publication*]
**J Jap Biochem Soc** ... Journal. Japanese Biochemical Society [*A publication*]
**J Jap Bot**.... Journal of Japanese Botany [*A publication*]

**J Jap Chem** ... Journal of Japanese Chemistry [*A publication*]
**J Jap For Soc** ... Journal. Japanese Forestry Society [*A publication*]
**J Jap Inst Light Metals** ... Journal. Japan Institute of Light Metals [*A publication*]
**J Jap Inst Met** ... Journal. Japan Institute of Light Metals [*A publication*]
**J Jap S Lub** ... Journal. Japan Society of Lubrication Engineers [*A publication*]
**J Jap Soc Air Pol** ... Journal. Japan Society of Air Pollution [*A publication*]
**J Jap Soc Civ Eng** ... Journal. Japan Society of Civil Engineers [*A publication*]
**J Jap Soc Fd Nutr** ... Journal. Japanese Society of Food and Nutrition [*A publication*]
**J Jap Soc Food Nutr** ... Journal. Japanese Society of Food and Nutrition [*A publication*]
**J Jap Soc Grassland Sci** ... Journal. Japanese Society of Grassland Science [*A publication*]
**J Jap Soc Grassld Sci** ... Journal. Japanese Society of Grassland Science [*A publication*]
**J Jap Soc Mech Eng** ... Journal. Japan Society of Mechanical Engineers [*A publication*]
**J Jap Soc Powder Met** ... Journal. Japan Society of Powder and Powder Metallurgy [*A publication*]
**J Jap Soc Precis Eng** ... Journal. Japan Society of Precision Engineering [*A publication*]
**J Jap Soc Technol Plast** ... Journal. Japan Society for Technology of Plasticity [*A publication*]
**J Jap Turfgrass Res Assoc** ... Journal. Japan Turfgrass Research Association [*A publication*]
**J Jap Vet Med Ass** ... Journal. Japan Veterinary Medical Association
**J Jap Wood Res Soc** ... Journal. Japan Wood Research Society [*A publication*]
**J Ja Stud** .... Journal of Japanese Studies [*A publication*]
**J Jazz Stud** ... Journal of Jazz Studies [*A publication*]
**J Jazz Studies** ... Journal of Jazz Studies [*A publication*]
**JJC** ............ Jackson Junior College [*Florida; Michigan*]
**JJC** ............ Jiffy Junction Connector
**JJC** ............ Joliet Junior College [*Illinois*]
**JJCL** .......... Jadavpur Journal of Comparative Literature [*A publication*]
**JJCRA** ......... Japanese Journal of Clinical Radiology [*A publication*]
**JJCS** .......... Journal of Jewish Communal Service [*A publication*]
**JJDP** .......... Juvenile Justice and Delinquency Prevention
**JJE** ............ Japanese Journal of Ethnology [*A publication*]
**JJeCoS** ...... Journal of Jewish Communal Service [*A publication*]
**J Jew Commun Serv** ... Journal of Jewish Communal Service [*A publication*]
**J Jewish Communal Service** ... Journal of Jewish Communal Service [*A publication*]
**J Jewish St** ... Journal of Jewish Studies [*A publication*]
**JJewLorePh** ... Journal of Jewish Lore and Philosophy [*New York*] [*A publication*]
**JJewS** ........ Journal of Jewish Studies [*A publication*]
**JJ FAD** ...... Just Jammin' Fresh and Def [*Rap recording group*]
**JJFC** .......... Jana Jae Fan Club (EA)
**JJFC** .......... Jim and Jesse Fan Club (EA)
**JJFC** .......... Joan Jett Fan Club (EA)
**JJFC** .......... Johnny and Jack Fan Club (EA)
**JJFED** ....... JFE. Journal du Four Electrique and des Industries Electrochimiques [*A publication*]
**JJGL** .......... Jahrbuch fuer Juedische Geschichte und Literatur [*Berlin*] [*A publication*]
**JJI** ............ Juanjui [*Peru*] [*Airport symbol*] (OAG)
**JJIND** ....... JNCI. Journal of the National Cancer Institute [*A publication*]
**J Jinsen Med Sci** ... Journal of Jinsen Medical Sciences [*A publication*]
**JJITC** ........ Jayco Jafari International Travel Club (EA)
**J Jiwaji Univ** ... Journal. Jiwaji University [*A publication*]
**J JJ Group Hosp Grant Med Coll** ... Journal. JJ Group of Hospitals and Grant Medical College [*A publication*]
**JJK** ............ Josai Jinbun Kenkyu [*Studies in the Humanities*] [*A publication*]
**JJLG** .......... Jahrbuch. Juedisch-Literarische Gesellschaft [*Frankfurt Am Main*] [*A publication*]
**JJM** ............ John Judkyn Memorial (EA)
**J J Mar** ...... [*J. J.*] Marshall's Kentucky Reports [*24-30 Kentucky*] [*A publication*] (DLA)
**J J Marsh** .. [*J. J.*] Marshall's Kentucky Supreme Court Reports [*1829-32*] [*A publication*] (DLA)
**JJ Marsh (KY)** ... Marshall's Reports [*Kentucky*] [*A publication*] (DLA)
**JJMAS** ...... Jack Jones Music Appreciation Society (EAIO)
**JJN** ............ Jinjiang [*China*] [*Airport symbol*] (OAG)
**JJO** ............ Mountain City, TN [*Location identifier*] [*FAA*] (FAAL)
**JJOGA** ...... Journal. Japanese Obstetrical and Gynecological Society [*A publication*]
**J Johannesburg Hist Found** ... Journal. Johannesburg Historical Foundation [*A publication*]
**J Joint Panel Nucl Mar Propul** ... Journal. Joint Panel on Nuclear Marine Propulsion [*A publication*]
**JJOMD** ..... JOM. Journal of Occupational Medicine [*A publication*]
**JJOPA7** ..... Japanese Journal of Ophthalmology [*A publication*]
**JJP** ............ Jatiya Janata Party [*National People's Party*] [*Bangladesh*] [*Political party*] (PPW)
**JJP** ............ Journal of Juristic Papyrology [*A publication*]
**JJPAA** ....... Japanese Journal of Pharmacology [*A publication*]
**JJPAAZ** .... Japanese Journal of Pharmacology [*A publication*]
**JJPES** ........ Journal. Jewish Palestine Exploration Society [*Jerusalem*] [*A publication*]
**JJPG** .......... Jahrbuch. Jean-Paul-Gesellschaft [*A publication*]
**JJPHA** ...... Japanese Journal of Physiology [*A publication*]
**JJPHAM** .. Japanese Journal of Physiology [*A publication*]
**JJPHDP** .... Japanese Journal of Phycology [*A publication*]
**J Jpn Accident Med Assoc** ... Journal. Japan Accident Medical Association [*A publication*]
**J Jpn Anodizing Assoc** ... Journal. Japanese Anodizing Association [*A publication*]
**J Jpn Assoc Automat Control Eng** ... Journal. Japan Association of Automatic Control Engineers [*A publication*]
**J Jpn Assoc Infect Dis** ... Journal. Japanese Association for Infectious Diseases [*A publication*]
**J Jpn Assoc Mineral Pet Econ Geol** ... Journal. Japanese Association of Mineralogists, Petrologists, and Economic Geologists [*A publication*]
**J Jpn Assoc Periodontol** ... Journal. Japanese Association of Periodontology [*A publication*]
**J Jpn Assoc Pet Technol** ... Journal. Japanese Association of Petroleum Technologists [*A publication*]
**J Jpn Assoc Phys Med Balneol Climatol** ... Journal. Japanese Association of Physical Medicine, Balneology, and Climatology [*A publication*]
**J Jpn Assoc Thorac Surg** ... Journal. Japanese Association for Thoracic Surgery [*A publication*]
**J Jpn Biochem Soc** ... Journal. Japanese Biochemical Society [*A publication*]
**J Jpn Boiler Assoc** ... Journal. Japan Boiler Association [*A publication*]
**J Jpn Bot** ... Journal of Japanese Botany [*A publication*]
**J Jpn Broncho-Esophagol Soc** ... Journal. Japan Broncho-Esophagological Society [*A publication*]
**J Jpn Chem** ... Journal of Japanese Chemistry [*A publication*]
**J Jpn Chem Suppl** ... Journal of Japanese Chemistry. Supplement [*A publication*]
**J Jpn Coll Angiol** ... Journal. Japanese College of Angiology [*A publication*]
**J Jpn Contact Lens Soc** ... Journal. Japan Contact Lens Society [*A publication*]
**J Jpn Crystallogr Soc** ... Journal. Japanese Crystallographical Society [*A publication*]
**J Jpn Dent Anesth Soc** ... Journal. Japanese Dental Anesthesia Society [*A publication*]
**J Jpn Dermatol Assoc** ... Journal. Japanese Dermatological Association [*A publication*]
**J Jpn Diabetes Soc** ... Journal. Japan Diabetes Society [*A publication*]
**J Jpn Diabetic Soc** ... Journal. Japan Diabetic Society [*A publication*]
**J Jpn Electr Assoc** ... Journal. Japan Electric Association [*A publication*]
**J Jpn For Soc** ... Journal. Japanese Forestry Society [*A publication*]
**J Jpn Gas Assoc** ... Journal. Japan Gas Association [*A publication*]
**J Jpn Geotherm Energy Assoc** ... Journal. Japan Geothermal Energy Association [*A publication*]
**J Jpn Health Phys Soc** ... Journal. Japan Health Physics Society [*A publication*]
**J Jpn Hosp Assoc** ... Journal. Japan Hospital Association [*A publication*]
**J Jpn Inst Landscape Archit** ... Journal. Japanese Institute of Landscape Architects [*A publication*]
**J Jpn Inst Light Met** ... Journal. Japan Institute of Light Metals [*A publication*]
**J Jpn Inst Met** ... Journal. Japan Institute of Metals [*A publication*]
**J Jpn Inst Met (Sendai)** ... Journal. Japan Institute of Metals (Sendai) [*A publication*]
**J Jpn Inst Navig** ... Journal. Japan Institute of Navigation [*A publication*]
**J Jpn Med Assoc** ... Journal. Japan Medical Association [*A publication*]
**J Jpn Med Coll** ... Journal. Japan Medical College [*A publication*]
**J Jpn Obstet Gynecol Soc (Engl Ed)** ... Journal. Japanese Obstetrical and Gynecological Society (English Edition) [*A publication*]
**J Jpn Obstet Gynecol Soc (Jpn Ed)** ... Journal. Japanese Obstetrical and Gynecological Society (Japanese Edition) [*A publication*]
**J Jpn Oil Chem Soc** ... Journal. Japan Oil Chemists Society [*A publication*]
**J Jpn Orthop Assoc** ... Journal. Japanese Orthopaedic Association [*A publication*]
**J Jpn Pet Inst** ... Journal. Japan Petroleum Institute [*A publication*]
**J Jpn Pharm Assoc** ... Journal. Japan Pharmaceutical Association [*A publication*]
**J Jpn Psychosom Soc** ... Journal. Japanese Psychosomatic Society [*A publication*]
**J Jpn Res Assoc Text End-Uses** ... Journal. Japan Research Association for Textile End-Uses [*A publication*]
**J Jpn Soc Aeronaut and Space Sci** ... Journal. Japan Society for Aeronautical and Space Sciences [*A publication*]
**J Jpn Soc Air Pollut** ... Journal. Japan Society of Air Pollution [*A publication*]
**J Jpn Soc Biomater** ... Journal. Japanese Society for Biomaterials [*A publication*]
**J Jpn Soc Blood Transfus** ... Journal. Japan Society of Blood Transfusion [*A publication*]
**J Jpn Soc Cancer Ther** ... Journal. Japan Society for Cancer Therapy [*A publication*]
**J Jpn Soc Colo-Proctol** ... Journal. Japan Society of Colo-Proctology [*A publication*]
**J Jpn Soc Compos Mater** ... Journal. Japan Society of Composite Materials [*A publication*]

**J Jpn Soc Dent Appar Mater** ... Journal. Japan Society for Dental Apparatus and Materials [*A publication*]
**J Jpn Soc Food Nutr** ... Journal. Japanese Society of Food and Nutrition [*A publication*]
**J Jpn Soc Food Sci Technol** ... Journal. Japan Society for Food Science and Technology [*A publication*]
**J Jpn Soc Grassl Sci** ... Journal. Japanese Society of Grassland Science [*A publication*]
**J Jpn Soc Herb Crops Grassl Farming** ... Journal. Japanese Society of Herbage Crops and Grassland Farming [*A publication*]
**J Jpn Soc Hortic Sci** ... Journal. Japanese Society for Horticultural Science [*A publication*]
**J Jpn Soc Lubr Eng** ... Journal. Japan Society of Lubrication Engineers [*A publication*]
**J Jpn Soc Powder Metall** ... Journal. Japan Society of Powder and Powder Metallurgy [*A publication*]
**J Jpn Soc Powder Powder Metall** ... Journal. Japan Society of Powder and Powder Metallurgy [*A publication*]
**J Jpn Soc Precis Eng** ... Journal. Japan Society of Precision Engineering [*A publication*]
**J Jpn Soc Reticuloendothel Syst** ... Journal. Japan Society of the Reticuloendothelial System [*A publication*]
**J Jpn Soc Simulation Technol** ... Journal. Japan Society for Simulation Technology [*A publication*]
**J Jpn Soc Strength Fract Mater** ... Journal. Japanese Society for Strength and Fracture of Materials [*A publication*]
**J Jpn Soc Technol Plast** ... Journal. Japan Society for Technology of Plasticity [*A publication*]
**J Jpn Stud** ... Journal of Japanese Studies [*A publication*]
**J Jpn Surg Soc** ... Journal. Japanese Surgical Society [*A publication*]
**J Jpn Tech Assoc Pulp Pap Ind** ... Journal. Japanese Technical Association of the Pulp and Paper Industry [*A publication*]
**J Jpn Turfgrass Res Assoc** ... Journal. Japan Turfgrass Research Association [*A publication*]
**J Jpn Vet Med Assoc** ... Journal. Japan Veterinary Medical Association [*A publication*]
**J Jpn Water Works Assoc** ... Journal. Japan Water Works Association [*A publication*]
**J Jpn Weld Soc** ... Journal. Japan Welding Society [*A publication*]
**J Jpn Wood Res Soc** ... Journal. Japan Wood Research Society [*A publication*]
**JJQ**............ James Joyce Quarterly [*A publication*]
**JJR**............ James Joyce Review [*A publication*]
**J Jr Inst Eng (London)** ... Journal. Junior Institution of Engineers (London) [*A publication*]
**JJS**............ James Joyce Society (EA)
**JJS**............ Jewish Journal of Sociology [*A publication*]
**JJS**............ Journal of Japanese Studies [*A publication*]
**JJS**............ Journal of Jewish Studies [*A publication*]
**JJS**............ Jumping-Jacks Shoes, Inc. [*AMEX symbol*] (SPSG)
**JJSAAG**.... Japanese Journal of Studies on Alcohol [*A publication*]
**JJSC**.......... Jefferson Smurfit Corporation [*NASDAQ symbol*] (NQ)
**JJSC**.......... Justices of the Supreme Court [*Legal term*] (DLA)
**JJSF**.......... J & J Snack Foods Corp. [*Pennsauken, NJ*] [*NASDAQ symbol*] (NQ)
**JJSGA**....... Japanese Journal of Surgery [*A publication*]
**JJSGAY**.... Japanese Journal of Surgery [*A publication*]
**J JSLE (Jpn Soc Lubr Eng) Int Ed** ... Journal. JSLE (Japan Society of Lubrication Engineers). International Edition [*A publication*]
**JJSO**.......... Jewish Journal of Sociology [*A publication*]
**J-J S-S**....... Jean-Jacques Servan-Schreiber [*French publisher*]
**JJSt**........... Journal of Jewish Studies [*London*] [*A publication*]
**JJSWC**...... Jiffy Junction Single Wire Connector
**JJT**............ Jumbo Jet Transport
**JJTCAR**.... Japanese Journal of Tuberculosis and Chest Diseases [*A publication*]
**J Jt Panel Nucl Mar Propul** ... Journal. Joint Panel on Nuclear Marine Propulsion [*England*] [*A publication*]
**J Jur**.......... Journal of Jurisprudence [*A publication*] (DLA)
**J Jur Pap** ... Journal of Juristic Papyrology [*A publication*]
**J Jur Papyrol** ... Journal of Juristic Papyrology [*A publication*] (DLA)
**J Juvenile Res** ... Journal of Juvenile Research [*A publication*]
**J Juv L**....... Journal of Juvenile Law [*A publication*]
**J Juzen Med Soc** ... Journal. Juzen Medical Society [*A publication*]
**JJV**............ Jahrbuch fuer Juedische Volkskunde [*A publication*]
**JJVRA**....... Japanese Journal of Veterinary Research [*A publication*]
**JJVRAE**.... Japanese Journal of Veterinary Research [*A publication*]
**JJWC**......... Jiffy Junction Wire Connector
**JJWFC**....... Jerry Jeff Walker Fan Club (EA)
**JJWUA**..... Journal. Jiwaji University [*A publication*]
**JJZOAP**.... Japanese Journal of Zoology [*A publication*]
**J & K**.......... All India Reporter, Jammu and Kashmir [*A publication*] (DLA)
**JK**.............. Central Caribbean Air Ltd. [*Antigua*] [*ICAO designator*] (FAAC)
**JK**.............. Flip-Flop Circuit [*Data processing*]
**JK**.............. Jack (MSA)
**JK**.............. Jishu Kanri [*Voluntary Management*] [*Japanese method for increasing productivity of industrial workers by involving them in planning*]
**J/K**............ Joule per Kelvin [*Physics*]
**JK**.............. Junk [*Ship's rigging*] (ROG)
**JK**.............. Trabajos Aereos y Enlaces SA [*Spain*] [*ICAO designator*] (ICDA)
**JK & A**....... John Krucek & Associates [*Telecommunications service*] (TSSD)
**JKAF**......... Jahrbuch fuer Kleinasiatische Forschung. Internationale Orientalistische Zeitschrift [*A publication*]
**J Kagawa Nutr Coll** ... Journal. Kagawa Nutrition College [*A publication*]
**JKAHS**...... Journal. Kerry Archaeological and Historical Society [*A publication*]
**J Kanagawa Prefect J Coll Nutr** ... Journal. Kanagawa Prefectural Junior College of Nutrition [*A publication*]
**J Kan BA** ... Journal. Kansas Bar Association [*A publication*]
**J Kan B Ass'n** ... Journal. Kansas Bar Association [*A publication*] (DLA)
**J Kan Med Soc** ... Journal. Kansas Medical Society [*A publication*]
**J Kansai Med Sch** ... Journal. Kansai Medical School [*Japan*] [*A publication*]
**J Kansai Med Univ** ... Journal. Kansai Medical University [*A publication*]
**J Kansas Geol Surv** ... Journal. Kansas Geological Survey [*A publication*]
**J Kansas Med Soc** ... Journal. Kansas Medical Society [*A publication*]
**J Kans Dent Assoc** ... Journal. Kansas Dental Association [*A publication*]
**J Kans Entomol Soc** ... Journal. Kansas Entomological Society [*A publication*]
**J Kans Ent Soc** ... Journal. Kansas Entomological Society [*A publication*]
**J Kans Med Soc** ... Journal. Kansas Medical Society [*A publication*]
**J Kans State Dent Assoc** ... Journal. Kansas State Dental Association [*A publication*]
**J Kanto-Tosan Agr Exp Sta** ... Journal. Kanto-Tosan Agricultural Experiment Station [*A publication*]
**J Karnatak U Hum** ... Journal. Karnatak University. Humanities [*A publication*]
**J Karnatak Univ** ... Journal. Karnatak University [*A publication*]
**J Karnatak Univ Sci** ... Journal. Karnatak University. Science [*A publication*]
**J Karnatak U Soc Sci** ... Journal. Karnatak University. Social Sciences [*A publication*]
**J Karyopathol Espec Tumor Tumorvirus** ... Journal of Karyopathology; Especially Tumor and Tumorvirus [*A publication*]
**J Karyopathol Tumor Tumorvirus** ... Journal of Karyopathology; Especially Tumor and Tumorvirus [*A publication*]
**JKAS**......... Jack Knight Airmail Society (EA)
**JKAUA**...... Journal. Karnatak University [*A publication*]
**JKAWA**..... Jaarboek. Koninklijke Academie van Wetenschappen (Amsterdam) [*A publication*]
**JKB**............ Justice of the King's Bench (ROG)
**JKBIR**........ Justice of the King's Bench, Ireland (ROG)
**JKC**............ Jidosha Kiki Company Ltd.
**JKC**............ Shreveport, LA [*Location identifier*] [*FAA*] (FAAL)
**JKE**............ Journal of Post Keynesian Economics [*A publication*]
**J Keio Med Soc** ... Journal. Keio Medical Society [*Japan*] [*A publication*]
**J Kel**........... [*Sir John*] Kelyng's English Crown Cases [*A publication*] (DLA)
**J Kelyng**..... [*Sir John*] Kelyng's English Crown Cases [*A publication*] (DLA)
**J Kelyng (Eng)** ... [*Sir John*] Kelyng's English Crown Cases [*A publication*] (DLA)
**J Kerala Acad Biol** ... Journal. Kerala Academy of Biology [*A publication*]
**J Kerry Archaeol Hist Soc** ... Journal. Kerry Archaeological and Historical Society [*A publication*]
**JKF**............ Jahrbuch fuer Kleinasiatische Forschung [*A publication*]
**JKFCFC**.... Jimmy Kish "The Flying Cowboy" Fan Club (EA)
**JKFSD**....... Journal. Korean Forestry Society [*A publication*]
**JKG**............ Jahrbuch. Kleist-Gesellschaft [*A publication*]
**JKG**............ Jidische Kultur Gezelschaft [*Argentina*] [*A publication*]
**JKG**............ Jonkoping [*Sweden*] [*Airport symbol*] (OAG)
**J/kg**............ Joule per Kilogram [*Physics*]
**JKG**............ Juedische Kulturgemeinschaft [*A publication*]
**J/(KG K)**.... Joules per Kilogram Kelvin
**JKGKA**...... Joho Kagaku Gijutsu Kenkyu Shukai Happyo Ronbunshu [*A publication*]
**JKGS**......... Jahrbuecher fuer Kultur und Geschichte der Slaven [*A publication*]
**JKGV**......... Jahrbuch. Koelnischer Geschichtsverein [*A publication*]
**JKH**............ Chios [*Greece*] [*Airport symbol*] (OAG)
**JKHHA**..... Journal. Korea Institute of Electronics Engineers [*A publication*]
**JKHY**......... Henry [*Jack*] & Associates, Inc. [*Monett, MO*] [*NASDAQ symbol*] (NQ)
**JKIEA**....... Journal. Korean Institute of Electrical Engineers [*Republic of Korea*] [*A publication*]
**JKKB**......... Jeunesse du Kwilu-Kwango-Bateke [*Kwilu-Kwango-Bateke Youth*]
**JKKNA**...... Jaarboek van Kankeronderzoek en Kankerbestrijding in Nederland [*A publication*]
**JKL**............ Jackson, KY [*Location identifier*] [*FAA*] (FAAL)
**JKMAD**..... Journal. Korea Military Academy [*A publication*]
**JKMG**........ Jahrbuch. Karl-May-Gesellschaft [*A publication*]
**JKMS**......... Jack Knight Air Mail Society (EA)
**JKMSA**..... Journal. Kansas Medical Society [*A publication*]
**JKMSD**..... Journal. Korean Mathematical Society [*A publication*]
**JKNA**......... Jaarboek. Koninklijke Nederlandsche Academie [*A publication*]
**JKNC**......... Jammu and Kashmir National Conference [*India*] [*Political party*] (PPW)

**JKNCD**...... Journal. Kongju National Teacher's College [*A publication*]
**J Kongju Natl Teach Coll** ... Journal. Kongju National Teacher's College [*Republic of Korea*] [*A publication*]
**J Korea Electr Assoc** ... Journal. Korea Electric Association [*Republic of Korea*] [*A publication*]
**J Korea Inf Sci Soc** ... Journal. Korea Information Science Society [*A publication*]
**J Korea Inst Electron Eng** ... Journal. Korea Institute of Electronics Engineers [*A publication*]
**J Korea Merch Mar Coll Nat Sci Ser** ... Journal. Korea Merchant Marine College. Natural Sciences Series [*Republic of Korea*] [*A publication*]
**J Korea Mil Acad** ... Journal. Korea Military Academy [*Republic of Korea*] [*A publication*]
**J Korean Acad Maxillofac Radiol** ... Journal. Korean Academy of Maxillofacial Radiology [*Republic of Korea*] [*A publication*]
**J Korean Agric Chem Soc** ... Journal. Korean Agricultural Chemical Society [*Republic of Korea*] [*A publication*]
**J Korean Cancer Res Assoc** ... Journal. Korean Cancer Research Association [*A publication*]
**J Korean Ceram Soc** ... Journal. Korean Ceramic Society [*Republic of Korea*] [*A publication*]
**J Korean Chem Soc** ... Journal. Korean Chemical Society [*A publication*]
**J Korean Dent Assoc** ... Journal. Korean Dental Association [*Republic of Korea*] [*A publication*]
**J Korean For Soc** ... Journal. Korean Forestry Society [*Republic of Korea*] [*A publication*]
**J Korean Inst Chem Eng** ... Journal. Korean Institute of Chemical Engineers [*Republic of Korea*] [*A publication*]
**J Korean Inst Electr Eng** ... Journal. Korean Institute of Electrical Engineers [*Republic of Korea*] [*A publication*]
**J Korean Inst Electron Eng** ... Journal. Korean Institute of Electronics Engineers [*A publication*]
**J Korean Inst Met** ... Journal. Korean Institute of Metals [*Republic of Korea*] [*A publication*]
**J Korean Inst Min** ... Journal. Korean Institute of Mining [*Republic of Korea*] [*A publication*]
**J Korean Inst Miner Mining Eng** ... Journal. Korean Institute of Mineral and Mining Engineers [*Republic of Korea*] [*A publication*]
**J Korean Inst Min Geol** ... Journal. Korean Institute of Mining Geology [*Republic of Korea*] [*A publication*]
**J Korean Math Soc** ... Journal. Korean Mathematical Society [*A publication*]
**J Korean Med Assoc** ... Journal. Korean Medical Association [*Republic of Korea*] [*A publication*]
**J Korean Meteorol Soc** ... Journal. Korean Meteorological Society [*Republic of Korea*] [*A publication*]
**J Korean Nucl Soc** ... Journal. Korean Nuclear Society [*Republic of Korea*] [*A publication*]
**J Korean Ophthalmol Soc** ... Journal. Korean Ophthalmological Society [*A publication*]
**J Korean Phys Soc** ... Journal. Korean Physical Society [*A publication*]
**J Korean Radiol Soc** ... Journal. Korean Radiological Society [*Republic of Korea*] [*A publication*]
**J Korean Res Soc Dent Hypn** ... Journal. Korean Research Society for Dental Hypnosis [*A publication*]
**J Korean Res Soc Radiol Technol** ... Journal. Korean Research Society of Radiological Technology [*Republic of Korea*] [*A publication*]
**J Korean Soc Agric Mach** ... Journal. Korean Society of Agricultural Machinery [*A publication*]
**J Korean Soc Civ Eng** ... Journal. Korean Society of Civil Engineers [*Republic of Korea*] [*A publication*]
**J Korean Soc Crop Sci** ... Journal. Korean Society of Crop Science [*Republic of Korea*] [*A publication*]
**J Korean Soc Hort Sci** ... Journal. Korean Society for Horticultural Science [*A publication*]
**J Korean Soc Mech Eng** ... Journal. Korean Society of Mechanical Engineers [*Republic of Korea*] [*A publication*]
**J Korean Soc Soil Sci Fert** ... Journal. Korean Society of Soil Science and Fertilizer [*A publication*]
**J Korean Soc Text Eng Chem** ... Journal. Korean Society of Textile Engineers and Chemists [*Republic of Korea*] [*A publication*]
**J Korean Statist Soc** ... Journal. Korean Statistical Society [*A publication*]
**J Korean Surg Soc** ... Journal. Korean Surgical Society [*A publication*]
**JKORS**...... Journal. Korean Operations Research Society [*A publication*]
**J Koyasan Univ** ... Journal. Koyasan University [*A publication*]
**JKP**........... James Knox Polk [*US president, 1795-1849*]
**JKPC**.......... Junior Knights of Peter Claver (EA)
**JKPT**......... [*The*] Mills-Jennings Co. [*NASDAQ symbol*] (NQ)
**JKR**........... Janakpur [*Nepal*] [*Airport symbol*] (OAG)
**JKS**........... Jacks Creek, TN [*Location identifier*] [*FAA*] (FAAL)
**JKS**........... Jahrbuch. Kunsthistorische Sammlungen [*A publication*]
**JKSCR**....... Jackscrew [*Mechanical engineering*]
**JKSW**........ Jahrbuch. Kunsthistorische Sammlungen (Wien) [*A publication*]
**JKT**........... Jacket (KSC)
**JKT**........... Jakarta [*Indonesia*] [*Airport symbol*] (OAG)
**JKT**........... Job Knowledge Test [*Military*] (AFM)
**JKU**........... Journal. Karnatak University [*Dharwar*] [*A publication*]
**JKU**........... Kyoto University, Kyoto, Japan [*Library symbol*] [*Library of Congress*] (LCLS)
**J Kukem**..... Journal of Kukem [*A publication*]
**J Kumamoto Women's Univ** ... Journal. Kumamoto Women's University [*A publication*]
**J Kumasi Univ Sci Technol** ... Journal. Kumasi University of Science and Technology [*A publication*]
**JKUR**......... Jammu and Kashmir University Review [*A publication*]
**J Kurume Med Assoc** ... Journal. Kurume Medical Association [*A publication*]
**J Kuwait Med Assoc** ... Journal. Kuwait Medical Association [*A publication*]
**JKVA**......... Jaarboek. Koninklijke Vlaamse Academie voor Wetenschappen. Letteren en Schone Kunsten van Belgie [*A publication*]
**JKW**........... Jahrbuch fuer Kunstwissenschaft [*A publication*]
**JKW**........... Juvonen, K. W., Winnipeg, Manitoba CDA [*STAC*]
**J KY Med Assoc** ... Journal. Kentucky Medical Association [*A publication*]
**JKYND**...... Journal. Materials Science Research Institute. Dongguk University [*A publication*]
**J Kyorin Med Soc** ... Journal. Kyorin Medical Society [*A publication*]
**J Kyoto Prefect Med Univ** ... Journal. Kyoto Prefectural Medical University [*Japan*] [*A publication*]
**J Kyoto Prefect Univ Med** ... Journal. Kyoto Prefectural University of Medicine [*A publication*]
**J Kyungpook Eng** ... Journal. Kyungpook Engineering [*Republic of Korea*] [*A publication*]
**J Kyungpook Eng Kyungpook Natl Univ** ... Journal. Kyungpook Engineering. Kyungpook National University [*A publication*]
**J Kyushu Dent Soc** ... Journal. Kyushu Dental Society [*Japan*] [*A publication*]
**J Kyushu Hematol Soc** ... Journal. Kyushu Hematological Society [*A publication*]
**JL**.............. JAG Listing [*Military*]
**JL**.............. Japan Air Lines [*ICAO designator*] (OAG)
**JL**.............. Javan LASER
**JL**.............. Jazz-Lift [*Provides jazz records to persons in Iron Curtain countries*] [*Defunct*] (EA)
**JL**.............. Jefferson Lyons [*Commercial firm*] [*British*]
**Jl**.............. Joel [*Old Testament book*]
**J & L**.......... Jones and La Touche's Irish Chancery Reports [*A publication*] (DLA)
**JL**.............. Jornal de Letras [*A publication*]
**JL**.............. Joule's Law [*Physics*]
**JL**.............. Journal [*Online database field identifier*]
**jl**.............. Journal [*Record Book*] [*Bookkeeping*] [*French*]
**JL**.............. Journal (ROG)
**JL**.............. Journal. American Liszt Society [*A publication*]
**JL**.............. Journal of Linguistics [*A publication*]
**JL**.............. Juedisches Lexikon [*A publication*]
**JL**.............. July
**JL**.............. July [*A publication*]
**JL**.............. Junior Leaders Regiment [*British military*] (DMA)
**JL**.............. Jurin Law [*Electronics*]
**JL**.............. Jurisprudence de la Cour d'Appel de Liege [*A publication*] (DLA)
**JL**.............. Just Looking [*A browser*] [*Retail slang*]
**JL**.............. JustLife (EA)
**JL**.............. Lab. Jacques Logeais [*France*] [*Research code symbol*]
**JLA**........... Cooper Landing, AK [*Location identifier*] [*FAA*] (FAAL)
**JLA**........... Jack L. Ahr [*Designer's mark on US bicentennial quarter*]
**JLA**........... Jalna Resources [*Vancouver Stock Exchange symbol*]
**JLA**........... Jet Lift Aircraft
**JLA**........... Jewish Librarians Association [*Later, AJL*] (EA)
**JLA**........... Jornal de Letras e Artes [*A publication*]
**J Lab Clin Med** ... Journal of Laboratory and Clinical Medicine [*A publication*]
**J Label Com** ... Journal of Labelled Compounds [*Later, Journal of Labelled Compounds and Radiopharmaceuticals*] [*A publication*]
**J Label Compound Radiopharm** ... Journal of Labelled Compounds and Radiopharmaceuticals [*A publication*]
**J Labelled Compd** ... Journal of Labelled Compounds [*Later, Journal of Labelled Compounds and Radiopharmaceuticals*] [*A publication*]
**J Labelled Compd Radiopharm** ... Journal of Labelled Compounds and Radiopharmaceuticals [*A publication*]
**J Labor Research** ... Journal of Labor Research [*A publication*]
**J Labour Hyg Iron Steel Ind** ... Journal of Labour Hygiene in Iron and Steel Industry [*A publication*]
**JLACBF**.... Justus Liebigs Annalen der Chemie [*A publication*]
**J La Cl Med** ... Journal of Laboratory and Clinical Medicine [*A publication*]
**J LA Dent Assoc** ... Journal. Louisiana Dental Association [*A publication*]
**JLAEA**...... Journal. Language Association of Eastern Africa [*A publication*]
**Jl Aesthetics** ... Journal of Aesthetics and Art Criticism [*A publication*]
**JLAL**......... Journal of Latin American Lore [*A publication*]
**J LA Med Soc** ... Journal. Louisiana State Medical Society [*A publication*]
**J-Lancet**..... Journal-Lancet [*A publication*]
**J Land & Pub Util Econ** ... Journal of Land and Public Utility Economics [*A publication*]
**J Land & PU Econ** ... Journal of Land and Public Utility Economics [*A publication*]
**J Landwirtsch** ... Journal fuer Landwirtschaft [*A publication*]
**J Lang Teach** ... Journal for Language Teaching [*A publication*]

**Jl Appl Photogr Engin** ... Journal of Applied Photographic Engineering [*A publication*]
**J Lar Otol** .. Journal of Laryngology and Otology [*A publication*]
**J Laryng**..... Journal of Laryngology and Otology [*A publication*]
**J Laryngol Otol** ... Journal of Laryngology and Otology [*A publication*]
**J Laryngol Otol Suppl** ... Journal of Laryngology and Otology. Supplement [*A publication*]
**J Laryng Ot** ... Journal of Laryngology and Otology [*A publication*]
**JLAS**.......... Journal of Latin American Studies [*A publication*]
**JLAS**.......... Journal. Linguistic Association of the Southwest [*A publication*]
**J LA State Med Soc** ... Journal. Louisiana State Medical Society [*A publication*]
**J & La T**..... Jones and La Touche's Irish Chancery Reports [*A publication*] (DLA)
**J Lat Am L** ... Journal of Latin American Lore [*A publication*]
**J Lat Am St** ... Journal of Latin American Studies [*A publication*]
**J Lat Am Stud** ... Journal of Latin American Studies [*A publication*]
**J Latin Amer Stud** ... Journal of Latin American Studies [*A publication*]
**J Law Econ** ... Journal of Law and Economics [*A publication*]
**J Law & Econ** ... Journal of Law and Economics [*A publication*]
**J Law & Econ Dev** ... Journal of Law and Economic Development [*A publication*]
**J Law & Ed** ... Journal of Law and Education [*A publication*] (DLA)
**J Law & Educ** ... Journal of Law and Education [*A publication*]
**J Law Reform** ... Journal of Law Reform [*A publication*] (DLA)
**J Law Soc**... Journal of Law and Society [*A publication*]
**J Law Soc Sc** ... Journal. Law Society of Scotland [*A publication*]
**J Law Soc Scot** ... Journal. Law Society of Scotland [*A publication*]
**J Law Soc'y Scotland** ... Law Society of Scotland. Journal [*A publication*] (DLA)
**JLB**............ Jewish Labor Bund (EA)
**JLB**............ Journal of Labor Economics [*A publication*]
**JLB**............ Juedisches Litteratur-Blatt [*A publication*]
**Jl Belge Radiol** ... Journal Belge de Radiologie [*A publication*]
**J Lbr Res** ... Journal of Labor Research [*A publication*]
**JLB Smith Inst Ichthyol Spec Publ** ... J. L. B. Smith Institute of Ichthyology. Special Publication [*A publication*]
**JLBTS**....... Japanese Land-Based Test Site (MCD)
**Jl Bus Fin**... Journal of Business Finance and Accounting [*A publication*]
**Jl Bus Strat** ... Journal of Business Strategy [*A publication*]
**JLC**............ Houston [*Texas*] Allen Center [*Airport symbol*] (OAG)
**JLC**............ Japanese Linear Collider [*High energy physics*]
**JLC**............ Jewish Labor Committee (EA)
**JLC**............ Joint Logistics Commanders [*Military*]
**JLC**............ Joint Logistics Committee [*Military*]
**JLC**............ Junction Latching Circulator
**JLCAT**....... Joint Logistics Commanders' Action Team [*Military*]
**JLCD**......... Joint Liaison Committee on Documents (DS)
**JLC & E**..... Jonesboro, Lake City & Eastern Railroad
**J L and Com** ... Journal of Law and Commerce [*A publication*]
**Jl Commun** ... Journal of Communication [*A publication*]
**JL & Com Soc** ... Journal. Law and Commerce Society [*Hong Kong*] [*A publication*] (DLA)
**Jl Con Mkt** ... Journal of Consumer Marketing [*A publication*]
**Jl Consmr R** ... Journal of Consumer Research [*A publication*]
**Jl Cont B**.... Journal of Contemporary Business [*A publication*]
**JLCPA**....... Journal of Counseling Psychology [*A publication*]
**J/L/Cpl**...... Junior Lance-Corporal [*British military*] (DMA)
**JLCRD**...... Journal of Labelled Compounds and Radiopharmaceuticals [*A publication*]
**JLCSA4**..... Journal. American Leather Chemists' Association. Supplement [*A publication*]
**JLD**............ Journal of Learning Disabilities [*A publication*]
**JLDIA** ....... Journal of Learning Disabilities [*A publication*]
**J/Ldr**......... Junior Leader [*British military*] (DMA)
**JLDS** ......... Journal. Lancashire Dialect Society [*A publication*]
**JLE**............ Jet Lift Engine
**JLE**............ Journal of Law and Economics [*A publication*]
**J Lear Disabil** ... Journal of Learning Disabilities [*A publication*]
**J Learn Di** ... Journal of Learning Disabilities [*A publication*]
**J Learn Dis** ... Journal of Learning Disabilities [*A publication*]
**J Learn Disab** ... Journal of Learning Disabilities [*A publication*]
**J Learn Disabil** ... Journal of Learning Disabilities [*A publication*]
**Jl E Asiat Stud** ... Journal of East Asiatic Studies [*A publication*]
**J L and Ec** ... Journal of Law and Economics [*A publication*]
**J L & Econ** ... Journal of Law and Economics [*A publication*]
**JL & Econ Dev** ... Journal of Law and Economic Development [*A publication*]
**J L & Econ Develop** ... Journal of Law and Economic Development [*A publication*]
**J L and Ed** ... Journal of Law and Education [*A publication*]
**J L & Educ** ... Journal of Law and Education [*A publication*]
**J Leeds Univ Text Stud Assoc** ... Journal. Leeds University Textile Students' Association [*A publication*]
**J Leeds Univ Union Chem Soc** ... Journal. Leeds University Union Chemical Society [*A publication*]
**J Legal Ed** ... Journal of Legal Education [*A publication*]
**J Legal Educ** ... Journal of Legal Education [*A publication*]
**J Legal Med** ... Journal of Legal Medicine [*A publication*]
**J Legal Prof** ... Journal of the Legal Profession [*A publication*]
**J Legal Stud** ... Journal of Legal Studies [*A publication*]
**J Leg Ed**..... Journal of Legal Education [*A publication*]
**J Leg Educ** ... Journal of Legal Education [*A publication*]
**J Leg Hist**.. Journal of Legal History [*A publication*]
**J Legis** ....... Journal of Legislation [*United States*] [*A publication*]
**J Legislation** ... Journal of Legislation [*A publication*]
**J Leg Med** ... Journal of Legal Medicine [*A publication*]
**J Leg Plur**.. Journal of Legal Pluralism and Unofficial Law [*A publication*]
**J Leg Stud** ... Journal of Legal Studies [*A publication*]
**J Leis Res**.. Journal of Leisure Research [*A publication*]
**J Leisur**...... Journal of Leisurability [*A publication*]
**J Leisurability** ... Journal of Leisurability [*A publication*]
**J Leisure**.... Journal of Leisure Research [*A publication*]
**J Leisure Res** ... Journal of Leisure Research [*A publication*]
**JLEMA**..... Journal of Engineering Mathematics [*A publication*]
**J Lepid Soc** ... Journal. Lepidopterists' Society [*A publication*]
**JLER** ......... Journal of Leisure Research [*A publication*]
**J Less-C Met** ... Journal of the Less-Common Metals [*A publication*]
**J Less Common Met** ... Journal of the Less-Common Metals [*A publication*]
**J Leukocyte Biol** ... Journal of Leukocyte Biology [*A publication*]
**JLF**............ Joint Landing Force
**JLFAA**....... Journal de la France Agricole [*A publication*]
**JLFB**.......... Joint Landing Force Board
**JLFC**.......... Joan Lunden Fan Club (EA)
**JLFC**.......... Johnny Lee Fan Club (EA)
**JLFC**.......... Johnny Len Fan Club (EA)
**JLG**............ Jahrbuch. Juedisch-Literarische Gesellschaft [*Frankfurt Am Main*] [*A publication*]
**JLG**............ Jewish Lawyers Guild (EA)
**JLGI**.......... JLG Industries, Inc. [*NASDAQ symbol*] (NQ)
**JLH** ........... Arlington Heights, IL [*Location identifier*] [*FAA*] (FAAL)
**JLH** ........... Jahrbuch fuer Liturgik und Hymnologie [*A publication*]
**JLH** ........... Journal of Library History [*Later, Journal of Library History, Philosophy, and Comparative Librarianship*] [*A publication*]
**JLH** ........... Journal of Library History, Philosophy, and Comparative Librarianship [*A publication*]
**JLHPA**...... Jan Liao Hsueh Pao [*A publication*]
**JLHYAD**... Journal of Hydrology [*Dunedin*] [*A publication*]
**JLi**............. Jewish Life [*A publication*]
**JLI** ............ Julian, CA [*Location identifier*] [*FAA*] (FAAL)
**J Lib Admin** ... Journal of Library Administration [*A publication*]
**J Lib Arts Sci Kitasato Univ** ... Journal of Liberal Arts and Sciences. Kitasato University [*A publication*]
**J Lib Arts Sci Sapporo Med Coll** ... Journal of Liberal Arts and Sciences. Sapporo Medical College [*A publication*]
**J Lib Automation** ... Journal of Library Automation [*A publication*]
**J Liber Stud** ... Journal of Libertarian Studies [*A publication*]
**J Lib Hist**... Journal of Library History [*Later, Journal of Library History, Philosophy, and Comparative Librarianship*] [*A publication*]
**J Lib Hist**... Journal of Library History, Philosophy, and Comparative Librarianship [*A publication*]
**J Lib and Info Science** ... Journal of Library and Information Science [*A publication*]
**J Lib Inf Sci** ... Journal of Library and Information Science [*A publication*]
**J Libnship** ... Journal of Librarianship [*A publication*]
**J Libr** ......... Journal of Librarianship [*A publication*]
**J Librarianship** ... Journal of Librarianship [*A publication*]
**J Libr Aut**.. Journal of Library Automation [*A publication*]
**J Libr Auto** ... Journal of Library Automation [*A publication*]
**J Libr Autom** ... Journal of Library Automation [*A publication*]
**J Libr Automn** ... Journal of Library Automation [*A publication*]
**J Libr Hist** ... Journal of Library History [*Later, Journal of Library History, Philosophy, and Comparative Librarianship*] [*A publication*]
**J Libr Hist** ... Journal of Library History, Philosophy, and Comparative Librarianship [*A publication*]
**J Libr Inf Sci** ... Journal of Library and Information Science [*A publication*]
**JLIEA**........ Journal of Industrial Engineering [*A publication*]
**J Life Sci R Dublin Soc** ... Journal of Life Sciences. Royal Dublin Society [*A publication*]
**J Light Met Weld Constr** ... Journal of Light Metal Welding and Construction [*A publication*]
**J Limnol Soc South Afr** ... Journal. Limnological Society of South Africa [*A publication*]
**JL & Information Science** ... Journal of Law and Information Science [*A publication*]
**J Ling**......... Journal of Linguistics [*A publication*]
**J Linguist**... Journal of Linguistics [*A publication*]
**J Linguistics** ... Journal of Linguistics [*A publication*]
**J Linn Soc Lond Bot** ... Journal. Linnean Society of London. Botany [*A publication*]
**J Linn Soc Lond Zool** ... Journal. Linnean Society of London. Zoology [*A publication*]
**J Lipid Mediators** ... Journal of Lipid Mediators [*A publication*]
**J Lipid Res** ... Journal of Lipid Research [*A publication*]
**J Lipid Research** ... Journal of Lipid Research [*A publication*]
**J Liq Chromatogr** ... Journal of Liquid Chromatography [*A publication*]
**J Liquid Chromatogr** ... Journal of Liquid Chromatography [*A publication*]
**JLIS**........... Journal of Law and Information Science [*A publication*] (APTA)

**J Lit Sem** ... Journal of Literary Semantics [*A publication*]
**J Li W** ... Jahrbuch fuer Liturgiewissenschaft [*A publication*]
**JLKNO** ... Jahrbuch fuer Landeskunde von Niederoesterreich [*A publication*]
**Jll** ... Juillet [*July*] [*French*]
**JLMC** ... Joint Labor Management Committee of the Retail Food Industry (EA)
**J L Med** ... Journal of Legal Medicine [*A publication*]
**JLMIC** ... Japan Light Machinery Information Center (EA)
**JLMPA** ... Journal of Microwave Power [*A publication*]
**JLMS** ... Journal. London Mathematical Society [*A publication*]
**JLMSA** ... Jewish Liturgical Music Society of America (EA)
**Jl Musicology** ... Journal of Musicology [*A publication*]
**JLN** ... Jack London Newsletter [*A publication*]
**JLN** ... Jaclyn, Inc. [*AMEX symbol*] (SPSG)
**JLN** ... Joplin [*Missouri*] [*Airport symbol*] (OAG)
**JLN** ... Joplin, MO [*Location identifier*] [*FAA*] (FAAL)
**JLN Oe** ... Jahrbuch fuer die Landeskunde von Nieder-Oesterreich [*A publication*]
**Jl NY Ent Soc** ... Journal. New York Entomological Society [*A publication*]
**Jl NZ Diet Ass** ... Journal. New Zealand Dietetic Association [*A publication*]
**JLO** ... Junction Light Output
**JLOIC** ... Joint Logistics, Operations, Intelligence Center [*NATO*] (NATG)
**J Lond Math** ... Journal. London Mathematical Society [*A publication*]
**J London Math Soc** ... Journal. London Mathematical Society [*A publication*]
**J London Math Soc (2)** ... Journal. London Mathematical Society. Second Series [*A publication*]
**J London School Trop Med** ... Journal. London School of Tropical Medicine [*A publication*]
**J Lond Soc** ... Journal. London Society [*A publication*]
**J Long Term Care** ... Journal of Long-Term Care Administration [*A publication*]
**J Long Term Care Adm** ... Journal of Long-Term Care Administration [*A publication*]
**J Long Term Care Admin** ... Journal of Long-Term Care Administration [*A publication*]
**JLOTA** ... Journal of Laryngology and Otology [*A publication*]
**JLOTS** ... Joint Logistics Over-the-Shore [*Military*] (RDA)
**J Louis St Med Soc** ... Journal. Louisiana State Medical Society [*A publication*]
**J Low Freq Noise Vib** ... Journal of Low Frequency Noise and Vibration [*A publication*]
**J Low Temp Phys** ... Journal of Low Temperature Physics [*A publication*]
**JLP** ... Jamaica Labour Party [*Political party*] (PPW)
**JLP** ... Jazz for Life Project (EA)
**JLPB** ... Joint Logistics Planning Board
**JLPC** ... Joint Logistics Plans Committee [*Military*]
**JLPG** ... Joint Logistics Plans Group [*Military*]
**JL & Pol** ... Journal of Law and Politics [*A publication*] (DLA)
**JLPPG** ... Joint Logistics and Personnel Policy Guidance [*Military*] (AFM)
**JLR** ... Jabalpur [*India*] [*Airport symbol*] (OAG)
**JLR** ... Jamaica Law Reports [*1953-55*] [*A publication*] (DLA)
**JLR** ... Jewish Language Review [*A publication*]
**JLR** ... Johore Law Reports [*India*] [*A publication*] (DLA)
**JLR** ... Journal of Labor Research [*A publication*]
**JLR** ... Journal of Linguistic Research [*A publication*]
**JLR** ... Junior Leaders Regiment [*British military*] (DMA)
**Jl R Agric Soc** ... Journal. Royal Agricultural Society of England [*A publication*]
**Jl R Anthrop Inst** ... Journal. Royal Anthropological Institute of Great Britain and Ireland [*A publication*]
**Jl R Aust Hist Soc** ... Royal Australian Historical Society. Journal [*A publication*] (APTA)
**JLRB** ... Joint Labor Relations Board
**JLRB** ... Joint Logistics Review Board [*Military*]
**JLRC** ... Jack London Research Center (EA)
**JLREID** ... Joint Long-Range Estimative Intelligence Document [*Military*]
**JL & Religion** ... Journal of Law and Religion [*A publication*] (DLA)
**Jl of Research** ... Journal of Research in Music Education [*A publication*]
**Jl R Hist Soc Qd** ... Royal Historical Society of Queensland. Journal [*A publication*] (APTA)
**Jl R Hort Soc** ... Journal. Royal Horticulture Society [*A publication*]
**Jl R Microsc Soc** ... Journal. Royal Microscopical Society [*A publication*]
**JLRPG** ... Joint Long-Range Proving Ground (KSC)
**JLRRT** ... Jordan Left-Right Reversal Test [*Educational test*]
**JLRSA** ... Joint Long-Range Strategic Appraisal [*Military*]
**JLRSE** ... Joint Long-Range Strategic Estimates [*Military*]
**Jl R Soc Arts** ... Journal. Royal Society of Arts [*A publication*]
**Jl R Soc NZ** ... Journal. Royal Society of New Zealand [*A publication*]
**JLRSS** ... Joint Long-Range Strategic Study [*Military*] (AFM)
**JLRU** ... Journal. Library of Rutgers University [*A publication*]
**JLS** ... Jet Lift System
**JLS** ... Jewels (ADA)
**JLS** ... Joint Least Squares [*Statistics*]
**JLS** ... Journal. Law Society of Scotland [*A publication*]
**JLS** ... Journal of Literary Semantics [*A publication*]
**Jl S Afr Bot** ... Journal of South African Botany [*A publication*]
**Jl S-East Agric Coll (Wye)** ... Journal. South-Eastern Agricultural College (Wye) [*Kent*] [*A publication*]
**J/L/Sgt** ... Junior Lance-Sergeant [*British military*] (DMA)
**JLSMA** ... Journal. Louisiana State Medical Society [*A publication*]
**Jl Small Bus** ... American Journal of Small Business [*A publication*]
**JL Soc** ... Journal. Law Society of Scotland [*A publication*] (DLA)
**Jl Soc Mot Pict Telev Engin** ... Journal. Society of Motion Picture and Television Engineers [*A publication*]
**Jl Soc Photogr Sci** ... Journal. Society of Photographic Science and Technology of Japan [*A publication*]
**Jl Soc Photogr Sci Technol Japan** ... Journal. Society of Photographic Science and Technology of Japan [*A publication*]
**J of the L Soc of Scotl** ... Journal. Law Society of Scotland [*A publication*]
**JL Soc Scotland** ... Journal. Law Society of Scotland [*A publication*]
**JL Soc'y** ... Journal. Law Society of Scotland [*A publication*]
**J L Socy Scot** ... Journal. Law Society of Scotland [*A publication*]
**JLSP** ... Joint Logistics Support Plan
**J L Studies** ... Journal of Legal Studies [*A publication*]
**JLT** ... Journal du Textile [*Paris*] [*A publication*]
**JLT** ... Junior Lord of the Treasury
**J L Temp Ph** ... Journal of Low Temperature Physics [*A publication*]
**Jl Test Eval** ... Journal of Testing and Evaluation [*A publication*]
**JLTF** ... Jewish Librarians Task Force (EA)
**JLTPB** ... Joint Logistics Techniques and Procedures Board [*Military*]
**JLUB** ... Jiffy Lube International, Inc. [*Baltimore, MD*] [*NASDAQ symbol*] (NQ)
**J Lubric Technol Trans ASME** ... Journal of Lubrication Technology. Transactions of the American Society of Mechanical Engineers [*A publication*]
**J Lubr Tech** ... Journal of Lubrication Technology [*A publication*]
**J Lubr Technol** ... Journal of Lubrication Technology [*A publication*]
**J Lubr Technol Trans ASME** ... Journal of Lubrication Technology. Transactions of the American Society of Mechanical Engineers [*A publication*]
**J Lub Tech** ... Journal of Lubrication Technology. Transactions of the American Society of Mechanical Engineers [*A publication*]
**J Lumin** ... Journal of Luminescence [*A publication*]
**J Luminesc** ... Journal of Luminescence [*A publication*]
**J Lute** ... Journal. Lute Society of America [*A publication*]
**J Lute Soc Amer** ... Journal. Lute Society of America [*A publication*]
**JLW** ... Jahrbuch fuer Liturgiewissenschaft [*A publication*]
**JLY** ... Jena, LA [*Location identifier*] [*FAA*] (FAAL)
**J Lymphol** ... Journal of Lymphology [*A publication*]
**JLZ** ... Jahresberichte des Literarischen Zentralblattes [*A publication*]
**JM** ... Air Jamaica Ltd. [*ICAO designator*] (OAG)
**JM** ... Jactitation of Marriage [*Legal*] [*British*] (ROG)
**jm** ... Jamaica [*MARC country of publication code*] [*Library of Congress*] (LCCP)
**JM** ... Jamaica [*ANSI two-letter standard code*] (CNC)
**Jm** ... James [*New Testament book*] (BJA)
**JM** ... James Madison [*US president, 1751-1836*]
**JM** ... James Monroe [*US president, 1758-1831*]
**JM** ... Jesuit Missions (EA)
**J/M** ... Jettison Motor (KSC)
**JM** ... Jewish Male [*Classified advertising*]
**JM** ... Jiyu-Minshuto [*Liberal-Democratic Party*] [*Japan*] [*Political party*]
**JM** ... John Mercanti [*Designer's mark, when appearing on US coins*]
**JM** ... Journal of Marketing [*A publication*]
**JM** ... Journal of Music Theory [*A publication*]
**JM** ... Julia MacRae [*Publisher*] [*British*]
**JM** ... Julian Messner [*Publisher's imprint*]
**JM** ... Junction Module [*Deep Space Instrumentation Facility, NASA*]
**JM** ... Juris Magister [*Master of Laws*]
**JM** ... Justizminister [*Minister of Justice*] [*German*] (ILCA)
**JM** ... Justizministerium [*Ministry of Justice*] [*German*] (ILCA)
**JM** ... Juxtamembrane Domain
**2JM** ... 2 June Movement [*West Germany*]
**J/M²** ... Joules per Square Meter
**J/M³** ... Joules per Cubic Meter [*Physics*]
**JMA** ... Houston [*Texas*] Astrodome [*Airport symbol*] (OAG)
**JMA** ... James Martin Associates [*Database consulting group*] [*British*]
**JMA** ... Jamming Modulation Analysis
**JMA** ... Japan Management Association
**JMA** ... Japan Meteorological Agency
**JMA** ... Japan Microphotography Association
**JMA** ... Japanese Military Administration
**JMA** ... Jewelry Manufacturers Association (EA)
**JMA** ... Jewish Music Alliance (EA)
**JMA** ... Joint Mission Analysis
**JMA** ... Journal of Macroeconomics [*A publication*]
**JMA** ... Julia Morgan Association [*Inactive*] (EA)
**JMA** ... Junior Management Assistant
**JMA** ... Junior Medical Assistant [*British military*] (DMA)
**JMA** ... Junior Military Aviator
**JMAAD** ... Joint Military Assistance Affairs Division (CINC)
**JMAC** ... Joint Munitions Allocation Committee
**J Macomb Dent Soc** ... Journal. Macomb Dental Society [*A publication*]
**J Macromol Chem** ... Journal of Macromolecular Chemistry [*A publication*]
**J Macromol Sci A** ... Journal of Macromolecular Science. Part A [*A publication*]
**J Macromol Sci B** ... Journal of Macromolecular Science. Part B. Physics [*A publication*]

**J Macromol Sci C** ... Journal of Macromolecular Science. Part C [*A publication*]
**J Macromol Sci Chem** ... Journal of Macromolecular Science. Chemistry [*A publication*]
**J Macromol Sci Chem A** ... Journal of Macromolecular Science. Part A. Chemistry [*A publication*]
**J Macromol Sci Part A** ... Journal of Macromolecular Science. Part A. Chemistry [*A publication*]
**J Macromol Sci Part B** ... Journal of Macromolecular Science. Part B. Physics [*A publication*]
**J Macromol Sci Phys** ... Journal of Macromolecular Science. Part B. Physics [*A publication*]
**J Macromol Sci Rev Macromol Chem** ... Journal of Macromolecular Science. Part C. Reviews in Macromolecular Chemistry [*A publication*]
**J Macromol Sci Rev Macromol Chem Phys** ... Journal of Macromolecular Science. Reviews in Macromolecular Chemistry and Physics [*A publication*]
**J Macromol Sci Rev Polym Technol** ... Journal of Macromolecular Science. Part D. Reviews in Polymer Technology [*A publication*]
**J Macr S Ch** ... Journal of Macromolecular Science. Part A. Chemistry [*A publication*]
**J Macr S Ph** ... Journal of Macromolecular Science. Part B. Physics [*A publication*]
**J Macr S Rm** ... Journal of Macromolecular Science. Part C. Reviews in Macromolecular Chemistry [*A publication*]
**J of MACT** ... Journal. Maulana Azad College of Technology [*A publication*]
**J MACT** .... Journal. Maulana Azad College of Technology [*India*] [*A publication*]
**J Madras Agric Stud Union** ... Journal. Madras Agricultural Students' Union [*A publication*]
**J Madras Inst Technol** ... Journal. Madras Institute of Technology [*A publication*]
**J Madras Univ** ... Journal. Madras University [*A publication*]
**J Madras Univ B** ... Journal. Madras University. Section B. Contributions in Mathematics, Physical and Biological Science [*A publication*]
**J Madras Univ Sect B** ... Journal. Madras University. Section B [*A publication*]
**J Madurai Kamaraj Univ** ... Journal. Madurai Kamaraj University [*A publication*]
**J Madurai Univ** ... Madurai University. Journal [*A publication*]
**JMAG**........ Journal of Molecular and Applied Genetics [*A publication*]
**J Magn Magn Mater** ... Journal of Magnetism and Magnetic Materials [*A publication*]
**J Magn and Magn Mater** ... Journal of Magnetism and Magnetic Materials [*A publication*]
**J Magn Res** ... Journal of Magnetic Resonance [*A publication*]
**J Magn Resonance** ... Journal of Magnetic Resonance [*A publication*]
**J Maharaja Sayajirao Univ Baroda** ... Journal. Maharaja Sayajirao University of Baroda [*A publication*]
**J Maharashtra Agric Univ** ... Journal. Maharashtra Agricultural Universities [*A publication*]
**J Mahar Sayayira Univ Baroda** ... Journal. Maharaja Sayayira University of Baroda [*A publication*]
**JMAHEP**.. Joint Military Aircraft Hurricane Evacuation Plan (AFM)
**J Maine Dent Assoc** ... Journal. Maine Dental Association [*A publication*]
**J Maine Med Assoc** ... Journal. Maine Medical Association [*A publication*]
**J Makromol Chem** ... Journal fuer Makromolekulare Chemie [*A publication*]
**J Malacol Soc Aust** ... Journal. Malacological Society of Australia [*A publication*]
**J Malac Soc Aust** ... Journal. Malacological Society of Australia [*A publication*] (APTA)
**J Malar Inst India** ... Journal. Malaria Institute of India [*A publication*]
**J Malaya Branch Br Med Assoc** ... Journal. Malayan Branch. British Medical Association [*A publication*]
**J Malay Branch Roy Asiatic Soc** ... Journal. Malaysian Branch. Royal Asiatic Society [*A publication*]
**J Malays Branch R Asiat Soc** ... Journal. Malaysian Branch. Royal Asiatic Society [*A publication*]
**J Mal Br Brit Med Ass** ... Journal. Malayan Branch. British Medical Association [*A publication*]
**J Mal Br Roy Asiat Soc** ... Journal. Malaysian Branch. Royal Asiatic Society [*A publication*]
**J Mal & Comp L** ... Journal of Malaysian and Comparative Law [*A publication*]
**J Mal Vasc** ... Journal des Maladies Vasculaires [*A publication*]
**J Mal Vet Med Ass** ... Journal. Malayan Veterinary Medical Association [*A publication*]
**JMAM**....... Journal of Mammalogy [*A publication*]
**JMAM**....... Journal. Music Academy (Madras) [*A publication*]
**J Mammal** ... Journal of Mammalogy [*A publication*]
**J Mammal Soc Jpn** ... Journal. Mammalogical Society of Japan [*A publication*]
**J Manage** ... Journal of Management [*A publication*]
**J Manage Stud** ... Journal of Management Studies [*A publication*]
**J Manag Stu** ... Journal of Management Studies [*A publication*]
**J Manch Geogr Soc** ... Journal. Manchester Geographical Society [*A publication*]
**J Manch Geol Ass** ... Journal. Manchester Geological Association [*A publication*]
**J MAN GS** ... Journal of the Manchester Geographical Society [*A publication*] (ROG)
**J Manip Physiol Ther** ... Journal of Manipulative and Physiological Therapeutics [*A publication*]
**J Manipulative Physiol Ther** ... Journal of Manipulative and Physiological Therapeutics [*A publication*]
**J Manx Mus** ... Journal. Manx Museum [*A publication*]
**JMAPD**..... Journal de Mecanique Appliquee [*A publication*]
**J Mar Biol Assoc (India)** ... Journal. Marine Biological Association (India) [*A publication*]
**J Mar Biol Assoc (UK)** ... Journal. Marine Biological Association (United Kingdom) [*A publication*]
**J Mar Biol Ass (UK)** ... Journal. Marine Biological Association (United Kingdom) [*A publication*]
**J Mar Fam** ... Journal of Marriage and the Family [*A publication*]
**J Marine Bi** ... Journal. Marine Biological Association [*United Kingdom*] [*A publication*]
**J Marine Biol Ass (United Kingdom)** ... Journal. Marine Biological Association (United Kingdom) [*A publication*]
**J Marine Re** ... Journal of Marine Research [*A publication*]
**J Marine Res** ... Journal of Marine Research [*A publication*]
**J Marital Fam Ther** ... Journal of Marital and Family Therapy [*A publication*]
**J Maritime L** ... Journal of Maritime Law and Commerce [*A publication*]
**J Maritime Law and Commer** ... Journal of Maritime Law and Commerce [*A publication*]
**J Marit Law** ... Journal of Maritime Law and Commerce [*A publication*]
**J of Marit L and Commerce** ... Journal of Maritime Law and Commerce [*A publication*]
**J Marit Saf Acad Part 2** ... Journal. Maritime Safety Academy. Part 2 [*Japan*] [*A publication*]
**J Mar J Prac & Proc** ... John Marshall Journal of Practice and Procedure [*A publication*]
**J Mark**....... Journal of Marketing [*A publication*]
**J Market**.... Journal of Marketing [*A publication*]
**J Marketing** ... Journal of Marketing [*A publication*]
**J Marketing Res** ... Journal of Marketing Research [*A publication*]
**J Market (L)** ... Journal. Market Research Society (London) [*A publication*]
**J Market R** ... Journal of Marketing Research [*A publication*]
**J Market Research Society Vic** ... Journal. Market Research Society of Victoria [*A publication*] (APTA)
**J Market Res Soc** ... Journal. Market Research Society [*A publication*]
**J Mark Prof** ... Journal of Marketing for Professions [*A publication*]
**J Mark Res** ... Journal of Marketing Research [*A publication*]
**J Marktforsch** ... Journal fuer Marktforschung [*A publication*]
**J Mar Law & Com** ... Journal of Maritime Law and Commerce [*A publication*]
**J Mar L and Com** ... Journal of Maritime Law and Commerce [*A publication*]
**J Mar LR**... John Marshall Law Review [*A publication*]
**J Mar L Rev** ... John Marshall Law Review [*A publication*]
**J Mar March** ... Journal de la Marine Marchande [*A publication*]
**J Mar Res** ... Journal of Marine Research [*A publication*]
**J Marr & Fam** ... Journal of Marriage and the Family [*A publication*]
**J Marriage** ... Journal of Marriage and the Family [*A publication*]
**J Marriage & Fam** ... Journal of Marriage and the Family [*A publication*]
**J Marriage Family** ... Journal of Marriage and the Family [*A publication*]
**J Marshall J** ... John Marshall Journal of Practice and Procedure [*A publication*]
**J Mar Technol Soc** ... Journal. Marine Technology Society [*A publication*]
**JMAS**........ Journal of Modern African Studies [*A publication*]
**J Mass Dent Soc** ... Journal. Massachusetts Dental Society [*A publication*]
**J Mass Spectrom** ... Journal of Mass Spectrometry and Ion Physics [*A publication*]
**J Mass Spectrom Ion Phys** ... Journal of Mass Spectrometry and Ion Physics [*A publication*]
**J Mass Sp Ion P** ... Journal of Mass Spectrometry and Ion Physics [*A publication*]
**J Mater**...... Journal of Materials [*A publication*]
**J Mater Energy Syst** ... Journal of Materials for Energy Systems [*A publication*]
**J Materials Sci** ... Journal of Materials Science [*A publication*]
**J Mater Sci** ... Journal of Materials Science [*A publication*]
**J Mater Sci Lett** ... Journal of Materials Science. Letters [*A publication*]
**J Mater Sci Res Inst Dongguk Univ** ... Journal. Materials Science Research Institute. Dongguk University [*A publication*]
**J Mater Sci Soc Jpn** ... Journal. Materials Science Society of Japan [*A publication*]
**J Mater Technol** ... Journal of Materials Technology [*A publication*]
**J Mater Test Res Assoc** ... Journal. Material Testing Research Association [*Japan*] [*A publication*]
**J Math Anal** ... Journal of Mathematical Analysis and Applications [*A publication*]
**J Math Anal Appl** ... Journal of Mathematical Analysis and Applications [*A publication*]
**J Math Anal and Appl** ... Journal of Mathematical Analysis and Applications [*A publication*]
**J Math Biol** ... Journal of Mathematical Biology [*A publication*]
**J Math Chem** ... Journal of Mathematical Chemistry [*A publication*]
**J Math Econom** ... Journal of Mathematical Economics [*A publication*]
**J Mathematical Phys** ... Journal of Mathematical Physics [*A publication*]
**J Mathematical and Physical Sci** ... Journal of Mathematical and Physical Sciences [*A publication*]

**J Mathematical Psychology** ... Journal of Mathematical Psychology [*A publication*]
**J Mathematical Sociology** ... Journal of Mathematical Sociology [*A publication*]
**J Math (Jabalpur)** ... Journal of Mathematics (Jabalpur) [*A publication*]
**J Math Jap** ... Journal. Mathematical Society of Japan [*A publication*]
**J Math Kyoto Univ** ... Journal of Mathematics. Kyoto University [*A publication*]
**J Math Mech** ... Journal of Mathematics and Mechanics [*A publication*]
**J Math Modelling Teach** ... Journal of Mathematical Modelling for Teachers [*A publication*]
**J Math NS** ... Journal of Mathematics. New Series [*A publication*]
**J Math P A** ... Journal de Mathematiques Pures et Appliquees [*A publication*]
**J Math Phys** ... Journal of Mathematical Physics [*A publication*]
**J Math Phys** ... Journal of Mathematics and Physics [*A publication*]
**J Math & Phys** ... Journal of Mathematics and Physics [*A publication*]
**J Math Phys (Cambridge Mass)** ... Journal of Mathematics and Physics (Cambridge, Massachusetts) [*A publication*]
**J Math Phys (NY)** ... Journal of Mathematical Physics (New York) [*A publication*]
**J Math and Phys Sci** ... Journal of Mathematical and Physical Sciences [*A publication*]
**J Math Phys Sci** ... Journal of Mathematical and Physical Sciences [*A publication*]
**J Math Psyc** ... Journal of Mathematical Psychology [*A publication*]
**J Math Psych** ... Journal of Mathematical Psychology [*A publication*]
**J Math Psychol** ... Journal of Mathematical Psychology [*A publication*]
**J Math Pures Appl** ... Journal de Mathematiques Pures et Appliquees [*A publication*]
**J Math Pures Appl 9** ... Journal de Mathematiques Pures et Appliquees. Neuvieme Serie [*A publication*]
**J Math Res Exposition** ... Journal of Mathematical Research and Exposition [*A publication*]
**J Math Sci** ... Journal of Mathematics and Sciences [*A publication*]
**J Math & Sci** ... Journal of Mathematics and Sciences [*A publication*]
**J Math Soci** ... Journal of Mathematical Sociology [*A publication*]
**J Math Sociol** ... Journal of Mathematical Sociology [*A publication*]
**J Math Soc Japan** ... Journal. Mathematical Society of Japan [*A publication*]
**J Math Soc Jpn** ... Journal. Mathematical Society of Japan [*A publication*]
**J Math Tokushima Univ** ... Journal of Mathematics. Tokushima University [*A publication*]
**J Mat Sci** ... Journal of Materials Science [*A publication*]
**J Mat Sci Lett** ... Journal of Materials Science. Letters [*A publication*]
**J Maulana Azad College Tech** ... Journal. Maulana Azad College of Technology [*A publication*]
**J Maxillofac Orthop** ... Journal of Maxillofacial Orthopedics [*A publication*]
**J Maxillofac Surg** ... Journal of Maxillofacial Surgery [*A publication*]
**JMB**.......... Japan Missionary Bulletin [*Tokyo*] [*A publication*]
**JMB**.......... Jewelers Memorandum Bureau (EA)
**JMB**.......... Johnson Matthey Bankers [*Commercial firm*] [*British*]
**JMB**.......... Joint Matriculation Board [*British*] (DCTA)
**JMB**.......... Joint Meteorological Board (AAG)
**JMB**.......... Joint Movements Branch [*NATO*] (NATG)
**JMB**.......... Journal of Molecular Biology [*A publication*]
**JMB**.......... Journal of Money, Credit, and Banking [*A publication*]
**JMBCD**...... Journal de Microscopie et de Biologie Cellulaire [*A publication*]
**JMBR**........ JMB Realty Trust [*NASDAQ symbol*] (NQ)
**JMBRAS**... Journal. Malayan Branch. Royal Asiatic Society [*A publication*]
**JMBXA**..... Journal de Medecine de Bordeaux [*A publication*]
**JMC**.......... Japan Medical Congress [*A publication*]
**JMC**.......... Joint Maritime Commission
**JMC**.......... Joint Maritime Congress [*Washington, DC*] (EA)
**JMC**.......... Joint Message Center
**JMC**.......... Joint Meteorological Committee
**JMC**.......... Joint Military Commission [*US, North Vietnam, South Vietnam, Viet Cong*]
**JMC**.......... Journal of Medicinal Chemistry [*A publication*]
**JMC**.......... Justice Mining Corporation [*Vancouver Stock Exchange symbol*]
**JMC**.......... Sausalito, CA [*Location identifier*] [*FAA*] (FAAL)
**JMCA**........ Jewish Ministers Cantors Association of America and Canada (EA)
**JMCA**........ Judges, Marshals, and Constables Association
**JMCAA**..... Jewish Minister and Cantors Association of America [*Later, JMCA*] (EA)
**JMCAAC**.. Jewish Ministers Cantors Association of America and Canada (EA)
**JMCAD**..... Journal of Molecular Catalysis [*A publication*]
**JMCC**........ Joint Mobile Communications Center [*NATO*] (NATG)
**JMCC**........ Joint Movements Coordinating Committee [*British*]
**JMCI**......... Journal of Molecular and Cellular Immunology [*A publication*]
**JMCI J Mol Cell Immunol** ... JMCI. Journal of Molecular and Cellular Immunology [*A publication*]
**JMCOL**..... JUMPS Monthly Compute Output Listing [*Military*] (AABC)
**JMCP**........ Jefferson Medical College of Philadelphia
**JMD**.......... Joint Managing Director (DCTA)
**JMD**.......... Joint Monitor Display
**JMD**.......... Journal of Management Development [*A publication*]
**J MD Acad Sci** ... Journal. Maryland Academy of Sciences [*A publication*]
**JMDC**........ Joint Manual Direction Center [*Air Force*]
**JMDR**........ Journal of Missile Defense Research [*A publication*]
**J MD State Dent Assoc** ... Journal. Maryland State Dental Association [*A publication*]
**JME**.......... James Industries [*Vancouver Stock Exchange symbol*]
**JME**.......... Joint Maximum Effort
**JME**.......... Journal of Mathematical Economics [*A publication*]
**JME**.......... Journal of Monetary Economics [*A publication*]
**JMEA**........ Jewish Music Educators Association (EA)
**J Mec**......... Journal de Mecanique [*A publication*]
**J Mecanique** ... Journal de Mecanique [*A publication*]
**J Mecan Phys Atm** ... Journal de Mecanique et Physique de l'Atmosphere [*A publication*]
**J Mec Appl** ... Journal de Mecanique Appliquee [*A publication*]
**J Mech**....... Journal of Mechanisms [*A publication*]
**J Mechanochem Cell Motil** ... Journal of Mechanochemistry and Cell Motility [*A publication*]
**J Mechanochem & Cell Motility** ... Journal of Mechanochemistry and Cell Motility [*A publication*]
**J Mechanochem Cell Motility** ... Journal of Mechanochemistry and Cell Motility [*A publication*]
**J Mech Des** ... Journal of Mechanical Design [*United States*] [*A publication*]
**J Mech Des Trans ASME** ... Journal of Mechanical Design. Transactions of the American Society of Mechanical Engineers [*A publication*]
**J Mech E** ... Journal of Mechanical Engineering Science [*A publication*]
**J Mech Eng** ... Journal of Mechanical Engineering Science [*A publication*]
**J Mech Eng Lab** ... Journal. Mechanical Engineering Laboratory [*Japan*] [*A publication*]
**J Mech Eng Lab (Tokyo)** ... Journal. Mechanical Engineering Laboratory (Tokyo) [*A publication*]
**J Mech Engng Lab** ... Journal. Mechanical Engineering Laboratory [*A publication*]
**J Mech Engng Sci** ... Journal of Mechanical Engineering Science [*A publication*]
**J Mech Eng Sci** ... Journal of Mechanical Engineering Science [*A publication*]
**J Mech Lab Jap** ... Journal. Mechanical Laboratory of Japan [*A publication*]
**J Mech Lab (Tokyo)** ... Journal. Mechanical Laboratory (Tokyo) [*A publication*]
**J Mech Phys** ... Journal of the Mechanics and Physics of Solids [*A publication*]
**J Mech Phys Solids** ... Journal of the Mechanics and Physics of Solids [*A publication*]
**J Mech Working Technol** ... Journal of Mechanical Working Technology [*A publication*]
**J Mech Work Technol** ... Journal of Mechanical Working Technology [*A publication*]
**J Mec Phys Atmos** ... Journal de Mecanique et Physique de l'Atmosphere [*France*] [*A publication*]
**J Mec Theor Appl** ... Journal de Mecanique Theorique et Appliquee [*Journal of Theoretical and Applied Mechanics*] [*A publication*]
**J Mec Theor et Appl** ... Journal de Mecanique Theorique et Appliquee [*Journal of Theoretical and Applied Mechanics*] [*A publication*]
**JMED**........ Jones Medical Industries, Inc. [*St. Louis, MO*] [*NASDAQ symbol*] (NQ)
**J Med**......... Jornal do Medico [*A publication*]
**J Med**......... Journal of Medicine [*A publication*]
**JMED**........ Jungle Message Encoder-Decoder (MCD)
**JMEDA**..... Journal of Medical Education [*A publication*]
**J Med A Alabama** ... Journal. Medical Association of the State of Alabama [*A publication*]
**J Med Ass Eire** ... Journal. Medical Association of Eire [*A publication*]
**J Med Ass Form** ... Journal. Medical Association of Formosa [*A publication*]
**J Med Assn GA** ... Journal. Medical Association of Georgia [*A publication*]
**J Med Assoc Eire** ... Journal. Medical Association of Eire [*A publication*]
**J Med Assoc GA** ... Journal. Medical Association of Georgia [*A publication*]
**J Med Assoc Iwate Prefect Hosp** ... Journal. Medical Association of Iwate Prefectural Hospital [*Japan*] [*A publication*]
**J Med Assoc Jam** ... Journal. Medical Association of Jamaica [*A publication*]
**J Med Assoc S Afr** ... Journal. Medical Association of South Africa [*A publication*]
**J Med Assoc State Ala** ... Journal. Medical Association of the State of Alabama [*A publication*]
**J Med Assoc State Alabama** ... Journal. Medical Association of the State of Alabama [*A publication*]
**J Med Assoc Thai** ... Journal. Medical Association of Thailand [*A publication*]
**J Med Assoc Thail** ... Journal. Medical Association of Thailand [*A publication*]
**J Med Ass Ok** ... Journal. Medical Association of Okayama [*A publication*]
**J Med Ass South Africa** ... Journal. Medical Association of South Africa [*A publication*]
**J Med Ass Thail** ... Journal. Medical Association of Thailand [*A publication*]
**J Med (Basel)** ... Journal of Medicine. Experimental and Clinical (Basel) [*A publication*]
**J Med Besancon** ... Journal de Medecine de Besancon [*A publication*]
**J Med Bord** ... Journal de Medecine de Bordeaux [*A publication*]
**J Med Bordeaux** ... Journal de Medecine de Bordeaux [*A publication*]
**J Med Bord Sud-Ouest** ... Journal de Medecine de Bordeaux et du Sud-Ouest [*A publication*]
**J Med Brux** ... Journal Medical de Bruxelles [*A publication*]
**J Med Caen** ... Journal de Medecine de Caen [*A publication*]

**J Med Chem** ... Journal of Medicinal Chemistry [*A publication*]
**J Med Chir** ... Journal de Medecine et de Chirurgie [*A publication*]
**J Med Chir** ... Journal Medico-Chirurgical [*A publication*]
**J Med Chir Pharm (Paris)** ... Journal de Medecine, Chirurgie, Pharmacie (Paris) [*A publication*]
**J Med Chir Prat** ... Journal de Medecine et de Chirurgie Pratiques [*A publication*]
**J Med et Chir Prat** ... Journal de Medecine et de Chirurgie Pratiques [*A publication*]
**J Med (Cincinnati)** ... Journal of Medicine (Cincinnati) [*A publication*]
**J Med Coll Keijo** ... Journal. Medical College in Keijo [*A publication*]
**J Med Dent Assoc Botswana** ... Journal. Medical and Dental Association of Botswana [*A publication*]
**J Med Ed** ... Journal of Medical Education [*A publication*]
**J Med Educ** ... Journal of Medical Education [*A publication*]
**J Med El** .... Journal of Medical Electronics [*A publication*]
**J Med Electron** ... Journal of Medical Electronics [*A publication*]
**J Med Eng and Technol** ... Journal of Medical Engineering and Technology [*A publication*]
**J Med Eng Technol** ... Journal of Medical Engineering and Technology [*A publication*]
**J Med Ent** ... Journal of Medical Entomology [*A publication*]
**J Med Entomol** ... Journal of Medical Entomology [*A publication*]
**J Med Entomol Suppl** ... Journal of Medical Entomology. Supplement [*A publication*]
**J Med Ethic** ... Journal of Medical Ethics [*A publication*]
**J Med Ethics** ... Journal of Medical Ethics [*A publication*]
**J Med Franc** ... Journal Medical Francais [*A publication*]
**J Med Genet** ... Journal of Medical Genetics [*A publication*]
**J Med Hait** ... Journal Medical Haitien [*A publication*]
**J Med Humanit Bioethics** ... Journal of Medical Humanities and Bioethics [*A publication*]
**J Med Hum Bioeth** ... Journal of Medical Humanities and Bioethics [*A publication*]
**J Medicaid Manage** ... Journal for Medicaid Management [*A publication*]
**J Medicaid Mgt** ... Journal for Medicaid Management [*A publication*]
**J Mediev Hi** ... Journal of Medieval History [*A publication*]
**J Mediev R** ... Journal of Medieval and Renaissance Studies [*A publication*]
**J Mediev Renaissance Stud** ... Journal of Medieval and Renaissance Studies [*A publication*]
**J Med Int Med Abstr Rev** ... Journal of Medicine and International Medical Abstracts and Reviews [*A publication*]
**J Mediterr Anthropol Archaeol** ... Journal of Mediterranean Anthropology and Archaeology [*A publication*]
**J Med Kosmet** ... Journal fuer Medizinische Kosmetik [*A publication*]
**J Med Lab Technol** ... Journal of Medical Laboratory Technology [*A publication*]
**J Med Leg Psych Anthr** ... Journal de Medecine Legale Psychiatrique et d'Anthropologie Criminelle [*A publication*]
**J Med Liban** ... Journal Medical Libanais [*A publication*]
**J Med Lyon** ... Journal de Medecine de Lyon [*A publication*]
**J Med Micro** ... Journal of Medical Microbiology [*A publication*]
**J Med Microbiol** ... Journal of Medical Microbiology [*A publication*]
**J Med Montp** ... Journal de Medecine de Montpellier [*A publication*]
**J Med Pa** ... Journal de Medecine de Paris [*A publication*]
**J Med Pernambuco** ... Jornal de Medicina de Pernambuco [*A publication*]
**J Med Pharm Chem** ... Journal of Medicinal and Pharmaceutical Chemistry [*A publication*]
**J Med Phil** ... Journal of Medicine and Philosophy [*A publication*]
**J Med Philos** ... Journal of Medicine and Philosophy [*A publication*]
**J Med Poitiers** ... Journal de Medecine de Poitiers [*A publication*]
**J Med (Porto)** ... Jornal do Medico (Porto) [*A publication*]
**J Med Prim** ... Journal of Medical Primatology [*A publication*]
**J Med Primatol** ... Journal of Medical Primatology [*A publication*]
**J Med Prof Ass** ... Journal. Medical Professions Association [*A publication*]
**J Med Sci**... Journal of Medical Sciences [*A publication*]
**J Med Sci Banaras Hindu Univ** ... Journal of Medical Sciences. Banaras Hindu University [*A publication*]
**J Med Soc New Jers** ... Journal. Medical Society of New Jersey [*A publication*]
**J Med Soc New Jersey** ... Journal. Medical Society of New Jersey [*A publication*]
**J Med Soc NJ** ... Journal. Medical Society of New Jersey [*A publication*]
**J Med Soc Toho Univ** ... Journal. Medical Society of Toho University [*A publication*]
**J Med Strasb** ... Journal de Medecine de Strasbourg [*A publication*]
**J Med Strasbourg** ... Journal de Medecine de Strasbourg [*France*] [*A publication*]
**J Med Syst** ... Journal of Medical Systems [*A publication*]
**J Med Technol** ... Journal of Medical Technology [*A publication*]
**J M Educ** ... Journal of Medical Education [*A publication*]
**J Med Vet et Comp** ... Journal de Medecine Veterinaire et Comparee [*A publication*]
**J Med Vet (Lyon)** ... Journal de Medecine Veterinaire (Lyon) [*A publication*]
**J Med Vet Mil** ... Journal de Medecine Veterinaire Militaire [*A publication*]
**J Med Vet Mycol** ... Journal of Medical and Veterinary Mycology [*A publication*]
**J Med Vet et Zootech (Lyon)** ... Journal de Medecine Veterinaire et de Zootechnie (Lyon) [*A publication*]
**J Med Virol** ... Journal of Medical Virology [*A publication*]
**J Med (Westbury NY)** ... Journal of Medicine (Westbury, New York) [*A publication*]
**J Med Wom Fed** ... Journal. Medical Women's Federation [*A publication*]
**JMeH** ........ Journal of Medieval History [*A publication*]
**JMEM** ....... Joint Munitions Effectiveness Manual [*Military*] (AFM)
**JMEM** ....... Junior Marine Engineering Mechanic [*British military*] (DMA)
**J Membrane Biol** ... Journal of Membrane Biology [*A publication*]
**J Membrane Sci** ... Journal of Membrane Science [*A publication*]
**J Membr Bio** ... Journal of Membrane Biology [*A publication*]
**J Membr Biol** ... Journal of Membrane Biology [*A publication*]
**J Membr Sci** ... Journal of Membrane Science [*A publication*]
**JMEMT** .... John Morgan Evans of Merthyr Tydil [*An association*] (EA)
**JMEMTF** ... Joint Munitions Effectiveness Manual Task Force (MCD)
**JMENS** ..... Joint Mission Element Need Statement (MCD)
**J Mental Def Research** ... Journal of Mental Deficiency Research [*A publication*]
**J Ment Def** ... Journal of Mental Deficiency Research [*A publication*]
**J Ment Defic Res** ... Journal of Mental Deficiency Research [*A publication*]
**J Ment Health** ... Journal of Mental Health [*A publication*]
**J Ment Health Adm** ... Journal. Mental Health Administration [*A publication*]
**J Ment Sc** .. Journal of Mental Science [*A publication*]
**J Ment Sci** ... Journal of Mental Science [*A publication*]
**J Ment Subnorm** ... Journal of Mental Subnormality [*A publication*]
**J Mercer Dent Soc** ... Journal. Mercer Dental Society [*A publication*]
**J Merioneth Hist Rec Soc** ... Journal. Merioneth Historical Record Society [*A publication*]
**JMES** ........ Journal. Middle East Society [*Jerusalem*] [*A publication*]
**J Met** ......... Journal of Metals [*A publication*]
**J Met** ......... Journal of Meteorology [*A publication*]
**J Metal Finish Soc Korea** ... Journal. Metal Finishing Society of Korea [*A publication*]
**J Metall Club R Coll Sci Technol** ... Journal. Metallurgical Club. Royal College of Science and Technology [*A publication*]
**J Metall Club Univ Strathclyde** ... Journal. Metallurgical Club. University of Strathclyde [*A publication*]
**J Metals**..... Journal of Metals [*A publication*]
**J Metamorph Geol** ... Journal of Metamorphic Geology [*A publication*]
**J Meteorol** ... Journal of Meteorology [*United States*] [*A publication*]
**J Meteorol Res** ... Journal of Meteorological Research [*Japan*] [*A publication*]
**J Meteorol Soc Jpn** ... Journal. Meteorological Society of Japan [*A publication*]
**J Met Finish Soc Jap** ... Journal. Metal Finishing Society of Japan [*A publication*]
**J Met Finish Soc Jpn** ... Journal. Metal Finishing Society of Japan [*A publication*]
**J Met Soc Jap** ... Journal. Meteorological Society of Japan [*A publication*]
**J Mex Am Hist** ... Journal of Mexican American History [*A publication*]
**JMF** ........... James Madison Foundation (EA)
**JMF** ........... Jet Mixing Flow
**JMF** ........... Jewish Music Forum
**JMF** ........... John Marshall Foundation (EA)
**JMF** ........... Journal of International Money and Finance [*A publication*]
**JMF** ........... Journal of Marriage and the Family [*A publication*]
**JMFC** ........ Jared Martin Fan Club (EA)
**JMFC** ........ Jayne Mansfield Fan Club (EA)
**JMFC** ........ Jimmy Murphy Fan Club (EA)
**JMFT** ........ Journal of Milk and Food Technology [*Later, Journal of Food Protection*] [*A publication*]
**J f MG** ....... Jahrbuch fuer Mineralogie und Geologie [*A publication*]
**JMG** .......... Jewelry Manufacturers Guild (EA)
**JMG** .......... Joint Meteorological Group [*DoD*]
**JMG** .......... Journal of Information and Image Management [*A publication*]
**JMG** .......... Journal of Management Consulting [*A publication*]
**JMG** .......... Journal of Metamorphic Geology [*A publication*]
**JMG** .......... Journal of Micrographics [*A publication*]
**JMG** .......... Journal of Molecular Graphics [*A publication*]
**JMGA**........ Jewellers and Metalsmiths Group of Australia
**JM Genet**... Journal of Medical Genetics [*A publication*]
**JMGS** ........ Journal of Modern Greek Studies [*A publication*]
**J Mgt** ......... Journal of Management [*A publication*]
**J Mgt Stud** ... Journal of Management Studies [*A publication*]
**J Mgt Studies** ... Journal of Management Studies [*A publication*]
**JMH** .......... Journal of Medieval History [*A publication*]
**JMH** .......... Journal of Mississippi History [*A publication*]
**JMH** .......... Journal of Modern History [*A publication*]
**JMI** ............ Jackson & Moreland, Incorporated (MCD)
**JMI** ............ Jan Mayen [*Jan Mayen Island*] [*Seismograph station code, US Geological Survey*] (SEIS)
**JMI** ............ John Muir Institute for Environmental Studies (EA)
**J Mich Dent Assoc** ... Journal. Michigan Dental Association [*A publication*]
**J Mich Med Soc** ... Journal. Michigan State Medical Society [*A publication*]
**J Mich State Dent Assoc** ... Journal. Michigan State Dental Association [*A publication*]
**J Mich State Dent Soc** ... Journal. Michigan State Dental Society [*A publication*]
**J Mich State Med Soc** ... Journal. Michigan State Medical Society [*A publication*]
**J Mich St Med Soc** ... Journal. Michigan State Medical Society [*A publication*]

**J Micr and Nat Sc** ... Journal of Microscopy and Natural Science [*A publication*]
**J Microb Biotechnol** ... Journal of Microbial Biotechnology [*A publication*]
**J Microbiol Epidem Immunobiol** ... Journal of Microbiology, Epidemiology, and Immunobiology [*A publication*]
**J Microbiol Epidemiol Immunobiol (USSR)** ... Journal of Microbiology, Epidemiology, and Immunobiology (USSR) [*A publication*]
**J Microbiol Methods** ... Journal of Microbiological Methods [*A publication*]
**J Microbiol UAR** ... Journal of Microbiology of the United Arab Republic [*A publication*]
**J Microcomput Appl** ... Journal of Microcomputer Applications [*A publication*]
**J Microencapsulation** ... Journal of Microencapsulation [*A publication*]
**J Microg** .... Journal de Micrographie [*A publication*]
**J Microgr**... Journal of Micrographics [*A publication*]
**J Micrographics** ... Journal of Micrographics [*A publication*]
**J Micronutr Anal** ... Journal of Micronutrient Analysis [*A publication*]
**J Microphotogr** ... Journal of Microphotography [*A publication*]
**J Microsc**... Journal de Microscopie [*France*] [*A publication*]
**J Microsc**... Journal of Microscopy [*A publication*]
**J Microsc B** ... Journal de Microscopie et de Biologie Cellulaire [*A publication*]
**J Microsc Biol Cell** ... Journal de Microscopie et de Biologie Cellulaire [*A publication*]
**J Microsc (O)** ... Journal of Microscopy (Oxford) [*A publication*]
**J Microscopie** ... Journal de Microscopie [*A publication*]
**J Microscopy** ... Journal of Microscopy [*A publication*]
**J Microsc (Oxf)** ... Journal of Microscopy (Oxford) [*A publication*]
**J Microsc (Paris)** ... Journal de Microscopie (Paris) [*A publication*]
**J Microsc Soc** ... Journal. Royal Microscopical Society [*A publication*]
**J Microsc et Spectrosc Electron** ... Journal de Microscopie et de Spectroscopie Electroniques [*A publication*]
**J Microsc Spectrosc Electron** ... Journal de Microscopie et de Spectroscopie Electroniques [*A publication*]
**J Microsc Spectrosc Electron (France)** ... Journal de Microscopie et de Spectroscopie Electroniques (France) [*A publication*]
**J Microsurg** ... Journal of Microsurgery [*A publication*]
**J Microwave Power** ... Journal of Microwave Power [*A publication*]
**J Microwave Pwr** ... Journal of Microwave Power [*A publication*]
**JMIE**......... Joint Maritime Information Element [*Coast Guard*]
**J Mie Med Coll** ... Journal. Mie Medical College [*A publication*]
**JMIFC**....... Jeanette MacDonald International Fan Club (EA)
**JMIFC**....... Johnny Mathis International Fan Club (EA)
**JMiH**......... Journal of Mississippi History [*A publication*]
**J Milk Food** ... Journal of Milk and Food Technology [*Later, Journal of Food Protection*] [*A publication*]
**J Milk & Food Tech** ... Journal of Milk and Food Technology [*Later, Journal of Food Protection*] [*A publication*]
**J Milk Food Technol** ... Journal of Milk and Food Technology [*Later, Journal of Food Protection*] [*A publication*]
**J Milk Tech** ... Journal of Milk Technology [*A publication*]
**J Mil Serv Inst** ... Journal. Military Service Institution [*A publication*]
**J Mil Soc**... Journal of Political and Military Sociology [*A publication*]
**J Min Coll Akita Univ Ser A** ... Journal. Mining College. Akita University. Series A. Mining Geology [*A publication*]
**J Mineral Petrol Econ Geol** ... Journal of Mineralogy, Petrology, and Economic Geology [*A publication*]
**J Mineral Soc Jpn** ... Journal. Mineralogical Society of Japan [*A publication*]
**J Mines Met Fuels** ... Journal of Mines, Metals, and Fuels [*A publication*]
**J Mines Met Fuels (Calcutta)** ... Journal of Mines, Metals, and Fuels (Calcutta) [*A publication*]
**J Mine Vent Soc S Afr** ... Journal. Mine Ventilation Society of South Africa [*A publication*]
**J Min Geol** ... Journal of Mining and Geology [*Nigeria*] [*A publication*]
**J Mining Met Inst Jap** ... Journal. Mining and Metallurgical Institute of Japan [*A publication*]
**J Min Inst Kyushu** ... Journal. Mining Institute of Kyushu [*Japan*] [*A publication*]
**J Minist Agric (GB)** ... Journal. Ministry of Agriculture (Great Britain) [*A publication*]
**J Minist Hlth** ... Journal. Ministry of Health [*A publication*]
**J Ministry Ag** ... Agriculture (Journal of the Ministry of Agriculture) [*A publication*]
**J Min Metall Inst Jap** ... Journal. Mining and Metallurgical Institute of Japan [*A publication*]
**J Minn Acad Sci** ... Journal. Minnesota Academy of Science [*A publication*]
**JMIR**......... Journal. Ministere de l'Instruction Publique en Russie [*A publication*]
**J Miss Acad Sci** ... Journal. Mississippi Academy of Sciences [*A publication*]
**JMissH**...... Journal of Mississippi History [*A publication*]
**J Miss Hist** ... Journal of Mississippi History [*A publication*]
**J Mississippi Med Ass** ... Journal. Mississippi State Medical Association [*A publication*]
**J Miss Med Ass** ... Journal. Mississippi State Medical Association [*A publication*]
**J Miss State Med Assoc** ... Journal. Mississippi State Medical Association [*A publication*]
**J Miss St Med Ass** ... Journal. Mississippi State Medical Association [*A publication*]
**JMJ**.......... Jesus, Mary, and Joseph
**JMJ**.......... John Marshall Journal of Practice and Procedure [*A publication*]
**JMJ**.......... Johnston Airways [*Chicago, IL*] [*FAA designator*] (FAAC)
**JMK**.......... Journal of Marketing [*A publication*]
**JMK**.......... Mikonos [*Greece*] [*Airport symbol*] (OAG)
**JMKNA2**... Annual Reports. Institute of Population Problems [*A publication*]
**JMKOA**..... Jemna Mechanika a Optika [*A publication*]
**J Mkt**........ Journal of Marketing [*A publication*]
**J Mktg**....... Journal of Marketing [*A publication*]
**J Mktg Res** ... Journal of Marketing Research [*A publication*]
**J Mkting**.... Journal of Marketing [*A publication*]
**J Mkting Res** ... Journal of Marketing Research [*A publication*]
**J Mkt Res** ... Journal of Marketing Research [*A publication*]
**JMKU** ....... Journal of Mathematics. Kyoto University [*A publication*]
**JML**.......... James Madison [*AMEX symbol*] (SPSG)
**JML**.......... Journal of Modern Literature [*A publication*]
**JMLC**........ James Madison Ltd. [*NASDAQ symbol*] (NQ)
**JM Ling**..... Journal of Mayan Linguistics [*A publication*]
**JMLR**........ John Marshall Law Review [*A publication*]
**JMLS** ........ John Marshall Law School [*Chicago, IL*] (DLA)
**JMLS** ........ John Menzies Library Services [*Information service or system*] (IID)
**JMM** ......... Jacobi Matrix Method [*Mathematics*]
**JMM** ......... Journal of Macromarketing [*A publication*]
**JMM** ......... Journal. Manx Museum [*A publication*]
**JMM** ......... Journal de la Marine Marchande et de la Navigation Aerienne [*A publication*]
**JMM** ......... Journal of Microbiological Methods [*A publication*]
**JMMAA**.... Journal. Maine Medical Association [*A publication*]
**JMMF**....... James Monroe Memorial Foundation (EA)
**JMMMD**.. Journal of Magnetism and Magnetic Materials [*A publication*]
**JMMNA**... Journal de la Marine Marchande et de la Navigation Aerienne [*A publication*]
**JMMSD**.... Journal. Korea Merchant Marine College. Natural Sciences Series [*A publication*]
**JMN**.......... Jeweled-Orifice Misting Nozzle
**JMN**.......... Johan Mangku Negara [*Malaysian Honour*]
**JMN**.......... Journal of Management Studies [*A publication*]
**JMNCL**..... Jeunesse du Mouvement National Congolaise - Lumumba [*Youth of the Lumumba Wing of the Congolese National Movement*]
**J/Mne**........ Junior Marine [*British military*] (DMA)
**JMO**.......... Jomsom [*Nepal*] [*Airport symbol*] (OAG)
**JMO**.......... Jugoslovenska Muslimanska Organizacija [*Yugoslav Moslem Organization*] [*Political party*] (PPE)
**J MO B**...... Journal. Missouri Bar [*A publication*]
**J MO Bar**.. Journal. Missouri Bar [*A publication*]
**J Mod Afric Stud** ... Journal of Modern African Studies [*A publication*]
**J Mod Afr S** ... Journal of Modern African Studies [*A publication*]
**J Mod Afr Stud** ... Journal of Modern African Studies [*A publication*]
**J MO Dent Assoc** ... Journal. Missouri Dental Association [*A publication*]
**J Mod Hist** ... Journal of Modern History [*A publication*]
**J Mod Lit**... Journal of Modern Literature [*A publication*]
**J/MOL**...... Joules per Mole [*Physics*]
**J Mol Appl Genet** ... Journal of Molecular and Applied Genetics [*A publication*]
**J Mol Biol** ... Journal of Molecular Biology [*A publication*]
**J Mol Catal** ... Journal of Molecular Catalysis [*A publication*]
**J Mol Catal (China)** ... Journal of Molecular Catalysis (China) [*A publication*]
**J Mol Cel C** ... Journal of Molecular and Cellular Cardiology [*A publication*]
**J Mol Cell Cardiol** ... Journal of Molecular and Cellular Cardiology [*A publication*]
**J Molec Biol** ... Journal of Molecular Biology [*A publication*]
**J Mol Endocrinol** ... Journal of Molecular Endocrinology [*A publication*]
**J Mol Evol** ... Journal of Molecular Evolution [*A publication*]
**J/(MOL K)** ... Joules per Mole Kelvin [*Physics*]
**J Mol Liq**... Journal of Molecular Liquids [*A publication*]
**J Molluscan Stud** ... Journal of Molluscan Studies [*A publication*]
**J Molluscan Stud Suppl** ... Journal of Molluscan Studies. Supplement [*A publication*]
**J Mol Med** ... Journal of Molecular Medicine [*A publication*]
**J Mol Spect** ... Journal of Molecular Spectroscopy [*A publication*]
**J Mol Spectrosc** ... Journal of Molecular Spectroscopy [*A publication*]
**J Mol Struct** ... Journal of Molecular Structure [*A publication*]
**J Mond Pharm** ... Journal Mondial de Pharmacie [*A publication*]
**J Monetary Econ** ... Journal of Monetary Economics [*A publication*]
**J Money Cred Bank** ... Journal of Money, Credit, and Banking [*A publication*]
**J Money Cred & Bank** ... Journal of Money, Credit, and Banking [*A publication*]
**J Money Credit Bank** ... Journal of Money, Credit, and Banking [*A publication*]
**J Money Credit & Banking** ... Journal of Money, Credit, and Banking [*A publication*]
**J Moral Ed** ... Journal of Moral Education [*A publication*]
**J Moral Educ** ... Journal of Moral Education [*A publication*]
**J Mormon Hist** ... Journal of Mormon History [*A publication*]
**J Morph**..... Journal of Morphology [*A publication*]
**J Morphol** ... Journal of Morphology [*A publication*]
**J Morphol Physiol** ... Journal of Morphology and Physiology [*A publication*]

**J Morph and Physiol** ... Journal of Morphology and Physiology [*A publication*]
**J Moscow Patr** ... Journal of the Moscow Patriarchate [*A publication*]
**J Mot Behav** ... Journal of Motor Behavior [*A publication*]
**J Motion Pict Soc India** ... Journal. Motion Picture Society of India [*A publication*]
**J Motor Beh** ... Journal of Motor Behavior [*A publication*]
**J MO Water Sewage Conf** ... Journal. Missouri Water and Sewage Conference [*A publication*]
**JMP**.......... Jack Morton Productions, Inc. [*New York, NY*] [*Telecommunications*] (TSSD)
**JMP**.......... John M. Poindexter [*National Security Advisor during the Reagan Administration*]
**JMP**.......... Johnson Matthey Public Ltd. Co. [*Toronto Stock Exchange symbol*]
**JMP**.......... Joint Manpower Program [*Military*] (CINC)
**J du MP**..... Journal du Ministere Public [*A publication*]
**JMP**.......... Journal of Public Policy and Marketing [*A publication*]
**JMP**.......... Jump [*Data processing*]
**JMP**.......... Peters [*J. M.*] [*AMEX symbol*] (SPSG)
**JMPAB**..... Joint Materiel Priorities and Allocation Board [*Military*] (AABC)
**JMPC**........ Joint Military Procurements Control [*World War II*]
**JMPMA**.... Journal of Medical Primatology [*A publication*]
**JMPO**........ Journal of Microwave Power [*A publication*]
**JMPP**........ Joint Munitions Production Panel (MCD)
**JMPPD**..... Journal of Marketing and Public Policy [*A publication*]
**JMPR**........ Jumper (MSA)
**JMPSB**...... Journal of Mathematical and Physical Sciences [*A publication*]
**JMPT**........ Joint Military Potential Test (MCD)
**JMPT**........ Journal of Manipulative and Physiological Therapeutics [*A publication*]
**JMPTC**..... Joint Military Packaging Training Center
**JmQ**.......... Journalism Quarterly [*A publication*]
**JMR**.......... Jamair, Inc. [*Camden, AR*] [*FAA designator*] (FAAC)
**JMR**.......... Johannesburg Mounted Rifles [*British military*] (DMA)
**JMR**.......... Journal of Marketing Research [*A publication*]
**JMRAS**..... Journal. Malayan Branch. Royal Asiatic Society [*A publication*]
**JMRC**........ Joint Mobile Relay Center (MCD)
**JMRE**........ JM Resources, Inc. [*NASDAQ symbol*] (NQ)
**JMRO**....... Joint Medical Regulating Office (AABC)
**JMRO**....... Joint Military Regulating Office
**JMRP**........ Joint Meteorological Radio Propagation Committee [*British*] (MCD)
**JMRPDC**.. Japan Medical Research Foundation. Publication [*A publication*]
**JMRS**........ Journal. Market Research Society [*A publication*]
**JMRS**........ Journal of Medieval and Renaissance Studies [*A publication*]
**JMRT**........ Junior Members Round Table [*American Library Association*]
**JMS**.......... Jacob More Society (EA)
**JMS**.......... Jamestown [*North Dakota*] [*Airport symbol*] (OAG)
**JMS**.......... Jamestown, ND [*Location identifier*] [*FAA*] (FAAL)
**JMS**.......... Jewish Media Service (EA)
**JMS**.......... John Milton Society for the Blind [*Later, JMSB*] (EA)
**JMS**.......... Joint Movements Staff [*British*]
**JMS**.......... Journal of Maltese Studies [*A publication*]
**JMS**.......... Journal of Management Studies [*A publication*]
**JMS**.......... Jump to Subroutine Instruction [*Data processing*]
**JMSAC**..... Joint Meteorological Satellite Advisory Committee
**JMSB**........ John Milton Society for the Blind (EA)
**JMSBA**..... Journal of Mental Subnormality [*A publication*]
**JmSC**......... Japan Microfilm Service Center Co. Ltd., Tokyo, Japan [*Library symbol*] [*Library of Congress*] (LCLS)
**JMSCA**..... Journal of Mental Science [*A publication*]
**JMSDC**..... Joint Merchant Shipping Defence Committee [*General Council of British Shipping*] (DS)
**JMSDF**...... Japanese Maritime Self-Defense Force
**JMSED**..... Journal de Microscopie et de Spectroscopie Electroniques [*A publication*]
**JMSJ**......... Journal. Mathematical Society of Japan [*A publication*]
**JMSLS**...... Joliet Three-Minute Speech and Language Screen [*Test*]
**JMSMD**.... Journal of Materials for Energy Systems [*A publication*]
**JMSNA**..... Journal. Medical Society of New Jersey [*A publication*]
**JMSNS**..... Justification of Major System New Start [*Military*]
**JMSPO**..... Joint Meteorological Satellite Program Office
**JMSUB**..... Journal. Maharaja Sayajirao University of Baroda [*A publication*]
**JMSX**........ Job Memory Switch Matrix
**JMT**.......... Job Methods Training
**JMT**.......... Joint Management Team (MCD)
**JMT**.......... Journal of Music Therapy [*A publication*]
**JMT**.......... Judgment (DCTA)
**JMTAA**..... Journal. Institute of Mathematics and Its Applications [*A publication*]
**JMTB**........ Joint Military Transportation Board
**JMTC**........ Joint Military Transportation Committee
**JMTE**........ Journal. Michigan Teachers of English [*A publication*]
**JMTG**........ Joint Military Task Group (MUGU)
**JMTG**........ Joint Military Terminology Group (AFM)
**JMTheory** ... Journal of Music Theory [*A publication*]
**JMTherapy** ... Journal of Music Therapy [*A publication*]
**J Mt Sinai Hosp** ... Journal. Mount Sinai Hospital [*A publication*]
**JMTSS**...... Joint Multichannel Trunking and Switching System (MCD)
**JMU**.......... James Madison University [*Virginia*]
**JMU**.......... Jamshedpur Mazdoor Union [*India*]
**JMUEOS**.. Journal. Manchester University. Egyptian and Oriental Society [*A publication*]
**JMultiAn**... Journal of Multivariate Analysis [*A publication*]
**J Multivar Anal** ... Journal of Multivariate Analysis [*A publication*]
**J Multivariate Anal** ... Journal of Multivariate Analysis [*A publication*]
**JMUSA**..... Journal. American Musicological Society [*A publication*]
**J Muscle Res Cell Motil** ... Journal of Muscle Research and Cell Motility [*A publication*]
**JMUSDC**.. Joint Mexican-United States Defense Commission
**J Mus Francais** ... Journal Musical Francais [*A publication*]
**J Music Res** ... Journal of Musicological Research [*A publication*]
**J Music Ther** ... Journal of Music Therapy [*A publication*]
**J Music Thr** ... Journal of Music Theory [*A publication*]
**J/Musn**...... Junior Musician [*British military*] (DMA)
**J Mus Theory** ... Journal of Music Theory [*A publication*]
**J Mus Ther** ... Journal of Music Therapy [*A publication*]
**J Mus Therapy** ... Journal of Music Therapy [*A publication*]
**JMUTA**..... Journal of Music Therapy [*A publication*]
**JMUTB**..... Journal of Music Theory [*A publication*]
**JMV**.......... Jahresschrift fuer Mitteldeutsche Vorgeschichte [*A publication*]
**JMVB**........ Joint Merchant Vessels Board [*World War II*]
**JMVL**........ Jahrbuch. Museum fuer Voelkerkunde zu Leipzig [*A publication*]
**JMW**......... James McNeill Whistler [*Nineteenth-century American painter and etcher*]
**JMX**.......... Jumbogroup Multiplex [*Bell System*]
**JMY**.......... Jamesway Corp. [*NYSE symbol*] (SPSG)
**J Mysore Agr Exp Union** ... Journal. Mysore Agricultural and Experimental Union [*A publication*]
**J Mysore Med Assoc** ... Journal. Mysore Medical Association [*A publication*]
**J Mysore U Arts** ... Journal. Mysore University. Section A. Arts [*A publication*]
**J Mysore Univ Sect B** ... Journal. Mysore University. Section B [*A publication*]
**J Mysore Univ Sect B Sci** ... Journal. Mysore University. Section B. Science [*India*] [*A publication*]
**JMYUAP**.. Journal. Mysore University. Section B. Science [*A publication*]
**jn**............... Jan Mayen [*MARC country of publication code*] [*Library of Congress*] (LCCP)
**JN**............. Jannock Ltd. [*Toronto Stock Exchange symbol*]
**J-N**............ Jet Navigation (AAG)
**JN**............. Jet Navigation Chart
**JN**............. Jewish Newsletter [*A publication*]
**JN**............. Jim's Neighbors (EA)
**JN**............. Job Number
**Jn**.............. John [*New Testament book*]
**JN**............. John Nurminen [*Finland*] [*ICAO designator*] (FAAC)
**JN**............. Johnson Noise [*Thermal noise, that made by a resistor at a temperature above absolute zero*]
**JN**............. Johnsonian Newsletter [*A publication*]
**JN**............. Join (MSA)
**JN**............. Journal Name [*Online database field identifier*]
**JN**............. Journal of Neuroscience [*A publication*]
**JN**............. Journal Numismatique [*A publication*]
**Jn**.............. Juglans nigra [*Eastern black walnut*]
**JN**............. Juilliard News Bulletin [*A publication*]
**JN**............. Junction
**JN**............. June (ROG)
**JN**............. Junior (ROG)
**Jn**.............. King John [*Shakespearean work*]
**JNA**........... Jena Nomina Anatomica [*Anatomy*]
**JNA**........... Jewish News Agency (BJA)
**JNA**........... Jordanian News Agency
**JNA**........... Junior Naval Airman [*British military*] (DMA)
**JNA**........... Northern Illinois University, De Kalb, IL [*OCLC symbol*] (OCLC)
**JNAA**........ Journal. National Academy of Administration [*India*] [*A publication*]
**JNABD**...... Journal of Nuclear Agriculture and Biology [*A publication*]
**JNAC**......... Japan-North American Commission on Cooperative Mission (EA)
**JNACC**...... Joint Nuclear Accident Coordinating Center
**JNAFS**....... Journal of Northwest Atlantic Fishery Science [*A publication*]
**J Nagoya City Univ Med Assoc** ... Journal. Nagoya City University Medical Association [*Japan*] [*A publication*]
**J Nagoya Med Assoc** ... Journal. Nagoya Medical Association [*A publication*]
**JNAL**......... Jackson National Life [*NASDAQ symbol*] (NQ)
**JNALA**...... Journal of the New African Literature and the Arts [*A publication*]
**JNAM**....... Junior Naval Air Mechanic [*British military*] (DMA)
**J Nanjing Inst For** ... Journal. Nanjing Institute of Forestry [*A publication*]
**J Nanjing Inst Technol** ... Journal. Nanjing Institute of Technology [*A publication*]
**J Nanjing Technol Coll For Prod** ... Journal. Nanjing Technological College of Forest Products [*A publication*]
**J Nara Gakugei Univ** ... Journal. Nara Gakugei University [*Japan*] [*A publication*]

**J Nara Med Ass** ... Journal. Nara Medical Association [*A publication*]
**J Nara Med Assoc** ... Journal. Nara Medical Association [*A publication*]
**JNA Referees Bank** ... Journal. National Association of Referees in Bankruptcy [*A publication*] (DLA)
**J Narr Tech** ... Journal of Narrative Technique [*A publication*]
**JNAT**......... Jefferson National Life [*NASDAQ symbol*] (NQ)
**J Natal Zulu Hist** ... Journal of Natal and Zulu History [*A publication*]
**J Nat Assn Col Adm Counsel** ... Journal. National Association of College Admissions Counselors [*A publication*]
**J Nat Canc** ... Journal. National Cancer Institute [*A publication*]
**J Nat Cancer Inst** ... Journal. National Cancer Institute [*A publication*]
**J Nat Chem Lab Ind** ... Journal. National Chemical Laboratory for Industry [*Japan*] [*A publication*]
**J Nat Chiao Tung Univ** ... National Chiao Tung University. Journal [*A publication*]
**J Nat Hist** ... Journal of Natural History [*A publication*]
**J Nat Inst Hospital Adm** ... Journal. National Institute of Hospital Administration [*A publication*]
**J Nat Inst Soc Sci** ... Journal. National Institute of Social Sciences [*A publication*]
**J Natl Acad Sci** ... Journal. National Academy of Sciences [*Republic of Korea*] [*A publication*]
**J Natl Acad Sci (Repub Korea) Nat Sci Ser** ... Journal. National Academy of Sciences (Republic of Korea). Natural Sciences Series [*A publication*]
**J Natl Agric Soc Ceylon** ... Journal. National Agricultural Society of Ceylon [*A publication*]
**J Natl Analg Soc** ... Journal. National Analgesia Society [*US*] [*A publication*]
**J Natl Assn Coll Adm Counsel** ... Journal. National Association of College Admissions Counselors [*A publication*]
**J Natl Assn Women Deans Adm & Counsel** ... Journal. National Association for Women Deans, Administrators, and Counselors [*A publication*]
**J Natl Assoc Hosp Dev** ... Journal. National Association for Hospital Development [*US*] [*A publication*]
**J Natl Assoc Priv Psychiatr Hosp** ... Journal. National Association of Private Psychiatric Hospitals [*US*] [*A publication*]
**J Natl Cancer Inst** ... Journal. National Cancer Institute [*A publication*]
**J Natl Chem Lab Ind** ... Journal. National Chemical Laboratory for Industry [*Japan*] [*A publication*]
**J Natl Chiao Tung Univ** ... Journal. National Chiao Tung University [*A publication*]
**J Natl Def Med Coll** ... Journal. National Defense Medical College [*A publication*]
**J Natl Inst Agric Bot** ... Journal. National Institute of Agricultural Botany [*A publication*]
**J Natl Inst Pers Res S Afr CSIR** ... Journal. National Institute for Personnel Research. South African Council for Scientific and Industrial Research [*A publication*]
**J Natl Med Assoc** ... Journal. [*US*] National Medical Association [*A publication*]
**J Natl Res Counc Thail** ... Journal. National Research Council of Thailand [*A publication*]
**J Natl Res Counc Thailand** ... Journal. National Research Council of Thailand [*A publication*]
**J Natl Sci Counc Sri Lanka** ... Journal. National Science Council of Sri Lanka [*A publication*]
**J Natl Tech Assoc** ... Journal. National Technical Association [*United States*] [*A publication*]
**J Natn Cancer Inst** ... Journal. National Cancer Institute [*A publication*]
**J Natn Inst Agric Bot** ... Journal. National Institute of Agricultural Botany [*A publication*]
**J Nat Prod** ... Journal of Natural Products [*A publication*]
**J Nat Prod (Lloydia)** ... Journal of Natural Products (Lloydia) [*A publication*]
**J Nat Res Coun Thai** ... Journal. National Research Council of Thailand [*A publication*]
**J Nat Rubber Res** ... Journal of Natural Rubber Research [*A publication*]
**J Nat Sci**.... Journal of Natural Sciences [*Malaysia*] [*A publication*]
**J Nat Sci Chonnam Natl Univ** ... Journal of Natural Science. Chonnam National University [*A publication*]
**J Nat Sci and Math** ... Journal of National Science and Mathematics [*A publication*]
**J Nat Sci Math** ... Journal of Natural Sciences and Mathematics [*A publication*]
**J Nat Sci Math (Lahore)** ... Journal of Natural Sciences and Mathematics (Lahore) [*A publication*]
**J Nat Sci Res Inst** ... Journal. Natural Science Research Institute. Yonsei University [*Republic of Korea*] [*A publication*]
**J Nat Sci Res Inst Yonsei Univ** ... Journal. Natural Science Research Institute. Yonsei University [*A publication*]
**J Nat Sci Soc Ichimura Gakuen J Coll** ... Journal. Natural Scientific Society. Ichimura Gakuen Junior College [*A publication*]
**J Nat Sci Soc Ichimura Gakuen Univ Ichimura Gakuen J Coll** ... Journal. Natural Scientific Society. Ichimura Gakuen University and Ichimura Gakuen Junior College [*A publication*]
**J Nat Sci Yeungnam Univ** ... Journal of Natural Sciences. Yeungnam University [*A publication*]
**J Natural Hist** ... Journal of Natural History [*A publication*]
**J Natur Sci and Math** ... Journal of Natural Sciences and Mathematics [*A publication*]
**J Natur Sci Math** ... Journal of Natural Sciences and Mathematics [*A publication*]
**J Naut Arch** ... International Journal of Nautical Archaeology and Underwater Exploration [*A publication*]
**J Naut Soc Jpn** ... Journal. Nautical Society of Japan [*A publication*]
**J Navig**....... Journal of Navigation [*A publication*]
**J Navigation** ... Royal Institute of Navigation. Journal of Navigation [*London*] [*A publication*]
**J NAWDAC** ... Journal. National Association for Women Deans, Administrators, and Counselors [*A publication*]
**JNB**............ Johannesburg [*South Africa*] [*Airport symbol*] (OAG)
**JNBIA**....... Journal. Newark Beth Israel Hospital [*A publication*]
**JNBK**......... Jefferson National Bank [*Watertown, NY*] [*NASDAQ symbol*] (NQ)
**JNBMDW** ... Journal. New Brunswick Museum [*A publication*]
**J NB Mus**.. Journal. New Brunswick Museum [*A publication*]
**JNC**........... Jet Navigation Chart
**JNC**........... Joint Negotiating Council [*British*] (DCTA)
**JNC**........... Journal. National Cancer Institute [*A publication*]
**JNC**........... Junction (ADA)
**J NC Dent Soc** ... Journal. North Carolina Dental Society [*A publication*]
**JNCG**......... Japan Nuclear Codes Group
**J N Ch R A S** ... Journal. North China Branch. Royal Asiatic Society [*A publication*]
**JNCI**.......... JNCI. Journal of the National Cancer Institute [*A publication*]
**JNCL**......... Joint National Committee for Languages (EA)
**JNCLA**...... Journal. National Chemical Laboratory for Industry [*A publication*]
**JNCO**........ Junior Non-Commissioned Officer [*British military*] (DMA)
**JNC Referees Bank** ... Journal. National Conference of Referees in Bankruptcy [*A publication*] (DLA)
**J NC Sect Am Water Works Assoc NC Water Pollut Control Assoc** ... Journal. North Carolina Section of the American Water Works Association and North Carolina Water Pollution Control Association [*A publication*]
**JNCUD**..... Journal of Natural Science. Chonnam National University [*A publication*]
**JNCYA**...... Journal of Neurocytology [*A publication*]
**JND**........... Just Noticeable Difference [*Psychology*]
**J NDI**......... Journal of NDI [*Japan*] [*A publication*]
**JNDRA**....... Journal of New Drugs [*A publication*]
**Jn D Rv**...... Jane's Defence Review [*A publication*]
**JNE**............ Ja Niin Edespain [*And So On*] [*Finnish*]
**Jne**............ Jeune [*Junior*] [*French*]
**JNE**............ Journal of Near Eastern Studies [*A publication*]
**JNE**............ Journal of Negro Education [*A publication*]
**JNE**............ Journal of Nursing Education [*A publication*]
**JNE**............ Journal of Nutrition Education [*A publication*]
**J Near East** ... Journal of Near Eastern Studies [*A publication*]
**J Near Eastern Stud** ... Journal of Near Eastern Studies [*A publication*]
**J Near East St** ... Journal of Near Eastern Studies [*A publication*]
**J Near East Stud** ... Journal of Near Eastern Studies [*A publication*]
**J Near E St** ... Journal of Near Eastern Studies [*A publication*]
**J Near E Stud** ... Journal of Near Eastern Studies [*A publication*]
**J Nebr Dent Assoc** ... Journal. Nebraska Dental Association [*A publication*]
**JNEEA**...... Journal of Negro Education [*A publication*]
**J Ne Exp Ne** ... Journal of Neuropathology and Experimental Neurology [*A publication*]
**J of Neg Ed** ... Journal of Negro Education [*A publication*]
**J Neg Hist** ... Journal of Negro History [*A publication*]
**J Negro Ed** ... Journal of Negro Education [*A publication*]
**J Negro Educ** ... Journal of Negro Education [*A publication*]
**J of Negro Educ** ... Journal of Negro Education [*A publication*]
**J Negro His** ... Journal of Negro History [*A publication*]
**J Negro Hist** ... Journal of Negro History [*A publication*]
**J of Negro Hist** ... Journal of Negro History [*A publication*]
**JNELDA** ... Journal of Nutrition for the Elderly [*A publication*]
**J Nematol** .. Journal of Nematology [*A publication*]
**J Ne Ne Psy** ... Journal of Neurology, Neurosurgery, and Psychiatry [*A publication*]
**J N Engl Water Pollut Control Assoc** ... Journal. New England Water Pollution Control Association [*A publication*]
**J N Engl Water Works Assoc** ... Journal. New England Water Works Association [*A publication*]
**J Nepal Chem Soc** ... Journal. Nepal Chemical Society [*A publication*]
**J Nephrol Nurs** ... Journal of Nephrology Nursing [*A publication*]
**J Nerv Ment** ... Journal of Nervous and Mental Disease [*A publication*]
**J Nerv Ment Dis** ... Journal of Nervous and Mental Disease [*A publication*]
**JNES**......... Journal of Near Eastern Studies [*A publication*]
**JNETD**...... Journal of Non-Equilibrium Thermodynamics [*A publication*]
**J Neural Tr** ... Journal of Neural Transmission [*A publication*]
**J Neural Transm** ... Journal of Neural Transmission [*A publication*]
**J Neural Transm Suppl** ... Journal of Neural Transmission. Supplementum [*A publication*]
**J Neurobiol** ... Journal of Neurobiology [*A publication*]
**J Neurochem** ... Journal of Neurochemistry [*A publication*]
**J Neurocyt** ... Journal of Neurocytology [*A publication*]
**J Neurocytol** ... Journal of Neurocytology [*A publication*]
**J Neuroendocrinol** ... Journal of Neuroendocrinology [*A publication*]
**J Neurogen** ... Journal of Neurogenetics [*A publication*]
**J Neurogenet** ... Journal of Neurogenetics [*A publication*]

**J Neuroimmunol** ... Journal of Neuroimmunology [*A publication*]
**J Neuroimmunol Suppl** ... Journal of Neuroimmunology. Supplement [*A publication*]
**J Neurol** ..... Journal of Neurology [*A publication*]
**J Neurol (Berlin)** ... Journal of Neurology (Berlin) [*A publication*]
**J Neurol Neurosurg Psychiat** ... Journal of Neurology, Neurosurgery, and Psychiatry [*A publication*]
**J Neurol Neurosurg Psychiatry** ... Journal of Neurology, Neurosurgery, and Psychiatry [*A publication*]
**J Neurol Sci** ... Journal of the Neurological Sciences [*A publication*]
**J Neuro-Oncol** ... Journal of Neuro-Oncology [*A publication*]
**J Neuropath Exper Neurol** ... Journal of Neuropathology and Experimental Neurology [*A publication*]
**J Neuropath Exp Neurol** ... Journal of Neuropathology and Experimental Neurology [*A publication*]
**J Neuropathol Exp Neurol** ... Journal of Neuropathology and Experimental Neurology [*A publication*]
**J Neurophysiol** ... Journal of Neurophysiology [*A publication*]
**J Neurophysiol (Bethesda)** ... Journal of Neurophysiology (Bethesda) [*A publication*]
**J Neuropsychiat** ... Journal of Neuropsychiatry [*A publication*]
**J Neuropsychiatr Suppl** ... Journal of Neuropsychiatry. Supplement [*A publication*]
**J Neuropsychiatry** ... Journal of Neuropsychiatry [*A publication*]
**J Neuroradiol** ... Journal of Neuroradiology [*A publication*]
**J Neurosci** ... Journal of Neuroscience [*A publication*]
**J Neurosci Methods** ... Journal of Neuroscience Methods [*A publication*]
**J Neurosci Nurs** ... Journal of Neuroscience Nursing [*A publication*]
**J Neurosci Res** ... Journal of Neuroscience Research [*A publication*]
**J Neurosurg** ... Journal of Neurosurgery [*A publication*]
**J Neurosurg Nurs** ... Journal of Neurosurgical Nursing [*A publication*]
**J Neurosurg Sci** ... Journal of Neurosurgical Sciences [*A publication*]
**J Neurotrauma** ... Journal of Neurotrauma [*A publication*]
**J Neuro-Visc Relat** ... Journal of Neuro-Visceral Relations [*A publication*]
**J Neurphysl** ... Journal of Neurophysiology [*A publication*]
**J Neur Sci**.. Journal of the Neurological Sciences [*A publication*]
**J Newark Beth Israel Hosp** ... Journal. Newark Beth Israel Hospital [*United States*] [*A publication*]
**J Newark Beth Isr Hosp** ... Journal. Newark Beth Israel Hospital [*A publication*]
**J Newark Beth Isr Med Cent** ... Journal. Newark Beth Israel Medical Center [*A publication*]
**J Newcastle Sch Arts** ... Newcastle School of Arts. Journal [*A publication*] (APTA)
**J New Drugs** ... Journal of New Drugs [*A publication*]
**J New Engl Water Works Ass** ... Journal. New England Water Works Association [*A publication*]
**JNF**............ Jewish National Fund (EA)
**JNFA**......... Journal of Numismatic Fine Arts [*A publication*]
**JNFC**......... Juice Newton Fan Club (EA)
**JNFS**......... Journal of Northwest Atlantic Fishery Science [*A publication*]
**JNG**........... Jahrbuch fuer Numismatik und Geldgeschichte [*A publication*]
**JNG**........... [*The*] Jews in NAZI Germany; A Handbook of Facts Regarding Their Present Situation [*A publication*] (BJA)
**JNG**........... Joining [*Also, J*]
**JNGG**........ Jahrbuch fuer Numismatik und Geldgeschichte [*A publication*]
**JNH**........... Journal of Negro History [*A publication*]
**JNHAC**..... Jewish National Home for Asthmatic Children
**J NH Dent Soc** ... Journal. New Hampshire Dental Society [*A publication*]
**JNI**............ Jahrbuch. Nordfriesisches Institut [*A publication*]
**J Niger Assoc Dent Stud** ... Journal. Nigeria Association of Dental Students [*A publication*]
**J Nigerian Inst Oil Palm Res** ... Journal. Nigerian Institute for Oil Palm Research [*A publication*]
**J Nihon Univ Med Assoc** ... Journal. Nihon University Medical Association [*A publication*]
**J Nihon Univ Sch Dent** ... Journal. Nihon University School of Dentistry [*A publication*]
**J Nippon Med Sch** ... Journal. Nippon Medical School [*A publication*]
**JNIPRMSI** ... Japan. National Institute of Polar Research. Memoirs. Special Issue [*A publication*]
**J Nissei Hosp** ... Journal. Nissei Hospital [*Japan*] [*A publication*]
**JNJ**........... Johnson & Johnson [*NYSE symbol*] (SPSG)
**J NJ Dent Assoc** ... Journal. New Jersey Dental Association [*A publication*]
**J NJ Dent Hyg Assoc** ... Journal. New Jersey Dental Hygienists Association [*A publication*]
**J NJ State Dent Soc** ... Journal. New Jersey State Dental Society [*A publication*]
**JNKVV Res J** ... JNKVV [*Jawaharlal Nehru Krishi Vishwa Vidyalaya*] Research Journal [*A publication*]
**JNL**............ Atchison, KS [*Location identifier*] [*FAA*] (FAAL)
**JNL**............ Japanese National Laboratory
**JNL**............ Jenolan [*Australia*] [*Seismograph station code, US Geological Survey*] (SEIS)
**JNL**............ Johnsonian News Letter [*A publication*]
**JNL**............ Journal
**JNL**............ Journal of Northern Luzon [*A publication*]
**JNL**............ Journalist. Orgaan van de Nederlandse Vereniging van Journalisten [*A publication*]
**Jnl Aesthetics** ... Journal of Aesthetics and Art Criticism [*A publication*]
**Jnl Aesthetics & Art Crit** ... Journal of Aesthetics and Art Criticism [*A publication*]
**Jnl Am Folklore** ... Journal of American Folklore [*A publication*]
**Jnl Am Hist** ... Journal of American History [*A publication*]
**Jnl of Archtl Education** ... Journal of Architectural Education [*A publication*]
**Jnl of Archtl Research** ... Journal of Architectural Research [*A publication*]
**Jnl Asian Stu** ... Journal of Asian Studies [*A publication*]
**Jnl Basque Stud** ... Journal of Basque Studies [*A publication*]
**Jnl Business Ed** ... Journal of Business Education [*A publication*]
**Jnl of Canadian Art History** ... Journal of Canadian Art History [*A publication*]
**Jnl Cardiac Rehab** ... Journal of Cardiac Rehabilitation [*A publication*]
**Jnl Counsel Psych** ... Journal of Counseling Psychology [*A publication*]
**Jnl Econ Hist** ... Journal of Economic History [*A publication*]
**Jnl Engl Ger Philol** ... Journal of English and Germanic Philology [*A publication*]
**Jnl of Environmental Psychology** ... Journal of Environmental Psychology [*A publication*]
**Jnl of Garden History** ... Journal of Garden History [*A publication*]
**Jnl Gen Ed** ... Journal of General Education [*A publication*]
**Jnl Higher Ed** ... Journal of Higher Education [*A publication*]
**Jnl Hist Ideas** ... Journal of the History of Ideas [*A publication*]
**Jnl Home Econ** ... Journal of Home Economics [*A publication*]
**Jnl Inst Eng (Fed Malaysia)** ... Journal. Institution of Engineers (Federation of Malaysia) [*A publication*]
**Jnl Ital Ling** ... Journal of Italian Linguistics [*A publication*]
**Jnl Lib Hist** ... Journal of Library History [*Later, Journal of Library History, Philosophy, and Comparative Librarianship*] [*A publication*]
**Jnl Life Sci** ... Journal of Life Sciences [*A publication*]
**Jnl Marketing** ... Journal of Marketing [*A publication*]
**Jnl Marr & Fam** ... Journal of Marriage and the Family [*A publication*]
**Jnl Mod Hist** ... Journal of Modern History [*A publication*]
**Jnl Negro Ed** ... Journal of Negro Education [*A publication*]
**Jnl Negro Hist** ... Journal of Negro History [*A publication*]
**JnlOBP**...... Journal of Black Poetry [*A publication*]
**Jnl Ocular Ther Surg** ... Journal of Ocular Therapy and Surgery [*A publication*]
**JnlONJP**... Journal of New Jersey Poets [*A publication*]
**JnlOPC**...... Journal of Popular Culture [*A publication*]
**Jnl Philos**... Journal of Philosophy [*A publication*]
**Jnl of Planning & Environment Law** ... Journal of Planning and Environment Law [*A publication*]
**Jnl Polit Econ** ... Journal of Political Economy [*A publication*]
**Jnl Politics** ... Journal of Politics [*A publication*]
**Jnl Relig**...... Journal of Religion [*A publication*]
**JNLS**......... Journals (ADA)
**JNLST**....... Journalist
**JNM**.......... JNM. Journal of Nuclear Medicine [*A publication*]
**JNMD**....... Journal of Nervous and Mental Disease [*A publication*]
**JNMDA**...... Journal of Nervous and Mental Disease [*A publication*]
**JNMED**..... Journal of Neuroscience Methods [*A publication*]
**JNMM**...... Journal of the Institute of Nuclear Materials Management [*A publication*] (EAAP)
**JNMR**....... Joint National Media Research [*Database producer*]
**JNMSD**..... Journal of Nuclear Medicine and Allied Sciences [*A publication*]
**JNMTA**..... Journal of Nonmetals [*Later, Semiconductors and Insulators*] [*England*] [*A publication*]
**JNND**........ Just Not Noticeable Difference (MSA)
**JNNPA**...... Journal of Neurology, Neurosurgery, and Psychiatry [*A publication*]
**JNNVA**..... Jaarboek. Nederlandse Natuurkundige Vereniging [*A publication*]
**JNOC**........ Japan National Oil Corporation
**J No Luzon** ... Journal of Northern Luzon [*A publication*]
**J Non-Cryst** ... Journal of Non-Crystalline Solids [*A publication*]
**J Non-Cryst Solids** ... Journal of Non-Crystalline Solids [*A publication*]
**J Nondestr Eval** ... Journal of Nondestructive Evaluation [*United States*] [*A publication*]
**J Non-Destr Insp** ... Journal of Non-Destructive Inspection [*A publication*]
**J Non-Equilib Thermodyn** ... Journal of Non-Equilibrium Thermodynamics [*A publication*]
**J Nonmet** ... Journal of Nonmetals [*Later, Semiconductors and Insulators*] [*A publication*]
**J Nonmet Semicond** ... Journal of Nonmetals and Semiconductors [*Later, Semiconductors and Insulators*] [*A publication*]
**J Nonmet and Semicond** ... Journal of Nonmetals and Semiconductors [*Later, Semiconductors and Insulators*] [*A publication*]
**J Non-Newtonian Fluid Mech** ... Journal of Non-Newtonian Fluid Mechanics [*A publication*]
**J Nonverbal Behav** ... Journal of Nonverbal Behavior [*A publication*]
**J Northampton Mus** ... Journal. Northampton Museum and Art Gallery [*A publication*]
**J Northamptonshire Natur Hist Soc Fld Club** ... Journal. Northamptonshire Natural History Society and Field Club [*A publication*]
**J Northeast Asian Studies** ... Journal of Northeast Asian Studies [*A publication*]
**J Northwest Atl Fish Sci** ... Journal of Northwest Atlantic Fishery Science [*A publication*]

**J Northwest Univ Nat Sci Ed** ... Journal. Northwest University. Natural Science Edition [*A publication*]
**J Norw Med Assoc** ... Journal. Norwegian Medical Association [*A publication*]
**JNOS**......... Jahrbuecher fuer Nationaloekonomie und Statistik [*A publication*]
**JNP**........... Joint Nuclear Plot (CINC)
**JNP**........... Newport Beach, CA [*Location identifier*] [*FAA*] (FAAL)
**JNPAB**...... Journal of Personality Assessment [*A publication*]
**JNPE**......... Joint Nuclear Planning Element (MCD)
**JNPI**.......... Jetevator Null Position Indicator
**JNPRD**....... Journal of Natural Products [*A publication*]
**JNPS**......... Journal. Nagari Pracarini Sabha [*A publication*]
**JNR**........... Hamilton Aeroservices [*Trenton, NJ*] [*FAA designator*] (FAAC)
**JNR**........... Japan National Railways
**JNR**........... June Resources, Inc. [*Vancouver Stock Exchange symbol*]
**JNR**........... Junior (EY)
**JNR**........... Unalakleet, AK [*Location identifier*] [*FAA*] (FAAL)
**JNRC**......... Joint Nuclear Research Center [*EURATOM*]
**JNRI**.......... Joint Nuclear Research Institute [*USSR*]
**JNRM**....... Journal of Natural Resources Management and Interdisciplinary Studies [*A publication*]
**JNROTC**... Junior Naval Reserve Officer Training Corps
**JNRREQ**... Journal of Natural Rubber Research [*A publication*]
**JNS**........... International Graduate School, St. Louis, MO [*OCLC symbol*] (OCLC)
**JNS**........... Jahrbuecher fuer National-Oekonomie und Statistik [*A publication*]
**JNS**........... Jet Noise Survey
**JNS**........... Jugoslovenska Nacionalna Stranka [*Yugoslav National Party*] [*Political party*] (PPE)
**JNS**........... Minneapolis, MN [*Location identifier*] [*FAA*] (FAAL)
**JNSC**......... Joint Navigation Satellite Committee
**JNSCA**...... Journal of the Neurological Sciences [*A publication*]
**JNSEL**....... Journal of the Northwest Semitic Languages [*Leiden*] [*A publication*]
**JNSI**.......... Journal. Numismatic Society of India [*A publication*]
**JNSL**......... Journal of the Northwest Semitic Languages [*Leiden*] [*A publication*]
**JNSMP**..... Journal. Numismatic Society of Madhya Pradesh [*A publication*]
**JNSNA**...... Journal of Neurosurgical Nursing [*A publication*]
**JNSSB**....... Journal of Neurosurgical Sciences [*A publication*]
**J f N St**...... Jahrbuecher fuer Nationaloekonomie und Statistik [*A publication*]
**JNSV**......... Jones & Vining, Inc. [*NASDAQ symbol*] (NQ)
**J NSW Council for Mentally Handicapped** ... Journal. New South Wales Council for the Mentally Handicapped [*A publication*] (APTA)
**JNT**........... Joint
**JNT**........... Journal of Narrative Technique [*A publication*]
**JNT**........... New York, NY [*Location identifier*] [*FAA*] (FAAL)
**JNTAD**...... Journal. National Technical Association [*A publication*]
**JNTO**........ Japan National Tourist Organization (EA)
**JNT STK CO**... Joint Stock Company (DLA)
**JNT VEN**.. Joint Venture [*Legal term*] (DLA)
**JNU**........... Juneau [*Alaska*] [*Airport symbol*] (OAG)
**JNU**........... Juneau, AK [*Location identifier*] [*FAA*] (FAAL)
**JNU**........... Universal Jet Navigation Charts [*Air Force*]
**JNUCA**...... Journal of Nuclear Energy [*New York*] [*1954-59*] [*A publication*]
**J Nucl Agric Biol** ... Journal of Nuclear Agriculture and Biology [*A publication*]
**J Nucl Biol** ... Journal of Nuclear Biology and Medicine [*A publication*]
**J Nucl Biol Med** ... Journal of Nuclear Biology and Medicine [*A publication*]
**J Nuclear Med** ... Journal of Nuclear Medicine [*A publication*]
**J Nuclear Sci Tech** ... Journal of Nuclear Science and Technology [*A publication*]
**J Nucl Energ** ... Journal of Nuclear Energy [*A publication*]
**J Nucl Energy** ... Journal of Nuclear Energy [*A publication*]
**J Nucl Energy Part A** ... Journal of Nuclear Energy. Part A. Reactor Science [*A publication*]
**J Nucl Energy Part B** ... Journal of Nuclear Energy. Part B. Reactor Technology [*A publication*]
**J Nucl Energy Part C** ... Journal of Nuclear Energy. Part C. Plasma Physics, Accelerators, Thermonuclear Research [*A publication*]
**J Nucl Energy Parts A/B** ... Journal of Nuclear Energy. Parts A/B. Reactor Science and Technology [*A publication*]
**J Nucl Mat** ... Journal of Nuclear Materials [*A publication*]
**J Nucl Mater** ... Journal of Nuclear Materials [*A publication*]
**J Nucl Med** ... Journal of Nuclear Medicine [*A publication*]
**J Nucl Med Allied Sci** ... Journal of Nuclear Medicine and Allied Sciences [*A publication*]
**J Nucl Med Pam** ... Journal of Nuclear Medicine. Pamphlet [*A publication*]
**J Nucl Med Suppl** ... Journal of Nuclear Medicine. Supplement [*A publication*]
**J Nucl Med Technol** ... Journal of Nuclear Medicine Technology [*A publication*]
**J Nucl Radiochem (Peking)** ... Journal of Nuclear and Radiochemistry (Peking) [*A publication*]
**J Nucl Sci (Seoul)** ... Journal of Nuclear Sciences (Seoul) [*A publication*]
**J Nucl Sci and Technol** ... Journal of Nuclear Science and Technology [*A publication*]
**J Nucl Sci Technol** ... Journal of Nuclear Science and Technology [*A publication*]
**J Nuc Sci T** ... Journal of Nuclear Science and Technology [*A publication*]
**JNUL**......... Jewish National and University Library
**J Number Th** ... Journal of Number Theory [*A publication*]
**J Number Theory** ... Journal of Number Theory [*A publication*]
**J Nurs Adm** ... Journal of Nursing Administration [*A publication*]
**J Nurs Admin** ... Journal of Nursing Administration [*A publication*]
**J Nurs Care** ... Journal of Nursing Care [*A publication*]
**J Nurs Ed**... Journal of Nursery Education [*A publication*]
**J Nurs Ed**... Journal of Nursing Education [*A publication*]
**J Nurs Educ** ... Journal of Nursing Education [*A publication*]
**J Nurse Midwife** ... Journal of Nurse Midwifery [*A publication*]
**J Nurs Ethics** ... Journal of Nursing Ethics [*A publication*]
**J Nurs Hist** ... Journal of Nursing History [*A publication*]
**J Nurs Midwife** ... Journal of Nurse Midwifery [*A publication*]
**J Nurs Staff Dev** ... Journal of Nursing Staff Development [*A publication*]
**J Nurs (Taipei)** ... Journal of Nursing (Taipei) [*A publication*]
**J Nutr**......... Journal of Nutrition [*A publication*]
**J Nutr Diet** ... Journal of Nutrition and Dietetics [*A publication*]
**J Nutr Educ** ... Journal of Nutrition Education [*A publication*]
**J Nutr Elderly** ... Journal of Nutrition for the Elderly [*A publication*]
**J Nutr Growth Cancer** ... Journal of Nutrition, Growth, and Cancer [*A publication*]
**J Nutr Sci**... Journal of Nutritional Sciences [*A publication*]
**J Nutr Sci Vitaminol** ... Journal of Nutritional Science and Vitaminology [*A publication*]
**J Nutr Sc V** ... Journal of Nutritional Science and Vitaminology [*A publication*]
**J Nutr Suppl** ... Journal of Nutrition. Supplement [*United States*] [*A publication*]
**JNVBDV**... Journal of Nonverbal Behavior [*A publication*]
**J NVCA**..... Journal. National Volleyball Coaches Association [*A publication*]
**JNVOA**..... Jewish Nazi Victims Organization of America (EA)
**JNW**.......... Joint Committee on New Weapons and Equipment
**JNW**.......... Newport, OR [*Location identifier*] [*FAA*] (FAAL)
**JNWOC**.... Joint Warfare Operations Center
**JNWPS**..... Joint Nuclear Weapons Publication Systems (MCD)
**JNWPU**..... Joint Numerical Weather Prediction Unit
**JNWSemL**... Journal of the Northwest Semitic Languages [*Leiden*] [*A publication*]
**J Nw SL**..... Journal of the Northwest Semitic Languages [*A publication*]
**JNY**.......... Jenney Beechcraft, Inc. [*East Bedford, MA*] [*FAA designator*] (FAAC)
**J NY Entomol Soc** ... Journal. New York Entomological Society [*A publication*]
**J NY Ent So** ... Journal. New York Entomological Society [*A publication*]
**J NY Med Coll Flower Fifth Ave Hosp** ... Journal. New York Medical College. Flower and Fifth Avenue Hospitals [*A publication*]
**J NY Med Coll Flower and Fifth Ave Hosp** ... Journal. New York Medical College. Flower and Fifth Avenue Hospitals [*A publication*]
**J NY State Nurses Assoc** ... Journal. New York State Nurses Association [*A publication*]
**J NY State Sch Nurse Teach Assoc** ... Journal. New York State School Nurse Teachers Association [*A publication*]
**JNZ**........... Jennings, LA [*Location identifier*] [*FAA*] (FAAL)
**J NZ Assoc Bacteriol** ... Journal. New Zealand Association of Bacteriologists [*A publication*]
**J NZ Diet Assoc** ... Journal. New Zealand Dietetic Association [*A publication*]
**J NZ Fed Hist Soc** ... Journal. New Zealand Federation of Historical Societies [*A publication*]
**J NZ Inst Chem** ... Journal. New Zealand Institute of Chemistry [*A publication*]
**J NZ Inst Med Lab Technol** ... Journal. New Zealand Institute of Medical Laboratory Technology [*A publication*]
**JNZKA**...... Jinko Zoki [*A publication*]
**J NZ Soc Periodontol** ... Journal. New Zealand Society of Periodontology [*A publication*]
**JO**............. Jewish Observer and Middle East Review [*London*] [*A publication*]
**JO**............. Job Order
**Jo**.............. Joel [*Old Testament book*] (BJA)
**Jo**.............. Johannes Faventinus [*Deceased circa 1187*] [*Authority cited in pre-1607 legal work*] (DSA)
**JO**............. Joint Organization
**JO**............. Joint Ownership [*Business term*]
**Jo**.............. Jones' Irish Exchequer Reports [*A publication*] (DLA)
**jo**............... Jordan [*MARC country of publication code*] [*Library of Congress*] (LCCP)
**JO**............. Jordan [*ANSI two-letter standard code*] (CNC)
**Jo**.............. Joseph (BJA)
**JO**............. Journal Officiel des Communautes Europeennes [*Official Journal of the European Communities*] [*A publication*] (ILCA)
**JO**............. Journalist [*Navy rating*]
**JO**............. Junior Officer

**JO** ............. Jupiter Orbiter [*NASA*]
**JO** ............. Juvenile Offenders
**JO** ............. SAT Fluggesellschoff mbH [*Germany*] [*ICAO designator*] (FAAC)
**JO1** ........... Journalist, First Class [*Navy rating*]
**JO2** ........... Journalist, Second Class [*Navy rating*]
**JO3** ........... Journalist, Third Class [*Navy rating*]
**JoA** ............ Jewel of Africa [*Zambia*] [*A publication*]
**JOA** ........... Joint Objective Area (NVT)
**JOA** ........... Joint Oceanographic Assembly [*Marine science*] (MSC)
**JOA** ........... Joint Operating Agreement
**JOA** ........... Journal of Advertising [*A publication*]
**JOABAW** ... Journal of Applied Behavior Analysis [*A publication*]
**Joa Bologne** ... Johannes Bolognetus [*Deceased, 1575*] [*Authority cited in pre-1607 legal work*] (DSA)
**JOAD** ........ Journal. American Dietetic Association [*A publication*]
**JOAD** ........ Junior Olympic Archery Development
**JOADE8** .... Journal of Adolescence [*A publication*]
**JOAEEB** ... Journal of Applied Entomology [*A publication*]
**JO AI** ......... Jahreshefte des Oesterreichischen Archaeologischen Instituts in Wien [*A publication*] (OCD)
**Joa Imo** ...... Johannes de Imola [*Deceased, 1436*] [*Authority cited in pre-1607 legal work*] (DSA)
**JOALAS** .... Journal of Allergy [*Later, Journal of Allergy and Clinical Immunology*] [*A publication*]
**JOAN** ........ Journal of Applied Nutrition [*A publication*]
**Jo de Ana** ... Johannes de Anania [*Deceased, 1457*] [*Authority cited in pre-1607 legal work*] (DSA)
**Joan Andr** .. Johannes Andreae [*Deceased, 1348*] [*Authority cited in pre-1607 legal work*] (DSA)
**JOANAY** ... Journal of Anatomy [*A publication*]
**Joan Bapt Villalob** ... Johannes Baptista Villalobos [*Authority cited in pre-1607 legal work*] (DSA)
**Joan Bologne** ... Johannes Bolognetus [*Deceased, 1575*] [*Authority cited in pre-1607 legal work*] (DSA)
**Joan Borcholt** ... Johannes Borcholten [*Deceased, 1593*] [*Authority cited in pre-1607 legal work*] (DSA)
**Joan de Ces** ... Johannes de Cesena [*Flourished, 13th century*] [*Authority cited in pre-1607 legal work*] (DSA)
**JOAND3** ... Journal of Andrology [*A publication*]
**Joan Fan** .... Johannes Faventinus [*Deceased circa 1187*] [*Authority cited in pre-1607 legal work*] (DSA)
**Joan de Lign** ... Johannes de Lignano [*Deceased, 1383*] [*Authority cited in pre-1607 legal work*] (DSA)
**Joan Mon** ... Johannes Monachus [*Deceased, 1313*] [*Authority cited in pre-1607 legal work*] (DSA)
**Joann** ......... Johannes Teutonicus [*Deceased circa 1246*] [*Authority cited in pre-1607 legal work*] (DSA)
**Jo de Anna** ... Johannes de Anania [*Deceased, 1457*] [*Authority cited in pre-1607 legal work*] (DSA)
**Joannes** ...... Johannes Franciscus Pavinus [*Flourished, 1448-82*] [*Authority cited in pre-1607 legal work*] (DSA)
**Joann Teut** ... Johannes Teutonicus [*Deceased, 1246*] [*Authority cited in pre-1607 legal work*] (DSA)
**Joan Vaud** ... Johannes Vaudus [*Flourished, 16th century*] [*Authority cited in pre-1607 legal work*] (DSA)
**JOAP** ......... Joint Oil Analysis Program [*Military*] (NVT)
**JOAP** ......... Journal of Applied Psychology [*A publication*]
**JOAP-CG** ... Joint Oil Analysis Program Coordinating Group (MCD)
**JOAP-TSC** ... Joint Oil Analysis Program Technical Support Center (MCD)
**JOB** ............ General Employment Enterprises, Inc. [*AMEX symbol*] (SPSG)
**Jo B** ............ Johannes Bassianus [*Flourished, 12th century*] [*Authority cited in pre-1607 legal work*] (DSA)
**JOB** ............ Journal of Broadcasting [*A publication*]
**JOB** ............ Journal of Business [*A publication*]
**JOB** ............ Journal of Business Administration [*A publication*]
**JOB** ............ Journal of Occupational Behaviour [*A publication*]
**JOB** ............ Judicial Officers Bulletin [*A publication*]
**JOB** ............ Just One Break (EA)
**JOBAPT** .... John the Baptist
**J Obes Weight Regul** ... Journal of Obesity and Weight Regulation [*A publication*]
**JOBG** ......... Jahrbuch. Oesterreichische Byzantinische Gesellschaft [*A publication*]
**JOBLIB** ..... Job Library [*Data processing*]
**JOBM** ........ Journal of Behavioral Medicine [*A publication*]
**Jo de Bor** .... Johannes de Borbonio [*Flourished, 1317-30*] [*Authority cited in pre-1607 legal work*] (DSA)
**Job Outlk** ... Job Outlook for College Graduates through 1990 [*A publication*]
**JOBS** ......... Job Oriented Basic Skills [*Program*] [*Military*]
**Job Safe & H** ... Job Safety and Health [*A publication*]
**JOBSDN** ... Journal of Biosciences [*Bangalore*] [*A publication*]
**JOBSEO** ... Journal. Orissa Botanical Society [*A publication*]
**Jobsons Invest Dig** ... Jobson's Investment Digest [*A publication*] (APTA)
**Jobsons Investment D** ... Jobson's Investment Digest [*A publication*] (APTA)
**Jobsons Min Yearb** ... Jobson's Mining Yearbook [*Australia*] [*A publication*]
**J Obstet Gynaec Br Commonw** ... Journal of Obstetrics and Gynaecology of the British Commonwealth [*A publication*]
**J Obstet Gynaec Brit Cmwlth** ... Journal of Obstetrics and Gynaecology of the British Commonwealth [*A publication*]
**J Obstet Gynaec Brit Common** ... Journal of Obstetrics and Gynaecology of the British Commonwealth [*A publication*]
**J Obstet Gynaec Brit Emp** ... Journal of Obstetrics and Gynaecology of the British Empire [*A publication*]
**J Obstet Gynaecol Br Commonw** ... Journal of Obstetrics and Gynaecology of the British Commonwealth [*A publication*]
**J Obstet Gynaecol Br Emp** ... Journal of Obstetrics and Gynaecology of the British Empire [*A publication*]
**J Obstet Gynaecol India** ... Journal of Obstetrics and Gynaecology of India [*A publication*]
**J Obstet Gynecol Neonatal Nurs** ... Journal of Obstetric, Gynecologic, and Neonatal Nursing [*A publication*]
**J Obst and Gynaec Brit Emp** ... Journal of Obstetrics and Gynaecology of the British Empire [*A publication*]
**JOBTAP** .... Job Training Assessment Program [*Vocational guidance test*]
**JOC** ........... Cambria County Library System, Johnstown, PA [*OCLC symbol*] (OCLC)
**JOC** ........... Chief Journalist [*Navy rating*]
**JOC** ........... Jewett Owners Club (EA)
**JOC** ........... Jewish Occupational Council [*Later, NAJVS*] (EA)
**JOC** ........... Job Order Contracting
**JOC** ........... Jocose [*or Jocular*]
**JOC** ........... John Coutts Library Services [*ACCORD*] [*UTLAS symbol*]
**JOC** ........... Joint Operations Center
**JOC** ........... Joint Organizing Committee [*Global Atmospheric Research Program*]
**JOC** ........... Journal of Communication Management [*A publication*]
**JOC** ........... Journal of Organic Chemistry [*A publication*]
**JOC** ........... Junior Officer Council [*Army*]
**JOC** ........... Junior Optimist Clubs (EA)
**JOC** ........... New York, NY [*Location identifier*] [*FAA*] (FAAL)
**Jo & Car** ..... Jones and Cary's Irish Exchequer Reports [*1838-39*] [*A publication*] (DLA)
**JOCARG** ... Joint Wideband Circuit Allocation and Requirement Group, Thailand [*Military*] (CINC)
**JOCAS** ...... Job Order Cost Accounting System (MCD)
**JOCC** ......... Jeunesse Ouvriere Catholique Canadienne [*Young Canadian Catholic Workers*] [*Established 1930*]
**JOCC** ......... Joint Operations Control Center
**J OCCA** ...... Journal. Oil and Colour Chemists' Association [*A publication*]
**J Occ Bhvr** ... Journal of Occupational Behaviour [*A publication*]
**J Occ Health Safety Aust** ... Journal of Occupational Health and Safety in Australia [*A publication*]
**J Occ Med** ... Journal of Occupational Medicine [*A publication*]
**J Occ Psy** ... Journal of Occupational Psychology [*A publication*]
**J Occup Accid** ... Journal of Occupational Accidents [*A publication*]
**J Occupa Med** ... Journal of Occupational Medicine [*A publication*]
**J Occupa Psychol** ... Journal of Occupational Psychology [*A publication*]
**J Occupational Accidents** ... Journal of Occupational Accidents [*A publication*]
**J Occupat Med** ... Journal of Occupational Medicine [*A publication*]
**J Occup Behav** ... Journal of Occupational Behaviour [*A publication*]
**J Occup Health Safety** ... Journal of Occupational Health and Safety - Australia and New Zealand [*A publication*]
**J Occup Med** ... Journal of Occupational Medicine [*A publication*]
**J Occup Psychol** ... Journal of Occupational Psychology [*A publication*]
**JOCE** ......... Journal Officiel des Communautes Europeennes [*A publication*] (DLA)
**J Oceanogr Soc Jpn** ... Journal. Oceanographical Society of Japan [*A publication*]
**J Oceanol Soc Korea** ... Journal. Oceanological Society of Korea [*A publication*]
**J Ocean Technol** ... Journal of Ocean Technology [*A publication*]
**JOCECA** ... Journal Officiel. Communaute Europeenne du Charbon et de l'Acier [*A publication*]
**Jo Ch** .......... Johnson's New York Chancery Reports [*A publication*] (DLA)
**JOCH** ........ Journal of Community Health [*A publication*]
**JOCI** .......... Jeunesse Ouvriere Chretienne Internationale [*International Young Christian Workers - IYCW*] (EAIO)
**JOCIT** ....... JOVIAL Compiler Implementation Tool [*Data processing*] (MCD)
**JOCM** ....... Master Chief Journalist [*Navy rating*]
**JOCMA** ..... Journal of Occupational Medicine [*A publication*]
**JOCNEE** ... Journal of Child Neurology [*A publication*]
**Jo Comm Eur** ... Journal Officiel des Communautes Europeennes [*Official Journal of the European Communities*] [*A publication*] (ILCA)
**JOCOTAS** ... Joint Committee on Tactical Shelters (MCD)
**Jo de Cre** .... Johannes Bassianus de Cremona [*Flourished, 12th century*] [*Authority cited in pre-1607 legal work*] (DSA)
**Jo Cre** ......... Johannes Bassianus de Cremona [*Flourished, 12th century*] [*Authority cited in pre-1607 legal work*] (DSA)
**JOCS** ......... Journal of Offender Counseling, Services, and Rehabilitation [*A publication*]
**JOCS** ......... Senior Chief Journalist [*Navy rating*]
**J-OCT** ........ Joint Operational Compatibility Tests
**JOD** ........... Joint Occupancy Date (MCD)
**JOD** ........... Journal of Development [*A publication*]
**JOD** ........... Journal of Documentation [*London*] [*A publication*]

**JOD**.......... Juedischer Ordnungsdienst [*A publication*]
**JOD**.......... Juvenile Onset Diabetes [*Medicine*]
**JODAC**...... Johannesburg Democratic Action Committee [*South Africa*]
**JODC**........ Japan Oceanographic Data Center [*Information service or system*] (IID)
**JODC**........ Journal of Dentistry for Children [*A publication*]
**JODC**........ Juvenile Osteochondritits Dissecans [*Medicine*]
**JODE**......... Journal of Drug Education [*A publication*]
**JODI**.......... Journal of Drug Issues [*A publication*]
**JODIN**...... Iodinium [*Iodine*] [*Chemical element*] [*Symbol is I*] [*Pharmacy*] (ROG)
**JODIV**....... John the Divine
**J Odor Control**... Journal of Odor Control [*A publication*]
**JODV**........ Journal of Divorce [*A publication*]
**JOE**........... Joensuu [*Finland*] [*Airport symbol*] (OAG)
**JOE**........... Joensuu [*Finland*] [*Seismograph station code, US Geological Survey*] [*Closed*] (SEIS)
**JOE**........... Juvenile Opportunities Endeavor
**JOEAI**....... Jahreshefte. Oesterreichisches Archaeologische Institut in Wien [*A publication*]
**JOEByz**..... Jahrbuch der Oesterreichischen Byzantinistik [*A publication*]
**JOEEA**...... Journal of Emotional Education [*A publication*]
**JOEG**......... Joint Operations Evaluation Group (AABC)
**JOEG-V**.... Joint Operations Evaluation Group, Vietnam [*Air Force*] (MCD)
**JOEM**........ Junior Ordnance Electrical Mechanic [*British military*] (DMA)
**JOENA**...... Journal of Endocrinology [*A publication*]
**Joenkoepings Laens Hushallningssaellsk Tidskr**... Joenkoepings Laens Hushallningssaellskaps. Tidskrift [*A publication*]
**Joensuun Korkeakoulun Julk Sar Bii**... Joensuun Korkeakoulun Julkaisuja. Sarja Bii [*A publication*]
**JOERA**...... Journal of Educational Research [*A publication*]
**JoES**.......... Journal of European Studies [*A publication*]
**JOET**......... Journal of Education for Teaching [*A publication*]
**JOEVANG**... John the Evangelist
**Jo Ex Ir**...... Jones' Irish Exchequer Reports [*A publication*] (DLA)
**Jo Ex Pro W**... Jones' Exchequer Proceedings Concerning Wales [*1939*] [*A publication*] (DLA)
**JOF**........... Japan OTC Equity Fund, Inc. [*NYSE symbol*] (SPSG)
**Jo F**........... Johannes de Fintona [*Flourished, 13th century*] [*Authority cited in pre-1607 legal work*] (DSA)
**Jo de F**....... Johannes de Fintona [*Flourished, 13th century*] [*Authority cited in pre-1607 legal work*] (DSA)
**JOF**........... Journal of Forecasting [*A publication*]
**Jo Fa**.......... Johannes Faventinus [*Deceased circa 1187*] [*Authority cited in pre-1607 legal work*] (DSA)
**Jo Fav**........ Johannes Faventinus [*Deceased circa 1187*] [*Authority cited in pre-1607 legal work*] (DSA)
**J Off Rech Pech Can**... Journal. Office des Recherches sur les Pecheries du Canada [*A publication*]
**J Off Repub Fr**... Journal Officiel de la Republique Francaise [*A publication*]
**JOFH**........ Journal of Family History. Studies in Family, Kinship, and Demography [*A publication*]
**Jo de Fi**...... Johannes de Fintona [*Flourished, 13th century*] [*Authority cited in pre-1607 legal work*] (DSA)
**JOFL**......... Johnstown Flood National Memorial
**JOG**........... Joggle [*Engineering*]
**JOG**........... Jogyakarta [*Indonesia*] [*Airport symbol*] (OAG)
**JOG**........... Joint Operating Group [*SLA/ASIS*]
**JOG**........... Joint Operations Graphics [*Military*]
**JOG**........... Joint Operations Group [*DoD*]
**JOGEA**...... Journal of Gerontology [*A publication*]
**JOGG A**..... Journal of Geography [*A publication*]
**JOGL**......... Journal of Glaciology [*A publication*]
**JOGM**........ Jord og Myr. Tidsskrift foer det Norske Jord og Myselskap [*A publication*]
**JOGNB**..... JOGN [*Journal of Obstetric, Gynecologic, and Neonatal Nursing*] Nursing [*A publication*]
**JOGNN**..... Journal of Obstetric, Gynecologic, and Neonatal Nursing [*A publication*]
**JOGN Nurs**... JOGN [*Journal of Obstetric, Gynecologic, and Neonatal Nursing*] Nursing [*A publication*]
**Jogtud Koezl**... Jogtudomanyi Koezloeny [*A publication*]
**JOH**........... Johannesburg [*South Africa*] [*Seismograph station code, US Geological Survey*] [*Closed*] (SEIS)
**Joh**............ Johannine (BJA)
**Joh**............ John [*New Testament book*] (BJA)
**JOH**........... Johnstone Point, AK [*Location identifier*] [*FAA*] (FAAL)
**JOH**........... Journal of Housing [*A publication*]
**JOH**........... St. John's College [*Cambridge, England*] (DAS)
**Joh Ch Rep**... Johnson's New York Chancery Reports [*A publication*] (DLA)
**JOHE**........ Journal of Health Economics [*A publication*]
**JOHEA**...... Journal of Heredity [*A publication*]
**JOHEEC**... Journal of Hepatology [*Amsterdam*] [*A publication*]
**JOHH**........ Journal of Holistic Health [*A publication*]
**J Ohio Herpetol Soc**... Journal. Ohio Herpetological Society [*A publication*]
**JOHJ**......... John O'Hara Journal [*A publication*]
**John**.......... Chase's United States Circuit Court Decisions, Edited by Johnson [*A publication*] (DLA)
**John**.......... Johnson's English Vice-Chancellors' Reports [*A publication*] (DLA)
**John**.......... Johnson's Maryland Chancery Reports [*A publication*] (DLA)
**John**.......... Johnson's New York Reports [*A publication*] (DLA)
**John**.......... Johnson's New York Supreme Court Reports [*A publication*] (DLA)
**John Alexander Monogr Ser Var Phases Thorac Surg**... John Alexander Monograph Series on Various Phases of Thoracic Surgery [*A publication*]
**John Am Not**... John's American Notaries [*A publication*] (DLA)
**John Cas**.... Johnson's New York Cases [*A publication*] (DLA)
**John Chan**... Johnson's New York Chancery Reports [*A publication*] (DLA)
**John Ch Rep**... Johnson's New York Chancery Reports [*A publication*] (DLA)
**John Dewey Soc Yrbk**... John Dewey Society. Yearbook [*A publication*]
**John Dict**... Johnson's English Dictionary [*A publication*] (DLA)
**John Eng Ch**... Johnson's English Vice-Chancellors' Reports [*A publication*] (DLA)
**John & H**... Johnson and Hemming's English Chancery Reports [*70 English Reprint*] [*A publication*] (DLA)
**John Herron Art Inst Bul**... John Herron Art Institute. Bulletin [*Indianapolis*] [*A publication*]
**John Innes Bull**... John Innes Bulletin [*A publication*]
**John Innes Hortic Inst Annu Rep**... John Innes Horticultural Institution. Annual Report [*A publication*]
**John Innes Inst Annu Rep**... John Innes Institute. Annual Report [*A publication*]
**John Mar J Prac & Proc**... John Marshall Journal of Practice and Procedure [*A publication*]
**John Marshall J**... John Marshall Journal of Practice and Procedure [*A publication*]
**John Marshall Jr**... John Marshall Journal of Practice and Procedure [*A publication*]
**John Marshall LQ**... John Marshall Law Quarterly [*A publication*] (DLA)
**John Marsh LJ**... John Marshall Law Journal [*A publication*] (DLA)
**John Marsh LQ**... John Marshall Law Quarterly [*A publication*] (DLA)
**John Marsh L Rev**... John Marshall Law Review [*A publication*]
**JOHNNIAC**... John's [*Von Neumann*] Integrator and Automatic Computer [*An early computer*]
**John Oxley J**... John Oxley Journal [*A publication*]
**John Rylands Lib Bul**... John Rylands Library. Bulletin [*A publication*]
**Johns**......... Chase's United States Circuit Court Decisions, Edited by Johnson [*A publication*] (DLA)
**Johns**......... Johnson's English Vice-Chancellors' Reports [*A publication*] (DLA)
**Johns**......... Johnson's Maryland Chancery Reports [*A publication*] (DLA)
**Johns**......... Johnson's New York Supreme Court Reports [*A publication*] (DLA)
**Johns Bills**... Johnson's Bills of Exchange [*2nd ed.*] [*1839*] [*A publication*] (DLA)
**Johns C**...... Johnson's New York Cases [*A publication*] (DLA)
**Johns Cas**.. Johnson's New York Cases [*A publication*] (DLA)
**Johns Cases**... Johnson's New York Cases [*A publication*] (DLA)
**Johns Cas (NY)**... Johnson's New York Cases [*A publication*] (DLA)
**Johns Ch**.... Johnson's English Vice-Chancellors' Reports [*A publication*] (DLA)
**Johns Ch**.... Johnson's Maryland Chancery Decisions [*A publication*] (DLA)
**Johns Ch**.... Johnson's New York Chancery Reports [*A publication*] (DLA)
**Johns Ch Cas**... Johnson's New York Chancery Reports [*A publication*] (DLA)
**Johns Ch (NY)**... Johnson's New York Chancery Reports [*A publication*] (DLA)
**Johns Civ L Sp**... Johnson's Civil Law of Spain [*A publication*] (DLA)
**Johns Ct Err**... Johnson's New York Court of Errors Reports [*A publication*] (DLA)
**Johns Dec**.. Johnson's Maryland Chancery Decisions [*A publication*] (DLA)
**Johns Eccl L**... Johnson's Ecclesiastical Law [*A publication*] (DLA)
**Johns Eng Ch**... Johnson's English Chancery Reports [*A publication*] (DLA)
**Johns & H**... Johnson and Hemming's English Chancery Reports [*70 English Reprint*] [*A publication*] (DLA)
**Johns & Hem**... Johnson and Hemming's English Chancery Reports [*70 English Reprint*] [*A publication*] (DLA)
**Johns & H (Eng)**... Johnson and Hemming's English Chancery Reports [*70 English Reprint*] [*A publication*] (DLA)
**Johns H Med**... Johns Hopkins Medical Journal [*A publication*]
**Johns Hopkins APL Tech Dig**... Johns Hopkins University. Applied Physics Laboratory. Technical Digest [*United States*] [*A publication*]
**Johns Hopkins APL Technical Digest**... Johns Hopkins University. Applied Physics Laboratory. Technical Digest [*A publication*]
**Johns Hopkins Hosp Bull**... Johns Hopkins Hospital. Bulletin [*A publication*]
**Johns Hopkins M**... Johns Hopkins Magazine [*A publication*]
**Johns Hopkins Med J**... Johns Hopkins Medical Journal [*A publication*]
**Johns Hopkins Med J Suppl**... Johns Hopkins Medical Journal. Supplement [*A publication*]
**Johns Hopkins Oceanogr Stud**... Johns Hopkins Oceanographic Studies [*A publication*]
**Johns Hopkins Ser in Math Sci**... Johns Hopkins Series in the Mathematical Sciences [*A publication*]

**Johns Hopkins Univ Appl Phys Lab Spec Rep** ... Johns Hopkins University. Applied Physics Laboratory. Special Report [*A publication*]
**Johns Hopkins Univ Chesapeake Bay Inst Tech Rept** ... Johns Hopkins University. Chesapeake Bay Institute. Technical Report [*A publication*]
**Johns Hopkins Univ Cir** ... Johns Hopkins University. Circular [*A publication*]
**Johns Hopkins Univ McCollum Pratt Inst Contrib** ... Johns Hopkins University. McCollum Pratt Institute. Contribution [*A publication*]
**Johns Hopkins Univ Stud** ... Johns Hopkins University. Studies in Historical and Political Science [*A publication*]
**Johns Hopkins Univ Studies in Geology** ... Johns Hopkins University. Studies in Geology [*A publication*]
**Johns HRV** ... Johnson's English Chancery Reports [*A publication*] (DLA)
**Johns H U Stud** ... Johns Hopkins University. Studies in Historical and Political Science [*A publication*]
**Johns Mar R** ... Johnson on Maritime Rights [*A publication*] (DLA)
**Johns (NY)** ... Johnson's New York Reports [*A publication*] (DLA)
**Johns NZ**... Johnson's New Zealand Reports [*A publication*] (DLA)
**Johnson**...... Johnson's English Vice-Chancellors' Reports [*A publication*] (DLA)
**Johnson**...... Johnson's Maryland Chancery Decisions [*A publication*] (DLA)
**Johnson**...... Johnson's New York Reports [*A publication*] (DLA)
**Johnson NYR** ... Johnson's New York Reports [*A publication*] (DLA)
**Johnson R** ... Johnson's New York Reports [*A publication*] (DLA)
**Johnson's Quarto Dict** ... Johnson's Quarto Dictionary [*A publication*] (DLA)
**Johnson's Rep** ... Johnson's New York Reports [*A publication*] (DLA)
**Johns Pat Man** ... Johnson's Patent Manual [*A publication*] (DLA)
**Johns R**...... Johnson's New York Reports [*A publication*] (DLA)
**Johns Rep**.. Johnson's New York Supreme Court Reports [*A publication*] (DLA)
**Johnst Inst** ... Johnston's Institutes of the Laws of Spain [*A publication*] (DLA)
**Johnst (NZ)** ... Johnston's New Zealand Reports [*A publication*] (DLA)
**Johns Tr** .... Johnson's Impeachment Trial [*A publication*] (DLA)
**Johns US** ... Johnson's Reports of Chase's United States Circuit Court Decisions [*A publication*] (DLA)
**Johns VC** ... Johnson's English Vice-Chancellors' Reports [*A publication*] (DLA)
**Johns VC (Eng)** ... Johnson's English Vice-Chancellors' Reports [*A publication*] (DLA)
**JOHOA**..... Journal of Housing [*A publication*]
**JOHPER**... Journal of Health, Physical Education, Recreation [*A publication*]
**Johs**........... Johannes Galensis [*Flourished, 13th century*] [*Authority cited in pre-1607 legal work*] (DSA)
**JoHS**.......... Journal of Hellenic Studies [*A publication*]
**Joh Teut**..... Johannes Teutonicus [*Deceased circa 1246*] [*Authority cited in pre-1607 legal work*] (DSA)
**JOHX**........ Johnson Flying Service [*Air carrier designation symbol*]
**JOHX**........ Journal of Homosexuality [*A publication*]
**JOI**............ Joint Oceanographic Institutions, Inc. [*Research center*] (RCD)
**JOI**............ Joinville [*Brazil*] [*Airport symbol*] (OAG)
**JOIB**.......... Journal. Oriental Institute (Baroda) [*A publication*]
**JOICA**........ Journal. Institution of Chemists [*A publication*]
**JOIDES**..... Joint Oceanographic Institutions for Deep Earth Sampling
**Joides J**...... Joides Journal [*A publication*]
**JOIDES Journal** ... Joint Oceanographic Institutions for Deep Earth Sampling. Journal [*A publication*]
**J Oil Col C** ... Journal. Oil and Colour Chemists' Association [*A publication*]
**J Oil Colour Chem Ass** ... Journal. Oil and Colour Chemists' Association [*A publication*]
**J Oil Colour Chem Assoc** ... Journal. Oil and Colour Chemists' Association [*A publication*]
**J Oil Fat Ind** ... Journal of Oil and Fat Industries [*A publication*]
**J Oilseeds Res** ... Journal of Oilseeds Research [*A publication*]
**J Oil Technol Assoc India** ... Journal. Oil Technologists' Association of India [*A publication*]
**J Oil Technol Assoc India (Bombay)** ... Journal. Oil Technologists' Association of India (Bombay) [*A publication*]
**J Oil Technol Assoc India (Kanpur India)** ... Journal. Oil Technologists' Association of India (Kanpur, India) [*A publication*]
**Jo de Imol**.. Johannes de Imola [*Deceased, 1436*] [*Authority cited in pre-1607 legal work*] (DSA)
**JOIN** ......... Jobs or Income Now [*Students for a Democratic Society*] [*Defunct*]
**JOIN** ......... Joinery (ADA)
**JOIN** ......... Joint Optical Information Network [*Army*]
**JOIN** ......... Jones Intercable, Inc. [*NASDAQ symbol*] (NQ)
**JOINREP** ... Joining Report (MCD)
**Joint Automat Contr Conf Prepr Tech Pap** ... Joint Automatic Control Conference. Preprints of Technical Papers [*A publication*]
**JOIP**.......... Joint Operations Interface Procedure (NASA)
**JOIS**.......... Japan Online Information System [*Database*]
**JOJA**......... July, October, January, and April [*Denotes quarterly payments of interest or dividends in these months*] [*Business term*]
**JOJAA**...... Journal of Otolaryngology of Japan [*A publication*]
**Jo Je S**....... Journal of Jewish Studies [*A publication*]
**JOJO**......... Jojoba Horizons, Inc. [*NASDAQ symbol*] (NQ)
**Jo Jur**......... Journal of Jurisprudence [*A publication*] (DLA)
**J Okayama Med Soc** ... Journal. Okayama Medical Society [*Japan*] [*A publication*]
**J Okayama Med Soc Suppl** ... Journal. Okayama Medical Society. Supplement [*Japan*] [*A publication*]
**JOKI**.......... John Fitzgerald Kennedy National Historical Site
**J Okla Dent Assoc** ... Journal. Oklahoma Dental Association [*A publication*]
**J Okla State Dent Assoc** ... Journal. Oklahoma State Dental Association [*A publication*]
**J Okla State Med Assoc** ... Journal. Oklahoma State Medical Association
**JOKU**........ Jokull [*A publication*]
**JOKUA**..... Joekull (Reykjavik) [*A publication*]
**JOL**........... Job Organization Language [*1979*] [*Data processing*] (CSR)
**JOL**........... Jolo [*Philippines*] [*Airport symbol*] (OAG)
**JOL**........... Jolon [*California*] [*Seismograph station code, US Geological Survey*] (SEIS)
**JOL**........... Joule, Inc. [*AMEX symbol*] (SPSG)
**JOL**........... Journal of Oriental Literature [*A publication*]
**J d'Ol**........ Les Jugements d'Oleron [*Laws of Oleron*] [*Maritime law*] [*A publication*] (DLA)
**JOLA**......... Journal of Library Automation [*A publication*]
**JOLAB**...... Journal-Lancet [*A publication*]
**Jo & La T**... Jones and La Touche's Irish Chancery Reports [*A publication*] (DLA)
**J Old Wexford Soc** ... Journal. Old Wexford Society [*A publication*]
**Jo Le**.......... Johannis Lectura [*A publication*] (DSA)
**JOLT**......... Juvenile Offenders Learn the Truth [*Program*]
**JOM**.......... Jeunesse Ouvriere Marocaine [*Moroccan Working Youth*]
**JOM**.......... Job Operation Manual (AAG)
**JOM**.......... Job-Oriented Manual (AAG)
**JOM**.......... Johnson-O'Malley Act [*1934*]
**JOM**.......... Journal of Management [*A publication*]
**JOM**.......... Journal of Metals [*A publication*]
**JOM**.......... Journal of Occupational Medicine [*A publication*]
**JOMA**....... Journal of Military Assistance [*A publication*]
**JOMER**..... Jewish Observer and Middle East Review [*A publication*]
**JOMF**........ Journal of Marriage and the Family [*A publication*]
**JOM J Occup Med** ... JOM. Journal of Occupational Medicine [*United States*] [*A publication*]
**JOML**........ Journal of Organometallic Chemistry Library [*Elsevier Book Series*] [*A publication*]
**JOMMA**... Journal of Mathematics and Mechanics [*A publication*]
**JOMN**....... Jeweled-Orifice Misting Nozzle
**Jo de Mo**.... Johannes de Monciaco [*Flourished, 1263-66*] [*Authority cited in pre-1607 legal work*] (DSA)
**Jo Mon**....... Johannes Monachus [*Deceased, 1313*] [*Authority cited in pre-1607 legal work*] (DSA)
**JOMS**........ Journal of Oral and Maxillofacial Surgery [*A publication*]
**JOMSD**..... Journal of Oral and Maxillofacial Surgery [*A publication*]
**JOMU**....... John Muir National Historic Site
**JOMV**....... Jahrbuch. Oberoesterreichischer Musealverein [*A publication*]
**JOMYA**..... Journal of Meteorology [*A publication*]
**JON**.......... Jeweled-Orifice Nozzle
**JON**.......... Job Order Number (MCD)
**JON**.......... Johnston Island [*Airport symbol*] (OAG)
**Jon**............ Jonah [*Old Testament book*]
**JON**.......... Jonas [*Old Testament book*] [*Douay version*]
**Jon**............ [*Sir William*] Jones' English King's Bench and Common Pleas Reports [*A publication*] (DLA)
**Jon**............ [*Sir Thomas*] Jones' English King's Bench and Common Pleas Reports [*A publication*] (DLA)
**Jon**............ Jones' Irish Exchequer Reports [*A publication*] (DLA)
**JON**.......... Jonpol Explorations Ltd. [*Toronto Stock Exchange symbol*]
**JONB**........ Joni Blair of California [*NASDAQ symbol*] (NQ)
**Jon & Car**... Jones and Cary's Irish Exchequer Reports [*1838-39*] [*A publication*] (DLA)
**J Oncol Tianjin Med J Suppl** ... Journal of Oncology. Tianjin Medical Journal. Supplement [*A publication*]
**JONE**........ Journal of Nutrition Education [*A publication*]
**JONEA**...... Journal of Neurophysiology [*A publication*]
**Jones**.......... Jones' Irish Exchequer Reports [*A publication*] (DLA)
**Jones**.......... Jones' North Carolina Equity Reports [*54-59*] [*1853-63*] [*A publication*] (DLA)
**Jones**.......... Jones' North Carolina Law Reports [*A publication*] (DLA)
**Jones**.......... Jones' Reports [*11, 12 Pennsylvania*] [*A publication*] (DLA)
**Jones**.......... Jones' Reports [*43-48, 52-57, 61, 62 Alabama*] [*A publication*] (DLA)
**Jones**.......... Jones' Reports [*22-30 Missouri*] [*A publication*] (DLA)
**Jones**.......... Jones' Upper Canada Common Pleas Reports [*A publication*] (DLA)
**Jones 1**....... [*Sir William*] Jones' English King's Bench Reports [*A publication*] (DLA)
**Jones 2**....... [*Sir Thomas*] Jones' English King's Bench Reports [*A publication*] (DLA)
**Jones B**...... Jones' Law of Bailments [*A publication*] (DLA)
**Jones Bailm** ... Jones' Law of Bailments [*A publication*] (DLA)
**Jones Barclay & Whittelsey** ... Jones, Barclay, and Whittelsey's Reports [*31 Missouri*] [*A publication*] (DLA)
**Jones B & W (MO)** ... Jones, Barclay, and Whittelsey's Reports [*31 Missouri*] [*A publication*] (DLA)

**Jones & C**... Jones and Cary's Irish Exchequer Reports [*1838-39*] [*A publication*] (DLA)
**Jones Ch Mort** ... Jones on Chattel Mortgages [*A publication*] (DLA)
**Jones Easem** ... Jones' Treatise on Easements [*A publication*] (DLA)
**Jones Eq** .... Jones' North Carolina Equity Reports [*54-59*] [*1853-63*] [*A publication*] (DLA)
**Jones Eq (NC)** ... Jones' North Carolina Equity Reports [*54-59*] [*1853-63*] [*A publication*] (DLA)
**Jones Exch** ... Jones' Irish Exchequer Reports [*A publication*] (DLA)
**Jones Fr Bar** ... Jones' History of the French Bar [*A publication*] (DLA)
**Jones French Bar** ... Jones' History of the French Bar [*A publication*] (DLA)
**Jones & H Hind Law** ... Jones and Haughton's Hindoo Law [*A publication*] (DLA)
**Jones Inst**... Jones' Institutes of Hindoo Law [*A publication*] (DLA)
**Jones Intr**... Jones' Introduction to Legal Science [*A publication*] (DLA)
**Jones Ir**...... Jones' Irish Exchequer Reports [*A publication*] (DLA)
**Jones & L**... Jones and La Touche's Irish Chancery Reports [*A publication*] (DLA)
**Jones L**....... Jones' Law Reports [*A publication*] (DLA)
**Jones & La T** ... Jones and La Touche's Irish Chancery Reports [*A publication*] (DLA)
**Jones Law**.. Jones' North Carolina Law Reports [*A publication*] (DLA)
**Jones Lib** ... Jones on Libel [*1812*] [*A publication*] (DLA)
**Jones & L (Ir)** ... Jones and La Touche's Irish Chancery Reports [*A publication*] (DLA)
**Jones L Of T** ... Jones on Land and Office Titles [*A publication*] (DLA)
**Jones & McM** ... Jones and McMurtrie's Pennsylvania Supreme Court Reports [*A publication*] (DLA)
**Jones & McM (PA)** ... Jones and McMurtrie's Pennsylvania Supreme Court Reports [*A publication*] (DLA)
**Jones Mort** ... Jones on Mortgages [*A publication*] (DLA)
**Jones NC** ... Jones' North Carolina Law Reports [*A publication*] (DLA)
**Jones PA**.... Jones' Reports [*11, 12 Pennsylvania*] [*A publication*] (DLA)
**Jones Pledges** ... Jones on Pledges and Collateral Securities [*A publication*] (DLA)
**Jones Ry Sec** ... Jones on Railway Securities [*A publication*] (DLA)
**Jones & S**... Jones and Spencer's Superior Court Reports [*33-61 New York*] [*A publication*] (DLA)
**Jones Salv** ... Jones' Law of Salvage [*A publication*] (DLA)
**Jones Securities** ... Jones on Railroad Securities [*A publication*] (DLA)
**Jones & Sp** ... Jones and Spencer's Superior Court Reports [*33-61 New York*] [*A publication*] (DLA)
**Jones & Spen** ... Jones and Spencer's Superior Court Reports [*33-61 New York*] [*A publication*] (DLA)
**Jones T** ...... [*Sir Thomas*] Jones' English King's Bench Reports [*A publication*] (DLA)
**Jones UC** ... Jones' Upper Canada Common Pleas Reports [*A publication*] (DLA)
**Jones Uses** ... Jones' Law of Uses [*A publication*] (DLA)
**Jones & V Laws** ... Jones and Varick's Laws of New York [*A publication*] (DLA)
**Jones W** ..... [*Sir William*] Jones' English King's Bench Reports [*A publication*] (DLA)
**Jon Ex**........ Jones' Irish Exchequer Reports [*A publication*] (DLA)
**Jon Exch**.... Jones' Irish Exchequer Reports [*A publication*] (DLA)
**Jon Ir Exch** ... Jones' Irish Exchequer Reports [*A publication*] (DLA)
**Jon & L**....... Jones and La Touche's Irish Chancery Reports [*A publication*] (DLA)
**Jon & La T** ... Jones and La Touche's Irish Chancery Reports [*A publication*] (DLA)
**JONS**......... Journal of Northern Studies [*A publication*]
**JONS**......... Juntas de Ofensiva Nacional Sindicalista [*Syndicalist Juntas of the National Offensive*] [*Spain*] [*Political party*] (PPE)
**J Ont Dent Assoc** ... Journal. Ontario Dental Association [*Canada*] [*A publication*]
**JONUDL**.. Journal. American College of Nutrition [*A publication*]
**Jonxis Lect** ... Jonxis Lectures [*A publication*]
**JOO**.......... Jonesboro, GA [*Location identifier*] [*FAA*] (FAAL)
**JOOD**........ Junior Officer of the Day [*or Deck*] [*Navy*]
**JOOFA**....... Journal Officiel de la Republique Francaise [*A publication*]
**JOOM**....... Journal of Occupational Medicine [*A publication*]
**JOOMS**..... Junior Observers of Meteorology [*Trainees for government service to replace Weather Bureau men who had gone to war*] [*World War II*]
**JOOS**......... Job-Oriented Organizational Structure (AAG)
**JOOW**....... Junior Officer of the Watch [*Navy*]
**JOP**........... Job Opportunity Program (OICC)
**JOP**........... Jobs Optional Program [*Combination job opportunities in the business sector and on the job training*] (OICC)
**JOP**........... Joint Observing Program [*NASA*]
**JOP**........... Joint Operating Plan
**JOP**........... Joint Operation Procedure (AAG)
**JOP**........... Journal of Occupational Psychology [*A publication*]
**JOp**........... Jupiter Orbiter Probe [*Later, Project Galileo*] [*NASA*]
**JOPA**......... Junior Officers and Professional Association
**JOPA**......... Juventud Organizada del Pueblo en Armas [*Armed People's Organized Youth*] [*Guatemala*] (PD)
**JOPC**......... Junior Olympic Pistol Championship [*National Rifle Association*]
**JO/PCN**.... Job Order/Program Control Number [*Army*]
**JOPD**......... Journal of Psychoactive Drugs [*A publication*]
**JOPDA**...... Journal of Pediatrics [*A publication*]
**J Open Educ Assoc Qld** ... Journal. Open Education Association of Queensland [*A publication*] (APTA)
**J Operational Psychiatr** ... Journal of Operational Psychiatry [*A publication*]
**J Operations Res Soc Japan** ... Journal. Operations Research Society of Japan [*A publication*]
**J Operator Theory** ... Journal of Operator Theory [*A publication*]
**J Oper Res Soc** ... Journal. Operational Research Society [*A publication*]
**J Oper Res Soc Am** ... Journal. Operation Research Society of America [*A publication*]
**J Oper Res Soc Jap** ... Journal. Operations Research Society of Japan [*A publication*]
**JOPES**....... Joint Operation Planning and Execution System [*DoD*]
**JOPES**....... Joint Operations Planning and Execution System [*Military*]
**JOPHA** ..... Journal de Physiologie [*A publication*]
**J Ophthalmic Nurs Technol** ... Journal of Ophthalmic Nursing and Technology [*A publication*]
**JOPID**....... Journal of Pipelines [*A publication*]
**JOPM**........ Joint Occupancy Plan Memorandum (AAG)
**JOPM**........ Joint Operation Procedure Memorandum (AAG)
**JOPP**......... Joint Operational Policies and Procedures (MCD)
**JOPP**......... Journal of Primary Prevention [*A publication*]
**JOPPA**...... Journal de Physiologie (Paris). Supplement [*A publication*]
**JOPR**......... Joint Operation Procedure Report (AAG)
**JOPREP**.... Joint Operational Report [*Military*] (AFM)
**J Op Res So** ... Journal. Operations Research Society of Japan [*A publication*]
**J Op Res Soc** ... Journal. Operational Research Society [*A publication*]
**JOPS**......... Joint Operational Planning System [*Military*]
**JOPSA**...... Journal of Psychology [*A publication*]
**J Opt**.......... Journal of Optics [*A publication*]
**J Opt Commun** ... Journal of Optical Communications [*A publication*]
**J Optimization Theory Appl** ... Journal of Optimization Theory and Applications [*A publication*]
**J Optimiz Theory and Appl** ... Journal of Optimization Theory and Applications [*A publication*]
**J Optim Th** ... Journal of Optimization Theory and Applications [*A publication*]
**J Optim Theory Appl** ... Journal of Optimization Theory and Applications [*A publication*]
**J Opt Soc**... Journal. Optical Society of America [*A publication*]
**J Opt Soc Am** ... Journal. Optical Society of America [*A publication*]
**J Opt Soc Am A** ... Journal. Optical Society of America. A. Optics and Image Science [*A publication*]
**J Opt Soc Am B Opt Phys** ... Journal. Optical Society of America. B. Optical Physics [*A publication*]
**J Opt Soc Amer** ... Journal. Optical Society of America [*A publication*]
**J Opt Soc Am Rev Sci Instrum** ... Journal. Optical Society of America and Review of Scientific Instruments [*A publication*]
**J Opt Soc Cum Ind** ... Journal. Optical Society of America. Cumulative Index [*A publication*]
**JOQ**.......... Job Order Quantity [*Military*] (AFIT)
**JOR**.......... Jet Operations Requirements
**JOR**.......... Job Operations Report
**JOR**.......... Job Order Request (AAG)
**JOR**.......... Joint Operations Requirements [*Military*] (AFM)
**JOR**.......... Jordan [*ANSI three-letter standard code*] (CNC)
**JOR**.......... Jorgensen [*Earle M.*] Co. [*NYSE symbol*] (SPSG)
**JOR**.......... Journal of Organizational Behavior Management [*A publication*]
**JOR**.......... Journal of Oriental Research [*A publication*]
**JORADF**... Journal de Radiologie [*Paris*] [*A publication*]
**Jo Radio Law** ... Journal of Radio Law [*A publication*] (DLA)
**J Oral Implantol** ... Journal of Oral Implantology [*A publication*]
**J Oral Implant Transplant Surg** ... Journal of Oral Implant and Transplant Surgery [*A publication*]
**J Oral Maxillofac Surg** ... Journal of Oral and Maxillofacial Surgery [*A publication*]
**J Oral Med** ... Journal of Oral Medicine [*A publication*]
**J Oral Pathol** ... Journal of Oral Pathology [*A publication*]
**J Oral Rehabil** ... Journal of Oral Rehabilitation [*A publication*]
**J Oral Surg** ... Journal of Oral Surgery [*A publication*]
**J Oral Surg Anesth Hosp Dent Serv** ... Journal of Oral Surgery, Anesthesia, and Hospital Dental Service [*A publication*]
**J Oral Therap Pharmacol** ... Journal of Oral Therapeutics and Pharmacology [*A publication*]
**J Oral Ther Pharmacol** ... Journal of Oral Therapeutics and Pharmacology [*A publication*]
**JORC**......... Junior Olympic Rifle Championship [*National Rifle Association*]
**Jordan Dent J** ... Jordan Dental Journal [*A publication*]
**Jordan Med J** ... Jordan Medical Journal [*A publication*]
**Jordan Minist Agric Annu Rep (Eng Ed)** ... Jordan. Ministry of Agriculture. Annual Report (English Edition) [*A publication*]
**Jordan Pln** ... Five-Year Plan for Economic and Social Development, 1981-85 (Jordan) [*A publication*]
**Jordbruksekon Meddel** ... Jordbruksekonomiska Meddelanden [*A publication*]
**Jordbruksekon Medd Statens Jordbruksnamned** ... Jordbruksekonomiska Meddelanden. Statens Jordbruksnamned [*A publication*]
**Jordbrukstek Inst Cirk** ... Jordbrukstekniska Institutet. Cirkulaer [*A publication*]

**Jord-Ekon Medd** ... Jordbruksekonomiska Meddelanden [*A publication*]
**Jord Jt St Comp** ... Jordan on Joint Stock Companies [*A publication*] (DLA)
**JORDM** .... Journal Officiel. Republique Democratique de Madagascar [*A publication*]
**Jord PJ** ...... Jordan's Parliamentary Journal [*A publication*] (DLA)
**JOREA**...... Journal of Rehabilitation [*A publication*]
**JOREDR**... Journal of Orthopaedic Research [*A publication*]
**JOREES**.... Journal of Oilseeds Research [*A publication*]
**J Oreg Dent Assoc** ... Journal. Oregon Dental Association [*A publication*]
**JORF**......... Journal Officiel de la Republique Francaise [*A publication*]
**JORG** ........ Joint Oceanographic Research Group
**J Organometal Chem** ... Journal of Organometallic Chemistry [*A publication*]
**J Organometallic Chem** ... Journal of Organometallic Chemistry [*A publication*]
**J Organomet Chem** ... Journal of Organometallic Chemistry [*A publication*]
**J Organomet Chem Libr** ... Journal. Organometallic Chemistry Library [*A publication*]
**J Org Chem** ... Journal of Organic Chemistry [*A publication*]
**J Org Chem USSR** ... Journal of Organic Chemistry of the USSR [*A publication*]
**J Orgl Bhvr Mgt** ... Journal of Organizational Behavior Management [*A publication*]
**J Orgl Com** ... Journal of Organizational Communication [*A publication*]
**J Orgmet Ch** ... Journal of Organometallic Chemistry [*A publication*]
**J Oriental Soc Aust** ... Journal. Oriental Society of Australia [*A publication*] (APTA)
**J Orient Inst (Baroda)** ... Journal. Oriental Institute (Baroda) [*A publication*]
**J Or Inst** .... Journal. Oriental Institute [*A publication*]
**J Orissa Bot Soc** ... Journal. Orissa Botanical Society [*A publication*]
**J Orissa Math Soc** ... Journal. Orissa Mathematical Society [*A publication*]
**JORITDS** ... Joint Optical Range Instrumentation Type Designation System
**Jornadas Agron Trab** ... Jornadas Agronomicas. Trabajos [*A publication*]
**Jornadas Agron Vet Univ Buenos Aires Fac Agron Vet** ... Jornadas Agronomicas y Veterinarias. Universidad de Buenos Aires. Facultad de Agronomia y Veterinaria [*A publication*]
**Jornand de Reb Get** ... Jornandes. De Rebus Geticis [*A publication*] (DLA)
**Jorn Bras Psicol** ... Jornal Brasileiro de Psicologia [*A publication*]
**J Ornithol** .. Journal fuer Ornithologie [*A publication*]
**JORRI**....... Journal. Operating Room Research Institute [*A publication*]
**JORS**........ Journal. Operational Research Society [*A publication*]
**JORSJ**....... Journal. Operations Research Society of Japan [*A publication*]
**J Or Soc Aust** ... Journal. Oriental Society of Australia [*A publication*]
**J Or Stud** ... Journal of Oriental Studies [*A publication*]
**J Orthomol Psychiatry** ... Journal of Orthomolecular Psychiatry [*A publication*]
**J Orthop R** ... Journal of Orthopaedic Research [*A publication*]
**J Orthop Res** ... Journal of Orthopaedic Research [*A publication*]
**J Orthop Sports Phys Ther** ... Journal of Orthopaedic and Sports Physical Therapy [*A publication*]
**J Ortho and Sports Phys Ther** ... Journal of Orthopaedic and Sports Physical Therapy [*A publication*]
**JOS**........... Jeunesse Ouvriere du Senegal [*Senegalese Working Youth*]
**JOS**........... Jezyki Obce w Szkole [*A publication*]
**JOS**........... Job Order Supplement (MCD)
**JOS**........... Jos [*Nigeria*] [*Airport symbol*] (OAG)
**Jos**............. Joseph (BJA)
**Jos**............. Joseph's Reports [*21 Nevada*] [*A publication*] (DLA)
**Jos**............. Josephus (BJA)
**Jos**............. Joshua [*Old Testament book*]
**Jos**............. Josiah (BJA)
**JOS**........... Joss Energy Ltd. [*Toronto Stock Exchange symbol*]
**JOS**........... Jostens, Inc. [*NYSE symbol*] (SPSG)
**JOS**........... Josvafo [*Hungary*] [*Seismograph station code, US Geological Survey*] (SEIS)
**JOS**........... Journal of Oriental Studies [*A publication*]
**JOSA**......... Journal. Optical Society of America [*A publication*]
**JOSA**......... Seaman Apprentice, Journalist, Striker [*Navy rating*]
**JOSAA**...... Journal. Optical Society of America [*A publication*]
**Josa Andras Muz Ev** ... Josa Andras Muzeum Evkoenyve [*A publication*]
**JOSAF**....... Joint Operations Support Activity Frankfurt [*National Security Agency*]
**J Osaka City Med Cent** ... Journal. Osaka City Medical Center [*A publication*]
**J Osaka Dent Univ** ... Journal. Osaka Dental University [*A publication*]
**J Osaka Inst Sci Technol Part 1** ... Journal. Osaka Institute of Science and Technology. Part 1 [*A publication*]
**J Osaka Med Coll** ... Journal. Osaka Medical College [*Japan*] [*A publication*]
**J Osaka Odontol Soc** ... Journal. Osaka Odontological Society [*A publication*]
**J Osaka Univ Dent Sch** ... Journal. Osaka University Dental School [*A publication*] 
**J Osaka Univ Dent Soc** ... Journal. Osaka University Dental Society [*Japan*] [*A publication*]
**JosAnt**........ Jewish Antiquities [*Josephus*] (BJA)
**Josan Zass** ... Josanpu Zasshi. Japanese Journal for Midwives [*A publication*]
**JosApion**.... Against Apion [*Josephus*] (BJA)
**Jos & Bev** ... Joseph and Beven's Digest of Decisions [*Ceylon*] [*A publication*] (DLA)
**JOSCO**...... Joint Overseas Shipping Control Office
**Joseph**........ Josephus [*First century AD*] [*Classical studies*] (OCD)
**JOSH** ........ Job Safety and Health [*Bureau of National Affairs*] [*Information service or system*] (CRD)
**Josh**........... Joshua [*Old Testament book*]
**JOSH** .......... Journal of School Health [*A publication*]
**JOSHA**...... Joho Shori [*A publication*]
**JOSHB**...... Journal. American Society for Horticultural Science [*A publication*]
**JOSHB5**.... Journal. American Society for Horticultural Science [*A publication*]
**JOSHUA**... Joint Sticking Hemoglobin Universal Assay [*Sickle cell anemia test*]
**JOSL** ......... Joslyn Corp. [*NASDAQ symbol*] (NQ)
**JO/SL**........ Jupiter Orbiter Satellite Lander [*NASA*]
**JosLife** ....... Life of Josephus (BJA)
**J Oslo City Hosp** ... Journal. Oslo City Hospital [*A publication*]
**JOSM**........ Jesuit Office of Social Ministry [*Later, NOJSM*] (EA)
**J Osmania Univ** ... Journal. Osmania University [*A publication*]
**JOSN**......... Seaman, Journalist, Striker [*Navy rating*]
**JOSO**......... Joint Organization for Solar Observations
**JOSP** ......... Junior Olympic Shooting Program [*National Rifle Association*]
**JOSPRO** ... Joint Ocean [*or Overseas*] Shipping Procedure
**JOSS** ......... JOHNNIAC [*John's Integrator and Automatic Computer*] Open Shop System [*Time-sharing language*] [*Rand Corp.*] [*1962*] [*Data processing*]
**JOSS** ......... Joint Ocean Surface Study
**JOSS** ......... Joint Overseas Switching System [*Military*] (AABC)
**JOstByzGes** ... Jahrbuch. Oesterreichische Byzantinische Gesellschaft [*Vienna*] [*A publication*]
**JosWars**..... Wars [*Josephus*] (BJA)
**JOT**........... Jam on Target
**Jo T**........... John of Tynemouth [*Deceased, 1221*] [*Authority cited in pre-1607 legal work*] (DSA)
**JOT**........... Joint Operational Test
**JOT**........... Joliet, IL [*Location identifier*] [*FAA*] (FAAL)
**Jo T** ........... [*Sir Thomas*] Jones' English King's Bench Reports [*A publication*] (DLA)
**JOT**........... Journal of Coatings Technology [*A publication*]
**JOT**........... Journal of Taxation [*A publication*]
**JOTA**......... Jamboree on the Air [*Boy Scouts of America*]
**JOTC**......... Joint Oil Targets Committee [*World War II*]
**JOTC**......... Jungle Operations Training Center [*Army*] (INF)
**Jo Te** ......... Johannes Teutonicus [*Deceased circa 1246*] [*Authority cited in pre-1607 legal work*] (DSA)
**JOT & E** .... Joint Operational Test and Evaluation (MCD)
**JOT J Oberflaechentech** ... JOT. Journal fuer Oberflaechentechnik [*A publication*]
**JOTOD** ..... Journal of Otolaryngology [*A publication*]
**JOTODX**... Journal d'Oto-Rhino-Laryngologie [*A publication*]
**J Otolaryngol** ... Journal of Otolaryngology [*A publication*]
**J Oto-Laryngol Soc Aust** ... Journal. Oto-Laryngological Society of Australia [*A publication*]
**J Otolaryngol Suppl** ... Journal of Otolaryngology. Supplement [*A publication*]
**J Oto-Rhino-Laryngol Soc Jpn** ... Journal. Oto-Rhino-Laryngological Society of Japan [*A publication*]
**JOTPA** ...... Journal of Oral Therapeutics and Pharmacology [*A publication*]
**JOTR**......... Joint Operational and Technical Reviews [*Military*] (AFIT)
**JOTR**......... Joshua Tree National Monument
**JOTS**......... Job-Oriented Training Standards (AFM)
**J Otto Rank** ... Journal. Otto Rank Association [*A publication*]
**jou** ............. Jouissance [*Payable Interest*] [*French*] [*Business term*]
**JOU**.......... Osaka University, Kita-ku, Osaka, Japan [*Library symbol*] [*Library of Congress*] (LCLS)
**JOU** .......... Sioux Falls, SD [*Location identifier*] [*FAA*] (FAAL)
**JOUAM** .... Junior Order United American Mechanics
**JOU-N**....... Osaka University, Nakanishima Library, Osaka, Japan [*Library symbol*] [*Library of Congress*] (LCLS)
**JOUR** ........ Journal
**JOUR** ........ Journeyman
**Jour Acoust Soc** ... Journal. Acoustical Society of America [*A publication*]
**Jour Aesthetics and Art Crit** ... Journal of Aesthetics and Art Criticism [*A publication*]
**Jour Am Folklore** ... Journal of American Folklore [*A publication*]
**Jour Am Inst Archit** ... Journal. American Institute of Architecture [*A publication*]
**Jour Am Jud Soc** ... Journal. American Judicature Society [*A publication*]
**Jour Am Studies** ... Journal of American Studies [*A publication*]
**Jour Brit Studies** ... Journal of British Studies [*A publication*]
**Jour Chem Physics** ... Journal of Chemical Physics [*A publication*]
**Jour Church and State** ... Journal of Church and State [*A publication*]
**Jour Comp Leg** ... Journal. Society of Comparative Legislation [*A publication*] (DLA)
**Jour Conat Law** ... Journal of Conational Law [*A publication*] (DLA)
**Jour Conchyliologie** ... Journal de Conchyliologie [*A publication*]
**Jour Conflict Resolution** ... Journal of Conflict Resolution [*A publication*]
**Jour Conseil** ... Journal du Conseil [*A publication*]
**Jour Contemp Hist** ... Journal of Contemporary History [*A publication*]
**Jour Crim L** ... Journal of Criminal Law and Criminology [*A publication*]
**Jour Crim Law** ... Journal of Criminal Law, Criminology, and Police Science [*Later, Journal of Criminal Law and Criminology*] [*A publication*]
**Jour Devel Areas** ... Journal of Developmental Areas [*A publication*]
**Jour Eccl Hist** ... Journal of Ecclesiastical History [*A publication*]

**Jour Ecology** ... Journal of Ecology [*A publication*]
**Jour Econ and Bus Hist** ... Journal of Economic and Business History [*A publication*]
**Jour Econ Hist** ... Journal of Economic History [*A publication*]
**Jour Farm Hist** ... Journal of Farm History [*A publication*]
**Jour Folklore Inst** ... Journal. Folklore Institute [*A publication*]
**Jour Gemmology** ... Journal of Gemmology and Proceedings of the Gemmological Association of Great Britain [*A publication*]
**Jour Geol Education** ... Journal of Geological Education [*A publication*]
**Jour Glaciology** ... Journal of Glaciology [*A publication*]
**Jour Hist Ideas** ... Journal of the History of Ideas [*A publication*]
**Jour Hist Med** ... Journal of the History of Medicine [*A publication*]
**Jour Hist Phil** ... Journal of the History of Philosophy [*A publication*]
**Jour Human Rel** ... Journal of Human Relations [*A publication*]
**Jour of Indian Art and Ind** ... Journal of Indian Art and Industry [*A publication*]
**Jour Inorganic and Nuclear Chemistry** ... Journal of Inorganic and Nuclear Chemistry [*A publication*]
**Jour of Int Affairs** ... Journal of International Affairs [*A publication*]
**Jour Interam Studies** ... Journal of Interamerican Studies and World Affairs [*A publication*]
**Jour Jur** ..... Journal of Jurisprudence [*A publication*] (DLA)
**Jour Juris**... Hall's Journal of Jurisprudence [*A publication*] (DLA)
**Jour Jur Sc** ... Journal of Jurisprudence and Scottish Law Magazine [*A publication*] (DLA)
**Jour Land Public Utility Econ** ... Journal of Land and Public Utility Economics [*A publication*]
**Jour Law**.... Journal of Law [*A publication*] (DLA)
**Jour Law and Econ** ... Journal of Law and Economic Development [*A publication*]
**Jour Legal Ed** ... Journal of Legal Education [*A publication*]
**Jour Lib Hist** ... Journal of Library History [*Later, Journal of Library History, Philosophy, and Comparative Librarianship*] [*A publication*]
**Jour Miss Hist** ... Journal of Mississippi History [*A publication*]
**Jour Mod Hist** ... Journal of Modern History [*A publication*]
**JOURN** ..... Journal
**Journ Adm Com** ... Journal des Administrations Communales [*A publication*]
**Journal Cork Hist Soc** ... Journal. Cork Historical and Archaeological Society [*A publication*]
**Journal Greater India Soc** ... Journal. Greater India Society [*A publication*]
**Journal Gujarat Research Soc** ... Journal. Gujarat Research Society [*India*] [*A publication*]
**Journalism Conf Workshop ADA** ... Journalism Conference and Workshop. American Dental Association Council on Journalism and American Association of Dental Editors [*A publication*]
**Journalism Educ** ... Journalism Educator [*A publication*]
**Journalism Q** ... Journalism Quarterly [*A publication*]
**Journal Q**... Journalism Quarterly [*A publication*]
**Journal of RPS** ... Journal. Royal Photographic Society [*A publication*]
**Journal Sadul Rajasthani Research Inst** ... Journal. Sadul Rajasthani Research Institute [*A publication*]
**Journal Soc Antiq** ... Journal. Royal Society of Antiquaries of Ireland [*A publication*]
**Journal Soc Finno-Ougr** ... Journal. Societe Finno-Ougrienne [*A publication*]
**Journ Annu Diabetol Hotel-Dieu** ... Journees Annuelles de Diabetologie Hotel-Dieu [*A publication*]
**Journ Ass Med Mut** ... Journal. Association Medicale Mutuelle [*A publication*]
**Journ Atmos Terr Phys** ... Journal of Atmospheric and Terrestrial Physics [*A publication*]
**Journ Be Neur Psych** ... Journal Belge de Neurologie et de Psychiatrie [*A publication*]
**Journ Be Radiol** ... Journal Belge de Radiologie [*A publication*]
**Journ Be Urol** ... Journal Belge d'Urologie [*A publication*]
**Journ Bib Lit** ... Journal of Biblical Literature [*A publication*] (OCD)
**Journ Biochem** ... Journal of Biochemistry [*A publication*]
**Journ Biochem Micr Tech Eng** ... Journal of Biochemical and Microbiological Technology and Engineering [*A publication*]
**Journ Biol Chem** ... Journal of Biological Chemistry [*A publication*]
**Journ Biophys Biochem Cytol** ... Journal of Biophysical and Biochemical Cytology [*A publication*]
**Journ Bot Brit For** ... Journal of Botany. British and Foreign [*A publication*]
**Journ Br Astr Ass** ... Journal. British Astronomical Association [*A publication*]
**Journ Calorim Anal Therm Prepr** ... Journees de Calorimetrie et d'Analyse Thermique. Preprints [*A publication*]
**Journ Ceyl Obstet Gyn Ass** ... Journal. Ceylon Obstetric and Gynaecological Association [*A publication*]
**Journ Chem Phys** ... Journal of Chemical Physics [*A publication*]
**Journ Chem Soc** ... Journal. Chemical Society [*A publication*]
**Journ Chim Phys Chim** ... Journal de Chimie Physique et de Physico-Chimie Biologique [*A publication*]
**Journ Chin Chem Soc** ... Journal. Chinese Chemical Society [*A publication*]
**Journ Chir** ... Journal de Chirurgie [*A publication*]
**Journ Clin Ophthal** ... Journal of Clinical Ophthalmology [*A publication*]
**Journ Clin Path** ... Journal of Clinical Pathology [*A publication*]
**Journ Clin Psychol** ... Journal of Clinical Psychology [*A publication*]
**Journ Fisc**.. Journal Pratique de Droit Fiscal et Financier [*A publication*]
**Journ Hist Behavioral Sci** ... Journal of the History of the Behavioral Sciences [*A publication*]
**Journ J Paix** ... Journal des Juges de Paix [*A publication*]
**Journ Jur** ... Journal of Jurisprudence [*A publication*] (DLA)
**Journ Med Fr** ... Journees Medicales de France et de l'Union Francaise [*A publication*]
**Journ Pharm Fr** ... Journees Pharmaceutiques Francaises [*A publication*]
**Journ Phil** ... Journal of Philology [*A publication*] (OCD)
**Journ Pr Chem** ... Journal fuer Praktische Chemie [*A publication*]
**Journ Q**...... Journalism Quarterly [*A publication*]
**Journ Rech Ovine Caprine** ... Journees de la Recherche Ovine et Caprine [*A publication*]
**Journ Sav**... Journal des Savants [*A publication*] (OCD)
**Journ Sci Cent Natl Coord Etud Rech Nutr Aliment** ... Journees Scientifiques. Centre National de Coordination des Etudes et Recherches sur la Nutrition et l'Alimentation [*A publication*]
**Journ Vinic Export** ... Journee Vinicole Export [*A publication*]
**Jour Pac Hist** ... Journal of Pacific History [*A publication*]
**Jour Palynology** ... Journal of Palynology [*A publication*]
**Jour Philos** ... Journal of Philosophy [*A publication*]
**Jour Pol Econ** ... Journal of Political Economy [*A publication*]
**Jour Politics** ... Journal of Politics [*A publication*]
**Jour Presby Hist** ... Journal of Presbyterian History [*A publication*]
**Jour Ps Med** ... Journal of Psychological Medicine and Medical Jurisprudence [*A publication*] (DLA)
**Jour f Psychol u Neurol** ... Journal fuer Psychologie und Neurologie [*A publication*]
**Jour Pub Law** ... Journal of Public Law [*A publication*]
**Jour of Relig** ... Journal of Religion [*A publication*]
**Jour Relig Hist** ... Journal of Religious History [*A publication*]
**Jour Soc Civ** ... Journal des Societes Civiles et Commerciales [*A publication*] (DLA)
**Jour Soc Hist** ... Journal of Social History [*A publication*]
**Jour Society Archit Historians** ... Journal. Society of Architectural Historians [*A publication*]
**Jour of Soc Issues** ... Journal of Social Issues [*A publication*]
**Jour Soc Philos** ... Journal of Social Philosophy [*A publication*]
**Jour Soc Sci** ... Journal of Social Sciences [*A publication*]
**Jour Speech Disorders** ... Journal of Speech Disorders [*A publication*]
**Jour Trib Com** ... Journal des Tribunaux de Commerce [*A publication*] (DLA)
**Jour of West** ... Journal of the West [*A publication*]
**JOUSD**...... Journal of Science. Busan National University [*A publication*]
**Jov**............ Hymnus in Jovem [*of Callimachus*] [*Classical studies*] (OCD)
**JOV** .......... Jahrbuch des Oesterreichischen Volksliedwerkes [*A publication*]
**JOV** .......... Jahrbuch fuer Ostdeutsche Volkskunde [*A publication*]
**JOVE**.......... Jupiter Orbiting Vehicle for Exploration (MCD)
**JOVIAL** .... Joule's Own Version of the International Algebraic [*or Algorithmic*] Language [*1958*] [*Data processing*]
**Jow Dict**..... Jowitt's Dictionary of English Law [*2nd ed.*] [*1977*] [*A publication*] (DLA)
**JOWOG**.... Joint Working Group
**JOWRDN** ... Journal of Obesity and Weight Regulation [*A publication*]
**JOY** .......... Job Opportunity for Youth [*NASA employment program*]
**JOY** .......... Joy Manufacturing Co. [*NYSE symbol*] (SPSG)
**JOYA**.......... Journal of Youth and Adolescence [*A publication*]
**Joy Acc** ...... Joy's Evidence of Accomplices [*1836*] [*A publication*] (DLA)
**Joyce Ins**.... Joyce on Insurance [*A publication*] (DLA)
**Joyce Lim**... Joyce on Limitations [*A publication*] (DLA)
**Joyce Prac Inj** ... Joyce's Law and Practice of Injunctions [*1872*] [*A publication*] (DLA)
**Joyce Prin Inj** ... Joyce's Doctrines and Principles of Injunctions [*1877*] [*A publication*] (DLA)
**Joy Chal**..... Joy's Peremptory Challenge of Jurors [*1844*] [*A publication*] (DLA)
**Joy Conf**..... Joy. Admissibility of Confessions [*1842*] [*A publication*] (DLA)
**Joy Ev** ........ Joy's Evidence of Accomplices [*1836*] [*A publication*] (DLA)
**Joy Leg Ed** ... Joy on Legal Education [*A publication*] (DLA)
**Joyn Lim**.... Joynes on Limitations [*A publication*] (DLA)
**JOYS**......... Journal of Youth Services in Libraries [*A publication*]
**JOZ** ........... Jozini [*South Africa*] [*Seismograph station code, US Geological Survey*] (SEIS)
**JP**.............. Die Juedische Presse [*The Jewish Press*] [*German*] (BJA)
**JP**.............. Fighter [*Russian aircraft symbol*]
**JP**.............. Inex Adria Aviopromet [*Yugoslavia*] [*ICAO designator*] (FAAC)
**JP**.............. Jack Panel
**JP**.............. Jacobi Polynomial [*Mathematics*]
**JP**.............. Jahrbuch fuer Philologie [*A publication*]
**JP**.............. James M. Peed [*Designer's mark when appearing on US coins*]
**JP**.............. Janata Party [*India*] [*Political party*] (PPW)
**JP**.............. Japan [*ANSI two-letter standard code*] (CNC)
**JP**.............. Japan Paper
**JP**.............. Jarrow Press, Inc.
**JP**.............. Jatiya Party [*Political party*] [*Bangladesh*]
**JP**.............. Jean Pierre Cosmetiques, Inc. [*Vancouver Stock Exchange symbol*]
**JP**.............. Jefferson-Pilot Corp. [*NYSE symbol*] (SPSG)
**JP**.............. Jerusalem Post [*A publication*]
**JP**.............. Jet Penetration
**JP**.............. Jet Petroleum (AFM)

**JP**.............. Jet Pilot
**JP**.............. Jet Pipe
**JP**.............. Jet Power
**JP**.............. Jet Propellant [*or Propulsion*]
**JP**.............. Jet Propulsion Fuel
**JP**.............. Jet Pump [*Bioinstrumentation*]
**JP**.............. Jewish Press [*Brooklyn, NY*] [*A publication*] (BJA)
**JP**.............. Jezyk Polski [*A publication*]
**J & P**.......... Joannou & Paraskevaides [*Construction company*] [*British*]
**JP**.............. Job the Patient (BJA)
**JP**.............. Job Placement [*Job Service*] (OICC)
**JP**.............. Job Processor
**JP**.............. Jobst Pump [*Medicine*]
**JP**.............. Joint Pacific [*Military*] (CINC)
**J & P**.......... Joists and Planks [*Technical drawings*]
**JP**.............. Jones Party [*Malta*] [*Political party*] (PPE)
**JP**.............. Joseph Pennell [*Specification-made paper*]
**JP**.............. Journal of Parapsychology [*A publication*]
**JP**.............. Journal of Philology [*A publication*]
**JP**.............. Journal of Philosophy [*A publication*]
**JP**.............. Journal of Politics [*A publication*]
**J & P**.......... Journal and Proceedings [*Australia*] [*A publication*]
**JP**.............. Journal de Psychologie Normale et Pathologique [*A publication*]
**JP**.............. Journal of Psychology [*A publication*]
**JP**.............. Judge of Probate [*British*] (ROG)
**JP**.............. Junction Panel [*or Point*] [*Electronics*]
**JP**.............. Junge Pioniero
**JP**.............. Junior Partner [*i.e., a husband*] [*Slang*]
**JP**.............. Junior Principal [*Freemasonry*] (ROG)
**JP**.............. Junior Probationer [*British*] (ROG)
**JP**.............. Juristische Praxis [*A publication*]
**JP**.............. Justice Party [*Turkey*] [*Political party*]
**JP**.............. Justice of the Peace
**JP**.............. Justice of the Peace and Local Government Review [*A publication*] (DLA)
**JP**.............. Justice of the Peace Reports [*United Kingdom*] [*A publication*]
**JP**.............. Justice of the Peace. Weekly Notes of Cases [*England*] [*A publication*] (DLA)
**JP**.............. Jute Protection [*Telecommunications*] (TEL)
**JP**.............. Juventud Peronista [*Peronist Youth*] [*Argentina*]
**JP**.............. Kim Jong Pil [*South Korean politician*]
**JPA**........... Jack Panel Assembly
**JPA**........... Japan Procurement Agency
**JPA**........... Jesuit Philosophical Association of the United States and Canada (EA)
**JPA**........... Jet Pioneers Association of the United States of America (EA)
**JPA**........... Jewish Palestinian Aramaic (BJA)
**JPA**........... Joao Pessoa [*Brazil*] [*Airport symbol*] (OAG)
**JPA**........... Job Pack Area [*Data processing*] (IBMDP)
**JPA**........... Job Performance Aid
**JPA**........... Joint Passover Association of the City of New York (EA)
**JPA**........... Joint Planning Activity [*DoD*]
**JPA**........... Journal of Policy Analysis and Management [*A publication*]
**JPA**........... Junior Philatelists of America (EA)
**JPA**........... Jurisprudence du Port D'Anvers [*Belgium*] [*A publication*]
**JPA**........... La Porte, TX [*Location identifier*] [*FAA*] (FAAL)
**J PA Acad Sci** ... Journal. Pennsylvania Academy of Science [*A publication*]
**J-PAAS**..... Jubilation - Paul Anka Admiration Society (EA)
**JPAC**......... ADMAC, Inc. [*Kent, WA*] [*NASDAQ symbol*] (NQ)
**J Pac H**...... Journal of Pacific History [*A publication*]
**J Pac Hist**.. Journal of Pacific History [*A publication*]
**J Pacif Hist** ... Journal of Pacific History [*A publication*] (APTA)
**J Pacific Hist** ... Journal of Pacific History [*A publication*] (APTA)
**J Paediatr Dent** ... Journal of Paediatric Dentistry [*A publication*]
**J Pain Symptom Manage** ... Journal of Pain and Symptom Management [*A publication*]
**J Paint Tec** ... Journal of Paint Technology [*A publication*]
**J Paix**......... Journal de la Paix [*A publication*]
**J Pak Hist Soc** ... Journal. Pakistan Historical Society [*A publication*]
**J Pak Med Ass** ... Journal. Pakistan Medical Association [*A publication*]
**J Pak Med Assoc** ... Journal. Pakistan Medical Association [*A publication*]
**J Palaegr Soc** ... Journal. Palaeographical Society [*A publication*]
**J Paleont**.... Journal of Paleontology [*A publication*]
**J Paleontol** ... Journal of Paleontology [*A publication*]
**J Pales Stu** ... Journal of Palestine Studies [*A publication*]
**J Palest Arab Med Ass** ... Journal. Palestine Arab Medical Association [*A publication*]
**J Palestine Stud** ... Journal of Palestine Studies [*A publication*]
**J Palestine Studies** ... Journal of Palestine Studies [*A publication*]
**J Palynol**.... Journal of Palynology [*A publication*]
**J Palynology** ... Journal of Palynology [*A publication*]
**J Palynol Palynol Soc India** ... Journal of Palynology. Palynological Society of India [*A publication*]
**JPAM**........ Joint Program Assessment Memorandum (MCD)
**JPAMD**..... Journal of Policy Analysis and Management [*A publication*]
**JPANDA**... Journal of Psychoanalytic Anthropology [*A publication*]
**J Pang Med Soc** ... Journal. Pangasinan Medical Society [*A publication*]
**JPaOrS**...... Journal. Palestine Oriental Society [*A publication*]
**JPAP**......... Jet Penetration Approach
**JPAPD**...... Journal of Experimental Psychology: Animal Behavior Processes [*A publication*]
**J Papua NG Society** ... Journal. Papua and New Guinea Society [*A publication*] (APTA)
**J Parapsych** ... Journal of Parapsychology [*A publication*]
**J Parapsychol** ... Journal of Parapsychology [*A publication*]
**J Parasit**..... Journal of Parasitology [*A publication*]
**J Parasitol** ... Journal of Parasitology [*A publication*]
**J Parasitology** ... Journal of Parasitology [*A publication*]
**J Par Distr** ... Journal of Parallel and Distributed Computing [*A publication*]
**J Parenter Drug Assoc** ... Journal. Parenteral Drug Association [*A publication*]
**J Parenter Sci Technol** ... Journal of Parenteral Science and Technology [*A publication*]
**J Park Rec Adm** ... Journal of Park and Recreation Administration [*A publication*]
**J Parlia Info** ... Journal of Parliamentary Information [*A publication*]
**J Past Care** ... Journal of Pastoral Care [*A publication*]
**J Past Coun** ... Journal of Pastoral Counseling [*A publication*]
**J Pastoral Care** ... Journal of Pastoral Care [*A publication*]
**J Path Bact** ... Journal of Pathology and Bacteriology [*A publication*]
**J Path and Bacteriol** ... Journal of Pathology and Bacteriology [*A publication*]
**J Pathol**...... Journal of Pathology [*A publication*]
**J Pathol Bacteriol** ... Journal of Pathology and Bacteriology [*A publication*]
**J Pathology** ... Journal of Pathology [*A publication*]
**J Patient Acc Manage** ... Journal of Patient Account Management [*A publication*]
**J Pat Off Soc'y** ... Journal. Patent Office Society [*A publication*]
**J Pat Of So** ... Journal. Patent Office Society [*A publication*]
**J PA Water Works Oper Assoc** ... Journal. Pennsylvania Water Works Operators' Association [*A publication*]
**JPB**........... Joint Planning Board
**JPB**........... Joint Procurement Board [*Military*] (AABC)
**JPB**........... Joint Production Board [*US and Great Britain*]
**JPB**........... Joint Purchasing Board
**JPB**........... Journal des Poetes (Brussels) [*A publication*]
**JPB**........... Junctional Premature Beat [*Cardiology*]
**JPBAEB**.... Journal of Psychopathology and Behavioral Assessment [*A publication*]
**JPBEA**....... Journal de Pharmacie de Belgique [*A publication*]
**JPBPB**....... Journal of Pharmacokinetics and Biopharmaceutics [*A publication*]
**JPBS**.......... Jettison Pushbutton Switch
**JPC**........... Jack Patch Cord
**JpC**............ Japanese Columbia [*Record label*]
**JPC**........... Jeunesse pour Christ [*Youth for Christ International - YFCI*] (EA)
**JPC**........... Jeunesse Progressiste Casamancaise [*Casamance Progressive Youth*] [*Senegal*]
**JPC**........... Johnson Products Company, Inc. [*AMEX symbol*] (SPSG)
**JPC**........... Joint Planning Committee
**JPC**........... Joint Power Conditioner
**JPC**........... Joint Production Committee [*British*] (DCTA)
**JPC**........... Journal of Pastoral Care [*A publication*]
**JPC**........... Journal of Planar Chromatography [*A publication*]
**JPC**........... Journal of Popular Culture [*A publication*]
**JPC**........... Judge of the Prize Court (DLA)
**JPC**........... Judicial Planning Council (OICC)
**JPC**........... Junctional Premature Contraction [*Cardiology*]
**JPC**........... Just Prior Condition [*Data processing*]
**JPC**........... Justice of the Peace Clerk [*British*] (ROG)
**JPCA**......... Jewish Penicillin Connoisseurs Association (EA)
**JPCAAC**.... Journal. Air Pollution Control Association [*A publication*]
**JPCC**......... Joint Pacific Command Control Network (MCD)
**JPCC**......... Joint Petroleum Coordination Center/Committee [*NATO*] (NATG)
**JPCCA**....... Journal of Physical and Colloid Chemistry [*A publication*]
**JPCD**......... Just Perceptible Color Difference [*Telecommunications*] (TEL)
**JPCG-CRM** ... Joint Policy Coordinating Group on Computer Resources Management (MCD)
**JPCG/DIMM** ... Joint Policy Coordinating Group on Defense Integrated Materiel Management (AFIT)
**JPCG-DMI** ... Joint Policy Coordinating Group on Depot Maintenance Interservicing
**JPCMA**..... Journal of Photochemistry [*A publication*]
**JPCRB**....... Journal of Physical and Chemical Reference Data [*A publication*]
**JPCRD**...... Journal of Physical and Chemical Reference Data [*A publication*]
**JPCSB**....... Journal of Physics and Chemistry of Solids. Supplement [*A publication*]
**JPCSC**....... Journal of Physical and Chemical Reference Data. Supplement [*A publication*]
**JP Ct**.......... Justice of the Peace's Court [*Legal term*] (DLA)
**JPD**........... Japan Publishers Directory [*Japan Publications Guide Service*] [*Japan*] [*Information service or system*] (CRD)
**JPDAAH**... Journal. American Podiatry Association [*A publication*]
**JPDADK**... Journal. Parenteral Drug Association [*A publication*]
**JPDC**......... Japan Petroleum Development Company
**JPDEA**...... Journal of Prosthetic Dentistry [*A publication*]
**JPDF**......... Journal Pratique de Droit Fiscal et Financier [*A publication*]

**JPDMB**..... American Society of Psychosomatic Dentistry and Medicine. Journal [*A publication*]
**JPDMBK**.. Journal. American Society of Psychosomatic Dentistry and Medicine [*A publication*]
**JPDPA**...... Journal of Periodontology - Periodontics [*A publication*]
**JPDR**......... Japan Power Demonstration Reactor
**J PE**.......... Journal of Physical Education and Program [*A publication*]
**JPE**............ Journal of Political Economy [*A publication*]
**J Peace Res**... Journal of Peace Research [*A publication*]
**J Peace Research**... Journal of Peace Research [*A publication*]
**J Peace Sci**... Journal of Peace Science [*A publication*]
**J Peasant Stud**... Journal of Peasant Studies [*A publication*]
**J Peasant Studies**... Journal of Peasant Studies [*A publication*]
**J Peas Stud**... Journal of Peasant Studies [*A publication*]
**JP ECON**.. Journal of Political Economy [*A publication*] (ROG)
**J Ped**.......... Jornal de Pediatria [*A publication*]
**J PED**........ Journal of Pedagogy [*New York*] [*A publication*] (ROG)
**J Ped**.......... Journal of Pediatrics [*A publication*]
**JPEDD**...... Journal of Physics Education [*A publication*]
**J Pediat**...... Journal of Pediatrics [*A publication*]
**J Pediat Psychol**... Journal of Pediatric Psychology [*A publication*]
**J Pediatr**.... Journal of Pediatrics [*A publication*]
**J Pediatr Endocr**... Journal of Pediatric Endocrinology [*A publication*]
**J Pediatr Gastroenterol Nutr**... Journal of Pediatric Gastroenterology and Nutrition [*A publication*]
**J Pediatr Nurs**... Journal of Pediatric Nursing. Nursing Care of Children and Families [*A publication*]
**J Pediatr Ophthalmol**... Journal of Pediatric Ophthalmology [*A publication*]
**J Pediatr Ophthalmol Strabismus**... Journal of Pediatric Ophthalmology and Strabismus [*A publication*]
**J Pediatr Orthop**... Journal of Pediatric Orthopedics [*A publication*]
**J Pediatr Psychol**... Journal of Pediatric Psychology [*A publication*]
**J Pediatr Surg**... Journal of Pediatric Surgery [*A publication*]
**J Pediat Surg**... Journal of Pediatric Surgery [*A publication*]
**J Pedod**...... Journal of Pedodontics [*A publication*]
**J Ped Surg**... Journal of Pediatric Surgery [*A publication*]
**JPEL**.......... Journal of Planning and Environment Law [*A publication*]
**JPEN**......... Journal of Parenteral and Enteral Nutrition [*A publication*]
**J Pendid UM**... Jurnal Pendidikan. University of Malaya [*A publication*]
**JPEN J Parent Enteral Nutr**... JPEN. Journal of Parenteral and Enteral Nutrition [*A publication*]
**J Pen Pl and Comp**... Journal of Pension Planning and Compliance [*A publication*]
**J Pension Plan and Compliance**... Journal of Pension Planning and Compliance [*A publication*]
**J Pension Planning and Compliance**... Journal of Pension Planning and Compliance [*A publication*]
**JPer**........... Journal of Personality [*A publication*]
**J PERD**...... Journal of Physical Education, Recreation, and Dance [*A publication*]
**J Perinat**.... Journal of Perinatology [*A publication*]
**J Perinat Med**... Journal of Perinatal Medicine [*A publication*]
**J Periodont**... Journal of Periodontology [*A publication*]
**J Periodontal Res**... Journal of Periodontal Research [*A publication*]
**J Periodontal Res Suppl**... Journal of Periodontal Research. Supplement [*A publication*]
**J Periodontol**... Journal of Periodontology [*A publication*]
**J Periodontol-Periodontics**... Journal of Periodontology - Periodontics [*A publication*]
**J Period Re**... Journal of Periodontal Research [*A publication*]
**J Perm Way Instn**... Permanent Way Institution. Journal [*A publication*]
**JPers**.......... Journal of Personality [*A publication*]
**J Pers Asse**... Journal of Personality Assessment [*A publication*]
**J Pers Assess**... Journal of Personality Assessment [*A publication*]
**J Personal**... Journal of Personality [*A publication*]
**J Personality & Social Psychol**... Journal of Personality and Social Psychology [*A publication*]
**J Person Soc Psychol**... Journal of Personality and Social Psychology [*A publication*]
**J Pers Soc**.. Journal of Personality and Social Psychology [*A publication*]
**J Pers Soc Psychol**... Journal of Personality and Social Psychology [*A publication*]
**J Perth Hosp**... Journal. Perth Hospital [*A publication*] (APTA)
**JPESB**....... Jewish Palestine Exploration Society. Bulletin [*A publication*]
**JPESJ**........ Jewish Palestine Exploration Society. Journal [*A publication*] (BJA)
**J Pestic Sci**... Journal of Pesticide Science [*A publication*]
**J Pestic Sci (Nihon Noyakugaku Kaishi)**... Journal of Pesticide Science (Nihon Noyakugaku Kaishi) [*A publication*]
**JPET**.......... Journal of Petroleum Technology [*A publication*]
**J Pet Geol**.. Journal of Petroleum Geology [*England*] [*A publication*]
**J Petrol**...... Journal of Petrology [*A publication*]
**J Petrol Geol**... Journal of Petroleum Geology [*A publication*]
**J Petrol Techn**... Journal of Petroleum Technology [*A publication*]
**J Petrol Technol**... Journal of Petroleum Technology [*A publication*]
**J Petro Tec**... Journal of Petroleum Technology [*A publication*]
**J Pet Tech**... Journal of Petroleum Technology [*A publication*]
**J Pet Technol**... Journal of Petroleum Technology [*A publication*]
**JPF**........... Jewish Peace Fellowship (EA)
**JPF**........... Jewish Philanthropic Fund of 1933 (EA)
**JPF**........... Job Planning Form
**JPF**........... Journal of Popular Film [*Later, Journal of Popular Film and Television*] [*A publication*]
**JPF**........... Justice of the Peace Fiscal [*British*] (ROG)
**JPFAEV**.... Journal of Psychotherapy and the Family [*A publication*]
**JPFC**.......... Jane Powell Fan Club (EA)
**JPFC**.......... Jeanne Pruett Fan Club (EA)
**JPFC**.......... Judas Priest Fan Club (EA)
**JPFMA**...... Journal of Physics. F: Metal Physics [*A publication*]
**JPFO**......... Jews for the Preservation of Firearms Ownership (EA)
**JPFT**.......... Joiner Pilaster Fumetight [*Technical drawings*]
**JPG**........... Jefferson Proving Ground [*Army*] [*Madison, IN*] (AABC)
**JPG**........... Job Performance [*or Proficiency*] Guide (AFM)
**JPG**........... Joint Planning Group [*NATO*] (NATG)
**JPGC**......... Joint Power Generation Conference
**JPGED**...... Journal of Experimental Psychology: General [*A publication*]
**JPGR**......... Journal of Plant Growth Regulation [*A publication*]
**JPGS**......... Japan Publications Guide Service [*Information service or system*] (IID)
**JPH**........... Jones, Paul H., Romulus MI [*STAC*]
**JPH**........... Journal of Pacific History [*A publication*]
**JPh**............ Journal of Philosophy [*A publication*]
**JPh**............ Journal of Phonetics [*A publication*]
**J Ph**........... Journal of Physiology [*A publication*]
**JPH**........... Journal of Presbyterian History [*A publication*]
**JPHA**......... John Pelham Historical Association (EA)
**JPHAA**...... Journal. American Pharmaceutical Association [*A publication*]
**JPHAA3**.... Journal. American Pharmaceutical Association [*A publication*]
**JPHAC**...... Journal of Physics. A: Mathematical and General [*A publication*]
**J Phar Biop**... Journal of Pharmacokinetics and Biopharmaceutics [*A publication*]
**J Pharm**..... Journal de Pharmacie [*A publication*]
**J Pharmacobio-Dyn**... Journal of Pharmacobio-Dynamics [*A publication*]
**J Pharmacokinet Biopharm**... Journal of Pharmacokinetics and Biopharmaceutics [*A publication*]
**J Pharmacol**... Journal de Pharmacologie [*A publication*]
**J Pharmacol Clin**... Journal de Pharmacologie Clinique [*A publication*]
**J Pharmacol Exper Therap**... Journal of Pharmacology and Experimental Therapeutics [*A publication*]
**J Pharmacol Exp Ther**... Journal of Pharmacology and Experimental Therapeutics [*A publication*]
**J Pharmacol Methods**... Journal of Pharmacological Methods [*A publication*]
**J Pharmacol (Paris)**... Journal de Pharmacologie (Paris) [*A publication*]
**J Pharm Assoc Thailand**... Journal. Pharmaceutical Association of Thailand [*A publication*]
**J Pharm B**... Journal of Pharmaceutical and Biomedical Analysis [*A publication*]
**J Pharm Belg**... Journal de Pharmacie de Belgique [*A publication*]
**J Pharm Biomed Anal**... Journal of Pharmaceutical and Biomedical Analysis [*A publication*]
**J Pharm Clin**... Journal de Pharmacie Clinique [*A publication*]
**J Pharm Els Lothr**... Journal der Pharmazie von Elsass-Lothringen [*A publication*]
**J Pharm Exp**... Journal of Pharmacology and Experimental Therapeutics [*A publication*]
**J Pharm Exp Ther**... Journal of Pharmacology and Experimental Therapeutics [*A publication*]
**J Pharm (Lahore)**... Journal of Pharmacy (Lahore) [*A publication*]
**J Pharm (Paris)**... Journal de Pharmacie et des Sciences Accessoires (Paris) [*A publication*]
**J Pharm Pha**... Journal of Pharmacy and Pharmacology [*A publication*]
**J Pharm Pharmac**... Journal of Pharmacy and Pharmacology [*A publication*]
**J Pharm Pharmacol**... Journal of Pharmacy and Pharmacology [*A publication*]
**J Pharm Pharmacol Suppl**... Journal of Pharmacy and Pharmacology. Supplement [*A publication*]
**J Pharm Sc**... Journal of Pharmaceutical Sciences [*A publication*]
**J Pharm Sci**... Journal of Pharmaceutical Sciences [*A publication*]
**J Pharm Sci Accessoires**... Journal de Pharmacie et des Sciences Accessoires [*A publication*]
**J Pharm Sci UAR**... Journal of Pharmaceutical Sciences of the United Arab Republic [*A publication*]
**J Pharm Soc Jap**... Journal. Pharmaceutical Society of Japan [*A publication*]
**J Pharm Soc Japan**... Journal. Pharmaceutical Society of Japan [*A publication*]
**J Pharm Soc Jpn**... Journal. Pharmaceutical Society of Japan [*A publication*]
**J Pharm Soc Korea**... Journal. Pharmaceutical Society of Korea [*A publication*]
**J Pharm Technol**... Journal of Pharmacy Technology [*A publication*]
**J Pharm Univ Karachi**... Journal of Pharmacy. University of Karachi [*A publication*]
**J Ph Ch Ref Data**... Journal of Physical and Chemical Reference Data [*A publication*]
**JPHD**........ Journal of Public Health Dentistry [*A publication*]
**J Phenomen**... Journal of Phenomenological Psychology [*A publication*]
**JPHGB**...... Journal of Physics. G: Nuclear Physics [*A publication*]
**J Ph GUW**... Jahrbuch der Philosophischen Gesellschaft an der Universitaet Wien [*A publication*]
**J Phil**......... Journal of Philosophy [*A publication*]
**J Phila Assoc Psychoanal**... Journal. Philadelphia Association for Psychoanalysis [*A publication*]

**J Phila Cty Dent Soc** ... Journal. Philadelphia County Dental Society [*A publication*]
**J Philadelphia Coll Pharm** ... Journal. Philadelphia College of Pharmacy [*A publication*]
**J Philadelphia Gen Hosp** ... Journal. Philadelphia General Hospital [*A publication*]
**J Phil Dev**.. Journal of Philippine Development [*A publication*]
**J Phil Educ** ... Journal of Philosophy of Education [*A publication*]
**J Philipp Dent Assoc** ... Journal. Philippine Dental Association [*A publication*]
**J Philipp Fed Priv Med Pract** ... Journal. Philippine Federation of Private Medical Practitioners [*A publication*]
**J Philippine Development** ... Journal of Philippine Development [*A publication*]
**J Philippine MA** ... Journal. Philippine Medical Association [*A publication*]
**J Philippine Statis** ... Journal of Philippine Statistics [*A publication*]
**J Philipp Isl Med Assoc** ... Journal. Philippine Islands Medical Association [*A publication*]
**J Philipp Med Assoc** ... Journal. Philippine Medical Association [*A publication*]
**J Philipp Pharm Assoc** ... Journal. Philippine Pharmaceutical Association [*A publication*]
**J Philipp Vet Med Assoc** ... Journal. Philippine Veterinary Medical Association [*A publication*]
**J Phil Log**.. Journal of Philosophical Logic [*A publication*]
**J Philos**...... Journal of Philosophy [*A publication*]
**J Philos Lo** ... Journal of Philosophical Logic [*A publication*]
**J Philos Logic** ... Journal of Philosophical Logic [*A publication*]
**J Philos Sport** ... Journal of the Philosophy of Sport [*A publication*]
**J Phil Sport** ... Journal of the Philosophy of Sport [*A publication*]
**J Phil Stat** ... Journal of Philippine Statistics [*A publication*]
**J Phil Stud** ... Journal of Philosophical Studies [*A publication*]
**JPHMD**..... Journal of Experimental Psychology: Human Learning and Memory [*A publication*]
**JPhon**......... Journal of Phonetics [*A publication*]
**J Photoacoust** ... Journal of Photoacoustics [*A publication*]
**J Photochem** ... Journal of Photochemistry [*A publication*]
**J Photochem Etching** ... Journal of Photochemical Etching [*A publication*]
**J Photogr Sci** ... Journal of Photographic Science [*A publication*]
**J Photogr Soc Am** ... Journal. Photographic Society of America [*A publication*]
**J Photomicrogr Soc** ... Journal. Photomicrographic Society [*A publication*]
**J Phot Sci**... Journal of Photographic Science [*A publication*]
**J Phot Soc Amer** ... Journal. Photographic Society of America [*A publication*]
**JPHP**......... Journal of Public Health Policy [*A publication*]
**JPHPD**...... Journal of Experimental Psychology: Human Perception and Performance [*A publication*]
**JPHS**......... Journal. Presbyterian Historical Society [*A publication*]
**JPHS**......... Pakistan Historical Society. Journal [*A publication*]
**JPhV**.......... Jahresbericht. Philologischer Verein [*A publication*]
**J Phy**.......... Journal de Physique, de Chimie, d'Histoire Naturelle, et des Arts [*A publication*]
**JPHYA**...... Journal of Physiology [*A publication*]
**J Phycol**..... Journal of Phycology [*A publication*]
**J Phycology** ... Journal of Phycology [*A publication*]
**J Phys**........ Journal of Physics [*A publication*]
**J Phys**........ Journal of Physiology [*A publication*]
**J Phys**........ Journal de Physique [*A publication*]
**J Phys A** .... Journal of Physics. A: Mathematical and General [*Bristol*] [*A publication*]
**J Phys A Gen Phys** ... Journal of Physics. A: General Physics [*A publication*]
**J Phys A (London)** ... Journal of Physics. A: General Physics (London) [*A publication*]
**J Phys A (London) Math Gen** ... Journal of Physics. A: Mathematical and General (London) [*A publication*]
**J Phys A (London) Proc Phys Soc Gen** ... Journal of Physics. A: Proceedings. Physical Society. General (London) [*A publication*]
**J Phys A Math Nucl Gen** ... Journal of Physics. A: Mathematical, Nuclear, and General [*A publication*]
**J Phys B**..... Journal of Physics. B: Atomic and Molecular Physics [*A publication*]
**J of Phys B At Mol Phys** ... Journal of Physics. B: Atomic and Molecular Physics [*A publication*]
**J Phys B (London)** ... Journal of Physics. B: Atomic and Molecular Physics (London) [*A publication*]
**J Phys C**..... Journal of Physics. C: Solid State Physics [*A publication*]
**J Phys Chem** ... Journal of Physical Chemistry [*A publication*]
**J Phys & Chem Ref Data** ... Journal of Physical and Chemical Reference Data [*A publication*]
**J Phys Chem Ref Data** ... Journal of Physical and Chemical Reference Data [*A publication*]
**J Phys Chem Ref Data Suppl** ... Journal of Physical and Chemical Reference Data. Supplement [*A publication*]
**J Phys Chem Sol** ... Journal of Physics and Chemistry of Solids [*A publication*]
**J Phys and Chem Solids** ... Journal of Physics and Chemistry of Solids [*A publication*]
**J Phys Chem Solids** ... Journal of Physics and Chemistry of Solids [*A publication*]
**J Phys Chem Solids Suppl** ... Journal of Physics and Chemistry of Solids. Supplement [*England*] [*A publication*]
**J Phys Chem (Wash)** ... Journal of Physical Chemistry (Washington, DC) [*A publication*]
**J Phys Ch S** ... Journal of Physics and Chemistry of Solids [*A publication*]
**J Phys C (London)** ... Journal of Physics. C: Solid State Physics (London) [*A publication*]
**J Phys Coll Chem** ... Journal of Physical and Colloid Chemistry [*A publication*]
**J Phys & Colloid Chem** ... Journal of Physical and Colloid Chemistry [*A publication*]
**J Phys Colloq** ... Journal de Physique. Colloque [*A publication*]
**J Phys C Solid State Phys** ... Journal of Physics. C: Solid State Physics [*A publication*]
**J Phys D Appl Phys** ... Journal of Physics. D: Applied Physics [*A publication*]
**J Phys D (London)** ... Journal of Physics. D: Applied Physics (London) [*A publication*]
**J Phys E**..... Journal of Physics. E: Scientific Instruments [*A publication*]
**J Phys Earth** ... Journal of Physics of the Earth [*A publication*]
**J Phys Ed**... Journal of Physical Education [*A publication*]
**J Phys Educ** ... Journal of Physical Education [*A publication*]
**J Phys Educ & Rec** ... Journal of Physical Education and Recreation [*Later, Journal of Physical Education, Recreation, and Dance*] [*A publication*]
**J Phys Educ Rec & Dance** ... Journal of Physical Education, Recreation, and Dance [*A publication*]
**J Phys Educ Recr** ... Journal of Physical Education and Recreation [*Later, Journal of Physical Education, Recreation, and Dance*] [*A publication*]
**J Phys E (London) Sci Instrum** ... Journal of Physics. E: Scientific Instruments (London) [*A publication*]
**J Phys E Sci Instrum** ... Journal of Physics. E: Scientific Instruments [*A publication*]
**J Phys F**..... Journal of Physics. F: Metal Physics [*A publication*]
**J Phys F Met Phys** ... Journal of Physics. F: Metal Physics [*A publication*]
**J Phys G** .... Journal of Physics. G: Nuclear Physics [*A publication*]
**J Phys G Nu** ... Journal of Physics. G: Nuclear Physics [*A publication*]
**J Physical Chem** ... Journal of Physical Chemistry [*A publication*]
**J Physiol**.... Journal of Physiology [*A publication*]
**J Physiol Exper** ... Journal de Physiologie Experimentale et Pathologique [*A publication*]
**J Physiol (Lond)** ... Journal of Physiology (London) [*A publication*]
**J Physiol (Paris)** ... Journal de Physiologie (Paris) [*A publication*]
**J Physiol (Paris) Suppl** ... Journal de Physiologie (Paris). Supplement [*France*] [*A publication*]
**J Physiol et Path Gen** ... Journal de Physiologie et de Pathologie Generale [*A publication*]
**J Physiol Soc Jpn** ... Journal. Physiological Society of Japan [*A publication*]
**J Physique** ... Journal de Physique [*A publication*]
**J Phys Jap** ... Journal. Physical Society of Japan [*A publication*]
**J Phys Lett** ... Journal de Physique. Lettres [*A publication*]
**J Physl (Lon)** ... Journal of Physiology (London) [*A publication*]
**J Physl (Par)** ... Journal de Physiologie (Paris) [*A publication*]
**J Phys (Moscow)** ... Journal of Physics (Moscow) [*USSR*] [*A publication*]
**J Phys Ocea** ... Journal of Physical Oceanography [*A publication*]
**J Phys Oceanogr** ... Journal of Physical Oceanography [*A publication*]
**J Phys Org Chem** ... Journal of Physical Organic Chemistry [*A publication*]
**J Phys (Orsay Fr)** ... Journal de Physique (Orsay, France) [*A publication*]
**J Phys (Paris)** ... Journal de Physique (Paris) [*A publication*]
**J Phys (Paris) Colloq** ... Journal de Physique (Paris). Colloque [*A publication*]
**J Phys (Paris) Lett** ... Journal de Physique. Lettres (Paris) [*A publication*]
**J Phys (Paris) Suppl** ... Journal de Physique (Paris). Supplement [*A publication*]
**J Phys Rad** ... Journal de Physique et le Radium [*A publication*]
**J Phys Radium** ... Journal de Physique et le Radium [*France*] [*A publication*]
**J Phys (Soc Fr Phys) Colloq** ... Journal de Physique (Societe Francaise de Physique). Colloque [*A publication*]
**J Phys Soc Jap** ... Journal. Physical Society of Japan [*A publication*]
**J Phys Soc Jpn Suppl** ... Journal. Physical Society of Japan. Supplement [*A publication*]
**J Phys Theor Appl** ... Journal de Physique Theorique et Appliquee [*A publication*]
**J Phytopathol (Berl)** ... Journal of Phytopathology (Berlin) [*A publication*]
**J Phytopathol (UAR)** ... Journal of Phytopathology (UAR) [*A publication*]
**JPI**............ Jackson Personality Inventory [*Personality development test*] [*Psychology*]
**JPI**............ Job Performance Illustrations (MCD)
**JPI**............ Joint Packaging Instruction
**JPI**............ Journal of Product Innovation Management [*A publication*]
**JPI**............ JP Industries, Inc. [*NYSE symbol*] (SPSG)
**JPI**............ Sitka, AK [*Location identifier*] [*FAA*] (FAAL)
**JPIC**........... Joint Program Integration Committee [*NASA*] (NASA)
**JPIFAN**..... Japan Pesticide Information [*A publication*]
**JPIM**......... Journal of Product Innovation Management [*Product Development and Management Association*] [*A publication*]
**J Pineal Res** ... Journal of Pineal Research [*A publication*]
**J Pipeline Div Am Soc Civ Eng** ... Journal. Pipeline Division. American Society of Civil Engineers [*A publication*]
**J Pipelines** ... Journal of Pipelines [*A publication*]
**JPJ**............ Justice of the Peace Journal [*A publication*]
**JPJ**............ Justice of the Peace and Local Government Review [*A publication*] (DLA)

**JPJ**........... Justice of the Peace. Weekly Notes of Cases [*England*] [*A publication*] (DLA)
**JPJ**........... Paterson, NJ [*Location identifier*] [*FAA*] (FAAL)
**JPJo**.......... Justice of the Peace. Weekly Notes of Cases [*England*] [*A publication*] (DLA)
**JPJu**.......... Journal of Psychology and Judaism [*A publication*]
**JPKS**.......... Jahrbuch. Preussische Kunstsammlungen [*A publication*]
**JPL**........... Jacksonville Public Library System, Jacksonville, FL [*OCLC symbol*] (OCLC)
**JPL**........... Jet Propulsion Laboratory [*Renamed H. Allen Smith Jet Propulsion Laboratory, 1973, after a retiring congressman. However, JPL is used officially*] [*California Institute of Technology*] [*Pasadena, CA*] [*NASA*] [*Research center*]
**JPL**........... Job Parts List (AAG)
**JPL**........... Journal of Philosophical Logic [*A publication*]
**J P L**.......... Journal of Planning Law [*A publication*]
**JPL**........... Journal of Products Liability [*A publication*]
**J P and L**.... Journal of Psychiatry and Law [*A publication*]
**J Plan Envir Law** ... Journal of Planning and Environment Law [*A publication*]
**J Plan & Environ L** ... Journal of Planning and Environment Law [*A publication*]
**J Planif Develop** ... Journal de la Planification du Developpement [*A publication*]
**J Plankton Res** ... Journal of Plankton Research [*England*] [*A publication*]
**J Plann Environ Law** ... Journal of Planning and Environment Law [*A publication*]
**J Planning and Environment Law** ... Journal of Planning and Environment Law [*A publication*]
**J Plann Property Law** ... Journal of Planning and Property Law [*A publication*]
**J Plan & Prop L** ... Journal of Planning and Property Law [*A publication*]
**J Plant Anat Morphol (Jodhpur)** ... Journal of Plant Anatomy and Morphology (Jodhpur) [*A publication*]
**J Plant Breed** ... Journal of Plant Breeding [*A publication*]
**J Plant Crops** ... Journal of Plantation Crops [*A publication*]
**J Plant Dis Prot** ... Journal of Plant Diseases and Protection [*A publication*]
**J Plant Growth Regul** ... Journal of Plant Growth Regulation [*A publication*]
**J Plantn Crops** ... Journal of Plantation Crops [*A publication*]
**J Plant Nut** ... Journal of Plant Nutrition [*A publication*]
**J Plant Nutr** ... Journal of Plant Nutrition [*A publication*]
**J Plant Nutr Soil Sci** ... Journal of Plant Nutrition and Soil Science [*A publication*]
**J Plant Physiol** ... Journal of Plant Physiology [*A publication*]
**J Plant Prot** ... Journal of Plant Protection [*A publication*]
**J Plas Age** ... Japan Plastics Age [*A publication*]
**J Plasma Ph** ... Journal of Plasma Physics [*A publication*]
**J Plasma Phys** ... Journal of Plasma Physics [*A publication*]
**J Plast An** .. Japan Plastics Industry Annual [*A publication*]
**J Plast Reconstr Surg Nurs** ... Journal of Plastic and Reconstructive Surgical Nursing [*A publication*]
**J Platn Crops** ... Journal of Plantation Crops [*A publication*]
**JPLE**.......... Journal of Professional Legal Education [*Australia*] [*A publication*]
**JPL/ETR**... Jet Propulsion Laboratory Field Station, Air Force Eastern Test Range
**J Pl L**......... Journal of Planning Law [*A publication*]
**JPL Publ 78** ... Jet Propulsion Laboratory. Publication 78 [*A publication*]
**JPL Q Tech Rev** ... JPL [*Jet Propulsion Laboratory*] Quarterly Technical Review [*A publication*]
**JPLSA**....... Journal. Polarographic Society [*A publication*]
**JPL Space Programs Summ** ... Jet Propulsion Laboratory. Space Programs Summary [*A publication*]
**JPL Tech Memo** ... JPL [*Jet Propulsion Laboratory*] Technical Memorandum [*A publication*]
**JPL Tech Rep** ... JPL [*Jet Propulsion Laboratory*] Technical Report [*A publication*]
**JPM**........... Jerusalem Post Magazine [*A publication*]
**JPM**........... Jet-Piercing Machine
**JPM**........... Job Performance Manual (MCD)
**JPM**........... Job Performance Measure
**JPM**........... Joint Project Manager
**JPM**........... Journal of Property Management [*A publication*]
**JPM**........... Journal of Purchasing and Materials Management [*A publication*]
**JPM**........... Morgan [*J. P.*] & Co., Inc. [*NYSE symbol*] (SPSG)
**JPM**........... Personnel Management [*A publication*]
**JPMA**........ Juvenile Products Manufacturers Association (EA)
**JPMA J Pak Med Assoc** ... JPMA. Journal. Pakistan Medical Association [*A publication*]
**JPMEA**..... Journal. Philippine Medical Association [*A publication*]
**JPMI**......... JPM Industries, Inc. [*Bridgeview, IL*] [*NASDAQ symbol*] (NQ)
**JPMO**........ Joint Program Management Office (MCD)
**JPMR**........ Joint Projected Manpower Requirements [*Military*] (AABC)
**JPMS**........ J. P. Morgan Securities
**JPMSA**...... Journal of Pharmaceutical Sciences [*A publication*]
**JPN**........... Japan [*ANSI three-letter standard code*] (CNC)
**JPN**........... Japan Fund, Inc. [*NYSE symbol*] (SPSG)
**jpn**............ Japanese [*MARC language code*] [*Library of Congress*] (LCCP)
**JPN**........... Japanese
**JPN**........... Journal of Personal Selling and Sales Management [*A publication*]
**JPN**........... Washington, DC [*Location identifier*] [*FAA*] (FAAL)
**Jpn Agric Res Q** ... Japan Agricultural Research Quarterly [*A publication*]
**Jpn Analyst** ... Japan Analyst [*A publication*]
**Jpn Annu Rev Electron Comput Telecommun** ... Japan Annual Reviews in Electronics, Computers, and Telecommunications [*A publication*]
**Jpn Arch Histol** ... Japanese Archives of Histology [*A publication*]
**Jpn Arch Intern Med** ... Japanese Archives of Internal Medicine [*A publication*]
**Jpn Archit** ... Japan Architect [*A publication*]
**Jpn At Energy Res Inst Annu Rep Acc** ... Japan. Atomic Energy Research Institute. Annual Report and Account [*A publication*]
**Jpn At Energy Res Inst Rep Res Rep** ... Japan. Atomic Energy Research Institute. Report. Research Report [*A publication*]
**Jpn Chem Ind** ... Japan Chemical Industry [*A publication*]
**Jpn Chem Q** ... Japan Chemical Quarterly [*A publication*]
**Jpn Chem Rev** ... Japan Chemical Review [*A publication*]
**Jpn Circ J** .. Japanese Circulation Journal [*A publication*]
**Jpn Dent J** ... Japanese Dental Journal [*A publication*]
**Jpn Dtsch Med Ber** ... Japanisch-Deutsche Medizinische Berichte [*A publication*]
**Jpn Eco A** .. Japan Economic Almanac
**Jpn Econ J** ... Japan Economic Journal [*A publication*]
**Jpn Elec I**... Japan Electronics Industry [*A publication*]
**Jpn Electron Eng** ... Japan Electronic Engineering [*A publication*]
**Jpn Energy Technol Intell** ... Japan Energy and Technology Intelligence [*A publication*]
**Jpn Export** ... Export Statistical Schedule (Japan) [*A publication*]
**Jpn Forcst** ... Five-Year Economic Forecast (Japan) [*A publication*]
**Jpn Gas Assoc J** ... Japan Gas Association. Journal [*A publication*]
**Jpn-Ger Med Rep** ... Japan-Germany Medical Reports [*A publication*]
**Jpn Heart J** ... Japanese Heart Journal [*A publication*]
**Jpn Hosp** ... Japan Hospitals [*A publication*]
**Jpn Import** ... Import Statistical Schedule (Japan) [*A publication*]
**Jpn Ind Technol Bull** ... Japan Industrial and Technological Bulletin [*A publication*]
**Jp Niv**........ Jurisprudence des Tribunaux de l'Arrondissement de Nivelles [*A publication*]
**Jpn J Aerosp Med Psychol** ... Japanese Journal of Aerospace Medicine and Psychology [*A publication*]
**Jpn J Alcohol Stud & Drug Depend** ... Japanese Journal of Alcohol Studies and Drug Dependence [*A publication*]
**Jpn J Allergol** ... Japanese Journal of Allergology [*A publication*]
**Jpn J Allergy** ... Japanese Journal of Allergy [*A publication*]
**Jpn J Anesthesiol** ... Japanese Journal of Anesthesiology [*A publication*]
**Jpn J Anim Reprod** ... Japanese Journal of Animal Reproduction [*A publication*]
**Jpn J Antibiot** ... Japanese Journal of Antibiotics [*A publication*]
**Jpn J Appl Entomol Zool** ... Japanese Journal of Applied Entomology and Zoology [*A publication*]
**Jpn J Appl Phys** ... Japanese Journal of Applied Physics [*A publication*]
**Jpn J Appl Phys 1** ... Japanese Journal of Applied Physics. Part 1 [*A publication*]
**Jpn J Appl Phys 2 Lett** ... Japanese Journal of Applied Physics. Part 2. Letters [*A publication*]
**Jpn J Appl Phys Part 1** ... Japanese Journal of Applied Physics. Part 1. Regular Papers and Short Notes [*A publication*]
**Jpn J Appl Phys Part 2** ... Japanese Journal of Applied Physics. Part 2. Letters [*A publication*]
**Jpn J Appl Phys Suppl** ... Japanese Journal of Applied Physics. Supplement [*A publication*]
**Jpn J Astron** ... Japanese Journal of Astronomy [*A publication*]
**Jpn J Astron Geophys** ... Japanese Journal of Astronomy and Geophysics [*A publication*]
**Jpn J Bacteriol** ... Japanese Journal of Bacteriology [*A publication*]
**Jpn J Bot** ... Japanese Journal of Botany [*A publication*]
**Jpn J Breed** ... Japanese Journal of Breeding [*A publication*]
**Jpn J Cancer Clin** ... Japanese Journal of Cancer Clinics [*A publication*]
**Jpn J Cancer Res** ... Japanese Journal of Cancer Research [*A publication*]
**Jpn J Cancer Res (Gann)** ... Japanese Journal of Cancer Research (Gann) [*A publication*]
**Jpn J Chem** ... Japanese Journal of Chemistry [*A publication*]
**Jpn J Chest Dis** ... Japanese Journal of Chest Diseases [*A publication*]
**Jpn J Child Adoles Psychiatry** ... Japanese Journal of Child and Adolescent Psychiatry [*A publication*]
**Jpn J Clin Electron Microsc** ... Japanese Journal of Clinical Electron Microscopy [*A publication*]
**Jpn J Clin Exp Med** ... Japanese Journal of Clinical and Experimental Medicine [*A publication*]
**Jpn J Clin Hematol** ... Japanese Journal of Clinical Hematology [*A publication*]
**Jpn J Clin Med** ... Japanese Journal of Clinical Medicine [*A publication*]
**Jpn J Clin Oncol** ... Japanese Journal of Clinical Oncology [*A publication*]
**Jpn J Clin Ophthalmol** ... Japanese Journal of Clinical Ophthalmology [*A publication*]
**Jpn J Clin Pathol** ... Japanese Journal of Clinical Pathology [*A publication*]
**Jpn J Clin Pathol Suppl** ... Japanese Journal of Clinical Pathology. Supplement [*A publication*]

**Jpn J Clin Pharmacol** ... Japanese Journal of Clinical Pharmacology [*A publication*]
**Jpn J Clin Radiol** ... Japanese Journal of Clinical Radiology [*A publication*]
**Jpn J Clin Urol** ... Japanese Journal of Clinical Urology [*A publication*]
**Jpn J Const Med** ... Japanese Journal of Constitutional Medicine [*A publication*]
**Jpn J Crop Sci** ... Japanese Journal of Crop Science [*A publication*]
**Jpn J Dairy Food Sci** ... Japanese Journal of Dairy and Food Science [*A publication*]
**Jpn J Dairy Sci** ... Japanese Journal of Dairy Science [*A publication*]
**Jpn J Dermatol** ... Japanese Journal of Dermatology [*A publication*]
**Jpn J Dermatol Ser B (Engl Ed)** ... Japanese Journal of Dermatology. Series B (English Edition) [*A publication*]
**Jpn J Ecol** ... Japanese Journal of Ecology [*A publication*]
**Jpn J Eng Abstr** ... Japanese Journal of Engineering. Abstracts [*A publication*]
**Jpn J Ergonomics** ... Japanese Journal of Ergonomics [*A publication*]
**Jpn J Ethnol** ... Japanese Journal of Ethnology [*A publication*]
**Jpn J Exp Med** ... Japanese Journal of Experimental Medicine [*A publication*]
**Jpn J Exp Morphol** ... Japanese Journal of Experimental Morphology [*A publication*]
**Jpn J Fertil Steril** ... Japanese Journal of Fertility and Sterility [*A publication*]
**Jpn J Gastroenterol** ... Japanese Journal of Gastroenterology [*A publication*]
**Jpn J Genet** ... Japanese Journal of Genetics [*A publication*]
**Jpn J Genet Suppl** ... Japanese Journal of Genetics. Supplement [*A publication*]
**Jpn J Geol Geogr** ... Japanese Journal of Geology and Geography [*A publication*]
**Jpn J Geriatr** ... Japanese Journal of Geriatrics [*A publication*]
**Jpn J Herpetol** ... Japanese Journal of Herpetology [*A publication*]
**Jpn J Hum Genet** ... Japanese Journal of Human Genetics [*A publication*]
**Jpn J Hyg** .. Japanese Journal of Hygiene [*A publication*]
**Jpn J Ichthyol** ... Japanese Journal of Ichthyology [*A publication*]
**Jpn J Ind Health** ... Japanese Journal of Industrial Health [*A publication*]
**Jpn J Lepr** ... Japanese Journal of Leprosy [*A publication*]
**Jpn J Limnol** ... Japanese Journal of Limnology [*A publication*]
**Jpn J Malacol** ... Japanese Journal of Malacology [*A publication*]
**Jpn J Math** ... Japanese Journal of Mathematics [*A publication*]
**Jpn J Med** ... Japanese Journal of Medicine [*A publication*]
**Jpn J Med Electron Biol Eng** ... Japanese Journal of Medical Electronics and Biological Engineering [*A publication*]
**Jpn J Med Electron and Biol Eng** ... Japanese Journal of Medical Electronics and Biological Engineering [*A publication*]
**Jpn J Med Mycol** ... Japanese Journal of Medical Mycology [*A publication*]
**Jpn J Med Sci 1** ... Japanese Journal of Medical Sciences. Part 1. Anatomy [*A publication*]
**Jpn J Med Sci 2** ... Japanese Journal of Medical Sciences. Part 2. Biochemistry [*A publication*]
**Jpn J Med Sci 3** ... Japanese Journal of Medical Sciences. Part 3. Biophysics [*A publication*]
**Jpn J Med Sci 4** ... Japanese Journal of Medical Sciences. Part 4. Pharmacology [*A publication*]
**Jpn J Med Sci 5** ... Japanese Journal of Medical Sciences. Part 5. Pathology [*A publication*]
**Jpn J Med Sci 6** ... Japanese Journal of Medical Sciences. Part 6. Bacteriology and Parasitology [*A publication*]
**Jpn J Med Sci 7** ... Japanese Journal of Medical Sciences. Part 7. Social Medicine and Hygiene [*A publication*]
**Jpn J Med Sci 8** ... Japanese Journal of Medical Sciences. Part 8. Internal Medicine, Pediatry, and Psychiatry [*A publication*]
**Jpn J Med Sci 9** ... Japanese Journal of Medical Sciences. Part 9. Surgery, Orthopedy, and Odontology [*A publication*]
**Jpn J Med Sci 10** ... Japanese Journal of Medical Sciences. Part 10. Ophthalmology [*A publication*]
**Jpn J Med Sci 11** ... Japanese Journal of Medical Sciences. Part 11. Gynecology and Tocology [*A publication*]
**Jpn J Med Sci 12** ... Japanese Journal of Medical Sciences. Part 12. Oto-Rhino-Laryngology [*A publication*]
**Jpn J Med Sci 13** ... Japanese Journal of Medical Sciences. Part 13. Dermatology and Urology [*A publication*]
**Jpn J Med Sci Biol** ... Japanese Journal of Medical Science and Biology [*A publication*]
**Jpn J Michurin Biol** ... Japanese Journal of Michurin Biology [*A publication*]
**Jpn J Microbiol** ... Japanese Journal of Microbiology [*A publication*]
**Jpn J Midwife** ... Japanese Journal for the Midwife [*A publication*]
**Jpn J Nephrol** ... Japanese Journal of Nephrology [*A publication*]
**Jpn J Neurol Psychiatry** ... Japanese Journal of Neurology and Psychiatry [*A publication*]
**Jpn J Nucl Med** ... Japanese Journal of Nuclear Medicine [*A publication*]
**Jpn J Nurs** ... Japanese Journal of Nursing [*A publication*]
**Jpn J Nurs Res** ... Japanese Journal of Nursing Research [*A publication*]
**Jpn J Nutr** ... Japanese Journal of Nutrition [*A publication*]
**Jpn J Obstet Gynecol** ... Japanese Journal of Obstetrics and Gynecology [*A publication*]
**Jpn J Ophthalmol** ... Japanese Journal of Ophthalmology [*A publication*]
**Jpn J Oral Biol** ... Japanese Journal of Oral Biology [*A publication*]
**Jpn J Palynol** ... Japanese Journal of Palynology [*A publication*]
**Jpn J Parasitol** ... Japanese Journal of Parasitology [*A publication*]
**Jpn J Pediat** ... Japanese Journal of Pediatrics [*A publication*]
**Jpn J Pediat Surg Med** ... Japanese Journal of Pediatric Surgery and Medicine [*A publication*]
**Jpn J Pharm** ... Japanese Journal of Pharmacognosy [*A publication*]
**Jpn J Pharmacogn** ... Japanese Journal of Pharmacognosy [*A publication*]
**Jpn J Pharmacognosy** ... Japanese Journal of Pharmacognosy [*A publication*]
**Jpn J Pharmacol** ... Japanese Journal of Pharmacology [*A publication*]
**Jpn J Pharm Chem** ... Japanese Journal of Pharmacy and Chemistry [*A publication*]
**Jpn J Phys** ... Japanese Journal of Physics [*A publication*]
**Jpn J Phys Educ** ... Japanese Journal of Physical Education [*A publication*]
**Jpn J Phys Fitness Sports Med** ... Japanese Journal of Physical Fitness and Sports Medicine [*A publication*]
**Jpn J Physiol** ... Japanese Journal of Physiology [*A publication*]
**Jpn J Plast Reconstr Surg** ... Japanese Journal of Plastic and Reconstructive Surgery [*A publication*]
**Jpn J Psychiatry Neurol** ... Japanese Journal of Psychiatry and Neurology [*A publication*]
**Jpn J Psychol** ... Japanese Journal of Psychology [*A publication*]
**Jpn J Psychopharmacol** ... Japanese Journal of Psychopharmacology [*A publication*]
**Jpn J Psychosom Med** ... Japanese Journal of Psychosomatic Medicine [*A publication*]
**Jpn J Public Health** ... Japanese Journal of Public Health [*A publication*]
**Jpn J Radiol Technol** ... Japanese Journal of Radiological Technology [*A publication*]
**Jpn J Relig** ... Japanese Journal of Religious Studies [*A publication*]
**Jpn J Sanit Zool** ... Japanese Journal of Sanitary Zoology [*A publication*]
**Jpn J Smooth Muscle Res** ... Japanese Journal of Smooth Muscle Research [*A publication*]
**Jpn J Stud Alcohol** ... Japanese Journal of Studies on Alcohol [*A publication*]
**Jpn J Surg** ... Japanese Journal of Surgery [*A publication*]
**Jpn J Thorac Dis** ... Japanese Journal of Thoracic Diseases [*A publication*]
**Jpn J Trop Agric** ... Japanese Journal of Tropical Agriculture [*A publication*]
**Jpn J Trop Med Hyg** ... Japanese Journal of Tropical Medicine and Hygiene [*A publication*]
**Jpn J Tuberc** ... Japanese Journal of Tuberculosis [*A publication*]
**Jpn J Tuberc Chest Dis** ... Japanese Journal of Tuberculosis and Chest Diseases [*A publication*]
**Jpn J Urol** ... Japanese Journal of Urology [*A publication*]
**Jpn J Vet R** ... Japanese Journal of Veterinary Research [*A publication*]
**Jpn J Vet Res** ... Japanese Journal of Veterinary Research [*A publication*]
**Jpn J Vet Sci** ... Japanese Journal of Veterinary Science [*A publication*]
**Jpn J Zool** ... Japanese Journal of Zoology [*A publication*]
**Jpn J Zootech Sci** ... Japanese Journal of Zootechnical Science [*A publication*]
**Jpn Light Met Weld** ... Japan Light Metal Welding [*A publication*]
**Jpn Market** ... Dentsu Japan Marketing/Advertising Yearbook [*A publication*]
**Jpn Med J** ... Japanese Medical Journal [*A publication*]
**Jpn Med Res Found Publ** ... Japan Medical Research Foundation. Publication [*A publication*]
**JPNNB** ...... Journal of Psychiatric Nursing and Mental Health Services [*A publication*]
**Jpn Nucl Med** ... Japanese Nuclear Medicine [*A publication*]
**JPNP** ......... Journal de Psychologie Normale et Pathologique [*A publication*]
**JPNPA** ...... Journal de Psychologie Normale et Pathologique [*A publication*]
**Jpn P Comp** ... Japanese Invasion of America's Personal Computer Market [*A publication*]
**Jpn Pestic Inf** ... Japan Pesticide Information [*A publication*]
**Jpn Petrol** .. Japan Petroleum and Energy Weekly [*A publication*]
**Jpn P Indx** ... Japan Price Indexes Annual, 1984 [*A publication*]
**Jpn Plast**.... Japan Plastics [*A publication*]
**Jpn Poult Sci** ... Japanese Poultry Science [*A publication*]
**Jpn Printer** ... Japan Printer [*A publication*]
**Jpn Psychol Res** ... Japanese Psychological Research [*A publication*]
**Jpn Quart**... Japan Quarterly [*A publication*]
**Jpn Railw Eng** ... Japanese Railway Engineering [*A publication*]
**Jpn Rev Clin Ophthalmol** ... Japanese Review of Clinical Ophthalmology [*A publication*]
**Jpn Sci Mon** ... Japanese Scientific Monthly [*A publication*]
**Jpn Sci Rev Med Sci** ... Japan Science Review. Medical Sciences [*A publication*]
**Jpn Sci Rev Min Metall** ... Japanese Science Review. Mining and Metallurgy [*A publication*]
**Jpn Soc Aeronaut Space Sci Trans** ... Japan Society for Aeronautical and Space Sciences. Transactions [*A publication*]
**Jpn Soc Tuberc Annu Rep** ... Japanese Society for Tuberculosis. Annual Report [*A publication*]
**Jpn Spectros Co Appl Notes** ... Japan Spectroscopic Company. Application Notes [*A publication*]
**Jpn Steel Bull** ... Japan Steel Bulletin [*A publication*]
**Jpn Steel Tube Tech Rev** ... Japan Steel and Tube Technical Review [*A publication*]
**Jpn Steel Works** ... Japan Steel Works [*A publication*]
**Jpn Steel Works Tech News** ... Japan Steel Works. Technical News [*A publication*]
**Jpn Steel Works Tech Rev** ... Japan Steel Works. Technical Review [*A publication*]
**Jpn Steel Works Tech Rev (Engl Ed)** ... Japan Steel Works. Technical Review (English Edition) [*A publication*]
**Jpn Stud Hist Sci** ... Japanese Studies in the History of Science [*A publication*]
**JP (NSW)** ... Justice of the Peace (New South Wales) [*A publication*] (APTA)

**JPNT**......... Joiner Pilaster Nontight [*Technical drawings*]
**Jpn TAPPI**... Japan TAPPI [*Technical Association of the Pulp and Paper Industry*] [*A publication*]
**Jpn Telecommun Rev**... Japan Telecommunications Review [*A publication*]
**Jpn Trade**.. Standard Trade Index of Japan [*A publication*]
**JPO**............ Joint Petroleum Office
**JPO**............ Joint Program Office [*Military*] (SDI)
**JPO**............ Joint Project Office [*or Officer*]
**JPO**............ Journal of Portfolio Management [*A publication*]
**JPO**............ Junior Professional Officer [*United Nations*]
**JPO**............ Juvenile Probation Officer (OICC)
**JPOAA**...... Junior Panel Outdoor Advertising Association [*Later, ESOAA*]
**JPOC**......... JSC [*Johnson Space Center*] Payload Operations Center (MCD)
**JPOCB**...... Journal of Popular Culture [*A publication*]
**J Podiatr Med Educ**... Journal of Podiatric Medical Education [*A publication*]
**JPOGDP**... Journal of Psychosomatic Obstetrics and Gynaecology [*A publication*]
**JPO J Prac Orthod**... JPO. Journal of Practical Orthodontics [*A publication*]
**JPol**........... Jezyk Polski [*A publication*]
**JPol**........... Journal of Politics [*A publication*]
**J Polarogr Soc**... Journal. Polarographic Society [*England*] [*A publication*]
**J Pol Econ**... Journal of Political Economy [*A publication*]
**J Pol Economy**... Journal of Political Economy [*A publication*]
**J Police Sci and Ad**... Journal of Police Science and Administration [*A publication*]
**J Police Sci & Adm**... Journal of Police Science and Administration [*A publication*]
**J Police Sci Adm**... Journal of Police Science and Administration [*A publication*]
**J Polic Sci**.. Journal of Police Science and Administration [*A publication*]
**J Policy Anal Manage**... Journal of Policy Analysis and Management [*A publication*]
**J Policy Analysis Manage**... Journal of Policy Analysis and Management [*A publication*]
**J Policy Analysis and Mgt**... Journal of Policy Analysis and Management [*A publication*]
**J Policy Model**... Journal of Policy Modeling [*A publication*]
**J Polit**........ Journal of Politics [*A publication*]
**J Polit Ec**... Journal of Political Economy [*A publication*]
**J Polit Econ**... Journal of Political Economy [*A publication*]
**J Politics**.... Journal of Politics [*A publication*]
**J Polit Mil**... Journal of Political and Military Sociology [*A publication*]
**J Polit Milit Sociol**... Journal of Political and Military Sociology [*A publication*]
**J Polit Stud**... Journal of Political Studies [*A publication*]
**J Pol and Military Sociol**... Journal of Political and Military Sociology [*A publication*]
**J Pol Mil Sociol**... Journal of Political and Military Sociology [*A publication*]
**J Pol Sci**..... Journal of Polymer Science [*A publication*]
**J Pol Sci & Admin**... Journal of Police Science and Administration [*A publication*] (DLA)
**J Pol Sci C**... Journal of Polymer Science. Part C: Polymer Symposia [*Later, Journal of Polymer Science. Polymer Symposia Edition*] [*A publication*]
**J Pol Sc PC**... Journal of Polymer Science. Polymer Chemistry Edition [*A publication*]
**J Pol Sc PL**... Journal of Polymer Science. Polymer Letters Edition [*A publication*]
**J Pol Sc PP**... Journal of Polymer Science. Polymer Physics Edition [*A publication*]
**J Pol Soc**.... Journal. Polynesian Society [*A publication*]
**J Pol Stud**.. Journal of Political Studies [*A publication*]
**J Polym Mater**... Journal of Polymer Materials [*A publication*]
**J Polym Sci**... Journal of Polymer Science [*A publication*]
**J Polym Sci A-1**... Journal of Polymer Science. Part A-1: Polymer Chemistry [*A publication*]
**J Polym Sci A-2**... Journal of Polymer Science. Part A-2: Polymer Physics [*A publication*]
**J Polym Sci B**... Journal of Polymer Science. Part B: Polymer Letters [*A publication*]
**J Polym Sci Macromol Rev**... Journal of Polymer Science. Macromolecular Reviews [*A publication*]
**J Polym Sci Part A-1: Polym Chem**... Journal of Polymer Science. Part A-1: Polymer Chemistry [*A publication*]
**J Polym Sci Part A-2: Polym Phys**... Journal of Polymer Science. Part A-2: Polymer Physics [*A publication*]
**J Polym Sci Part B: Polym Lett**... Journal of Polymer Science. Part B: Polymer Letters [*A publication*]
**J Polym Sci Part C**... Journal of Polymer Science. Part C: Polymer Symposia [*Later, Journal of Polymer Science. Polymer Symposia Edition*] [*A publication*]
**J Polym Sci Part C: Polym Symp**... Journal of Polymer Science. Part C: Polymer Symposia [*Later, Journal of Polymer Science. Polymer Symposia Edition*] [*A publication*]
**J Polym Sci Part D**... Journal of Polymer Science. Part D: Macromolecular Reviews [*A publication*]
**J Polym Sci Part D: Macromol Rev**... Journal of Polymer Science. Part D: Macromolecular Reviews [*A publication*]
**J Polym Sci Polym Chem**... Journal of Polymer Science. Polymer Chemistry Edition [*A publication*]
**J Polym Sci Polym Chem Ed**... Journal of Polymer Science. Polymer Chemistry Edition [*A publication*]
**J Polym Sci Polym Lett**... Journal of Polymer Science. Polymer Letters Edition [*A publication*]
**J Polym Sci Polym Lett Ed**... Journal of Polymer Science. Polymer Letters Edition [*A publication*]
**J Polym Sci Polym Phys**... Journal of Polymer Science. Polymer Physics Edition [*A publication*]
**J Polym Sci Polym Phys Ed**... Journal of Polymer Science. Polymer Physics Edition [*A publication*]
**J Polym Sci Polym Symp**... Journal of Polymer Science. Polymer Symposia Edition [*A publication*]
**J Polynesia**... Journal. Polynesian Society [*A publication*]
**J Polynes Soc**... Journal. Polynesian Society [*A publication*]
**J Polyn Soc**... Journal. Polynesian Society [*A publication*]
**J Pomol**...... Journal of Pomology [*A publication*]
**J Pomology**... Journal of Pomology and Horticultural Science [*A publication*]
**JPONED**... Journal of Psychosocial Oncology [*A publication*]
**J Pop Cul**... Journal of Popular Culture [*A publication*]
**J Pop Cult**... Journal of Popular Culture [*A publication*]
**J Pop Culture**... Journal of Popular Culture [*A publication*]
**J Pop Film & TV**... Journal of Popular Film and Television [*A publication*]
**J Pop Fi TV**... Journal of Popular Film and Television [*A publication*]
**J Pop F & TV**... Journal of Popular Film and Television [*A publication*]
**J Pop Res**... Journal of Population Research [*A publication*]
**J Popul**....... Journal of Population [*A publication*]
**J Popular F**... Journal of Popular Film and Television [*A publication*]
**J Popul Behav Soc Environ Issues**... Journal of Population. Behavioral, Social, and Environmental Issues [*A publication*]
**J Port Econ e Fins**... Jornal Portugues de Economia e Financas [*A publication*]
**J Portf Manage**... Journal of Portfolio Management [*A publication*]
**J Portfolio Mgt**... Journal of Portfolio Management [*A publication*]
**JPOS**......... Journal. Palestine Oriental Society [*A publication*]
**J POS**........ Journal. Patent Office Society [*A publication*]
**J Post Anesth Nurs**... Journal of Post Anesthesia Nursing [*A publication*]
**J Postgrad Med (Bombay)**... Journal of Postgraduate Medicine (Bombay) [*A publication*]
**J Post Grad Sch Indian Agric Res Inst**... Journal. Post Graduate School. Indian Agricultural Research Institute [*A publication*]
**J Post Keynes Econ**... Journal of Post Keynesian Economics [*A publication*]
**J Powder Bulk Solids Tech**... Journal of Powders and Bulk Solids Technology [*A publication*]
**J Powder Bulk Solids Technol**... Journal of Powder and Bulk Solids Technology [*A publication*]
**J Power Div Am Soc Civ Eng**... Journal. Power Division. American Society of Civil Engineers [*A publication*]
**J Power Sources**... Journal of Power Sources [*A publication*]
**JPP**............ Jalkeen Puolenpaiuan [*Afternoon*] [*Finland*]
**JPP**............ Japan Paper Proofs
**JPP**............ Joint Planning Process [*Military*] (NVT)
**JPP**............ Joint Program Plan (NASA)
**JPP**............ Journal of Pastoral Practice [*A publication*]
**JPPDA**...... Journal of Child Psychology and Psychiatry and Allied Disciplines [*Later, Journal of Child Psychology and Psychiatry*] [*A publication*]
**JPPIAX**..... Jugoslovenska Pediajatrija [*A publication*]
**JPPL**.......... Joint Personnel Priority List
**JPPL**.......... Journal of Planning and Property Law [*A publication*]
**JPPMB**...... Jahrbuch fuer Psychologie, Psychotherapie, und Medizinische Anthropologie [*A publication*]
**JpPol**.......... Japanese Polydor-Deutsche Grammophon [*Record label*]
**JPPP**.......... Jewish People, Past and Present [*Jewish Encyclopedic Handbooks*] [*A publication*] (BJA)
**JPPRI**........ Jewish Policy Planning and Research Institute [*Synagogue Council of America*]
**JPPS**.......... Jack Point Preservation Society (EA)
**JPPSA**....... Journal of Pharmacy and Pharmacology. Supplement [*A publication*]
**JPPSOWA**... Joint Personal Property Shipping Office, Washington, DC [*Military*] (AABC)
**JPPSST**..... Joseph Preschool and Primary Self-Concept Screening Test [*Child development test*] [*Psychology*]
**JpPV**.......... Japanese Polydor Variable Microgroove [*Record label*]
**JPQ**............ Jung Personality Questionnaire [*Personality development test*] [*Psychology*]
**JPQCA**...... Journal de Physique. Colloque [*A publication*]
**JPQSA**...... Journal de Physique. Supplement [*A publication*]
**JPr**............ Die Juedische Presse [*Berlin*] [*A publication*]
**JPR**............ Joint Procurement Regulations [*of Army and Air Force*]
**JPR**............ Journal of Peace Research [*A publication*]
**JPR**............ Journal of Psycholinguistic Research [*A publication*]
**JPR**............ Journal of Purchasing and Materials Management [*A publication*]
**jpr**............. Judaeo-Persian [*MARC language code*] [*Library of Congress*] (LCCP)
**JPR**............ Justice of the Peace and Local Government Review Reports [*A publication*] (DLA)

**J of Prac App** ... Journal of Practical Approaches to Developmental Handicap [*A publication*]
**J Pract Nurs** ... Journal of Practical Nursing [*A publication*]
**J Prag**......... Journal of Pragmatics [*A publication*]
**J Prak Chem** ... Journal fuer Praktische Chemie [*A publication*]
**J Prakt Chem** ... Journal fuer Praktische Chemie [*A publication*]
**J Prat de Droit Fiscal** ... Journal Pratique de Droit Fiscal et Financier [*A publication*]
**JPRC**......... Joint Personnel Recovery Center [*Military*]
**J PR CT**..... Judge Prerogative Court, Canterbury [*British*] (ROG)
**JPREA**....... Japanese Psychological Research [*A publication*]
**JPREAV**.... Japanese Psychological Research [*A publication*]
**J Pre Concr** ... Journal. Prestressed Concrete Institute [*A publication*]
**J Pre-Med Course Sapporo Med Coll** ... Journal of Pre-Medical Course. Sapporo Medical College [*A publication*]
**J Pre-Raph** ... Journal of Pre-Raphaelite Studies [*A publication*]
**J Presby H** ... Journal of Presbyterian History [*A publication*]
**J Presby Hist Soc** ... Journal. Presbyterian Historical Society [*A publication*]
**J Pres H**..... Journal of Presbyterian History [*A publication*]
**J Pressure Vessel Technol** ... Journal of Pressure Vessel Technology [*A publication*]
**J Pressure Vessel Technol Trans ASME** ... Journal of Pressure Vessel Technology. Transaction. ASME [*American Society of Mechanical Engineers*] [*A publication*]
**J Prestressed Concr Inst** ... Journal. Prestressed Concrete Institute [*A publication*]
**J Prev**......... Journal of Prevention [*A publication*]
**J Prev Dent** ... Journal of Preventive Dentistry [*A publication*]
**J Prev Psychiatry** ... Journal of Preventive Psychiatry [*A publication*]
**JPRGA**...... Journal de Chimie Physique et Revue Generale des Colloides [*A publication*]
**JPRH**......... Journal of Prison Health [*A publication*]
**J Print Hist Soc** ... Journal. Printing Historical Society [*A publication*]
**J Prison Jail Health** ... Journal of Prison and Jail Health [*A publication*]
**JPrKS**........ Jahrbuch. Preussische Kunstsammlungen [*A publication*]
**JPRLB**....... Journal of Psycholinguistic Research [*A publication*]
**JPRO**......... Joint Photographic Reconnaissance Organization [*World War II*]
**JPROB**...... Judge of Probate [*British*] (ROG)
**J Proc Am Hort Soc** ... Journal of Proceedings. American Horticultural Society [*A publication*]
**J & Proc A'sian Methodist Historical Soc** ... Australasian Methodist Historical Society. Journal and Proceedings [*A publication*] (APTA)
**J Proc Asiat Soc Bengal** ... Journal and Proceedings. Asiatic Society of Bengal [*A publication*]
**J Proc Aust Hist Soc** ... Australian Historical Society. Journal and Proceedings [*A publication*] (APTA)
**J Proc Aust Jewish Hist Soc** ... Australian Jewish Historical Society. Journal and Proceedings [*A publication*] (APTA)
**J & Proc Aust Methodist Hist Soc** ... Australasian Methodist Historical Society. Journal and Proceedings [*A publication*] (APTA)
**J Proc Australas Meth Hist Soc** ... Australasian Methodist Historical Society. Journal and Proceedings [*A publication*] (APTA)
**J Proc Broken Hill Hist Soc** ... Broken Hill Historical Society. Journal and Proceedings [*A publication*] (APTA)
**J Proc Inst Chem (India)** ... Journal and Proceedings. Institution of Chemists (India) [*A publication*]
**J Proc Instn Chem (India)** ... Journal and Proceedings. Institution of Chemists (India) [*A publication*]
**J Proc Inst Rd Transp Engrs** ... Journal and Proceedings. Institute of Road Transport Engineers [*A publication*]
**J Proc Inst Sewage Purif** ... Journal and Proceedings. Institute of Sewage Purification [*A publication*]
**J Proc Newcastle Hunter Dist Hist Soc** ... Newcastle and Hunter District Historical Society. Journal and Proceedings [*A publication*] (APTA)
**J Proc Oil Technol Assoc** ... Journal and Proceedings. Oil Technologists' Association [*A publication*]
**J Proc Parramatta Dist Hist Soc** ... Parramatta and District Historical Society. Journal and Proceedings [*A publication*] (APTA)
**J Proc R Aust Hist Soc** ... Royal Australian Historical Society. Journal and Proceedings [*A publication*] (APTA)
**J Proc Roy Soc NSW** ... Journal and Proceedings. Royal Society of New South Wales [*A publication*]
**J Proc R Soc NSW** ... Journal and Proceedings. Royal Society of New South Wales [*A publication*]
**J Proc R Soc West Aust** ... Journal and Proceedings. Royal Society of Western Australia [*A publication*]
**J Proc Sydney Tech Coll Chem Soc** ... Journal and Proceedings. Sydney Technical College. Chemical Society [*A publication*]
**J Proc W Aust Hist Soc** ... Western Australian Historical Society. Journal and Proceedings [*A publication*] (APTA)
**J Prod L**..... Journal of Products Law (DLA)
**J Prod Liab** ... Journal of Products Liability [*A publication*]
**J Prod Liability** ... Journal of Products Liability [*A publication*]
**J Prof Nurs** ... Journal of Professional Nursing [*A publication*]
**J Prof Serv Mark** ... Journal of Professional Services Marketing [*A publication*]
**J Project Techniques** ... Journal of Projective Techniques and Personality Assessment [*Later, Journal of Personality Assessment*] [*A publication*]
**J Property Mgt** ... Journal of Property Management [*A publication*]
**J Prop Manage** ... Journal of Property Management [*A publication*]
**J Prop Mgt** ... Journal of Property Management [*A publication*]
**J Propul P** ... Journal of Propulsion and Power [*A publication*]
**J Pros Dent** ... Journal of Prosthetic Dentistry [*A publication*]
**J Prosthet Dent** ... Journal of Prosthetic Dentistry [*A publication*]
**J Protozool** ... Journal of Protozoology [*A publication*]
**JPRS**......... Joint Publications Research Service [*Department of Commerce*]
**JPRSA**....... Journal and Proceedings. Royal Society of New South Wales [*A publication*]
**J Prsbyt Hist** ... Journal of Presbyterian History [*A publication*]
**JPRS-GUO** ... Joint Publications Research Service Translations - Government Use Only [*Department of Commerce*]
**JPS**........... Japan Press Service
**JPS**........... Jean Piaget Society [*Later, JPSSSKD*] (EA)
**JPS**........... Jet Plume Simulation
**JPS**........... Jeunesse Populaire Senegalaise [*Senegalese People's Youth*]
**JPS**........... Jewish Publication Society (EA)
**JPS**........... Joint Planning Staff [*US and Great Britain*] [*World War II*]
**JPS**........... Joint Position Sense [*Medicine*]
**JPS**........... Jones Plumbing Systems [*AMEX symbol*] (SPSG)
**JPS**........... Journal of Collective Negotiations in the Public Sector [*A publication*]
**JPS**........... Journal of Palestine Studies [*A publication*]
**JPS**........... Journal of Peasant Studies [*A publication*]
**JPS**........... Journal of Personal Selling and Sales Management [*A publication*]
**JPS**........... Journal of Polymer Science [*A publication*]
**JPS**........... Journal. Polynesian Society [*A publication*]
**JPs**........... Journal of Psychology [*A publication*]
**JPSA**......... Jacob's Prevocational Skills Assessment
**JPSA**......... Jewish Pharmaceutical Society of America (EA)
**JPSA**......... Joint Program for the Study of Abortion
**JPSA**......... Journal. Photographic Society of America [*A publication*]
**JPSA**......... Junior Philatelic Society of America [*Later, JPA*] (EA)
**JPSBA**....... Journal of Psychology of the Blind [*A publication*]
**JPSC**......... Joint Production Survey Committee
**JPSCD**....... Journal of Polymer Science. Part C. Polymer Symposia [*Later, Journal of Polymer Science. Polymer Symposia Edition*] [*A publication*]
**JPSG**......... Joint Planning and Scheduling Group
**J P Sm**........ [*J. P.*] Smith's English King's Bench Reports [*1803-06*] [*A publication*] (DLA)
**J P Smith**... [*J. P.*] Smith's English King's Bench Reports [*A publication*] (DLA)
**J P Smith (Eng)** ... [*J. P.*] Smith's English King's Bench Reports [*A publication*] (DLA)
**JPsNP**....... Journal de Psychologie Normale et Pathologique [*A publication*]
**JPSO**......... Journal of Psychosocial Oncology [*A publication*]
**JPSP**......... Journal of Personality and Social Psychology [*A publication*]
**JPSPB**....... Journal of Personality and Social Psychology [*A publication*]
**JPSRB**....... Journal of Psychological Researches [*A publication*]
**JPSS**......... Journal of Personality and Social Systems [*A publication*]
**JPSS**......... Just, Participatory, and Sustainable Society [*World Council of Churches*]
**JPSSSKD** ... Jean Piaget Society: Society for the Study of Knowledge and Development (EA)
**JPST**......... Jahrbuch fuer Philosophie und Spekulative Theologie [*A publication*]
**JPST**......... Journal of Parenteral Science and Technology [*A publication*] (EAAP)
**JPsy**......... Journal of Psychology [*A publication*]
**JPsych**....... Journal de Psychologie Normale et Pathologique [*A publication*]
**J Psychedel Drugs** ... Journal of Psychedelic Drugs [*A publication*]
**J Psychedelic Drugs** ... Journal of Psychedelic Drugs [*A publication*]
**J Psychiatr Law** ... Journal of Psychiatry and Law [*A publication*]
**J Psychiatr Nurs** ... Journal of Psychiatric Nursing and Mental Health Services [*A publication*]
**J Psychiatr Res** ... Journal of Psychiatric Research [*A publication*]
**J Psychiatr Treat Eval** ... Journal of Psychiatric Treatment and Evaluation [*A publication*]
**J Psychiatry & L** ... Journal of Psychiatry and Law [*A publication*]
**J Psych and L** ... Journal of Psychiatry and Law [*A publication*]
**J Psych & Law** ... Journal of Psychiatry and Law [*A publication*]
**J Psych Law** ... Journal of Psychiatry and Law [*A publication*]
**J Psychoact Drugs** ... Journal of Psychoactive Drugs [*A publication*]
**J Psychoanal Anthropol** ... Journal of Psychoanalytic Anthropology [*A publication*]
**J Psychohist** ... Journal of Psychohistory [*A publication*]
**J Psychol** ... Journal of Psychology [*A publication*]
**J Psycholin** ... Journal of Psycholinguistic Research [*A publication*]
**J Psycholing Res** ... Journal of Psycholinguistic Research [*A publication*]
**J Psycholinguist Res** ... Journal of Psycholinguistic Research [*A publication*]
**J Psychol u Neurol** ... Journal fuer Psychologie und Neurologie [*A publication*]

**J Psychol Norm Path** ... Journal de Psychologie Normale et Pathologique [*A publication*]
**J Psychol Norm Pathol (Paris)** ... Journal de Psychologie Normale et Pathologique (Paris) [*A publication*]
**J Psychological Medicine** ... Journal of Psychological Medicine and Medical Jurisprudence [*A publication*] (DLA)
**J Psychol Res** ... Journal of Psychological Researches [*A publication*]
**J Psychol T** ... Journal of Psychology and Theology [*A publication*]
**J Psychopathol Behav Assess** ... Journal of Psychopathology and Behavioral Assessment [*A publication*]
**J Psychopharmacol (Oxford)** ... Journal of Psychopharmacology (Oxford) [*A publication*]
**J Psychosocial Nurs** ... Journal of Psychosocial Nursing and Mental Health Services [*A publication*]
**J Psychosoc Nurs** ... Journal of Psychosocial Nursing and Mental Health Services [*A publication*]
**J Psychosoc Nurs Ment Healt Serv** ... Journal of Psychosocial Nursing and Mental Health Services [*A publication*]
**J Psychosoc Oncol** ... Journal of Psychosocial Oncology [*A publication*]
**J Psychosom** ... Journal of Psychosomatic Research [*A publication*]
**J Psychosom Obstet Gynaecol** ... Journal of Psychosomatic Obstetrics and Gynaecology [*A publication*]
**J Psychosom Res** ... Journal of Psychosomatic Research [*A publication*]
**J Psychother & Fam** ... Journal of Psychotherapy and the Family [*A publication*]
**J Psych Res** ... Journal of Psychiatric Research [*A publication*]
**J Psych Th** ... Journal of Psychology and Theology [*A publication*]
**JPsyR** ........ Journal of Psycholinguistic Research [*A publication*]
**JPT** ........... Houston [*Texas*] Park-Ten [*Airport symbol*] (OAG)
**JPT** ........... Jahrbuch fuer Philosophie und Spekulative Theologie [*A publication*]
**JPT** ........... Jahrbuecher fuer Protestantische Theologie [*Leipzig/Braunschweig*] [*A publication*]
**JPT** ........... Japanese Proficiency Test [*Educational test*]
**JPT** ........... Jet Pipe Temperature
**JPT** ........... Job Progress Ticket
**JPT** ........... Journal of Partnership Taxation [*A publication*]
**JPT** ........... Journal of Petroleum Technology [*A publication*]
**JPT** ........... Journal of Psychology and Theology [*A publication*]
**JPT** ........... Jupitor Resources Ltd. [*Vancouver Stock Exchange symbol*]
**JPTDS** ....... Joint Photographic Type Designation System [*Military*]
**JPTDS** ....... Junior Participating Tactical Data System [*Also known as "Jeep"*] (MCD)
**JPTEA** ....... Journal of Projective Techniques [*Later, Journal of Personality Assessment*] [*A publication*]
**JPTF** ......... Joint Parachute Test Facility [*DoD*]
**JPT J Pet Technol** ... JPT. Journal of Petroleum Technology [*A publication*]
**JPTL** ......... Jet Pipe Temperature Limiter (MCD)
**JPTO** ......... Jet-Propelled Takeoff
**JPTUAL** .... Japanese Journal of Tuberculosis [*A publication*]
**JPU** ........... Job Processing Unit
**JPU** ........... Journal. Poona University [*A publication*]
**JPU** ........... Journal of Public Economics [*A publication*]
**JPU** ........... Just Publishable Unit
**J Pub L** ...... Journal of Public Law [*A publication*]
**J Publ Econ** ... Journal of Public Economics [*A publication*]
**J Public Econ** ... Journal of Public Economics [*A publication*]
**J Public Health** ... Journal of Public Health [*A publication*]
**J Public Health Dent** ... Journal of Public Health Dentistry [*A publication*]
**J Public Health Med Technol Korea Univ** ... Journal of Public Health and Medical Technology. Korea University [*A publication*]
**J Public Health Policy** ... Journal of Public Health Policy [*A publication*]
**J Public Health Pract** ... Journal of Public Health Practice [*Japan*] [*A publication*]
**J Public and Internat Affairs** ... Journal of Public and International Affairs [*A publication*]
**J Public Policy** ... Journal of Public Policy [*A publication*]
**J Public Service Papua & NG** ... Journal. Public Service of Papua and New Guinea [*A publication*] (APTA)
**J Pulp and Pap Sci** ... Journal of Pulp and Paper Science [*A publication*]
**J Purch** ....... Journal of Purchasing [*Later, Journal of Purchasing and Materials Management*] [*A publication*]
**J Purchasing & Materials Mgt** ... Journal of Purchasing and Materials Management [*A publication*]
**J Purch Mater Manage** ... Journal of Purchasing and Materials Management [*A publication*]
**J Pure Appl Algebra** ... Journal of Pure and Applied Algebra [*A publication*]
**J Pure Appl Sci** ... Journal of Pure and Applied Sciences [*A publication*]
**J Pure Appl Sci (Ankara)** ... Journal of Pure and Applied Sciences (Ankara) [*A publication*]
**J Pusan Med Coll** ... Journal. Pusan Medical College [*A publication*]
**JpV** ........... Japanese Victor [*Record label*]
**JPV** ........... Joint Pacific Voice [*Military*] (CINC)
**JPVDA** ...... Journal of Preventive Dentistry [*A publication*]
**JPVTA** ....... Journal of Pressure Vessel Technology [*A publication*]
**JPW** ........... Jerusalem Post Weekly [*A publication*]
**JPW** ........... Job Processing Word
**JP (WA)** ..... Justice of the Peace (Western Australia) [*A publication*] (APTA)
**JPWC** ......... Joint Postwar Committee
**JPY** ........... Journal of Political Economy [*A publication*]
**JPYABL** .... Annals. Japan Association for Philosophy of Science [*A publication*]
**JPYBA** ....... Journal of Polymer Science. Polymer Letters Edition [*A publication*]
**JPYCA** ...... Journal of Polymer Science. Polymer Symposia Edition [*A publication*]
**JQ** ............. J-Q Resources, Inc. [*Toronto Stock Exchange symbol*]
**JQ** ............. Japan Quarterly [*A publication*]
**JQ** ............. Jewish Quarterly [*A publication*]
**JQ** ............. Job Questionnaire
**JQ** ............. Journalism Quarterly [*A publication*]
**JQ** ............. Trans Jamaican Airlines Ltd. [*ICAO designator*] (FAAC)
**JQA** .......... John Quincy Adams [*US president, 1767-1848*]
**JQB** .......... Justice of the Queen's Bench [*Legal term*] (DLA)
**JQC** ........... Dayton, OH [*Location identifier*] [*FAA*] (FAAL)
**JQE** ........... Jaque [*Panama*] [*Airport symbol*] (OAG)
**JQE** ........... Journal of Quantum Electronics [*A publication*]
**J Qing Hua Univ** ... Journal. Qing Hua University [*A publication*]
**JQR** .......... Jewish Quarterly Review [*A publication*]
**JQT** ........... Journal of Quality Technology [*A publication*]
**J Quality Tech** ... Journal of Quality Technology [*A publication*]
**J Qual Tech** ... Journal of Quality Technology [*A publication*]
**J Qual Technol** ... Journal of Quality Technology [*A publication*]
**J Quan Spec** ... Journal of Quantitative Spectroscopy and Radiative Transfer [*A publication*]
**J Quant Spectrosc Radiat Transfer** ... Journal of Quantitative Spectroscopy and Radiative Transfer [*A publication*]
**J Quant Spectrosc and Radiat Transfer** ... Journal of Quantitative Spectroscopy and Radiative Transfer [*A publication*]
**J Quekett Microsc Club** ... Journal. Quekett Microscopical Club [*A publication*]
**JR** .............. Air Yugoslavia [*ICAO designator*] (FAAC)
**JR** .............. Jacobus Rex [*King James*]
**JR** .............. Jam Resistant
**JR** .............. James River Corp. of Virginia [*NYSE symbol*] (SPSG)
**JR** .............. Jar (MCD)
**Jr** ............... Jeremiah [*Old Testament book*] (BJA)
**J e R** .......... Jeta e Re
**JR** .............. [*The*] Jewish Right (EA)
**JR** .............. Jezyk Rosyjski [*A publication*]
**JR** .............. Jigger [*Ship's rigging*] (ROG)
**JR** .............. Job Routed [*Military*] (AFIT)
**JR** .............. John Ross Ewing, Jr. [*Character in TV series "Dallas"*]
**JR** .............. Johnson's New York Reports [*A publication*] (DLA)
**JR** .............. Joint Resolution [*Usually, of the US Senate and House of Representatives*]
**JR** .............. Joint Review
**JR** .............. Jordan Register (EA)
**JR** .............. Jour [*Day*] [*French*]
**JR** .............. Journal (ADA)
**JR** .............. Journal of Religion [*A publication*]
**JR** .............. Judges' Rules [*A publication*] (DLA)
**JR** .............. Juedische Rundschau [*Berlin*] [*A publication*]
**Jr** ............... Juglans regia [*Persian walnut*]
**JR** .............. Jugoslav Register [*Yugoslavian ship classification society*] (DS)
**JR** .............. Junction Rack (KSC)
**JR** .............. Junctional Rhythm [*Cardiology*]
**JR** .............. Junior
**JR** .............. Juridical Review [*A publication*]
**JR** .............. Jurist Reports [*1873-78*] [*New Zealand*] [*A publication*] (DLA)
**JR** .............. Juror
**JRA** ........... Jam-Resistant Antenna
**JRA** ........... Jewish Royalty Association (EA)
**JRA** ........... Job Release Analysis
**Jr A** ........... Journal of Arizona History [*A publication*]
**JRA** ........... Journal. Society of Research Administrators [*A publication*]
**JRA** ........... Juvenile Rheumatoid Arthritis [*Medicine*]
**JRA** ........... New York, NY [*Location identifier*] [*FAA*] (FAAL)
**J Race Dev** ... Journal of Race Development [*A publication*]
**J Racial Aff** ... Journal of Racial Affairs [*A publication*]
**JRAD** ......... Joint Resource Assessment Data
**JRADA** ...... Journal of Radiology [*A publication*]
**J Rad Chem** ... Journal of Radioanalytical Chemistry [*Later, Journal of Radioanalytical and Nuclear Chemistry*] [*A publication*]
**J Radiat Curing** ... Journal of Radiation Curing [*A publication*]
**J Radiat Res** ... Journal of Radiation Research [*A publication*]
**J Radiat Res Radiat Process** ... Journal of Radiation Research and Radiation Processing [*A publication*]
**J Radiat Res (Tokyo)** ... Journal of Radiation Research (Tokyo) [*A publication*]
**J Radioanal Chem** ... Journal of Radioanalytical Chemistry [*Later, Journal of Radioanalytical and Nuclear Chemistry*] [*A publication*]
**J Radioanal Nucl Chem** ... Journal of Radioanalytical and Nuclear Chemistry [*A publication*]
**J Radio L** ... Journal of Radio Law [*A publication*] (DLA)
**J Radiol** ...... Journal de Radiologie [*A publication*]
**J Radiol Electrol** ... Journal de Radiologie et d'Electrologie [*A publication*]
**J Radiol Electrol Med Nucl** ... Journal de Radiologie, d'Electrologie, et de Medecine Nucleaire [*Later, Journal de Radiologie*] [*A publication*]

**J Radiol (Paris)** ... Journal de Radiologie (Paris) [*A publication*]
**J Radiol Phys Ther Univ Kanazawa** ... Journal of Radiology and Physical Therapy. University of Kanazawa [*A publication*]
**J Radiol Prot** ... Journal of Radiological Protection [*A publication*]
**J Radio Res Lab** ... Journal. Radio Research Laboratories [*Japan*] [*A publication*]
**J Rad Res L** ... Journal. Radio Research Laboratories [*Japan*] [*A publication*]
**J R Aeronaut Soc** ... Journal. Royal Aeronautical Society [*England*] [*A publication*]
**J R Afr Soc** ... Journal. Royal African Society [*A publication*]
**JRAfS** ........ Journal. Royal African Society [*A publication*]
**JRAGAY** ... Journal. Royal Agricultural Society of England [*A publication*]
**J R Agric Soc** ... Journal. Royal Agricultural Society [*A publication*]
**J R Agric Soc Engl** ... Journal. Royal Agricultural Society of England [*A publication*]
**JRAHS** ...... Journal. Royal Australian Historical Society [*A publication*] (APTA)
**JRAI** .......... Journal. Royal Anthropological Institute of Great Britain and Ireland [*A publication*]
**J Raj Inst Hist Res** ... Journal. Rajasthan Institute of Historical Research [*A publication*]
**J Rakuno Gakuen Univ Nat Sci** ... Journal. Rakuno Gakuen University. Natural Science [*A publication*]
**JRAMA** ..... Journal. Royal Army Medical Corps [*A publication*]
**J Raman Sp** ... Journal of Raman Spectroscopy [*A publication*]
**J Raman Spectrosc** ... Journal of Raman Spectroscopy [*A publication*]
**J Range Man** ... Journal of Range Management [*A publication*]
**J Range Manage** ... Journal of Range Management [*A publication*]
**J Range Mgt** ... Journal of Range Management [*A publication*]
**J R Anthropol Inst GB Irel** ... Journal. Royal Anthropological Institute of Great Britain and Ireland [*A publication*]
**JRAPDU** ... Journal of Research APAU [*Andhra Pradesh Agricultural University*] [*A publication*]
**JRARA** ...... Journal of Radiation Research [*A publication*]
**J R Army Med Corps** ... Journal. Royal Army Medical Corps [*A publication*]
**J R Army Vet Corps** ... Journal. Royal Army Veterinary Corps [*A publication*]
**JRAS** ......... Journal of the Royal Agricultural Society [*A publication*] (ROG)
**JRAS** ......... Journal. Royal Asiatic Society of Great Britain and Ireland [*A publication*]
**JRASA** ...... Journal. Royal Astronomical Society of Canada [*A publication*]
**JRASBB** .... Journal. Royal Asiatic Society. Bombay Branch [*A publication*]
**JRASBengal** ... Journal. Royal Asiatic Society of Bengal [*A publication*]
**JRAS Bombay** ... Journal. Bombay Branch. Royal Asiatic Society [*A publication*]
**JRASCB** .... Journal. Royal Asiatic Society. Ceylon Branch [*A publication*]
**JRASHKB** ... Journal. Royal Asiatic Society. Hong Kong Branch [*A publication*]
**JR Asiat Soc GB Irel** ... Journal. Royal Asiatic Society of Great Britain and Ireland [*A publication*]
**JRASM** ..... Journal. Royal Asiatic Society. Malayan Branch [*A publication*]
**JRASMB** ... Journal. Royal Asiatic Society. Malayan Branch [*A publication*]
**J R Astron Soc Can** ... Journal. Royal Astronomical Society of Canada [*A publication*]
**JRATA** ...... Joint Research and Test Activity (MCD)
**JRATA** ...... Joint Research and Test Agency [*Terminated, 1966*] [*Military*]
**J R Aust Hist Soc** ... Journal. Royal Australian Historical Society [*A publication*]
**JRB** ........... Joint Radio Board
**JRB** ........... Joint Reconnaissance Board [*Military*] (AABC)
**JRB** ........... Joint Review Board (MCD)
**JRB** ........... Journal of Retail Banking [*A publication*]
**jrb** .............. Judaeo-Arabic [*MARC language code*] [*Library of Congress*] (LCCP)
**JRB** ........... New York, NY [*Location identifier*] [*FAA*] (FAAL)
**JRBA-A** ..... Journal. Royal Institute of British Architects [*A publication*]
**JRBED2** .... Journal of Reproductive Biology and Comparative Endocrinology [*A publication*]
**Jr Bkshelf** .. Junior Bookshelf [*A publication*]
**JRBM** ........ Journal of Renaissance and Baroque Music [*A publication*]
**Jr Br Assoc Teach Deaf** ... Journal. British Association of Teachers of the Deaf [*A publication*]
**JRBSDA** .... British Columbia Forest Service-Canadian Forestry Service. Joint Report [*A publication*]
**JRC** ........... Jet Reaction Control
**JRC** ........... Jewish Refugees Committee (EAIO)
**JrC** ............ Johnson Reprint Corporation, New York, NY [*Library symbol*] [*Library of Congress*] (LCLS)
**JRC** ........... Joint Railroad Conference
**JRC** ........... Joint Reconnaissance Center [*Military*] (AFM)
**JRC** ........... Joint Recovery Center (MCD)
**JRC** ........... Joint Representation Committee [*British*] (DCTA)
**JRC** ........... Joint Research Center [*Commission of the European Communities*]
**JRC** ........... Junior Red Cross
**JRCAS** ....... Journal. Royal Central Asian Society [*A publication*]
**JRCC** ......... Joint Reconnaissance Control Center (MCD)
**JRCC** ......... Joint Regional Continuing Committee [*Later, RCEAC*] [*Civil Defense*]
**JRCC** ......... Joint Rescue Coordination Center [*Military*] (AFM)
**JRCDMS** ... Joint Review Committee on Education in Diagnostic Medical Sonography (EA)
**JRCE-A** ..... Journal. Irrigation and Drainage Division. Proceedings of the American Society of Civil Engineers [*A publication*]
**JRCEMT-P** ... Joint Review Committee on Educational Programs for the EMT [*Emergency Medical Technician*]-Paramedic (EA)
**JRCEPEP** ... Joint Review Committee on Educational Programs for the EMT [*Emergency Medical Technician*]-Paramedic (EA)
**JRCEPPA** ... Joint Review Committee on Educational Programs for Physician Assistants (EA)
**JRCERT** .... Joint Review Committee on Education in Radiologic Technology (EA)
**JRCEST** .... Joint Review Committee on Education for the Surgical Technologist (EA)
**JRCI** .......... Jamming RADAR Coverage Indicator (MSA)
**JRCI** .......... Journal. Regional Cultural Institute [*A publication*]
**JRCI** .......... Journal of the Royal Colonial Institute (ROG)
**J R Coll Gen Pract** ... Journal. Royal College of General Practitioners [*A publication*]
**J R Coll Gen Pract Occas Pap** ... Journal. Royal College of General Practitioners. Occasional Paper [*A publication*]
**Jr Coll J** ..... Junior College Journal [*A publication*]
**Jr Coll Jnl** ... Junior College Journal [*A publication*]
**J R Coll Physicians** ... Journal. Royal College of Physicians of London [*A publication*]
**J R Coll Physicians Lond** ... Journal. Royal College of Physicians of London [*A publication*]
**J R Coll Surg Edinb** ... Journal. Royal College of Surgeons of Edinburgh [*A publication*]
**J R Coll Surg Edinburg** ... Journal. Royal College of Surgeons of Edinburg [*A publication*]
**J R Coll Surg Irel** ... Journal. Royal College of Surgeons in Ireland [*A publication*]
**JRCOMA** ... Joint Review Committee for the Ophthalmic Medical Assistant (EA)
**JRCOMP** .. Joint Review Committee for Ophthalmic Medical Personnel (EA)
**JRC-PA** ..... Joint Review Committee on Educational Programs for Physician Assistants (EA)
**JRCRTE** .... Joint Review Committee for Respiratory Therapy Education (EA)
**JRCS** ......... Jet Reaction Control System
**JRCS** ......... John Reich Collectors Society (EA)
**JRCSA** ....... Journal. Royal College of Surgeons of Edinburgh [*A publication*]
**JRD** ........... Jahrbuch der Rheinischen Denkmalpflege [*A publication*]
**JRd** ............ Juedische Rundschau [*Berlin*] [*A publication*]
**JRD** ........... Riverside, CA [*Location identifier*] [*FAA*] (FAAL)
**JRDA** ......... Jeunesse du Rassemblement Democratique Africain [*Youth of the African Democratic Rally*]
**JRDACI** .... Jeunesse du Rassemblement Democratique Africain de Cote d'Ivoire [*Youth of the African Democratic Rally of the Ivory Coast*]
**JRDB** ......... Joint Research and Development Board [*1946-1947*]
**JRDC** ......... Japan Research Development Corporation
**JRDCA** ...... Journal of Radiation Curing [*A publication*]
**JRDOD** ..... Joint Research and Development Objectives Document [*Military*] (AABC)
**JRDP** ......... Jahrbuch der Rheinischen Denkmalpflege [*A publication*]
**JRE** ........... Journal of Econometrics [*A publication*]
**JRE** ........... Journal of Real Estate Taxation [*A publication*]
**JRe** ............ Journal of Religion [*A publication*]
**JRE** ........... Journal of Religious Ethics [*A publication*]
**JRE** ........... JR Energy Ltd. [*Vancouver Stock Exchange symbol*]
**JRE** ........... New York [*New York*] E. 60th Street [*Airport symbol*] (OAG)
**JREA** ......... James Robison Evangelistic Association (EA)
**J Read** ........ Journal of Reading [*A publication*]
**J Read Beh** ... Journal of Reading Behavior [*A publication*]
**J Read Behav** ... Journal of Reading Behavior [*A publication*]
**J Read Behavior** ... Journal of Reading Behavior [*A publication*]
**J Read Writ Learn Disabil Int** ... Journal of Reading, Writing, and Learning Disabilities International [*A publication*]
**J Real Est Tax** ... Journal of Real Estate Taxation [*A publication*]
**J Recept Res** ... Journal of Receptor Research [*A publication*]
**J Rech Atmos** ... Journal de Recherches Atmospheriques [*A publication*]
**J Rech Cent Natl Rech Sci Lab Bellevue (Paris)** ... Journal des Recherches. Centre National de la Recherche Scientifique. Laboratoires de Bellevue (Paris) [*A publication*]
**J Rech CNRS** ... Journal des Recherches. Centre National de la Recherche Scientifique [*France*] [*A publication*]
**J Rech Oceanogr** ... Journal de Recherche Oceanographique [*A publication*]
**J Reconstr Microsurg** ... Journal of Reconstructive Microsurgery [*A publication*]
**J Recreational Math** ... Journal of Recreational Mathematics [*A publication*]
**J Refrig** ...... Journal of Refrigeration [*A publication*]
**J Regional Science** ... Journal of Regional Science [*A publication*]
**J Region Sci** ... Journal of Regional Science [*A publication*]
**J Reg Sc** ..... Journal of Regional Science [*A publication*]
**J Reg Sci** .... Journal of Regional Science [*A publication*]
**J Rehab** ...... Journal of Rehabilitation [*A publication*]
**J Rehabil** .... Journal of Rehabilitation [*A publication*]

**J Rehabil Asia** ... Journal of Rehabilitation in Asia [*A publication*]
**J Rehabil D** ... Journal of Rehabilitation of the Deaf [*A publication*]
**J Rehabil R D** ... Journal of Rehabilitation R and D [*Research and Development*] [*A publication*]
**J Rehabil Res Dev** ... Journal of Rehabilitation Research and Development [*A publication*]
**J Rehabil Res Dev Clin Suppl** ... Journal of Rehabilitation Research and Development. Clinical Supplement [*A publication*]
**J Reine Angew Math** ... Journal fuer die Reine und Angewandte Mathematik [*A publication*]
**J Reinf Plast Comp** ... Journal of Reinforced Plastics and Composites [*A publication*]
**J Reinf Plast Compos** ... Journal of Reinforced Plastics and Composites [*A publication*]
**J Rein Math** ... Journal fuer die Reine und Angewandte Mathematik [*A publication*]
**J Rel**.......... Journal of Religion [*A publication*]
**J Rel Africa** ... Journal of Religion in Africa [*A publication*]
**JR Electr and Mech Eng** ... Journal. Royal Electrical and Mechanical Engineers [*A publication*]
**J R Electr Mech Eng** ... Journal. Royal Electrical and Mechanical Engineers [*England*] [*A publication*]
**J Rel Ethics** ... Journal of Religious Ethics [*A publication*]
**J Rel H**....... Journal of Religious History [*A publication*]
**J Rel Health** ... Journal of Religion and Health [*A publication*]
**J Rel Hist**... Journal of Religious History [*A publication*]
**J Relig**....... Journal of Religion [*A publication*]
**J Relig Afr** ... Journal of Religion in Africa [*A publication*]
**J Relig Educ** ... Journal of Religious Education [*A publication*]
**J Relig Ethics** ... Journal of Religious Ethics [*A publication*]
**J Relig H**.... Journal of Religion and Health [*A publication*]
**J Relig His** ... Journal of Religious History [*A publication*]
**J Relig Hist** ... Journal of Religious History [*A publication*] (APTA)
**J Religion Health** ... Journal of Religion and Health [*A publication*]
**J Religious History** ... Journal of Religious History [*A publication*] (APTA)
**J of Relig Thought** ... Journal of Religious Thought [*A publication*]
**J Rel Psych Res** ... Journal of Religion and Psychical Research [*A publication*]
**J Rel St**...... Journal of Religious Studies [*A publication*]
**J Rel Thot** ... Journal of Religious Thought [*A publication*]
**J Rel Thought** ... Journal of Religious Thought [*A publication*]
**J of Rel Thought** ... Journal of Religious Thought [*A publication*]
**JREM**........ Junior Radio Electrical Mechanic [*British military*] (DMA)
**J Remote Sensing** ... Journal of Remote Sensing [*A publication*]
**J Remount Vet Corps** ... Journal of the Remount and Veterinary Corps [*A publication*]
**J Ren & Bar Mus** ... Journal of Renaissance and Baroque Music [*A publication*]
**J Rep**.......... Johnson's Maryland Chancery Reports [*A publication*] (DLA)
**J Rep**.......... Johnson's New York Reports [*A publication*] (DLA)
**J Rep**.......... Johnson's Reports of Chase's United States Circuit Court Decisions [*A publication*] (DLA)
**J Reprd & Fert** ... Journal of Reproduction and Fertility [*A publication*]
**J Repr Fert** ... Journal of Reproduction and Fertility [*A publication*]
**J Reprints Antitrust L & Econ** ... Journal of Reprints for Antitrust Law and Economics [*A publication*] (DLA)
**J Reprod Biol Comp Endocrinol** ... Journal of Reproductive Biology and Comparative Endocrinology [*A publication*]
**J Reprod Fertil** ... Journal of Reproduction and Fertility [*A publication*]
**J Reprod Fertil** ... Journal of Reproductive Fertility [*A publication*]
**J Reprod Fertil Suppl** ... Journal of Reproduction and Fertility. Supplement [*A publication*]
**J Reprod Immunol** ... Journal of Reproductive Immunology [*A publication*]
**J Reprod Med** ... Journal of Reproductive Medicine [*A publication*]
**J Reprod Med Lying-In** ... Journal of Reproductive Medicine. Lying-In [*A publication*]
**JRERDM**.. Journal of Receptor Research [*A publication*]
**J Re S**......... Journal of Religious Studies [*A publication*]
**JRES-A** ..... Journal of Regional Science [*A publication*]
**J Res APAU (Andhra Pradesh Agric Univ)** ... Journal of Research APAU (Andhra Pradesh Agricultural University) [*A publication*]
**J Res Assam Agric Univ** ... Journal of Research. Assam Agricultural University [*A publication*]
**J Res Crime** ... Journal of Research in Crime and Delinquency [*A publication*]
**J Res Crime & Del** ... Journal of Research in Crime and Delinquency [*A publication*]
**J Res Crime & Delinq** ... Journal of Research in Crime and Delinquency [*A publication*]
**J Res Dev E** ... Journal of Research and Development in Education [*A publication*]
**J Res & Devel Educ** ... Journal of Research and Development in Education [*A publication*]
**J Res Develop Educ** ... Journal of Research and Development in Education [*A publication*]
**J Res Dev Lab Portland Cem Assoc** ... Journal. Research and Development Laboratories. Portland Cement Association [*A publication*]
**J Research M Education** ... Journal of Research in Music Education [*A publication*]
**J Res Haryana Agric Univ** ... Haryana Agricultural University. Journal of Research [*A publication*]
**J Res Indian Med** ... Journal of Research in Indian Medicine [*A publication*]
**J Res Indian Med Yoga Homoeopathy** ... Journal of Research in Indian Medicine, Yoga, and Homoeopathy [*A publication*]
**J Res Inst Catal Hokkaido Univ** ... Journal. Research Institute for Catalysis. Hokkaido University [*A publication*]
**J Res Inst Catalysis Hokkaido Univ** ... Journal. Research Institute for Catalysis. Hokkaido University [*A publication*]
**J Res Inst Med Sci Korea** ... Journal. Research Institute of Medical Science of Korea [*Republic of Korea*] [*A publication*]
**J Res Inst Sci and Technol Nihon Univ** ... Journal. Research Institute of Science and Technology. Nihon University [*A publication*]
**J Res Inst Sci Technol Nihon Univ** ... Journal. Research Institute of Science and Technology. Nihon University [*Japan*] [*A publication*]
**J Res (Jpn)** ... Journal of Research (Japan) [*A publication*]
**J Res Lepid** ... Journal of Research on the Lepidoptera [*A publication*]
**J Res (Ludhiana)** ... Journal of Research (Ludhiana) [*India*] [*A publication*]
**J Res Math Educ** ... Journal for Research in Mathematics Education [*A publication*]
**J Res M & T** ... Journal of Resource Management and Technology [*A publication*]
**J Res Mus Ed** ... Journal of Research in Music Education [*A publication*]
**J Res Mus Educ** ... Journal of Research in Music Education [*A publication*]
**J Res Music** ... Journal of Research in Music Education [*A publication*]
**J Res Music Educ** ... Journal of Research in Music Education [*A publication*]
**J Res Nat Bur Stand** ... Journal of Research. [*US*] National Bureau of Standards [*A publication*]
**J Res Nat Bur Standards** ... Journal of Research. [*US*] National Bureau of Standards [*A publication*]
**J Res Nat Bur Stand Sect A Phys Chem** ... Journal of Research. [*US*] National Bureau of Standards. Section A. Physics and Chemistry [*A publication*]
**J Res Nat Bur Stand Sect B Math Sci** ... Journal of Research. [*US*] National Bureau of Standards. Section B. Mathematical Sciences [*A publication*]
**J Res Nat Bur Stand Sect C** ... Journal of Research. [*US*] National Bureau of Standards. Section C. Engineering and Instrumentation [*A publication*]
**J Res Nat Bur Stand Sect C Eng Instrum** ... Journal of Research. [*US*] National Bureau of Standards. Section C. Engineering and Instrumentation [*A publication*]
**J Res Nat Bur Stand Sect D** ... Journal of Research. [*US*] National Bureau of Standards. Section D. Radio Science [*A publication*]
**J Res Natl Bur Stand A** ... Journal of Research. [*US*] National Bureau of Standards. Section A. Physics and Chemistry [*A publication*]
**J Res Natl Bur Stand B** ... Journal of Research. [*US*] National Bureau of Standards. Section B. Mathematics and Mathematical Physics [*A publication*]
**J Res Natl Bur Stand C** ... Journal of Research. [*US*] National Bureau of Standards. Section C. Engineering and Instrumentation [*A publication*]
**J Res Natl Bur Stand (US)** ... Journal of Research. National Bureau of Standards (United States) [*A publication*]
**J Res NBS** ... Journal of Research. [*US*] National Bureau of Standards [*A publication*]
**J Res NBS A** ... Journal of Research. [*US*] National Bureau of Standards. Section A. Physics and Chemistry [*A publication*]
**J Res NBS B** ... Journal of Research. [*US*] National Bureau of Standards. Section B. Mathematical Sciences [*A publication*]
**J Res Pers** ... Journal of Research in Personality [*A publication*]
**J Res Punjab Agric Univ** ... Journal of Research. Punjab Agricultural University [*A publication*]
**J Res Punjab Agr Univ** ... Journal of Research. Punjab Agricultural University [*A publication*]
**J Res Read** ... Journal of Research in Reading [*A publication*]
**J Res Sci Agra Univ** ... Journal of Research in Science. Agra University [*A publication*]
**J Res Sci Teach** ... Journal of Research in Science Teaching [*A publication*]
**J Res Singing** ... Journal of Research in Singing [*A publication*]
**J Res Soc Pak** ... Journal. Research Society of Pakistan [*A publication*]
**J Res US Geol Surv** ... Journal of Research. United States Geological Survey [*A publication*]
**J Res US G S** ... Journal of Research. United States Geological Survey [*A publication*]
**J Retail**....... Journal of Retailing [*A publication*]
**J Retail Bank** ... Journal of Retail Banking [*A publication*]
**J Retail Banking** ... Journal of Retail Banking [*A publication*]
**J Retailing** ... Journal of Retailing [*A publication*]
**J Retail Traders Assn NSW** ... Journal of the Retail Traders' Association of New South Wales [*A publication*] (APTA)
**J Retail Traders Assoc NSW** ... Journal of the Retail Traders' Association of New South Wales [*A publication*] (APTA)
**J Retic Soc** ... Journal. Reticuloendothelial Society [*A publication*]
**J Reticuloendothel Soc** ... Journal. Reticuloendothelial Society [*A publication*]
**JRF**............ Jackie Robinson Foundation (EA)
**JRF**............ Jewish Reconstructionist Foundation (EA)
**JRF**............ John-Roger Foundation (EA)
**JRF**............ Judicial Research Foundation [*Defunct*]
**JRFC**......... Jerry Reed Fan Club (EA)
**JRFC**......... Johnny Rodriguez Fan Club (EA)
**JRFS**.......... Janssen Research Foundation Series [*Elsevier Book Series*] [*A publication*]

**JRFTNG** ... Jet Refresher Training [*Navy*] (NVT)
**JRG** ... Jahrbuch. Raabe-Gesellschaft [*A publication*]
**JRG** ... Journal of Regional Science [*A publication*]
**JRGZ** ... Jahrbuch. Roemisch-Germanisches Zentralmuseum [*Mainz*] [*A publication*]
**JRGZMainz** ... Jahrbuch. Roemisch-Germanisches Zentralmuseum (Mainz) [*A publication*]
**JRH** ... Jorhat [*India*] [*Airport symbol*] (OAG)
**JRH** ... Journal of Religious History [*A publication*]
**J Rheol** ... Journal of Rheology [*A publication*]
**J Rheology** ... Journal of Rheology [*A publication*]
**J Rheumatol** ... Journal of Rheumatology [*A publication*]
**J Rheumatol Suppl** ... Journal of Rheumatology. Supplement [*A publication*]
**J R Hortic Soc** ... Journal. Royal Horticulture Society [*A publication*]
**JRHSQ** ... Journal. Royal Historical Society of Queensland [*A publication*]
**JRI** ... Jail Release Information
**JRI** ... Jewel Resources [*Vancouver Stock Exchange symbol*]
**JRI** ... Journal of Risk and Insurance [*A publication*]
**JRIHDC** ... Journal of Research in Indian Medicine, Yoga, and Homoeopathy [*A publication*]
**JRIMD** ... Journal of Reproductive Immunology [*A publication*]
**JRINA** ... Journal. Research Institute for Catalysis. Hokkaido University [*A publication*]
**J R Inst Br Archit** ... Journal. Royal Institute of British Architects [*A publication*]
**J R Inst Chem** ... Journal. Royal Institute of Chemistry [*A publication*]
**J R Inst Public Health** ... Journal. Royal Institute of Public Health [*England*] [*A publication*]
**J R Inst Public Health Hyg** ... Journal. Royal Institute of Public Health and Hygiene [*A publication*]
**J Rio Grande Val Hortic Soc** ... Journal. Rio Grande Valley Horticulture Society [*A publication*]
**JRISDON** ... Jurisdiction (ROG)
**J Risk Ins** ... Journal of Risk and Insurance [*A publication*]
**J Risk & Insur** ... Journal of Risk and Insurance [*A publication*]
**J Risk Insur** ... Journal of Risk and Insurance [*A publication*]
**J RI State Dent Soc** ... Journal. Rhode Island State Dental Society [*A publication*]
**JRJ** ... JAVA [*Jamaica Association of Villas and Apartments*] Reservations Jamaica (EA)
**JRJ** ... Journal of Reform Judaism [*A publication*]
**JRL** ... Jarvis Resources [*Vancouver Stock Exchange symbol*]
**JRL** ... Jet Research Laboratory (MCD)
**JRL** ... Journal of Retailing [*A publication*]
**Jrl Ad Res** ... Journal of Advertising Research [*A publication*]
**Jrl Advtg** ... Journal of Advertising [*A publication*]
**Jrl Audit** ... Journal of Accounting Auditing and Finance [*A publication*]
**JRLB** ... John Rylands Library. Bulletin [*A publication*]
**Jrl Bldg S** ... Journal. Chartered Institution of Building Services [*A publication*]
**Jrl Bus** ... Journal of Business [*A publication*]
**Jrl Coatng** ... Journal of Coatings Technology [*A publication*]
**Jrl Comm** ... Journal of Commerce [*A publication*]
**Jrl Def & D** ... Journal of Defense and Diplomacy [*A publication*]
**Jrl Elec I** ... Journal of the Electronics Industry [*A publication*]
**Jrl Eng Pwr** ... Journal of Engineering for Power [*A publication*]
**Jr Lib** ... Junior Libraries [*A publication*]
**Jrl Int B** ... Journal of International Business Studies [*A publication*]
**Jrl Irrep** ... Journal of Irreproducible Results [*A publication*]
**Jrl Market** ... Journal of Marketing [*A publication*]
**Jrl Metals** ... Journal of Metals [*A publication*]
**Jrl Mkt R** ... Journal of Marketing Research [*A publication*]
**Jrl P** ... Journal. Patent Office Society [*A publication*]
**Jrl Petro** ... Journal of Petroleum Technology [*A publication*]
**Jrl P Mgmt** ... Journal of Portfolio Management [*A publication*]
**Jrl Retail** ... Journal of Retailing [*A publication*]
**Jrl RE Tax** ... Journal of Real Estate Taxation [*A publication*]
**Jr LS** ... Junior Life Saving [*Red Cross*]
**Jrl Solar** ... Journal of Solar Energy Engineering [*A publication*]
**J Rly Div Instn Mech Engrs** ... Institution of Mechanical Engineers. Railway Division. Journal [*A publication*]
**JRM** ... Jettison Release Mechanism
**JRM** ... Joule-Rowland Method [*Physics*]
**JRM** ... Journal of Research in Music Education [*A publication*]
**JRMB** ... Joint Requirements and Management Board [*Later, JROC*] [*Military*]
**JRME** ... Journal of Research in Music Education [*A publication*]
**JRMEA** ... Journal of Research in Music Education [*A publication*]
**JRMF** ... Joseph R. McCarthy Foundation (EA)
**J R Microsc Soc** ... Journal. Royal Microscopical Society [*A publication*]
**JRMIE2** ... Journal of Reconstructive Microsurgery [*A publication*]
**JRMMRA** ... Journal. Rocky Mountain Medieval and Renaissance Association [*A publication*]
**JRMS** ... Journal. Royal Meteorological Society [*A publication*]
**JRMTO** ... Joint Rail Military Traffic Office (AABC)
**JRMX** ... JRM Holdings, Inc. [*NASDAQ symbol*] (NQ)
**JrNAD** ... Junior National Association for the Deaf (EA)
**J R Nav Med Serv** ... Journal. Royal Naval Medical Service [*A publication*]
**JRNBA** ... Journal of Research. [*US*] National Bureau of Standards [*A publication*]
**JRNCDM** ... Journal of Radioanalytical and Nuclear Chemistry [*A publication*]
**JRNDEX** ... Journal Index
**Jr N H** ... Journal of Negro History [*A publication*]
**JRNIST** ... Journalist
**JRNL** ... Journal
**JRNMA** ... Journal. Royal Naval Medical Service [*A publication*]
**JRNSCA** ... Jurist Reports, New Series, Court of Appeal [*New Zealand*] [*A publication*] (DLA)
**JRNSML** ... Jurist Reports, New Series, Cases in Mining Law [*New Zealand*] [*A publication*] (DLA)
**JRNSSC** ... Jurist Reports, New Series, Supreme Court [*New Zealand*] [*A publication*] (DLA)
**JRO** ... Junior Radio Operator [*British military*] (DMA)
**JRO** ... Kilimanjaro [*Tanzania*] [*Airport symbol*] (OAG)
**JROC** ... Joint Requirements Oversight Council [*Military*]
**JROFC** ... James "Rebel" O'Leary Fan Club (EA)
**JROJATC** ... James "Rebel" O'Leary and Jammie Ann Tape Club (EA)
**J Roman Stud** ... Journal of Roman Studies [*A publication*]
**J Rom S** ... Journal of Roman Studies [*A publication*]
**J Rom Stud** ... Journal of Roman Studies [*A publication*]
**J Root Crops** ... Journal of Root Crops [*A publication*]
**J Rossica Soc** ... Journal. Rossica Society of Russian Philately [*A publication*]
**JROTC** ... Junior Reserve Officers' Training Corps (AABC)
**J Roy Agr S** ... Journal. Royal Agricultural Society of England [*A publication*]
**J Royal Aust Hist Soc** ... Journal. Royal Australian Historical Society [*A publication*] (APTA)
**J Royal Military College Aust** ... Journal. Royal Military College of Australia [*A publication*] (APTA)
**J Royal Soc New Zeal** ... Journal. Royal Society of New Zealand [*A publication*]
**J Royal Soc WA** ... Journal. Royal Society of Western Australia [*A publication*] (APTA)
**J Roy Artil** ... Journal of the Royal Artillery [*A publication*]
**J Roy Arty** ... Journal of the Royal Artillery [*A publication*]
**J Roy Asia** ... Journal. Royal Asiatic Society of Great Britain and Ireland [*A publication*]
**J Roy Asiatic Soc** ... Journal. Royal Asiatic Society [*A publication*]
**J Roy Asiat Soc** ... Journal. Royal Asiatic Society [*A publication*]
**J Roy Astro** ... Journal. Royal Astronomical Society of Canada [*A publication*]
**J Roy Aust** ... Journal. Royal Australian Historical Society [*A publication*]
**J Roy Col P** ... Journal. Royal College of Physicians of London [*A publication*]
**J Roy Inst Cornwall N Ser** ... Journal. Royal Institution of Cornwall. New Series [*A publication*]
**J Roy Microscop Soc** ... Journal. Royal Microscopical Society [*A publication*]
**J Roy Micr Soc** ... Journal. Royal Microscopical Society [*A publication*]
**J Roy Soc Antiq Ir** ... Journal. Royal Society of Antiquaries of Ireland [*A publication*]
**J Roy Soc Arts** ... Journal. Royal Society of Arts [*A publication*]
**J Roy Soc NSW** ... Royal Society of New South Wales. Journal and Proceedings [*A publication*] (APTA)
**J Roy Soc W Aust** ... Royal Society of Western Australia. Journal [*A publication*] (APTA)
**J Roy Sta A** ... Journal. Royal Statistical Society. Series A. General [*A publication*]
**J Roy Sta B** ... Journal. Royal Statistical Society. Series B. Methodological [*A publication*]
**J Roy Sta C** ... Journal. Royal Statistical Society. Series C. Applied Statistics [*A publication*]
**J Roy Statis** ... Journal. Royal Statistical Society [*A publication*]
**J Roy Statist Soc Ser A** ... Journal. Royal Statistical Society. Series A. General [*A publication*]
**J Roy Statist Soc Ser B** ... Journal. Royal Statistical Society. Series B. Methodological [*A publication*]
**J Roy Statist Soc Ser C** ... Journal. Royal Statistical Society. Series C. Applied Statistics [*A publication*]
**J Roy Statist Soc Ser C Appl Statist** ... Journal. Royal Statistical Society. Series C. Applied Statistics [*A publication*]
**J Roy Stat Soc A J Verb Learn Verb Beh** ... Journal. Royal Statistical Society. A Journal of Verbal Learning and Verbal Behavior [*A publication*]
**JRP** ... Job Readiness Posture (OICC)
**JRPFA** ... Journal of Reproduction and Fertility [*A publication*]
**JRPG** ... Joint RADAR Planning Group [*Military*] (CET)
**JRPM** ... Joint Registered Publications Memorandum
**JRPUA** ... Journal of Research. Punjab Agricultural University [*A publication*]
**JRR** ... Japanese Research Reactor
**JRRC** ... Joint Regional Reconnaissance Center [*NATO*] (NATG)
**JRRIAN** ... Journal. Rubber Research Institute of Malaysia [*A publication*]
**J RRI Malaysia** ... Journal. Rubber Research Institute of Malaysia [*A publication*]
**J RRI Sri Lanka** ... Journal. Rubber Research Institute of Sri Lanka [*A publication*]
**JRRLA** ... Journal. Radio Research Laboratories [*Tokyo*] [*A publication*]
**JRRT** ... John Ronald Renel Tolkien [*British author, 1892-1973*]
**JRS** ... Japanese Rocket Society
**JRS** ... Jersey [*Channel Islands*] [*Seismograph station code, US Geological Survey*] [*Closed*] (SEIS)
**JRS** ... Jerusalem [*Airport symbol*] (OAG)

**JRS**........... Jet Repair Service
**JRS**........... John R. Sinnock [*Designer's mark, when appearing on US coins*]
**JRS**........... Joint Reporting Structure [*Military*] (AFM)
**JRS**........... Journal. Market Research Society [*A publication*]
**JRS**........... Journal of Regional Science [*A publication*]
**JRS**........... Journal of Research in Singing [*A publication*]
**JRS**........... Journal. Roentgen Society [*A publication*] (ROG)
**JRS**........... Journal of Roman Studies [*A publication*]
**JRS**........... Journal of Russian Studies [*A publication*]
**JRSAA**...... Journal. Royal Society of Arts [*A publication*]
**JRSAI**........ Journal. Royal Society of Antiquaries of Ireland [*A publication*]
**J R Sanit Inst**... Journal. Royal Sanitary Institute [*England*] [*A publication*]
**JRSAntI**.... Journal. Royal Society of Antiquaries of Ireland [*A publication*]
**JRSC**......... Jam-Resistant Secure Communications
**Jr Sch Mines**... Journal. Royal School of Mines [*A publication*]
**Jr Schol**...... Junior Scholastic [*A publication*]
**JRSHDS**.... Journal. Royal Society of Health [*A publication*]
**JR Signals Inst**... Journal. Royal Signals Institution [*A publication*]
**J/RSM**....... Junior Regimental Sergeant-Major [*British military*] (DMA)
**J RSNZ**...... Journal. Royal Society of New Zealand [*A publication*]
**JRSO**......... Jewish Restitution Successor Organization (EA)
**J R Soc Arts**... Journal. Royal Society of Arts [*England*] [*A publication*]
**J R Soc Encour Arts Manuf Commer**... Journal. Royal Society for the Encouragement of Arts, Manufactures, and Commerce [*A publication*]
**J R Soc Health**... Journal. Royal Society of Health [*A publication*]
**J R Soc Hlth**... Journal. Royal Society of Health [*A publication*]
**J R Soc Med**... Journal. Royal Society of Medicine [*A publication*]
**J R Soc NZ**... Journal. Royal Society of New Zealand [*A publication*]
**J R Soc W Aust**... Royal Society of Western Australia. Journal [*A publication*] (APTA)
**J R Soc West Aust**... Journal. Royal Society of Western Australia [*A publication*]
**JRSOD**...... Journal. Reticuloendothelial Society [*A publication*]
**JRSS**......... Journal. Royal Statistical Society [*A publication*]
**J R Stat Soc**... Journal. Royal Statistical Society [*England*] [*A publication*]
**JRSUA**...... Journal. Royal Society of Western Australia [*A publication*]
**JRS/USA**.. Jesuit Refugee Service/USA (EA)
**JRSVC**....... Jam-Resistant Secure Voice Communications (MCD)
**JRSWG**..... Joint Reentry System Working Group
**JRT**........... Job Relations Training
**JRT**........... Journal of Religious Thought [*A publication*]
**JRT**........... Journal of Retailing [*A publication*]
**JRT**........... Jugoslovenska Radio-Televizija [*Radio and television network*] [*Yugoslavia*]
**JRT**........... Tampa, FL [*Location identifier*] [*FAA*] (FAAL)
**JRTC**......... Joint Readiness Training Center [*Fort Chaffee, AR*] (INF)
**JR Telev Soc**... Journal. Royal Television Society [*A publication*]
**J R Th**........ Journal of Religious Thought [*A publication*]
**J Rubber Res Inst Malays**... Journal. Rubber Research Institute of Malaysia [*A publication*]
**J Rubber Res Inst Sri Lanka**... Journal. Rubber Research Institute of Sri Lanka [*A publication*]
**J Rubb Res Inst Malaya**... Journal. Rubber Research Institute of Malaya [*A publication*]
**JRUL**......... Journal. Rutgers University Library [*A publication*]
**J R United Serv Inst**... Journal. Royal United Service Institution [*Later, Journal. Royal United Services Institute for Defense Studies*] [*A publication*]
**J Rural Coop Int Res Cent Rural Coop Communities**... Journal of Rural Cooperation. International Research Center on Rural Cooperative Communities [*A publication*]
**J Rural Dev**... Journal of Rural Development [*A publication*]
**J Rural Econ and Development**... Journal of Rural Economics and Development [*A publication*]
**J Rural Educ**... Journal of Rural Education [*A publication*]
**J Rural Eng Dev**... Journal of Rural Engineering and Development [*A publication*]
**J Rur Coop**... Journal of Rural Cooperation [*A publication*]
**JRuS**.......... Journal of Russian Studies [*A publication*]
**JRUSI**........ Journal of the Royal United Service Institution [*A publication*] (ROG)
**J Rutgers Univ Libr**... Journal. Rutgers University Library [*A publication*]
**JRV**........... Javelin Rocket Vehicle
**JRVSB**....... Jena Review. Supplement [*A publication*]
**JRX**........... Joint Readiness Exercise (MCD)
**JRZ**........... Jugoslovenska Radikalna Zajednica [*Yugoslav Radical Union*] [*Political party*] (PPE)
**JS**.............. Chosonminhang - CAA of DPR of Korea [*ICAO designator*] (FAAC)
**JS**.............. Jack Screw
**J/S**............ Jam to Signal Ratio
**JS**.............. Jam Strobe (IEEE)
**JS**.............. Jamestowne Society (EA)
**J/S**............ Jamming to Signal
**JS**.............. Janus. Supplements [*A publication*]
**JS**.............. Japan Society (EA)
**JS**.............. Jargon Society (EA)
**JS**.............. Jazykovedny Sbornik [*A publication*]
**JS**.............. Jazykovedny Studie [*A publication*]
**J & S**......... Jebb and Symes' Irish Queen's Bench Reports [*A publication*] (DLA)
**JS**.............. Jet Stabilization
**JS**.............. Jet Stream
**JS**.............. Jet Study (AAG)
**JS**.............. Jetevator Sensor
**JS**.............. Jettison Signal
**JS**.............. Job Search [*Job Training and Partnership Act*] (OICC)
**JS**.............. Job Service (OICC)
**JS**.............. Job Specification [*Department of Labor*]
**JS**.............. Job Stream [*Data processing*]
**JS**.............. John R. Sinnock [*Designer's mark, when appearing on US coins*]
**JS**.............. Johnson Society (EA)
**JS**.............. Joint Services [*British military*] (DMA)
**JS**.............. Joint Staff [*Military*] (CINC)
**JS**.............. Joint Support [*Military*] (AFM)
**JS**.............. Jones and Spencer's Superior Court Reports [*33-61 New York*] [*A publication*] (DLA)
**J & S**......... Jones and Spencer's Superior Court Reports [*33-61 New York*] [*A publication*] (DLA)
**JS**.............. Jourdain Society [*British*]
**JS**.............. Journal. Arnold Schoenberg Institute [*A publication*]
**JS**.............. Journal des Savants [*A publication*]
**J & S**......... Judah and Swan's Jamaica Reports [*1839*] [*A publication*] (DLA)
**JS**.............. Judaic Studies [*A publication*]
**JS**.............. Judaisme Sepharadi (BJA)
**JS**.............. Judean Society (EA)
**JS**.............. Judgment Summons [*British*] (ROG)
**JS**.............. Judicial Separation [*British*] (ROG)
**JS**.............. Junior Scholastic [*A publication*]
**JS**.............. Junior Seaman [*British military*] (DMA)
**JS**.............. Jury Sittings (Faculty Cases) [*Scotland*] [*A publication*] (DLA)
**JS**.............. Just Scale
**J/S**............ Justified
**JS**.............. Sea of Japan
**JSA**........... Jammer System Analysis
**JSA**........... Japan Silk Association (EA)
**JSA**........... Jesuit Seismological Association (EA)
**JSA**........... Jet Show Assembly
**JSA**........... Jewelers Security Alliance of the US (EA)
**JSA**........... Jewelers Shipping Association (EA)
**JSA**........... Jewish Society of America
**JSA**........... Job Safety Analysis
**JSA**........... Joint Security Area (MCD)
**JSA**........... Journal. Societe des Africanistes [*A publication*]
**JSA**........... Journal. Societe des Americanistes [*A publication*]
**JSA**........... Journeymen Stone Cutters Association of North America [*Defunct*]
**JSA**........... Junior Statesmen of America (EA)
**JSAC**......... Jet Strategic Airlift Capability [*of Military Air Command*] (AAG)
**JSAC**......... Joint Strategy and Action Committee (EA)
**JSACA**....... Journal. South African Chemical Institute [*A publication*]
**J SA Chem I**... Journal. South African Chemical Institute [*A publication*]
**JSAED**...... Journal of Strain Analysis for Engineering Design [*A publication*]
**JSAf**.......... Journal. Societe des Africanistes [*A publication*]
**JSAFA4**..... Journal. South African Forestry Association [*A publication*]
**JSAFE**....... Journal of South-East Asia and the Far East [*A publication*]
**J Safe Res**.. Journal of Safety Research [*A publication*]
**J SA For Assoc**... Journal. South African Forestry Association [*A publication*]
**JSAfr**......... Journal. Societe des Africanistes [*A publication*]
**J S Afr Assoc Anal Chem**... Journal. South African Association of Analytical Chemists [*A publication*]
**J S Afr Biol Soc**... Journal. South African Biological Society [*A publication*]
**J S Afr Bot**... Journal of South African Botany [*A publication*]
**J S Afr Bot Suppl Vol**... Journal of South African Botany. Supplementary Volume [*A publication*]
**J Saf Res**.... Journal of Safety Research [*A publication*]
**J S Afr For Assoc**... Journal. South African Forestry Association [*A publication*]
**J S Afr Inst Eng**... Journal. South African Institution of Engineers [*A publication*]
**J S Afr Inst Mining Met**... Journal. South African Institute of Mining and Metallurgy [*A publication*]
**J S Afr Inst Min Metall**... Journal. South African Institute of Mining and Metallurgy [*A publication*]
**J S Afr Speech Hear Assoc**... Journal. South African Speech and Hearing Association [*A publication*]
**J S Afr Vet Assoc**... Journal. South African Veterinary Association [*A publication*]
**J S Afr Vet Med Assoc**... Journal. South African Veterinary Medical Association [*Later, South African Veterinary Association. Journal*] [*A publication*]
**JSAG**......... Joint Service Advisory Group
**JSAH**......... Journal. Society of Architectural Historians [*A publication*]
**JSAH**......... Journal of Southeast Asian History [*A publication*]

**J SA I Min** ... Journal. South African Institute of Mining and Metallurgy [*A publication*]
**J Sains Malays** ... Jernel Sains Malaysia [*A publication*]
**J Sains Nukl** ... Jernal Sains Nuklear [*A publication*]
**JSAIS** ........ Junior South African Individual Scales [*Intelligence test*]
**J Saitama Univ Fac Ed Math Natur Sci** ... Journal. Saitama University. Faculty of Education. Mathematics and Natural Science [*A publication*]
**J Saitama Univ Nat Sci** ... Journal. Saitama University. Natural Science [*Japan*] [*A publication*]
**JSAL** .......... Journal of South African Law [*A publication*] (ILCA)
**JSAL** .......... Journal of South Asian Languages [*A publication*]
**JSALO** ...... Journal of Studies on Alcohol [*A publication*]
**JSAM** ........ Joint Security Assistance Memorandum [*Military*]
**JSAM** ........ Joint Service Achievement Medal [*Military decoration*]
**JSAm** ......... Journal. Societe des Americanistes de Paris [*A publication*]
**JSAMA** ..... Journal. South African Institute of Mining and Metallurgy [*A publication*]
**JSAmP** ...... Journal. Societe des Americanistes de Paris [*A publication*]
**JSAMSA** ... Joint Security Assistance Memorandum Supporting Analysis (MCD)
**J San Antonio Dent Soc** ... Journal. San Antonio District Dental Society [*A publication*]
**J Sanit Eng Div Proc Am Soc Civ Eng** ... Journal. Sanitary Engineering Division. Proceedings. American Society of Civil Engineers [*A publication*]
**J San'yo Assoc Adv Sci Technol** ... Journal. San'yo Association for Advancement of Science and Technology [*Japan*] [*A publication*]
**JSAP** .......... Joint Statement of Agreed Principles [*US-USSR*]
**JSAP** .......... Journal. Societe des Americanistes de Paris [*A publication*]
**J Sapporo Munic Gen Hosp** ... Journal. Sapporo Municipal General Hospital [*Japan*] [*A publication*]
**JSAR** ......... Joint Service Agreement Report [*Defense Supply Agency*]
**JSARC** ........ Joint Search and Rescue Center [*Military*] (AABC)
**J S Archit** ... Journal. Society of Architectural Historians [*A publication*]
**JSAS** .......... Jammer System Analysis Simulator
**JSAS** .......... Journal of Southeast Asian Studies [*A publication*]
**JSAS** .......... Journal Supplement Abstract Service [*American Psychological Association*]
**J S Asia L** .. Journal of South Asian Literature [*A publication*]
**JSAT** ......... Joint System Acceptance Test (MCD)
**JSATG** ...... Joint Services Actions Task Group (MCD)
**JSav** .......... Journal des Savants [*A publication*]
**J Savants** ... Journal des Savants [*A publication*]
**JSB** ............ Bachelor of Judicial Science
**JSB** ............ Jaswant Singh and Bhattacharji [*Staining method for blood cells, named for its discoverers*] [*Medicine*]
**JSB** ............ Jewish Society for the Blind (EA)
**JSB** ............ Jewish Statistical Bureau (EA)
**JSB** ............ Joint-Stock Bank [*Banking*]
**JSB** ............ Journal of Small Business Management [*A publication*]
**JSBCD3** ..... Journal. American Society of Brewing Chemists [*A publication*]
**JSBK** .......... Johnstown Savings Bank FSB [*Johnstown, PA*] [*NASDAQ symbol*] (NQ)
**JSBS** .......... Joint Strategic Bomber Study
**JSC** ............ Jackson State College [*Later, Jackson State University*] [*Mississippi*]
**JSC** ............ Jascan Resources, Inc. [*Toronto Stock Exchange symbol*]
**JSC** ............ Jenkinsville [*South Carolina*] [*Seismograph station code, US Geological Survey*] (SEIS)
**JSC** ............ Job-Site Component
**JSC** ............ [*Lyndon B.*] Johnson Space Center [*Formerly, Manned Spacecraft Center*] [*NASA*] [*Houston, TX*]
**JSC** ............ Johnstown & Stony Creek Rail Road Co. [*AAR code*]
**JSC** ............ Joint Scientific Committee [*WMO/ICSU*]
**JSC** ............ Joint Security Control
**JSC** ............ Joint Service Committee [*Military*]
**JSC** ............ Joint Setup Cost
**JSC** ............ Joint Staff Council [*Japanese*] [*Military*] (CINC)
**JSC** ............ Joint Standing Committee (ADA)
**JSC** ............ Joint-Stock Company
**JSC** ............ Joint Strategic Capabilities [*Military*]
**JSC** ............ Joint Strategic Committee [*Military*]
**JSC** ............ Joint Support Command [*Navy*]
**JSC** ............ Joly Steam Calorimeter
**JSC** ............ Journal. Institute for Socioeconomic Studies [*A publication*]
**JSC** ............ Journal of Structural Chemistry [*A publication*]
**JSC** ............ Judgments of the Supreme Court of Cyprus [*A publication*] (ILCA)
**JSC** ............ Junior Staff Course [*British*]
**JSC** ............ Justice of the Supreme Court
**JSCA** ......... Japanese Spaniel Club of America [*Later, JCCA*] (EA)
**JSCA** ......... Journeymen Stone Cutters Association of North America [*Defunct*] (EA)
**JSCAEN** .... Joint Schools Committee for Academic Excellence Now (EA)
**JSCB** ......... Job Step Control Block [*Data processing*] (BUR)
**JSCBT** ....... Joint Steering Committee of the Book Trade [*Australia*]
**JSCC** .......... Japanese Securities Clearing Corporation
**JSCC** .......... Scott Cable Communications, Inc. [*NASDAQ symbol*] (NQ)
**JSCCB** ....... Joint Services Configuration Control Board [*Military*] (AFIT)
**J Sc D** ......... Doctor of Juridical Science
**JScE** ........... Eimac [*Division of Varian Associates*] Technical Library, San Carlos, CA [*Library symbol*] [*Library of Congress*] (LCLS)
**JSCERDCG** ... Joint Service Civil Engineering Research and Development Coordination Group [*Military*] (RDA)
**J Sc Food Agriculture** ... Journal of the Science of Food and Agriculture [*A publication*]
**J Sch Healt** ... Journal of School Health [*A publication*]
**J Sch Health** ... Journal of School Health [*A publication*]
**J Sch Hlth** ... Journal of School Health [*A publication*]
**J Sc Hiroshima Univ S B Div 1 Zool** ... Journal of Science. Hiroshima University. Series B. Division 1. Zoology [*A publication*]
**J Sch Lib Assoc Qld** ... Journal. School Library Association of Queensland [*A publication*] (APTA)
**J Sch Lib Ass Q** ... Journal. School Library Association of Queensland [*A publication*] (APTA)
**J Sch Libr Assoc Qld** ... Journal. School Library Association of Queensland [*A publication*] (APTA)
**J School Libr Ass Qd** ... Journal. School Library Association of Queensland [*A publication*]
**J Sch Pharm Univ Tehran** ... Journal. School of Pharmacy. University of Tehran [*A publication*]
**J Sch Psych** ... Journal of School Psychology [*A publication*]
**J Sch Psychol** ... Journal of School Psychology [*A publication*]
**Jschr Mitteldtsch Vorgesch** ... Jahresschrift fuer Mitteldeutsche Vorgeschichte [*A publication*]
**J Schr Vg (Halle)** ... Jahresschrift fuer Mitteldeutsche Vorgeschichte (Halle) [*A publication*]
**J Sci** .......... Journal of Science [*A publication*]
**J Sci Agric Res** ... Journal for Scientific Agricultural Research [*A publication*]
**J Sci Agric Soc Finl** ... Journal. Scientific Agricultural Society of Finland [*A publication*]
**J Sci Agr Res** ... Journal for Scientific Agricultural Research [*A publication*]
**J Sci Assoc Maharajah's Coll** ... Journal. Science Association. Maharajah's College [*A publication*]
**J Sci Busan Natl Univ** ... Journal of Science. Busan National University [*A publication*]
**J Sci Club** ... Journal of the Science Club [*A publication*]
**J Sci Coll Gen Educ Univ Tokushima** ... Journal of Science. College of General Education. University of Tokushima [*A publication*]
**J Sci Educ Chonnam Natl Univ** ... Journal of Science Education. Chonnam National University [*A publication*]
**J Sci Educ Chungbuk Natl Univ** ... Journal of Science Education. Chungbuk National University [*A publication*]
**J Sci Educ Jeonbug Natl Univ** ... Journal of Science Education. Jeonbug National University [*A publication*]
**J Sci Educ (Jeonju)** ... Journal of Science Education (Jeonju) [*A publication*]
**J Sci Educ Sci Educ Res Inst Teach Coll Kyungpook Univ** ... Journal of Science Education. Science Education Research Institute Teacher's College. Kyungpook University [*A publication*]
**J Sci Eng Res** ... Journal of Science and Engineering Research [*India*] [*A publication*]
**J Sci Engrg Res** ... Journal of Science and Engineering Research [*A publication*]
**J Scient Agric Soc Finl** ... Journal. Scientific Agricultural Society of Finland [*A publication*]
**J Scient Ind Res** ... Journal of Scientific and Industrial Research [*A publication*]
**J Scient Instrum** ... Journal of Scientific Instruments [*A publication*]
**J Scient Stud Relig** ... Journal for the Scientific Study of Religion [*A publication*]
**J Sci Fd Agric** ... Journal of the Science of Food and Agriculture [*A publication*]
**J Sci Food** .. Journal of the Science of Food and Agriculture [*A publication*]
**J Sci Food Agr** ... Journal of the Science of Food and Agriculture [*A publication*]
**J Sci Food Agric** ... Journal of the Science of Food and Agriculture [*A publication*]
**J Sci Food Agric Abstr** ... Journal of the Science of Food and Agriculture. Abstracts [*A publication*]
**J Sci Hiroshima Univ** ... Journal of Science. Hiroshima University [*A publication*]
**J Sci Hiroshima Univ A** ... Journal of Science. Hiroshima University. Series A. Physics and Chemistry [*A publication*]
**J Sci Hiroshima Univ Ser A** ... Journal of Science. Hiroshima University. Series A. Physics and Chemistry [*A publication*]
**J Sci Hiroshima Univ Ser A-II** ... Journal of Science. Hiroshima University. Series A-II [*A publication*]
**J Sci Hiroshima Univ Ser A Math Phys Chem** ... Journal of Science. Hiroshima University. Series A. Mathematics, Physics, Chemistry [*A publication*]
**J Sci Hiroshima Univ Ser A Phys Chem** ... Journal of Science. Hiroshima University. Series A. Physics and Chemistry [*A publication*]
**J Sci Hiroshima Univ Ser B Div 2 Bot** ... Journal of Science. Hiroshima University. Series B. Division 2. Botany [*A publication*]
**J Sci Hiroshima Univ Ser B Div 1 Zool** ... Journal of Science. Hiroshima University. Series B. Division 1. Zoology [*A publication*]
**J Sci Hiroshima Univ Ser C** ... Journal of Science. Hiroshima University. Series C. Geology and Mineralogy [*A publication*]

**J Sci Hiroshima Univ Ser C (Geol Mineral)** ... Journal of Science. Hiroshima University. Series C. Geology and Mineralogy [*A publication*]
**J Sci Ind R** ... Journal of Scientific and Industrial Research [*A publication*]
**J Sci and Ind Res** ... Journal of Scientific and Industrial Research [*A publication*]
**J Sci Ind Res** ... Journal of Scientific and Industrial Research [*A publication*]
**J Sci Ind Res (India)** ... Journal of Scientific and Industrial Research (India) [*A publication*]
**J Sci Ind Res Sect A** ... Journal of Scientific and Industrial Research. Section A. General [*A publication*]
**J Sci Ind Res Sect B** ... Journal of Scientific and Industrial Research. Section B [*A publication*]
**J Sci Ind Res Sect C** ... Journal of Scientific and Industrial Research. Section C. Biological Sciences [*A publication*]
**J Sci Ind Res Sect D** ... Journal of Scientific and Industrial Research. Section D. Technology [*A publication*]
**J Sci Instr** .. Journal of Scientific Instruments [*A publication*]
**J Sci Instrum** ... Journal of Scientific Instruments [*A publication*]
**J Sci Instrum Phys Ind** ... Journal of Scientific Instruments and Physics in Industry [*A publication*]
**J Sci Instrum Suppl** ... Journal of Scientific Instruments. Supplement [*A publication*]
**J Sci (Karachi)** ... Journal of Science (Karachi) [*A publication*]
**J Sci Lab D** ... Journal. Scientific Laboratories. Denison University [*A publication*]
**J Sci Lab Denison Univ** ... Journal. Scientific Laboratories. Denison University [*A publication*]
**J Sci Labor** ... Journal of Science of Labor [*Japan*] [*A publication*]
**J Sci Labour Part 2** ... Journal of Science of Labour. Part 2 [*A publication*]
**J Sci Med Lille** ... Journal des Sciences Medicales de Lille [*A publication*]
**J Sci Meteorol** ... Journal Scientifique de la Meteorologie [*A publication*]
**J Sci Nutr**... Journal des Sciences de la Nutrition [*A publication*]
**J Sci Res** .... Journal of Scientific Research [*A publication*]
**J Sci Res Banaras Hindu Univ** ... Journal of Scientific Research. Banaras Hindu University [*A publication*]
**J Sci Res (Bhopal)** ... Journal of Scientific Research (Bhopal) [*A publication*]
**J Sci Res Counc Jam** ... Journal. Scientific Research Council of Jamaica [*A publication*]
**J Sci Res (Hardwar)** ... Journal of Scientific Research (Hardwar, India) [*A publication*]
**J Sci Res (Hardwar India)** ... Journal of Scientific Research (Hardwar, India) [*A publication*]
**J Sci Res (Indones)** ... Journal of Scientific Research (Indonesia) [*A publication*]
**J Sci Res Inst (Tokyo)** ... Journal. Scientific Research Institute (Tokyo) [*A publication*]
**J Sci Res (Lahore)** ... Journal of Scientific Research (Lahore) [*A publication*]
**J Sci Res Plants & Med** ... Journal of Scientific Research in Plants and Medicines [*A publication*]
**J Sci Soc Thailand** ... Journal. Science Society of Thailand [*A publication*]
**J Sci Soil Manure (Jap)** ... Journal of the Science of Soil and Manure (Japan) [*A publication*]
**J Sci St Re** ... Journal for the Scientific Study of Religion [*A publication*]
**J Sci Stud Rel** ... Journal for the Scientific Study of Religion [*A publication*]
**J Sci Stud Relig** ... Journal for the Scientific Study of Religion [*A publication*]
**J Sci Tech** .. Journal of Science and Technology [*A publication*]
**J Sci Technol** ... Journal of Science and Technology [*A publication*]
**J Sci and Technol** ... Journal of Science and Technology [*A publication*]
**J Sci Technol (Aberdeen Scotl)** ... Journal of Science Technology (Aberdeen, Scotland) [*A publication*]
**J Sci Technol (London)** ... Journal of Science and Technology (London) [*A publication*]
**J Sci Technol (Peshawar)** ... Journal of Science and Technology (Peshawar) [*A publication*]
**JSCJA** ....... Journal. Society of Chemical Industry (Japan) [*A publication*]
**JSCM** ........ Joint Service Commendation Medal [*Military decoration*] (AFM)
**JSCM** ........ JSC [*Johnson Space Center*] Manual [*NASA*] (NASA)
**JSCMA** ..... Journal. South Carolina Medical Association [*A publication*]
**J SC Med Assoc** ... Journal. South Carolina Medical Association [*A publication*]
**JSCMPO**... Joint Service Cruise Missile Program Office (MCD)
**JSCO** ......... Joint Staff Communications Office [*Military*] (AABC)
**JSCOD** ...... Job Safety Consultant [*A publication*]
**JSCOM** ..... Joint Services Commendation Medal (RDA)
**JS Com Ind L** ... Journal. Society of Commercial and Industrial Law [*A publication*] (ILCA)
**J S Cosm Ch** ... Journal. Society of Cosmetic Chemists [*A publication*]
**J Scott** ........ Reporter, English Common Bench Reports [*A publication*] (DLA)
**J Scott Assoc Geogr Teach** ... Journal. Scottish Association of Geography Teachers [*A publication*]
**JSCP** .......... Joint Strategic Capabilities Plan [*Military*]
**JSCPB** ........ Proceedings. Japan Society of Civil Engineers [*A publication*]
**JSCR** ......... Job Schedule Change Request
**JSCS** .......... Joint Strategic Connectivity Committee [*Joint Chiefs of Staff*]
**JSCS** .......... Junior Slovak Catholic Sokol (EA)
**JSCSA** ....... Journal of Statistical Computation and Simulation [*A publication*]
**JScStRel** .... Journal for the Scientific Study of Religion [*New Haven, CT*] [*A publication*]
**JSCU** ......... Joint Supply Council for Union of South Africa [*World War II*]
**JSCUD** ...... Journal of Science Education. Chungbuk National University [*A publication*]
**J Scunthorpe Mus Soc** ... Journal. Scunthorpe Museum Society [*A publication*]
**JSD** ........... Doctor of Judicial [*or Juridical*] Science [*or Doctor of the Science of Law*]
**JSD** ........... Jatiya Samajtantrik Dal [*National Socialist Party*] [*Bangladesh*] [*Political party*] (PPW)
**JSD** ........... Jeunesse Social Democrate [*Social Democratic Youth*] [*Malagasy*]
**JSD** ........... Jewish Society for the Deaf [*Later, New York Society for the Deaf*] (EA)
**JSD** ........... JiJi Securities Data Service [*JiJi Press Ltd.*] [*Japan*] [*Information service or system*] (CRD)
**JSD** ........... Justification Service Digit [*Telecommunications*] (TEL)
**JSD** ........... Stratford, CT [*Location identifier*] [*FAA*] (FAAL)
**JSDA** ......... Japanese Self-Defense Agency
**JSDC** ......... Journal. Society of Dyers and Colourists [*A publication*]
**JSDF** ......... Japan Self-Defense Force (CINC)
**JSDF** ......... Jin Shin Do Foundation for Bodymind Acupressure (EA)
**JSDM** ........ June, September, December, and March [*Denotes quarterly payments of interest or dividends in these months*] [*Business term*]
**JSDP** ......... Jewish Social Democratic Party [*Political party*] (BJA)
**J S Dye Col** ... Journal. Society of Dyers and Colourists [*A publication*]
**JSE** ........... Jam Strobe Extractor
**JSEA** ......... Japan Ship Exporters Association (DS)
**JSEA** ......... Jesuit Secondary Education Association (EA)
**JSEAC** ........ Joint Societies Employment Advisory Committee
**J-SEAD** ..... Joint Suppression of Enemy Air Defenses [*Military*] (INF)
**J SE Asian Hist** ... Journal of Southeast Asian History [*A publication*]
**J SE Asian Stud** ... Journal of Southeast Asian Studies [*A publication*]
**J SE Asia S** ... Journal of Southeast Asian Studies [*A publication*]
**J Se As Stud** ... Journal of Southeast Asian Studies [*A publication*]
**J Seattle King Cty Dent Soc** ... Journal. Seattle-King County Dental Society [*A publication*]
**J Sec Ed** ..... Journal of Secondary Education [*A publication*]
**J Sediment Petrol** ... Journal of Sedimentary Petrology [*A publication*]
**J Sediment Petrology** ... Journal of Sedimentary Petrology [*A publication*]
**J Sed Petrol** ... Journal of Sedimentary Petrology [*A publication*]
**J Seed Technol** ... Journal of Seed Technology [*A publication*]
**JSEI** .......... Joint Second Echelon Interdiction
**J Sej** .......... Jernal Sejarah [*A publication*]
**J Semitic S** ... Journal of Semitic Studies [*A publication*]
**JSemS** ........ Journal of Semitic Studies [*Manchester*] [*A publication*]
**J Sem St** ..... Journal of Semitic Studies [*A publication*]
**J Seoul Woman's Coll** ... Journal. Seoul Woman's College [*A publication*]
**JSEP** .......... Job Skills Education Program [*Military*]
**JSEP** .......... Joint Services Electronics Program [*Military*]
**J Separ Proc Technol** ... Journal of Separation and Process Technology [*A publication*]
**J Serb Chem Soc** ... Journal. Serbian Chemical Society [*A publication*]
**J Seric Sci Jpn** ... Journal of Sericultural Science of Japan [*A publication*]
**JSeS** ........... Journal of Semitic Studies [*Manchester*] [*A publication*]
**JSESPO** .... Joint [*Maritime Administration - Navy*] Surface-Effects Ship Program Office
**JSET** .......... Journal of Sex Education and Therapy [*A publication*]
**J Severance Union Med Coll** ... Journal. Severance Union Medical College [*A publication*]
**J Sex Marital Ther** ... Journal of Sex and Marital Therapy [*A publication*]
**JSEXP** ....... Joint Services Explosives Program (MCD)
**J Sex Res** ... Journal of Sex Research [*A publication*]
**JSEY** .......... Jersey [*One of the Channel Islands*] (ROG)
**JSF** ............ Japan Scholarship Foundation (EA)
**JSF** ............ Jesse Stuart Foundation (EA)
**JSF** ............ Job Services File
**JSF** ............ Joint Security Force [*Army*] (INF)
**JSF** ............ Junctor Switch Frame [*Telecommunications*] (TEL)
**JSF** ............ Junior Statesmen Foundation (EA)
**JSFA** .......... Journal of the Science of Food and Agriculture [*A publication*]
**JSFC** .......... Jack Scalia Fan Club (EA)
**JSFC** .......... Japanese-Soviet Fisheries Commission for the Northwest Pacific
**JSFC** .......... Joe Stampley Fan Club (EA)
**JSFOu** ....... Journal. Societe Finno-Ougrienne [*A publication*]
**JSFP** .......... Joint Service Fuze Plan [*Army*]
**JSFWUB** ... Jahrbuch. Schlesische Friedrich-Wilhelm Universitaet zu Breslau [*A publication*]
**JSG** ............ Jahrbuch. Schiller-Gesellschaft [*A publication*]
**JSG** ............ Jamaica (BWI) Study Group (EA)
**JSG** ............ Job Seekers Guide to Private and Public Companies [*A publication*]
**JSG** ............ Jugoslavia Study Group (EA)
**JSGCC** ....... Joint Service Guidance and Control Committee
**JSGLL** ....... Japanese Studies in German Language and Literature [*A publication*]
**JSGOMRAM** ... Joint Study Group on Military Resources Allocation Methodology (MCD)

**J S Gr**......... [*J. S.*] Green's Law Reports [*13-15 New Jersey*] [*A publication*] (DLA)
**JSGRP**....... Jewish Symbols in the Greco-Roman Period [*A publication*] (BJA)
**JSGU**......... Jahrbuch. Schweizerische Gesellschaft fuer Urgeschichte [*A publication*]
**JSH**............ Jihocesky Sbornik Historicky [*A publication*]
**JSH**............ Journal of Social History [*A publication*] (ADA)
**JSH**............ Journal of Southern History [*A publication*]
**JSHA**......... Johannes Schwalm Historical Association (EA)
**JSHABP**.... Journal. South African Speech and Hearing Association [*A publication*]
**J Shanghai Coll Text Technol** ... Journal. Shanghai College of Textile Technology [*A publication*]
**J Shanghai Jiaotong Univ** ... Journal of Shanghai Jiaotong University/ Shanghai Jiaotong Daxue Xuebao [*A publication*]
**J Shanghai Sci Inst** ... Journal. Shanghai Science Institute [*A publication*]
**J Shanghai Sci Inst Sect 1** ... Journal. Shanghai Science Institute. Section 1. Experimental Biology and Medicine [*A publication*]
**J Shanghai Sci Inst Sect 1** ... Journal. Shanghai Science Institute. Section 1. Mathematics, Astronomy, Physics, Geophysics, Chemistry, and Allied Sciences [*A publication*]
**J Shanghai Sci Inst Sect 2** ... Journal. Shanghai Science Institute. Section 2. Geology, Palaeontology, Mineralogy, and Petrology [*A publication*]
**J Shanghai Sci Inst Sect 3** ... Journal. Shanghai Science Institute. Section 3. Systematic and Morphological Biology [*A publication*]
**J Shanghai Sci Inst Sect 5** ... Journal. Shanghai Science Institute. Section 5. General [*A publication*]
**J Shanxi Univ Nat Sci Ed** ... Journal. Shanxi University. Natural Science Edition [*A publication*]
**J SHASE**... Journal. Society of Heating, Air Conditioning, and Sanitary Engineers of Japan [*A publication*]
**J Shaw** ....... John Shaw's Justiciary Reports [*1848-52*] [*Scotland*] [*A publication*] (DLA)
**J Shaw Just** ... John Shaw's Justiciary Reports [*1848-52*] [*Scotland*] [*A publication*] (DLA)
**JSHD**......... Journal of Speech and Hearing Disorders [*A publication*]
**JSHDA**...... Journal of Speech and Hearing Disorders [*A publication*]
**JSHEA**...... Journal of School Health [*A publication*]
**J Sheffield Univ Met Soc** ... Journal. Sheffield University Metallurgical Society [*A publication*]
**J Shellfish Res** ... Journal of Shellfish Research [*A publication*]
**JSHG**......... Hokkai Gakuen University, Sapporo, Japan [*Library symbol*] [*Library of Congress*] (LCLS)
**J Shimane Med Assoc** ... Journal. Shimane Medical Association [*Japan*] [*A publication*]
**J Shimonoseki Coll Fish** ... Journal. Shimonoseki College of Fisheries [*A publication*]
**J Shimonoseki Univ Fish** ... Journal. Shimonoseki University of Fisheries [*A publication*]
**J Ship Res** ... Journal of Ship Research [*A publication*]
**J S Hist**...... Journal of Southern History [*A publication*]
**J Shivaji Univ** ... Journal. Shivaji University [*A publication*]
**J Shivaji Univ Sci** ... Journal. Shivaji University (Science) [*A publication*]
**J Shoreline Manage** ... Journal of Shoreline Management [*A publication*]
**J Showa Med Assoc** ... Journal. Showa Medical Association [*Japan*] [*A publication*]
**JSHR**......... Journal of Speech and Hearing Research [*A publication*]
**JSHS**......... Jewish Society for Human Service [*British*]
**JSHS**......... Junior Science and Humanities Symposia [*Terminated, 1977*]
**J-S H Sch Clearing House** ... Junior-Senior High School Clearing House [*A publication*]
**JSI**............. Job Satisfaction Inventory [*Guidance*]
**JSI**............. Job Schedule Items (MCD)
**JSI**............. Job Search Information
**JSI**............. Job Sensitivity Inventory [*Interpersonal skills and attitudes test*]
**JSI**............. Journal. American Society for Information Science [*A publication*]
**JSI**............. Journal of Social Issues [*A publication*]
**JSI**............. Journal of Societal Issues [*A publication*] (ADA)
**JSI**............. Skiathos [*Greece*] [*Airport symbol*] (OAG)
**JSIA**........... Joint Service Induction Area
**JSIA**........... Justice System Improvement Act [*1979*]
**JSIAM**....... Journal. Society of Industrial and Applied Mathematics [*A publication*]
**J Siam Soc** ... Journal. Siam Society [*A publication*]
**J-SIDS**....... Joint Service Intrusion Detection System [*Military*] (INF)
**J Signalaufzeichnungsmater** ... Journal fuer Signalaufzeichnungsmaterialien [*A publication*]
**J Signalaufzeichnungsmaterialien** ... Journal fuer Signalaufzeichnungsmaterialien [*A publication*]
**JSIID**......... Joint Service Interior Intrusion Detection Devices [*Military*] (MCD)
**JSIIDS**...... Joint Service Interior Intrusion Detection System [*Military*]
**JSIM**......... Joint Service Intelligence Manual
**JSIN**.......... Journal. Society for International Numismatics [*A publication*]
**J Singapore Nat Acad Sci** ... Journal. Singapore National Academy of Science [*A publication*]
**J Singapore Natl Acad Sci** ... Journal. Singapore National Academy of Science [*A publication*]
**J Singapore Paediatr Soc** ... Journal. Singapore Paediatric Society [*A publication*]
**JSIP**........... Job Service Improvement Program [*Department of Labor*]
**JSIPS**........ Joint Services Imagery Processing System [*Military*]
**JSIPS**........ Joint Systems Integration Planning Staff [*Air Force*]
**JSISD**........ Journal of Current Social Issues [*A publication*]
**JSJ**............. Journal for the Study of Judaism [*Later, Journal for the Study of Judaism in thePersian, Hellenistic, and Roman Periods*] [*A publication*]
**J & S Jam**.. Judah and Swan's Jamaica Reports [*1839*] [*A publication*] (DLA)
**JSK**............ Jahrbuch. Sammlung Kippenberg Duesseldorf [*A publication*]
**JSK**............ St. Cloud, MN [*Location identifier*] [*FAA*] (FAAL)
**JSL**............ Jet Select Logic (MCD)
**JSL**............ Job Specification Language
**JSL**............ Johnson Society of London (EA)
**JSL**............ Joint Stock List [*Military*] (AFIT)
**JSL**............ Joint Support List [*Military*]
**JSL**............ Journal. School of Languages [*A publication*]
**JSL**............ Journal of Symbolic Logic [*A publication*]
**JSLB**.......... Japan Society of London. Bulletin [*A publication*]
**JSLCA**....... Journal of Solution Chemistry [*A publication*]
**JslF**............ Juznoslovenski Filolog [*A publication*]
**JSLGWCM** ... Joint Services LASER-Guided Weapons Countermeasures (MCD)
**JSLI**........... Johnson-Sea-Link I [*A submersible for deep sea studies*]
**JSLQ**......... Journal of Symbolic Logic. Quarterly [*A publication*]
**JSLS**.......... Joint Services Liaison Staff [*British*]
**JSLWG**...... Joint Spacelab Working Group [*NASA*] (NASA)
**JSM**........... Jesus Salvator Mundi [*Jesus the Savior of the World*] [*Latin*] (ROG)
**JSM**........... Joint Staff Memorandum (MCD)
**JSM**........... Joint Staff Mission [*British*] [*World War II*]
**JSM**........... Jose De San Martin [*Argentina*] [*Airport symbol*] (OAG)
**JSM**........... Journal of Synagogue Music [*A publication*]
**JSM**........... Journal of Systems Management [*A publication*]
**JSM**........... Master of Judicial Science
**JSMA**........ Joint Sealer Manufacturers Association
**J Small Anim Pract** ... Journal of Small Animal Practice [*A publication*]
**J Small Bus Manage** ... Journal of Small Business Management [*A publication*]
**J Small Bus Mgt** ... Journal of Small Business Management [*A publication*]
**J Sm Anim P** ... Journal of Small Animal Practice [*A publication*]
**JSMB**........ Joint Sealift Movements Board [*Military*] (AFM)
**JSME**........ Japan Society of Mechanical Engineers
**JSME**........ Joint Soil Moisture Experiment
**JSMMART** ... Journal. Society for Mass Media and Resource Technology [*A publication*] (APTA)
**JSMPE**...... Journal. Society of Motion Picture Engineers [*A publication*]
**J SMPTE**.. Journal. SMPTE [*Society of Motion Picture and Television Engineers*] [*A publication*]
**JSMS**......... Job Service Matching Systems [*US Employment Service*] [*Department of Labor*]
**JSMSM**..... Joint Service Meritorious Service Medal [*Military decoration*]
**JSN**............ Job Sequence Number
**JSN**............ Joint Space Narrowing [*Medicine*]
**JSNA**......... Jaspers Society of North America (EA)
**JSNOOFC** ... Judson Scott Is Number 1 Official Fan Club (EA)
**JSNPE**....... Joint Staff Nuclear Planning Element (MCD)
**JSNT**......... Journal for the Study of the New Testament [*A publication*]
**JSNTDC** ... Annuaire. Societe Helvetique des Sciences Naturelles. Partie Scientifique [*A publication*]
**JSO**............ Jacksonville, TX [*Location identifier*] [*FAA*] (FAAL)
**JSO**............ Jerusalem Symphony Orchestra (BJA)
**JSO**............ Joint Service Office
**JSO**............ Journal. Societe des Oceanistes [*A publication*]
**J So AL**...... Journal of South Asian Literature [*A publication*]
**JSOC**......... Joint Ship Operations Center
**JSOC**......... Joint Ship Operations Committee
**JSOC**......... Joint Special Operations Center (MCD)
**JSOC**......... Joint Special Operations Command [*Military*]
**JSOC**......... Joint Strategic Operations Command (MCD)
**JSOc**.......... Journal. Societe des Oceanistes [*A publication*]
**J Soc African** ... Journal. Societe des Africanistes [*A publication*]
**J Soc Air-Cond Refrig Eng Korea** ... Journal. Society of Air-Conditioning and Refrigerating Engineers of Korea [*Republic of Korea*] [*A publication*]
**J Soc Amer** ... Journal. Societe des Americanistes [*A publication*]
**J Soc Arch** ... Journal. Society of Archivists [*A publication*]
**J Soc Archer-Antiq** ... Journal. Society of Archer-Antiquaries [*A publication*]
**J Soc Arch Hist** ... Journal. Society of Architectural Historians [*A publication*]
**J Soc Architect Hist** ... Journal. Society of Architectural Historians [*A publication*]
**J Soc Army Hist Res** ... Journal. Society for Army Historical Research [*A publication*]
**J Soc Arts**.. Journal. Society of Arts [*A publication*]
**J Soc Automot Eng** ... Journal. Society of Automotive Engineers [*A publication*]

**J Soc Automot Eng Jpn Inc** ... Journal. Society of Automotive Engineers of Japan, Incorporated [*A publication*]
**J Soc Automot Engrs Australas** ... Society of Automotive Engineers of Australasia. Journal [*A publication*] (APTA)
**J Soc Bibliogr Nat Hist** ... Journal. Society for the Bibliography of Natural History [*A publication*]
**J Soc Brew (Japan)** ... Journal. Society of Brewing (Japan) [*A publication*]
**J Soc Brew (Tokyo)** ... Journal. Society of Brewing (Tokyo) [*A publication*]
**J Soc Can Anesth** ... Journal. Societe Canadienne des Anesthesistes [*A publication*]
**J Soc Can Sci Judiciaires** ... Journal. Societe Canadienne des Sciences Judiciaires [*A publication*]
**J Soc Casework** ... Social Casework Journal [*A publication*]
**J Soc Chem Ind (Jpn)** ... Journal. Society of Chemical Industry (Japan) [*A publication*]
**J Soc Chem Ind (Lond)** ... Journal. Society of Chemical Industry (London) [*A publication*]
**J Soc Chem Ind (London)** ... Journal. Society of Chemical Industry (London) [*A publication*]
**J Soc Chem Ind (London) Abstr** ... Journal. Society of Chemical Industry (London). Abstracts [*A publication*]
**J Soc Chem Ind (London) Rev Sect** ... Journal. Society of Chemical Industry (London). Review Section [*A publication*]
**J Soc Chem Ind (London) Trans Commun** ... Journal. Society of Chemical Industry (London). Transactions and Communications [*A publication*]
**J Soc Chem Ind Vic** ... Journal. Society of Chemical Industry of Victoria [*A publication*] (APTA)
**J Soc Cienc Med Lisb** ... Jornal. Sociedade das Ciencias Medicas de Lisboa [*A publication*]
**J Soc Cosmet Chem** ... Journal. Society of Cosmetic Chemists [*A publication*]
**J Soc Dairy Technol** ... Journal. Society of Dairy Technology [*A publication*]
**J Soc Dy Colour** ... Journal. Society of Dyers and Colourists [*A publication*]
**J Soc Dyers Colourists** ... Journal. Society of Dyers and Colourists [*A publication*]
**J Soc Eng (Lond)** ... Journal. Society of Engineers (London) [*A publication*]
**J Soc Eng Miner Springs** ... Journal. Society of Engineers for Mineral Springs [*Japan*] [*A publication*]
**J Soc Env Engrs** ... Journal. Society of Environmental Engineers [*A publication*]
**J Soc Environ Eng** ... Journal. Society of Environmental Engineers [*A publication*]
**J Soc Environ Engrs** ... Journal. Society of Environmental Engineers [*A publication*]
**J Soc Exp Agric** ... Journal. Society of Experimental Agriculturists [*A publication*]
**J Soc Glass Technol** ... Journal. Society of Glass Technology [*A publication*]
**J Soc Hist**.. Journal of Social History [*A publication*]
**J Soc Hygiene** ... Journal of Social Hygiene [*A publication*]
**J Social Casework** ... Journal of Social Casework [*A publication*]
**J Social and Econ Studies** ... Journal of Social and Economic Studies [*A publication*]
**J Social Forces** ... Journal of Social Forces [*A publication*]
**J Social Hyg** ... Journal of Social Hygiene [*A publication*]
**J Social Issues** ... Journal of Social Issues [*A publication*]
**J Social Pol and Econ Studies** ... Journal of Social, Political, and Economic Studies [*A publication*]
**J Social Policy** ... Journal of Social Policy [*A publication*]
**J Social and Pol Studies** ... Journal of Social and Political Studies [*A publication*]
**J Social Psychol** ... Journal of Social Psychology [*A publication*]
**J Soc Ind Appl Math** ... Journal. Society of Industrial and Applied Mathematics [*United States*] [*A publication*]
**J Soc Instrum and Control** ... Journal. Society of Instrument and Control Engineers [*A publication*]
**J Soc Iss**..... Journal of Social Issues [*A publication*]
**J Soc Issue** ... Journal of Social Issues [*A publication*]
**J Soc Issues** ... Journal of Societal Issues [*A publication*] (APTA)
**J Soc Leath Technol Chem** ... Journal. Society of Leather Technologists and Chemists [*A publication*]
**J Soc Leath Trades Chem** ... Journal. Society of Leather Trades Chemists [*A publication*]
**J Soc Mater Sci (Jpn)** ... Journal. Society of Materials Science (Japan) [*A publication*]
**J Soc Motion Pict Eng** ... Journal. Society of Motion Picture Engineers [*A publication*]
**J Soc Motion Pict Telev Eng** ... Journal. Society of Motion Picture and Television Engineers [*A publication*]
**J Soc Motion Pict and Telev Eng** ... Journal. Society of Motion Picture and Television Engineers [*A publication*]
**J Soc Mot Pict Eng** ... Journal. Society of Motion Picture Engineers [*A publication*]
**J Soc Mot Pict Tel Eng** ... Journal. Society of Motion Picture and Television Engineers [*A publication*]
**J Soc Nav Archit Jpn** ... Journal. Society of Naval Architects of Japan [*A publication*]
**J Soc Nav Arch Japan** ... Journal. Society of Naval Architects of Japan [*A publication*]
**J Soc Non-Destr Test** ... Journal. Society for Non-Destructive Testing [*A publication*]
**J Soc Occup Med** ... Journal. Society of Occupational Medicine [*A publication*]
**J Soc Ocean** ... Journal. Societe des Oceanistes [*A publication*]
**J Soc Oceanistes** ... Journal. Societe des Oceanistes [*A publication*]
**J Soc Org Syn Chem (Jpn)** ... Journal. Society of Organic Synthetic Chemistry (Japan) [*A publication*]
**J Soc Org Synth Chem** ... Journal. Society of Organic Synthetic Chemistry [*A publication*]
**J Soc Osteopaths (Lond)** ... Journal. Society of Osteopaths (London) [*A publication*]
**J Soc Pet Eng** ... Journal. Society of Petroleum Engineers [*A publication*]
**J Soc Phil**... Journal of Social Philosophy [*A publication*]
**J Soc Photogr Sci and Technol Jpn** ... Journal. Society of Photographic Science and Technology of Japan [*A publication*]
**J Soc Photo Opt Instrum Eng** ... Journal. Society of Photo-Optical Instrumentation Engineers [*A publication*]
**J Soc Pol**.... Journal of Social Policy [*A publication*]
**J Soc Polic** ... Journal of Social Policy [*A publication*]
**J Soc Policy** ... Journal of Social Policy [*A publication*]
**J Soc Psych** ... Journal of Social Psychology [*A publication*]
**J Soc Psychol** ... Journal of Social Psychology [*A publication*]
**J Soc Psych Res** ... Journal. Society for Psychical Research [*A publication*]
**J Soc Pub Teach Law N S** ... Journal. Society of Public Teachers of Law. New Series [*A publication*]
**J Soc Pub T L** ... Journal. Society of Public Teachers of Law [*A publication*]
**J Soc Radiol Prot** ... Journal. Society for Radiological Protection [*A publication*]
**J Soc Res** ... Journal of Social Research [*A publication*]
**J Soc Rubber Ind (Jpn)** ... Journal. Society of Rubber Industry (Japan) [*A publication*]
**J Soc Sci** .... Journal of Social Sciences [*A publication*]
**J Soc Sci Hum** ... Journal of Social Sciences and Humanities [*A publication*]
**J Soc Sci Photogr Jpn** ... Journal. Society of Scientific Photography of Japan [*A publication*]
**J Soc Statist Paris** ... Journal. Societe Statistique de Paris [*A publication*]
**J Soc Ther** ... Journal of Social Therapy [*A publication*]
**J Soc Underwater Technol** ... Journal. Society for Underwater Technology [*A publication*]
**J Soc Welfare L** ... Journal of Social Welfare Law [*A publication*]
**J Soc Work & Hum Sex** ... Journal of Social Work and Human Sexuality [*A publication*]
**J Soc'y Comp Leg** ... Journal. Society of Comparative Legislation [*A publication*] (DLA)
**J Socy Pub Tchrs L** ... Journal. Society of Public Teachers of Law [*A publication*]
**J So Hist**.... Journal of Southern History [*A publication*]
**J Soil Biol & Ecol** ... Journal of Soil Biology and Ecology [*A publication*]
**J Soil Conservation Serv NSW** ... Journal. Soil Conservation Service of New South Wales [*A publication*] (APTA)
**J Soil Conserv NSW** ... Journal. Soil Conservation Service of New South Wales [*A publication*] (APTA)
**J Soil Conserv Service NSW** ... Journal. Soil Conservation Service of New South Wales [*A publication*] (APTA)
**J Soil Conserv Serv NSW** ... Journal. Soil Conservation Service of New South Wales [*A publication*] (APTA)
**J Soil Mech Found Div Am Soc Civ Eng** ... Journal. Soil Mechanics and Foundations Division. American Society of Civil Engineers [*A publication*]
**J Soil Sci**.... Journal of Soil Science [*A publication*]
**J Soil Sci Soc Am** ... Journal. Soil Science Society of America [*A publication*]
**J Soil Sci Soc Philipp** ... Journal. Soil Science Society of the Philippines [*A publication*]
**J Soil Sci UAR** ... Journal of Soil Science of the United Arab Republic [*A publication*]
**J Soil Sci Un Arab Repub** ... Journal of Soil Science of the United Arab Republic [*A publication*]
**J Soil Wat** ... Journal of Soil and Water Conservation [*US*] [*A publication*]
**J Soil & Water Conser** ... Journal of Soil and Water Conservation [*A publication*]
**J Soil Water Conserv** ... Journal of Soil and Water Conservation [*US*] [*A publication*]
**J Soil Water Conserv India** ... Journal of Soil and Water Conservation in India [*A publication*]
**J Sol Chem** ... Journal of Solution Chemistry [*A publication*]
**J Sol Energy Eng** ... Journal of Solar Energy Engineering [*United States*] [*A publication*]
**J Sol Energy Res** ... Journal of Solar Energy Research [*A publication*]
**J Sol Energy Sci Eng** ... Journal of Solar Energy Science and Engineering [*United States*] [*A publication*]
**J Sol Energy Soc Korea** ... Journal. Solar Energy Society of Korea [*Republic of Korea*] [*A publication*]
**J Sol En Sci** ... Journal of Solar Energy Science and Engineering [*A publication*]
**J Solid Lubr** ... Journal of Solid Lubrication [*A publication*]
**J Solid-Phase Biochem** ... Journal of Solid-Phase Biochemistry [*A publication*]
**J Solid State Chem** ... Journal of Solid State Chemistry [*A publication*]
**J Solid Wastes** ... Journal of Solid Wastes [*A publication*]
**J Solid Wastes Manage** ... Journal of Solid Wastes Management [*Japan*] [*A publication*]
**J Soln Chem** ... Journal of Solution Chemistry [*A publication*]

**J Sol St Ch** ... Journal of Solid State Chemistry [*A publication*]
**J Solut Chem** ... Journal of Solution Chemistry [*A publication*]
**J Solution Chem** ... Journal of Solution Chemistry [*A publication*]
**J Somerset Mines Res Group** ... Journal. Somerset Mines Research Group [*A publication*]
**JSON**......... Joint Services Operational Notice
**JSON**......... Josephson International, Inc. [*NASDAQ symbol*] (NQ)
**J Soonchunhyang Coll** ... Journal. Soonchunhyang College [*A publication*]
**JSOP**......... Joint Strategic Objectives Plan [*Military*]
**JSOR**......... Joint Services Operational Requirement [*Military*]
**JSOR**......... Journal. Society of Oriental Research [*A publication*]
**JSORS**....... Joint Service Operational Requirement Statement (MCD)
**JSOSE**....... Joint Special Operations Support Element [*DoD*]
**JSOT**......... Journal for the Study of the Old Testament [*A publication*]
**J Sound and Vib** ... Journal of Sound and Vibration [*A publication*]
**J Sound Vib** ... Journal of Sound and Vibration [*A publication*]
**J Sound Vibration** ... Journal of Sound and Vibration [*A publication*]
**J South Afr Chem Inst** ... Journal. South African Chemical Institute [*A publication*]
**J South Afr Stud** ... Journal of Southern African Studies [*A publication*]
**J South Afr Vet Assoc** ... Journal. South African Veterinary Association [*A publication*]
**J South Afr Vet Med Ass** ... Journal. South African Veterinary Medical Association [*Later, South African Veterinary Association. Journal*] [*A publication*]
**J South Afr Wildl Manage Assoc** ... Journal. Southern African Wildlife Management Association [*A publication*]
**J South Asian Lit** ... Journal of South Asian Literature [*A publication*]
**J South As Lit** ... Journal of South Asian Literature [*A publication*]
**J South Calif Dent Assistants Assoc** ... Journal. Southern California Dental Assistants Association [*A publication*]
**J South Calif Dent Assoc** ... Journal. Southern California Dental Association [*A publication*]
**J South California Dent A** ... Journal. Southern California Dental Association [*A publication*]
**J South Calif State Dent Assoc** ... Journal. Southern California State Dental Association [*A publication*]
**J Southeast Agric Coll (Wye England)** ... Journal. Southeastern Agricultural College (Wye, England) [*A publication*]
**J Southeast Asian Stud** ... Journal of Southeast Asian Studies [*A publication*]
**J Southeast Sect Am Water Works Assoc** ... Journal. Southeastern Section. American Water Works Association [*A publication*]
**J Southern Hist** ... Journal of Southern History [*A publication*]
**J South His** ... Journal of Southern History [*A publication*]
**J South Hist** ... Journal of Southern History [*A publication*]
**J South Res** ... Journal of Southern Research [*A publication*]
**J South West Afr Sci Soc** ... Journal. South West African Scientific Society [*A publication*]
**J Sov Cardiovasc Res** ... Journal of Soviet Cardiovascular Research [*A publication*]
**J Soviet Math** ... Journal of Soviet Mathematics [*A publication*]
**J Sov Laser Res** ... Journal of Soviet Laser Research [*A publication*]
**J Sov Oncol** ... Journal of Soviet Oncology [*A publication*]
**JSOW**........ Joint Standoff Weapons Program
**JSP**............ Jacketed Soft-Point [*Ammunition*]
**JSP**............ Japan Socialist Party [*Nikon Shakaito*] [*Political party*] (PPW)
**JSP**............ Joint Services Development Program
**JSP**............ Joint Staff Planners [*Joint Chiefs of Staff*]
**JSP**............ Journal of Social Psychology [*A publication*]
**JSP**............ Journal of Statistical Planning and Inference [*A publication*]
**JSP**............ Judicial Selection Project (EA)
**JSP**............ Jurisdictional Separation Process
**J Spacecr Rockets** ... Journal of Spacecraft and Rockets [*A publication*]
**J Spacecr and Rockets** ... Journal of Spacecraft and Rockets [*A publication*]
**J Space L** ... Journal of Space Law [*A publication*]
**J Space Law** ... Journal of Space Law [*A publication*]
**J Spac Rock** ... Journal of Spacecraft and Rockets [*A publication*]
**J Span Stud** ... Journal of Spanish Studies. Twentieth Century [*A publication*]
**JSPB**.......... Joint Staff Pension Board [*United Nations*]
**JSPC**.......... Joint Sobe Processing Center [*Okinawa*] [*Military*]
**JSPC**.......... Joint Strategic Plans Committee [*Military*]
**JSPD**......... Joint Strategic Planning Document (MCD)
**JSPD**......... Joint Subsidiary Plans Division [*Military*] (MUGU)
**JSPDA5**..... Journal. American Society of Psychosomatic Dentistry [*A publication*]
**J Sp Disorders** ... Journal of Speech and Hearing Disorders [*A publication*]
**JSPDSA**.... Joint Strategic Planning Document Supporting Analysis [*Military*] (AABC)
**JSPEB**....... Journal of Special Education [*A publication*]
**J Spec**......... Jewish Spectator [*A publication*]
**J Spec Ed** ... Journal of Special Education [*A publication*]
**J Spec Ed Men Retard** ... Journal for Special Educators of the Mentally Retarded [*Later, Journal for Special Educators*] [*A publication*]
**J Spec Educ** ... Journal of Special Education [*A publication*]
**J Spec Philos** ... Journal of the Speculative Philosophy [*A publication*]
**J Spectros Soc Jpn** ... Journal. Spectroscopical Society of Japan [*A publication*]
**J Sp Educ**... Journal of Special Education [*A publication*]
**J Sp Educators** ... Journal for Special Educators [*A publication*]
**J Sp Educ Men Retard** ... Journal for Special Educators of the Mentally Retarded [*Later, Journal for Special Educators*] [*A publication*]
**J Speech D** ... Journal of Speech and Hearing Disorders [*A publication*]
**J Speech He** ... Journal of Speech and Hearing Research [*A publication*]
**J Speech & Hear Dis** ... Journal of Speech and Hearing Disorders [*A publication*]
**J Speech Hear Disord** ... Journal of Speech and Hearing Disorders [*A publication*]
**J Speech & Hear Disord** ... Journal of Speech and Hearing Disorders [*A publication*]
**J Speech Hearing Dis** ... Journal of Speech and Hearing Disorders [*A publication*]
**J Speech & Hear Res** ... Journal of Speech and Hearing Research [*A publication*]
**J Speech Hear Res** ... Journal of Speech and Hearing Research [*A publication*]
**JSPF**.......... Joint Staff Pension Fund [*United Nations*]
**JSPFL**....... Jointly Sponsored Program for Foreign Libraries [*Defunct*]
**JSPG**.......... Joint Strategic Plans Group [*Military*]
**JSPHA**...... Journal of Speech and Hearing Research [*A publication*]
**JSPIJ**......... Journal of Social and Political Ideas in Japan [*A publication*]
**JSPMA**...... Journal of Supramolecular Structure [*Later, Journal of Cellular Biochemistry*] [*A publication*]
**JSPMRC**... Joint Service Program Management Review Committee [*Military*]
**JSPOG**...... Joint Strategic Plans and Operations Group
**J Sport Beh** ... Journal of Sport Behavior [*A publication*]
**J Sport Behav** ... Journal of Sport Behavior [*A publication*]
**J Sport Hist** ... Journal of Sport History [*A publication*]
**J Sport Med** ... Journal of Sports Medicine and Physical Fitness [*A publication*]
**J Sport Psy** ... Journal of Sport Psychology [*A publication*]
**J Sport Psychol** ... Journal of Sport Psychology [*A publication*]
**J Sport Sci** ... Journal of Sports Sciences [*A publication*]
**J Sports Med** ... Journal of Sports Medicine [*A publication*]
**J Sports Med and P Fit** ... Journal of Sports Medicine and Physical Fitness [*A publication*]
**J Sports Med Phys Fit** ... Journal of Sports Medicine and Physical Fitness [*A publication*]
**J Sports Med Phys Fitness** ... Journal of Sports Medicine and Physical Fitness [*A publication*]
**J Sport and Soc Iss** ... Journal of Sport and Social Issues [*A publication*]
**J Sport Soc Iss** ... Journal of Sport and Social Issues [*A publication*]
**J Sports Turf Res Inst** ... Journal of the Sports Turf Research Institute [*A publication*]
**JSPR**.......... Journal. Society for Psychical Research [*A publication*]
**JSPS**.......... Japan Society for the Promotion of Science
**JSPS**.......... Jewish Student Press Service (EA)
**JSPS**.......... Joint Strategic Planning System [*Military*]
**JSPs**.......... Journal of Social Psychology [*A publication*]
**JSPSA**....... Journal of Social Psychology [*A publication*]
**JSPSE**....... Journal. Society of Photographic Scientists and Engineers [*A publication*]
**JSPTL**....... Journal. Society of Public Teachers of Law [*A publication*]
**JSR**............ Jackson Resources Ltd. [*Vancouver Stock Exchange symbol*]
**JSR**............ Jam to Signal Ratio (MCD)
**JSR**............ Japan Science Review [*A publication*]
**JSR**............ Japan Socialist Review [*A publication*]
**JSR**............ Japan Synthetic Rubber Co. Ltd.
**JSR**............ Japanese Sociological Review [*A publication*]
**JSR**............ Jessore [*Bangladesh*] [*Airport symbol*] (OAG)
**JSR**............ Jewish Student Review [*A publication*]
**JSR**............ Journal of Social Research [*A publication*]
**JSR**............ Journal of Spacecraft and Rockets [*A publication*]
**JSR**............ Jump to Subroutine [*Data processing*] (BUR)
**JSRA**......... Job Search and Relocation Assistance Projects (OICC)
**JSRBA**....... Journal of Scientific Research. Banaras Hindu University [*A publication*]
**JSRC**......... Joint Ship Repair Committee
**JSRCC**....... Joint Search and Rescue Coordination Center (MCD)
**JSRHS**....... Japan Science Review. Humanistic Studies [*A publication*]
**JSRK**......... Jeunesse Socialiste Royale Khmere [*Royal Cambodian Socialist Youth*]
**JSR LPH**... Japan Science Review. Literature, Philosophy, and History [*A publication*]
**JSRP**.......... Joint Services Reading Panel [*Military*] [*British*]
**JSRS**.......... Jewish Social Research Series [*A publication*]
**JSRS**.......... Jury System Reform Society [*British*]
**JSRSA**....... JARE [*Japanese Antarctic Research Expedition*] Scientific Reports. Special Issue [*A publication*]
**JSRT**.......... Joint Short-Range Technology (MCD)
**JSS**............ Jet Steering System
**JSS**............ Jewish Social Studies [*A publication*]
**JSS**............ Jim Smith Society (EA)
**JSS**............ Job Shop Simulator
**JSS**............ Joint Surveillance System [*FAA*] [*Air Force*]
**JSS**............ Journal of Semitic Studies [*A publication*]
**JSS**............ Journal. Siam Society [*Bangkok*] [*A publication*]
**JSS**............ Journal of Social Sciences [*A publication*]
**JSS**............ Journal of Spanish Studies. Twentieth Century [*A publication*]
**JSS**............ Journal of Sports Sciences [*A publication*]

**JSS**............ Journal of Systems and Software [*A publication*]
**JSS**............ Junior Secondary School
**JSSA**.......... John Steinbeck Society of America (EA)
**JSSAM**...... Joint Service Small Arms Management Committee (MCD)
**JSSAP**....... Joint Service Small Arms Panel (MCD)
**JSSAP**....... Joint Service Small Arms Program (RDA)
**JSSB**.......... Journal. Siam Society (Bangkok) [*A publication*]
**JSSC**.......... Joint Services Staff College [*or Course*] [*Obsolete*] [*British*]
**JSSC**.......... Joint Shop Stewards Committee [*British*]
**JSSC**.......... Joint Strategic Survey Committee [*or Council*] [*DoD*]
**JSSC**.......... Journal of Solid-State Circuits [*IEEE*] [*A publication*]
**JSSEA**....... Journal. American Society of Safety Engineers [*A publication*]
**JSSM**......... Joint Services Staff Manual [*Military*] [*British*]
**JSSPG**....... Job Shop Simulation Program Generator (KSC)
**JSSP News** ... JSSP [*Junior Secondary Science Project*] Newsletter [*A publication*] (APTA)
**JSSQ** ......... Jewish Social Service Quarterly [*A publication*]
**JSSR**.......... Journal for the Scientific Study of Religion [*A publication*]
**JSSR**.......... Journal of Social Services Research [*A publication*]
**JSSRel**....... Journal for the Scientific Study of Religion [*A publication*]
**JSSSG** ....... Journal. Society for the Study of State Governments [*Varanasi*] [*A publication*]
**JSST**.......... Job Seeking Skills Training (OICC)
**JSSTC** ....... Journal of Spanish Studies. Twentieth Century [*A publication*]
**JSSUP**....... Japanese Space Shuttle Utilization Program (MCD)
**JSS/US** ..... Japanese Sword Society of the United States (EA)
**JST** ............ Japanese Standard Time (DEN)
**JST** ............ Jet STOL [*Short Takeoff and Landing*] Transport [*Aircraft*]
**JST** ............ Johnson Society. Transactions [*A publication*]
**JST** ............ Johnstown [*Pennsylvania*] [*Airport symbol*] (OAG)
**JST** ............ Johnstown, PA [*Location identifier*] [*FAA*] (FAAL)
**JST** ............ Joint Systems Test (KSC)
**JST** ............ Journal of Business Strategy [*A publication*]
**JST** ............ Journal of Science and Technology [*A publication*]
**JSTA** ......... Justice System Training Association (EA)
**JSTAA**....... Journal. Royal Statistical Society. Series A. General [*A publication*]
**J Starch Sweet Technol Res Soc Japan** ... Journal. Starch Sweetener Technological Research Society of Japan [*A publication*]
**J Starch Technol Res Soc Jpn** ... Journal of Starch Technology. Research Society of Japan [*A publication*]
**JSTARS** .... Joint Surveillance and Target Attack RADAR System
**J Stat Comput Simul** ... Journal of Statistical Computation and Simulation [*A publication*]
**J Statis Soc** ... Journal. Statistical Society [*A publication*]
**J Statist Comp and Simulation** ... Journal of Statistical Computation and Simulation [*A publication*]
**J Statist Comput Simulation** ... Journal of Statistical Computation and Simulation [*A publication*]
**J Statist Phys** ... Journal of Statistical Physics [*A publication*]
**J Statist Plann Inference** ... Journal of Statistical Planning and Inference [*A publication*]
**J Statist Res** ... Journal of Statistical Research [*A publication*]
**J Stat Phys** ... Journal of Statistical Physics [*A publication*]
**J Stat Plann Inference** ... Journal of Statistical Planning and Inference [*A publication*]
**J Stat Plann and Inference** ... Journal of Statistical Planning and Inference [*A publication*]
**J Stat Rsr** ... Journal of Statistical Research [*A publication*]
**JSTBA**....... Journal. Royal Statistical Society. Series B. Methodological [*A publication*]
**J St Bar Calif** ... Journal. State Bar of California [*A publication*] (DLA)
**J St Barnabas Med Cent** ... Journal. Saint Barnabas Medical Center [*A publication*]
**J Ster Biochem** ... Journal of Steroid Biochemistry [*A publication*]
**J Sterile Serv Manage** ... Journal of Sterile Services Management [*A publication*]
**J Steroid B** ... Journal of Steroid Biochemistry [*A publication*]
**J Steroid Biochem** ... Journal of Steroid Biochemistry [*A publication*]
**J Steward Anthropol Soc** ... Journal. Steward Anthropological Society [*A publication*]
**J Steward Anthro Soc** ... Journal. Steward Anthropological Society [*A publication*]
**J Sth Afr Vet Med Ass** ... Journal. South African Veterinary Medical Association [*Later, South African Veterinary Association. Journal*] [*A publication*]
**JStJu** ......... Journal for the Study of Judaism in the Persian, Hellenistic, and Roman Periods [*Leiden*] [*A publication*]
**J St Jud**...... Journal for the Study of Judaism [*Later, Journal for the Study of Judaism in the Persian, Hellenistic, and Roman Periods*] [*A publication*]
**J St Med** .... Journal of State Medicine [*A publication*]
**JSTN** ......... Justin Industries, Inc. [*NASDAQ symbol*] (NQ)
**JSTNA** ....... Journal. American Statistical Association [*A publication*]
**J St N T** ..... Journal for the Study of the New Testament [*A publication*]
**J Stomat**..... Journal de Stomatologie [*A publication*]
**J Stomatol Belg** ... Journal de Stomatologie de Belgique [*A publication*]
**J Stomatol Soc (Jpn)** ... Journal. Stomatological Society (Japan) [*A publication*]
**J Stored Pr** ... Journal of Stored Products Research [*A publication*]
**J Stored Prod Res** ... Journal of Stored Products Research [*A publication*]
**J St OT** ...... Journal for the Study of the Old Testament [*A publication*]
**JSTPA** ....... Joint Strategic Target Planning Agency (NATG)
**JSTPD**....... Journal of Science and Technology (Peshawar, Pakistan) [*A publication*]
**JSTPS** ....... Joint Strategic Target Planning Staff [*DoD*]
**JSTR**.......... Joint Systematic Troop Review [*Military*]
**J Strain Anal** ... Journal of Strain Analysis [*A publication*]
**J Strain Anal Eng Des** ... Journal of Strain Analysis for Engineering Design [*A publication*]
**J Strain Anal Engng Des** ... Journal of Strain Analysis for Engineering Design [*A publication*]
**J Strain Analysis** ... Journal of Strain Analysis [*A publication*]
**J Struc Mec** ... Journal of Structural Mechanics [*A publication*]
**J Struct Ch** ... Journal of Structural Chemistry [*A publication*]
**J Struct Chem** ... Journal of Structural Chemistry [*A publication*]
**J Struct Di** ... Journal. Structural Division. Proceedings of the American Society of Civil Engineers [*A publication*]
**J Struct Div Amer Soc Civil Eng Proc** ... Journal. Structural Division. Proceedings of the American Society of Civil Engineers [*A publication*]
**J Struct Div Proc ASCE** ... Journal. Structural Division. Proceedings of the American Society of Civil Engineers [*A publication*]
**J Struct Geol** ... Journal of Structural Geology [*A publication*]
**J Struct Le** ... Journal of Structural Learning [*A publication*]
**J Struct Mech** ... Journal of Structural Mechanics [*A publication*]
**J Structural Learning** ... Journal of Structural Learning [*A publication*]
**J Structural Mech** ... Journal of Structural Mechanics [*A publication*]
**J St Tax'n** .. Journal of State Taxation [*A publication*] (DLA)
**JSTU** ......... Tohoku University, Sendai, Japan [*Library symbol*] [*Library of Congress*] (LCLS)
**J Stud Alc** .. Journal of Studies on Alcohol [*A publication*]
**J Stud Alcohol** ... Journal of Studies on Alcohol [*A publication*]
**J Stud Alcohol (Suppl)** ... Journal of Studies on Alcohol (Supplement) [*A publication*]
**J Stud Amer Med Ass** ... Journal. Student American Medical Association [*A publication*]
**J Stud Econ Economet** ... Journal for Studies in Economics and Econometrics [*A publication*]
**J Studies Alcohol** ... Journal of Studies on Alcohol [*A publication*]
**J Studies Econ and Econometrics** ... Journal for Studies in Economics and Econometrics [*A publication*]
**JSTX**.......... Joro Spider Toxin [*Biochemistry*]
**JSU**............ Hokkaido University, Sapporo, Japan [*Library symbol*] [*Library of Congress*] (LCLS)
**JSU**............ Jacksonville State University [*Jacksonville, AL*]
**JSU**............ Junta Socialista Unida [*United Socialist Party*] [*Spain*]
**JSUB** ......... Jahrbuch. Schlesische Friedrich-Wilhelm Universitaet zu Breslau [*A publication*]
**J Submic Cy** ... Journal of Submicroscopic Cytology [*A publication*]
**J Submicrosc Cytol** ... Journal of Submicroscopic Cytology [*A publication*]
**J Submicrosc Cytol Pathol** ... Journal of Submicroscopic Cytology and Pathology [*A publication*]
**J Subst Abuse Treat** ... Journal of Substance Abuse Treatment [*A publication*]
**J Suffolk Acad L** ... Journal. Suffolk Academy of Law [*A publication*]
**J Sui Pharm** ... Journal Suisse de Pharmacie [*A publication*]
**J Suisse Apic** ... Journal Suisse d'Apiculture [*A publication*]
**J Suisse Horlog** ... Journal Suisse d'Horlogerie [*A publication*]
**J Suisse Horlog Bijout** ... Journal Suisse d'Horlogerie et de Bijouterie [*A publication*]
**J Suisse Med** ... Journal Suisse de Medecine [*A publication*]
**J Sul-Am Med** ... Jornal Sul-Americano de Medicina [*A publication*]
**J Supervision** ... Journal of Supervision and Training in Ministry [*A publication*]
**J Supervision Tr Min** ... Journal of Supervision and Training in Ministry [*A publication*]
**J Supramolecular Struct** ... Journal of Supramolecular Structure [*Later, Journal of Cellular Biochemistry*] [*A publication*]
**J Supramol Struct** ... Journal of Supramolecular Structure [*Later, Journal of Cellular Biochemistry*] [*A publication*]
**J Supramol Struct Cell Biochem** ... Journal of Supramolecular Structure and Cellular Biochemistry [*Later, Journal of Cellular Biochemistry*] [*A publication*]
**J Supramol Struct (Suppl)** ... Journal of Supramolecular Structure (Supplement) [*A publication*]
**J Supram St** ... Journal of Supramolecular Structure [*Later, Journal of Cellular Biochemistry*] [*A publication*]
**J Surg Oncol** ... Journal of Surgical Oncology [*A publication*]
**J Surg Res** ... Journal of Surgical Research [*A publication*]
**J Surv Mapp** ... Journal. Surveying and Mapping Division. Proceedings of the American Society of Civil Engineers [*A publication*]
**J Surv & Mapp Div Proc ASCE** ... Journal. Surveying and Mapping Division. Proceedings of the American Society of Civil Engineers [*A publication*]
**J Surv Mapping Div Amer Soc Civil Eng Proc** ... Journal. Surveying and Mapping Division. Proceedings of the American Society of Civil Engineers [*A publication*]
**JSVA** ......... Jewish Socialist Verband of America [*Defunct*] (EA)
**JSVIA**........ Journal of Sound and Vibration [*A publication*]
**J SWA Sci Soc** ... Journal. South West African Scientific Society [*A publication*]

**J SWA (South West Afr) Sci Soc** ... Journal SWA (South West Africa) Scientific Society [*A publication*]
**JSWC** ......... Journal of Soil and Water Conservation [*A publication*]
**JSWDL** ...... Joint Services Weapon Data Link (MCD)
**JSWL** ......... Journal of Social Welfare Law [*A publication*]
**JSWPB** ...... Joint Special Weapons Publications Board
**JSWS** ......... Journal of Social Work and Human Sexuality [*A publication*]
**JSW Tech Rev** ... JSW [*Japan Steel Works*] Technical Review [*A publication*]
**JSY** ............ New Jersey Airways, Inc. [*East Orange, NJ*] [*FAA designator*] (FAAC)
**JSYB** .......... Jewish Socialist Youth Bund [*Later, MJSG*] (EA)
**J Symb Anthropol** ... Journal of Symbolic Anthropology [*A publication*]
**J Symb Log** ... Journal of Symbolic Logic [*A publication*]
**J Symb Logic** ... Journal of Symbolic Logic [*A publication*]
**J Symbolic Logic** ... Journal of Symbolic Logic [*A publication*]
**J Symbol Logic** ... Journal of Symbolic Logic [*A publication*]
**J Sym Log** ... Journal of Symbolic Logic [*A publication*]
**J Syn Org J** ... Journal of Synthetic Organic Chemistry (Japan) [*A publication*]
**J Synth Lubr** ... Journal of Synthetic Lubrication [*A publication*]
**J Synth Org Chem (Jpn)** ... Journal of Synthetic Organic Chemistry (Japan) [*A publication*]
**J Synth Rubber Ind (Lanzhou People's Repub China)** ... Journal of Synthetic Rubber Industry (Lanzhou, People's Republic of China) [*A publication*]
**J Sys Mgmt** ... Journal of Systems Management [*A publication*]
**J Sys Mgt** .. Journal of Systems Management [*A publication*]
**J Sys and Soft** ... Journal of Systems and Software [*A publication*]
**J System J** ... Justice System Journal [*A publication*]
**J Systems Mgt** ... Journal of Systems Management [*A publication*]
**J Systems Software** ... Journal of Systems and Software [*A publication*]
**J Syst Eng** ... Journal of Systems Engineering [*A publication*]
**J Syst Engng** ... Journal of Systems Engineering [*A publication*]
**J Syst Man** ... Journal of Systems Management [*A publication*]
**J Syst Manage** ... Journal of Systems Management [*A publication*]
**J Syst Mgt** ... Journal of Systems Management [*A publication*]
**J Syst and Software** ... Journal of Systems and Software [*A publication*]
**JT** .............. Jahrbuch der Technik [*A publication*]
**JT** .............. James Taylor [*Singer*]
**JT** .............. Jerusalem Talmud (BJA)
**JT** .............. Jewish Tribune [*Bombay*] [*A publication*]
**JT** .............. Jig Template (MSA)
**JT** .............. John Tyler [*US president, 1790-1862*]
**JT** .............. Joint
**J-T** ............ Joule-Thomson [*Physics*]
**JT** .............. Journal of Music Therapy [*A publication*]
**JT** .............. Journal des Tribunaux [*A publication*]
**JT** .............. Juridisk Tidsskrift [*A publication*] (ILCA)
**JT** .............. Juvenile Templar [*Freemasonry*]
**JT** .............. Societe de Transports Services et Travaux Aeriens [*Tunisavia*] [*ICAO designator*] (FAAC)
**JTA** ........... Azia Keizai Kenkyujo [*Institute for Developing Economies*], Tokyo, Japan [*Library symbol*] [*Library of Congress*] (LCLS)
**JTA** ........... Japanese Technical Abstracts [*A publication*]
**JTA** ........... Jewish Telegraphic Agency (EA)
**JTA** ........... Job Task Analysis
**JTA** ........... Joint Table of Allowance
**JTA** ........... Joint Tenancy Agreement [*Military*]
**JTA** ........... Journal of Thermal Analysis [*A publication*]
**JTAC** ......... Joint Technical Advisory Committee [*Electronics*]
**JTACC** ...... Joint Tactical Air Control Center
**JTACMIS-A** ... Joint Tactical Missile System - Army
**JTACMS** ... Joint Tactical Missile System
**JTACMS-A** ... Joint Tactical Missile System - Army
**JTAD** ......... Joint Tactical Aids Detachment [*Military*]
**JTAG** ......... Japan Trade Advisory Group [*British Overseas Trade Board*] (DS)
**J Taiwan Agric Res** ... Journal of Taiwan Agricultural Research [*A publication*]
**J Taiwan Agr Res** ... Journal of Taiwan Agricultural Research [*A publication*]
**J Taiwan Mus** ... Journal. Taiwan Museum [*A publication*]
**J Takeda Res Lab** ... Journal. Takeda Research Laboratories [*A publication*]
**J Takeda Res Labs** ... Journal. Takeda Research Laboratories [*Japan*] [*A publication*]
**JTA-M** ....... Jewish Teachers Association - Morim (EA)
**J Tamil Stud** ... Journal of Tamil Studies [*A publication*]
**J Tam S** ...... Journal of Tamil Studies [*A publication*]
**JTASA** ....... Journal. Tennessee Academy of Science [*A publication*]
**JTASB** ....... Joint Tactical Air Support Board
**jt auth** ......... Joint Author
**JTAWG** ..... Joint Targeting and Weapon Guidance (MCD)
**J Tax** .......... Journal of Taxation [*A publication*]
**J Taxation** ... Journal of Taxation [*A publication*]
**J Tax'n** ....... Journal of Taxation [*A publication*]
**JTB** ............ Joint Bar
**JTB** ............ Joint Transportation Board [*Military*]
**JTB** ............ Journal of Theoretical Biology [*A publication*]
**JTBBD7** .... Journal of Chemical Technology and Biotechnology. B. Biotechnology [*A publication*]
**JTBSMHS** ... Jacques Timothe Boucher Sieur de Montbrun Heritage Society (EA)
**JTC** ............ Houston [*Texas*] Town/Country [*Airport symbol*] (OAG)
**JTC** ............ Jewish Thought and Civilization (BJA)
**JTC** ............ Joint Telecommunications Committee [*Military*] (AFM)
**JTC** ............ Joule-Thomson Coefficient [*Physics*]
**JTC** ............ Journal for Theology and the Church [*A publication*]
**JTC** ............ Junior Training Corps [*British*]
**JTC³A** ........ Joint Tactical Command, Control, and Communications Agency [*Military*]
**JTCC** ......... Joint Test Coordinating Committee (MCD)
**JTCCCS** .... Joint Tactical Command, Control, and Communications System [*Military*] (MCD)
**JTCCG** ...... Joint Technical Configuration Control Group [*Military*] (AABC)
**JTCE** ......... Journal of Transportation Engineering. Proceedings. American Society of Civil Engineers [*A publication*]
**JTCG** ......... Joint Technical Coordinating Group [*Military*] (MCD)
**JTCG/ALNNO** ... Joint Technical Coordinating Group for Air Launched Non-Nuclear Ordnance [*Military*] (AFM)
**JTCG/AS** .. Joint Technical Coordinating Group for Aircraft Survivability [*Military*]
**JTCG-DLA** ... Joint Technical Coordinating Group for Data Link Acquisitions (MCD)
**JTCG-DMI** ... Joint Technical Coordinating Group for Depot Maintenance Interservicing [*Military*] (AFIT)
**JTCG-EER** ... Joint Technical Coordinating Group for Electronic Equipment Reliability (MCD)
**JTCG-ESR** ... Joint Technical Coordinating Group for Electronics Systems Reliability (MCD)
**JTCG/MD** ... Joint Technical Coordinating Group for Munitions Development [*Military*]
**JTCG/ME** ... Joint Technical Coordinating Group for Munitions Effectiveness [*Military*] (AFM)
**JTCG/MS** ... Joint Technical Coordinating Group on Munitions Survivability [*Military*] (RDA)
**JTCGP** ...... Joint Technical Coordinating Group [*Military*]
**JTCGP/ME** ... Joint Technical Coordinating Group for Munitions Effectiveness [*Military*]
**JTCGP-TACS** ... Joint Technical Coordinating Group for Tactical Air Control System [*Military*]
**JTCG-STD** ... Joint Technical Coordinating Group on Simulators and Training Devices (MCD)
**JTCh** .......... Journal for Theology and the Church [*A publication*]
**JTCMD** ..... Journal of Tissue Culture Methods [*A publication*]
**JTCMEC** ... Journal of Traditional Chinese Medicine [*A publication*]
**JTCO** ......... Jacksonville Terminal Company [*AAR code*]
**JTC³S** ........ Joint Tactical Command and Control and Communications System [*Military*] (RDA)
**JTCY-P** ..... Jig Transit Central Y-Plane
**JTD** ........... Joint Table of Distribution [*Military*] (AFM)
**JTD** ........... Joint Test Directorate [*Military*] (CAAL)
**JTDA** ......... Joint Track Data Storage
**JTDAA** ...... Journal. Tennessee Dental Association [*A publication*]
**JTDE** ......... Joint Technology Demonstrator Engine [*Air Force*] (MCD)
**JTDP** ......... Joint Technical Development Plan
**JTDS** ......... Joint Track Data Storage
**JTE** ........... Jamming Tactics Evaluation
**JTE** ........... Joint Technical Evaluation (MCD)
**JTE** ........... Joint Test Element
**JT & E** ........ Joint Test and Evaluation [*DoD*]
**JTE** ........... Joule-Thomson Effect [*Physics*]
**JTE** ........... Journal of Teacher Education [*A publication*]
**JTE** ........... Journal of Transport Economics and Policy [*A publication*]
**J Teach Ed** ... Journal of Teacher Education [*A publication*]
**J Teach Educ** ... Journal of Teacher Education [*A publication*]
**J Teaching PE** ... Journal of Teaching in Physical Education [*A publication*]
**J Teach Learn** ... Journal of Teaching and Learning [*A publication*]
**JTEC** ......... Japan Telecommunications Engineering and Consultancy (TEL)
**JTEC** ......... Joint Training Enhancement Committee [*Military*]
**J Tech Assoc Fur Ind** ... Journal. Technical Association of the Fur Industry [*A publication*]
**J Tech Bengal Engrg College** ... Journal of Technology. Bengal Engineering College [*A publication*]
**J Tech Councils ASCE Proc ASCE** ... Journal. Technical Councils of ASCE. Proceedings of the American Society of Civil Engineers [*A publication*]
**J Tech Lab (Tokyo)** ... Journal. Technical Laboratory (Tokyo) [*A publication*]
**J Techn** ...... Journal of Technology [*A publication*]
**J Techn Meth** ... Journal of Technical Methods and Bulletin. International Association of Medical Museums [*A publication*]
**J Technol** ... Journal of Technology [*A publication*]
**J Technol Eng** ... Journal of Technology and Engineering [*A publication*]
**J Tech Phys** ... Journal of Technical Physics [*A publication*]
**J Tech Vocat Educ S Afr** ... Journal for Technical and Vocational Education in South Africa [*A publication*]
**J Tech Writ Commun** ... Journal of Technical Writing and Communication [*A publication*]
**JT ED** ........ Joint Editor
**J Teflon** ...... Journal of Teflon [*A publication*]

**J Telecommun Networks** ... Journal of Telecommunication Networks [*A publication*]
**J Telecom Net** ... Journal of Telecommunication Networks [*A publication*]
**J Tenn Acad Sci** ... Journal. Tennessee Academy of Science [*A publication*]
**J Tenn Dent Assoc** ... Journal. Tennessee Dental Association [*A publication*]
**J Tenn Med Ass** ... Journal. Tennessee Medical Association [*A publication*]
**J Tenn Med Assoc** ... Journal. Tennessee Medical Association [*A publication*]
**J Tenn State Dent Assoc** ... Journal. Tennessee State Dental Association [*A publication*]
**JTEP**.......... Journal of Transport Economics and Policy [*A publication*]
**J Terramech** ... Journal of Terramechanics [*A publication*]
**J Terramechanics** ... Journal of Terramechanics [*A publication*]
**J Tert Ed Admin** ... Journal of Tertiary Educational Administration [*A publication*]
**J Tertiary Educ Adm** ... Journal of Tertiary Educational Administration [*A publication*] (APTA)
**J Test and Eval** ... Journal of Testing and Evaluation [*A publication*]
**J Test Eval** ... Journal of Testing and Evaluation [*A publication*]
**JTETF**.......... Joint Test and Evaluation Task Force [*Air Force*]
**JTEVA**.......... Journal of Testing and Evaluation [*A publication*]
**JTEX**.......... Jaytex Oil & Gas [*NASDAQ symbol*] (NQ)
**J Texas Dent Hyg Assoc** ... Journal. Texas Dental Hygienists Association [*A publication*]
**J Textile Inst** ... Journal. Textile Institute [*A publication*]
**J Text Inst** ... Journal. Textile Institute [*A publication*]
**J Text Inst Abstr** ... Journal. Textile Institute. Abstracts [*A publication*]
**J Text Inst Proc** ... Journal. Textile Institute. Proceedings [*A publication*]
**J Text Inst Proc Abstr** ... Journal. Textile Institute. Proceedings and Abstracts [*A publication*]
**J Text Inst Trans** ... Journal. Textile Institute. Transactions [*A publication*]
**J Text Mach Soc Jap** ... Journal. Textile Machinery Society of Japan [*A publication*]
**J Text Stud** ... Journal of Texture Studies [*A publication*]
**J Texture Stud** ... Journal of Texture Studies [*A publication*]
**JTF**.......... Japan Textile Federation
**JTF**.......... Jet Tear-Down Facility (MCD)
**JTF**.......... Joint Tactical Fusion [*Army*] (RDA)
**JTF**.......... Joint Task Force [*Military*]
**JTF**.......... Joint Test Force [*Military*]
**JTF**.......... Joule-Thomson Flow [*Physics*]
**JTFAK**.......... Joint Task Force Alaska [*Military*]
**JTFHQ**.......... Joint Task Force Headquarters [*Military*] (MCD)
**JTFOA**.......... Joint Task Force Operating Area [*Military*] (NVT)
**JTFP**.......... Joint Tactical Fusion Program [*Military*] (RDA)
**JTFPMO**... Joint Tactical Fusion Program Management Office [*Army*] (RDA)
**JTFREP**.... Joint Task Force Report [*Military*]
**JTG**.......... Joint Task Group [*Military*]
**JTG**.......... Joint Test Group [*Nuclear energy*] (NRCH)
**JTG**.......... Joint Training Group [*NASA*] (NASA)
**JTG**.......... Journal of Tropical Geography [*A publication*]
**JTGG-A**.......... Journal of Tropical Geography [*A publication*]
**JTGGAA**... Journal of Tropical Geography [*A publication*]
**Jth**.......... Judith [*Old Testament book*] [*Roman Catholic canon*] (BJA)
**J Thanatol** ... Journal of Thanatology [*A publication*]
**J Theol St** .. Journal of Theological Studies [*A publication*]
**J Theol Sthn Afr** ... Journal of Theology for Southern Africa [*A publication*]
**J Theor Bio** ... Journal of Theoretical Biology [*A publication*]
**J Theor Biol** ... Journal of Theoretical Biology [*A publication*]
**J Theoret Biol** ... Journal of Theoretical Biology [*A publication*]
**J Theor N** .. Journal of Theoretical Neurobiology [*A publication*]
**J Theor Soc Behav** ... Journal for the Theory of Social Behavior [*A publication*]
**J Thermal Anal** ... Journal of Thermal Analysis [*A publication*]
**J Thermal Insulation** ... Journal of Thermal Insulation [*A publication*]
**J Therm Ana** ... Journal of Thermal Analysis [*A publication*]
**J Therm Anal** ... Journal of Thermal Analysis [*A publication*]
**J Therm Bio** ... Journal of Thermal Biology [*A publication*]
**J Therm Biol** ... Journal of Thermal Biology [*A publication*]
**J Therm Eng** ... Journal of Thermal Engineering [*A publication*]
**J Therm Engng** ... Journal of Thermal Engineering [*A publication*]
**J Therm Insul** ... Journal of Thermal Insulation [*A publication*]
**J Therm Stresses** ... Journal of Thermal Stresses [*A publication*]
**J Thora Cardiovasc Surg** ... Journal of Thoracic and Cardiovascular Surgery [*A publication*]
**J Thorac Cardiovasc Surg** ... Journal of Thoracic and Cardiovascular Surgery [*A publication*]
**J Thorac Cardiov Surg** ... Journal of Thoracic and Cardiovascular Surgery [*A publication*]
**J Thoracic Cardiovas Surg** ... Journal of Thoracic and Cardiovascular Surgery [*A publication*]
**J Thoracic Surg** ... Journal of Thoracic Surgery [*A publication*]
**J Thorac Surg** ... Journal of Thoracic Surgery [*A publication*]
**J Thor Surg** ... Journal of Thoracic and Cardiovascular Surgery [*A publication*]
**J Thought** .. Journal of Thought [*A publication*]
**JTHP**.......... Joule-Thomson High Pressure [*Physics*]
**JThS**.......... Journal of Theological Studies [*A publication*]
**J Th So Africa** ... Journal of Theology for Southern Africa [*A publication*]
**J Th St**.......... Journal of Theological Studies [*A publication*]
**JTI**.......... Journal of Taxation of Investments [*A publication*]
**JTI**.......... Jydsk Teknologisk Institut [*Technological Institute of Jutland*] [*Denmark*]
**JTIDS**.......... Joint Tactical Information Distribution System [*DoD*]
**J-TIES**.......... Japan Technology Information and Evaluation Service (EISS)
**JTIG**.......... Joint Target Intelligence Group [*Military*] (CINC)
**J Timber Dev Assoc India** ... Journal. Timber Development Association of India [*A publication*]
**J Timber Dryers Preserv Assoc India** ... Journal. Timber Dryers' and Preservers' Association of India [*A publication*]
**J Time Ser Anal** ... Journal of Time Series Analysis [*A publication*]
**Jt Inst Lab Astrophy Rep** ... Joint Institute for Laboratory Astrophysics. Report [*A publication*]
**JTIS**.......... Japanese Technical Information Service [*University Microfilms International*] [*Information service or system*] (IID)
**JTJ**.......... Japan Information Center of Science and Technology, Tokyo, Japan [*Library symbol*] [*Library of Congress*] (LCLS)
**JTKU**.......... Keio University, Tokyo, Japan [*Library symbol*] [*Library of Congress*] (LCLS)
**JTL**.......... Josephson Transmission Line [*Physics*]
**JTL**.......... Joutel Resources Ltd. [*Toronto Stock Exchange symbol*]
**JTLAS**.......... Jet Transport Landing Approach Simulator
**JTLY**.......... Jointly
**JTMA**.......... Joint Traffic Management Agency (MCD)
**JTMB**.......... Joint Transportation Movements Board [*Military*] (CINC)
**JTMC**.......... J. T. Moran Financial Corp. [*NASDAQ symbol*] (NQ)
**JTML**.......... Junior Town Meeting League (EA)
**JTMLS**.......... Joint Tactical Microwave Landing System (MCD)
**JTMMA**.... Journal. Tennessee Medical Association [*A publication*]
**JTMSS**.......... Joint Tactical Multichannel Switch System (MCD)
**JTMTDE**.. Journal of Trace and Microprobe Techniques [*A publication*]
**JTN**.......... Jewish Television Network
**JTNDL**.......... Kokuritsu Kokkai Toshokan [*National Diet Library*], Tokyo, Japan [*Library symbol*] [*Library of Congress*] (LCLS)
**JTNS**.......... Nihon Shinbun Kyokai [*Japanese Newspaper Association*], Tokyo, Japan [*Library symbol*] [*Library of Congress*] (LCLS)
**JTO**.......... Jeunesse Travailleuse Oubanguienne [*Ubangi Working Youth*]
**JTO**.......... Joint Technical Operations (AAG)
**JTO**.......... Journal des Tribunaux d'Outre-Mer [*A publication*]
**JTO**.......... Junction Temperature, Operating
**JTOC**.......... Joint Tactical Operations Center
**J Tohoku Dent Univ** ... Journal. Tohoku Dental University [*A publication*]
**J Tohoku Min Soc** ... Journal. Tohoku Mining Society [*Japan*] [*A publication*]
**J Tokyo Coll Fish** ... Journal. Tokyo College of Fisheries [*A publication*]
**J Tokyo Dent Coll Soc** ... Journal. Tokyo Dental College Society [*A publication*]
**J Tokyo Med Assoc** ... Journal. Tokyo Medical Association [*A publication*]
**J Tokyo Med Coll** ... Journal. Tokyo Medical College [*A publication*]
**J Tokyo Univ Fish** ... Journal. Tokyo University of Fisheries [*A publication*]
**J Tokyo Women's Med Coll** ... Journal. Tokyo Women's Medical College [*A publication*]
**J Tongji Med Univ** ... Journal. Tongji Medical University [*A publication*]
**JTOR**.......... Joint Terms of Reference (MCD)
**J Tottori Daigaku Nogaku** ... Journal. Tottori Daigaku Nogaku-Buo [*A publication*]
**J Town Pl I** ... Journal of Town Planning Institute [*A publication*]
**J Town Reg Plann** ... Journal for Town and Regional Planning [*A publication*]
**J Tox Env H** ... Journal of Toxicology and Environmental Health [*A publication*]
**J Toxicol**.... Journal of Health Toxicology [*A publication*]
**J Toxicol Clin Exp** ... Journal de Toxicologie Clinique et Experimentale [*A publication*]
**J Toxicol Clin Toxicol** ... Journal of Toxicology. Clinical Toxicology [*A publication*]
**J Toxicol Cutaneous Ocul Toxicol** ... Journal of Toxicology. Cutaneous and Ocular Toxicology [*A publication*]
**J Toxicol Environ Health** ... Journal of Toxicology and Environmental Health [*A publication*]
**J Toxicol Sci** ... Journal of Toxicological Sciences [*A publication*]
**J Toxicol Toxin Rev** ... Journal of Toxicology. Toxin Reviews [*A publication*]
**JTP**.......... Job Training Package
**JTP**.......... Job Training Program (OICC)
**JTP**.......... Joint Technical Panel [*Aerospace*]
**JTP**.......... Joint Training Package
**JTP**.......... Journal of Transport Economics and Policy [*A publication*]
**JTP**.......... Journeyman Training Program
**JTP**.......... Juventud Trabajadora Peronista [*Working Peronist Youth*] [*Argentina*]
**JTPA**.......... Job Training Partnership Act [*Formerly, CETA*] [*1982*]
**JTPA**.......... Job Training Partnership Administration
**JT Ph**.......... Jahrbuch fuer Technische Physik [*A publication*]
**JTPS**.......... Job and Tape Planning System
**JTPT**.......... Job Task Performance Test
**JTQ**.......... Wrightstown, NJ [*Location identifier*] [*FAA*] (FAAL)
**JTR**.......... Joint Termination Regulation
**JTR**.......... Joint Travel Regulations
**JTR**.......... Journal of European Industrial Training [*A publication*]
**JTR**.......... Journal of Travel Research [*A publication*]
**JTR**.......... Journal of Typographic Research [*A publication*]
**JTR**.......... Santorini [*Thira Islands*] [*Airport symbol*] (OAG)

**JTRAC** ...... JPL [*Jet Propulsion Laboratory*] Transient Radiation Analysis by Computer Program [*NASA*]
**J Trace Elem Exp Med** ... Journal of Trace Elements in Experimental Medicine [*A publication*]
**J Trace Microprobe Tech** ... Journal of Trace and Microprobe Techniques [*A publication*]
**J Tradit Chin Med** ... Journal of Traditional Chinese Medicine [*A publication*]
**J Transp Ec** ... Journal of Transport Economics and Policy [*A publication*]
**J Transp Econ Policy** ... Journal of Transport Economics and Policy [*A publication*]
**J Transp Eng Div Amer Soc Civil Eng Proc** ... Journal. Transportation Engineering Division. American Society of Civil Engineers. Proceedings [*A publication*]
**J Transpersonal Psychol** ... Journal of Transpersonal Psychology [*A publication*]
**J Transpers Psych** ... Journal of Transpersonal Psychology [*A publication*]
**J Transp Hist** ... Journal of Transport History [*A publication*]
**J Transp Med** ... Journal of Transportation Medicine [*Japan*] [*A publication*]
**J Transport Econ Pol** ... Journal of Transport Economics and Policy [*A publication*]
**J Transport Econ and Policy** ... Journal of Transport Economics and Policy [*A publication*]
**J Trans Soc Eng (London)** ... Journal and Transactions. Society of Engineers (London) [*A publication*]
**J Trauma** ... Journal of Trauma [*A publication*]
**J Trav INSERM-DPHM** ... Journees de Travail INSERM [*Institut National de la Sante et de la Recherche Medicale*]-DPHM [*A publication*]
**J Travis County Med Soc** ... Journal. Travis County Medical Society [*Michigan*] [*A publication*]
**JTRB** ......... Joint Telecommunications Resource Board [*Office of Science and Technology Policy*] [*Washington, DC*] (EGAO)
**JTRC** ......... Joint Theatre Reconnaissance Committee [*NATO*] (NATG)
**JTRCP** ....... Joint Travel Regulations, Department of Defense Civilian Personnel
**JTRE** ......... Joint Tsunami Research Effort
**J Trib** ......... Journal des Tribunaux [*A publication*]
**J Tribol** ...... Journal of Tribology [*A publication*]
**J Trop For** ... Journal of Tropical Forestry [*A publication*]
**J Trop Geog** ... Journal of Tropical Geography [*A publication*]
**J Trop Geogr** ... Journal of Tropical Geography [*A publication*]
**J Tropical Geography** ... Journal of Tropical Geography [*A publication*]
**J Trop Med** ... Journal of Tropical Medicine and Hygiene [*A publication*]
**J Trop Med Hyg** ... Journal of Tropical Medicine and Hygiene [*A publication*]
**J Trop Med and Hyg (London)** ... Journal of Tropical Medicine and Hygiene (London) [*A publication*]
**J Trop Med (London)** ... Journal of Tropical Medicine (London) [*A publication*]
**J Trop Pediat** ... Journal of Tropical Pediatrics [*A publication*]
**J Trop Pediatr** ... Journal of Tropical Pediatrics [*A publication*]
**J Trop Pediatr Afr Child Health** ... Journal of Tropical Pediatrics and African Child Health [*A publication*]
**J Trop Pediatr Environ Child Health** ... Journal of Tropical Pediatrics and Environmental Child Health [*A publication*]
**J Trop Pediatr Environ Child Health Monogr** ... Journal of Tropical Pediatrics and Environmental Child Health. Monograph [*A publication*]
**J Trop Vet Sc** ... Journal of Tropical Veterinary Science [*A publication*]
**JTRS** .......... Joint Tenant with Right of Survivorship [*Legal term*] (DLA)
**JTRS** .......... Journal. Thailand Research Society [*A publication*]
**JTRUS** ...... Joint Travel Regulations
**JTS** ............ Japan Troposcatter Systems
**JTS** ............ Job Training Standard
**JTS** ............ Joint Training Standards [*Military*] (KSC)
**JTS** ............ Journal of Theological Studies [*A publication*]
**JTS** ............ Justice Telecommunications Service [*Department of Justice*] (TSSD)
**JTSA** ......... Jewish Theological Seminary of America
**JTSA** ......... Joint Tactical Support Activity
**JTSA** ......... Joint Technical Support Activity
**J T S Behav** ... Journal for the Theory of Social Behavior [*A publication*]
**JTSCC** ....... Joint Telecommunications Standards Coordinating Committee [*American National Standards Institute*] [*Telecommunications*]
**JTSG** ......... Joint Trials Subgroup [*NATO*] (NATG)
**J Tsing Hua Univ** ... Journal. Tsing Hua University [*A publication*]
**JTSN** ......... Jettison (MSA)
**JTST** .......... Jet Stream
**JTSTR** ....... Jet Stream
**J Tsuda College** ... Journal. Tsuda College [*A publication*]
**JTSV** .......... Jahresbericht des Thueringisch-Saechsischen Vereins fuer Erforschung des Vaterlaendischen Altertums [*A publication*]
**JTT** ............ Executive Aircraft Leasing, Inc. [*Albertville, AL*] [*FAA designator*] (FAAC)
**JTTCW** ..... Jesus to the Communist World [*Later, CMCW*] (EA)
**JTTPRG** .... Joint Tactics, Techniques, and Procedures Review Group
**JTTRD9** .... Journal of Toxicology. Toxin Reviews [*A publication*]
**JTTRE** ....... Joint Tropical Trials Research Establishment [*Australia*] (RDA)
**JTTU** ......... Jet Transitional Training Unit [*Navy*]
**JTU** ............ Jackson Turbidity Unit [*Water pollution*]
**JTU** ............ Jet Training Unit
**JTUAC** ...... Joint Trade Union Advisory Committee
**J Tuberc Lepr** ... Journal of Tuberculosis and Leprosy [*Japan*] [*A publication*]
**JTUFA** ...... Journal. Tokyo University of Fisheries [*A publication*]
**J Tung-Chi Univ** ... Journal. Tung-Chi University [*A publication*]
**J Turk Phytopathol** ... Journal of Turkish Phytopathology [*A publication*]
**JTV** ............ Jet Test Vehicle
**JTV** ............ Jones Intercable Investors LP Class A [*AMEX symbol*] (SPSG)
**JTVI** .......... Journal of Transactions. Victoria Institute [*A publication*]
**JTW** ........... Journey-to-Work Database [*Computer Sciences of Australia Pty. Ltd.*] [*Information service or system*] (CRD)
**JTWC** ........ Joint Typhoon Warning Center
**JTWO** ........ J2 Communications [*Los Angeles, CA*] [*NASDAQ symbol*] (NQ)
**JTWROS** .. Joint Tenants with Right of Survivorship [*Legal term*]
**JTX** ............ Joint Test Exercises
**JTX** ............ Joint Training Exercise [*Military*]
**JTX** ............ Journal of Taxation [*A publication*]
**J Typogr Res** ... Journal of Typographic Research [*A publication*]
**JTZ** ............ Oklahoma City, OK [*Location identifier*] [*FAA*] (FAAL)
**JTZ** ............ Zantop Airways, Inc. [*Detroit, MI*] [*FAA designator*] (FAAC)
**JU** .............. Jeunesse Universelle
**JU** .............. Joint Use [*Military*] (AFIT)
**JU** .............. Joint User [*Telecommunications*] (TEL)
**JU** .............. Joygerms Unlimited (EA)
**Ju** .............. Judaism [*A publication*]
**Ju** .............. Judges [*Old Testament book*] (BJA)
**JU** .............. Jugoslovenski Aerotransport [*Yugoslavia*] [*ICAO designator*] (FAAC)
**JU** .............. Juilliard Review. Annual [*A publication*]
**JU** .............. Julep (ROG)
**JU** .............. Jump Unit
**JU** .............. June
**JU** .............. Junker [*German aircraft type*] [*World War II*]
**JU** .............. Jure Uxoris [*In Right of His Wife*] [*Latin*] (ROG)
**JUA** ........... Joint Underwriting Association [*Generic term*] (DHSM)
**JUAG** ......... Jahrbuch. Ungarische Archaeologische Gesellschaft [*A publication*]
**JUARA** ...... Journal of Chemistry. United Arab Republic [*A publication*]
**JUB** ............ Journal. Bombay University [*A publication*]
**JUB** ............ Juba [*Sudan*] [*Airport symbol*] (OAG)
**JUB** ............ Jubilate
**Jub** ............ Jubilees [*Pseudepigrapha*] (BJA)
**JUB** ............ Justice of the Upper Bench [*Legal term*] (DLA)
**JUBU** ......... Journalistutbildningsutredningen [*Sweden*]
**JUCG** ......... Joint Utilization Coordination Group [*DoD*]
**Ju Ch** ......... Junyj Chudoznik [*A publication*]
**JUCO** ........ Junior College (OICC)
**JUCO Rev** ... JUCO [*National Junior College Athletic Association*] Review [*A publication*]
**JUCUND** .. Jucunde [*Pleasantly*] [*Latin*]
**JUD** ........... Duluth, MN [*Location identifier*] [*FAA*] (FAAL)
**JUD** ........... Jahrbuch. Universitaet Duesseldorf [*A publication*]
**JUD** ........... Jeunesse d'Union Dahomeene [*Dahomean Youth Union*]
**Jud** ............ Judaic (BJA)
**Jud** ............ Judaica [*Zurich*] [*A publication*]
**Jud** ............ Judaism [*A publication*]
**Jud** ............ Judean (BJA)
**JUD** ........... Judges [*Old Testament book*] (ROG)
**JUD** ........... Judgment
**JUD** ........... Judicial
**Jud** ............ Judith [*Old Testament book*] [*Roman Catholic canon*]
**JUD** ........... Juris Utriusque Doctor [*Doctor of Both Laws; i.e., Canon and Civil Law*]
**Jud** ............ [*Sir R.*] Phillimore's Ecclesiastical Judgments [*1867-75*] [*A publication*] (DLA)
**Jud Chr** ...... Judicial Chronicle [*A publication*] (DLA)
**Jud Com PC** ... Judicial Committee of the Privy Council [*A publication*] (DLA)
**Jud Conduct Rep** ... Judicial Conduct Reporter [*A publication*] (DLA)
**Jud Coun (NY)** ... Judicial Council (New York). Annual Reports [*A publication*] (DLA)
**Judd** ........... Judd's Reports [*4 Hawaii*] [*A publication*] (DLA)
**JUDE** ......... Judicature (ROG)
**JUDG** ........ Judge
**Judg** ........... Judges [*Old Testament book*]
**JUDG** ......... Judicate, Inc. [*Philadelphia, PA*] [*NASDAQ symbol*] (NQ)
**Jud GCC** .... Judgments, Gold Coast Colony [*A publication*] (DLA)
**JUDGE** ...... Judged Utility Decision Generator
**Judge Advo J** ... Judge Advocate Journal [*A publication*]
**Judges J** ..... Judges' Journal [*A publication*]
**JUDGT** ...... Judgment
**Judg UB** .... Judgments of Upper Bench [*England*] [*A publication*] (DLA)
**Judic** .......... Judicature [*A publication*]
**JUDIC** ....... Judicial
**Judicature** .. Journal. American Judicature Society [*A publication*]
**Judicature J Am Jud Soc'y** ... Judicature. Journal of the American Judicature Society [*A publication*]
**Jud J** .......... Judges' Journal [*A publication*]

**JUDL**......... Judicial (ROG)
**Jud Pan Mult Lit** ... Rulings of the Judicial Panel on Multidistrict Litigation [*A publication*] (DLA)
**Jud QR**....... Judicature Quarterly Review [*1896*] [*A publication*] (DLA)
**JUDr**......... Juris Utriusque Doctor [*Doctor of Both Laws; i.e., Canon and Civil Law*]
**JUDRE**...... Judicature
**Jud Rep**...... New York Judicial Repository [*A publication*] (DLA)
**Jud Repos**.. Judicial Repository [*New York*] [*A publication*] (DLA)
**Jud & Sw**.... Judah and Swan's Jamaica Reports [*1839*] [*A publication*] (DLA)
**JUDY**........ Judy's, Inc. [*NASDAQ symbol*] (NQ)
**JUE**........... Journal of Urban Economics [*A publication*]
**JUE**........... Julich [*Federal Republic of Germany*] [*Seismograph station code, US Geological Survey*] (SEIS)
**J U Film As** ... Journal. University Film Association [*A publication*]
**JUG**........... Joint Users Group [*Data processing*]
**JUG**........... Jugenheim [*Federal Republic of Germany*] [*Seismograph station code, US Geological Survey*] [*Closed*] (SEIS)
**JUG**........... Jugoslav (DSUE)
**Jug**............ Jugoton [*Yugoslavia*] [*Record label*]
**JUG**........... Jugulo [*To the Throat*] [*Pharmacy*]
**Jug et Delib** ... Jugements et Deliberations du Conseil Souverain de la Nouvelle France [*A publication*] (DLA)
**JUGFET**.... Junction Gate Field-Effect Transistor (TEL)
**Jug Ist Cas** ... Jugoslovenski Istorijski Casopis [*A publication*]
**Jugosl Drus Prouc Zemljista Posebne Publ** ... Jugoslovensko Drustvo za Proucavanje Zemljista. Posebne Publikacije [*A publication*]
**Jugosl Ginekol Opstet** ... Jugoslovenska Ginekologija i Opstetricija [*A publication*]
**Jugosl Med Biokem** ... Jugoslavenska Medicinska Biokemija [*A publication*]
**Jugosl Pcelarstvo** ... Jugoslovensko Pcelarstvo [*A publication*]
**Jugosl Pedijatr** ... Jugoslovenska Pediajatrija [*A publication*]
**Jugosl Pregl** ... Jugoslovenski Pregled [*A publication*]
**Jugosl Pronalazastvo** ... Jugoslovensko Pronalazastvo [*A publication*]
**Jugosl Simp Hmeljarstvo Ref** ... Jugoslovanski Simpozij za Hmeljarstvo Referati [*A publication*]
**Jugosl Vet Glasn** ... Jugoslovenski Veterinarski Glasnik [*A publication*]
**Jugosl Vinograd Vinar** ... Jugoslovensko Vinogradarstvo i Vinarstvo [*A publication*]
**Jugosl Vocarstvo** ... Jugoslovensko Vocarstvo [*A publication*]
**JUI**............ Jamiatul Ulama-i-Islam [*Political party*] [*Pakistan*] (FEA)
**JUI**............ Juist [*West Germany*] [*Airport symbol*] [*Obsolete*] (OAG)
**Juilliard R** ... Juilliard Review [*A publication*]
**JUJ**............ Jujuy [*Argentina*] [*Airport symbol*] (OAG)
**JUJ**............ Jujuy [*Argentina*] [*Seismograph station code, US Geological Survey*] (SEIS)
**JUJAMCYN** ... Jujamcyn Theaters [*Established by William McKnight, and named for his three grandchildren, Judy, James, and Cynthia*]
**JUKE**......... Video Jukebox Network, Inc. [*NASDAQ symbol*] (NQ)
**JUKGS**...... Journal of Ukrainian Graduate Studies [*A publication*]
**J Ukr Stud** ... Journal of Ukrainian Studies [*A publication*]
**JUL**............ Joint University Libraries
**JUL**............ Journal of Urban Law [*A publication*]
**JUL**............ Julepus [*Julep*] [*Pharmacy*] (ROG)
**JUL**............ Juliaca [*Peru*] [*Airport symbol*] (OAG)
**JUL**............ Julian [*Calendar*]
**JUL**............ Julianehab [*Denmark*] [*Later, NAQ*] [*Geomagnetic observatory code*]
**JUL**............ July (AFM)
**JUL**............ Juris Utriusque Licentiatus [*Licentiate in Both Laws; i.e., Canon and Civil Law*]
**JULAC**...... Joint-Use Libraries Advisory Committee [*South Australia*]
**Jul Frontin** ... Julius Frontinus [*Roman soldier and author, 40-103*] (DLA)
**Juli**............ [*Salvius*] Julianus [*Flourished, 2nd century*] [*Authority cited in pre-1607 legal work*] (DSA)
**Julia**........... [*Salvius*] Julianus [*Flourished, 2nd century*] [*Authority cited in pre-1607 legal work*] (DSA)
**Julian**......... Julianus Imperator [*332-363AD*] [*Classical studies*] (OCD)
**JULIE**........ Joint Utility Locating Information for Excavators [*Telecommunications*] (TEL)
**Ju Lieb Ann Chem** ... Justus Liebigs Annalen der Chemie [*A publication*]
**JULIEX**..... Julie [*Sonobuoy System*] Exercise [*Navy*] (NVT)
**Julk Oulu Yliopisto Ydintek Laitos** ... Julkaisuja-Oulu Yliopisto. Ydintekniikkan Laitos [*A publication*]
**J Ultra Res** ... Journal of Ultrastructure Research [*A publication*]
**J Ultrasound Med** ... Journal of Ultrasound in Medicine [*A publication*]
**J Ultrastruct Mol Struct Res** ... Journal of Ultrastructure and Molecular Structure Research [*A publication*]
**J Ultrastruct Res** ... Journal of Ultrastructure Research [*A publication*]
**J Ultrastruct Res Suppl** ... Journal of Ultrastructure Research. Supplement [*A publication*]
**JUM**.......... Judaism [*A publication*]
**JUM**.......... Jumla [*Nepal*] [*Airport symbol*] (OAG)
**JUMO**....... Junkers-Motor [*Junkers aircraft engine*] [*German military - World War II*]
**JUMP**........ Joint UHF Modernization Project (MCD)
**JUMPS**..... Joint Uniform Military Pay Service [*or System*]
**JUMPS-RC** ... Joint Uniform Military Pay System - Reserve Components (MCD)
**JUN**........... Jump Unconditionally [*Data processing*]
**JUN**........... June (AFM)
**JUN**........... Junior
**JUN**........... Junius (ROG)
**JUNA**........ Juedische Nachrichten [*A publication*]
**JUNAC**...... Grupo Andino - Junta del Acuerdo de Cartagena [*Andean Group - Cartagena Agreement Board - ANCOM*] (EAIO)
**JUNC**........ Jeunesse d'Union Nationale Congolaise [*Congolese National Youth Union*]
**JUNC**........ Junction
**Jun Col J**.... Junior College Journal [*A publication*]
**JUNCT**...... Junction
**JUNE**........ Joint Utility Notification for Excavators (IEEE)
**Jung Wirt**... Junge Wirtschaft [*A publication*]
**Junior Coll J** ... Junior College Journal [*A publication*]
**Junior Inst Eng (London) J Rec Trans** ... Junior Institution of Engineers (London). Journal and Record of Transactions [*A publication*]
**JUNIP**....... Juniperus [*Juniper*] [*Pharmacy*] (ROG)
**J United Ser Inst Ind** ... Journal. United Service Institution of India [*A publication*]
**J United Serv Inst India** ... Journal. United Service Institution of India [*A publication*]
**J Univ Bombay** ... Journal. University of Bombay [*A publication*]
**J Univ Bombay NS** ... Journal. University of Bombay. New Series [*A publication*]
**J Univ Durban-Westville** ... Journal. University of Durban-Westville [*A publication*]
**J Univ F Assoc** ... Journal. University Film Association [*Carbondale*] [*A publication*]
**J Univ Gauhati** ... Journal. University of Gauhati [*A publication*]
**J Univ Geol Soc (Nagpur)** ... Journal. University Geological Society (Nagpur) [*A publication*]
**J Univ Kuwait (Sci)** ... Journal. University of Kuwait (Science) [*A publication*]
**J Univ Peshawar** ... Journal. University of Peshawar [*A publication*]
**J Univ Poona** ... Journal. University of Poona [*A publication*]
**J Univ Poona Sci Technol** ... Journal. University of Poona. Science and Technology [*A publication*]
**J Univ Saugar** ... Journal. University of Saugar [*A publication*]
**J Univ Saugar Part 2 Sect A** ... Journal. University of Saugar. Part 2. Section A. Physical Sciences [*A publication*]
**J Univ Sheffield Geol Soc** ... Journal. University of Sheffield. Geological Society [*A publication*]
**J Univ S Med Soc** ... Journal. University of Sydney. Medical Society [*A publication*]
**J Univ Stud** ... Journal of University Studies [*A publication*]
**JUNKA**..... Junkatsu [*A publication*]
**JUNO**........ Juno Lighting, Inc. [*NASDAQ symbol*] (NQ)
**JUNR**........ Junior
**JUNT**........ Juntae (ROG)
**Junta del Acuer** ... Grupo Andino - Junta del Acuerdo de Cartagena [*Andean Group - Cartagena Agreement Board - ANCOM*] (EA)
**Junta Energ Nucl Rep (Spain)** ... Junta de Energia Nuclear. Report (Spain) [*A publication*]
**Junta Invest Cient Ultramar Estud Ensaios Doc (Port)** ... Junta de Investigacoes Cientificas do Ultramar. Estudos, Ensaios, e Documentos (Portugal) [*A publication*]
**Junta Invest Ultramar Estud Ens Doc** ... Junta de Investigacoes do Ultramar. Estudos, Ensaios, e Documentos [*A publication*]
**JUO**.......... Junior Under-Officer [*British military*] (DMA)
**J UOEH**.... Journal of UOEH [*University of Occupational and Environmental Health*] [*Japan*] [*A publication*]
**JUP**........... Jamiatul Ulama-i-Pakistan [*Political party*] [*Pakistan*] (FEA)
**JUP**........... Journal. University of Poona. Humanities Section [*A publication*]
**JUP**........... Jupiter (KSC)
**JUP**........... Juventud Universitaria Peronista [*University Peronist Youth*] [*Argentina*]
**JUP**........... Juventud Uruguaya de Pie [*Upstanding Uruguayan Youth*] (PD)
**JUP**........... Upland, CA [*Location identifier*] [*FAA*] (FAAL)
**JUPD-A**..... Journal. Urban Planning and Development Proceedings. American Society of Civil Engineers [*A publication*]
**JUPITER**.. Judicial Precedent Information Trace by Electronic Retrieval [*Database*] [*Toyo Information Systems Co.*] [*Information service or system*] (CRD)
**JUPOA**...... Journal of Undergraduate Psychological Research [*A publication*]
**JUPOA**...... Journal. University of Poona. Science and Technology [*A publication*]
**JUPSA**...... Journal. Physical Society of Japan [*A publication*]
**JUr**............ Journal of Urology [*A publication*]
**JUR**........... Julia Resources [*Vancouver Stock Exchange symbol*]
**JUR**........... Jurassic [*Period, era, or system*] [*Geology*]
**JUR**........... Juridical (ROG)
**JUR**........... Jurisprudence (ROG)
**Jur**............. Jurisprudentie van het Hof van Justitie van de Europese Gemeenschappen [*A publication*]
**Jur**............. [*The*] Jurist [*Washington, DC*] [*A publication*] (DLA)

**JUR** .......... Jurist (ROG)
**Jur** .......... Jurist. Quarterly Journal of Jurisprudence [*A publication*]
**Jur** .......... Jurist Reports [*18 vols.*] [*England*] [*A publication*] (DLA)
**Jur** .......... London Jurist [*1854*] [*A publication*] (DLA)
**Jur A** .......... Jurisprudence du Port D'Anvers [*A publication*]
**Jura Riv** ..... Jura. Rivista Internazionale di Diritto Romano e Antico [*A publication*]
**J Urban** ...... Journal of Urban Law [*A publication*]
**J Urban Affairs** ... Journal of Urban Affairs [*A publication*]
**J Urban Anal** ... Journal of Urban Analysis [*A publication*]
**J Urban Analysis** ... Journal of Urban Analysis [*A publication*]
**J Urban Ec** ... Journal of Urban Economics [*A publication*]
**J Urban Econ** ... Journal of Urban Economics [*A publication*]
**J Urban H** ... Journal of Urban History [*A publication*]
**J Urban His** ... Journal of Urban History [*A publication*]
**J Urban Hist** ... Journal of Urban History [*A publication*]
**J Urban L** .. Journal of Urban Law [*A publication*]
**J Urban Law** ... Journal of Urban Law [*A publication*]
**J Urban Living Health Assoc** ... Journal. Urban Living and Health Association [*Japan*] [*A publication*]
**J Urban Pla** ... Journal. Urban Planning and Development Division. Proceedings of the American Society of Civil Engineers [*A publication*]
**J Urban Planning & Dev Div Proc ASCE** ... Journal. Urban Planning and Development Division. Proceedings of the American Society of Civil Engineers [*A publication*]
**Jur Bl** ......... Juristische Blaetter [*A publication*]
**Jur Com Brux** ... Jurisprudence Commerciale de Bruxelles [*A publication*]
**Jur Comm Fl** ... Jurisprudence Commerciale des Flandres [*A publication*]
**Jur Congo** .. Jurisprudence et Droit du Congo [*A publication*]
**JUR D** ........ Juris Doctor [*Doctor of Law*] [*Latin*] (ADA)
**JUR DIG** ... Jure Dignitatis [*By Right of Rank*] [*Latin*] (ROG)
**JURE** .......... Junta Revolucionaria Cubana [*Exile action group*]
**Jur Etat** ...... Jurisprudence de l'Etat Independant du Congo [*A publication*]
**Jur Ex** ........ Hargrave's Francis-Jurisconsult Exercitations [*A publication*] (DLA)
**JURG** ......... Joint Users Requirements Group (NASA)
**JURG** ......... Jurgensen's [*NASDAQ symbol*] (NQ)
**Juridical Rev** ... Juridical Review [*A publication*]
**Jurid R** ....... Juridical Review [*A publication*]
**Jurid Rev** .... Juridical Review [*A publication*]
**Jurid Soc'y Pap** ... Juridical Society Papers [*England*] [*A publication*] (DLA)
**Juri J** .......... Jurimetrics Journal [*A publication*]
**Jurimetrics** ... Jurimetrics Journal [*A publication*]
**Jurimetrics J** ... Jurimetrics Journal [*A publication*]
**JURIS** ........ Jurisdiction (AABC)
**JURIS** ........ Jurisprudence (ADA)
**JURIS** ........ Juristisches Informationssystem [*Judicial Information System*] [*Federal Ministry of Justice*] [*Legal database*] [*Federal Republic of Germany*] (IID)
**JURIS** ........ Justice Retrieval and Inquiry System [*Department of Justice*] [*Legal databank*] [*Information service or system*] (IID)
**JURISD** ..... Jurisdiction
**JURISDN** ... Jurisdiction (ROG)
**JURISDON** ... Jurisdiction (ROG)
**JURISP** ..... Jurisprudence
**Jurispr** ....... Jurisprudence (DLA)
**Jurist Sch** .... Juristische Schulung [*A publication*]
**Jur Liege** .... Jurisprudence de la Cour d'Appel de Liege [*A publication*] (DLA)
**Jur M** ......... Master of Jurisprudence
**Jur Mar** ...... Molloy's De Jure Maritimo [*A publication*] (DLA)
**Jur NY** ....... Jurist, or Law and Equity Reporter [*New York*] [*A publication*] (DLA)
**J Urol** ......... Journal of Urology [*A publication*]
**J Urol Med Chir** ... Journal d'Urologie Medicale et Chirurgicale [*A publication*]
**J Urol Neph** ... Journal d'Urologie et de Nephrologie [*A publication*]
**J Urol Nephrol** ... Journal d'Urologie et de Nephrologie [*A publication*]
**Jur Ouv** ...... Jurisprudence de Louage d'Ouvrage [*A publication*]
**Jur Port Anv** ... Jurisprudence du Port D'Anvers [*A publication*]
**JUR R** ........ Juridical Review [*A publication*]
**Jur R** ......... Juristische Rundschau [*A publication*]
**Jur Rev** ....... Juridical Review [*A publication*]
**Jur Ros** ....... Roscoe's Jurist [*London*] [*A publication*] (DLA)
**Jur (Sc)** ...... [*The*] Scottish Jurist [*Edinburgh*] [*A publication*] (DLA)
**Jur Sc D** ...... Doctor of Judicial Science [*or Doctor of the Science of Jurisprudence*]
**Jur Soc P** .... Juridical Society Papers [*1858-74*] [*Scotland*] [*A publication*] (DLA)
**Jur St** ......... Juridical Styles [*Scotland*] [*A publication*] (DLA)
**JURT** ......... Juneau Report [*A publication*]
**JURUE** ...... Joint Unit for Research on the Urban Environment [*British*]
**J Urusvati Himalayan Res Inst Roerich Mus** ... Journal. Urusvati Himalayan Research Institute of Roerich Museum [*A publication*]
**Jur Utr Dr** ... Juris Utriusque Doctor [*Doctor of Both Laws; i.e., Canon and Civil Law*]
**JUS** ........... Department of Justice Library [*UTLAS symbol*]
**Jus** ............. Jacobus de Porta Ravennate [*Deceased, 1178*] [*Authority cited in pre-1607 legal work*] (DSA)
**Ju S** ........... Juristische Schulung [*A publication*]
**Jus** ............. Jus; Rivista di Scienze Giuridiche [*A publication*]
**JUS** ........... Justice
**JUS** ........... Nenana, AK [*Location identifier*] [*FAA*] (FAAL)
**J US Artillery** ... Journal. United States Artillery [*A publication*]
**JUS AVEN** ... Jusculum Avenaceum [*Gruel*] [*Pharmacy*] (ROG)
**JUSC** ......... Jusculum [*Broth*] [*Pharmacy*] (ROG)
**JUSCIMPC** ... Joint United States/Canada Industrial Mobilization Planning Committee [*NATO*] (NATG)
**Jus Code** .... Code of Justinian [*A publication*] (DLA)
**Jus Code** .... Justices' Code [*Oregon*] [*A publication*] (DLA)
**Juscul** ......... Jusculum [*Broth*] [*Pharmacy*]
**Jus Eccl** ...... Jus Ecclesiasticum [*A publication*]
**JUSII** ......... Journal. United Service Institution of India [*A publication*]
**J Usines Gaz** ... Journal des Usines a Gaz [*France*] [*A publication*]
**Jus Inst** ...... Institutes of Justinian [*Roman law*] [*A publication*] (DLA)
**JUSMAAG** ... Joint United States Military Assistance Advisory Group
**JUSMAG** .. Joint United States Military Advisory Group
**JUSMAGG** ... Joint United States Military Aid Group, Greece
**JUSMAGPHIL** ... Joint United States Military Advisory Group to the Republic of the Philippines [*World War II*]
**JUSMAGTHAI** ... Joint United States Military Assistance Group, Thailand
**JUSMAP** ... Joint United States Military Advisory and Planning Group
**JUSMG** ..... Joint United States Military Group
**JUSMGP** .. Joint United States Military Group
**JUSMMAT** ... Joint United States Military Mission for Aid to Turkey
**Jus Nav Rhod** ... Jus Navale Rhodiorum [*A publication*] (DLA)
**JUSNC** ...... Journal. United States National Committee [*A publication*]
**JUSO** ........ Jungsozialist [*Young Socialist*] [*Germany*]
**JUSPAO** ... Joint United States Public Affairs Office [*Vietnam*]
**Jus Rom MA** ... Jus Romanum Medii Aevi [*A publication*]
**JUSS** ......... Jussien (ROG)
**JUSS** ......... Jussive
**JUSSC** ....... Joint United States Strategic Committee
**JUST** ......... Justice (ROG)
**Just** ............ Justices' Law Reporter [*Pennsylvania*] [*A publication*] (DLA)
**Just** ............ Justiciary [*Legal term*] (DLA)
**JUST** ......... Justification (AABC)
**Just** ............ Justin (BJA)
**JUST** ......... Justinian (ROG)
**JUST ANGL** ... Justiciarius Anglie [*Chief Justiciary of England*] [*Latin*] (ROG)
**JUST CP** ... Justice of the Common Pleas (ROG)
**Just Dig** ..... Digest of Justinian [*A publication*] (DLA)
**Just Econ** ... Just Economics [*A publication*]
**Justices' LR (PA)** ... Justices' Law Reporter [*Pennsylvania*] [*A publication*] (DLA)
**Justice System J** ... Justice System Journal [*A publication*]
**JUSTIFON** ... Justification (ROG)
**Justin** ......... Justinian [*483-565, Byzantine emperor*] [*Authority cited in pre-1607 legal work*] (DSA)
**Just Inst** ..... Justinian's Institutes [*A publication*] (DLA)
**JUSTIS** ..... Judicial State Information System (OICC)
**JUST ITIN** ... Justice Itinerant [*Legal term*] (DLA)
**JUST KB** ... Justice of the King's Bench [*British*] (ROG)
**Just Lieb Ann Chem** ... Justus Liebigs Annalen der Chemie [*A publication*]
**Just LR** ...... Justices' Law Reporter [*Pennsylvania*] [*A publication*] (DLA)
**Justn** .......... Justinian [*483-565, Byzantine emperor*]
**Just P** ......... Justice of the Peace [*A publication*]
**Just P** ......... Justice of the Peace and Local Government Review [*A publication*] (DLA)
**Just Peace** ... Justice of the Peace and Local Government Review [*A publication*] (DLA)
**Just SL** ....... Justice's Sea Law [*A publication*] (DLA)
**Just Sys J** .. Justice System Journal [*A publication*]
**Just Syst J** ... Justice System Journal [*A publication*]
**Justus Liebigs Ann Chem** ... Justus Liebigs Annalen der Chemie [*A publication*]
**JUT** ............ Jet Utility Transport
**JUT** ............ Jeunesse de l'Unite Togolaise [*Togolese Unity Youth*]
**Juta** ............ Juta's Daily Reporter [*South Africa*] [*A publication*] (DLA)
**Juta** ............ Juta's Prize Cases [*South Africa*] [*A publication*] (DLA)
**Juta** ............ Juta's Supreme Court Reports [*1880-1910*] [*Cape Of Good Hope, South Africa*] [*A publication*] (DLA)
**Jute Bull** ..... Jute Bulletin [*A publication*]
**Jute Jute Fabr Bangladesh Newsl** ... Jute and Jute Fabrics. Bangladesh Newsletter [*A publication*]
**Jutendo Med** ... Jutendo Medicine [*Japan*] [*A publication*]
**J Utiliz Agr Prod** ... Journal of Utilization of Agricultural Products [*A publication*]
**Ju V** ........... Justiz und Verwaltung [*A publication*]
**JUV** ........... Juvenal [*Roman poet, 60-140AD*] [*Classical studies*] (ROG)
**JUV** ........... Juvenile
**JUV** ........... Juvenis [*Young*] [*Latin*]
**Juv Ct J** ...... Juvenile Court Journal [*A publication*] (DLA)
**Juv Ct JJ** ... Juvenile Court Judges Journal [*A publication*]
**Juv Ct Judges J** ... Juvenile Court Judges Journal [*A publication*]
**Juv & Dom Rel Ct** ... Juvenile and Domestic Relations Court [*Legal term*] (DLA)
**JUVE** ......... Juvenile
**Juven Just** ... Juvenile Justice [*A publication*]
**Juv and Fam Courts J** ... Juvenile and Family Court Journal [*A publication*]

**Juv & Fam Ct J** ... Juvenile and Family Court Journal [*A publication*]
**JUV JUST** ... Juvenile Justice [*Legal term*] (DLA)
**JUVOS**...... Joint Unemployment, Vacancy, and Operating Statistics [*Department of Employment*] [*British*]
**JUWAT**..... Joint Unconventional Warfare Assessment Team [*Military*]
**JUWC**........ Joint Unconventional Warfare Command (MCD)
**JUWTF**..... Joint Unconventional Warfare Task Force
**JUWTFA** .. Joint Unconventional Warfare Task Force, Atlantic
**JUXT**......... Juxta [*Near*] [*Pharmacy*]
**JUY**........... Andalusia, AL [*Location identifier*] [*FAA*] (FAAL)
**Juz Fil**........ Juznoslovenski Filolog. Povremeni Spis za Slovensku Filologiju i Lingvistiku [*A publication*]
**JUZIAG**.... Juzen Igakkai Zasshi [*A publication*]
**JV**.............. Air Charters [*Senegal*] [*ICAO designator*] (ICDA)
**JV**.............. Jagdverband [*German aircraft fighter unit*] [*World War II*]
**JV**.............. Jahrbuch fuer Volksliedforschung [*A publication*]
**JV**.............. Jamahiriya Airways [*Libyan Arab Jamahiriya*] [*ICAO designator*] (FAAC)
**JV**.............. Janesbury Valve [*Aerospace*] (KSC)
**jv**................ Janvier [*January*] [*French*]
**JV**.............. Japanese Vellum
**JV**.............. Jet Ventilation [*Medicine*]
**JV**.............. Jewish Vegetarians of North America (EA)
**JV**.............. Joint Venture [*Legal term*] [*Business term*]
**J & V**......... Jones and Varick's Laws of New York [*A publication*] (DLA)
**j/v**............... Jour de Vue [*Days after Sight*] [*French*]
**JV**.............. Journal. Violin Society of America [*A publication*]
**JV**.............. Journal Voucher [*Accounting*]
**JV**.............. Jugular Vein [*Anatomy*]
**JV**.............. Junior Varsity
**JVA**........... Ankavandra [*Madagascar*] [*Airport symbol*] (OAG)
**JVA**........... Jaarboek. Vereeniging Amstelodanum [*A publication*]
**JVA**........... Jahrbuch. Verein von Altertumsfreunden im Rheinland [*A publication*]
**JVA**........... Jet Vane Actuators
**JVA**........... Jewish Vacation Association [*Superseded by Association of Jewish Sponsored Camps*] (EA)
**JVA**........... Journal of Volunteer Administration [*A publication*]
**JVA**........... Junior Victory Army [*World War II*]
**JVAA**......... Jewish Visual Artists Association (EA)
**J Vac Sci T** ... Journal of Vacuum Science and Technology [*A publication*]
**J Vac Sci Tech** ... Journal of Vacuum Science and Technology [*A publication*]
**J Vac Sci and Technol** ... Journal of Vacuum Science and Technology [*A publication*]
**J Vac Sci Technol** ... Journal of Vacuum Science and Technology [*A publication*]
**J Vac Sci and Technol A** ... Journal of Vacuum Science and Technology. A. Vacuum, Surfaces, and Films [*A publication*]
**J Vac Sci and Technol B** ... Journal of Vacuum Science and Technology. B. Micro-Electronics Processing and Phenomena [*A publication*]
**J Vac Soc Jpn** ... Journal. Vacuum Society of Japan [*A publication*]
**J Value Eng** ... Journal of Value Engineering [*A publication*]
**J Value Inq** ... Journal of Value Inquiry [*A publication*]
**JVARh**....... Jahrbuch. Verein von Altertumsfreunden im Rheinland [*A publication*]
**JVAS**......... Jandel Video Analysis System
**J Vasc Surg** ... Journal of Vascular Surgery [*A publication*]
**JVB**........... James V. Brown Library of Williamsport and Lycoming County, Williamsport, PA [*OCLC symbol*] (OCLC)
**JVB**........... Joint Vulnerability Board
**JVB**........... Juedisches Volksblatt (Breslau) [*A publication*]
**JV Bl**.......... Justizverwaltungsblatt [*A publication*]
**JVC**........... Japan Victor Company
**JVC**........... Jesuit Volunteer Corps: Northwest (EA)
**JVC**........... Jet Vane Control (MCD)
**JVC**........... Jewelers Vigilance Committee (EA)
**JVC**........... Jules Verne Circle (EA)
**JVC**........... Junior Vice Commander
**JVD**........... Jugular Venous Distention [*Medicine*]
**JVD**........... Juris Utriusque Doctor [*Doctor of Both Laws; i.e., Canon and Civil Law*]
**JVDHS**...... Jahresverzeichnis der Deutschen Hochschulschriften [*A bibliographic publication*] [*Germany*]
**JVE**........... Jeans Viscosity Equation [*Physics*]
**JVEG**......... Jaarbericht. Vooraziatische-Egyptisch Genootschap "Ex Oriente Lux" [*A publication*]
**J Vener Dis Inf** ... Journal of Venereal Disease Information [*A publication*]
**JVER**......... Journal of Vocational Education Research [*A publication*] (EAAP)
**J Verbal Learn** ... Journal of Verbal Learning and Verbal Behavior [*A publication*]
**J Verb Learn** ... Journal of Verbal Learning and Verbal Behavior [*A publication*]
**J Verb Learn Verb Behav** ... Journal of Verbal Learning and Verbal Behavior [*A publication*]
**J Vertebr Paleontol** ... Journal of Vertebrate Paleontology [*A publication*]
**J Ver Vaterl Naturk Wuertt** ... Jahresheft. Verein fuer Vaterlaendische Naturkunde in Wuerttemberg [*A publication*]
**J Vet Anim Husb Res (India)** ... Journal of Veterinary and Animal Husbandry Research (India) [*A publication*]
**J Vet Fac Univ Tehran** ... Journal. Veterinary Faculty. University of Tehran [*A publication*]
**J Vet Med**.. Journal of Veterinary Medicine [*Japan*] [*A publication*]
**J Vet Med Educ** ... Journal of Veterinary Medical Education [*A publication*]
**J Vet Med Ser A** ... Journal of Veterinary Medicine. Series A [*A publication*]
**J Vet Med Ser B** ... Journal of Veterinary Medicine. Series B [*A publication*]
**J Vet Midi** ... Journal des Veterinaires du Midi [*A publication*]
**J Vet Pharmacol Ther** ... Journal of Veterinary Pharmacology and Therapeutics [*A publication*]
**J Vet Pharm Ther** ... Journal of Veterinary Pharmacology and Therapeutics [*A publication*]
**J Vet Sci UAR** ... Journal of Veterinary Science of the United Arab Republic [*A publication*]
**JVF**........... Jahrbuch fuer Volksliedforschung [*A publication*]
**JV Gew R Schutz** ... Jahrbuch der Internationalen Vereinigung fuer Gewerblichen Rechtsschutz [*A publication*]
**JVH**........... Bangor, ME [*Location identifier*] [*FAA*] (FAAL)
**JVH**........... Jahrbuch fuer Volkskunde der Heimatvertriebenen [*A publication*]
**JVH**........... Jahresverzeichnis der Deutschen Hochschulschriften [*A publication*]
**JVIBDM**... Journal of Visual Impairment and Blindness [*A publication*]
**J Vic Teachers Union** ... Journal of the Victorian Teachers' Union [*A publication*] (APTA)
**J Vinyl Technol** ... Journal of Vinyl Technology [*A publication*]
**J Viola da Gamba Soc Amer** ... Journal. Viola da Gamba Society of America [*A publication*]
**J Violin S**... Journal. Violin Society of America [*A publication*]
**J Violin Soc Amer** ... Journal. Violin Society of America [*A publication*]
**J Virol**........ Journal of Virology [*A publication*]
**J Virol Methods** ... Journal of Virological Methods [*A publication*]
**J Virology**.. Journal of Virology [*A publication*]
**JVIS**.......... Jackson Vocational Interest Survey [*Vocational guidance test*]
**J Visual Impairment & Blind** ... Journal of Visual Impairment and Blindness [*A publication*]
**JVita**.......... Life of Josephus (BJA)
**J Vitaminol** ... Journal of Vitaminology [*A publication*]
**J Vitaminol (Kyoto)** ... Journal of Vitaminology (Kyoto) [*A publication*]
**JVJE**.......... Jahrbuch. Vereinigung Juedischer Exportakademiker [*A publication*]
**JVJGL**....... Jahrbuch. Verein fuer Juedische Geschichte und Literatur [*A publication*]
**JVL**........... Beloit/Janesville [*Wisconsin*] [*Airport symbol*] (OAG)
**JVL**........... Janesville, WI [*Location identifier*] [*FAA*] (FAAL)
**JVLBA**....... Journal of Verbal Learning and Verbal Behavior [*A publication*]
**JVLHOD**... Jahrbuch. Verein fuer Landeskunde und Heimatpflege im Gau Oberdonau [*A publication*]
**JVLVB**....... Journal of Verbal Learning and Verbal Behavior [*A publication*]
**JVMAE6**... Journal of Veterinary Medicine. Series A [*A publication*]
**JVMBE9**... Journal of Veterinary Medicine. Series B [*A publication*]
**JVMED**..... Journal of Virological Methods [*A publication*]
**JVNC**......... John Von Neumann National Supercomputer Center [*Princeton, NJ*] (GRD)
**J V N M**..... Jaarboek. Vereeniging voor Nederlandsche Muziekgeschiedenis [*A publication*]
**JVNS**......... Jahrbuch. Verein fuer Niederdeutsche Sprachforschung [*A publication*]
**J Vocat Beh** ... Journal of Vocational Behavior [*A publication*]
**J Vocat Behav** ... Journal of Vocational Behavior [*A publication*]
**J Voc Behav** ... Journal of Vocational Behavior [*A publication*]
**J Voet Com ad Pand** ... Jan Voet's Commentarius ad Pandectas [*A publication*] (DLA)
**J Volcanol Geotherm Res** ... Journal of Volcanology and Geothermal Research [*A publication*]
**J Volun Act** ... Journal of Voluntary Action Research [*A publication*]
**J Volunteer Adm** ... Journal of Volunteer Administration [*A publication*]
**JVP**........... Janatha Vimukhti Peramuna [*People's Liberation Front*] [*Sri Lanka*] [*Political party*] (PPW)
**JVP**........... Japanese Vellum Proofs
**JVP**........... Journal of Vertebrate Paleontology [*A publication*]
**JVP**........... Juedische Volkspartei (BJA)
**JVP**........... Jugular Vein [*or Venous*] Pulse [*Medicine*]
**JVP**........... Junior Vice-President [*Freemasonry*] (ROG)
**JVPADK**... Journal of Vertebrate Paleontology [*A publication*]
**JVPT**......... Jugular Venous Pulse Tracing [*Medicine*]
**JVPTD9**.... Journal of Veterinary Pharmacology and Therapeutics [*A publication*]
**JVR**........... Jury Verdict Research, Inc. [*Information service or system*] (IID)
**JVS**........... Jewish Vegetarian Society - America [*Later, JVSNA*] (EA)
**JVS**........... Jewish Vocational Services
**JVS**........... Joint Vocational School
**JVSch**........ Jahrbuch. Verein Schweizerischer Gymnasial-Lehrer [*A publication*]
**JVSNA**...... Jewish Vegetarian Society-North America (EA)
**JVSPLNMQNSC** ... Je Vous Salue par les Noms Maconniques que Nous Seul Connoissons [*I Salute You by the Masonic Names, Which We Only Know*] [*French*] [*Freemasonry*]
**JVSUES**.... Journal of Vascular Surgery [*A publication*]
**JVVVA**...... Justice for Veteran Victims of the Veterans Administration (EA)

**JVWK**........ Jahrbuch. Verein fuer Westfaelische Kirchengeschichte [*A publication*]
**JVWP**........ Jahrbuch des Vereins fuer Wissenschaftliche Paedagogik [*A publication*]
**JVX**........... Joint Service Vertical-Lift Aircraft, Experimental [*Military*] (RDA)
**JVY**........... Jeffersonville, IN [*Location identifier*] [*FAA*] (FAAL)
**JVZ**........... Juedische Volkszeitung [*Oberingelheim/Leipzig*] [*A publication*]
**JW**............ Arrow Airways, Inc. [*ICAO designator*] (FAAC)
**JW**............ Jacket Water
**J & W**........ Jacob and Walker's English Chancery Reports [*A publication*] (DLA)
**JW**............ Jahrbuch der Kunsthistorischen Sammlungen in Wien [*A publication*]
**JW**............ Jehovah's Witnesses (ADA)
**JW**............ [*The*] Jewish War [*A publication*] (BJA)
**JW**............ [*The*] Jewish Week [*A publication*]
**JW**............ John Wiley [*& Sons*] [*Publisher*]
**JW**............ Jordan Watch [*Database*] [*Jordan & Sons Ltd.*] [*Information service or system*] (CRD)
**JW**............ Journal of the West [*A publication*]
**JW**............ Junior Warden [*Freemasonry*]
**JW**............ Junior Wolf [*A young philanderer*] [*Slang*]
**JW**............ Junior Woodward [*Ancient Order of Foresters*]
**JWA**.......... Jwalamukhi [*India*] [*Seismograph station code, US Geological Survey*] [*Closed*] (SEIS)
**JWABAQ**... Journal for Water and Wastewater Research [*A publication*]
**JWADF**..... Joint Western Air Defense Force (MUGU)
**JWAfrL**..... Journal of West African Languages [*A publication*]
**JW Afr Sci Ass**... Journal. West African Science Association [*A publication*]
**JWAG**........ Journal. Walters Art Gallery [*A publication*]
**J Wagga Wagga Dist Hist Soc**... Wagga Wagga and District Historical Society. Journal [*A publication*] (APTA)
**JWAI**......... Johnson Worldwide Associates, Inc. [*NASDAQ symbol*] (NQ)
**J Wakayama Med Soc**... Journal. Wakayama Medical Society [*A publication*]
**JWAL**........ Journal of West African Languages [*A publication*]
**JWalt**......... Journal. Walters Art Gallery [*A publication*]
**J Walters Art Gal**... Journal. Walters Art Gallery [*A publication*]
**J WA Nurses**... Journal. Western Australian Nurses Association [*A publication*] (APTA)
**JWarb**........ Journal. Warburg and Courtauld Institute [*A publication*]
**J Warburg C**... Journal. Warburg and Courtauld Institute [*A publication*]
**J Warburg Courtauld Inst**... Journal. Warburg and Courtauld Institute [*A publication*]
**J Warburg and Courtauld Inst**... Journal. Warburg and Courtauld Institute [*A publication*]
**JWAS**........ Journal. Washington Academy of Sciences [*A publication*]
**JWASA**..... Journal. Washington Academy of Sciences [*A publication*]
**J Wash Acad Sci**... Journal. Washington Academy of Sciences [*A publication*]
**J Washington Acad Sci**... Journal. Washington Academy of Sciences [*A publication*]
**JWAT**........ Jamaica Water Properties [*NASDAQ symbol*] (NQ)
**J Water P C**... Journal. Water Pollution Control Federation [*A publication*]
**J Water Pollut Contr Fed**... Journal. Water Pollution Control Federation [*A publication*]
**J Water Pollut Control Fed**... Journal. Water Pollution Control Federation [*A publication*]
**J Water Pollut Control Fed**... Water Pollution Control Federation. Journal [*A publication*]
**J Water Resour**... Journal of Water Resources [*A publication*]
**J Water Resour Planning & Manage Div Proc ASCE**... Journal. Water Resources Planning and Management Division. Proceedings of the American Society of Civil Engineers [*A publication*]
**J Water Resour Plann Manage Div Am Soc Civ Eng**... Journal. Water Resources Planning and Management Division. Proceedings of the American Society of Civil Engineers [*A publication*]
**J Water Resour Plann Manage Div ASCE**... Journal. Water Resources Planning and Management Division. Proceedings of the American Society of Civil Engineers [*A publication*]
**J Water Waste**... Journal of Water and Waste [*Japan*] [*A publication*]
**J Water Wastewater Res**... Journal for Water and Wastewater Research [*A publication*]
**J Waterway**... Journal. Waterways, Harbors, and Coastal Engineering Division. American Society of Civil Engineers [*A publication*]
**J Waterway Port Coastal Ocean Div Amer Soc Civil Eng Proc**... Journal. Waterways, Port, Coastal, and Ocean Division. American Society of Civil Engineers. Proceedings [*A publication*]
**J Waterway Port Coastal & Ocean Div Proc ASCE**... Journal. Waterways, Port, Coastal, and Ocean Division. Proceedings. American Society of Civil Engineers [*A publication*]
**J Waterw Harbors Div Am Soc Civ Eng**... Journal. Waterways and Harbors Division. American Society of Civil Engineers [*A publication*]
**J Water Works Assoc**... Journal. Water Works Association [*Japan*] [*A publication*]
**J Waterw Port Coastal Ocean Div ASCE**... Journal. Waterways, Port, Coastal, and Ocean Division. American Society of Civil Engineers [*A publication*]
**JWB**.......... Jahrbuch der Wittheit zu Bremen [*A publication*]
**JWB**.......... Joint Wages Board (DAS)
**JWB**.......... National Jewish Welfare Board [*Later, JCCANA*] (EA)
**JWBC**........ Joint Whole Blood Center [*Military*]
**JWBCA**..... Joint Whole Blood Control Agency (MCD)
**JWBJBC**... JWB [*Jewish Welfare Board*] Jewish Book Council (EA)
**JWBS**........ Journal. Welsh Bibliographic Society [*A publication*]
**JWC**.......... Jim Walter Corporation [*NYSE symbol*] (SPSG)
**JWC**.......... Junction Wire Connector
**JWC**.......... Jungle Warfare Course [*Military*] (MCD)
**JWCBRS**... Journal. West China Border Research Society [*A publication*]
**JWCI**......... Journal. Warburg and Courtauld Institute [*A publication*]
**JWCTD**..... Journal of Wood Chemistry and Technology [*A publication*]
**JWCTDJ**... Journal of Wood Chemistry and Technology [*A publication*]
**JWE**.......... Joint Warfare Establishment [*British*]
**JWEC**........ Jefferson-Williams Energy Corporation [*NASDAQ symbol*] (NQ)
**J West**........ Journal of the West [*A publication*]
**J West Afr Inst Oil Palm Res**... Journal. West African Institute for Oil Palm Research [*A publication*]
**J West Afr Sci Assoc**... Journal. West African Science Association [*A publication*]
**J West Aust Nurses**... Journal. West Australian Nurses [*A publication*]
**J West Scot Iron Steel Inst**... Journal. West of Scotland Iron and Steel Institute [*A publication*]
**J West Soc Eng**... Journal. Western Society of Engineers [*A publication*]
**J West Soc Periodont**... Journal. Western Society of Periodontology [*A publication*]
**J West Soc Periodontol**... Journal. Western Society of Periodontology [*A publication*]
**JWF**.......... Job Work Folder (AABC)
**JWFC**........ Jacky Ward Fan Club (EA)
**JWFC**........ Jimmy Wakely Fan Club (EA)
**JWFC**........ Joe Waters Fan Club (EA)
**JWG**.......... Jahrbuch fuer Wirtschaftsgeschichte [*A publication*]
**JWG**.......... Joint Working Group [*Military*]
**JWG**.......... Jugendwohlfahrtsgesetz [*Youth Welfare Law*] [*German*] (ILCA)
**JWGA**........ Joint War Games Agency [*JCS*] [*DoD*]
**JWGCG**..... Joint War Games Control Group [*Military*] (CINC)
**JWGL**........ Jahrbuch der Wissenschaftlichen Gesellschaft fuer Luftfahrt [*A publication*]
**JWGM**...... Joint Working Group Meeting [*NASA*] (KSC)
**JWGV**........ Jahrbuch. Wiener Goethe-Verein [*A publication*]
**JWH**.......... Journal of World History [*A publication*]
**JWI**........... Jehovah's Witnesses Information (EAIO)
**JWI**........... Journal. Warburg and Courtauld Institute [*London*] [*A publication*]
**JWIDA**...... Journal of Wildlife Diseases [*A publication*]
**J Wildl Dis**... Journal of Wildlife Diseases [*A publication*]
**J Wildlife Mgt**... Journal of Wildlife Management [*A publication*]
**J Wildl Man**... Journal of Wildlife Management [*A publication*]
**J Wildl Manage**... Journal of Wildlife Management [*A publication*]
**JWIM**........ Journal of Wildlife Management [*A publication*]
**J Wind Eng and Ind**... Journal of Wind Engineering and Industrial Aerodynamics [*A publication*]
**J Wind Engng & Ind Aerodyn**... Journal of Wind Engineering and Industrial Aerodynamics [*A publication*]
**J Wind Engng Ind Aerodynam**... Journal of Wind Engineering and Industrial Aerodynamics [*A publication*]
**J Wis Dent Assoc**... Journal. Wisconsin Dental Association [*A publication*]
**J Wis State Dent Soc**... Journal. Wisconsin State Dental Society [*A publication*]
**JWKB**........ Jordan-Wentzel-Kramers-Brillouin [*Physics*]
**J Wld Trade Law**... Journal of World Trade Law [*A publication*]
**JWLR**........ Jeweller [*British*] (ADA)
**JWMS**....... Journal. William Morris Society [*A publication*]
**JWNS**........ Jewish News Service (BJA)
**J & WO**...... Jettison and Washing Overboard
**JWO**.......... Job Work Order
**J Won Kwang Public Health Jr Coll**... Journal. Won Kwang Public Health Junior College [*A publication*]
**J Wood Chem Technol**... Journal of Wood Chemistry and Technology [*A publication*]
**J World Hist**... Journal of World History [*A publication*]
**J World Tr**... Journal of World Trade Law [*A publication*]
**J World Trade L**... Journal of World Trade Law [*A publication*]
**J World Trade Law**... Journal of World Trade Law [*A publication*]
**J World Tr L**... Journal of World Trade Law [*A publication*]
**JWP**.......... Jamaican Workers' Party [*Political party*] (PPW)
**JWP**.......... Joint Working Party (ADA)
**JWP**.......... JWP, Inc. [*NYSE symbol*] (SPSG)
**JWPC**........ Joint War Plans Committee
**JWPC**........ Joint War Production Committee
**JWPCF**...... Journal. Water Pollution Control Federation [*A publication*]
**JWPFA**...... Journal. Water Pollution Control Federation [*A publication*]
**JWPNN**..... Jobs with Peace National Network [*Later, NJWPC*] (EA)
**JWPS**........ Joint War Production Staff

**JWPT**........ Jersey Wildlife Preservation Trust (EAIO)
**JWPZK**..... Jahrbuch fuer Wissenschaftliche und Praktische Zuechtungskunde [*A publication*]
**JWR**.......... Joint War Room [*Military*]
**JWRA**........ Joint War Room Annex [*Military*] (CINC)
**JWRC**........ Jewish Women's Resource Center (EA)
**JWREEG**.. Journal of Water Resources [*A publication*]
**JWS**.......... Jahrbuch fuer Wirtschafts und Sozialpaedagogik [*A publication*]
**JW u S**....... Jahrbuch fuer Wirtschafts und Sozialpaedagogik [*A publication*]
**JWS**.......... Japanese Weekend School
**JWS**.......... Jazz World Society (EA)
**JwS**.......... John Wiley & Sons, New York, NY [*Library symbol*] [*Library of Congress*] (LCLS)
**JWS**.......... Joint Warfare Staff [*British*]
**JWS**.......... Journal of Western Speech [*A publication*]
**JWS**.......... Judson Welliver Society (EA)
**JWSL**........ Journal of Women's Studies in Literature [*A publication*]
**JWSO**........ Joint Wool Selling Organisation [*Australia*]
**JWSS**......... James Willard Schultz Society (EA)
**JWT**.......... Journal of World Trade Law [*A publication*]
**JWT**.......... JWT Group, Inc. [*Formerly, J. Walter Thompson Co.*] [*NYSE symbol*] (SPSG)
**JWTC**........ Jungle Warfare Training Center [*Army*]
**JWTL**........ Journal of World Trade Law [*A publication*]
**JWU**.......... International Jewelry Workers Union [*Later, Service Employees International Union*]
**JWU**.......... Sumter, SC [*Location identifier*] [*FAA*] (FAAL)
**JWV**.......... Jewish War Veterans of the USA (EA)
**JWVA**........ Jewish War Veterans of the USA - National Ladies Auxiliary (EA)
**J W Vir Phil Soc** ... Journal. West Virginia Philosophical Society [*A publication*]
**JWVUSANM** ... Jewish War Veterans USA National Memorial (EA)
**JWWJA**.... Journal. Japan Water Works Association [*A publication*]
**JWY**.......... Jet Way, Inc. [*Ypsilanti, MI*] [*FAA designator*] (FAAC)
**JWYCC**..... Jamestown-Williamsburg-Yorktown Celebration Committee
**JWZ**.......... Juedische Wochenzeitung [*A publication*]
**JX**............. International Jet Air Ltd. [*ICAO designator*] (FAAC)
**JX**............. Jesus Christus [*Jesus Christ*] [*Latin*] (ROG)
**JX**............. Jorex Ltd. [*Toronto Stock Exchange symbol*]
**JXCG**......... Joint Exercise Control Group [*Military*] (AABC)
**JXG**........... Juvenile Xanthogranuloma [*Ophthalmology*]
**JXN**........... Jackson [*Michigan*] [*Airport symbol*] (OAG)
**J X-Ray Technol** ... Journal of X-Ray Technology [*A publication*]
**JXT**........... Morristown, TN [*Location identifier*] [*FAA*] (FAAL)
**J XXII**........ Extravagantes Johannes XXII [*A publication*] (DSA)
**Jy**............. Jansky [*A unit of electromagnetic flux density*]
**JY**............. Japanese Yen [*Monetary unit*]
**JY**............. Jersey European Airways [*Great Britain*] [*ICAO designator*] (FAAC)
**JY**............. Jordan [*Aircraft nationality and registration mark*] (FAAC)
**JY**............. July
**JY**............. Jury [*Ship's rigging*] (ROG)
**JYA**........... Junior Year Abroad [*Collegiate term*]
**JYADA6**.... Journal of Youth and Adolescence [*A publication*]
**J Yamagata Agric For Soc** ... Journal. Yamagata Agriculture and Forestry Society [*A publication*]
**J Yamashina Inst Ornithol** ... Journal. Yamashina Institute for Ornithology [*A publication*]
**JYB**........... Jewish Year Book [*A publication*]
**JYC**........... Interstate Helicopters, Inc. [*Roseland, NJ*] [*FAA designator*] (FAAC)
**JYC**........... Jacques-Yves Cousteau [*French marine explorer*] [*Initialism pronounced "Jheek" when used as nickname*]
**JYCE-A**..... Journal. Hydraulics Division. Proceedings of the American Society of Civil Engineers [*A publication*]
**JYEP**......... Jubilee Youth Employment Program [*South Australia*]
**JYM**........... Journal of Property Management [*A publication*]
**J Yokohama Munic Univ** ... Journal. Yokohama Municipal University [*A publication*]
**J Yonago Med Assoc** ... Journal. Yonago Medical Association [*A publication*]
**J Youth Ado** ... Journal of Youth and Adolescence [*A publication*]
**J Youth Adolesc** ... Journal of Youth and Adolescence [*A publication*]
**J Youth & Adolescence** ... Journal of Youth and Adolescence [*A publication*]
**JYV**........... Houston, TX [*Location identifier*] [*FAA*] (FAAL)
**JYV**........... Jyvaskyla [*Finland*] [*Airport symbol*] (OAG)
**JZ**............. Jazykovedny Zbornik [*A publication*]
**Jz**............. Jazz Magazine [*A publication*]
**Jz**............. Jezykoznawca [*A publication*]
**JZ**............. Jinruigaku Zasshi [*Anthropological Journal*] [*A publication*]
**JZ**............. Juedische Zeitung [*A publication*]
**JZ**............. Juedische Zeremonialkunst [*A publication*] (BJA)
**JZ**............. Juristenzeitung [*A publication*]
**JZ**............. Zaire Aero Services [*ICAO designator*] (FAAC)
**JZ Bl**.......... Juedisches Zentralblatt [*A publication*]
**JZF**........... Jannasch-Zafirion-Farrington [*Marine sediment trap*]
**JZG**........... Juedische Zeitschrift fuer Wissenschaft und Leben (A. Geiger) [*A publication*] (BJA)
**J Zhejiang Med Univ** ... Journal. Zhejiang Medical University [*A publication*]
**JZI**............ Charleston, SC [*Location identifier*] [*FAA*] (FAAL)
**JZM**........... Jazzman Resources, Inc. [*Vancouver Stock Exchange symbol*]
**JZO**........... Juedische Zeitung fuer Ostdeutschland [*Breslau*] [*A publication*]
**JZOOAE**... Journal of Zoology [*London*] [*A publication*]
**J Zoo Anim Med** ... Journal of Zoo Animal Medicine [*A publication*]
**J Zool**........ Journal of Zoology [*A publication*]
**J Zool (Lond)** ... Journal of Zoology (London) [*A publication*]
**J Zool Res** ... Journal of Zoological Research [*A publication*]
**J Zool Res (Aligarh)** ... Journal of Zoological Research (Aligarh) [*A publication*]
**J Zool Ser A** ... Journal of Zoology. Series A [*A publication*]
**J Zool Ser B** ... Journal of Zoology. Series B [*A publication*]
**J Zool Soc India** ... Journal. Zoological Society of India [*A publication*]
**JZQ**........... Norfolk, VA [*Location identifier*] [*FAA*] (FAAL)
**JZRED2**.... Journal of Zoological Research [*Aligarh*] [*A publication*]
**JZSAEU**.... Journal of Zoology. Series A [*A publication*]
**JZSBEX**.... Journal of Zoology. Series B [*A publication*]
**JZWL**........ Juedische Zeitschrift fuer Wissenschaft und Leben [*A publication*]

# K

**K** ........ Amphibious [*JETDS*]
**k** ........ Boltzmann Constant [*Symbol*] [*IUPAC*]
**k** ........ Bulk Modulus of Elasticity [*Symbol*] (DEN)
**K** ........ Capacity (AAG)
**K** ........ Cara [*Dear One*] [*Latin*]
**K** ........ Carat [*Unit of measure for precious stones or gold*]
**K** ........ Care
**K** ........ Carissimus [*Dearest*] [*Latin*]
**K** ........ Carlo Erba [*Italy*] [*Research code symbol*]
**K** ........ Carus
**K** ........ Cathode [*Electron device*] (MSA)
**K** ........ Cellophane (AAG)
**K** ........ Certified Kosher [*Food labeling*]
**K** ........ Circuses [*Public-performance tariff class*] [*British*]
**k** ........ Coefficient of Alienation [*Psychology*]
**K** ........ Cold [*Air mass*] (FAAC)
**K** ........ Computer [*JETDS nomenclature*]
**K** ........ Consonantal [*Linguistics*]
**K** ........ Constant
**K** ........ Cretaceous [*Period, era, or system*] [*Geology*]
**K** ........ Cumulus [*Cloud*] [*Meteorology*]
**°K** ........ Degrees Kelvin
**K** ........ Dielectric Constant
**K** ........ Equilibrium Constant [*Symbol*] [*Chemistry*]
**K** ........ Invitation to Transmit [*Communications*] (FAAC)
**K** ........ Ionization Constant [*Symbol*] [*Chemistry*]
**K** ........ K Capture [*A type of radioactive decay*]
**K** ........ Kadenz [*Cadence*] [*Music*]
**K** ........ Kaempferol [*Biochemistry*]
**K** ........ Kainic Acid [*Biochemistry*]
**K** ........ Kaiser [*In radio call signs west of the Mississippi River*] (ROG)
**K** ........ Kaken Chemical Co. [*Japan*] [*Research code symbol*]
**K** ........ Kalendas [*Calends*]
**K** ........ Kalium [*Potassium*] [*Chemical element*]
**K** ........ Kallikrein [*or Kininogenin*] Inhibiting Unit [*Hematology*]
**K** ........ Kammer [*Chamber, Division*] [*German*] (ILCA)
**K** ........ Kanamycin [*Antibacterial compound*]
**K** ........ Kanone [*Gun*] [*German military - World War II*]
**K** ........ Kansas State Library, Topeka, KS [*Library symbol*] [*Library of Congress*] (LCLS)
**K** ........ Karat [*A twenty-fourth part; unit of value for gold*]
**K** ........ Karolus de Tocco [*Flourished, 13th century*] [*Authority cited in pre-1607 legal work*] (DSA)
**K** ........ Karyotype [*Clinical chemistry*]
**K** ........ Kathode [*Cathode*]
**K** ........ Kayak
**K** ........ Kayser
**K** ........ Keel
**K** ........ Keg
**K** ........ Kell [*Blood group*]
**K** ........ Kellogg Co. [*NYSE symbol*] (SPSG)
**K** ........ Kelp [*Quality of the Bottom*] [*Nautical charts*]
**K** ........ Kelvin [*Symbol*] [*SI unit of thermodynamic temperature*]
**K** ........ Kensal Press [*Publisher*] [*British*]
**K** ........ Kentish
**K** ........ Kenyon's English King's Bench Reports [*A publication*] (DLA)
**K** ........ Kern Wave [*Earthquakes*]
**K** ........ Kerosene (AAG)
**K** ........ Kerr Constant [*Optics*]
**K** ........ Ketamine [*An anesthetic*]
**K** ........ Ketch (ROG)
**k** ........ Ketib (BJA)
**K** ........ Ketotifen [*Pharmacology*]
**K** ........ Key
**K** ........ Keyboard [*A publication*]
**K** ........ Keyes' New York Court of Appeals Reports [*A publication*] (DLA)
**K** ........ KGB [*Komitet Gossudarstvennoi Bezopasnosti*] Agent
**K** ........ Kicker [*Football*]
**K** ........ Killed
**K** ........ Kilo [*Phonetic alphabet*] [*International*] (DSUE)
**k** ........ Kilo [*A prefix meaning multiplied by $10^3$ SI symbol*]
**K** ........ Kilobyte [*$10^3$ bytes*] [*Data processing*]
**K** ........ Kilocycles per Second [*Aviation code*] (FAAC)
**k** ........ Kilogram [*Also, kg*] [*Symbol*] [*SI unit for mass*]
**k** ........ Kilohm
**K** ........ Kindergarten
**K** ........ Kinesthetic (AAG)
**K** ........ Kinetic Energy [*Symbol*] [*IUPAC*]
**K** ........ King [*Phonetic alphabet*] [*Royal Navy*] [*World War I*] [*Pre-World War II*] [*World War II*] (DSUE)
**K** ........ King [*Chess, card games*]
**K** ........ Kingdom (ROG)
**K** ........ Kings [*Old Testament book*] (BJA)
**K** ........ [*Georg*] Kinsky [*When used in identifying Beethoven's compositions, refers to cataloging of his works by musicologist Kinsky*]
**K** ........ Kip [*Monetary unit*] [*Laos*]
**K** ........ Kip [*1000 lbs.*]
**K** ........ Kirk (ROG)
**K** ........ [*Ralph*] Kirkpatrick [*When used in identifying D. Scarlatti's compositions, refers to cataloging of his works by musicologist Kirkpatrick*]
**K** ........ Kitchen
**K** ........ Klinge [*Germany*] [*Research code symbol*]
**K** ........ Klio. Beitraege zur Alten Geschichte [*A publication*]
**K** ........ Klystron
**K** ........ Knight [*Chess, card games*]
**K** ........ Knighthood
**K** ........ Knit
**K** ........ Knjizevnost [*A publication*]
**K** ........ Knock [*Cardiology*]
**K** ........ Knots [*Also, KT*] [*Nautical speed unit*]
**K** ........ Knowledge [*A publication*]
**K** ........ Knudsen Number
**K** ........ [*Ludwig Ritter von*] Koechel [*When used in identifying Mozart's compositions, refers to cataloging of his works by musicologist Koechel*]
**K** ........ Kollaborateur [*Nickname given Alain Robbe-Grillet*] [*World War II*]
**K** ........ Kollsman [*When followed by altimeter setting*] [*See also KOL*] [*Aviation*] (FAAC)
**K** ........ Kontra [*Contra*] [*Music*]
**K** ........ Kopeck [*Monetary unit*] [*USSR*]
**K** ........ Koruna [*Monetary unit*] [*Czechoslovakia*]
**K** ........ Kosher
**K** ........ Kosmos [*Publisher*] [*Holland*]
**K** ........ Kotze's Transvaal High Court Reports [*South Africa*] [*A publication*] (DLA)
**K** ........ Kouyunjik [*or Kuyounjik*] [*Collection of cuneiform tablets from Kuyounjik in the British Museum, London*] (BJA)
**K** ........ Kraftfahrwesen [*Motor transport*] [*German military - World War II*]
**K** ........ Kraftrad [*Motorcycle*] [*German military - World War II*]
**K** ........ Krazy Kat [*Cartoon character by George Herriman*]
**K** ........ Krona [*Monetary unit*] [*Iceland, Sweden*]
**K** ........ Krone [*Crown*] [*Monetary unit*] [*Denmark, Norway*]
**K** ........ Kroon [*Monetary unit*] [*Estonia*]
**K** ........ Krupp Gun
**K** ........ Kultur [*A publication*]
**K** ........ Kunststoffe [*A publication*]
**K** ........ Kurus [*Monetary unit*] [*Turkey*]
**K** ........ Kwacha [*Monetary unit*] [*Malawi, Zambia*]
**K** ........ Kyat [*Monetary unit*] [*Burma*]
**K** ........ Lysine [*One-letter symbol; see Lys*]
**k** ........ Mass Transfer Coefficient [*Symbol*] [*IUPAC*]
**K** ........ Modified for use as target aircraft [*Suffix to Navy plane designation*]
**k** ........ Multiplication Factor [*or Constant*]
**K** ........ NCO Logistics Program [*Army skill qualification identifier*] (INF)
**K** ........ One Thousand (NASA)

**K**............... Phylloquinone [*Vitamin K*] [*Also, PMQ*] [*Biochemistry*]
**K**............... Potassium [*Chemical element*]
**K**............... Promotional Fare [*Also, L, Q, V*] [*Airline fare code*]
**k**............... Rate Constant [*Symbol*] [*Chemistry*]
**K**............... Relay (CET)
**K**............... Required Rate of Return [*Finance*]
**K**............... Smoke [*Weather charts*]
**K**............... Solar Absorption Index (CET)
**K**............... Strikeout [*Baseball symbol*]
**K**............... Tanker [*Designation for all US military aircraft*]
**K**............... Telemetering [*JETDS*]
**k**............... Thermal Conductivity [*Symbol*] [*IUPAC*]
**K**............... Thousand (ADA)
**K**............... United Kingdom [*IYRU nationality code*] (IYR)
**K**............... Wetboek van Koophandel [*Commercial Code*] [*Dutch*] (ILCA)
**K1**............... Kayak, Single Person (ADA)
**K2**............... Kayak, Two Person (ADA)
**K2**............... Mount Godwin-Austen [*Initialism denotes that mountain is second highest (to Everest) in the Karakoram range in the Himalayas*] [*Initialism also used as brand name of skiing equipment*]
**K-3**............... Kummer, Kneser, and Kodaira [*Surfaces*] [*Mathematics*]
**K4**............... Kayak, Four Person (ADA)
**K9**............... Canine [*K9 Corps - Army Dogs*] [*World War II*]
**9K**............... Kuwait [*Aircraft nationality and registration mark*] (FAAC)
**K25**............... Oak Ridge Uranium Separation Plant [*Code designation*] (DEN)
**3K's**............... Kingsley, Kinsella, and Keeney [*Prominent citizens of Brooklyn; all three died within a year of each other, 1884-1885*]
**K (Cars)**..... Designation for certain Chrysler front-wheel-drive cars [*Aries, Reliant*]
**K (Day)**...... Day set for strike or assault by a carrier's aircraft; corresponds to D-Day [*Navy*]
**KA**............... Alaska International Industries, Inc. [*ICAO designator*] (FAAC)
**KA**............... Alkair [*Denmark*] [*ICAO designator*] (ICDA)
**Ka**............... Auroral Absorption Index (CET)
**KA**............... Australia [*IYRU nationality code*] (IYR)
**KA**............... Concrete Arch [*Bridges*]
**KA**............... Eha-Kibbuts ha-Artsi (BJA)
**KA**............... HMS King Alfred [*British military*] (DMA)
**KA**............... Kainic Acid [*Biochemistry*]
**KA**............... Kamov [*USSR*] [*ICAO aircraft manufacturer identifier*] (ICAO)
**KA**............... Kansas Music Review [*A publication*]
**Ka**............... Kaolinite [*A mineral*]
**Ka**............... Karolus de Tocco [*Flourished, 13th century*] [*Authority cited in pre-1607 legal work*] (DSA)
**KA**............... Kathode [*Cathode*] (AAG)
**KA**............... Keren Ami (BJA)
**KA**............... Ketoacidosis [*Medicine*]
**K/A**............... Ketogenic to Anti-Ketogenic [*Ratio*] [*In diets*]
**KA**............... Keyed Alike [*Locks*] (ADA)
**ka**............... Killed in Action
**kA**............... Kiloampere
**KA**............... King of Arms
**KA**............... King-Armstrong Unit [*Clinical chemistry*]
**KA**............... Knight of St. Andrew [*Obsolete*] [*Russia*]
**K/A**............... Knights of the Altar (EA)
**KA**............... Know-All [*Australian*] [*Slang*] (DSUE)
**KA**............... Korean Affairs [*A publication*]
**K-A**............... Kuhlmann-Anderson Intelligence Tests [*Education*]
**KA**............... Kultura [*A publication*]
**KA**............... Kulturarbeit [*A publication*]
**KA**............... Kunstmuseets Arsskrift [*A publication*]
**KA**............... Kuwait Airways Corp.
**KA**............... Kypriakes Aerogrammes [*Cyprus Airlines*]
**KA**............... Kyrkohistorisk Arsskrift [*A publication*]
**KA**............... Start-of-Message Signal in Morse Telegraphy [*Aviation code*] (FAAC)
**Ka A**............... Kansas Appeals Reports [*A publication*] (DLA)
**kaa**............... Karakalpak [*MARC language code*] [*Library of Congress*] (LCCP)
**KAA**............... Karratha [*Australia*] [*Seismograph station code, US Geological Survey*] [*Closed*] (SEIS)
**KAA**............... Kasama [*Zambia*] [*Airport symbol*] (OAG)
**KAA**............... Keep-Alive Anode
**KAAA**........ Kingman, AZ [*AM radio station call letters*]
**KAAB**........ Batesville, AR [*AM radio station call letters*]
**KAAK**........ Great Falls, MT [*FM radio station call letters*]
**KAAL**........ Austin, MN [*Television station call letters*]
**KAAM**........ Dallas, TX [*AM radio station call letters*]
**KAAN**........ Bethany, MO [*AM radio station call letters*]
**KAAN-FM**... Bethany, MO [*FM radio station call letters*]
**KAAO**........ Kabul [*Afghanistan*] [*Seismograph station code, US Geological Survey*] (SEIS)
**KAAP**........ Kansas Army Ammunition Plant (AABC)
**KAAQ**........ Alliance, NE [*FM radio station call letters*]
**KAAR**........ Medical Lake, WA [*FM radio station call letters*]
**KAAS-TV**... Salina, KS [*Television station call letters*]
**KAAT**........ Oakhurst, CA [*FM radio station call letters*]
**KAAY**........ Little Rock, AR [*AM radio station call letters*]
**KAb**........... Abilene Free Public Library, Abilene, KS [*Library symbol*] [*Library of Congress*] (LCLS)
**KAB**........... Kabansk [*USSR*] [*Seismograph station code, US Geological Survey*] (SEIS)
**KAB**........... Kaneb Services, Inc. [*NYSE symbol*] (SPSG)
**KAB**........... Kariba Dam [*Zimbabwe*] [*Airport symbol*] (OAG)
**KAB**........... Katholieke Arbeidersbeweging [*Netherlands*]
**KAB**........... Keep America Beautiful (EA)
**Kabard Balkar Gos Univ Sb Nauchn Rab Aspir**... Kabardino-Balkarskii Gosudarstvennyi Universitet. Sbornik Nauchnykh Rabot Aspirantov [*A publication*]
**Kabardino-Balkarsk Gos Univ Ucen Zap**... Kabardino-Balkarskii Gosudarstvennyi Universitet. Ucenyi Zapiski [*A publication*]
**KABB**......... San Antonio, TX [*Television station call letters*]
**KABC**......... Kaufman Assessment Battery for Children
**KABC**......... Los Angeles, CA [*AM radio station call letters*]
**KABC-TV**... Los Angeles, CA [*Television station call letters*]
**KAbE**......... Dwight D. Eisenhower Library, Abilene, KS [*Library symbol*] [*Library of Congress*] (LCLS)
**Kabel Tekh**... Kabel'naya Tekhnika [*A publication*]
**KABF**......... Little Rock, AR [*FM radio station call letters*]
**K Abg G**..... Kommunalabgabengesetz [*A publication*]
**K d Abg Sten Ber**... Verhandlungen. Kammer der Abgeordneten des Bayerischen Landtags. Stenographische Berichte [*A publication*]
**KABI**......... Abilene, KS [*AM radio station call letters*]
**KABI**......... Abilene/Municipal [*Texas*] [*ICAO location identifier*] (ICLI)
**KABIR**........ Kapitalist Birokrat [*Capitalist Bureaucrat*] [*Term for foreigner*] [*Indonesia*]
**KABK-FM**... Augusta, AR [*FM radio station call letters*]
**KABL**......... Oakland, CA [*AM radio station call letters*]
**KABL-FM**... San Francisco, CA [*FM radio station call letters*]
**KABN**......... Long Island, AK [*AM radio station call letters*]
**KABQ**......... Albuquerque/International [*New Mexico*] [*ICAO location identifier*] (ICLI)
**KABQ**......... Albuquerque, NM [*AM radio station call letters*]
**KABR**......... Alamo Community, NM [*AM radio station call letters*]
**Kab Seb**...... Kabar Sebarang. Sulating Maphilindo [*A publication*]
**Kabul Univ Fac Agric Res Note**... Kabul University. Faculty of Agriculture. Research Notes [*A publication*]
**Kabul Univ Fac Agric Tech Bull**... Kabul University. Faculty of Agriculture. Technical Bulletin [*A publication*]
**KABX-FM**... Merced, CA [*FM radio station call letters*]
**KABY-TV**... Aberdeen, SD [*Television station call letters*]
**kac**............... Kachin [*MARC language code*] [*Library of Congress*] (LCCP)
**KAC**........... Kaman Aircraft Corporation (MCD)
**KAC**........... Kameshli [*Syria*] [*Airport symbol*] (OAG)
**KAC**........... Kapper [*A publication*]
**KAC**........... Kinetics and Catalysis
**KAC**........... Komatsu America Corporation
**KAC**........... Korean American Coalition (EA)
**KAC**........... Kuwait Airways Corporation (MENA)
**KACA**......... Prosser, WA [*FM radio station call letters*]
**K Acad Belg Jaarb**... Koninklijk Academie van Belgie. Jaarboek [*A publication*]
**KACB-TV**... San Angelo, TX [*Television station call letters*]
**KACC**......... Alvin, TX [*FM radio station call letters*]
**KACC**......... Kaiser Aluminum & Chemical Corporation (MCD)
**KACC**......... Korean-American Chamber of Commerce [*Later, AAACC*]
**KACE**......... Inglewood, CA [*FM radio station call letters*]
**KACF**......... Korean-American Cultural Foundation (EA)
**KACH**......... Preston, ID [*AM radio station call letters*]
**KACH-FM**... Peston, ID [*FM radio station call letters*]
**KACI**......... The Dalles, OR [*AM radio station call letters*]
**KACIA**....... Korea-American Commerce and Industry Association [*Later, KS*]
**KACI-FM**... The Dalles, OR [*FM radio station call letters*]
**KACJ**......... Greenwood, AR [*AM radio station call letters*]
**KACK**......... Nantucket [*Massachusetts*] [*ICAO location identifier*] (ICLI)
**KACO**......... Bellville, TX [*AM radio station call letters*]
**KACT**......... Andrews, TX [*AM radio station call letters*]
**KACT**......... Waco/Waco Municipal [*Texas*] [*ICAO location identifier*] (ICLI)
**KACT-FM**... Andrews, TX [*FM radio station call letters*]
**KACU**......... Abilene, TX [*FM radio station call letters*]
**KACV-FM**... Amarillo, TX [*FM radio station call letters*]
**KACV-TV**... Amarillo, TX [*Television station call letters*]
**KACY**......... Atlantic City/Atlantic City [*New Jersey*] [*ICAO location identifier*] (ICLI)
**KACY**......... Payette, ID [*AM radio station call letters*]
**KAD**........... Kadena Air Base, Ryuku Islands (NASA)
**KAD**........... Kadrey Energy [*Vancouver Stock Exchange symbol*]
**KAD**........... Kaduna [*Nigeria*] [*Airport symbol*] (OAG)
**KAD**........... Karad [*India*] [*Seismograph station code, US Geological Survey*] (SEIS)
**KAD**........... Keyboard and Display [*Data processing*]
**KADA**......... Ada, OK [*AM radio station call letters*]
**KADA-FM**... Ada, OK [*FM radio station call letters*]

**Kadel R** ...... Kadelpian Review [*A publication*]
**KaDeWe** .... Kaufhaus des Westens [*Department Store of the West*] [*Germany*]
**KADF** ........ Kuwait Air Defense Force (MCD)
**KADI** ......... Republic, MO [*FM radio station call letters*]
**KADM** ....... Ardmore [*Oklahoma*] [*ICAO location identifier*] (ICLI)
**KADN** ........ Lafayette, LA [*Television station call letters*]
**KADQ** ........ Rexburg, ID [*FM radio station call letters*]
**KADR** ........ Elkader, IA [*AM radio station call letters*]
**Kadry Selsk Khoz** ... Kadry Sel'sko Khoziaistva [*A publication*]
**KADS** ........ Elk City, OK [*AM radio station call letters*]
**KADS** ........ Korea Air Defense System (CINC)
**KADU** ........ Kenya African Democratic Union [*Political party*] (PPW)
**KADV** ........ Modesto, CA [*FM radio station call letters*]
**KADW** ....... Camp Springs/Andrews Air Force Base [*Maryland*] [*ICAO location identifier*] (ICLI)
**KADY-TV** ... Oxnard, CA [*Television station call letters*]
**KAE** ........... Kaena [*Hawaii*] [*Seismograph station code, US Geological Survey*] (SEIS)
**KAE** ........... Kake [*Alaska*] [*Airport symbol*] (OAG)
**KAE** ........... Knitting Arts Expo (TSPED)
**KAEF** ......... Arcata, CA [*Television station call letters*]
**Kaelte-Klima-Prakt** ... Kaelte-Klima-Praktiker [*A publication*]
**Kaelte Klimatech** ... Kaelte und Klimatechnik [*A publication*]
**Kaeltetech-Klim** ... Kaeltetechnik-Klimatisierung [*A publication*]
**KAER** ........ Sacramento, CA [*FM radio station call letters*]
**KAET** ......... Phoenix, AZ [*Television station call letters*]
**KAEX** ........ Alexandria/England Air Force Base [*Louisiana*] [*ICAO location identifier*] (ICLI)
**KAEZ** ......... Gilmer, TX [*FM radio station call letters*]
**KAF** ........... Karato [*Papua New Guinea*] [*Airport symbol*] (OAG)
**KAF** ........... Kenya Air Force
**KAF** ........... Kleinasiatische Forschungen [*A publication*]
**KAFB** ......... Keesler Air Force Base [*Mississippi*]
**KAFB** ......... Kirtland Air Force Base [*New Mexico*]
**KAFC** ......... Kenny Antcliff Fan Club (EA)
**KAFF** ......... Flagstaff, AZ [*AM radio station call letters*]
**KAFF-FM** ... Flagstaff, AZ [*FM radio station call letters*]
**KAFFR** ...... Kaffaria [*South Africa*] (ROG)
**KAFH** ......... Ku-Band Antenna Feed Horn
**KAFM** ........ Red Lodge, MT [*FM radio station call letters*]
**KAFO** ........ Knee-Ankle-Foot Orthosis [*Medicine*]
**KAFPAC** ... Catalogus Faunae Poloniae [*A publication*]
**KAFT** ......... Fayetteville, AR [*Television station call letters*]
**KAFX** ......... Diboll, TX [*AM radio station call letters*]
**KAFX-FM** ... Diboll, TX [*FM radio station call letters*]
**KAFY** ......... Bakersfield, CA [*AM radio station call letters*]
**KAG** ........... Cryptographic Aid, General Publication (CET)
**KAG** ........... Kagoshima [*Japan*] [*Seismograph station code, US Geological Survey*] (SEIS)
**KAG** ........... Kagoshima Space Center [*Japan*]
**KAG** ........... Kelvin Astatic Galvanometer [*Electronics*]
**KAGB** ........ Honolulu, HI [*FM radio station call letters*]
**KAGC** ........ Bryan, TX [*AM radio station call letters*]
**KAGE** ........ Winona, MN [*AM radio station call letters*]
**KAGE-FM** ... Winona, MN [*FM radio station call letters*]
**KAGG** ........ Madisonville, TX [*FM radio station call letters*]
**KAGH** ........ Crossett, AR [*AM radio station call letters*]
**KAGH-FM** ... Crossett, AR [*FM radio station call letters*]
**KAGI** ......... Grants Pass, OR [*AM radio station call letters*]
**KAGI** ......... Kesatuan Aksi Guru Indonesia [*Action Front of Indonesian Teachers*]
**Kag Kog** ..... Kagaku Kogaku [*A publication*]
**KAGL** ........ San Bernardino, CA [*Television station call letters*]
**KAGN** ........ Abilene, TX [*FM radio station call letters*]
**KAGO** ........ Klamath Falls, OR [*AM radio station call letters*]
**KagoBH** ..... Kagoshima Daigaku Bunka Hokoku [*Cultural Science Reports. Kagoshima University*] [*A publication*]
**KAGO-FM** ... Klamath Falls, OR [*FM radio station call letters*]
**KAGR** ........ Ventura, CA [*FM radio station call letters*]
**KAGU** ........ Spokane, WA [*FM radio station call letters*]
**KAGY** ........ Port Sulphur, LA [*AM radio station call letters*]
**KAH** ........... Keilschrifttexte aus Assur Historischen Inhalts [*A publication*] (BJA)
**KAHI** ......... Auburn, CA [*AM radio station call letters*]
**KAHI** ......... Keilschrifttexte aus Assur Historischen Inhalts [*A publication*] (BJA)
**KAHM** ....... Prescott, AZ [*FM radio station call letters*]
**KAHR** ........ Poplar Bluff, MO [*FM radio station call letters*]
**KAHRP** ..... Knob-Associated Histidine-Rich Protein [*Cytology*]
**KAHSLC** ... Knoxville Area Health Science Consortium [*Library network*]
**KAHU** ........ Hilo, HI [*AM radio station call letters*]
**KAI** ........... Kaieteur [*Guyana*] [*Airport symbol*] (OAG)
**KAI** ........... Kaimata [*New Zealand*] [*Seismograph station code, US Geological Survey*] (SEIS)
**KAI** ........... Kanaanaeische und Aramaeische Inschriften [*A publication*] (BJA)
**KAI** ........... Kazan Aviation Institute
**KAI** ........... Keep America Independent [*Defunct*] (EA)
**KAI** ........... Korean Affairs Institute (EA)
**KAIB** ......... Kaibab Industries [*NASDAQ symbol*] (NQ)
**KAIC** ......... Komatsu America Industries Corporation
**KAID** ......... Boise, ID [*Television station call letters*]
**KAIG** ......... Kearfott Acceleration Integrating Gyroscope
**KAIGBZ** .... Japanese Journal of Nuclear Medicine [*A publication*]
**KAII-TV** .... Wailuku, HI [*Television station call letters*]
**KAIL** .......... Fresno, CA [*Television station call letters*]
**KAIM** ........ Honolulu, HI [*AM radio station call letters*]
**KAIM-FM** ... Honolulu, HI [*FM radio station call letters*]
**KAIN** ......... Vidalia, LA [*AM radio station call letters*]
**KAIO-FM** ... Russellville, AR [*FM radio station call letters*]
**Kair** ........... Kairos. Zeitschrift fuer Religionswissenschaft und Theologie [*A publication*]
**KAIS** ......... Korean Air Intelligence System (MCD)
**Kais Akad d Wiss Denksch Philos-Hist Kl** ... Kaiserliche Akademie der Wissenschaften in Wien. Philosophisch-Historische Klasse. Denkschriften [*A publication*]
**Kais Akad d Wissensch Sitzungsb Philos-Hist Klasse** ... Kaiserliche Akademie der Wissenschaften in Wien. Philosophisch-Historische Klasse. Sitzungsberichte [*A publication*]
**Kais-Deutsch Archaol Inst Jahrb** ... Kaiserlich-Deutsches Archaeologisches Institut. Jahrbuch [*A publication*]
**Kaiser Fdn Med Bull** ... Kaiser Foundation Medical Bulletin [*A publication*]
**Kaiser Found Med Bull** ... Kaiser Foundation Medical Bulletin [*A publication*]
**Kaiser Found Med Bull Abstr Issue** ... Kaiser Foundation Medical Bulletin. Abstract Issue [*A publication*]
**KAIST** ....... Korea Advanced Institute of Science and Technology [*Seoul*] [*Information service or system*] (IID)
**KAIT-TV** ... Jonesboro, AR [*Television station call letters*]
**KAIZAN** .... Acta Anatomica Nipponica [*A publication*]
**KAJ** ............ Kajaani [*Finland*] [*Airport symbol*] (OAG)
**KAJ** ............ Kashiwara [*Japan*] [*Seismograph station code, US Geological Survey*] (SEIS)
**KAJ** ............ Keilschrifttexte aus Assur Juridischen Inhalts [*A publication*] (BJA)
**KAJA** ......... San Antonio, TX [*FM radio station call letters*]
**KAJD** ......... Juneau, AK [*AM radio station call letters*]
**Kaj Ekon Mal** ... Kajian Ekonomi Malaysia [*A publication*]
**KAJH** ......... Lake Arthur, LA [*FM radio station call letters*]
**KAJI** .......... Keilschrifttexte aus Assur Juridischen Inhalts [*A publication*] (BJA)
**Kajian Vet** ... Kajian Veterinaire [*A publication*]
**KAJJ** ......... Greenwood, AR [*FM radio station call letters*]
**KAJKA** ...... Kagaku Kojo [*A publication*]
**KAJN-FM** ... Crowley, LA [*FM radio station call letters*]
**KAJO** ......... Grants Pass, OR [*AM radio station call letters*]
**Kaju Shikenjo Hokoku Bull Fruit Tree Res Stn Ser A Yatabe** ... Kaju Shikenjo Hokoku. Bulletin of the Fruit Tree Research Station. Series A. Yatabe [*A publication*]
**KAJX** ......... Aspen, CO [*FM radio station call letters*]
**KAK** ........... Kakioka [*Japan*] [*Seismograph station code, US Geological Survey*] (SEIS)
**KAK** ........... Kakioka [*Japan*] [*Geomagnetic observatory code*]
**KAK** ........... Key-Auto-Key [*Data processing*]
**KAK** ........... Kungliga Automobil Klubben
**Kakao Zuck** ... Kakao und Zucker [*A publication*]
**Kakatiya J Eng Stud** ... Kakatiya Journal of English Studies [*A publication*]
**KAKC** ........ Tulsa, OK [*AM radio station call letters*]
**KAKEA** ...... Kakuyugo Kenkyu [*A publication*]
**KAKE-TV** ... Wichita, KS [*Television station call letters*]
**KAKI** ......... Benton, AR [*FM radio station call letters*]
**KAKM** ....... Anchorage, AK [*Television station call letters*]
**KAKN** ........ Naknek, AK [*FM radio station call letters*]
**KAKOA** ..... Kagaku Kogyo [*A publication*]
**KAKR** ........ Akron [*Ohio*] [*ICAO location identifier*] (ICLI)
**KAKS** ......... Canyon, TX [*AM radio station call letters*]
**KAKS-FM** ... Canyon, TX [*FM radio station call letters*]
**Kakteen Orchideen Rundsch** ... Kakteen und Orchideen Rundschau [*A publication*]
**Kakteen Sukkulenten** ... Kakteen und Andere Sukkulenten [*A publication*]
**Kakuriken Kenkyu Hokoku Suppl** ... Kakuriken Kenkyu Hokoku. Supplement [*Japan*] [*A publication*]
**K Ak Wiss Mat-Nat Cl Szb** ... Kaiserliche Akademie der Wissenschaften. Mathematische-Naturwissenschaftliche Klasse. Sitzungsberichte [*A publication*]
**KAKYA** ..... Kagaku (Kyoto) [*A publication*]
**KAKZA** ...... Kagaku Keizai [*A publication*]
**KAL** ........... Caltech Data Ltd. [*Vancouver Stock Exchange symbol*]
**KAL** ........... Kalamein [*Trademark*]
**KAL** ........... Kalendae [*The Kalends*] [*First day of the ancient Roman month*]
**KAL** ........... Kalgoorlie [*Australia*] (DSUE)
**KAL** ........... Kalium [*Potassium*] [*Pharmacy*]
**Kal** ............. Kallah (BJA)
**KAL** ........... Kalocsa [*Hungary*] [*Seismograph station code, US Geological Survey*] [*Closed*] (SEIS)
**KAL** ........... Kaltag [*Alaska*] [*Airport symbol*] (OAG)
**KAL** ........... Korean Air Lines, Inc.
**KAL** ........... Kyushu American Literature [*Fukuoka, Japan*] [*A publication*]
**KALA** ........ Davenport, IA [*FM radio station call letters*]
**Kalamazoo Med** ... Kalamazoo Medicine [*A publication*]

**KALB**......... Albany/Albany [*New York*] [*ICAO location identifier*] (ICLI)
**KALB**......... Alexandria, LA [*AM radio station call letters*]
**KALB-TV**.. Alexandria, LA [*Television station call letters*]
**KALC**......... Krypton Absorption in Liquid Carbon Dioxide [*Nuclear energy*] (NRCH)
**KALD**........ Kalamein [*Trademark*] Door
**KALDAS**... Kidsgrove ALGOL [*Algorithmic Language*] Digital Analogue Simulation [*Data processing*] [*British*]
**KALE**......... Richland, WA [*AM radio station call letters*]
**KALF**......... Red Bluff, CA [*FM radio station call letters*]
**KALI**.......... Alice/International [*Texas*] [*ICAO location identifier*] (ICLI)
**KALI**.......... San Gabriel, CA [*AM radio station call letters*]
**Kalinin Gos Ped Inst Ucen Zap** ... Kalininskii Gosudarstvennyi Pedagogiceskii Institut Imeni M. I. Kalinina Ucenye Zapiski [*A publication*]
**Kaliningrad Gos Ped Inst Ucen Zap** ... Kaliningradskii Gosudarstvennyi Pedagogiceskii Institut Ucenye Zapiski [*A publication*]
**Kaliningrad Gos Univ Differencial'naja Geom Mnogoobraz Figur** ... Kaliningradskogo Gosudarstvennogo Universitet Differencial'naja Geometrija Mnogoobrazii Figur [*A publication*]
**Kaliningrad Gos Univ Trudy Kaf Teoret i Eksper Fiz** ... Kaliningradskii Gosudarstvennyi Universitet Trudy Kafedry Teoreticeskoi i Eksperimental'noi Fiziki [*A publication*]
**Kaliningrad Gos Univ Ucen Zap** ... Kaliningradskii Gosudarstvennyi Universitet Ucenye Zapiski [*A publication*]
**Kal Inser**.... Kaleidoscope Insert [*A publication*]
**KALL**......... Salt Lake City, UT [*AM radio station call letters*]
**KALM**........ Thayer, MO [*AM radio station call letters*]
**Kal Mad**...... Kaleidoscope-Madison [*A publication*]
**Kal Mil**....... Kaleidoscope-Milwaukee [*A publication*]
**KALO**........ Port Arthur, TX [*AM radio station call letters*]
**KALP**......... Alpine, TX [*FM radio station call letters*]
**KAL PPT**... Kali Praeparatum [*Prepared Kali*] [*Carbonate of potash*] [*Pharmacy*] (ROG)
**KALQ-FM** ... Alamosa, CO [*FM radio station call letters*]
**KALR**......... Hot Springs, AR [*FM radio station call letters*]
**KalR**.......... Kallah Rabbati (BJA)
**KALS**......... Kalispell, MT [*FM radio station call letters*]
**Kal Schweiz Imkers** ... Kalender des Schweizer Imkers [*A publication*]
**Kal Sver Bergh** ... Kalender foer Sveriges Berghandtering [*A publication*]
**KALT**......... Atlanta, TX [*AM radio station call letters*]
**KALU**........ Langston, OK [*FM radio station call letters*]
**KALV**......... Alva, OK [*AM radio station call letters*]
**KALV**......... Kalvar Corp. [*NASDAQ symbol*] (NQ)
**KALW**........ San Francisco, CA [*FM radio station call letters*]
**KALX**......... Berkeley, CA [*FM radio station call letters*]
**KALY**......... Albuquerque, NM [*AM radio station call letters*]
**KAM**.......... Benedictine College, South Campus, Atchison, KS [*Library symbol*] [*Library of Congress*] (LCLS)
**kam**............ Kamba [*MARC language code*] [*Library of Congress*] (LCCP)
**Kam**............ Kamena [*A publication*]
**Kam**............ Kames' Dictionary of Decisions, Scotch Court of Session [*A publication*] (DLA)
**Kam**............ Kames' Remarkable Decisions, Scotch Court of Session [*2 vols.*] [*1716-52*] [*A publication*] (DLA)
**KAM**.......... Kameyama [*Japan*] [*Seismograph station code, US Geological Survey*] (SEIS)
**KAM**.......... Keep-Alive Memory [*Data processing*]
**KAM**.......... Kehillath Anshe Mayriv (BJA)
**KAM**.......... Kenya African Movement
**KAM**.......... Kinematic Analysis Method
**KAM**.......... Knudsen Absolute Manometer [*Physics*]
**KAM**.......... Kolmogorov-Arnold-Moser [*Statistical mechanics*]
**KAMA**....... Amarillo/Amarillo Air Terminal [*Texas*] [*ICAO location identifier*] (ICLI)
**KAMA**....... El Paso, TX [*AM radio station call letters*]
**KAMB**....... Merced, CA [*FM radio station call letters*]
**KAMC**....... Komatsu America Manufacturing Corporation [*Chattanooga, TN*]
**KAMC**....... Lubbock, TX [*Television station call letters*]
**KAMD**....... Camden, AR [*AM radio station call letters*]
**Kam Eluc** ... Kames' Elucidation of the Laws of Scotland [*A publication*] (DLA)
**Kam Eq**...... Kames' Principles of Equity [*A publication*] (DLA)
**Kames**........ Kames' Dictionary of Decisions, Scotch Court of Session [*A publication*] (DLA)
**Kames**........ Kames' Remarkable Decisions, Scotch Court of Session [*2 vols.*] [*1716-52*] [*A publication*] (DLA)
**Kames Dec** ... Kames' Dictionary of Decisions, Scotch Court of Session [*A publication*] (DLA)
**Kames Dict Dec** ... Kames' Dictionary of Decisions, Scotch Court of Session [*A publication*] (DLA)
**Kames Elucid** ... Kames' Elucidation of the Laws of Scotland [*A publication*] (DLA)
**Kames Eq**... Kames' Principles of Equity [*A publication*] (DLA)
**Kames Rem** ... Kames' Remarkable Decisions, Scotch Court of Session [*2 vols.*] [*1716-52*] [*A publication*] (DLA)
**Kames Rem Dec** ... Kames' Remarkable Decisions [*Scotland*] [*A publication*] (DLA)
**Kames Sel Dec** ... Kames' Select Decisions [*Scotland*] [*A publication*] (DLA)
**KAME-TV** ... Reno, NV [*Television station call letters*]
**KAMG**....... Victoria, TX [*AM radio station call letters*]
**KAMI**........ Cozad, NE [*AM radio station call letters*]
**KAMI-FM** ... Cozad, NE [*FM radio station call letters*]
**Kaminshu**... Kakyu Saibansho Minji Saibanreishu [*A publication*]
**KAMJ**........ Phoenix, AZ [*AM radio station call letters*]
**KAMJD**..... Kawasaki Medical Journal [*A publication*]
**KAMJ-FM** ... Phoenix, AZ [*FM radio station call letters*]
**KAML**....... Kenedy-Karnes, TX [*AM radio station call letters*]
**KAML-FM** ... Gillette, WY [*FM radio station call letters*]
**Kam L Tr**... Kames' Historical Law Tracts [*Scotland*] [*A publication*] (DLA)
**KAMN**....... Kaman Corp. [*NASDAQ symbol*] (NQ)
**KAMO**....... Rogers, AR [*AM radio station call letters*]
**KAMO-FM** ... Rogers, AR [*FM radio station call letters*]
**KAMP**....... El Centro, CA [*AM radio station call letters*]
**Kamp's Paed Tb** ... Kamp's Paedagogische Taschenbuecher [*A publication*]
**KAMQ**....... Carlsbad, NM [*AM radio station call letters*]
**Kam Rem**... Kames' Remarkable Decisions, Scotch Court of Session [*2 vols.*] [*1716-52*] [*A publication*] (DLA)
**KAMR-TV** ... Amarillo, TX [*Television station call letters*]
**KAMS**........ Korea Ammunition Management System (MCD)
**KAMS**........ Mammoth Spring, AR [*FM radio station call letters*]
**Kam Sel**...... Kames' Select Decisions [*Scotland*] [*A publication*] (DLA)
**Kam Sel Dec** ... Kames' Select Decisions [*Scotland*] [*A publication*] (DLA)
**KAMU-FM** ... College Station, TX [*FM radio station call letters*]
**KAMU-TV** ... College Station, TX [*Television station call letters*]
**KAMX**....... Albuquerque, NM [*AM radio station call letters*]
**KAMY**....... Lubbock, TX [*FM radio station call letters*]
**KAMZ**....... El Paso, TX [*FM radio station call letters*]
**KAN**........... Kanazawa [*Japan*] [*Seismograph station code, US Geological Survey*] (SEIS)
**kan**............. Kannada [*MARC language code*] [*Library of Congress*] (LCCP)
**KAN**........... Kano [*Nigeria*] [*Airport symbol*] (OAG)
**KAN**........... Kansas
**KAN**........... Kansas Power & Light Co. [*NYSE symbol*] (SPSG)
**Kan**............. Kansas Reports [*A publication*]
**Kan**............. Kansas Supreme Court Reports [*A publication*] (DLA)
**Kan**............. Kantorei [*Record label*] [*Germany*]
**KAN**........... Knight of St. Alexander Nevsky [*Obsolete*] [*Russian*]
**KAN**........... Kriegsausruestungsnachweisung [*Table of Basic Allowances*] [*German military - World War II*]
**KANA**........ Anaconda, MT [*AM radio station call letters*]
**Kan Acad Sci Trans** ... Kansas Academy of Science. Transactions [*A publication*]
**Kan Admin Regs** ... Kansas Administration Regulations [*A publication*] (DLA)
**Kanagawa Prefect Mus Bull** ... Kanagawa Prefectural Museum. Bulletin [*A publication*]
**Kan Ag Exp** ... Kansas State Agricultural College. Agricultural Experiment Station. Publications [*A publication*]
**Kan Ann**..... Vernon's Kansas Statutes, Annotated [*A publication*] (DLA)
**Kan App**..... Kansas Appeals Reports [*A publication*] (DLA)
**Kan App**..... Kansas Court of Appeals Reports [*A publication*]
**Kan App 2d** ... Kansas Court of Appeals Reports. Second Series [*A publication*]
**Kanazawa Univ Res Inst Tuberc Annu Rep** ... Kanazawa University. Research Institute of Tuberculosis. Annual Report [*A publication*]
**KanazHB**... Kanazawa Daigaku Hobungakubu Ronshu. Bungakuhen [*Studies and Essays. Faculty of Law and Literature. Kanazawa University. Literature*] [*A publication*]
**KanazJK**.... Kanazawa Daigaku Kyoyobu Ronshu. Jinbunkagakuhen [*Studies in Humanities. College of Liberal Arts. Kanazawa University*] [*A publication*]
**Kan BAJ**.... Kansas Bar Association. Journal [*A publication*]
**Kan B Ass'n J** ... Kansas Bar Association. Journal [*A publication*]
**Kan City L Rep** ... Kansas City Law Reporter [*A publication*] (DLA)
**Kan City L Rev** ... Kansas City Law Review [*A publication*] (DLA)
**Kan Civ Proc Code Ann (Vernon)** ... Vernon's Kansas Statutes, Annotated, Code of Civil Procedure [*A publication*]
**Kan Civ Pro Stat Ann** ... Vernon's Kansas Statutes, Annotated, Code of Civil Procedure [*A publication*] (DLA)
**Kan Civ Pro Stat Ann (Vernon)** ... Vernon's Kansas Statutes, Annotated, Code of Civil Procedure [*A publication*] (DLA)
**Kan CL & IWC** ... Kansas Commission of Labor and Industry Workmen's Compensation Department Reports [*A publication*] (DLA)
**Kan CL Rep** ... Kansas City Law Reporter [*A publication*] (DLA)
**Kan Corp Code Ann (Vernon)** ... Vernon's Kansas Statutes, Annotated, Corporation Code [*A publication*]
**Kan Crim Code Ann (Vernon)** ... Vernon's Kansas Statutes, Annotated, Criminal Code [*A publication*]
**Kan Crim Code & Code of Crim Proc** ... Criminal Code and Code of Criminal Procedure [*Kansas*] [*A publication*] (DLA)
**Kan Crim Code & Code of Crim Proc (Vernon)** ... Vernon's Kansas Statutes, Annotated, Criminal Code and Code of Criminal Procedure [*A publication*] (DLA)
**Kan Crim Proc Code Ann (Vernon)** ... Vernon's Kansas Statutes, Annotated, Code of Criminal Procedure [*A publication*]
**Kan Ct App** ... Kansas Appellate Reports [*A publication*] (DLA)
**KAND**........ Corsicana, TX [*AM radio station call letters*]

**KAND-FM** ... Corsicana, TX [*FM radio station call letters*]
**KANDIDATS** ... Kansas Digital Data System
**Kan Dig**...... Hatcher's Kansas Digest [*A publication*] (DLA)
**KANE**........ New Iberia, LA [*AM radio station call letters*]
**KANGA**..... Kangaroo (DSUE)
**Kan Hist Quar** ... Kansas Historical Quarterly [*A publication*]
**KANI**........ Wharton, TX [*AM radio station call letters*]
**Kan Jud Council Bull** ... Kansas Judicial Council. Bulletin [*A publication*]
**Kan Law**..... Kansas Lawyer [*A publication*] (DLA)
**Kan Law Rev** ... Kansas Law Review [*A publication*]
**Kan Lib Bull** ... Kansas Library Bulletin [*A publication*]
**Kan Libr Bull** ... Kansas Library Bulletin [*A publication*]
**Kan LJ**....... Kansas Law Journal [*A publication*] (DLA)
**Kan L Rev**.. Kansas Law Review [*A publication*]
**KANN**........ Roy, UT [*AM radio station call letters*]
**KANO**........ Brooklyn Park, MN [*AM radio station call letters*]
**Kano S**........ Kano Studies [*Nigeria*] [*A publication*]
**Kan Prob Code Ann (Vernon)** ... Vernon's Kansas Statutes, Annotated, Probate Code [*A publication*]
**KanQ**.......... Kansas Quarterly [*A publication*]
**KANr**......... Kanamycin Resistant [*Genetics*]
**Kan Reg**..... Kansas Register [*A publication*]
**KANS**........ Kansas (AFM)
**Kans**.......... Kansas Reports [*A publication*] (DLA)
**KANS**........ Larned, KS [*AM radio station call letters*]
**Kans Acad Sci Trans** ... Kansas Academy of Science. Transactions [*A publication*]
**Kans Ac Sc Tr** ... Kansas Academy of Science. Transactions [*A publication*]
**Kans Agric Exp Stn Bienn Rep Dir** ... Kansas Agricultural Experiment Station. Biennial Report of the Director [*A publication*]
**Kans Agric Exp Stn Bull** ... Kansas Agricultural Experiment Station. Bulletin [*A publication*]
**Kans Agric Exp Stn Circ** ... Kansas Agricultural Experiment Station. Circular [*A publication*]
**Kans Agric Exp Stn Res Publ** ... Kansas Agricultural Experiment Station. Research Publication [*A publication*]
**Kans Agric Exp Stn Tech Bull** ... Kansas Agricultural Experiment Station. Technical Bulletin [*A publication*]
**Kans Agr Situation** ... Kansas Agricultural Situation. Kansas State University of Agriculture and Applied Science. Extension Service [*A publication*]
**Kansai Soc NA Jnl** ... Kansai Society of Naval Architects. Journal [*A publication*]
**Kansallis-Osake-Pankki Econ R** ... Kansallis-Osake-Pankki. Economic Review [*A publication*]
**Kansantal Aikakausk** ... Kansantaloudellinen Aikakauskirja [*A publication*]
**Kans App** ... Kansas Appeals Reports [*A publication*] (DLA)
**Kansas Acad Sci Trans** ... Kansas Academy of Science. Transactions [*A publication*]
**Kansas Bus Tchr** ... Kansas Business Teacher [*A publication*]
**Kansas City L Rev** ... University of Kansas City. Law Review [*A publication*]
**Kansas City Rv Sc** ... Kansas City Review of Science and Industry [*A publication*]
**Kansas Geol Survey Map** ... Kansas Geological Survey. Map [*A publication*]
**Kansas J Sociol** ... Kansas Journal of Sociology [*A publication*]
**Kansas Lib Bul** ... Kansas Library Bulletin [*A publication*]
**Kansas LJ** ... Kansas Law Journal [*A publication*] (DLA)
**Kansas R**.... Kansas City Review [*A publication*]
**Kansas R**.... Kansas Reports [*A publication*] (DLA)
**Kansas Univ Mus Nat History Misc Pub** ... Kansas University. Museum of Natural History. Miscellaneous Publication [*A publication*]
**Kansas Univ Paleont Contr** ... Kansas University. Paleontological Contributions [*A publication*]
**Kansas Water Resources Board Bull** ... Kansas State Water Resources Board. Bulletin [*A publication*]
**Kans BA**..... Kansas City Bar Journal [*A publication*] (DLA)
**Kan SCC**.... Kansas State Corporation Commission Reports [*A publication*] (DLA)
**Kans Ci Med J** ... Kansas City Medical Journal [*A publication*]
**Kans Cy Med J** ... Kansas City Medical Journal [*A publication*]
**Kans Eng Exp Stn Bull** ... Kansas Engineering Experiment Station. Bulletin [*A publication*]
**Kans Eng Exp Stn (Manhattan Kans) Spec Rep** ... Kansas. Engineering Experiment Station (Manhattan, Kansas). Special Report [*A publication*]
**Kans Environ Health Serv Bull** ... Kansas Environmental Health Services Bulletin [*A publication*]
**Kan Sess Laws** ... Session Laws of Kansas [*A publication*] (DLA)
**Kans Geol Surv Bull** ... Kansas Geological Survey. Bulletin [*A publication*]
**Kans Geol Surv Ser Spat Anal** ... Kansas Geological Survey. Series on Spatial Analysis [*A publication*]
**Kans Ground Water Basic-Data Release** ... Kansas Ground Water. Basic-Data Release [*A publication*]
**Kans Hist Q** ... Kansas Historical Quarterly [*A publication*]
**Kans Med**.. Kansas Medicine [*A publication*]
**Kans Nurse** ... Kansas Nurse [*A publication*]
**Kans R**....... Kansas Reports [*A publication*] (DLA)
**Kans Sch Nat** ... Kansas School Naturalist [*A publication*]
**Kans State Board Agric Div Entomol Act** ... Kansas State Board of Agriculture. Division of Entomology. Activities [*A publication*]
**Kans State Geol Surv Bull** ... Kansas State Geological Survey. Bulletin [*A publication*]
**Kans State Geol Surv Comput Contrib** ... Kansas State Geological Survey. Computer Contribution [*A publication*]
**Kans State Geol Surv Computer Contrib** ... Kansas State Geological Survey. Computer Contribution [*A publication*]
**Kans State Geol Surv Spec Distrib Publ** ... Kansas State Geological Survey. Special Distribution Publication [*A publication*]
**Kans State Geol Surv Spec Distribution Publication** ... Kansas State Geological Survey. Special Distribution Publication [*A publication*]
**Kans State Hortic Soc Trans** ... Kansas State Horticultural Society. Transactions [*A publication*]
**Kans State Univ Bull Kans Eng Exp Sta Bull** ... Kansas State University Bulletin. Kansas Engineering Experiment Station. Bulletin [*A publication*]
**Kans State Univ Eng Exp Stn Bull** ... Kansas State University. Engineering Experiment Station. Bulletin [*A publication*]
**Kans State Univ Eng Exp Stn Repr** ... Kansas State University. Engineering Experiment Station. Reprint [*A publication*]
**Kans State Univ Inst Syst Des Optim Rep** ... Kansas State University. Institute for Systems Design and Optimization. Report [*A publication*]
**Kans St Bd Agr Tr An Rp Bien Rp** ... Kansas State Board of Agriculture. Transactions. Annual Report. Biennial Report [*A publication*]
**Kans Stockman** ... Kansas Stockman [*A publication*]
**Kan Stat**..... Kansas Statutes [*A publication*] (DLA)
**Kan Stat Ann** ... Kansas Statutes, Annotated [*A publication*] (DLA)
**Kan State Hist Soc Coll** ... Kansas State Historical Society. Collections [*A publication*]
**Kan State Univ Inst Syst Des Optim Rep** ... Kansas State University. Institute for Systems Design and Optimization. Report [*A publication*]
**Kans Teach** ... Kansas Teacher and Western School Journal [*A publication*]
**Kan St LJ**... Kansas State Law Journal [*A publication*] (DLA)
**Kan Subject Ann Vernon's** ... Vernon's Kansas Statutes, Annotated [*A publication*] (DLA)
**Kans Univ B Ed** ... Kansas University. Bulletin of Education [*A publication*]
**Kans Univ Mus Nat History Pub Paleont Contr Sci Bull** ... Kansas University. Museum of Natural History. Publications. Paleontological Contributions. Science Bulletin [*A publication*]
**Kans Univ Paleontol Contrib Pap** ... Kansas University. Paleontology Contribution Paper [*A publication*]
**Kans Univ Q** ... Kansas University. Quarterly [*A publication*]
**Kans Univ Sc B** ... Kansas University. Science Bulletin [*A publication*]
**Kans Univ Sci Bull** ... Kansas University. Science Bulletin [*A publication*]
**Kans Water Res Board Bull** ... Kansas Water Resources Board. Bulletin [*A publication*]
**Kans Wheat Qual Kans State Board Agr** ... Kansas Wheat Quality. Kansas State Board of Agriculture [*Kansas Wheat Commission*] [*A publication*]
**Kanto J Orthop Traumatol** ... Kanto Journal of Orthopedics and Traumatology [*Japan*] [*A publication*]
**Kant-Stud**.. Kant-Studien [*A publication*]
**KANU**........ Kenya African National Union [*Political party*] (PPW)
**KANU**........ Lawrence, KS [*FM radio station call letters*]
**Kan UCC Ann (Vernon)** ... Vernon's Kansas Statutes, Annotated, Uniform Commercial Code [*A publication*] (DLA)
**Kan U Lawy** ... Kansas University Lawyer [*A publication*] (DLA)
**Kan Univ Kan Studies Ed** ... Kansas University. Kansas Studies in Education [*A publication*]
**Kan Univ Lawy** ... Kansas University Lawyer [*A publication*] (DLA)
**KANW**....... Albuquerque, NM [*FM radio station call letters*]
**KANZ**........ Garden City, KS [*FM radio station call letters*]
**KAnz**......... Kunstgeschichtliche Anzeigen [*A publication*]
**KANZUS**... Korea, Australia, New Zealand, and the United States (CINC)
**KAO**.......... Kappa Alpha Order
**KAO**.......... Kinesthetic Anharmonic Oscillator [*Facetious term for a swing*]
**KAO**.......... Knights of Aquarius Order (EAIO)
**KAO**.......... Kuiper Airborne Observatory [*NASA*]
**KAO**.......... Kuusamo [*Finland*] [*Airport symbol*] (OAG)
**KAOI**......... Wailuku, HI [*FM radio station call letters*]
**KAOK**........ Lake Charles, LA [*AM radio station call letters*]
**KAOL**........ Carrollton, MO [*AM radio station call letters*]
**KAOR**........ Vermillion, SD [*FM radio station call letters*]
**KAOS**........ Fictitious organization of enemy agents in TV series "Get Smart." Although designed to look like an acronym, the letters in KAOS do not actually represent words.
**KAOS**........ Killer as an Organized Sport [*Campus game*]
**KAOS**........ Olympia, WA [*FM radio station call letters*]
**KAP**.......... Kampioen [*A publication*]
**KAP**.......... Kaphearst Resources [*Vancouver Stock Exchange symbol*]
**KAP**.......... Kinematical Analysis Program
**KAP**.......... Knowledge, Attitudes, and Practice [*Sociology*]
**KAPA**........ Potassium Aminopropylamide [*Organic chemistry*]
**KAPA**........ Raymond, WA [*AM radio station call letters*]
**Kapala Cruise Rep** ... Kapala Cruise Report [*A publication*]
**KAPB**........ Marksville, LA [*AM radio station call letters*]
**KAPB-FM** ... Marksville, LA [*FM radio station call letters*]
**KAPE**........ Cape Girardeau, MO [*AM radio station call letters*]
**KAPE**........ Keeping the Army in the Public Eye [*British military*] (DMA)

**KAPH** ........ Kingman, KS [*FM radio station call letters*]
**Kapital** ....... Kapitalistate [*A publication*]
**Kapitalis** .... Kapitalistate [*A publication*]
**KAPL** ......... Kaplan Industries, Inc. [*NASDAQ symbol*] (NQ)
**KAPL** ......... Kennedy Approved Parts List [*NASA*] (KSC)
**KAPL** ......... Knolls Atomic Power Laboratory [*Schenectady, NY*] [*Department of Energy*]
**K-APN** ....... KSC [*Kennedy Space Center*] Automated Payloads Notice [*NASA*] (NASA)
**KAPO** ........ Kameradschaftpolizei (BJA)
**KAPP** ......... Knolls Atomic Power Plant
**KAPP** ......... Yakima, WA [*Television station call letters*]
**KAPPI** ....... Kesatuan Aksi Pemuda Peladjar Indonesia
**K-APPS** ..... KSC [*Kennedy Space Center*] Automated Payloads Project Specification [*NASA*] (NASA)
**KAPR** ......... Douglas, AZ [*AM radio station call letters*]
**KAPS** ......... Mount Vernon, WA [*AM radio station call letters*]
**KAPSE** ...... Kernel APSE [*ADA Program Support Environment*] [*Data processing*]
**KAPT** ......... Luling, TX [*FM radio station call letters*]
**KAPY** ......... Port Angeles, WA [*AM radio station call letters*]
**KAPZ** ......... Bald Knob, AR [*AM radio station call letters*]
**KAQQ** ........ Spokane, WA [*AM radio station call letters*]
**KAQU** ........ Huntington, TX [*FM radio station call letters*]
**Kar** ............ Indian Law Reports, Karachi Series [*A publication*] (DLA)
**KAR** ........... Kamarang [*Guyana*] [*Airport symbol*] (OAG)
**KAR** ........... Kansas Administrative Regulations [*A publication*]
**K Ar** .......... Kansatieteellinen Arkisto [*A publication*]
**KAR** ........... Kap Resources [*Vancouver Stock Exchange symbol*]
**KAR** ........... Karabiner [*Carbine*] [*German military - World War II*]
**KAR** ........... Karachi [*Pakistan*] [*Seismograph station code, US Geological Survey*] (SEIS)
**kar** ............. Karen [*MARC language code*] [*Library of Congress*] (LCCP)
**Kar** ............. Karolus de Tocco [*Flourished, 13th century*] [*Authority cited in pre-1607 legal work*] (DSA)
**KAR** ........... Keilschrifttexte aus Assur Religioesen Inhalts [*A publication*] (BJA)
**KAR** ........... King's African Rifles [*Military unit*] [*British*]
**Kar** ............. Pakistan Law Reports, Karachi Series [*A publication*] (DLA)
**KAR** ........... URCARCO, Inc. [*NYSE symbol*] (SPSG)
**KARA** ........ Santa Clara, CA [*FM radio station call letters*]
**KARAC** ...... Kustoms and Rodders Association of Canada
**Karachi Math Assoc Riazi Souvenir** ... Riazi Souvenir. Karachi Mathematics Association [*A publication*]
**Karachi Univ J Sci** ... Karachi University. Journal of Science [*A publication*]
**KARB** ........ Price, UT [*FM radio station call letters*]
**KARD** ........ West Monroe, LA [*Television station call letters*]
**Kardiol Pol** ... Kardiologia Polska [*A publication*]
**Kardiol Pol Tow Internistow Pol Sek Kardiol** ... Kardiologia Polska. Towarzystwo Internistow Polskich. Sekeja Kardiologiczna [*A publication*]
**KARE** ........ Care Enterprises [*NASDAQ symbol*] (NQ)
**KARE** ........ Minneapolis, MN [*Television station call letters*]
**KARF** ......... Washington [*District of Columbia*] [*ICAO location identifier*] (ICLI)
**Karger Biobehav Med Ser** ... Karger Biobehavioral Medicine Series [*A publication*]
**Karger Contin Educ Ser** ... Karger Continuing Education Series [*A publication*]
**KARI** .......... Blaine, WA [*AM radio station call letters*]
**KARI** .......... Keilschrifttexte aus Assur Religioesen Inhalts [*A publication*] (BJA)
**Kariba Stud** ... Kariba Studies [*A publication*]
**KARJA** ...... Karjantuote [*A publication*]
**KARKA** ..... Karada No Kagaku [*A publication*]
**KARK-TV** ... Little Rock, AR [*Television station call letters*]
**KARL** ......... Karlsruhe Architectural Language [*Data processing*] (CSR)
**KARL** ......... Tracy, MN [*FM radio station call letters*]
**Karl-August-Forster-Lect** ... Karl-August-Forster-Lectures [*A publication*]
**Kar LJ** ........ Karachi Law Journal [*A publication*]
**Karlov Laz Cas** ... Karlovarsky Lazensky Casopis [*A publication*]
**Karlsruher Beitr Entwicklungsphysiol Pflanz** ... Karlsruher Beitraege zur Entwicklungsphysiologie der Pflanzen [*A publication*]
**Karlsruher Geogr Hefte** ... Karlsruher Geographische Hefte [*A publication*]
**KARM** ....... Visalia, CA [*FM radio station call letters*]
**KARN** ........ Little Rock, AR [*AM radio station call letters*]
**Karnataka Med J** ... Karnataka Medical Journal [*A publication*]
**Karnatak Univ J Sci** ... Karnatak University. Journal of Science [*A publication*]
**KARO** ........ Columbia, MO [*FM radio station call letters*]
**Karolinska Symp Res Methods Reprod Endocrinol** ... Karolinska Symposia on Research Methods in Reproductive Endocrinology [*A publication*]
**Karpato Balk Geol Assots Mater Kom Mineral Geokhim** ... Karpato-Balkanskaya Geologicheskaya Assotsiatsiya. Materialy Komissii Mineralogii i Geokhimii [*A publication*]
**KARPEN** ... Karyawan Pegawai Negeri [*Indonesia*]
**KARQ** ........ Ashdown, AR [*FM radio station call letters*]
**KARR** ........ Kirkland, WA [*AM radio station call letters*]
**KARRAA** ... Kenya. Department of Agriculture. Annual Report [*A publication*]
**KARS** ......... Belen, NM [*AM radio station call letters*]
**KARS** ......... Kansas Applied Remote Sensing Program [*University of Kansas*] [*Research center*] (RCD)
**KARS** ......... Kennedy Athletic Recreation and Social [*NASA*] (KSC)
**KARS-FM** ... Belen, NM [*FM radio station call letters*]
**KART** ........ Jerome, ID [*AM radio station call letters*]
**KART** ........ Watertown/International [*New York*] [*ICAO location identifier*] (ICLI)
**Kartogr Let** ... Kartograficeskaja Letopis [*A publication*]
**Kartogr Nachr** ... Kartographische Nachrichten [*A publication*]
**Kartogr Nachr (Stuttg)** ... Kartographische Nachrichten (Stuttgart) [*A publication*]
**Kartogr Pr** ... Kartograficky Prehled [*A publication*]
**Kartonagen Papierwaren Ztg** ... Kartonagen und Papierwaren-Zeitung [*A publication*]
**KARV** ........ Russellville, AR [*AM radio station call letters*]
**KARY** ........ Prosser, WA [*AM radio station call letters*]
**KARY-FM** ... Grandview, WA [*FM radio station call letters*]
**KARZ** ........ Burney, CA [*FM radio station call letters*]
**KAS** ........... Benedictine College, North Campus, Atchison, KS [*Library symbol*] [*Library of Congress*] (LCLS)
**KAS** ........... Kansas [*Obsolete*] (ROG)
**Kas** ............. Kansas Reports [*A publication*] (DLA)
**kas** ............. Kashmiri [*MARC language code*] [*Library of Congress*] (LCCP)
**KAS** ........... Kaskada Resources Ltd. [*Vancouver Stock Exchange symbol*]
**KAS** ........... Kastamonu [*Turkey*] [*Seismograph station code, US Geological Survey*] (SEIS)
**KAS** ........... Katz Adjustment Scales [*Psychology*]
**KAS** ........... Knowledge Access System [*Interface*]
**KAS** ........... Knowledge Acquisition System
**KAS** ........... Konrad Adenauer Stiftung [*Political party*] [*Federal Republic of Germany*]
**KAS** ........... Kroeber Anthropological Society (EA)
**KAS** ........... Kulanka Afka Somalyed
**KASA** ......... Phoenix, AZ [*AM radio station call letters*]
**KASB** ......... Bellevue, WA [*FM radio station call letters*]
**KASC** ......... Knowledge Availability Systems Center [*University of Pittsburgh*]
**KASE** ......... Austin, TX [*FM radio station call letters*]
**KASEA** ....... Kagaku To Seibutsu [*A publication*]
**Kaseigaku Zasshi J Home Econ Jap** ... Kaseigaku Zasshi. Journal of Home Economics of Japan [*A publication*]
**Kasetsart J** ... Kasetsart Journal [*A publication*]
**Kasetsart Univ Fish Res Bull** ... Kasetsart University. Fishery Research Bulletin [*A publication*]
**KASF** ......... Alamosa, CO [*FM radio station call letters*]
**KASH** ........ Knowledge, Attitude, Skills, Habits [*Formula*] [*LIMRA*]
**KASH** ........ Modesto, CA [*AM radio station call letters*]
**KASH-FM** ... Anchorage, AK [*FM radio station call letters*]
**Kas His S** ... Kansas State Historical Society. Collections [*A publication*]
**Kashmir LJ** ... Kashmir Law Journal [*India*] [*A publication*] (DLA)
**Kashmir Sci** ... Kashmir Science [*A publication*]
**Kashmir Univ Fac Sci Res J** ... Kashmir University. Faculty of Science. Research Journal [*A publication*]
**KASI** .......... Ames, IA [*AM radio station call letters*]
**KASI** .......... Kesatuan Aksi Sardjana Indonesia [*Action Front of Indonesian Scholars*]
**KASK** ......... Las Cruces, NM [*FM radio station call letters*]
**KASK-TV** .. Las Cruces, NM [*Television station call letters*]
**KASL** ......... Kasler Corp. [*NASDAQ symbol*] (NQ)
**KASL** ......... Kasseler Arbeiten zur Sprache und Literatur. Anglistik-Germanistik-Romanistik [*A publication*]
**KASL** ......... Newcastle, WY [*AM radio station call letters*]
**KASM** ........ Albany, MN [*AM radio station call letters*]
**KASN** ........ Pine Bluff, AR [*Television station call letters*]
**KASO** ........ Minden, LA [*AM radio station call letters*]
**KASO-FM** ... Minden, LA [*FM radio station call letters*]
**KASP** ......... Chamber Ensemble for Free Dance [*Yugoslavia*]
**Kas R** .......... Kansas Reports [*A publication*] (DLA)
**Kasr El-Aini J Surg** ... Kasr El-Aini Journal of Surgery [*A publication*]
**KASRP** ...... Kaiser Steel Corp. Pfd [*NASDAQ symbol*] (NQ)
**Kass** ........... Kassinin [*Biochemistry*]
**Kassenzahnarzt Colloq Med Dent** ... Kassenzahnarzt. Colloquium Med Dent [*A publication*]
**KAST** ......... Astoria, OR [*AM radio station call letters*]
**KAST** ......... Kalman Automatic Sequential TMA [*Military*] (CAAL)
**KAST-FM** ... Astoria, OR [*FM radio station call letters*]
**KASU** ........ Jonesboro, AR [*FM radio station call letters*]
**KAT** ........... Asbury Theological Seminary, Wilmore, KY [*OCLC symbol*] (OCLC)
**KAT** ........... Die Keilinschriften und das Alte Testament [*A publication*] (BJA)
**KAT** ........... Kaitaia [*New Zealand*] [*Airport symbol*] (OAG)
**KAT** ........... Kanamycin Acetyltransferase [*An enzyme*]
**KAT** ........... Kappa Alpha Theta [*Sorority*]
**kat** ............. Katal [*Unit of enzyme activity*]
**Kat** ............. Katholiek [*A publication*]
**KAT** ........... Kizyl-Arvat [*USSR*] [*Seismograph station code, US Geological Survey*] (SEIS)
**KAT** ........... Kommentar zum Alten Testament [*A publication*] (BJA)

**KATA**........ Arcata, CA [*AM radio station call letters*]
**Katal**........ Katallagete [*A publication*]
**Katal Katal**... Kataliz i Katalizatory [*USSR*] [*A publication*]
**Katal Pererab Uglevodorodnogo Syr'ya**... Kataliticheskaya Pererabotka Uglevodorodnogo Syr'ya [*A publication*]
**KATB**........ Anchorage, AK [*FM radio station call letters*]
**Kat Bl**........ Katechetische Blaetter [*A publication*]
**KATC**........ Korean Army Training Center
**KATC**........ Lafayette, LA [*Television station call letters*]
**KATCA**...... Korean-American Technical Cooperation Association
**Katch Pr Law**... Katchenovsky's Prize Law [*2nd ed.*] [*1867*] [*A publication*] (DLA)
**Kat Datamater Nor Berggrunn**... Katalog over Datamateriale for Norges Berggrunn [*A publication*]
**KATE**........ Albert Lea, MN [*AM radio station call letters*]
**KatechBR**... Katechetische Blaetter [*Berlin-Grunewald*] [*A publication*] (BJA)
**KATF**........ Dubuque, IA [*FM radio station call letters*]
**Kat Fauny Pol**... Katalog Fauny Polski [*A publication*]
**Kath**.......... Katholiek [*A publication*]
**Kath Cult Tijdsch**... Katholiek Cultureel Tijdschrift [*A publication*]
**KATH-FM**... Douglas, WY [*FM radio station call letters*]
**KathM**....... Die Katholischen Missionen (BJA)
**Kath MJS**... Katholisches Missionsjahrbuch der Schweiz [*A publication*]
**KATI**......... Casper, WY [*AM radio station call letters*]
**Katilolehti**... Katilolehti. Tidskrift foer Barnmorskor [*A publication*]
**KATJ**........ George, CA [*FM radio station call letters*]
**KATK**........ Carlsbad, NM [*AM radio station call letters*]
**KATK-FM**... Carlsbad, NM [*FM radio station call letters*]
**KATL**........ Atlanta/The William B. Hartsfield Atlanta International [*Georgia*] [*ICAO location identifier*] (ICLI)
**KATL**........ Miles City, MT [*AM radio station call letters*]
**Katl Prevrashch Uglevodorodov**... Kataliticheskie Prevrascheniya Uglevodorodov [*A publication*]
**KATM**....... Katmai National Monument
**KATM-FM**... Pueblo, CO [*FM radio station call letters*]
**KATN**........ Fairbanks, AK [*Television station call letters*]
**KATO**........ Kahtou: a Publication of the Native Communications Society of British Columbia [*A publication*]
**KATO**........ Safford, AZ [*AM radio station call letters*]
**KATQ**....... Plentywood, MT [*AM radio station call letters*]
**KATQ-FM**... Plentywood, MT [*FM radio station call letters*]
**KATS**........ Kennedy Space Center Avionics Test Set [*NASA*] (NASA)
**KATS**........ Yakima, WA [*FM radio station call letters*]
**KatShing**.... Katorikku Shingaku [*Catholic Theology*] [*Tokyo*] [*A publication*] (BJA)
**KATSl**....... Kommentar zum Alten Testament [*E. Sellin*] [*A publication*] (BJA)
**KATT-FM**... Oklahoma City, OK [*FM radio station call letters*]
**KATU**........ Portland, OR [*Television station call letters*]
**KATUSA**... Korean Augmentation to the United States Army
**KATV**........ Little Rock, AR [*Television station call letters*]
**KATW**....... Lewiston, ID [*FM radio station call letters*]
**KATX**........ Plainview, TX [*FM radio station call letters*]
**KATY**........ San Luis Obispo, CA [*AM radio station call letters*]
**KATY-FM**... Idyllwild, CA [*FM radio station call letters*]
**KATZ**........ St. Louis, MO [*AM radio station call letters*]
**KATZ-FM**... Alton, IL [*FM radio station call letters*]
**kau**........... Kanuri [*MARC language code*] [*Library of Congress*] (LCCP)
**KAU**.......... Kaohsiung [*Takao*] [*Republic of China*] [*Seismograph station code, US Geological Survey*] (SEIS)
**KAU**.......... Kenya African Union [*1944*] [*Political party*] (PPW)
**KAU**.......... Keystation Adapter Unit [*Data processing*]
**KAU**.......... Kilo Accounting Units (NASA)
**KAU**.......... King-Armstrong Unit [*Clinical chemistry*]
**KAUB-FM**... Auburn, NE [*FM radio station call letters*]
**Kauch i Rezina**... Kauchuk i Rezina [*A publication*]
**Kauf Mack**... Kaufmann's Edition of Mackeldey's Civil Law [*A publication*] (DLA)
**Kaufm Mackeld Civ Law**... Kaufmann's Edition of Mackeldey's Civil Law [*A publication*] (DLA)
**KAUG**........ Augusta [*Maine*] [*ICAO location identifier*] (ICLI)
**KAUI**........ Kekaha, HI [*FM radio station call letters*]
**KAUM**....... Colorado City, TX [*FM radio station call letters*]
**Kauno Politech Inst Darb**... Kauno Politechnikos Instituto Darbai [*A publication*]
**Kauno Valstybinio Med Inst Darb**... Kauno Valstybinio Medicinos Instituto Darbai [*A publication*]
**KAUP**........ Kauppalehti [*A publication*]
**KAUR**........ Sioux Falls, SD [*FM radio station call letters*]
**KAUS**........ Austin, MN [*AM radio station call letters*]
**KAUS**........ Austin/Robert Mueller Municipal [*Texas*] [*ICAO location identifier*] (ICLI)
**KAUS-FM**... Austin, MN [*FM radio station call letters*]
**KAUT**........ Oklahoma City, OK [*Television station call letters*]
**Kautch Gummi Kunstst Asbest**... Kautschuk und Gummi. Kunststoffe. Asbest [*A publication*]
**Kaut Gum Ku**... Kautschuk und Gummi. Kunststoffe [*A publication*]
**Kaut Gummi**... Kautschuk und Gummi. Kunststoffe [*A publication*]
**Kaut u Gummi Kunst**... Kautschuk und Gummi. Kunststoffe [*A publication*]
**Kautsch Gummi Kunstst**... Kautschuk und Gummi. Kunststoffe [*A publication*]
**Kautsch Gummi Kunstst Plastomere Elastomere Duromere**... Kautschuk und Gummi. Kunststoffe. Plastomere, Elastomere, Duromere [*A publication*]
**KAUZ-TV**... Wichita Falls, TX [*Television station call letters*]
**KAV**.......... Cambourne Resources [*Vancouver Stock Exchange symbol*]
**KAV**.......... Kavieng [*New Ireland*] [*Seismograph station code, US Geological Survey*] [*Closed*] (SEIS)
**KAV**.......... Keilschrifttexte aus Assur Verschiedenen Inhalts [*A publication*] (BJA)
**kav**............ Koste, Assuransie, Vrag [*Cost, Insurance, Freight*] [*Afrikaans*] [*Business term*]
**KAVA**........ Burney, CA [*AM radio station call letters*]
**KAVC**........ Rosamond, CA [*FM radio station call letters*]
**KAVI**......... Keilschrifttexte aus Assur Verschiedenen Inhalts [*A publication*] (BJA)
**KAVI**......... Rocky Ford, CO [*AM radio station call letters*]
**KAVI-FM**... Rocky Ford, CO [*FM radio station call letters*]
**Kavk Etnogr Sb**... Kavkazskij Etnograficeskij Sbornik [*A publication*]
**KAVL**........ Lancaster, CA [*AM radio station call letters*]
**KAVS**........ Mojave, CA [*FM radio station call letters*]
**KAVT-FM**... Austin, MN [*FM radio station call letters*]
**KAVU-TV**... Victoria, TX [*Television station call letters*]
**KAVV**........ Benson, AZ [*FM radio station call letters*]
**KAW**.......... Kawthaung [*Burma*] [*Airport symbol*] (OAG)
**Kawasaki Med J**... Kawasaki Medical Journal [*A publication*]
**Kawasaki Rozai Tech Rep**... Kawasaki Rozai Technical Report [*A publication*]
**Kawasaki Steelmaking Tech Rep**... Kawasaki Steelmaking Technical Report [*Japan*] [*A publication*]
**Kawasaki Steel Tech Bull**... Kawasaki Steel Technical Bulletin [*A publication*]
**Kawasaki Steel Tech Rep**... Kawasaki Steel Technical Report [*Japan*] [*A publication*]
**Kawasaki Tech Rev**... Kawasaki Technical Review [*Japan*] [*A publication*]
**KAWB**....... Brainerd, MN [*Television station call letters*]
**KAWC**....... Yuma, AZ [*AM radio station call letters*]
**KAWC-FM**... Yuma, AZ [*FM radio station call letters*]
**KAWE**....... Bemidji, MN [*Television station call letters*]
**KAWJ**........ Korrespondenzblatt des Vereins zur Gruendung und Erhaltung der Akademie fuer die Wissenschaft des Judentums [*A publication*] (BJA)
**KAWL**....... York, NE [*AM radio station call letters*]
**KAWL-FM**... York, NE [*FM radio station call letters*]
**KAWN**....... Carswell [*Texas*] [*ICAO location identifier*] (ICLI)
**KAWS**........ Hemphill, TX [*AM radio station call letters*]
**KAWV**....... Oracle, AZ [*FM radio station call letters*]
**KAWW**...... Heber Springs, AR [*AM radio station call letters*]
**KAWW-FM**... Heber Springs, AR [*FM radio station call letters*]
**KAWZ**....... Twin Falls, ID [*FM radio station call letters*]
**KAX**.......... Kalbarri [*Australia*] [*Airport symbol*] (OAG)
**KAXE**........ Grand Rapids, MN [*FM radio station call letters*]
**KAXL**........ Green Acres, CA [*FM radio station call letters*]
**KAY**.......... Katlanovo [*Yugoslavia*] [*Seismograph station code, US Geological Survey*] (SEIS)
**Kay**............ Kay's English Vice-Chancellors' Reports [*69 English Reprint*] [*A publication*] (DLA)
**KAY**.......... Wakaya [*Fiji*] [*Airport symbol*] [*Obsolete*] (OAG)
**KAYC**........ Beaumont, TX [*AM radio station call letters*]
**KAYD**........ Beaumont, TX [*FM radio station call letters*]
**KAYE-FM**... Tonkawa, OK [*FM radio station call letters*]
**Kay (Eng)**... Kay's English Vice-Chancellors' Reports [*69 English Reprint*] [*A publication*] (DLA)
**KAYI**......... Muskogee, OK [*FM radio station call letters*]
**Kay & J**...... Kay and Johnson's English Vice-Chancellors' Reports [*69, 70 English Reprint*] [*A publication*] (DLA)
**KAYJ**......... San Angelo, TX [*AM radio station call letters*]
**Kay & J (Eng)**... Kay and Johnson's English Vice-Chancellors' Reports [*69, 70 English Reprint*] [*A publication*] (DLA)
**Kay & John**... Kay and Johnson's English Vice-Chancellors' Reports [*69, 70 English Reprint*] [*A publication*] (DLA)
**Kay & Johns**... Kay and Johnson's English Vice-Chancellors' Reports [*69, 70 English Reprint*] [*A publication*] (DLA)
**KAYL**........ Storm Lake, IA [*AM radio station call letters*]
**KAYL-FM**... Storm Lake, IA [*FM radio station call letters*]
**KAYM**....... Yuma, AZ [*FM radio station call letters*]
**KAYN**....... Nogales, AZ [*FM radio station call letters*]
**KAYO**........ Aberdeen, WA [*AM radio station call letters*]
**KAYO-FM**... Aberdeen, WA [*FM radio station call letters*]
**KAYQ**........ Warsaw, MO [*FM radio station call letters*]
**KAYR**........ Van Buren, AR [*AM radio station call letters*]
**KAYS**........ Hays, KS [*AM radio station call letters*]
**KAYSEE**... Kansas City [*Missouri*] [*Slang*]
**Kay Ship**.... Kay. Shipmasters, and Seamen [*2nd ed.*] [*1894*] [*A publication*] (DLA)
**KAYU-TV**... Spokane, WA [*Television station call letters*]
**KAYX**........ Richmond, MO [*FM radio station call letters*]
**KAYY**........ Fairbanks, AK [*FM radio station call letters*]
**KAYZ**........ El Dorado, AR [*FM radio station call letters*]

**KAZ** .......... Karuizawa [*Also, KRZ*] [*Japan*] [*Seismograph station code, US Geological Survey*] (SEIS)
**kaz** .......... Kazakh [*MARC language code*] [*Library of Congress*] (LCCP)
**KAZ** .......... Konsument. Test Magazine der Konsumenteninformation [*A publication*]
**KAZA** .......... Gilroy, CA [*AM radio station call letters*]
**Kazah Gos Ped Inst Ucen Zap** ... Kazakhskii Gosudarstvennyi Pedagogiceskii Institut Imeni Abaja Ucenye Zapiski [*A publication*]
**Kazak Ak Habarlary** ... Kazak SSR Gylym Akademijasynyn Habarlary. Izvestija Akademii Nauk Kazachskoj SSR [*A publication*]
**Kazan Gos Univ Ucen Zap** ... Kazanskii Ordena Trudovogo Krasnogo Znameni Gosudarstvennyi Universitet Imeni V. I. Ul'janova-Lenina Ucenye Zapiski [*A publication*]
**Kazan Med Z** ... Kazanskii Meditsinskii Zhurnal [*A publication*]
**Kazan Med Zh** ... Kazanskii Meditsinskii Zhurnal [*A publication*]
**Kazan Med Zhurnal** ... Kazanskii Meditsinskii Zhurnal [*A publication*]
**KAZI** .......... Austin, TX [*FM radio station call letters*]
**KAZM** .......... Sedona, AZ [*AM radio station call letters*]
**KAZN** .......... Pasadena, CA [*AM radio station call letters*]
**Kaz Nauchno-Issled Inst Lesn Khoz Agrolesomelio Tr** ... Kazakhskii Nauchno-Issledovatel'skii Institut Lesnogo Khozyaistva i Agrolesomelioratsii Trudy [*A publication*]
**Kaz Nauchno-Issled Inst Lesn Khoz Tr** ... Kazakhskii Nauchno-Issledovatel'skii Institut Lesnogo Khozyaistva Trudy [*A publication*]
**KAZQ** .......... Albuquerque, NM [*Television station call letters*]
**KazSSR** .......... Kazakh Soviet Socialist Republic
**KAZU** .......... Pacific Grove, CA [*FM radio station call letters*]
**KAZY** .......... Denver, CO [*FM radio station call letters*]
**KAZZ** .......... Deer Park, WA [*FM radio station call letters*]
**KB** .......... Bermuda [*IYRU nationality code*] (IYR)
**KB** .......... Cadabo Gestione Servizi Aeronautici [*Italy*] [*ICAO designator*] (FAAC)
**KB** .......... Cruisair Ltd. [*Kenya*] [*ICAO designator*] (FAAC)
**KB** .......... English Law Reports, King's Bench Division [*1901-52*] [*A publication*] (DLA)
**KB** .......... Kasboek [*Cash Book*] [*Afrikaans*] [*Business term*]
**KB** .......... Kauri-Butanol Value [*Measure of relative solvent power*]
**KB** .......... Keilinschriftliche Bibliothek [*Berlin*] [*A publication*] (BJA)
**KB** .......... Ketone Bodies [*Clinical chemistry*]
**KB** .......... Kew Bulletin [*A publication*]
**KB** .......... Keyboard [*Data processing*]
**KB** .......... Kilo BTU [*British Thermal Unit*]
**kb** .......... Kilobar
**kb** .......... Kilobase
**kb** .......... KiloBIT [*Binary Digit*] [*Data processing*]
**KB** .......... Kilobyte [*$10^3$ bytes*] [*Data processing*]
**KB** .......... Kincheng Banking Corp. [*Hong Kong*]
**KB** .......... King's Bench [*of law courts*] [*British*]
**KB** .......... King's Bishop [*Chess*]
**KB** .......... Kitchen and Bathroom
**KB** .......... Kitchen Biddy [*Female kitchen worker*] [*Restaurant slang*]
**KB** .......... Kite Balloon [*Air Force*]
**KB** .......... Knee Bearing
**KB** .......... Knee Brace [*Technical drawings*]
**KB** .......... Knight Bachelor [*or Knight Companion*] of the Order of the Bath [*British*]
**KB** .......... Knowledgeability Brief (MCD)
**KB** .......... Kommanditbolaget [*Limited Partnership*] [*German*] (ILCA)
**KB** .......... Komunist (Belgrade) [*A publication*]
**KB** .......... Koninklijk Besluit [*Royal Decree*] [*Dutch*] (ILCA)
**KB** .......... Kontrabass [*Double Bass*] [*Music*]
**KB** .......... Korpus Bezpieczenstwa (BJA)
**KB** .......... Korrespondenz-Blatt des Verbandes der Deutschen Juden [*A publication*] (BJA)
**K & B** .......... Kotze and Barber's Transvaal (High Court) Reports [*1885-88*] [*A publication*] (DLA)
**KB** .......... Kredietbrief [*Letter of Credit*] [*Afrikaans*] [*Business term*]
**KB** .......... Kulturbund
**KB** .......... Kulturbund der Deutsche Demokratische Republik [*German League of Culture*] [*German Democratic Republic*] (EY)
**KB** .......... Kulturos Barai [*A publication*]
**KB** .......... Kunstgeschichte in Bildern [*A publication*] (OCD)
**KBA** .......... Barbados [*IYRU nationality code*] (IYR)
**KBA** .......... Kabala [*Sierra Leone*] [*Airport symbol*] (OAG)
**KBA** .......... Kenn Borek Air Ltd. [*Dawson Creek, BC*] [*FAA designator*] (FAAC)
**KBA** .......... Ketobutyraldehyde Dimethyl Acetal [*Biochemistry*]
**KBA** .......... Killed by Air [*Military*]
**KBA** .......... Kleinwort Benson Australian Income Fund, Inc. [*NYSE symbol*] (SPSG)
**KBA** .......... Knight of St. Benedict of Avis
**kba** .......... Kontant by Aflewering [*Cash on Delivery*] [*Afrikaans*] [*Business term*]
**KBA** .......... Korte Berichten voor de Machinebranche en Apparatenbranche [*A publication*]
**KBAA** .......... Kieler Beitraege zur Anglistik und Amerikanistik [*A publication*]
**KBAA** .......... Ortonville, MN [*FM radio station call letters*]
**KBAB** .......... Marysville/Beale Air Force Base [*California*] [*ICAO location identifier*] (ICLI)
**KBAC** .......... Kennedy Booster Assembly Contractor (MCD)
**KBAD** .......... Shreveport/Barksdale Air Force Base [*Louisiana*] [*ICAO location identifier*] (ICLI)
**KBAI** .......... Morro Bay, CA [*AM radio station call letters*]
**KBAK-TV** ... Bakersfield, CA [*Television station call letters*]
**KBAL** .......... Kimball International, Inc. [*NASDAQ symbol*] (NQ)
**KBAL** .......... Kleine Beitraege zum Assyrischen Lexikon [*A publication*]
**KBAL** .......... San Saba, TX [*AM radio station call letters*]
**KBAL-FM** ... San Saba, TX [*FM radio station call letters*]
**K-BALL** .......... Cannibalize (MCD)
**KBAM** .......... Longview, WA [*AM radio station call letters*]
**KBAMA** .......... Kosmicheskaya Biologiya i Aviakosmicheskaya Meditsina [*A publication*]
**KBAR** .......... Burley, ID [*AM radio station call letters*]
**KBAR** .......... Kilobar
**KBART** .......... Kings Bay Army Terminal
**KBAS** .......... Bullhead City, AZ [*AM radio station call letters*]
**KBAT** .......... Midland, TX [*FM radio station call letters*]
**KBAU** .......... Golden Meadow, LA [*FM radio station call letters*]
**KBAY** .......... San Jose, CA [*FM radio station call letters*]
**K-Bayer Ak Wiss Muenchen Mat-Phys Kl Szb Abh** ... Koeniglich-Bayerische Akademie der Wissenschaften zu Muenchen. Mathematisch-Physikalische Klasse. Sitzungsberichte. Abhandlungen [*A publication*]
**KBAZ** .......... Basile, LA [*FM radio station call letters*]
**KBAZ** .......... Kitchen Bazaar, Inc. [*NASDAQ symbol*] (NQ)
**KBB** .......... Baker University, Baldwin City, KS [*Library symbol*] [*Library of Congress*] (LCLS)
**KBB** .......... Kentucky Bench and Bar [*A publication*]
**KBB** .......... King's Bad Bargain [*Undesirable serviceman*] [*Slang*] [*British*] (DSUE)
**KBB** .......... Kitchens, Bedrooms, and Bathrooms Equipment Exhibition [*British*] (ITD)
**KBB** .......... Kulturas Biroja Biletins [*Bulletin. Cultural Bureau of the American Latvian Association in the US*] [*A publication*]
**KBBA** .......... Benton, AR [*AM radio station call letters*]
**KBBB** .......... Borger, TX [*AM radio station call letters*]
**KBBC** .......... Lake Havasu City, AZ [*FM radio station call letters*]
**KBBD** .......... Beaver, UT [*FM radio station call letters*]
**KBBE** .......... McPherson, KS [*FM radio station call letters*]
**KBBF** .......... Santa Rosa, CA [*FM radio station call letters*]
**KBBG** .......... Waterloo, IA [*FM radio station call letters*]
**KBBH** .......... Holbrook, AZ [*FM radio station call letters*]
**KBBI** .......... Homer, AK [*AM radio station call letters*]
**KBBK** .......... Rupert, ID [*AM radio station call letters*]
**KBBL** .......... Big Bear Lake, CA [*Television station call letters*]
**KBBM** .......... Waldport, OR [*AM radio station call letters*]
**KBBN-FM** ... Broken Bow, NE [*FM radio station call letters*]
**KBBO** .......... Yakima, WA [*AM radio station call letters*]
**KBBQ** .......... Santa Barbara, CA [*AM radio station call letters*]
**KBBQ-FM** ... Fort Smith, AR [*FM radio station call letters*]
**KBBR** .......... North Bend, OR [*AM radio station call letters*]
**KBBS** .......... Buffalo, WY [*AM radio station call letters*]
**KBBU** .......... Los Lunas, NM [*FM radio station call letters*]
**KBBV** .......... Big Bear Lake, CA [*AM radio station call letters*]
**KBBW** .......... Waco, TX [*AM radio station call letters*]
**KBBX** .......... Centerville, UT [*AM radio station call letters*]
**KBBY** .......... Ventura, CA [*FM radio station call letters*]
**KBBZ** .......... Kalispell, MT [*FM radio station call letters*]
**KBC** .......... Bellarmine College, Louisville, KY [*OCLC symbol*] (OCLC)
**KBC** .......... Birch Creek [*Alaska*] [*Airport symbol*] (OAG)
**KBC** .......... K-Band Circulator
**KBC** .......... King's Bench Court [*British*]
**KBCA** .......... Keystone Bituminous Coal Association
**KBCB** .......... Bellingham, WA [*Television station call letters*]
**KBCE** .......... Boyce, LA [*FM radio station call letters*]
**KBCH** .......... Lincoln City, OR [*AM radio station call letters*]
**KBCH-FM** ... Kings Beach, CA [*FM radio station call letters*]
**KBCI-TV** ... Boise, ID [*Television station call letters*]
**KBCJ** .......... Koninklijke Belgische Commissie voor Volkskunde, Vlaamse Afdeling Jaarboek [*A publication*]
**KBCL** .......... Shreveport, LA [*AM radio station call letters*]
**KBCN** .......... Fairbanks, AK [*AM radio station call letters*]
**KBCO** .......... Boulder, CO [*AM radio station call letters*]
**KBCO-FM** ... Boulder, CO [*FM radio station call letters*]
**KBCP** .......... Paradise, CA [*Television station call letters*]
**KBCQ** .......... Roswell, NM [*FM radio station call letters*]
**KBCR** .......... Steamboat Springs, CO [*AM radio station call letters*]
**KBCS** .......... Bellevue, WA [*FM radio station call letters*]
**KBCT** .......... Boca Raton [*Florida*] [*ICAO location identifier*] (ICLI)
**KBCU** .......... North Newton, KS [*FM radio station call letters*]
**KBCV** .......... Bentonville, AR [*FM radio station call letters*]
**KBD** .......... Kaschin-Beck Disease [*Medicine*]
**KBD** .......... Keyboard
**KBD** .......... King's Bench Division [*of law courts*] [*British*] (ROG)
**KBD** .......... Thousand Barrels per Day [*Also, TBD*]
**KBDA** .......... Korrespondenzblatt. Gesamtverein der Deutschen Geschichte und Altertumsvereine [*A publication*]
**KBDC** .......... King's Bench Divisional Court [*British*]
**KBDE** .......... Baudette [*Minnesota*] [*ICAO location identifier*] (ICLI)

**KBDF**........ Kleine Beitraege zur Droste-Forschung [*Munster*] [*A publication*]
**KBDG**........ Turlock, CA [*FM radio station call letters*]
**K & B Dig**... Kerford and Box's Victorian Digest [*A publication*] (DLA)
**KBDI-TV**... Broomfield, CO [*Television station call letters*]
**KB Div'l Ct**... King's Bench Divisional Court [*England*] (DLA)
**KBDL**........ Windsor Locks/Bradley International [*Connecticut*] [*ICAO location identifier*] (ICLI)
**KBDY**........ St. Louis, MO [*FM radio station call letters*]
**KBE**........... Bell Island, AK [*Location identifier*] [*FAA*] (FAAL)
**KBE**........... Berea College, Berea, KY [*OCLC symbol*] (OCLC)
**KBE**........... Key British Enterprises [*Dun & Bradstreet Ltd.*] [*Information service or system*] (IID)
**KBE**........... Keyboard Encoder [*Data processing*]
**KBE**........... Keyboard Entry [*Data processing*]
**KBE**........... Knight of the Black Eagle [*Obsolete*] [*Russia*]
**KBE**........... Knight Commander of the [*Order of the*] British Empire
**KBE**........... Korean Business Review [*A publication*]
**KBE**........... Kratka Bulgarska Enciklopedija [*A publication*]
**KBEA**......... Mission, KS [*AM radio station call letters*]
**KBEA J**...... Kentucky Business Education Association. Journal [*A publication*]
**KBEBD**...... Kvartalsskrift. Bergen Bank [*A publication*]
**KBEC**......... Waxahachie, TX [*AM radio station call letters*]
**KBED**........ Bedford/Laurence G. Hanscom Field [*Massachusetts*] [*ICAO location identifier*] (ICLI)
**KBEE-FM**... Modesto, CA [*FM radio station call letters*]
**KBEH**........ Bellevue, WA [*Television station call letters*]
**KBEL**......... Idabel, OK [*AM radio station call letters*]
**K Belg Inst Natuurwet Studiedoc**... Koninklijk Belgisch Instituut voor Natuurwetenschappen. Studiedocumenten [*A publication*]
**K Belg Inst Natuurwet Verh**... Koninklijk Belgisch Instituut voor Natuurwetenschappen. Verhandelingen [*A publication*]
**KBEMD**.... Kultuurpatronen. Bulletin Etnografisch Museum (Delft) [*A publication*]
**KBEM-FM**... Minneapolis, MN [*FM radio station call letters*]
**KBEN**........ Carrizo Springs, TX [*AM radio station call letters*]
**KB (Eng)**.... English Law Reports, King's Bench Division [*1901-52*] [*A publication*] (DLA)
**KBEQ**........ Kansas City, MO [*FM radio station call letters*]
**KBER**........ Spanish Fork, UT [*FM radio station call letters*]
**KBES**......... Ceres, CA [*FM radio station call letters*]
**KBES**......... Knowledge-Based Expert System
**KBET**......... Canyon Country, CA [*AM radio station call letters*]
**KBEV-FM**... Millbank, SD [*FM radio station call letters*]
**KBEW**........ Blue Earth, MN [*AM radio station call letters*]
**KBEZ**......... Tulsa, OK [*FM radio station call letters*]
**KBF**........... K-Band Feed
**KBF**........... Kyburz Flat [*California*] [*Seismograph station code, US Geological Survey*] (SEIS)
**KBFC**......... Forrest City, AR [*FM radio station call letters*]
**KBFC**......... Karen Brooks Fan Club (EA)
**KBFC**......... Kippe Brannon Fan Club (EA)
**KBFD**......... Honolulu, HI [*Television station call letters*]
**KBFI**.......... Bonners Ferry, ID [*AM radio station call letters*]
**KBFI**.......... Seattle Boeing Field/King Country International [*Washington*] [*ICAO location identifier*] (ICLI)
**KBFL**......... Bakersfield/Meadows Field [*California*] [*ICAO location identifier*] (ICLI)
**KBFL**......... Buffalo, MO [*FM radio station call letters*]
**KBFM**........ Edinburg, TX [*FM radio station call letters*]
**KBFM**........ Mobile/Aerospace [*Alabama*] [*ICAO location identifier*] (ICLI)
**KBFN**........ Berkeley, CA [*AM radio station call letters*]
**KBFS**......... Belle Fourche, SD [*AM radio station call letters*]
**KBFT**......... Browning, MT [*FM radio station call letters*]
**KBFW**........ Bellingham-Ferndale, WA [*AM radio station call letters*]
**KBFX**......... Anchorage, AK [*FM radio station call letters*]
**KBGE**........ Bellevue, WA [*Television station call letters*]
**KBGL**......... Kopenhagener Beitraege zur Germanistischen Linguistik [*A publication*]
**KBGN**........ Caldwell, ID [*AM radio station call letters*]
**KBGR**........ Bangor/International [*Maine*] [*ICAO location identifier*] (ICLI)
**KBGS**......... Big Spring/Webb Air Force Base [*Texas*] [*ICAO location identifier*] (ICLI)
**KBGWAB**... Koninklijk Museum voor Midden-Afrika [*Tervuren, Belgie*]. Annalen. Reeks in Octavo. Geologische Wetenschappen [*A publication*]
**KBH**........... Killed by Helicopter [*In reference to the enemy*] [*Vietnam*]
**KBHB**......... Sturgis, SD [*AM radio station call letters*]
**KBHC**......... Nashville, AR [*AM radio station call letters*]
**KBHE-FM**... Rapid City, SD [*FM radio station call letters*]
**KBHE-TV**... Rapid City, SD [*Television station call letters*]
**KBHK-TV**... San Francisco, CA [*Television station call letters*]
**KBHL**......... Osakis, MN [*FM radio station call letters*]
**KBHM**........ Birmingham [*Alabama*] [*ICAO location identifier*] (ICLI)
**KBHP**......... Bemidji, MN [*FM radio station call letters*]
**KBHS**......... Hot Springs, AR [*AM radio station call letters*]
**KBHS-FM**... Hot Springs, AR [*FM radio station call letters*]
**KBHT**......... Crockett, TX [*FM radio station call letters*]
**KBHU-FM**... Spearfish, SD [*FM radio station call letters*]
**KBHW**........ International Falls, MN [*FM radio station call letters*]
**KBI**............ Keyboard Immortals [*Recording label*]
**KBI**............ Kribi [*Cameroon*] [*Airport symbol*] (OAG)
**KBIA**.......... Columbia, MO [*FM radio station call letters*]
**KBIB**.......... Marion, TX [*AM radio station call letters*]
**KBIC**.......... Alice, TX [*FM radio station call letters*]
**KBIF**.......... El Paso/Biggs Air Force Base [*Texas*] [*ICAO location identifier*] (ICLI)
**KBIF**.......... Fresno, CA [*AM radio station call letters*]
**KBIG**.......... Los Angeles, CA [*FM radio station call letters*]
**KBIL**.......... San Angelo, TX [*AM radio station call letters*]
**KBIL-FM**.. San Angelo, TX [*FM radio station call letters*]
**KBIM**......... Keyboard Interface Module (MCD)
**KBIM**......... Kongres Buruh Islam Merdeka [*Free Islamic Trade Union Congress*] [*Indonesia*]
**KBIM**......... Roswell, NM [*AM radio station call letters*]
**KBIM-FM**... Roswell, NM [*FM radio station call letters*]
**KBIM-TV**... Roswell, NM [*Television station call letters*]
**KBIN**.......... Council Bluffs, IA [*Television station call letters*]
**KBIS**.......... Kitchen and Bath Industry Show West (ITD)
**KBIS**.......... Little Rock, AR [*AM radio station call letters*]
**KBIT**.......... Sonora, TX [*Television station call letters*]
**KBIT/S**...... KiloBITS [*Binary Digits*] per Second [*Transmission rate*] [*Data processing*] (TEL)
**KBIU**.......... Lake Charles, LA [*FM radio station call letters*]
**KBIX**.......... Biloxi/Keesler Air Force Base [*Mississippi*] [*ICAO location identifier*] (ICLI)
**KBIX**.......... Muskogee, OK [*AM radio station call letters*]
**KBIX-FM**.. Wagoner, OK [*FM radio station call letters*]
**KBIZ**.......... Ottumwa, IA [*AM radio station call letters*]
**KBJ**............ Kentucky Bar Journal [*A publication*]
**KBJ**............ Kentucky State Bar Journal [*A publication*] (DLA)
**KBJJ**.......... Marshall, MN [*FM radio station call letters*]
**KBJM**......... Lemmon, SD [*AM radio station call letters*]
**KBJR-TV**.. Superior, WI [*Television station call letters*]
**KBJS**.......... Jacksonville, TX [*FM radio station call letters*]
**KBJT**.......... Fordyce, AR [*AM radio station call letters*]
**KBK**........... Korte Berichten voor de Kledingbranche [*A publication*]
**KBKA**......... Kongres Buruh Karata Api [*Congress of Railway Workers*] [*Indonesia*]
**KBKB**......... Fort Madison, IA [*AM radio station call letters*]
**KBKB-FM**... Fort Madison, IA [*FM radio station call letters*]
**KBKE**......... Bakersfield, CA [*FM radio station call letters*]
**KBKL**......... Kritische Berichte zur Kunstgeschichtlichen Literatur [*A publication*]
**KBKOD**..... Steinkohlenbergbauverein Kurznachrichten [*A publication*]
**KBKR**......... Baker, OR [*AM radio station call letters*]
**KBL**............ Hebraeisches und Aramaeisches Lexikon zum Alten Testament [*L. Koehler and W. Baumgarther*] [*A publication*] (BJA)
**KBL**............ Kabul [*Afghanistan*] [*Seismograph station code, US Geological Survey*] (SEIS)
**KBL**............ Kabul [*Afghanistan*] [*Airport symbol*] (OAG)
**KBL**............ Kilusan ng Bangong Lipunan [*New Society Movement*] [*Philippines*] (PD)
**Kbl**............. Korrespondenzblatt. Verein fuer Niederdeutsche Sprachforschung [*A publication*]
**KBL**............ Kraft Black Liquor [*Pulping technology*]
**KBL**............ Kredietbank Luxembourgeoise [*Luxembourg*]
**KBL**............ Lexicon in Veteris Testamenti Libros. Supplementum [*L. Koehler and W. Baumgartner*] [*A publication*] (BJA)
**K Bl BE**...... Koelner Blaetter fuer Berufserziehung [*A publication*]
**KBLE**......... Seattle, WA [*AM radio station call letters*]
**KBLF**......... Red Bluff, CA [*AM radio station call letters*]
**KBLG**......... Billings, MT [*AM radio station call letters*]
**KBLG**......... Kritische Blaetter zur Literatur der Gegenwart [*A publication*]
**KBLH**......... Keel Blade Height [*Botany*]
**KBLI**.......... Bellingham/International [*Washington*] [*ICAO location identifier*] (ICLI)
**KBLI**.......... Blackfoot, ID [*AM radio station call letters*]
**KBLJ**.......... La Junta, CO [*FM radio station call letters*]
**KBLL**.......... Helena, MT [*AM radio station call letters*]
**KBLL**.......... Keel Blade Length [*Botany*]
**KBLL-FM**... Helena, MT [*FM radio station call letters*]
**KBLN**......... Sherman, TX [*AM radio station call letters*]
**KBLP**......... Lindsay, OK [*FM radio station call letters*]
**KBLQ-FM**... Logan, UT [*FM radio station call letters*]
**KBl Ref**...... Kirchenblatt fuer die Reformierte Schweiz [*Basel*] [*A publication*]
**Kbl RS**........ Kirchenblatt fuer die Reformierte Schweiz [*A publication*]
**KBLR-TV**.. Paradise, NV [*Television station call letters*]
**KBLU**......... Yuma, AZ [*AM radio station call letters*]
**KBLV**......... Bellerville/Scott Air Force Base [*Illinois*] [*ICAO location identifier*] (ICLI)
**KBLX-FM**... Berkeley, CA [*FM radio station call letters*]
**KBLZ**......... Lufkin, TX [*AM radio station call letters*]
**KBM**........... Kabwum [*Papua New Guinea*] [*Airport symbol*] (OAG)
**KBM**........... Karissimo Bene Merenti [*To the Most Dear and Well-Deserving*] [*Correspondence*]
**KBM**........... Keyboard Monitor [*Data processing*]
**KBM**........... Knowledge Base Machine [*Data processing*]

**KBM**.......... Korte Berichten voor de Meubelbranche en Stofferingsbranche [*A publication*]
**KBME**........ Bismarck, ND [*Television station call letters*]
**KBMEA**...... Kosmicheskaya Biologiya i Meditsina [*A publication*]
**KBMEDO**... Karger Biobehavioral Medicine Series [*A publication*]
**KBMG**........ Hamilton, MT [*FM radio station call letters*]
**KBMI**.......... Roma, TX [*FM radio station call letters*]
**KBMN**........ Bozeman, MT [*AM radio station call letters*]
**KBMO**........ Benson, MN [*AM radio station call letters*]
**KBMR**........ Bismarck, ND [*AM radio station call letters*]
**KBMS**........ Vancouver, WA [*AM radio station call letters*]
**KBMT**........ Beaumont, TX [*Television station call letters*]
**KBMV**........ Birch Tree, MO [*AM radio station call letters*]
**KBMV-FM**... Birch Tree, MO [*FM radio station call letters*]
**KBMW**....... Breckenridge, MN [*AM radio station call letters*]
**KBMX**........ Eldon, MO [*FM radio station call letters*]
**KBMY**........ Bismarck, ND [*Television station call letters*]
**KBNA**......... El Paso, TX [*AM radio station call letters*]
**KBNA**......... Nashville/Metropolitan [*Tennessee*] [*ICAO location identifier*] (ICLI)
**KBNA-FM**... El Paso, TX [*FM radio station call letters*]
**KBND**......... Bend, OR [*AM radio station call letters*]
**KBNJ**.......... Corpus Christi, TX [*FM radio station call letters*]
**KBNL**.......... Laredo, TX [*FM radio station call letters*]
**KBNN**......... Julian, CA [*FM radio station call letters*]
**KBNO**......... Denver, CO [*AM radio station call letters*]
**KBNP**......... Portland, OR [*AM radio station call letters*]
**KBNR**......... Brownsville, TX [*FM radio station call letters*]
**KBO**........... Berichten uit het Buitenland [*A publication*]
**KBO**........... Keep Buggering On [*Perseverance*] [*Slang*] [*British*] (DSUE)
**KBo**............ Keilschrifttexte aus Boghazkoi [*A publication*] (BJA)
**KBO**........... Kite and Balloon Officer [*Navy*]
**KBO**........... Kommunistischer Bund Oesterreichs [*Communist League of Austria*] [*Political party*] (PPW)
**KBO**........... Organization for the Management and Development of the Kagera River Basin (EA)
**KBOA**......... Kennett, MO [*AM radio station call letters*]
**KBOB**......... West Covina, CA [*FM radio station call letters*]
**KBOE**......... Oskaloosa, IA [*AM radio station call letters*]
**K-Boehm Ges Wiss Mat-Nat Cl Szb**... Koeniglich-Boehmische Gesellschaft der Wissenschaften in Prag. Mathematisch-Naturwissenschaftliche Klasse. Sitzungsberichte [*A publication*]
**KBOF**......... Washington/Bolling Air Force Base [*District of Columbia*] [*ICAO location identifier*] (ICLI)
**KBOI**.......... Boise/Boise Air Terminal [*Idaho*] [*ICAO location identifier*] (ICLI)
**KBOI**.......... Boise, ID [*AM radio station call letters*]
**KBOK**......... Malvern, AR [*AM radio station call letters*]
**KBOK-FM**... Malvern, AR [*FM radio station call letters*]
**KBOL**......... Boulder, CO [*AM radio station call letters*]
**KBOM**........ Los Alamos, NM [*FM radio station call letters*]
**KBON**......... Lake Arrowhead, CA [*FM radio station call letters*]
**KBOO**......... Portland, OR [*FM radio station call letters*]
**KBOP**......... Pleasanton, TX [*AM radio station call letters*]
**KBOP-FM**... Pleasanton, TX [*FM radio station call letters*]
**KBOQ**......... Marina, CA [*FM radio station call letters*]
**KBOS**......... Boston/Logan International [*Massachusetts*] [*ICAO location identifier*] (ICLI)
**KBOS**......... Tulare, CA [*FM radio station call letters*]
**KBOT**......... Kansas City Board of Trade
**KBOV**......... Bishop, CA [*AM radio station call letters*]
**KBOW**........ Butte, MT [*AM radio station call letters*]
**KBOX**......... Lompoc, CA [*FM radio station call letters*]
**KBOY-FM**... Medford, OR [*FM radio station call letters*]
**KBOZ**......... Bozeman, MT [*AM radio station call letters*]
**KBOZ-FM**... Bozeman, MT [*FM radio station call letters*]
**KBP**............ Kainate-Binding Protein [*Biochemistry*]
**KBP**............ Kappa Beta Pi [*Society*]
**KBP**............ Kent-Barlow Publications Ltd. [*Information service or system*] (IID)
**KBP**............ Keyboard Process [*Data processing*]
**KBP**............ Kiev [*USSR*] Borispol Airport [*Airport symbol*] (OAG)
**kbp**............ Kilobase Pairs [*Genetics*]
**KBP**............ Kite Balloon Pilot
**KBP**............ Korte Berichten voor de Verpakkingsbranche [*A publication*]
**KBPI-FM**.. Denver, CO [*FM radio station call letters*]
**KBPK**......... Buena Park, CA [*FM radio station call letters*]
**KBPL**......... Communist League Proletarian Left [*Netherlands*] [*Political party*] (PPW)
**KBP Q**........ Kappa Beta Pi Quarterly [*A publication*]
**KBPR**......... Brainerd, MN [*FM radio station call letters*]
**kbps**........... KiloBITS [*Binary Digits*] per Second [*Transmission rate*] [*Data processing*]
**KBPS**......... Portland, OR [*AM radio station call letters*]
**KBPS-FM**... Portland, OR [*FM radio station call letters*]
**KBPT**......... Beaumont Port-Arthur/Jefferson County [*Texas*] [*ICAO location identifier*] (ICLI)
**KBQC**......... Davenport, IA [*AM radio station call letters*]
**KBQC-FM**... Bettendorf, IA [*FM radio station call letters*]
**KBQN**......... Pago Pago, AS [*AM radio station call letters*]
**KBQQ**......... Minot, ND [*FM radio station call letters*]
**KBR**........... Kaaba Resources [*Vancouver Stock Exchange symbol*]
**KBR**........... Keio Business Review [*A publication*]
**KBR**........... Kota Bharu [*Malaysia*] [*Airport symbol*] (OAG)
**KBR**........... Rheinisch-Westfaelisches Institut fuer Wirtschaftsforschung. Konjunkturberichte [*A publication*]
**KBRA**......... Freer, TX [*FM radio station call letters*]
**KBRB**......... Ainsworth, NE [*AM radio station call letters*]
**KBRB-FM**... Ainsworth, NE [*FM radio station call letters*]
**KBRC**......... Mount Vernon, WA [*AM radio station call letters*]
**KBRD**......... Tacoma, WA [*FM radio station call letters*]
**KBRE**......... Cedar City, UT [*AM radio station call letters*]
**KBRE-FM**... Cedar City, UT [*FM radio station call letters*]
**KBRF**......... Fergus Falls, MN [*AM radio station call letters*]
**KBRF-FM**... Fergus Falls, MN [*FM radio station call letters*]
**KBRG**......... Fremont, CA [*FM radio station call letters*]
**KBRI**.......... Brinkley, AR [*AM radio station call letters*]
**KBRK**......... Brookings, SD [*AM radio station call letters*]
**KBRL**......... McCook, NE [*AM radio station call letters*]
**KBRN**......... Boerne, TX [*AM radio station call letters*]
**KBRO**......... Bremerton, WA [*AM radio station call letters*]
**KBRO**......... Brownsville/International [*Texas*] [*ICAO location identifier*] (ICLI)
**KBRR**......... Thief River Falls, MN [*Television station call letters*]
**KBRS**......... Springdale, AR [*AM radio station call letters*]
**KBRT**......... Avalon, CA [*AM radio station call letters*]
**KBRU**......... Fort Morgan, CO [*FM radio station call letters*]
**KBRV**......... Soda Springs, ID [*AM radio station call letters*]
**KBRW**........ Barrow, AK [*AM radio station call letters*]
**KBRX**......... O'Neill, NE [*AM radio station call letters*]
**KBRX-FM**... O'Neill, NE [*FM radio station call letters*]
**KBRZ**......... Freeport, TX [*AM radio station call letters*]
**KBS**........... Bo [*Sierra Leone*] [*Airport symbol*] [*Obsolete*] (OAG)
**KBS**........... Kellogg Biological Station [*Michigan State University*]
**kbs**............ KiloBITS [*Binary Digits*] per Second [*Transmission rate*] [*Data processing*]
**KBS**........... Kilobytes per Second [*Data processing*]
**KBS**........... Kinematic Bombing System
**KBS**........... Kingsbay [*Spitsbergen*] [*Seismograph station code, US Geological Survey*] (SEIS)
**KBS**........... Knight of the Blessed Sacrament
**KBS**........... Korean Broadcasting System
**KBS**........... Stites, McElwain & Fowler, Bellarmine College Library, Louisville, KY [*OCLC symbol*] (OCLC)
**KBSA**......... El Dorado, AR [*FM radio station call letters*]
**KBSA**......... Kassian Benevolent Society in America (EA)
**KBSA**......... Knowledge-Based Software Assistant [*Data processing*]
**KBSB**......... Bemidji, MN [*FM radio station call letters*]
**KBSC**......... Knowledge-Based Systems Centre [*Polytechnic of the South Bank*] [*British*] (CB)
**KBSD-TV**.. Ensign, KS [*Television station call letters*]
**KBSEA**....... Bulletin. Kyoto Educational University. Series B. Mathematics and Natural Science [*A publication*]
**KBSF**......... Springhill, LA [*AM radio station call letters*]
**KBSG**......... Auburn, WA [*AM radio station call letters*]
**KBSG-FM**... Tacoma, WA [*FM radio station call letters*]
**KBSH-TV**... Hays, KS [*Television station call letters*]
**KBSI**.......... Cape Girardeau, MO [*Television station call letters*]
**KBSI**.......... Kongres Buruh Seluruh Indonesia [*All Indonesia Congress of Workers*]
**KBSL-TV**.. Goodland, KS [*Television station call letters*]
**KBSM**........ Austin/Bergstrom Air Force Base [*Texas*] [*ICAO location identifier*] (ICLI)
**KBSM**........ McCall, ID [*FM radio station call letters*]
**KBSN**......... Moses Lake, WA [*AM radio station call letters*]
**KBSP-TV**.. Salem, OR [*Television station call letters*]
**KBSR**......... Kankakee, Beaverville & Southern Railroad Co. [*AAR code*]
**KBSS-FM**... Booneville, AR [*FM radio station call letters*]
**KBST**......... Big Spring, TX [*AM radio station call letters*]
**KBST-FM**... Big Spring, TX [*FM radio station call letters*]
**KBSU**......... Boise, ID [*FM radio station call letters*]
**KBSW**........ Twin Falls, ID [*FM radio station call letters*]
**KBTA**......... Batesville, AR [*AM radio station call letters*]
**KBTB**......... Bethel, AK [*FM radio station call letters*]
**KBTC**......... Houston, MO [*AM radio station call letters*]
**KBTD**......... Knee Board Training Device [*Military*] (MCD)
**KBTG**......... Keep Britain Tidy Group (DCTA)
**KBTG**......... Tidy Britain Group [*An association*] (EAIO)
**KBTM**........ Jonesboro, AR [*AM radio station call letters*]
**KBTN**......... Neosho, MO [*AM radio station call letters*]
**KBTO**......... Bottineau, ND [*FM radio station call letters*]
**KBTR**......... Baton Rouge/Ryan Field [*Louisiana*] [*ICAO location identifier*] (ICLI)
**KBTS-FM**... Killeen, TX [*FM radio station call letters*]
**KBTT**......... Bridgeport, TX [*FM radio station call letters*]
**KBTV**......... Burlington/International [*Vermont*] [*ICAO location identifier*] (ICLI)
**KBTV**......... Des Moines, IA [*Television station call letters*]
**KBTX-TV**.. Bryan, TX [*Television station call letters*]
**KBU**........... Keyboard Unit [*Data processing*] (NASA)
**KBU**........... Knuckle Buster University [*Facetious term*]

**KBUB** ........ Brownwood, TX [*FM radio station call letters*]
**KBUC** ........ Cibolo, TX [*AM radio station call letters*]
**KBUC** ........ Upper Canada King's Bench Reports [*A publication*] (DLA)
**KBUF**......... Buffalo/Greater Buffalo International [*New York*] [*ICAO location identifier*] (ICLI)
**KBUF**......... Holcomb, KS [*AM radio station call letters*]
**KBUK** ........ La Grange TX [*FM radio station call letters*]
**KBUL** ........ Carson City, NV [*FM radio station call letters*]
**KBUN**........ Bemidji, MN [*AM radio station call letters*]
**KBUR** ........ Burbank/Hollywood-Burbank [*California*] [*ICAO location identifier*] (ICLI)
**KBUR** ........ Burlington, IA [*AM radio station call letters*]
**KBUS**......... Paris, TX [*FM radio station call letters*]
**KBUT** ........ Crested Butte, CO [*FM radio station call letters*]
**KBUX** ........ Quartzsite, AZ [*FM radio station call letters*]
**KBUY** ........ Ruidoso, NM [*AM radio station call letters*]
**KBUY-FM** ... Ruidoso, NM [*FM radio station call letters*]
**KBUZ** ........ El Dorado, KS [*FM radio station call letters*]
**KBV** ........... Kobold Resources Ltd. [*Vancouver Stock Exchange symbol*]
**KBV** ........... Korte Berichten voor de Verfbranche [*A publication*]
**KBVM** ....... Portland, OR [*FM radio station call letters*]
**KBVO** ........ Austin, TX [*Television station call letters*]
**KBVR**........ Corvallis, OR [*FM radio station call letters*]
**KBVV**........ Enid, OK [*FM radio station call letters*]
**KBW** .......... Kommunistischer Bund Westdeutschland [*Communist League of West Germany*] [*Political party*] (PPW)
**KBW** .......... Korrespondenzblatt fuer die Hoeheren Schulen Wuerttembergs [*A publication*]
**KBWC** ....... Marshall, TX [*FM radio station call letters*]
**KBWD** ....... Brownwood, TX [*AM radio station call letters*]
**KBWH**....... Blair, NE [*FM radio station call letters*]
**KBWI**......... Baltimore/Baltimore-Washington International [*Maryland*] [*ICAO location identifier*] (ICLI)
**KBWL**........ Roosevelt, UT [*FM radio station call letters*]
**KBWS-FM** ... Sisseton, SD [*FM radio station call letters*]
**KBXB**......... Canton, MO [*FM radio station call letters*]
**KBXG** ........ Denver, CO [*AM radio station call letters*]
**KBXL**......... Caldwell, ID [*FM radio station call letters*]
**KBXR**......... Weatherford, OK [*FM radio station call letters*]
**KBXS** ......... Ely, NV [*FM radio station call letters*]
**KBY** ........... Streaky Bay [*Australia*] [*Airport symbol*] (OAG)
**KBYE**......... Oklahoma City, OK [*AM radio station call letters*]
**KBYG** ........ Big Spring, TX [*AM radio station call letters*]
**KBYH**........ Blytheville Air Force Base [*Arkansas*] [*ICAO location identifier*] (ICLI)
**KBYO** ........ Tallulah, LA [*FM radio station call letters*]
**KBYR**......... Anchorage, AK [*AM radio station call letters*]
**KBYU-FM** ... Provo, UT [*FM radio station call letters*]
**KBYU-TV** ... Provo, UT [*Television station call letters*]
**KBYZ**......... Bismarck, ND [*FM radio station call letters*]
**KBZB**......... Bisbee, AZ [*AM radio station call letters*]
**KBZE**......... Security, CO [*FM radio station call letters*]
**KBZR**......... Blue Springs, MO [*AM radio station call letters*]
**KBZT-FM** ... La Quinta, CA [*FM radio station call letters*]
**KBZY**......... Salem, OR [*AM radio station call letters*]
**KBZZ**......... La Junta, CO [*AM radio station call letters*]
**KC**.............. Canada [*IYRU nationality code*] (IYR)
**KC**.............. [*The*] Kanawha Central Railway Co. [*AAR code*]
**KC**.............. Kansas City [*Missouri*] [*Slang*]
**KC**.............. Karman Constant [*Physics*]
**KC**.............. Kartell Convent Deutscher Studenten Juedischen Glaubens (BJA)
**KC**.............. Kathodal Closing [*Medicine*]
**KC**.............. Kennel Club
**KC**.............. Keratoconjunctivitis [*Ophthalmology*]
**KC**.............. Kerr Cell [*Optics*]
**KC**.............. Keston College [*Formerly, Centre for the Study of Religion and Communism*] (EA)
**KC**.............. Key Company [*AMEX symbol*] (SPSG)
**KC**.............. Keyboard Classics [*A publication*]
**kc**............... Kilocalorie
**KC**.............. Kilocharacter (BUR)
**kc**............... Kilocycle [*Radio*]
**KC**.............. Kilocycles per Second [*Aviation code*] (FAAC)
**kc**............... Kilograms per Square Centimeter (DS)
**KC**.............. King's Colonials [*British military*] (DMA)
**KC**.............. King's Counsel [*British*]
**KC**.............. Kings County [*Sussex, New Brunswick*] (DAS)
**KC**.............. King's Cross [*British*] (ADA)
**KC**.............. Knight Club (EA)
**KC**.............. Knight Commander
**KC**.............. Knight of the Crescent [*Turkey*]
**KC**.............. Knights of Columbus
**K of C** ......... Knights of Columbus (EA)
**KC**.............. Kritika Chronika [*A publication*]
**K & C** .......... Kunst en Cultuur [*A publication*]
**KC**.............. Kunstchronik [*A publication*]
**Kc**............... Kupffer Cell [*Histology*]
**KC**.............. Kyle Classification [*Library science*]
**KC**.............. Sky Charter (Malton) Ltd. [*ICAO designator*] (FAAC)
**KCA**........... Keeshond Club of America (EA)
**KCA**........... Keesings Contemporary Archives [*A publication*] [*Also, an information service or system*]
**KCA**........... Kentucky Callers Association (EA)
**KCA**........... Komondor Club of America (EA)
**KCA**........... Kuvasz Club of America (EA)
**KCAB**......... Dardanelle, AR [*AM radio station call letters*]
**KCAC** ......... Korean Civil Action Corps (CINC)
**KCAG** ........ Korean Civic Action Group
**KCAH**........ Watsonville, CA [*Television station call letters*]
**kcal**............. Kilocalorie
**KCAL**......... Norwalk, CA [*Television station call letters*]
**KCAL**......... Redlands, CA [*AM radio station call letters*]
**KCAL-FM** ... Redlands, CA [*FM radio station call letters*]
**KCAM** ....... Glennallen, AK [*AM radio station call letters*]
**KCAN** ........ Albion, NE [*Television station call letters*]
**KCAO** ........ Kansas City Area Office [*Energy Research and Development Administration*]
**KCAP**......... Helena, MT [*AM radio station call letters*]
**KCAQ** ........ Oxnard, CA [*FM radio station call letters*]
**KCAR** ........ Caribou [*Maine*] [*ICAO location identifier*] (ICLI)
**KCAR** ........ Clarksville, TX [*AM radio station call letters*]
**KCAS**......... Knots Calibrated Airspeed (MCD)
**KCAS**......... Slaton, TX [*AM radio station call letters*]
**KCAT**......... Kemptville College of Agricultural Technology [*Canada*] (ARC)
**KCAT**......... Pine Bluff, AR [*AM radio station call letters*]
**KCAU-TV** ... Sioux City, IA [*Television station call letters*]
**KCAW** ....... Sitka, AK [*FM radio station call letters*]
**KCAY** ........ Russell, KS [*FM radio station call letters*]
**KCB** ........... Kansas City Ballet
**KCB** ........... Kartell Convent Blaetter (BJA)
**KCB** ........... Keyboard Change Button [*Data processing*]
**KCB** ........... Knight Commander of the [*Order of the*] Bath [*British*] (GPO)
**KCBA**......... Salinas, CA [*Television station call letters*]
**KCBB**......... Stratmoor, CO [*AM radio station call letters*]
**KCBD-TV** ... Lubbock, TX [*Television station call letters*]
**KCBF**......... Fairbanks, AK [*AM radio station call letters*]
**KCBI-FM**.. Dallas, TX [*FM radio station call letters*]
**KCBM** ....... Colombus Air Force Base [*Mississippi*] [*ICAO location identifier*] (ICLI)
**KCBNAY**... Annals. Kurashiki Central Hospital [*A publication*]
**KCBQ** ........ San Diego, CA [*AM radio station call letters*]
**KCBQ-FM** ... San Diego, CA [*FM radio station call letters*]
**KCBS**......... San Francisco, CA [*AM radio station call letters*]
**KC Bsns Jl** ... Kansas City Business Journal [*A publication*]
**KCBS-TV**.. Los Angeles, CA [*Television station call letters*]
**KCBT**......... Board of Trade of Kansas City, MO (EA)
**KCBW** ....... Sedalia, MO [*FM radio station call letters*]
**KCBX**......... San Luis Obispo, CA [*FM radio station call letters*]
**KCBY-TV** ... Coos Bay, OR [*Television station call letters*]
**KCBZ**......... Clarksville, TX [*FM radio station call letters*]
**KCC** ........... Centre College of Kentucky, Danville, KY [*OCLC symbol*] (OCLC)
**KCC** ........... Coffman Cove, AK [*Location identifier*] [*FAA*] (FAAL)
**KCC** ........... Kansas City Connecting Railroad Co. [*AAR code*]
**KCC** ........... Kathodal Closure Contraction [*Medicine*]
**KCC** ........... Keokuk Community College [*Iowa*]
**KCC** ........... Keyboard Common Contact [*Data processing*]
**KCC** ........... Knapp Communications Corporation
**KCC** ........... Knife Collectors Club (EA)
**KCC** ........... Knight Commander of the [*Order of the*] Crown [*Belgium*]
**KCC** ........... Kona Coffee Council (EA)
**KCC** ........... Koplar Communications Center [*St. Louis, MO*] [*Telecommunications*] (TSSD)
**KCCB**......... Corning, AR [*AM radio station call letters*]
**KCCC**......... Carlsbad, NM [*AM radio station call letters*]
**KCCC**......... Key Chain Collectors Club (EA)
**KCCH**........ Knight Commander of Court of Honor [*British*]
**KCCI-TV** ... Des Moines, IA [*Television station call letters*]
**KCCK-FM** ... Cedar Rapids, IA [*FM radio station call letters*]
**KCCL**......... Paris, AR [*AM radio station call letters*]
**KCCL-FM** ... Paris, AR [*FM radio station call letters*]
**KCCM** ....... Kupffer Cell Conditioned Medium
**KCCM-FM** ... Moorhead, MN [*FM radio station call letters*]
**KCCN** ........ Honolulu, HI [*AM radio station call letters*]
**KCCN-FM** ... Honolulu, HI [*FM radio station call letters*]
**KCCO-TV** ... Alexandria, MN [*Television station call letters*]
**KCCQ** ........ Ames, IA [*FM radio station call letters*]
**KCCR**......... Pierre, SD [*AM radio station call letters*]
**KCCS**......... Salem, OR [*AM radio station call letters*]
**KCCT**......... Corpus Christi, TX [*AM radio station call letters*]
**KCCU** ........ Lawton, OK [*FM radio station call letters*]
**KCCV**......... Independence, MO [*AM radio station call letters*]
**KCCW-TV** ... Walker, MN [*Television station call letters*]
**KCCX**......... Commerce, OK [*FM radio station call letters*]
**KCCY**......... Pueblo, CO [*FM radio station call letters*]
**KCCZ**......... Cedar City, UT [*Television station call letters*]
**KCDA** ........ Coeur D'Alene, ID [*FM radio station call letters*]
**KCDC** ........ Longmont, CO [*FM radio station call letters*]
**KCDH**........ Nephi, UT [*FM radio station call letters*]
**KCDN**........ Shreveport, LA [*Television station call letters*]

**KCDS**......... Angwin, CA [*FM radio station call letters*]
**KCDS**......... Childress [*Texas*] [*ICAO location identifier*] (ICLI)
**KCDX**......... Kearney, AZ [*FM radio station call letters*]
**KCDY**......... Carlsbad, NM [*FM radio station call letters*]
**KCDZ**......... Twentynine Palms, CA [*FM radio station call letters*]
**KCE**........... Collinsville [*Australia*] [*Airport symbol*] (OAG)
**KCE**........... KC Piper Sales, Inc. [*Olathe, KS*] [*FAA designator*] (FAAC)
**KCE**........... Kultura Centro Esperantista [*Esperanto Cultural Center - ECC*] (EAIO)
**KCEA**......... Atherton, CA [*FM radio station call letters*]
**KCEB**......... Casper, WY [*FM radio station call letters*]
**KCED**......... Centralia-Chehalis, WA [*FM radio station call letters*]
**KCEE**......... Tucson, AZ [*AM radio station call letters*]
**KCEF**......... Chicopee Falls/Westover Air Force Base [*Massachusetts*] [*ICAO location identifier*] (ICLI)
**KCEM**......... Aztec, NM [*AM radio station call letters*]
**KCEM-FM**... Bloomfield, NM [*FM radio station call letters*]
**KCEN-TV**... Temple, TX [*Television station call letters*]
**KCEP**......... Las Vegas, NV [*FM radio station call letters*]
**KCEQ**......... Walnut Creek, CA [*FM radio station call letters*]
**KCER**......... Kananaskis Centre for Environmental Research [*University of Calgary*] [*Research center*] (RCD)
**KCES**......... Eufaula, OK [*FM radio station call letters*]
**KCESDX**... Karger Continuing Education Series [*A publication*]
**KCET**......... Los Angeles, CA [*Television station call letters*]
**KCEV-FM**... Wichita, KS [*FM radio station call letters*]
**KCEW**......... Crestview/Bob Sikes [*Florida*] [*ICAO location identifier*] (ICLI)
**KCEZ**......... Corning, CA [*FM radio station call letters*]
**KCF**........... Key-Click Filter
**KCF**........... Thousand Cubic Feet
**KCFA**......... Eagle River, AK [*AM radio station call letters*]
**KCFB**......... King City Federal Savings Bank [*Mount Vernon, IL*] [*NASDAQ symbol*] (NQ)
**KCFB**......... St. Cloud, MN [*FM radio station call letters*]
**KCFC**......... Karen Carpenter Fan Club [*Defunct*] (EA)
**KCFD**......... Bryan/Coulter Field [*Texas*] [*ICAO location identifier*] (ICLI)
**KCFF**......... Korean Cultural and Freedom Foundation (EA)
**KCFI**......... Cedar Falls, IA [*AM radio station call letters*]
**KCFM**......... Lexington, MO [*FM radio station call letters*]
**KCFMC**..... Kevin Collins Foundation for Missing Children (EA)
**KCFO**......... Tulsa, OK [*AM radio station call letters*]
**KCFP**......... Austin, TX [*Television station call letters*]
**KCFR**......... Denver, CO [*FM radio station call letters*]
**KCFS**......... Sioux Falls, SD [*FM radio station call letters*]
**KCFV**......... Ferguson, MO [*FM radio station call letters*]
**KCFW-TV**... Kalispell, MT [*Television station call letters*]
**KCFX**......... Harrisonville, MO [*FM radio station call letters*]
**KCG**........... Chignik, AK [*Location identifier*] [*FAA*] (FAAL)
**KCG**........... Kinetocardiogram [*Cardiology*]
**KCGB**......... Hood River, OR [*FM radio station call letters*]
**KCGL**......... Centerville, UT [*FM radio station call letters*]
**KCGM**......... Scobey, MT [*FM radio station call letters*]
**KCGN**......... Ortonville, MN [*FM radio station call letters*]
**KCGS**......... Marshall, AR [*AM radio station call letters*]
**KCGY-FM**... Laramie, WY [*FM radio station call letters*]
**KCH**........... Ketch
**KCH**........... Ketchum & Co., Inc. [*AMEX symbol*] (SPSG)
**KCH**........... King's College Hospital
**KCH**........... Knight Commander of the Guelphic Order of Hanover [*British*]
**KCH**........... Korte Berichten voor de Chemiebranche [*A publication*]
**K Ch**........... Kritika Chronika [*A publication*]
**KCH**........... Kuching [*Malaysia*] [*Airport symbol*] (OAG)
**KCHA**......... Charles City, IA [*AM radio station call letters*]
**KCHA**......... Chattanooga/Lovell [*Tennessee*] [*ICAO location identifier*] (ICLI)
**KCHA-FM**... Charles City, IA [*FM radio station call letters*]
**KCHC**......... Central Point, OR [*FM radio station call letters*]
**KCHD**......... Chandler/Williams Air Force Base [*Arizona*] [*ICAO location identifier*] (ICLI)
**KCHE**......... Cherokee, IA [*AM radio station call letters*]
**KCHE-FM**... Cherokee, IA [*FM radio station call letters*]
**KCHF**......... Santa Fe, NM [*Television station call letters*]
**KCHG**......... Somerset, TX [*AM radio station call letters*]
**KCHI**......... Chicago/Metropolitan Area [*Illinois*] [*ICAO location identifier*] (ICLI)
**KCHI**......... Chillicothe, MO [*AM radio station call letters*]
**KCHI-FM**... Chillicothe, MO [*FM radio station call letters*]
**KCHJ**......... Delano, CA [*AM radio station call letters*]
**KCHK**......... New Prague, MN [*AM radio station call letters*]
**KCHK-FM**... New Prague, MN [*FM radio station call letters*]
**KCHL**......... San Antonio, TX [*AM radio station call letters*]
**KCHN**......... Jeffers, MN [*AM radio station call letters*]
**KCHO**......... Chico, CA [*FM radio station call letters*]
**KCHR**......... Charleston, MO [*AM radio station call letters*]
**KCHS**......... Charleston/Municipal and Air Force Base [*South Carolina*] [*ICAO location identifier*] (ICLI)
**KCHS**......... Knight Commander of the Holy Sepulchre
**KCHS**......... Truth Or Consequences, NM [*AM radio station call letters*]
**KCHT**......... Kechabta [*Tunisia*] [*Seismograph station code, US Geological Survey*] (SEIS)
**KCHU**......... Valdez, AK [*AM radio station call letters*]
**KCHV**......... Coachella, CA [*FM radio station call letters*]
**KCHX**......... Midland, TX [*FM radio station call letters*]
**KCI**........... Aeromech Commuter Airlines [*Clarksburg, WV*] [*FAA designator*] (FAAC)
**KCI**........... Key Club International (EA)
**KCI**........... Key Collectors International (EA)
**kCi**........... Kilocurie (DEN)
**KCI**........... Kit Collectors International (EA)
**KCIA**......... South Korean Central Intelligence Agency [*Later, Agency for National Security Planning*] (PD)
**KCIB**......... Central Valley, CA [*FM radio station call letters*]
**KCIC**......... Grand Junction, CO [*FM radio station call letters*]
**KCID**......... Caldwell, ID [*AM radio station call letters*]
**KCID-FM**... Caldwell, ID [*FM radio station call letters*]
**KCIE**......... Knight Commander of the [*Order of the*] Indian Empire [*British*]
**KCII**......... Washington, IA [*AM radio station call letters*]
**KCII-FM**... Washington, IA [*FM radio station call letters*]
**KCIJ**......... North Fort Polk, LA [*FM radio station call letters*]
**KCIK**......... El Paso, TX [*Television station call letters*]
**KCIL**......... Houma, LA [*FM radio station call letters*]
**KCIM**......... Carroll, IA [*AM radio station call letters*]
**KCIN**......... Victorville, CA [*AM radio station call letters*]
**KCIO**......... King's Commissioned Indian Officer [*British military*] (DMA)
**KCIR**......... Twin Falls, ID [*FM radio station call letters*]
**KCIS**......... Edmonds, WA [*AM radio station call letters*]
**KCIT**......... Amarillo, TX [*Television station call letters*]
**KCIV**......... Mount Bullion, CA [*FM radio station call letters*]
**KCIX**......... Garden City, ID [*FM radio station call letters*]
**KCIZ**......... Springdale, AR [*FM radio station call letters*]
**KCJB**......... Minot, ND [*AM radio station call letters*]
**KCJF**......... Kellogg, ID [*FM radio station call letters*]
**KCJH**......... Stockton, CA [*FM radio station call letters*]
**KCJJ**......... Iowa City, IA [*AM radio station call letters*]
**KCK**........... Kansas City, KS [*Location identifier*] [*FAA*] (FAAL)
**KCKA**......... Centralia, WA [*Television station call letters*]
**KCKC**......... San Bernardino, CA [*AM radio station call letters*]
**KCKJ**......... Fairfield, IA [*FM radio station call letters*]
**KCKK**......... Kanab, UT [*FM radio station call letters*]
**KCKL**......... Malakoff, TX [*FM radio station call letters*]
**KCKM**......... Kansas City, KS [*AM radio station call letters*]
**KCKN**......... Roswell, NM [*AM radio station call letters*]
**KCKS**......... Concordia, KS [*FM radio station call letters*]
**KCKX**......... Stayton, OR [*AM radio station call letters*]
**KCKY**......... Coolidge, AZ [*AM radio station call letters*]
**KCL**........... Chignik, AK [*Location identifier*] [*FAA*] (FAAL)
**K & CL**....... Kensington and Chelsea Law Group [*British*]
**KCL**........... King's College, London
**KCL**........... Klamath County Library, Klamath Falls, OR [*OCLC symbol*] (OCLC)
**KCL**........... Knudsen Cosine Law [*Physics*]
**KCLA**......... Pine Bluff, AR [*AM radio station call letters*]
**KCLB**......... Coachella, CA [*AM radio station call letters*]
**KCLC**......... St. Charles, MO [*FM radio station call letters*]
**KCLD**......... St. Cloud, MN [*AM radio station call letters*]
**KCLD-FM**... St. Cloud, MN [*FM radio station call letters*]
**KCLE**......... Cleburne, TX [*AM radio station call letters*]
**KCLE**......... Cleveland/Cleveland-Hopkins International [*Ohio*] [*ICAO location identifier*] (ICLI)
**KCLE**......... Continuing Legal Education, University of Kentucky College of Law (DLA)
**KCLF**......... New Roads, LA [*AM radio station call letters*]
**KCLH**......... Colby, KS [*FM radio station call letters*]
**KCLI**......... Clinton, OK [*FM radio station call letters*]
**KCLI**......... Kansas City Life Insurance Co. [*NASDAQ symbol*] (NQ)
**KCLK**......... Asotin, WA [*AM radio station call letters*]
**KCLK-FM**... Clarkston, WA [*FM radio station call letters*]
**KCLL**......... College Station/Easterwood Field [*Texas*] [*ICAO location identifier*] (ICLI)
**KCLN**......... Clinton, IA [*AM radio station call letters*]
**KCLN-FM**... Clinton, IA [*FM radio station call letters*]
**KCLO-TV**... Rapid City, SD [*Television station call letters*]
**KCLP**......... Claude, TX [*AM radio station call letters*]
**KCLQ-FM**... Hanford, CA [*FM radio station call letters*]
**KCLR**......... Ralls, TX [*AM radio station call letters*]
**KCLS**......... Flagstaff, AZ [*AM radio station call letters*]
**KCLS**......... Kern County Library System [*Library network*]
**KCLS**......... Knight Commander of the Lion and the Sun
**KCLT**......... West Helena, AR [*FM radio station call letters*]
**KCLU**......... Korean Council of Organization [*South Korea*]
**KCLV**......... Clovis, NM [*AM radio station call letters*]
**KCLV-FM**... Clovis, NM [*FM radio station call letters*]
**KCLW-FM**... Hamilton, TX [*FM radio station call letters*]
**KCLX**......... Colfax, WA [*AM radio station call letters*]
**KCLY**......... Clay Center, KS [*FM radio station call letters*]
**KCLY**......... Kent and County of London Yeomanry [*Military unit*] [*British*]
**KCM**........... Kam Creed Mines Ltd. [*Vancouver Stock Exchange symbol*] [*Toronto Stock Exchange symbol*]
**KCM**........... Keratinocyte-Conditioned Medium [*Biochemistry*]

**KCM** .......... Kilenge Mission [*New Britain*] [*Seismograph station code, US Geological Survey*] (SEIS)
**KCM** .......... Kupffer Cell Medium
**KCMA** ....... Broken Arrow, OK [*FM radio station call letters*]
**KCMA** ....... Kitchen Cabinet Manufacturers Association (EA)
**KCMB** ....... Baker, OR [*FM radio station call letters*]
**KCM & B**... Kansas City, Memphis & Birmingham Railroad
**KCMC** ....... Texarkana, TX [*AM radio station call letters*]
**KCME** ....... Manitou Springs, CO [*FM radio station call letters*]
**KCMG** ....... Knight Commander of St. Michael and St. George [*Facetiously translated, "Kindly Call Me God"*] [*British*]
**KCMG** ....... Mountain Grove, MO [*AM radio station call letters*]
**KCMG-FM** ... Mountain Grove, MO [*FM radio station call letters*]
**KCMH**....... Columbus/Port Columbus International [*Ohio*] [*ICAO location identifier*] (ICLI)
**KCMH**....... Mountain Home, AR [*FM radio station call letters*]
**KCMI** ........ Terrytown, NE [*FM radio station call letters*]
**KCMJ** ........ Palm Springs, CA [*AM radio station call letters*]
**KCMJ-FM** ... Indio, CA [*FM radio station call letters*]
**KCMLN** .... Kansas City Metropolitan Library Network Council [*Library network*]
**KCMN**....... Colorado Springs, CO [*AM radio station call letters*]
**KCMO**....... Kansas City, Mexico & Orient [*AAR code*]
**KCMO**....... Kansas City, MO [*AM radio station call letters*]
**KCMO-FM** ... Kansas City, MO [*FM radio station call letters*]
**KCMQ**....... Columbia, MO [*FM radio station call letters*]
**KCMR** ....... Mason City, IA [*FM radio station call letters*]
**KCMS**........ Edmonds, WA [*FM radio station call letters*]
**KCMT** ....... Chester, CA [*FM radio station call letters*]
**KCMT** ....... Keystone Portland Cement [*NASDAQ symbol*] (NQ)
**KCMU**....... Seattle, WA [*FM radio station call letters*]
**KCMW-FM** ... Warrensburg, MO [*FM radio station call letters*]
**KCMX** ....... Ashland, OR [*AM radio station call letters*]
**KCMX** ....... Keyset Central Multiplexer
**KCMX-FM** ... Ashland, OR [*FM radio station call letters*]
**KCMY** ....... Sacramento, CA [*Television station call letters*]
**KCN**........... Chernofski Harbor, AK [*Location identifier*] [*FAA*] (FAAL)
**KCN**........... Kit Configuration Notice (MCD)
**KCN**........... Kit Control Number [*Navy*] (NG)
**KCNA** ........ Cave Junction, OR [*FM radio station call letters*]
**KCNA** ........ Korean Central News Agency [*North Korea*]
**KCNC-TV** ... Denver, CO [*Television station call letters*]
**KCND**........ Bismarck, ND [*FM radio station call letters*]
**KCNF** ........ Fort Worth [*Texas*] [*ICAO location identifier*] (ICLI)
**KCNI** ......... Broken Bow, NE [*AM radio station call letters*]
**KCNM**....... Carlsbad/Cavern City Air Terminal [*New Mexico*] [*ICAO location identifier*] (ICLI)
**KCNM**....... San Jose, CM [*AM radio station call letters*]
**KCNN**........ East Grand Forks, MN [*AM radio station call letters*]
**KCNO**........ Alturas, CA [*AM radio station call letters*]
**KCNT** ........ Hastings, NE [*FM radio station call letters*]
**KCNW**....... Fairway, KS [*AM radio station call letters*]
**KCNW**....... Kelly's Creek & Northwestern Railroad Co. [*AAR code*]
**KCNW**....... Waco/James Connally [*Texas*] [*ICAO location identifier*] (ICLI)
**KCNY** ........ Moab, UT [*AM radio station call letters*]
**KCO**........... Keep Cost Order [*Telecommunications*] (TEL)
**KCOB** ........ Newton, IA [*AM radio station call letters*]
**KCOF** ........ Cocoa/Patrick Air Force Base [*Florida*] [*ICAO location identifier*] (ICLI)
**KCOG**........ Centerville, IA [*AM radio station call letters*]
**KCOH**........ Houston, TX [*AM radio station call letters*]
**KCOL** ........ Fort Collins, CO [*AM radio station call letters*]
**KColC** ....... Colby Community College, Colby, KS [*Library symbol*] [*Library of Congress*] (LCLS)
**KCOM**....... Comanche, TX [*AM radio station call letters*]
**KCOMZ**.... Korean Communications Zone [*Military*]
**KCON**........ Conway, AR [*AM radio station call letters*]
**KCOO**........ Coos Bay, OR [*FM radio station call letters*]
**KCOP** ........ Kencope Energy Companies [*NASDAQ symbol*] (NQ)
**KCOP** ........ Los Angeles, CA [*Television station call letters*]
**KCOR** ........ San Antonio, TX [*AM radio station call letters*]
**KCOS** ........ Colorado Springs/Peterson Field [*Colorado*] [*ICAO location identifier*] (ICLI)
**KCOS** ........ El Paso, TX [*Television station call letters*]
**KCOT** ........ Cotulla/Municipal [*Texas*] [*ICAO location identifier*] (ICLI)
**KCOU**........ Columbia, MO [*FM radio station call letters*]
**KCOW**....... Alliance, NE [*AM radio station call letters*]
**KCOY-TV** ... Santa Maria, CA [*Television station call letters*]
**KCP** ........... Kansas City Public Library, Kansas City, MO [*OCLC symbol*] (OCLC)
**KCP** ........... Keene's Cement Plaster [*Technical drawings*]
**KCP** ........... Key Crude Prices [*Database*] [*Petroleum Intelligence Weekly*] [*Information service or system*] (CRD)
**KCP** ........... Knight Commander of [*the Order of*] Pius IX
**KCP** ........... Korean Communist Party [*Political party*] [*Democratic People's Republic of Korea*] (FEA)
**KCPB**......... Thousand Oaks, CA [*FM radio station call letters*]
**KCPC**......... Collins [*Keith*] Petroleum [*NASDAQ symbol*] (NQ)
**KCPC**......... Keene's Cement Plaster Ceiling [*Technical drawings*]
**KCP & G**.... Kansas City, Pittsburgh & Gulf Railroad
**KC Phil** ...... Kansas City Philharmonic Program Notes [*A publication*]
**KCPI-FM** .. Albert Lea, MN [*FM radio station call letters*]
**KCPM**........ Chico, CA [*Television station call letters*]
**KCPQ** ........ Tacoma, WA [*Television station call letters*]
**KCPR**......... San Luis Obispo, CA [*FM radio station call letters*]
**KCPS** ......... Burlington, IA [*AM radio station call letters*]
**KCPS** ......... Kansas City Public Service R. R. [*AAR code*]
**kcps**............ Kilocycles per Second
**KCPT**......... Kansas City, MO [*Television station call letters*]
**KCPX-FM** ... Salt Lake City, UT [*FM radio station call letters*]
**KCQR** ........ Ellwood, CA [*FM radio station call letters*]
**KCR** ........... Colorado Creek, AK [*Location identifier*] [*FAA*] (FAAL)
**KCR** ........... Kansas City Law Review [*A publication*] (DLA)
**KCR** ........... Key Call Receiver [*Telecommunications*] (TEL)
**KCR** ........... [*The*] Kowloon Canton Railway [*Hong Kong*] (DCTA)
**KCR** ........... Reports Tempore Chancellor King [*A publication*] (DLA)
**KCR** ........... University of Missouri at Kansas City. Law Review [*A publication*]
**KCRAB8**.... Annual Report. Cancer Research Institute. Kanazawa University [*A publication*]
**KCRA-TV** ... Sacramento, CA [*Television station call letters*]
**KCRB-FM** ... Bemidji, MN [*FM radio station call letters*]
**KCRC**......... Enid, OK [*AM radio station call letters*]
**KCRC**......... Kansas City Records Center [*Military*]
**KCRCHE**... Kansas City Regional Council for Higher Education [*Library network*]
**KCRE**......... Crescent City, CA [*AM radio station call letters*]
**KCREEN**... Kapala Cruise Report [*A publication*]
**KCRE-FM** ... Crescent City, CA [*FM radio station call letters*]
**KCRF**......... Korean Conflict Research Foundation [*Defunct*]
**KCRF-FM** ... Lincoln City, OR [*FM radio station call letters*]
**KCRG**......... Cedar Rapids, IA [*AM radio station call letters*]
**KCRG-TV** ... Cedar Rapids, IA [*Television station call letters*]
**KCRH** ........ Hayward, CA [*FM radio station call letters*]
**KCRI-FM**.. Helena, AR [*FM radio station call letters*]
**KCRK-FM** ... Colville, WA [*FM radio station call letters*]
**KCRM** ........ Cameron, TX [*FM radio station call letters*]
**KCRN** ........ Santa Rosa, CA [*FM radio station call letters*]
**KCRO** ........ Omaha, NE [*AM radio station call letters*]
**KCRP**......... Corpus Christi/International [*Texas*] [*ICAO location identifier*] (ICLI)
**KCRS**......... Midland, TX [*AM radio station call letters*]
**KCRT**......... KCR Technology, Inc. [*East Hartford, CT*] [*NASDAQ symbol*] (NQ)
**KCRT**......... Keyboard Cathode Ray Tube (MCD)
**KCRT**......... Trinidad, CO [*AM radio station call letters*]
**KCRT-FM** ... Trinidad, CO [*FM radio station call letters*]
**KCRV** ........ Caruthersville, MO [*AM radio station call letters*]
**KCRW** ....... Santa Monica, CA [*FM radio station call letters*]
**KCRX**......... Roswell, NM [*AM radio station call letters*]
**KCS**............ Conston Corp. [*AMEX symbol*] (SPSG)
**KCS**............ [*The*] Kansas City Southern Railway Co. [*AAR code*]
**KCS**............ Keratoconjunctivitis Sicca [*Ophthalmology*]
**KCS**............ Key Configuration Studies (NASA)
**KCS**............ Keyboard Configuration Studies (NASA)
**KCS**............ Keyboard Controlled Sequencer [*Data processing*]
**KCS**............ Keyboards, Computers, and Software [*A publication*]
**kcs**.............. Kilocycles per Second
**KCS**............ King's College School [*British*]
**KCS**............ Knight of [*the Order of*] Charles III of Spain
**KCS**............ Knight of the Order of Charles XIII of Sweden [*Freemasonry*]
**KCS**............ Knoxville Air Courier Service, Inc. [*Knoxville, TN*] [*FAA designator*] (FAAC)
**KCS**............ Thousand Characters per Second
**KCSB-FM** ... Santa Barbara, CA [*FM radio station call letters*]
**KCSC**......... Edmond, OK [*FM radio station call letters*]
**KCSC**......... Kansas City Service Center [*IRS*]
**KCSC**......... Kansas Cosmosphere and Space Center [*Hutchinson, KS*]
**KCSD**......... Sioux Falls, SD [*FM radio station call letters*]
**KCSF** ......... Stanton Foundation (EA)
**KCSG**......... KCS Group, Inc. [*NASDAQ symbol*] (NQ)
**KCSG**......... Knight Commander of [*the Order of*] St. Gregory [*British*]
**KCSI** .......... Knight Commander of the [*Order of the*] Star of India [*British*]
**KCSJ** .......... Pueblo, CO [*AM radio station call letters*]
**KCSJ-FM** ... Pueblo, CO [*FM radio station call letters*]
**KCSM**........ San Mateo, CA [*FM radio station call letters*]
**KCSM-TV** ... San Mateo, CA [*Television station call letters*]
**KCSN**......... Kralovska Ceska Spolecnost Nauk [*A publication*]
**KCSN**......... Northridge, CA [*FM radio station call letters*]
**KCSO** ......... Modesto, CA [*Television station call letters*]
**KCSP**......... Casper, WY [*FM radio station call letters*]
**KCSR**......... Chadron, NE [*AM radio station call letters*]
**KCSS** ......... Knight Commander of [*the Order of*] St. Sylvester
**KCSS** ......... Turlock, CA [*FM radio station call letters*]
**KCST** ......... Florence, OR [*AM radio station call letters*]
**KC Star** ...... Kansas City Star [*A publication*]
**KCStJ & CB** ... Kansas City, St. Joseph & Council Bluffs Railroad
**KCSU-FM** ... Fort Collins, CO [*FM radio station call letters*]
**KCSY** ......... Soldotna, AK [*AM radio station call letters*]
**KCT** ........... Kansas City Terminal Railway Co. [*AAR code*]
**KCT** ........... Kaolin Cephalin Time [*Clinical chemistry*]

**KCT** .......... Kaolin Clotting Time [*Clinical chemistry*]
**KCT** .......... Kathodal Closing Tetanus [*Medicine*]
**KCT** .......... Katholiek Cultureel Tijdschrift [*A publication*]
**KCT** .......... Kelvin Circulation Theorem [*Physics*]
**KCT** .......... Knight Commander of the Temple [*Freemasonry*] (ROG)
**KCT** .......... Knox's Cube Test [*Short-term memory and attention span test*]
**KCTA**......... Corpus Christi, TX [*AM radio station call letters*]
**KCTB**......... Cut Bank [*Montana*] [*ICAO location identifier*] (ICLI)
**KCTB**......... Cut Bank, MT [*FM radio station call letters*]
**KCTC**......... Sacramento, CA [*FM radio station call letters*]
**KCTE**......... Kathodal Closure Tetanus [*Medicine*]
**KCTF**......... Waco, TX [*Television station call letters*]
**KCTI**......... Gonzales, TX [*AM radio station call letters*]
**KC Times**... Kansas City Times [*A publication*]
**KCTM**....... Rio Grande City, TX [*FM radio station call letters*]
**KCTMLPCC** ... Key Chain Tag and Mini License Plate Collectors Club [*Later, LPKCMLPCC*] (EA)
**KCTN**......... Garnavillo, IA [*FM radio station call letters*]
**KCTO**......... Columbia, LA [*AM radio station call letters*]
**KCTO-FM** ... Columbia, LA [*FM radio station call letters*]
**KCTP**......... Poplar Bluff, MO [*Television station call letters*]
**KCTR**......... Billings, MT [*AM radio station call letters*]
**KCTR-FM** ... Billings, MT [*FM radio station call letters*]
**KCTS**......... Knight Commander of the Tower and Sword [*Portugal*] (ROG)
**KCTS-TV**.. Seattle, WA [*Television station call letters*]
**KCTT**......... Yellville, AR [*AM radio station call letters*]
**KCTT-FM** ... Yellville, AR [*FM radio station call letters*]
**KCTV**......... Kansas City, MO [*Television station call letters*]
**KCTX**......... Childress, TX [*AM radio station call letters*]
**KCTY**......... Salinas, CA [*AM radio station call letters*]
**KCTZ**......... Bozeman, MT [*Television station call letters*]
**KCU**.......... Keyboard Control Unit
**KCUB**......... Tucson, AZ [*AM radio station call letters*]
**KCUE**......... Red Wing, MN [*AM radio station call letters*]
**KCUI**......... Pella, IA [*FM radio station call letters*]
**KCUK**......... Chevak, AK [*FM radio station call letters*]
**KCUL**......... Marshall, TX [*AM radio station call letters*]
**KCUR-FM** ... Kansas City, MO [*FM radio station call letters*]
**KCUS**......... Columbus/Municipal [*New Mexico*] [*ICAO location identifier*] (ICLI)
**KCUS**......... Sartell, MN [*AM radio station call letters*]
**KCUZ**......... Clifton, AZ [*AM radio station call letters*]
**KCV**.......... Kancana Ventures Ltd. [*Vancouver Stock Exchange symbol*]
**KCV**.......... Knight of Gustavus Vasa [*Sweden*]
**KCVF**......... Portland, OR [*Television station call letters*]
**KCVG**......... Cincinnati/Greater Cincinnati [*Ohio*] [*ICAO location identifier*] (ICLI)
**KCVL**......... Colville, WA [*AM radio station call letters*]
**KCVO**......... Knight Commander of the Royal Victorian Order [*British*]
**KCVO-FM** ... Camdenton, MO [*FM radio station call letters*]
**KCVP**......... Konservativ-Christlichsoziale Volkspartei [*Conservative Christian-Social Party*] [*Switzerland*] [*Political party*] (PPE)
**KCVR**......... Lodi, CA [*AM radio station call letters*]
**KCVS**......... Clovis/Cannon Air Force Base [*New Mexico*] [*ICAO location identifier*] (ICLI)
**KCVS**......... Salina, KS [*FM radio station call letters*]
**KCWA-FM** ... Arnold, MO [*FM radio station call letters*]
**KCWB**......... Glendale, AZ [*FM radio station call letters*]
**KCWB**......... Kansas City Westport Belt [*AAR code*]
**KCWC-FM** ... Riverton, WY [*FM radio station call letters*]
**KCWC-TV** ... Lander, WY [*Television station call letters*]
**KCWD**......... Harrison, AR [*FM radio station call letters*]
**KCWD**......... Kaleidoscope: Current World Data [*ABC-CLIO*] [*Information service or system*] (IID)
**KCWM**....... Barstow, CA [*FM radio station call letters*]
**KCWT**......... Wenatchee, WA [*Television station call letters*]
**KCWW**....... Tempe, AZ [*AM radio station call letters*]
**KCXL**......... Calexico/International [*California*] [*ICAO location identifier*] (ICLI)
**KCXL**......... Liberty, MO [*AM radio station call letters*]
**KCXY**......... Camden, AR [*FM radio station call letters*]
**KCYC**......... King's Cheshire Yeomanry Cavalry [*British military*] (DMA)
**KCYL**......... Lampasas, TX [*AM radio station call letters*]
**KCYN**......... Pocahontas, AR [*FM radio station call letters*]
**KCYS**......... Cheyenne [*Wyoming*] [*ICAO location identifier*] (ICLI)
**KCYX**......... McMinnville, OR [*AM radio station call letters*]
**KCYY**......... San Antonio, TX [*FM radio station call letters*]
**KCZ**.......... Kochi [*Japan*] [*Airport symbol*] (OAG)
**KCZE**......... New Hampton, IA [*FM radio station call letters*]
**KCZO**......... Carrizo Springs, TX [*FM radio station call letters*]
**KCZP**......... Kenai, AK [*FM radio station call letters*]
**KCZQ**......... Cresco, IA [*FM radio station call letters*]
**KCZY**......... Osage, IA [*FM radio station call letters*]
**KD**............ British Island Airways Ltd. [*Great Britain*] [*ICAO designator*] (FAAC)
**KD**............ Kathodal Duration [*Medicine*]
**KD**............ Kawasaki Disease [*Also, KS, MLNS*] [*Medicine*]
**KD**............ Keep It Dark [*Say nothing about it*] [*Slang*]
**KD**............ Kentucky Dam [*TVA*]
**K D**........... Kerygma und Dogma [*A publication*]
**KD**............ Kettledrum
**KD**............ Keyed to Differ [*Locks*] (ADA)
**KD**............ Khaki Drill [*British military*] (DMA)
**KD**............ Killed (AABC)
**KD**............ Kiln-Dried [*Lumber*]
**kD**............ Kilodalton [*Molecular mass measure*]
**KD**............ Kilter Diagram
**KD**............ Kirchliche Dogmatik [*A publication*]
**KD**............ Klinge [*Germany*] [*Research code symbol*]
**KD**............ Knee Disarticulation [*Medicine*]
**KD**............ Knocked Down [*i.e., disassembled*]
**KD**............ Known-Distance [*Range*] [*Weaponry*] (INF)
**KD**............ Komitet Domowy. Warsaw Ghetto (BJA)
**KD**............ Korsakoff's Disease [*Medicine*]
**KD**............ Kriegs Dekoration [*War Decoration*] [*German*]
**KD**............ Kristeligt Dagblad [*A publication*]
**KD**............ Kuwaiti Dinar [*Monetary unit*] (BJA)
**KD**............ Pilotless Aerial Target [*Navy*]
**KDA**.......... Kit Design Approach
**KDA**.......... Kuranda [*Australia*] [*Seismograph station code, US Geological Survey*] [*Closed*] (SEIS)
**KDAB**......... Ogden, UT [*FM radio station call letters*]
**KDAC**......... Fort Bragg, CA [*AM radio station call letters*]
**KDAE**......... Sinton, TX [*AM radio station call letters*]
**KDAF**......... Dallas, TX [*Television station call letters*]
**KDAK**......... Carrington, ND [*AM radio station call letters*]
**KDAL**......... Dallas/Dallas-Love Field [*Texas*] [*ICAO location identifier*] (ICLI)
**KDAL**......... Duluth, MN [*AM radio station call letters*]
**KDAL-FM** ... Duluth, MN [*FM radio station call letters*]
**KDAM**....... Monroe City, MO [*FM radio station call letters*]
**K Danske Vidensk Selsk Skr** ... Kongelige Danske Videnskabernes Selskab. Skrifter [*A publication*]
**K Dan Vidensk Selsk Biol Skr** ... Kongelige Danske Videnskabernes Selskab. Biologiske Skrifter [*A publication*]
**K Dan Vidensk Selsk Mat Fys Medd** ... Kongelige Danske Videnskabernes Selskab. Matematisk-Fysisk Meddelelser [*Denmark*] [*A publication*]
**K Dan Vidensk Selsk Mat Fys Skr** ... Kongelige Danske Videnskabernes Selskab. Matematisk-Fysisk Skrifter [*Denmark*] [*A publication*]
**K Dan Vidensk Selsk Over Selsk Virksomhed** ... Kongelige Danske Videnskabernes Selskab. Oversigt Selskabets Virksomhed [*A publication*]
**K Dan Vidensk Selsk Skr Naturvidensk Mat Afd** ... Kongelige Danske Videnskabernes Selskab. Skrifter. Naturvidenskabelig og Mathematisk Afdeling [*A publication*]
**KDAO**......... Marshalltown, IA [*AM radio station call letters*]
**KDAP**......... Douglas, AZ [*AM radio station call letters*]
**KDAQ**......... Shreveport, LA [*FM radio station call letters*]
**KDAR**......... Oxnard, CA [*FM radio station call letters*]
**KDAT**......... Kiln-Dried After Treatment [*Lumber*]
**KDAT**......... Merced, CA [*FM radio station call letters*]
**KDAY**......... Dayton/James M. Coxdayton Municipal [*Ohio*] [*ICAO location identifier*] (ICLI)
**KDAY**......... Santa Monica, CA [*AM radio station call letters*]
**KDAZ**......... Albuquerque, NM [*AM radio station call letters*]
**KDB**.......... Kambalda [*Australia*] [*Airport symbol*] (OAG)
**KDB**.......... Keller-Dorian, Berthon [*Method*] [*Photography*]
**KDB**.......... Kelvin Double Bridge [*Physics*]
**KDB**.......... Konedobu [*Papua New Guinea*] [*Seismograph station code, US Geological Survey*] (SEIS)
**KDB**.......... Korea Development Bank
**KDB**.......... Santa Barbara, CA [*AM radio station call letters*]
**KDBB**......... Bonne Terre, MO [*FM radio station call letters*]
**KDBC-TV** ... El Paso, TX [*Television station call letters*]
**KDB-FM** ... Santa Barbara, CA [*FM radio station call letters*]
**KDBH**......... Natchitoches, LA [*FM radio station call letters*]
**KDBM**......... Dillon, MT [*AM radio station call letters*]
**KDBM-FM** ... Dillon, MT [*FM radio station call letters*]
**KDBN**......... Dallas, TX [*AM radio station call letters*]
**KDBX**......... Boonville, MO [*FM radio station call letters*]
**KDc**........... Dodge City Public Library, Dodge City, KS [*Library symbol*] [*Library of Congress*] (LCLS)
**KDC**.......... Kathodal Duration Contraction [*Medicine*]
**KDC**.......... Keil and Delitzsch Commentaries [*A publication*] (BJA)
**KDC**.......... Key Distribution Center (MCD)
**KDC**.......... Keyed Display Console
**KDC**.......... Kodiak [*Alaska*] [*Seismograph station code, US Geological Survey*] (SEIS)
**KDC**.......... Kosher Dining Club (BJA)
**KDCA**......... Washington/National [*District of Columbia*] [*ICAO location identifier*] (ICLI)
**KDCC**......... Washington [*District of Columbia*] [*ICAO location identifier*] (ICLI)
**KDCE**......... Espanola, NM [*AM radio station call letters*]
**KDCG**......... San Diego Coast Guard Air Base [*California*] [*ICAO location identifier*] (ICLI)
**KDCK**......... Cadec Systems, Inc. [*NASDAQ symbol*] (NQ)
**KDCK**......... Dodge City, KS [*FM radio station call letters*]
**KDCL**......... Knocked Down, in Carloads

**KDCP** ........ Kidney Disease Control Program [*Public Health Service*]
**KDCR** ........ Sioux Center, IA [*FM radio station call letters*]
**KDCV-FM** ... Blair, NE [*FM radio station call letters*]
**KDCY** ........ Cotulla, TX [*FM radio station call letters*]
**KDCZ** ........ Delta Junction, AK [*FM radio station call letters*]
**KDD** ........... Kokusai Denshin Denwa Co. Ltd. [*Telegraph & Telephone Corp.*] [*Tokyo, Japan*] [*Telecommunications*]
**KDDA** ........ Dumas, AR [*AM radio station call letters*]
**KDDA-FM** ... Dumas, AR [*FM radio station call letters*]
**KDDB** ........ Paso Robles, CA [*FM radio station call letters*]
**KDDD** ........ Dumas, TX [*AM radio station call letters*]
**KDDGAU** ... Deutsche Dendrologische Gesellschaft. Kurzmitteilungen [*A publication*]
**KDDQ** ........ Comanche, OK [*FM radio station call letters*]
**KDDR** ........ Oakes, ND [*AM radio station call letters*]
**KDDR-FM** ... Oakes, ND [*FM radio station call letters*]
**KDD Tech J** ... KDD Technical Journal [*A publication*]
**KDDYF** ...... Kennedy Resources [*NASDAQ symbol*] (NQ)
**KDe** ........... Derby Public Library, Derby, KS [*Library symbol*] [*Library of Congress*] (LCLS)
**KDE** ........... Keyboard Data Entry
**KDE** ........... Kidde, Inc. [*NYSE symbol*] (SPSG)
**KDE** ........... Koroba [*Papua New Guinea*] [*Airport symbol*] [*Obsolete*] (OAG)
**KDEA** ........ New Iberia, LA [*FM radio station call letters*]
**KDEB-TV** ... Springfield, MO [*Television station call letters*]
**KDEC** ........ Decorah, IA [*AM radio station call letters*]
**KDEE** ........ Cameron, MO [*FM radio station call letters*]
**KDEF** ........ Albuquerque, NM [*AM radio station call letters*]
**KDEL-FM** ... Arkadelphia, AR [*FM radio station call letters*]
**KDEM** ....... Deming, NM [*FM radio station call letters*]
**KDEM** ....... Kurzweil Data Entry Machine [*for optical character recognition*]
**KDEN** ........ Denver, CO [*AM radio station call letters*]
**KDEN** ........ Denver/Stapleton International [*Colorado*] [*ICAO location identifier*] (ICLI)
**KDEO** ........ Waipahu, HI [*AM radio station call letters*]
**KDEO-FM** ... Waipahu, HI [*FM radio station call letters*]
**KDES** ......... Palm Springs, CA [*AM radio station call letters*]
**KDES-FM** ... Palm Springs, CA [*FM radio station call letters*]
**KDET** ........ Center, TX [*AM radio station call letters*]
**KDET** ........ Detroit/Detroit City [*Michigan*] [*ICAO location identifier*] (ICLI)
**KDEV** ........ Juneau, AK [*FM radio station call letters*]
**KDEW** ....... De Witt, AR [*AM radio station call letters*]
**KDEW-FM** ... De Witt, AR [*FM radio station call letters*]
**KDEX** ........ Dexter, MO [*AM radio station call letters*]
**KDEX-FM** ... Dexter, MO [*FM radio station call letters*]
**KDEZ** ........ Jonesboro, AR [*FM radio station call letters*]
**KDF** ........... Kalamein [*Trademark*] Door and Frame
**KDF** ........... Knob Door Fastener
**KDF** ........... Knocked Down Flat
**KDF** ........... Koenigsberger Deutsche Forschungen [*A publication*]
**KDF** ........... Kraft durch Freude [*Strength through Joy Movement*] [*Pre-World War II*] [*German*]
**KDFC** ......... Kenny Dale Fan Club (EA)
**KDFC** ......... Korea Development Finance Corporation
**KDFC** ......... Palo Alto, CA [*AM radio station call letters*]
**KDFC-FM** ... San Francisco, CA [*FM radio station call letters*]
**KDFI-TV** ... Dallas, TX [*Television station call letters*]
**KDFM** ....... Silverton, CO [*FM radio station call letters*]
**KDFN** ........ Doniphan, MO [*AM radio station call letters*]
**KDFR** ........ Des Moines, IA [*FM radio station call letters*]
**KDFT** ......... Ferris, TX [*AM radio station call letters*]
**KDFW** ....... Dallas-Fort Worth/Regional Airport [*Texas*] [*ICAO location identifier*] (ICLI)
**KDFW-TV** ... Dallas, TX [*Television station call letters*]
**KDFX** ......... Dubuque, IA [*FM radio station call letters*]
**KDG** ........... Kedougou [*Senegal*] [*Seismograph station code, US Geological Survey*] [*Closed*] (SEIS)
**KDG** ........... King's Dragoon Guards [*Later, QDG*] [*Military unit*] [*British*]
**KDGB** ........ Dodge City, KS [*FM radio station call letters*]
**KDGE** ........ Gainesville, TX [*FM radio station call letters*]
**KDGNB** ..... Kinki Daigaku Genshiryoku Kenkyusho Nenpo [*A publication*]
**KDGNBX** .. Annual Report. Kinki University. Atomic Energy Research Institute [*A publication*]
**KDGO** ........ Durango, CO [*AM radio station call letters*]
**KDH** .......... Kandahar [*Afghanistan*] [*Airport symbol*] (OAG)
**KDH** .......... Korean Direct Hire
**KDH** .......... Kosher Dining Hall (BJA)
**KDHB** ........ Las Vegas, NV [*AM radio station call letters*]
**KDHI** ......... Twentynine Palms, CA [*AM radio station call letters*]
**KDHL** ........ Faribault, MN [*AM radio station call letters*]
**KDHN** ........ Dimmitt, TX [*AM radio station call letters*]
**KDHN** ........ Dothan [*Alabama*] [*ICAO location identifier*] (ICLI)
**KDHS** ........ Modesto, CA [*FM radio station call letters*]
**KDHT** ........ Dalhart [*Texas*] [*ICAO location identifier*] (ICLI)
**KDHT** ........ Greeley, CO [*FM radio station call letters*]
**KDHX** ........ St. Louis, MO [*FM radio station call letters*]
**KDI** ............ KDI Corp. [*NYSE symbol*] (SPSG)
**KDI** ............ Kendari [*Indonesia*] [*Airport symbol*] (OAG)
**KDI** ............ Kuwaiti Dinar [*Monetary unit*] (DS)
**KDIA** ......... Oakland, CA [*AM radio station call letters*]
**KDIC** ......... Grinnell, IA [*FM radio station call letters*]
**KDIF** ......... Riverside, CA [*AM radio station call letters*]
**KDII** .......... Key Defense Intelligence Issue (MCD)
**KDIN-TV** .. Des Moines, IA [*Television station call letters*]
**KDIO** ......... Ortonville, MN [*AM radio station call letters*]
**KDIU** ......... Dimmitt, TX [*FM radio station call letters*]
**KDIX** ......... Dickinson, ND [*AM radio station call letters*]
**KDJI** .......... Holbrook, AZ [*AM radio station call letters*]
**KDJK** ......... Oakdale, CA [*FM radio station call letters*]
**KDJQ** ......... Red Bluff, CA [*FM radio station call letters*]
**KDJS** ......... Willmar, MN [*AM radio station call letters*]
**KDJW** ........ Amarillo, TX [*AM radio station call letters*]
**KDJW-FM** ... Amarillo, TX [*FM radio station call letters*]
**KDK** ........... Khodzhikent [*USSR*] [*Seismograph station code, US Geological Survey*] [*Closed*] (SEIS)
**KDK** ........... Kodiak Airways, Inc. [*Kodiak, AK*] [*FAA designator*] (FAAC)
**KDK** ........... Kodiak [*Alaska*] Municipal Airport [*Airport symbol*] [*Obsolete*] (OAG)
**KDKA** ........ Pittsburgh, PA [*AM radio station call letters*] [*First station to broadcast a baseball game, August 5, 1921*]
**KDKA-TV** ... Pittsburgh, PA [*Television station call letters*]
**KDKB** ........ Mesa-Phoenix, AZ [*FM radio station call letters*]
**KDKD** ........ Clinton, MO [*AM radio station call letters*]
**KDKD-FM** ... Clinton, MO [*FM radio station call letters*]
**KDKF-TV** ... Klamath Falls, OR [*Television station call letters*]
**KDKHB** ..... Kyoto Daigaku Kogyo Kyoin Yoseijo Kenkyu Hokoku [*A publication*]
**KDKIA** ....... Kyoto Daigaku Kogaku Kenkyusho Iho [*A publication*]
**KDKKB** ...... Kagoshima Daigaku Kogakubu Kenkyu Hokoku [*A publication*]
**KDKK-FM** ... Park Rapids, MN [*FM radio station call letters*]
**KDKO** ........ Littleton, CO [*AM radio station call letters*]
**KDKS** ........ Benton, LA [*FM radio station call letters*]
**KDKSB** ...... Kyushu Daigaku Kogaku Shuho [*A publication*]
**KDL** ........... Kerrisdale Resources Limited [*Vancouver Stock Exchange symbol*]
**KDL** ........... Kreisinger Development Laboratory (KSC)
**KDLA** ........ De Ridder, LA [*AM radio station call letters*]
**KDLB** ........ Henryetta, OK [*AM radio station call letters*]
**KDLCL** ...... Knocked Down, in Less than Carloads
**KDLF** ......... Del Rio/Laughlin Air Force Base [*Texas*] [*ICAO location identifier*] (ICLI)
**KDLF** ......... Port Neches, TX [*AM radio station call letters*]
**KDLG** ........ Dillingham, AK [*AM radio station call letters*]
**KDLH** ........ Duluth/International [*Minnesota*] [*ICAO location identifier*] (ICLI)
**KDLH-TV** ... Duluth, MN [*Television station call letters*]
**KDLK** ........ Del Rio, TX [*FM radio station call letters*]
**KDLM** ........ Detroit Lakes, MN [*AM radio station call letters*]
**KDLO-FM** ... Watertown, SD [*FM radio station call letters*]
**KDLO-TV** ... Florence, SD [*Television station call letters*]
**KDLP** ......... Bayou Vista, LA [*AM radio station call letters*]
**KDLR** ......... Devils Lake, ND [*AM radio station call letters*]
**KDLS** ......... Perry, IA [*AM radio station call letters*]
**KDLS-FM** ... Perry, IA [*FM radio station call letters*]
**KDLT** ......... Mitchell, SD [*Television station call letters*]
**KDLY** ......... Lander, WY [*FM radio station call letters*]
**KDMA** ........ Montevideo, MN [*AM radio station call letters*]
**KDMA** ........ Tucson/Davis Monthan Air Force Base [*Arizona*] [*ICAO location identifier*] (ICLI)
**KDMD** ....... Anchorage, AK [*Television station call letters*]
**KDMG-FM** ... Pella, IA [*FM radio station call letters*]
**KDMI** ......... Des Moines, IA [*FM radio station call letters*]
**KDMI** ......... Thousands of Delivered Machine Instructions [*Data processing*]
**KDMN** ....... Buena Vista, CO [*AM radio station call letters*]
**KDMO** ....... Carthage, MO [*AM radio station call letters*]
**KDMS** ........ El Dorado, AR [*AM radio station call letters*]
**KDMS** ........ Kennedy Space Center Data Management System [*NASA*] (NASA)
**K/DN** ......... Kickdown [*Automotive engineering*]
**KDN** ........... Kinetically Designed Nozzle (NASA)
**KDN** ........... N'Dende [*Gabon*] [*Airport symbol*] (OAG)
**K-DNA** ....... Deoxyribonucleic Acid - Kinetoplast [*Biochemistry, genetics*]
**KDNA** ........ Yakima, WA [*FM radio station call letters*]
**KDNC** ........ Denver City, TX [*FM radio station call letters*]
**KDNK** ........ Carbondale, CO [*FM radio station call letters*]
**KDNKDR** .. Proceedings. Faculty of Agriculture. Kyushu Tokai University [*A publication*]
**KDNL-TV** ... St. Louis, MO [*Television station call letters*]
**KDNO** ........ Delano, CA [*FM radio station call letters*]
**KDNT** ........ Denton, TX [*AM radio station call letters*]
**KDNW** ....... Duluth, MN [*FM radio station call letters*]
**KDNY** ........ Home Intensive Care, Inc. [*NASDAQ symbol*] (NQ)
**KDO** ........... Ketodeoxyoctonate [*Biochemistry*]
**KDO** ........... Key District Office [*IRS*]
**KDOA** ........ Tulia, TX [*FM radio station call letters*]
**KDOB-TV** ... Bakersfield, CA [*Television station call letters*]
**KDOC-TV** ... Anaheim, CA [*Television station call letters*]

**KDOE**........ Brigham City, UT [*FM radio station call letters*]
**KDOG**........ North Mankato, MN [*FM radio station call letters*]
**KDOK**........ Tyler, TX [*AM radio station call letters*]
**KDOM**....... Windom, MN [*AM radio station call letters*]
**KDOM-FM** ... Windom, MN [*FM radio station call letters*]
**KDON** ....... Kaydon Corp. [*Muskegon, MI*] [*NASDAQ symbol*] (NQ)
**KDON-FM** ... Salinas, CA [*FM radio station call letters*]
**KDOR**........ Bartlesville, OK [*Television station call letters*]
**KDOS**........ Key to Disk Operating System
**KDOS**........ Key Display Operating System
**KDOS**........ Laredo, TX [*AM radio station call letters*]
**KDOV**........ Dover Air Force Base [*Delaware*] [*ICAO location identifier*] (ICLI)
**KDP**........... Kandep [*Papua New Guinea*] [*Airport symbol*] [*Obsolete*] (OAG)
**KDP**........... Key Data Points (MCD)
**KDP**........... Key Development Plan [*Telecommunications*] (TEL)
**KDP**........... Keyboard, Display, and Printer [*Data processing*]
**KDP**........... Known Datum Point
**KDP**........... Korean Democratic Party [*Political party*] [*Democratic People's Republic of Korea*] (FEA)
**KDP**........... Kurdish Democratic Party [*Iran*] [*Political party*]
**KDP**........... Potassium Dideuterium Phosphate
**KDP**........... Potassium [*Kalium*] Dihydrogen Phosphate [*Inorganic chemistry*]
**KDPA**........ Knitgoods Dyers and Processors Association
**KDPA**........ West Chicago/Du Page County [*Illinois*] [*ICAO location identifier*] (ICLI)
**KDPI**.......... Kurdish Democratic Party of Iran [*Political party*] (PPW)
**KDPM**....... Kleine Deutsche Prosadenkmaeler des Mittelalters [*A publication*]
**K-DPN**....... KSC [*Kennedy Space Center*] DOD [*Department of Defense*] Payloads Notice [*NASA*] (NASA)
**K-DPPS**..... KSC [*Kennedy Space Center*] DOD [*Department of Defense*] Payloads Projects Specification [*NASA*] (NASA)
**KDPR**........ Dickinson, ND [*FM radio station call letters*]
**KDPS**......... Des Moines, IA [*FM radio station call letters*]
**KDPS**......... Kurdish Democratic Party of Syria [*Political party*]
**KDQN**........ De Queen, AR [*AM radio station call letters*]
**KDQN-FM** ... De Queen, AR [*FM radio station call letters*]
**KDR**........... Kandrian [*Papua New Guinea*] [*Airport symbol*] (OAG)
**KDR**........... Kangeld Resources Ltd. [*Vancouver Stock Exchange symbol*]
**KDR**........... Kappa Delta Rho [*Fraternity*]
**KDR**........... Keyboard Data Recorder [*Data processing*]
**KDR**........... Kidderminster [*British depot code*]
**K/DR**......... Kitchen/Dining Room [*Classified advertising*] (ADA)
**KDR**........... Knockdown Resistance [*Pesticide technology*]
**KDRF**......... Deer Lodge, MT [*FM radio station call letters*]
**KDRG**........ Deer Lodge, MT [*AM radio station call letters*]
**KDRK-FM** ... Spokane, WA [*FM radio station call letters*]
**KDRM**....... Moses Lake, WA [*FM radio station call letters*]
**KDRNBK** .. Annual Report. Noto Marine Laboratory [*A publication*]
**KDRO**........ Sedalia, MO [*AM radio station call letters*]
**KDRQ**........ Wishek, ND [*AM radio station call letters*]
**KDRS**......... Paragould, AR [*AM radio station call letters*]
**KDRT**........ Del Rio/International [*Texas*] [*ICAO location identifier*] (ICLI)
**KDRV**........ Medford, OR [*Television station call letters*]
**KDRW**....... Silverton, CO [*AM radio station call letters*]
**KDRY**........ Alamo Heights, TX [*AM radio station call letters*]
**KDS**........... Kamad Silver Co. Ltd. [*Vancouver Stock Exchange symbol*]
**KDS**........... Kathode Dark Space
**KDS**........... Kaufman Developmental Scale [*Child development test*]
**KDS**........... Kedougou [*Senegal*] [*Seismograph station code, US Geological Survey*] (SEIS)
**KDS**........... Keel Depth Simulator
**KDS**........... Key to Disc System
**KDS**........... Key Display System [*Data processing*] (MDG)
**KDS**........... Komma Dimokratikou Sosialismou [*Party for Democratic Socialism*] [*Greek*] [*Political party*] (PPE)
**KDS**........... Kristen Demokratisk Samling [*Christian Democratic Union*] [*Sweden*] [*Political party*] (PPE)
**KDSD-FM** ... Pierpont, SD [*FM radio station call letters*]
**KDSD-TV** ... Aberdeen, SD [*Television station call letters*]
**KDSE**......... Dickinson, ND [*Television station call letters*]
**KDSGA**...... Kagoshima Daigaku Suisangakubu Kiyo [*A publication*]
**KDSI**.......... Alice, TX [*AM radio station call letters*]
**KDSI**.......... Knowledge Data System, Inc. [*NASDAQ symbol*] (NQ)
**KDSI**.......... Thousands of Delivered Source Instructions [*Data processing*]
**KDSJ**.......... Deadwood, SD [*AM radio station call letters*]
**KDSL**......... Konzepte der Sprack- und Literaturwissenschaft [*A publication*]
**KDSL**......... Thousands of Delivered Source Lines of Code [*Data processing*]
**KDSM**....... Des Moines [*Iowa*] [*ICAO location identifier*] (ICLI)
**KDSM**....... Keratinizing Desquamative Squamous Metaplasia [*Medicine*]
**KDSM-TV** ... Des Moines, IA [*Television station call letters*]
**KDSN**........ Denison, IA [*AM radio station call letters*]
**KDSN-FM** ... Denison, IA [*FM radio station call letters*]
**KDSQ**........ Denison-Sherman, TX [*FM radio station call letters*]
**KDSR**......... Williston, ND [*FM radio station call letters*]
**KDSRA2**.... Annals of Science. Kanazawa University. Part 2. Biology-Geology [*A publication*]
**KDST**......... Dyersville, IA [*FM radio station call letters*]
**KDSU**......... Fargo, ND [*FM radio station call letters*]
**KDSX**......... Denison-Sherman, TX [*AM radio station call letters*]
**KDT**........... Kammer der Technik
**KDT**........... Kathodal Duration Tetanus [*Medicine*]
**KDT**........... Key Data Terminal
**KDT**........... Key-to-Disk-to-Tape (MCD)
**KDT**........... Keyboard Display Terminal (MCD)
**KDT**........... Keyboard and Display Test (MCD)
**KDTA**........ Delta, CO [*AM radio station call letters*]
**KDTD**........ Plainview, TX [*FM radio station call letters*]
**KDTE**......... Kathodal Duration Tetanus [*Medicine*] (ROG)
**KDTH**........ Dubuque, IA [*AM radio station call letters*]
**KDTIA**....... Kumamoto Daigaku Taishitsu Igaku Kenkyusho Hokoku [*A publication*]
**KDTN**........ Denton, TX [*Television station call letters*]
**KDTV**........ San Francisco, CA [*Television station call letters*]
**KDTW**....... Detroit/Metropolitan Wayne County [*Michigan*] [*ICAO location identifier*] (ICLI)
**KDTX-TV** ... Dallas, TX [*Television station call letters*]
**KDU**........... Keyboard Display Unit (MCD)
**KDUB-TV** ... Dubuque, IA [*Television station call letters*]
**KDUC**........ Barstow, CA [*FM radio station call letters*]
**KDUG**........ Douglas/Bisbee International [*Arizona*] [*ICAO location identifier*] (ICLI)
**KDUH-TV** ... Scottsbluff, NE [*Television station call letters*]
**KDUK**........ Eugene, OR [*AM radio station call letters*]
**KDUN**........ Reedsport, OR [*AM radio station call letters*]
**KDUO**........ Riverside, CA [*FM radio station call letters*]
**KDUR**........ Durango, CO [*FM radio station call letters*]
**KDUX-FM** ... Aberdeen, WA [*FM radio station call letters*]
**KDUZ**........ Hutchinson, MN [*AM radio station call letters*]
**KDV**........... Kalender der Detuschen Volksgemeinschaft fuer Rumaenien [*A publication*]
**KDV**........... Kandavu [*Fiji*] [*Airport symbol*] (OAG)
**KdV**........... Korteweg-deVries [*Equation*] [*Mathematics*]
**kDVC**........ Kilovolts, Direct Current (KSC)
**KDVL**........ Devils Lake, ND [*FM radio station call letters*]
**KDVR**........ Denver, CO [*Television station call letters*]
**KDVS**......... Davis, CA [*FM radio station call letters*]
**KDVS**......... Kongelige Danske Videnskabernes Selskab. Historisk-Filosofiske Meddelelser [*Copenhagen*] [*A publication*]
**KDVSA**...... Kongelige Danske Videnskabernes Selskab. Matematisk-Fysisk Meddelelser [*A publication*]
**KDVV**........ Topeka, KS [*FM radio station call letters*]
**KDWA**....... Hastings, MN [*AM radio station call letters*]
**KDWB**....... St. Paul, MN [*AM radio station call letters*]
**KDWB-FM** ... Richfield, MN [*FM radio station call letters*]
**KDWD**....... Burlington, IA [*FM radio station call letters*]
**KDWN**....... Las Vegas, NV [*AM radio station call letters*]
**KDWZ**....... Des Moines, IA [*FM radio station call letters*]
**KDX**........... Klondex Mines [*Vancouver Stock Exchange symbol*]
**KDX**........... Knock Down Export [*Automotive engineering*]
**KDXA**........ Virginia City, NV [*AM radio station call letters*]
**KDXE**........ Sulphur Springs, TX [*FM radio station call letters*]
**KDXI**......... Mansfield, LA [*AM radio station call letters*]
**KDXL**........ St. Louis Park, MN [*FM radio station call letters*]
**KDXR**........ Borger, TX [*FM radio station call letters*]
**KDXT**........ Missoula, MT [*FM radio station call letters*]
**KDXU**........ St. George, UT [*AM radio station call letters*]
**KDXY**........ Paragould, AR [*FM radio station call letters*]
**KDY**........... Kennedy Resources [*Vancouver Stock Exchange symbol*]
**KDYL**........ Salt Lake City, UT [*AM radio station call letters*]
**KDYN**........ Ozark, AR [*AM radio station call letters*]
**KDYN-FM** ... Ozark, AR [*FM radio station call letters*]
**KDYS**......... Abilene/Dyess Air Force Base [*Texas*] [*ICAO location identifier*] (ICLI)
**KDZ**........... Kurdzhali [*Bulgaria*] [*Seismograph station code, US Geological Survey*] (SEIS)
**KDZA**........ Pueblo, CO [*AM radio station call letters*]
**KDZN**........ Glendive, MT [*FM radio station call letters*]
**KE**.............. Kaiser Engineers (NRCH)
**Ke**.............. Keen's English Rolls Court Reports [*48 English Reprint*] [*A publication*] (DLA)
**KE**.............. Keewatin Echo [*A publication*]
**KE**.............. Kendall's Compound E [*Cortisone*]
**ke**............... Kenya [*MARC country of publication code*] [*Library of Congress*] (LCCP)
**KE**.............. Kenya [*ANSI two-letter standard code*] (CNC)
**KE**.............. Kerr Effect [*Optics*]
**KE**.............. Key Equipment [*Telecommunications*] (TEL)
**KE**.............. Kinetic Energy
**KE**.............. King Edward (ROG)
**KE**.............. Knight of the Eagle
**KE**.............. Knight of the Elephant [*Denmark*]
**KE**.............. Knights of Equity (EA)
**KE**.............. Knowledge Engineer [*Data processing*]
**KE**.............. Koger Equity, Inc. [*AMEX symbol*] (CTT)
**KE**.............. Korean Air Lines, Inc. [*ICAO designator*] (FAAC)
**KEA**........... Kanada Esperanto-Asocio [*Canadian Esperanto Association*]

**KEA** .......... Kealakomo [*Hawaii*] [*Seismograph station code, US Geological Survey*] [*Closed*] (SEIS)
**KEA** .......... Keane, Inc. [*AMEX symbol*] (SPSG)
**KEA** .......... Knitwear Employers Association (EA)
**KEAA** ........ Kearney, NE [*FM radio station call letters*]
**KEAG** ........ Anchorage, AK [*FM radio station call letters*]
**KEAN** ........ Abilene, TX [*AM radio station call letters*]
**Keane & Gr** ... Keane and Grant's English Registration Appeal Cases [*1854-62*] [*A publication*] (DLA)
**Keane & GRC** ... Keane and Grant's English Registration Appeal Cases [*1854-62*] [*A publication*] (DLA)
**KEAN-FM** ... Abilene, TX [*FM radio station call letters*]
**KEAP** ........ Fresno, CA [*AM radio station call letters*]
**KEAR** ........ San Francisco, CA [*FM radio station call letters*]
**KEAS** ........ Eastland, TX [*AM radio station call letters*]
**KEAS** ........ Knots Equivalent Airspeed (MCD)
**KEAS-FM** ... Eastland, TX [*FM radio station call letters*]
**Keat Fam Sett** ... Keatinge's Family Settlements [*1810*] [*A publication*] (DLA)
**Keats-Shell** ... Keats-Shelley Journal [*A publication*]
**Keats-Shelley J** ... Keats-Shelley Journal [*A publication*]
**Keats-Shelley J Ann Bibl** ... Keats-Shelley Journal. Annual Bibliography [*A publication*]
**Keats Sh M** ... Keats-Shelley Memorial Association. Bulletin [*A publication*]
**KEB** .......... English Bay, AK [*Location identifier*] [*FAA*] (FAAL)
**KEB** .......... Keban [*Turkey*] [*Seismograph station code, US Geological Survey*] (SEIS)
**Keb** .......... Keble's English King's Bench Reports [*83, 84 English Reprint*] [*A publication*] (DLA)
**KEB** .......... Korea Exchange Bank (IMH)
**KEBC** ........ Oklahoma City, OK [*FM radio station call letters*]
**KEB COLL** ... Keble College [*Oxford University*] (ROG)
**KEBE** ........ Jacksonville, TX [*AM radio station call letters*]
**Keb J** ........ Keble's Justice of the Peace [*A publication*] (DLA)
**Kebl** .......... Keble's English King's Bench Reports [*83, 84 English Reprint*] [*A publication*] (DLA)
**Keble** ........ Keble's English King's Bench Reports [*83, 84 English Reprint*] [*A publication*] (DLA)
**Keble (Eng)** ... Keble's English King's Bench Reports [*83, 84 English Reprint*] [*A publication*] (DLA)
**KEBR** ........ Kobe Economic and Business Review [*A publication*]
**KEBR** ........ Rocklin, CA [*AM radio station call letters*]
**Keb Stat** ..... Keble's Statutes [*A publication*] (DLA)
**KEC** .......... Kecskemet [*Hungary*] [*Seismograph station code, US Geological Survey*] (SEIS)
**KECC** ........ Miles City, MT [*FM radio station call letters*]
**KECG** ........ El Cerrito, CA [*FM radio station call letters*]
**KECG** ........ Elizabeth City Coast Guard Air Base/Municipal [*North Carolina*] [*ICAO location identifier*] (ICLI)
**KECH-FM** ... Sun Valley, ID [*FM radio station call letters*]
**KECI-TV** ... Missoula, MT [*Television station call letters*]
**KECO** ........ Elk City, OK [*FM radio station call letters*]
**K & E Conv** ... Key and Elphinstone's Conveyancing [*15th ed.*] [*1953-54*] [*A publication*] (DLA)
**KECP** ........ Kit Engineering Change Proposal (KSC)
**KECR** ........ El Cajon, CA [*FM radio station call letters*]
**KECU** ........ Eureka, CA [*FM radio station call letters*]
**KECY-TV** ... Yuma, AZ [*Television station call letters*]
**KED** .......... Kaedi [*Mauritania*] [*Airport symbol*] (OAG)
**KED** .......... Kedougou [*Senegal*] [*Seismograph station code, US Geological Survey*] [*Closed*] (SEIS)
**KED** .......... Known Enemy Dead [*Military*]
**KEDA** ........ San Antonio, TX [*AM radio station call letters*]
**KEDB** ........ Las Vegas, NV [*FM radio station call letters*]
**KEDD** ........ Dodge City, KS [*AM radio station call letters*]
**Ke Do** ........ Kerygma und Dogma [*A publication*]
**KEDO** ........ Longview, WA [*AM radio station call letters*]
**KEDP** ........ Las Vegas, NM [*FM radio station call letters*]
**KEDT** ........ Corpus Christi, TX [*Television station call letters*]
**KEDW** ........ Edwards Air Force Base [*California*] [*ICAO location identifier*] (ICLI)
**KEDY** ........ Mount Shasta, CA [*FM radio station call letters*]
**KEE** .......... Emporia State University, School of Library Science, Emporia, KS [*OCLC symbol*] (OCLC)
**KEE** .......... Kantoor en Efficiency [*A publication*]
**KEE** .......... Kelle [*Congo*] [*Airport symbol*] (OAG)
**KEE** .......... Kerr Electro-Optical Effect [*Optics*]
**KEE** .......... Keychart Educational Equipment [*for use with an electronic typewriter*]
**KEE** .......... Knowledge Engineering Environment [*An artificial intelligence system*]
**KEED** ........ Eugene, OR [*AM radio station call letters*]
**KEEE** ........ Nacogdoches, TX [*AM radio station call letters*]
**KEEF-TV** .. Los Angeles, CA [*Television station call letters*]
**KEEI** ........ Key Energy Enterprises, Incorporated [*NASDAQ symbol*] (NQ)
**KEEI** ........ Winslow, AZ [*FM radio station call letters*]
**KEEL** ........ Kent European Enterprises Limited [*British*]
**KEEL** ........ Shreveport, LA [*AM radio station call letters*]
**Keen** .......... Keen's English Rolls Court Reports [*48 English Reprint*] [*A publication*] (DLA)
**KEEN** ........ San Jose, CA [*AM radio station call letters*]
**Keen Ch** ..... Keen's English Rolls Court Reports [*48 English Reprint*] [*A publication*] (DLA)
**Keen (Eng)** ... Keen's English Rolls Court Reports [*48 English Reprint*] [*A publication*] (DLA)
**Keener Quasi Contr** ... Keener's Cases on Quasi Contracts [*A publication*] (DLA)
**KEEP** ........ Kyosato Education Experiment Project [*Self-help program for Japanese farmers established by Americans in 1948*]
**KEEP** ........ Marshall, TX [*FM radio station call letters*]
**Keep Abreast J** ... Keeping Abreast. Journal of Human Nurturing [*A publication*]
**Keep Abreast J Hum Nurt** ... Keeping Abreast. Journal of Human Nurturing [*A publication*]
**KEEPS** ...... Kodak Ektaprint Electronic Publishing System [*Hardware and software components*] [*Eastman Kodak Co.*]
**KEES** ........ Gladewater, TX [*AM radio station call letters*]
**KEET** ........ Eureka, CA [*Television station call letters*]
**KEEX** ........ Kee Exploration, Inc. [*NASDAQ symbol*] (NQ)
**KEEY-FM** ... Minneapolis, MN [*FM radio station call letters*]
**KEEZ-FM** ... Mankato, MN [*FM radio station call letters*]
**KEF** .......... Reykjavik [*Iceland*] Keflavik Airport [*Airport symbol*] (OAG)
**KEFD** ........ Houston/Ellington Air Force Base [*Texas*] [*ICAO location identifier*] (ICLI)
**KEFM** ........ Omaha, NE [*FM radio station call letters*]
**KEFR** ........ Le Grand, CA [*FM radio station call letters*]
**KEG** .......... Keg Restaurants Ltd. [*Toronto Stock Exchange symbol*] [*Vancouver Stock Exchange symbol*]
**KEGEAC** ... Japanese Journal of Plastic and Reconstructive Surgery [*A publication*]
**KEGG** ........ Daingerfield, TX [*AM radio station call letters*]
**KEGL** ........ Fort Worth, TX [*FM radio station call letters*]
**KEGP** ........ Eagle Pass/Municipal [*Texas*] [*ICAO location identifier*] (ICLI)
**KEGS** ........ Emporia, KS [*FM radio station call letters*]
**KEGS** ........ Kenworth Engine Governing System [*Automotive engineering*]
**KEH** .......... King Edward's Horse Regiment [*Military unit*] [*British*]
**KEH** .......... Kurzgefasstes Exegetisches Handbuch zum Alten Testament [*Leipzig*] [*A publication*] (BJA)
**Kehutanan Indones** ... Kehutanan Indonesia [*A publication*]
**KEI** .......... Keidanren Review of Japanese Economy [*A publication*]
**KEI** .......... Keithley Instruments [*AMEX symbol*] (SPSG)
**KEI** .......... Kepi [*Indonesia*] [*Airport symbol*] (OAG)
**KEI** .......... Kresge Eye Institute
**KEIA** ........ Korea Economic Institute of America (EA)
**KEIKA** ...... Keikinzoku [*A publication*]
**Keil** .......... Keilway's English King's Bench Reports [*72 English Reprint*] [*A publication*] (DLA)
**KEIL** ........ Key Essential Item List [*Defense Supply Agency*]
**Keilw** ........ Keilway's English King's Bench Reports [*72 English Reprint*] [*A publication*] (DLA)
**Keilway** ...... Keilway's English King's Bench Reports [*72 English Reprint*] [*A publication*] (DLA)
**Keilw (Eng)** ... Keilway's English King's Bench Reports [*72 English Reprint*] [*A publication*] (DLA)
**KEIN** ........ Great Falls, MT [*AM radio station call letters*]
**Keio Bus R** ... Keio Business Review [*Tokyo*] [*A publication*]
**Keio Econ S** ... Keio Economic Studies [*A publication*]
**Keio Econ Stud** ... Keio Economic Studies [*Tokyo*] [*A publication*]
**Keio Eng Rep** ... Keio Engineering Reports [*A publication*]
**Keio Engrg Rep** ... Keio Engineering Reports [*A publication*]
**Keio J Med** ... Keio Journal of Medicine [*A publication*]
**Keio J Polit** ... Keio Journal of Politics [*A publication*]
**Keio Math Sem Rep** ... Keio Mathematical Seminar. Reports [*A publication*]
**Keio Sci Tech Rep** ... Keio Science and Technology Reports [*A publication*]
**KEIS** ........ Kentucky Economic Information System [*University of Kentucky*] [*Lexington*] [*Database producer*] [*Information service or system*]
**Keisai Geppo** ... Keiji Saiban Geppo [*A publication*]
**Keishu** ........ Saiko Saibansho Keiji Hanreishu [*A publication*]
**Keith Ch PA** ... Registrar's Book, Keith's Court of Chancery [*Pennsylvania*] [*A publication*] (DLA)
**Keith Shipton Dev Spec Study** ... Keith Shipton Developments. Special Study [*A publication*]
**KEJO** ........ Corvallis, OR [*FM radio station call letters*]
**KEJO** ........ Kelly-Johnston Enterprises [*NASDAQ symbol*] (NQ)
**KEJS** ........ Lubbock, TX [*FM radio station call letters*]
**KEK** .......... Ekwok [*Alaska*] [*Airport symbol*] (OAG)
**KEK** .......... Kappa Eta Kappa [*Fraternity*]
**Ke K** .......... Keiryo Kokugogaku [*Mathematical Linguistics*] [*A publication*]
**KEK** .......... Konferenz Europaeischer Kirchen [*Conference of European Churches - CEC*] (EA)
**KEK** .......... Kypriakon Ethnikon Komma [*Cypriot National Party (1944-1960)*] [*Greek Cypriot*] [*Political party*] (PPE)
**KEKA-FM** ... Eureka, CA [*FM radio station call letters*]
**KEK Annu Rep (Natl Lab High Energy Phys)** ... KEK Annual Report (National Laboratory for High Energy Physics) [*A publication*]
**KEKB** ........ Fruita, CO [*FM radio station call letters*]
**KEKHA** ..... Koshu Eiseiin Kenkyu Hokoku [*A publication*]

**KEL**.......... Karntner Einheitsliste [*Carinthian Unity List*] [*Austria*] [*Political party*] (PPE)
**KEL**.......... Keles [*USSR*] [*Later, TKT*] [*Geomagnetic observatory code*]
**Kel**.......... Kelim (BJA)
**KEL**.......... Kelsey-Hayes Canada Ltd. [*Toronto Stock Exchange symbol*]
**KEL**.......... Kelud [*Java*] [*Seismograph station code, US Geological Survey*] [*Closed*] (SEIS)
**Kel**.......... [*Sir John*] Kelyng's English Crown Cases [*A publication*] (DLA)
**KEL**.......... Known Enemy Location [*Military*]
**KEL**.......... Koroska Enotna Lista [*Carinthian Unity List*] [*Austria*] [*Political party*] (PPE)
**Kel 1**.......... [*Sir John*] Kelyng's English Crown Cases [*A publication*] (DLA)
**Kel 2**.......... [*William*] Kelynge's English Chancery Reports [*A publication*] (DLA)
**KELA**.......... Centralia-Chehalis, WA [*AM radio station call letters*]
**Kel An**.......... Kelly's Life Annuities [*1835*] [*A publication*] (DLA)
**Kel CC**.......... [*Sir John*] Kelyng's English Crown Cases [*A publication*] (DLA)
**Kel Cont**.......... Kelly on Contracts of Married Women [*A publication*] (DLA)
**KELD**.......... El Dorado, AR [*AM radio station call letters*]
**KELD**.......... El Dorado/Goodwin Field [*Arkansas*] [*ICAO location identifier*] (ICLI)
**Kel Draft**.......... Kelly's Draftsman [*14th ed.*] [*1978*] [*A publication*] (DLA)
**KELE**.......... Aurora, MO [*FM radio station call letters*]
**KELG**.......... Elgin, TX [*AM radio station call letters*]
**Kel GA**.......... Kelly's Reports [*1-3 Georgia*] [*A publication*] (DLA)
**Kelh**.......... Kelham's Norman French Law Dictionary [*A publication*] (DLA)
**Kelham**.......... Kelham's Norman French Law Dictionary [*A publication*] (DLA)
**Kelh Dict**.......... Kelham's Norman French Law Dictionary [*A publication*] (DLA)
**KELI**.......... Kristana Esperantista Ligo Internacia [*International Christian Esperanto Association*] (EAIO)
**KELI**.......... San Angelo, TX [*FM radio station call letters*]
**Kel J**.......... [*Sir John*] Kelyng's English Crown Cases [*A publication*] (DLA)
**KELK**.......... Elko, NV [*AM radio station call letters*]
**Kelk Jud Acts** ... Kelke's Judicature Acts [*A publication*] (DLA)
**Kellen**.......... Kellen's Reports [*146-55 Massachusetts*] [*A publication*] (DLA)
**Kell GA R**.. [*James M.*] Kelly's Georgia Reports [*A publication*] (DLA)
**Kel Life Ann** ... Kelly on Life Annuities [*A publication*] (DLA)
**Kelly**.......... Kelly's Reports [*1-3 Georgia*] [*A publication*] (DLA)
**Kelly & C** ... Kelly and Cobb's Reports [*4, 5 Georgia*] [*A publication*] (DLA)
**Kelly & Cobb** ... Kelly and Cobb's Reports [*4, 5 Georgia*] [*A publication*] (DLA)
**KELN**.......... North Platte, NE [*FM radio station call letters*]
**KELO**.......... Sioux Falls, SD [*AM radio station call letters*]
**KELO-FM** ... Sioux Falls, SD [*FM radio station call letters*]
**KELO-TV** ... Sioux Falls, SD [*Television station call letters*]
**KELP**.......... El Paso/International [*Texas*] [*ICAO location identifier*] (ICLI)
**KELP**.......... El Paso, TX [*AM radio station call letters*]
**KELP**.......... Kindergarten Evaluation for Learning Potential [*McGraw Hill*]
**KELR-FM** ... Chariton, IA [*FM radio station call letters*]
**KELS**.......... Kohlman Evaluation of Living Skills [*Occupational therapy*]
**Kel Sc Fac**.. Kelly's Scire Facias [*2nd ed.*] [*1849*] [*A publication*] (DLA)
**KELT**.......... Harlingen, TX [*FM radio station call letters*]
**KELU**.......... Kuching Employees and Labourers' Union [*Sarawak*]
**Kel Us**.......... Kelly on Usury [*1835*] [*A publication*] (DLA)
**Kel W**.......... [*William*] Kelynge's English Chancery Reports [*A publication*] (DLA)
**KELY**.......... Ely, NV [*AM radio station call letters*]
**KELY**.......... Kelly Services, Inc. [*NASDAQ symbol*] (NQ)
**KELY-FM** ... Ely, NV [*FM radio station call letters*]
**Kelynge W** ... [*William*] Kelynge's English Chancery Reports [*A publication*] (DLA)
**Kelynge W (Eng)** ... [*William*] Kelynge's English Chancery Reports [*A publication*] (DLA)
**Kelyng J**..... [*Sir John*] Kelyng's English Crown Cases [*A publication*] (DLA)
**Kelyng J (Eng)** ... [*Sir John*] Kelyng's English Crown Cases [*A publication*] (DLA)
**KEm**.......... Emporia Public Library, Emporia, KS [*Library symbol*] [*Library of Congress*] (LCLS)
**KEM**.......... Kemi [*Finland*] [*Airport symbol*] (OAG)
**KEM**.......... Kemper Corp. [*NYSE symbol*] (SPSG)
**KEMA Publ** ... KEMA [*Keuring van Elektrotechnische Materialen Arnhem*] Publikaties [*A publication*]
**KEMAR**..... Knowles Electronics Manikin for Acoustic Research
**KEMA Sci Tech Rep** ... KEMA [*Keuring van Elektrotechnische Materialen Arnhem*] Scientific and Technical Reports [*A publication*]
**KEMB**.......... Emmetsburg, IA [*FM radio station call letters*]
**Kemble Sax** ... Kemble's The Saxons in England [*A publication*] (DLA)
**KEMC**.......... Billings, MT [*FM radio station call letters*]
**KEmC**.......... College of Emporia, Emporia, KS [*Library symbol*] [*Library of Congress*] (LCLS)
**KEMEDB** ... Infection, Inflammation, and Immunity [*A publication*]
**Kemerov Gos Ped Inst Ucen Zap** ... Kemerovskii Gosudarstvennyi Pedagogiceskii Institut Ucenye Zapiski [*A publication*]
**Kem Ind**..... Kemija u Industriji [*Yugoslavia*] [*A publication*]
**Kem-Kemi** ... Kemia-Kemi [*A publication*]
**Kem Kozl**.... Kemiai Kozlemenyek [*A publication*]
**Kem Kozlem** ... Kemiai Kozlemenyek [*A publication*]
**KEMM**...... Commerce, TX [*FM radio station call letters*]
**Kem Maandesbl Nord Handelsbl Kem Ind** ... Kemisk Maandesblad. Nordisk Handelsblad foer Kemisk Industri [*A publication*]
**KEMO**....... Kennesaw Mountain National Battlefield Park
**KEmT**........ Kansas State Teachers College, Emporia, KS [*Library symbol*] [*Library of Congress*] [*Obsolete*] (LCLS)
**Kem-Talajt** ... Kemia-Talajtani Tanszek [*A publication*]
**Kem Teollisuus** ... Kemian Teollisuus [*Finland*] [*A publication*]
**Kem Tidskr** ... Kemisk Tidskrift [*A publication*]
**KEmU**........ Emporia State University, Emporia, KS [*Library symbol*] [*Library of Congress*] (LCLS)
**KEM-V**...... Kinetic Energy Missile Vehicle [*Army*]
**KEMV**....... Mountain View, AR [*Television station call letters*]
**Ken**.......... Kendall [*Record label*]
**KEN**.......... Kenema [*Sierra Leone*] [*Airport symbol*] (OAG)
**KEN**.......... Kennedy Air Service [*Valdez, AK*] [*FAA designator*] (FAAC)
**KEN**.......... Kenridge Mineral [*Vancouver Stock Exchange symbol*]
**KEN**.......... Kentucky
**KEN**.......... Kenya [*ANSI three-letter standard code*] (CNC)
**KEN**.......... Kenyon College, Gambier, OH [*OCLC symbol*] (OCLC)
**Ken**.......... Kenyon's English King's Bench Reports [*A publication*] (DLA)
**KENA**........ Kenai Corp. [*NASDAQ symbol*] (NQ)
**KENA**........ Mena, AR [*AM radio station call letters*]
**KENA-FM** ... Mena, AR [*FM radio station call letters*]
**Kenan**........ Kenan's Reports [*76-91 North Carolina*] [*A publication*] (DLA)
**Kenana Res Stn Annu Rep** ... Kenana Research Station. Annual Report [*A publication*]
**KENC**........ Kentucky Central Life Insurance Co. [*NASDAQ symbol*] (NQ)
**KENCLIP** ... Kentucky Cooperative Library and Information Project [*Library network*]
**KENCO**..... Kendrick & Company [*Telecommunications service*] (TSSD)
**KEND**........ Enid/Vance Air Force Base [*Oklahoma*] [*ICAO location identifier*] (ICLI)
**Ken Dec**...... Kentucky Decisions (Sneed) [*2 Kentucky*] [*A publication*] (DLA)
**KENE**........ Toppenish, WA [*AM radio station call letters*]
**KENI**.......... Anchorage, AK [*AM radio station call letters*]
**Kenkyu Hokoku Bull Fac Agric Tamagawa Univ** ... Kenkyu Hokoku. Bulletin. Faculty of Agriculture. Tamagawa University [*A publication*]
**Kenkyu Hokoku J Niigata Agricultural Experiment Station** ... Kenkyu Hokoku. Journal. Niigata Agricultural Experiment Station [*A publication*]
**Kenkyu Hokoku J Tottori Univ Nat Sci** ... Kenkyu Hokoku. Journal. Faculty of Education. Tottori University. Natural Science [*A publication*]
**Kenkyu Hokoku Res Bull Hokkaido Natl Agric Exp Stn** ... Kenkyu Hokoku. Research Bulletin. Hokkaido National Agricultural Experiment Station [*A publication*]
**Kenkyu Hokoku Sci Pap Cent Res Inst Jap Tob Salt Public Corp** ... Kenkyu Hokoku. Scientific Papers. Central Research Institute. Japan Tobacco and Salt Public Corporation [*A publication*]
**Kenley Abstr** ... Kenley Abstracts [*A publication*]
**Ken LR**....... Kentucky Law Reporter [*A publication*] (DLA)
**Ken L Re**.... Kentucky Law Reporter [*A publication*] (DLA)
**KENN**........ Farmington, NM [*AM radio station call letters*]
**KENN**........ Kennecott Co. Railroad [*AAR code*]
**KENN**........ Kennington Ltd. [*NASDAQ symbol*] (NQ)
**Kenn Ch**..... Kennedy's Chancery Practice [*2nd ed.*] [*1852-53*] [*A publication*] (DLA)
**Kenn C Mar** ... Kennedy on Courts-Martial [*A publication*] (DLA)
**Kennett**....... Kennett upon Impropriations [*A publication*] (DLA)
**Kennett**....... Kennett's Glossary [*A publication*] (DLA)
**Kennett Gloss** ... Kennett's Glossary [*A publication*] (DLA)
**Kennett Par Ant** ... Kennett's Parochial Antiquities [*A publication*] (DLA)
**Kenn Gloss** ... Kennett's Glossary [*A publication*] (DLA)
**Kenn Imp** ... Kennett upon Impropriations [*A publication*] (DLA)
**Kenn Jur**.... Kennedy on Juries [*A publication*] (DLA)
**Kenn Par Antiq** ... Kennett's Parochial Antiquities [*A publication*] (DLA)
**Kenn Pr**...... Kennedy's Chancery Practice [*2nd ed.*] [*1852-53*] [*A publication*] (DLA)
**KENO**........ Las Vegas, NV [*AM radio station call letters*]
**Ken Opin**.... Kentucky Opinions [*A publication*] (DLA)
**KenR**.......... Kenyon Review [*A publication*]
**KENS**......... Kenilworth Systems Corp. [*NASDAQ symbol*] (NQ)
**KENS**......... Kensington [*West London*] (ROG)
**KENSO**..... Kensington Racecourse [*Australia*] (DSUE)
**KENS-TV** ... San Antonio, TX [*Television station call letters*]
**KENT**......... Kent Financial Services [*NASDAQ symbol*] (SPSG)
**Kent**.......... Kent's Commentaries on American Law [*A publication*] (DLA)
**KENT**......... Odessa, TX [*AM radio station call letters*]
**Kent A R**.... Kent Archaeological Review [*A publication*]
**Kent Archaeol Rev** ... Kent Archaeological Review [*A publication*]
**Kent Com**.... Kent's Commentaries on American Law [*A publication*] (DLA)

**Kent Comm** ... Kent's Commentaries on American Law [*A publication*] (DLA)
**KENT-FM** ... Odessa, TX [*FM radio station call letters*]
**Kent Rev**..... Kent Review [*A publication*]
**Kent & R St** ... Kent and Radcliff's Law of New York, Revision of 1801 [*A publication*] (DLA)
**Kent's Commen** ... Kent's Commentaries on American Law [*A publication*] (DLA)
**Kent Tech Rev** ... Kent Technical Review [*A publication*]
**Kentucky Acad Sci Trans** ... Kentucky Academy of Science. Transactions [*A publication*]
**Kentucky Geol Surv Bull** ... Kentucky. Geological Survey. Bulletin [*A publication*]
**Kentucky Geol Survey Bull** ... Kentucky. Geological Survey. Bulletin [*A publication*]
**Kentucky Geol Survey County Rept** ... Kentucky. Geological Survey. County Report [*A publication*]
**Kentucky Geol Survey Inf Circ** ... Kentucky. Geological Survey. Information Circular [*A publication*]
**Kentucky Geol Survey Rept Inv** ... Kentucky. Geological Survey. Report of Investigations [*A publication*]
**Kentucky Geol Survey Spec Pub** ... Kentucky. Geological Survey. Special Publication [*A publication*]
**Kentucky LJ** ... Kentucky Law Journal [*A publication*]
**Kentucky Med J** ... Kentucky Medical Journal [*A publication*]
**KENU**........ Enumclaw, WA [*AM radio station call letters*]
**KENV**........ Wendover/Wendover Auxiliary Air Base [*Utah*] [*ICAO location identifier*] (ICLI)
**KENW**....... Portales, NM [*Television station call letters*]
**KENW-FM** ... Portales, NM [*FM radio station call letters*]
**Ke:nx**.......... Connects [*Macintosh*] [*Data processing*]
**KENY**........ Kenai, AK [*AM radio station call letters*]
**Keny**.......... Kenyon's English King's Bench Reports [*A publication*] (DLA)
**Kenya Colony Prot Geol Surv Mem** ... Kenya. Colony and Protectorate. Geological Survey. Memoir [*A publication*]
**Kenya Dep Agric Annu Rep** ... Kenya. Department of Agriculture. Annual Report [*A publication*]
**Kenya and East African Med J** ... Kenya and East African Medical Journal [*A publication*]
**Kenya Fmr** ... Kenya Farmer [*A publication*]
**Kenya Inform Serv Bull** ... Kenya Information Services. Bulletin [*A publication*]
**Kenya J Sci Technol Ser B Biol Sci** ... Kenya Journal of Science and Technology. Series B. Biological Sciences [*A publication*]
**Kenya LR**... Kenya Law Reports [*A publication*] (DLA)
**Kenya Med J** ... Kenya Medical Journal [*A publication*]
**Kenya Nurs J** ... Kenya Nursing Journal [*A publication*]
**Kenya R**..... Kenya Review [*A publication*]
**Kenya Tuberc Invest Cent Annu Rep** ... Kenya. Tuberculosis Investigation Centre. Annual Report [*A publication*]
**Kenya Tuberc Respir Dis Res Cent Ann Rep** ... Kenya. Tuberculosis and Respiratory Diseases Research Centre. Annual Report [*A publication*]
**Keny Ch**..... Chancery Cases [*2 Notes of King's Bench Cases*] [*England*] [*A publication*] (DLA)
**Kenyon R**... Kenyon Review [*A publication*]
**Kenyon Rev** ... Kenyon Review [*A publication*]
**KEO**.......... Keld'Or Resources, Inc. [*Vancouver Stock Exchange symbol*]
**KEO**.......... King Edward's Own [*British military*] (DMA)
**KEO**.......... Odienne [*Ivory Coast*] [*Airport symbol*] (OAG)
**KEOC**........ King Edward's Own Cavalry [*British military*] (DMA)
**KEOJ**........ Caney, KS [*FM radio station call letters*]
**KEOK**........ Tahlequah, OK [*FM radio station call letters*]
**KEOL**........ King Edward's Own Lancers [*British military*] (DMA)
**KEOL**........ La Grande, OR [*FM radio station call letters*]
**KEOM**....... Mesquite, TX [*FM radio station call letters*]
**KEOR**........ Atoka, OK [*AM radio station call letters*]
**KEP**........... Kellner Eye Piece
**KEP**........... Key Entry Processing
**KEP**........... King Edward Point [*South Georgia Island*] [*Seismograph station code, US Geological Survey*] (SEIS)
**KEP**........... Knight of the Eagle and Pelican [*Freemasonry*]
**KEP**........... Nepalganj [*Nepal*] [*Airport symbol*] (OAG)
**KEPC**......... Colorado Springs, CO [*FM radio station call letters*]
**KEPE**......... Kentron Programmatismou kai Oikonomikon Ereunon [*Indonesia*]
**KEPG**......... Victoria, TX [*FM radio station call letters*]
**KEPH**........ Ephraim, UT [*FM radio station call letters*]
**Kep es Hangtech** ... Kep- es Hangtechnika [*A publication*]
**KEPO**........ Eagle Point, OR [*FM radio station call letters*]
**KEPOA**....... Keep This Office Advised
**KEPROM** ... Keyed-Access, Erasable, Programmable Read-Only Memory [*Data processing*]
**KEPR-TV**... Pasco, WA [*Television station call letters*]
**KEPS**......... Eagle Pass, TX [*AM radio station call letters*]
**KEPT**......... Prescott, AZ [*FM radio station call letters*]
**KEPZ**......... Kaohsiung Export Processing Zone [*Reexport manufacturing complex*] [*Taiwan*]
**KEQ**........... Kebar [*Indonesia*] [*Airport symbol*] (OAG)
**KEQU**........ Kewaunee Scientific Corp. [*Formerly, Kewaunee Science Equipment*] [*NASDAQ symbol*] (NQ)
**Ker**............ Indian Law Reports, Kerala Series [*A publication*] (DLA)
**Ker**............ Kerithoth (BJA)
**KER**........... Kerman [*Iran*] [*Airport symbol*] (OAG)
**KER**........... Kermanshah [*Iran*] [*Seismograph station code, US Geological Survey*] (SEIS)
**KER**........... Kern [*A publication*]
**KER**........... Kerr Addison Mines Ltd. [*Toronto Stock Exchange symbol*]
**KER**........... Kerry [*County in Ireland*] (ROG)
**KER**........... Kinetic Energy Release
**KERA**........ Dallas, TX [*FM radio station call letters*]
**Kerala**........ All Indian Law Reports, Kerala Series [*A publication*] (DLA)
**Kerala J Vet Sci** ... Kerala Journal of Veterinary Science [*A publication*]
**Kerala LJ**... Kerala Law Journal [*A publication*] (DLA)
**Keram Rundsch Kunst-Keram** ... Keramische Rundschau und Kunst-Keramik [*A publication*]
**Keram Sb**... Keramicheskii Sbornik [*A publication*]
**Keram Z**..... Keramische Zeitschrift [*A publication*]
**KERA-TV** ... Dallas, TX [*Television station call letters*]
**KERB**......... Kermit, TX [*AM radio station call letters*]
**KERB-FM** ... Kermit, TX [*FM radio station call letters*]
**KerC**........... Kerkyraika Chronika [*A publication*]
**KERD**........ Kinetic Energy Release Distribution [*Of ions for spectral studies*]
**KerDo**......... Kerygma und Dogma [*A publication*]
**KERE**......... Atchison, KS [*AM radio station call letters*]
**KEREN-OR** ... Jerusalem Institutions for the Blind (EA)
**KERI**.......... Green Acres-Wasco, CA [*AM radio station call letters*]
**Ker LT**....... Kerala Law Times [*A publication*]
**KERM**....... Torrington, WY [*FM radio station call letters*]
**KERMA**..... Kinetic Energy Released per Unit Mass (DEN)
**KERN**........ Bakersfield, CA [*AM radio station call letters*]
**Kern**........... Kernan's Reports [*11-14 New York*] [*A publication*] (DLA)
**Kern**........... Kern's Reports [*100-116 Indiana*] [*A publication*] (DLA)
**Kernenerg**.. Kernenergie [*A publication*]
**Kernenerg Beil** ... Kernenergie. Beilage [*East Germany*] [*A publication*]
**KERN-FM** ... Bakersfield, CA [*FM radio station call letters*]
**Kernforschungsz Karlsruhe Ber** ... Kernforschungszentrum Karlsruhe. Bericht [*A publication*]
**Kerntechnik Isotpentech Chem** ... Kerntechnik, Isotopentechnik, und Chemie [*A publication*]
**Kerntech Normung Inf** ... Kerntechnische Normung Informationen [*West Germany*] [*A publication*]
**KERO**........ Kerosine [*British*]
**KERO-TV** ... Bakersfield, CA [*Television station call letters*]
**KERP**......... Pueblo, CO [*FM radio station call letters*]
**KERR**......... Kerrier [*England*]
**Kerr**............ Kerr's New Brunswick Reports [*A publication*] (DLA)
**Kerr**............ Kerr's Reports [*18-22 Indiana*] [*A publication*] (DLA)
**Kerr**............ Kerr's Reports [*27-29 New York Civil Procedure*] [*A publication*] (DLA)
**KERR**......... Polson, MT [*AM radio station call letters*]
**Kerr Act**..... Kerr's Actions at Law [*3rd ed.*] [*1861*] [*A publication*] (DLA)
**Kerr Anc L**... Kerr on Ancient Lights [*A publication*] (DLA)
**Kerr Black**... Kerr's Blackstone [*12th ed.*] [*1895*] [*A publication*] (DLA)
**Kerr Disc**.... Kerr's Discovery [*1870*] [*A publication*] (DLA)
**Kerr Ext**..... Kerr on Inter-State Extradition [*A publication*] (DLA)
**Kerr F & M**... Kerr's Fraud and Mistake [*7th ed.*] [*1952*] [*A publication*] (DLA)
**Kerr Fr**....... Kerr's Fraud and Mistake [*7th ed.*] [*1952*] [*A publication*] (DLA)
**Kerr Inj**...... Kerr on Injunctions [*A publication*] (DLA)
**Kerr (NB)**... Kerr's New Brunswick Reports [*A publication*] (DLA)
**Kerr Rec**..... Kerr on Receivers [*A publication*] (DLA)
**Kerr Stu Black** ... Kerr's Student's Blackstone [*A publication*] (DLA)
**Kerr W & M Cas** ... Kerr's Water and Mineral Cases [*A publication*] (DLA)
**Kerse**.......... Kerse's Manuscript Decisions, Scotch Court of Session [*A publication*] (DLA)
**Kersey Dict** ... [*John*] Kersey's English Dictionary [*1708*] [*A publication*] (DLA)
**Kert Egy Kozl** ... Kerteszeti Egyetem Kozlemenyei [*A publication*]
**Kertesz Egyet Kozl** ... Kerteszeti Egyetem Kozlemenyei [*A publication*]
**Kertesz Szolesz Foisk** ... Kerteszeti es Szoleszeti Foiskola Evkoryve [*A publication*]
**Kertesz Szolesz Foisk Kozl** ... Kerteszeti es Szoleszeti Foiskola Kozlemenyei [*A publication*]
**Kert Szolesz Foiskola Evk** ... Kerteszeti es Szoleszeti Foiskola Evkoryve [*A publication*]
**Kert Szolesz Foiskola Kozl** ... Kerteszeti es Szoleszeti Foiskola Kozlemenyei [*A publication*]
**KERUK-NASI** ... Kerukunan Nasional [*Campaign for National Harmony*] [*Indonesia*]
**KERV**......... Kerrville, TX [*AM radio station call letters*]
**KES**............ Keio Economic Studies [*A publication*]
**KES**............ Key Element Search (MCD)
**KES**............ Keystone Consolidated Industries, Inc. [*NYSE symbol*] (SPSG)
**KES**............ Ksar Es Souk [*Seismograph station code, US Geological Survey*] [*Closed*] (SEIS)
**KES**............ Kvakera Esperantista Societo [*Quaker Esperanto Society - QES*] (EAIO)
**KESD**......... Brookings, SD [*FM radio station call letters*]
**KESD-TV**.. Brookings, SD [*Television station call letters*]

**KESE**......... Amarillo, TX [*FM radio station call letters*]
**KESF**......... Alexandria/Esler Field [*Louisiana*] [*ICAO location identifier*] (ICLI)
**KESM**......... El Dorado Springs, MO [*AM radio station call letters*]
**KESM-FM**... El Dorado Springs, MO [*FM radio station call letters*]
**KESO**......... South Padre Island, TX [*FM radio station call letters*]
**KESP**......... Santa Barbara, CA [*AM radio station call letters*]
**KESQ-TV**... Palm Springs, CA [*Television station call letters*]
**KESS**......... Fort Worth, TX [*AM radio station call letters*]
**KESS**......... Kartvelur Enata St'rukt'uris Sak'itxebi [*A publication*]
**KESS**......... Kinetic Energy Storage System
**KEST**......... San Francisco, CA [*AM radio station call letters*]
**Keston News**... Keston News Service [*A publication*]
**KESY**......... Omaha, NE [*AM radio station call letters*]
**KESY-FM**... Omaha, NE [*FM radio station call letters*]
**KESZ**......... Phoenix, AZ [*FM radio station call letters*]
**Keszthelyi Mezogazd Akad Kiad**... Keszthelyi Mezogazdasagi Akademia Kiadvanyai [*A publication*]
**Keszthelyi Mezogazdasagtud Kar Kozl**... Keszthelyi Mezogazdasagtudomanyi Kar Kozlemenyei [*A publication*]
**KET**......... Kengtung [*Burma*] [*Airport symbol*] (OAG)
**KET**......... Keravat [*New Britain*] [*Seismograph station code, US Geological Survey*] [*Closed*] (SEIS)
**KET**......... Ketamine [*An anesthetic*]
**Ket**......... Kethuboth (BJA)
**KET**......... Krypton Exposure Technique (MCD)
**KETA**......... Oklahoma City, OK [*Television station call letters*]
**KETAL**......... Kalamazoo Area Library Consortium [*Library network*]
**KETB**......... Coeur D'Alene, ID [*FM radio station call letters*]
**KETC**......... St. Louis, MO [*Television station call letters*]
**KETG**......... Arkadelphia, AR [*Television station call letters*]
**KETH**......... Houston, TX [*Television station call letters*]
**Keth**......... Kethuboth (BJA)
**KETK-TV**... Jacksonville, TX [*Television station call letters*]
**keto**......... Ketosteroid [*Endocrinology*]
**KETR**......... Commerce, TX [*FM radio station call letters*]
**KETRI**......... Kenya Trypanosomiasis Research Institute
**KETS**......... Little Rock, AR [*Television station call letters*]
**KETT**......... Kettering Industries [*NASDAQ symbol*] (NQ)
**K'ETTE**......... Kitchenette [*Classified advertising*] (ADA)
**KETV**......... Omaha, NE [*Television station call letters*]
**KETX**......... Livingston, TX [*AM radio station call letters*]
**KETX-FM**... Livingston, TX [*FM radio station call letters*]
**KEU**......... Eastern Kentucky University, Richmond, KY [*OCLC symbol*] (OCLC)
**KEUN**......... Eunice, LA [*AM radio station call letters*]
**Keuring Elektrotech Mater Sci Tech Rep**... Keuring van Elektrotechnische Materialen. Scientific and Technical Reports [*A publication*]
**KEV**......... Kevo [*Finland*] [*Seismograph station code, US Geological Survey*] (SEIS)
**keV**......... Kiloelectron Volt
**KEV**......... King's Empire Veterans [*British military*] (DMA)
**KEV**......... Komisarstvo za Evreiskiie Vuprosi [*Bulgaria*] (BJA)
**KEVA**......... Evanston, WY [*AM radio station call letters*]
**KEVII**......... King Edward VII [*British*]
**KEVIII**......... King Edward VIII [*British*]
**KEVN**......... Kevo Notes [*A publication*]
**KEVN-TV**... Rapid City, SD [*Television station call letters*]
**KEVU**......... Eugene, OR [*Television station call letters*]
**KEVX**......... Kevex Corp. [*NASDAQ symbol*] (NQ)
**KEW**......... Kew [*England*] [*Seismograph station code, US Geological Survey*] [*Closed*] (SEIS)
**KEW**......... Kewatin
**keW**......... Kiloelectron Watt
**KEW**......... Kinetic Energy Weapons [*Military*] (RDA)
**KEWB**......... Anderson, CA [*FM radio station call letters*]
**KEWB**......... Kinetic Experiment on Water Boiler [*Nuclear reactor*]
**Kew Bull**......... Kew Bulletin [*A publication*]
**Kew Bull Addit Ser**... Kew Bulletin. Additional Series [*A publication*]
**KEWE**......... Oroville, CA [*FM radio station call letters*]
**KEWI**......... Topeka, KS [*AM radio station call letters*]
**KEWN**......... New Bern/Simmons-Nott [*North Carolina*] [*ICAO location identifier*] (ICLI)
**KEWR**......... Newark/International [*New Jersey*] [*ICAO location identifier*] (ICLI)
**KEWU-FM**... Cheney, WA [*FM radio station call letters*]
**KEX**......... Kanabea [*Papua New Guinea*] [*Airport symbol*] (OAG)
**KEX**......... Kirby Corp. [*AMEX symbol*] (SPSG)
**KEX**......... Portland, OR [*AM radio station call letters*]
**KEXC**......... Eager, AZ [*FM radio station call letters*]
**KEXD**......... Kirby Exploration Co., Inc. [*NASDAQ symbol*] (NQ)
**KEXI**......... Walla Walla, WA [*FM radio station call letters*]
**KEXL**......... Norfolk, NE [*FM radio station call letters*]
**KEXO**......... Grand Junction, CO [*AM radio station call letters*]
**KEXS**......... Excelsior Springs, MO [*AM radio station call letters*]
**Kexue Tongbao (Foreign Lang Ed)**... Kexue Tongbao (Foreign Language Edition) [*A publication*]
**KEY**......... Key Airlines [*Salt Lake City, UT*] [*FAA designator*] (FAAC)
**KEY**......... Key Anacon Mines Ltd. [*Toronto Stock Exchange symbol*]
**Key**......... Key to Christian Education [*A publication*]
**KEY**......... KeyCorp [*NYSE symbol*] (SPSG)
**Key**......... Keyes' New York Court of Appeals Reports [*A publication*] (DLA)
**KEYA**......... Belcourt, ND [*FM radio station call letters*]
**KEYB**......... Altus, OK [*FM radio station call letters*]
**KEYBD**......... Keyboard [*Data processing*]
**Keybd Mag**... Keyboard Magazine [*A publication*]
**KEYC**......... Key Centurion Bancshares, Inc. [*Huntington, WV*] [*NASDAQ symbol*] (NQ)
**Key Ch**......... Keyes on Future Interest in Chattels [*A publication*] (DLA)
**KEYC-TV**... Mankato, MN [*Television station call letters*]
**KEYE**......... Perryton, TX [*AM radio station call letters*]
**Key Econ Sci**... Key to Economic Science [*A publication*]
**Key Econ Sci Manage Sci**... Key to Economic Science and Managerial Sciences [*A publication*]
**KEYE-FM**... Perryton, TX [*FM radio station call letters*]
**Key & Elph Conv**... Key and Elphinstone's Conveyancing [*15th ed.*] [*1953-54*] [*A publication*] (DLA)
**Keyes**......... Keyes' New York Court of Appeals Reports [*A publication*] (DLA)
**KEYF**......... Dishman, WA [*AM radio station call letters*]
**KEYF-FM**... Cheney, WA [*FM radio station call letters*]
**KEYG**......... Grand Coulee, WA [*AM radio station call letters*]
**KEYG-FM**... Grand Coulee, WA [*FM radio station call letters*]
**KEYH**......... Houston, TX [*AM radio station call letters*]
**KEYI-FM**.. San Marcos, TX [*FM radio station call letters*]
**KEYJ**......... Abilene, TX [*AM radio station call letters*]
**KEYJ-FM**... Abilene, TX [*FM radio station call letters*]
**Keyl**......... Keylway's [*or Keilway's*] English King's Bench Reports [*A publication*] (DLA)
**KEYL**......... Long Prairie, MN [*AM radio station call letters*]
**Key Lands**... Keyes on Future Interest in Lands [*A publication*] (DLA)
**Keylway**......... Keylway's [*or Keilway's*] English King's Bench Reports [*A publication*] (DLA)
**KEYMAT**... Keying Material [*Data processing*] (NVT)
**KEYN-FM**... Wichita, KS [*FM radio station call letters*]
**Key Notes**... Key Notes Donemus [*A publication*]
**Key Oceanogr Rec Doc**... Key to Oceanographic Records Documentation [*A publication*]
**KEYPER**... Keywords Permuted (DIT)
**KEYRA**......... Keyboard [*A publication*]
**Key Rem**......... Keyes on Remainders [*A publication*] (DLA)
**KEYS**......... Corpus Christi, TX [*AM radio station call letters*]
**Keys St Ex**... Keyser's Stock Exchange [*1850*] [*A publication*] (DLA)
**Keystone News Bull**... Keystone News Bulletin [*United States*] [*A publication*]
**KEYT-TV**.. Santa Barbara, CA [*Television station call letters*]
**KEYV**......... Las Vegas, NV [*FM radio station call letters*]
**KEYW**......... Key West/Key West International [*Florida*] [*ICAO location identifier*] (ICLI)
**KEYW**......... Pasco, WA [*FM radio station call letters*]
**Keyword Index Intern Med**... Keyword Index in Internal Medicine [*A publication*]
**Keyword Index Med Lit**... Keyword Index for the Medical Literature [*A publication*]
**Key Word Index Wildl Res**... Key Word Index of Wildlife Research [*A publication*]
**KEYY**......... Provo, UT [*AM radio station call letters*]
**KEYZ**......... Williston, ND [*AM radio station call letters*]
**KEZA**......... Fayetteville, AR [*FM radio station call letters*]
**KEZB**......... El Paso, TX [*AM radio station call letters*]
**KEZB-FM**... El Paso, TX [*FM radio station call letters*]
**KEZC**......... Yuma, AZ [*AM radio station call letters*]
**KEZD**......... Windsor, CA [*AM radio station call letters*]
**KEZE-FM**... Spokane, WA [*FM radio station call letters*]
**KEZF**......... Portland, OR [*AM radio station call letters*]
**KEZG**......... Lincoln, NE [*FM radio station call letters*]
**KEZH**......... Hastings, NE [*FM radio station call letters*]
**KEZI**......... Eugene, OR [*Television station call letters*]
**KEZJ**......... Twin Falls, ID [*AM radio station call letters*]
**KEZJ-FM**... Twin Falls, ID [*FM radio station call letters*]
**KEZK**......... St. Louis, MO [*FM radio station call letters*]
**KEZL**......... Fowler, CA [*FM radio station call letters*]
**KEZM**......... Sulphur, LA [*AM radio station call letters*]
**KEZN**......... Palm Desert, CA [*FM radio station call letters*]
**KEZO**......... Omaha, NE [*AM radio station call letters*]
**KEZO-FM**... Omaha, NE [*FM radio station call letters*]
**KEZP**......... Canadian, TX [*FM radio station call letters*]
**KEZQ**......... North Little Rock, AR [*AM radio station call letters*]
**KEZQ-FM**... Jacksonville, AR [*FM radio station call letters*]
**KEZR**......... San Jose, CA [*FM radio station call letters*]
**KEZS-FM**... Cape Girardeau, MO [*FM radio station call letters*]
**KEZT**......... Ames, IA [*FM radio station call letters*]
**KEZU**......... Scott City, KS [*FM radio station call letters*]
**KEZV**......... Spearfish, SD [*FM radio station call letters*]
**KEZW**......... Aurora, CO [*AM radio station call letters*]
**KEZX**......... Seattle, WA [*AM radio station call letters*]
**KEZX-FM**... Seattle, WA [*FM radio station call letters*]
**KEZY**......... Anaheim, CA [*FM radio station call letters*]
**KEZZ**......... Aitkin, MN [*FM radio station call letters*]

**KF** ............ Air Flight, Luftfahrt GmbH, Dusseldorf [*West Germany*] [*ICAO designator*] (FAAC)
**KF** ............ Fiji [*IYRU nationality code*] (IYR)
**KF** ............ Gold Coast Judgments and the Masai Cases, by King-Farlow [*1915-17*] [*Ghana*] [*A publication*] (DLA)
**KF** ............ Karl Fischer [*Reagent*] [*Analytical chemistry*]
**KF** ............ Key Field
**KF** ............ KIDS Fund (EA)
**KF** ............ Kleinasiatische Forschungen [*A publication*]
**KF** ............ Kleine Flote [*Piccolo*] [*German*]
**KF** ............ Knight of Ferdinand [*Spain*]
**KF** ............ Knudsen Flow [*Physics*]
**KF** ............ Koff [*Type of ship*] (DS)
**KF** ............ Koinonia Foundation (EA)
**KF** ............ Konservative Folkeparti [*Conservative People's Party (Commonly called the Conservative Party)*] [*Denmark*] [*Political party*] (PPE)
**KF** ............ Kontrafagott [*Double Bassoon*] [*Organ stop*] [*Music*]
**KF** ............ Korea Fund, Inc. [*NYSE symbol*] (SPSG)
**KF** ............ Kosciuszko Foundation (EA)
**KF** ............ Kossuth Foundation (EA)
**KF** ............ Rhine Air AG [*Sweden*] [*ICAO designator*] (ICDA)
**KFA** .......... Keep Fit Association [*British*]
**KFA** .......... Kernforschungsanlage [*Julich, Germany*]
**KFA** .......... Kiffa [*Mauritania*] [*Airport symbol*] (OAG)
**KFA** .......... Kinesthetic Figural Aftereffects [*Also, KFAE*] [*Psychometrics*]
**KFA** .......... Krishnamurti Foundation of America (EA)
**KFAA** ......... Rogers, AR [*Television station call letters*]
**KFAB** ......... Kidney-Fixing Antibody [*Immunology*]
**KFAB** ......... Omaha, NE [*AM radio station call letters*]
**KFAE** ......... Kinesthetic Figural Aftereffects [*Also, KFA*] [*Psychometrics*]
**KFAED** ....... Kuwait Fund for Arab Economic Development
**KFAE-FM** ... Richland, WA [*FM radio station call letters*]
**KFAI** ......... Minneapolis, MN [*FM radio station call letters*]
**KFAL** ......... Fulton, MO [*AM radio station call letters*]
**KFAM** ........ North Salt Lake City, UT [*AM radio station call letters*]
**KFAN** ........ Fredericksburg, TX [*FM radio station call letters*]
**KFAR** ......... Fairbanks, AK [*AM radio station call letters*]
**KFAS** ......... Casa Grande, AZ [*AM radio station call letters*]
**KFAS** ......... Keyed File Access System
**KFAS-FM** ... Casa Grande, AZ [*FM radio station call letters*]
**KFAT** ......... Corvallis, OR [*FM radio station call letters*]
**KFAT** ......... Fresno/Fresno Air Terminal [*California*] [*ICAO location identifier*] (ICLI)
**KFAX** ......... San Francisco, CA [*AM radio station call letters*]
**KFAY** ......... Farmington, AR [*AM radio station call letters*]
**KFAY-FM** ... Huntsville, AR [*FM radio station call letters*]
**KFB** ........... Bethany College, Lindsborg, KS [*OCLC symbol*] (OCLC)
**KFBB-TV** .. Great Falls, MT [*Television station call letters*]
**KFBC** ......... Cheyenne, WY [*AM radio station call letters*]
**KFBD-FM** ... Waynesville, MO [*FM radio station call letters*]
**KFBG** ......... Fort Bragg/Simons Auxiliary Air Base [*North Carolina*] [*ICAO location identifier*] (ICLI)
**KFBK** ......... Sacramento, CA [*AM radio station call letters*]
**KFBN** ......... Laurel, MT [*AM radio station call letters*]
**KFBQ** ......... Cheyenne, WY [*FM radio station call letters*]
**KFBR** ......... Nogales, AZ [*AM radio station call letters*]
**KFBT** ......... Las Vegas, NV [*Television station call letters*]
**KFBU** ......... McCook, NE [*FM radio station call letters*]
**KFC** ........... Kajagoogoo Fan Club (EA)
**KFC** ........... Katholieke Film-Centrale [*Netherlands*]
**KFC** ........... Kentfield [*California*] [*Seismograph station code, US Geological Survey*] (SEIS)
**KFC** ........... Kentucky Fried Chicken Corp. [*Later, KFC Corp.*] (ADA)
**KFCA** ......... Conway, AR [*AM radio station call letters*]
**KFCB** ......... Concord, CA [*Television station call letters*]
**KFCF** ......... Fresno, CA [*FM radio station call letters*]
**KFCI** ......... Knife and Fork Club International (EA)
**KFCM** ........ Cherokee Village, AR [*FM radio station call letters*]
**KFCR** ......... Custer, SD [*AM radio station call letters*]
**KFD** ........... Key Financial Data (ADA)
**KFD** ........... Kinetic Family Drawing [*Psychology*]
**KFD** ........... Kyasanur Forest Disease
**KFDA-TV** ... Amarillo, TX [*Television station call letters*]
**KFDC** ......... Fort Dodge, IA [*FM radio station call letters*]
**KFDC** ......... Washington/National Flight Data Center [*District of Columbia*] [*ICAO location identifier*] (ICLI)
**KFDF** ......... Van Buren, AR [*AM radio station call letters*]
**KFDI** ......... Wichita, KS [*AM radio station call letters*]
**KFDI-FM** .. Wichita, KS [*FM radio station call letters*]
**KFDM-TV** ... Beaumont, TX [*Television station call letters*]
**KfdO** .......... Komitee fuer den Osten (BJA)
**KFDX-TV** ... Wichita Falls, TX [*Television station call letters*]
**KFE** ........... Kathode Flicker Effect
**KFEA** ......... Korean Federation of Education Associations
**KFEL** ......... Pueblo, CO [*AM radio station call letters*]
**KFEQ** ......... St. Joseph, MO [*AM radio station call letters*]
**KFER** ......... Santa Cruz, CA [*FM radio station call letters*]
**KFF** ........... Kvinnenes Frie Folkevalgte [*Women's Freely Elected Representatives*] [*Norway*] [*Political party*] (PPE)
**KFFA** ......... Helena, AR [*AM radio station call letters*]
**KFFB** ......... Fairfield Bay, AR [*FM radio station call letters*]
**KFFLBA** .... Konglomerati Florida Foundation for Literature and the Book Arts (EA)
**KFFM** ........ Yakima, WA [*FM radio station call letters*]
**KFFMA** ...... Klepzig Fachberichte fuer die Fuehrungskraefte aus Maschinenbau und Huettenwesen [*A publication*]
**KFFN** ......... Sierra Vista, AZ [*FM radio station call letters*]
**KFFO** ......... Dayton/Wright-Patterson Air Force Base [*Ohio*] [*ICAO location identifier*] (ICLI)
**KFFUA** ...... Kraftfutter [*A publication*]
**KFFX** ......... Emporia, KS [*FM radio station call letters*]
**KFGG** ........ Corpus Christi, TX [*FM radio station call letters*]
**KFGO** ........ Fargo, ND [*AM radio station call letters*]
**KFGO-FM** ... Fargo, ND [*FM radio station call letters*]
**KFGQ** ........ Boone, IA [*AM radio station call letters*]
**KFGQ-FM** ... Boone, IA [*FM radio station call letters*]
**KFH** ........... Fort Hays State University, Hays, KS [*OCLC symbol*] (OCLC)
**KFH** ........... Ku-Band Feed Horn
**KFH** ........... Wichita, KS [*AM radio station call letters*]
**KFHM** ........ San Antonio, TX [*AM radio station call letters*]
**KFI** ............ Los Angeles, CA [*AM radio station call letters*]
**KFIA** .......... Carmichael, CA [*AM radio station call letters*]
**KFIA** .......... King Fahd International Airport [*Saudi Arabia*]
**KFIG** .......... Fresno, CA [*AM radio station call letters*]
**KFIG-FM** .. Fresno, CA [*FM radio station call letters*]
**KFIL** .......... Preston, MN [*AM radio station call letters*]
**KFIL-FM** ... Preston, MN [*FM radio station call letters*]
**KFIN** .......... Jonesboro, AR [*FM radio station call letters*]
**KFIR** .......... American Kefir Corp. [*Fairlawn, NJ*] [*NASDAQ symbol*] (NQ)
**KFIR** .......... Sweet Home, OR [*AM radio station call letters*]
**KFIS** .......... Soda Springs, ID [*FM radio station call letters*]
**KFIT** .......... Lockhart, TX [*AM radio station call letters*]
**KFIX** .......... Ada, OK [*FM radio station call letters*]
**KFIZ** .......... Fond Du Lac, WI [*AM radio station call letters*]
**KFIZA** ........ Kyoto Furitsu Ika Daigaku Zasshi [*A publication*]
**KFJB** .......... Marshalltown, IA [*AM radio station call letters*]
**KFJC** .......... Los Altos, CA [*FM radio station call letters*]
**KFJM** ......... Grand Forks, ND [*AM radio station call letters*]
**KFJM-FM** ... Grand Forks, ND [*FM radio station call letters*]
**KFJZ** .......... Fort Worth, TX [*AM radio station call letters*]
**KFKA** ......... Greeley, CO [*AM radio station call letters*]
**KFKF-FM** ... Kansas City, KS [*FM radio station call letters*]
**KFK Hausmitt** ... KFK [*Kernforschungszentrum Karlsruhe*] Hausmitteilungen [*A publication*]
**KFKI Kozl** ... KFKI [*Kozponti Fizikai Kutato Intezet*] Kozlemenyek [*A publication*]
**KFK Nachr** ... KFK [*Kernforschungszentrum Karlsruhe*] Nachrichten [*A publication*]
**KFKQ** ......... New Holstein, WI [*FM radio station call letters*]
**KFKU** ......... Lawrence, KS [*AM radio station call letters*]
**KFL** ........... Kenya Federation of Labour
**KFL** ........... Key Facilities List [*AEC*]
**KFL** ........... University of Kansas, Law Library, Lawrence, KS [*OCLC symbol*] (OCLC)
**KFLA** ......... Scott City, KS [*AM radio station call letters*]
**KFlAH** ........ United States Army Hospital, Fort Leavenworth, KS [*Library symbol*] [*Library of Congress*] (LCLS)
**KFLG** ......... Bullhead City, AZ [*FM radio station call letters*]
**KFlGS** ........ United States Army, Command and General Staff College Library, Fort Leavenworth, KS [*Library symbol*] [*Library of Congress*] (LCLS)
**KFLI** .......... Eureka, CA [*AM radio station call letters*]
**KFLJ** .......... Walsenburg, CO [*AM radio station call letters*]
**KFLL** .......... Bridgeport, NE [*FM radio station call letters*]
**KFLL** .......... Fort Lauderdale/Fort Lauderdale-Hollywood International [*Florida*] [*ICAO location identifier*] (ICLI)
**KFLN** ......... Baker, MT [*AM radio station call letters*]
**KFLN-FM** ... Baker, MT [*FM radio station call letters*]
**KFLO** ......... Florence/Municipal [*South Carolina*] [*ICAO location identifier*] (ICLI)
**KFLO** ......... Shreveport, LA [*AM radio station call letters*]
**KFLQ** ......... Albuquerque, NM [*FM radio station call letters*]
**KFLQ** ......... Kentucky Foreign Language Quarterly [*A publication*]
**KFLR-FM** ... Phoenix, AZ [*FM radio station call letters*]
**KFLS** ......... Klamath Falls, OR [*AM radio station call letters*]
**KFLT** ......... Tucson, AZ [*AM radio station call letters*]
**KFLY** ......... Corvallis, OR [*AM radio station call letters*]
**KFLZ** ......... Bishop, TX [*FM radio station call letters*]
**KFM** ........... Klystron Frequency Multiplier
**KFM** ........... Knight of St. Ferdinand and Merit [*Italy*]
**KFMA** ........ Jerome, ID [*FM radio station call letters*]
**KFMB** ........ San Diego, CA [*AM radio station call letters*]
**KFMB-FM** ... San Diego, CA [*FM radio station call letters*]
**KFMB-TV** ... San Diego, CA [*Television station call letters*]
**KFMC** ........ Fairmont, MN [*FM radio station call letters*]
**KFME** ........ Fargo, ND [*Television station call letters*]
**KFMF** ........ Chico, CA [*FM radio station call letters*]
**KFMG** ........ Albuquerque, NM [*FM radio station call letters*]
**KFMH** ........ Falmouth/Otis Air Force Base [*Massachusetts*] [*ICAO location identifier*] (ICLI)

**KFMH**....... Muscatine, IA [*FM radio station call letters*]
**KFMI**........ Eureka, CA [*FM radio station call letters*]
**KFMJ**........ Grants Pass, OR [*FM radio station call letters*]
**KFMK**........ Houston, TX [*FM radio station call letters*]
**KFML**........ Kommunistiska Foerbundet Marxist-Leninisterna [*Communist League of Marxist-Leninists*] [*Sweden*] [*Political party*] (PPE)
**KFML**........ Little Falls, MN [*FM radio station call letters*]
**KFMM**...... Thatcher, AZ [*FM radio station call letters*]
**KFMN**....... Farmington [*New Mexico*] [*ICAO location identifier*] (ICLI)
**KFMN**....... Lihue, HI [*FM radio station call letters*]
**KFMO**....... Flat River, MO [*AM radio station call letters*]
**KFMQ**....... Lincoln, NE [*FM radio station call letters*]
**KFMR**....... Stockton, CA [*FM radio station call letters*]
**KFMS**........ North Las Vegas, NV [*AM radio station call letters*]
**KFMS-FM** ... Las Vegas, NV [*FM radio station call letters*]
**KFMT**........ Fremont, NE [*FM radio station call letters*]
**KFMU-FM** .. Oak Creek, CO [*FM radio station call letters*]
**KFMV**........ Franklin, LA [*FM radio station call letters*]
**KFMW**...... Waterloo, IA [*FM radio station call letters*]
**KFMX**........ Lubbock, TX [*AM radio station call letters*]
**KFMX-FM** ... Lubbock, TX [*FM radio station call letters*]
**KFMY**........ Fort Myers/Page Field [*Florida*] [*ICAO location identifier*] (ICLI)
**KFMY**........ Provo, UT [*AM radio station call letters*]
**KFMZ**........ Columbia, MO [*FM radio station call letters*]
**KFNA**........ El Paso, TX [*AM radio station call letters*]
**KFNB-TV** ... Casper, WY [*Television station call letters*]
**KFNC**........ Sulphur, OK [*FM radio station call letters*]
**KFNE**........ Riverton, WY [*Television station call letters*]
**KFNF**........ Oberlin, KS [*FM radio station call letters*]
**KFNN**........ Mesa, AZ [*AM radio station call letters*]
**KFNO**........ Fresno, CA [*FM radio station call letters*]
**KFNR**........ Rawlins, WY [*Television station call letters*]
**KFNS**........ Amarillo, TX [*AM radio station call letters*]
**K & F NSW** ... Knox and Fitzhardinge's New South Wales Reports [*A publication*] (DLA)
**KFNV**........ Ferriday, LA [*AM radio station call letters*]
**KFNV-FM** ... Ferriday, LA [*FM radio station call letters*]
**KFNW**....... Fargo, ND [*AM radio station call letters*]
**KFNW-FM** ... Fargo, ND [*FM radio station call letters*]
**KFO**........... Killing Federal Officer
**KFO**........... King Solomon Resources [*Vancouver Stock Exchange symbol*]
**KFO**........... Klamath Falls [*Oregon*] [*Seismograph station code, US Geological Survey*] (SEIS)
**KFOC**........ Kaiser-Frazer Owners Clubs of America [*Later, KFOCI*] (EA)
**KFOCI**....... Kaiser-Frazer Owners Club International (EA)
**KFOE**......... Topeka/Forbes Air Force Base [*Kansas*] [*ICAO location identifier*] (ICLI)
**KFOG**........ San Francisco, CA [*FM radio station call letters*]
**KFOK**........ West Hampton Beach/Suffolk County [*New York*] [*ICAO location identifier*] (ICLI)
**KFOM**....... Sulphur, OK [*FM radio station call letters*]
**KFOR**........ Lincoln, NE [*AM radio station call letters*]
**KFOX**........ Redondo Beach, CA [*FM radio station call letters*]
**KFP**........... False Pass [*Alaska*] [*Airport symbol*] (OAG)
**KFP**........... Konstitutionella Folkpartiet [*Constitutional People's Party*] [*Finland*] [*Political party*] (PPE)
**KFP**........... Pittsburg State University, Pittsburg, KS [*OCLC symbol*] (OCLC)
**KFPS**........ Salem, MO [*AM radio station call letters*]
**KFPW**........ Fort Smith, AR [*AM radio station call letters*]
**KFQ**........... Keystone Folklore Quarterly [*A publication*]
**KFQD**........ Anchorage, AK [*AM radio station call letters*]
**KFQX-FM** ... Merkel, TX [*FM radio station call letters*]
**KFR**........... Keefer Resources, Inc. [*Vancouver Stock Exchange symbol*]
**KFR**........... Kentucky Folklore Record [*A publication*]
**KFRA**........ Franklin, LA [*AM radio station call letters*]
**KFRC**........ San Francisco, CA [*AM radio station call letters*]
**KFRD**........ Rosenberg-Richmond, TX [*AM radio station call letters*]
**KFRD-FM** ... Rosenberg-Richmond, TX [*FM radio station call letters*]
**KFRE**......... Fresno, CA [*AM radio station call letters*]
**KFRG**........ San Bernardino, CA [*FM radio station call letters*]
**KFRK**........ Hutchinson, KS [*FM radio station call letters*]
**KFRL**......... Kansas Flight Research Laboratory
**KFRLF**....... Keeley-Frontier Resources [*NASDAQ symbol*] (NQ)
**KFRM**........ Salina, KS [*AM radio station call letters*]
**KFRN**........ Long Beach, CA [*AM radio station call letters*]
**KFRO**........ Longview, TX [*AM radio station call letters*]
**KFRR**........ Thornton, CO [*AM radio station call letters*]
**KFRS**........ Sumner, WA [*AM radio station call letters*]
**KFRST**....... Killing Frost [*Meteorology*] (FAAC)
**KFRU**........ Columbia, MO [*AM radio station call letters*]
**KFRX**........ Lincoln, NE [*FM radio station call letters*]
**KFS**........... Kalman Filtering System
**KFS**........... Kentucky Folklore Series [*A publication*]
**KFS**........... Keyed File System [*Data processing*]
**KFS**........... Klippel-Feil Syndrome [*Medicine*]
**KFS**........... Kohles, F. S., Montebello CA [*STAC*]
**KFS**........... University of Kansas, Spencer Library, Lawrence, KS [*OCLC symbol*] (OCLC)
**KFSA**......... Fort Smith, AR [*AM radio station call letters*]
**KFSAAX** ... Kungliga Fysiografiska Sallskapets i Lund. Arsbok [*A publication*]
**KFSB**......... Joplin, MO [*AM radio station call letters*]
**KFSC**......... Waterloo, IA [*Television station call letters*]
**KFSD-FM** ... San Diego, CA [*FM radio station call letters*]
**KFSG**......... Los Angeles, CA [*FM radio station call letters*]
**KFSH**......... Hilo, HI [*FM radio station call letters*]
**KFSH & RC** ... King Faisal Specialist Hospital and Research Center [*Saudi Arabia*]
**KFSI**.......... Rochester, MN [*FM radio station call letters*]
**KFSK**......... Petersburg, AK [*FM radio station call letters*]
**KFSLAW**... Kungliga Fysiografiska Sallskapets i Lund. Foerhandlingar [*A publication*]
**KFSM**........ Fort Smith/Municipal [*Arkansas*] [*ICAO location identifier*] (ICLI)
**KFSM-TV** ... Fort Smith, AR [*Television station call letters*]
**KFSN-TV**.. Fresno, CA [*Television station call letters*]
**KFSO**......... Visalia, CA [*FM radio station call letters*]
**KFSR**......... Fresno, CA [*FM radio station call letters*]
**KFSR**......... Karakul Fur Sheep Registry [*Later, AKFSR*] (EA)
**KFST**......... Fort Stockton, TX [*AM radio station call letters*]
**KFST-FM** ... Fort Stockton, TX [*FM radio station call letters*]
**KFT**............ Kalman Filter Theory
**KFT**............ KFT. Kraftfahrzeugtechnik [*A publication*]
**KFTCIC**..... Kuwait Foreign Trading, Contracting & Investment Company
**KFTH**........ Marion, AR [*FM radio station call letters*]
**KFTL**......... Stockton, CA [*Television station call letters*]
**KFTM**........ Fort Morgan, CO [*AM radio station call letters*]
**KFTR-TV**.. International Falls, MN [*Television station call letters*]
**KFTS**......... Klamath Falls, OR [*Television station call letters*]
**KFTTA**...... Kao Fen Tzu T'ung Hsun [*A publication*]
**KFTU**......... Korean Federation of Trade Unions [*Democratic People's Republic of Korea*]
**KFTV**......... Hanford, CA [*Television station call letters*]
**KFTW**........ Fort Worth/Meacham [*Texas*] [*ICAO location identifier*] (ICLI)
**KFTW**........ Fredericktown, MO [*AM radio station call letters*]
**KFTY**......... Santa Rosa, CA [*Television station call letters*]
**KFTZ**......... Idaho Falls, ID [*FM radio station call letters*]
**KFU**........... Friends University, Wichita, KS [*OCLC symbol*] (OCLC)
**KFUK**........ Kristelig Forening for Unge Kvinder [*Young Women's Christian Associations - YWCA*] [*Denmark*]
**KFUM**....... Kristelig Forening for Unge Maend [*Young Men's Christian Associations - YMCA*] [*Denmark*]
**KFUN**........ Las Vegas, NM [*AM radio station call letters*]
**KFUO**........ Clayton, MO [*AM radio station call letters*]
**KFUO-FM** ... Clayton, MO [*FM radio station call letters*]
**KFV**............ Quest for Value Dual Fund [*NYSE symbol*] (SPSG)
**KFVE**......... Honolulu, HI [*Television station call letters*]
**KFVS-TV**.. Cape Girardeau, MO [*Television station call letters*]
**KFW**........... Wichita Public Library, Wichita, KS [*OCLC symbol*] (OCLC)
**KFWB**........ Los Angeles, CA [*AM radio station call letters*]
**KFWD**....... Fort Worth, TX [*Television station call letters*]
**KFWH**....... Fort Worth/Carswell Air Force Base [*Texas*] [*ICAO location identifier*] (ICLI)
**KFWJ**........ Lake Havasu City, AZ [*AM radio station call letters*]
**KFWU**....... Fort Bragg, CA [*Television station call letters*]
**KFX**............ Korean Foreign Exchange (IMH)
**KFXD**........ Nampa, ID [*AM radio station call letters*]
**KFXD-FM** ... Nampa, ID [*FM radio station call letters*]
**KFXE**......... Camdenton, MO [*AM radio station call letters*]
**KFXE**......... Fort Lauderdale/Executive [*Florida*] [*ICAO location identifier*] (ICLI)
**KFXI**.......... Marlow, OK [*FM radio station call letters*]
**KFXJ**......... Abilene, TX [*FM radio station call letters*]
**KFXT-TV**.. Sioux Falls, SD [*Television station call letters*]
**KFXX**......... Oregon City, OR [*AM radio station call letters*]
**KFXX-FM** ... Hugoton, KS [*FM radio station call letters*]
**KFXY**......... Morgan City, LA [*FM radio station call letters*]
**KFXZ**......... Maurice, LA [*FM radio station call letters*]
**KFY**............ KISS [*Knights in the Service of Satan*] - Flaming Youth [*Defunct*] (EA)
**KFYE**......... Fresno, CA [*FM radio station call letters*]
**KFYI**.......... Phoenix, AZ [*AM radio station call letters*]
**KFYN**........ Bonham, TX [*AM radio station call letters*]
**KFYO**........ Lubbock, TX [*AM radio station call letters*]
**KFYR**......... Bismarck, ND [*AM radio station call letters*]
**KFYR-TV**.. Bismarck, ND [*Television station call letters*]
**K Fysiogr Sallsk Lund Arsb** ... Kungliga Fysiografiska Sallskapets i Lund. Arsbok [*A publication*]
**K Fysiogr Sallsk Lund Forh** ... Kungliga Fysiografiska Sallskapets i Lund. Foerhandlingar [*A publication*]
**KFYV**......... Fayetteville/Drake Field [*Arkansas*] [*ICAO location identifier*] (ICLI)
**KFYZ-FM** ... Bonham, TX [*FM radio station call letters*]
**KfZ**............. Katalysatorfahrzeugen [*Catalyst-Outfitted Auto*] [*German*]
**KFZTA**...... Kraftfahrzeugtechnik [*A publication*]
**KG**.............. Center of Gravity above Keel (MCD)
**KG**.............. Kammergericht [*District Court, Berlin*] [*German*] (DLA)

**KG** ........ Kampfgeschwader [*Bombardment wing*] [*German military - World War II*]
**KG** ........ Katholische Gedanken [*A publication*]
**K & G** ........ Keane and Grant's English Registration Appeal Cases [*1854-62*] [*A publication*] (DLA)
**KG** ........ Keg
**K & G** ........ Kerbing and Guttering [*British*] (ADA)
**KG** ........ Ketoglutaric [*Biochemistry*]
**KG** ........ Key Generator (MCD)
**kG** ........ Kilogauss
**kg** ........ Kilogram [*Also, k*] [*Symbol*] [*SI unit for mass*]
**KG** ........ Kinder, Gentler [*America*] [*In a George Bush speech during the 1989 Republican Convention*]
**KG** ........ Kindergarten
**KG** ........ King
**KG** ........ Knifemakers Guild (EA)
**KG** ........ Knight of [*the Order of*] the Garter [*British*]
**KG** ........ Known Gambler [*Police slang*]
**KG** ........ Kommanditgesellschaft [*Limited Partnership*] [*German*]
**KG** ........ Kultusgemeinde (BJA)
**KG** ........ Orion Airways Ltd. [*Great Britain*] [*ICAO designator*] (FAAC)
**1 KG** ........ I Kings [*Old Testament book*]
**2 KG** ........ II Kings [*Old Testament book*]
**KG5** ........ HMS King George V [*British military*] (DMA)
**KGA** ........ Kananga [*Zaire*] [*Airport symbol*] (OAG)
**KGA** ........ King's German Artillery [*British military*] (DMA)
**KGA** ........ Kitchen Guild of America
**KGA** ........ Kunstgeschichtliche Anzeigen [*A publication*]
**KGA** ........ Spokane, WA [*AM radio station call letters*]
**KGaA** ........ Kommanditgesellschaft auf Aktien [*Limited Partnership with Shares*] [*German*]
**KGAAM** .... Kungliga Gustav Adolfs Akademiens. Minnesbok [*A publication*]
**KGAC** ........ St. Peter, MN [*FM radio station call letters*]
**K Gad** ........ Kritikas Gadagramata [*A publication*]
**KGAF** ........ Gainesville, TX [*AM radio station call letters*]
**KGAG** ........ Gage [*Oklahoma*] [*ICAO location identifier*] (ICLI)
**KgAG** ........ Kurzgefasste Assyrische Grammatik [*A publication*] (BJA)
**KGAK** ........ Gallup, NM [*AM radio station call letters*]
**KGAL** ........ Lebanon, OR [*AM radio station call letters*]
**KGAL/MIN** ... Kilogallons per Minute (MCD)
**KGAM** ........ Wichita, KS [*FM radio station call letters*]
**KGAN** ........ Cedar Rapids, IA [*Television station call letters*]
**KGAP** ........ Gurdon, AR [*FM radio station call letters*]
**KGAS** ........ Carthage, TX [*AM radio station call letters*]
**KGB** ........ Kewaunee, Green Bay & Western R. R. [*AAR code*]
**KGB** ........ Kindly Gunn Bunch [*Refers to the Metropolitan Transit Authority of New York City; Gunn is the MTA chairman*]
**KGB** ........ Komitet Gosudarstvennoi Bezopasnosti [*Committee of State Security*] [*Russian Secret Police*] [*Also satirically interpreted as Kontora Grubykh Banditov, or "Office of Crude Bandits"*]
**KGB** ........ Konge [*Papua New Guinea*] [*Airport symbol*] (OAG)
**KGBA-FM** ... Holtville, CA [*FM radio station call letters*]
**KGbB** ........ Barton County Community College, Great Bend, KS [*Library symbol*] [*Library of Congress*] (LCLS)
**KGBC** ........ Galveston, TX [*AM radio station call letters*]
**KGB-FM** ... San Diego, CA [*FM radio station call letters*]
**KGBI-FM** ... Omaha, NE [*FM radio station call letters*]
**KGbLS** ........ Central Kansas Library System, Great Bend, KS [*Library symbol*] [*Library of Congress*] (LCLS)
**KGbMC** ........ Central Kansas Medical Center, Great Bend, KS [*Library symbol*] [*Library of Congress*] (LCLS)
**KGBM-FM** ... Randsburg, CA [*FM radio station call letters*]
**KGBR** ........ Gold Beach, OR [*FM radio station call letters*]
**KGBS** ........ Krypton Gas Bottling Station [*Nuclear energy*] (NRCH)
**KGBT** ........ Harlingen, TX [*AM radio station call letters*]
**KGBT-TV** ... Harlingen, TX [*Television station call letters*]
**KGBX** ........ Springfield, MO [*AM radio station call letters*]
**KGBX-FM** ... Bolivar, MO [*FM radio station call letters*]
**KGC** ........ Kingscote [*Australia*] [*Airport symbol*] (OAG)
**KGC** ........ Kiwi Growers of California (EA)
**KGC** ........ Knight of the Golden Circle
**KGC** ........ Knight Grand Commander
**KGC** ........ Knight of the Grand Cross
**KGC** ........ W. M. Krogman Center for Research in Child Growth and Development [*University of Pennsylvania*] [*Research center*] (RCD)
**KGCA** ........ Del Norte, CA [*AM radio station call letters*]
**kgcal** ........ Kilogram-Calorie
**KGCB** ........ Knight Grand Cross of the [*Order of the*] Bath [*British*]
**KGCC** ........ Douglas, AZ [*Television station call letters*]
**KGCF** ........ Kahlil Gibran Centennial Foundation (EA)
**KGCH-FM** ... Sidney, MT [*FM radio station call letters*]
**KGCI** ........ Grundy Center, IA [*FM radio station call letters*]
**KGCK** ........ Garden City [*Kansas*] [*ICAO location identifier*] (ICLI)
**KGCR** ........ Goodland, KS [*FM radio station call letters*]
**KGCSG** ........ Knight Grand Cross of the Order of St. Gregory the Great [*British*] (ADA)
**KGCT-TV** ... Tulsa, OK [*Television station call letters*]
**kg/cum** ........ Kilograms per Cubic Meter
**KGCX** ........ Sidney, MT [*AM radio station call letters*]
**KGD** ........ Karaganda [*USSR*] [*Geomagnetic observatory code*]
**KGDN** ........ Ephrata, WA [*FM radio station call letters*]
**KGE** ........ Kansas Gas & Electric Co. [*NYSE symbol*] (SPSG)
**KGE** ........ King-Errington Resources Ltd. [*Vancouver Stock Exchange symbol*]
**KGE** ........ Klein-Gordon Equation [*Physics*]
**KGE** ........ Knights of the Golden Eagle (EA)
**KGEE** ........ Monahans, TX [*FM radio station call letters*]
**KGEG** ........ Spokane/International [*Washington*] [*ICAO location identifier*] (ICLI)
**KGEM** ........ Boise, ID [*AM radio station call letters*]
**KGEN** ........ Tulare, CA [*AM radio station call letters*]
**KGEO** ........ Bakersfield, CA [*AM radio station call letters*]
**KGER** ........ Long Beach, CA [*AM radio station call letters*]
**K Ges Wiss Goettingen Abh** ... Koenigliche Gesellschaft der Wissenschaften zu Goettingen. Abhandlungen [*A publication*]
**KGET** ........ Bakersfield, CA [*Television station call letters*]
**KGEZ** ........ Kalispell, MT [*AM radio station call letters*]
**KGF** ........ Keilinschriften und Geschichtsforschung [*A publication*] (BJA)
**KGF** ........ Keratinocyte Growth Factor [*Biochemistry*]
**kg-f** ........ Kilogram-Foot
**kgf** ........ Kilogram-Force [*Unit of force*]
**KGF** ........ Knight of the Golden Fleece [*Spain and Austria*]
**KGF** ........ Kriegsgefangener [*Prisoner of War*] [*German*]
**KGFA** ........ Great Falls/Malmstrom Air Force Base [*Montana*] [*ICAO location identifier*] (ICLI)
**KGF/CM²** ... Kilogram Force per Square Centimeter
**KGFE** ........ Grand Forks, ND [*Television station call letters*]
**KGFF** ........ Shawnee, OK [*AM radio station call letters*]
**KGFJ** ........ Los Angeles, CA [*AM radio station call letters*]
**KGFK** ........ Grand Forks/International [*North Dakota*] [*ICAO location identifier*] (ICLI)
**KGFL** ........ Clinton, AR [*AM radio station call letters*]
**KGFM** ........ Bakersfield, CA [*FM radio station call letters*]
**KGF/M** ........ Kilogram Force per Meter
**KGF/M²** .... Kilogram Force per Square Meter
**KGFS** ........ King George's Fund for Sailors [*British*]
**KGFW** ........ Kearney, NE [*AM radio station call letters*]
**KGFX** ........ Pierre, SD [*AM radio station call letters*]
**KGFX-FM** ... Pierre, SD [*FM radio station call letters*]
**KGG** ........ Consolidated Goldwest [*Vancouver Stock Exchange symbol*]
**KGG** ........ Kedougou [*Senegal*] [*Airport symbol*] (OAG)
**KgGBAS** .... Kurzgefasste Grammatik der Biblisch Aramaeischen Sprache [*A publication*] (BJA)
**KGGF** ........ Coffeyville, KS [*AM radio station call letters*]
**KGGG** ........ Longview/Gregg County [*Texas*] [*ICAO location identifier*] (ICLI)
**KGGG-FM** ... Rapid City, SD [*FM radio station call letters*]
**KGGI** ........ Riverside, CA [*FM radio station call letters*]
**KGGJ** ........ Klaus-Groth-Gesellschaft. Jahresgabe [*A publication*]
**KGGM-TV** ... Albuquerque, NM [*Television station call letters*]
**KGGN** ........ Gladstone, MO [*AM radio station call letters*]
**KGGO** ........ Des Moines, IA [*AM radio station call letters*]
**KGGO-FM** ... Des Moines, IA [*FM radio station call letters*]
**KGH** ........ Kanbum Gakkai Kaiho [*Journal. Sinological Society*] [*A publication*]
**KGH** ........ Kidney Goldblatt Hypertension Scale
**KGH** ........ Knight of the Guelphic Order of Hanover [*British*]
**KGHKA** ..... Kogyo Gijutsuin. Hakko Kenkyusho Kenkyu Hokoku [*A publication*]
**KGHL** ........ Billings, MT [*AM radio station call letters*]
**KGHO** ........ Hoquiam, WA [*AM radio station call letters*]
**KGHO-FM** ... Hoquiam, WA [*FM radio station call letters*]
**KGHP** ........ Gig Harbor, WA [*FM radio station call letters*]
**KGHS** ........ International Falls, MN [*AM radio station call letters*]
**KGHT** ........ Sheridan, AR [*AM radio station call letters*]
**KGI** ........ Cryderman Gold, Inc. [*Vancouver Stock Exchange symbol*]
**KGI** ........ Kalgoorlie [*Australia*] [*Airport symbol*] (OAG)
**KGI** ........ Kellogg [*Idaho*] [*Seismograph station code, US Geological Survey*] (SEIS)
**KGI** ........ Komeet [*A publication*]
**KGID** ........ Giddings, TX [*FM radio station call letters*]
**KGII** ........ King George II [*British*]
**KGIL** ........ San Fernando, CA [*AM radio station call letters*]
**KGIM** ........ Aberdeen, SD [*AM radio station call letters*]
**KGIM-FM** ... Aberdeen, SD [*AM radio station call letters*]
**KGIN** ........ Grand Island, NE [*Television station call letters*]
**KGIR** ........ Cape Girardeau, MO [*AM radio station call letters*]
**KGIW** ........ Alamosa, CO [*AM radio station call letters*]
**KGJ** ........ Karonga [*Malawi*] [*Airport symbol*] (OAG)
**KG/J** ........ Kilograms per Joule
**KGJ** ........ King Jack Resources [*Vancouver Stock Exchange symbol*]
**KGK** ........ Kabushiki Goshi Kaisha [*Partnership*] [*Japan*]
**KGK** ........ Koliganek [*Alaska*] [*Airport symbol*] (OAG)
**KGKG** ........ Brookings, SD [*FM radio station call letters*]
**KGKK** ........ Kangaku Kenkyu [*Sinological Studies*] [*A publication*]
**KGKL** ........ San Angelo, TX [*AM radio station call letters*]
**KGKL-FM** ... San Angelo, TX [*FM radio station call letters*]
**KGKO** ........ Benton, AR [*AM radio station call letters*]

**KGKR**........ Kansai Gaidai Kenkyu Ronshu [*Journal. Kansai University of Foreign Studies*] [*A publication*]
**KGKZA**..... Kogyo Kagaku Zasshi [*A publication*]
**KGL**........... Kaufel Group Ltd. [*Toronto Stock Exchange symbol*]
**KGL**........... Kigali [*Rwanda*] [*Airport symbol*] (OAG)
**KGL**........... King's German Legion [*British military*] (DMA)
**KGL**........... Koeniglich [*Royal*] [*German*]
**KGL**........... Port-Aux-Francais [*Formerly, Kerguelen*] [*France*] [*Geomagnetic observatory code*]
**KGLA**........ Gretna, LA [*AM radio station call letters*]
**KGLB-TV**... Okmulgee, OK [*Television station call letters*]
**KGLC**......... Miami, OK [*AM radio station call letters*]
**KGLD**......... St. Louis, MO [*AM radio station call letters*]
**Kgl Danske Vidensk Selsk Oversigt**... Kongelige Danske Videnskabernes Selskab. Oversigt Selskabets Virksomhed [*A publication*]
**KGLE**......... Glendive, MT [*AM radio station call letters*]
**KGLF-FM**... Freeport, TX [*FM radio station call letters*]
**KGLI**......... Sioux City, IA [*FM radio station call letters*]
**KGLM-FM**... Anaconda, MT [*FM radio station call letters*]
**KGLN**......... Glenwood Springs, CO [*AM radio station call letters*]
**KGLO**......... Mason City, IA [*AM radio station call letters*]
**KGLS**......... Galveston/Scholes Field [*Texas*] [*ICAO location identifier*] (ICLI)
**KGLS**......... Pratt, KS [*FM radio station call letters*]
**KGLT**......... Bozeman, MT [*FM radio station call letters*]
**KGLX**......... Gallup, NM [*FM radio station call letters*]
**KGLY**......... Tyler, TX [*FM radio station call letters*]
**KGM**.......... Keratinocyte Growth Medium [*Cell culture*]
**KGM**.......... Kerr Glass Manufacturing Corp. [*NYSE symbol*] (SPSG)
**KGM**.......... Key Generator Module
**KGM**.......... Kiena Gold Mines Ltd. [*Toronto Stock Exchange symbol*]
**kg-m**.......... Kilogram-Meter
**KGM**.......... Kluang [*Malaysia*] [*Seismograph station code, US Geological Survey*] (SEIS)
**KG/M²**....... Kilograms per Square Meter
**KG/M³**....... Kilograms per Cubic Meter
**KGMB**........ Honolulu, HI [*Television station call letters*]
**KGMC**........ Oklahoma City, OK [*Television station call letters*]
**KGMD-TV**... Hilo, HI [*Television station call letters*]
**KGMG**........ Oceanside, CA [*AM radio station call letters*]
**KGMG-FM**... Oceanside, CA [*FM radio station call letters*]
**KGMI**........ Bellingham, WA [*AM radio station call letters*]
**KGMN**........ Kingman, AZ [*FM radio station call letters*]
**KGMO**........ Cape Girardeau, MO [*FM radio station call letters*]
**KGMR**........ Clarksville, AR [*FM radio station call letters*]
**KGMT**........ Fairbury, NE [*AM radio station call letters*]
**KGMV**........ Wailuku, HI [*Television station call letters*]
**KGNB**........ New Braunfels, TX [*AM radio station call letters*]
**KGNBA**..... Kenritsu Gan Senta Niigata Byoin Ishi [*A publication*]
**KGNC**........ Amarillo, TX [*AM radio station call letters*]
**KGND**........ Ketchum, OK [*FM radio station call letters*]
**KGNG**........ Brookfield, MO [*AM radio station call letters*]
**KGNM**........ St. Joseph, MO [*AM radio station call letters*]
**KGNN**........ Cuba, MO [*AM radio station call letters*]
**KGNO**........ Dodge City, KS [*AM radio station call letters*]
**KGNR**........ Sacramento, CA [*AM radio station call letters*]
**KGNS-TV**... Laredo, TX [*Television station call letters*]
**KGNT**........ Grants/Grants-Milan [*New Mexico*] [*ICAO location identifier*] (ICLI)
**KGNU**........ Boulder, CO [*FM radio station call letters*]
**KGNV**........ Gainesville [*Florida*] [*ICAO location identifier*] (ICLI)
**KGNW**........ Burien-Seattle, WA [*AM radio station call letters*]
**KGNZ**........ Abilene, TX [*FM radio station call letters*]
**KGO**.......... King's Gurkha Officer [*British military*] (DMA)
**KGO**.......... San Francisco, CA [*AM radio station call letters*]
**KGOK**........ Pauls Valley, OK [*FM radio station call letters*]
**KGOL**........ Humble, TX [*AM radio station call letters*]
**KGON**........ Portland, OR [*FM radio station call letters*]
**KGOR**........ Omaha, NE [*FM radio station call letters*]
**KGOS**........ Torrington, WY [*AM radio station call letters*]
**KGOT**........ Anchorage, AK [*FM radio station call letters*]
**KGO-TV**..... San Francisco, CA [*Television station call letters*]
**KGOU**........ Norman, OK [*FM radio station call letters*]
**KGP**.......... Komma Georgiou Papandreou [*Party of George Papandreou*] [*Greek*] [*Political party*] (PPE)
**KG/(PA S M²)**... Kilograms per Pascal Second Square Meter
**KGPD**........ Lahoma, OK [*FM radio station call letters*]
**KGPR**........ Great Falls, MT [*FM radio station call letters*]
**kgps**.......... Kilograms per Second
**KGR**.......... Kanonengranate [*Shell for a gun*] [*German military - World War II*]
**K & Gr**........ Keane and Grant's English Registration Appeal Cases [*1854-62*] [*A publication*] (DLA)
**KGR**.......... Kengate Resources [*Vancouver Stock Exchange symbol*]
**KGR**.......... Key Generator Receiver (MCD)
**kgr**............ Kirghiz Soviet Socialist Republic [*MARC country of publication code*] [*Library of Congress*] (LCCP)
**KGR**.......... Kobe Gaidai Ronso [*Kobe City University Journal*] [*A publication*]
**KGR**.......... [*The*] Koger Co. [*AMEX symbol*] (SPSG)
**KGRA**........ Known Geothermal Resource Area [*Department of the Interior*]
**KGRB**........ Greenbay/Austin Straubel [*Wisconsin*] [*ICAO location identifier*] (ICLI)
**KGRB**........ West Covina, CA [*AM radio station call letters*]
**KGRC**........ Hannibal, MO [*FM radio station call letters*]
**K & GRC**.... Keane and Grant's English Registration Appeal Cases [*1854-62*] [*A publication*] (DLA)
**KGRD**........ Orchard, NE [*FM radio station call letters*]
**KGRE**........ Greeley, CO [*AM radio station call letters*]
**KGRE-FM**... Wray, CO [*FM radio station call letters*]
**KGRG**........ Auburn, WA [*FM radio station call letters*]
**KGRI-FM**... Henderson, TX [*FM radio station call letters*]
**KGRK**........ Killeen/Robert Gray Army Air Field [*Texas*] [*ICAO location identifier*] (ICLI)
**KGRL**........ Bend, OR [*AM radio station call letters*]
**KGRM**........ Grambling, LA [*FM radio station call letters*]
**KGRN**........ Grinnell, IA [*AM radio station call letters*]
**KGRO**........ Pampa, TX [*AM radio station call letters*]
**KGRR**........ Grand Rapids/Kent County Cascade [*Michigan*] [*ICAO location identifier*] (ICLI)
**KGRS**......... Burlington, IA [*FM radio station call letters*]
**KGRT**......... Las Cruces, NM [*AM radio station call letters*]
**KGRT-FM**... Las Cruces, NM [*FM radio station call letters*]
**KGRV**........ Winston, OR [*AM radio station call letters*]
**KGRW**........ Friona, TX [*FM radio station call letters*]
**KGRX**........ Globe, AZ [*FM radio station call letters*]
**KGRZ**........ Missoula, MT [*AM radio station call letters*]
**KGS**.......... Kate Greenaway Society (EA)
**KGS**.......... Ketogenic Steroid [*Endocrinology*]
**kg/s**.......... Kilograms per Second
**KGS**.......... King George Sound [*Indian Ocean*] (ADA)
**Kgs**........... Kings [*Old Testament book*]
**KGS**.......... Koelner Germanistische Studien [*A publication*]
**KGS**.......... Kos [*Greece*] [*Airport symbol*] (OAG)
**KGSB**........ Goldsboro/Seymour-Johnson Air Force Base [*North Carolina*] [*ICAO location identifier*] (ICLI)
**KGSP**........ Parkville, MO [*FM radio station call letters*]
**KGSR**........ Bastrop, TX [*FM radio station call letters*]
**KGST**........ Fresno, CA [*AM radio station call letters*]
**KGStJ**........ Knight of Grace, Order of St. John of Jerusalem
**KGSU-FM**... Cedar City, UT [*FM radio station call letters*]
**KGSW-TV**... Albuquerque, NM [*Television station call letters*]
**KGT**.......... Kemper Intermediate Government Trust [*NYSE symbol*] (SPSG)
**KGTF**........ Agana, GU [*Television station call letters*]
**KGTF**........ Great Falls/International [*Montana*] [*ICAO location identifier*] (ICLI)
**KGTL**........ Homer, AK [*AM radio station call letters*]
**KGTM**........ Wichita Falls, TX [*AM radio station call letters*]
**KGTN**........ Georgetown, TX [*AM radio station call letters*]
**KGTO**........ Tulsa, OK [*AM radio station call letters*]
**KGTS**........ College Place, WA [*FM radio station call letters*]
**KGTV**........ San Diego, CA [*Television station call letters*]
**KGTW**........ Ketchikan, AK [*FM radio station call letters*]
**KGU**.......... Honolulu, HI [*AM radio station call letters*]
**KGU**.......... Keningau [*Malaysia*] [*Airport symbol*] (OAG)
**KGU**.......... Kobe Gakuin University [*UTLAS symbol*]
**KGU**.......... Kwansei Gakuin University [*A publication*]
**KGUAS**..... Kwansei Gakuin University. Annual Studies [*A publication*]
**KGUC**........ Gunnison, CO [*AM radio station call letters*]
**KGUC-FM**... Gunnison, CO [*FM radio station call letters*]
**KGUL**........ Port Lavaca, TX [*AM radio station call letters*]
**KGUM**........ Agana, GU [*AM radio station call letters*]
**KGUN**........ Tucson, AZ [*Television station call letters*]
**KGUS**........ Florence, AZ [*AM radio station call letters*]
**KGUS**........ Peru/Grisson Air Force Base [*Indiana*] [*ICAO location identifier*] (ICLI)
**KGV**.......... King George V [*British*]
**KGV**.......... Knight of Gustavus Vasa [*Sweden*]
**KGVE**........ Grove, OK [*FM radio station call letters*]
**KGVH**........ Gunnison, CO [*FM radio station call letters*]
**KGVL**........ Greenville, TX [*AM radio station call letters*]
**KGVM**........ Gardnerville-Minden, NV [*FM radio station call letters*]
**KGVO**........ King George the Fifth's Own [*British military*] (DMA)
**KGVO**........ Missoula, MT [*AM radio station call letters*]
**KGVT**........ Greenville/Majors Field [*Texas*] [*ICAO location identifier*] (ICLI)
**KGVW**........ Belgrade, MT [*AM radio station call letters*]
**KGVW**........ Grandview/Richards-Gebaur Air Force Base [*Missouri*] [*ICAO location identifier*] (ICLI)
**KGVW-FM**... Belgrade, MT [*FM radio station call letters*]
**KGVY**........ Green Valley, AZ [*AM radio station call letters*]
**KGW**.......... Kagi [*Papua New Guinea*] [*Airport symbol*] (OAG)
**KGW**.......... Kreeger, George W., Atlanta GA [*STAC*]
**KGW**.......... Portland, OR [*AM radio station call letters*]
**KGWA**........ Enid, OK [*AM radio station call letters*]
**KGWB**........ Wahpeton, ND [*FM radio station call letters*]
**KGWC**........ Offutt Air Force Base, Omaha [*Nebraska*] [*ICAO location identifier*] (ICLI)
**KGWC-TV**... Casper, WY [*Television station call letters*]
**KGWL-TV**... Lander, WY [*Television station call letters*]
**KGWN-TV**... Cheyenne, WY [*Television station call letters*]

**KGWO**....... Greenwood-Leflore [*Mississippi*] [*ICAO location identifier*] (ICLI)
**KGWR-TV** ... Rock Spring, WY [*Television station call letters*]
**KGW-TV**... Portland, OR [*Television station call letters*]
**KGWY**....... Gillette, WY [*FM radio station call letters*]
**KGX**........... Grayling [*Alaska*] [*Airport symbol*] (OAG)
**kGy**............ Kilo Gray [*Absorbed dose*] [*Radiology*]
**kGy**............ Kilogray [*Radiation dose*]
**KGY**........... Kingaroy [*Australia*] [*Airport symbol*] (OAG)
**KGY**........... Olympia, WA [*AM radio station call letters*]
**KGYN**........ Guymon, OK [*AM radio station call letters*]
**KGZ**........... Glacier Creek, AK [*Location identifier*] [*FAA*] (FAAL)
**KH**............. Cambodia [*ANSI two-letter standard code*] (CNC)
**KH**............. Cook Island Airways Ltd. [*New Zealand*] [*ICAO designator*] (FAAC)
**KH**............. Hong Kong [*IYRU nationality code*] (IYR)
**KH**............. Hungary [*License plate code assigned to foreign diplomats in the US*]
**KH**............. Kadosh [*Freemasonry*] (ROG)
**KH**............. Kawasaki Heavy Industries Ltd. [*Japan*] [*ICAO aircraft manufacturer identifier*] (ICAO)
**KH**............. Kelvin-Helmholtz [*Waves*] [*Meteorology*]
**KH**............. Keren Hayesod (BJA)
**KH**............. Kersten Hurik Group [*Commercial firm*] [*British*]
**KH**............. Keyhole Series [*Optical reconnaissance satellites*]
**Kh**.............. Khirbet (BJA)
**KH**............. Kilohenry
**KH**............. King's Hussars [*Military unit*] [*British*]
**KH**............. Kneller Hall [*British military*] (DMA)
**KH**............. Knight of the Guelphic Order of Hanover [*British*]
**K of H**......... Knight of Hanover
**KH**............. Knight of Honor
**KH**............. Kupat Holim (BJA)
**KH**............. Kwartalnik Historyczny [*A publication*]
**KHA**........... Khancoban [*Australia*] [*Seismograph station code, US Geological Survey*] (SEIS)
**kha**............ Khasi [*MARC language code*] [*Library of Congress*] (LCCP)
**KHA**........... Killed by Hostile Action [*Military*]
**KHA**........... Kitty Hawk Airways, Inc. [*Dallas, TX*] [*FAA designator*] (FAAC)
**KHAC**........ Window Rock, AZ [*AM radio station call letters*]
**KHAD**........ De Soto, MO [*AM radio station call letters*]
**Khadi Gram** ... Khadi Gramodyong [*India*] [*A publication*]
**KHAI-TV**.. Honolulu, HI [*Television station call letters*]
**KHAK**........ Cedar Rapids, IA [*AM radio station call letters*]
**KHAK-FM** ... Cedar Rapids, IA [*FM radio station call letters*]
**KHalH**....... Hertzler Research Foundation, Halstead, KS [*Library symbol*] [*Library of Congress*] (LCLS)
**KHAM**....... Horseshoe Bend, AR [*AM radio station call letters*]
**KHAP**........ Chico, CA [*FM radio station call letters*]
**KHAR**........ Anchorage, AK [*AM radio station call letters*]
**KHAR**........ Harrisburg/Capital City [*Pennsylvania*] [*ICAO location identifier*] (ICLI)
**Kharchova Promst** ... Kharchova Promyslovist [*A publication*]
**Khar'k Inst Mekh Elektrif Sel'sk Khoz Nauchn Zap** ... Khar'kovskii Institut Mekhanizatsii i Elektrifikatsii Sel'skogo Khozyaistva Nauchnye Zapiski [*A publication*]
**Khar'k Med Inst Tr** ... Khar'kovskii Meditsinskii Institut Trudy [*A publication*]
**KHAS**........ Hastings, NE [*AM radio station call letters*]
**KHAS-TV** ... Hastings, NE [*Television station call letters*]
**KHAT**........ Kurzer Handkommentar zum Alten Testament [*Tuebingen*] [*A publication*] (BJA)
**KHAT**........ Lincoln, NE [*AM radio station call letters*]
**KHAT-FM** ... Lincoln, NE [*FM radio station call letters*]
**KHAW-TV** ... Hilo, HI [*Television station call letters*]
**KHAY**........ Ventura, CA [*FM radio station call letters*]
**KHayF**....... Fort Hays State University, Hays, KS [*Library symbol*] [*Library of Congress*] (LCLS)
**KHayv**........ Haysville Community Library, Haysville, KS [*Library symbol*] [*Library of Congress*] (LCLS)
**KHAZ**........ Hays, KS [*FM radio station call letters*]
**KHB**........... Khabarovsk [*USSR*] [*Geomagnetic observatory code*]
**KHB**........... King's Hard Bargain [*British military slang for undesirable sailor or soldier*]
**KHB**........... Krebs-Henseleit Bicarbonate [*A buffer*] [*Analytical biochemistry*]
**KHB**........... KSC [*Kennedy Space Center*] Handbook [*NASA*] (KSC)
**KHB**........... Kurzgefasstes Exegetisches Handbuch zum Alten Testament [*Leipzig*] [*A publication*] (BJA)
**KHBC-TV** ... Hilo, HI [*Television station call letters*]
**KHBM**....... Monticello, AR [*AM radio station call letters*]
**KHBM-FM** ... Monticello, AR [*FM radio station call letters*]
**KHBR**........ Hillsboro, TX [*AM radio station call letters*]
**KHBR**........ Hobart [*Oklahoma*] [*ICAO location identifier*] (ICLI)
**KHBS**........ Fort Smith, AR [*Television station call letters*]
**KHBT**........ Humboldt, IA [*FM radio station call letters*]
**KHC**........... Karen Horney Clinic (EA)
**KHC**........... Kasperske Hory [*Czechoslovakia*] [*Seismograph station code, US Geological Survey*] (SEIS)
**KHC**........... King's Honorary Chaplain [*British*]
**KHCB-FM** ... Houston, TX [*FM radio station call letters*]
**KHCC-FM** ... Hutchinson, KS [*FM radio station call letters*]
**KHCD**........ Kenya High Court Digest [*A publication*] (DLA)
**KHCD**........ Salina, KS [*FM radio station call letters*]
**KHCE**........ San Antonio, TX [*Television station call letters*]
**KHCLA**...... K'o Hsueh Chi Lu [*A publication*]
**KHCR**........ Paauilo, HI [*FM radio station call letters*]
**KHCV**........ Seattle, WA [*Television station call letters*]
**KHD**.......... Klockner-Humboldt-Deutz [*Diesel engine manufacturer*] [*Federal Republic of Germany*]
**KHDC**........ Chualar, CA [*FM radio station call letters*]
**KHDL**........ Opportunity, WA [*AM radio station call letters*]
**KHDS**........ King's Honorary Dental Surgeon [*British*]
**KHDX**........ Conway, AR [*FM radio station call letters*]
**KHE**........... Kheis [*USSR*] [*Seismograph station code, US Geological Survey*] (SEIS)
**Kheberleri Izv** ... Kheberleri Izvestiya [*USSR*] [*A publication*]
**KHEI**......... Kihei, HI [*AM radio station call letters*]
**Khematol Kruvoprelivane** ... Khematologiya i Kruvoprelivane [*A publication*]
**KHEN**........ Caldwell, TX [*FM radio station call letters*]
**KHEP**........ Phoenix, AZ [*AM radio station call letters*]
**KHER**........ Crystal City, TX [*FM radio station call letters*]
**KHET**........ Honolulu, HI [*Television station call letters*]
**KHEY**........ El Paso, TX [*AM radio station call letters*]
**KHEY-FM** ... El Paso, TX [*FM radio station call letters*]
**KHEZ**........ Caldwell, ID [*FM radio station call letters*]
**KHF**........... Korean Hemorrhagic Fever [*Medicine*]
**KHFD**........ Hartford/Brainard Field [*Connecticut*] [*ICAO location identifier*] (ICLI)
**KHFI-FM** ... Austin, TX [*FM radio station call letters*]
**KHFM**....... Albuquerque, NM [*FM radio station call letters*]
**KHFT**........ Hobbs, NM [*Television station call letters*]
**KHFX**........ Honolulu, HI [*FM radio station call letters*]
**KHG**.......... Kashi [*China*] [*Airport symbol*] (OAG)
**KHGI**......... Keystone Heritage Group, Incorporated [*Lebanon, PA*] [*NASDAQ symbol*] (NQ)
**KHGI-TV**.. Kearney, NE [*Television station call letters*]
**KHH**.......... Kaohsiung [*Taiwan*] [*Airport symbol*] (OAG)
**KHH**.......... Kirchoff, H. H., St. Paul MN [*STAC*]
**KHHF**........ Victoria, TX [*FM radio station call letters*]
**KHHH**....... Honolulu, HI [*FM radio station call letters*]
**KHHI**......... Hilo, HI [*FM radio station call letters*]
**KHHT**........ Minot, ND [*FM radio station call letters*]
**KHI**............ Kakhk [*Iran*] [*Seismograph station code, US Geological Survey*] (SEIS)
**KHi**............ Kansas State Historical Society, Topeka, KS [*Library symbol*] [*Library of Congress*] (LCLS)
**KHI**............ Karachi [*Pakistan*] [*Airport symbol*] (OAG)
**KHI**............ Kemper High Income [*NYSE symbol*] (SPSG)
**KHIB**......... Durant, OK [*FM radio station call letters*]
**KHIB**......... Hibbing/Chisholm-Hibbing [*Minnesota*] [*ICAO location identifier*] (ICLI)
**Khidrol Met** ... Khidrologiya i Meteorologiya [*A publication*]
**Khidrol Meteorol** ... Khidrologiya i Meteorologiya [*A publication*]
**KHIF**.......... Keeping House of Ill Fame
**KHIF**.......... Ogden/Hill Air Force Base [*Utah*] [*ICAO location identifier*] (ICLI)
**KHIGA**...... Khirurgiya [*A publication*]
**Khig Epidemiol Mikrobiol** ... Khigiena. Epidemiologiya i Mikrobiologiya [*A publication*]
**Khig Zdraveopaz** ... Khigiena i Zdraveopazvane [*A publication*]
**Khig Zdraveopazvane** ... Khigiena i Zdraveopazvane [*A publication*]
**KHIH**......... Boulder, CO [*FM radio station call letters*]
**KHIL**.......... Willcox, AZ [*AM radio station call letters*]
**KHilT**......... Tabor College, Hillsboro, KS [*Library symbol*] [*Library of Congress*] (LCLS)
**KHIM**........ Flagstaff, AZ [*FM radio station call letters*]
**Khim Belka** ... Khimiya Belka [*A publication*]
**Khim Drev** ... Khimiya Drevesiny [*A publication*]
**Khim Elementoorg Soedin** ... Khimiya Elementoorganicheskikh Soedinenii [*A publication*]
**Khim Farm Promst** ... Khimiko Farmatsevticheskaya Promyshlennost [*A publication*]
**Khim-Farm Zh** ... Khimiko-Farmatsevticheskii Zhurnal [*A publication*]
**Khim-Far Zh** ... Khimiko-Farmatsevticheskii Zhurnal [*A publication*]
**Khim Fiz-Khim Prir Sint Polim** ... Khimiya i Fiziko-Khimiya Prirodnykh i Sinteticheskikh Polimerov [*A publication*]
**Khim Geogr Gidrogeokhim** ... Khimicheskaya Geografiya i Gidrogeokhimiya [*A publication*]
**Khim Getero** ... Khimiya Geterotsiklicheskikh Soedineniya [*A publication*]
**Khim Geterotsiklich Soedin** ... Khimiya Geterotsiklicheskikh Soedinenii [*A publication*]
**Khim Geterotsikl Soedin Akad Nauk Latv SSR** ... Khimiya Geterotsiklicheskikh Soedinenii Akademiya Nauk Latviiskoi SSR [*Latvian SSR*] [*A publication*]
**Khim Geterotsikl Soedin Sb** ... Khimiya Geterotsiklicheskikh Soedinenii Sbornik [*A publication*]
**Khim Ind**.... Khimiya i Industriya [*A publication*]
**Khim Khim Tekhnol (Alma-Ata)** ... Khimiya i Khimicheskaya Tekhnologiya (Alma-Ata) [*A publication*]

**Khim Khim Tekhnol Drev** ... Khimiya i Khimicheskaya Tekhnologiya Drevesiny [*USSR*] [*A publication*]
**Khim Khim Tekhnol (Lvov)** ... Khimiya i Khimicheskaya Tekhnologiya (Lvov) [*A publication*]
**Khim Khim Teknol (Cheboksary USSR)** ... Khimiya i Khimicheskaya Tekhnologiya (Cheboksary, USSR) [*A publication*]
**Khim Mashinostr Mosk Inst Khim Mashinostr** ... Khimicheskoe Mashinostroenie Moskovskii Institut Khimicheskogo Mashinostroeniya [*A publication*]
**Khim Med** ... Khimiya i Meditsina [*A publication*]
**Khim Nauka Prom-St** ... Khimicheskaya Nauka i Promyshlennost [*A publication*]
**Khim i Neft Mashinostr** ... Khimicheskoe i Neftyanoe Mashinostroenie [*A publication*]
**Khim Neft Mashinostr** ... Khimicheskoe i Neftyanoe Mashinostroenie [*A publication*]
**Khim Pererab Drev** ... Khimicheskaya Pererabotka Drevesiny [*A publication*]
**Khim Pererab Drev Nauchno-Tekh Sb** ... Khimicheskaya Pererabotka Drevesiny Nauchno-Tekhnicheskii Sbornik [*USSR*] [*A publication*]
**Khim Plazmy** ... Khimiya Plazmy Sbornik Statej [*A publication*]
**Khim Prirod Soed** ... Khimiya Prirodnykh Soedinenii [*A publication*]
**Khim Prir S** ... Khimiya Prirodnykh Soedinenii [*A publication*]
**Khim Prir Soedin (Tashk)** ... Khimiya Prirodnykh Soedinenii (Tashkent) [*A publication*]
**Khim Prod Koksovaniya Uglei Vostoka SSSR** ... Khimicheskie Produkty Koksovaniya Uglei Vostoka SSSR [*A publication*]
**Khim Prom** ... Khimicheskaya Promyshlennost [*A publication*]
**Khim Promst (Moscow)** ... Khimicheskaya Promyshlennost (Moscow) [*A publication*]
**Khim Promst Ser Fosfornaya Promst** ... Khimicheskaya Promyshlennost Seriya Fosfornaya Promyshlennost [*A publication*]
**Khim Promst Ser Okhr Okruzh Sredy Ratsion Ispol'z Prir Resur** ... Khimicheskaya Promyshlennost Seriya Okhrana Okruzhayushchei Sredy i Ratsional'noe Ispol'zovanie Prirodnykh Resursov [*A publication*]
**Khim Prom-St' Ukr** ... Khimicheskaya Promyshlennost' Ukrainy [*A publication*]
**Khim Reakt Prep** ... Khimicheskie Reaktivy i Preparaty [*A publication*]
**Khim Redk Elem** ... Khimiya Redkikh Elementov [*A publication*]
**Khim Sel'Khoz** ... Khimiya v Sel'skom Khozyaistve [*A publication*]
**Khim Sel'sk Khoz** ... Khimiya v Sel'skom Khozyaistve [*A publication*]
**Khim Sel'sk Khoz Bashk** ... Khimizatsiya Sel'skogo Khozyaistva Bashkirii [*A publication*]
**Khim Sera Azotorg Soedin Soderzh Neftyakh Nefteprod** ... Khimiya Sera- i Azotorganicheskikh Soedinenii Soderzhashchikhsiya v Neftyakh i Nefteproduktakh [*A publication*]
**Khim Seraorg Soedin Soderzh Neftyakh Nefteprod** ... Khimiya Seraorganicheskikh Soedinenii, Soderzhashchikhsya v Neftyakh i Nefteproduktakh [*USSR*] [*A publication*]
**Khim Signal Zhivotn** ... Khimicheskie Signaly Zhivotnykh [*A publication*]
**Khim Sots Zemled** ... Khimizatsiya Sotsialisticheskogo Zemledeliya [*A publication*]
**Khim Svyaz' Krist Fiz Svoj** ... Khimicheskaya Svyaz' v Kristallakh i Ikh Fizicheskie Svojstva [*A publication*]
**Khim Tekhnol** ... Khimicheskaia Tekhnologiia [*A publication*]
**Khim Tekhnol Drev Tsellyul Bum** ... Khimiya i Tekhnologiya Drevesiny Tsellyulozy i Bumagi [*A publication*]
**Khim Tekhnol Goryuch Slantsev Prod Ikh Pererab** ... Khimiya i Tekhnologiya Goryuchikh Slantsev i Produktov Ikh Pererabotki [*USSR*] [*A publication*]
**Khim Tekhnol (Kharkov)** ... Khimicheskaya Tekhnologiya (Kharkov) [*Ukrainian SSR*] [*A publication*]
**Khim Tekhnol (Kiev)** ... Khimicheskaya Tekhnologiya (Kiev) [*Ukrainian SSR*] [*A publication*]
**Khim Tekhnol Molbdena Vol'frama** ... Khimiya i Tekhnologiya Molibdena i Vol'frama [*A publication*]
**Khim Tekhnol Neorg Proizvod** ... Khimiya i Tekhnologiya Neorganicheskikh Proizvodstv [*A publication*]
**Khim Tekhnol Svoistva Primen Plastmass** ... Khimicheskaya Tekhnologiya Svoistva i Primenenie Plastmass [*A publication*]
**Khim i Tekhnol Topliv i Masel** ... Khimiya i Tekhnologiya Topliv i Masel [*A publication*]
**Khim Tekhnol Topl Masel** ... Khimiya i Tekhnologiya Topliv i Masel [*A publication*]
**Khim Tekhnol Topl Prod Ego Pererab** ... Khimiya i Tekhnologiya Topliva i Produktov Ego Pererabotki [*A publication*]
**Khim Tekhnol Top Masel** ... Khimiya i Tekhnologiya Topliv i Masel [*USSR*] [*A publication*]
**Khim Termodin Rastvorov** ... Khimiya i Termodinamika Rastvorov [*A publication*]
**Khim Tverd Topl (Leningrad)** ... Khimiya Tverdogo Topliva (Leningrad) [*A publication*]
**Khim Tverd Topl (Moscow)** ... Khimiya Tverdogo Topliva (Moscow) [*A publication*]
**Khim Volokna** ... Khimicheskie Volokna [*A publication*]
**Khim Vys Ehnerg** ... Khimiya Vysokikh Ehnergij [*A publication*]
**KHIN** ......... Red Oak, IA [*Television station call letters*]
**KHIP** ......... Hollister, CA [*FM radio station call letters*]
**KHIRAE**.... Khirurgiya [*Moscow*] [*A publication*]
**Khir Lietop** ... Khirurgicheskaia Lietopis [*A publication*]
**Khir Zhelchevyvodyashchikh Putei** ... Khirurgiya Zhelchevyvodyashchikh Putei [*A publication*]
**KHIS** ......... Bakersfield, CA [*AM radio station call letters*]
**KHIS-FM** ... Bakersfield, CA [*FM radio station call letters*]
**KHIT** ......... Sun Valley, NV [*AM radio station call letters*]
**KHI Tech Rev** ... KHI [*Kawasaki Heavy Industries*] Technical Review [*Japan*] [*A publication*]
**KHJJ** ......... Lancaster, CA [*AM radio station call letters*]
**KHK**........... Khark [*Iran*] [*Airport symbol*] [*Obsolete*] (OAG)
**KHK**........... Kurzer Handkommentar zum Alten Testament [*A publication*] (BJA)
**KHKC-FM** ... Atoka, OK [*FM radio station call letters*]
**KHKE**........ Cedar Falls, IA [*FM radio station call letters*]
**KHKR**........ East Helena, MT [*AM radio station call letters*]
**KHKR-FM** ... East Helena, MT [*FM radio station call letters*]
**KHKY**........ Hickory/Municipal [*North Carolina*] [*ICAO location identifier*] (ICLI)
**KHL**........... Kennedy-Heaviside Layer [*Electronics*]
**KHL**........... Keren Hajesod Ljisroel (BJA)
**KHL**........... Kupat Holim Le-'Ovdim Le'umiyim [*A publication*] (BJA)
**KHLA** ........ Lake Charles, LA [*FM radio station call letters*]
**KHLB** ........ Burnet, TX [*AM radio station call letters*]
**KHLB-FM** ... Burnet, TX [*FM radio station call letters*]
**KHLC** ........ Bandera, TX [*FM radio station call letters*]
**Khlebopekar Konditer Prom** ... Khlebopekarnaya i Konditerskaya Promyshlennost [*A publication*]
**Khlebopek Kondter Promst** ... Khlebopekarnaya i Konditerskaya Promyshlennost [*A publication*]
**Khlebopek Promst** ... Khlebopekarnaya Promyshlennost [*A publication*]
**KHLO**........ Hilo, HI [*AM radio station call letters*]
**Khlopehatobuma Promst** ... Khlopehatobumazhnaya Promyshlennost [*A publication*]
**Khlopkovod** ... Khlopkovodstvo [*A publication*]
**KHLR**........ Kahler Corp. [*NASDAQ symbol*] (NQ)
**KHLS**......... Blytheville, AR [*FM radio station call letters*]
**KHLT** ........ Little Rock, AR [*AM radio station call letters*]
**KHM** ......... Cambodia [*ANSI three-letter standard code*] (CNC)
**KHM** ......... Khamtis [*Burma*] [*Airport symbol*] (OAG)
**KHM** ......... King's Harbour Master [*Obsolete*] [*British*]
**KH-M**......... Yad V'Kidush Hashem, House of Martyrs (EA)
**KHMEA**.... Khidrologiya i Meteorologiya [*A publication*]
**KHMN** ...... Alamogordo/Holloman Air Force Base [*New Mexico*] [*ICAO location identifier*] (ICLI)
**KHMO** ...... Hannibal, MO [*AM radio station call letters*]
**KHN** .......... Knoop Hardness Number
**KHN** .......... Nanchang [*China*] [*Airport symbol*] (OAG)
**KHN** .......... Northern Kentucky University, Highland Heights, KY [*OCLC symbol*] (OCLC)
**KHNC**........ Johnstown, CO [*AM radio station call letters*]
**KHND** ........ Harvey, ND [*AM radio station call letters*]
**KHNE-FM** ... Hastings, NE [*FM radio station call letters*]
**KHNE-TV** ... Hastings, NE [*Television station call letters*]
**KHNL**......... Honolulu, HI [*Television station call letters*]
**KHNS**......... Haines, AK [*FM radio station call letters*]
**KHNS**......... King's Honorary Nursing Sister [*British*]
**KHO** .......... Khorog [*USSR*] [*Seismograph station code, US Geological Survey*] (SEIS)
**kho** ............. Khotanese [*MARC language code*] [*Library of Congress*] (LCCP)
**KHOB**........ Hobbs/Les County [*New Mexico*] [*ICAO location identifier*] (ICLI)
**KHOC**........ Levelland, TX [*FM radio station call letters*]
**KHOG-TV** ... Fayetteville, AR [*Television station call letters*]
**KHOK** ....... Hoisington, KS [*FM radio station call letters*]
**KHOL**........ Beulah, ND [*AM radio station call letters*]
**Kholod Tekh** ... Kholodil'naya Tekhnika [*USSR*] [*A publication*]
**Kholod Tekhn** ... Kholodil'naya Tekhnika [*A publication*]
**Kholod Tekh Tekhnol** ... Kholodil'naya Tekhnika i Tekhnologiya [*Ukrainian SSR*] [*A publication*]
**KHOM** ...... Houma, LA [*FM radio station call letters*]
**KHON-TV** ... Honolulu, HI [*Television station call letters*]
**KHOP**........ Hopkinsville/Campbell Army Air Field [*Kentucky*] [*ICAO location identifier*] (ICLI)
**KHOP**........ Modesto, CA [*FM radio station call letters*]
**KHOS**........ Sonora, TX [*AM radio station call letters*]
**KHOS-FM** ... Sonora, TX [*FM radio station call letters*]
**KHOT**........ Madera, CA [*AM radio station call letters*]
**KHOU** ....... Houston/William P. Hobby [*Texas*] [*ICAO location identifier*] (ICLI)
**KHOU-TV** ... Houston, TX [*Television station call letters*]
**KHOW** ...... Denver, CO [*AM radio station call letters*]
**KHOX**........ Hoxie, AR [*FM radio station call letters*]
**KHOY**........ Laredo, TX [*FM radio station call letters*]
**KHOZ**........ Harrison, AR [*AM radio station call letters*]
**KHP**........... Honorary Physician to the King [*British*]
**KHP**........... Koppers Hydrate Process
**KHPA** ........ Hope, AR [*FM radio station call letters*]
**KHPE** ........ Albany, OR [*FM radio station call letters*]
**KHPN**........ White Plains/Westchester [*New York*] [*ICAO location identifier*] (ICLI)
**KHPQ**........ Clinton, AR [*FM radio station call letters*]

**KHPR** ........ Honolulu, HI [*FM radio station call letters*]
**KHQ** ......... Kansas Historical Quarterly [*A publication*]
**KHQA-TV** ... Hannibal, MO [*Television station call letters*]
**KHQN** ....... Spanish Fork, UT [*AM radio station call letters*]
**KHQT** ........ Los Altos, CA [*FM radio station call letters*]
**KHQ-TV** .... Spokane, WA [*Television station call letters*]
**KHR** .......... Khorongon [*USSR*] [*Seismograph station code, US Geological Survey*] [*Closed*] (SEIS)
**Khranitelna Prom-St** ... Khranitelna Promishlenost [*A publication*]
**Khranit Prom** ... Khranitelna Promishlenost [*A publication*]
**Khranit Prom-St** ... Khranitelna Promishlenost [*A publication*]
**KHRI** ......... Kresge Hearing Research Institute [*University of Michigan*] [*Research center*]
**KHRL** ........ Harlingen/Industrial Airpack [*Texas*] [*ICAO location identifier*] (ICLI)
**KHRN** ........ Hearne, TX [*FM radio station call letters*]
**KHRO** ........ Harrison/Boone County [*Arkansas*] [*ICAO location identifier*] (ICLI)
**Khron VOZ** ... Khronika VOZ [*Vsemirnoj Organisatsij Zdravookhraneniya*] [*A publication*]
**KHRT** ........ Mary Esther/Eglin Air Field Auxiliary [*Florida*] [*ICAO location identifier*] (ICLI)
**KHRT** ........ Minot, ND [*AM radio station call letters*]
**KHS** .......... Honorary Surgeon to the King [*British*]
**KHS** .......... Kentucky Historical Society. Register [*A publication*]
**KHS** .......... Knight of the Holy Sepulchre
**KHSC** ........ Ontario, CA [*Television station call letters*]
**KHSD-TV** ... Lead, SD [*Television station call letters*]
**KHSH** ........ Alvin, TX [*Television station call letters*]
**KHSJ** ......... Hemet, CA [*AM radio station call letters*]
**KHSL** ......... Chico, CA [*AM radio station call letters*]
**KHSL-TV** ... Chico, CA [*Television station call letters*]
**KHSN** ........ Coos Bay, OR [*AM radio station call letters*]
**KHSR** ........ Kentucky Historical Society. Register [*A publication*]
**KHSS** ......... Walla Walla, WA [*FM radio station call letters*]
**KHST** ........ Homestead/Homestead Air Force Base [*Florida*] [*ICAO location identifier*] (ICLI)
**KHST** ........ Lamar, MO [*FM radio station call letters*]
**KHSU-FM** ... Arcata, CA [*FM radio station call letters*]
**KHSX** ........ Irving, TX [*Television station call letters*]
**KHSYA** ..... Kexue Shiyan [*A publication*]
**KHT** .......... Kathode Heating Time
**KHT** .......... Khost [*Afghanistan*] [*Airport symbol*] [*Obsolete*] (OAG)
**KHTH** ....... Dillon, CO [*AM radio station call letters*]
**KHTK** ........ Florissant, MO [*FM radio station call letters*]
**KHTL** ........ Houghton Lake/Roscommon [*Michigan*] [*ICAO location identifier*] (ICLI)
**KHTN** ........ Placerville, CA [*FM radio station call letters*]
**KHTPBU** ... Kexue Tongbao [*Foreign Language Edition*] [*A publication*]
**KHTR** ........ Pullman, WA [*FM radio station call letters*]
**KHTT** ........ Healdsburg, CA [*FM radio station call letters*]
**KHTV** ........ Houston, TX [*Television station call letters*]
**KHTX** ........ Truckee, CA [*AM radio station call letters*]
**KHTY** ........ Santa Barbara, CA [*FM radio station call letters*]
**KHTZ** ........ Visalia, CA [*AM radio station call letters*]
**KHu** .......... Hutchinson Public Library, Hutchinson, KS [*Library symbol*] [*Library of Congress*] (LCLS)
**KHU** .......... Kahuku [*Hawaii*] [*Seismograph station code, US Geological Survey*] (SEIS)
**KHUB** ........ Fremont, NE [*AM radio station call letters*]
**KHuC** ......... Hutchinson Community Junior College, Hutchinson, KS [*Library symbol*] [*Library of Congress*] (LCLS)
**KHUG** ....... Phoenix, OR [*AM radio station call letters*]
**KHUG-FM** ... Phoenix, OR [*FM radio station call letters*]
**KHUI** ......... Kahului, HI [*FM radio station call letters*]
**KHUL** ........ Houlton/International [*Maine*] [*ICAO location identifier*] (ICLI)
**KHUM** ...... Ottawa, KS [*FM radio station call letters*]
**KHUN** ....... Huntsville, TX [*FM radio station call letters*]
**KHUT** ........ Hutchinson, KS [*FM radio station call letters*]
**KHV** .......... Khabarovsk [*USSR*] [*Airport symbol*] (OAG)
**KhV** .......... Khristianski Vostok (BJA)
**KHVH** ........ Honolulu, HI [*AM radio station call letters*]
**KHVN** ........ Fort Worth, TX [*AM radio station call letters*]
**KHVO** ....... Hilo, HI [*Television station call letters*]
**KHVR** ........ Havre [*Montana*] [*ICAO location identifier*] (ICLI)
**KHVSU** ..... Kungliga Humanistiska Vetenskapssamfundet i Uppsala [*A publication*]
**KHWO** ...... Hollywood/North Perry [*Florida*] [*ICAO location identifier*] (ICLI)
**KHWY** ....... Santa Rosa, NM [*FM radio station call letters*]
**KHXS** ........ Abilene, TX [*FM radio station call letters*]
**KHYB** ........ Kupat Holim Year Book [*A publication*] (BJA)
**KHYE** ........ Hemet, CA [*FM radio station call letters*]
**KHYI** ......... Arlington, TX [*FM radio station call letters*]
**KHYL** ........ Auburn, CA [*FM radio station call letters*]
**KHYM** ....... Gilmer, TX [*AM radio station call letters*]
**KHYS** ........ Port Arthur, TX [*FM radio station call letters*]
**KHYT** ........ Toppenish, WA [*FM radio station call letters*]
**kHz** ........... Kilohertz [*Electronics*]
**KHZAD** ..... Kachiku Hanshokugaku Zasshi [*A publication*]
**KI** .............. Absorption index for the daylight end of a day-night electromagnetic transmission path (CET)
**KI** .............. Contactair Flugdienst & Co. [*ICAO designator*] (FAAC)
**KI** .............. Kach International (EA)
**KI** .............. Kanaanaeische Inschriften [*A publication*] (BJA)
**KI** .............. Karyotype Instability [*Genetics*]
**KI** .............. Key Industry [*Business term*]
**KI** .............. Keyette International (EA)
**KI** .............. Khmer Insurgents [*Cambodian rebel force*]
**Ki** .............. Kierunki [*A publication*]
**KI** .............. Kinase Insert
**KI** .............. Kinatuinamot Illengajuk [*A publication*]
**Ki** .............. Kings [*Old Testament book*]
**KI** .............. Kitchen (AABC)
**KI** .............. Kiwanis International (EA)
**KI** .............. Knesset Israel (BJA)
**KI** .............. Know, Incorporated (EA)
**KI** .............. Knowledge Integrity [*Electronic information*] (IT)
**KI** .............. Kovats [*Retention*] Index
**KI** .............. Kroenig's Isthmus [*Of resonance*] [*Medicine*]
**KiA** ............ Die Keilinschriften der Achaemeniden [*A publication*] (BJA)
**KIA** ............ Kachin Independence Army [*Burma*] (PD)
**KIA** ............ Kent International Airport [*British*]
**KIA** ............ Killed in Action [*Military*]
**KIA** ............ Kligler Iron Agar [*Medium*]
**KIAB** .......... Wichita/McConnell Air Force Base [*Kansas*] [*ICAO location identifier*] (ICLI)
**KIA - BNR** ... Killed in Action - Body Not Recovered (MCD)
**KIAC** .......... Kansai International Airport Company [*Japan*]
**KIAC** .......... Kerr Industrial Applications Center [*Southeastern Oklahoma State University*] [*Durant*] [*Information service or system*] (IID)
**KIAD** ......... Washington/Dulles International [*District of Columbia*] [*ICAO location identifier*] (ICLI)
**KIAG** ......... Mountain View, MO [*FM radio station call letters*]
**KIAG** ......... Niagara Falls/International [*New York*] [*ICAO location identifier*] (ICLI)
**KIAH** ......... Houston/Intercontinental [*Texas*] [*ICAO location identifier*] (ICLI)
**KIAK** .......... Fairbanks, AK [*AM radio station call letters*]
**KIAL** .......... Unalaska, AK [*AM radio station call letters*]
**KIAM** ........ Nenana, AK [*AM radio station call letters*]
**KIAR** .......... Kuzell Institute for Arthritis Research [*Medical Research Institute at Pacific Medical Center*] [*Research center*] (RCD)
**KIAS** .......... Knots Indicated Airspeed (MCD)
**KIAS** .......... Korea Advanced Institute of Science
**KIB** ............ Ivanof Bay, AK [*Location identifier*] [*FAA*] (FAAL)
**KiB** ............ Keilinschriftliche Bibliothek [*A publication*] (BJA)
**KIBBA** ....... Konstruktiver Ingenieurbau Berichte [*A publication*]
**KIBC** .......... Burney, CA [*FM radio station call letters*]
**Kibern Avtom** ... Kibernetika i Avtomatika [*A publication*]
**Kibernet i Vychisl Tekhn** ... Akademiya Nauk Ukrainskoi SSR. Institut Kibernetiki. Kibernetika i Vychislitelnaya Tekhnika [*A publication*]
**Kibernet i Vychisl Tekhn** ... Kibernetika i Vychislitel'naya Tekhnika [*A publication*]
**Kibernet i Vycisl Tehn** ... Kibernetika i Vycislitel'naya Tehnika [*A publication*]
**Kibern i Vychisl Tekh** ... Kibernetika i Vychislitel'naya Tekhnika [*A publication*]
**Kibern Vychisl Tekh** ... Kibernetika i Vychislitel'naya Tekhnika [*Ukrainian SSR*] [*A publication*]
**KIBIC** ........ Karolinska Institutets Bibliotek och Informationscentral [*Karolinska Institute Library and Information Center*] [*Sweden*] [*Information service or system*] (IID)
**KIBL** .......... Beeville, TX [*AM radio station call letters*]
**KIBL-FM** .. Beeville, TX [*FM radio station call letters*]
**KIBS** .......... Bishop, CA [*FM radio station call letters*]
**KIC** ............ Kansas Information Circuit [*Library network*]
**KIC** ............ Karlsruhe Isochronous Cyclotron
**KIC** ............ Ketoisocaproate [*Biochemistry*]
**KIC** ............ King City, CA [*Location identifier*] [*FAA*] (FAAL)
**KIC** ............ Knight of the Iron Crown [*British*] (ROG)
**KIC** ............ Kosan Boka [*Ivory Coast*] [*Seismograph station code, US Geological Survey*] (SEIS)
**KICA** .......... Clovis, NM [*AM radio station call letters*]
**KICB** .......... Fort Dodge, IA [*FM radio station call letters*]
**KICC** .......... International Falls, MN [*FM radio station call letters*]
**KICD** ......... Spencer, IA [*AM radio station call letters*]
**KICD-FM** ... Spencer, IA [*FM radio station call letters*]
**KICE** .......... Bend, OR [*FM radio station call letters*]
**KICK** .......... Springfield, MO [*AM radio station call letters*]
**KICL** .......... Grinnell, IA [*FM radio station call letters*]
**KICM** ........ Healdton, OK [*FM radio station call letters*]
**KICO** ......... Calexico, CA [*AM radio station call letters*]
**KICR** .......... Oakdale, LA [*AM radio station call letters*]
**KICR-FM** .. Oakdale, LA [*FM radio station call letters*]
**KICS** .......... Hastings, NE [*AM radio station call letters*]
**KICT** .......... Wichita/Mid-Continent [*Kansas*] [*ICAO location identifier*] (ICLI)

**KICT-FM** .. Wichita, KS [*FM radio station call letters*]
**KICU** ......... Keyboard Interface Control Unit [*Data processing*]
**KICU-TV**... San Jose, CA [*Television station call letters*]
**KICX**.......... McCook, NE [*AM radio station call letters*]
**KICX-FM**.. McCook, NE [*FM radio station call letters*]
**KICY**.......... Nome, AK [*AM radio station call letters*]
**KICY-FM**.. Nome, AK [*FM radio station call letters*]
**KICZ**.......... Elk City, OK [*FM radio station call letters*]
**KID** ........... Idaho Falls, ID [*AM radio station call letters*]
**KID** ........... Key Industry [*Business term*] (DS)
**KID** ........... Keyboard Input Device (MCD)
**KID** ........... Kidd Resources Ltd. [*Vancouver Stock Exchange symbol*]
**Kid**............. Kiddushin (BJA)
**KID** ........... Kidnaping [*FBI standardized term*]
**KID** ........... Kildare [*County in Ireland*] (ROG)
**KID** ........... Kristianstad [*Sweden*] [*Airport symbol*] (OAG)
**KIDA-FM** ... Ida Grove, IA [*FM radio station call letters*]
**KIDD** ......... Kiddie Products, Inc. [*NASDAQ symbol*] (NQ)
**KIDD-FM** ... Bend, OR [*FM radio station call letters*]
**KIDE**.......... Hoopa, CA [*FM radio station call letters*]
**KIDI**........... Albuquerque, NM [*FM radio station call letters*]
**KIDID6**...... Kidney Disease [*A publication*]
**KIDK** ......... Idaho Falls, ID [*Television station call letters*]
**Kidma Isr J Dev** ... Kidma. Israel Journal of Development [*A publication*]
**Kidney Dis** ... Kidney Disease [*A publication*]
**Kidney Int**.. Kidney International [*A publication*]
**Kidney Int Suppl** ... Kidney International. Supplement [*A publication*]
**KIDO**.......... Boise, ID [*AM radio station call letters*]
**KIDS**.......... Kestrel Interactive Development System [*Data processing*]
**KIDS**.......... Kindergarten Inventory of Developmental Skills [*Child development test*]
**KIDS**.......... Magic Years Child Care & Learning Centers, Inc. [*NASDAQ symbol*] (NQ)
**KIDS**.......... Palmyra, MO [*FM radio station call letters*]
**Kidult**......... Kid-Adult [*Television viewer aged 12-34*]
**KIDX** ......... Billings, MT [*FM radio station call letters*]
**KIDY** ......... San Angelo, TX [*Television station call letters*]
**KIDZ** ......... Direct Connection International, Inc. [*NASDAQ symbol*] (NQ)
**KIDZD** ...... Kanazawa Ika Daigaku Zasshi [*A publication*]
**KIE**............ Kennedy Institute of Ethics, Washington, DC [*OCLC symbol*] (OCLC)
**Kie**............. Kierkegaardiana [*A publication*]
**KIE**............ Kieta [*Papua New Guinea*] [*Airport symbol*] (OAG)
**KIE**............ Kinetic Isotope Effect [*Physical chemistry*]
**Kie**............. Kompanjie [*Company*] [*Afrikaans*]
**KIEA**.......... Ethete, WY [*FM radio station call letters*]
**KIEE**.......... Knoxville International Energy Exposition [*1982*]
**Kieferchir**... Kieferchirurgie [*A publication*]
**KIEI**........... Kundu Introversion-Extraversion Inventory [*Personality development test*] [*Psychology*]
**Kieler Rechtswiss Abh** ... Kieler Rechtswissenschaftliche Abhandlungen [*A publication*]
**Kieler Studien** ... Kieler Studien zur Deutschen Literaturgeschichte [*A publication*]
**Kiel Meeresforsch** ... Kieler Meeresforschungen [*A publication*]
**Kiel Milchwirtsch Forschungsber** ... Kieler Milchwirtschaftliche Forschungsberichte [*A publication*]
**Kiel Not Pflanzenkd Schleswig Holstein** ... Kieler Notizen zur Pflanzenkunde in Schleswig Holstein [*A publication*]
**KIEM-TV** ... Eureka, CA [*Television station call letters*]
**KIER Bulletin** ... Korea. Institute of Energy and Resources. Bulletin [*A publication*]
**KIET**.......... Korea Institute for Industrial Economics and Technology [*South Korea*] [*Research center*] [*Also, an information service or system*] (IRC)
**KIEV**.......... Glendale, CA [*AM radio station call letters*]
**Kiev Univ Visn Ser Geogr** ... Kiev Universitet Visnik Seriya Geografi [*A publication*]
**KIEZ**.......... Brusly, LA [*FM radio station call letters*]
**KIF**............ Kodak Industrial Film
**KIF**............ Name and Address Key Index File [*IRS*]
**KIFG**.......... Iowa Falls, IA [*AM radio station call letters*]
**KIFG-FM**.. Iowa Falls, IA [*FM radio station call letters*]
**KIFIS**......... Kollsman Integrated Flight Instrumentation System [*Aviation*]
**KIFI-TV** .... Idaho Falls, ID [*Television station call letters*]
**KIFM**......... San Diego, CA [*FM radio station call letters*]
**KIFTSG**..... Kiftsgate [*England*]
**KIFW**......... Sitka, AK [*AM radio station call letters*]
**KIG** ........... Koingnaas [*South Africa*] [*Airport symbol*] (OAG)
**KIGAM Bull** ... KIGAM [*Korea Research Institute of Geoscience and Mineral Resources*] Bulletin [*A publication*]
**KIGC** ......... Oskaloosa, IA [*FM radio station call letters*]
**KIGO** ......... St. Anthony, ID [*AM radio station call letters*]
**KIGS**.......... Hanford, CA [*AM radio station call letters*]
**KIH**............ Coast Independent Hi-Tech [*Vancouver Stock Exchange symbol*]
**KIH**............ Kaisar-I-Hind [*Indian medal*]
**KIH**............ Kilometres in the Hour [*Rate of march*] [*Military*] [*British*]
**KIH**............ Kish Island [*Iran*] [*Airport symbol*] (OAG)
**KIHN**......... Hugo, OK [*AM radio station call letters*]
**KIHR** ......... Hood River, OR [*AM radio station call letters*]
**KIHR** ......... Korean Institute for Human Rights (EA)
**KIHS** ......... Yakima, WA [*FM radio station call letters*]
**KIHX-FM** ... Prescott Valley, AZ [*FM radio station call letters*]
**KII**............. Keystone International, Incorporated [*NYSE symbol*] (SPSG)
**KII**............. Kuder Interest Inventory [*Occupational information*] (OICC)
**KII**............. Kwartaalreeks over Informatie en Informatie Beleid [*A publication*]
**KIIC**........... Kuwait International Investment Company
**KIID-TV**.... Huron, SD [*Television station call letters*]
**KIIGD**........ Kitasato Igaku [*A publication*]
**KIII** ........... Corpus Christi, TX [*Television station call letters*]
**KIIK-FM** ... Fairfield, IA [*FM radio station call letters*]
**KIIM**.......... Tucson, AZ [*FM radio station call letters*]
**KIIN-TV**.... Iowa City, IA [*Television station call letters*]
**KIIQ-FM**... Reno, NV [*FM radio station call letters*]
**KIIS** .......... Korean Institute of International Studies
**KIIS** .......... Los Angeles, CA [*AM radio station call letters*]
**KIIS-FM**.... Los Angeles, CA [*FM radio station call letters*]
**Kiito Kensajo Kenkyu Hokoku Res Rep Silk Cond** ... Kiito Kensajo Kenkyu Hokoku. Research Reports of the Silk Conditioning Houses [*A publication*]
**Kiiv Derzh Univ Im T G Shevchenka Nauk Shchorichnik** ... Kiivs'kii Derzhavnii Universitet Imeni T. G. Shevchenka Naukovii Shchorichnik [*A publication*]
**Kiiv Derzh Univ Stud Nauk Pr** ... Kiivs'kii Derzhavnii Universitet Students'ki Naukovi Pratsi [*A publication*]
**KIIX**........... Wellington, CO [*AM radio station call letters*]
**KIIZ**........... Killeen, TX [*AM radio station call letters*]
**KIJ** ............ Independence Community Junior College, Independence, KS [*Library symbol*] [*Library of Congress*] (LCLS)
**KIJ** ............ Kawah Idjen [*Java*] [*Seismograph station code, US Geological Survey*] [*Closed*] (SEIS)
**KiJ** ............ Knjizevnost i Jezik [*A publication*]
**KIJ** ............ Niigata [*Japan*] [*Airport symbol*] (OAG)
**KIJK**.......... Prineville, OR [*FM radio station call letters*]
**KIJN**.......... Farwell, TX [*AM radio station call letters*]
**KIJN-FM**.. Farwell, TX [*FM radio station call letters*]
**KIJV** .......... Huron, SD [*AM radio station call letters*]
**kik**............. Kikuyu [*MARC language code*] [*Library of Congress*] (LCCP)
**KIK** ........... Kozawa, Iwatsuru, and Kawaguchi [*Factor involving injection of cancerous gastric juices into rabbits, named for its discoverers*] [*Medicine*]
**KIKC**.......... Forsyth, MT [*AM radio station call letters*]
**KIKC-FM**.. Forsyth, MT [*FM radio station call letters*]
**KIKF** .......... Garden Grove, CA [*FM radio station call letters*]
**KIKI**........... Honolulu, HI [*AM radio station call letters*]
**KIKI-FM** ... Honolulu, HI [*FM radio station call letters*]
**KIKK**.......... Pasadena, TX [*AM radio station call letters*]
**KIKK-FM** ... Houston, TX [*FM radio station call letters*]
**KIKM-FM** ... Sherman, TX [*FM radio station call letters*]
**KIKN** ......... Pharr, TX [*AM radio station call letters*]
**KIKO** ......... Miami, AZ [*AM radio station call letters*]
**KIKR**.......... Conroe, TX [*AM radio station call letters*]
**KIKS**.......... Iola, KS [*AM radio station call letters*]
**KIKS-FM** .. Iola, KS [*FM radio station call letters*]
**KIKT**.......... Greenville, TX [*FM radio station call letters*]
**KIKV-FM** ... Alexandria, MN [*FM radio station call letters*]
**KIKX-FM** ... Manitou Springs, CO [*FM radio station call letters*]
**KIKZ**.......... Seminole, TX [*AM radio station call letters*]
**KIL**............ Keyed Input Language
**Kil** ............ Kil'aim (BJA)
**KIL**............ Kilderkin [*Unit of measurement*] [*British*] (ROG)
**KIL**............ Kilembe Resources Ltd. [*Vancouver Stock Exchange symbol*]
**KIL**............ Kilogram
**KIL**............ Kilometer
**KIL**............ Krypton Ion LASER
**KILA**.......... Las Vegas, NV [*FM radio station call letters*]
**Kilb** ........... Kilburn's English Magistrates' Cases [*A publication*] (DLA)
**KILD**.......... Kildare [*County in Ireland*] (ROG)
**KILD**.......... Kilderkin [*Unit of measurement*] [*British*]
**KILE** .......... Kile Technology Corp. [*NASDAQ symbol*] (NQ)
**KILG**.......... Wilmington/Greater Wilmington [*Delaware*] [*ICAO location identifier*] (ICLI)
**KILJ** .......... Mount Pleasant, IA [*AM radio station call letters*]
**KILJ-FM**... Mount Pleasant, IA [*FM radio station call letters*]
**KILK**.......... Kilkenny [*County in Ireland*]
**Kilk** ........... Kilkerran's Scotch Court of Session Decisions [*A publication*] (DLA)
**Kilkerran** ... Kilkerran's Scotch Court of Session Decisions [*A publication*] (DLA)
**KILLS**........ Ka-Inertial Launch and Leave System
**KILM**......... Wilmington/New Hannover County [*North Carolina*] [*ICAO location identifier*] (ICLI)
**KILO** ......... Colorado Springs, CO [*FM radio station call letters*]
**KILO** ......... Kilogram
**KILO** ......... Kilometer
**Kilobaud Microcomput** ... Kilobaud Microcomputing [*A publication*]
**KILOL**........ Kiloliter
**KILOM**...... Kilometer
**KILR**.......... Estherville, IA [*AM radio station call letters*]

**KILR-FM**.. Estherville, IA [*FM radio station call letters*]
**KILS**.......... Keller Industries Ltd. [*NASDAQ symbol*] (NQ)
**KILT**.......... Houston, TX [*AM radio station call letters*]
**KILT-FM**.. Houston, TX [*FM radio station call letters*]
**KIM**........... Keyboard Input Matrix [*Data processing*]
**KIM**........... Kimberley [*South Africa*] [*Seismograph station code, US Geological Survey*] (SEIS)
**KIM**........... Kimberley [*South Africa*] [*Airport symbol*] (OAG)
**KIMA-TV**... Yakima, WA [*Television station call letters*]
**KIMB**......... Kimball, NE [*AM radio station call letters*]
**KIMB**......... Kimbark Oil & Gas Co. [*NASDAQ symbol*] (NQ)
**Kimball's D F**... Kimball's Dairy Farmer [*A publication*]
**KIMC**......... Kimco Energy Corp. [*NASDAQ symbol*] (NQ)
**KIMCODE**... Kimble Method for Controlled Devacuation
**KIMG**......... Key Image Systems, Inc. [*NASDAQ symbol*] (NQ)
**KIML**......... Gillette, WY [*AM radio station call letters*]
**KIMM**......... Rapid City, SD [*AM radio station call letters*]
**KIMMA**..... Kongres Indian Muslim Malaysia [*Malaysia Indian Moslem Congress*] [*Political party*] (PPW)
**Kim Muhendisligi**... Kimya Muhendisligi [*Turkey*] [*A publication*]
**KIMN-FM**... Fort Collins, CO [*FM radio station call letters*]
**KIMO**......... Anchorage, AK [*Television station call letters*]
**KIMO**......... Kings Mountain National Military Park
**KIMP**......... Mount Pleasant, TX [*AM radio station call letters*]
**Kim Sanayi**... Kimya ve Sanayi [*Turkey*] [*A publication*]
**KiMSV**....... Kirsten Murine Sarcoma Virus
**KIMT**......... Mason City, IA [*Television station call letters*]
**KI MUSV**.. Kirsten Murine Sarcoma Virus
**KIMX**......... Laramie, WY [*FM radio station call letters*]
**KIMY**......... Watonga, OK [*FM radio station call letters*]
**KIN**........... Association of Kinsmen Clubs (EA)
**KIN**........... Kinark Corp. [*AMEX symbol*] (SPSG)
**KIN**........... Kinescope
**KIN**........... Kingston [*Jamaica*] [*Airport symbol*] (OAG)
**KIN**........... Kingston [*Jamaica*] [*Seismograph station code, US Geological Survey*] (SEIS)
**Kin**........... Kinnim (BJA)
**kin**........... Kinyarwanda [*MARC language code*] [*Library of Congress*] (LCCP)
**KINA**......... Salina, KS [*AM radio station call letters*]
**KIND**......... Independence, KS [*AM radio station call letters*]
**KIND**......... Indianapolis/International [*Indiana*] [*ICAO location identifier*] (ICLI)
**KIND**......... Kinder-Care Learning Centers, Inc. [*NASDAQ symbol*] (NQ)
**KIND**......... Kindness in Nature's Defense [*Elementary school course*]
**Kinderaerztl Prax**... Kinderaerztliche Praxis [*A publication*]
**Kind and First Grade**... Kindergarten and First Grade [*A publication*]
**KIND-FM**... Independence, KS [*FM radio station call letters*]
**Kindler Tb**... Kindler Taschenbuecher Geist und Psyche [*A publication*]
**Kind M**....... Kindergarten Primary Magazine [*A publication*]
**KINE**......... Kinescope
**KINE**......... Kingsville, TX [*AM radio station call letters*]
**Kinesither Sci**... Kinesitherapie Scientifique [*A publication*]
**Kinet Catal**... Kinetics and Catalysis [*A publication*]
**Kinet Goreniya Iskop Topl**... Kinetika Goreniya Iskopaemykh Topliv [*A publication*]
**Kinet Katal**... Kinetika i Kataliz [*A publication*]
**Kinet Mech Polym**... Kinetics and Mechanisms of Polymerization [*A publication*]
**KINF**......... Dodge City, KS [*FM radio station call letters*]
**KING**......... Kinetic Intense Neutron Generator
**King**........... King's Reports [*5, 6 Louisiana*] [*A publication*] (DLA)
**KING**......... Seattle, WA [*AM radio station call letters*]
**King**........... Select Cases in Chancery Tempore King, Edited by Macnaghten [*1724-33*] [*England*] [*A publication*] (DLA)
**King Abdulaziz Med J**... King Abdulaziz Medical Journal [*A publication*]
**King Cas**.... Cases in King's Colorado Civil Practice [*A publication*] (DLA)
**King Cas Temp**... Select Cases in Chancery Tempore King [*1724-33*] [*England*] [*A publication*] (DLA)
**KINGD**....... Kingdom
**King Dig**..... King's Tennessee Digest [*A publication*] (DLA)
**King Faisal Spec Hosp Med J**... King Faisal Specialist Hospital. Medical Journal [*A publication*]
**King-Farlow**... Gold Coast Judgments and the Masai Cases, by King-Farlow [*1915-17*] [*Ghana*] [*A publication*] (DLA)
**KING-FM**... Seattle, WA [*FM radio station call letters*]
**Kings**......... Kingsway [*Record label*]
**KINGSBR**... Kingsbridge [*England*]
**King's Con Cs**... King's Conflicting Cases [*Texas*] [*A publication*] (DLA)
**King's Conf Ca**... King's Conflicting Cases [*Texas*] [*A publication*] (DLA)
**Kingston Geol Rev**... Kingston Geology Review [*United Kingdom*] [*A publication*]
**Kingston LR**... Kingston Law Review [*A publication*]
**Kingston L Rev**... Kingston Law Review [*A publication*]
**Kingston-On-Hull Mus Bull**... Kingston-On-Hull Museums. Bulletin [*A publication*]
**KING-TV**.. Seattle, WA [*Television station call letters*]
**KINI**......... Crookston, NE [*FM radio station call letters*]
**Kininy Kininovaya Sist Krovi**... Kininy i Kininovaya Sistema Krovi. Biokhimiya, Farmakologiya, Patfiziologiya, Metody Issledovaniya. Rol V. Patologii [*A publication*]
**KINK**......... Portland, OR [*FM radio station call letters*]
**KINK**......... Wink/Winkler County [*Texas*] [*ICAO location identifier*] (ICLI)
**Kin Kei**....... Kinyu Keizai [*A publication*]
**KINL**......... Eagle Pass, TX [*FM radio station call letters*]
**KINL**......... International Falls [*Minnesota*] [*ICAO location identifier*] (ICLI)
**KINN**......... Kinnard Investments, Inc. [*NASDAQ symbol*] (NQ)
**Kinney Law Dict & Glos**... Kinney's Law Dictionary and Glossary [*A publication*] (DLA)
**KINN-FM**... Alamogordo, NM [*FM radio station call letters*]
**KINO**......... Winslow, AZ [*AM radio station call letters*]
**Kino Photo Ind**... Kino-Photo Industry [*A publication*]
**Kinotech**..... Kinotechnik [*A publication*]
**Kinotech Filmtech Ausg A**... Kinotechnik und Filmtechnik. Ausgabe A [*A publication*]
**Kinotech Filmtech Ausg B**... Kinotechnik und Filmtechnik. Ausgabe B [*A publication*]
**KINQ**......... Fairbanks, AK [*FM radio station call letters*]
**KINS**......... Eureka, CA [*AM radio station call letters*]
**KINS**......... Indian Springs/Indian Springs Army Air Field [*Nevada*] [*ICAO location identifier*] (ICLI)
**KINSA**....... Kodak International Newspaper Snapshot Awards
**K Inst Tropen Meded Afd Tropische Producten**... Koninklijk Instituut voor de Tropen. Mededeling. Afdeling Tropische Producten [*A publication*]
**KINT**......... Winston Salem/Smith-Reynolds [*North Carolina*] [*ICAO location identifier*] (ICLI)
**KINTB**....... Kintbury [*England*]
**KINT-TV**... El Paso, TX [*Television station call letters*]
**Kintyre Antiqu Nat Hist Soc Mag**... Kintyre Antiquarian and Natural History Society. Magazine [*A publication*]
**KINV**......... Kentucky Investors, Inc. [*NASDAQ symbol*] (NQ)
**KINW**......... Wallace, ID [*FM radio station call letters*]
**KINY**......... Juneau, AK [*AM radio station call letters*]
**KINY**......... Kinney System, Inc. [*NASDAQ symbol*] (NQ)
**KIo**........... Iola Free Public Library, Iola, KS [*Library symbol*] [*Library of Congress*] (LCLS)
**KIO**........... Kili [*Marshall Islands*] [*Airport symbol*] (OAG)
**KIO**........... Kuwait Investment Office (ECON)
**KIOA**......... Des Moines, IA [*AM radio station call letters*]
**KIOB**......... Grand Junction, CO [*FM radio station call letters*]
**KIOC**......... Orange, TX [*FM radio station call letters*]
**KIOI**......... San Francisco, CA [*FM radio station call letters*]
**KIOK**......... Richland, WA [*FM radio station call letters*]
**KIOL-FM**... Lamesa, TX [*FM radio station call letters*]
**KIOO**......... Porterville, CA [*FM radio station call letters*]
**KIOPI**....... Kienzle Input/Output Peripheral Interface
**KIoS**......... Southeast Kansas Library System, Iola, KS [*Library symbol*] [*Library of Congress*] (LCLS)
**KIOS-FM**... Omaha, NE [*FM radio station call letters*]
**KIOT**......... Barstow, CA [*AM radio station call letters*]
**KIOU**......... Shreveport, LA [*AM radio station call letters*]
**KIOW**......... Forest City, IA [*FM radio station call letters*]
**KIOX**......... Bay City, TX [*AM radio station call letters*]
**KIP**........... Key Indigenous Personnel (MCD)
**KIP**........... Key Intelligence Position (AFM)
**KIP**........... Keyboard Input Processor [*Data processing*] (NASA)
**KIP**........... Kipapa [*Hawaii*] [*Seismograph station code, US Geological Survey*] (SEIS)
**KIP**........... Knowledge Industry Publications, Inc. [*Telecommunications*]
**KIP**........... Knowledge Information Processing [*Data processing*]
**KIP**........... Thousand Pounds
**KIPA**......... Hilo, HI [*AM radio station call letters*]
**KIPA-FM**.. Hilo, HI [*FM radio station call letters*]
**KIPC**......... Lubbock, TX [*Television station call letters*]
**KIP-FT**...... Thousand Foot-Pounds
**KIPI**......... Knowledge Industry Publications, Incorporated [*White Plains, NY*] [*Telecommunications*] [*Information service or system*]
**KIPL**......... Imperial/Imperial County [*California*] [*ICAO location identifier*] (ICLI)
**KIPO**......... Honolulu, HI [*FM radio station call letters*]
**KIPO**......... Keyboard Input Printout [*Data processing*] (IEEE)
**KIPOB**....... Kompleksnye Issledovaniya Prirody Okeana [*A publication*]
**KIPR**......... Kwartalnik Institutu Polsko-Radzieckiego [*A publication*]
**KIPR**......... Pine Bluff, AR [*FM radio station call letters*]
**KIPS**......... Kaufman Infant and Preschool Scale [*Child development test*] [*Psychology*]
**KIPS**......... Kilo-Instructions per Second
**KIPS**......... Kilowatt Isotope Power System (IEEE)
**KIPS**......... Knowledge Information Processing Systems [*Data processing*]
**KIQ**........... Key Intelligence Question [*CIA*]
**KIQ**........... Kira [*Papua New Guinea*] [*Airport symbol*] (OAG)
**KIQI**......... San Francisco, CA [*AM radio station call letters*]
**KIQO**......... Atascadero, CA [*FM radio station call letters*]
**KIQQ**......... Lenwood, CA [*FM radio station call letters*]
**KIQS**......... Willows, CA [*AM radio station call letters*]
**KIQS-FM**.. Willows, CA [*FM radio station call letters*]
**KIQX**......... Durango, CO [*FM radio station call letters*]
**KIQY**......... Lebanon, OR [*FM radio station call letters*]

**KIQZ** ......... Rawlins, WY [*FM radio station call letters*]
**KIR** ........... Key Intelligence Requirement (MCD)
**Kir** ............. Kirby's Connecticut Reports and Supplement [*1785-89*] [*A publication*] (DLA)
**kir**............... Kirghiz [*MARC language code*] [*Library of Congress*] (LCCP)
**KIR** ........... Kiruna [*Sweden*] [*Seismograph station code, US Geological Survey*] (SEIS)
**KIR** ........... Kiruna [*Sweden*] [*Geomagnetic observatory code*]
**KiR**............ Kniga i Revoljucija [*A publication*]
**KIR** ........... Knight's Industrial Reports [*A publication*] (DLA)
**KI Rapp** ..... Korrosionsinstitutet. Rapport [*A publication*]
**Kirb**............ Kirby's Connecticut Reports and Supplement [*1785-89*] [*A publication*] (DLA)
**KIRBS** ....... Korean Institute for Research in the Behavioral Sciences
**Kirby**.......... Kirby's Connecticut Reports and Supplement [*1785-89*] [*A publication*] (DLA)
**Kirby's Conn R** ... Kirby's Connecticut Reports [*A publication*] (DLA)
**Kirby's R**.... Kirby's Connecticut Reports [*A publication*] (DLA)
**Kirby's Rep** ... Kirby's Connecticut Reports [*A publication*] (DLA)
**Kirchor**....... Kirchenchor [*A publication*]
**Kirch PA**.... Kirchner, Prosopographia Attica [*A publication*]
**Kirin Univ J Nat Sci** ... Kirin University Journal. Natural Sciences [*People's Republic of China*] [*A publication*]
**KIRK**.......... Kirkcaldy [*Seaport in Scotland*]
**KIRK**.......... Lebanon, MO [*FM radio station call letters*]
**KIRKCUDB** ... Kirkcudbrightshire [*County in Scotland*]
**Kirkus** ........ Virginia Kirkus' Service. Bulletin [*A publication*]
**Kirkus R**..... Kirkus Reviews [*A publication*]
**KIRL**.......... St. Charles, MO [*AM radio station call letters*]
**Kirmus** ....... Kirchenmusiker [*A publication*]
**KIRO** ......... Seattle, WA [*AM radio station call letters*]
**KIRO-TV**... Seattle, WA [*Television station call letters*]
**Kirov Gos Pedagog Inst Uch Zap** ... Kirovskii Gosudarstvennyi Pedagogicheskii Institut. Uchenye Zapiski [*A publication*]
**KIRP**.......... Kodak Infrared Phosphor
**KIRS**.......... Kodak Infrared Scope
**KIRS**.......... San Diego, CA [*AM radio station call letters*]
**KirSeph**...... Kirjath Sepher [*Jerusalem*] (BJA)
**KirSSR**....... Kirghiz Soviet Socialist Republic
**KIRT**.......... Mission, TX [*AM radio station call letters*]
**Kirt Sur Pr** ... Kirtland on Practice in Surrogates' Courts [*A publication*] (DLA)
**KIRV**.......... Fresno, CA [*AM radio station call letters*]
**KIRX**.......... Kirksville, MO [*AM radio station call letters*]
**KIS**............ Keep It Simple (ADA)
**KIS**............ Kenny Information Systems [*Database producer*] (IID)
**KIS**............ Kenya Independent Squadron [*British military*] (DMA)
**KIS**............ Key Independent System [*Instant photo development company*] [*France*]
**KIS**............ Keyboard Input Simulation [*Data processing*]
**KIS**............ Kishinev [*USSR*] [*Seismograph station code, US Geological Survey*] (SEIS)
**KIS**............ Kisumu [*Kenya*] [*Airport symbol*] (OAG)
**KIS**............ Kitting Instruction Sheet [*NASA*] (NASA)
**KIS**............ Kodak Infrared Scope
**KiS** ............ Kultura i Spoleczenstwo [*A publication*]
**KISA**.......... Honolulu, HI [*AM radio station call letters*]
**KISA**.......... Voluntary International Service Assignments [*of the Society of Friends*]
**Kisb Ir Land L** ... Kisbey on the Irish Land Law [*A publication*] (DLA)
**KISC**.......... Kimmins Corporation [*Tampa, FL*] [*NASDAQ symbol*] (NQ)
**KISC**.......... Knowledge Industry Systems Concept [*Publishing and education*] [*Pronounced "kiss"*]
**KISC**.......... Spokane, WA [*FM radio station call letters*]
**KISD**.......... Pipestone, MN [*FM radio station call letters*]
**KISDA**....... Report. Institute for Systems Design and Optimization. Kansas State University [*A publication*]
**Kiserletugyi Koezlem** ... Kiserletugyi Koezlemenyek [*A publication*]
**Kiserletugyi Kozl A** ... Kiserletugyi Koezlemenyek. A Kotet. Novenytermesztes [*A publication*]
**Kiserletugyi Kozl B** ... Kiserletugyi Koezlemenyek. B Kotet. Allattenyesztes [*A publication*]
**Kiserletugyi Kozl C** ... Kiserletugyi Koezlemenyek. C Kotet. Kerteszet [*A publication*]
**Kiserl Koezl Erdogazdasag** ... Kiserletugyi Koezlemenyek. Erdogazdasag [*A publication*]
**Kiserl Kozl** ... Kiserletugyi Koezlemenyek [*A publication*]
**Kiserl Orvostud** ... Kiserletes Orvostudomany [*A publication*]
**KISI**.......... Malvern, AR [*FM radio station call letters*]
**Kisinev Gos Univ Ucen Zap** ... Kisinevskii Gosudarstvennyi Universitet. Ucenye Zapiski [*A publication*]
**KISJ-FM**... Brownwood, TX [*FM radio station call letters*]
**KISM**.......... Bellingham, WA [*FM radio station call letters*]
**KISMIF**...... Keep It Simple, Make It Fun
**KISN**.......... Salt Lake City, UT [*AM radio station call letters*]
**KISN**.......... Williston/International [*North Dakota*] [*ICAO location identifier*] (ICLI)
**KISN-FM**.. Salt Lake City, UT [*FM radio station call letters*]
**KISP**.......... Islip/MacArthur Field [*New York*] [*ICAO location identifier*] (ICLI)
**KISR**.......... Fort Smith, AR [*FM radio station call letters*]
**KISS**.......... Keep It Short and Simple (MCD)
**KISS**.......... Keep It Short and Sweet [*Radio messages*]
**KISS**.......... Keep It Simple, Stupid [*Bridge bidding term*]
**KISS**.......... Keep It Straight and Simple [*Data processing*]
**KISS**.......... Key Integrative Social Systems
**KISS**.......... Keyed Indexed Sequential Search
**KISS**.......... Knights in the Service of Satan [*Rock music group*]
**KISS**.......... San Antonio, TX [*FM radio station call letters*]
**KISSNIX**... [*Henry*] Kissinger and [*Richard*] Nixon [*Term coined by columnist William Safire*]
**KIST**.......... Keyword Index to Serial Titles [*A publication*]
**KIST**.......... Korean Institute for Science and Technology
**KIST**.......... Santa Barbara, CA [*AM radio station call letters*]
**KISU-TV**... Pocatello, ID [*Television station call letters*]
**KiSV**.......... Kirsten Sarcoma Virus
**KISW**......... Seattle, WA [*FM radio station call letters*]
**KISX**.......... Whitehouse, TX [*FM radio station call letters*]
**KISY**.......... Tioga, LA [*FM radio station call letters*]
**KISZ**.......... Cortez, CO [*AM radio station call letters*]
**KISZ**.......... Kommunista Ifjusagi Szovetseg [*Communist Youth Organization*] [*Hungary*]
**KISZAR**..... Japanese Journal of Parasitology [*A publication*]
**KISZ-FM**.. Cortez, CO [*FM radio station call letters*]
**KIT**............ Kaufman Ion Thrustor
**KIT**............ Kentucky & Indiana Terminal Railroad Co. [*AAR code*]
**KIT**............ Kermit [*Texas*] [*Seismograph station code, US Geological Survey*] (SEIS)
**KIT**............ Key Issue Tracking [*Database*]
**KIT**............ Kit Manufacturing Co. [*AMEX symbol*] (SPSG)
**KIT**............ Kitchen (ADA)
**Kit**............. Kitchin's Retourna Brevium [*4 eds.*] [*1581-92*] [*A publication*] (DLA)
**KIT**............ Kithira [*Greece*] [*Airport symbol*] (OAG)
**KIT**............ Kittrell Junior College, Kittrell, NC [*OCLC symbol*] [*Inactive*] (OCLC)
**KIT**............ Koninklijk Instituut voor de Tropen. Centrale Bibliotheek. Aanwinstenlijst [*A publication*]
**KIT**............ Yakima, WA [*AM radio station call letters*]
**KITA**.......... Kesatuan Insaf Tanah Air [*National Consciousness Party*] [*Malaysia*] [*Political party*] (PPW)
**KITA**.......... Kick in the Afterdeck [*Bowdlerized version*]
**KITA**.......... Little Rock, AR [*AM radio station call letters*]
**Kitakanto Med J** ... Kitakanto Medical Journal [*A publication*]
**Kitano Hosp J Med** ... Kitano Hospital Journal of Medicine [*A publication*]
**Kit Arch Exp Med** ... Kitasato Archives of Experimental Medicine [*A publication*]
**Kitasato Arch Exp Med** ... Kitasato Archives of Experimental Medicine [*A publication*]
**Kitasato Med** ... Kitasato Medicine [*A publication*]
**Kitch** .......... Kitchin on Jurisdictions of Courts-Leet, Courts-Baron, Etc. [*A publication*] (DLA)
**Kitch Courts** ... Kitchin on Jurisdictions of Courts-Leet, Courts-Baron, Etc. [*A publication*] (DLA)
**Kitch Cts**.... Kitchin on Courts [*A publication*] (DLA)
**Kitchen**....... Griqualand West Reports [*Cape Colony, South Africa*] [*A publication*] (DLA)
**Kit Ct**......... Kitchin on Jurisdictions of Courts-Leet, Courts-Baron, Etc. [*A publication*] (DLA)
**KITE**.......... Kerrville, TX [*FM radio station call letters*]
**KITES**........ Kinescope Image Test and Evaluation System (MCD)
**KITH**.......... Apple Valley, CA [*AM radio station call letters*]
**KITI**........... Centralia-Chehalis, WA [*AM radio station call letters*]
**Kit Jik Igaku** ... Kitasato Jikken Igaku [*Kitasato Archives of Experimental Medicine*] [*A publication*]
**Kit Jur**........ Kitchin on Jurisdictions of Courts-Leet, Courts-Baron, Etc. [*A publication*] (DLA)
**KITK**.......... Kit Karson Corp. [*NASDAQ symbol*] (NQ)
**KITL**.......... King International Corp. [*NASDAQ symbol*] (NQ)
**KITM**.......... Mission, TX [*FM radio station call letters*]
**KITN**.......... Minneapolis, MN [*Television station call letters*]
**KITO**.......... Vinita, OK [*FM radio station call letters*]
**KITR**.......... Creston, IA [*FM radio station call letters*]
**Kit Rd Trans** ... Kitchin's Road Transport Law [*19th ed.*] [*1978*] [*A publication*] (DLA)
**KITS**.......... Meridian Diagnostics, Inc. [*Cincinnati, OH*] [*NASDAQ symbol*] (NQ)
**KITS**.......... San Francisco, CA [*FM radio station call letters*]
**KITT**.......... Knight Industries Two Thousand [*Acronym is name of computerized car in TV series "Knight Rider"*]
**KITT**.......... Shreveport, LA [*FM radio station call letters*]
**Kitto**.......... Kitto's Journal of Sacred Literature [*A publication*]
**KITU**.......... Beaumont, TX [*Television station call letters*]
**KITV**.......... Honolulu, HI [*Television station call letters*]
**KITX**.......... Hugo, OK [*FM radio station call letters*]
**KITY**.......... San Antonio, TX [*FM radio station call letters*]
**KITZ**.......... Silverdale, WA [*AM radio station call letters*]
**KIU**........... Kallikrein Inactivator Unit [*Analytical biochemistry*]
**KIUL**.......... Garden City, KS [*AM radio station call letters*]
**KIUN**......... Pecos, TX [*AM radio station call letters*]
**KIUP**.......... Durango, CO [*AM radio station call letters*]
**KIV**........... Kali Venture Corp. [*Vancouver Stock Exchange symbol*]

**KIV** ............ Keep in View
**KIV** ............ Ketoisovalerate [*Biochemistry*]
**KIV** ............ Kiev [*USSR*] [*Geomagnetic observatory code*]
**KIV** ............ Kishinev [*USSR*] [*Airport symbol*] (OAG)
**KIVA-FM** ... Santa Fe, NM [*FM radio station call letters*]
**KIVI** .......... Nampa, ID [*Television station call letters*]
**KIVR** .......... Cave Junction, OR [*AM radio station call letters*]
**KIVS** .......... Goldendale, WA [*FM radio station call letters*]
**KIVV-TV** ... Lead, SD [*Television station call letters*]
**KIVY** .......... Crockett, TX [*AM radio station call letters*]
**KIVY-FM** ... Crockett, TX [*FM radio station call letters*]
**KIW** ........... Kitwe [*Zambia*] [*Airport symbol*] (OAG)
**KiW** ............ Ksiazka i Wiedza [*A publication*]
**KIWA** ......... Keuringsinstituut voor Waterleidingartikelen
**KIWA** ......... Sheldon, IA [*AM radio station call letters*]
**KIWA-FM** ... Sheldon, IA [*FM radio station call letters*]
**KIWI** .......... Bakersfield, CA [*FM radio station call letters*]
**KIWR** ......... Council Bluffs, IA [*FM radio station call letters*]
**KIWW** ....... Harlingen, TX [*FM radio station call letters*]
**KIX** ............ Kerkhoff Industries, Inc. [*AMEX symbol*] [*Toronto Stock Exchange symbol*] (SPSG)
**KIXA** .......... Pittsburg, CA [*AM radio station call letters*]
**KIXC** .......... Quanah, TX [*AM radio station call letters*]
**KIXC-FM** .. Quanah, TX [*FM radio station call letters*]
**KIXE-TV** ... Redding, CA [*Television station call letters*]
**KIXF** .......... Kodak Industrial X-Ray Film
**KIXI** ........... Mercer Island-Seattle, WA [*AM radio station call letters*]
**KIXK** .......... El Dorado, AR [*FM radio station call letters*]
**KIXL** .......... Del Valle, TX [*AM radio station call letters*]
**KIXQ** ......... Webb City, MO [*FM radio station call letters*]
**KIXR** .......... Ponca City, OK [*FM radio station call letters*]
**KIXS** .......... Harker Heights, TX [*FM radio station call letters*]
**KIXT** .......... Hot Springs, AR [*AM radio station call letters*]
**KIXV** .......... Brady, TX [*FM radio station call letters*]
**KIXX** .......... Watertown, SD [*FM radio station call letters*]
**KIXY-FM** .. San Angelo, TX [*FM radio station call letters*]
**KIXZ** .......... Amarillo, TX [*AM radio station call letters*]
**KIY** ............ Kilwa [*Tanzania*] [*Airport symbol*] (OAG)
**KIY** ............ Kiyosumi [*Japan*] [*Seismograph station code, US Geological Survey*] [*Closed*] (SEIS)
**Kiyo J Fac Sci Hokkaido Univ Ser VI Zool** ... Kiyo. Journal of the Faculty of Science. Hokkaido University. Series VI. Zoology [*A publication*]
**KIYS** .......... Boise, ID [*FM radio station call letters*]
**KIYU** .......... Galena, AK [*AM radio station call letters*]
**KIZN** .......... Boise, ID [*AM radio station call letters*]
**KIZN-FM** ... New Plymouth, ID [*FM radio station call letters*]
**KIZRA** ....... Kinzoku Zairyo [*A publication*]
**KIZV** .......... Kieler Zeitschriftenverzeichnis [*A publication*]
**KIZZ** .......... Minot, ND [*FM radio station call letters*]
**KJ** .............. Crescent Air Transport Ltd. [*Pakistan*] [*ICAO designator*] [*Obsolete*] (FAAC)
**KJ** .............. Iscargo Ltd. [*Iceland*] [*ICAO designator*] (FAAC)
**KJ** .............. Jamaica [*IYRU nationality code*] (IYR)
**K & J** .......... Kay and Johnson's English Vice-Chancellors' Reports [*69, 70 English Reprint*] [*A publication*] (DLA)
**kJ** .............. Kilojoule
**KJ** .............. Kipling Journal [*A publication*]
**KJ** .............. Kirchenmusikalisches Jahrbuch [*A publication*]
**KJ** .............. Knee Jerk [*Medicine*]
**KJ** .............. Knight of St. Joachim
**KJ** .............. Knights of Jurisprudence
**KJ** .............. Knjizevnost i Jezik [*A publication*]
**KJ** .............. Koloniales Jahrbuch [*A publication*]
**KJ** .............. Korea Journal [*A publication*]
**KJAB-FM** ... Mexico, MO [*FM radio station call letters*]
**KJAC-TV** .. Port Arthur, TX [*Television station call letters*]
**KJAE** ......... Leesville, LA [*FM radio station call letters*]
**KJAK** ......... Slaton, TX [*FM radio station call letters*]
**KJAM** ........ Madison, SD [*AM radio station call letters*]
**KJAM-FM** ... Madison, SD [*FM radio station call letters*]
**KJAN** ......... Atlantic, IA [*AM radio station call letters*]
**KJAN** ......... Jackson/Allen C. Thompson Field [*Mississippi*] [*ICAO location identifier*] (ICLI)
**KJAS** ......... Jasper, TX [*FM radio station call letters*]
**KJAT** ......... Dulce, NM [*FM radio station call letters*]
**KJAV** ......... Alamo, TX [*FM radio station call letters*]
**KJAX** ......... Jacksonville/International [*Florida*] [*ICAO location identifier*] (ICLI)
**KJAX** ......... Stockton, CA [*AM radio station call letters*]
**KJAY** ......... Sacramento, CA [*AM radio station call letters*]
**KJAZ** ......... Alameda, CA [*FM radio station call letters*]
**K Jb** ........... Kirchenmusikalisches Jahrbuch [*A publication*]
**K Jb** ........... Koelner Jahrbuch fuer Vor- und Fruehgeschichte [*A publication*]
**KJBC** ......... Midland, TX [*AM radio station call letters*]
**KJBR** ......... Jonesboro, AR [*FM radio station call letters*]
**KJBS** ......... Julesburg, CO [*FM radio station call letters*]
**KJBX** ......... Lubbock, TX [*AM radio station call letters*]
**KJBZ** ......... Laredo, TX [*FM radio station call letters*]
**KJC** ........... Jefferson Community College, Louisville, KY [*OCLC symbol*] (OCLC)
**KJC** ........... Keystone Junior College [*Pennsylvania*]
**KJCB** ......... Lafayette, LA [*AM radio station call letters*]
**KJCF** ......... Festus, MO [*AM radio station call letters*]
**KJCK** ......... Junction City, KS [*AM radio station call letters*]
**KJCK-FM** ... Junction City, KS [*FM radio station call letters*]
**KJCO** ......... Yuma, CO [*FM radio station call letters*]
**KJCPL** ....... Koninklijke Java-China-Paketvaart Lijnen
**KJCR** ......... Keene, TX [*FM radio station call letters*]
**KJCS** ......... Nacogdoches, TX [*FM radio station call letters*]
**KJCT** ......... Grand Junction, CO [*Television station call letters*]
**KJDE** ......... Sandpoint, ID [*FM radio station call letters*]
**KJDJ** ......... San Luis Obispo, CA [*AM radio station call letters*]
**KJDY** ......... John Day, OR [*AM radio station call letters*]
**KJEF** ......... Jennings, LA [*AM radio station call letters*]
**KJEF-FM** ... Jennings, LA [*FM radio station call letters*]
**KJEL** ......... Lebanon, MO [*AM radio station call letters*]
**KJEM** ........ Bentonville, AR [*AM radio station call letters*]
**KJEM-FM** ... Seligman, MO [*FM radio station call letters*]
**KJEO** ......... Fresno, CA [*Television station call letters*]
**KJET** ......... Kingsburg, CA [*FM radio station call letters*]
**KJEZ** ......... Poplar Bluff, MO [*FM radio station call letters*]
**KJF** ........... Kajaani [*Finland*] [*Seismograph station code, US Geological Survey*] (SEIS)
**KJF** ........... Karl-Jaspers Foundation (EA)
**KJF** ........... Kutta-Joukowski Force
**KJFA** ......... Grass Valley, CA [*FM radio station call letters*]
**KJFK** ......... New York/John F. Kennedy International [*New York*] [*ICAO location identifier*] (ICLI)
**KJFK** ......... Perry, OK [*FM radio station call letters*]
**KJFM** ........ Louisiana, MO [*FM radio station call letters*]
**KJFP** ......... Yakutat, AK [*FM radio station call letters*]
**KJG** ........... Kunstwissenschaftliches Jahrbuch. Gorresgesellschaft [*A publication*]
**KJGEDG** ... Korean Journal of Genetics [*A publication*]
**KJHA** ......... Houston, AK [*FM radio station call letters*]
**KJHK** ......... Lawrence, KS [*FM radio station call letters*]
**KJHKD5** ... Bulletin. Fruit Tree Research Station. Series D [*Kuchinotsu*] [*A publication*]
**KJHY** ......... Emmett, ID [*FM radio station call letters*]
**KJI** ............ Kay Jewelers, Incorporated [*NYSE symbol*] (SPSG)
**KJIA** .......... Sioux Falls, SD [*AM radio station call letters*]
**KJIB** .......... South Padre Island, TX [*FM radio station call letters*]
**KJIC** .......... Pasadena, TX [*FM radio station call letters*]
**KJIL** .......... Bethany, OK [*FM radio station call letters*]
**KJIM** ......... Englewood, CO [*AM radio station call letters*]
**KJIN** .......... Houma, LA [*AM radio station call letters*]
**KJIW** ......... West Helena, AR [*AM radio station call letters*]
**KJIW-FM** ... West Helena, AR [*FM radio station call letters*]
**KJJ** ............ Kuhner, J. J., Cleveland OH [*STAC*]
**KJJB** .......... Eunice, LA [*FM radio station call letters*]
**KJJC** .......... Osceola, IA [*FM radio station call letters*]
**KJJG** .......... Spencer, IA [*FM radio station call letters*]
**KJJI** ........... Shamrock, TX [*FM radio station call letters*]
**KJJJ** ........... Clifton, AZ [*FM radio station call letters*]
**KJJK** .......... Fergus Falls, MN [*AM radio station call letters*]
**KJJK-FM** ... Fergus Falls, MN [*FM radio station call letters*]
**KJJO** .......... St. Louis Park, MN [*AM radio station call letters*]
**KJJQ** .......... Volga, SD [*AM radio station call letters*]
**KJJR** .......... Whitefish, MT [*AM radio station call letters*]
**KJJY** .......... Des Moines, IA [*AM radio station call letters*]
**KJJY-FM** ... Ankeny, IA [*FM radio station call letters*]
**KJJZ** .......... Kodiak, AK [*FM radio station call letters*]
**KjK** ............ Keel ja Kirjandus [*A publication*]
**KJKC** ......... Portland, TX [*FM radio station call letters*]
**KJKJ** .......... Grand Forks, ND [*FM radio station call letters*]
**KJKS** ......... Cameron, TX [*FM radio station call letters*]
**KJL** ............ Kenneth J. Lane [*Jewelry designer*]
**KJLA** ......... Kansas City, MO [*AM radio station call letters*]
**KJLF** .......... Butte, MT [*FM radio station call letters*]
**KJLF-TV** ... El Paso, TX [*Television station call letters*]
**KJLH** ......... Compton, CA [*FM radio station call letters*]
**KJLO** ......... Monroe, LA [*AM radio station call letters*]
**KJLO-FM** ... Monroe, LA [*FM radio station call letters*]
**KJLR** ......... Olney, TX [*FM radio station call letters*]
**KJLS** ......... Hays, KS [*FM radio station call letters*]
**KJLT** ......... North Platte, NE [*AM radio station call letters*]
**KJLY** ......... Blue Earth, MN [*FM radio station call letters*]
**KJMB** ........ Blythe, CA [*AM radio station call letters*]
**KJMB-FM** ... Blythe, CA [*FM radio station call letters*]
**KJMD** ........ Laneville, TX [*AM radio station call letters*]
**KJMDA** ..... Kobe Journal of Medical Sciences [*A publication*]
**KJME** ........ Denver, CO [*AM radio station call letters*]
**KJMH** ........ Burlington, IA [*Television station call letters*]
**KJMM** ....... Tucson, AZ [*AM radio station call letters*]
**KJMO** ........ Jefferson City, MO [*FM radio station call letters*]
**KJMZ** ........ Dallas, TX [*FM radio station call letters*]
**KJN** ........... Kajaani [*Finland*] [*Closed*] [*Seismograph station code, US Geological Survey*] [*Closed*] (SEIS)
**KJNA** ......... Jena, LA [*AM radio station call letters*]

**KJNA-FM** ... Jena, LA [*FM radio station call letters*]
**KJNE** ........ Hillsboro, TX [*FM radio station call letters*]
**KJNNA** ..... Koku Igaku Jikkentai Hokoku [*A publication*]
**KJNO** ........ Juneau, AK [*AM radio station call letters*]
**KJNP** ........ North Pole, AK [*AM radio station call letters*]
**KJNP-FM** ... North Pole, AK [*FM radio station call letters*]
**KJNP-TV** .. North Pole, AK [*Television station call letters*]
**KJNT** ........ Hempsted [*New York*] [*ICAO location identifier*] (ICLI)
**KJO** .......... Kommunistische Jugend Oesterreich [*Communist Youth of Austria*]
**KJOI** ......... Los Angeles, CA [*FM radio station call letters*]
**KJOJ** ......... Conroe, TX [*FM radio station call letters*]
**KJOK** ........ Yuma, AZ [*FM radio station call letters*]
**KJOL** ........ Grand Junction, CO [*FM radio station call letters*]
**KJOP** ........ Lemoore, CA [*AM radio station call letters*]
**KJOR** ........ Sun Valley, NV [*AM radio station call letters*]
**KJOT** ........ Boise, ID [*FM radio station call letters*]
**KJOY** ........ Stockton, CA [*AM radio station call letters*]
**KJPW** ........ Waynesville, MO [*AM radio station call letters*]
**KJPW-FM** ... Waynesville, MO [*FM radio station call letters*]
**KJQN** ........ Ogden, UT [*AM radio station call letters*]
**KJQN-FM** ... Ogden, UT [*FM radio station call letters*]
**KJQY** ........ San Diego, CA [*FM radio station call letters*]
**KJR** .......... Seattle, WA [*AM radio station call letters*]
**KJRB** ........ Spokane, WA [*AM radio station call letters*]
**KJRC** ........ South Lake Tahoe, CA [*AM radio station call letters*]
**KJRG** ........ Newton, KS [*AM radio station call letters*]
**KJRH** ........ Tulsa, OK [*Television station call letters*]
**KJRR** ........ Jamestown, ND [*Television station call letters*]
**KJS** .......... Kansas Journal of Sociology
**KJS** .......... Karl-Jaspers Stiftung [*Karl-Jaspers Foundation - KJF*] (EA)
**KJS** .......... Knjizevnost i Jezik u Skoli [*A publication*]
**KJS** .......... Kodak Job Sheet
**KJS** .......... V-Groove on One Side [*Lumber*]
**KJSA** ........ Mineral Wells, TX [*AM radio station call letters*]
**KJSAA** ...... Kumamoto Journal of Science. Series A. Mathematics, Physics, and Chemistry [*A publication*]
**KJSBA** ...... Kumamoto Journal of Science. Series B. Section 2. Biology [*A publication*]
**KJSK** ........ Columbus, NE [*AM radio station call letters*]
**KJSM** ........ Sequim, WA [*AM radio station call letters*]
**KJSN** ........ Modesto, CA [*FM radio station call letters*]
**KJStJ** ....... Knight of Justice, Order of St. John of Jerusalem
**KJTH** ........ Hiawatha, KS [*FM radio station call letters*]
**KJTL** ........ Wichita Falls, TX [*Television station call letters*]
**KJTT** ........ Oak Harbor, WA [*AM radio station call letters*]
**KJTV** ........ Lubbock, TX [*Television station call letters*]
**KJTY** ........ Topeka, KS [*FM radio station call letters*]
**KJU** .......... Kamiraba [*Papua New Guinea*] [*Airport symbol*] [*Obsolete*] (OAG)
**KJUD** ........ Juneau, AK [*Television station call letters*]
**KJUG** ........ Tulare, CA [*AM radio station call letters*]
**KJUG-FM** ... Tulare, CA [*FM radio station call letters*]
**KJUL** ........ North Las Vegas, NV [*FM radio station call letters*]
**KJUN** ........ Puyallup, WA [*AM radio station call letters*]
**KJUS** ........ Beaumont, TX [*AM radio station call letters*]
**KJV** .......... King James Version [*or Authorized Version of the Bible, 1611*]
**KJVC** ........ Mansfield, LA [*FM radio station call letters*]
**KJVD** ........ Kommunistischer Jugendverband Deutschlands [*Communist Youth Club of Germany*]
**KJVH** ........ Longview, WA [*FM radio station call letters*]
**KJVI** ......... Jackson, WY [*Television station call letters*]
**KJVS** ........ Baker, OR [*FM radio station call letters*]
**KJVSA** ...... Kerala Journal of Veterinary Science [*A publication*]
**KJWH** ........ Camden, AR [*AM radio station call letters*]
**KJWL** ........ Georgetown, TX [*FM radio station call letters*]
**KJYE** ........ Grand Junction, CO [*AM radio station call letters*]
**KJYE-FM** ... Grand Junction, CO [*FM radio station call letters*]
**KJYK** ........ Tucson, AZ [*AM radio station call letters*]
**KJYO** ........ Oklahoma City, OK [*FM radio station call letters*]
**KJZY** ........ Denton, TX [*FM radio station call letters*]
**KJZZ** ........ Phoenix, AZ [*FM radio station call letters*]
**KK** ............ Arab International Aviation Co. [*Egypt*] [*ICAO designator*] (FAAC)
**KK** ............ Die Welt der Bibel. Kleinkommentare zur Heiligen Schrift [*Duesseldorf*] [*A publication*] (BJA)
**KK** ............ Kabushiki Kaishi [*Joint stock company*] [*Japan*]
**KK** ............ Kahal Kadosh. Holy Congregation (BJA)
**KK** ............ Kaiser Koenigliche
**KK** ............ Kaluza-Klein [*Theories*] [*Physics*]
**KK** ............ Kenya [*IYRU nationality code*] (IYR)
**KK** ............ Keren Kayemeth (BJA)
**kK** ............ Kilokayser
**KK** ............ Kings
**KK** ............ Kingston Korner (EA)
**KK** ............ Kirke og Kultur [*A publication*]
**K-K** ........... Kirov-Kiev [*USSR*]
**KK** ............ Kleinkaliber [*Small Caliber*] [*German military*]
**KK** ............ Knee Kick [*Neurology*]
**KK** ............ Kokugo To Kokubungaku [*Japanese Language and Literature*] [*A publication*]
**KK** ............ Komisja Koordynacyjna. Zydowskie Instytucje Opiekuncze (BJA)
**KK** ............ Kosher Kitchen (BJA)
**KK** ............ Kremlin Kommandant
**KK** ............ Kulutusosuuskuntien Keskusliitto [*Co-Operative Union*] [*Finland*] (EY)
**K & K** ........ Kunst und Kuenstler [*A publication*]
**KK** ............ Kurzgefasster Kommentar zu den Heiligen Schriften Alten und Neuen Testaments [*Munich*] [*A publication*] (BJA)
**KK** ............ Kwartalnik Klasyczny [*A publication*]
**KK** ............ Welt der Bibel. Kleinkommentare zur Heiligen Schrift [*A publication*]
**KKA** .......... Benedictine College, Atchison, KS [*OCLC symbol*] (OCLC)
**KKA** .......... Kamer van Koophandel en Fabrieken te Paramaribo. Bulletin [*A publication*]
**KKA** .......... Kitchen Klutzs of America [*Inactive*] (EA)
**KKA** .......... Knights of King Arthur (EA)
**KKA** .......... Koyukuk [*Alaska*] [*Airport symbol*] (OAG)
**KKAA** ........ Aberdeen, SD [*AM radio station call letters*]
**KKAJ** ........ Ardmore, OK [*FM radio station call letters*]
**KKAK** ........ Porterville, CA [*Television station call letters*]
**KKAL** ........ Arroyo Grande, CA [*AM radio station call letters*]
**KKAM** ....... Fresno, CA [*AM radio station call letters*]
**KKAN** ........ Phillipsburg, KS [*AM radio station call letters*]
**KKAP** ........ Floydada, TX [*AM radio station call letters*]
**KKAP-FM** ... Floydada, TX [*FM radio station call letters*]
**KKAQ** ........ Thief River Falls, MN [*AM radio station call letters*]
**KKAR** ........ Bellevue, NE [*AM radio station call letters*]
**KKAS** ........ Silsbee, TX [*AM radio station call letters*]
**KKAT** ........ Ogden, UT [*FM radio station call letters*]
**KKATD** ..... Klima-Kaelte-Technik [*A publication*]
**KKAY** ........ White Castle, LA [*AM radio station call letters*]
**KKAY-FM** ... Donaldsonville, LA [*FM radio station call letters*]
**KKAZ** ........ Cheyenne, WY [*FM radio station call letters*]
**KKB** .......... Baker University, Baldwin City, KS [*OCLC symbol*] (OCLC)
**KKB** .......... Kitoi [*Alaska*] [*Airport symbol*] (OAG)
**KKBB** ........ Shafter, CA [*FM radio station call letters*]
**KKBC-FM** ... Baker, OR [*FM radio station call letters*]
**KKBG** ........ Hilo, HI [*FM radio station call letters*]
**KKBI** ......... Broken Bow, OK [*FM radio station call letters*]
**KKBJ** ........ Bemidji, MN [*AM radio station call letters*]
**KKBJ-FM** ... Bemidji, MN [*FM radio station call letters*]
**KKBL** ........ Monett, MO [*FM radio station call letters*]
**KKBN** ........ Twain Harte, CA [*FM radio station call letters*]
**KKBQ** ........ Houston, TX [*AM radio station call letters*]
**KKBQ-FM** ... Pasadena, TX [*FM radio station call letters*]
**KKBR** ........ Los Alamos, NM [*FM radio station call letters*]
**KKBS** ........ Guymon, OK [*FM radio station call letters*]
**KKBT** ........ Los Angeles, CA [*FM radio station call letters*]
**KKBZ** ........ White Rock, NM [*FM radio station call letters*]
**KKc** .......... Kansas City Public Library, Kansas City, KS [*Library symbol*] [*Library of Congress*] (LCLS)
**KKC** .......... Kansas City Public Library, Kansas City, KS [*OCLC symbol*] (OCLC)
**KKC** .......... Khon Kaen [*Thailand*] [*Airport symbol*] (OAG)
**KKC** .......... Knox College Library, University of Toronto [*UTLAS symbol*]
**KKCA** ........ Fulton, MO [*FM radio station call letters*]
**KKcB** ......... Central Baptist Theological Seminary, Kansas City, KS [*Library symbol*] [*Library of Congress*] (LCLS)
**KKCB** ........ San Luis Obispo, CA [*AM radio station call letters*]
**KKcBM** ...... Bethany Medical Center, Kansas City, KS [*Library symbol*] [*Library of Congress*] (LCLS)
**KKCC-FM** ... Clinton, OK [*FM radio station call letters*]
**KKCI** ......... Goodland, KS [*FM radio station call letters*]
**KKcJS** ....... Jensen-Salsbery Laboratories, Kansas City, KS [*Library symbol*] [*Library of Congress*] (LCLS)
**KKCK** ........ Marshall, MN [*FM radio station call letters*]
**KKCL** ........ Lorenzo, TX [*FM radio station call letters*]
**KKCM** ....... Shakopee, MN [*AM radio station call letters*]
**KKcP** ......... Providence - Saint Margaret Health Center, Kansas City, KS [*Library symbol*] [*Library of Congress*] (LCLS)
**KKCQ** ........ Fosston, MN [*AM radio station call letters*]
**KKCS-FM** ... Colorado Springs, CO [*FM radio station call letters*]
**KKCW** ....... Beaverton, OR [*FM radio station call letters*]
**KKCY** ........ Portland, OR [*FM radio station call letters*]
**KKD** .......... Kokoda [*Papua New Guinea*] [*Airport symbol*] (OAG)
**KKD** .......... Korintji-Kaba-Dempo [*Sumatra*] [*Seismograph station code, US Geological Survey*] [*Closed*] (SEIS)
**KKDA** ........ Grand Prairie, TX [*AM radio station call letters*]
**KKDA-FM** ... Dallas, TX [*FM radio station call letters*]
**KKDD** ........ Brush, CO [*FM radio station call letters*]
**KKDD** ........ Katalog Kandidatskikh i Doktorskikh Dissertatsii [*A bibliographic publication*]
**K K-D-H** .... Knight Kadosch [*Freemasonry*]
**KKDJ** ........ Fresno, CA [*FM radio station call letters*]
**KKDKA** ..... Bulletin. Kyushu Institute of Technology [*A publication*]
**KKDL** ........ Detroit Lakes, MN [*FM radio station call letters*]
**KKDQ** ........ Fosston, MN [*FM radio station call letters*]
**KKDV** ........ Fields Landing, CA [*AM radio station call letters*]
**KKDY** ........ West Plains, MO [*FM radio station call letters*]
**KKE** .......... Kerikeri [*New Zealand*] [*Airport symbol*] (OAG)

**KKE** ........... Kleena Kleene Gold Mines [*Vancouver Stock Exchange symbol*]
**KKE** ........... Kommunistiko Komma Ellados [*Communist Party of Greece*] [*Political party*] (PPW)
**KKED-FM** ... Corpus Christi, TX [*FM radio station call letters*]
**KKEE**......... Long Beach, WA [*FM radio station call letters*]
**KKEes**........ Kommunistiko Komma Ellados - Esoterikou [*Communist Party of Greece - Interior*] [*Political party*] (PPE)
**KKEex** ....... Kommunistiko Komma Ellados - Exoterikou [*Communist Party of Greece - Exterior*] [*Political party*] (PPE)
**KKEG** ........ Fayetteville, AR [*FM radio station call letters*]
**KKEHA**..... Kobayashi Rigaku Kenkyusho Hokoku [*A publication*]
**KKEI**.......... Imperial, NE [*FM radio station call letters*]
**KKEL**.......... Hobbs, NM [*AM radio station call letters*]
**KKES**......... Kommunistiko Komma Ellados - Esoterikou [*Communist Party of Greece - Interior*] [*Political party*] (PPW)
**KKEY**......... Portland, OR [*AM radio station call letters*]
**KKEZ**......... Fort Dodge, IA [*FM radio station call letters*]
**KKF**........... Kleiner Kirchenfuehrer [*A publication*]
**KKFC**......... KISS [*Knights in the Service of Satan*] Konnection Fan Club (EA)
**KKFI**.......... Kansas City, MO [*FM radio station call letters*]
**KKFM**........ Colorado Springs, CO [*FM radio station call letters*]
**KKFN** ........ Sioux Falls, SD [*AM radio station call letters*]
**KKFO** ........ Coalinga, CA [*AM radio station call letters*]
**KKFR**......... Glendale, AZ [*FM radio station call letters*]
**KKFT**......... Fort Scott, KS [*Television station call letters*]
**KKFX**......... Seattle, WA [*AM radio station call letters*]
**KKG**........... Kappa Kappa Gamma [*Sorority*]
**KKG**........... Konawaruk [*Guyana*] [*Airport symbol*] [*Obsolete*] (OAG)
**KKG**........... Kootenay King Resources [*Vancouver Stock Exchange symbol*]
**KKGD**......... Rifle, CO [*AM radio station call letters*]
**K-K Geog Ges Wien Mitt** ... Kaiserlich-Koenigliche Geographische Gesellschaft in Wien. Mitteilungen [*A publication*]
**KKGG**........ Waimea, HI [*FM radio station call letters*]
**KKGL**......... Pinetop, AZ [*FM radio station call letters*]
**KKGO**........ Hesperia, CA [*AM radio station call letters*]
**KKGO-FM** ... Los Angeles, CA [*FM radio station call letters*]
**KKGR**......... Gresham, OR [*AM radio station call letters*]
**KKGZ**......... Brush, CO [*AM radio station call letters*]
**KKH**........... Kailua-Kona [*Hawaii*] [*Seismograph station code, US Geological Survey*] (SEIS)
**KKH**........... Karakoram Highway [*Asia*]
**KKH**........... Kongiganak [*Alaska*] [*Airport symbol*] (OAG)
**KKH**........... Kunst und Kultur der Hethiter [*A publication*]
**KKHI**.......... San Francisco, CA [*AM radio station call letters*]
**KKHI-FM** ... San Francisco, CA [*FM radio station call letters*]
**KKHJ** ......... Ennis, MT [*FM radio station call letters*]
**KKHKA**..... Kagaku Keisatsu Kenkyusho Hokoku, Hokagaku Hen [*A publication*]
**KKHL**......... Klung Kidney-Heart-Lung [*Machine*]
**KKHQ**........ Odem, TX [*FM radio station call letters*]
**KKHR**......... Anson, TX [*FM radio station call letters*]
**KKI** ............ Akiachak [*Alaska*] [*Airport symbol*] (OAG)
**KKI** ............ Karkar Island [*Papua New Guinea*] [*Seismograph station code, US Geological Survey*] (SEIS)
**KKIC**.......... Boise, ID [*AM radio station call letters*]
**KKID** .......... Sallisaw, OK [*AM radio station call letters*]
**KKID-FM** ... Sallisaw, OK [*FM radio station call letters*]
**KKIFC** ....... Kris Kristofferson International Fan Club (EA)
**KKIK**.......... Lubbock, TX [*FM radio station call letters*]
**KKIM** ......... Albuquerque, NM [*AM radio station call letters*]
**KKIN** .......... Aitkin, MN [*AM radio station call letters*]
**KKIP**.......... Lowell, AR
**KKIQ** .......... Livermore, CA [*FM radio station call letters*]
**KKIS-FM**.. Walnut Creek, CA [*FM radio station call letters*]
**KKIT**........... Taos, NM [*AM radio station call letters*]
**KKIU** .......... Keele ja Kirjanduse Instituudi Uurimused [*A publication*]
**KKIX**.......... Fayetteville, AR [*FM radio station call letters*]
**KKJ**............ Kita Kyushu [*Japan*] [*Airport symbol*] [*Obsolete*] (OAG)
**KKJHD** ..... Koseisho Gan Kenkyu Joseikin Ni Yoru Kenkyu Hokoku [*A publication*]
**KKJI** .......... Gallup, NM [*FM radio station call letters*]
**KKJO**......... St. Joseph, MO [*FM radio station call letters*]
**KKJQ**......... Garden City, KS [*FM radio station call letters*]
**KKJR**......... Hutchison, MN [*FM radio station call letters*]
**KKJY-FM** ... Albuquerque, NM [*FM radio station call letters*]
**KKJZ**.......... Soledad, CA [*AM radio station call letters*]
**KKK**........... Invisible Empire Knights of the Ku Klux Klan (EA)
**KKK**........... Kissel Kar Klub (EA)
**KKK**........... Kokugo Kokubun No Kenkyu [*Studies in Japanese Language and Literature*] [*A publication*]
**KKKDB**...... Kyushu Ketsueki Kenkyu Dokokaishi [*A publication*]
**KKKEA6**.... Tuberculosis Research [*A publication*]
**KKKK** ........ Odessa, TX [*FM radio station call letters*]
**KKL** ........... Kam-Kotia Mines Ltd. [*Toronto Stock Exchange symbol*]
**KKL** ........... Karluk Lake, AK [*Location identifier*] [*FAA*] (FAAL)
**KKL** ........... Keren Kayemeth Leisrael (BJA)
**KKL** ........... Kwartalnik Klasyczny [*A publication*]
**KKLA**.......... Los Angeles, CA [*FM radio station call letters*]
**KKLC**......... Pineville, LA [*AM radio station call letters*]
**KKLD** ........ Tucson, AZ [*FM radio station call letters*]
**KKLI**.......... Widefield, CO [*FM radio station call letters*]
**KKLL**......... Webb City, MO [*AM radio station call letters*]
**KKLO** ........ Leavenworth, KS [*AM radio station call letters*]
**KKLQ** ........ San Diego, CA [*AM radio station call letters*]
**KKLQ-FM** ... San Diego, CA [*FM radio station call letters*]
**KKLR**......... Poplar Bluff, MO [*FM radio station call letters*]
**KKLS**.......... Rapid City, SD [*AM radio station call letters*]
**KKLS-FM** ... Sioux Falls, SD [*FM radio station call letters*]
**KKLT**......... Phoenix, AZ [*FM radio station call letters*]
**KKLU** ........ Colusa, CA [*FM radio station call letters*]
**KKLV**......... Anchorage, AK [*FM radio station call letters*]
**KKLY**......... Delta, CO [*FM radio station call letters*]
**KKLZ**......... Las Vegas, NV [*FM radio station call letters*]
**KKM**.......... Kota Kinabalu [*Malaysia*] [*Seismograph station code, US Geological Survey*] (SEIS)
**KKM**.......... North Central Kansas Library, Manhattan, KS [*OCLC symbol*] (OCLC)
**KKMA** ....... Le Mars, IA [*FM radio station call letters*]
**KKMC** ....... Gonzales, CA [*AM radio station call letters*]
**KKMG**....... Pueblo, CO [*FM radio station call letters*]
**KKMJ**........ Austin, TX [*FM radio station call letters*]
**KKMK** ....... Rapid City, SD [*FM radio station call letters*]
**KKMO**....... Tacoma, WA [*AM radio station call letters*]
**KKMT** ....... Ennis, MT [*AM radio station call letters*]
**KKMX**....... Hayden, CO [*AM radio station call letters*]
**KKMX-FM** ... Hayden, CO [*FM radio station call letters*]
**KKMY** ....... Orange, TX [*FM radio station call letters*]
**KKN**.......... Kansas Newman College, Wichita, KS [*OCLC symbol*] (OCLC)
**KKN**.......... Kirkenes [*Norway*] [*Airport symbol*] (OAG)
**K-K Naturh Hofmus An** ... Kaiserlich-Koenigliche Naturhistorische Hofmuseum. Annalen [*A publication*]
**KKNB** ........ Crete, NE [*FM radio station call letters*]
**KKNC** ........ Sun Valley, NV [*AM radio station call letters*]
**KKND**........ Stillwater, OK [*FM radio station call letters*]
**KKNG**........ Oklahoma City, OK [*FM radio station call letters*]
**KKNK**........ Carson City, NV [*AM radio station call letters*]
**KKNO**........ Gretna, LA [*AM radio station call letters*]
**KKNX**........ Huntsville, TX [*AM radio station call letters*]
**KKO**........... Kaikohe [*New Zealand*] [*Airport symbol*] [*Obsolete*] (OAG)
**KKO**........... Ottawa University, Ottawa, KS [*OCLC symbol*] (OCLC)
**KKOA**........ Kearney, NE [*AM radio station call letters*]
**KKOA**........ Kustom Kemps of America (EA)
**KKOB** ........ Albuquerque, NM [*AM radio station call letters*]
**KKOB-FM** ... Albuquerque, NM [*FM radio station call letters*]
**KKOJ**......... Jackson, MN [*AM radio station call letters*]
**KKOK-FM** ... Morris, MN [*FM radio station call letters*]
**KKOL** ........ Hampton, AR [*FM radio station call letters*]
**KKON**........ Kealakekua, HI [*AM radio station call letters*]
**KKOR**........ Gallup, NM [*FM radio station call letters*]
**KKOS** ........ Carlsbad, CA [*FM radio station call letters*]
**KKOSB**...... Kagaku Kogyo. Supplement [*A publication*]
**KKOW**........ Pittsburg, KS [*AM radio station call letters*]
**KKOY**......... Chanute, KS [*AM radio station call letters*]
**KKOY-FM** ... Chanute, KS [*FM radio station call letters*]
**KKOZ** ........ Ava, MO [*AM radio station call letters*]
**KKOZ-FM** ... Ava, MO [*FM radio station call letters*]
**KKP** ........... Kappa Kappa Psi [*Society*]
**KKP** ........... University of Kansas, Medical Library, Kansas City, KS [*OCLC symbol*] (OCLC)
**KKPL-FM** ... Opportunity, WA [*FM radio station call letters*]
**KKPR**......... Kearney, NE [*FM radio station call letters*]
**KKQ**........... Sterling College, Sterling, KS [*OCLC symbol*] (OCLC)
**KKQQ**........ Volga, SD [*FM radio station call letters*]
**KKQV** ........ Wichita Falls, TX [*FM radio station call letters*]
**KKR** ........... Emporia State University, Emporia, KS [*OCLC symbol*] (OCLC)
**KKR** ........... Kaukura [*French Polynesia*] [*Airport symbol*] (OAG)
**KKR** ........... Kohlberg Kravis Roberts & Co.
**KKR** ........... Kokanee Resources Ltd. [*Vancouver Stock Exchange symbol*]
**KKR** ........... Kurtis-Kraft Register [*Defunct*] (EA)
**KKR** ........... Kurukshetra [*India*] [*Seismograph station code, US Geological Survey*] (SEIS)
**KKRB**......... Klamath Falls, OR [*FM radio station call letters*]
**KKRC-FM** ... Sioux Falls, SD [*FM radio station call letters*]
**KKRD** ........ Wichita, KS [*FM radio station call letters*]
**KKRE**......... Monument, CO [*AM radio station call letters*]
**K Krigsvetenskapakad Handlingar Tidskr** ... Kungliga Krigsvetenskapsakademiens. Handlingar och Tidskrift [*A publication*]
**KKRK** ........ Douglas, AZ [*FM radio station call letters*]
**KKRL**......... Carroll, IA [*FM radio station call letters*]
**KKRP**......... Delhi, LA [*FM radio station call letters*]
**KKRQ** ........ Iowa City, IA [*FM radio station call letters*]
**KKRS**......... Burns, OR [*FM radio station call letters*]
**KKRT**......... Wenatchee, WA [*AM radio station call letters*]
**KKRTD**...... KFT. Kraftfahrzeugtechnik [*A publication*]
**KKRV** ........ Kernville, CA [*FM radio station call letters*]
**KKRX** ........ Lawton, OK [*AM radio station call letters*]
**KKRX-FM** ... Lawton, OK [*FM radio station call letters*]
**KKRZ**......... Portland, OR [*FM radio station call letters*]

**KKS**........... Kansas State University, Farrell Library, Manhattan, KS [*OCLC symbol*] (OCLC)
**KKSA**......... Folsom, CA [*AM radio station call letters*]
**KKSA**......... Keith Keating Society for the Arts [*Inactive*] (EA)
**KKSD**......... Anchorage, AK [*AM radio station call letters*]
**KKSF**......... San Francisco, CA [*FM radio station call letters*]
**KKSKA**...... Kanagawa-Ken Kogyo Shikenjo Kenkyu Hokoku [*A publication*]
**KKSN**........ Vancouver, WA [*AM radio station call letters*]
**KKSN-FM** ... Portland, OR [*FM radio station call letters*]
**KKSR**......... Sartell, MN [*FM radio station call letters*]
**KKSS**......... Santa Fe, NM [*FM radio station call letters*]
**KKSU**........ Manhattan, KS [*AM radio station call letters*]
**KKSY**......... Bald Knob, AR [*FM radio station call letters*]
**KKT**........... King's Knight [*Chess*]
**KKTC**......... Brownfield, TX [*FM radio station call letters*]
**KKTM**........ Flagstaff, AZ [*Television station call letters*]
**KKTO**........ Santa Fe, NM [*Television station call letters*]
**KKTT**......... Bernallillo, NM [*AM radio station call letters*]
**KKTU**........ Cheyenne, WY [*Television station call letters*]
**KKTV**......... Colorado Springs, CO [*Television station call letters*]
**KKTX**......... Kilgore, TX [*AM radio station call letters*]
**KKTX-FM** ... Kilgore, TX [*FM radio station call letters*]
**KKTZ**......... Mountain Home, AR [*FM radio station call letters*]
**KKU**........... Ekuk [*Alaska*] [*Airport symbol*] (OAG)
**KKU**........... Keanakolu [*Hawaii*] [*Seismograph station code, US Geological Survey*] (SEIS)
**KKU**........... University of Kansas, Lawrence, KS [*OCLC symbol*] (OCLC)
**KKUA**........ Wailuku, HI [*FM radio station call letters*]
**KKUB**........ Brownfield, TX [*AM radio station call letters*]
**KKUC**........ La Grande, OR [*FM radio station call letters*]
**KKUL**........ Hardin, MT [*AM radio station call letters*]
**KKUL**........ King Kullen Grocery Co., Inc. [*NASDAQ symbol*] (NQ)
**KKUL-FM** ... Hardin, MT [*FM radio station call letters*]
**KKUP**........ Cupertino, CA [*FM radio station call letters*]
**KKUR**........ Ojai, CA [*FM radio station call letters*]
**KKUS**........ San Luis Obispo, CA [*FM radio station call letters*]
**KKUZ**........ Joplin, MO [*FM radio station call letters*]
**KKV**........... Central Kansas Library System, Book Processing Center, Great Bend, KS [*OCLC symbol*] (OCLC)
**KKV**........... Kinetic-Kill Vehicle [*Military*] (SDI)
**KKVI**.......... Twin Falls, ID [*Television station call letters*]
**KKVO**........ Altus, OK [*FM radio station call letters*]
**KKVU**........ Tremonton, UT [*AM radio station call letters*]
**KKVU-FM** ... Tremonton, UT [*FM radio station call letters*]
**KKVV**........ Las Vegas, NV [*AM radio station call letters*]
**KKW**.......... Kainokawa [*Japan*] [*Seismograph station code, US Geological Survey*] (SEIS)
**KKW**.......... Kikwit [*Zaire*] [*Airport symbol*] (OAG)
**KKW**.......... Washburn University of Topeka, Topeka, KS [*OCLC symbol*] (OCLC)
**KKWC**....... Watford, ND [*AM radio station call letters*]
**KKWK**....... Muskogee, OK [*FM radio station call letters*]
**KKWQ**....... Warroad, MN [*FM radio station call letters*]
**KKWS**........ Wadena, MN [*FM radio station call letters*]
**KKWY**....... Ogden, UT [*FM radio station call letters*]
**KKWZ**....... Richfield, UT [*FM radio station call letters*]
**KKX**........... Kikaiga Shima [*Japan*] [*Airport symbol*] (OAG)
**KKX**........... Southwestern College, Winfield, KS [*OCLC symbol*] (OCLC)
**KKXK**........ Montrose, CO [*FM radio station call letters*]
**KKXL**......... Grand Forks, ND [*AM radio station call letters*]
**KKXL-FM** ... Grand Forks, ND [*FM radio station call letters*]
**KKXO**........ Eugene, OR [*AM radio station call letters*]
**KKXX**........ Paradise, CA [*AM radio station call letters*]
**KKXX-FM** ... Delano, CA [*FM radio station call letters*]
**KKYA**........ Yankton, SD [*FM radio station call letters*]
**KKYHB**..... Kakuriken Kenkyu Hokoku [*A publication*]
**KKYK-FM** ... Little Rock, AR [*FM radio station call letters*]
**KKYN**........ Plainview, TX [*AM radio station call letters*]
**KKYN-FM** ... Plainview, TX [*FM radio station call letters*]
**KKYR**........ Texarkana, AR [*AM radio station call letters*]
**KKYR-FM** ... Texarkana, TX [*FM radio station call letters*]
**KKYS**......... Bryan, TX [*FM radio station call letters*]
**KKYX**........ San Antonio, TX [*AM radio station call letters*]
**KKYY**........ San Diego, CA [*FM radio station call letters*]
**KKZIS**....... Komisja Koordynacyjna Zydowskich Instytucji Spolecznych (BJA)
**KKZN**........ Kanab, UT [*AM radio station call letters*]
**KKZR**........ Houston, TX [*AM radio station call letters*]
**KKZX**......... Spokane, WA [*FM radio station call letters*]
**KKZZ**......... Lancaster, CA [*FM radio station call letters*]
**KL**............. Kaliszer Leben (BJA)
**KL**............. Kansalaisvallen Liitto [*League of Civil Power*] [*Finland*] [*Political party*] (PPW)
**K-L**............ Kansas State Library, Law Department, Topeka, KS [*Library symbol*] [*Library of Congress*] (LCLS)
**KL**............. Karl Lagerfeld [*Fashion designer*]
**K-L**............ Karl-Lorimar Home Video, Inc.
**KL**............. Kaufmaennische Leitung [*Business Management*] [*German*]
**KL**............. Keel (ROG)
**KL**............. Keller's Language [*1977*] [*Data processing*] (CSR)
**KL**............. Kelvin Law [*Physics*]
**KL**............. Kerley Lines [*Radiology*]
**KL**............. Key Length [*Data processing*] (BUR)
**KL**............. Key Locker
**KL**............. Kidney Lobe
**kL**............. Kilolambert
**kL**............. Kiloliter
**KL**............. Klaeger [*Plaintiff*] [*German*] (ILCA)
**KL**............. Klasse [*Class*] [*German*]
**KL**............. Klebs-Loeffler [*Bacteriology*]
**KL**............. Kleinmann-Low [*Astronomy*]
**KL**............. Klemm Flugzeugbau GmbH & Apparatebau Nabern [*Federal Republic of Germany*] [*ICAO aircraft manufacturer identifier*] (ICAO)
**Kl**............. Klio. Beitraege zur Alten Geschichte [*A publication*]
**KL**............. KLM [*Koninklijke Luchtvaart Maatschappij*] Royal Dutch Airlines [*ICAO designator*] (OAG)
**KL**............. Knight of Leopold [*Austria, Belgium*] (ROG)
**KL**............. Knight of [*the Order of*] Leopold of Austria
**K of L**......... Knights of Labor
**KL**............. Knights of Lithuania
**K of L**......... Knights of Lithuania (EA)
**KL**............. Konzentrationslager [*Concentration Camp*] [*German*] (BJA)
**KL**............. Kuala Lumpur [*Malaysia*]
**KL**............. Kullback-Leibler [*Mathematics*]
**KL**............. Kultur in Literatur [*A publication*]
**KL**............. Kunst und Literatur [*A publication*]
**Kl**............. Kunstliteratur [*A publication*]
**KL**............. Kypriakos Logos [*A publication*]
**KLA**........... Ka-Ahari Resources [*Vancouver Stock Exchange symbol*]
**KLA**........... Klystron Amplifier
**KLA**........... Knight of [*the Order of*] Leopold of Austria
**KLAC**......... KLA Instruments Corporation [*NASDAQ symbol*] (NQ)
**KLAC**......... Los Angeles, CA [*AM radio station call letters*]
**KLAD**........ Klamath Falls, OR [*AM radio station call letters*]
**KLAD-FM** ... Klamath Falls, OR [*FM radio station call letters*]
**KLAK**......... Durant, OK [*FM radio station call letters*]
**KLAL**......... Lamoni, IA [*FM radio station call letters*]
**KLAM**........ Cordova, AK [*AM radio station call letters*]
**KLAN**........ Glasgow, MT [*FM radio station call letters*]
**KLAN**........ Lansing/Capital Region [*Michigan*] [*ICAO location identifier*] (ICLI)
**Klank**......... Klank en Weerklank [*A publication*]
**KLANSS**... Keep That Local Area Network Simple, Stupid [*Telecommunications*]
**K Lantbrhogsk Annlr** ... Kungliga Lantbrukshoegskolans. Annaler [*A publication*]
**K Lantbruksakad Tidskr** ... Kungliga Lantbruksakademiens. Tidskrift [*A publication*]
**K Lantbrukshoegsk Statens Lantbruksfoers Jordbruksfoers Medd** ... Kungliga Lantbrukshoegskolan och Statens Lantbruksfoersoek. Statens Jordbruksfoersoek Meddelande [*A publication*]
**K Lantbrukshogsk Ann** ... Kungliga Lantbrukshoegskolans. Annaler [*A publication*]
**KLAQ**........ El Paso, TX [*FM radio station call letters*]
**KLAR**........ Laredo, TX [*AM radio station call letters*]
**KLAS**......... Las Vegas/McCarran International [*Nevada*] [*ICAO location identifier*] (ICLI)
**KLaSH**....... Larned State Hospital, Larned, KS [*Library symbol*] [*Library of Congress*] (LCLS)
**Klasicni Naucn Spisi Mat Inst (Beograd)** ... Klasicni Naucn. Spisi. Matematicki Institut (Beograd) [*A publication*]
**Klass Phil Stud** ... Klassische Philologische Studien [*A publication*] (OCD)
**KLAS-TV**.. Las Vegas, NV [*Television station call letters*]
**KLAT**......... Houston, TX [*AM radio station call letters*]
**KLATA8**.... Kungliga Lantbruksakademiens. Tidskrift [*A publication*]
**KLAU**........ Capitola, CA [*AM radio station call letters*]
**KLAV**......... Las Vegas, NV [*AM radio station call letters*]
**KLaw**.......... Lawrence Free Public Library, Lawrence, KS [*Library symbol*] [*Library of Congress*] (LCLS)
**KLAW**....... Lawton, OK [*FM radio station call letters*]
**K Law Rep** ... Kentucky Law Reporter [*A publication*] (DLA)
**KLAX**......... Los Angeles/International [*California*] [*ICAO location identifier*] (ICLI)
**KLAX-TV** ... Alexandria, LA [*Television station call letters*]
**KLAY**......... Lakewood, WA [*AM radio station call letters*]
**KLAZ**......... Hot Springs, AR [*FM radio station call letters*]
**KLB**........... Kalabo [*Zambia*] [*Airport symbol*] (OAG)
**KLB**........... Kilopound (MCD)
**KLB**........... Knight of [*the Order of*] Leopold [*Belgium*]
**KLB**........... Kulturhistorische Liebhaberbibliothek [*A publication*]
**KLBA**......... Albia, IA [*AM radio station call letters*]
**KLBB**......... Lubbock/Regional [*Texas*] [*ICAO location identifier*] (ICLI)
**KLBB**......... St. Paul, MN [*AM radio station call letters*]
**KLBC**......... Durant, OK [*FM radio station call letters*]
**KLBJ**......... Austin, TX [*AM radio station call letters*]
**KLBJ-FM** ... Austin, TX [*FM radio station call letters*]
**KLBK-TV**.. Lubbock, TX [*Television station call letters*]
**KLBM**........ La Grande, OR [*AM radio station call letters*]
**KLBN**........ Albion, NE [*FM radio station call letters*]
**KLBO**........ Monahans, TX [*AM radio station call letters*]

**KLBQ** ........ El Dorado, AR [*FM radio station call letters*]
**KLBS** ........ Los Banos, CA [*AM radio station call letters*]
**KLBY** ........ Colby, KS [*Television station call letters*]
**KLC** ........... Kern County Library System, Bakersfield, CA [*OCLC symbol*] (OCLC)
**KLC** ........... Kirkland Lake [*Ontario*] [*Seismograph station code, US Geological Survey*] [*Closed*] (SEIS)
**KLCB** ........ Libby, MT [*AM radio station call letters*]
**KLCC** ........ Eugene, OR [*FM radio station call letters*]
**KLCD** ........ Decorah, IA [*FM radio station call letters*]
**KLCE** ........ Blackfoot, ID [*FM radio station call letters*]
**KLCH** ........ Lake Charles/Lake Charles [*Louisiana*] [*ICAO location identifier*] (ICLI)
**KLCI** .......... Nampa, ID [*FM radio station call letters*]
**KLCK** ........ Goldendale, WA [*AM radio station call letters*]
**KLCK** ........ Rickenbacker Air Force Base [*Ohio*] [*ICAO location identifier*] (ICLI)
**KLCL** ........ Lake Charles, LA [*AM radio station call letters*]
**KLCM** ........ Lewistown, MT [*FM radio station call letters*]
**KLCN** ........ Blytheville, AR [*AM radio station call letters*]
**KLCR** ........ Center, TX [*FM radio station call letters*]
**KLCS** ........ Los Angeles, CA [*Television station call letters*]
**KLCX** ........ Florence, OR [*FM radio station call letters*]
**KLCY** ........ East Missoula, MT [*AM radio station call letters*]
**KLCY-FM** ... Salt Lake City, UT [*FM radio station call letters*]
**KLCZ** ........ Corcoran, CA [*FM radio station call letters*]
**KLD** ........... Kelly, Douglas & Co. Ltd. [*Toronto Stock Exchange symbol*]
**KLD** ........... King's Light Dragoons [*British military*] (DMA)
**KLDD** ........ Dallas, TX [*AM radio station call letters*]
**KLDE** ........ Houston, TX [*FM radio station call letters*]
**KLDI** .......... Laramie, WY [*AM radio station call letters*]
**KLDO-TV** ... Laredo, TX [*Television station call letters*]
**KLDT** ........ Lake Dallas, TX [*Television station call letters*]
**KLDY** ........ Lacey, WA [*AM radio station call letters*]
**KLDZ** ........ Lincoln, NE [*FM radio station call letters*]
**KLE** ........... Kala Explorations [*Vancouver Stock Exchange symbol*]
**KLE** ........... Kratkaja Literaturnaja Enciklopedija [*A publication*]
**KLe** ........... Leavenworth Public Library, Leavenworth, KS [*Library symbol*] [*Library of Congress*] (LCLS)
**KLEA** ........ Lovington, NM [*AM radio station call letters*]
**KLEA-FM** ... Lovington, NM [*FM radio station call letters*]
**KLEB** ........ Golden Meadow, LA [*AM radio station call letters*]
**KleBl** ......... Klerusblatt [*Munich*] [*A publication*] (BJA)
**Klebs** ......... Klebsiella [*A genus of bacteria*]
**KLEE** ........ Ottumwa, IA [*AM radio station call letters*]
**KLEF** ........ Anchorage, AK [*FM radio station call letters*]
**KLEH** ........ Anamosa, IA [*AM radio station call letters*]
**KLEI** .......... Kailua, HI [*AM radio station call letters*]
**Klei Keram** ... Klei en Keramiek [*Netherlands*] [*A publication*]
**Kleine Ergaenzungsreihe Hochschulbuechern Math** ... Kleine Ergaenzungsreihe zu den Hochschulbuechern fuer Mathematik [*A publication*]
**Kleine Naturwiss Bibliothek** ... Kleine Naturwissenschaftliche Bibliothek [*A publication*]
**Kleinheubacher Ber** ... Kleinheubacher Berichte [*East Germany*] [*A publication*]
**Kleintier Prax** ... Kleintier-Praxis [*A publication*]
**KLEL** ........ San Jose, CA [*FM radio station call letters*]
**KLEM** ........ Le Mars, IA [*AM radio station call letters*]
**KLEN** ........ Cheyenne, WY [*FM radio station call letters*]
**KLEO** ........ Wichita, KS [*AM radio station call letters*]
**KLEP** ........ Newark, AR [*Television station call letters*]
**KLEPA** ...... Kleintier-Praxis [*A publication*]
**Klepzig Fachber** ... Klepzig Fachberichte fuer die Fuehrungskraefte aus Maschinenbau und Huettenwesen [*A publication*]
**Klepzig Fachber Fuehrungskraefte Ind Tech** ... Klepzig Fachberichte fuer die Fuehrungskraefte aus Industrie und Technik [*A publication*]
**KLER** ........ Orofino, ID [*AM radio station call letters*]
**KLER-FM** ... Orofino, ID [*FM radio station call letters*]
**KLeS** .......... Saint Mary College, Leavenworth, KS [*Library symbol*] [*Library of Congress*] (LCLS)
**KLES** ........ Worthington, MN [*FM radio station call letters*]
**KLEV** ........ Cleveland, TX [*AM radio station call letters*]
**KLeVA** ....... United States Veterans Administration Center, Leavenworth, KS [*Library symbol*] [*Library of Congress*] (LCLS)
**KLEW-TV** ... Lewiston, ID [*Television station call letters*]
**KLEX** ........ Lexington, MO [*AM radio station call letters*]
**KLEY** ........ Wellington, KS [*AM radio station call letters*]
**KLF** ........... Kleinasiatische Forschungen [*Weimar*] [*A publication*]
**KLFA** ........ King City, CA [*FM radio station call letters*]
**KLFB** ........ Lubbock, TX [*AM radio station call letters*]
**KLFC** ........ Branson, MO [*FM radio station call letters*]
**KLFD** ........ Litchfield, MN [*AM radio station call letters*]
**KLFD-FM** ... Litchfield, MN [*FM radio station call letters*]
**KLFE** ........ San Bernardino, CA [*AM radio station call letters*]
**KLFF** ........ Glendale, AZ [*AM radio station call letters*]
**KLFI** .......... Hampton/Langley Air Force Base [*Virginia*] [*ICAO location identifier*] (ICLI)
**KLFJ** .......... Springfield, MO [*AM radio station call letters*]
**KLFK** ........ Lufkin/Angelina County [*Texas*] [*ICAO location identifier*] (ICLI)
**KLFM** ........ Great Falls, MT [*FM radio station call letters*]
**KLFO** ........ Junction, TX [*FM radio station call letters*]
**KLFO** ........ Kleinasiatische Forschungen [*Weimar*] [*A publication*]
**KlForsch** .... Kleinasiatische Forschungen [*Weimar*] [*A publication*]
**KLFT** ........ Lafayette/Regional [*Louisiana*] [*ICAO location identifier*] (ICLI)
**KLFV** ........ Missoula, MT [*Television station call letters*]
**KLFY-TV** .. Lafayette, LA [*Television station call letters*]
**KLG** ........... Kalgoorlie [*Australia*] [*Seismograph station code, US Geological Survey*] (SEIS)
**KLG** ........... Kalskag [*Alaska*] [*Airport symbol*] (OAG)
**KLG** ........... Keto-L-glutonic (Acid) [*Biochemistry*]
**KLG** ........... Keto-Laevo-Gulonic Acid [*Organic chemistry*]
**KLG** ........... Knudsen Leaf Gauge [*Physics*]
**KLG** ........... University of Louisville, Louisville, KY [*OCLC symbol*] (OCLC)
**KLGA** ........ Algona, IA [*AM radio station call letters*]
**KLGA** ........ New York/La Guardia [*New York*] [*ICAO location identifier*] (ICLI)
**KLGA-FM** ... Algona, IA [*FM radio station call letters*]
**KLGB** ........ Long Beach [*California*] [*ICAO location identifier*] (ICLI)
**KLGG** ........ Delta, UT [*FM radio station call letters*]
**KLGN** ........ Logan, UT [*AM radio station call letters*]
**KLGR** ........ Knight's Local Government Reports [*A publication*] (DLA)
**KLGR** ........ Redwood Falls, MN [*AM radio station call letters*]
**KLGR-FM** ... Redwood Falls, MN [*FM radio station call letters*]
**KLGS** ........ Versailles, MO [*FM radio station call letters*]
**KLGT** ........ Buffalo, WY [*FM radio station call letters*]
**KLGV** ........ Longview, TX [*AM radio station call letters*]
**KLH** ........... Kapapala Ranch [*Hawaii*] [*Seismograph station code, US Geological Survey*] (SEIS)
**KLH** ........... Keyhole Limpet Hemocyanin [*Immunology*]
**KLH** ........... Kloss, Low, and Hofmann [*Initialism is name of electronics company and brand name of its products*]
**KLH** ........... Knight of the Legion of Honor [*France*]
**KLHAAK** .. Kungliga Lantbrukshoegskolans. Annaler [*A publication*]
**KLHI-FM** ... Lahaina, HI [*FM radio station call letters*]
**KLHO** ........ Thayer, MO [*FM radio station call letters*]
**KLHS-FM** ... Lewiston, ID [*FM radio station call letters*]
**KLHT** ........ Honolulu, HI [*AM radio station call letters*]
**KLI** ............ Herrenjournal International. Fachzeitschrift fuer Herrenmode [*A publication*]
**KLI** ............ Kaliber Resources Ltd. [*Vancouver Stock Exchange symbol*]
**KLI** ............ King's Light Infantry [*Military unit*] [*British*]
**Kliatt** .......... Kliatt Paperback Book Guide [*A publication*]
**KLIC** .......... Keyletter-in-Context [*Data processing*]
**KLIC** .......... Korumburra Living for Independence Centre [*Australia*]
**KLIC** .......... Kulicke & Soffa Industries, Inc. [*NASDAQ symbol*] (NQ)
**KLID** .......... Poplar Bluff, MO [*AM radio station call letters*]
**KLIF** .......... Dallas, TX [*AM radio station call letters*]
**KLIK** .......... Jefferson City, MO [*AM radio station call letters*]
**KLIL** .......... Moreauville, LA [*FM radio station call letters*]
**KLIM** .......... Limon, CO [*AM radio station call letters*]
**Klima Kaelte Heiz** ... Klima, Kaelte, Heizung [*A publication*]
**Klima Kaelteing** ... Klima und Kaelteingenieur [*A publication*]
**Klima-Kaelte-Tech** ... Klima-Kaelte-Technik [*A publication*]
**Klima Schn D** ... Klima-Schnellmeldedienst [*A publication*]
**Klima-Tech** ... Klima-Technik [*A publication*]
**Klim Grej Hlad** ... Klimatisacija Grejanje Hladenje [*A publication*]
**Klim Kaelte Ing** ... Klima und Kaelte Ingenieur [*A publication*]
**Klin** ............ Klinikus [*A publication*]
**KLIN** .......... Lincoln, NE [*AM radio station call letters*]
**KLINA** ....... K, Li, and Na [*For the chemical elements potassium, lithium, and sodium*] [*Beckman flame system*] [*Trademark*]
**Klin Anaesthesiol Intensivther** ... Klinische Anaesthesiologie und Intensivtherapie [*A publication*]
**KLindB** ...... Bethany College, Lindsborg, KS [*Library symbol*] [*Library of Congress*] (LCLS)
**Kline Chem** ... Kline Guide to the Chemical Industry [*A publication*]
**Klin Eksp Med** ... Kliniska un Eksperimentala Medicina [*A publication*]
**Klin Jahrb** ... Klinisches Jahrbuch [*A publication*]
**Klin Khir** .... Klinicheskaya Khirurgiya [*Kiev*] [*A publication*]
**Klin Lech Zlokach Novoobraz** ... Klinika i Lechenie Zlokachestvennykh Novoobrazovanii [*A publication*]
**Klin Med (Mosc)** ... Klinicheskaya Meditsina (Moscow) [*A publication*]
**Klin Med Osterr Z Wiss Prakt Med** ... Klinische Medizin. Oesterreichische Zeitschrift fuer Wissenschaftliche und Praktische Medizin [*A publication*]
**Klin Med (Vienna)** ... Klinische Medizin (Vienna) [*A publication*]
**Klin Monats** ... Klinische Monatsblaetter fuer Augenheilkunde [*A publication*]
**Klin Monatsbl Augenheilkd** ... Klinische Monatsblaetter fuer Augenheilkunde [*A publication*]
**Klin Oczna** ... Klinika Oczna [*A publication*]
**Klin Paediat** ... Klinische Paediatrie [*A publication*]
**Klin Paediatr** ... Klinische Paediatrie [*A publication*]
**Klin Rentgenol Resp Mezhved Sb** ... Klinicheskoi Rentgenologii Respublikanskoi Mezhvedomstvennyi Sbornik [*A publication*]

**Klin Therap Wchnschr** ... Klinisch-Therapeutische Wochenschrift [*A publication*]
**Klin Wchnschr** ... Klinische Wochenschrift [*A publication*]
**Klin Woch** ... Klinische Wochenschrift [*A publication*]
**Klin Wochenschr** ... Klinische Wochenschrift [*A publication*]
**Klin Ws** ...... Klinische Wochenschrift [*A publication*]
**Klin Wschr** ... Klinische Wochenschrift [*A publication*]
**Klio** ............ Klio. Beitraege zur Alten Geschichte [*A publication*]
**KLIQ** ......... Shingle Springs, CA [*FM radio station call letters*]
**KLIR** ......... Columbus, NE [*FM radio station call letters*]
**KLIS** ......... Palestine, TX [*FM radio station call letters*]
**KLIT** ......... Glendale, CA [*FM radio station call letters*]
**KLIT** ......... Little Rock/Adams Field [*Arkansas*] [*ICAO location identifier*] (ICLI)
**KLIT-FM** .. Carpinteria, CA [*FM radio station call letters*]
**KLIV** ......... San Jose, CA [*AM radio station call letters*]
**KLIX** ......... Twin Falls, ID [*AM radio station call letters*]
**KLIX-FM** .. Twin Falls, ID [*FM radio station call letters*]
**KLIZ** ......... Brainerd, MN [*AM radio station call letters*]
**KLIZ** ......... Korea Limited Identification Zone
**KLIZ** ......... Limestone/Loring Air Force Base [*Maine*] [*ICAO location identifier*] (ICLI)
**KLIZ-FM** .. Brainerd, MN [*FM radio station call letters*]
**KLJ** ........... Jewish Hospital, Louisville, KY [*OCLC symbol*] (OCLC)
**KLJ** ........... Kentucky Law Journal [*A publication*]
**KLJ** ........... Knight of [*the Order of*] St. Lazarus of Jerusalem [*British*]
**KLJB-TV** ... Davenport, IA [*Television station call letters*]
**KLJC** ......... Kansas City, MO [*FM radio station call letters*]
**KLK** ........... Kealakekua [*Hawaii*] [*Seismograph station code, US Geological Survey*] [*Closed*] (SEIS)
**KLK** ........... Killick Gold Co. [*Vancouver Stock Exchange symbol*]
**KLKC** ......... Parsons, KS [*AM radio station call letters*]
**KLKC-FM** ... Parsons, KS [*FM radio station call letters*]
**KLKE** ......... Del Rio, TX [*AM radio station call letters*]
**Kl KF** ......... Kleinen Kirchenfuehrer [*A publication*]
**KLKHA** ..... Klinicheskaya Khirurgiya [*A publication*]
**KLKI** ......... Anacortes, WA [*AM radio station call letters*]
**KLKIA** ....... Ki, Klima + Kaelte-Ingenieur [*A publication*]
**KLKM** ....... Llano, TX [*FM radio station call letters*]
**KLKO** ....... Elko, NV [*FM radio station call letters*]
**KLKS** ......... Breezy Point, MN [*FM radio station call letters*]
**KLKT** ......... Incline Village, NV [*FM radio station call letters*]
**KLKY** ......... Prescott Valley, AZ [*AM radio station call letters*]
**KLL** ........... Kalltalsperre [*Federal Republic of Germany*] [*Seismograph station code, US Geological Survey*] (SEIS)
**KLL** ........... Levelock [*Alaska*] [*Airport symbol*] (OAG)
**KLLA** ......... Leesville, LA [*AM radio station call letters*]
**KLLF** ......... Wichita Falls, TX [*AM radio station call letters*]
**KLLI** ......... Hooks, TX [*FM radio station call letters*]
**KLLK** ......... Willits, CA [*AM radio station call letters*]
**KLLL** ......... Lubbock, TX [*AM radio station call letters*]
**KLLL-FM** ... Lubbock, TX [*FM radio station call letters*]
**KLLM** ........ Forks, WA [*FM radio station call letters*]
**KLLM** ........ KLLM Transport Services, Inc. [*NASDAQ symbol*] (NQ)
**KLLN** ......... Newark, AR [*FM radio station call letters*]
**KLLR** ......... Walker, MN [*AM radio station call letters*]
**KLLR-FM** ... Walker, MN [*FM radio station call letters*]
**KLLT** ......... Grants, NM [*FM radio station call letters*]
**KLLV** ......... Breen, CO [*AM radio station call letters*]
**KLLY** ......... Oildale, CA [*FM radio station call letters*]
**KL/M** ......... Kiloliters per Minute
**KLM** .......... Kilometer
**KLM** .......... KLM [*Koninklijke Luchtvaart Maatschappij*] Royal Dutch Airlines [*NYSE symbol*] (SPSG)
**KLM** .......... Koninklijke Luchtvaart Maatschappij [*Royal Dutch Airlines*]
**KLM** .......... Kuala Lumpur [*Malaysia*] [*Seismograph station code, US Geological Survey*] (SEIS)
**KLM** .......... University of Louisville, School of Music Library, Louisville, KY [*OCLC symbol*] (OCLC)
**KLMG-TV** ... Longview, TX [*Television station call letters*]
**KLMIA** ...... Klinicheskaya Meditsina [*A publication*]
**KLMK** ....... Poteau, OK [*FM radio station call letters*]
**KLMN** ....... Amarillo, TX [*FM radio station call letters*]
**KLMO** ....... Longmont, CO [*AM radio station call letters*]
**KLMR** ....... Lamar, CO [*AM radio station call letters*]
**KLMS** ....... Lincoln, NE [*AM radio station call letters*]
**KLMX** ....... Clayton, NM [*AM radio station call letters*]
**KLN** .......... Kelan Resources [*Vancouver Stock Exchange symbol*]
**KLN** .......... Larsen Bay [*Alaska*] [*Airport symbol*] (OAG)
**KLN** .......... Norton-Children's Hospital Medical Library, Louisville, KY [*OCLC symbol*] (OCLC)
**KLNA** ........ West Palm Beach/Palm Beach County Park [*Florida*] [*ICAO location identifier*] (ICLI)
**KLNE-FM** ... Lexington, NE [*FM radio station call letters*]
**KLNE-TV** ... Lexington, NE [*Television station call letters*]
**KLNG** ........ Council Bluffs, IA [*AM radio station call letters*]
**KLNI** ......... Pearl City, HI [*AM radio station call letters*]
**KLNK** ........ Lincoln/Municipal [*Nebraska*] [*ICAO location identifier*] (ICLI)
**KLNM** ....... Las Vegas, NM [*FM radio station call letters*]
**KLNO** ........ Llano, TX [*Television station call letters*]
**KLO** .......... Kalibo [*Philippines*] [*Airport symbol*] (OAG)
**KLO** .......... Klystron Oscillator
**KLO** .......... Ogden, UT [*AM radio station call letters*]
**KLOA** ........ Ridgecrest, CA [*AM radio station call letters*]
**KLOA-FM** ... Ridgecrest, CA [*FM radio station call letters*]
**KLOC** ........ Ceres, CA [*AM radio station call letters*]
**KLOC** ........ [*The*] Kushner-Locke Company [*NASDAQ symbol*] (NQ)
**KLOE** ........ Goodland, KS [*AM radio station call letters*]
**KLOF** ......... Kloof Gold Mining Co. Ltd. [*NASDAQ symbol*] (NQ)
**KLOG** ........ Kelso, WA [*AM radio station call letters*]
**KLOH** ........ Pipestone, MN [*AM radio station call letters*]
**KLOK** ........ San Jose, CA [*AM radio station call letters*]
**KLOL** ......... Houston, TX [*FM radio station call letters*]
**KLOM** ....... Lompoc, CA [*AM radio station call letters*]
**KLON** ........ Long Beach, CA [*FM radio station call letters*]
**KLOO** ........ Corvallis, OR [*AM radio station call letters*]
**KLOQ** ........ Merced, CA [*AM radio station call letters*]
**KLOR-FM** ... Ponca City, OK [*FM radio station call letters*]
**KLOS** ......... Kloss Video Corp. [*NASDAQ symbol*] (NQ)
**KLOS** ......... Los Angeles, CA [*FM radio station call letters*]
**KLOU** ........ Louisville/Bowman [*Kentucky*] [*ICAO location identifier*] (ICLI)
**KLOU** ........ St. Louis, MO [*FM radio station call letters*]
**KLOV** ........ Loveland, CO [*AM radio station call letters*]
**KLOW** ....... Caruthersville, MO [*FM radio station call letters*]
**KLOZ** ........ Eldon, MO [*FM radio station call letters*]
**KLP** ........... Korean Labor Party [*Communist*] [*Political party*] (CINC)
**KLP** ........... Louisville Free Public Library, Louisville, KY [*OCLC symbol*] (OCLC)
**KLPA** ......... Khan-Lewis Phonological Analysis [*Speech evaluation test*]
**KLPA-TV** .. Alexandria, LA [*Television station call letters*]
**Kl Pauly** ..... Der Kleine Pauly [*A publication*] (OCD)
**KLPB-TV** .. Lafayette, LA [*Television station call letters*]
**KLPI-FM** .. Ruston, LA [*FM radio station call letters*]
**KLPL** ......... Lake Providence, LA [*AM radio station call letters*]
**KLPL-FM** ... Lake Providence, LA [*FM radio station call letters*]
**KLPR** ......... Valley City, ND [*FM radio station call letters*]
**KLPW** ........ Union, MO [*AM radio station call letters*]
**KLPW-FM** ... Union, MO [*FM radio station call letters*]
**KLPX** ......... Tucson, AZ [*FM radio station call letters*]
**KLPZ** ......... Parker, AZ [*AM radio station call letters*]
**KLQL** ......... Luverne, MN [*FM radio station call letters*]
**KLQP** ......... Madison, MN [*FM radio station call letters*]
**KLQZ** ........ Paragould, AR [*FM radio station call letters*]
**KLR** ........... Columbus Air Transport, Inc. [*Columbus, OH*] [*FAA designator*] (FAAC)
**KLR** ........... Kalmar [*Sweden*] [*Airport symbol*] (OAG)
**KLR** ........... Kathiawar Law Reports [*India*] [*A publication*] (DLA)
**KLR** ........... Kentucky Law Reporter [*A publication*] (DLA)
**KLRA** ......... England, AR [*AM radio station call letters*]
**KLRA-FM** ... England, AR [*FM radio station call letters*]
**KLRB** ......... Wolfforth, TX [*Television station call letters*]
**KLRC** ......... Siloam Springs, AR [*FM radio station call letters*]
**KLRD** ........ Laredo/International [*Texas*] [*ICAO location identifier*] (ICLI)
**KLRD** ........ Yucaipa, CA [*FM radio station call letters*]
**KLRE-FM** ... Little Rock, AR [*FM radio station call letters*]
**KLRF** ......... Jacksonville/Little Rock Air Force Base [*Arkansas*] [*ICAO location identifier*] (ICLI)
**KLRK** ......... Vandalia, MO [*FM radio station call letters*]
**KLRN** ........ San Antonio, TX [*Television station call letters*]
**KLRQ** ........ Clinton, MO [*FM radio station call letters*]
**KLRR** ......... Redmond, OR [*FM radio station call letters*]
**KLRT** ......... Kleinert's, Inc. [*NASDAQ symbol*] (NQ)
**KLRT** ......... Little Rock, AR [*Television station call letters*]
**KLRU-TV** ... Austin, TX [*Television station call letters*]
**KLS** ........... Faculty of Library and Information Science, University of Toronto [*UTLAS symbol*]
**KLS** ........... Karlskrona [*Sweden*] [*Seismograph station code, US Geological Survey*] [*Closed*] (SEIS)
**KLS** ........... Kaskaskia Library System [*Library network*]
**KLS** ........... Kelso Resources [*Vancouver Stock Exchange symbol*]
**KLS** ........... Kelso, WA [*Location identifier*] [*FAA*] (FAAL)
**KLS** ........... Key Lock Switch
**KLS** ........... Kidney, Liver, Spleen [*Medicine*]
**KLS** ........... Knight of the Lion and Sun [*Persia*] (ROG)
**KLS** ........... Knotted List Structure (BUR)
**KLS** ........... Krypton LASER System
**KLSA** ......... Alexandria, LA [*FM radio station call letters*]
**KLSC** ......... Korean Logistic Service Corps (CINC)
**KLSC** ......... Lamesa, TX [*FM radio station call letters*]
**Kl Schr** ....... Kleine Schriften [*of various authors*] [*Classical studies*] (OCD)
**KLSE** ......... Kuala Lumpur Stock Exchange
**KLSE-FM** ... Rochester, MN [*FM radio station call letters*]
**KLSF** ......... Amarillo, TX [*FM radio station call letters*]
**KLSI** .......... Kansas City, MO [*FM radio station call letters*]
**KLSIFC** ..... Kathy Lynn Sacra International Fan Club (EA)
**KLSK** ......... Santa Fe, NM [*FM radio station call letters*]
**KLSN** ......... Jefferson, IN [*FM radio station call letters*]
**KLSP** ......... Angola, LA [*FM radio station call letters*]
**KLSR** ......... Memphis, TX [*AM radio station call letters*]
**KLSR-FM** ... Memphis, TX [*FM radio station call letters*]

**KLSS** ......... Mason City, IA [*AM radio station call letters*]
**KLSSAR**.... Kungliga Lantbrukshoegskolan och Statens Lantbruksfoersoek. Statens Husdjursforsok Meddelande [*A publication*]
**KLSS-FM** ... Mason City, IA [*FM radio station call letters*]
**KLST** ......... Kindergarten Language Screening Test
**KLST** ......... San Angelo, TX [*Television station call letters*]
**KLSU**......... Baton Rouge, LA [*FM radio station call letters*]
**KLSV** ......... Las Vegas/Nellis Air Force Base [*Nevada*] [*ICAO location identifier*] (ICLI)
**KLSX** ......... Los Angeles, CA [*FM radio station call letters*]
**KLSY** ......... Bellevue, WA [*AM radio station call letters*]
**KLSY-FM** ... Bellevue, WA [*FM radio station call letters*]
**KLSZ-FM** ... Van Buren, AR [*FM radio station call letters*]
**KLT**............ Kansas City Power & Light Co. [*NYSE symbol*] (SPSG)
**KLT**............ Kerala Law Times [*A publication*]
**KLT**............ Kiloton [*Nuclear equivalent of 1000 tons of high explosives*] (AAG)
**KlT**............ Kleine Texte fuer Theologische und Philosophische Vorlesungen [*A publication*] (BJA)
**KLT**............ Klystron Life Test
**KLTA**......... Breckenridge, MN [*FM radio station call letters*]
**KLTB**......... Boise, ID [*FM radio station call letters*]
**KLTC**......... Dickinson, ND [*AM radio station call letters*]
**KLTD**......... Lampasas, TX [*FM radio station call letters*]
**KLTE**......... Oklahoma City, OK [*FM radio station call letters*]
**KLTF**......... Little Falls, MN [*AM radio station call letters*]
**KLTG**......... Corpus Christi, TX [*FM radio station call letters*]
**KLTI**.......... Macon, MO [*AM radio station call letters*]
**KLTJ** ......... Galveston, TX [*Television station call letters*]
**KLTK**......... Southwest City, MO [*AM radio station call letters*]
**KLTL-TV**.. Lake Charles, LA [*Television station call letters*]
**KLTM-TV** ... Monroe, LA [*Television station call letters*]
**KLTN** ......... Las Vegas, NV [*FM radio station call letters*]
**KLTO** ......... El Paso, TX [*FM radio station call letters*]
**KLTO** ......... Knurling Tool
**KLTQ** ......... Sparta, MO [*FM radio station call letters*]
**KLTR**......... Houston, TX [*FM radio station call letters*]
**KLTS** ......... Altus Air Force Base [*Oklahoma*] [*ICAO location identifier*] (ICLI)
**KLTS-TV**.. Shreveport, LA [*Television station call letters*]
**KLTT**......... Brighton, CO [*AM radio station call letters*]
**KLTV**......... Tyler, TX [*Television station call letters*]
**KLTW**......... El Dorado, AR [*FM radio station call letters*]
**KLTX**......... Seattle, WA [*FM radio station call letters*]
**KLTY**......... Fort Worth, TX [*FM radio station call letters*]
**KLTZ**......... Glasgow, MT [*AM radio station call letters*]
**KLU**........... KaiserTech Limited [*Formerly, Kaiser Aluminum & Chemical Corp.*] [*NYSE symbol*] (SPSG)
**KLU**........... Key and Lamp Units [*Telecommunications*]
**KLU**........... Klagenfurt [*Austria*] [*Airport symbol*] (OAG)
**KLU**........... Klutina [*Alaska*] [*Seismograph station code, US Geological Survey*] (SEIS)
**KLUA**......... Kailua-Kona, HI [*FM radio station call letters*]
**KLUB**......... Milton-Freewater, OR [*FM radio station call letters*]
**Kluber Dr des Gens** ... Kluber's Droit des Gens [*A publication*] (DLA)
**KLUC**......... Las Vegas, NV [*AM radio station call letters*]
**KLUC-FM** ... Las Vegas, NV [*FM radio station call letters*]
**Klucze Oznaczania Owadow Pol** ... Klucze do Oznaczania Owadow Polski [*A publication*]
**KLUE**......... Muskogee, OK [*AM radio station call letters*]
**KLUF**......... Brenham, TX [*FM radio station call letters*]
**KLUF**......... Phoenix/Luke Air Force Base [*Arizona*] [*ICAO location identifier*] (ICLI)
**KLUH**......... Poplar Bluff, MO [*FM radio station call letters*]
**KLUJ**......... Harlingen, TX [*Television station call letters*]
**KLUK**......... Cincinnati/Municipal-Lunken Field [*Ohio*] [*ICAO location identifier*] (ICLI)
**KLUK**......... Laughlin, NV [*FM radio station call letters*]
**KLUM-FM** ... Jefferson City, MO [*FM radio station call letters*]
**KLUR**......... Wichita Falls, TX [*FM radio station call letters*]
**KLUV**......... Dallas, TX [*FM radio station call letters*]
**KLUX**......... Robstown, TX [*FM radio station call letters*]
**KLUZ-TV** ... Albuquerque, NM [*Television station call letters*]
**KLV**........... Karlovy Vary [*Czechoslovakia*] [*Airport symbol*] (OAG)
**KLVE**......... Los Angeles, CA [*FM radio station call letters*]
**KLVF**......... Las Vegas, NM [*FM radio station call letters*]
**KLVI**......... Beaumont, TX [*AM radio station call letters*]
**KLVJ**......... Mountain Home, ID [*AM radio station call letters*]
**KLVJ-FM** ... Mountain Home, ID [*FM radio station call letters*]
**KLVL**......... Pasadena, TX [*AM radio station call letters*]
**KLVM**......... Prunedale, CA [*FM radio station call letters*]
**KLVN**......... Newton, IA [*FM radio station call letters*]
**KLVQ**......... Athens, TX [*AM radio station call letters*]
**KLVR**......... Santa Rosa, CA [*FM radio station call letters*]
**KLVS**......... Lake Oswego, OR [*AM radio station call letters*]
**KLVS**......... Las Vegas [*New Mexico*] [*ICAO location identifier*] (ICLI)
**KLVT**......... Levelland, TX [*AM radio station call letters*]
**KLVU**......... Haynesville, LA [*AM radio station call letters*]
**KLVU-FM** ... Haynesville, LA [*FM radio station call letters*]
**KLVV**......... Bountiful, UT [*FM radio station call letters*]
**KLVX**......... Las Vegas, NV [*Television station call letters*]
**KLW**.......... Claw Resources Ltd. [*Vancouver Stock Exchange symbol*]
**KLW**.......... Faculty of Law Library, University of Toronto [*UTLAS symbol*]
**KLW**.......... Klawock [*Alaska*] [*Airport symbol*] (OAG)
**KLWD**........ Sheridan, WY [*FM radio station call letters*]
**KLWJ**........ Umatilla, OR [*AM radio station call letters*]
**KLWN**........ Lawrence, KS [*AM radio station call letters*]
**KLWOA**.... Klinische Wochenschrift [*A publication*]
**Kl Ws**........ Klinische Wochenschrift [*A publication*]
**KLWT**........ Lebanon, MO [*AM radio station call letters*]
**KLWT-FM** ... Lebanon, MO [*FM radio station call letters*]
**KLWY**........ Cheyenne, WY [*Television station call letters*]
**KLX**........... Kalamata [*Greece*] [*Airport symbol*] (OAG)
**KLX**........... Kidney and Lung Extract
**KLXK**......... Minneapolis, MN [*FM radio station call letters*]
**KLXQ**......... Uvalde, TX [*FM radio station call letters*]
**KLXR**......... Redding, CA [*AM radio station call letters*]
**KLXS-FM** ... Pierre, SD [*FM radio station call letters*]
**KLXV-TV** ... San Jose, CA [*Television station call letters*]
**KLXX**......... Bismarck-Mandan, ND [*AM radio station call letters*]
**KLY**........... Kelley Oil & Gas Partnership Ltd. [*AMEX symbol*] (SPSG)
**KLY**........... Klei en Keramiek [*A publication*]
**KLY**........... Klyuchi [*USSR*] [*Seismograph station code, US Geological Survey*] (SEIS)
**KLYD**......... Bakersfield, CA [*AM radio station call letters*]
**KLYF**......... Des Moines, IA [*FM radio station call letters*]
**KLYK**......... Longview, WA [*FM radio station call letters*]
**KLYN**......... Lynden, WA [*FM radio station call letters*]
**KLYQ**......... Hamilton, MT [*AM radio station call letters*]
**KLYR**......... Clarksville, AR [*AM radio station call letters*]
**KLYR-FM** ... Clarksville, AR [*FM radio station call letters*]
**KLYT**......... Albuquerque, NM [*FM radio station call letters*]
**KLYV**......... Dubuque, IA [*FM radio station call letters*]
**KLYX**......... Thermopolis, WY [*FM radio station call letters*]
**KLZ**........... Denver, CO [*AM radio station call letters*]
**KLZ**........... Kleinzee [*South Africa*] [*Airport symbol*] (OAG)
**KLZE**......... Owensville, MO [*FM radio station call letters*]
**KLZK**......... Farwell, TX [*FM radio station call letters*]
**KLZR**......... Lawrence, KS [*FM radio station call letters*]
**KLZX**......... Salt Lake City, UT [*AM radio station call letters*]
**KLZX-FM** ... Salt Lake City, UT [*FM radio station call letters*]
**KLZY**......... Powell, WY [*FM radio station call letters*]
**KLZZ**......... Los Osos-Baywood Park, CA [*FM radio station call letters*]
**KM**............ Air Malta [*ICAO designator*] (FAAC)
**KM**............ Comoros [*ANSI two-letter standard code*] (CNC)
**KM**............ Ha-Kibbuts ha-Me'uhad (BJA)
**KM**............ K Mart Corp. [*NYSE symbol*] (SPSG)
**KM**............ Kabataang Makabayan [*Nationalist Youth*] [*Philippines*]
**KM**............ Kanamycin [*Antibacterial compound*]
**KM**............ Kansas Magazine [*A publication*]
**KM**............ [*The*] Kansas & Missouri Railway & Terminal Co. [*Formerly, KMRT*] [*AAR code*]
**KM**............ Kent Messenger [*A publication*]
**KM**............ Kieler Meeresforschungen [*A publication*]
**kM**............ Kilomega
**km**............ Kilometer
**KM**............ Kinetic Momentum
**KM**............ King and Martyr [*Church calendars*]
**KM**............ Kingdom
**KM**............ King's Medal [*or Medallist*] [*British*]
**KM**............ King's Messenger [*British*] (ROG)
**Km**............ Kirchenmusiker [*A publication*]
**KM**............ Kitchen Mechanic [*Restaurant slang*]
**KM**............ Klystron Mount
**KM**............ Knight of Malta
**KM**............ Kubelka-Munk [*Optics*]
**KM**............ Kurram Militia [*British military*] (DMA)
**KM**............ Kwartalnik Muzyczny [*A publication*]
**KM**............ Manhattan Public Library, Manhattan, KS [*Library symbol*] [*Library of Congress*] (LCLS)
**KM2**.......... Kermit [*Texas*] [*Seismograph station code, US Geological Survey*] (SEIS)
**KM$^3$**.......... Cubic Kilometer
**KM5**.......... Kermit [*Texas*] [*Seismograph station code, US Geological Survey*] (SEIS)
**KM6**.......... Kermit [*Texas*] [*Seismograph station code, US Geological Survey*] (SEIS)
**KM9**.......... Kermit [*Texas*] [*Seismograph station code, US Geological Survey*] (SEIS)
**KMA**.......... Kerema [*Papua New Guinea*] [*Airport symbol*] (OAG)
**KMA**.......... Koopman [*A publication*]
**KMA**.......... Korea Military Academy
**KMA**.......... Ku-Band Multiple Access (MCD)
**KMA**.......... Shenandoah, IA [*AM radio station call letters*]
**KMAA**........ Kart Marketing Association of America (EA)
**KMAD**........ Madill, OK [*AM radio station call letters*]
**KMADF**.... Kamad Silver Co. Ltd. [*NASDAQ symbol*] (NQ)
**KMAD-FM** ... Madill, OK [*FM radio station call letters*]
**KMAF**........ Midland/Regional Air Terminal [*Texas*] [*ICAO location identifier*] (ICLI)
**KMAG**........ Fort Smith, AR [*FM radio station call letters*]

**KMAG**....... Komag, Inc. [*NASDAQ symbol*] (NQ)
**KMAG**....... Korea Military Advisory Group [*United States*]
**KMAGA**.... Konstruktion im Maschinen-, Apparate-, und Geraetebau [*A publication*]
**KMAJ**........ Topeka, KS [*FM radio station call letters*]
**KMAK**........ Orange Grove, CA [*FM radio station call letters*]
**KMAL**........ Malden, MO [*FM radio station call letters*]
**KMAM**...... Butler, MO [*AM radio station call letters*]
**KMAN**....... Manhattan, KS [*AM radio station call letters*]
**KMAP**....... South St. Paul, MN [*AM radio station call letters*]
**KMAQ**....... Maquoketa, IA [*AM radio station call letters*]
**KMAQ-FM**... Maquoketa, IA [*FM radio station call letters*]
**KMAR**....... Winnsboro, LA [*AM radio station call letters*]
**KMAR-FM**... Winnsboro, LA [*FM radio station call letters*]
**KMAS**........ Korean Medical Association of America (EA)
**KMAS**........ Shelton, WA [*AM radio station call letters*]
**KMAU**....... Wailuku, HI [*Television station call letters*]
**KMAUA**.... Klinische Monatsblaetter fuer Augenheilkunde [*A publication*]
**KMAV**....... Mayville, ND [*AM radio station call letters*]
**KMAV-FM**... Mayville, ND [*FM radio station call letters*]
**KMAX**....... Arcadia, CA [*FM radio station call letters*]
**KMB**.......... Kaspar, Melchior, and Balthazar [*Initials of the three Wise Men placed on Polish homes during the Christmas season*]
**KMB**.......... Kimbe [*New Britain*] [*Seismograph station code, US Geological Survey*] [*Closed*] (SEIS)
**KMB**.......... Kimberly-Clark Corp. [*NYSE symbol*] (SPSG)
**KMB**.......... Koinambe [*Papua New Guinea*] [*Airport symbol*] (OAG)
**kmb**............ Kontant met Bestelling [*Cash with Order*] [*Business term*] [*Afrikaans*]
**KMBC-TV**... Kansas City, MO [*Television station call letters*]
**KMBH**....... Harlingen, TX [*Television station call letters*]
**KMBI**........ Spokane, WA [*AM radio station call letters*]
**KMBI-FM**... Spokane, WA [*FM radio station call letters*]
**KMBL**........ Junction, TX [*AM radio station call letters*]
**KMBO**....... Keith Martin Ballet Oregon
**KMBR**....... Kansas City, MO [*FM radio station call letters*]
**KMBS**....... West Monroe, LA [*AM radio station call letters*]
**KMBU**....... Powell, WY [*FM radio station call letters*]
**KMBY-FM**... Seaside, CA [*FM radio station call letters*]
**KMBZ**....... Kansas City, MO [*AM radio station call letters*]
**KMC**.......... Kamloops CableNet [*Vancouver Stock Exchange symbol*]
**kMc**........... Kilomegacycle
**KMC**.......... Korean Marine Corps [*North Korea*]
**KMCC**....... Sacremento/McClellan Air Force Base [*California*] [*ICAO location identifier*] (ICLI)
**KMCC**....... Thoreau, NM [*FM radio station call letters*]
**KMCD**....... Fairfield, IA [*AM radio station call letters*]
**KMCE**....... Rancho Cordova, CA [*AM radio station call letters*]
**KMCF**........ Tampa/MacDill Air Force Base [*Florida*] [*ICAO location identifier*] (ICLI)
**KMCH**....... Manchester, IA [*FM radio station call letters*]
**KMCI**........ Kansas City/International [*Missouri*] [*ICAO location identifier*] (ICLI)
**KMCI**........ Lawrence, KS [*Television station call letters*]
**KMCK**....... Siloam Springs, AR [*FM radio station call letters*]
**KMCL**........ McCall, ID [*FM radio station call letters*]
**KMCM-FM**... Miles City, MT [*FM radio station call letters*]
**KMCO**....... McAlester, OK [*FM radio station call letters*]
**KMCO**....... Orlando/McCoy Air Force Base [*Florida*] [*ICAO location identifier*] (ICLI)
**KMcpC**...... McPherson College, McPherson, KS [*Library symbol*] [*Library of Congress*] (LCLS)
**KMCQ**....... The Dalles, OR [*FM radio station call letters*]
**KMCR**....... Montgomery City, MO [*FM radio station call letters*]
**kMcs**......... Kilomegacycles per Second (AABC)
**KMCT-TV**... West Monroe, LA [*Television station call letters*]
**KMCW**...... Great Falls, MT [*AM radio station call letters*]
**KMCX**....... Ogallala, NE [*FM radio station call letters*]
**KMCY**....... Minot, ND [*Television station call letters*]
**KMD**.......... Kamlode Resources, Inc. [*Vancouver Stock Exchange symbol*]
**KMDAT**.... KeyMath Diagnostic Arithmetic Test
**KMDC**....... Kirschner Medical Corporation [*Timonium, MD*] [*NASDAQ symbol*] (NQ)
**KMDL**....... Kaplan, LA [*FM radio station call letters*]
**KMDO**....... Fort Scott, KS [*AM radio station call letters*]
**KMDT**....... Middletown/Harrisburg International-Olmsted Field [*Pennsylvania*] [*ICAO location identifier*] (ICLI)
**KMDW**...... Chicago/Chicago Midway [*Illinois*] [*ICAO location identifier*] (ICLI)
**KMDX**....... Parker, AZ [*FM radio station call letters*]
**KMDY**....... Thousand Oaks, CA [*AM radio station call letters*]
**KME**.......... Kappa Mu Epsilon [*Society*]
**KME**.......... Kermit [*Texas*] [*Seismograph station code, US Geological Survey*] [*Closed*] (SEIS)
**KME**.......... Kerr Magneto-Optical Effect [*Optics*]
**KME**.......... Kraft Mill Effluent [*Pulp and paper processing*]
**KME**.......... Media Center, Audio Visual Library, University of Toronto [*UTLAS symbol*]
**KMEB**....... Wailuku, HI [*Television station call letters*]
**KMEC**....... Keystone Medical Corporation [*NASDAQ symbol*] (NQ)
**KMED**....... K MED Centers, Inc. [*NASDAQ symbol*] (NQ)
**KMED**....... Medford, OR [*AM radio station call letters*]
**KMEF**........ Keratin, Myosin, Epidermin, Fibrin [*Biochemistry*]
**KMEG**....... Sioux City, IA [*Television station call letters*]
**KMEL**........ San Francisco, CA [*FM radio station call letters*]
**KMEM**...... Memphis/International [*Tennessee*] [*ICAO location identifier*] (ICLI)
**KMEM**...... Memphis, MO [*FM radio station call letters*]
**KMEN**....... San Bernardino, CA [*AM radio station call letters*]
**KMEO**....... Phoenix, AZ [*AM radio station call letters*]
**KMEO-FM**... Phoenix, AZ [*FM radio station call letters*]
**KMER**....... Kemmerer, WY [*AM radio station call letters*]
**KMER**....... Kodak Metal Etch Resist
**KMER**....... Merced/Castle Air Force Base [*California*] [*ICAO location identifier*] (ICLI)
**KMES**........ Jonesville, LA [*FM radio station call letters*]
**KMET**....... Banning, CA [*AM radio station call letters*]
**KMEX-TV**... Los Angeles, CA [*Television station call letters*]
**KMEZ-FM**... Fort Worth, TX [*FM radio station call letters*]
**KMF**.......... Kamina [*Papua New Guinea*] [*Airport symbol*] (OAG)
**KMF**.......... Koussevitzky Music Foundation (EA)
**KMFA**....... Austin, TX [*FM radio station call letters*]
**KMFB**........ Kieler Milchwirtschaftliche Forschungsberichte [*A publication*]
**KMFB**........ Mendocino, CA [*FM radio station call letters*]
**KMFC**........ Centralia, MO [*FM radio station call letters*]
**KMFC**........ Kimberly McCullough Fan Club (EA)
**KMFE**........ McAllen/Miller International [*Texas*] [*ICAO location identifier*] (ICLI)
**KMFI**......... Sierra Vista, AZ [*AM radio station call letters*]
**KMFM**...... Premont, TX [*FM radio station call letters*]
**KMFR**........ Phoenix, OR [*AM radio station call letters*]
**KMG**.......... Kerr-McGee Corp. [*NYSE symbol*] [*Toronto Stock Exchange symbol*] (SPSG)
**KMG**.......... Kumagaya [*Japan*] [*Seismograph station code, US Geological Survey*] (SEIS)
**KMG**.......... Kunming [*Republic of China*] [*Airport symbol*] (OAG)
**KMGA**....... Albuquerque, NM [*FM radio station call letters*]
**KMGC**....... Dallas, TX [*FM radio station call letters*]
**KMGE**....... Eugene, OR [*FM radio station call letters*]
**KMGE**....... Marietta/Dobbins Air Force Base [*Georgia*] [*ICAO location identifier*] (ICLI)
**KMGG**....... Monte Rio, CA [*FM radio station call letters*]
**KMGH-TV**... Denver, CO [*Television station call letters*]
**KMGI**........ Seattle, WA [*FM radio station call letters*]
**KMGL**....... Oklahoma City, OK [*FM radio station call letters*]
**KMGM**...... Montevideo, MN [*FM radio station call letters*]
**KMGN**....... Flagstaff, AZ [*FM radio station call letters*]
**KMGO**....... Centerville, IA [*FM radio station call letters*]
**KMGP**....... Monahans, TX [*FM radio station call letters*]
**KMGQ**....... Goleta, CA [*FM radio station call letters*]
**KMGR**....... Murray, UT [*AM radio station call letters*]
**KMGR-FM**... Orem, UT [*FM radio station call letters*]
**KMGT**....... Honolulu, HI [*Television station call letters*]
**KMGW**...... Casper, WY [*FM radio station call letters*]
**KMGX**....... San Fernando, CA [*FM radio station call letters*]
**KMGZ**....... Lawton, OK [*FM radio station call letters*]
**kmh**........... Kilometers per Hour
**KMH**......... Knight of Merit of Holstein
**KMHA**....... Four Bears, ND [*FM radio station call letters*]
**KMHD**...... Gresham, OR [*FM radio station call letters*]
**KMHL**....... Marshall, MN [*AM radio station call letters*]
**KMHP**....... K'ung Meng Msueh-Pao [*Journal. Confucius Mencius Society*] [*A publication*]
**KMHR**....... Sacramento/Mather Air Force Base [*California*] [*ICAO location identifier*] (ICLI)
**KMHT**....... Marshall, TX [*AM radio station call letters*]
**KMHT-FM**... Marshall, TX [*FM radio station call letters*]
**kMHZ**....... Kilomega Hertz (MCD)
**KMI**........... Commercium. Maandblad voor Economisch, Administratief, en Ondernemersonderwijs [*A publication*]
**KMI**........... Keilschrifttexte Medizinischen Inhalts [*A publication*] (BJA)
**KMI**........... Kessler Marketing Intelligence [*Information service or system*] (IID)
**KMI**........... KSC [*Kennedy Space Center*] Management Instruction [*NASA*] (KSC)
**KMI**........... Miyazaki [*Japan*] [*Airport symbol*] (OAG)
**KMIA**....... Miami/International [*Florida*] [*ICAO location identifier*] (ICLI)
**KMIB**......... Minot/Minot Air Force Base [*North Dakota*] [*ICAO location identifier*] (ICLI)
**KMID-TV**... Midland, TX [*Television station call letters*]
**KMIH**........ Mercer Island, WA [*FM radio station call letters*]
**KMiJ**......... Johnson County Mental Health Center, Mission, KS [*Library symbol*] [*Library of Congress*] (LCLS)
**KMIK**........ Santa Fe, NM [*AM radio station call letters*]
**KMIL**......... Cameron, TX [*AM radio station call letters*]
**KMIN**........ Grants, NM [*AM radio station call letters*]
**KMIO-FM**... Espanola, NM [*FM radio station call letters*]
**KMIQ**........ Robstown, TX [*FM radio station call letters*]
**KMIR-TV**... Palm Springs, CA [*Television station call letters*]
**KMIS**......... Portageville, MO [*AM radio station call letters*]
**KMIS-FM**... Portageville, MO [*FM radio station call letters*]

**KMIT**......... Mitchell, SD [*FM radio station call letters*]
**KMIV**......... Millville/Millville [*New Jersey*] [*ICAO location identifier*] (ICLI)
**KMIX**......... Turlock, CA [*AM radio station call letters*]
**KMIX-FM**... Turlock, CA [*FM radio station call letters*]
**KMIY**......... Grand Junction, CO [*AM radio station call letters*]
**KMIZ**......... Columbia, MO [*Television station call letters*]
**KMJ**......... Fresno, CA [*AM radio station call letters*]
**Km J**......... Kirchenmusikalisches Jahrbuch [*A publication*]
**KMJ**......... Knight of Maximilian Joseph [*Bavaria*]
**KMJ**......... Kumamoto [*Japan*] [*Airport symbol*] (OAG)
**KMJ**......... Kume Jima [*Ryukyu Islands*] [*Seismograph station code, US Geological Survey*] (SEIS)
**Km Jb**......... Kirchenmusikalisches Jahrbuch [*A publication*]
**KMJC**......... El Cajon, CA [*AM radio station call letters*]
**KMJC-FM**... Clinton, IA [*FM radio station call letters*]
**KMJI**......... Shreveport, LA [*AM radio station call letters*]
**KMJJ-FM**... Shreveport, LA [*FM radio station call letters*]
**KMJK-FM**... Lake Oswego, OR [*FM radio station call letters*]
**KMJM**......... St. Louis, MO [*FM radio station call letters*]
**KMJO**......... Lewiston, ID [*FM radio station call letters*]
**KMJQ**......... Houston, TX [*FM radio station call letters*]
**KMJX**......... Conway, AR [*FM radio station call letters*]
**KMJY**......... Newport, WA [*AM radio station call letters*]
**KMK**......... Kamakura [*Japan*] [*Seismograph station code, US Geological Survey*] [*Closed*] (SEIS)
**KMK**......... Kansas State University, Manhattan, KS [*Library symbol*] [*Library of Congress*] (LCLS)
**KMK**......... Keren Mif'alim Konstruktiviyim [*Constructive Enterprises Fund*] (BJA)
**KMK**......... Konyvtartudomanyi es Modszertani Kozpont [*Center for Library Science and Methodology*] [*Hungary*] [*Information service or system*] (IID)
**KMKC**......... Kansas City/Kansas City [*Missouri*] [*ICAO location identifier*] (ICLI)
**KMKE**......... Milwaukee/General Mitchell Field [*Wisconsin*] [*ICAO location identifier*] (ICLI)
**KMKF**......... Manhattan, KS [*FM radio station call letters*]
**KMKM**......... Kansas City [*Missouri*] [*ICAO location identifier*] (ICLI)
**KMKO**......... Muskogee/Davis [*Oklahoma*] [*ICAO location identifier*] (ICLI)
**KMKRY**.... Kvutzat Mesahake Kadur Regel Yehudit (BJA)
**KMKS**......... Bay City, TX [*FM radio station call letters*]
**KMKT-FM**... Denison, TX [*FM radio station call letters*]
**KMK-V**......... Kansas State University, Veterinary Medicine Library, Manhattan, KS [*Library symbol*] [*Library of Congress*] (LCLS)
**KML**......... Carmel Container Systems Ltd. [*AMEX symbol*] (SPSG)
**KML**......... Kamileroi [*Australia*] [*Airport symbol*] [*Obsolete*] (OAG)
**KML**......... Kamuela [*Hawaii*] [*Seismograph station code, US Geological Survey*] [*Closed*] (SEIS)
**KMLA**......... Texarkana, TX [*AM radio station call letters*]
**KMLA-FM**... Ashdown, AR [*FM radio station call letters*]
**KMLB**......... Melbourne/Cape Kennedy Regional [*Florida*] [*ICAO location identifier*] (ICLI)
**KMLC**......... McAlester/Municipal [*Oklahoma*] [*ICAO location identifier*] (ICLI)
**KMLE**......... Chandler, AZ [*FM radio station call letters*]
**KMLM**......... Odessa, TX [*Television station call letters*]
**KMLO**......... Fallbrook, CA [*FM radio station call letters*]
**KMLT**......... Amarillo, TX [*FM radio station call letters*]
**KMLT**......... Millinocket/Millinocke [*Maine*] [*ICAO location identifier*] (ICLI)
**KMLU**......... Monroe/Monroe Municipal [*Louisiana*] [*ICAO location identifier*] (ICLI)
**KMLWA**... Kommunalwirtschaft [*A publication*]
**KMM**......... Kamigamo [*Japan*] [*Seismograph station code, US Geological Survey*] [*Closed*] (SEIS)
**KMM**......... Kemper Multi-Market Income [*NYSE symbol*] (SPSG)
**KMM**......... Kimam [*Indonesia*] [*Airport symbol*] (OAG)
**KMM**......... Knight of the Order of Military Merit [*Prussia*] (ROG)
**KMM**......... Morehead State University, Morehead, KY [*OCLC symbol*] (OCLC)
**KMMA**......... Knitting Machine Manufacturers Association [*Defunct*] (EA)
**KMMC**......... Salem, MO [*FM radio station call letters*]
**KMMJ**......... Grand Island, NE [*AM radio station call letters*]
**KMML**......... Amarillo, TX [*FM radio station call letters*]
**KMMO**......... Marshall, MO [*AM radio station call letters*]
**KMMO-FM**... Marshall, MO [*FM radio station call letters*]
**KMMR**......... Malta, MT [*FM radio station call letters*]
**KMMRA**... Khimicheskoe Mashinostroenie [*A publication*]
**K-MMSEN**... KSC [*Kennedy Space Center*] MMSE [*Multiuse Mission Support Equipment*] Notice [*NASA*] (NASA)
**K-MMSEPS**... KSC [*Kennedy Space Center*] MMSE [*Multiuse Mission Support Equipment*] Project Specification [*NASA*] (NASA)
**KMMT**......... Mammoth Lakes, CA [*FM radio station call letters*]
**KMMX-FM**... Terrell Hills, TX [*FM radio station call letters*]
**KMMZ**......... Greybull, WY [*AM radio station call letters*]
**KMN**......... Kamina [*Zaire*] [*Airport symbol*] (OAG)
**KMN**......... Kumano [*Japan*] [*Seismograph station code, US Geological Survey*] (SEIS)
**Km Nachrichten**... Kirchenmusikalische Nachrichten [*A publication*]
**KMNC**......... North Central Kansas Libraries, Manhattan, KS [*Library symbol*] [*Library of Congress*] (LCLS)
**KMND**......... Midland, TX [*AM radio station call letters*]
**KMNE-TV**... Bassett, NE [*Television station call letters*]
**KMNL**......... Kinetic Minerals, Inc. [*NASDAQ symbol*] (NQ)
**KMNR**......... Rolla, MO [*FM radio station call letters*]
**KMNS**......... Sioux City, IA [*AM radio station call letters*]
**KMNT**......... Centralia-Chehalis, WA [*FM radio station call letters*]
**KMNY**......... Pomona, CA [*AM radio station call letters*]
**KMNZ**......... Oklahoma City, OK [*Television station call letters*]
**KMO**......... Manokotak [*Alaska*] [*Airport symbol*] (OAG)
**KMOA**......... Kensett, AR [*AM radio station call letters*]
**KMOB**......... Mobile/Bates Field [*Alabama*] [*ICAO location identifier*] (ICLI)
**KMOC**......... Wichita Falls, TX [*FM radio station call letters*]
**KMOD-FM**... Tulsa, OK [*FM radio station call letters*]
**KMOE**......... Butler, MO [*FM radio station call letters*]
**KMOG**......... Payson, AZ [*AM radio station call letters*]
**KMOH-TV**... Kingman, AZ [*Television station call letters*]
**KMOJ**......... Minneapolis, MN [*FM radio station call letters*]
**KMOK**......... Lewiston, ID [*FM radio station call letters*]
**KMOL-TV**... San Antonio, TX [*Television station call letters*]
**KMOM**......... Monticello, MN [*AM radio station call letters*]
**KMON**......... Great Falls, MT [*AM radio station call letters*]
**KMON**......... Keyboard Monitor [*Digital Equipment Corp.*]
**KMON-FM**... Great Falls, MT [*FM radio station call letters*]
**KMOO**......... Mineola, TX [*AM radio station call letters*]
**KMOO-FM**... Mineola, TX [*FM radio station call letters*]
**KMOQ**......... Baxter Springs, KS [*FM radio station call letters*]
**KMOR**......... Scottsbluff, NE [*FM radio station call letters*]
**KMOS-TV**... Sedalia, MO [*Television station call letters*]
**KMOT**......... Minot/International [*North Dakota*] [*ICAO location identifier*] (ICLI)
**KMOT**......... Minot, ND [*Television station call letters*]
**KMOV**......... St. Louis, MO [*Television station call letters*]
**KMOW**......... Austin, TX [*AM radio station call letters*]
**KMOX**......... St. Louis, MO [*AM radio station call letters*]
**KMOZ**......... Rolla, MO [*AM radio station call letters*]
**KMP**......... Keetmanshoop [*South-West Africa*] [*Airport symbol*] (OAG)
**KMP**......... Kilusang Mabubukid ng Pilipnas [*Philippine Peasant Federation*] [*Political party*]
**KMP**......... Kommunistak Magyarorszagi Partja [*Communist Party of Hungary*] [*Political party*] (PPE)
**KMP**......... Koyala Mazdoor Panchayat [*India*]
**KMPC**......... Los Angeles, CA [*AM radio station call letters*]
**KMPG**......... Hollister, CA [*AM radio station call letters*]
**kmph**......... Kilometers per Hour (AABC)
**KMPH**......... Visalia, CA [*Television station call letters*]
**KMPL**......... Sikeston, MO [*AM radio station call letters*]
**KMPO**......... Modesto, CA [*FM radio station call letters*]
**KMPP**......... Kisan Mazdoor Praja Party [*India*] [*Political party*]
**KMPR**......... Minot, ND [*FM radio station call letters*]
**KMPS**......... Kernel Multiple Processing System [*Data processing*]
**kmps**......... Kilometers per Second
**KMPS**......... Seattle, WA [*AM radio station call letters*]
**KMPS-FM**... Seattle, WA [*FM radio station call letters*]
**KMPV**......... Montpelier/Edward F. Knapp [*Vermont*] [*ICAO location identifier*] (ICLI)
**KMPX**......... Decatur, TX [*Television station call letters*]
**KMPZ**......... Osceola, AR [*FM radio station call letters*]
**KMQ**......... Komatsu [*Japan*] [*Airport symbol*] (OAG)
**KMQT**......... Marquette/Marquette County [*Michigan*] [*ICAO location identifier*] (ICLI)
**KMQX**......... Springtown, TX [*FM radio station call letters*]
**KMR**......... Cambria Resources Ltd. [*Vancouver Stock Exchange symbol*]
**KMR**......... Kafrarian Mounted Rifles [*British military*] (DMA)
**KMR**......... Karimui [*Papua New Guinea*] [*Airport symbol*] (OAG)
**KMR**......... Kremsmuenster [*Austria*] [*Seismograph station code, US Geological Survey*] (SEIS)
**KMR**......... Kwajalein Missile Range (AABC)
**KMRA**......... Knitwear Mill Representatives Association [*Defunct*] (EA)
**KMRC**......... Morgan City, LA [*AM radio station call letters*]
**KMRE**......... Dumas, TX [*FM radio station call letters*]
**KMRF**......... Marshfield, MO [*AM radio station call letters*]
**KMrJ**......... Johnson County Library, Merriam, KS [*Library symbol*] [*Library of Congress*] (LCLS)
**KMRJ**......... Ukiah, CA [*FM radio station call letters*]
**KMRK**......... Odessa, TX [*FM radio station call letters*]
**KMRN**......... Cameron, MO [*AM radio station call letters*]
**KMRO**......... Camarillo, CA [*FM radio station call letters*]
**KMRR**......... South Tucson, AZ [*AM radio station call letters*]
**KMRS**......... Morris, MN [*AM radio station call letters*]
**KMrS**......... Shawnee Mission Medical Center, Merriam, KS [*Library symbol*] [*Library of Congress*] (LCLS)
**KMRT**......... [*The*] Kansas & Missouri Railway & Terminal Co. [*Later, KM*] [*AAR code*]
**KMRY**......... Cedar Rapids, IA [*AM radio station call letters*]
**KMS**......... Camas Resources Ltd. [*Vancouver Stock Exchange symbol*]

**KMS** .......... Keysort Multiple Selector
**km/s** .......... Kilometers per Second
**KMS** .......... King's Magnetic Ore Separator (ROG)
**K Ms** .......... Kirchliche Monatsschrift [*A publication*]
**KMS** .......... Knowledge Management System [*Data processing*]
**KMS** .......... Kumasi [*Ghana*] [*Airport symbol*] (OAG)
**KMS** .......... Murray State University, Murray, KY [*OCLC symbol*] (OCLC)
**KMSA** ........ Grand Junction, CO [*FM radio station call letters*]
**KMSB-TV** ... Nogales, AZ [*Television station call letters*]
**KMSC** ........ Sioux City, IA [*FM radio station call letters*]
**KMSD** ....... Milbank, SD [*AM radio station call letters*]
**KMSD-FM** ... Millbank, SD [*FM radio station call letters*]
**KMSG-TV** ... Sanger, CA [*Television station call letters*]
**KMSI** ......... KMS Industries, Inc. [*NASDAQ symbol*] (NQ)
**KMSL** ........ Stamps, AR [*FM radio station call letters*]
**KMSM-FM** ... Butte, MT [*FM radio station call letters*]
**KMSN** ....... Madison/Truax Field [*Wisconsin*] [*ICAO location identifier*] (ICLI)
**KMSO** ....... Missoula, MT [*FM radio station call letters*]
**KMSP** ........ Minneapolis/Minneapolis-St. Paul International [*Minnesota*] [*ICAO location identifier*] (ICLI)
**KMSP-TV** ... Minneapolis, MN [*Television station call letters*]
**KMSR** ........ Sauk Centre, MN [*FM radio station call letters*]
**KMSS** ........ Massena/Richards Field [*New York*] [*ICAO location identifier*] (ICLI)
**KMSS-TV** ... Shreveport, LA [*Television station call letters*]
**KMST** ........ Monterey, CA [*Television station call letters*]
**KMSU** ....... Mankato, MN [*FM radio station call letters*]
**KMSY** ........ New Orleans/International [*Louisiana*] [*ICAO location identifier*] (ICLI)
**KMT** .......... Kennametal, Inc. [*NYSE symbol*] (SPSG)
**KMT** .......... Kinomoto [*Japan*] [*Seismograph station code, US Geological Survey*] [*Closed*] (SEIS)
**KMT** .......... Knight of St. Maria Theresa [*Austria*] (ROG)
**KMT** .......... Kuomintang [*Nationalist Party of Taiwan*] [*Political party*] (PD)
**KMTA** ....... Kinsey, MT [*AM radio station call letters*]
**KMTB** ....... Kibris Milli Turk Birligi [*Cypriot National Turkish Union*] (PPE)
**KMTB** ....... Murfreesboro, AR [*FM radio station call letters*]
**KMTC** ....... Mount Clemens/Selfridge Air Force Base [*Michigan*] [*ICAO location identifier*] (ICLI)
**KMTC** ....... Russellville, AR [*FM radio station call letters*]
**KMTF** ........ Fresno, CA [*Television station call letters*]
**KMTH** ....... Maljamar, NM [*FM radio station call letters*]
**KMTI** ......... Manti, UT [*AM radio station call letters*]
**KMTL** ........ Sherwood, AR [*AM radio station call letters*]
**KMTN** ....... Jackson, WY [*FM radio station call letters*]
**KMTP** ........ Mount Pleasant, UT [*FM radio station call letters*]
**KMTPS** ..... Key Makers' Trade Protection Society [*A union*] [*British*]
**KMTR-TV** ... Eugene, OR [*Television station call letters*]
**KMTS** ........ Glenwood Springs, CO [*FM radio station call letters*]
**KMTV** ....... Omaha, NE [*Television station call letters*]
**KMTW** ...... Las Vegas, NV [*AM radio station call letters*]
**KMTX** ....... Helena, MT [*AM radio station call letters*]
**KMTX-FM** ... Helena, MT [*FM radio station call letters*]
**KMTY** ....... Aurora, NE [*FM radio station call letters*]
**KMU** .......... Kamikineusu Station [*Japan*] [*Seismograph station code, US Geological Survey*] (SEIS)
**KMU** .......... Kilusang Mayo Uno [*May First Movement*] [*Philippines*] [*Political party*]
**KMU** .......... Kismayu [*Somalia*] [*Airport symbol*] (OAG)
**KMU** .......... Kit Munition Unit [*Air Force*] (MCD)
**KMUD** ....... Garberville, CA [*FM radio station call letters*]
**KMUL** ....... Muleshoe, TX [*AM radio station call letters*]
**KMUL-FM** ... Muleshoe, TX [*FM radio station call letters*]
**KMUN** ....... Astoria, OR [*FM radio station call letters*]
**KMUO** ....... Mountain Home/Mountain Home Air Force Base [*Idaho*] [*ICAO location identifier*] (ICLI)
**K Mus Midden-Afr (Tervuren Belg) Ann Reeks Octavo Geol Wet** ... Koninklijk Museum voor Midden-Afrika (Tervuren, Belgie). Annalen. Reeks in Octavo. Geologische Wetenschappen [*A publication*]
**K Mus Midden-Afr (Tervuren Belg) Ann Reeks Octavo Zool Wet** ... Koninklijk Museum voor Midden-Afrika (Tervuren, Belgie). Annalen. Reeks in Octavo. Zoologische Wetenschappen [*A publication*]
**K Mus Midden-Afr (Tervuren Belg) Ann Reeks 8o Geol Wet** ... Koninklijk Museum voor Midden-Afrika (Tervuren, Belgie). Annalen. Reeks in Octavo. Geologische Wetenschappen [*A publication*]
**K Mus Midden-Afr (Tervuren Belg) Rapp Annu Dep Geol Mineral** ... Koninklijk Museum voor Midden-Afrika (Tervuren, Belgie). Rapport Annuel. Departement de Geologie et de Mineralogie [*A publication*]
**K Mus Midden-Afr (Tervuren Belg) Zool Doc** ... Koninklijk Museum voor Midden-Afrika (Tervuren, Belgie). Zoologische Documentatie [*A publication*]
**KMUW** ...... Wichita, KS [*FM radio station call letters*]
**KMV** .......... Kalemyo [*Burma*] [*Airport symbol*] (OAG)
**KMV** .......... Keen Mountain [*Virginia*] [*Seismograph station code, US Geological Survey*] [*Closed*] (SEIS)
**KMV** .......... Killed Measles-Virus Vaccine
**KMVC** ....... Wishek, ND [*FM radio station call letters*]
**KMVI** ........ Wailuku, HI [*AM radio station call letters*]
**KMVI-FM** ... Pukalani, HI [*FM radio station call letters*]
**KMVL** ....... Madisonville, TX [*AM radio station call letters*]
**KMVP** ....... Commerce City, CO [*AM radio station call letters*]
**KMVR** ....... Mesilla Park, NM [*FM radio station call letters*]
**KMVT** ....... Twin Falls, ID [*Television station call letters*]
**KMW** ......... KMW Systems Corp. [*AMEX symbol*] (SPSG)
**K M²/W** ..... Kelvin Square Meters per Watt
**KMWC** ...... Hayden, ID [*FM radio station call letters*]
**KMWL** ...... Mineral Wells [*Texas*] [*ICAO location identifier*] (ICLI)
**KMWX** ...... Yakima, WA [*AM radio station call letters*]
**KMXF** ........ Montgomery/Maxwell Air Force Base [*Alabama*] [*ICAO location identifier*] (ICLI)
**KMXO** ....... Merkel, TX [*AM radio station call letters*]
**KMXQ** ....... Socorro, NM [*FM radio station call letters*]
**KMXR** ....... Corpus Christi, TX [*FM radio station call letters*]
**KMXT** ....... Kodiak, AK [*FM radio station call letters*]
**KMXU** ....... Manti, UT [*FM radio station call letters*]
**KMXX** ....... Sterling, CO [*FM radio station call letters*]
**KMY** .......... Moser Bay [*Alaska*] [*Airport symbol*] (OAG)
**KMYB** ....... Pawhuska, OK [*FM radio station call letters*]
**KMYI** ........ Armijo, NM [*FM radio station call letters*]
**KMYQ** ....... Bastrop, LA [*AM radio station call letters*]
**KMYQ-FM** ... Bastrop, LA [*FM radio station call letters*]
**KMYR** ....... Myrtle Beach/Myrtle Beach Air Force Base [*South Carolina*] [*ICAO location identifier*] (ICLI)
**KMYZ** ....... Pryor, OK [*AM radio station call letters*]
**KMYZ-FM** ... Pryor, OK [*FM radio station call letters*]
**KMZQ-FM** ... Henderson, NV [*FM radio station call letters*]
**KMZU** ....... Carrollton, MO [*FM radio station call letters*]
**KN** ............. GKN Group Services Ltd. [*United Kingdom*] [*ICAO designator*] (ICDA)
**KN** ............. Kainai News [*A publication*]
**KN** ............. Kennedy Notice [*NASA*] (KSC)
**KN** ............. Kenya Navy
**kN** ............. Kilonewton
**KN** ............. Kinetics of Neutralization [*Chemistry*]
**KN** ............. Kings Norton Mint [*British*]
**KN** ............. Kitting Notice [*NASA*] (NASA)
**KN** ............. Klamath Northern Railway Co. [*Later, KNOR*] [*AAR code*]
**Kn** ............. Knapp's Privy Council Appeal Cases [*1829-36*] [*England*] [*A publication*] (DLA)
**kn** ............. Knee
**KN** ............. Knot
**KN** ............. Known
**Kn** ............. Knox's Supreme Court Reports [*A publication*] (APTA)
**Kn** ............. Knudsen Number [*IUPAC*]
**KN** ............. Kol Nidre (BJA)
**kn** ............. Korea, North [*MARC country of publication code*] [*Library of Congress*] (LCCP)
**KN** ............. Krasnaja Nov' [*A publication*]
**KN** ............. KSC [*Kennedy Space Center*] Notice (NASA)
**KN** ............. Kunst der Nederlanden [*A publication*]
**KN** ............. Kwartalnik Neofilologiczny [*A publication*]
**KN** ............. St. Christopher-Nevis [*ANSI two-letter standard code*] (CNC)
**KNA** ........... Katholische Nachrichten-Agentur [*Catholic Press Agency*] [*Federal Republic of Germany*]
**KNA** ........... Kenar Resources [*Vancouver Stock Exchange symbol*]
**KNA** ........... Kenya News Agency
**KNA** ........... Kex National Association (EA)
**KNA** ........... Killed; Not Enemy Action [*Military*]
**KNA** ........... Korean National Airlines
**KNA** ........... Korean National Association (EA)
**KNA** ........... Kuki National Assembly [*India*] [*Political party*] (PPW)
**KNA** ........... Kununurra [*Australia*] [*Seismograph station code, US Geological Survey*] (SEIS)
**KNA** ........... St. Christopher-Nevis [*ANSI three-letter standard code*] (CNC)
**KNAB** ........ Albany/Albany Naval Air Station [*Georgia*] [*ICAO location identifier*] (ICLI)
**KNAB** ........ Burlington, CO [*AM radio station call letters*]
**KNAB-FM** ... Burlington, CO [*FM radio station call letters*]
**Kn AC** ........ Knapp's Privy Council Appeal Cases [*1829-36*] [*England*] [*A publication*] (DLA)
**KNAC** ........ Long Beach, CA [*FM radio station call letters*]
**KNAF** ........ Fredericksburg, TX [*AM radio station call letters*]
**KNAI** ......... Phoenix, AZ [*FM radio station call letters*]
**KNAIR** ....... Kuehne & Nagel Air Cargo Ltd. [*British*]
**KNAK** ........ Delta, UT [*AM radio station call letters*]
**KNAL** ........ Victoria, TX [*AM radio station call letters*]
**KNAN** ........ Monroe, LA [*FM radio station call letters*]
**KNAP** ........ Knape & Vogt Manufacturing Co. [*NASDAQ symbol*] (NQ)
**KNAP** ........ Knapwell [*England*]
**Knapp** ......... Knapp's Privy Council Reports [*England*] [*A publication*] (DLA)
**Knapp & O** ... Knapp and Ombler's English Election Cases [*A publication*] (DLA)
**KNAQ** ........ Rupert, ID [*FM radio station call letters*]

**KNAS**........ Nashville, AR [*FM radio station call letters*]
**KNAT**........ Albuquerque, NM [*Television station call letters*]
**KNAU**........ Flagstaff, AZ [*FM radio station call letters*]
**Knaur Tb**.... Knaur Taschenbuecher [*A publication*]
**Knaur Vis**... Knaur Visuell [*A publication*]
**KNAV-FM** ... Navasota, TX [*FM radio station call letters*]
**KNAX**........ Fresno, CA [*FM radio station call letters*]
**KNAZ-TV** ... Flagstaff, AZ [*Television station call letters*]
**KNB**.......... Kanab [*Utah*] [*Seismograph station code, US Geological Survey*] (SEIS)
**KNB**.......... Kanab [*Utah*] [*Airport symbol*] (OAG)
**KNB**.......... Kanab, UT [*Location identifier*] [*FAA*] (FAAL)
**KNBA**........ Vallejo, CA [*AM radio station call letters*]
**KNBC**........ Beaufort/Beaufort Marine Corps Air Station [*South Carolina*] [*ICAO location identifier*] (ICLI)
**KNBC-TV** ... Los Angeles, CA [*Television station call letters*]
**KNBE**........ Dallas/Hensley Field Naval Air Station [*Texas*] [*ICAO location identifier*] (ICLI)
**KNBG**........ New Orleans/Alvin Callender Naval Air Station [*Louisiana*] [*ICAO location identifier*] (ICLI)
**KNBL**........ Knife Blade
**KNBO**........ New Boston, TX [*AM radio station call letters*]
**KNBR**........ San Francisco, CA [*AM radio station call letters*]
**KNBT**........ New Braunfels, TX [*FM radio station call letters*]
**KNBU**........ Baldwin City, KS [*FM radio station call letters*]
**KNBW**........ Kirin Brewery Co. Ltd. [*NASDAQ symbol*] (NQ)
**KNBY**........ Newport, AR [*AM radio station call letters*]
**KNBZ**........ Wasilla, AK [*FM radio station call letters*]
**KNC**.......... Canadian Crew Energy [*Vancouver Stock Exchange symbol*]
**KNC**.......... Kamerun National Congress
**KNC**.......... Kansas Newman College [*Formerly, Sacred Heart College*] [*Wichita*]
**KNC**.......... Kingcome Navigation [*AAR code*]
**KNCA**........ Jacksonville/New River Marine Corps Air Station [*North Carolina*] [*ICAO location identifier*] (ICLI)
**KNCB**........ Vivian, LA [*AM radio station call letters*]
**KNCC**........ Tsaile, AZ [*FM radio station call letters*]
**KNCD**........ Kincaid Furniture Co., Inc. [*NASDAQ symbol*] (NQ)
**KNCI**........ Kinetic Concepts, Inc. [*NASDAQ symbol*] (NQ)
**KNCI**........ Overland Park, KS [*AM radio station call letters*]
**Kn Civ Proc** ... Knox on Civil Procedure in India [*A publication*] (DLA)
**KNCK**........ Concordia, KS [*AM radio station call letters*]
**KNCN**........ Sinton, TX [*FM radio station call letters*]
**KNCO**........ Grass Valley, CA [*AM radio station call letters*]
**KNCO**........ Quonset Point/Quonset Point Naval Air Station [*Rhode Island*] [*ICAO location identifier*] (ICLI)
**KNCO-FM** ... Grass Valley, CA [*FM radio station call letters*]
**KNCQ**........ Redding, CA [*FM radio station call letters*]
**KNCR**........ Fortuna, CA [*AM radio station call letters*]
**Kn Cr Law** ... Knox on Bengal Criminal Law [*A publication*] (DLA)
**KNCT**........ Belton, TX [*Television station call letters*]
**KNCT-FM** ... Killeen, TX [*FM radio station call letters*]
**KNCY**........ Nebraska City, NE [*AM radio station call letters*]
**KNCY-FM** ... Nebraska City, NE [*FM radio station call letters*]
**KND**.......... Kindu [*Zaire*] [*Airport symbol*] (OAG)
**KNDA**........ Odessa, TX [*AM radio station call letters*]
**KNDC**........ Hettinger, ND [*AM radio station call letters*]
**KNDI**........ Honolulu, HI [*AM radio station call letters*]
**KNDK**........ Langdon, ND [*AM radio station call letters*]
**KNDN**........ Farmington, NM [*AM radio station call letters*]
**KNDO**........ Karen National Defense Organization [*Burma*]
**KNDO**........ Yakima, WA [*Television station call letters*]
**KNDP**........ Kamerun National Democratic Party [*Later, UNC*]
**KNDR**........ Kinder-Care, Inc. [*NASDAQ symbol*] (NQ)
**KNDR**........ Mandan, ND [*FM radio station call letters*]
**KNDU**........ Richland, WA [*Television station call letters*]
**KNDY**........ Marysville, KS [*AM radio station call letters*]
**KNDY-FM** ... Marysville, KS [*FM radio station call letters*]
**KNE**.......... KN Energy, Inc. [*NYSE symbol*] (SPSG)
**KNE**.......... Knie Resources, Inc. [*Vancouver Stock Exchange symbol*]
**KNEA**........ Brunswick/Glynco Naval Air Station [*Georgia*] [*ICAO location identifier*] (ICLI)
**KNEA**........ Jonesboro, AR [*AM radio station call letters*]
**KNEB**........ Scottsbluff, NE [*AM radio station call letters*]
**KNEB-FM** ... Scottsbluff, NE [*FM radio station call letters*]
**KNED**........ Knife Edge
**KNED**........ McAlester, OK [*AM radio station call letters*]
**K Ned Akad Wet Proc Ser A** ... Koninklijke Nederlandse Akademie van Wetenschappen. Proceedings. Series A. Mathematical Sciences [*Netherlands*] [*A publication*]
**K Ned Akad Wet Proc Ser B Palaeontol Geol Phys Chem** ... Koninklijke Nederlandse Akademie van Wetenschappen. Proceedings. Series B. Palaeontology, Geology, Physics, and Chemistry [*A publication*]
**K Ned Akad Wet Proc Ser B Phys Sci** ... Koninklijke Nederlandse Akademie van Wetenschappen. Proceedings. Series B. Physical Sciences [*Later, Koninklijke Nederlandse Akademie van Wetenschappen. Proceedings. Series B. Palaeontology, Geology, Physics, and Chemistry*] [*Netherlands*] [*A publication*]
**K Ned Akad Wet Proc Ser C** ... Koninklijke Nederlandse Akademie van Wetenschappen. Proceedings. Series C. Biological and Medical Sciences [*Netherlands*] [*A publication*]
**K Ned Akad Wet Versl Gewone Vergad Afd Natuurkd** ... Koninklijke Nederlandse Akademie van Wetenschappen. Verslag van de Gewone Vergadering van de Afdeling Natuurkunde [*A publication*]
**K Nederlandsch Aardrijkskundig Genootschap Tijdschrift** ... Koninklijk Nederlandsch Aardrijkskundig Genootschap. Tijdschrift [*A publication*]
**K Nederlandsch Geol-Mijn Genootschap Verh Geol Ser** ... Koninklijk Nederlandsch Geologisch-Mijnbouwkundig Genootschap Verhandelingen. Geologische Serie [*A publication*]
**K Nederlandse Akad Wetensch Afd Natuurk Verh Proc** ... Koninklijke Nederlandse Akademie van Wetenschappen. Afdeling Natuurkunde. Verhandelingen. Proceedings [*A publication*]
**K Ned Natuurhist Ver Uitg** ... Koninklijke Nederlandse Natuurhistorische Vereniging. Uitgave [*A publication*]
**KNEI**........ Waukon, IA [*AM radio station call letters*]
**KNEI-FM** ... Waukon, IA [*FM radio station call letters*]
**KNEK**........ Washington, LA [*AM radio station call letters*]
**KNEK-FM** ... Washington, LA [*FM radio station call letters*]
**KNEL**........ Brady, TX [*AM radio station call letters*]
**KNEL**........ Lakehurst/Lakehurst Naval Air Station [*New Jersey*] [*ICAO location identifier*] (ICLI)
**KNEM**........ Nevada, MO [*AM radio station call letters*]
**KNEN**........ Norfolk, NE [*FM radio station call letters*]
**KNEO**........ Neosho, MO [*FM radio station call letters*]
**KNeo**.......... W. A. Rankin Memorial Library, Neodesha, KS [*Library symbol*] [*Library of Congress*] (LCLS)
**KNES**........ Fairfield, TX [*FM radio station call letters*]
**KNET**........ Palestine, TX [*AM radio station call letters*]
**KNEU**........ Roosevelt, UT [*AM radio station call letters*]
**KNEV**........ Reno, NV [*FM radio station call letters*]
**KNEW**........ New Orleans [*Louisiana*] [*ICAO location identifier*] (ICLI)
**KNEW**........ Oakland, CA [*AM radio station call letters*]
**KNEZ**........ Lompoc, CA [*AM radio station call letters*]
**KNF**.......... Klein-Nishina Formula [*Physics*]
**KNf**.......... Kwartalnik Neofilologiczny [*A publication*]
**KNFB**........ Nowata, OK [*FM radio station call letters*]
**KNFM**........ Midland, TX [*FM radio station call letters*]
**KNFO**........ Waco, TX [*FM radio station call letters*]
**KNFT**........ Bayard, NM [*AM radio station call letters*]
**KNFT-FM** ... Bayard, NM [*FM radio station call letters*]
**KNG**.......... Kaimana [*Indonesia*] [*Airport symbol*] (OAG)
**KNG**.......... Kaliningrad [*USSR*] [*Geomagnetic observatory code*]
**KNG**.......... Konigsberg [*Kaliningrad*] [*USSR*] [*Seismograph station code, US Geological Survey*] [*Closed*] (SEIS)
**KNGL**........ McPherson, KS [*AM radio station call letters*]
**KNGM**........ Emporia, KS [*FM radio station call letters*]
**KNGP**........ Corpus Christi/Corpus Christi Naval Air Station [*Texas*] [*ICAO location identifier*] (ICLI)
**KNGS**........ Coalinga, CA [*FM radio station call letters*]
**KNGT**........ Jackson, CA [*FM radio station call letters*]
**KNGU**........ Norfolk/Norfolk Naval Air Station [*Virginia*] [*ICAO location identifier*] (ICLI)
**KNGX**........ Claremore, OK [*FM radio station call letters*]
**KNGYA**..... K'uang Yeh [*A publication*]
**KNGZ**........ Alameda/Alameda Naval Air Station [*California*] [*ICAO location identifier*] (ICLI)
**KNH**.......... Kipuka Nene [*Hawaii*] [*Seismograph station code, US Geological Survey*] (SEIS)
**KNHC**........ Seattle, WA [*FM radio station call letters*]
**KNHK**........ Patuxent River/Patuxent River Naval Air Station [*Maryland*] [*ICAO location identifier*] (ICLI)
**KNHS**........ Torrance, CA [*FM radio station call letters*]
**KNHZ**........ Brunswick/Brunswick Naval Air Station [*Maryland*] [*ICAO location identifier*] (ICLI)
**KNI**.......... Koyna Nagar [*India*] [*Seismograph station code, US Geological Survey*] [*Closed*] (SEIS)
**KNI**.......... Kyodo News International, Inc. [*Information service or system*] (IID)
**KNIA**........ Knoxville, IA [*AM radio station call letters*]
**KNIC**........ Lamar, CO [*FM radio station call letters*]
**Knick**........ Knickerbocker Magazine [*A publication*]
**KNID**........ Enid, OK [*FM radio station call letters*]
**Knight Mech Dict** ... Knight's American Mechanical Dictionary [*A publication*] (DLA)
**Knight's Ind** ... Knight's Industrial Reports [*A publication*] (DLA)
**Knight's Local Govt R** ... Knight's Local Government Reports [*United Kingdom*] [*A publication*]
**Knih Ustred Ustavu Geol** ... Knihovna Ustredniho Ustavu Geologickeho [*A publication*]
**Knih Ustred Ust Geol** ... Knihovna Ustredniho Ustavu Geologickeho [*A publication*]
**KNIK-FM** ... Anchorage, AK [*FM radio station call letters*]
**KNIM**........ Maryville, MO [*AM radio station call letters*]
**KNIM-FM** ... Maryville, MO [*FM radio station call letters*]
**KNIN-FM** ... Wichita Falls, TX [*FM radio station call letters*]

**KNIP**.......... Jacksonville/Jacksonville Naval Air Station [*Florida*] [*ICAO location identifier*] (ICLI)
**KNIQ**......... Mason City, IA [*FM radio station call letters*]
**KNIR**......... Beeville/Chase Field Naval Air Station [*Texas*] [*ICAO location identifier*] (ICLI)
**KNIR**......... New Iberia, LA [*AM radio station call letters*]
**KNIS**.......... Carson City, NV [*FM radio station call letters*]
**KNIT**......... TechKnits, Inc. [*NASDAQ symbol*] (NQ)
**Knit Times** ... Knitting Times [*A publication*]
**Knitting Int** ... Knitting International [*A publication*]
**KNIX-FM** ... Phoenix, AZ [*FM radio station call letters*]
**Knizhnaya Letopis Dopl Vyp** ... Knizhnaya Letopis. Dopolnitel'nyi Vypusk [*A publication*]
**Knizhnaya Letopis Ukazatel Ser Izdanii** ... Knizhnaya Letopis Ukazatel Seriinykh Izdanii [*A publication*]
**Kniznaja Letopis Dopl Vyp** ... Kniznaja Letopis Dopolnitelnyi Vypusk [*A publication*]
**Kniznice Odborn Ved Spisu Vysoke Uceni Tech v Brne** ... Kniznice Odbornych a Vedeckych Spisu Vysokeho Uceni Technickeho v Brne [*A publication*]
**Kniznice Odb Ved Spisu Vys Uceni Tech Brne** ... Kniznice Odbornych a Vedeckych Spisu Vysokeho Uceni Technickeho v Brne [*Czechoslovakia*] [*A publication*]
**Kniznice Odb Ved Spisu Vys Uceni Tech Brne B** ... Kniznice Odbornych a Vedeckych Spisu Vysokeho Uceni Technickeho v Brne. Rada B [*Czechoslovakia*] [*A publication*]
**Kniznice & Ved Inf** ... Kniznice a Vedecke Informacie [*A publication*]
**KNJ**........... Kindamba [*Congo*] [*Airport symbol*] (OAG)
**Knji**............ Knjizevnost [*A publication*]
**KnjiK**.......... Knjizevna Kritika. Casopis za Estetiku Knjizevnosti [*A publication*]
**KnjiNov**...... Knjizevne Novine [*A publication*]
**KnjIst**......... Knjizevna Istorija [*A publication*]
**Knjiz**........... Knjizevnost [*A publication*]
**Knjiz Sigma** ... Knjizica Sigma [*A publication*]
**Knj J**........... Knjizevnost i Jezik [*A publication*]
**KNJK**......... El Centro Naval Air Station [*California*] [*ICAO location identifier*] (ICLI)
**KNJO**........ Thousand Oaks, CA [*FM radio station call letters*]
**KNK**........... Kakhonak [*Alaska*] [*Airport symbol*] (OAG)
**KNK**........... Klondike Air, Inc. [*Anchorage, AK*] [*FAA designator*] (FAAC)
**KNK**........... Knik Glacier [*Alaska*] [*Seismograph station code, US Geological Survey*] (SEIS)
**KNKA**........ Kansas City [*Missouri*] [*ICAO location identifier*] (ICLI)
**KNKC**........ Post, TX [*FM radio station call letters*]
**KNKK**........ Brigham City, UT [*AM radio station call letters*]
**KNKT**........ Cherry Point Marine Corps Air Station [*North Carolina*] [*ICAO location identifier*] (ICLI)
**KNKX**........ Miramar Naval Air Station [*California*] [*ICAO location identifier*] (ICLI)
**KNL**........... Centaur Resources Ltd. [*Vancouver Stock Exchange symbol*]
**KNL**........... Keller, N. L., Washington DC [*STAC*]
**KNL**........... Knight of the Netherlands Lion
**KNLA**........ Karen National Liberation Army [*Burma*] [*Political party*]
**KNLB**........ Lake Havasu City, AZ [*FM radio station call letters*]
**KNLC**........ Hanford/Lemorre Naval Air Station [*California*] [*ICAO location identifier*] (ICLI)
**KNLC**........ St. Louis, MO [*Television station call letters*]
**KNLE-FM** ... Round Rock, TX [*FM radio station call letters*]
**Kn Let**........ Kniznaja Letopis [*A publication*]
**Kn Letopis Dop Vyp** ... Knizhnaya Letopis. Dopolnitel'nyi Vypusk [*USSR*] [*A publication*]
**KNLF**......... Karen National Liberation Front [*Burma*] (PD)
**KNLF**......... Quincy, CA [*FM radio station call letters*]
**Kn LGR**...... Knight's Local Government Reports [*A publication*] (DLA)
**KNLJ**......... Jefferson City, MO [*Television station call letters*]
**KNLR**........ Bend, OR [*FM radio station call letters*]
**KNLS**......... Knolls (MCD)
**KNLT**........ Walla Walla, WA [*FM radio station call letters*]
**KNLU**........ Monroe, LA [*FM radio station call letters*]
**KNLV**........ Ord, NE [*AM radio station call letters*]
**KNLV-FM** ... Ord, NE [*FM radio station call letters*]
**KNM**.......... Keene State College, Keene, NH [*OCLC symbol*] (OCLC)
**KNM**.......... Kenya National Museum
**KNM**.......... Mennonite Historical Society, Newton, KS [*Library symbol*] [*Library of Congress*] (LCLS)
**KNM**.......... Ondernemersvisie [*A publication*]
**KNMB**........ Koninklijke Nederlandse Middenstandsbond [*A publication*]
**KNMC**....... Havre, MT [*FM radio station call letters*]
**KNMC**....... Knutson Mortgage Corporation [*Bloomington, MN*] [*NASDAQ symbol*] (NQ)
**KNME-TV** ... Albuquerque, NM [*Television station call letters*]
**KNMH**...... Coast Guard Station, Washington [*District of Columbia*] [*ICAO location identifier*] (ICLI)
**KNMI**........ Farmington, NM [*FM radio station call letters*]
**KNMO**....... Nevada, MO [*FM radio station call letters*]
**Kn & Moo** .. 3 Knapp's Privy Council Reports [*England*] [*A publication*] (DLA)
**KNMP**....... Koninklijke Nederlandse Maatschappij ter Bevordering der Pharmacie [*Royal Dutch Society for Advancement of Pharmacy*] [*Information service or system*] (IID)
**KNMQ**....... Santa Fe, NM [*FM radio station call letters*]
**KNMX**....... Las Vegas, NM [*AM radio station call letters*]
**KNN**.......... K-Nearest-Neighbor [*Algorithm*]
**KNN**.......... Kenton Natural Resources Corp. [*Vancouver Stock Exchange symbol*]
**KnN**............ Knjizevne Novine [*A publication*]
**KNnB**......... Bethel College, North Newton, KS [*Library symbol*] [*Library of Congress*] (LCLS)
**KNNB**........ Whiteriver, AZ [*FM radio station call letters*]
**KNND**....... Cottage Grove, OR [*AM radio station call letters*]
**KNNG-FM** ... Sterling, CO [*FM radio station call letters*]
**KNNS**........ Grand Rapids, MN [*FM radio station call letters*]
**Kn NSW**..... Knox's New South Wales Reports [*A publication*] (DLA)
**Kn (NSW)** ... Knox's Supreme Court Reports (New South Wales) [*A publication*] (APTA)
**KNNT**........ Kennett, MO [*AM radio station call letters*]
**KNNUDP** ... Koninklijke Nederlandse Natuurhistorische Vereniging. Uitgave [*A publication*]
**KNO**.......... Kano, Nigeria [*Remote site*] [*NASA*] (NASA)
**Kn & O**....... Knapp and Ombler's English Election Cases [*A publication*] (DLA)
**KNO**.......... Knogo Corp. [*NYSE symbol*] (SPSG)
**KNO**.......... Knox Ranch [*California*] [*Seismograph station code, US Geological Survey*] [*Closed*] (SEIS)
**KNO**.......... Korrespondenzblatt der Nachrichtenstelle fuer den Orient [*A publication*] (BJA)
**KNO**.......... Kwartalnik Naucyzciela Opolskiego [*A publication*]
**KNOB**........ Frazier Park, CA [*AM radio station call letters*]
**KNOBF**..... Knobby Lake Mines [*NASDAQ symbol*] (NQ)
**KNOBS**..... Knowledge-Based System
**KNOC**........ Natchitoches, LA [*AM radio station call letters*]
**KNOD**....... Harlan, IA [*FM radio station call letters*]
**KNOE**........ Monroe, LA [*AM radio station call letters*]
**KNOE-FM** ... Monroe, LA [*FM radio station call letters*]
**KNOE-TV** ... Monroe, LA [*Television station call letters*]
**KNOF**........ St. Paul, MN [*FM radio station call letters*]
**KNOK**........ Belle Chasse, LA [*FM radio station call letters*]
**KNOM**...... Nome, AK [*AM radio station call letters*]
**Kn & Omb** ... Knapp and Ombler's English Election Cases [*A publication*] (DLA)
**KNON**....... Dallas, TX [*FM radio station call letters*]
**KNOP-TV** ... North Platte, NE [*Television station call letters*]
**KNOR**........ Klamath Northern Railway Co. [*AAR code*]
**KNOR**........ Norman, OK [*AM radio station call letters*]
**K Nor Vidensk Selsk Foerhandl** ... Kongelige Norske Videnskabers Selskab. Foerhandlinger [*A publication*]
**K Nor Vidensk Selsk Forh** ... Kongelige Norske Videnskabers Selskab. Foerhandlinger [*A publication*]
**K Nor Vidensk Selsk Mus Bot Avd Rapp** ... Kongelige Norske Videnskabers Selskab Museet. Botanisk Avdeling Rapport [*A publication*]
**K Nor Vidensk Selsk Mus Misc** ... Kongelige Norske Videnskabers Selskab. Museet. Miscellanea [*A publication*]
**K Nor Vidensk Selsk Skr** ... Kongelige Norske Videnskabers Selskab. Skrifter [*A publication*]
**KNOS**........ Marshall, MO [*FM radio station call letters*]
**KNoSH**...... Norton State Hospital, Norton, KS [*Library symbol*] [*Library of Congress*] (LCLS)
**KNOT**........ Prescott, AZ [*AM radio station call letters*]
**KNOT-FM** ... Prescott, AZ [*FM radio station call letters*]
**Know**.......... Knowledge [*Record label*]
**KNOW**....... KnowledgeWare Inc. [*NASDAQ symbol*] (NQ)
**KNOW**....... Minneapolis, MN [*AM radio station call letters*]
**KNOW**....... Port Angeles Coast Guard Air Station [*Washington*] [*ICAO location identifier*] (ICLI)
**Knowl**......... Knowledge [*A publication*]
**Knowledge Practice Math** ... Knowledge and Practice of Mathematics [*A publication*]
**Knowles**...... Knowles' Reports [*3 Rhode Island*] [*A publication*] (DLA)
**KNOWLT** ... Knowlton [*England*]
**KNOX**........ Grand Forks, ND [*AM radio station call letters*]
**Knox**........... Knox's New South Wales Reports [*A publication*] (DLA)
**Knox & F**.... Knox and Fitzhardinge's New South Wales Reports [*A publication*] (DLA)
**Knox & Fitz** ... Knox and Fitzhardinge's Reports [*New South Wales*] [*A publication*] (APTA)
**KNOX-FM** ... Grand Forks, ND [*FM radio station call letters*]
**Knox (NSW)** ... Knox's Supreme Court Reports (New South Wales) [*A publication*] (APTA)
**KNP**........... Katholieke Nationale Partij [*Catholic National Party*] [*Netherlands*] [*Political party*] (PPE)
**KNP**........... Katholisk Nederlands Persbureau [*Catholic Netherlands Press Agency*] [*Netherlands*]
**KNP**........... Korea National Party [*Republic of Korea*] [*Political party*] (PPW)
**KNP**........... Koshkonong Nuclear Plant (NRCH)
**KNPA**........ Pensacola/Pensacola Naval Air Station [*Florida*] [*ICAO location identifier*] (ICLI)
**KNPB**........ Reno, NV [*Television station call letters*]
**Kn PC**......... Knapp's Privy Council Appeal Cases [*1829-36*] [*England*] [*A publication*] (DLA)

**KNPC** ........ Kuwait National Petroleum Company
**KNPI**.......... Kundu's Neurotic Personality Inventory [*Psychology*]
**KNPJB** ...... Konepajamies [*A publication*]
**KNPP**......... Kewaunee Nuclear Power Plant (NRCH)
**KNPR** ........ Las Vegas, NV [*FM radio station call letters*]
**KNPT** ........ Newport, OR [*AM radio station call letters*]
**KNQ**.......... Kone [*New Caledonia*] [*Airport symbol*] [*Obsolete*] (OAG)
**KNQI** ......... Kingsville Naval Air Station [*Texas*] [*ICAO location identifier*] (ICLI)
**KNQX**........ Key West/Key West Naval Air Station [*Florida*] [*ICAO location identifier*] (ICLI)
**KNR**........... King's National Roll
**KNR**........... Koninklijke Nederlandsche Reedersvereeniging [*A publication*]
**KNR**........... Korean National Railroad (DCTA)
**KNRB** ........ Fort Worth, TX [*AM radio station call letters*]
**KNRB** ........ Mayport/Mayport Naval Station [*Florida*] [*ICAO location identifier*] (ICLI)
**KNRJ**......... Houston, TX [*FM radio station call letters*]
**KNRL** ........ Knurl [*Engineering*]
**KNRR**........ Pembina, ND [*Television station call letters*]
**KNRY** ........ Monterey, CA [*AM radio station call letters*]
**KNS** ........... Kazan [*Formerly, Kazanskaya*] [*USSR*] [*Geomagnetic observatory code*]
**KNS** ........... King Island [*Tasmania*] [*Airport symbol*] (OAG)
**KNS** ........... Knight of [*the Order of*] the Royal Northern Star [*Sweden*]
**KNSA** ........ Unalakleet, AK [*AM radio station call letters*]
**KNSD** ........ San Diego, CA [*Television station call letters*]
**KNSE**......... Ontario, CA [*AM radio station call letters*]
**KNSF**......... Washington Naval Air Facility [*District of Columbia*] [*ICAO location identifier*] (ICLI)
**KNSFA2**.... Kongelige Norske Videnskabers Selskab. Foerhandlinger [*A publication*]
**KNSI**.......... San Nicolas Island/San Nicolas Auxiliary Air Base [*California*] [*ICAO location identifier*] (ICLI)
**KNSJA** ...... Journal. Korean Nuclear Society [*A publication*]
**KNSM** ....... Koninklijke Nederlandsche Stoomboot Maatschappij [*A publication*]
**KNSN** ........ Walla Walla, WA [*FM radio station call letters*]
**KNSP**......... Staples, MN [*AM radio station call letters*]
**KNSP-FM** ... Staples, MN [*FM radio station call letters*]
**KNSR** ........ Collegeville, MN [*FM radio station call letters*]
**KNST**......... Tucson, AZ [*AM radio station call letters*]
**KNSU** ........ Thibodaux, LA [*FM radio station call letters*]
**KNSW** ....... Knife Switch
**KNSX** ........ Steelville, MO [*FM radio station call letters*]
**KNT**........... Kent Electronics Corp. [*NYSE symbol*] (SPSG)
**KNT**........... Knight [*British title*]
**KNTA** ........ Santa Clara, CA [*AM radio station call letters*]
**KNTB** ........ Los Alamitos/Los Alamitos Naval Air Station [*California*] [*ICAO location identifier*] (ICLI)
**KNTD**........ Point Mugu Naval Air Station [*California*] [*ICAO location identifier*] (ICLI)
**KNTF**......... Ontario, CA [*FM radio station call letters*]
**KNTI** ......... Lakeport, CA [*FM radio station call letters*]
**KNTO**........ Livingston, CA [*FM radio station call letters*]
**KNTR** ........ Ferndale, WA [*AM radio station call letters*]
**KNTS**......... Abilene, TX [*AM radio station call letters*]
**KNTU**........ Denton, TX [*FM radio station call letters*]
**KNTU**........ Virginia Beach/Oceana Naval Air Station [*Virginia*] [*ICAO location identifier*] (ICLI)
**KNTV** ........ San Jose, CA [*Television station call letters*]
**KNTX-FM** ... Norton, KS [*FM radio station call letters*]
**KNU**........... Kanpur [*India*] [*Airport symbol*] (OAG)
**KNU**........... Karen National Union [*Burma*] (PD)
**KNU**........... Knuckle [*Automotive engineering*]
**KNUA**........ Bremerton, WA [*FM radio station call letters*]
**KNUE**........ Tyler, TX [*FM radio station call letters*]
**KNUFNS**... Kampuchean National United Front for National Salvation (PD)
**KNUI**......... Kahului, HI [*AM radio station call letters*]
**KNUJ** ........ New Ulm, MN [*AM radio station call letters*]
**KNUP**........ Karen National Unity Party [*Burma*]
**KNUQ** ....... Mountain View/Moffett Naval Air Station [*California*] [*ICAO location identifier*] (ICLI)
**KNUU** ....... Paradise, NV [*AM radio station call letters*]
**KNUW**....... Whidbey Island/Whidbey Island Naval Air Station [*Washington*] [*ICAO location identifier*] (ICLI)
**KNUZ**........ Houston, TX [*AM radio station call letters*]
**KNVO**........ McAllen, TX [*Television station call letters*]
**KNVR**........ Paradise-Chico, CA [*FM radio station call letters*]
**KNVS** ........ Kongelige Norske Videnskabers Selskab [*A publication*]
**KNW**.......... Konawaena [*Hawaii*] [*Seismograph station code, US Geological Survey*] [*Closed*] (SEIS)
**KNW**.......... New Stuyahok [*Alaska*] [*Airport symbol*] (OAG)
**KNWA**....... Bellefonte, AR [*AM radio station call letters*]
**KNWAA**.... Koninklijke Nederlandse Akademie van Wetenschappen. Proceedings. Series A. Mathematical Sciences [*A publication*]
**KNWBA**.... Proceedings. Koninklijke Nederlandse Akademie van Wetenschappen. Series B. Physical Sciences [*A publication*]
**KNWC**....... Sioux Falls, SD [*AM radio station call letters*]
**KNWCA**.... Koninklijke Nederlandse Akademie van Wetenschappen. Proceedings. Series C. Biological and Medical Sciences [*A publication*]
**KNWC-FM** ... Sioux Falls, SD [*FM radio station call letters*]
**KNWD**....... Natchitoches, LA [*FM radio station call letters*]
**KNWR**....... Bellingham, WA [*FM radio station call letters*]
**KNWS** ....... Waterloo, IA [*AM radio station call letters*]
**KNWS-FM** ... Waterloo, IA [*FM radio station call letters*]
**KNWZ**....... Thousand Palms, CA [*AM radio station call letters*]
**KNX**.......... Kununurra [*Australia*] [*Airport symbol*] (OAG)
**KNX**.......... Los Angeles, CA [*AM radio station call letters*]
**KNXN**....... Quincy, CA [*FM radio station call letters*]
**KNXR**....... Rochester, MN [*FM radio station call letters*]
**KNXT** ....... Visalia, CA [*Television station call letters*]
**KNXV-TV** ... Phoenix, AZ [*Television station call letters*]
**KNXX**........ Willow Grove/Willow Grove Naval Air Station [*Pennsylvania*] [*ICAO location identifier*] (ICLI)
**KNY**........... Kanoya [*Japan*] [*Geomagnetic observatory code*]
**KNY**........... Kearney National, Inc. [*AMEX symbol*] (SPSG)
**KNY**........... Kenergy Resource Corp. [*Vancouver Stock Exchange symbol*]
**KNYC**........ New York (City) [*New York*] [*ICAO location identifier*] (ICLI)
**KNYD**........ Broken Arrow, OK [*FM radio station call letters*]
**KNYL**........ Yuma/Vincent Marine Corps Air Station [*Arizona*] [*ICAO location identifier*] (ICLI)
**KNYN**........ Santa Fe, NM [*FM radio station call letters*]
**KNYO**........ Independence, CA [*AM radio station call letters*]
**KNZ**........... Kanozan [*Japan*] [*Geomagnetic observatory code*]
**KNZ**........... Kenieba [*Mali*] [*Airport symbol*] (OAG)
**KNZA** ........ Hiawatha, KS [*FM radio station call letters*]
**KNZJ**......... El Toro Marine Corps Air Station [*California*] [*ICAO location identifier*] (ICLI)
**KNZS**......... Montecito, CA [*AM radio station call letters*]
**KNZW** ....... South Weymouth/South Weymouth Naval Air Station [*Massachusetts*] [*ICAO location identifier*] (ICLI)
**KNZY** ........ San Diego/North Island Naval Air Station [*California*] [*ICAO location identifier*] (ICLI)
**KO**.............. Aerolineas Colonia SA [*Uruguay*] [*ICAO designator*] (FAAC)
**Ko**.............. C. H. Boehringer Sohn, Ingelheim [*Germany*] [*Research code symbol*]
**KO**.............. [*The*] Coca-Cola Co. [*NYSE symbol*] (SPSG)
**KO**.............. Commanding Officer [*Military slang*]
**KO**.............. Contracting Officer [*Also, CO, CONTRO*]
**KO**.............. Kashrut Observance (BJA)
**KO**.............. Kattoo [*Ship's rigging*] (ROG)
**KO**.............. Keep Off [*i.e., avoid assuming the risk on an application, pending further investigation*] [*Insurance*]
**K/O**............ Keep Open [*Medicine*]
**KO**.............. Kickoff (MSA)
**KO**.............. Kilogram (ROG)
**KO**.............. King's Own [*Military unit*] [*British*]
**K i O**.......... Kirche im Osten [*A publication*]
**KO**.............. Klystron Oscillator
**K & O**......... Knapp and Ombler's English Election Cases [*A publication*] (DLA)
**KO**.............. Knee Orthosis [*Medicine*]
**KO**.............. Knockout [*Partly cut out or loosened area which can be easily removed, as in a junction box*] [*Technical drawings*]
**KO**.............. Knockout [*Boxing*]
**KO**.............. Kodiak-Western Alaska Airlines, Inc. [*CAB official abbreviation*]
**KO**.............. Kolloidnyi Zhurnal [*A publication*]
**Ko**.............. Kompanjie [*Company*] [*Afrikaans*]
**KO**.............. Kongo-Overzee. Tijdschrift voor en Over Belgisch-Kongo en Andere Overzeese Gewesten [*A publication*]
**KO**.............. Konkursordnung [*Bankruptcy*] [*German*] (ILCA)
**ko** .............. Korea, South [*MARC country of publication code*] [*Library of Congress*] (LCCP)
**Ko**.............. Kovcezic [*A publication*]
**KO**.............. Kraus-Thomson Organization [*Publisher*]
**KO**.............. Kunst des Orients [*A publication*]
**KO**.............. Opposite of OK [*Slang*] [*German*]
**KO's**........... Knockout Drops [*A drug producing unconsciousness*] [*Slang*]
**KOA**........... Communications on Alternatives in Education [*Defunct*] (EA)
**KOA**........... Denver, CO [*AM radio station call letters*]
**KOA**........... Kailua-Kona, HI [*Location identifier*] [*FAA*] (FAAL)
**KOA**........... Kampground Owners Association [*Phoenix, AZ*] (EA)
**KOA**........... Kampgrounds of America
**KOA**........... Karate and Oriental Arts [*A publication*]
**KOA**........... Knocked-on-Atom
**KOA**........... Koala Technologies [*AMEX symbol*] (SPSG)
**KOA**........... Kobuan [*Solomon Islands*] [*Seismograph station code, US Geological Survey*] [*Closed*] (SEIS)
**KOA**........... Kona [*Hawaii*] [*Airport symbol*] (OAG)
**koa** ............ Kontant op Aflewering [*Cash on Delivery*] [*Business term*] [*Afrikaans*]
**KOAA-TV** ... Pueblo, CO [*Television station call letters*]
**KOAB-FM** ... Bend, OR [*FM radio station call letters*]
**KOAB-TV** ... Bend, OR [*Television station call letters*]
**KOAC**........ Corvallis, OR [*AM radio station call letters*]
**KOAC-TV** ... Corvallis, OR [*Television station call letters*]

**KOAI**......... Denton, TX [*FM radio station call letters*]
**KOAK**........ Oakland/Metropolitan Oakland International [*California*] [*ICAO location identifier*] (ICLI)
**KOAK**........ Red Oak, IA [*AM radio station call letters*]
**KOAK-FM** ... Red Oak, IA [*FM radio station call letters*]
**KOAL**........ Price, UT [*AM radio station call letters*]
**KOAM-TV** ... Pittsburg, KS [*Television station call letters*]
**KOAOA**..... Klinika Oczna [*A publication*]
**KOAQ**........ Terrytown, NE [*AM radio station call letters*]
**KOARER**... Korean Arachnology [*A publication*]
**KOAS**........ Kealakekua, HI [*FM radio station call letters*]
**KOAT-TV** ... Albuquerque, NM [*Television station call letters*]
**KOAX**........ Mason, TX [*FM radio station call letters*]
**KOB**........... King's Own Borderers [*British military*] (DMA)
**KOB**........... Kobe [*Japan*] [*Seismograph station code, US Geological Survey*] (SEIS)
**KoB**........... Koehler and Baumgartner Lexikon in Veteris Testamenti Libros [*Leiden*] [*A publication*] (BJA)
**KOB**........... Koutaba [*Cameroon*] [*Airport symbol*] (OAG)
**KOB**........... Kriegsoffizier-Bewerber [*Applicant for Wartime Commission*] [*German military - World War II*]
**KOBC**........ Joplin, MO [*FM radio station call letters*]
**KOBE**........ Las Cruces, NM [*AM radio station call letters*]
**Kobe Econ Bus R** ... Kobe Economic and Business Review [*A publication*]
**Kobe J Med Sci** ... Kobe Journal of Medical Sciences [*A publication*]
**Kobe Kogyo Tech Rep** ... Kobe Kogyo Technical Report [*Japan*] [*A publication*]
**Kobelco Tech Bull** ... Kobelco Technical Bulletin [*A publication*]
**Kobe Res Dev** ... Kobe Research Development [*A publication*]
**Kobe Steel Rep** ... Kobe Steel Report [*A publication*]
**Kobe U Econ R** ... Kobe University. Economic Review [*A publication*]
**Kobe U Law R** ... Kobe University. Law Review [*A publication*]
**Kobe UL Rev** ... Kobe University. Law Review [*A publication*] (DLA)
**Kobe Univ Econ R** ... Kobe University. Economic Review [*A publication*]
**Kobe Univ Law R** ... Kobe University. Law Review [*A publication*]
**Kobe Univ L Rev** ... Kobe University. Law Review [*A publication*]
**KOBF**........ Farmington, NM [*Television station call letters*]
**KOBG**........ Wasilla, AK [*AM radio station call letters*]
**KOBH-FM** ... Hot Springs, SD [*FM radio station call letters*]
**KOBI**......... Medford, OR [*Television station call letters*]
**Ko Bl A f A** ... Korrespondenzblaetter des Archivs fuer Anthropologie und Urgeschichte [*A publication*]
**Ko Bl DAG** ... Korrespondenzblatt der Deutschen Anthropologischen Gesellschaft [*A publication*]
**Ko Bl VSL** ... Korrespondenzblatt des Vereins fuer Siebenbuergische Landeskunde [*A publication*]
**KOBO**........ Yuba City, CA [*AM radio station call letters*]
**KOBOL**..... Keystation On-Line Business-Oriented Language [*Data processing*]
**KOBPDP**... Klucze do Oznaczania Bezkregowcow Polski [*A publication*]
**KOBR**........ Roswell, NM [*Television station call letters*]
**KOB-TV**.... Albuquerque, NM [*Television station call letters*]
**Kobunshi Ronbun** ... Kobunshi Ronbunshu [*A publication*]
**Kobunsh Ron** ... Kobunshi Ronbunshu [*A publication*]
**KOC**........... Kathodal Opening Contraction [*Medicine*]
**KOC**........... Knight of the [*Order of the*] Oak Crown
**KOC**........... Kochi [*Japan*] [*Seismograph station code, US Geological Survey*] (SEIS)
**KOC**........... Koumac [*New Caledonia*] [*Airport symbol*] (OAG)
**KOC**........... Kuwait Oil Company
**KOC**........... Occupational and Environmental Health Unit, University of Toronto [*UTLAS symbol*]
**KOC**........... TCC Beverages Ltd. [*Toronto Stock Exchange symbol*]
**KOCC**........ Oklahoma City, OK [*FM radio station call letters*]
**KOCCCG**.. Kunia Operations Control Center Coordination Group (CINC)
**KOCE-TV** ... Huntington Beach, CA [*Television station call letters*]
**Koch**........... Koch's Supreme Court Decisions [*Ceylon*] [*A publication*] (DLA)
**KOCM**....... Newport Beach, CA [*FM radio station call letters*]
**KOCMA**.... Koroze a Ochrana Materialu [*A publication*]
**KOCN**........ Pacific Grove, CA [*FM radio station call letters*]
**KOCO**........ Korea Oil Corporation
**KOCO-TV** ... Oklahoma City, OK [*Television station call letters*]
**KOCR**........ Cedar Rapids, IA [*Television station call letters*]
**KOCTY**...... Smoke over City [*Aviation*] (FAAC)
**KOCV**........ Odessa, TX [*FM radio station call letters*]
**KOCV-TV** ... Odessa, TX [*Television station call letters*]
**KOD**........... Kodaikanal [*India*] [*Geomagnetic observatory code*]
**KOD**........... Kodaikanal [*India*] [*Seismograph station code, US Geological Survey*] (SEIS)
**KODA**........ Houston, TX [*FM radio station call letters*]
**Kodaikanal Obs Bull A** ... Kodaikanal Observatory Bulletin. Series A [*A publication*]
**Kodaikanal Obs Bull B** ... Kodaikanal Observatory Bulletin. Series B [*A publication*]
**Kodaikanal Obs Bull Ser A** ... Kodaikanal Observatory Bulletin. Series A [*India*] [*A publication*]
**Kodai Math J** ... Kodai Mathematical Journal [*A publication*]
**Kodai Math Sem Rep** ... Kodai Mathematical Seminar Reports [*A publication*]
**Kodak Data Book of Applied Phot** ... Kodak Data Book of Applied Photography [*A publication*]
**Kodak Internat Fotogr** ... Kodak International Fotografie [*A publication*]
**Kodak Publ G 47** ... Kodak Publication. G-47 [*A publication*]
**Kodak Publ G 49** ... Kodak Publication. G-49 [*A publication*]
**Kodak Publ G 102** ... Kodak Publication. G-102 [*A publication*]
**Kodak Res Lab Mon Abstr Bull** ... Kodak Research Laboratories. Monthly Abstract Bulletin [*A publication*]
**KODCO**..... Korean Overseas Development Company [*Korean government agency*]
**KODE-TV** ... Joplin, MO [*Television station call letters*]
**KODI**......... Cody, WY [*AM radio station call letters*]
**KODJ**........ Los Angeles, CA [*FM radio station call letters*]
**KODK**........ Kingsville, TX [*FM radio station call letters*]
**KODL**........ The Dalles, OR [*AM radio station call letters*]
**KODM**....... Odessa, TX [*FM radio station call letters*]
**KODR**........ King's Overseas Dominions Regiment [*British military*] (DMA)
**KODS**........ Carnelian Bay, CA [*FM radio station call letters*]
**KODY**........ North Platte, NE [*AM radio station call letters*]
**KOE**........... Kilograms Oil Equivalent [*Petroleum industry*]
**kOe**........... Kilooersted
**KOE**........... Koppel [*Federal Republic of Germany*] [*Seismograph station code, US Geological Survey*] (SEIS)
**KOE**........... Kupang [*Indonesia*] [*Airport symbol*] (OAG)
**KOEA**........ Doniphan, MO [*FM radio station call letters*]
**Koe D Bl**..... Koelner Domblatt [*A publication*]
**Koedoe Monogr** ... Koedoe Monograph [*A publication*]
**KOED-TV** ... Tulsa, OK [*Television station call letters*]
**Koe Geogr Arb** ... Koelner Geographische Arbeiten [*A publication*]
**K d Oe L**..... Kritik des Oeffentlichen Lebens [*A publication*]
**KOEL**........ Oelwein, IA [*AM radio station call letters*]
**KOEL-FM** ... Oelwein, IA [*FM radio station call letters*]
**Koeln**.......... Koeln. Vierteljahreschrift fuer Freunde der Stadt [*A publication*]
**Koeln Dombl** ... Koelner Domblatt [*A publication*]
**Koelner Z** ... Koelner Zeitschrift fuer Soziologie und Sozial-Psychologie [*A publication*]
**Koelner Z Soz** ... Koelner Zeitschrift fuer Soziologie und Sozial-Psychologie [*A publication*]
**Koelner Z Soziol u Soz-Psychol** ... Koelner Zeitschrift fuer Soziologie und Sozial-Psychologie [*A publication*]
**Koeln Geogr Arb** ... Koelner Geographische Arbeiten [*A publication*]
**Koeln Geol H** ... Koelner Geologische Hefte [*A publication*]
**Koeln JB V Frueh Gesch** ... Koelner Jahrbuch fuer Vor- und Fruehgeschichte [*A publication*]
**KOEN**........ Koenig, Inc. [*NASDAQ symbol*] (NQ)
**KOERA**..... Kolorisztikai Ertesito [*A publication*]
**Koerp St G** ... Koerperschaftssteuergesetz [*A publication*]
**KOES**......... Hamilton, TX [*AM radio station call letters*]
**KOET**........ Eufaula, OK [*Television station call letters*]
**Koe T**......... Koelner Tageblatt [*A publication*]
**KOEX**........ Oklahoma City [*Oklahoma*] [*ICAO location identifier*] (ICLI)
**KOEZ**........ Newton, KS [*FM radio station call letters*]
**Koezgazd Szle** ... Koezgazdasagi Szemle [*A publication*]
**Koezlekedes Tud Sz** ... Koezlekedes Tudomanyi Szemle [*A publication*]
**Koezlemenyek-MTA Szamitastechn Automat Kutato Int (Budapest)** ... Koezlemenyek-MTA Szamitastechnikai es Automatizalasi Kutato Intezet (Budapest) [*A publication*]
**Koezl Magy Tud Akad Musz Fiz Kut Intez** ... Koezlemenyei Magyar Tudomanyos Akademia Muszaki Fizikai Kutato Intezetenek [*A publication*]
**Koezl-MTA Szamitastech Automat Kutato Int (Budapest)** ... Koezlemenyek-MTA Szamitastechnikai es Automatizalasi Kutato Intezet (Budapest) [*A publication*]
**Koezn**......... Koezneveles [*A publication*]
**Koe Z Soz Soz Psych** ... Koelner Zeitschrift fuer Soziologie und Sozial-Psychologie [*A publication*]
**KOF**........... Knitted Outerwear Foundation (EA)
**KOF**........... Kofu [*Japan*] [*Seismograph station code, US Geological Survey*] (SEIS)
**KOF**........... Kultur og Folkeminder [*A publication*]
**KOFC**........ Fayetteville, AR [*AM radio station call letters*]
**KOFE**......... St. Maries, ID [*AM radio station call letters*]
**KOFF**......... Offutt Air Force Base, Omaha [*Nebraska*] [*ICAO location identifier*] (ICLI)
**KOFI**.......... Kalispell, MT [*AM radio station call letters*]
**KOFI-FM** ... Kalispell, MT [*FM radio station call letters*]
**KOFK**........ Milan, NM [*AM radio station call letters*]
**KOFM**........ Enid, OK [*FM radio station call letters*]
**KOFO**........ Ottawa, KS [*AM radio station call letters*]
**KOFS**......... Key Officers of Foreign Service Posts [*A publication*]
**KOFX**........ El Paso, TX [*FM radio station call letters*]
**KOFY**........ San Mateo, CA [*AM radio station call letters*]
**KOFY-FM** ... San Francisco, CA [*FM radio station call letters*]
**KOFY-TV** ... San Francisco, CA [*Television station call letters*]
**KO & G**...... Kansas, Oklahoma & Gulf Railway Co.
**KOG**........... Kansas, Oklahoma & Gulf Railway Co. [*AAR code*]
**KOG**........... Kindly Old Gentleman [*Slang*]
**KOG**........... Koger Properties, Inc. [*NYSE symbol*] (SPSG)
**KOGA**........ Ogallala, NE [*AM radio station call letters*]

**KOGAA**..... Koatsu Gasu [*A publication*]
**KOGA-FM**... Ogallala, NE [*FM radio station call letters*]
**KOGG**........ Wailuku, HI [*Television station call letters*]
**KOGJA**...... Kogyo Gijutsu [*A publication*]
**KOGM**....... Opelousas, LA [*FM radio station call letters*]
**KOGO**....... Ventura, CA [*AM radio station call letters*]
**KOGS**........ Ogdensburg [*New York*] [*ICAO location identifier*] (ICLI)
**KOGT**........ Orange, TX [*AM radio station call letters*]
**KOH**.......... King's Own Hussars [*British military*] (DMA)
**KOH**.......... Kohala [*Hawaii*] [*Seismograph station code, US Geological Survey*] (SEIS)
**Koh**............ Kohelet (BJA)
**KOH**.......... Konjunkturpolitik. Zeitschrift fuer Angewandte Konjunkturforschung. Beihefte [*A publication*]
**KOH**.......... Koolatah [*Australia*] [*Airport symbol*] [*Obsolete*] (OAG)
**KOH**.......... Reno, NV [*AM radio station call letters*]
**Kohasz Lapok**... Kohaszati Lapok [*Hungary*] [*A publication*]
**KOHED**..... Kohle und Heizoel [*A publication*]
**KOHEPFC**... King of Our Hearts Elvis Presley Fan Club (EA)
**KOHI**......... St. Helens, OR [*AM radio station call letters*]
**KOHL**........ Fremont, CA [*FM radio station call letters*]
**KOHM**...... Kilohm (MCD)
**KOHM**...... Lubbock, TX [*FM radio station call letters*]
**KOHO**....... Honolulu, HI [*AM radio station call letters*]
**KohR**.......... Kohelet Rabbah (BJA)
**KOHS**........ Orem, UT [*FM radio station call letters*]
**K'o Hsueh T'Ung PAO (Foreign Lang Ed)**... K'o Hsueh T'Ung PAO (Foreign Language Edition) [*A publication*]
**KOHU**....... Hermiston, OR [*AM radio station call letters*]
**KOHZ**........ Billings, MT [*FM radio station call letters*]
**KOI**............ Kennedy Operating Instructions [*NASA*] (KSC)
**KOI**............ Kirkwall [*Orkney Islands*] [*Airport symbol*] (OAG)
**KOI**............ KSC [*Kennedy Space Center*] Operation Instruction [*NASA*] (NASA)
**KOI**............ Ontario Institute for Studies in Education Library [*UTLAS symbol*]
**KOIA-TV**.. Ottumwa, IA [*Television station call letters*]
**KOIL**......... Kelley Oil Corp. [*NASDAQ symbol*] (NQ)
**KOIL**......... Omaha, NE [*AM radio station call letters*]
**Koinonike Epitheor**... Koinonike Epitheoresis [*A publication*]
**KOIN-TV**.. Portland, OR [*Television station call letters*]
**KOIR**......... Edinburg, TX [*FM radio station call letters*]
**KOIS**.......... Kuder Occupational Interest Survey [*Aptitude and skills test*]
**KOISA**....... Kosmicheskie Issledovaniya [*A publication*]
**KOIT**......... San Francisco, CA [*AM radio station call letters*]
**KOIT-FM**... San Francisco, CA [*FM radio station call letters*]
**KOJ**........... Kagoshima [*Japan*] [*Airport symbol*] (OAG)
**KOJ**........... Keen on the Job (ADA)
**KOJ**........... Konjunkturpolitik. Zeitschrift fuer Angewandte Konjunkturforschung [*A publication*]
**KoJ**............ Korea Journal [*A publication*]
**KOJAA**...... Konkurito Janaru [*A publication*]
**KOJC**......... Cedar Rapids, IA [*FM radio station call letters*]
**Ko Jis**......... Kostnicke Jiskry [*A publication*]
**KOJM**........ Havre, MT [*AM radio station call letters*]
**KOJUA**..... Kokyu To Junkan [*A publication*]
**KOJY**......... Dinuba, CA [*FM radio station call letters*]
**KOK**.......... Horizon Air Service [*Honolulu, HI*] [*FAA designator*] (FAAC)
**KOK**.......... Kansallinen Kokoomus [*National Coalition Party*] [*Finland*] [*Political party*] (EAIO)
**KOK**.......... Keukenkompas. Vakblad voor Inbouwkeukens, Inbouwapparatuur, en Accessoires [*A publication*]
**KoK**........... Kirke og Kultur [*A publication*]
**KOK**.......... Kokkola [*Finland*] [*Airport symbol*] (OAG)
**kok**............ Konkani [*MARC language code*] [*Library of Congress*] (LCCP)
**KOKA**........ Shreveport, LA [*AM radio station call letters*]
**KOKAA**..... Kobunshi Kagaku [*A publication*]
**KOKAB**..... Kobunshi Kako [*A publication*]
**Kokalos**...... Kokalos Studi Pubblicati. Istituto di Storia Antica. Universita di Palermo [*A publication*]
**KOKB**........ Blackwell, OK [*AM radio station call letters*]
**KOKC**........ Guthrie, OK [*AM radio station call letters*]
**KOKC**........ Oklahoma City/Will Rogers World [*Oklahoma*] [*ICAO location identifier*] (ICLI)
**KOKE**........ Rollingwood, TX [*AM radio station call letters*]
**Kokeishu**.... Koto Saibansho Keiji Hanreishu [*A publication*]
**KOKF**........ Edmond, OK [*FM radio station call letters*]
**Kok Gak Zas**... Kokka Gakkai Zassi [*Journal. Association of Political and Social Science*] [*A publication*]
**KOKH-TV**... Oklahoma City, OK [*Television station call letters*]
**KOKI-TV**... Tulsa, OK [*Television station call letters*]
**KOKK**........ Huron, SD [*AM radio station call letters*]
**KOKKA**..... Koks i Khimiya [*A publication*]
**KOKL**........ Okmulgee, OK [*AM radio station call letters*]
**KOKL-FM**... Okmulgee, OK [*FM radio station call letters*]
**KOKN**........ Hobbs, NM [*FM radio station call letters*]
**KOKO**........ Warrensburg, MO [*AM radio station call letters*]
**KOKR**........ Newport, AR [*FM radio station call letters*]
**KOKS**........ Poplar Bluff, MO [*FM radio station call letters*]
**Koks Khim**... Koks i Khimiya [*USSR*] [*A publication*]
**KOKU**........ Agana, GU [*FM radio station call letters*]
**KOKX**........ Keokuk, IA [*AM radio station call letters*]
**KOKX-FM**... Keokuk, IA [*FM radio station call letters*]
**KOKY**........ Jacksonville, AR [*AM radio station call letters*]
**KOKZ**........ Waterloo, IA [*FM radio station call letters*]
**KOL**........... King's College, Wilkes-Barre, PA [*OCLC symbol*] (OCLC)
**KOL**........... Knights of Lithuania (EA)
**KOL**........... Kollmorgen Corp. [*NYSE symbol*] (SPSG)
**KOL**........... Kollsman [*See also K*] [*Aviation*] (FAAC)
**KOl**............ Olathe Public Library, Olathe, KS [*Library symbol*] [*Library of Congress*] (LCLS)
**KOLA**........ San Bernardino, CA [*FM radio station call letters*]
**Kolch Proizv**... Kolchoznoe Proizvodstvo [*A publication*]
**KOLD-TV**... Tucson, AZ [*Television station call letters*]
**KOLE**........ Port Arthur, TX [*AM radio station call letters*]
**Koleopterol Rundsch**... Koleopterologische Rundschau [*A publication*]
**KOLF**......... Kolff Medical, Inc. [*NASDAQ symbol*] (NQ)
**KOlH**......... Olathe Commumity Hospital, Olathe, KS [*Library symbol*] [*Library of Congress*] (LCLS)
**Kolhospnyk Ukr**... Kolhospnyk Ukrainy [*A publication*]
**KOLI**......... King's Own Light Infantry [*Military unit*] [*British*]
**KOlJL**........ Johnson County Law Library, Olathe, KS [*Library symbol*] [*Library of Congress*] (LCLS)
**Kolkhozno-Sovkhoznoe Proizod Turkm**... Kolkhozno-Sovkhoznoe Proizvodstvo Turkmenistana [*A publication*]
**Kolkhoz Proizvod**... Kolkhoznoe Proizvodstvo [*A publication*]
**Kolkhoz-Sovkhoz Proizvod**... Kolkhozno-Sovkhoznoe Proizvodstvo [*A publication*]
**Kolkhoz-Sovkhoz Proizvod Kirgizii**... Kolkhozno-Sovkhoznoe Proizvodstvo Kirgizii [*A publication*]
**Kolkhoz-Sovkhoz Proizvod Mold**... Kolkhozno-Sovkhoznoe Proizvodstvo Moldavil [*A publication*]
**Kolkhoz-Sovkhoz Proizvod RSFSR**... Kolkhozno-Sovkhoznoe Proizvodstvo RSFSR [*A publication*]
**KOLL**......... Pine Bluff, AR [*FM radio station call letters*]
**Koll Azerb**... Kollektsioner Azerbaidzhana [*A publication*]
**Koll Bl Neuburg**... Neuburger Kollektaneenblatt [*A publication*]
**Kolloidnyi Zh**... Kolloidnyi Zhurnal [*A publication*]
**Kolloid-Z**.... Kolloid-Zeitschrift [*West Germany*] [*A publication*]
**Kolloid-Z**.... Kolloid-Zeitschrift und Zeitschrift fuer Polymere [*A publication*]
**Kolloid Zh**... Kolloidnyi Zhurnal [*A publication*]
**Kolloid-Z & Z Polym**... Kolloid-Zeitschrift und Zeitschrift fuer Polymere [*A publication*]
**Koll Z**......... Kolloidnyi Zhurnal [*A publication*]
**Koll Zh**....... Kolloidnyi Zhurnal [*A publication*]
**KOLM**........ Rochester, MN [*AM radio station call letters*]
**KOlMN**..... Mid-America Nazarene College, Olathe, KS [*Library symbol*] [*Library of Congress*] (LCLS)
**KOLN**......... Lincoln, NE [*Television station call letters*]
**Koln Jb Vor Fruh Gesch**... Koelner Jahrbuch fuer Vor- und Fruehgeschichte [*A publication*]
**Kolomen Ped Inst Ucen Zap**... Kolomenskii Pedagogiceskii Institut Ucenye Zapiski [*A publication*]
**Kolor Ert**.... Kolorisztikai Ertesito [*A publication*]
**KOLO-TV**... Reno, NV [*Television station call letters*]
**KOLR**........ Springfield, MO [*Television station call letters*]
**KOLS**........ De Soto, MO [*FM radio station call letters*]
**KOLS**........ Nogales/International [*Arizona*] [*ICAO location identifier*] (ICLI)
**KOLT**........ Scottsbluff, NE [*AM radio station call letters*]
**KOLU**........ Pasco, WA [*FM radio station call letters*]
**KOLV**........ Olivia, MN [*FM radio station call letters*]
**KOLY**........ Mobridge, SD [*AM radio station call letters*]
**KOLY-FM**... Mobridge, SD [*FM radio station call letters*]
**Kolze**.......... Transvaal Reports, by Kolze [*A publication*] (DLA)
**KOM**.......... Kentucky, Ohio, Michigan [*Medical library network*]
**KOM**.......... Kilometric Wavelength [*Radio astronomy*]
**KOM**.......... Komaba [*Japan*] [*Seismograph station code, US Geological Survey*] [*Closed*] (SEIS)
**KOM**.......... Komitet Opiekunczy Miejski (BJA)
**KOM**.......... Komo-Manda [*Papua New Guinea*] [*Airport symbol*] [*Obsolete*] (OAG)
**KoM**........... Korea Microforms, Seoul, Korea [*Library symbol*] [*Library of Congress*] (LCLS)
**KOM**.......... KSC [*Kennedy Space Center*] Organizational Manual [*NASA*] (NASA)
**KOM**.......... Tijdschrift voor Effectief Directiebeleid [*A publication*]
**KOMA**....... Oklahoma City, OK [*AM radio station call letters*]
**KOMA**....... Omaha/Eppley Air Field [*Nebraska*] [*ICAO location identifier*] (ICLI)
**KOMAA**.... Kovove Materialy [*A publication*]
**KOMAB**.... Korean Medical Abstracts [*A publication*]
**Komarom Meg Muz Koz**... Komarom Megyei Muzeumok Koezlemenei [*A publication*]
**Komarovskie Chteniya Bot Inst Akad Nauk SSSR**... Komarovskie Chteniya Botanicheskogo Instituta Academii Nauk SSSR [*A publication*]
**KOMB**....... Fort Scott, KS [*FM radio station call letters*]
**KomBeiANT**... Kommentare und Beitraege zum Alten und Neuen Testament [*Duesseldorf*] [*A publication*] (BJA)
**Kombin Anal**... Kombinatornyi Analiz [*A publication*]

**Kombinatornyi Anal** ... Kombinatornyi Analiz [*A publication*]
**KOMC** ....... Branson, MO [*AM radio station call letters*]
**KOME** ....... San Jose, CA [*FM radio station call letters*]
**KOMJ** ....... Atlantic, IA [*FM radio station call letters*]
**Kom Krystalogr PAN Biul Inf** ... Komisja Krystalogradfii PAN [*Polska Akademia Nauk*]. Biuletyn Informacyjny [*A publication*]
**Komm Abg G** ... Kommunalabgabengesetz [*A publication*]
**Kom Mazur-Warmin** ... Komunikaty Mazursko-Warminskie [*A publication*]
**Komm Kass Z** ... Kommunal-Kassen-Zeitschrift [*A publication*]
**Komm Sov Latv** ... Kommunist Sovetskoj Latvii [*A publication*]
**Komm St Z** ... Kommunale Steuer-Zeitschrift [*A publication*]
**Kommunal'n Khoz** ... Kommunal'nvoe Khozyaistvo [*A publication*]
**Kommunist Azerbajd** ... Kommunist Azerbajdzana [*A publication*]
**Kommunist Sov Latvii** ... Kommunist Sovetskoj Latvii [*A publication*]
**Kommun u Klassenkampf** ... Kommunismus und Klassenkampf [*A publication*]
**KOMO** ...... Seattle, WA [*AM radio station call letters*]
**KOMO-TV** ... Seattle, WA [*Television station call letters*]
**KOMP** ....... Las Vegas, NV [*FM radio station call letters*]
**KompH** ...... Komparatistische Hefte [*A publication*]
**Kompleksn Ispol'z Miner Syr'ya** ... Kompleksnoe Ispol'zovanie Mineral'nogo Syr'ya [*A publication*]
**Kompleksn Issled Kasp Morya** ... Kompleksnye Issledovaniya Kaspiiskogo Morya [*A publication*]
**Kompleksn Issled Prir Okeana** ... Kompleksnye Issledovaniya Prirody Okeana [*A publication*]
**Kompleksn Issled Vodokhran** ... Kompleksnye Issledovaniya Vodokhranilishch [*A publication*]
**KOMRMLN** ... Kentucky-Ohio-Michigan Regional Medical Library [*Library network*]
**KOMSOMOL** ... Communist Youth League [*From the Russian*]
**Komspol** ..... Komanditni Spolecnost [*Limited Partnership Company*] [*Czechoslovakian*]
**Kom Ukr** .... Kommunist Ukrainy [*A publication*]
**KOMU-TV** ... Columbia, MO [*Television station call letters*]
**KOMW** ...... Omak, WA [*AM radio station call letters*]
**KOMW-FM** ... Omak, WA [*FM radio station call letters*]
**KOMX** ....... Pampa, TX [*FM radio station call letters*]
**KOMY** ....... Watsonville, CA [*AM radio station call letters*]
**kon** ............ Kongo [*MARC language code*] [*Library of Congress*] (LCCP)
**KON** .......... Kongsberg [*Norway*] [*Seismograph station code, US Geological Survey*] (SEIS)
**KONA** ........ Kennewick, WA [*AM radio station call letters*]
**KONA-FM** ... Kennewick, WA [*FM radio station call letters*]
**Konan Women's Coll Res** ... Konan Women's College. Researches [*A publication*]
**Koncar Strucne Inf** ... Koncar Strucne Informacije [*A publication*]
**KONC-FM** ... Sun City, AZ [*FM radio station call letters*]
**KONE** ........ Reno, NV [*AM radio station call letters*]
**Konf Int Ges Biol Rhythm Forsch** ... Konferenz der Internationalen Gesellschaft fuer Biologische Rhythmusforschung [*A publication*]
**Kongr Zbl Ges Inn Med** ... Kongresszentralblatt fuer die Gesamte Innere Medizin und Ihre Grenzgebiete [*A publication*]
**KONG-TV** ... Everett, WA [*Television station call letters*]
**Kong Zentralbl Ges Innere Med** ... Kongresszentralblatt fuer die Gesamte Innere Medizin und Ihre Grenzgebiete [*A publication*]
**Konigsberg Univ Jahrb** ... Koenigsberg Universitaet. Jahrbuch [*A publication*]
**Koninkl Nederlandse Akad Wetensch Proc** ... Koninklijke Nederlandse Akademie van Wetenschappen. Proceedings [*A publication*]
**Koninkl Nederlandse Akad Wetensch Verh Afd Natuurk** ... Koninklijke Nederlandse Akademie van Wetenschappen. Verhandelingen. Afdeling Natuurkunde [*A publication*]
**KONJD** ..... Konjunkturberichte [*A publication*]
**Konj Pol** ..... Konjunkturpolitik [*A publication*]
**Konjunkturber** ... Konjunkturberichte [*A publication*]
**Konjunkturpol** ... Konjunkturpolitik [*A publication*]
**KONO** ....... San Antonio, TX [*AM radio station call letters*]
**KONP** ........ Port Angeles, WA [*AM radio station call letters*]
**KONPA** ..... Konzerv- es Paprikaipar [*A publication*]
**Konservn Ovoshchesush Prom-St** ... Konservnaya i Ovoshchesushil'naya Promyshlennost' [*A publication*]
**Konservn Plodoovoschchn Prom** ... Konservnaya i Plodoovoshchchnaya Promyshlennost [*A publication*]
**Konservn Promst** ... Konservnaya Promyshlennost [*A publication*]
**Konserv Ovoshchesush Prom** ... Konservnaya i Ovoshchesushil'naya Promyshlennost' [*A publication*]
**Konsthist T** ... Konsthistorisk Tidskrift [*A publication*]
**Konsthist Tid** ... Konsthistorisk Tidskrift [*A publication*]
**Konsthist Tidskrift** ... Konsthistorisk Tidskrift [*A publication*]
**Konsthist Ts** ... Konsthistorisk Tidskrift [*A publication*]
**Konstit Med** ... Konstitutionelle Medizin [*A publication*]
**Konstit Med Neur Ther** ... Konstitutionelle Medizin und Neuraltherapie [*A publication*]
**Konst Rat App** ... Konstam's Rating Appeals [*1904-08*] [*A publication*] (DLA)
**Konstr Elem Methoden** ... Konstruktion, Elemente, Methoden [*A publication*]
**Konstr Giessen** ... Konstruieren und Giessen [*West Germany*] [*A publication*]
**Konstr Ingenieurbau Ber** ... Konstruktiver Ingenieurbau Berichte [*A publication*]
**Konstr Masch-Appar- Geraetebau** ... Konstruktion im Maschinen-, Apparate-, und Geraetebau [*A publication*]
**Konstr Masch App Geraetebau** ... Konstruktion im Maschinen-, Apparate-, und Geraetebau [*A publication*]
**Konstr Mater Osn Grafita** ... Konstruktsionnye Materialy na Osnove Grafita [*A publication*]
**Konstr Mater Osn Ugleroda** ... Konstruktsionnye Materialy na Osnove Ugleroda [*A publication*]
**Konstr Uglegrafitovye Mater Sb Tr** ... Konstruktsionnye Uglegrafitovye Materialy Sbornik Trudov [*A publication*]
**Konst Svoistva Miner** ... Konstitutsiya i Svoistva Mineralov [*A publication*]
**Konst Svoj Miner** ... Konstitutsiya i Svoistva Mineralov [*A publication*]
**Konst & W Rat App** ... Konstam and Ward's Rating Appeals [*1909-12*] [*A publication*] (DLA)
**Konsult Mater Ukr Gos Inst Eksp Farm** ... Konsultatsionnye Materialy Ukrainskii Gosudarstvennyi Institut Eksperimental'noi Farmatsii [*A publication*]
**KONT** ........ Ontario/International [*California*] [*ICAO location identifier*] (ICLI)
**Kontrol'no Izmer Tekh** ... Kontrol'no Izmeritel'naya Tekhnika [*A publication*]
**Kontrol Tekhnol Protsessov Obogashch Polezn Iskop** ... Kontrol i Tekhnologiya Protsessov Obogashcheniya Poleznykh Iskopaemykh [*A publication*]
**KONX** ........ Elkonix Corp. [*NASDAQ symbol*] (NQ)
**KONY** ........ Washington, UT [*AM radio station call letters*]
**Konyvtari Figy** ... Konyvtari Figyelo [*A publication*]
**konyvvizsg** ... Konyvvizsgalo [*Auditor, Accountant*] [*Hungarian*]
**Konzepte Zeitgemaess Physikunterrichts** ... Konzepte eines Zeitgemaessen Physikunterrichts [*A publication*]
**Konzerv-Paprikaip** ... Konzerv- es Paprikaipar [*A publication*]
**KOO** .......... Kongolo [*Zaire*] [*Airport symbol*] (OAG)
**KOOD** ....... Hays, KS [*Television station call letters*]
**KOOG-TV** ... Ogden, UT [*Television station call letters*]
**KOOI-FM** ... Jacksonville, TX [*FM radio station call letters*]
**KOOK** ........ Modesto, CA [*AM radio station call letters*]
**KOOL** ........ Insta Cool, Inc. of North America [*NASDAQ symbol*] (NQ)
**KOOL** ........ Phoenix, AZ [*AM radio station call letters*]
**KOOL-FM** ... Phoenix, AZ [*FM radio station call letters*]
**KOOO** ....... Onawa, IA [*FM radio station call letters*]
**KOOPA** ....... Kozhevenno-Obuvnaya Promyshlennost [*A publication*]
**Kooper Zemed** ... Kooperativno Zemedelie [*A publication*]
**KOOQ** ....... North Platte, NE [*AM radio station call letters*]
**Koord Khim** ... Koordinatsionnaya Khimiya [*A publication*]
**KOOS** ........ North Bend, OR [*FM radio station call letters*]
**KOOV** ........ Copperas Cove, TX [*FM radio station call letters*]
**KOOZ** ........ Great Falls, MT [*FM radio station call letters*]
**KOP** ........... Kansallis-Osake-Pankki [*National Capital Stock Bank*] [*Finland*]
**KOP** ........... Kansallis-Osake-Pankki. Economic Review [*A publication*]
**KOP** ........... Kickoff Point [*Diamond drilling*]
**KOP** ........... Kopeck [*Monetary unit in Russia*]
**KOP** ........... Koppers Co., Inc. [*NYSE symbol*] (SPSG)
**KOP** ........... Nakhon Phanom [*Thailand*] [*Airport symbol*] [*Obsolete*] (OAG)
**KOPA** ........ Scottsdale, AZ [*AM radio station call letters*]
**KOPB-FM** ... Portland, OR [*FM radio station call letters*]
**KOPB-TV** ... Portland, OR [*Television station call letters*]
**KOPCC** ...... Kunzang Odsal Palyul Changchub Choling [*An association*] (EA)
**KOPE** ........ Medford, OR [*FM radio station call letters*]
**KOPF** ......... Miami/Opa Locka [*Florida*] [*ICAO location identifier*] (ICLI)
**KopGS** ....... Kopenhagener Germanistische Studien [*A publication*]
**KOPN** ........ Columbia, MO [*FM radio station call letters*]
**KOPR** ........ Butte, MT [*FM radio station call letters*]
**Ko Pr** .......... Komsomol'skaja Pravda [*A publication*]
**KOPRA** ..... Konservnaya i Ovoshchesushil'naya Promyshlennost' [*A publication*]
**KOPS** ......... Keep Off Pounds Sensibly [*Club*]
**KOPS** ......... Thousands of Operations per Second (NASA)
**KOPY-FM** ... Alice, TX [*FM radio station call letters*]
**KOQI** ......... Soquel, CA [*AM radio station call letters*]
**KOQO** ....... Clovis, CA [*AM radio station call letters*]
**KOQO-FM** ... Fresno, CA [*FM radio station call letters*]
**KOR** ........... Contracting Officer
**KOR** ........... King's Own Royal [*Military unit*] [*British*]
**KOR** ........... Knowledge of Results [*Visual monitoring*]
**KOR** ........... Koala Resources Ltd. [*Vancouver Stock Exchange symbol*]
**KOR** ........... Kodak Ortho Resist
**KOR** ........... Kokoro [*Papua New Guinea*] [*Airport symbol*] (OAG)
**KOR** ........... Koran (ROG)
**kor** ............. Korean [*MARC language code*] [*Library of Congress*] (LCCP)
**KOR** ........... Koror [*Palau Islands*] [*Seismograph station code, US Geological Survey*] [*Closed*] (SEIS)
**KOR** ........... Republic of Korea [*ANSI three-letter standard code*] (CNC)
**KOR** ........... Seaplane [*Russian symbol*]
**KOR** ........... Social Self-Defense Committee [*Also, SSDC*] [*Poland*] (PD)
**KORADQ** ... Key to Oceanographic Records Documentation [*A publication*]
**KORA-FM** ... Bryan, TX [*FM radio station call letters*]
**Koranyi Sandor Tarsasag Tud Ulesei** ... Koranyi Sandor Tarsasag Tudomanyos Ulesei [*A publication*]
**KORD** ........ Chicago/O'Hare [*Illinois*] [*ICAO location identifier*] (ICLI)

**KORD**........ Pasco, WA [*AM radio station call letters*]
**KORE**........ Kinetic Analysis Using Over-Relaxation [*FORTRAN computer program*] [*Physical chemistry*]
**KORE**........ Springfield-Eugene, OR [*AM radio station call letters*]
**Korea Exchange Bank Mo R** ... Monthly Review. Korea Exchange Bank [*A publication*]
**Korea Geol and Miner Inst Rep of Geol Miner Explor** ... Korea. Geological and Mineral Institute. Report of Geological and Mineral Exploration [*A publication*]
**Korea Inst Forest Genet Res Rept** ... Korea. Institute of Forest Genetics. Research Reports [*A publication*]
**Korea J**....... Korea Journal [*A publication*]
**Korea LR**.... Korea Law Review [*A publication*] (DLA)
**Korea Med J** ... Korea Medical Journal [*A publication*]
**Koreana Quart** ... Koreana Quarterly [*A publication*]
**Korean Arachnol** ... Korean Arachnology [*A publication*]
**Korean Bee J** ... Korean Bee Journal [*A publication*]
**Korean Biochem J** ... Korean Biochemical Journal [*A publication*]
**Korean Cent J Med** ... Korean Central Journal of Medicine [*A publication*]
**Korean Inst Miner Min Eng J** ... Korean Institute of Mineral and Mining Engineers. Journal [*Republic of Korea*] [*A publication*]
**Korean J Agric Econ** ... Korean Journal of Agricultural Economics [*A publication*]
**Korean J Anim Sci** ... Korean Journal of Animal Sciences [*A publication*]
**Korean J Appl Entomol** ... Korean Journal of Applied Entomology [*A publication*]
**Korean J Appl Microbiol Bioeng** ... Korean Journal of Applied Microbiology and Bioengineering [*Republic of Korea*] [*A publication*]
**Korean J Biochem** ... Korean Journal of Biochemistry [*A publication*]
**Korean J Bot** ... Korean Journal of Botany [*A publication*]
**Korean J Breed** ... Korean Journal of Breeding [*Republic of Korea*] [*A publication*]
**Korean J Chem Eng** ... Korean Journal of Chemical Engineering [*A publication*]
**Korean J Comp L** ... Korean Journal of Comparative Law [*A publication*] (DLA)
**Korean J Dermatol** ... Korean Journal of Dermatology [*A publication*]
**Korean J Entomol** ... Korean Journal of Entomology [*A publication*]
**Korean J Environ Health Soc** ... Korean Journal of Environmental Health Society [*Republic of Korea*] [*A publication*]
**Korean J Fd Sci Technol** ... Korean Journal of Food Science and Technology [*A publication*]
**Korean J Food Sci Technol** ... Korean Journal of Food Science and Technology [*A publication*]
**Korean J Genet** ... Korean Journal of Genetics [*A publication*]
**Korean J Hortic Sci** ... Korean Journal of Horticultural Science [*A publication*]
**Korean J Hort Sci** ... Korean Journal of Horticultural Science [*South Korea*] [*A publication*]
**Korean J of Internat L** ... Korean Journal of International Law [*A publication*] (DLA)
**Korean J Intern Med** ... Korean Journal of Internal Medicine [*A publication*]
**Korean J Int'l L** ... Korean Journal of International Law [*A publication*] (DLA)
**Korean J Microbiol** ... Korean Journal of Microbiology [*A publication*]
**Korean J Mycol** ... Korean Journal of Mycology [*A publication*]
**Korean J Nucl Med** ... Korean Journal of Nuclear Medicine [*A publication*]
**Korean J Nutr** ... Korean Journal of Nutrition [*A publication*]
**Korean J Obstet Gynecol** ... Korean Journal of Obstetrics and Gynecology [*A publication*]
**Korean J Parasitol** ... Korean Journal of Parasitology [*A publication*]
**Korean J Pharmacogn** ... Korean Journal of Pharmacognosy [*A publication*]
**Korean J Pharmacol** ... Korean Journal of Pharmacology [*A publication*]
**Korean J Physiol** ... Korean Journal of Physiology [*South Korea*] [*A publication*]
**Korean J Plant Pathol** ... Korean Journal of Plant Pathology [*A publication*]
**Korean J Plant Prot** ... Korean Journal of Plant Protection [*South Korea*] [*A publication*]
**Korean J Public Health** ... Korean Journal of Public Health [*A publication*]
**Korean J Urol** ... Korean Journal of Urology [*Republic of Korea*] [*A publication*]
**Korean J Vet Res** ... Korean Journal of Veterinary Research [*Republic of Korea*] [*A publication*]
**Korean J Zool** ... Korean Journal of Zoology [*A publication*]
**Korean L**.... Korean Law [*A publication*] (DLA)
**Korean R**.... Korean Review [*A publication*]
**Korean Sci Abstr** ... Korean Scientific Abstracts [*South Korea*] [*A publication*]
**Korean Sci Abstracts** ... Korean Scientific Abstracts [*A publication*]
**Korean Soc Anim Nutr & Feedstuffs** ... Korean Society of Animal Nutrition and Feedstuffs [*A publication*]
**Korean Stud For** ... Korean Studies Forum [*Republic of Korea*] [*A publication*]
**Korea Res Inst Geosci Miner Resour KIGAM Bull** ... Korea Research Institute of Geoscience and Mineral Resources. KIGAM Bulletin [*A publication*]
**Korea Univ Med J** ... Korea University. Medical Journal [*A publication*]
**KORF**........ Norfolk/Norfolk Regional Airport [*Virginia*] [*ICAO location identifier*] (ICLI)
**KORG**........ Anaheim, CA [*AM radio station call letters*]
**Korh Orvostech** ... Korhaz- es Orvostechnika [*Hungary*] [*A publication*]
**Kor J**.......... Korea Journal [*Republic of Korea*] [*A publication*]
**Kor J Comp Law** ... Korea Journal of Comparative Law [*Republic of Korea*] [*A publication*]
**Kor J Int Stud** ... Korea Journal of International Studies [*Republic of Korea*] [*A publication*]
**KORK**........ Las Vegas, NV [*AM radio station call letters*]
**KORL**........ Honolulu, HI [*AM radio station call letters*]
**KORL**........ Orlando [*Florida*] [*ICAO location identifier*] (ICLI)
**Korma Korml Skh Zhivotn** ... Korma i Kormlenie Sel'skokhozyaitvennykh Zhivotnykh [*A publication*]
**Kor Med**..... Korean Medicine [*A publication*]
**Kormi Godivlya Sil's'kogospod Tvarin** ... Kormi ta Godivlya Sil's'kogospodars'kikh Tvarin [*A publication*]
**Korml Skh Zhivotn** ... Kormlenie Sel'skokhozyaistvennykh Zhivotnykh [*A publication*]
**Kormoproizvod Sb Nauchn Rab** ... Kormoproizvodstvo Sbornik Nauchnykh Rabot [*A publication*]
**KORN**........ Mitchell, SD [*AM radio station call letters*]
**Korn Mag**... Korn Magasinet [*A publication*]
**KORO**........ Corpus Christi, TX [*Television station call letters*]
**Kor Obs**...... Korea Observer [*Republic of Korea*] [*A publication*]
**Koroze Ochr Mater** ... Koroze a Ochrana Materialu [*A publication*]
**Koroz Zast** ... Korozija i Zastita [*A publication*]
**KORP**........ Corporate Management Group, Inc. [*North Miami Beach, FL*] [*NASDAQ symbol*] (NQ)
**KORQ**........ Abilene, TX [*AM radio station call letters*]
**KORQ-FM** ... Abilene, TX [*FM radio station call letters*]
**KORR**........ King's Own Royal Regiment [*Military unit*] [*British*]
**Korr Bl Nd S** ... Korrespondenzblatt des Vereins fuer Niederdeutsche Sprachforschung [*A publication*]
**Korresp Abwasser** ... Korrespondenz Abwasser [*A publication*]
**Korrespondenzbriefe Zuckerfabr** ... Korrespondenzbriefe fuer Zuckerfabriken [*A publication*]
**Korrosionsinst Rapp** ... Korrosionsinstitutet. Rapport [*A publication*]
**Korroz Figyelo** ... Korrozios Figyelo [*A publication*]
**Korroz Khim Proizvod Sposoby Zashch** ... Korroziya v Khimicheskikh Proizvodstvakh i Sposoby Zashchity [*A publication*]
**Korroz Met Splavov** ... Korroziya Metallov i Splavov [*USSR*] [*A publication*]
**Korroz Zashch** ... Korroziya i Zashchita v Neftegazovoi Promyshlennosti Nauchno-Tekhnicheskii Sbornik [*A publication*]
**Korroz Zashch Neftegazov Prom-St** ... Korroziya i Zashchita v Neftegazovoi Promyshlennosti [*USSR*] [*A publication*]
**Kors J Neur Psych** ... Korsakov Journal of Neurology and Psychiatry [*A publication*]
**KORSTIC** ... Korea Scientific and Technological Information Center [*INSPEC operator*]
**Kor Stud Forum** ... Korea Studies Forum [*Pittsburg*] [*A publication*]
**KORT**........ Grangeville, ID [*AM radio station call letters*]
**Korte Meded Bosbouwproefsta** ... Korte Mededeling Stichting Bosbouwproefstation "De Dorschkamp" [*A publication*]
**Korte Meded Sticht Bosbproefstn Dorschkamp** ... Korte Mededelingen Stichting Bosbouwproefstation "De Dorschkamp" [*A publication*]
**KORT-FM** ... Grangeville, ID [*FM radio station call letters*]
**KORV**........ Oroville, CA [*AM radio station call letters*]
**Kor World Aff** ... Korea and World Affairs [*A publication*]
**KOS**.......... Kansallis-Osake-Pankki. Economic Review [*A publication*]
**KOS**.......... Kosmodemyansk [*USSR*] [*Seismograph station code, US Geological Survey*] [*Closed*] (SEIS)
**KOSAB**...... Korean Scientific Abstracts [*A publication*]
**KOSA-TV** ... Odessa, TX [*Television station call letters*]
**KOSB**........ King's Own Scottish Borderers [*Military unit*] [*British*]
**KOSBA**...... Kosmos. Seria A. Biologia (Warsaw) [*A publication*]
**KOSC**........ Oscoda/Wurtsmith Air Force Base [*Michigan*] [*ICAO location identifier*] (ICLI)
**KOSCO**..... Korea Oil Storage Company (CINC)
**KOSCOT**... Cosmetics for the Community of Tomorrow [*Acronym used as brand name*]
**KOSE**........ Osceola, AR [*AM radio station call letters*]
**KOSH**........ Osawatomie State Hospital, Osawatomie, KS [*Library symbol*] [*Library of Congress*] (LCLS)
**KOSI**......... Denver, CO [*FM radio station call letters*]
**KOSK**........ Oskaloosa, IA [*FM radio station call letters*]
**KOSM**....... Cascade International, Inc. [*NASDAQ symbol*] (NQ)
**Kosm B Av M** ... Kosmicheskaya Biologiya i Aviakosmicheskaya Meditsina [*A publication*]
**Kosm Bd**..... Kosmos-Baendchen [*A publication*]
**Kosm Biol Aviakosm Med** ... Kosmicheskaya Biologiya i Aviakosmicheskaya Meditsina [*A publication*]
**Kosm Biol Med** ... Kosmicheskaya Biologiya i Meditsina [*A publication*]
**Kosmet J**.... Kosmetik Journal [*A publication*]
**Kosmetol**.... Kosmetologie. Zeitschrift fuer Kosmetik in Wissenschaft und Praxis [*A publication*]
**Kosmet Parfum Drogen Rundsch** ... Kosmetik-Parfum-Drogen Rundschau [*A publication*]
**Kosmices Issled** ... Kosmiceskie Issledovanija [*A publication*]
**Kosmic Issled** ... Kosmiceskie Issledovanija [*A publication*]
**Kosm Issled** ... Kosmicheskie Issledovaniya [*A publication*]
**Kosm Issled Ukr** ... Kosmicheskie Issledovaniya na Ukraine [*Ukrainian SSR*] [*A publication*]

**Kosm Issled Zemnykh Resur** ... Kosmicheskie Issledovaniya Zemnykh Resursov Metody i Sredstva Izmerenii i ObrAabotki Informatsii [*A publication*]
**Kosmos Bibl** ... Kosmos Bibliothek [*A publication*]
**Kosmos Ser A Biol (Warsaw)** ... Kosmos. Seria A. Biologia (Warsaw) [*A publication*]
**Kosmos Ser A (Warsaw)** ... Kosmos. Seria A. Biologia (Warsaw) [*A publication*]
**Kosmos (Warsaw) Ser B** ... Kosmos. Seria B. Przyroda Nieozywiona (Warsaw) [*A publication*]
**KoSNU** ...... Seoul National University, Seoul, Korea [*Library symbol*] [*Library of Congress*] (LCLS)
**KOSO** ........ Patterson, CA [*FM radio station call letters*]
**KOSS** ........ Koss Corp. [*NASDAQ symbol*] (NQ)
**K Ost** ......... Kirche im Osten [*A publication*]
**KOST** ......... Los Angeles, CA [*FM radio station call letters*]
**Kostrom Gos Ped Inst Ucen Zap** ... Kostromskoi Gosudarstvennyi Pedagogiceskii Institut Imeni N. A. Nekrasova UcenyEe Zapiski [*A publication*]
**KOSU-FM** ... Stillwater, OK [*FM radio station call letters*]
**KoSYU** ....... Yonsei University, Seoul, Korea [*Library symbol*] [*Library of Congress*] (LCLS)
**KOT** ........... Kotlik [*Alaska*] [*Airport symbol*] (OAG)
**KOTA** ........ Rapid City, SD [*AM radio station call letters*]
**KOTA-TV** ... Rapid City, SD [*Television station call letters*]
**KOTB** ........ Evanston, WY [*FM radio station call letters*]
**KOTD** ........ Plattsmouth, NE [*AM radio station call letters*]
**KOTE** ........ Eureka, KS [*FM radio station call letters*]
**KOTI** ......... Klamath Falls, OR [*Television station call letters*]
**KOTM-FM** ... Ottumwa, IA [*FM radio station call letters*]
**KOTN** ........ Keep on Truckin' News [*A publication*] (EAAP)
**KOTN** ........ Pine Bluff, AR [*AM radio station call letters*]
**KOTO** ........ Telluride, CO [*FM radio station call letters*]
**KOTR** ........ Cambria, CA [*FM radio station call letters*]
**KOTRA** ..... Korea Trade Promotion Center (EA)
**KOTS** ........ Deming, NM [*AM radio station call letters*]
**KOtU** ........ Ottawa University, Ottawa, KS [*Library symbol*] [*Library of Congress*] (LCLS)
**KOTV** ........ Tulsa, OK [*Television station call letters*]
**KOTY-FM** ... Richland, WA [*FM radio station call letters*]
**KOTZ** ........ Kotzebue, AK [*AM radio station call letters*]
**Kotze** ......... Kotze's Transvaal High Court Reports [*South Africa*] [*A publication*] (DLA)
**Kotze & B** ... Supreme Court Reports, Transvaal [*1885-88*] [*South Africa*] [*A publication*] (DLA)
**Kotze & Barb** ... Supreme Court Reports, Transvaal [*1885-88*] [*South Africa*] [*A publication*] (DLA)
**Kotze & Barber** ... Transvaal Court Reports [*A publication*] (DLA)
**KOU** .......... Koula Moutou [*Gabon*] [*Airport symbol*] (OAG)
**KOU** .......... Koumac [*New Caledonia*] [*Seismograph station code, US Geological Survey*] (SEIS)
**KOUD** ....... Douglas, AZ [*FM radio station call letters*]
**KOUL** ........ Sinton, TX [*FM radio station call letters*]
**KOUR** ........ Independence, IA [*AM radio station call letters*]
**KOUR-FM** ... Independence, IA [*FM radio station call letters*]
**KOUS-TV** ... Hardin, MT [*Television station call letters*]
**KOV** ........... Key Operated Valve
**Kov** ............ Kovcezic [*A publication*]
**KOV** ........... Kriegsopferversorgung [*A publication*]
**Kov** ............ N. A. Kovach, Los Angeles, CA [*Library symbol*] [*Library of Congress*] (LCLS)
**KOVC** ........ Valley City, ND [*AM radio station call letters*]
**KOVE** ........ Lander, WY [*AM radio station call letters*]
**KOVI** ......... King of Video [*NASDAQ symbol*] (NQ)
**Kovove Mater** ... Kovove Materialy [*A publication*]
**KOvpJ** ........ Johnson County Community College, Overland Park, KS [*Library symbol*] [*Library of Congress*] (LCLS)
**KOVR** ........ Stockton, CA [*Television station call letters*]
**KOW** .......... Ghanzhou [*China*] [*Airport symbol*] (OAG)
**KOW** .......... Keen on Waller [*A coterie of women admirers of British stage actor, Lewis Waller (1860-1915)*] (ROG)
**KOW** .......... Kowkash Gold [*Vancouver Stock Exchange symbol*]
**KOWA** ....... Escondido, CA [*AM radio station call letters*]
**KOWB** ....... Laramie, WY [*AM radio station call letters*]
**KOWF** ....... Escondido, CA [*FM radio station call letters*]
**KOWL** ....... South Lake Tahoe, CA [*AM radio station call letters*]
**KOWO** ...... Waseca, MN [*AM radio station call letters*]
**KOWO-FM** ... Waseca, MN [*FM radio station call letters*]
**KOXE** ........ Brownwood, TX [*FM radio station call letters*]
**KOXR** ........ Oxnard, CA [*AM radio station call letters*]
**KOY** ........... Koyama [*Japan*] [*Seismograph station code, US Geological Survey*] [*Closed*] (SEIS)
**KOY** ........... Olga Bay [*Alaska*] [*Airport symbol*] (OAG)
**KOY** ........... Phoenix, AZ [*AM radio station call letters*]
**KOYE** ........ Laredo, TX [*FM radio station call letters*]
**KOY-FM** ... Phoenix, AZ [*FM radio station call letters*]
**KOYL** ........ Odessa, TX [*AM radio station call letters*]
**KOYLI** ....... King's Own Yorkshire Light Infantry [*Military unit*] [*British*]
**KOYN** ........ Paris, TX [*FM radio station call letters*]
**KOZ** ........... Kozyrevsk [*USSR*] [*Seismograph station code, US Geological Survey*] (SEIS)
**KOZ** ........... Ouzinkie [*Alaska*] [*Airport symbol*] (OAG)
**KOZ** ........... Ouzinkie, AK [*Location identifier*] [*FAA*] (FAAL)
**KOZA** ........ Odessa, TX [*AM radio station call letters*]
**KOZAA** ..... Kozarstvi [*A publication*]
**KOZE** ........ Lewiston, ID [*AM radio station call letters*]
**KOZE-FM** ... Lewiston, ID [*FM radio station call letters*]
**Kozgazd Szle** ... Kozgazdasagi Szemle [*A publication*]
**KOZHA** ..... Kolloidnyi Zhurnal [*A publication*]
**Kozh-Obuvn Prom-st** ... Kozhevenno-Obuvnaya Promyshlennost [*USSR*] [*A publication*]
**Kozh Obuvn Prom SSSR** ... Kozhevenno Obuvnaya Promyshlennost SSSR [*A publication*]
**KOZI** ......... Chelan, WA [*AM radio station call letters*]
**KOZI-FM** ... Chelan, WA [*FM radio station call letters*]
**KOZJ** ......... Joplin, MO [*Television station call letters*]
**KOZK** ........ Springfield, MO [*Television station call letters*]
**Kozlem Agrartud Oszt Magy Tud Akad** ... Koezlemenyei. Agrartudomanyok Osztalyanak. Magyar Tudomanyos Akademia [*A publication*]
**Kozlemenyek-MTA Szamitastechn Automat Kutato Int (Budapest)** ... Koezlemenyek-MTA Szamitastechnikai es Automatizalasi Kutato Intezet (Budapest) [*A publication*]
**Kozlem Mosonmagyoarovari Agrartud Foiskola** ... Koezlemenyei. Mosonmagyoarovari Agrartudomanyi Foiskola [*A publication*]
**KOZN** ........ Imperial, CA [*FM radio station call letters*]
**KOZQ** ........ Waynesville, MO [*AM radio station call letters*]
**KOZT** ........ Fort Bragg, CA [*FM radio station call letters*]
**KOZX** ........ Cabool, MO [*FM radio station call letters*]
**KOZY** ........ Grand Rapids, MN [*AM radio station call letters*]
**KOZZ** ........ Reno, NV [*FM radio station call letters*]
**KP** ............. Air Cape [*South Africa*] [*ICAO designator*] (FAAC)
**KP** ............. Democratic People's Republic of Korea [*ANSI two-letter standard code*] (CNC)
**K-P** ............ Kaiser-Permanente
**kp** .............. Kaliophilite [*CIPW classification*] [*Geology*]
**KP** ............. Kensington Palace [*British*]
**KP** ............. Keogh Plan [*Business term*]
**KP** ............. Keratitic Precipitate [*Ophthalmology*]
**KP** ............. Keratitis Punctata [*Ophthalmology*]
**KP** ............. Keskustapuolue [*Center Party of Finland*] [*Political party*] (PPW)
**KP** ............. Key Personnel
**KP** ............. Key Pulsing
**KP** ............. Keyboard Perforator
**KP** ............. Keypunch [*Data processing*]
**KP** ............. Kick Plate
**KP** ............. Kickpipe [*Building construction*]
**KP** ............. Kidney Pore
**KP** ............. Kids of Preachers
**KP** ............. Kill Probability (MCD)
**KP** ............. Kilometer Post
**KP** ............. Kilopond
**kp** .............. Kilopulse
**KP** ............. Kinetic Percolation
**KP** ............. Kinetic Potential
**KP** ............. King Post
**KP** ............. King's Parade [*British*] (DSUE)
**KP** ............. King's Pawn [*Chess*] (ADA)
**KP** ............. King's Pleasure [*British*]
**KP** ............. King's Proctor [*British*]
**KP** ............. Kitchen Police [*Kitchen helpers*] [*Military*]
**KP** ............. Klein Paradox [*Physics*]
**KP** ............. Knight of Pius IX
**KP** ............. Knight of St. Patrick [*British*]
**KP** ............. Knights of Pythias (EA)
**K of P** ........ Knights of Pythias
**KP** ............. Knotty Pine
**KP** ............. Komma Proodeftikon [*Progressive Party*] [*Greek*] [*Political party*] (PPE)
**KP** ............. Kommunistesch Partei [*Communist Party*] [*Luxembourg*] [*Political party*] (PPE)
**KP** ............. Kommunistische Partei [*Communist Party*] [*German*] [*Political party*]
**KP** ............. Kritika Phylla [*A publication*]
**KP** ............. Kulturni Politika [*A publication*]
**KP** ............. Kurdish Program (EA)
**KP** ............. Kurie Plot [*Physics*]
**KP** ............. Kwartalnik Prasoznawczy [*A publication*]
**KP** ............. Papua New Guinea [*IYRU nationality code*] (IYR)
**KPA** ........... Kappa Networks, Inc. [*AMEX symbol*] (SPSG)
**KPA** ........... Key Pulse Adapter [*Telecommunications*] (TEL)
**KPA** ........... Kidney Plasminogen Activator [*Anticlotting agent*]
**kPa** ............ Kilopascal
**KPA** ........... Klystron Power Amplifier
**KPA** ........... Kopiago [*Papua New Guinea*] [*Airport symbol*] (OAG)
**KPA** ........... Korea Procurement Agency
**KPA** ........... Kraft Paper Association [*Later, API*] (EA)
**KPAB** ......... Kentucky Philological Association. Bulletin [*A publication*]
**KPAC** ......... San Antonio, TX [*FM radio station call letters*]
**KPAE** ......... Erwinville, LA [*FM radio station call letters*]

**KPAE**......... Everett/Snohomish County-Paine Field [*Washington*] [*ICAO location identifier*] (ICLI)
**KPAG**......... Pagosa Springs, CO [*AM radio station call letters*]
**KPAH**......... Tonopah, NV [*FM radio station call letters*]
**KPAL**......... North Little Rock, AR [*AM radio station call letters*]
**KPAM**......... Panama City/Tyndall Air Force Base [*Florida*] [*ICAO location identifier*] (ICLI)
**KPAN**......... Hereford, TX [*AM radio station call letters*]
**KPAN-FM**... Hereford, TX [*FM radio station call letters*]
**KPAR**......... Granbury, TX [*AM radio station call letters*]
**KParSH**..... Parsons State Hospital, Parsons, KS [*Library symbol*] [*Library of Congress*] (LCLS)
**KPAS**......... Fabens, TX [*FM radio station call letters*]
**KPAT**......... Sioux Falls, SD [*FM radio station call letters*]
**KPAX-TV**... Missoula, MT [*Television station call letters*]
**KPAY**......... Chico, CA [*AM radio station call letters*]
**KPAY-FM**... Chico, CA [*FM radio station call letters*]
**KPAZ-TV**... Phoenix, AZ [*Television station call letters*]
**KPB**........... Kenai Peninsula Borough [*Alaska*]
**KPB**........... Kommunistische Partij van Belgie [*Communist Party of Belgium*] [*See also PCB*] [*Political party*] (PPE)
**KPB**........... Point Baker, AK [*Location identifier*] [*FAA*] (FAAL)
**KPBA**......... Pine Bluff, AR [*AM radio station call letters*]
**KPBC**......... Dallas, TX [*AM radio station call letters*]
**KPBF**......... Pine Bluff/Grider Field [*Arkansas*] [*ICAO location identifier*] (ICLI)
**KPBG**......... Plattsburg/Plattsburg Air Force Base [*New York*] [*ICAO location identifier*] (ICLI)
**KPBI**......... West Palm Beach/Palm Beach International [*Florida*] [*ICAO location identifier*] (ICLI)
**KPBQ-FM**... Pine Bluff, AR [*FM radio station call letters*]
**KPBS-FM**... San Diego, CA [*FM radio station call letters*]
**KPBS-TV**.. San Diego, CA [*Television station call letters*]
**KPBX-FM**... Spokane, WA [*FM radio station call letters*]
**KPC**........... Kappa Resources [*Vancouver Stock Exchange symbol*]
**KPC**........... Keratinocyte Precursor Cell
**KPC**........... Key Personnel Course (MCD)
**KPC**........... Keyboard/Printer Control [*Data processing*]
**KPC**........... Keypunch Cabinet [*Data processing*]
**KPC**........... Khapcheranga [*USSR*] [*Seismograph station code, US Geological Survey*] (SEIS)
**kpc**........... Kiloparsec [*Astronomy*]
**KPC**........... Kinetic Process Control
**KPC**........... Klystron Phase Control
**KPC**........... Knights of Peter Claver (EA)
**KPC**........... Koblenz Procurement Center [*Military*] [*Federal Republic of Germany*] (NATG)
**KPC**........... Kodak Photofabrication Center
**KPC**........... Kuwait Petroleum Corporation
**KPC**........... Paducah Junior College, Paducah, KY [*OCLC symbol*] (OCLC)
**KPC**........... Port Clarence [*Alaska*] [*Airport symbol*] (OAG)
**KPC**........... Port Clarence, AK [*Location identifier*] [*FAA*] (FAAL)
**KPCA**......... Marked Tree, AR [*AM radio station call letters*]
**KPCB**......... Rockport, TX [*FM radio station call letters*]
**KPCC**......... Pasadena, CA [*FM radio station call letters*]
**KPCE**......... Eunice, NM [*FM radio station call letters*]
**KPCH**......... Dubach, LA [*FM radio station call letters*]
**KPCI**......... Key Production Company, Incorporated [*NASDAQ symbol*] (NQ)
**KPCL**......... Farmington, NM [*FM radio station call letters*]
**KPCO**......... Quincy, CA [*AM radio station call letters*]
**KPCR**......... Bowling Green, MO [*AM radio station call letters*]
**KPCR-FM**... Bowling Green, MO [*FM radio station call letters*]
**KPCS**......... Pueblo, CO [*Television station call letters*]
**KPCW**......... Park City, UT [*FM radio station call letters*]
**KPD**........... Kennedy Program Directive [*NASA*] (NASA)
**KP & D**....... Kick Plate and Drip (AAG)
**KPD**........... Kommunistische Partei Deutschlands [*Communist Party of Germany*] [*Federal Republic of Germany*] [*Political party*] (PPW)
**KPD-ML**... Kommunistische Partei Deutschlands/Marxisten-Leninisten [*Communist Party of Germany/Marxists-Leninists*] [*Federal Republic of Germany*] [*Political party*] (PPW)
**KPDN**......... Pampa, TX [*AM radio station call letters*]
**KPDQ**......... Portland, OR [*AM radio station call letters*]
**KPDQ-FM**... Portland, OR [*FM radio station call letters*]
**KPDR**......... Wheeler, TX [*FM radio station call letters*]
**KPDX**......... Portland/International [*Oregon*] [*ICAO location identifier*] (ICLI)
**KPDX**......... Vancouver, WA [*Television station call letters*]
**KPE**........... Columbia Pictures Entertainment [*NYSE symbol*] (SPSG)
**kpe**........... Kpelle [*MARC language code*] [*Library of Congress*] (LCCP)
**KPEJ**......... Odessa, TX [*Television station call letters*]
**KPEL**......... Lafayette, LA [*AM radio station call letters*]
**KPEN-FM**... Soldotna, AK [*FM radio station call letters*]
**KPEQ**......... Jal, NM [*FM radio station call letters*]
**KPER**......... Hobbs, NM [*FM radio station call letters*]
**KPET**......... Lamesa, TX [*AM radio station call letters*]
**KPEZ**......... Austin, TX [*FM radio station call letters*]
**KPF**........... Kangaroo Protection Foundation (EA)
**KPF**........... Katadyn Pocket Filter
**KPF**........... Key Pulse on Front Cord [*Telecommunications*] (TEL)
**KPFA**......... Berkeley, CA [*FM radio station call letters*]
**KPFB**......... Berkeley, CA [*FM radio station call letters*]
**KPFK**......... Los Angeles, CA [*FM radio station call letters*]
**KPFM**......... Mountain Home, AR [*FM radio station call letters*]
**KPFR**......... Pueblo, CO [*FM radio station call letters*]
**KPFT**......... Houston, TX [*FM radio station call letters*]
**KPFX**......... Killeen, TX [*FM radio station call letters*]
**KPG**........... Keeping
**KPG**........... Kliatt Paperback Book Guide [*A publication*]
**KPG**........... Kurupung [*Guyana*] [*Airport symbol*] (OAG)
**KPGA**......... Pismo Beach, CA [*FM radio station call letters*]
**KPGE**......... Page, AZ [*AM radio station call letters*]
**KPGR**......... Pleasant Grove, UT [*FM radio station call letters*]
**KPH**........... Kaena Point [*Hawaii*] [*Seismograph station code, US Geological Survey*] [*Closed*] (SEIS)
**kph**........... Kilometers per Hour
**KPH**........... Know Problems of Hydrocephalus (EA)
**KPH**........... Komunisticka Partija Hrvatske [*Communist Party of Croatia*] [*Political party*]
**KPH**........... Ktav Publishing House, Inc. [*New York*] (BJA)
**KPH**........... Pauloff Harbor/Sanak Island, AK [*Location identifier*] [*FAA*] (FAAL)
**KPHF**......... Newport News/Patrick Henry [*Virginia*] [*ICAO location identifier*] (ICLI)
**KPHF**......... Phoenix, AZ [*FM radio station call letters*]
**KPHL**......... Philadelphia/International [*Pennsylvania*] [*ICAO location identifier*] (ICLI)
**KPHN**......... Barling, AR [*FM radio station call letters*]
**KPHN**......... Port Huron [*Michigan*] [*ICAO location identifier*] (ICLI)
**KPHO-TV**... Phoenix, AZ [*Television station call letters*]
**KPHX**......... Phoenix, AZ [*AM radio station call letters*]
**KPHX**......... Phoenix/Sky Harbor International [*Arizona*] [*ICAO location identifier*] (ICLI)
**KPI**........... Kapit [*Malaysia*] [*Airport symbol*] (OAG)
**KPI**........... Karyopyknotic Index [*Cytology*]
**KPI**........... Killearn Properties, Incorporated [*AMEX symbol*] (SPSG)
**KPI**........... King Pin Inclination [*Automotive engineering*]
**kpi**........... Kips [*Thousands of Pounds*] per Square Inch
**KPI**........... Kunitz Protease Inhibitor [*Medicine*]
**KPI**........... Kuwait Petroleum International (ECON)
**KPI**........... KWIK Products International Corp. [*Vancouver Stock Exchange symbol*]
**KPIA**......... Keep Printing in Australia Campaign
**KPIC**......... Key Phrase in Context
**KPIC**......... Roseburg, OR [*Television station call letters*]
**KPIE**......... St. Petersburg/Clearwater International [*Florida*] [*ICAO location identifier*] (ICLI)
**KPIG**......... Freedom, CA [*FM radio station call letters*]
**KPIT**......... Pittsburgh/Greater Pittsburgh [*Pennsylvania*] [*ICAO location identifier*] (ICLI)
**KPIX**......... San Francisco, CA [*Television station call letters*]
**KPJ**........... Komunisticka Partija Jugoslavije [*Communist Party of Yugoslavia*] [*Political party*] (PPE)
**KPJN**......... Gonzales, TX [*FM radio station call letters*]
**KPJO**......... Avalon, CA [*FM radio station call letters*]
**KPK**........... Kampeer + Caravan Kampioen [*A publication*]
**KPK**........... Kanaka Peak [*California*] [*Seismograph station code, US Geological Survey*] (SEIS)
**KPK**........... Kappa Phi Kappa [*Fraternity*]
**KPK**........... Parks [*Alaska*] [*Airport symbol*] (OAG)
**KPK**........... Parks, AK [*Location identifier*] [*FAA*] (FAAL)
**KPKY**......... Pocatello, ID [*FM radio station call letters*]
**KPL**........... Copeland Resources [*Vancouver Stock Exchange symbol*]
**KPL**........... Kick Plate [*Building construction*]
**KPL**........... Kommunistisch Partei vu Leetzebuerg [*Communist Party of Luxembourg*] [*Political party*] (PPW)
**KPLA**......... Riverbank, CA [*AM radio station call letters*]
**K Pl B**......... Klein Placaatboek [*A publication*]
**KPLC-TV**.. Lake Charles, LA [*Television station call letters*]
**KPLE**......... Temple, TX [*FM radio station call letters*]
**KPLM**......... Palm Springs, CA [*FM radio station call letters*]
**KPLN-FM**... Plains, TX [*FM radio station call letters*]
**KPLO-FM**... Reliance, SD [*FM radio station call letters*]
**KPLO-TV**... Reliance, SD [*Television station call letters*]
**KPLR-TV**.. St. Louis, MO [*Television station call letters*]
**KPLS**......... Key Pulsing (MSA)
**KPLT**......... Paris, TX [*AM radio station call letters*]
**KPLU-FM**... Tacoma, WA [*FM radio station call letters*]
**KPLV**......... Port Lavaca, TX [*FM radio station call letters*]
**KPLX**......... Fort Worth, TX [*FM radio station call letters*]
**KPLY**......... Sparks, NV [*AM radio station call letters*]
**KPLZ**......... Seattle, WA [*FM radio station call letters*]
**KPM**........... Kathode Pulse Modulation
**Kpm**........... Kilopondmeter
**KPM**........... King's Police Medal
**KPM**........... Kronig-Penny Model
**KPMA**......... Altamont, OR [*FM radio station call letters*]
**KPMB**......... Pembina [*North Dakota*] [*ICAO location identifier*] (ICLI)
**KPMC**......... Bakersfield, CA [*AM radio station call letters*]

**KPMD** ....... Palmdale/Air Force Plant No. 42 [*California*] [*ICAO location identifier*] (ICLI)
**KPMG** ....... Klynveld Peat Marwick Goerdeler [*Commercial firm*] [*British*]
**KPMI** ......... Kraner Preschool Math Inventory [*Educational test*]
**KPMO** ....... Mendocino, CA [*AM radio station call letters*]
**KPN** .......... Confederation for an Independent Poland (PD)
**KPN** .......... Kipnuk [*Alaska*] [*Airport symbol*] (OAG)
**KPN** .......... Kipnuk, AK [*Location identifier*] [*FAA*] (FAAL)
**KPN** .......... Kupiano [*Papua New Guinea*] [*Seismograph station code, US Geological Survey*] (SEIS)
**KPNC** ........ Ponca City [*Oklahoma*] [*ICAO location identifier*] (ICLI)
**KPNC-FM** ... Ponca City, OK [*FM radio station call letters*]
**KPND** ........ Sandpoint, ID [*FM radio station call letters*]
**KPNE** ........ Philadelphia/North Philadelphia [*Pennsylvania*] [*ICAO location identifier*] (ICLI)
**KPNE-TV** ... North Platte, NE [*Television station call letters*]
**KPNLF** ...... Khmer People's National Liberation Front [*Kampuchea*] (PD)
**KPNO** ........ Kitt Peak National Observatory [*Tucson, AZ*] [*National Science Foundation*]
**KPNOB** ..... Kitt Peak National Observatory [*Tucson, AZ*]
**KPNS** ........ Pensacola/Regional [*Florida*] [*ICAO location identifier*] (ICLI)
**KPNW** ....... Eugene, OR [*AM radio station call letters*]
**KPNW-FM** ... Eugene, OR [*FM radio station call letters*]
**KPNX-TV** ... Mesa, AZ [*Television station call letters*]
**KPNY** ........ Alliance, NE [*FM radio station call letters*]
**KPO** .......... Keypunch Operator [*Data processing*]
**KPO** .......... Kitt Peak National Observatory, Tucson, AZ [*OCLC symbol*] (OCLC)
**KPO** .......... Kommunistische Partei Oesterreichs [*Communist Party of Austria*] [*Political party*] (PPW)
**KPOA** ........ Lahaina, HI [*FM radio station call letters*]
**KPOB** ........ Fayetteville/Pope Air Force Base [*North Carolina*] [*ICAO location identifier*] (ICLI)
**KPOB-TV** ... Poplar Bluff, MO [*Television station call letters*]
**KPOC** ........ Key Prep on Campus [*Slang*]
**KPOC** ........ Pocahontas, AR [*AM radio station call letters*]
**KPOD** ........ Crescent City, CA [*AM radio station call letters*]
**KPOD-FM** ... Crescent North, CA [*FM radio station call letters*]
**KPOF** ......... Denver, CO [*AM radio station call letters*]
**KPOI-FM** ... Honolulu, HI [*FM radio station call letters*]
**KPOK** ........ Bowman, ND [*AM radio station call letters*]
**KPOL** ......... Tucson, AZ [*Television station call letters*]
**KPOM-TV** ... Fort Smith, AR [*Television station call letters*]
**KPOO** ........ San Francisco, CA [*FM radio station call letters*]
**KPOP** ........ San Diego, CA [*AM radio station call letters*]
**KPOR** ........ East Porterville, CA [*FM radio station call letters*]
**KPOS** ......... Post, TX [*AM radio station call letters*]
**KPOW** ....... Powell, WY [*AM radio station call letters*]
**KPOWU** ..... Kenya Petroleum and Oil Workers' Union
**KPP** ........... Kaneb Pipeline Partnership LP [*NYSE symbol*] (SPSG)
**KPP** ........... Keeper of the Privy Purse [*British*]
**KPP** ........... Komunistyczna Partia Polski [*Communist Party of Poland (1925-1938)*] [*Political party*] (PPE)
**KPPC** ......... Pasadena, CA [*AM radio station call letters*]
**KPPR** ......... Williston, ND [*FM radio station call letters*]
**kpps** .......... Kilopulses per Second
**KPQ** .......... Wenatchee, WA [*AM radio station call letters*]
**KPQ-FM** ... Wenatchee, WA [*FM radio station call letters*]
**KPQI** ......... Presque Isle/Presque Isle [*Maine*] [*ICAO location identifier*] (ICLI)
**KPQX** ........ Havre, MT [*FM radio station call letters*]
**KPR** .......... Kniga i Proletarskaya Revolyutsiya [*A publication*]
**KPR** .......... Knight of Polonia Restituta [*British*]
**KPR** .......... Knots per Revolution
**KPR** .......... Kodak Photo Resist
**KPR** .......... Krasnaya Polyana [*USSR*] [*Seismograph station code, US Geological Survey*] [*Closed*] (SEIS)
**KPR** .......... Port Williams [*Alaska*] [*Airport symbol*] (OAG)
**KPR** .......... Port Williams, AK [*Location identifier*] [*FAA*] (FAAL)
**KPRA** ......... Ukiah, CA [*FM radio station call letters*]
**KPRB** ......... Redmond, OR [*AM radio station call letters*]
**KPRC** ......... Houston, TX [*AM radio station call letters*]
**KPRC-TV** .. Houston, TX [*Television station call letters*]
**KPRD** ........ Kennedy Program Requirements Document [*NASA*] (NASA)
**KPRE** ........ Paris, TX [*AM radio station call letters*]
**KPRK** ......... Livingston, MT [*AM radio station call letters*]
**KPRL** ......... Paso Robles, CA [*AM radio station call letters*]
**KPRM** ....... Park Rapids, MN [*AM radio station call letters*]
**KPRN** ........ Grand Junction, CO [*FM radio station call letters*]
**KPRO** ........ Kaypro Corp. [*NASDAQ symbol*] (NQ)
**KPRO** ........ Riverside, CA [*AM radio station call letters*]
**KPRP** ......... Kampuchean People's Revolutionary Party [*Political party*] (PD)
**KPR-P** ........ Kuder Preference Record - Personal [*Psychology*]
**KPRQ** ........ Price, UT [*FM radio station call letters*]
**KPRR** ......... El Paso, TX [*FM radio station call letters*]
**KPRS** ......... Kansas City, MO [*FM radio station call letters*]
**KPRT** ......... Kansas City, MO [*AM radio station call letters*]
**KPRV-FM** ... Heavener, OK [*FM radio station call letters*]
**KPRW** ........ Oklahoma City, OK [*AM radio station call letters*]
**KPRX** ......... Bakersfield, CA [*FM radio station call letters*]
**KPRY-TV** .. Pierre, SD [*Television station call letters*]
**KPRZ** ......... San Marcos, CA [*AM radio station call letters*]
**KPS** ........... Kempsey [*Australia*] [*Airport symbol*] (OAG)
**KPS** ........... Kilometers per Second (NASA)
**KPS** ........... Kirbati Philatelic Society (EA)
**KPS** ........... Klystron Power Supply
**KPS** ........... Knight of the (Order of the) Polar Star [*Sweden*] (ROG)
**KPS** ........... Kommunistische Partei der Schweiz [*Communist Party of Switzerland*] [*Political party*] (PPE)
**KPS** ........... Kommunistische Partij Suriname [*Communist Party of Surinam*] [*Political party*] (PPW)
**KPS** ........... One Thousand Pulses per Second (KSC)
**KPSA** ......... Alamogordo, NM [*AM radio station call letters*]
**KPSA-FM** ... La Luz, NM [*FM radio station call letters*]
**KPSC** ......... Palm Springs, CA [*FM radio station call letters*]
**KPSD** ......... Faith, SD [*FM radio station call letters*]
**KPSD-TV** .. Eagle Butte, SD [*Television station call letters*]
**KPSI** .......... Kip [*Thousands of Pounds*] per Square Inch
**KPSI** .......... Palm Springs, CA [*AM radio station call letters*]
**KPSI-FM** ... Palm Springs, CA [*FM radio station call letters*]
**KPSJA** ....... Journal. Korean Physical Society [*Republic of Korea*] [*A publication*]
**KPSL** ......... Thousand Palms, CA [*AM radio station call letters*]
**KPSM** ........ Brownwood, TX [*FM radio station call letters*]
**KPSM** ........ Klystron Power Supply Modulator
**KPSM** ........ Portsmouth/Pease Air Force Base [*New Hampshire*] [*ICAO location identifier*] (ICLI)
**KPSO** ......... Falfurrias, TX [*AM radio station call letters*]
**KPSO-FM** ... Falfurrias, TX [*FM radio station call letters*]
**KPSS** ......... Kommunisticheskaya Partiya Sovietskogo Soyuza [*Communist Party of the Soviet Union*] [*Political party*]
**KPST-TV** .. Vallejo, CA [*Television station call letters*]
**KPSU** ......... Goodwell, OK [*FM radio station call letters*]
**KPSX** ......... Palacios [*Texas*] [*ICAO location identifier*] (ICLI)
**KPT** ........... Keeping Posted for Teachers [*New York*] [*A publication*]
**KPT** ........... Keeprite, Inc. [*Toronto Stock Exchange symbol*]
**KPT** ........... Kenner Parker Toys, Inc. [*NYSE symbol*] (SPSG)
**KPT** ........... Pittsburg State University, Pittsburg, KS [*Library symbol*] [*Library of Congress*] (LCLS)
**KPTL** ......... Carson City, NV [*AM radio station call letters*]
**KPTL** ......... Keptel, Inc. [*NASDAQ symbol*] (NQ)
**KPTM** ........ Omaha, NE [*Television station call letters*]
**KPTO** ........ Citrus Heights, CA [*AM radio station call letters*]
**KPTS** ......... Hutchinson, KS [*Television station call letters*]
**KPTV** ......... Portland, OR [*Television station call letters*]
**KPTX** ......... Pecos, TX [*FM radio station call letters*]
**KPU** ........... Kommunisticheskaia Partiia Ukrainy [*Communist Party of the Ukraine*] [*Political party*]
**KPUA** ........ Hilo, HI [*AM radio station call letters*]
**KPUB** ........ Pueblo Memorial [*Colorado*] [*ICAO location identifier*] (ICLI)
**KPUB** ........ Winters, TX [*AM radio station call letters*]
**KPUB-FM** ... Winters, TX [*FM radio station call letters*]
**KPUC** ........ Korean Presidential Unit Citation [*Military award*]
**KPUG** ........ Bellingham, WA [*AM radio station call letters*]
**KPUP** ......... Carmel Valley, CA [*AM radio station call letters*]
**KPUP** ......... Key Personnel Upgrade Program [*National Guard*]
**KPUR** ........ Amarillo, TX [*AM radio station call letters*]
**KPUR-FM** ... Canyon, TX [*FM radio station call letters*]
**KPUZ** ........ Kommunisticheskaia Partiia Uzbekistana [*Communist Party of Uzbekistan*] [*Political party*]
**KPV** ........... Kid-Powered Vehicle
**KPVD** ........ Providence/Theodore Francis Greene State [*Rhode Island*] [*ICAO location identifier*] (ICLI)
**KPVI** .......... Pocatello, ID [*Television station call letters*]
**KPVU** ......... Prairie View, TX [*FM radio station call letters*]
**KPWA** ....... Korean Patriotic Women's Association in America (EA)
**KPWB** ........ Piedmont, MO [*AM radio station call letters*]
**KPWB-FM** ... Piedmont, MO [*FM radio station call letters*]
**KPWM** ...... Portland/International Jetport [*Maine*] [*ICAO location identifier*] (ICLI)
**KPWN** ....... Parowan, UT [*FM radio station call letters*]
**KPWR** ........ Los Angeles, CA [*FM radio station call letters*]
**KPWS** ........ Crowley, LA [*AM radio station call letters*]
**KPXE** ......... Liberty, TX [*AM radio station call letters*]
**KPXI** .......... Mount Pleasant, TX [*FM radio station call letters*]
**KPXR** ......... Anchorage, AK [*FM radio station call letters*]
**KPY** ........... Port Bailey [*Alaska*] [*Airport symbol*] (OAG)
**KPY** ........... Port Bailey, AK [*Location identifier*] [*FAA*] (FAAL)
**KPYN** ........ Atlanta, TX [*FM radio station call letters*]
**KQ** ............. Air South, Inc. [*Airline code*]
**KQ** ............. Kansas Quarterly [*A publication*]
**KQ** ............. Kenya Airways Ltd. [*ICAO designator*] (FAAC)
**KQ** ............. Koreana Quarterly [*A publication*]
**KQA** .......... Akutan [*Alaska*] [*Airport symbol*] (OAG)
**KQA** .......... Akutan, AK [*Location identifier*] [*FAA*] (FAAL)
**KQAA** ........ Aberdeen, SD [*FM radio station call letters*]
**KQAD** ........ Luverne, MN [*AM radio station call letters*]
**KQAL** ........ Winona, MN [*FM radio station call letters*]
**KQAM** ....... Wichita, KS [*AM radio station call letters*]
**KQAQ** ........ Austin, MN [*AM radio station call letters*]
**KQAY-FM** ... Tucumcari, NM [*FM radio station call letters*]

**KQAZ**........ Springerville-Eager, AZ [*FM radio station call letters*]
**KQBE**........ Ellensburg, WA [*FM radio station call letters*]
**KQC**.......... King's College London [*British*] (IRUK)
**KQCD-TV**... Dickinson, ND [*Television station call letters*]
**KQCL**........ Faribault, MN [*FM radio station call letters*]
**KQCP**........ King's and Queen's College of Physicians [*Ireland*]
**KQCR**........ Cedar Rapids, IA [*FM radio station call letters*]
**KQCV**........ Oklahoma City, OK [*AM radio station call letters*]
**KQDF-FM**... Larned, KS [*FM radio station call letters*]
**KQDI**......... Great Falls, MT [*AM radio station call letters*]
**KQDI-FM**... Great Falls, MT [*FM radio station call letters*]
**KQDJ**........ Jamestown, ND [*AM radio station call letters*]
**KQDJ-FM**... Jamestown, ND [*FM radio station call letters*]
**KQDS**........ Duluth, MN [*AM radio station call letters*]
**KQDS-FM**... Duluth, MN [*FM radio station call letters*]
**KQDY**........ Bismarck, ND [*FM radio station call letters*]
**KQEA**........ Lake Charles, LA [*FM radio station call letters*]
**KQEC**........ San Francisco, CA [*Television station call letters*]
**KQED**........ San Francisco, CA [*Television station call letters*]
**KQED-FM**... San Francisco, CA [*FM radio station call letters*]
**KQEG**........ La Crescent, MN [*FM radio station call letters*]
**KQEN**........ Roseburg, OR [*AM radio station call letters*]
**KQEO**........ Albuquerque, NM [*AM radio station call letters*]
**KQEU**........ Olympia, WA [*AM radio station call letters*]
**KQEW**........ Fordyce, AR [*FM radio station call letters*]
**KQEZ**........ Coolidge, AZ [*FM radio station call letters*]
**KQF**.......... Krupp Quick-Firing Gun
**KQFC**........ Boise, ID [*FM radio station call letters*]
**KQFE**......... Springfield, OR [*FM radio station call letters*]
**KQFM**........ Hermiston, OR [*FM radio station call letters*]
**KQFX**........ Georgetown, TX [*FM radio station call letters*]
**KQHK**........ Hutchinson, KS [*FM radio station call letters*]
**KQHT**........ Crookston, MN [*FM radio station call letters*]
**KQHU**........ Yankton, SD [*FM radio station call letters*]
**KQIC**........ Willmar, MN [*FM radio station call letters*]
**KQID**........ Alexandria, LA [*FM radio station call letters*]
**KQIK**........ Lakeview, OR [*AM radio station call letters*]
**KQIK-FM**... Lakeview, OR [*FM radio station call letters*]
**KQIL**......... Grand Junction, CO [*AM radio station call letters*]
**KQIP**......... Odessa, TX [*FM radio station call letters*]
**KQIQ**......... Lemoore, CA [*AM radio station call letters*]
**KQIX-FM**... Grand Junction, CO [*FM radio station call letters*]
**KQIZ-FM**... Amarillo, TX [*FM radio station call letters*]
**KQJM**........ King, Queen, Jack Meld [*Canasta*]
**KQKD**........ Redfield, SD [*AM radio station call letters*]
**KQKI**........ Bayou Vista, LA [*FM radio station call letters*]
**KQKL**........ Apple Valley, CA [*AM radio station call letters*]
**KQKQ-FM**... Council Bluffs, IA [*FM radio station call letters*]
**KQKS**........ Longmont, CO [*FM radio station call letters*]
**KQKX**........ Woodlake, CA [*FM radio station call letters*]
**KQKY**........ Kearney, NE [*FM radio station call letters*]
**KQL**.......... Kol [*Papua New Guinea*] [*Airport symbol*] (OAG)
**KQLA**........ Ogden, KS [*FM radio station call letters*]
**KQLD**........ Port Sulphur, LA [*FM radio station call letters*]
**KQLI**......... Lawton, OK [*FM radio station call letters*]
**KQLO**........ Reno, NV [*AM radio station call letters*]
**KQLS**......... Colby, KS [*FM radio station call letters*]
**KQLT**........ Casper, WY [*FM radio station call letters*]
**KQLV**........ Sheridan, AR [*FM radio station call letters*]
**KQLX**........ Lisbon, ND [*AM radio station call letters*]
**KQLX-FM**... Lisbon, ND [*FM radio station call letters*]
**KQLZ-FM**... Los Angeles, CA [*FM radio station call letters*]
**KQM**.......... Kolson Quick Modality Test [*Education*]
**KQMA-FM**... Phillipsburg, KS [*FM radio station call letters*]
**KQMC-FM**... Brinkley, AR [*FM radio station call letters*]
**KQMG**........ Carrizo Springs, TX [*FM radio station call letters*]
**KQMJ**........ Henryetta, OK [*FM radio station call letters*]
**KQMQ**........ Honolulu, HI [*AM radio station call letters*]
**KQMQ-FM**... Honolulu, HI [*FM radio station call letters*]
**KQMS**........ Redding, CA [*AM radio station call letters*]
**KQMX**........ Rolla, MO [*FM radio station call letters*]
**KQNG**........ Lihue, HI [*AM radio station call letters*]
**KQNG-FM**... Lihue, HI [*FM radio station call letters*]
**KQNK**........ Norton, KS [*AM radio station call letters*]
**KQNM**........ Gallup, NM [*FM radio station call letters*]
**KQNS-FM**... Lindsborg, KS [*FM radio station call letters*]
**KQPD**........ Payette, ID [*FM radio station call letters*]
**KQPR-FM**... Albert Lea, MN [*FM radio station call letters*]
**KQPT**........ Sacramento, CA [*FM radio station call letters*]
**KQQF**........ Coffeyville, KS [*FM radio station call letters*]
**KQQK**........ Galveston, TX [*FM radio station call letters*]
**KQQL**........ Anoka, MN [*FM radio station call letters*]
**KQQQ**........ Pullman, WA [*AM radio station call letters*]
**KQR**.......... Cobequid Resources Ltd. [*Vancouver Stock Exchange symbol*]
**KQR**.......... Kit Quotation Request (MCD)
**KQRK**........ Ronan, MT [*FM radio station call letters*]
**KQRN**........ Mitchell, SD [*FM radio station call letters*]
**KQRO**........ Cuero, TX [*AM radio station call letters*]
**KQRO-FM**... Cuero, TX [*FM radio station call letters*]
**KQRS**........ Golden Valley, MN [*AM radio station call letters*]
**KQRS-FM**... Golden Valley, MN [*FM radio station call letters*]
**KQRZ**........ Fairbanks, AK [*FM radio station call letters*]
**KQSD-TV**... Lowry, SD [*Television station call letters*]
**KQSK**........ Chadron, NE [*FM radio station call letters*]
**KQSR**......... Williston, ND [*AM radio station call letters*]
**KQSS**......... Miami, AZ [*FM radio station call letters*]
**KQST**......... Sedona, AZ [*FM radio station call letters*]
**KQSW**........ Rock Springs, WY [*FM radio station call letters*]
**KQT**.......... Konkordanz zu den Qumrantexten [*A publication*] (BJA)
**KQTL**........ Sahuarita, AZ [*AM radio station call letters*]
**KQTV**........ St. Joseph, MO [*Television station call letters*]
**KQTY**........ Borger, TX [*AM radio station call letters*]
**KQTZ**........ Hobart, OK [*FM radio station call letters*]
**KQUE**........ Houston, TX [*FM radio station call letters*]
**KQUL**........ Seattle, WA [*AM radio station call letters*]
**KQUS-FM**... Hot Springs, AR [*FM radio station call letters*]
**KQUY-FM**... Butte, MT [*FM radio station call letters*]
**KQV**.......... Pittsburgh, PA [*AM radio station call letters*]
**KQVO**........ Calexico, CA [*FM radio station call letters*]
**KQWB**........ Fargo, ND [*AM radio station call letters*]
**KQWB-FM**... Moorhead, MN [*FM radio station call letters*]
**KQWC**........ Webster City, IA [*AM radio station call letters*]
**KQWC-FM**... Webster City, IA [*FM radio station call letters*]
**KQXI**......... Arvada, CO [*AM radio station call letters*]
**KQXK**........ Springdale, AR [*AM radio station call letters*]
**KQXL-FM**... New Roads, LA [*FM radio station call letters*]
**KQXT**........ San Antonio, TX [*FM radio station call letters*]
**KQXX**........ McAllen, TX [*FM radio station call letters*]
**KQXY**........ Nederland, TX [*AM radio station call letters*]
**KQXY-FM**... Beaumont, TX [*FM radio station call letters*]
**KQYB**........ Spring Grove, MN [*FM radio station call letters*]
**KQYK**........ Kalikaq Yugnek. Bethel Regional High School [*A publication*]
**KQYN**........ Twentynine Palms, CA [*FM radio station call letters*]
**KQYT**........ Green Valley, AZ [*FM radio station call letters*]
**KQYX**........ Joplin, MO [*AM radio station call letters*]
**KQYZ**........ Lemoore, CA [*FM radio station call letters*]
**KQZE**........ St. Johns, AZ [*FM radio station call letters*]
**KQZY**........ Dallas, TX [*FM radio station call letters*]
**KQZZ**........ Silverton, CO [*FM radio station call letters*]
**KR**............. Contractor [*Navy*]
**KR**............. Kallah Rabbati (BJA)
**KR**............. Kar-Air [*Finland*] [*ICAO designator*] (FAAC)
**KR**............. Keesom Relationship
**K & R**......... Kent and Radcliff's Law of New York, Revision of 1801 [*A publication*] (DLA)
**K-R**............ Kent-Rosanoff Free Association Test [*Psychology*]
**KR**............. Kenyon Review [*A publication*]
**KR**............. Key Records [*Record label*]
**KR**............. Key Register
**KR**............. Keying Relay
**K and R**...... Kidnaping and Ransom [*Insurance policy*]
**kR**.............. Kilorayleigh
**kR**.............. Kiloroentgen
**KR**............. Kinetic Reaction
**KR**............. King's Regiment [*Military unit*] [*British*]
**KR**............. King's Regulations for the Army and the Army Reserves [*British*]
**KR**............. King's Remembrancer [*British*]
**KR**............. King's Rook [*Chess*]
**KR**............. Kipp Relay
**KR**............. Kirkus Reviews [*A publication*]
**KR**............. Knight of the [*Order of the*] Redeemer [*Greece*]
**KR**............. Knowledge Representation [*Data processing*]
**KR**............. Knowledge of Results
**KR**............. Koleopterologische Rundschau [*A publication*]
**KR**............. Koloniale Rundschau (BJA)
**KR**............. Korean Register [*Korean ship classification society*] (DS)
**kr**.............. Krediteur [*Creditor*] [*Business term*] [*Afrikaans*]
**KR**............. Kreuzer [*Monetary unit*] [*German*]
**KR**............. [*The*] Kroger Co. [*NYSE symbol*] (SPSG)
**Kr**.............. Krokodil [*A publication*]
**KR**............. Krona [*Crown*] [*Monetary unit*] [*Iceland, Sweden*] (EY)
**KR**............. Krone [*Crown*] [*Monetary unit*] [*Denmark, Norway*] (EY)
**K-R**............ Krueger-Ringier [*Book manufacturer*]
**Kr**.............. Krypton [*Chemical element*]
**KR**............. Republic of Korea [*ANSI two-letter standard code*] (CNC)
**KRA**........... Contractor Responsible Action (MCD)
**KRA**........... Key Result Area
**KRA**........... Kickback Racket Act
**KRA**........... Koelner Romanistische Arbeiten [*A publication*]
**KRA**........... Kraft, Inc. [*NYSE symbol*] (SPSG)
**KRA**........... Krakow [*Poland*] [*Seismograph station code, US Geological Survey*] (SEIS)
**KRA**........... Kroniek van het Ambacht/Kleinbedrijf en Middenbedrijf [*A publication*]
**KRAA**........ Perryville, MO [*FM radio station call letters*]
**KRAB**........ Green Acres, CA [*FM radio station call letters*]
**KRAC**........ Morgan Hill, CA [*FM radio station call letters*]
**KR & ACI**.. King's Regulations and Air Council Instructions [*British military*] (DMA)
**KRAD**........ Perry, OK [*AM radio station call letters*]
**KRAE**........ Cheyenne, WY [*AM radio station call letters*]

**Kraeved Zap Kamc Obl Kraeved Muzeja** ... Kraevedceskie Zapiski Kamcatskaja Oblastnajakraevedceskaja Muzeja [*A publication*]
**Kraeved Zap Obl Kraeved Muz Upr Magadan Oblispolkoma** ... Kraevedcheskie Zapiski Oblastnoi Kraevedcheskoi Muzei Upravleniya Magadanskogo Oblispolkoma [*A publication*]
**Kraev Zadachi Differ Uravn** ... Kraevye Zadachi dlya Differentsial'nykh Uravnenij [*A publication*]
**KRAF** ........ Holdenville, OK [*AM radio station call letters*]
**Kraftfahrtech Forschungsarb** ... Kraftfahrtechnische Forschungsarbeiten [*A publication*]
**KRAG-JORG** ... Krag-Jorgensen Rifle
**KRAI** .......... Craig, CO [*AM radio station call letters*]
**KR & AI** ..... King's Regulations and Admiralty Instructions [*Navy*] [*British*]
**KRAI-FM** ... Craig, CO [*FM radio station call letters*]
**KR Air** ........ King's Regulations and Orders for the Royal Canadian Air Force
**KRAJ** ......... Johannesburg, CA [*FM radio station call letters*]
**KRAK** ........ Sacramento, CA [*AM radio station call letters*]
**KRAK-FM** ... Sacramento, CA [*FM radio station call letters*]
**KRAL** ......... Rawlins, WY [*AM radio station call letters*]
**KRAN** ........ Morton, TX [*AM radio station call letters*]
**Krankenpfl Soins Infirm** ... Krankenpflege. Soins Infirmiers [*A publication*]
**Krank Hs** ... Krankenhaus [*A publication*]
**KRAO** ........ Colfax, WA [*FM radio station call letters*]
**KRAQ** ........ Jackson, MN [*FM radio station call letters*]
**KRAR** ........ Erath, LA [*FM radio station call letters*]
**Kra Soob** .... Kratkie Soobscenija o Doklakach i Polevych Issledovanijach Instituta Archeologii [*A publication*]
**Kratkije Soobscenija Inst Eth** ... Kratkije Soobscenija Instituta Ethnografiji Akademiji Nauk SSSR [*A publication*]
**Kratk Soobshch Buryat Kompleksn Nauchno-Issled Inst** ... Kratkie Soobshcheniya Buryatskogo Kompleksnogo Nauchno-Issledovatel'skogo Instituta [*A publication*]
**Kratk Soobshch Fiz** ... Kratkie Soobshcheniya po Fizike [*A publication*]
**Krat Soob Inst Ark A N SSSR** ... Kratkie Soobshcheniia Instituta Arkheologii Akademii Nauk SSSR [*A publication*]
**Krat Soob Inst Etnogr** ... Kratkie Soobshcheniia Institut Etnografii Akademiia Nauk SSSR [*A publication*]
**Krat Soob Inst Ist Mater Kul't** ... Kratkie Soobshcheniia Institut Istorii Material'noi Kul'tury Akademiia Nauk SSSR [*A publication*]
**Krat Soob OGAM** ... Kratkie Soobshcheniia o Polevykh Arkheologicheskikh Issledovaniiakh Odesskogo Gosudarstvennogo Arkheologicheskogo Muzeia [*A publication*]
**KRAV** ........ Tulsa, OK [*FM radio station call letters*]
**KRAX** ........ Rapid City, SD [*FM radio station call letters*]
**KRAY-FM** ... Salinas, CA [*FM radio station call letters*]
**KRAZ** ........ Farmington, NM [*FM radio station call letters*]
**KRB** ........... Kansas River Basin
**KRB** ........... Kariba [*Rhodesia*] [*Seismograph station code, US Geological Survey*] [*Closed*] (SEIS)
**KRB** ........... Karumba [*Australia*] [*Airport symbol*] (OAG)
**KRB** ........... Krebs-Ringer-Bicarbonate [*Buffer solution*]
**KRB** ........... Kredietbank. Weekberichten [*A publication*]
**KRB** ........... MBNA Corp. [*NYSE symbol*] (SPSG)
**KRBA** ........ Lufkin, TX [*AM radio station call letters*]
**KRBB** ......... Wichita, KS [*FM radio station call letters*]
**KRBC-TV** ... Abilene, TX [*Television station call letters*]
**KRBD** ........ Ketchikan, AK [*FM radio station call letters*]
**KRBE-FM** ... Houston, TX [*FM radio station call letters*]
**KRBF** ......... Bonners Ferry, ID [*FM radio station call letters*]
**KRBFC** ...... Kenny Roberts and Bettyanne Fan Club [*Defunct*] (EA)
**KRBG** ........ Bunkie, LA [*FM radio station call letters*]
**KRB-GA** .... Krebs-Ringer-Bicarbonate Glucose-Albumin [*Buffer solution*]
**KRBH** ........ Hondo, TX [*FM radio station call letters*]
**KRBI** .......... St. Peter, MN [*AM radio station call letters*]
**KRBI-FM** .. St. Peter, MN [*FM radio station call letters*]
**KRBJ** ......... Taos, NM [*FM radio station call letters*]
**KRBK-TV** ... Sacramento, CA [*Television station call letters*]
**KRBM** ........ Pendleton, OR [*FM radio station call letters*]
**KRBN** ........ Boston [*Massachusetts*] [*ICAO location identifier*] (ICLI)
**KRBN** ........ Red Lodge, MT [*AM radio station call letters*]
**KRBO** ........ Las Vegas, NV [*FM radio station call letters*]
**KRBQ** ........ Sheridan, WY [*Television station call letters*]
**KRBR** ......... Duluth, MN [*Television station call letters*]
**KRBS** ......... Krebs-Ringer Bicarbonate Solution
**KRBSG** ...... Krebs-Ringer Bicarbonate Solution with Glucose
**KRBT** ......... Missoula, MT [*Television station call letters*]
**KRBU-TV** ... Cedar Rapids, IA [*Television station call letters*]
**KRBZ** ......... Tusayan, AZ [*FM radio station call letters*]
**KRC** ........... Keweenaw Research Center [*Army*] [*Houghton, MI*] [*Research center*] (GRD)
**KRC** ........... King Ranch [*California*] [*Seismograph station code, US Geological Survey*] [*Closed*] (SEIS)
**KRC** ........... Knight of the Red Cross [*Freemasonry*]
**KRC** ........... Knowledge Resource Center [*Computer-based information delivery system in libraries*] [*Generic term*]
**KRC** ........... Kodak Reflex Camera
**KRC** ........... Regis College Library, University of Toronto [*UTLAS symbol*]
**KRCA** ........ Rapid City/Ellsworth Air Force Base [*South Dakota*] [*ICAO location identifier*] (ICLI)
**KRCB-TV** ... Cotati, CA [*Television station call letters*]
**KRCC** ......... Colorado Springs, CO [*FM radio station call letters*]
**KRCD** ........ Chubbuck, ID [*AM radio station call letters*]
**KRCD-FM** ... Chubbuck, ID [*FM radio station call letters*]
**KRCG** ........ Jefferson City, MO [*Television station call letters*]
**KRCH** ........ Rochester, MN [*FM radio station call letters*]
**Kr Chron** .... Kritika Chronika [*A publication*]
**KRCK** ........ Burbank, CA [*AM radio station call letters*]
**KRCL** ......... Salt Lake City, UT [*FM radio station call letters*]
**KRCN** ........ King's Regulations and Orders for the Royal Canadian Navy
**KRCO** ........ Prineville, OR [*AM radio station call letters*]
**KRCR-TV** ... Redding, CA [*Television station call letters*]
**KRCS** ......... Sturgis, SD [*FM radio station call letters*]
**KRCU** ........ Cape Girardeau, MO [*FM radio station call letters*]
**KRCV** ........ Reno, NV [*AM radio station call letters*]
**KRCX** ......... Roseville, CA [*AM radio station call letters*]
**KRCY** ......... Kingman, AZ [*FM radio station call letters*]
**KRD** ........... Kourday [*USSR*] [*Seismograph station code, US Geological Survey*] [*Closed*] (SEIS)
**KRD** ........... Krieger Data International Corp. [*Vancouver Stock Exchange symbol*]
**KRDA** ........ Springville, UT [*AM radio station call letters*]
**KRDC-FM** ... St. George, UT [*FM radio station call letters*]
**KRDD** ........ Roswell, NM [*AM radio station call letters*]
**KRDE** ........ Denver [*Colorado*] [*ICAO location identifier*] (ICLI)
**KRDF-FM** ... Spearman, TX [*FM radio station call letters*]
**KRDG** ........ Redding, CA [*AM radio station call letters*]
**KRDI-FM** ... Decorah, IA [*FM radio station call letters*]
**KRDM** ........ Ardmore, OK [*FM radio station call letters*]
**KRDO** ........ Colorado Springs, CO [*AM radio station call letters*]
**KRDO-FM** ... Colorado Springs, CO [*FM radio station call letters*]
**KRDO-TV** ... Colorado Springs, CO [*Television station call letters*]
**KRDR** ........ Red River/Grand Forks Air Force Base [*North Dakota*] [*ICAO location identifier*] (ICLI)
**KRDS** ......... Tolleson, AZ [*AM radio station call letters*]
**KRDU** ........ Dinuba, CA [*AM radio station call letters*]
**KRDU** ........ Raleigh/Raleigh-Durham [*North Carolina*] [*ICAO location identifier*] (ICLI)
**KRDZ** ........ Wray, CO [*AM radio station call letters*]
**KRE** ........... Consolidated Regal Resources Ltd. [*Vancouver Stock Exchange symbol*]
**KRE** ........... Knight of the Red Eagle [*Prussia*]
**KRE** ........... Korea Exchange Bank. Monthly Review [*A publication*]
**KRE** ........... Kure [*Japan*] [*Seismograph station code, US Geological Survey*] [*Closed*] (SEIS)
**Krebs A** ...... Krebsarzt [*A publication*]
**Krebsforsch** ... Krebsforschung [*A publication*]
**Krebsforsch Krebsbekaempf** ... Krebsforschung und Krebsbekaempfung [*West Germany*] [*A publication*]
**KREC** ......... Brian Head, UT [*FM radio station call letters*]
**KRED** ........ Eureka, CA [*AM radio station call letters*]
**KRED-FM** ... Eureka, CA [*FM radio station call letters*]
**Kredietbank W Bul** ... Kredietbank. Weekly Bulletin [*A publication*]
**Kredietbnk** ... Weekly Bulletin. Kredietbank [*A publication*]
**KREE** ......... Lubbock/Reese Air Force Base [*Texas*] [*ICAO location identifier*] (ICLI)
**KREEP** ...... Potassium [*Chemical symbol: K*], Rare-Earth Elements, and Phosphorus [*Acronym used to describe crust material brought from the moon by astronauts*]
**KREG-TV** ... Glenwood Springs, CO [*Television station call letters*]
**KREH** ........ Sisseton, SD [*FM radio station call letters*]
**KREI** .......... Farmington, MO [*AM radio station call letters*]
**KREJ** ......... Medicine Lodge, KS [*FM radio station call letters*]
**KREK** ......... Bristow, OK [*FM radio station call letters*]
**KREL** ......... Henderson, NV [*AM radio station call letters*]
**KREMS** ..... Kiernan Reentry Measurement Site
**KREM-TV** ... Spokane, WA [*Television station call letters*]
**KREMU** .... Kenya Rangeland Ecological Monitoring Unit
**KREN** ........ Kings Road Entertainment, Inc. [*Los Angeles, CA*] [*NASDAQ symbol*] (NQ)
**KREN-TV** ... Reno, NV [*Television station call letters*]
**KREP** ......... Belleville, KS [*FM radio station call letters*]
**KRES** ......... Moberly, MO [*FM radio station call letters*]
**Kresge Art Bull** ... Kresge Art Center. Bulletin [*A publication*]
**KRESS** ....... Kinetic Ring Energy Storage System
**Kress** .......... Kress' Reports [*2-12 Pennsylvania Superior Court*] [*166-194 Pennsylvania*] [*A publication*] (DLA)
**KrestR** ........ Krestanska Revue [*Prague*] [*A publication*]
**KrestRTPril** ... Krestanska Revue. Theologicka Priloha [*Prague*] [*A publication*]
**Kret Chron** ... Kretika Chronika [*A publication*]
**KREUZ** ...... Kreuzer [*Monetary unit*] [*German*] (ROG)
**KRev** .......... Kentucky Review [*A publication*]
**KREW** ....... Sunnyside, WA [*AM radio station call letters*]
**KREW-FM** ... Sunnyside, WA [*FM radio station call letters*]
**KREX** ......... Keel Blade Tip Reflex [*Botany*]
**KREX-TV** ... Grand Junction, CO [*Television station call letters*]
**KREY-TV** ... Montrose, CO [*Television station call letters*]
**KREZ-TV** ... Durango, CO [*Television station call letters*]

**KRF**........... Kathode Ray Furnace
**KRF**........... Kerf Petroleums [*Vancouver Stock Exchange symbol*]
**KRF**........... Knowledge of Results Feedback
**KRF**........... Kramfors [*Sweden*] [*Airport symbol*] (OAG)
**KrF**........... Kristelig Folkpartiet [*Christian People's Party*] [*Norway*] [*Political party*] (PPE)
**KrF**........... Kristeligt Folkeparti [*Christian People's Party*] [*Denmark*] [*Political party*] (PPE)
**KRFA-FM** ... Moscow, ID [*FM radio station call letters*]
**KRFC**......... KISS [*Knights in the Service of Satan*] Rocks Fan Club (EA)
**KRFD**......... Marysville, CA [*AM radio station call letters*]
**KRFD-FM** ... Marysville, CA [*FM radio station call letters*]
**KRFM**......... Show Low, AZ [*FM radio station call letters*]
**KRFN**......... Knight-Ridder Financial News [*Database*] (IT)
**KRFO**......... Owatonna, MN [*AM radio station call letters*]
**KRFO-FM** ... Owatonna, MN [*FM radio station call letters*]
**KRFS**......... Superior, NE [*AM radio station call letters*]
**KRFS-FM** ... Superior, NE [*FM radio station call letters*]
**KRFW**......... Fort Worth [*Texas*] [*ICAO location identifier*] (ICLI)
**KRFX**......... Denver, CO [*FM radio station call letters*]
**KRG**........... Karasabai [*Guyana*] [*Airport symbol*] (OAG)
**KRG**........... Kerema [*Papua New Guinea*] [*Seismograph station code, US Geological Survey*] [*Closed*] (SEIS)
**KRG**........... Knight of the Redeemer of Greece (ROG)
**KRG**........... Krebs-Ringer-Glucose [*Buffer solution and growth medium*]
**KRG**........... KRG Management, Inc. [*Toronto Stock Exchange symbol*]
**KrG**........... Kriegsgericht [*War Tribunal*] [*German*]
**KRGA**......... Kemmerer, WY [*FM radio station call letters*]
**KRGC**......... Chicago [*Illinois*] [*ICAO location identifier*] (ICLI)
**KRGE**......... Weslaco, TX [*AM radio station call letters*]
**KRGF**......... Greenfield, CA [*FM radio station call letters*]
**KRGI**......... Grand Island, NE [*AM radio station call letters*]
**KRGI-FM** ... Grand Island, NE [*FM radio station call letters*]
**KRGK**......... Carthage, MO [*FM radio station call letters*]
**KRGN**......... Amarillo, TX [*FM radio station call letters*]
**KRGO**......... Fowler, CA [*AM radio station call letters*]
**KRGS**......... West Yellowstone, MT [*FM radio station call letters*]
**KRGT**......... Hutto, TX [*FM radio station call letters*]
**KRGV-TV** ... Weslaco, TX [*Television station call letters*]
**KRH**........... Redhill [*England*] [*Airport symbol*]
**KRHD**......... Duncan, OK [*AM radio station call letters*]
**KRHD-FM** ... Duncan, OK [*FM radio station call letters*]
**KRHS**......... Bullhead City, AZ [*AM radio station call letters*]
**Kr Hs A**...... Krankenhausarzt [*A publication*]
**Kr Hs Umsch** ... Krankenhaus-Umschau [*A publication*]
**KRI**........... Karin Lake Explorations [*Vancouver Stock Exchange symbol*]
**KRI**........... Kikori [*Papua New Guinea*] [*Airport symbol*] (OAG)
**KRI**........... King Research, Incorporated [*Computer consultant*] [*Information service or system*] (IID)
**KRI**........... King's Royal Irish [*Military unit*] [*British*]
**KRI**........... Knight-Ridder, Inc. [*NYSE symbol*] (SPSG)
**KRIA**......... Terrell Hills, TX [*AM radio station call letters*]
**KRIB**......... Mason City, IA [*AM radio station call letters*]
**KRIC**......... Rexburg, ID [*FM radio station call letters*]
**KRIC**......... Richmond/Richard Evelyn Byrd International [*Virginia*] [*ICAO location identifier*] (ICLI)
**KRIH**......... King's Royal Irish Hussars [*British military*] (DMA)
**KRIJ**......... Paradise, CA [*FM radio station call letters*]
**KRIL**......... Odessa, TX [*AM radio station call letters*]
**KRIM**......... Payson, AZ [*FM radio station call letters*]
**Krim Forensische Wiss** ... Kriminalistik und Forensische Wissenschaften [*A publication*]
**KRIN**......... Waterloo, IA [*Television station call letters*]
**KRIO**......... McAllen, TX [*AM radio station call letters*]
**Kriog Vak Tekh** ... Kriogennaya i Vakuumnaya Tekhnika [*Ukrainian SSR*] [*A publication*]
**KRIPO**....... Kriminalpolizei [*Ordinary Criminal Police*] [*German*]
**KRISA**....... Kristallografiya [*A publication*]
**KRISP**....... Kenya Rift International Seismic Project
**Kris Study Group NY Psychoanal Inst Monogr** ... Kris Study Group of the New York Psychoanalytic Institute. Monograph [*A publication*]
**Kristallogr** ... Kristallografiya [*A publication*]
**Kristallogr Grundl Anwend** ... Kristallographie. Grundlagen und Anwendung [*A publication*]
**Kristall Tech** ... Kristall und Technik [*A publication*]
**Krist und Tech** ... Kristall und Technik [*A publication*]
**Krist Tech**.. Kristall und Technik [*A publication*]
**KRIS-TV** ... Corpus Christi, TX [*Television station call letters*]
**KRIT**......... Clarion, IA [*FM radio station call letters*]
**Krit**........... Kriterion [*A publication*]
**KritC**......... Kritik (Copenhagen) [*A publication*]
**Krit Justiz**.. Kritische Justiz [*A publication*]
**KRIV**......... Houston, TX [*Television station call letters*]
**KRIV**......... Riverside/March Air Force Base [*California*] [*ICAO location identifier*] (ICLI)
**KRIX**......... Brownsville, TX [*FM radio station call letters*]
**KRIZ**......... Renton, WA [*AM radio station call letters*]
**KRJ**........... Kamimuroga [*Japan*] [*Seismograph station code, US Geological Survey*] (SEIS)
**KRJB**......... Ada, MN [*FM radio station call letters*]
**KRJC**......... Elko, NV [*FM radio station call letters*]
**KRJH**......... Hallettsville, TX [*AM radio station call letters*]
**KRJT**......... Bowie, TX [*AM radio station call letters*]
**KRJT-FM** ... Bowie, TX [*FM radio station call letters*]
**KRJUD**...... Kritische Justiz [*A publication*]
**KRJY**......... St. Louis, MO [*FM radio station call letters*]
**KRK**........... Kirkenes [*Norway*] [*Seismograph station code, US Geological Survey*] [*Closed*] (SEIS)
**KRK**........... Krakow [*Poland*] [*Airport symbol*] (OAG)
**KrK**........... Krestanska Revue [*Prague*] [*A publication*]
**KRKC**......... Kansas City [*Missouri*] [*ICAO location identifier*] (ICLI)
**KRKC**......... King City, CA [*AM radio station call letters*]
**KRKC-FM** ... King City, CA [*FM radio station call letters*]
**KRKHB**...... Krankenhaus-Umschau [*A publication*]
**KRKK**......... Rock Springs, WY [*AM radio station call letters*]
**KRKL**......... Yountville, CA [*AM radio station call letters*]
**KRKM**......... Kremmling, CO [*FM radio station call letters*]
**KRKN**......... Pittsburg, KS [*FM radio station call letters*]
**KRKO**......... Everett, WA [*AM radio station call letters*]
**KRKQ**......... Chester, CA [*FM radio station call letters*]
**KRKR**......... Tucson Estates, CA [*AM radio station call letters*]
**KRKS**......... Denver, CO [*AM radio station call letters*]
**KRKT**......... Albany, OR [*AM radio station call letters*]
**KRKT-FM** ... Albany, OR [*FM radio station call letters*]
**KRKX**......... Billings, MT [*FM radio station call letters*]
**KRKY**......... Granby, CO [*AM radio station call letters*]
**KRKZ**......... Altus, OK [*FM radio station call letters*]
**KRL**........... Karlsruhe [*Federal Republic of Germany*] [*Seismograph station code, US Geological Survey*] (SEIS)
**KRL**........... Kathode Ray Lamp
**KRL**........... Kingdom Resources Limited [*Vancouver Stock Exchange symbol*]
**KRL**........... Kirchhoff Radiation Law [*Physics*]
**KRL**........... Knowledge Representation Language
**KRL**........... Korla [*China*] [*Airport symbol*] (OAG)
**KRLA**......... Los Angeles [*California*] [*ICAO location identifier*] (ICLI)
**KRLA**......... Pasadena, CA [*AM radio station call letters*]
**KRLB-FM** ... Lubbock, TX [*FM radio station call letters*]
**KRLC**......... Lewiston, ID [*AM radio station call letters*]
**KRLD**......... Dallas, TX [*AM radio station call letters*]
**KRLN**......... Canon City, CO [*AM radio station call letters*]
**KRLN-FM** ... Canon City, CO [*FM radio station call letters*]
**KRLR**......... Las Vegas, NV [*Television station call letters*]
**KRLS**......... Keweenaw Rocket Launch Site [*University of Michigan*]
**KRLS**......... Knoxville, IA [*FM radio station call letters*]
**KRLT**......... South Lake Tahoe, CA [*FM radio station call letters*]
**KRLU**......... Lost Cabin, WY [*FM radio station call letters*]
**KRLV**......... Las Vegas, NV [*FM radio station call letters*]
**KRLW**......... Walnut Ridge, AR [*AM radio station call letters*]
**KRLW-FM** ... Walnut Ridge, AR [*FM radio station call letters*]
**KRLX**......... Northfield, MN [*FM radio station call letters*]
**KRLZ**......... Krelitz Industries, Inc. [*Minneapolis, MN*] [*NASDAQ symbol*] (NQ)
**KRM**........... Klein-Rydberg Method [*Physics*]
**KRM**........... Kurmenty [*USSR*] [*Seismograph station code, US Geological Survey*] (SEIS)
**KRM**........... Kurzweil Reading Machine
**KRM**........... Royal Ontario Museum Library [*UTLAS symbol*]
**KRMA-TV** ... Denver, CO [*Television station call letters*]
**KRMB**......... Roseau, MN [*FM radio station call letters*]
**KRMD-FM** ... Shreveport, LA [*FM radio station call letters*]
**KRME**......... Hondo, TX [*AM radio station call letters*]
**KRME**......... Rome/Griffiss Air Force Base [*New York*] [*ICAO location identifier*] (ICLI)
**KRMG**......... Tulsa, OK [*AM radio station call letters*]
**KRMH**......... Leadville, CO [*AM radio station call letters*]
**KRMH-FM** ... Leadville, CO [*FM radio station call letters*]
**KRMJA**...... Kurme Medical Journal [*A publication*]
**KRMK**......... Cordell, OK [*FM radio station call letters*]
**KRML**......... Carmel, CA [*AM radio station call letters*]
**KRMM**......... Payson, AZ [*FM radio station call letters*]
**KRMNA**...... Kriminalistik [*A publication*]
**KRMO**......... Monett, MO [*AM radio station call letters*]
**KRMS**......... Osage Beach, MO [*AM radio station call letters*]
**KRMW**......... Silt, CO [*AM radio station call letters*]
**KRMX**......... Pueblo, CO [*AM radio station call letters*]
**KRN**........... Food Magazine [*A publication*]
**KRN**........... Kiruna [*Sweden*] [*Airport symbol*] (OAG)
**KRNA**......... Iowa City, IA [*FM radio station call letters*]
**KRNB**......... Memphis, TN [*FM radio station call letters*]
**KRND**......... San Antonio/Randolf Air Force Base [*Texas*] [*ICAO location identifier*] (ICLI)
**KRNE-TV** ... Merriman, NE [*Television station call letters*]
**KRNL-FM** ... Mount Vernon, IA [*FM radio station call letters*]
**KRNO**......... Reno/International [*Nevada*] [*ICAO location identifier*] (ICLI)
**KRNO**......... Reno, NV [*AM radio station call letters*]
**KRNO-FM** ... Reno, NV [*FM radio station call letters*]
**KRNQ**......... Des Moines, IA [*FM radio station call letters*]
**KRNR**......... Roseburg, OR [*AM radio station call letters*]
**KRNS**......... San Antonio, TX [*AM radio station call letters*]

**KRNT** ........ Des Moines, IA [*AM radio station call letters*]
**KRNU** ........ Lincoln, NE [*FM radio station call letters*]
**KRNV** ........ Reno, NV [*Television station call letters*]
**KRNY** ........ Kearney, NE [*FM radio station call letters*]
**KRNY** ........ New York [*New York*] [*ICAO location identifier*] (ICLI)
**KRO** .......... Kathode Ray Oscilloscope
**KRO** .......... Katholieke Radio Omroep [*Catholic Broadcasting Association*] [*Netherlands*]
**kro** ............ Kru [*MARC language code*] [*Library of Congress*] (LCCP)
**KROA** ........ Grand Island, NE [*FM radio station call letters*]
**KROB** ........ Robstown, TX [*AM radio station call letters*]
**KROB-FM** ... Robstown, TX [*FM radio station call letters*]
**KROC** ........ Knight Royalty Corporation [*NASDAQ symbol*] (NQ)
**KROC** ........ Rochester, MN [*AM radio station call letters*]
**KROC** ........ Rochester/Rochester-Monroe County [*New York*] [*ICAO location identifier*] (ICLI)
**KR & O (Can)** ... King's Regulations and Orders for the Royal Canadian Army
**KROC-FM** ... Rochester, MN [*FM radio station call letters*]
**Kroc Found Ser** ... Kroc Foundation Series [*A publication*]
**Kroc Found Symp** ... Kroc Foundation Symposia [*A publication*]
**KROD** ........ El Paso, TX [*AM radio station call letters*]
**KROE** ........ Sheridan, WY [*AM radio station call letters*]
**Kroeber Anthro Soc Pap** ... Kroeber Anthropological Society. Papers [*A publication*]
**KROE-FM** ... Sheridan, WY [*FM radio station call letters*]
**KROF** ........ Abbeville, LA [*AM radio station call letters*]
**KROF-FM** ... Abbeville, LA [*FM radio station call letters*]
**KROI** ........ Sparks, NV [*FM radio station call letters*]
**KROK** ........ De Ridder, LA [*FM radio station call letters*]
**KROL** ........ Laughlin, NV [*AM radio station call letters*]
**Krolikovod Zverovod** ... Krolikovodstvo i Zverovodstvo [*A publication*]
**Kron** .......... Kronika [*A publication*]
**Kronobergsboken** ... Kronobergsboken Arsbok foer Hylten-Cavallius Foereningen [*A publication*]
**KRON-TV** ... San Francisco, CA [*Television station call letters*]
**KROO** ........ Breckenridge, TX [*FM radio station call letters*]
**KROP** ........ Brawley, CA [*AM radio station call letters*]
**KROQ** ........ Burbank, CA [*AM radio station call letters*]
**KROQ-FM** ... Pasadena, CA [*FM radio station call letters*]
**KROR** ........ Yucca Valley, CA [*FM radio station call letters*]
**KROS** ........ Clinton, IA [*AM radio station call letters*]
**KROU** ........ Spencer, OK [*FM radio station call letters*]
**KROW** ....... Reno, NV [*AM radio station call letters*]
**KROW** ....... Roswell/Industrial Air Center [*New Mexico*] [*ICAO location identifier*] (ICLI)
**KROX** ........ Crookston, MN [*AM radio station call letters*]
**KROY** ........ Kroy, Inc. [*NASDAQ symbol*] (NQ)
**KROY** ........ Sacramento, CA [*FM radio station call letters*]
**KROZ** ........ Tyler, TX [*FM radio station call letters*]
**KRP** .......... Karapiro [*New Zealand*] [*Seismograph station code, US Geological Survey*] (SEIS)
**KRP** .......... Karup [*Denmark*] [*Airport symbol*] (OAG)
**KRP** .......... Key Resource People [*US Chamber of Commerce*]
**KRP** .......... King's Rook's Pawn [*Chess*]
**KRP** .......... Kodak Relief Plate
**KRP** .......... Kolmer [*Test with*] Reiter Protein [*Serology*]
**KRP** .......... Krebs-Ringer-Phosphate [*Buffer solution*]
**KRP** .......... Kurdistan Revolutionary Party [*Iraq*] [*Political party*] (PPW)
**KRPA** ........ Rancho Palos Verdes, CA [*Television station call letters*]
**KRPB** ........ Krebs-Ringer-Phosphate Buffer [*Solution*]
**KRPL** ........ Moscow, ID [*AM radio station call letters*]
**KRPM** ....... Seattle, WA [*AM radio station call letters*]
**KRPM-FM** ... Tacoma, WA [*FM radio station call letters*]
**KRPN** ........ Roy, UT [*FM radio station call letters*]
**KRPQ** ........ Rohnert Park, CA [*FM radio station call letters*]
**KRPR** ........ Rochester, MN [*FM radio station call letters*]
**KRPS** ........ Weir, KS [*FM radio station call letters*]
**KRPT** ........ Anadarko, OK [*AM radio station call letters*]
**KRPT-FM** ... Anadarko, OK [*FM radio station call letters*]
**KRPV** ........ Roswell, NM [*Television station call letters*]
**KRPX** ........ Price, UT [*AM radio station call letters*]
**KRQ** .......... Crimsonstar Resources [*Vancouver Stock Exchange symbol*]
**KRQ** .......... Kentucky Romance Quarterly [*A publication*]
**KRQK** ........ Lompoc, CA [*FM radio station call letters*]
**KRQO** ........ Pittsburg, TX [*FM radio station call letters*]
**KRQQ** ........ Tucson, AZ [*FM radio station call letters*]
**KRQR** ........ San Francisco, CA [*FM radio station call letters*]
**KRQS** ........ Pagosa Springs, CO [*FM radio station call letters*]
**KRQU** ........ Laramie, WY [*FM radio station call letters*]
**KRQX** ........ Mexia, TX [*AM radio station call letters*]
**KRQY** ........ Coburg, OR [*AM radio station call letters*]
**KRR** .......... Kansai Research Reactor [*Japan*]
**KRR** .......... Karoi [*Rhodesia*] [*Seismograph station code, US Geological Survey*] (SEIS)
**KRR** .......... Kettle River Resources Ltd. [*Vancouver Stock Exchange symbol*]
**KRR** .......... King's Royal Rifles [*Military unit*] [*British*]
**KRR** .......... Krasnodar [*USSR*] [*Airport symbol*] (OAG)
**KRRB** ........ Dickinson, ND [*FM radio station call letters*]
**KRRC** ........ King's Royal Rifle Corps [*Military unit*] [*British*]
**KRRC** ........ Portland, OR [*FM radio station call letters*]
**KRRG** ........ Laredo, TX [*FM radio station call letters*]
**KRRI** ......... Boulder City, NV [*FM radio station call letters*]
**KRRK** ........ Bennington, NE [*FM radio station call letters*]
**KRRP** ........ Coushatta, LA [*AM radio station call letters*]
**KRRQ** ........ Lafayette, LA [*FM radio station call letters*]
**KRRS** ........ Santa Rosa, CA [*AM radio station call letters*]
**KRRT** ........ Kerrville, TX [*Television station call letters*]
**KrRThPr** .... Krestanska Revue. Theologicka Priloha [*Prague*] [*A publication*]
**KRRU** ........ Pueblo, CO [*AM radio station call letters*]
**KRRV** ........ Alexandria, LA [*AM radio station call letters*]
**KRRV-FM** ... Alexandria, LA [*FM radio station call letters*]
**KRRZ** ........ Minot, ND [*AM radio station call letters*]
**KRS** .......... Kearney State College, Kearney, NE [*OCLC symbol*] (OCLC)
**KRS** .......... Kentucky Revised Statutes [*A publication*]
**KRS** .......... Kerato-Refractive Society (EA)
**KRS** .......... Kinematograph Renter's Society
**KRS** .......... Knowledge Retrieval System [*KnowledgeSet Corp.*]
**KRS** .......... Krasnogorka [*USSR*] [*Seismograph station code, US Geological Survey*] [*Closed*] (SEIS)
**KRS** .......... Kristiansand [*Norway*] [*Airport symbol*] (OAG)
**KRSA** ........ Petersburg, AK [*AM radio station call letters*]
**KRSB-FM** ... Roseburg, OR [*FM radio station call letters*]
**KRSC** ........ Othello, WA [*AM radio station call letters*]
**KRSD** ........ Sioux Falls, SD [*FM radio station call letters*]
**KRSE** ........ Seattle [*Washington*] [*ICAO location identifier*] (ICLI)
**KRSE** ........ Yakima, WA [*FM radio station call letters*]
**KRSH** ........ Overland, MO [*FM radio station call letters*]
**KRSHB3** .... Annals of Science. Kanazawa University [*A publication*]
**KRSJ** ........ Durango, CO [*FM radio station call letters*]
**KRS Jugosl/Carsus Iugosl** ... KRS Jugoslavije/Carsus Iugoslaviae [*A publication*]
**KRSK** ........ Spokane, WA [*Television station call letters*]
**KRSL** ........ Kreisler Manufacturing Co. [*NASDAQ symbol*] (NQ)
**KRSL** ........ Russell, KS [*AM radio station call letters*]
**KRSM** ........ Dallas, TX [*FM radio station call letters*]
**KRSN** ........ Kerosene (MSA)
**KRSN** ........ Los Alamos, NM [*AM radio station call letters*]
**KRSO** ........ San Bernardino, CA [*AM radio station call letters*]
**KRS-ONE** ... Knowledge Reigns Supreme Over Nearly Everyone [*Rap recording artist*]
**KrSoob(Kiev)** ... Kratkije Soobscenija Breves Communications de l'Institute d'Archeologie (Kiev) [*A publication*]
**Kr Soobsc Inst Arheol** ... Kratkie Soobscenija Instituta Arheologii [*A publication*]
**KRSP** ........ South Salt Lake, UT [*AM radio station call letters*]
**KRSP-FM** ... Salt Lake City, UT [*FM radio station call letters*]
**KRSS** ........ Spokane, WA [*AM radio station call letters*]
**KRST** ........ Albuquerque, NM [*FM radio station call letters*]
**KRSTL** ...... Knowledge Representation Systems Trials Laboratory [*Pronounced "crystal"*] [*Artificial intelligence*]
**KRSU** ........ Appleton, MN [*FM radio station call letters*]
**KRSV** ........ Afton, WY [*AM radio station call letters*]
**KRSV-FM** ... Afton, WY [*FM radio station call letters*]
**KRSW-FM** ... Worthington-Marshall, MN [*FM radio station call letters*]
**KRSY** ........ Roswell, NM [*AM radio station call letters*]
**KRT** .......... Kathode Ray Tube (AAG)
**KRT** .......... Keravat [*New Britain*] [*Seismograph station code, US Geological Survey*] [*Closed*] (SEIS)
**KRT** .......... Khartoum [*Sudan*] [*Airport symbol*] (OAG)
**KRTEA** ...... Kristall und Technik [*A publication*]
**KRTH** ........ Los Angeles, CA [*AM radio station call letters*]
**KRTH-FM** ... Los Angeles, CA [*FM radio station call letters*]
**KRTL** ........ Atlanta [*Georgia*] [*ICAO location identifier*] (ICLI)
**KRTM** ........ Temecula, CA [*FM radio station call letters*]
**KRTN** ........ Raton, NM [*AM radio station call letters*]
**KRTN-FM** ... Raton, NM [*FM radio station call letters*]
**KRTO** ........ Kathode Ray Tube Oscillograph
**KRTRA** ...... Krupp Technical Review [*English Translation*] [*A publication*]
**KRTR-FM** ... Kailua, HI [*FM radio station call letters*]
**KRTS** ........ Kathode Ray Tube Shield
**KRTS** ........ Seabrook, TX [*FM radio station call letters*]
**KRTT** ........ Kathode Ray Tube Tester
**KRTU** ........ San Antonio, TX [*FM radio station call letters*]
**KRTV** ........ Great Falls, MT [*Television station call letters*]
**KRTW** ....... Baytown, TX [*Television station call letters*]
**KRTX** ........ Galveston, TX [*FM radio station call letters*]
**KRTZ** ........ Cortez, CO [*FM radio station call letters*]
**KRU** .......... Karasu [*USSR*] [*Seismograph station code, US Geological Survey*] (SEIS)
**kru** ............ Kurukh [*MARC language code*] [*Library of Congress*] (LCCP)
**KRUE** ........ Krueger [*W. A.*] Co. [*NASDAQ symbol*] (NQ)
**KRUG** ........ KRUG International Corp. [*NASDAQ symbol*] (NQ)
**KRUI** ........ Ruidoso Downs, NM [*AM radio station call letters*]
**KRUI-FM** ... Iowa City, IA [*FM radio station call letters*]
**Krummeck** ... Decisions of the Water Courts [*1913-36*] [*South Africa*] [*A publication*] (DLA)
**KRUN** ........ Ballinger, TX [*AM radio station call letters*]
**KRUN-FM** ... Ballinger, TX [*FM radio station call letters*]
**Krupp Tech Rev (Engl Transl)** ... Krupp Technical Review (English Translation) [*West Germany*] [*A publication*]

**KRUS**........ Ruston, LA [*AM radio station call letters*]
**KRUX**........ Las Cruces, NM [*FM radio station call letters*]
**KRUZ**........ Santa Barbara, CA [*FM radio station call letters*]
**KRV**.......... Kirovabad [*USSR*] [*Seismograph station code, US Geological Survey*] (SEIS)
**KRVC**........ Medford, OR [*AM radio station call letters*]
**KRVE**........ Santa Rosa, CA [*AM radio station call letters*]
**KRVH**........ Rio Vista, CA [*FM radio station call letters*]
**KRVK-FM**... Leavenworth, KS [*FM radio station call letters*]
**KRVL**........ Kerrville, TX [*FM radio station call letters*]
**KRVM**........ Eugene, OR [*FM radio station call letters*]
**KRVN**........ Lexington, NE [*AM radio station call letters*]
**KRVN-FM**... Lexington, NE [*FM radio station call letters*]
**KRVR**........ Davenport, IA [*FM radio station call letters*]
**KRVS**........ Lafayette, LA [*FM radio station call letters*]
**KRVZ**........ Springerville/Eager, AZ [*AM radio station call letters*]
**KRW**.......... Karlsruhe - West [*Federal Republic of Germany*] [*Seismograph station code, US Geological Survey*] (SEIS)
**KRWA**........ Washington [*District of Columbia*] [*ICAO location identifier*] (ICLI)
**KRWA-FM**... Waldron, AR [*FM radio station call letters*]
**KRWB**........ Roseau, MN [*AM radio station call letters*]
**KRWC**........ Buffalo, MN [*AM radio station call letters*]
**KRWF**........ Redwood Falls, MN [*Television station call letters*]
**KRWG**........ Las Cruces, NM [*FM radio station call letters*]
**KRWG-TV**... Las Cruces, NM [*Television station call letters*]
**KRWL**........ Butte, MT [*Television station call letters*]
**KRWN**........ Farmington, NM [*FM radio station call letters*]
**KRWQ**........ Gold Hill, OR [*FM radio station call letters*]
**KRWR**........ Carson City, NV [*FM radio station call letters*]
**KRX**.......... Christina Exploration [*Vancouver Stock Exchange symbol*]
**KRX**.......... Kar Kar [*Papua New Guinea*] [*Airport symbol*] (OAG)
**KRXA**........ Seward, AK [*AM radio station call letters*]
**KRXK**........ Rexburg, ID [*AM radio station call letters*]
**KRXK-FM**... Rexburg, ID [*FM radio station call letters*]
**KRXL**........ Kirksville, MO [*FM radio station call letters*]
**KRXO**........ Oklahoma City, OK [*FM radio station call letters*]
**KRXQ**........ Roseville, CA [*FM radio station call letters*]
**KRXR**........ Gooding, ID [*AM radio station call letters*]
**KRXT**........ Rockdale, TX [*FM radio station call letters*]
**KRXV**........ Yermo, CA [*FM radio station call letters*]
**KRXX**........ Marlin, TX [*FM radio station call letters*]
**KRXY**........ Lakewood, CO [*AM radio station call letters*]
**KRXY-FM**... Lakewood, CO [*FM radio station call letters*]
**KRY**.......... Karamay [*China*] [*Airport symbol*] (OAG)
**KRYK**........ Chinook, MT [*FM radio station call letters*]
**KRYL**........ Gatesville, TX [*FM radio station call letters*]
**Krym Gos Med Inst Tr**... Krymskii Gosudarstvennyi Meditsinskii Institut Trudy [*A publication*]
**KRYS**........ Corpus Christi, TX [*AM radio station call letters*]
**KRYS-FM**... Corpus Christi, TX [*FM radio station call letters*]
**KRYT**........ Pueblo, CO [*AM radio station call letters*]
**KRYT-FM**... Pueblo, CO [*FM radio station call letters*]
**KRZ**.......... Karuizawa [*Japan*] [*Also, KAZ*] [*Seismograph station code, US Geological Survey*] (SEIS)
**KRZ**.......... Kiri [*Zaire*] [*Airport symbol*] (OAG)
**KRZA**........ Alamosa, CO [*FM radio station call letters*]
**KRZB-TV**... Hot Springs, AR [*Television station call letters*]
**KRZE**........ Farmington, NM [*AM radio station call letters*]
**KRZI**........ Waco, TX [*AM radio station call letters*]
**KRZK**........ Branson, MO [*FM radio station call letters*]
**KRZQ-FM**... Tahoe City, CA [*FM radio station call letters*]
**KRZR**........ Hanford, CA [*FM radio station call letters*]
**KRZY**........ Albuquerque, NM [*AM radio station call letters*]
**KRZZ**........ Wichita, KS [*AM radio station call letters*]
**KRZZ-FM**... Derby, KS [*FM radio station call letters*]
**KS**............ Akademiia Nauk SSSR. Institut Narodov Azii. Kratkie Soobshcheniia [*Moscow*] [*A publication*]
**KS**............ Casair Aviation Ltd. [*Great Britain*] [*ICAO designator*] (FAAC)
**KS**............ Kansas [*Postal code*]
**KS**............ Kansas Reports [*A publication*] (DLA)
**KS**............ Kant-Studien [*A publication*]
**KS**............ Kaposi's Sarcoma [*Medicine*]
**KS**............ Katoptric System [*Optics*]
**KS**............ Kawasaki Syndrome [*Also, KD, MLNS*]
**KS**............ Keep Type Standing [*Printing*]
**KS**............ Keltic Society and the College of Druidism (EA)
**KS**............ Ketosteroid [*Endocrinology*]
**KS**............ Key Seated [*Freight*]
**KS**............ Keyset [*Navy*] (NVT)
**K/S**........... Kick Stage [*NASA*] (NASA)
**KS**............ Kidney Sac
**KS**............ Kilostere
**KS**............ King Solomon [*Freemasonry*] (ROG)
**KS**............ King's Scholar [*British*]
**KS**............ King's Serjeant [*British*] (ROG)
**KS**............ King's Speech [*British*]
**KS**............ Kipling Society of North America - USA and Canada (EA)
**KS**............ Kirjath Sepher [*Jerusalem*] (BJA)
**KS**............ Kiting Stock [*Investment term*]
**KS**............ Klinefelter's Syndrome [*Medicine*]
**KS**............ Knife Switch
**KS**............ Knight of the Sword [*of Sweden*]
**KS**............ Knock Sensor [*Automotive engineering*]
**KS**............ Kodak Standard [*Photography*]
**KS**............ Kokoxili Suture [*Paleogeography*]
**KS**............ Kolmogorov - Smirnov Test [*Statistics*]
**KS**............ Koloniale Studien [*A publication*]
**KS**............ Korea Society (EA)
**KS**............ Korean Survey [*A publication*]
**KS**............ Kraemer System
**KS**............ Kreditsaldo [*Credit Balance*] [*Afrikaans*]
**KS**............ Kultura Slova [*A publication*]
**K & S**........ Kunst und Sprache [*A publication*]
**KS**............ Kurze Sicht [*Short Sight*] [*German*]
**Ks**............ Kush (BJA)
**KS**............ Kveim-Seltzback (Test) [*Medicine*]
**ks**............. Potassium Metasilicate [*CIPW classification*] [*Geology*]
**KS**............ Singapore [*IYRU nationality code*] (IYR)
**KSA**.......... Kafka Society of America (EA)
**KSA**.......... Kansas Motor Carriers Association, Topeka KS [*STAC*]
**KSA**.......... Kansas Statutes, Annotated [*A publication*]
**KSA**.......... Kite-Supported Antenna
**KSA**.......... Knight of St. Anne [*Obsolete*] [*Russia*]
**KSA**.......... Ksara [*Lebanon*] [*Seismograph station code, US Geological Survey*] (SEIS)
**KSA**.......... Ksara [*Lebanon*] [*Geomagnetic observatory code*]
**KSA**.......... Ku-Band Single Access (MCD)
**KSA**.......... Kwajalein Standard Atmosphere
**KSA**.......... St. Augustine's Seminary Library, University of Toronto [*UTLAS symbol*]
**KSAA**........ Keats-Shelley Association of America (EA)
**KSABD**...... Korean Scientific Abstracts [*A publication*]
**KSAC**........ Sacramento, CA [*AM radio station call letters*]
**KSAC**........ Sacramento/Executive [*California*] [*ICAO location identifier*] (ICLI)
**KSAE**........ Korean Scientists and Engineers Abroad [*Republic of Korea*] [*Information service or system*] (IID)
**K-Saechs Ges Wiss Leipzig Mat-Phys Cl Ber**... Koeniglich-Saechsische Gesellschaft der Wissenschaften zu Leipzig. Mathematisch-Physische Klasse. Berichte ueber die Verhandlungen [*A publication*]
**KSAF**........ Knob Noster, MO [*FM radio station call letters*]
**KSAF**........ Santa Fe [*New Mexico*] [*ICAO location identifier*] (ICLI)
**KSAH**........ Universal City, TX [*AM radio station call letters*]
**KSAI**......... Saipan, CM [*AM radio station call letters*]
**KSAJ-FM**... Abilene, KS [*FM radio station call letters*]
**KSAK**........ Walnut, CA [*FM radio station call letters*]
**KSAL**........ Salina, KS [*AM radio station call letters*]
**KSal**.......... Salina Public Library, Salina, KS [*Library symbol*] [*Library of Congress*] (LCLS)
**KSalM**....... Marymount College, Salina, KS [*Library symbol*] [*Library of Congress*] (LCLS)
**KSalW**....... Kansas Wesleyan University, Salina, KS [*Library symbol*] [*Library of Congress*] (LCLS)
**KSAM**........ Huntsville, TX [*AM radio station call letters*]
**KSAM**........ Keyed Sequential Access Method [*Data processing*] (CMD)
**KSAN**........ San Diego/International-Lindbergh Field [*California*] [*ICAO location identifier*] (ICLI)
**KSAN-FM**... San Francisco, CA [*FM radio station call letters*]
**KSAQ**........ San Antonio, TX [*FM radio station call letters*]
**KSAR**........ Salem, AR [*FM radio station call letters*]
**KSAS-TV**.. Wichita, KS [*Television station call letters*]
**KSAT**........ San Antonio/International [*Texas*] [*ICAO location identifier*] (ICLI)
**KSAT-TV**.. San Antonio, TX [*Television station call letters*]
**KSAU**........ Nacogdoches, TX [*FM radio station call letters*]
**KSAV**........ Savannah/Municipal [*Georgia*] [*ICAO location identifier*] (ICLI)
**KSAW**........ Gwinn/K. I. Sawyer Air Force Base [*Michigan*] [*ICAO location identifier*] (ICLI)
**KSAX**........ Alexandria, MN [*Television station call letters*]
**KSAY**........ Fort Bragg, CA [*FM radio station call letters*]
**KSB**.......... Kradschuetzen-Bataillon [*Motorcycle Battalion*] [*German military - World War II*]
**KSBA**........ Coos Bay, OR [*FM radio station call letters*]
**KSBC**........ Hot Springs, AR [*FM radio station call letters*]
**KSBD**........ San Bernardino/Norton Air Force Base [*California*] [*ICAO location identifier*] (ICLI)
**KSBH**........ Coushatta, LA [*FM radio station call letters*]
**KSBI**......... Oklahoma City, OK [*Television station call letters*]
**KSBJ**......... Humble, TX [*FM radio station call letters*]
**KSBQ**........ Santa Maria, CA [*AM radio station call letters*]
**KSBR**........ Mission Viejo, CA [*FM radio station call letters*]
**KSBS-FM**... Pago Pago, AS [*FM radio station call letters*]
**KSBS-TV**... Steamboat Springs, CO [*Television station call letters*]
**KSBT**........ Steamboat Springs, CO [*FM radio station call letters*]
**KSB Tech Ber**... KSB [*Klein, Schanzlin, Becker*] Technische Berichte [*West Germany*] [*A publication*]

**KSBurNII** ... Kratkir Soobscenija Burjatskogo Kompleksnogo Naucnoissledovatel'skogo Instituta Serija Storiko-Filologiceskaja [*A publication*]
**KSBW** ........ Salinas, CA [*Television station call letters*]
**KSBY** ........ Salisbury/Wicomico County [*Maryland*] [*ICAO location identifier*] (ICLI)
**KSBY-TV** .. San Luis Obispo, CA [*Television station call letters*]
**KSC** ........... Council of State Governments, Lexington, KY [*OCLC symbol*] (OCLC)
**KSC** ........... Kennedy Space Center [*NASA*]
**KSC** ........... King's School, Canterbury (ROG)
**KSC** ........... Knight of St. Columba
**KSC** ........... Komunisticka Strana Ceskoslovenska [*Communist Party of Czechoslovakia*] [*Political party*] (PPW)
**KSC** ........... Korea Shipping Corporation (DS)
**KSC** ........... Korean Service Corps
**KSC** ........... Kosice [*Czechoslovakia*] [*Airport symbol*] (OAG)
**KSCA** ......... Santa Barbara, CA [*FM radio station call letters*]
**KSCAP** ...... Kennedy Space Center Area Permit [*NASA*] (MCD)
**KSCB** ......... Liberal, KS [*AM radio station call letters*]
**KSCB-FM** ... Liberal, KS [*FM radio station call letters*]
**KSCC** ......... Berryville, AR [*FM radio station call letters*]
**KSCE** ......... El Paso, TX [*Television station call letters*]
**KSCF** ......... Thousand Standard Cubic Feet
**KSCGH** ..... Kyushu Chugokugakkaiho [*Journal of the Sinological Society of Kyushu*] [*A publication*]
**KSch (Alt)** ... Kleine Schriften zur Geschichte de Volkes Israel [*A. Alt*] [*A publication*] (BJA)
**KSCH-TV** ... Stockton, CA [*Television station call letters*]
**KSCI** .......... San Bernardino, CA [*Television station call letters*]
**KSCI** .......... San Clemente Naval Auxiliary Air Base [*California*] [*ICAO location identifier*] (ICLI)
**KSCJ** ......... Sioux City, IA [*AM radio station call letters*]
**KSCK** ......... Stockton/Stockton Metropolitan [*California*] [*ICAO location identifier*] (ICLI)
**KSCL** ......... Shreveport, LA [*FM radio station call letters*]
**KSCO** ......... Santa Cruz, CA [*AM radio station call letters*]
**KSCO-FM** ... Santa Cruz, CA [*FM radio station call letters*]
**KSCQ** ......... Silver City, NM [*FM radio station call letters*]
**KSCR** ......... Benson, MN [*FM radio station call letters*]
**KSCS** ......... Fort Worth, TX [*FM radio station call letters*]
**KSCU** ......... Santa Clara, CA [*FM radio station call letters*]
**KSC/ULO** ... Kennedy Space Center/Unmanned Launch Operations [*NASA*]
**KSCV** ......... Kearney, NE [*FM radio station call letters*]
**KSC-WTROD** ... Kennedy Space Center - Western Test Range Operations Division [*NASA*]
**KSD** ........... C. H. Boehringer Sohn, Ingelheim [*Germany*] [*Research code symbol*]
**KSD** ........... Karlstad [*Sweden*] [*Airport symbol*] (OAG)
**KSDB** ......... Kommunal Statistisk DataBank [*Danmarks Statistik*] [*Denmark*] [*Information service or system*] (CRD)
**KSDB-FM** ... Manhattan, KS [*FM radio station call letters*]
**KSD-FM** .... St. Louis, MO [*FM radio station call letters*]
**KSDK** ......... St. Louis, MO [*Television station call letters*]
**KSDKA** ....... Kobe Shosen Daigaku Kiyo. Dai-2-Rui. Kokai, Kikan, Rigaku-Hen [*A publication*]
**KSDL** ......... Kieler Studien zur Deutschen Literaturgeschichte [*A publication*]
**KSDM** ......... International Falls, MN [*FM radio station call letters*]
**KSDN** ......... Aberdeen, SD [*AM radio station call letters*]
**KSDN-FM** ... Aberdeen, SD [*FM radio station call letters*]
**KSDO** ......... San Diego, CA [*AM radio station call letters*]
**KSDO-FM** ... San Diego, CA [*FM radio station call letters*]
**KSDP** ......... Sand Point, AK [*AM radio station call letters*]
**KSDR** ......... Watertown, SD [*AM radio station call letters*]
**KSDS** ......... Key Sequenced Data Set (CMD)
**KSDS** ......... San Diego, CA [*FM radio station call letters*]
**KSDZ** ......... Gordon, NE [*FM radio station call letters*]
**KSE** ........... Kasese [*Uganda*] [*Airport symbol*] (OAG)
**KSE** ........... Knight of Saint-Esprit [*France*]
**KSE** ........... Knight of the Star of the East (ROG)
**KSE** ........... Korea Stock Exchange (ECON)
**KSEA** ......... Korean Scientists and Engineers Association in America (EA)
**KSEA** ......... Seattle/Seattle-Tacoma International [*Washington*] [*ICAO location identifier*] (ICLI)
**KSEA** ......... Seattle, WA [*FM radio station call letters*]
**K & SEAFA** ... Korea and South East Asia Forces Association of Australia
**KSEC** ......... Lamar, CO [*FM radio station call letters*]
**KSED** ......... Sedona, AZ [*FM radio station call letters*]
**KSEE** ......... Fresno, CA [*Television station call letters*]
**KSEI** .......... Pocatello, ID [*AM radio station call letters*]
**KSEI-FM** .. Pocatello, ID [*FM radio station call letters*]
**KSEK** ......... Pittsburg, KS [*AM radio station call letters*]
**KSEL** ......... Portales, NM [*AM radio station call letters*]
**KSEL-FM** ... Portales, NM [*FM radio station call letters*]
**KSEM** ......... Selma/Craig Air Force Base [*Alabama*] [*ICAO location identifier*] (ICLI)
**KSEM-FM** ... Seminole, TX [*FM radio station call letters*]
**KSEN** ......... Shelby, MT [*AM radio station call letters*]
**KSEO** ......... Durant, OK [*AM radio station call letters*]
**KSEQ** ......... Visalia, CA [*FM radio station call letters*]
**KSER** ......... Everett, WA [*FM radio station call letters*]
**KSES** ......... Selma/Selfield [*Alabama*] [*ICAO location identifier*] (ICLI)
**KSES** ......... Yucca Valley, CA [*AM radio station call letters*]
**KSEV** ......... Tomball, TX [*AM radio station call letters*]
**KSEY** ......... Seymour, TX [*AM radio station call letters*]
**KSEY-FM** ... Seminole, TX [*FM radio station call letters*]
**KSEZ** ......... Sioux City, IA [*FM radio station call letters*]
**KSF** ........... Karen Silkwood Fund (EA)
**KSF** ........... Kassel [*West Germany*] [*Airport symbol*] (OAG)
**KSF** ........... Keel Shock Factor (NATG)
**ksf** ............ Kips [*Thousands of Pounds*] per Square Foot
**KSF** ........... Knight of St. Ferdinand [*Sicily*] (ROG)
**KSF** ........... Knight of San Fernando [*Spain*]
**KSF** ........... Quaker State Corp. [*NYSE symbol*] (SPSG)
**KSFA** ......... Nacogdoches, TX [*AM radio station call letters*]
**KSFC** ......... Keith Sewell Fan Club (EA)
**KSFC** ......... Spokane, WA [*FM radio station call letters*]
**KSFE** ......... Needles, CA [*AM radio station call letters*]
**KSFF** ......... Spokane/Felts [*Washington*] [*ICAO location identifier*] (ICLI)
**KSFH** ......... Mountain View, CA [*FM radio station call letters*]
**KSFI** .......... Salt Lake City, UT [*FM radio station call letters*]
**KSFM** ......... Knight of St. Ferdinand and Merit [*Italy*]
**KSFM** ......... Woodland, CA [*FM radio station call letters*]
**KSFO** ......... San Francisco, CA [*AM radio station call letters*]
**KSFO** ......... San Francisco/International [*California*] [*ICAO location identifier*] (ICLI)
**KSFR** ......... Santa Fe, NM [*FM radio station call letters*]
**KSFS** ......... San Francisco Coast Guard Air Station [*California*] [*ICAO location identifier*] (ICLI)
**KSFT** ......... St. Joseph, MO [*AM radio station call letters*]
**KSFUS** ...... Korean Student Federation of the United States (EA)
**KSFX** ......... Roswell, NM [*FM radio station call letters*]
**KSFY-TV** .. Sioux Falls, SD [*Television station call letters*]
**KSG** ........... Harvard University, Kennedy School for Government, Cambridge, MA [*OCLC symbol*] (OCLC)
**KSG** ........... Knight of St. George [*Russia*] [*Obsolete*]
**KSG** ........... Knight of St. Gregory
**KSGB** ......... Fort Worth, TX [*AM radio station call letters*]
**KSGI** .......... St. George, UT [*AM radio station call letters*]
**KSGL** ......... Wichita, KS [*AM radio station call letters*]
**KSGM** ......... Chester, IL [*AM radio station call letters*]
**KSGN** ......... Riverside, CA [*FM radio station call letters*]
**KSGR** ......... Nampa, ID [*AM radio station call letters*]
**KSGT** ......... Jackson, WY [*AM radio station call letters*]
**KSGT** ......... Kleine Schriften. Gesellschaft fuer Theatergeschichte [*A publication*]
**KSGW-TV** ... Sheridan, WY [*Television station call letters*]
**KSH** ........... Kenya Shilling [*Monetary unit*] (IMH)
**KSH** ........... Key Strokes per Hour
**KSH** ........... Knight of St. Hubert [*Bavaria*]
**KSH** ........... Kolel Shomre Hachomos [*An association*] (EA)
**KSH** ........... Kuh Shi [*Republic of China*] [*Seismograph station code, US Geological Survey*] (SEIS)
**KSHA** ......... Redding, CA [*FM radio station call letters*]
**KSHAB2** .... Bulletin. Fruit Tree Research Station. Series A [*Yatabe*] [*A publication*]
**KSHB-TV** ... Kansas City, MO [*Television station call letters*]
**KSHE** ......... Crestwood, MO [*FM radio station call letters*]
**KSHI** .......... Zuni, NM [*FM radio station call letters*]
**KShm** ......... Johnson County Public Library, Shawnee Mission, KS [*Library symbol*] [*Library of Congress*] (LCLS)
**KSHR-FM** ... Coquille, OR [*FM radio station call letters*]
**KSH/RMBH** ... Kolel Shomre Hachomos/Reb Meir Baal Haness (EA)
**KSHSR** ...... Kentucky State Historical Society. Register [*A publication*]
**KSHU** ......... Huntsville, TX [*FM radio station call letters*]
**KSHV** ......... Shreveport/Regional Airport [*Louisiana*] [*ICAO location identifier*] (ICLI)
**KSHY** ......... Cheyenne, WY [*AM radio station call letters*]
**KSI** ............ Karsanskaya [*USSR*] [*Later, TFS*] [*Geomagnetic observatory code*]
**KSI** ............ Kemgas Sydney, Inc. [*Vancouver Stock Exchange symbol*]
**KSI** ............ Kips [*Thousands of Pounds*] per Square Inch (MCD)
**KSI** ............ Kleine Schriften zur Geschichte des Volkes Israel [*A. Alt*] [*A publication*] (BJA)
**KSI** ............ Knight of [*the Order of*] the Star of India [*British*]
**KSIB** ......... Creston, IA [*AM radio station call letters*]
**KSID** ......... Sidney, NE [*AM radio station call letters*]
**KSID-FM** .. Sidney, NE [*FM radio station call letters*]
**KSIF** .......... Idaho Falls, ID [*FM radio station call letters*]
**KSIG** ......... Crowley, LA [*AM radio station call letters*]
**KSIIMK** .... Kratkie Soobshcheniia o Dokladakh i Polevykh Issledovaniiakh Instituta Istorii Materialnoi Kulturi [*A publication*] (BJA)
**KSIL** .......... Silver City, NM [*AM radio station call letters*]
**KSIM** ......... Sikeston, MO [*AM radio station call letters*]
**KSIN** ......... Sioux City, IA [*Television station call letters*]
**KSINA** ....... Kratkije Soobscenija Instituta Narodov Azii [*A publication*]
**KSIP** .......... Kent Scientific & Industrial Projects Ltd. [*British*] (IRUK)
**KSIQ** ......... Brawley, CA [*FM radio station call letters*]
**KSIR** ......... Estes Park, CO [*AM radio station call letters*]
**KSIS** ......... Sedalia, MO [*AM radio station call letters*]

**KSISL**........ Kratkije Soobscenija Instituta Slajanovednija Akademija Nauk SSSR [*A publication*]
**KSIT**.......... Rock Springs, WY [*FM radio station call letters*]
**KSIV**.......... Clayton, MO [*AM radio station call letters*]
**KSIV**.......... Kratkije Soobscenija Instituta Vostokovedenija Akademija Nauk SSSR [*A publication*]
**KSIW**......... Woodward, OK [*AM radio station call letters*]
**KSIX**.......... Corpus Christi, TX [*AM radio station call letters*]
**KSJ**............ Kashima [*Japan*] [*Seismograph station code, US Geological Survey*] (SEIS)
**KSJ**............ Kasos Island [*Greece*] [*Airport symbol*] (OAG)
**KSJ**............ Keats-Shelley Journal [*A publication*]
**KSJ**............ Knight of St. Januarius [*Naples*]
**KSJ**............ Knights of St. John (EA)
**KSJB**.......... Jamestown, ND [*AM radio station call letters*]
**KSJC-FM**... Stockton, CA [*FM radio station call letters*]
**KSJD**.......... Cortez, CO [*FM radio station call letters*]
**KSJE**.......... Farmington, NM [*FM radio station call letters*]
**KSJJ**........... Redmond, OR [*FM radio station call letters*]
**KSJK**.......... Talent, OR [*AM radio station call letters*]
**KSJL**........... San Antonio, TX [*AM radio station call letters*]
**KSJM**.......... Jamestown, ND [*FM radio station call letters*]
**KSJN**.......... Minneapolis-St. Paul, MN [*FM radio station call letters*]
**KSJO**.......... San Jose, CA [*FM radio station call letters*]
**KSJR-FM**... Collegeville, MN [*FM radio station call letters*]
**KSJS**........... San Jose, CA [*FM radio station call letters*]
**KSJSC**........ Knights of St. John Supreme Commandery (EA)
**KSJT**........... San Angelo/Mathis Field [*Texas*] [*ICAO location identifier*] (ICLI)
**KSJT-FM**... San Angelo, TX [*FM radio station call letters*]
**KSJU**.......... Collegeville, MN [*FM radio station call letters*]
**KSJV**.......... Fresno, CA [*FM radio station call letters*]
**KSJX**.......... San Jose, CA [*AM radio station call letters*]
**KSJY**.......... Lafayette, LA [*FM radio station call letters*]
**KSK**........... Kappa Sigma Kappa [*Later, Theta Xi*] [*Fraternity*]
**KSK**........... Karlskoga [*Sweden*] [*Airport symbol*] (OAG)
**KSKA**......... Anchorage, AK [*FM radio station call letters*]
**KSKA**......... Spokane/Fairchild Air Force Base [*Washington*] [*ICAO location identifier*] (ICLI)
**KSKB**......... Brooklyn, IA [*FM radio station call letters*]
**KSKD**......... Sweet Home, OR [*FM radio station call letters*]
**KSKF**.......... Klamath Falls, OR [*FM radio station call letters*]
**KSKF**.......... San Antonio/Kelly Air Force Base [*Texas*] [*ICAO location identifier*] (ICLI)
**KSKG**......... Salina, KS [*FM radio station call letters*]
**KSKI**.......... Hailey, ID [*AM radio station call letters*]
**KSKI-FM**.. Sun Valley, ID [*FM radio station call letters*]
**KSKJ**.......... American Slovenian Catholic Union of the USA (EA)
**KSKM**......... Bethel, AK [*AM radio station call letters*]
**KSKN**......... Spokane, WA [*Television station call letters*]
**KSKO**......... McGrath, AK [*AM radio station call letters*]
**K Skogs o Lantbr Akad Tidskr**... Kungliga Skogs- och Lantbruksakademiens. Tidskrift [*A publication*]
**KSKQ**......... Los Angeles, CA [*AM radio station call letters*]
**KSKQ-FM**... Long Beach, CA [*FM radio station call letters*]
**KSKR**......... Whitefish, MT [*AM radio station call letters*]
**KSKS**......... Tulsa, OK [*AM radio station call letters*]
**KSKT**......... Wamego, KS [*FM radio station call letters*]
**KSKU**......... Hutchinson, KS [*FM radio station call letters*]
**KSKY**......... Balch Springs, TX [*AM radio station call letters*]
**KSKY**......... Sandusky/Griffing [*Ohio*] [*ICAO location identifier*] (ICLI)
**KSL**........... Kanadska Slovenska Liga [*Canadian Slovak League - CSL*]
**KSL**........... Kassala [*Sudan*] [*Airport symbol*] (OAG)
**KSL**........... Keio University [*EDUCATSS*] [*UTLAS symbol*]
**KSL**........... Kentucky Department of Libraries, Library Extension Division, Frankfort, KY [*OCLC symbol*] (OCLC)
**KSL**........... Keyboard Simulated Lateral Telling [*Data processing*]
**KSL**........... Knight of the Sun and Lion [*Persia*]
**KSl**............ Kultura Slova [*A publication*]
**KSL**........... Salt Lake City, UT [*AM radio station call letters*]
**KSLA-TV**.. Shreveport, LA [*Television station call letters*]
**KSLC**......... McMinnville, OR [*FM radio station call letters*]
**KSLC**......... Salt Lake City/International [*Utah*] [*ICAO location identifier*] (ICLI)
**KSLD**......... Riverside, CA [*Television station call letters*]
**KSLE**......... Seminole, OK [*FM radio station call letters*]
**KSLH**......... St. Louis, MO [*FM radio station call letters*]
**KSLI**.......... King's Shropshire Light Infantry [*Military unit*] [*British*]
**KSLJ**.......... Knight of [*the Order of*] St. Lazarus of Jerusalem [*British*]
**KSLL**......... Richardson, TX [*FM radio station call letters*]
**KSLM**........ Salem, OR [*AM radio station call letters*]
**K-SLN**....... KSC [*Kennedy Space Center*] Spacelab Notice [*NASA*] (NASA)
**KSLO**......... Opelousas, LA [*AM radio station call letters*]
**K-SLPS**...... KSC [*Kennedy Space Center*] Spacelab Project Specification [*NASA*] (NASA)
**KSLQ**......... Washington, MO [*AM radio station call letters*]
**KSLQ-FM**... Washington, MO [*FM radio station call letters*]
**KS LR**........ Kansas Law Review [*A publication*]
**KSLR**......... San Antonio, TX [*AM radio station call letters*]
**KSLS**......... Liberal, KS [*FM radio station call letters*]
**KSLT**......... Spearfish, SD [*FM radio station call letters*]
**KSLTA**....... Kungliga Skogs- och Lantbruksakademiens. Tidskrift [*A publication*]
**KSL-TV**..... Salt Lake City, UT [*Television station call letters*]
**KSLU**......... Hammond, LA [*FM radio station call letters*]
**KSLV**......... Monte Vista, CO [*AM radio station call letters*]
**KSLV-FM**... Monte Vista, CO [*FM radio station call letters*]
**KSLX**......... Scottsdale, AZ [*FM radio station call letters*]
**KSLY-FM**... San Luis Obispo, CA [*FM radio station call letters*]
**KSM**.......... Katubsanan sa Mamumio [*Philippine United Labor Congress*]
**KSM**.......... Kemper Strategic Municipal Trust [*NYSE symbol*] (SPSG)
**KSM**.......... Korean Service Medal [*Military decoration*]
**K-SM**......... KSC [*Kennedy Space Center*] Shuttle Management [*Document*] [*NASA*] (NASA)
**KSM**.......... Saint Mary's [*Alaska*] [*Airport symbol*] (OAG)
**KSM**.......... Saint Mary's, AK [*Location identifier*] [*FAA*] (FAAL)
**KSM**.......... St. Michael's College Library, University of Toronto [*UTLAS symbol*]
**KSM**.......... Shawnee Medical Center Medical Library, Shawnee Mission, KS [*OCLC symbol*] (OCLC)
**KSMA**........ Santa Maria, CA [*AM radio station call letters*]
**KSMB**........ Keats-Shelley Memorial Bulletin [*Rome*] [*A publication*]
**KSMB**........ Lafayette, LA [*FM radio station call letters*]
**KSMBR**..... Keats-Shelley Memorial Bulletin (Rome) [*A publication*]
**KSMC**........ Moraga, CA [*FM radio station call letters*]
**KSMF**........ Ashland, OR [*FM radio station call letters*]
**KSMF**........ Sacramento/Sacramento Metropolitan [*California*] [*ICAO location identifier*] (ICLI)
**KSMG**....... Seguin, TX [*FM radio station call letters*]
**KSMGA**..... Koks, Smola, Gaz [*A publication*]
**KSMI**......... Orcutt, CA [*AM radio station call letters*]
**KSMJ**........ Sacramento, CA [*AM radio station call letters*]
**KSMK-FM**... Cottonwood, AZ [*FM radio station call letters*]
**KSML**........ Kosher Meal [*Airline notation*]
**KSML**........ Salem, SD [*FM radio station call letters*]
**KSMM**....... Fargo, ND [*FM radio station call letters*]
**KSMMP**.... Kin Seeking Missing Military Personnel [*Organization of parents with sons missing in action with purpose of supplementing US government search for missing personnel*] [*Post-World War II*]
**KSMO**....... Salem, MO [*AM radio station call letters*]
**KSMQ-TV**... Austin, MN [*Television station call letters*]
**KSMR**........ Winona, MN [*FM radio station call letters*]
**KSMSA**..... Kosmos [*Stuttgart*] [*A publication*]
**KSM & SG**... Knight of Saint Michael and Saint George [*Ionian Islands*]
**KSMS-TV**... Monterey, CA [*Television station call letters*]
**KSMT**........ Breckenridge, CO [*FM radio station call letters*]
**KSMU**....... Komunistycha Spilka Molodi Ukrainy
**KSMU**....... Springfield, MO [*FM radio station call letters*]
**KSMX**........ Walla Walla, WA [*AM radio station call letters*]
**KSN**........... Kassan Resources [*Vancouver Stock Exchange symbol*]
**KSN**........... Kit Shortage Notice
**KSNB-TV**... Superior, NE [*Television station call letters*]
**KSNC**........ Great Bend, KS [*Television station call letters*]
**KSND**........ Springfield-Eugene, OR [*FM radio station call letters*]
**KSNE**......... Marshall, AR [*FM radio station call letters*]
**KSNF**......... Joplin, MO [*Television station call letters*]
**KSNG**........ Garden City, KS [*Television station call letters*]
**KSNI-FM**.. Santa Maria, CA [*FM radio station call letters*]
**KSNK**........ McCook, NE [*Television station call letters*]
**KSNM**....... Truth Or Consequences, NM [*FM radio station call letters*]
**KSNN**........ Los Banos, CA [*FM radio station call letters*]
**KSNO**........ Aspen, CO [*AM radio station call letters*]
**KSNO-FM**... Snowmass Village, CO [*FM radio station call letters*]
**KSNR**........ Thief River Falls, MN [*FM radio station call letters*]
**KSNT**......... Topeka, KS [*Television station call letters*]
**KSNW**....... Wichita, KS [*Television station call letters*]
**KSNY**........ Snyder, TX [*AM radio station call letters*]
**KSNY-FM**... Snyder, TX [*FM radio station call letters*]
**KSO**........... Kastoria [*Greece*] [*Airport symbol*] (OAG)
**KSOC**........ Key Symbol Out of Context [*Data processing*] (DIT)
**KSOF**........ Wichita, KS [*FM radio station call letters*]
**KSOK**........ Arkansas City, KS [*AM radio station call letters*]
**KSOL**......... San Mateo, CA [*FM radio station call letters*]
**KSON**........ San Diego, CA [*AM radio station call letters*]
**KSON-FM**... San Diego, CA [*FM radio station call letters*]
**KSOO**........ Sioux Falls, SD [*AM radio station call letters*]
**KSOP**......... Salt Lake City, UT [*AM radio station call letters*]
**KSOP-FM**... Salt Lake City, UT [*FM radio station call letters*]
**KSOR**........ Ashland, OR [*FM radio station call letters*]
**KSOS**......... Brigham City, UT [*FM radio station call letters*]
**KSOX**........ Raymondville, TX [*AM radio station call letters*]
**KSOX-FM**... Raymondville, TX [*FM radio station call letters*]
**KSOZ**......... Point Lookout, MO [*FM radio station call letters*]
**KSP**........... Kentucky Department of Libraries, Processing Center, Frankfort, KY [*OCLC symbol*] (OCLC)
**KSP**........... Keyset Panel
**KSP**........... Knight of St. Stanislaus of Poland
**KSP**........... Kodak Special Plate
**KSP**........... Ksiaz [*Poland*] [*Seismograph station code, US Geological Survey*] (SEIS)

**KSPB**......... Pebble Beach, CA [*FM radio station call letters*]
**KSPC**......... Claremont, CA [*FM radio station call letters*]
**KSPD**......... Boise, ID [*AM radio station call letters*]
**KSPG**......... El Dorado, KS [*AM radio station call letters*]
**KSPG**......... St. Petersburg/Albert Whitted [*Florida*] [*ICAO location identifier*] (ICLI)
**KSPI**......... Stillwater, OK [*AM radio station call letters*]
**KSPI-FM**... Stillwater, OK [*FM radio station call letters*]
**KSPK**......... Walsenburg, CO [*FM radio station call letters*]
**KSPL**......... San Marcos, TX [*AM radio station call letters*]
**K-SPN**....... KSC [*Kennedy Space Center*] Shuttle Project Notice [*NASA*] (NASA)
**KSPN**......... Vail, CO [*AM radio station call letters*]
**KSPN-FM**... Aspen, CO [*FM radio station call letters*]
**KSPO**......... Dishman, WA [*FM radio station call letters*]
**KSPQ**......... West Plains, MO [*FM radio station call letters*]
**KSPR**......... Springfield, MO [*Television station call letters*]
**KSPRA**...... Kuznechno-Shtampovochnoe Proizvodstvo [*A publication*]
**KSPS**......... Kilo Symbols per Second (MCD)
**K-SPS**....... KSC [*Kennedy Space Center*] Shuttle Project Specification [*NASA*] (NASA)
**KSPS**......... Wichita Falls/Sheppard Air Force Base and Municipal [*Texas*] [*ICAO location identifier*] (ICLI)
**KSPS-TV**... Spokane, WA [*Television station call letters*]
**KSPT**......... Sandpoint, ID [*AM radio station call letters*]
**KSPZ**......... Colorado Springs, CO [*FM radio station call letters*]
**KsQ**........... Kansas Quarterly [*A publication*]
**KSQD-FM**... Lowry, SD [*FM radio station call letters*]
**KSQI**......... Greeley, CO [*FM radio station call letters*]
**KSQY**......... Deadwood, SD [*FM radio station call letters*]
**KSR**........... Keyboard Send and Receive [*Data processing*]
**KSR**........... Koster [*South Africa*] [*Seismograph station code, US Geological Survey*] (SEIS)
**KSR**........... Sandy River, AK [*Location identifier*] [*FAA*] (FAAL)
**KSRA**......... Salmon, ID [*AM radio station call letters*]
**KSRA-FM**... Salmon, ID [*FM radio station call letters*]
**KSRB**......... Hardy, AR [*AM radio station call letters*]
**KSRC**......... Socorro, NM [*AM radio station call letters*]
**KSRE**......... Minot, ND [*Television station call letters*]
**KSRF**......... Santa Monica, CA [*FM radio station call letters*]
**KSRG**......... Sac City, IA [*FM radio station call letters*]
**KSRH**......... San Rafael, CA [*FM radio station call letters*]
**KSRM**......... Soldotna, AK [*AM radio station call letters*]
**KSRNA**...... Kiso To Rinsho [*A publication*]
**KSRO**......... Santa Rosa, CA [*AM radio station call letters*]
**KSRQ**......... Thief River Falls, MN [*FM radio station call letters*]
**KSRR**......... Provo, UT [*AM radio station call letters*]
**KSRS**......... Kevo Subarctic Research Station. Reports [*A publication*]
**KSRS**......... Roseburg, OR [*FM radio station call letters*]
**KSRT**......... Orange, CA [*AM radio station call letters*]
**KSRV**......... Ontario, OR [*AM radio station call letters*]
**KSRV-FM**... Ontario, OR [*FM radio station call letters*]
**KSRW**......... Childress, TX [*FM radio station call letters*]
**KSRZ-FM**... North Platte, NE [*FM radio station call letters*]
**KSS**........... Kearns-Sayre Syndrome [*Ophthalmology*]
**KSS**........... Kearns-Sayres Syndrome [*Medicine*]
**KSS**........... Kellogg Switchboard and Supply
**KSS**........... Kent State University, School of Library Science, Kent, OH [*OCLC symbol*] (OCLC)
**KSS**........... Keying Switching Station
**KSS**........... Knee Signature System [*Orthopedics*]
**KSS**........... Knight of St. Sylvester
**KSS**........... Knight of the Southern Star [*Brazil*]
**KSS**........... Knight of the Sword of Sweden
**KSS**........... Komunisticka Strane Slovenska [*Communist Party of Slovakia*] [*Czechoslovakia*] [*Political party*] (PPW)
**KSS**........... Korea Stamp Society (EA)
**KSSA**......... Plano, TX [*AM radio station call letters*]
**KSSA-FM**... McKinney, TX [*FM radio station call letters*]
**KSSB**......... Calipatria, CA [*FM radio station call letters*]
**KSSBI**........ Konfederasi Serikat Serikat Buruh Islam [*Confederation of Islamic Trade Unions of Indonesia*]
**KSSC**......... Columbus, KS [*FM radio station call letters*]
**KSSC**......... Joplin, MO [*AM radio station call letters*]
**KSSC**......... Sumter/Shaw Air Force Base [*South Carolina*] [*ICAO location identifier*] (ICLI)
**KSSD**......... Cedar City, UT [*FM radio station call letters*]
**KSSI**......... China Lake, CA [*FM radio station call letters*]
**KSSK**......... Honolulu, HI [*AM radio station call letters*]
**KSSK-FM**... Waipahu, HI [*FM radio station call letters*]
**KSSM**......... Miami, OK [*FM radio station call letters*]
**KSSM**......... Sault Ste. Marie/Sault Ste. Marie Municipal [*Michigan*] [*ICAO location identifier*] (ICLI)
**KSSN**......... Little Rock, AR [*FM radio station call letters*]
**KSSQ**......... Conroe, TX [*AM radio station call letters*]
**KSSR**......... Santa Rosa, NM [*AM radio station call letters*]
**KSSS**......... Colorado Springs, CO [*AM radio station call letters*]
**K-SSS**....... KSC [*Kennedy Space Center*] Shuttle Project Station Set Specification [*NASA*] (NASA)
**KSST**......... Sulphur Springs, TX [*AM radio station call letters*]
**KSSY**......... Wenatchee, WA [*FM radio station call letters*]
**KSt**............ Kant-Studien [*A publication*]
**KST**........... Katholiek Sociaal Tijdschrift [*A publication*]
**KST**........... Keilinschriftliche Studien [*A publication*] (BJA)
**KST**........... Key Station Terminal [*Data processing*]
**KST**........... Keyseat (KSC)
**KST**........... King Solomon's Temple [*Freemasonry*]
**KST**........... Kolcsonos Segito Takarekpenztarak [*Mutual Savings Banks*] [*Hungarian*]
**KSTA**......... Coleman, TX [*AM radio station call letters*]
**KSTA-FM**... Coleman, TX [*FM radio station call letters*]
**KSTB**......... Breckenridge, TX [*AM radio station call letters*]
**KSTC**......... Kansas State Teachers College
**KSTC**......... Sterling, CO [*AM radio station call letters*]
**KSteC**........ Sterling College, Sterling, KS [*Library symbol*] [*Library of Congress*] (LCLS)
**KSTF**......... Scottsbluff, NE [*Television station call letters*]
**KstG**.......... Korperschaftsteuergesetz [*German Corporation Taxation Act*] (DLA)
**KSTG**......... Sikeston, MO [*FM radio station call letters*]
**KStJ**.......... Knight Commander of [*the Order of*] St. John of Jerusalem [*British*]
**K ST J of J**... Knight of St. John of Jerusalem [*Freemasonry*] (ROG)
**KSTK**......... Wrangell, AK [*FM radio station call letters*]
**KSTKBO**.... Clean Air. Special Edition [*A publication*]
**KSTL**......... St. Louis/Lambert-St. Louis International [*Missouri*] [*ICAO location identifier*] (ICLI)
**KSTL**......... St. Louis, MO [*AM radio station call letters*]
**KSTN**......... Keystone Financial, Inc. [*NASDAQ symbol*] (NQ)
**KSTN**......... Kriegsstaerke-Nachweisung [*Table of Organization*] [*German military - World War II*]
**KSTN**......... Stockton, CA [*AM radio station call letters*]
**KSTN-FM**... Stockton, CA [*FM radio station call letters*]
**KSTO**......... Agana, GU [*FM radio station call letters*]
**KSTP**......... St. Paul, MN [*AM radio station call letters*]
**KSTP-FM**... St. Paul, MN [*FM radio station call letters*]
**KSTP-TV**.. St. Paul, MN [*Television station call letters*]
**KSTQ**......... Alexandria, MN [*FM radio station call letters*]
**KSTR**......... Grand Junction, CO [*AM radio station call letters*]
**KSTR**......... Kema Suspension Test Reactor [*Netherlands*]
**KSTR-FM**... Montrose, CO [*FM radio station call letters*]
**KSTS**......... San Jose, CA [*Television station call letters*]
**KSTSDG**... Kenya Journal of Science and Technology. Series B. Biological Sciences [*A publication*]
**K-STSM**.... KSC [*Kennedy Space Center*] Space Transportation System Management [*Document*] [*NASA*] (NASA)
**KSTT**......... Davenport, IA [*AM radio station call letters*]
**KSTU**......... Salt Lake City, UT [*Television station call letters*]
**KSTV**......... Stephenville, TX [*AM radio station call letters*]
**KSTV-FM**... Stephenville, TX [*FM radio station call letters*]
**KSTV-TV**.. Ventura, CA [*Television station call letters*]
**KSTW**......... Tacoma, WA [*Television station call letters*]
**KSTX**......... San Antonio, TX [*FM radio station call letters*]
**KSTZ**......... Ste. Genevieve, MO [*FM radio station call letters*]
**ksu**............ Kansas [*MARC country of publication code*] [*Library of Congress*] (LCCP)
**KSU**........... Kansas City Southern Industries, Inc. [*NYSE symbol*] (SPSG)
**KSU**........... Kansas State University
**KSU**........... Kent State University [*Ohio*]
**KSU**........... Kent State University, Kent, OH [*OCLC symbol*] (OCLC)
**KSU**........... Key Service Unit (IEEE)
**KSU**........... Key System Control Unit [*Telecommunications*]
**KSU**........... Kousour [*Djibouti*] [*Seismograph station code, US Geological Survey*] (SEIS)
**KSU**........... Kristiansund [*Norway*] [*Airport symbol*] (OAG)
**KSU**........... Kyoto Sangyo University [*UTLAS symbol*]
**KSUA**......... College, AK [*FM radio station call letters*]
**KSUB**......... Cedar City, UT [*AM radio station call letters*]
**KSUD**......... West Memphis, AR [*AM radio station call letters*]
**KSUE**......... Susanville, CA [*AM radio station call letters*]
**KSUE-FM**... Susanville, CA [*FM radio station call letters*]
**KSUI**......... Iowa City, IA [*FM radio station call letters*]
**KSU (Kyoto Sangyo Univ) Econ and Bus R**... KSU (Kyoto Sangyo University). Economic and Business Review [*A publication*]
**KSUM**......... Fairmont, MN [*AM radio station call letters*]
**KSUN**......... Phoenix, AZ [*AM radio station call letters*]
**KSUP**......... Juneau, AK [*FM radio station call letters*]
**KSUR-FM**... Greenfield, CA [*FM radio station call letters*]
**KSUT**......... Ignacio, CO [*FM radio station call letters*]
**KSUU**......... Fairfield/Travis Air Force Base [*California*] [*ICAO location identifier*] (ICLI)
**KSUV**......... McFarland, CA [*FM radio station call letters*]
**KSUX**......... Sioux City [*Iowa*] [*ICAO location identifier*] (ICLI)
**KSUX**......... Winnebago, NE [*FM radio station call letters*]
**KSUZ-TV**... Abilene, TX [*Television station call letters*]
**KSV**........... Kirjallisuudentutkijain Seuran Vuosikirja [*A publication*]
**KSV**........... Knight of St. Vladimir [*Obsolete*] [*Russian*]
**KSVA**......... Corrales, NM [*FM radio station call letters*]
**KSVC**......... Richfield, UT [*AM radio station call letters*]
**KSVD**......... Kennewick, WA [*FM radio station call letters*]

**K Svenska Vet-Ak Hdl Oefv** ... Kungliga Svenska Vetenskaps-Akademiens. Handlingar. Oefversigt til Handlingar [*A publication*]
**K Sven Vetenskapsakad Avh Naturskyddsarenden** ... Kungliga Svenska Vetenskapsakademiens. Avhandlingar i Naturskyddsarenden [*A publication*]
**K Sven Vetenskapsakad Handl** ... Kungliga Svenska Vetenskapsakademiens. Handlingar [*A publication*]
**K Sven Vetenskapsakad Skr Naturskyddsarenden** ... Kungliga Svenska Vetenskapsakademiens. Skrifter i Naturskyddsarenden [*A publication*]
**KSVK** ......... Kalevalaseuran Vuosikirja [*A publication*]
**KSVN** ........ Ogden, UT [*AM radio station call letters*]
**KSVP** ......... Artesia, NM [*AM radio station call letters*]
**KSVR** ......... Mount Vernon, WA [*FM radio station call letters*]
**KSVY** ......... Opportunity, WA [*AM radio station call letters*]
**KSW** .......... C. H. Boehringer Sohn, Ingelheim [*Germany*] [*Research code symbol*]
**KSW** .......... Knight of St. Wladimir [*Obsolete*] [*Russian*]
**KSW** .......... Wichita State University, Wichita, KS [*OCLC symbol*] (OCLC)
**KSWA** ........ Graham, TX [*AM radio station call letters*]
**KSWA** ........ Swan Islands [*ICAO location identifier*] (ICLI)
**KSWB** ........ Seaside, OR [*AM radio station call letters*]
**KSWC** ........ Winfield, KS [*FM radio station call letters*]
**KSWF** ........ Newburgh/Stewart [*New York*] [*ICAO location identifier*] (ICLI)
**KSWH** ........ Arkadelphia, AR [*FM radio station call letters*]
**KSWK** ........ Lakin, KS [*Television station call letters*]
**KSWM** ...... Aurora, MO [*AM radio station call letters*]
**KSWO** ....... Lawton, OK [*AM radio station call letters*]
**KSWO-TV** ... Lawton, OK [*Television station call letters*]
**KSWP** ........ Lufkin, TX [*FM radio station call letters*]
**KSWT** ........ Liberal, KS [*Television station call letters*]
**KSWW** ...... Raymond, WA [*FM radio station call letters*]
**KSXM** ........ Pendleton, OR [*FM radio station call letters*]
**KSXY** ......... Reno, NV [*FM radio station call letters*]
**KSYC** ......... Yreka, CA [*AM radio station call letters*]
**KSYD** ......... Reedsport, OR [*FM radio station call letters*]
**KSYE** ......... Frederick, OK [*FM radio station call letters*]
**KSYL** ......... Alexandria, LA [*AM radio station call letters*]
**KSYM** ........ Smyrna/Sewart Air Force Base [*Tennessee*] [*ICAO location identifier*] (ICLI)
**KSYM-FM** ... San Antonio, TX [*FM radio station call letters*]
**KSYN** ........ Joplin, MO [*FM radio station call letters*]
**KSYR** ......... Syracuse/Hancock International [*New York*] [*ICAO location identifier*] (ICLI)
**KSYS** ......... Medford, OR [*Television station call letters*]
**KSYV** ......... Solvang, CA [*FM radio station call letters*]
**KSYY** ......... Denver, CO [*FM radio station call letters*]
**KSYZ-FM** ... Grand Island, NE [*FM radio station call letters*]
**KSZL** ......... Barstow, CA [*AM radio station call letters*]
**KSZL** ......... Knobnoster/Whiteman Air Force Base [*Missouri*] [*ICAO location identifier*] (ICLI)
**KT** ............. British Airtours Ltd. [*United Kingdom*] [*ICAO designator*] (ICDA)
**KT** ............. Canadian-Tech Industries, Inc. [*Vancouver Stock Exchange symbol*]
**KT** ............. Contract [*Navy*]
**KT** ............. Cretaceous-Tertiary [*Geology*]
**KT** ............. Kangmar Thrust [*Geophysics*]
**KT** ............. Karat [*Also, CT*]
**KT** ............. Katy Industries, Inc. [*Formerly, Missouri-Kansas-Texas R. R. Co., with Wall Street slang name of "Kathy"*] [*NYSE symbol*] (SPSG)
**KT** ............. Kentucky & Tennessee Railway [*AAR code*]
**KT** ............. Ketamine [*An anesthetic*]
**KT** ............. Keying Time [*Computer order entry*]
**KT** ............. Khaksar Tehrik [*Political party*] [*Pakistan*] (FEA)
**KT** ............. Khaleej Times [*A publication*]
**KT** ............. Khotanese Texts (BJA)
**KT** ............. Khristianskoe Tchtenie [*A publication*]
**kt** ............... Kiloton [*Nuclear equivalent of 1000 tons of high explosives*]
**KT** ............. Kinetic Theory
**KT** ............. Kinetin [*Plant growth regulator*]
**KT** ............. Kit
**KT** ............. Knight [*Chess*]
**KT** ............. Knight [*British title*]
**KT** ............. Knight of Tabor [*Freemasonry*] (ROG)
**KT** ............. Knight of the Thistle [*British*]
**KT** ............. Knighted
**KT** ............. Knights Templar
**KT** ............. Knots [*Also, K*] [*Nautical speed unit*]
**KT** ............. Koloniaal Tijdschrift [*A publication*]
**KT** ............. Kredit [*Credit*] [*Afrikaans*]
**KT** ............. Topeka Public Library, Topeka, KS [*Library symbol*] [*Library of Congress*] (LCLS)
**KT** ............. Trinidad and Tobago [*IYRU nationality code*] (IYR)
**KT1** ........... Kermit [*Texas*] [*Seismograph station code, US Geological Survey*] (SEIS)
**KT2** ........... Kermit [*Texas*] [*Seismograph station code, US Geological Survey*] [*Closed*] (SEIS)
**KT4** ........... Kermit [*Texas*] [*Seismograph station code, US Geological Survey*] (SEIS)
**KT5** ........... Kermit [*Texas*] [*Seismograph station code, US Geological Survey*] [*Closed*] (SEIS)
**KT7** ........... Kermit [*Texas*] [*Seismograph station code, US Geological Survey*] (SEIS)
**KT8** ........... Kermit [*Texas*] [*Seismograph station code, US Geological Survey*] (SEIS)
**KT9** ........... Kermit [*Texas*] [*Seismograph station code, US Geological Survey*] [*Closed*] (SEIS)
**KTA** ........... Karratha [*Australia*] [*Airport symbol*] (OAG)
**KTA** ........... Key Telephone Adapter [*Telecommunications*] (TEL)
**KTA** ........... Keyboard Teachers Association (EA)
**KTA** ........... Kite Trade Association International (EA)
**KTA** ........... Knitted Textile Association (EA)
**KTA** ........... Knots True Airspeed
**KTA** ........... Kotzebue [*Alaska*] [*Seismograph station code, US Geological Survey*] (SEIS)
**KTA** ........... Potassium Turbo-Alternator
**KTAA** ........ Kerman, CA [*FM radio station call letters*]
**KTAB-TV** ... Abilene, TX [*Television station call letters*]
**KTAC** ........ Tacoma, WA [*AM radio station call letters*]
**KTAE** ......... Taylor, TX [*AM radio station call letters*]
**KTAG** ........ Cody, WY [*FM radio station call letters*]
**KTAG** ........ Korea Trade Advisory Group [*British Overseas Trade Board*] (DS)
**KTAI** .......... Kingsville, TX [*FM radio station call letters*]
**KTAI** .......... Kite Trade Association International [*Later, KTA*] (EA)
**KTAJ** ......... St. Joseph, MO [*Television station call letters*]
**KTAK** ........ Riverton, WY [*FM radio station call letters*]
**KTAL-FM** ... Texarkana, TX [*FM radio station call letters*]
**KTAL-TV** .. Texarkana, TX [*Television station call letters*]
**KTAM** ....... Bryan, TX [*AM radio station call letters*]
**KTAN** ........ Sierra Vista, AZ [*AM radio station call letters*]
**KTAO** ........ Taos, NM [*FM radio station call letters*]
**KTAP** ........ Santa Maria, CA [*AM radio station call letters*]
**KTAQ** ........ Greeneville, TX [*Television station call letters*]
**KTAR** ........ Phoenix, AZ [*AM radio station call letters*]
**KTAS** ......... Knots True Airspeed [*Navy*] (NVT)
**KTAT** ......... Frederick, OK [*AM radio station call letters*]
**KTAV** ........ Knoxville, IA [*FM radio station call letters*]
**Ktavim Rec Agric Res Stn** ... Ktavim Records of the Agricultural Research Station [*A publication*]
**KTB** ........... Kriegstagebuch [*War Diary*] [*German military - World War II*]
**KTB** ........... Thorne River, AK [*Location identifier*] [*FAA*] (FAAL)
**KTBA** ......... Ketothiomethylbutyric Acid [*Organic chemistry*]
**KTBA** ......... Tuba City, AZ [*AM radio station call letters*]
**Kt Bach** ...... Knight Bachelor
**KTBA-FM** ... Tuba City, AZ [*FM radio station call letters*]
**KTBB** ......... Tyler, TX [*AM radio station call letters*]
**KTBC-TV** .. Austin, TX [*Television station call letters*]
**KTBI** .......... Ephrata, WA [*AM radio station call letters*]
**KTBN-TV** .. Santa Ana, CA [*Television station call letters*]
**KTBO-TV** ... Oklahoma City, OK [*Television station call letters*]
**KTBQ** ........ Nacogdoches, TX [*FM radio station call letters*]
**KTBR** ......... Roseburg, OR [*AM radio station call letters*]
**KTBS-TV** .. Shreveport, LA [*Television station call letters*]
**KTBW-TV** ... Tacoma, WA [*Television station call letters*]
**KTBY** ......... Anchorage, AK [*Television station call letters*]
**KTC** ........... Kellogg Telecommunications Corporation [*Littleton, CO*] [*Telecommunications*] (TSSD)
**KTC** ........... Kutchino [*USSR*] [*Later, MOS*] [*Geomagnetic observatory code*]
**KTC** ........... Somerset Community College, Somerset, KY [*OCLC symbol*] (OCLC)
**KTC** ........... Trinity College Library, University of Toronto [*UTLAS symbol*]
**KTCA-TV** ... St. Paul, MN [*Television station call letters*]
**KTCB** ......... Malden, MO [*AM radio station call letters*]
**KTCC** ......... Colby, KS [*FM radio station call letters*]
**KTCC** ......... Key Tronic Corporation [*NASDAQ symbol*] (NQ)
**KTCC** ......... Tucumcari [*New Mexico*] [*ICAO location identifier*] (ICLI)
**KTCD** ........ Eureka, CA [*AM radio station call letters*]
**KTCE** ......... Payson, UT [*FM radio station call letters*]
**KTCF** ......... Crosby, MN [*FM radio station call letters*]
**KTCH** ........ Wayne, NE [*AM radio station call letters*]
**KTCH-FM** ... Wayne, NE [*FM radio station call letters*]
**KTCI-TV** ... St. Paul, MN [*Television station call letters*]
**KTCJ** ......... Minneapolis, MN [*AM radio station call letters*]
**KTCL** ......... Fort Collins, CO [*FM radio station call letters*]
**KTCM** ....... Tacoma/McChord Air Force Base [*Washington*] [*ICAO location identifier*] (ICLI)
**KTCN** ........ Eureka Springs, AR [*FM radio station call letters*]
**KTCO** ........ Kenan Transport Company [*Chapel Hill, NC*] [*NASDAQ symbol*] (NQ)
**KTCP** ......... Taft, OK [*FM radio station call letters*]
**KTCR** ......... Kennewick, WA [*AM radio station call letters*]
**KTCS** ......... Fort Smith, AR [*AM radio station call letters*]
**KTCS** ......... Truth Or Consequences/Municipal [*New Mexico*] [*ICAO location identifier*] (ICLI)
**KTCS-FM** ... Fort Smith, AR [*FM radio station call letters*]

**KTCU-FM** ... Fort Worth, TX [*FM radio station call letters*]
**KTCV** ......... Kennewick, WA [*FM radio station call letters*]
**KTCZ-FM** ... Minneapolis, MN [*FM radio station call letters*]
**KTD** .......... Kita-Daito [*Japan*] [*Airport symbol*] (OAG)
**KTDB** ........ Ramah, NM [*FM radio station call letters*]
**KTDL** ........ Farmerville, LA [*AM radio station call letters*]
**KTDN** ........ Palestine, TX [*FM radio station call letters*]
**KTDO** ........ Toledo, OR [*AM radio station call letters*]
**KTDO-FM** ... Toledo, OR [*FM radio station call letters*]
**KTDR** ........ Del Rio, TX [*FM radio station call letters*]
**KTDS** ........ Key to Disk Software
**KTDX** ........ Winslow, AZ [*FM radio station call letters*]
**KTDY** ........ Lafayette, LA [*FM radio station call letters*]
**KTDZ-TV** ... Portland, OR [*Television station call letters*]
**KTE** ........... Kennedy-Thorndike Experiment
**KTE** ........... Kermit [*Texas*] [*Seismograph station code, US Geological Survey*] (SEIS)
**K-TEA** ....... Kaufman Test of Educational Achievement
**KTEB** ......... Teterboro [*New Jersey*] [*ICAO location identifier*] (ICLI)
**KTEC** ......... Klamath Falls, OR [*FM radio station call letters*]
**KTEE** ......... Idaho Falls, ID [*AM radio station call letters*]
**KTEH** ........ San Jose, CA [*Television station call letters*]
**KTEI** ......... Piggott, AR [*FM radio station call letters*]
**KTEJ** ......... Jonesboro, AR [*Television station call letters*]
**KTEK** ......... Alvin, TX [*AM radio station call letters*]
**K Tek Hoegsk Handl** ... Kungliga Tekniska Hoegskolans. Handlingar [*Sweden*] [*A publication*]
**K-TEL** ........ Kives-Television [*In company name K-Tel International. Derived from name of company president and fact that it markets its products on television*]
**KTEL** ......... Walla Walla, WA [*AM radio station call letters*]
**KTEM** ....... Temple, TX [*AM radio station call letters*]
**KTEN** ........ Ada, OK [*Television station call letters*]
**KTEO** ........ San Angelo, TX [*AM radio station call letters*]
**KTEO-FM** ... San Angelo, TX [*FM radio station call letters*]
**KTEP** ......... El Paso, TX [*FM radio station call letters*]
**KTEQ** ........ Rapid City, SD [*FM radio station call letters*]
**KTER** ......... Terrell, TX [*AM radio station call letters*]
**KTEZ** ......... Lubbock, TX [*FM radio station call letters*]
**KTF** ............ Kansas Turfgrass Foundation (EA)
**KTF** ............ Kauai Test Facility [*AEC*]
**KTF** ............ Kemper Municipal Income Fund [*NYSE symbol*] (CTT)
**KTF** ............ Kwartaalfacetten. Informatie over Krediet en Financiering [*A publication*]
**KTFA** ......... Groves, TX [*FM radio station call letters*]
**KTFC** ......... Sioux City, IA [*FM radio station call letters*]
**KTFH** ......... Conroe, TX [*Television station call letters*]
**KTFI** .......... Twin Falls, ID [*AM radio station call letters*]
**KTFJ** .......... Dakota City, NE [*AM radio station call letters*]
**KTFM** ......... San Antonio, TX [*FM radio station call letters*]
**KTFR** ......... Kodak Thin-Film Resist [*Cathode coating*]
**KTFX** ......... Tulsa, OK [*FM radio station call letters*]
**KTG** ........... Kap Tobin [*Greenland*] [*Seismograph station code, US Geological Survey*] (SEIS)
**KTG** ........... Ketapang [*Indonesia*] [*Airport symbol*] (OAG)
**KTGE** ......... Salinas, CA [*AM radio station call letters*]
**KTGF** ......... Great Falls, MT [*Television station call letters*]
**KTGF** ......... Keratinocyte T-Cell Growth Factor [*Immunology*]
**KTGG** ......... Spring Arbor, MI [*AM radio station call letters*]
**KTGIFC** .... Karen Taylor-Good International Fan Club (EA)
**KTGL** ......... Beatrice, NE [*FM radio station call letters*]
**KTGM** ........ Tamuning, GU [*Television station call letters*]
**KTGO** ......... Tioga, ND [*AM radio station call letters*]
**KTGR** ......... Columbia, MO [*AM radio station call letters*]
**KTh** ............ Kerk en Theologie [*Wageningen*] [*A publication*]
**KTH** ........... Kungliga Tekniska Hoegskolan [*Royal Institute of Technology*] [*Stockholm, Sweden*] (ARC)
**KTHB** ......... Kungliga Tekniska Hogskolans Bibliotek [*Royal Institute of Technology Library*] [*Information service or system*] (IID)
**KTHE** ......... Thermopolis, WY [*AM radio station call letters*]
**KTheol** ....... Kerk en Theologie [*Wageningen*] [*A publication*]
**KTHI-TV** ... Fargo, ND [*Television station call letters*]
**KTHO** ......... South Lake Tahoe, CA [*AM radio station call letters*]
**KTHO-FM** ... South Lake Tahoe, CA [*FM radio station call letters*]
**KTHP** ......... Longview, TX [*Television station call letters*]
**KTHS** ......... Berryville, AR [*AM radio station call letters*]
**KTHT** ......... Fresno, CA [*FM radio station call letters*]
**KTHV** ......... Little Rock, AR [*Television station call letters*]
**KTI** ............. Kinai Technologies, Inc. [*Formerly, Kinai Resources Corp.*] [*Vancouver Stock Exchange symbol*]
**KTI** ............. Kirsch Technologies, Incorporated [*Software manufacturer*] [*St. Clair, MI*]
**KTI** ............. Kitchen Table International [*David D. Busch's vaporware software company*]
**KTIB** .......... Thibodaux, LA [*AM radio station call letters*]
**KTID** .......... San Rafael, CA [*AM radio station call letters*]
**KTID-FM** ... San Rafael, CA [*FM radio station call letters*]
**KTIG** .......... Pequot Lakes, MN [*FM radio station call letters*]
**KTII** ........... K-Tron International, Incorporated [*NASDAQ symbol*] (NQ)
**KTIJ** ........... Elk City, OK [*FM radio station call letters*]
**KTIK** .......... Oklahoma City/Tinker Air Force Base [*Oklahoma*] [*ICAO location identifier*] (ICLI)
**KTIL** ........... Tillamook, OR [*AM radio station call letters*]
**KTIL-FM** .. Tillamook, OR [*FM radio station call letters*]
**KTIM** .......... Wickenburg, AZ [*AM radio station call letters*]
**KTIM-FM** ... Wickenburg, AZ [*FM radio station call letters*]
**KTIN** .......... Fort Dodge, IA [*Television station call letters*]
**KTIP** .......... Porterville, CA [*AM radio station call letters*]
**KTIS** .......... Minneapolis, MN [*AM radio station call letters*]
**KTIS-FM** .. Minneapolis, MN [*FM radio station call letters*]
**KTIV** .......... Sioux City, IA [*Television station call letters*]
**KTIX** .......... Pendleton, OR [*AM radio station call letters*]
**KTJA** ......... Mount Vernon, MO [*FM radio station call letters*]
**KTJB** ......... New Boston, TX [*FM radio station call letters*]
**KTJC** ......... Rayville, LA [*FM radio station call letters*]
**KTJJ** .......... Farmington, MO [*FM radio station call letters*]
**KTJO-FM** ... Ottawa, KS [*FM radio station call letters*]
**KTKA-TV** ... Topeka, KS [*Television station call letters*]
**KTKC** ......... Springhill, LA [*FM radio station call letters*]
**KTKK** ......... Sandy, UT [*AM radio station call letters*]
**KTKN** ......... Ketchikan, AK [*AM radio station call letters*]
**KTKR** ......... Taft, CA [*AM radio station call letters*]
**KTKS** ......... Waco, TX [*FM radio station call letters*]
**KTKT** ......... Tucson, AZ [*AM radio station call letters*]
**KTKU** ......... Juneau, AK [*FM radio station call letters*]
**KTL** ............ K-Tel International, Inc. [*Toronto Stock Exchange symbol*] (SPSG)
**KTL** ............ Kuratorium fuer Technik in der Landwirtschaft
**KTLA** ......... Los Angeles, CA [*Television station call letters*]
**KTLB** ......... Twin Lakes, IA [*FM radio station call letters*]
**KTL Ber Landtech** ... Kuratorium fuer Technik in der Landwirtschaft. Berichte ueber Landtechnik [*A publication*]
**KTLC** ......... Tye, TX [*FM radio station call letters*]
**KTLE** ......... Tooele, UT [*AM radio station call letters*]
**KTLE-FM** ... Tooele, UT [*FM radio station call letters*]
**KTLF** ......... Colorado Springs, CO [*FM radio station call letters*]
**KTLH** ......... Tallahassee/Dale Mabry Field [*Florida*] [*ICAO location identifier*] (ICLI)
**KTLK** ......... Lubbock, TX [*AM radio station call letters*]
**KTLM** ......... Taft, CA [*FM radio station call letters*]
**KTLO** ......... Mountain Home, AR [*AM radio station call letters*]
**KTLO-FM** ... Mountain Home, AR [*FM radio station call letters*]
**KTLQ** ......... Tahlequah, OK [*AM radio station call letters*]
**KTLR-FM** ... Terrell, TX [*FM radio station call letters*]
**KTLS** ......... Ada, OK [*FM radio station call letters*]
**KTLT** ......... Wichita Falls, TX [*FM radio station call letters*]
**KTLU** ......... Rusk, TX [*AM radio station call letters*]
**KTLV** ......... Midwest City, OK [*AM radio station call letters*]
**KTLX** ......... Columbus, NE [*FM radio station call letters*]
**KTM** .......... Katmai [*Alaska*] [*Seismograph station code, US Geological Survey*] (SEIS)
**KTM** .......... Katmandu [*Nepal*] [*Airport symbol*] (OAG)
**KTM** .......... Ketema, Inc. [*AMEX symbol*] (CTT)
**KTM** .......... Key Transport Module
**KTM** .......... Menninger Clinic Library, Topeka, KS [*Library symbol*] [*Library of Congress*] (LCLS)
**KTM** .......... Thomas More College, Fort Mitchell, KY [*OCLC symbol*] (OCLC)
**KTMA** ....... Ketema, Inc. [*NASDAQ symbol*] (NQ)
**KT MAR SC** ... Knight Mareschal of Scotland (ROG)
**KTMA-TV** ... Minneapolis, MN [*Television station call letters*]
**KTMB** ....... Miami/New Tamiami [*Florida*] [*ICAO location identifier*] (ICLI)
**KTMC** ....... McAlester, OK [*AM radio station call letters*]
**KTMD** ....... Galveston, TX [*Television station call letters*]
**KTME** ....... Lompoc, CA [*AM radio station call letters*]
**KTMG** ....... Deer Trail, CO [*AM radio station call letters*]
**KTMK** ....... Katimavik. Faculty of Physical Education. University of Alberta [*A publication*]
**KTMO** ....... Kennett, MO [*FM radio station call letters*]
**KTMP** ....... Heber City, UT [*AM radio station call letters*]
**KTMS** ....... Knapp Time Metaphor Scale
**KTMS** ....... Santa Barbara, CA [*AM radio station call letters*]
**KTMT** ....... Medford, OR [*FM radio station call letters*]
**KTMX** ....... Colusa, CA [*FM radio station call letters*]
**KTN** .......... Keltic, Inc. [*Toronto Stock Exchange symbol*]
**KTN** .......... Ketchikan [*Alaska*] [*Airport symbol*] (OAG)
**KTN** .......... Ketchikan, AK [*Location identifier*] [*FAA*] (FAAL)
**KTN** .......... Kuratorium fuer die Tagungen der Nobelpreistrager [*Standing Committee for Nobel Prize Winners' Congresses - SCNPWC*] (EA)
**KTN** .......... Potassium Tantalate Niobate (MCD)
**KTNC** ....... Falls City, NE [*AM radio station call letters*]
**KTNC-FM** ... Falls City, NE [*FM radio station call letters*]
**KTNE-TV** ... Alliance, NE [*Television station call letters*]
**KTNF** ....... Kodak Timing Negative Film
**KTNI** ........ Kansas Neurological Institute, Topeka, KS [*Library symbol*] [*Library of Congress*] (LCLS)
**KTNL** ....... Sitka, AK [*Television station call letters*]
**KTNM** ...... Tucumcari, NM [*AM radio station call letters*]
**KTNN** ....... Window Rock, AZ [*AM radio station call letters*]

**KTNQ**........ Los Angeles, CA [*AM radio station call letters*]
**KTNR**........ Kenedy-Karnes, TX [*FM radio station call letters*]
**KTNS**......... Oakhurst, CA [*AM radio station call letters*]
**KTNT**........ Miami/Dade-Collier Training and Transition Airport [*Florida*] [*ICAO location identifier*] (ICLI)
**KTNT-FM**... Edmund, OK [*FM radio station call letters*]
**KTNV**........ Las Vegas, NV [*Television station call letters*]
**KTNW**....... Richland, WA [*Television station call letters*]
**KTNY**........ Libby, MT [*FM radio station call letters*]
**KTO**.......... Kato [*Guyana*] [*Airport symbol*] (OAG)
**KTO**.......... Konto [*Account on Credit*] [*German*]
**KTO**.......... Kraus-Thomson Organization [*Publishing*]
**KtO**........... KTO Microform, Millwood, NY [*Library symbol*] [*Library of Congress*] (LCLS)
**KTO**.......... Kuwaiti Theatre of Operation [*Operation Desert Storm*]
**KTOB**........ Petaluma, CA [*AM radio station call letters*]
**KTOC**........ Jonesboro, LA [*AM radio station call letters*]
**KTOC-FM**... Jonesboro, LA [*FM radio station call letters*]
**KTOD-FM**... Conway, AR [*FM radio station call letters*]
**KTOE**........ Mankato, MN [*AM radio station call letters*]
**KTOF**......... Cedar Rapids, IA [*FM radio station call letters*]
**KtoK**.......... Kokugo To Kokubungaku [*Japanese Language and Literature*] [*A publication*]
**KTOK**........ Oklahoma City, OK [*AM radio station call letters*]
**KTOL**........ Lacey, WA [*AM radio station call letters*]
**KTOM**....... Salinas, CA [*AM radio station call letters*]
**KTOM-FM**... Salinas, CA [*FM radio station call letters*]
**KTON**........ Belton, TX [*AM radio station call letters*]
**KTOO**........ Juneau, AK [*FM radio station call letters*]
**KTOO-TV**... Juneau, AK [*Television station call letters*]
**KTOP**........ Topeka, KS [*AM radio station call letters*]
**KTOS**......... Kratos, Inc. [*NASDAQ symbol*] (NQ)
**KTOT**........ Big Bear Lake, CA [*FM radio station call letters*]
**KTOW**....... Sand Springs, OK [*AM radio station call letters*]
**KTOW-FM**... Sand Springs, OK [*FM radio station call letters*]
**KTOZ**........ Springfield, MO [*AM radio station call letters*]
**KTOZ-FM**... Marshfield, MO [*FM radio station call letters*]
**KTP**........... Kentucky Truck Plant [*Ford Motor Co.*]
**KTP**........... Kingston-Tinson [*Jamaica*] [*Airport symbol*] (OAG)
**KT P**.......... Knight's Pawn [*Chess*] (ROG)
**KTPA**......... Prescott, AR [*AM radio station call letters*]
**KTPA**......... Tampa/International [*Florida*] [*ICAO location identifier*] (ICLI)
**KTPB**......... Kilgore, TX [*FM radio station call letters*]
**KTPH**........ Tonopah, NV [*FM radio station call letters*]
**KTPI**.......... Kaum-Tani Persatuan Indonesia [*Indonesian Farmers' Party*] [*Surinam*] [*Political party*] (PPW)
**KTPI**.......... Tehachapi, CA [*FM radio station call letters*]
**KTPK**......... Topeka, KS [*FM radio station call letters*]
**KTPR**......... Fort Dodge, IA [*FM radio station call letters*]
**KTPS**......... Tacoma, WA [*Television station call letters*]
**KTPS-FM**... Tacoma, WA [*FM radio station call letters*]
**KTPX**......... Odessa, TX [*Television station call letters*]
**KTQM-FM**... Clovis, NM [*FM radio station call letters*]
**KTQN**......... Belton, TX [*FM radio station call letters*]
**KTQQ**......... Sulphur, LA [*FM radio station call letters*]
**KTQX**......... Bakersfield, CA [*FM radio station call letters*]
**KTR**........... Contractor
**KTR**........... K-2 Resources, Inc. [*Vancouver Stock Exchange symbol*]
**KTR**........... Katherine [*Australia*] [*Airport symbol*] (OAG)
**KTR**........... Katuura [*Japan*] [*Later, HTY*] [*Geomagnetic observatory code*]
**KTR**........... Katuura [*Japan*] [*Seismograph station code, US Geological Survey*] [*Closed*] (SEIS)
**KTR**........... Keyboard Typing Reperforator [*Data processing*]
**KTR**........... Korea Trade Report [*A publication*]
**KTRA**......... Farmington, NM [*FM radio station call letters*]
**KTRB**......... Modesto, CA [*AM radio station call letters*]
**KTRC**......... Santa Fe, NM [*AM radio station call letters*]
**KTRE-TV**.. Lufkin, TX [*Television station call letters*]
**KTRF**......... Thief River Falls, MN [*AM radio station call letters*]
**KTRH**......... Houston, TX [*AM radio station call letters*]
**KTRI-FM**.. Mansfield, MO [*FM radio station call letters*]
**KTRK-TV**... Houston, TX [*Television station call letters*]
**KTRO**........ Port Hueneme, CA [*AM radio station call letters*]
**KTRQ-FM**... Tri City, OR [*FM radio station call letters*]
**KTRR**......... Loveland, CO [*FM radio station call letters*]
**KTRS**......... Casper, WY [*FM radio station call letters*]
**KTRU**........ Houston, TX [*FM radio station call letters*]
**KTRV**......... Nampa, ID [*Television station call letters*]
**KTRW**........ Spokane, WA [*AM radio station call letters*]
**KTRX**......... Tarkio, MO [*FM radio station call letters*]
**KTRY**......... Bastrop, LA [*AM radio station call letters*]
**KTRY-FM**... Bastrop, LA [*FM radio station call letters*]
**KTRZ**......... Riverton, WY [*FM radio station call letters*]
**KTS**........... Brevig Mission [*Alaska*] [*Airport symbol*] (OAG)
**KTS**........... Kelvin Temperature Scale
**KTS**........... Key Telephone System [*Telecommunications*] (AAG)
**KTS**........... Knight of the Tower and Sword [*Portugal*]
**KTS**........... Knots (ADA)
**KTS**........... Kodiak Tracking Station [*NASA*] (MCD)
**KTS**........... Kwajalein Test Site (MCD)
**KTS**........... Southern Baptist Theological Seminary, Louisville, KY [*OCLC symbol*] (OCLC)
**KTS**........... Teller Mission, AK [*Location identifier*] [*FAA*] (FAAL)
**KTSA**......... Kahn Test of Symbol Arrangement [*Psychology*]
**KTSA**......... San Antonio, TX [*AM radio station call letters*]
**KTSB**......... Sioux Center, IA [*FM radio station call letters*]
**KTSC**......... Pueblo, CO [*Television station call letters*]
**KTSC-FM**... Pueblo, CO [*FM radio station call letters*]
**KTSD-FM**... Reliance, SD [*FM radio station call letters*]
**KTSD-TV**.. Pierre, SD [*Television station call letters*]
**KTSF**......... San Francisco, CA [*Television station call letters*]
**KTSH**........ Topeka State Hospital, Topeka, KS [*Library symbol*] [*Library of Congress*] (LCLS)
**KTSJ**.......... Pomona, CA [*AM radio station call letters*]
**KTSM**........ El Paso, TX [*AM radio station call letters*]
**KTSM-FM**... El Paso, TX [*FM radio station call letters*]
**KTSM-TV**... El Paso, TX [*Television station call letters*]
**KTSP-TV**.. Phoenix, AZ [*Television station call letters*]
**KTSR**......... College Station, TX [*FM radio station call letters*]
**KTSS**......... Aiea, HI [*FM radio station call letters*]
**KTSU**......... Houston, TX [*FM radio station call letters*]
**KTSV**......... Stormont-Vail Hospital, Topeka, KS [*Library symbol*] [*Library of Congress*] (LCLS)
**KTT**........... Kermit [*Texas*] [*Seismograph station code, US Geological Survey*] [*Closed*] (SEIS)
**KTT**........... Kittila [*Finland*] [*Airport symbol*] (OAG)
**KTTC**......... Keesler Technical Training Center
**KTTC**......... Rochester, MN [*Television station call letters*]
**KTTD**......... Claypool, AZ [*FM radio station call letters*]
**KTTI**.......... Yuma, AZ [*FM radio station call letters*]
**KTTK**......... Lebanon, MO [*FM radio station call letters*]
**KTTL**......... Alva, OK [*FM radio station call letters*]
**KTTL**......... Korea Tactical Target List (MCD)
**KTTN**......... Trenton/Mercer County [*New Jersey*] [*ICAO location identifier*] (ICLI)
**KTTN**......... Trenton, MO [*AM radio station call letters*]
**KTTN-FM**... Trenton, MO [*FM radio station call letters*]
**KTTR**......... Rolla, MO [*AM radio station call letters*]
**KTTS**......... Springfield, MO [*AM radio station call letters*]
**KTTS-FM**... Springfield, MO [*FM radio station call letters*]
**KTTT**......... Columbus, NE [*AM radio station call letters*]
**KTTU-TV**... Tucson, AZ [*Television station call letters*]
**KTTV**......... Los Angeles, CA [*Television station call letters*]
**KTTW**........ Sioux Falls, SD [*Television station call letters*]
**KTTX**......... Brenham, TX [*AM radio station call letters*]
**KTTY**......... San Diego, CA [*Television station call letters*]
**KTTZ**......... Ajo, AZ [*FM radio station call letters*]
**KTU**........... Key Telephone Unit
**KTU**........... Kota [*India*] [*Airport symbol*] (OAG)
**KTU**........... Transylvania University, Lexington, KY [*OCLC symbol*] (OCLC)
**KTUC**......... Tucson, AZ [*AM radio station call letters*]
**KTUE**......... Tulia, TX [*AM radio station call letters*]
**KTUF**......... Kirksville, MO [*FM radio station call letters*]
**KTUH**......... Honolulu, HI [*FM radio station call letters*]
**KTUI**.......... Sullivan, MO [*AM radio station call letters*]
**KTUI-FM**... Sullivan, MO [*FM radio station call letters*]
**KTUL**......... Tulsa/International [*Oklahoma*] [*ICAO location identifier*] (ICLI)
**KTUL-TV**... Tulsa, OK [*Television station call letters*]
**KTUO**......... Sonora, CA [*FM radio station call letters*]
**KTUS**......... Galveston, TX [*AM radio station call letters*]
**KTUS**......... Tucson/International [*Arizona*] [*ICAO location identifier*] (ICLI)
**KTUU-TV**... Anchorage, AK [*Television station call letters*]
**KTUX**......... Carthage, TX [*FM radio station call letters*]
**KTV**........... Kamarata [*Venezuela*] [*Airport symbol*] (OAG)
**KTV**........... Kuwait Television
**KTVA**......... Anchorage, AK [*Television station call letters*]
**KTVA**......... United States Veterans Administration Hospital, Topeka, KS [*Library symbol*] [*Library of Congress*] (LCLS)
**KTVB**......... Boise, ID [*Television station call letters*]
**KTVD**......... Denver, CO [*Television station call letters*]
**KTVE**......... El Dorado, AR [*Television station call letters*]
**KTVF**......... Fairbanks, AK [*Television station call letters*]
**KTVG**......... Grand Island, NE [*Television station call letters*]
**KTVH**......... Helena, MT [*Television station call letters*]
**KTVI**.......... St. Louis, MO [*Television station call letters*]
**KTVJ**.......... Boulder, CO [*Television station call letters*]
**KTVK**......... Phoenix, AZ [*Television station call letters*]
**KTVL**......... Medford, OR [*Television station call letters*]
**KTVM**........ Butte, MT [*Television station call letters*]
**KTVN**......... Reno, NV [*Television station call letters*]
**KTVO**......... Kirksville, MO [*Television station call letters*]
**KTVQ**......... Billings, MT [*Television station call letters*]
**KTVR**......... La Grande, OR [*Television station call letters*]
**KTVS**......... Sterling, CO [*Television station call letters*]
**KTVT**......... Fort Worth, TX [*Television station call letters*]
**KTVU**......... Kleine Texte fuer Vorlesungen und Uebungen [*A publication*]
**KTVU**......... Oakland, CA [*Television station call letters*]
**KTVW-TV**... Phoenix, AZ [*Television station call letters*]

**KTVX**......... Salt Lake City, UT [*Television station call letters*]
**KTVY**......... Oklahoma City, OK [*Television station call letters*]
**KTVZ**......... Bend, OR [*Television station call letters*]
**KTW**.......... Katowice [*Poland*] [*Airport symbol*] (OAG)
**KTW**.......... Washburn University of Topeka, Topeka, KS [*Library symbol*] [*Library of Congress*] (LCLS)
**KTWA**....... Ottumwa, IA [*FM radio station call letters*]
**KTWG**....... Agana, GU [*AM radio station call letters*]
**KTW-L**....... Washburn University of Topeka, School of Law, Topeka, KS [*Library symbol*] [*Library of Congress*] (LCLS)
**KTWN**....... Texarkana, AR [*FM radio station call letters*]
**KTWN**....... Texarkana, TX [*AM radio station call letters*]
**KTWO**....... Casper, WY [*AM radio station call letters*]
**KTWO-TV**... Casper, WY [*Television station call letters*]
**KTWU**....... Topeka, KS [*Television station call letters*]
**KTWV-FM**... Los Angeles, CA [*FM radio station call letters*]
**KTX**.......... Keith Railway Equipment Co. [*AAR code*]
**KTX**.......... Kermit [*Texas*] [*Seismograph station code, US Geological Survey*] (SEIS)
**KTXA**........ Fort Worth, TX [*Television station call letters*]
**KTXB**......... Beaumont, TX [*FM radio station call letters*]
**KTXF**......... Brownsville, TX [*FM radio station call letters*]
**KTXH**......... Houston, TX [*Television station call letters*]
**KTXI**.......... Gordonville, MO [*FM radio station call letters*]
**KTXJ**.......... Jasper, TX [*AM radio station call letters*]
**KTXK**......... Texarkana/Municipal-Webb Field [*Arkansas*] [*ICAO location identifier*] (ICLI)
**KTXK**......... Texarkana, TX [*FM radio station call letters*]
**KTXL**......... Sacramento, CA [*Television station call letters*]
**KTXN-FM**... Victoria, TX [*FM radio station call letters*]
**KTXO**........ Sherman, TX [*AM radio station call letters*]
**KTXQ**........ Fort Worth, TX [*FM radio station call letters*]
**KTXR**........ Springfield, MO [*FM radio station call letters*]
**KTXS-TV**.. Sweetwater, TX [*Television station call letters*]
**KTXT-FM**... Lubbock, TX [*FM radio station call letters*]
**KTXT-TV**.. Lubbock, TX [*Television station call letters*]
**KTXU**........ Paris, TX [*FM radio station call letters*]
**KTXX**........ Devine, TX [*FM radio station call letters*]
**KTXY**......... Jefferson City, MO [*FM radio station call letters*]
**KTXZ**......... West Lake Hills, TX [*AM radio station call letters*]
**KTY**.......... Terror Bay [*Alaska*] [*Airport symbol*] (OAG)
**KTY**.......... Terror Bay, AK [*Location identifier*] [*FAA*] (FAAL)
**KTYD**........ Santa Barbara, CA [*FM radio station call letters*]
**KTYL-FM**... Tyler, TX [*FM radio station call letters*]
**KTYM**....... Inglewood, CA [*AM radio station call letters*]
**KTYN**........ Minot, ND [*AM radio station call letters*]
**KTYR**......... Tyler/Pounds Field [*Texas*] [*ICAO location identifier*] (ICLI)
**KTYS**......... Knoxville/McGee Tyson [*Tennessee*] [*ICAO location identifier*] (ICLI)
**KTYZ**......... Wolf Point, MT [*AM radio station call letters*]
**KTYZ-FM**... Wolf Point, MT [*FM radio station call letters*]
**KTZ**.......... Kutztown [*Pennsylvania*] [*Seismograph station code, US Geological Survey*] (SEIS)
**KTZA**......... Artesia, NM [*FM radio station call letters*]
**KTZR**......... Tucson, AZ [*AM radio station call letters*]
**KTZZ-TV**.. Seattle, WA [*Television station call letters*]
**KU**.............. Kapuskasing Uplift [*Canada*] [*Geology*]
**KU**.............. Kentucky Utilities Co. [*NYSE symbol*] (SPSG)
**KU**.............. Keyboard Unit [*Data processing*] (NASA)
**KU**.............. Kitvei Ugarit (BJA)
**KU**.............. Krebs Unit
**Ku**.............. Kurchatovium [*See also Rf*] [*Proposed name for chemical element 104*]
**Ku**.............. Kurtosis [*The relative degree of flatness in the region about the mode of a frequency curve*]
**ku**.............. Kuwait [*MARC country of publication code*] [*Library of Congress*] (LCCP)
**KU**.............. Kuwait Airways Corp. [*ICAO designator*] (FAAC)
**KU**.............. University of Kansas, Lawrence, KS [*Library symbol*] [*Library of Congress*] (LCLS)
**KUA**........... Kit Upkeep Allowance [*British*]
**KUA**........... Kobe University. Economic Review [*A publication*]
**KUA**........... Kuantan [*Malaysia*] [*Airport symbol*] (OAG)
**KUAA**........ Custer, SD [*FM radio station call letters*]
**KUAC-FM**... Fairbanks, AK [*FM radio station call letters*]
**KUAC-TV**... Fairbanks, AK [*Television station call letters*]
**KUAD-FM**... Windsor, CO [*FM radio station call letters*]
**KUAF**........ Fayetteville, AR [*FM radio station call letters*]
**KUAI**......... Eleele, HI [*AM radio station call letters*]
**KUAM**....... Agana, GU [*AM radio station call letters*]
**KUAM-FM**... Agana, GU [*FM radio station call letters*]
**KUAM-TV**... Agana, GU [*Television station call letters*]
**KUAR**........ Little Rock, AR [*FM radio station call letters*]
**KUAS-TV**... Tucson, AZ [*Television station call letters*]
**KUAT**........ Tucson, AZ [*AM radio station call letters*]
**KUAT-FM**... Tucson, AZ [*FM radio station call letters*]
**KUAT-TV**... Tucson, AZ [*Television station call letters*]
**KUB**........... Keilschrifturkunden aus Boghazkoi [*A publication*] (BJA)
**KUB**........... Kidney and Upper Bladder
**KUB**........... Kidney, Ureter, Bladder [*X-ray*]
**KUB**........... Kubota Corp. ADR [*NYSE symbol*] (SPSG)
**KUBA**........ Yuba City, CA [*AM radio station call letters*]
**Kuban Gos Univ Naucn Trudy**... Kubanskii Gosudarstvennyi Universitet Naucnyi Trudy [*A publication*]
**KUBB**........ Mariposa, CA [*FM radio station call letters*]
**KUBC**........ Montrose, CO [*AM radio station call letters*]
**KUBD**........ Denver, CO [*Television station call letters*]
**KUBE**........ Seattle, WA [*FM radio station call letters*]
**KUBEA**...... Kunststoff-Berater [*A publication*]
**KUBES**...... Ku-Ring-Gai Bushland and Environmental Society [*Australia*]
**Kubota Tech Rep**... Kubota Technical Reports [*A publication*]
**KUBR**........ San Juan, TX [*AM radio station call letters*]
**KUBS**......... Newport, WA [*FM radio station call letters*]
**KUC**........... Kucino [*USSR*] [*Seismograph station code, US Geological Survey*] [*Closed*] (SEIS)
**KUC**........... Kuria [*Kiribati*] [*Airport symbol*] (OAG)
**KUCA**........ Conway, AR [*FM radio station call letters*]
**KUCB-FM**... Des Moines, IA [*FM radio station call letters*]
**KUCI**......... Irvine, CA [*FM radio station call letters*]
**KUCR**........ Riverside, CA [*FM radio station call letters*]
**KUCV**........ Lincoln, NE [*FM radio station call letters*]
**KuD**............ Kerygma und Dogma [*Goettingen*] [*A publication*]
**KUD**........... Kudat [*Malaysia*] [*Airport symbol*] (OAG)
**KUDA**........ Pahrump, NV [*FM radio station call letters*]
**KUDKA**..... Kumamoto Daigaku Kogakubu Kenkyu Hokoku [*A publication*]
**KUDL**........ Kansas City, KS [*FM radio station call letters*]
**KUDY**........ Spokane, WA [*AM radio station call letters*]
**KUED**........ Kodak Unitized Engineering Data
**KUED**........ Salt Lake City, UT [*Television station call letters*]
**Kuehn-Arch**... Kuehn-Archiv [*A publication*]
**Kuelfoeldi Mehesz Szemle**... Kuelfoeldi Meheszeti Szemle [*A publication*]
**KUER**........ Kobe University. Economic Review [*A publication*]
**KUER**........ Salt Lake City, UT [*FM radio station call letters*]
**KUET**........ Black Canyon City, AZ [*AM radio station call letters*]
**KUEZ**........ Lufkin, TX [*FM radio station call letters*]
**KUFM**....... Missoula, MT [*FM radio station call letters*]
**KUFNCD**.. Kampuchean United Front for National Construction and Defence [*Political party*] (PPW)
**KUFR**........ Salt Lake City, UT [*FM radio station call letters*]
**KUFW**....... Woodlake, CA [*FM radio station call letters*]
**KUG**........... Kupang [*Timor*] [*Seismograph station code, US Geological Survey*] (SEIS)
**KUGB**........ Karate Union of Great Britain
**KUGBNC**.. Karate Union of Great Britain National Championship
**Kugellager-Z**... Kugellager-Zeitschrift [*A publication*]
**KUGN**........ Eugene, OR [*AM radio station call letters*]
**KUGN-FM**... Eugene, OR [*FM radio station call letters*]
**KUGR**........ Green River, WY [*AM radio station call letters*]
**KUGS**........ Bellingham, WA [*FM radio station call letters*]
**KUGT**........ Jackson, MO [*AM radio station call letters*]
**KUH**........... Kaapuna [*Hawaii*] [*Seismograph station code, US Geological Survey*] (SEIS)
**KUH**........... Kuhlman Corp. [*NYSE symbol*] (SPSG)
**KUH**........... Kushiro [*Japan*] [*Airport symbol*] (OAG)
**KUHB**........ St. Paul Island, AK [*FM radio station call letters*]
**KUHCA**..... Journal. Korean Institute of Metals [*Republic of Korea*] [*A publication*]
**KUHF**........ Houston, TX [*FM radio station call letters*]
**KUHL**........ Santa Maria, CA [*AM radio station call letters*]
**KUHT**........ Houston, TX [*Television station call letters*]
**KUIB**......... Vernal, UT [*FM radio station call letters*]
**Kuibysev Gos Ped Inst Naucn Trudy**... Kuibysevskii Gosudarstvennyi Pedagogiceskii Institut Naucnyi Trudy [*A publication*]
**Kuibysev Gos Ped Inst Ucen Zap**... Ministerstvo Prosvescenija RSFSR Kuibysevskii Gosudarstvennyi Pedagogiceskii Institut Imeni V. V. Kuibyseva Ucenyi Zapiski [*Kuybyshev*] [*A publication*]
**Kuibyshev Inzh Stroit Inst Tr**... Kuibyshevskii Inzhenerno-Stroitel'nyi Institut Trudy [*A publication*]
**KUIC**......... Vacaville, CA [*FM radio station call letters*]
**KUID-TV**.. Moscow, ID [*Television station call letters*]
**KUIK**......... Hillsboro, OR [*AM radio station call letters*]
**KUIN**......... Vernal, UT [*FM radio station call letters*]
**KUISA**....... Japanese Journal of Aerospace Medicine and Psychology [*A publication*]
**KUJ**........... Walla Walla, WA [*AM radio station call letters*]
**KUK**........... Kasigluk [*Alaska*] [*Airport symbol*] (OAG)
**KUK**........... Temperatur Technik. Zeitschrift fuer das Gesamte Temperaturgebiet Kaltetechnik, Klimatechnik, und Heizungstechnik Einschliesslich Isolierung Lueftung, Kuehltransport, und Tiefkuehltransport [*A publication*]
**KUK**........... University of Kentucky, Lexington, KY [*OCLC symbol*] (OCLC)
**KUKI**......... Ukiah, CA [*AM radio station call letters*]
**KUKI-FM**... Ukiah, CA [*FM radio station call letters*]
**Ku Kl**.......... Kultur og Klasse [*A publication*]
**KUKQ**........ Tempe, AZ [*AM radio station call letters*]
**KUKU**........ Willow Springs, MO [*AM radio station call letters*]
**KUKUA**...... Kukuruza [*A publication*]
**KUKU-FM**... Willow Springs, MO [*FM radio station call letters*]
**KuKv**.......... Klassizismus und Kulturverfall [*A publication*]

**KUL**........... Kinjo Gakuin University Library [*UTLAS symbol*]
**KUL**........... Kuala Lumpur [*Malaysia*] [*Airport symbol*] (OAG)
**KUL**........... Kulyab [*USSR*] [*Seismograph station code, US Geological Survey*] (SEIS)
**KuL**........... Kunst und Literatur [*A publication*]
**KUL**........... Sterling Central Union List of Serials, Sterling, KS [*OCLC symbol*] (OCLC)
**KU-L**.......... University of Kansas, School of Law, Lawrence, KS [*Library symbol*] [*Library of Congress*] (LCLS)
**KULA**........ Maunawili, HI [*AM radio station call letters*]
**KULC**........ Ogden, UT [*Television station call letters*]
**KULE**........ Ephrata, WA [*AM radio station call letters*]
**KULM**....... Columbus, TX [*FM radio station call letters*]
**KULP**......... El Campo, TX [*AM radio station call letters*]
**Kulp**........... Kulp's Luzerne Legal Register Reports [*Pennsylvania*] [*A publication*] (DLA)
**KULR-TV**... Billings, MT [*Television station call letters*]
**KULS**......... Kentucky Union List of Serials [*Library network*]
**Kult es Jozosseg**... Kultura es Jozosseg [*A publication*]
**Kult i Spolecz**... Kultura i Spoleczenstwo [*A publication*]
**KulturaW**... Kultura (Warsaw) [*A publication*]
**Kulturen**..... Kulturen Arsbok till Medlemmerna av Kulturhistoriska Foerening foer Soedra Sverige [*A publication*]
**Kulturpflanze Beih**... Kulturpflanze Beiheft [*A publication*]
**KULU**........ Kvindernes u Landsudvalg [*Women and Development*] [*Copenhagen, Denmark*] (EAIO)
**KULY**........ Ulysses, KS [*AM radio station call letters*]
**KUM**.......... Kumamoto [*Japan*] [*Seismograph station code, US Geological Survey*] (SEIS)
**KU-M**........ University of Kansas, School of Medicine, Kansas City, KS [*Library symbol*] [*Library of Congress*] (LCLS)
**KUM**.......... University of Kentucky, Medical Center, Lexington, KY [*OCLC symbol*] (OCLC)
**KUM**.......... Yaku Shima [*Japan*] [*Airport symbol*] (OAG)
**KUMA**....... Pendleton, OR [*AM radio station call letters*]
**Kumamoto Jour Sci Ser A Mathematics Physics and Chemistry**... Kumamoto Journal of Science. Series A. Mathematics, Physics, and Chemistry [*A publication*]
**Kumamoto J Sci**... Kumamoto Journal of Science [*A publication*]
**Kumamoto J Sci Biol**... Kumamoto Journal of Science. Biology [*A publication*]
**Kumamoto J Sci Geol**... Kumamoto Journal of Science. Geology [*A publication*]
**Kumamoto J Sci Math**... Kumamoto Journal of Science. Mathematics [*A publication*]
**Kumamoto J Sci Ser A**... Kumamoto Journal of Science. Series A. Mathematics, Physics, and Chemistry [*A publication*]
**Kumamoto J Sci Ser B Sect 1**... Kumamoto Journal of Science. Series B. Section 1. Geology [*A publication*]
**Kumamoto J Sci Ser B Sect 2 Biol**... Kumamoto Journal of Science. Series B. Section 2. Biology [*A publication*]
**Kumamoto Med J**... Kumamoto Medical Journal [*A publication*]
**Kumamoto Pharm Bull**... Kumamoto Pharmaceutical Bulletin [*A publication*]
**KUMD-FM**... Duluth, MN [*FM radio station call letters*]
**KUMJA**..... Kumamoto Medical Journal [*A publication*]
**KUMJB**..... Kyungpook University. Medical Journal [*A publication*]
**KUMM**...... Morris, MN [*FM radio station call letters*]
**KUMMI**..... Kobe University Medical Mission to Indonesia
**KUMR**....... Rolla, MO [*FM radio station call letters*]
**KUMU**....... Honolulu, HI [*AM radio station call letters*]
**KUMU-FM**... Honolulu, HI [*FM radio station call letters*]
**KUMV-TV**... Williston, ND [*Television station call letters*]
**KUN**........... Kunia, Oahu, HI [*Location identifier*] [*FAA*] (FAAL)
**KUN**........... Kunming [*Republic of China*] [*Seismograph station code, US Geological Survey*] (SEIS)
**KUN**........... Kunststoffe [*A publication*]
**KUNA**........ Indio, CA [*AM radio station call letters*]
**KUNC-FM**... Greeley, CO [*FM radio station call letters*]
**Kun Chung Hseuh Pao Acta Entomol Sin**... Kun Chung Hseuh Pao. Acta Entomologica Sinica [*A publication*]
**KUNI**......... Cedar Falls, IA [*FM radio station call letters*]
**KUNM**....... Albuquerque, NM [*FM radio station call letters*]
**KUNO**....... Corpus Christi, TX [*AM radio station call letters*]
**KUNQ**....... Houston, MO [*FM radio station call letters*]
**KUNR**........ Reno, NV [*FM radio station call letters*]
**KUNSA**..... Kunststoffe. Organ der Deutschen Kunststoff-Fachverbaende [*A publication*]
**Kunst-Ber**... Kunststoff-Berater [*A publication*]
**Kunst u Lit**... Kunst und Literatur. Sowjetwissenschaft Zeitschrift zur Verbreitung Sowjetischer Erfahrungen [*A publication*]
**Kunstof Rub**... Kunststof en Rubber [*A publication*]
**Kunstst**....... Kunststoffe [*A publication*]
**Kunstst Bau**... Kunststoffe im Bau [*A publication*]
**Kunstst-Berat**... Kunststoff-Berater [*A publication*]
**Kunstst-Berat Rundsch Tech**... Kunststoff-Berater Vereinigt mit Kunststoff-Rundschau und Kunststoff-Technik [*A publication*]
**Kunstst Ger Plast**... Kunststoffe - German Plastics [*A publication*]
**Kunstst J**.... Kunststoff Journal [*A publication*]
**Kunststoff**.. Kunststoffe. German Plastics, Including Kunststoffe im Bau [*A publication*]
**Kunststoffberat Rundsch Tech**... Kunststoffberater, Rundschau, und Technik [*A publication*]
**Kunstst-Plast**... Kunststoffe-Plastics [*A publication*]
**Kunstst-Rundsch**... Kunststoff-Rundschau [*A publication*]
**Kunstst Tech Kunstst Anwend**... Kunststoff-Technik und Kunststoff-Anwendung [*A publication*]
**KUNV**........ Las Vegas, NV [*FM radio station call letters*]
**KUNY**........ Mason City, IA [*FM radio station call letters*]
**KUO**........... Kuopio [*Finland*] [*Airport symbol*] (OAG)
**KUOA**........ Siloam Springs, AR [*AM radio station call letters*]
**KUOI-FM**... Moscow, ID [*FM radio station call letters*]
**KUOM**....... Minneapolis, MN [*AM radio station call letters*]
**KUON-TV**... Lincoln, NE [*Television station call letters*]
**KUOO**....... Spirit Lake, IA [*FM radio station call letters*]
**KUOP**....... Stockton, CA [*FM radio station call letters*]
**Ku Or**......... Kunst des Orients [*A publication*]
**KUOR-FM**... Redlands, CA [*FM radio station call letters*]
**KUOW**....... Seattle, WA [*FM radio station call letters*]
**KUP**........... Kunststoffe-Plastics; Schweizerische Fachzeitschrift fuer Herstellung, Verarbeitung, und Anwendung von Kunststoffen [*A publication*]
**KUP**........... Kupang [*Timor*] [*Seismograph station code, US Geological Survey*] [*Closed*] (SEIS)
**KUP**........... Kupiano [*Papua New Guinea*] [*Airport symbol*] (OAG)
**KUP**........... University of Kentucky, Prestonburg Community College, Prestonburg, KY [*OCLC symbol*] (OCLC)
**KUPD-FM**... Tempe, AZ [*FM radio station call letters*]
**KUPI**.......... Idaho Falls, ID [*AM radio station call letters*]
**KUPI-FM**... Idaho Falls, ID [*FM radio station call letters*]
**KUPK-TV**... Garden City, KS [*Television station call letters*]
**KUPL**.......... Portland, OR [*AM radio station call letters*]
**KUPLA**....... Kunststoffe-Plastics [*A publication*]
**KUPL-FM**... Portland, OR [*FM radio station call letters*]
**KUPS**......... Tacoma, WA [*FM radio station call letters*]
**KUR**........... Kit Use Ratio [*Statistics*]
**kur**.............. Kurdish [*MARC language code*] [*Library of Congress*] (LCCP)
**KUR**........... Kurilsk [*USSR*] [*Seismograph station code, US Geological Survey*] (SEIS)
**KUR**........... Kyoto University Reactor
**KURA**........ Ouray, CO [*FM radio station call letters*]
**KURAAV**.. Annual Reports. Research Reactor Institute. Kyoto University [*A publication*]
**Kurator Tech Landwirt Flugschr**... Kuratorium fuer Technik in der Landwirtschaft. Flugschrift [*A publication*]
**KURL**........ Billings, MT [*AM radio station call letters*]
**KURM**....... Kurzweil Music Systems, Inc. [*Waltham, MA*] [*NASDAQ symbol*] (NQ)
**KURM**....... Rogers, AR [*AM radio station call letters*]
**Kurme Med J**... Kurme Medical Journal [*A publication*]
**KURO**....... Huron, SD [*FM radio station call letters*]
**Kurortol Fizioter**... Kurortologiya i Fizioterapiya [*Bulgaria*] [*A publication*]
**Kurortol Uurim**... Kurortoloogilised Uurimused [*A publication*]
**Kursk Gos Med Inst Sb Tr**... Kurskii Gosudarstvennyi Meditsinskii Institut. Sbornik Trudov [*A publication*]
**Kursk Gos Ped Inst Ucen Zap**... Kurskii Gosudarstvennyi Pedagogiceskii Institut. Ucenye Zapiski [*A publication*]
**Kurtrier Jb**... Kurtrierisches Jahrbuch [*A publication*]
**KURUA**..... Kunststoff-Rundschau [*A publication*]
**Kurume Med J**... Kurume Medical Journal [*A publication*]
**Kurume Univ J**... Kurume University. Journal [*A publication*]
**KURY**........ Brookings, OR [*AM radio station call letters*]
**KURY-FM**... Brookings, OR [*FM radio station call letters*]
**Kurzmitt Dtsch Dendrol Ges**... Kurzmitteilungen Deutsche Dendrologische Gesellschaft [*A publication*]
**Kurznachr Akad Wiss Goettingen**... Kurznachrichten. Akademie der Wissenschaften in Goettingen [*Federal Republic of Germany*] [*A publication*]
**Kurznachr Akad Wiss Goettingen Sammelh**... Kurznachrichten. Akademie der Wissenschaften in Goettingen. Sammelheft [*A publication*]
**KUS**........... Kushiro [*Japan*] [*Seismograph station code, US Geological Survey*] (SEIS)
**KU-S**.......... University of Kansas, Kenneth Spencer Research Library, Lawrence, KS [*Library symbol*] [*Library of Congress*] (LCLS)
**KUS**........... University of Kentucky, Southeast Center, Cumberland, KY [*OCLC symbol*] (OCLC)
**KUSA**........ St. Louis, MO [*AM radio station call letters*]
**KUSA-TV**... Denver, CO [*Television station call letters*]
**KUSC**........ Los Angeles, CA [*FM radio station call letters*]
**KUSD**........ Vermillion, SD [*AM radio station call letters*]
**KUSD-FM**... Vermillion, SD [*FM radio station call letters*]
**KUSD-TV**... Vermillion, SD [*Television station call letters*]
**KUSEB**...... Kuki Seijo [*A publication*]
**KUSF**........ San Francisco, CA [*FM radio station call letters*]
**KUSG**........ St. George, UT [*Television station call letters*]
**KUSH**........ Cushing, OK [*AM radio station call letters*]
**KUSI-TV**... San Diego, CA [*Television station call letters*]
**KUSK**........ Prescott, AZ [*Television station call letters*]
**KUSM**....... Bozeman, MT [*Television station call letters*]
**KUSP**......... Ku-Band Signal Processor (MCD)

**KUSP**......... Santa Cruz, CA [*FM radio station call letters*]
**KUSR**......... Ames, IA [*FM radio station call letters*]
**KUST**......... Kustom Electronics, Inc. [*NASDAQ symbol*] (NQ)
**KUSU-FM** ... Logan, UT [*FM radio station call letters*]
**KUT**........... Austin, TX [*FM radio station call letters*]
**kut**............ Kutenai [*MARC language code*] [*Library of Congress*] (LCCP)
**KUT**........... Kutsu-Ga-Hara [*Japan*] [*Seismograph station code, US Geological Survey*] (SEIS)
**Kut**............ Kuttim (BJA)
**KUT**........... Lexington Technical Institute, Lexington, KY [*OCLC symbol*] (OCLC)
**KUT**........... University of Toronto Union Catalogue Section [*UTLAS symbol*]
**KUTA**......... Blanding, UT [*AM radio station call letters*]
**KUTA-FM** ... Blanding, UT [*FM radio station call letters*]
**Kutch**.......... All India Reporter, Kutch [*1949-56*] [*A publication*] (DLA)
**KUTD**......... Keep Up to Date (KSC)
**KUTE**......... Desert Hot Springs, CA [*AM radio station call letters*]
**KUTF**......... Salem, OR [*Television station call letters*]
**KUTGW**..... Keep Up the Good Work
**KUTI**......... Selah, WA [*AM radio station call letters*]
**KUTP**......... Phoenix, AZ [*Television station call letters*]
**KUTR**......... Salt Lake City, UT [*AM radio station call letters*]
**KUTT**......... Fairbury, NE [*FM radio station call letters*]
**KUTV**......... Salt Lake City, UT [*Television station call letters*]
**KUTY**......... Palmdale, CA [*AM radio station call letters*]
**KUUB**......... Bozeman, MT [*AM radio station call letters*]
**KUUB-FM** ... Bozeman, MT [*FM radio station call letters*]
**KUUL**......... Davenport, IA [*FM radio station call letters*]
**KUUS**......... Billings, MT [*AM radio station call letters*]
**KUUY**......... Orchard Valley, WY [*AM radio station call letters*]
**KUUZ**......... Lake Village, AR [*FM radio station call letters*]
**KUVN-TV** ... Garland, TX [*Television station call letters*]
**KUVO**......... Denver, CO [*FM radio station call letters*]
**KUVR**......... Holdrege, NE [*AM radio station call letters*]
**KUVR-FM** ... Holdrege, NE [*FM radio station call letters*]
**Kuwait Bull Mar Sci** ... Kuwait Bulletin of Marine Science [*A publication*]
**Ku Welt Berl Mus** ... Kunst der Welt in den Berliner Museen [*A publication*]
**KUWL**......... Fairbanks, AK [*FM radio station call letters*]
**KUWR**......... Laramie, WY [*FM radio station call letters*]
**KUWS**......... Superior, WI [*FM radio station call letters*]
**KUX**........... Kumix Resources Corp. [*Vancouver Stock Exchange symbol*]
**KUY**........... Kuyper [*Indonesia*] [*Later, TNG*] [*Geomagnetic observatory code*]
**KUY**........... Uyak [*Alaska*] [*Airport symbol*] (OAG)
**KUY**........... Uyak, AK [*Location identifier*] [*FAA*] (FAAL)
**KUYO**......... Evansville, WY [*AM radio station call letters*]
**Kuz**............ Kuznica [*A publication*]
**KUZN**......... Palmer, AK [*FM radio station call letters*]
**Kuznechno-Shtampov** ... Kuznechno-Shtampovochnoe Proizvodstvo [*A publication*]
**KUZZ**......... Bakersfield, CA [*AM radio station call letters*]
**KUZZ-FM** ... Bakersfield, CA [*FM radio station call letters*]
**KV**............. British Virgin Island [*IYRU nationality code*] (IYR)
**KV**............. Compagnia Aeronautica Italiana [*Italy*] [*ICAO designator*] (FAAC)
**KV**............. K-V Pharmaceutical Co. [*AMEX symbol*] (SPSG)
**KV**............. Kalevalaseuran Vuosikirja [*A publication*]
**KV**............. Kerr Vector [*Optics*]
**KV**............. Key Verifier [*Data processing*]
**KV**............. Kidney Valve
**KV**............. Kill Vehicle
**kV**............. Kilovolt
**KV**............. Kinematic Viscosity
**KV**............. Kirkens Verden [*A publication*]
**KV**............. Knights of Vartan (EA)
**KV**............. Korte Verklaring der Heilige Schrift [*Kampen*] [*A publication*]
**KV**............. Kriegsverwendungsfaehig [*Fit for Active Service*] [*German military - World War II*]
**KVA**........... Karavia [*Zaire*] [*Geomagnetic observatory code*]
**KVA**........... Kavala [*Greece*] [*Airport symbol*] (OAG)
**kVA**........... Kilovolt Ampere
**KVAC**......... Forks, WA [*AM radio station call letters*]
**KVAD**......... Valdosta/Moody Air Force Base [*Georgia*] [*ICAO location identifier*] (ICLI)
**kVAH**......... Kilovolt-Ampere Hour
**kVAhm**....... Kilovolt-Ampere Hour Meter (MSA)
**KVAK**......... Valdez, AK [*AM radio station call letters*]
**KVAL-TV** ... Eugene, OR [*Television station call letters*]
**kVAM**......... Kilovolt-Ampere Meter
**KVAN**......... Vancouver, WA [*AM radio station call letters*]
**Kvan Elektr** ... Kvantovia Elektronika [*A publication*]
**Kvant**.......... Akademija Nauk SSSR i Akademija Pedagogiceskih Nauk SSSR. Kvant [*A publication*]
**Kvantovaya Ehlektron** ... Kvantovaya Ehlektronika [*A publication*]
**Kvantovaya Elektron (Kiev)** ... Kvantovaya Elektronika (Kiev) [*A publication*]
**Kvantovaya Elektron (Moskva)** ... Kvantovaya Elektronika (Moskva) [*A publication*]
**KVAO**......... Eager, AZ [*FM radio station call letters*]
**kvar**........... Kilovar
**kVAr**.......... Kilovolt-Ampere Reactive
**kvarh**.......... Kilovar-Hour
**Kvartalsskrift (Stockh)** ... Kvartalsskrift (Stockholm) [*A publication*]
**KVAS**......... Astoria, OR [*AM radio station call letters*]
**Kvasny Prum** ... Kvasny Prumysl [*Czechoslovakia*] [*A publication*]
**KVATL**....... Koninklijke Vlaamse Academie voor Taal- en Letterkunde [*A publication*]
**KVAW**........ Eagle Pass, TX [*Television station call letters*]
**KVAZ**......... Henryetta, OK [*FM radio station call letters*]
**KVBA**......... Kanamycin-Vancomycin Blood Agar [*Microbiology*]
**KVBC**......... Las Vegas, NV [*Television station call letters*]
**KVBG**......... Lompoc/Vandenberg Air Force Base [*California*] [*ICAO location identifier*] (ICLI)
**KVBMAS**.. Biologiske Meddelelser Kongelige Danske Videnskabernes Selskab [*A publication*]
**KVBM-TV** ... Minneapolis, MN [*Television station call letters*]
**KVBR**......... Brainerd, MN [*AM radio station call letters*]
**KVC**........... King Cove [*Alaska*] [*Airport symbol*] (OAG)
**KVC**........... King Cove, AK [*Location identifier*] [*FAA*] (FAAL)
**KVCE**......... Fallon, NV [*FM radio station call letters*]
**KVCL**......... Winnfield, LA [*AM radio station call letters*]
**KVCL-FM** ... Winnfield, LA [*FM radio station call letters*]
**KVCO**......... Concordia, KS [*FM radio station call letters*]
**kVCP**......... Kilovolt Constant Potential
**KVCR**......... San Bernardino, CA [*FM radio station call letters*]
**KVCR-TV** ... San Bernardino, CA [*Television station call letters*]
**KVCS**......... KXE6S Verein Chess Society (EA)
**KVCT**......... Victoria, TX [*Television station call letters*]
**KVCU**......... Redfield, SD [*FM radio station call letters*]
**KVCV**......... Victorville/George Air Force Base [*California*] [*ICAO location identifier*] (ICLI)
**KVCX**......... Gregory, SD [*FM radio station call letters*]
**KVCY**......... Fort Scott, KS [*FM radio station call letters*]
**KVDA**......... San Antonio, TX [*Television station call letters*]
**KVDB**......... Sioux Center, IA [*AM radio station call letters*]
**kVdc**........... Kilovolt Direct Current (IEEE)
**KVDP**......... Dry Prong, LA [*FM radio station call letters*]
**KVDT**......... Keyboard Visual Display Terminal (MCD)
**KVEA**......... Corona, CA [*Television station call letters*]
**KVEC**......... San Luis Obispo, CA [*AM radio station call letters*]
**KVEG**......... North Las Vegas, NV [*AM radio station call letters*]
**KVEL**......... Vernal, UT [*AM radio station call letters*]
**KVEN**......... Ventura, CA [*AM radio station call letters*]
**KVEO**......... Brownsville, TX [*Television station call letters*]
**KVET**......... Austin, TX [*AM radio station call letters*]
**K Vetensk Akad Handl** ... Kungliga Vetenskaps-Akademiens. Handlingar [*A publication*]
**K Vetensk Akad N Handl (Stockholm)** ... Kungliga Vetenskaps-Akademiens. Nya Handlingar (Stockholm) [*A publication*]
**K Vetenskapssamh Uppsala Arsb** ... Kungliga Vetenskapssamhaellets i Uppsala. Arsbok [*A publication*]
**K Vetensk-Soc Arsb** ... Kungliga Vetenskaps-Societetens. Arsbok [*A publication*]
**K Vet-Landbohojsk Arsskr** ... Kongelige Veterinaer-og Landbohojskole Arsskrift [*A publication*]
**K Vet Landbohojsk Inst Sterilitetsforsk Arsberet** ... Kongelige Veterinaer og Landbohojskole Institut foer Sterilitetsforskning Arsberetning [*A publication*]
**KVEW**........ Kennewick, WA [*Television station call letters*]
**KVEZ**......... Smithfield, UT [*FM radio station call letters*]
**KVF**........... Kent Volunteer Fencibles [*British military*] (DMA)
**KVFD**......... Fort Dodge, IA [*AM radio station call letters*]
**KVFM**......... Logan, UT [*FM radio station call letters*]
**KVFW**......... Winfield, KS [*AM radio station call letters*]
**KVFX**......... Manteca, CA [*FM radio station call letters*]
**KVG**........... Kavieng [*Papua New Guinea*] [*Airport symbol*] (OAG)
**KVG**........... Kavieng [*Papua New Guinea*] [*Seismograph station code, US Geological Survey*] (SEIS)
**KVG**........... Keyed Video Generator
**KVG**........... Kritische Vierteljahresschrift fuer Gesetzgebung [*A publication*]
**KVGB**......... Great Bend, KS [*AM radio station call letters*]
**KVGB-FM** ... Great Bend, KS [*FM radio station call letters*]
**KVGO**......... Pineville, LA [*AM radio station call letters*]
**KVGR**......... Templeton, CA [*AM radio station call letters*]
**KVHAAH** ... Kungliga Vitterhets Historie och Antikvitets Akademiens. Handlingar [*A publication*]
**KVHF**......... Kailua-Kona, HI [*Television station call letters*]
**KVHP**......... Lake Charles, LA [*Television station call letters*]
**KVHS**......... Concord, CA [*FM radio station call letters*]
**KVI**............ Carlsbad Ventures [*Vancouver Stock Exchange symbol*]
**KVI**............ Korean Veterans International (EA)
**KVI**............ Seattle, WA [*AM radio station call letters*]
**KVIA-TV**... El Paso, TX [*Television station call letters*]
**KVIB**......... Makawao, HI [*FM radio station call letters*]
**KVIC**......... Victoria, TX [*FM radio station call letters*]
**KVIE**......... Sacramento, CA [*Television station call letters*]
**KVIH-TV** .. Clovis, NM [*Television station call letters*]
**KVII-TV**.... Amarillo, TX [*Television station call letters*]
**KVIJ-TV** ... Sayre, OK [*Television station call letters*]
**KVIK**......... Travis Air Force Base, CA [*FM radio station call letters*]
**KVIL**......... Highland Park, TX [*AM radio station call letters*]
**KVIL-FM** .. Highland Park-Dallas, TX [*FM radio station call letters*]

**KVIN** ........ Vinita, OK [*AM radio station call letters*]
**KVIO-TV**... Carlsbad, NM [*Television station call letters*]
**KVIP**......... Redding, CA [*AM radio station call letters*]
**KVIP-FM**.. Redding, CA [*FM radio station call letters*]
**KVIQ**......... Eureka, CA [*Television station call letters*]
**KVIV**......... El Paso, TX [*AM radio station call letters*]
**KVJS**......... Kritische Vierteljahresschrift [*A publication*]
**KVK**.......... Kriegsverdienstkreuz [*War Service Cross*] [*German military decoration - World War II*]
**KVKEK**...... Kroniek van Kunst en Kultur [*A publication*]
**KVKI**......... Shreveport, LA [*AM radio station call letters*]
**KVKI-FM**... Shreveport, LA [*FM radio station call letters*]
**KVL**.......... Kingsvale Resources [*Vancouver Stock Exchange symbol*]
**KVL**.......... Kivalina [*Alaska*] [*Airport symbol*] (OAG)
**KVL**.......... Kivalina, AK [*Location identifier*] [*FAA*] (FAAL)
**KVLA**........ Vidalia, LA [*AM radio station call letters*]
**KVLBA**...... Kanamycin-Vancomycin Labeled Blood Agar [*Microbiology*]
**KVLC**........ Las Cruces, NM [*FM radio station call letters*]
**KVLD**........ Valdez, AK [*AM radio station call letters*]
**KVLE**........ Gunnison, CO [*FM radio station call letters*]
**KVLF**........ Alpine, TX [*AM radio station call letters*]
**KVLG**........ La Grange, TX [*AM radio station call letters*]
**KVLH**........ Pauls Valley, OK [*AM radio station call letters*]
**KVLI**......... Lake Isabella, CA [*AM radio station call letters*]
**KVLL**......... Woodville, TX [*AM radio station call letters*]
**KVLM**........ Kevlin Microwave Corp. [*NASDAQ symbol*] (NQ)
**KVLT-FM**... Owasso, OK [*FM radio station call letters*]
**KVLU**........ Beaumont, TX [*FM radio station call letters*]
**KVLV**........ Fallon, NV [*AM radio station call letters*]
**KVLV-FM**... Fallon, NV [*FM radio station call letters*]
**KVLY**........ Edinburg, TX [*FM radio station call letters*]
**kVM**.......... Kilovolt Meter
**KVMA**........ Magnolia, AR [*AM radio station call letters*]
**KVMA-FM**... Magnolia, AR [*FM radio station call letters*]
**KVMC**........ Colorado City, TX [*AM radio station call letters*]
**KVMFA**..... Kongelige Danske Videnskabernes Selskab. Matematisk-Fysisk Skrifter [*A publication*]
**KVMR**........ Nevada City, CA [*FM radio station call letters*]
**KVMT**........ Vail, CO [*FM radio station call letters*]
**KVMV**........ McAllen, TX [*FM radio station call letters*]
**KVMX**........ Eastland, TX [*FM radio station call letters*]
**KVN**.......... Kaiserville [*Nevada*] [*Seismograph station code, US Geological Survey*] (SEIS)
**KVN**.......... Kimmins Environmental Services [*NYSE symbol*] (SPSG)
**KVNA**........ Flagstaff, AZ [*AM radio station call letters*]
**KVNA-FM**... Flagstaff, AZ [*FM radio station call letters*]
**KVNE-FM**... Tyler, TX [*FM radio station call letters*]
**KVNF**........ Paonia, CO [*FM radio station call letters*]
**KVNI**......... Coeur D'Alene, ID [*AM radio station call letters*]
**KVNO**........ Omaha, NE [*FM radio station call letters*]
**KVNS**........ Korrespondenzblatt. Verein fuer Niederdeutsche Sprachforschung [*A publication*]
**KVNU**........ Logan, UT [*AM radio station call letters*]
**KVO**.......... Keep Vein Open [*Medicine*]
**KVO**.......... Kraftverkehrsordnung fuer den Gueterfernverkehr mit Kraftfahrzeugen [*Regulation for the Carriage of Goods by Motor Vehicles*] [*German*] [*Business term*] (ILCA)
**KVOA-TV**... Tucson, AZ [*Television station call letters*]
**KVOC**........ Casper, WY [*AM radio station call letters*]
**KVOD**........ Denver, CO [*FM radio station call letters*]
**KVOE**........ Emporia, KS [*AM radio station call letters*]
**KVOI**......... Oro Valley, AZ [*AM radio station call letters*]
**KVOJ**......... Edna, TX [*AM radio station call letters*]
**KVOK**........ Kodiak, AK [*AM radio station call letters*]
**KVOL**........ Lafayette, LA [*AM radio station call letters*]
**KVOL-FM**... Opelousas, LA [*FM radio station call letters*]
**KVOM**....... Morrilton, AR [*AM radio station call letters*]
**KVOM-FM**... Morrilton, AR [*FM radio station call letters*]
**KVON**........ Napa, CA [*AM radio station call letters*]
**KVOO**........ Tulsa, OK [*AM radio station call letters*]
**KVOO-FM**... Tulsa, OK [*FM radio station call letters*]
**KVOP**........ Plainview, TX [*AM radio station call letters*]
**KVOR**........ Colorado Springs, CO [*AM radio station call letters*]
**KVOS-TV**... Bellingham, WA [*Television station call letters*]
**KVOU**........ Uvalde, TX [*AM radio station call letters*]
**KVOW**....... Riverton, WY [*AM radio station call letters*]
**KVOX**........ Moorhead, MN [*AM radio station call letters*]
**KVOX-FM**... Moorhead, MN [*FM radio station call letters*]
**KVOY**........ Mojave, CA [*AM radio station call letters*]
**KVP**.......... Katholieke Volkspartij [*Catholic People's Party*] [*Netherlands*] [*Political party*] (PPE)
**kVP**.......... Kilovolt Peak
**KVP**.......... Kodak Vacuum Probe
**KVP**.......... Kodak Versamat Processor
**KVPA**........ Port Isabel, TX [*FM radio station call letters*]
**KVPC-FM**... San Joaquin, CA [*FM radio station call letters*]
**KVPH**........ Bismarck, ND [*FM radio station call letters*]
**KVPH**........ KV Pharmaceutical Co. [*NASDAQ symbol*] (NQ)
**KVPI**......... Ville Platte, LA [*AM radio station call letters*]
**KVPI-FM**.. Ville Platte, LA [*FM radio station call letters*]
**KVPO**........ Berwick, LA [*FM radio station call letters*]
**KVPR**........ Fresno, CA [*FM radio station call letters*]
**KVPRA**...... Kvasny Prumysl [*A publication*]
**KVPS**......... Valparaiso/Eglin Air Force Base [*Florida*] [*ICAO location identifier*] (ICLI)
**KVQB**........ Cabot, AR [*AM radio station call letters*]
**KVQC**........ Stephenville, TX [*FM radio station call letters*]
**KVRA**........ Vermillion, SD [*AM radio station call letters*]
**KVRB**........ Vero Beach/Vero Beach [*Florida*] [*ICAO location identifier*] (ICLI)
**KVRC**........ Arkadelphia, AR [*AM radio station call letters*]
**KVRD**........ Cottonwood, AZ [*AM radio station call letters*]
**KVRD-FM**... Cottonwood, AZ [*FM radio station call letters*]
**KVRF**........ Vermillion, SD [*FM radio station call letters*]
**KVRH**........ Salida, CO [*AM radio station call letters*]
**KVRH-FM**... Salida, CO [*FM radio station call letters*]
**KVRK**........ Atwater, CA [*FM radio station call letters*]
**KVRP**........ Stamford, TX [*AM radio station call letters*]
**KVRP-FM**... Haskell, TX [*FM radio station call letters*]
**KVRR**........ Fargo, ND [*Television station call letters*]
**KVS**.......... Kabelvisie Onafhankelijk Tijdschrift voor Kabel en Lokale Televisie [*A publication*]
**KVS**.......... Kelvin-Varley Slide [*Electronics*]
**KVS**.......... Kurzweil VoiceSystem [*Voice-recognition computer device*]
**KVSA**........ McGehee, AR [*AM radio station call letters*]
**KVSC**........ St. Cloud, MN [*FM radio station call letters*]
**KVSD**........ Vista, CA [*AM radio station call letters*]
**KVSF**........ Santa Fe, NM [*AM radio station call letters*]
**KVSH**........ Valentine, NE [*AM radio station call letters*]
**KVSI**......... Montpelier, ID [*AM radio station call letters*]
**KVSL**........ Show Low, AZ [*AM radio station call letters*]
**KVSN**........ Tumwater, WA [*AM radio station call letters*]
**KVSO**........ Ardmore, OK [*AM radio station call letters*]
**KVSR**........ Rapid City, SD [*FM radio station call letters*]
**KVST**........ Keystone Visual Survey Test [*Ophthalmology*]
**KVSV**........ Beloit, KS [*AM radio station call letters*]
**KVSV-FM**... Beloit, KS [*FM radio station call letters*]
**KVT**.......... Kavak [*Turkey*] [*Seismograph station code, US Geological Survey*] (SEIS)
**KVTI**......... Tacoma, WA [*FM radio station call letters*]
**KVTN**........ Pine Bluff, AR [*Television station call letters*]
**KVTT**........ Dallas, TX [*FM radio station call letters*]
**KVTV**........ Laredo, TX [*Television station call letters*]
**KVU**.......... Kleer-Vu Industries, Inc. [*AMEX symbol*] (SPSG)
**KVU**.......... Victoria University Library, University of Toronto [*UTLAS symbol*]
**KVUE-TV**... Austin, TX [*Television station call letters*]
**KVUU**........ Pueblo, CO [*FM radio station call letters*]
**KVVA**........ Phoenix, AZ [*AM radio station call letters*]
**KVVA-FM**... Apache Junction, AZ [*FM radio station call letters*]
**KVVL**......... Thief River Falls, MN [*FM radio station call letters*]
**KVVP**........ Leesville, LA [*FM radio station call letters*]
**KVVQ**........ Hesperia, CA [*AM radio station call letters*]
**KVVQ-FM**... Victorville, CA [*FM radio station call letters*]
**KVVS**........ Windsor, CO [*AM radio station call letters*]
**KVVT**........ Barstow, CA [*Television station call letters*]
**KVVU-TV**... Henderson, NV [*Television station call letters*]
**KVW**.......... Kansas City, Kaw Valley R. R., Inc. [*AAR code*]
**KVW**.......... Kurzweil Voice Writer
**KVWC**........ Vernon, TX [*AM radio station call letters*]
**KVWC-FM**... Vernon, TX [*FM radio station call letters*]
**KVWG**........ Pearsall, TX [*AM radio station call letters*]
**KVWG-FM**... Pearsall, TX [*FM radio station call letters*]
**KVWM**....... Show Low, AZ [*AM radio station call letters*]
**KVWM-FM**... Show Low, AZ [*FM radio station call letters*]
**KVXO**........ Spokane, WA [*FM radio station call letters*]
**KVYN**........ St. Helena, CA [*FM radio station call letters*]
**KVZK-2**..... Pago Pago, AS [*Television station call letters*]
**KVZK-4**..... Pago Pago, AS [*Television station call letters*]
**KVZK-5**..... Pago Pago, AS [*Television station call letters*]
**KW**........... Afrikan Airlines Ltd. [*Ghana*] [*ICAO designator*] (FAAC)
**KW**........... Dorado Wings [*Airline code*]
**KW**........... Kaiser Wilhelm [*King William*] [*Name of two Prussian kings and emperor of Germany*] (ROG)
**KW**........... Kaliszer Woch (BJA)
**K & W**........ Kames and Woodhouselee's Folio Dictionary, Scotch Court of Session [*A publication*] (DLA)
**KW**........... Kampfwagen [*Tank*] [*German military - World War II*]
**KW**........... Katabatic Wind
**KW**........... Keith-Wagener [*Ophthalmology*]
**KW**........... Kenworth Truck Co.
**KW**........... Key West [*Florida*]
**KW**........... Key Word [*Online database field identifier*]
**kW**........... Kilowatt
**KW**........... Kiloword (BUR)
**KW**........... Kimmelstiel-Wilson [*Medicine*]
**K i W**........ Kirche in der Welt [*A publication*]
**KW**........... Knight of William [*Netherlands*]
**KW**........... Knight of Windsor (ROG)
**KW**........... Knitwise [*Knitting*]
**KW**........... Koloniaal Weekblad [*A publication*]
**KW**........... Korean War

**KW**............ Kraftwagen [*Motor Vehicle*] [*German*]
**KW**............ Kruskal-Wallis Test [*Fisheries*]
**KW**............ Kuwait [*ANSI two-letter standard code*] (CNC)
**KWA**.......... Keyword Adapted [*Data processing*]
**KWA**.......... Kwajalein [*Marshall Islands*] [*Airport symbol*] (OAG)
**KWA**.......... Kwantlen College Library [*UTLAS symbol*]
**KWA**.......... Kweiyang [*Republic of China*] [*Seismograph station code, US Geological Survey*] (SEIS)
**KWAB**....... Big Spring, TX [*Television station call letters*]
**KWAC**....... Bakersfield, CA [*AM radio station call letters*]
**KWAC**....... Keyword and Context [*Indexing*] (DIT)
**KWAD**....... Wadena, MN [*AM radio station call letters*]
**KWAI**........ Honolulu, HI [*AM radio station call letters*]
**KWAJ**........ Kwajalein Atoll (AABC)
**KWAK**....... Stuttgart, AR [*AM radio station call letters*]
**KWAL**....... Wallace, ID [*AM radio station call letters*]
**KWAL**....... Wallops Island/Wallops Station [*Virginia*] [*ICAO location identifier*] (ICLI)
**KWAM**...... Memphis, TN [*AM radio station call letters*]
**Kwangju Teach Coll Sci Educ Cent Rev** ... Kwangju Teachers College. Science Education Center. Review [*A publication*]
**Kwansei Gak L Rev** ... Kwansei Gakuin University. Law Review [*A publication*] (DLA)
**Kwansei Gakuin Sociol Dept Stud** ... Kwansei Gakuin University. Sociology Department Studies [*A publication*]
**Kwansei Gakuin U Ann Stud** ... Kwansei Gakuin University. Annual Studies [*A publication*]
**Kwansei Gakuin Univ Annual Stud** ... Kwansei Gakuin University. Annual Studies [*A publication*]
**KWAR**....... Waverly, IA [*FM radio station call letters*]
**Kwar Hist Kul Mat** ... Kwartalnik Historii Kultury Materialnej [*A publication*]
**Kwartalnik Geol** ... Kwartalnik Geologiczny [*A publication*]
**Kwart Geol** ... Kwartalnik Geologiczny [*A publication*]
**Kwart Geol (Pol Inst Geol)** ... Kwartalnik Geologiczny (Poland. Instytut Geologiczny) [*A publication*]
**Kwart Hist Kult** ... Kwartalnik Historii Kultury [*A publication*]
**Kwart Hist Kult Mater** ... Kwartalnik Historii Kultury Materialnej [*A publication*]
**Kwart Hist Nauki Tech** ... Kwartalnik Historii Nauki i Techniki [*A publication*]
**Kwart Hist Nauki i Tech** ... Kwartalnik Historii Nauki i Techniki [*A publication*]
**Kwart Opolski** ... Kwartalnik Opolski [*A publication*]
**KWAT**....... Watertown, SD [*AM radio station call letters*]
**KWAV**....... Monterey, CA [*FM radio station call letters*]
**KWAX**....... Eugene, OR [*FM radio station call letters*]
**KWAY**....... Waverly, IA [*AM radio station call letters*]
**KWAY-FM** ... Waverly, IA [*FM radio station call letters*]
**KWAZ**....... Needles, CA [*FM radio station call letters*]
**KWB**.......... Keith, Wagener, Barker [*Ophthalmology*]
**KWBB**........ San Francisco, CA [*Television station call letters*]
**KWBC**....... Navasota, TX [*AM radio station call letters*]
**KWBC**....... Washington [*District of Columbia*] [*ICAO location identifier*] (ICLI)
**KWBE**........ Beatrice, NE [*AM radio station call letters*]
**KWBF**........ Katholische Welt-Bibelfoderation [*World Catholic Federation for the Biblical Apostolate - WCFBA*] (EAIO)
**KWBG**....... Boone, IA [*AM radio station call letters*]
**KWBG-FM** ... Boone, IA [*FM radio station call letters*]
**KWBI**......... Morrison, CO [*FM radio station call letters*]
**KWBI-TV** ... Denver, CO [*Television station call letters*]
**KWBU**....... Waco, TX [*FM radio station call letters*]
**KWBW**...... Hutchinson, KS [*AM radio station call letters*]
**KWBX**....... Bend, OR [*FM radio station call letters*]
**KWBY**....... Woodburn, OR [*AM radio station call letters*]
**KWC**.......... K-Band Waveguide Circulator
**KWC**.......... Kentucky Wesleyan College [*Owensboro*]
**KWC**.......... Kierownictwo Walki Cywilnej (BJA)
**KWC**.......... Wycliffe College Library, University of Toronto [*UTLAS symbol*]
**KWCB**....... Floresville, TX [*FM radio station call letters*]
**KWCD**....... Grover City, CA [*FM radio station call letters*]
**KWCH-TV** ... Hutchinson, KS [*Television station call letters*]
**KWCK**....... Searcy, AR [*AM radio station call letters*]
**KWCK-FM** ... Searcy, AR [*FM radio station call letters*]
**KWCL**........ Oak Grove, LA [*AM radio station call letters*]
**KWCL-FM** ... Oak Grove, LA [*FM radio station call letters*]
**KWCM-TV** ... Appleton, MN [*Television station call letters*]
**KWCO**....... Chickasha, OK [*AM radio station call letters*]
**KWCR-FM** ... Ogden, UT [*FM radio station call letters*]
**KWCS**........ Bridgeport, TX [*FM radio station call letters*]
**KWCV**....... Wichita, KS [*Television station call letters*]
**KWCW**...... Walla Walla, WA [*FM radio station call letters*]
**KWCX**....... Wilcox, AZ [*FM radio station call letters*]
**KWD**.......... Consolidated Westrex Development [*Vancouver Stock Exchange symbol*]
**KWD**.......... Draco [*Sweden*] [*Research code symbol*]
**KWD**.......... Kellwood Co. [*NYSE symbol*] (SPSG)
**KWDF**....... Ball, LA [*AM radio station call letters*]
**KWDG**....... Idabel, OK [*FM radio station call letters*]
**K & W Dic** ... Kames and Woodhouselee's Folio Dictionary, Scotch Court of Session [*A publication*] (DLA)
**KWDJ**........ Riverside, CA [*FM radio station call letters*]
**KWDM**...... West Des Moines, IA [*FM radio station call letters*]
**KWDQ**....... Woodward, OK [*FM radio station call letters*]
**KWDR**....... Kwandur Newsletter. Council for Yukon Indians [*A publication*]
**KWDX**....... Silsbee, TX [*FM radio station call letters*]
**KWE**.......... Guiyang [*China*] [*Airport symbol*] (OAG)
**kWe**........... Kilowatts of Electric Energy
**KWE**.......... Knight of the White Eagle [*Poland*]
**KWEB**........ Rochester, MN [*AM radio station call letters*]
**KWED**....... Seguin, TX [*AM radio station call letters*]
**KWEH**....... Camden, AR [*FM radio station call letters*]
**KWEI**......... Weiser, ID [*AM radio station call letters*]
**KWEI-FM** ... Weiser, ID [*FM radio station call letters*]
**KWEL**........ Midland, TX [*AM radio station call letters*]
**KWEN**....... Tulsa, OK [*FM radio station call letters*]
**KWES**........ Colorado Springs, CO [*AM radio station call letters*]
**KWET**........ Cheyenne, OK [*Television station call letters*]
**KWEW**...... Coalinga, CA [*Television station call letters*]
**KWEX-TV** ... San Antonio, TX [*Television station call letters*]
**KWEY**....... Weatherford, OK [*AM radio station call letters*]
**KWF**.......... Waterfall, AK [*Location identifier*] [*FAA*] (FAAL)
**KWFC**........ Kelli Warren Fan Club (EA)
**KWFC**........ Springfield, MO [*FM radio station call letters*]
**KWFH**....... Parker, AZ [*FM radio station call letters*]
**KWFL**........ Roswell, NM [*FM radio station call letters*]
**KWFM**...... Kurt Weill Foundation for Music (EA)
**KWFM**...... Tucson, AZ [*FM radio station call letters*]
**KWFN**....... Fredonia, KS [*FM radio station call letters*]
**KWFT**........ Wichita Falls, TX [*AM radio station call letters*]
**KWFX**........ Woodward, OK [*FM radio station call letters*]
**KWG**.......... Stockton, CA [*AM radio station call letters*]
**KWGEA**.... Kwartalnik Geologiczny [*A publication*]
**KWGG**....... Hampton, IA [*FM radio station call letters*]
**KWGH**....... Big Lake, TX [*AM radio station call letters*]
**KWGH-FM** ... Big Lake, TX [*FM radio station call letters*]
**KWGN-TV** ... Denver, CO [*Television station call letters*]
**KWGS**........ Tulsa, OK [*FM radio station call letters*]
**kWh**........... Kilowatt-Hour
**KWHB**....... Tulsa, OK [*Television station call letters*]
**KWHCA**.... Kwangsan Hakhoe Chi [*A publication*]
**KWHD**...... Castle Rock, CO [*Television station call letters*]
**KWHE**....... Honolulu, HI [*Television station call letters*]
**kWhe**......... Kilowatt-Hour Electric
**KWHH**...... Hilo, HI [*Television station call letters*]
**KWHI-FM** ... Brenham, TX [*FM radio station call letters*]
**KWHK**....... Hutchinson, KS [*AM radio station call letters*]
**KWHL**....... Anchorage, AK [*FM radio station call letters*]
**KWHM**...... Kilowatt-Hour Meter
**KWHN**...... Fort Smith, AR [*AM radio station call letters*]
**KWHO**...... Weed, CA [*FM radio station call letters*]
**KWHQ-FM** ... Kenai, AK [*FM radio station call letters*]
**kWhr**.......... Kilowatt-Hour
**KWHT**....... Pendleton, OR [*FM radio station call letters*]
**KWHW**...... Altus, OK [*AM radio station call letters*]
**KWHY-TV** ... Los Angeles, CA [*Television station call letters*]
**KWHZ**....... Ferndale, CA [*FM radio station call letters*]
**KWI**........... Kosher Wine Institute (EA)
**KWI**........... Kuwait [*Kuwait*] [*Airport symbol*] (OAG)
**KWi**............ Wichita Public Library, Wichita, KS [*Library symbol*] [*Library of Congress*] (LCLS)
**KWiB**......... [*The*] Boeing Co., Wichita Division Library, Wichita, KS [*Library symbol*] [*Library of Congress*] (LCLS)
**KWIC**......... Keyword in Context [*Indexing*]
**KWIC-FM** ... Beaumont, TX [*FM radio station call letters*]
**KWiF**......... Friends University, Wichita, KS [*Library symbol*] [*Library of Congress*] (LCLS)
**KWiGS**...... Church of Jesus Christ of Latter-Day Saints, Genealogical Society Library, Wichita Branch, Wichita, KS [*Library symbol*] [*Library of Congress*] (LCLS)
**KWiIL**........ Institute of Logopedics, Wichita, KS [*Library symbol*] [*Library of Congress*] (LCLS)
**KWiK**......... Kansas Newman College, Wichita, KS [*Library symbol*] [*Library of Congress*] (LCLS)
**KWIK**........ KWIK Products International Corp. [*NASDAQ symbol*] (NQ)
**KWIK**........ Pocatello, ID [*AM radio station call letters*]
**KWIL**......... Albany, OR [*AM radio station call letters*]
**KWIN**........ Lodi, CA [*FM radio station call letters*]
**KWIP**......... Dallas, OR [*AM radio station call letters*]
**KWIQ**........ Moses Lake, WA [*AM radio station call letters*]
**KWIQ-FM** ... Moses Lake, WA [*FM radio station call letters*]
**KWiSF**....... Saint Francis Hospital, Wichita, KS [*Library symbol*] [*Library of Congress*] (LCLS)
**KWiSJ**....... Saint Joseph Hospital, Wichita, KS [*Library symbol*] [*Library of Congress*] (LCLS)
**KWIT**......... Keyword in Title [*Indexing*]
**KWIT**......... Sioux City, IA [*FM radio station call letters*]
**KWiU**......... Wichita State University, Wichita, KS [*Library symbol*] [*Library of Congress*] (LCLS)

**KWIV** ....... Douglas, WY [*AM radio station call letters*]
**KWiVA** ....... United States Veterans Administration Hospital, Wichita, KS [*Library symbol*] [*Library of Congress*] (LCLS)
**KWiWC** ..... Wichita Clinic, Wichita, KS [*Library symbol*] [*Library of Congress*] (LCLS)
**KWiWM** .... Wesley Medical Center, Wichita, KS [*Library symbol*] [*Library of Congress*] (LCLS)
**KWIX** ........ Moberly, MO [*AM radio station call letters*]
**KWIY** ........ Brady, TX [*Television station call letters*]
**KWIZ** ......... Santa Ana, CA [*AM radio station call letters*]
**KWIZ-FM** ... Santa Ana, CA [*FM radio station call letters*]
**KWJC** ........ Liberty, MO [*FM radio station call letters*]
**KWJJ** ........ Portland, OR [*AM radio station call letters*]
**KWJJ-FM** ... Portland, OR [*FM radio station call letters*]
**KWJM** ....... Farmerville, LA [*FM radio station call letters*]
**KWJY** ........ Woodward, OK [*FM radio station call letters*]
**KWK** .......... Kampfwagenkanone [*Tank Gun*] [*German military - World War II*]
**KWK** .......... Kurs Wynikowy Kalkulacyjny [*Calculated Effective Rate*] [*Foreign trade*] [*Polish*]
**KWK** .......... Kwigillingok [*Alaska*] [*Airport symbol*] (OAG)
**KWK** .......... Kwigillingok, AK [*Location identifier*] [*FAA*] (FAAL)
**KWKA** ....... Clovis, NM [*AM radio station call letters*]
**KWKH** ....... Shreveport, LA [*AM radio station call letters*]
**KWKH-FM** ... Shreveport, LA [*FM radio station call letters*]
**KWKI** ........ Big Spring, TX [*AM radio station call letters*]
**KWKK** ....... Dardanelle, AR [*FM radio station call letters*]
**KWKL** ....... Arkansas City, KS [*FM radio station call letters*]
**KWKQ** ....... Graham, TX [*FM radio station call letters*]
**KWKR** ....... Leoti, KS [*FM radio station call letters*]
**KWKS** ........ Winfield, KS [*FM radio station call letters*]
**KWKT** ........ Waco, TX [*Television station call letters*]
**KWKW** ...... Los Angeles, CA [*AM radio station call letters*]
**KWKY** ....... Des Moines, IA [*AM radio station call letters*]
**KWL** .......... Guilin [*China*] [*Airport symbol*] (OAG)
**KWLA** ....... Many, LA [*AM radio station call letters*]
**KWLC** ........ Decorah, IA [*AM radio station call letters*]
**KWLD** ....... Plainview, TX [*FM radio station call letters*]
**KWLF** ........ Fairbanks, AK [*FM radio station call letters*]
**KWLF** ........ Kodak Wratten Light Filter
**KWLI** ......... Eagle, CO [*FM radio station call letters*]
**KWLL** ........ Casa Grande, AZ [*AM radio station call letters*]
**KWLM** ...... Willmar, MN [*AM radio station call letters*]
**KWLO** ....... Waterloo, IA [*AM radio station call letters*]
**KWLS** ........ Pratt, KS [*AM radio station call letters*]
**KWLT** ........ North Crossett, AR [*FM radio station call letters*]
**KWLV** ....... Many, LA [*FM radio station call letters*]
**kWm** .......... Kilowatt Meter
**KWM** ......... Korean War Memorial (EA)
**KWM** ......... Kowanyama [*Australia*] [*Airport symbol*] (OAG)
**KW/M²** ..... Kilowatts per Square Meter
**KWMB** ...... Wabasha, MN [*AM radio station call letters*]
**KWMC** ...... Del Rio, TX [*AM radio station call letters*]
**KWMG** ...... Columbus, NE [*FM radio station call letters*]
**KWMJ** ....... Midland, TX [*FM radio station call letters*]
**KWMQ** ...... Southwest City, MO [*FM radio station call letters*]
**KWMT** ...... Fort Dodge, IA [*AM radio station call letters*]
**KWMU** ...... St. Louis, MO [*FM radio station call letters*]
**KWMW** .... Maljamar, NM [*FM radio station call letters*]
**KWN** .......... Kenwin Shops, Inc. [*AMEX symbol*] (SPSG)
**KWN** .......... Korean Wideband Network [*Communications*] [*Military*] (MCD)
**KWN** .......... Quinhagak [*Alaska*] [*Airport symbol*] (OAG)
**KWN** .......... Quinhagak, AK [*Location identifier*] [*FAA*] (FAAL)
**KWNA** ....... Winnemucca, NV [*AM radio station call letters*]
**KWNA-FM** ... Winnemucca, NV [*FM radio station call letters*]
**KWNB-TV** ... Hayes Center, NE [*Television station call letters*]
**KWNC** ....... Quincy, WA [*AM radio station call letters*]
**KWND** ....... Saratoga, WY [*FM radio station call letters*]
**KWNE** ....... Ukiah, CA [*FM radio station call letters*]
**KWNG** ....... Red Wing, MN [*FM radio station call letters*]
**KWNK** ....... Simi Valley, CA [*AM radio station call letters*]
**KWNM-TV** ... Silver City, NM [*Television station call letters*]
**KWNN** ....... Little Rock, AR [*AM radio station call letters*]
**KWNO** ....... Winona, MN [*AM radio station call letters*]
**KWNQ** ....... Harrison, AR [*FM radio station call letters*]
**KWNS** ....... Winnsboro, TX [*FM radio station call letters*]
**KWNZ** ....... Carson City, NV [*FM radio station call letters*]
**KwO** .......... Kwartalnik Opolski [*A publication*]
**KWOA** ....... Worthington, MN [*AM radio station call letters*]
**KWOA-FM** ... Worthington, MN [*FM radio station call letters*]
**KWOC** ....... Keyword out of Context [*Indexing*]
**KWOC** ....... Poplar Bluff, MO [*AM radio station call letters*]
**KWOCA** .... Key Word Online Catalogue Access
**KWOD** ....... Sacramento, CA [*FM radio station call letters*]
**KWOF** ....... Waterloo, IA [*AM radio station call letters*]
**KWOM** ...... Watertown, MN [*AM radio station call letters*]
**KWON** ....... Bartlesville, OK [*AM radio station call letters*]
**KWOR** ....... Worland, WY [*AM radio station call letters*]
**KWOR-FM** ... Worland, WY [*AM radio station call letters*]
**KWOS** ....... Jefferson City, MO [*AM radio station call letters*]
**KWOT** ....... Keyword out of Title [*Indexing*]
**KWOT** ....... Kilometer-Wave Orbiting Telescope [*NASA*]
**KWOW** ...... Clifton, TX [*FM radio station call letters*]
**KWOX** ....... Woodward, OK [*FM radio station call letters*]
**KWOZ** ....... Mountain View, AR [*FM radio station call letters*]
**KWP** .......... Kierowinctwo Walki Podziemnej (BJA)
**KWP** .......... King World Productions, Inc. [*NYSE symbol*] (SPSG)
**KWP** .......... Korean Workers' Party [*Democratic People's Republic of Korea*] [*Political party*] (PD)
**KWP** .......... West Point [*Alaska*] [*Airport symbol*] (OAG)
**KWP** .......... West Point, AK [*Location identifier*] [*FAA*] (FAAL)
**KWPC** ........ Muscatine, IA [*AM radio station call letters*]
**KWPM** ...... West Plains, MO [*AM radio station call letters*]
**KWPN** ....... West Point, NE [*AM radio station call letters*]
**KWPN-FM** ... West Point, NE [*FM radio station call letters*]
**KWPR** ........ Claremore, OK [*AM radio station call letters*]
**KWQC-TV** ... Davenport, IA [*Television station call letters*]
**KWQQ** ....... Hatch, NM [*FM radio station call letters*]
**kWr** ........... Kilowatts Reactive
**KWR** .......... KW Resources Ltd. [*Vancouver Stock Exchange symbol*]
**KWRB** ....... Macon/Robins Air Force Base [*Georgia*] [*ICAO location identifier*] (ICLI)
**KWRD** ....... Henderson, TX [*AM radio station call letters*]
**KWRE** ....... Warrenton, MO [*AM radio station call letters*]
**KWRF** ........ Warren, AR [*AM radio station call letters*]
**KWRF-FM** ... Warren, AR [*FM radio station call letters*]
**KWRI** ........ Wrightstown/McGuire Air Force Base [*New Jersey*] [*ICAO location identifier*] (ICLI)
**KWRL** ........ La Grande, OR [*FM radio station call letters*]
**KWRM** ....... Corona, CA [*AM radio station call letters*]
**KWRO** ....... Coquille, OR [*AM radio station call letters*]
**KWRP** ........ San Jacinto, CA [*FM radio station call letters*]
**KWRRI** ...... Kansas Water Resources Research Institute [*Department of the Interior*] [*Kansas State University*] [*Research center*] (RCD)
**KWRRI** ...... Kentucky Water Resources Research Institute [*Department of the Interior*] [*University of Kentucky*] [*Lexington, KY*] [*Research center*] (RCD)
**KWRS** ........ Spokane, WA [*FM radio station call letters*]
**KWRT** ........ Boonville, MO [*AM radio station call letters*]
**KWRW** ...... Rusk, TX [*FM radio station call letters*]
**KWS** .......... Southwestern College, Winfield, KS [*Library symbol*] [*Library of Congress*] (LCLS)
**KWSA** ........ West Klamath, OR [*AM radio station call letters*]
**KWSB-FM** ... Gunnison, CO [*FM radio station call letters*]
**KWSC** ........ Wayne, NE [*FM radio station call letters*]
**KWSD** ....... Mount Shasta, CA [*AM radio station call letters*]
**KWSD** ....... White Sands/Condron Army Air Field [*New Mexico*] [*ICAO location identifier*] (ICLI)
**KWSE** ........ Williston, ND [*Television station call letters*]
**KWSH** ....... Wewoka, OK [*AM radio station call letters*]
**KWSI** ......... Warm Springs, OR [*FM radio station call letters*]
**KWSJ** ........ Saint John's College, Winfield, KS [*Library symbol*] [*Library of Congress*] (LCLS)
**KWSK** ........ Daingerfield, TX [*FM radio station call letters*]
**KWSL** ........ Sioux City, IA [*AM radio station call letters*]
**KWSM** ....... Sherman, TX [*FM radio station call letters*]
**KWSO** ....... Warm Springs, OR [*FM radio station call letters*]
**KWSP** ........ Santa Margarita, CA [*FM radio station call letters*]
**KWSS** ........ Gilroy, CA [*FM radio station call letters*]
**KWST** ........ Brawley, CA [*FM radio station call letters*]
**KWSU** ....... Pullman, WA [*AM radio station call letters*]
**KWSU-TV** ... Pullman, WA [*Television station call letters*]
**kWt** ........... Kilowatt, Thermal
**KWT** .......... Kuwait [*ANSI three-letter standard code*] (CNC)
**KWT** .......... Kuwait Times [*A publication*]
**KWT** .......... Kwethluk [*Alaska*] [*Airport symbol*] (OAG)
**KWT** .......... Kwethluk, AK [*Location identifier*] [*FAA*] (FAAL)
**KWTA** ....... Electra, TX [*FM radio station call letters*]
**KWTD** ....... Lonoke, AR [*FM radio station call letters*]
**kW(th)** ....... Kilowatt, Thermal
**KWTN** ....... Keewatin [*FAA*] (FAAC)
**KWTO** ....... Springfield, MO [*AM radio station call letters*]
**KWTO-FM** ... Springfield, MO [*FM radio station call letters*]
**KWTR** ....... Lakeport, CA [*AM radio station call letters*]
**KWTS** ........ Canyon, TX [*FM radio station call letters*]
**KWTV** ....... Oklahoma City, OK [*Television station call letters*]
**KWTX** ....... Waco, TX [*AM radio station call letters*]
**KWTX-FM** ... Waco, TX [*FM radio station call letters*]
**KWTX-TV** ... Waco, TX [*Television station call letters*]
**KWTY** ....... Cartago, CA [*FM radio station call letters*]
**KWU** .......... Kansas Wesleyan University [*Salina*]
**KWU** .......... Kraftwerksunion [*Federal Republic of Germany*]
**KWUN** ....... Concord, CA [*AM radio station call letters*]
**KWUR** ....... Clayton, MO [*FM radio station call letters*]
**KWURA** .... KWU [*Kraftwerk Union AG, Muehlheim*] Report [*A publication*]
**KWU Rep** .. KWU [*Kraftwerk Union AG, Muehlheim*] Report [*A publication*]
**KWVA** ....... Korean War Veterans Association (EA)
**KWVE** ....... San Clemente, CA [*FM radio station call letters*]

**KWVM**...... Korean War Veterans Memorial (EA)
**KWVR**....... Enterprise, OR [*AM radio station call letters*]
**KWVR-FM**... Enterprise, OR [*FM radio station call letters*]
**KWVS**....... Kingsville, TX [*FM radio station call letters*]
**KWVV-FM**... Homer, AK [*FM radio station call letters*]
**KWW**......... Asbury College, Wilmore, KY [*OCLC symbol*] (OCLC)
**KWWC-FM**... Columbia, MO [*FM radio station call letters*]
**KWWD**...... Wildwood/Cape May County [*New Jersey*] [*ICAO location identifier*] (ICLI)
**KWWJ**....... Baytown, TX [*AM radio station call letters*]
**KWWK**...... Rochester, MN [*FM radio station call letters*]
**KWWL**...... Waterloo, IA [*Television station call letters*]
**KWWR**...... Mexico, MO [*FM radio station call letters*]
**KWWW**..... Wenatchee, WA [*AM radio station call letters*]
**KWWW-FM**... Quincy, WA [*FM radio station call letters*]
**KWX**......... Kiwai Island [*Papua New Guinea*] [*Airport symbol*] (OAG)
**KWXE**....... Glenwood, AR [*FM radio station call letters*]
**KWXI**....... Glenwood, AR [*AM radio station call letters*]
**KWXX-FM**... Hilo, HI [*FM radio station call letters*]
**KWXY**....... Cathedral City, CA [*AM radio station call letters*]
**KWXY-FM**... Cathedral City, CA [*FM radio station call letters*]
**KWY**......... Key Way
**KWYD**....... Colorado Springs, CO [*AM radio station call letters*]
**KWYK-FM**... Aztec, NM [*FM radio station call letters*]
**KWYN**....... Wynne, AR [*AM radio station call letters*]
**KWYN-FM**... Wynne, AR [*FM radio station call letters*]
**KWYO**....... Sheridan, WY [*AM radio station call letters*]
**KWYR**....... Winner, SD [*AM radio station call letters*]
**KWYR-FM**... Winner, SD [*FM radio station call letters*]
**KWYS**........ West Yellowstone, MT [*AM radio station call letters*]
**KWYX**....... Jasper, TX [*FM radio station call letters*]
**KWYZ**....... Everett, WA [*AM radio station call letters*]
**KWZD**....... Hamlin, TX [*FM radio station call letters*]
**KX**............. Cayman Airways Ltd. [*ICAO designator*] (FAAC)
**KX**............. [*The*] Holy Bible (1955) [*R.A. Knox*] [*A publication*] (BJA)
**KXA**.......... Kasaan, AK [*Location identifier*] [*FAA*] (FAAL)
**KXAA**........ Rock Island, WA [*FM radio station call letters*]
**KXAL-FM**... Pittsburg, TX [*FM radio station call letters*]
**KXAN-TV**... Austin, TX [*Television station call letters*]
**KXAR**........ Hope, AR [*AM radio station call letters*]
**KXAR-FM**... Hope, AR [*FM radio station call letters*]
**KXAS-TV**.. Fort Worth, TX [*Television station call letters*]
**KXAX**........ St. James, MN [*FM radio station call letters*]
**KXAZ**........ Page, AZ [*FM radio station call letters*]
**KXBR**........ Greenfield, MO [*FM radio station call letters*]
**KXBX**........ Lakeport, CA [*FM radio station call letters*]
**KXC**........... Keleket X-Ray Corporation
**KXCI**......... Tucson, AZ [*FM radio station call letters*]
**KXCL**........ Yuba City, CA [*FM radio station call letters*]
**KXCR**........ El Paso, TX [*FM radio station call letters*]
**KXCV**........ Maryville, MO [*FM radio station call letters*]
**KXDC**........ Monterey, CA [*AM radio station call letters*]
**KXDC-FM**... Carmel, CA [*FM radio station call letters*]
**KXDD**........ Yakima, WA [*FM radio station call letters*]
**KXDX**........ Stuttgart, AR [*FM radio station call letters*]
**KXDZ**........ Anchorage, AK [*FM radio station call letters*]
**KXEG**........ Tolleson, AZ [*AM radio station call letters*]
**KXEI**......... Havre, MT [*FM radio station call letters*]
**KXEL**......... Waterloo, IA [*AM radio station call letters*]
**KXEM**....... McFarland, CA [*AM radio station call letters*]
**KXEN**........ Festus-St. Louis, MO [*AM radio station call letters*]
**KXEO**........ Mexico, MO [*AM radio station call letters*]
**KXER**......... Templeton, CA [*AM radio station call letters*]
**KXEW**....... South Tucson, AZ [*AM radio station call letters*]
**KXEX**........ Fresno, CA [*AM radio station call letters*]
**KXF**........... Kodak X-Ray Film
**KXF**........... Koro [*Fiji*] [*Airport symbol*] (OAG)
**KXFM**........ Santa Maria, CA [*FM radio station call letters*]
**KXFX**........ Santa Rosa, CA [*FM radio station call letters*]
**KXGC-FM**... El Campo, TX [*FM radio station call letters*]
**KXGF**........ Great Falls, MT [*AM radio station call letters*]
**KXGN**........ Glendive, MT [*AM radio station call letters*]
**KXGN-TV**... Glendive, MT [*Television station call letters*]
**KXGO**........ Arcata, CA [*FM radio station call letters*]
**KXIA**......... Marshalltown, IA [*FM radio station call letters*]
**KXIC**......... Iowa City, IA [*AM radio station call letters*]
**KXII**.......... Ardmore, OK [*Television station call letters*]
**KXIQ**......... Bend, OR [*FM radio station call letters*]
**KXIT**......... Dalhart, TX [*AM radio station call letters*]
**KXIT-FM**.. Dalhart, TX [*FM radio station call letters*]
**KXIV**......... Salt Lake City, UT [*Television station call letters*]
**KXJB-TV**.. Valley City, ND [*Television station call letters*]
**KXJK**........ Forrest City, AR [*AM radio station call letters*]
**KXKK**........ Lordsburg, NM [*FM radio station call letters*]
**KXKL**........ Denver, CO [*AM radio station call letters*]
**KXKL-FM**... Denver, CO [*FM radio station call letters*]
**KXKQ**........ Safford, AZ [*FM radio station call letters*]
**KXKS**........ Albuquerque, NM [*AM radio station call letters*]
**KXKW**....... Lafayette, LA [*AM radio station call letters*]
**KXKZ**........ Ruston, LA [*FM radio station call letters*]
**KXL**.......... Portland, OR [*AM radio station call letters*]
**KXLA**......... Rayville, LA [*AM radio station call letters*]
**KXLE**......... Ellensburg, WA [*AM radio station call letters*]
**KXLE-FM**... Ellensburg, WA [*FM radio station call letters*]
**KXL-FM**.... Portland, OR [*FM radio station call letters*]
**KXLF-TV**.. Butte, MT [*Television station call letters*]
**KXLI**......... St. Cloud, MN [*Television station call letters*]
**KXLK**........ Haysville, KS [*FM radio station call letters*]
**KXLN-TV**... Rosenburg, TX [*Television station call letters*]
**KXLO**........ Lewistown, MT [*AM radio station call letters*]
**KXLP**........ New Ulm, MN [*FM radio station call letters*]
**KXLQ**........ Indianola, IA [*AM radio station call letters*]
**KXLS**......... Alva, OK [*FM radio station call letters*]
**KXLT**......... Denver, CO [*FM radio station call letters*]
**KXLT-TV**.. Rochester, MN [*Television station call letters*]
**KXLU**........ Los Angeles, CA [*FM radio station call letters*]
**KXLV-FM**... Cambridge, MN [*FM radio station call letters*]
**KXLY**........ Spokane, WA [*AM radio station call letters*]
**KXLY-FM**... Spokane, WA [*FM radio station call letters*]
**KXLY-TV**.. Spokane, WA [*Television station call letters*]
**KXMA-TV**... Dickinson, ND [*Television station call letters*]
**KXMB-TV**... Bismarck, ND [*Television station call letters*]
**KXMC-TV**... Minot, ND [*Television station call letters*]
**KXMD-TV**... Williston, ND [*Television station call letters*]
**KXMG**....... Marana, AZ [*FM radio station call letters*]
**KXMK**....... Arizona City, AZ [*FM radio station call letters*]
**KXMS**........ Joplin, MO [*FM radio station call letters*]
**KXMX**....... Madera, CA [*FM radio station call letters*]
**KXNE-FM**... Norfolk, NE [*FM radio station call letters*]
**KXNE-TV**... Norfolk, NE [*Television station call letters*]
**KXNP**........ North Platte, NE [*FM radio station call letters*]
**KXO**.......... El Centro, CA [*AM radio station call letters*]
**KXOA**........ Sacramento, CA [*AM radio station call letters*]
**KXOA-FM**... Sacramento, CA [*FM radio station call letters*]
**KXOF**........ Bloomfield, IA [*FM radio station call letters*]
**KXO-FM**... El Centro, CA [*FM radio station call letters*]
**KXOI**......... Crane, TX [*AM radio station call letters*]
**KXOJ**......... Sapulpa, OK [*AM radio station call letters*]
**KXOJ-FM**... Sapulpa, OK [*FM radio station call letters*]
**KXOK**........ St. Louis, MO [*AM radio station call letters*]
**KXOL**........ Clinton, OK [*AM radio station call letters*]
**KXON-TV**... Claremore, OK [*Television station call letters*]
**KXOR**........ Thibodaux, LA [*FM radio station call letters*]
**KXOX**........ Sweetwater, TX [*AM radio station call letters*]
**KXOX-FM**... Sweetwater, TX [*FM radio station call letters*]
**KXOZ**........ Mountain View, MO [*FM radio station call letters*]
**KXPO**........ Grafton, ND [*AM radio station call letters*]
**KXPO-FM**... Grafton, ND [*FM radio station call letters*]
**KXPR**......... Sacramento, CA [*FM radio station call letters*]
**KXPT**......... Santa Paula, CA [*FM radio station call letters*]
**KXPZ**......... Lytle, TX [*FM radio station call letters*]
**KXRA**........ Alexandria, MN [*AM radio station call letters*]
**KXRA-FM**... Alexandria, MN [*FM radio station call letters*]
**KXRB**......... Sioux Falls, SD [*AM radio station call letters*]
**KXRE**......... Manitou Springs, CO [*AM radio station call letters*]
**KXRJ**......... Russellville, AR [*FM radio station call letters*]
**KXRM-TV**... Colorado Springs, CO [*Television station call letters*]
**KXRO**........ Aberdeen, WA [*AM radio station call letters*]
**KXRQ**........ Trumann, AR [*AM radio station call letters*]
**KXRX**........ Seattle, WA [*FM radio station call letters*]
**KXSA**......... Dermott, AR [*AM radio station call letters*]
**KXSA-FM**... Dermott, AR [*FM radio station call letters*]
**KXSM**........ Saint Mary College, Xavier, KS [*Library symbol*] [*Library of Congress*] (LCLS)
**KXSS**......... Waite Park, MN [*AM radio station call letters*]
**KXSS-FM**... Waite Park, MN [*FM radio station call letters*]
**KXTD**........ Wagoner, OK [*AM radio station call letters*]
**KXTL**......... Butte, MT [*AM radio station call letters*]
**KXTN**........ San Antonio, TX [*AM radio station call letters*]
**KXTO**........ Reno, NV [*AM radio station call letters*]
**KXTP**......... Superior, WI [*AM radio station call letters*]
**KXTQ**........ Lubbock, TX [*AM radio station call letters*]
**KXTR**......... Kansas City, MO [*FM radio station call letters*]
**KXTV**......... Sacramento, CA [*Television station call letters*]
**KXTX-TV**... Dallas, TX [*Television station call letters*]
**KXTZ**......... Henderson, NV [*FM radio station call letters*]
**KXUS**......... Springfield, MO [*FM radio station call letters*]
**KXVQ**........ Pawhuska, OK [*AM radio station call letters*]
**KXVR**........ Mountain Pass, CA [*FM radio station call letters*]
**KXXK**........ Chickasha, OK [*FM radio station call letters*]
**KXXO**........ Olympia, WA [*FM radio station call letters*]
**KXXR**........ Liberty, MO [*FM radio station call letters*]
**KXXV**........ Waco, TX [*Television station call letters*]
**KXXX**........ Colby, KS [*AM radio station call letters*]
**KXXX-FM**... San Francisco, CA [*FM radio station call letters*]
**KXXY**........ Oklahoma City, OK [*AM radio station call letters*]
**KXXY-FM**... Oklahoma City, OK [*FM radio station call letters*]
**KXXZ**......... Barstow, CA [*FM radio station call letters*]
**KXYL**......... Brownwood, TX [*AM radio station call letters*]
**KXYQ**........ Salem, OR [*FM radio station call letters*]
**KXYZ**......... Houston, TX [*AM radio station call letters*]
**KXZZ**......... Lake Charles, LA [*AM radio station call letters*]

**KY**............. Cayman Islands [*ANSI two-letter standard code*] (CNC)
**KY**............. Kabaka Yekka [*The King Alone*] [*Uganda*] [*Suspended*] [*Political party*]
**KY**............. Kent Yeomanry [*Military unit*] [*British*]
**KY**............. Kentucky [*Postal code*] (AFM)
**Ky**............. Kentucky Department of Libraries, Frankfort, KY [*Library symbol*] [*Library of Congress*] (LCLS)
**KY**............. Kentucky Reports [*A publication*]
**KY**............. Kentucky Supreme Court Reports [*1879-1951*] [*A publication*] (DLA)
**KY**............. Key (MCD)
**KY**............. Keying Devices [*JETDS nomenclature*] [*Military*] (CET)
**KY**............. Kyrie [*Liturgical*]
**KY**............. West Africa Airlines Ltd. [*Ghana*] [*ICAO designator*] (FAAC)
**KyA**........... Ashland Public Library, Ashland, KY [*Library symbol*] [*Library of Congress*] (LCLS)
**KYA**........... Kyakhta [*USSR*] [*Seismograph station code, US Geological Survey*] [*Closed*] (SEIS)
**KYA**........... San Francisco, CA [*FM radio station call letters*]
**KY Acts**...... Kentucky Acts [*A publication*]
**KY Admin Reg** ... Kentucky Administrative Register [*A publication*] (DLA)
**KY Admin Regs** ... Kentucky Administration Regulations Service [*A publication*] (DLA)
**KY Ag Exp** ... Kentucky. Agricultural Experiment Station. Publications [*A publication*]
**KY Agri-Bus Q** ... Kentucky Agri-Business Quarterly [*A publication*]
**KY AgriBus Spotlight** ... Kentucky Agri-Business Spotlight [*A publication*]
**KY Agric Exp Stn Annu Rep** ... Kentucky. Agricultural Experiment Station. Annual Report [*A publication*]
**KY Agric Exp Stn Bull** ... Kentucky. Agricultural Experiment Station. Bulletin [*A publication*]
**KY Agric Exp Stn Misc Pubs** ... Kentucky. Agricultural Experiment Station. Miscellaneous Publications [*A publication*]
**KY Agric Exp Stn Prog Rep** ... Kentucky. Agricultural Experiment Station. Progress Report [*A publication*]
**KY Agric Exp Stn Regul Bull** ... Kentucky. Agricultural Experiment Station. Regulatory Bulletin [*A publication*]
**KY Agric Exp Stn Results Res** ... Kentucky. Agricultural Experiment Station. Results of Research [*A publication*]
**KYAK**........ Anchorage, AK [*AM radio station call letters*]
**KYAX**........ Alturas, CA [*FM radio station call letters*]
**KYAY**........ Los Gatos, CA [*FM radio station call letters*]
**Kyb**............ Kybernetik [*A publication*]
**Kyb**............ Kybernetika [*A publication*]
**KyBB**.......... Berea College, Berea, KY [*Library symbol*] [*Library of Congress*] (LCLS)
**KYBB**......... Tracy, CA [*FM radio station call letters*]
**KYBD**........ Keyboard (MSA)
**KYBE**......... Frederick, OK [*FM radio station call letters*]
**KY Bench and B** ... Kentucky Bench and Bar [*A publication*]
**Kybernetika Suppl** ... Kybernetika. Supplement [*A publication*]
**KYBG**........ Aurora, CO [*AM radio station call letters*]
**KYBG-FM** ... Castle Rock, CO [*FM radio station call letters*]
**KyBgW**...... Western Kentucky University, Bowling Green, KY [*Library symbol*] [*Library of Congress*] (LCLS)
**KyBgW-K**.. Western Kentucky University, Kentucky Library, Bowling Green, KY [*Library symbol*] [*Library of Congress*] (LCLS)
**KY B J**....... Kentucky Bar Journal [*A publication*]
**KYBNA**..... Kybernetika [*A publication*]
**Ky-BPH**..... Kentucky Library for the Blind and Physically Handicapped, Frankfort, KY [*Library symbol*] [*Library of Congress*] (LCLS)
**KYBS**......... Livingston, MT [*FM radio station call letters*]
**KY Bus Led** ... Kentucky Business Ledger [*A publication*]
**KyBvU**....... Union College, Barbourville, KY [*Library symbol*] [*Library of Congress*] (LCLS)
**KYC**........... Keystone Camera Products Corp. [*AMEX symbol*] (SPSG)
**KYC**........... Know Your Customer [*Business term*]
**KyC**............ Kypriaka Chronika [*A publication*]
**KYCA**......... Prescott, AZ [*AM radio station call letters*]
**KyCambC**.. Campbellsville College, Campbellsville, KY [*Library symbol*] [*Library of Congress*] (LCLS)
**KyCarD**...... Dow Corning Corp., TIS Library, Carrollton, KY [*Library symbol*] [*Library of Congress*] (LCLS)
**KYCH**........ Convent General of the Knights York Cross of Honour (EA)
**KYCK**........ Crookston, MN [*FM radio station call letters*]
**KYCN**........ Wheatland, WY [*AM radio station call letters*]
**KYCN-FM** ... Wheatland, WY [*FM radio station call letters*]
**Ky Coal J**... Kentucky Coal Journal [*A publication*]
**KyColW**..... Lindsey Wilson College, Columbia, KY [*Library symbol*] [*Library of Congress*] (LCLS)
**KY Comment'r** ... Kentucky Commentator [*A publication*] (DLA)
**KyCov**........ Kenton County Public Library, Covington, KY [*Library symbol*] [*Library of Congress*] (LCLS)
**KyCovStE**.. Saint Elizabeth Medical Center, Covington, KY [*Library symbol*] [*Library of Congress*] (LCLS)
**KYCP**......... Keystone Camera Products Corporation [*NASDAQ symbol*] (NQ)
**KYCR**......... Golden Valley, MN [*AM radio station call letters*]
**KYCS**......... Rock Springs, WY [*FM radio station call letters*]
**KYCSA**...... K'uang Yeh Chi Shu [*A publication*]
**KYCX-FM** ... Mexia, TX [*FM radio station call letters*]
**KYD**........... Kilo Yard
**Kyd**............ Kyd on Bills of Exchange [*A publication*] (DLA)
**Kyd Aw**...... Kyd on Awards [*A publication*] (DLA)
**Kyd Bills**.... Kyd on Bills of Exchange [*A publication*] (DLA)
**KyDC**......... Centre College of Kentucky, Danville, KY [*Library symbol*] [*Library of Congress*] (LCLS)
**Kyd Corp**.... Kyd on Corporations [*A publication*] (DLA)
**KYDE**........ Pine Bluff, AR [*AM radio station call letters*]
**KY Dec**....... Sneed's Kentucky Decisions [*2 Kentucky*] [*A publication*] (DLA)
**KY Dent J** ... Kentucky Dental Journal [*A publication*]
**KY Dep Fish Wildl Resour Fish Bull** ... Kentucky. Department of Fish and Wildlife Resources. Fisheries Bulletin [*A publication*]
**KY Dep Mines Miner Geol Div Ser 8 Bull** ... Kentucky. Department of Mines and Minerals. Geological Division. Series 8. Bulletin [*A publication*]
**KYDKAJ** ... Annual Report. Kyoritsu College of Pharmacy [*A publication*]
**KYDS**......... Kiloyards (MCD)
**KYDS**......... Sacramento, CA [*FM radio station call letters*]
**KYDZ**........ Cody, WY [*FM radio station call letters*]
**KYEA**........ West Monroe, LA [*FM radio station call letters*]
**KY Economy** ... Kentucky Economy [*A publication*]
**KYEE**......... Alamogordo, NM [*FM radio station call letters*]
**KYEL-TV**.. Yuma, AZ [*Television station call letters*]
**KYERI**....... Know Your Endorsers - Require Identification [*Advice to businessmen and others who cash checks for the public*]
**KyErP**........ Seminary of Saint Pius X, Erlanger, KY [*Library symbol*] [*Library of Congress*] (LCLS)
**KYES**......... Anchorage, AK [*Television station call letters*]
**KYEZ**......... Salina, KS [*FM radio station call letters*]
**KYF**........... Yeelirie [*Australia*] [*Airport symbol*] (OAG)
**KY Farm Home Sci** ... Kentucky Farm and Home Science [*A publication*]
**KYFC**......... Kansas City, MO [*Television station call letters*]
**KyFc**........... United States Army, Fort Campbell Post Library (R. F. Sink Memorial Library), Fort Campbell, KY [*Library symbol*] [*Library of Congress*] (LCLS)
**KyFkAS**..... United States Army Armor School, Fort Knox, KY [*Library symbol*] [*Library of Congress*] (LCLS)
**KYFM**........ Bartlesville, OK [*FM radio station call letters*]
**KyFmTM**... Thomas More College, Fort Mitchell, KY [*Library symbol*] [*Library of Congress*] (LCLS)
**KY Folkl Rec** ... Kentucky Folklore Record [*A publication*]
**KY Folk Rec** ... Kentucky Folklore Record [*A publication*]
**KYFR**......... Shenandoah, IA [*AM radio station call letters*]
**KyFSC**....... Kentucky State University, Frankfort, KY [*Library symbol*] [*Library of Congress*] (LCLS)
**KyGeC**....... Georgetown College, Georgetown, KY [*Library symbol*] [*Library of Congress*] (LCLS)
**KY Geol Survey Bull Inf Circ Rept Inv Special Pub** ... Kentucky. Geological Survey. Bulletin. Information Circular. Report of Investigations. Special Publication [*A publication*]
**KY Geol Surv Rep Invest** ... Kentucky. Geological Survey. Report of Investigations [*A publication*]
**KY Geol Surv Ser 9 Bull** ... Kentucky. Geological Survey. Series 9. Bulletin [*A publication*]
**KY Geol Surv Ser 10 Cty Rep** ... Kentucky. Geological Survey. Series 10. County Report [*A publication*]
**KY Geol Surv Ser 9 Rep Invest** ... Kentucky. Geological Survey. Series 9. Report of Investigation [*A publication*]
**KY Geol Surv Ser 10 Rep Invest** ... Kentucky. Geological Survey. Series 10. Report of Investigation [*A publication*]
**KY Geol Surv Ser 9 Spec Publ** ... Kentucky. Geological Survey. Series 9. Special Publication [*A publication*]
**Ky Geol Surv Spec Publ** ... Kentucky. Geological Survey. Special Publication [*A publication*]
**KY Geol Surv Thesis Ser** ... Kentucky. Geological Survey. Thesis Series [*A publication*]
**KYGO**........ Denver, CO [*FM radio station call letters*]
**KY G S Rp Prog B** ... Kentucky. Geological Survey. Report of Progress. Bulletin [*A publication*]
**KyHaHi**..... Harrodsburg Historical Society, Harrodsburg, KY [*Library symbol*] [*Library of Congress*] (LCLS)
**KyHhN**...... Northern Kentucky University, Highland Heights, KY [*Library symbol*] [*Library of Congress*] (LCLS)
**KyHhN-L**.. Northern Kentucky University, B. P. Chase College of Law, Covington, KY [*Library symbol*] [*Library of Congress*] (LCLS)
**KyHi**.......... Kentucky Historical Society, Frankfort, KY [*Library symbol*] [*Library of Congress*] (LCLS)
**KY Hist Soc Reg** ... Kentucky Historical Society. Register [*A publication*]
**KYHS**........ Kentucky Historical Society. Register [*A publication*]
**KyHzC**....... Hazard Community College, Hazard, KY [*Library symbol*] [*Library of Congress*] (LCLS)
**KYIA**.......... Goshen, CA [*FM radio station call letters*]
**KYII**........... Burkburnett, TX [*FM radio station call letters*]
**KYIN**.......... Mason City, IA [*Television station call letters*]
**KYIP**.......... Detroit/Willow Run [*Michigan*] [*ICAO location identifier*] (ICLI)
**KYJC**......... Medford, OR [*AM radio station call letters*]

**KYK**.......... Karluk [*Alaska*] [*Airport symbol*] (OAG)
**KYK**.......... Karluk, AK [*Location identifier*] [*FAA*] (FAAL)
**KYK**.......... Kayak Island [*Alaska*] [*Seismograph station code, US Geological Survey*] (SEIS)
**KYK**.......... Kelley-Kerr Energy [*Vancouver Stock Exchange symbol*]
**Kyk**.......... Kyklos [*A publication*]
**KYKA**........ Naches, WA [*FM radio station call letters*]
**KYKD**........ Bethel, AK [*FM radio station call letters*]
**KYKK**........ Hobbs, NM [*AM radio station call letters*]
**Kyklos Int Z Sozialwiss Int Rev Soc Sci** ... Kyklos. Internationale Zeitschrift fuer Sozialwissenschaften. Revue International des Sciences Sociales. International Review for Social Sciences [*A publication*]
**KYKM**........ Winfield, TX [*FM radio station call letters*]
**KYKN**........ Keizer, OR [*AM radio station call letters*]
**KYKR-FM** ... Port Arthur, TX [*FM radio station call letters*]
**KYKS**........ Lufkin, TX [*FM radio station call letters*]
**KYKX**........ Longview, TX [*FM radio station call letters*]
**KYKY**........ St. Louis, MO [*FM radio station call letters*]
**KYKZ**........ Lake Charles, LA [*FM radio station call letters*]
**KY L**.......... Kentucky Law Reporter [*A publication*] (DLA)
**KYL**.......... Kyle Resources, Inc. [*Vancouver Stock Exchange symbol*]
**KY Law J**... Kentucky Law Journal [*A publication*]
**KY Law Rep** ... Kentucky Law Reporter [*A publication*] (DLA)
**KYLC**........ Osage Beach, MO [*FM radio station call letters*]
**KYLE**........ Kyle Technology Corp. [*NASDAQ symbol*] (NQ)
**KY Lib Assn Bull** ... Kentucky Library Association. Bulletin [*A publication*]
**KY Libr Ass Bull** ... Kentucky Library Association. Bulletin [*A publication*]
**KY L J**........ Kentucky Law Journal [*A publication*]
**KYLO**........ Davis, CA [*FM radio station call letters*]
**KyLo**.......... Louisville Free Public Library, Louisville, KY [*Library symbol*] [*Library of Congress*] (LCLS)
**KyLoB**........ Bellarmine College, Louisville, KY [*Library symbol*] [*Library of Congress*] (LCLS)
**KyLoB-M**.. Bellarmine College, Thomas Merton Studies Center, Louisville, KY [*Library symbol*] [*Library of Congress*] (LCLS)
**KyLoBW**.... Brown & Williamson Tobacco Corp., Research Department Library, Louisville, KY [*Library symbol*] [*Library of Congress*] (LCLS)
**KyLoC**........ Courier-Journal & Louisville Times Co., Inc., Louisville, KY [*Library symbol*] [*Library of Congress*] (LCLS)
**KyLoF**........ Filson Club, Louisville, KY [*Library symbol*] [*Library of Congress*] (LCLS)
**KyLoJ**........ Jefferson Community College, Louisville, KY [*Library symbol*] [*Library of Congress*] (LCLS)
**KyLoL**........ Louisville Presbyterian Seminary, Louisville, KY [*Library symbol*] [*Library of Congress*] (LCLS)
**KyLoM**........ Louisville Medical Library, Louisville, KY [*Library symbol*] [*Library of Congress*] (LCLS)
**KyLoN**........ Spalding College, Louisville, KY [*Library symbol*] [*Library of Congress*] (LCLS)
**KyLoS**........ Southern Baptist Theological Seminary, Louisville, KY [*Library symbol*] [*Library of Congress*] (LCLS)
**KyLoU**........ University of Louisville, Louisville, KY [*Library symbol*] [*Library of Congress*] (LCLS)
**KyLoU-Ar** ... University of Louisville, University Archives and Records Center, Louisville, KY [*Library symbol*] [*Library of Congress*] (LCLS)
**KyLoU-HS** ... University of Louisville, Health Sciences Library, Louisville, KY [*Library symbol*] [*Library of Congress*] (LCLS)
**KyLoV**........ United States Veterans Administration Hospital, Louisville, KY [*Library symbol*] [*Library of Congress*] (LCLS)
**KY LR**........ Kentucky Law Reporter [*A publication*] (DLA)
**KY L Rep**... Kentucky Law Reporter [*A publication*] (DLA)
**KY L Rev**... Kentucky Law Review [*A publication*] (DLA)
**KY L Rptr**.. Kentucky Law Reporter [*A publication*] (DLA)
**KYLS**........ Ironton, MO [*FM radio station call letters*]
**KYLT**........ Missoula, MT [*AM radio station call letters*]
**KyLx**.......... Lexington Public Library, Lexington, KY [*Library symbol*] [*Library of Congress*] (LCLS)
**KyLxCB**..... Lexington Theological Seminary, Lexington, KY [*Library symbol*] [*Library of Congress*] (LCLS)
**KyLxCS**..... Council of State Governments, State Information Center, Lexington, KY [*Library symbol*] [*Library of Congress*] (LCLS)
**KyLxI**........ IBM Corp., Office Products Division, Lexington, KY [*Library symbol*] [*Library of Congress*] (LCLS)
**KyLxIMM** ... Institute for Mining and Minerals Research, Lexington, KY [*Library symbol*] [*Library of Congress*] (LCLS)
**KyLxK**........ Keeneland Association, Inc., Lexington, KY [*Library symbol*] [*Library of Congress*] (LCLS)
**KyLxT**........ Transylvania University, Lexington, KY [*Library symbol*] [*Library of Congress*] (LCLS)
**KyLxTI**...... Lexington Technical Institute, Lexington, KY [*Library symbol*] [*Library of Congress*] (LCLS)
**KyLxV**........ United States Veterans Administration Hospital, Lexington, KY [*Library symbol*] [*Library of Congress*] (LCLS)
**KYMA**........ Yuma, AZ [*Television station call letters*]
**KyMadC**.... Madisonville Community College, Media Center, Madisonville, KY [*Library symbol*] [*Library of Congress*] (LCLS)
**KyMan**....... Clay County Public Library, Manchester, KY [*Library symbol*] [*Library of Congress*] (LCLS)
**KYMC**........ Ballwin, MO [*FM radio station call letters*]
**KYMD**........ Kentucky Medical Insurance Co. [*Louisville, KY*] [*NASDAQ symbol*] (NQ)
**KyMdC**...... Midway Junior College and Pinkerton High School, Midway, KY [*Library symbol*] [*Library of Congress*] (LCLS)
**KYMG**........ Anchorage, AK [*FM radio station call letters*]
**KYMN**........ Northfield, MN [*AM radio station call letters*]
**KYMO**........ East Prairie, MO [*AM radio station call letters*]
**KyMoreU**... Morehead State University, Morehead, KY [*Library symbol*] [*Library of Congress*] (LCLS)
**KYMS**........ Keep Your Mouth Shut
**KYMS**........ Santa Ana, CA [*FM radio station call letters*]
**KyMurT**..... Murray State University, Murray, KY [*Library symbol*] [*Library of Congress*] (LCLS)
**KYN**.......... Kynurenine [*Biochemistry*]
**KyNaM**...... Nazareth Mother House Archives, Nazareth, KY [*Library symbol*] [*Library of Congress*] (LCLS)
**KY Nat Preserv Comm Tech Rep** ... Kentucky. Nature Preserves Commission. Technical Report [*A publication*]
**KYND**........ Cypress, TX [*AM radio station call letters*]
**KYNE-TV** ... Omaha, NE [*Television station call letters*]
**KYNG**........ Coos Bay, OR [*AM radio station call letters*]
**KYNG**........ Youngstown [*Ohio*] [*ICAO location identifier*] (ICLI)
**KYNG-FM** ... Coos Bay, OR [*FM radio station call letters*]
**KYNO**........ Fresno, CA [*AM radio station call letters*]
**KYNO-FM** ... Fresno, CA [*FM radio station call letters*]
**KYNT**........ Yankton, SD [*AM radio station call letters*]
**KY Nurse**... Kentucky Nurse [*A publication*]
**KY Nurses Assoc Newsl** ... Kentucky Nurses' Association. Newsletter [*A publication*]
**KY Nurses Assoc News Lett** ... Kentucky Nurses' Association. Newsletter [*A publication*]
**KYNZ**........ Lone Grove, OK [*FM radio station call letters*]
**KYO**.......... Kyocera Corp. [*NYSE symbol*] (SPSG)
**KYO**.......... Kyoto [*Japan*] [*Seismograph station code, US Geological Survey*] (SEIS)
**Kyo**.......... Kyoto University. Economic Review [*A publication*]
**KYOC**........ Yoakum, TX [*FM radio station call letters*]
**KYOK**........ Houston, TX [*AM radio station call letters*]
**KYOO**........ Bolivar, MO [*AM radio station call letters*]
**KY Op**........ Kentucky Court of Appeals Opinions [*A publication*] (DLA)
**KY Op**........ Kentucky Opinions [*A publication*]
**KY Opin**..... Kentucky Opinions [*A publication*] (DLA)
**KYOR**........ Globe, AZ [*AM radio station call letters*]
**Kyorin J Med Med Technol** ... Kyorin Journal of Medicine and Medical Technology [*A publication*]
**KYOS**........ Merced, CA [*AM radio station call letters*]
**KYOT-FM** ... Granbury, TX [*FM radio station call letters*]
**Kyoto Daigaku Nogaku-Bu Enshurin Hokoku Bull Kyoto Univ For** ... Kyoto Daigaku Nogaku-Bu Enshurin Hokoku/Bulletin. Kyoto University Forests [*A publication*]
**Kyoto L Rev** ... Kyoto Law Review [*A publication*] (DLA)
**Kyoto Univ Afr Stud** ... Kyoto University. African Studies [*A publication*]
**Kyoto Univ Econ R** ... Kyoto University. Economic Review [*A publication*]
**Kyoto Univ Fac Sci Mem Ser Geol Mineral** ... Kyoto University. Faculty of Science. Memoirs. Series of Geology and Mineralogy [*A publication*]
**Kyoto Univ Geophys Res Stn Rep** ... Kyoto University. Geophysical Research Station. Reports [*A publication*]
**KYOU**........ Wendover, NV [*FM radio station call letters*]
**KyOw**........ Owensboro-Daviess County Public Library, Owensboro, KY [*Library symbol*] [*Library of Congress*] (LCLS)
**KyOwB**...... Brescia College, Owensboro, KY [*Library symbol*] [*Library of Congress*] (LCLS)
**KyOwK**...... Kentucky Wesleyan College, Owensboro, KY [*Library symbol*] [*Library of Congress*] (LCLS)
**KYP**.......... Kyaukpyu [*Burma*] [*Airport symbol*] (OAG)
**KyPad**........ Paducah Public Library, Paducah, KY [*Library symbol*] [*Library of Congress*] (LCLS)
**KyPadC**...... Paducah Community College, Paducah, KY [*Library symbol*] [*Library of Congress*] (LCLS)
**KyParF**...... John Fox, Jr. Memorial Library, Paris, KY [*Library symbol*] [*Library of Congress*] (LCLS)
**KYPG**........ Girard, KS [*FM radio station call letters*]
**KyPikC**...... Pikeville College, Pikeville, KY [*Library symbol*] [*Library of Congress*] (LCLS)
**KYQT**........ Newport, OR [*FM radio station call letters*]
**KYQX**........ Weatherford, TX [*FM radio station call letters*]
**KY R**.......... Kentucky Reports [*A publication*] (DLA)
**KYR**.......... Kentucky Review [*A publication*]
**KYR**.......... Kyber Resources [*Vancouver Stock Exchange symbol*]
**KyRE**........ Eastern Kentucky University, Richmond, KY [*Library symbol*] [*Library of Congress*] (LCLS)
**KYRE**........ Yreka, CA [*FM radio station call letters*]
**KY Reg**....... Kentucky State Historical Society. Register [*A publication*]
**KY Rev Stat** ... Kentucky Revised Statutes [*A publication*] (DLA)
**KY Rev Stat Ann** ... Baldwin's Kentucky Revised Statutes, Annotated [*A publication*] (DLA)

**KY Rev Stat Ann (Baldwin)** ... Baldwin's Official Edition. Kentucky Revised Statutes, Annotated [*A publication*]
**KY Rev Stat Ann (Michie/Bobbs-Merrill)** ... Kentucky Revised Statutes, Annotated. Official Edition (Michie/Bobbs-Merrill) [*A publication*]
**KY Rev Stat & R Serv (Baldwin)** ... Kentucky Revised Statutes and Rules Service (Baldwin) [*A publication*]
**KY Rev Stat & Rules Serv** ... Kentucky Revised Statutes and Rules Service (Baldwin) [*A publication*] (DLA)
**KYRK-FM** ... Las Vegas, NV [*FM radio station call letters*]
**Kyrkohist Arsskr** ... Kyrkohistorisk Arsskrift [*A publication*]
**KYRO** ........ Potosi, MO [*AM radio station call letters*]
**KY Roman Q** ... Kentucky Romance Quarterly [*A publication*]
**KYRS** ......... Atwater, NM [*FM radio station call letters*]
**KYS** ........... Kayes [*Mali*] [*Airport symbol*] (OAG)
**KYS** ........... Kentucky State University, Frankfort, KY [*OCLC symbol*] (OCLC)
**KYS** ........... Keycorp Industries [*Vancouver Stock Exchange symbol*]
**KYS** ........... Kiyosumi - Telemeter [*Japan*] [*Seismograph station code, US Geological Survey*] (SEIS)
**KyS** ............ Kypriakai Spoudai [*A publication*]
**KY SBJ** ...... Kentucky State Bar Journal [*A publication*] (DLA)
**KYSC** ......... Yakima, WA [*FM radio station call letters*]
**KY Sch J** .... Kentucky School Journal [*A publication*]
**Kyshe** ......... Kyshe's Reports [*1808-90*] [*A publication*] (DLA)
**KYSL** ......... Frisco, CO [*FM radio station call letters*]
**KYSM** ........ Mankato, MN [*AM radio station call letters*]
**KYSM-FM** ... Mankato, MN [*FM radio station call letters*]
**KYSN** ........ East Wenatchee, WA [*FM radio station call letters*]
**KySoC** ........ Somerset Community College, Somerset, KY [*Library symbol*] [*Library of Congress*] (LCLS)
**KYSS-FM** ... Missoula, MT [*FM radio station call letters*]
**KYST** ......... Texas City, TX [*AM radio station call letters*]
**KY St BJ** .... Kentucky State Bar Journal [*A publication*] (DLA)
**KY St Law** ... Morehead and Brown. Digest of Kentucky Statute Laws [*A publication*] (DLA)
**KYT** ........... Keystone Explorations [*Vancouver Stock Exchange symbol*]
**KYT** ........... Kyauktaw [*Burma*] [*Airport symbol*] (OAG)
**KYTE** ......... Portland, OR [*AM radio station call letters*]
**KYTOON** ... Kite Balloon [*Air Force*]
**KyTrA** ........ Abbey of Gethsemani, Trappist, KY [*Library symbol*] [*Library of Congress*] (LCLS)
**KYTT-FM** ... Coos Bay, OR [*FM radio station call letters*]
**KYTV** ......... Springfield, MO [*Television station call letters*]
**KYTX** ......... Beeville, TX [*FM radio station call letters*]
**kyu** ............ Kentucky [*MARC country of publication code*] [*Library of Congress*] (LCCP)
**KYU** ........... Koyukuk [*Alaska*] [*Airport symbol*] (OAG)
**KYU** ........... Koyukuk, AK [*Location identifier*] [*FAA*] (FAAL)
**KyU** ........... University of Kentucky, Lexington, KY [*Library symbol*] [*Library of Congress*] (LCLS)
**KyU-A** ........ University of Kentucky, Ashland Community College, Ashland, KY [*Library symbol*] [*Library of Congress*] (LCLS)
**KyU-ASC** .. University of Kentucky, Agricultural Science Center, Lexington, KY [*Library symbol*] [*Library of Congress*] (LCLS)
**KyU-C** ........ University of Kentucky, Southeast Center, Cumberland, KY [*Library symbol*] [*Library of Congress*] (LCLS)
**KyU-E** ........ University of Kentucky, Elizabethtown Community College, Elizabethtown, KY [*Library symbol*] [*Library of Congress*] (LCLS)
**KyU-F** ........ University of Kentucky, Fort Knox Center, Fort Knox, KY [*Library symbol*] [*Library of Congress*] (LCLS)
**KYUF** ........ Uvalde, TX [*FM radio station call letters*]
**KyU-H** ....... University of Kentucky, Northwest Center, Henderson, KY [*Library symbol*] [*Library of Congress*] (LCLS)
**KYUK** ........ Bethel, AK [*AM radio station call letters*]
**KYUK-TV** ... Bethel, AK [*Television station call letters*]
**KyU-L** ........ University of Kentucky, Law Library, Lexington, KY [*Library symbol*] [*Library of Congress*] (LCLS)
**KyU-M** ...... University of Kentucky, Medical Center, Lexington, KY [*Library symbol*] [*Library of Congress*] (LCLS)
**KYUM** ....... Yuma/Yuma Marine Corps Air Station, Yuma International [*Arizona*] [*ICAO location identifier*] (ICLI)
**KyU-N** ....... University of Kentucky, Northern Center, Covington, KY [*Library symbol*] [*Library of Congress*] (LCLS)
**Kyungpook Educ Forum** ... Kyungpook Education Forum [*A publication*]
**Kyungpook Math J** ... Kyungpook Mathematical Journal [*A publication*]
**Kyungpook Univ Med J** ... Kyungpook University. Medical Journal [*A publication*]
**KY Univ Office Res Eng Services Bull** ... Kentucky University. Office of Research and Engineering Services. Bulletin [*A publication*]
**KY Univ Off Res Eng Serv Bull** ... Kentucky University. Office of Research and Engineering Services. Bulletin [*A publication*]
**KyU-P** ........ University of Kentucky, Prestonburg Community College, Prestonburg, KY [*Library symbol*] [*Library of Congress*] (LCLS)
**Kyush J Med Sci** ... Kyushu Journal of Medical Science [*A publication*]
**Kyushu Agr Res** ... Kyushu Agricultural Research [*A publication*]
**Kyushu J Med Sci** ... Kyushu Journal of Medical Science [*A publication*]
**Kyushu Univ Coll Gen Educ Rep Earth Sci** ... Kyushu University. College of General Education. Reports on Earth Science [*A publication*]
**Kyushu Univ Dep Geol Sci Rep** ... Kyushu University. Department of Geology. Science Reports [*A publication*]
**Kyushu Univ Fac Agr Sci Bull** ... Kyushu University. Faculty of Agriculture. Science Bulletin [*A publication*]
**Kyushu Univ Fac Sci Mem Ser D** ... Kyushu University. Faculty of Science. Memoirs. Series D. Geology [*A publication*]
**Kyushu Univ Faculty Sci Mem** ... Kyushu University. Faculty of Science. Memoirs [*A publication*]
**KYUS-TV** ... Miles City, MT [*Television station call letters*]
**KYUU** ........ Liberal, KS [*AM radio station call letters*]
**KYVA** ........ Gallup, NM [*AM radio station call letters*]
**KYVE** ........ Yakima, WA [*Television station call letters*]
**KYW** .......... Philadelphia, PA [*AM radio station call letters*]
**KyWA** ........ Asbury College, Wilmore, KY [*Library symbol*] [*Library of Congress*] (LCLS)
**KY Warbler** ... Kentucky Warbler [*A publication*]
**KyWAT** ..... Asbury Theological Seminary, Wilmore, KY [*Library symbol*] [*Library of Congress*] (LCLS)
**KyWavH** .... Waverly Hills Tuberculosis Sanatorium, Waverly Hills, KY [*Library symbol*] [*Library of Congress*] (LCLS)
**KY WC Dec** ... Kentucky Workmen's Compensation Board Decisions [*A publication*] (DLA)
**KyWilC** ...... Cumberland College, Williamsburg, KY [*Library symbol*] [*Library of Congress*] (LCLS)
**KyWn** ......... Clark County Public Library, Winchester, KY [*Library symbol*] [*Library of Congress*] (LCLS)
**KyWnS** ...... Southeastern Christian College, Winchester, KY [*Library symbol*] [*Library of Congress*] (LCLS)
**KYW-TV** ... Philadelphia, PA [*Television station call letters*]
**KYX** .......... Yalumet [*Papua New Guinea*] [*Airport symbol*] (OAG)
**KYXE** ......... Selah, WA [*AM radio station call letters*]
**KYXI** .......... Yuma, AZ [*FM radio station call letters*]
**KYXS-FM** ... Mineral Wells, TX [*FM radio station call letters*]
**KYXX** ........ Ozona, TX [*FM radio station call letters*]
**KYXY** ........ San Diego, CA [*FM radio station call letters*]
**KYYA** ........ Billings, MT [*FM radio station call letters*]
**KYYC** ......... Shelby, MT [*FM radio station call letters*]
**KYYK** ........ Palestine, TX [*FM radio station call letters*]
**KYYN** ........ Poteau, OK [*AM radio station call letters*]
**KYYS** ......... Kansas City, MO [*FM radio station call letters*]
**KYYY** ........ Bismarck, ND [*FM radio station call letters*]
**KYYZ** ......... Williston, ND [*FM radio station call letters*]
**KZ** ............. Karakulevodstvo i Zverovodstvo [*A publication*]
**KZ** ............. Killing Zone [*Military*] [*British*]
**KZ** ............. Kilohertz [*Preferred form is kHz*] [*Electronics*] (MCD)
**K & Z** ......... Kipp and Zonen Recorders
**KZ** ............. Kirchliche Zeitschrift [*A publication*]
**KZ** ............. Konzentrationslager [*Concentration Camp*] [*Initials also used in medicine to indicate a psychiatric syndrome found in surviving victims of the World War II camps*] [*German*]
**KZ** ............. Kuhns Zeitschrift fuer Vergleichende Sprachforschung [*A publication*] (BJA)
**KZ** ............. Kulturny Zivot [*Bratislava*] [*A publication*]
**KZ** ............. Kurszettel [*Stock Exchange List*] [*German*]
**kZ** ............. Kurze Sicht [*Short Sight*] [*German*] [*Business term*]
**KZ** ............. Kysor Industrial Corp. [*NYSE symbol*] (SPSG)
**KZ** ............. New Zealand [*IYRU nationality code*] (IYR)
**KZ** ............. Trans Europe Air [*France*] [*ICAO designator*] (FAAC)
**KZAB** ......... Albuquerque [*New Mexico*] [*ICAO location identifier*] (ICLI)
**KZAIA** ........ Kogyo Zairyo [*A publication*]
**KZAK** ......... Tyler, TX [*AM radio station call letters*]
**KZAL** ......... Desert Center, CA [*FM radio station call letters*]
**KZAM** ........ Springfield, OR [*AM radio station call letters*]
**KZAM-FM** ... Creswell, OR [*FM radio station call letters*]
**KZAO** ......... Dardanelle, AR [*AM radio station call letters*]
**KZAP** ......... Sacramento, CA [*FM radio station call letters*]
**KZAT** ......... Kommentar zum Alten Testament [*A publication*] (BJA)
**KZAU** ......... Chicago, Aurora [*Illinois*] [*ICAO location identifier*] (ICLI)
**KZAZ** ......... Bellingham, WA [*FM radio station call letters*]
**KZB** ........... Zachar Bay [*Alaska*] [*Airport symbol*] (OAG)
**KZB** ........... Zachar Bay, AK [*Location identifier*] [*FAA*] (FAAL)
**KZBB** ......... Poteau, OK [*FM radio station call letters*]
**KZBK** ......... Brookfield, MO [*FM radio station call letters*]
**KZBL** ......... Natchitoches, LA [*FM radio station call letters*]
**KZBQ** ......... Pocatello, ID [*AM radio station call letters*]
**KZBQ-FM** ... Pocatello, ID [*FM radio station call letters*]
**KZBS** ......... Oklahoma City, OK [*FM radio station call letters*]
**KZBW** ........ Boston, Nashua [*New Hampshire*] [*ICAO location identifier*] (ICLI)
**KZBX** ......... McAlester, OK [*FM radio station call letters*]
**KZDC** ......... Washington, Leesburg [*Virginia*] [*ICAO location identifier*] (ICLI)
**KZDV** ......... Denver, Longmont [*Colorado*] [*ICAO location identifier*] (ICLI)
**KZDX** ......... Burley, ID [*FM radio station call letters*]
**KZED** ......... Wellington, KS [*FM radio station call letters*]
**KZEE** ......... Weatherford, TX [*AM radio station call letters*]
**KZEL-FM** ... Eugene, OR [*FM radio station call letters*]

**KZEN** ........ Central City, NE [*FM radio station call letters*]
**KZEP** ........ San Antonio, TX [*FM radio station call letters*]
**KZEU** ........ Victoria, TX [*FM radio station call letters*]
**KZEV** ........ Clear Lake, IA [*FM radio station call letters*]
**KZEW** ........ Dallas, TX [*FM radio station call letters*]
**KZEY** ........ Tyler, TX [*AM radio station call letters*]
**KZEZ** ........ St. George, UT [*FM radio station call letters*]
**KZF** ........ Kaintiba [*Papua New Guinea*] [*Airport symbol*] (OAG)
**KZFM** ........ Corpus Christi, TX [*FM radio station call letters*]
**KZFN** ........ Moscow, ID [*FM radio station call letters*]
**KZFR** ........ Chico, CA [*FM radio station call letters*]
**KZFW** ........ Fort Worth, Euless [*Texas*] [*ICAO location identifier*] (ICLI)
**KZFX** ........ Lake Jackson, TX [*FM radio station call letters*]
**KZGKA** ..... Kinzoku Zairyo Gijutsu Kenkyusho Kenkyu Hokoku [*A publication*]
**KZGT** ........ Great Falls [*Montana*] [*ICAO location identifier*] (ICLI)
**KZGZ** ........ Agana, GU [*FM radio station call letters*]
**KZHT** ........ Provo, UT [*FM radio station call letters*]
**KZHU** ........ Houston, Humble [*Texas*] [*ICAO location identifier*] (ICLI)
**KZI** ........ Kozani [*Greece*] [*Airport symbol*] (OAG)
**KZID** ........ Indianapolis [*Indiana*] [*ICAO location identifier*] (ICLI)
**KZID** ........ McCall, ID [*AM radio station call letters*]
**KZIG** ........ Cave City, AR [*FM radio station call letters*]
**KZII-FM** ... Lubbock, TX [*FM radio station call letters*]
**KZIM** ........ Cape Girardeau, MO [*AM radio station call letters*]
**KZIN-FM** ... Shelby, MT [*FM radio station call letters*]
**KZIO** ........ Superior, WI [*FM radio station call letters*]
**KZIP** ........ Amarillo, TX [*AM radio station call letters*]
**KZIQ** ........ Ridgecrest, CA [*AM radio station call letters*]
**KZIQ-FM** ... Ridgecrest, CA [*FM radio station call letters*]
**KZIX** ........ Humnoke, AR [*FM radio station call letters*]
**KZJA** ........ Eureka, CA [*Television station call letters*]
**KZJB** ........ Newton, IA [*Television station call letters*]
**KZJC** ........ Flagstaff, AZ [*Television station call letters*]
**KZJE** ........ Clovis, CA [*Television station call letters*]
**KZJF** ........ Paris, TX [*Television station call letters*]
**KZJG** ........ Longmont, CO [*Television station call letters*]
**KZJH** ........ Jackson, WY [*FM radio station call letters*]
**KZJI** ........ Victoria, TX [*Television station call letters*]
**KZJL** ........ Houston, TX [*Television station call letters*]
**KZJX** ........ Jacksonville Hillard [*Florida*] [*ICAO location identifier*] (ICLI)
**KZKC** ........ Kansas City, MO [*Television station call letters*]
**KZKC** ........ Kansas City Olathe [*Kansas*] [*ICAO location identifier*] (ICLI)
**KZKQ** ........ Mangum, OK [*FM radio station call letters*]
**KZKS** ........ Rifle, CO [*FM radio station call letters*]
**KZKX** ........ Seward, NE [*FM radio station call letters*]
**KZLA** ........ Los Angeles Palmdale [*California*] [*ICAO location identifier*] (ICLI)
**KZLA-FM** ... Los Angeles, CA [*FM radio station call letters*]
**KZLC** ........ Salt Lake City [*Utah*] [*ICAO location identifier*] (ICLI)
**KZLE** ........ Batesville, AR [*FM radio station call letters*]
**KZLN-FM** ... Othello, WA [*FM radio station call letters*]
**KZLS** ........ Billings, MT [*FM radio station call letters*]
**KZLT-FM** ... East Grand Forks, MN [*FM radio station call letters*]
**KZMA** ....... Miami [*Florida*] [*ICAO location identifier*] (ICLI)
**KZMC-FM** ... McCook, NE [*FM radio station call letters*]
**KZME** ....... Memphis [*Tennessee*] [*ICAO location identifier*] (ICLI)
**KZMI** ....... San Jose, CM [*FM radio station call letters*]
**KZMK** ....... Bisbee, AZ [*FM radio station call letters*]
**KZMO** ....... California, MO [*AM radio station call letters*]
**KZMO-FM** ... California, MO [*FM radio station call letters*]
**KZMP** ....... Minneapolis, Farmington [*Minnesota*] [*ICAO location identifier*] (ICLI)
**KZMQ** ....... Greybull, WY [*FM radio station call letters*]
**KZMT** ....... Helena, MT [*FM radio station call letters*]
**KZMTLG** ... Koninklijke Zuidnederlandse Maatschappij voor Taal- en Letterkunde en Geschiedenis [*A publication*]
**KZMX** ....... Hot Springs, SD [*AM radio station call letters*]
**KZMZ** ....... Alexandria, LA [*FM radio station call letters*]
**KZN** ........ Kazan [*USSR*] [*Airport symbol*] (OAG)
**KZN** ........ Kozani [*Greece*] [*Seismograph station code, US Geological Survey*] (SEIS)
**KZN** ........ Zaimische [*USSR*] [*Later, KNS*] [*Geomagnetic observatory code*]
**KZNA** ....... Hill City, KS [*FM radio station call letters*]
**KZNE** ....... Chadron, NE [*AM radio station call letters*]
**KZNG** ....... Hot Springs, AR [*AM radio station call letters*]
**KZNN** ....... Rolla, MO [*FM radio station call letters*]
**KZNY** ....... New York, Ronkonkoma [*New York*] [*ICAO location identifier*] (ICLI)
**KZO** ........ Komise pro Zahranicni Obchod [*Foreign Trade Commission*] [*Czechoslovakian*]
**KZOA** ....... KZ Owners' Association [*Defunct*] (EA)
**KZOA** ....... Oakland, Freemont [*California*] [*ICAO location identifier*] (ICLI)
**KZOB** ....... Cleveland, Oberlin [*Ohio*] [*ICAO location identifier*] (ICLI)
**KZOC** ....... Osage City, KS [*FM radio station call letters*]
**KZOE** ....... Longview, WA [*FM radio station call letters*]
**KZOK** ....... Seattle, WA [*FM radio station call letters*]
**KZOL** ....... Provo, UT [*FM radio station call letters*]
**KZOO** ....... Honolulu, HI [*AM radio station call letters*]
**KZOQ** ....... Missoula, MT [*FM radio station call letters*]
**KZOR** ....... Hobbs, NM [*FM radio station call letters*]
**KZOT** ....... Marianna, AR [*AM radio station call letters*]
**KZOU** ....... Little Rock, AR [*AM radio station call letters*]
**KZOU-FM** ... Little Rock, AR [*FM radio station call letters*]
**KZOW** ....... St. Louis Park, MN [*AM radio station call letters*]
**KZOX** ....... Macon, MO [*FM radio station call letters*]
**KZOZ** ....... San Luis Obispo, CA [*FM radio station call letters*]
**KZP** ........ Kwartalnik dla Historji Zydow w Polsce [*A publication*] (BJA)
**KZPR** ....... Minot, ND [*FM radio station call letters*]
**KZPS** ....... Dallas, TX [*FM radio station call letters*]
**KZQQ** ....... West Valley City, UT [*AM radio station call letters*]
**kzr** ........ Kazakh Soviet Socialist Republic [*MARC country of publication code*] [*Library of Congress*] (LCCP)
**KZRC** ....... Milwaukie, OR [*AM radio station call letters*]
**KZRO** ....... South Fort Polk, LA [*FM radio station call letters*]
**KZRQ** ....... Corrales, NM [*AM radio station call letters*]
**KZRR** ....... Albuquerque, NM [*FM radio station call letters*]
**KZS** ........ Koelner Zeitschrift fuer Soziologie [*A publication*]
**KZS** ........ Kutztown State College, Kutztown, PA [*OCLC symbol*] (OCLC)
**KZSC** ....... Santa Cruz, CA [*FM radio station call letters*]
**KZSD-TV** ... Martin, SD [*Television station call letters*]
**KZSE** ....... Rochester, MN [*FM radio station call letters*]
**KZSE** ....... Seattle, Auburn [*Washington*] [*ICAO location identifier*] (ICLI)
**KZSN** ....... Hutchinson, KS [*FM radio station call letters*]
**KZSQ-FM** ... Sonora, CA [*FM radio station call letters*]
**KZSS** ....... Albuquerque, NM [*AM radio station call letters*]
**KZSS** ....... Koelner Zeitschrift fuer Soziologie und Sozial-Psychologie [*A publication*]
**KZST** ....... Santa Rosa, CA [*FM radio station call letters*]
**KZSU** ....... Stanford, CA [*FM radio station call letters*]
**KZTA** ....... Yakima, WA [*AM radio station call letters*]
**KZTL** ....... Atlanta, Hampton [*Georgia*] [*ICAO location identifier*] (ICLI)
**KZTR** ....... Santa Paula, CA [*AM radio station call letters*]
**KZTR-FM** ... Camarillo, CA [*FM radio station call letters*]
**KZTV** ....... Corpus Christi, TX [*Television station call letters*]
**KZTX** ....... Refugio, TX [*FM radio station call letters*]
**KZUE** ....... El Reno, OK [*AM radio station call letters*]
**KZUL-FM** ... Lake Havasu City, AZ [*FM radio station call letters*]
**KZUM** ....... Lincoln, NE [*FM radio station call letters*]
**KZUN** ....... Zuni Pueblo/Blackrock [*New Mexico*] [*ICAO location identifier*] (ICLI)
**KZUU** ....... Pullman, WA [*FM radio station call letters*]
**KZV** ........ Kartell Zionistischer Verbindungen (BJA)
**KZVE** ....... San Antonio, TX [*FM radio station call letters*]
**KZXL** ....... Great Bend, KS [*FM radio station call letters*]
**KZXR** ....... Salinas, CA [*AM radio station call letters*]
**KZXY-FM** ... Apple Valley, CA [*FM radio station call letters*]
**KZYP** ....... Pine Bluff, AR [*FM radio station call letters*]
**KZYQ** ....... St. James, MO [*FM radio station call letters*]
**KZYR** ....... Avon, CO [*FM radio station call letters*]
**KZYX** ....... Philo, CA [*FM radio station call letters*]
**KZZA** ....... Glenwood, MN [*FM radio station call letters*]
**KZZB** ....... Beaumont, TX [*AM radio station call letters*]
**KZZB-FM** ... Beaumont, TX [*FM radio station call letters*]
**KZZI** ....... West Jordan, UT [*AM radio station call letters*]
**KZZJ** ....... Rugby, ND [*AM radio station call letters*]
**KZZJ-FM** ... Rugby, ND [*FM radio station call letters*]
**KZZK-FM** ... Richland, WA [*FM radio station call letters*]
**KZZL** ....... Pullman, WA [*FM radio station call letters*]
**KZZM** ....... Tallulah, LA [*AM radio station call letters*]
**KZZN** ....... Littlefield, TX [*AM radio station call letters*]
**KZZO** ....... Clovis, NM [*FM radio station call letters*]
**KZZP** ....... Mesa, AZ [*AM radio station call letters*]
**KZZPA** ...... Kolloid-Zeitschrift und Zeitschrift fuer Polymere [*A publication*]
**KZZP-FM** ... Mesa, AZ [*FM radio station call letters*]
**KZZQ** ....... Mirando City, TX [*FM radio station call letters*]
**KZZR** ....... Burns, OR [*AM radio station call letters*]
**KZZT** ....... Moberly, MO [*FM radio station call letters*]
**KZZU-FM** ... Spokane, WA [*FM radio station call letters*]
**KZZX** ....... Alamogordo, NM [*AM radio station call letters*]
**KZZY-FM** ... Devils Lake, ND [*FM radio station call letters*]
**KZZZ** ....... Kingman, AZ [*FM radio station call letters*]

# L

L.................. Angle
L.................. Angular Momentum [*Symbol*] [*IUPAC*]
l-------........... Atlantic Ocean [*MARC geographic area code*] [*Library of Congress*] (LCCP)
L.................. Avogadro Constant [*Symbol*] [*IUPAC*]
l.................. Azimuthal Quantum Number [*or Orbital Angular Momentum Quantum Number*] [*Symbol*]
L.................. Azimuthal Quantum Number [*or Orbital Angular Momentum Quantum Number*] - Total [*Symbol*]
L.................. Cleared to Land [*Aviation*] (FAAC)
L.................. Cold-weather aircraft with special equipment such as skis or extra insulation [*Designation for all US military aircraft*]
L.................. Concerts and Recitals of Serious Music (Permits) [*Public-performance tariff class*] [*British*]
L.................. Countermeasures [*JETDS nomenclature*]
L-................. Days before Launch [*Usually followed by a number*] [*NASA*] (KSC)
L.................. Difference of Latitude [*Navigation*]
L.................. Drizzle [*Meteorology*]
L.................. Electrical [*in British naval officers' ranks*]
L.................. Element
L.................. Elevated [*Railway*] [*Also, EL*]
L.................. Equipped with Search Light [*Suffix to plane designation*] [*Navy*]
L.................. Fifty [*Roman numeral*]
L.................. Finland [*IYRU nationality code*] (IYR)
L.................. Glider Aircraft [*When first letter in Navy aircraft designation*]
L.................. Inductance [*Symbol*] (AAG)
L.................. Kinetic Potential [*Symbol*]
L.................. L-Asparaginase [*Also, A, L-ase, L-asnase, L-Asp*] [*An enzyme, an antineoplastic*]
L.................. Labaz [*Belgium, France*] [*Research code symbol*]
L.................. Label (MDG)
L.................. Labetalol [*Pharmacology*]
L.................. Labor
L.................. Laboratory
L.................. Laboratory Attendant [*Ranking title*] [*British Royal Navy*]
L.................. Lactobacillus
L.................. Ladestreifen [*Ammunition Clip*] [*German military - World War II*]
L.................. Ladinian [*Geology*]
L.................. Lady [*or Ladyship*]
L.................. Lagrangian Function
L.................. Lake [*Maps and charts*]
L.................. Lambert [*Unit of luminance*] [*Preferred unit is lx, Lux*]
L.................. Lameness [*Used by immigration officials*] [*Obsolete*]
L.................. Laminated
L.................. Lamp
L.................. Lancashire Flats [*British*] (DCTA)
L.................. Lancers
L.................. Lancet [*London*] [*A publication*]
L.................. Land
L.................. Landing
L.................. Landplane
L.................. Landulfus Acconzaioco [*Flourished, 13th century*] [*Authority cited in pre-1607 legal work*] (DSA)
L.................. Langmuir [*Unit of measure*]
L.................. Language
L.................. Language [*A publication*]
L.................. Lansing's New York Supreme Court Reports [*A publication*] (DLA)
L.................. Lansing's Select Cases in Chancery [*1824, 1826*] [*New York*] [*A publication*] (DLA)
L.................. Lanthanum [*Chemical element; symbol is La*]
L.................. Larceny [*FBI standardized term*]
L.................. Large [*Size designation for clothing, etc.*]
L.................. Larva [*Biology*]
L.................. Lat [*Monetary unit*] [*Latvia*]
L.................. Latching [*Electronics*]
L.................. Late
L.................. Latent Heat
L.................. Latin
L.................. Latitude
L.................. Latomus [*A publication*]
L.................. Launch [*or Launcher*]
L.................. Laurentius Hispanus [*Deceased, 1248*] [*Authority cited in pre-1607 legal work*] (DSA)
L.................. Lavender [*Botany*]
L.................. Law
L.................. Lawson's Notes of Decisions, Registration [*A publication*] (DLA)
L.................. "Lay" Source (BJA)
L.................. Layer [*Officer's rating*] [*British Royal Navy*]
L.................. Lead Sheath (AAG)
L.................. Leader (ADA)
L.................. Leaf [*Bibliography*] [*Botany*]
L.................. Leaflet
L.................. League
L.................. Learner
L.................. Learning [*Denotes learning drivers before they receive their automobile driving licenses*] [*British*]
L.................. Leasehold (ROG)
L.................. Leather
L.................. Leave
L.................. Lederle Laboratories [*Research code symbol*]
L.................. Leeward
L.................. Left [*Direction*]
L.................. Left [*Politics*]
L.................. Left [*side of a stage*] [*A stage direction*]
L.................. Left Hand [*Music*] (ROG)
L.................. Legal Division [*Coast Guard*]
L.................. Leges [*Laws*] [*Latin*] (ROG)
L.................. Legge [*Law, Act, Statute*] [*Italian*] (ILCA)
L.................. Legitimate
L.................. Lempira [*Monetary unit*] [*Honduras*]
L.................. Lenad Subgroup [*Leucite, nephelite, halite, thenardite*] [*CIPW classification*] [*Geology*]
L.................. Length [*or Lengthwise*]
l.................. Length [*Symbol*] [*IUPAC*]
L.................. Lens
L.................. Leodium [*A publication*]
L.................. Leonardo [*A publication*]
L.................. Lepetit [*Italy*] [*Research code symbol*]
L.................. Lepidocrocite [*A mineral*]
L.................. Lethal
L.................. Letter
L.................. Leu [*Monetary unit*] [*Romania*]
L.................. Leucine [*One-letter symbol; see Leu*] [*An amino acid*]
l/................. Leur [*Their, Your*] [*Business term*] [*French*]
L.................. Lev [*Monetary unit*] [*Bulgaria*]
L.................. Level (KSC)
L.................. Levo [*or Laevo*] [*Configuration in chemical structure*]
l.................. Levorotary [*or Levorotatory*] [*Chemistry*]
L.................. Lewisite [*War gas*] [*Army symbol*]
L.................. Lexical Rule [*Linguistics*]
L.................. Liaison [*Airplane designation*]
L.................. Liber [*Book*] [*Latin*]
L.................. Liberal [*Politics*]
L.................. Libra [*Pound*]
L.................. Library
L.................. Libration [*Space exploration*]
L.................. License
L.................. Licensed to Practice [*Medicine*]
L.................. Licentiate
L.................. Lidocaine [*Topical anesthetic*]
L.................. Lidoflazine [*A vasodilator*]
L.................. Lies [*Read*] [*German*]
L.................. Lieutenant [*Navy*] [*British*]
L.................. Life [*Insurance*]
L.................. Lift
L.................. Ligament [*or Ligamentum*]
L.................. Ligand [*Chemistry*]

L ........ Light [*Chain*] [*Biochemistry, immunochemistry*]
L ........ Light
L ........ Light Sense
L ........ Lighting [*As part of a code*]
L ........ Lightning [*Meteorology*]
L ........ Lilac
L ........ Lima [*Phonetic alphabet*] [*International*] (DSUE)
L ........ Lime
L ........ Limen or Threshold [*Psychology*]
L ........ Limestone [*Petrology*]
L ........ Limit
L ........ Limited (DLA)
L ........ Line
L ........ Line Assembly (AAG)
L ........ Linen [*Deltiology*]
L ........ Liner [*Nautical*]
L ........ Lines Dose [*Medicine*]
L ........ Lingual [*Dentistry*]
L ........ Link
L ........ Linnaean
L ........ Lip
L ........ Lipoid [*Biochemistry*]
L ........ Liquid
(l) ........ Liquid [*Chemistry*]
l ........ Liquidation [*Liquidation*] [*Business term*] [*French*]
L ........ Lira [*Monetary unit*] [*Italy*]
L ........ List (MSA)
L ........ Listed [*Stock exchange term*]
L ........ Listening Post [*In symbol only*]
L ........ Lit
L ........ Litas [*Monetary unit*] [*Lithuania*]
L ........ Liter [*Also, l*] [*Metric measure of volume*]
L ........ Literate
L ........ Lithium [*Chemical element*] (ROG)
L ........ Little
L ........ Live [*Wiring code*] [*British*]
L ........ Living Room (ROG)
L ........ Livre [*Monetary unit*] [*French*] [*Obsolete*]
L ........ Load (MDG)
L ........ Loam [*Agronomy*]
L ........ Lobe [*Of a leaf*] [*Botany*]
L ........ Loblaw Companies Ltd. [*Toronto Stock Exchange symbol*] [*Vancouver Stock Exchange symbol*]
L ........ Local
l ........ Locative (Case) [*Linguistics*]
L ........ Locator [*Compass*]
L ........ Locator Beacon
L ........ Loch
L ........ Lockheed Aircraft Corp. [*ICAO aircraft manufacturer identifier*] (ICAO)
L ........ Locus [*Place*] [*Latin*]
L ........ Lodge
L ........ Logair [*Air Force contract aircraft identification prefix*] (FAAC)
L ........ Logarithm [*Mathematics*]
L ........ Logistics (FAAC)
L ........ Loi [*Law, Statute, Act*] [*French*] (ILCA)
L ........ London [*England*]
L ........ London [*Phonetic alphabet*] [*Royal Navy*] [*World War I*] [*Pre-World War II*] (DSUE)
L ........ Long
L ........ Long, Rolling Sea [*Meteorology*]
L ........ Longacre [*James B.*] [*Designer's mark, when appearing on US coins*]
L ........ Longitude
L ........ [*Alessandro*] Longo [*When used in identifying D. Scarlatti's compositions, refers to cataloging of his works by musicologist Longo*]
L ........ Loop [*Fingerprint description*]
L ........ Looper [*Data processing*] (MDG)
L ........ Lorazepam [*A tranquilizer*]
L ........ Lord [*or Lordship*]
L ........ Lorentz Unit [*Electronics*]
L ........ Lost [*Sports statistics*]
L ........ Lost [*RADAR*]
L ........ Lough [*Maps and charts*]
L ........ Louisiana Reports [*A publication*] (DLA)
L ........ Louisiana State Library, Baton Rouge, LA [*Library symbol*] [*Library of Congress*] (LCLS)
L ........ Love [*Phonetic alphabet*] [*World War II*] (DSUE)
L ........ Low [*or Lower*]
L ........ Low Season [*Airline fare code*]
L ........ Lower Bow [*Music*] (ROG)
l ........ Lower Limit of a Class Interval [*Psychology*]
L ........ Loyalty
L ........ Luitingh [*Holland*]
L ........ Lumbar [*Medicine*]
L ........ Lumen [*Unit of luminous flux*]
L ........ Luteolin [*Botany*]
L ........ Luxembourg
L ........ Luxury [*In automobile model name "Cordia L"*]
l ........ Lyxose [*One-letter symbol; see Lyx*]
l ........ Lyxose [*As substituent on nucleoside*] [*Biochemistry*]
l ........ Mean Free Path [*Symbol*] [*IUPAC*]
L ........ Merck & Co., Inc. [*Research code symbol*]
L ........ Promotional Fare [*Also, K, Q, V*] [*Airline fare code*]
L ........ Radiance [*Symbol*] [*IUPAC*]
L ........ Refusal to Extend Decision of Cited Case beyond Precise Issues Involved [*Used in Shepard's Citations*] [*Legal term*] (DLA)
L ........ Requires Fuel and Oil [*Search and rescue symbol that can be stamped in sand or snow*]
L ........ Sandoz Pharmaceuticals [*Research code symbol*]
L ........ Searchlight Control [*JETDS nomenclature*]
L ........ Self-Inductance [*Symbol*] [*IUPAC*]
L ........ Shape Descriptor [*Dining el, for example. The shape resembles the letter for which it is named*]
L ........ Silo Launched [*Missile launch environment symbol*]
L ........ Single Acetate (AAG)
L ........ Timber [*Lumber*] [*Vessel load line mark*]
L ........ Time of Launch [*NASA*]
L1 ........ First Language (ADA)
$L_1$ ........ First Lumbar Vertebra [*Second lumbar vertebra is $L_2$, etc., through $L_5$*] [*Medicine*]
L5 ........ Long Quinto [*Pt. 10 of Year Books*] [*A publication*] (DSA)
L6 ........ Laboratories Low-Level Linked List Language [*Bell Systems*] (DIT)
L7 ........ Square [*A slang term of the 1950's, derived from juxtaposing these two characters to form a square*]
9L ........ Sierra Leone [*Aircraft nationality and registration mark*] (FAAC)
3L's ........ Legislators, Lawyers, and Lead [*Forces mustered by opponents of proposed nuclear-waste burial sites*]
3L's ........ Luxury, Leisure, Longevity [*Economics*]
LA ........ Concerts and Recitals of Serious Music (Annual Licence) [*Public-performance tariff class*] [*British*]
LA ........ Fighter [*Russian aircraft symbol*]
LA ........ Hoffmann-La Roche, Inc. [*Research code symbol*]
La ........ [*The*] Holy Bible from Ancient Eastern Manuscripts [*G. M. Lamsa*] [*A publication*] (BJA)
LA ........ LA Gear, Inc. [*NYSE symbol*] (CTT)
LA ........ Lab. Aron [*France*] [*Research code symbol*]
La ........ Labial [*Dentistry*]
LA ........ Labor Arbitration Reports [*A publication*] (DLA)
LA ........ Labor Area
La ........ Laches [*of Plato*] [*Classical studies*] (OCD)
LA ........ Lactalbumin [*Biochemistry*]
LA ........ Lactic Acid [*Biochemistry*]
LA ........ Lag Amplifier
La ........ Lagulanda (BJA)
LA ........ Laira [*Plymouth*] [*British depot code*]
LA ........ Lake Aircraft [*ICAO aircraft manufacturer identifier*] (ICAO)
LA ........ Lama Foundation (EA)
LA ........ Lambda Alpha
La ........ Lambert [*Unit of luminance*] [*Preferred unit is lx, Lux*] (ADA)
La ........ Lamentations [*Old Testament book*] (BJA)
LA ........ Lancastrian [*Of the royal house of Lancaster*] [*British*] (ROG)
LA ........ Land Agent [*Ministry of Agriculture, Fisheries, and Food*] [*British*]
L/A ........ Landing Account [*Shipping*]
L & A ........ Landing and Ascent [*NASA*]
La ........ Landulfus Acconzaioco [*Flourished, 13th century*] [*Authority cited in pre-1607 legal work*] (DSA)
LA ........ Lane
La ........ Lane's English Exchequer Reports [*1605-12*] [*A publication*] (DLA)
La ........ Lanfrancus [*Deceased, 1089*] [*Authority cited in pre-1607 legal work*] (DSA)
La ........ Lanfrancus Cremensis [*Deceased, 1229*] [*Authority cited in pre-1607 legal work*] (DSA)
LA ........ Language [*Online database field identifier*]
LA ........ Language Age [*Score*]
LA ........ Language Arts [*A publication*]
La ........ Lanthanum [*Chemical element*]
LA ........ Laos [*or Lao People's Democratic Republic*] [*ANSI two-letter standard code*] (CNC)
La ........ Lapus de Castiglionchio [*Flourished, 1353-81*] [*Authority cited in pre-1607 legal work*] (DSA)
La ........ Lapus Tatti [*Flourished, 14th century*] [*Authority cited in pre-1607 legal work*] (DSA)
LA ........ Large Amount [*Medicine*]
LA ........ Large Aperture [*Photography*] (ROG)
LA ........ LASER Altimeter [*NASA*]
LA ........ LASER [*Gyro*] Axis (IEEE)
LA ........ Last [*Wool weight*]
LA ........ Lastenausgleich [*A publication*]
LA ........ Latex Agglutination [*Test*] [*Clinical chemistry*]
LA ........ Lathe [*Division in the county of Kent*] [*British*]
LA ........ Latin America
LA ........ Launch Abort [*NASA*] (KSC)
LA ........ Launch Aft
LA ........ Launch Analyst [*Aerospace*] (AAG)

**LA** ............. Launch Area [*NASA*] (KSC)
**LA** ............. Launch Azimuth [*NASA*] (KSC)
**LA** ............. Laureate in Arts
**La** ............. Laurentius Hispanus [*Deceased, 1248*] [*Authority cited in pre-1607 legal work*] (DSA)
**LA** ............. Lava [*Maps and charts*]
**LA** ............. Lavatory (DSUE)
**LA** ............. Lavochkin [*USSR aircraft type*] [*World War II*]
**LA** ............. Law Agent
**LA** ............. Lawyers' Reports, Annotated [*A publication*] (DLA)
**LA** ............. Le Arti [*A publication*]
**LA** ............. Lead Adapter [*Electric equipment*]
**LA** ............. Lead Amplifier
**LA** ............. Lead Angle (MSA)
**LA** ............. Leading Aircraftsman [*RAF*] [*British*]
**LA** ............. Leading Article (ROG)
**LA** ............. Leaf Abscission [*Botany*]
**LA** ............. Learning Activity (ADA)
**LA** ............. Leasehold Area (ADA)
**L/A** ............. Leave Advance [*Military*]
**LA** ............. Lebensalter [*Chronological Age*] [*Psychology*]
**LA** ............. Ledger Account (ROG)
**LA** ............. Ledger Asset
**L & A**......... Leembruggen and Asirvatham's Appeal Court Reports [*Ceylon*] [*A publication*] (DLA)
**LA** ............. Left Angle
**LA** ............. Left Arm [*Medicine*]
**LA** ............. Left Ascension
**LA** ............. Left Atrium [*Anatomy*]
**LA** ............. Left Auricle [*Anatomy*]
**LA** ............. Left Axilla (KSC)
**LA** ............. Legal Adviser
**LA** ............. Legal Asset [*Business term*]
**LA** ............. Lege Artis [*According to the Art*] [*Pharmacy*]
**LA** ............. Legislative Affairs
**LA** ............. Legislative Assembly
**LA** ............. Legitimate Access [*British police term*]
**LA** ............. Legum Allegoriae [*Philo*] (BJA)
**LA** ............. LeMans America (EA)
**LA** ............. Lemko Association of US and Canada (EA)
**LA** ............. Leschetizky Association (EA)
**LA** ............. Lethal Area [*Of indirect-fire weapon systems*] [*Military*]
**LA** ............. Letter of Activation [*Military*]
**L/A** ............. Letter of Authority
**La** ............. Letteratura [*A publication*]
**LA** ............. Letters Abroad (EA)
**L/A** ............. Lettre d'Avis [*Letter of Advice*] [*French*]
**LA** ............. Leucine Aminopeptidase [*Also, LP, LPAP*] [*An enzyme*]
**LA** ............. Leukoagglutinating [*Immunochemistry*]
**LA** ............. Levator Ani [*Anatomy*]
**LA** ............. Liberal Arts
**LA** ............. Libertarian Alliance [*London, England*] (EAIO)
**LA** ............. Library of Art [*A publication*]
**LA** ............. Library Association [*British*]
**LA** ............. Library Automation
**LA** ............. Licensing Act (DLA)
**LA** ............. Licensing Assistant (NRCH)
**LA** ............. Licensing Authority (DCTA)
**LA** ............. Licentiate in Arts
**LA** ............. Lieutenant-at-Arms [*British*]
**L & A**......... Light and Accommodation [*Optometry*]
**LA** ............. Light Ale (ADA)
**LA** ............. Light Alloy
**LA** ............. Light Armor [*Telecommunications*] (TEL)
**LA** ............. Light Artillery
**LA** ............. Lighter-than-Air [*Aircraft*]
**LA** ............. Lighter Association (EA)
**LA** ............. Lightning Arrester
**LA** ............. Lincoln Annex [*A publication*]
**LA** ............. Line Adapter [*Data processing*] (CMD)
**LA** ............. Linea Aerea Nacional de Chile [*Chilean airline*] [*ICAO designator*] (OAG)
**LA** ............. Linear Arithmetic [*Data processing*]
**LA** ............. Linear Assembly
**LA** ............. Linguistica Antverpiensia [*A publication*]
**LA** ............. Linguistische Arbeiten [*A publication*]
**LA** ............. Linguoaxial [*Dentistry*]
**LA** ............. Link Allotter
**LA** ............. Link Analysis
**LA** ............. Linnaean Society
**LA** ............. Liquid Asset [*Business term*]
**LA** ............. Lisan Al-'Arabi [*A publication*]
**LA** ............. Listed Address [*Telecommunications*] (TEL)
**LA** ............. Listing Agent [*Classified advertising*] (ADA)
**LA** ............. Literarische Anzeiger [*A publication*]
**LA** ............. Literate in Arts
**LA** ............. Literaturanzeiger fuer das Allgemeine Wissenschaftliche Schrifttum [*A publication*]
**LA** ............. Liverpool Academy [*British*]
**LA** ............. Living Age [*A publication*]
**L/A** ............. Lloyd's Agent
**LA** ............. Load Adjuster (CET)
**LA** ............. Local Address
**LA** ............. Local Agent
**LA** ............. Local Alarm (NRCH)
**LA** ............. Local Anesthetic [*Medicine*]
**LA** ............. Local Authority
**LA** ............. Lock Actuator (MCD)
**LA** ............. Locus Allowed (ROG)
**LA** ............. Lodging Allowance [*British military*] (DMA)
**LA** ............. Log Analyzer Processor [*Data processing*]
**LA** ............. Logarithmic Amplifier
**LA** ............. Logical Address
**LA** ............. Loners of America [*An association*] (EA)
**LA** ............. Long-Acting [*Pharmacy*]
**LA** ............. Longitudinal Acoustic [*Spectroscopy*]
**LA** ............. Loop Antenna (DEN)
**LA** ............. Lord Advocate of Scotland (DLA)
**LA** ............. Los Alamos Scientific Laboratory [*USAEC*] (MCD)
**LA** ............. Los Angeles [*California*] [*Slang*]
**LA** ............. Louisiana [*Postal code*] (AFM)
**L & A**......... Louisiana & Arkansas Railway Co.
**LA** ............. Louisiana & Arkansas Railway Co. [*AAR code*]
**LA** ............. Louisiana Reports [*A publication*] (DLA)
**LA** ............. Louisiana Supreme Court Reports [*A publication*] (DLA)
**LA** ............. Low Alcohol [*Trademark of Anheuser-Busch, Inc.*]
**LA** ............. Low Altitude
**LA** ............. Low Angle [*RADAR*] (DEN)
**LA** ............. Low Approach [*Aviation*] (FAAC)
**LA** ............. Lower Arm
**LA** ............. Luscombe Association (EA)
**LA** ............. Lymphadenopathy [*Medicine*]
**La** ............. Old Latin Version (BJA)
**£A** ............. Pounds Australian [*Monetary unit*]
**LAA** ........... Lamar [*Colorado*] [*Airport symbol*] (OAG)
**LAA** ........... Lamar, CO [*Location identifier*] [*FAA*] (FAAL)
**La A** ........... Landarzt [*A publication*]
**LAA** ........... Laser Association of America [*Later, LEMA*] (EA)
**LAA** ........... LASER Attenuator Assembly
**LAA** ........... Launch Area Antenna (MCD)
**LAA** ........... League of Advertising Agencies [*New York, NY*] (EA)
**LAA** ........... Library Association of Australia
**LAA** ........... Lieutenant-at-Arms [*British*] (DMA)
**LAA** ........... Life Insurance Advertisers Association [*Later, LCA*] (EA)
**LAA** ........... Light Antiaircraft [*Guns*]
**LAA** ........... Light Army Aircraft
**LAA** ........... Lighterage Assembly Area
**LAA** ........... Lipizzan Association of America (EA)
**LAA** ........... Lithuanian Alliance of America (EA)
**LAA** ........... Little America [*Antarctica*] [*Seismograph station code, US Geological Survey*] [*Closed*] (SEIS)
**LAA** ........... Live Assembly Area (MCD)
**LAA** ........... Liverpool Academy of Arts [*England*]
**LAA** ........... Los Angeles Airways, Inc.
**LA A** ........... Louisiana Annual Reports [*A publication*] (DLA)
**LA A** ........... Louisiana Courts of Appeal Reports [*A publication*] (DLA)
**LAA** ........... Low-Altitude Attack
**LAAA** ........ Latin American Association of Archives [*See also ALA*] (EAIO)
**LAAA** ........ Liverpool Annuals of Archaeology and Anthropology [*A publication*]
**LAAAAS**... Latin American Association for Afro-Asian Studies (EAIO)
**LAAAS**...... Low-Altitude Airfield Attack System (MCD)
**LAAB**......... Light Armored Assault Battalion [*Marine Corps*]
**LAABAM** ... Latin American Association of Behavior Analysis and Modification (EAIO)
**LAABF** ...... Ladies' Auxiliary of the American Beekeeping Federation (EA)
**LAAC**......... Library Association's Annual Conference [*British*]
**LAAC**......... Lloyd's Acceptance Corp. [*NASDAQ symbol*] (NQ)
**LAAC**......... Lord Chancellor's Legal Aid Advisory Committee [*British*] (DLA)
**LAACB**...... Langenbecks Archiv fuer Chirurgie [*A publication*]
**LAACC**...... Light Antiaircraft Control Center (NATG)
**LA Acts**...... State of Louisiana: Acts of the Legislature [*A publication*] (DLA)
**LAAD** ........ Latin American Agribusiness Development Corp.
**LAADIW**... Latin American Association for the Development and Integration of Women [*See also ALADIM*] [*Santiago, Chile*] (EAIO)
**LA Admin Code** ... Louisiana Administrative Code [*A publication*] (DLA)
**LA Admin Reg** ... Louisiana Administrative Register [*A publication*] (DLA)
**LAADS**...... Los Angeles Air Defense Sector [*ADC*]
**LAADS**...... Low-Altitude Air Defense [*or Delivery*] System
**LAADS**...... Low-Altitude Air Dropped Stores (MCD)
**LAAEMCTS** ... Latin American Association of Environmental Mutagens, Carcinogens, and Teratogens Societies [*Mexico City, Mexico*] (EAIO)
**LAAF**......... Lawson Army Airfield [*Fort Benning, GA*] (MCD)
**LAAF**......... Libby Army Airfield
**LAAFS** ...... Los Angeles Air Force Station
**LAAG** ........ Latin American Anthropology Group (EA)

**LA Ag Exp** ... Louisiana. Agricultural Experiment Station. Publications [*A publication*]
**LA Agr** ....... Louisiana Agriculture [*A publication*]
**LA Agric** .... Louisiana Agriculture [*A publication*]
**LA Agric Exp Stn Bull** ... Louisiana. Agricultural Experiment Station. Bulletin [*A publication*]
**LAAI** .......... Licentiate of the Institute of Administrative Accountants [*British*] (DBQ)
**LAAIB** ....... Latin American Air Intelligence Brief (MCD)
**L A of Alta Bul** ... Library Association of Alberta. Bulletin [*A publication*]
**LAAM** ....... Large-Animal Anesthesia Machine [*Instrumentation*]
**LAAM** ....... Levo-alpha-Acetylmethadol [*Drug alternative to methadone*]
**LAAM** ....... Light Antiaircraft Missile
**LAAMBN** ... Light Antiaircraft Missile Battalion (MUGU)
**LAAMSF**... Latin American Association of Medical Schools and Faculties [*See also ALAFEM*] [*Quito, Ecuador*] (EAIO)
**La An** ......... Lawyers' Reports, Annotated [*A publication*] (DLA)
**LAANAQ** .. Ecole Superieure d'Agriculture de la Suede. Annales [*A publication*]
**LA Ann** ...... Louisiana Annual Reports [*A publication*] (DLA)
**LA Ann Reps** ... Louisiana Annual Reports [*A publication*] (DLA)
**LA An R**..... Louisiana Annual Reports [*A publication*] (DLA)
**LA An Rep** ... Louisiana Annual Reports [*A publication*] (DLA)
**LAAO** ........ L-Amino Acid Oxidase [*An enzyme*]
**LAAO** ........ Los Alamos Area Office [*Energy Research and Development Administration*]
**LA A (Orleans)** ... Louisiana Court of Appeals (Parish of Orleans) (DLA)
**LAAP**......... Longhorn Army Ammunition Plant (MCD)
**LAAP**......... Louisiana Army Ammunition Plant (AABC)
**LAAPD**...... Los Angeles Air Procurement District
**LAAPI** ....... Latin American Association of Pharmaceutical Industries [*See also ALIFAR*] (EAIO)
**LA App** ...... Louisiana Courts of Appeal Reports [*A publication*] (DLA)
**LA App (Orleans)** ... Louisiana Court of Appeals (Parish of Orleans) (DLA)
**LAAR**......... Liquid Air Accumulator Rocket
**LAAS**......... Light Armor Antitank System (MCD)
**LAAS**......... Los Angeles Air Service, Inc.
**LAAS**......... Low-Altitude Alerting System
**LAASCA** ... Long-Range Antisubmarine Capability Aircraft
**LAASP** ...... Latin American Association for Social Psychology [*Formerly, Latinamerican Social Psychology Committee*] (EA)
**LAAT**......... LASER-Augmented Airborne TOW Sight [*Army*] (MCD)
**LAAT**......... Logistics Assessment and Assistance Team (MCD)
**LAA Univ & Coll Lib Sec News** ... Library Association of Australia. University and College Libraries Section. News Sheet [*A publication*] (APTA)
**LAA Univ Lib Sec News** ... Library Association of Australia. University Libraries Section. News Sheet [*A publication*] (APTA)
**LAA Univ Lib Sec News Sheet** ... Library Association of Australia. University Libraries Section. News Sheet [*A publication*] (APTA)
**LAAV** ........ Light Airborne ASW [*Antisubmarine Warfare*] Vehicle
**LAAW** ....... Legal Automated Army-Wide
**LAAW** ....... Light Assault Antitank Weapon
**LAAW** ....... Local Antiair Warfare (NVT)
**LAAW** ....... Lotus. Afro-Asian Writings [*A publication*]
**LAAWC**..... Local Antiair Warfare Commander (NVT)
**La B**........... La Bas [*A publication*]
**LAB** .......... LAB Flying Service [*Haines, AK*] [*FAA designator*] (FAAC)
**Lab**............ Labatt's California District Court Reports [*1857-58*] [*A publication*] (DLA)
**Lab**............ Labeo. Rassegna di Diritto Romano [*A publication*]
**LAB** .......... Lablab [*Papua New Guinea*] [*Airport symbol*] (OAG)
**LAB** .......... Labmin Resources Ltd. [*Toronto Stock Exchange symbol*]
**LAB** .......... Labor
**Lab**............ Laboratorio [*A publication*]
**LAB** .......... Laboratory (AFM)
**LAB** .......... Laboratory for Applied Biophysics [*MIT*] (MCD)
**LAB** .......... Labour Party [*Great Britain*] [*Political party*]
**LAB** .......... Labrador [*Canada*]
**LAB** .......... Labuan [*Island in Malaysia*] (ROG)
**LAB** .......... Lactic Acid Bacteria [*Food microbiology*]
**Lab**............ Lambertus de Ramponibus [*Deceased, 1304*] [*Authority cited in pre-1607 legal work*] (DSA)
**LAB** .......... Latin America Bureau [*London, England*] (EAIO)
**LAB** .......... Lead Acid Battery
**LAB** .......... Leave Authorization Balance [*Air Force*] (AFM)
**LAB** .......... Leisure Activities Blank [*Vocational guidance test*]
**LAB** .......... Level of Aspiration Board [*Psychology*]
**LAB** .......... Liber Antiquitatum Biblicarum. Pseudo-Philo (BJA)
**LAB** .......... Licentiate of the Associated Board of Royal Schools of Music [*British*]
**LAB** .......... Light Attack Battalion (INF)
**LAB** .......... Linear Alkylbenzene [*Organic chemistry*]
**LAB** .......... Liquor Administration Board [*New South Wales, Australia*]
**LAB** .......... Lithosphere-Asthenosphere Boundary [*Geology*]
**LAB** .......... Live Animals Board [*IATA*] (DS)
**LAB** .......... Lloyd Aereo Boliviano SA [*Lloyd Bolivian Air Line*]
**LAB** .......... Local Area Broadcast (NVT)
**LAB** .......... Los Angeles Bar Bulletin [*A publication*]
**LAB** .......... Los Angeles Branch [*AEC*]
**LAB** .......... Low-Altitude Bombing [*Military*]
**LAB** .......... Nichols Institute [*AMEX symbol*] (SPSG)
**LABA**......... Laboratory Animal Breeders Association (EA)
**Lab AC**....... Labour Appeal Cases [*India*] [*A publication*] (DLA)
**LABAC**...... Licentiate Member of the Association of Business and Administrative Computing [*British*] (DBQ)
**LABAN**...... Lakas ng Bayan [*Peoples' Power Movement - Fight*] [*Philippines*] [*Political party*] (PPW)
**Lab Anim** ... Laboratory Animals [*A publication*]
**Lab Anim Care** ... Laboratory Animal Care [*A publication*]
**Lab Anim Handb** ... Laboratory Animal Handbooks [*A publication*]
**Lab Anim Sc** ... Laboratory Animal Science [*A publication*]
**Lab Anim Sci** ... Laboratory Animal Science [*A publication*]
**Lab Anim Symp** ... Laboratory Animal Symposia [*A publication*]
**LA Bar** ....... Louisiana Bar. Official Publication of the Louisiana State Bar Association [*A publication*] (DLA)
**Lab Arb**...... Labor Arbitration Reports [*Bureau of National Affairs*] [*A publication*] (DLA)
**Lab Arb Awards** ... Labor Arbitration Awards [*Commerce Clearing House*] [*A publication*] (DLA)
**Lab Arb BNA** ... Labor Arbitration Reports. Bureau of National Affairs [*A publication*]
**Lab Arb & Disp Settl** ... Labor Arbitration and Dispute Settlements [*A publication*] (DLA)
**LA Bar J** .... Louisiana Bar Journal [*A publication*]
**Lab & Auto Bull** ... Labor and Automation Bulletin [*A publication*] (DLA)
**LABB**......... Beauty Labs, Inc. [*NASDAQ symbol*] (NQ)
**LABB**......... Los Angeles Bar Bulletin [*A publication*]
**Lab Biochim Nutr Publ Univ Cathol Louvain Fac Sci Agron** ... Laboratoire de Biochimie de la Nutrition. Publication. Universite Catholique de Louvain. Faculte des Sciences Agronomiques [*A publication*]
**Lab-Bl**........ Laboratoriums-Blaetter [*A publication*]
**LAB Bull**.... Los Angeles Bar Bulletin [*A publication*]
**Lab Cent Ponts Chaussees Bull Liaison Lab Ponts Chaussees** ... Laboratoire Central des Ponts et Chaussees. Bulletin de Liaison des Laboratoires des Ponts et Chaussees [*A publication*]
**Lab Cent Ponts Chaussees Note Inf Tech** ... Laboratoire Central des Ponts et Chaussees. Note d'Information Technique [*A publication*]
**Lab Cent Ponts Chaussees Rapp Rech** ... Laboratoire Central des Ponts et Chaussees. Rapport de Recherche [*A publication*]
**Lab Central Ensayo Mater Constr Madrid Publ** ... Laboratorio Central de Ensayo de Materiales de Construccion. Madrid. Publicacion [*A publication*]
**Lab Clin Stress Res Karolinska Sjukhuset Rep** ... Laboratory for Clinical Stress Research. Karolinska Sjukhuset. Reports [*A publication*]
**LABCOM** ... Laboratory Command [*Army*] [*Adelphi, MD*] (RDA)
**LAB-CO-OP** ... Labour and Co-Operative Party [*British*]
**LABDA**...... Laboratornoe Delo [*A publication*]
**Lab Del** ...... Laboratornoe Delo [*A publication*]
**Lab Delo** .... Laboratornoe Delo [*A publication*]
**Labden J Sci Technol** ... Labden. Journal of Science and Technology [*India*] [*A publication*]
**LABDET** ... [*Isotopic*] Label [*Incorporation*] Determination
**Labdev J Sci Technol** ... Labdev Journal of Science and Technology [*A publication*]
**Labdev J Sci & Technol A** ... Labdev Journal of Science and Technology. Part A. Physical Sciences [*A publication*]
**Labdev J Sci & Technol B** ... Labdev Journal of Science and Technology. Part B. Life Sciences [*A publication*]
**Labdev J Sci Technol Part B Life Sci** ... Labdev Journal of Science and Technology. Part B. Life Sciences [*A publication*]
**Labdev J Sci Tech Part A** ... Labdev Journal of Science and Technology. Part A. Physical Sciences [*A publication*]
**Labdev Part A** ... Labdev Journal of Science and Technology. Part A. Physical Sciences [*A publication*]
**Labdev Part B** ... Labdev Journal of Science and Technology. Part B. Life Sciences [*A publication*]
**Lab Diagn**.. Laboratoriumi Diagnosztika [*A publication*]
**Lab Dig** ...... Laboratory Digest [*A publication*]
**LABE**......... Lava Beds National Monument
**LABEL** ...... Law Students Association for Buyers' Education in Labeling [*Student legal action organization*]
**Lab and Emp** ... Labour and Employment Gazette [*A publication*]
**Lab and Empl** ... Labour and Employment Gazette [*A publication*]
**Lab and Empl L** ... Labor and Employment Law [*A publication*]
**Lab Ensayo Mater Invest Tecnol An** ... Laboratorio de Ensayo de Materiales e Investigaciones Tecnologicas. Anales [*A publication*]
**Lab Equip Dig** ... Laboratory Equipment Digest [*A publication*]
**LABEX** ...... Laboratory Equipment Exhibition (TSPED)
**LABF** ......... Latin American Banking Federation [*Bogota, Colombia*] (EA)
**Lab Gaz**...... Labour Gazette [*A publication*]
**Lab Gov Chem (GB) Misc Rep** ... Laboratory of the Government Chemist (Great Britain). Miscellaneous Report [*A publication*]
**Lab Gov Chem (GB) Occas Pap** ... Laboratory of the Government Chemist (Great Britain). Occasional Paper [*A publication*]
**L Abh** ......... Abhandlungen. Saechsische Gesellschaft der Wissenschaften zu Leipzig [*A publication*]
**Lab His** ...... Labour History [*A publication*]
**Lab Hist**..... Labor History [*A publication*]
**Lab Hist**..... Labour History [*A publication*] (APTA)

**LABIB**....... LASER Bibliography (MCD)
**LABIL**....... Light Aircraft Binary Information Link
**Lab Ind**...... Labour and Industry [*A publication*]
**Lab Inf Rec**... Labour Information Record [*A publication*]
**Lab Instrum Tech Ser**... Laboratory Instrumentation and Techniques Series [*A publication*]
**Lab Inv**....... Laboratory Investigation [*A publication*]
**Lab Invest**.. Laboratory Investigation [*A publication*]
**LABJ**......... Los Angeles Bar Journal [*A publication*]
**LA B J**........ Louisiana Bar Journal [*A publication*]
**Lab J Australas**... Laboratory Journal of Australasia [*A publication*] (APTA)
**LABL**......... Australian Company Secretary's Business Law Manual [*A publication*]
**LABL**......... Multi-Color Corp. [*NASDAQ symbol*] (NQ)
**LABLD**...... Laboratoriums-Blaetter [*A publication*]
**Lab L J**....... Labor Law Journal [*A publication*]
**Lab L Rep**.. Labor Law Reporter [*Commerce Clearing House*] [*A publication*] (DLA)
**Lab L Rep CCH**... Labor Law Reports. Commerce Clearing House [*A publication*]
**LABMA**..... Laboratory Management [*A publication*]
**Lab Manage**... Laboratory Management [*A publication*]
**Lab Manage Today**... Lab Management Today [*A publication*]
**Lab Med**.... Labor Medica [*Mexico*] [*A publication*]
**Lab Med**.... Laboratory Medicine [*A publication*]
**Lab Microcomput**... Laboratory Microcomputer [*A publication*]
**LABMIS**.... Laboratories Management Information System
**Lab Mo**...... Labour Monthly [*A publication*]
**Lab N**......... Labor News [*A publication*]
**Lab Nac Eng Civ (Port) Mem**... Laboratorio Nacional de Engenharia Civil (Portugal). Memoria [*A publication*]
**Laboratoriumsbl Med Diagn E Behring**... Laboratoriumsblaetter fuer die Medizinische Diagnostik E. V. Behring [*A publication*]
**Labor C**...... Labor Code [*A publication*] (DLA)
**LABORDOC**... International Labour Documentation [*International Labour Office*] [*Geneva, Switzerland*] [*Bibliographic database*]
**Labor His**... Labor History [*A publication*]
**Labor Hist**... Labor History [*A publication*]
**Labor Hyg Occup Dis (Engl Transl)**... Labor Hygiene and Occupational Diseases (English Translation) [*A publication*]
**Labor Hyg Occup Dis (USSR)**... Labor Hygiene and Occupational Diseases (USSR) [*A publication*]
**LABORINFO**... Labour Information Database [*International Labour Office*] [*Information service or system*] (IID)
**Labor Law J**... Labor Law Journal [*A publication*]
**Labor L J**... Labor Law Journal [*A publication*]
**Labor Med**... Labor-Medizin [*A publication*]
**Labor Nts**... Labor Notes [*A publication*]
**LaborPraxis Med**... LaborPraxis in der Medizin [*A publication*]
**Labor Tdy**.. Labor Today [*A publication*]
**Labour**........ Labour/Le Travailleur [*A publication*]
**Labour and Employment Gaz**... Labour and Employment Gazette [*A publication*]
**Labour Gaz**... Labour Gazette [*A publication*]
**Labour Hist**... Labour History [*A publication*] (APTA)
**Labour Mo**... Labour Monthly [*A publication*]
**Labour Res**... Labour Research [*A publication*]
**Labour Research Bul**... Labour Research Bulletin [*A publication*]
**Labour Soc**... Labour and Society [*A publication*]
**Labour Wkly**... Labour Weekly [*A publication*]
**LABP**......... Latin American Book Programs [*Defunct*]
**LABP**......... Lethal Aid for Bomber Penetration (MCD)
**LABPA**...... Laboratory Practice [*A publication*]
**LABPIE**..... Low-Altitude Bombing Position Indicator Equipment [*Military*]
**Lab Ponts Chaussees Bull Liaison**... Laboratoire des Ponts et Chaussees. Bulletin de Liaison [*A publication*]
**Lab Ponts Chaussees Rapp Rech**... Laboratoire des Ponts et Chaussees. Rapport de Recherche [*A publication*]
**LABPR**...... Local Advisory Board Procedural Regulation (Office of Rent Stabilization) [*Economic Stabilization Agency*] [*A publication*] (DLA)
**Lab Pract**... Laboratory Practice [*A publication*]
**Lab Practice**... Laboratory Practice [*A publication*]
**Lab Prax**.... Laboratoriumspraxis [*A publication*]
**Lab Prod For Est (Can) Rapp**... Laboratoire des Produits Forestiers de l'Est (Canada). Rapport [*A publication*]
**LABR**......... Laborer
**L Abr**.......... Lilly's Abridgment [*England*] [*A publication*] (DLA)
**Lab Radiol Dozim Cesk Akad Ved Report**... Laborator Radiologicke Dozimetrie. Ceskoslovenska Akademie Ved. Report [*A publication*]
**LABRAPS**... Laboratoire de Recherche en Administration et Politique Scolaires [*Canada*]
**LABRDR**... Labrador [*Canada*] [*FAA*] (FAAC)
**Lab Rel and Empl News**... Labor Relations and Employment News [*A publication*]
**Lab Rel Guide (P-H)**... Labor Relations Guide (Prentice-Hall, Inc.) [*A publication*] (DLA)
**Lab Rel Rep**... Labor Relations Reporter [*A publication*]
**Lab Rel Rep BNA**... Labor Relations Reporter. Bureau of National Affairs [*A publication*]
**Lab Rep Franklin Inst**... Laboratory Report. Franklin Institute [*A publication*]
**Lab Rep Transp Road Res Lab**... Laboratory Report. Transport and Road Research Laboratory [*Crowthorne*] [*A publication*]
**Lab Res Methods Biol Med**... Laboratory and Research Methods in Biology and Medicine [*A publication*]
**LABREV**... Laboratoire de Recherche sur l'Emploi, la Repartition, et la Securite du Revenu [*University of Quebec at Montreal*] [*Research center*] (RCD)
**Labr Hist**... Labour History [*A publication*]
**LABROC**... Laboratory Rocket
**LABS**......... Laboratory Admission Baseline Studies
**LABS**......... Louisiana Bancshares, Inc. [*Baton Rouge, LA*] [*NASDAQ symbol*] (NQ)
**LABS**......... Low-Altitude Bombing System [*Air Force*]
**LABSAP**.... Laboratoire des Sciences de l'Activite Physique [*Laval University*] [*Canada*] [*Research center*] (RCD)
**LA Bsns Jl**... Los Angeles Business Journal [*A publication*]
**LABSTAT**... Labor Statistics [*Database*] [*Department of Lab r*]
**Lab Tech**.... Laboratoire et Technique [*A publication*]
**Lab Tech Rep Div Mech Eng Natl Res Counc Can**... Laboratory Technical Report. Division of Mechanical Engineering. National Research Council of Canada [*A publication*]
**Lab Tuinbouwplantenteelt Landbouwhogesch Wageningen Publ**... Laboratorium voor Tuinbouwplantenteelt Landbouwhogeschool Wageningen Publikatie [*A publication*]
**LABU**........ Latin American Blind Union [*See also ULAC*] [*Montevideo, Uruguay*] (EAIO)
**LA Bus R**... Louisiana Business Review [*A publication*]
**LA Bus Survey**... Louisiana Business Survey [*A publication*]
**LA Bus Svy**... Louisiana Business Survey [*A publication*]
**LABUT**...... Labor Utilization (MCD)
**LAbV**......... Vermilion Parish Library, Abbeville, LA [*Library symbol*] [*Library of Congress*] (LCLS)
**LabVIEW**.. Laboratory Virtual Instrument Engineering Workbench
**LAC**........... AB Bofors [*Sweden*] [*Research code symbol*]
**LAC**........... Fort Lewis, WA [*Location identifier*] [*FAA*] (FAAL)
**LAC**........... La Crosse [*A bunyavirus*]
**LaC**........... Labiocervical [*Dentistry*]
**LAC**........... Labour Appeal Cases [*India*] [*A publication*] (ILCA)
**LAC**........... Labour Arbitration Cases [*Canada Law Book, Inc.*] [*Information service or system*] [*A publication*] [*A publication*] (CRD)
**LAC**........... Lac Minerals Ltd. [*NYSE symbol*] [*Toronto Stock Exchange symbol*] (SPSG)
**LAC**........... Laceration [*Medicine*]
**Lac**............ Lacerta [*Constellation*]
**LAC**........... LaCrosse [*A virus*]
**LAC**........... Lae-City [*Papua New Guinea*] [*Airport symbol*] (OAG)
**LAC**........... Landers [*California*] [*Seismograph station code, US Geological Survey*] (SEIS)
**LAC**........... Large Acrocentric Chromosome [*Medicine*]
**LAC**........... Large-Area-Counter [*Astronomy*] [*Instrumentation*]
**LAC**........... LASER Amplifier Chain
**LAC**........... Launch Analyst's Console [*Aerospace*] (AAG)
**LAC**........... Launcher Assignment Console
**LAC**........... Leading Aircraftsman [*RAF*] [*British*]
**LAC**........... Learning Assistance Center [*Stanford University*]
**LAC**........... Legal Advisory Committee [*of NYSE*]
**LAC**........... Lemon Administrative Committee (EA)
**LAC**........... Letteratura ed Arte Contemporanea [*A publication*]
**LAC**........... Liberal Academic Complex
**LAC**........... Liberated Areas Committee [*World War II*]
**LAC**........... Liberty Amendment Committee of the USA (EA)
**LAC**........... Licentiate of the Apothecaries' Compan British*]
**LAC**........... Lights Advisory Committee [*General Council of British Shipping*] (DS)
**LAC**........... Limited Area Coverage [*Data*]
**LAC**........... Limiting Admissible Concentration
**LAC**........... Lindamood Auditory Conceptualization Test
**LAC**........... Linear Absorption Coefficient
**LAC**........... Linguoaxiocervical [*Dentistry*]
**LAC**........... Liposome-Antibody-Complement [*Immunochemistry*]
**LAC**........... Liquid Affinity Chromatography
**LAC**........... List of Assessed Contractors [*Military*] (RDA)
**LAC**........... Lithuanian American Community (EA)
**LAC**........... Load Accumulator
**LAC**........... Local Advisory Council [*British labor*]
**LAC**........... Local Agency Check (AFM)
**LAC**........... Local Area Coverage [*Meteorology*]
**LAC**........... Lockheed Aircraft Corporation
**LAC**........... Logistics Area Coordinator (MCD)
**LAC**........... Long-Run Average Cost Curve [*Economics*]
**LAC**........... Longitudinal Aerodynamic Characteristics
**LAC**........... Lunar Aeronautical Chart [*Air Force*]
**LACA**......... Ladies Apparel Contractors Association (EA)
**LACA**......... Life Agency Cashiers Association of the United States and Canada (EA)

**LACA**......... Low-Altitude Control Area
**LACAC**...... Latin American Civil Aviation Commission [*See also CLAC*] (EAIO)
**LAC of AMFC** ... Library Affairs Committee of the Associated Mid-Florida Colleges [*Library network*]
**LACAP**...... Latin American Cooperative Acquisitions Program [*or Project*]
**LACAS**...... LASER Applications in Close Air Support [*Air Force*]
**LACAS**...... Low-Altitude Close Air Support [*Military*]
**LACASA** ... Latin American and Caribbean Solidarity Association (EA)
**La de Castigl** ... Lapus de Castiglionchio [*Flourished, 1353-81*] [*Authority cited in pre-1607 legal work*] (DSA)
**LACAT**...... Legislative Alliance of Creative Arts Therapies (EA)
**LACATA**... Laundry and Cleaners Allied Trades Association [*Later, TCATA*] (EA)
**LACATE**... Lower Atmosphere Composition and Temperature Experiment [*National Science Foundation*]
**LACB**......... Landing Aids Control Building [*NASA*] (NASA)
**LACB**......... Legal Aid Clearinghouse. Bulletin [*A publication*] (APTA)
**LACB**......... Look Angles of Celestial Bodies (KSC)
**LACBWR**.. LaCrosse Boiling Water Reactor [*Also, LCBWR*]
**LACC**......... Latin American and Caribbean Center [*Florida International University*] [*Research center*] (RCD)
**LACC**......... Lloyd's Aviation Claims Centre (AIA)
**LACC**......... Los Angeles City College [*California*]
**LACCB**...... Latin American Confederation of Clinical Biochemistry (EAIO)
**LACCSM**.. Latin American and Caribbean Council for Self-Management (EAIO)
**LACE**......... Language for ALGOL [*Algorithmic Language*] Compiler Extension [*Data processing*] (CSR)
**LACE**......... LASER Aerospace Communications Experiment
**LACE**......... Launch Angle Condition Evaluator
**LACE**......... Launch Automatic Checkout Equipment
**LACE**......... [*The*] Lingerie and Corsetry Exhibition [*British*] (ITD)
**LACE**......... Liquid Air Collection Engine
**LACE**......... Liquid Air Cycle Engine [*Aerospace plane engine concept*]
**LACE**......... Local Automatic Circuit Exchange [*Telecommunications*]
**LACE**......... Lunar Atmospheric Composition Experiment [*Apollo*] [*NASA*]
**LACE**......... Luton Analogue Computing Engine [*British*] (DEN)
**LACES**...... London Airport Cargo Electronic-Data-Processing Scheme
**Lacey Dig**... Lacey's Digest of Railroad Decisions [*A publication*] (DLA)
**Lach**......... Laches [*of Plato*] [*Classical studies*] (OCD)
**LACH**........ Lightweight Amphibious Container Handler (MCD)
**LACHD**..... Liebigs Annalen der Chemie [*A publication*]
**LACHSA**... Licentiate of the Australian College of Health Service Administrators
**LACI**.......... Lipoprotein-Associated Coagulation Inhibitor [*Hematology*]
**LACIE**....... Large Area Crop Inventory Experiment [*NASA*]
**LACIP**....... Large Area Crop Inventory Program [*NASA*] (NASA)
**LA Civ Code Ann (West)** ... West's Louisiana Civil Code, Annotated [*A publication*]
**LA Civ Code Ann (West)** ... West's Louisiana Code of Civil Procedure, Annotated [*A publication*] (DLA)
**Lac Jur**....... Lackawanna Jurist [*A publication*]
**Lacka Leg News** ... Lackawanna Legal News [*Pennsylvania*] [*A publication*] (DLA)
**Lackawanna B** ... Lackawanna Bar Reporter [*Pennsylvania*] [*A publication*] (DLA)
**Lackawanna Inst Pr** ... Lackawanna Institute of History and Science. Proceedings and Collections [*A publication*]
**Lack Bar R** ... Lackawanna Bar Reporter [*Pennsylvania*] [*A publication*] (DLA)
**Lack Co (PA)** ... Lackawanna County Reports [*Pennsylvania*] [*A publication*] (DLA)
**Lack Farben Chem** ... Lack- und Farben-Chemie
**Lack Farben Z** ... Lack- und Farben-Zeitschrift [*A publication*]
**Lack Jur**..... Lackawanna Jurist [*A publication*]
**Lack Jurist** ... Lackawanna Jurist [*A publication*]
**Lack Leg N** ... Lackawanna Legal News [*Pennsylvania*] [*A publication*] (DLA)
**Lack Leg News (PA)** ... Lackawanna Legal News [*Pennsylvania*] [*A publication*] (DLA)
**Lack Leg R** ... Lackawanna Legal Record [*Pennsylvania*] [*A publication*] (DLA)
**Lack Leg Rec** ... Lackawanna Legal Record [*Pennsylvania*] [*A publication*] (DLA)
**Lack LN**..... Lackawanna Legal News [*Pennsylvania*] [*A publication*] (DLA)
**Lack LR**..... Lackawanna Legal Record [*Pennsylvania*] [*A publication*] (DLA)
**LACLA**...... Latin American Constitutional Law Association (EAIO)
**LACM**....... Latin America Common Market [*Proposed*]
**LACMA**..... Latin American and Caribbean Movers Association (EAIO)
**LACMA**..... Los Angeles County Museum of Art
**LACMN**.... Leading Aircrewman [*British military*] (DMA)
**lac-mRNA** ... Ribonucleic Acid, Messenger - lac operon [*Biochemistry, genetics*]
**LACO**........ Liberty American Corporation [*Lincoln, NE*] [*NASDAQ symbol*] (NQ)
**LACO**........ Los Angeles College of Optometry [*California*]
**LA Code Civ Pro Ann** ... West's Louisiana Code of Civil Procedure, Annotated [*A publication*] (DLA)
**LA Code Civ Proc Ann (West)** ... West's Louisiana Code of Civil Procedure, Annotated [*A publication*]
**LA Code Crim Pro Ann** ... West's Louisiana Code of Criminal Procedure, Annotated [*A publication*] (DLA)
**LA Code Crim Proc Ann (West)** ... West's Louisiana Code of Criminal Procedure, Annotated [*A publication*]
**LA Code Juv Proc Ann (West)** ... West's Louisiana Code of Juvenile Procedure, Annotated [*A publication*]
**LACOM**.... Low-Altitude Contour Matching (MCD)
**LACONIQ** ... Laboratory Computer Online Inquiry
**LA Const Art** ... Louisiana Constitution [*A publication*] (DLA)
**LACOTS**... Local Authorities' Coordinating Body on Training Standards [*British*]
**LACP**......... Lignes Aeriennes Canadiennes Pacifiques
**Lacr**........... Lacerta [*Constellation*]
**LACR**......... Latin America Commodities Report [*A publication*]
**LACR**......... Low-Altitude Coverage RADAR
**LACRC**...... Locally Assigned Convoy Route Carrier Code
**LAC REC** .. Lactis Recentis [*New Milk*] [*Pharmacy*] (ROG)
**La Cros Bsn** ... La Crosse City Business [*A publication*]
**Lac RR Dig** ... Lacey's Digest of Railroad Decisions [*A publication*] (DLA)
**LACS**......... Laboratory Automated Calibration System (MCD)
**LACS**......... League Against Cruel Sports (EA)
**LACS**......... Lithuanian-American Catholic Services (EA)
**LACS**......... Los Angeles Catalyst Study [*Environmental Protection Agency*]
**LACS**......... Los Angeles Copyright Society (EA)
**LACSA**...... Lineas Aereas Costarricenses Sociedad Anonima [*Airline*] [*Costa Rica*]
**LACSAB**.... Local Authorities' Conditions of Service Advisory Board [*British*] (DCTA)
**LACSD**...... Los Angeles Council of Engineers and Scientists. Proceedings Series [*A publication*]
**LACT**......... Lease Automatic Custody Transfer
**LACT**......... Low-Affinity Choline Transport
**Lactation Rev** ... Lactation Review [*A publication*]
**LACUNY J** ... LACUNY [*Library Association. City University of New York*] Journal [*A publication*]
**LACUS**...... Linguistic Association of Canada and the United States (EA)
**LACUSA**... Liberty Amendment Committee of the USA (EA)
**LACUSA**... Lithuanian-American Community of the USA [*Later, LAC*] (EA)
**LACV**......... Legal Aid Commission of Victoria [*Australia*]
**LACV**......... Light Amphibious Cargo Vehicle (MCD)
**LACV**......... Light Armored Combat Vehicle
**LACV**......... Lighter, Air-Cushion Vehicle [*Usually used in combination with numerals*] [*Military*] (RDA)
**LACV-30** ... Lighter, Air Cushion Vehicle, 30 Tons [*Military*] (MCD)
**LACW**....... Leading Aircraft Woman [*RAF*] [*British*]
**LACYMCA** ... Latin American Confederation of YMCAs [*See also CLACJ*] (EAIO)
**LAD**.......... Lactate Dehydrogenase [*Also, LD, LDH*] [*An enzyme*]
**LAD**.......... Lactic Acid Dehydrogenase [*See also LDH*] [*An enzyme*]
**LAD**.......... Ladder (MSA)
**lad**............ Ladino [*MARC language code*] [*Library of Congress*] (LCCP)
**LAD**.......... Ladron Mountain [*New Mexico*] [*Seismograph station code, US Geological Survey*] (SEIS)
**LAD**.......... Landing Assist Device [*Aviation*] (NG)
**LAD**.......... Language Acquisition Device
**LAD**.......... Large Area Display
**LAD**.......... LASER Acoustic Delay
**LAD**.......... LASER Acquisition Device (MCD)
**LAD**.......... LASER Acquisition and Direction
**LAD**.......... LASER Air Defense
**LAD**.......... Last Appearance Datum [*Geology*]
**LAD**.......... Lateral Awareness and Directionality Test [*Sensorimotor skills test*]
**LAD**.......... Latest Arrival Date (AABC)
**LAD**.......... Leaf Area Duration [*Botany*]
**LAD**.......... Lebanon Airport Development Corp. [*West Lebanon, NH*] [*FAA designator*] (FAAC)
**LAD**.......... Left Anterior Descending [*Artery*]
**LAD**.......... Left Anterior Digestive [*Gland*]
**LAD**.......... Left Axis Deviation [*Medicine*]
**LAD**.......... Les Amis de Delage [*An association*] (EAIO)
**LAD**.......... Leukocyte Adhesion Deficiency [*Medicine*]
**LAD**.......... Library Administration Division [*American Library Association*] [*Later, LAMA*] (EA)
**LAD**.......... Ligament Augmentation Device [*Sports medicine*]
**LAD**.......... Light Aid Detachment [*Military*] [*British*]
**LAD**.......... Light Area Defense (MCD)
**LAD**.......... Lipoamide Dehydrogenase [*An enzyme*]
**LAD**.......... Liquid Agent Detector (AABC)
**LAD**.......... Lithium Aluminum Deuteride [*Inorganic chemistry*]
**LAD**.......... Lloyd's Aviation Department (AIA)
**LAD**.......... Location Aid Device (MCD)
**LAD**.......... Logical Analysis Device
**LAD**.......... Logical Aptitude Device (BUR)
**LAD**.......... Logistic Approval Data
**LAD**.......... Low-Accuracy Data/Designation [*System*] (MUGU)
**LAD**.......... Low-Altitude Dispenser
**LAD**.......... Low-Angle Dolly

**LAD**.......... Luanda [*Angola*] [*Airport symbol*] (OAG)
**LAD**.......... Lunar Atmosphere Detector [*Aerospace*]
**LAD**.......... Our Lady of Angels College, Aston, PA [*OCLC symbol*] (OCLC)
**LADA**........ Left Acromio-Dorso-Anterior [*A fetal position*] [*Obstetrics*]
**LADA**........ Lesson Analysis Design Approach
**LADA**........ Light Air Defense Artillery [*Army*]
**LADA**........ London Air Defence Area [*British military*] (DMA)
**LA Daily J**... Los Angeles Daily Journal [*A publication*]
**LADAPT**... Lookup Dictionary Adaptor Program (IEEE)
**LADAR**...... LASER Detection and Ranging
**LADAR**...... LASER Doppler RADAR (MCD)
**LADB**........ Laboratory Animal Data Bank [*Battelle Memorial Institute*] [*Columbus, OH*] [*Information service or system*] [*No longer available online*] (IID)
**LADB**........ Latin American Data Bank [*University of Florida*] (IID)
**LADB**........ Latin American Data Base [*An association*] (EA)
**LADC**........ Left Anterior Descending Coronary Artery [*Anatomy*]
**Ladd**.......... Ladd's Reports [*59-64 New Hampshire*] [*A publication*] (DLA)
**LADD**........ Low-Altitude Drogue Delivery (AFM)
**LADDER**... Language Access to Distributed Data with Error Recovery
**LADDER**... Leisure, Activities, Disadvantaged, Disabled, Elderly Resources [*Australia*]
**LADE**........ Lineas Aereas del Estada [*Argentine Air Force airline*]
**LA Dep Conserv Geol Surv Miner Resour Bull**... Louisiana. Department of Conservation. Geological Survey. Mineral Resources Bulletin [*A publication*]
**LA Dep Public Works Basic Rec Rep**... Louisiana. Department of Public Works. Basic Records Report [*A publication*]
**LA Dep Public Works Tech Rep**... Louisiana. Department of Public Works. Technical Report [*A publication*]
**LA Dept Conserv Bienn Rept**... Louisiana. Department of Conservation. Biennial Report [*A publication*]
**LA Dept Public Works Water Res Pamph**... Louisiana. Department of Public Works. Water Resources Pamphlet [*A publication*]
**LADF**......... Ladd Furniture, Inc. [*NASDAQ symbol*] (NQ)
**LADH**......... Liver Alcohol Dehydrogenase [*An enzyme*]
**Lad HJ**....... Ladies' Home Journal [*A publication*]
**LADIES**..... Life after Divorce Is Eventually Sane (EA)
**LADIES**..... Low-Altitude Air Defense Identification and Engagement Study
**Ladies' H J**... Ladies' Home Journal [*A publication*]
**Ladies Home J**... Ladies' Home Journal [*A publication*]
**LADIZ**....... Leaving Air Defense Identification Zone
**LADLE**...... Librarians Antidefamation League
**LADM**........ Laboratory Automated Data Management
**LADP**......... Left Acromio-Dorso-Posterior [*A fetal position*] [*Obstetrics*]
**LADPOP**... Lethal Agent Disposal Process Optimization Program (MCD)
**LADS**......... LASER Air Defense System
**LADS**......... LASER Airborne Depth Sounder
**LADS**......... Light Area Defense System (MCD)
**LADS**......... Lightweight Air Defense System (MCD)
**LADS**......... Limited Attack Defense System
**LADS**......... Local Area Data Set
**LADS**......... Low-Altitude Defense System (MCD)
**LADS**......... Low-Altitude Detection System [*Air Force*]
**LADS**......... Low-Altitude Dispensing System [*Missiles*]
**Lad Schl G**... Ladenschlussgesetz [*A publication*]
**LADT**......... Local Area Data Transport [*AT & T*]
**LADT**......... Low-Altitude Drop Test [*NASA*]
**L Adv**......... Lord Advocate [*British*] (DAS)
**L Advertiser**... Law Advertiser [*1823-31*] [*A publication*] (DLA)
**LADY**......... Tennis Lady, Inc. [*Dallas, TX*] [*NASDAQ symbol*] (NQ)
**LAE**........... Lae [*Papua New Guinea*] [*Airport symbol*] (OAG)
**LAE**........... Lae [*Papua New Guinea*] [*Seismograph station code, US Geological Survey*] [*Closed*] (SEIS)
**LAE**........... Launcher Adapter Electronics (MCD)
**LAE**........... Lead Angle Error
**LAE**........... Leadership Ability Evaluation [*Psychology*]
**LAE**........... Left Arithmetic Element
**LAE**........... Left Atrial Enlargement [*Cardiology*]
**LAE**........... Lethal Area Estimate
**LAE**........... Linear Alcohol Ethoxylate [*Surfactant*]
**LAE**........... "Love Is All" for Enge (EA)
**LAEADA**... Alabama. Agricultural Experiment Station. Leaflet (Auburn University) [*A publication*]
**LAEC**......... Law and Aboriginal and Ethnic Communities [*Curriculum Development Project*] [*Australia*]
**LAECA**...... Land Economics [*A publication*]
**LAECC**...... Groupe International Laicat et Communaute Chretienne [*International Laity and Christian Community Group - ILCCG*] (EA)
**LA Economy**... Louisiana Economy [*A publication*]
**LAED**........ Large Area Electronic Display
**LAEDP**...... Large Area Electronic Display Panel
**LAEF**......... Luso-American Education Foundation (EA)
**LA Eng**...... Louisiana Engineer [*A publication*]
**LAEP**......... Large Area Electronic Panel
**LAER**......... Latin America Economic Report [*A publication*]
**LAER**......... Lowest Achievable Emission Rate [*Environmental Protection Agency*]
**LAET**......... Limiting Actual Exposure Time (KSC)
**LAETRILE**... Laevo-Mandelonitrile-beta-glucuronic Acid [*Possible anticancer compound*]
**LAEV**......... Laevus [*Left*] [*Pharmacy*]
**LAF**........... Lafarge Corp. [*NYSE symbol*] (SPSG)
**LAF**........... Lafayette [*Indiana*] [*Airport symbol*] (OAG)
**LAF**........... Lafayette [*Rhode Island*] [*Seismograph station code, US Geological Survey*] [*Closed*] (SEIS)
**LAF**........... Lafayette College, Easton, PA [*OCLC symbol*] (OCLC)
**LAF**........... Lafayette, IN [*Location identifier*] [*FAA*] (FAAL)
**LAF**........... Laminar Airflow (KSC)
**LAF**........... Landscape Architecture Foundation (EA)
**Laf**............ Lanfrancus [*Deceased, 1089*] [*Authority cited in pre-1607 legal work*] (DSA)
**Laf**............ Lanfrancus Cremensis [*Deceased, 1229*] [*Authority cited in pre-1607 legal work*] (DSA)
**LaF**........... Langue Francaise [*A publication*]
**LAF**........... Left Anterior Fascicle [*Anatomy*]
**LAF**........... Leukocyte-Activating Factor [*Immunochemistry*]
**LAF**........... Limited Amplifier Filter
**LAF**........... Limits and Fits [*System*] [*Precision of tolerance*] [*Automotive engineering*]
**LAF**........... Live Aid Foundation (EA)
**LAF**........... Living Arts Foundation (EA)
**LAF**........... Logistic Availability Factor (CAAL)
**LAF**........... Luteal Angiogenic Factor [*Biochemistry*]
**LAF**........... Lymphocyte Activating Factor [*Immunology*]
**LAF**........... Lyophilized Allantoic Fluid [*Endocrinology*]
**LAFacTLima**... Libro Anual. Facultad de Teologia. Universidad Pontificia y Civil [*Lima, Peru*] [*A publication*]
**Lafayette Clin Stud Schizophr**... Lafayette Clinic. Studies on Schizophrenia [*A publication*]
**LAFB**......... Langley Air Force Base (MCD)
**LAFB**......... Left Anterior Fascicular Block [*Cardiology*]
**LAFB**......... Libyan Arab Foreign Bank
**LAFB**......... Light Assault Floating Bridge [*British military*] (DMA)
**LAFB**......... Lincoln Air Force Base (AAG)
**LAFB**......... Local Authority Fire Brigade [*British*]
**LAFC**......... Latin-American Forestry Commission
**LAFC**......... Loan America Financial Corporation [*Miami Lakes, FL*] [*NASDAQ symbol*] (NQ)
**LAFC**......... Lynn Anderson Fan Club (EA)
**LAFF**......... Launcher Air Filtration Facility
**LAFF**......... Luso-American Fraternal Federation (EA)
**LAFL**......... Latin American Football League [*London, England*]
**LAFOA**...... Laser Focus [*A publication*]
**LA FONT**... La Fontaine [*French author, 1621-1695*] (ROG)
**LA Free P**.. Los Angeles Free Press [*A publication*]
**LAFTA**...... Latin American Association of Freight and Transport Agents (EA)
**LAFTA**...... Latin-American Free Trade Association [*Later, LAIA*]
**LAFTC**...... Latin American Federation of Thermalism and Climatism [*See also FLT*] [*Buenos Aires, Argentina*] (EAIO)
**LAFTO**...... Latin American Confederation of Tourist Organizations [*Buenos Aires, Argentina*] (EAIO)
**LAFTS**....... LASER and FLIR [*Forward-Looking Infrared*] Test Set [*Air Force*]
**LAFTS**....... Los Alamos Fourier Transform Spectrometer [*Department of Energy*] (GRD)
**LAFUS**...... Latvian Association of Foresters in the United States (EA)
**LAFV**......... Light Armoured Fighting Vehicle [*British military*] (DMA)
**LAFY**......... Lafayette United [*NASDAQ symbol*] (NQ)
**LaG**........... La Giustizia [*A publication*]
**LaG**........... Labiogingival [*Dentistry*]
**Lag**........... Lagena [*Flask*] [*Latin*]
**LAG**........... Lagging [*Engineering*]
**LAG**........... Lagoon [*Maps and charts*]
**LAG**........... LaGuardia Community College Library [*UTLAS symbol*]
**LAG**........... Langila [*Cape Gloucester*] [*New Britain*] [*Seismograph station code, US Geological Survey*] (SEIS)
**LAG**........... LASER Absolute Gravimeter
**LAG**........... Lastenausgleichsgesetz (BJA)
**LAG**........... Liga Armada Gallega [*Armed Galician League*] [*Spain*] (PD)
**LAG**........... Linguoaxiogingival [*Dentistry*]
**LAG**........... [*A*] Literary Atlas and Gazetteer of the British Isles [*A publication*]
**LAG**........... Livermore Action Group (EA)
**LAG**........... Load and Go Assembler (BUR)
**LAG**........... Logical Applications Group [*Social Security Administration*]
**LAG**........... London Amusement Guide
**LAG**........... Lymphangiogram [*or Lymphangiography*]
**LAGB**......... Linguistics Association of Great Britain
**LAGB**......... Linhas Aereas da Guine-Bissau [*Airline*] [*Guinea-Bissau*]
**Lag Bull**..... Lag Bulletin [*A publication*]
**LAGE**......... Location of Australian Government Employment Committee
**LAGE**......... Los Angeles Grain Exchange (EA)
**La Geog**...... La Geographie [*A publication*]
**LA Geol Surv Clay Resour Bull**... Louisiana. Geological Survey. Clay Resources Bulletin [*A publication*]
**LA Geol Surv Geol Bull**... Louisiana. Geological Survey. Geological Bulletin [*A publication*]

**LA Geol Surv Miner Resour Bull** ... Louisiana. Geological Survey. Mineral Resources Bulletin [*A publication*]
**LA Geol Surv Water Resour Bull** ... Louisiana. Geological Survey and Department of Public Works. Water Resources Bulletin [*A publication*]
**LA Geol Surv Water Resour Pam** ... Louisiana. Geological Survey and Department of Public Works. Water Resources Pamphlet [*A publication*]
**LAGEOS** ... LASER Geodynamic Satellite [*NASA*]
**LAGG** ........ Fighter [*Russian aircraft symbol*]
**LaGIN** ....... Louisiana Government Information Network [*Louisiana State Library*] [*Baton Rouge*] [*Information service or system*] (IID)
**LAGMA** .... Lawn and Garden Manufacturers Association [*Defunct*] (EA)
**LAGN** ........ Lagoon [*Board on Geographic Names*]
**Lagos HCR** ... Lagos High Court Reports [*A publication*] (DLA)
**Lagos Notes Rec** ... Lagos Notes and Records [*A publication*]
**Lagos R** ...... Judgments in the Supreme Court, Lagos [*1884-92*] [*Nigeria*] [*A publication*] (DLA)
**LAGR** ........ Los Angeles Gear, Inc. [*Los Angeles, CA*] [*NASDAQ symbol*] (NQ)
**LAGS** ......... LASER-Activated Geodetic Satellite [*AFCRL*]
**LAGS** ......... Launch Abort Guide Simulation [*NASA*] (NASA)
**LAGS** ......... Linguistic Atlas of the Gulf States
**LAGUMS** ... LASER-Guided Missile System (MCD)
**Lah** ............ Indian Law Reports, Lahore Series [*A publication*] (DLA)
**Lah** ............ Indian Rulings, Lahore Series [*A publication*] (DLA)
**La H** ........... Labor History [*A publication*]
**LAH** ........... Labuha [*Indonesia*] [*Airport symbol*] (OAG)
**lah** ............ Lahnda [*MARC language code*] [*Library of Congress*] (LCCP)
**LAH** ........... Lahore [*Pakistan*] [*Seismograph station code, US Geological Survey*] [*Closed*] (SEIS)
**LAH** ........... Launch Axis, Horizontal (MCD)
**LAH** ........... Lebanon, NH [*Location identifier*] [*FAA*] (FAAL)
**LAH** ........... Left Anterior Hemiblock [*Cardiology*]
**LAH** ........... Left Atrial Hypertrophy [*Cardiology*]
**LAH** ........... Licentiate of the Apothecaries' Hall [*Dublin*]
**LAH** ........... Lithium Aluminum Hydride [*Inorganic chemistry*]
**LAH** ........... Logical Analyzer of Hypothesis (IEEE)
**LaH** ........... Louisiana History [*A publication*]
**LAH** ........... Low-Altitude Hold [*Military*] (CAAL)
**Lah** ............ Pakistan Law Reports, Lahore Series [*A publication*] (DLA)
**LAHB** ........ Local Authorities Historic Buildings Act [*Town planning*] [*British*]
**Lah Cas** ...... Lahore Cases [*India*] [*A publication*] (DLA)
**Lahey Clin Found Bull** ... Lahey Clinic Foundation. Bulletin [*A publication*]
**LAHF** ........ Latin American Hospital Federation (EAIO)
**LA His Q** ... Louisiana Historical Quarterly [*A publication*]
**LA His S** .... Louisiana Historical Society. Publications [*A publication*]
**LA Hist** ...... Louisiana History [*A publication*]
**LA Hist Quar** ... Louisiana Historical Quarterly [*A publication*]
**LAHIVE** .... Low-Altitude/High-Velocity Experiment
**Lah LJ** ....... Lahore Law Journal [*India*] [*A publication*] (DLA)
**Lah LT** ....... Lahore Law Times [*India*] [*A publication*] (DLA)
**Lahore** ....... All India Reporter, Lahore Series [*A publication*] (ILCA)
**Lahore L Times** ... Lahore Law Times [*India*] [*A publication*] (DLA)
**LAHS** ........ Local Authority Health Services [*British*]
**LAHS** ........ Low-Altitude, High-Speed
**LAI** ............ Labioincisal [*Dentistry*]
**LAI** ............ Lact-Aid International [*Commercial firm*] (EA)
**LAI** ............ Lannion [*France*] [*Airport symbol*] (OAG)
**LAI** ............ Lasir Gold, Inc. [*Vancouver Stock Exchange symbol*]
**LAI** ............ Latin American Institute [*University of New Mexico*] [*Research center*] (RCD)
**LAI** ............ Leaf Area Index [*Forestry*]
**LAI** ............ League Against Imperialism [*Australia*]
**LAI** ............ Lesson Administrative Instructions [*Military*]
**LAI** ............ Leukocyte Adherence Inhibition [*Immunochemistry*]
**LAI** ............ Library Association of Ireland (EAIO)
**LAI** ............ Life Adjustment Inventory [*Psychology*]
**LAI** ............ Load Address Immediate (BUR)
**LAI** ............ Loaded Applicator Impedance
**LAI** ............ Love Attitudes Inventory [*Premarital relations test*] [*Psychology*]
**LAI** ............ Low-Altitude Indicator
**LAIA** .......... Latin American Industrialists Association [*Montevideo, Uruguay*] (EAIO)
**LAIA** .......... Latin American Integration Association [*Formerly, LAFTA*] [*See also ALADI*] (EAIO)
**LAIC** .......... Lithuanian-American Information Center [*Defunct*]
**LAIEC** ....... Latin American Institute of Educational Communication [*Mexico City, Mexico*] (EAIO)
**LAIFS** ........ Los Angeles International Fern Society (EA)
**LAIL** .......... Latin American Indian Literatures [*A publication*]
**LAILA** ....... Latin American Indian Literatures Association (EA)
**LAIMP** ...... Lunar-Anchored Interplanetary Monitoring Platform [*Aerospace*] (MCD)
**LAINA** ....... Laboratory Investigation [*A publication*]
**LAINS** ....... Low-Altitude Inertial Navigation System [*Air Force*]
**LAIR** .......... Letterman Army Institute of Research [*San Francisco, CA*]
**LAIR** .......... Liquid Air (NASA)
**LAIRS** ....... Labor Agreement Information Retrieval System [*Office of Management and Budget*]
**LAIRS** ....... Land-Air Integrated Reduction System (MUGU)
**LAIRS** ....... Lightweight Advanced Inertial Reference Sphere
**LAIRTS** ..... Large Aperture Infrared Telescope System
**LAIS** .......... Labor Arbitration Information System [*LRP Publications*] [*Information service or system*] (CRD)
**LAIS** .......... Leiter Adult Intelligence Scale [*Intelligence test*] [*Psychology*]
**LAIS** .......... Library Acquisitions Information System
**LAIS** .......... Loan Accounting Information System [*Agency for International Development*]
**LAIT** .......... Latex Agglutination Inhibition Test [*for pregnancy*] [*Medicine*]
**LAIT** .......... Logistics Assistance and Instruction Team [*Military*] (AABC)
**LAITS** ........ Latin American Institute for Transnational Studies (EA)
**LAIU** ......... Launch Abort Interface Unit [*NASA*] (MCD)
**LAIWS** ...... Land-Air White Sands (MUGU)
**LAJ** ............ Lajes [*Brazil*] [*Airport symbol*] (OAG)
**LAJ** ............ Los Angeles Junction Railway Co. [*AAR code*]
**LAJPEL** .... Latin American Journal of Politics, Economics, and Law [*A publication*] (DLA)
**LAK** ........... Aklavik [*Canada*] [*Airport symbol*] (OAG)
**LAK** ........... G & E Aviation [*Traverse City, MI*] [*FAA designator*] (FAAC)
**LAK** ........... Laker Resources [*Vancouver Stock Exchange symbol*]
**LAK** ........... Lightweight Antenna Kit
**LaK** ........... Literatur als Kunst [*A publication*]
**LAK** ........... Lymphokine-Activated Killer [*Cells*] [*Immunotherapy*]
**LAKAA** ...... Laekartidningen [*A publication*]
**LAKE** ......... Lakeland Industries, Inc. [*NASDAQ symbol*] (NQ)
**Lakeside** ..... Lakeside Monthly [*A publication*]
**Lakes Lett** ... Lakes Letter [*United States*] [*A publication*]
**LAKFC** ...... Los Angeles Kings Fan Club (EA)
**Lakokras Mater Ikh Primen** ... Lakokrasochnye Materialy i Ikh Primenenie [*A publication*]
**L Akt** .......... Linguistik Aktuell [*A publication*]
**LaL** ............ Labiolingual [*Dentistry*]
**LAL** ............ Lakeland, FL [*Location identifier*] [*FAA*] (FAAL)
**LAL** ............ Lana Gold Corp. [*Vancouver Stock Exchange symbol*]
**LAL** ............ Langley Aeronautical Laboratory [*NASA*]
**LAL** ............ Limulus Amebocyte Lysate
**LAL** ............ Livonia, Avon & Lakeville Railroad Corp. [*AAR code*]
**LAL** ............ Loudspeaker Acoustical Labyrinth
**LAL** ............ Low Air Loss
**LAL** ............ Lower Acceptance Level
**LAL** ............ Lysinoalanine [*An amino acid*]
**LA(L)A** ...... Local Authorities (Land) Act [*Town planning*] [*British*]
**LALA** ......... Low-Altitude Alert [*Air traffic control*]
**LA Law** ...... Los Angeles Lawyer [*A publication*]
**LA Law Rev** ... Louisiana Law Review [*A publication*]
**LALD** ......... Low-Angle Low-Drag
**L Alem** ....... Law of the Alemanni [*A publication*] (DLA)
**LALI** .......... Labiolingual [*Dentistry*]
**LALI** .......... Latin American-Caribbean Labor Institute (EA)
**LA Lib Assn Bull** ... Louisiana Library Association. Bulletin [*A publication*]
**LA Lib Bul** ... Louisiana Library Association. Bulletin [*A publication*]
**LA LJ** ......... Louisiana Law Journal [*New Orleans*] [*A publication*] (DLA)
**LALLL** ....... Low-Altitude Low-Light Level
**LALLS** ....... Low-Angle LASER Light Scattering
**LALM** ........ Limulus Amebocyte Lysate Method
**LALO** ......... Low-Altitude Observation
**Lalor** .......... Lalor's Supplement to Hill and Denio's New York Reports [*A publication*] (DLA)
**Lalor Pol Econ** ... Lalor's Cyclopaedia of Political Science, Political Economy, Etc. [*A publication*] (DLA)
**Lalor's Supp** ... Lalor's Supplement to Hill and Denio's New York Reports [*A publication*] (DLA)
**Lalor's Supp (Hill and Denio)** ... Lalor's Supplement to Hill and Denio's New York Reports [*A publication*] (DLA)
**Lalor Supp** ... Lalor's Supplement to Hill and Denio's New York Reports [*A publication*] (DLA)
**LALP** ......... Longest Activity from Longest Project
**LALR** ......... Latin American Literary Review [*A publication*]
**LALR** ......... Lookahead Left to Right [*Data processing*]
**LA LR** ....... Louisiana Law Review [*A publication*]
**LAlR** ......... Rapides Parish Library, Alexandria, LA [*Library symbol*] [*Library of Congress*] (LCLS)
**LA L Rev** .... Louisiana Law Review [*A publication*]
**Lal RP** ........ Lalor's Law of Real Property [*A publication*] (DLA)
**LALS** ......... LaGuardia Automated Library System [*LaGuardia Community College*] [*Information service or system*] (IID)
**LALS** ......... LASER Alarm Locator System
**LALS** ......... Linkless Ammunition Loading System (MCD)
**LALSD** ...... Language for Automated Logic and System Design [*Data processing*] (CSR)
**lam** ............ Lamba [*MARC language code*] [*Library of Congress*] (LCCP)
**Lam** ............ Lambert [*Unit of luminance*] [*Preferred unit is lx, Lux*]
**Lam** ............ Lambertus de Ramponibus [*Deceased, 1304*] [*Authority cited in pre-1607 legal work*] (DSA)
**Lam** ............ Lamentations [*Old Testament book*]
**LAM** ........... Laminate (MSA)
**LAM** ........... Laminectomy [*Medicine*]
**Lam** ............ Lampas. Tijdschrift voor Nederlandse Classici [*A publication*]

**LAM** .......... Land Attack Mode [*Navy*] (CAAL)
**LaM** .......... Langues Modernes [*A publication*]
**LAM** .......... L'Approdo Musicale [*A publication*]
**LAM** .......... Laramide Resources Ltd. [*Vancouver Stock Exchange symbol*]
**LAM** .......... Late Ambulatory Monitoring [*Medicine*]
**LAM** .......... Latin America Mission (EA)
**LAM** .......... Latin American Investment Fund [*NYSE symbol*] (SPSG)
**LAM** .......... Latin American Mission [*Air Force*]
**LAM** .......... Leading Air Mechanic [*British military*] (DMA)
**LAM** .......... Liberalium Artium Magister [*Master of the Liberal Arts*]
**LA & M** .......... Library Administration and Management
**LAM** .......... Life Action Ministries (EA)
**LAM** .......... Limpet Assembly Modular [*Navy*] (CAAL)
**LAM** .......... Load Accumulator with Magnitude
**LAM** .......... London Academy of Music
**LAM** .......... London's Australian Magazine [*A publication*]
**LAM** .......... Long Aerial Mine [*Military*]
**LAM** .......... Longitudinal Acoustic [*or Acoustical*] Mode [*Spectroscopy*]
**LAM** .......... Loop Addition and Modification [*Data processing*]
**LAM** .......... Los Alamos [*New Mexico*] [*Airport symbol*] (OAG)
**LAM** .......... Los Alamos, NM [*Location identifier*] [*FAA*] (FAAL)
**LAM** .......... Louisiana Motor Freight Bureau [*STAC*]
**LAM** .......... Low-Altitude Missile (MCD)
**LAM** .......... Lymphangioleiomyomatosis [*Medicine*]
**LAM** .......... Master of Liberal Arts
**LAMA** .......... Laboratory Animal Management Association (EA)
**LAMA** .......... Latin American Manufacturers Association [*Washington, DC*] (EA)
**LAMA** .......... Lead Air Materiel Area [*Air Force*]
**LAMA** .......... Legal Assistant Management Association (EA)
**LAMA** .......... Library Administration and Management Association (EA)
**LAMA** .......... Light Aircraft Manufacturers' Association (EA)
**LAMA** .......... Livestock Auction Markets Association (EA)
**LAMA** .......... Local Automatic Message Accounting [*Telecommunications*] (TEL)
**LAMAA** .... Lakokrasochnye Materialy i Ikh Primenenie [*A publication*]
**LAMA BES** ... LAMA [*Library Administration and Management Association*] Buildings and Equipment Section
**LAMACHA** ... Louisiana-Alabama-Mississippi Automated Clearing House Association
**LAMA FRFDS** ... LAMA [*Library Administration and Management Association*] Fund Raising and Financial Development Section
**LAMA LOMS** ... LAMA [*Library Administration and Management Association*] Library Organization and Management Section
**LAMA PAS** ... LAMA [*Library Administration and Management Association*] Personnel Administration Section
**LAMA PRS** ... LAMA [*Library Administration and Management Association*] Public Relations Section
**Lamar** .......... Lamar's Reports [*25-40 Florida*] [*A publication*] (DLA)
**LAMAR** ..... Large Area Modular Array of Reflectors [*Astronomy*]
**LAMAR** ..... Linear-Elastic Matrix Analysis Routine
**LAMARS** .. Large Amplitude Multimode Aerospace Research Simulator
**LAMAS** ..... Location and Movement Analysis System (MCD)
**LAMA SASS** ... LAMA [*Library Administration and Management Association*] Systems and Services Section
**LAMA SS** ... LAMA [*Library Administration and Management Association*] Statistics Section
**LAMA SSS** ... LAMA [*Library Administration and Management Association*] Systems and Services Section
**Lamb** .......... [*William*] Lambard [*Deceased, 1601*] [*Authority cited in pre-1607 legal work*] (DSA)
**Lamb** .......... Lambard's Archaionomia [*A publication*] (DLA)
**Lamb** .......... Lambard's Archeion [*1635*] [*A publication*] (DLA)
**Lamb** .......... Lambard's Eirenarcha [*A publication*] (DLA)
**Lamb** .......... Lambard's Explication [*A publication*] (DLA)
**LAMB** .......... Lambeth [*Degrees granted by Archbishop of Canterbury*] [*British*] (ROG)
**LAMB** .......... Lambourne [*England*]
**Lamb** .......... Lamb's Reports [*103-105 Wisconsin*] [*A publication*] (DLA)
**LAMB** .......... Light Armoured Motor Brigade [*British military*] (DMA)
**LAMB** .......... Local Area Multiuser Board [*American Micronics*] [*Data processing*]
**LAMB** .......... Los Alamos Water Boiler (NRCH)
**Lamb Arch** ... Lambard's Archaionomia [*A publication*] (DLA)
**Lamb Arch** ... Lambard's Archeion [*1635*] [*A publication*] (ILCA)
**Lamb Archaion** ... Lambard's Archaionomia [*A publication*] (DLA)
**Lamb Const** ... Lambard's Duties of Constables, Etc. [*A publication*] (DLA)
**Lamb Dow** ... Lambert's Law of Dower [*A publication*] (DLA)
**Lamb Eir** .... Lambard's Eirenarcha [*A publication*] (DLA)
**Lamb Eiren** ... Lambard's Eirenarcha [*A publication*] (DLA)
**Lamber de Sal** ... Lambertus de Salinis [*Flourished, 14th century*] [*Authority cited in pre-1607 legal work*] (DSA)
**Lamb Explic** ... Lambard's Explication [*A publication*] (DLA)
**Lamb de Ramp** ... Lambertus de Ramponibus [*Deceased, 1304*] [*Authority cited in pre-1607 legal work*] (DSA)
**LAMBS** ..... Laboratory Animal Management and Business Systems [*Data processing*]
**LAMC** .......... Language and Mode Converter [*Data processing*] (TEL)
**LAMC** .......... Last Maneuver Calculation [*Orbit identification*]
**LAMC** .......... Letterman Army Medical Center (AABC)
**LAMC** .......... Lima Army Modification Center (RDA)
**LAMCO** .... Liberian American-Swedish Minerals Company
**LAMCS** ..... Latin American Military Communications System
**LAMDA** .... [*The*] London Academy of Music and Dramatic Art
**LAME** .......... Lake Mead National Recreation Area
**LAME** .......... Licensed Aircraft Maintenance Engineer (ADA)
**LAMEA** ..... Laval Medical [*A publication*]
**LAMEF** ..... Los Alamos Medium Energy Facility
**LAMG** .......... Laban Art of Movement Guild [*Later, LG*] (EA)
**LAMIE7** .... Letters in Applied Microbiology [*A publication*]
**LAMIT** ...... Local Authorities' Mutual Investment Trust [*British*]
**LAMM** ...... Leitfaeden fuer Angewandte Mathematik und Mechanik [*A publication*]
**LAMMA** ... LASER Microprobe Mass Analyzer [*Spectrometry*]
**LAMMR** ... Large Antenna Multifrequency Microwave Radiometer (MCD)
**LAMMS** .... LASER Microprobe Mass Spectrometry [*or Spectroscopy*]
**La Molina Peru Estac Exp Agric Inf** ... La Molina Peru Estacion Experimental Agricola. Informe [*A publication*]
**LAMOPH** ... Ladies Auxiliary, Military Order of the Purple Heart, United States of America (EA)
**LAMP** .......... Center for the Study of Legal Authority and Mental Patient Status (EA)
**LAMP** .......... Laos Ammunition Procedures (CINC)
**LAMP** .......... Large Advanced Mirror Program [*Military*] (SDI)
**LAMP** .......... LASER and MASER Patents
**LAMP** .......... Laser Microbeam Program [*Research center*] (RCD)
**LAMP** .......... LASER and Mixing Program
**LAMP** .......... Leap and Stamp [*Dance terminology*]
**LAMP** .......... Library Addition and Maintenance Program
**LAMP** .......... Life Agency Management Program [*GAMC*]
**LAMP** .......... Light Airborne Multipurpose System [*Navy*] (MCD)
**LAMP** .......... Logistics Automation Master PLan [*Military*]
**LAMP** .......... Louis Armstrong Memorial Project
**LAMP** .......... Low-Altitude Manned Penetrator
**LAMP** .......... SOI Industries, Inc. [*NASDAQ symbol*] (NQ)
**LAMPF** ..... Los Alamos Meson Physics Facility [*Later, Clinton P. Anderson Meson Physics Facility at Los Alamos*] [*Department of Energy*]
**LAMP-H** ... Lighter, Amphibian Heavy Lift
**LAMPP** ..... Los Alamos Molten Plutonium Program
**LAMPRE** .. Los Alamos Molten Plutonium Reactor Experiment
**LAMPS** ..... Large Amplitude SLOSH [*Sea, Lake, Overland Surge from Hurricanes*] [*NASA*]
**LAMPS** ..... Light Airborne Multiple Package System
**LAMPS** ..... Light Airborne Multipurpose System [*Navy*]
**LamR** .......... Lamentations Rabbah (BJA)
**LAMR** .......... Latin American Music Review [*A publication*]
**LAMRL** ..... Logistic Area Material Readiness List [*Military*] (AFIT)
**LAMRTPI** ... Legal Associate Member of the Royal Town Planning Institute [*British*] (DBQ)
**LAMS** .......... Land Acoustical Monitoring System [*NASA*]
**LAMS** .......... Land Acquisition and Management Schemes [*British*]
**LAMS** .......... Large Atypical Mole Syndrome [*Medicine*]
**LAMS** .......... Load Alleviation and Mode Stabilization
**LAMS** .......... London Aero Motor Services
**LAMSA** ..... Lineas Aereas Mexicana, Sociedad Anonima
**LAMSAC** .. Local Authorities' Management Services and Computer Committee [*British*]
**LAMSIM** .. Launcher and Missile Simulator
**L Am Soc** ... Law in American Society [*A publication*] (DLA)
**L Am Soc'y** ... Law in American Society [*A publication*] (DLA)
**LAmT** .......... Tangipahoa Parish Library, Amite, LA [*Library symbol*] [*Library of Congress*] (LCLS)
**LAMTD** ..... Laminated
**LAMTS** ..... Launcher Adapter Missile Test Set
**LAN** .......... Inland [*Aviation code*]
**LAN** .......... Lanarkshire [*County in Scotland*]
**LAN** .......... Lancer Corp. [*AMEX symbol*] (SPSG)
**LAN** .......... Lanchow [*Republic of China*] [*Seismograph station code, US Geological Survey*] [*Closed*] (SEIS)
**Lan** .......... Landulfus Acconzaioco [*Flourished, 13th century*] [*Authority cited in pre-1607 legal work*] (DSA)
**Lan** .......... Lanfrancus [*Deceased, 1089*] [*Authority cited in pre-1607 legal work*] (DSA)
**Lan** .......... Lanfrancus Cremensis [*Deceased, 1229*] [*Authority cited in pre-1607 legal work*] (DSA)
**lan** .......... Langue d'Oc [*MARC language code*] [*Library of Congress*] (LCCP)
**LAN** .......... Lansing [*Michigan*] [*Airport symbol*] (OAG)
**LAN** .......... Lansing, MI [*Location identifier*] [*FAA*] (FAAL)
**LAN** .......... Latin America Newsletters [*A publication*]
**LAN** .......... Latin American Newsletters [*Latin American Newsletters Ltd.*] [*Great Britain*] [*Information service or system*] (IID)
**LAN** .......... Library Automation and Networks
**LAN** .......... Life Association News [*A publication*]
**LAN** .......... Lime-Ammonium-Nitrate [*Fertilizer*]
**LAN** .......... Linea Aerea Nacional [*National Airline*] [*Chile*]
**LAN** .......... Linked Access Network
**LAN** .......... Local Apparent Noon [*Navigation*]
**LAN** .......... Local Area Network [*Telecommunications*]

**LAN**.......... Local Area Networks [*Information Gatekeepers, Inc.*] [*Information service or system*] [*No longer available online*] (CRD)
**LAN**.......... Longitude of the Ascending Node
**LAN**.......... Mesa Public Library, Los Alamos, NM [*OCLC symbol*] (OCLC)
**LAN**.......... Panorama Air Tour, Inc. [*Honolulu, HI*] [*FAA designator*] (FAAC)
**LANA**........ Language Analog [*Project*]
**LANA**........ Liquid Air Corp. [*Formerly, Liquid Air of North America*] [*NASDAQ symbol*] (NQ)
**LANA**........ Lithuanian American National Alliance (EA)
**LANA**........ Llama Association of North America (EA)
**LANABS**... Light Attack Navigation and Bombing System (MCD)
**LANAC**..... Laminar Air Navigation and Anticollision [*Air Force*]
**LANAC**..... Lawyers Alliance for Nuclear Arms Control [*Later, LAWS*] (EA)
**Lan Acon**.... Landulfus Acconzaioco [*Flourished, 13th century*] [*Authority cited in pre-1607 legal work*] (DSA)
**Lanbau Vol**... Lanbauforschung Volkenrode [*A publication*]
**LANBY**...... Large Automatic Navigational Buoy [*Shipping*] (DS)
**LANC**........ Lancaster [*England*] (ROG)
**LANC**........ Lancaster Colony Corp. [*NASDAQ symbol*] (NQ)
**Lanc**........... Lancellottus [*Authority cited in pre-1607 legal work*] (DSA)
**LANC**........ Lancer [*Military*] [*British*] (ROG)
**LANC**........ Land. Newsletter. Lands Directorate. Environment Canada [*A publication*]
**LANC**........ Liga Apararii Nationale Crestine [*League of National Christian Defense*] [*Romania*] [*Political party*] (PPE)
**LANCA**..... Lancet [*A publication*]
**Lancell Galiaul**... Lancellottus Galiaula [*Flourished, 16th century*] [*Authority cited in pre-1607 legal work*] (DSA)
**Lanchow Univ J Nat Sci**... Lanchow University Journal. Natural Sciences [*People's Republic of China*] [*A publication*]
**Lanc Law Rev**... Lancaster Law Review [*A publication*] (DLA)
**Lanc L Rev**... Lancaster Law Review [*A publication*] (DLA)
**LANCO**..... Landscape Nursery Council (EA)
**LANCRA**... Landing Craft
**LANCRAB**... Landing Craft and Bases [*Military*]
**LANCRABEU**... Landing Craft and Bases, Europe [*Navy*]
**LANCRABNAW**... Landing Craft and Bases, Northwest African Waters [*World War II*] [*Navy*]
**Lan Cre**...... Lanfrancus Cremensis [*Deceased, 1229*] [*Authority cited in pre-1607 legal work*] (DSA)
**Lanc Rev**.... Lancaster Review [*Pennsylvania*] [*A publication*] (DLA)
**LANCS**...... Lancashire [*County in England*]
**Land**.......... Land. Bureau of Land Management [*Alaska*] [*A publication*]
**Land**.......... Land and Land News [*A publication*]
**LAND**........ Lane Wood, Inc. [*NASDAQ symbol*] (NQ)
**LAND**........ League Against Nuclear Dangers [*Defunct*] (EA)
**LANDA**..... Ladies Auxiliary to the National Dental Association [*Later, ANDA*] (EA)
**Land A**....... Landarzt [*A publication*]
**Land App Ct Cas**... Land Appeal Court Cases [*New South Wales*] [*A publication*] (APTA)
**Landarb**..... Landarbeit [*A publication*]
**Landarb Tech**... Landarbeit und Technik [*A publication*]
**Land Arch**... Landscape Architecture [*A publication*]
**Landbauforsch Voelkenrode**... Landbauforschung Voelkenrode [*A publication*]
**Landbauforsch Voelkenrode Sonderh**... Landbauforschung Voelkenrode. Sonderheft [*A publication*]
**Landbouwkd Tijdschr**... Landbouwkundig Tijdschrift [*A publication*]
**Landbouwmechan**... Landbouwmechanisatie [*A publication*]
**Landbouwproefstn Suriname Bull**... Landbouwproefstation Suriname. Bulletin [*A publication*]
**Landbouwproefstn Suriname Meded**... Landbouwproefstation Suriname. Mededeling [*A publication*]
**Landbouwvoorl**... Landbouwvoorlichting [*A publication*]
**Landbouwvoorlichting**... Rijkslandbouwvoorlichtingsdienst [*A publication*]
**Landbrugsokonomiske Stud Copenh Vet Landbohojsk Okon Inst**... Landbrugsokonomiske. Studier. Copenhagen Veterinaer. Og Landbohojskole. Okonomisk Institut [*A publication*]
**LANDCENT**... Allied Land Forces Central Europe [*NATO*]
**Land Comp Rep**... Land Reports, by Roche, Dillon, and Kehoe [*1881-82*] [*Ireland*] [*A publication*] (DLA)
**Land Com Rep**... Land Reports, by Roche, Dillon, and Kehoe [*1881-82*] [*Ireland*] [*A publication*] (DLA)
**Land Conserv Ser Dep NT**... Land Conservation Series. Department of the Northern Territory [*A publication*] (APTA)
**LANDCRA**... Landing Craft and Bases [*Military*] (AFIT)
**LANDCRAB**... Landing Craft and Bases [*Military*] (AABC)
**Land Dec**... Land Decisions, United States [*A publication*] (DLA)
**Land Econ**... Land Economics [*A publication*]
**LANDENMARK**... Allied Land Forces Denmark [*NATO*]
**Landerbank**... Landerbank Economic Bulletin [*A publication*]
**Land Est C**... Landed Estates Court [*England*] (DLA)
**LANDEX**... Landing Exercise [*Navy*] (CAAL)
**LANDFAE**... Large Area Nozzle Delivery of Fuel Air Explosive (RDA)
**LANDFOR**... Landing Force [*Military*]
**LANDFORASCU**... Landing Force Air Support Control Unit [*Navy*]
**LANDIS**.... Low-Approach Navigation Director System [*Aircraft landing aid*] [*Air Force*]
**Landis & Gyr Rev**... Landis and Gyr Review [*A publication*]
**Land Issues Probl VA Polytech Inst State Univ Coop Ext Serv**... Land Issues and Problems. Virginia Polytechnic Institute and State University. Cooperative Extension Service [*A publication*]
**LANDJUT**... Allied Land Forces Schleswig-Holstein and Jutland [*NATO*] (NATG)
**LANDLD**.. Landlord (ROG)
**Land Loon**... Het Oude Land van Loon. Jaarboek van de Federatie der Geschied- en Oudheidkundige Kringen van Limburg [*A publication*]
**Land L Serv**... Land Laws Service [*A publication*] (APTA)
**Landmasch-Markt**... Landmaschinen-Markt [*A publication*]
**Landmasch Rundsch**... Landmaschinen-Rundschau [*A publication*]
**Landmasch-Rundschau**... Landmaschinen-Rundschau [*West Germany*] [*A publication*]
**Land Miner Surv**... Land and Minerals Surveying [*London*] [*A publication*]
**LANDNON**... Allied Land Forces North Norway [*NATO*] (NATG)
**LANDNORTH**... Allied Land Forces Northern Europe [*NATO*] (NATG)
**LANDNORWAY**... Allied Land Forces Norway [*NATO*]
**Landoekonom Forsoglab Aarbog (Copenhagen)**... Landoekonomisk Forsogslaboratorium Aarbog (Copenhagen) [*A publication*]
**Landokon Forsogslab Efterars**... Landoekonomisk Forsogslaboratoriums Efterarsmode [*A publication*]
**Landowning in Scot**... Landowning in Scotland [*A publication*]
**Land Reform**... Land Reform, Land Settlement, and Cooperatives [*A publication*]
**Land Resour Dev Cent Tech Bull**... Land Resources Development Centre. Technical Bulletin [*A publication*]
**Land Resour Div Dir Overseas Surv Land Resour Study**... Land Resources Division. Directorate of Overseas Surveys. Land Resource Study [*A publication*]
**Land Resour Div Dir Overseas Surv Tech Bull**... Land Resources Division. Directorate of Overseas Surveys. Technical Bulletin [*A publication*]
**Land Resour Manage Ser Div Land Resour Manage CSIRO**... Land Resources Management Series. Division of Land Resources Management. Commonwealth Scientific and Industrial Research Organisation [*A publication*] (APTA)
**Land Resour Mgmt Ser Div Land Resour Mgmt CSIRO**... Land Resources Management Series. Division of Land Resources Management. Commonwealth Scientific and Industrial Research Organisation [*A publication*] (APTA)
**Land Resour Stud Land Resour Div Dir Overseas Surv**... Land Resource Study. Land Resources Division. Directorate of Overseas Surveys [*A publication*]
**Land Res Ser Commonw Sci Industr Res Organ (Aust)**... Land Research Series. Commonwealth Scientific and Industrial Research Organisation (Melbourne, Australia) [*A publication*]
**Land Res Ser CSIRO**... Land Research Series. Commonwealth Scientific and Industrial Research Organisation [*A publication*] (APTA)
**Land Res Ser CSIRO (Aust)**... Land Research Series. Commonwealth Scientific and Industrial Research Organisation (Australia) [*A publication*]
**LANDS**...... Landsearch [*Database*] [*Australia*]
**LANDSC**... Landscape
**Landscape Arch**... Landscape Architecture [*A publication*]
**Landscape Archre**... Landscape Architecture [*A publication*]
**Landscape Des**... Landscape Design [*A publication*]
**Landscape Intl**... Landscape International [*A publication*]
**Landscape Plann**... Landscape Planning [*A publication*]
**Landscape Res**... Landscape Research [*A publication*]
**Landsc Arch**... Landscape Architecture [*A publication*]
**LANDSONOR**... Allied Land Forces South Norway [*NATO*] (NATG)
**LANDSOUTH**... Allied Land Forces Southern Europe [*NATO*]
**LANDSOUTHEAST**... Allied Land Forces Southeastern Europe [*NATO*]
**Land of Sun**... Land of Sunshine [*A publication*]
**Landtech**... Landtechnik [*A publication*]
**Landtech Forsch**... Landtechnische Forschung [*A publication*]
**Land-Tuinbouw Jaarb**... Land en Tuinbouw Jaarboek [*A publication*]
**LANDUP**.. Alberta Land Use Planning Data Bank [*Alberta Municipal Affairs*] [*Information service or system*] [*Defunct*] (IID)
**Land U Pl Rep**... Land Use Planning Reports [*A publication*] (DLA)
**Land Use Built Form Stud Inf Notes**... Land Use Built Form Studies. Information Notes [*A publication*]
**Land Use Built Form Stud Reps**... Land Use Built Form Studies. Reports [*A publication*]
**Land Use Built Form Stud Wking Paps**... Land Use Built Form Studies. Working Papers [*A publication*]
**Land Use Built Form Tech Notes**... Land Use Built Form Studies. Technical Notes [*A publication*]
**Land Use and Env L Rev**... Land Use and Environment Law Review [*A publication*]
**Land Use & Env't L Rev**... Land Use and Environment Law Review [*A publication*] (DLA)
**Land Use Law and Zoning Dig**... Land Use Law and Zoning Digest [*A publication*]
**Land & Water LR**... Land and Water Law Review [*A publication*]
**Land & Water L Rev**... Land and Water Law Review [*A publication*]
**Landw Fo**... Landwirtschaftliche Forschung [*A publication*]

**Landw Forsch** ... Landwirtschaftliche Forschung [*A publication*]
**Landw G**..... Landwirtschaftsgesetz [*A publication*]
**Landwirt** .... Landwirtschaft [*A publication*]
**Landwirt-Angew Wiss Bundesmin Ernahr Landwirt Forsten** ... Landwirtschaft-Angewandte Wissenschaft. Bundesministerium fuer Ernaehrung, Landwirtschaft, und Forsten [*A publication*]
**Landwirt Forsch Sonderh** ... Landwirtschaftliche Forschung. Sonderheft [*A publication*]
**Landwirtsch Angew Wiss** ... Landwirtschaft-Angewandte Wissenschaft [*A publication*]
**Landwirtsch Chem Bundesversuchsanst (Linz) Veroeff** ... Landwirtschaftlich-Chemische Bundesversuchsanstalt (Linz). Veroeffentlichungen [*A publication*]
**Landwirtsch Forsch** ... Landwirtschaftliche Forschung [*A publication*]
**Landwirtsch Jahrb** ... Landwirtschaftliche Jahrbuecher [*A publication*]
**Landwirtsch Jahrb Schweiz** ... Landwirtschaftliches Jahrbuch der Schweiz [*A publication*]
**Landwirt Schriftenr Boden Pflanze** ... Landwirtschaftliche Schriftenreihe Boden und Pflanze [*A publication*]
**Landwirtsch Ver Stn** ... Landwirtschaftlichen Versuchs-Stationen [*A publication*]
**Landwirt Zentralbl** ... Landwirtschaftliches Zentralblatt [*A publication*]
**Landw Jb Bay** ... Landwirtschaftliches Jahrbuch fuer Bayern [*A publication*]
**Landw Jb Schweiz** ... Landwirtschaftliches Jahrbuch der Schweiz [*A publication*]
**Landw Mh** ... Landwirtschaftliche-Monatshefte [*A publication*]
**Landw Wbl Kurhessen-Waldeck** ... Landwirtschaftliches Wochenblatt fuer Kurhessen-Waldeck [*A publication*]
**Landw Wbl (Muenchen)** ... Landwirtschaftliches Wochenblatt (Muenchen) [*A publication*]
**Landw Wbl Westf Lippe** ... Landwirtschaftliches Wochenblatt fuer Westfalen und Lippe [*A publication*]
**LANDZEALAND** ... Allied Land Forces Zealand [*NATO*] (NATG)
**LANE** ........ Labrador Nor-Eastern [*A publication*]
**LANE** ........ [*The*] Lane Co., Inc. [*NASDAQ symbol*] (NQ)
**Lane** ........... Lane's English Exchequer Reports [*1605-12*] [*A publication*] (DLA)
**LANE** ........ Linguistic Atlas of New England
**LANFORTRACOMLANT** ... Landing Force Training Command, Atlantic [*Navy*]
**Lang** ........... Langages [*Paris*] [*A publication*]
**LANG** ........ Langley [*England*]
**LANG** ........ Language (AFM)
**Lang** ........... Language [*A publication*]
**L Ang** ......... Los Angeles Medical Journal [*A publication*]
**LangA** ........ Language and Automation [*A publication*]
**LangAb** ...... Language and Language Behavior Abstracts [*A publication*]
**Lang Arts** ... Language Arts [*A publication*]
**Lang Autom** ... Language and Automation [*A publication*]
**Lang and C** ... Language and Culture [*Hokkaido University*] [*A publication*]
**Lang Ca Cont** ... Langdell's Cases on Contracts [*A publication*] (DLA)
**Lang Ca Sales** ... Langdell's Cases on the Law of Sales [*A publication*] (DLA)
**Lang and Commun** ... Language and Communication [*A publication*]
**Lang Cont** .. Langdell's Cases on Contracts [*A publication*] (DLA)
**Lang Cont** .. Langdell's Summary of the Law of Contracts [*A publication*] (DLA)
**Langd Cont** ... Langdell's Cases on Contracts [*A publication*] (DLA)
**Langd Cont** ... Langdell's Summary of the Law of Contracts [*A publication*] (DLA)
**Langenbeck** ... Langenbecks Archiv fuer Chirurgie [*A publication*]
**Langenbecks Arch Chir** ... Langenbecks Archiv fuer Chirurgie [*A publication*]
**Lang Eq Pl** ... Langdell's Cases in Equity Pleading [*A publication*] (DLA)
**Lang Eq Pl** ... Langdell's Summary of Equity Pleading [*A publication*] (DLA)
**Lang Fr** ...... Langue Francaise [*A publication*]
**LangL** ......... Language Learning [*A publication*]
**Lang & L** .... Language and Literature [*A publication*]
**Lang Lang Behav Abstr** ... Language and Language Behavior Abstracts. LLBA [*A publication*]
**Lang Learn** ... Language Learning [*A publication*]
**Lang Mod** .. Langues Modernes [*A publication*]
**LangMono** ... Language Monographs [*A publication*]
**LangQ** ........ Language Quarterly [*A publication*]
**Lang R** ....... Language Research [*A publication*]
**LangS** ......... Language Sciences [*A publication*]
**Lang & S** .... Language and Style [*A publication*]
**Lang S** ........ Language and Style [*A publication*]
**Lang Sales** ... Langdell's Cases on the Law of Sales [*A publication*] (DLA)
**Lang Soc** .... Language in Society [*London*] [*A publication*]
**Lang Speech** ... Language and Speech [*A publication*]
**Lang & Speech** ... Language and Speech [*A publication*]
**Lang Speech & Hearing Serv Sch** ... Language, Speech, and Hearing Services in Schools [*A publication*]
**Lang Speech Hear Serv Sch** ... Language, Speech, and Hearing Services in Schools [*A publication*]
**Lang Style** ... Language and Style [*A publication*]
**Lang Sum Cont** ... Langdell's Summary of the Law of Contracts [*A publication*] (DLA)
**LangTAb** .... Language Teaching Abstracts [*Later, Language Teaching and Linguistics Abstracts*] [*A publication*]
**Lang Teach** ... Language Teaching [*A publication*]
**Lang Teach & Ling Abstr** ... Language Teaching and Linguistics Abstracts [*A publication*]
**Lang Teach Linguist Abstr** ... Language Teaching and Linguistics Abstracts [*A publication*]
**Lang Tr** ...... Langley's Trustees' Act [*A publication*] (DLA)
**Langue et Culture** ... Notre Langue et Notre Culture [*A publication*]
**Langues et L** ... Langues et Linguistique [*A publication*]
**LANH** ........ Launch (MSA)
**LAN Harris** ... Local Area Networks. A Harris Perspective [*A publication*]
**LANIC** ....... LAN [*Local Area Network*] Interface Card (PCM)
**LANICA** .... Lineas Aereas de Nicaragua, SA [*Nicaraguan airline*]
**LANL** ........ Los Alamos National Laboratory [*Department of Energy*] [*Los Alamos, NM*]
**LanM** ......... Langues Modernes [*A publication*]
**L Ann** ......... Louisiana Annual Reports [*A publication*] (DLA)
**LANNET** ... Large Artificial Nerve [*or Neuron*] Network
**LAnP** .......... Louisiana State Penitentiary, Angola, LA [*Library symbol*] [*Library of Congress*] (LCLS)
**LAN/RM** ... Local Area Network Reference Model
**Lans** ........... Lansing's New York Supreme Court Reports [*A publication*] (DLA)
**Lans** ........... Lansing's Reports [*New York*] [*A publication*]
**LANS** ......... Large Atypical Nevus Syndrome [*Medicine*]
**LANS** ......... Lightweight Airborne Navigation System (MCD)
**LANS** ......... Local Area Network System [*Telecommunications*]
**LANS** ......... LORAN Airborne Navigation System (IEEE)
**LANSA** ...... Lineas Aereas Nacionales Consolidadas Sociedad Anonima
**LANSCE** ... Los Alamos Neutron Scattering Center
**Lans Ch** ...... Lansing's Select Cases in Chancery [*1824, 1826*] [*New York*] [*A publication*] (DLA)
**Lansg** ......... New York Supreme Court Reports (Lansing) [*A publication*] (DLA)
**LANSHIPRON** ... Landing Ship Squadron (CINC)
**Lansing** ...... New York Supreme Court Reports (Lansing) [*A publication*] (DLA)
**Lans Sel Cas** ... Lansing's Select Cases in Chancery [*1824, 1826*] [*New York*] [*A publication*] (DLA)
**LANT** ........ Atlantic
**Lantbrhogsk Annlr** ... Lantbrukshogskolans Annaler [*A publication*]
**Lantbrhogsk Meddn** ... Lantbrukshogskolans Meddelanden [*A publication*]
**Lantbruks-Hoegsk Ann** ... Lantbruks-Hoegskolans Annaler [*A publication*]
**Lantbrukshoegsk Jordbruksfoersoeksanst Medd** ... Lantbrukshoegskolan Jordbruksfoersoeksanstalten Meddelands [*A publication*]
**Lantbrukshogsk Ann** ... Lantbrukshogskolans Annaler [*A publication*]
**Lantbrukshogsk Husdjursforsoksanst Medd** ... Lantbrukshogskolan Husdjursforsoksanstalten Meddelande [*A publication*]
**Lantbrukshogsk Meddel** ... Lantbrukshogskolans Meddelanden [*A publication*]
**Lantbrukshogsk Medd Ser A** ... Lantbrukshogskolans Meddelanden. Series A [*A publication*]
**Lantbrukshogsk Medd Ser B** ... Lantbrukshogskolans Meddelanden. Series B [*A publication*]
**Lantbrukshogsk Vaxtskyddsrapp Tradg** ... Lantbrukshogskolan Vaxtskyddsrapporter Tradgard [*A publication*]
**Lantbrukstidskr Stockholms Lan Stad** ... Lantbrukstidskrift foer Stockholms Lan och Stad [*A publication*]
**LANTCOM** ... Atlantic Command [*Navy*]
**LANTCOMOPCONCEN** ... Atlantic [*Fleet*] Commander Operational Control Center [*Navy*]
**Lanterne Med** ... Lanterne Medicale [*A publication*]
**LANTFAP** ... Allied Command Atlantic Frequency Allocation Panel [*Obsolete*] [*NATO*] (NATG)
**LANTFLEASWTACSCOL** ... Atlantic Fleet Antisubmarine Warfare Tactical School [*Navy*]
**LANTFLT** ... Atlantic Fleet
**LANTFLTRANSUPPFAC** ... Atlantic Fleet Training Support Facilities
**LANTFLTWPNRAN** ... Atlantic Fleet Weapons Range [*Later, AFRSF*] [*Navy*]
**LANTICOMIS** ... LANTCOM Integrated Command and Control Management Information System (MCD)
**LANTINTCEN** ... Atlantic Intelligence Center [*Navy*]
**LANTIRN** ... Low-Altitude Navigation and Targeting Infrared [*System*] for Night [*Aviation*]
**Lantm Andelsfolk** ... Lantman och Andelsfolk [*A publication*]
**LANTNAVFACENGCOM** ... Atlantic Division Naval Facilities Engineering Command
**LANTOPS** ... Atlantic Operations Supply Facilities (MCD)
**LANTOPSSUPFAC** ... Atlantic Operations Supply Facilities
**LANTREADEX** ... Atlantic Readiness Exercise (MCD)
**LANTRESFLT** ... Atlantic Reserve Fleet
**LANV** ........ Landsing Institutional Properties Trust V [*Menlo Park, CA*] [*NASDAQ symbol*] (NQ)
**LANX** ........ LAN Systems, Inc. [*NASDAQ symbol*] (NQ)
**LANX** ........ Local Area Network Exchange
**LANZ** ........ Lancer Orthodontics, Inc. [*NASDAQ symbol*] (NQ)
**LANZA** ..... Landarzt [*A publication*]
**LAO** ........... La Teko Resources Ltd. [*Vancouver Stock Exchange symbol*]
**lao** .............. Lao [*MARC language code*] [*Library of Congress*] (LCCP)
**LAO** ........... Laoag [*Philippines*] [*Airport symbol*] (OAG)
**LAO** ........... Laos [*or Lao People's Democratic Republic*] [*ANSI three-letter standard code*] (CNC)

**LAO** .......... Large Assembly Order (MCD)
**LAO** .......... Lasa Array [*Montana*] [*Seismograph station code, US Geological Survey*] (SEIS)
**LAO** .......... Left Anterior Oblique [*Cardiology*]
**LAO** .......... Legal Assistance Officer
**LAO** .......... Les Amis de l'Orgue [*An association*] (EAIO)
**LAO** .......... Licensing Authorities Office
**LAO** .......... Licentiate of the Art of Obstetrics [*British*]
**LAO** .......... Logistics Assistance Office [*or Officer*] [*Army Materiel Command*]
**LAOAR** ..... Latin American Office of Aerospace Research [*Air Force*]
**LAOCIF** .... Logistic Assistance Office Command Interest Flasher [*Military*] (AABC)
**LAOD** ........ Los Angeles Ordnance District [*Military*] (AAG)
**LA Off Public Works Water Resour Basic Rec Rep** ... Louisiana. Office of Public Works. Water Resources. Basic Records Report [*A publication*]
**LAOOC** ..... Los Angeles Olympic Organizing Committee (EA)
**LAOR** ........ La Teko Resources Ltd. [*NASDAQ symbol*] (NQ)
**LAOS** ........ Laymen's Overseas Service [*Acronym is now used as official name of the organization*]
**LAOSC** ...... Local Authorities Ordnance Survey Committee [*British*]
**LAP** .......... La Paz [*Mexico*] [*Airport symbol*] (OAG)
**LAP** .......... La Paz [*Mexico*] [*Seismograph station code, US Geological Survey*] (SEIS)
**LAP** .......... Laboratory Accreditation Program [*Department of Commerce*]
**LAP** .......... Laboratory of Advertising Performance [*McGraw-Hill*]
**LAP** .......... Laboratory of Architecture and Planning [*Massachusetts Institute of Technology*] [*Research center*] (RCD)
**LAP** .......... Lakewood Public Library, Lakewood, OH [*OCLC symbol*] (OCLC)
**lap** .......... Laparoscopy [*Medicine*]
**LAP** .......... Laparotomy [*Medicine*]
**LAP** .......... Lapland
**lap** .......... Lapp [*MARC language code*] [*Library of Congress*] (LCCP)
**Lap** .......... Lapus de Castiglionchio [*Flourished, 1353-81*] [*Authority cited in pre-1607 legal work*] (DSA)
**LAP** .......... Large Area Panel
**LAP** .......... Latin American Parliament [*See also PLA*] [*Bogota, Colombia*] (EAIO)
**LAP** .......... Latin American Perspectives [*A publication*]
**LAP** .......... Lattice Assessment Program [*Civil Defense*]
**LAP** .......... Launch Analyst Panel [*Aerospace*] (AAG)
**LAP** .......... Learning Accomplishment Profile [*Psychology*]
**LAP** .......... Left Atrial Pressure [*Cardiology*]
**LAP** .......... Lesson Assembly Program (IEEE)
**LAP** .......... Lethality Assessment Program
**LAP** .......... Leucine Aminopeptidase [*Also, LA, LP*] [*An enzyme*]
**LAP** .......... Leukocyte Alkaline Phosphatase [*An enzyme*]
**LAP** .......... Liberation Action Party [*Trinidad and Tobago*] [*Political party*] (PPW)
**LAP** .......... Liberian Action Party [*Political party*]
**LAP** .......... Library Access Program
**LAP** .......... Library Awareness Program [*FBI*]
**LAP** .......... Line Access Point [*Telecommunications*] (TEL)
**LAP** .......... Link Access Procedure [*Telecommunications*] (TEL)
**LAP** .......... Link Access Protocol [*Telecommunications*]
**LAP** .......... List Assembly Programming [*Data processing*]
**LAP** .......... Load, Assemble, Pack [*Army*] (AABC)
**LAP** .......... Location Audit Program [*Navy*] (NG)
**LAP** .......... Logistics Assistance Program
**LAP** .......... Loide Aereo Nacional, SA [*Brazilian airline*]
**LAP** .......... London Airport
**LAP** .......... Lord's Acre Plan (EA)
**LAP** .......... Loudspeaker Acoustical Phase-Inverter
**L Ap** .......... Louisiana Courts of Appeal Reports [*A publication*] (DLA)
**LAP** .......... Low-Altitude Penetration
**LAP** .......... Low-Altitude Performance
**LAP** .......... Lyophilized Anterior Pituitary [*Endocrinology*]
**LAPA** ......... Latin America Parents Association (EA)
**LAPA** ......... Leukocyte Alkaline Phosphatase Activity [*Biochemistry*]
**LAPA** ......... Lightweight Aggregate Producers Association (EA)
**LAPA** ......... Los Angeles Procurement Agency [*Army*]
**LAPAC** ...... Life Amendment Political Action Committee [*Defunct*] (EA)
**LAPADS** ... Lightweight Acoustic Processing and Display System [*British military*] (DMA)
**LAPAM** ..... Low-Altitude Penetrating Attack Missile [*Proposed*]
**LaPar** ......... La Parisienne [*A publication*]
**LAPB** ......... Laboratories' Applied Physiology Branch [*Army*]
**LAPB** ......... Link Access Procedure Balanced [*Telecommunications*]
**LAPB** ......... Link Access Protocol, B Channel [*Telecommunications*]
**LAPC** ......... Los Angeles Pacific College [*California*]
**LAPD** ......... Limited Axial Power Distribution (IEEE)
**LAPD** ......... Link Access Protocol, D Channel [*Telecommunications*]
**LAPD** ......... Los Angeles Air Procurement District
**Lap Dec** ...... Laperriere's Speaker's Decisions [*Canada*] [*A publication*] (DLA)
**LAPDOG** .. Low-Altitude Pursuit Dive on Ground (MCD)
**LAPE** ......... Lineas Aereas Postales Espanoles [*Airline*] [*Spain*]
**LAPERS** .... Labor and Production Effectiveness Reporting System [*DoD*]
**LAPES** ....... Low-Altitude Parachute Extraction System [*Military*]
**LAPFO** ...... Los Angeles Procurement Field Office
**LA Phil** ...... Los Angeles Philharmonic. Program Notes [*A publication*]
**LA Phil Sym Mag** ... Los Angeles Philharmonic Orchestra. Symphony Magazine [*A publication*]
**Lapid** ......... Lapideum [*Stony*] [*Latin*]
**Lapidary Jour** ... Lapidary Journal [*A publication*]
**LAPIS** ........ LASER Photoionization Spectroscopy
**LAPIS** ........ Legislative Authorization Program Information System [*General Accounting Office*] [*Defunct*] (IID)
**LAPL** ......... Lead Allowance Parts Lists
**LAPL** ......... Los Angeles Public Library
**LA Plant Sugar Manuf** ... Louisiana. Planter and Sugar Manufacturer [*A publication*]
**LAPLD** ...... Landscape Planning [*A publication*]
**Lap Lemb Penelit Kehutanan** ... Laporan. Lembaga Penelitian Kehutanan [*A publication*]
**LAPM** ........ Last Premidcourse Orbit
**LAPMAU** ... Lectures in Applied Mathematics [*A publication*]
**LAPMS** ..... Latin American Paper Money Society (EA)
**LAPOCA** ... L-Asparaginase, Prednisone, Oncovin [*Vincristine*], Cytarabine, Adriamycin [*Antineoplastic drug regimen*]
**LAPP** ......... Lappish [*Language, etc.*] (ROG)
**LAPP** ......... Lower Achieving Pupils Project [*British*]
**LAPPES** .... Large Power Plant Effluent Study (NRCH)
**Lappie** ........ Live-Alone Person [*Lifestyle classification*]
**LAPR** ......... Latin America Political Report [*A publication*]
**LAPR** ......... Los Alamos Power Reactor
**LAPRE** ...... Los Alamos Power Reactor Experiment
**LAPS** ......... LASER Profile System
**LAPS** ......... Latin American Philatelic Society (EA)
**LAPS** ......... Latin American, Portuguese, and Spanish [*Division*] [*Library of Congress*]
**LAPS** ......... Left Aft Propulsion System [*or Subsystem*] (NASA)
**LAPS** ......... Light-Addressable Potentiometric Sensor [*Semiconductor*]
**LAPS** ......... Literary, Artistic, Political, or Scientific [*Value*] [*In obscenity law, a criterion established by the 1973 case of Miller Versus California*]
**LAPS** ......... Loan Application Processing System
**LAPS** ......... Louis-Allen Power Supply
**LAPS** ......... Low-Altitude Proximity Sensor (MCD)
**LAPSA** ...... Lineas Aereas Paraguayas Sociedad Anonima [*Airline*] [*Paraguay*]
**LAPSS** ....... LASER Airborne Photographic Scanning System [*Navy*]
**LAPSS** ....... Low-Angle Polycrystalline Silicon Sheet [*Photovoltaic energy systems*]
**LAPT** ......... Library Acquisitions: Practice and Theory [*A publication*]
**LAPT** ......... Local Apparent Time (MSA)
**LAPT** ......... Los Angeles Union Passenger Terminal [*AAR code*]
**LAPUT** ...... Light-Activated Programmable Unijunction Transistor
**LAQ** .......... Beida [*Libya*] [*Airport symbol*] (OAG)
**LAQ** .......... Lacquer (KSC)
**LAQ** .......... Library Administration Quarterly
**LAQ** .......... Livres et Auteurs Quebecois [*A publication*]
**LAQT** ........ Low-Altitude Qualification Test [*Balloon*]
**LaR** .......... La Rassegna [*A publication*]
**LAR** .......... Labor Arbitration Reports [*Bureau of National Affairs*] [*A publication*] (DLA)
**LAR** .......... Land Registry [*British*]
**LAR** .......... Laramie [*Wyoming*] [*Airport symbol*] (OAG)
**LAR** .......... Laramie [*Wyoming*] [*Seismograph station code, US Geological Survey*] (SEIS)
**LAR** .......... Laramie, WY [*Location identifier*] [*FAA*] (FAAL)
**LAR** .......... Lariat Oil & Gas Ltd. [*Toronto Stock Exchange symbol*]
**LAR** .......... Laryngology
**LAR** .......... LASER-Aided Rocket (MCD)
**LAR** .......... Launch Acceptability Region (MCD)
**LAR** .......... Launcher Adapter Rail (MCD)
**LAR** .......... Lawrence Aviation, Inc. [*Lawrence, KS*] [*FAA designator*] (FAAC)
**LAR** .......... Leaf Area Ratio [*Botany*]
**LAR** .......... Left Arm Reclining [*or Recumbent*] [*Medicine*]
**LAR** .......... Leukocyte Adhesion Receptor [*Immunology*]
**LAR** .......... Library Association. Record [*A publication*]
**LAR** .......... Life Assurance Relief [*British*]
**LAR** .......... Light Artillery Rocket (MCD)
**LAR** .......... Light Attendant Station [*Coast Guard*]
**LAR** .......... Limit Address Register [*Data processing*]
**LAR** .......... Liquid Air Rocket
**LAR** .......... Local Acquisition RADAR (CET)
**LAR** .......... Loita Armada Revolucionaria [*Armed Revolutionary Struggle*] [*Spain*] (PD)
**LAR** .......... Long-Range Aircraft Rocket (NG)
**LAR** .......... Long-Range Assessments and Research [*Program*] [*Department of State*] [*Washington, DC*]
**L-Ar** .......... Louisiana Department of State, State Archives and Records, Baton Rouge, LA [*Library symbol*] [*Library of Congress*] (LCLS)
**LA R** .......... Louisiana Reports [*A publication*] (DLA)
**LAR** .......... Low-Altitude Release
**LAR** .......... Low-Angle Reentry [*Aerospace*] (MCD)
**LAR** .......... Low-Aspect Ratio

**LARA**......... Latin American Railways Association (EA)
**LARA**......... Light Armed Reconnaissance Aircraft [*Air Force*]
**LARA**......... Low-Altitude RADAR Altimeter [*Air Force*]
**LARAM**..... Line Addressable Random Access Memory [*Data processing*] (MDG)
**La de Rampo** ... Lambertus de Ramponibus [*Deceased, 1304*] [*Authority cited in pre-1607 legal work*] (DSA)
**LArB**.......... Bienville Parish Library, Arcadia, LA [*Library symbol*] [*Library of Congress*] (LCLS)
**L Arb**.......... Linguistische Arbeiten [*A publication*]
**LArbG**........ Landesarbeitsgericht [*Provincial Labor Court of Appeal*] [*German*] (ILCA)
**LARC**......... Association for Library Automation Research Communications (EA)
**LARC**......... Langley Research Center [*NASA*]
**LARC**......... Larceny [*FBI standardized term*]
**LARC**......... Large Automatic Research Computer [*or Calculator*]
**LARC**......... LASER-Activated Recession Compensator (MCD)
**LARC**......... Laser Applications Research Center [*Research center*] (RCD)
**LARC**......... Leukocyte Automatic Recognition Computer [*Blood counting*]
**LARC**......... Libyan-American Reconstruction Commission
**LARC**......... Lighter, Amphibious, Resupply Cargo [*Vessel*]
**LARC**......... Lindheimer Astronomical Research Center [*Northwestern University*]
**LARC**......... Livermore Atomic Research Computer
**LARC**......... Local Alcoholism Reception Center
**LARC**......... Locally Assigned Reporting Code [*Munitions reports*] (AFM)
**LARC**......... Loose Actors Revolving Company [*for producing plays; members include actors George C. Scott and Rod Steiger*]
**LARC**......... Los Alamitos Race [*NASDAQ symbol*] (NQ)
**LARC**......... Low-Altitude Ride Control [*Shock-absorbing system*] [*Aviation*] (MCD)
**LARC**......... Regional Conference for Latin America [*UN Food and Agriculture Organization*]
**LARCAE** ... Ligeia Association pour le Renouvellement de la Culture Artistique Europeenne [*Paris, France*] (EAIO)
**LARCCH**... Latin America Resource Center and Clearinghouse (EA)
**LARCF** ...... Lithuanian American Roman Catholic Federation (EA)
**LARC Med** ... LARC Medical [*A publication*]
**LARC Rep** ... LARC Reports [*A publication*]
**LARCT** ...... Last Radio Contact [*Aviation*]
**LARDS**...... Low-Accuracy RADAR Data Transmission System
**LARE**........ Local Asymptotic Relative Efficiency [*Statistics*]
**LA Reg**....... Louisiana Register [*A publication*]
**LAREHS** ... Laboratory of Research in Human and Social Ecology [*University of Quebec at Montreal*] [*Canada*] [*Research center*] (RCD)
**LA Rep**....... Louisiana Reports [*A publication*] (DLA)
**LA Rev Stat Ann (West)** ... West's Louisiana Revised Statutes, Annotated [*A publication*] (DLA)
**LARF**......... Lebanese Armed Revolutionary Faction
**LARF**......... Low-Altitude RADAR Fuzing (CET)
**LARFEN** ... Agricultural Research Organization. Division of Forestry. Ilanot Leaflet [*A publication*]
**LARG** ........ Largamente [*Easily*] [*Music*]
**LARG** ........ Largo [*Very Slow*] [*Music*] (ROG)
**LARG** ........ Library-Anthropology Resource Group
**Large Scale Syst Theory and Appl** ... Large Scale Systems. Theory and Applications [*A publication*]
**LARGO** ..... Larghetto [*Slow*] [*Music*] (ROG)
**LARGOS**... LASER-Activated Reflecting Geodetic Optical Satellite
**LARIA** ....... Local Authorities Research and Intelligence Association [*British*]
**LARIAT** .... LASER RADAR Intelligence Acquisition Technology
**LARIAT** .... Long-Range Area RADAR for Intrusion Detection and Tracking
**LARIS** ....... Low-Altitude RADAR Interface System (MCD)
**LARL**......... Laurel Savings Association [*NASDAQ symbol*] (NQ)
**LArm**.......... Literaturnaia Armeniia. Ezhemesiachnyi Literaturno-Khudozhestvennyi i Obshchestvenno-Politicheskii Zhurnal [*A publication*]
**LARMC**..... Landstuhl Army Regional Medical Center [*Federal Republic of Germany*]
**LARP**......... Line Automatic Reperforator (CET)
**LARP**......... Local and Remote Printing [*Data processing*]
**LARPS** ...... Local and Remote Printing Station [*Data processing*]
**LARR**......... Latin American Research Review [*A publication*]
**LARRL**...... Fort Keogh Livestock and Range Research Laboratory [*Miles City, MT*] [*Department of Agriculture*] (GRD)
**LARRS** ...... Livestock and Range Research Station [*Department of Agriculture*] (GRD)
**LARS**......... Laboratory for Agricultural Remote Sensing
**LARS**......... Laboratory for Applications of Remote Sensing [*Purdue University*] [*Research center*] (RCD)
**LARS**......... Laminar Angular Rate Sensor [*Navy*]
**LARS**......... Language-Structured Auditory Retention Span Test
**LARS**......... Larsen Co. [*NASDAQ symbol*] (NQ)
**LARS**......... LASER-Aided Rocket System [*Military*] (CAAL)
**LARS**......... LASER Angular Rate Sensor [*or Scanner*]
**LARS**......... LASER-Articulated Robotic System
**LARS**......... Launch and Recovery System [*NASA*]
**LARS**......... Left Add, Right Subtract [*Army field artillery technique*] (INF)
**LARS**......... Light Artillery Rocket System (NATG)
**LARS**......... Low-Altitude RADAR System (NATG)
**LARSA** ...... Latin American Rural Sociological Association (EAIO)
**LARSI** ....... Laboratoire de Recherche en Sciences Immobilieres [*University of Quebec at Montreal*] [*Research center*] (RCD)
**LARSP** ...... Language Assessment Remediation and Screening Procedure [*for the language impaired*]
**LA Rural Econ** ... Louisiana Rural Economist. Louisiana State University. Department of Agriculture and Agribusiness [*A publication*]
**LARVA**...... Low-Altitude Research Vehicular Advancements
**LARY**......... Larry's Ice Cream, Inc. [*NASDAQ symbol*] (NQ)
**LARYA**...... Laryngoscope [*A publication*]
**Laryng**........ Laryngology
**LARYNGOL** ... Laryngology
**Laryngol Rhinol Otol** ... Laryngologie, Rhinologie, Otologie [*A publication*]
**Laryngol Rhinol Otol Ihre Grenzeb** ... Laryngologie, Rhinologie, Otologie, und Ihre Grenzebiete [*A publication*]
**Laryngol Rhinol Otol (Stuttg)** ... Laryngologie, Rhinologie, Otologie (Stuttgart) [*A publication*]
**Laryngo-Rhino-Otol** ... Laryngo- Rhino- Otologie [*A publication*]
**Laryngoscop** ... Laryngoscope [*A publication*]
**LAS**........... Almirall [*Spain*] [*Research code symbol*]
**LAS**........... La Salle College, Philadelphia, PA [*OCLC symbol*] (OCLC)
**LAS**........... Labor Area Summary [*Employment and Training Administration*] [*Department of Labor*]
**LAS**........... Laboratories of Applied Sciences [*University of Chicago*] (MCD)
**LAS**........... Laboratory of Atmospheric Sciences [*National Science Foundation*]
**LAS**........... Laboratory Automation System
**LAS**........... Landing Approach Simulator
**LAS**........... Language Assessment Scales [*Test*]
**La S**........... Language and Style [*A publication*]
**LAS**........... Large Amplitude Simulator
**LAS**........... Large Astronomical Satellite [*ESRO*]
**LAS**........... Large-Probe Atmospheric Structure [*NASA*]
**LAS**........... Las Vegas [*Nevada*] [*Airport symbol*] (OAG)
**LAS**........... Las Vegas, NV [*Location identifier*] [*FAA*] (FAAL)
**LAS**........... LASER Absorption Spectrometer
**LAS**........... LASER Antiflash System
**LAS**........... Laser Industries Ltd. [*AMEX symbol*] (SPSG)
**LAS**........... Launch Area Supervisor (AFM)
**LAS**........... Launch Auxiliary System
**LAS**........... Leadership Appraisal Survey [*Interpersonal skills and attitudes test*]
**LAS**........... League of Arab States [*Tunis, Tunisia*]
**LAS**........... Lebanese-American Society of Greater New York [*Defunct*] (EA)
**LAS**........... Leipziger Aegyptologische Studien [*A publication*] (BJA)
**LAS**........... Life Association News [*A publication*]
**LAS**........... Life Assurance of Scotland [*Commercial firm*]
**LAS**........... Light-Activated Switch
**LAS**........... Limited Assignment Status [*Military*]
**LAS**........... Linear Alkylbenzene Sulfonate [*Surfactant*]
**LAS**........... Litha-Alumina-Silicate [*Inorganic chemistry*]
**LAS**........... Liturgical Arts Society (EA)
**LAS**........... Local Adaptation Syndrome [*Medicine*]
**LAS**........... Local Address Space
**LAS**........... Local Area Screening
**LAS**........... Logical Address Strobe
**LAS**........... London Appreciation Society
**LAS**........... Long-Range Assistance Strategy (CINC)
**LAS**........... Longitudinal Air Spring
**LAS**........... Lord Advocate of Scotland
**LaS**........... Louisiana Studies [*A publication*]
**LAS**........... Low-Alloy Steel
**LAS**........... Low-Altitude Satellite
**LAS**........... Lunar Attitude System [*Aerospace*]
**LAS**........... Lutheran Academy for Scholarship [*Defunct*] (EA)
**LAS**........... Lymphadenopathy Syndrome [*Medicine*]
**LAS**........... Lysine Acetylsalicylate [*Biochemistry*]
**LAS**........... Saskatchewan Libraries Retrospective Conversion [*UTLAS symbol*]
**LASA**......... Laboratory Animal Science Association [*British*]
**LASA**......... Large Aperture Seismic Array [*Nuclear detection device*]
**LASA**......... Large Area Solar Array
**LASA**......... Latin American Studies Association (EA)
**LASA**......... LIDAR [*Light Detection and Ranging*] Atmospheric Sounder and Altimeter
**LASAM**..... LASER Semiactive Missile
**LASAR**...... Logic Automated Stimulus and Response (MCD)
**LASAS**....... Latin American Secretariat for Academic Services [*Defunct*]
**LASB**......... Lackawaxen & Stourbridge Railroad Corp. [*AAR code*]
**LASC**......... Light Armored Squad Carrier
**LASCA** ...... Large Area Solar Cell Array
**LASCAR** ... Language for Simulation of Computer Architecture (CSR)
**Lasc H War** ... Lascelles' Horse Warranty [*2nd ed.*] [*1880*] [*A publication*] (DLA)
**Lasc Juv Off** ... Lascelles on Juvenile Offenders [*A publication*] (DLA)

**LASCo**....... Larkin Aircraft Supply Co. [*Australia*]
**LASCO**...... Latin America Science Cooperation Office (MSC)
**LASCODOCS**... Linguistic Analysis of Spanish Colonial Documents
**LASCOT**... Large Screen Color Television System (NASA)
**LASCR**...... Light-Activated Silicon-Controlled Rectifier
**LASCS**...... Light-Activated Silicon-Controlled Switch (MCD)
**LASD**........ Labor Agreement Settlement Data [*Cast Metals Association*] [*A publication*]
**LASD**........ Latin American Serial Documents
**L-Ase**........ L-Asparaginase [*Also, A, L, L-Asp, L-asnase*] [*An enzyme, an antineoplastic*]
**LASE**......... Large Aperture Seismic Experiment [*Geophysical survey*]
**LASE**......... Laser-Scan International, Inc. [*NASDAQ symbol*] (NQ)
**LASE**......... LIDAR [*Light Detection and Ranging*] Atmosphere Sensing Experiment
**LASER**...... League for the Advancement of States' Equal Rights (EA)
**LASER**...... Learning Achievement through Saturated Educational Resources
**LASER**...... Light Amplification by Stimulated Emission of Radiation [*Acronym was coined in 1957 by scientist Gordon Gould*]
**LASER**...... London and South Eastern Library Region [*Information service or system*] (IID)
**Laser und Angew Strahlentech**... Laser und Angewandte Strahlentechnik [*A publication*]
**Laser Appl Med Biol**... Laser Applications in Medicine and Biology [*A publication*]
**LASERCOM**... LASER Communications (MCD)
**Laser Elektro-Opt**... Laser und Elektro-Optik [*A publication*]
**Laser und Elektro-Opt**... Laser und Elektro-Optik [*A publication*]
**Laser Foc**... Laser Focus Buyers Guide [*A publication*]
**Laser Focus Fiberoptic Commun**... Laser Focus with Fiberoptic Communications [*A publication*]
**Laser Focus Fiberoptic Technol**... Laser Focus with Fiberoptic Technology [*A publication*]
**Laser F Wld**... Laser Focus World [*A publication*]
**Laser J**....... Laser Journal [*A publication*]
**Laser Opt Non Conv**... Lasers et Optique Non Conventionelle [*France*] [*A publication*]
**Laser Optoelektron**... Laser und Optoelektronik [*A publication*]
**Laser und Optoelektron**... Laser und Optoelektronik [*A publication*]
**Laser Part**.. Laser and Particle Beams [*A publication*]
**Laser Rep**... Laser Report [*A publication*]
**Laser Rev**... Laser Review [*A publication*]
**Lasers & App**... Lasers and Applications. A High Tech Publication [*A publication*]
**Lasers Med Sci**... Lasers in Medical Science [*A publication*]
**Lasers Surg Med**... Lasers in Surgery and Medicine [*A publication*]
**Laser Surg**... Lasers in Surgery and Medicine [*A publication*]
**Laser & Unconv Opt J**... Laser and Unconventional Optics Journal [*A publication*]
**LA Sess Law Serv**... Louisiana Session Law Service [*A publication*] (DLA)
**LA Sess Law Serv (West)**... Louisiana Session Law Service (West) [*A publication*]
**LASH**........ LASER Antitank Semiactive Homing
**LASH**........ Latin American Society of Hepatology [*See also SLH*] (EAIO)
**LASH**........ Legislative Action on Smoking and Health (EA)
**LASH**........ Lighter Aboard Ship [*Barge-carrying ship*]
**LASH**........ List of Australian Subject Headings [*A publication*] (APTA)
**LA Ship**...... Latin American Shipping [*A publication*]
**LASI**.......... Landing-Site Indicator [*Aviation*]
**LASI**.......... Laser Industries Ltd. [*NASDAQ symbol*] (NQ)
**LASI**.......... Library of Ancient Semitic Inscriptions (BJA)
**LASI**.......... Licentiate of the Ambulance Service Institute [*British*] (DBQ)
**LASIE**........ Information Bulletin. Library Automated Systems Information Exchange [*A publication*]
**LASIL**........ Land and Sea Interaction Laboratory [*Environmental Science Services Administration*]
**LASINT**.... LASER Intelligence (MCD)
**LASL**......... Los Alamos Scientific Laboratory [*USAEC*]
**LASLA**...... Laboratoire d'Analyse Statistique des Langues Anciennes [*Laboratory for the Statistical Analysis of Ancient Languages*] [*University of Liege, Belgium*]
**LASMEC**.. Local Authorities School Meals Equipment Consortium
**LASMO**..... London & Scottish Marine Oil [*British*]
**L-Asnase**.... L-Asparaginase [*Also, A, L, L-ase, L-Asp*] [*An enzyme, an antineoplastic*]
**LASO**......... Low-Altitude Search Option [*Search mode of the BOMARC guidance system*]
**LASOR**...... LASER Spillover and Reflectivity (MCD)
**LASORS**... Literature Analysis System on Road Safety [*Australia Department of Transport and Communications*] [*Information service or system*] (CRD)
**L-Asp**......... L-Asparaginase [*Also, A, L, L-ase, L-asnase*] [*An enzyme, an antineoplastic*]
**LASP**......... Laboratory for Atmospheric and Space Physics [*University of Colorado*] [*Research center*]
**LASP**......... Local Attached Support Processor
**LASP**......... Low-Altitude Space Platform (MCD)
**LASP**......... Low-Altitude Surveillance Platform (MCD)
**LASPAC**.... Landing Gear, Avionics Systems Package (MCD)
**LASPAU**... Latin American Scholarship Program of American Universities (EA)
**LASR**......... Laboratories for Astrophysics and Space Research [*University of Chicago*] [*Research center*]
**LASR**......... Laser Precision Corp. [*NASDAQ symbol*] (NQ)
**LASR**......... Literature Analysis System of the Office of Road Safety [*Department of Transport*] [*Australia*] [*Information service or system*] (CRD)
**LASR**......... Low-Altitude Surveillance RADAR
**LASRAM**.. Low-Altitude Short-Range Missile
**LASRB**...... Laser Review [*A publication*]
**LASRM**..... Low-Altitude Short-Range Missile
**LASRM**..... Low-Altitude Supersonic Research Missile
**LASS**......... Labile Aggregation-Stimulating Substance [*Hematology*]
**LASS**......... Large Aperture Solenoid Spectrometer [*Stanford Linear Accelerator Center*]
**LASS**......... Large Area Screening Systems (MCD)
**LASS**......... Large Area Sky Survey
**LASS**......... LASER-Activated Silicon Switch (MCD)
**LASS**......... Launch Area Support Ship
**LASS**......... Light-Activated Silicon Switch
**LASS**......... Lighter-than-Air Submarine Simulator
**LASS**......... Line Amplifier and Super Sync Mixer
**LASS**......... Line Automatic Sensing and Switching (FAAC)
**LASS**......... Local Area Signaling Service [*Bell Laboratories*]
**LASS**......... Local Authority Social Services [*British*]
**LASS**......... Logistics Analysis Simulation System
**LASS**......... Logistics Automated Supply System
**LASS**......... Low-Angle Silicon Sheet [*Photovoltaic energy systems*]
**LASS**......... Lunar Applications of a Spent Stage [*Aerospace*] (MCD)
**LASSC**....... Latin American Social Sciences Council [*Argentina*] [*Database producer*] (EA)
**LASSII**...... Low-Altitude Satellite Studies of Ionospheric Irregularities
**LASSM**..... Line Amplifier and Super Sync Mixer (MSA)
**LASSO**...... Landing and Approach System, Spiral-Oriented
**LASSO**...... LASER Search and Secure Observer (CET)
**LASSO**...... LASER Synchronization from Stationary Orbit (IEEE)
**LASSO**...... Library Acquisition Services System Online [*Suggested name for the Library of Cogress computer system*]
**LASSO**...... Light Air-to-Surface Semiautomatic Optical [*French missile*]
**LASSO**...... Light Aviation Special Support Operations
**LASSO**...... Lunar Applications of a Spent Stage in Orbit [*Aerospace*] (MCD)
**LASSP**....... Laboratory for Atomic and Solid State Physics [*Cornell University*] [*Research center*] (RCD)
**LASST**....... Laboratory for Surface Science and Technology [*University of Maine at Orono*] [*Research center*] (RCD)
**LASSV**....... Land and Approach System for Space Vehicles [*NASA*] (KSC)
**LAST**......... Language and Systems Together [*Programming language*] [*Baytec*] [*Bay City, MI*]
**LAST**......... Large Aperture Scanning Telescope (TEL)
**LAST**......... Liberty Acquisitions Corp. [*Tampa, FL*] [*NASDAQ symbol*] (NQ)
**LAST**......... Low-Altitude Supersonic Target (RDA)
**LA State Dep Conserv Geol Bull**... Louisiana State Department of Conservation. Geological Bulletin [*A publication*]
**LA State Med Soc J**... Louisiana State Medical Society. Journal [*A publication*]
**LA State Univ Agric Mech Coll Eng Exp Stn Repr Ser**... Louisiana State University and Agricultural and Mechanical College. Engineering Experiment Station. Reprint Series [*A publication*]
**LA State Univ and Agr Mech Coll Tech Rept**... Louisiana State University and Agricultural and Mechanical College. Technical Reports [*A publication*]
**LA State Univ Div Eng Res Bull**... Louisiana State University. Division of Engineering Research. Bulletin [*A publication*]
**LA State Univ Div Eng Res Eng**... Louisiana State University. Division of Engineering Research. Engineering Research Bulletin [*A publication*]
**LA State Univ Div Eng Res Eng Res Bull**... Louisiana State University. Division of Engineering Research. Engineering Research Bulletin. [*A publication*]
**LA State Univ Eng Expt Sta Bull Studies Phys Sci Ser**... Louisiana State University. Engineering Experiment Station. Bulletin. Studies. Physical Science Series [*A publication*]
**LA State Univ Proc Annu For Symp**... Louisiana State University. Proceedings. Annual Forestry Symposium [*A publication*]
**LA State Univ Stud Biol Sci Ser**... Louisiana State University. Studies. Biological Science Series [*A publication*]
**LA State Univ Stud Coastal Stud Ser**... Louisiana State University. Studies. Coastal Studies Series [*A publication*]
**LA St Exp Sta G Agr LA**... Louisiana State Experiment Stations. Geology and Agriculture of Louisiana [*A publication*]
**LA Stud**...... Louisiana Studies [*A publication*]
**LA St Univ An Rp Sup**... Louisiana State University. Annual Report of the Superintendent [*A publication*]
**LASU**......... Local Air Supply Unit [*British military*] (DMA)
**LA SUQ**..... Louisiana State University. Quarterly [*A publication*] (DLA)
**LASV**......... Low-Altitude Supersonic Vehicle [*Formerly, SLAM*] [*Air Force*]

**Las Vegas Rev J** ... Las Vegas Review. Journal [*A publication*]
**LASVEM** .. Lightly Armored Structure Vulnerability Estimation Methodology (MCD)
**LASX** ......... Lasertechnics, Inc. [*NASDAQ symbol*] (NQ)
**LaT** ........... La Torre [*A publication*]
**LAT** ........... Lae [*Papua New Guinea*] [*Seismograph station code, US Geological Survey*] (SEIS)
**LAT** ........... Language Aptitude Test [*Military*] (AFM)
**LAT** ........... Large Angle Torque (MCD)
**LAT** ........... Latch (NASA)
**Lat** ............. Latch's English King's Bench Reports [*1625-28*] [*A publication*] (DLA)
**LAT** ........... Latent
**LAT** ........... Lateral (KSC)
**LAT** ........... Latex Agglutination Test [*Clinical chemistry*]
**LAT** ........... Lathwell Resources Ltd. [*Vancouver Stock Exchange symbol*]
**lat** ............. Latin [*MARC language code*] [*Library of Congress*] (LCCP)
**LAT** ........... Latin
**LAT** ........... Latin America Regional Reports [*A publication*]
**LAT** ........... Latitude
**Lat** ............. Latomus [*A publication*]
**LAT** ........... Latrine (DSUE)
**LAT** ........... Latshaw Enterprises [*AMEX symbol*] (SPSG)
**LAT** ........... Latus [*Wide*] [*Pharmacy*]
**LAT** ........... Latvia
**LAT** ........... Learning Ability Test [*Military*] (AFM)
**LAT** ........... Left Anterior Thigh [*Medicine*]
**LAT** ........... Lcvcl abovc Threshold
**LAT** ........... Light Artillery Tractor [*British military*] (DMA)
**LAT** ........... Linear Accelerator Tube
**LAT** ........... Linseed Association Terms [*Shipping*]
**LAT** ........... Local Apparent Time
**LAT** ........... Lockheed Air Terminal, Inc. [*Subsidiary of Lockheed Aircraft Corp.*]
**LAT** ........... Logistics Assistance Team (MCD)
**LAT** ........... Long-Acting Theophylline [*Pharmacology*]
**LAT** ........... Los Angeles Times [*A publication*]
**LAT** ........... Lot Acceptance Test (NASA)
**LAT** ........... Low-Angle Track (CAAL)
**Lat** ............. Valsts Biblioteka [*State Library of Latvia*], Riga, Latvia [*Library symbol*] [*Library of Congress*] (LCLS)
**LAT-A** ....... Latrunculin-A [*A toxin*]
**LATA** ......... Local Access Transport Area [*Telecommunications*]
**LATA** ......... London Amenity and Transport Association
**LAT ADMOV** ... Lateri Admoveatum [*Let It Be Applied to the Side*] [*Pharmacy*]
**LATAF** ...... Logistics Activation Task Force [*Air Force*] (MCD)
**LATAG** ...... LASER Air-to-Air Gunnery Simulator [*Military*] (CAAL)
**LATAG** ...... Latin American Trade Advisory Group [*British Overseas Trade Board*] (DS)
**LatAm** ........ Index to Latin American Periodicals [*A publication*]
**Lat Am** ....... Latin America [*A publication*]
**Lat Amer** .... Latin American Perspectives [*A publication*]
**Lat Amer Mg** ... Latin American Monographs [*A publication*]
**Lat Am Ind** ... Latin American Indian Literatures [*A publication*]
**Lat Am Ind Lit** ... Latin American Indian Literatures [*A publication*]
**Lat Am J Chem Engng Appld Chem** ... Latin American Journal of Chemical Engineering and Applied Chemistry [*A publication*]
**Lat Am J Heat Mass Transfer** ... Latin American Journal of Heat and Mass Transfer [*A publication*]
**Lat Am Lit** ... Latin American Literary Review [*A publication*]
**Lat Am Min Lett** ... Latin American Mining Letter [*A publication*]
**Lat Am Mon Econ Indic** ... Latin American Monthly Economic Indicators [*A publication*]
**Lat Am Mus** ... Latin American Music Review [*A publication*]
**Lat Am Mus R** ... Latin American Music Review [*A publication*]
**Lat Am Res** ... Latin American Research Review [*A publication*]
**Lat Am Res R** ... Latin American Research Review [*A publication*]
**Lat Am Thea** ... Latin American Theater Review [*A publication*]
**LATAR** ...... LASER-Augmented Target Acquisition and Recognition System (MCD)
**LATAS** ...... LASER-Augmented Target Acquisition System
**LAT-B** ....... Latrunculin-B [*A toxin*]
**LATB** ......... Lithium Aluminum Tri-tert-Butoxyhydride [*Organic chemistry*]
**LATBR** ...... Los Angeles Times Book Review [*A publication*]
**LATC** ........ Los Angeles Theater Center [*California*]
**LATCC** ...... London Air-Traffic Control Center
**Latch** .......... Latch's English King's Bench Reports [*1625-28*] [*A publication*] (DLA)
**LATCH** ..... Literature Attached to Charts [*Nursing program*]
**LATD** ........ Large Area Transmission Density (MCD)
**LATD** ........ Latitude (ADA)
**LATDISP** .. Lateral Dispersion (MCD)
**LAT DOL** ... Lateri Dolente [*To the Painful Side*] [*Pharmacy*]
**LATE** ......... Legal Assistance for the Elderly
**Lateinam Anders** ... Lateinamerika Anders [*A publication*]
**Lateinam-Studien** ... Lateinamerika-Studien [*A publication*]
**LATER** ...... Ladies' After Thoughts on Equal Rights [*Acronym is used as name of association*] [*Defunct*] (EA)
**LATER** ...... [*The*] Life and Times of Eddie Roberts [*TV program*]
**Later Rom Emp** ... [*The*] Later Roman Empire [*A publication*] (OCD)
**LATF** ......... Lloyd's American Trust Fund (AIA)
**La Th** ......... La Themis [*A publication*] (DLA)
**LATH** ........ Laos and Thailand Military Assistance
**Lath** ............ Lathrop's Reports [*115-145 Massachusetts*] [*A publication*] (DLA)
**LATH** ........ Libraries of Affiliated Teaching Hospitals - School of Medicine [*Library network*]
**La Them LC** ... La Themis (Lower Canada) [*A publication*] (DLA)
**Lathrop** ...... Lathrop's Reports [*115-145 Massachusetts*] [*A publication*] (DLA)
**Lath Wind L** ... Latham on the Law of Window Lights [*A publication*] (DLA)
**LATI** ......... Linee Aeree Transcontinentali Italiane
**LATIA** ....... Landbouwkundig Tijdschrift [*A publication*]
**LA Times** ... Los Angeles Times [*A publication*]
**Latin Am and Empire Rept** ... NACLA's [*North American Congress on Latin America*] Latin America and Empire Report [*A publication*]
**Latin Amer** ... Latinskaja Amerika [*A publication*]
**Latin Amer P** ... Latin American Perspectives [*A publication*]
**Latin Amer Perspect** ... Latin American Perspectives [*A publication*]
**Latin Amer Res R** ... Latin American Research Review [*A publication*]
**Latin Am Perspectives** ... Latin American Perspectives [*A publication*]
**Latin Am Research R** ... Latin American Research Review [*A publication*]
**Latin Am Res R** ... Latin American Research Review [*A publication*]
**Latin Am Times** ... Latin American Times [*A publication*]
**Latinsk Amer** ... Latinskaja Amerika [*A publication*]
**LATIS** ........ Lightweight Airborne Thermal Imaging System (MCD)
**LATIS** ........ Loop Activity Tracking Information System [*Telecommunications*] (TEL)
**Lat Jus** ....... Latrobe's Justice [*A publication*] (DLA)
**LATL** ......... Lateral (MSA)
**LATLI** ....... Latin American Tax Law Institute (EAIO)
**LATN** ........ Low-Altitude Tactical Navigation
**LATNS** ...... Los Angeles Times News Service
**LATO** ........ List of Applicable Technical Orders [*Military*] (AFIT)
**Latomus** ..... Latomus; Revue d'Etudes Latines [*A publication*]
**LATP** ......... League of American Theatres and Producers (EA)
**LATP** ......... Lima Army Tank Plant [*Ohio*]
**LATR** ......... Latin American Theater Review [*A publication*]
**LA TR** ........ Louisiana Term Reports (Martin) [*A publication*] (DLA)
**LATREC** ... LASER-Acoustic Time Reversal Expansion and Compression (MCD)
**LATRL** ...... Lateral
**LA TR (NS)** ... Louisiana Term Reports, New Series (Martin) [*1823-30*] [*A publication*] (DLA)
**La Trobe Library J** ... La Trobe Library Journal [*A publication*] (APTA)
**LATS** ......... LDEF [*Long-Duration Exposure Facility*] Assembly and Transportation System [*NASA*] (NASA)
**LATS** ......... Leather and Associated Trades Show [*British*] (ITD)
**LATS** ......... Light Armored Turret System (MCD)
**LATS** ......... Light Attack Turbofan Single Aircraft [*Aviation*]
**LATS** ......... Lightweight Antenna Terminal Seeker
**LATS** ......... Long-Acting Thyroid Stimulator [*Endocrinology*]
**LATS-P** ...... Long Acting Thyroid Stimulator-Protector [*Endocrinology*]
**LatSSR** ...... Latvian Soviet Socialist Republic
**LATT** ......... LASER Atmospheric Transmission Test
**LatT** .......... Latin Teaching [*A publication*]
**Latt Pr C Pr** ... Lattey's Privy Council Practice [*1869*] [*A publication*] (DLA)
**LATUF** ...... Latin America Trade Union Federation (NATG)
**Latv** ............ Latvian
**Latv Ent** ..... Latvijas Entomologs [*A publication*]
**Latv Fil Vses Ova Pochvovedov Sb Tr** ... Latviiskii Filial Vsesoyuznogo Obshchestva Pochvovedov Sbornik Trudov [*A publication*]
**Latviisk Gos Univ Ucen Zap** ... Latviiskii Gosudarstvennyi Universitet Imeni Petra Stucki Ucenyi Zapiski [*A publication*]
**Latviisk Mat Ezegodnik** ... Latviiskii Matematiceskii Ezegodnik [*A publication*]
**Latvijas PSR Zinatn Akad Vestis** ... Latvijas PSR Zinatnu Akademijas. Vestis [*A publication*]
**Latvijas PSR Zinatn Akad Vestis Fiz Tehn Zinatn Ser** ... Latvijas PSR Zinatnu Akademijas. Vestis. Fizikas un Tehnisko Zinatnu Serija [*A publication*]
**Latvijas Valsts Univ Zinatn Raksti** ... PSRS Augstakas Izglitibas Ministrija. Petera Stuckas Latvijas Valsts Universitate. Zinatniskie Raksti [*A publication*]
**Latv Lauksaimn Akad Raktsi** ... Latvijas Lauksaimniecibas Akademijas Raktsi [*A publication*]
**Latv Lopkopibas Vet Inst Raksti** ... Latvijas Lopkopibas un Veterinarijas Zinatniski Petnieciska Instituta Raksti [*A publication*]
**Latv Lopkopibas Vet Zinat Petnieciska Inst Raksti** ... Latvijas Lopkopibas un Veterinarijas Zinatniski Petnieciska Instituta Raksti [*A publication*]
**Latv Mat Ezheg** ... Latvijskij Matematicheskij Ezhegodnik [*A publication*]
**Latv Mat Ezhegodnik** ... Latviiskii Gosudarstvennyi Universitet Imeni Petra Stucki Latviiskii Matematicheskii Ezhegodnik [*A publication*]
**Latv PSR Zinat Akad Biol Inst Dzivnieku Fiziol Sekt Raksti** ... Latvijas PSR Zinatnu Akademija. Biologijas Instituts. Dzivnieku Fiziologijas Sektora Raksti [*A publication*]

**Latv PSR Zinat Akad Biol Inst Raksti** ... Latvijas PSR Zinatnu Akademija Biologijas Instituta Raksti [*A publication*]
**Latv PSR Zinat Akad Kim Inst Zinat Raksti** ... Latvijas PSR Zinatnu Akademija Kimijas Instituta Zinatniskie Raksti [*A publication*]
**Latv PSR Zinat Akad Mezsaimn Probl Koksnes Kim Inst Raksti** ... Latvijas PSR Zinatnu Akademija Mezsaimniecibas Problemu un Koksnes Kimijas Instituta Raksti [*A publication*]
**Latv PSR Zinat Akad Vestis** ... Latvijas PSR Zinatnu Akademijas. Vestis [*Riga*] [*A publication*]
**Latv PSR Zinat Akad Vestis Fiz Teh Ser** ... Latvijas PSR Zinatnu Akademijas. Vestis. Fizikas un Tehnisko Zinatnu Serija [*A publication*]
**Latv PSR Zinat Akad Vestis Fiz Teh Zinat Ser** ... Latvijas PSR Zinatnu Akademijas. Vestis. Fizikas un Tehnisko Zinatnu Serija [*A publication*]
**Latv PSR Zinat Akad Vestis Kim Ser** ... Latvijas PSR Zinatnu Akademijas. Vestis. Kimijas Serija [*A publication*]
**Latv Univ Raksti Kim Fak Ser** ... Latvijas Universitates Raksti. Kimijas Fakultates Serijas [*A publication*]
**Latv Univ Raksti Lauksaimn Fak Ser** ... Latvijas Universitates Raksti. Lauksaimniecibas Fakultates Serija [*A publication*]
**Latv Univ Raksti Mat Dabas Zinat Fak Ser** ... Latvijas Universitates Raksti. Matematikas un Dabas Zinatnu. Fakultates Serija [*A publication*]
**Latv Univ Raksti Med Fak Ser** ... Latvijas Universitates Raksti. Medicinas Fakultates Serija [*A publication*]
**Latv Valsts Univ Bot Darza Raksti** ... Latvijas Valsts Universitates Botaniska Darza Raksti [*A publication*]
**LATWING** ... Light Attack Wing [*Navy*] (NVT)
**LAU** .......... Lamu [*Kenya*] [*Airport symbol*] (OAG)
**LAU** .......... Lauder [*New Zealand*] [*Geomagnetic observatory code*]
**LAU** .......... Laumontite [*A zeolite*]
**LAU** .......... Launcher Aircraft Unit
**LAU** .......... Laundry (MSA)
**LAU** .......... Laurentian University Library [*UTLAS symbol*]
**Lau** .......... Laurentius Hispanus [*Deceased, 1248*] [*Authority cited in pre-1607 legal work*] (DSA)
**LAU** .......... Line Adapter Unit [*Data processing*]
**lau** .......... Louisiana [*MARC country of publication code*] [*Library of Congress*] (LCCP)
**Laud** .......... [*Guillelmus de Monte*] Lauduno [*Deceased, 1343*] [*Authority cited in pre-1607 legal work*] (DSA)
**LAUD** ........ League of Americans of Ukrainian Descent (EA)
**Lauder** ........ Fountainhall's Session Cases [*1678-1712*] [*Scotland*] [*A publication*] (DLA)
**LAUK** ........ Library Association of the United Kingdom
**LAUM** ....... Linguistic Atlas of the Upper Midwest
**LAUNC** ..... Launceston [*Municipal borough in England*]
**Laund News** ... Laundry News [*A publication*]
**Laundry Dry Clean J Can** ... Laundry and Dry Cleaning Journal of Canada [*A publication*]
**Lau de Pin** ... Laurentius de Pinu [*Deceased, 1397*] [*Authority cited in pre-1607 legal work*] (DSA)
**LAUR** ........ Laurel Entertainment, Inc. [*NASDAQ symbol*] (NQ)
**Lau R** ......... Laurel Review [*A publication*]
**Laur** .......... Laurentian Library [*Classical studies*] (OCD)
**Laur** .......... Laurentius Hispanus [*Deceased, 1248*] [*Authority cited in pre-1607 legal work*] (DSA)
**Laur** .......... Reports of the High Court of Griqualand [*1882-1910*] [*South Africa*] [*A publication*] (DLA)
**Lauren** ........ Laurentius Hispanus [*Deceased, 1248*] [*Authority cited in pre-1607 legal work*] (DSA)
**Laurence** .... Laurence's Reports of the High Court of Griqualand [*1882-1910*] [*South Africa*] [*A publication*] (DLA)
**Lauren de Rodul** ... Laurentius de Rodulphis [*Flourished, 15th century*] [*Authority cited in pre-1607 legal work*] (DSA)
**Laur HC Ca** ... Lauren's High Court Cases [*South Africa*] [*A publication*] (DLA)
**Laur de Palat** ... Laurentius de Pallatis [*Flourished, 16th century*] [*Authority cited in pre-1607 legal work*] (DSA)
**Laur Prim** .. Laurence's Primogeniture [*1878*] [*A publication*] (DLA)
**LAUS** ......... Local Area Unemployment Statistics (OICC)
**LAUSC** ...... Linguistic Atlas of the United States and Canada [*1930*]
**Lauss Eq** .... Laussat's Equity Practice in Pennsylvania [*A publication*] (DLA)
**LAUTRO** ... Life Assurance and Unit Trust Regulatory Organisation [*British*]
**lav** .......... Latvian [*MARC language code*] [*Library of Congress*] (LCCP)
**LAV** .......... Launch Axis, Vertical (MCD)
**LAV** .......... Lavatory (KSC)
**lav** .......... Lavender [*Philately*]
**LAV** .......... Lifting Ascent Vehicle
**LAV** .......... Light Armored Vehicle [*Army*] (RDA)
**LAV** .......... Linea Aeropostal Venezolana [*Venezuelan airline*]
**LAV** .......... Lymphadenopathy-Associated Virus
**LAV** .......... Lymphocyte-Associated Virus
**LAV** .......... Varah [*L. A.*] Ltd. [*Toronto Stock Exchange symbol*]
**LAVA** ........ Linear Acoustic Vernier Analyzer (CAAL)
**LAVA** ........ Linear Amplifier for Various Applications (IEEE)
**LAVA** ........ Low-Frequency Acoustic Vernier Analyzer (NVT)
**LAV/ADS** ... Light Armored Vehicle/Air Defense System [*Army*]
**Laval Med** ... Laval Medical [*A publication*]
**Laval Theol** ... Laval Theologique et Philosophique [*A publication*]
**Laval Theol Phil** ... Laval Theologique et Philosophique [*A publication*]
**LavalTPh** ... Laval Theologique et Philosophique [*Quebec*] [*A publication*] (BJA)
**Laval Univ For Res Found Contrib** ... Laval University Forest Research Foundation. Contributions [*A publication*]
**Lav Arroz** ... Lavoura Arrozeira [*A publication*]
**LAV-AT** .... Light Armored Vehicle - Antitank [*Canada*]
**LAVE** ......... Association Vocanologique Europeenne [*European Volcanological Association*] [*Paris, France*] (EAIO)
**LAVEND** ... Lavendula [*Lavender*] [*Pharmacology*] (ROG)
**LAVEPA** ... Local Administration of Vocational Education and Practical Arts (OICC)
**LAVERS** .... Lake Vessel Reporting System
**LAVFWUS** ... Ladies Auxiliary to the Veterans of Foreign Wars of the United States (EA)
**Lav Ist Anat Istol Patol (Perugia)** ... Lavori. Istituto di Anatomia e Istologia Patologica. Universita degli Studi (Perugia) [*A publication*]
**Lav Ist Anat Istol Patol Univ Studi (Perugia)** ... Lavori. Istituto di Anatomia e Istologia Patologica. Universita degli Studi (Perugia) [*A publication*]
**Lav Ist Bot Giardino Colon Palermo** ... Lavori. Istituto Botanico Giardino Coloniale di Palermo [*A publication*]
**LAVM** ....... Low-Altitude Vulnerability Model [*Aerospace*] (MCD)
**LAVMA** ..... Lavoro e Medicina [*A publication*]
**Lav Med** .... Lavoro e Medicina [*A publication*]
**Lav Neuropsichiatr** ... Lavoro Neuropsichiatrico [*A publication*]
**LAVO** ........ Lassen Volcanic National Park
**LAVO** ........ Lavatory [*Slang*] (DSUE)
**Lavori Ist Anat Istol Patol Univ Studi (Perugia)** ... Lavori. Istituto di Anatomia e Istologia Patologica. Universita degli Studi (Perugia) [*Italy*] [*A publication*]
**Lav Pall** ...... Lavacrum Palladis [*of Callimachus*] [*Classical studies*] (OCD)
**LavTP** ........ Laval Theologique et Philosophique [*A publication*]
**Lav Um** ...... Lavoro Umano [*A publication*]
**Lav Um Suppl** ... Lavoro Umano. Supplemento [*Italy*] [*A publication*]
**Law** .......... Alabama Lawyer [*A publication*]
**LAW** .......... Ladies Against Women (EA)
**LAW** .......... Land Authority for Wales
**LAW** .......... Lawrence [*Kansas*] [*Seismograph station code, US Geological Survey*] (SEIS)
**LAW** .......... Lawter International, Inc. [*NYSE symbol*] (SPSG)
**LAW** .......... Lawton [*Oklahoma*] [*Airport symbol*] (OAG)
**LAW** .......... Lawton, OK [*Location identifier*] [*FAA*] (FAAL)
**LAW** .......... Lawyer (ADA)
**LAW** .......... Leading Aircraft Woman [*RAF*] [*British*]
**LAW** .......... League of American Wheelmen
**LAW** .......... Left Attack Wing [*Women's lacrosse position*]
**LAW** .......... Left-Handers Against the World [*Defunct*] (EA)
**LAW** .......... Legal Advocates for Women (EA)
**LAW** .......... Legal Aid Warranty [*Fund providing legal services in case of arrest*]
**LAW** .......... Light Antiarmor Weapon [*Military*] (RDA)
**LAW** .......... Light Antitank Weapon
**LAW** .......... Light Area Weapon
**LAW** .......... Light Assault Weapon
**LAW** .......... Local Air Warning
**LAW** .......... Logistics Action Worksheet
**Law** .......... London Law Magazine [*A publication*]
**LAW** .......... Low-Acid Waste [*Nuclear energy*] (NRCH)
**LAW** .......... Low-Altitude Warning (MCD)
**LAW** .......... Loyalist Association of Workers [*Trade union*] [*Northern Ireland*]
**LAW** .......... Quaere Legal Resources Ltd. [*UTLAS symbol*]
**LAW** .......... United States Supreme Court Library, Washington, DC [*OCLC symbol*] (OCLC)
**Law Advert** ... Law Advertiser [*1823-31*] [*A publication*] (DLA)
**Law Alm** ..... Law Almanac [*New York*] [*A publication*] (DLA)
**Law Am** ...... Lawyer of the Americas [*A publication*]
**Law Amdt J** ... Law Amendment Journal [*1855-58*] [*A publication*] (DLA)
**Law Amer** .. Lawyer of the Americas [*A publication*]
**Law Americas** ... Lawyer of the Americas [*A publication*]
**Law Am Jour** ... Law Amendment Journal [*1855-58*] [*A publication*] (DLA)
**LAWASIA** ... Law Association for Asia and the Pacific [*Australia*] (EAIO)
**LAWASIA** ... LAWASIA. Journal of the Law Association for Asia and the Western Pacific [*A publication*] (DLA)
**LAWASIA CLB** ... LAWASIA [*Law Association for Asia and the Pacific*] Commercial Law Bulletin [*A publication*] (APTA)
**LAWASIA HRB** ... LAWASIA [*Law Association for Asia and the Pacific*] Human Rights Bulletin [*A publication*]
**LAWASIA LJ** ... LAWASIA [*Law Association for Asia and the Pacific*] Law Journal [*A publication*] (DLA)
**LAWASIA (NS)** ... LAWASIA [*Law Association for Asia and the Pacific*] (New Series) [*A publication*] (APTA)
**LA Water Resour Res Inst Bull** ... Louisiana Water Resources Research Institute. Bulletin [*A publication*]
**LAWB** ........ Los Alamos Water Boiler [*Nuclear reactor*] (NRCH)
**Law & Bank** ... Lawyer and Banker [*New Orleans*] [*A publication*] (DLA)
**Law & Bank** ... Lawyers' and Bankers' Quarterly [*A publication*] (DLA)

**Law & Banker** ... Lawyer and Banker and Central Law Journal [*A publication*] (DLA)
**Law & Bk Bull** ... Weekly Law and Bank Bulletin [*Ohio*] [*A publication*] (DLA)
**Law Bk Rev Dig** ... Law Book Review Digest and Current Legal Bibliography [*A publication*] (DLA)
**Law Bul**...... Law Bulletin [*A publication*]
**Law Bul & Br** ... Law Bulletin and Brief [*A publication*] (DLA)
**Law Bul IA** ... Law Bulletin. State University of Iowa [*A publication*] (DLA)
**Law Bull**..... Law Bulletin [*Zambia*] [*A publication*] (DLA)
**Law Bull**..... Weekly Law Bulletin [*Ohio*] [*A publication*] (DLA)
**LAW/BUSA** ... League of American Wheelman/Bicycle USA (EA)
**Law Cas Wm I** ... Law Cases, William I to Richard I [*England*] [*A publication*] (DLA)
**Law Ch Bdg Soc** ... Law on Church Building Societies [*A publication*] (DLA)
**Law Ch P** ... Lawes on Charterparties [*1813*] [*A publication*] (DLA)
**Law Chr** ..... Law Chronicle [*England*] [*A publication*] (DLA)
**Law Chr** ..... Law Chronicle [*South Africa*] [*A publication*] (ILCA)
**Law Chr & Auct Rec** ... Law Chronicle and Auction Record [*A publication*] (DLA)
**Law Chr & Jour Jur** ... Law Chronicle and Journal of Jurisprudence [*A publication*] (DLA)
**Law Ch Ward** ... Law on Church Wardens [*A publication*] (DLA)
**Law Cl**........ Law Clerk (DLA)
**Law Cl Rec** ... Law Clerk Record [*1910-11*] [*A publication*] (DLA)
**Law Com**.... Law Commission (DLA)
**Law Com**.... Law Commission Report [*A publication*] (DLA)
**Law Committee News** ... Lawyers' Committee News [*A publication*] (DLA)
**Law & Comp Tech** ... Law and Computer Technology [*Later, Law/Technology*] [*A publication*]
**Law & Comput Tech** ... Law and Computer Technology [*Later, Law/Technology*] [*A publication*]
**Law & Comput Technol** ... Law and Computer Technology [*Later, Law/Technology*] [*A publication*]
**Law Con**..... Lawson on Contracts [*A publication*] (DLA)
**Law and Con Pr** ... Law and Contemporary Problems [*A publication*]
**Law in Cont** ... Law in Context [*A publication*]
**Law & Contemp Prob** ... Law and Contemporary Problems [*A publication*]
**Law Contemp Probl Ser** ... Law and Contemporary Problems Series [*A publication*]
**Law Cont Pr** ... Law and Contemporary Problems [*A publication*]
**Law Council Newsl** ... Law Council Newsletter [*A publication*] (APTA)
**Law Dept Bull** ... Law Department Bulletin, Union Pacific Railroad Co. [*A publication*] (DLA)
**Law Dig**...... Law Digest [*A publication*]
**LAWDS**..... LORAN-Aided Weapons Delivery System
**LAWEB**..... Lake Warning [*or Weather*] Bulletin [*National Weather Service*] [*A publication*]
**Law Ecc Law** ... Law's Ecclesiastical Law [*2nd ed.*] [*1844*] [*A publication*] (DLA)
**Law Ed**....... Lawyer's Edition, United States Supreme Court Reports [*A publication*] (DLA)
**Law Ed Adv Op** ... United States Supreme Court Reports, Lawyers' Edition, Advance Opinions [*A publication*] (DLA)
**Law Ed 2d** ... United States Supreme Court Reports, Lawyers' Edition, Second Series [*A publication*] (DLA)
**Law & Eq Rep** ... Law and Equity Reporter [*New York*] [*A publication*] (DLA)
**Lawes Ch** ... Lawes on Charterparties [*1813*] [*A publication*] (DLA)
**Lawes Pl**..... Lawes on Pleading [*A publication*] (DLA)
**Law Ex J**.... Law Examination Journal [*A publication*] (DLA)
**Law Ex Rep** ... Law Examination Reporter [*A publication*] (DLA)
**LAWFA**..... Landwirtschaftliche Forschung [*A publication*]
**Law Fr Dict** ... Law French Dictionary [*A publication*] (DLA)
**Law Gaz**..... Law Gazette [*A publication*] (DLA)
**Law Guild M** ... Lawyers' Guild Monthly [*A publication*] (DLA)
**Law Guild Rev** ... Lawyers Guild Review [*A publication*]
**LAWH**....... Lawhon [*John F.*] Furniture [*NASDAQ symbol*] (NQ)
**Law & Hist Rev** ... Law and History Review [*A publication*] (DLA)
**Law and Housing J** ... Law and Housing Journal [*A publication*]
**Law and Hum Behav** ... Law and Human Behavior [*A publication*]
**Law Hum Behav** ... Law and Human Behavior [*A publication*]
**Law Inst J** ... Law Institute Journal [*A publication*] (APTA)
**Law Int**....... Law Intelligencer [*United States*] [*A publication*] (DLA)
**Law & Int Aff** ... Law and International Affairs [*A publication*]
**Law J** ......... Law Journal Reports [*A publication*] (DLA)
**Law J** ......... Lawyers Journal [*A publication*]
**Law Ja** ....... Law in Japan [*A publication*]
**Law J Ch**.... Law Journal, New Series, Chancery [*A publication*] (DLA)
**Law J Exch** ... Law Journal, New Series, Exchequer [*A publication*] (DLA)
**Law Jour**.... Law Journal [*A publication*]
**Law Jour**.... Law Journal Reports [*A publication*] (DLA)
**Law Jour (M & W)** ... Morgan and Williams' Law Journal [*London*] [*A publication*] (DLA)
**Law Jour (Smith's)** ... [*J. P.*] Smith's Law Journal [*London*] [*A publication*] (DLA)
**Law JPD**.... Law Journal, Probate Division [*A publication*] (DLA)
**Law JPD & A** ... Law Journal Reports, New Series, Probate, Divorce, and Admiralty [*1875-1946*] [*A publication*] (DLA)
**Law JQB**.... Law Journal, New Series, English Queen's Bench [*A publication*] (DLA)
**Law Jr QB** ... Law Journal, New Series, English Queen's Bench [*A publication*] (DLA)
**Law Jur**...... Law's Jurisdiction of the Federal Courts [*A publication*] (DLA)
**Law and Just** ... Law and Justice [*A publication*]
**Law Lat Dic** ... Law Latin Dictionary [*A publication*] (DLA)
**Law & Legisl in the German Dem Rep** ... Law and Legislation in the German Democratic Republic [*A publication*] (DLA)
**Law & Lib**.. Law and Liberty [*A publication*] (DLA)
**Law Lib**...... Law Librarian [*A publication*]
**Law Lib J**... Law Library Journal [*A publication*]
**Law Libn**.... Law Librarian [*A publication*]
**Law Lib N**... Law Library News [*A publication*] (DLA)
**Law Lib NS** ... Law Library, New Series [*Philadelphia, PA*] [*A publication*] (DLA)
**Law Libr J** ... Law Library Journal [*A publication*]
**Law Librn**.. Law Librarian [*A publication*]
**Law LJ**....... Lawrence Law Journal [*A publication*] (DLA)
**Law & L N** ... Lawyer and Law Notes [*A publication*]
**LAW M**..... Law Magazine and Review [*A publication*] (ROG)
**LawM** ........ Lawrence Microfilming Service, Fuquay-Varina, NC [*Library symbol*] [*Library of Congress*] (LCLS)
**LAWM**...... Light All-Weather Missile (MCD)
**Law Mag**.... Law Magazine [*A publication*] (DLA)
**Law & Mag** ... Lawyer and Magistrate Magazine [*1898-99*] [*Dublin*] [*A publication*] (DLA)
**Law & Magis Mag** ... Lawyer's and Magistrate's Magazine [*A publication*] (DLA)
**Law Mag & Law Rev** ... Law Magazine and Law Review [*A publication*] (DLA)
**Law & Mag Mag** ... Lawyer and Magistrate Magazine [*1898-99*] [*Dublin*] [*A publication*] (DLA)
**Law Mag & R** ... Law Magazine and Review [*A publication*] (DLA)
**Law Mag & Rev** ... Law Magazine and Review [*A publication*] (DLA)
**Law Man on Prof Conduct ABA/BNA** ... Lawyers' Manual on Professional Conduct. American Bar Association/Bureau of National Affairs [*A publication*]
**Law Med Health Care** ... Law, Medicine, and Health Care [*A publication*]
**Law Med & Health Care** ... Law, Medicine, and Health Care [*A publication*]
**Law Med J** ... Lawyer's Medical Journal [*A publication*]
**Law Mo**...... Western Law Monthly (Reprint) [*Ohio*] [*A publication*] (DLA)
**Law N** ........ Law News [*A publication*] (DLA)
**Law N** ........ Law Notes [*A publication*]
**Lawn Gard Mark** ... Lawn and Garden Marketing [*A publication*]
**Lawn Gardn** ... Lawn and Garden Marketing [*A publication*]
**Law Off Econ & Management** ... Law Office Economics and Management [*A publication*]
**Law Off Econ and Mgt** ... Law Office Economics and Management [*A publication*]
**Law Off Information Service** ... Law Office Information Service [*A publication*]
**Law Pat**...... Law's United States Patent Cases [*A publication*] (DLA)
**Law Pat Dig** ... Law's Digest of United States Patent Cases [*A publication*] (DLA)
**Law Phil**..... Law and Philosophy [*A publication*]
**Law Pl**........ Lawes' Pleading in Assumpsit [*1810*] [*A publication*] (DLA)
**Law Pl**........ Lawes' Pleading in Civil Actions [*1806*] [*A publication*] (DLA)
**Law and Policy Internat Bus** ... Law and Policy in International Business [*A publication*]
**Law and Pol Int Bus** ... Law and Policy in International Business [*A publication*]
**Law & Pol Int'l Bus** ... Law and Policy in International Business [*A publication*]
**Law and Poly Intl Bus** ... Law and Policy in International Business [*A publication*]
**Law and Poly Q** ... Law and Policy Quarterly [*A publication*]
**Law Pr**........ Law's Practice in United States Courts [*A publication*] (DLA)
**Law & Psychology Rev** ... Law and Psychology Review [*A publication*] (DLA)
**Law and Psych Rev** ... Law and Psychology Review [*A publication*]
**Law Q**......... Law Quarterly Review [*A publication*]
**Law Q R**..... Law Quarterly Review [*A publication*]
**Law Q Rev** ... Law Quarterly Review [*A publication*]
**Law Quar Rev** ... Law Quarterly Review [*A publication*]
**Law Quart** ... Law Quarterly Review [*A publication*]
**Law Quart R** ... Law Quarterly Review [*A publication*]
**Law Quart Rev** ... Law Quarterly Review [*A publication*]
**Law R**......... Law Review [*A publication*] (APTA)
**Lawr**........... Lawrence High Court Reports [*Griqualand*] [*A publication*] (DLA)
**LAWR** ....... Weekly Report (Latin American) [*A publication*]
**Law Rec** ..... Ceylon Law Recorder [*A publication*] (DLA)
**Law Rec** ..... Irish Law Recorder [*1827-38*] [*A publication*] (ILCA)
**Law Rec** ..... Law Recorder [*1827-31*] [*Ireland*] [*A publication*] (DLA)
**Law Rec (NS)** ... Law Recorder, New Series [*Ireland*] [*A publication*] (DLA)
**Law Rec (OS)** ... Law Recorder, First Series [*Ireland*] [*A publication*] (DLA)
**Law Ref Com** ... Law Reform Committee (DLA)
**Law Ref Cttee** ... Law Reform Committee (DLA)
**Law Reg**..... American Law Register [*Philadelphia*] [*A publication*] (DLA)
**Law Reg**..... Law Register, Chicago [*A publication*] (DLA)
**Law Reg Cas** ... Lawson's Registration Cases [*England*] [*A publication*] (DLA)
**Lawrence**.... Lawrence's Reports [*20 Ohio*] [*A publication*] (DLA)

**Lawrence Comp Dec** ... Lawrence's First Comptroller's Decisions [*United States*] [*A publication*] (DLA)
**Lawrence Compt Dec** ... Lawrence's First Comptroller's Decisions [*United States*] [*A publication*] (DLA)
**Lawrence Livermore Lab Rep** ... Lawrence Livermore Laboratory. Report [*A publication*]
**Lawrence Rev Nat Prod** ... Lawrence Review of Natural Products [*A publication*]
**Lawrence Rev Nat Prod Monogr Syst** ... Lawrence Review of Natural Products. Monograph System [*A publication*]
**Law Rep**..... Law Reporter [*England*] [*A publication*] (DLA)
**Law Rep**..... Law Reporter (Ramsey and Morin) [*Canada*] [*A publication*] (DLA)
**Law Rep**..... Law Reports [*England*] [*A publication*] (DLA)
**Law Rep**..... Louisiana Reports [*A publication*] (DLA)
**Law Rep**..... New Zealand Law Reports [*A publication*] (DLA)
**Law Rep**..... Ohio Law Reporter [*A publication*] (DLA)
**Law Rep A & E** ... Law Reports, Admiralty and Ecclesiastical Cases [*1865-75*] [*A publication*] (DLA)
**Law Rep App Cas** ... Law Reports, Appeal Cases [*England*] [*A publication*] (DLA)
**Law Rep CC** ... Law Reports, Crown Cases [*A publication*] (DLA)
**Law Rep Ch** ... Law Reports, Chancery Appeal Cases [*England*] [*A publication*] (DLA)
**Law Rep Ch App** ... Law Reports, Chancery Appeal Cases [*England*] [*A publication*] (DLA)
**Law Rep Ch D** ... Law Reports, Chancery Division [*A publication*] (DLA)
**Law Rep CP** ... Law Reports, Common Pleas [*England*] [*A publication*] (DLA)
**Law Rep CPD** ... Law Reports, Common Pleas Division [*England*] [*A publication*] (DLA)
**Law Rep Dig** ... Law Reports Digest [*A publication*] (DLA)
**Law Rep Eq** ... Law Reports, Equity Cases [*A publication*] (DLA)
**Law Rep Ex** ... Law Reports, Exchequer [*A publication*] (DLA)
**Law Rep Ex D** ... Law Reports, Exchequer Division [*England*] [*A publication*] (DLA)
**Law Rep HL** ... Law Reports, House of Lords, English and Irish Appeal Cases [*A publication*] (DLA)
**Law Rep HL Sc** ... Law Reports, Scotch and Divorce Appeal Cases, House of Lords [*A publication*] (DLA)
**Law Rep Ind App** ... Law Reports, Indian Appeals [*A publication*] (DLA)
**Law Rep Ir** ... Law Reports, Irish [*A publication*] (DLA)
**Law Rep Misc D** ... Law Reports, Miscellaneous Division [*A publication*] (DLA)
**Law Rep NS** ... Law Reports, New Series [*New York*] [*A publication*] (DLA)
**Law Repos** ... Carolina Law Repository [*North Carolina*] [*A publication*] (DLA)
**Law Rep P** ... Law Reports, Probate [*A publication*] (DLA)
**Law Rep PC** ... Law Reports, Privy Council, Appeal Cases [*England*] [*A publication*] (DLA)
**Law Rep P & D** ... Law Reports, Probate and Divorce Cases [*A publication*] (DLA)
**Law Rep QB** ... Law Reports, Queen's Bench [*A publication*] (DLA)
**Law Rep QBD** ... Law Reports, Queen's Bench Division [*A publication*] (DLA)
**Law Repr**.... Law Reporter (Ramsey and Morin) [*Canada*] [*A publication*] (DLA)
**Law Rep (Tor)** ... Law Reporter (Toronto) [*A publication*] (DLA)
**Law Rev**..... Law Review [*A publication*]
**Law Rev J**.. Law Review Journal [*A publication*] (DLA)
**Law Rev Qu** ... Law Review Quarterly [*Albany, NY*] [*A publication*] (DLA)
**Law Rev & Qu J** ... Law Review and Quarterly Journal [*London*] [*A publication*] (DLA)
**Law Rev U Det** ... Law Review. University of Detroit [*A publication*] (DLA)
**LAWRS**..... Limited Aviation Weather Reporting Station [*FAA*] (FAAC)
**Lawr Wh**.... Lawrence's Edition of Wheaton on International Law [*A publication*] (DLA)
**LAWS**........ LASER Atmospheric Wind Sounder [*NASA*]
**LAWS**........ Lawson Products, Inc. [*NASDAQ symbol*] (NQ)
**LAWS**........ Lawyers Alliance for World Security (EA)
**LAWS**........ Leadership and World Society [*Defunct*]
**LAWS**........ Low-Altitude Warning System (NVT)
**Laws Austl Cap Terr** ... Laws of the Australian Capital Territory [*1911-59*] [*In force on 1 January 1960*] [*A publication*] (DLA)
**Law School Rec** ... Law School Record [*Chicago*] [*A publication*] (DLA)
**Law School Rev** ... Law School Review. Toronto University [*A publication*] (DLA)
**Laws Cont** ... Lawson on Contracts [*A publication*] (DLA)
**Law Ser MO Bull** ... University of Missouri. Bulletin. Law Series [*A publication*] (DLA)
**LAWSO**..... Lockheed Antisubmarine Warfare Systems Organization
**Law & Soc** ... Law and Social Change [*A publication*] (DLA)
**Law Soc ACT NL** ... Law Society of the Australian Capital Territory. Newsletter [*A publication*]
**Law Soc Bull** ... Law Society. Bulletin [*South Australia*] [*A publication*] (APTA)
**Law Soc G** ... Law Society. Gazette [*A publication*]
**Law Soc Gaz** ... Law Society's Gazette [*A publication*]
**Law and Society R** ... Law and Society Review [*A publication*]
**Law Soc J**... Law Society. Journal [*A publication*] (APTA)
**Law Soc Jo** ... Law Society of Massachusetts. Journal [*A publication*] (DLA)
**Law & Soc Ord** ... Law and the Social Order [*A publication*]
**Law & Soc Order** ... Law and the Social Order [*A publication*]
**Law Soc Prob** ... Law and Social Problems [*Pondicherry*] [*A publication*]
**Law & Soc R** ... Law and Society Review [*A publication*]
**Law Soc R**.. Law and Society Review [*A publication*]
**Law & Soc Rev** ... Law and Society Review [*A publication*]
**Law Soc Tas NL** ... Law Society of Tasmania. Newsletter [*A publication*]
**Law Socy Gaz** ... Law Society. Gazette [*A publication*]
**Law Socy J** ... Law Society. Journal [*A publication*]
**Law and Socy Rev** ... Law and Society Review [*A publication*]
**Law Soc'y Scotl** ... Law Society of Scotland. Journal [*A publication*] (DLA)
**Lawson Exp Ev** ... Lawson on Expert and Opinion Evidence [*A publication*] (DLA)
**Lawson Pres Ev** ... Lawson on Presumptive Evidence [*A publication*] (DLA)
**Lawson Rights Rem & Pr** ... Lawson on Rights, Remedies, and Practice [*A publication*] (DLA)
**Lawson Usages & Cust** ... Lawson on the Law of Usages and Customs [*A publication*] (DLA)
**Laws Reg Cas** ... Lawson's Registration Cases, Irish [*1885-1914*] [*A publication*] (DLA)
**Law State**... Law and State [*A publication*]
**Law Stud**.... Law Student [*A publication*] (ILCA)
**Law Stud Mag** ... Law Students' Magazine [*A publication*] (DLA)
**Law Stud Mag NS** ... Law Students' Magazine. New Series [*A publication*] (DLA)
**Law Stu H** ... Law Students' Helper [*A publication*] (ILCA)
**Law Stu Mag** ... Law Students' Magazine [*A publication*] (DLA)
**Laws Wom** ... Laws of Women [*A publication*] (DLA)
**Law T**......... Law Times Reports [*A publication*] (DLA)
**Law Tcher** ... Law Teacher [*A publication*]
**Law Tchr**.... Law Teacher [*A publication*] (DLA)
**Law Tech** ... Law/Technology [*A publication*]
**Law/Technol** ... Law/Technology [*A publication*]
**Law Tenn Rep** ... Tennessee Reports [*A publication*] (DLA)
**Law Times (NS)** ... Law Times. New Series [*Pennsylvania*] [*A publication*] (DLA)
**Law Times (OS)** ... Law Times, Old Series [*Luzerne, PA*] [*A publication*] (DLA)
**Law Title Guar Funds News** ... Lawyers Title Guaranty Funds News [*A publication*]
**Law T NS**... Law Times. New Series [*Pennsylvania*] [*A publication*] (DLA)
**Law T NS**... Law Times Reports, New Series [*England*] [*A publication*] (DLA)
**Law Tr**....... Law Tracts [*A publication*] (DLA)
**Law T Rep NS** ... Law Times Reports, New Series [*England*] [*A publication*] (DLA)
**Law T Rep OS** ... Law Times Reports, Old Series [*England*] [*A publication*] (DLA)
**Law of Trusts Tiff & Bul** ... Tiffany and Bullard on Trusts and Trustees [*A publication*] (DLA)
**Law US Cts** ... Law's Practice in United States Courts [*A publication*] (DLA)
**LAWV**....... [*The*] Lorain & West Virginia Railway Co. [*AAR code*]
**Law V & S** ... Lawrence's Visitation and Search [*A publication*] (DLA)
**Law W**........ Law Weekly [*A publication*] (DLA)
**Law Wheat** ... Lawrence's Edition of Wheaton on International Law [*A publication*] (DLA)
**Lawy**........... Lawyer (DLA)
**Lawyer & Banker** ... Lawyer and Banker and Central Law Journal [*A publication*] (DLA)
**Lawyers Co-Op** ... Lawyers Co-Operative Publishing Co. (DLA)
**Lawyers Med J** ... Lawyer's Medical Journal [*A publication*]
**Lawyers' Rep Ann** ... Lawyers' Reports, Annotated [*A publication*] (DLA)
**Lawyers' Rep Annotated** ... Lawyers' Reports, Annotated [*A publication*] (DLA)
**Lawyers' Rev** ... Lawyers' Review [*A publication*] (DLA)
**Lawy & LN** ... Lawyer and Law Notes [*A publication*]
**Lawy Mag** ... Lawyers' Magazine [*A publication*] (DLA)
**Lawy Med J** ... Lawyer's Medical Journal [*A publication*]
**Lawy Rep Ann** ... Lawyers' Reports, Annotated [*A publication*] (DLA)
**Lawy Rev** ... Lawyers' Review [*A publication*] (DLA)
**LAX**........... Bahia De Los Angeles [*Mexico*] [*Seismograph station code, US Geological Survey*] (SEIS)
**LAX**........... Lacrosse [*British*] (ROG)
**LAX**........... Laurel Explorations Ltd. [*Vancouver Stock Exchange symbol*]
**lax**............. Laxative [*Pharmacy*]
**LAX**........... Los Angeles [*California*] [*Airport symbol*] (OAG)
**LAY**........... Ladysmith [*South Africa*] [*Airport symbol*] (OAG)
**LAY**........... Lanyu [*Republic of China*] [*Seismograph station code, US Geological Survey*] (SEIS)
**Lay**............ Lay's English Chancery Reports [*A publication*] (DLA)
**La-Yaaran For Israel For Assoc** ... La-Ya'aran/The Forester. Israel Forestry Association [*A publication*]
**LAYGEN**... Layout Generator [*Ergonomics*]
**Layos**......... Layos, Hollywood [*Record label*]
**LAZ**........... Bom Jesus Da Lapa [*Brazil*] [*Airport symbol*] (OAG)
**LAZ**........... La Luz Mines Ltd. [*Toronto Stock Exchange symbol*]
**LAZR**........ Laser Photonics, Inc. [*NASDAQ symbol*] (NQ)
**LB**............. Baccalaureus Literarum [*Bachelor of Literature*]
**LB**............. Farbwerke Hoechst AG [*Germany*] [*Research code symbol*]
**LB**............. Graduate in Letters
**LB**............. LaBarge, Inc. [*AMEX symbol*] (SPSG)

**LB** ............. Laboratory Bulletin
**LB** ............. Labrador [*Canada*] [*Postal code*]
**LB** ............. Lactose Broth [*Microbiology*]
**L/B**............. Ladingsbrief [*Bill of Lading*] [*Afrikaans*]
**LB** ............. Lady Boss
**LB** ............. Lag Bolt [*Technical drawings*]
**LB** ............. Lamellar Body [*Physiology*]
**LB** ............. Land Based
**LB** ............. Landing Barge
**LB** ............. Landing Beach [*Navy*]
**L/B**............. Landing Book [*Tea trade*] (ROG)
**LB** ............. Lane Bryant, Inc.
**LB** ............. Large Bowel [*Anatomy*]
**LB** ............. Last Brochure
**LB** ............. Late Babylonian (BJA)
**LB** ............. Late Bronze [*Age*] (BJA)
**LB** ............. Launch Boost (MCD)
**LB** ............. Launch Bunker (MUGU)
**LB** ............. Launch Bus (NASA)
**LB** ............. Laurentian Bank of Canada [*Toronto Stock Exchange symbol*]
**LB** ............. Lavatory Basin
**L & B**.......... Leadam and Baldwin's Select Cases before the King's Council [*England*] [*A publication*] (DLA)
**LB** ............. Lebanon [*ANSI two-letter standard code*] (CNC)
**LB** ............. Lectori Benevolo [*To the Kind (or Gentle) Reader*] [*Latin*]
**LB** ............. Lecture Bottle [*Shipment of gas products*] [*Union Carbide Corp.*]
**LB** ............. Left on Base [*Baseball*]
**L & B**.......... Left and Below [*Medicine*]
**LB** ............. Left Border [*Genetics*]
**LB** ............. Left Buttock [*Medicine*]
**LB** ............. Left Fullback [*Soccer*]
**LB** ............. Leg Bye [*Cricket*]
**LB** ............. Legal Bond [*Investment term*]
**LB** ............. Legum Baccalaureus [*Bachelor of Laws*]
**LB** ............. Leiomyoblastoma [*Medicine*]
**Lb** ............. Leptosphaerulinia briosiana [*A fungus*]
**LB** ............. Letter Box
**LB** ............. Leuvense Bijdragen [*Bijblad*] [*A publication*]
**LB** ............. Levende Billeder [*A publication*]
**LB** ............. Levobunolol [*Also, LBUN*] [*Biochemistry*]
**LB** ............. Liaison Branch [*BUPERS*]
**LB** ............. Liberalized Imports [*Yugoslavia*] (IMH)
**lb** ............. Liberia [*MARC country of publication code*] [*Library of Congress*] (LCCP)
**lb** ............. Libra [*Pound*] [*Unit of weight*] (AAG)
**LB** ............. Library Bulletin
**LB** ............. Lifeboat (AAG)
**LB** ............. Ligand Binding Domain [*Genetics*]
**LB** ............. Light Battalion [*British military*] (DMA)
**LB** ............. Light Bombardment [*Air Force*]
**LB** ............. Light Bomber [*Air Force*]
**LB** ............. Light Bracket (AAG)
**LB** ............. Limited Base [*Air Force*] (AFM)
**LB** ............. Limited Benefits [*Unemployment insurance*] (OICC)
**LB** ............. Limited Partner in Brokers Firm [*London Stock Exchange*]
**LB** ............. Line Buffer [*Data processing*]
**LB** ............. Line Busy
**LB** ............. Linebacker [*Football*]
**LB** ............. Linguistica Biblica [*A publication*]
**LB** ............. Linoleum Base [*Technical drawings*]
**L & B**.......... Literature and Belief [*A publication*]
**LB** ............. Litter Bearer (AABC)
**LB** ............. Litterarum Baccalaureus [*Bachelor of Letters or Literature*]
**LB** ............. Live Birth
**LB** ............. Living Bank (EA)
**LB** ............. Lloyd Aereo Boliviano SA [*Bolivia*] [*ICAO designator*] (FAAC)
**LB** ............. Load Bank [*Data processing*] (KSC)
**LB** ............. Local Battery [*Radio*]
**LB** ............. Local Board
**LB** ............. Log Book
**LB** ............. Logan Brothers Book Co.
**LB** ............. Logical Block
**LB** ............. London Borough [*England*]
**LB** ............. London Bridge
**LB** ............. Long Bill [*Business term*]
**LB** ............. Long Binh [*Vietnam*]
**LB** ............. Loose Body [*Medicine*]
**L & B**.......... Lothians and Border Horse [*British military*] (DMA)
**LB** ............. Low Back [*Disorder*] [*Medicine*]
**LB** ............. Low Band (AAG)
**LB** ............. Low Bay (KSC)
**LB** ............. Lower Bearing
**LB** ............. Lower Bound [*Data processing*]
**LB** ............. Lower Brace (MCD)
**LB** ............. Lunch Break
**LB** ............. Photographic Laboratory Specialist [*Navy*]
**lb** ............. Pound [*Libra*] [*Unit of weight*]
**LB1** ............ Lasa B Ring [*Montana*] [*Seismograph station code, US Geological Survey*] (SEIS)
**LB2** ............ Lasa B Ring [*Montana*] [*Seismograph station code, US Geological Survey*] (SEIS)
**LB3** ............ Lasa B Ring [*Montana*] [*Seismograph station code, US Geological Survey*] (SEIS)
**LB4** ............ Lasa B Ring [*Montana*] [*Seismograph station code, US Geological Survey*] (SEIS)
**LBA** ........... Lahr/Bader Area [*Federal Republic of Germany*]
**LBA** ........... Leeds/Bradford [*England*] [*Airport symbol*] (OAG)
**LBA** ........... Ligand-Binding Assay [*Analytical biochemistry*]
**LBA** ........... Lima Bean Agar [*Microbiology*]
**LBA** ........... Limit of Basic Aircraft (MCD)
**LBA** ........... Linear-Bounded Automaton
**LBA** ........... Little Books on Art [*A publication*]
**LBA** ........... Load-Bearing Axis
**LBA** ........... Local Battery Apparatus
**LBA** ........... Local Bus Adapter [*Data processing*]
**LBA** ........... London Boroughs Association [*British*] (DCTA)
**LBA** ........... Lutheran Benevolent Association (EA)
**LBA** ........... Luxembourg Brotherhood of America (EA)
**LBAB** ......... Lima Bean Advisory Board [*Superseded by California Dry Bean Advisory Board*] (EA)
**LBAD** ......... Lexington-Blue Grass Army Depot [*Kentucky*] (AABC)
**LBAF** ......... Line Width, Black-to-White-Ratio, Area, Fixation Point
**L Bai** ......... Leges Baiarum [*A publication*] (DLA)
**LBAK**......... Lightweight Broadband Antenna Kit
**LBANA**...... Laboratory Animals [*A publication*]
**L & Bank**.... Lawyer and Banker [*A publication*] (DLA)
**LBASA** ...... Laboratory Animal Science [*A publication*]
**LBAT** ........ Late Babylonian Astronomical and Related Texts (BJA)
**LBB**............ Lancaster Bible College, Lancaster, PA [*OCLC symbol*] (OCLC)
**Lbb**............ Leishmania braziliensis braziliensis [*Microbiology*]
**LBB**............ Leuvense Bijdragen (Bijblad) [*A publication*]
**LBB**............ Life Blower Bearing
**LBB**............ Linear Ball Bushing
**LBB**............ [*The*] Little Black Book [*Cygnet Technologies, Inc.*] [*Database software*]
**LBB**............ Lubbock [*Texas*] [*Airport symbol*] (OAG)
**LBB**............ Lubbock, TX [*Location identifier*] [*FAA*] (FAAL)
**LBBA** ......... London Bacon Buyers' Association Ltd. [*British*]
**LBBB** ......... Left Bundle Branch Block [*Cardiology*]
**LBBG**......... Burgas [*Bulgaria*] [*ICAO location identifier*] (ICLI)
**LBBP** ......... Laboratory of Blood and Blood Products [*Public Health Service*]
**LBBSB**....... Left Bundle Branch System Block [*Cardiology*]
**L & B Bull** ... Daily Law and Bank Bulletin [*Ohio*] [*A publication*] (DLA)
**LBC**........... Laboratoires Bruneau & Cie [*France*] [*Research code symbol*]
**LBC**........... Land Bank Commission
**LBC**........... Landmark Bancshares Corporation [*NYSE symbol*] (SPSG)
**LBC**........... Large Bore Cannon (MCD)
**LBC**........... LASER Beam Cutting [*Welding*]
**LBC**........... Law Book Company [*Australia*]
**LBC**........... Layman's Bible Commentary [*London*] [*A publication*] (BJA)
**LBC**........... Left Book Club [*Founded in the 1930's by publisher Victor Gollancz*] [*Defunct*] [*British*]
**LBC**........... Levesque, Beaubien & Company [*Toronto Stock Exchange symbol*]
**LBC**........... Liberty Baptist College [*Virginia*]
**LBC**........... Liberty Bell Communications, Inc. [*Detroit, MI*] [*Telecommunications*] (TSSD)
**LBC**........... Lilliputian Bottle Club (EA)
**LBC**........... Line Balance Converter
**LBC**........... Load Bus Contactor [*Aviation*]
**LBC**........... Local Baggage Committee [*IATA*] (DS)
**LBC**........... Local Bus Controller
**LBC**........... Logistical Base Command [*Korea*]
**LBC**........... London Ballet Circle
**LBC**........... London Bankruptcy Court
**LBC**........... London Broadcasting Company
**LBC**........... Lothian and Berwick Cavalry [*British military*] (DMA)
**LBC**........... Lubudi [*Zaire*] [*Seismograph station code, US Geological Survey*] (SEIS)
**LBC**........... Lummer-Brodhun Cube [*Physics*]
**LBC-A** ....... LASER Beam Cutting - Air
**LBCC**......... Long Beach City College [*California*]
**LBC/CML** ... Lymphoid Blast Crisis of Chronic Myeloid Leukemia [*Oncology*]
**LBCD**......... Left Border Cardiac Dullness [*Cardiology*]
**LBC-EV**..... LASER Beam Cutting - Evaporative
**LBCF** ......... Laboratory Branch Complement Fixation [*Clinical chemistry*]
**LBC-IG**...... LASER Beam Cutting - Inert Gas
**LBCL**......... Louisville Behavior Check List [*Psychology*]
**LBCL** ......... Lymphoblastoid B-Cell Line [*Genetics*]
**LBC News** ... Law Book Company Ltd. Newsletter [*A publication*] (APTA)
**LBCO** ......... Lanthanum-Barium-Copper-Oxide [*Inorganic chemistry*]
**LBC-O** ....... LASER Beam Cutting - Oxygen
**LB Co**......... Law Book Co. [*Australia*]
**LB Cos Indust Arb Serv** ... Law Book Company's Industrial Arbitration Service [*A publication*] (APTA)
**LB Cos Practical Forms** ... Law Book Company's Practical Forms and Precedents [*A publication*] (APTA)

**LB Cos Tax Serv** ... Law Book Company's Taxation Service [*A publication*] (APTA)
**LBcS** .......... Belle Chasse State School, Belle Chasse, LA [*Library symbol*] [*Library of Congress*] (LCLS)
**LBD** .......... Left Border of Dullness [*Cardiology*]
**LBD** .......... Lifting Body Development
**LBD** .......... Light Beam Deflection
**LBD** .......... Little Black Devils [*Nickname given to the 90th Battalion of the Winnipeg Rifles during the Northwest Rebellion in 1885*]
**LBD** .......... Little Black Dress [*Women's fashions*]
**LBDQ** ........ Leader Behavior Description Questionnaire [*Psychology*]
**L/Bdr** ........ Lance-Bombardier [*British military*] (DMA)
**LBDT** ........ Low Bay Dolly Tug (NASA)
**LBE** .......... Lakewood Board of Education, Lakewood, OH [*OCLC symbol*] [*Inactive*] (OCLC)
**LBE** .......... Lance-Bubbling-Equilibrium [*Steelmaking*]
**LBE** .......... Land-Bearing Equipment [*Military*] (INF)
**LBE** .......... Landing Barge, Emergency Repair
**LBE** .......... Latrobe [*Pennsylvania*] [*Airport symbol*] (OAG)
**LBE** .......... Latrobe, PA [*Location identifier*] [*FAA*] (FAAL)
**LBE** .......... Libra Energy, Inc. [*Vancouver Stock Exchange symbol*]
**LBE** .......... Load-Bearing Equipment (INF)
**LBEA** ........ Lutheran Braille Evangelism Association (EA)
**LBeB** ........ Bossier Parish Library, Benton, LA [*Library symbol*] [*Library of Congress*] (LCLS)
**LBEB** ........ Laboratory of Brain Evolution and Behavior [*National Institute of Mental Health*]
**LBEF** ........ Land-Based Evaluation Facility [*Military*] (CAAL)
**LBEI** ........ Licentiate of the Institution of Body Engineers [*British*] (DBQ)
**L Bella** ....... Lingua Bella [*A publication*]
**LBEN** ........ Low-Byte Enable
**LBer** .......... Linguistische Berichte [*A publication*]
**Lber** .......... Literaturbericht (BJA)
**LBES** ........ Laboratory of Biomedical and Environmental Sciences [*Research center*] (RCD)
**LBF** .......... Lactobacillus bulgaricus Factor [*Biochemistry*]
**LBF** .......... Landing Barge Flak [*British military*] (DMA)
**LBF** .......... Les Buteaux [*France*] [*Seismograph station code, US Geological Survey*] (SEIS)
**LBF** .......... Liver Blood Flow [*Physiology*]
**LBF** .......... London Book Fair [*England*]
**LBF** .......... Louis Braille Foundation for Blind Musicians (EA)
**LBF** .......... Lyme Borreliosis Foundation (EA)
**LBF** .......... North Platte [*Nebraska*] [*Airport symbol*] (OAG)
**LBF** .......... North Platte, NE [*Location identifier*] [*FAA*] (FAAL)
**LBF** .......... Pounds, Force (MCD)
**LBFA** ........ Official Martin Landau-Barbara Bain Fan Association (EA)
**LBFC** ........ Landmark Financial Corporation [*Hartford, CT*] [*NASDAQ symbol*] (NQ)
**LBFC** ........ Lane Brody Fan Club (EA)
**LBFC** ........ Laura Branigan Fan Club (EA)
**LBFC** ........ Lauralee Bell Fan Club (EA)
**LB Free P**... Long Beach Free Press [*A publication*]
**LBF S/FT²** ... Pound-Force Seconds per Square Foot
**LB/FT**........ Pounds per Foot
**LB/FT²**...... Pounds per Square Foot
**LB/FT³**...... Pounds per Cubic Foot
**LB/(FT H)** ... Pounds per Foot-Hour
**LB/(FT S)** ... Pounds per Foot-Second
**LBG** .......... Le Bourget Airport [*France*]
**LBG** .......... Left Buccal Ganglion [*Medicine*]
**LBG** .......... Lucky Break Gold [*Vancouver Stock Exchange symbol*]
**LB/GAL** .... Pounds per Gallon
**LBGO** ........ Gorna Orechovitsa [*Bulgaria*] [*ICAO location identifier*] (ICLI)
**LBH** .......... Length, Breadth, Height
**LBH** .......... Local Board of Health [*British*]
**LBH** .......... Lyman-Birge-Hopfield [*System*] [*Physics*] (MUGU)
**LB/H** ......... Pounds per Hour
**LBH** .......... Sydney [*Australia*] [*Airport symbol*] (OAG)
**LBHA** ........ Little Big Horn Associates (EA)
**LB/(HP H)** ... Pounds per Horsepower-Hour
**LBI** .......... Albi [*France*] [*Airport symbol*] (OAG)
**LBI** .......... Leo Baeck Institute (EA)
**LBI** .......... Libra Industries, Inc. [*Vancouver Stock Exchange symbol*]
**LBI** .......... Library Bibliographies and Indexes [*A publication*]
**LBI** .......... Library Binding Institute (EA)
**LBI** .......... Licensed Beverage Industries [*Later, DISCUS*] (EA)
**LBI** .......... Lima Bean (trypsin) Inhibitor [*Biochemistry*]
**LBI** .......... Lloyds Bank International (ADA)
**LBI** .......... Lloyds & BOLSA [*Bank of London & South America*] International Bank Ltd. [*British*]
**LBIB** ........ Linguistica Biblica [*A publication*]
**LBibel** ....... Im Lande der Bibel [*Berlin-Dahlem*] [*A publication*] (BJA)
**LBIC** ........ Licensed Beverage Information Council (EA)
**LBIMS** ...... Laban/Bartenieff Institute of Movement Studies (EA)
**LBIN** .......... Pound-Force per Inch (MSA)
**LB/IN²**...... Pounds per Square Inch
**LB/IN³**...... Pounds per Cubic Inch
**L & B Ins Dig** ... Littleton and Blatchley's Insurance Digest [*A publication*] (DLA)
**LBIPP** ........ Licentiate of the British Institute of Professional Photography (DBQ)
**LBIR** .......... LASER Beam Image Reproducer
**LBIST** ........ Licentiate of the British Institute of Surgical Technologists (DBQ)
**LBIYB** ........ Leo Baeck Institute. Year Book [*A publication*]
**LBJ** .......... Lady Bird Johnson [*Mrs. Lyndon Baines Johnson*]
**LBj** .......... Leksykohraficny j Bjuleten [*A publication*]
**LBJ** .......... Load Bank and Jump [*Data processing*]
**LBJ** .......... Long Binh Jail [*Vietnam*]
**LBJ** .......... Lyndon Baines Johnson [*US president, 1908-1973*]
**LBJL** .......... Lyndon B. Johnson Library
**LBJSC** ....... Lyndon B. Johnson Space Center (MSC)
**LBK** .......... Landing Barge, Kitchen
**LBK** .......... Left Bank
**LBKF** ........ Landmark Banking of Florida [*NASDAQ symbol*] (NQ)
**LBL** .......... Label (MSA)
**LBL** .......... Laminar Boundary Layer
**LBL** .......... Lawrence Berkeley Laboratory [*Berkeley, CA*] [*Department of Energy*] (GRD)
**LBL** .......... Left Buttock Line (MCD)
**LBL** .......... Liberal [*Kansas*] [*Airport symbol*] (OAG)
**LBL** .......... Liberal, KS [*Location identifier*] [*FAA*] (FAAL)
**LBL** .......... Literaturblatt fuer Germanische und Romanische Philologie [*A publication*]
**LBl** .......... Living Blues [*A publication*]
**LBL** .......... Lymphoblastic Lymphoma [*Oncology*]
**LBL Comput Cent Newsl** ... LBL [*Lawrence Berkeley Laboratory*] Computer Center Newsletter [*A publication*]
**LBLJA** ....... Labor Law Journal [*A publication*]
**LBL Newsmag** ... LBL [*Lawrence Berkeley Laboratory*] Newsmagazine [*United States*] [*A publication*]
**LBLS** .......... Laminar Boundary-Layer Separation
**LBM** .......... Lean Body Mass [*Exercise*]
**LBM** .......... Liberty-Bell Mines, Inc. [*Vancouver Stock Exchange symbol*]
**LBM** .......... Little Butte [*Montana*] [*Seismograph station code, US Geological Survey*] [*Closed*] (SEIS)
**LBM** .......... Load Buffer Memory [*Data processing*]
**LBM** .......... Local Board Memoranda
**LBM** .......... Logic Bus Monitor [*Data processing*] (CET)
**LBM** .......... Morehouse Parish Library, Bastrop, LA [*Library symbol*] [*Library of Congress*] (LCLS)
**LBM** .......... Pounds, Mass (MCD)
**LB/M** ......... Pounds per Minute (AAG)
**LBMC** ........ Liberty Bell Matchcover Club (EA)
**LB/MIN** ..... Pounds per Minute
**LBMP** ........ Land-Based Marine Pollution
**LbN** .......... Labial Nerve [*Anatomy*]
**LBN** .......... Lebanon [*ANSI three-letter standard code*] (CNC)
**LBN** .......... Letter Box Number [*Viet Cong equivalent to the US APO*]
**LBN** .......... Lewis x Brown Norway [*Rat strain*]
**LBN** .......... Liberty Broadcasting Network [*Cable-television system*]
**LBN** .......... Line Balancing Network [*Telecommunications*] (TEL)
**LBNK** ........ Lafayette Bancorp, Inc. [*Bridgeport, CT*] [*NASDAQ symbol*] (NQ)
**LBNP** ........ Lower Body Negative Pressure [*Boots*] [*Space flight equipment*] [*NASA*]
**LBNPD** ...... Lower Body Negative Pressure Device [*Space flight equipment*] [*NASA*]
**LBNSY** ...... Long Beach Naval Shipyard (MUGU)
**LBO** .......... Landing Barge Oiler [*British military*] (DMA)
**LBO** .......... Lebanon, MO [*Location identifier*] [*FAA*] (FAAL)
**LBO** .......... Leveraged Buy-Out
**LBO** .......... Light Beam Oscillograph
**LBO** .......... Line Building Out
**LBocNS** ..... Northwest State School, Bossier City, LA [*Library symbol*] [*Library of Congress*] (LCLS)
**L Book Adviser** ... Law Book Adviser [*A publication*] (DLA)
**LBP** .......... Land-Based Plant (NRCH)
**LBP** .......... Length Between Perpendiculars [*Technical drawings*]
**LBP** .......... Leucine-Binding Protein [*Biochemistry*]
**LBP** .......... Light Beam Pickup
**LBP** .......... Low-Back Pain [*Medicine*]
**LBP** .......... Low Blood Pressure [*Medicine*]
**LBP** .......... Personnel Landing Boat [*Navy symbol*] [*Obsolete*]
**LBPD** ........ Plovdiv [*Bulgaria*] [*ICAO location identifier*] (ICLI)
**LBPH** ........ Libraries for the Blind and Physically Handicapped [*Automated system*]
**L-BPH** ....... Louisiana State Library, Department for the Blind and Physically Handicapped, Baton Rouge, LA [*Library symbol*] [*Library of Congress*] (LCLS)
**LBPI** .......... LASER Beam Position Indicator
**LBPIS** ........ LASER Beam Position Indicator System
**LBPO** ........ Lifting Body Program Office [*NASA*]
**LBPR** ........ Lumped Burnable Poison Rod [*Assembly*] [*Nuclear energy*] (NRCH)
**L & B Prec** ... Leake and Bullen's Precedents of Pleading [*A publication*] (DLA)
**LBQ** .......... Lambarene [*Gabon*] [*Airport symbol*] (OAG)
**LBQUDZ**... Living Bird Quarterly [*A publication*]

**LBr**............ East Baton Rouge Parish Public Library, Baton Rouge, LA [*Library symbol*] [*Library of Congress*] (LCLS)
**LBR**............ L-Band Radiometer (MCD)
**Lbr**............ Labor
**LBR**............ LASER Beam Recorder [*or Recording*]
**LBR**............ LASER Beam Rider (RDA)
**LBR**............ Liberia [*ANSI three-letter standard code*] (CNC)
**LbR**............ Limba Romana [*Bucuresti*] [*A publication*]
**LBR**............ Line of Bomb Release (NATG)
**LBR**............ Little Bear Resources [*Vancouver Stock Exchange symbol*]
**LBR**............ Little Books on Religion [*A publication*]
**LBR**............ Lloyds Bank Review [*A publication*]
**LBR**............ Local Base Rescue [*Air Force*] (AFM)
**L & BR**....... London & Blackwall Railway [*British*] (ROG)
**LBR**............ Low Birth Rate
**LBR**............ Low BIT [*Binary Digit*] Rate [*Data processing*] (MCD)
**LBR**............ Low Rurning Rate (KSC)
**LBR**............ Lower Burma Rulings [*India*] [*A publication*] (DLA)
**LBR**............ [*The*] Lowville & Beaver River Railroad Co. [*AAR code*]
**LBR**............ Lumber (KSC)
**LBR**............ Luso-Brazilian Review [*A publication*]
**LBrAg**........ Louisiana State Department of Agriculture, Research Library, Baton Rouge, LA [*Library symbol*] [*Library of Congress*] (LCLS)
**LBRC**......... Loft Bomb Release Computer (MCD)
**LBrC**.......... Louisiana Commerce Department, Research Library, Baton Rouge, LA [*Library symbol*] [*Library of Congress*] (LCLS)
**LBrCJIS**.... Commission on Law Enforcement and Criminal Justice, Criminal Justice Information System, Baton Rouge, LA [*Library symbol*] [*Library of Congress*] (LCLS)
**LBrcTI**....... Louisiana Training Institute, Bridge City Library, Bridge City, LA [*Library symbol*] [*Library of Congress*] (LCLS)
**LBrE**.......... Ethyl Corp., Chemical Development Library, Baton Rouge, LA [*Library symbol*] [*Library of Congress*] (LCLS)
**LBrEd**........ Louisiana Education Department, Baton Rouge, LA [*Library symbol*] [*Library of Congress*] (LCLS)
**LBRF**......... Lower Branchial Filament
**LBrG**.......... Gulf South Research Institute, Baton Rouge, LA [*Library symbol*] [*Library of Congress*] (LCLS)
**LBRG**......... LASER Beam Rider Guidance (MCD)
**LBrGS**....... Church of Jesus Christ of Latter-Day Saints, Genealogical Society Library, Baton Rouge Branch, Baton Rouge, LA [*Library symbol*] [*Library of Congress*] (LCLS)
**Lbr Hist (Australia)**... Labour History (Australia)
**Lbr Hist (US)**... Labor History (United States) [*A publication*]
**LBrHR**....... Louisiana Department of Health and Human Resources, Policy Planning and Evaluation Office, Baton Rouge, LA [*Library symbol*] [*Library of Congress*] (LCLS)
**LBrHR-Y**... Louisiana Department of Health and Human Resources, Office of Youth Services, Baton Rouge, LA [*Library symbol*] [*Library of Congress*] (LCLS)
**LBrIPA**...... Louisiana Information Processing Authority, Baton Rouge, LA [*Library symbol*] [*Library of Congress*] (LCLS)
**LBrJ**........... Louisiana Justice Department, Huey P. Long Library, Baton Rouge, LA [*Library symbol*] [*Library of Congress*] (LCLS)
**LBrL**........... Labor Department, Research Library, Baton Rouge, LA [*Library symbol*] [*Library of Congress*] (LCLS)
**Lbr Law J**.. Labor Law Journal [*A publication*]
**LBrLC**........ Louisiana Legislative Council, Reference Division, Baton Rouge, LA [*Library symbol*] [*Library of Congress*] (LCLS)
**LBrLH**....... Earl K. Long Hospital, Medical Library, Baton Rouge, LA [*Library symbol*] [*Library of Congress*] (LCLS)
**LBrNR**....... Natural Resources Department, Research and Development Library, Baton Rouge, LA [*Library symbol*] [*Library of Congress*] (LCLS)
**LBrNR-F**... Natural Resources Department, Office of Forestry, Baton Rouge, LA [*Library symbol*] [*Library of Congress*] (LCLS)
**LBrPS**........ Public Service Commission, Baton Rouge, LA [*Library symbol*] [*Library of Congress*] (LCLS)
**LBrR**.......... Louisiana Revenue Department, Research Department, Baton Rouge, LA [*Library symbol*] [*Library of Congress*] (LCLS)
**LBRS**......... Rousse [*Bulgaria*] [*ICAO location identifier*] (ICLI)
**LBrSP**........ State Planning Office, Library, Baton Rouge, LA [*Library symbol*] [*Library of Congress*] (LCLS)
**Lbr Studies J**... Labor Studies Journal [*A publication*]
**LBRT**......... Liberty
**LBrTD-Av**... Department of Transportation and Development, Aviation Office, Baton Rouge, LA [*Library symbol*] [*Library of Congress*] (LCLS)
**LBrTD-H**... Department of Transportation and Development, Office of Highways, Research and Development Library, Baton Rouge, LA [*Library symbol*] [*Library of Congress*] (LCLS)
**LBrTD-Pw**... Department of Transportation and Development, Office of Public Works, Baton Rouge, LA [*Library symbol*] [*Library of Congress*] (LCLS)
**Lbr Today**.. Labor Today [*A publication*]
**LBrUC**....... Department of Urban and Community Affairs, Office of Planning and Technical Assistance, Baton Rouge, LA [*Library symbol*] [*Library of Congress*] (LCLS)
**LBRV**......... Lifting Body Research Vehicle
**LBRV**......... Low BIT [*Binary Digit*] Rate Voice [*Telecommunications*]
**LBrWF-S**... Department of Wildlife and Fisheries, Louisiana Stream Control Commission, Baton Rouge, LA [*Library symbol*] [*Library of Congress*] (LCLS)
**LBRY**......... Library (MSA)
**LBS**............ Labasa [*Fiji*] [*Airport symbol*] (OAG)
**LBS**............ Labour and Society [*A publication*]
**LBS**............ Laminar Boundary-Layer Separation
**LBS**............ Landing Boat, Support [*Navy symbol*]
**LBS**............ Large Blast Simulator
**LBS**............ Large Bulb Ship
**LBS**............ LASER Beam Surgery
**LBS**............ LASER Bombing System
**LBS**............ Launch Blast Simulator (MUGU)
**LBS**............ Lecithin Bile State [*Medicine*]
**LBS**............ Lectori Benevolo Salutem [*To the Kind (or Gentle) Reader, Greeting*] [*Latin*]
**LBS**............ Liberation Broadcasting Station (CINC)
**LBS**............ Light Bomber Strike [*Air Force*] (NATG)
**LBS**............ Line Buffer System [*Data processing*]
**LBS**............ Lithuanian Boy Scouts (EA)
**LBS**............ Load Balance System [*Telecommunications*] (TEL)
**LBS**............ Load-Bearing Surface (MCD)
**LBS**............ Load Bearing System
**LBS**............ Loire Base Section [*World War II*]
**LBS**............ London Business School [*England*]
**LBS**............ Lopende Betaalstelsel [*Pay as You Earn*] [*Afrikaans*]
**LBS**............ Lysine-Binding Site [*Hematology*]
**LB/S**.......... Pounds per Second
**LBSA**......... Lipid-Bound Sialic Acid [*Analytical biochemistry*]
**LBSA**......... Long Binh Subarea [*Vietnam*]
**LBSC**......... Licentiate of the British Society of Commerce (DBQ)
**LBSC**......... LSB Bancshares, Incorporated of South Carolina [*Lexington, SC*] [*NASDAQ symbol*] (NQ)
**LBSCR**....... London, Brighton & South Coast Railway [*British*]
**LBSD**......... Lightweight Battlefield Surveillance Device
**LBSEDV**.... Leiden Botanical Series [*A publication*]
**LBSF**.......... Lions Blind Sports Foundation (EA)
**LBSF**.......... Sofia [*Bulgaria*] [*ICAO location identifier*] (ICLI)
**LBSS**.......... Local Boards of the Selective Service System
**LBSZ**......... Stara Zagora [*Bulgaria*] [*ICAO location identifier*] (ICLI)
**LBT**............ Chemical Laboratory Technician [*or Technology*] [*Navy*]
**LBT**............ L-Band Tetrode
**LBT**............ L-Band Transmitter
**LBT**............ Labatt [*John*] Ltd. [*Toronto Stock Exchange symbol*] [*Vancouver Stock Exchange symbol*]
**LBT**............ Labete [*Solomon Islands*] [*Seismograph station code, US Geological Survey*] (SEIS)
**LBT**............ Landbouwkundig Tijdschrift [*A publication*]
**lbt**.............. Librettist [*MARC relator code*] [*Library of Congress*] (LCCP)
**LBT**............ Linear Beam Tube
**LBT**............ Low Bandpass Transformer
**LBT**............ Low BIT [*Binary Digit*] Test [*Data processing*] (IEEE)
**LBT**............ Lumberton, NC [*Location identifier*] [*FAA*] (FAAL)
**LBT**............ Lutheran Bible Translators (EA)
**LBT**............ Pound Troy
**LBT**............ Pounds Thrust [*NASA*] (KSC)
**LBT CBS**.... Local-Battery Talking, Common-Battery Signaling [*Telecommunications*] (TEL)
**LBTF**......... Long Beach Test Facility [*Missiles*]
**LBTI**.......... Long-Burning Target Indicator [*British military*] (DMA)
**LBTS**......... Land-Based Test Site
**LBTY**......... Liberty Petroleum Co. [*NASDAQ symbol*] (NQ)
**LBU**........... Labuan [*Malaysia*] [*Airport symbol*] (OAG)
**LBU**........... Large Base Unit [*Telecommunications*]
**LBU**........... Launcher Booster Unit
**LBUN**........ Levobunolol [*Also, LB*] [*Biochemistry*]
**LBuP**.......... Plaquemines Parish Library, Buras, LA [*Library symbol*] [*Library of Congress*] (LCLS)
**LBUR**......... Library Bureau, Inc. [*Herkimer, NY*] [*NASDAQ symbol*] (NQ)
**LBV**............ La Belle, FL [*Location identifier*] [*FAA*] (FAAL)
**LBV**............ Landing Boat, Vehicle [*Navy symbol*] [*Obsolete*]
**LBV**............ Libreville [*Gabon*] [*Airport symbol*] (OAG)
**LBW**........... Landing Barge Water [*British military*] (DMA)
**LBW**........... LASER Beam Welding
**LBW**........... Leg before Wicket [*Cricket*]
**LBW**........... Long Bawan [*Indonesia*] [*Airport symbol*] (OAG)
**LBW**........... Low Birth Weight [*Obstetrics*]
**LBW**........... Low Body Weight
**LBW**........... Low-Speed Black and White [*Photography*]
**LBW**........... Lutheran Braille Workers (EA)
**LBWN**........ Varna [*Bulgaria*] [*ICAO location identifier*] (ICLI)
**LBWTAP**.. Food Science and Technology [*Zurich*] [*A publication*]
**LBX**............ Lake Jackson, TX [*Location identifier*] [*FAA*] (FAAL)
**LBY**............ Hattiesburg, MS [*Location identifier*] [*FAA*] (FAAL)
**LBY**............ Libya [*ANSI three-letter standard code*] (CNC)
**LB/YD²**...... Pounds per Square Yard
**LB/YD³**...... Pounds per Cubic Yard
**LBYR**......... Labyrinth [*Engineering*]
**LBYRPK**.... Labyrinth Pack [*Engineering*]
**LC**.............. Ewell's Leading Cases on Infancy, Etc. [*A publication*] (DLA)

**L/C** ........ Inductance/Capacitance (AAG)
**LC** ........ Label Clause
**LC** ........ Labor Cases [*A publication*] (DLA)
**L & C** ........ Laboratory and Checkout (NASA)
**LC** ........ Laboratory Craftsman (ADA)
**LC** ........ Labour Canada [*See also TRAVC*]
**LC** ........ Labour Corps [*British military*] (DMA)
**LC** ........ Lagonda Club, US Section (EA)
**LC** ........ Lake Central Airlines
**LC** ........ Lakey Clinic Medical Center [*Burlington, MA*]
**LC** ........ Lamb Committee (EA)
**LC** ........ Lancaster & Chester Railway Co. [*AAR code*]
**LC** ........ Lance Corporal
**LC** ........ Land Commission [*British*]
**LC** ........ Land Court [*Legal*] [*British*]
**LC** ........ Landing Craft
**LC** ........ Langerhans' Cells [*Medicine*]
**LC** ........ Langmuir Circulation [*Geophysics*]
**LC** ........ Language Code [*Online database field identifier*]
**L and C** ........ Language and Communication [*A publication*]
**LC** ........ Large Case [*Indicator*] [*IRS*]
**LC** ........ Large Cell [*Lymphoma classification*]
**LC** ........ Larval Chamber [*Botany*]
**LC** ........ Last Card
**LC** ........ Late Clamped [*Umbilical cord*]
**LC** ........ Late Commitment [*Reason for missed interception*] [*Military*]
**LC** ........ Lateral Component
**LC** ........ Launch Center
**LC** ........ Launch Complex
**LC** ........ Launch Conference [*Aerospace*] (AAG)
**L/C** ........ Launch Control [*Aerospace*] (AAG)
**LC** ........ Launch Coordinator [*NASA*]
**LC** ........ Launch Corridor [*Aerospace*] (AAG)
**LC** ........ Launch Cost [*Aerospace*]
**LC** ........ Launch Count [*NASA*] (KSC)
**LC** ........ Launch Countdown [*NASA*] (NASA)
**LC** ........ Launch Critical (MCD)
**LC** ........ Launching Control [*Military*]
**LC** ........ Laundry Chute (MSA)
**LC** ........ Laureate of Arts
**LC** ........ Laureate of Letters
**LC** ........ Law Commission (DLA)
**LC** ........ Law Courts
**LC** ........ Lead Covered [*or Coated*]
**LC** ........ Leading Cases (DLA)
**LC** ........ League of Communists [*Yugoslavia*]
**LC** ........ League of Composers (EA)
**LC** ........ League of the Cross [*Roman Catholic religious order*] (ROG)
**LC** ........ Learning Curve (MSA)
**LC** ........ Least Count
**LC** ........ Leesona Corporation (KSC)
**L & C** ........ Lefroy and Cassel's Practice Cases [*1881-83*] [*Ontario*] [*A publication*] (ILCA)
**LC** ........ Left Center [*A stage direction*]
**LC** ........ Left Chest [*Medicine*] (KSC)
**LC** ........ Left Circumflex (Artery) [*Anatomy*]
**LC** ........ Legal Committee (MCD)
**LC** ........ Legal Currency (ADA)
**LC** ........ Legionaries of Christ [*Roman Catholic men's religious order*]
**LC** ........ Legislative Council [*British*]
**LC** ........ Legitimate Child
**L & C** ........ Leigh and Cave's English Crown Cases Reserved [*1861-65*] [*A publication*] (DLA)
**LC** ........ Length of Chord (MSA)
**LC** ........ Lethal Concentration
**LC** ........ Letter Contract
**LC** ........ Letter of Credit
**L/C** ........ Lettera di Credito [*Letter of Credit*] [*Italian*] [*Business term*]
**LC** ........ Letterature Contemporanea [*A publication*]
**LC** ........ Letters and Cards [*US Postal Service*]
**LC** ........ Lettre de Credit [*Letter of Credit*] [*French*]
**lc** ........ Leucite [*CIPW classification*] [*Geology*]
**l/c** ........ Leur Compte [*Their Account*] [*French*]
**LC** ........ Level Control
**LC** ........ Level Crossing
**LC** ........ Leverage Contract [*Business term*]
**LC** ........ Leydig's Cells [*Endocrinology*]
**LC** ........ Liaison-Cargo [*Air Force*]
**LC** ........ Liberal Conservative
**LC** ........ Liberalt Centrum [*Liberal Center*] [*Denmark*] [*Political party*] (PPE)
**LC** ........ Libertarisch Centrum [*Libertarian Center Netherlands*] (EAIO)
**LC** ........ Liberty Corporation [*NYSE symbol*] (SPSG)
**LC** ........ Library Chronicle [*A publication*]
**L of C** ........ Library of Congress
**LC** ........ Library of Congress [*Online database field identifier*]
**LC** ........ Library of Congress Classification
**LC** ........ Lieutenant Commander
**LC** ........ Light Car [*British*]
**LC** ........ Light Case [*Military*] (NATG)
**LC** ........ Light Chain [*Immunoglobulin*]
**LC** ........ Light Company [*British military*] (DMA)
**LC** ........ Light Control [*Technical drawings*]
**LC** ........ Lightly Canceled
**LC** ........ Limited Coordinating (NG)
**LC** ........ Line-Carrying
**LC** ........ Line Circuit [*Telecommunications*]
**LC** ........ Line Collector
**L of C** ........ Line of Communication [*Military*]
**LC** ........ Line of Communication [*Military*]
**LC** ........ Line Concentrator
**LC** ........ Line Connection
**LC** ........ Line Construction Tools [*JETDS nomenclature*] [*Military*] (CET)
**LC** ........ Line of Contact [*Military*]
**LC** ........ Line Contractor (MCD)
**LC** ........ Line Control
**L/C** ........ Line of Credit [*Business term*]
**LC** ........ Line Crosser [*Deserter*] [*Military*]
**LC** ........ Linear Combination
**LC** ........ Linguocervical [*Dentistry*]
**LC** ........ Link Circuit
**LC** ........ Links and Chargers (NATG)
**LC** ........ Liquid Capacity
**LC** ........ Liquid Chromatography
**LC** ........ Liquid Crystal
**LC** ........ Literature Criticism from 1400 to 1800 [*A publication*]
**LC** ........ Lithocholate [*Biochemistry*]
**LC** ........ Liturgical Conference (EA)
**LC** ........ Liver Cirrhosis [*Medicine*]
**LC** ........ Living Children
**LC** ........ Load Carrier
**LC** ........ Load Cell
**LC** ........ Load Center (MSA)
**LC** ........ Load-Compensating (MSA)
**LC** ........ Load Computer [*or Controller*] (MCD)
**LC** ........ Load Contactor
**LC** ........ Loading Coil [*Telecommunications*] (TEL)
**LC** ........ Loan Capital [*Business term*]
**LC** ........ Loan Crowd [*Investment term*]
**LC** ........ Local Call [*Followed by telephone number*]
**LC** ........ Local Channel (CET)
**LC** ........ Local Control (FAAC)
**LC** ........ Location Counter [*Data processing*]
**LC** ........ Locked Closed
**LC** ........ Loco Citato [*In the Place Cited*] [*Latin*]
**LC** ........ Locus Ceruleus [*Brain anatomy*]
**LC** ........ Locus of Control [*Psychology*]
**LC** ........ Loganair Ltd. [*British*] [*ICAO designator*] (FAAC)
**LC** ........ Logic Corporation
**LC** ........ London Clause [*Business term*]
**LC** ........ London Club (EA)
**L/C** ........ Loop Check (MUGU)
**LC** ........ Loose Coupler
**LC** ........ Lord Chamberlain [*British*]
**LC** ........ Lord Chancellor [*British*]
**LC** ........ Los Californianos (EA)
**LC** ........ Lotta Continua [*Continuous Struggle*] [*Italy*] [*Political party*] (PPE)
**LC** ........ Loud and Clear
**LC** ........ [A] Lover's Complaint [*Shakespearean work*]
**LC** ........ Low Carbon [*Content, as low-carbon steel*]
**L/C** ........ Low Compression [*Automotive engineering*]
**LC** ........ Low Conditioners [*Psychology*]
**LC** ........ Lower California
**LC** ........ Lower Canada
**LC** ........ Lower Cylinder
**LC** ........ Lowercase [*i.e., small letters*] [*Typography*]
**LC** ........ LOX [*Liquid Oxygen*] Clean
**LC** ........ Lubrication Chart
**LC** ........ Lymphocyte-Mediated Cytotoxicity [*Also, LMC*] [*Immunology*]
**LC** ........ Lytic Capacity [*Clinical chemistry*]
**LC** ........ St. Lucia [*ANSI two-letter standard code*] (CNC)
**LC** ........ Scottish Land Court Reports [*A publication*] (DLA)
**L/C** ........ Single Acetate Single Cotton [*Wire insulation*] (AAG)
**LC1** ........ Lasa C Ring [*Montana*] [*Seismograph station code, US Geological Survey*] (SEIS)
**LC2** ........ Lasa C Ring [*Montana*] [*Seismograph station code, US Geological Survey*] (SEIS)
**LC3** ........ Lasa C Ring [*Montana*] [*Seismograph station code, US Geological Survey*] (SEIS)
**LC4** ........ Lasa C Ring [*Montana*] [*Seismograph station code, US Geological Survey*] (SEIS)
**$LC_{50}$** ........ Lethal Concentration, Median [*Lethal for 50% of test group*]
**LCA** ........ Lacana Mining Corp. [*Toronto Stock Exchange symbol*]
**LCA** ........ Lake Carriers' Association (EA)
**LCA** ........ Lake Central Airlines
**LCA** ........ Lamborghini Club America (EA)
**LCA** ........ Laminate Council of America (EA)
**LCA** ........ Land Compensation Act [*Town planning*] [*British*]
**LCA** ........ Landing Craft, Assault [*Navy ship symbol*]

**LCA** ........... Landscape Contractors Association [*Australia*]
**LCA** ........... Larnaca [*Cyprus*] [*Airport symbol*] (OAG)
**LCA** ........... Launch Control Amplifier [*NASA*] (NASA)
**LCA** ........... Launch Control Analyst [*NASA*] (AAG)
**LCA** ........... Launch [*or Launcher*] Control Area [*Missiles*]
**LCA** ........... Law Council of Australia
**LCA** ........... Leadership Councils of America (EA)
**LCA** ........... Leading Cases, Annotated [*A publication*] (DLA)
**LCA** ........... Leading Catering Accountant [*British military*] (DMA)
**LCA** ........... LeConte Airlines [*Wrangell, AK*] [*FAA designator*] (FAAC)
**LCA** ........... Left Coronary Artery [*Cardiology*]
**LCA** ........... Lesson Content Analysis
**LCA** ........... Leukocyte Common Antigen [*Immunochemistry*]
**LCA** ........... Leveling Control Amplifier
**LCA** ........... Library Club of America [*Defunct*] (EA)
**LCA** ........... Library-College Associates (EA)
**LCA** ........... Library of Congress Authority File [*Source file*] [*UTLAS symbol*]
**LCA** ........... Licensed Company Auditor [*British*]
**LCA** ........... Life Communicators Association [*Des Moines, IA*] (EA)
**LCA** ........... Light Combat Aircraft [*Military*]
**LCA** ........... Lighting Control Assembly [*NASA*] (KSC)
**LCA** ........... Line Clearance Airdrome [*Air Force*]
**LCA** ........... Line Control Adapter
**LCA** ........... Liquid Crystal Analog
**LCA** ........... Lithocholic Acid [*Biochemistry*]
**LCA** ........... Lithuanian Catholic Alliance (EA)
**LCA** ........... Load Controller Assembly (NASA)
**LCA** ........... Local Coal Authority [*Australia*]
**LCA** ........... Local Communications Adapter [*IBM Corp.*]
**LCA** ........... Local Communications Area (KSC)
**LCA** ........... Log Cabin [*Alabama*] [*Seismograph station code, US Geological Survey*] (SEIS)
**LCA** ........... Logistic Control Activity (AABC)
**LCA** ........... London City Airport [*British*]
**LCA** ........... Longitudinal Chromatic Aberration
**LCA** ........... Lowercase Alphabet
**LCA** ........... Lussazione Congenita dell'Anca [*Congenital Hip Dislocation*] [*Italian*] [*Medicine*]
**LCA** ........... Lutheran Church in America [*Later, ELCA*]
**LCA** ........... Lutheran Church of Australia
**LCA** ........... Lutheran Collegiate Association [*Defunct*] (EA)
**LCA** ........... St. Lucia [*ANSI three-letter standard code*] (CNC)
**LCAAJ** ........ Language and Culture Atlas of Ashkenazic Jewry [*A publication*] (BJA)
**LCAAP** ...... Lake City Army Ammunition Plant (AABC)
**LCaC** ......... Cameron Parish Library, Cameron, LA [*Library symbol*] [*Library of Congress*] (LCLS)
**LCAC** ......... Landing Craft, Air Cushion [*Navy symbol*]
**LCAC** ......... Library of Congress Classification - Additions and Changes [*A publication*]
**LCAC** ......... Listed Company Advisory Committee [*of NYSE*]
**LCAC** ......... Low-Cost Automation Centre [*British*]
**LCACCC** ... Laymen's Commission of the American Council of Christian Churches (EA)
**LCAD** ........ Logistics Cost Analysis Data (MCD)
**LC-ADD** .... Library of Congress - American Doctoral Dissertations [*A bibliographic publication*]
**LCAF** ......... Lutheran Church in America Foundation
**LCA(FT)** .... Landing Craft, Assault (Flamethrower) [*British military*] (DMA)
**LCA(H)** ...... Landing Craft, Assault (Hedgerow)
**LCAH** ........ London and Continental Advertising Holdings [*British*]
**LCAM** ....... Liver Cell Adhesion Molecule [*Cytology*]
**LCAO** ........ Leadership Council of Aging Organizations (EA)
**LCAO** ........ Linear Combination of Atomic Orbitals
**LCA(OC)** ... Landing Craft, Assault (Obstacle Clearance) [*British military*] (DMA)
**LCAO-MO-SCF** ... Linear Combination of Atomic Orbitals to Form Molecular Orbitals by a Self-Consistent Field [*Quantum mechanics*]
**LCAP** ......... Local Combat Air Patrol
**LCAP** ......... Loop Carrier Analysis Program [*Bell System*]
**LCAR** ......... Late Cutaneous Anaphylactic Reaction [*Immunology*]
**LCAR** ......... Launch Complex Assessment Report [*NASA*] (KSC)
**LCAR** ......... Lescarden, Inc. [*NASDAQ symbol*] (NQ)
**LCAR** ......... Lotus Cortina of America Register (EA)
**LCAR** ......... Low-Cost Attack RADAR
**LCar** ........... United States Public Health Service Hospital, Carville, LA [*Library symbol*] [*Library of Congress*] (LCLS)
**LCAS** ......... Lithuanian Catholic Academy of Sciences (EA)
**LCAT** ......... Lecithin-Cholesterol Acyltransferase [*An enzyme*]
**LCATA** ...... Laundry and Cleaners Allied Trades Association [*Later, TCATA*]
**LCAUS** ...... Latvian Choir Association of the US (EA)
**LCAV** ......... Licensed Clubs Association of Victoria [*Australia*]
**LCAVAT** ... Landing Craft and Amphibious Vehicle Assignment Table
**LCAX** ......... Landing Craft, Assault, Experimental [*Navy ship symbol*]
**LCB** ............ Centraal Bureau voor de Statistiek. Bibliotheek en Documentatiedienst. Lijst van Aanwinsten [*A publication*]
**LCB** ............ Landing Craft, Vehicle [*Navy symbol*]
**LCB** ............ Launch Control Building [*NASA*]
**LCB** ............ Least-Common Bigram [*Data processing*] (BYTE)
**LCB** ............ Least Common BIT [*Binary Digit*] (MCD)
**LCB** ............ Left Cornerback [*Football*]
**LCB** ............ Liefdezusters van de H. Carolus Borromeus [*Sisters of Charity of St. Charles Borromeo - SCSCB*] (EAIO)
**LCB** ............ Limited Capability Buoy
**LCB** ............ Line Control Block [*Data processing*]
**LCB** ............ Liquor Control Board [*Canada*]
**LCB** ............ Living Country Blues [*A publication*]
**LCB** ............ Logic Control Block
**LCB** ............ London Centre for Biotechnology [*British*] (IRUK)
**LCB** ............ Longitudinal Position of Center of Buoyancy
**LCB** ............ Lord Chief Baron [*British*]
**LCBA** .......... Loyal Christian Benefit Association [*Erie, PA*] (EA)
**LCBB** .......... "Life Can Be Beautiful" [*Old radio program; nicknamed "Elsie Beebee"*]
**LCBF** .......... Local Cerebral Blood Flow [*Medicine*]
**LCBI** ........... Landmark Community Bancorp, Incorporated [*NASDAQ symbol*] (NQ)
**LCBM** ......... LifeCore Biomedical, Inc. [*NASDAQ symbol*] (NQ)
**LCBO** ......... Linear Combination of [*Semi-localized*] Band Orbitals [*Atomic physics*]
**LCBWR** ..... LaCrosse Boiling Water Reactor [*Also, LACBWR*]
**LCC** ............ Amphibious Command Ship [*Formerly, AGC*] [*Navy symbol*]
**LCC** ............ Charles A. Lindbergh Collectors Club (EA)
**LCC** ............ Labor Case Comments [*Cast Metals Association*] [*A publication*]
**LCC** ............ Labour Coordinating Committee [*British*]
**LCC** ............ Land Capability Classes [*Agriculture*]
**LCC** ............ Land Conservation Council of New South Wales [*Australia*]
**LCC** ............ Land Court Cases [*New South Wales*] [*A publication*] (DLA)
**LCC** ............ Landing Control Center
**LCC** ............ Landing Craft, Control
**LCC** ............ Langley Complex Coordination [*Device*] [*NASA*]
**LCC** ............ Language for Conversational Computing (MDG)
**LCC** ............ Large-Capacity Cassette [*Photocopier technology*]
**LCC** ............ Launch Command and Control
**LCC** ............ Launch Commit Criteria (MCD)
**LCC** ............ Launch Control Center [*NASA*]
**LCC** ............ Launch Control Console
**LCC** ............ Le Cercle Concours d'Elegance (EA)
**LCC** ............ Leach's English Crown Cases [*1730-1815*] [*A publication*] (DLA)
**LCC** ............ Lead Covered Cable [*Telecommunications*] (TEL)
**LCC** ............ Leadless Chip Carrier [*Motorola, Inc.*]
**LCC** ............ Levo-Carnitine Chloride [*Biochemistry*]
**LCC** ............ Liang-Chow [*Republic of China*] [*Seismograph station code, US Geological Survey*] [*Closed*] (SEIS)
**LCC** ............ Libertarian Council of Churches (EA)
**LCC** ............ Library of Congress Classification
**LCC** ............ Life-Cycle Costing [*or Costs*] [*DoD*]
**LCC** ............ Ligue Canadienne des Composeurs [*Canadian League of Composers - CLC*]
**LCC** ............ Lincoln Capital Corp. [*Toronto Stock Exchange symbol*]
**LCC** ............ Liquid Crystal Cell (IEEE)
**LCC** ............ Liquid-Cushion Electroplating Cell [*Steel production*]
**LCC** ............ Liquor Control Commission
**LCC** ............ Lithophane Collectors Club (EA)
**LCC** ............ Little Carter Cay [*NASA*] (KSC)
**LCC** ............ Load Controlling Crewman [*Helicopter*] [*Navy*]
**LCC** ............ Loading Coil Case [*Telecommunications*] (TEL)
**LCC** ............ Local Communications Complex
**LCC** ............ Local Communications Console
**LCC** ............ Local Control Console (CAAL)
**LCC** ............ Local Coordinating Committee
**LCC** ............ Lockheed-California Company [*Division of Lockheed Aircraft Corp.*]
**LCC** ............ Logistic Control Code [*Military*] (AABC)
**LCC** ............ Logistics Control Center [*Military*] (INF)
**LCC** ............ Logistics Coordination Center [*NATO*]
**LCC** ............ London Chamber of Commerce [*British*] (DAS)
**LCC** ............ London Communications Committee [*World War II*]
**LCC** ............ London County Council [*or Councillor*] [*Later, GLC*]
**LCC** ............ Lost Chord Clubs (EA)
**LCC** ............ Low-Cost Classifier (MCD)
**LCC** ............ Lundy Collectors Club (EA)
**LCCA** .......... Late Cortical Cerebellar Atrophy [*Neurology*]
**LCCA** .......... Lawyers Committee on Central America (EA)
**LCCA** .......... Left Circumflex Coronary Artery [*Anatomy*]
**LCCA** .......... Life Cycle Cost Analysis (MCD)
**LCCA** .......... Lionel Collectors Club of America (EA)
**LCCA** .......... Lithuanian Chamber of Commerce of America (EA)
**LCCA** .......... Load Current Contacting Aiding
**LCCA** .......... London Church Choir Association
**LCCB** .......... Local Change Control Board (MCD)
**LCCB** .......... Local Configuration Control Board (AABC)
**LCCC** .......... Leadless Ceramic Chip Carrier [*Electronics*]
**L & CCC** .... Leigh and Cave's English Crown Cases Reserved [*1861-65*] [*A publication*] (DLA)
**LCCC** .......... Life Care Communities Corporation [*NASDAQ symbol*] (NQ)

**LCCC**......... Lower Canada Civil Code [*A publication*] (DLA)
**LCCC**......... Luzerne County Community College [*Nanticoke, PA*] (TSSD)
**LCCC**......... Nicosia [*Cyprus*] [*ICAO location identifier*] (ICLI)
**LCCD**......... Launch Commit Criteria Document [*NASA*] (NASA)
**LCCE**......... Lee County Central Electric [*AAR code*]
**LCCE**......... Life-Cycle Cost Estimate (AABC)
**LCCEP**...... Logistics Civilian Career Enhancement Program [*Military*]
**LCCI**.......... London Chamber of Commerce and Industry [*British*] (DCTA)
**LCCID**....... Life Cycle Cost in Design [*Computer program released by US Army Construction Engineering Research Laboratory*] (RDA)
**LCCMS**..... Launch Control Center Measuring Station [*NASA*] (KSC)
**LCCN**........ Library of Congress Catalog-Card Number
**LCC (NSW)**... Land Appeal Court Cases (New South Wales) [*A publication*] (APTA)
**LCCO**........ Life Cycle Cost of Ownership (MCD)
**LCCOGA**... Liaison Committee of Cooperating Oil and Gas Associations (EA)
**LC Cont**..... Langdell's Cases on Contracts [*A publication*] (DLA)
**LCCP**......... LASER Code Control Panel (MCD)
**LCCP**......... Launch Captain's Control Panel [*Navy*] (CAAL)
**LCCP**......... Linguistic Circle of Canberra. Publications [*A publication*]
**LCCP**......... Lower Canada Civil Procedure [*A publication*] (DLA)
**LCCPT**...... Low-Cost Cockpit Procedures Trainer (MCD)
**LCCR**......... Laboratory for Computer and Communications Research [*Simon Fraser University*] [*Canada*] [*Research center*] (RCD)
**LCCR**......... Leadership Conference on Civil Rights (EA)
**LCCRUL**... Lawyers' Committee for Civil Rights under Law (EA)
**LCCS**......... Large Capacity Core Storage [*Data processing*] (MDG)
**LCCS**......... Launcher Captain Control System [*Military*] (NVT)
**LCCS**......... Library of Congress Classification Schedules [*A publication*]
**LCCS**......... Logistics Control Center System
**LCCS**......... Low Cervical Caesarean Section
**LCCTS**....... Life Cycle Cost Tracking System [*Social Security Administration*]
**LCCU**........ Lightweight Crewman Communication Umbilical (MCD)
**LCCV**......... Large-Component Cleaning Vessel [*Nuclear energy*] (NRCH)
**LCD**........... Language for Computer Design (CSR)
**LCD**........... Launch Control Design [*NASA*] (AAG)
**LCD**........... Launch Countdown [*NASA*] (NASA)
**LCD**........... Least [*or Lowest*] Common Denominator [*or Divisor*] [*Mathematics*]
**LCD**........... Lightweight Ceramic Dome
**LCD**........... Liquid Crystal Digital [*Battery-powered wristwatch*]
**LCD**........... Liquid Crystal Diode
**LCD**........... Liquid Crystal Display
**LCD**........... Liquor Carbonis Detergens [*Coal tar solution*] [*Medicine*]
**LCD**........... Litterarisches Centralblatt fuer Deutschland [*A publication*]
**LCD**........... Liver Cell Dysplasia [*Medicine*]
**LCD**........... LM [*Lunar Module*] Change Directive [*NASA*] (KSC)
**LCD**........... Local Climatological Data [*A publication*]
**LCD**........... London College of Divinity
**LCD**........... Lord Chancellor's Department [*British*]
**LCD**........... Loss of Clock Detector
**LCD**........... Louis Trichardt [*South Africa*] [*Airport symbol*] (OAG)
**LCD**........... Lumped Constant Dispersion
**LCD**........... Ohio Lower Court Decisions [*A publication*] (DLA)
**LCDC**......... Laboratory Centre for Disease Control [*Canada*]
**LCDHWIU**... Laundry, Cleaning, and Dye House Workers' International Union [*Later, Textile Processors, Service Trades, Health Care, Professional, and Technical Employees International Union*] (EA)
**LCDR**......... Lieutenant Commander (AAG)
**LCDR**......... London, Chatham & Dover Railway [*British*]
**LCDS**......... Lefschetz Center for Dynamical Systems [*Brown University*] [*Research center*] (RCD)
**LCDS**......... Low-Cost Development System [*National Semiconductor Corp.*]
**LCDT**......... London Contemporary Dance Theatre
**LCDTL**...... Load-Compensated Diode Transistor Logic [*Data processing*]
**LCE**........... La Ceiba [*Honduras*] [*Airport symbol*] (OAG)
**LCE**........... Landing Craft, Emergency Repair
**LCE**........... Latest Cost Estimate (NATG)
**LCE**........... Launch Complex Engineer [*NASA*] (KSC)
**LCE**........... Launch Complex Equipment
**LCE**........... Launch Control Equipment (AAG)
**LCE**........... Launch Countdown Exercise [*NASA*] (AFM)
**LCE**........... Legal Counsel for the Elderly (EA)
**LCE**........... Load-Carrying Equipment (MCD)
**LCE**........... Load Circuit Efficiency
**LCE**........... Logistic Capability Estimate (MCD)
**LCE**........... Lone Star Industries, Inc. [*Formerly, Lone Star Cement Corp.*] [*NYSE symbol*] (SPSG)
**LCE**........... Low-Cost Expendable [*Refers to payload type*] [*NASA*]
**LCEA**......... Licentiate of the Association of Cost and Executive Accountants [*British*] (DBQ)
**LCEAPL**.... Lawyers Committee for the Enforcement of Animal Protection Law (EA)
**LCEB**......... Launch Control Equipment Building (AFM)
**LCEC**......... Liquid Chromatographs with Electrochemical Detection
**LCEECSTI**... Liaison Committee of the European Economic Community Steel Tube Industry (EAIO)
**LCEHV**...... Low-Cost Expendable Harassment Vehicle [*Air Force*] (MCD)
**LCEM**........ Leading Control Electrical Mechanic [*British military*] (DMA)
**LCEOP**...... Landing Craft, Engine Overhaul Parties
**LCEP**......... Lower Critical End Points [*Supercritical extraction*]
**LCEPS**....... Labor Cooperative Educational and Publishing Society (EA)
**LC Eq**......... White and Tudor's Leading Cases in Equity [*A publication*] (DLA)
**LCEWS**..... Low-Cost Electronic Warfare Suite (NVT)
**LCF**........... Landing Craft, Flak
**LCF**........... Language Central Facility [*Data processing*] (IEEE)
**LCF**........... Last Chance Filter (MCD)
**LCF**........... Last Chance Forever (EA)
**LCF**........... Launch Control Facility
**LCF**........... Lawyers Christian Fellowship (EA)
**LCF**........... Least [*or Lowest*] Common Factor [*Mathematics*]
**LCF**........... Least Cost Feed Formulation System (ADA)
**LCF**........... Lederberg-Coxeter-Frucht [*Notation*] [*Graph theory, mathematics*]
**LCF**........... Left Circumflex Artery [*Anatomy*]
**LCF**........... Level Control Function [*Data processing*]
**LCF**........... Library of Congress Films [*Source file*] [*UTLAS symbol*]
**LCF**........... Lincomycin Cosynthetic Factor [*Biochemistry*]
**LCF**........... Little City Foundation (EA)
**LCF**........... Living Church Foundation (EA)
**LCF**........... Local Cycle Fatigue (IEEE)
**LCF**........... Logical Channel Fill
**LCF**........... Longitudinal Position of Center of Flotation
**LCF**........... Low Cab Forward [*Automotive engineering*]
**LCF**........... Low-Carbon Ferrochrome [*Metallurgy*]
**LCF**........... Low-Cycle Fatigue [*Rocket engine*]
**LCF**........... Lymphocyte Chemoattractant Factor [*Biochemistry*]
**LCFA**......... Lithuanian Catholic Federation Ateitis (EA)
**LCFA**......... Long-Chain Fatty Acids [*Organic chemistry*]
**LCFBA**...... Lahey Clinic Foundation. Bulletin [*A publication*]
**LCFC**......... Leslie Charleson Fan Club (EA)
**LC(FF)**....... Landing Craft, Infantry (Flotilla Flagship) [*Navy symbol*]
**LCFLOLS**... Laterally Compounded Fresnel Lens Optical Landing System
**LCFLOTSPAC**... Landing Craft, Flotilla, Pacific Fleet
**LCFNM**..... Lawyers' Campaign to Free Nelson Mandela (EA)
**LCFS**......... Last-Come, First-Served
**LCFS**......... Lil' Champ Food Stores, Inc. [*NASDAQ symbol*] (NQ)
**LCFU**......... Laboratory Configured Fire Units (MCD)
**LCG**........... La Coruna [*Spain*] [*Airport symbol*] (OAG)
**LCG**........... Landing Craft Gun (MCD)
**LCG**........... Landing Craft, Gunboat
**LCG**........... Langerhans' Cell Granule [*Anatomy*]
**LCG**........... Langerhans' Cell Granulomatosis [*Oncology*]
**LCG**........... Lead Computing Gyro (MCD)
**LCG**........... Left Cerebral Ganglion [*Medicine*]
**LCG**........... Leon Cerro Gordo [*Mexico*] [*Seismograph station code, US Geological Survey*] (SEIS)
**LCG**........... Liquid-Cooled Garment [*Spacesuit*]
**LCG**........... Loads Control Group [*Prepares supplies to be airlifted*] [*Military*]
**LCG**........... Logistics Control Group [*Air Materiel Command*] (AAG)
**LCG**........... Longitudinal Position of Center of Gravity
**LCG**........... Low Center of Gravity [*Tractor engineering*]
**LCG**........... Low-Cost Generator
**LCG**........... Lower Courts Gazette [*Ontario*] [*A publication*] (DLA)
**LCG**........... Wayne, NE [*Location identifier*] [*FAA*] (FAAL)
**LCGB**......... Letzeburger Chreschtliche Gewerkschaftsbond [*Confederation of Christian Trade Unions of Luxembourg*]
**LCGF**......... Longitudinal Ciliated Groove of Filament
**LCGIL**....... Libera Confederazione Generale Italiana dei Lavoratori [*Free Italian General Confederation of Workers*]
**LCG(L)**...... Landing Craft, Gun (Large)
**LCG(M)**..... Landing Craft, Gun (Medium)
**LCGME**..... Liaison Committee on Graduate Medical Education
**LCGO**........ Linear Combination of Gaussian Orbitals [*Atomic physics*]
**LCGP**........ Landing Craft, Group
**LCG(S)**...... Landing Craft, Gun (Small) [*British military*] (DMA)
**LCGS**......... Lead Computing Gun Sight
**LCGT**......... Listening Comprehension Group Test
**LCGU**........ Lead Computing Gyroscope Unit (MCD)
**LCGU**........ Local Cerebral Glucose Utilization [*Biochemistry*]
**LCH**........... Lake Charles [*Louisiana*] [*Airport symbol*] (OAG)
**LCH**........... Lake Charles, LA [*Location identifier*] [*FAA*] (FAAL)
**LCH**........... Landing Craft Headquarters [*British military*] (DMA)
**LCH**........... Landing Craft (Heavy) (ADA)
**LCH**........... Landing Craft Hospital [*British military*] (DMA)
**LCH**........... Larch Resources Ltd. [*Vancouver Stock Exchange symbol*]
**LCH**........... Latch (MSA)
**LCH**........... Launch
**LCH**........... Launching Charging Header
**LCh**........... Liberte Chretienne [*A publication*]
**LCh**........... Licentiate of the Institute of Chiropodists [*British*]
**L Ch**........... Licentiatus Chirurgiae [*Licentiate in Surgery*]
**LCH**........... Life Cycle Hypothesis [*Economics*]
**LCH**........... Logical Channel Queue [*Data processing*]

**L CH**......... Lord Chancellor [*British*] (ROG)
**LCHA**........ Love Canal Homeowners Association (EA)
**LCHM**....... Life Chemistry, Inc. [*NASDAQ symbol*] (NQ)
**LCHNB8**... Lichenologist [*Oxford*] [*A publication*]
**LCHP**........ Lancaster County Historical Society. Papers [*A publication*]
**LCHP**........ Local Control Hydraulic Panel
**LCHQ**........ Local Command Headquarters [*NATO*] (NATG)
**LChQ**......... Lutheran Church Quarterly [*A publication*]
**LCHR**........ Launcher (AAG)
**L Chr**......... Law Chronicle [*England*] [*A publication*] (DLA)
**LCHR**........ Lawyers Committee for Human Rights (EA)
**LChr**.......... Liberte Chretienne [*A publication*] (BJA)
**LChr**.......... Logotechnika Chronika [*A publication*]
**LChR**......... [*The*] Lutheran Church Review [*A publication*]
**L Chron**...... Law Chronicle [*England*] [*A publication*] (DLA)
**L Chron & L Stud Mag**... Law Chronicle and Law Students' Magazine [*A publication*] (DLA)
**L Chron & L Stud Mag (NS)**... Law Chronicle and Law Students' Magazine (New Series) [*A publication*] (DLA)
**LCHS**......... Lancaster County Historical Society. Papers [*A publication*]
**LCHS**......... Large Component Handling System [*Nuclear energy*] (NRCH)
**LChSt**........ Saint Bernard Parish Library, Chalmette, LA [*Library symbol*] [*Library of Congress*] (LCLS)
**LCHTF**...... Low-Cycle High-Temperature Fatigue [*Rocket engine*]
**LCI**............ Labor Cost Index
**LCI**............ Laboratory of Cellular Immunology [*University of Arizona*] [*Research center*] (RCD)
**LCI**............ Laconia [*New Hampshire*] [*Airport symbol*] (OAG)
**LCI**............ Laconia, NH [*Location identifier*] [*FAA*] (FAAL)
**LCI**............ Lafarge Canada, Inc. [*Toronto Stock Exchange symbol*]
**LCI**............ Landing Craft, Infantry [*Obsolete*]
**LCI**............ Launcher Control Indicator [*Missiles*] (AABC)
**LCI**............ Legally Correct Interpretation [*of the ABM treaty*]
**LCI**............ Liga Comunista Internacionalista [*International Communist League*] [*Portugal*] [*Political party*] (PPE)
**LCI**............ Lions Clubs International (EA)
**LCI**............ Literary Criticism Index [*A publication*]
**LCI**............ Livestock Conservation Institute (EA)
**LCI**............ Locus of Control Interview [*Psychology*]
**LCI**............ Low-Cost Inertial
**LCI**............ Lummus Crest, Inc. [*Telecommunications service*] (TSSD)
**LCI**............ United States Central Intelligence Agency, McLean, VA [*OCLC symbol*] (OCLC)
**LCI(A)**....... Landing Craft, Infantry (Ammunition)
**LCIA**.......... London Court of International Arbitration
**LCIB**.......... Library of Congress. Information Bulletin [*A publication*]
**LCIC**.......... Leisure Concepts, Incorporated [*New York, NY*] [*NASDAQ symbol*] (NQ)
**LCICD**....... Liquid Crystal Induced Circular Dichroism [*Spectroscopy*]
**LCI(D)**....... Landing Craft, Infantry (Demolition) [*British military*] (DMA)
**LCIDIV**..... Landing Craft, Infantry, Division
**LCIFC**........ Lou Christie International Fan Club (EA)
**LCIFLOT**.. Landing Craft, Infantry, Flotilla [*Obsolete*]
**LCI(G)**....... Landing Craft, Infantry, Gunboat [*Obsolete*]
**LCIGRP**.... Landing Craft, Infantry, Group
**LCIGS**....... Low-Cost Inertial Guidance Subsystem (MCD)
**LCIHR**....... Lawyers Committee for International Human Rights (EA)
**LCII**.......... Laser Master International, Incorporated [*Formerly, Laser Craft Industries, Incorporated*] [*NASDAQ symbol*] (NQ)
**LCIL**.......... Landing Craft, Infantry, Large [*Obsolete*]
**LCILFLOT**... Landing Craft, Infantry, Large, Flotilla [*Obsolete*]
**LCI(M)**...... Landing Craft, Infantry (Medium) [*British military*] (DMA)
**LCI(M)**...... Landing Craft, Infantry (Mortar Ship) [*Obsolete*]
**LC Inf Bul**... United States. Library of Congress. Information Bulletin [*A publication*]
**LCI(R)**....... Landing Craft, Infantry (Rocket Ship) [*Obsolete*]
**LC/IR**........ Liquid Chromatography/Infrared
**LCI(S)**....... Landing Craft, Infantry (Small) [*British military*] (DMA)
**LCIS**.......... Lighter Collectors' International Society (EA)
**LCJ**........... Lawyers for Civil Justice (EA)
**LCJ**........... Lord Chief Justice [*British*]
**LCJ**........... Lower Canada Jurist, Montreal [*1848-91*] [*A publication*] (DLA)
**LC Jur**....... Lower Canada Jurist [*A publication*] (DLA)
**LCK**........... Columbus, OH [*Location identifier*] [*FAA*] (FAAL)
**LCK**........... Landing Craft, Kitchen
**L Ck**.......... Leading Cook [*British military*] (DMA)
**LCK**........... Legion of Christ the King [*Defunct*] (EA)
**LCKS**......... Locks
**LCL**............ Labor Congress of Liberia
**LCL**............ Lambert Cosine Law [*Physics*]
**LCL**............ Landing Craft, Logistic [*British military*] (DMA)
**LCL**............ Lateral Collateral Ligament [*Anatomy*]
**LCL**............ Leading Catholic Layman
**LCL**............ Lens Culinaris Lectin
**LCL**............ Less-than-Carload [*Under 60,000 pounds*]
**LCL**............ Less-than-Container Load [*Shipping*]
**LCL**............ Levinthal-Coles-Lillie Bodies [*Microbiology*]
**LCL**............ Library of Congress, Interlibrary Loan Department [*UTLAS symbol*]
**LCL**............ Licentiate of Canon Law [*British*]
**LCL**............ Licentiate of Civil Law
**LCL**............ Lifting Condensation Level [*Meteorology*]
**LCL**............ Light Center Length
**LCL**............ Limited Channel Logout
**LCL**............ Linkage Control Language [*Data processing*] (BUR)
**LCL**............ Local (AFM)
**LCL**............ Localizer (CET)
**LCL**............ Loeb Classical Library. Harvard University Press [*A publication*] (BJA)
**LCL**............ Logical Comparative LOFAR
**LCL**............ Loose Container Load [*Shipping*] (IMH)
**LCL**............ Lot-Car Load
**LCL**............ Lower Confidence Limit [*Statistics*]
**LCL**............ Lower Control Limit [*QCR*]
**LCL**............ Lymphoblastoid Cell Line
**LCL**............ Lymphocytic Lymphosarcoma [*Oncology*]
**LCL**............ Lymphoma Cell Line [*Oncology*]
**LCLA**......... Lutheran Church Library Association (EA)
**LCLAA**...... Labor Council for Latin American Advancement (EA)
**LCL/CI**...... Limited Calendar Life, Controlled Item
**LCLD**......... Laclede Steel Co. [*NASDAQ symbol*] (NQ)
**LCli**........... Audubon Regional Library, Clinton, LA [*Library symbol*] [*Library of Congress*] (LCLS)
**LC Listy Cukrov**... LC. Listy Cukrovarnicke [*A publication*]
**LCLJ**.......... Lower Canada Law Journal [*A publication*] (DLA)
**LCL Jo**....... Lower Canada Law Journal [*A publication*] (DLA)
**LCLK**......... Larnaca [*Cyprus*] [*ICAO location identifier*] (ICLI)
**LCLM**........ Low-Cost Lightweight Missile (MCD)
**LCLS**......... Lewis and Clark Library System [*Library network*]
**LCL(SAust)**... Liberal and Country League (South Australia)
**LCLV**......... Liberace Club of Las Vegas (EA)
**LCLV**......... Liquid-Crystal Light Valve (IEEE)
**LCLV**......... Low-Cost Launch Vehicle [*NASA*] (KSC)
**LCL(WA)**.. Liberal and Country League (Western Australia)
**LCM**.......... Laboratory Contract Manager (MCD)
**LCM**.......... Lake Champlain & Moriah Rail Road Co. [*AAR code*]
**LCM**.......... Land Combat Missile
**LCM**.......... Landing Craft, Mechanized [*Navy symbol*]
**LCM**.......... Landing Craft, Medium [*Navy*]
**LCM**.......... Large-Core Memory [*Data processing*]
**LCM**.......... LASER Countermeasure
**LCM**.......... Launch Control Monitor (MCD)
**LCM**.......... Launch Crew Member (AAG)
**LCM**.......... Lead-Coated Metal [*Technical drawings*]
**LCM**.......... Least Common Multiple [*Mathematics*]
**LCM**.......... Least Concave Majorant [*Statistics*]
**LCM**.......... Left Costal Margin [*Medicine*]
**LCM**.......... Leukocyte-Conditioned Medium [*Microbiology*]
**LCM**.......... Libertarian Center Netherlands (EAIO)
**LCM**.......... Library of Congress Maps [*Source file*] [*UTLAS symbol*]
**LCM**.......... Life Cycle Manager (MCD)
**LCM**.......... Lightning Creek Mines Ltd. [*Vancouver Stock Exchange symbol*]
**LCM**.......... Line Concentrator Module
**LCM**.......... Line Control Module [*Telecommunications*] (TEL)
**LCM**.......... Liquid Curing Medium
**LCM**.......... Literary Criterion (Mysore) [*A publication*]
**LCM**.......... Little Company of Mary, Nursing Sisters [*Roman Catholic religious order*]
**LCM**.......... LOCA [*Loss-of-Coolant Accident*] Core Melt [*Nuclear energy*] (NRCH)
**LCM**.......... Loer, C. M., Reno NV [*STAC*]
**LCM**.......... London City Mission
**LCM**.......... London College of Music (ROG)
**LCM**.......... Lost Circulation Material [*Oil well drilling*]
**LCM**.......... Lower of Cost or Market
**LCM**.......... Lowest Common Multiple [*Mathematics*]
**LCM**.......... Lymphocyte Conditioned Medium [*Hematology*]
**LCM**.......... Lymphocytic Choriomeningitis [*Medicine*]
**LCM(2)**...... Landing Craft, Mechanized, MKII [*Navy symbol*]
**LCM(3)**...... Landing Craft, Mechanized, MKIII [*Navy symbol*]
**LCM6**........ Landing Craft, Mechanized, MKVI [*Navy symbol*]
**LCM8**........ Landing Craft, Mechanized, MKVIII [*Navy symbol*]
**LCMA**....... Lutheran Campus Ministry Association (EA)
**LCMA**....... Lutheran Church Men of America
**LC MARC**... Library of Congress Machine Readable Catalog [*Library of Congress*] [*Washington, DC*] [*Bibliographic database*]
**LCMCFC**.. Liaison Committee for Mediterranean Citrus Fruit Culture [*See also CLAM*] [*Madrid, Spain*] (EAIO)
**LCMCS**..... Liquid Conditioned Microclimate System [*Army*] (RDA)
**LCME**........ Large Climate-Moderating Envelope [*Energy-conserving form of architecture*]
**LCME**........ Liaison Committee on Medical Education (EA)
**LCMF**........ Lettre aux Communautes de la Mission de France [*A publication*]
**LCM(G)**..... Landing Craft, Mechanised (Gun) [*British military*] (DMA)
**LC & M Gaz**... Lower Courts and Municipal Gazette [*Canada*] [*A publication*] (DLA)
**LCMH**....... Lake Charles Memorial Hospital [*Lake Charles, LA*]
**LCMI**......... Licentiate of Cost and Management Institute [*British*]

**LCML**........ Library of Congress Minimal Level Cataloguing [*Source file*] [*UTLAS symbol*]
**LCML**........ Low-Capacity Microwave Link
**LC(ML)C**.. Ligue Communiste (Marxiste-Leniniste) du Canada [*Canadian Communist League (Marxist-Leninist)*]
**LCMM**...... Life-Cycle Management Model (AABC)
**LCMM**...... Life Cycle Material Manager (MCD)
**LCMP**........ Launcher Control and Monitoring Panel
**LCMP**........ Life Cycle Management Planning [*Army*]
**LCMP**........ Local Commandant, Military Police [*British military*] (DMA)
**LCM(R)**..... Landing Craft, Mechanised (Rocket) [*British military*] (DMA)
**LCMRGlc**... Local Cerebral Metabolic Rate for Glucose [*Brain research*]
**LCMS**........ Launch Control and Monitoring System [*NASA*] (AAG)
**LCMS**........ Life-Cycle Management System
**LC/MS**...... Liquid Chromatography/Mass Spectrometry
**LCMS**........ Logistics Command Management System
**LCMS**........ Low-Cost Modular Spacecraft [*NASA*]
**LCMS**........ Lutheran Church - Missouri Synod
**LCMSO**...... Landing Craft, Material Supply Officer
**LCMT**........ London Centre for Marine Technology [*British*] (IRUK)
**LCMV**........ Lymphocytic Choriomeningitis Virus
**LCN**........... La Cosa Nostra [*Our Thing*]
**LCN**........... Landing Craft, Navigation [*Obsolete*]
**LCN**........... Large Co-Ops Network [*British*]
**LCN**........... Law Council Newsletter [*A publication*] (APTA)
**LCN**........... Liaison Change Notice
**LCN**........... Load Classification Number (AFM)
**LCN**........... Local Civil Noon (ADA)
**LCN**........... Local Computer Network
**LCN**........... Local Control Number (MCD)
**LCN**........... Logistics Control Number (MCD)
**LCNA**........ Lacana Mining Corp. [*NASDAQ symbol*] (NQ)
**LCNA**........ Lewis Carroll Society of North America (EA)
**LC/NA**....... Lutherans Concerned/North America (EA)
**LCNC**........ Local Cartage National Conference [*Later, LSHCNC*]
**LCNC**........ Nicosia [*Cyprus*] [*ICAO location identifier*] (ICLI)
**LCNGO-EC**... Liaison Committee of Development Non-Governmental Organizations to the European Communities (EAIO)
**LCNN**........ Land Commander, North Norway [*NATO*] (NATG)
**LCNP**........ Lawyers' Committee on Nuclear Policy (EA)
**LCNP**........ Licentiate of the National Council of Psychotherapists [*British*]
**LCNR**........ Liquid Core Nuclear Rocket
**LCNT**........ Link Celestial Navigation Trainer
**LCNTR**...... Location Counter [*Data processing*]
**LC/NUC**.... Library of Congress and National Union Catalog Author Lists, 1942-1962 [*A publication*]
**LCNVA**...... Low-Cost Night Vision Aid (MCD)
**LCNVG**..... Low-Cost Night Vision Goggles (MCD)
**LCO**........... Landing Craft Officer [*British*] (ADA)
**LCO**........... Landmark America [*AMEX symbol*] (SPSG)
**LCO**........... Launch Control Operation (MCD)
**LCO**........... Launching Control Office [*or Officer*] [*Military*]
**LCO**........... Light Cycle Oil [*Petrochemical technology*]
**LCO**........... Limiting Conditions for Operation [*Nuclear energy*] (NRCH)
**LCO**........... Logistics Control Office [*Military*] (AABC)
**LCO**........... Lord Chancellor's Office [*British*] (DLA)
**LCO**........... Low Cardiac Output [*Cardiology*]
**LCO**........... Lowest Cost of Ownership
**LCOA**........ Logistics Control Office, Atlantic [*Military*]
**LCOC**........ Launch Control Officer's Console (AAG)
**LCOC**........ Lincoln Continental Owners Club (EA)
**LCOCC**...... Atlantic [*Fleet*] Commander Operational Control Center [*Navy*]
**LCOCU**..... Landing Craft, Obstruction Clearance Unit
**L/COH**...... Lance-Corporal of Horse [*British military*] (DMA)
**LCOL**........ Lieutenant Colonel
**LColC**........ Caldwell Parish Library, Columbia, LA [*Library symbol*] [*Library of Congress*] (LCLS)
**LColfG**....... Grant Parish Library, Colfax, LA [*Library symbol*] [*Library of Congress*] (LCLS)
**LCOLNT**... Low Coolant
**LCOM**....... Local Committee Operations Manual [*A publication*] (EAAP)
**LCOM**....... Logic Control Output Module (MCD)
**LCOM**....... Logistics Composite Model
**L & Comm**... Law and Communication [*A publication*] (DLA)
**LCOMM**... Library Council of Metropolitan Milwaukee [*Wisconsin*] [*Library network*]
**L Comment**... Law Commentary [*A publication*] (DLA)
**L Comment'y**... Law Commentary [*A publication*] (DLA)
**L COMP RAM**... Licentiate in Composition, Royal Academy of Music [*British*] (ROG)
**L/COMPT**... Luggage Compartment [*Automotive engineering*]
**L & Comp Tech**... Law and Computer Technology [*Later, Law/Technology*] [*A publication*]
**L & Comp Technol**... Law and Computer Technology [*Later, Law/Technology*] [*A publication*]
**L & Computer Tech**... Law and Computer Technology [*A publication*] (DLA)
**LCON**........ Lexicon Resources Corp. [*NASDAQ symbol*] (NQ)
**L & Contemp Prob**... Law and Contemporary Problems [*A publication*]
**L and Contemp Probl**... Law and Contemporary Problems [*A publication*]
**LCOP**........ Launch Control Officer's Panel (AAG)
**LCOP**........ Logistics Control Office, Pacific [*Military*] (AABC)
**LCOR**........ Langley Corporation [*NASDAQ symbol*] (NQ)
**LCOR**........ Lincoln Cosmopolitan Owners Registry (EA)
**L-CORP**..... Lance-Corporal [*Military*] [*British*] (ROG)
**LCOS**........ Lead Computing Optical Sight
**LCOSE**....... Launch Complex Operational Support Equipment
**LCOSS**...... Lead Computing Optical Sighting System (MCD)
**LCouRR**..... Red River Parish Library, Coushata, LA [*Library symbol*] [*Library of Congress*] (LCLS)
**LCovD**........ Delta Regional Primate Research Center, Science Information Service, Covington, LA [*Library symbol*] [*Library of Congress*] (LCLS)
**LCovSt**....... Saint Tammany Parish Library, Covington, LA [*Library symbol*] [*Library of Congress*] (LCLS)
**LCP**........... Galbraith Lake Camp, AK [*Location identifier*] [*FAA*] (FAAL)
**LCP**........... Landing Craft, Personnel
**LCP**........... Language Conversion Program [*Data processing*] (BUR)
**LCP**........... Large Coil Program [*Physics*]
**LCP**........... Latinitas Christianorum Primaeva [*A publication*]
**LCP**........... Launch Control Panel
**LCP**........... Law and Contemporary Problems [*A publication*]
**LCP**........... Lawyers Co-Operative Publishing Co. [*Rochester, NY*]
**LCP**........... Leader, Company Procurement [*Military*] (AFIT)
**LCP**........... Left Circular Polarization
**L-C-P**........ Leg-Calve-Perthes Disease [*Medicine*]
**LCP**........... Legislative Council for Photogrammetry [*Later, MAPPS*] (EA)
**LCP**........... Lehndorff Canadian Prop. [*Limited Partnership Units*] [*Toronto Stock Exchange symbol*]
**LCP**........... Library Chronicle. University of Pennsylvania [*A publication*]
**LCP**........... Licentiate of the College of Preceptors [*British*]
**LCP**........... Link Control Procedure [*Telecommunications*]
**LCP**........... Liquid-Crystal Polymer [*Organic chemistry*]
**LCP**........... Liquid Cyclone Process [*for making high-protein edible cottonseed flour*]
**LCP**........... Little Computer Person [*Activision computer game*]
**LCP**........... Load Cell Platform
**LCP**........... Local Calibration Procedure
**LCP**........... Local Collaborative Projects [*Between business and education*] [*British*]
**LCP**........... Local Control Panel (CAAL)
**LCP**........... Local Control Point [*Telecommunications*] (TEL)
**LCP**........... Logistic Capability Plan [*Navy*]
**LCP**........... London College of Printing
**LCP**........... Lost Cause Press, Louisville, KY [*Library symbol*] [*Library of Congress*] (LCLS)
**LCP**........... Lower Cost Processor (MCD)
**LCPA**........ Lincoln Center for the Performing Arts (EA)
**LC-PAD**..... Liquid Chromatography plus Pulsed Amperometric Detection [*Analytical chemistry*]
**LCPC**........ Liquid Cyclone Processed Cottonseed Flour
**LCPC**........ Low-Cost-to-Produce Classifier (MCD)
**LCPC Note Inf Tech**... Laboratoire Central des Ponts et Chaussees. Note d'Information Technique [*A publication*]
**LCP-FY**..... Logistic Capability Plan - Fiscal Year [*Navy*] (NG)
**LCPG**........ Logic Clock Pulse Generator [*Data processing*]
**LCPH**........ Paphos [*Cyprus*] [*ICAO location identifier*] (ICLI)
**LCPIS**........ Low-Cost Propulsion Integration Study (MCD)
**LCPL**........ Lance Corporal
**LCPL**........ Landing Craft, Personnel, Large [*Navy symbol*]
**LCPL**........ Left Circularly Polarized Light
**LCPL**........ Leon-Jefferson Library System [*Library network*]
**LCPLR**...... Landing Craft, Personnel Leader
**LCP(M)**..... Landing Craft, Personnel (Medium)
**LCP(N)**...... Landing Craft, Personnel (Nested) [*Obsolete*]
**LCP(P)**....... Landing Craft, Personnel (Plastic)
**LCPR**........ Landing Craft, Personnel, Ramped [*Navy symbol*]
**LC Pract**..... LC [*Liquid Chromatography*] in Practice [*A publication*]
**LCP(S)**....... Landing Craft, Personnel (Small) [*British military*] (DMA)
**LCPS**........ Large Cloud Particle-Size Spectrometer
**LCPS**........ Licentiate of the College of Physicians and Surgeons [*British*]
**LCPS**........ Lithuanian Catholic Press Society (EA)
**LCP & SA**... Licentiate of Physicians and Surgeons of America
**LCP(SY)**.... Landing Craft, Personnel (Survey)
**LCPTT**...... Low-Cost Part Task Trainer (MCD)
**LCP(U)**...... Landing Craft, Personnel (Utility) [*British military*] (DMA)
**LCQ**........... Launch Crew Quarters (AFM)
**LCQ**........... Logical Channel Queue [*Data processing*] (BUR)
**LCQ**........... Lutheran Church Quarterly [*A publication*]
**LCQJCA**... Library of Congress. Quarterly Journal of Current Acquisitions [*A publication*]
**LCR**........... Inductance-Capacitance-Resistance (CET)
**LCR**........... La Lucha [*Costa Rica*] [*Seismograph station code, US Geological Survey*] (SEIS)
**LCR**........... Land Compensation Reports [*A publication*] (ILCA)
**LCR**........... Landing Craft, Raiding [*British*]
**LCR**........... Landing Craft, Rocket [*British military*] (DMA)
**LCR**........... Landing Craft, Rubber
**LCR**........... Las Cruces, NM [*Location identifier*] [*FAA*] (FAAL)
**LCR**........... Late Cutaneous Reaction [*Immunology*]
**LCR**........... Launch Control Room (MCD)
**LCR**........... Least-Cost Routing [*Telecommunications*]

**LCr**.......... Letter of Credit
**L/CR**......... Lettre de Credit [*Letter of Credit*] [*French*]
**LCR**.......... Leurocristine [*Oncovin, Vincristine*] [*Also, O, V, VC, VCR*] [*Antineoplastic drug*]
**LCr**.......... Lieutenant Commander [*Navy*] [*British*]
**LCR**.......... Light Chopping Reticle
**LCR**.......... Ligue Communiste Revolutionnaire [*Revolutionary Communist League*] [*France*] [*Political party*] (PPW)
**LCR**.......... Liquid Chromatographic Reactor
**LCR**.......... Liquide Cephalo-Rachidien [*Cerebrospinal Fluid*] [*French*]
**LCR**.......... Liquido Cefaloraquideo [*Cerebrospinal Fluid*] [*Spanish*]
**LCR**.......... Log Count Rate [*Nuclear energy*] (NRCH)
**LCR**.......... Logistic Change Report [*Military*] (AFM)
**LCR**.......... Low-Cost Reusable [*Refers to payload type*] [*NASA*]
**LCR**.......... Low Cross Range
**LCR**.......... Lower Canada Reports [*A publication*] (DLA)
**LCR**.......... Lucero Resources Corp. [*Vancouver Stock Exchange symbol*]
**LCR**.......... Lung Configuration Recorder
**LCR**.......... Lutheran Churches of the Reformation
**LCrA**......... Acadia Parish Library, Crowley, LA [*Library symbol*] [*Library of Congress*] (LCLS)
**LCRA**......... Akrotiri [*Cyprus*] [*ICAO location identifier*] (ICLI)
**LCRA**......... Lithuanian Catholic Religious Aid (EA)
**LCRA**......... Lower Colorado River Authority
**LCRC**......... Laotian Cultural and Research Center (EA)
**LCRC**......... Lenawee County Railroad Company, Inc. [*AAR code*]
**LCRE**......... Lithium Cooled Reactor Experiment
**LC Rep S Qu**... Lower Canada Seignorial Questions Reports [*A publication*] (DLA)
**LCRES**........ Letter Carrier Route Evaluation System [*Postal Service*]
**LCRIS**........ Loop Cable Record Inventory System (MCD)
**LCrit**........ Literary Criterion [*Mysore*] [*A publication*]
**LCR(L)**....... Landing Craft, Rubber (Large) [*Obsolete*]
**LCRL**......... Lewis and Clark Regional Library [*Library network*]
**LCRM**......... Launch Control Room (AAG)
**LCRM**......... Linear Count Rate Meter (NRCH)
**LCRO**......... Episkopi [*Cyprus*] [*ICAO location identifier*] (ICLI)
**LCRO**......... Linear Combination of Rydberg Orbitals [*Atomic physics*]
**LCRO**......... Low Cross-Range Orbiter (KSC)
**LCR(R)**....... Landing Craft, Rubber (Rocket)
**LCRR**......... Nicosia [*Cyprus*] [*ICAO location identifier*] (ICLI)
**LCR(S)**....... Landing Craft, Rubber (Small) [*Obsolete*]
**LCRS**......... Low-Cost Readout Station [*NASA*]
**LCRSMEEC**... Liaison Committee of the Rice Starch Manufacturers of the EEC [*Louvain, Belgium*] (EAIO)
**LCRT**......... Low-Contrast Resolution Test [*Optics*]
**LCRU**......... Landing Craft, Recovery Unit
**LCRU**......... Lunar Communications Relay Unit [*Apollo*] [*NASA*]
**LCRV**......... Length of Curve (MSA)
**LCRVR**........ Little Change in River Stage (FAAC)
**LCS**.......... Laboratory-Certifying Scientist [*Analytical chemistry*]
**LCS**.......... Laboratory for Computer Science [*Massachusetts Institute of Technology*] [*Research center*] (RCD)
**LCS**.......... Lancaster Resources [*Vancouver Stock Exchange symbol*]
**LCS**.......... Land Combat System
**LCS**.......... Landing Craft, Support
**LCS**.......... Large Capacity [*or Core*] Storage [*Data processing*]
**LCS**.......... LASER Communications System
**LCS**.......... LASER Crosswind System (RDA)
**LCS**.......... Lateral Control System (MUGU)
**LCS**.......... Lathe Control System
**LCS**.......... Launch Complex Set
**LCS**.......... Launch Control Sequence (AAG)
**LCS**.......... Launch Control Simulator
**LCS**.......... Launch Control Station
**LCS**.......... Launch Control System [*or Subsystem*]
**LCS**.......... Law of Corresponding States [*Physics*]
**LCS**.......... League Championship Series [*Baseball*]
**LCS**.......... Leak Control System [*Nuclear energy*] (NRCH)
**LCS**.......... Leakage Collection System [*Nuclear energy*] (NRCH)
**LCS**.......... Learning Classifier System [*Data processing*]
**LCS**.......... Leveling Control System
**LCS**.......... Liaison Call Sheet
**LCS**.......... Library Cat Society (EA)
**LCS**.......... Library Catalogue System [*Australia*]
**LCS**.......... Library Computer System [*University of Illinois*] [*Library network*]
**LCS**.......... Library Control System [*Ohio State Library*] [*Columbus*] [*Information service or system*] (IID)
**LCS**.......... Life Care Services
**LCS**.......... Life-Cycle Survivability (MSA)
**LCS**.......... Light Cruiser Squadron [*British military*] (DMA)
**LCS**.......... Lincoln Calibration Sphere
**LCS**.......... Line Coding Storage
**LCS**.......... Liquid Controlled Solid (KSC)
**LCS**.......... Liquid Cooling System
**LCS**.......... Liquid Crystal Shutter [*Epson*] [*Printer technology*]
**LCS**.......... List of Command Signals (MCD)
**LCS**.......... Lithuanian Cultural Society [*Defunct*] (EA)
**LCS**.......... Litton Computer Services [*Information service or system*] (IID)
**LCS**.......... Lladro Collectors Society (EA)
**LCS**.......... Local Communications Services [*British*]
**LCS**.......... London Controlling Section [*British military*] (DMA)
**LCS**.......... Loop Control System [*Nuclear energy*] (NRCH)
**LCS**.......... LOPO [*Local Post*] Collectors Society (EA)
**LCS**.......... Lottery Collectors Society (EA)
**LCS**.......... Loudness Contour Selector
**LCS**.......... Low-Cost LASER Seeker (MCD)
**LCS**.......... Statewide Library Computer System [*University of Illinois*] [*Information service or system*] (IID)
**LCSA**......... Lewis and Clark Society of America (EA)
**LC Sales**..... Langdell's Cases on the Law of Sales [*A publication*] (DLA)
**LCSB**......... Launch Control Support Building [*Missiles*]
**LCSCF**........ Libera Cattedra di Storia della Civilta Fiorentina [*A publication*]
**LCSCU**........ Launch Coolant System Control Unit (AAG)
**LCSE**......... LASER Communication Satellite Experiment [*NASA*]
**LCSEC**........ Life-Cycle Software Engineering Center [*Army*]
**LCSEFE**....... Labor Committee for Safe Energy and Full Employment (EA)
**LCSH**......... Library of Congress Subject Headings [*Formerly, SHDC*] [*A publication*]
**LCSI**......... Launch Critical Support Items [*NASA*] (KSC)
**LCSI**......... LCS Industries, Inc. [*NASDAQ symbol*] (NQ)
**LCSI**......... Licentiate of the Construction Surveyors' Institute [*British*] (DBQ)
**LCSI**......... Logistic Control Shipping Instruction (AAG)
**LCS(L)**....... Landing Craft, Support (Large) [*Obsolete*]
**LCS(M)**....... Landing Craft, Support (Medium)
**LCSMM**........ Life-Cycle Systems Management Model
**LCSN**......... Local Circuit Switched Network
**LCSO**......... Launch Control Safety Officer (MCD)
**LCSO**......... Local Communications Service Order
**LCSPL**........ Launch Critical Spare Parts List [*NASA*] (KSC)
**LCSR**......... Laboratory for Computer Science Research [*Rutgers University*] [*Research center*] (RCD)
**LCS(R)**....... Landing Craft, Support (Rocket)
**LCSR**......... Landing Craft, Swimmer Reconnaissance [*Navy symbol*]
**LCSR**......... Large Caliber Soft Recoil [*Weaponry*] (MCD)
**LCSR(L)**...... Landing Craft, Swimmer Recovery (Light) [*Navy symbol*] (NVT)
**LCSRM**........ Loop Current Step Response Method (IEEE)
**LCSS**......... Land Combat Support Set (NATG)
**LCSS**......... Land Combat Support Systems
**LCSS**......... Land Combat System Study (AFIT)
**LCS(S)**....... Landing Craft, Support (Small), MKI [*Navy symbol*] [*Obsolete*]
**LCSS**......... Launch Control and Sequencer System
**LCSS**......... Lightweight Camouflage Screen System (MCD)
**LCSS**......... London Council of Social Service
**LCSSAP**....... Low-Cost Silicon Solar Array Project
**LCSSC**........ Life-Cycle Software Support Center [*Army*]
**LCSSE**........ Life-Cycle Software Support Environment [*Army*]
**LCSSP**........ Laboratory of Chemical and Solid-State Physics [*MIT*] (MCD)
**LCST**......... Licentiate of the College of Speech Therapists [*British*]
**LCST**......... Lower Critical-Solution-Temperature
**LCSU**......... Lao Civil Servants' Union
**LCSU**......... Local Concentrator Switching Unit [*Telecommunications*] (TEL)
**LCSVF**........ Logistics Combat Support Vehicle Family (MCD)
**LCSW**......... Latch Checking Switch (MSA)
**LCT**.......... Landing Craft, Tank [*Navy symbol*]
**LCT**.......... Laplace-Carson Transform [*Mathematics*]
**LCT**.......... Latest Closing Time
**LCT**.......... Launch Control Trailer
**LCT**.......... Launch Countdown [*NASA*] (NASA)
**L Ct**......... Law Court (DLA)
**LCT**.......... Lencourt Ltd. [*Toronto Stock Exchange symbol*]
**LCT**.......... Life Component Tester
**LCT**.......... Ligue Communiste des Travailleurs [*Communist Workers' League*] [*Senegal*] [*Political party*] (PPW)
**LCT**.......... Liquid Crystal Thermography
**LCT**.......... Local Civil Time
**LCT**.......... Local Correlation-Tracking [*Instrumental technique*]
**LCT**.......... Locate (MSA)
**LCT**.......... Locust (MSA)
**LCT**.......... Logical Channel Termination
**LCT**.......... Long Calcined Ton [*Bauxite, etc.*]
**LCT**.......... Long-Chain Triglyceride [*Biochemistry*]
**LCT**.......... Louis Comfort Tiffany [*Signature on the art glass designed by Tiffany*]
**LCT**.......... Lymphocytotoxicity Test [*Hematology*]
**LCT-1**........ Lunar Cycle Test One [*Aerospace*]
**LCT(A)**....... Landing Craft, Tank (Armored)
**LCTA**......... London Corn Trade Association
**LCTA**......... Lymphocytotoxic Antibodies [*Immunochemistry*]
**LCTD**......... Located (AFM)
**LCTF**......... Large Coil Test Facility (MCD)
**LCTF**......... Lloyd's Canadian Trust Fund (AIA)
**LCT(H)**....... Landing Craft, Tank (Hospital) [*British military*] (DMA)
**LCTHF**........ Lewis and Clark Trail Heritage Foundation (EA)
**LCTI**......... Large Components Test Installation [*Nuclear energy*] (NRCH)
**LCTL**......... Large Component Test Loop [*Nuclear energy*]

**LCTMP**..... Little Change in Temperature [*Meteorology*] (FAAC)
**LCTN**......... Location
**LCTP**......... Launcher Control Test Panel
**LCT(R)**....... Landing Craft, Tank (Rocket)
**LCTR**......... Locator
**LCT(S)**....... Landing Craft, Tank (Slow)
**LCTS**......... LASER Coherence Techniques Section
**LCTSU**...... Launch Control Transfer Switching Unit [*Aerospace*] (AAG)
**LCTT**......... Launch Complex Telemetry Trailer
**LCU**........... Lac-Coated Urea Fertilizer
**LCU**........... Landing Craft, Utility [*Navy symbol*]
**LCU**........... Large Close-Up (ADA)
**LCU**........... Launch Control Unit (MCD)
**LCU**........... Library of Congress Music [*Source file*] [*UTLAS symbol*]
**LCU**........... Life Change Unit [*Psychometrics*]
**LCU**........... Line Control Unit [*Data communications*]
**LCU**........... Line Coupling Unit (NASA)
**LCU**........... Link Control Unit [*Telecommunications*] (TEL)
**LCU**........... Lucin, UT [*Location identifier*] [*FAA*] (FAAL)
**LCUC**......... Letter Carriers' Union of Canada
**LCuC**......... Liver Copper Concentration [*Physiology*]
**LCUG**........ Liquid-Cooled Undergarment (MCD)
**LCUP**......... Library Chronicle. University of Pennsylvania [*A publication*]
**LC/USA**.... Lutheran Council in the USA [*Defunct*] (EA)
**LCUT**......... Library Chronicle. University of Texas [*A publication*]
**LCV**........... La Cueva [*New Mexico*] [*Seismograph station code, US Geological Survey*] (SEIS)
**LCV**........... Landing Craft, Vehicle [*Navy symbol*]
**LCV**........... LASER Compatible Vidicon
**LCV**........... League of Conservation Voters (EA)
**LCV**........... Level Control Valve (MCD)
**LCV**........... Local Control Valve [*Nuclear energy*] (NRCH)
**LCV**........... Longer Combination Vehicle [*Trucks hauling multiple trailers*]
**LCV**........... Lorry Command Vehicle [*British military*] (DMA)
**LCV**........... Low Calorific Value [*of a fuel*]
**LCVA**......... Light Commercial Vehicle Association (EA)
**LCVAO**..... Linear Combination of Virtual Atomic Orbitals [*Physical chemistry*]
**LCVD**........ LASER Chemical Vapor Deposition [*Coating technology*]
**LCVD**........ Least Coincidence Voltage Detection (MDG)
**LCVG**......... Liquid Cooling and Ventilation Garment [*NASA*] (NASA)
**LCVIP**....... Licensee Contractor Vendor Inspection Report Program [*Nuclear energy*] (NRCH)
**LCVM**........ Log Conversion Voltmeter
**LCVP**......... Landing Craft, Vehicle, Personnel [*Navy symbol*] [*NATO*]
**LCW**.......... Line Control Word
**LCW**.......... Lithuanian Catholic Women (EA)
**LCW**.......... Lutheran Church Women [*Defunct*] (EA)
**LCWHN**.... Latin American and Caribbean Women's Health Network (EAIO)
**LCWI**......... Left Ventricular Cardiac Work Index [*Physiology*]
**LCWP**........ Law Commission Working Paper [*A publication*] (DLA)
**LCWR**........ Leadership Conference of Women Religious of the USA (EA)
**LCWSL**..... Large Caliber Weapon Systems Laboratory [*ARRADCOM*] (RDA)
**LCX**........... Higginsville, MO [*Location identifier*] [*FAA*] (FAAL)
**LCX**........... Launch Complex
**LCY**........... Guthrie, OK [*Location identifier*] [*FAA*] (FAAL)
**LCY**........... League of Communists of Yugoslavia [*Savez Komunista Jugoslavije*] [*Political party*] (PPW)
**LCZ**........... Laws of the Canal Zone [*A publication*] (DLA)
**LCZR**......... Localizer
**LD**............. Decisions Lost [*Boxing*]
**LD**............. Doctor of Letters
**LD**............. Lab. Dausse [*France*] [*Research code symbol*]
**L & D**......... Labor and Delivery [*Area of a hospital*]
**LD**............. Labor Department
**LD**............. Labor Dispute (DLA)
**LD**............. Lactate Dehydrogenase [*Also, LAD, LDH*] [*An enzyme*]
**LD**............. Lady Day [*March 25, the Feast of the Annunciation*] [*British*]
**LD**............. Lamina Densa [*Dermatology*]
**LD**............. Lamp Driver
**LD**............. Land
**LD**............. Land Office Decisions, United States [*A publication*] (DLA)
**L & D**......... Landing and Deceleration [*NASA*] (NASA)
**LD**............. Language Dissertations [*A publication*]
**LD**............. Large Dollar [*Indicator*] [*IRS*]
**LD**............. LASER Desorption [*of ions for analysis*]
**LD**............. LASER Diode
**LD**............. Lateral Direction (MCD)
**LD**............. Lateral Dorsal [*Anatomy*]
**LD**............. Lateral Drift
**LD**............. Lateralis Dorsalis [*Neuroanatomy*]
**LD**............. Launch Director [*NASA*] (KSC)
**LD**............. Launching Division [*Missiles*] (MUGU)
**LD**............. Laus Deo [*Praise to God*] [*Latin*]
**LD**............. Law Dictionary [*A publication*] (DLA)
**LD**............. Layer Depth
**LD**............. Lead [*or Leads*] [*Publishing*]
**LD**............. Leading (MSA)
**LD**............. Learning Disability [*or Learning-Disabled*]
**LD**............. Least Depth [*Nautical charts*]
**LD**............. Lectio Divina [*Paris*] [*A publication*] (BJA)
**LD**............. Left Defense
**LD**............. Left Deltoid [*Medicine*]
**LD**............. Left Door [*Theater*]
**LD**............. Legal Deposit (ADA)
**LD**............. Legal Discriminator (MCD)
**LD**............. Legionnaire's Disease
**LD**............. Legislative Department [*Generic term*] (ROG)
**LD**............. Legislative Digest. Forecast and Review [*Anchorage, AK*] [*A publication*]
**L-D**............ Leishman-Donovan (Bodies) [*Microbiology*]
**LD**............. Length-Diameter Ratio
**LD**............. Lepide Dictum [*Wittily Said*] [*Latin*] (ADA)
**LD**............. Letdown [*Nuclear energy*] (NRCH)
**LD**............. Lethal Dose
**LD**............. Let's Discuss
**L/D**............ Letter of Deposit [*Banking*]
**LD**............. Level Detector
**LD**............. Level Discriminator
**LD**............. Library of Devotion [*A publication*]
**LD**............. Libyan Dinar [*Monetary unit*] (BJA)
**L en D**........ Licencie en Droit [*Licentiate in Law*] [*French*]
**LD**............. Licentiate in Dentistry [*British*] (ROG)
**LD**............. Licentiate in Divinity (DAS)
**LD**............. Lifeboat Deck
**L:D**............ Lift-Drag [*Ratio*]
**LD**............. Light on Dark
**LD**............. Light-Dark [*Cycles*]
**LD**............. Light Difference [*Difference between amounts of light perceptible to the two eyes*] [*Ophthalmology*]
**LD**............. Light Dragoons [*Military unit*] [*British*]
**L/D**............ Light Duty [*Automotive engineering*]
**LD**............. Limited
**LD**............. Limited Disease [*Medicine*]
**LD**............. Limited Partner in Dual Capacity Firm [*London Stock Exchange*]
**LD**............. Line of Departure [*Military*]
**LD**............. Line Dolly (MCD)
**LD**............. Line Drawing (MSA)
**LD**............. Line Driver
**LD**............. Line of Duty [*Military*]
**LD**............. Linear Decision
**LD**............. Linear Dichroism [*Spectra*]
**LD**............. Lineas Aereas del Estada [*Argentine Air Force airline*] [*ICAO designator*] (FAAC)
**LD**............. Linguodistal [*Dentistry*]
**LD**............. Linker Directive [*Telecommunications*] (TEL)
**LD**............. Linz and Donawetz [*Furnace*] [*Metallurgy*] [*Named after two plant sites in Austria*]
**LD**............. Liquid Drop
**LD**............. List Down
**LD**............. List of Drawings [*USN*] (MCD)
**LD**............. Litera Dominicalis [*Sunday Letter*]
**LD**............. Literary Digest [*A publication*]
**LD**............. Lithuanian Days [*A publication*]
**LD**............. Litterarum Doctor [*Doctor of Letters or Literature*] [*Latin*] (ROG)
**LD**............. Lituanistikos Darbai [*Chicago*] [*A publication*]
**LD**............. Living Donor [*Medicine*]
**LD**............. Livres Disponibles [*A publication*]
**LD**............. Load [*or Loader*] (AAG)
**LD**............. Loading Dock (MCD)
**LD**............. Loading Dose
**L & D**......... Loans and Discounts [*Banking*]
**LD**............. Local Delivery
**LD**............. Local Director (DCTA)
**LD**............. Logic Driver [*Data processing*]
**LD**............. Logical Design
**LD**............. Logistics Demonstration (MCD)
**LD**............. Logistics Document (MCD)
**LD**............. Lombard-Dowell [*Broth medium*] [*Microbiology*]
**LD**............. London Docks
**LD**............. Long Day [*Botany*]
**LD**............. Long Delay
**LD**............. Long Distance
**LD**............. Long Duration
**LD**............. Longitudinal Diameter
**LD**............. Longitudinal Division [*Cytology*]
**LD**............. Loop Diagram
**LD**............. Loop-Disconnect [*Telecommunications*] (TEL)
**LD**............. Lord
**L & D**......... Loss and Damage
**LD**............. Low Density
**LD**............. Low Dose [*Medicine*]
**LD**............. Low Drag
**LD**............. Low Dutch [*Language, etc.*]
**LD**............. Low Dynamic
**LD**............. Lower Deck
**LD**............. Lunar Day (KSC)
**LD**............. Lunar Drill [*NASA*] (KSC)

**LD** ........ Lyme Disease [*Medicine*]
**LD** ........ Lymphocyte Defined [*Immunology*]
**LD** ........ Lymphocyte Depletion [*Hematology*]
**LD** ........ Vietnam [*License plate code assigned to foreign diplomats in the US*]
**LD1** ........ Lasa D Ring [*Montana*] [*Seismograph station code, US Geological Survey*] (SEIS)
**LD2** ........ Lasa D Ring [*Montana*] [*Seismograph station code, US Geological Survey*] (SEIS)
**LD3** ........ Lasa D Ring [*Montana*] [*Seismograph station code, US Geological Survey*] (SEIS)
**LD4** ........ Lasa D Ring [*Montana*] [*Seismograph station code, US Geological Survey*] (SEIS)
**$LD_{50}$** ........ Lethal Dose, Median [*Also, MLD*] [*Lethal for 50% of test group*]
**LDA** ........ Ascension Parish Library, Donaldsonville, LA [*Library symbol*] [*Library of Congress*] (LCLS)
**LDA** ........ Labor Developments Abroad [*A publication*]
**LDA** ........ Laboratory Designated Area (AFIT)
**LDA** ........ Landing Distance Available [*Aviation*] (FAAC)
**LDA** ........ LASER Doppler Anemometry
**LDA** ........ Late-Differentiation Antigen [*Immunology*]
**LDA** ........ Lauryl Diethanolamide [*Also, LDE*] [*Organic chemistry*]
**LDA** ........ Lead Development Association [*London, England*] (EAIO)
**LDA** ........ Learning Disabilities Association of America (EA)
**LDA** ........ Left Dorso-Anterior [*A fetal position*] [*Obstetrics*]
**LDA** ........ Legitimacy Declaration Act [*British*] (ROG)
**LDA** ........ Lesson Design Approach (MCD)
**LDA** ........ Limiting Dilution Analyses [*Analytical biochemistry*]
**LDA** ........ Line Driving Amplifier
**LDA** ........ Linear Discriminant Analysis
**LDA** ........ Lithium Diisopropylamide [*Organic chemistry*]
**LDA** ........ Local Data Administrator
**LDA** ........ Local-Density (Functional) Approximation [*Physical chemistry*]
**LDA** ........ Local Design Agency (MCD)
**LDA** ........ Localizer Directional Aid [*Aviation*]
**LDA** ........ Locate Drum Address (CET)
**LDA** ........ Logical Device Address [*Data processing*] (IBMDP)
**LDA** ........ Lord's Day Alliance of the United States (EA)
**LDA** ........ Lower-Deck Attitude [*British military*] (DMA)
**LDA** ........ Lowest Designated Assembly
**LDA** ........ Lutheran Deaconess Association (EA)
**LDA** ........ Lymphocyte-Dependent Antibody [*Immunology*]
**LDAA** ........ Lexikographikon Deltion Akademias Athenon [*A publication*]
**LDAC** ........ Learning Disabilities Association of Canada (EAIO)
**LDAC** ........ Lunar Surface Data Acquisition Camera [*Aerospace*]
**LDA J** ........ Louisiana Dental Association. Journal [*A publication*]
**LDAL** ........ Landall Corp. [*NASDAQ symbol*] (NQ)
**LDAO** ........ Lauryldimethylamine Oxide [*Detergent*]
**LDAPS** ........ Long-Duration Auxiliary Power System (NG)
**LDAR** ........ Lightning Detection and Ranging System [*Meteorology*]
**LDAS** ........ LASER Detection and Analysis System (MCD)
**LdB** ........ Das Land der Bibel (BJA)
**LDB** ........ Launch Data Bus [*Data processing*] (MCD)
**LDB** ........ Leader Dogs for the Blind (EA)
**LDB** ........ Legionnaire's Disease Bacterium
**LDB** ........ Legislative Data Base [*Department of Energy*] [*Information service or system*] (IID)
**LDB** ........ Light Distribution Box (AAG)
**LDB** ........ Limited Data Block (KSC)
**LDB** ........ Load Determining Bolt
**LDB** ........ Logical Database
**LDB** ........ Logistics Data Bank (NASA)
**LDB** ........ Londrina [*Brazil*] [*Airport symbol*] (OAG)
**LDB** ........ Low-Drag Bomb
**LDBC** ........ LDB Corporation [*NASDAQ symbol*] (NQ)
**LDBE** ........ London Diocesan Board of Education
**Ld Birk** ........ Lord Birkenhead's Judgments, House of Lords [*England*] [*A publication*] (DLA)
**LDBLC** ........ Low-Drag Boundary Layer Control [*Military*]
**LDBMA** ........ Landbouwmechanisatie [*A publication*]
**LDBOS** ........ LASER Designation Battlefield Obscuration Simulator (RDA)
**Ld Br Sp** ........ Lord Brougham's Speeches [*A publication*] (DLA)
**LDC** ........ Labor Data Collection (MCD)
**LDC** ........ Laboratory Data Control [*Commercial firm*]
**LDC** ........ Latitude Data Computer
**LDC** ........ Laundry and Dry Cleaning International Union
**LDC** ........ Learning Disability Center
**LDC** ........ Learning Disordered Children
**LDC** ........ Less Developed Country
**LDC** ........ Level Decision Circuit
**LDC** ........ Libertarian Defense Caucus (EA)
**LDC** ........ Library Development Center [*Columbia University*]
**LDC** ........ Library Development Consultants, Inc. [*Information service or system*] (IID)
**LDC** ........ Light Direction Center [*Military*]
**LDC** ........ Lindeman Island [*Australia*] [*Airport symbol*]
**LDC** ........ Line Directional Coupler
**LDC** ........ Line-Drop Compensator (MSA)
**LDC** ........ Linear Detonating Cord (MSA)
**LDC** ........ Load Drawer Computer (MCD)
**LDC** ........ Local Data Concentrator [*Telecommunications*]
**LDC** ........ Local Defense Center
**LDC** ........ Local Departmental Committee [*British labor*]
**LDC** ........ Local Development Company
**LDC** ........ Local Display Controller
**LDC** ........ Logistics Data Center [*Army*] (AABC)
**LDC** ........ London Dumping Convention [*Sets standards for disposal of wastes in oceans*]
**LDC** ........ Long-Distance Call
**LDC** ........ Long-Distance Communications
**LDC** ........ Low-Speed Data Channel
**LDC** ........ Lower Dead Center
**LDC** ........ Lutheran Deaconess Conference (EA)
**LDCC** ........ Large Diameter Component Cask [*Nuclear energy*] (NRCH)
**LDCC** ........ Lectin-Dependent Cell-Mediated Cytotoxicity [*Biochemistry*]
**LDCF** ........ Lymphocyte Derived Chemotactic Factor [*Biochemistry*]
**LDCO** ........ Laundry and Dry Cleaning Operations [*Military*]
**LDCO** ........ Leader Development Corporation [*NASDAQ symbol*] (NQ)
**L & D Conv** ... Leigh and Dalzell. Conversion of Property [*1825*] [*A publication*] (DLA)
**LDCP** ........ Landing Dynamics Computer Program [*NASA*]
**LDCS** ........ Long-Distance Control System (IEEE)
**LDCV** ........ Large Dense-Core Vesicle [*Neurobiology*]
**LDD** ........ LASER Detector Diode
**LdD** ........ Letras de Deusto [*A publication*]
**LDD** ........ Letter of Determination of Dependency
**LDD** ........ Light-Dark Discrimination [*Ophthalmology*]
**LDD** ........ Little Diomede Island, AK [*Location identifier*] [*FAA*] (FAAL)
**LDD** ........ Loaded
**LDD** ........ Local Data Distribution
**LDD** ........ Local Development District
**LDD** ........ Logic Design Data [*Telecommunications*] (TEL)
**LDD** ........ Logical Database Designer [*Data processing*]
**LDD** ........ Long-Distance Dispersal [*Botany*]
**LDD** ........ Low-Density Data (KSC)
**LDD** ........ Lunar Dust Detector [*NASA*]
**LDDC** ........ Least-Developed Developing Country [*Trade status*]
**LDDC** ........ London Docklands Development Corp. [*British*] (ECON)
**LDDI** ........ Local Distributed Data Interface [*AMP Products Corp.*]
**LDDS** ........ LDDS Communications, Inc. (NQ)
**LDDS** ........ Light Division Direct Support [*Artillery system*] (MCD)
**LDDS** ........ Limited Distance Data Service [*Telecommunications*]
**LDDS** ........ Local Digital Distribution Subsystem
**LDDS** ........ Low-Density Data System
**LDE** ........ Lagrange Differential Equation
**LDE** ........ Laminar Defect Examination (IEEE)
**LDE** ........ Lauryl Diethanolamide [*Also, LDA*] [*Organic chemistry*]
**LDE** ........ Les Dames d'Escoffier (EA)
**LDE** ........ Linear Differential Equation
**LDE** ........ Local Dynamics Experiment [*Marine science*] (MSC)
**LDE** ........ Long-Delayed Echo
**LDE** ........ Long-Duration Exposure
**LDE** ........ Lourdes/Tarbes [*France*] [*Airport symbol*] (OAG)
**LDeB** ........ Beauregard Parish Library, DeRidder, LA [*Library symbol*] [*Library of Congress*] (LCLS)
**L Dec** ........ Land Office Decisions, United States [*A publication*] (DLA)
**LDEC** ........ Lunar Docking Events Controller [*NASA*] (MCD)
**LDEF** ........ Long-Duration Exposure Facility [*NASA*]
**LDEG** ........ Laus Deo et Gloria [*Praise and Glory Be to God*] [*Latin*]
**LDERRY** ... Londonderry [*County in Ireland*] (ROG)
**LDET** ........ Level Detector (MSA)
**LDEX** ........ Landing Exercise [*Navy*] (NVT)
**LD-EYA** .... Lombard-Dowell Egg Yolk Agar [*Microbiology*]
**LDF** ........ Light Digital FACSIMILE [*Machine*]
**LDF** ........ Linear Discriminant Function [*Mathematics*]
**LDF** ........ Linear Driving Force
**LDF** ........ Load Division Fault
**LDF** ........ Local Defense Forces
**LDF** ........ Local Density Functional Theory [*Chemistry*]
**LDF** ........ London Diocesan Fund
**LDF** ........ NAACP [*National Association for the Advancement of Colored People*] Legal Defense and Educational Fund (EA)
**LDFC** ........ Lew DeWitt Fan Club (EA)
**LD is FFD** ... Line of Departure Is Friendly Forward Disposition [*Army*] (AABC)
**LDG** ........ Korte Berichten over Handel, Ambacht, Dienstverlening, Toerisme, Middenbedrijf, en Kleinbedrijf [*A publication*]
**LDG** ........ Landing [*Maps and charts*] (AFM)
**LDG** ........ Leading
**LDG** ........ Left Digestive Gland
**LDG** ........ Libyan Desert Glass [*Archeology*]
**LDG** ........ Linear Displacement Gauge
**LDG** ........ Loading
**LDG** ........ Lodge (MCD)
**LDG** ........ Longs Drug Stores Corp. [*NYSE symbol*] (SPSG)
**LDG** ........ Low-Density Gas
**Ldg & Dly** .. Landing and Delivery [*Shipping*] (DS)
**LDGE** ........ LEM [*Lunar Excursion Module*] Dummy Guidance Equipment [*NASA*] (KSC)
**LDGLT** ...... Leading Light [*Navigation signal*]

**L-DGO**....... Lamont-Doherty Geological Observatory [*Formerly, LGO*] [*Columbia University*]
**LDGP**........ Low-Drag General Purpose (MCD)
**Ldg Tel**....... Leading Telegraphist
**LDGV**........ Light-Duty Gasoline Vehicle
**LDGX**........ Lodgistix, Inc. [*NASDAQ symbol*] (NQ)
**LDH**........... Lactate Dehydrogenase [*Also, LAD, LD*] [*An enzyme*]
**LDH**........... Lord Howe Island [*Australia*] [*Airport symbol*] (OAG)
**LDHC**........ Locker Door Hydraulic Cylinder
**LDHD**........ Lymphocyte-Depletion Hodgkin's Disease [*Medicine*]
**LDHM**....... London Diocesan Home Mission [*or Missionary*]
**LDHR**........ League for the Defense of Human Rights in Romania (EAIO)
**LDHRR**..... League for the Defense of Human Rights in Romania [*Paris, France*] (EAIO)
**LDI**........... Landing Direction Indicator [*Aviation*] (FAAC)
**LDI**........... LASER Desorption Ionization [*Spectroscopy*]
**LDI**........... Life Detection Instrument
**LDI**........... Lindi [*Tanzania*] [*Airport symbol*] (OAG)
**LDI**........... Linear Displacement Indicator
**LDI**........... Load Indicator
**LDI**........... Lockheed DataPlan, Incorporated [*Information service or system*] (IID)
**LDI**........... Loredi Resources Ltd. [*Vancouver Stock Exchange symbol*]
**LDIC**.......... LDI Corp. [*NASDAQ symbol*] (NQ)
**L Dict**......... Law Dictionary [*A publication*] (DLA)
**LDII**........... Larson-Davis, Incorporated [*NASDAQ symbol*] (NQ)
**LDIM**......... Luminescence Digital Imaging Microscopy
**LDIN**.......... Lead-In Lighting [*or Lights*] [*Aviation*]
**L-Dink**....... Lower Class - Double [*or Dual*] Income, No Kids [*Lifestyle classification*]
**LDISCR**..... Level Discriminator (MSA)
**LDIU**.......... Launch Data Interface Unit (MCD)
**L Div**.......... Law Division (DLA)
**L Div**.......... Licentiate in Divinity
**LDJ**........... Linden, NJ [*Location identifier*] [*FAA*] (FAAL)
**LDJ**........... Load D-Bank and Jump [*Data processing*]
**LDJU**......... Luvers of David Jones United (EA)
**LDK**........... Lower Deck
**Ld Ken**....... Lord Kenyon's English King's Bench Reports [*1753-59*] [*A publication*] (DLA)
**Ld Kenyon**... Lord Kenyon's English King's Bench Reports [*1753-59*] [*A publication*] (DLA)
**Ld Kenyon (Eng)**... Lord Kenyon's English King's Bench Reports [*1753-59*] [*A publication*] (DLA)
**LDL**........... Language Description Language [*Data processing*]
**LDL**........... Learned Doctor of Laws
**LDL**........... Letopis Doma Literatorov [*A publication*]
**LDL**........... Liquid Delay Line
**LDL**........... Logical Display List (MCD)
**LDL**........... Long Distance Love [*An association*] (EA)
**LDL**........... Low-Density Lipoprotein [*Biochemistry*]
**LDL**........... Lower Detectable Limit [*Chemical analysis*]
**LDL**........... Lower Deviation Level (AABC)
**LDL**........... Lydall, Inc. [*NYSE symbol*] (SPSG)
**LDL**........... University of Nebraska, Lincoln, Lincoln, NE [*OCLC symbol*] (OCLC)
**LDLA**......... Limited Distance Line Adapter
**LDL-C**....... Low-Density Lipoprotein-Cholesterol [*Biochemistry*]
**LDLE**......... Light-Duty Lathe Engine
**LDLN**........ Lumieres dans la Nuit [*Unidentified flying objects*] [*French*]
**LDLR**......... Land Development Law Reporter [*A publication*] (DLA)
**LDLR**......... Low-Density Lipoprotein Receptor [*Biochemistry*]
**LDM**.......... Laidlaw Transportation Ltd. [*Toronto Stock Exchange symbol*]
**LDM**.......... LASER Drilling Machine
**LDM**.......... Last Day of the Month (AFM)
**LdM**.......... Lautbibliothek der Deutschen Mundarten [*A publication*]
**LDM**.......... Lee, David M., Los Angeles CA [*STAC*]
**LDM**.......... Libby Dam [*Montana*] [*Seismograph station code, US Geological Survey*] (SEIS)
**LDM**.......... Licentiate of Dental Medicine
**LDM**.......... Limited-Distance MODEM [*Data processing*]
**LDM**.......... Linear Delta Modulation
**LDM**.......... Lingue del Mondo [*A publication*]
**LDM**.......... Local Data Manager
**LDM**.......... Long-Delay Monostable [*Circuitry*]
**LDM**.......... Lord Mayor
**LDM**.......... Low-Density Microsome [*Cytology*]
**LDM**.......... Ludington, MI [*Location identifier*] [*FAA*] (FAAL)
**LDMC**........ Livestock Development and Marketing Corporation [*Burma*] (DS)
**LDMI**......... LASER Distance Measuring Instrument
**LDMK**........ Landmark (KSC)
**LDMK**........ Landmark Bank for Savings [*Whitman, MA*] [*NASDAQ symbol*] (NQ)
**LDMM**....... Leadville Mining & Milling Corp. [*New York, NY*] [*NASDAQ symbol*] (NQ)
**LDMOS**.... Lateral Double-Diffused Metal-Oxide Semiconductor (MCD)
**LD-MPT**.... Ligue Democratique - Mouvement pour le Parti des Travailleurs [*Democratic League - Movement for the Workers' Party*] [*Senegal*] [*Political party*] (PPW)
**LDMS**........ Laboratory Data Management System [*IBM Corp.*]
**LDMS**........ LASER Desorption Mass Spectrometry
**LDMS**........ LASER Distance Measuring System
**LDMS**........ Lunar Distance Measuring System [*Aerospace*]
**LDMWR**... Limited Depot Maintenance Work Requirements
**LDMX**........ Local Digital Message Exchange (AABC)
**LDN**........... Lamidanda [*Nepal*] [*Airport symbol*] (OAG)
**LDN**........... Lightning Detection Network [*Electric Power Research Institute*]
**LDN**........... Linden, VA [*Location identifier*] [*FAA*] (FAAL)
**LDN**........... Listed Directory Number [*Bell System*]
**LDN**........... Locally Defined Neighborhood
**LDN**........... London [*Ontario*] [*Seismograph station code, US Geological Survey*] (SEIS)
**LDN**........... London [*England*]
**LDN**........... London Daily News [*A publication*]
**LDN**........... London Silver Corp. [*Vancouver Stock Exchange symbol*]
**LDNA**........ Long-Distance Navigation Aid
**LD-NEYA**... Lombard-Dowell Neomycin Egg Yolk Agar [*Microbiology*]
**Ldnpr**......... Ladenpreis [*List Price*] [*German*]
**LDNS**......... Lightweight Doppler Navigation System (MCD)
**LDNS**......... London Silver Corp. [*NASDAQ symbol*] (NQ)
**LDO**........... Documentatiecentrum voor Overheidspersoneel. Literatuuroverzicht [*A publication*]
**LDO**........... Ladouanie [*Suriname*] [*Airport symbol*] (OAG)
**LDO**........... Launch Division Officer [*Missiles*] (MUGU)
**LDO**........... Limited Duty Officer [*Navy*]
**LDO**........... Linear Diophantine Object
**LDO**........... Logical Device Order [*Data processing*] (IBMDP)
**LDO**........... Low-Density Oil [*Petroleum industry*]
**LDO**........... Low-Density Overlay [*Plywood*]
**LDO**........... St. Mary's Dominican College, New Orleans, LA [*OCLC symbol*] (OCLC)
**LDOM**....... Lorenz Domination [*Statistics*]
**L-DOPA**.... Levo-Dihydroxyphenylalanine [*Pharmacology*]
**LDOS**........ Leather Dressers' Old Society [*A union*] [*British*]
**LDOS**........ Lord's Day Observance Society [*British*]
**LDP**........... Laban ng Demokratikong Pilipino [*Democratic Filipino's Struggle*] [*Political party*]
**LDP**........... Laboratory Distribution Panel
**LDP**........... Ladyship [*or Lordship*]
**LDP**........... Langmuir Diffusion Pump [*Engineering*]
**LDP**........... Language Data Processing (MSA)
**LDP**........... Large Developmental Plant [*Project*] [*Department of Energy*]
**LDP**........... Leadership Development Projects [*National Science Foundation*]
**LDP**........... Leaflet Dispensing Pod
**LDP**........... Left Dorso-Posterior [*A fetal position*] [*Obstetrics*]
**LDP**........... Liberal-Democratic Party of Japan [*Jiyu-Minshuto*] [*Political party*] (PPW)
**LDP**........... Liberal Demokratische Partei [*Liberal Democratic Party*] [*Federal Republic of Germany*] [*Political party*] (PPE)
**LDP**........... Lietuviy Demokraty Partija [*Lithuanian Democratic Party*] [*Political party*] (PPE)
**L/DP**......... Living/Dying Project (EA)
**LdP**........... Livros de Portugal [*A publication*]
**LDP**........... Local Data Package (KSC)
**LDP**........... Local Data Processor (AABC)
**LDP**........... Logistics Data Package
**LDP**........... Lomas Data Products [*Marlboro, MA*] [*Computer manufacturer*]
**LDP**........... London Daily Price [*British*]
**LDP**........... Long-Day Plant [*Botany*]
**LDP**........... Lordship [*British*]
**LDP**........... Lorentz Doppler Profile [*Physics*]
**LDPD**........ Liberal-Demokratische Partei Deutschlands [*Liberal Democratic Party of Germany*] [*German Democratic Republic*] [*Political party*] (PPW)
**LDPE**......... Low-Density Polyethylene [*Polymer*]
**LDPN**........ Low-Density Phenolic Nylon [*Polymer*]
**LD is PPOS**... Line of Departure Is Present Positions [*Military*] (AABC)
**LdProv**....... Lettore de Provincia [*A publication*]
**LDPS**......... L-Band Digital Phase Shifter
**LDQ**........... Leaders Equity Corp. [*Vancouver Stock Exchange symbol*]
**LDR**........... Labor, Delivery, Recovery Room [*Medicine*]
**LDR**........... Landmark Resources Ltd. [*Vancouver Stock Exchange symbol*]
**LDR**........... Large Deployable Reflector [*Astronomy*]
**LDR**........... LASER Designator Range (MCD)
**LDR**........... Leader (AFM)
**LDR**........... Ledger (ADA)
**LDR**........... Length-Diameter Ratio
**LDR**........... Level Distribution Recorder
**LDR**........... Light-to-Dark Ratio
**LDR**........... Light Dependent Resistor
**LDR**........... Line Driver-Receiver [*Computer communication*] (TEL)
**LDR**........... Linear Decision Rule
**LDR**........... Linear Dynamic Range
**LDR**........... Llandore [*Welsh depot code*]
**LDR**........... Loader (MSA)
**LDR**........... Log Dose Response [*Biochemical analysis*]
**LDR**........... Lorentz Double Refraction [*Physics*]
**L/DR**......... Lounge/Dining Room [*Classified advertising*] (ADA)

**LDR** .......... Low Data Rate [*RADAR*]
**LDR** .......... Low Data Register [*Data processing*]
**LDR** .......... Low-Density, Recorder
**LDR** .......... Low Dose Rate [*Medicine*]
**LDRA** ........ Low Data Rate Auxiliary [*RADAR*]
**Ld Ray** ....... Lord Raymond's King's Bench and Common Pleas Reports [*1694-1732*] [*A publication*] (DLA)
**Ld Raym** .... Lord Raymond's King's Bench and Common Pleas Reports [*1694-1732*] [*A publication*] (DLA)
**LDRC**......... Libel Defense Resource Center (EA)
**LDRC**......... Lumber Dealers Research Council [*Defunct*] (EA)
**LDRC Bulletin** ... LDRC (Libel Defense Resource Center) Bulletin [*A publication*]
**LDRDA** ..... Long Distance Running Directors Association (EA)
**LDRG** ........ Liberal, Democratic and Reformist Group [*See also GLDR*] (EAIO)
**LDRI**.......... Low Data Rate Input [*RADAR*]
**LDRIACS** ... Low-Data Rate Integrated Acoustic Communications System [*Military*] (CAAL)
**LDRM** ....... LASER Designator Rangefinding Module (RDA)
**LDRP**......... Learning Disability Rating Procedure [*Educational test*]
**LDRS**......... LASER Discrimination RADAR System
**L/DRS** ....... Level and Density Recorder Switch [*Nuclear energy*] (NRCH)
**LDRSHP**... Leadership
**LDRSP** ...... Leadership (AFM)
**LDRT**......... [*The*] Lake Front Dock & Railroad Terminal Co. [*Formerly, LDT*] [*AAR code*]
**LDRY** ........ Laundry (AFM)
**LDS**............ Havre, MT [*Location identifier*] [*FAA*] (FAAL)
**LDS**............ Landing/Deceleration Subsystem [*NASA*] (NASA)
**LDS**............ Landing, Deservicing, and Safing [*NASA*] (KSC)
**LDS**............ Langmuir Dark Space [*Electronics*]
**LDS**............ Large Disk Storage [*Data processing*] (IEEE)
**LDS**............ LASER Deep Space
**LDS**............ LASER Designator System [*Rangefinder*] (MCD)
**LDS**............ LASER Drilling System
**LDS**............ Latter-Day Saints [*Mormons*]
**LDS**............ Launch Data System [*NASA*] (KSC)
**LDS**............ Launch Detection Satellite [*USSR*]
**LDS**............ Laus Deo Semper [*Praise to God Always*] [*Latin*]
**LDS**............ Layered Defense System (MCD)
**LDS**............ Leader Development Study [*Army*]
**LDS**............ Leadership [*A publication*]
**LDS**............ Leak Detection System [*Nuclear energy*] (NRCH)
**LDS**............ Lethal Defense System (MCD)
**LDS**............ Lexington Developmental Scales [*Child development test*]
**LDS**............ Licentiate in Dental Surgery
**LDS**............ Lietuviu Darbininku Susivienijimas [*Association of Lithuanian Workers*] (EA)
**LDS**............ Linear Dynamic System
**LDS**............ Liquid, Diesel-Cycle, Supercharged
**LDS**............ Local Digital Switch [*Telecommunications*] (TEL)
**LDS**............ Local Distribution System [*Cable television*] (MDG)
**LDS**............ Logistics Data Sheet
**LDS**............ Long Distance Swimmer
**LDS**............ Lunar Drill System [*NASA*]
**LDSA**......... Logistics Doctrine and Systems Agency [*Army*] (MCD)
**LDSc**......... Licentiate in Dental Science [*British*]
**LDSD**......... Lookdown/Shootdown (MCD)
**LDSI**.......... Licentiate in Dental Surgery (Ireland)
**LDSJ** ......... Little Daughters of St. Joseph [*Roman Catholic religious order*]
**LDSO** ........ Logistics Doctrine and Systems Office [*Army*]
**LDSR**......... League of Distilled Spirits Rectifiers [*Defunct*]
**LDSRA**...... Logistics Doctrine Systems and Readiness Agency [*Army*] (AABC)
**LDSRCPS Glas** ... Licentiate in Dental Surgery of the Royal College of Physicians and Surgeons of Glasgow [*British*]
**LDSRCS**.... Licentiate in Dental Surgery of the Royal College of Surgeons [*British*]
**LDSRCS Edin** ... Licentiate in Dental Surgery of the Royal College of Surgeons of Edinburgh [*British*]
**LDSRCS Eng** ... Licentiate in Dental Surgery of the Royal College of Surgeons of England
**LDSRCS Irel** ... Licentiate in Dental Surgery of the Royal College of Surgeons in Ireland
**LDSS** ......... LASER Designator Search System
**LDSS** ......... Lunar Deep Seismic Sounding [*Aerospace*] (MCD)
**LDSSIG**..... Learning Disabled Student SIG [*Special Interest Group*] (EA)
**LDST** ......... Letdown Storage Tank [*Nuclear energy*] (NRCH)
**LDT** ........... L-DOPA Test [*Endocrinology*]
**LDT** ........... [*The*] Lake Front Dock & Railroad Terminal Co. [*Later, LDRT*] [*AAR code*]
**LDT** ........... Language Dependent Translator
**LDT** ........... LASER Discharge Tube
**LDT** ........... Lateral Dorsal Tract [*Neuroanatomy*]
**LDT** ........... Level Delay Time
**LDT** ........... Level Detector (KSC)
**LDT** ........... Library Development Team
**LDT** ........... Licensed Deposit-Taking Institution [*British*]
**LDT** ........... Light-Duty Truck
**LDT** ........... Linear Differential Transformer
**LDT** ........... Linear Displacement Transduced (MCD)
**LDT** ........... Local Daylight Saving Time
**LDT** ........... Local Descriptor Table [*Data processing*]
**LDT** ........... Logic Design Translator [*Data processing*]
**LDT** ........... Logistic Delay Time (CAAL)
**LDT** ........... London Dipole Theory
**LDT** ........... Long Distance Transmission (BUR)
**LDT** ........... Long Dry Ton
**LDT** ........... Lubbock, TX [*Location identifier*] [*FAA*] (FAAL)
**LDTA** ........ Leak Detection Technology Association (EA)
**LDTC**......... Lawndale Transportation Company [*AAR code*]
**LDTC**......... Learning Disabilities Teacher Consultant
**LD/TE** ....... Line Driver/Terminal Equipment (MCD)
**LDTF** ........ Light of Divine Truth Foundation (EA)
**LDTM** ....... Lander Dynamic Test Model [*NASA*]
**LDTR**........ Long Dwell Time RADAR (NATG)
**LDTTY**...... Landing Line Teletype
**LDU**........... Lahad Datu [*Malaysia*] [*Airport symbol*] (OAG)
**LDU**........... Lamp Dimmer Unit (MCD)
**LdU**........... Landesring der Unabhaengigen [*Independent Party*] [*Switzerland*] [*Political party*] (PPE)
**LDU**........... Leather Dressers' Union [*British*]
**LDU**........... Line Driver Unit [*Computer communication*] (MCD)
**LDUB** ........ Long Double Upright Brace [*Medicine*]
**LD/USA**.... Long Distance/USA, Inc. [*Honolulu, HI*] [*Telecommunications*] (TSSD)
**LDV** ........... Lactic Dehydrogenase Virus
**LDV** ........... LASER Doppler Velocimeter
**LDV** ........... Leadville [*Nevada*] [*Seismograph station code, US Geological Survey*] [*Closed*] (SEIS)
**LDV** ........... League of Disabled Voters (EA)
**LDV** ........... Lectus Developments Ltd. [*Vancouver Stock Exchange symbol*]
**LDV** ........... Light-Duty Vehicle
**LDV** ........... Linear Differential Vector
**LDV** ........... Local Defence Volunteers [*Later called Home Guards*] [*British*] [*World War II*]
**LDV** ........... Low-Dollar Value
**LDVA** ........ Lodi District Vintners Association (EA)
**LDVE**........ Linear Differential Vector Equation
**LDW** .......... Left Defense Wing [*Women's lacrosse position*]
**LDWB** ....... Laidlaw, Inc. Class B [*NYSE symbol*] (SPSG)
**LDWSS** ..... LASER Designator Weapon System Simulation (RDA)
**LDX** ........... Long-Distance Xerography [*Xerox Corp.*] [*Communications facsimile system*]
**LDY** ........... Leicestershire and Derbyshire Yeomanry [*Military unit*] [*British*]
**LDY** ........... Londonderry [*Northern Ireland*] [*Airport symbol*] (OAG)
**LDZ** ........... St. Louis, MO [*Location identifier*] [*FAA*] (FAAL)
**LE** .............. Antenna Effective Length for Electric-Field Antennas (IEEE)
**Le** .............. Asia-Philippines Leader [*A publication*]
**L & E**.......... English Law and Equity Reports [*American Reprint*] [*A publication*] (DLA)
**LE** .............. Eunice Public Library, Eunice, LA [*Library symbol*] [*Library of Congress*] (LCLS)
**LE** .............. Labor Exchange
**LE** .............. Laboratory of Electronics [*Rockefeller University*] [*Research center*] (RCD)
**LE** .............. Laboratory Evaluation (MUGU)
**LE** .............. Lagina Ephemeris Aegyptiaca et Universa [*A publication*]
**LE** .............. Land Economics [*A publication*]
**LE** .............. Lands' End [*NYSE symbol*] (SPSG)
**LE** .............. Lateral Element
**LE** .............. Lateral Epicondyle [*Anatomy*]
**LE** .............. Latest Estimate [*Business term*]
**L/E**............. Launch Encounter [*NASA*] (KSC)
**LE** .............. Launch Escape [*NASA*] (KSC)
**LE** .............. Launching Equipment
**LE** .............. Law Enforcement
**LE** .............. Laws of Eshnunna (BJA)
**LE** .............. Lawyers' Edition, United States Supreme Court Reports [*A publication*] (DLA)
**LE** .............. Lead Engineer (AAG)
**LE** .............. Leading Edge [*Aerospace*]
**LE** .............. Learning Exchange [*A publication*] (APTA)
**LE** .............. Lease
**le**................ Lebanon [*MARC country of publication code*] [*Library of Congress*] (LCCP)
**LE** .............. Lector
**Le** .............. Ledge
**LE** .............. Lee-Enfield [*British military*] (DMA)
**LE** .............. Left End
**LE** .............. Left Extremity
**LE** .............. Left Eye
**LE** .............. Leg Exercise [*Sports medicine*]
**Le** .............. Leonard [*Unit for cathode rays*]
**LE** .............. Leone [*Monetary unit*] [*Sierra Leone*]
**LE** .............. Les Echos [*A publication*]
**LE** .............. Less than or Equal
**LE** .............. Leucine Enkephalin [*Biochemistry*]
**LE** .............. Leucocyte Elastase [*An enzyme*]
**LE** .............. Leukemia [*Oncology*]

**LE** ........ Levy Industries Ltd. [*Toronto Stock Exchange symbol*]
**Le** ........ Lewis [*Blood group*]
**Le** ........ Lewis Number [*IUPAC*]
**LE** ........ Liberal Education [*A publication*]
**LE** ........ Library Edition (ADA)
**LE** ........ Lifting Eye
**LE** ........ Light Equipment
**LE** ........ Limited Edition (ADA)
**LE** ........ Limits of Error
**LE** ........ Line Equipment [*Telecommunications*] (TEL)
**LE** ........ Linear Expansion [*Physics*]
**LE** ........ Linguistica Extranea [*A publication*]
**LE** ........ Literarisches Echo [*A publication*]
**LE** ........ Local Exchange [*Telecommunications*] (TEL)
**LE** ........ Locally Engaged
**LE** ........ Locally Excited [*Physical chemistry*]
**LE** ........ Logic Element
**LE** ........ Logistic Effectiveness (CAAL)
**LE** ........ Logistic Evaluation
**LE** ........ Long-Evans Rat
**LE** ........ Loop Extender [*Telecommunications*] (TEL)
**LE** ........ Louisiana Eastern Railroad [*AAR code*]
**LE** ........ Low Efficiency
**LE** ........ Low Energy (CAAL)
**LE** ........ Low Entry [*Truck cab*]
**LE** ........ Low Explosive [*Military*]
**LE** ........ Lower Epidermis [*Botany*]
**LE** ........ Lower Extremity [*Medicine*]
**LE** ........ Lugalbanda and Enmerkar (BJA)
**LE** ........ Lugalbanda Epos (BJA)
**LE** ........ Lunar Ephemeris
**LE** ........ Lupus Erythematosus [*Hematology*]
**LE** ........ Magnum Airlines [*Pty.*] Ltd. [*South Africa*] [*ICAO designator*] (FAAC)
**£E** ........ Pounds Egyptian [*Monetary unit*]
**Le** ........ [*The*] Twenty-Four Books of the Holy Scriptures (1853) [*I. Leeser*] (BJA)
**LEA** ........ Landes-Entschaedigungsamt (BJA)
**LEA** ........ Language Experience Approach [*Education*]
**LEA** ........ Latest Epicardial Activation [*Cardiology*]
**LEA** ........ Launch Enable Alarm (MCD)
**LEA** ........ Launch Escape Assembly [*NASA*] (KSC)
**LEA** ........ Law Enforcement Assistance Program (EA)
**LEA** ........ Lead [*South Dakota*] [*Seismograph station code, US Geological Survey*] [*Closed*] (SEIS)
**LEA** ........ Leader Resources, Inc. [*Vancouver Stock Exchange symbol*]
**Lea** ........ Leadership [*A publication*]
**LEA** ........ League [*Unit of measurement*]
**LEA** ........ Learmonth [*Australia*] [*Airport symbol*] (OAG)
**Lea** ........ Lea's Tennessee Reports [*A publication*] (DLA)
**LEA** ........ Leather
**LEA** ........ Leathergoods [*A publication*]
**LEA** ........ Leave
**LEA** ........ Letter Enjoyers Association (EA)
**LEA** ........ Light-Emitting Array
**LEA** ........ Line Equalizing Amplifier (AFM)
**LEA** ........ Load Effective Address [*Data processing*]
**LEA** ........ Local Education Agency [*School district*] [*HEW*] (OICC)
**LEA** ........ Local Education Authority [*British*]
**LEA** ........ Local Employment Act [*Town planning*] [*British*]
**LEA** ........ Logistic Evaluation Agency [*Army*]
**LEA** ........ Logistics Engineering Analysis (NASA)
**LEA** ........ Long-Endurance Aircraft
**LEA** ........ Loop Extension Amplifier
**LEA** ........ Loss Executives Association [*Parsippany, NJ*] (EA)
**LEA** ........ Lower Excess Air [*Combustion technology*]
**LEA** ........ Lutheran Education Association (EA)
**LEAA** ........ Lace and Embroidery Association of America [*Later, Lace Importers Association*] (EA)
**LEAA** ........ Law Enforcement Assistance Act
**LEAA** ........ Law Enforcement Assistance Administration [*Closed, functions transferred to Office of Justice Assistance, Research, and Statistics*] [*Department of Justice*]
**LEAA Legal Op** ... Law Enforcement Assistance Administration. Legal Opinions [*A publication*] (DLA)
**LEAB** ........ Albacete [*Spain*] [*ICAO location identifier*] (ICLI)
**LEA/BZ** ..... Vessel Leased to Brazil [*Navy*]
**LEAC** ........ Levelized Energy Adjustment Clause (NRCH)
**LEAC** ........ Madrid [*Spain*] [*ICAO location identifier*] (ICLI)
**Leach** ........ Leach's English Crown Cases [*1730-1815*] [*A publication*] (DLA)
**LEA/CH** .... Vessel Leased to China [*Navy*]
**Leach CC** ... Leach's Crown Cases, King's Bench [*England*] [*A publication*] (DLA)
**Leach CL** ... Leach's Cases in Crown Law [*A publication*] (DLA)
**Leach Cl Cas** ... Leach's Club Cases [*London*] [*A publication*] (DLA)
**Leach Cr Cas** ... Leach's English Crown Cases [*1730-1815*] [*A publication*] (DLA)
**LEAD** ........ Law Students Exposing Advertising Deceptions [*Student legal action organization*]
**LEAD** ........ Leader Effectiveness and Adaptability Description [*Test*]
**Lead** ........ Leader Law Reports [*Ceylon*] [*A publication*] (DLA)
**LEAD** ........ Leadville Corp. [*NASDAQ symbol*] (NQ)
**LEAD** ........ Learn, Execute, and Diagnose
**LEAD** ........ Letterkenny Army Depot [*Pennsylvania*] (AABC)
**Lead Abstr** ... Lead Abstracts [*A publication*]
**Leadam** ...... Leadam's Select Cases before King's Council in the Star Chamber [*Selden Society Publications, Vols. 16, 25*] [*A publication*] (DLA)
**Leadam Req** ... Select Cases in the Court of Requests, Edited by I. S. Leadam [*Selden Society Publications, Vol. 12*] [*A publication*] (DLA)
**Lead Cas Am** ... American Leading Cases, Edited by Hare and Wallace [*A publication*] (DLA)
**Lead Cas Eq** ... Leading Cases in Equity, by White and Tudor [*A publication*] (DLA)
**Lead Cas in Eq** ... Leading Cases in Equity, by White and Tudor [*A publication*] (DLA)
**Lead Cas in Eq (Eng)** ... Leading Cases in Equity, by White and Tudor [*England*] [*A publication*] (DLA)
**LEADER** ... Lehigh Automatic Device for Efficient Retrieval [*Center for Information Sciences, Lehigh University*] [*Bethlehem, PA*] [*Data processing*]
**LEADER** ... Logistics Echelons above Division in Europe (MCD)
**Lead LR** ..... Leader Law Reports [*South Africa*] [*A publication*] (DLA)
**Lead Res Dig** ... Lead Research Digest [*A publication*]
**LEADS** ...... Law Enforcement Automated Data System (IEEE)
**LEADS** ...... Library Experimental Automated Demonstration System [*Data processing*]
**LEADS** ...... Line Equipment Assignment and Display System [*GTE Corp.*]
**LEA/EC** .... Vessel Leased to Ecuador [*Navy*]
**LEAF** ........ Interleaf, Inc. [*Cambridge, MA*] [*NASDAQ symbol*] (NQ)
**LEAF** ........ Ladies Environmentally Aware of Forests [*Australia*]
**LEAF** ........ Land Educational Associates Foundation (EA)
**LEAF** ........ Liberal Education for Adoptive Families (EA)
**LEAF** ........ LISP Extended Algebraic Facility
**LEAF** ........ Lotus Extended Applications Facility
**LEAF** ........ Women's Legal Education and Action Fund [*Canada*]
**Leafl Amat Ent Soc** ... Leaflet. Amateur Entomologist's Society [*A publication*]
**Leafl Anim Prod Div Kenya Minist Agric** ... Leaflet. Animal Production Division. Kenya Ministry of Agriculture [*A publication*]
**Leafl Br Isles Bee Breeders Ass** ... Leaflet. British Isles Bee Breeders' Association [*A publication*]
**Leafl Calif Agric Exp Stn** ... Leaflet. California Agricultural Experiment Station [*A publication*]
**Leafl Calif Agric Exp Stn Ext Serv** ... Leaflet. California Agricultural Experiment Station. Extension Service [*A publication*]
**Leafl Commonw For Timb Bur (Canberra)** ... Leaflet. Commonwealth Forestry and Timber Bureau (Canberra) [*A publication*]
**Leafl Coop Ext Serv Univ GA** ... Leaflet. Cooperative Extension Service. University of Georgia [*A publication*]
**Leafl Coop Ext Univ Calif** ... Leaflet. Cooperative Extension. University of California [*A publication*]
**Leafl Dep Agric (Ceylon)** ... Leaflet. Department of Agriculture (Ceylon) [*A publication*]
**Leafl Dep Agric Fish (Ire)** ... Leaflet. Department of Agriculture and Fisheries (Irish Republic) [*A publication*]
**Leafl Dep Agric Tech Instruct Ire** ... Leaflet. Department of Agriculture and Technical Instruction for Ireland [*A publication*]
**Leafl Div Agric Sci Univ Calif** ... Leaflet. Division of Agricultural Sciences. University of California [*A publication*]
**Leaflet US Dep Agric** ... Leaflet. United States Department of Agriculture [*A publication*]
**Leafl Ext Serv Utah St Univ** ... Leaflet. Extension Service. Utah State University [*A publication*]
**Leafl Forests Dep West Aust** ... Leaflet. Forests Department. Western Australia [*A publication*] (APTA)
**Leafl For Timb Bur** ... Leaflet. Forestry and Timber Bureau [*A publication*] (APTA)
**Leafl Israel Agric Res Organ Div For (Ilanot)** ... Leaflet. Israel Agricultural Research Organization. Division of Forestry (Ilanot) [*A publication*]
**Leafl L Tex Agric Ext Serv Tex AM Univ Syst** ... Leaflet L. Texas Agricultural Extension Service. Texas A & M University System [*A publication*]
**Leafl Minist Agric (Nth Ire)** ... Leaflet. Ministry of Agriculture (Northern Ireland) [*A publication*]
**Leafl Montreal Bot Gdn** ... Leaflet. Montreal Botanical Garden [*A publication*]
**Leafl Okla State Univ Agr Appl Sci Agr Ext Serv** ... Leaflet. Oklahoma State University of Agriculture and Applied Science. Agricultural Extension Service [*A publication*]
**Leafl PA State Univ Ext Serv** ... Leaflet. Cooperative Extension Service. Pennsylvania State University [*A publication*]
**Leafl Rutgers State Univ Coll Agr Environ Sci Ext Serv** ... Leaflet. Rutgers State University. College of Agriculture and Environmental Science. Extension Service [*A publication*]
**Leafl Univ Calif Coop Ext Serv** ... Leaflet. University of California. Cooperative Extension Service [*A publication*]
**Leafl Univ Hawaii Coop Ext Serv** ... Leaflet. University of Hawaii. Cooperative Extension Service [*A publication*]

**Leafl US Dep Agric** ... Leaflet. United States Department of Agriculture [*A publication*]
**Leafl VBBA** ... Leaflet. Village Bee Breeders Association [*A publication*]
**Leafl West Bot** ... Leaflets of Western Botany [*A publication*]
**LEA/FR**..... Vessel Leased to France [*Navy*]
**LEAFS**....... LASER-Excited Atomic Fluorescent Spectrometry
**LEAG**......... Legislative Extended Assistance Group [*University of Iowa*] [*Research center*] (RCD)
**LEA/GR**.... Vessel Leased to Greece [*Navy*]
**League Exch** ... League Exchange [*A publication*]
**League Int Food Educ Newsl** ... League for International Food Education. Newsletter [*A publication*]
**League Nations Bull Health Org** ... League of Nations. Bulletin of the Health Organization [*A publication*]
**League of Nations Off J** ... League of Nations. Official Journal [*A publication*] (DLA)
**League of Nations OJ** ... League of Nations. Official Journal [*A publication*] (DLA)
**League of Nations OJ Spec Supp** ... League of Nations. Official Journal. Special Supplement [*A publication*] (DLA)
**LEAH**........ Lulov, Esrog, Arrovos, Hadassim (BJA)
**LEAK**......... Leak-X Corp. [*NASDAQ symbol*] (NQ)
**LEAK**......... Liposome-Encapsulated Amikacin [*Bactericide*]
**Leake**......... Leake on Contracts [*1861-1931*] [*A publication*] (DLA)
**Leake**......... Leake's Digest of the Law of Property in Land [*A publication*] (DLA)
**Leake Cont** ... Leake on Contracts [*1861-1931*] [*A publication*] (DLA)
**Leake Land** ... Leake's Digest of the Law of Property in Land [*A publication*] (DLA)
**LEAL**......... Alicante [*Spain*] [*ICAO location identifier*] (ICLI)
**LEAM**........ Almeria [*Spain*] [*ICAO location identifier*] (ICLI)
**LEAM**........ Lunar Ejecta and Meteorites [*Experiment*] [*NASA*]
**Leam & Spic** ... Leaming and Spicer's Laws, Grants, Concessions, and Original Constitutions [*New Jersey*] [*A publication*] (DLA)
**LEA/MX**... Vessel Leased to Mexico [*Navy*]
**LEA/NE**.... Vessel Leased to Netherlands [*Navy*]
**LEA/NO**.... Vessel Leased to Norway [*Navy*]
**LEANON**.. Lupus Erythematosus Anonymous (EA)
**LEAO**........ Almagro [*Spain*] [*ICAO location identifier*] (ICLI)
**LEAP**......... Labor Education Advancement Program
**LEAP**......... Laboratory Education Advancement Program [*Department of Labor*]
**LEAP**......... Laboratory Evaluation and Accreditation Program
**LEAP**......... Language for Expressing Associative Procedures [*Data processing*]
**LEAP**......... Large Einsteinium Activation Program
**LEAP**......... Leadership and Education for Advancement of Phoenix [*Arizona*]
**LEAP**......... Leading Edge Airborne PANAR
**LEAP**......... Lease/Purchase Corp. [*White Plains, NY*] [*NASDAQ symbol*] (NQ)
**LEAP**......... Legal and Educational Aid to the Poor [*Center*]
**LEAP**......... Lewis Expandable Adjustable Prosthesis [*Orthopedics*]
**LEAP**......... [*Pershing Missile*] Life Extension Assessment Program [*Army*] (MCD)
**LEAP**......... Lifetime Element Advancing Program
**LEAP**......... Lift-Off Elevation and Azimuth Programmer
**LEAP**......... Lightweight Exoatmospheric Advanced Projectile [*Military*] (SDI)
**LEAP**......... Liquid Engine Air-Augmented Package (MCD)
**LEAP**......... Loaned Executives Assignment Program [*American Association of Advertising Agencies lobbying group*]
**LEAP**......... Lockheed Electronics Assembly Program
**LEAP**......... Logistic Element Action Proposal (MCD)
**LEAP**......... Logistic Event and Assessment Program
**LEAP**......... Logistics Efficiencies to Increase Army Power (MCD)
**LEAP**......... Low-Energy All-Purpose (Collimator) [*Radiology*]
**LEAP**......... Lower Eastside Action Project [*New York City*]
**LEAP**......... Lunar Escape Ambulance Pack [*Aerospace*]
**LEA/PA**.... Vessel Leased to Panama [*Navy*]
**LEA/PE**..... Vessel Leased to Peru [*Navy*]
**LEA/PG**.... Vessel Leased to Paraguay [*Navy*]
**Leap Rom Civ L** ... Leapingwell on the Roman Civil Law [*A publication*] (DLA)
**LEAPS**....... LASER Electro-Optical Alignment Pole for Surveying [*NASA*]
**LEAPS**....... LASER Engineering and Application of Prototype System (MCD)
**LEAPS**....... Local Exchange Area Planning Simulation [*Bell Laboratories*]
**LEAR**......... Lear Petroleum Corp. [*NASDAQ symbol*] (NQ)
**LEAR**......... Logistics Evaluation and Review
**LEAR**......... Low-Energy Antiproton Ring [*Particle physics*]
**LEAR**......... Low Erucic Acid Rapeseed [*Plant variety*]
**Learn**.......... Learning [*A publication*]
**Learn Exch** ... Learning Exchange [*A publication*] (APTA)
**Learn & L**... Learning and the Law [*A publication*] (DLA)
**Learn & Law** ... Learning and the Law [*A publication*] (DLA)
**Learn & Motiv** ... Learning and Motivation [*A publication*]
**Learn Motiv** ... Learning and Motivation [*A publication*]
**Learn Res Bull** ... Learning Resources Bulletin [*A publication*]
**Learn Today** ... Learning Today [*A publication*]
**LEA/RU**.... Vessel Leased to Russia [*Navy*]
**LEAS**......... Aviles/Asturias [*Spain*] [*ICAO location identifier*] (ICLI)
**LEAS**......... Lease Electronic Accounting System (IEEE)
**LEAS**......... Lower Echelon Automatic Switchboard
**LEASAT**.... Leased Satellite Communications (NVT)
**L in Eastern Eur** ... Law in Eastern Europe [*A publication*] (DLA)
**L East Eur** ... Law in Eastern Europe [*A publication*] (DLA)
**LEAT**......... Lea Transit Compendium [*A publication*]
**LEATH**...... Leather (ROG)
**LEATH**...... Leatherhead [*City in England*]
**Leather Chem** ... Leather Chemistry [*Japan*] [*A publication*]
**Leather Sci (Madras)** ... Leather Science (Madras) [*A publication*]
**Leath Sci**.... Leather Science [*A publication*]
**Leath Shoe** ... Leather and Shoes [*A publication*]
**LEA/UK**.... Vessel Leased to United Kingdom [*Navy*]
**LEA/UR**.... Vessel Leased to Uruguay [*Navy*]
**LEAVERATS** ... Leave Rations [*Military*]
**Leaves Paint Res Noteb** ... Leaves from a Paint Research Notebook [*A publication*]
**LEB**............ East Baton Rouge Parish Public Library, Baton Rouge, LA [*OCLC symbol*] (OCLC)
**LEB**............ Lateral Efferent Bundle [*Neuroanatomy*]
**LEB**............ Lebanon [*New Hampshire*] [*Airport symbol*] (OAG)
**LEB**............ Lebanon, NH [*Location identifier*] [*FAA*] (FAAL)
**LEB**............ London Electricity Board
**LEB**............ Lower Equipment Bay [*Apollo*] [*NASA*]
**LEBA**......... Cordoba [*Spain*] [*ICAO location identifier*] (ICLI)
**Leban Med J** ... Lebanese Medical Journal [*A publication*]
**Lebanon**..... Lebanon County Legal Journal [*Pennsylvania*] [*A publication*] (DLA)
**Lebanon Co LJ (PA)** ... Lebanon County Legal Journal [*Pennsylvania*] [*A publication*] (DLA)
**Leban Pharm J** ... Lebanese Pharmaceutical Journal [*A publication*]
**LeBAU**....... American University of Beirut, Beirut, Lebanon [*Library symbol*] [*Library of Congress*] (LCLS)
**LEBB**......... Bilbao [*Spain*] [*ICAO location identifier*] (ICLI)
**Leben Erde** ... Lebendige Erde [*A publication*]
**Lebensm Ernaehrung** ... Lebensmittel und Ernaehrung [*A publication*]
**Lebensm Ind** ... Lebensmittel-Industrie [*A publication*]
**Lebensmittelchem Gerichtl Chem** ... Lebensmittelchemie und Gerichtliche Chemie [*A publication*]
**Lebensmittelchemie u Gerichtl Chemie** ... Lebensmittelchemie und Gerichtliche Chemie [*A publication*]
**Lebensmittelchem Lebensmittelqual** ... Lebensmittelchemie, Lebensmittelqualitaet [*A publication*]
**Lebensmittel-Ind** ... Lebensmittel-Industrie [*A publication*]
**Lebensm-Wiss Technol** ... Lebensmittel-Wissenschaft Technologie [*A publication*]
**Lebensversicher Med** ... Lebensversicherungs Medizin [*A publication*]
**Leben Umwelt (Aarau)** ... Leben und Umwelt (Aarau) [*A publication*]
**Leben Umwelt (Wiesb)** ... Leben und Umwelt (Wiesbaden) [*A publication*]
**Leber Mag D** ... Leber Magen Darm [*A publication*]
**LEBG**......... Burgos [*Spain*] [*ICAO location identifier*] (ICLI)
**LEBL**......... Barcelona [*Spain*] [*ICAO location identifier*] (ICLI)
**LEBNAP**... Lebanese Kidnap [*Victims*] [*American hostages held in Beirut*]
**Leb Pharm J** ... Lebanese Pharmaceutical Journal [*A publication*]
**LEBR**......... Bardenas Reales [*Spain*] [*ICAO location identifier*] (ICLI)
**LebSeels**..... Lebendige Seelsorge (BJA)
**LEBT**......... Betera [*Spain*] [*ICAO location identifier*] (ICLI)
**LEBU**......... Large Eddy Breakup Device [*Aerodynamics*]
**LEBZ**......... Badajoz/Talavera La Real [*Spain*] [*ICAO location identifier*] (ICLI)
**LEC**............ Lake Erie College [*Painesville, OH*]
**LEC**............ Lake Erie College, Painesville, OH [*OCLC symbol*] (OCLC)
**LEC**............ LAMPS [*Light Airborne Multipurpose System*] Element Coordinator [*Navy*] (CAAL)
**LEC**............ Land Economics [*A publication*]
**LEC**............ Landed Estates Courts Commission [*England*] (DLA)
**LEC**............ LANTCOM ELINT Center (MCD)
**LEC**............ LASER Electronic Computer
**LEC**............ Launch Escape Control [*NASA*] (KSC)
**LEC**............ Lecture
**LEC**............ Les Etudes Classiques [*A publication*]
**LEC**............ Library of English Classics [*A publication*]
**LEC**............ Life Education Centre [*Australia*]
**LEC**............ Light Energy Converter [*Telecommunications*] (TEL)
**LEC**............ Limited Editions Club
**LeC**............ Lingua e Cultura [*A publication*]
**LEC**............ Liquid Encapsulated Czochralski [*Crystal growing technique*] (IEEE)
**LEC**............ Livestock Equipment Council [*Defunct*] (EA)
**LEC**............ Local Employment Committee [*Department of Employment*] [*British*]
**LEC**............ Local Engineering Change [*DoD*]
**LEC**............ Local Export Control [*British*] (DS)
**LEC**............ Lockheed Electronics Corporation [*Subsidiary of Lockheed Aircraft Corp.*]
**LEC**............ Low-Echo-Centroid [*Geology*]
**LEC**............ Lumped Element Circulator
**LEC**............ Lunar Equipment Conveyor [*Aerospace*]
**LECA**......... Launch Escape Control Area [*NASA*] (KSC)
**LECA**......... Lehman Caves National Monument

**Le & Ca** ...... Leigh and Cave's English Crown Cases Reserved [*1861-65*] [*A publication*] (DLA)
**LECA** ......... Madrid [*Spain*] [*ICAO location identifier*] (ICLI)
**LECAPSR** ... Llano Estacado Center for Advanced Professional Studies and Research [*Eastern New Mexico University*] [*Research center*] (RCD)
**LECB** ......... Barcelona [*Spain*] [*ICAO location identifier*] (ICLI)
**LECC** ......... Lake Erie Cleanup Committee (EA)
**Lec El Dr Civ Rom** ... Lecons Elementaires du Droit Civil Romain [*A publication*] (DLA)
**Lec Elm** ...... Lecons Elementaires du Droit Civil [*A publication*] (DLA)
**LECH** ........ Calamocha [*Spain*] [*ICAO location identifier*] (ICLI)
**LECH** ........ Lechters, Inc. [*NASDAQ symbol*] (NQ)
**Lech Kurortakh Zabaik** ... Lechenie na Kurortakh Zabaikal'ya [*A publication*]
**Lech Kurortakh Zabaikalya** ... Lechenie na Kurortakh Zabaikal'ya [*A publication*]
**LECL** ......... Valencia [*Spain*] [*ICAO location identifier*] (ICLI)
**LECM** ......... Madrid [*Spain*] [*ICAO location identifier*] (ICLI)
**LECNA** ...... Lutheran Educational Conference of North America (EA)
**LECO** ........ La Coruna [*Spain*] [*ICAO location identifier*] (ICLI)
**LECO** ........ Leeco Diagnostics, Inc. [*NASDAQ symbol*] (NQ)
**LECO** ........ Local Engineering Control Office [*Telecommunications*] (TEL)
**LECP** ......... Low-Energy Charged Particle [*Atomic physics*]
**LECP** ......... Palma [*Spain*] [*ICAO location identifier*] (ICLI)
**LECS** ......... Launching Equipment Checkout Set
**LECS** ......... Local Economic Consequences Study [*Military*]
**LECS** ......... Sevilla [*Spain*] [*ICAO location identifier*] (ICLI)
**Lec Ser Div Appl Geomech CSIRO** ... Lecture Series. Division of Applied Geomechanics. Commonwealth Scientific and Industrial Research Organisation [*A publication*] (APTA)
**LECT** ......... League for the Exchange of Commonwealth Teachers (EA)
**LECT** ......... LecTec Corp. [*Minnetonka, MN*] [*NASDAQ symbol*] (NQ)
**LECT** ......... Lectern (ROG)
**Lect** ............ Lecturas [*A publication*]
**LECT** ......... Lecture [*or Lecturer*]
**Lect Appl Math** ... Lectures in Applied Mathematics [*A publication*]
**Lect Biblioth** ... Lecture et Bibliotheques [*A publication*]
**Lect Cent Ass Beekrps** ... Lecture to Central Association of Bee-Keepers [*A publication*]
**Lect Coral Gables Conf Fundam Interact High Energy** ... Lectures from the Coral Gables Conference on Fundamental Interactions at High Energy [*A publication*]
**Lect Hall Chem Pharmacol** ... Lecture Hall for Chemistry and Pharmacology [*Japan*] [*A publication*]
**Lect Int Symp Migr** ... Lectures. International Symposium on Migration [*A publication*]
**Lect LSUC** ... Special Lectures. Law Society of Upper Canada [*A publication*] (DLA)
**Lect Math Life Sci** ... Lectures on Mathematics in the Life Sciences [*A publication*]
**Lect Monogr Rep R Inst Chem** ... Lectures, Monographs, and Reports. Royal Institute of Chemistry [*A publication*]
**Lect Notes Biomath** ... Lecture Notes in Biomathematics [*A publication*]
**Lect Notes Chem** ... Lecture Notes in Chemistry [*A publication*]
**Lect Notes Coastal Estuarine Stud** ... Lecture Notes on Coastal and Estuarine Studies [*A publication*]
**Lect Notes Comput Sci** ... Lecture Notes in Computer Science [*A publication*]
**Lect Notes Div Tech Conf Soc Plast Eng Vinyl Plast Div** ... Lecture Notes Division. Technical Conference. Society of Plastics Engineers. Vinyl Plastics Divisions [*A publication*]
**Lect Notes Math** ... Lecture Notes in Mathematics [*A publication*]
**Lect Notes Phys** ... Lecture Notes in Physics [*A publication*]
**Lect Notes Suppl Phys** ... Lecture Notes and Supplements in Physics [*A publication*]
**LECTR** ...... Lecturer
**Lect Sci Basis Med** ... Lectures on the Scientific Basis of Medicine [*A publication*]
**Lect Theor Phys** ... Lectures in Theoretical Physics [*A publication*]
**Lecturas Econ** ... Lecturas de Economia [*A publication*]
**Lecture Notes in Biomath** ... Lecture Notes in Biomathematics [*A publication*]
**Lecture Notes in Chem** ... Lecture Notes in Chemistry [*Berlin*] [*A publication*]
**Lecture Notes in Comput Sci** ... Lecture Notes in Computer Science [*A publication*]
**Lecture Notes in Control and Information Sci** ... Lecture Notes in Control and Information Sciences [*A publication*]
**Lecture Notes in Econom and Math Systems** ... Lecture Notes in Economics and Mathematical Systems [*A publication*]
**Lecture Notes in Math** ... Lecture Notes in Mathematics [*A publication*]
**Lecture Notes in Med Inform** ... Lecture Notes in Medical Informatics [*A publication*]
**Lecture Notes in Phys** ... Lecture Notes in Physics [*A publication*]
**Lecture Notes in Pure and Appl Math** ... Lecture Notes in Pure and Applied Mathematics [*A publication*]
**Lecture Notes in Statist** ... Lecture Notes in Statistics [*A publication*]
**Lecture Notes and Suppl in Phys** ... Lecture Notes and Supplements in Physics [*A publication*]
**Lectures in Appl Math** ... Lectures in Applied Mathematics [*A publication*]
**Lectures LSUC** ... Special Lectures. Law Society of Upper Canada [*A publication*]
**Lectures in Math** ... Lectures in Mathematics [*Tokyo*] [*A publication*]
**Lectures Math Life Sci** ... Lectures on Mathematics in the Life Sciences [*A publication*]
**LECV** ......... Colmenar Viejo [*Spain*] [*ICAO location identifier*] (ICLI)
**LED** ........... Large Electronic Display
**LED** ........... Law Enforcement Division [*National Park Service*]
**L Ed** ........... Lawyers' Edition, United States Supreme Court Reports [*A publication*] (DLA)
**LED** ........... Leaded
**LED** ........... League for Ecological Democracy (EA)
**LED** ........... Ledger
**LED** ........... Leningrad [*USSR*] [*Airport symbol*] (OAG)
**LED** ........... Library Education Division [*American Library Association*] [*Defunct*]
**LED** ........... Light-Emitting Diode [*Display component*]
**LED** ........... Line Embossing Device [*Data processing*]
**LED** ........... Literatuuroverzicht Medezeggenschap [*A publication*]
**LED** ........... Local Employment Development [*Australia*]
**LED** ........... Logical Error Detection
**LED** ........... Logistics Engineering Directorate [*ARRCOM*] (RDA)
**LED** ........... Low-Energy Detector
**LED** ........... Low-Energy Diffraction
**LED** ........... Lower Emissions Dispatch [*Environmental Protection Agency*]
**LED** ........... Lupus Erythematosus Disseminatus [*Medicine*]
**LED** ........... North Platte, NE [*Location identifier*] [*FAA*] (FAAL)
**LE 2d** ......... Lawyer's Edition, United States Supreme Court Reports, Second Series [*A publication*] (DLA)
**LEDA** ........ LANDSAT Earthnet Data Availability [*ESA-Earthnet Programme Office*] [*Database*]
**LEDA** ........ Low-Energy Deasphalting [*Petroleum refining*]
**L Ed (Adv Ops)** ... United States Supreme Court Reports, Lawyers' Edition, Advance Opinions [*A publication*] (DLA)
**LEDC** ......... League for Emotionally Disturbed Children
**LEDC** ......... Local Economic Development Corporation
**LEDC** ......... Logistics Executive Development Course [*Army*]
**LEDD** ........ Light-Emitting Diode Display
**L Ed 2d** ...... Lawyers' Edition, United States Supreme Court Reports, Second Series [*A publication*] (DLA)
**LEDET** ...... Law Enforcement Detachment [*Coast Guard*]
**LED FO** ..... Ledger Folio (ROG)
**LEDM** ....... Valladolid [*Spain*] [*ICAO location identifier*] (ICLI)
**LEDP** ......... Large Electronic Display Panel
**LEDR** ......... Laboratory for Environmental Data Research [*National Oceanic and Atmospheric Administration*]
**LEDR** ......... Leadership Properties, Inc. [*NASDAQ symbol*] (NQ)
**LEDR** ......... Light-Emitting Diode Recorder (MCD)
**LEDS** ......... Law Enforcement Data System
**LEDSHP** ... Leadership
**LEDT** ......... Limited Entry Decision Table
**L Ed (US)** ... Lawyers' Edition, United States Supreme Court Reports [*A publication*] (DLA)
**LEE** ............ [*The*] Lake Erie & Eastern Railroad Co. [*AAR code*]
**LEE** ............ Lee Enterprises, Inc. [*NYSE symbol*] (SPSG)
**LEE** ............ Leeds [*Utah*] [*Seismograph station code, US Geological Survey*] (SEIS)
**LEE** ............ Leefmilieu [*A publication*]
**Lee** ............. Lee's English Ecclesiastical Reports [*A publication*] (DLA)
**Lee** ............. Lee's Reports [*9-12 California*] [*A publication*] (DLA)
**LEE** ............ Leesburg, FL [*Location identifier*] [*FAA*] (FAAL)
**LEE** ............ Logistics Evaluation Exercise
**Lee Abs** ...... Lee's Abstracts of Title [*1843*] [*A publication*] (DLA)
**Lee Bank** .... Lee's Law and Practice of Bankruptcy [*3rd ed.*] [*1887*] [*A publication*] (DLA)
**LEEC** ......... Sevilla-El Copero Base [*Spain*] [*ICAO location identifier*] (ICLI)
**Lee Cap** ...... Lee on Captures [*A publication*] (DLA)
**LEED** ......... LASER-Energized Explosive Device
**LEED** ......... Longitudinal Employer-Employee Data File [*Social Security Administration*]
**LEED** ......... Low-Energy Electron Diffraction [*Spectroscopy*]
**Lee Dict** ...... Lee's Dictionary of Practice [*A publication*] (DLA)
**Leeds Dent J** ... Leeds Dental Journal [*A publication*]
**Leeds G As Tr** ... Leeds Geological Association. Transactions [*A publication*]
**Leeds Northr Tech J** ... Leeds and Northrup Technical Journal [*A publication*]
**LeedsSE** ..... Leeds Studies in English [*A publication*]
**LEEE** ......... Madrid [*Spain*] [*ICAO location identifier*] (ICLI)
**Lee Eccl** ...... Lee's English Ecclesiastical Reports [*A publication*] (DLA)
**Lee Found Nutr Res Rep** ... Lee Foundation for Nutritional Research. Report [*A publication*]
**Lee G** .......... [*Sir George*] Lee's English Ecclesiastical Reports [*A publication*] (DLA)
**Lee & H** ...... Lee's English King's Bench Reports Tempore Hardwicke [*1733-38*] [*A publication*] (DLA)
**LEEIXS** ..... Low-Energy-Electron-Induced X-Ray Spectrometry
**LEEP** ......... Law Enforcement Education Program [*Department of Justice*]
**LEEP** ......... Law Enforcement Explorer Post [*Boy Scouts*]
**LEEP** ......... Library Education Experimental Project [*Syracuse University*]
**LEER** ......... Low-Energy Electron Reflection (IEEE)
**LEES** ......... Laboratory for Electromagnetic and Electronic Systems [*Massachusetts Institute of Technology*] [*Research center*] (RCD)

**LEES** ......... Lake Erie Environmental Studies
**LEES** ......... Launch Equipment Evaluation Set (MCD)
**Leese** ......... Leese's Reports [*26 Nebraska*] [*A publication*] (DLA)
**Lee Ship** ..... Lee's Laws of Shipping [*A publication*] (DLA)
**LEET** ......... Limiting Equivalent Exposure Time (MUGU)
**Lee T Hard** ... Lee's English King's Bench Cases Tempore Hardwicke [*1733-38*] [*England*] [*A publication*] (DLA)
**Lee T Hardw** ... Lee's English King's Bench Cases Tempore Hardwicke [*1733-38*] [*England*] [*A publication*] (DLA)
**Leeuwenhoek Ned Tijdschr** ... Leeuwenhoek Nederlandsch Tijdschrift [*A publication*]
**LEF** ........... Lake Erie, Franklin & Clarion Railroad Co. [*AAR code*]
**LEF** ........... Landpower Education Fund
**LEF** ........... LASER Excited Fluorescence
**LEF** ........... Leading Edge Flap [*Aviation*]
**LEF** ........... Left-In Telephone [*Telecommunications*] (TEL)
**LEF** ........... Life Extension Foundation (EA)
**LEF** ........... Light-Emitting Film (IEEE)
**LEF** ........... Lincoln Educational Foundation [*Defunct*] (EA)
**LEF** ........... Line Expansion Function
**LEF** ........... Linear-Energy Spectrophotofluorometry
**LEF** ........... Liquid Expanded Film
**LEF** ........... Loss Entry Form [*Insurance*]
**LEFC** ......... L-Band Electronic Frequency Converter
**Lef & Cas** ... Lefroy and Cassel's Practice Cases [*1881-83*] [*Ontario*] [*A publication*] (DLA)
**Lef Cr L** ..... Lefroy's Irish Criminal Law [*A publication*] (DLA)
**LEFCS** ....... Leading Edge Flap Control System [*Aviation*]
**Lef Dec** ....... Lefevre's Parliamentary Decisions, by Bourke [*England*] [*A publication*] (DLA)
**LEFM** ........ Linear-Elastic Fracture Mechanics
**LEFO** ......... Land's End for Order [*Shipping*]
**Lefroy** ......... Lefroy's Railroad and Canal Cases [*England*] [*A publication*] (DLA)
**LEFU** ......... Light Ends Fractionating Unit [*Petroleum technology*]
**LEFW** ........ Lake Erie & Fort Wayne Railroad Co. [*AAR code*]
**Leg** ............ De Legibus [*of Cicero*] [*Classical studies*] (OCD)
**LEG** ........... Legal (AFM)
**LEG** ........... Legate
**Leg** ............ Legatio ad Gaium [*of Philo Judaeus*] [*Classical studies*] (OCD)
**LEG** ........... Legato [*Smoothly and Connectedly*] [*Music*]
**LEG** ........... Legend [*Numismatics*]
**Leg** ............ Leges [*Laws of Plato*] [*Classical studies*] (OCD)
**Leg** ............ Leges [*Laws*] [*Latin*] (ILCA)
**LEG** ........... Leggett & Platt, Inc. [*NYSE symbol*] (SPSG)
**LEG** ........... Legislation [*or Legislature*]
**LEG** ........... Legislative Library of British Columbia [*UTLAS symbol*]
**LEG** ........... Legit [*He, or She, Reads*] [*Latin*]
**LEG** ........... Legunt [*They Read*] [*Latin*] (ADA)
**LEG** ........... Liquefied Energy Gas
**LEG** ........... Logistic Evaluation Group
**LEG** ........... Logistical Expediting Group
**LEGA** ......... Granada/Armilla [*Spain*] [*ICAO location identifier*] (ICLI)
**Leg Adv** ...... Legal Adviser [*Chicago*] [*A publication*] (DLA)
**Leg Agr** ...... De Lege Agraria [*of Cicero*] [*Classical studies*] (OCD)
**Leg Aid Rev** ... Legal Aid Review [*A publication*]
**LEGAL** ...... League for Equitable General Aviation Legislation (EA)
**Legal Adv** ... Legal Advertiser [*Chicago*] [*A publication*] (DLA)
**Legal Adv** ... Legal Adviser [*Denver*] [*A publication*] (DLA)
**Legal Aid Rev** ... Legal Aid Review [*A publication*]
**Legal Aspects Med Prac** ... Legal Aspects of Medical Practice [*A publication*]
**Legal Asp Med Prac** ... Legal Aspects of Medical Practice [*A publication*] (DLA)
**Legal Econ** ... Legal Economics [*A publication*]
**Legal Educ Newsl** ... Legal Education Newsletter [*A publication*]
**Leg Alfred** ... Leges Alfredi [*Laws of King Alfred*] [*Latin*] [*A publication*] (DLA)
**Legal Gaz (PA)** ... Legal Gazette (Pennsylvania) [*A publication*] (DLA)
**Legal Int** .... Legal Intelligencer [*A publication*] (DLA)
**Legal Intel** ... Legal Intelligencer [*A publication*] (DLA)
**Legal Intell** ... Legal Intelligencer [*A publication*] (DLA)
**Legal Med Ann** ... Legal Medicine Annual [*A publication*]
**Legal Med Q** ... Legal Medical Quarterly [*A publication*]
**Legal Obser** ... Legal Observer [*London*] [*A publication*] (DLA)
**Legal Observer** ... New York Legal Observer [*A publication*] (DLA)
**Legal Rep** ... Legal Reporter [*Australia*] [*A publication*]
**Legal Rep** ... Legal Reporter, New Series [*Tennessee*] [*A publication*] (DLA)
**Legal Res J** ... Legal Research Journal [*A publication*]
**Legal Resp Child Adv Protection** ... Legal Response; Child Advocacy and Protection [*A publication*] (DLA)
**Legal Serv Bull** ... Legal Service Bulletin [*A publication*] (APTA)
**Legal Service Bul** ... Legal Service Bulletin [*A publication*]
**Legal Services Bul** ... Legal Services Bulletin [*A publication*]
**Legal Stud** ... Legal Studies [*A publication*]
**Legal Times Wash** ... Legal Times of Washington [*A publication*]
**Leg Aspects Med Pract** ... Legal Aspects of Medical Practice [*A publication*]
**Legat** .......... De Lagatione ad Caium [*Philo*] (BJA)
**LEGAT** ...... Legal Attache [*FBI agent posted at an American embassy*]
**Leg Bibl** ...... Legal Bibliography [*A publication*] (DLA)
**Leg Canut** .. Leges Canuti [*Laws of King Canute or Knut*] [*Latin*] [*A publication*] (DLA)
**Leg Ch Forms** ... Leggo's Chancery Forms [*Ontario*] [*A publication*] (DLA)
**Leg Ch Pr** ... Leggo's Chancery Practice [*Ontario*] [*A publication*] (DLA)
**Leg Chron** .. Legal Chronicle Reports, Edited by Foster [*Pennsylvania*] [*A publication*] (DLA)
**Leg Chron Rep** ... Legal Chronicle Reports [*Pottsville, PA*] [*A publication*] (DLA)
**LEGCO** ...... Legislative Council [*Hong Kong*] (ECON)
**Leg Contents LC** ... Legal Contents. LC [*A publication*]
**legd** ............ Legend
**LEGE** ......... Gerona/Costa Brava [*Spain*] [*ICAO location identifier*] (ICLI)
**Leg Ec** ........ Legal Economics [*A publication*]
**Leg Econ** .... Legal Economics [*A publication*]
**Leg Edm** ..... Leges Edmundi [*Laws of King Edmund*] [*Latin*] [*A publication*] (DLA)
**LEGEN** ...... Liposome-Encapulated Gentamicin [*Bactericide*]
**LEGEND** ... Legal Electronic Network and Database (EISS)
**Leg Ethel** ... Leges Ethelredi [*Laws of King Ethelred*] [*Latin*] [*A publication*] (DLA)
**Leg Exam** ... Legal Examiner [*London or New York*] [*1831-35; 1862-68; 1869-72*] [*A publication*] (DLA)
**Leg Exam & LC** ... Legal Examiner and Law Chronicle [*London*] [*A publication*] (DLA)
**Leg Exam & Med J** ... Legal Examiner and Medical Jurist [*London*] [*A publication*] (DLA)
**Leg Exam NS** ... Legal Examiner, New Series [*England*] [*A publication*] (DLA)
**Leg Exam WR** ... Legal Examiner Weekly Reporter [*A publication*] (DLA)
**Leg Exch** .... Legal Exchange [*Des Moines, IA*] [*A publication*] (DLA)
**Leg Exec** .... Legal Executive [*A publication*]
**Leg G** ......... Legal Guide [*A publication*] (DLA)
**Legg** ........... Leggett's Reports [*India*] [*A publication*] (DLA)
**LEGG** ........ Leggiero [*Light and Rapid*] [*Music*]
**Leg Gaz** ...... Legal Gazette [*A publication*] (DLA)
**Leg Gaz R** .. Campbell's Legal Gazette Reports [*Pennsylvania*] [*A publication*] (DLA)
**Leg Gaz Re** ... Campbell's Legal Gazette Reports [*Pennsylvania*] [*A publication*] (ILCA)
**Leg Gaz Rep** ... Campbell's Legal Gazette Reports [*Pennsylvania*] [*A publication*] (DLA)
**Legg Bills L** ... Leggett on Bills of Lading [*A publication*] (DLA)
**Legge** .......... Legge's Supreme Court Cases [*A publication*] (APTA)
**Leggo** ......... Leggiero [*Light and Rapid*] [*Music*]
**Legg Out** .... Legge on Outlawry [*A publication*] (DLA)
**LEGGS** ...... Loyal Escorts of the Green Garters (EA)
**Leg HI** ......... Laws of King Henry the First [*A publication*] (DLA)
**Leg Inf Bul** ... Legal Information Bulletin [*A publication*] (DLA)
**Leg Inf Manage Index** ... Legal Information Management Index [*A publication*]
**Leg Inq** ....... Legal Inquirer [*London*] [*A publication*] (DLA)
**Leg & Ins R** ... Legal and Insurance Reporter [*Pennsylvania*] [*A publication*] (DLA)
**Leg & Ins Rep** ... Legal and Insurance Reporter [*Philadelphia, PA*] [*A publication*] (DLA)
**Leg & Ins Rept** ... Legal and Insurance Reporter [*Philadelphia, PA*] [*A publication*] (DLA)
**Leg Int** ........ Legal Intelligencer [*A publication*] (DLA)
**Leg Intel** ..... Legal Intelligencer [*A publication*] (DLA)
**Leg Intell** .... Legal Intelligencer [*A publication*] (DLA)
**Leg Intl** ....... Legal Intelligencer [*A publication*] (DLA)
**LEGIS** ....... Legislative [*or Legislature*]
**LEGIS** ....... Legislative Information and Status System [*for House of Representatives*]
**Legis e Giurispr Trib** ... Legislazione e Giurisprudenza Tributaria [*Milan, Italy*] [*A publication*] (DLA)
**LEGISL** ..... Legislative (ADA)
**LEGISLN** ... Legislation
**Legisl Netw Nurses** ... Legislative Network for Nurses [*A publication*]
**Legisl Stud Quart** ... Legislative Studies Quarterly [*A publication*]
**LEGISNET** ... National Legislative Network [*National Conference of State Legislatures*] [*Information service or system*] (IID)
**Legis Roundup** ... Legislative Roundup [*A publication*]
**Legis Stud Q** ... Legislative Studies Quarterly [*A publication*] (DLA)
**Leg Issues** .. Legal Issues of European Integration [*A publication*] (ILCA)
**LEGIT** ....... Legitimate (DSUE)
**Leg J** .......... Pittsburgh Legal Journal [*Pennsylvania*] [*A publication*] (DLA)
**Leg Jour** ..... Pittsburgh Legal Journal [*Pennsylvania*] [*A publication*] (DLA)
**Legka Tekst Promst** ... Legka i Tekstilna Promislovist [*A publication*]
**Legk Pishch Promst Podmoskov'ya** ... Legkaya i Pishchevaya Promyshlennost Podmoskov'ya [*A publication*]
**Legk Promst (Kaz)** ... Legkaya Promyshlennost (Kazakhstana) [*A publication*]
**Legk Promst (Kiev)** ... Legkaya Promyshlennost (Kiev) [*A publication*]
**Legk Promst (Moscow)** ... Legkaya Promyshlennost (Moscow) [*A publication*]
**LEGM** ........ Low-Energy Gamma Monitor
**Leg M Dig** ... Legal Monthly Digest [*Australia*] [*A publication*] (DLA)
**Leg Med** ..... Legal Medicine [*A publication*]
**Leg Med Annu** ... Legal Medicine Annual [*Later, Legal Medicine*] [*A publication*]
**Leg Med Annual** ... Legal Medicine Annual [*A publication*]
**Leg Med Q** ... Legal Medicine Quarterly [*A publication*]

**Leg Misc**.... Legal Miscellany [*Ceylon*] [*A publication*] (DLA)
**Leg Misc & Rev**... Legal Miscellany and Review [*India*] [*A publication*] (DLA)
**Leg News**... Legal News [*Canada*] [*A publication*] (DLA)
**Leg Notes**... Legal Notes on Local Government [*New York*] [*A publication*] (DLA)
**Leg Notes and View Q**... Legal Notes and Viewpoints Quarterly [*A publication*]
**LEGO**........ Leg Godt [*Play Well*] [*Denmark*] [*Acronym is brand of child's building toy*]
**Leg Obs**...... Legal Observer [*London*] [*A publication*] (DLA)
**Leg Obs**...... Legal Observer and Solicitor's Journal [*London*] [*A publication*] (DLA)
**Leg Oler**..... Laws of Oleron [*Maritime law*] [*A publication*] (DLA)
**Leg Op**....... Legal Opinion [*Pennsylvania*] [*A publication*] (DLA)
**Leg Ops (PA)**... Legal Opinion [*Pennsylvania*] [*A publication*] (DLA)
**Leg Out**...... Legge on Outlawry [*A publication*] (DLA)
**LegPer**........ Index to Legal Periodicals [*A publication*]
**Leg Period Dig**... Legal Periodical Digest [*A publication*]
**Leg Port**..... Leges Portuum [*A publication*] (DLA)
**Leg Pract & Sol J**... Legal Practitioner and Solicitor's Journal [*1846-47, 1849-51*] [*A publication*] (DLA)
**LEGR**......... Granada [*Spain*] [*ICAO location identifier*] (ICLI)
**Leg R**.......... Legal Record Reports [*Pennsylvania*] [*A publication*] (DLA)
**Leg Rec**...... Legal Record [*Detroit, MI*] [*A publication*] (DLA)
**Leg Rec Rep**... Legal Record Reports [*Pennsylvania*] [*A publication*] (DLA)
**Leg Ref**....... Legal Reformer [*1819-20*] [*A publication*] (DLA)
**Leg Ref Serv Q**... Legal Reference Services Quarterly [*A publication*]
**Leg Rem**..... Legal Remembrancer [*Calcutta*] [*A publication*] (DLA)
**Leg Rep**...... Legal Reporter [*1840-43*] [*Ireland*] [*A publication*] (DLA)
**Leg Rep (Ir)**... Legal Reporter, Irish Courts [*A publication*] (DLA)
**Leg Rep SL**... Legal Reporter Special Leave Supplement [*A publication*]
**Leg Res J**... Legal Research Journal [*A publication*]
**Leg Resour Index**... Legal Resource Index [*A publication*]
**Leg Rev**...... Legal Review [*1812-13*] [*London*] [*A publication*] (DLA)
**Leg R (Tenn)**... Legal Reporter Parallel to Shannon Cases [*Tennessee*] [*A publication*] (DLA)
**LEGS**......... Learning Experience Guides for Nursing Students [*Series of films, games, slides, etc.*]
**LEGS**......... Legacies (ROG)
**LEGS**......... Lethality End Game Simulation (MCD)
**LEGS**......... Lighter Electronics Guidance System (MCD)
**Leg Ser B**... Legal Service Bulletin [*A publication*] (APTA)
**Leg Serv Bull**... Legal Service Bulletin [*A publication*]
**Leg Stud Q**... Legislative Studies Quarterly [*A publication*]
**LEGT**......... Madrid/Getafe [*Spain*] [*ICAO location identifier*] (ICLI)
**Leg T Cas**... Legal Tender Cases [*A publication*] (DLA)
**Legul**.......... Leguleian [*1850-65*] [*A publication*] (DLA)
**Legume Res**... Legume Research [*A publication*]
**LEG (UN)**... Department of Legal Affairs of the United Nations
**Legve**.......... Legislative
**Leg W**......... Legal World [*India*] [*A publication*] (DLA)
**Leg Wisb**.... Laws of Wisby [*Maritime law*] [*A publication*] (DLA)
**LEGY**......... Legacy (ROG)
**Leg YB**....... Legal Year Book [*London*] [*A publication*] (DLA)
**LEH**........... Launch/Entry Helmet (MCD)
**LEH**........... Le Havre [*France*] [*Airport symbol*] (OAG)
**Leh**............ Lehigh County Law Journal [*Pennsylvania*] [*A publication*] (DLA)
**LEHC**........ Huesca [*Spain*] [*ICAO location identifier*] (ICLI)
**Leh Co LJ (PA)**... Lehigh County Law Journal [*Pennsylvania*] [*A publication*] (DLA)
**LEHI**......... Hinojosa Del Duque [*Spain*] [*ICAO location identifier*] (ICLI)
**Lehigh**........ Lehigh Valley Law Reporter [*Pennsylvania*] [*A publication*] (DLA)
**Lehigh Alumni Bull**... Lehigh Alumni Bulletin [*A publication*]
**Lehigh Co LJ**... Lehigh County Law Journal [*Pennsylvania*] [*A publication*] (DLA)
**Lehigh LJ**.. Lehigh County Law Journal [*Pennsylvania*] [*A publication*] (DLA)
**Lehigh Val Law Rep**... Lehigh Valley Law Reporter [*Pennsylvania*] [*A publication*] (DLA)
**Lehigh Val LR**... Lehigh Valley Law Reporter [*Pennsylvania*] [*A publication*] (DLA)
**Lehigh Val L Rep**... Lehigh Valley Law Reporter [*Pennsylvania*] [*A publication*] (DLA)
**Leh LJ**....... Lehigh County Law Journal [*A publication*] (DLA)
**LEHR**........ Laboratory for Energy-Related Health Research [*Department of Energy*] [*University of California-Davis*] (GRD)
**Lehrb Allg Geogr**... Lehrbuch der Allgemeinen Geographie [*A publication*]
**Lehrb Anthropol**... Lehrbuch der Anthropologie [*A publication*]
**Lehrb Handb Ingenieurwiss**... Lehr- und Handbuecher der Ingenieurwissenschaften [*A publication*]
**Lehrbuecher Monograph Geb Exakten Wissensch Math Reihe**... Lehrbuecher und Monographien aus dem Gebiete der Exakten Wissenschaften [*LMW*]. Mathematische Reihe [*A publication*]
**Leh VLR (PA)**... Lehigh Valley Law Reporter [*Pennsylvania*] [*A publication*] (DLA)
**LEI**............ Almeria [*Spain*] [*Airport symbol*] (OAG)
**LEI**............ LASER-Enhanced Ionization [*Spectrometry*]
**LEI**............ Leading Economic Indicator
**LEI**............ Legal Expense Insurance Ltd. [*Australia*]
**Lei**............. Leijona [*Record label*] [*Finland*]
**LEI**............ Leipzig [*German Democratic Republic*] [*Seismograph station code, US Geological Survey*] [*Closed*] (SEIS)
**Lei**............. Leitura [*A publication*]
**LEI**............ Library Equipment Institute [*American Library Association*]
**LEI**............ Life Events [*or Expectancy*] Inventory
**LEI**............ Literacy and Evangelism International (EA)
**LEI**............ Local Employment Initiative [*Australia*]
**LEI**............ Locher Evers International Ltd.
**LEI**............ Raleigh, NC [*Location identifier*] [*FAA*] (FAAL)
**LEIA**.......... Luminescence Enzyme Immunoassay [*Clinical chemistry*]
**LEIAC**........ Livestock Exports Industry Advisory Committee [*Australia*]
**LEIB**.......... Ibiza [*Spain*] [*ICAO location identifier*] (ICLI)
**LEIC**.......... Leicestershire [*County in England*] (ROG)
**Leica Fot**.... Leica Fotographie [*A publication*]
**Leica Fotogr (Engl Ed)**... Leica Fotografie (English Edition) [*A publication*]
**Leichhardt Hist J**... Leichhardt Historical Journal [*A publication*] (APTA)
**LEICS**........ Leicestershire [*County in England*]
**LEICSC**..... Legal Education Institute, United States Civil Service Commission (DLA)
**LEID**.......... Limit of Error on Inventory Difference
**LEID**.......... Low-Energy Ion Detector
**Leiden Bot Ser**... Leiden Botanical Series [*A publication*]
**LEIDS**....... Logistics Electronic Information Delivery System
**Leidsche Geol Meded**... Leidsche Geologische Mededeelingen [*Later, Leidse Geologische Mededelingen*] [*A publication*]
**Leidse Geol Meded**... Leidse Geologische Mededelingen [*A publication*]
**Leiegouw**.... Verslagen en Mededeelingen van de Leiegouw [*A publication*]
**LeIF**........... Leukocyte Interferon [*Genetics*]
**Leigh**.......... Leigh's Virginia Supreme Court Reports [*1829-42*] [*A publication*] (DLA)
**Leigh**.......... Ley's English King's Bench Reports [*1608-29*] [*A publication*] (DLA)
**Leigh Abr**... Leigh's Abridgment of the Law of Nisi Prius [*1838*] [*A publication*] (DLA)
**Leigh & C**... Leigh and Cave's English Crown Cases Reserved [*1861-65*] [*A publication*] (DLA)
**Leigh & CCC**... Leigh and Cave's English Crown Cases Reserved [*1861-65*] [*A publication*] (DLA)
**Leigh & D Conv**... Leigh and Dalzell. Conversion of Property [*1825*] [*A publication*] (DLA)
**Leigh GA**... Leigh's Game Act [*A publication*] (DLA)
**Leigh & LM Elec**... Leigh and Le Marchant. Elections [*4th ed.*] [*1885*] [*A publication*] (DLA)
**Leigh NP**.... Leigh's Abridgment of the Law of Nisi Prius [*1838*] [*A publication*] (DLA)
**Leigh (VA)**... Leigh's Virginia Supreme Court Reports [*1829-42*] [*A publication*] (DLA)
**LEIN**.......... Law Enforcement Information Network
**LEINS R**.... Leinster Regiment [*Military unit*] [*British*] (ROG)
**LEIP**.......... Leipzig [*City in East Germany*] (ROG)
**Leipzig Bienenztg**... Leipziger Bienenzeitung [*A publication*]
**Leipz Monatsschr Text Ind**... Leipziger Monatsschrifter fuer Textil-Industrie [*A publication*]
**Leipz Stud**... Leipziger Studien zur Klassischen Philosophie [*A publication*] (OCD)
**LEIS**.......... Lander Electrical Interface Simulator [*NASA*]
**LEIS**.......... LeisureLine [*Footscray Institute of Technology Library*] [*Database*] [*Information service or system*] (IID)
**LEIS**.......... Low-Energy Ion Scattering [*For study of surfaces*]
**Leis Hour**... Leisure Hour [*A publication*]
**Leis and Move**... Leisure and Movement [*A publication*]
**Leis Recreat Tour Abstr**... Leisure, Recreation, and Tourism Abstracts [*A publication*]
**Leis Rec Tourism Abs**... Leisure, Recreation, and Tourism Abstracts [*A publication*]
**Leis Stud**.... Leisure Studies [*A publication*]
**Leis Stud Centre Rev**... Leisure Studies Centre. Review [*A publication*]
**Leistung**..... Leistung in Zahlen [*A publication*]
**Leisure Ele**... Leisure Time Electronics [*A publication*]
**Leisure Mgmt**... Leisure Management [*A publication*]
**LEIT**.......... Leitrim [*County in Ireland*] (ROG)
**Leitfaden Elektrotech**... Leitfaeden der Elektrotechnik [*A publication*]
**Leitfaeden Angew Math Mech**... Leitfaeden der Angewandten Mathematik und Mechanik [*A publication*]
**Leith Black**... Leith. Blackstone on Real Property [*2nd ed.*] [*1880*] [*A publication*] (DLA)
**Leith R Pr**.. Leith's Real Property Statutes [*Ontario*] [*A publication*] (DLA)
**LEITR**....... Leitrim [*County in Ireland*] (ROG)
**Leitz-Mitt Wissen Technik**... Leitz-Mitteilungen fuer Wissenschaft und Technik [*A publication*]
**Leitz-Mitt Wiss & Tech**... Leitz-Mittcilungen fuer Wissenschaft und Technik [*A publication*]
**Leitz Sci and Tech Inf**... Leitz Scientific and Technical Information [*A publication*]
**LEIU**.......... Law Enforcement Intelligence Units [*An association*] (EA)
**LEIX**.......... Lowrance Electronics, Incorporated [*Tulsa, OK*] [*NASDAQ symbol*] (NQ)
**LEJ**........... Leipzig [*East Germany*] [*Airport symbol*] (OAG)

**LEJ**........... Longitudinal Expansion Joint [*Technical drawings*]
**LEJR**........ Jerez [*Spain*] [*ICAO location identifier*] (ICLI)
**LEK**........... Laiko Enotiko Komma [*Populist Union Party*] [*Greece*] [*Political party*] (PPE)
**LEK**........... LASER Experimental Package
**LEK**........... Lexington [*Kentucky*] [*Seismograph station code, US Geological Survey*] (SEIS)
**LEK**........... Liquid Encapsulated Kyropoulos [*Crystal growing technique*]
**Lek Obz**..... Lekarsky Obzor [*A publication*]
**LEKOTEK**... Leksaker, Bibliotek [*Program providing meaningful toys for mentally disturbed children; operates on the same principle as a lending library.*] [*Name formed from Swedish words for "playthings" and "library"*]
**Lek Pr**........ Lekarske Prace [*A publication*]
**Lek Sredstva Dal'nego Vostoka**... Lekarstvennye Sredstva Dal'nego Vostoka [*A publication*]
**Lek Syrevye Resur Irkutsk Obl**... Lekarstvennye i Syrevye Resursy Irkutskoi Oblasti [*A publication*]
**Lek Veda Zahr**... Lekarska Veda v Zahranici [*A publication*]
**Lek Wojsk**... Lekarz Wojskowy [*Poland*] [*A publication*]
**Lek Zpr**...... Lekarsky Zpravy [*A publication*]
**Lek Zpr Lek Fak Karlovy Univ Hradci Kralove**... Lekarske Zpravy Lekarske Fakulty Karlovy University v Hradci Kralove [*A publication*]
**LEL**........... Labour Educational League [*Australia*]
**LEL**........... Lake Evella [*Australia*] [*Airport symbol*] (OAG)
**LEL**........... Lancashire Enterprise Ltd. [*British*] (ECON)
**LEL**........... Large Engineering Loop [*NASA*] (NRCH)
**LEL**........... League of Empire Loyalists [*British*]
**LEL**........... Learning Expectancy Level [*Education*]
**LEL**........... Lens-End-Lamp
**LEL**........... Letitia Elizabeth Landon [*English poet and novelist, 1802-1839*]
**LEL**........... Link-Edit Language [*Data processing*]
**LEL**........... Lower Electrical Limit (NRCH)
**LEL**........... Lower Explosive Limit [*of fuel vapor*]
**LEL**........... Lowest Effect Level [*Toxicology*]
**Leland Stanford Jr Univ Pub**... Leland Stanford Junior University. Publications [*A publication*]
**LELC**......... Murcia/San Javier [*Spain*] [*ICAO location identifier*] (ICLI)
**LELL**......... Sabadell [*Spain*] [*ICAO location identifier*] (ICLI)
**LELN**......... Leon [*Spain*] [*ICAO location identifier*] (ICLI)
**LELO**......... Logrono [*Spain*] [*ICAO location identifier*] (ICLI)
**LELS**......... Low-Energy LASER System
**LELTS**....... Lightweight Electronic Locating and Tracking System
**LELU**......... Launch Enable Logic Unit
**LELU**......... Lugo [*Spain*] [*ICAO location identifier*] (ICLI)
**Lely & F Elec**... Lely and Foulkes' Elections [*3rd ed.*] [*1887*] [*A publication*] (DLA)
**Lely & F Jud Acts**... Lely and Foulkes' Judicature Acts [*4th ed.*] [*1883*] [*A publication*] (DLA)
**Lely & F Lic Acts**... Lely and Foulkes' Licensing Acts [*3rd ed.*] [*1887*] [*A publication*] (DLA)
**Lely Railw**... Lely's Regulation of Railway Acts [*1873*] [*A publication*] (DLA)
**LEM**.......... Antenna Effective Length for Magnetic-Field Antennas (IEEE)
**LEM**.......... Laboratory of Electro-Modeling [*USSR*]
**LEM**.......... Laboratory Environment Model (MCD)
**LEM**.......... Lake Exploration Module [*University of Wisconsin*]
**LEM**.......... LASER Energy Monitor
**LEM**.......... LASER Exhaust Measurement
**LEM**.......... Lateral Eye Movement
**LEM**.......... Launch Escape Monitor (MCD)
**LEM**.......... Launch Escape Motor [*NASA*]
**LEM**.......... Launcher Electronic Module [*Military*] (RDA)
**LEM**.......... Law Enforcement Manual [*IRS*]
**LEM**.......... Le Matin [*Morocco*] [*A publication*]
**LEM**.......... Leading Electrical Mechanician
**LEM**.......... Leibovitz-Emory Medium [*Microbiology*]
**LEM**.......... Lembang [*Java*] [*Seismograph station code, US Geological Survey*] (SEIS)
**LEM**.......... Lemmon, SD [*Location identifier*] [*FAA*] (FAAL)
**lem**............. Lemon [*Philately*]
**LEM**.......... Length of Effectiveness for Magnetic-Field Antennae
**LEM**.......... Leukocytic Endogenous Mediator [*Immunochemistry*]
**LEM**.......... Light Effector Mediator System [*Plant physiology*]
**LEM**.......... Light Equipment Maintenance (MCD)
**LEM**.......... Liquid Emulsion Membrane [*Separation technology*]
**LEM**.......... Logic Enhanced Memory
**LEM**.......... Logical End of Media
**LEM**.......... Logistic Element Manager
**LEM**.......... Luminescences Emission Monitor
**LEM**.......... Lunar Excursion Module [*Later, LM*] [*NASA*]
**LEMA**........ Laser and Electro-Optics Manufacturers' Association (EA)
**LEM(A)**...... Leading Electrical Mechanic (Air) [*British military*] (DMA)
**LEMAC**..... Leading Edge Mean Aerodynamic Chord
**Le Mar**....... Le Marchant's Gardner Peerage Case [*A publication*] (DLA)
**LEMAR**..... Legalize Marijuana [*Acronym is used for name of an organization*]
**LEM(AW)**... Leading Electrical Mechanic (Air Weapon) [*British military*] (DMA)
**LEMD**....... Madrid/Barajas [*Spain*] [*ICAO location identifier*] (ICLI)
**LEMDA**..... Lighting-Electrical Materials Distributors Association (EA)
**LEMDE**..... Lunar Excursion Module Descent Engine [*NASA*] (MCD)
**LEMF**........ Labour Exchange Managers' Federation [*A union*] [*British*]
**LEMF**........ Law Enforcement Memorial Foundation (EA)
**LEMF**........ Local Effective Mole Fraction [*Chemistry*]
**LEMG**....... Malaga [*Spain*] [*ICAO location identifier*] (ICLI)
**LEMH**....... Mahon/Menorca [*Spain*] [*ICAO location identifier*] (ICLI)
**LEMIT An**... LEMIT [*Laboratorio de Ensayo de Materiales e Investigaciones Tecnologicas*] Anales [*A publication*]
**LEMIT An Ser 2**... LEMIT [*Laboratorio de Ensayo de Materiales e Investigaciones Tecnologicas*] Anales. Serie 2 [*A publication*]
**LEML & AIA**... Locomotive Engineers Mutual Life and Accident Insurance Association (EA)
**LEMM**...... Madrid [*Spain*] [*ICAO location identifier*] (ICLI)
**LeMo**........ Letterature Moderne [*A publication*]
**LEMO**....... Sevilla/Moron [*Spain*] [*ICAO location identifier*] (ICLI)
**LEMPA**..... Low-Energy Magnetospheric Particle Analyzer [*Atomic physics*]
**LEMRAS**.. Law Enforcement Manpower Resources Allocation [*IBM program product*]
**LEMRP**..... Law Enforcement Memorial Research Project (EA)
**LEMS**........ Linear Econometric Modeling System (BUR)
**LEMSIP**.... Laboratory for Experimental Medicine and Surgery in Primates [*New York University*] [*Research center*]
**LEMUF**..... Limits of Error on Material Unaccounted For
**LEN**........... [*The*] Lake Erie & Northern Railway Co. [*AAR code*]
**LEN**........... Land and Environment Notes [*A publication*] (APTA)
**LEN**........... Legal Electronic Network [*Australia*]
**LEN**........... Length
**LEN**........... Leninakan [*USSR*] [*Seismograph station code, US Geological Survey*] (SEIS)
**LEN**........... Lennar Corp. [*NYSE symbol*] (SPSG)
**LEN**........... Lenora Explorations Ltd. [*Toronto Stock Exchange symbol*]
**LEN**........... Lentini Aviation, Inc. [*Pontiac, MI*] [*FAA designator*] (FAAC)
**LEN**........... Leon [*Mexico*] [*Airport symbol*] (OAG)
**LEN**........... Library of Early Novelists [*A publication*]
**LEN**........... Light-Emitting Numerics
**LEN**........... Ligue Europeenne de Natation [*European Swimming Federation*] [*Loughborough, England*] (EAIO)
**LEN**........... Linear Electrical Network
**LEN**........... Load Equalization Net [*Aircraft arresting barrier*] [*Trademark*]
**LenauA**...... Lenau Almanach [*A publication*]
**Lenauf**........ Lenau Forum [*A publication*]
**LenC**.......... Lenguaje y Ciencias [*A publication*]
**Lend a H**.... Lend a Hand [*A publication*]
**Lending LF**... Lending Law Forum [*A publication*]
**Lend LF**..... Lending Law Forum [*A publication*]
**LengM**....... Lenguas Modernas [*A publication*]
**LENGTHD**... Lengthened (ROG)
**Leninabad Gos Ped Inst Ucen Zap**... Leninabadskii Gosudarstvennyi Pedagogiceskii Institut Ucenye Zapiski [*A publication*]
**Leningrad Gorn Inst Zap**... Leningrad Gornyy Institut Zapiski [*A publication*]
**Leningrad Gos Ped Inst Ucen Zap**... Leningradskii Gosudarstvennyi Pedagogiceskii Institut Imeni A. I. Gercena Ucenye Zapiski [*A publication*]
**Leningrad Gos Univ Ucen Zap**... Leningradskii Gosudarstvennyi Ordena Lenina Universitet Imeni A. A. Zdanova Ucenyi Zapiski [*A publication*]
**Leningrad Gos Univ Ucen Zap Ser Mat Nauk**... Leningradskii Gosudarstvennyi Ordena Lenina Universitet Imeni A. A. Zdanova Ucenye Zapiski Serija Matematiceskih Nauk [*A publication*]
**Leningrad Inz-Ekonom Inst Trudy**... Leningradskii Inzenerno-Ekonomiceskii Institut Imeni Pal'miro Tol'jatti Trudy [*A publication*]
**Leningrad Inz-Stroitel Inst Sb Trudov**... Leningradskii Inzhenerno-Stroitel'skii Institut Sbornik Trudov [*A publication*]
**Leningrad Meh Inst Sb Trudov (LMI)**... Leningradskii Mekhanicheskii Institut Sbornik Trudov (LMI) [*A publication*]
**Leningrad Politehn Inst Trudy**... Leningradskii Politehniceskii Institut Imeni M. I. Kalinina Trudy LPI [*A publication*]
**Leningrad Univ Vestn Geol Geogr**... Leningradskii Universitet Vestnik Geologiya i Geografiya [*A publication*]
**Leningr Inst Sov Torg Sb Tr**... Leningradskii Institut Sovetskoi Torgovli Sbornik Trudov [*A publication*]
**Leningr Inst Tochn Mekh Opt Tr**... Leningradskii Institut Tochnoi Mekhaniki i Optiki Trudy [*A publication*]
**Leningr Inzh Mezhvuz Temat Sb Tr**... Leningradskii Inzhenerno-Stroitel'nyi Institut Mezhvuzovskii Tematicheskii Sbornik Trudov [*A publication*]
**Leningr Inzh Stroit Inst Mezhvuz Temat Sb**... Leningradskii Inzhenerno-Stroitel'nyi Institut Mezhvuzovskii Tematicheskii Sbornik [*A publication*]
**Leningr Inzh Stroit Inst Sb Tr**... Leningradskii Inzhenerno-Stroitel'nyii Institut Sbornik Trudov [*A publication*]
**Leningr Mekh Inst Sb Tr**... Leningradskii Mekhanicheskii Institut Sbornik Trudov [*A publication*]
**Leningr Met Zavod Tr**... Leningradskii Metallicheskii Zavod Trudy [*A publication*]

**Leningr Nauchno Issled Inst Gematol Pereliv Krovi Sb Tr** ... Leningradskii Nauchno-Issledovatel'skii Institut Gematologii i Perelivaniya Krovi Sbornik Trudov [*A publication*]
**Leningr Nauchno Issled Inst Lesn Khoz Sb Nauchn Tr** ... Leningradskii Nauchno-Issledovatel'skii Institut Lesnogo Khozyaistva Sbornik Nauchnykh Trudov [*A publication*]
**Leningr Nauchno Issled Konstr Inst Khim Mashinostr Tr** ... Leningradskii Nauchno-Issledovatel'skii i Konstruktorskii Institut Khimicheskogo Mashinostroeniya Trudy [*A publication*]
**Leningr Tekhnol Inst Tsellyul Bum Promsti Tr** ... Leningradskii Tekhnologicheskii Institut Tsellyulozno-Bumazhnoi Promyshlennosti Trudy [*A publication*]
**LENIT** ....... Leniter [*Gently*] [*Pharmacy*]
**Len Konop** ... Len i Konopliya [*A publication*]
**LENS** ......... Concord Camera Corp. [*NASDAQ symbol*] (NQ)
**LEntA** ........ London Enterprise Agency
**LENTO** ..... Lentando [*With Increasing Slowness*] [*Music*] (ROG)
**LENWID**... Length to Width Ratio [*Of a leaf*] [*Botany*]
**LENZ** ......... Vision Sciences, Inc. [*Monrovia, CA*] [*NASDAQ symbol*] (NQ)
**Lenzinger Ber** ... Lenzinger Berichte [*A publication*]
**LEO** ........... Dreyfus Strategic Municipals [*NYSE symbol*] (SPSG)
**LEO** ........... Lear Oil & Gas Corp. [*Vancouver Stock Exchange symbol*]
**Leo** ............ Leonardo [*A publication*]
**Leo** ............ Leonard's King's Bench Reports [*1540-1615*] [*England*] [*A publication*] (DLA)
**Leo** ............ Leonardus [*Authority cited in pre-1607 legal work*] (DSA)
**LEO** ........... Leoncito [*Argentina*] [*Seismograph station code, US Geological Survey*] (SEIS)
**LEO** ........... Liaison Engineering Order
**LEO** ........... Librating Equidistant Observer
**LEO** ........... Littoral Environment Observation [*Program*] [*Oceanography*]
**LEO** ........... Local Elected Official (OICC)
**LEO** ........... Low Earth Orbit
**LEO** ........... Lunar Exploration Office [*NASA*]
**LEO** ........... Lyon's Electronic Office
**Leo Baeck Inst Jews Germ Yrbk** ... Leo Baeck Institute of Jews from Germany. Yearbook [*A publication*]
**Leoc** ............ Against Leocrates [*of Lycurgus*] [*Classical studies*] (OCD)
**LEOC** ........ Ocana [*Spain*] [*ICAO location identifier*] (ICLI)
**LEOMA** .... LASER/Electro/Optic Measurement Alignment System
**LEOMA** .... LASER and Electro-Optics Manufacturers' Association
**Leon** ........... Leonardo [*A publication*]
**Leon** ........... Leonard's King's Bench, Common Pleas, and Exchequer Reports [*England*] [*A publication*] (DLA)
**Leonhar Eul Opera Omnia Ser 2** ... Leonharki Euleri Opera Omnia. Series Secunda [*A publication*]
**Leon LA Dig** ... Leonard's Louisiana Digest of United States Cases [*A publication*] (DLA)
**Leon Prec**... Leonard's Precedents in County Courts [*1869*] [*A publication*] (DLA)
**LEOPCID** ... Local Elected Officials Project of the Center for Innovative Diplomacy (EA)
**LEOS** ......... IEEE [*Institute of Electrical and Electronics Engineers*] Lasers and Electro-Optics Society (EA)
**LEOT** ......... Left-End-of-Tape
**LEOV** ........ Oviedo [*Spain*] [*ICAO location identifier*] (ICLI)
**LEP** ............ Large Electron-Positron [*Accelerator*] [*in Europe*]
**LEP** ............ Large Electronic Panel
**LEP** ............ Latin America Weekly Report [*A publication*]
**LEP** ............ Least Energy Principle
**Lep** ............ Lepidoptera [*Entomology*]
**Lep** ............ Lepus [*Constellation*]
**LEP** ............ Library of Exact Philosophy
**LEP** ............ [*Pershing Missile*] Life Extension Program [*Army*] (MCD)
**LEP** ............ Light Evaluation Plan (MCD)
**LEP** ............ Lightning-Induced Electron Precipitation [*Atmospheric physics*]
**LEP** ............ Limited English Proficiency
**LEP** ............ Lipoprotein Electrophoresis [*Biochemistry*]
**LEP** ............ List of Effective Pages (NVT)
**LEP** ............ Local Environment Plan [*Australia*]
**LEP** ............ Locally Enlisted Personnel [*British military*] (DMA)
**LEP** ............ Low Egg Passage [*Rabies vaccine*]
**LEP** ............ Lower End Plug (IEEE)
**LEP** ............ Lowest Effective Power
**LEPA** ......... Laboratoire d'Etudes Politiques et Administratives [*Universite Laval, Quebec*] [*Canada*]
**LEPA** ......... Palma De Mallorca [*Spain*] [*ICAO location identifier*] (ICLI)
**LEPC** ......... Law Enforcement Planning Commission
**LEPC** ......... Local Emergency Planning Committee [*Hazardous waste*]
**LEPD** ......... Low-Energy Photon Detector [*Environmental Protection Agency*]
**LEPDAV** ... Lepidoptera [*Copenhagen*] [*A publication*]
**LEPEDEA** ... Low-Energy Proton-Electron Differential Energy Analyzer [*NASA*]
**LEPG** ......... Lep Group PLC [*NASDAQ symbol*] (NQ)
**LEPI** .......... Litton Educational Publishing, Incorporated
**LEPMA** ..... Lithographic Engravers and Plate Makers Association (EA)
**LEPO** ......... Pollensa [*Spain*] [*ICAO location identifier*] (ICLI)
**LEPOR** ...... Long-Term and Expanded Program of Oceanic Exploration and Research
**LEPP** ......... Pamplona/Noain-Pamplona [*Spain*] [*ICAO location identifier*] (ICLI)
**LEPR** ......... LASER Electron Paramagnetic Resonance
**LEPRA** ...... British Leprosy Relief Association (IRUK)
**Lep Rev** ...... Leprosy Review [*A publication*]
**Lepr India** .. Leprosy in India [*A publication*]
**Leprosy Rev** ... Leprosy Review [*A publication*]
**Lepr Rev** ..... Leprosy Review [*A publication*]
**LEPS** ......... Launch Escape Propulsion System [*NASA*]
**Leps** ........... Lepus [*Constellation*]
**LEPS** ......... London-Eyring-Polanyi-Sato Method [*Reaction dynamics*]
**LEPSOC** .... Lepidopterists' Society (EA)
**Lept** ............ Against Leptines [*of Demosthenes*] [*Classical studies*] (OCD)
**Lept** ............ Leptospira [*Genus of bacteria*]
**LEPT** ......... Long-Endurance Patrolling Torpedo
**LEPT** ......... Low-Energy Particle Telescope
**LEPW** ........ Longitudinal Electric Pressure Wave
**LEQ** ........... Line of Equipment [*Telecommunications*] (TEL)
**LEQ** ........... Line Equipped [*Telecommunications*] (TEL)
**L & Eq Rep** ... Law and Equity Reporter [*United States*] [*A publication*] (DLA)
**LER** ............ Land Equivalent Ratio [*Agriculture*]
**LER** ............ Launcher Equipment Room [*Missiles*]
**LER** ............ Leading Edge Radius (MSA)
**LER** ............ Lease Expenditure Request (MCD)
**LER** ............ Leinster [*Australia*] [*Airport symbol*] (OAG)
**LER** ............ Lerwick [*United Kingdom*] [*Geomagnetic observatory code*]
**LER** ............ Licensee Event Report [*Nuclear energy*] (NRCH)
**LER** ............ Light Efficiency Radiator [*General Motors Corp.*] [*Automotive engineering*]
**LER** ............ London Electric Railway
**LER** ............ Long Eye Relief (MCD)
**LER** ............ Loss Exchange Ratio (MCD)
**LERA** ......... Limited Employee Retirement Account (IEEE)
**LERB** ......... Line Error Recording Block (MCD)
**LERC** ......... Laramie Energy Research Center [*Department of Energy*]
**LERC** ......... Lewis Research Center [*NASA*] (KSC)
**LEREA** ...... Leprosy Review [*A publication*]
**L & E Rep** .. English Law and Equity Reports [*American Reprint*] [*A publication*] (DLA)
**LERF** ......... Laboratory Experimental Research Facility [*Army*] (RDA)
**LERI** .......... Murcia/Alcantarilla [*Spain*] [*ICAO location identifier*] (ICLI)
**LERK** ......... LASER Experimental Research Kit
**LERN** ........ Learning Resources Network (EA)
**LERN** ........ Learning Technology, Inc. [*Westport, CT*] [*NASDAQ symbol*] (NQ)
**LERN** ........ Literacy and Education Resource Network [*Australia*]
**LERP** ......... Labor Education and Research Project (EA)
**LERS** ......... Reus [*Spain*] [*ICAO location identifier*] (ICLI)
**LERS (Lab Etud Rech Synthelabo) Monogr Ser** ... LERS (Laboratoires d'Etudes et de Recherches Synthelabo) Monograph Series [*A publication*]
**LERT** ......... Rota [*Spain*] [*ICAO location identifier*] (ICLI)
**LERTCON** ... Alert Condition [*Military*] (AABC)
**LERX** ......... Leading Edge Root Extension [*Aviation*]
**LERY** ......... Leroy Pharmacies, Inc. [*NASDAQ symbol*] (CTT)
**LES** ............ Laboratory for Environmental Studies [*Ohio State University*] [*Research center*] (RCD)
**LES** ............ Lambert-Eaton Myasthenic Syndrome [*Medicine*]
**LES** ............ LASER Excitation Spectroscopy
**LES** ............ Launch Effects Simulator
**LES** ............ Launch Enabling System
**LES** ............ Launch Environmental Simulator (MCD)
**LES** ............ Launch Equipment Shop (MCD)
**LES** ............ Launch Escape System [*or Subsystem*] [*NASA*]
**LES** ............ Leading Edge Slats (MCD)
**LES** ............ Leave and Earnings Statement [*Military*] (AABC)
**LES** ............ Legal Electronic System [*Australia*]
**LES** ............ Lesbian (DSUE)
**LES** ............ [*The*] Leslie Fay Companies [*NYSE symbol*]
**LES** ............ Lesobeng [*Lesotho*] [*Airport symbol*] (OAG)
**Les** ............. Lesonenu. Quarterly of Hebrew [*A publication*]
**LES** ............ Lesozavodsk [*USSR*] [*Seismograph station code, US Geological Survey*] [*Closed*] (SEIS)
**LES** ............ Licensing Executives Society (EA)
**LES** ............ Life Experiences Survey [*Psychology*]
**LES** ............ Light Experimental Supercruiser (MCD)
**LES** ............ Lilliput Edison Screw
**LES** ............ Limited Early Site [*Nuclear energy*] (NRCH)
**LES** ............ Limited English Speaking (OICC)
**LES** ............ Lincoln Experimental Satellite [*Lincoln Laboratory, MIT*]
**LeS** ............ Lingua e Stile [*Bologna*] [*A publication*]
**LES** ............ Loaded Equipment Section
**LES** ............ Local Engineering Specifications [*DoD*]
**LES** ............ Local Excitatory State
**LES** ............ London Evening Standard [*A publication*]
**LES** ............ Loop Error Signal
**LES** ............ Low-Energy Sputter
**LES** ............ Lower Esophageal Sphincter [*Medicine*]

**LES**........... Lunar Escape System [*NASA*]
**LES**........... Support Landing Boat [*Navy symbol*] [*Obsolete*]
**LESA**......... Lake Erie Steam Association [*Defunct*]
**LESA**......... Land Evaluation and Site Assessment System [*Department of Agriculture*]
**LESA**......... Lunar Exploration System for Apollo [*NASA*]
**LESA**......... Salamanca [*Spain*] [*ICAO location identifier*] (ICLI)
**LESAT**...... Leased Satellite [*Military*] (CAAL)
**Lesbian T**... Lesbian Tide [*A publication*]
**LESC**......... Launch Escape System Control [*NASA*] (KSC)
**LESC**......... LE [*Lupus Erythematosus*] Support Club (EA)
**LESC**......... Lunar-Environment Sample Container [*Apollo*] [*NASA*]
**LESG**......... Late Effects Study Group [*for Hodgkins disease*]
**Lesh**.......... Leshonenu [*Jerusalem*] (BJA)
**LESI**.......... Leif Ericson Society International (EA)
**LESJ**......... Son San Juan Air Force Base [*Spain*] [*ICAO location identifier*] (ICLI)
**Les Khoz**.... Lesnoe Khozyaistvo [*A publication*]
**LESL**......... Law Enforcement Standards Laboratory [*National Institute of Standards and Technology*]
**LESM**........ Longman's Elementary Science Manuals [*A publication*]
**LESM**........ Murcia [*Spain*] [*ICAO location identifier*] (ICLI)
**Les Miz**...... Les Miserables [*Musical based on Victor Hugo's novel*]
**Lesnaya Prom**... Lesnaya Promyshlennost [*A publication*]
**Lesn Bum Derevoobrab Promst (Kiev)**... Lesnaya Bumazhnaya i Derevoobrabatyvayushchaya Promyshlennost (Kiev) [*A publication*]
**Lesn Cas**.... Lesnicky Casopis [*A publication*]
**Lesn Hoz**.... Lesnoe Hozjajstvo [*A publication*]
**Lesnictvi Cesk Akad Zemed Ustav Vedeckotech Inf Zemed**... Lesnictvi. Ceskoslovenska Akademie Zemedelska Ustav Vedeckotechnickych Informaci pro Zemedelstvi [*A publication*]
**Lesn Khoz**.. Lesnoe Khozyaistvo [*A publication*]
**Lesnoe Khoz**... Lesnoe Khozyaistvo [*A publication*]
**Lesn Pr**....... Lesnicka Prace [*A publication*]
**Lesn Prace**... Lesnicka Prace [*A publication*]
**Lesn Prom**... Lesnaja Promyslennost [*A publication*]
**Lesn Prom-St**... Lesnaya Promyshlennost [*USSR*] [*A publication*]
**LESNW**..... Lesnwith [*England*]
**Lesn Zh (Archangel USSR)**... Lesnoi Zhurnal (Archangel, USSR) [*A publication*]
**LESO**......... San Sebastian [*Spain*] [*ICAO location identifier*] (ICLI)
**LESOC**...... Lincoln Experimental Satellite Operations Center (MCD)
**Lesokhim Promst**... Lesokhimicheskaya Promyshlennost [*A publication*]
**LESOP**...... Leveraged Employee Stock Ownership Plan [*Procter & Gamble Co.*]
**Lesoved**...... Lesovedenie [*A publication*]
**Lesovod Agrolesomelior**... Lesovodstvo i Agrolesomelioratsiia [*A publication*]
**Lesovod Agrolesomelior Resp Mezhved Temat Sb**... Lesovodstvo i Agrolesomelioratsiya Respublikanskii Mezhvedomstvennyi Tematicheskii Sbornik [*A publication*]
**LESP**......... Law Enforcement Standards Program [*National Institute of Law Enforcement and Criminal Justice*]
**LESP**......... Lower Esophageal Sphincter Pressure [*Medicine*]
**LESP**......... Madrid [*Spain*] [*ICAO location identifier*] (ICLI)
**L'Esprit**...... L'Esprit Createur [*A publication*]
**Les Prom**.... Lesnaya Promyshlennost [*A publication*]
**LESR**......... Limited Early Site Review [*Nuclear energy*] (NRCH)
**LESS**.......... LASER-Excited Shpol'skii Spectrometry
**LESS**.......... Law Encounter Severity Scale [*Personality development test*] [*Psychology*]
**LESS**.......... Leading Edge Structure Subsystem [*Aviation*] (NASA)
**LESS**.......... Least-Cost Estimating and Scheduling System
**L/ESS**......... Loads/Environmental Spectra Survey (MCD)
**LESS**.......... Lunar Escape System Simulator [*NASA*]
**LEST**......... Large Earth-Based [*formerly, European*] Solar Telescope
**LEST**......... Large Earth Survey Telescope
**LEst**.......... Le Lingue Estere [*A publication*]
**LEST**......... Low-Energy Speech Transmission
**LEST**......... Santiago [*Spain*] [*ICAO location identifier*] (ICLI)
**Lest & But**... Lester and Butler's Supplement to Lester's Georgia Reports [*A publication*] (DLA)
**Lester**........ Lester's Reports [*31-33 Georgia*] [*A publication*] (DLA)
**Lester & B**... Lester and Butler's Supplement to Lester's Georgia Reports [*A publication*] (DLA)
**Lester Supp**... Lester and Butler's Supplement to Lester's Georgia Reports [*A publication*] (DLA)
**Lest PL**...... Lester's Decisions in Public Land Cases [*A publication*] (DLA)
**LESU**......... Law Enforcement Study Unit [*of the American Topical Association*] (EA)
**LESU**......... Seo De Urgel [*Spain*] [*ICAO location identifier*] (ICLI)
**Les Zh**........ Lesnoi Zhurnal [*A publication*]
**LET**........... Launch Effects Trainer [*Weaponry*] (MCD)
**LET**........... Launch Escape Tower [*NASA*] (MCD)
**LET**........... Leader Effectiveness Training [*A course of study*]
**LET**........... Leading Edge Tracker
**LET**........... Learning Efficiency Test [*Educational test*]
**LET**........... Leticia [*Colombia*] [*Airport symbol*] (OAG)
**LET**........... Letter
**Let**............ Letteratura [*A publication*]
**LET**........... Lettish [*Latvian*] (ROG)
**let**............. Lettre [*Letter, Draft*] [*Business term*] [*French*]
**LET**........... Light Equipment Transporter (MCD)
**LET**........... Limited Environmental Test (MCD)
**LET**........... Lincoln Experimental Terminal [*NASA*]
**LET**........... Linear Energy Transfer [*Radiology*]
**LET**........... Lithium Excretion Test [*Clinical chemistry*]
**LET**........... Live Environment Testing
**LET**........... Local Enterprise Trust [*British*]
**LET**........... Logical Equipment Table
**LET**........... Logistic Escape Trunk (CAAL)
**LET**........... London and Edinburgh Trust [*British*]
**LET**........... Low-End Torque [*Automotive engineering*]
**LET**........... Low-Energy Telescope [*Geophysics*]
**LET**........... Lux e Tenebris [*Light Out of Darkness*] [*Latin*] [*Freemasonry*]
**LETA**......... Sevilla/Tablada [*Spain*] [*ICAO location identifier*] (ICLI)
**LETB**......... Local Exchange Test Bed [*Telecommunications*] (TEL)
**LETC**......... Laramie Energy Technology Center [*Department of Energy*] (GRD)
**Let D**.......... Doctor of Letters
**LetD**.......... Letras de Deusto [*A publication*]
**LE-TE**........ Leading Edge - Trailing Edge [*Aerodynamics*]
**LETF**......... Launch Equipment Test Facility [*NASA*] (NASA)
**LETFO**...... Letter Follows (NOAA)
**LETHR**...... Leather
**Let It**.......... Lettere Italiane [*A publication*]
**LetM**.......... Lettres Modernes [*A publication*]
**LetMs**......... Letopis Matice Srpske [*A publication*]
**LETN**......... Law Enforcement Television Network
**LetN**.......... Lettres Nouvelles [*A publication*]
**LETO**......... Madrid/Torrejon [*Spain*] [*ICAO location identifier*] (ICLI)
**Letopisi Khig-Epidemiol Inst**... Letopisi na Khigienno-Epidemiologichnite Instituti [*A publication*]
**Letopisi Khig-Epidemiol Sluzhba**... Letopisi na Khigienno-Epidemiologichnata Sluzhba [*Bulgaria*] [*A publication*]
**Letopis Jschr Serb Volksforsch**... Letopis Jahresschrift des Instituts fuer Serbische Volksforschung [*A publication*]
**Letop Nauc Rad Poljopriv Fak Novi Sad**... Letopis Naucnih Radova. Poljoprivredni Fakultet. Novi Sad [*A publication*]
**Let Rom**..... Lettres Romanes [*A publication*]
**LETS**......... Large, External Transformation Sensitive [*Glycoprotein*] [*Also known as CSP*] [*Cytochemistry*]
**LETS**......... Launch Equipment Test Set (MCD)
**LETS**......... Law Enforcement Teletype [*or Teletypewriter*] Service [*Phoenix, AZ*]
**LETS**......... Leading Edge Tracker System
**LETS**......... Learning Experience for Technical Students [*NASA*]
**LETS**......... Linear-Energy Transfer Spectrometer [*Radiology*] (KSC)
**LETS**......... Linear-Energy Transfer System [*Radiology*]
**LETS**......... Live Environment Testing with SAGE (MCD)
**LETS**......... Low-Energy Telescope System [*Geophysics*]
**LETS**......... Lunar Experiment Telemetry System [*Aerospace*]
**Lett**........... Letteratura [*A publication*]
**LETT**......... Letters
**LETT**......... Lettish [*Latvian*] (ROG)
**Lett Appl Eng Sci**... Letters in Applied and Engineering Sciences [*A publication*]
**Lett Appl and Eng Sci**... Letters in Applied and Engineering Sciences [*A publication*]
**Lett Appl Microbiol**... Letters in Applied Microbiology [*A publication*]
**Lett Heat Mass Transf**... Letters in Heat and Mass Transfer [*A publication*]
**Lett Heat Mass Transfer**... Letters in Heat and Mass Transfer [*A publication*]
**Lett Heat and Mass Transfer**... Letters in Heat and Mass Transfer [*A publication*]
**Lett Inf Bur Rech Geol Min**... Lettre d'Information. Bureau de Recherches Geologiques et Minieres [*Paris*] [*A publication*]
**Lett Ital**...... Lettere Italiane [*A publication*]
**Lett Math Phys**... Letters in Mathematical Physics [*A publication*]
**Lett Mod**.... Letterature Moderne [*A publication*]
**Lett Nuov C**... Lettere al Nuovo Cimento [*A publication*]
**Lett Nuovo Cim**... Lettere al Nuovo Cimento [*A publication*]
**Lett Nuovo Cimento**... Lettere al Nuovo Cimento [*A publication*]
**Lett Nuovo Cimento Soc Ital Fis**... Lettere al Nuovo Cimento. Societa Italiana di Fisica [*Italy*] [*A publication*]
**Lettre Inf**.... Lettre d'Information [*A publication*]
**Lett Roman**... Lettres Romanes [*A publication*]
**Lettura Oft**... Lettura Oftalmologica [*A publication*]
**LEU**........... Emory University, Division of Librarianship, Atlanta, GA [*OCLC symbol*] (OCLC)
**LEU**........... Launch Enable Unit
**LEU**........... Launcher Electronic Unit (MCD)
**Leu**............ Leucine [*Also, L*] [*An amino acid*]
**LEU**........... Lewis, IN [*Location identifier*] [*FAA*] (FAAL)
**LEU**........... License to Export Uranium (NRCH)
**LEU**........... Low-Enriched Uranium [*Nuclear energy*]
**LEU**........... Seo De Urgel [*Spain*] [*Airport symbol*] (OAG)
**Leu Bij**........ Leuvense Bijdragen [*A publication*]
**LEUC**......... Leucotomy [*European term for lobotomy*] (DSUE)
**Leuk**........... Leukemia [*Medicine*]
**Leukemia Abstr**... Leukemia Abstracts [*A publication*]

**leuko**.......... Leukocyte [*Hematology*]
**Leuk Res**.... Leukemia Research [*A publication*]
**Leuk Soc Am Res Inc Annu Scholar Fellow Meet** ... Leukemia Society of America Research, Inc. Annual Scholar Fellow Meeting [*A publication*]
**Leuv Bijdr**.. Leuvense Bijdragen [*A publication*]
**LEV**........... Bureta [*Fiji*] [*Airport symbol*] (OAG)
**LEV**........... Grand Isle, LA [*Location identifier*] [*FAA*] (FAAL)
**LEV**........... Launch Escape Vehicle [*NASA*]
**LEV**........... Leibovitz-Emory Medium for Viral Cultures [*Microbiology*]
**LEV**........... Leichtverwundet; Leichtverwundeter [*Slightly wounded; minor casualty*] [*German military - World War II*]
**LEV**........... Lev Scientific Industries Ltd. [*Vancouver Stock Exchange symbol*]
**LEV**........... Level
**LEV**........... Lever
**Lev**............ Levinz's King's Bench and Common Pleas Reports [*1660-97*] [*England*] [*A publication*] (DLA)
**LEV**........... Levis [*Light*] [*Pharmacy*]
**Lev**............ Leviticus [*Old Testament book*]
**LEV**........... Levyne [*A zeolite*]
**LEV**........... Lifting Entry Vehicle
**LEV**........... Loader/Editor/Verifier [*Telecommunications*] (TEL)
**LEV**........... Local Exhaust Ventilation [*Hazardous material control*]
**LEV**........... Logistics Entry Vehicle
**LEV**........... Loyal Edinburgh Volunteers [*British military*] (DMA)
**LEV**........... Lunar Excursion Vehicle [*Aerospace*]
**Levant Recursos Nat Proj Radam (Bras)** ... Levantamento de Recursos Naturais. Projecto Radam (Brasil) [*A publication*]
**LEVC**......... Valencia [*Spain*] [*ICAO location identifier*] (ICLI)
**LEVCB**...... Low-Emission Vehicle Certification Board [*Terminated, 1980*] [*Environmental Protection Agency*]
**LEVD**......... Valladolid [*Spain*] [*ICAO location identifier*] (ICLI)
**Leveltari Kozlem** ... Leveltari Kozlemenyei [*A publication*]
**Leveltari Sz** ... Leveltari Szemle [*A publication*]
**Levende Nat** ... Levende Natuur [*A publication*]
**Lev Ent**....... Levinz's Entries [*England*] [*A publication*] (DLA)
**Levi Com L** ... Levi's International Commercial Law [*2nd ed.*] [*1863*] [*A publication*] (DLA)
**LEVID**....... Leviathan [*A publication*]
**Levi Merc L** ... Levi's Mercantile Law [*1854*] [*A publication*] (DLA)
**LEVIT**....... Leviter [*Lightly*] [*Pharmacy*]
**LEVIT**....... Leviticus [*Old Testament book*] (ROG)
**Lev JP**........ Levinge's Irish Justice of the Peace [*A publication*] (DLA)
**LEVM**........ Valencia [*Spain*] [*ICAO location identifier*] (ICLI)
**LEVMETR** ... Levelometer
**LEVN**........ Levin Computer Corp. [*NASDAQ symbol*] (NQ)
**LevR**.......... Leviticus Rabbah (BJA)
**LEVS**......... Leaves
**LEVS**......... Lev Scientific Industries Ltd. [*NASDAQ symbol*] (NQ)
**LEVS**......... Madrid/Cuatro Vientos [*Spain*] [*ICAO location identifier*] (ICLI)
**LevT**........... Levende Talen [*A publication*]
**LEVT**......... Vitoria [*Spain*] [*ICAO location identifier*] (ICLI)
**LEVVA**...... Lunar Extravehicular Visor Assembly [*NASA*] (KSC)
**LEVX**......... Vigo [*Spain*] [*ICAO location identifier*] (ICLI)
**Levy WTM** ... Woerterbuch ueber die Talmudim und Midraschim [*J. Levy*] [*A publication*] (BJA)
**LEW**.......... Auburn/Lewiston, ME [*Location identifier*] [*FAA*] (FAAL)
**Lew**............ Lewin's English Crown Cases Reserved [*1822-38*] [*A publication*] (DLA)
**LEW**.......... Lewis [*Rat strain*]
**Lew**............ Lewis' Reports [*Missouri*] [*A publication*] (DLA)
**Lew**............ Lewis' Reports [*Nevada*] [*A publication*] (DLA)
**LEW**.......... Lewiston [*Maine*] [*Airport symbol*] (OAG)
**LE & W**...... Literature East and West [*A publication*]
**Lew App**..... Lewin's Appportionment [*1869*] [*A publication*] (DLA)
**Lew B & S**.. Lewis on Bonds and Securities [*A publication*] (DLA)
**Lew CC**...... Lewin's English Crown Cases [*A publication*] (DLA)
**Lew CL**....... Lewis' Criminal Law [*A publication*] (DLA)
**Lew Conv** ... Lewis' Principles of Conveyancing [*A publication*] (DLA)
**Lew Dig Cr L** ... Lewis' Digest of United States Criminal Law [*A publication*] (DLA)
**Lew Elec**..... Lewis' Election Manual [*A publication*] (DLA)
**Lew Eq Dr** ... Lewis on Equity Drafting [*A publication*] (DLA)
**Lewin**......... Lewin on Trusts [*A publication*] (DLA)
**Lewin CC** ... Lewin's English Crown Cases Reserved [*1822-38*] [*A publication*] (DLA)
**Lewin CC (Eng)** ... Lewin's English Crown Cases [*A publication*] (DLA)
**Lewin Cr Cas** ... Lewin's English Crown Cases Reserved [*A publication*] (DLA)
**Lew Ind Pen** ... Lewis' East India Penal Code [*A publication*] (DLA)
**Lewis**.......... Lewis' Appeals Reports [*29-35 Missouri*] [*A publication*] (DLA)
**Lewis**.......... Lewis' Kentucky Law Reporter [*A publication*] (DLA)
**Lewis**.......... Lewis' Reports [*Nevada*] [*A publication*] (DLA)
**Lewis Em Dom** ... Lewis on Eminent Domain [*A publication*] (DLA)
**Lewis Perp** ... Lewis' Law of Perpetuities [*A publication*] (DLA)
**Lew L Cas**.. Lewis' Leading Cases on Public Land Law [*A publication*] (DLA)
**Lew LT**....... Lewis on Land Titles in Philadelphia [*A publication*] (DLA)
**LEW Nachr** ... LEW [*Lokomotivbau-Elektrotechnische Werke*] Nachrichten [*A publication*]
**LEWP**........ Line Echo Wave Pattern
**Lew Perp**.... Lewis' Law of Perpetuities [*A publication*] (DLA)
**Lew St**........ Lewis on Stocks, Bonds, Etc. [*A publication*] (DLA)
**Lew Tr**........ Lewin on Trusts [*A publication*] (DLA)
**LEWU**....... Lanka Estate Workers' Union [*Ceylon*]
**Lew US Cr L** ... Lewis' Digest of United States Criminal Law [*A publication*] (DLA)
**LEX**........... Cary Memorial Library, Lexington, MA [*OCLC symbol*] (OCLC)
**LEX**........... Land Exercise [*Marine Corps*]
**LEX**........... Leading Edge Extension [*Aviation*]
**LEX**........... Letter Exchange (EA)
**Lex**............ Lexical (BJA)
**LEX**........... Lexicon
**LEX**........... Lexington [*Virginia*] [*Seismograph station code, US Geological Survey*] [*Closed*] (SEIS)
**LEX**........... Lexington/Frankfort [*Kentucky*] [*Airport symbol*] (OAG)
**Lex**............ Lexis [*A publication*]
**LEX**........... Line Exchange [*Telecommunications*]
**LEx**........... Liver Extract [*Protein/lipid substance*] [*Immunology*]
**LEXB**........ Lexington Savings Bank [*Lexington, MA*] [*NASDAQ symbol*] (NQ)
**Lex Cust**..... Lex Custumaria [*Latin*] [*A publication*] (DLA)
**LEXD**........ Lexden [*England*]
**LEXD**........ Lexidata Corp. [*NASDAQ symbol*] (NQ)
**LEXI**.......... Lexicon Corp. [*NASDAQ symbol*] (NQ)
**LEXICOG** ... Lexicography
**LEXIS**........ Legal Research Service [*Registered service mark*] (IID)
**LEXIS**........ Lexicography Information Service [*Federal Republic of Germany*] [*Data processing*]
**LEXJ**......... Santander [*Spain*] [*ICAO location identifier*] (ICLI)
**Lex Man**.... Lex Maneriorum [*Latin*] [*A publication*] (DLA)
**Lex Mer Am** ... Lex Mercatoria Americana [*Latin*] [*A publication*] (DLA)
**Lex Merc Red** ... Lex Mercatoria Rediviva, by Beawes [*A publication*] (DLA)
**Lex Mess** ... Lexicon Messanense [*Classical studies*] (OCD)
**LEXP**......... Language Experience
**LEXP**......... Lexington Precision Corp. [*NASDAQ symbol*] (SPSG)
**Lex Parl**..... Lex Parliamentaria [*Latin*] [*A publication*] (DLA)
**L Exr**.......... Launceston Examiner [*A publication*] (APTA)
**L Exr (Newspr) (Tas)** ... Launceston Examiner (Newspaper) (Tasmania) [*A publication*] (APTA)
**Lex Sci**....... Lex et Scientia [*A publication*]
**LexSyr**....... Lexicon Syriacum [*A publication*] (BJA)
**LEXT**......... Lexitech International Documentation Network, Inc. [*Jericho, NY*] [*NASDAQ symbol*] (NQ)
**L/EXT**....... Lower Extremity [*Medicine*]
**Lex Th Q**.... Lexington Theological Quarterly [*A publication*]
**Ley**............ Ley's English Court of Wards Reports [*A publication*] (DLA)
**Ley**............ Ley's English King's Bench Reports [*1608-29*] [*A publication*] (DLA)
**LEY**........... Liberal European Youth
**LEYD**........ Leyden [*Netherlands*] (ROG)
**Leyte-Samar Stud** ... Leyte-Samar Studies [*A publication*]
**Ley Wards** ... Ley's English Court of Wards Reports [*A publication*] (DLA)
**LEZ**........... Lunar Equatorial Zone [*Army Map Service*]
**LEZA**......... Zaragoza [*Spain*] [*ICAO location identifier*] (ICLI)
**LEZG**......... Zaragoza [*Spain*] [*ICAO location identifier*] (ICLI)
**LEZL**......... Sevilla [*Spain*] [*ICAO location identifier*] (ICLI)
**LF**.............. Fighter Aircraft Fitted with Engine Rated for Low-Altitude Performance
**LF**.............. La Fosse Platinum Group, Inc. [*Toronto Stock Exchange symbol*]
**LF**.............. Lacrimatory Factor [*Food technology*]
**LF**.............. Lacrosse Foundation (EA)
**LF**.............. Lactoferrin [*Biochemistry*]
**LF**.............. Lama Foundation (EA)
**LF**.............. [*The*] Lancashire Fusiliers [*Military unit*] [*British*]
**LF**.............. Land Forces [*Military*] [*British*]
**LF**.............. Landing Force [*Navy*] (NVT)
**LF**.............. Latex Fixation [*Test*] [*Medicine*]
**LF**.............. Lathe Fixture (MCD)
**LF**.............. Laucks Foundation (EA)
**LF**.............. Launch Facility
**LF**.............. Launch Forward
**LF**.............. Law French (DLA)
**LF**.............. Lawn Faucet (MSA)
**LF**.............. Le Figaro [*A publication*]
**LF**.............. Leaf [*Bibliography*] (ROG)
**LF**.............. League of Friendship (EA)
**LF**.............. Leapfrog Configuration [*Circuit theory*] (IEEE)
**LF**.............. Lebanese Forces
**LF**.............. Lederer Foundation (EA)
**LF**.............. Ledger Folio
**LF**.............. Left Field [*or Fielder*] [*Baseball*]
**LF**.............. Left Foot
**LF**.............. Left Forward [*Football*]
**LF**.............. Left Front
**LF**.............. Left Fullback [*Soccer*]
**LF**.............. Legion of Frontiersmen [*British military*] (DMA)

**LF**.............. Lettering Faded
**LF**.............. Lettres Francaises [*A publication*]
**LF**.............. Lia Fail [*A publication*]
**LF**.............. Liberty Federation (EA)
**LF**.............. Liederkranz Foundation (EA)
**LF**.............. Life Float
**LF**.............. Lifeline Foundation (EA)
**LF**.............. Lifting Fan [*Hovercraft*]
**LF**.............. Lightface [*Type*]
**LF**.............. Ligue de Foyer [*Salvation Army Home League - SAHL*] (EAIO)
**LF**.............. Limit of Flocculation
**LF**.............. Line Feed [*Control character*] [*Data processing*]
**LF**.............. Line Finder [*Teletype*]
**LF**.............. Lineal Feet
**LF**.............. Linear Filter
**LF**.............. Linear Foot
**LF**.............. Linjeflyg AB [*Sweden*] [*ICAO designator*] (FAAC)
**LF**.............. Linoleum Floor [*Technical drawings*]
**LF**.............. Lisle Fellowship (EA)
**LF**.............. Listy Filologicke [*A publication*]
**LF**.............. Literaturen Front [*Sofia*] [*A publication*]
**LF**.............. Lituanus Foundation (EA)
**LF**.............. Live Fire
**LF**.............. Live Flying (NATG)
**LF**.............. Load Factor
**LF**.............. Loaf
**LF**.............. Local Film
**LF**.............. Local Force [*Viet Cong combat force*]
**LF**.............. Locally Funded (AFM)
**LF**.............. Lock Forward
**LF**.............. Logic Function
**LF**.............. Logical File [*Data processing*] (BUR)
**LF**.............. Lost on Foul [*Boxing*]
**LF**.............. Lovelace Foundation for Medical Education and Research [*Reorganized to form Lovelace Medical Foundation and Lovelace Biomedical and Environmental Research Institute*]
**LF**.............. Low Fat [*Diet*]
**LF**.............. Low-Fluence [*Physics*]
**LF**.............. Low Foliage Forager [*Ecology*]
**LF**.............. Low Food Density [*Ecology*]
**LF**.............. Low Force
**LF**.............. Low Forceps [*Delivery*] [*Obstetrics*]
**LF**.............. Low Frequency
**lf**.............. Low Rate Forward [*Ecology*]
**LF**.............. Siebelwerke ATG GmbH [*Federal Republic of Germany*] [*ICAO aircraft manufacturer identifier*] (ICAO)
**LF**.............. University of Illinois. Law Forum [*A publication*]
**LFA**............ Klamath Falls, OR [*Location identifier*] [*FAA*] (FAAL)
**LFA**............ Land Force Adriatic [*British Royal Marines*] [*World War II*]
**LFA**............ Land Force, Airmobility [*NATO*] (NATG)
**LFA**............ Landing Force Aviation
**LFA**............ Large Families of America [*Defunct*] (EA)
**LFA**............ Left Femoral Artery [*Anatomy*]
**LFA**............ Left Frontoanterior [*A fetal position*] [*Obstetrics*]
**LFA**............ Light Freight Agent (ADA)
**LFA**............ Littlefield, Adams & Co. [*AMEX symbol*] (SPSG)
**LFA**............ Local Freight Agent
**LFA**............ Low Flow Alarm (IEEE)
**LFA**............ Lupus Foundation of America (EA)
**LFA**............ Lutheran Fraternities of America (EA)
**LFA**............ Lymphocyte Function-Associated Antigen [*Immunochemistry*]
**LFAA**......... Ambleteuse [*France*] [*ICAO location identifier*] (ICLI)
**LFAAV**....... Landing Force Assault Amphibious Vehicle (MCD)
**LFAB**......... Dieppe/Saint-Aubin [*France*] [*ICAO location identifier*] (ICLI)
**LFAC**......... Calais/Dunkerque [*France*] [*ICAO location identifier*] (ICLI)
**LFACS**....... Light Future Armored Combat System [*Tank*]
**LFAD**......... Compiegne/Margny [*France*] [*ICAO location identifier*] (ICLI)
**LFAE**......... Eu-Mers/Le Treport [*France*] [*ICAO location identifier*] (ICLI)
**LFAF**......... Laon/Chambry [*France*] [*ICAO location identifier*] (ICLI)
**LFAF**......... Low-Frequency Accelerometer Flutter (MCD)
**LFAG**......... Peronne/Saint-Quentin [*France*] [*ICAO location identifier*] (ICLI)
**LFAH**......... Soissons/Cuffies [*France*] [*ICAO location identifier*] (ICLI)
**LFAI**.......... Lifting Fair Air Intake [*Hovercraft*]
**LFAI**.......... Nangis/Les Loges [*France*] [*ICAO location identifier*] (ICLI)
**LFAJ**.......... Argentan [*France*] [*ICAO location identifier*] (ICLI)
**LFAK**......... Dunkerque-Ghyvelde [*France*] [*ICAO location identifier*] (ICLI)
**LFAL**......... La Fleche/Thoree-Les-Pins [*France*] [*ICAO location identifier*] (ICLI)
**LFAM**........ Berck-Sur-Mer [*France*] [*ICAO location identifier*] (ICLI)
**LFAM**........ Life of America Insurance Corp. of Boston [*NASDAQ symbol*]
**LFAM**........ Low-Frequency Accelerometer Modes (MCD)
**LFAN**......... Conde-Sur-Noireau [*France*] [*ICAO location identifier*] (ICLI)
**LFAO**......... Bagnole-De-L'Orne [*France*] [*ICAO location identifier*] (ICLI)
**LFAP**......... Low-Frequency Accelerometer POGO [*Polar Orbiting Geophysical Observatory*] [*NASA*] (NASA)
**LFAP**......... Rethel-Perthes [*France*] [*ICAO location identifier*] (ICLI)
**LFAQ**......... Albert/Bray [*France*] [*ICAO location identifier*] (ICLI)
**LFAR**......... Last Frame Address Register
**LFAR**......... Liberal and Fine Arts Review [*A publication*]
**LFAR**......... Libertarians for Animal Rights (EA)
**LFAR**......... Montdidier [*France*] [*ICAO location identifier*] (ICLI)
**LFAS**......... Falaise-Monts-D'Eraines [*France*] [*ICAO location identifier*] (ICLI)
**LFAS**......... League of Finnish-American Societies (EA)
**LFAT**......... Le Touquet/Paris-Plage [*France*] [*ICAO location identifier*] (ICLI)
**LFaU**.......... Union Parish Library, Farmerville, LA [*Library symbol*] [*Library of Congress*] (LCLS)
**LFAU**......... Vauville [*France*] [*ICAO location identifier*] (ICLI)
**LFAV**......... Valenciennes/Denain [*France*] [*ICAO location identifier*] (ICLI)
**LFAW**........ Villerupt [*France*] [*ICAO location identifier*] (ICLI)
**LFAX**......... Mortagne-Au-Perche [*France*] [*ICAO location identifier*] (ICLI)
**LFAY**......... Amiens/Glisy [*France*] [*ICAO location identifier*] (ICLI)
**LFB**............ Lafayette, TN [*Location identifier*] [*FAA*] (FAAL)
**LFB**............ Landing Force Bulletin [*Marine Corps*]
**LFB**............ Lateral Forebrain Bundle
**LFB**............ Left Fullback [*Soccer*]
**LFB**............ Light Field Battery [*British military*] (DMA)
**LFB**............ Limited Frequency Band
**LFB**............ London Festival Ballet
**LFB**............ London Fire Brigade
**LFB**............ Longview Fibre Co. [*NYSE symbol*] (CTT)
**LFB**............ Loop Fluidized Bed [*Chemical engineering*]
**LFB**............ Low-Frequency Beacon
**LFB**............ Luxol Fast Blue [*Biological stain*]
**LFB2**.......... London Festival Ballet's Ensemble Group
**LFBA**......... Agen/La Garenne [*France*] [*ICAO location identifier*] (ICLI)
**LFBA**......... Licentiate of the Corporation of Executives and Administrators [*British*] (DBQ)
**LFBB**......... Bordeaux [*France*] [*ICAO location identifier*] (ICLI)
**LFBC**......... Cazaux [*France*] [*ICAO location identifier*] (ICLI)
**LFBD**......... Bordeaux/Merignac [*France*] [*ICAO location identifier*] (ICLI)
**LFBD**......... Letters of the First Babylonian Dynasty [*A publication*] (BJA)
**LFBE**......... Bergerac/Roumaniere [*France*] [*ICAO location identifier*] (ICLI)
**LFBF**......... Toulouse/Francazal [*France*] [*ICAO location identifier*] (ICLI)
**LFBG**......... Cognac/Chateau Bernard [*France*] [*ICAO location identifier*] (ICLI)
**LFBH**......... La Rochelle/Laleu [*France*] [*ICAO location identifier*] (ICLI)
**LFBI**.......... Poitiers/Biard [*France*] [*ICAO location identifier*] (ICLI)
**LFBJ**.......... Saint-Junien [*France*] [*ICAO location identifier*] (ICLI)
**LFBK**......... Lincoln First Banks [*NASDAQ symbol*] (NQ)
**LFBK**......... Montlucon-Gueret [*France*] [*ICAO location identifier*] (ICLI)
**LFBL**......... Limoges/Bellegarde [*France*] [*ICAO location identifier*] (ICLI)
**LFBM**........ Mont-De-Marsan [*France*] [*ICAO location identifier*] (ICLI)
**LFBN**......... Niort/Souche [*France*] [*ICAO location identifier*] (ICLI)
**LFBO**......... Toulouse/Blagnac [*France*] [*ICAO location identifier*] (ICLI)
**LFBP**......... Pau/Pont-Long-Uzein [*France*] [*ICAO location identifier*] (ICLI)
**LFBQ**......... Toulouse [*France*] [*ICAO location identifier*] (ICLI)
**LFBR**......... Liquid Fluidized Bed Reactor
**LFBR**......... Muret/Lherm [*France*] [*ICAO location identifier*] (ICLI)
**LFBR-CX**.. Liquid Fluidized Bed Reactor Critical Experiment
**LFBS**......... Biscarosse/Parentis [*France*] [*ICAO location identifier*] (ICLI)
**LFBT**......... Tarbes/Ossun-Lourdes [*France*] [*ICAO location identifier*] (ICLI)
**LFBU**......... Angouleme/Brie-Champniers [*France*] [*ICAO location identifier*] (ICLI)
**LFBV**......... Brive/La Roche [*France*] [*ICAO location identifier*] (ICLI)
**LFBW**........ Mont-De-Marsan [*France*] [*ICAO location identifier*] (ICLI)
**LFBX**......... Perigeux/Bassillac [*France*] [*ICAO location identifier*] (ICLI)
**LFBY**......... Dax/Seyresse [*France*] [*ICAO location identifier*] (ICLI)
**LFBZ**......... Biarritz-Bayonne/Anglet [*France*] [*ICAO location identifier*] (ICLI)
**LFC**............ Concordia Parish Library, Ferriday, LA [*Library symbol*] [*Library of Congress*] (LCLS)
**LFC**............ L-Band Frequency Converter
**LFC**............ Lafayette Flying Corps [*World War I*]
**LFC**............ Lake Forest College [*Illinois*]
**LFC**............ Lake Fork Canyon [*New Mexico*] [*Seismograph station code, US Geological Survey*] (SEIS)
**LFC**............ Laminar Flow Control [*Aerodynamics*]
**LFC**............ Large Format Camera [*Space exploration*]
**LFC**............ Lateral Femoral Condyle [*Anatomy*]
**LFC**............ Level of Free Convection [*Meteorology*]
**LFC**............ Light Fighter Course [*Army*]
**LFC**............ Live Fire Component (MCD)
**LFC**............ Load Frequency Control (IEEE)
**LFC**............ Local Files Check
**LFC**............ Local Forms Control [*Data processing*] (CMD)
**LFC**............ Logic Flow Chart [*Data processing*]
**LFC**............ Logo Forum on Compuserve [*Inactive*] (EA)
**LFC**............ Lomas Financial Corp. [*NYSE symbol*] (SPSG)
**LFC**............ Loverboy Fan Club (EA)
**LFC**............ Low-Frequency Choke (DEN)
**LFC**............ Low-Frequency Correction (CET)

**LFC** Low-Frequency Current
**LFC** Lunar Facsimile Capsule [*NASA*] (KSC)
**LFC** Lunar Farside Chart [*Air Force*]
**LFCA** Chatellerault/Targe [*France*] [*ICAO location identifier*] (ICLI)
**LFCB** Bagneres De Luchon [*France*] [*ICAO location identifier*] (ICLI)
**LF & CB** Legal Fees and Costs Board [*Australia*]
**LFCC** Cahors/Lalbenque [*France*] [*ICAO location identifier*] (ICLI)
**LFCD** Andernos-Les-Bains [*France*] [*ICAO location identifier*] (ICLI)
**LFCE** Gueret/Saint-Laurent [*France*] [*ICAO location identifier*] (ICLI)
**LFCF** Figeac/Livernon [*France*] [*ICAO location identifier*] (ICLI)
**LFCG** Saint-Girons/Antichan [*France*] [*ICAO location identifier*] (ICLI)
**LFCH** Arcachon/La Teste De Buch [*France*] [*ICAO location identifier*] (ICLI)
**LFCI** Albi/Le Sequestre [*France*] [*ICAO location identifier*] (ICLI)
**LFCI** Licentiate of the Faculty of Commerce and Industry [*British*] (DBQ)
**LFCJ** Jonzac/Neulles [*France*] [*ICAO location identifier*] (ICLI)
**LFCK** Castres/Mazamet [*France*] [*ICAO location identifier*] (ICLI)
**LFCL** Toulouse/Lasbordes [*France*] [*ICAO location identifier*] (ICLI)
**LFCM** Millau/Larzac [*France*] [*ICAO location identifier*] (ICLI)
**LFCN** Nogaro [*France*] [*ICAO location identifier*] (ICLI)
**LFCO** Oloron/Herrere [*France*] [*ICAO location identifier*] (ICLI)
**LFCP** Pons/Avy [*France*] [*ICAO location identifier*] (ICLI)
**LFCQ** Graulhet/Mondragon [*France*] [*ICAO location identifier*] (ICLI)
**LFCR** Rodez/Marcillac [*France*] [*ICAO location identifier*] (ICLI)
**LFCS** Bordeaux/Saucats [*France*] [*ICAO location identifier*] (ICLI)
**LFCS** Land Forces Classification System (AABC)
**LFCS** LASER Fire Control System
**LFCS** Licentiate of the Faculty of Secretaries [*British*] (DBQ)
**LFCT** Thouars [*France*] [*ICAO location identifier*] (ICLI)
**LFCU** Ussel/Thalamy [*France*] [*ICAO location identifier*] (ICLI)
**LFCV** Villefranche-De-Rouergue [*France*] [*ICAO location identifier*] (ICLI)
**LFCW** Villeneuve-Sur-Lot [*France*] [*ICAO location identifier*] (ICLI)
**LFCX** Castelsarrasin/Moissac [*France*] [*ICAO location identifier*] (ICLI)
**LFCY** Royan/Medis [*France*] [*ICAO location identifier*] (ICLI)
**LFCZ** Mimizan [*France*] [*ICAO location identifier*] (ICLI)
**LFD** Lactose-Free Diet
**LFD** Latest Finish Date
**LFD** Launch and Flight Division [*Ballistic Research Laboratory*] (RDA)
**LFD** Least Fatal Dose
**LFD** Line Fault Detector [*Telecommunications*] (TEL)
**LFD** Litchfield, MI [*Location identifier*] [*FAA*] (FAAL)
**LFD** Local Frequency Distribution
**LFD** Longford [*County in Ireland*] (ROG)
**LFD** Low-Fat Diet
**LFD** Low-Forceps Delivery [*Obstetrics*]
**LFD** Low-Frequency Decoy
**LFD** Low-Frequency Disturbance
**LFD** Lutheran Foundation for Religious Drama (EA)
**LFDA** Aire-Sur-L'Addour [*France*] [*ICAO location identifier*] (ICLI)
**LFDA** Land and Facilities Development Administration [*HUD*]
**LFDB** Montauban [*France*] [*ICAO location identifier*] (ICLI)
**LFDC** Montendre/Marcillac [*France*] [*ICAO location identifier*] (ICLI)
**LFDE** Egletons [*France*] [*ICAO location identifier*] (ICLI)
**LFDF** Low-Frequency Direction Finder (MCD)
**LFDF** Sainte-Foy-La-Grande [*France*] [*ICAO location identifier*] (ICLI)
**LFDG** Gaillac/Lisle Sur Tarn [*France*] [*ICAO location identifier*] (ICLI)
**LFDH** Auch/Lamothe [*France*] [*ICAO location identifier*] (ICLI)
**LFDI** Libourne/Artiques De Lussac [*France*] [*ICAO location identifier*] (ICLI)
**LFDJ** Pamiers/Les Pujols [*France*] [*ICAO location identifier*] (ICLI)
**LFDK** Soulac-Sur-Mer [*France*] [*ICAO location identifier*] (ICLI)
**LFDL** Loudun [*France*] [*ICAO location identifier*] (ICLI)
**LFDM** Low Flyer, Defense Mode
**LFDM** Marmande/Virazeil [*France*] [*ICAO location identifier*] (ICLI)
**LFDN** Rochefort/Saint-Agnant [*France*] [*ICAO location identifier*] (ICLI)
**LFDO** Bordeaux/Souge [*France*] [*ICAO location identifier*] (ICLI)
**LFDP** Saint-Pierre D'Oleron [*France*] [*ICAO location identifier*] (ICLI)
**LFDQ** Castelnau-Magnoac [*France*] [*ICAO location identifier*] (ICLI)
**LFDR** La Reole/Floudes [*France*] [*ICAO location identifier*] (ICLI)
**LFDS** Sarlat/Domme [*France*] [*ICAO location identifier*] (ICLI)
**LFDT** Tarbes/Laloubere [*France*] [*ICAO location identifier*] (ICLI)
**LFDU** Lesparre/St. Laurent Du Medoc [*France*] [*ICAO location identifier*] (ICLI)
**LFDV** Couhe/Verac [*France*] [*ICAO location identifier*] (ICLI)
**LFDW** Chauvigny [*France*] [*ICAO location identifier*] (ICLI)
**LFDX** Fumel/Montayral [*France*] [*ICAO location identifier*] (ICLI)
**LFDY** Bordeaux-Yvrac [*France*] [*ICAO location identifier*] (ICLI)
**LFDZ** Condat-Sur-Vezere [*France*] [*ICAO location identifier*] (ICLI)
**LFE** Brotherhood of Locomotive Firemen and Enginemen [*Later, United Transportation Union*] [*AFL-CIO*]
**LFE** Logarithmic Feedback Element [*Data processing*]
**LFEA** Delle-Ile [*France*] [*ICAO location identifier*] (ICLI)
**LFEB** Dinan/Trelivan [*France*] [*ICAO location identifier*] (ICLI)
**LFEB** Launch Facility Equipment Building [*Missiles*]
**LFEC** Ouessant [*France*] [*ICAO location identifier*] (ICLI)
**LFED** Liberty Federal Savings & Loan [*NASDAQ symbol*] (NQ)
**LFED** Pontivy [*France*] [*ICAO location identifier*] (ICLI)
**LFEE** Reims [*France*] [*ICAO location identifier*] (ICLI)
**LFEF** Amboise/Dierre [*France*] [*ICAO location identifier*] (ICLI)
**LFEG** Argenton-Sur-Creuse [*France*] [*ICAO location identifier*] (ICLI)
**LFEH** Aubigny-Sur-Nere [*France*] [*ICAO location identifier*] (ICLI)
**LFEI** Briare/Chatillon [*France*] [*ICAO location identifier*] (ICLI)
**LFEJ** Chateauroux/Villers [*France*] [*ICAO location identifier*] (ICLI)
**LFEK** Issoudun/Le Fay [*France*] [*ICAO location identifier*] (ICLI)
**LFEL** Le Blanc [*France*] [*ICAO location identifier*] (ICLI)
**L Fem** Letras Femeninas [*A publication*]
**LFEM** Montargis/Vimory [*France*] [*ICAO location identifier*] (ICLI)
**LFEN** Laboratorio de Fisica e Engenharia Nucleores [*Portugal*]
**LFEN** Tours/Sorigny [*France*] [*ICAO location identifier*] (ICLI)
**LFEO** Saint-Malo/Saint-Servan [*France*] [*ICAO location identifier*] (ICLI)
**LFEP** Pouilly-Maconge [*France*] [*ICAO location identifier*] (ICLI)
**LFEQ** Quiberon [*France*] [*ICAO location identifier*] (ICLI)
**LFER** Linear Free Energy Relationship
**LFER** Redon/Bains-Sur-Oust [*France*] [*ICAO location identifier*] (ICLI)
**LFES** Guiscriff-Scaer [*France*] [*ICAO location identifier*] (ICLI)
**LFET** Til-Chatel [*France*] [*ICAO location identifier*] (ICLI)
**LFETS** Live Fire Evasive Target System [*Army*] (INF)
**LFEU** Bar-Le-Duc [*France*] [*ICAO location identifier*] (ICLI)
**LFEV** Gray-Saint-Adrien [*France*] [*ICAO location identifier*] (ICLI)
**LFEW** Saulieu-Liernais [*France*] [*ICAO location identifier*] (ICLI)
**LF-EX** Life Expectancy [*Military*]
**LFEX** Nancy-Azelot [*France*] [*ICAO location identifier*] (ICLI)
**LFEY** Ile-D'Yeu/Le Grand Phare [*France*] [*ICAO location identifier*] (ICLI)
**LFEZ** Nancy-Malzeville [*France*] [*ICAO location identifier*] (ICLI)
**LFF** La Frestal [*France*] [*Seismograph station code, US Geological Survey*] (SEIS)
**LFF** Light Filter Factor
**LFF** London Film Festival
**LFFA** CORTA (Orly Ouest) [*France*] [*ICAO location identifier*] (ICLI)
**LFFB** Buno-Bonnevaux [*France*] [*ICAO location identifier*] (ICLI)
**LFFC** Mantes-Cherence [*France*] [*ICAO location identifier*] (ICLI)
**LFFD** Saint-Andre-De L'Eure [*France*] [*ICAO location identifier*] (ICLI)
**LFFE** Enghien-Moisselles [*France*] [*ICAO location identifier*] (ICLI)
**LFFF** Paris [*France*] [*ICAO location identifier*] (ICLI)
**LFFG** La Ferte-Gaucher [*France*] [*ICAO location identifier*] (ICLI)
**LFFH** Chateau-Thierry-Belleau [*France*] [*ICAO location identifier*] (ICLI)
**LFFI** Ancenis [*France*] [*ICAO location identifier*] (ICLI)
**LFFJ** Joinville-Mussey [*France*] [*ICAO location identifier*] (ICLI)
**LFFK** Fontenay-Le-Conte [*France*] [*ICAO location identifier*] (ICLI)
**LFFL** Bailleau-Armenonville [*France*] [*ICAO location identifier*] (ICLI)
**LFFM** La Motte-Beuvron [*France*] [*ICAO location identifier*] (ICLI)
**LFFN** Brienne-Le-Chateau [*France*] [*ICAO location identifier*] (ICLI)
**LFFO** Tonnerre-Moulins [*France*] [*ICAO location identifier*] (ICLI)
**LFFP** LASER Fusion Feasibility Project [*Nuclear fusion*]
**LFFP** Pithiviers [*France*] [*ICAO location identifier*] (ICLI)
**LFFQ** La Ferte-Alais [*France*] [*ICAO location identifier*] (ICLI)
**LFFR** Bar-Sur-Seine [*France*] [*ICAO location identifier*] (ICLI)
**LFFS** Suippes [*France*] [*ICAO location identifier*] (ICLI)
**LFFT** Neufchateau-Roucaux [*France*] [*ICAO location identifier*] (ICLI)
**LFFTD** Laser Focus with Fiberoptic Technology [*A publication*]
**LFFU** Chateauneuf-Sur-Cher [*France*] [*ICAO location identifier*] (ICLI)
**LFFV** Vierzon-Mereau [*France*] [*ICAO location identifier*] (ICLI)
**LFFW** Montaigu-Saint-Georges [*France*] [*ICAO location identifier*] (ICLI)
**LFFX** Tournus-Cuisery [*France*] [*ICAO location identifier*] (ICLI)
**LFFY** Etrepagny [*France*] [*ICAO location identifier*] (ICLI)
**LFFZ** Sezanne-Saint-Remy [*France*] [*ICAO location identifier*] (ICLI)
**LFG** Landfill Gas
**LFG** Lead-Free Glass
**LFG** Lexical Functional Grammar [*Artificial intelligence*]
**LFG** Liberty Financial Group, Inc. [*AMEX symbol*] (SPSG)
**LFG** Low-Frequency Generator
**LFGA** Colmar/Houssen [*France*] [*ICAO location identifier*] (ICLI)
**LFGB** Mulhouse/Habsheim [*France*] [*ICAO location identifier*] (ICLI)
**LFGC** Strasbourg/Neuhof [*France*] [*ICAO location identifier*] (ICLI)

**LFGD** ......... Arbois [*France*] [*ICAO location identifier*] (ICLI)
**LFGE** ......... Avallon [*France*] [*ICAO location identifier*] (ICLI)
**LFGF** ......... Beaune/Challanges [*France*] [*ICAO location identifier*] (ICLI)
**LFGG** ......... Belfort/Chaux [*France*] [*ICAO location identifier*] (ICLI)
**LFGG** ......... Low-Frequency Gravity Gradiometer
**LFGH** ......... Cosne-Sur-Loire [*France*] [*ICAO location identifier*] (ICLI)
**LFGI** ......... Dijon/Val Suzon [*France*] [*ICAO location identifier*] (ICLI)
**LFGJ** ......... Dole/Tavaux [*France*] [*ICAO location identifier*] (ICLI)
**LFGK** ......... Joigny [*France*] [*ICAO location identifier*] (ICLI)
**LFGL** ......... Lons Le Saunier/Courlaoux [*France*] [*ICAO location identifier*] (ICLI)
**LFGM** ......... Montceau Les Mines/Pouilloux [*France*] [*ICAO location identifier*] (ICLI)
**LFGN** ......... Paray Le Monial [*France*] [*ICAO location identifier*] (ICLI)
**LFGO** ......... Pont-Sur-Yonne [*France*] [*ICAO location identifier*] (ICLI)
**LFGP** ......... Saint-Florentin/Cheu [*France*] [*ICAO location identifier*] (ICLI)
**LFGQ** ......... Semur-En-Auxois [*France*] [*ICAO location identifier*] (ICLI)
**LFGR** ......... Doncourt-Les-Conflans [*France*] [*ICAO location identifier*] (ICLI)
**LFGS** ......... Longuyon/Villette [*France*] [*ICAO location identifier*] (ICLI)
**LFGT** ......... Sarrebourg/Buhl [*France*] [*ICAO location identifier*] (ICLI)
**LFGU** ......... Sarreguemines/Neunkirch [*France*] [*ICAO location identifier*] (ICLI)
**LFGV** ......... Thionville/Yutz [*France*] [*ICAO location identifier*] (ICLI)
**LFGW** ......... Verdun/Rozelier [*France*] [*ICAO location identifier*] (ICLI)
**LFGX** ......... Champagnole/Crotenay [*France*] [*ICAO location identifier*] (ICLI)
**LFGY** ......... Saint-Die/Remoneix [*France*] [*ICAO location identifier*] (ICLI)
**LFGZ** ......... Nuits-Saint-Georges [*France*] [*ICAO location identifier*] (ICLI)
**LFH** ........... Left Femoral Hernia [*Medicine*]
**LFH** ........... Lower Fascial Height [*Medicine*]
**LFH** ........... Lunar Far Horizon (KSC)
**LFHA** ......... Issoire/Le Broc [*France*] [*ICAO location identifier*] (ICLI)
**LFHB** ......... Moulins/Avermes [*France*] [*ICAO location identifier*] (ICLI)
**LFHC** ......... Perouges/Meximieux [*France*] [*ICAO location identifier*] (ICLI)
**LFHD** ......... Pierrelatte [*France*] [*ICAO location identifier*] (ICLI)
**LFHE** ......... Romans/Saint-Paul [*France*] [*ICAO location identifier*] (ICLI)
**LFHF** ......... Ruoms [*France*] [*ICAO location identifier*] (ICLI)
**LFHG** ......... Saint-Chamond/L'Horme [*France*] [*ICAO location identifier*] (ICLI)
**LFHH** ......... Vienne/Reventin [*France*] [*ICAO location identifier*] (ICLI)
**LFHI** ......... Morestel [*France*] [*ICAO location identifier*] (ICLI)
**LFHJ** ......... Lyon/Corbas [*France*] [*ICAO location identifier*] (ICLI)
**LFHK** ......... Camp De Canjuers [*France*] [*ICAO location identifier*] (ICLI)
**LFHL** ......... Langogne/L'Esperon [*France*] [*ICAO location identifier*] (ICLI)
**LFHM** ......... Megeve [*France*] [*ICAO location identifier*] (ICLI)
**LFHN** ......... Bellegarde/Vouvray [*France*] [*ICAO location identifier*] (ICLI)
**LFHO** ......... Aubenas-Vals-Lanas [*France*] [*ICAO location identifier*] (ICLI)
**LFHP** ......... Le Puy/Loudes [*France*] [*ICAO location identifier*] (ICLI)
**LFHQ** ......... Saint-Flour/Coltines [*France*] [*ICAO location identifier*] (ICLI)
**LFHR** ......... Brioude-Beaumont [*France*] [*ICAO location identifier*] (ICLI)
**LFHS** ......... Bourg/Ceyreziat [*France*] [*ICAO location identifier*] (ICLI)
**LFHT** ......... Ambert-Le-Poyet [*France*] [*ICAO location identifier*] (ICLI)
**LFHU** ......... L'Alpe D'Huez [*France*] [*ICAO location identifier*] (ICLI)
**LFHV** ......... Villefrance/Tarare [*France*] [*ICAO location identifier*] (ICLI)
**LFHW** ......... Belleville-Villie-Morgon [*France*] [*ICAO location identifier*] (ICLI)
**LFHX** ......... Lapalisse-Perigny [*France*] [*ICAO location identifier*] (ICLI)
**LFHY** ......... Moulins/Montbeugny [*France*] [*ICAO location identifier*] (ICLI)
**LFHZ** ......... Sallanches-Mont-Blanc [*France*] [*ICAO location identifier*] (ICLI)
**LFI** ............ Hampton, VA [*Location identifier*] [*FAA*] (FAAL)
**LFI** ............ Last Frame Indicator
**LFI** ............ Let's Face It [*An association*] [*Later, AFLFI*] (EA)
**LFI** ............ Lifting Fan Intake [*Hovercraft*]
**LFI** ............ Linear Function Interpolator
**L-FI** ........... Live-Free, Incorporated [*An association*] (EA)
**LFI** ............ Low-Frequency Inductor
**LFIA** .......... Luminescence and Fluorescence Immunoassay [*Clinical chemistry*]
**LFIB** .......... Belves-Saint-Pardoux [*France*] [*ICAO location identifier*] (ICLI)
**LFIC** .......... Cross Corsen [*France*] [*ICAO location identifier*] (ICLI)
**LFICS** ........ Landing Force Integrated Communications System [*Marine Corps*]
**LFID** .......... Condom-Valence-Sur-Baise [*France*] [*ICAO location identifier*] (ICLI)
**LFIE** .......... Cross Etel [*France*] [*ICAO location identifier*] (ICLI)
**LFIF** .......... Saint-Afrique-Belmont [*France*] [*ICAO location identifier*] (ICLI)
**LFIG** .......... Cassagnes-Begonhes [*France*] [*ICAO location identifier*] (ICLI)
**LFIH** .......... Chalais [*France*] [*ICAO location identifier*] (ICLI)
**LFIINST** ... Life Fellow Imperial Institute [*British*] (ROG)
**LFIJ** .......... Cross Jobourg [*France*] [*ICAO location identifier*] (ICLI)
**LFIK** .......... Riberac-Saint-Aulaye [*France*] [*ICAO location identifier*] (ICLI)
**LFiI** ........... Listy Filologicke [*A publication*]
**LFIL** .......... Rion-Des-Landes [*France*] [*ICAO location identifier*] (ICLI)
**LFILIE** ...... Libera Federazione Italiana Lavoratori Industrie Estrattive [*Free Italian Federation of Workers in Mining Industries*]
**LFIM** ......... Low-Frequency Instruments and Measurement (MCD)
**LFIM** ......... Saint Gaudens Montrejeau [*France*] [*ICAO location identifier*] (ICLI)
**LFIN** .......... Cross Gris-Nez [*France*] [*ICAO location identifier*] (ICLI)
**LFIN** .......... Lincoln Financial Corp. [*NASDAQ symbol*] (NQ)
**LFINT** ....... Low-Frequency Intersection
**LFIP** .......... Peyresourde-Balestas [*France*] [*ICAO location identifier*] (ICLI)
**LFIPA** ........ Laminated Fiberglass Insulation Producers Association (EA)
**LFIR** .......... Revel-Montgey [*France*] [*ICAO location identifier*] (ICLI)
**LFIRSS** ...... Louis Finkelstein Institute for Religious and Social Studies (EA)
**LFISWB** .... Loyal, Free, Industrious Society of Wheelwrights and Blacksmiths [*A union*] [*British*]
**LFIT** .......... Toulouse-Bourg-Saint-Bernard [*France*] [*ICAO location identifier*] (ICLI)
**LFIV** .......... Vendays-Montalivet [*France*] [*ICAO location identifier*] (ICLI)
**LFIX** .......... Itxassou [*France*] [*ICAO location identifier*] (ICLI)
**LFIY** .......... Saint-Jean-D'Angely [*France*] [*ICAO location identifier*] (ICLI)
**LFJ** ............ Low-Frequency Jammer
**LFJG** ......... Cross La Garde [*France*] [*ICAO location identifier*] (ICLI)
**LFJV** ......... Low Frequency Jet Ventilation [*Medicine*]
**LFK** ........... Lufkin/Nacogdoches [*Texas*] [*Airport symbol*] (OAG)
**LFK** ........... Lufkin, TX [*Location identifier*] [*FAA*] (FAAL)
**LFKA** ......... Albertville [*France*] [*ICAO location identifier*] (ICLI)
**LFKB** ......... Bastia/Poretta, Corse [*France*] [*ICAO location identifier*] (ICLI)
**LFKC** ......... Calvi/Sainte-Catherine, Corse [*France*] [*ICAO location identifier*] (ICLI)
**LFKD** ......... Sollieres-Sardieres [*France*] [*ICAO location identifier*] (ICLI)
**LFKE** ......... Saint-Jean-En-Royans [*France*] [*ICAO location identifier*] (ICLI)
**LFKF** ......... Figari, Sud-Corse [*France*] [*ICAO location identifier*] (ICLI)
**LFKG** ......... Ghisonaccia-Alzitone [*France*] [*ICAO location identifier*] (ICLI)
**LFKH** ......... Saint-Jean-D'Avelanne [*France*] [*ICAO location identifier*] (ICLI)
**LFKJ** ......... Ajaccio/Campo Dell'Oro, Corse [*France*] [*ICAO location identifier*] (ICLI)
**LFKL** ......... Lyon-Brindas [*France*] [*ICAO location identifier*] (ICLI)
**LFKM** ......... Saint-Galmier [*France*] [*ICAO location identifier*] (ICLI)
**LFKO** ......... Propriano [*France*] [*ICAO location identifier*] (ICLI)
**LFKP** ......... La Tour-Du-Pin-Cessieu [*France*] [*ICAO location identifier*] (ICLI)
**LFKS** ......... Solenzara, Corse [*France*] [*ICAO location identifier*] (ICLI)
**LFKT** ......... Corte [*France*] [*ICAO location identifier*] (ICLI)
**LFKY** ......... Belley-Peyrieu [*France*] [*ICAO location identifier*] (ICLI)
**LFKZ** ......... Saint-Claude-Pratz [*France*] [*ICAO location identifier*] (ICLI)
**LFL** ............ LASER Flash Lamp
**LFL** ............ League for Liberty (EA)
**LFL** ............ Length of Flowering Period [*Botany*]
**LFL** ............ Lesbian Feminist Liberation (EA)
**LFL** ............ Libertarians for Life (EA)
**LFL** ............ Linear Field Line
**LFl** ............ Long Flashing Light [*Navigation signal*]
**LFL** ............ Lower Flammable Limit
**LFL** ............ Lutherans for Life (EA)
**LFLA** ......... Auxerre/Moneteau [*France*] [*ICAO location identifier*] (ICLI)
**LFLA** ......... Landing Force Logistics Afloat (MCD)
**LFlAA** ....... Laut-und Formenlehre des Aegyptisch-Aramaeisch [*A publication*] (BJA)
**LFLB** ......... Chambery/Aix-Les-Bains [*France*] [*ICAO location identifier*] (ICLI)
**LFLC** ......... Clermont-Ferrand/Aulnat [*France*] [*ICAO location identifier*] (ICLI)
**LFLD** ......... Bourges [*France*] [*ICAO location identifier*] (ICLI)
**LFLE** ......... Chambery/Challes-Les-Eaux [*France*] [*ICAO location identifier*] (ICLI)
**LFLEN** ...... Leaf Length [*Botany*]
**LFLF** ......... Orleans [*France*] [*ICAO location identifier*] (ICLI)
**LFLG** ......... Grenoble/Le Versoud [*France*] [*ICAO location identifier*] (ICLI)
**LFLGTH** ... Leaf Length [*Botany*]
**LFLH** ......... Chalon/Champforgeuil [*France*] [*ICAO location identifier*] (ICLI)
**LFLI** .......... Annemasse [*France*] [*ICAO location identifier*] (ICLI)
**LFLJ** .......... Courchevel [*France*] [*ICAO location identifier*] (ICLI)
**LFLK** ......... Oyonnax/Arbent [*France*] [*ICAO location identifier*] (ICLI)
**LFLL** .......... Lyon/Satolas [*France*] [*ICAO location identifier*] (ICLI)
**LFLM** ......... Macon/Charnay [*France*] [*ICAO location identifier*] (ICLI)
**LFLN** ......... Saint-Yan [*France*] [*ICAO location identifier*] (ICLI)
**LFLO** ......... Roanne/Renaison [*France*] [*ICAO location identifier*] (ICLI)
**LFLP** ......... Annecy/Meythet [*France*] [*ICAO location identifier*] (ICLI)

**LFLPU** ...... Libyan Federation of Labor and Professional Unions
**LFLQ** ......... Montelimar/Ancone [*France*] [*ICAO location identifier*] (ICLI)
**LFLR** ......... Saint-Rambert-D'Albon [*France*] [*ICAO location identifier*] (ICLI)
**LFLS** .......... Grenoble/Saint-Geoirs [*France*] [*ICAO location identifier*] (ICLI)
**LFLT** ......... Montlucon/Domerat [*France*] [*ICAO location identifier*] (ICLI)
**LFLU** ......... Valence/Chabeuil [*France*] [*ICAO location identifier*] (ICLI)
**LFLV** ......... Vichy/Charmeil [*France*] [*ICAO location identifier*] (ICLI)
**LFLW** ........ Aurillac [*France*] [*ICAO location identifier*] (ICLI)
**LFLWP** ...... Land Forces Logistics Working Party (MCD)
**LFLX** ......... Chateauroux/Deols [*France*] [*ICAO location identifier*] (ICLI)
**LFLY** ......... Lyon/Bron [*France*] [*ICAO location identifier*] (ICLI)
**LFLZ** ......... Feurs/Chambeon [*France*] [*ICAO location identifier*] (ICLI)
**LFM** ........... Franklin and Marshall College, Lancaster, PA [*OCLC symbol*] (OCLC)
**LFM** ........... Landing Force Manual [*Marine Corps, Navy*]
**LFM** ........... LASER Force Microscope
**LFM** ........... Launch First Motion
**LFM** ........... Limited Fine Mesh
**LFM** ........... Linear Feet per Minute
**LFM** ........... Linear Frequency Modulation (CAAL)
**LFM** ........... Local File Manager
**LFM** ........... Loss Frequency Method [*Insurance*]
**LFM** ........... Low-Field Magnetometer [*Instrumentation*]
**LFM** ........... Low-Frequency Magnetic [*Field*]
**LFM** ........... Low-Frequency Modulation
**LFM** ........... Low-Powered Fan Marker (MUGU)
**LFM** ........... Lower Figure of Merit
**LFM** ........... Lubrecht Forest [*Montana*] [*Seismograph station code, US Geological Survey*] [*Closed*] (SEIS)
**LFMA** ......... Aix-Les-Milles [*France*] [*ICAO location identifier*] (ICLI)
**LFMA** ......... Laminated Foil Manufacturers' Association [*Defunct*]
**LFMB** ......... Aix-En-Provence [*France*] [*ICAO location identifier*] (ICLI)
**LFMC** ......... Le Luc/Le Cannet [*France*] [*ICAO location identifier*] (ICLI)
**LFMD** ......... Cannes/Mandelieu [*France*] [*ICAO location identifier*] (ICLI)
**LFME** ......... Nimes/Courbessac [*France*] [*ICAO location identifier*] (ICLI)
**LFMER** ...... Lovelace Foundation for Medical Education and Research [*Reorganized to form Lovelace Medical Foundation and Lovelace Biomedical and Environmental Research Institute*] (MCD)
**LFMF** ......... Fayence [*France*] [*ICAO location identifier*] (ICLI)
**LF/MF** ....... Low Frequency, Medium Frequency
**LFMG** ......... La Montagne Noire [*France*] [*ICAO location identifier*] (ICLI)
**LFMH** ......... Saint-Etienne/Boutheon [*France*] [*ICAO location identifier*] (ICLI)
**LFMI** .......... Istres/Le Tube [*France*] [*ICAO location identifier*] (ICLI)
**LFMI** .......... Lasers for Medicine, Incorporated [*NASDAQ symbol*] (NQ)
**LFMJ** ......... Nice/Mont Agel [*France*] [*ICAO location identifier*] (ICLI)
**LFMK** ......... Carcassonne/Salvaza [*France*] [*ICAO location identifier*] (ICLI)
**LFML** ......... Little Flower Mission League (EA)
**LFML** ......... Marseille/Marignane [*France*] [*ICAO location identifier*] (ICLI)
**LFMM** ........ Aix-En-Provence [*France*] [*ICAO location identifier*] (ICLI)
**LFMN** ........ Nice/Cote D'Azur [*France*] [*ICAO location identifier*] (ICLI)
**LFMO** ........ Orange/Caritat [*France*] [*ICAO location identifier*] (ICLI)
**LFMOP** ...... Linear Frequency Modulation on Pulse (MCD)
**LFMP** ......... Perpignan/Rivesaltes [*France*] [*ICAO location identifier*] (ICLI)
**LFMQ** ........ Le Castellet [*France*] [*ICAO location identifier*] (ICLI)
**LFMR** ......... Barcelonnette/Saint-Pons [*France*] [*ICAO location identifier*] (ICLI)
**LFMR** ......... Low-Frequency Microwave Radiometer
**LFMS** ......... Ales/Deaux [*France*] [*ICAO location identifier*] (ICLI)
**LFMS** ......... Laminated Ferrite Memory System (MCD)
**LFMT** ......... Montpellier/Frejorgues [*France*] [*ICAO location identifier*] (ICLI)
**LFMU** ......... Beziers/Vias [*France*] [*ICAO location identifier*] (ICLI)
**LFMV** ......... Avignon/Caumont [*France*] [*ICAO location identifier*] (ICLI)
**LFMW** ........ Castelnaudary/Villeneuve [*France*] [*ICAO location identifier*] (ICLI)
**LFMX** ......... Chateau-Arnoux/Saint-Auban [*France*] [*ICAO location identifier*] (ICLI)
**LFMY** ......... Salon [*France*] [*ICAO location identifier*] (ICLI)
**LFMZ** ......... Lezignan-Corbieres [*France*] [*ICAO location identifier*] (ICLI)
**LFN** ........... Logical File Name
**LFN** ........... Logical File Number
**LFN** ........... Louisburg, NC [*Location identifier*] [*FAA*] (FAAL)
**LFNA** ......... Gap/Tallard [*France*] [*ICAO location identifier*] (ICLI)
**LFNB** ......... Mende/Brenoux [*France*] [*ICAO location identifier*] (ICLI)
**LFNC** ......... Mont-Dauphin/Saint-Crepin [*France*] [*ICAO location identifier*] (ICLI)
**LFND** ......... Pont-Saint-Esprit [*France*] [*ICAO location identifier*] (ICLI)
**LFNE** ......... Salon/Eyguieres [*France*] [*ICAO location identifier*] (ICLI)
**LFNF** ......... Vinon [*France*] [*ICAO location identifier*] (ICLI)
**LFNG** ......... Montpellier/L'Or [*France*] [*ICAO location identifier*] (ICLI)
**LFNGFT** ... Landing Force Naval Gunfire Team
**LFNH** ......... Carpentras [*France*] [*ICAO location identifier*] (ICLI)
**LFNI** .......... Conqueyrac [*France*] [*ICAO location identifier*] (ICLI)
**LFNJ** .......... Aspres-Sur-Buech [*France*] [*ICAO location identifier*] (ICLI)
**LFNK** ......... Vars-Les-Crosses-Et-Les-Tronches [*France*] [*ICAO location identifier*] (ICLI)
**LFNL** ......... Saint-Martin-De-Londres [*France*] [*ICAO location identifier*] (ICLI)
**LFNM** ........ La Mole [*France*] [*ICAO location identifier*] (ICLI)
**LFNO** ........ Florac-Sainte-Enimie [*France*] [*ICAO location identifier*] (ICLI)
**LFNP** ......... Pezenas-Nizas [*France*] [*ICAO location identifier*] (ICLI)
**LFNQ** ........ Mont-Louis-La-Quillane [*France*] [*ICAO location identifier*] (ICLI)
**LFNR** ......... Berre-La-Fare [*France*] [*ICAO location identifier*] (ICLI)
**LFNS** ......... Low-Frequency Navigation System (NG)
**LFNS** ......... Sisteron-Theze [*France*] [*ICAO location identifier*] (ICLI)
**LFNT** ......... Avignon-Pujaut [*France*] [*ICAO location identifier*] (ICLI)
**LFNT** ......... Low-Frequency Intersection (FAAC)
**LFNU** ......... Uzes [*France*] [*ICAO location identifier*] (ICLI)
**LFNV** ......... Valreas-Visan [*France*] [*ICAO location identifier*] (ICLI)
**LFNW** ........ Puivert [*France*] [*ICAO location identifier*] (ICLI)
**LFNX** ......... Bedarieux-La-Tour-Sur-Orb [*France*] [*ICAO location identifier*] (ICLI)
**LFNY** ......... Saint-Etienne-En-Devoluy [*France*] [*ICAO location identifier*] (ICLI)
**LFNZ** ......... Le Mazet-De-Romanin [*France*] [*ICAO location identifier*] (ICLI)
**LFO** ........... Low-Frequency Oscillator
**LFOA** ......... Avord [*France*] [*ICAO location identifier*] (ICLI)
**LFOB** ......... Beauvais/Tille [*France*] [*ICAO location identifier*] (ICLI)
**LFOC** ......... Crateaudun [*France*] [*ICAO location identifier*] (ICLI)
**LFOC** ......... Landing Force Operation Center [*Navy*] (CAAL)
**LFOC** ......... Lea-Francis Owners Club [*South Mimms, Hertfordshire, England*] (EAIO)
**LFOD** ......... Saumur/Saint-Florent [*France*] [*ICAO location identifier*] (ICLI)
**LFOE** ......... Evreux/Fauville [*France*] [*ICAO location identifier*] (ICLI)
**LFOF** ......... Alencon/Valframbert [*France*] [*ICAO location identifier*] (ICLI)
**LFOG** ......... Flers/Saint-Paul [*France*] [*ICAO location identifier*] (ICLI)
**LFOH** ......... Le Havre/Octeville [*France*] [*ICAO location identifier*] (ICLI)
**LFOI** .......... Abbeville [*France*] [*ICAO location identifier*] (ICLI)
**LFOJ** .......... Orleans/Bricy [*France*] [*ICAO location identifier*] (ICLI)
**LFOK** ......... Chalons/Vatry [*France*] [*ICAO location identifier*] (ICLI)
**LFOL** ......... L'Aigle/Saint-Michel [*France*] [*ICAO location identifier*] (ICLI)
**LFOM** ........ Lessay [*France*] [*ICAO location identifier*] (ICLI)
**LFOM** ........ Low-Frequency Outer Marker (MSA)
**LFON** ......... Dreux/Vernouillet [*France*] [*ICAO location identifier*] (ICLI)
**LFOO** ......... Les Sables D'Olonne/Talmont [*France*] [*ICAO location identifier*] (ICLI)
**LFOP** ......... Landing and Ferry Operations Panel [*NASA*] (NASA)
**LFOP** ......... Rouen/Boos [*France*] [*ICAO location identifier*] (ICLI)
**LFOQ** ......... Blois/Le Breuil [*France*] [*ICAO location identifier*] (ICLI)
**LFOR** ......... Chartres/Champhol [*France*] [*ICAO location identifier*] (ICLI)
**LFORM** ...... Landing Force Operational Reserve Material [*Navy*] (NVT)
**LFOS** ......... Launch and Flight Operations System
**LFOS** ......... Saint-Valery/Vittefleur [*France*] [*ICAO location identifier*] (ICLI)
**LFOT** ......... Tours/Saint-Symphorien [*France*] [*ICAO location identifier*] (ICLI)
**LFOU** ......... Cholet/Le Pontreau [*France*] [*ICAO location identifier*] (ICLI)
**LFOV** ......... Laval/Entrammes [*France*] [*ICAO location identifier*] (ICLI)
**LFOW** ........ Saint-Quentin/Roupy [*France*] [*ICAO location identifier*] (ICLI)
**LFOX** ......... Etampes/Mondesir [*France*] [*ICAO location identifier*] (ICLI)
**LFOY** ......... Le Havre/Saint-Romain [*France*] [*ICAO location identifier*] (ICLI)
**LFOZ** ......... Orleans/Saint-Denis-De-L'Hotel [*France*] [*ICAO location identifier*] (ICLI)
**LFP** ........... Labor-Force Participation
**LFP** ........... Large Flat Plate
**LFP** ........... Late Flight Plan
**LFP** ........... Left Frontoposterior [*A fetal position*] [*Obstetrics*]
**LFP** ........... LFP Holdings, Inc. [*Toronto Stock Exchange symbol*]
**LFP** ........... Liberala Folkpartiet [*Liberal People's Party*] [*Finland*] [*Political party*] (PPE)
**LFP** ........... Libraries for Prisons [*An association*] (EA)
**LFP** ........... Listen for Pleasure [*Audio books*]
**LFP** ........... Livestock Feed Program
**LFPA** ......... Persan-Beaumont [*France*] [*ICAO location identifier*] (ICLI)
**LFPAG** ...... Live Firing Program Analysis Group [*Military*] (CAAL)
**LFPB** ......... Paris/Le Bourget [*France*] [*ICAO location identifier*] (ICLI)
**LFPC** ......... Creil [*France*] [*ICAO location identifier*] (ICLI)
**LFPD** ......... Bernay/Saint-Martin [*France*] [*ICAO location identifier*] (ICLI)
**LFPE** ......... Meaux/Esbly [*France*] [*ICAO location identifier*] (ICLI)
**LFPEF** ....... Low-Frequency Pulsed Electromagnetic Field
**LFPER** ....... Leaf Persistence [*Botany*]
**LFPF** ......... Beynes/Thiverval [*France*] [*ICAO location identifier*] (ICLI)
**LFPG** ......... Paris/Charles-De-Gaulle [*France*] [*ICAO location identifier*] (ICLI)

**LFPH**......... Chelles/Le Pin [*France*] [*ICAO location identifier*] (ICLI)
**LFPI**.......... Paris/Issy-Les-Moulineaux [*France*] [*ICAO location identifier*] (ICLI)
**LFPJ**.......... Taverny [*France*] [*ICAO location identifier*] (ICLI)
**LFPK**......... Coulommiers/Voisins [*France*] [*ICAO location identifier*] (ICLI)
**LFPL**.......... Lewis Flight Propulsion Laboratory [*NASA*]
**LFPL**.......... Lognes/Emerainville [*France*] [*ICAO location identifier*] (ICLI)
**LFPM**........ Melun/Villaroche [*France*] [*ICAO location identifier*] (ICLI)
**LFPN**......... Toussus-Le-Noble [*France*] [*ICAO location identifier*] (ICLI)
**LFPO**......... Paris/Orly [*France*] [*ICAO location identifier*] (ICLI)
**LFPP**.......... Le Plessis-Belleville [*France*] [*ICAO location identifier*] (ICLI)
**LFPQ**......... Fontenay-Tresigny [*France*] [*ICAO location identifier*] (ICLI)
**LFPR**......... Guayancourt [*France*] [*ICAO location identifier*] (ICLI)
**LFPRL**....... Lewis Flight Propulsion Research Laboratory [*NASA*] (MUGU)
**LFPS**.......... Licentiate of the Faculty of Physicians and Surgeons [*British*]
**LFPS**.......... Low-Frequency Phase Shifter [*Telecommunications*]
**LFPS**.......... Paris [*France*] [*ICAO location identifier*] (ICLI)
**LFPSG**....... Licentiate of the Faculty of Physicians and Surgeons, Glasgow (ROG)
**LFPT**......... Pontoise/Cormeilles-En-Vexin [*France*] [*ICAO location identifier*] (ICLI)
**LFPU**......... Moret/Episy [*France*] [*ICAO location identifier*] (ICLI)
**LFPUB**...... Leaf Pubescence [*Botany*]
**LFPV**......... Villacoublay/Velizy [*France*] [*ICAO location identifier*] (ICLI)
**LFPW**........ Low-Frequency Plasma Wave
**LFPW**........ Paris, Centre Meteorologique [*France*] [*ICAO location identifier*] (ICLI)
**LFPX**......... Chavenay/Villepreux [*France*] [*ICAO location identifier*] (ICLI)
**LFPY**......... Bretigny-Sur-Orge [*France*] [*ICAO location identifier*] (ICLI)
**LFPZ**......... Saint-Cyre-L'Ecole [*France*] [*ICAO location identifier*] (ICLI)
**LFQ**........... Light Foot Quantizer
**LFQ**........... Limited Flying Quality
**LFQ**........... Literature/Film Quarterly [*A publication*]
**LFQA**......... Reims/Prunay [*France*] [*ICAO location identifier*] (ICLI)
**LFQB**......... Troyes/Barberey [*France*] [*ICAO location identifier*] (ICLI)
**LFQC**......... Luneville/Croismare [*France*] [*ICAO location identifier*] (ICLI)
**LFQD**......... Arras/Roclincourt [*France*] [*ICAO location identifier*] (ICLI)
**LFQE**......... Etain/Rouvres [*France*] [*ICAO location identifier*] (ICLI)
**LFQF**......... Autun/Bellevue [*France*] [*ICAO location identifier*] (ICLI)
**LFQG**......... Nevers/Fourchambault [*France*] [*ICAO location identifier*] (ICLI)
**LFQH**......... Chatillon-Sur-Seine [*France*] [*ICAO location identifier*] (ICLI)
**LFQI**.......... Cambrai/Epinoy [*France*] [*ICAO location identifier*] (ICLI)
**LFQJ**......... Maubeuge/Elesmes [*France*] [*ICAO location identifier*] (ICLI)
**LFQK**......... Chalons/Ecury-Sur-Coole [*France*] [*ICAO location identifier*] (ICLI)
**LFQL**......... Lens/Benifontaine [*France*] [*ICAO location identifier*] (ICLI)
**LFQM**........ Besancon-La-Veze [*France*] [*ICAO location identifier*] (ICLI)
**LFQN**......... Saint-Omer/Wizernes [*France*] [*ICAO location identifier*] (ICLI)
**LFQO**......... Lille/Marcq-En-Baroeul [*France*] [*ICAO location identifier*] (ICLI)
**LFQP**......... Phalsbourg/Bourscheid [*France*] [*ICAO location identifier*] (ICLI)
**LFQQ**......... Lille/Lesquin [*France*] [*ICAO location identifier*] (ICLI)
**LFQR**......... Romilly-Sur-Seine [*France*] [*ICAO location identifier*] (ICLI)
**LFQS**......... Vitry-En-Artois [*France*] [*ICAO location identifier*] (ICLI)
**LFQT**......... Merville/Calonne [*France*] [*ICAO location identifier*] (ICLI)
**LFQU**......... Sarre-Union [*France*] [*ICAO location identifier*] (ICLI)
**LFQV**......... Charleville/Mezieres [*France*] [*ICAO location identifier*] (ICLI)
**LFQW**........ Vesoul-Frotey [*France*] [*ICAO location identifier*] (ICLI)
**LFQY**......... Saverne-Steinbourg [*France*] [*ICAO location identifier*] (ICLI)
**LFQZ**......... Dieuze-Gueblange [*France*] [*ICAO location identifier*] (ICLI)
**L FR**.......... Franc [*Monetary unit*] [*Luxembourg*]
**LFR**........... Inshore Fire Support Ship [*Navy symbol*]
**LFR**........... La Fria [*Venezuela*] [*Airport symbol*] (OAG)
**LFR**........... Laboratory Facilities Request (MCD)
**LFR**........... Laminar-Flow Reactor [*Engineering*]
**LFr**........... Langue Francaise [*A publication*]
**L Fr**.......... Law French (DLA)
**LFR**........... Linear Flow Reactor [*Chemical engineering*]
**LFR**........... Low-Flux Reactor
**LFR**........... Low-Frequency Range (MCD)
**LFR**........... Lowest Fare Routing [*Travel industry*]
**LFr**........... Saint Mary Parish Library, Franklin, LA [*Library symbol*] [*Library of Congress*] (LCLS)
**LFRA**......... Angers/Avrille [*France*] [*ICAO location identifier*] (ICLI)
**LFRA**......... League of Federal Recreation Associations (EA)
**LFRA**......... Leatherhead Food Research Association [*British*] (ARC)
**LF(RA)**...... Listy Filologicke. Supplement. Revue Archeologique [*A publication*]
**LFRAP**...... Long Feeder Route Analysis Program [*Bell System*]
**LFRAPI**..... Life Fellow of the Royal Australian Planning Institute
**LFRB**......... Brest/Guipavas [*France*] [*ICAO location identifier*] (ICLI)
**LFRC**......... Cherbourg/Maupertus [*France*] [*ICAO location identifier*] (ICLI)
**LFRC**......... Latex Foam Rubber Council [*Defunct*] (EA)
**LFRC**......... Laurentian Forest Research Center [*Canadian Forestry Service*] [*Research center*] (RCD)
**LFRD**......... Dinard/Pleurtuit-Saint-Malo [*France*] [*ICAO location identifier*] (ICLI)
**LFRD**......... Lot Fraction Reliability Deviation [*Quality control*]
**LFRE**......... La Baule/Escoublac [*France*] [*ICAO location identifier*] (ICLI)
**LFRF**......... Granville [*France*] [*ICAO location identifier*] (ICLI)
**LFRG**......... Deauville/Saint-Gatien [*France*] [*ICAO location identifier*] (ICLI)
**LFRH**......... Lorient/Lann-Bihoue [*France*] [*ICAO location identifier*] (ICLI)
**LFRI**.......... La Roche-Sur-Yon/Les Ajoncs [*France*] [*ICAO location identifier*] (ICLI)
**LFRJ**.......... Landivisiau [*France*] [*ICAO location identifier*] (ICLI)
**LFRK**......... Caen/Carpiquet [*France*] [*ICAO location identifier*] (ICLI)
**LFRL**......... Lanveoc/Poulmic [*France*] [*ICAO location identifier*] (ICLI)
**LFRM**........ Le Mans/Arnage [*France*] [*ICAO location identifier*] (ICLI)
**LFRN**......... Rennes/Saint-Jacques [*France*] [*ICAO location identifier*] (ICLI)
**LFRO**......... Lannion/Servel [*France*] [*ICAO location identifier*] (ICLI)
**L Front**...... Literaturen Front [*A publication*]
**LFRP**......... Ploermel-Loyat [*France*] [*ICAO location identifier*] (ICLI)
**LFRQ**......... Quimper/Pluguffan [*France*] [*ICAO location identifier*] (ICLI)
**LFRR**......... Brest [*France*] [*ICAO location identifier*] (ICLI)
**LFRR**......... Low-Frequency Radio Range (MCD)
**LFRS**......... Nantes/Chateau Bougon [*France*] [*ICAO location identifier*] (ICLI)
**LFRT**......... Saint-Brieuc Armor [*France*] [*ICAO location identifier*] (ICLI)
**LFrtW**........ Washington Parish Library, Franklinton, LA [*Library symbol*] [*Library of Congress*] (LCLS)
**LFRU**......... Morlaix/Ploujean [*France*] [*ICAO location identifier*] (ICLI)
**LFRV**......... Vannes/Meucon [*France*] [*ICAO location identifier*] (ICLI)
**LFRW**........ Avranches/Le Val Saint-Pere [*France*] [*ICAO location identifier*] (ICLI)
**LFRX**......... Brest [*France*] [*ICAO location identifier*] (ICLI)
**LFRY**......... Cherbourg [*France*] [*ICAO location identifier*] (ICLI)
**LFRZ**......... Saint-Nazaire/Montoir [*France*] [*ICAO location identifier*] (ICLI)
**LFS**........... Amphibious Fire Support Ship [*Navy symbol*]
**LFS**........... Labour Force Survey [*Canada*]
**LFS**........... Lancaster Finishing School [*British military*] (DMA)
**LFS**........... LASER Fluorescence Spectroscopy
**LFS**........... Launch Facility Simulator
**LFS**........... League of Filipino Students
**LFS**........... Leather Finishers' Society [*A union*] [*British*]
**LFS**........... Lettres Francaises [*A publication*]
**LFS**........... Libertarian Futurist Society (EA)
**LFS**........... Licentiate of the Faculty of Architects and Surveyors [*British*] (DBQ)
**LFS**........... Liquid Flow System
**LFS**........... Liver Function Series [*Clinical chemistry*]
**LFS**........... Local Format Storage
**LFS**........... Logic Fault Simulator [*Data processing*]
**LFS**........... Logistics Feasibility System
**LFS**........... Logistics/Ferry Station
**LFS**........... Loop Feedback Signal
**LFSA**......... Besancon/Thise [*France*] [*ICAO location identifier*] (ICLI)
**LFSA**......... First Federal Savings & Loan Association of Lenawee County [*NASDAQ symbol*] (NQ)
**LFSA**......... Logistical Force Structure Assessment (MCD)
**LFSB**......... Bale/Mulhouse [*France/Switzerland*] [*ICAO location identifier*] (ICLI)
**LFSC**......... Colmar/Meyenheim [*France*] [*ICAO location identifier*] (ICLI)
**LfSC**.......... Librarians for Social Change. Journal [*A publication*]
**LFSC**......... Life Sciences, Inc. [*NASDAQ symbol*] (NQ)
**LFSC**......... Limited First-Strike Capability
**LFSC**......... Louisville Fear Survey for Children [*Psychology*]
**LFSCWW**... Live Food Singles Club - World Wide (EA)
**LFSD**......... Dijon/Longvic [*France*] [*ICAO location identifier*] (ICLI)
**LFSE**......... Epinal/Dogneville [*France*] [*ICAO location identifier*] (ICLI)
**LFSF**......... Metz/Frescaty [*France*] [*ICAO location identifier*] (ICLI)
**LFSG**......... Epinal/Mirecourt [*France*] [*ICAO location identifier*] (ICLI)
**LFSH**......... Haguenau [*France*] [*ICAO location identifier*] (ICLI)
**LFSI**.......... Saint-Dizier/Robinson [*France*] [*ICAO location identifier*] (ICLI)
**LFSJ**.......... Sedan/Douzy [*France*] [*ICAO location identifier*] (ICLI)
**LFSK**......... Vitry-Le-Francois/Vauclerc [*France*] [*ICAO location identifier*] (ICLI)
**LFSL**.......... Toul/Rosieres [*France*] [*ICAO location identifier*] (ICLI)
**LFSM**........ Montbeliard/Courcelles [*France*] [*ICAO location identifier*] (ICLI)
**LFSMT/S**... Liquid Fuel Systems Maintenance Technician/Specialist [*Aerospace*] (AAG)
**LFSN**......... Nancy/Essey [*France*] [*ICAO location identifier*] (ICLI)
**LFSO**......... Nancy/Ochey [*France*] [*ICAO location identifier*] (ICLI)
**LFSP**......... Pontarlier [*France*] [*ICAO location identifier*] (ICLI)
**LFSQ**......... Belfort/Fontaine [*France*] [*ICAO location identifier*] (ICLI)

**LFSR** ......... Linear Feedback Shift Register
**LFSR** ......... Reims/Champagne [*France*] [*ICAO location identifier*] (ICLI)
**LFSS** ......... Landing Force Support Ship [*Navy*]
**LFSS** ......... Launch Facility Security System [*NASA*] (KSC)
**LFST** ......... Largest Feasible Steerable Telescope
**LFST** ......... Strasbourg/Entzheim [*France*] [*ICAO location identifier*] (ICLI)
**LFSU** ......... Rolampont [*France*] [*ICAO location identifier*] (ICLI)
**LFSV** ......... Landing Force Support Vehicle (MCD)
**LFSV** ......... Pont-Saint-Vincent [*France*] [*ICAO location identifier*] (ICLI)
**LFSW** ......... Epernay/Plivot [*France*] [*ICAO location identifier*] (ICLI)
**LFSW** ......... Landing Force Support Weapon
**LFSX** ......... Luxeuil/Saint-Sauveur [*France*] [*ICAO location identifier*] (ICLI)
**LFSY** ......... Chaumont-La Vendue [*France*] [*ICAO location identifier*] (ICLI)
**LFSZ** ......... Vittel/Champ De Courses [*France*] [*ICAO location identifier*] (ICLI)
**LFT** ......... Ladd-Franklin Theory [*Color vision*]
**LFT** ......... Lafayette [*Louisiana*] [*Airport symbol*] (OAG)
**LFT** ......... Lafayette, LA [*Location identifier*] [*FAA*] (FAAL)
**LFT** ......... Laminar Flow Torch [*For plasma generation*]
**LFT** ......... LASER Flash Tube
**LFT** ......... Late Finish Time
**LFT** ......... Latex Fixation Test [*Medicine*]
**LFT** ......... Latex Flocculation Test [*Clinical chemistry*]
**LFT** ......... Launch Facility Trainer
**LFT** ......... Leaflet (ADA)
**LFT** ......... Leap-Frog Test
**LFT** ......... Left Frontotransverse [*A fetal position*] [*Obstetrics*]
**LFT** ......... Ley Federal de Trabajo [*Mexico*] [*A publication*]
**LFT** ......... Lifetime Corp. [*NYSE symbol*] (SPSG)
**LFT** ......... Lifting (MSA)
**LFT** ......... Ligand-Field Theory [*Physical chemistry*]
**LFT** ......... Light Fire Team [*Military*] (CINC)
**LFT** ......... Linear Flash Tube
**LFT** ......... Linear Foot (ADA)
**LFT** ......... Live Fire Test
**LFT** ......... Liver Function Test [*Medicine*]
**LFT** ......... Low-Frequency Transduction
**LFTC** ......... Landing Force Training Command [*Navy*] (NVT)
**LFTC** ......... Toulon [*France*] [*ICAO location identifier*] (ICLI)
**LFTDWP** .. Land Force Tactical Doctrine Working Party [*NASA*] (MCD)
**LFTF** ......... Cuers/Pierrefeu [*France*] [*ICAO location identifier*] (ICLI)
**LFTH** ......... Hyeres/Le Palyvestre [*France*] [*ICAO location identifier*] (ICLI)
**LFTM** ......... Lifetime Communities [*NASDAQ symbol*] (NQ)
**LFTN** ......... La Grand'Combe [*France*] [*ICAO location identifier*] (ICLI)
**LFtp** ......... Library Program, Cataloging Department, Recreation Service, Fort Polk, LA [*Library symbol*] [*Library of Congress*] (LCLS)
**LFTR** ......... Toulon/Saint-Mandrier [*France*] [*ICAO location identifier*] (ICLI)
**LFTS** ......... Toulon [*France*] [*ICAO location identifier*] (ICLI)
**LFTU** ......... Frejus/Saint-Raphael [*France*] [*ICAO location identifier*] (ICLI)
**LFTU** ......... Landing Force Training Unit [*Marine Corps*]
**LFTW** ......... Nimes/Garons [*France*] [*ICAO location identifier*] (ICLI)
**LFU** ......... Least Frequently Used [*Data processing*]
**LFU** ......... Lunar Flying Unit [*NASA*]
**LFV** ......... Lassa-Fever Virus
**LFV** ......... Low-Frequency Vibration
**LFV** ......... Lunar Flying Vehicle [*NASA*]
**LFV** ......... Northhampton, MA [*Location identifier*] [*FAA*] (FAAL)
**LFVM** ......... Miquelon [*France*] [*ICAO location identifier*] (ICLI)
**LFVO** ......... Library Foundation for Voluntary Organizations [*Defunct*] (EA)
**LFVP** ......... Saint-Pierre, Saint-Pierre-Et Miquelon [*France*] [*ICAO location identifier*] (ICLI)
**LFW** ......... Lome [*Togo*] [*Airport symbol*] (OAG)
**LFW** ......... Looking for Work
**LFWB** ......... Sccom Sud-Ouest [*France*] [*ICAO location identifier*] (ICLI)
**LFWID** ...... Length of Leaf at Widest Portion [*Botany*]
**LFXA** ......... Amberieu [*France*] [*ICAO location identifier*] (ICLI)
**LFXB** ......... Saintes/Thenac [*France*] [*ICAO location identifier*] (ICLI)
**LFXC** ......... Contrexeville [*France*] [*ICAO location identifier*] (ICLI)
**LFXD** ......... Doullens/Lucheux [*France*] [*ICAO location identifier*] (ICLI)
**LFXE** ......... Camp De Mourmelon [*France*] [*ICAO location identifier*] (ICLI)
**LFXF** ......... Limoges/Romanet [*France*] [*ICAO location identifier*] (ICLI)
**LFXG** ......... Camp De Bitche [*France*] [*ICAO location identifier*] (ICLI)
**LFXH** ......... Camp Du Valdahon [*France*] [*ICAO location identifier*] (ICLI)
**LFXI** ......... Apt/Saint-Christol [*France*] [*ICAO location identifier*] (ICLI)
**LFXJ** ......... Bordeaux [*France*] [*ICAO location identifier*] (ICLI)
**LFXK** ......... Camp De Suippes [*France*] [*ICAO location identifier*] (ICLI)
**LFXL** ......... Mailly-Le-Camp [*France*] [*ICAO location identifier*] (ICLI)
**LFXM** ......... Mourmelon [*France*] [*ICAO location identifier*] (ICLI)
**LFXN** ......... Narbonne [*France*] [*ICAO location identifier*] (ICLI)
**LFXO** ......... Tours/Cinq-Mars La Pile [*France*] [*ICAO location identifier*] (ICLI)
**LFXP** ......... Camp De Sissonne [*France*] [*ICAO location identifier*] (ICLI)
**LFXQ** ......... Camp De Coetquidan [*France*] [*ICAO location identifier*] (ICLI)
**LFXR** ......... Rochefort/Soubise [*France*] [*ICAO location identifier*] (ICLI)
**LFXS** ......... Camp De La Courtine [*France*] [*ICAO location identifier*] (ICLI)
**LFXT** ......... Camp De Caylus [*France*] [*ICAO location identifier*] (ICLI)
**LFXU** ......... Les Mureaux [*France*] [*ICAO location identifier*] (ICLI)
**LFXV** ......... Lyon/Mont-Verdun [*France*] [*ICAO location identifier*] (ICLI)
**LFXW** ......... Camp Du Larzac [*France*] [*ICAO location identifier*] (ICLI)
**LFYA** ......... Drachenbronn [*France*] [*ICAO location identifier*] (ICLI)
**LFYD** ......... Damblain [*France*] [*ICAO location identifier*] (ICLI)
**LFYF** ......... Centre Meteorologique de Concentration et de Diffusion, French Air Force [*France*] [*ICAO location identifier*] (ICLI)
**LFYG** ......... Cambrai/Niergnies [*France*] [*ICAO location identifier*] (ICLI)
**LFYH** ......... Broye-Les-Pesmes [*France*] [*ICAO location identifier*] (ICLI)
**LFYL** ......... Lure/Malbouhans [*France*] [*ICAO location identifier*] (ICLI)
**LFYM** ......... Marigny-Le-Grand [*France*] [*ICAO location identifier*] (ICLI)
**LFYO** ......... Villacoublay [*France*] [*ICAO location identifier*] (ICLI)
**LFYR** ......... Romorantin/Pruniers [*France*] [*ICAO location identifier*] (ICLI)
**LFYS** ......... Sainte-Leocadie [*France*] [*ICAO location identifier*] (ICLI)
**LFYT** ......... Saint-Simon/Clastres [*France*] [*ICAO location identifier*] (ICLI)
**LFYX** ......... Paris [*France*] [*ICAO location identifier*] (ICLI)
**LFZ** ......... Laminar Flow Zone
**LG** ......... Guidotti & C. [*Italy*] [*Research code symbol*]
**LG** ......... La Geographie [*A publication*]
**LG** ......... Laban Guild [*Formerly, LAMG*] (EA)
**LG** ......... Laclede Gas Co. [*NYSE symbol*] (SPSG)
**LG** ......... Lagoon [*Maps and charts*] (ROG)
**L/G** ......... Land Grant (DLA)
**LG** ......... Landed Gentry
**LG** ......... Landgericht [*Regional Court*] [*German*] (ILCA)
**LG** ......... Landing Gear [*Aircraft*]
**LG** ......... Landing Ground [*Navy*]
**LG** ......... Landing Group [*Navy*] (NVT)
**Lg** ......... Language [*A publication*]
**LG** ......... Language [*Online database field identifier*]
**LG** ......... Large
**LG** ......... Large Grain
**LG** ......... Lateral Gastrocnemius
**L & G** ......... Latina et Graeca [*A publication*]
**LG** ......... Launcher Group [*Army*]
**LG** ......... Law Glossary (DLA)
**LG** ......... Leathercraft Guild (EA)
**LG** ......... Left Gluteus [*Medicine*]
**LG** ......... Left Guard [*Football*]
**LG** ......... Leichtgeschuetz [*Light gun for airborne operations*] [*German military - World War II*]
**LG** ......... Length (MSA)
**LG** ......... Level Gauge
**LG** ......... Lewis Gun
**LG** ......... Lieutenant General [*British*] (ROG)
**LG** ......... Life Guards [*Military unit*] [*British*]
**LG** ......... Light Green
**LG** ......... Light Gun
**LG** ......... Line Generator [*Data processing*]
**LG** ......... Linear Gate
**LG** ......... Linguogingival [*Dentistry*]
**LG** ......... Lining
**LG** ......... Liquid Gas
**LG** ......... Literary Guide [*A publication*]
**LG** ......... [*The*] Literary Guild
**LG** ......... Literaturnaya Gazeta [*A publication*]
**LG** ......... Little Guides [*A publication*]
**LG** ......... Local Government (ADA)
**LG** ......... Loganiar Ltd. [*British*]
**LG** ......... London Gazette [*A publication*]
**LG** ......... Long (KSC)
**LG** ......... Longold Resources, Inc. [*Vancouver Stock Exchange symbol*]
**LG** ......... Longwood Gardens [*Kennett Square, PA*]
**LG** ......... Loop Gain
**LG** ......... Low German [*Language, etc.*]
**LG** ......... Low Glucose [*Medicine*]
**LG** ......... Lumen Gentium [*Dogmatic Constitution on the Church*] [*Vatican II document*]
**LG** ......... Luxembourgoise de Navigation Aerienne [*LUXAIR*] [*Luxembourg airline*] [*ICAO designator*] (FAAC)
**LG** ......... Lymph Glands [*Medicine*]
**LGA** ......... Large for Gestational Age [*Pediatrics*]
**LGA** ......... LGA: Local Government Administration [*A publication*]
**LGA** ......... Light-Gun Amplifier
**LGA** ......... Local Government Administration
**LGA** ......... Local Government Area (ADA)
**LGA** ......... Local Government Audit [*British*]
**LgA** ......... Lodging Allowance [*British military*] (DMA)
**LGA** ......... Low-Gain Antenna
**LGA** ......... New York [*New York*] La Guardia [*Airport symbol*] (OAG)
**LGAC** ......... Athinai [*Greece*] [*ICAO location identifier*] (ICLI)

**LGACHP**... Local Government and Community Housing Program [*Australia*]
**LGAD**........ Andravida [*Greece*] [*ICAO location identifier*] (ICLI)
**LGAES**...... Lesbian and Gay Associated Engineers and Scientists [*Later, NOGLSTP*] (EA)
**LGAF**......... Light Ground-Attack Fighter
**LGAG**........ Agrinion [*Greece*] [*ICAO location identifier*] (ICLI)
**LGAL**......... Alexandroupolis [*Greece*] [*ICAO location identifier*] (ICLI)
**LGAM**....... Amphiali [*Greece*] [*ICAO location identifier*] (ICLI)
**LGAR**........ Ladies of the Grand Army of the Republic (EA)
**LGAS**......... Low-G Accelerometer System [*NASA*]
**LGAT**......... Athinai [*Greece*] [*ICAO location identifier*] (ICLI)
**LGATR**...... Local Government Appeals Tribunal Reports [*A publication*] (APTA)
**LGATR (NSW)**... Local Government Appeals Tribunal Reports (New South Wales) [*A publication*] (APTA)
**LGAX**........ Alexandria [*Greece*] [*ICAO location identifier*] (ICLI)
**L Gaz**.......... Law Gazette [*A publication*] (DLA)
**LGB**........... Landry-Guillain-Barre (Syndrome) [*Medicine*]
**LGB**........... LASER-Guided Bomb
**LGB**........... Lateral Geniculate Body
**LGB**........... Local Government Board
**LGB**........... Local Government Bulletin [*A publication*] (APTA)
**LGB**........... Long Beach [*California*] [*Airport symbol*] (OAG)
**LGB**........... Long Beach, CA [*Location identifier*] [*FAA*] (FAAL)
**LGBA**......... Lesbian and Gay Bands of America (EA)
**LGBBA3**.... Acta Botanica Horti Bucurestiensis [*A publication*]
**LGBCE**...... Local Government Boundary Commission for England
**LGBL**......... Nea Anghialos [*Greece*] [*ICAO location identifier*] (ICLI)
**LGBO**........ Local Government Board Office [*British*]
**LGBPM**..... Lesbian, Gay, and Bisexual People in Medicine (EA)
**LGC**........... La Grange, GA [*Location identifier*] [*FAA*] (FAAL)
**LGC**........... Laboratory of the Government Chemist [*Research center*] [*British*] (IRC)
**LGC**........... Lakewood Golf Course [*California*] [*Seismograph station code, US Geological Survey*] (SEIS)
**LGC**........... Large-Probe Gas Chromatograph [*NASA*]
**LGC**........... Launch Guidance Computer
**LGC**........... Laurentian Group Corp. [*Toronto Stock Exchange symbol*]
**LGC**........... Leafy Greens Council (EA)
**LGC**........... LM [*Lunar Module*] Guidance Computer [*NASA*]
**LGC**........... Local Government Center [*Database producer*] (EA)
**LGC**........... Local Government Chronicle [*1855*] [*A publication*] (DLA)
**LGC**........... Logic (MSA)
**LGC**........... Lord Great Chamberlain [*British*] [*A publication*] (DLA)
**LGC**........... Lorry with Gas Containers [*British*]
**LGC**........... Lunar Gas Chromatograph
**LGC**........... Lunar Geological Camera [*NASA*] (KSC)
**LGCA**........ Late Great Chevrolet Association (EA)
**LGCA**........ London Gregorian Choral Association
**LGCL**......... Licentiate of the Guild of Cleaners and Launderers [*British*] (DBQ)
**LGCP**......... Lexical-Graphical Composer Printer [*Photocomposition*]
**LGCPHW**... Lesbian and Gay Caucus of Public Health Workers (EA)
**LGd**............ Dorsal Lateral Geniculate Nucleus [*Also, dLGN*] [*Anatomy*]
**LGD**........... La Grande, OR [*Location identifier*] [*FAA*] (FAAL)
**LGD**........... Lambda Gamma Delta [*Society*]
**LGD**........... Large Group Display (MCD)
**LGD**........... Leaderless Group Discussion
**LGD**........... Low-Grade Dysplasia [*Medicine*]
**LGDA**........ National Lawn and Garden Distributors Association (EA)
**LGE**........... Food and Nonfood. Fachzeitschrift fuer Unternehmer und Fuhrungskrafte Moderner Grossformen in Lebensmittelhandel [*A publication*]
**LGE**........... Landing Ground, Emergency [*British military*] (DMA)
**LGE**........... Large (MSA)
**LGE**........... LEM [*Lunar Excursion Module*] Guidance Equipment [*NASA*] (KSC)
**LGE**........... LG & E Energy [*NYSE symbol*] (SPSG)
**LGE**........... Logic Gate Expander [*Data processing*]
**LGE**........... Lunar Geological Equipment [*NASA*]
**LGEAQ**..... Local Government Engineers Association of Queensland [*Australia*]
**LGEL**......... Elefsis [*Greece*] [*ICAO location identifier*] (ICLI)
**LGen**.......... Lieutenant General [*Navy*] [*British*]
**LGER**......... Low German [*Language, etc.*] (ROG)
**LGF**............ Lunder Germanistische Forschungen [*A publication*]
**LGF**............ Yuma/Yuma Proving Ground, AZ [*Location identifier*] [*FAA*] (FAAL)
**LGFC**......... Lesley Gore Fan Club (EA)
**LGG**........... Liege [*Belgium*] [*Airport symbol*] (OAG)
**LGG**........... Light Gas Gun
**LGG**........... Light-Gun Pulse Generator
**LGGBFC**... Larry Gatlin and the Gatlin Brothers Fan Club (EA)
**LGGBIFC**... Larry Gatlin and the Gatlin Brothers International Fan Club (EA)
**LGGG**........ Athinai [*Greece*] [*ICAO location identifier*] (ICLI)
**LGH**........... Lactogenic Hormone [*Also, LTH, PR, PRL*] [*Endocrinology*]
**LGH**........... Lansing General Hospital [*Michigan*]
**LGH**........... Leigh Creek [*Australia*] [*Airport symbol*] (OAG)
**LGH**........... Length
**LGH**........... Logarithmic Histogram Scanning [*Mass spectrometry*]
**LGHCS**...... Lutheran General Health Care System (EA)
**LGHI**......... Khios [*Greece*] [*ICAO location identifier*] (ICLI)
**LGHL**........ Porto Heli [*Greece*] [*ICAO location identifier*] (ICLI)
**LGI**............ Deadman's Cay [*Bahamas*] [*Airport symbol*] (OAG)
**LGI**............ Large Glucagon Immunoreactivity [*Immunochemistry*]
**LGI**............ Lateral Giant Interneuron [*Neurobiology*]
**LGI**............ Locally Generated Income (MCD)
**LGI**............ Lunar Geology Investigation [*NASA*]
**LGIEE**....... Liaison Group for International Educational Exchange (EA)
**LGIO**......... Ioannina [*Greece*] [*ICAO location identifier*] (ICLI)
**LGIR**.......... Iraklion [*Greece*] [*ICAO location identifier*] (ICLI)
**LGIU**......... LASER Gyro Interface Unit (NASA)
**LGIU**......... Local Government Information Unit [*British*]
**LGJ**............ Local Government Journal [*A publication*] (ROG)
**LGJ**............ Lost Generation Journal [*A publication*]
**LGK**........... Langkawi [*Malaysia*] [*Airport symbol*] (OAG)
**LGKA**........ Kastoria [*Greece*] [*ICAO location identifier*] (ICLI)
**LGKC**........ Kithira [*Greece*] [*ICAO location identifier*] (ICLI)
**LGKF**......... Kefallinia [*Greece*] [*ICAO location identifier*] (ICLI)
**LGKJ**......... Kastelorizo [*Greece*] [*ICAO location identifier*] (ICLI)
**LGKL**......... Kalamata [*Greece*] [*ICAO location identifier*] (ICLI)
**LGKM**....... Kavala/Amigdhaleon [*Greece*] [*ICAO location identifier*] (ICLI)
**LGKO**........ Kos [*Greece*] [*ICAO location identifier*] (ICLI)
**LGKP**......... Karpathos [*Greece*] [*ICAO location identifier*] (ICLI)
**LGKR**........ Kerkira [*Greece*] [*ICAO location identifier*] (ICLI)
**LGKS**......... Kasos [*Greece*] [*ICAO location identifier*] (ICLI)
**LGKV**........ Kavala/Khrisoupolis [*Greece*] [*ICAO location identifier*] (ICLI)
**LGKZ**......... Kozani [*Greece*] [*ICAO location identifier*] (ICLI)
**LGL**............ Large Granular Leukocyte [*Hematology*]
**LGL**............ Large Granular Lymphocyte [*Hematology*]
**LGL**............ Local Government Library [*A publication*]
**LGL**............ Long Lellang [*Malaysia*] [*Airport symbol*] (OAG)
**LGL**............ Lown-Ganong-Levine [*Syndrome*] [*Medicine*]
**LGL**............ Lynch Corp. [*AMEX symbol*] (SPSG)
**LGLC**......... Libertarians for Gay and Lesbian Concerns (EA)
**LGLE**......... Leros [*Greece*] [*ICAO location identifier*] (ICLI)
**LGL & P**.... Local Government Law and Practice [*Gifford*] [*A publication*] (APTA)
**LGLR**......... Larissa [*Greece*] [*ICAO location identifier*] (ICLI)
**LGM**.......... LASER Ground Mapper
**LGM**.......... LASER-Guided Munition
**LGM**.......... Last Glacial Maximum [*Climatology*]
**LGM**.......... Liberty Godparent Ministry (EA)
**LGM**.......... Little Green Men [*British term for space signals*]
**LGM**.......... Little Green Mountain [*Idaho*] [*Seismograph station code, US Geological Survey*] [*Closed*] (SEIS)
**LGM**.......... Local Government Management [*A publication*]
**LGM**.......... Logistic Guidance Memorandum
**LGM**.......... Loop Ground Multiplexer (MCD)
**LGMA**....... Lesbian and Gay Medical Association (EAIO)
**LGMC**....... Local Government Ministers' Conference [*Australia*]
**LGMG**....... Megara [*Greece*] [*ICAO location identifier*] (ICLI)
**LGMK**....... Mikonos [*Greece*] [*ICAO location identifier*] (ICLI)
**LGML**........ Milos [*Greece*] [*ICAO location identifier*] (ICLI)
**LGMR**....... Marathon [*Greece*] [*ICAO location identifier*] (ICLI)
**LGMS**........ LASER Ground Mapping System
**LGMT**........ Mitilini [*Greece*] [*ICAO location identifier*] (ICLI)
**LGN**........... Lagoon (ADA)
**LGN**........... Lagunillas [*Venezuela*] [*Seismograph station code, US Geological Survey*] (SEIS)
**LGN**........... Lateral Geniculate Nucleus
**LGN**........... Legion Resources Ltd. [*Vancouver Stock Exchange symbol*]
**LGN**........... Line Gate Number [*Data processing*]
**LGN**........... Logical Group Number [*Data processing*] (IBMDP)
**LGN**........... Logicon, Inc. [*NYSE symbol*] (SPSG)
**LGND**........ Lateral Geniculate Nucleus Dorsal [*Neuroanatomy*]
**LGND**........ Legends Co. of Chicago, Inc. [*NASDAQ symbol*] (NQ)
**LGNMVTE**... Lignum Vitae [*Botany*]
**LGNT**........ LEGENT Corp. [*NASDAQ symbol*] (NQ)
**LGO**........... Lamont Geological Observatory [*Later, L-DGO*] [*Columbia University*]
**LGO**........... Light Gas Oil [*Fuel technology*]
**LGO**........... Local Government Officer [*A publication*] (APTA)
**LGO**........... Local Government Ordinances [*A publication*] (APTA)
**LGO**........... Logo Resources Ltd. [*Vancouver Stock Exchange symbol*]
**LGO**........... Low Gravity Orbit
**LGOC**........ London General Omnibus Company [*British*] (DCTA)
**Lgoru Inf Bull**... Lgoru Information Bulletin [*A publication*]
**LGP**........... Laboratory Graduate Participation [*Oak Ridge National Laboratory*]
**LGP**........... LASER-Guided Projectile (MCD)
**LGP**........... Legaspi [*Philippines*] [*Seismograph station code, US Geological Survey*] (SEIS)
**LGP**........... Legaspi [*Philippines*] [*Airport symbol*] (OAG)
**LGP**........... Low Ground Pressure
**LGP**........... Lummer-Gehreke Plate [*Physics*]
**LGPA**......... Local Government Planners Association [*Australia*]
**LGPA**......... Paros [*Greece*] [*ICAO location identifier*] (ICLI)

**LGPIM** ...... Lesbian and Gay People in Medicine [*Later, LGBPM*] (EA)
**LGPIT** ....... Leningrad Pedagogical Institute of Foreign Languages. Transactions [*A publication*]
**LGPN** ........ International Leather Goods, Plastic, and Novelty Workers' Union (EA)
**LGPZ**......... Preveza [*Greece*] [*ICAO location identifier*] (ICLI)
**LGQ**........... Lago Agrio [*Ecuador*] [*Airport symbol*] (OAG)
**LGR**........... Knight's Local Government Reports [*A publication*] (DLA)
**LGR**........... Laird Group, Inc. [*Toronto Stock Exchange symbol*]
**LGR**........... Leasehold Ground Rent (ROG)
**LGR**........... Lethal Ground Range (MCD)
**LGR**........... Light-Water-Cooled, Graphite-Moderated Reactor (NRCH)
**LGr**............ Literaturnaya Gruziya [*Tbilisi*] [*A publication*]
**LGR**........... Local Government Reorganization [*British*]
**LGR**........... Local Government Reports [*England*] [*A publication*] (DLA)
**LGR**........... Local Government Reports, New South Wales [*Australia*] [*A publication*] (DLA)
**LGR**........... Logrono [*Spain*] [*Seismograph station code, US Geological Survey*] (SEIS)
**LGR**........... London Grand Rank [*Freemasonry*]
**LGR**........... Low Greek [*Language, etc.*]
**LGR**........... Low Group Receiving Unit
**LGR**........... New South Wales Local Government Reports [*A publication*] (APTA)
**LGra**........... Grambling State University, Grambling, LA [*Library symbol*] [*Library of Congress*] (LCLS)
**LGRA**......... Local Government Reports of Australia [*A publication*] (APTA)
**LGRD**......... Rodos/Maritsa [*Greece*] [*ICAO location identifier*] (ICLI)
**LGRED**...... Local Government Review [*A publication*]
**LGR (Eng)** ... Local Government Reports [*England*] [*A publication*] (DLA)
**LG Rev**....... Local Government Review [*A publication*]
**LGRF**......... Loan Guaranty Revolving Fund
**LGrJ**.......... Jefferson Parish Public Library, Gretna, LA [*Library symbol*] [*Library of Congress*] (LCLS)
**LGRMG**.... Lesbian/Gay Rights Monitoring Group (EA)
**LGRNG**..... Long Range (FAAC)
**LGR (NSW)** ... Local Government Law Reports (New South Wales) [*A publication*] (APTA)
**LGRP**......... Literaturblatt fuer Germanische und Romanische Philologie [*A publication*]
**LGRP**......... Rodos/Paradisi [*Greece*] [*ICAO location identifier*] (ICLI)
**LGRPh**....... Literaturblatt fuer Germanische und Romanische Philologie [*A publication*]
**LGRX**......... Araxos [*Greece*] [*ICAO location identifier*] (ICLI)
**LGS**........... Grambling State University, Grambling, LA [*OCLC symbol*] (OCLC)
**LGS**........... Lagoons [*Maps and charts*] (ROG)
**LGS**........... Landing Guidance System [*Aerospace*]
**LGS**........... Large Gray Ship [*Slang*] [*Navy*]
**LGS**........... Late Glacial Stage [*Paleontology*]
**LGS**........... Lebowa Granite Suite [*Bushveld Complex, South Africa*] [*Geology*]
**LGS**........... Lega dei Giovani Somali [*Somali Youth League*]
**LGS**........... Limerick Generation Station [*Nuclear energy*] (NRCH)
**LGS**........... Liquid Asset and Government Securities (ADA)
**LGS**........... Louisiana General Services, Inc. [*NYSE symbol*] (SPSG)
**LGS**........... Lower Group Stop (NRCH)
**LGS**........... Lunar Geophysical Surface
**LGS**........... Lunar Gravity Simulator [*Aerospace*]
**LGSA**......... Khania/Souda [*Greece*] [*ICAO location identifier*] (ICLI)
**LGSA**......... Local Government and Shires Association [*Australia*]
**LGSD**......... Sedes [*Greece*] [*ICAO location identifier*] (ICLI)
**LGSHA** ..... Language, Speech, and Hearing Services in Schools [*A publication*]
**LGSK**......... Skiathos [*Greece*] [*ICAO location identifier*] (ICLI)
**LGSM**........ Licentiate of Guildhall School of Music [*British*]
**LGSM**........ Samos [*Greece*] [*ICAO location identifier*] (ICLI)
**LGSP**......... Sparti [*Greece*] [*ICAO location identifier*] (ICLI)
**LGSR**......... Santorini [*Greece*] [*ICAO location identifier*] (ICLI)
**LGsSH**....... Greenwell Springs State Hospital, Greenwell Springs, LA [*Library symbol*] [*Library of Congress*] (LCLS)
**LGST**......... Sitia [*Greece*] [*ICAO location identifier*] (ICLI)
**LGSV**......... Stefanovikion [*Greece*] [*ICAO location identifier*] (ICLI)
**LGSY**......... Skyros [*Greece*] [*ICAO location identifier*] (ICLI)
**LGT**........... Langat Encephalitis [*Medicine*]
**LGT**........... Late Generalized Tuberculosis [*Medicine*]
**LGT**........... Light
**LGT**........... Liquid Gas Tank
**LGT**........... Local Geomagnetic Time
**LGT**........... Logistec Corp. [*Toronto Stock Exchange symbol*]
**LGT**........... Low Gelling Temperature [*Analytical biochemistry*]
**LGT**........... Low Group Transmitting Unit
**LGTA**......... Ligue Generale des Travailleurs Angolais [*General League of Angolan Workers in Exile*]
**LGTB**......... Local Government Training Board [*British*]
**LGTD**......... Lighted
**L & G Temp Plunk** ... Lloyd and Goold's Irish Chancery Reports Tempore Plunkett [*A publication*] (DLA)
**L & G Temp Sugd** ... Lloyd and Goold's Irish Chancery Reports Tempore Sugden [*1835*] [*A publication*] (DLA)
**LGTG**......... Tanagra [*Greece*] [*ICAO location identifier*] (ICLI)
**LGTH**......... Length (AFM)
**LGTH**......... Lexington Group in Transportation History (EA)
**LGTH**......... Lightning Hole [*Electronics*]
**LGTK**......... Logitek, Inc. [*NASDAQ symbol*] (NQ)
**LGTL**......... Kasteli [*Greece*] [*ICAO location identifier*] (ICLI)
**L & GTP** .... Lloyd and Goold's Irish Chancery Reports Tempore Plunkett [*A publication*] (DLA)
**LGTP**......... Tripolis [*Greece*] [*ICAO location identifier*] (ICLI)
**L & GT Plunk** ... Lloyd and Goold's Irish Chancery Reports Tempore Plunkett [*A publication*] (DLA)
**LGTRA**...... Logistics and Transportation Review [*A publication*]
**L & GTS** .... Lloyd and Goold's Irish Chancery Reports Tempore Sugden [*1835*] [*A publication*] (DLA)
**LGTS**......... Thessaloniki [*Greece*] [*ICAO location identifier*] (ICLI)
**L & GT Sug** ... Lloyd and Goold's Irish Chancery Reports Tempore Sugden [*1835*] [*A publication*] (DLA)
**LGTT**......... Dekeleia/Tatoi [*Greece*] [*ICAO location identifier*] (ICLI)
**LGU**........... Ladies Golf Union
**LGU**........... Leningrad State University. Philology Series. Transactions [*A publication*]
**LGU**........... Local Glucose Utilization [*Physiology*]
**LGU**........... Logan [*Utah*] [*Airport symbol*] (OAG)
**LGU**........... Logan, UT [*Location identifier*] [*FAA*] (FAAL)
**L Guard**...... Law Guardian [*A publication*] (DLA)
**LGUM**........ Legume, Inc. [*Montville, NJ*] [*NASDAQ symbol*] (NQ)
**LGV**........... Lymphogranuloma Venereum [*Medicine*]
**LGVD**......... Large Group View Display (MCD)
**LGVO**......... Volos [*Greece*] [*ICAO location identifier*] (ICLI)
**LGW**.......... Gatwick [*England*] [*Airport symbol*]
**LGW**.......... Landing Gear Warning
**LGW**.......... London-Gatwick [*England*] [*Airport symbol*] (OAG)
**LGW**.......... Love Games Won [*Tennis*]
**LGWF**........ Libyan General Workers' Federation
**LGWS**........ LASER-Guided Weapons Systems (IEEE)
**LGWV**........ Long Wave [*Radio*] (FAAC)
**LGX**........... Lovington, NM [*Location identifier*] [*FAA*] (FAAL)
**LGZA**......... Zakinthos [*Greece*] [*ICAO location identifier*] (ICLI)
**LH**.............. Deutsche Lufthansa AG [*Germany*] [*ICAO designator*] (OAG)
**LH**.............. L. Hungerford [*Record label*] [*Great Britain*]
**LH**.............. Labor Historians [*Inactive*] (EA)
**LH**.............. Labor Hour [*In contract work*]
**LH**.............. Labour History [*A publication*] (APTA)
**LH**.............. Laetolil Hominid
**LH**.............. Langmuir-Hinshelwood Mechanism [*Chemistry*]
**LH**.............. Large Heavy Seeds [*Botany*]
**LH**.............. Larval Heart
**LH**.............. Las Hermanas [*Later, LH-USA*] (EA)
**LH**.............. Last Half [*of month*] [*Business term*] (DS)
**LH**.............. Late Helladic (BJA)
**LH**.............. Lateral Hypothalamic [*or Hypothalamus*]
**L & H**......... Laurel and Hardy [*The film comedy team of Stan Laurel and Oliver Hardy*]
**LH**.............. Learning Handicapped
**L/H**............ Leasehold [*Legal term*] (DLA)
**LH**.............. Left Halfback [*Soccer*]
**LH**.............. Left Hand
**LH**.............. Left Hyperphoria [*Ophthalmology*]
**Ld'H**.......... Legion d'Honneur [*French decoration*]
**LH**.............. Legion d'Honneur [*French decoration*]
**LH**.............. Lewisite-Mustard Gas Mix [*for land mines*] [*Army symbol*]
**lh**............... Liechtenstein [*MARC country of publication code*] [*Library of Congress*] (LCCP)
**LH**.............. Light Horse [*Cavalry*]
**LH**.............. Lighthawk [*An association*] (EA)
**LH**.............. Lighthouse [*Maps and charts*]
**LH**.............. Lightly Hinged [*Philately*]
**LH**.............. Limited Hold
**LH**.............. Lincoln Herald [*A publication*]
**LH**.............. Linear Hybrid
**LH**.............. Link House Books [*Publisher*] [*Great Britain*]
**LH**.............. Lipid Hydrocarbon [*Biochemistry*]
**LH**.............. Liquid Hydrogen
**LH**.............. Literarischer Handweiser [*A publication*]
**L & H**......... Literature and History [*A publication*]
**LH**.............. Litter Hook
**LH**.............. Livres Hebdomadaires [*A publication*]
**LH**.............. Local Horizontal
**LH**.............. Loch's Horse [*British military*] (DMA)
**LH**.............. Lodging Hospitality [*A publication*]
**LH**.............. Lone Hand [*A publication*] (APTA)
**LH**.............. Low Head [*Nuclear energy*] (NRCH)
**L/H**............ Low-to-High (MDG)
**LH**.............. Lower Half
**LH**.............. Lower Hemispherical (MCD)
**LH**.............. Lower Hold [*Shipping*]
**LH**.............. Lues Hereditaria [*Medicine*]
**LH**.............. Luteinizing-Hormone [*Also, ICSH, LSH*] [*Endocrinology*]
**$LH_2$**............ Liquid Hydrogen [*NASA*]
**LHA**........... Amphibious Assault Carrier [*or Ship*] (Landing Helicopter Assault Ship) [*Navy symbol*]

**LHA** ... Ladies' Hermitage Association (EA)
**LHA** ... Landing Helicopter Assault
**LHA** ... Lanham Housing Act (DLA)
**LHA** ... Lateral Hypothalamic Area
**LHA** ... Lay Helpers' Association [*British*]
**LHA** ... Left Heart Assistance [*Cardiology*]
**LHA** ... Leisure & Hotel Appointments [*Recruitment for the hotel, leisure, and travel industries*] [*British*]
**LHA** ... Lhasa [*Tibet*] [*Seismograph station code, US Geological Survey*] [*Closed*] (SEIS)
**LHA** ... Libertarian Humanist Association (EA)
**LHA** ... Licentiate of the Institute of Health Service Administrators [*British*] (DBQ)
**LHA** ... Light Helicopter, Attack [*Computer test vehicle*]
**LHA** ... Livestock Husbandry Adviser [*Ministry of Agriculture, Fisheries, and Food*] [*British*]
**LHA** ... Local Health Authority [*British*]
**LHA** ... Local Hour Angle [*Navigation*]
**LHA** ... Local Housing Authority
**LHA** ... Lord High Admiral [*British*]
**LHA** ... Lower-Half Assembly
**LHA** ... Lower Hour Angle [*Navigation*]
**LHA** ... Lutheran Hospital Association of America (EA)
**LHA** ... McNeese State University, Lake Charles, LA [*OCLC symbol*] (OCLC)
**LHAA** ... Budapest [*Hungary*] [*ICAO location identifier*] (ICLI)
**LHAAP** ... Longhorn Army Ammunition Plant (AABC)
**L/Hadr** ... Lance Havidar [*Military*] [*British*]
**LHAMS** ... Local Hour Angle of Mean Sun
**LHAR** ... London, Havre, Antwerp, Rouen [*Shipping route*] (ROG)
**LHAR** ... London, Hull, Antwerp, or Rotterdam [*Shipping route*]
**LHarC** ... Catahoula Parish Library, Harrisonburg, LA [*Library symbol*] [*Library of Congress*] (LCLS)
**LHAS** ... Luteinizing Hormone Antiserum [*Endocrinology*]
**LHaSC** ... Saint Charles Parish Library, Hahnville, LA [*Library symbol*] [*Library of Congress*] (LCLS)
**LHAT** ... League of Historic American Theatres (EA)
**LHATS** ... Local Hour Angle of True Sun
**LHB** ... Bachelor of Humane Letters [*or Bachelor of Literature or Bachelor of the More Humane Letters*]
**LHB** ... Laboratory Hazards Bulletin [*Royal Society of Chemistry*] [*Information service or system*] (IID)
**LHb** ... Lateral Habenular (Nucleus) [*Neuroanatomy*]
**LHB** ... Left Halfback [*Soccer*]
**LHB** ... Lock Haven Bulletin [*A publication*]
**LHB** ... Lost Heartbeat [*An attractive girl*] [*Slang*]
**LHBANA** .. Log House Builder's Association of North America (EA)
**LHBEDM** ... Law and Human Behavior [*A publication*]
**LHBMA** ... Let's Have Better Mottoes Association [*A mythical association*] (EA)
**LHBP** ... Budapest/Ferihegy [*Hungary*] [*ICAO location identifier*] (ICLI)
**LHC** ... Arlington, TN [*Location identifier*] [*FAA*] (FAAL)
**LHC** ... L & N Housing Corporation [*NYSE symbol*] (SPSG)
**LHC** ... Lakehead University [*Thunder Bay*] [*Ontario*] [*Seismograph station code, US Geological Survey*] (SEIS)
**LHC** ... Large Hadron Collider [*High-energy physics*]
**LHC** ... Left-Hand Circular [*Polarization*] (IEEE)
**LHC** ... Left Hypochondrium [*Medicine*]
**LHC** ... Light Harvesting Complex
**LHC** ... Light Hydrocarbon [*Organic chemistry*]
**LHC** ... Lignin-Hemicellulose-Cellulose [*A complex found in plants*]
**LHC** ... Lined Hollow Charge
**LHC** ... Liquid Hydrogen Container
**LHC** ... Log Homes Council (EA)
**LHC** ... Lord High Chancellor [*British*]
**LHC** ... Loretto Heights College [*Denver, CO*]
**LHC** ... Louis, Holland, Callaway [*Advertising agency*]
**LHC** ... Lutheran Historical Conference (EA)
**LHCA** ... Longshoremen's and Harbor Workers' Compensation Act (DLA)
**LHCC** ... Budapest [*Hungary*] [*ICAO location identifier*] (ICLI)
**LHCIMA** ... Licentiate of the Hotel, Catering, and Institutional Management Association [*British*] (DBQ)
**LHCP** ... Left-Hand Circularly Polarized [*LASER waves*]
**LHCP** ... Local History Coordination Project [*Australia*]
**LHD** ... Anchorage, AK [*Location identifier*] [*FAA*] (FAAL)
**LHD** ... Lakehead University Library [*UTLAS symbol*]
**LHD** ... Left-Hand Drive [*AEC*]
**LHD** ... Licentiate in Health, Dublin (ROG)
**LHD** ... Litterarum Humaniorum Doctor [*Doctor of Humane Letters; Doctor of Humanities; Doctor of Letters; Doctor of Letters of Humanity; Doctor of Polite Literature; or Doctor of the More Humane Letters*] [*Latin*]
**LHD** ... Load, Haul, Dump [*Mining*]
**LHD** ... Multipurpose Amphibious Assault Ship
**LHDC** ... Debrecen [*Hungary*] [*ICAO location identifier*] (ICLI)
**LHDC** ... Lateral Homing Depth Charge
**LHDR** ... Left-Hand Drive [*AEC*]
**LHDS** ... LASER Hole Drilling System
**LHE** ... Lagrange-Helmholtz Equation
**LHE** ... Lahore [*Pakistan*] [*Airport symbol*] (OAG)
**LHE** ... Liquid Helium
**LHEA** ... Laboratory for High Energy Astrophysics [*Greenbelt, MD*] [*NASA*] (GRD)
**LHEB** ... Left-Hand Equipment Bay [*NASA*] (KSC)
**LHEF** ... Lesbian Herstory Educational Foundation (EA)
**LHF** ... Labor Heritage Foundation (EA)
**LHF** ... Lamp Heat Flux
**LHF** ... Left Heart Failure [*Medicine*]
**LHF** ... Lighthouse, Fixed [*Maps and charts*] (ROG)
**LHF** ... List Handling Facility
**LHFC** ... Laura Hendler Fan Club (EA)
**LHFEB** ... Left-Hand Forward Equipment Bay [*NASA*] (KSC)
**LHFl** ... Lighthouse, Floating [*Maps and charts*] (ROG)
**LHFS** ... Ligand Hyperfine Structure
**LHFT** ... Light Helicopter Fireteam [*Navy*] (NVT)
**LHG** ... Licentiate of the Institute of Heraldic and Genealogical Studies [*British*] (DBQ)
**LHGR** ... Linear Heat Generation Rate [*Nuclear energy*] (NRCH)
**LHH** ... Left-Hand Head
**LHH** ... Lower Hybrid Resonance Heating (MCD)
**LHHS** ... Lutheran Hospitals and Homes Society of America (EA)
**LHHW** ... Langmuir-Hinshelwood-Hougen-Watson Rate Equation [*Chemical kinetics*]
**LHI** ... Fort Lauderdale, FL [*Location identifier*] [*FAA*] (FAAL)
**LHI** ... Lefthanders International (EA)
**LHI** ... Leigh Instruments Ltd. [*Toronto Stock Exchange symbol*]
**LHI** ... Lighthouse, Intermittent [*Maps and charts*] (ROG)
**LHI** ... Lord Howe Island [*Australia*] (ADA)
**LHi** ... Louisiana Historical Society, New Orleans, LA [*Library symbol*] [*Library of Congress*] (LCLS)
**LHJ** ... Ladies' Home Journal [*A publication*]
**LHK** ... Lebenshaltungskosten [*Cost of Living*] [*German*]
**LHL** ... Left Hepatic Lobe [*Anatomy*]
**LHM** ... Lake Helena [*Montana*] [*Seismograph station code, US Geological Survey*] [*Closed*] (SEIS)
**LHM** ... Licensed Hotel Motel
**LHM** ... Lisuride Hydrogen Maleate [*Pharmacology*]
**LHM** ... Loop Handling Machine [*Nuclear energy*] (NRCH)
**LHM** ... Master of Humane Letters [*or Master of the More Humane Letters*]
**LHME** ... LASER HELLFIRE Missile Evaluation (MCD)
**LHMM** ... Laymen's Home Missionary Movement (EA)
**LHN** ... Lillehammer [*Norway*] [*Seismograph station code, US Geological Survey*] (SEIS)
**LHN** ... Localized Hypertrophic Neuropathy [*Medicine*]
**LHNCBC** ... Lister Hill National Center for Biomedical Communications [*National Library of Medicine*] [*Information service or system*] (IID)
**LHO** ... Local Head Office [*British*] (DCTA)
**LHOB** ... Longworth House Office Building
**LHoC** ... Clairborne Parish Library, Homer, LA [*Library symbol*] [*Library of Congress*] (LCLS)
**LHOLD** ... Leasehold (ROG)
**LHON** ... Leber's Hereditary Optic Neuropathy [*Ophthalmology*]
**LHouT** ... Terrebonne Parish Library, Houma, LA [*Library symbol*] [*Library of Congress*] (LCLS)
**LHOX** ... Low- and High-Pressure Oxygen
**LHP** ... Larval Hemolymph Protein [*Entomology*]
**LHP** ... Late Hyperpolarizing Potential [*Neurophysiology*]
**LHP** ... Launcher Handling Procedure
**LHP** ... Left-Hand Panel
**LHP** ... Left-Handed Pitcher [*Baseball*]
**LHP** ... Lehu [*Papua New Guinea*] [*Airport symbol*] (OAG)
**LHPC** ... Light-Harvesting Chlorophyll Protein Complex [*Botany*]
**LHPG** ... LASER-Heated Pedestal Growth [*Crystal growing technology*]
**LHPS** ... Lead Hydrogen Purge System [*Nuclear energy*] (IEEE)
**LHQ** ... Allied Land Headquarters [*World War II*]
**LHQ** ... Lancaster, OH [*Location identifier*] [*FAA*] (FAAL)
**LHQ** ... Louisiana Historical Quarterly [*A publication*]
**LHR** ... Heathrow [*England*] [*Airport symbol*]
**LHR** ... Left-Hand Rule
**LHR** ... [*The*] Lehigh & Hudson River Railway Co. [*Absorbed into Consolidated Rail Corp.*] [*AAR code*]
**L & HR** ... [*The*] Lehigh & Hudson River Railway Co. [*Absorbed into Consolidated Rail Corp.*]
**LHR** ... Leukocyte Histamine Release [*Test*]
**LHR** ... Lighthouse, Revolving [*Maps and charts*] (ROG)
**LHR** ... Liquid-Holding Recovery [*of bacterial cells*]
**LHR** ... Lock Haven Review [*A publication*]
**LHR** ... London-Heathrow [*England*] [*Airport symbol*] (OAG)
**LHR** ... Lower Hybrid Resonance
**LHR** ... Lumen Hour (ADA)
**LHRAA** ... Lutheran Human Relations Association of America (EA)
**LHRBI** ... Luteinizing Hormone Receptor Binding Inhibitor [*Endocrinology*]
**LHRE** ... Low Heat Rejection Engine [*Mechanical engineering*]
**LH-RF** ... Luteinizing-Hormone Releasing Factor [*Also, GnRF, GnRH, LH-RH, LH-RH/FSH-RH, LRF, LRH*] [*Endocrinology*]
**LH-RH** ... Luteinizing-Hormone Releasing Hormone

**LH-RH/FSH-RH** ... Luteinizing-Hormone Releasing Hormone/Follicle-Stimulating Hormone Releasing Hormone [*Also, GnRF, GnRH, LH-RF, LH-RH, LRF, LRH*] [*Endocrinology*]
**LHRL** ........ Lucas Heights Research Laboratories [*Australia*]
**LHRS**........ Life History Recorder Set [*or System*] (MCD)
**LHRT** ........ Library History Round Table [*American Library Association*]
**LHS** .......... Lake Hughes, CA [*Location identifier*] [*FAA*] (FAAL)
**LHS** .......... Layered Half Space
**LHS** .......... Left-Hand Side
**LHS** .......... Left Heart Strain [*Medicine*]
**LHS** .......... Liberty Hill [*South Carolina*] [*Seismograph station code, US Geological Survey*] (SEIS)
**LHS** .......... Library History Seminar
**LHS** .......... Lightweight Hydraulic System [*Navy aviation*]
**LHS** .......... Loop Handling System [*Nuclear energy*] (NRCH)
**LHS** .......... Lunar Horizon Sensor [*Aerospace*]
**LHS** .......... Southeastern Louisiana University, Hammond, LA [*Library symbol*] [*Library of Congress*] (LCLS)
**LHSb** ......... Literarnohistoricky Sbornik [*A publication*]
**LHSC**......... Left-Hand Side Console [*NASA*] (KSC)
**LHSC**......... Liquid Hydrogen System Complex [*NASA*] (KSC)
**LHSC**......... Luther Hospital Sentence Completions [*Nursing school test*]
**LHSI**.......... Low-Head Safety Injection [*Nuclear energy*] (NRCH)
**LHSl**.......... Litteraria Historica Slovaca [*A publication*]
**LHSLG**...... Lincoln Health Sciences Library Group [*Library network*]
**LHSSC** ...... Left-Hand Side Storage Container [*NASA*] (KSC)
**LHSSP** ...... Les Houches Summer School Proceedings [*Elsevier Book Series*] [*A publication*]
**LHSV**........ Liquid Hourly Space Velocity [*Fluid dynamics*]
**LHT** .......... Left Hypertropia [*Ophthalmology*]
**LHT** .......... Library Hi Tech [*Pierian Press, Inc.*] [*Information service or system*] [*A publication*] (IID)
**LHT** .......... Lighthouse Tender
**LHT** .......... Lord High Treasurer [*British*]
**LHT** .......... Lunar Hand Tool [*NASA*]
**LHTEC**...... Light Helicopter Turbine Engine Co. [*US Army contractor*]
**LHTF**........ Lincoln Heritage Trail Foundation (EA)
**LHTH**........ Left-Hand Thread
**L-HTL**....... L-Histidinol [*Biochemistry*]
**LHTN**........ Library Hi Tech News [*A publication*]
**LHU**.......... Lake Havasu City [*Arizona*] [*Airport symbol*] (OAG)
**L & Human Behav** ... Law and Human Behavior [*A publication*]
**LH-USA** .... Las Hermanas-United States of America (EA)
**LHUSA** ..... Likud-Herut USA (EA)
**LHV**.......... Light Horse Volunteers [*British military*] (DMA)
**LHV**.......... Liquid Hydrogen Vessel
**LHV**.......... Lock Haven, PA [*Location identifier*] [*FAA*] (FAAL)
**LHV**.......... Low Heat [*or Heating*] Value (MCD)
**LHV**.......... Luchtvaart Historische Vereniging [*Society of Aeronautical Historians - SAH*] [*Defunct*] (EAIO)
**LHW**.......... Hinesville, GA [*Location identifier*] [*FAA*] (FAAL)
**LHW**.......... Lanzhou [*China*] [*Airport symbol*] (OAG)
**LHW**.......... Lees-Hromas-Webb [*Theory*]
**LHW**.......... Left Half Word
**LHW**.......... Literarischer Handweiser [*A publication*]
**LHW**.......... Lower High Water [*Tides and currents*]
**LHWI** ........ Lower High-Water Interval [*Tides and currents*]
**LHX**.......... La Junta, CO [*Location identifier*] [*FAA*] (FAAL)
**LHX**.......... Light Helicopter, Experimental [*Army*] (RDA)
**LHX**.......... Light Helicopters [*Army*] (RDA)
**LHX**.......... Lochiel Exploration Ltd. [*Toronto Stock Exchange symbol*]
**LHY**.......... Lancashire Hussars Yeomanry [*British military*] (DMA)
**LHY**.......... Literary Half-Yearly [*A publication*]
**LHY**.......... Lohame Herut Yisrael (BJA)
**L Hy**.......... Registered Hypnotist
**LHY**.......... Wilkes-Barre, PA [*Location identifier*] [*FAA*] (FAAL)
**LI** .............. Labeling Index [*Measurement of cell labeling*]
**L/I**............. Labindustries [*Commercial firm*]
**LI** .............. Landscape Institute [*British*]
**LI** .............. Late Iron [*Age*] (BJA)
**L & I**.......... Launch and Impact (AFM)
**LI** .............. Lawn Institute (EA)
**LI** .............. (Laws of) Lipit-Ishtar (BJA)
**LI** .............. Leadership Institute (EA)
**LI** .............. Leakage of Information [*British*] [*World War II*]
**LI** .............. Leeward Islands Air Transport [*1974*] Ltd. [*Antigua, Barbuda*] [*ICAO designator*] (FAAC)
**LI** .............. Left in Place [*Telecommunications*] (TEL)
**LI** .............. Legal Intelligencer [*A publication*] (DLA)
**LI** .............. Legislative Instrument [*Ghana*] [*1960-*] [*A publication*] (ILCA)
**LI** .............. Leitender Ingenieur [*Chief Engineer*] [*German military - World War II*]
**LI** .............. Leo's Industries, Inc. [*AMEX symbol*] (SPSG)
**L/I**............. Letter of Indemnity (DS)
**LI** .............. Letter of Intent
**LI** .............. Letter of Introduction (ADA)
**LI** .............. Lettere Italiane [*A publication*]
**LI** .............. Level Indicator
**LI** .............. Liability [*Insurance*]
**LI** .............. Liberal International [*World Liberal Union*] [*London, England*] (EAIO)
**LI** .............. Libertarian International (EA)
**LI** .............. Libro Italiano [*A publication*]
**LI** .............. License Inquiry [*Police*]
**LI** .............. Licentiate of Instruction [*or Licentiate Instructor*]
**LI** .............. Liechtenstein [*ANSI two-letter standard code*] (CNC)
**LI** .............. Lifegain Institute (EA)
**LI** .............. Liga International (EA)
**LI** .............. Light Infantry
**LI** .............. Lightly Included [*Colored gemstone grade*]
**LI** .............. Ligue Internationale de la Representation Commerciale [*International League of Commercial Travelers and Agents - ILCTA*] (EAIO)
**LI** .............. Lilac (ROG)
**LI** .............. Lincoln's Inn [*London*] [*One of the Inns of Court*]
**LI** .............. Line Item (AABC)
**Li** .............. Lingua [*A publication*]
**LI** .............. Linguoincisal [*Dentistry*]
**LI** .............. Link
**LI** .............. Lions International [*Later, LCI*] (EA)
**LI** .............. Liquid Ionization [*Spectrometric instrumentation*]
**Li** .............. Listener [*A publication*]
**LI** .............. Litchfield Institute (EA)
**LI** .............. Liter [*Metric measure of volume*] (MCD)
**LI** .............. Literature and Art [*Russia*] [*A publication*]
**L & I**.......... Literature and Ideology [*A publication*]
**Li**............... Lithium [*Chemical element*]
**LI** .............. Lithographer [*Navy rating*]
**LI** .............. Local Interneuron [*Neuroanatomy*]
**LI** .............. Logistic Index (CAAL)
**LI** .............. Logistics Instructions [*Military*]
**LI** .............. Loglan Institute (EA)
**LI** .............. Loitering with Intent [*British*] (DSUE)
**LI** .............. London International [*Record label*] [*Great Britain, USA, etc.*]
**LI** .............. Long Island
**LI** .............. [*The*] Long Island Rail Road Co. [*AAR code*]
**LI** .............. Longitudinal Interval (ADA)
**LI** .............. Loop of Intestine
**LI** .............. Lot Indices
**LI** .............. Low Intensity
**LI** .............. Lubrication Instructions [*Marine Corps*]
**LI** .............. Luce Intellettuale [*A publication*]
**LI** .............. Luteinization Inhibitor [*Endocrinology*]
**LI** .............. Lymphoid Cellular Infiltration [*Oncology*]
**LI1** ............ Lithographer, First Class [*Navy rating*]
**LI2** ............ Lithographer, Second Class [*Navy rating*]
**LI3** ............ Lithographer, Third Class [*Navy rating*]
**LIA**............ International Union of Life Insurance Agents
**LIA**............ Label Information Area (CMD)
**LIA**............ Land Information and Analysis [*Program*] [*Department of the Interior*]
**LIA**............ Laser Institute of America (EA)
**LIA**............ Lead Industries Association [*New York, NY*] (EA)
**LIA**............ Leather Industries of America (EA)
**LIA**............ Leukemia-Associated Inhibiting Activity [*Medicine*]
**LIA**............ Liaison
**LIA**............ Licensing Industry Association [*Later, ILMA*] (EA)
**LIA**............ Lima [*Ohio*] [*Airport symbol*] (OAG)
**LIA**............ Limiting Interval Availability
**LIA**............ Linear Induction Accelerator (MCD)
**LIA**............ Liposome Immunoassay [*Clinical chemistry*]
**LIA**............ Liver Infusion Agar [*Germination medium*]
**LIA**............ Loop Interface Address
**LIA**............ Low-Impact Aerobics
**LIA**............ Luminescence Immunoassay [*Clinical chemistry*]
**LIA**............ Lymphocyte-Induced Angiogenesis [*Immunology*]
**LIA**............ Lysine Iron Agar [*Microbiology*]
**LIAA**.......... Library and Information Association of Australia [*Proposed*]
**LIAA**.......... Life Insurance Association of America [*Later, ACLI*] (EA)
**LIAB**.......... Liability
**LIAB**.......... Life Insurance Adjustment Bureau [*Defunct*] (EA)
**LIAC**.......... Legal Industry Advisory Council (EA)
**LIAC**.......... Liberian International American Corporation [*New York*]
**LIAC**.......... Light-Induced Absorbance Change
**LIAC**.......... Local Industry Advisory Committee [*Civil defense*]
**LIADA**....... Liga Ibero-Americana de Astronomia [*Ibero-American Astronomy League*] (EAIO)
**Liaison Rep Commonw Geol Liaison Off** ... Liaison Report. Commonwealth Geological Liaison Office [*A publication*]
**Liaisons Soc** ... Liaisons Sociales [*A publication*]
**Liais Serv Note For Res Lab (Winnipeg)** ... Liaison and Services Note. Forest Research Laboratory (Winnipeg) [*A publication*]
**LIAMA**...... Life Insurance Agency Management Association [*Later, LIMRA*]
**LIANEI** ..... Liver Annual [*A publication*]
**LIAR**.......... Lexicon of Inconspicuously Ambiguous Recommendations [*Term coined by Robert J. Thornton of Lehigh University*]
**LIAR**.......... Report. Labrador Inuit Association [*A publication*]
**LIAS** .......... Library Information Access System [*Pennsylvania State University Libraries*] [*University Park*] [*Information service or system*] (IID)

**LIAT** .......... Leeward Islands Air Transport Services Ltd. [*Humorous interpretation: Luggage in Another Town*] [*Airline*]
**LIB** .......... Federal Liberal Agency of Canada Library [*UTLAS symbol*]
**LIB** .......... Left Inboard (MCD)
**LIB** .......... Liber [*Book*]
**LIB** .......... Liberal
**LIB** .......... Liberation
**LIB** .......... Liberator Bomber Aircraft [*British*] (DSUE)
**Lib** .......... Liberia
**LIB** .......... Liberty [*Geographical division*] [*British*]
**LIB** .......... Liberty Aviation, Inc. [*New Castle, DE*] [*FAA designator*] (FAAC)
**LIB** .......... Liberty, NC [*Location identifier*] [*FAA*] (FAAL)
**Lib** .......... Libra [*Constellation*]
**LIB** .......... Libra [*Pound*]
**Lib** .......... Librarian (DLA)
**LIB** .......... Library [*A publication*]
**LIB** .......... Library (AFM)
**LIB** .......... Libretto [*Music*]
**Lib** .......... Libya [*A publication*]
**LIB** .......... Line Interface Base [*Telecommunications*]
**LIBA** .......... Amendola [*Italy*] [*ICAO location identifier*] (ICLI)
**LIBA** .......... Long Island Biological Association
**LIBACC** .......... Library Acquisition Program [*Computer program*]
**LibAnt** .......... Libya Antiqua [*A publication*]
**Lib Ass** .......... Liber Assisarum [*Book of Assizes, or pleas of the crown*] [*Pt. 5 of Year Books*] [*A publication*] (DLA)
**Lib Assn Alta Bull** ... Library Association of Alberta. Bulletin [*A publication*]
**Lib Assn R** ... Library Association. Record [*A publication*]
**Lib Assn Rec** ... Library Association. Record [*A publication*]
**Lib Assn Yrbk** ... Library Association. Yearbook [*A publication*]
**Lib Assoc Rec** ... Library Association. Record [*A publication*]
**LIBB** .......... Brindisi [*Italy*] [*ICAO location identifier*] (ICLI)
**Lib Binder** ... Library Binder [*A publication*]
**Lib Brow** .... Librarians' Browser [*A publication*]
**LIBC** .......... Crotone [*Italy*] [*ICAO location identifier*] (ICLI)
**LIBC** .......... Latent Iron-Binding Capacity [*Clinical chemistry*]
**LibC** .......... Library Chronicle [*A publication*]
**LIBC** .......... Lloyd's Insurance Brokers Committee (AIA)
**Lib Chron** ... Library Chronicle [*A publication*]
**LIBCO** .......... Liberty Investors Benefit Insurance Co.
**Lib Coll J** ... Library College Journal [*A publication*]
**Lib Colon** ... Libri Coloniarum [*Classical studies*] (OCD)
**LIBCON** .... Libertarian Conservative
**LIBCON** .... Library of Congress
**Lib Cong Inf Bull** ... Library of Congress. Information Bulletin [*A publication*]
**Lib Cong Q** ... Library of Congress. Quarterly Journal [*A publication*] (DLA)
**Lib Cong Q J** ... Library of Congress. Quarterly Journal [*A publication*]
**Lib Cong Q J Cur Acq** ... Library of Congress. Quarterly Journal of Current Acquisitions [*A publication*]
**LIBD** .......... Bari/Palese Macchie [*Italy*] [*ICAO location identifier*] (ICLI)
**LIBE** .......... Ligo Internacia de Blindaj Esperantistoj [*International League of Blind Esperantists - ILBE*] (EAIO)
**LIBE** .......... Monte S. Angelo [*Italy*] [*ICAO location identifier*] (ICLI)
**LIBEC** .......... Light Behind Camera [*Photographic technique*]
**LIB ED** .......... Libertarian Education: A Magazine for the Liberation of Learning [*A publication*]
**Lib Educ** .......... Liberal Education [*A publication*]
**Lib Ent** .......... Old Books of Entries [*A publication*] (DLA)
**Liber** .......... Liberation [*A publication*]
**LIBER** .......... Ligue des Bibliotheques Europeennes de Recherche [*League of European Research Libraries*] (EAIO)
**Liberal Ed** ... Liberal Education [*A publication*]
**Liberal Educ** ... Liberal Education [*A publication*]
**Liberal Geol Soc Cross Sec Type Log** ... Liberal Geological Society. Cross Sections. Type Log [*A publication*]
**LIBER Bull** ... Ligue des Bibliotheques Europeennes de Recherche. Bulletin [*A publication*]
**Liberian L** .. Liberian Law [*A publication*] (DLA)
**Liberian LJ** ... Liberian Law Journal [*A publication*]
**LiberianSJ** ... Liberian Studies Journal [*A publication*]
**Liber Stud J** ... Liberian Studies Journal [*A publication*]
**Libertas Math** ... Libertas Mathematica [*A publication*]
**LIBF** .......... Foggia [*Italy*] [*ICAO location identifier*] (ICLI)
**LIBF** .......... London International Book Fair [*England*]
**Lib Feud** .......... Liber Feudorum [*Book of Feuds*] [*At the end of the Corpus Juris Civilis*] [*A publication*] (DLA)
**LIBG** .......... Grottaglie [*Italy*] [*ICAO location identifier*] (ICLI)
**LIBGIS** .......... Library General Information Survey [*of the National Center for Educational Statistics*]
**LIBH** .......... Liberty Homes, Inc. [*NASDAQ symbol*] (NQ)
**LIBH** .......... Marina Di Ginosa [*Italy*] [*ICAO location identifier*] (ICLI)
**Lib Hist** .......... Library History [*A publication*]
**LIBI** .......... Vieste [*Italy*] [*ICAO location identifier*] (ICLI)
**LIBID** .......... London Interbank Bid Rate [*for Eurodollar deposits*] [*London Stock Exchange*]
**Lib Inf Bull** ... Library Information Bulletin [*A publication*]
**Lib Inf Sci** .. Library and Information Science [*A publication*]
**Lib Int** .......... Liber Intrationum [*Book of Entries*] [*1510*] [*A publication*] (DLA)
**Lib Intr** .......... Liber Intrationum [*Book of Entries*] [*A publication*] (DLA)
**LIBISAC** ... Livres Bibliotheque Saclay Database [*Commissariat a l'Energie Atomique*] [*France*] [*Information service or system*] (CRD)
**LibJ** .......... Library Journal [*A publication*]
**LIBJ** .......... Vibo Valentia [*Italy*] [*ICAO location identifier*] (ICLI)
**LIBK** .......... Caraffa Di Catanzaro [*Italy*] [*ICAO location identifier*] (ICLI)
**LIBL** .......... Liberal
**LIBL** .......... Palascia [*Italy*] [*ICAO location identifier*] (ICLI)
**LIB LAB** .... Liberal-Labour Alliance [*British*] (DSUE)
**Lib Leaves** ... Library Leaves from the Library of Long Island University [*A publication*]
**Lib L & Eq** ... Library of Law and Equity [*A publication*] (DLA)
**LibLit** .......... Library Literature [*A publication*]
**Lib (London)** ... Library (London)
**LIBM** .......... Grottammare [*Italy*] [*ICAO location identifier*] (ICLI)
**LIBMAS** .... Library Master File [*FORTRAN program*]
**LIBMISH** ... Liberia Military Mission [*US*]
**LIBMRG** ... Library Merge Program [*Computer program*]
**LIBN** .......... Lecce [*Italy*] [*ICAO location identifier*] (ICLI)
**LIBN** .......... Liberty National Corp. [*NASDAQ symbol*] (NQ)
**LibN** .......... Library Notes [*A publication*]
**LIBNAT** .... Library Network Analysis Theory
**Libn & Bk W** ... Librarian and Book World [*A publication*]
**Lib News Bul** ... Library News Bulletin [*A publication*]
**Lib Nig** .......... Liber Niger [*Black Book*] [*A publication*] (DLA)
**Lib Nig Scacc** ... Liber Niger Scaccarii [*Black Book of the Exchequer*] [*A publication*] (DLA)
**LIBO** .......... Lincoln Boyhood National Memorial
**LIBO** .......... London Interbank Offered [*Rate*] [*Reference point for syndicated bank loans*]
**LIBO** .......... Ortanova [*Italy*] [*ICAO location identifier*] (ICLI)
**Lib Occurrent** ... Library Occurrent [*A publication*]
**Lib Op** .......... Library Opinion [*A publication*] (APTA)
**Lib Opinion** ... Liberal Opinion [*A publication*] (APTA)
**Lib Opinion** ... Library Opinion [*A publication*] (APTA)
**LIBOR** .......... London Interbank Offered Rate [*Reference point for syndicated bank loans*]
**LIBORS** .... LASER Ionization Based on Resonant Saturation [*Physics*]
**LIBP** .......... Pescara [*Italy*] [*ICAO location identifier*] (ICLI)
**Lib Period Round Table Newsletter** ... Library Periodicals Round Table. Newsletter [*A publication*]
**Lib Pl** .......... Liber Placitandi [*Book of Pleading*] [*A publication*] (DLA)
**Lib Plac** .......... Lilly's Assize Reports [*1688-93*] [*A publication*] (DLA)
**Lib Pty Aust NSW Div Res Bull** ... Liberal Party of Australia. New South Wales Division. Research Bulletin [*A publication*] (APTA)
**Lib Q** .......... Library Quarterly [*A publication*]
**LIBQ** .......... Monte Scuro [*Italy*] [*ICAO location identifier*] (ICLI)
**LIBR** .......... Brindise/Casale [*Italy*] [*ICAO location identifier*] (ICLI)
**Libr** .......... Libra [*Constellation*]
**LIBR** .......... Librarian (EY)
**LIBR** .......... Library
**Lib R** .......... Library Review [*A publication*]
**Libr Acquis Pract and Theory** ... Library Acquisitions. Practice and Theory [*A publication*]
**Lib Rames** ... Liber Ramesiensis [*Book of Ramsey*] [*A publication*] (DLA)
**Libr AR** .......... Library Association. Record [*A publication*]
**Library Op** ... Library Opinion [*A publication*] (APTA)
**Library Sci (Japan)** ... Library Science (Japan) [*A publication*]
**Libr Ass Aust Univ Coll Libr Sect News Sh** ... Library Association of Australia. University and College Libraries Section. News Sheet [*A publication*]
**Libr Assoc Rec** ... Library Association. Record [*A publication*]
**Libr Ass Rec** ... Library Association. Record [*A publication*]
**Libr Binder** ... Library Binder [*A publication*]
**Libr Bull Univ Lond** ... Library Bulletin. University of London [*A publication*]
**Libr Chron** ... Library Chronicle [*A publication*]
**Libr Chron Univ Tex** ... Library Chronicle. University of Texas [*A publication*]
**Libr Coll J** ... Library College Journal [*A publication*]
**Libr Comput Equip Rev** ... Library Computer Equipment Review [*A publication*]
**Libr Congr Inf Bull** ... Library of Congress. Information Bulletin [*A publication*]
**Lib Reg** .......... Register Book [*A publication*] (DLA)
**Lib Res** .......... Library Research [*A publication*]
**Lib Resources & Tech Serv** ... Library Resources and Technical Services [*A publication*]
**Lib Resources and Tech Services** ... Library Resources and Technical Services [*A publication*]
**Lib Res Tec** ... Library Resources and Technical Services [*A publication*]
**Lib Rev** .......... Library Review [*A publication*]
**Libr Her** .......... Library Herald [*A publication*]
**Libr Hist** .......... Library History [*A publication*]
**Libr Inf Bull** ... Library and Information Bulletin [*A publication*]
**Libr and Inf Sci** ... Library and Information Science [*A publication*]
**Libr Inf Sci Abstr** ... Library and Information Science Abstracts [*A publication*]
**Libri Oncol** ... Libri Oncologici [*Yugoslavia*] [*A publication*]
**LIBRIS** .......... Library Information Service [*or System*] [*The Royal Library*] [*Database*] [*Information service or system*] (IID)

**LIBRIS** ...... Library Realtime Information System [*South Australian College of Advanced Education*]
**Libr J** ......... Library Journal [*A publication*]
**Libr Lit** ....... Library Literature [*A publication*]
**Libr Mater Afr** ... Library Materials on Africa [*A publication*]
**LIBRN** ....... Librarian
**Libr News Bull** ... Library News Bulletin [*A publication*]
**Libr Newsl** ... Librarians' Newsletter [*United States*] [*A publication*]
**Libr Q** ........ Library Quarterly [*A publication*]
**Libr Resources Tech Serv** ... Library Resources and Technical Services [*A publication*]
**Libr Resour and Tech Serv** ... Library Resources and Technical Services [*A publication*]
**Libr Resour Tech Serv** ... Library Resources and Technical Services [*A publication*]
**Libr Rev** ..... Library Review [*A publication*]
**Libr Rev For Comm (Lond)** ... Library Review. Forestry Commission (London) [*A publication*]
**Libr Sci Abstr** ... Library Science Abstracts [*A publication*]
**Libr Sci Slant Docum** ... Library Science with a Slant to Documentation [*A publication*]
**Libr Technol Rep** ... Library Technology Reports [*A publication*]
**Libr Trends** ... Library Trends [*A publication*]
**Lib Rub** ...... Liber Ruber [*Red Book*] [*A publication*] (DLA)
**Lib Rub Scacc** ... Liber Ruber Scaccarii [*Red Book of the Exchequer*] [*A publication*] (DLA)
**Libr W** ........ Library World [*A publication*]
**Libr Wld** ..... Library World [*A publication*]
**LIBS** .......... Campobasso [*Italy*] [*ICAO location identifier*] (ICLI)
**LIBS** .......... LASER-Induced Breakdown Spectroscopy
**Lib Scene** ... Library Scene [*A publication*]
**LibSciAb** .... Library and Information Science Abstracts [*A publication*]
**Lib Sci Slant Doc** ... Library Science with a Slant to Documentation [*A publication*]
**LIBSET** ..... Library Set [*Computer program*]
**LibSIG** ....... Libertarian SIG [*Special Interest Group*] (EA)
**LIB & SL** ... Libel and Slander [*Legal term*] (DLA)
**LIBSTAD** ... Working Party on Library and Book Trade Relations [*Great Britain*]
**LIBSYS** ..... Library System [*Computer program*]
**LIBT** ......... Termoli [*Italy*] [*ICAO location identifier*] (ICLI)
**Lib Tech Rep** ... Library Technology Reports [*A publication*]
**Lib Trends** ... Library Trends [*A publication*]
**LIBU** .......... Latronico [*Italy*] [*ICAO location identifier*] (ICLI)
**LIB (UN)** ... Headquarters Library of the United Nations
**LIBV** .......... Gioia Del Colle [*Italy*] [*ICAO location identifier*] (ICLI)
**LibVT** ........ Libri Veteris Testamenti (BJA)
**LIBW** ......... Bonifati [*Italy*] [*ICAO location identifier*] (ICLI)
**Lib W** ......... Library World [*A publication*]
**LIBX** .......... Martina Franca [*Italy*] [*ICAO location identifier*] (ICLI)
**LIBY** .......... Santa Maria Di Leuca [*Italy*] [*ICAO location identifier*] (ICLI)
**Libya Ant** ... Libya Antiqua [*A publication*]
**Libya Minist Ind Geol Sec Bull** ... Libya. Ministry of Industry. Geological Section. Bulletin [*A publication*]
**Libya Minist Ind Geol Sect Bull** ... Libya. Ministry of Industry. Geological Section. Bulletin [*A publication*]
**Libyan J Agric** ... Libyan Journal of Agriculture [*A publication*]
**Libyan J Earth Sci** ... Libyan Journal of Earth Science [*A publication*]
**Libyan J Sci** ... Libyan Journal of Science [*A publication*]
**LIBZ** .......... Potenza [*Italy*] [*ICAO location identifier*] (ICLI)
**LIC** ............ Chief Lithographer [*Navy rating*]
**LIC** ............ Lacquer Insulating Compound
**LIC** ............ Lamto [*Ivory Coast*] [*Seismograph station code, US Geological Survey*] (SEIS)
**LIC** ............ Language Identity Code [*Army*] (INF)
**LIC** ............ LASER Image Converter
**LIC** ............ LASER-Induced Chemistry (RDA)
**LIC** ............ LASER Intercept Capability [*Military*] (CAAL)
**LIC** ............ Law in Context [*Australia*] [*A publication*]
**LIC** ............ Lawson, I. C., St. Paul MN [*STAC*]
**LIC** ............ League International for Creditors (DCTA)
**LIC** ............ Lecturer in Charge (ADA)
**LIC** ............ Level Indicator Controller (NRCH)
**LIC** ............ Library Information Center [*Lunar and Planetary Institute*] [*Information service or system*] (IID)
**LIC** ............ License (KSC)
**LIC** ............ Licentiate
**LIC** ............ Life Insurance in Canada [*A publication*]
**LIC** ............ Life Insurers Conference [*Richmond, VA*] (EA)
**LIC** ............ Limiting Isorrheic Concentration [*Medicine*]
**LIC** ............ Limon, CO [*Location identifier*] [*FAA*] (FAAL)
**LIC** ............ Linear Integrated Circuit
**LIC** ............ Lithuanian Information Center (EA)
**LIC** ............ Load Interface Circuit (MCD)
**LIC** ............ Local Import Control [*British*] (DS)
**LIC** ............ London International College [*British*]
**LIC** ............ Loop Insertion Cell [*Nuclear energy*] (NRCH)
**LIC** ............ Low Income Country
**LIC** ............ Low Inertia Clutch
**LIC** ............ Low-Intensity Conflict [*Military*]
**LIC** ............ Lunar Instrument Carrier [*NASA*] (KSC)
**LICA** .......... Lamezia/Terme [*Italy*] [*ICAO location identifier*] (ICLI)
**LICA** .......... Land Improvement Contractors of America (EA)
**LICA** .......... Ligue Internationale Contre le Racisme et l'Antisemitisme [*International League Against Racism and Antisemitism*]
**LicAc** .......... Licentiate in Acupuncture [*British*]
**Lic Agro** ..... Licentiate in Agronomy [*British*]
**LICALM** ..... LORAN Inertial Command Air-Launched Missile
**LICB** .......... Comiso [*Italy*] [*ICAO location identifier*] (ICLI)
**LICC** .......... Catania/Fontanarossa [*Italy*] [*ICAO location identifier*] (ICLI)
**LICC** .......... League for Innovation in the Community College (EA)
**LICCD** ....... Ligue Internationale Contre la Concurrence Deloyale [*International League Against Unfair Competition*] (EAIO)
**LICD** .......... Lampedusa [*Italy*] [*ICAO location identifier*] (ICLI)
**LICD** .......... Licensed (ROG)
**Lic en Der** .. Licenciado en Derecho [*Licentiate in Law*] [*Spanish*]
**LICE** .......... Enna [*Italy*] [*ICAO location identifier*] (ICLI)
**LICE** .......... License (ROG)
**Licensing L and Bus Rep** ... Licensing Law and Business Report [*A publication*]
**Licens Int** ... Licensing International [*A publication*]
**Licentiate All-India Mon J Med Surg** ... Licentiate All-India Monthly Journal of Medicine and Surgery [*A publication*]
**LICET** ........ Library of Industrial and Commercial Education and Training
**LICF** .......... [*The*] Long Island City Financial Corporation [*NASDAQ symbol*] (NQ)
**LICF** .......... Messina [*Italy*] [*ICAO location identifier*] (ICLI)
**Lic en Fil** .... Licenciado en Filosofia [*Licentiate in Philosophy*] [*Spanish*]
**LICG** .......... Pantelleria [*Italy*] [*ICAO location identifier*] (ICLI)
**LICH** .......... Capo Spartivento [*Italy*] [*ICAO location identifier*] (ICLI)
**LICH** .......... Lichenologist [*A publication*]
**LICH** .......... Lichfield [*City in England*] (ROG)
**Licht-Forsch** ... Licht-Forschung [*A publication*]
**Lichttech** .... Lichttechnik [*A publication*]
**LICI** ........... Finale [*Italy*] [*ICAO location identifier*] (ICLI)
**LICI** ........... Lilly Industrial Coatings, Incorporated [*NASDAQ symbol*] (NQ)
**LICIT** ......... Labor-Industry Coalition for International Trade [*Washington, DC*] (EA)
**LICITA** ...... Life Insurance Company Income Tax Act of 1959
**LICJ** .......... Palermo/Punta Raisi [*Italy*] [*ICAO location identifier*] (ICLI)
**LICK** .......... Lightweight Communication Kit (MCD)
**LICL** .......... Gela [*Italy*] [*ICAO location identifier*] (ICLI)
**LICM** ......... Calopezzati [*Italy*] [*ICAO location identifier*] (ICLI)
**LICM** ......... Left Intercostal Margin [*Anatomy*]
**LICM** ......... Master Chief Lithographer [*Navy rating*]
**Lic Med** ...... Licentiate in Medicine
**LICND** ....... Life Insurance Committee for a Nuclear Disarmament (EA)
**LICNWF** ... Life Insurance Committee for a Nuclear Weapons Freeze [*Later, LICND*] (EA)
**LICO** .......... Cozzo Spadaro [*Italy*] [*ICAO location identifier*] (ICLI)
**LICO** .......... Lifesurance Corporation [*NASDAQ symbol*] (NQ)
**LICOF** ........ Land Lines Communications Facilities [*Aviation*] (FAAC)
**LICOR** ....... Lightning Correlation
**LICP** .......... Lead Inventory Control Point (NG)
**LicP** ........... Liceus de Portugal [*A publication*]
**LICP** .......... Palermo/Boccadifalco [*Italy*] [*ICAO location identifier*] (ICLI)
**Lic Phil** ...... Licentiate in Philosophy [*British*]
**LICR** .......... Reggio Calabria [*Italy*] [*ICAO location identifier*] (ICLI)
**LICROSS** .. League of International Red Cross Societies
**LiCrOx** ...... Lithium/Chromium-Oxide [*Type of battery*]
**LICS** .......... Lotus International Character Set [*Printer technology*] (PCM)
**LICS** .......... Sciacca [*Italy*] [*ICAO location identifier*] (ICLI)
**LICS** .......... Senior Chief Lithographer [*Navy rating*]
**LICT** .......... Trapani/Birgi [*Italy*] [*ICAO location identifier*] (ICLI)
**LICTA** ....... Life Insurance Company Tax Act of 1955
**Lic Tech** .... Licentiate in Technology [*British*]
**Lic Theol** .... Licentiate in Theology [*British*]
**LICU** .......... League of IBM [*International Business Machines Corp.*] Employee Credit Unions (EA)
**LICU** .......... Ustica [*Italy*] [*ICAO location identifier*] (ICLI)
**LICVD** ....... LASER-Induced Chemical Vapor Deposition [*Photovoltaic energy systems*]
**LICW** ......... Licentiate of the Institute of Clerks of Works of Great Britain, Inc. (DBQ)
**LICX** .......... Prizzi [*Italy*] [*ICAO location identifier*] (ICLI)
**LICZ** .......... Sigonella [*Italy*] [*ICAO location identifier*] (ICLI)
**LID** ........... Labor Information Database [*International Labor Office*] [*Information service or system*] (IID)
**LID** ........... Laboratory of Infectious Diseases [*Later, Laboratory of Viral Diseases*] [*NIAID*]
**LID** ........... LASER Image Display (MCD)
**LID** ........... LASER Intrusion Detector
**LID** ........... LASER Intrusion Device (MCD)
**LID** ........... LASER Isotope Dating
**LID** ........... Leadless Inverted Device
**LID** ........... League for Industrial Democracy (EA)
**LID** ........... Letters in Digit Strings [*Psychology*]
**LID** ........... Library Issue Document (NVT)
**LID** ........... Lidco Industries, Inc. [*Toronto Stock Exchange symbol*]
**LID** ........... Lift Improvement Device (MCD)

**LID** ........... Light Infantry Division [*Army*] (INF)
**LID** ........... Limited Instrument Departure (MCD)
**LID** ........... Line Item Description (MCD)
**LID** ........... Linear Imaging Device (MCD)
**LID** ........... Liquid Immersion Development [*Reprography*]
**LID** ........... Liquid Interface Diffusion
**LiD** ........... Literatur im Dialog [*A publication*]
**LID** ........... Literaturdienst Medizin und Umwelt [*Literature Service in Medicine and Environment*] [*Austrian National Institute for Public Health*] [*Information service or system*] (IID)
**LID** ........... Local Issue Data [*Telecommunications*] (TEL)
**LID** ........... Locked-In Device (MSA)
**LID** ........... Logical Identification (MCD)
**LID** ........... Logistics Identification Document (NASA)
**L & ID** ........ London and India Docks [*Shipping*] [*British*] (ROG)
**LID** ........... Low-Iodine Diet [*Medicine*]
**LIDA** .......... Ligue Internationale des Droits de l'Animal [*International League for Animal Rights*] (EAIO)
**LIDA** .......... Lodzer Idishe Dramatishe Aktyorn (BJA)
**LIDAR** ....... Atmospheric Light Detection and Ranging Facility [*Los Alamos, NM*] [*Los Alamos National Laboratory*] [*Department of Energy*] (GRD)
**LIDAR** ....... LASER Infrared RADAR (IEEE)
**LIDAR** ....... LASER Intensity Direction and Ranging (IEEE)
**LIDAR** ....... Light Detection and Ranging
**LIDAS** ....... Laboratory Instrument Data Acquisition
**LIDB** .......... Logistics Intelligence Data Base (AABC)
**LIDC** .......... Lead Industries Development Council [*British*] (DAS)
**LIDC** .......... Ligue Internationale du Droit de la Concurrence [*International League for Competition Law*] [*Paris, France*] (EA)
**LIDC** .......... Low Intensity - Direct Current
**LIDF** .......... Line Intermediate Distributing Frame
**LIDIA** ........ Liaison Internationale des Industries de l'Alimentation [*International Liaison for the Food Industries*]
**LIDIA** ........ Licentiate of the Industrial Design Institute of Australia
**LIDO** ......... Logistics Inventory Disposition Order (AAG)
**LIDS** .......... Laboratory for Information and Decision Systems [*Massachusetts Institute of Technology*] [*Research center*] (RCD)
**LIDS** .......... LASER Illumination Detection System
**LIDS** .......... LASER Infrared Countermeasures Demonstration System [*Air Force*]
**LIDS** .......... Lithium Ion Drift Semiconductor
**LIDS** .......... Logistics Item Data Systems [*DoD*]
**LIDUS** ....... Liberal-Demokratische Union der Schweiz [*Liberal Democratic Union of Switzerland*] [*Political party*] (PPE)
**LIE** ............ Lectures in Economics. Theory, Institutions, Policy [*Elsevier Book Series*] [*A publication*]
**LIE** ............ Left Inboard Elevon [*Aviation*] (MCD)
**LIE** ............ Legal Issues of European Integration [*A publication*]
**LIE** ............ Libenge [*Zaire*] [*Airport symbol*] [*Obsolete*] (OAG)
**LIE** ............ Liechtenstein [*ANSI three-letter standard code*] (CNC)
**LIE** ............ Limited Information Estimation
**LIE** ............ Line Islands Experiment [*National Science Foundation*]
**LIEA** .......... Alghero [*Italy*] [*ICAO location identifier*] (ICLI)
**LIEA** .......... Low Income Energy Assistance [*Later, LIHEAP*] [*Block grant*]
**LIEB** .......... Capo Bellavista [*Italy*] [*ICAO location identifier*] (ICLI)
**LIEB** .......... Liebert Corp. [*NASDAQ symbol*] (NQ)
**Lieber Civ Lib** ... Lieber on Civil Liberty and Self Government [*A publication*] (DLA)
**Lieb Herm** ... Lieber's Hermeneutics [*A publication*] (DLA)
**Liebigs Ann Chem** ... Liebigs Annalen der Chemie [*A publication*]
**LIEC** .......... Capo Carbonara [*Italy*] [*ICAO location identifier*] (ICLI)
**Liecht** ........ Liechtenstein
**LIECU** ....... League of IBM [*International Business Machines Corp.*] Employee Credit Unions [*Later, LICU*] (EA)
**LIED** .......... Decimomannu [*Italy*] [*ICAO location identifier*] (ICLI)
**LIED** .......... LASER Initiating Explosive Device
**LIED** .......... Linkage Editor [*Data processing*]
**LIEE** .......... Cagliari/Elmas [*Italy*] [*ICAO location identifier*] (ICLI)
**LIEE** .......... Law in Eastern Europe [*A publication*] (DLA)
**LIEF** .......... Capo Frasca [*Italy*] [*ICAO location identifier*] (ICLI)
**LIEF** .......... Launch Information Exchange Facility [*NASA*]
**LIEFC** ........ Long Island Early Fliers Club (EA)
**LIEG** .......... Guardiavecchia [*Italy*] [*ICAO location identifier*] (ICLI)
**Lie Groups Hist Frontiers and Appl** ... Lie Groups. History. Frontiers and Applications [*A publication*]
**LIEH** .......... Capo Caccia [*Italy*] [*ICAO location identifier*] (ICLI)
**LIEL** .......... Capo S. Lorenzo [*Italy*] [*ICAO location identifier*] (ICLI)
**LIEM** .......... Macomer [*Italy*] [*ICAO location identifier*] (ICLI)
**LIEN** .......... Fonni [*Italy*] [*ICAO location identifier*] (ICLI)
**LIENS** ........ Ligue Europeenne pour une Nouvelle Societe [*European League for a New Society - ELNS*] [*Paris, France*] (EAIO)
**LIEO** .......... Olbia/Costa Smeralda [*Italy*] [*ICAO location identifier*] (ICLI)
**LIEP** .......... LORAN Integrated Engineering Program
**LIEP** .......... Perdasdefogu [*Italy*] [*ICAO location identifier*] (ICLI)
**LIEPS** ........ LORAN Integrated Engineering Program, Shed Light
**Liet Fiz Rink** ... Lietuvos Fizikos Rinkinys [*A publication*]
**Liet Fiz Rinkinys** ... Lietuvos Fizikos Rinkinys [*Lithuanian SSR*] [*A publication*]
**Liet Gyvulinink Mokslinio Tyrimo Inst Darb** ... Lietuvos Gyvulininkystes Mokslinio Tyrimo Instituto Darbai [*A publication*]
**Liet Gyvulinink Vet Mokslinio Tyrimo Inst Darb** ... Lietuvos Gyvulininkystes ir Veterinarijos Mokslinio Tyrimo Instituto Darbai [*A publication*]
**Liet Hidrotech Melior Mokslinio Tyrimo Inst Darb** ... Lietuvos Hidrotechnikas ir Melioracijos Mokslinio Tyrimo Instituto Darbai [*A publication*]
**Liet Mat Rink** ... Lietuvos Matematikos Rinkinys [*A publication*]
**Liet Misku Ukio Mokslinio Tyrimo Inst Darb** ... Lietuvos Misku Ukio Mokslinio Tyrimo Instituto Darbai [*A publication*]
**LIETS** ........ Land Integrated Equipment for Tactical Systems (MCD)
**Liet TSR Aukst Mokslo Darb Chem Chem Technol** ... Lietuvos TSR Aukstuju Mokyklu Mokslo Darbai. Chemija ir Chemine Technologija [*Lithuanian SSR*] [*A publication*]
**Liet TSR Aukst Mokyklu Moksl Darb Ultragarsas** ... Lietuvos TSR Aukstuju Mokyklu Mokslo Darbai. Ultragarsas [*A publication*]
**Liet TSR Aukst Mokyklu Mokslo Darb Biol** ... Lietuvos TSR Aukstuju Mokyklu Mokslo Darbai. Biologija [*A publication*]
**Liet TSR Aukst Mokyklu Mokslo Darb Chem Chem Technol** ... Lietuvos TSR Aukstuju Mokyklu Mokslo Darbai. Chemija ir Chemine Technologija [*A publication*]
**Liet TSR Aukst Mokyklu Mokslo Darb Elektrotech Autom** ... Lietuvos TSR Aukstuju Mokyklu Mokslo Darbai. Elektrotechnika ir Automatika [*A publication*]
**Liet TSR Aukst Mokyklu Mokslo Darb Elektrotech Mech** ... Lietuvos TSR Aukstuju Mokyklu Mokslo Darbai. Elektrotechnika ir Mechanika [*A publication*]
**Liet TSR Aukst Mokyklu Mokslo Darb Geogr Geol** ... Lietuvos TSR Aukstuju Mokyklu Mokslo Darbai. Geografija ir Geologija [*A publication*]
**Liet TSR Aukst Mokyklu Mokslo Darb Mech** ... Lietuvos TSR Aukstuju Mokyklu Mokslo Darbai. Mechanika [*A publication*]
**Liet TSR Aukst Mokyklu Mokslo Darb Mech Technol** ... Lietuvos TSR Aukstuju Mokyklu Mokslo Darbai. Mechanine Technologija [*A publication*]
**Liet TSR Aukst Mokyklu Mokslo Darb Med** ... Lietuvos TSR Aukstuju Mokyklu Mokslo Darbai. Medicina [*A publication*]
**Liet TSR Aukst Mokyklu Mokslo Darb Statyba Archit** ... Lietuvos TSR Aukstuju Mokyklu Mokslo Darbai. Statyba ir Architektura [*A publication*]
**Liet TSR Aukst Mokyklu Mokslo Darb Tekst Odos Technol** ... Lietuvos TSR Aukstuju Mokyklu Mokslo Darbai. Tekstiles ir Odos Technologija [*A publication*]
**Liet TSR Mokslu Akad Bot Inst Bot Klausimai** ... Lietuvos TSR Mokslu Akademiya Botanikos Institutas. Botanikos Klausimai [*A publication*]
**Liet TSR Mokslu Akad Bot Inst Straipsniu Rinkinys** ... Lietuvos TSR Mokslu Akademija Botanikos Institutas Straipsniu Rinkinys [*A publication*]
**Liet TSR Mokslu Akad Darb** ... Lietuvos TSR Mokslu Akademijos Darbai [*A publication*]
**Liet TSR Mokslu Akad Darbai B** ... Lietuvos TSR Mokslu Akademijos Darbai. Serija B [*A publication*]
**Liet TSR Mokslu Akad Darb Ser B** ... Lietuvos TSR Mokslu Akademijos Darbai. Serija B [*A publication*]
**Liet TSR Mokslu Akad Darb Ser C** ... Lietuvos TSR Mokslu Akademijos Darbai. Serija C [*A publication*]
**Liet TSR Mokslu Akad Darb Ser C Biol Mokslai** ... Lietuvos TSR Mokslu Akademijos Darbai. Serija C. Biologijos Mokslai [*A publication*]
**Liet TSR Mokslu Akad Eksp Med Inst Darb** ... Lietuvos TSR Mokslu Akademijos Eksperimentines Medicinos Instituto Darbai [*A publication*]
**Liet TSR Mokslu Akad Geogr Skyrius Moksliniai Pranesimai** ... Lietuvos TSR Mokslu Akademija Geografijos Skyrius Moksliniai Pranesimai [*A publication*]
**Liet TSR Mokslu Akad Geol Geogr Inst Moksliniai Pranesimai** ... Lietuvos TSR Mokslu Akademija Geologijos Geografijos Instituta Moksliniai Pranesimai [*A publication*]
**Liet TSR Mokslu Akad Zinynas** ... Lietuvos TSR Mokslu Akademijas Zinynas [*A publication*]
**Lietuvos Mok Akad Darbai** ... Lietuvos TSR Mokslu Akademijos Darbai [*A publication*]
**Liet Vet Akad Darb** ... Lietuvos Veterinarijos Akademijos Darbai [*A publication*]
**Liet Zemdir Moks Tyrimo Inst Darb** ... Lietuvos Zemdirbystes Mokslinio Tyrimo Instituto Darbai [*A publication*]
**Liet Zemes Ukio Akad Mokslo Darb** ... Lietuvos Zemes Ukio Akademija Mokslo Darbai [*A publication*]
**LIEUT** ....... Lieutenant (EY)
**Lieut-Col** .... Lieutenant-Colonel [*British military*] (DMA)
**Lieut-Gen** ... Lieutenant-General [*British military*] (DMA)
**LIF** ............ LASER-Induced Fluorescence [*Physical chemistry*]
**LIF** ............ LASER Interference Filter
**LIF** ............ Layaway of Industrial Facilities (AABC)
**LIF** ............ Left Iliac Fossa [*Medicine*]
**LIF** ............ Leukemia Inhibitory Factor [*Oncology*]
**LIF** ............ Leukocyte Inhibition Factor [*Hematology*]
**LIF** ............ Lifestyle Restaurants, Inc. [*AMEX symbol*] (SPSG)
**LIF** ............ Lifu [*Loyalty Islands*] [*Airport symbol*] (OAG)

**LIF**............ Logistics Intelligence File (AABC)
**LIF**............ Lone Indian Fellowship [*Later, Lone Indian Fellowship and Lone Scout Alumni*] (EA)
**LIF**............ Low-Ionization Filament Component [*Galactic science*]
**LIFA**.......... Licentiate of the International Faculty of Arts [*British*]
**LIFE**.......... Laboratory for International Fuzzy Engineering Research [*Japan*]
**LIFE**.......... Language Improvement to Facilitate Education of Hearing-Impaired Children [*A project of NEA*]
**LIFE**.......... LASER-Induced Fluorescence Emission
**LIFE**.......... League for International Food Education (EA)
**LIFE**.......... Lear Integrated Flight Equipment (MCD)
**LIFE**.......... Learning in a Free Environment [*Education program*]
**LIFE**.......... Less Infant Fatality Everywhere [*In association name, Project LIFE*]
**LIFE**.......... Liberia International Foundation for Elevation
**LIFE**.......... Life Issues in Formal Education (EA)
**LIFE**.......... Lifeline Systems, Inc. [*NASDAQ symbol*] (NQ)
**LIFE**.......... Logistics Intelligence File Europe
**LIFE**.......... Love Is Feeding Everyone (EA)
**LIFE**.......... Low Income Family Emancipation Society
**LIFE**.......... Low Income Family Emergency Center
**Life and Acc Ins R** ... Bigelow's Life and Accident Insurance Reports [*A publication*] (DLA)
**Life Aust**.... Life Australia [*A publication*] (APTA)
**Life C**......... Life (Health and Accident) Cases [*Commerce Clearing House*] [*A publication*] (DLA)
**Life Cas**...... Life (Health and Accident) Cases [*Commerce Clearing House*] [*A publication*] (DLA)
**Life Cas 2d** ... Life (Health and Accident) Cases, Second Series [*Commerce Clearing House*] [*A publication*] (DLA)
**Life Chem Rep Suppl Ser** ... Life Chemistry Reports. Supplement Series [*A publication*]
**Life D**......... Life Digest [*A publication*] (APTA)
**Life Dig**...... Life Digest [*A publication*] (APTA)
**Life Environ** ... Life and Environment [*Japan*] [*A publication*]
**Life Health & Accid Ins Cas 2d CCH** ... Life, Health, and Accident Insurance Cases. Second. Commerce Clearing House [*A publication*]
**Life Ins Courant** ... Life Insurance Courant [*A publication*]
**Life Insur Index** ... Life Insurance Index [*A publication*]
**LIFEL**........ Limited Functional English Literacy
**Life & Lett** ... Life and Letters [*A publication*]
**Lifelong Learn** ... Lifelong Learning [*A publication*]
**Lifelong Learn Adult Years** ... Lifelong Learning: The Adult Years [*A publication*]
**LIFEMAN** ... Live Fire Evaluation Manikin [*Perceptronics, Inc.*] [*Military*]
**Life with Mus** ... Life with Music [*A publication*]
**LIFES**........ LASER-Induced Fluorescence and Environmental Sensing [*NASA*]
**Life Sci**....... Life Sciences [*A publication*]
**Life Sci Adv** ... Life Science Advances [*A publication*]
**Life Sci Agric Exp Stn Tech Bull (Maine)** ... Life Sciences and Agriculture Experiment Station. Technical Bulletin (Maine) [*A publication*]
**Life Sci Collect** ... Life Sciences Collection [*A publication*]
**Life Sci Inst Kivo Jochi Daigaku Seimei Kagaku Kenkyusho** ... Life Science Institute Kivo/Jochi Daigaku Seimei Kagaku Kenkyusho [*A publication*]
**Life Sci Monogr** ... Life Sciences Monographs [*A publication*]
**Life Sci Part I** ... Life Sciences. Part I. Physiology and Pharmacology [*A publication*]
**Life Sci Part II** ... Life Sciences. Part II. Biochemistry. General and Molecular Biology [*A publication*]
**Life Sci Part II Biochem Gen Mol Biol** ... Life Sciences. Part II. Biochemistry. General and Molecular Biology [*A publication*]
**Life Sci Part I Physiol Pharmacol** ... Life Sciences. Part I. Physiology and Pharmacology [*A publication*]
**Life Sci Res Rep** ... Life Sciences Research Reports [*A publication*]
**Life Sci Space Res** ... Life Sciences and Space Research [*Netherlands*] [*A publication*]
**Lifeskills Teach Mag** ... Lifeskills Teaching Magazine [*A publication*]
**LifeSpir**...... [*The*] Life of the Spirit [*London*] [*A publication*] (BJA)
**LIFESTA**... Lifeboat Station [*Coast Guard*]
**Life Support Syst** ... Life Support Systems [*A publication*]
**Life-Threat** ... Life-Threatening Behavior [*A publication*]
**LIFFE**........ London International Financial Futures Exchange Ltd. [*London, England*]
**LiFHAS**..... Libertarian Foundation for Human Assistance (EAIO)
**LiFHAS**..... Libertarische Fonds voor Hulp Acties [*Libertarian Foundation for Human Assistance*] (EAIO)
**LIFI**........... Life of Indiana Corp. [*Indianapolis, IN*] [*NASDAQ symbol*] (NQ)
**LIFLSA**..... Lone Indian Fellowship and Lone Scout Alumni (EA)
**LIFMOP**... Linearly Frequency-Modulated Pulse
**LIFO**.......... Last In, First Out [*Queuing technique*] [*Accounting*]
**LIFO**.......... Life Orientation (Survey)
**LIFPL**........ Ligue Internationale de Femmes pour la Paix et la Liberte [*Women's International League for Peace and Freedom - WILPF*] (EAIO)
**LIFRAM** ... Liquid-Fueled Ramjet [*Navy*] (MCD)
**LIFS**........... London International Furniture Show [*British*] (ITD)
**LIFS**........... Lowell Institution for Savings [*Lowell, MA*] [*NASDAQ symbol*] (NQ)
**LIFSA**........ Life Sciences [*A publication*]
**LIFSUM**.... Airlift Summary Report [*Air Force*]
**LIFT**.......... [*The*] Aviation Group, Inc. [*NASDAQ symbol*] (NQ)
**LIFT**.......... Link Intellectual Functions Tester
**LIFT**.......... Logically Integrated FORTRAN Translator [*UNIVAC*]
**LIFT**.......... London International Festival of Theatre [*British*]
**LIFT**.......... London International Freight Terminal (DS)
**LIFT**.......... Low Interfacial Tension [*Physical chemistry*]
**LIFT**.......... Lower Inventory for Tomorrow [*A program of the Canadian government to bring heavy stocks of wheat into line with demand by paying farmers not to produce*]
**Lift Elevator Lift Ropeway Eng** ... Lift, Elevator Lift, and Ropeway Engineering [*A publication*]
**LIG**............ LASER Image Generator (MCD)
**LIG**............ Leichte Infanteriegeschuetz [*Light Infantry Howitzer*] [*German military - World War II*]
**lig**.............. Ligacao [*Union*] [*Portuguese*]
**LIG**............ Ligament [*or Ligamentum*]
**LIG**............ Ligated [*or Ligation*] [*Medicine*]
**LIG**............ Limoges [*France*] [*Airport symbol*] (OAG)
**LiG**............ Literatur in der Gesellschaft [*A publication*]
**LIG**............ London Industrial Group [*British*]
**Lig**............ Pro Ligario [*of Cicero*] [*Classical studies*] (OCD)
**LIGA**.......... Liquid Granule Applicator [*Device used to disperse pesticides*]
**Ligand Q**.... Ligand Quarterly [*A publication*]
**LIGCM**...... Licentiate of the Incorporated Guild of Church Musicians [*British*] (ROG)
**Lig Dig**....... Ligon's Digest [*Alabama*] [*A publication*] (DLA)
**LIGG**.......... Ligaments [*or Ligamenti*]
**LIGHT**....... Light Industrial Gas Heat Transfer
**Light Aust** ... Lighting in Australia [*A publication*]
**Light Des Appl** ... Lighting Design and Application [*A publication*]
**Light Equip News** ... Lighting Equipment News [*A publication*]
**LIGHTEX** ... Searchlight Illumination Exercise [*Also, LITEX*] [*Military*] (NVT)
**Lighting Des Applic** ... Lighting Design and Application [*A publication*]
**Lighting Design & Appl** ... Lighting Design and Application [*A publication*]
**Lighting Equip News** ... Lighting Equipment News [*A publication*]
**Lighting Res Tech** ... Lighting Research and Technology [*A publication*]
**Light Light** ... Light and Lighting [*A publication*]
**Light and Light** ... Light and Lighting [*A publication*]
**Light and Light and Environ Des** ... Light and Lighting and Environmental Design [*A publication*]
**Light Light Environ Des** ... Light and Lighting and Environmental Design [*A publication*]
**Light Met Age** ... Light Metal Age [*A publication*]
**Light Met (London)** ... Light Metals (London) [*A publication*]
**Light Met Met Ind** ... Light Metals and Metal Industry [*England*] [*A publication*]
**Light Met (New York)** ... Light Metals: Proceedings of Sessions. American Institute of Mining, Metallurgical, and Petroleum Engineers. Annual Meeting (New York) [*A publication*]
**Light Met (Tokyo)** ... Light Metals (Tokyo) [*A publication*]
**Light Mtl** ... Light Metal Age [*A publication*]
**LIGHTPHOTORON** ... Light Photographic Squadron
**Light Res and Technol** ... Lighting Research and Technology [*A publication*]
**Light Res Technol** ... Lighting Research and Technology [*A publication*]
**Lignite Symp Proc** ... Lignite Symposium. Proceedings [*A publication*]
**LIGO**.......... LASER Interferometry Gravitational Wave Observatory [*Proposed*]
**LIH**............ LASER Interferometric Holography
**LIH**............ Left Inguinal Hernia [*Medicine*]
**LIH**............ Letters and Inscriptions of Hammurabi [*A publication*] (BJA)
**LIH**............ Light Intensity High
**LIH**............ Lihue [*Hawaii*] [*Airport symbol*] (OAG)
**LIH**............ Line Interface Handler
**LIHDC**...... Low Income Housing Development Corporation [*North Carolina*] (EA)
**LIHE**.......... Lutheran Institute of Human Ecology (EA)
**LIHEAP**.... Low Income Home Energy Assistance Program [*Formerly, LIEA*] [*Block grant*]
**LIHG**.......... Ligue Internationale de Hockey sur Glace [*International Ice Hockey Federation*]
**LIHIS**........ Low Income Housing Information Service (EA)
**LI Hist Soc Memoirs** ... Long Island Historical Society. Memoirs [*A publication*]
**LIHN**.......... Hieronymi Liber Interpretationis Hebraicorum Nominum (BJA)
**LII**............. Larizza Industries, Incorporated [*AMEX symbol*] (SPSG)
**LII**............. Life Insurance Index [*A publication*]
**LII**............. Livestock Industry Institute (EA)
**LII**............. Mulia [*Indonesia*] [*Airport symbol*] (OAG)
**LII**............. Nieuwe Linie [*A publication*]
**LIIA**........... Italy International NOTAM Office [*Italy*] [*ICAO location identifier*] (ICLI)
**LIIB**........... Roma [*Italy*] [*ICAO location identifier*] (ICLI)
**LIIC**........... Italy Military International NOTAM Office [*Italy*] [*ICAO location identifier*] (ICLI)
**LIIG**........... Logistics Item Identification Guide [*Military*] (AFM)

**LIII**........... Roma [*Italy*] [*ICAO location identifier*] (ICLI)
**Liiketal Aikakausk** ... Liiketaloudellinen Aikakauskirja [*Journal of Business Economics*] [*A publication*]
**LIINEO**..... Livestock International [*A publication*]
**LIIP**........... LASER-Induced Infrared Photochemistry
**LIIR**........... Italian Agency for Air Navigation Services [*Italy*] [*ICAO location identifier*] (ICLI)
**LIJ**............ Law Institute Journal [*A publication*] (APTA)
**LIJ**............ Lawyers for an Independent Judiciary (EA)
**Lijec Vjesn** ... Lijecnicki Vjesnik [*A publication*]
**LIJJ**........... Roma [*Italy*] [*ICAO location identifier*] (ICLI)
**LIK**............ Leichte Infanteriekolonne [*Light Infantry Supply Column*] [*German military - World War II*]
**LiK**............ Liaudies Kuryba [*A publication*]
**LIK**............ Likiep [*Marshall Islands*] [*Airport symbol*] (OAG)
**LiK**............ Literatura ir Kalba [*A publication*]
**LIL**............ Laboratory Interface Language [*Programming language*]
**LIL**............ Large Immersion Lens
**LIL**............ Large-Ion Lithophile
**LIL**............ Lead-In Light-System [*Aviation*]
**LIL**............ Light Intensity Low
**LIL**............ Lilac (ROG)
**LIL**............ Lille [*France*] [*Airport symbol*] (OAG)
**LIL**............ Lille [*France*] [*Seismograph station code, US Geological Survey*] [*Closed*] (SEIS)
**Lil**............ Lilly's English Assize Reports [*1688-93*] [*A publication*] (DLA)
**LiL**............ Limba si Literatura [*A publication*]
**LIL**............ Lincoln's Inn Library [*A publication*] (DLA)
**LIL**............ Live-In Lover [*Slang*] (DSUE)
**LIL**............ Long Island Lighting Co. [*Formerly, LLT*] [*NYSE symbol*] (SPSG)
**LIL**............ Low-Input Landscaping
**LIL**............ Lunar International Laboratory
**LILA**.......... Ligue Internationale de la Librairie Ancienne [*International League of Antiquarian Booksellers - ILAB*] (EAIO)
**Lil Abr**....... Lilly's Abridgment [*England*] [*A publication*] (DLA)
**LILAC**......... Low-Intensity Large Area [*Headlight*]
**LILAM**......... Licentiate of the Institute of Leisure and Amenity Management [*British*] (DBQ)
**LILCO**......... Long Island Lighting Company
**Lil Conv**..... Lilly's Conveyancer [*A publication*] (DLA)
**LILE**.......... Large Ion Lithophile Element [*Geochemistry*]
**LiLi**........... Zeitschrift fuer Literaturwissenschaft und Linguistik [*A publication*]
**Lilla**.......... Lillabulero [*A publication*]
**Lille Chir** ... Lille Chirurgical [*A publication*]
**Lille Med** ... Lille Medical [*A publication*]
**Lille Med Actual** ... Lille Medical. Actualites [*A publication*]
**Lill Ent**....... Lilly's Entries [*England*] [*A publication*] (DLA)
**Lilly**........... Lilly's Reports and Pleadings of Cases in Assize [*170 English Reprint*] [*1688-93*] [*A publication*] (DLA)
**Lilly Abr**.... Lilly's Abridgment [*England*] [*A publication*] (DLA)
**Lilly Assize** ... Lilly's Reports and Pleadings of Cases in Assize [*170 English Reprint*] [*1688-93*] [*A publication*] (DLA)
**Lilly Assize (Eng)** ... Lilly's Reports and Pleadings of Cases in Assize [*170 English Reprint*] [*1688-93*] [*A publication*] (DLA)
**LILO**.......... Last-In, Last-Out [*Accounting*]
**LILOC**........ Light Lyne Optical Correlation (MCD)
**LILRC**........ Long Island Library Resources Council [*Bellport, NY*] [*Library network*]
**Lil Reg**....... Lilly's Practical Register [*A publication*] (ILCA)
**Lily Yearb North Am Lily Soc** ... Lily Yearbook. North American Lily Society [*A publication*]
**LIM**........... Compass Locator of Inner Marker Site
**LIM**........... Laboratory Institute of Merchandising [*New York, NY*]
**LIM**........... Language Interpretation Module
**LIM**........... Latent Image Memory
**LIM**........... Leg-Inducing Membrane [*Entomology*]
**LIM**........... Leningrad Institute of Metals [*USSR*] (MCD)
**LIM**........... Light Intensity Medium
**LIM**........... Lima [*Peru*] [*Seismograph station code, US Geological Survey*] (SEIS)
**LIM**........... Lima [*Peru*] [*Airport symbol*] (OAG)
**LIM**........... Lima Public Library, Lima, OH [*OCLC symbol*] (OCLC)
**LIM**........... Limber (MSA)
**LIM**........... Limerick [*County in Ireland*] (ROG)
**LIM**........... Limit
**LIM**........... Limonene [*Organic chemistry*]
**LIM**........... Line Interface Module
**LIM**........... Linear Induction Motor [*Magnetic rapid-transit car*]
**LiM**........... Lingue del Mondo [*A publication*]
**LIM**........... Liquid Injection Molding
**LiM**........... Literatura i Marksizm [*A publication*]
**LiM**........... Literatura i Mastatsva [*A publication*]
**LIM**........... Losing Inventory Manager [*Army*] (AABC)
**LIM**........... Lotus/Intel/Microsoft [*Data processing*]
**LIM**........... Lower Inlet Module [*Nuclear energy*] (NRCH)
**LIMA**......... LASER-Induced Ion-Mass Analyzer [*Instrumentation*]
**LIMA**......... Licentiate of the Institute of Mathematics and Its Applications [*British*] (DBQ)
**LIMA**......... Logic-in-Memory Array
**LIMA**......... Torino [*Italy*] [*ICAO location identifier*] (ICLI)
**LIMAC**....... Large Integrated Monolithic Array Computer (MCD)
**LIM ACT**.. Limitation of Action [*Legal term*] (DLA)
**LIMAS**....... Lightweight Marking System [*British Army*]
**LIMB**......... Library Instruction Materials Bank [*Loughborough University of Technology*] [*Information service or system*] (IID)
**LIMB**......... Limestone Injection/Multistage Burner
**LIMB**......... Liquid Metal Breeder [*Reactor*]
**LIMB**......... Milano/Bresso [*Italy*] [*ICAO location identifier*] (ICLI)
**LIMC**......... Lexicon Iconographicum Mythologiae Classicae [*A publication*]
**LIMC**......... Milano/Malpensa [*Italy*] [*ICAO location identifier*] (ICLI)
**LIMD**......... Grigna Settentrionale [*Italy*] [*ICAO location identifier*] (ICLI)
**LIMD**......... Limited (ROG)
**LIMDAT**... Limiting Date
**LIMDIS**..... Limited Distribution [*Military*] (AFIT)
**LIME**......... Bergamo/Orio Al Serio [*Italy*] [*ICAO location identifier*] (ICLI)
**LIME**......... Low-Iron, Manganese-Enriched [*Meteorite*]
**LIMEA**....... Low-Iron-Content Monoethanolamine
**LIMEAN**.... London Interbank Median Average Rate
**Li Men**....... Literatura ir Menas [*A publication*]
**limest**......... Limestone [*Petrology*]
**LIMF**......... Licentiate of the Institute of Metal Finishing [*British*] (DBQ)
**LIMF**......... Torino/Caselle [*Italy*] [*ICAO location identifier*] (ICLI)
**LIMFAC**... Limiting Factor (MCD)
**LIMG**......... Albenga [*Italy*] [*ICAO location identifier*] (ICLI)
**LIMH**......... Pian Rosa [*Italy*] [*ICAO location identifier*] (ICLI)
**LIMI**.......... Colle Del Gigante [*Italy*] [*ICAO location identifier*] (ICLI)
**LIMIRIS**... LASER-Induced Modulation of Infrared in Silicon
**LIMIT**....... Lot-Size Inventory Management Interpolation Technique (BUR)
**LIMJ**......... Genova/Sestri [*Italy*] [*ICAO location identifier*] (ICLI)
**LIMK**......... Torino/Bric Della Croce [*Italy*] [*ICAO location identifier*] (ICLI)
**LIML**......... Limited Information Maximum Likelihood [*Econometrics*]
**LIML**......... Milano/Linate [*Italy*] [*ICAO location identifier*] (ICLI)
**LIMM**........ Milano [*Italy*] [*ICAO location identifier*] (ICLI)
**LIMN**......... Cameri [*Italy*] [*ICAO location identifier*] (ICLI)
**Limn Ocean** ... Limnology and Oceanography [*A publication*]
**LIMNOL**... Limnology
**Limnol Donau** ... Limnologie der Donau [*A publication*]
**Limnol & Oceanog** ... Limnology and Oceanography [*A publication*]
**Limnol Oceanogr** ... Limnology and Oceanography [*A publication*]
**Limnol & Oceanogr** ... Limnology and Oceanography [*A publication*]
**Limnol Oceanogr Suppl** ... Limnology and Oceanography. Supplement [*A publication*]
**LIMO**......... Least Input for the Most Output [*Business term*]
**LIMO**......... Limousine (DSUE)
**LIMO**......... Monte Bisbino [*Italy*] [*ICAO location identifier*] (ICLI)
**LIMON**...... Limonis [*Of Lemon*] [*Pharmacy*] (ROG)
**LIMOSO**... Limitation of Supplies Order [*World War II*]
**LIMP**......... Louis XIV, James II, Mary, Prince of Wales [*Jacobite toast*]
**LIMP**......... Lunar-Anchored Interplanetary Monitoring Platform [*Aerospace*]
**LIMP**......... Parma [*Italy*] [*ICAO location identifier*] (ICLI)
**LIMPS**....... Linear Induction Motor Propulsion System
**LIMQ**......... Govone [*Italy*] [*ICAO location identifier*] (ICLI)
**LimR**......... Limba Romana [*Bucuresti*] [*A publication*]
**LIMR**......... Limiter
**LIMR**......... Novi Ligure [*Italy*] [*ICAO location identifier*] (ICLI)
**LIMRA**....... Life Insurance Marketing and Research Association [*Hartford, CT*] (EA)
**LIMRC**....... LRU [*Line Replaceable Unit*] Identification and Maintenance Requirements Catalog (NASA)
**LIMRF**....... Life Insurance Medical Research Fund [*Defunct*]
**LIMRV**....... Linear Induction Motor Research Vehicle [*Magnetic rapid-transit car*]
**LIMS**......... Laban Institute of Movement Studies [*Later, LBIMS*] (EA)
**LIMS**......... Laboratory Information Management System
**LIMS**......... Library Information Management System [*University of Maryland*]
**LIMS**......... Limb Infrared Monitor of the Stratosphere
**LIMS**......... Limb-Motion Sensor [*System*]
**LIMS**......... Logistic Inventory Management System [*North American Rockwell*]
**LIMS**......... Piacenza/San Damiano [*Italy*] [*ICAO location identifier*] (ICLI)
**LIMSS**....... Logistics Information Management Support System [*Military*]
**LIMSW**..... Limit Switch (NRCH)
**LIMT**......... Passo Della Cisa [*Italy*] [*ICAO location identifier*] (ICLI)
**LIMTV**....... Linear Induction Motor Test Vehicle [*Magnetic rapid-transit car*]
**LIMU**......... Capo Mele [*Italy*] [*ICAO location identifier*] (ICLI)
**LIMV**......... Passo Dei Giovi [*Italy*] [*ICAO location identifier*] (ICLI)
**LIMW**........ Aosta [*Italy*] [*ICAO location identifier*] (ICLI)
**LIMY**......... Monte Malanotte [*Italy*] [*ICAO location identifier*] (ICLI)
**LIMZ**......... Levaldigi [*Italy*] [*ICAO location identifier*] (ICLI)
**LIN**........... Law Institute News [*Australia*] [*A publication*]
**LIN**........... Lincoln [*Nebraska*] [*Seismograph station code, US Geological Survey*] [*Closed*] (SEIS)
**Lin**............ Linden [*Record label*]

**LIN** ........ Linden, CA [*Location identifier*] [*FAA*] (FAAL)
**LIN** ........ Line Item Number (AABC)
**LIN** ........ Lineal (MSA)
**LIN** ........ Linear (KSC)
**LIN** ........ Linen (ADA)
**LIN** ........ Liniment
**LIN** ........ Liquid Nitrogen (AFM)
**LIN** ........ Massachusetts Institute of Technology, Lincoln Laboratory, Lexington, MA [*OCLC symbol*] (OCLC)
**LIN** ........ Milan [*Italy*] Forlanini-Linate [*Airport symbol*] (OAG)
**LIN** ........ Nitlyn Airways, Inc. [*Shirley, NY*] [*FAA designator*] (FAAC)
**LINA** ........ Literaturnachweise [*Literature Compilations Database*] [*Fraunhofer Society*] (IID)
**LINAC** ........ Linear [*Electron*] Accelerator
**Linacre** ........ Linacre Quarterly [*A publication*]
**Linacre Q** ... Linacre Quarterly [*A publication*]
**Lin Alg App** ... Linear Algebra and Its Applications [*A publication*]
**LINAS** ........ LASER-Integrated Navigation/Attack System (MCD)
**LINB** ........ LIN Broadcasting Corp. [*NASDAQ symbol*] (NQ)
**LINC** ........ Laboratory Instrument Computer [*Medical analyzer*]
**LINC** ........ Learning Institute of North Carolina
**LINC** ........ Legislative Information Network Corp. [*Information service or system*] (IID)
**LINC** ........ Library & Information Consultants Ltd. [*Information service or system*] (IID)
**LINC** ........ Lincoln Income Life [*NASDAQ symbol*] (NQ)
**LINC** ........ Lincolnshire [*County in England*]
**LINC** ........ Lucas Industries Noise Centre [*British*] (IRUK)
**Linc Farm Conf Proc** ... Lincoln College. Farmers' Conference. Proceedings [*A publication*]
**LINCLOE** ... Lightweight Individual Combat Clothing and Equipment (AABC)
**Linc LR** ........ Lincoln Law Review [*A publication*]
**LINCO** ........ Linearly Organized Chemical Code for Use in Computer Systems (DIT)
**Lincoln L Rev** ... Lincoln Law Review [*A publication*]
**Lincoln Rec Soc** ... Lincoln Record Society [*A publication*]
**Lincolnshire Hist Arch** ... Lincolnshire History and Archaeology [*A publication*]
**LINCOMPEX** ... Linked Compressor and Expander (NATG)
**LINCOS** ........ Lingua Cosmica [*Artificial language consisting of radio signals of varying lengths and frequencies*]
**LINCOTT** ... Liaison, Interface, Coupling, Technology Transfer
**LINCS** ........ Language Information Network and Clearinghouse System [*Center for Applied Linguistics*] [*Washington, DC*]
**LINCS** ........ Lincolnshire [*County in England*]
**LINCT** ........ Linctus [*Tincture*] [*Pharmacy*] (ROG)
**LIND** ........ Lindberg Corp. [*NASDAQ symbol*] (NQ)
**LINDA** ........ Line Drawing Analyzer [*Cybernetics*]
**Lindbergia J Bryol** ... Lindbergia. A Journal of Bryology [*A publication*]
**Linde-Ber Tech Wiss** ... Linde-Berichte aus Technik und Wissenschaft [*A publication*]
**Linde Reports Sci & Technol** ... Linde Reports on Science and Technology [*A publication*]
**Linde Rep Sci and Technol** ... Linde Reports on Science and Technology [*A publication*]
**Linde Rep Sci Technol** ... Linde Reports on Science and Technology [*A publication*]
**L'Ind Ital del Cemento** ... L'Industria Italiana del Cemento [*A publication*]
**Lind Jur** ........ Lindley's Study of Jurisprudence [*A publication*] (DLA)
**Lindl Copartn** ... Lindley on Partnership [*A publication*] (DLA)
**Lindley** ........ Lindley's Law of Companies [*A publication*] (DLA)
**Lindley Comp** ... Lindley's Law of Companies [*A publication*] (DLA)
**Lindley P** .... Lindley on Partnership [*A publication*] (DLA)
**Lindley Part** ... Lindley on Partnership [*A publication*] (DLA)
**Lindl Partn** ... Lindley on Partnership [*A publication*] (DLA)
**Lind Part** .... Lindley on Partnership [*A publication*] (DLA)
**Lind Pr** ........ Lindewoode's Provinciales [*A publication*] (DLA)
**Lind Prob** ... Lindsay on Probates [*A publication*] (DLA)
**LINE** ........ Linear Corp. [*NASDAQ symbol*] (NQ)
**LINE** ........ Long Interspersed Element Sequence [*Genetics*]
**Linear Algebra and Appl** ... Linear Algebra and Its Applications [*A publication*]
**Linear Algebra Appl** ... Linear Algebra and Its Applications [*A publication*]
**Linear Algebra Its Appl** ... Linear Algebra and Its Applications [*A publication*]
**Linen News** ... Linen Supply News [*A publication*]
**LINER** ........ Low-Ionization Nuclear Emission-Line Region [*Spectroscopy*]
**LINES** ........ Library Information Network Exchange Services [*Australia*] [*A publication*]
**Lines Rev** ... Lines Review [*A publication*]
**LINFT** ........ Linear Foot
**Ling** ........ De Lingua Latina [*of Varro*] [*Classical studies*] (OCD)
**Ling** ........ Linguistica [*A publication*]
**LING** ........ Linguistics
**Ling A** ........ Linguistic Analysis [*A publication*]
**LingB** ........ Linguistische Berichte [*A publication*]
**LingBib** ........ Linguistica Biblica [*Bonn*] [*A publication*]
**Ling Bibl** .... Linguistica Biblica [*A publication*]
**LingC** ........ Linguistic Communications [*A publication*]
**Ling Cal** ........ Linguistic Calculation [*A publication*]
**Ling Est** ........ Lingue Estere [*A publication*]
**LingH** ........ Linguistics (The Hague) [*A publication*]
**LingI** ........ Linguistic Inquiry [*A publication*]
**Ling Inq** ........ Linguistic Inquiry [*A publication*]
**Ling Inquiry** ... Linguistic Inquiry [*A publication*]
**Ling Inv** ........ Linguisticae Investigationes [*A publication*]
**Ling e L** ........ Lingua e Literatura [*A publication*]
**Ling Lit** ........ Linguistics in Literature [*A publication*]
**Ling Litt** ........ Linguistica et Litteraria [*A publication*]
**Lingnan Sci J** ... Lingnan Science Journal [*A publication*]
**LINGO** ........ [*A*] programming language [*1978*] (CSR)
**Ling & P** ........ Linguistics and Philosophy [*A publication*]
**LingP** ........ Linguistique (Paris) [*A publication*]
**Ling Phil** .... Linguistics and Philosophy [*A publication*]
**Ling Philos** ... Linguistics and Philosophy [*A publication*]
**Ling R** ........ Linguistic Reporter [*A publication*]
**Ling Stile** ... Lingua e Stile [*A publication*]
**Linguist An** ... Linguistic Analysis [*A publication*]
**Linguist Ber** ... Linguistische Berichte [*A publication*]
**Linguistic Circle Manitoba and N Dak Proc** ... Linguistic Circle of Manitoba and North Dakota. Proceedings [*A publication*]
**Linguist In** ... Linguistic Inquiry [*A publication*]
**Linguist Lang Behav Abstr** ... Linguistics and Language Behavior Abstracts. LLBA [*A publication*]
**Lingv Sb** ........ Lingvisticeskij Sbornik [*A publication*]
**LINIM** ........ Liniment
**Lin Ins** ........ De Lineis Insecabilibus [*of Aristotle*] [*Classical studies*] (OCD)
**Lin Invest** ... Linguisticae Investigationes. Supplementa. Studies in French and General Linguistics [*A publication*]
**LINJET** ........ Liquid Injection Electric Thruster [*NASA*] (NASA)
**LINK** ........ Lawyers Information Network [*Australia*]
**LINK** ........ Library and Information Network [*Planned Parenthood Federation of America, Inc.*] [*Information service or system*] (IID)
**LINK** ........ Literature in Nursing Kardex
**Lin Lit S** ........ Linguistic and Literary Studies in Eastern Europe [*A publication*]
**LINLOG** ........ Linear-Logarithmic (IEEE)
**LINN** ........ Lincoln Foodservice Products, Inc. [*Fort Wayne, IN*] [*NASDAQ symbol*] (NQ)
**LINN** ........ Linnaeus
**Linn Belg** ... Linneana Belgica [*A publication*]
**Linneana Belg** ... Linneana Belgica [*A publication*]
**Linnean Soc Biol J** ... Linnean Society. Biological Journal [*A publication*]
**Linnean Soc NSW Proc** ... Proceedings. Linnean Society of New South Wales [*A publication*] (APTA)
**Linn Ind** ........ Linn's Index of Pennsylvania Reports [*A publication*] (DLA)
**Linn Laws Prov PA** ... Linn on the Laws of the Province of Pennsylvania [*A publication*] (DLA)
**Linn Soc J Zool** ... Linnean Society. Journal. Zoology [*A publication*]
**Linn Soc Lond Biol J** ... Linnean Society of London. Biological Journal [*A publication*]
**Linn Soc Lond Zool J** ... Linnean Society of London. Zoological Journal [*A publication*]
**Linn Soc NSW Proc** ... Linnean Society of New South Wales. Proceedings [*A publication*]
**Linn Soc Symp Ser** ... Linnean Society. Symposium Series [*A publication*]
**LINO** ........ Liaison Officer [*Military*]
**LINO** ........ Linoleum
**LINO** ........ Linotype
**LINOL** ........ Linoleum (MSA)
**LINOS** ........ Learning and Information Needs of Schools [*Australia*]
**LINQ** ........ Literature in North Queensland [*A publication*]
**LINR** ........ Linear Instruments Corp. [*NASDAQ symbol*] (NQ)
**LINS** ........ Labrador Institute of Northern Studies [*Memorial University of Newfoundland*] [*Canada*] [*Research center*] (RCD)
**LINS** ........ LASER Inertial Navigation System (MCD)
**LINS** ........ Lightweight Inertial Navigation System [*Air Force*]
**LINS** ........ LORAN Inertial System
**LInstBB** ........ Licentiate of the Institute of British Bakers (DBQ)
**LInstBCA** .. Licentiate of the Institute of Burial and Cremation Administration [*British*] (DBQ)
**L Inst J** ........ Law Institute Journal [*A publication*]
**L Inst J Vict** ... Law Institute Journal of Victoria [*A publication*]
**L Inst P** ........ Licentiate of the Institute of Physics [*British*]
**L Intell** ........ Law Intelligencer [*United States*] [*A publication*] (DLA)
**LINUS** ........ Local Information Network for Universal Service [*Telecommunications service*] (TSSD)
**LINUS** ........ Logical Inquiry and Update System
**LINV** ........ Life Investors, Inc. [*NASDAQ symbol*] (NQ)
**LINZ** ........ Lindsay Manufacturing Co. [*NASDAQ symbol*] (CTT)
**Linz AF** ........ Linzer Archaeologische Forschungen [*A publication*]
**Linzer Biol Beitr** ... Linzer Biologische Beitraege [*A publication*]
**LIO** ........ Lesser Included Offense
**LIO** ........ Liberian Iron Ore Ltd. [*Toronto Stock Exchange symbol*]
**LIO** ........ Limon [*Costa Rica*] [*Airport symbol*] (OAG)
**LIO** ........ Lionel Corp. [*AMEX symbol*] (SPSG)
**LIO** ........ Liottite [*A zeolite*]
**LiO** ........ Lithium Organic Battery
**LIO** ........ Local Interconnect Option [*Wang Laboratories, Inc.*] (BYTE)

**LIO** ........... National Restaurant Association Large Independent Operators [*Defunct*] (EA)
**LIOAS** ....... LASER-Induced Optoacoustic Spectroscopy
**LIOC** .......... Lighted Independent of Computer
**LIOCS** ....... Logical Input/Output Control System [*Data processing*]
**LIOD** ......... Lightweight Optronic Director (MCD)
**LIODD** ...... LASER In-Flight Obstacle Detection Device
**Liofilizzazione Criobiol Appl Criog** ... Liofilizzazione Criobiologia Applicazioni Criogeniche [*A publication*]
**LiOH** ......... Lithium Hydroxide (NASA)
**LIOL** .......... Legal Information On-Line [*Ministry of Labour*] [*Hamilton, ON*] [*Information service or system*] (IID)
**LION** ......... Lehman Investment Opportunity Note
**LI/ON** ....... Logicon Input/Output Network
**LION** ......... Lunar International Observer Network [*NASA*]
**LIONS** ....... Library Information and On-Line Network Service [*New York Public Library*] [*Information service or system*] (IID)
**Lion Unicor** ... Lion and the Unicorn [*A publication*]
**LIOP** .......... Life in One Position [*Telecommunications*] (TEL)
**LIOP** .......... Limited Initial Operating Production (MCD)
**LIP** ............ Boston, MA [*Location identifier*] [*FAA*] (FAAL)
**LIP** ............ Label Integrity Program [*Australia*]
**LIP** ............ LASER-Induced Plasma [*Spectroscopy*]
**LIP** ............ Latent Information Parameter
**LIP** ............ Legal Inverse Path [*Physics*]
**LIP** ............ Life Insurance Policy
**LIP** ............ Lipkovo [*Yugoslavia*] [*Seismograph station code, US Geological Survey*] (SEIS)
**LIP** ............ [*Construction*] Loan in Process [*Banking*]
**LIP** ............ Local Initiatives Program [*Canada*]
**LIP** ............ Low Internal Phase [*Emulsion chemistry*]
**LIP** ............ Lunar Impact Probe [*Aerospace*]
**LIP** ............ Lymphoid Interstitial Pneumonitis [*Medicine*]
**LIPA** .......... Aviano [*Italy*] [*ICAO location identifier*] (ICLI)
**LIPA** .......... Labor Institute of Public Affairs (EA)
**LIPA** .......... Lauric [*or Lauroyl or Lauryl*] Isopropanolamide [*Also, LPA*] [*Organic chemistry*]
**LIPA** .......... List of Interchangeable Parts and Assemblies
**LIPAS** ........ LASER-Induced Photoacoustic Spectroscopy
**LIPB** .......... Bolzano [*Italy*] [*ICAO location identifier*] (ICLI)
**LIPB** .......... Lloyd's International Private Banking [*Finance*]
**Lip Bib Jur** ... Lipenius' Bibliotheca Juridica [*A publication*] (DLA)
**LIPC** .......... Cervia [*Italy*] [*ICAO location identifier*] (ICLI)
**LIPD** .......... Udine/Campoformido [*Italy*] [*ICAO location identifier*] (ICLI)
**LIPE** .......... Bologna/Borgo Panigale [*Italy*] [*ICAO location identifier*] (ICLI)
**LIPE** .......... Lipe-Rollway Corp. [*NASDAQ symbol*] (NQ)
**LIPES** ........ Les Informations Politiques et Sociales [*A publication*]
**LIPF** .......... Ferrara [*Italy*] [*ICAO location identifier*] (ICLI)
**LIPG** .......... Gorizia [*Italy*] [*ICAO location identifier*] (ICLI)
**LIPH** .......... Treviso/San Angelo [*Italy*] [*ICAO location identifier*] (ICLI)
**LIPHE** ........ Life Interpersonal History Enquiry [*Test*] [*Psychology*]
**LIPI** ........... Rivolto [*Italy*] [*ICAO location identifier*] (ICLI)
**LIPID** ........ Logical Page Identifier
**LIPJ** .......... Bassano Del Grappa [*Italy*] [*ICAO location identifier*] (ICLI)
**LIPK** .......... Forli [*Italy*] [*ICAO location identifier*] (ICLI)
**LIPL** .......... Ghedi [*Italy*] [*ICAO location identifier*] (ICLI)
**LIPL** .......... Linear Information Processing Language [*High-order programming language*] [*Data processing*] (IEEE)
**LIPL** .......... Living Places [*A publication*]
**LIPN** .......... Verona/Boscomantico [*Italy*] [*ICAO location identifier*] (ICLI)
**LIPO** .......... [*The*] Liposome Co., Inc. [*Princeton, NJ*] [*NASDAQ symbol*] (NQ)
**LIPO** .......... Local Industry Promotion Organisation [*Australia*]
**LIPO** .......... Montichiari [*Italy*] [*ICAO location identifier*] (ICLI)
**LIPP** .......... Lippincott's Monthly [*A publication*]
**LIPP** .......... Padova [*Italy*] [*ICAO location identifier*] (ICLI)
**Lippay Janos Tud Ulesszak Eloadasai** ... Lippay Janos Tudomanyos Ulesszak Eloadasai [*A publication*]
**Lipp Cr L** ... Lippitt's Massachusetts Criminal Law [*A publication*] (DLA)
**Lippinc** ....... Lippincott's Magazine [*A publication*]
**Lippincott's Med Sci** ... Lippincott's Medical Science [*A publication*]
**LIPQ** .......... Ronchi De'Legionari [*Italy*] [*ICAO location identifier*] (ICLI)
**LIPR** .......... Rimini [*Italy*] [*ICAO location identifier*] (ICLI)
**LIPS** .......... Laboratory Interface Peripheral Subsystem [*Data processing*]
**LIPS** .......... Leiter International Performance Scale [*Psychology*]
**LIPS** .......... Library and Information Plans [*British*]
**LIPS** .......... Litton Industries Privacy System
**Lips** ........... Low Income, Parents Supporting [*Lifestyle classification*]
**LIPS** .......... Showcase Cosmetics, Inc. [*NASDAQ symbol*] (NQ)
**LIPS** .......... Treviso/Istrana [*Italy*] [*ICAO location identifier*] (ICLI)
**LIPT** .......... Vicenza [*Italy*] [*ICAO location identifier*] (ICLI)
**LIPU** .......... Padova [*Italy*] [*ICAO location identifier*] (ICLI)
**LIPV** .......... Venezia/San Nicolo [*Italy*] [*ICAO location identifier*] (ICLI)
**LIPX** .......... Villafranca [*Italy*] [*ICAO location identifier*] (ICLI)
**LIPY** .......... Ancona/Falconara [*Italy*] [*ICAO location identifier*] (ICLI)
**LIPZ** .......... Venezia/Tessera [*Italy*] [*ICAO location identifier*] (ICLI)
**LIQ** ............ Athens, TX [*Location identifier*] [*FAA*] (FAAL)
**LIQ** ............ Liquest International Marketing [*Vancouver Stock Exchange symbol*]
**liq** ............. Liqueur [*Solution*] [*Pharmacy*]
**LIQ** ............ Liquid (AAG)
**LIQ** ............ Liquidation (MCD)
**LIQ** ............ Liquor
**LIQ** ............ Lisala [*Zaire*] [*Airport symbol*] (OAG)
**LIQ** ............ Lower Inner Quadrant [*Anatomy*]
**LIQB** .......... Arezzo [*Italy*] [*ICAO location identifier*] (ICLI)
**LIQB** .......... Liqui-Box Corp. [*NASDAQ symbol*] (NQ)
**LIQC** .......... Capri [*Italy*] [*ICAO location identifier*] (ICLI)
**Liq Cryst Ordered Fluids** ... Liquid Crystals and Ordered Fluids [*A publication*]
**LIQD** .......... Passo Della Porretta [*Italy*] [*ICAO location identifier*] (ICLI)
**LIQDTE** .... Liquidate (ROG)
**LIQI** ........... Gran Sasso [*Italy*] [*ICAO location identifier*] (ICLI)
**LIQJ** .......... Civitavecchia [*Italy*] [*ICAO location identifier*] (ICLI)
**LIQK** .......... Capo Palinuro [*Italy*] [*ICAO location identifier*] (ICLI)
**LIQM** ......... Rifredo Mugello [*Italy*] [*ICAO location identifier*] (ICLI)
**LIQN** .......... Rieti [*Italy*] [*ICAO location identifier*] (ICLI)
**LIQO** .......... Monte Argentario [*Italy*] [*ICAO location identifier*] (ICLI)
**LIQOR** ....... Liquidator (ROG)
**LIQP** .......... Palmaria [*Italy*] [*ICAO location identifier*] (ICLI)
**LIQQ** .......... Monte Cavo [*Italy*] [*ICAO location identifier*] (ICLI)
**LIQR** .......... Radicofani [*Italy*] [*ICAO location identifier*] (ICLI)
**LIQS** .......... Siena [*Italy*] [*ICAO location identifier*] (ICLI)
**Liq Scintill Count** ... Liquid Scintillation Counting [*A publication*]
**Liq Scintill Counting** ... Liquid Scintillation Counting [*A publication*]
**LIQT** .......... Circeo [*Italy*] [*ICAO location identifier*] (ICLI)
**Liquefied Nat Gas** ... Liquefied Natural Gas [*A publication*]
**LIQUID** ..... Liquidus [*Liquid*] [*Pharmacy*] (ROG)
**LIQUON** ... Liquidation
**Liquor Cont L Rep CCH** ... Liquor Control Law Reports. Commerce Clearing House [*A publication*]
**Liquor Cont L Serv (CCH)** ... Liquor Control Law Service (Commerce Clearing House) [*A publication*] (DLA)
**Liquor Hbk** ... Liquor Handbook [*A publication*]
**LIQV** .......... Volterra [*Italy*] [*ICAO location identifier*] (ICLI)
**LIQW** ......... Sarzana/Luni [*Italy*] [*ICAO location identifier*] (ICLI)
**LIQZ** .......... Ponza [*Italy*] [*ICAO location identifier*] (ICLI)
**LIR** ............ Dover, DE [*Location identifier*] [*FAA*] (FAAL)
**LIR** ............ Laboratory for Insulation Research [*MIT*] (MCD)
**LIR** ............ Leader Internode Ratio [*Botany*]
**LIR** ............ Liberia [*Costa Rica*] [*Airport symbol*] (OAG)
**LIR** ............ Licentiate of the Institute of Population Registration [*British*] (DBQ)
**LiR** ............ Limba Romana [*Bucuresti*] [*A publication*]
**LIR** ............ Limiting Interval Reliability
**LIR** ............ Line Integral Refractometer
**lir** .............. Lira [*Monetary unit*] [*Italy*]
**Li R** ........... Literaturnaja Rossija [*A publication*]
**lir** .............. Lithuanian Soviet Socialist Republic [*MARC country of publication code*] [*Library of Congress*] (LCCP)
**LIR** ............ Longitude Independent Reset
**LIR** ............ Lost Item Replacement (MCD)
**LIRA** .......... Lambeg Industrial Research Association [*United Kingdom*] (IRUK)
**LIRA** .......... Liberal Industrial Relations Association [*British*]
**LIRA** .......... Little Italy Restoration Association
**LIRA** .......... Roma/Ciampino [*Italy*] [*ICAO location identifier*] (ICLI)
**LIRB** .......... Vigna Di Valle [*Italy*] [*ICAO location identifier*] (ICLI)
**LIRBM** ...... Liver, Iron, Red Bone Marrow
**LIRC** .......... Centocelle [*Italy*] [*ICAO location identifier*] (ICLI)
**LIRC** .......... Lebanese Information and Research Center (EA)
**LIRC** .......... Ligue Internationale de la Representation Commerciale [*International League of Commercial Travelers and Agents - ILCTA*] (EAIO)
**LIRE** .......... Lincoln Institute for Research and Education (EA)
**LIRE** .......... Pratica Di Mare [*Italy*] [*ICAO location identifier*] (ICLI)
**LIRES** ........ Literature Retrieval System [*Data processing*]
**LIRES-MC** ... Literature Retrieval System - Multiple Searching, Complete Text [*Data processing*]
**LIRF** .......... Low-Intensity Reciprocity Failure [*Of photographic emulsions*]
**LIRF** .......... Roma/Fiumicino [*Italy*] [*ICAO location identifier*] (ICLI)
**LIRG** .......... Guidonia [*Italy*] [*ICAO location identifier*] (ICLI)
**LIRG** .......... Landesverband der Israelitischen Religionsgemeinde (BJA)
**LIRG** .......... Library and Information Research Group [*Bristol Polytechnic Library*] [*Great Britain*] [*Information service or system*] (IID)
**LIRH** .......... Frosinone [*Italy*] [*ICAO location identifier*] (ICLI)
**LIRI** ........... Salerno/Pontecagnano [*Italy*] [*ICAO location identifier*] (ICLI)
**LIRJ** .......... Marina Di Campo [*Italy*] [*ICAO location identifier*] (ICLI)
**LIRK** .......... Monte Terminillo [*Italy*] [*ICAO location identifier*] (ICLI)
**LIRL** .......... Latina [*Italy*] [*ICAO location identifier*] (ICLI)
**LIRL** .......... Low Intensity Runway Lighting
**LIRLY** ....... Load-Indicating Relay (MSA)
**LIRM** ......... Grazzanise [*Italy*] [*ICAO location identifier*] (ICLI)
**LIRN** .......... Library and Information for the Northwest [*Program of the Fred Meyer Charitable Trust*]
**LIRN** .......... Napoli/Capodichino [*Italy*] [*ICAO location identifier*] (ICLI)
**LIRP** .......... Pisa [*Italy*] [*ICAO location identifier*] (ICLI)
**LIRQ** .......... Firenze [*Italy*] [*ICAO location identifier*] (ICLI)
**LIRR** .......... [*The*] Long Island Rail Road Co.

**LIRR**.......... Roma [*Italy*] [*ICAO location identifier*] (ICLI)
**LIRS**.......... Grosseto [*Italy*] [*ICAO location identifier*] (ICLI)
**LIRS**.......... Lance Information Retrieval System
**LIRS**.......... Legal Information and Reference Services [*General Accounting Office*] (IID)
**LIRS**.......... Level Indicator Recording Switch (NRCH)
**LIRS**.......... Library Information Retrieval Service [*Oregon State University*] [*Information service or system*]
**LIRS**.......... Library Information Retrieval System [*California Institute of Technology*] [*Pasadena, CA*]
**LIRS**.......... Lutheran Immigration and Refugee Service (EA)
**LIRSH**....... List of Items Requiring Special Handling
**LIRT**.......... Library Instruction Round Table [*American Library Association*]
**LIRT**.......... Trevico [*Italy*] [*ICAO location identifier*] (ICLI)
**LIRTS**........ Large Infrared Telescope
**LIRU**.......... Roma/Urbe [*Italy*] [*ICAO location identifier*] (ICLI)
**LIRV**.......... Viterbo [*Italy*] [*ICAO location identifier*] (ICLI)
**LIRZ**.......... Perugia [*Italy*] [*ICAO location identifier*] (ICLI)
**LIS**............ Laboratory Information Systems
**LIS**............ Land Information System [*New South Wales, Australia*]
**LIS**............ Land Inquiry Service [*Australia*]
**LIS**............ Lanthanide-Ion Induced Chemical Shift [*Spectroscopy*]
**LIS**............ LARC Instruction Simulator
**LIS**............ Large Interactive Surface [*Automated drafting table that serves as a computer input and output device*]
**LIS**............ LASER Illuminator System
**LIS**............ LASER-Induced Separation (MCD)
**LIS**............ LASER Interferometer System
**LIS**............ LASER Isotope Separation
**LIS**............ Launch Instant Selector
**LIS**............ Left Intercostal Space [*Cardiology*]
**LIS**............ Legislative Information Service [*New Jersey State Legislature*] [*Trenton*] [*Information service or system*] (IID)
**LIS**............ Legislative Information System [*National Conference of State Legislatures*] [*Information service or system*] (IID)
**LIS**............ Library and Information Science
**LIS**............ Library and Information Service
**LIS**............ Library and Information Services [*Institution of Mining and Metallurgy*] [*Great Britain*] [*Information service or system*] (IID)
**LIS**............ Library Information Services [*Information service or system*] (IID)
**LIS**............ Library Information System [*Georgetown University*] [*Information service or system*]
**LIS**............ Licensure Information System [*Public Health Service*] [*Georgetown University Medical Center*] (IID)
**LIS**............ Life Insurance Selling [*A publication*]
**LIS**............ Line Information Store [*Telecommunications*] (TEL)
**LIS**............ Line Isolation Switch [*Reactor level switch*] (IEEE)
**LIs**............ Lingua Islandica [*A publication*]
**LIS**............ Linguisticae Investigationes. Supplementa. Studies in French and General Linguistics [*A publication*]
**LIS**............ Link Information Sciences (BUR)
**LIS**............ Liposome Immunosensor [*Electrochemistry*]
**LIS**............ Lisbon [*Portugal*] [*Seismograph station code, US Geological Survey*] (SEIS)
**LIS**............ Lisbon [*Portugal*] [*Airport symbol*] (OAG)
**Lis**............ Listener [*A publication*]
**LIS**............ Lithium Diodosalicylate [*Organic chemistry*]
**LIS**............ LM [*Lunar Module*] Interface Control Specification [*NASA*] (KSC)
**LIS**............ Load I-Bank and Jump [*Data processing*]
**LIS**............ Lobular in Situ [*Medicine*]
**LIS**............ Locate in Scotland [*Investment group*] (ECON)
**LIS**............ Loop Input Signal
**LIS**............ Loss Information Service [*Insurance*]
**LIS**............ Low-Impact Switch (MCD)
**LIS**............ Low Intensity Sonication [*Chemistry*]
**LIS**............ Lutheran Immigration Service [*Later, LIRS*] (EA)
**LIS**............ Luxembourg Income Study [*Economics*]
**LISA**.......... Laboratory for Information Science in Agriculture [*Research center*] [*Defunct*] (RCD)
**LISA**.......... LARC Instruction Assembly
**LISA**.......... Library and Information Science Abstracts [*Library Association Publishing Ltd.*] [*Bibliographic database*] [*A publication*] [*England*]
**LISA**.......... Library Systems Analysis
**LISA**.......... Licht Sammler [*Light Collector*] [*Fluorescent plastic used in commercial displays*] [*German*]
**LISA**.......... Life Insurance Society of America (EA)
**LISA**.......... Line Impedance Stabilization Network
**LISA**.......... Linear Systems Analysis
**LISA**.......... Linked Indexed Sequential Access
**Li Sa**.......... Litteratur og Samfund [*A publication*]
**LISA**.......... Locally Integrated Software Architecture [*Apple microcomputer*] [*Data processing*]
**LISA**.......... London and International School of Acting [*British*]
**LISA**.......... Low-Impact Sustainable Agriculture
**LISA**.......... Seaman Apprentice, Lithographer, Striker [*Navy rating*]
**LISC**.......... Library and Information Services Council [*British*]
**LISC**.......... Lions International Stamp Club (EA)
**LISC**.......... Local Initiatives Support Corporation (EA)
**LISDOK**.... Literaturinformationssystem [*Literature Information System*] [*North Rhine-Westphalia Institute for Air Pollution Control*] [*Information service or system*] (IID)
**LISFA**........ Lost in Space Fannish Alliance (EA)
**LISH**.......... Last In, Still Here [*Accounting*] (ADA)
**LISI**........... Library Interface Systems, Incorporated [*Information service or system*] (IID)
**LISK**.......... Liskeard [*Municipal borough in England*]
**LiSk**........... Literary Sketches [*A publication*]
**LISL**........... Amsterdam Studies in the Theory and History of Linguistic Science. Series V. Library and Information Sources in Linguistics [*A publication*]
**LISL**........... Letopis Instituta za Serbski Iudospyt w Budysinje pri Nemskej Akademiji Wedo-Moscow w Berlinje Rjad A Rec A Literatura [*A publication*]
**LISM**......... Licentiate of the Incorporated Society of Musicians (ROG)
**LISM**......... Licentiate, Institute of Sales and Marketing Executives (ADA)
**LISN**.......... Library Services Network [*Library network*]
**LISN**.......... Line Impedance Stabilization Network
**LISN**.......... Long Island Sports Network [*Cable-television system*]
**LISN**.......... Seaman, Lithographer, Striker [*Navy rating*]
**LISP**.......... LASER Isotope Separation Program
**LISP**.......... Lightweight Individual Special Purpose [*Weaponry*]
**LISP**.......... List Processing [*Programming language*] [*Facetious translation: "Lots of Insane, Stupid Parentheses"*] [*Data processing*]
**LISP**.......... List Processor [*Standard programming language*] [*1958*] [*Data processing*]
**LISPD**........ Library and Information Services for People with Disabilities [*Australia*]
**LISR**.......... Legal Information Service. Reports. Native Law Centre. University of Saskatchewan [*A publication*]
**LISRB**........ Life Insurance Sales Research Bureau [*Later, LIMRA*]
**LISST**........ Library and Information Scholarship Today [*A publication*]
**LIST**.......... [*Office of*] LASER and Isotope Separation Technology [*Energy Research and Development Administration*]
**LIST**.......... Last In, Still There [*Accounting*]
**LIST**.......... Library Index Search and Transcribe
**LIST**.......... Library and Information Services, Tees-Side (IEEE)
**LIST**.......... Library and Information Services Today [*A publication*]
**List**........... List Sdruzeni Moravskych Spisovatelu [*A publication*]
**List**........... Listener [*A publication*]
**LIST**.......... Low Isotonic Strength Titrator
**LISTAR**..... Lincoln Information Storage and Retrieval [*MIT*]
**LISTD**....... Licentiate of the Imperial Society of Teachers of Dancing [*British*]
**Liste Abbrev Mots Titres** ... Liste d'Abbreviations de Mots des Titres de Periodiques [*A publication*]
**Listprokatnoe Proizvod** ... Listoprokatnoe Proizvodstvo [*A publication*]
**LISTS**........ Library Information System Time-Sharing
**List of Stat Instr** ... List of Statutory Instruments [*A publication*]
**Listy Cukrov** ... Listy Cukrovarnicke [*A publication*]
**Listy Fil**..... Listy Filologicke [*A publication*]
**LISU**.......... Library and Information Staff Union [*Australia*]
**LISV**.......... Loyal Independent Sheffield Volunteers [*British military*] (DMA)
**LISWG**...... Land Interface Sub-Working Group [*NATO*] (NATG)
**LIT**............ Language Imitation Test
**LIT**............ Language Inventory for Teachers [*Child development test*]
**LIT**............ Lawrence Institute of Technology [*Later, Lawrence Technological University*]
**LIt**............. Lettere Italiane [*A publication*]
**LIT**............ Librarians Inquiry Terminal (IT)
**LIt**............. Libro Italiano [*A publication*]
**Lit**............. Lietuvos TSR Valstybine Respublikine Biblioteka [*National Library of Lithuania*], Vilnius, Lithuania [*Library symbol*] [*Library of Congress*] (LCLS)
**LIT**............ Life Insurance Trust (DLA)
**LIT**............ Light Interface Technology [*Signal transmission*]
**LIT**............ Light Intratheater Transport [*Air Force*]
**LIT**............ Light Ion Trough
**LIT**............ Line Insulation Test [*Telecommunications*]
**LIT**............ Liquid Injection Technique (IEEE)
**Lit**............. Lire Italiane [*Italian Lire*] [*Monetary unit*]
**LIT**............ Litany (ROG)
**LIT**............ Liter [*Metric measure of volume*]
**LIT**............ Literacy
**LIT**............ Literal
**Lit**............. Literarisches [*A publication*]
**Lit**............. Literarium [*A publication*]
**LIT**............ Literary
**Lit**............. Literatur [*A publication*]
**LIT**............ Literature
**lit**.............. Lithuanian [*MARC language code*] [*Library of Congress*] (LCCP)
**Lit**............. Litigation [*A publication*]
**Lit**............. Littell's Kentucky Reports [*A publication*] (DLA)
**LIT**............ Litterae [*Letters*] [*Latin*] (ADA)
**Lit**............. Litterature [*University of Paris*] [*A publication*]
**Lit**............. Litteris [*A publication*]

**Lit**.............. Little
**LIT**............ Little Rock [*Arkansas*] [*Airport symbol*] (OAG)
**Lit**.............. Littleton's English Common Pleas Reports [*A publication*] (DLA)
**Lit**.............. Littleton's Tenures [*A publication*] (DLA)
**LIT**............ Litton Industries, Inc. [*NYSE symbol*] (SPSG)
**Lit**.............. Liturgia [*A publication*]
**LIT**............ Liturgy
**LIT**............ Local Inclusive Tour (DCTA)
**LIT**............ Location/Identification Transmitter [*NASA*]
**LIT**............ London Investment Trust [*British*]
**LIT**............ Low-Impedance Transmission
**LITA**.......... Library and Information Technology Association (EA)
**LitA**........... Literaturnaya Armeniya [*Erevan*] [*A publication*]
**LITA ITAL** ... LITA [*Library and Information Technology Association*] Information Technology and Libraries [*A publication*]
**LItal**........... Lettere Italiane [*A publication*]
**LitAP**......... Literarni Archiv Pamatniku Narodniho Pisemnictvi [*A publication*]
**Lit Arts**...... Liturgical Arts [*A publication*]
**Lit AS**......... Literatur als Sprache. Literaturtheorie-Interpretation-Sprachkritik [*A publication*]
**Lit Automat** ... New Literature on Automation [*A publication*]
**Lit B**........... Litterarum Baccalaureus [*Bachelor of Letters or Literature*]
**Lit Ber Dent Med** ... Literaturbericht ueber Neue Veroeffentlichungen auf dem Gebiete der Dentalmedizin [*A publication*]
**Lit & Bl Dig** ... Littleton and Blatchley's Insurance Digest [*A publication*] (DLA)
**Lit Brooke** ... Brooke's New Cases, English King's Bench [*1515-58*] [*A publication*] (DLA)
**Lit C**........... Literarisches Zentralblatt fuer Deutschland [*A publication*]
**LITCA**....... Licensing, Innovation, and Technology Consultants' Association (EAIO)
**Lit Criterion** ... Literary Criterion [*A publication*]
**Lit Crit Regist** ... Literary Criticism Register. LCR [*A publication*]
**Lit D**........... Literary Digest [*A publication*]
**Lit D**........... Litterarum Doctor [*Doctor of Letters or Literature*]
**Lit Dig**......... Literary Digest [*A publication*]
**LitDokAB**.. Literaturdokumentation zur Arbeitsmarkt- und Berufsforschung [*Deutsche Bundesanstalt fuer Arbeit*] [*Federal Republic of Germany*] [*Information service or system*] (CRD)
**LITE**.......... BMC International Corp. [*NASDAQ symbol*] (NQ)
**LITE**.......... LASER Illuminator Targeting Equipment
**LITE**.......... LASER In-Space Technology Experiment
**LITE**.......... Legal Information Through Electronics [*Air Force*]
**LITE**.......... Let's Improve Today's Education [*Newsletter*]
**Lit E**........... Literary Endeavour [*A publication*]
**Liteinoe Proizvod** ... Liteinoe Proizvodstvo [*USSR*] [*A publication*]
**Liteinoe Prozvod** ... Liteinoe Proizvodstvo [*A publication*]
**Literature**... Literature East and West [*A publication*]
**Liter Discussion** ... Literacy Discussion [*A publication*]
**LITES**........ LASER Intercept and Technical Exploitation System (MCD)
**LitEW**........ Literature East and West [*A publication*]
**LITEX**....... Searchlight Illumination Exercise [*Also, LIGHTEX*] [*Military*] (NVT)
**Lit/Film Q** ... Literature/Film Quarterly [*A publication*]
**Lit/F Q**....... Literature/Film Quarterly [*A publication*]
**Lit/F Quarterly** ... Literature/Film Quarterly [*A publication*]
**LITFUND** ... Fund for the Relief of Russian Writers and Scientists in Exile (EA)
**Lit Gaz**....... Literaturnaja Gazeta [*A publication*]
**LITH**......... Lithograph [*or Lithography*] (ROG)
**LITH**......... Lithuania (ROG)
**LITH**......... Lithuanian [*Language, etc.*]
**Lit Half**....... Literary Half-Yearly [*A publication*]
**LITHD**...... Lithographed (ROG)
**Lit Hist**...... Literature and History [*A publication*]
**Lit Hist Soc Quebec Tr** ... Literary and Historical Society of Quebec. Transactions [*A publication*]
**Lith Min Resour** ... Lithology and Mineral Resources [*A publication*]
**LITHO**...... Lithograph (AABC)
**LITHOG**... Lithography
**Lithol Issled Kaz** ... Lithologicheskie Issledovanniya v Kazakhstane [*USSR*] [*A publication*]
**Lithol Miner Resour** ... Lithology and Mineral Resources [*A publication*]
**LITHOT**.... Lithotomy [*Medicine*]
**LithSSR**..... Lithuanian Soviet Socialist Republic
**LITHUAN** ... Lithuanian
**Lithuanian Math J** ... Lithuanian Mathematical Journal [*A publication*]
**Lithuanian Math Trans** ... Lithuanian Mathematical Transactions [*A publication*]
**LIT HUM** ... Litera Humaniores [*Classic literature*] (ROG)
**LIT HUM** ... Literae Humanitores [*Latin*]
**Litig**........... Litigation [*A publication*] (DLA)
**LITIGON**.. Litigation (ROG)
**LITINT**..... Literacy International
**LITINT**..... Literature Intelligence (MCD)
**LITIR**........ Literary Information and Retrieval [*Data processing*]
**Lit Jb**.......... Liturgisches Jahrbuch [*A publication*]
**Lit Krit**....... Literatur und Kritik [*A publication*]
**LItL**........... Letteratura Italiana Laterza [*A publication*]
**LitL**........... Literarni Listy [*A publication*]
**LitL**........... Literatura Ludowa [*A publication*]
**Lit Letter**.... Literary Letter [*A publication*] (APTA)
**LIT-LIT**..... Committee on World Literacy and Christian Literature [*Later, Intermedia*] (EA)
**LitM**.......... Literarni Mesicnik [*A publication*]
**LitM**.......... Literaturnaya Mysl [*A publication*]
**Lit M**.......... Master of Literature
**Lit Mat Sb** ... Litovskij Matematiceskij Sbornik [*A publication*]
**LitMo**......... Liturgie und Moenchtum [*A publication*] (BJA)
**Lit Mod Art** ... LOMA. Literature on Modern Art [*A publication*]
**Lit Mus Fin** ... Literature, Music, Fine Arts [*A publication*]
**Lit Mys**...... Literatura i Mystectvo [*A publication*]
**LitN**........... Literarni Noviny [*Praha*] [*A publication*]
**Litol Geokhim Paleogeogr Neftegazonosn Osad Form Uzb** ... Litologiya, Geokhimiya, i Paleogeografiya Neftegazonosn Osadochnykh Formatsii Uzbekistana [*A publication*]
**Litol i Polez Iskop** ... Litologiya i Poleznye Iskopaemye [*A publication*]
**Litov Fiz Sb** ... Litovskii Fizicheskii Sbornik [*A publication*]
**Litov Mekh Sb** ... Litovskii Mekhanicheskii Sbornik [*A publication*]
**Litovsk Mat Sb** ... Litovskii Matematiceskii Sbornik [*A publication*]
**LitP**............ Literature in Perspective [*A publication*]
**LitP**............ Literature and Psychology [*A publication*]
**Lit Per**........ Literary Perspectives [*A publication*] (APTA)
**Lit Ph Soc NY Tr** ... Literary and Philosophical Society of New York. Transactions [*A publication*]
**Lit Psych**.... Literature and Psychology [*A publication*]
**Lit & Psychol** ... Literature and Psychology [*A publication*]
**Lit Psychol** ... Literature and Psychology [*A publication*]
**Lit R**........... Literary Review [*A publication*]
**LITR**.......... Low-Cost Indirect-Fire Training Round [*Army*] (INF)
**LITR**.......... Low-Intensity Test Reactor [*ORNL*]
**Lit Res New** ... Literary Research Newsletter [*A publication*]
**Lit Rev**....... Literary Review [*A publication*]
**Lit Rev Oils Fats** ... Literature Review on Oils and Fats [*A publication*]
**LitS**............ Literatura i Sucanist [*A publication*]
**Lit Sel Ca**... Littell's Select Kentucky Cases [*A publication*] (DLA)
**Lit Steam Pwr** ... Light Steam Power [*A publication*]
**Litt**............ Littell's Kentucky Supreme Court Reports [*1822-24*] [*A publication*] (DLA)
**Litt**............ Litteraria [*A publication*]
**LITT**.......... Litterateur [*French*] (ROG)
**Litt**............ Litteratures [*A publication*]
**Litt**............ Litteris [*A publication*]
**Litt**............ Littleton's English Common Pleas Reports [*A publication*] (DLA)
**Litt B**......... Litterarum Baccalaureus [*Bachelor of Letters or Literature*]
**Litt Comp Laws** ... Littell's Statute Law [*Kentucky*] [*A publication*] (DLA)
**Litt D**......... Litterarum Doctor [*Doctor of Letters or Literature*]
**LittD(Econ)** ... Doctor of Letters in Economic Studies (ADA)
**Littell**........ Littell's Kentucky Reports [*A publication*] (DLA)
**LittHD**....... Doctor of Hebrew Letters (BJA)
**Lit & Theo R** ... Literary and Theological Review [*A publication*]
**LittK**.......... Litterae (Kuemmerle) [*A publication*]
**Litt (KY)**.... Littell [*Kentucky*] [*A publication*] (DLA)
**Litt L**......... Licentiate in Letters
**LITTLE**..... [*A*] programming language [*1970-1973*] (CSR)
**Little Brooke** ... Brooke's New Cases, English King's Bench [*1515-58*] [*A publication*] (DLA)
**Little M**...... Little Magazine [*A publication*]
**LittleR**........ Little Review [*A publication*]
**Littleton**..... Littleton's English Common Pleas and Exchequer Reports [*A publication*] (DLA)
**Litt M**........ Master of Letters
**Litt Rep**...... Littleton's English Common Pleas and Exchequer Reports [*A publication*] (DLA)
**LITTS**........ Large Inventory Top-Tier Site [*Industrial hazard designation*] [*British*]
**Litt Sel Cas** ... Littell's Select Kentucky Cases [*A publication*] (DLA)
**Litt & S St Law** ... Littell and Swigert's Digest of Statute Law [*Kentucky*] [*A publication*] (DLA)
**Litt Ten**...... Littleton's Tenures [*A publication*] (DLA)
**LITTY**....... Libraries of Idaho Teletype Network - Academics [*Library network*]
**Lit U**........... Literaturna Ukrajina [*A publication*]
**LITURG**.... Liturgies (ROG)
**Liturg Arts** ... Liturgical Arts [*A publication*]
**Liturgical Rev** ... Liturgical Review [*A publication*]
**LITVC**....... Liquid Injection Thrust Vector Control
**LitW**.......... Literatura (Warsaw, Poland) [*A publication*]
**LITW**......... Longitudinally in Homogeneous Traveling Waves (MCD)
**Lit W (Bost)** ... Literary World (Boston) [*A publication*]
**Lit Wiss Ling** ... Literaturwissenschaft und Linguistik [*A publication*]
**LITZ**.......... Litzendraht [*Wire*] [*German*]
**Lit ZentB** ... Literarisches Zentralblatt [*A publication*]
**LIU**............ Line Interface Unit [*Data communications*]
**LIU**............ Littlefield, TX [*Location identifier*] [*FAA*] (FAAL)
**LIU**............ Long Island University [*Brooklyn, NY*]
**LIU**............ Wood, Wire, and Metal Lathers' International Union [*Later, UBC*]
**LIUNA**...... Laborers' International Union of North America (EA)

**LIV**............ Law of Initial Value [*Joseph Wilder*]
**LIV**............ Legislative Indexing Vocabulary
**LIV**............ Light Infantry Volunteers [*Military unit*] [*British*]
**LIV**............ Line Item Value
**LIV**............ Lived [*or Living*]
**LIV**............ Livengood, AK [*Location identifier*] [*FAA*] (FAAL)
**LIV**............ Liverpool (ROG)
**LIV**............ Livingstone Energy [*Vancouver Stock Exchange symbol*]
**Liv**............ Livingston's Mayor's Court Reports [*New York*] [*A publication*] (DLA)
**LIV**............ Livorno [*Italy*] [*Seismograph station code, US Geological Survey*] [*Closed*] (SEIS)
**LIV**............ Livraison [*Delivery*] [*French*]
**LIV**............ Livre [*Book or Pound*] [*French*]
**LIV**............ Livy [*Roman historian, c. 10BC*] (ROG)
**LIV**............ Low-Input Voltage (KSC)
**LIV**............ Low Investment Vehicle
**LIV**............ Lunar and Interplanetary Vehicle [*Aerospace*] (AFM)
**Liv Ag**........ Livermore on Principal and Agent [*A publication*] (DLA)
**Liv Age**....... Littell's Living Age [*A publication*]
**LIVB**.......... Passo Del Brennero [*Italy*] [*ICAO location identifier*] (ICLI)
**Liv Blues**.... Living Blues [*A publication*]
**LIVC**.......... Low-Input Voltage Converter
**LIVC**.......... Monte Cimone [*Italy*] [*ICAO location identifier*] (ICLI)
**Liv Cas**....... Livingston's Cases in Error [*New York*] [*A publication*] (DLA)
**Liv Condit Hlth** ... Living Conditions and Health [*A publication*]
**LIVCR**....... Low-Input Voltage Conversion and Regulation
**LIVD**.......... Dobbiaco [*Italy*] [*ICAO location identifier*] (ICLI)
**Liv Dis**....... Livermore's Dissertation on the Contrariety of Laws [*A publication*] (DLA)
**LIVE**.......... Learning through Industry and Voluntary Educators [*Community education program*]
**LIVE**.......... Lunar Impact Vehicle [*NASA*] (KSC)
**LIVE**.......... Passo Resia [*Italy*] [*ICAO location identifier*] (ICLI)
**Liver Ann**... Liver Annual [*A publication*]
**Liverm Ag**.. Livermore on Principal and Agent [*A publication*] (DLA)
**Livermore Ag** ... Livermore on Principal and Agent [*A publication*] (DLA)
**Liverp Manch Geol J** ... Liverpool and Manchester Geological Journal [*A publication*]
**Liverpool G As Tr J** ... Liverpool Geological Association. Transactions. Journal [*A publication*]
**Liverpool Geog Soc Tr An Rp** ... Liverpool Geographical Society. Transactions and Annual Report of the Council [*A publication*]
**Liverpool G Soc Pr** ... Liverpool Geological Society. Proceedings [*A publication*]
**Liverpool L Rev** ... Liverpool Law Review [*A publication*]
**Liverpool and Manchester Geol Jour** ... Liverpool and Manchester Geological Journal [*A publication*]
**Liverpool Med Inst Trans Rep** ... Liverpool Medical Institution. Transactions and Reports [*A publication*]
**Liverpool School Trop Med Mem** ... Liverpool School of Tropical Medicine. Memoirs [*A publication*]
**Liver Quant Aspects Struct Func** ... Liver: Quantitative Aspects of Structure and Function. Proceedings of the International Gstaad Symposium [*A publication*]
**Livest Advis** ... Livestock Adviser [*A publication*]
**Livest Int**.... Livestock International [*A publication*]
**Live Stock Bul** ... Live Stock Bulletin [*A publication*] (APTA)
**Live Stock J and Fancier's Gaz** ... Live Stock Journal and Fancier's Gazette [*A publication*]
**Livest Prod Sci** ... Livestock Production Science [*A publication*]
**LIVEX**....... Live Exercise [*Military exercise in which live forces participate*] (NATG)
**LIVF**.......... Frontone [*Italy*] [*ICAO location identifier*] (ICLI)
**LIVG**.......... Monte Grappa [*Italy*] [*ICAO location identifier*] (ICLI)
**Living Bird Q** ... Living Bird Quarterly [*A publication*]
**Living Cold Int Symp** ... Living in the Cold. International Symposium [*A publication*]
**Living Mus** ... Living Museum [*A publication*]
**LIVJA5**...... Lijecnicki Vjesnik [*A publication*]
**Liv Jud Cas** ... Livingston's Judicial Opinions [*New York*] [*A publication*] (DLA)
**Liv Judic Op** ... Livingston's Judicial Opinions [*New York*] [*A publication*] (DLA)
**Liv Jud Op** ... Livingston's Judicial Opinions [*New York*] [*A publication*] (DLA)
**Liv La Cr Code** ... Livingston's Louisiana Criminal Code [*A publication*] (DLA)
**Liv Law Mag** ... Livingston's Law Magazine [*New York*] [*A publication*] (DLA)
**Liv L Mag** ... Livingston's Law Magazine [*New York*] [*A publication*] (DLA)
**Liv L Reg** ... Livingston's Law Register [*New York*] [*A publication*] (DLA)
**LIVM**......... Marino Di Ravenna [*Italy*] [*ICAO location identifier*] (ICLI)
**Liv Med Chir J** ... Liverpool Medico-Chirurgical Journal [*A publication*]
**LIVO**......... Tarvisio [*Italy*] [*ICAO location identifier*] (ICLI)
**LIVP**.......... Paganella [*Italy*] [*ICAO location identifier*] (ICLI)
**LIVR**.......... Low-Input Voltage Regulation
**LIVR**.......... Passo Rolle [*Italy*] [*ICAO location identifier*] (ICLI)
**LIVT**.......... Trieste [*Italy*] [*ICAO location identifier*] (ICLI)
**Liv US Pen Co** ... Livingston's System of United States Penal Codes [*A publication*] (DLA)
**LIVV**.......... Monte Venda [*Italy*] [*ICAO location identifier*] (ICLI)
**Liv Wild**..... Living Wilderness [*A publication*]
**Liv Wildn**... Living Wilderness [*A publication*]
**Liv for Young Home** ... Living for Young Homemakers [*A publication*]
**LIW**........... Letters in Words [*Psychology*]
**LIW**........... Loikaw [*Burma*] [*Airport symbol*] (OAG)
**LIW**........... Long Instruction Word [*Teraplex*] [*Data processing*]
**LIW**........... Loss in Weight
**LIWA/YWA** ... Yearbook of World Affairs. London Institute of World Affairs [*A publication*]
**LIWB**......... Livermore Water Boiler [*Nuclear reactor*] [*Dismantled*]
**LIWMS**..... Laura Ingalls Wilder Memorial Society (EA)
**LIXISCOPE** ... Low-Intensity X-Ray Imaging Scope
**LIY**............ Leicestershire Imperial Yeomanry [*British military*] (DMA)
**LIY**............ Limay [*Nicaragua*] [*Seismograph station code, US Geological Survey*] (SEIS)
**LIYP**.......... Legacy International Youth Program [*Later, LIYTP*] (EA)
**LIYTP**........ Legacy International Youth Training Program (EA)
**LIYV**.......... Lettuce Infectious Yellows Virus
**LIYW**......... Aviano [*Italy*] [*ICAO location identifier*] (ICLI)
**LIZ**............ Limestone, ME [*Location identifier*] [*FAA*] (FAAL)
**LIZ**............ Lizard (MSA)
**LIZARDS** ... Library Information Search and Retrieval Data System (IEEE)
**Lizars**......... Lizar's Scotch Exchequer Cases [*A publication*] (DLA)
**LIZC**.......... Liz Claiborne, Inc. [*NASDAQ symbol*] (NQ)
**Liz Sc Exch** ... Lizar's Scotch Exchequer Cases [*A publication*] (DLA)
**LJ**.............. British Guiana Limited Jurisdiction (Official Gazette) [*1899-1955*] [*A publication*] (DLA)
**LJ**.............. Hall's American Law Journal [*A publication*] (DLA)
**LJ**.............. House of Lords Journals [*England*] [*A publication*] (DLA)
**LJ**.............. Jennings Public Library, Jennings, LA [*Library symbol*] [*Library of Congress*] (LCLS)
**LJ**.............. Joullie [*France*] [*Research code symbol*]
**LJ**.............. Law Journal. New Series [*A publication*]
**LJ**.............. Law Journal Newspaper [*1866-1965*] [*A publication*]
**LJ**.............. Law Judge (DLA)
**LJ**.............. Lawson & Jones Ltd. [*Toronto Stock Exchange symbol*]
**LJ**.............. Lennard-Jones [*Physical chemistry*]
**LJ**.............. Library Journal [*A publication*]
**LJ**.............. Life Jacket
**LJ**.............. Limburg's Jaarboek [*A publication*]
**LJ**.............. Limited Partner in Jobbers Firm [*London Stock Exchange*]
**LJ**.............. Line Judge [*Football*]
**LJ**.............. Little Joe [*Early developmental spacecraft*] [*NASA*]
**LJ**.............. Little John [*Rocket*] [*Military*] (AABC)
**LJ**.............. Liturgisches Jahrbuch [*A publication*]
**LJ**.............. Long Jump
**LJ**.............. Lord Justice
**L-J**............ Lowenstein-Jensen [*Growth medium*]
**LJ**.............. Lower Canada Law Journal [*A publication*] (DLA)
**LJ**.............. Luther-Jahrbuch [*A publication*]
**LJ**.............. New York Law Journal [*A publication*]
**LJ**.............. Ohio State Law Journal [*A publication*]
**LJ**.............. Sierra Leone Airways Ltd. [*ICAO designator*] (FAAC)
**LJA**........... Ljetopis Jugoslavenske Akademije [*A publication*]
**LJA**........... Lodja [*Zaire*] [*Airport symbol*] (OAG)
**LJA**........... Lord Justice of Appeal
**LJaD**......... Dixon Correctional Institute, Jackson, LA [*Library symbol*] [*Library of Congress*] (LCLS)
**LJ Adm**...... Law Journal, New Series, Admiralty [*A publication*] (DLA)
**LJ Adm NS** ... Law Journal Reports, Admiralty, New Series [*1865-75*] [*A publication*] (DLA)
**LJ Adm NS (Eng)** ... Law Journal Reports, New Series, Admiralty [*England*] [*A publication*] (DLA)
**L in Japan** ... Law in Japan [*A publication*]
**LJ App**....... Law Journal Reports, New Series, Appeals [*A publication*] (DLA)
**LJb**............ Literaturwissenschaftliches Jahrbuch der Goerres-Gesellschaft [*A publication*]
**L-Jb**........... Luther-Jahrbuch [*A publication*]
**LJ Bank**..... Law Journal Reports, Bankruptcy [*A publication*] (DLA)
**LJ Bank NS** ... Law Journal Reports, New Series, Bankruptcy [*A publication*] (DLA)
**LJ Bankr**.... Law Journal Reports, Bankruptcy [*A publication*] (DLA)
**LJ Bankr NS (Eng)** ... Law Journal Reports, New Series, Bankruptcy [*England*] [*A publication*] (DLA)
**LJ Bcy**........ Law Journal Reports, New Series, Bankruptcy [*A publication*] (DLA)
**LJ Bk**......... Law Journal Reports, Bankruptcy [*A publication*] (DLA)
**LJC**............ La Jolla [*California*] [*Seismograph station code, US Geological Survey*] [*Closed*] (SEIS)
**LJC**............ La Jolla Bancorp [*AMEX symbol*] (SPSG)
**LJC**............ Laredo Junior College [*Texas*]
**LJC**............ Lasell Junior College [*Newton, MA*]
**LJC**............ Law Journal Reports, New Series, Common Pleas [*England*] [*A publication*] (DLA)
**LJC**............ Lees Junior College [*Jackson, KY*]
**LJC**............ London Juvenile Court (DAS)
**LJC**............ Lord Jesus Christ (ROG)
**LJC**............ Loretto Junior College [*Kentucky*]
**LJC**............ Louisville, KY [*Location identifier*] [*FAA*] (FAAL)

**LJCC**......... Law Journal, County Courts Reporter [*A publication*] (DLA)
**LJCC**......... Local Joint Consultative Committee [*British*] (DCTA)
**LJCCA**....... Law Journal Newspaper, County Court Appeals [*England*] [*A publication*] (DLA)
**LJCCR**....... Law Journal Reports, New Series, Crown Cases Reserved [*England*] [*A publication*] (DLA)
**LJCCR (NS)**... Law Journal Reports, New Series, Crown Cases Reserved [*England*] [*A publication*] (DLA)
**LJ Ch**......... Law Journal Reports, New Series, Chancery [*A publication*] (DLA)
**LJ Ch (Eng)**... Law Journal Reports, New Series, Chancery [*England*] [*A publication*] (DLA)
**LJ Ch NS (Eng)**... Law Journal Reports, New Series, Chancery [*England*] [*A publication*] (DLA)
**LJ Ch (OS)**... Law Journal Reports, Chancery, Old Series [*1822-31*] [*England*] [*A publication*] (DLA)
**LJCP**......... Law Journal Reports, Common Pleas Decisions [*England*] [*A publication*] (DLA)
**LJCPD**....... Law Journal Reports, Common Pleas Decisions [*England*] [*A publication*] (DLA)
**LJCP (Eng)**... Law Journal Reports, Common Pleas Decisions [*England*] [*A publication*] (DLA)
**LJCP NS**... Law Journal Reports, Common Pleas Decisions, New Series [*1831-75*] [*A publication*] (DLA)
**LJCP NS (Eng)**... Law Journal Reports, Common Pleas, New Series [*England*] [*A publication*] (DLA)
**LJCP (OS)**... Law Journal Reports, Common Pleas, Old Series [*England*] [*A publication*] (DLA)
**LJCRF**....... La Jolla Cancer Research Foundation [*Research center*] (RCD)
**LJCS**......... Lord Justice Clerk of Scotland (DAS)
**LJD**........... Doctor of Letters of Journalism
**LJDFC**....... Lacy J. Dalton Fan Club (EA)
**LJD & M**... Law Journal Reports, New Series, Divorce and Matrimonial [*England*] [*A publication*] (DLA)
**LJE**........... Local Job Entry
**LJ Ecc**....... Law Journal Reports, New Series, Ecclesiastical Cases [*A publication*] (DLA)
**LJ Eccl**....... Law Journal Reports, New Series, Ecclesiastical Cases [*A publication*] (DLA)
**LJED**......... Large Jet Engine Department [*NASA*] (KSC)
**LJeL**.......... LaSalle Parish Library, Jena, LA [*Library symbol*] [*Library of Congress*] (LCLS)
**LJ Eq**......... Law Journal Reports, Chancery, New Series [*1831-1946*] [*A publication*] (DLA)
**LJEWU**..... Lanka Jatika Estate Workers' Union [*Ceylon National Estate Workers' Union*]
**LJ Ex**......... Law Journal Reports, New Series, Exchequer Division [*England*] [*A publication*] (DLA)
**LJ Exch**..... Law Journal Reports, New Series, Exchequer Division [*England*] [*A publication*] (DLA)
**LJ Exch (Eng)**... Law Journal Reports, New Series, Exchequer Division [*England*] [*A publication*] (DLA)
**LJ Exch in Eq (Eng)**... English Law Journal. Exchequer in Equity [*A publication*] (DLA)
**LJ Exch NS**... Law Journal Reports, New Series, Exchequer [*1831-75*] [*A publication*] (DLA)
**LJ Exch NS (Eng)**... Law Journal Reports, New Series, Exchequer Division [*England*] [*A publication*] (DLA)
**LJ Exch (OS)**... Law Journal Reports, Exchequer, Old Series [*A publication*] (DLA)
**LJ Ex D**..... Law Journal Reports, New Series, Exchequer Division [*England*] [*A publication*] (DLA)
**LJ Ex Eq**.... Law Journal, Exchequer in Equity [*England*] [*A publication*] (DLA)
**LJFC**......... Leon Jordan Fan Club (EA)
**LJG**........... Landesjagdgesetz [*A publication*]
**LJG**........... Levend Joods Geloof (Liberaal Joodse Gemeente) (BJA)
**LJG**........... Lord Justice General [*British*]
**LJGG**......... Literaturwissenschaftliches Jahrbuch der Goerres-Gesellschaft [*A publication*]
**LJH**........... Legon Journal of the Humanities [*A publication*]
**LJHL**......... Law Journal Reports, New Series, House of Lords [*England*] [*A publication*] (DLA)
**L J Hum**..... Lamar Journal of the Humanities [*A publication*]
**LJI**............ Library of Jewish Information (BJA)
**LJIFS**........ Law Journal, Irish Free State [*1931-32*] [*A publication*] (DLA)
**LJ Ir**......... Law Journal, Irish [*1933-34*] [*A publication*] (DLA)
**LJJ**............ Jefferson Davis Parish Library, Jennings, LA [*Library symbol*] [*Library of Congress*] (LCLS)
**LJJ**............ Lords Justices
**LJK**........... Ashland, VA [*Location identifier*] [*FAA*] (FAAL)
**LJKB**......... Law Journal Reports, King's Bench [*A publication*] (DLA)
**LJKB**......... Law Journal Reports. King's Bench. New Series [*United Kingdom*] [*A publication*]
**LJKB (Eng)**... Law Journal Reports, King's Bench [*England*] [*A publication*] (DLA)
**LJKB NS**... Law Journal Reports, King's Bench, New Series [*A publication*] (DLA)
**LJKB NS (Eng)**... Law Journal Reports, King's Bench, New Series [*England*] [*A publication*] (DLA)
**LJKB OS**... Law Journal, King's Bench, Old Series [*England*] [*A publication*] (DLA)
**LJKBOS**.... Law Journal Reports. King's Bench. Old Series [*United Kingdom*] [*A publication*]
**LJL**........... Little John Launcher [*Military*]
**LJLC**......... Law Journal (Lower Canada) [*A publication*] (DLA)
**LJLT**......... Law Journal (Law Tracts) [*England*] [*A publication*] (DLA)
**LJLV**......... Little Joe Launch Vehicle [*NASA*]
**LJ Mag**...... Law Journal, New Series, Common Law, Magistrates Cases (Discontinued) [*A publication*] (DLA)
**LJ Mag Cas**... Law Journal Reports, Magistrates' Cases [*1822-31*] [*A publication*] (DLA)
**LJ Mag Cas (Eng)**... Law Journal Reports, Magistrates' Cases [*England*] [*A publication*] (DLA)
**LJ Mag Cas NS**... Law Journal Reports, Magistrates' Cases, New Series [*1831-96*] [*A publication*] (DLA)
**LJ Mag Cas NS (Eng)**... Law Journal Reports, Magistrates' Cases, New Series [*England*] [*A publication*] (DLA)
**LJ of the Marut Bunnag Internat L Off**... Law Journal. Marut Bunnag International Law Office [*A publication*] (DLA)
**LJ Mat**....... Law Journal, Matrimonial [*England*] [*A publication*] (DLA)
**LJ Mat Cas**... Law Journal, New Series, Divorce and Matrimonial [*England*] [*A publication*] (DLA)
**LJ Mat (Eng)**... Law Journal, Matrimonial [*England*] [*A publication*] (DLA)
**LJMC**........ Law Journal Reports, New Series, Magistrates' Cases [*England*] [*A publication*] (DLA)
**LJM Cas**.... Law Journal Reports, New Series, Magistrates' Cases [*England*] [*A publication*] (DLA)
**LJMCOS**... Law Journal Reports, Old Series, Magistrates' Cases [*England*] [*A publication*] (DLA)
**LJMPA**..... Law Journal Reports, Matrimonial, Probate, and Admiralty [*England*] [*A publication*] (DLA)
**LJM & W**.. Morgan and Williams' Law Journal [*London*] [*A publication*] (DLA)
**LJN**........... Lake Jackson [*Texas*] [*Airport symbol*] (OAG)
**LJNC**......... Law Journal, Notes of Cases [*A publication*] (DLA)
**LJNCCA**... Law Journal Newspaper, County Court Appeals [*England*] [*A publication*] (DLA)
**LJNCCR**.... Law Journal Newspaper, County Court Reports [*England*] [*A publication*] (DLA)
**LJNC (Eng)**... Law Journal, Notes of Cases [*England*] [*A publication*] (DLA)
**LJ News**..... Law Journal Newspaper [*1866-1965*] [*A publication*] (DLA)
**LJ News (Eng)**... Law Journal Newspaper [*England*] [*A publication*] (DLA)
**LJ Newsp**... Law Journal Newspaper [*1866-1965*] [*A publication*] (DLA)
**LJ NS**........ Law Journal, New Series [*England*] [*A publication*] (DLA)
**LJo**............ Jackson Parish Library, Jonesboro, LA [*Library symbol*] [*Library of Congress*] (LCLS)
**L Jo**........... Law Journal Newspaper [*England*] [*A publication*] (DLA)
**L Jo NC**..... Law Journal, Notes of Cases [*England*] [*A publication*] (DLA)
**LJ OS**........ Law Journal, Old Series [*1822-31*] [*London*] [*A publication*] (DLA)
**LJ OS Ch**... Law Journal, Old Series, Chancery [*1822-23*] [*A publication*] (DLA)
**LJ OS CP**.. Law Journal, Old Series, Common Pleas [*1822-31*] [*A publication*] (DLA)
**LJ OS Ex**... Law Journal, Old Series, Exchequer [*1830-31*] [*A publication*] (DLA)
**LJ OS KB**.. Law Journal, Old Series, King's Bench [*1822-31*] [*A publication*] (DLA)
**LJOSMC**... Law Journal, Old Series, Magistrates' Cases [*1826-31*] [*A publication*] (ILCA)
**LJP**........... Law Journal Reports, New Series, Privy Council [*England*] [*A publication*] (DLA)
**LJP**........... Law Journal Reports, Probate, Divorce, and Admiralty [*England*] [*A publication*] (DLA)
**LJP**........... Liquid Junction Potential
**LJP**........... Localized Juvenile Periodontitis [*Dentistry*]
**LJPC**......... Law Journal Reports, Privy Council [*England*] [*A publication*] (DLA)
**LJ PC (Eng)**... Law Journal Reports, Privy Council [*England*] [*A publication*] (DLA)
**LJ PC NS**.. Law Journal Reports, New Series, Privy Council [*England*] [*A publication*] (DLA)
**LJPD & A**... Law Journal Reports, New Series, Probate, Divorce, and Admiralty [*1875-1946*] [*A publication*] (DLA)
**LJPD & Adm**... Law Journal Reports, New Series, Probate, Divorce, and Admiralty [*England*] [*A publication*] (DLA)
**LJP & M**.... Law Journal, Probate and Matrimonial [*England*] [*A publication*] (DLA)
**LJPM & A**... Law Journal Reports, New Series, Probate, Matrimonial, and Admiralty [*England*] [*A publication*] (DLA)
**LJ Prob**...... Law Journal Reports, New Series, Probate and Matrimonial [*1858-59, 1866-75*] [*A publication*] (DLA)
**LJ Prob (Eng)**... Law Journal, Probate and Matrimonial [*England*] [*A publication*] (DLA)
**LJ Prob & Mat**... Law Journal, Probate and Matrimonial [*England*] [*A publication*] (DLA)
**LJ Prob NS**... Law Journal Reports, New Series, Probate and Matrimonial [*1858-59, 1866-75*] [*A publication*] (DLA)
**LJ Prob NS (Eng)**... Law Journal, Probate and Matrimonial, New Series [*England*] [*A publication*] (DLA)

**LJQB**......... Law Journal Reports, New Series, Queen's Bench [*England*] [*A publication*] (DLA)
**LJQBD**...... Law Journal Reports, New Series, Queen's Bench Division [*England*] [*A publication*] (DLA)
**LJQBD NS** ... Law Journal Reports, New Series, Queen's Bench Division [*England*] [*A publication*] (DLA)
**LJQB (Eng)** ... Law Journal Reports, New Series, Queen's Bench [*England*] [*A publication*] (DLA)
**LJQB NS**... Law Journal Reports, New Series, Queen's Bench [*1831-1946*] [*A publication*] (DLA)
**LJQB NS (Eng)** ... Law Journal Reports, Queen's Bench, New Series [*England*] [*A publication*] (DLA)
**LJR**............ Law Journal Reports [*A publication*]
**LJR**............ Lead Joint Runner
**LJR**............ Little John Rocket [*Military*]
**LJR**............ Lone Jack Resources Ltd. [*Vancouver Stock Exchange symbol*]
**LJR**............ Low Jet Route (ADA)
**LJR**............ Low Jet Routes [*A publication*] (APTA)
**LJR (Eng)** ... Law Journal Reports [*England*] [*A publication*] (DLA)
**LJ Rep** ....... Law Journal Reports [*A publication*] (DLA)
**LJ Rep NS** ... Law Journal Reports, New Series [*A publication*] (DLA)
**LJS** ............ Lap Joint Strength
**LJSCAA**.... Annuaire Agricole de la Suisse [*A publication*]
**LJSI**........... L. J. Simone, Inc. [*NASDAQ symbol*] (NQ)
**LJ/SLJ** ...... Library Journal/School Library Journal [*A publication*]
**LJ Sm** ........ Smith's Law Journal [*London*] [*A publication*] (DLA)
**LJ Spec Rep** ... LJ [*Library Journal*] Special Report [*A publication*]
**LJSU** ......... Local Junction Switching Unit [*Telecommunications*] (TEL)
**L & J Tr Mar** ... Ludlow and Jenkyns on the Law of Trade-Marks [*A publication*] (DLA)
**LJU**............ Ljubljana [*Yugoslavia*] [*Airport symbol*] (OAG)
**LJU**............ Ljubljana [*Laibach*] [*Yugoslavia*] [*Seismograph station code, US Geological Survey*] (SEIS)
**LJU**............ Oscoda, MI [*Location identifier*] [*FAA*] (FAAL)
**LJUC**......... Law Journal of Upper Canada [*A publication*] (DLA)
**L & Just**..... Law and Justice [*A publication*]
**LJZ**............ Leipziger Juedische Zeitung [*A publication*]
**LK**............. Arawak Airlines (OAG)
**LK**............. Laaste Kwartier [*Last Quarter*] [*Business term*] [*Afrikaans*]
**LK**............. Laiko Komma [*Populist Party*] [*Greece*] [*Political party*] (PPE)
**LK**............. Lake [*Board on Geographic Names*] (MCD)
**LK**............. Leak (KSC)
**LK**............. Left Kidney [*Medicine*]
**LK**............. Leipziger Kommentar das Reichsstrafgesetzbuch [*A publication*]
**LK**............. Lek [*Monetary unit*] [*Albania*]
**Lk**.............. Leptosphaeria korrea [*A fungus*]
**lk**............... Lewenskoste [*Cost of Living*] [*Afrikaans*]
**LK**............. Liederkranz [*Type of cheese*] (BJA)
**L-K**............ Linguistic-Kinesic [*Psychiatry*]
**LK**............. Link (KSC)
**LK**............. Literatur und Kritik [*A publication*]
**LK**............. Literatur als Kunst [*A publication*]
**LK**............. Literatura ir Kalba [*A publication*]
**LK**............. Literaturnyj Kritik [*A publication*]
**LK**............. Lock [*Automotive engineering*]
**LK**............. Lockheed Corp. [*NYSE symbol*] (SPSG)
**LK**............. Looking for Party [*Telecommunications*] (TEL)
**LK**............. Lord Keeper [*of the Great Seal*] [*British*] (ROG)
**L & K**......... Love and Kisses [*Correspondence*]
**LK**............. Low-Priority Key [*Data processing*]
**LK**............. Lowenfeld Kaleidoblocs [*Psychological testing*]
**LK**............. Lucas Air Societes [*ICAO designator*] (FAAC)
**Lk**.............. Luke [*New Testament book*]
**LK**............. Lymphokine [*Immunochemistry*]
**LK**............. Sri Lanka [*ANSI two-letter standard code*] (CNC)
**LK1**........... Ladies' Kayak, Single Person (ADA)
**LK2**........... Ladies' Kayak, Two Person (ADA)
**LK4**........... Ladies' Kayak, Four Person (ADA)
**LKA**.......... Amphibious Cargo Ship [*Navy symbol*]
**LKA**.......... Larantuka [*Indonesia*] [*Airport symbol*] (OAG)
**LKA**.......... Lighthouse Keepers Association (EA)
**LKA**.......... Literarische Keilschrifttexte aus Assur [*A publication*] (BJA)
**LKA**.......... Miraloma, CA [*Location identifier*] [*FAA*] (FAAL)
**LKA**.......... Sri Lanka [*ANSI three-letter standard code*] (CNC)
**LKA of A**.... Ladies Kennel Association of America (EA)
**LKAA**........ Ladies Kennel Association of America (EA)
**LKAA**........ Praha [*Czechoslovakia*] [*ICAO location identifier*] (ICLI)
**LKAAAN**.... Annual Report. Laboratory of Algology [*Trebon*] [*A publication*]
**LKAI**......... LKA International, Inc. [*NASDAQ symbol*] (NQ)
**LKartB**....... Landeskartellbehoerde [*Provincial Cartel Authority*] [*German*] (DLA)
**LKB**.......... Lakeba [*Fiji*] [*Airport symbol*] (OAG)
**LKBB**........ Bratislava [*Czechoslovakia*] [*ICAO location identifier*] (ICLI)
**LKC**.......... Lake Chabot [*California*] [*Seismograph station code, US Geological Survey*] (SEIS)
**LKC**.......... Lancaster County Library, Lancaster, PA [*OCLC symbol*] (OCLC)
**LKC**.......... Lekana [*Congo*] [*Airport symbol*] (OAG)
**LKCL**......... LASER Kit Combination Lock
**LKD**.......... Locked (KSC)
**LKDP**......... Lietuviu Krikscioniu Demokratu Partija [*Lithuanian Christian Democratic Party*] [*Political party*] (PPE)
**LKF**.......... Linear Kalman Filter
**LKG**.......... League of the Kingdom of God [*Church of England*]
**LKG**.......... Leakage (MSA)
**LKG**.......... Locking (KSC)
**LKG**.......... Looking (MSA)
**LKG**.......... Loop Key Generator (MCD)
**LKGE**........ Linkage (MSA)
**LKHO**........ Holesov [*Czechoslovakia*] [*ICAO location identifier*] (ICLI)
**LKHOAW** ... Lesnoe Khozyaistvo [*A publication*]
**LKI**........... Duluth, MN [*Location identifier*] [*FAA*] (FAAL)
**LKI**........... Is Lietuviu Kulturos Istorijos [*A publication*]
**LKI**........... Lazare Kaplan International, Inc. [*AMEX symbol*] (SPSG)
**LKI**........... Loki Gold Corp. [*Vancouver Stock Exchange symbol*]
**LKIB**......... Bratislava/Ivanka [*Czechoslovakia*] [*ICAO location identifier*] (ICLI)
**LKK**.......... Kulik Lake, AK [*Location identifier*] [*FAA*] (FAAL)
**LKK**.......... Lake Shore Mines Ltd. [*Toronto Stock Exchange symbol*]
**LKK**.......... Lietuviu Kalbotyros Klausimai [*A publication*]
**LKKV**......... Karlovy Vary [*Czechoslovakia*] [*ICAO location identifier*] (ICLI)
**LKKZ**......... Kosice [*Czechoslovakia*] [*ICAO location identifier*] (ICLI)
**LKL**........... Lakselv [*Norway*] [*Airport symbol*] (OAG)
**LKLY**......... Likely (FAAC)
**LKM**.......... Lafayette, LA [*Location identifier*] [*FAA*] (FAAL)
**LKM**.......... Locke Rich Minerals [*Vancouver Stock Exchange symbol*]
**LKM**.......... Low-Key Maintenance
**LKMT**........ Ostrava [*Czechoslovakia*] [*ICAO location identifier*] (ICLI)
**LKN**.......... Leknes [*Norway*] [*Airport symbol*] (OAG)
**LKN**.......... Lock-In
**LK-NDV**.... Newcastle Disease Virus, L-Kansas Strain
**LKNPOS**... Last Known Position (MCD)
**LKNPT**...... Last Known Port (MCD)
**LKNT**........ Locknut (MSA)
**LKO**.......... Billings, MT [*Location identifier*] [*FAA*] (FAAL)
**LKO**.......... Lucknow [*India*] [*Airport symbol*] (OAG)
**LKP**.......... Lake Placid, NY [*Location identifier*] [*FAA*] (FAAL)
**LKP**.......... Lamellar Keratoplasty [*Ophthalmology*]
**LKP**.......... Landelijke Knokplogen [*Netherlands Regional Action Groups*] [*World War II*]
**LKP**.......... Last Known Position [*Aviation*] (NVT)
**LKP**.......... Liberaalinen Kansanpuolue [*Liberal People's Party*] [*Finland*] [*Political party*] (PPE)
**LKP**.......... Lietuvos Komunisty Partija [*Communist Party of Lithuania*] [*Political party*] (PPE)
**LKPP**......... Piestany [*Czechoslovakia*] [*ICAO location identifier*] (ICLI)
**LKPR**......... Praha/Ruzyne [*Czechoslovakia*] [*ICAO location identifier*] (ICLI)
**LK & PRR** ... Lahaina-Kaanapali & Pacific Railroad [*Hawaii*]
**LKQ**.......... Like Kind and Quality (Metal) [*Auto repair*]
**LKQCP**...... Licentiate of the King's and Queen's College of Physicians [*Australia*]
**LKQCPI**.... Licentiate of the King's and Queen's College of Physicians of Ireland
**LKR**.......... Lancaster, SC [*Location identifier*] [*FAA*] (FAAL)
**LKR**.......... Left Knee Right [*Guitar playing*]
**LKR**.......... LK Resources Ltd. [*Toronto Stock Exchange symbol*]
**LKR**.......... Locker (KSC)
**LKROT**...... Locked Rotor
**LKRT**........ Loyal Knights of the Round Table (EA)
**LKS**.......... Lambda Kappa Sigma (EA)
**LKS**.......... Liberation Kanake Socialiste [*Socialist Kanak Liberation*] [*New Caledonia*] (PD)
**LKS**.......... Liver, Kidney, Spleen [*Medicine*]
**LKS**.......... Logan-Keck-Stickney [*Method*]
**LKS**.......... Louisville, KY [*Location identifier*] [*FAA*] (FAAL)
**LKS**.......... Lucky 7 Exploration [*Vancouver Stock Exchange symbol*]
**LKS**.......... Lucky Stores, Inc. [*NYSE symbol*] (SPSG)
**LKSCR**...... Lockscrew
**LKSL**......... Sliac [*Czechoslovakia*] [*ICAO location identifier*] (ICLI)
**LKT**.......... Locket (ROG)
**LKT**.......... Lookout (MSA)
**LKT**.......... Salmon, ID [*Location identifier*] [*FAA*] (FAAL)
**LKTRD**...... Elektro-Tehniek [*A publication*]
**LKTT**......... Poprad/Tatry [*Czechoslovakia*] [*ICAO location identifier*] (ICLI)
**LKU**.......... Literarische Keilschrifttexte aus Uruk [*A publication*] (BJA)
**LKUP**........ Lockup
**LKV**.......... Lake Ventures Ltd. [*Vancouver Stock Exchange symbol*]
**LKV**.......... Laked Kanamycin-Vancomycin [*Agar*] [*Microbiology*]
**LKV**.......... Lakeview, OR [*Location identifier*] [*FAA*] (FAAL)
**LKV**.......... Left Knee Vertical [*Guitar playing*]
**LKVY**......... Lykens Valley Railroad Co. [*AAR code*]
**LKW**.......... Lake Wisdom [*Papua New Guinea*] [*Seismograph station code, US Geological Survey*] (SEIS)
**LKW**.......... Lakewood Mining [*Vancouver Stock Exchange symbol*]
**LK/WA**...... Lock Washer [*Automotive engineering*]
**LKWASH** ... Lock Washer [*Automotive engineering*]

**LKX** .......... La Pryor, TX [*Location identifier*] [*FAA*] (FAAL)
**LKY** .......... Lucky Strike Resources [*Vancouver Stock Exchange symbol*]
**LL** .......... Aero Lloyd Flugreisen GmbH & Co. KG, Frankfurt [*West Germany*] [*ICAO designator*] (FAAC)
**LL** .......... All Is Well [*Search and rescue symbol that can be stamped in sand or snow*]
**LL** .......... Double-Loop Magnetic Mine Sweep [*Navy*] [*British*]
**LL** .......... La Ley. Revista Juridica Argentina [*A publication*]
**LL** .......... Lab. Lafon [*France*] [*Research code symbol*]
**LL** .......... Labor Letter [*Cast Metals Association*] [*A publication*]
**LL** .......... Lakeside Leader [*Slave Lake, Alberta*] [*A publication*]
**LL** .......... Lamina Lucida [*Dermatology*]
**LL** .......... Land-Line [*Telecommunications*] (TEL)
**LL** .......... Land Locomotion Laboratory [*Army*]
**LL** .......... Landline [*Aviation*]
**LL** .......... Language Learning [*A publication*]
**LL** .......... Large Letter
**LL** .......... Large Light Seeds [*Botany*]
**LL** .......... Large Lymphocyte [*Medicine*]
**LL** .......... Last (ROG)
**LL** .......... Late Latin [*Language, etc.*]
**LL** .......... Latent Lethality [*Radiation casualty criterion*] [*Army*]
**LL** .......... Lateral Lemniscus [*Neuroanatomy*]
**LL** .......... Lateral Line [*Invertebrate zoology*]
**LL** .......... Lateral Lip
**L/L** .......... Latitude/Longitude (IEEE)
**LL** .......... Laugh Lovers (EA)
**LL** .......... Launch and Landing [*NASA*] (NASA)
**LL** .......... Launch Left (MCD)
**LL** .......... Laurentian Life Insurance Co., Inc. [*Toronto Stock Exchange symbol*]
**LL** .......... Law Latin
**L-L** .......... Law Library of Louisiana, New Orleans, LA [*Library symbol*] [*Library of Congress*] (LCLS)
**LL** .......... Law List (ILCA)
**LL** .......... Laws (ROG)
**LL** .......... Laymen's League (EA)
**LL** .......... League (ROG)
**LL** .......... Lean Line (EA)
**LL** .......... Lease or Loan
**LL** .......... Leased Line [*Private telephone or Teletype line*] [*Telecommunications*]
**LL** .......... Leaves [*Bibliography*]
**L£** .......... Lebanese Pound [*Monetary unit*] (IMH)
**LL** .......... Lederle Laboratories [*Research code symbol*]
**LL** .......... Left Lower [*Medicine*]
**LL** .......... Left Lung [*Medicine*]
**LL** .......... Leges [*Laws*] [*Latin*]
**LL** .......... Legislative Liaison
**L & L** .......... Legislative and Liaison [*Military*]
**LL** .......... Legum [*Of Laws*] [*Latin*] (ADA)
**L & L** .......... Lehrproben und Lehrgaenge [*A publication*]
**L/L** .......... Leigh Light [*British military*] (DMA)
**LL** .......... Lend-Lease [*Bill*] [*World War II*]
**LL** .......... Lending Library
**LL** .......... Lepromatous-Type Leprosy [*Animal pathology*]
**LL** .......... Lessons Learned
**LL** .......... Letras (Lima) [*A publication*]
**LL** .......... Lever Lock (MCD)
**L & L** .......... Lewd and Lascivious
**LL** .......... Liber Lovaniensis [*A publication*]
**LL** .......... Liberty Lobby (EA)
**L/L** .......... Library Labels [*Antiquarian book trade*]
**LL** .......... Library Literature [*A publication*]
**L es L** .......... Licencie es Lettres [*Licentiate in Letters*] [*French*] (EY)
**LL** .......... License in Civil Law
**LL** .......... Life and Letters [*A publication*]
**LL** .......... Lifelong Learning: The Adult Years [*A publication*]
**LL** .......... Light Line [*Military*]
**LL** .......... Light Load (AAG)
**LL** .......... Light Lock
**LL** .......... Light Lorry [*British*]
**LL** .......... Lighterage Limits
**L si L** .......... Limba si Literatura [*A publication*]
**LL** .......... Limba si Literatura [*A publication*]
**LL** .......... Limited Liability [*Finance*]
**LL** .......... Limiting Level
**LL** .......... Lincoln Laboratory [*MIT*] (MCD)
**LL** .......... Lincoln Library of Essential Information
**LL** .......... Line Leg [*Telegraph*] [*Telecommunications*] (TEL)
**L-L** .......... Line-to-Line (MCD)
**LL** .......... Lines
**LL** .......... Lines Layout (MCD)
**L & L** .......... Lingua e Literatura [*A publication*]
**L & L** .......... Linguistica et Litteraria [*A publication*]
**LL** .......... Link Level [*Telecommunications*]
**LL** .......... Liquid Limit (IEEE)
**L/L** .......... Liquid/Liquid Extraction [*Laboratory procedure*]
**LL** .......... Liquor Law
**LL** .......... Literary Lives [*A publication*]
**LL** .......... Literatur und Leben [*A publication*]
**LL** .......... Litre (ROG)
**LL** .......... Little League [*Baseball*]
**LL** .......... Live Load
**LL** .......... Livres et Lectures [*A publication*]
**LL** .......... Lloyd's List [*A publication*]
**LL** .......... Load Line [*Shipping*] (DS)
**LL** .......... Load List (MSA)
**LL** .......... Local Lesion [*Pathology*]
**LL** .......... Local Line [*Telecommunications*]
**LL** .......... Local Linearization
**LL** .......... Locator Lists [*Army*]
**LL** .......... Loco Laudato [*In the Place Quoted*] [*Latin*]
**LL** .......... Lodges [*Freemasonry*] (ROG)
**LL** .......... Loft Line (MSA)
**LL** .......... Long Lead (NASA)
**LL** .......... Long Line [*Telecommunications*] (MCD)
**LL** .......... Loose Leaf
**LL** .......... Lord Lieutenant
**LL** .......... Lords
**LL** .......... Loudness Level
**LL** .......... Low Latin [*Language, etc.*]
**LL** .......... Low Level
**LL** .......... Low Load [*Finance*]
**LL** .......... Lower Laterals [*Botany*]
**LL** .......... Lower Left
**LL** .......... Lower Leg
**LL** .......... Lower Lid [*Ophthalmology*]
**LL** .......... Lower Limb [*Lower edge of sun, moon, etc.*] [*Navigation*]
**LL** .......... Lower Limen [*Psychology*]
**LL** .......... Lower Limit
**LL** .......... Lower Lobe [*Medicine*]
**LL** .......... Lunar Landing [*NASA*] (KSC)
**LL** .......... Luther League (EA)
**LL** .......... Lutlag [*Limited Company*] [*Norwegian*]
**L/L** .......... Lymphoma/Leukemia [*Oncology*]
**LL** .......... Lysolecithin [*Biochemistry*]
**3LL** .......... Lewis Lung Carcinoma [*Oncology*]
**LLA** .......... Lady Licentiate of Arts [*Scotland*]
**LLA** .......... Lady Literate in Arts [*British*]
**LLA** .......... Lakeland Aviation [*Rice Lake, WI*] [*FAA designator*] (FAAC)
**LLA** .......... Latin Liturgy Association (EA)
**LLA** .......... Laubach Literacy Action (EA)
**LLA** .......... Leased Line Adapter [*Telecommunications*]
**LLA** .......... Lend-Lease Administration [*Defunct*]
**LLA** .......... Leshonenu La'am [*A publication*]
**LLA** .......... Lesotho Liberation Army (PD)
**LLA** .......... Limited Locus Allowed [*Legal*] (ROG)
**LLA** .......... Limiting Lines of Approach [*Navy*] (NVT)
**LLA** .......... Literary Landmarks Association (EA)
**LLA** .......... Little Library [*A publication*]
**LLA** .......... Llanada [*California*] [*Seismograph station code, US Geological Survey*] (SEIS)
**LLA** .......... Low-Level Analog (MCD)
**LLA** .......... Lower Left Abdomen [*Injection Site*]
**LLA** .......... Lulea [*Sweden*] [*Airport symbol*] (OAG)
**LLA** .......... Luther League of America [*Later, LL*]
**LLA** .......... White Lake, LA [*Location identifier*] [*FAA*] (FAAL)
**LLAA** .......... Israel Airports Authority Headquarters [*Israel*] [*ICAO location identifier*] (ICLI)
**LLAII** .......... Leurs Altesses Imperiales [*Their Imperial Highnesses*] [*French*]
**LLAARR** ... Leurs Altesses Royales [*Their Royal Highnesses*] [*French*]
**LLAD** .......... Ben Gurion [*Israel*] [*ICAO location identifier*] (ICLI)
**LLAD** .......... Low-Level Air Defence [*Navy*] [*British*]
**LLafL** .......... Lafayette Public Library, Lafayette, LA [*Library symbol*] [*Library of Congress*] (LCLS)
**LLafS** .......... University of Southwestern Louisiana, Lafayette, LA [*Library symbol*] [*Library of Congress*] (LCLS)
**LL Alfredi** ... Leges Alfredi [*Laws of King Alfred*] [*Latin*] [*A publication*] (DLA)
**LLAMA** .......... Low-Level Acceleration Measurement Apparatus
**LLAN** .......... Llandaff (ROG)
**LLap** .......... Saint John Parish Library, La Place, LA [*Library symbol*] [*Library of Congress*] (LCLS)
**LLAT** .......... Law Latin
**LLAT** .......... Lawrence Lowery Apperception Test
**LL Athelst** ... Laws of Athelstan [*A publication*] (DLA)
**LLB** .......... Computrac, Inc. [*AMEX symbol*] (SPSG)
**LLB** .......... Lawyers' Law Books [*1977*] [*A publication*] (ILCA)
**LLB** .......... Lawyers Liberation Bulletin [*A publication*] (APTA)
**LLB** .......... Legum Baccalaureus [*Bachelor of Laws*]
**LLB** .......... Little League Baseball (EA)
**LLB** .......... Long Leg Brace [*Orthopedics*]
**LLB** .......... Lower Leg Brace [*Medicine*]
**LLBA** .......... Linguistics and Language Behavior Abstracts [*Sociological Abstracts, Inc.*] [*San Diego, CA*] [*Bibliographic database*] [*A publication*]
**LLBBMA** .. Loose Leaf and Blank Book Manufacturers Association [*Later, ABPM*] (EA)
**LLBC** .......... Liquid Large-Bore Cannon (MCD)
**LLBCD** .......... Left Lower Border of Cardiac Dullness [*Cardiology*]

**LLBD**........ Meteorological Service [*Israel*] [*ICAO location identifier*] (ICLI)
**LLBG**........ Tel Aviv/D. Ben Gurion [*Israel*] [*ICAO location identifier*] (ICLI)
**LLBS**......... Beersheba/Teyman [*Israel*] [*ICAO location identifier*] (ICLI)
**LLBS**......... Low-Level Bombsight (NATG)
**LL Burgund** ... Laws of Burgundians [*A publication*] (DLA)
**LLC**........... La Lucha Farm [*Costa Rica*] [*Seismograph station code, US Geological Survey*] (SEIS)
**LLc**............ Lake Charles Public Library, Lake Charles, LA [*Library symbol*] [*Library of Congress*] (LCLS)
**LLC**........... Lakeland Library Cooperative [*Library network*]
**LL and C**.... Language Learning and Communication [*A publication*]
**LLC**........... Law Certificate
**L & LC**...... Leeds and Liverpool Canal [*Shipping*] [*British*] (ROG)
**L & LC**...... Lift and Lift Cruise (MCD)
**LLC**........... Limited Life Component (MCD)
**LLC**........... Liquid Level Control
**LLC**........... Liquid-Liquid Chromatography
**LlC**............ Llen Cymru [*A publication*]
**LLC**........... Logical Link Control [*Telecommunications*]
**LLC**........... Long Leg Cast [*Orthopedics*]
**LLC**........... Long Lines Coordination (NATG)
**LLC**........... Low Liquid Cutoff
**LLC**........... Loyola University, Career Information Center, New Orleans, LA [*OCLC symbol*] (OCLC)
**LLC**........... Luneberg Lens Commutator [*Physics*]
**LL Canuti R** ... Laws of King Canute [*or Knut*] [*A publication*] (DLA)
**LLcC**......... Calcasieu Parish Public Library, Lake Charles, LA [*Library symbol*] [*Library of Congress*] (LCLS)
**Ll CC Pr**..... Lloyd's County Courts Practice [*A publication*] (DLA)
**LLCF**......... Launch and Landing Computational Facilities [*NASA*] (NASA)
**LLCFR**....... Lobbyists and Lawyers for Campaign Finance Reform (EA)
**LLCM**........ Licentiate of the London College of Music [*British*] (DBQ)
**LLCM**........ Master of Comparative Law (DLA)
**LLcM**......... McNeese State University, Lake Charles, LA [*Library symbol*] [*Library of Congress*] (LCLS)
**LLCM(TD)** ... Licentiate of the London College of Music (Teacher's Diploma) [*British*]
**LLCO**......... Licentiate of the London College of Osteopathy
**Ll Comp**..... Lloyd's Compensation for Lands, Etc. [*6th ed.*] [*1895*] [*A publication*] (DLA)
**LL COOL J** ... Ladies Love Cool James [*Rap recording artist, James Todd Smith*]
**LLCS**......... Link Level Communications Subsystem [*NCR Corp.*]
**LLCS**......... Liquid Level Control Switch
**LLCS**......... Low-Level Compaction Station [*Nuclear energy*] (NRCH)
**LLCSC**....... Lower Level Computer Software Component
**LLCUNAE** ... Law Library of Congress United Association of Employees
**LLD**.......... Lactobacillus Lactis Dorner Factor [*Vitamin $B_{12}$ Also, APA, APAF, EF*]
**LLD**.......... Lamp Lumen Depreciation
**LLD**.......... LASER Light Detector
**LLD**.......... Launcher Load Dolly
**LLD**.......... Legum Doctor [*Doctor of Laws*]
**LLD**.......... Live Letter-Drop [*Espionage*]
**LLD**.......... Logic Level Driver [*Data processing*] (MCD)
**LLD**.......... Long-Lasting Depolarization [*Neurophysiology*]
**LLD**.......... Low-Level Detector (IEEE)
**LLD**.......... Low-Level Dose [*Nuclear energy*] (NRCH)
**LLD**.......... Lower Limit of Detection [*Spectrometry*]
**LLDEF**....... Lambda Legal Defense and Education Fund (EA)
**LLDPE**...... Linear Low-Density Polyethylene [*Plastics technology*]
**LLDS**......... Low-Level Weapons Delivery System (MCD)
**LLDV**......... Luc-Luong Dac-Viet [*Vietnamese special forces*]
**LLE**........... Laboratory for LASER Energetics [*University of Rochester*] [*Research center*]
**LLE**........... Large Local Exchange [*Telecommunications*] (TEL)
**LLE**........... Left Lower Extremity [*Medicine*]
**LLE**........... Lightning Loss Exclusion [*Insurance*]
**LLE**........... Liquid-Liquid Equilibria [*Physical chemistry*]
**LLE**........... Liquid-Liquid Extraction
**LLE**........... Long Line Effect
**LLE**........... Long Line Equipment [*Telecommunications*] (TEL)
**LLE**........... West Bend, WI [*Location identifier*] [*FAA*] (FAAL)
**LLEC**......... Long Lake Energy Corporation [*New York, NY*] [*NASDAQ symbol*] (NQ)
**LL Edw Conf** ... Laws of Edward the Confessor [*A publication*] (DLA)
**LLEE**......... Leurs Eminences [*Their Eminences*] [*French*]
**LLEE**......... Leurs Excellences [*Their Excellencies*] [*French*]
**L & Leg GDR** ... Law and Legislation in the German Democratic Republic [*A publication*] (DLA)
**L & Legis in GDR** ... Law and Legislation in the German Democratic Republic [*A publication*] (DLA)
**LLEIS**........ Lower Level End Item Subdivision [*Army*] (AABC)
**L & LeM**.... Leigh and Le Marchant. Elections [*4th ed.*] [*1885*] [*A publication*] (DLA)
**LLES**......... Eyn-Shemer [*Israel*] [*ICAO location identifier*] (ICLI)
**LLeS**......... Leesville State School, Leesville, LA [*Library symbol*] [*Library of Congress*] (LCLS)
**LLET**......... Elat/J. Hozman [*Israel*] [*ICAO location identifier*] (ICLI)
**LLeV**......... Vernon Parish Library, Leesville, LA [*Library symbol*] [*Library of Congress*] (LCLS)
**LLF**........... Lag Line Filter
**LLF**........... Laki-Lorand Factor [*Factor XIII*] [*Also, FSF*] [*Hematology*]
**LLF**........... Land Level Facility [*Navy*]
**LLF**........... Laubach Literacy Fund [*Later, LLI*] (EA)
**LLF**........... Left Lateral Femoral [*Site of injection*] [*Medicine*]
**LLF**........... Les Lettres Francaises [*A publication*]
**LLF**........... Line Link Frame [*Telecommunications*] (TEL)
**LLF**........... Little League Foundation (EA)
**LLF**........... Load List File (AFIT)
**LLFC**......... Laryssa Lauret Fan Club (EA)
**LLFC**......... Loretta Lynn Fan Club (EA)
**LLFM**........ Land Line Frequency Modulation (AAG)
**LLFM**........ Low-Level Flux Monitor [*Nuclear energy*] (NRCH)
**LLFPB**....... Linear, Lumped, Finite, Passive, Bilateral
**LLG**.......... Chillagoe [*Australia*] [*Airport symbol*] [*Obsolete*] (OAG)
**LlG**............ [*David*] Lloyd George [*Liberal party leader and Prime Minister of Great Britain*]
**LLG**.......... Logical Language Group [*An association*] (EA)
**LLG**.......... Logical Line Group [*Data processing*] (IBMDP)
**LLG**.......... Luggage and Leather Goods Salesmen's Association of America (EA)
**LLG**.......... Luggage and Travelware [*A publication*]
**LLGDS**...... Landlocked and Geographically Disadvantaged States [*Developing countries*]
**LLGF**......... Leather, Leather Goods, Fur [*Department of Employment*] [*British*]
**LLGMA**..... Luggage and Leather Goods Manufacturers of America (EA)
**Ll & GTP**... Lloyd and Goold's Irish Chancery Reports Tempore Plunkett [*A publication*] (DLA)
**Ll & GT Pl** ... Lloyd and Goold's Irish Chancery Reports Tempore Plunkett [*A publication*] (DLA)
**Ll & GTS**... Lloyd and Goold's Irish Chancery Reports Tempore Sugden [*1835*] [*A publication*] (DLA)
**LLH**.......... Lahore Light Horse [*British military*] (DMA)
**LLH**.......... Library of Literary History [*A publication*]
**LLHA**........ Haifa/U. Michaeli [*Israel*] [*ICAO location identifier*] (ICLI)
**LL Hen I**.... Laws of Henry I [*A publication*] (DLA)
**LLHZ**........ Herzlia [*Israel*] [*ICAO location identifier*] (ICLI)
**LLI**............ Lalibella [*Ethiopia*] [*Airport symbol*] (OAG)
**LLI**............ Late Latent Infection [*Medicine*]
**LLI**............ Latitude and Longitude Indicator
**LLI**............ Laubach Literacy International (EA)
**LLI**............ Life Line International (EA)
**LLI**............ Ligula Length Index
**LLI**............ Limited Life Item (MCD)
**LLI**............ Lipari [*Lipari Islands*] [*Seismograph station code, US Geological Survey*] (SEIS)
**LLI**............ Liquid Level Indicator
**LLI**............ Long Lead Item (MUGU)
**LLI**............ Longitude and Latitude Indicator
**LLI**............ Lord Lieutenant of Ireland
**LLI**............ Low-Level Interface
**L & Lib**...... Law and Liberty [*A publication*] (DLA)
**L Lib**......... Law Librarian [*A publication*]
**LLIB**......... Rosh Pina/Mahanaim-I. Ben-Yaakov [*Israel*] [*ICAO location identifier*] (ICLI)
**L Lib J**....... Law Library Journal [*A publication*]
**L Libr J**...... Law Library Journal [*A publication*]
**LLIC**......... Lamar Life Corporation [*NASDAQ symbol*] (NQ)
**LLIL**......... Long Lead Item List
**LLIL**......... Long Lead Time Items List (NASA)
**LLiLi**......... Livingston Parish Library, Livingston, LA [*Library symbol*] [*Library of Congress*] (LCLS)
**L and Lin M** ... Language and Linguistics in Melanesia [*A publication*]
**LL Inse**...... Laws of Ina [*A publication*] (DLA)
**LLIT**......... Liquid-Like Intermediate Transistory
**LLIU**......... Launch and Landing Interface Unit (MCD)
**LLIV**......... Low-Level Input Voltage
**LLJ**........... Challis, ID [*Location identifier*] [*FAA*] (FAAL)
**LLJ**........... Labor Law Journal [*A publication*]
**LLJ**........... Lahore Law Journal [*India*] [*A publication*] (DLA)
**LLJ**........... LaTrobe Library Journal [*A publication*]
**LLJ**........... Law Library Journal [*A publication*]
**LLJJ**......... Lords Justices
**LLJM**........ Ministry of Transport [*Israel*] [*ICAO location identifier*] (ICLI)
**Ll Jud Act**.. Lloyd's Supreme Court of Judicature Acts [*1875*] [*A publication*] (DLA)
**LLK**........... Liberator Lake, AK [*Location identifier*] [*FAA*] (FAAL)
**LLK**........... Little Lake Resources Ltd. [*Vancouver Stock Exchange symbol*]
**LLK**........... Louis Leakey - Korongo [*Anthropological skull*]
**LLL**........... La Leche League [*Local affiliates of LLLI*] (EA)
**LLL**........... Land Locomotion Laboratory [*Army*]
**LLL**........... Lawrence Livermore Laboratory [*Also, LLNL*] [*University of California*]
**LLL**........... Lawyers, Layers, and Limos [*Television broadcasting industry*]
**LLL**........... Left Lower Eyelid [*Medicine*]
**LLL**........... Left Lower Lobe [*of lung*] [*Medicine*]

**LLL**........... Liberte, Liberation, et Liberation Nationale [*French resistance movement*] [*World War II*]
**LLL**........... Licentiate in Laws
**LLL**........... Light Living Library (EA)
**LLL**........... Lillooet [*British Columbia*] [*Seismograph station code, US Geological Survey*] [*Closed*] (SEIS)
**LLL**........... Long Lead List (MCD)
**LLL**........... Long Line Loiter [*Aircraft*]
**LLL**........... Loose Leaf Ledger
**LLL**........... Love's Labour's Lost [*Shakespearean work*]
**LLL**........... Low-Level Logic
**LLL**........... Low Light Level
**LLL**........... Lower Lip Length [*Medicine*]
**LLL**........... Loyal Lusitanian League [*British military*] (DMA)
**LLL**........... Lutheran Laymen's League [*Later, ILLL*] (EA)
**LLL**........... University of Nebraska, Lincoln College of Law, Lincoln, NE [*OCLC symbol*] (OCLC)
**LLLB**......... Left Long Leg Brace [*Medicine*]
**LLLGB**...... Low-Level-LASER Guided Bomb
**LLLI**.......... La Leche League International (EA)
**Ll List LR**.. Lloyd's List Law Reports [*England*] [*A publication*] (DLA)
**LLLLLL**.... Laboratories Low-Level Linked List Language [*Bell Systems*] (MCD)
**Ll LLR**....... Lloyd's List Law Reports [*England*] [*A publication*] (DLA)
**LLLO**......... Lend-Lease Liaison Office [*World War II*]
**LL Longobard** ... Laws of the Lombards [*A publication*] (DLA)
**Ll L Pr Cas** ... Lloyd's List Prize Cases Reports [*England*] [*A publication*] (DLA)
**Ll LR**.......... Lloyd's List Law Reports [*England*] [*A publication*] (DLA)
**Ll L Rep**..... Lloyd's List Law Reports [*England*] [*A publication*] (DLA)
**LLLT**......... Low-Light-Level Television [*Night vision device*] [*Military*] (RDA)
**LLLTV**....... Low-Level LASER Television
**LLLTV**....... Low-Light-Level Television [*Night vision device*] [*Military*]
**LLLWT**..... Low-Level Liquid Waste Tank [*Nuclear energy*] (NRCH)
**LLM**.......... Langues et Lettres Modernes [*A publication*]
**LLM**.......... Launcher Loader Module
**LLM**.......... Lawyers Linked by MODEM [*Computer bulletin board system*] [*FIDO*]
**LLM**.......... Legum Magister [*Master of Laws*] [*Latin*]
**LLM**.......... Limb Load Monitor
**LLM**.......... Limba si Literatura Moldovencasca Chisinau [*A publication*]
**LLM**.......... Load Line Method
**LLM**.......... Localized Leukocyte Mobilization
**LLM**.......... Low-Level Multiplexer
**LLM**.......... Loyola University, New Orleans, LA [*OCLC symbol*] (OCLC)
**LLM**.......... Lunar Landing Mission [*NASA*]
**LLM**.......... Lunar Landing Module [*NASA*] (MCD)
**LLM**.......... Master of Laws
**LLMA**........ Leavers Lace Manufacturers of America [*Defunct*] (EA)
**LL Malcom R Scott** ... Laws of Malcolm, King of Scotland [*A publication*] (DLA)
**Ll Mar LN** ... Lloyd's Maritime Law Newsletter [*A publication*] (DLA)
**LLM (CL)** ... Master of Laws in Comparative Law
**LLM Com** ... Master of Commercial Law
**LLMD**........ Lifeline Healthcare Group, Ltd. [*NASDAQ symbol*] (NQ)
**LLMFC**..... Laura Lee McBride Fan Club (EA)
**LLM (Int L)** ... Master of Laws in International Law
**LLMM**....... Leurs Majestes [*Their Majesties*] [*French*]
**LLMPP**..... Liquid Level Monitor Port Plug [*Nuclear energy*] (NRCH)
**LLMR**........ Mitzpe-Ramon [*Israel*] [*ICAO location identifier*] (ICLI)
**LLMZ**........ Metzada/I. Bar Yehuda [*Israel*] [*ICAO location identifier*] (ICLI)
**LLN**.......... League for Less Noise
**LLN**.......... Levelland, TX [*Location identifier*] [*FAA*] (FAAL)
**LLN**.......... Line Link Network [*Bell System*]
**LLNL**......... Lawrence Livermore National Laboratory [*Also, LLL*] [*Livermore, CA*] [*Department of Energy*] (GRD)
**LLNO**........ Low-Level Night Operations [*Aviation*]
**LL NS**........ Law Library, New Series [*Philadelphia Reprint of English Treatises*] [*A publication*] (DLA)
**LLO**.......... Legionella-Like Organisms [*Medicine*]
**LLO**.......... Llano, TX [*Location identifier*] [*FAA*] (FAAL)
**LLO**.......... Low Lunar Orbit
**LLOC**......... Land Line of Communications [*Military*]
**LLOG**........ Lincoln Logs Ltd. [*Chestertown, NY*] [*NASDAQ symbol*] (NQ)
**LLOS**......... Landmark Line of Sight (KSC)
**LLOV**......... Low-Level Output Voltage
**LLOV**......... Ovda [*Israel*] [*ICAO location identifier*] (ICLI)
**LLOYA2**.... Lloydia [*Cincinnati*] [*A publication*]
**Lloyd & Goold (T Plunkett) (Ir)** ... Lloyd and Goold's Irish Chancery Reports Tempore Plunkett [*A publication*] (DLA)
**Lloyd & Goold (T Sugden) (Ir)** ... Lloyd and Goold's Irish Chancery Reports Tempore Sugden [*A publication*] (DLA)
**Lloydia**....... Lloydia. Lloyd Library and Museum [*A publication*]
**Lloydia J Nat Prod** ... Lloydia. Journal of Natural Products [*A publication*]
**Lloyd LR**.... Lloyd's List Law Reports [*England*] [*A publication*] (DLA)
**Lloyd Pr Cas** ... Lloyd's List Prize Cases Reports [*England*] [*A publication*] (DLA)
**Lloyd Pr Cas NS** ... Lloyd's List Prize Cases Reports, Second Series [*1939-53*] [*A publication*] (DLA)
**Lloyds AE** ... Lloyd's Aviation Economist [*A publication*]
**Lloyds Bank R** ... Lloyds Bank Review [*A publication*]
**Lloyds Bk**... Lloyds Bank Review [*A publication*]
**Lloyd's List LR** ... Lloyd's List Law Reports [*England*] [*A publication*] (DLA)
**Lloyds Mar and Com LQ** ... Lloyd's Maritime and Commercial Law Quarterly [*A publication*]
**Lloyd's Mar LN** ... Lloyd's Maritime Law Newsletter [*A publication*] (DLA)
**Lloyds Mex** ... Lloyd's Mexican Economic Report [*A publication*]
**Lloyd's Pr Cas** ... Lloyd's List Prize Cases Reports [*England*] [*A publication*] (DLA)
**Lloyd's Prize Cas** ... Lloyd's List Prize Cases Reports [*London*] [*A publication*] (DLA)
**Lloyd's Rep** ... Lloyd's List Law Reports [*England*] [*A publication*] (DLA)
**Lloyd & W** ... Lloyd and Welsby's English Mercantile Cases [*A publication*] (DLA)
**LLP**........... Lambda Limiting Process
**LLP**........... LASER Light Pump
**LLP**........... Launch and Landing Project [*NASA*] (NASA)
**LLP**........... Law and Liberty Project [*Defunct*] (EA)
**LLP**........... Leased Long Lines Program (NATG)
**LLP**........... Line Link Pulsing [*Telecommunications*]
**LLP**........... Linear Log Potentiometer
**LLP**........... Live Load Punch
**LLP**........... Lloyd's of London Press [*British*]
**LLP**........... Lollipop Daycare [*Vancouver Stock Exchange symbol*]
**LLP**........... London Labour Party [*London, England*] [*Political party*]
**LLP**........... Long Lead Part
**LLP**........... Lunar Landing Program [*NASA*]
**LLP**........... Lyman Laboratory of Physics [*Harvard*] (MCD)
**LLPDD**...... Late Luteal Phase Dysphoric Disorder [*Gynecology*]
**LLPE**......... Labor's League for Political Education [*AFL*] [*Later merged into Committee on Political Education of AFL-CIO*]
**LLpEC**....... East Carroll Parish Library, Lake Providence, LA [*Library symbol*] [*Library of Congress*] (LCLS)
**LLPI**.......... Linen and Lace Paper Institute [*Later, SSI*] (EA)
**LLPL**......... Low Low Pond Level (IEEE)
**LLPN**......... Lumped, Linear, Parametric Network
**LLPO**......... Launch and Landing Project Office [*NASA*] (NASA)
**Ll Pr**........... Lloyd on Prohibition [*1849*] [*A publication*] (DLA)
**Ll Pr Cas**.... Lloyd's List Prize Cases Reports [*England*] [*A publication*] (DLA)
**Ll Pr Cas NS** ... Lloyd's List Prize Cases Reports, New Series [*1939-53*] [*A publication*] (DLA)
**LLPS**.......... Low-Level Pumping Station (ADA)
**LLQ**........... Left Lower Quadrant [*of abdomen*] [*Medicine*]
**LLQA**......... Limiting Lines of Quiet Approach [*Navy*] (NVT)
**LLR**........... High Court of Lagos Law Reports [*Nigeria*] [*A publication*] (ILCA)
**LLR**........... Lancaster Law Review [*A publication*] (DLA)
**LLR**........... Leader Law Reports [*South Africa*] [*A publication*] (DLA)
**LLR**........... Left Lateral Rotation [*Medicine*]
**LLR**........... Leukemia-Like Reaction [*Hematology*]
**LLR**........... Liberian Law Reports [*A publication*] (ILCA)
**LLR**........... Line of Least Resistance
**LLR**........... Load-Limiting Resistor
**LLR**........... Low-Level Radiation
**LLR**........... Low-Level Resistance [*to disease*]
**LLR**........... Lunar LASER Ranging [*Aerospace*]
**LLR**........... Luzerne Legal Register [*A publication*]
**LLRC**......... Luneberg Lens Rapid Commutator [*Physics*]
**Ll Rep**........ Lloyd's List Law Reports [*England*] [*A publication*] (DLA)
**LLRES**....... Load-Limiting Resistor (MSA)
**LLRF**......... Low-Level Radio Frequency
**LLRF**......... Lunar Landing Research Facility [*Aerospace*]
**LLRF**......... Lunar LASER Range-Finder [*Aerospace*]
**LLRGDY**... Allergy [*Copenhagen*] [*A publication*]
**LLRI**.......... Low-Level-Run-In (MCD)
**LLRM**........ Low-Level Radio Modulator
**LLRP**......... Long Lead Repair Part
**Ll R Pr Cas** ... Lloyd's List Prize Cases Reports, Second Series [*1939-53*] [*A publication*] (DLA)
**LLRT**......... Local Leak Rate Test [*Nuclear energy*] (NRCH)
**LLRT**......... Low-Level Reactor Test (IEEE)
**LLRTD5**.... Allertonia [*A publication*]
**LLRV**......... Lunar Landing Research Vehicle [*Aerospace*]
**LLS**........... Land Laws Service [*Australia*] [*A publication*]
**LLS**........... LASER Light Source
**LLS**........... LASER Line Scanner
**LLS**........... Launch and Landing Site (MCD)
**LLS**........... Lazy Leukocyte Syndrome [*Medicine*]
**LLS**........... Liquid Level Sensor
**LLS**........... Local Library System [*OCLC*]
**LLS**........... Louisiana State University, Graduate School of Library Science, Baton Rouge, LA [*OCLC symbol*] (OCLC)
**LLS**........... Low-Level Sensor (KSC)
**LLS**........... Low-Level Service [*Data processing*]
**LLS**........... Low-Level Solid [*Nuclear energy*] (NRCH)
**LLS**........... Lunar Landing Simulator [*Aerospace*] (AAG)
**LLS**........... Lunar Logistics System [*NASA*]

**LLSA** ......... Land Lines Assembly [*Ground Communications Facility, NASA*]
**LLSA** ......... Latin Languages Speaking Allergists [*See also GAILL*] (EAIO)
**LLSA** ......... Limiting Lines of Surfaced Approach [*Navy*] (NVT)
**LLSAC** ....... LASER Line Scanner Aerial Camera
**LLSC** ......... Israel South Control Area Control Center Unit [*Israel*] [*ICAO location identifier*] (ICLI)
**LLSD** ......... Tel Aviv/Sde Dov [*Israel*] [*ICAO location identifier*] (ICLI)
**LLSEE** ....... Linguistic and Literary Studies in Eastern Europe [*A publication*]
**LLSIL** ........ Lower Living Standard Income Level [*CETA*] [*Department of Labor*]
**LLSL** .......... Lakeland First Financial Group, Inc. [*NASDAQ symbol*] (NQ)
**LLSNA** ...... Limiting Lines of Snorkel Approach [*Navy*] (NVT)
**LLSPT** ....... Licentiateship of the London School of Polymer Technology [*British*] (DBQ)
**LLSS** .......... LASER Light Scattering Spectroscopy
**LLSS** .......... LASER Light Source Station
**LLSS** .......... Low-Level Sounding System [*for measuring weather conditions*]
**Ll St** .......... Lloyd's Statutes of Practical Utility [*A publication*] (DLA)
**LLSU** ......... Low-Level Signaling Unit [*Telecommunications*] (TEL)
**LLSUA** ...... Limiting Lines of Submerged Approach [*Navy*] (NVT)
**Ll Suc** ........ Lloyd on Succession Laws [*1877*] [*A publication*] (DLA)
**LLSV** ......... Low-Level Storage Vault [*Nuclear energy*] (NRCH)
**LLSV** ......... Lunar Logistics System Vehicle [*NASA*]
**LLSWV** ..... Low-Level Solid Waste Storage Vault [*Nuclear energy*] (NRCH)
**LLT** ........... Lahore Law Times [*India*] [*A publication*] (DLA)
**LLT** ........... Lander Local Time [*NASA*]
**LLT** ........... Left Lateral Thigh [*Medicine*]
**LLT** ........... Library of Living Thought [*A publication*]
**LLT** ........... London Landed Terms [*Shipping*]
**LLT** ........... Long Lead Time
**LLT** ........... Low-Level Terminal
**LLT** ........... Low-Level Turbulence
**LLT** ........... Low-Light Television
**LLT** ........... Loyola University, Law Library, New Orleans, LA [*OCLC symbol*] (OCLC)
**LLTA** ......... Tel Aviv [*Israel*] [*ICAO location identifier*] (ICLI)
**LLTC** ......... Linear Technology Corporation [*Milpitas, CA*] [*NASDAQ symbol*] (NQ)
**LLTCS** ....... Low-Limit Temperature Control Systems
**LLTD** ......... Lightweight LASER Target Designator
**LLTDS** ...... Launch Landing Test Data System (MCD)
**LLTI** .......... Long Lead Time Items (AAG)
**LLTIL** ........ Long Lead Time Items List [*Military*] (CAAL)
**LLTR** ......... Large Leak Test Rig [*Nuclear energy*] (NRCH)
**Ll Tr M** ...... Lloyd on Trade-Marks [*A publication*] (DLA)
**LLTT** ......... Landline Teletypewriter [*Military*]
**LLTTY** ...... Landline Teletypewriter [*Military*]
**LLTV** ......... Low-Light-Level Television [*Night vision device*] [*Military*]
**LLTV** ......... Lunar Landing Training Vehicle [*Aerospace*]
**LLTWP** ..... Low-Level Tritiated Water Processing Subsystem (MCD)
**LLU** .......... Lamar, MO [*Location identifier*] [*FAA*] (FAAL)
**LLU** .......... Lending Library Unit
**LLU** .......... Loma Linda University, Loma Linda, CA [*OCLC symbol*] (OCLC)
**LLu** ........... Saint James Parish Library, Lutcher, LA [*Library symbol*] [*Library of Congress*] (LCLS)
**LLud** .......... Literatura Ludowa [*A publication*]
**LLV** ........... Long Life Valve
**LLV** ........... Long Life Vehicle [*Automotive engineering*]
**LLV** ........... Loyal London Volunteers [*British military*] (DMA)
**LLV** ........... Lunar Landing Vehicle [*NASA*]
**LLV** ........... Lunar Logistics Vehicle [*NASA*]
**LLV** ........... Lymphocytic Leukemia Virus
**LLVPG** ...... Large Launch Vehicle Planning Group [*NASA*]
**LLW** .......... Lilongwe [*Malawi*] [*Airport symbol*] (OAG)
**Ll & W** ....... Lloyd and Welsby's English Mercantile Cases [*A publication*] (DLA)
**LLW** .......... Low-Level Radioactive Waste
**LLW** .......... Low-Level Waste [*Nuclear energy*] (NRCH)
**LLW** .......... Lower Low Water [*Tides and currents*]
**LLWAS** ..... Low-Level Wind Shear Alert System [*Pronounced "elwaas"*] [*Meteorology*] (FAAC)
**LLWDDD** ... Low-Level Waste Disposal Development and Demonstration
**Ll & Wels**... Lloyd and Welsby's English Commercial Cases [*A publication*] (DLA)
**LLWI** ......... Lower Low-Water Interval [*Tides and currents*]
**LL Wisegotho** ... Laws of the Visigoths [*A publication*] (DLA)
**LL Wm Conq** ... Laws of William the Conqueror [*A publication*] (DLA)
**LL Wm Noth** ... Laws of William the Bastard [*A publication*] (DLA)
**LLWP** ........ Local Liaison Working Party [*Australian Atomic Energy Commission*]
**LLWS** ........ Low-Level Wind Shear [*Meteorology*] (FAAC)
**LLWSAS** ... Low-Level Wind Shear Alert System [*Meteorology*] (FAAC)
**LLWSV** ..... Low-Level Waste Storage Vault [*Nuclear energy*] (NRCH)
**LLX** ........... Louisiana Land & Exploration Co. [*NYSE symbol*] [*Toronto Stock Exchange symbol*]
**LLX** ........... Lyndonville, VT [*Location identifier*] [*FAA*] (FAAL)
**LLY** ........... Lilly [*Eli*] & Co. [*NYSE symbol*] (SPSG)
**LLY** ........... Llanelly [*Welsh depot code*]
**LLYP** ......... Long Leaf Yellow Pine [*Lumber*]
**LLZ** ........... Localizer [*ICAO designator*] (CET)
**LL Zt** ......... Leipziger Lehrerzeitung [*A publication*]
**LM** ............ Antilliaanse Luchtvaart Maatschappi [*Netherlands*] [*ICAO designator*] (FAAC)
**L & M** ........ Labor and Material Bond
**LM** ............ Laboratory Manager
**LM** ............ Laboratory Microscope
**LM** ............ Laboratory Module (MCD)
**LM** ............ Labour Mobility [*British*]
**LM** ............ Lactose Malabsorption [*Gastroenterology*]
**LM** ............ Lacus Mortis [*Lunar area*]
**LM** ............ Lady's Magazine [*A publication*]
**LM** ............ Lamentations [*Old Testament book*]
**LM** ............ Land Mine [*Military*]
**LM** ............ Land Mobile
**LM** ............ Landmark (KSC)
**LM** ............ Language Monographs [*A publication*]
**LM** ............ Langues Modernes [*A publication*]
**LM** ............ Large Memory [*Data processing*]
**LM** ............ Large Mouth Bass [*Pisciculture*]
**LM** ............ Lateral Malleolus [*Anatomy*]
**LM** ............ Lateral Meniscus [*Anatomy*]
**LM** ............ Laufenden Monats [*Of the Current Month*] [*German*]
**LM** ............ Launch Mount (AFM)
**LM** ............ Le Monde [*A publication*]
**LM** ............ Leading Mechanician
**LM** ............ Leave Message [*Word processing*]
**LM** ............ Lee-Metford [*British military*] (DMA)
**LM** ............ Left Male (MSA)
**LM** ............ Left Mid (NASA)
**LM** ............ Leg Multiple [*Telegraph*] [*Telecommunications*] (TEL)
**LM** ............ Legal Medicine
**LM** ............ Legg Mason, Inc. [*NYSE symbol*] (SPSG)
**LM** ............ Legion of Merit [*Military decoration*]
**LM** ............ Leisure Monthly Magazine [*A publication*]
**LM** ............ Leptomeningeal Metastasis
**LM** ............ Lethal Material
**LM** ............ Letterature Moderne [*A publication*]
**LM** ............ Level Meter
**LM** ............ Lexikon der Marienkunde [*A publication*]
**L & M** ........ [*The*] Librarian and the Machine [*A publication*]
**LM** ............ Licentiate in Medicine
**LM** ............ Licentiate in Midwifery
**LM** ............ Light Maintenance
**LM** ............ Light Metal
**LM** ............ Light Microscope
**LM** ............ Light Minimum [*Medicine*]
**LM** ............ Light Music [*Canadian Broadcasting Corporation record series prefix*]
**LM** ............ Lindenmaier-Moehring, Nachschlagewerk des Bundesgerichtshofes [*Collection of Decisions of the Federal Supreme Court, Together with Comments*] [*A publication*] (ILCA)
**LM** ............ Linear Modulation
**L/M** ........... Lines per Minute [*Data processing*]
**LM** ............ Linguomesial [*Dentistry*]
**LM** ............ Link Manager
**LM** ............ Lipid Mobilizing Hormone [*Endocrinology*]
**LM** ............ Liquid Membrane
**LM** ............ Liquid Metal
**LM** ............ List of Material [*DoD*]
**L/M** ........... List of Materials (AAG)
**LM** ............ Listeria Monocytogenes [*Microorganism*]
**LM** ............ Litchfield & Madison [*AAR code*]
**L and M** ..... Literature and Medicine [*A publication*]
**L & M** ........ Literature and Medicine [*A publication*]
**L/M** ........... Liters per Minute
**LM** ............ Liturgie und Moenchtum [*A publication*] (BJA)
**LM** ............ Load Module (MCD)
**LM** ............ Local Manufacture (AAG)
**LM** ............ Local Memory
**LM** ............ Local Militia [*British military*] (DMA)
**LM** ............ Locator, Middle [*Aviation*] (FAAC)
**LM** ............ Locus Monumenti [*Place of the Monument*] [*Latin*]
**LM** ............ Logic Module [*Data processing*] (MCD)
**LM** ............ Logistics Manager (MCD)
**LM** ............ London Law Magazine [*A publication*]
**LM** ............ London Magazine [*A publication*]
**LM** ............ London Mercury [*A publication*]
**LM** ............ Long Measure (ROG)
**LM** ............ Long Meter [*Music*]
**LM** ............ Long Module (MCD)
**LM** ............ Longitudinal Muscle [*Anatomy*]
**LM** ............ Loop Multiplexer
**LM** ............ Lord Mayor
**L-M** ........... Louisiana State Museum, New Orleans, LA [*Library symbol*] [*Library of Congress*] (LCLS)
**LM** ............ Low Meaningfulness [*Psychology*]

**L/M** .......... Low/Medium (MCD)
**LM** .......... Low Molecular [*Chemistry*]
**LM** .......... Lower Magazine [*Typography*]
**LM** .......... Lower Motor [*Neurology*]
**L & M** ........ Lowndes and Maxwell's English Practice Cases [*1852-54*] [*A publication*] (DLA)
**LM** .......... Lucrari de Muzicologie [*A publication*]
**LM** .......... Ludus Magistralis [*A publication*]
**LM** .......... Luftmine [*Aerial mine*] [*German military - World War II*]
**LM** .......... Lumen [*Symbol*] [*SI unit of luminous flux*]
**L/M** .......... Luminosity to Mass [*Ratio*] [*Astronomy*]
**LM** .......... Luna Monthly [*A publication*]
**LM** .......... Lunar Mission
**LM** .......... Lunar Module [*Formerly, LEM*] [*NASA*]
**LM** .......... Lutherische Monatshefte [*A publication*]
**LM** .......... Maestretti [*Italy*] [*Research code symbol*]
**LM** .......... Middle Latitude [*Navigation*]
**LM2** .......... Lima [*Magdalena*] [*Peru*] [*Seismograph station code, US Geological Survey*] (SEIS)
**LM2** .......... Liver Microsomal Band 2
**LMA** .......... Labor Market Area
**LMA** .......... Lake Minchumina [*Alaska*] [*Airport symbol*] (OAG)
**LMA** .......... Laminating Materials Association [*Oradell, NJ*] (EA)
**LMA** .......... Large Model Access (MCD)
**LMA** .......... LASER Microspectral Analysis
**LMA** .......... Last Manufacturers Association [*Defunct*] (EA)
**LMA** .......... Le Moyen Age [*A publication*]
**LMA** .......... Leading Medical Assistant [*British military*] (DMA)
**LMA** .......... League for Mutual Aid [*Defunct*] (EA)
**LMA** .......... Left Mentoanterior [*A fetal position*] [*Obstetrics*]
**LMA** .......... Licensed Merchandisers' Association [*Later, ILMA*] (EA)
**LMA** .......... Lingerie Manufacturers Association [*Later, IAMA*] (EA)
**LMA** .......... Liver Membrane Autoantibody [*Immunochemistry*]
**LMA** .......... Livestock Marketing Association (EA)
**LMA** .......... Local Marshalling Areas (MCD)
**LMA** .......... Lock Museum of America (EA)
**LMA** .......... Logsplitter Manufacturers Association (EA)
**LMA** .......... Lunar Meteoroid Analyzer [*NASA*]
**LMA** .......... Lunar Module Adapter [*NASA*] (MCD)
**LM1A** ........ Late Minoan 1A [*Archaeology*]
**LMAB** ........ London Munitions Assignments Board [*World War II*]
**LMAC** ........ Labor-Management Advisory Committee [*Terminated, 1974*] [*Cost of Living Council*] (EGAO)
**LMAC** ........ Labor Market Advisory Councils [*Department of Labor and Department of Health, Education, and Welfare*] [*Terminated, 1982*] (EGAO)
**LMAC** ........ Landmark American Corporation [*NASDAQ symbol*] (NQ)
**LMaD** ........ DeSoto Parish Library, Mansfield, LA [*Library symbol*] [*Library of Congress*] (LCLS)
**LMAD** ........ Let's Make a Deal [*TV program*]
**LMAD** ........ Lietuvos TSR Mokslu Akademijos Darbai. Serija A [*Vilnius*] [*A publication*]
**LMAE** ........ Lunar Module Ascent Engine [*NASA*]
**LMAF** ........ Live Missile Assembly Facility
**LMAFS** ...... Lookout Mountain Air Force Station
**LM-Ag** ....... Liver Membrane Antigen [*Immunochemistry*]
**L Mag** ........ London Law Magazine [*A publication*]
**L Mag** ........ London Magazine [*A publication*]
**L Mag & LR** ... Law Magazine and Law Review [*A publication*] (DLA)
**L Mag & Rev** ... Law Magazine and Review [*A publication*] (DLA)
**LMags** ....... Index to Little Magazines [*A publication*]
**LMAL** ........ Langley Memorial Aeronautical Laboratory [*NASA*] (AAG)
**LMAMA** ... Louisa May Alcott Memorial Association (EA)
**LManyS** ..... Sabine Parish Library, Many, LA [*Library symbol*] [*Library of Congress*] (LCLS)
**LMAOS** ...... Liverpool Monographs in Archaeology and Oriental Studies
**LMarA** ....... Avoyelles Parish Library, Marksville, LA [*Library symbol*] [*Library of Congress*] (LCLS)
**LMARS** ...... Library Management and Retrieval System [*Navy*] [*Information service or system*] (IID)
**LM/ATM** ... Lunar Module Apollo Telescope Mount [*NASA*] (MCD)
**LMAV** ........ LASER Maverick (MCD)
**LMB** .......... Labor Market Bulletin (OICC)
**LMB** .......... Laurence-Moon-Biedl [*Medicine*]
**LMB** .......... Linear Motion Bearing
**LMB** .......... Local Message Box (NATG)
**LMB** .......... Low-Maintenance Battery (MCD)
**LM1B** ........ Late Minoan 1B [*Archaeology*]
**LMBBS** ...... Laurence-Moon-Bardet-Biedl Syndrome [*Medicine*]
**LMBBSN** .. Laurence-Moon-Bardet-Biedl Syndrome Network [*An association*] (EA)
**LMBC** ........ Lady Margaret Boat Club [*of St. John's College, Cambridge*] [*British*]
**LMBC** ........ Landmark Bancorp [*NASDAQ symbol*] (NQ)
**LMBF** ........ Low and Medium Bleeding Frequency [*Medicine*]
**LMBI** ......... Local Memory Bus Interface [*Data processing*]
**LM Bl** ........ Lueneburger Museumsblaetter [*A publication*]
**LMBO** ........ Leveraged Management Buy-Out
**LMBS** ........ Laurence-Moon-Biedl Syndrome [*Medicine*]
**LMC** .......... Cleveland-Marshall College of Law, Cleveland, OH [*OCLC symbol*] (OCLC)
**LMC** .......... Labor Market Characteristics (OICC)
**LMC** .......... Lamacarena [*Colombia*] [*Airport symbol*] [*Obsolete*] (OAG)
**LMC** .......... Lamina Monopolar Cell [*Cytology*]
**LMC** .......... Lamocks [*Republic of China*] [*Seismograph station code, US Geological Survey*] (SEIS)
**LMC** .......... Lancia Motor Club [*Ledbury, Herefordshire, England*] (EAIO)
**LMC** .......... Large Magellanic Cloud [*Astronomy*]
**LMC** .......... LASER Mirror Coating
**LMC** .......... Lateral Motor Column [*of the spinal cord*] [*Neurobiology*]
**LMC** .......... Least Material Condition (MSA)
**LMC** .......... Ligue Monarchiste du Canada [*Monarchist League of Canada*] (EAIO)
**LMC** .......... Lime-Magnesium Carbonate
**LMC** .......... Liquid Metal Cycle
**LMC** .......... Literature, Meaning, Culture [*A publication*]
**LMC** .......... Lloyd's Machinery Certificate [*Shipping*]
**LMC** .......... Local Mate Competition [*Entomology*]
**LMC** .......... Local Medical Committee [*British*]
**LMC** .......... Logistic Movement Center [*Military*] (CAAL)
**LMC** .......... Logistics Management Center [*Army*] (MCD)
**LMC** .......... Lomas Mortgage Corp. [*NYSE symbol*] [*Later, CMO*] (SPSG)
**LMC** .......... Lon Morris College [*Texas*]
**LMC** .......... Long-Run Marginal Cost Curve [*Economics*]
**LMC** .......... Louisville Municipal College [*Kentucky*]
**LMC** .......... Low Middling Clause [*Business term*]
**LMC** .......... Lymphocyte-Mediated Cytotoxicity [*Also, LC*] [*Immunology*]
**LMC** .......... Lymphomyeloid Complex [*Medicine*]
**LMc** .......... Morgan City Public Library, Morgan City, LA [*Library symbol*] [*Library of Congress*] (LCLS)
**LMCA** ....... Laboratory Materiel Control Activity (AFIT)
**LMCA** ....... Left Main Coronary Artery [*Anatomy*]
**LMCA** ....... Logistics Management Course for Auditors [*Army*]
**LMCA** ....... Logistics Material Control Activity [*Military*]
**LMCAD** .... Left Main Coronary Artery Disease
**LMCC** ........ Land Mobile Communications Council (EA)
**LMCC** ........ Licentiate of Medical Council of Canada
**LMCC** ........ Low-Mintage Coin Club (EA)
**LMCLQ** ..... Lloyds Maritime and Commercial Law Quarterly [*A publication*] (DLA)
**LM/CM$^2$** ... Lumens per Square Centimeter
**LMCMS** .... Licentiate Ministers and Certified Mediums Society (EA)
**LMCN** ....... Launch Maintenance Conference Network [*Aerospace*] (AAG)
**LMCP** ........ Laboratory Module Computer Program
**LMCR** ........ Liquid Metal Cooled Reactor
**LMCS** ........ Legal Management Consultancy Services [*Australia*]
**LMCSS** ...... Letter Mail Code Sort System [*Postal Service*]
**LMCT** ........ Ligand-to-Metal Charge Transfer [*Physical chemistry*]
**LMD** .......... Australian Legal Monthly Digest [*A publication*] (APTA)
**LMD** .......... La Maison-Dieu [*A publication*]
**LMD** .......... Labor Mobility Demonstration
**LMD** .......... LASER Microwave Division [*Army*]
**LMD** .......... Leaf-Mold (ROG)
**LMD** .......... Left Medial Deltoid [*Injection Site*]
**LMD** .......... Legal Monthly Digest [*Australia*] [*A publication*] (DLA)
**LMD** .......... Liquid Metal Detector
**L/(M D)** ..... Liter per Meter Day
**LMD** .......... Local Medical Doctor
**LMD** .......... Long Meter Double [*Music*]
**LMD** .......... Louisiana Midland Railway Co. [*Later, LMT*] [*AAR code*]
**LMD** .......... Low Modulus Direction [*Mechanical testing*]
**LMD** .......... Low-Molecular-Weight Dextran [*Medicine*]
**LMD** .......... Lunar Meteoroid Detector [*NASA*]
**L/(M$^2$ D)** ... Liters per Square Meter Day
**LMDA** ....... Lee's Multidifferential Agar [*Brewery bacteria culture medium*]
**LMDA** ....... Lunar Meteoroid Detector-Analyzer [*NASA*]
**LMDE** ....... Lunar Module Descent Engine [*NASA*]
**LMDM** ...... Little Mission for the Deaf-Mute [*See also PMS*] [*Rome, Italy*] (EAIO)
**LME** .......... L. M. Ericsson [*Swedish telecommunications company*] (TEL)
**LME** .......... Labor Market Exposure [*Work Incentive Program*]
**LME** .......... Lambda Mercantile Corp. [*Toronto Stock Exchange symbol*]
**LME** .......... Large Marine Ecosystem
**LME** .......... Launch Monitor Equipment [*NASA*] (KSC)
**LME** .......... Layer Management Entity
**LME** .......... Link Monitor Equipment (MCD)
**LME** .......... Liquid Membrane Extraction [*Separation science and technology*]
**LME** .......... Liquid Mercury Engine
**LME** .......... Liquid Metal Embrittlement (MCD)
**LME** .......... Locally Manufactured Equipment
**LME** .......... Logistics Management Engineering, Inc. [*Annapolis, MD*] [*Telecommunications*] (TSSD)
**LME** .......... London Metal Exchange
**LME** .......... Lunar Module Engine [*NASA*]
**LME** .......... Lysine Methyl Ester [*Biochemistry*]
**LMEC** ........ Lambda Mercantile Corporation [*Toronto, ON*] [*NASDAQ symbol*] (NQ)
**LMEC** ........ Line Map Editing Console
**LMEC** ........ Liquid Metal Engineering Center [*Energy Research and Development Administration*]
**LMED** ....... Lyphomed, Inc. [*NASDAQ symbol*] (NQ)

**L Med and Health** ... Law, Medicine, and Health Care [*A publication*]
**L Med Q** .... Legal Medical Quarterly [*A publication*]
**LMEE** ....... Light Military Electronics Equipment
**LMEIC** ...... Life Member of Engineering Institute of Canada
**L Mer** ......... London Mercury [*A publication*]
**LMES** ........ Laboratory for Meteorology and Earth Sciences [*NASA*]
**LMET** ........ Leadership and Management Education and Training [*Navy*]
**LMetJ** ........ Jefferson Parish Library, Metairie, LA [*Library symbol*] [*Library of Congress*] (LCLS)
**LMetR** ....... Jefferson Parish Recreation Department, Metairie, LA [*Library symbol*] [*Library of Congress*] (LCLS)
**LMF** .......... Lack of Moral Fibre [*British military*] (DMA)
**LMF** .......... Lake Michigan Federation (EA)
**LMF** .......... Language Media Format (CET)
**LMF** .......... Large Myelinated Fiber [*Neuroanatomy*]
**LMF** .......... Large-Scale Melt Facility [*Nuclear reactor test unit*]
**LMF** .......... Last Meal Furnished
**LMF** .......... Last Month's Forecast (MCD)
**LMF** .......... Le Mans [*France*] [*Seismograph station code, US Geological Survey*] [*Closed*] (SEIS)
**LMF** .......... Le Monde Francais [*A publication*]
**LMF** .......... Leukeran [*Chlorambucil*], Methotrexate, Fluorouracil [*Antineoplastic drug regimen*]
**LMF** .......... Leukocyte Mitogenic Factor [*Medicine*]
**LMF** .......... Linear Matched Filter (IEEE)
**LMF** .......... Liquid Metal Fuel
**LMF** .......... Low and Medium Frequency
**LMF** .......... Lower Mid Fuselage (NASA)
**LMF** .......... Lymphocyte Mitogenic Factor [*Endocrinology, hematology*]
**LMFA** ........ Lucky Mee Family Association (EA)
**LMFBR** ..... Liquid Metal Fast Breeder Reactor
**LMFC** ........ Leigh McCloskey Fan Club (EA)
**LMFC** ........ Liza Minnelli Fan Club (EA)
**LMFC** ........ Louise Mandrell Fan Club (EA)
**LMFE** ........ London Meat Futures Exchange [*British*]
**LMFR** ........ Liquid Metal Fueled Reactor
**LMFRE** ..... Liquid Metal Fueled Reactor Experiment
**LMG** .......... Lamington [*Papua New Guinea*] [*Seismograph station code, US Geological Survey*] (SEIS)
**LMG** .......... LASER Milling Gauge
**LMG** .......... Lauerer Markin Gibbs, Inc. [*Maumee, OH*] [*Telecommunications*] (TSSD)
**LMG** .......... Lawson Mardon Group Ltd. [*AMEX symbol*] (SPSG)
**LMG** .......... Left Main Gear (MCD)
**LMG** .......... Light Machine Gun
**LMG** .......... Liquid Methane Gas
**LMG** .......... Louisiana Mining Corp. [*Vancouver Stock Exchange symbol*]
**LMGC** ........ Lunar Module Guidance Computer [*NASA*] (KSC)
**LMGR** ....... Liberation Movement of the German Reich [*An association*] (EAIO)
**LMG Rep Data and Word Process Libr** ... LMG [*Library Management Group*] Report on Data and Word Processing for Libraries [*A publication*]
**LMGSM** .... Latin and Mediterranean Group for Sport Medicine (EA)
**LMH** .......... Lady Margaret Hall [*Oxford University*]
**LMH** .......... Lebensmittelzeitung [*A publication*]
**LMH** .......... Lewis, M. H., Winchester VA [*STAC*]
**LMH** .......... Light Metal Hydride
**LMH** .......... Lipid Mobilizing Hormone [*Endocrinology*]
**LMHA** ........ Lay Mission-Helpers Association (EA)
**LMHF** ........ Lauritz Melchior Heldentenor Foundation (EA)
**LMHI** ........ Liga Medicorum Homoeopathica Internationalis [*International Homoeopathic Medical League*] (EA)
**LMHS** ........ Lancaster Mennonite Historical Society (EA)
**LMHX** ........ Liquid Metal Heat Exchanger (NRCH)
**LMI** ........... Labor Market Information [*Department of Labor*]
**LMI** ........... Lawn Mower Institute [*Later, OPEI*]
**LMi** ........... Leo Minor [*Constellation*]
**LMI** ........... Leukocyte Migration Inhibition [*Hematology*]
**LMI** ........... Life Management Institute [*Life Office Management Association*]
**LMI** ........... Liquid Mercury Isolator
**LMI** ........... Liquid Metal Ionization [*Spectrometry*]
**LMi** ........... Literaturna Misel [*Sofia*] [*A publication*]
**LMI** ........... Livestock Merchandising Institute [*Later, LII*] (EA)
**LMI** ........... Loaded Motional Impedance
**LMI** ........... Local Memory Image
**LMI** ........... Logistics Management Institute [*Bethesda, MD*] [*Research center*] (AFM)
**LMI** ........... Low-Molecular-Weight Inhibitor [*of protease activity*]
**LMI** ........... Lumi [*Papua New Guinea*] [*Airport symbol*] (OAG)
**LMI** ........... Lymphocyte Migration Index
**LMIAA** ...... Licentiate Architect Member of the Incorporated Association of Architects and Surveyors [*British*] (DAS)
**LMIAS** ...... Licentiate Surveyor Member of the Incorporated Association of Architects and Surveyors [*British*] (DAS)
**LMI-ATS** .. Labor Market Information - Analytical Table Series [*Department of Labor - Employment and Training Administration*] (OICC)
**LMIB** ........ Light Motorized Infantry Battalion (INF)
**LMIC** ........ Liberty Mutual Insurance Company
**LMIC** ........ Liquid Metals Information Center [*AEC*]
**LMin** ......... Leo Minor [*Constellation*]
**L/MIN** ....... Liters per Minute
**LMIS** ........ Labor Market Information System [*Department of Labor*]
**LMIS** ........ Liquid Metal Ion Source
**LMIS** ........ Lloyd's Maritime Information Services Ltd. [*Information service or system*] (IID)
**LMiW** ........ Webster Parish Library, Minden, LA [*Library symbol*] [*Library of Congress*] (LCLS)
**LMJ** .......... Greer, SC [*Location identifier*] [*FAA*] (FAAL)
**LMJ** .......... Lutherisches Missions Jahrbuch [*A publication*]
**LMK** .......... [*Jean Baptiste*] Lamarck [*French naturalist, 1744-1829*] (ROG)
**LMK** .......... Landmark (NASA)
**LMK** .......... Landmark Corp. [*Toronto Stock Exchange symbol*]
**LML** .......... Lae [*Marshall Islands*] [*Airport symbol*] (OAG)
**LML** .......... Landmark Land Co., Inc. [*AMEX symbol*] (SPSG)
**LML** .......... Large and Medium Lymphocytes [*Medicine*]
**LML** .......... Leesona Moos Laboratory
**LML** .......... Left Mediolateral [*Episiotomy*] [*Obstetrics*]
**LML** .......... Left Mentolateral [*Episiotomy*] [*Obstetrics*]
**LML** .......... Logical Memory Level
**LMLE** ........ Local Maximum Likelihood Estimates [*Statistics*]
**LMLE** ........ Long Magazine Lee-Enfield [*British military*] (DMA)
**LMLG** ........ Luther. Mitteilungen der Luthergesellschaft [*A publication*]
**LMLP** ........ La Monda Lingvo-Problemo [*A publication*]
**LM & LR** ... Law Magazine and Law Review [*A publication*] (DLA)
**LMLR** ........ Load Memory Lockout Register
**LM/LRV** ... Lunar Module/Lunar Roving Vehicle [*NASA*]
**LMLSA** ..... Language Monographs. Linguistic Society of America [*A publication*]
**LMM** ......... Compass location station when combined with middle marker of the instrument landing system [*FAA term*] (CET)
**LMM** ......... Lactobacillus Maintenance Medium [*Microbiology*]
**LMM** ......... Lemming Resources, Inc. [*Vancouver Stock Exchange symbol*]
**LMM** ......... Lentigo Maligna Melanoma [*Oncology*]
**LMM** ......... Library Microfilm & Materials Co.
**LMM** ......... Light Meromyosin [*Biochemistry*]
**LMM** ......... Lines per Millimeter (AAG)
**LMM** ......... Liquid Money Market [*Banking*]
**LMM** ......... Living Masters of Music [*A publication*]
**LMM** ......... Llanelly & Mynydd Mawr Railway [*Wales*]
**LMM** ......... Locator at Middle Marker [*Aviation*]
**LMM** ......... Los Mochis [*Mexico*] [*Airport symbol*] (OAG)
**LMM** ......... Lourenco Marques [*Mozambique*] [*Seismograph station code, US Geological Survey*] (SEIS)
**LMMA** ...... Lutheran Medical Mission Association [*Defunct*] (EA)
**LMMCI** ..... Labor Management Maritime Committee, Incorporated (EA)
**LMMF** ....... Local Maintenance and Management of Facilities [*Military*] (AABC)
**LMMFHR** ... Letelier-Moffitt Memorial Fund for Human Rights [*Later, LMMFHR/IPS*] (EA)
**LMMFHR/IPS** ... Letelier-Moffitt Memorial Fund for Human Rights/ Institute for Policy Studies (EA)
**LMMHD** ... Liquid Metal Magnetohydrodynamics
**LMML** ....... Malta/Luqa [*Malta*] [*ICAO location identifier*] (ICLI)
**LMMM** ..... Malta [*Malta*] [*ICAO location identifier*] (ICLI)
**LMMS** ....... LASER Microprobe Mass Spectrometry [*or Spectroscopy*]
**LMMS** ....... Lightweight Multipurpose Missile System (MCD)
**LMMS** ....... Local Message Metering Service [*Telecommunications*] (TEL)
**LMMU** ...... Latin Mediterranean Medical Union [*See also UMML*] [*Mantua, Italy*] (EAIO)
**LMN** .......... Lamoni, IA [*Location identifier*] [*FAA*] (FAAL)
**LMN** .......... Lanthanum Magnesium Double Nitrate
**LMN** .......... Lateral Mesencephalic Nucleus [*Brain anatomy*]
**LMN** .......... Lateral Motoneuron [*Neurobiology*]
**LMN** .......... Library Management Network, Inc. [*Information service or system*] (IID)
**LMN** .......... Limbang [*Malaysia*] [*Airport symbol*] (OAG)
**LMN** .......... Lineman (AABC)
**LMN** .......... Load Matching Network
**LMN** .......... Locomotor Neuron [*Neurology*]
**LMN** .......... Lornex Mining Corp. [*Vancouver Stock Exchange symbol*]
**LMN** .......... Lost Music Network [*Defunct*] (EA)
**LMN** .......... Lower Motor Neuron [*Anatomy*]
**LMN** .......... Northeast Louisiana University, Monroe, LA [*Library symbol*] [*Library of Congress*] (LCLS)
**LMNA** ....... Label Manufacturers National Association [*Defunct*]
**LMNA** ....... Land-Based Multimission Naval Aircraft (MCD)
**LMNDF** .... Lesbian Mothers National Defense Fund (EA)
**LMNED** .... Laboratories for Molecular Neuroendocrinology and Diabetes [*Tulane University*] [*Research center*] (RCD)
**LMNL** ....... Lower Motor Neuron Lesion [*Medicine*]
**LMNT** ....... Aris Corp. [*NASDAQ symbol*] (NQ)
**LMNTD** .... Elements [*A publication*]
**LMO** .......... LASER Master Oscillator
**LMO** .......... Lasmo Canada, Inc. [*Toronto Stock Exchange symbol*]
**LMO** .......... Lens-Modulated Oscillator
**LMO** .......... Linear Master Oscillator
**LMO** .......... Logistics Management Office [*Army*]
**LMO** .......... Lookout Mountain Observatory [*California*] [*Seismograph station code, US Geological Survey*] [*Closed*] (SEIS)

**LMO**.......... Ouachita Parish Public Library, Monroe, LA [*Library symbol*] [*Library of Congress*] (LCLS)
**LMOA**....... Locomotive Maintenance Officers' Association (EA)
**L Mod**........ Langues Modernes [*A publication*]
**LMod**......... Lettres Modernes [*A publication*]
**LMOI**......... Labor Market and Occupational Information (OICC)
**LMold**........ Limba si Literatura Moldoveneasca [*A publication*]
**LMOS**....... Loop Maintenance Operations System [*Formerly, MLR*] [*Bell System*]
**LMP**.......... Labor Mobility Project [*Department of Labor*]
**LMP**.......... Lamap [*New Hebrides*] [*Seismograph station code, US Geological Survey*] (SEIS)
**LMP**.......... Laminated Metal Part
**LMP**.......... Lampedusa [*Italy*] [*Airport symbol*] (OAG)
**LMP**.......... Last Menstrual Period [*Medicine*]
**LMP**.......... Latent Membrane Protein [*Genetics*]
**LMP**.......... Lawson Mardon Group Ltd. [*Toronto Stock Exchange symbol*]
**LMP**.......... Left Mentoposterior [*A fetal position*] [*Obstetrics*]
**LMP**.......... Library Material Processed
**LMP**.......... Light Marching Pack [*Military*]
**LMP**.......... Light Metal Products
**LMP**.......... Liquid Monopropellant
**LMP**.......... Liquid Oxygen Maintenance Panel (AAG)
**LMP**.......... List of Measurement Points (NASA)
**LMP**.......... Literary Market Place [*A publication*]
**LMP**.......... LM [*Lunar Module*] Mission Programmer [*NASA*] (KSC)
**LMP**.......... Longitudinal Muscles of Pinnule
**LMP**.......... Low Melting Point
**LMP**.......... Low-Molecular-Weight Polypeptide [*Biochemistry*]
**LM & P**...... Lowndes, Maxwell, and Pollock's English Bail Court Practice Reports [*1850-51*] [*A publication*] (DLA)
**LMP**.......... Lumbar Puncture [*Medicine*]
**LMP**.......... Lunar Module Pilot [*Apollo*] [*NASA*]
**LMPA**........ Qualified Member of the Master Photographers Association [*British*] (DBQ)
**LMPBLK**... Lampblack
**LMPG**........ Light Mobile Protected Gun (INF)
**LMPM**....... Library Material Preservation Manual
**LMPRT**..... Locally Most Powerful Rank Test [*Statistics*]
**LMPS**........ Lunar Module Procedures Simulator [*NASA*]
**LMPT**........ Logistics and Material Planning Team (NATG)
**LMQ**.......... La Malbaie [*Quebec*] [*Seismograph station code, US Geological Survey*] (SEIS)
**LMQ**.......... Legal Medical Quarterly [*A publication*]
**LMR**.......... La Mourre [*France*] [*Seismograph station code, US Geological Survey*] (SEIS)
**LMR**.......... Labor-Management Relations
**LMR**.......... Lamaur, Inc. [*NYSE symbol*] (SPSG)
**LMR**.......... LASER Magnetic Resonance (MCD)
**LMR**.......... Launch Mission Rules [*NASA*] (KSC)
**LMR**.......... Launch Monitor Room [*NASA*] (MCD)
**LMR**.......... Light Modulation Recording
**LMR**.......... Ligue Marxiste Revolutionnaire [*Revolutionary Marxist League*] [*Switzerland*] [*Political party*] (PPW)
**LMR**.......... Line Monitor/Recorder (MCD)
**LMR**.......... Liquid Metal Reactor
**LMR**.......... Longmoor Military Railway [*British military*] (DMA)
**LMR**.......... Lowest Maximum Range
**LMR**.......... St. Louis, MO [*Location identifier*] [*FAA*] (FAAL)
**LMRA**....... Labor-Management Relations Act [*1947*]
**LMRCP**..... Licenciate in Midwifery of the Royal College of Physicians [*British*]
**LMRD**....... Launch Mission Rules Document [*NASA*] (KSC)
**LMRDA**..... Labor-Management Reporting and Disclosure Act [*1959*]
**LMRDA-IM**... Labor-Management Reporting and Disclosure Act - Investigative Matter [*FBI standardized term*]
**LMRK**....... Landmark Graphics Corp. [*NASDAQ symbol*] (CTT)
**LMRP**........ Lunar Module Replaceable Package [*NASA*] (KSC)
**LMRPC**..... Linear-Motor Resonant-Piston Compressor [*Navy*]
**LMRR**........ Lunar Module Rendezvous RADAR [*NASA*]
**LMRS**........ Labor-Management Relations Service of the US Conference of Mayors (EA)
**LMRS**........ Lockheed Maintenance Recording System
**LMRSH**..... Licentiate Member of the Royal Society of Health [*British*]
**LMRTPI**.... Legal Member of the Royal Town Planning Institute [*British*] (DBQ)
**LMS**........... Laboratory for Mathematics and Statistics [*University of California at San Diego*] [*Research center*] (RCD)
**LMS**........... Laboratory of Molecular Structure [*Massachusetts Institute of Technology*]
**LMS**........... [*The*] Lamson & Sessions Co. [*NYSE symbol*] (SPSG)
**LMS**........... Land Mass Simulator
**LMS**........... LASER Bank Management System [*Data processing*]
**LMS**........... LASER Magnetic Stage
**LMS**........... LASER Magnetic Storage International
**LMS**........... LASER Mapping System
**LMS**........... LASER Mass Spectrometer
**LMS**........... Latin Mass Society (EAIO)
**LMS**........... Laurence-Moon Syndrome [*Medicine*]
**LMS**........... Least Mean Square (IEEE)
**LMS**........... Leiomyosarcoma [*Oncology*]
**LMS**........... LEM [*Lunar Excursion Module*] Mission Simulator [*NASA*]
**LMS**........... Letopis Matice Srpske. Novi Sad [*A publication*]
**LMS**........... Level Measuring Set [*for test signals*] [*Telecommunications*] (TEL)
**LMS**........... Library Management System
**LMS**........... Licentiate in Medicine and Surgery [*British*]
**LMS**........... Lightning Mapper Sensor [*NASA*]
**LMS**........... Limestone [*Technical drawings*]
**LMS**........... Limited Mass Search [*Chromatography*]
**LMS**........... Linear Measuring System
**LMS**........... Liquid Metal System
**LMS**........... List Management System
**LMS**........... Literature Management System
**LMS**........... Load Matching Switch
**LMS**........... Load Measurement System (NASA)
**LMS**........... Loadmaster Systems, Inc. [*Vancouver Stock Exchange symbol*]
**LMS**........... Local Management of Schools [*British*]
**LMS**........... Local Measured Service [*Telecommunications*] (TEL)
**LMS**........... Lockheed Missile System (MCD)
**LMS**........... Logistics Management Specialist (MCD)
**LMS**........... Logistics Master Schedules (MCD)
**LMS**........... London Mediaeval Studies [*A publication*]
**LmS**........... London Microfilming Services Ltd., London, ON, Canada [*Library symbol*] [*Library of Congress*] (LCLS)
**LMS**........... London, Midland & Scottish Railway [*British*]
**LMS**........... London Missionary Society
**LMS**........... Lookout Mountain Observatory [*California*] [*Seismograph station code, US Geological Survey*] (SEIS)
**LMS**........... Louisville, MS [*Location identifier*] [*FAA*] (FAAL)
**LM/S**......... Lumens per Second (MCD)
**LMS**........... Lunar Mass Spectrometer [*NASA*]
**LMS**........... Lunar Measuring System [*Aerospace*]
**LMS**........... Lutheran Mission Societies (EA)
**LMSA**........ Labor-Management Services Administration [*Department of Labor*]
**LMSC**........ Let Me See Correspondence [*Business term*]
**LMSC**........ Liquid Metals Safety Committee [*AEC*] (MCD)
**LMSC**........ Lockheed Missiles & Space Corporation [*Subsidiary of Lockheed Aircraft Corp.*]
**LMSC**........ Logistics Management Systems Center [*Military*]
**LMSCEZ**... Lasers in Medical Science [*A publication*]
**LM & Sc R**... London, Midland & Scottish Railway [*British*] (DCTA)
**LMSE**........ Laboratory Module Simulation Equipment
**LMSE**........ Liquid Metal Slip Ring
**LMSG**........ Low Magnetic Saturation Garnet
**LMSI**......... Association of Lithuanian Foresters in Exile [*Defunct*] (EA)
**LMSLA**..... Lantmannen (Sweden) [*A publication*]
**LMSN**........ Local Message Switched Network
**LMSR**........ London, Midland & Scottish Railway [*British*]
**LMSS**........ Land Mobile Satellite Service [*Rockwell International Corp.*]
**LMSS**........ Lunar Mapping and Survey System [*NASA*] (MCD)
**LM & SS**.... Lunar Mapping and Survey System [*NASA*] (KSC)
**LMSSA**..... Licentiate in Medicine and Surgery of the Society of Apothecaries [*British*]
**LMST**........ Learning of Middle Size Task [*Psychology*]
**LMT**.......... Klamath Falls [*Oregon*] [*Airport symbol*] (OAG)
**LMT**.......... LASER Marksmanship Trainer (MCD)
**LMT**.......... Launch Motor Test
**LMT**.......... Leadership and Management Training [*Navy*] (NVT)
**LMT**.......... Learning Methods Test [*Mills*] [*Education*]
**LMT**.......... Left Mentotransverse [*A fetal position*] [*Obstetrics*]
**LMT**.......... Lemonthyme [*Tasmania*] [*Seismograph station code, US Geological Survey*] [*Closed*] (SEIS)
**LMT**.......... Length, Mass, Time [*Physics*]
**LMT**.......... Length of Mean Turn
**LMT**.......... Levtech Medical Technologies Ltd. [*Vancouver Stock Exchange symbol*]
**LMT**.......... Library Management [*A publication*]
**LMT**.......... Lifetime Medical Television
**LMT**.......... Limit (AFM)
**LMT**.......... Local Mean Time (AFM)
**LMT**.......... Log Mean Temperature
**LMT**.......... Logical Mapping Table
**LMT**.......... Logistic Management of the Turnaround (MCD)
**LMT**.......... Logistics Management Team [*Navy*]
**LMT**.......... Louisiana Midland Transport [*AAR code*]
**LMT**.......... Lowenfeld Mosaic Test [*Psychology*]
**LMTA**........ Language Modalities Test for Aphasia [*Psychology*]
**LMTA**........ Library/Media Technical Assistant
**LMTBR**..... Liquid Metal Thorium Breeder Reactor
**LMTBS**..... Lightweight Multifunction Tactical Beacon System (MCD)
**LMTC**....... Launcher Maintenance Trainer Course
**LMTD**....... Logarithmic Mean Temperature Difference
**LMTDNS**... Launch Environment, Mission, Type, Design Number, and Series [*Missiles*] (AFM)
**LMTG**....... Limiting (MSA)
**LMTI**......... Louisiana Training Institute, Monroe, LA [*Library symbol*] [*Library of Congress*] (LCLS)
**LMTN**....... Leamington [*British depot code*]
**LMTO**....... Linear Combination of Muffin Tin Orbitals [*Atomic physics*]
**LMTPI**...... Legal Member of the Town Planning Institute [*British*] (DLA)

**LMTR**........ Limiter [*Electronics*]
**LMTS**........ LaserMaster Technologies, Inc. [*NASDAQ symbol*] (SPSG)
**LMU**.......... Lake Mountain [*Utah*] [*Seismograph station code, US Geological Survey*] (SEIS)
**LMU**.......... Latin Monetary Union [*Established in 1865*]
**LMU**.......... Lincoln Memorial University [*Tennessee*]
**LMU**.......... Line Monitor Unit
**LMU**.......... Loyola Marymount University [*Los Angeles, CA*]
**LMU**.......... University of Missouri, Law School, Columbia, MO [*OCLC symbol*] (OCLC)
**LMus**......... Licentiate of Music
**LMusA**...... Licentiate in Music, Australia (ADA)
**LMusLCM**... Licentiate in Music of the London College of Music [*British*] (DBQ)
**LMusSAA**... Licentiate in Music, Society of Australasian Arts (ADA)
**LMusTCL**... Licentiate in Music, Trinity College of Music, London [*British*] (DBQ)
**L de Muz**.... Lucrari de Muzicologie [*A publication*]
**LMV**.......... Lettuce Mosaic Virus
**LMV**.......... Long Market Value [*Investment term*]
**LMVD**....... Lower Mississippi Valley Division [*Army Engineers*]
**LMW**......... Ladd Mountain [*Washington*] [*Seismograph station code, US Geological Survey*] (SEIS)
**LMW**......... LASER Microwelder
**LMW**......... Low Molecular Weight [*Chemistry*]
**LMW**......... Lower Midwest
**lm/W**......... Lumens per Watt
**LMWH**....... Low-Molecular-Weight Heparin [*Biochemistry*]
**LMWP**....... Labor-Management Welfare-Pension [*Reports*] [*Department of Labor*]
**LMX**.......... L-Type Multiplex [*Telecommunications*] (TEL)
**LMX**.......... LMX Resources Ltd. [*Vancouver Stock Exchange symbol*]
**LMXB**........ Low-Mass X-Ray Binary [*Star system*]
**LMY**.......... Lake Murray [*Papua New Guinea*] [*Airport symbol*] (OAG)
**LN**............. Background Noise Level (CAAL)
**ln**.............. Central and Southern Line Islands [*gb (Gilbert Islands) used in records cataloged after October 1978*] [*MARC country of publication code*] [*Library of Congress*] (LCCP)
**LN**............. Jamahiriya Libyan Arab Airlines [*Libyan Arab Jamahiriya*] [*ICAO designator*] (FAAC)
**LN**............. Lane (MCD)
**LN**............. Large-Probe Nephelometer [*NASA*]
**LN**............. LASER Nephelometry [*Analytical biochemistry*]
**LN**............. Lateen [*Ship's rigging*] (ROG)
**LN**............. Lateral Neuropil [*Neurology*]
**LN**............. Law Notes [*A publication*]
**LN**............. Law Notes, American Bar Association Section of General Practice [*A publication*] (DLA)
**LN**............. Law Notes, London [*A publication*] (DLA)
**LN**............. Leading Note [*Music*] (ROG)
**L of N**......... League of Nations [*1919-1946*]
**LN**............. League of Nations [*1919-1946*]
**LN**............. Legal News [*Canada*] [*A publication*] (DLA)
**LN**............. Legal Notice (OICC)
**LN**............. Legal Notification [*Ghana*] [*A publication*] (DLA)
**LN**............. Lepista Nuda [*A fungus*]
**L-N**............ Lesch-Nyhan [*Medicine*]
**LN**............. Lesion Number [*Pathology*]
**LN**............. Lettres Nouvelles [*A publication*]
**LN**............. Liaison (AFM)
**LN**............. Liber Niger [*Black Book*] [*A publication*] (DLA)
**LN**............. Library Notes [*A publication*]
**LN**............. Lien
**LN**............. Line (AAG)
**LN**............. Lingua Nostra [*A publication*]
**LN**............. Lip Nerve
**LN**............. Liquid Nitrogen
**LN**............. Lira Nuova [*Monetary unit*] [*Italy*] (ROG)
**LN**............. Literaturnoe Nasledstvo [*A publication*]
**LN**............. Load Number
**LN**............. Loan
**LN**............. Local National
**ln**.............. Logarithm (Natural) [*Mathematics*]
**LN**............. Lot Number
**L & N**......... Louisville & Nashville Railroad Co.
**LN**............. Low Foliage Nester [*Ecology*]
**LN**............. Luminometer Number [*Hydrocarbon fuel rating*]
**LN**............. Lupus Network (EA)
**LN**............. Lymph Node [*Medicine*]
**LN**............. New Orleans Public Library, New Orleans, LA [*Library symbol*] [*Library of Congress*] (LCLS)
**ln-----**......... North Atlantic Ocean [*MARC geographic area code*] [*Library of Congress*] (LCCP)
**LN**............. Norway [*Aircraft nationality and registration mark*] (FAAC)
**$LN_2$**........... Liquid Nitrogen [*NASA*] (NASA)
**LNA**........... Launch Numerical Aperture [*Telecommunications*] (TEL)
**LNA**........... Leading National Advertiser
**LNA**........... League of the Norden Associations (EA)
**LNA**........... Leucine Nitroanilide [*Biochemistry*]
**LNA**........... Liberation News Agency [*Vietnam*]
**LNA**........... Lithium Nitrate Ammoniate [*Inorganic chemistry*]
**LNA**........... Lithographers National Association
**LNA**........... Lithuanian Numismatic Association (EA)
**LNA**........... Local Navy Authority
**LNA**........... Local Numbering Area [*Telecommunications*] (TEL)
**LnA**............ London Allowance [*British military*] (DMA)
**LnA**............ London Aphrodite [*A publication*]
**LNA**........... Love-N-Addiction [*An association*] (EA)
**LNA**........... Low-Noise Amplifier [*Satellite communications*]
**LNA**........... Low-Noise Antenna
**LNA**........... Lunar Resources Ltd. [*Vancouver Stock Exchange symbol*]
**LNA**........... New Orleans City Archives, New Orleans, LA [*Library symbol*] [*Library of Congress*] (LCLS)
**LNA**........... West Palm Beach, FL [*Location identifier*] [*FAA*] (FAAL)
**LNAC**......... Librarians for Nuclear Arms Control (EA)
**LNAC**......... Limited National Agency Check (AFM)
**LNAC**......... Louisville, New Albany & Corydon Railroad Co. [*AAR code*]
**LNAH**......... League of Night Adoration in the Home [*Later, NAH*] (EA)
**LNaN**......... Northwestern State University of Louisiana, Natchitoches, LA [*Library symbol*] [*Library of Congress*] (LCLS)
**LNaNa**....... Natchitoches Parish Library, Natchitoches, LA [*Library symbol*] [*Library of Congress*] (LCLS)
**LNAP**......... Low Nonessential Air Pressure (IEEE)
**LNapA**....... Assumption Parish Library, Napoleonville, LA [*Library symbol*] [*Library of Congress*] (LCLS)
**lnaz---**........ Azores Islands [*MARC geographic area code*] [*Library of Congress*] (LCCP)
**LNB**........... Lamen Bay [*Vanuata*] [*Airport symbol*] (OAG)
**LNB**........... Large Navigation Buoy [*Marine science*] (MSC)
**LNB**........... Leipziger Namenkundliche Beitraege [*A publication*]
**LNB**........... Local Name Base [*Data processing*]
**LNB**........... Loteria. Loteria Nacional de Beneficencia [*A publication*]
**LNB**........... Louisiana National Bank [*Baton Rouge*] (TSSD)
**LNB**........... Low-Noise Block [*Satellite communications*]
**LNB**........... New Orleans Baptist Theological Seminary, New Orleans, LA [*Library symbol*] [*Library of Congress*] (LCLS)
**LNBA**......... Bell Aerospace Co., New Orleans, LA [*Library symbol*] [*Library of Congress*] (LCLS)
**LNBA**......... Laymen's National Bible Association (EA)
**LNBC**......... Laymen's National Bible Committee [*Formerly, LNC*] [*Later, LNBA*] (EA)
**LNBC**......... Liberty National Bancorp, Inc. [*Louisville, KY*] [*NASDAQ symbol*] (NQ)
**LNBD**......... Lens Board [*Mechanical engineering*]
**LNBF**......... Low-Noise Block Feed [*Satellite communications*]
**LNBK**......... Lane Financial, Inc. [*Northbrook, IL*] [*NASDAQ symbol*] (NQ)
**lnbm---**....... Bermuda [*MARC geographic area code*] [*Library of Congress*] (LCCP)
**LNBS**......... Lesotho National Broadcasting Service [*South Africa*]
**LNC**........... Lancaster, TX [*Location identifier*] [*FAA*] (FAAL)
**LNC**........... Lancer Resources [*Vancouver Stock Exchange symbol*]
**LNC**........... Landscape Nursery Council (EA)
**LNC**........... Laymen's National Committee [*Later, LNBC*] (EA)
**LNC**........... Lincoln National Corporation [*NYSE symbol*] (SPSG)
**LNC**........... Local Naval Commander
**LNC**........... LORAN Navigation Chart [*Air Force*]
**LNC**........... Low-Noise Cable
**LNC**........... Low-Noise Converter [*Satellite communications*]
**LNC**........... Lunacharskoye [*USSR*] [*Seismograph station code, US Geological Survey*] [*Closed*] (SEIS)
**LNC**........... Lymph Node Cell [*Medicine*]
**LNC**........... Midway Aviation [*Arlington, TX*] [*FAA designator*] (FAAC)
**LNC**........... New Orleans Public Library, New Orleans, LA [*OCLC symbol*] (OCLC)
**lnca---**........ Canary Islands [*MARC geographic area code*] [*Library of Congress*] (LCCP)
**LNCE**......... Lance, Inc. [*NASDAQ symbol*] (NQ)
**LNCH**......... Launch (AAG)
**LNCHR**...... Launcher
**L-NCP**....... Liberal-National Country Party [*Australia*] [*Political party*] (PPW)
**LNCR**......... Lincoln Resources, Inc. [*NASDAQ symbol*] (NQ)
**LNCSEA**... Lecture Notes on Coastal and Estuarine Studies [*A publication*]
**lncv---**......... Cape Verde [*Islands*] [*MARC geographic area code*] [*Library of Congress*] (LCCP)
**LNCY**......... Lunacy [*FBI standardized term*]
**LND**........... Dillard University, New Orleans, LA [*Library symbol*] [*Library of Congress*] (LCLS)
**LND**........... Hawaii Landair [*Honolulu, HI*] [*FAA designator*] (FAAC)
**LND**........... Land (FAAC)
**LND**........... Lander, WY [*Location identifier*] [*FAA*] (FAAL)
**LND**........... Lawyers for Nuclear Disarmament (EAIO)
**LND**........... Limiting Nose Dive [*Aerospace*]
**LND**........... Lincoln National Income Fund, Inc. [*Formerly, Lincoln National Direct Placement Fund, Inc.*] [*NYSE symbol*] (SPSG)
**LND**........... Lined
**LND**........... Local Number Dialed [*Telecommunications*] (TEL)
**LND**........... London [*Ontario*] [*Seismograph station code, US Geological Survey*] (SEIS)
**LND**........... Lymph Node Dissection [*Medicine*]

**LNDC**........ Delgado Community College, New Orleans, LA [*Library symbol*] [*Library of Congress*] (LCLS)
**LNDC**........ Lesotho National Development Corporation
**LNDE**........ Lundy Electronics & Systems, Inc. [*NASDAQ symbol*] (NQ)
**LNDG**........ Landing [*Maps and charts*] (KSC)
**LNDH**........ Local Nationals, Direct Hire [*Military*] (AABC)
**LNDIS**....... Landing Intermediate Station [*Aviation*] (FAAC)
**LNDK**........ Landmark Oil & Gas [*NASDAQ symbol*] (NQ)
**LNDL**........ Lindal Cedar Homes, Inc. [*NASDAQ symbol*] (NQ)
**LNDO**........ Local Neglect of Differential Overlap [*Physical chemistry*]
**LNDR**........ Land Reform [*Italy*] [*A publication*]
**L & NE**....... Lehigh & New England Railway Co. [*Absorbed into Consolidated Rail Corp.*]
**LNE**........... Lehigh & New England Railway Co. [*Absorbed into Consolidated Rail Corp.*] [*AAR code*]
**LNE**........... Liquid Nitrogen Evaporator
**LNE**........... Local Network Emulator
**LNE**........... Lonorore [*Vanuata*] [*Airport symbol*] (OAG)
**LNE**........... Northeast Louisiana University, Monroe, LA [*OCLC symbol*] (OCLC)
**LNER**........ Linear Films, Inc. [*Tulsa, OK*] [*NASDAQ symbol*] (NQ)
**LNER**........ London & North Eastern Railway [*British*]
**LNERG**....... London & North Eastern Railway Group [*British*]
**LNESC**...... LULAC [*League of United Latin American Citizens*] National Educational Service Centers (EA)
**LNewr**........ Pointe Coupee Parish Library, New Roads, LA [*Library symbol*] [*Library of Congress*] (LCLS)
**LNF**........... Latvian National Foundation [*Stockholm, Sweden*] (EAIO)
**LNF**........... Leon's Furniture Ltd. [*Toronto Stock Exchange symbol*]
**LNF**........... Linfen [*Republic of China*] [*Seismograph station code, US Geological Survey*] (SEIS)
**LNF**........... Lithuanian National Foundation (EA)
**LNF**........... Little-Known Fan [*of science fiction or fantastic literature*] [*See also BNF*]
**LNF**........... Local National Forces [*SEATO*] (CINC)
**LNF**........... Lomas & Nettleton Financial Corp. [*NYSE symbol*] (SPSG)
**LNF**........... Low-Noise Feed [*Satellite communications*]
**LNFC**......... Leonard Nimoy Fan Club (EA)
**LNFCS**...... Leonard Nimoy Fan Club, Spotlight (EAIO)
**LNFM**....... Louisiana Masonic Grand Lodge, New Orleans, LA [*Library symbol*] [*Library of Congress*] (LCLS)
**LNG**.......... Lateral Nasal Gland [*Anatomy*]
**LNG**.......... Lese [*Papua New Guinea*] [*Airport symbol*] (OAG)
**LNG**.......... Lining (MSA)
**LNG**.......... Liquefied Natural Gas
**LNG**.......... Liste de Noms Geographiques [*A publication*] (BJA)
**LNG**.......... Long
**LNG**.......... Luning [*Nevada*] [*Seismograph station code, US Geological Survey*] [*Closed*] (SEIS)
**Lnge**.......... Lounge [*Classified advertising*] (ADA)
**LNH**.......... Lunar Near Horizon [*NASA*] (KSC)
**LNHA**........ Louisiana Historical Association, Memorial Hall, New Orleans, LA [*Library symbol*] [*Library of Congress*] (LCLS)
**LNHiC**....... [*The*] Historic New Orleans Collection, New Orleans, LA [*Library symbol*] [*Library of Congress*] (LCLS)
**LNI**............ Inland Library System, Redlands, CA [*OCLC symbol*] (OCLC)
**LNI**............ La Nuova Italia [*A publication*]
**LNI**............ Log Neutralization Index [*Microbiology*]
**LNI**............ Lonely, AK [*Location identifier*] [*FAA*] (FAAL)
**LNIAC**........ Los Ninos International Adoption Center (EA)
**LNIB**.......... Loch Ness Investigation Bureau [*Inactive*] (EA)
**LNiI**........... Iberia Parish Library, New Iberia, LA [*Library symbol*] [*Library of Congress*] (LCLS)
**LNIS**.......... Atlantic Naval Intelligence Summary (MCD)
**LNIT**.......... Local Nasal Immunotherapy
**lnjn---**......... Jan Mayen [*MARC geographic area code*] [*Library of Congress*] (LCCP)
**LNK**........... Air Link Corp. [*Ft. Collins, CO*] [*FAA designator*] (FAAC)
**L/Nk**.......... Lance-Naik [*British military*] (DMA)
**LNK**........... Lenkoran [*USSR*] [*Seismograph station code, US Geological Survey*] (SEIS)
**LNK**........... Lincoln [*Nebraska*] [*Airport symbol*] (OAG)
**LNK**........... Link
**LNL**........... Land O' Lakes, WI [*Location identifier*] [*FAA*] (FAAL)
**LNL**........... Langues Neo-Latines [*A publication*]
**LNL**........... Law Library of Louisiana, New Orleans, LA [*OCLC symbol*] (OCLC)
**LNL**........... Les Nouvelles Litteraires [*A publication*]
**LNL**........... Let Nicaragua Live [*An association*] (EA)
**LNL**........... Loyola University, New Orleans, LA [*Library symbol*] [*Library of Congress*] (LCLS)
**LNLA**........ Lithuanian National League of America (EA)
**LNLI**.......... League for National Labor in Israel (EA)
**LNLJ**......... Linguistic Notes from La Jolla [*A publication*]
**LNL-L**........ Loyola University, Law Library, New Orleans, LA [*Library symbol*] [*Library of Congress*] (LCLS)
**LNLM**....... Low-Noise Level Margin
**LNLM**....... United States Bureau of Land Management, New Orleans Outer Continental Shelf Office, New Orleans, LA [*Library symbol*] [*Library of Congress*] (LCLS)
**LNL-Phar**... Loyola University, Pharmacy Library, New Orleans, LA [*Library symbol*] [*Library of Congress*] (LCLS)
**LNM**.......... Langimar [*Papua New Guinea*] [*Airport symbol*] (OAG)
**LNM**.......... Lansdowne Minerals [*Vancouver Stock Exchange symbol*]
**LNM**.......... Lebanese National Movement [*Political party*] (PPW)
**LNM**.......... Leon [*Mexico*] [*Seismograph station code, US Geological Survey*] (SEIS)
**LNM**.......... Level of No Motion [*Oceanography*]
**LNM**.......... Library Cooperative of Macomb [*Library network*]
**LNM**.......... Lithium Nuclear Microprobe
**LNM**.......... Local Notice to Mariners
**LnM**........... London Mercury [*A publication*]
**LNM**.......... Lymph Node Metastases [*Oncology*]
**LNM**.......... Margaret C. Hanson Normal School, New Orleans, LA [*Library symbol*] [*Library of Congress*] [*Obsolete*] (LCLS)
**lnma---**....... Madeira Islands [*MARC geographic area code*] [*Library of Congress*] (LCCP)
**LNMA**....... New Orleans Museum of Art, New Orleans, LA [*Library symbol*] [*Library of Congress*] (LCLS)
**LNMC**....... Monaco [*Monaco*] [*ICAO location identifier*] (ICLI)
**LNMP**....... Last Normal Menstrual Period [*Medicine*]
**LNMRB**..... Laboratory of Nuclear Medicine and Radiation Biology
**LNMS**....... Large-Probe Neutral Mass Spectrometer [*NASA*]
**LNMVA**.... Learning and Motivation [*A publication*]
**LNN**.......... Leipziger Neueste Nachrichten [*A publication*]
**LNN**.......... Leningrad [*USSR*] [*Seismograph station code, US Geological Survey*] [*Closed*] (SEIS)
**LNN**.......... Leningrad [*USSR*] [*Geomagnetic observatory code*]
**LNN**.......... Lincoln Resources, Inc. [*Vancouver Stock Exchange symbol*]
**LNN**.......... Willoughby, OH [*Location identifier*] [*FAA*] (FAAL)
**LNNB**....... Luria-Nebraska Neuropsychological Battery
**LNND**....... Notre Dame Seminary, New Orleans, LA [*Library symbol*] [*Library of Congress*] (LCLS)
**LNO**.......... Laona & Northern Railway Co. [*AAR code*]
**LNO**.......... Leonora [*Australia*] [*Airport symbol*] (OAG)
**LNO**.......... Liaison Officer [*Military*]
**LNO**.......... Limited Nuclear Option [*Military*] (MCD)
**LNo**........... Lingua Nostra [*A publication*]
**LNOC**....... Libya National Oil Company
**LNOP**....... Orleans Parish Medical Society, New Orleans, LA [*Library symbol*] [*Library of Congress*] (LCLS)
**Lno Penko-Dzhutovaya Promst**... Lno Penko-Dzhutovaya Promyshlennost [*A publication*]
**LNos**.......... Lingua Nostra [*A publication*]
**L Notes**...... Law Notes, England [*A publication*] (DLA)
**L Notes Gen Pract**... Law Notes for the General Practitioner [*A publication*] (DLA)
**L Notes (NY)**... Law Notes (New York) [*A publication*]
**LNouv**........ Lettres Nouvelles [*A publication*]
**LNP**........... Bibliotheca Parsoniana, New Orleans, LA [*Library symbol*] [*Library of Congress*] [*Obsolete*] (LCLS)
**LNP**........... Lecture Notes in Physics [*A publication*]
**LNP**........... Libertarian Party [*Australia*] [*Political party*]
**LNP**........... Liquefied Natural Petroleum
**LNP**........... Liquid Nitrogen Processing
**LNP**........... Loss of Normal Power (IEEE)
**LNP**........... Low Needle Position [*on dial*]
**LNP**........... Lunar Neutron Probe [*NASA*] (KSC)
**LNP**........... Lunping [*Taiwan*] [*Geomagnetic observatory code*]
**LNP**........... Wise, VA [*Location identifier*] [*FAA*] (FAAL)
**LNPF**......... Lebanese National Patriotic Forces [*Political party*]
**LNPF**......... Lymph Node Permeability Factor [*Immunology*]
**LNPIB**....... Loch Ness Phenomena Investigation Bureau [*Later, LNIB*]
**LNPo**......... Polyanthos, New Orleans, LA [*Library symbol*] [*Library of Congress*] (LCLS)
**LNQ**.......... Lincolnshire Notes and Queries [*A publication*]
**LNQ**.......... Longest Queue
**LNR**.......... Lagos Notes and Records [*A publication*]
**LNR**.......... Linamar Machine Ltd. [*Toronto Stock Exchange symbol*]
**LNR**.......... Liner
**LNR**.......... Liquid Nitrogen Refrigeration
**LNR**.......... Lone Rock, WI [*Location identifier*] [*FAA*] (FAAL)
**LNR**.......... Lonorore [*New Hebrides*] [*Seismograph station code, US Geological Survey*] (SEIS)
**LNR**.......... Louisiana Numerical Register [*Louisiana State Library*] [*Baton Rouge, LA*] [*Library network*]
**LNR**.......... Low-Noise Receiver
**LNR**.......... Luftnachrichten-Regiment [*Air forces signal regiment*] [*German military - World War II*]
**LNRC**....... Little Nash Rambler Club (EA)
**L & NRR**.... Louisville & Nashville Railroad Co.
**LNS**........... Laboratory for Nuclear Science [*MIT*] (MCD)
**LNS**........... Lancaster [*Pennsylvania*] [*Airport symbol*] (OAG)
**LNS**........... Land Navigation System
**LNS**........... Lansco Resources [*Vancouver Stock Exchange symbol*]
**LNS**........... Lanslevillard [*France*] [*Seismograph station code, US Geological Survey*] (SEIS)
**LNS**........... LASER Night Sensor
**LNS**........... Lesch-Nyhan Syndrome [*Medicine*]
**LNS**........... Liberation News Service (EA)
**LNS**........... London Normal School

**LNS** ........... Long Normal Superchron [*Geology*]
**LNS** ........... Lundastudier i Nordisk Sprakvetenskap [*A publication*]
**LNS** ........... Lutheran News Service [*Lutheran Church in America*] [*Information service or system*] (IID)
**LNS** ........... Nicholls State University, Ellender Memorial Library, Thibodaux, LA [*OCLC symbol*] (OCLC)
**LNSA** ......... Local Navy Supervising Activity
**LNSB** ......... Lincoln Savings Bank [*Carnegie, PA*] [*NASDAQ symbol*] (NQ)
**lnsb---** ......... Svalbard and Jan Mayen [*MARC geographic area code*] [*Library of Congress*] (LCCP)
**LNSF** ......... Light Night Striking Force [*British military*] (DMA)
**LNSL** ......... Southeast Louisiana Library Network Cooperative (SEALLING), New Orleans, LA [*Library symbol*] [*Library of Congress*] (LCLS)
**LNSM** ......... Saint Mary's Dominican College, New Orleans, LA [*Library symbol*] [*Library of Congress*] (LCLS)
**LNSN** ......... Local Non-Switched Network
**LNSO** ......... Shell Oil Co., New Orleans, LA [*Library symbol*] [*Library of Congress*] (LCLS)
**LNSP** ......... Lens Speed [*Mechanical engineering*]
**LNSU** ......... Library Network of SIBIL Users (EAIO)
**LNSU** ......... United States Department of Agriculture, Southern Utilization and Development Division, Agricultural Research Service, New Orleans, LA [*Library symbol*] [*Library of Congress*] (LCLS)
**LNT** ........... Launch Network Test
**LNT** ........... Millinocket, ME [*Location identifier*] [*FAA*] (FAAL)
**LNT** ........... Tulane University, New Orleans, LA [*Library symbol*] [*Library of Congress*] (LCLS)
**LNT-BA** .... Tulane University, Graduate School of Business Administration, New Orleans, LA [*Library symbol*] [*Library of Congress*] (LCLS)
**LNTC** ......... International House, Cunningham Library, New Orleans, LA [*Library symbol*] [*Library of Congress*] (LCLS)
**LNTL** ......... Lane Telecommunications, Inc. [*NASDAQ symbol*] (NQ)
**LNTL** ......... Lintel
**LNT-L** ....... Tulane University, Law Library, New Orleans, LA [*Library symbol*] [*Library of Congress*] (LCLS)
**LNT-M** ...... Tulane University, Medical Library, New Orleans, LA [*Library symbol*] [*Library of Congress*] (LCLS)
**LNT-MC** ... Greater New Orleans Microform Cooperative, Tulane University, New Orleans, LA [*Library symbol*] [*Library of Congress*] (LCLS)
**LNTO** ......... Lento [*Very Slow*] [*Music*] (ROG)
**LNTP** ......... New Orleans Times-Picayune, New Orleans, LA [*Library symbol*] [*Library of Congress*] (LCLS)
**LNTS** ......... League of Nations Treaty Series [*A publication*] (DLA)
**LNTS** ......... Liquid Nitrogen Transfer System
**LNTWA** .... Low-Noise Traveling Wave Amplifier
**LNU** ........... Last Name Unknown
**LNU** ........... League of Nations Union
**LNU** ........... Negentien Nu [*A publication*]
**LNU** ........... University of New Orleans, New Orleans, LA [*Library symbol*] [*Library of Congress*] [*OCLC symbol*] (LCLS)
**LNUCA** ..... United States Circuit Court of Appeals, Fifth Circuit Law Library, New Orleans, LA [*Library symbol*] [*Library of Congress*] (LCLS)
**LNUrs** ........ Ursuline Academy, New Orleans, LA [*Library symbol*] [*Library of Congress*] (LCLS)
**LNV** ........... Lincoln National Convertible Securities Fund, Inc. [*NYSE symbol*] (SPSG)
**LNV** ........... Londolovit [*Papua New Guinea*] [*Airport symbol*] [*Obsolete*] (OAG)
**LNV** ........... Longovilo [*Chile*] [*Seismograph station code, US Geological Survey*] (SEIS)
**LNV** ........... Lonvest Corp. [*Toronto Stock Exchange symbol*] [*Vancouver Stock Exchange symbol*]
**LNVA** ......... United States Veterans Administration Hospital, New Orleans, LA [*Library symbol*] [*Library of Congress*] (LCLS)
**LNVI** ......... Landsing Institutional Properties Trust VI [*Menlo Park, CA*] [*NASDAQ symbol*] (NQ)
**LNW** ........... [*The*] Louisiana & North West Railroad Co. [*AAR code*]
**LNWR** ....... London & North Western Railway [*British*]
**LNX** ........... Xavier University, New Orleans, LA [*Library symbol*] [*Library of Congress*] [*OCLC symbol*] (LCLS)
**LNY** ........... Lanai City [*Hawaii*] [*Airport symbol*] (OAG)
**LNY** ........... Laws of New York [*A publication*] (DLA)
**LNYD** ......... Lanyard
**LNYL** ......... Leksikon fun der Nayer Yidisher Literatur [*New York*] [*A publication*] (BJA)
**LNYT** ......... League of New York Theatres [*Later, LNYTP*] (EA)
**LNYTP** ...... League of New York Theatres and Producers (EA)
**LNYV** ......... Lettuce Necrotic Yellows Virus
**LNZ** ........... Linz [*Austria*] [*Airport symbol*] (OAG)
**ŁNZ** ........... Pounds New Zealand [*Monetary unit*]
**LO** ............. Connect Me to a Perforator Receiver [*Communications*] (FAAC)
**LO** ............. Lamp Oil
**LO** ............. Landelijke Organistatie [*Netherlands underground organization*] [*World War II*]
**LO** ............. Landsorganisasjonen i Norge [*Norwegian Federation of Trade Unions*]
**LO** ............. Landsorganisationen i Sverige [*Swedish Federation of Trade Unions*]
**LO** ............. Larval Operculum
**LO** ............. Launch Operations [*or Operator*] [*NASA*]
**LO** ............. Law Observer [*1872*] [*India*] [*A publication*] (DLA)
**LO** ............. Law Officer
**LO** ............. Law Opinions [*A publication*] (DLA)
**LO** ............. Lay Observer (ILCA)
**LO** ............. Layout [*Graphic arts*]
**LO** ............. Learning Objective
**LO** ............. Left Outboard (MCD)
**LO** ............. Legal Observer [*British*]
**LO** ............. Legal Officer
**LO** ............. Legal Opinion [*1870-73*] [*A publication*] (DLA)
**lo** ............... Lesotho [*MARC country of publication code*] [*Library of Congress*] (LCCP)
**L/O** ........... Letter of Offer
**LO** ............. Letter Orders
**LO** ............. Level Off
**LO** ............. Liaison Office [*or Officer*]
**LO** ............. Licensed Officer [*US Merchant Marine*]
**LO** ............. [*The*] Lifestyles Organization (EA)
**LO** ............. Lift-Off (AAG)
**LO** ............. Limerent Object [*One who is the object of obsessional romantic love*]
**LO** ............. Limited Order [*Business term*]
**LO** ............. Limnology and Oceanography [*A publication*]
**LO** ............. Line Occupancy
**LO** ............. Linguoocclusal [*Dentistry*]
**LO** ............. Liquid Oxygen
**LO** ............. Literaturnoe Obozrenie [*A publication*]
**LO** ............. Loam [*Type of soil*] (ROG)
**LO** ............. Local Office
**LO** ............. Local Order
**LO** ............. Local Origination [*Television programming*]
**LO** ............. Local Oscillator [*Electronics*]
**LO** ............. Locator File [*Information retrieval*]
**LO** ............. Locator, Outer [*Aviation*] (FAAC)
**Lo** ............. Lochlann [*A publication*]
**LO** ............. Lock-On
**LO** ............. Lock-Out
**LO** ............. Locked Open [*Technical drawings*]
**LO** ............. Locked Oscillator
**LO** ............. Loco [*Place*] [*Latin*]
**LO** ............. Loco [*As Written*] [*Music*]
**LO** ............. Logical Operation (AAG)
**LO** ............. Logistics Offensive
**LO** ............. London Office
**LO** ............. Longitude
**LO** ............. Longitudinal Optic
**LO** ............. Look-Out [*Navy*] [*British*]
**Lo** ............. Lotarius [*Flourished, 1191-1212*] [*Authority cited in pre-1607 legal work*] (DSA)
**LO** ............. Louisiana Musician [*A publication*]
**LO** ............. Louisville Orchestra [*Record label*]
**LO** ............. Louth [*County in Ireland*] (ROG)
**LO** ............. Love Object
**LO** ............. Low (KSC)
**LO** ............. Low Loaders (DCTA)
**LO** ............. Low Oblique [*Aerospace*]
**LO** ............. Lowest Offer [*Business term*]
**LO** ............. Lubricating Oil
**LO** ............. Lubrication Order
**LO** ............. Lunar Orbiter [*Aerospace*] (MCD)
**LO** ............. Lutte Ouvriere [*Workers' Struggle*] [*France*] [*Political party*] (PPW)
**LO** ............. Opelousas-Eunice Public Library, Opelousas, LA [*Library symbol*] [*Library of Congress*] (LCLS)
**LO** ............. Polskie Linie Lotnicze [*Poland*] [*ICAO designator*] (FAAC)
**LO** ............. Solicitor's Law Opinion, United States Internal Revenue Bureau [*A publication*] (DLA)
**$LO_2$** ........... Liquid Oxygen [*Also, LOX*] [*NASA*] (KSC)
**LO2** ........... Pahute Mesa [*Nevada*] [*Seismograph station code, US Geological Survey*] [*Closed*] (SEIS)
**LOA** ........... Landing Operations Area [*NASA*] (NASA)
**LOA** ........... Launch on Assessment [*Military*]
**LOA** ........... Launch on Attack [*Military*]
**LOA** ........... Launch Operations Agency [*NASA*] (KSC)
**LOA** ........... Launch Operations Area (MCD)
**LOA** ........... Leave of Absence
**LOA** ........... Left Occipitoanterior [*A fetal position*] [*Obstetrics*]
**LOA** ........... Length Over-All [*Technical drawings*]
**LOA** ........... Leona, TX [*Location identifier*] [*FAA*] (FAAL)
**LOA** ........... Letter of Agreement
**LOA** ........... Letter of Offer and Acceptance (MCD)
**LOA** ........... Level of Authority [*Military*] (AFIT)
**LOA** ........... Life Offices' Association [*British*] (DCTA)
**LOA** ........... Light Observation Aircraft
**LOA** ........... Line of Assurance

**LOA** .......... Local Overseas Allowance [*British military*] (DMA)
**LOA** .......... London Orphan Asylum (ROG)
**LOA** .......... Lorcan Resources Ltd. [*Vancouver Stock Exchange symbol*]
**LOA** .......... Lorraine [*Australia*] [*Airport symbol*] [*Obsolete*] (OAG)
**LOA** .......... Los Alamos [*New Mexico*] [*Seismograph station code, US Geological Survey*] (SEIS)
**LOA** .......... Low Oil Agglomeration [*Coal processing*]
**LOAA** ........ Letter of Agreement and Acceptance
**LOAC** ........ Low Accuracy
**LOAD** ........ LASER Optoacoustic Detection
**LOAD** ........ Low-Altitude Defense (MCD)
**LOADEX**... Loading Exercise [*Military*] (NVT)
**LOADS**...... Low-Altitude Defense System
**LOAF**........ Large Open-Area Floor
**LOAF**........ Look at Finland [*A publication*]
**LOAL** ........ Lock-On after Launch [*Weaponry*] (CAAL)
**LOAM** ....... List of Applicable Material (MCD)
**LOAMP** .... Logarithmic Amplifier (IEEE)
**LOAN**........ Surety Capital Corp. [*NASDAQ symbol*] (NQ)
**LOAN/A** ... Vessels Loaned to Army [*Navy*]
**LOAN/C** ... Vessels Loaned to Coast Guard [*Navy*]
**LOAN/M** .. Vessels Loaned to Miscellaneous Activities [*US Maritime Academy, etc.*] [*Navy*]
**LOAN/S**.... Vessels Loaned to States [*Navy*]
**LOAN/W** .. Vessels Loaned to War Shipping Administration [*Terminated, 1946*] [*Navy*]
**LOAP** ........ List of Applicable Publications [*Air Force*]
**LOAS**......... Lift-Off Acquisition System
**LOAT** ........ Trausdorf [*Austria*] [*ICAO location identifier*] (ICLI)
**LOAV** ........ Voslau [*Austria*] [*ICAO location identifier*] (ICLI)
**LOAVF**...... Lorcan Resources Ltd. [*NASDAQ symbol*] (NQ)
**LOB** .......... [*The*] Land of the Bible: A Historical Geography [*A publication*] (BJA)
**LOB** .......... Launch Operations Branch [*NASA*]
**LOB** .......... Launch Operations Building [*NASA*]
**LOB** .......... Left on Base [*Baseball*]
**LOB** .......... Left of Baseline
**LOB** .......... Left Out of Battle [*British*]
**LOB** .......... Left Outboard (MCD)
**LOB** .......... Limited Operating Base (AFM)
**LOB** .......... Line of Balance
**LOB** .......... Line of Bearing [*Navy*] (NVT)
**LOB** .......... Line of Business [*Used in corporate reports to Federal Trade Commission*]
**LOB** .......... [*Raymond E.*] Linn Operations Building [*National Security Agency*]
**LOB** .......... List of Bidders (FAAC)
**LOB** .......... Location of Offices Bureau [*British*]
**LOB** .......... Logistics Operating Base
**LOB** .......... Loyal Order of the Boar (EA)
**LObA**......... Allen Parish Library, Oberlin, LA [*Library symbol*] [*Library of Congress*] (LCLS)
**LOBA** ........ Last Offer Binding Arbitration [*Labor negotiations*]
**LOBAR**...... Long Baseline RADAR
**LOBI**.......... Library Orientation/Bibliographic Instruction [*Florida Library Association caucus*]
**Lobin**.......... Lobingier's Extra-Territorial Cases [*United States Court for China*] [*A publication*] (DLA)
**LOBSTER** ... Long-Term Ocean Bottom Settlement Test for Engineering Research [*Navy project*]
**LOBTP**...... League of Off-Broadway Theatres and Producers [*Later, OBL*] (EA)
**LOC** .......... Landing Operations Center (MCD)
**LOC** .......... Large Optical Cavity [*LASER design*]
**LOC** .......... Launch Operations Center [*NASA*]
**LOC** .......... Launch Operations Complex
**LOC** .......... Launch Operator's Console [*Aerospace*] (AAG)
**LOC** .......... Laverda Owner's Club (EA)
**LOC** .......... Le Groupe Opus Communications, Inc. [*Vancouver Stock Exchange symbol*]
**LOC** .......... LeMoyne-Owen College, Memphis, TN [*OCLC symbol*] (OCLC)
**LOC** .......... Letter of Comment
**LOC** .......... Letter of Compliance [*Program*] [*Coast Guard*]
**LOC** .......... Letters of Credit
**LOC** .......... Level of Consciousness [*Medicine*]
**LOC** .......... Liaison Officer Coordinator [*Air Force*] (AFM)
**LOC** .......... Library of Congress
**LOC** .......... Limited Operational Capability (CET)
**LOC** .......... Lincoln Owners Club (EA)
**LOC** .......... Lincoln School [*California*] [*Seismograph station code, US Geological Survey*] (SEIS)
**LOC** .......... Line of Communication [*Military*]
**LOC** .......... Line of Contact (MCD)
**LOC** .......... Line of Correction
**LOC** .......... Linked Object Code (TEL)
**LOC** .......... Liquid Organic Compound
**LOC** .......... Load Overcurrent
**LOC** .......... Local
**LOC** .......... Localizer (MSA)
**LOC** .......... Localizer Line of Sight
**LOC** .......... Locate (MSA)
**LOC** .......... Location (AFM)
**LOC** .......... Location Counter [*Data processing*]
**LOC** .......... Locative (Case) [*Linguistics*]
**LOC** .......... Lock-On Completed (MCD)
**LOC** .......... Loctite Corporation [*NYSE symbol*] (SPSG)
**Loc** ............ Locus [*A publication*]
**LOC** .......... Logistic Operation Center [*Military*]
**LOC** .......... Lord of Creation
**LOCA** ........ Late Onset Cerebellar Ataxia [*Medicine*]
**LOCA** ........ Loss-of-Coolant Accident [*Nuclear energy*]
**LOCAL**...... Load On-Call [*Data processing*]
**Local Ct & Mun Gaz** ... Local Courts and Municipal Gazette [*Toronto, ON*] [*A publication*] (DLA)
**Local Fin**.... Local Finance [*A publication*]
**Local Fin (The Hague)** ... Local Finance (The Hague) [*A publication*]
**Local Gov**... Local Government and Magisterial Reports [*England*] [*A publication*] (DLA)
**Local Gov Adm** ... Local Government Administration [*A publication*] (APTA)
**Local Gov J of Western Aust** ... Local Government Journal of Western Australia [*A publication*] (APTA)
**Local Gov R Aust** ... Local Government Reports of Australia [*A publication*] (DLA)
**Local Gov Rev** ... Local Government Review [*United Kingdom*] [*A publication*]
**Local Gov South Aust** ... Local Government in South Australia [*A publication*] (APTA)
**Local Gov in South Aust** ... Local Government in South Australia [*A publication*] (APTA)
**Local Gov in Sthn Afr** ... Local Government in Southern Africa [*A publication*]
**Local Gov Stud** ... Local Government Studies [*A publication*]
**Local Govt** ... Local Government [*A publication*] (APTA)
**Local Gov't** ... Local Government and Magisterial Reports [*England*] [*A publication*] (DLA)
**Local Govt Adm** ... Local Government Administration [*A publication*] (APTA)
**Local Govt Admin** ... Local Government Administration [*A publication*] (APTA)
**Local Govt B** ... Local Government Bulletin [*Manila*] [*A publication*]
**Local Govt Chron** ... Local Government Chronicle [*A publication*]
**Local Govt Eng** ... Local Government Engineer [*A publication*] (APTA)
**Local Govt Forum** ... Local Government Forum [*A publication*]
**Local Govt IULA Newsl** ... Local Government - IULA [*International Union of Local Authorities*] Newsletter [*A publication*]
**Local Govt Jl WA** ... Local Government Journal of Western Australia [*A publication*]
**Local Govt Manpower** ... Local Government Manpower [*A publication*]
**Local Govt News** ... Local Government News [*A publication*]
**Local Govt Policy Making** ... Local Government Policy Making [*A publication*]
**Local Govt Q** ... Local Government Quarterly [*Dacca*] [*A publication*]
**Local Govt R Austl** ... Local Government Reports of Australia [*A publication*]
**Local Govt Rev** ... Local Government Review [*A publication*]
**Local Govt R Japan** ... Local Government Review in Japan [*A publication*]
**Local Govt R (NSW)** ... Local Government Reports, New South Wales [*Australia*] [*A publication*] (DLA)
**Local Govt Stud** ... Local Government Studies [*A publication*]
**Local Hist**.. Local Historian [*A publication*]
**Local Popul Stud** ... Local Population Studies Magazine and Newsletter [*A publication*]
**LOCALS** ... Low-Cost Alternate LASER Seeker (MCD)
**LOCAM** .... Logistics Cost Analysis Model (MCD)
**LOCAP**...... Low Capacitance [*Cable*] [*Bell System*]
**LOCAP**...... Low [*Altitude*] Combat Air Patrol (NVT)
**LOCAT**...... Low-Altitude Clear-Air Turbulence (MCD)
**LOCAT**...... Low-Cost Air Target (MCD)
**LOCATE**... Library of Congress Automation Techniques Exchange
**LOCATE**... Local Area Telecommunications, Inc. [*Digital microwave carrier*] [*New York, NY*] (TSSD)
**LOCATE**... LORAN/OMEGA Course and Tracking Equipment (MCD)
**Locat Rep Div Miner Chem CSIRO** ... Location Report. Division of Mineral Chemistry. Commonwealth Scientific and Industrial Research Organisation [*A publication*] (APTA)
**LOCATS**... Lockheed Optical Communications and Tracking System
**LOCC** ........ Launch Operations Control Center
**LOCC** ........ Launcher Order and Capture Computer (MCD)
**Locc**............ Loccenius. De Jure Maritimo [*A publication*] (DLA)
**LOCC** ........ Logistical Operations Control Center [*Army*]
**Locc De Jur Mar** ... Loccenius. De Jure Maritimo [*A publication*] (DLA)
**LOC CIT** ... Loco Citato [*In the Place Cited*] [*Latin*]
**LOCCOZO** ... Line of Communication Combat Zone [*Military*]
**Locc Prot**.... Loccumer Protokolle [*A publication*]
**Loc Ct Gaz** ... Local Courts and Municipal Gazette [*Toronto, ON*] [*A publication*] (DLA)
**LOCD** ........ Lines of Communication Designators (MCD)
**LOCD** ........ Local Disease
**LOC DOL** ... Loco Dolenti [*To the Painful Spot*] [*Pharmacy*]
**LOCE** ........ Limited Operational Capability for Europe [*DoD*]
**LOCE** ........ Loss-of-Coolant Experiment [*Nuclear energy*]

**LOCF**......... Location File (MCD)
**LOCF**......... Loss-of-Coolant Flow [*Nuclear energy*] (NRCH)
**Loc Finance** ... Local Finance [*A publication*]
**Loc Gov Chron** ... Local Government Chronicle [*London, England*] [*A publication*] (DLA)
**Locgov Dig** ... Locgov Digest [*A publication*] (APTA)
**Loc Gov Rev** ... Local Government Review [*A publication*]
**Loc Govt Chr & Mag Rep** ... Local Government Chronicle and Magisterial Reporter [*London*] [*A publication*] (DLA)
**Loc Govt Rev** ... Local Government Review [*A publication*]
**LOCH**......... Loch Exploration, Inc. [*NASDAQ symbol*] (NQ)
**LOCH**......... London Option Clearing House [*A clearing corporation created in April 1978 by the London Stock Exchange*]
**LOCI**.......... Ligue des Originaires de Cote d'Ivoire [*League of Ivory Coast Natives*]
**LOCI**.......... List of Cancelled Items
**LOCI**.......... Logarithmic Computing Instrument
**LOCI**.......... Low-Cost Interceptor (MCD)
**LOCIS**....... Library of Congress Information System [*Library of Congress*] [*Information service or system*] (IID)
**LO CIT**...... Loco Citato [*In the Place Cited*] [*Latin*]
**LOCK**......... Logistical Operational Control Key [*Army*] (AABC)
**Locke News** ... Locke Newsletter [*A publication*]
**Lock GL**...... Locke's Game Laws [*5th ed.*] [*1866*] [*A publication*] (DLA)
**Lockheed GA Q** ... Lockheed Georgia Quarterly [*A publication*]
**Lockheed Horiz** ... Lockheed Horizons [*A publication*]
**Lockheed Symp Magnetohydrodyn** ... Lockheed Symposia on Magnetohydrodynamics [*A publication*]
**Lock Rev Ca** ... Lockwood's Reversed Cases [*New York*] [*A publication*] (DLA)
**Lock Rev Cas** ... Lockwood's Reversed Cases [*New York*] [*A publication*] (DLA)
**Lockwood Dir** ... Lockwood's Directory of the Paper and Allied Trades [*A publication*]
**LOCL**......... Local Federal Savings & Loan Association [*NASDAQ symbol*] (NQ)
**LOCL**......... Loyal Order of Catfish Lovers (EA)
**LOC LAUD** ... Loco Laudato [*In the Place Quoted*] [*Latin*]
**LOCN**......... Location
**LOCO**......... Locomotive (AABC)
**LOCO**......... Long Core [*Drilling program*]
**LOCO**......... Love Oil Company [*NASDAQ symbol*] (NQ)
**Loco J**......... Locomotive Journal [*A publication*] (APTA)
**LOCOM**.... Local Community (ADA)
**LOCOR**..... Local Coordinator [*Aviation*] (FAAC)
**LOCOS**...... Local Oxidation of Silicon [*Transistor technology*]
**LOCP**......... Launcher Operation Control Panel
**LOCP**......... Loss-of-Coolant Protection [*Nuclear energy*] (NRCH)
**LOCPOD**.. Low-Cost Powered Dispenser
**LOCPORT** ... Lines of Communications Ports (AABC)
**Loc Primo Cit** ... Loco Primo Citato [*In the Place First Cited*] [*Latin*] (ILCA)
**LOC PRIUS CIT** ... Loco Prius Citato [*In the Place First Cited*] [*Latin*] (ADA)
**LOCPURO** ... Local Purchase Order
**LOCS**......... Librascope Operations Control System
**LOCS**......... Logic and Control Simulator [*Data processing*] (BUR)
**Loc Self Gov** ... Local Self-Government [*A publication*]
**LOCTRACS** ... Lockheed Tracking and Control System
**Locus Standi** ... Locus Standi Reports [*England*] [*A publication*] (DLA)
**LOD**........... Large Organic Debris [*Pisciculture*]
**LOD**........... Launch Operations Directive [*or Director*] [*NASA*]
**LOD**........... Launch Operations Division [*NASA*] (KSC)
**LOD**........... Law Officers' Department [*British*]
**LOD**........... Leadership and Organization Development Journal [*A publication*]
**LOD**........... Leading Ones Detector [*Data processing*]
**LOD**........... Length of Day
**L & OD**...... Lester & Orpen Dennys [*Canadian publisher*]
**LOD**........... Level of Detail (MCD)
**LOD**........... Light-Off Detector [*Military*] (CAAL)
**LOD**........... Limit of Detection
**LOD**........... Line of Dance
**LOD**........... Line of Departure [*Military*] (AFM)
**LOD**........... Line of Direction
**LOD**........... Line of Duty [*Military*]
**LOD**........... List of Drawings
**LOD**........... Little Oxford Dictionary [*A publication*]
**LOD**........... Location Dependent
**LOD**........... Lodi Metals, Inc. [*Vancouver Stock Exchange symbol*]
**LOD**........... Logarithm of the Odds
**LOD**........... Longana [*Vanuata*] [*Airport symbol*] (OAG)
**LODACS**... Low-Dispersion Automatic Cannon System
**LODC**......... Local Defense District Craft
**LODCS**...... Lunar Orbiter Data Conversion System [*Aerospace*]
**LODE**......... Large Optics Demonstration Experiment [*DoD*]
**LODEM**.... Loading Dock Equipment Manufacturers Association (EA)
**LODESMP** ... Logistics Data Element Standardization and Management Process (IEEE)
**LODESTAR** ... Logically Organized Data Entry, Storage, and Recording
**Lodg Ind**..... United States Lodging Industry [*A publication*]
**LODI**......... List of Deleted Items (NG)
**LODISNAV** ... Long-Distance Navigation (FAAC)
**LODOR**...... Loaded, Waiting Orders or Assignment [*Navy*]
**LODP**......... Lunar Orbiter Data Printer [*Aerospace*]
**LO & DS**.... London Operatic and Dramatic Society (ROG)
**LODTM**.... Large Optics Diamond Turning Machine (SDI)
**LODUS**..... Low Data Rate UHF [*Ultra-High Frequency*] Satellite [*RADAR*] (MCD)
**Lodzki Num** ... Lodzki Numizmatyk [*A publication*]
**Lodzk Stud Etnogr** ... Lodzkie Studia Etnograficzne [*A publication*]
**Lodz Stud Etnogr** ... Lodzkie Studia Etnograficzne [*A publication*]
**Lodz Tow Nauk Pr Wydz 3** ... Lodzkie Towarzystwo Naukowe Prace Wydzialu 3. Nauk Matematyczno-Przyrodniczych [*A publication*]
**Lodz Tow Nauk Pr Wydz 4** ... Lodzkie Towarzystwo Naukowe Prace Wydzialu 4. Nauk Lekarskich [*A publication*]
**Lodz Tow Nauk Pr Wydz 3 Nauk Mat-Przyr** ... Lodzkie Towarzystwo Naukowe Prace Wydzialu 3. Nauk Matematyczno-Przyrodniczych [*A publication*]
**LOE**........... Left Outboard Elevon [*Aviation*] (MCD)
**LOE**........... Letter of Evaluation
**LOE**........... Letter of Execution (MCD)
**LOE**........... Level of Effort (KSC)
**LOE**........... Light-Off Examination [*Navy*] (NVT)
**LOE**........... Line of Effort (MCD)
**LOE**........... Loei [*Thailand*] [*Airport symbol*] [*Obsolete*] (OAG)
**LOEAT**...... Lowest Temperature Exceeded for All Time [*Meteorology*] (FAAC)
**LOEC**......... List of Effective Cards (NVT)
**LOEFM**..... Lowest Temperature Exceeded for the Month [*Meteorology*] (FAAC)
**LOEM(A)** ... Leading Ordnance Electrical Mechanic (Air) [*British military*] (DMA)
**LOEP**......... List of Effective Pages (NVT)
**LOEP**......... Loss of Electric Power
**LOERO**..... Large Orbiting Earth Resources Observatory (IEEE)
**LOESE**...... Lowest Temperature Exceeded So Early [*Meteorology*] (FAAC)
**LOESL**...... Lowest Temperature Equaled So Late [*Meteorology*] (FAAC)
**LOEX**........ Library Orientation/Instruction Exchange [*Library network*]
**LOF**........... Lack of Fusion
**LOF**........... Lecherous Old Fool [*Slang*]
**LOF**........... Line of Fire
**LOF**........... Line-of-Flight (MCD)
**LOF**........... Line of Force
**LOF**........... Local Oscillator Filter [*Electronics*]
**LOF**........... Local Oscillator Frequency [*Electronics*]
**LOF**........... London and Overseas Freighter
**LOF**........... Longest Operation First
**LOF**........... Loss of Feedwater [*Nuclear energy*] (NRCH)
**LOF**........... Loss of Flow [*Nuclear energy*] (NRCH)
**LOF**........... Lowest Operating Frequency (IEEE)
**LOF**........... Resort Air [*St. Louis, MO*] [*FAA designator*] (FAAC)
**LOFA**......... Loss of Flow Accident [*Nuclear energy*] (NRCH)
**LOFAAD**... Low-Altitude Forward Area Air Defense (AABC)
**LOFAADS** ... Low-Altitude Forward Area Anti-Aircraft Defense System [*Army*]
**LOFAR**...... Low-Frequency Acquisition and Ranging
**LOFAR**...... Low-Frequency Analysis and Recording [*Sonobuoys*] [*Navy*]
**LOFAT**...... Low-Flying Aerial Target [*Military*] (CAAL)
**LOFC**......... Ligues Ouvrieres Feminines Chretiennes [*Bruessel*] [*A publication*]
**LOFC**......... Loss of Forced Circulation [*Nuclear energy*] (NRCH)
**LOFES**...... Load Factor Error Sensor (MCD)
**LOFF**......... Leakoff [*Mechanical engineering*]
**L Off Ec and Mgmt** ... Law Office Economics and Management [*A publication*]
**L Off Econ & Man** ... Law Office Economics and Management [*A publication*]
**L Off Econ & Mgt** ... Law Office Economics and Management [*A publication*] (DLA)
**Lofft**........... Lofft's English King's Bench Reports [*1772-74*] [*A publication*] (DLA)
**Lofft Append** ... Lofft's Maxims, Appended to Lofft's Reports [*A publication*] (DLA)
**Lofft Lib**..... Lofft on the Law of Libels [*A publication*] (DLA)
**Lofft Max**.. Maxims Appended to Lofft's Reports [*A publication*] (DLA)
**Lofft's Rep** ... Lofft's English King's Bench Reports [*1772-74*] [*A publication*] (DLA)
**Lofft Un L** ... Lofft's Elements of Universal Law [*A publication*] (DLA)
**LOFO**......... Low-Frequency Oscillation (MCD)
**LOFRECO** ... Low Front End Cost [*Engineering*]
**Lofred**......... [*Sigismundus*] Lofredus [*Deceased, 1539*] [*Authority cited in pre-1607 legal work*] (DSA)
**LOFT**......... Line Oriented Flight Training (MCD)
**Loft**............ Lofft's English King's Bench Reports [*1772-74*] [*A publication*] (DLA)
**LOFT**......... Loss of Flow [*or Fluid*] Test Facility [*Nuclear energy*]
**LOFT**......... Low-Frequency Telescope [*NASA*]
**LOFTI**....... Low-Frequency Transionospheric Satellite
**LOFW**....... Loss of Feedwater [*Nuclear energy*] (NRCH)
**LOG**.......... Lawn-O-Gram [*A publication*] (EAAP)
**LOG**.......... Legion of Guardsmen (EA)

**LOG**.......... Logan [*Utah*] [*Seismograph station code, US Geological Survey*] [*Closed*] (SEIS)
**LOG**.......... Logan Mines Ltd. [*Vancouver Stock Exchange symbol*]
**LOG**.......... Logarithm [*Mathematics*]
**LOG**.......... Logic
**LOG**.......... Logistics (KSC)
**log**.......... Logogram (BJA)
**log**.......... Logographic (BJA)
**Log**.......... Logos. Internationale Zeitschrift fuer Philosophie und Kultur [*A publication*]
**LOG**.......... Pago Pago, AQ [*Location identifier*] [*FAA*] (FAAL)
**LOG**.......... Rayonier Timberlands LP [*NYSE symbol*] (SPSG)
**LOGACS**... Low-G Accelerometer Calibration System [*NASA*]
**LOGAIR**.... Logistics Airlift [*Military*]
**LOGAIRNET**... Logistics Air Network [*Air Force*]
**LOGAL**..... Logical Algorithmic Language [*Data processing*] (CSR)
**LOGALGOL**... Logical Algorithmic Language [*Data processing*]
**LOGAM**.... Logistics Analysis Model [*Army*] (RDA)
**LOGAMP**... Logistics and Acquisition Management Program [*Army*] (RDA)
**Log Anal**.... Log Analyst [*A publication*]
**Log Anal**.... Logique et Analyse [*A publication*]
**LOGANDS**... Logical Commands
**LOGATAK**... Logistics Attack Model [*BDM Corp.*] (MCD)
**LOGBALNET**... Logistics Ballistic Missile Network [*Air Force*]
**LOGC**........ Logic Devices, Inc. [*NASDAQ symbol*] (CTT)
**LOGC**........ Logistics Center [*Army*]
**LOGCAB**... Logistics Center Advisory Board (MCD)
**LOGC-AMIP**... Logistics Center Involvement in Army Model Improvement Program
**LOGCAP**... Logistic and Command Assessment of Projects [*Army*]
**LOGCAP**... Logistics Civil Augmentation Program [*Army*]
**LOGCCIS**... Logistics Command Central Information System [*United Kingdom*]
**LOGCEN**.. Logistics Center (MCD)
**LOGCMD**... Logistical Command
**LOGCOM**... Logistic Communications (CET)
**LOGCOM**... Logistics Command (MCD)
**LOGCOMD**... Logistical Command
**Log Comp**... Logan's Compendium of Ancient Law [*A publication*] (DLA)
**LOGCON**... Logistics Readiness Condition System [*DARCOM*] (MCD)
**LOGCOR**... Logistics Coordination (NVT)
**LOGDB**..... Logistics Database
**LOGDESMAP**... Logistics Data Element Standardization and Management Program [*DoD*] (AABC)
**LOGDESMO**... Logistics Data Element Standardization and Management Office [*DoD*] (AABC)
**LOGDIV**.... Logistics Division [*Supreme Headquarters, Allied Powers Europe*] (NATG)
**LOGE**........ Logetronics, Inc. [*NASDAQ symbol*] (NQ)
**LOGEL**....... Logic Generating Language [*Data processing*]
**LOGEST**... Annual Logistic Estimate (NATG)
**LOGEX**..... Logistical Exercise [*Army*] (AABC)
**LOGFED**... Log File Editor Processor [*Data processing*]
**LOGFOR**... Logistics Force [*Military*]
**LOGFTC**... Logarithmic Fast Time Constant
**Loggers Handb Pac Logging Congr**... Loggers Handbook. Pacific Logging Congress [*A publication*]
**LOGHELO**... Logistics Helicopter (NVT)
**LOGI**......... Logimetrics, Incorporated [*NASDAQ symbol*] (NQ)
**LOGIC**....... LASER Optical Guidance Integration Concept [*Missile guidance*]
**LOGIC**....... Level of Greatest Item Control [*DoD*]
**LOGIC**....... Local Government Information Center
**LOGICOM**... Logical Communications, Inc. [*East Norwalk, CT*] [*Telecommunications*] (TSSD)
**Logik Grundlagen Math**... Logik und Grundlagen der Mathematik [*A publication*]
**LOGIMP**... Logistic Improvement Program [*Military*]
**LOGIN**...... Local Government Information Network [*Information service or system*]
**LOGIPAC**... Logical Processor and Computer
**Logique et Anal NS**... Logique et Analyse. Nouvelle Serie [*A publication*]
**Logist Spectrum**... Logistics Spectrum [*A publication*]
**Logist & Transp Rev**... Logistics and Transportation Review [*A publication*]
**LOGIT**....... Logical Inference Tester [*NASA*]
**LOGK**........ Kapfenberg [*Austria*] [*ICAO location identifier*] (ICLI)
**LOGLAN**.. Logical Language
**LOGLAND**... Logistics Transport by Land [*Military*]
**LOGLISP**... Prolog and List Processing
**LOGMAP**... Logistics System Master Plan [*Army*]
**LOGMARS**... Logistic Applications of Automated Marking and Reading Symbols [*DoD*]
**LOGMIS**... Logistics Management Information System [*USACC*]
**LOGMOD**... Logic Model [*Fault isolation device*] [*Army*] (MCD)
**LOGMOD**... Logistics Module [*Simulation games*] [*Army*] (INF)
**LOGNET**.. Logistics Network (MCD)
**LOGO**........ [*A*] programming language [*For schoolchildren*] [*1967*] (CSR)
**LOGO**........ Limitation of Government Obligation (MCD)
**LOGO**........ Logotype [*Advertising*] (DSUE)
**LOGOIS**.... Logistics Operating Information System (AABC)
**Logos**.......... Logos Journal [*A publication*]
**LOGP**......... Logistics Plans
**LOGPAC**... Logistics Package [*Army*] (INF)
**LOG PLAN**... Logistics System Plan [*Navy*] [*DoD*]
**LOGR**........ Logistical Ratio [*Army*]
**LOGRAM**... Logical Program
**LOGREC**... Log Recording [*Data processing*]
**LOGREP**... Logistics Replenishment (NVT)
**LOGREP**... Logistics Representative [*Navy*] (NVT)
**LOGREQ**.. Logistics Requirements (NVT)
**LOGS**........ Logistics Supportability (AABC)
**LOGS**........ Logos Scientific, Inc. [*NASDAQ symbol*] (NQ)
**LOGSACS**... Logistics Structure and Composition System (AABC)
**LOGSAM**... Logistics Support Alternative [*or Analysis*] Model (MCD)
**LOGSAR**... Logistics Storage and Retrieval System (MCD)
**LOGSAT**... Logistics Special Assistance Team (MCD)
**Log & Saw**... Logging and Sawmilling Journal [*A publication*]
**LOGSEA**... Logistics Transport by Sea [*Military*]
**Log Spec**... Logistics Spectrum [*A publication*]
**LOGSTAT**... Logistical Status Report [*Military*] (INF)
**LOGSUM**... Logistics Summary (NVT)
**LOGSUP**... Logistics Support
**LOGSVC**... Logistics Service [*Military*] (NVT)
**LOGTAB**... Logic Tables (IEEE)
**LOgWC**..... West Carroll Parish Library, Oak Grove, LA [*Library symbol*] [*Library of Congress*] (LCLS)
**LOH**.......... League of Housewives [*Also known as HOW*]
**LOH**.......... Length of Hospitalization
**LOH**.......... Light Observation Helicopter
**LOH**.......... Local Osteolytic Hypercalcemia [*Endocrinology*]
**LOH**.......... Loja [*Ecuador*] [*Airport symbol*] (OAG)
**LOH**.......... Loss of Heterozygosity [*Genetics*]
**LOHA**........ Loch Harris, Inc. [*NASDAQ symbol*] (NQ)
**LOHAC**..... Loading and Handling Corrective Action Program
**LOHAP**..... Light Observation Helicopter Avionics Package (MCD)
**Lohnuntern Land-Forstwirt**... Lohnunternehmen in Land- und Forstwirtschaft [*A publication*]
**LOHS**........ Loss of Heat Sink [*Nuclear energy*] (NRCH)
**LOHTADS**... Light Observation Helicopter Target Acquisition Designation System (MCD)
**LOI**........... Laboratory Operating Instructions (MCD)
**LOI**........... Laredo, TX [*Location identifier*] [*FAA*] (FAAL)
**LOI**........... Letter of Instruction
**LOI**........... Letter of Intent (MCD)
**LOI**........... Letter of Interest (NG)
**LOI**........... Letter of Introduction
**LOI**........... Limit of Impurities
**LOI**........... Limiting Oxygen Index
**LOI**........... Line of Induction
**LOI**........... List of Items (AABC)
**LOI**........... Lock-On Initiated (MCD)
**LOI**........... Lodge of Instruction [*Freemasonry*]
**LOI**........... Loss on Ignition [*Analytical chemistry*]
**LOI**........... Lunar Orbit Insertion [*NASA*]
**LOID**......... Location Identifiers [*A publication*] [*FAA*]
**LOIH**......... Hohenems-Dornbirn [*Austria*] [*ICAO location identifier*] (ICLI)
**LOIJ**.......... St. Johann, Tirol [*Austria*] [*ICAO location identifier*] (ICLI)
**LOIS**.......... Langsam Library Online Information Services [*University of Cincinnati*] (OLDSS)
**LOIS**.......... Library Online Information Services [*Morehead State University*] (OLDSS)
**LOIS**.......... Library Order Information System [*Computer system*] [*Library of Congress*] [*Obsolete*]
**LOIS**.......... Loss of Interim Status [*Environmental Protection Agency*]
**Lois Batim**... Lois des Batiments [*A publication*] (DLA)
**Lois Rec**..... Lois Recentes du Canada [*A publication*] (DLA)
**LOIT**.......... Loitering [*FBI standardized term*]
**LOIUSA**.... Loyal Orange Institution of United States of America (EA)
**LOJN**......... Lo-Jack Corp. [*Braintree, MA*] [*NASDAQ symbol*] (NQ)
**LOK**........... Lockwood Petroleum, Inc. [*Vancouver Stock Exchange symbol*]
**LOL**........... League of Lefthanders (EA)
**LOL**........... Left Occipitolateral [*A fetal position*] [*Obstetrics*]
**LOL**........... Length of Lead [*Actual*] [*Technical drawings*]
**LOL**........... Limit of Liability (MCD)
**LOL**........... Limited Operating Life
**LOL**........... Line of Launch [*Navy*] (CAAL)
**LOL**........... Little Old Lady [*Slang*]
**lol**............ Lolo (Bantu) [*MARC language code*] [*Library of Congress*] (LCCP)
**LOL**........... London-Oiseau-Lyre [*Record label*] [*Great Britain, USA, etc.*]
**LOL**........... Lovelock [*Nevada*] [*Airport symbol*] [*Obsolete*] (OAG)
**LOL**........... Loyal Orange Lodge
**LOLA**........ Library On-Line Acquisitions [*Washington State University*] [*Data processing system*]
**LOLA**........ Light Observation Light-Armored Aircraft
**LOLA**........ Long Line Azimuth [*Survey*]
**LOLA**........ Lower Leg Artery [*Anatomy*]
**LOLA**........ Lunar Orbit and Landing Approach [*Simulator*] [*NASA*]
**LOLAD**..... Low-Altitude LASER Air Defense System
**LOLAS**...... Location of Launching Site [*Army*]

**LOLEX**...... Low-Level Extraction [*Military aviation*]
**LOLI**.......... Limited Operational-Life Items [*NASA*] (NASA)
**LOLI**.......... Loyal Orange Ladies Institution (EA)
**LOLIS**....... Literature of Librarianship and Information Science [*Australia*]
**LOLITA**.... Language for the On-Line Investigation and Transformation of Abstractions [*Data processing*]
**LOLITA**.... Library On-Line Information and Text Access [*Oregon State University*] [*Corvallis, OR*] [*Data processing system*]
**Lollipops**.... Lollipops, Ladybugs, and Lucky Stars [*A publication*]
**LO/LO**...... Lift-On/Lift-Off
**LOLP**......... Loss of Load Probability [*Nuclear energy*] (IEEE)
**Lo LR**......... Loyola Law Rcvicw [*A publication*]
**LOLS**......... Land of Lincoln Savings & Loan [*NASDAQ symbol*] (NQ)
**LOLV**......... Lower Leg Vein [*Anatomy*]
**LOLVE**....... Lower Leg Venule [*Anatomy*]
**LOLW**....... Laid Off, Lack of Work [*Unemployment insurance and the Bureau of Labor Statistics*] (OICC)
**LOLW**....... Wels [*Austria*] [*ICAO location identifier*] (ICLI)
**LOM**.......... Laminated Object Manufacturing [*Desktop manufacturing*]
**LOM**.......... LASER Optical Modulator
**LOM**.......... Launch Operations Manager [*NASA*]
**LOM**.......... League of Mercy [*Salvation Army*]
**LOM**.......... Legion of Merit [*Military award*]
**LOM**.......... Level of Maintenance (MCD)
**LOM**.......... Light-Optic Microscope (MSA)
**LOM**.......... Limitation of Movement
**LOM**.......... List of Materials (CET)
**LOM**.......... List of Modifications (AFM)
**LOM**.......... Locator at Outer Marker [*Aviation*]
**LOM**.......... Loewen, Ondaatje, McCutcheon, Inc. [*Toronto Stock Exchange symbol*] [*Vancouver Stock Exchange symbol*]
**LOM**.......... Lomas & Nettleton Mortgage Investors [*NYSE symbol*] (SPSG)
**LOM**.......... Lome [*Togo*] [*Seismograph station code, US Geological Survey*] (SEIS)
**LOM**.......... Loss of Motion [*Medicine*]
**LOM**.......... Low-Frequency Outer Marker
**LOM**.......... Low-Order Memory (CET)
**LOM**.......... Loyal Order of Moose (EA)
**LOM**.......... Lunar Orbital Map [*Air Force*]
**LOM**.......... Lunar Orbital Mission [*NASA*] (KSC)
**LOMA**....... Life Office Management Association [*Atlanta, GA*] (EA)
**LOMA**....... Literature on Modern Art
**LOMA**....... Lutheran Outdoors Ministry Association [*Later, NLOMA*] (EA)
**LOMAC**.... Logistic Management Advisory Committee
**LOMAD**.... Low-to-Medium-Altitude Air Defense (AABC)
**LOMAH**.... Location of Miss and Hit [*Marksmanship training*] [*Army*] (INF)
**LOMAR**.... Local Manual Attempt Recording (TEL)
**Lomax Ex'rs**... Lomax on Executors [*A publication*] (DLA)
**Lombard**.... Loads of Money but a Real Dolt [*Bowdlerized version*] [*Lifestyle classification*] [*Australia*]
**Lom CH Rep**... Lomas's City Hall Reporter [*New York*] [*A publication*] (DLA)
**Lom Dig**..... Lomax's Digest of Real Property [*A publication*] (DLA)
**Lom Ex**...... Lomax on Executors [*A publication*] (DLA)
**LOMF**....... Loss of Main Feedwater [*Nuclear energy*] (NRCH)
**LOMI**........ Letter of Moral Intent [*Business term*]
**LOMK**....... Lomak Petroleum, Inc. [*NASDAQ symbol*] (NQ)
**LOMO**....... London Overseas Mail Office
**LOMS**....... Library Organization and Management Section [*Library Administration Division of ALA*]
**LOMSA**..... Left Otitis Media Suppurative Acute [*Medicine*]
**LOMSCH**... Left Otitis Media Suppurative Chronic [*Medicine*]
**LOMUSS**.. Lockheed Multiprocessor Simulation System (IEEE)
**LON**.......... Letter of Notification
**LON**.......... Line of Nodes
**LON**.......... London [*England*] [*Airport symbol*] (OAG)
**Lon**............ London [*Record label*] [*Export issues of English Decca - mainly USA, Canada, etc.*]
**LON**.......... London [*England*]
**LON**.......... Longitude (KSC)
**LON**.......... Longmire [*Washington*] [*Seismograph station code, US Geological Survey*] (SEIS)
**LON**.......... Tupelo, MS [*Location identifier*] [*FAA*] (FAAL)
**LON**.......... University College, London, England [*OCLC symbol*] (OCLC)
**LONAL**..... Local Off-Net Access Line [*Telecommunications*] (TEL)
**LOND**........ London
**Lond**.......... London Encyclopedia [*A publication*] (DLA)
**LOND**........ London House, Inc. [*Park Ridge, IL*] [*NASDAQ symbol*] (NQ)
**Lond A**....... London Archaeologist [*A publication*]
**Lond Clin Med J**... London Clinic Medical Journal [*A publication*]
**L'Ondes Electr**... L'Ondes Electronique [*A publication*]
**Lond Gaz**.... London Gazette [*A publication*]
**Lond J**........ London Journal [*A publication*]
**Lond Jur**.... London Jurist Reports [*England*] [*A publication*] (DLA)
**Lond Jur NS**... London Jurist, New Series [*A publication*] (DLA)
**Lond LM**.... London Law Magazine [*A publication*] (DLA)
**Lond M**...... London Magazine [*A publication*]
**Lond Mag**.. London Magazine [*A publication*]
**Lond Math Soc Lect Note Ser**... London Mathematical Society. Lecture Note Series [*A publication*]
**Lond Math Soc Monogr**... London Mathematical Society. Monographs [*A publication*]
**Lond Med Gaz**... London Medical Gazette [*A publication*]
**Lond Med St**... London Mediaeval Studies [*A publication*]
**Lond Mercury**... London Mercury [*A publication*]
**Lond Nat**.... London Naturalist [*A publication*]
**London Archaeol**... London Archaeologist [*A publication*]
**London Archit**... London Architect [*A publication*]
**London Archt**... London Architect [*A publication*]
**London Bus Mag**... London Bus Magazine [*A publication*]
**London Bus School J**... London Business School. Journal [*A publication*]
**London Commun Wk Serv Newsl**... London Community Work Service Newsletter [*A publication*]
**London Docklands Dev Newsl**... London Docklands Development Newsletter [*A publication*]
**London Ednl R**... London Educational Review [*A publication*]
**London Hlth News**... London Health News [*A publication*]
**London Ind Centre News**... London Industrial Centre News [*A publication*]
**London J**.... London Journal [*A publication*]
**London Jnl**... London Journal [*A publication*]
**London Labour Brief**... London Labour Briefing [*A publication*]
**London Lesbian Newsl**... London Lesbian Newsletter [*A publication*]
**London L Rev**... City of London Law Review [*A publication*]
**London Mag**... London Magazine [*A publication*]
**London Math Soc Lecture Note Ser**... London Mathematical Society. Lecture Note Series [*A publication*]
**London Math Soc Monographs**... London Mathematical Society. Monographs [*A publication*]
**London Meas Rates Mat Prices**... London Measured Rates and Materials Prices [*A publication*]
**London Middlesex Archaeol Soc Spec Pap**... London and Middlesex Archaeological Society. Special Papers [*A publication*]
**London Natur**... London Naturalist [*A publication*]
**London Passenger Transp**... London Passenger Transport [*A publication*]
**London Rev Public Admin**... London Review of Public Administration [*A publication*]
**London Shellac Res Bur Bull**... London Shellac Research Bureau. Bulletin [*A publication*]
**London Shellac Res Bur Tech Pap**... London Shellac Research Bureau. Technical Paper [*A publication*]
**London Soc Jnl**... London Society. Journal [*A publication*]
**London Stud**... London Studies [*A publication*]
**London Volunt News**... London Voluntary News [*A publication*]
**Lond Q**....... London Quarterly Review [*A publication*]
**LondQHolbR**... London Quarterly and Holborn Review [*A publication*]
**Lond QHR**... London Quarterly and Holborn Review [*A publication*]
**Lond Q R**... London Quarterly and Holborn Review [*A publication*]
**Lond School Trop Med Research Mem Ser**... London School of Tropical Medicine. Research Memoir Series [*A publication*]
**Lond Studio**... London Studio [*A publication*]
**Lond Topog Rec**... London Topographical Record [*A publication*]
**LONESHS**... Limited- or Non-English Speaking Handicapped Student
**LONEX**..... Laboratory Office Network Experiment [*DoD*]
**LONG**........ Longitude (AFM)
**LONG**........ Longus [*Long*] [*Pharmacy*]
**LONG**........ [*The*] Longwood Group Ltd. [*NASDAQ symbol*] (NQ)
**Long Ashton Res Stn Rep**... Long Ashton Research Station. Report [*A publication*]
**Long Beach B Bull**... Long Beach Bar Bulletin [*A publication*] (DLA)
**Long Dst L**... Long-Distance Letter [*A publication*]
**Longest R**... Longest Revolution [*A publication*]
**Longev**........ Longevita [*A publication*]
**LONGF**..... Longford [*County in Ireland*] (ROG)
**LONGFD**.. Longford [*County in Ireland*]
**Longf Dist**... Longfield on Distress and Replevin [*A publication*] (DLA)
**Longf & T**... Longfield and Townsend's Irish Exchequer Reports [*1841-42*] [*A publication*] (DLA)
**Long Irr**...... Long on Irrigation [*A publication*] (DLA)
**Long Isl B**.. Long Island Business [*A publication*]
**Long Isl Forum**... Long Island Forum [*A publication*]
**LONGL**..... Longitudinal (FAAC)
**Longm**........ Longman's Magazine [*A publication*]
**LONGN**..... Longeron [*Aerospace engineering*]
**Longovall**... [*Johannes*] Longovallius [*Flourished, 16th century*] [*Authority cited in pre-1607 legal work*] (DSA)
**Long Point Bird Obs Annu Rep**... Long Point Bird Observatory. Annual Report [*A publication*]
**Long Q**....... Long Quinto [*Pt. 10 of Year Books*] [*A publication*] (DLA)
**Long Quinto**... Year Books, Part X [*5 Edw. 4, 1465*] [*A publication*] (DLA)
**Long & R**.... Long and Russell's Election Cases [*Massachusetts*] [*A publication*] (DLA)
**Long Range Plan**... Long-Range Planning [*A publication*]
**Long Range Plann**... Long-Range Planning [*A publication*]
**Long-Rang P**... Long-Range Planning [*A publication*]
**Long Rev**.... Longest Revolution [*A publication*]
**Long S**........ Long on Sales of Personal Property [*A publication*] (DLA)
**Long & T**.... Longfield and Townsend's Irish Exchequer Reports [*1841-42*] [*A publication*] (DLA)
**LONGT**..... Longtree [*England*]

**Long Term Care Health Serv Adm Q** ... Long Term Care and Health Services Administration. Quarterly [*A publication*]
**Long Term Care Q** ... Long-Term Care Quarterly [*A publication*]
**LONGV**..... Longevity (AFM)
**LonM**......... London Magazine [*A publication*]
**Lon Mag**.... London Magazine [*A publication*]
**LONO**........ Low Noise
**Lon R Bks**.. London Review of Books [*A publication*]
**LONS**........ Laboratory Office Network System [*DoD*]
**LONS**........ Light of the Night Sky [*Galaxy*]
**LONS**........ Local Online Network System
**Lons Cr L**... Lonsdale's Statute Criminal Law [*A publication*] (DLA)
**LOO**.......... Loumic Resources Ltd. [*Vancouver Stock Exchange symbol*]
**Loodusuurijate Selts Tappistead Sekts Toim** ... Loodusuurijate Selts Tappisteaduste Sektsiooni Toimetised [*A publication*]
**Loodusuur Seltsi Aastar** ... Loodusuurijate. Seltsi Aastaraaman [*A publication*]
**LOOK**........ Opticorp, Inc. [*NASDAQ symbol*] (NQ)
**Look Ahead Proj Highlights** ... Looking Ahead and Projection Highlights [*A publication*]
**Look Jpn**.... Look Japan [*A publication*]
**Look Lab (Hawaii)** ... Look Laboratory (Hawaii) [*A publication*]
**LOOM**....... Light Opera of Manhattan
**LOOM**....... Loyal Order of Moose (EA)
**Loonb Land-Tuinbouw** ... Loonbedrijf in Land- en Tuinbouw [*A publication*]
**LOOP**........ Long-Range Open Ocean Patrol [*Navy*] (NVT)
**LOOP**........ Loss of Offsite Power [*Nuclear energy*] (NRCH)
**LOOP**........ Louisiana Offshore Oil Port [*Group of major oil companies*]
**LOOPS**...... Local Office Online Payment System [*Unemployment insurance*]
**LOOW**....... Lake Ontario Ordnance Works
**LOP**.......... Lake Ontario Cement Ltd. [*Toronto Stock Exchange symbol*]
**LOP**.......... Last Operation Completed [*Data processing*]
**LOP**.......... Launch Operations [*or Operator's*] Panel [*NASA*]
**LOP**.......... Learning Opportunity [*Education*]
**LOP**.......... Least Objectionable Program [*Television*]
**LOP**.......... Leave on Pass
**LOP**.......... Left Occipitoposterior [*A fetal position*] [*Obstetrics*]
**LOP**.......... Left Outside Position [*Dancing*]
**LOP**.......... Letter of Promulgation [*Navy*] (NVT)
**LOP**.......... Letter of Proposal [*Military*] (AFM)
**LOP**.......... Levels-of-Processing [*Psychology*]
**LOp**.......... Lex Operator Gene
**LOP**.......... Life of Program
**LOP**.......... Line-Oriented Protocol
**LOP**.......... Line of Position [*Electronics*]
**LOP**.......... Local Office Project [*Department of Health and Social Security*] [*British*]
**LOP**.......... Local Operating Procedures (AFM)
**LOP**.......... Local Operational Plot
**LOP**.......... Logistics Officer Program [*Army*]
**LOP**.......... Loss of Offsite Power [*Nuclear energy*] (NRCH)
**LOP**.......... Low-Order Position [*Military*] (AFIT)
**LOP**.......... Lubricating Oil Pump (MSA)
**LOPA**........ Layout of Passenger Accommodation (MCD)
**LOPA**........ Local Payment of Airline (MCD)
**LOPAC**...... Load Optimization and Passenger Acceptance Control [*Airport computer*]
**LOPAD**..... Logarithmic Outline [*or Online*] Processing System for Analog Data (IEEE)
**LOPAIR**.... Long Path Infrared
**LOPAR**...... Long Baseline Position and Rates [*Guidance and tracking system*] [*Air Force*]
**LOPAR**...... Low-Power Acquisition RADAR
**Lopatochnye Mash Struinye Appar** ... Lopatochnye Mashiny i Struinye Apparaty [*A publication*]
**LOPC**........ Lunar Orbit Plane Change [*NASA*]
**LOPG**........ Launch Operations Planning Group
**LOP-GAP** ... Liquid Oxygen Petrol, Guided Aircraft Projectile
**LOPI**.......... Loss of Pipe Integrity [*Nuclear energy*] (NRCH)
**LOPKGS**... Loose or in Packages [*Freight*]
**LOPO**........ Local Post (EA)
**LOPO**........ Low-Power Boiler [*US reactor*]
**LOPOS**...... Local Oxidation of Polysilicon over Silicon [*Transistor technology*]
**LOPP**........ Lunar Orbiter Photographic Project [*Aerospace*]
**LOPRA**...... Low-Power Reactor Assembly [*University of Illinois*] (NRCH)
**LO-PRO**.... Low-Profile
**LOPS**........ Length of Patient Stay [*Medicine*] (AABC)
**LOPS**........ Limited Offer to Purchase Scheme [*Australia*]
**LOPS**........ Lunar Orbiting Photographic System [*Aerospace*]
**LOPU**........ Logistics Organization Planning Unit
**LOQ**.......... Leadership Opinion Questionnaire [*Test*]
**LOQ**.......... Loquitur [*He, or She, Speaks*] [*Latin*]
**LOQ**.......... Lower Outer Quadrant [*Anatomy*]
**LO-QG**...... Locked Oscillator-Quadrature Grid [*Data processing*]
**LOR**.......... Ladies of Retreads (EA)
**LOR**.......... Large Optical Reflector
**LOR**.......... Letter of Request (AFIT)
**LOR**.......... Level of Repair
**LOR**.......... Lockout Relay (MCD)
**LOR**.......... Long Open Reading [*Frame*] [*Genetics*]
**LOR**.......... Long-Range Planning [*A publication*]
**LOR**.......... Loral Corp. [*NYSE symbol*] (SPSG)
**LOR**.......... Lorazepam [*A tranquilizer*]
**LOR**.......... Lorcha [*Ship's rigging*] (ROG)
**LOR**.......... Lormes [*Somee*] [*France*] [*Seismograph station code, US Geological Survey*] (SEIS)
**LOR**.......... Low-Frequency Omnidirectional Radio Range
**LOR**.......... Lower Operator Rate [*Telecommunications*] [*British*]
**LOR**.......... Lunar Orbit [*or Orbital*] Rendezvous [*NASA*]
**LOR**.......... Ozark, Fort Rucker, AL [*Location identifier*] [*FAA*] (FAAL)
**LORA**........ Level of Repair Analysis (MCD)
**LORA**........ Long-Range Adaption (MCD)
**LORA**........ Long-Range Addition (NVT)
**LORAC**...... Long-Range Accuracy [*RADAR*]
**LORAD**..... Long-Range Active Detection
**LORAD**..... Long-Range Air Defense (AABC)
**LORADAC** ... Long-Range Active Detection and Communications System
**LORAE**...... Long-Range Attitude and Event [*Instrumentation system*]
**LORAH**..... Long-Range Area Homing
**LORA-HOJ** ... Long-Range - Home on Jam
**LORAMS**... Long-Range Automatic Measuring Station [*Meteorology*]
**LORAN**..... Long-Range Navigation
**LORAN DM** ... Long-Range Navigation Double Master
**LORAN DS** ... Long-Range Navigation Double Slave
**LORAN M** ... Long-Range Navigation Master
**LORAN S** ... Long-Range Navigation Slave
**LORAPH**.. Long-Range Passive Homing System
**LORAS**...... Low-Range Airspeed System (MCD)
**LORBAS**... Large Off-Line Retrieval Text Base Access System
**LORBI**....... Locked-On RADAR Bearing Indicator
**LORC**........ Lockheed Radio Command (MUGU)
**LORCS**...... League of Red Cross Societies
**LORD**........ Licensing Online Retrieval Data (NRCH)
**LORD**........ List of Required Documents (NVT)
**LORD**........ Long-Range and Detection RADAR (NATG)
**LORD**........ Lordosis [*Medicine*]
**L & Order**.. Law and Order [*A publication*] (DLA)
**LORDF**...... Loredi Resources Ltd. [*NASDAQ symbol*] (NQ)
**LORDS**...... Licensing On-Line Retrieval Data System (NRCH)
**Lords Jour** ... Journals of the House of Lords [*England*] [*A publication*] (DLA)
**LOREC**...... Long-Range Earth Current Communications
**Lore & L**.... Lore and Language [*A publication*]
**LORELCO** ... Lower Elevated Serum Cholesterol [*Acronym is trade name of Dow Chemical*]
**LORELEI** ... Long-Range Echo Level Indicator
**Lorenz**........ Lorenz's Ceylon Reports [*A publication*] (DLA)
**Lorenz App R** ... Lorenz's Appeal Reports [*Ceylon*] [*A publication*] (DLA)
**Lorenz Rep** ... Lorenz's Ceylon Reports [*A publication*] (ILCA)
**LOREORS**... Long-Range, Electro-Optical Reconnaissance System
**LORES**...... Long-Route Engineering Study [*Bell System*]
**LO-RES**.... Low Resolution [*Data processing*]
**LORI**.......... Limited Operational Readiness Inspection (MCD)
**Lori**............ [*Petrus*] Loriotus [*Deceased circa 1580*] [*Authority cited in pre-1607 legal work*] (DSA)
**Loring & Russel El Cases** ... Loring and Russell's Election Cases in Massachusetts [*A publication*] (DLA)
**Loring & Russell** ... Loring and Russell's Election Cases in Massachusetts [*A publication*] (DLA)
**Lor Inst**...... Lorimer. Institutes of Law [*A publication*] (ILCA)
**Loriot**......... [*Petrus*] Loriotus [*Deceased circa 1580*] [*Authority cited in pre-1607 legal work*] (DSA)
**LORL**......... Large Orbital Research Laboratory [*NASA*]
**LORMODS** ... Long-Range Metal Object Detection System (MCD)
**LORMONSTA** ... LORAN Monitor Station
**LORO**........ Lobe-On Receive Only [*Electronic counter-countermeasures*]
**LOROP**...... Long-Range Oblique Photography
**LORPGAC** ... Long-Range Proving Ground Automatic Computer (IEEE)
**LORRE**...... Laboratory of Renewable Resources Engineering [*Purdue University*]
**Lor & Russ** ... Loring and Russell's Election Cases in Massachusetts [*A publication*] (DLA)
**LORS**......... LM [*Lunar Module*] Optical Rendezvous System [*NASA*]
**LORS**......... Long-Range SONAR
**LORS**......... Lunar Orbiting Reconnaissance System [*Aerospace*]
**LORSA**....... Long-Range Steerable Antenna (MCD)
**LORSAC**.... Long-Range Submarine Communications (AAG)
**Lor Sc L**..... Lorimer's Handbook of Scotch Law [*A publication*] (DLA)
**LORSTA**.... LORAN Transmitting Station
**LORSU**...... Long-Range Special Unit [*Military*]
**LORT**........ League of Resident Theaters (EA)
**LORTAN**.. Long-Range and Tactical Navigation System
**LORTRAP** ... Long-Range Training and Rotation Plan
**LORV**........ Low-Observability Reentry Vehicle
**LOS**.......... Laboratory Operating System [*NASA*]
**LOS**.......... Lagos [*Nigeria*] [*Airport symbol*] (OAG)
**LOS**.......... Land Ownership Survey
**LOS**.......... Latin Old Style (ADA)
**LOS**.......... Launch Operations System [*NASA*] (KSC)
**LOS**.......... Launch on Search [*Navy*] (CAAL)

**LOS** .......... Launcher Operation Station (MCD)
**LOS** .......... Law of the Sea [*United Nations*] (ASF)
**LOS** .......... Length of Service
**LOS** .......... Length of Stay
**LOS** .......... Liaison Office Support
**LOS** .......... Licentiate in Obstetrical Science
**LOS** .......... Lift-Off Simulator [*NASA*] (NASA)
**LOS** .......... Line Out of Service [*Telecommunications*] (TEL)
**LOS** .......... Line of Scrimmage [*Football*]
**LOS** .......... Line of Sight
**LOS** .......... Line of Supply
**LOS** .......... Literary Onomastics Studies [*A publication*]
**LOS** .......... Live Oak Society (EA)
**LOS** .......... Logistic Operation - Streamline [*Military*] (AABC)
**LOS** .......... Logistic Oriented Schools [*Army*]
**LOS** .......... Loop Output Signal (CET)
**LOS** .......... Loss of Sight
**LOS** .......... Loss of Signal
**LOS** .......... Loss of Synchronization
**LOS** .......... Lunar Orbiting Satellite [*or Spacecraft*] [*Aerospace*] (MCD)
**LOS** .......... Midwestern Baptist Theological Seminary, Kansas City, MO [*OCLC symbol*] (OCLC)
**LOS-AD** .... Line-of-Sight - Air Defense [*DoD*]
**LOSAM**..... Low-Altitude Surface-to-Air Missiles (NATG)
**Los Ang Cty Mus Contrib Sci** ... Los Angeles County Museum. Contributions in Science [*A publication*]
**Los Angeles BAB** ... Los Angeles Bar Association. Bulletin [*A publication*] (DLA)
**Los Angeles B Bull** ... Los Angeles Bar Bulletin [*A publication*]
**Los Angeles Bus and Econ** ... Los Angeles Business and Economics [*A publication*]
**Los Angeles Counc Eng Sci Proc Ser** ... Los Angeles Council of Engineers and Scientists. Proceedings Series [*A publication*]
**Los Angeles County Mus Contr Sci** ... Los Angeles County Museum. Contributions in Science [*A publication*]
**Los Angeles County Mus Nat History Quart** ... Los Angeles County Museum of Natural History. Quarterly [*A publication*]
**Los Angeles Ed Res B** ... Los Angeles Educational Research Bulletin [*A publication*]
**Los Angeles L Rev** ... Los Angeles Law Review [*A publication*] (DLA)
**Los Angeles Mus Art Bull** ... Los Angeles County Museum. Bulletin of the Art Division [*A publication*]
**Los Angeles Mus Bul** ... Los Angeles County Museum. Bulletin of the Art Division [*A publication*]
**Los Angeles Mus Q** ... Los Angeles County Museum of History, Science, and Art. Quarterly [*A publication*]
**LOS-AT**..... Line-of-Sight - Antitank [*DoD*]
**LOSC**......... Law of the Sea Conference [*United Nations*] (MSC)
**LOSD** ........ League of St. Dymphna (EA)
**LOSE**......... Let Others Share Equally [*Slogan opposing President Gerald R. Ford's anti-inflation WIN campaign*]
**LOSE**......... Let's Omit Superfluous Expenses [*Slogan opposing President Gerald R. Ford's anti-inflation WIN campaign*]
**LOS-F**........ Line-of-Sight - Forward [*DoD*]
**LOS-FH** .... Line-of-Sight - Forward Heavy [*DoD*]
**LOSL**......... Saint Landry Parish Library, Opelousas, LA [*Library symbol*] [*Library of Congress*] (LCLS)
**LOSM** ....... Launch Operations Simulation Model
**LOS of NA** ... Ladies Oriental Shrine of North America (EA)
**LOSP**......... Loss of Offsite Power [*Nuclear energy*] (NRCH)
**LOSP**......... Loss of System Pressure [*Nuclear energy*] (NRCH)
**LOSR**......... Limit of Stack Register
**LOSR**......... Line-of-Sight Rate (MCD)
**LOS-R** ....... Line-of-Sight - Rear [*DoD*]
**LOSREP**.... Loss Report [*Aircrew/aircraft*]
**LOSS** ......... Landing Observer Signal System (MSA)
**LOSS** ......... Large Object Salvage System [*Navy*]
**LOSS** ......... Lunar Orbit Space Station [*NASA*]
**LOSS** ......... Lunar Orbital Survey System [*NASA*] (KSC)
**Loss & Dam Rev** ... Loss and Damage Review [*A publication*] (DLA)
**Loss Pre** ..... Loss Prevention [*A publication*]
**Loss Prev** ... Loss Prevention: A CEP Technical Manual [*A publication*]
**Loss Sec Reg** ... Loss' Security Regulations [*A publication*] (DLA)
**LOSSYS**.... Landing Observer Signal System
**LOST**......... Law of the Sea Treaty (MCD)
**LOST**......... Linear One-Step Transition [*Mathematical model for social grouping*]
**LOST**......... Lommel and Steinkopf [*German name for mustard gas, taken from two of the chemists who helped develop it as a chemical warfare agent*]
**LOST**......... Lube Oil Storage Tank (NRCH)
**LOST/A** .... Vessels Lost by Accident, Collision, or Similar Methods [*Navy*]
**LOST/E**..... Vessels Lost through Enemy Action [*Navy*]
**LOSTF** ...... Line-of-Sight Test Fixture
**LOSTFC**.... Line-of-Sight Task Force Communications [*Military*] (CAAL)
**LOSTFCS** ... Line-of-Sight Task Force Communications System [*Military*]
**LOST/P**..... Vessels Lost Due to Weather, Perils of the Sea, or Similar Reasons [*Navy*]
**LOSTW**..... Lostwithiel [*Municipal borough in England*]
**LOT** .......... Large Orbiting Telescope (MCD)
**LOT** .......... Lateral Olfactory Tract
**LOT** .......... Leadership and Organization Development Journal [*A publication*]
**LOT** .......... Left Occipitotransverse [*A fetal position*] [*Obstetrics*]
**LOT** .......... Left Outer Thigh [*Injection site*]
**LOT** .......... Letter of Transmittal (MCD)
**LOT** .......... Life of Type (AFIT)
**LOT** .......... Lift-Off Time [*Aerospace*] (MCD)
**LOT** .......... Light-Off Temperature [*For steady-state combustion*]
**LOT** .......... Light Operated Typewriter
**LOT** .......... Load on Top [*Oil tankers*]
**LOT** .......... Lock on Track
**LOT** .......... Lodestar Energy, Inc. [*Vancouver Stock Exchange symbol*]
**Lot**............. Lotarius Rosario de Cremona [*Deceased, 1227*] [*Authority cited in pre-1607 legal work*] (DSA)
**LOT** .......... Lotio [*Lotion*] [*Pharmacy*]
**LOT** .......... Lotru [*Romania*] [*Seismograph station code, US Geological Survey*] (SEIS)
**LOT** .......... Lower Outer Tube
**LOT** .......... Romeoville, IL [*Location identifier*] [*FAA*] (FAAL)
**LOTADS**... Long-Term Worldwide Air Defense Study [*Army*] (AABC)
**LOTAS**...... Large Optical Tracker - Aerospace
**LOTAWS**.. LASER Obstacle Terrain Avoidance Warning System
**LOTC** ........ London Over-the-Counter Market [*Information service or system*] (IID)
**LOTCIP** .... Long-Term Communications Improvement Plan (NATG)
**LOTE**......... Languages Other than English (ADA)
**LOTE**......... Lesser of Two Evils [*Politics*]
**LOTH R** .... Lotharian Regiment [*Military*] [*British*] (ROG)
**LOTIS** ....... Logical Structure: The Timing and the Sequencing of Synchronous/Asynchronous Machines [*Data processing*] (CSR)
**LOTMP**..... Lowest Temperature [*Meteorology*] (FAAC)
**LOTON**..... Long Tons Discharged or Loaded
**LOTOS**...... Language of Temporal Ordering of Specifications [*Data processing*]
**LOTR** ........ [*The*] Lord of the Rings [*A trilogy*]
**LOTS**......... Land Ownership and Tenure System [*Australia*]
**LOTS**......... Large Overland Transporter System (MCD)
**LOTS**......... Launch Operations Television System
**LOTS**......... LEM [*Lunar Excursion Module*] Optical Tracking System [*NASA*] (KSC)
**LOTS**......... Lighter, Over-the-Shore [*Missions*] [*For air-cushion vehicles*] (RDA)
**LOTS**......... Load over the Side
**LOTS**......... Logistics over the Shore [*Military*]
**LOTS**......... LORAN Operational Training School
**LOTS**......... Lotus Development Corp. [*NASDAQ symbol*] (NQ)
**Lotta Antiparass** ... Lotta Antiparassitaria [*A publication*]
**Lotta Contro Tuberc** ... Lotta Contro la Tubercolosi [*A publication*]
**Lotta Tuberc** ... Lotta Contro la Tubercolosi [*A publication*]
**Lotta Tuberc Mal Polm Soc** ... Lotta Contro la Tubercolosi e le Malattie Polmonari Sociali [*A publication*]
**LOTUS**...... Long-Term Upper Ocean Study
**Lotus Int** .... Lotus International [*A publication*]
**LOTV** ........ Launch Operations and Test Vehicle [*NASA*] (KSC)
**LOTW** ....... Loaded on Trailers or Wagons [*Freight*]
**LOU**........... Letter of Understanding [*Nuclear energy*] (NRCH)
**LOU**........... Louisiana
**LOU**........... Louisville Gas & Electric Co. [*Kentucky*] [*NYSE symbol*] (SPSG)
**LOU**........... Louisville, KY [*Location identifier*] [*FAA*] (FAAL)
**Loughborough Univ Technol Chem Eng J** ... Loughborough University of Technology. Chemical Engineering Journal [*A publication*]
**Loughborough Univ Technol Chem Eng Soc J** ... Loughborough University of Technology. Chemical Engineering Society. Journal [*A publication*]
**Loughborough Univ Technol Dep Transp Technol TT Rep** ... Loughborough University of Technology. Department of Transport Technology. TT Report [*A publication*]
**LOUH** ........ Light Observation Utility Helicopter (NATG)
**Louisiana Ann** ... Louisiana Annual Reports [*A publication*] (DLA)
**Louisiana Ann Rep** ... Louisiana Annual Reports [*A publication*] (DLA)
**Louisiana Geol Surv Bull** ... Louisiana. Geological Survey. Bulletin [*A publication*]
**Louisiana L Rev** ... Louisiana Law Review [*A publication*]
**Louisiana Rep** ... Louisiana Reports [*A publication*] (DLA)
**Louisiana Water Resources Research Inst Bull** ... Louisiana Water Resources Research Institute. Bulletin [*A publication*]
**Louis Rep** ... Louisiana Reports [*A publication*] (DLA)
**Louisville Law** ... Louisville Lawyer [*A publication*]
**Louisville Med** ... Louisville Medicine [*A publication*]
**Louisville Med News** ... Louisville Medical News [*A publication*]
**Louisvl Mg** ... Louisville Magazine [*A publication*]
**Lou Leg N**.. Louisiana Legal News [*A publication*] (DLA)
**Lou LJ**....... Louisiana Law Journal [*New Orleans*] [*A publication*] (DLA)
**Lou L Jour** ... Louisiana Law Journal [*A publication*] (DLA)
**Lou L Rev**... Louisiana Law Review [*A publication*]
**LOUO**........ Limited Official Use Only [*Military*]
**Lou R** ......... Louisiana Reports [*A publication*] (DLA)
**Lou Rep NS** ... Martin's Louisiana Reports, New Series [*A publication*] (DLA)

**Lou Reps**.... Louisiana Reports [*A publication*] (DLA)
**Louvain Stds** ... Louvain Studies [*A publication*]
**Louvain Univ Inst Geol Mem** ... Louvain Universite. Institut Geologique. Memoires [*A publication*]
**Louv Med**... Louvain Medical [*A publication*]
**LouvSt**........ Louvain Studies [*Leuven*] [*A publication*]
**Louv Univ Inst Geol Mem** ... Louvain Universite. Institut Geologique. Memoires [*A publication*]
**LOV**........... Limit of Visibility
**LOV**........... Loss of Vehicle (KSC)
**LOV**........... Loss of Visibility (NASA)
**LOV**........... Lovo [*Sweden*] [*Geomagnetic observatory code*]
**LOV**........... Societe Miniere Louvem, Inc. [*Toronto Stock Exchange symbol*]
**LOVA**........ Low Vulnerability Ammunition [*Military*] (RDA)
**Lov Arb**...... Lovesy on Arbitration [*1867*] [*A publication*] (DLA)
**LOVE**........ Language Organization Voicing Esperanto
**LOVE**........ Linguistics of Visual English [*Sign language system for the hearing impaired*]
**Love Bank** ... Lovesy's Bankruptcy Act [*1869, 1870*] [*A publication*] (DLA)
**LOVISIM** ... Low-Visibility Landing Simulation [*Program*] [*Air Force*]
**LOVV**........ Wien [*Austria*] [*ICAO location identifier*] (ICLI)
**LOW**.......... Launch on Warning [*Missiles*]
**LOW**.......... Laws of War (MCD)
**LOW**.......... Link Orderwire Project
**LOW**.......... Loners on Wheels (EA)
**Low**........... Lowell's District Court Reports [*United States, Massachusetts District*] [*A publication*] (DLA)
**LOW**.......... Lowe's Companies, Inc. [*NYSE symbol*] (SPSG)
**LOW**.......... West Yellowstone, MT [*Location identifier*] [*FAA*] (FAAL)
**LOWBI**...... Low-Birth-Weight Infant [*Obstetrics*]
**Low Can**..... Lower Canada Reports [*A publication*] (DLA)
**Low Can Jur** ... Lower Canada Jurist [*A publication*] (DLA)
**Low Can Jurist** ... Lower Canada Jurist [*A publication*] (DLA)
**Low Can LJ** ... Lower Canada Law Journal [*A publication*] (DLA)
**Low Can R** ... Lower Canada Reports [*A publication*] (DLA)
**Low Can Rep** ... Lower Canada Reports [*A publication*] (DLA)
**Low Can Rep SQ** ... Lower Canada Seignorial Questions Reports [*A publication*] (DLA)
**Low Count H** ... Low Countries History. Yearbook [*Acta Historiae Neerlandicae*] [*A publication*]
**Low C Seign** ... Lower Canada Seignorial Questions Reports [*A publication*] (DLA)
**Low Dec (F)** ... Lowell's Decisions [*A publication*] (DLA)
**Low Dis**...... Lowell's District Court Reports [*United States, Massachusetts District*] [*A publication*] (DLA)
**Low-E**......... Low-Elevation (CAAL)
**LOW-E**...... Low-Emissivity [*Glass*]
**Lowell**........ Lowell's District Court Reports [*United States, Massachusetts District*] [*A publication*] (DLA)
**Lower Can Jur** ... Lower Canada Jurist [*A publication*] (DLA)
**Lower Can SQ** ... Lower Canada Seignorial Questions Reports [*A publication*] (DLA)
**Lower Ct Dec** ... Ohio Lower Court Decisions [*A publication*] (DLA)
**LOWFAR** ... Low-Frequency Analysis and Recording (MCD)
**LOWG**....... Graz [*Austria*] [*ICAO location identifier*] (ICLI)
**LOWG**....... Landing Operations Working Group [*NASA*] (NASA)
**LOWI**........ Innsbruck [*Austria*] [*ICAO location identifier*] (ICLI)
**LOWK**....... Klagenfurt [*Austria*] [*ICAO location identifier*] (ICLI)
**LOWL**....... Linz [*Austria*] [*ICAO location identifier*] (ICLI)
**LOWL**....... Low-Level Language [*Computer programming*]
**Low-Level Radioact Waste Technol Newsl** ... Low-Level Radioactive Waste Technology Newsletter [*A publication*]
**LOWM**...... Wien [*Austria*] [*ICAO location identifier*] (ICLI)
**Lownd Av**... Lowndes' General Average [*10th ed.*] [*1975*] [*A publication*] (DLA)
**Lownd Col** ... Lowndes on Collisions at Sea [*A publication*] (DLA)
**Lownd Cop** ... Lowndes on Copyright [*A publication*] (DLA)
**Lowndes & M** ... Lowndes and Maxwell's English Bail Court Reports [*1852-54*] [*A publication*] (DLA)
**Lowndes & M (Eng)** ... Lowndes and Maxwell's English Bail Court Reports [*1852-54*] [*A publication*] (DLA)
**Lowndes M & P** ... Lowndes, Maxwell, and Pollock's English Bail Court Reports [*1850-51*] [*A publication*] (DLA)
**Lownd Ins**.. Lowndes on Insurance [*A publication*] (DLA)
**Lownd Leg** ... Lowndes on Legacies [*A publication*] (DLA)
**Lownd & M** ... Lowndes and Maxwell's English Bail Court Reports [*1852-54*] [*A publication*] (DLA)
**Lownd M & P** ... Lowndes, Maxwell, and Pollock's English Bail Court Reports [*1850-51*] [*A publication*] (DLA)
**LownInST** ... P. W. Lown Institute. Brandeis University. Studies and Texts (BJA)
**Lown Leg** ... Lowndes on Legacies [*A publication*] (DLA)
**Lown & M** ... Lowndes and Maxwell's English Bail Court Reports [*1852-54*] [*A publication*] (DLA)
**Lown M & P** ... Lowndes, Maxwell, and Pollock's English Bail Court Reports [*1850-51*] [*A publication*] (DLA)
**Low Pay Bull** ... Low Pay Bulletin [*A publication*]
**Low Pay Rev** ... Low Pay Review [*A publication*]
**Low Pr Code** ... Lower Provinces Code [*India*] [*A publication*] (DLA)
**LOWS**........ Salzburg [*Austria*] [*ICAO location identifier*] (ICLI)
**Low Temp Phys (Kiev)** ... Low Temperature Physics (Kiev) [*A publication*]
**Low Temp Res Stn (Camb) Annu Rep** ... Low Temperature Research Station (Cambridge). Annual Report [*A publication*]
**Low Temp Sci Ser A** ... Low Temperature Science. Series A. Physical Sciences [*A publication*]
**Low Temp Sci Ser B Biol Sci** ... Low Temperature Science. Series B. Biological Sciences [*A publication*]
**LOWW**...... Wien/Schwechat [*Austria*] [*ICAO location identifier*] (ICLI)
**LOWZ**....... Zell Am See [*Austria*] [*ICAO location identifier*] (ICLI)
**LOX**.......... Liquid Oxygen [*Also,* $LO_2$
***LO-X***.......... *Low Thermal Expansion [Synthetic ceramic]*
**LOXA**........ Aigen/Ennstal [*Austria*] [*ICAO location identifier*] (ICLI)
**LOXAT**...... Lowest Temperature Exceeded for All Time [*Meteorology*] (FAAC)
**LOXFM**..... Lowest Temperature Exceeded for the Month [*Meteorology*] (FAAC)
**LOXG**........ Graz [*Austria*] [*ICAO location identifier*] (ICLI)
**LOXK**........ Klagenfurt [*Austria*] [*ICAO location identifier*] (ICLI)
**LOXL**........ Horsching [*Austria*] [*ICAO location identifier*] (ICLI)
**LOX/LH**.... Liquid Oxygen and Liquid Hydrogen
**LOXN**........ Wiener Neustadt [*Austria*] [*ICAO location identifier*] (ICLI)
**Lox-PLD**.... Loxoseles reclusus - Phospholipase D [*An enzyme*]
**LOXS**........ Schwaz, Tirol [*Austria*] [*ICAO location identifier*] (ICLI)
**LOXSE**....... Lowest Temperature Exceeded So Early [*Meteorology*] (FAAC)
**LOXSL**...... Lowest Temperature Exceeded So Late [*Meteorology*] (FAAC)
**LOXT**........ Langenlebarn [*Austria*] [*ICAO location identifier*] (ICLI)
**LOXT**........ Large Orbital X-Ray Telescope [*NASA*]
**LOXZ**........ Zeltweg [*Austria*] [*ICAO location identifier*] (ICLI)
**LOY**.......... Loyalty (AABC)
**LOY**.......... Loyola - Notre Dame Library, Inc., Baltimore, MD [*OCLC symbol*] (OCLC)
**LOYC**........ Loyola Capital Corp. [*Baltimore, MD*] [*NASDAQ symbol*] (NQ)
**Loy Chi LJ** ... Loyola University of Chicago. Law Journal [*A publication*]
**Loy Con Prot J** ... Loyola Consumer Protection Journal [*Los Angeles*] [*A publication*] (DLA)
**Loy Dig**...... Loyola Digest [*A publication*] (DLA)
**Loy LA Int'l and Comp L Ann** ... Loyola of Los Angeles. International and Comparative Law Annual [*A publication*]
**Loy LA Int'l & Comp LJ** ... Loyola of Los Angeles. International and Comparative Law Journal [*A publication*]
**Loy LA L Rev** ... Loyola University of Los Angeles [*later, Loyola Marymount University*]. Law Review [*A publication*]
**Loy Law**..... Loyola Lawyer [*A publication*] (DLA)
**Loy LJ**........ Loyola Law Journal [*New Orleans*] [*1920-32*] [*A publication*] (DLA)
**Loy LR**....... Loyola Law Review [*A publication*]
**Loy L Rev**... Loyola Law Review [*A publication*]
**Loy LR LA** ... Loyola of Los Angeles. Law Review [*A publication*]
**Loyola Dig** ... Loyola Digest [*A publication*] (DLA)
**Loyola LJ**... Loyola Law Journal [*A publication*] (DLA)
**Loyola Los A L Rev** ... Loyola of Los Angeles. Law Review [*A publication*]
**Loyola of Los Angeles L Rev** ... Loyola of Los Angeles. Law Review [*A publication*]
**Loyola Los Ang Int'l & Comp L Ann** ... Loyola of Los Angeles. International and Comparative Law Annual [*A publication*]
**Loyola L Rev** ... Loyola Law Review [*A publication*]
**Loyola U Chi LJ** ... Loyola University of Chicago. Law Journal [*A publication*]
**Loyola ULA L Rev** ... Loyola University of Los Angeles [*later, Loyola Marymount University*]. Law Review [*A publication*]
**Loyola ULJ (Chicago)** ... Loyola University Law Journal (Chicago) [*A publication*]
**Loyola ULJ (Chicago)** ... Loyola University. Law Review (Chicago) [*A publication*] (DLA)
**Loyola UL Rev (LA)** ... Loyola University of Los Angeles [*later, Loyola Marymount University*]. Law Review [*A publication*]
**Loyola Univ of Chicago LJ** ... Loyola University of Chicago. Law Journal [*A publication*]
**Loyola Univ L Rev** ... Loyola University. Law Review [*Chicago*] [*A publication*] (DLA)
**Loy R**......... Loyola Law Review [*A publication*]
**Loy U Chi LJ** ... Loyola University of Chicago. Law Journal [*A publication*]
**LOZ**.......... Liquid Ozone
**LOZ**.......... London [*Kentucky*] [*Airport symbol*] (OAG)
**LOZ**.......... Lovozero [*USSR*] [*Geomagnetic observatory code*]
**Lozar Vinar** ... Lozarstvo Vinarstvo [*A publication*]
**LP**............. Laboratory Procedure
**LP**............. Labour Party of South Africa [*Political party*] (PPW)
**L/P**............ Lactate/Pyruvate [*Ratio*]
**LP**............. Ladyship [*or Lordship*]
**LP**............. Laminated Polyethylene Film
**LP**............. Lamp [*Automotive engineering*]
**LP**............. Land Plane
**LP**............. Landing Point [*British military*] (DMA)
**LP**............. Large-Paper Edition [*of a book*]
**LP**............. Large Particle
**LP**............. Large Post
**LP**............. Laryngeal Pharyngeal [*Medicine*]
**LP**............. Last Paid [*Military*]
**LP**............. Last Performance

**LP** ............ Latent Period [*Physiology*]
**LP** ............ Lateral Pyloric [*Neuron*]
**LP** ............ Launch Pad (KSC)
**LP** ............ Launch Platform
**LP** ............ Launching Platoon [*Army*]
**LP** ............ Laureate of Philosophy
**LP** ............ Law Pamphlet (ROG)
**LP** ............ Lay Preacher
**LP** ............ Leadership Project [*Defunct*] (EA)
**LP** ............ Leaf Protein [*Food industry*]
**LP** ............ Leathery Pocket [*of pineapple*]
**LP** ............ Left Pectoral Fin [*Fish anatomy*]
**LP** ............ Left Traffic Pattern [*Aviation*] (FAAC)
**LP** ............ Legal Process [*British*]
**LP** ............ Lempira [*Monetary unit*] [*Honduras*]
**LP** ............ Lesnaja Promyslennost [*A publication*]
**LP** ............ Lesnicka Prace [*A publication*]
**Lp** ............ Letopis [*A publication*]
**LP** ............ Lettering Piece (ROG)
**L/P** ............ Letterpress (ADA)
**LP** ............ Letters Patent (ROG)
**LP** ............ Leucine Aminopeptidase [*Also, LA, LAP*] [*An enzyme*]
**LP** ............ Leucocyte Pyrogen [*Immunology*]
**LP** ............ Leukocyte-Poor [*Hematology*]
**LP** ............ Liberal Party [*Canada*] (PPW)
**LP** ............ Liberator Party [*Guyana*] [*Political party*] (PPW)
**LP** ............ Libertarian Party (EA)
**LP** ............ Library of Parliament [*Canada*]
**LP** ............ Library of Philosophy [*A publication*]
**L/P** ............ Life Policy [*Insurance*]
**LP** ............ Light Pen
**LP** ............ Light Perception [*Ophthalmology*]
**LP** ............ Light Pulse [*Embryology*]
**LP** ............ Lightproof [*Technical drawings*]
**LP** ............ Limited Partnership
**LP** ............ Limited Planning (MCD)
**LP** ............ Limited Procurement
**LP** ............ Limited Production (AABC)
**LP** ............ Limited Proprietorship [*Business term*]
**LP** ............ Limp [*Binding*] [*Publishing*]
**lp** ............ Line Pair [*Philately*]
**LP** ............ Line Printer [*Data processing*]
**LP** ............ Linear Phase
**LP** ............ Linear Polarization
**LP** ............ Linear Prediction [*Data processing*]
**LP** ............ Linear Programming [*Data processing*]
**LP** ............ Linen Press (ADA)
**LP** ............ Lingua Portuguesa [*A publication*]
**LP** ............ Lingua Posnaniensis [*A publication*]
**LP** ............ Linguistic Problems
**LP** ............ Linguopulpal [*Dentistry*]
**LP** ............ Linker Polypeptide [*Biochemistry*]
**Lp** ............ Lipoprotein [*Biochemistry*]
**LP** ............ Liquefied Petroleum [*Gas*]
**LP** ............ Liquid Phase [*Chemistry*]
**LP** ............ Liquid Propane (FAAC)
**LP** ............ Liquid Propellant
**LP** ............ Liquid Propellant Missile
**LP** ............ Liquidity Preference [*Economics*]
**LP** ............ List Processor [*Standard programming language*] [*1958*] [*Data processing*] (BUR)
**LP** ............ List of Publications [*National Institute of Standards and Technology*]
**LP** ............ Listening Post
**LP** ............ Lists of Parts (NATG)
**LP** ............ Literature and Psychology [*A publication*]
**L & P** ............ Literature and Psychology [*A publication*]
**LP** ............ Litho-Printer Magazine [*A publication*] [*British*]
**LP** ............ Litter Patient
**LP** ............ Livens Projector [*Military*]
**LP** ............ Liver Protein [*Medicine*]
**LP** ............ Load Point (BUR)
**LP** ............ Local Pastors [*British*]
**LP** ............ Local Procurement [*Military*]
**LP** ............ Local Purchase (AFM)
**LP** ............ Locating Point [*Optical tooling*]
**L of P** ............ Lodge of Perfection [*Freemasonry*] (DAS)
**LP** ............ Lodge-Pole Pine [*Utility pole*] [*Telecommunications*] (TEL)
**LP** ............ Loewenthal Papers [*Shanghai/Washington, DC*] [*A publication*] (BJA)
**LP** ............ Log Periodic [*Antenna*] (NATG)
**LP** ............ Logic Probe
**LP** ............ Lollipop Power [*An association*] (EA)
**LP** ............ London Particular [*Marsala*]
**LP** ............ Long-Pass [*Absorption cell*]
**LP** ............ Long Period
**LP** ............ Long Persistence
**LP** ............ Long Picot
**LP** ............ Long Playing [*Phonograph record*]
**LP** ............ Long Position [*Investment term*]
**LP** ............ Long Primer
**LP** ............ Long Provost
**LP** ............ Longest Path
**LP** ............ Longitudinal Parity [*Telecommunications*] (TEL)
**LP** ............ Loop [*Knitting*]
**LP** ............ Lord President of the Court of Session, Scotland (DLA)
**LP** ............ Lord Provost [*British*]
**LP** ............ Lorentz-Polarization [*Optics*]
**LP** ............ Losing Pitcher [*Baseball*]
**LP** ............ Loss of Pay [*Court-martial sentence*] [*Marine Corps*]
**LP** ............ Love Project (EA)
**LP** ............ Low Pass [*Electronics*]
**LP** ............ Low Performance
**LP** ............ Low Point
**LP** ............ Low Power [*Microscopy*]
**LP** ............ Low Pressure
**LP** ............ Low-Pressure Cylinder [*Especially, a locomotive cylinder*]
**LP** ............ Low Protein [*Nutrition*]
**LP** ............ Lower Peninsula [*Michigan*]
**LP** ............ Lumbar Puncture [*Medicine*]
**L/P** ............ Lymphocyte to Polymorph Ratio [*Hematology*]
**LP** ............ Lythway Press [*British*]
**LP** ............ Popular Concerts [*Public-performance tariff class*] [*British*]
**ɫP** ............ Pounds Palestine [*Monetary unit*]
**LP** ............ Societe Air Alpes [*France*] [*ICAO designator*] (FAAC)
**LP-28** ............ Ligas Populares de 28 de Febrero [*February 28 Popular Leagues*] [*El Salvador*] (PD)
**LPA** ............ Amphibious Transport [*Navy ship symbol*]
**LPA** ............ La Plata [*Argentina*] [*Seismograph station code, US Geological Survey*] (SEIS)
**LPA** ............ La Posada Airways [*Texas*] (FAAC)
**LPA** ............ Labor Policy Association (EA)
**LPA** ............ Las Palmas [*Canary Islands*] [*Airport symbol*] (OAG)
**LPA** ............ LASER Printer Adapter
**LPA** ............ Launch Phase Analyst
**LPA** ............ Lauric [*or Lauroyl or Lauryl*] Isopropanolamide [*Also, LIPA*] [*Organic chemistry*]
**LPA** ............ Leaky Pipe Antenna
**LPA** ............ Left Pulmonary Artery [*Anatomy*]
**LPA** ............ Light Pulser Array
**LPA** ............ Limited Period Appointment [*Short-term employment*] [*British*]
**LPA** ............ Limited Purpose Agency (OICC)
**LPA** ............ Linear Power Amplifier
**LPA** ............ Link Pack Area [*Data processing*] (MCD)
**LpA** ............ Lipoprotein A [*Biochemistry*]
**LPA** ............ Liquid Propellant Analysis
**LPA** ............ Literature Primers [*A publication*]
**LPA** ............ Lithium Perchlorate Ammoniate [*Inorganic chemistry*]
**LPA** ............ Little People of America (EA)
**LPA** ............ Local Planning Assistance (OICC)
**LPA** ............ Local Planning Authority [*British*] (DCTA)
**LPA** ............ Local Public Agency
**L & PA** ............ Lodging and Pay Allowance [*British military*] (DMA)
**LPA** ............ Log Periodic Antenna
**LPA** ............ Low-Power Amplifier (CET)
**LPA** ............ Low-Pressure Alarm (IEEE)
**LPA** ............ Lysophosphatidic Acid [*Biochemistry*]
**LPA** ............ Sky West, Inc. [*Page, AZ*] [*FAA designator*] (FAAC)
**LPAA** ............ League of Pace Amendment Advocates (EA)
**LPAA** ............ Log Periodic Array Antenna
**LPAC** ............ Labor Policy Advisory Committee for Multilateral Trade Negotiations [*Terminated, 1980*] (EGAO)
**LPAC** ............ Lancer Pacific, Inc. [*Carlsbad, CA*] [*NASDAQ symbol*] (NQ)
**LPAC** ............ Libertarian Party Abolitionist Caucus (EA)
**L Paed (B)** ... Lexikon fuer Paedagogik (Bern) [*A publication*]
**L Paed (F)** ... Lexikon fuer Paedagogik (Freiburg) [*A publication*]
**LPAI** ............ La Petite Academy, Incorporated [*NASDAQ symbol*] (NQ)
**LPAI** ............ Ligue Populaire Africaine pour l'Independance [*African People's League for Independence*] [*Djibouti*]
**L-PAM** ............ L-Phenylalanine Mustard [*Melphalan*] [*Also, A, M, MPH, MPL*] [*Antineoplastic drug*]
**LPAM** ............ Lisboa [*Portugal*] [*ICAO location identifier*] (ICLI)
**LPAR** ............ Alverca [*Portugal*] [*ICAO location identifier*] (ICLI)
**LPAR** ............ Large Phased-Array RADAR
**LPARM** ............ Liquid Propellant Applied Research Motor
**L/PAT** ............ Letters Patent (ROG)
**LPAT** ............ Lopat Industries, Inc. [*Wanamassa, NJ*] [*NASDAQ symbol*] (NQ)
**LPAV** ............ Aveiro [*Portugal*] [*ICAO location identifier*] (ICLI)
**LPAZ** ............ Santa Maria, Santa Maria Island [*Portugal*] [*ICAO location identifier*] (ICLI)
**LPB** ............ La Paz [*Bolivia*] [*Geomagnetic observatory code*]
**LPB** ............ La Paz [*Bolivia*] [*Airport symbol*] (OAG)
**LPB** ............ La Paz [*Bolivia*] [*Seismograph station code, US Geological Survey*] (SEIS)
**LPB** ............ Laser and Particle Beams [*A publication*]
**LpB** ............ Lipoprotein B [*Biochemistry*]
**LPB** ............ Loan Policy Board [*of SBA*] [*Abolished, 1965*]
**LPB** ............ Lollipop Power Books (EA)
**LPB** ............ [*The*] Louisiana & Pine Bluff Railway Co. [*AAR code*]
**LPB** ............ Low-Level Penetration Bomb

**LPB** ........... Low-Probability Behavior
**LPB** ........... Lunar and Planetary Bibliography [*Lunar and Planetary Institute*] [*Information service or system*] (IID)
**LPB** ........... Paper Book of Laurence, J., in Lincoln's Inn Library [*A publication*] (DLA)
**LPBA** ......... Lawyer-Pilots Bar Association (EA)
**LPBBA** ...... Log Periodic Broadband Antenna
**LPBE** ......... Beja [*Portugal*] [*ICAO location identifier*] (ICLI)
**LPBE** ......... Linear Poisson-Boltzmann Equation [*Physical chemistry*]
**LPBG** ......... Braganca [*Portugal*] [*ICAO location identifier*] (ICLI)
**LPBJ** ......... Beja [*Portugal*] [*ICAO location identifier*] (ICLI)
**LPBR** ......... Braga [*Portugal*] [*ICAO location identifier*] (ICLI)
**LPBT** ......... Ladies Professional Bowlers Tour (EA)
**LPC** ........... La Cumbre Peak [*California*] [*Seismograph station code, US Geological Survey*] (SEIS)
**LPC** ........... Laboratory Pulse Compression
**LPC** ........... Landmarks Preservation Commission [*New York City*]
**LPC** ........... Launch Pod Container [*General Support Rocket System*] (MCD)
**LPC** ........... Laurylpyridinium Chloride [*Also, DPC*] [*Organic chemistry*]
**LPC** ........... Leader Preparation Course
**LPC** ........... Leaf Protein Concentrate [*Food industry*]
**LPC** ........... Least-Preferred Co-Worker [*Management term*]
**LPC** ........... Leather Personnel Carriers [*i.e., boots*] [*Slang*] [*Army*]
**LPC** ........... Leukocyte Particle Counter [*Instrumentation*]
**LPC** ........... Library Practice Certificate [*Australia*] (ADA)
**LPC** ........... Light Patrol Car [*British*]
**LPC** ........... Linear Power Controller
**LPC** ........... Linear Predictive Coding [*Digital coding technique*] [*Telecommunications*]
**LPC** ........... Link Priority Change [*NASA*] (KSC)
**LpC** ........... Lipoprotein C [*Biochemistry*]
**LPC** ........... Livestock Publications Council (EA)
**LPC** ........... Lockheed Propulsion Company [*Division of Lockheed Aircraft Corp.*] (KSC)
**LPC** ........... Lompoc, CA [*Location identifier*] [*FAA*] (FAAL)
**LPC** ........... Loop-Control [*Relay*] (IEEE)
**LPC** ........... Loop Preparation Cask [*Nuclear energy*] (NRCH)
**LPC** ........... Lord President's Committee [*British*]
**LPC** ........... Lords of the Privy Council Lower Provinces Code [*India*] [*A publication*] (DLA)
**LPC** ........... Low-Power Counter
**LPC** ........... Low-Pressure Chamber Technician [*Navy*]
**LPC** ........... Low-Pressure Composite
**LPC** ........... Low-Pressure Compressor
**LPC** ........... Lower Pump Cubicle (IEEE)
**LPC** ........... Lumped-Parameter Calorimeter [*Heat measure*]
**LPC** ........... Lysophosphatidylcholine [*Also, Lyso-PC*] [*Biochemistry*]
**LPCA** ......... Lunar Pyrotechnic Control Assembly [*Aerospace*]
**LPCAT** ...... Laboratory for Pest Control Application Technology [*Ohio State University*] [*Research center*] (RCD)
**LPCC** ......... Library Practice Certificate Course [*Australia*]
**LPCC** ......... Low-Pressure Combustion Chamber
**LPCG** ......... LASER Planning and Coordination Group [*Energy Research and Development Administration*]
**LPCH** ......... Chaves [*Portugal*] [*ICAO location identifier*] (ICLI)
**LPCI** .......... Low-Pressure Coolant Injection [*Nuclear energy*] (NRCH)
**LPCIS** ........ Low-Pressure Coolant Injection System [*Nuclear energy*] (NRCH)
**LPCL** ......... Laboratory Pulse Compression Loop
**LPCM** ........ Linear Phase Code Modulation
**LPCO** ......... Coimbra [*Portugal*] [*ICAO location identifier*] (ICLI)
**LPCP** ......... Launcher Preparation Control Panel
**LPCRS** ....... Low-Pressure Coolant Recirculation System [*Nuclear energy*] (IEEE)
**LPCS** ......... Cascais [*Portugal*] [*ICAO location identifier*] (ICLI)
**LPCS** ......... Laterally to the Pedunculus Cerebellaris Superior [*Medicine*]
**LPCS** ......... Local Post Collectors Society (EA)
**LPCS** ......... Low-Pressure Core Spray System [*Nuclear energy*] (NRCH)
**LPCV** ......... Covilha [*Portugal*] [*ICAO location identifier*] (ICLI)
**LPCVD** ...... Liquid Phase Chemical Vapor Deposition [*Photovoltaic energy systems*]
**LPCVD** ...... Low-Pressure Chemical Vapor Deposition [*Semiconductor technology*]
**LP-CW** ....... Long Pulse - Continuous Wave (NG)
**LPD** ........... Amphibious Transport Dock [*Landing Platform, Dock*] [*Navy ship symbol*]
**LPD** ........... La Pedrera [*Colombia*] [*Airport symbol*] (OAG)
**LPD** ........... Landing Platform, Dock
**LPD** ........... Landing Point Designator [*Apollo*] [*NASA*]
**LPD** ........... Language Processing and Debugging [*Data processing*] (BUR)
**LPD** ........... Laredo Petroleums [*Vancouver Stock Exchange symbol*]
**LPD** ........... LASER Polarization Detector
**LPD** ........... Launch Platform Detected [*Navy*] (CAAL)
**LPD** ........... Launch Point Determination
**LPD** ........... Launch Procedure Document [*NASA*] (KSC)
**LPD** ........... Least Perceptible Difference [*Psychology*]
**LPD** ........... Lighting-Power Density
**LPD** ........... Linear Power Density [*Nuclear energy*] (NRCH)
**LpD** ........... Lipoprotein D [*Biochemistry*]
**LPD** ........... Liquid-Protein Diet
**LPD** ........... Liters per Day (KSC)
**LPD** ........... Local Power Density (NRCH)
**LPD** ........... Local Procurement Direct [*Military*]
**LPD** ........... Log Periodic Dipole
**LPD** ........... Low-Performance Drone
**LPD** ........... Low Period Dipole
**LPD** ........... Low-Power Difference (IEEE)
**LPD** ........... Low-Pressure Difference (IEEE)
**LPD** ........... Low Protein Diet
**LPD** ........... Lymphoproliferative Disease [*Oncology*]
**LPDA** ......... Linear Photodiode Array [*Instrumentation*]
**LPDA** ......... Log Periodic Dipole Antenna [*Military*] (CAAL)
**LPDA** ......... Log Periodic Dipole Array
**LPDC** ......... LASER Plasmadynamic Converter
**LPDC** ......... London Parcels Delivery Company
**LpDH** ......... Lysopine Dehydrogenase [*An enzyme*]
**LPDM** ........ List of Physical Dimensions (NASA)
**LPDR** ......... Lao People's Democratic Republic
**LPDS** ......... Lipoprotein Deficient Human Serum
**LPDX** ......... Landing Platform Dock
**LPE** ........... Launch Preparation Equipment (AABC)
**LPE** ........... Limited Paperback Editions
**LPE** ........... Linear Parameter Estimation [*Physical chemistry*]
**LPE** ........... Linear Polyethylene [*Organic chemistry*]
**LpE** ........... Lipoprotein E [*Biochemistry*]
**LPE** ........... Lipoprotein Electrophoresis [*Biochemistry*]
**LPE** ........... Liquid Phase Epitaxy [*Magnetic film*]
**LPE** ........... London Press Exchange
**LPE** ........... Loop Preparation Equipment [*Nuclear energy*] (NRCH)
**LPE** ........... Lunar and Planetary Ephemerides Assembly [*Space Flight Operations Facility, NASA*]
**LPE** ........... Lysophosphatidylethanolamine [*Biochemistry*]
**LPEA** ......... Luis Palau Evangelistic Association (EA)
**LPEC** ......... Launch Preparation Equipment Compartment (AABC)
**LPEO** ......... Local Public Employment Office
**LPEP** ......... Le Peep Restaurants, Inc. [*Denver, CO*] [*NASDAQ symbol*] (NQ)
**LPer** ........... Literature in Performance [*A publication*]
**LPerc** ......... Light Perception [*Ophthalmology*]
**LPES** ......... Launch Preparation Equipment Set (AABC)
**LPEV** ......... Evora [*Portugal*] [*ICAO location identifier*] (ICLI)
**LPEV** ......... Launch Preparation Equipment Vault (MCD)
**LPF** ........... Landsing Pacific Fund [*AMEX symbol*] (CTT)
**LPF** ........... Le Pertre [*France*] [*Seismograph station code, US Geological Survey*] (SEIS)
**LPF** ........... Left Posterior Fascicle [*Anatomy*]
**LPF** ........... Leukocytosis-Promoting Factor [*Hematology*]
**LPF** ........... Life Probability Function
**LPF** ........... Light Patrol Frigate (ADA)
**LPF** ........... Liquid Pressure Filter
**LPF** ........... Logically Passive Function
**LPF** ........... Low-Pass Filter [*Electronics*]
**LPF** ........... Low-Power Field [*Microscopy*]
**LPF** ........... Low-Profile Flange
**LPF** ........... Lowest Possible Airfare
**LPF** ........... Lutheran Peace Fellowship (EA)
**LPF** ........... Pop Festivals [*Public-performance tariff class*] [*British*]
**LPFA** ......... London Potato Futures Association [*London Stock Exchange*]
**LPFB** ......... Left Posterior Fascicular Block [*Cardiology*]
**LPFL** ......... Flores, Flores Island [*Portugal*] [*ICAO location identifier*] (ICLI)
**LPFL** ......... Lowpass Filter (MSA)
**LPFM** ........ Low-Powered Fan Marker (MSA)
**LPFMRD** .. Lingvisticheskie Problemy Funktsional'nogo Modelirovaniia Rechevoi Deiatel'nosti [*A publication*]
**LPFO** ......... London Procurement Field Office
**LPFP** ......... Low-Pressure Fuel Pump (KSC)
**LPFR** ......... Faro [*Portugal*] [*ICAO location identifier*] (ICLI)
**LPFR** ......... Liquid Phase Flow Reactor (KSC)
**LPFRT** ....... Limited Preliminary Flight Rating Test
**LPFT** ......... Low-Pressure Fuel Turbopump
**LPFTP** ....... Low-Pressure Fuel Turbopump (NASA)
**LPFU** ......... Funchal, Madeira Island [*Portugal*] [*ICAO location identifier*] (ICLI)
**LPG** ........... La Plata [*Argentina*] [*Airport symbol*] (OAG)
**LPG** ........... Lake Ponask Gold Corp. [*Toronto Stock Exchange symbol*]
**LPG** ........... Landpachtgesetz [*A publication*]
**LPG** ........... Langage de Programmation et de Gestion [*French computer language*] (IEEE)
**LPG** ........... Lapping [*Electricity*]
**LPG** ........... Last Page Generator (NASA)
**LPG** ........... Launch Preparations Group [*NASA*]
**LPG** ........... Licentiate of the Physicians Guild [*British*]
**LPG** ........... Liquefied Petroleum Gas
**LPG** ........... Liquid Propane Gas
**LPG** ........... Liquid Propellant Gun (NASA)
**LPG** ........... Long Path Gas [*Spectroscopy*]
**LPG** ........... Lousy Paying Guest [*Hotel slang*]
**LPG** ........... Low-Pressure Gas (NRCH)
**LPG** ........... Petrolane Partners LP [*NYSE symbol*] (SPSG)
**LPGA** ......... Ladies Professional Golf Association (EA)

**LPGA**......... Living Plant Growers Association (EA)
**LPGA**......... Louisiana Pecan Growers' Association (EA)
**LPGE**......... LEM [*Lunar Excursion Module*] Partial Guidance Equipment [*NASA*] (KSC)
**LPGG**......... Liquid Propellant Gas Generator
**LPGITA**.... Liquefied Petroleum Gas Industry Technical Association [*British*]
**LPGITC**..... Liquified Petroleum Gas Industry Technical Committee
**LPGR**......... Graciosa, Graciosa Island [*Portugal*] [*ICAO location identifier*] (ICLI)
**LPGS**......... Liquid Pathway Generic Study [*Nuclear energy*] (NRCH)
**LPGS**......... Liquified Petroleum Gas Report [*American Petroleum Institute*] [*Database*]
**LPH**........... Amphibious Assault Ship (Landing Platform, Helicopter) [*Navy symbol*]
**LPH**........... Laboratory of Physiological Hygiene [*University of Minnesota*] [*Research center*] (RCD)
**LPH**........... Landing Personnel Helicopter [*British*] (NATG)
**LPh**........... Late Phoenician (BJA)
**LPH**........... Lee Pharmaceuticals [*AMEX symbol*] (SPSG)
**LPH**........... Left Posterior Hemiblock [*Cardiology*]
**LPH**........... Legrest Pin Handle
**LPh**........... Licentiate of Philosophy
**LPH**........... Lines per Hour [*Printing*]
**LPH**........... Lipotropin Hormone [*Endocrinology*]
**LPH**........... Liters per Hour (KSC)
**LPH**........... Lochgilphead [*Scotland*] [*Airport symbol*] (OAG)
**LPHB**......... Low-Pressure Heating Boiler
**LPHLA**....... Laporan. Lembaga Penelitian Hasil Hutan [*A publication*]
**LPHLDR**... Lampholder
**LPHR**......... Horta, Faial Island [*Portugal*] [*ICAO location identifier*] (ICLI)
**LPHS**......... Lunar and Planetary Horizon Scanner [*Aerospace*]
**LPI**............ Colorado Springs, CO [*Location identifier*] [*FAA*] (FAAL)
**LPI**............ Latent Photographic Image
**LPI**............ Launching Position Indicator
**LPI**............ Law and Policy in International Business [*A publication*]
**LPI**............ Leaf Plastochron Index [*Botany*]
**LPI**............ Learning Preference Inventory
**LPI**............ Lightning Protection Institute (EA)
**LPI**............ Lines per Inch [*Printing*]
**LPI**............ Linkoeping [*Sweden*] [*Airport symbol*] (OAG)
**LPI**............ Linus Pauling Institute of Science and Medicine [*Research center*] (RCD)
**LPI**............ Lomond Publications, Inc. [*Telecommunications service*] (TSSD)
**LPI**............ Longitudinally Applied Paper Insulation [*Telecommunications*] (TEL)
**LPI**............ Louisiana Polytechnical Institute
**LPI**............ Low-Power Illuminator (NATG)
**LPI**............ Low-Power Injection [*Nuclear energy*] (NRCH)
**LPI**............ Low-Pressure Index
**LPI**............ Low-Pressure Injection [*Nuclear energy*] (NRCH)
**LPI**............ Low Probability of Intercept (NVT)
**LPI**............ Low Probability of Interest
**LPI**............ Lunar and Planetary Institute [*University Space Research Association*] [*Research center*] (RCD)
**LPIA**.......... Label Printing Industries of America (EA)
**LPIA**.......... Liquid Propellant Information Agency [*Johns Hopkins Univeristy*]
**LPIBSS**...... Lunar and Planetary Institute Bibliographic Search Service [*University Space Research Association*] [*Information service or system*] (IID)
**LPiC**........... Central Louisiana State Hospital, Medical Library, Pineville, LA [*Library symbol*] [*Library of Congress*] (LCLS)
**LPI Contribution**... Lunar and Planetary Institute. Contribution [*A publication*]
**LPID**.......... Logical Page Identifier (BUR)
**LPiL**........... Louisiana College, Pineville, LA [*Library symbol*] [*Library of Congress*] (LCLS)
**LPIN**.......... Espinho [*Portugal*] [*ICAO location identifier*] (ICLI)
**LPIR**.......... Limited Partnership Investment Review [*Information service or system*] (EISS)
**LPIR**.......... Low-Probability Intercept RADAR
**LPIS**.......... Low-Pressure Injection System [*Nuclear energy*] (NRCH)
**LPISS**........ Low-Power Illuminator Signal Source (MCD)
**LPI Technical Report**... Lunar and Planetary Institute. Technical Report [*A publication*]
**LPIU**.......... Lithographers and Photoengravers International Union [*Later, Graphic Arts International Union*]
**LPJF**.......... Leiria [*Portugal*] [*ICAO location identifier*] (ICLI)
**LPJO**.......... Alijo [*Portugal*] [*ICAO location identifier*] (ICLI)
**LPK**........... Lao Pen Kang [*Laotian Neutralist Party*] (CINC)
**LPKCMLPCC**... License Plate, Key Chain, and Mini License Plate Collectors Club (EA)
**LPL**............ Laborers Political League (EA)
**LPL**............ Labour Protection League [*A union*] [*British*]
**LPL**............ Lamina Propria Lymphocyte [*Hematology*]
**LPL**............ LASER-Pumped-LASER
**LPL**............ Lawton Public Library, Lawton, OK [*OCLC symbol*] (OCLC)
**LPL**............ Lease-A-Plane International [*Northbrook, IL*] [*FAA designator*] (FAAC)
**LPL**............ Lethbridge Public Library [*UTLAS symbol*]
**LPL**............ Lightproof Louver [*Technical drawings*]
**LPL**............ Linear Programming Language [*Intertechnique*] [*French*] [*Data processing*] (BUR)
**LPL**............ Lipoprotein Lipase [*An enzyme*]
**LPL**............ List Processing Language [*Data processing*] (IEEE)
**LPL**............ Liverpool [*England*] [*Airport symbol*] (OAG)
**LPL**............ LM [*Lunar Module*] Plan [*NASA*] (KSC)
**LPL**............ Local Processor Link
**LPL**............ Long Pulse LASER
**LPL**............ Louisiana Power & Light Co. [*NYSE symbol*] (SPSG)
**LPL**............ Low Polar Latitude [*Geophysics*]
**LPL**............ Low-Power Logic
**LPL**............ Lunar and Planetary Laboratory [*University of Arizona*] [*Research center*] (MCD)
**LPL**............ Lunar Projects Laboratory
**LPL**............ Lysophospholipase [*An enzyme*]
**LPLA**.......... Lajes, Terceira Island [*Portugal*] [*ICAO location identifier*] (ICLI)
**LPLA**.......... Lao Peoples Liberation Army (CINC)
**LPlaI**.......... Iberville Parish Library, Plaquemine, LA [*Library symbol*] [*Library of Congress*] (LCLS)
**LPLG**.......... Lagos [*Portugal*] [*ICAO location identifier*] (ICLI)
**L Pl G**......... Landesplanungsgesetz [*A publication*]
**LPLG**.......... Left Pleural Ganglion [*Medicine*]
**LPLI**........... LPL Technologies, Inc. [*NASDAQ symbol*] (NQ)
**LPLNG**....... Low-Pressure Liquefied Natural Gases (NRCH)
**LPLP**.......... Language Problems and Language Planning [*A publication*]
**LPLR**.......... Lock Pillar (AAG)
**LPLWS**...... Launch Pad Lightning Warning System [*NASA*] (KSC)
**LPM**........... Lamap [*Vanuatu*] [*Airport symbol*] (OAG)
**LPM**........... Lane Photograph Method
**LPM**........... LASER Phase Macroscope
**LPM**........... Leipziger Messe Journal [*A publication*]
**LPM**........... Licensing Project Manager [*Nuclear energy*] (NRCH)
**LPM**........... Light Pulser Matrix
**LPM**........... Linearly Polarized Mode [*Telecommunications*] (TEL)
**LPM**........... Lines per Minute [*Data processing*]
**LPM**........... Liquid Phase Methanation [*Fuel chemistry*]
**LPM**........... Liters per Minute (MCD)
**LPM**........... Liver Plasma Membrane
**LP & M**...... Liverpool Post and Mercury [*A publication*] (ROG)
**LPM**........... Long Particular [*or Peculiar*] Metre [*Music*]
**LPM**........... Los Pinos Mountain [*New Mexico*] [*Seismograph station code, US Geological Survey*] (SEIS)
**LPM**........... Lunar Payload Module [*Aerospace*] (MCD)
**LPM**........... Lunar Portable Magnetometer [*Apollo*] [*NASA*]
**LPMA**......... Lead Pencil Manufacturers Association [*Later, Pencil Makers Association*] (EA)
**LPMA**......... Loose-Parts-Monitor Assembly [*Nuclear energy*] (NRCH)
**LPMAD**..... Living Personnel Management Authorization Document [*DoD*]
**LPMES**...... Logistics Performance Measurement and Evaluation System (AABC)
**LPMF**......... Monfortinho [*Portugal*] [*ICAO location identifier*] (ICLI)
**LPMG**......... Lisboa [*Portugal*] [*ICAO location identifier*] (ICLI)
**LPMI**.......... Mirandela [*Portugal*] [*ICAO location identifier*] (ICLI)
**LPMR**......... Monte Real [*Portugal*] [*ICAO location identifier*] (ICLI)
**LPM/S**....... Liquid Phase Methanation/Shift Reaction [*Fuel chemistry*]
**LPMS**......... Logistics Program Management System [*Air Force*] (AFIT)
**LPMS**......... Loose-Parts Monitoring System [*Nuclear energy*] (NRCH)
**LPMT**......... Montijo [*Portugal*] [*ICAO location identifier*] (ICLI)
**LPN**........... Licensed Practical Nurse
**LPN**........... Logical Page Number (BUR)
**LPN**........... Long Part Number
**LPN**........... Longview, Portland & Northern Railway Co. [*AAR code*]
**LPN**........... Low-Pass Network [*Electronics*]
**LPN**........... National Federation of Licensed Practical Nurses
**LPNA**......... Lithographers and Printers National Association [*Later, PIA*] (EA)
**LPNGP**...... Low-Pressure Noble Gas Processing (NRCH)
**LPO**........... La Porte [*Indiana*] [*Airport symbol*] (OAG)
**LPO**........... Laramie Project Office [*Laramie, WY*] [*Department of Energy*] (GRD)
**LPO**........... Lateral Preoptic [*Brain anatomy*]
**LPO**........... Le Pouchou [*France*] [*Seismograph station code, US Geological Survey*] (SEIS)
**LPO**........... Liberal Party Organization [*British*]
**LPO**........... Liberale Partei Oesterreichs [*Liberal Party of Austria*] [*Political party*] (PPE)
**LPO**........... Light Perception Only [*Ophthalmology*]
**LPO**........... Linpro Specified Properties SBI [*AMEX symbol*] (SPSG)
**LPO**........... Liquid Phase Oxidation [*Chemical processing*]
**LPO**........... Loan Production Office [*Banking*]
**LPO**........... Local Purchase Order
**LPO**........... London Philharmonic Orchestra
**LPO**........... Low Power Output (MSA)
**LPO**........... Low-Pressure Oxygen
**LPO**........... Lunar Parking Orbit [*Apollo*] [*NASA*]
**LPO**........... Lunar Polar Orbiter [*NASA*]

**LPOC**......... Labile Particulate Organic Carbon [*Environmental science*]
**L/POL**........ Life Policy [*Insurance*] (DCTA)
**L & Pol Int'l Bus** ... Law and Policy in International Business [*A publication*]
**L'POOL**..... Liverpool (ROG)
**LPOP**......... Low-Pressure Oxidizer Turbopump (NASA)
**LPosn**......... Lingua Posnaniensis [*A publication*]
**LPOT**......... Low-Pressure Oxidizer Turbopump (MCD)
**LPOT**......... Ota [*Portugal*] [*ICAO location identifier*] (ICLI)
**LPOTP**...... Low-Pressure Oxidizer Turbopump (NASA)
**LPOX**......... Low-Pressure Oxygen (AFM)
**LPP**........... La Parola del Passato [*A publication*]
**LPP**........... Labor Protection Plan
**LPP**........... Labour Progressive Party [*Canadian communist party*]
**LPP**........... Lanka Prajatantrawadi Party [*Ceylon*]
**LPP**........... Lappeenranta [*Finland*] [*Airport symbol*] (OAG)
**LPP**........... Large Paper Proofs
**LPP**........... LASER-Produced Plasma
**LPP**........... Launcher Preparation Control Panel
**LPP**........... Leader Preparation Program
**LPP**........... Lear Petroleum Partners LP [*AMEX symbol*] (SPSG)
**LPP**........... Lebowa People's Party [*South Africa*] [*Political party*] (PPW)
**LPP**........... Length of Perpendiculars
**LPP**........... Lines per Page
**LPP**........... Local Patching Panel
**LP & P**....... Logistics Policy and Procedures for Contingency Operations [*DARCOM*] (CINC)
**LPP**........... Long Periodic Perturbation
**LPP**........... Low-Power Physics (IEEE)
**LPP**........... Low-Pressure-Pipe System [*Waste water treatment*]
**L & PP**....... Lunar and Planetary Program
**LPP**........... Lunar Precepts Positioner [*Aerospace*]
**LPPC**......... Lisboa [*Portugal*] [*ICAO location identifier*] (ICLI)
**LPPC**......... Load Point Photocell
**LPPD**......... Ponta Delgada, Sao Miguel Island [*Portugal*] [*ICAO location identifier*] (ICLI)
**LPPG**......... Liquid Paperboard Packaging Group of Australia
**LPPH**......... Leningrad Prison Psychiatric Hospital [*Later, LSPH*]
**LPPI**.......... Pico, Pico Island [*Portugal*] [*ICAO location identifier*] (ICLI)
**LPPM**......... Portimao [*Portugal*] [*ICAO location identifier*] (ICLI)
**LPPMUL**.. Lawyers Protecting People from Malicious and Unjustified Lawsuits (EA)
**LPPO**......... Santa Maria [*Portugal*] [*ICAO location identifier*] (ICLI)
**LPPR**......... Porto [*Portugal*] [*ICAO location identifier*] (ICLI)
**LPPS**.......... Low-Pressure Plasma Sprayed [*Thermal barrier coating*]
**LPPS**.......... Porto Santo, Porto Santo Island [*Portugal*] [*ICAO location identifier*] (ICLI)
**LPPT**......... Lisboa [*Portugal*] [*ICAO location identifier*] (ICLI)
**LPPT**......... Low Pressurization Pressure Test Transmitter (IEEE)
**LPPTS**........ [*The*] Library of the Palestine Pilgrims' Text Society (BJA)
**LPPV**......... Praia Verde [*Portugal*] [*ICAO location identifier*] (ICLI)
**LPR**........... Amphibious Transport (Small) [*Navy ship symbol*]
**LPR**........... La Peregrina [*Puerto Rico*] [*Seismograph station code, US Geological Survey*] (SEIS)
**LPR**........... Lanpar Technologies, Inc. [*Toronto Stock Exchange symbol*]
**LPR**........... Late Phase Reaction [*or Response*] [*Medicine*]
**LPR**........... Late Position Report [*Report of a flight which is off flight plan*]
**LPR**........... Late Procurement Request [*Air Force*] (AFM)
**LPR**........... Leadership Potential Rating [*Army*] (AABC)
**LPR**........... Licensed Preacher
**LPR**........... Lilly's Practical Register [*A publication*] (DLA)
**LPR**........... Line Printer [*Data processing*] (NASA)
**LPR**........... Liquid Propellant Rocket [*Air Force*]
**LPR**........... Local Payment Receipt (AABC)
**LPR**........... London Property Register [*London Research Centre*] [*London, England*] [*Information service or system*] (IID)
**LPR**........... Long-Playing Rocket [*Aerospace*]
**LPR**........... Looper Position Regulator
**LPR**........... Lymphocyte Proliferative Response [*Immunology*]
**LPR**........... Lynchburg Pool Reactor
**LPR-5**........ Lease Production Revenue System - 5 File [*Petroleum Information Corp.*] [*Information service or system*] (CRD)
**LPR-10**...... Lease Production Revenue System - 10 File [*Petroleum Information Corp.*] [*Information service or system*] (CRD)
**LPRA**......... Laws of Puerto Rico Annotated [*A publication*]
**LPRA**......... Lost Parts Replacement Authorization (MCD)
**LPRB**......... Loaded Program Request Block [*Data processing*] (BUR)
**LPRC**......... Launch Pitch Rate Control
**LPRC**......... Library Public Relations Council (EA)
**LPRCO**...... Logistics Planning and Reporting Code [*Military*]
**LPRE**......... Liquid Propellant Rocket Engine [*Air Force*]
**LPRF**......... Low-Power Radio Frequency (MCD)
**LPRF**......... Low Pulse Recurrence Frequency (MCD)
**LPRI**.......... Licentiate of the Plastics and Rubber Institute [*British*] (DBQ)
**LPRINT**.... Lookup Dictionary Print Program (IEEE)
**LPRL**......... Lentz Peace Research Laboratory (EA)
**LPRM**........ Local Power Range Monitor (NRCH)
**LPRM**........ Low-Power Range Monitor [*Nuclear energy*] (NRCH)
**LProj**......... Light Projection [*Ophthalmology*]
**LPRP**......... Lao People's Revolutionary Party [*Phak Pasason Pativat Lao*] [*Political party*] (PPW)
**LPRR**......... Low-Power Research Reactor
**LPRS**......... Low-Pressure Recirculation System (NRCH)
**LPRSVR**.... Life Preserver
**LPRT**......... Low Power Relay Transmitter
**LPS**........... L-Band Phase Shifter
**LPS**........... La Palma [*El Salvador*] [*Seismograph station code, US Geological Survey*] (SEIS)
**LPS**........... Laboratory Peripheral System
**LPS**........... Laboratory Program Summary (MCD)
**LPS**........... Landing Performance Score (MCD)
**LPS**........... LASER Particulate Spectrometer [*NASA*]
**LPS**........... LASER Power Supply
**LPS**........... Last Period Satisfied [*IRS*]
**LPS**........... Laterality Preference Schedule [*Psychology*]
**LPS**........... Launch Phase Simulator [*NASA*]
**LPS**........... Launch Processing System [*NASA*] (KSC)
**LPS**........... Liberale Partei der Schweiz [*Liberal Party of Switzerland*] [*Political party*] (PPE)
**LPS**........... Liberian Philatelic Society [*Defunct*] (EA)
**LPS**........... Library Processes System [*Educomp*] [*Information service or system*] (IID)
**LPS**........... Lightproof Shade [*Technical drawings*]
**LPS**........... Line Procedure Specifications (CMD)
**LPS**........... Linear Programming System [*Data processing*]
**LPS**........... Lines per Second [*Data processing*]
**LPS**........... Lipopolysaccharide [*Biochemistry*]
**LPS**........... Liters per Second (KSC)
**LPS**........... Loan Production System [*Department of Veterans Affairs*]
**LPS**........... Local Process Specification (NG)
**LPS**........... Logicon Products [*Vancouver Stock Exchange symbol*]
**LPS**........... Logistic Policy Statement [*Navy*]
**LPS**........... Logistics Planning Study (MCD)
**LPS**........... London & Port Stanley Railway Co. [*AAR code*]
**LPS**........... London Press Service
**LPS**........... Longfellow Poetry Society (EA)
**Lps**............ Loops [*Military decoration*] (AABC)
**LPS**........... Lopez Island [*Washington*] [*Airport symbol*] (OAG)
**LPS**........... Lord Privy Seal [*British*]
**LPS**........... Low-Power Schottky [*Electronics*]
**LPS**........... Low-Pressure Sand [*Casting*] [*Automotive engineering*]
**LPS**........... Low-Pressure Scram [*Nuclear energy*] (IEEE)
**LPS**........... Low-Pressure Separator [*Chemical engineering*]
**LPS**........... Low-Pressure Sodium
**LPS**........... Lunar Penetrometer System [*Aerospace*]
**LPS**........... Lunar Pilotage System [*Aerospace*]
**LPSA**......... Lithographic Preparatory Services Association [*Later, GPA*] (EA)
**LPSA**......... Log Periodic Scattering Array
**LPSC**......... Luxembourg Philatelic Study Club [*Defunct*] (EA)
**LPSC**......... Santa Cruz [*Portugal*] [*ICAO location identifier*] (ICLI)
**LPSCU**...... Ladies Pennsylvania Slovak Catholic Union (EA)
**LPSD**......... Logically Passive Self-Dual
**LPSG**......... Live Oak, Perry & South Georgia Railway Co. [*AAR code*]
**LPSI**.......... Low-Pressure Safety Injection [*Nuclear energy*] (NRCH)
**LPSI**.......... Sines [*Portugal*] [*ICAO location identifier*] (ICLI)
**LPSIP**........ Low-Pressure Safety Injection Pump [*Nuclear energy*] (NRCH)
**LPSJ**......... Sao Jorge, Sao Jorge Island [*Portugal*] [*ICAO location identifier*] (ICLI)
**LPSN**......... Local Packet Switched Network
**LPSNY**...... Lithuanian Philatelic Society of New York (EA)
**LPSO**......... Laboratory Procurement Supply Office
**LPSO**......... Lloyd's Policy Signing Office [*Lloyd's of London*]
**LPSS**.......... Amphibious Transport Submarine [*Landing Platform, Submarine*] [*Navy ship symbol*]
**LPSS**.......... Law and Political Science Section [*Association of College and Research Libraries*]
**LPSS**.......... Line Protection Switching System [*Bell System*]
**LPSS**.......... Local Population Studies Society [*British*]
**LPSSNJ**.... Low-Power Self-Screening Noise Jammer [*Military*] (CAAL)
**LPST**......... Sintra [*Portugal*] [*ICAO location identifier*] (ICLI)
**LPSVD**...... Linear Prediction with Singular Value Decomposition [*Data processing*]
**LPSW**........ Low-Pressure Service Water [*Nuclear energy*] (NRCH)
**L & Psychology Rev** ... Law and Psychology Review [*A publication*] (DLA)
**L & Psych Rev** ... Law and Psychology Review [*A publication*] (DLA)
**L Psy R**...... Law and Psychology Review [*A publication*]
**LPT**............ Lampang [*Thailand*] [*Seismograph station code, US Geological Survey*] (SEIS)
**LPT**............ Lampang [*Thailand*] [*Airport symbol*] (OAG)
**LPT**............ Language Proficiency Test [*Military*] (AFM)
**LPT**............ Latest Recommended Posting Times [*Business term*] (DCTA)
**LPT**............ Leading Physical Trainer [*British military*] (DMA)
**LPT**............ Lear Petroleum Corp. [*NYSE symbol*] (SPSG)
**LPT**............ Licensed Physical Therapist
**LPT**............ Light Pen Tracking (MCD)
**LPT**............ Limited Procurement Test
**LP-T**.......... Limited Production - Test (AABC)
**LPT**............ Line Printer [*Data processing*]

**LPT**............ Liquid Penetrant Testing [*or Examination*] [*Nuclear energy*] (NRCH)
**LPT**............ Lock Pointer Table
**LPT**............ Low Point [*Technical drawings*]
**LPT**............ Low-Power Test
**LPT**............ Low-Pressure Test
**LPT**............ Low-Pressure Transducer
**LPT**............ Low-Pressure Turbine [*Nuclear energy*] (NRCH)
**LPtaW**....... West Baton Rouge Parish Library, Port Allen, LA [*Library symbol*] [*Library of Congress*] (LCLS)
**LPTB**......... London Passenger Transport Board
**LPTB**......... Low-Pressure Turbine [*on a ship*] (DS)
**LPTC**......... Lower Primary Teaching Certificate [*Australia*]
**LPTD**......... Linear Programmed Thermal Degradation [*Instrumentation*]
**LPTD**......... Long Play Talkdown
**LPTD-MS**... Linear Programmed Thermal Degradation - Mass Spectroscopy [*Instrumentation*]
**LPTF**......... Low-Power Test Facility [*Nuclear energy*]
**LPTIS**........ Laguna Peak Tracking and Injection Station
**LPTN**......... Tancos [*Portugal*] [*ICAO location identifier*] (ICLI)
**LPTR**......... Line Printer [*Data processing*] (MSA)
**LPTR**......... Livermore Pool Type Reactor
**LPTS**......... Louisiana Presbyterian Theological Seminary
**LPTTL**........ Low-Power Transistor-Transistor Logic
**LPTTP**........ League of Professional Theatre Training Programs [*Defunct*] (EA)
**LPTV**......... Channel America LPTV Holdings, Inc. [*NASDAQ symbol*] (NQ)
**LPTV**......... Lapin Tutkimusseura Vuosikirja [*Research Society of Lapland. Yearbook*] [*A publication*]
**LPTV**......... Large Payload Test Vehicle [*Air Force*]
**LPTV**......... Low-Power Television
**LPTW**......... Lake Providence, Texarkana & Western R. R. [*AAR code*]
**LPU**........... Language Processor Unit
**LPu**........... Late Punic (BJA)
**LPU**........... League of Prayer for Unity [*Defunct*] (EA)
**LPU**........... Least Publishable Unit [*of research data*]
**LPU**........... Legal Practices Update [*A publication*]
**LPU**........... Life Preserver Unit
**LP-U**.......... Limited Production - Urgent (AABC)
**LPU**........... Line Processing Unit
**LPU**........... Lions Philatelic Unit (EA)
**LPU**........... Liquid Processing Unit
**LPU**........... Low Pay Unit [*British*]
**LPU**........... Low-Power Unit (CAAL)
**LPUG**......... Lasers in Publishing Users Group (EA)
**LPUU**......... Linear Programming under Uncertainty [*Data processing*]
**LPV**........... Houston, TX [*Location identifier*] [*FAA*] (FAAL)
**LPV**........... Landing Platform Vehicle [*Navy*] [*British*]
**LPV**........... Launching Point Vertical (NATG)
**LPV**........... Left Pulmonary Vein [*Anatomy*]
**LPV**........... Lightproof Vent [*Technical drawings*]
**LPV**........... Log Periodic V [*Antenna*]
**LPV**........... Lymphotropic Papovavirus
**LPVR**......... Vila Real [*Portugal*] [*ICAO location identifier*] (ICLI)
**LPVT**......... Large Print Video Terminal
**LPVZ**......... Viseu [*Portugal*] [*ICAO location identifier*] (ICLI)
**LPW**........... [*The*] Age. Large Print Weekly [*A publication*] (APTA)
**LPW**........... Liberal Party of Wales [*Political party*]
**LPW**........... Linear Polarized Wave
**LPW**........... Local Point Warning [*Military*]
**LPW**........... Longitudinal Pressure Wave
**lp/W**.......... Lumens per Watt (CET)
**LPWA**......... Local Public Works Act (OICC)
**LPX**........... Louisiana-Pacific Corp. [*NYSE symbol*] (SPSG)
**LPYS**......... Labour Party Young Socialists [*British*] [*Political party*]
**LPZ**........... La Paz [*San Calixto*] [*Bolivia*] [*Seismograph station code, US Geological Survey*] (SEIS)
**LPZ**........... Leipzig [*City and district in East Germany*] (ROG)
**LPZ**........... Low Population Zone (NRCH)
**LPZ**........... Ruston, LA [*Location identifier*] [*FAA*] (FAAL)
**Lpz Bien Zt**... Leipziger Bienenzeitung [*A publication*]
**LQ**............. Argentina [*Aircraft nationality and registration mark*] (FAAC)
**LQ**............. International and Comparative Law Quarterly [*A publication*]
**LQ**............. Last Quarter [*Moon phase*]
**LQ**............. Laterality Quotient [*Neuropsychology*]
**LQ**............. Laurentian Capital Corp. [*AMEX symbol*] (SPSG)
**LQ**............. Learning Quotient
**LQ**............. Lebanese Air Transport [*ICAO designator*] (FAAC)
**LQ**............. Lege Quaeso [*Please Read*] [*Latin*]
**LQ**............. Letter Quality (PCM)
**LQ**............. Library Quarterly [*A publication*]
**LQ**............. Linear Quadratic [*Mathematics*]
**lq**............. Liquid
**LQ**............. London Quarterly [*A publication*]
**LQ**............. Longevity Quotient [*Demography*]
**LQ**............. Lordosis Quotients [*Medicine*]
**Lq**............. Love Wave [*Earthquakes*]
**LQ**............. Lowest Quadrant
**LQ**............. Lowest Quadrille
**LQ**............. Lutheran Quarterly [*A publication*]
**LQA**........... La Quiaca [*Argentina*] [*Geomagnetic observatory code*]
**LQA**........... La Quiaca [*Argentina*] [*Seismograph station code, US Geological Survey*] [*Closed*] (SEIS)
**LQA**........... Living Quarters Allowance [*Air Force*] (AFM)
**LQD**........... Liquid
**LQD**........... Lowest Quantity Determinable [*Analytical chemistry*]
**LQDR**......... Liquidator
**LQF**........... Liturgiegeschichtliche Quellen und Forschungen [*Muenster*] [*A publication*]
**LQFD**......... Liquefied
**LQG**........... Linear Quadratic Gaussian (MCD)
**LQG**........... Lorain, OH [*Location identifier*] [*FAA*] (FAAL)
**LQGLS**....... Liquid in Glass
**LQHR**......... London Quarterly and Holborn Review [*A publication*]
**LQK**........... Pickens, SC [*Location identifier*] [*FAA*] (FAAL)
**LQL**........... Willoughby, OH [*Location identifier*] [*FAA*] (FAAL)
**LQM**........... La Quinta Motor Inns, Inc. [*NYSE symbol*] (SPSG)
**LQM**........... Puerto Leguizamo [*Colombia*] [*Airport symbol*] (OAG)
**LQMETR**... Liquidometer
**LQN**........... Boston, MA [*Location identifier*] [*FAA*] (FAAL)
**LQN**........... Qala-Nau [*Afghanistan*] [*Airport symbol*] [*Obsolete*] (OAG)
**LQP**........... Fort Collins, CO [*Location identifier*] [*FAA*] (FAAL)
**LQP**........... La Quinta Motor LP [*NYSE symbol*] (SPSG)
**LQP**........... Letter Quality Printer [*Data processing*]
**LQP**........... Linear Quadratic Problem [*Mathematics*]
**LQQ**........... Chicago, IL [*Location identifier*] [*FAA*] (FAAL)
**LQR**........... Larned, KS [*Location identifier*] [*FAA*] (FAAL)
**LQR**........... Law Quarterly Review [*A publication*]
**LQR**........... Liquor
**LQR**........... London Quarterly Review [*A publication*]
**L Q Rev**...... Law Quarterly Review [*A publication*]
**LQS**........... Les Quatre Saisons [*Record label*] [*France*]
**LQS**........... Lock Haven State College, Lock Haven, PA [*OCLC symbol*] (OCLC)
**LQST**......... Leadership Q-Sort Test [*Psychology*]
**LQT**........... Liverpool Quay Terms (DS)
**LQT**........... Los Queltehues [*Chile*] [*Seismograph station code, US Geological Survey*] (SEIS)
**LQUADW**... Ligand Quarterly [*A publication*]
**LQUT**......... Queensland Unit and Group Titles Law and Practice [*Australia*] [*A publication*]
**LQV**........... Pennington Gap, VA [*Location identifier*] [*FAA*] (FAAL)
**LQX**........... Lehighton, PA [*Location identifier*] [*FAA*] (FAAL)
**LQY**........... Springfield, IL [*Location identifier*] [*FAA*] (FAAL)
**LR**............. Alabama Law Review [*A publication*]
**LR**............. Congregation of La Retraite [*Saint Germain-En-Laye, France*] (EAIO)
**Lr**............. King Lear [*Shakespearean work*]
**LR**............. Labeled Release [*Mars life detection experiment*]
**LR**............. Labor Reports (OICC)
**LR**............. Labor Review [*A publication*]
**LR**............. Labor Room [*Obstetrics*]
**LR**............. Laboratory Reactor
**LR**............. Laboratory Reagent
**LR**............. Laboratory Report
**LR**............. Lactated Ringer [*Medicine*]
**LR**............. Ladder Rung (AAG)
**LR**............. Lady's Realm [*A publication*] (ROG)
**L & R**.......... Lake and Rail
**Lr**............. Lancer [*Military*] [*British*] (DMA)
**LR**............. Land Registry (DLA)
**LR**............. Landing RADAR
**L & R**.......... Landing and Recovery (KSC)
**LR**............. Lapse Ratio [*Insurance*]
**L & R**.......... Larceny and Receiving
**LR**............. Large Ring
**LR**............. LASER-RADAR (MCD)
**LR**............. [*The*] Last Message Received by Me Was ____ [*Aviation code*] (FAAC)
**LR**............. Last Renewal
**LR**............. Latency Relaxation
**LR**............. Lateral Rectus [*Muscle*] [*Anatomy*]
**LR**............. Lateral Root [*Botany*]
**lR**............. Laufend Rechnung [*Current Account*] [*German*] [*Business term*]
**L/R**............ Launch/Reentry (MCD)
**LR**............. Launch Reliability (MCD)
**LR**............. Launch Right (MCD)
**LR**............. Law Record [*1911-12*] [*India*] [*A publication*] (DLA)
**LR**............. Law Recorder [*1827-38*] [*Ireland*] [*A publication*] (DLA)
**LR**............. Law Register [*1880-1909*] [*A publication*] (DLA)
**LR**............. Law Reporter [*1821-22*] [*A publication*] (DLA)
**LR**............. Law Reports [*A publication*]
**LR**............. Law Review [*A publication*]
**LR**............. Lawesson Reagent [*Organic chemistry*]
**Lr**............. Lawrencium [*Original symbol, Lw, changed in 1963*] [*Chemical element*]
**LR**............. Lay Reader (ROG)
**LR**............. Layer Rating [*British military*] (DMA)
**LR**............. Leaders of Religion [*A publication*]
**LR**............. Leaf Rust [*Plant Pathology*]

**LR** ... Lear [*ICAO aircraft manufacturer identifier*] (ICAO)
**LR** ... Leave to Appeal Refused [*Legal term*] (ADA)
**LR** ... Leave Rations [*Military*]
**LR** ... Ledger (ROG)
**LR** ... Left Rear
**L & R** ... Left and Right
**L-R** ... Left to Right
**LR** ... Left Rudder (MCD)
**LR** ... Leicestershire Regiment [*Military unit*] [*British*]
**LR** ... Lent Reading (ROG)
**LR** ... Les Lettres Romanes [*A publication*]
**LR** ... Lesion Expansion Rate [*Pathology*]
**LR** ... Letter [*Online database field identifier*]
**LR** ... Letter Report
**LR** ... Letter Requirement
**LR** ... Level Recorder
**LR** ... Level Regulator (NRCH)
**LR** ... Leviticus Rabbah (BJA)
**LR** ... Liaison Report (AAG)
**LR** ... Liaison Request (AAG)
**LR** ... Liberaal Reveil [*A publication*]
**LR** ... Liberia [*ANSI two-letter standard code*] (CNC)
**LR** ... Library Review [*A publication*]
**LR** ... Licensing Registration [*British*]
**L/R** ... Life/Revisit [*NASA*] (KSC)
**LR** ... Lifespan Resources [*An association*] (EA)
**LR** ... Likelihood Ratio [*Statistics*]
**LR** ... Limba Romina [*A publication*]
**LR** ... Limit Register
**LR** ... Limited Recoverable (IEEE)
**LR** ... Line Receiver
**LR** ... Line Relay
**LR** ... Linear Regression [*Mathematics*]
**LR** ... Lineas Aereas Costarricenses, Sociedad Anonima (LACSA) [*Costa Rica*] [*ICAO designator*] (ICDA)
**LR** ... Link Resources, Inc. [*Vancouver Stock Exchange symbol*]
**LR** ... Liquid Rocket
**LR** ... Listing Requirement [*Investment term*]
**LR** ... Literary Review [*A publication*]
**LR** ... Literaturnaya Rossiya [*A publication*]
**LR** ... Living Room
**LR** ... Lloyd's Register of Shipping
**LR** ... Load Ratio
**LR** ... Load Rejection (NRCH)
**LR** ... Load-Resistor Relay (MSA)
**LR** ... Loading Ramp
**LR** ... Loan Rate [*Banking*]
**L/R** ... Local/Remote [*Telecommunications*] (TEL)
**LR** ... Lock Rail
**L/R** ... Locus of Radius
**LR** ... Log Run [*Lumber*]
**LR** ... Logical Record
**LR** ... Logistic Regression [*Medicine*]
**LR** ... Logistical Reassignment [*Military*] (AFIT)
**LR** ... London Rank [*Freemasonry*]
**LR** ... Long Range
**LR** ... Long Rifle
**LR** ... Long Run [*Economics*]
**lr** ... Lopende Rekening [*Current Account*] [*Business term*] [*Afrikaans*]
**L & R** ... Loring and Russell's Election Cases in Massachusetts [*A publication*] (DLA)
**LR** ... Louisiana Reports [*A publication*] (DLA)
**lr** ... Low Rate Reverse [*Ecology*]
**LR** ... Low Risk
**LR** ... Lower (ADA)
**LR** ... Lower Rail [*Typography*]
**LR** ... Lower Right
**LR** ... Lower Rule
**LR** ... Loyal Regiment [*Military*] [*British*]
**LR** ... Lugger [*Ship's rigging*] (ROG)
**LR** ... Lutherische Rundschau [*A publication*]
**LR** ... New Zealand Law Reports [*A publication*] (DLA)
**LR** ... Ohio Law Reporter [*A publication*] (DLA)
**LR** ... Radiolocation Land Station [*ITU designation*]
**Lr** ... Rayleigh Wave [*Earthquakes*]
**LR3** ... LASER Ranging Retroreflection [*Also, LRRR*] [*Initialism pronounced "LR-cubed"*] [*Apollo 11 experiment*] [*NASA*]
**LR$^3$** ... Logistics Readiness Rating Report [*DoD*]
**LRA** ... Labor Research Association (EA)
**LRA** ... Lace Research Association [*British*]
**LRA** ... Lagged Reserve Accounting [*Banking*]
**LRA** ... Landing Rights Airport [*US Customs*]
**LRA** ... Larissa [*Greece*] [*Airport symbol*] (OAG)
**LRA** ... LASER [*Gyro*] Reference Axis (IEEE)
**LRA** ... Last Return Amount [*IRS*]
**LRA** ... Launcher Relay Assembly [*Navy*] (CAAL)
**LRA** ... Lawyers' Reform Association [*Australia*]
**LRA** ... Lawyers' Reports, Annotated [*A publication*] (DLA)
**LRA** ... Least Restrictive Alternative [*For the education of the handicapped*]
**LRA** ... Libertarian Republican Alliance (EA)
**LRA** ... Library Record of Australasia [*A publication*] (APTA)
**LRA** ... Library of Romance [*A publication*]
**LRA** ... Light Replaceable Assemblies
**LRA** ... Line Receiving Amplifier (MSA)
**LRA** ... Lithuanian Regeneration Association (EA)
**LRA** ... Little Rock [*Arkansas*] [*Seismograph station code, US Geological Survey*] [*Closed*] (SEIS)
**LRA** ... Load Reference Axis
**LRA** ... Locked-Rotor Amperes (MSA)
**LRA** ... Long-Range Aviation [*Army*] (AABC)
**LRA** ... Lord Ruthven Assembly [*An association*] (EA)
**LRA** ... Lower Right Abdomen [*Injection site*]
**LRA** ... North Carolina Union List of Serials for Community Colleges [*Library network*]
**LRAA** ... Long-Range Air Army [*USSR*] (MCD)
**LRAAM** ... Long Range Air-to-Air Missile [*Air Force*]
**LRAAS** ... Long-Range Airborne ASW [*Antisubmarine Warfare*] System (MCD)
**Lrab Hasarakakan Gitutyun** ... Lraber Hasarakakan Gitutyunneri [*A publication*]
**LRAC** ... English Law Reports, Appeal Cases [*A publication*] (DLA)
**LRAC** ... Labrador. Resources Advisory Council. Newsletter [*A publication*]
**LRAC** ... Long-Run Average Costs [*Marketing*]
**LRAD** ... Licentiate of the Royal Academy of Dancing [*British*]
**LR Adm & Ecc** ... Law Reports, Admiralty and Ecclesiastical Cases [*1865-75*] [*A publication*] (DLA)
**LR Adm & Eccl** ... Law Reports, Admiralty and Ecclesiastical Cases [*1865-75*] [*A publication*] (DLA)
**LR Adm & Eccl (Eng)** ... Law Reports, Admiralty and Ecclesiastical Cases [*England*] [*A publication*] (DLA)
**LRADP** ... Long-Range Active Duty Program [*Army*]
**LRA & E** ... English Law Reports, Admiralty and Ecclesiastical [*A publication*] (DLA)
**LRAF** ... Long-Range Air Force
**LRAM** ... Licentiate of the Royal Academy of Music [*British*] (EY)
**LRAN** ... Local Regional Access Node (MCD)
**LR Ann** ... Lawyers' Reports, Annotated [*A publication*] (DLA)
**LRA NS** ... Lawyers' Reports, Annotated, New Series [*A publication*] (DLA)
**LRAO** ... Logistics Review and Analysis Office [*US Army Defense Ammunition Center and School*]
**LRAOP** ... Long-Range Aerospace Observation Platform
**LRAP** ... Leucine-Rich Amelogenin Polypeptide [*Biochemistry of dental enamel*]
**LRAP** ... Long-Range Acoustic Propagation
**LR App** ... English Law Reports, Appeal Cases, House of Lords [*A publication*] (DLA)
**LRAPP** ... Long-Range Acoustic Propagation Project
**LR App Cas** ... English Law Reports, Appeal Cases, House of Lords [*A publication*] (DLA)
**LR App Cas (Eng)** ... English Law Reports, Appeal Cases, House of Lords [*A publication*] (DLA)
**LRAR** ... Arad [*Romania*] [*ICAO location identifier*] (ICLI)
**LRaR** ... Richland Parish Library, Rayville, LA [*Library symbol*] [*Library of Congress*] (LCLS)
**LRAS** ... Long-Range Autonomous Submersible
**LRAT** ... Long-Range Antitank [*Army*] (INF)
**LRATC** ... Long-Run Average Total Costs [*Economics*]
**LRATGW** ... Long-Range Antitank Guided Weapon [*British military*] (DMA)
**LRB** ... La Revue Bibliographique [*A publication*]
**LRB** ... Labour Relations Board [*Canada*]
**LRB** ... Level Reference Base
**LRB** ... Lissamine Rhodamine B [*Fluorescent dye*]
**LRB** ... Local Reference Beam [*Holography*]
**LRB** ... London Rifle Brigade [*Military unit*] [*British*]
**LRB** ... Loyalty Review Board [*Abolished, 1953*] [*Civil Service Commission*]
**L Rb** ... Lutherischer Rundblick [*A publication*]
**LRBB** ... Bucuresti [*Romania*] [*ICAO location identifier*] (ICLI)
**LRBC** ... Bacau [*Romania*] [*ICAO location identifier*] (ICLI)
**LRBC** ... Lloyd's Registry Building Certificate
**LRBF** ... Longitudinal Ridge of Basal Fold
**LRBFM** ... National Labor Relations Board Field Manual
**LRBG** ... Law Reports, British Guiana [*1890-1955*] [*A publication*] (DLA)
**LRBM** ... Baia Mare/Tauti Magherusi [*Romania*] [*ICAO location identifier*] (ICLI)
**LRBM** ... Long-Range Ballistic Missile
**LRBR** ... Long-Range Ballistic Rocket
**LRBR** ... Long-Range Bombardment Round
**LRBS** ... Bucuresti/Baneasa [*Romania*] [*ICAO location identifier*] (ICLI)
**LRBS** ... LASER Ranging Bombing System
**LR Burm** ... Law Reports, British Burma [*A publication*] (DLA)
**LR Burma** ... Law Reports, British Burma [*A publication*] (DLA)
**LRC** ... Labour Representation Committee [*Northern Ireland*] (PPW)
**LRC** ... Labrador Retriever Club (EA)
**LRC** ... Langley Research Center [*NASA*]

**LRC**.......... Law Reform Commission [*Canada*]
**LRC**.......... Law Reform Committee (DLA)
**LRC**.......... Lead Resistance Compensator
**LRC**.......... Leaders Reaction Course [*Military training*] (INF)
**LRC**.......... Learning Resource Center
**L or RC** ...... Leather or Rubber Covered [*Freight*]
**LRC**.......... Lenoir Rhyne College [*Hickory, NC*]
**LRC**.......... Lesbian Resource Center (EA)
**LRC**.......... Level Recording Controller
**LRC**.......... Lewis Research Center [*NASA*]
**LRC**.......... Liberia Refining Company
**LRC**.......... Library Research Center [*University of Illinois*] (IID)
**LRC**.......... Light Rapid Comfortable [*Train system*]
**LRC**.......... Light Repair Car [*British*]
**LRC**.......... Limnological Research Center [*University of Minnesota*] [*Research center*] (RCD)
**LRC**.......... Line Rectifier Circuit
**LRC**.......... Linguistics Research Center [*University of Texas at Austin*] [*Research center*] (RCD)
**LRC**.......... Lionel Railroader Club (EA)
**LRC**.......... Lipid Research Center [*Washington University*] [*Research center*] (RCD)
**LRC**.......... Lipid Research Clinics
**LRC**.......... Load Ratio Control (MSA)
**LRC**.......... Locomotor Respiratory Coupling [*Physiology*]
**LRC**.......... Lode Resources Corp. [*Vancouver Stock Exchange symbol*]
**LRC**.......... Logistics Readiness Center [*Air Force*]
**LRC**.......... Logistics to Relay Converter (MCD)
**LRC**.......... London Rowing Club
**LRC**.......... Lone Oak Road [*California*] [*Seismograph station code, US Geological Survey*] (SEIS)
**LRC**.......... Long-Range Climb (MCD)
**LRC**.......... Long-Range Cruise [*Aircraft speed*]
**LRC**.......... Longitudinal Redundancy Check [*Data processing*]
**LRC**.......... Lori Corporation [*AMEX symbol*] (SPSG)
**LRC**.......... Lower Rib Cage [*Anatomy*]
**LRC**.......... Luneberg Rapid Commutator [*Physics*]
**LRC**.......... Lung Rate Counter
**LRC**.......... Lutheran Resources Commission (EA)
**LRCA**......... Law Reports, Court of Appeals of New Zealand [*A publication*] (DLA)
**LRCA**......... Lithuanian Roman Catholic Alliance of America [*Later, LCA*] (EA)
**LRCA**......... Long-Range Combat Aircraft
**LRCA**......... Lop Rabbit Club of America (EA)
**LRCC**......... English Law Reports, Crown Cases Reserved [*2 vols.*] [*1865-75*] [*A publication*] (DLA)
**LRCC**......... Longitudinal Redundancy Check Character [*Telecommunications*] (TEL)
**LRCC (Eng)** ... English Law Reports, Crown Cases Reserved [*2 vols.*] [*1865-75*] [*A publication*] (DLA)
**LRCCPPT** ... Lipid Research Clinics Coronary Primary Prevention Trial [*Cardiology*]
**LRCCR**...... Law Reports, Crown Cases Reserved [*England*] [*A publication*] (DLA)
**LRCE**......... LASER Relay Communication Equipment
**LRCE**......... Little Rock Cotton Exchange [*Defunct*]
**LRCFA**...... Lithuanian Roman Catholic Federation of America (EA)
**LR Ch** ........ Law Reports, Chancery Appeal Cases [*England*] [*A publication*] (DLA)
**LR Ch App** ... Chancery Appeal Cases [*1865-75*] [*A publication*] (DLA)
**LR Ch D**..... English Law Reports, Chancery Division [*A publication*] (DLA)
**LR Ch D (Eng)** ... Law Reports, Chancery Division, English Supreme Court of Judicature [*A publication*] (DLA)
**LR Ch Div (Eng)** ... Law Reports, Chancery Division, English Supreme Court of Judicature [*A publication*] (DLA)
**LR Ch (Eng)** ... Law Reports, Chancery Appeal Cases [*England*] [*A publication*] (DLA)
**LRCK**......... Constanta/M. Kogalniceau [*Romania*] [*ICAO location identifier*] (ICLI)
**LRCL**......... Cluj-Napoca/Someseni [*Romania*] [*ICAO location identifier*] (ICLI)
**LRCM**........ Licentiate of the Royal College of Music [*British*]
**LRCM**........ Long-Range Cruise Missile [*Navy*]
**LRCO** ........ Limited Remote [*or Radio*] Communication Outlet
**LRCO** ........ Long-Range Capability Objective [*Air Force*]
**LRCOM** .... Long-Range Very-High-Frequency/Ultrahigh-Frequency Communications (FAAC)
**LRCP**......... Laboratory Research Cooperative Program [*Scientific Services Program*] [*Army*] (RDA)
**LRCP**......... Law Reports, Common Pleas [*1865-75*] [*England*] [*A publication*] (DLA)
**LRCP**......... Licentiate of the Royal College of Physicians [*British*]
**LRCP**......... Long-Range Construction Program [*Military*]
**LRCPD**...... English Law Reports, Common Pleas Division [*A publication*] (DLA)
**LRCP Div** .. Law Reports, Common Pleas Division [*England*] [*A publication*] (DLA)
**LRCP Div (Eng)** ... English Law Reports, Common Pleas Division [*A publication*] (DLA)
**LRCPE** ...... Licentiate of the Royal College of Physicians (Edinburgh)
**LRCP (Eng)** ... Law Reports, Common Pleas [*England*] [*A publication*] (DLA)
**LRCPI** ....... Licentiate of the Royal College of Physicians of Ireland
**LRCP Irel** .. Licentiate of the Royal College of Physicians of Ireland
**LRCPLA**.... Lithuanian Roman Catholic Priests' League of America (EA)
**LRCP & S** .. Licentiate of the Royal College of Physicians and the College of Surgeons of Edinburgh, and of the Faculty of Physicians and Surgeons of Glasgow (ROG)
**LR Cr Cas Res** ... Law Reports, Crown Cases Reserved [*England*] [*A publication*] (DLA)
**LRCS**......... Caransebes/Caransebes [*Romania*] [*ICAO location identifier*] (ICLI)
**LRCS**......... LASER RADAR Cross Section
**LRCS**......... League of Red Cross and Red Crescent Societies [*Switzerland*] (EA)
**LRCS**......... League of Red Cross Societies
**LRCS**......... Licentiate of the Royal College of Surgeons [*British*]
**LRCS**......... Load Relief Control System
**LRCSE**....... Licentiate of the Royal College of Surgeons (Edinburgh)
**LRCSI**........ Licentiate of the Royal College of Surgeons in Ireland
**LRCS Irel** .. Licentiate of the Royal College of Surgeons in Ireland
**LRCT**......... Licentiate of the Royal Conservatory of Toronto [*Canada*]
**LRCV**......... Craiova [*Romania*] [*ICAO location identifier*] (ICLI)
**LRCVS** ...... Licentiate of the Royal College of Veterinary Surgeons [*British*]
**LRC-W** ...... Lutheran Resources Commission - Washington [*Later, LRC*] (EA)
**LRCX**......... Lam Research Corporation [*Fremont, CA*] [*NASDAQ symbol*] (NQ)
**LRD** .......... Labour Research Department [*Trade union*] [*British*]
**LRD** .......... Landing and Recovery Division [*NASA*]
**LRD** .......... Laredo [*Texas*] [*Airport symbol*] (OAG)
**LRD** .......... LASER Ranger and Designator (MCD)
**LRD** .......... Launch Readiness Demonstration [*NASA*] (KSC)
**LRD** .......... Living Related Donor [*Medicine*]
**LRD** .......... Logistics Requirements Determination (MCD)
**LRD** .......... Long-Range Data [*RADAR*]
**LRD** .......... Long-Reach Detonator [*Explosive*]
**LRD** .......... Lord River Gold [*Vancouver Stock Exchange symbol*]
**LRD** .......... Lysinated Rhodamine Dextran [*Cytology*]
**LRDC**......... Land Resources Development Centre [*British*] (ARC)
**LRDC**......... Learning Research and Development Center [*University of Pittsburgh*] [*Research center*]
**LRDD** ........ Limited Rights to Delivered Data
**LRDE**......... Long-Run Deal Effect [*Marketing*]
**LRDG**......... Long Range Desert Group [*British Army*] [*World War II*]
**LR Dig** ....... Law Reports Digest [*A publication*] (DLA)
**LRDL**......... Longitudinal Ridge of Dorsal Lip
**LRDMM** ... Long-Range Dual-Mission Missile (MCD)
**LRDR** ........ Last Revision Date Routine
**LRDS**......... LASER Ranging and Designation System [*Military*] (CAAL)
**LRDU** ........ Long-Range Development Unit
**LRE**........... La Recherche [*A publication*]
**LRE**........... Lafayette Radio Electronics Corp.
**LRE**........... Latest Revised Estimate (MCD)
**LRE**........... Least Restrictive Environment [*For the education of the handicapped*]
**LRE**........... Licentiate in Religious Education
**LRE**........... Light Responsive Element [*Chemistry*]
**LRe** ........... Linguistische Reihe [*A publication*]
**LRE**........... Liquid Rocket Engine
**LRE**........... Local Resource Enhancement [*Biology*]
**LRE**........... Logistics Readiness Elements (MCD)
**LRE**........... Longreach [*Australia*] [*Airport symbol*] (OAG)
**LRE**........... Lunar Retrograde Engine [*NASA*] (KSC)
**LREA**......... Law Reports, East Africa [*A publication*] (DLA)
**L Rec** ......... Law Recorder [*Dublin, Ireland*] [*A publication*] (DLA)
**LREC**......... Liaison Residency Endorsement Committee [*Superseded by RRCEM*] (EA)
**LRECL** ...... Logical Records of Fixed Length (MCD)
**L Rec NS** ...... Law Recorder, New Series [*Ireland*] [*A publication*] (DLA)
**L Record**..... Law Recorder [*Dublin, Ireland*] [*A publication*] (DLA)
**L Rec OS**.... Law Recorder, First Series [*Ireland*] [*A publication*] (DLA)
**LREDA**...... Liberal Religious Educators Association (EA)
**LREE**......... Light Rare Earth Elements [*Chemistry*]
**LREG**......... Leading Regulator [*British*]
**LREH** ........ Low-Renin Essential Hypertension [*Medicine*]
**LR E & I App** ... Law Reports. English and Irish Appeals [*United Kingdom*] [*A publication*]
**LRE & I App** ... Law Reports, House of Lords, English and Irish Appeals [*1866-75*] [*A publication*] (DLA)
**L & R Election Cases** ... Loring and Russell's Election Cases in Massachusetts [*A publication*] (DLA)
**LREM(A)** .. Leading Radio Electrical Mechanic (Air) [*British military*] (DMA)
**LR Eng & Ir App** ... Law Reports, English and Irish Appeals [*1866-75*] [*A publication*] (DLA)
**L Rep**.......... Carolina Law Repository (Reprint) [*North Carolina*] [*A publication*] (DLA)
**L Rep Mont** ... Law Reporter, Montreal [*A publication*] (DLA)
**L Repos**...... Law Repository [*A publication*] (DLA)

**LR Eq**......... English Law Reports, Equity [*1866-75*] [*A publication*] (DLA)
**LR Eq (Eng)**... English Law Reports, Equity [*1866-75*] [*A publication*] (DLA)
**LRES**......... Land Resources Corp. [*NASDAQ symbol*] (NQ)
**LRES**......... Letters
**LRES**......... Long-Range Earth Sensor
**LRESDD**... Legume Research [*A publication*]
**L Rev**......... Law Review [*A publication*]
**L Rev Dig**... Law Review Digest [*A publication*] (DLA)
**L Rev & Quart J**... Law Review and Quarterly Journal [*London*] [*A publication*] (DLA)
**L Rev U Detroit**... Law Review. University of Detroit [*A publication*] (DLA)
**LREW**........ Long-Range Early Warning (NATG)
**LREWP**..... Long-Range Electronic Warfare Plan [*Military*] (CAAL)
**LREWS**..... Long-Range Early Warning System (NATG)
**LR Ex**......... English Law Reports, Exchequer [*1866-75*] [*A publication*] (DLA)
**LREX**......... L Rex International, Inc. [*NASDAQ symbol*] (NQ)
**LR Ex Cas**... English Law Reports, Exchequer [*1866-75*] [*A publication*] (DLA)
**LR Exch**..... English Law Reports, Exchequer [*1866-75*] [*A publication*] (DLA)
**LR Exch D**... English Law Reports, Exchequer Division [*A publication*] (DLA)
**LR Exch Div**... Law Reports, Exchequer Division [*England*] [*A publication*] (DLA)
**LR Exch Div (Eng)**... English Law Reports, Exchequer Division [*A publication*] (DLA)
**LR Exch (Eng)**... English Law Reports, Exchequer [*1866-75*] [*A publication*] (DLA)
**LR Ex D**..... Law Reports, Exchequer Division [*England*] [*A publication*] (DLA)
**LR Ex Div**... English Law Reports, Exchequer Division [*A publication*] (DLA)
**LRF**........... Jacksonville, AR [*Location identifier*] [*FAA*] (FAAL)
**LRF**........... LASER Range-Finder
**LRF**........... Last Return Filed [*IRS*]
**LRF**........... Late Renal Failure [*Medicine*]
**LRF**........... Latex and Resorcinol Formaldehyde
**LRF**........... Launch Rate Factor
**LRF**........... Lepidoptera Research Foundation (EA)
**LRF**........... Lincoln NC Realty Fund, Inc. [*AMEX symbol*] (SPSG)
**LRF**........... Liquid Rocket Fuel (MCD)
**LRF**........... Liver Residue Factor [*Molybdenum*] [*Medicine*]
**LRF**........... London Regional Federation [*League of Nations Union*]
**LRF**........... Long-Range Facility [*Telecommunications*] (TEL)
**LRF**........... Long-Range Flight
**LRF**........... Low Refraction Layer
**LRF**........... Lumber Recovery Factor
**LRF**........... Luteinizing-Hormone Releasing Factor [*Also, GnRF, GnRH, LH-RF, LH-RH, LH-RH/FSH-RH, LRH*] [*Endocrinology*]
**LRFAX**...... Low-Resolution Facsimile [*Telecommunications*] (TEL)
**LRFC**......... LASER Range-Finder Controller (MCD)
**LRFG**......... Low-Range Force Gauge
**LRFI**.......... League for Religious Freedom in Israel [*Later, American Friends of Religious Freedom in Israel*] (EA)
**LRF/MTR**... LASER Range-Finder and Marked Target Receiver (MCD)
**LRFPS**....... Licentiate of the Royal Faculty of Physicians and Surgeons [*British*]
**LRFPS(G)**... Licentiate of the Royal Faculty of Physicians and Surgeons, Glasgow
**LRFS**......... Long-Range Forecasting System (TEL)
**LRF/SSC**... LASER Ranger Finder/Solid State Computer (MCD)
**LRG**........... Land Resources Group
**LRG**........... Landscape Research Group [*Lutterworth, Leicestershire, England*] (EAIO)
**LRG**........... Large (FAAC)
**LRG**........... Leucine-Rich Glycoprotein
**LRG**........... License Review Group [*Nuclear energy*] (NRCH)
**LRG**........... Lincoln, ME [*Location identifier*] [*FAA*] (FAAL)
**LRG**........... Liquefied Refinery Gas
**LRG**........... Logistic Review Group [*Military*] (CAAL)
**LRG**........... Long Range
**LRG**........... Long-Range Guidance (MCD)
**LRG**........... Lorgues [*France*] [*Seismograph station code, US Geological Survey*] (SEIS)
**LRGB**......... Long-Range Guided Bomb (MCD)
**LRGPP**...... Long-Range Generation Planning Problem [*Energy*]
**LRH**........... La Rochelle [*France*] [*Airport symbol*] (OAG)
**LRh**........... Liquid Rheostat
**LRH**........... Luteinizing-Hormone Releasing Hormone [*Also, GnRF, GnRH, LH-RF, LH-RH, LH-RH/FSH-RH, LRF*] [*Endocrinology*]
**LRHL**......... Law Reports, English and Irish Appeals and Peerage Claims, House of Lords [*England*] [*A publication*] (DLA)
**LRHL (Eng)**... Law Reports, English and Irish Appeals and Peerage Claims, House of Lords [*England*] [*A publication*] (DLA)
**LRHL Sc**.... English Law Reports, House of Lords, Scotch and Divorce Appeal Cases [*1866-75*] [*A publication*] (DLA)
**LRHL Sc App Cas**... Law Reports, House of Lords, Scotch and Divorce Appeal Cases [*1866-75*] [*A publication*] (DLA)
**LRHL Sc App Cas (Eng)**... English Law Reports, House of Lords, Scotch and Divorce Appeal Cases [*1866-75*] [*A publication*] (DLA)
**LRHSC**...... Large Radioisotope Heat Source Capsule [*NASA*] (KSC)
**LRI**............ Big Lost River [*Idaho*] [*Seismograph station code, US Geological Survey*] [*Closed*] (SEIS)
**LRI**............ Lawndale Railway & Industrial Co. [*Terminated*] [*AAR code*]
**LRI**............ Learning Resources Institute (EA)
**LRI**............ LeaRonal, Incorporated [*NYSE symbol*] (SPSG)
**LRI**............ Left-Right Indicator
**LRI**............ Legal Resource Index [*Information Access Corp.*] [*Bibliographic database*] [*Information service or system*] (IID)
**LRI**............ Library Resources, Incorporated [*Subsidiary of Encyclopaedia Britannica*]
**LrI**............. Library Resources, Incorporated, Chicago, IL [*Library symbol*] [*Library of Congress*] (LCLS)
**LRI**............ Libri e Riviste d'Italia [*A publication*]
**LRI**............ Lighting Research Institute (EA)
**LRI**............ Literature and Religion of Israel [*A publication*]
**LRI**............ Long-Range Indicator
**LRI**............ Long-Range Input (CET)
**LRI**............ Long-Range Inspector
**LRI**............ Long-Range Interceptor
**LRI**............ Long-Range RADAR Input
**LRI**............ Longboat Resources, Incorporated [*Vancouver Stock Exchange symbol*]
**LRI**............ Lower Respiratory Infection [*Medicine*]
**LRIA**.......... English Law Reports, Indian Appeals [*A publication*] (DLA)
**LRIA**.......... Iasi [*Romania*] [*ICAO location identifier*] (ICLI)
**LRIA**.......... Level Removable Instrument Assembly [*Nuclear energy*] (IEEE)
**LRIBA**....... Licentiate of the Royal Institute of British Architects
**LRIC**.......... Licentiate of the Royal Institute of Chemistry [*British*]
**LRIC**.......... Long-Run Incremental Cost [*Business term*] (ADA)
**LRIF**.......... Logos. Rivista Internazionale di Filosofia [*A publication*]
**LRIM**......... Long-Range Input Monitor [*RADAR*]
**LR Ind App**... English Law Reports, Indian Appeals [*A publication*] (DLA)
**LR Ind App Supp**... English Law Reports, Indian Appeals, Supplement [*A publication*] (DLA)
**LR Indian App**... English Law Reports, Indian Appeals [*A publication*] (DLA)
**LR Indian App (Eng)**... English Law Reports, Indian Appeals [*A publication*] (DLA)
**LRINF**....... Longer-Range Intermediate-Range Nuclear Forces
**LRIP**.......... Language Research in Progress (DIT)
**LRIP**.......... Long-Range Impact Point (MUGU)
**LRIP**.......... Low-Rate Initial Production (RDA)
**L Ripuar**...... Law of the Ripuarians [*A publication*] (DLA)
**LRIr**.......... Law Reports, Ireland [*1878-1893*] [*A publication*]
**LR Ir**.......... Law Reports, Irish [*A publication*] (DLA)
**LRIR**.......... Limb Radiance Inversion Radiometer
**LRIR**.......... Low-Resolution Infrared Radiometer
**LRIRR**....... Low-Resolution Infrared Radiometer (MSA)
**LRJ**............ Lemars, IA [*Location identifier*] [*FAA*] (FAAL)
**LRK**........... Kenya Law Reports [*A publication*] (DLA)
**LRK**........... LASER Research Kit
**LRKB**......... English Law Reports, King's Bench Division [*1901-52*] [*A publication*] (DLA)
**LRKB**......... Quebec Official Reports, King's Bench [*A publication*] (ILCA)
**LRKD**........ Literarische Rundschau fuer das Katholische Deutschland [*A publication*]
**LRL**............ Lawrence Radiation Laboratory [*Livermore*] [*Later, Lawrence Livermore Laboratory*] [*University of California*]
**LRL**............ Leakage Resistance Limit
**LRL**............ Light Railway Loads [*British*]
**LRL**............ Limited Raman LASER
**LRL**............ Linguistics Research Laboratory [*Gallaudet College*] [*Research center*] (RCD)
**LRL**............ Linking Relocating Loader
**LRL**............ Livermore Research Laboratory [*University of California*] (KSC)
**LRL**............ Logical Record Length
**LRL**............ Logical Record Location
**LRL**............ Lunar Receiving Laboratory [*NASA*]
**LRL**............ Tulane University, Law Library, New Orleans, LA [*OCLC symbol*] (OCLC)
**LR/LD**....... Line Receiver/Line Driver (MCD)
**LRLEI**........ League for Religious Labor in Eretz Israel (EA)
**LRLF**......... Local Radio Luminosity Function [*Cosmology*]
**LRLG**......... Long-Range Logistics Guidance [*Air Force*]
**LRL-L**........ Lawrence Radiation Laboratory, Livermore [*Later, Lawrence Livermore Laboratory*] [*University of California*]
**LRLL**......... Longitudinal Ridge of Lateral Lip
**LRLTRAN**... Lawrence Radiation Laboratory FORTRAN [*Programming language*] [*1961*] (CSR)
**LRLTRAN**... Lawrence Radiation Laboratory Translator (IEEE)
**LRM**.......... La Rassegna Musicale [*A publication*]
**LRM**.......... La Romana [*Dominican Republic*] [*Airport symbol*] (OAG)
**LRM**.......... Labor Relations Reference Manual [*A publication*] (DLA)

**LRM** .......... Latching Relay Matrix
**LRM** .......... Lead Reactor Manufacturer (NRCH)
**LRM** .......... Limited Register Machine
**LRM** .......... Line Replacement Module
**LRM** .......... Liquid Reaction Molding
**LRM** .......... Liquid Rocket Motor (KSC)
**LRM** .......... Logarithmic Radiation Monitor (NRCH)
**LRM** .......... Logarithmic Ratio Module
**LRM** .......... Long-Range Missile Launcher
**LRM** .......... Lower Reject Limit Median
**LRM** .......... Lunar Reconnaissance [*or Rendezvous*] Mission [*Aerospace*]
**LRM** .......... Lunar Reconnaissance Module [*Aerospace*]
**LR Mad** ..... Indian Law Reports, Madras Series [*A publication*] (DLA)
**LRMC**......... Long-Run Marginal Costs
**LRMG** ....... Hughes Lockless Rifle/Machine Gun (MCD)
**LR Misc D** ... Law Reports, Miscellaneous Division [*A publication*] (DLA)
**LRMP**........ Long-Range Maritime Patrol [*Aircraft*] (NATG)
**LRMPDA** ... Australia. Commonwealth Scientific and Industrial Research Organisation. Land Resources Management. Technical Paper [*A publication*]
**LRMS**........ Library Routine Management System
**LRMTS**..... LASER Range-Finder and Marked Target Seeker (MCD)
**LRN**........... Literary Research Newsletter [*A publication*]
**LRN**........... Long-Range Navigation
**LRN**........... Long Reference Number
**LRN**........... LORAN [*Long-Range Aid to Navigation*]
**LRNA** ........ Laws Relating to the Navy Annotated [*Military law*]
**LRNBA**....... La Raza National Bar Association (EA)
**LRNC** ........ Long Reference Number Code
**LRNG** ........ Learning
**LRNOD**..... Long-Range Night Observation Device [*Army*] (AABC)
**LRNPDF** ... Lawrence Review of Natural Products [*A publication*]
**LRNR** ........ Low-Resolution Non-Scanning Radiometer (MCD)
**LRNS**......... Nova Scotia Law Reports [*A publication*] (DLA)
**LRNSEP**.... Lawrence Review of Natural Products. Monograph System [*A publication*]
**LR (NSW)** ... Law Reports (New South Wales) [*A publication*] (APTA)
**LRNSW**..... Law Reports, New South Wales Supreme Court [*A publication*] (DLA)
**LR (NSW) B & P** ... Law Reports (New South Wales). Bankruptcy and Probate [*A publication*] (APTA)
**LR (NSW) D** ... Law Reports (New South Wales). Divorce [*A publication*] (APTA)
**LR (NSW) Eq** ... Law Reports (New South Wales). Equity [*A publication*] (APTA)
**LR (NSW) Vice-Adm** ... Law Reports (New South Wales). Vice-Admiralty [*A publication*] (APTA)
**LRNZ** ........ Law Reports, New Zealand [*A publication*] (DLA)
**LRO** ........... Laboratory Review Office [*Army*] (RDA)
**LRO** ........... Large Radio Observatory (KSC)
**LRO** ........... Lathrop, CA [*Location identifier*] [*FAA*] (FAAL)
**LRO** ........... Leading Radio Operator [*British military*] (DMA)
**LRO** ........... Logistics Readiness Officer [*Military*] (AABC)
**LRO** ........... Long-Range Objectives [*Navy*]
**LRO** ........... Long-Range Order
**LRO** ........... Low-Resistance Ohmmeter
**LROA** ........ Land Rover Owners Association (EA)
**LROA USA** ... Land Rover Owners Association, USA (EA)
**LROC** ........ Libertarian Republican Organizing Committee (EA)
**LROD**........ Oradea [*Romania*] [*ICAO location identifier*] (ICLI)
**LRO(G)**...... Leading Radio Operator (General) [*British military*] (DMA)
**LROG** ........ Long-Range Objectives Group [*Navy*] (MCD)
**LROL**......... Laboratoire de Recherches en Optique et Laser [*Laval University*] [*Canada*] [*Research center*] (RCD)
**L Rom** ........ Limba Romana [*A publication*]
**LROP**......... Bucuresti/Otopeni [*Romania*] [*ICAO location identifier*] (ICLI)
**LROR** ........ Low-Resolution Omnidirectional Radiometer (MCD)
**LROTD** ..... Laryngologie, Rhinologie, Otologie [*A publication*]
**LRO(W)**..... Leading Radio Operator (Warfare) [*British military*] (DMA)
**LROY** ........ Leroy Properties & Development Corp. [*NASDAQ symbol*] (NQ)
**LRP**............ English Law Reports, Probate Division [*A publication*] (DLA)
**LRP**............ Lancaster, PA [*Location identifier*] [*FAA*] (FAAL)
**LRP**............ Large Repairs to Hull
**LRP**............ Large Rotating Plug [*Nuclear energy*] (NRCH)
**LRP**............ LASER Retinal Photocoagulator
**LRP**............ Late Receptor Potential [*Photoreceptor*] [*Physiology*]
**LRP**............ Launching Reference Point
**LRP**............ LDI [*Low Density Lipoprotein*] Receptor-Related Protein [*Biochemistry*]
**LRP**............ Lebanese Revolutionary Party [*Political party*] (PD)
**LRP**............ Lesbian Rights Project [*Later, NCLR*] (EA)
**LRP**............ Limited Rate Production
**LRP**............ LM [*Lunar Module*] Replaceable Package [*NASA*]
**LRP**............ Logistics Release Point [*Army*] (INF)
**LRP**............ Long-Range Path (IEEE)
**LRP**............ Long-Range Patrol [*Pronounced "lurp"*] [*Formerly, LRRP*] [*Army*] (AABC)
**LRP**............ Long-Range Penetration
**LRP**............ Long-Range Planning [*A publication*]
**LRP**............ Long-Range Plans (NVT)
**LRPA**......... Little Rock Port Railroad [*AAR code*]
**LRPA**......... Long-Range Patrol Aircraft (MCD)
**LRPC**......... English Law Reports, Privy Council, Appeal Cases [*1866-75*] [*A publication*] (DLA)
**LRPC**......... London Regional Passengers Committee [*British*] (ECON)
**LR PC** ........ Privy Council. Law Reports [*United Kingdom*] [*A publication*]
**LRPC (Eng)** ... English Law Reports, Privy Council, Appeal Cases [*1866-75*] [*A publication*] (DLA)
**LRPD**......... Law Reports, Probate Division [*A publication*] (DLA)
**LRP & D**.... Probate and Divorce Cases [*1865-75*] [*England*] [*A publication*] (DLA)
**LRP Div**..... English Law Reports, Probate, Divorce, and Admiralty Division [*A publication*] (DLA)
**LRPDS** ...... Long-Range Position-Determining System [*Army*] (RDA)
**LRPE**......... Long-Run Price Effect [*Marketing*]
**LRPF** ......... Liberal Religious Peace Fellowship (EA)
**LRPG**......... Long-Range Penetration Group [*Military*] [*World War II*]
**LRPG**......... Long-Range Proving Ground [*Air Force*]
**LRPGD**...... Long-Range Proving Ground Division [*Air Force*]
**LRPGR**...... Long-Range Planning Ground Rules (AAG)
**LRP/GWU** ... Logistics Research Project, George Washington University
**LRPL**......... Liquid Rocket Propulsion Laboratory [*Army*] (IEEE)
**LRP & M**... Law Reports, Probate and Matrimonial [*1866-75*] [*A publication*] (DLA)
**LRPP** ......... Long-Range Propulsion Plan (MCD)
**LRPPD** ...... Long-Range Planning Purpose Document
**LR Prob Div** ... English Law Reports, Probate, Divorce, and Admiralty Division [*A publication*] (DLA)
**LR Prob Div (Eng)** ... English Law Reports, Probate, Divorce, and Admiralty Division [*A publication*] (DLA)
**LR Prob & M (Eng)** ... English Law Reports, Probate, Divorce, and Admiralty Division [*A publication*] (DLA)
**LRPS** ......... Licentiate of the Royal Photographic Society [*British*] (DBQ)
**LRPS** ......... Long-Range Planning Service [*Stanford Research Institute*] [*Assists businesses in investment activities*] (IID)
**LRPS** ......... Long-Range Positioning System
**LRPT**......... Large Repair Parts Transporter (MCD)
**LRQB**......... English Law Reports, Queen's Bench Division [*1865-75*] [*A publication*] (DLA)
**LRQB**......... Quebec Queen's Bench Reports [*Canada*] [*A publication*] (DLA)
**LRQBD**...... English Law Reports, Queen's Bench Division [*1865-75*] [*A publication*] (DLA)
**LRQB Div** ... English Law Reports, Queen's Bench Division [*1865-75*] [*A publication*] (DLA)
**LRQB Div (Eng)** ... English Law Reports, Queen's Bench Division [*1865-75*] [*A publication*] (DLA)
**LRQB (Eng)** ... English Law Reports, Queen's Bench Division [*1865-75*] [*A publication*] (DLA)
**LR-QR**....... Letter Requirement - Quick Reaction [*Army*]
**LRR** ........... Labor Relations Reporter [*Bureau of National Affairs*] [*A publication*]
**LRR** ........... Labyrinthine Righting Reflex [*Physiology*]
**LRR** ........... Land-Rover Register 1947-1951 [*Petersfield, Hampshire, England*] (EAIO)
**LRR** ........... LASER Radiation Receiver
**LRR** ........... Launch Readiness Report [*or Review*] [*NASA*] (KSC)
**LRR** ........... Logistic Readiness Review [*Navy*]
**LRR** ........... Long-Range RADAR
**LRR** ........... Long-Range Reconnaissance (MCD)
**LRR** ........... Long-Range Requirements [*Navy*]
**LRR** ........... Long-Range Rocket (MUGU)
**LRR** ........... Longreach Resources Ltd. [*Vancouver Stock Exchange symbol*]
**LRR** ........... Loop Regenerative Repeater
**LRR** ........... Loss of Righting Reflex [*Medicine*]
**LRR** ........... Lot Rejection Report
**LRRC**......... Labor Relations and Research Center [*University of Massachusetts*]
**LRRD** ........ Long-Range Reconnaissance Detachment
**LRRDAP**... Long-Range Research, Development, and Acquisition Plan (RDA)
**LRRI**.......... Land Resources Research Institute [*Agriculture Canada*] [*Formerly, Soil Research Institute*] [*Research center*] (RCD)
**LRRI**.......... Long-Range Reference Retroreflectance Instrument [*Bicycle test*] [*National Institute of Standards and Technology*]
**LRRM**........ Labor Relations Reference Manual [*Bureau of National Affairs*] [*A publication*] (DLA)
**LRRM**........ Loss Ratio Reserve Method [*Insurance*]
**LRRM BNA** ... Labor Relations Reference Manual. Bureau of National Affairs [*A publication*]
**LRR & MF** ... Long-Range Resource and Management Forecast
**lrRNA**........ Ribonucleic Acid, Light Ribosomal [*Biochemistry, genetics*]
**LRRO** ........ Land Revenue Records and Enrollments Office [*British*]
**LRRP** ........ Law Reports, Restrictive Practices Cases [*1958-72*] [*A publication*] (DLA)
**LRRP**......... Long-Range Reconnaissance Patrol [*Pronounced "lurp"*] [*Later, LRP*] [*Army*] (AABC)
**LRRP**......... Lowest Required Radiated Power

**LRRPC**...... Restrictive Practices Cases [*1958-72*] [*England*] [*A publication*] (DLA)
**LRRR**......... LASER Ranging Retroreflection [*Also, LR3*] [*Pronounced "LR-cubed"*] [*Apollo 11 experiment*] [*NASA*]
**LRRS**......... Library Reports & Research Service, Inc. [*Information service or system*] (IID)
**LRRS**......... Limited Remaining Radiation Service [*Unit*] [*Military*]
**LRRT**......... Library Research Round Table [*American Library Association*]
**LRS**........... Laboratory Release System (MCD)
**LRS**........... Lactated Ringer's Solution [*Intravenous solution*]
**LRS**........... Lake Reporting Service
**LRS**........... Lamb-Retherford Shift [*Physics*]
**LRS**........... Lander Radio Subsystem [*NASA*]
**LRS**........... Lanyard Release Switch
**LRS**........... Larder Resources, Inc. [*Toronto Stock Exchange symbol*]
**LRS**........... Lares [*Puerto Rico*] [*Seismograph station code, US Geological Survey*] (SEIS)
**LRS**........... LASER Raman Scattering
**LRS**........... LASER Raman Spectroscopy
**LRS**........... LASER Ranging System
**LRS**........... LASER Raster Scanner
**LRS**........... Launch Recoil Simulator
**LRS**........... Laurinburg & Southern Railroad Co. [*AAR code*]
**LRS**........... Lawyer Referral Service
**LRS**........... League of Religious Settlements (EA)
**LRS**........... Legislative Reference Service [*Later, Congressional Research Service*] [*Library of Congress*]
**LRS**........... Legislative Research Service [*Commonwealth Parliamentary Library*] [*Australia*]
**LRS**........... Leipziger Rechtswissenschaftliche Studien [*A publication*]
**LRS**........... Leipziger Romanistischer Studien [*A publication*]
**LRS**........... Level Recording Switch (NRCH)
**LRS**........... Library Reproduction Service, Microfilm Co. of California, Los Angeles, CA [*Library symbol*] [*Library of Congress*] (LCLS)
**L/R/S**......... Library Rubber Stamps [*Antiquarian book trade*]
**LRS**........... Lifetime Reproductive Success [*Demographics*]
**LRS**........... Light Radiation Sensor
**LRS**........... Light Repair Section [*British military*] (DMA)
**LRS**........... Light's Retention Scale [*Test*]
**LRS**........... Lightweight RADAR Set
**LRS**........... Limited Resources Specialty (AFM)
**LRS**........... Lincoln Record Society [*A publication*]
**LRS**........... Linguistics Research System
**LRS**........... Liquid RADWASTE System (NRCH)
**LRS**........... Ljudska Republika Slovenije [*A publication*]
**LRS**........... Lloyd's Register of Shipping
**LRS**........... Logistics Requirements System [*Navy*]
**LRS**........... London Record Society [*British*] (ILCA)
**LRS**........... Long-Range Search
**LRS**........... Long-Range Study
**LRS**........... Long Reversed Superchron [*Geology*]
**LRS**........... Long Right Shift
**LRS**........... Low-Rate Station
**LRSA**......... Laboratoire de Recherche en Sciences de l'Administration [*Laval University*] [*Canada*] [*Research center*] (RCD)
**LR(SA)**...... Law Reports (South Australia) [*A publication*] (DLA)
**LRSA**......... South Australian Law Reports [*A publication*] (APTA)
**LRSAM**...... Long-Range Surface-to-Air Missile (NATG)
**LRSB**......... Sibiu/Turnisor [*Romania*] [*ICAO location identifier*] (ICLI)
**LRSC**......... Law Reports, New Zealand Supreme Court [*A publication*] (DLA)
**LRSC**......... Licentiate of the Royal Society of Chemistry [*British*] (DBQ)
**LRSC**......... Long-Range Surveillance Company [*Military*] (INF)
**LRSCA**...... Large Retractable Solar Cell Array
**LR Sc App**... Law Reports, Scotch Appeals [*A publication*] (DLA)
**LR Sc & D**... English Law Reports, House of Lords, Scotch and Divorce Appeal Cases [*1866-75*] [*A publication*] (DLA)
**LR Sc & D App**... Scottish and Divorce Appeals [*1866-75*] [*A publication*] (DLA)
**LR Sc & D App**... Scottish and Divorce Cases before the House of Lords [*A publication*] (DLA)
**LR Sc & Div**... Scotch and Divorce Appeals [*1866-75*] [*A publication*] (DLA)
**LR Sc Div App**... Law Reports, Scotch Appeals [*A publication*] (DLA)
**LRsch**......... Lutherische Rundschau [*Stuttgart*] [*A publication*]
**LRSD**......... Long-Range Surveillance Detachment [*Military*] (INF)
**LRS & D App**... Law Reports, Scotch and Divorce Appeals [*1866-75*] [*A publication*] (DLA)
**LRSDC**...... Lakes Region Sled Dog Club (EA)
**LR Sess Cas**... English Law Reports, Sessions Cases [*A publication*] (DLA)
**LRSF**......... Lactating Rat Serum Factor [*Immunology*]
**LRSF**......... Long-Range Systems Forecast
**LRSI**.......... Low-Temperature Reusable Surface Insulation (NASA)
**LRSIFC**..... Lori Robin Smith International Fan Club (EA)
**LRSK**......... Long-Range Station Keeping (NG)
**LRSL**......... Law Reports, Sierra Leone Series [*A publication*] (DLA)
**LRSLP**....... Lietuvos Revoliuciniu Socialistu Liaudininkai Partija [*Revolutionary Socialist Populists Party of Lithuania*] [*Political party*] (PPE)
**LRSM**........ Laboratory for Research on the Structure of Matter [*University of Pennsylvania*]
**LRSM**........ Licentiate of the Royal School of Music, London [*British*]
**LRSM**........ Satu Mare [*Romania*] [*ICAO location identifier*] (ICLI)
**LRSO**......... Long-Range Surveillance Outpost (MCD)
**LRSOM**..... Long-Range Stand-Off Missile
**LRSS**......... Long-Range Strategic Studies [*Military*] (AFIT)
**LRSS**......... Long-Range Survey System [*Military*]
**LR Stat**....... English Law Reports, Statutes [*A publication*] (DLA)
**LRS & TP**.. Long-Range Science and Technology Plan [*Army*]
**LRSTPP**.... Long-Range Scientific Technical Planning Program (NG)
**LRSU**......... Long-Range Surveillance Unit [*Military*] (INF)
**LRSV**......... Suceava/Salcea [*Romania*] [*ICAO location identifier*] (ICLI)
**LRT**........... LASER Range-Finder Theodolite
**LRT**........... Last Resort Target [*Military*]
**LRT**........... Launch, Recovery, and Transport [*Vehicle*]
**LRT**........... Lawrenceburg, TN [*Location identifier*] [*FAA*] (FAAL)
**LRT**........... Light Rail Transit
**LRT**........... Light Repair Truck [*British*]
**LRT**........... Likelihood Ratio Test [*Statistics*]
**LRT**........... LL & E Royalty Trust UBI [*NYSE symbol*] (SPSG)
**LRT**........... Local Leak Rate Test [*Nuclear energy*] (IEEE)
**LRT**........... Local Radiotherapy
**LRT**........... Loki Ranging Transponder
**LRT**........... London Reading Test [*Educational test*]
**LRT**........... London Regional Transport
**LRT**........... Long-Range Radiotelephone
**LRT**........... Long-Range Transport [*Navy*] [*British*]
**LRT**........... Long-Range Typhon [*Navy*] (NG)
**LRT**........... Long Ring Timer
**LRT**........... Lorient [*France*] [*Airport symbol*] (OAG)
**LRT**........... Lower Respiratory Tract [*Medicine*]
**LRTA**......... Lath Renders' Trade Association [*A union*] [*British*]
**LRTA**......... Leisure, Recreation, and Tourism Abstracts [*Database*] [*Commonwealth Agricultural Bureaux International*] [*Information service or system*] (CRD)
**LRTA**......... Light Rail Transit Association [*Milton, Keynes, England*] (EAIO)
**LRTAP**...... Long-Range Transport of Atmospheric Pollutants
**LRTC**......... Tulcea/Cataloi [*Romania*] [*ICAO location identifier*] (ICLI)
**LRTF**......... Linear Radial Transmission Filter [*Photography*]
**LRTF**......... Long-Range Technical Forecast (IEEE)
**LRTG**......... Logistics Reassignment Task Group [*DoD*] (MCD)
**LRTGT**...... Last Resort Target [*Military*]
**LRTI**.......... Lower Respiratory Tract Infection [*Medicine*] (ADA)
**LRTL**......... Light Railway Transport League [*British*] (DCTA)
**LRTM**........ Long-Range Training Mission [*Military*]
**LRTM**........ Tirgu Mures/Vidrasau [*Romania*] [*ICAO location identifier*] (ICLI)
**LRTNF**...... Long-Range Theater Nuclear Force [*Military*]
**LRTNW**..... Long-Range Theater Nuclear Weapons [*Military*]
**LRTR**......... Timisoara/Giarmata [*Romania*] [*ICAO location identifier*] (ICLI)
**LRTS**......... LASER Ranging and Tracking System (RDA)
**LRTS**......... Library Resources and Technical Services [*A publication*]
**LRU**........... Las Cruces [*New Mexico*] [*Airport symbol*] (OAG)
**LRU**........... Las Cruces, NM [*Location identifier*] [*FAA*] (FAAL)
**LRU**........... Least Recently Used [*Replacement algorithm*] [*Data processing*]
**LRU**........... Less than Release Unit [*Army*] (AABC)
**LRU**........... Line Removable Unit
**LRU**........... Line Replaceable Unit (AFM)
**LRU**........... Link Retraction Unit (KSC)
**LRU**........... Little Rock University [*Merged with University of Arkansas*]
**LRU**........... Lone Replaceable Unit (MCD)
**LRU**........... Lowest Repairable Unit (MCD)
**LRU**........... Lowest Replacement Unit (MCD)
**LRU**........... Tulane University, New Orleans, LA [*OCLC symbol*] (OCLC)
**LRuL**.......... Louisiana Technical University, Ruston, LA [*Library symbol*] [*Library of Congress*] (LCLS)
**LRuLP**....... Lincoln Parish Library, Ruston, LA [*Library symbol*] [*Library of Congress*] (LCLS)
**LRUP**......... La Raza Unida Party (EA)
**LRUPS**...... Line Replaceable Unit Power Supply (MCD)
**LRV**........... Lanarkshire Rifle Volunteers [*British military*] (DMA)
**LRV**........... Lancashire Rifle Volunteers [*British military*] (DMA)
**LRV**........... Launch Readiness Verification [*NASA*] (NASA)
**LRV**........... Leirvogur [*Iceland*] [*Geomagnetic observatory code*]
**LRV**........... Lifting Reentry Vehicle (MCD)
**LRV**........... Light Rail Vehicle
**LRV**........... Little Rabbit Valley [*California*] [*Seismograph station code, US Geological Survey*] (SEIS)
**LRV**........... Long-Range Video (MCD)
**LRV**........... Lunar Rover [*or Roving*] Vehicle [*NASA*]
**LRVEP**...... League of Rural Voters Education Project (EA)
**LRVSA**...... Landmaschinen-Rundschau [*A publication*]
**LRW**.......... Labor Relations Week [*Bureau of National Affairs*] [*Information service or system*] (CRD)
**LRW**.......... London Radio Workshop [*Independent Local Radio*] [*British*]
**LRWE**........ Long-Range Weapons Establishment [*Australia*]
**LRWES**...... Long-Range Weapons Experimental Station [*Australia*] (ADA)
**LRWRE**..... Long-Range Weapons Research Establishment [*Australia*] (ADA)

**LRY** ........ Lady Robyn Resources, Inc. [*Vancouver Stock Exchange symbol*]
**LRY** ........ Liberal Religious Youth
**LS**.......... Channel Express [*Air Services*] Ltd. [*Great Britain*] [*ICAO designator*] (FAAC)
**LS**.......... Labologists Society [*Farnborough, Hampshire, England*] (EAIO)
**LS**.......... Labor Service [*Military*]
**LS**.......... Laboratory System
**L/S**.......... Lactose/Sucrose [*Ratio*]
**LS**.......... Lacus Somniorum [*Lunar area*]
**LS**.......... Lamellar Strip [*Botany*]
**LS**.......... Land Service
**LS**.......... Land Surveying Program [*Association of Independent Colleges and Schools specialization code*]
**LS**.......... Land Surveyor
**LS**.......... Landesschuetzeneinheit [*Regional defense force*] [*German military - World War II*]
**LS**.......... Landing Ship
**LS**.......... Landing Site (KSC)
**LS**.......... Lange Sicht [*Long Sight*] [*German*]
**LS**.......... Language Specification (IEEE)
**LS**.......... Language and Speech [*A publication*]
**L and S**...... Language and Speech [*England*] [*A publication*]
**LS**.......... Lantern Slide [*Photography*]
**ls**.......... Laos [*MARC country of publication code*] [*Library of Congress*] (LCCP)
**LS**.......... LASER System
**LS**.......... [*The*] Last Message Sent by Me Was ____ [*Aviation code*] (FAAC)
**LS**.......... Lastensegler; Lastensegelflugzeug [*Cargo transport glider*] [*German military - World War II*]
**LS**.......... Latch Side
**LS**.......... Late Scramble [*Reason for missed interception*] [*Military*]
**LS**.......... Late Shock [*Medicine*]
**LS**.......... Lateral Septum
**LS**.......... Lateral Subsylvian Cortex [*Neuroanatomy*]
**LS**.......... Launch Sequence (MCD)
**LS**.......... Launch Service
**L & S**........ Launch and Servicing (AAG)
**LS**.......... Launch Set
**LS**.......... Launch Simulator (MUGU)
**LS**.......... Launch Site [*NASA*] (MCD)
**LS**.......... Launch Station (MCD)
**LS**.......... Launching System
**L & S**........ Laverne and Shirley [*Television program*]
**LS**.......... Law Student (DLA)
**LS**.......... Le Gros Scouts [*British military*] (DMA)
**LS**.......... Le Soir [*A publication*]
**LS**.......... Le Soleil [*Dakar*] [*A publication*]
**LS**.......... Lead Sheet [*Military*]
**LS**.......... Leaders of Science [*A publication*]
**LS**.......... Leading Seaman [*Navy*] [*British*]
**LS**.......... Leading Stoker
**L-S**.......... Leap-Second
**LS**.......... Learning Step
**LS**.......... Least Significant (IEEE)
**LS**.......... Least Squares [*Mathematical statistics*]
**LS**.......... Lebendige Schule [*A publication*]
**LS**.......... Lebendige Seelsorge [*A publication*]
**L/S**.......... Lecithin/Sphingomyelin [*Ratio*] [*Clinical chemistry*]
**LS**.......... Left Sacrum [*Medicine*] (KSC)
**LS**.......... Left Safety [*Sports*]
**LS**.......... Left Shift
**LS**.......... Left Side
**LS**.......... Legal Scroll
**LS**.......... Leiomyosarcoma [*Medicine*]
**LS**.......... Leksikograficeskij Sbornik [*A publication*]
**LS**.......... Length of Stroke
**LS**.......... Lepidopterists' Society
**LS**.......... Lesotho [*ANSI two-letter standard code*] (CNC)
**LS**.......... Less
**LS**.......... Lessing Society (EA)
**LS**.......... Letter Service
**LS**.......... Letter Signed [*Manuscript descriptions*]
**LS**.......... Letter Stock
**LS**.......... Leukemia Society of America
**LS**.......... Level Setter
**LS**.......... Level Switch
**LS**.......... Library Science
**LS**.......... Library Search
**LS**.......... Library Services
**LS**.......... Licensed Surveyor [*British*] (ADA)
**LS**.......... Licentiate in Science
**LS**.......... Licentiate in Surgery
**LS**.......... Life Science (NASA)
**LS**.......... Life Support (AAG)
**LS**.......... Life System (MCD)
**LS**.......... Lifesaving Service [*Coast Guard*]
**LS**.......... Light Ship
**LS**.......... Light Source
**LS**.......... Light Sussex [*Poultry*]
**LS**.......... Light Switch
**LS**.......... Lighthouse Service [*Coast Guard*]
**LS**.......... Lighting Supervisor [*Television*]
**LS**.......... Lighting System
**LS**.......... Lightning Sensor [*Aviation*]
**LS**.......... Lignosulfonate [*Pulp and paper processing*]
**LS**.......... Like-Sexed
**LS**.......... Limbic System [*Brain anatomy*]
**LS**.......... Limestone [*Petrology*] (AAG)
**LS**.......... Liminal [*or Least*] Sensation [*Psychology*]
**LS**.......... Limit Switch [*Electronics*]
**LS**.......... Line Scan (DEN)
**LS**.......... Line Stretcher
**LS**.......... Line Switch [*Telecommunications*] (TEL)
**LS**.......... Lingua e Stile [*A publication*]
**L & S**........ Lingua e Stile [*A publication*]
**LS**.......... Lingue Straniere [*A publication*]
**LS**.......... Linguistica Slovaca [*A publication*]
**LS**.......... Linker Scanning [*Mutants*] [*Genetics*]
**LS**.......... Linksozialisten [*Left Socialists*] [*Austria*] [*Political party*] (PPE)
**LS**.......... Liquid Scintillation [*Chemical analysis*]
**LS**.......... Liquid Sensor (AAG)
**LS**.......... List of Specifications (NATG)
**LS**.......... List Total [*Banking*]
**LS**.......... Listed Securities
**LS**.......... Literatura v Shkole [*A publication*]
**LS**.......... Literature Search
**LS**.......... Literaturny Sovremennik [*A publication*]
**l/s**.......... Liters per Second [*SI symbol*]
**LS**.......... Liver and Spleen [*Medicine*]
**LS**.......... Livestock (DCTA)
**L/S**.......... Load System (MCD)
**LS**.......... Loading Splice [*Telecommunications*] (TEL)
**LS**.......... Loca Sancta [*A publication*] (BJA)
**LS**.......... Local Store
**LS**.......... Local Sunset
**LS**.......... Locked Shut (NRCH)
**LS**.......... Lockheed Standards
**LS**.......... Locus Sepulchri [*Place of the Sepulchre*] [*Latin*]
**LS**.......... Locus Sigilli [*Place of the Seal*] [*Legal term*] [*Latin*]
**LS**.......... Logistical Support [*Army*]
**L & S**........ Logistics and Support (NASA)
**LS**.......... London Scottish [*Army regiment*]
**LS**.......... [*The*] London Sinfonietta
**LS**.......... Long Service (ADA)
**LS**.......... Long Shot [*A photograph or motion picture sequence taken from a distance*]
**LS**.......... Long Sleeves [*Dressmaking*]
**Ls**.......... Longear Sunfish [*Ichthyology*]
**LS**.......... Longitudinal Section
**LS**.......... Loose Shot
**LS**.......... Lost Seska (EA)
**LS**.......... Loudspeaker
**LS**.......... Lovat Scouts [*British military*] (DMA)
**LS**.......... Low-Power Schottky [*Electronics*]
**LS**.......... Low Salt [*Dietetics*]
**LS**.......... Low Similarity [*Psychology*]
**LS**.......... Low-Speed
**LS**.......... Lower Structure
**LS**.......... Lumbosacral [*Medicine*]
**LS**.......... Lump Sum
**LS**.......... Lunar Surface (KSC)
**LS**.......... Lung Sounds [*Medicine*]
**LS**.......... Lusitania Sacra [*A publication*]
**LS**.......... Lute Society [*Harrow, England*] (EAIO)
**LS**.......... Lute Society of America. Journal [*A publication*]
**LS**.......... Luteinization Stimulator [*Endocrinology*]
**LS**.......... Luxury Sport [*In automobile model name "Cordia LS"*]
**LS**.......... Lymphosarcoma [*Medicine*]
**ls-----**....... South Atlantic Ocean [*MARC geographic area code*] [*Library of Congress*] (LCCP)
**LS**.......... Spectator (London) [*A publication*]
**LS**.......... Sudanese Pound (IMH)
**LS**.......... Summer [*Vessel load line mark*]
**L3S**.......... LNG [*Liquefied Natural Gas*] Seabed Supported System
**LSA**.......... Labor Services Agency (AABC)
**LSA**.......... Labor Surplus Area
**LSA**.......... Labour Staff Association [*National Coal Board*] [*British*]
**LSA**.......... Lamesa, TX [*Location identifier*] [*FAA*] (FAAL)
**LSA**.......... Land Service Assistant [*Ministry of Agriculture, Fisheries, and Food*] [*British*]
**LSA**.......... Land Settlement Association [*British*]
**LSA**.......... Landing Ship, Assault [*Navy*] [*British*]
**LSA**.......... Landing Supply Activity
**LSA**.......... Landmark Savings Association [*AMEX symbol*] (SPSG)
**LSA**.......... Language Sampling and Analysis [*Educational test*]
**LSA**.......... Large Spherical Array
**LSA**.......... Late Stone Age
**LSA**.......... Lateral Spherical Aberration

**LSA**........... Launch Services Agreement (MCD)
**LSA**........... Law and Society Association (EA)
**LSA**........... Layton School of Art [*Wisconsin*]
**LSA**........... Lead Spring Assembly
**LSA**........... Leading Stores Accountant [*British military*] (DMA)
**LSA**........... League for Socialist Action [*Canada*]
**LSA**........... Leaving Scene of an Accident [*Traffic offense charge*]
**LSA**........... Lebende Sprachen. Zeitschrift fuer Fremde Sprachen in Wissenschaft und Praxis [*A publication*]
**LSA**........... Left Sacroanterior [*A fetal position, the breech position*] [*Obstetrics*]
**LSA**........... Leisure Studies Association [*British*]
**LSA**........... Leukemia Society of America (EA)
**LSA**........... Level Shift Amplifier
**LSA**........... Lhasa [*Tibet*] [*Seismograph station code, US Geological Survey*] (SEIS)
**LSA**........... Library Science Abstracts [*A publication*]
**LSA**........... Library Services Act [*1956*]
**LSA**........... Libre Service Actualites [*A publication*]
**LSA**........... Licensed Stores Association of Western Australia
**LSA**........... Licentiate in Agricultural Science
**LSA**........... Licentiate of the Society of Apothecaries [*British*]
**LSA**........... Lichen Sclerosis et Atrophicus [*Dermatology*]
**LSA**........... Life Saving Appliance [*or Apparatus*] (DS)
**LSA**........... Life Style Analysis [*Psychology*]
**LSA**........... Limited Space-Charge Accumulation [*Electronics*]
**LSA**........... Line-Sharing Adapter
**LSA**........... Linear Servo Actuator
**LSA**........... Linguistic Society of America (EA)
**LSA**........... Liquid Scintillation Analyzer [*Chemistry*]
**LSA**........... Lithuanian Scouts Association (EA)
**LSA**........... Lithuanian Students Association (EA)
**LSA**........... Little Sisters of the Assumption [*See also PSA*] [*Paris, France*] (EAIO)
**LSA**........... Livestock Agent
**LSA**........... Local Supervising Authority
**LSA**........... Locksmith Security Association (EA)
**LSA**........... Logistic Support Agreement [*Military*] (CAAL)
**LSA**........... Logistic Support Aircraft (MCD)
**LSA**........... Logistic Support Analysis
**LSA**........... Logistic Support Area (NVT)
**LSA**........... Logistic System Analysis [*Navy*]
**LSA**........... Logistics Supply Area
**LSA**........... Logistics Support Analysis
**LSA**........... Longitudinal Spherical Aberration
**LSA**........... Losuia [*Papua New Guinea*] [*Airport symbol*] (OAG)
**LSA**........... Louisiana Statutes, Annotated [*A publication*] (DLA)
**LSA**........... Low-Cost Solar Array (IEEE)
**LSA**........... Low-Intensity Lighting System [*Aviation code*] (FAAC)
**LSA**........... Low Specific Activity [*Radioisotope*]
**LSA**........... Lowe's Syndrome Association (EA)
**LSa**........... Lusitania Sacra [*A publication*]
**LSA**........... Lute Society of America (EA)
**LSa**........... Lymphosarcoma [*Medicine*]
**LSA**........... University of Arizona, Graduate Library School, Tucson, AZ [*OCLC symbol*] (OCLC)
**LSAA**......... Linen Supply Association of America [*Later, TRSA*] (EA)
**LSAAP**....... Lone Star Army Ammunition Plant (AABC)
**LSAB**......... Linguistic Society of America. Bulletin [*A publication*]
**LSAC**......... Labor Sector Advisory Committee [*Terminated, 1980*] (EGAO)
**LSAC**......... London Small Arms Company [*Military*]
**L-SACA**..... Larkin-Sopwith Aviation Co. of Australasia Ltd.
**LSAC/LSAS** ... Law School Admission Council/Law School Admission Services (EA)
**LSACN**...... Logistic Support Analysis Control Number (MCD)
**LSADDN**... Life Science Advances [*A publication*]
**LSA Exp Stn Tech Bull (Maine)** ... LSA [*Life Sciences and Agricultural*] Experiment Station. Technical Bulletin (Maine) [*A publication*]
**LSAG**......... Geneve [*Switzerland*] [*ICAO location identifier*] (ICLI)
**LSAH**......... Launch Site Accommodations Handbook [*NASA*] (NASA)
**lsai---**......... Ascension Island [*MARC geographic area code*] [*Library of Congress*] (LCCP)
**LSA/L**........ Language. Journal of the Linguistic Society of America [*A publication*]
**LSAL**......... Left Salivary [*Gland*]
**L Salic**........ Salic Law [*A publication*] (DLA)
**LSA/LSAR** ... Logistic Support Analysis/Logistic Support Analysis Record [*Army*] (RDA)
**LSAM**........ Launcher System Angles Matched [*Navy*] (CAAL)
**LSAM**........ Logistics Support Alternative [*or Analysis*] Model (MCD)
**LSAM**........ Lumped Shell Analysis Method
**LSAO**......... Line Station Assembly Order (MCD)
**LSAP**......... Laboratory Space Allocation Plan (MCD)
**LSAP**......... Launch Sequence Applications Program (MCD)
**LSAP**......... Letzeburger Sozialistesch Arbechter Partei [*Socialist Workers' Party of Luxembourg*] [*Political party*] (PPE)
**LSAP**......... Linear Systems Analysis Program [*Statistics*]
**LSAP**......... Link Layer Service Access Point
**LSAP**......... Logistic Support Analysis Plan [*or Program*] [*Army*]
**LSAP**......... Logistic Support Analysis Process [*Navy*]
**LSAPT**....... Lunar Sample Analysis Planning Team [*NASA*]
**LSAR**......... Logistic Support Analysis Record (RDA)
**LSARA**...... Landscape Architecture [*A publication*]
**LSARS**....... West's Louisiana Revised Statutes [*A publication*] (DLA)
**LSAT**......... Law School Admission Test
**LSAT**......... Logistic Shelter Air Transportable
**LSAZ**......... Zurich [*Switzerland*] [*ICAO location identifier*] (ICLI)
**LSB**........... Bachelor of Life Science
**LSB**........... High-Intensity Lighting System [*Aviation code*] (FAAC)
**LSB**........... La Sacra Bibbia (BJA)
**LSB**........... La Sainte Bible [*A publication*]
**LSB**........... Labour Supply Board [*British*]
**LSB**........... Landing Ship, Bombardment
**LSB**........... Launch Service Building
**LSB**........... Launcher Support Building
**LSB**........... Least Significant BIT [*or Byte*] [*Data compaction*]
**LSB**........... Left Sternal Border
**LSB**........... Legal Service Bulletin [*A publication*] (APTA)
**LSb**........... Leksikograficeskij Sbornik [*A publication*]
**LSB**........... Library of Standard Biographies [*A publication*]
**LSB**........... Lifestyle Beverage Corp. [*Vancouver Stock Exchange symbol*]
**LSB**........... Line Segment Block [*Data processing*]
**LSB**........... Linguistic Survey Bulletin [*A publication*]
**LSB**........... List of Successful Bidders [*DoD*]
**LSB**........... Logistic Support Base (NVT)
**LSB**........... Logistics Sustaining Base [*Military*] (RDA)
**LSB**........... London School Board
**LSB**........... Lordsburg, NM [*Location identifier*] [*FAA*] (FAAL)
**LSB**........... Low Silhouette Blade [*Aircraft*]
**LSB**........... Low-Speed Breaker Relay (IEEE)
**LSB**........... Low-Speed Buffer (CET)
**LSB**........... Lower Sideband [*Data transmission*]
**LSB**........... LSB Industries, Inc. [*AMEX symbol*] (SPSG)
**LSB**........... Lunar Surface Base [*NASA*] (KSC)
**LSB**........... Sitzungsberichte. Saechsische Akademie der Wissenschaften (Leipzig) [*A publication*]
**LSB**........... Southern University, Library, Baton Rouge, LA [*OCLC symbol*] (OCLC)
**LSBA**......... Leading Sick Bay Attendant [*Navy*] [*British*]
**LSBC**......... [*The*] La Salle & Bureau County Railroad Co. [*AAR code*]
**LSBCA**...... Lucrari Stiintifice ale Institutului Agronomic "Nicolae Balcescu" (Bucuresti). Seria C [*A publication*]
**LSBPHF**.... Library Service to the Blind and Physically Handicapped Forum [*Association of Specialized and Cooperative Library Agencies*]
**LSBR**......... Large Seed-Blanket Reactor
**LSBRT**....... Library Service to the Blind Round Table
**LSB (SA)**... Law Society. Bulletin (South Australia) [*A publication*] (APTA)
**lsbv---**......... Bouvet Island [*MARC geographic area code*] [*Library of Congress*] (LCCP)
**LSBX**......... Lawrence Savings Bank [*Lawrence, MA*] [*NASDAQ symbol*] (NQ)
**LSBY**......... Least Significant Byte [*Data compaction*] [*Data processing*]
**LSC**........... Labor Studies Center [*AFL-CIO*]
**LSC**........... Lake Survey Center [*National Oceanic and Atmospheric Administration*]
**LSC**........... Landing Ship Carrier [*British military*] (DMA)
**LSC**........... Large-Scale Computer
**LSC**........... Large Single Copy Region [*Of a chromosome*] [*Genetics*]
**LSC**........... Large Submetacentric Chromosome [*Medicine*]
**LSC**........... LASER Spectral Control
**LSC**........... Launch Sequence Control
**L Sc**........... Laureate of Science
**LSC**........... Law of the Sea Conference [*United Nations*]
**LSC**........... Learning Skills Center Reading and Study Skills Program [*Cornell University*] [*Research center*] (RCD)
**LSC**........... Least Significant Character (IEEE)
**LSC**........... Least Squares Circle [*Manufacturing term*]
**LSC**........... Least-Squares Collocation [*Mathematics*]
**LSC**........... Left-Sided Colon Cancer [*Oncology*]
**LSC**........... Left Stage Center [*A stage direction*]
**LSC**........... Legal Services for Children (EA)
**LSC**........... Legal Services Corporation [*Government agency*]
**LSC**........... Legislative Service Center [*Washington State Legislature*] [*Information service or system*] (IID)
**LSC**........... Lens Sign Convention
**LSC**........... Liberian Shipowners Council (EA)
**LSC**........... Library Services Center, Midwestern Regional Library System [*UTLAS symbol*]
**LSC**........... Library Services Center of Missouri [*Library network*]
**LSC**........... Library Store Catalogue [*Australia*]
**LSC**........... Libre Service Actualites [*A publication*]
**L es SC**....... Licencie es Sciences [*Licentiate of Sciences*] [*French*]
**LSC**........... Life Safety Code
**LSC**........... Limit Signaling Comparator
**LSC**........... Lincoln Sesquicentennial Committee [*Terminated, 1960*] [*Government agency*]
**LSC**........... Linear Sequential Circuit
**LSC**........... Linear-Shaped Charge
**LSC**........... Liquid Scintillation Cocktail [*Analytical chemistry*]
**LSC**........... Liquid Scintillation Counter [*or Counting*]

**LSC**........... Liquid Smoke Condensate
**LSC**........... Liquid Solid Chromatography
**LSC**........... Load Standardization Crew (MCD)
**LSC**........... Lobbyist Systems Corporation [*Information service or system*] (IID)
**LSC**........... Local Supercluster [*Cosmology*]
**LSC**........... Loco Sub Citato [*In the Place Cited Below*] [*Latin*] (ROG)
**LSC**........... Loco Supra Citato [*In the Place Cited Above*] [*Latin*]
**LSC**........... Logistic Support Cadre (MCD)
**LSC**........... Logistical Support Center [*Army*]
**LSC**........... London Salvage Corps
**LSC**........... Low-Speed Concentrator
**LSC**........... LSI Logic Corp. of Canada, Inc. [*Toronto Stock Exchange symbol*]
**LSC**........... Luminescent Solar Concentrator
**LSC**........... Luminescent Stamp Club (EA)
**LSC**........... Lump-Sum Contract
**LSC**........... Luxury Sport Coupe
**LSC**........... Shopco Laurel Centre LP [*AMEX symbol*] (SPSG)
**LSC**........... Southern University, Law Library, Baton Rouge, LA [*OCLC symbol*] (OCLC)
**LScA**......... Left Scapuloanterior [*A fetal position*] [*Obstetrics*]
**LSCA**......... Library Services and Construction Act [*1963*]
**LSCA**......... Logistics Support Cost Analysis (NASA)
**L'scape**...... Landscape [*A publication*]
**LSCC**......... Lattice Semiconductor Corp. [*NASDAQ symbol*] (NQ)
**LSCC**......... Liberty Seated Collectors Club (EA)
**LSCC**......... Line-Sequential Color Composite (IEEE)
**LSCC**......... Local Servicing Control Center [*Telecommunications*] (TEL)
**LSCC**......... London Scottish Cadet Corps [*British military*] (DMA)
**LScCom**..... Licentiate in Commercial Science
**L Sc D**........ Doctor of the Science of Law
**LSCD**......... Leading Seaman Clearance Diver
**LSCE**......... Launch Sequence and Control Equipment
**LSCE**......... Least Square Complex Exponential [*Mathematics*]
**LSCE**......... Licentiate of the Sydney College of Elocution [*Australia*]
**LSCG**......... Law School Computer Group (EA)
**LSci**.......... Language Sciences [*A publication*]
**LSCI**.......... Large-Scale Compound Integration
**LSCL**......... Lower Surface Center Line
**LSCM**........ Logistic Support Coordination Meeting [*Military*] (MCD)
**LSCO**......... Lanthanum Strontium Copper Oxide [*Inorganic chemistry*]
**LSCO**......... LESCO, Inc. [*Rocky River, OH*] [*NASDAQ symbol*] (NQ)
**LSCP**......... Laserscope, Inc. [*NASDAQ symbol*] (NQ)
**LScP**......... Left Scapuloposterior [*A fetal position*] [*Obstetrics*]
**LSCP**......... Logistic Support Control Point [*Military*] (AFM)
**LSCP**......... Low-Speed Card Punch [*Data processing*] (AABC)
**LSCP(Assoc)**... Associate of the London and Counties Society of Physiologists [*British*] (DBQ)
**LSCRRC**.... Law Students Civil Rights Research Council (EA)
**LSCS**......... Lower Segment Caesarean Section [*Medicine*]
**LScS**.......... Southern University, Scotlandville, Baton Rouge, LA [*Library symbol*] [*Library of Congress*] (LCLS)
**LSCSE**....... Lady Southern Cross Search Expedition [*Australia*]
**LScS-N**...... Southern University at New Orleans, New Orleans, LA [*Library symbol*] [*Library of Congress*] (LCLS)
**LScSoc**....... Licence in Social Science [*British*]
**LSCT**......... LASER Spectral Control Technique
**LSCT**......... Low-Speed Compound Terminal (CET)
**LSCU**......... Local Servicing Control Unit [*Telecommunications*] (TEL)
**LSD**........... Amphibious Ship, Dock
**LSD**........... Doctor of Library Science
**LSD**........... Doctor of Life Science
**LSD**........... Landing Ship Deck
**LSD**........... Landing Ship, Dock [*Navy symbol*]
**LSD**........... Landing-Site Determination [*NASA*] (KSC)
**LSD**........... Landing, Storage, Delivery [*Business term*]
**LSD**........... Language for Systems Development
**LSD**........... Large Screen Display
**LSD**........... Large Steel Desk [*Position given to ex-astronauts*]
**LSD**........... LASER-Selective Demagnetization [*Analytical technique*]
**LSD**........... LASER Signal Device
**LSD**........... [*Boris*] Laskin, [*Willard*] Spence, and [*Brian*] Dickson [*Canada Supreme Court justices known for their minority liberal positions*]
**LSD**........... Last Safe Date [*Marine insurance*] (DS)
**LSD**........... Latching Semiconductor Diode
**LSD**........... Latest Start Date
**LSD**........... Launch Support Division [*NASA*] (KSC)
**LSD**........... Launch Systems Data
**LSD**........... Lead Sulfide Detection
**LSD**........... Least Significant Difference [*Statistics*]
**LSD**........... Least Significant Digit [*Data compaction*] (MUGU)
**LSD**........... Lesson Specification Document (MCD)
**LSD**........... Level Sensor Demonstration
**LSD**........... Lexington, KY [*Location identifier*] [*FAA*] (FAAL)
**£SD**........... Librae, Solidi, Denarii [*Pounds, Shillings, Pence*] [*Latin*]
**LSD**........... Library Service to the Disadvantaged Committee
**LSD**........... Life, Sport, and Drama [*A publication*] [*British*]
**LSD**........... Lightermen, Stevedores, and Dockers
**LSD**........... Limited-Slip Differential [*Automotive engineering*]
**LSD**........... Line-Sharing Device
**LSD**........... Line Signal Detector
**LSD**........... Litteraria; Studie a Dokumenty [*A publication*]
**LSD**........... Local Spin Density [*Physics*]
**LSD**........... Log-Slope Difference [*Statistics*]
**LSD**........... Logarithmic Series Distribution [*Statistics*]
**LSD**........... Logistics Systems Division [*Air Force*]
**LSD**........... Lomir Shoyn Davenen (BJA)
**LSD**........... Long Side
**LSD**........... Long, Slow Distance [*Training method for runners*]
**LSD**........... Low-Speed Data
**LSD**........... Lowest Significant Dose [*Toxicology*]
**LSD**........... Lump-Sum Distribution [*Banking*]
**LSD**........... Lunar Surface Drill [*Aerospace*]
**LSD**........... Lysergic Acid Diethylamide [*or Lysergsaeure Diethylamid*] [*Hallucinogenic drug*]
**LSDA**......... Licentiate of the Speech and Drama Association (ADA)
**LSDF**......... Large Sodium Disposal Facility [*Nuclear energy*] (NRCH)
**LSDF**......... Library Service to the Deaf Forum [*Association of Specialized and Cooperative Library Agencies*]
**LSDP**......... Lietuvos Socialdemokratu Partija [*Lithuanian Social Democratic Party*] [*Political party*] (PPE)
**LSDR**......... Local Store Data Register
**LSDRM**..... Logistic Support Data Responsibility Matrix (MCD)
**LSDS**......... Large Screen Display System
**LSDS**......... Low-Speed Data Service [*RCA Global Communications, Inc.*] [*Telecommunications*] [*Piscataway, NJ*] (TSSD)
**LSDS**......... Low-Speed Digital System
**LSDSP**....... Latvijas Socialdemokratiska Stradnieku Partija [*Latvian Social Democratic Workers' Party*] [*Political party*] (EAIO)
**LSDT**......... Local Sidereal Time (MSA)
**LSDU**......... Link Layer Service Data Unit
**LSE**........... La Crosse [*Wisconsin*]/Winona [*Minnesota*] [*Airport symbol*] (OAG)
**LSE**........... Landing Ship, Emergency Repair
**LSE**........... Landing Signal Enlisted [*Military*]
**LSE**........... Large-Scale Equipment (MCD)
**LSE**........... Lattice Screen Editor [*Program editor*]
**LSE**........... Launch Sequencer Equipment [*NASA*]
**LSE**........... Launch Support Equipment [*NASA*] (AAG)
**LSE**........... Lease (ROG)
**LSE**........... Least Squares Estimator [*Statistics*]
**LSE**........... Leeds Studies in English and Kindred Languages [*A publication*]
**LSE**........... Left Second Entrance [*Theater*]
**LSE**........... Left Sternal Edge [*Cardiology*]
**LSE**........... Legal Services for the Elderly (EA)
**LSE**........... Lexikon Strassenverkehrsrechtlicher Entscheidungen [*A publication*]
**lse**............. Licensee [*MARC relator code*] [*Library of Congress*] (LCCP)
**LSE**........... Life Science Experiment (MUGU)
**LSE**........... Life Support Equipment (KSC)
**LSE**........... Limited Signed Edition (ADA)
**LSE**........... Liquid-Solid Extraction [*Chemistry*]
**LSE**........... Living Skin Equivalent [*Synthetic organ*]
**LSE**........... Logistics Support Element
**LSE**........... London School of Economics
**LSE**........... London Stock Exchange
**LSE**........... Longitudinal-Section Electric (IEEE)
**LSE**........... Loose
**LSE**........... Louisiana Sugar Exchange (EA)
**LSE**........... Lower Sternal Edge [*Cardiology*]
**LSE**........... Lunar Surface Experiment [*NASA*]
**LSE**........... Lund Studies in English [*A publication*]
**LSE**........... Queen's Bench Library [*Alberta*] [*UTLAS symbol*]
**LSEBA**...... LSE [*Laurence, Scott, & Electromotors Ltd.*] Engineering Bulletin [*A publication*]
**LSEC**......... Australian Company Secretary's Practice Manual [*A publication*]
**LSECS**....... Life Support and Environmental Control System (IEEE)
**LSEED**...... Launch Support Equipment - Engineering Division [*NASA*] (KSC)
**LSE Eng Bull**... LSE [*Laurence, Scott, & Electromotors Ltd.*] Engineering Bulletin [*A publication*]
**LSEIF**........ Lodestar Energy, Incorporated [*NASDAQ symbol*] (NQ)
**LSEMSA**... London School of Economics. Monographs on Social Anthropology [*A publication*]
**LSEP**......... Legal Services for the Elderly Poor [*Later, LSE*] (EA)
**LSEP**......... Lifetime Sports Education Project [*of Lifetime Sports Foundation*]
**LSEP**......... Lunar Surface Experiment Package [*NASA*]
**LSEQ**......... Launch Sequencer [*Navy*] (CAAL)
**LSER**......... Laser Corp. [*Salt Lake City, UT*] [*NASDAQ symbol*] (NQ)
**LSER**......... Raron [*Switzerland*] [*ICAO location identifier*] (ICLI)
**LSES**......... [*Salamon-Conte*] Life Satisfaction in the Elderly Scale
**LSE SKDS**... Loose or on Skids [*Freight*]
**LSET**......... Logistics Supportability Evaluation Team [*Military*] (AFIT)
**LSEV**......... Lunar Surface Exploration Vehicle [*Aerospace*]
**LSEZ**......... Zermatt [*Switzerland*] [*ICAO location identifier*] (ICLI)
**LSF**........... Fort Benning (Columbus), GA [*Location identifier*] [*FAA*] (FAAL)

**LSF** ........... La Souterraine [*France*] [*Seismograph station code, US Geological Survey*] (SEIS)
**LSF** ........... Laboratory Simulation Facility (MCD)
**LSF** ........... Lande Splitting Factor
**LSF** ........... Landing Ship, Fighter Direction [*British military*] (DMA)
**LSF** ........... Launch Support Facility [*NASA*] (KSC)
**LSF** ........... Least Square Fit
**LSF** ........... Lightweight Strike Fighter [*NATO Air Forces*]
**LSF** ........... Line Spread Function (MCD)
**LSF** ........... Line Switch Frame [*Telecommunications*] (TEL)
**LSF** ........... Literary Society Foundation (EA)
**LSF** ........... Lloyd Shaw Foundation (EA)
**LSF** ........... Lomas Mortgage Securities Fund, Inc. [*NYSE symbol*] (CTT)
**LSF** ........... Lunar Scientific Facility [*NASA*] (KSC)
**LSF** ........... Lymphocyte-Stimulating Factor [*Biochemistry*]
**LSFA** ......... Logistic System Feasibility Analysis (AABC)
**LSFAE** ....... Low-Speed Fuel Air Explosive
**LSFC** ......... Lennon Sisters Fan Club (EA)
**LSFE** ......... Life Sciences Flight Experiment [*NASA*] (NASA)
**LSFF** ......... Landing Ship, Flotilla Flagship [*Navy symbol*] [*Obsolete*]
**LSFFAR** .... Low-Spin Folding Fin Aircraft Rocket (IEEE)
**lsfk---** ......... Falkland Islands [*MARC geographic area code*] [*Library of Congress*] (LCCP)
**LSFN** ......... List of Selected File Numbers (AABC)
**LSFO** ......... Logistics Support Field Office [*Federal disaster planning*]
**LSFO** ......... Low-Sulfur Fuel Oil
**LSFR** ......... Large-Probe Solar Net Flux Radiometer [*NASA*]
**LSFR** ......... Local Storage Function Register
**LSFT** ......... Low Steamline Flow Test (IEEE)
**LSG** ........... Landing Ship, Gantry
**LSG** ........... Landing Ship, Gun [*British military*] (DMA)
**LSG** ........... Language Structure Group [*CODASYL*]
**LSG** ........... Lateral Superior Geniculate Artery [*Anatomy*]
**LSG** ........... Law Society. Gazette [*A publication*]
**LSG** ........... Legislative Strategy Group [*Reagan administration*]
**LSG** ........... Level Sensor Gradiometer
**LSG** ........... Ligo Samseksamaj Geesperantistoj [*Richmond, Surrey, England*] (EAIO)
**LSG** ........... Limited Subgroup (NATG)
**LSG** ........... Logistics Support Group (AAG)
**LSG** ........... Loh's Sinfully Good Ice Cream & Cookies, Inc. [*Vancouver Stock Exchange symbol*]
**LSG** ........... Lunar Surface Gravimeter [*Apollo*] [*NASA*]
**LSGA** ......... Laminators Safety Glass Association (EA)
**LSGA** ......... Los Angeles Securities Group [*NASDAQ symbol*] (NQ)
**LS Gaz** ....... Law Society's Gazette [*A publication*]
**LSGC** ......... Les Eplatures [*Switzerland*] [*ICAO location identifier*] (ICLI)
**LSGC** ......... Long Service and Good Conduct (ADA)
**LS & GCM** ... Long Service and Good Conduct Medal [*Military decoration*] [*British*]
**LSGD** ......... Lymphocyte Specific Gravity Distribution [*Medicine*]
**LSGE** ......... Ecuvillens [*Switzerland*] [*ICAO location identifier*] (ICLI)
**LSGG** ......... Geneve/Cointrin [*Switzerland*] [*ICAO location identifier*] (ICLI)
**LSGK** ......... Saanen [*Switzerland*] [*ICAO location identifier*] (ICLI)
**LSGL** ......... Lausanne/Blecherette [*Switzerland*] [*ICAO location identifier*] (ICLI)
**LSGM** ........ Long Service and Good Conduct Medal [*Australia*] [*Military decoration*]
**LSGN** ......... Neuchatel [*Switzerland*] [*ICAO location identifier*] (ICLI)
**LSGP** ......... La Cote [*Switzerland*] [*ICAO location identifier*] (ICLI)
**LSGP** ......... Large-Scale General Purpose
**LSGR** ......... Loose Granular Snow [*Skiing condition*]
**LSGS** ......... Left Stellate Ganglion Stimulation [*Physiology*]
**LSGS** ......... Sion [*Switzerland*] [*ICAO location identifier*] (ICLI)
**LSGT** ......... Gruyeres [*Switzerland*] [*ICAO location identifier*] (ICLI)
**L/Sgt** .......... Lance Sergeant [*British military*] (DMA)
**LSGU** ......... Local Spinal Glucose Utilization [*Medicine*]
**LSH** ........... Landing Ship, Headquarters
**LSH** ........... Landing Ship, Heavy
**LSH** ........... Lashio [*Burma*] [*Airport symbol*] (OAG)
**LSH** ........... Library Services to the Handicapped, Alberta Culture [*UTLAS symbol*]
**LSh** ........... Literatura v Shkole [*Moscow*] [*A publication*]
**LSH** ........... London School of Hygiene
**LSH** ........... Low Section Height [*Automotive engineering*]
**LSH** ........... Lowland-Southern Hybrid [*Hemoglobin phenotype of Rana pipiens*]
**LSH** ........... Loyal Suffolk Hussars [*British military*] (DMA)
**LSH** ........... Lutein-Stimulating Hormone [*Also, ICSH, LH*] [*Endocrinology*]
**LSH** ........... Lymphocytosis-Stimulating Hormone [*Endocrinology*]
**LSh** ........... Shreve Memorial and Caddo Parish Extension Library, Shreveport, LA [*Library symbol*] [*Library of Congress*] (LCLS)
**LSH** ........... Southeastern Louisiana University, Hammond, LA [*OCLC symbol*] (OCLC)
**LSHA** ........ Gstaad-Inn Grund [*Switzerland*] [*ICAO location identifier*] (ICLI)
**LShC** ......... Centenary College of Louisiana, Shreveport, LA [*Library symbol*] [*Library of Congress*] (LCLS)
**LSHC** ......... Light-Saturated Hydrocarbon [*Organic chemistry*]
**LShCa** ........ Caddo Parish Library, Shreveport, LA [*Library symbol*] [*Library of Congress*] (LCLS)
**LSHCNC** ... Local and Short Haul Carriers National Conference (EA)
**LSHG** ........ Gampel [*Switzerland*] [*ICAO location identifier*] (ICLI)
**LSHG** ........ Lashing [*Engineering*]
**LSHI** ......... Large-Scale Hybrid Integration
**LSHIP** ....... Leadership
**LSH(L)** ...... Landing Ship, Headquarters (Large)
**LSHLD** ...... Leasehold
**LShN** ......... R. W. Norton Art Foundation, Shreveport, LA [*Library symbol*] [*Library of Congress*] (LCLS)
**LSHQ** ........ Landing Ship, Headquarters [*British military*] (DMA)
**LSH(S)** ...... Landing Ship, Headquarters (Small)
**LSHS** ......... Sezegnin [*Switzerland*] [*ICAO location identifier*] (ICLI)
**LShTE** ....... Texas Eastern Transmission Corp., Shreveport, LA [*Library symbol*] [*Library of Congress*] (LCLS)
**LShUG** ...... United Gas Corp., Shreveport, LA [*Library symbol*] [*Library of Congress*] (LCLS)
**LsHUP** ...... Pennzoil United, Inc., Shreveport, LA [*Library symbol*] [*Library of Congress*] (LCLS)
**LSHV** ......... Laminated Synthetic High Voltage
**LSI** ............ Labour Supply Inspector [*British*]
**LSI** ............ Lake Superior & Ishpeming Railroad Co. [*AAR code*]
**LSI** ............ Landing Ship, Infantry [*Navy symbol*]
**LSI** ............ Large-Scale Integration [*of circuits*] [*Electronics*]
**LSI** ............ Largest Single Item (AFM)
**LSI** ............ LASER Surface Interaction
**LSI** ............ Launch Success Indicator
**LSI** ............ Law of the Sea Institute (EA)
**LSI** ............ Laws of the State of Israel (BJA)
**LSI** ............ Learning Style Inventory [*Occupational therapy*]
**LSI** ............ Learning Systems Institute [*Florida State University*] [*Research center*] (RCD)
**LSI** ............ Lerwick [*Scotland*] [*Airport symbol*] (OAG)
**LSI** ............ Lexique Stratigraphique International [*A publication*]
**LSI** ............ Life Space Interviewing [*Teaching technique*]
**LSI** ............ Light Scatter Index
**LSI** ............ Little Sitkin Island [*Alaska*] [*Seismograph station code, US Geological Survey*] [*Closed*] (SEIS)
**LSI** ............ Logistic Support Impact
**LSI** ............ Logistic Supportability Index
**LSI** ............ LSI Logic Corp. [*NYSE symbol*] (SPSG)
**LSI** ............ Lunar Science Institute [*Houston*]
**LSI** ............ Lunar Surface Instrument [*Aerospace*]
**LSIA** .......... Lamp and Shade Institute of America (EA)
**LSIA** .......... Licentiate of the Society of Industrial Artists [*British*]
**LSIB** .......... London Stage Information Bank [*Lawrence University*] [*Information service or system*] (IID)
**LSIC** .......... Large-Scale Integrated Circuit [*Electronics*] (KSC)
**LSIC** .......... LSI Corporation [*NASDAQ symbol*] (NQ)
**LSI Contrib** ... LSI [*Lunar Science Institute*] Contribution [*A publication*]
**LSID** .......... Launch Sequence and Interlock Document [*NASA*] (NASA)
**LSID** .......... Local Session Identification [*Data processing*] (IBMDP)
**LSidFW** ..... United States Fish and Wildlife Service, Sidell, LA [*Library symbol*] [*Library of Congress*] (LCLS)
**LSIEF** ........ Library Service to the Impaired Elderly Forum [*Association of Specialized and Cooperative Library Agencies*]
**LSI(G)** ....... Landing Craft, Infantry (Gunboat) [*Navy symbol*] [*Obsolete*]
**LSI(H)** ....... Landing Ship, Infantry (Hand-Hoisted Boats) [*British*]
**LSIL** .......... Land and Sea Interaction Laboratory [*Environmental Science Services Administration*] (NOAA)
**LSI(L)** ........ Landing Ship, Infantry (Large) [*Obsolete*]
**LSI(M)** ...... Landing Craft, Infantry (Mortar) [*Navy symbol*] [*Obsolete*]
**LSI(M)** ...... Landing Ship, Infantry (Medium) [*British*]
**LSIMS** ....... Liquid Secondary Ion Mass Spectrometry
**LSIO** .......... Lumbosacroiliac Orthosis [*Medicine*]
**LSI(R)** ....... Landing Craft, Infantry (Rocket) [*Navy symbol*] [*Obsolete*]
**LSIR** .......... Limb-Scanning Infrared Radiometer
**LSIR** .......... Low-Ship Impact Ranging [*Navy*] (CAAL)
**LSI(S)** ........ Landing Ship, Infantry (Small)
**LSIS** .......... LASER Shutterable Image Sensor
**LSIS** .......... League of Shut-In Sodalists (EA)
**LSIS** .......... Learning Style Identification Scale [*Educational test*]
**LSIT** .......... Linear Strip Ion Thruster
**LSITT** ........ Let's Stick It to Them [*Acronym used as book title*]
**LSJ** ............ La Societe Jersiaise (EAIO)
**LSJ** ............ Labor Studies Journal [*A publication*]
**LSJ** ............ Law Society. Journal [*A publication*] (APTA)
**LSJ** ............ Liddell and Scott [*Greek-English Lexicon, 9th ed., revised by H. Stuart Jones*] [*A publication*] (OCD)
**LSJ** ............ Little Sisters of Jesus [*See also PSJ*] [*Rome, Italy*] (EAIO)
**LSJ** ............ Lute Society. Journal [*A publication*]
**LSJM** ......... Laus Sit Jesu et Mariae [*Praise Be to Jesus and Mary*] [*Latin*]
**LSJS** .......... Law Society Judgement Scheme [*South Australia*] [*A publication*] (APTA)
**LS Judg Sch** ... Law Society Judgement Scheme [*South Australia*] [*A publication*] (APTA)
**LSK** ........... Leucosulfakinin [*Biochemistry*]
**LSK** ........... Liquid Sample Kit
**LSK** ........... Liver, Spleen, Kidney [*Medicine*]

**LSK**.......... Lusk, WY [*Location identifier*] [*FAA*] (FAAL)
**LSL**.......... Ladder Static Logic
**LSL**.......... Landing Ship, Logistic [*British*]
**LSL**.......... Left Sacrolateral [*A fetal position*] [*Obstetrics*]
**LSL**.......... Life Sciences Laboratory (AAG)
**LsL**.......... Limba si Literatura [*A publication*]
**LSl**.......... Linguistica Slovaca [*A publication*]
**LSL**.......... Link and Selector Language
**LSL**.......... Link Support Layer
**LSL**.......... Linnaean Society of London
**LSL**.......... Logical Shift Left [*Data processing*]
**LSL**.......... Logistics Spares List (KSC)
**LSL**.......... Logistics Systems Laboratory
**LSL**.......... Long Service Leave (ADA)
**LSL**.......... Los Chiles [*Costa Rica*] [*Airport symbol*] (OAG)
**LSL**.......... Louisiana State Library, Baton Rouge, LA [*OCLC symbol*] (OCLC)
**LSL**.......... Low Sight Lobe
**LSLA**.......... Lincoln Savings & Loan Association [*NASDAQ symbol*] (NQ)
**LSLB**.......... Left Short Leg Brace [*Medicine*]
**LSLDP**.......... Lietuvos Socialistu Liaudininkai Demokratu Partija [*Socialist Populists Democratic Party of Lithuania*] [*Political party*] (PPE)
**LSlov**.......... Livre Slovene [*Yugoslavia*] [*A publication*]
**LSLP**.......... Lietuvos Socialistu Liaudininkai Partija [*Socialist Populists Party of Lithuania*] [*Political party*] (PPE)
**LSLP**.......... Lump-Sum Leave Payment [*Air Force*] (AFM)
**LSLT**.......... League to Save Lake Tahoe (EA)
**LSLT**.......... Li-Shih Lun-Ts'ung [*Collection of Articles on History*] [*A publication*]
**LSM**.......... Lakeside & Marblehead R. R. [*AAR code*]
**LSM**.......... Landing Ship, Medium [*Navy symbol*]
**LSM**.......... Large Solid Motor [*Aerospace*]
**LSM**.......... LASER Scanning Microscope
**LSM**.......... LASER Slicing Machine
**LSM**.......... Launcher Status Multiplexer (MSA)
**LSM**.......... Launching System Module
**LSM**.......... Layered Synthetic Microstructure [*For optical instruments*]
**LSM**.......... Least Square Mean [*Mathematical statistics*]
**LSM**.......... Letter Sorting Machine [*US Postal Service*]
**LSM**.......... Liberation Support Movement Information Center (EA)
**LSM**.......... Life Science Module [*NASA*] (NASA)
**LSM**.......... Line-Scanning Mode [*Microscopy*]
**LSM**.......... Line Selection Module [*Telecommunications*] (TEL)
**LSM**.......... Linear Select Memory
**LSM**.......... Linear Sequential Machine
**LSM**.......... Litera Scripta Manet [*The Written Word Remains*] [*Latin*] (ADA)
**LSM**.......... Little Skull Mountain [*Nevada*] [*Seismograph station code, US Geological Survey*] (SEIS)
**LSM**.......... Logistic Support Manager
**LSM**.......... Long Semado [*Malaysia*] [*Airport symbol*] (OAG)
**LSM**.......... Loop Sampling Module
**LSM**.......... Louisiana State Library, Processing Center, Baton Rouge, LA [*OCLC symbol*] (OCLC)
**LSM**.......... Low-Sulfate Medium [*Microbiology*]
**LSM**.......... Lunar Surface Magnetometer [*NASA*]
**LSM**.......... Lymphocyte Separation Medium [*Medicine*]
**LSM**.......... Lysergic Acid Morpholide
**LSM**.......... Master of Life Science
**LSMA**.......... Low-Speed Multiplexer Arrangement
**LSMC**.......... Launching System Module Console [*Navy*] (CAAL)
**LSMD**.......... Dubendorf [*Switzerland*] [*ICAO location identifier*] (ICLI)
**LSME**.......... Emmen [*Switzerland*] [*ICAO location identifier*] (ICLI)
**LSME**.......... Logistic Support Maintenance Equipment (MCD)
**LSMEDI**... Lasers in Surgery and Medicine [*A publication*]
**LS/MFT**... Lucky Strike Means Fine Tobacco [*Advertising slogan*]
**LSMI**.......... Loadmaster Systems, Incorporated [*Tucson, AZ*] [*NASDAQ symbol*] (NQ)
**LSMI**.......... Logistics Support Management Information [*NASA*] (NASA)
**LSMITH**... Locksmith
**L/Smn**.......... Leading Seaman [*Navy*] [*British*] (DMA)
**LSM News**... Liberation Support Movement News [*A publication*]
**l/smos**.......... Logariasmos [*Account*] [*Greek*]
**LSMP**.......... Logistic Support and Mobilization Plan [*Military*] (NVT)
**LSMP**.......... Payerne [*Switzerland*] [*ICAO location identifier*] (ICLI)
**LSM(R)**..... Landing Ship, Medium (Rocket) [*Later, LFR*] [*Navy symbol*]
**LS & MS**.... Lake Shore & Michigan Southern Railway
**LS and MS**... Less Sleep and More Speed [*Hobo slang*]
**LSMS**.......... Living Standards Management Study [*International Monetary Fund*]
**LSMSO**..... Landing Ship, Material Supply Officer
**LSMU**.......... LASERcom Space Measurement Unit (IEEE)
**LSM-USA**... Lutheran Student Movement - USA (EA)
**LSMW**.......... London School of Medicine for Women (ROG)
**LSN**.......... Line Stabilization Network
**LSN**.......... Linear Sequential Network (MUGU)
**LSN**.......... Load Sharing Network
**LSN**.......... Local Stock Number
**LSN**.......... Los Banos, CA [*Location identifier*] [*FAA*] (FAAL)
**LSNB**.......... Lake Shore Bancorp, Inc. [*NASDAQ symbol*] (NQ)
**LSNS**.......... Lundastudier i Nordisk Sprakvetenskap [*A publication*]
**LSNSR**...... Line of Bearing Sensor
**LSNY**.......... Linnaean Society of New York (EA)
**LSO**.......... Kelso, WA [*Location identifier*] [*FAA*] (FAAL)
**LSO**.......... Landing Safety Officer (MCD)
**LSO**.......... Landing Signal Officer
**LSO**.......... Landing Support Officer [*Navy*]
**LSO**.......... Large Solar Observatory [*NASA*]
**LSO**.......... Last Standing Order
**LSO**.......... Lateral Superior Olive [*Brain anatomy*]
**LSO**.......... Launch/Safety Officer [*NASA*]
**LSO**.......... Lesotho [*ANSI three-letter standard code*] (CNC)
**lso**.......... Licensor [*MARC relator code*] [*Library of Congress*] (LCCP)
**LSO**.......... Life Systems Officer [*NASA*] (KSC)
**LSO**.......... Line Stabilized Oscillator
**LSO**.......... Logistics Studies Office [*Army*] (RDA)
**LSO**.......... London Symphony Orchestra
**LSO**.......... Lost Lake Resources Ltd. [*Vancouver Stock Exchange symbol*]
**LSO**.......... Louisiana Southern Railway Co. [*AAR code*]
**LSO**.......... Lumbosacral Orthosis [*Medicine*]
**LSOAD**...... Life Sciences Organizations and Agencies Directory [*A publication*]
**LSoc**.......... Language in Society [*A publication*]
**LSOC**.......... Lockheed Space Operations Co.
**LSOC**.......... Logistical Support Operations Center [*Army*]
**LSOCE**...... Linear Stochastic Optimal Control and Estimation [*Computer program*]
**L Soc Gaz**... Law Society's Gazette [*A publication*]
**L Soc J**....... Law Society. Journal [*A publication*]
**L & Soc Order**... Law and the Social Order [*A publication*]
**L and Soc Rev**... Law and Society Review [*A publication*]
**L in Soc'y**... Law in Society [*A publication*] (DLA)
**L Soc'y Gaz**... Law Society. Gazette [*A publication*]
**LSOMT**..... Large-Scale Operations Management Test (RDA)
**LSOP**.......... L-Serine-O-Phosphate [*Biochemistry*]
**LSOP**.......... Lunar Surface Operations Planning [*NASA*] (KSC)
**LSOT**.......... Landing Signal Officer Trainer [*Navy*]
**LSOV**.......... Linguistic Survey of the Ottawa Valley [*Carleton University*] [*Canada*] [*Research center*] (RCD)
**LSP**.......... Landing Ship Personnel [*British military*] (DMA)
**LSp**.......... Language and Speech [*A publication*]
**LSP**.......... Las Mesas [*Puerto Rico*] [*Seismograph station code, US Geological Survey*] (SEIS)
**LSP**.......... Las Piedras [*Venezuela*] [*Airport symbol*] (OAG)
**LSP**.......... Launcher Status Panel (MCD)
**LSP**.......... Least Significant Portion (MCD)
**LSP**.......... Least Significant Position (CMD)
**LSp**.......... Lebende Sprachen [*A publication*]
**LSP**.......... Left Sacroposterior [*A fetal position, the breech position*] [*Obstetrics*]
**LSP**.......... Leitsaetze fuer die Preisermittlung [*A publication*]
**LSP**.......... Level Set Point (NRCH)
**LSP**.......... Liberal Socialist Party [*Egypt*] [*Political party*] (PPW)
**LSP**.......... Liberale Staatspartij [*Liberal State Party*] [*Netherlands*] [*Political party*] (PPE)
**LSP**.......... Library Software Package (ADA)
**LSp**.......... Life Span
**LSP**.......... Life Support Package [*Diving apparatus*]
**LSP**.......... Light Scattering Photometer
**LSP**.......... Lincoln Society of Philately [*Defunct*] (EA)
**LSP**.......... Line Synchronizing Pulse
**LSP**.......... Linear Selenium Photocell
**LSP**.......... Lingvisticeskij Sbornik. Petrozavodsk [*A publication*]
**LSP**.......... Linked Systems Project [*of the Library of Congress*]
**lsp**.......... Liters per Second per Person (ECON)
**LSP**.......... Little Sisters of the Poor [*Roman Catholic religious order*]
**LSP**.......... Liver-Specific Protein
**LSP**.......... LM [*Lunar Module*] Specification [*NASA*] (KSC)
**LSP**.......... Local Store Pointer
**LSP**.......... Logistics Support Plan
**LSP**.......... Low-Salinity Plume [*Oceanography*]
**LSP**.......... Low-Speed Printer
**LSP**.......... Low Support Program (OICC)
**LSP**.......... Lower Sequential Permissive (NRCH)
**LSP**.......... Lower Solution Point
**LSP**.......... Lucas-Sargent Proposition [*Economics*]
**LSP**.......... Lumbar Spine [*Medicine*] (DHSM)
**LSP**.......... Lunar Spectral Photometrics [*Aerospace*]
**LSP**.......... Lunar Surface Probe [*Aerospace*]
**LSPA**.......... Amlikon [*Switzerland*] [*ICAO location identifier*] (ICLI)
**LSPAFRO**... Lump-Sum Payment to Air Force Reserve Officers
**LSPC**.......... Legal Services for Prisoners with Children (EA)
**LSPC**.......... Lewis Space Flight Center (MCD)
**LSPC**.......... Linear Selenium Photocell
**LSPC**.......... Living Stream Prayer Circle (EA)
**LSPC**.......... Logistics Systems Policy Committee [*Navy*]
**LSPC**.......... Long Service Payments Corporation [*Australia*]
**LSPC**.......... Louisiana Sweet Potato Commission
**LSPD**.......... Dittingen [*Switzerland*] [*ICAO location identifier*] (ICLI)
**LSPDF**...... Life Science Payloads Development Facility (MCD)
**LSPE**.......... Lunar Seismic Profiling Experiment [*NASA*]

**LSPET**....... Lunar Sample Preliminary Examination Team [*NASA*]
**LSPF**.......... Library Service to Prisoners Forum [*Association of Specialized and Cooperative Library Agencies*]
**LSPF**.......... Schaffhausen [*Switzerland*] [*ICAO location identifier*] (ICLI)
**LSPH**......... Leningrad Special Psychiatric Hospital [*Formerly, LPPH*]
**LSPH**......... Winterthur [*Switzerland*] [*ICAO location identifier*] (ICLI)
**LSPK**......... Hasenstrick [*Switzerland*] [*ICAO location identifier*] (ICLI)
**LSPK**......... Loudspeaker (TEL)
**LSPL**.......... Langenthal [*Switzerland*] [*ICAO location identifier*] (ICLI)
**LSPN**......... Triengen [*Switzerland*] [*ICAO location identifier*] (ICLI)
**LSPO**......... Lunar Surface Project Office [*NASA*] (KSC)
**LSPP**.......... Step-by-Step Precedents and Procedures. Companies, Trusts, Superannuation Funds [*Australia*] [*A publication*]
**LSPPA**....... Life Sciences. Part I. Physiology and Pharmacology [*A publication*]
**LSPPO** ...... Lead Screw Position Pick-Off
**LSPPS** ....... Logistic Support Plan for Preoperational Support (MCD)
**L Spr** .......... Lebende Sprachen [*A publication*]
**LSPR** ......... Low-Speed Pulse Restorer (MCD)
**LSPS**.......... Limited Serial Project Slip
**LSPS**.......... Local Service Planning System [*Telecommunications*] (TEL)
**LSPTP** ....... Low-Speed Paper Tape Punch [*Telecommunications*] (AABC)
**LSPTR**....... Low-Speed Paper Tape Reader [*Telecommunications*] (TEL)
**LSPUD**...... Lietuvos Socialdemokratu Partijos Uzsienio Delegatura [*Lithuanian Social Democratic Party*] (EAIO)
**LSPV** ......... Wangen-Lachen [*Switzerland*] [*ICAO location identifier*] (ICLI)
**LSPZ** ......... Luzern-Beromunster [*Switzerland*] [*ICAO location identifier*] (ICLI)
**LSQ**............ Line Squall [*Meteorology*] (FAAC)
**LSQ**............ L'Octogone, Bibliotheque Municipale de LaSalle, Quebec [*UTLAS symbol*]
**LSQ**............ Newark, NJ [*Location identifier*] [*FAA*] (FAAL)
**LSQA**......... Local System Queue Area [*Data processing*] (BUR)
**LSQCP** ...... Logistic System Quality Control Program [*Military*] (AFIT)
**LSR**............ Laboratory for Space Research [*Netherlands*]
**LSR**............ Land Sea Rescue (NASA)
**LSR**............ Landing Ship, Rocket (NATG)
**LSR**............ Lanthanide Shift Reagent [*Spectroscopy*]
**LSR**............ Large Ship Reactor
**LSR**............ Last Speed Rating [*of a horse*]
**LSR**............ Launch Signal Responder (AAG)
**LSR**............ Launch Site Recovery [*NASA*] (KSC)
**LSR**............ Launch Support Requirement [*NASA*] (KSC)
**LSR**............ League for Socialist Reconstruction [*Later, IUP*] (EA)
**LSR**............ Lettera di Sociologia Religiosa [*A publication*]
**LSR**............ Life Science Research Ltd. [*British*] (IRUK)
**LSR**............ Light-Scattering Response [*Biology*]
**LSR**............ Light-Sensitive Relay
**LSR**............ Light-Sensitive Resistor
**LSR**............ Light Stopping Reticle
**LSR**............ Light, Straight Run [*Petroleum technology*]
**LSR**............ Lighthouse Resources, Inc. [*Vancouver Stock Exchange symbol*]
**LSR**............ Limited to Searches (MCD)
**LSR**............ LINAC Stretcher Ring [*Design for an electron accelerator*]
**LSR**............ Linear Seal Ring
**LSR**............ Linear Sedimentation Rate [*Geology*]
**LSR**............ Lingual Skills Required [*Civil service*]
**LSR**............ Liquid Slip Ring
**LSR**............ Load Shifting Resistor (MSA)
**LSR**............ Load Storage Register
**LSR**............ Local Shared Resources [*Data processing*] (IBMDP)
**LSR**............ Local Standard of Rest [*Galactic science*]
**LSR**............ Local Sunrise
**LSR**............ Location Stack Register
**LSR**............ Locus Standi Reports [*A publication*] (DLA)
**LSR**............ Logical Shift Right [*Data processing*]
**LSR**............ Logistics Support Requirements (NG)
**LSR**............ Lone Star Review [*A publication*]
**LSR**............ Loop Shorting Relay (MCD)
**LSR**............ Loose Snow on Runway [*Aviation*] (FAAC)
**LSR**............ Lost River, AK [*Location identifier*] [*FAA*] (FAAL)
**LSR**............ Lovers of the Stinking Rose (EA)
**LSR**............ Low-Speed Reader
**LSR**............ Luftschutzraum [*Air-Raid Shelter*] [*German military - World War II*]
**LSR**............ Lunar Surface Rendezvous [*NASA*] (KSC)
**LSR**............ Luttrell Society. Reprints [*A publication*]
**LSR**............ Lynchburg Source Reactor
**LSRA**......... Logistic Support Requirement Analysis (MCD)
**LSRC**......... Launch Site Recovery Commander [*NASA*] (KSC)
**LSRC**......... Logistics Systems Review Committee [*DARCOM*] (MCD)
**LSRC**......... Lunar Surface Return Container [*NASA*] (KSC)
**LSRD**......... Logistic Support Readiness Date
**LSRE**......... Leisure
**LSRF** ......... LASER Submarine Range-Finder
**LSRF** ......... Logistic Support Resource Funds [*Army*]
**LSRI** .......... Large Screen RADAR Indicator
**LSRM**........ Lasermetrics, Inc. [*NASDAQ symbol*] (NQ)
**LSRM**........ Life Science Research Module (MCD)
**LSRO**......... Life Sciences Research Office [*NASA*] (KSC)
**LSRP** ......... Local Switching Replacement Planning [*Telecommunications*] (TEL)
**LSRV** ......... London and Scottish Rifle Volunteers [*Military*] [*British*] (ROG)
**LSRV** ......... Lunar Surface Roving Vehicle [*Aerospace*]
**LSS** ............ Laboratory Support Service
**LSS** ............ Laboratory for Surface Studies [*University of Wisconsin, Milwaukee*] [*Research center*] (RCD)
**LSS** ............ Ladies Shoemakers' Society [*A union*] [*British*]
**LSS** ............ Landing, Separation Simulator (MCD)
**LSS** ............ Landing Ship Sternchute [*British military*] (DMA)
**LSS** ............ Landing Ship, Support (NATG)
**LSS** ............ Landing-Site Supervisor
**LSS** ............ Language for Symbolic Simulation
**LSS** ............ Large-Scale Structure [*Cosmology*]
**LSS** ............ Large Space Structure (IEEE)
**LSS** ............ Large Space System (IEEE)
**LSS** ............ Lateral Series Servo (MCD)
**LSS** ............ Launch Sequence Simulator
**LSS** ............ Launch Signature Simulator (MCD)
**LSS** ............ Launch Status Summarizer
**LSS** ............ Launch Support Section [*NASA*]
**LSS** ............ Launch Support System [*NASA*] (KSC)
**LSS** ............ Launcher Support Structure [*Navy*] (CAAL)
**LSS** ............ Law Society of Scotland
**LSS** ............ Leipziger Semitische Studien [*A publication*] (BJA)
**LSS** ............ Leopold Stokowski Society (EA)
**LSS** ............ Les Saintes [*Guadeloupe*] [*Airport symbol*] (OAG)
**Ls S** ............ Letopis' Zurnal'nych Statej [*A publication*]
**LSS** ............ Leyte-Samar Studies [*A publication*]
**LSS** ............ Life Services System [*For the disabled*]
**LSS** ............ Life Support System [*or Subsystem*]
**LSS** ............ Lifesaving Station [*Nautical charts*]
**LSS** ............ Light Spot Scanner
**LSS** ............ Limited Storage Site (AABC)
**LSS** ............ Line Scanner System
**LSS** ............ Linking Segment Subprogram
**LSS** ............ Liquid Scintillation Spectrometer
**LSS** ............ Local Synchronization Subsystem [*Telecommunications*] (TEL)
**LSS** ............ Logistic Support Squadron (AAG)
**LSS** ............ Logistic Support System (AABC)
**LSS** ............ Longitudinal Static Stability
**LSS** ............ Loop Switching System [*Telecommunications*]
**LSS** ............ Lunar Soil Stimulant [*NASA*] (KSC)
**LSS** ............ Lunar Survey Sensor [*NASA*] (KSC)
**LSS** ............ Lunar Surveying System [*Aerospace*]
**LSS** ............ Lutheran Social Service System [*An association*]
**LSSA** ......... Leopold Stokowski Society of America (EA)
**LSSA** ......... Lipid Soluble Secondary Antioxidants [*Biochemistry*]
**LSSA** ......... Lithuanian Student Scout Association [*Later, Lithuanian Scouts Association College Division*] (EA)
**LSSA** ......... Logistic System Support Agency
**LSSAS**....... Longitudinal Static Stability Augmentation System (MCD)
**LSSB**......... Bern Radio [*Switzerland*] [*ICAO location identifier*] (ICLI)
**LSSB**......... Lake Sunapee Savings Bank FSB [*Newport, NH*] [*NASDAQ symbol*] (NQ)
**LSSB**......... Legal Support Services Branch [*General Accounting Office*] [*Information service or system*] (IID)
**LSSC**......... Lake Superior State College [*Sault Ste. Marie, MI*]
**LSSc**.......... Licentiate in Sacred Scriptures
**LSSC**......... Licentiate in Sanitary Science [*British*] (ROG)
**LSSC**......... Light SEAL [*Sea, Air, and Land*] Support Craft [*Navy symbol*]
**LSSC**......... Logistic Support System Characteristics (AAG)
**LSSC**......... Logistic System Support Center [*Army*]
**LSSD** ......... Level Sensitive Scan Design (MCD)
**LSSD** ......... Lower-Speed Service-Deriving [*Telecommunications*] (TSSD)
**LSSD** ......... Lunar Surface Sampling Device [*Aerospace*]
**LSSF**.......... Land Special Security Force [*Army*] (AABC)
**LSSF**.......... Life Sciences Support Facility [*NASA*] (NASA)
**LSSF**.......... Limited Service Storage Facility
**LSSG**......... Logistics Studies Steering Group (AABC)
**LSSGR**....... Local Switching System General Requirement [*Telecommunications*]
**LSSI**........... Legal Software Solutions, Incorporated [*NASDAQ symbol*] (NQ)
**LSSI**........... Library Systems and Services, Incorporated [*Information service or system*] (IID)
**LSSL**.......... Life Sciences Space Laboratory [*NASA*] (NASA)
**LSSL**.......... Support Landing Ship (Large) MK III
**LSSM** ........ Launch Site Support Manager [*NASA*] (NASA)
**LSSM** ........ Local Scientific Survey Module [*NASA*]
**LSSM** ........ Lunar Surface Scientific Module [*NASA*]
**LSSO** ......... Bern. Office Federal de l'Air [*Switzerland*] [*ICAO location identifier*] (ICLI)
**LSSO** ......... Library Science Student Organization
**LSSP**.......... Lanka Sama Samaja Party [*Sri Lanka Equal Society Party*] [*Political party*] (PPW)
**LSSP**.......... Latest Scram Set Point (NRCH)
**LSSP**.......... Launch Site Support Plan (MCD)

**LSSP**.......... Lunar Surveying System Program [*Aerospace*]
**LSSPO**........ Life Support Systems Project Office [*NASA*] (MCD)
**LSSPS**........ Libraries Serving Special Populations Section [*Association of Specialized and Cooperative Library Agencies*]
**LSSPSC**..... Life Sciences Strategic Planning Study Committee [*NASA*]
**LSSR**.......... Amphibious Coastal Reconnaissance Ship [*Navy symbol*]
**LSSR**.......... Berne/Radio Suisse SA [*Switzerland*] [*ICAO location identifier*] (ICLI)
**LSSRC**....... Life Sciences Shuttle Research Centrifuge [*NASA*] (NASA)
**LSSS**.......... Geneve [*Switzerland*] [*ICAO location identifier*] (ICLI)
**LSSS**.......... LASER Source Signature Simulator
**LSSS**.......... Lightweight Ship SATCOM Set [*Navy*] (CAAL)
**LSSS**.......... Limiting Safety System Setting [*Nuclear energy*] (NRCH)
**LSST**.......... Launch Site Support Team (MCD)
**lsst**............ Lead-Sheathed Steel-Taped
**LS/ST**........ Light Shield/Star Tracker (NASA)
**LSST**.......... List of Specifications and Standards (MSA)
**LSST**.......... Lone Star Technologies, Inc. [*Dallas, TX*] [*NASDAQ symbol*] (NQ)
**LSSW**......... Zurich [*Switzerland*] [*ICAO location identifier*] (ICLI)
**LSSYD6**.... Life Support Systems [*A publication*]
**LSSZB7**..... Institutul Agronomic Timisoara Lucrari Stiintifice. Seria Zootehnie [*A publication*]
**LST**............ Amphibious Ship, Tank
**LST**............ Lakewood Forest Products Ltd. [*Vancouver Stock Exchange symbol*]
**LST**............ Laminated SONAR Transistor
**LST**............ Landing Ship, Tank [*Navy symbol*]
**LST**............ Landing Ship Transport (MCD)
**LST**............ Laplace-Stieltjes Transform
**LST**............ Large Space Telescope [*Later, Space Telescope*] [*NASA*]
**LST**............ Large Stellar Telescope (KSC)
**LST**............ Large Subsonic Tunnel [*NASA*]
**LST**............ LASER Spot Tracker (MCD)
**LST**............ Last (BUR)
**LST**............ Late Start Time
**LST**............ Launceston [*Tasmania*] [*Airport symbol*] (OAG)
**LST**............ Launch Support Team [*NASA*] (KSC)
**LST**............ Lauryl Sulfate Tryptose [*Growth medium*]
**LST**............ Left Sacrotransverse [*A fetal position*] [*Obstetrics*]
**LST**............ Licentiate in Sacred Theology [*British*]
**LST**............ Light-Sensitive Tube
**LST**............ Line Scan Tube
**LST**............ Liquid Oxygen Start Tank (AAG)
**LST**............ Liquid Storage Tank (AAG)
**Lst**............. Lire Sterline [*Pounds Sterling*] [*Italian*]
**LST**............ Listener [*A publication*]
**LST**............ Listing of a Program in a File [*Data processing*]
**LST**............ Local Sidereal Time
**LST**............ Local Solar Time
**LST**............ Local Standard Time
**LST**............ Lone Star [*Missouri*] [*Seismograph station code, US Geological Survey*] (SEIS)
**LST**............ Lone Star, TX [*Location identifier*] [*FAA*] (FAAL)
**LST**............ Lunar Surface Telescope [*NASA*]
**LST**............ Lunar Surface Transponder [*Aerospace*]
**LSTAR**....... Limited Scientific and Technical Aerospace Reports [*NASA*] (MCD)
**LSTB**.......... Bellechasse [*Switzerland*] [*ICAO location identifier*] (ICLI)
**LSTB**.......... Long Shoot Terminal Bud [*Botany*]
**LStBA**........ Saint Joseph's Abbey, St. Benedict, LA [*Library symbol*] [*Library of Congress*] (LCLS)
**LSTD**.......... Leading Steward [*British military*] (DMA)
**LSTD**.......... Lunar Satellite Tracking Data [*NASA*] (KSC)
**lstd---**.......... Tristan da Cunha Island [*MARC geographic area code*] [*Library of Congress*] (LCCP)
**LSTE**.......... Launch Site Transportation Equipment [*NASA*] (NASA)
**LSTF**.......... Lead Sulfide Thin Film
**LST-G**........ Large Steam Turbine-Generator
**LStgH**........ Hunt Correctional Center (Louisiana Correctional Institute for Women), St. Gabriel, LA [*Library symbol*] [*Library of Congress*] (LCLS)
**LST(H)**...... Landing Ship, Tank (Casualty Evacuation) [*Navy symbol*] [*Obsolete*]
**LST(H)**...... Landing Ship, Tank (Hospital) [*British military*] (DMA)
**LSTI**........... Lakewood Forest Products Ltd. [*NASDAQ symbol*] (NQ)
**LStjT**.......... Tensas Parish Library, St. Joseph, LA [*Library symbol*] [*Library of Congress*] (LCLS)
**LSTM**......... Lander Static Test Model [*NASA*]
**LSTM**......... Low Steam
**LStmSM**.... St. Martin Parish Library, St. Martinville, LA [*Library symbol*] [*Library of Congress*] (LCLS)
**LSTO**.......... Motiers [*Switzerland*] [*ICAO location identifier*] (ICLI)
**LSTR**.......... Montricher [*Switzerland*] [*ICAO location identifier*] (ICLI)
**LSTS**.......... Landing Ship (Utility) [*Navy symbol*]
**LSTS**.......... Launch Station Test Set (MCD)
**LSTS**.......... Lunar Surface Thermal Simulator [*NASA*] (KSC)
**LSTSRFA**... Launch Station Test Set Radio Frequency Adapter (MCD)
**LSTT**.......... Lake Superior Terminal & Transfer Railway Co. [*AAR code*]
**LSTTL**........ Low-Power Schottky Transistor-Transistor Logic [*Electronics*]
**L Stud H**.... Law Students' Helper [*A publication*] (DLA)
**L Stud Helper**... Law Students' Helper [*A publication*] (DLA)
**L Stud J**..... Law Students' Journal [*A publication*] (DLA)
**L Stu Mag**... Law Students' Magazine [*A publication*] (DLA)
**L Stu Mag NS**... Law Students' Magazine. New Series [*A publication*] (ILCA)
**L Stu Mag OS**... Law Students' Magazine. Old Series [*A publication*] (ILCA)
**L St VG**...... Bayerisches Landesstraf- und Verordnungsgesetz [*A publication*]
**LSTX**.......... Bex [*Switzerland*] [*ICAO location identifier*] (ICLI)
**LSty**........... Language and Style [*A publication*]
**LSTY**.......... Yverdon [*Switzerland*] [*ICAO location identifier*] (ICLI)
**LSU**............ Institute of Continuing Legal Education, Louisiana State University Law Center (DLA)
**LSU**............ Labor Service Unit [*Military*]
**LSU**............ Lactose Saccharose Urea [*Cell growth medium*]
**LSU**............ Lamentation over the Destruction of Sumer and Ur (BJA)
**LSU**............ Landing Ship, Utility [*Navy symbol*] [*Obsolete*]
**LSU**............ Launcher Selector Unit
**LSU**............ Launcher Switching Unit [*Navy*] (CAAL)
**LSU**............ Law Society of Upper Canada [*UTLAS symbol*]
**LSU**............ Leading Signal Unit [*Telecommunications*] (TEL)
**LSU**............ Liberalsoziale Union [*Liberal Social Union*] [*Federal Republic of Germany*] [*Political party*] (PPW)
**LSU**............ Library Storage Unit
**LSU**............ Life Support Umbilical [*NASA*]
**LSU**............ Life Support Unit [*NASA*] (KSC)
**LSU**............ Lighthouse Study Unit (EA)
**LSU**............ Line-Sharing Unit
**LSU**............ Load Storage Unit [*Data processing*]
**LSU**............ Local Storage Unit [*Data processing*]
**LSU**............ Local Switching Unit [*Telecommunications*] (TEL)
**LSU**............ Local Synchronization Utility [*Telecommunications*] (TEL)
**LSU**............ Logistics Support Unit [*Military*] (NVT)
**LSU**............ Lone Signal Unit [*Telecommunications*] (TEL)
**LSU**............ Long Sukang [*Malaysia*] [*Airport symbol*] (OAG)
**LSU**............ Louisiana State University
**LSU**............ Southern University at New Orleans, New Orleans, LA [*OCLC symbol*] (OCLC)
**LSU For Note LA Sch For**... LSU Forestry Notes. Louisiana State University. School of Forestry and Wildlife Management [*A publication*]
**LSU For Notes LA Agric Exp Stn**... LSU [*Louisiana State University*] Forestry Notes. Louisiana Agricultural Experiment Station [*A publication*]
**LSUHS**...... Louisiana State University. Humanistic Series [*A publication*]
**LSUNO**..... Louisiana State University in New Orleans [*Later, University of New Orleans*]
**L Sup H & D**... Lalor's Supplement to Hill and Denio's New York Reports [*A publication*] (DLA)
**L Sup M Inst Pr**... Lake Superior Mining Institute. Proceedings [*A publication*]
**LSUSHS**... Louisiana State University. Studies. Humanities Series [*A publication*]
**LSUV**......... Lunar Surface Ultraviolet [*Camera*] [*NASA*]
**LSU Wood Util Note LA Sch For**... LSU Wood Utilization Notes. Louisiana State University. School of Forestry and Wildlife Management [*A publication*]
**LSV**............ Landing Ship, Vehicle [*Navy symbol*]
**LSV**............ Las Vegas, NV [*Location identifier*] [*FAA*] (FAAL)
**LSV**............ Left Subclavian Vein [*Anatomy*]
**LSV**............ Line Status Verifier [*Telecommunications*] (TEL)
**LSV**............ Linear Sweep Voltammograms [*Electrochemistry*]
**LSV**............ Logistics Support Vessel [*Military*]
**LSV**............ Lunar Shuttle Vehicle [*Aerospace*] (AAG)
**LSV**............ Lunar Surface Vehicle [*Aerospace*]
**LSV**............ Lunar Survey Viewfinder [*Aerospace*]
**LSVC**.......... Lunar Surface Vehicle Communications [*Aerospace*]
**LSVG**.......... Lifesaving (MSA)
**Lsvl Orch**... Louisville Orchestra Program Notes [*A publication*]
**LSVP**.......... Landing Ship, Vehicle and Personnel [*Navy symbol*]
**LSW**........... Detroit, MI [*Location identifier*] [*FAA*] (FAAL)
**LSW**........... Labrador Sea Water [*Oceanography*]
**LSW**........... Landslide [*Washington*] [*Seismograph station code, US Geological Survey*] [*Closed*] (SEIS)
**LSW**........... LASER Spot Welder
**LSW**........... Least Significant Word (MCD)
**LSW**........... Light Support Weapon (MCD)
**LSW**........... Limit Switch [*Electronics*]
**LSW**........... Ludowa Spoldzielnia Wydawnicza [*A publication*]
**LSWA**......... Large-Amplitude, Slow Wave Activity [*Encephalography*]
**LSWMA**.... Lutheran Society for Worship, Music, and the Arts [*Later, Liturgical Conference*]
**LSWP**......... Lump Sum Wage Payments (MCD)
**LSWR**......... London & South-Western Railway (ROG)
**L & SWR**.... London & South-Western Railway (ROG)
**LSWT**......... Low-Speed Wind Tunnel (MCD)
**LSX**............ Landing Ship, Experimental
**LSXB**.......... Balzers/FL [*Switzerland*] [*ICAO location identifier*] (ICLI)
**LSXD**.......... Domat-Ems [*Switzerland*] [*ICAO location identifier*] (ICLI)
**LSXE**.......... Erstfeld [*Switzerland*] [*ICAO location identifier*] (ICLI)
**LSXH**.......... Holziken [*Switzerland*] [*ICAO location identifier*] (ICLI)

**lsxj---** ......... St. Helena [*MARC geographic area code*] [*Library of Congress*] (LCCP)
**LSXL** ......... Lauterbrunnen [*Switzerland*] [*ICAO location identifier*] (ICLI)
**LSXM** ......... St. Moritz [*Switzerland*] [*ICAO location identifier*] (ICLI)
**LSXO** ......... Gossau SG [*Switzerland*] [*ICAO location identifier*] (ICLI)
**LSXS** ......... Schindellegi [*Switzerland*] [*ICAO location identifier*] (ICLI)
**LSXT** ......... Trogen [*Switzerland*] [*ICAO location identifier*] (ICLI)
**LSXU** ......... Untervaz [*Switzerland*] [*ICAO location identifier*] (ICLI)
**LSXV** ......... San Vittore [*Switzerland*] [*ICAO location identifier*] (ICLI)
**LSXW** ......... Wurenlingen [*Switzerland*] [*ICAO location identifier*] (ICLI)
**LSY** ......... Lismore [*Australia*] [*Airport symbol*] (OAG)
**LSZA** ......... Lugano [*Switzerland*] [*ICAO location identifier*] (ICLI)
**LSZB** ......... Bern/Belp [*Switzerland*] [*ICAO location identifier*] (ICLI)
**LSZC** ......... Bad Ragaz [*Switzerland*] [*ICAO location identifier*] (ICLI)
**LSZD** ......... Ascona [*Switzerland*] [*ICAO location identifier*] (ICLI)
**LSZE** ......... Bad Ragaz [*Switzerland*] [*ICAO location identifier*] (ICLI)
**LSZF** ......... Birrfeld [*Switzerland*] [*ICAO location identifier*] (ICLI)
**LSZG** ......... Grenchen [*Switzerland*] [*ICAO location identifier*] (ICLI)
**LSZH** ......... Zurich [*Switzerland*] [*ICAO location identifier*] (ICLI)
**LSZI** ......... Fricktal-Schupfart [*Switzerland*] [*ICAO location identifier*] (ICLI)
**LSZJ** ......... Courtelary [*Switzerland*] [*ICAO location identifier*] (ICLI)
**LSZK** ......... Speck-Fehraltorf [*Switzerland*] [*ICAO location identifier*] (ICLI)
**LSZL** ......... Locarno [*Switzerland*] [*ICAO location identifier*] (ICLI)
**LSZM** ......... Bale [*Switzerland*] [*ICAO location identifier*] (ICLI)
**LSZN** ......... Hausen Am Albis [*Switzerland*] [*ICAO location identifier*] (ICLI)
**LSZODB** ... Lehrbuch der Speziellen Zoologie [*A publication*]
**LSZP** ......... Biel/Kappelen [*Switzerland*] [*ICAO location identifier*] (ICLI)
**LSZR** ......... Altenrhein [*Switzerland*] [*ICAO location identifier*] (ICLI)
**LSZS** ......... Samedan [*Switzerland*] [*ICAO location identifier*] (ICLI)
**LSZT** ......... Lommis [*Switzerland*] [*ICAO location identifier*] (ICLI)
**LSZU** ......... Buttwil [*Switzerland*] [*ICAO location identifier*] (ICLI)
**LSZV** ......... Sitterdorf [*Switzerland*] [*ICAO location identifier*] (ICLI)
**LSZW** ......... Thun [*Switzerland*] [*ICAO location identifier*] (ICLI)
**LSZX** ......... Schanis [*Switzerland*] [*ICAO location identifier*] (ICLI)
**LSZY** ......... Porrentruy [*Switzerland*] [*ICAO location identifier*] (ICLI)
**LSZZ** ......... Collective address for NOTAM and SNOWTAM [*Switzerland*] [*ICAO location identifier*] (ICLI)
**LT** ......... La Torre [*A publication*]
**L & T** ......... Laboratories and Test (NASA)
**LT** ......... [*The*] Lake Terminal Railroad Co. [*AAR code*]
**LT** ......... Laminated TEFLON
**LT** ......... Landed Terms
**LT** ......... Landing Team
**L & T** ......... Landlord and Tenant [*A publication*] (DLA)
**LT** ......... Lands Tribunal [*Legal*] [*British*]
**LT** ......... Language Translation [*Data processing*]
**LT** ......... Laplace Transform [*Mathematics*]
**LT** ......... Large Tug [*Army*]
**LT** ......... Last (ROG)
**LT** ......... Lateral Tooth
**LT** ......... Lateral Triceps Brachii [*Medicine*]
**LT** ......... Laughter Therapy (EA)
**LT** ......... Laundry Tray
**L T** ......... Law Times [*A publication*]
**LT** ......... Law Times Journal [*A publication*] (DLA)
**LT** ......... Law Times Newspaper [*A publication*] (DLA)
**LT** ......... Law Times Reports [*British*]
**LT** ......... Lawn Tennis
**LT** ......... Lead Time (NG)
**L/T** ......... Leading Telegraphist
**LT** ......... Leading Torpedoman [*Navy*] [*British*]
**LT** ......... League of Tarcisians (EA)
**LT** ......... Left
**LT** ......... Left Tackle [*Football*]
**LT** ......... Left Thigh
**LT** ......... Legal Tender [*Currency*]
**LT** ......... Legal Title [*Business term*]
**lt** ......... Legal Training [*Navy*] [*British*]
**Lt** ......... Leptosphaerulina Trifolii [*A fungus*]
**LT** ......... Less Than (IBMDP)
**LT** ......... Letter
**LT** ......... Letter Telegram
**LT** ......... Letter of Transmittal (MCD)
**LT** ......... Leukotriene [*Clinical pharmacology*]
**LT** ......... Level Transmitter (NRCH)
**LT** ......... Level Trigger
**LT** ......... Levende Talen [*A publication*]
**LT** ......... Levin Tube [*Medicine*]
**LT** ......... Levothyroxine [*Pharmacy*]
**LT** ......... Licentiate in Teaching [*British*]
**LT** ......... Licentiate in Theology
**LT** ......... Lid Tank
**LT** ......... Lieutenant (EY)
**LT** ......... Light (AAG)
**LT** ......... Light Tank
**LT** ......... Light Trap
**LT** ......... Light Truck [*British*]
**LT** ......... Limit (DEN)
**LT** ......... Limited Term Employee (OICC)
**L/T** ......... Line Telecommunications
**LT** ......... Line Telegraphy
**L & T** ......... Line and Terminal [*Telecommunications*] (TEL)
**LT** ......... Line Terminator
**LT** ......... Link Terminal [*Telecommunications*] (TEL)
**LT** ......... Link Trainer Instructor
**LT** ......... Linked Term [*Online database field identifier*]
**LT** ......... Liquid Toned [*Copier*] [*Reprography*]
**LT** ......... Lira Toscana [*Tuscany Pound*] [*Monetary unit*] [*Italian*] (ROG)
**LT** ......... Lira Turca [*Turkish Pound*] [*Monetary unit*] [*Italian*] (ROG)
**LT** ......... Lo Ta'aseh (BJA)
**L/T** ......... Load Test (MCD)
**LT** ......... Loader Trainer (MCD)
**LT** ......... Loader-Transporter [*British military*] (DMA)
**LT** ......... Local Time
**LT** ......... Locum Tenens [*In the Place Of*] [*Latin*]
**LT** ......... Logic Theorist [*or Theory*] [*Data processing*]
**LT** ......... Logic Tree
**LT** ......... London-Ducretet-Thomson [*Record label*] [*Great Britain, USA, etc.*]
**LT** ......... London Transport
**LT** ......... Long Term
**LT** ......... Long-Term Stay [*in hospital*] [*British*]
**LT** ......... Long Ton [*2240 pounds*]
**LT** ......... Long Treble [*Crocheting*] (ROG)
**L & T** ......... Longfield and Townsend's Irish Exchequer Reports [*1841-42*] [*A publication*] (DLA)
**L/T** ......... Loop Test [*Aerospace*] (AAG)
**LT** ......... Lorimar-Telepictures Corp. [*AMEX symbol*] (SPSG)
**LT** ......... Lot
**LT** ......... Low Temperature
**LT** ......... Low Tension
**LT** ......... Low Torque
**LT** ......... Lower Torso
**LT** ......... Lucis Trust (EA)
**LT** ......... Lufttransport Unternehmen [*Germany*] [*ICAO designator*] (FAAC)
**LT** ......... Lug Terminal
**LT** ......... Lymphocyte Transformation [*Hematology*]
**LT** ......... Lymphotoxin [*Immunochemistry*]
**LT** ......... Turn Left after Takeoff [*Aviation*] (FAAC)
**1LT** ......... First Lieutenant [*Army*]
**2LT** ......... Second Lieutenant [*Army*]
**LTA** ......... Lady Teachers' Association [*Australia*]
**LTA** ......... Land Trust Alliance (EA)
**LTA** ......... Large Transport Airplane
**LTA** ......... Lawn Tennis Association (EAIO)
**LTA** ......... Lead Tetraacetate [*Organic chemistry*]
**LTA** ......... Leave Travel Allowance
**LTA** ......... Legionarios del Trabajo in America (EA)
**LTA** ......... Leisure Time Activity
**LTA** ......... Lettera di Transporto Aereo [*Air Waybill*] [*Italian*] [*Business term*]
**LTA** ......... Lettre de Transport Aerien [*Air Waybill*] [*French*] [*Business term*]
**LTA** ......... Leucotriene A [*Clinical pharmacology*]
**LTA** ......... Leveling Torquer Amplifier
**LTA** ......... Library Technical Assistant
**LTA** ......... Lighter-than-Air [*Aircraft*]
**LTA** ......... Linen Trade Association (EA)
**LTA** ......... Lipoate Transacetylase [*An enzyme*]
**LTA** ......... Lipoteichoic Acid [*Biochemistry*]
**LTA** ......... Living Together Arrangement
**LTA** ......... LM [*Lunar Module*] Test Article [*NASA*]
**LTA** ......... Local Training Area (MCD)
**LTA** ......... Logical Transient Area
**LTA** ......... Long-Term Arrangements [*Department of State*]
**LTA** ......... Long-Term Average (CAAL)
**LTA** ......... Low Temperature Aftercooled [*Automotive engineering*]
**LTA** ......... Low-Temperature Ashing [*Analytical chemistry*]
**LTA** ......... Lower Torso Assembly [*Aerospace*] (MCD)
**LTA** ......... South Lake Tahoe, CA [*Location identifier*] [*FAA*] (FAAL)
**LTA** ......... Tzaneen [*South Africa*] [*Airport symbol*] (OAG)
**LTAA** ......... Ankara [*Turkey*] [*ICAO location identifier*] (ICLI)
**LTAB** ......... Guvercinlik [*Turkey*] [*ICAO location identifier*] (ICLI)
**LTAB** ......... League to Abolish Billionaires [*Fictitious organization mentioned in Donald Duck comic by Carl Barks*]
**LTAC** ......... Ankara/Esenboga [*Turkey*] [*ICAO location identifier*] (ICLI)
**LTACFIRE** ... Lightweight Tactical Fire Direction System [*Artillery*] [*Army*] (INF)
**LTAD** ......... Ankara/Etimesgut [*Turkey*] [*ICAO location identifier*] (ICLI)
**LTADL** ......... Launcher Tube Azimuth Datum Line
**LTAE** ......... Ankara/Murted [*Turkey*] [*ICAO location identifier*] (ICLI)
**LTAF** ......... Adana/Sakirpasa [*Turkey*] [*ICAO location identifier*] (ICLI)
**LTAG** ......... Adana/Incirlik [*Turkey*] [*ICAO location identifier*] (ICLI)
**LTAH** ......... Afyon [*Turkey*] [*ICAO location identifier*] (ICLI)
**LTAI** ......... Antalya [*Turkey*] [*ICAO location identifier*] (ICLI)
**LTAJ** ......... Gaziantep [*Turkey*] [*ICAO location identifier*] (ICLI)
**LTAK** ......... Iskenderun [*Turkey*] [*ICAO location identifier*] (ICLI)

**LTAL**........ Kastamonu [*Turkey*] [*ICAO location identifier*] (ICLI)
**LTAM**........ Kayseri [*Turkey*] [*ICAO location identifier*] (ICLI)
**LTaM** ........ Madison Parish Library, Tallulah, LA [*Library symbol*] [*Library of Congress*] (LCLS)
**LTAN** ........ Konya [*Turkey*] [*ICAO location identifier*] (ICLI)
**LTAO** ........ Malatya/Erhac [*Turkey*] [*ICAO location identifier*] (ICLI)
**LTAP**........ Merzifon [*Turkey*] [*ICAO location identifier*] (ICLI)
**LTAQ** ........ Samsun [*Turkey*] [*ICAO location identifier*] (ICLI)
**LTAR**........ Sivas [*Turkey*] [*ICAO location identifier*] (ICLI)
**LTAS** ........ Lead Tetraacetate-Schiff (Reaction) [*Clinical chemistry*]
**LTAS** ........ Zonguldak [*Turkey*] [*ICAO location identifier*] (ICLI)
**LTAT**........ Malatya/Erhac [*Turkey*] [*ICAO location identifier*] (ICLI)
**LTAU** ........ Kayseri/Erkilet [*Turkey*] [*ICAO location identifier*] (ICLI)
**LTAV**........ Sivrihisar [*Turkey*] [*ICAO location identifier*] (ICLI)
**LTAVD**...... Low-Temperature Arc Vapor Deposition [*Coating technology*]
**Lt B** ........... Bachelor of Literature
**LTB**........... Laboratory Techniques in Biochemistry and Molecular Biology [*Elsevier Book Series*] [*A publication*]
**LTB**........... Laryngo-Tracheal Bronchitis
**LTB**........... Last Trunk Busy [*Telecommunications*] (TEL)
**LTB**........... Law Times Bankruptcy Reports [*United States*] [*A publication*] (DLA)
**LTB**........... Lawrence Traffic Bureau Inc., Kansas City MO [*STAC*]
**LTB**........... Leucotriene B [*Clinical pharmacology*]
**LTB**........... Light Bay [*Horse racing*]
**LTB**........... Limited Test Ban [*Nuclear testing*]
**LTB**........... Line Term Buffer [*Data processing*] (AABC)
**LTB**........... London Tourist Board [*British*] (DCTA)
**LTB**........... London Transport Board [*British*]
**LT(B)**........ Low-Tension (Battery) (DEN)
**LTBA**........ Die Lexikalischen Tafelserien der Babylonier und Assyrer in den Berliner Museen [*A publication*] (BJA)
**LTBA**........ Istanbul/Yesilkoy [*Turkey*] [*ICAO location identifier*] (ICLI)
**LTBA**........ Lexikalischen Tafelserien der Babylonier und Assyrer [*A publication*]
**LTBA**........ Linguistics of the Tibeto-Burman Area [*A publication*]
**LTBB**........ Istanbul [*Turkey*] [*ICAO location identifier*] (ICLI)
**LTBC**........ Alasehir [*Turkey*] [*ICAO location identifier*] (ICLI)
**LTBD**........ Aydin [*Turkey*] [*ICAO location identifier*] (ICLI)
**LTBE**........ Bursa [*Turkey*] [*ICAO location identifier*] (ICLI)
**LTBF**........ Balikesir [*Turkey*] [*ICAO location identifier*] (ICLI)
**LTBG**........ Bandirma [*Turkey*] [*ICAO location identifier*] (ICLI)
**LTBH** ........ Canakkale [*Turkey*] [*ICAO location identifier*] (ICLI)
**LTBI** ........ Eskisehir [*Turkey*] [*ICAO location identifier*] (ICLI)
**LTBJ**........ Izmir/Cumaovasi [*Turkey*] [*ICAO location identifier*] (ICLI)
**LTBK**........ Izmir/Gaziemir [*Turkey*] [*ICAO location identifier*] (ICLI)
**LTBL**........ Izmir/Cigli [*Turkey*] [*ICAO location identifier*] (ICLI)
**LtBl**........... Light Blend [*Horticulture*]
**LTBM**........ Isparta [*Turkey*] [*ICAO location identifier*] (ICLI)
**LTBMC**..... Long-Term Bone Marrow Culture [*Cell culture*]
**LTBN**........ Kutahya [*Turkey*] [*ICAO location identifier*] (ICLI)
**LTBO**........ Linear Time Base Oscillator
**LTBO**........ Usak [*Turkey*] [*ICAO location identifier*] (ICLI)
**LTBP**........ London Tanker Broker Panel
**LTBP**........ Yalova [*Turkey*] [*ICAO location identifier*] (ICLI)
**LTBQ**........ Topel [*Turkey*] [*ICAO location identifier*] (ICLI)
**LTBR**........ Yenisehir [*Turkey*] [*ICAO location identifier*] (ICLI)
**LTBS** ........ Dalaman [*Turkey*] [*ICAO location identifier*] (ICLI)
**LTBT**........ Akhisar [*Turkey*] [*ICAO location identifier*] (ICLI)
**LTBT**........ Limited Test Ban Treaty [*Signed in 1963; prohibits testing of nuclear devices in certain environments*]
**LTC**........... Lafferty Transportation [*AAR code*]
**LTC**........... Land Tenure Center [*University of Wisconsin*] [*Research center*]
**LTC**........... Land Transport Corps [*British military*] (DMA)
**LTC**........... Lattice (MSA)
**LTC**........... Launch Vehicle Test Conductor [*NASA*] (KSC)
**LTC**........... Lawn Tennis Club [*British*]
**LTC**........... Lead Telluride Crystal [*Photoconductor*]
**LTC**........... Leaseway Transportation Corporation [*NYSE symbol*] (SPSG)
**LTC**........... Lesotho Telecommunications Corporation [*Ministry of Transport and Communications*] [*Lesotho*] (TSSD)
**LTC**........... Less than Truckload Cargo (MCD)
**LTC**........... Leukotriene C [*Clinical pharmacology*]
**LTC**........... Liberia Telecommunications Corporation (IMH)
**LTC**........... Liberty to the Captives [*Later, ACAT*] (EA)
**LTC**........... Lieutenant Colonel (AABC)
**LTC**........... Light Terminal Complexes
**LTC**........... Lightly Treated Coated [*Papermaking*]
**LTC**........... Line Time Clock
**LTC**........... Line Traffic Coordinator (CET)
**LTC**........... Linear Transmission Channel
**LTC**........... Living Tree Center (EA)
**LTC**........... Livros Tecnicos e Cientificos Editora Ltda. [*Brazil*]
**LTC**........... Load Tap Changing
**LTC**........... Local Telephone Circuit [*Telecommunications*] (TEL)
**LTC**........... Local Terminal Controller
**LTC**........... Lockwood Torday & Carlisle Ltd. [*British*]
**LTC**........... Long-Term Care [*Medicine*]
**LTC**........... Long-Term Contract (ADA)
**LTC**........... Long Term Costing [*Military*] (RDA)
**LTC**........... Long Time Constant (IEEE)
**LTC**........... Longitudinal Time Constant
**LTC**........... Loop Test Conference [*Aerospace*] (AAG)
**LTC**........... Lotus Cosmetics International Ltd. [*Vancouver Stock Exchange symbol*]
**LTC**........... Low-Tar Content [*of cigarettes*]
**LTC**........... Low-Temperature Carbonization
**LTC**........... Low-Temperature Catalyst
**LTC**........... Low-Temperature Coefficient
**LTC**........... Low-Temperature Cooling
**LTC**........... Lunar Terrain [*or Topographic*] Camera [*NASA*]
**L(TC)**........ Tax Cases Leaflets [*Legal*] [*British*]
**LTCA**........ Elazig [*Turkey*] [*ICAO location identifier*] (ICLI)
**LTCB**........ Agri [*Turkey*] [*ICAO location identifier*] (ICLI)
**LTCC**........ Diyarbakir [*Turkey*] [*ICAO location identifier*] (ICLI)
**LTCD**........ Erzincan [*Turkey*] [*ICAO location identifier*] (ICLI)
**LTCDR**...... Lieutenant Commander
**LTCE**........ Erzurum [*Turkey*] [*ICAO location identifier*] (ICLI)
**LTCF**........ Kars [*Turkey*] [*ICAO location identifier*] (ICLI)
**LTCF**........ Long-Term Care Facility [*Medicine*]
**LTCG**........ Long-Term Capital Gain
**LTCG**........ Trabzon [*Turkey*] [*ICAO location identifier*] (ICLI)
**LTCH**........ Urfa [*Turkey*] [*ICAO location identifier*] (ICLI)
**LTCI**........ Van [*Turkey*] [*ICAO location identifier*] (ICLI)
**LTCJ**........ Batman [*Turkey*] [*ICAO location identifier*] (ICLI)
**LTCL**........ Licentiate of Trinity College of Music, London [*British*]
**LTCL**........ Long-Term Capital Loss
**LTCM**........ Licentiate of the Toronto Conservatory of Music [*Canada*]
**LTCMDR**... Lieutenant Commander (FAAC)
**LTCO**........ Landmark Technology Corporation [*Marietta, GA*] [*NASDAQ symbol*] (NQ)
**LTCO**........ London Transactions. International Congress of Orientalists [*A publication*]
**LTCOL**...... Lieutenant Colonel
**Lt-Comm**.... Lieutenant-Commander [*British military*] (DMA)
**LT/COR/WR**... Light Corner Wear [*Deltiology*]
**LT/CR**....... Light Crease [*Deltiology*]
**LTCT**........ Lower Thermal Comfort Threshold [*Environmental heating*]
**LTD**.......... Air O'Hare Ltd. [*Chicago, IL*] [*FAA designator*] (FAAC)
**LTD**.......... Ghadames [*Libya*] [*Airport symbol*] (OAG)
**LTD**.......... LASER Target Designator
**LTD**.......... Launch Test Directive [*NASA*] (KSC)
**LTD**.......... Letdown [*Nuclear energy*] (NRCH)
**LTD**.......... Leukotriene D [*Clinical pharmacology*]
**LTD**.......... Lift-Drag [*Ratio*] (MCD)
**LTD**.......... Lightweight Target Designator
**LTD**.......... Limited [*British corporation*] (EY)
**LTD**.......... [*The*] Limited, Inc. [*NYSE symbol*] (SPSG)
**LTD**.......... Line Transfer Device
**LTD**.......... Linear Transport Drive
**LTD**.......... Linear Tumor Diameter [*Oncology*]
**LTD**.......... Litchfield, IL [*Location identifier*] [*FAA*] (FAAL)
**LTD**.......... Live Test Demonstration
**LTD**.......... Local Test Desk [*Telecommunications*] (KSC)
**LTD**.......... Logistic Technical Data [*Navy*]
**LTD**.......... Long Tank Delta
**LTD**.......... Long-Term Depression [*Neurophysiology*]
**LTD**.......... Long-Term Disability
**LT & D**...... Love, Togetherness, and Devotion [*Rock music group*]
**LTD**.......... Low-Temperature Drying
**LTD**.......... Lumber Transfer and Distribution
**Ltda**.......... Limitada [*Limited*] [*Spanish*]
**Ltda**.......... Limitada [*Limited*] [*Portuguese*]
**LTDA**........ Localizer Type Directional Aid [*Aviation*] (FAAC)
**LTD ED**..... Limited Edition [*Publishing*]
**LTDL**........ Life Test Data Logger (CAAL)
**LTDM**........ Light Transmittance Difference Meter
**LTDP**........ Long-Term Defense Program [*NATO*] (MCD)
**LTDR**........ LASER Target Designator Receiver
**LTDS**........ LASER Target Designator System (MCD)
**LTDS**........ Launch Tracking [*or Trajectory*] Data System
**Ltd S**......... Limited Sirketi [*Limited Company, Corporation*] [*See also Sti, TAS*] [*Turkish*] (CED)
**LTDSS**...... LASER Target Designator Scoring System (MCD)
**Ltd Sti**....... Limited Sirketi [*Limited Company, Corporation*] [*See also Sti, TAS*] [*Turkish*]
**LTDT**........ Langley Transonic Dynamics Tunnel [*NASA*] (KSC)
**LTE**........... Land Trust Exchange [*Later, LTA*] (EA)
**LTE**........... Laplace Transformation Estimator
**LTE**........... Large Table Electroplotter [*Data processing*]
**LTE**........... Large Thrust per Element
**LTE**........... Launch to Eject
**LTE**........... Letter to the Editor
**LTE**........... Leucotriene E [*Clinical pharmacology*]
**LT(E)**........ Lieutenant (Engineer)
**LTE**........... Limited Technical Evaluation (MCD)
**LTE**........... Limited Test Equipment
**LTE**........... Line Termination Equipment [*Telecommunications*] (TEL)
**LTE**........... Linear Threshold Element [*Data processing*]
**LTE**........... Local Thermal Equilibrium [*Physical chemistry*]

**LTE**........... Local Thermodynamic Equilibrium [*Astronautics, astrophysics*]
**LTE**........... London Transport Executive
**LTE**........... Long-Term Effect
**LTE**........... Long-Term Enhancement [*Neurophysiology*]
**LTE**........... Long-Term Equilibration [*Analytical chemistry*]
**LTE**........... Low-Thrust Engine
**LTE**........... Tunisie Economique [*A publication*]
**LTEA**......... Leaf Tobacco Exporters Association (EA)
**L Teach**...... Law Teacher [*A publication*]
**L Teacher**... Law Teacher. Journal of the Association of Law Teachers, London [*A publication*]
**LTEC**......... Lincoln Telecommunications Company [*NASDAQ symbol*] (NQ)
**LTECA**...... Landtechnik [*A publication*]
**LTED**......... Long-Term Economic Deterioration [*Department of Commerce*]
**LT/ED/WR**... Light Edge Wear [*Deltiology*]
**Ltee**........... Limitee [*Limited*] [*French*]
**LTEK**......... Life Technologies, Inc. [*Gaithersburg, MD*] [*NASDAQ symbol*] (NQ)
**LTEL**......... Lorain Telecom Corp. [*Dallas, TX*] [*NASDAQ symbol*] (NQ)
**LTEMP**..... Low Temperature
**L T (Eng)**... Law Times Journal (England) [*A publication*] (DLA)
**LTEP**......... Long-Term Equipment Plan [*Military*] (RDA)
**LTER**......... Long Term Ecological Research [*National Science Foundation*]
**LTERR**...... Lunar Terrestrial Age
**LTF**........... LASER Terrain Follower
**LTF**........... Layman Tithing Foundation (EA)
**LTF**........... Leucotriene F [*Clinical pharmacology*]
**LTF**........... Ligand-Responsive Transcription Factor [*Genetics*]
**LTF**........... Light-Float [*Navigation*]
**LTF**........... Lightning Training Flight [*British military*] (DMA)
**LTF**........... Lipotropic Factor [*Choline*] [*Biochemistry*]
**LTF**........... Liquid Thermal Flowmeter
**LTF**........... Lithographic Technical Foundation [*Later, GATF*] (MSA)
**LTF**........... Local Training Flight
**LTF**........... Lymphocyte Transforming Factor [*Immunology*]
**LTF**........... Nicholls State University, Thibodaux, LA [*Library symbol*] [*Library of Congress*] (LCLS)
**LTFC**......... Landing Traffic [*Aviation*] (FAAC)
**LTFC**......... Low-Temperature Fuel Cell [*Energy source*]
**LTFCS**...... LASER Tank Fire Control System
**LTFD**......... Logic and Test Function Drawer [*Data processing*] (MCD)
**LT/FM**....... Long-Term/Frequency Modulation
**LTFRD**...... Lot Tolerance Fraction Reliability Deviation [*Quality control*]
**LTF Res Progr**... LTF [*Lithographic Technical Foundation*] Research Progress [*A publication*]
**LTFS**......... LASER Terrain Following System
**LTFT**......... Low-Temperature Flow Test [*Lubricant technology*]
**LTFV**......... Less Than Fair Value [*Business term*]
**LTG**........... Catalina Lighting [*AMEX symbol*] (SPSG)
**LTG**........... Legal Technology Group [*Information service or system*] (IID)
**LTG**........... Lettering (ADA)
**LTG**........... Lieutenant General (AABC)
**LTG**........... Lightening
**LTG**........... Lighting
**LTG**........... Lightning [*Meteorology*]
**LTG**........... Lightning Minerals [*Vancouver Stock Exchange symbol*]
**LTG**........... Line Trunk Group [*Telecommunications*]
**LTG**........... Linear Tangent Guidance (MCD)
**ltg**............. Lithographer [*MARC relator code*] [*Library of Congress*] (LCCP)
**LTG**........... Local Tactical Grid [*Military*] (NVT)
**LTG**........... Lunar Traverse Gravimeter [*Experiment*] [*NASA*]
**LTGC**......... Lieutenant Grand Commander [*Freemasonry*]
**LTGCC**....... Lightning Cloud-to-Cloud [*Meteorology*] (FAAC)
**LTGCCCG**... Lightning Cloud-to-Cloud, Cloud-to-Ground [*Meteorology*] (FAAC)
**LTGCG**...... Lightning Cloud-to-Ground [*Meteorology*] (FAAC)
**LTGCW**..... Lightning Cloud-to-Water [*Meteorology*] (FAAC)
**Ltg Des Appl**... Lighting Design and Application [*A publication*]
**LTGE**......... Lighterage
**LTGEN**...... Lieutenant General
**Ltg Equip News**... Lighting Equipment News [*A publication*]
**LTGF Newl**... Lawyers' Title Guaranty Funds Newsletter [*A publication*] (DLA)
**LTGH**........ Lightening Hole [*Engineering*]
**LTGIC**....... Lightning in Clouds [*Meteorology*] (FAAC)
**Ltg J (Thorn)**... Lighting Journal (Thorn) [*A publication*]
**LTGL**......... Lee-Tse-Goldberg-Lowe [*Theory*]
**Ltg Res Tech**... Lighting Research and Technology [*A publication*]
**L Th**........... La Themis [*Lower Canada*] [*A publication*] (DLA)
**LTH**........... Laboratory Test Handbook
**LTH**........... Lactogenic Hormone [*Also, LGH, PR, PRL*] [*Endocrinology*]
**LTH**........... Lethality and Target Hardening [*Military*] (SDI)
**L & TH**....... Lethality and Target Hardening [*Military*] (SDI)
**L Th**........... Licentiate in Theology
**LTH**........... Logical Track Header
**LTH**........... Low-Temperature Holding
**LTH**........... Low Turret Half
**LTH**........... Luteotrophic Hormone [*Also, PR, PRL*] [*Endocrinology*]
**Lth**............. Martin Luther's German Version of the Bible [*A publication*] (BJA)
**LTHA**........ Long-Term Heat Aging
**L Th K**........ Lexikon fuer Theologie und Kirche [*A publication*]
**LTHO**........ Lighthouse
**LTHPA**...... Lectures in Theoretical Physics [*A publication*]
**LThPh**....... Laval Theologique et Philosophique [*A publication*]
**LTHR**........ Leather (KSC)
**LTHS**......... La Trobe Historical Studies [*A publication*] (APTA)
**LTHV**........ Lucke Tumor Herpesvirus
**LTI**............ Land Training Installations (NATG)
**LTI**............ Licentiate of the Textile Institute [*British*] (DBQ)
**LTI**............ Light Transmission Index
**LTI**............ Limited to Interrogations (MCD)
**LTI**............ Linear Technology, Incorporated [*Toronto Stock Exchange symbol*]
**LTI**............ Long-Term Integration (CAAL)
**LTI**............ Lost Time Injury [*Industrial plant safety*]
**LTI**............ Low-Temperature Isomerization [*Organic chemistry*]
**LTI**............ Low-Temperature Isotope
**LTI**............ Lowell Technological Institute [*Massachusetts*]
**LTIC**.......... Language Teaching Information Centre [*British*] (CB)
**LTID**.......... Light-Intensity Detector (MSA)
**LTIED**....... Ekspress-Informatsiya Laboratornye Tekhnologicheskie Issledovaniya i Obogashchenie Mineral'nogo Syr'ya [*A publication*]
**LTimesLS**... Times Literary Supplement (London) [*A publication*]
**Lt Inf**.......... Light Infantry [*British military*] (DMA)
**LTIOV**....... Latest Time Information of Value [*Military*] (AFM)
**LTIP**.......... Long-Term Incentive Plan
**LTIRF**........ Lowell Technological Institute Research Foundation (MCD)
**LTIS**.......... LASER Target Interface System
**LTIV**.......... Lunar Trajectory Injection Vehicle [*NASA*] (KSC)
**LTIZ**.......... Liposome Technology, Inc. [*NASDAQ symbol*] (NQ)
**LTJ**............ Law Times Journal [*A publication*] (DLA)
**LTJ**............ Lutheran Theological Journal [*A publication*] (APTA)
**LTJC**......... Lyons Township Junior College [*Illinois*]
**LTJG**......... Lieutenant Junior Grade [*Navy*]
**LT Jo**......... Law Times [*A publication*]
**LT Jo (Eng)**... Law Times Journal (England) [*A publication*] (DLA)
**LT Jour**...... Law Times [*A publication*]
**LTK**........... Latakia [*Syria*] [*Airport symbol*] (OAG)
**LTK**........... Lexikon fuer Theologie und Kirche [*A publication*]
**LTK1**......... Ladies' Touring Kayak, Single Person (ADA)
**LTL**............ Aerie Airlines [*Nashville, TN*] [*FAA designator*] (FAAC)
**LTL**............ Lafourche Parish Library, Thibodaux, LA [*Library symbol*] [*Library of Congress*] (LCLS)
**LTL**............ Lastourville [*Gabon*] [*Airport symbol*] (OAG)
**Lt L**............ Leksykolohiia ta Leksykohrafiia Mizhvidomchyi Zbirnyk [*A publication*]
**LTL**............ Less than Truckload [*Under 24,000 pounds*]
**LTL**............ Line-to-Line
**LTL**............ Lintel [*Technical drawings*]
**LTL**............ Listing-Time Limit (MSA)
**LTL**............ Little
**LTL**............ Lot-Truck Load
**LTL**............ Lytton Minerals Ltd. [*Toronto Stock Exchange symbol*] [*Vancouver Stock Exchange symbol*]
**LTLA**......... Language Teaching and Linguistics Abstracts [*A publication*]
**LTLA**......... Launcher Tube Longitudinal Axis
**LTLCG**...... Little Change (FAAC)
**LTLE**......... Little [*Arthur D.*], Inc. [*NASDAQ symbol*] (NQ)
**LTLJ**.......... La Trobe Library Journal [*A publication*] (APTA)
**LTLP**......... Little Prince Productions Limited [*NASDAQ symbol*] (NQ)
**LTLS**......... Lincoln Trail Libraries System [*Library network*]
**LTLS**......... (London) Times Literary Supplement [*A publication*]
**LTLS**......... Long-Term Lapse Survey [*LIMRA*]
**LTLT**......... Long Time Low Temperature [*Food processing*]
**Lt Ltg**........ Light and Lighting [*A publication*]
**LTM**........... LASER Target Marker (RDA)
**LTM**........... Lead Time Matrix (MCD)
**LTM**........... Leading Torpedoman [*Navy*] [*British*]
**LTM**........... Leeds Texts and Monographs [*A publication*]
**LTM**........... Lethem [*Guyana*] [*Airport symbol*] (OAG)
**LTM**........... Licentiate in Tropical Medicine [*British*]
**LTM**........... Lient Trief Mixed [*Cement*]
**LTM**........... Life Test Model
**LTM**........... Line Type Modulation [*Radio*]
**LTM**........... Little Maria Mountains [*California*] [*Seismograph station code, US Geological Survey*] (SEIS)
**LTM**........... Live Traffic Model [*Telecommunications*] (TEL)
**LTM**........... Long-Term Memory
**LTM**........... Low-Trajectory Missiles (NRCH)
**LTMED**..... Low-Temperature Multieffect Distillation [*Chemical engineering*]
**LTMS**........ Lunar Terrain Measuring System [*Aerospace*]
**LTN**........... Alaska Legislative Teleconference Network [*Alaska State Legislative Affairs Agency*] [*Juneau, AK*] [*Telecommunications service*] (TSSD)
**LTN**........... Liberty Tree Network [*An association*] (EA)

LTN ........... Lightning (ADA)
LTN ........... Linear Time-Varying Network
LTN ........... Long-Term Nephelometer [*Instrumentation*]
LTN ........... Luton [*England*] [*Airport symbol*] (OAG)
LTNG ........ Lightning [*Meteorology*]
LTNGP ...... Low-Temperature Noble Gas Process [*Nuclear energy*] (NRCH)
LTNIF ....... Low-Temperature Neutron Irradiation Facility [*Oak Ridge, TN*] [*Oak Ridge National Laboratory*] [*Department of Energy*] (GRD)
LT NS ........ Law Times. New Series [*Pennsylvania*] [*A publication*] (DLA)
LT NS ........ Law Times Reports, New Series [*England*] [*A publication*] (DLA)
LT NS (Eng) ... Law Times. New Series [*England*] [*A publication*] (DLA)
LTO ........... Land Titles Office [*Australia*]
LTO ........... Landing and Takeoff
LTO ........... Lead-Tin Overlay [*Automotive engineering*]
LTO ........... Leading Torpedoman [*Navy*] [*British*] (DMA)
LTO ........... Local Tax Office [*British*]
LTO ........... Loreto [*Mexico*] [*Airport symbol*] (OAG)
LTO ........... Lot Time Order
LTOE ......... Living Table of Organization and Equipment [*Army*] (INF)
LTOF ......... Low-Temperature Optical Facility
LTOM ....... London's Traded Options Market [*British*] (ECON)
LTON ........ Long Ton [*2240 pounds*]
LTOS ......... Law Times, Old Series [*British*]
LT OS ........ Law Times Reports, Old Series [*England*] [*A publication*] (DLA)
LTOT ......... Latest Time over Target (AFM)
LT-P ........... Large Transmitter Coated with Paraffin
LTP ............ Laval Theologique et Philosophique [*A publication*]
LTP ............ LEM [*Lunar Excursion Module*] Test Procedure [*NASA*] (KSC)
LTP ............ Let's Tax Plutocrats [*Humorous interpretation of LTP - Limit on Tax Preferences*]
LTP ............ Letterpress
LTP ............ Library Technology Program [*Formerly, Library Technology Project*] [*ALA*] [*Defunct*]
LTP ............ Lient Trief Pure [*Cement*]
LTP ............ Limit on Tax Preferences
LTP ............ Line-Throwing Projectile (NG)
LTP ............ Linear Time Plot (MUGU)
LTP ............ Lipid Transfer Protein [*Biochemistry*]
LTP ............ Living Together Partner [*Lifestyle classification*]
LTP ............ Local Training Plan [*Job Training and Partnership Act*] (OICC)
LTP ............ Long-Term Potentiation [*Neurophysiology*]
LTP ............ Long Term Projections [*Townsend-Greenspan & Co., Inc.*] [*Database*]
LTP ............ Low-Temperature Phosphorimetry [*Analytical chemistry*]
LTP ............ Low-Temperature Physics
LTP ............ Lower Trip Point
LTP ............ Lunar Tidal Perturbation
LTPB ......... Lactone Terminated Polybutadiene [*Organic chemistry*] (MCD)
LTPD ......... Lot Tolerance Percent Defective [*Quality control*] (MSA)
LTPE ......... Long-Term Public Expenditure [*British*]
LTPHOTORON ... Light Photographic Squadron
LTPL ......... Long-Term Procedural Language
LTPO ......... LASER Technology Program Office [*Navy*]
LTPP ......... Lipothiamide-Pyrophosphate
LTPR ......... Long Taper
LTPR ......... Long-Term Prime Rate [*Finance*]
Lt Prod Engng ... Light Production Engineering [*A publication*]
LTPT ......... Low-Turbulence Pressure Tunnel [*NASA*]
LTQ ........... Le Touquet [*France*] [*Airport symbol*] (OAG)
LTQ ........... Lexington Theological Quarterly [*A publication*]
LTQ ........... Local Track Quality (NVT)
LTQ ........... Low Torque
LTQC ......... Long-Term Quality-Control [*Analytical chemistry*]
LTR ............ Lander Trajectory Reconstruction [*Program*] [*NASA*]
LTR ............ Lands Tribunal Rules [*Town planning*] [*British*]
LTR ............ LASER Tank Range-Finder
LTR ............ LASER Target Recognition [*Military*] (CAAL)
LTR ............ Later (FAAC)
LTR ............ Lattice Test Reactor
LTR ............ Law Times Reports [*United Kingdom*] [*A publication*]
LTR ............ Law Times Reports, New Series [*England*] [*A publication*] (DLA)
LTR ............ [*The*] Learning Tree [*UTLAS symbol*]
LTR ............ Leather. International Journal of the Industry [*A publication*]
LTR ............ Letter (AFM)
LTR ............ Levant Trade Review [*A publication*]
LTR ............ Library Technology Reports [*A publication*]
L-TR ........... Licensing Technical Review [*Nuclear energy*] (NRCH)
LTR ............ Light Tactical Raft
LTR ............ Lighter
LTR ............ Liquid Test Rig [*Apollo*] [*NASA*]
LTR ............ Living Together Relationship
LTR ............ Lockheed Training Reactor
LTR ............ Loew's Corp. [*Formerly, Loew's Theatres, Inc.*] [*NYSE symbol*] (SPSG)
LTR ............ Logistics and Transportation Review [*A publication*]
LTR ............ Lone Tree Road [*California*] [*Seismograph station code, US Geological Survey*] (SEIS)
LTR ............ Long-Term Reserve [*British military*] (DMA)
LTR ............ Long Terminal Repeat [*or Redundancy*] [*Genetics*]
LTR ............ Long Treble [*Knitting*]
LTR ............ Long-Tube Recirculation [*Evaporator*]
LTR ............ Longitudinal Triangular Ripples [*Oceanography*]
LTR ............ Lord Treasurer's Remembrancer [*British*]
LTR ............ Low-Temperature Reactor [*Chemical engineering*]
LTRA ......... Lands Tribunal Rating Appeals [*Legal*] [*British*]
L-TRAN .... Lesson Translator (NVT)
L in Trans .. Law in Transition [*A publication*]
L in Trans J ... Law in Transition Journal [*A publication*] (DLA)
L Trans Q .. Law in Transition Quarterly [*A publication*] (DLA)
L in Trans Q ... Law in Transition Quarterly [*A publication*] (DLA)
LTRC ......... Landing Traffic [*Aviation*] (FAAC)
LTRC ......... Louisiana Transportation Research Center [*Louisiana State University*] [*Research center*] (RCD)
LT Rep ....... Law Times Reports, New Series [*England*] [*A publication*] (DLA)
LT Rep NS ... Law Times Reports, New Series [*England*] [*A publication*] (DLA)
LTRF ......... LASER Tank Range-Finder
LTRI .......... Lightning and Transients Research Institute [*St. Paul, MN*] (MCD)
LTRN ........ Lantern (MSA)
LTR NS ..... Law Times Reports, New Series [*England*] [*A publication*] (DLA)
LTROS ...... Law Times Reports. Old Series [*United Kingdom*] [*A publication*]
LTRP ......... Long-Term Requirement Plan (NATG)
LTRPRS .... Letterpress
LTRS ......... LASER Target Recognition System
LTRS ......... Letters Shift [*Teleprinters*]
LTRS ......... Low Temperature Research Station [*British*]
LT Rulings ... Land Tax Rulings [*Australia*] [*A publication*]
LTS ............ Altus, OK [*Location identifier*] [*FAA*] (FAAL)
LTS ............ Labor Turnover Statistics (OICC)
LTS ............ Laboratory Test Set
LTS ............ Landfall Technique School [*Navy*]
LTS ............ Language Teaching System
LTS ............ Language Translation System
LTS ............ LASER Target Simulator (MCD)
LTS ............ LASER Test Set (MCD)
LTS ............ LASER-Triggered Switch (MCD)
LTS ............ Launch Telemetry Station
LTS ............ Launch Telemetry System
LTS ............ Launch Tracking Station
LTS ............ Launch Tracking System
LTS ............ Library Technical Services [*Library network*]
LTS ............ Library Technicians Section [*Library Association of Australia*]
LTS ............ Lifetrends Behavioral Systems, Inc. [*Vancouver Stock Exchange symbol*]
LTS ............ Lighting Test Set (KSC)
LTS ............ Line Transient Suppression
LTS ............ Linearity Test Set
LTS ............ Link Terminal Simulator
LTS ............ Llantrisant [*Welsh depot code*]
LTS ............ Load Transfer Switch
LT & S ....... London, Tilbury & Southend Railway [*British*]
LTS ............ (London) Times Literary Supplement [*A publication*]
LTS ............ Long-Term Stability
LTS ............ Long-Term Standard [*Lamp for spectrometry*]
LTS ............ Long-Term Storage [*Memory*] [*Data processing*]
LTS ............ Love Token Society (EA)
LTS ............ Low-Temperature Separation
LTS ............ Low Threshold Spike [*Neurochemistry*]
LTS ............ Lufttransport-Sud [*Airline*] [*Federal Republic of Germany*]
LTS ............ Trinity Lutheran Seminary, Columbus, OH [*OCLC symbol*] (OCLC)
LTSB ......... Low Temperature Science. Series B. Biological Sciences [*A publication*]
LTSC ......... Licentiate in the Technology of Surface Coatings [*British*] (DBQ)
LTSEM ..... Low-Temperature Scanning Electron Microscopy
LTSF ......... Lid Tank Shielding Facility [*Nuclear energy*] (NRCH)
LTSG ......... LASER-Triggered Spark Gap
LTSH ......... League of Tarcisians of the Sacred Heart [*Later, LT*] (EA)
LTSM ........ Long-Range Tactical Strike Missile (MCD)
LT(Sp) ....... Lieutenant (Special)
LTSPC ....... L'Union Territoriale des Syndicats Professionelles Caledoniens [*Territorial Federation of New Caledonian Unions of Private Employees*]
LT-SR ........ Large Transmitter Coated with Silicon Rubber
LT & SR ..... London, Tilbury & Southend Railway [*British*] (ROG)
LTSS ......... Long-Term Scientific Study [*NATO Defense Research Group*] (MCD)
LTSTA ...... Light Station [*Coast Guard*]

**LTSV**......... Lucerne Transient Streak Virus
**LTSW**......... Light Switch
**LTT**......... Land Title Trust (DLA)
**LTT**......... Landline Teletypewriter [*Military*]
**LTT**......... LASER Target Tracker
**LTT**......... Latakia Type Tobacco [*Shipping*]
**LT T**......... Lieutenant of Treasury [*British*]
**LTT**......... Light Tactical Transport (MCD)
**LTT**......... Light-Travel-Time [*Astronomy*]
**LTT**......... Long-Term Training (MCD)
**LTT**......... Louis Trichardt [*South Africa*] [*Seismograph station code, US Geological Survey*] (SEIS)
**LTT**......... Low-Temperature Test
**LTT**......... Lunar Test Table [*Aerospace*]
**LTT**......... Lymphocyte Transformation Test [*Medicine*]
**LTTAS**...... Light Tactical Transport Aircraft System [*Helicopter*] [*Military*] (RDA)
**LTTAT**...... Long Tank Thrust-Augmented Thor
**LTTB**......... Listen to the Band (EA)
**LTTBT**...... Low-Threshold Test Ban Treaty [*Proposed*]
**LTTC**......... Lowry Technical Training Center [*Air Force*] (AFM)
**LTTD**......... Letter-Type Technical Directive [*Navy*] (NG)
**LTTE**......... Liberation Tigers of Tamil Eelam [*Sri Lanka*]
**LTTL**......... Low-Power Transistor-Transistor Logic (IEEE)
**LTTMT**..... Low-Temperature Thermomechanical Treatment
**LTTR**......... Latter (FAAC)
**LTTR**......... Long-Term Tape Recorder
**LTU**......... Land Treatment Unit [*Waste disposal*]
**LTU**......... Lawrence Technological University
**LTU**......... Less Than
**LTU**......... Lift-Off Time and Update
**LTU**......... Line Terminating Unit (CET)
**LTU**......... Little Mountain [*Utah*] [*Seismograph station code, US Geological Survey*] (SEIS)
**LTU**......... Long Ton Unit
**LTU**......... Spencer, IA [*Location identifier*] [*FAA*] (FAAL)
**LTV**......... Land Transport Vehicle (NVT)
**LTV**......... Large Test Vessel [*Nuclear energy*] (NRCH)
**LTV**......... Launch Test Vehicles
**LTV**......... Life Test Vehicle
**LTV**......... Light-Vessel [*Navigation*]
**LTV**......... Ling-Temco-Vought Co.
**LTV**......... Loan-to-Value Ratio [*Finance*]
**LTV**......... Long-Term Vibration
**LTV**......... Long Tube Vertical
**LTVC**......... Launcher Tube Vertical Centerline
**LTW**......... List Taschenbuecher der Wissenschaft [*A publication*]
**LTW**......... Los Trancos Woods [*California*] [*Seismograph station code, US Geological Survey*] (SEIS)
**LTWA**......... Lawn Tennis Writers' Association of America [*Later, USTWA*] (EA)
**LTWG**......... Launch Test Working Group
**LTWT**......... Lightweight
**LTX**......... Lap-Top Expansion [*Data processing*]
**LTX**......... Lintronics International Ltd. [*Vancouver Stock Exchange symbol*]
**LTXRD**...... Low-Temperature X-Ray Diffraction [*Instrumentation*]
**LTXX**......... LTX Corp. [*NASDAQ symbol*] (NQ)
**LTYR**......... Light Year
**LTYX**......... Liberty Military Sales, Inc. [*NASDAQ symbol*] (NQ)
**Lu**......... H. Lundbeck [*Denmark*] [*Research code symbol*]
**LU**......... Labor Union (OICC)
**LU**......... Lamentations over the Destruction of Ur (BJA)
**LU**......... Laws of Ur Nammu (BJA)
**LU**......... Left Upper [*Medicine*]
**LU**......... Liberal-Unionist [*British*] (ROG)
**LU**......... Libraries Unlimited [*Library network*]
**LU**......... Library Utility [*Data processing*]
**LU**......... Ligue Universelle [*Esperantiste*]
**LU**......... Line-Up
**L & U**......... Lion and the Unicorn [*A publication*]
**LU**......... List Up
**LU**......... Load Unit
**L & U**......... Loading and Unloading
**LU**......... Lock Up (ADA)
**LU**......... Logical Unit [*Data processing*]
**LU**......... Logistical Unit (NATG)
**LU**......... Loudness Unit
**LU**......... Louisiana State University, Baton Rouge, LA [*Library symbol*] [*Library of Congress*] (LCLS)
**L & U**......... Lower and Upper [*Anatomy*]
**Lu**......... Lumen [*Anatomy*]
**Lu**......... Lusiada [*A publication*]
**Lu**......... Lutetium [*Chemical element*]
**Lu**......... Lutheran [*Blood group*]
**LU**......... Luxembourg [*ANSI two-letter standard code*] (CNC)
**lu**......... Luxembourg [*MARC country of publication code*] [*Library of Congress*] (LCCP)
**LU**......... St. Luke's Gospel [*New Testament book*] (ROG)
**LU**......... Transjet SA [*Belgium*] [*ICAO designator*] (FAAC)
**LU**......... Upper Limen [*Psychology*]
**LUA**......... Launch under Attack [*Nuclear warfare option*]
**LUA**......... Left Upper Arm [*Medicine*]
**LUA**......... Library Users of America (EA)
**LUA**......... Liverpool Underwriters Association (DS)
**LU-A**......... Louisiana State University in Alexandria, Alexandria, LA [*Library symbol*] [*Library of Congress*] (LCLS)
**LUA**......... Luanda [*Angola*] [*Seismograph station code, US Geological Survey*] [*Closed*] (SEIS)
**LUA**......... Luanda Belas [*Angola*] [*Geomagnetic observatory code*]
**LUA**......... Lukla [*Nepal*] [*Airport symbol*] (OAG)
**LUA**......... Lunds Universitet. Arsskrift [*A publication*]
**LUA**......... Luray, VA [*Location identifier*] [*FAA*] (FAAL)
**LUAC**......... Life Underwriters Association of Canada
**LUAMC**.... Leading Underwriters' Agreement for Marine Cargo Business (DS)
**LUAMH**.... Leading Underwriters' Agreement for Marine Hull Business (DS)
**LUAP**......... Land Use Adjustment Program
**LUAR**......... Liga de Uniao e Acao Revolucionaria [*Portugal*]
**LU-Ar**......... Louisiana State University, Department of Archives and Manuscripts, Baton Rouge, LA [*Library symbol*] [*Library of Congress*] (LCLS)
**LUB**......... Least [*or Lowest*] Upper Bound
**LUB**......... Left Upper Lobe Bronchus [*Anatomy*]
**LUB**......... Logical Unit Block [*Data processing*]
**lub**......... Luba [*MARC language code*] [*Library of Congress*] (LCCP)
**LUB**......... Lubbock [*Texas*] [*Seismograph station code, US Geological Survey*] (SEIS)
**LUB**......... Lubricate (AAG)
**LUB**......... Luby's Cafeterias, Inc. [*NYSE symbol*] (SPSG)
**LUBA**......... Limited Underwater Breathing Apparatus (NG)
**LUBC**......... Liberty United Bancorp [*NASDAQ symbol*] (NQ)
**LUBE**......... AutoSpa Corp. [*Woodside, NY*] [*NASDAQ symbol*] (NQ)
**LUBE**......... Lubricate (ADA)
**Lube Eq**...... Lube on Equity Pleading [*A publication*] (DLA)
**Lube PL**...... Lube on Equity Pleading [*A publication*] (DLA)
**LUBO**......... Lubricating Oil
**LUBR**......... Lubricate (ADA)
**Lubr Eng**.... Lubrication Engineering [*A publication*]
**Lubric Eng**... Lubrication Engineering [*A publication*]
**Lubric Engng**... Lubrication Engineering [*A publication*]
**LUBT**......... Lubricant (MSA)
**LUC**......... Land Use Concurrence [*Acquisition of real estate for the use of US forces on a rent-free basis*] [*Vietnam*]
**LUC**......... Large Unstained Cells [*Cytology*]
**LUC**......... Laucala Island [*Fiji*] [*Airport symbol*] (OAG)
**LUC**......... League of Ukrainian Catholics of America (EA)
**LUC**......... Living under Canvas [*British military*] (DMA)
**LU-C**......... Louisiana State University, Chemistry Library, Baton Rouge, LA [*Library symbol*] [*Library of Congress*] (LCLS)
**LUC**......... Louisiana Union Catalog [*Library network*]
**Luc**......... Lucan [*39-65AD*] [*Classical studies*] (OCD)
**Luc**......... Lucas: an Evangelical History Review [*A publication*] (APTA)
**Luc**......... Lucas' Reports [*Modern Reports, Part X*] [*A publication*] (DLA)
**Luc**......... Luceafarul [*A publication*]
**Luc**......... Lucullus [*of Plutarch*] [*Classical studies*] (OCD)
**Luc**......... Lucullus or Academica Posteriora [*of Cicero*] [*Classical studies*] (OCD)
**LUC**......... Lukens, Inc. [*NYSE symbol*] (SPSG)
**Luc**......... [*The*] Rape of Lucrece [*Shakespearean work*]
**LUCALOX**... Translucent Aluminum Oxide [*Ceramic*]
**LUCAS**...... Line Utilization Cable Assignment System (MCD)
**Lucas**...... Lucas' Reports [*Modern Reports, Part X*] [*A publication*] (DLA)
**Lucas Engng Rev**... Lucas Engineering Review [*A publication*]
**Lucas Eng Rev**... Lucas Engineering Review [*A publication*]
**LUCC**......... Lehigh University Computing Center [*Pennsylvania*] [*Research center*] (RCD)
**LUCHIP**.... Lutheran Church and Indian People [*An association*] [*Defunct*] (EA)
**LUCID**....... Language Used to Communicate Information System Design
**LUCID**....... Language for Utility Checkout and Instrumentation Development
**Lucil**......... Lucilius [*Second century BC*] [*Classical studies*] (OCD)
**Luck**......... Indian Law Reports, Lucknow Series [*A publication*] (DLA)
**LUCKN**..... Lucknow [*City in India*] (ROG)
**Luck Ser**..... Indian Law Reports, Lucknow Series [*A publication*] (DLA)
**LUCO**......... Lloyd's Underwriters Claims Office (AIA)
**LUCOLA**... Lutheran Coalition on Latin America (EA)
**LUCOM**.... Lunar Communication [*System*] [*Aerospace*]
**LUCP**......... League to Uphold Congregational Principles [*Defunct*] (EA)
**LUC PRIM**... Luce Primo [*At Daybreak*] [*Pharmacy*]
**LUCR**......... Lucretius [*Roman poet, 96-55BC*] [*Classical studies*] (ROG)
**Lucrari Muzicol**... Lucrari de Muzicologie [*A publication*]
**Lucrari Sti Inst Ped Galati**... Lucrari Stiintifice. Institutul Pedagogic Galati [*A publication*]
**Lucr Cercet Inst Cercet Ind Chim Aliment**... Lucrari de Cercetare. Institutul de Cercetari pentru Industrie si Chimie Alimentara [*A publication*]

**Lucr Cercet Inst Cercet Project Aliment** ... Lucrari de Cercetare. Institutul de Cercetari si Projectari Alimentare [*A publication*]
**Lucr Cercet Inst Chim Aliment** ... Lucrari de Cercetare. Institutul de Chimie Alimentara [*A publication*]
**Lucr Grad Bot (Bucuresti)** ... Lucrarile Gradinii Botanice (Bucuresti) [*A publication*]
**Lucr Gradinii Bot (Bucur)** ... Lucrarile Gradinii Botanice (Bucuresti) [*A publication*]
**Lucr ICPE** ... Lucrarile ICPE [*Institutul de Cercetare si Proiectare pentru Industria Electrotehnica*] [*Romania*] [*A publication*]
**Lucr Inst Cercet Alim** ... Lucrarile Institutului de Cercetari Alimentare [*A publication*]
**Lucr Inst Cercet Aliment** ... Lucrarile Institutului de Cercetari Alimentare [*A publication*]
**Lucr Inst Cercet Vet Bioprep Pasteur** ... Lucrarile Institutului de Cercetari Veterinare si Biopreparate Pasteur [*A publication*]
**Lucr Inst Pet Gaze Bucuresti** ... Lucrarile Institutului de Petrol si Gaze din Bucuresti [*A publication*]
**Lucr Inst Pet Gaz Geol Bucuresti** ... Lucrarile Institutului de Petrol, Gaze, si Geologie din Bucuresti [*A publication*]
**Lucr Semin Mat Fiz Inst Politeh "Traian Vuia" (Timisoara)** ... Lucrarile Seminarului de Matematica si Fizica. Institutului Politehnic "Traian Vuia" (Timisoara) [*A publication*]
**Lucr Ses Stiint Inst Agron Nicolae Balcescu** ... Lucrarile Sesiunii Stiintifice. Institutul Agronomic "Nicolae Balcescu" [*A publication*]
**Lucr Ses Stiint Inst Agron Nicolae Balcescu Ser C** ... Lucrarile Sesiunii Stiintifice. Institutul Agronomic "Nicolae Balcescu" (Bucuresti). Seria C. Zootehnie si Medicina Veterinara [*A publication*]
**Lucr Simp Biodeterior Clim** ... Lucrarile. Simpozion de Biodeteriorare si Climatizare [*A publication*]
**Lucr Simp Clim Biodeterior** ... Lucrarile. Simpozion de Climatizare si Biodeteriorare [*A publication*]
**Lucr Sti Inst Agron Dr Petru Groza (Cluj)** ... Lucrari Stiintifice. Institutul Agronomic "Dr. Petru Groza" (Cluj) [*A publication*]
**Lucr Sti Inst Agron Dr Petru Groza (Cluj) Ser Agr** ... Lucrari Stiintifice. Institutul Agronomic "Dr. Petru Groza" (Cluj). Seria Agricultura [*A publication*]
**Lucr Sti Inst Agron Ion Ionescu de la Brad (Iasi)** ... Lucrari Stiintifice. Institutul Agronomic "Ion Ionescu de la Brad" (Iasi) [*A publication*]
**Lucr Sti Inst Agron N Balcescu (Bucuresti) Ser A B C** ... Lucrari Stiintifice. Institutul Agronomic "Nicolae Balcescu" (Bucuresti). Seria A, B, C [*A publication*]
**Lucr Sti Inst Agron Professor Ion Ionescu de la Brad** ... Lucrari Stiintifice. Institutul Agronomic "Professor Ion Ionescu de la Brad" [*A publication*]
**Lucr Sti Inst Agron Timisoara (Bucuresti)** ... Lucrari Stiintifice. Institutul Agronomic Timisoara (Bucuresti) [*A publication*]
**Lucr Sti Inst Agron "T Vladimirescu" (Craiova)** ... Lucrari Stiintifice. Institutul Agronomic "T. Vladimirescu" (Craiova) [*A publication*]
**Lucr Sti Inst Cercet Zooteh** ... Lucrarile Stiintifice. Institutului de Cercetari Zootehnice [*A publication*]
**Lucr Stiint Cent Exp Ingrasaminte Bact (Bucharest)** ... Lucrari Stiintifice. Centrul Experimental de Ingrasaminte Bacteriene (Bucharest) [*A publication*]
**Lucr Stiint Inst Agron (Bucuresti) Ser A** ... Lucrari Stiintifice. Institutul Agronomic "Nicolae Balcescu" (Bucuresti). Seria A. Agronomie [*Romania*] [*A publication*]
**Lucr Stiint Inst Agron (Bucuresti) Ser B** ... Lucrari Stiintifice. Institutul Agronomic "Nicolae Balcescu" (Bucuresti). Seria B. Horticultura [*A publication*]
**Lucr Stiint Inst Agron (Bucuresti) Ser C** ... Lucrari Stiintifice. Institutul Agronomic "Nicolae Balcescu" (Bucuresti). Seria C. Zootehnie si Medicina Veterinara [*A publication*]
**Lucr Stiint Inst Agron (Bucuresti) Ser D Zooteh** ... Lucrari Stiintifice. Institutul Agronomic "Nicolae Balcescu" (Bucuresti). Seria D. Zootehnie [*A publication*]
**Lucr Stiint Inst Agron (Cluj)** ... Lucrari Stiintifice. Institutul Agronomic "Dr. Petru Groza" (Cluj) [*A publication*]
**Lucr Stiint Inst Agron (Cluj) Ser Agric** ... Lucrari Stiintifice. Institutul Agronomic "Dr. Petru Groza" (Cluj). Seria Agricultura [*A publication*]
**Lucr Stiint Inst Agron (Cluj) Ser Med Vet** ... Lucrari Stiintifice. Institutul Agronomic "Dr. Petru Groza" (Cluj). Seria Medicina Veterinari [*A publication*]
**Lucr Stiint Inst Agron (Cluj) Ser Med Vet Zooteh** ... Lucrari Stiintifice. Institutul Agronomic "Dr. Petru Groza" (Cluj). Seria Medicina Veterinara si Zootehnie [*A publication*]
**Lucr Stiint Inst Agron (Cluj) Ser Zooteh** ... Lucrari Stiintifice. Institutul Agronomic "Dr. Petru Groza" (Cluj). Seria Zootehnie [*A publication*]
**Lucr Stiint Inst Agron (Iasi)** ... Lucrarile Stiintifice. Institutul Agronomic "Professor Ion Ionescu de la Brad" (Iasi) [*A publication*]
**Lucr Stiint Inst Agron Ion Ionescu de la Brad (Iasi)** ... Lucrarile Stiintifice. Institutul Agronomic "Professor Ion Ionescu de la Brad" (Iasi) [*Romania*] [*A publication*]
**Lucr Stiint Inst Agron N Balcescu (Bucuresti) Ser C** ... Lucrari Stiintifice ale Institutului Agronomic "Nicolae Balcescu" (Bucuresti). Seria C [*Romania*] [*A publication*]
**Lucr Stiint Inst Agron N Balcescu (Bucur) Ser C** ... Lucrari Stiintifice ale Institutului Agronomic "Nicolae Balcescu" (Bucuresti). Seria C [*A publication*]
**Lucr Stiint Inst Agron "Nicolae Balcescu" Agron** ... Lucrari Stiintifice. Institutul Agronomic "Nicolae Balcescu." Agronomie [*A publication*]
**Lucr Stiint Inst Agron "Nicolae Balcescu" Hortic** ... Lucrari Stiintifice. Institutul Agronomic "Nicolae Balcescu." Horticultura [*A publication*]
**Lucr Stiint Inst Agron "Nicolae Balcescu" Imbunatatiri Fun** ... Lucrari Stiintifice. Institutul Agronomic "Nicolae Balcescu." Imbunatatiri Funciare [*A publication*]
**Lucr Stiint Inst Agron "Nicolae Balcescu" Med Vet** ... Lucrari Stiintifice. Institutul Agronomic "Nicolae Balcescu." Medicina Veterinara [*A publication*]
**Lucr Stiint Inst Agron "Nicolae Balcescu" Zooteh** ... Lucrari Stiintifice. Institutul Agronomic "Nicolae Balcescu." Zootehnie [*A publication*]
**Lucr Stiint Inst Agron (Timisoara) Seri Medna Vet** ... Lucrari Stiintifice. Institutul Agronomic (Timisoara). Seria Medicina Veterinara [*A publication*]
**Lucr Stiint Inst Agron (Timisoara) Ser Med Vet** ... Lucrari Stiintifice. Institutul Agronomic (Timisoara). Seria Medicina Veterinara [*A publication*]
**Lucr Stiint Inst Agron (Timisoara) Ser Zooteh** ... Lucrari Stiintifice. Institutul Agronomic (Timisoara). Seria Zootehnie [*A publication*]
**Lucr Stiint Inst Cercet Zooteh** ... Lucrarile Stiintifice. Institutului de Cercetari Zootehnice [*A publication*]
**Lucr Stiint Inst Cerc Zooteh** ... Lucrarile Stiintifice. Institutului de Cercetari Zootehnice [*A publication*]
**Lucr Stiint Inst Mine Petrosani** ... Lucrarile Stiintifice. Institutului de Mine Petrosani [*A publication*]
**Lucr Stiint Inst Mine Petrosani Ser 4** ... Lucrarile Stiintifice. Institutului de Mine Petrosani. Seria 4. Stiinte de Cultura Tehnica Generala [*A publication*]
**Lucr Stiint Inst Mine Petrosani Ser 5** ... Lucrarile Stiintifice. Institutului de Mine Petrosani. Seria 5. Geologie [*A publication*]
**Lucr Stiint Inst Mine Petrosani Ser 6** ... Lucrarile Stiintifice. Institutului de Mine Petrosani. Seria 6. Stiinte Sociale [*A publication*]
**Lucr Stiint Inst Patol Ig Anim** ... Lucrarile Stiintifice. Institutului de Patologie si Igiena Animala [*A publication*]
**Lucr Stiint Inst Pedagog Oradea Ser Mat Fiz Chim** ... Lucrari Stiintifice. Institutul Pedagogic din Oradea. Seria Matematica, Fizica, Chimie [*A publication*]
**Lucr Stiint Inst Politeh (Cluj)** ... Lucrarile Stiintifice. Institutul Politehnic (Cluj) [*A publication*]
**Lucr Stiint Inst Politeh (Galati)** ... Lucrari Stiintifice. Institutul Politehnic (Galati) [*A publication*]
**Lucr Stiint Inst Seruri Vacc Pasteur (Bucur)** ... Lucrarile Stiintifice. Institutului de Seruri si Vaccinuri Pasteur (Bucuresti) [*A publication*]
**Lucr Stiint Ser C VII** ... Lucrari Stiintifice. Seria C VII. Zootehnie si Medicina Veterinara [*Bucuresti*] [*A publication*]
**Lucr Stiint Ser Zooteh Med Vet** ... Lucrari Stiintifice. Seria Zootehnie si Medicina Veterinara [*A publication*]
**Lucr Stint Inst Agron (Timisoara) Ser Agron** ... Lucrari Stiintifice. Institutul Agronomic (Timisoara). Seria Agronomie [*A publication*]
**LUCS** ......... Land Use in Canada Series [*A publication*]
**LUD** ........... Lift-Up Door [*Technical drawings*]
**LuD** ........... Linguistik und Didaktik [*A publication*]
**LUD** ........... Luderitz [*South-West Africa*] [*Airport symbol*] (OAG)
**LUD** ........... Lundin Explorations [*Vancouver Stock Exchange symbol*]
**LUDA** ........ Land Use Data
**Lud Bolog**... Ludovicus Bolognnius [*Deceased, 1508*] [*Authority cited in pre-1607 legal work*] (DSA)
**Ludd** ........... Ludden's Reports [*43, 44 Maine*] [*A publication*] (DLA)
**Ludden** ....... Ludden's Reports [*43, 44 Maine*] [*A publication*] (DLA)
**Lud EC**........ Luder's Election Cases [*England*] [*A publication*] (DLA)
**Lud El Cas** ... Luder's Election Cases [*England*] [*A publication*] (DLA)
**Luder Elec Cas** ... Luder's Election Cases [*England*] [*A publication*] (DLA)
**Luders Elec Cas (Eng)** ... Luder's Election Cases [*England*] [*A publication*] (DLA)
**Lud Gozad** ... Ludovicus Gozzadini [*Deceased, 1536*] [*Authority cited in pre-1607 legal work*] (DSA)
**Lud & J Tr M** ... Ludlow and Jenkyns on Trade-Marks [*A publication*] (DLA)
**Ludo** ........... Ludovicus Pontanus de Roma [*Deceased, 1439*] [*Authority cited in pre-1607 legal work*] (DSA)
**Ludo Bolog** ... Ludovicus Bolognnius [*Deceased, 1508*] [*Authority cited in pre-1607 legal work*] (DSA)
**Ludo Ro**...... Ludovicus Pontanus de Roma [*Deceased, 1439*] [*Authority cited in pre-1607 legal work*] (DSA)
**Ludo de Ro** ... Ludovicus Pontanus de Roma [*Deceased, 1439*] [*Authority cited in pre-1607 legal work*] (DSA)
**Lud de Ro**... Ludovicus Pontanus de Roma [*Deceased, 1439*] [*Authority cited in pre-1607 legal work*] (DSA)
**LUE** ........... Dallas, TX [*Location identifier*] [*FAA*] (FAAL)
**LUE** ........... Left Upper Entrance [*Theater*]
**LUE** ........... Left Upper Extremity [*Medicine*]
**LUE** ........... Linear Unbiased Estimator [*Statistics*]
**LUE** ........... Link Utilization Efficiency

**LU-E**.......... Louisiana State University in Eunice, Eunice, LA [*Library symbol*] [*Library of Congress*] (LCLS)
**LU-ECT**..... Louisiana State at Baton Rouge, Eighteenth Century Short Title Catalogue, Baton Rouge, LA [*Library symbol*] [*Library of Congress*] (LCLS)
**Lueneburger B** ... Lueneburger Blaetter [*A publication*]
**LUF** ........... Glendale, AZ [*Location identifier*] [*FAA*] (FAAL)
**LUF** ........... Librairie Universelle de France [*A publication*]
**LUF** ........... Lift Unit Frame [*Shipping*] (DS)
**LUF** ........... Local Utah Freight Bureau, Omaha NE [*STAC*]
**LUF** ........... Lowest Usable [*or Useful*] Frequency [*Radio*]
**LUFBBK** ... Fonds de Recherches Forestieres. Universite Laval. Bulletin [*A publication*]
**LUFO** ........ Least Used, First Out [*Data processing*]
**Luftfahrttech Raumfahrttech** ... Luftfahrttechnik, Raumfahrttechnik [*A publication*]
**Luft- Kaeltetech** ... Luft- und Kaeltetechnik [*A publication*]
**Luft und Kaeltetech** ... Luft und Kaltetechnik [*A publication*]
**LUG**........... Lewisburg, TN [*Location identifier*] [*FAA*] (FAAL)
**LUG**........... Light Utility Glider
**LuG**........... Literatur und Geschichte. Eine Schriftenreihe [*A publication*]
**lug** ............. Luganda [*MARC language code*] [*Library of Congress*] (LCCP)
**LUG**........... Lugano [*Switzerland*] [*Airport symbol*] (OAG)
**LUG**........... Lugano Resources Ltd. [*Vancouver Stock Exchange symbol*]
**LUG**........... Luganville [*New Hebrides*] [*Seismograph station code, US Geological Survey*] (SEIS)
**LUG**........... Lugger [*Boat*]
**LUG BAT** ... Lugdunum Batavorum [*Leyden*] [*Imprint*] (ROG)
**LUGD**........ Lugdunum [*Lyons*] [*Imprint*] (ROG)
**LUGG**........ Luggage
**LUGS**......... Land Use Game Simulation
**LUH**........... Ledermarkt und Hautemarkt mit Gerbereiwissenschaft und Praxis. Das Wochenjournal fuer die Lederindustrie, den Hautegrosshandel und Ledergrosshandel [*A publication*]
**LUH**........... Lumen Hour
**LUHF**........ Lowest Usable [*or Useful*] High-Frequency [*Radio*]
**LUI** ........... La Union [*Honduras*] [*Airport symbol*] [*Obsolete*] (OAG)
**LUI** ........... London United Investments [*British*]
**lui** .............. Luiseno [*MARC language code*] [*Library of Congress*] (LCCP)
**LUIS**.......... Library User Information System [*Detroit, MI*] [*Library network*]
**LUJ**............ Big Lake, TX [*Location identifier*] [*FAA*] (FAAL)
**LUJB**......... Left Umbilical Junction Box [*Aerospace*] (AAG)
**LUK**........... Cincinnati, OH [*Location identifier*] [*FAA*] (FAAL)
**LUK**........... Leucadia National Corp. [*NYSE symbol*] (SPSG)
**LUK**........... Literatur und Kritik [*Wien*] [*A publication*]
**LUKY**........ Lucky Chance Mining Co. [*NASDAQ symbol*] (NQ)
**LUL**........... Laurel, MS [*Location identifier*] [*FAA*] (FAAL)
**LUL**........... Lease Underwriting Ltd. [*Australia*]
**LUL**........... Left Upper Eyelid [*Medicine*]
**LUL**........... Left Upper Limb [*Medicine*]
**LUL**........... Left Upper Lobe [*of lung*] [*Medicine*]
**LuL**........... Literatur und Leben [*A publication*]
**LUL**........... London Underground Ltd. [*British*] (ECON)
**LU-L**.......... Louisiana State University, Law Library, Baton Rouge, LA [*Library symbol*] [*Library of Congress*] (LCLS)
**LUL**........... Louisiana State University, Law Library, Baton Rouge, LA [*OCLC symbol*] (OCLC)
**LULA**......... Loyola University of Los Angeles [*Later, Loyola Marymount University*]
**LULAC**...... League of United Latin American Citizens (EA)
**LULOP**...... London Union List of Periodicals
**LULS**......... Lunar Logistics System [*NASA*]
**LULU**........ Locally Unwanted Land Use [*i.e. garbage incinerators, prisons, roads, etc.*]
**LULU**........ Logical Unit to Logical Unit
**LUM**.......... Bellingham, WA [*Location identifier*] [*FAA*] (FAAL)
**LuM**.......... Literatura un Maksla [*A publication*]
**LUM**.......... Living Utility Module [*NASA*] (KSC)
**LUM**.......... Local Urgent Mail [*British*]
**LU-M**......... Louisiana State University, Medical Center, New Orleans, LA [*Library symbol*] [*Library of Congress*] (LCLS)
**Lum**........... Lumen [*Record label*] [*France*]
**LUM**.......... Lumex, Inc. [*AMEX symbol*] (SPSG)
**Lum**........... Lumiere [*A publication*] (APTA)
**LUM**.......... Luminous (MSA)
**LUM**.......... Lumonics, Inc. [*Toronto Stock Exchange symbol*]
**LUM**.......... Maputo [*Mozambique*] [*Airport symbol*]
**LUM**.......... University of Maryland, School of Law, Baltimore, MD [*OCLC symbol*] (OCLC)
**Lum Ann**.... Lumley on the Law of Annuities [*A publication*] (DLA)
**LUMAS**..... Lunar Mapping System [*Aerospace*]
**Lum Bast**.... Lumley on Bastardy [*A publication*] (DLA)
**Lum BL**...... Lumley on Bye-Laws [*A publication*] (DLA)
**LUME**....... Light Utilization More Efficient (MCD)
**Lumen**........ Lumen Vitae [*A publication*]
**LUMF**........ Lockheed Underwater Missile Facility (AAG)
**Lumiere**...... Lumiere et Vie [*A publication*]
**LUMIS**...... Land Use Management Information System [*NASA*]
**Lumley PLC** ... Lumley's Poor Law Cases [*1834-42*] [*A publication*] (DLA)
**LUMO**....... Lowest Unoccupied Molecular Orbital [*Atomic physics*]
**Lum Parl Pr** ... Lumley's Parliamentary Practice [*A publication*] (DLA)
**Lumpkin**.... Lumpkin's Reports [*59-77 Georgia*] [*A publication*] (DLA)
**Lum PLC**... Lumley's Poor Law Cases [*1834-42*] [*A publication*] (DLA)
**Lum PL Cas** ... Lumley's Poor Law Cases [*1834-42*] [*A publication*] (DLA)
**Lumps**........ Life-Giving Unselfish Middle-Class Parent Survivors [*Lifestyle classification*] [*Facetious term coined by columnist Erma Bombeck to describe the Yuppies' progenitors*]
**Lum Pub H** ... Lumley's Public Health Acts [*12th ed.*] [*1950-55 and supplements*] [*A publication*] (DLA)
**Lum Sett**.... Lumley on the Law of Settlements [*A publication*] (DLA)
**LumVie**...... Lumiere et Vie [*Lyons*] [*A publication*]
**LumViSup** ... Lumiere et Vie. Supplement Biblique [*A publication*]
**LumVit**....... Lumen Vitae [*Brussels*] [*A publication*]
**LUN**........... Logical Unit Number
**LUN**........... Ludington & Northern Railway [*AAR code*]
**LUN**........... Lunar (KSC)
**LUN**........... Lund [*Sweden*] [*Seismograph station code, US Geological Survey*] [*Closed*] (SEIS)
**LUN**........... Lunette
**LUN**........... Lusaka [*Zambia*] [*Airport symbol*] (OAG)
**LUNARG**.. Lunar Gravity Simulator [*Aerospace*] (MCD)
**Lunar and Planetary Explor Colloquium Proc** ... Lunar and Planetary Exploration Colloquium. Proceedings [*A publication*]
**Lunar Sci Inst Contrib** ... Lunar Science Institute. Contribution [*A publication*]
**LUNCO**..... Lloyd's Underwriters Non-Marine Claims Office (AIA)
**LUND**........ Lund International Holdings, Inc. [*NASDAQ symbol*] (NQ)
**Lund Pat**.... Lund on Patents [*A publication*] (DLA)
**Lunds Univ Arsskr Avd 2** ... Lunds Universitets Arsskrift. Avdelningen 2. Kungliga Fysiografiska Salskapets i Lund. Handlinger [*A publication*]
**LUNG**........ CA Blockers, Inc. [*NASDAQ symbol*] (NQ)
**Lung Biol Health Dis** ... Lung Biology in Health and Disease [*A publication*]
**Lun Ger For**... Lunder Germanistische Forschungen [*A publication*]
**LUNK**........ Line/Trunk (MCD)
**LUNN**........ Lunn Industries, Inc. [*NASDAQ symbol*] (NQ)
**LUO**........... Laboratory Unit Operation
**LUO**........... Left Ureteral Orifice [*Medicine*]
**LUO**........... Luena [*Angola*] [*Airport symbol*] (OAG)
**LUO**........... Luogo [*As Written*] [*Music*]
**Luonnon Tutk** ... Luonnon Tutkija [*A publication*]
**LUOQ**........ Left Upper Outer Quadrant [*of abdomen*] [*Medicine*]
**LUOTC**..... London University Officers Training Corps [*British military*] (DMA)
**LUP**........... Kalaupapa [*Hawaii*] [*Airport symbol*] (OAG)
**LUP**........... Land Use and Planning [*British*]
**LUP**........... Laying-Up Position [*British military*] (DMA)
**LUP**........... Liberia Unification Party [*Political party*]
**Lup**........... Lupus [*Constellation*]
**LUPAC**...... Life Underwriters Political Action Committee
**LUPF**......... Linear Utility Prediction Function [*Mathematics*]
**Lupi**........... Lupus [*Constellation*]
**LUPS**......... Logistics Unit Productivity Study [*or System*] [*Army*]
**LUPUL**...... Lupulus [*Hops*] [*Pharmacy*] (ROG)
**LUPWT**..... Langley Unitary Plan Wind Tunnel [*NASA*] (KSC)
**LUQ**........... Left Upper Quadrant [*of abdomen*] [*Medicine*]
**LuQ**........... Lutheran Quarterly [*A publication*]
**LUQ**........... San Luis [*Argentina*] [*Airport symbol*] (OAG)
**LUR**........... Cape Lisburne [*Alaska*] [*Airport symbol*] (OAG)
**LUR**........... Laurasia Resources Ltd. [*Toronto Stock Exchange symbol*]
**LUR**........... Laureate [*Numismatics*]
**LuR**........... Literature und Reflexion [*A publication*]
**LUR**........... London Underground Railway
**LUR**........... Luria [*L.*] & Son, Inc. [*AMEX symbol*] (SPSG)
**LUR**........... Petera Stuckas Latvijas Valsts Universitate Zinatniskie Raksti. Filologijas Zinatnes. A Serija (Riga) [*A publication*]
**LURB**......... List of Unlocated Research Books [*A publication*] (APTA)
**LURE**......... Laboratoire d'Utilisation du Rayonnement Electromagnetique [*Laboratory for the Utilization of Electromagnetic Radiation*] [*Orsay, France*]
**LURE**......... Lunar Ranging Experiment [*Aerospace*]
**LURS**......... Land Use and Requirements Study (MCD)
**LUS**........... Large Ultimate Size [*Telecommunications*] (TEL)
**LUS**........... Latch Up Screen
**LUS**........... Laws of the United States [*A publication*] (DLA)
**LUS**........... Library of Useful Stories [*A publication*]
**LUS**........... Liquid Upper Stage (NASA)
**LUS**........... Load, Update, Subset
**LUS**........... Louisiana State University in Shreveport, Library, Shreveport, LA [*OCLC symbol*] (OCLC)
**LU-S**.......... Louisiana State University in Shreveport, Shreveport, LA [*Library symbol*] [*Library of Congress*] (LCLS)
**LUS**........... Lusaka [*Zambia*] [*Seismograph station code, US Geological Survey*] (SEIS)
**LUSCC**...... Latymer Upper School Cadet Corps [*British military*] (DMA)
**LUSEX**...... Lunar Surface Explorer Simulation Program [*Aerospace*] (MCD)
**Lush**.......... Lushington's English Admiralty Reports [*1859-62*] [*A publication*] (DLA)
**Lush Adm**.. Lushington's English Admiralty Reports [*1859-62*] [*A publication*] (DLA)

**Lush Pr**...... Lush's Common Law Practice [*A publication*] (DLA)
**Lush Pr L**... Lushington on Prize Law [*A publication*] (DLA)
**LUSI**.......... Lunar Surface Inspection [*Aerospace*]
**LUSING**.... Lusingando [*Coaxingly*] [*Music*]
**LUSK**......... Luskin's, Inc. [*NASDAQ symbol*] (NQ)
**LUSL**......... Loyola University School of Law (DLA)
**LU-SM**...... Louisiana State University in Shreveport, Medical Center Library, Shreveport, LA [*Library symbol*] [*Library of Congress*] (LCLS)
**Luso J Sci Tech**... Luso Journal of Science and Technology [*A publication*]
**LUSOLT**... Lakehead University School of Library Technology [*Canada*]
**LUST**......... Latrine Urinal Shower Toilet [*A unit of mobility equipment*] [*Military*]
**LUST**......... Leaking Underground Storage Tank [*Environmental chemistry*]
**LUT**........... Launch Umbilical Tower [*NASA*]
**LUT**........... Laura Station [*Australia*] [*Airport symbol*] [*Obsolete*] (OAG)
**LUT**........... Line Unit [*Data processing*] (BUR)
**LUT**........... Local User Terminal
**LUT**........... Lookup Table [*Data processing*] (BYTE)
**LUT**........... Loughborough University of Technology [*British*] (IRUK)
**LUT**........... Luteum [*Yellow*] [*Latin*]
**Lut**.............. [*E.*] Lutwyche's Entries and Reports, Common Pleas [*1682-1704*] [*A publication*] (DLA)
**LUTC**......... Life Underwriter Training Council [*Washington, DC*] (EA)
**LUTC**......... Life Underwriter Training Course
**LUTCAM**... Language Used to Conceal Actual Meaning
**Lut E**.......... [*E.*] Lutwyche's Entries and Reports, Common Pleas [*A publication*] (DLA)
**Lut Elec Cas**... Lutwyche's English Election Cases [*A publication*] (DLA)
**Lut Ent**....... Lutwyche's Entries [*1704; 1718*] [*A publication*] (DLA)
**Lute Soc J**.. Lute Society. Journal [*A publication*]
**LUTET**...... Lutetia Parisiorum [*Paris*] [*Imprint*] (ROG)
**LUTFCSUSTC**... Librarians United to Fight Costly, Silly, Unnecessary Serial Title Changes [*Defunct*] (EA)
**LUTH**........ Luther Medical Products, Inc. [*NASDAQ symbol*] (NQ)
**LUTH**........ Lutheran
**Luth**............ Lutheran [*A publication*]
**LuthChQ**.... Lutheran Church Quarterly [*A publication*]
**Luth Educ**.. Lutheran Education [*A publication*]
**Luther-Jahrb**... Luther-Jahrbuch [*A publication*]
**Luth H Conf**... Lutheran Historical Conference. Essays and Reports [*A publication*]
**LuthJB**....... Luther-Jahrbuch [*Hamburg*] [*A publication*]
**LuthMonh**... Lutherische Monatshefte [*Hamburg*] [*A publication*]
**LuthQ**........ Lutheran Quarterly [*A publication*]
**LuthRu**....... Lutherische Rundschau [*Geneva*] [*A publication*]
**Luth S**........ Lutheran Standard [*A publication*]
**Luth Th J**... Lutheran Theological Journal [*A publication*]
**Luth W**....... Lutheran Witness [*A publication*]
**LuthW**........ Lutheran World [*A publication*]
**LUTIRO**.... Life and Unit Trust Intermediaries Regulatory Organisation [*British*]
**LUTP**......... Land Use and Transport Planning [*British*]
**LUT PAR**.. Lutetia Parisiorum [*Paris*] [*Imprint*] (ROG)
**Lut RC**....... Lutwyche's English Registration Appeal Cases [*1843-45*] [*A publication*] (DLA)
**Lut Reg Cas**... [*A. J.*] Lutwyche's Registration Cases [*England*] [*A publication*] (DLA)
**LUTS**......... Light Units, Times Square [*Electronics*]
**LUTT**......... Launcher Umbilical Tower Transporter [*NASA*] (KSC)
**Lutte Cancer**... Lutte Contre le Cancer [*France*] [*A publication*]
**Lutw**........... [*E.*] Lutwyche's Entries and Reports, Common Pleas [*A publication*] (DLA)
**Lutw**........... [*A. J.*] Lutwyche's Registration Cases [*England*] [*A publication*] (DLA)
**Lutw E**........ Lutwyche's English Common Pleas Reports [*A publication*] (DLA)
**Lutw Reg Cas**... Lutwyche's English Registration Cases [*A publication*] (DLA)
**LUU**........... Illumination Unit (MCD)
**LUU**........... Laura [*Australia*] [*Airport symbol*] [*Obsolete*] (OAG)
**LUU**........... Louisiana State University, Baton Rouge, LA [*OCLC symbol*] (OCLC)
**LUV**........... Langgur [*Indonesia*] [*Airport symbol*] (OAG)
**LUV**........... Large Unilamellar Vesicle [*Pharmacy*] [*Biochemistry*]
**LUV**........... Light Utility Vehicle [*Pickup truck*]
**LU-V**.......... Louisiana State University, School of Veterinary Medicine, Medical Library, Baton Rouge, LA [*Library symbol*] [*Library of Congress*] (LCLS)
**LUV**........... Southwest Airlines Co. [*NYSE symbol*] (SPSG)
**LUVO**........ Luftvorwaermer [*Air Preheater*] [*German*]
**LUVO**........ Lunar Ultraviolet Observatory [*NASA*]
**LUVS**......... Southwest Airlines Co. [*NASDAQ symbol*] (NQ)
**LuW**.......... Literatur und Wirklichkeit [*A publication*]
**LUW**.......... Logical Units of Work [*Data processing*] (BYTE)
**LUW**.......... Luwuk [*Indonesia*] [*Airport symbol*] (OAG)
**LUX**........... Laurens, SC [*Location identifier*] [*FAA*] (FAAL)
**LUX**........... Luxembourg [*Luxembourg*] [*Airport symbol*] (OAG)
**LUX**........... Luxembourg [*Luxembourg*] [*Seismograph station code, US Geological Survey*] (SEIS)
**LUX**........... Luxembourg [*ANSI three-letter standard code*] (CNC)
**LUX**........... Luxottica Group ADS [*NYSE symbol*] (SPSG)
**LUX**........... Luxury [*or Luxurious*] [*Classified advertising*] (ADA)
**LUXAIR**.... Luxembourgeoise de Navigation Aerienne [*Airline*] [*Luxembourg*] (FAAC)
**Luxem**........ Luxembourg
**Luxemb Bienenztg**... Luxemburgische Bienen-Zeitung [*A publication*]
**LuxLBN**..... Bibliotheque Nationale de Luxembourg, Service du Pret, Luxembourg, Luxembourg [*Library symbol*] [*Library of Congress*] (LCLS)
**LUXT**......... Luxtec Corp. [*Sturbridge, MA*] [*NASDAQ symbol*] (NQ)
**LUZED**...... Luzon Engineer District [*Army*] [*World War II*]
**Luzerne Leg Obs (PA)**... Luzerne Legal Observer [*Pennsylvania*] [*A publication*] (DLA)
**Luzerne Leg Reg (PA)**... Luzerne Legal Register [*Pennsylvania*] [*A publication*]
**Luzerne Leg Reg R (PA)**... Luzerne Legal Register Reports [*Pennsylvania*] [*A publication*] (DLA)
**Luzerne LJ (PA)**... Luzerne Law Journal [*Pennsylvania*] [*A publication*] (DLA)
**Luz Law T**... Luzerne Law Times [*Pennsylvania*] [*A publication*] (DLA)
**Luz Leg Obs**... Luzerne Legal Observer [*Pennsylvania*] [*A publication*] (DLA)
**Luz Leg Reg**... Luzerne Legal Register [*A publication*]
**Luz Leg Reg Rep**... Luzerne Legal Register Reports [*Pennsylvania*] [*A publication*] (DLA)
**Luz LJ**........ Luzerne Law Journal [*Pennsylvania*] [*A publication*] (DLA)
**Luz LO**....... Luzerne Legal Observer [*Pennsylvania*] [*A publication*] (DLA)
**Luz LR**....... Luzerne Legal Register [*A publication*]
**Luz L Reg Rep**... Luzerne Legal Register Reports (Continuation of Kulp) [*Pennsylvania*] [*A publication*] (DLA)
**Luz LT (NS)**... Luzerne Law Times. New Series [*Pennsylvania*] [*A publication*] (DLA)
**Luz LT (OS)**... Luzerne Law Times. Old Series [*Pennsylvania*] [*A publication*] (DLA)
**LUZR**........ Petera Stuckas Latvijas Valsts Universitate Zinatniskie Raksti [*A publication*]
**LV**............. Argentina [*Aircraft nationality and registration mark*] (FAAC)
**LV**............. La Vanguardia [*Spain*] [*A publication*]
**LV**............. Laboratory Vehicle (MCD)
**LV**............. Lancastrian Volunteers [*British military*] (DMA)
**LV**............. Land Value (ADA)
**LV**............. Landing Vehicle
**LV**............. Largest Vessel [*British*] (ADA)
**LV**............. LASER Velocimeter
**LV**............. LaserVision [*Videodisc system*]
**LV**............. Last Vehicle [*Railroads*] (ROG)
**LV**............. Lateral Ventricle [*Neuroanatomy*]
**LV**............. Lateral Vestibular Nucleus [*Neuroanatomy*]
**LV**............. Launch Vehicle (MCD)
**LV**............. Laverda SpA [*Italy*] [*ICAO aircraft manufacturer identifier*] (ICAO)
**LV**............. Laws of Virginia [*A publication*] (DLA)
**LV**............. Leaky Valve [*Nuclear energy*] (NRCH)
**LV**............. Leave (AFM)
**LV**............. Leeds Volunteers [*British military*] (DMA)
**LV**............. Left Ventral Fin [*Fish anatomy*]
**LV**............. Left Ventricle [*Cardiology*]
**LV**............. Legal Volt
**LV**............. Lehigh Valley Railroad Co. [*Absorbed into Consolidated Rail Corp.*] [*AAR code*]
**LV**............. Leningradskij Universitet Vestnik Serija Istorii, Literatury, i Jazyka [*A publication*]
**LV**............. Lev [*Monetary unit*] [*Bulgaria*]
**LV**............. Level of Study [*Online database field identifier*]
**Lv**.............. Leviticus [*Old Testament book*]
**LV**............. Licensed Victualer
**LV**............. Lift Vector (NASA)
**LV**............. Light and Variable [*Referring to wind*]
**LV**............. Light Variegated Maize
**LV**............. Light Vehicle [*British military*] (DMA)
**LV**............. Light-Vessel [*Navigation*]
**LV**............. Limit Value
**LV**............. Limited Visibility Study (MCD)
**LV**............. Linea Aeropostal Venezolana [*Venezuelan airline*] [*ICAO designator*] (FAAC)
**LV**............. Linear Velocity
**LV**............. Live Vaccine [*Medicine*]
**LV**............. Livre [*Monetary unit*] [*Obsolete*] [*French*] (ROG)
**LV**............. Loading Valve (MCD)
**L/V**............ Local Vertical (KSC)
**LV**............. Louis Vuitton [*Initials used as a pattern on Vuitton luggage, handbags, etc.*]
**LV**............. Low Velocity [*British military*] (DMA)
**LV**............. Low in Volatiles [*Commercial grading*]
**LV**............. Low Voltage
**LV**............. Low Volume
**LV**............. Lumbar Vertebra [*Medicine*]
**LV**............. Lumen Vitae [*A publication*]
**LV**............. Lumiere et Vie [*Lyons*] [*A publication*]
**LV**............. Luncheon Voucher [*British*]
**LV**............. Valda [*France*] [*Research code symbol*]

**LVA** .......... Lancashire Volunteer Artillery [*British military*] (DMA)
**LVA** .......... Landing Vehicle, Airfoil
**LVA** .......... Landing Vehicle, Assault [*Navy symbol*]
**LVA** .......... Large Vertical Aperture Antenna [*Aviation*]
**LVA** .......... Launch Vehicle Availability [*NASA*]
**LVA** .......... Lava Capital Corp. [*Toronto Stock Exchange symbol*]
**LVA** .......... Left Ventricular Aneurysm [*Cardiology*]
**LVA** .......... Left Ventricular Assistance [*Cardiology*]
**LVA** .......... Left Visual Acuity [*Medicine*]
**LVA** .......... Literacy Volunteers of America (EA)
**LVA** .......... Local Virtual Address
**LVA** .......... Low Vision Aid [*Ophthalmology*]
**LVA** .......... Low-Voltage Activated [*Neurochemistry*]
**LV (A) (2)** .. Landing Vehicle, Tracked (Armored) (Mark II) ["*Water Buffalo,*" *Canopy Type*]
**LVAD** ........ Left Ventricle Assist Device [*Cardiology*]
**LVAIC** ....... Lehigh Valley Association of Independent College Libraries [*Library network*]
**LVAR** ......... Launch Vehicle Assessment Report [*or Review*] [*NASA*] (KSC)
**LVAR** ......... Lithuanian Veterans Association Ramove (EA)
**LVAS** ......... Left Ventricle Assist System [*Cardiology*]
**LVB** ........... Left Ventricular Bypass [*Cardiology*]
**LVB** ........... Liquid-Vapor Bubble [*Chemical engineering*]
**LVB** ........... Livramento [*Brazil*] [*Airport symbol*] (OAG)
**LVB** ........... Low-Voltage Bias
**LVC** .......... Decisions of the Lands Tribunal (Rating) [*A publication*] (DLA)
**LVC** .......... Enid, OK [*Location identifier*] [*FAA*] (FAAL)
**LVC** .......... Large Vacuum Chamber [*Army*]
**LVC** .......... Lebanon Valley College [*Pennsylvania*]
**LVC** .......... Lebanon Valley College, Annville, PA [*OCLC symbol*] (OCLC)
**LVC** .......... Lillian Vernon Corporation [*AMEX symbol*] (SPSG)
**LVC** .......... Log Voltmeter Converter
**LVC** .......... Low-Voltage Capacitor
**LVC** .......... Low-Voltage Cutoff [*Battery*]
**LVCD** ........ Least Voltage Coincidence Detector
**LVCM** ........ Licentiate of the Victoria College of Music [*London*] (ROG)
**LVCP** ........ Laboratory Vehicle Checkout Procedure
**LVCT** ........ Low-Voltage Circuit Tester (MCD)
**LVD** .......... Laboratory Vehicle Development
**lvd** ............ Leaved
**LVD** .......... Left Ventricular Assist Device [*An artificial organ*]
**LVD** .......... Level Island, AK [*Location identifier*] [*FAA*] (FAAL)
**LVD** .......... Light Valve Display
**LVD** .......... Louvered Door (AAG)
**LVD** .......... Low-Velocity Detonation [*or Drop*]
**LVD** .......... Low-Voltage Drop (CET)
**LVDA** ........ Launch Vehicle Data Adapter [*NASA*]
**LVDA** ........ Launch Vehicle Deployment Assembly [*NASA*] (MCD)
**LVDC** ........ Launch Vehicle Data Center [*NASA*] (KSC)
**LVDC** ........ Launch Vehicle Digital Computer [*NASA*]
**LVDC** ........ Low-Voltage Direct Current
**LVDG** ........ Las Vegas Discount Golf & Tennis, Inc. [*NASDAQ symbol*] (NQ)
**LVDIFC** ..... Leroy Van Dyke International Fan Club (EA)
**LVDP** ........ Left Ventricular Diastolic Pressure [*Cardiology*]
**LVDS** ........ Liquid, Vee, Diesel-Cycle, Supercharged
**LVDT** ........ Linear Variable Differential Transformer
**LVDT** ........ Linear Velocity Displacement Transformer (IEEE)
**LVDT** ........ Linear Voltage Differential Transformer (NASA)
**LVDT-PRIM** ... Linear Variable Differential Transformer - Primary
**LVDT-SEC** ... Linear Variable Differential Transformer - Secondary
**LVE** ........... Left Ventricular Enlargement [*Cardiology*]
**LVE** ........... Linear Vector Equation
**LVE** ........... Liquid Vapor Equilibrium
**LVE** ........... LIVE Entertainment, Inc. [*NYSE symbol*] (SPSG)
**LVE** ........... Liverpool Echo [*A publication*]
**LVED** ........ Left Ventricular End-Diastolic [*Cardiology*]
**LVEDD** ...... Left Ventricular End-Diastolic Dimension [*Cardiology*]
**LVEDP** ...... Left Ventricular End-Diastolic Pressure [*Cardiology*]
**LVEDV** ...... Left Ventricular End-Diastolic Volume [*Cardiology*]
**LVEF** ........ Left Ventricular Ejection Fraction [*Time*] [*Cardiology*]
**LVER** ........ Local Veterans Employment Representative [*Department of Labor*]
**LVES** ........ Low-Voltage Electrical Stimulation [*Meat treatment*]
**LVET** ........ Left Ventricular Ejection Time [*Cardiology*]
**LVETI** ....... Left Ventricular Ejection Time Index [*Cardiology*]
**LVF** ........... Dallas, TX [*Location identifier*] [*FAA*] (FAAL)
**LVF** ........... Left Ventricular Failure [*Cardiology*]
**LVF** ........... Left Visual Field [*Psychometrics*]
**LVF** ........... Linear Vector Function
**LVF** ........... Low-Voltage Fast [*Electronics*]
**LVFC** ........ Launch Vehicle Flight Control
**LVFCS** ...... Launch Vehicle Flight Control System
**LVFP** ........ Left Ventricular Filling Pressure [*Cardiology*]
**LVFS** ........ Large Volume Filtration System [*Environmental chemistry*]
**LVG** .......... Lauro/Viceroy/Global Joint Service [*Shipping*] (DS)
**LVG** .......... Leaving
**LVG** .......... Left Ventral Gluteal [*Injection site*]
**LVG** .......... Left Visceral Ganglion [*Medicine*]
**LVG** .......... Levengood Oil & Gas, Inc. [*Vancouver Stock Exchange symbol*]
**LVGC** ........ Launch Vehicle Guidance Computer [*NASA*]
**LVGO** ........ Light Vacuum Gas Oil [*Petroleum technology*]
**LVGSE** ...... Launch Vehicle Ground Support Equipment [*NASA*] (KSC)
**LVH** .......... Landing Vehicle, Hydrofoil
**LVH** .......... Left Ventricular Hypertrophy [*Cardiology*]
**LVHV** ........ Low-Volume High-Velocity (IEEE)
**LVHX** ........ Landing Craft, Hydrofoil, Experimental [*Navy symbol*]
**LVI** ........... Laus Verbo Incarnato [*Praise to the Incarnate Word*] [*Latin*]
**LVI** ........... Lavalin Industries, Inc. [*Toronto Stock Exchange symbol*]
**LVI** ........... Liquid Vapor Interface
**LVI** ........... Livingstone [*Zambia*] [*Airport symbol*] (OAG)
**LVI** ........... Local Veterinary Inspector [*British*]
**LVI** ........... LVI Group, Inc. [*NYSE symbol*] (SPSG)
**LVID** ......... Left Ventricle Internal Diameter [*Cardiology*]
**LVIS** ......... Launch Vehicle Instrumentation Systems [*NASA*] (KSC)
**LVIT** ......... Linear Variable Inductance Transducer
**L'viv Zootekh Vet Inst Nauk Pr** ... L'vivskii Zootekhnichno-Veterinarnii Institut. Naukovi Pratsi [*A publication*]
**LVJ** ........... Cleveland, OH [*Location identifier*] [*FAA*] (FAAL)
**LVK** ........... Livermore, CA [*Location identifier*] [*FAA*] (FAAL)
**LVK** ........... Lovelock [*Nevada*] [*Seismograph station code, US Geological Survey*] [*Closed*] (SEIS)
**LVKJ** ......... Latviesu Valodas Kulturas Jautajumi [*A publication*]
**LVL** ........... Laminated-Veneer Lumber
**LVL** ........... Lawrenceville, VA [*Location identifier*] [*FAA*] (FAAL)
**LVL** ........... Level (AAG)
**LVL** ........... Levelland Energy [*Vancouver Stock Exchange symbol*]
**LVL** ........... Lex Vehicle Leasing [*British*]
**LVL** ........... Long Vertical Left
**LVL** ........... Universite Laval, Bibliotheque [*UTLAS symbol*]
**LVLG** ......... Left Ventrolateral Gluteal [*Site of injection*] [*Medicine*]
**LVLG** ......... Luther. Vierteljahresschrift der Luthergesellschaft [*A publication*]
**LVLH** ........ Local Vertical/Local Horizontal (NASA)
**Lv Lns** ........ Live Lines [*A publication*]
**LVLO** ........ Local Vehicle Licensing Office [*British*]
**LVLOF** ...... Level Off [*Aviation*] (FAAC)
**LVM** .......... Launch Vehicle Monitor
**LVM** .......... Light Vehicle Mine [*Military*]
**LVM** .......... Line Voltage Monitor
**LVM** .......... Livingston, MT [*Location identifier*] [*FAA*] (FAAL)
**LVM** .......... Low-Value Materiel (MCD)
**LVMH** ....... Louis Vuitton Moet-Hennessy [*Commercial firm*] [*Belgium*]
**LVMH** ....... LVMH Moet Hennessy Louis Vuitton [*NASDAQ symbol*] (NQ)
**LVMP** ........ Launch Vehicle Mission Peculiar
**LVMS** ........ LEG [*Liquefied Energy Gas*] Volume Measuring System
**LVMS** ........ Limb Volume Measuring System
**LVMTAS** .. Low-Visibility, Moving Target Acquisition and Strike [*Military*]
**LVN** .......... Carnegie Public Library, Las Vegas, NM [*OCLC symbol*] (OCLC)
**LVN** .......... Lakeville, MN [*Location identifier*] [*FAA*] (FAAL)
**LVN** .......... Las Vegas [*Nevada*] [*Seismograph station code, US Geological Survey*] (SEIS)
**LVN** .......... Levon Resources Ltd. [*Toronto Stock Exchange symbol*] [*Vancouver Stock Exchange symbol*]
**LVN** .......... Library Video Network [*Video producer*]
**LVN** .......... Licensed Visiting Nurse
**LVN** .......... Licensed Vocational Nurse
**LVN** .......... Limiting Viscosity Number
**LVN** .......... Low-Voltage Neon
**LVNJ** ........ Long Valley [*New Jersey*] [*Seismograph station code, US Geological Survey*] (SEIS)
**LVNV** ........ Levon Resources Ltd. [*Vancouver, BC*] [*NASDAQ symbol*] (NQ)
**LVO** .......... Launch Vehicle Operations
**LVO** .......... Laverton [*Australia*] [*Airport symbol*] (OAG)
**LVO** .......... Lithiated Vanadium Oxide [*Battery technology*]
**LVO** .......... Louver Opening
**LVOP** ........ Local Vertical and Orbit Plane
**LVOR** ........ Low-Powered, Low-Very-High-Frequency Omnirange
**L'vov Politehn Inst Naucn Zap Ser Fiz-Mat** ... L'vovskii Politehniceskii Institut. Naucnye Zapiski. Serija Fiziko-Matematiceskaja [*A publication*]
**L'vov Torg Ekon Inst Nauchn Zap** ... L'vovskii Torgovo-Ekonomicheskii Institut. Nauchnye Zapiski [*A publication*]
**LVP** ........... Large Volume Parenterals [*Medicine*]
**LVP** ........... Left Ventricular Pressure [*Cardiology*]
**LVP** ........... Left Ventricular Pump [*Cardiology*]
**LVP** ........... Light Valve Projector
**LVP** ........... Low-Value Product
**LVP** ........... Low-Voltage Plate
**LVP** ........... Low-Voltage Protection [*Electronics*]
**LVP** ........... Lysine Vasopressin [*Antidiuretic hormone*]
**LVPD** ........ Launch Vehicle Pressure Display [*NASA*] (KSC)
**LVpE** ......... Evangeline Parish Library, Ville Platte, LA [*Library symbol*] [*Library of Congress*] (LCLS)
**LVPG** ........ Launch Vehicle Planning Group [*Aerospace*] (AAG)
**LVPL** ........ Liverpool [*England*]
**LVPP** ........ Launch Vehicle and Propulsion Program [*NASA*]

**LVPS** ........ Laboratory Vehicle Procedure Simulator
**LVPS** ........ Low-Voltage Power Supply
**LVPTG** ...... Lateral Vascularized Patellar Tendon Graft [*Orthopedics*]
**LVR** .......... Laboratory of Virology and Rickettsial Diseases
**LVR** .......... Land and Valuation Court Reports [*New South Wales*] [*A publication*] (APTA)
**lvr** ............ Latvian Soviet Socialist Republic [*MARC country of publication code*] [*Library of Congress*] (LCCP)
**LVR** .......... Lever (MSA)
**LVR** .......... Line Voltage Regulator
**LVR** .......... Liverpool [*England*] [*Seismograph station code, US Geological Survey*] [*Closed*] (SEIS)
**LVR** .......... London Volunteer Regiment [*British military*] (DMA)
**LVR** .......... Long Vertical Right
**LVR** .......... Longitudinal Video Recording
**LVR** .......... Louver (MSA)
**LVR** .......... Low-Voltage Rack
**LVR** .......... Low-Voltage Relay
**LVR** .......... Low-Voltage Release [*Electronics*]
**LVRC** ........ Lamoille Valley Railroad Company [*AAR code*]
**LVRE** ........ Low-Voltage Release Effect [*Electronics*] (MSA)
**LV Rep** ...... Lehigh Valley Law Reporter [*Pennsylvania*] [*A publication*] (DLA)
**LVRIS** ........ Low-Volume Ramjet Inlet System
**LVRJ** ........ Low-Voltage Ramjet
**LVRJ** ........ Low-Volume Ramjet
**LVRL** ........ Latrobe Valley Regional Library [*Australia*]
**LVRLSE** .... Low-Voltage Release [*Electronics*]
**LVRR** ........ Lehigh Valley Railroad Co. [*Absorbed into Consolidated Rail Corp.*]
**LV/RVV** .... Local Vertical/Relative Velocity Vector
**LVS** .......... Las Vegas Airlines, Inc. [*Las Vegas, NV*] [*FAA designator*] (FAAC)
**LVS** .......... Las Vegas, NM [*Location identifier*] [*FAA*] (FAAL)
**LVS** .......... Leaves (MSA)
**LVS** .......... Left Ventricular Strain [*Cardiology*]
**LvS** .......... Literatura v Shkole [*A publication*]
**LVS** .......... Logistics Vehicle System
**LVS** .......... Low-Velocity Scanning
**LVSC** ........ London Voluntary Service Council [*British*]
**LVSF** ........ Laboratory Vehicle Support Facility
**LVSG** ........ Launch Vehicle Study Group [*NASA*] (KSC)
**LVS/ITS** .... LASER Vibration Sensor Inspection Test System [*Army*] (RDA)
**LvSK** ........ Literatura v Shkole [*A publication*]
**LVSP** ........ Left Ventricular Systolic Pressure [*Cardiology*]
**LVSS** ........ Laboratory Vehicle System Segment
**LVST** ........ Longitudinal Velocity Sorting Tube
**LVSTK** ...... Livestock
**LVSV** ........ Left Ventricular Stroke Volume [*Cardiology*]
**LVSW** ........ Left Ventricular Stroke Work [*Cardiology*]
**LVSWI** ...... Left Ventricular Stroke Work Index [*Cardiology*]
**LVT** .......... Landing Vehicle, Tracked (Unarmored) [*Navy symbol*]
**LVT** .......... Levitt Corp. [*AMEX symbol*] (SPSG)
**LVT** .......... Lexicon Hebraicum et Aramaicum Veteris Testamenti [*Rome*] [*A publication*] (BJA)
**LVT** .......... Licensed Veterinary Technician
**LVT** .......... Linear Velocity Transducer
**LVT** .......... Livingston, TN [*Location identifier*] [*FAA*] (FAAL)
**LVT** .......... Low-Voltage Tubular
**LVT** .......... Lysine Vasotonin [*Adrenergic agent*]
**LVT (1)** ...... Landing Vehicle, Tracked (Unarmored) (Mark I) [*"Alligator"*] [*Navy symbol*]
**LVT (2)** ...... Landing Vehicle, Tracked (Unarmored) (Mark II) [*"Water Buffalo"*] [*Navy symbol*]
**LVT (3)** ...... Landing Vehicle, Tracked (Unarmored) (Mark III) [*Navy symbol*]
**LVT (4)** ...... Landing Vehicle, Tracked (Unarmored) (Mark IV)
**LVT (A)** ..... Landing Vehicle, Tracked (Armored) [*Turret Type*]
**LVTA** ........ London Vintage Taxi Association - American Section (EA)
**LVT (A) (1)** ... Landing Vehicle, Tracked (Armored) (Mark I) [*"Water Buffalo," Turret Type*]
**LVT (A) (4)** ... Landing Vehicle, Tracked (Armored) (Mark IV)
**LVT (A) (5)** ... Landing Vehicle, Tracked (Armored) (Mark V)
**LVTC** ........ Landing Vehicle, Tracked, Command (NVT)
**LVTC** ........ Launch Vehicle Test Conductor [*NASA*] (KSC)
**LVTCX** ...... Landing Vehicle, Tracked, Command, Experimental (MCD)
**LVTE** ........ Landing Vehicle, Tracked, Engineer [*Model 1*]
**LVTH** ........ Landing Vehicle, Tracked, Howitzer [*Model 6*]
**LVTL** ........ Lexicon in Veteris Testamenti Libros [*A publication*] (BJA)
**LVTN** ........ Louis Vuitton SA [*France*] [*NASDAQ symbol*] (NQ)
**LVTP** ........ Landing Vehicle, Tracked, Personnel (AABC)
**LVTPX** ...... Landing Vehicle, Tracked, Personnel, Experimental (MCD)
**LVTR** ........ Landing Vehicle, Tracked, Retriever (NVT)
**LVT(R)** ...... Landing Vehicle, Tracked (Rocket) [*British military*] (DMA)
**LVTR** ........ Low-VHF [*Very-High-Frequency*] Transmitter-Receiver
**LVTRX** ...... Landing Vehicle, Tracked, Recovery, Experimental (MCD)
**LVTU** ........ Landing Vehicle, Tracked (Unarmored)
**LVUPK** ...... Leave and Upkeep Period [*Military*] (NVT)
**LVUSA** ...... Legion of Valor of the United States of America (EA)
**LVV** .......... Delavan, WI [*Location identifier*] [*FAA*] (FAAL)
**LVV** .......... Left Ventricular Volume [*Cardiology*]
**LVV** .......... Lvov [*USSR*] [*Geomagnetic observatory code*]
**LVV** .......... Lvov [*Lemberg*] [*USSR*] [*Seismograph station code, US Geological Survey*] (SEIS)
**LVVC** ........ Lincolnshire Vintage Vehicle Club [*British*] (DCTA)
**LVW** ........ Landing Vehicle, Wheeled
**LVW** ........ Las Vegas [*Nevada*] [*Seismograph station code, US Geological Survey*] (SEIS)
**LVW** ........ Left Ventricular Wall [*Anatomy*]
**LVW** ........ Left Ventricular Work [*Cardiology*]
**LVWI** ........ Left Ventricular Work Index [*Cardiology*]
**LVWN** ...... Livable Winter Newsletter [*A publication*]
**LVX** .......... Leisure & Technology, Inc. [*NYSE symbol*] (SPSG)
**LVY** .......... La Verendrye Management Corp. [*Toronto Stock Exchange symbol*]
**LVY** .......... Levy [*Alaska*] [*Seismograph station code, US Geological Survey*] (SEIS)
**LVZ** .......... Low-Viscosity Zone
**LW** .......... Griechische und Lateinische Lehnwoerter im Talmud, Midrasch und Targum [*A publication*] (BJA)
**LW** .......... Lab. Wander [*France*] [*Research code symbol*]
**LW** .......... Lacerated Wound
**LW** .......... Landsteiner-Wiener [*Serum*]
**L-W** .......... Landsverk-Wollan [*Radiation survey meter*]
**LW** .......... Langwelle [*Long Wave*] [*German*] (MCD)
**LW** .......... Late Warning
**LW** .......... Lauda Air [*Austria*] [*ICAO designator*] (FAAC)
**LW** .......... Launch Window [*Aerospace*] (AAG)
**LW** .......... Law Weekly [*A publication*] (DLA)
**LW** .......... Lawrence Welk
**Lw** .......... Lawrencium [*Symbol changed, 1963, to Lr*] [*Chemical element*]
**LW** .......... Leave Word [*Telecommunications*] (TEL)
**LW** .......... Left Wing
**LW** .......... Light Wall
**LW** .......... Light Warning
**LW** .......... Light Weight [*Technical drawings*]
**LW** .......... Lightweight RADAR (NATG)
**LW** .......... Limited War
**LW** .......... Literarische Wochenschrift [*A publication*]
**LW** .......... Literatures of the World [*A publication*]
**LW** .......... Lives With (ADA)
**L & W** ...... Living and Well
**LW** .......... Living Wilderness [*A publication*]
**L & W** ...... Lloyd and Welsby's English Commercial and Mercantile Cases [*1829-30*] [*A publication*] (DLA)
**lw** .......... Loan Word (BJA)
**LW** .......... Logical Weakness [*Used in correcting manuscripts, etc.*]
**LW** .......... Long Wave [*Radio*]
**LW** .......... Lotus West (EA)
**LW** .......... Louisville & Wadley Railway Co. [*AAR code*]
**LW** .......... Low Water [*Tides and currents*]
**LW** .......... Low Wing [*Aviation*] (AIA)
**Lw** .......... Lower Hold [*Shipping*] (DS)
**LW** .......... Lumens per Watt (ADA)
**LW** .......... Lung Water
**L-10-W** ...... Levulose (10 Percent) in Water
**LWA** ........ Last Word Address
**LWA** ........ Lightly Wounded in Action
**LWA** ........ Lightweight Armor
**LWA** ........ Limited Work Authorizations [*Nuclear energy*]
**LWA** ........ Local Welfare Authority [*British*]
**LWA** ........ Long Wire Antenna
**LWA** ........ University of Southwestern Louisiana, Lafayette, LA [*OCLC symbol*] (OCLC)
**LWAR** ...... Lightweight Attack and/or Reconnaissance (NATG)
**LWASV** .... Lightweight Aircraft-to-Surface Vessel [*Military*]
**LWAY** ...... Lifeway Foods, Inc. [*NASDAQ symbol*] (NQ)
**LWB** ........ Greenbrier [*West Virginia*] [*Airport symbol*] (OAG)
**LWB** ........ Laboratory Workbench
**LWB** ........ Lewisburg, WV [*Location identifier*] [*FAA*] (FAAL)
**LWB** ........ Light-Water Breeder [*Reactor*]
**LWB** ........ Long Wheelbase
**LWB** ........ Lower Bound [*Data processing*]
**LWBR** ...... Light-Water Breeder Reactor
**LWBS** ...... Loyal Wheelwrights' and Blacksmiths' Society [*A union*] [*British*]
**LWC** ........ Lawrence [*Kansas*] [*Airport symbol*] (OAG)
**LWC** ........ League of Women Composers [*Later, ILWC*] (EA)
**LWC** ........ Lightweight Coated [*Paper*]
**LWC** ........ Lightweight Concrete [*Technical drawings*]
**LWC** ........ Lindsey Wilson College [*Columbia, KY*]
**LWC** ........ Liquid Water Content
**LWC** ........ Lithuanian World Community (EA)
**LWC** ........ Living with Cancer [*An association*] (EA)
**LWCA** ...... Light-Water Critical Assembly [*Nuclear reactor*] [*Japan*]
**LWCA** ...... Longwave Club of America (EA)
**LWCF** ...... Land and Water Conservation Fund [*Department of the Interior*]
**LWCH** ...... Lightweight Container Handler (MCD)
**LWCHW** ... Light-Water-Cooled, Heavy-Water-Moderated Reactor (NRCH)

**LWCMD** ... Licentiate of the Welsh College of Music and Drama [*British*] (DBQ)
**LWCMS** .... Lightweight Company Mortar System
**LW-COIN** ... Limited War - Counterinsurgency
**LWCS** ........ Limited War Capabilities Study
**LWCSS** ...... Lightweight Camouflage Screen System (MCD)
**LWCT** ........ Lee-White Clotting Time [*Hematology*]
**LWD** .......... Large Woody Debris [*Pisciculture*]
**LWD** .......... Larger Word [*Data processing*]
**LWD** .......... Launch Window Display [*Aerospace*] (MCD)
**LWD** .......... Left Wing Down [*Aviation*]
**LWD** .......... Long-Working Distance [*Microscopy*]
**LWD** .......... Loomis-Wood Diagram [*Physics*]
**LWD** .......... Low-Water Datum
**LWDG** ........ Lightweight Director Group [*Military*] (CAAL)
**LWE** .......... Lawrence Mining [*Vancouver Stock Exchange symbol*]
**LWE** .......... Liquid Whole Egg
**LWeJ** ......... Welsh Public Library, Welsh, LA [*Library symbol*] [*Library of Congress*] (LCLS)
**L & Welsb** ... Lloyd and Welsby's English Commercial and Mercantile Cases [*1829-30*] [*A publication*] (DLA)
**LWF** .......... Lightweight Fighter [*Air Force*]
**LWF** .......... Local Welfare Authority Full Time [*British*]
**LWF** .......... Lutheran World Federation [*See also FLM*] [*Geneva, Switzerland*] (EAIO)
**LWFC** ........ Lloyd Wood Fan Club [*Defunct*] (EA)
**LWF & C** ... Low Water Full and Change [*Tides and currents*]
**LWFCS** ...... Lightweight Fire Control System [*Military*] (CAAL)
**LWF Doc** ... LWF [*Lutheran World Federation*] Documentation [*A publication*]
**LWFJTF** ... Lightweight Fighter Joint Test Force [*Air Force*]
**LWF Rep** ... LWF [*Lutheran World Federation*] Report [*A publication*]
**LWFUSANC** ... Lutheran World Federation United States of America National Committee (EA)
**LWG** .......... Corvallis, OR [*Location identifier*] [*FAA*] (FAAL)
**LWG** .......... Lightweight Gun (NG)
**LWG** .......... Logistic Work Group [*NATO*] (NATG)
**LWG** .......... Longwood Gardens Library, Kennett Square, PA [*OCLC symbol*] (OCLC)
**LWGM** ...... Lightweight Gun Mount [*Military*] (CAAL)
**LWH** .......... Lawn Hill [*Australia*] [*Airport symbol*] [*Obsolete*] (OAG)
**LWHS** ....... Lightweight Headset [*Apollo*] [*NASA*]
**LWHVR** .... Lightweight High-Velocity Rifle
**LWI** .......... Load Wear Index
**LWI** .......... Low-Water Interval
**LWI** .......... Lwiro [*Zaire*] [*Seismograph station code, US Geological Survey*] (SEIS)
**LWI** .......... Lwiro [*Zaire*] [*Geomagnetic observatory code*]
**LWIC** ........ Lightweight Insulating Concrete [*Technical drawings*]
**LWII** ......... Long Wavelength Infrared Illuminator
**LWinF** ....... Franklin Parish Library, Winnsboro, LA [*Library symbol*] [*Library of Congress*] (LCLS)
**LWIR** ......... Long Wavelength Infrared
**LWIRC** ...... Limited Warfare Intelligence Reduction Complex
**LWIS** ......... Lewis [*Palmer G.*] Co., Inc. [*NASDAQ symbol*] (NQ)
**LWIU** ........ Laundry, Dry Cleaning, and Dye House Workers' International Union [*Later, Textile Processors, Service Trades, Health Care, Professional, and Technical Employees International Union*]
**LWIU** ........ Leather Workers International Union of America (EA)
**LWiW** ........ Winn Parish Library, Winnfield, LA [*Library symbol*] [*Library of Congress*] (LCLS)
**LWJ** .......... Lucas, William J., Albuquerque NM [*STAC*]
**LWK** .......... Leerblad. Vakblad voor de Lederwarenbranche en Reisartikelenbranche in de Beneluxlanden [*A publication*]
**LWK** .......... Lerwick [*Scotland*] Tingwall Airport [*Airport symbol*] (OAG)
**LWL** .......... Lambair Ltd. [*Winnipeg, MB*] [*FAA designator*] (FAAC)
**LWL** .......... Land Warfare [*formerly, Limited War*] Laboratory [*Army*]
**LWL** .......... Length [*of a boat*] at Waterline
**LWL** .......... Lightweight Launcher (MCD)
**LWL** .......... Load Waterline
**LWL** .......... Low Waterline
**LWL** .......... Wells [*Nevada*] [*Airport symbol*] [*Obsolete*] (OAG)
**LWLD** ........ Lightweight LASER Designator
**LWLR** ........ Land and Water Law Review [*A publication*]
**L and W LR** ... Land and Water Law Review [*A publication*]
**LWLRD** ...... Land and Water Law Review [*A publication*]
**LWM** ......... Larrimore, William M., San Francisco CA [*STAC*]
**LWM** ......... Lawrence, MA [*Location identifier*] [*FAA*] (FAAL)
**LWM** ......... Leonard Wood Memorial [*American Leprosy Foundation*] (EA)
**LWM** ......... Liquid Waste Monitor [*Nuclear energy*] (IEEE)
**LWM** ......... Low Watermark
**LWMB** ....... Local Works Managing Budget [*British Armed Forces*]
**LWMEL** .... Leonard Wood Memorial for the Eradication of Leprosy [*Later, LWM*] (EA)
**LWML** ....... Lutheran Women's Missionary League [*Later, ILWML*] (EA)
**LWMS** ....... Liquid Waste Management System [*Nuclear energy*] (NRCH)
**LWN** ......... Landbouwwereldnieuws [*A publication*]
**LWN** ......... Loewen Group, Inc. [*Toronto Stock Exchange symbol*]
**LWNA** ....... Lumber [*Timber*], Winter, North Atlantic [*Vessel load line mark*]
**LWO** ......... Layout Work Order (MCD)
**LWO** ......... Limited War Office [*Air Force*] (MCD)
**LWO** ......... Limited Warning Operation
**LWO** ......... Lubavitch Women's Organization (EA)
**LWO** ......... Lwow [*USSR*] [*Airport symbol*] (OAG)
**LWOFC** ..... Lindsay Wagner's Official Fan Club (EA)
**LWOP** ....... Leave without Pay
**LWorld** ...... Lutheran World [*A publication*]
**LWOS** ....... Low-Water Ordinary Spring [*Tides*]
**LWOST** ..... Low-Water Ordinary Spring Tides
**LWP** .......... Langley Working Paper [*NASA*]
**LWP** .......... Leave with Pay (KSC)
**LWP** .......... Limited War Plan
**LWP** .......... Liquid Waste Processing [*Nuclear energy*] (NRCH)
**LWP** .......... Load Water Plane
**LWPS** ........ Liquid Waste Processing System [*Nuclear energy*] (NRCH)
**LWQ** .......... Low-Water Quadrature
**LWQ** .......... Walnut Ridge, AR [*Location identifier*] [*FAA*] (FAAL)
**LWR** .......... Land and Water Law Review [*A publication*]
**LWR** .......... LASER Warning Receiver (MCD)
**LWR** .......... Lawrence Insurance Group [*AMEX symbol*] (SPSG)
**LWR** .......... Light-Water Reactor
**LWR** .......... Limited War Capability (AAG)
**LWR** .......... Liquid Waste Release [*Nuclear energy*] (IEEE)
**LWR** .......... Local Wage Rate
**LWR** .......... Long-Wave Radiation
**LWR** .......... Long Wavelength Redundant [*Camera for spectra*]
**LWR** .......... Lower (AAG)
**LWR** .......... Lutheran World Relief (EA)
**LWRECCE** ... Lightweight Reconnaissance Aircraft (NATG)
**LWRENAM** ... Leading WREN [*Women's Royal Naval Service*] Air Mechanic [*British military*] (DMA)
**LWRENCINE** ... Leading WREN [*Women's Royal Naval Service*] Cinema Operator [*British military*] (DMA)
**LWRENDHYG** ... Leading WREN [*Women's Royal Naval Service*] Dental Hygienist [*British military*] (DMA)
**LWRENDSA** ... Leading WREN [*Women's Royal Naval Service*] Dental Surgery Assistant [*British military*] (DMA)
**LWRENEDUC** ... Leading WREN [*Women's Royal Naval Service*] Education Assistant [*British military*] (DMA)
**LWRENMET** ... Leading WREN [*Women's Royal Naval Service*] Meteorologist [*British military*] (DMA)
**LWRENMT** ... Leading WREN [*Women's Royal Naval Service*] Motor Transport Driver [*British military*] (DMA)
**LWRENPHOT** ... Leading WREN [*Women's Royal Naval Service*] Photographer [*British military*] (DMA)
**LWRENQA** ... Leading WREN [*Women's Royal Naval Service*] Quarters Assistant [*British military*] (DMA)
**LWRENREM** ... Leading WREN [*Women's Royal Naval Service*] Radio Electrical Mechanic [*British military*] (DMA)
**LWRENRO(M)** ... Leading WREN [*Women's Royal Naval Service*] Radio Operator (Morse) [*British military*] (DMA)
**LWRENS(C)** ... Leading WREN [*Women's Royal Naval Service*] Stores Assistant (Clothes) [*British military*] (DMA)
**LWRENS(S)** ... Leading WREN [*Women's Royal Naval Service*] Stores Assistant (Stores) [*British military*] (DMA)
**LWRENSTD** ... Leading WREN [*Women's Royal Naval Service*] Steward [*British military*] (DMA)
**LWRENS(V)** ... Leading WREN [*Women's Royal Naval Service*] Stores Assistant (Victualling) [*British military*] (DMA)
**LWRENTEL** ... Leading WREN [*Women's Royal Naval Service*] Telephonist [*British military*] (DMA)
**LWRENTSA** ... Leading WREN [*Women's Royal Naval Service*] Training Support Assistant [*British military*] (DMA)
**LWRENWA** ... Leading WREN [*Women's Royal Naval Service*] Weapon Analyst [*British military*] (DMA)
**LWRENWTR(G)** ... Leading WREN [*Women's Royal Naval Service*] Writer (General) [*British military*] (DMA)
**LWRENWTR(P)** ... Leading WREN [*Women's Royal Naval Service*] Writer (Pay) [*British military*] (DMA)
**LWRENWTR(S)** ... Leading WREN [*Women's Royal Naval Service*] Writer (Shorthand) [*British military*] (DMA)
**LWRM** ...... Lightweight RADAR Missile (MCD)
**LWRRI** ...... Louisiana Water Resources Research Institute [*Department of the Interior*] [*Louisiana State University*] [*Research center*] (RCD)
**LWRS** ........ Lightweight Weather RADAR Set
**LWRU** ....... Lightweight RADAR Unit (NATG)
**LWS** .......... LASER Weapon System (MCD)
**LWS** .......... Lewiston [*Idaho*] [*Airport symbol*] (OAG)
**LWS** .......... Library Wholesale Services [*Information service or system*] (IID)
**LWS** .......... Light-Warning RADAR Set (NATG)
**LWS** .......... Lightning Warning Set [*Air Force*]
**LWS** .......... Lightning Warning System [*NASA*] (NASA)
**LWS** .......... Lightweight Sight
**LWS** .......... Lightweight System
**LWS** .......... Low-Water Sensitivity [*Brake fluid designation*]
**LWS** .......... Low Water of Spring Tide

**LWSC**........ Library Workforce Standing Committee [*Australia*]
**LWSD**........ LASER Weapon System Demonstrator [*Military*]
**LWSF**........ Lightweight Strike Fighter [*NATO Air Forces*]
**LWSI**........ Laidlaw Industries, Inc. [*NASDAQ symbol*] (NQ)
**LWSR**........ Lightweight Strike and Reconnaissance Aircraft (NATG)
**LWSR(R)**... Lightweight Strike and Reconnaissance Aircraft (Reconnaissance Role) (NATG)
**LWSR(S)**... Lightweight Strike and Reconnaissance Aircraft (Strike Role) (NATG)
**LWST**........ Light Waste Storage Tank (IEEE)
**LWST**........ Lowest (MSA)
**LW(STA)**... Light Warning (Station)
**LWSTC**...... Liquid Waste and Sludge Transporter Council (EA)
**Lw Stu H**.... Law Students' Helper [*A publication*] (DLA)
**LWT**.......... Amphibious Warping Tug [*Navy symbol*]
**LWT**.......... Lamb Weather Type [*Meteorology*]
**LWT**.......... Lewistown [*Montana*] [*Airport symbol*] (OAG)
**LWT**.......... Lightweight Transponder
**LWT**.......... Lightweight Type [*Anchor gear*]
**LWT**.......... Liquid Waste Treatment (MCD)
**LWT**.......... London Weekend Television [*England*]
**LWTA**........ LASER Window Test Apparatus [*Air Force*]
**LWTR**........ Leading Writer [*British military*] (DMA)
**LWTS**........ Laundry Waste Treatment System [*Nuclear energy*] (NRCH)
**LWTT**........ Liquid Waste Test Tank [*Nuclear energy*] (IEEE)
**LWU**.......... LASER Welder Unit
**LWU**.......... Leather Workers International Union of America
**LWU**.......... Literatur in Wissenschaft und Unterricht [*A publication*]
**LWUA**........ Local Water Utilities Administration [*Philippines*] (DS)
**LWUI**........ Longshoremen's and Warehousemen's Union International
**LWV**.......... Lackawanna & Wyoming Valley Railway Co. [*AAR code*] [*Absorbed into Consolidated Rail Corp.*]
**LWV**.......... Landwirtschaftsversorgungsamt [*German Land Economic Supply Office*] [*Post-World War II*]
**LWV**.......... Lawrenceville [*Illinois*] [*Airport symbol*] [*Obsolete*] (OAG)
**LWV**.......... League of Women Voters of the United States
**LWV**.......... Light-Weight Van
**LWVEF**...... League of Women Voters Education Fund (EA)
**LWVUS**..... League of Women Voters of the United States (EA)
**LWW**.......... Launch Window Width [*Aerospace*]
**LWW**.......... Lightweight Weapon
**LWWS**........ Lightweight Weapons Sight
**LWY**.......... Lawas [*Malaysia*] [*Airport symbol*] (OAG)
**LWYACC**.. Lithuanian World Youth Association Communications Center (EA)
**LWZ**.......... Lederwaren Zeitung [*A publication*]
**LX**.............. Cross Air [*Switzerland*] [*ICAO designator*] (FAAC)
**LX**.............. La Crosse, WI
**LX**.............. Liver Extract [*Protein/lipid substance*] [*Immunology*]
**LX**.............. Low Index [*Aviation*] (FAAC)
**lx**............... Lux [*Symbol*] [*SI unit of luminance*]
**LX**.............. Lux [*Light*] [*Latin*]
**LX**.............. Luxembourg [*Aircraft nationality and registration mark*] [*IYRU nationality code*] (FAAC)
**LXA**........... Lhasa [*China*] [*Airport symbol*] (OAG)
**LXA**........... Lipoxin A [*Biochemistry*]
**LXA**........... Load Index from Address
**LXAAAC**... Annual Report. Laboratory of Experimental Algology and Department of Applied Algology [*Trebon*] [*A publication*]
**LXAD**........ Lexington Army Depot [*Kentucky*] (AFIT)
**LXB**........... Lipoxin B [*Biochemistry*]
**LXB**........... Pittsburgh, PA [*Location identifier*] [*FAA*] (FAAL)
**LXBK**......... LSB Bancshares, Inc. [*Lexington, NC*] [*NASDAQ symbol*] (NQ)
**LXD**........... LASER Transceiver Device
**LXD**........... Load Index from Decrement
**LXFT**......... Linear Xenon Flash Tube
**LXGB**......... Gibraltar/North Front [*Gibraltar*] [*ICAO location identifier*] (ICLI)
**LXL**........... Little Falls, MN [*Location identifier*] [*FAA*] (FAAL)
**LXM**........... Lintex Minerals [*Vancouver Stock Exchange symbol*]
**LXMAR**..... Load External Memory Address Register
**LXN**........... Lexington, NE [*Location identifier*] [*FAA*] (FAAL)
**LXN**........... Lexington Resources Ltd. [*Vancouver Stock Exchange symbol*]
**LXP**........... Lorain Public Library, Lorain, OH [*OCLC symbol*] (OCLC)
**LXR**........... Luxor [*Egypt*] [*Airport symbol*] (OAG)
**LXS**........... Lemnos [*Greece*] [*Airport symbol*] (OAG)
**LX S**.......... Lux Second
**LXT**........... Left Exotropia [*Ophthalmology*]
**LXT**........... Linear Xenon Tube
**LXV**........... Leadville, CO [*Location identifier*] [*FAA*] (FAAL)
**LXX**........... Septuagint [*Version of the Bible*]
**LXY**........... Mexia, TX [*Location identifier*] [*FAA*] (FAAL)
**LY**.............. El Al - Israel Airlines Ltd. [*ICAO designator*] (FAAC)
**LY**.............. Lactoalbumin-Yeastolate [*Cell growth medium*]
**LY**.............. Langley [*Unit of sun's heat*]
**LY**.............. Last Year's Model [*Merchandising slang*]
**LY**.............. League for Yiddish [*Later, LYI*] (EA)
**LY**.............. Leicestershire Yeomanry (Prince Albert's Own) [*British military*] (DMA)
**LY**.............. Lessing Yearbook [*A publication*]
**LY**.............. Lethal Yellowing [*Plant pathology*]
**LY**.............. Liberal Youth [*Political party*] (EAIO)
**LY**.............. Libya [*ANSI two-letter standard code*] (CNC)
**ly**............... Libya [*MARC country of publication code*] [*Library of Congress*] (LCCP)
**LY**.............. Light Year
**LY**.............. Linear Yard (AFM)
**LY**.............. Lucifer Yellow [*A dye*] [*Organic chemistry*]
**Ly**.............. Lychnos [*A publication*]
**Ly**.............. Lyman [*Spectrography*]
**LY**.............. Lynngold Resources, Inc. [*Toronto Stock Exchange symbol*]
**LY**.............. Queen's Own Lowland Yeomanry [*Military unit*] [*British*]
**LYA**........... Lynch, Young & Associates [*Newport Beach, CA*] [*Telecommunications*] (TSSD)
**LYB**........... Little Cayman [*West Indies*] [*Airport symbol*] (OAG)
**LYBA**......... Beograd [*Yugoslavia*] [*ICAO location identifier*] (ICLI)
**LYBB**......... Beograd [*Yugoslavia*] [*ICAO location identifier*] (ICLI)
**LYBE**......... Beograd [*Yugoslavia*] [*ICAO location identifier*] (ICLI)
**LYBK**......... Banja Luka [*Yugoslavia*] [*ICAO location identifier*] (ICLI)
**LYC**........... Leicestershire Yeomanry Cavalry (Prince Albert's Own) [*British military*] (DMA)
**LyC**........... Lenguaje y Ciencias [*A publication*]
**LYC**........... Lycoming College, Williamsport, PA [*OCLC symbol*] (OCLC)
**Lyc**............ Lycurgus [*of Plutarch*] [*Fourth century BC*] [*Classical studies*] (OCD)
**Lychnos Lardomshist Samf Arsb** ... Lychnos Lardomshistoriska Samfundets Arsbok [*A publication*]
**Lyc N H NY An Pr** ... Lyceum of Natural History of New York. Annals. Proceedings [*A publication*]
**Lycoming** ... Lycoming Reporter [*Pennsylvania*] [*A publication*] (DLA)
**Lycoming R (PA)** ... Lycoming Reporter [*Pennsylvania*] [*A publication*] (DLA)
**Lycoph**....... Lycophron [*Third century BC*] [*Classical studies*] (OCD)
**Lycurg**........ Lycurgus [*of Plutarch*] [*Fourth century BC*] [*Classical studies*] (OCD)
**LYD**........... Houston, TX [*Location identifier*] [*FAA*] (FAAL)
**LYD**........... Lydney [*British depot code*]
**LydgN**........ Lydgate Newsletter [*A publication*]
**LYDMA**.... Lymphocyte Determined Membrane Antigen [*Immunology*]
**LYDP**......... Lydenburg Platinum Ltd. [*NASDAQ symbol*] (NQ)
**LYDU**........ Dubrovnik [*Yugoslavia*] [*ICAO location identifier*] (ICLI)
**LYF**........... Lutheran Youth Fellowship (EA)
**LYG**........... Lymphomatoid Granulomatosis [*Medicine*]
**LYH**........... Lynchburg [*Virginia*] [*Airport symbol*] (OAG)
**LYI**............ League for Yiddish, Inc. (EA)
**LYI**............ Libby, MT [*Location identifier*] [*FAA*] (FAAL)
**Lying-In J Reprod Med** ... Lying-In Journal of Reproductive Medicine [*A publication*]
**LYL**........... League of Young Liberals [*British*] (ROG)
**LYL**........... Lima, OH [*Location identifier*] [*FAA*] (FAAL)
**LYLJ**.......... Ljubljana [*Yugoslavia*] [*ICAO location identifier*] (ICLI)
**LYM**.......... Lymphocyte
**LYMB**........ Maribor [*Yugoslavia*] [*ICAO location identifier*] (ICLI)
**LYMBS**...... Lodzer Young Men's Benevolent Society (EA)
**LYMO**....... Mostar [*Yugoslavia*] [*ICAO location identifier*] (ICLI)
**LYMPH**..... Lymphocyte
**Lymphokine Res** ... Lymphokine Research [*A publication*]
**LYN**........... Atlanta, GA [*Location identifier*] [*FAA*] (FAAL)
**Lyn**............ Lynx [*Constellation*]
**LYND**........ Lynden, Inc. [*NASDAQ symbol*] (NQ)
**Lynd**.......... Lyndwood's Provinciales [*A publication*] (DLA)
**Lynd Prov**.. Lyndwood's Provinciales [*A publication*] (DLA)
**Lyndw Prov** ... Lyndwood's Provinciales [*A publication*] (DLA)
**Lyne**.......... Lyne's Irish Chancery Cases (Wallis) [*1766-91*] [*A publication*] (DLA)
**Lyne Lea**.... Lyne on Leases for Lives [*A publication*] (DLA)
**Lyne on Renew** ... Lyne on Renewals [*A publication*] (DLA)
**Lyne (Wall)** ... Wallis' Select Cases, Edited by Lyne [*1766-91*] [*Ireland*] [*A publication*] (DLA)
**LYNG**........ Lynton Group, Inc. [*NASDAQ symbol*] (NQ)
**LYNX**........ Lynx Exploration Co. [*NASDAQ symbol*] (NQ)
**Lynx Suppl (Prague)** ... Lynx Supplementum (Prague) [*A publication*]
**LYO**........... Lubavitch Youth Organization (EA)
**LYO**........... Lyondell Petrochemical [*NYSE symbol*] (SPSG)
**LYO**........... Lyons, KS [*Location identifier*] [*FAA*] (FAAL)
**LYOH**........ Ohrid [*Yugoslavia*] [*ICAO location identifier*] (ICLI)
**LYON**........ Liquid-Yield Option Note [*Merrill Lynch & Co.*] [*Finance*]
**LYON**........ Lyon Metal Products, Inc. [*NASDAQ symbol*] (NQ)
**Lyon Chir**... Lyon Chirurgical [*A publication*]
**Lyon Ind L** ... Lyon on the Laws of India [*A publication*] (DLA)
**Lyon Just**... Lyon's Institutes of Justinian [*A publication*] (DLA)
**Lyon Med**.. Lyon Medical [*A publication*]
**Lyon Pharm** ... Lyon Pharmaceutique [*A publication*]
**Lyon & R BS** ... Lyon and Redman on Bills of Sale [*A publication*] (DLA)
**Lyons Fac Sci Lab Geol Doc** ... Lyons. Faculte des Sciences. Laboratoires de Geologie. Documents [*A publication*]
**LYOS**......... Osijek [*Yugoslavia*] [*ICAO location identifier*] (ICLI)
**LYP**........... Faisalabad [*Pakistan*] [*Airport symbol*] (OAG)
**LyP**........... Libro y Pueblo [*A publication*]

**LYpAS**....... Logicheskii Yazyk dlia Predstavleniya Algoritmov Sinteza Releinykh Ustroistv [*A Programming Language for Logic and Coding Algorithm*] [*Book title*]
**LYPL**......... Pula [*Yugoslavia*] [*ICAO location identifier*] (ICLI)
**LYPR**......... Pristina [*Yugoslavia*] [*ICAO location identifier*] (ICLI)
**LYPW**......... Legion of Young Polish Women (EA)
**LYPZ**......... Portoroz [*Yugoslavia*] [*ICAO location identifier*] (ICLI)
**LYR**.......... Lancashire & Yorkshire Railway [*British*]
**LYR**.......... Layer (MSA)
**LYR**.......... Longyear [*Norway*] [*Airport symbol*] (OAG)
**Lyr**............ Lyra [*Constellation*]
**LYR**.......... Lyric
**Lyr**............ Lyrichord [*Record label*]
**lyr**............. Lyricist [*MARC relator code*] [*Library of Congress*] (LCCP)
**LYRC**......... Lyric Energy, Inc. [*NASDAQ symbol*] (NQ)
**LYRI**.......... Rijeka [*Yugoslavia*] [*ICAO location identifier*] (ICLI)
**LYRIC**....... Language for Your Remote Instruction by Computer [*Data processing*] (MDG)
**Lys**............ De Lysia [*of Dionysius Halicarnassensis*] [*Classical studies*] (OCD)
**LYS**........... Light of Yoga Society (EA)
**LYS**........... Lycksele [*Sweden*] [*Geomagnetic observatory code*]
**LYS**........... Lyon [*France*] [*Airport symbol*] (OAG)
**Lys**............ Lysander [*of Plutarch*] [*Classical studies*] (OCD)
**LYS**........... Lysander Gold [*Vancouver Stock Exchange symbol*]
**Lys**............ Lysias [*Fifth century BC*] [*Classical studies*] (OCD)
**Lys**............ Lysine [*Also, K*] [*An amino acid*]
**Lys**............ Lysistrata [*of Aristophanes*] [*Classical studies*] (OCD)
**LYS**........... Lysosome [*Cytology*]
**LYS**........... Lysozyme [*Also, LZM*] [*An enzyme*]
**LYS**........... Lysyl [*Enzymology*]
**LYS**........... Olean, NY [*Location identifier*] [*FAA*] (FAAL)
**LYSA**......... Sarajevo [*Yugoslavia*] [*ICAO location identifier*] (ICLI)
**LYSK**......... Skopje [*Yugoslavia*] [*ICAO location identifier*] (ICLI)
**Lyso-PC**..... Lysophosphatidylcholine [*Also, LPC*] [*Biochemistry*]
**Lysosomes Biol Pathol** ... Lysosomes in Biology and Pathology [*A publication*]
**LYSP**......... Split [*Yugoslavia*] [*ICAO location identifier*] (ICLI)
**LYT**........... Layout (MSA)
**LYTBT**...... Low-Yield Test Ban Treaty
**LYTI**.......... Titograd [*Yugoslavia*] [*ICAO location identifier*] (ICLI)
**LYTS**......... LSI Industries, Inc. [*NASDAQ symbol*] (NQ)
**LYTT**......... Lytta [*A Blistering Fly*] [*Pharmacy*] (ROG)
**LYTV**......... Tivat [*Yugoslavia*] [*ICAO location identifier*] (ICLI)
**LYU**........... Lehigh University, Bethlehem, PA [*OCLC symbol*] (OCLC)
**Lyumin Mater Osobo Chist Veshchestva** ... Lyuminestsentnye Materialy i Osobo Chistye Veshchestva. Sbornik Nauchnykh Trudov [*A publication*]
**LYVR**......... Vrsac [*Yugoslavia*] [*ICAO location identifier*] (ICLI)
**LYW**.......... Lyman [*Washington*] [*Seismograph station code, US Geological Survey*] (SEIS)
**LYX**........... Lydd [*England*] [*Airport symbol*]
**LYX**........... Lynx-Canada Explorations Ltd. [*Toronto Stock Exchange symbol*]
**Lyx**............ Lyxose [*Also, l*] [*A sugar*]
**LYY**........... Batesville, AR [*Location identifier*] [*FAA*] (FAAL)
**LYYY**......... Beograd [*Yugoslavia*] [*ICAO location identifier*] (ICLI)
**LYZA**......... Zagreb [*Yugoslavia*] [*ICAO location identifier*] (ICLI)
**LYZB**......... Zagreb [*Yugoslavia*] [*ICAO location identifier*] (ICLI)
**LYZD**......... Zadar [*Yugoslavia*] [*ICAO location identifier*] (ICLI)
**LZ**.............. Balkan-Bulgarian Airlines [*ICAO designator*] (FAAC)
**LZ**.............. Bulgaria [*Aircraft nationality and registration mark*] (FAAC)
**LZ**.............. Landing Zone
**LZ**.............. Literarisches Zentralblatt fuer Deutschland [*A publication*]
**LZ**.............. Literaturen Zbor [*A publication*]
**LZ**.............. Literaturnye Zapiski [*A publication*]
**LZ**.............. Loading Zone
**LZ**.............. [*The*] Lubrizol Corp. [*NYSE symbol*] (SPSG)
**LZ1**............ Luftschiff Zeppelin 1
**LZA**........... Labor Zionist Alliance (EA)
**LZAV**......... Latvijas PSR Zinatnu Akademijas. Vestis [*Riga*] [*A publication*]
**LZB**........... La-Z Boy Chair Co. [*NYSE symbol*] (SPSG)
**LZB**........... Literarisches Zentralblatt fuer Deutschland [*A publication*]
**LZCO**........ Landing Zone Control Officer [*Air Force*] (AFM)
**LZD**........... Launch Zone Display
**LZD**........... Literarisches Zentralblatt fuer Deutschland [*A publication*]
**LZDF**......... Launch Zone Display Flag
**LZEEBE**.... Long-Term Zonal Earth Energy Budget Experiment [*Spacecraft*] [*NASA*]
**LZER**......... LaserLand Corporation USA [*Aurora, CO*] [*NASDAQ symbol*] (NQ)
**LZF**........... Launch Zone Flag
**LZGF**......... Lewis Zero Gravity Facility
**LZGR**......... Lezak Group, Inc. [*NASDAQ symbol*] (NQ)
**LZH**........... Lanchow [*Republic of China*] [*Geomagnetic observatory code*]
**LZH**........... Lanchow [*Republic of China*] [*Seismograph station code, US Geological Survey*] (SEIS)
**LZIF**.......... Lyudmila Zhivkova International Foundation (EAIO)
**LZL**........... Landing Zone Locator
**LZL**........... Launcher, Zero Length [*British military*] (DMA)
**LZM**.......... Lysozyme [*An enzyme*]
**LZNAAN**.. Acta Zoologica Colombiana [*A publication*]
**LZO**........... Launch Zone Override
**LZOA**........ Labor Zionist Organization of America - Poale Zion [*Later, LZA*] (EA)
**LZOC**........ Lincoln Zephyr Owner's Club (EA)
**LZPC**......... Lead-Zinc Producers Committee (EA)
**LZR**........... Lazurus Distributors [*Vancouver Stock Exchange symbol*]
**LZR**........... Lizard Island [*Australia*] [*Airport symbol*] (OAG)
**LZT**........... Lead Zirconate Titanate [*Ferroelectric material*]
**LzT**........... Listy z Teatru [*A publication*]
**LZT**........... Local Zone Time
**LZU**........... Lincoln University, Lincoln University, PA [*OCLC symbol*] (OCLC)
**LZV**........... Lazarev [*USSR*] [*Later, NVL*] [*Geomagnetic observatory code*]
**LZW**.......... Olney-Noble, IL [*Location identifier*] [*FAA*] (FAAL)
**LZY**........... Greensboro, NC [*Location identifier*] [*FAA*] (FAAL)
**LZZ**........... Lampasas, TX [*Location identifier*] [*FAA*] (FAAL)

# M

M............... Absolute Magnitude [*Astronomy*]
M............... All India Reporter, Madras Series [*A publication*] (ILCA)
M............... Angular Momentum [*Symbol*] [*Physics*]
M............... Bending Moment [*Aerospace*] (AAG)
M-............... Days before Move Operation [*Usually followed by a number*] [*NASA*] (KSC)
M$............... Dollar [*Monetary unit*] [*Malaya*]
M............... Emma [*Phonetic alphabet*] [*In use in 1904 and 1914*] (DSUE)
M............... Field Goals Missed [*Football, basketball*]
M............... First Sergeant [*Army skill qualification identifier*] (INF)
M............... Ground, Mobile [*JETDS nomenclature*]
M............... Human Being Movement [*Rorschach*] [*Psychology*]
M............... Hungary [*IYRU nationality code*] (IYR)
M............... Imperial Chemical Industries [*Great Britain*] [*Research code symbol*]
M............... Indian Law Reports, Madras Series [*A publication*] (DLA)
M............... Instrumental Magnitude [*Earthquakes*]
M............... Intensity of Magnetization [*Symbol*] (DEN)
m------......... Intercontinental Areas (Eastern Hemisphere) [*MARC geographic area code*] [*Library of Congress*] (LCCP)
M............... J. F. Macfarlan & Co. [*Scotland*] [*Research code symbol*]
M............... M; the Civilized Man [*A publication*]
M............... M. Gentle Men for Gender Justice [*A publication*]
M............... Maasbode [*A publication*]
M............... Macerare [*Macerate*] [*Pharmacy*]
M............... Mach Number
M............... Machine
M............... MacNeil [*Herman A.*] [*Designer's mark, when appearing on US coins*]
M............... Macpherson's Scotch Session Cases [*1862-73*] [*A publication*] (DLA)
M............... Magister [*Master*] [*Latin*]
M............... Magistrate
M............... Magistratuur [*A publication*]
M............... Magnaflux
M............... Magnetic
M............... Magnetic Moment [*Symbol*] (DEN)
M............... Magnetic Polarization [*Symbol*] (DEN)
m ............... Magnetic Quantum Number [*Atomic physics*] [*Symbol*]
M............... Magnetron (MDG)
M............... Magnitude
M............... Maiden
M............... Mail
M............... Main
M............... Maintainability [*or Maintenance*] (MCD)
M............... Maintenance and Test Assemblies [*JETDS nomenclature*]
M............... Majesty
M............... Make
M............... Male [*Electronics*]
M............... Male
M............... Malignant [*Medicine*]
M............... Mammato [*Cloud formation*] (FAAC)
M............... Man
M............... Mandatory (KSC)
M............... Mane [*Morning*] [*Pharmacy*]
M............... Maneuvering Ship [*In speed triangle of relative movement problems*]
M............... Manichaean Middle Persian
M............... Manila [*Rope*]
M............... Manipulus [*A Handful*] [*Pharmacy*]
M............... Mannitol [*Organic chemistry*]
M............... Mano [*Hand*] [*Spanish*]
M............... Mantissa [*Decimal portion of a logarithm*]
M............... Manual
M............... Manuscripts [*A publication*]
M............... Map
M............... March
M............... Mare [*Thoroughbred racing*]
m ............... Marginal Propensity to Import [*Economics*]
M............... Maria [*Mary*]
M............... Marine [*Insurance*]
M............... Marine Corps [*When used as prefix with plane designation*]
M............... Marinus de Caramanico [*Flourished, 1269-85*] [*Authority cited in pre-1607 legal work*] (DSA)
M............... Maritime [*Air mass*] (FAAC)
M............... Maritus [*Bridegroom*] [*Latin*]
M............... Mark [*Monetary unit*] [*German*] (GPO)
M............... Marker [*Beacon*] (AFM)
M............... Marketing [*A publication*]
M............... Markka [*Monetary unit*] [*Finland*]
M............... Marksman [*British military*] (DMA)
M............... Maroon (FAAC)
M............... Marquis [*or Marquess*]
M............... Married
M............... Mars
M............... Marshal
M............... Martin Co. Division [*Martin-Marietta Corp.*] [*ICAO aircraft manufacturer identifier*] (ICAO)
M............... Martinus Gosia [*Authority cited in pre-1607 legal work*] (DSA)
M............... Martinus Zamorensis [*Flourished, 13th century*] [*Authority cited in pre-1607 legal work*] (DSA)
M............... Martyr
M............... Marxist [*Politics*]
M............... Masculine
M............... Mason (ROG)
M............... Mass
m ............... Mass [*Symbol*] [*IUPAC*]
M............... Massachusetts State Library, Boston, MA [*Library symbol*] [*Library of Congress*] (LCLS)
M............... Massage
M............... Masseur [*Ranking title*] [*British Royal Navy*]
M............... Massive [*Agriculture*]
M............... Master
M............... Mate [*of a ship*]
M............... Mater [*Mother*] [*Latin*]
M............... Mathematics [*Secondary school course*] [*British*]
M............... Matinee
M............... Matins [*Early morning prayers*]
M............... Matrix
M............... Matron [*British military*] (DMA)
M............... Mature
M............... Mature Audiences [*Movie rating*] [*Replaced by GP*]
M............... Mauthner [*Cell*] [*Neurology*]
M............... Maximal [*or Maximum*] [*Medicine*]
M............... Maximum Value [*Electronics*]
M............... Maxwell [*Electronics*] (DEN)
M............... May
M............... Mean [*Arithmetic average*]
M............... Mean Active Maintenance Downtime [*Data processing*]
M............... Mean Square
M............... Meaningfulness [*Psychology*]
M............... Measure [*Music*]
M............... Measured Ceiling [*Aviation*]
M............... Mechanical
M............... Mechlorethamine [*Also, HN, HN2, MBA, NM*] [*Mustargen, nitrogen mustard*] [*Antineoplastic drug*]
M............... Medal (ADA)
(M)............. Median
M............... Mediator
M............... Medical
M............... Medicinae [*Of Medicine*] [*Latin*]
M............... Medicine
M............... Medieval
M............... Medium [*Size designation for clothing, etc.*]
m ............... Medium [*Spectral*]
M............... Medium [*or 2-engine*] Plane
M............... Mega [*A prefix meaning multiplied by one million*] [*Symbol*]
M............... Megabyte [*Data storage capacity*] [*Data processing*]
M............... Megohm (AAG)
m ............... Mein [*My*] [*German*]
M............... Melbourne [*Mint mark*] [*Australia*]

**M**............... Melendus [*Flourished, 1188-1209*] [*Authority cited in pre-1607 legal work*] (DSA)

**M**............... Melittin [*Bee venom*]

**M**............... Melphalan [*Also, A, L-PAM, MPH, MPL*] [*Antineoplastic drug*]

**M**............... Melts At _____ [*Followed by a temperature*]

**M**............... Member

**M**............... Membrana [*Membrane*] [*Anatomy*]

**M**............... Memorandum

**M**............... Memoria [*Memory*] [*Latin*]

**M**............... Memorial; Journal Officiel du Grand Duche de Luxembourg [*A publication*] (ILCA)

**M**............... Memory

**M**............... Mensura [*By Measure*] [*Pharmacy*] (ROG)

**M**............... Mentum [*Chin*]

**M**............... Menzies' Cape Colony Supreme Court Reports [*A publication*] (DLA)

**M**............... Meperidine [*Also, MEP*] [*An analgesic*]

**M**............... Mercaptopurine [*Purinethol*] [*Also, MP, P*] [*Antineoplastic drug*]

**M**............... Mercury [*Chemical symbol is Hg*] (KSC)

**M**............... Merehurst [*Publisher*] [*British*]

**M**............... Merge [*Data processing*] (IBMDP)

**m** ............... Meridian (Lower Branch)

**M**............... Meridian (Upper Branch)

**M**............... Meridies [*Noon*] [*Latin*]

**M**............... Meridional Part [*Navigation*]

**M**............... Merkur [*A publication*]

**m** ............... Mes [*Month*] [*Business term*] [*Spanish*]

**M**............... Mesangium [*Anatomy*]

**M**............... Mesh

**M**............... Mesial [*Dentistry*]

**M**............... Mesomeric [*Organic chemistry*]

**M**............... Mesophyll [*Botany*]

**M**............... [*Admiral Sir Miles*] Messervy [*James Bond's superior in the Ian Fleming series of books and movies*]

**m** ............... Meta [*Chemistry*]

**M**............... Metabolite

**M**............... Metacenter

**M**............... Metal

**M**............... Metalsmith [*Navy*]

**M**............... Metamorphosis [*Phylogeny*]

**M**............... Metaproterenol [*Pharmacology*]

**M**............... Metastasis [*Oncology*]

**M**............... Meteorological [*JETDS nomenclature*]

**m** ............... Meter [*SI unit of length*]

**M**............... Methionine [*One-letter symbol; see Met*]

**M**............... Method

**M**............... Methodist

**M**............... Methotrexate [*Antineoplastic drug*]

**m** ............... Methyl [*As substituent on nucleoside*] [*Biochemistry*]

**M**............... Metoclopramide [*An antiemetic*]

**M**............... Metronome

**M**............... Metropolitan

**M**............... Mews

**M**............... Mezzo [*Moderate*] [*Music*]

**m** ............... Mi [*My*] [*Business term*] [*Spanish*]

**M**............... Michaelmas Term [*British*] [*Legal term*] (ILCA)

**M**............... Micrococcus [*Genus of bacteria*]

**M**............... Microphones [*JETDS nomenclature*] [*Military*] (CET)

**M**............... Microprocessor

**M**............... Microsporum [*Genus of fungi*]

**M**............... Microtubule [*Cytology*]

**M**............... Midazolan [*An anesthetic*]

**M**............... Midday (ADA)

**M**............... Middle

**M**............... Middle School [*British*]

**M**............... Midfield [*Men's lacrosse position*]

**M**............... Midline

**M**............... Midnight (ROG)

**m** ............... Midship [*Shipping*] (DS)

**M**............... Midwest Stock Exchange [*Chicago, IL*]

**M**............... Mike [*Phonetic alphabet*] [*World War II*] [*International*] (DSUE)

**M**............... Miles

**M**............... Miles' Pennsylvania Reports [*A publication*] (DLA)

**M**............... Military

**M**............... Military Airlift Command [*Military aircraft identification prefix*] (FAAC)

**M**............... Militia

**M**............... Milk (ROG)

**M**............... Mill

**M**............... Mille [*Thousand*] [*Roman numeral*]

**m** ............... Milli- [*A prefix meaning divided by 1000*] [*SI symbol*]

**M**............... Millime [*Monetary unit*] [*Tunisia*]

**M**............... Million

**M**............... Mine

**M**............... Minesweeper [*Navy*]

**M**............... Miniature [*Horticulture*]

**M**............... Minim

**M**............... Minimum (ADA)

**M**............... Ministry

**M**............... Minor

**M**............... Mint [*Condition*] [*Numismatics, etc.*]

**M**............... Minus

**M**............... Minute

**M**............... Miotic [*Biology*]

**M**............... Misce [*Mix*] [*Pharmacy*]

**M**............... Miscellaneous

**M**............... Miscible

**M**............... Mishnah [*Basis of the Talmud*] (BJA)

**M**............... Missile [*Air Force*]

**M**............... Missile Carrier Aircraft [*Designation for all US military aircraft*]

**M**............... Missing (FAAC)

**M**............... Missiology [*A publication*]

**M**............... Mission

**M**............... Mist [*Meteorology*]

**M**............... Mistura [*Mixture*] [*Pharmacy*]

**M**............... Mitic Subgroup [*Magnetite, chromite, hematite, ilmenite, titanite, perofskite, rutile*] [*CIPW classification*] [*Geology*]

**M**............... Mitochondrion [*Cytology*]

**M**............... Mitomycin [*Also, MC, MT*] [*Antineoplastic drug*]

**M**............... Mitosis [*Cytology*]

**M**............... Mitte [*Send*] [*Latin*]

**M**............... Mix [*or Mixture*]

**M**............... Mixed School [*British*]

**M**............... Mnemosyne [*A publication*]

**M**............... Mobile [*Missile launch environment symbol*] [*Biology*]

**M**............... Mobilization [*as in M-Day*] [*Military*] (AABC)

**M**............... Modal (Verb) [*Linguistics*]

**M**............... Mode

**M**............... Model [*in military nomenclature*]

**M**............... MODEM [*Data processing*]

**M**............... Moderate

**M**............... Moderate Sea or Swell [*Meteorology*]

**M**............... Modern [*Post-1920*] [*Deltiology*]

**M**............... Modified

**m** ............... Modified [*Regulation or order modified*] [*Used in Shepard's Citations*] [*Legal term*] (DLA)

**M**............... Modulation Depth [*Broadcasting*]

**M**............... Modulus

**M**............... Moisture

**m** ............... Molal [*Solute concentration by weight*] [*Chemistry*]

**M**............... Molar [*Permanent*] [*Dentistry*]

**M**............... Molar [*Solute concentration by volume*] [*Chemistry*]

**M**............... Molar Mass [*Symbol*] [*IUPAC*]

**M**............... Mole

**M**............... Molecular Weight [*Also, MOL WT, MW*]

**M**............... Moment

**M**............... Moment of Force [*Symbol*] [*IUPAC*]

**m/**.............. Mon [*My*] [*French*]

**M**............... Monastery

**M**............... Monday

**M**............... Monde [*A publication*]

**M**............... Money [*Economics*]

**M**............... Monitor (MDG)

**M**............... Monkey [*Phonetic alphabet*] [*Royal Navy*] [*World War I*] [*Pre-World War II*] (DSUE)

**M**............... Monoclonal [*Biochemistry*]

**M**............... Monocyte [*Hematology*]

**M**............... Monophage [*Biology*]

**M**............... Monoplane

**M**............... Monsieur [*Mister*] [*French*]

**M**............... Monsoon

**M**............... Mont [*Monte, etc.*] [*Italy and Sicily only*]

**M**............... Montana (DLA)

**M**............... Montavit Co. [*Austria*] [*Research code symbol*]

**M**............... Month

**M**............... Monthly

**M**............... Montmorillonite [*A mineral*]

**M**............... Montreal Stock Exchange

**M**............... Monumentum [*Monument*] [*Latin*]

**M**............... Moon

**M**............... Morgan [*George T.*] [*Designer's mark, when appearing on US coins*]

**M**............... Morison's Dictionary of Decisions, Scotch Court of Session [*1540-1808*] [*A publication*] (DLA)

**M**............... Morning

**m** ............... Morpha [*Form*] [*Biology*]

**M**............... Morphine [*Slang*]

**M**............... Morphological Rule [*Linguistics*]

**M**............... Morphometric Analysis [*Botany*]

**M**............... Mort [*Dead*] [*French*] (ROG)

**M**............... Mortar

**M**............... Mortgage

**M**............... Mortis [*Of Death*] [*Latin*]

**M**............... Motel

**M**............... Mother

**M**............... Motivational Ability

**M**............... Motor

**M**............... Motorship (DS)

M............... Motorway [*Traffic sign*] [*British*]
M............... Moulder [*Navy rating*] [*British*]
M............... Mound (MSA)
M............... Mountain
M............... Mountain Standard Time (FAAC)
M............... Mouth
M............... Move Being Made [*Data processing*]
M............... Movement [*Neurology*]
M............... Mucoid
M............... Mud
M............... Muddy [*Track condition*] [*Thoroughbred racing*]
M............... Muddy [*Quality of the bottom*] [*Nautical charts*]
M............... Multiplier
M............... Municipal Premises [*Public-performance tariff class*] [*British*]
M............... Murmur [*Heart*] [*Medicine*]
M............... Musculus [*Muscle*] [*Anatomy*]
M............... Museon. Revue d'Etudes Orientales [*A publication*]
M............... Music [*Films, television, etc.*]
M............... Musica [*A publication*]
M............... Musicology [*A publication*]
M............... Mustard Gas [*Also, H, HD, HS, HT*] [*Poison gas*] [*US Chemical Corps symbol*]
M............... Muster
M............... Mutitas [*Dullness*] [*Latin*]
M............... Mutual Companies
M............... Mutual Inductance [*Symbol*] [*IUPAC*]
M............... Mycelium [*Biology*]
M............... Mycobacterium [*Genus of microorganisms*]
M............... Myopia
M............... Myosin [*Muscle physiology*]
M............... New York Miscellaneous Reports [*A publication*] (DLA)
M............... Nomina [*Names*] [*Latin*] [*Probably a misprint for NN, by some supposed to denote St. Mary, patron saint of girls*] (ROG)
M............... Noon [*Meridies*]
M............... Ohio Miscellaneous Reports [*A publication*] (DLA)
M............... One Thousand [*Roman numeral*]
M............... Ordered Multistate [*Botany*]
M............... Queen Mary (DLA)
M............... Radiant Exitance [*Symbol*] [*IUPAC*]
M............... Reckitt & Sons Ltd. [*Great Britain*] [*Research code symbol*]
m ............... Response to Human Being Movement [*Rorschach*] [*Psychology*]
M............... Thioinosine [*One-letter symbol; see SIno, Sno*]
/M............... Thousand
M............... Time of Maneuver
1 M............ 1 Maccabees [*Old Testament book*]
$M_1$............ Mitral First Sound [*Cardiology*]
$M_1$............ Money Supply of a Country, Consisting of Currency and Demand Deposits [*Economics*]
2 M............ 2 Maccabees [*Old Testament book*]
M2............ Masterspec 2 [*Production Systems for Architects & Engineers, Inc.*] [*Information service or system*] (IID)
$M_2$............ Money Supply of a Country, Including $M_1$ and Commercial Time Deposits [*Economics*]
$M^2$............ Square Meter
$M^3$............ Cubic Meter
3M............ Maintenance and Material Management [*Navy*]
M3............ Military Manpower Models
3M............ Minnesota Mining & Manufacturing Co. [*Also, MMM*]
$M_3$............ Money Supply of a Country, Including $M_2$, Savings and Loan Association Deposits, and Certificates of Deposit [*Economics*]
9M............ Malaysia [*Aircraft nationality and registration mark*] (FAAC)
M12............ M12 [*Hawaii*] [*Seismograph station code, US Geological Survey*] [*Closed*] (SEIS)
M19............ Movimiento 19 de Abril [*Leftist guerrilla group*] [*Colombia*]
M50............ Mean of 1950 [*Coordinate system*] [*NASA*] (NASA)
3M's............ Manpower, Materials, Money
3M's............ Method, Meat, and Morality [*Cure for insanity, according to Victorian medical theory*]
4M's............ Medals, Muscles, Master's Degrees, and Marathons [*Means to advancement in the armed forces*]
M (Day)..... Mobilization Day [*Military*] (AFM)
M (Days).... Metrication Days [*Sponsored by the Metrication Board to educate merchants and public on metric system*] [*British*]
M (Way).... Motorway [*British*]
MA............ Aircraft Stations [*ITU designation*] (CET)
MA............ Amherst College, Amherst, MA [*Library symbol*] [*Library of Congress*] (LCLS)
ma----........ Arab States [*MARC geographic area code*] [*Library of Congress*] (LCCP)
MA............ Hungarian Airlines [*ICAO designator*] (FAAC)
MA............ Maandblad voor Accountancy en Bedrijfshuishoudkunde [*A publication*]
Ma............ Ma'arbae (BJA)
Ma............ Ma'aserot (BJA)
Ma............ Mach Number [*IUPAC*]
MA............ Machine Accountant [*Navy*]
MA............ Mackenzie News [*A publication*]
MA............ Madison Avenue [*A publication*]
MA............ Madras Artillery [*British military*] (DMA)
MA............ Magazine of Art [*A publication*]
MA............ Magister Artium [*Master of Arts*] [*Latin*]
MA............ Magma Arizona Railroad Co. [*Later, MAA*] [*AAR code*]
MA............ Magnesium Association [*Later, IMA*] (EA)
MA............ Magnetic Amplifier
MA............ Mahogany Association (EA)
MA............ Maids of Athena (EA)
MA............ Maintenance
MA............ Maintenance Ability (KSC)
MA............ Maintenance Actions
M/A.......... Maintenance Analysis (KSC)
MA............ Maintenance Area [*Military*] [*British*]
M & A........ Maintenance and Assembly (MCD)
MA............ Major (DSUE)
MA............ Maleic Anhydride [*Also, MAH*] [*Organic chemistry*]
MA............ Malignant Angioendotheliomatosis [*Oncology*]
MA............ Malonaldehyde [*Organic chemistry*]
MA............ Malpractice Association (EA)
MA............ Mamma (DSUE)
MA............ Management Abstracts [*A publication*]
MA............ Management Administration [*Department of Labor Statistics*] (OICC)
M & A........ Management and Administration
MA............ Management Adviser
MA............ Manager of Aviation
MA............ Manager's Assistant (DCTA)
MA............ Mangels Annahme [*For Non-Acceptance*] [*Business term*] [*German*]
MA............ Manifest Anxiety
MA............ Maniilaq Association (EA)
MA............ Manpower Administration [*Later, Employment and Training Administration*] [*Department of Labor*]
MA............ Manual
M/A.......... Manual or Automatic (NRCH)
MA............ Manufacturing Assembly
MA............ Manure (ROG)
MA............ Manx Airlines Ltd.
MA............ Map Analysis
MA............ March
Ma............ March's Action for Slander and Arbitrament [*A publication*] (DLA)
MA............ Margin Account [*Investment term*]
MA............ Marine Class
MA............ Maritime Administration [*Also, MARAD, MARITADMIN*] [*Department of Transportation*]
MA............ Mark [*Coin*] (ROG)
MA............ Market Average [*Investment term*]
MA............ Marketing Assistance (MCD)
MA............ Marriage Analysis [*Psychology*]
Ma............ Marsh [*Maps and charts*]
MA............ Marshaling Area [*Military*]
MA............ Martingana [*Ship's rigging*] (ROG)
Ma............ Martinus de Caramanico [*Flourished, 1269-85*] [*Authority cited in pre-1607 legal work*] (DSA)
Ma............ Martinus Gosia [*Authority cited in pre-1607 legal work*] (DSA)
Ma............ Maryland Music Educator [*A publication*]
MA............ Mass Analyzer
MA............ Massachusetts [*Postal code*]
MA............ Massachusetts Reports [*A publication*] (DLA)
MA............ Master (MSA)
MA............ Master Alarm
MA............ Master-at-Arms [*Navy*]
MA............ Master of Arts
MA............ Master Assistant [*British military*] (DMA)
MA............ Masters Abstracts [*A publication*]
MA............ Masurium
MA............ Mater [*Mother*] [*Latin*] (ADA)
MA............ Material Authorization (KSC)
Ma............ Matheus de Mathesillanis [*Flourished, 1381-1402*] [*Authority cited in pre-1607 legal work*] (DSA)
Ma............ Mattes [*Quality of the bottom*] [*Nautical charts*]
MA............ May
MA............ May Department Stores Co. [*NYSE symbol*] (SPSG)
MA............ Mazdaznan Association (EA)
MA............ Measurement Accuracy
MA............ Mechanical Accessories (MCD)
MA............ Mechanical Advantage
MA............ Mechanically Alloyed [*Metallurgy*]
MA............ Mechanician Apprentice [*British military*] (DMA)
MA............ Mechanoacoustic
MA............ Media Alliance (EA)
MA............ Medicaid (DLA)
MA............ Medical Annual [*A publication*]
MA............ Medical Assistance [*HEW*]
MA............ Medical Authority
M/A.......... Mediterranean/Adriatic [*Shipping*] (DS)
MA............ Mediterranean Area
MA............ Medium Aevum [*A publication*]
MA............ Medium Artillery
MA............ Mega [*A prefix meaning multiplied by one million*]
MA............ Megampere (IEEE)

**MA**............ Melanesian Alliance [*Political party*] [*Papua New Guinea*] (FEA)
**MA**............ Melodious Accord (EA)
**MA**............ Membrane Antigen [*Immunology*]
**MA**............ Memory Address [*Data processing*]
**MA**............ Menorah Association [*Defunct*] (EA)
**MA**............ Menstrual Age [*Medicine*]
**MA**............ Mental Age [*Psychology*]
**MA**............ Mentum Anterior [*In reference to the chin*]
**MA**............ Mercenary Association (EA)
**MA**............ Mercer Associates (EA)
**MA**............ Mercury Arc (MSA)
**MA**............ Mercury-Atlas [*Spacecraft*] [*NASA*]
**M & A**........ Mergers and Acquisitions
**M & A**........ Mergers & Acquisitions Data Base [*MLR Publishing Co.*] [*Information service or system*] (CRD)
**M/A**.......... Mess Attendant
**MA**............ Message Assembler
**MA**............ Messies Anonymous [*Commercial firm*] (EA)
**MA**............ Messing Allowance [*British military*] (DMA)
**MA**............ Metabolic Activity
**MA**............ Metabolic Analyzer
**MA**............ Metal Anchor (AAG)
**MA**............ Meter Amplifier
**MA**............ Meter Angle
**M/A**.......... Meters per Year
**MA**............ Methamphetamine [*Pharmacology*]
**MA**............ Methoxylamine [*Organic chemistry*]
**MA**............ Methyl Acrylate [*Organic chemistry*]
**MA**............ Methylanthranilic Acid
**MA**............ Metric Association [*Later, USMA*] (EA)
**MA**............ Mexican-American
**MA**............ Michigan Amber [*Variety of wheat*]
**MA**............ Microalloy
**MA**............ Microfilm Abstracts [*A publication*]
**MA**............ Microphone Amplifier
**MA**............ Microwave Associates, Inc. [*Later, M/A-Com*] (AAG)
**M-A**.......... Mid-America: An Historical Review [*A publication*]
**MA**............ Middeck Aft (MCD)
**MA**............ Middle Ages
**MA**............ Middle Assyrian [*Language, etc.*] (BJA)
**MA**............ Midmarch Associates (EA)
**MA**............ Midwest Academy (EA)
**MA**............ Mike Amplifier (NASA)
**MA**............ Mikes of America (EA)
**MA**............ Mileage Allowance
**MA**............ Miles Laboratories, Inc. [*Research code symbol*]
**MA**............ Military Academy
**MA**............ Military Accountant [*British military*] (DMA)
**MA**............ Military Administration
**MA**............ Military Affairs [*A publication*]
**MA**............ Military Aircraft
**MA**............ Military Assistance [*or Assistant*]
**MA**............ Military Attache [*Diplomacy*]
**MA**............ Military Aviator
**MA**............ Mill Annealed
**MA**............ Miller-Abbot (Tube) [*Medicine*]
**mA**............ Milliampere [*or Milliamperage*]
**Ma**............ Million Years Ago
**MA**............ Mind Association (EA)
**MA**............ Minimum Aircraft [*Powered hang gliders, replicas of early flying machines, etc.*] [*British*]
**MA**............ Ministry of Aviation [*British*]
**MA**............ Minnesota [*Obsolete*] (ROG)
**MA**............ Miscellaneous at Anchor [*Navy*] (NVT)
**MA**............ Miss Angle
**MA**............ Missed Appointment
**MA**............ Missed Approach [*Aviation*] (FAAC)
**MA**............ Missile Airframe (AAG)
**MA**............ Missile Away
**MA**............ Mission Accomplished [*Air Force*]
**MA**............ Mission Analysis (MCD)
**MA**............ Missionarius Apostolicus [*Missionary Apostolic*] [*Latin*]
**MA**............ Missouri Appeal Reports [*A publication*] (DLA)
**M & A**........ Missouri & Arkansas Railway Co.
**MA**............ Mistresses Anonymous (EA)
**MA**............ Mitotic Apparatus [*Cytology*]
**MA**............ Mobile Airlock (MCD)
**MA**............ Mobilization for Animals (EA)
**MA**............ Mobilization Augmentee [*Military*] (AFM)
**MA**............ Modern Age [*A publication*]
**MA**............ Modified Atmosphere [*Food technology*]
**MA**............ Modify Address (IEEE)
**MA**............ Monarchist Alliance (EA)
**MA**............ Monarticular Arthritis [*Medicine*]
**M/A**.......... Monetary Allowance
**M & A**........ Money and Advice
**MA**............ Monitoring Agency
**MA**............ Monoamine [*Chemistry*]
**MA**............ Monographs in Anaesthesiology [*Elsevier Book Series*] [*A publication*]
**M & A**........ Montagu and Ayrton's English Bankruptcy Reports [*1833-38*] [*A publication*] (DLA)
**MA**............ Monte Carlo Resources [*Vancouver Stock Exchange symbol*]
**MA**............ Moored Alongside [*Navy*] (NVT)
**MA**............ Moral Alternatives [*An association*] (EA)
**MA**............ Moreshet Archives [*Jerusalem*] (BJA)
**MA**............ Morocco [*ANSI two-letter standard code*] [*IYRU nationality code*] (CNC)
**MA**............ Mother's Aide [*Red Cross Nursing Services*]
**MA**............ Mothers of Asthmatics (EA)
**MA**............ Mountain Artillery
**MA**............ Moving Average [*Statistics*]
**MA**............ Moyen Age [*A publication*]
**MA**............ Multiple Access (NASA)
**MA**............ Multiple Application [*Military*] (AFIT)
**MA**............ Munitions Australia (DMA)
**MA**............ Munitions Tribunals Appeals, Great Britain High Court of Justice [*A publication*] (DLA)
**MA**............ Munitionsanstalt [*Ammunition Depot*] [*German military - World War II*]
**MA**............ Music Alliance (EA)
**MA**............ Musical Antiquary [*A publication*]
**MA**............ Musical Appreciation [*Record label*]
**MA**............ Mutagenic Activity
**MA**............ My Account [*Business term*]
**ma**............ Myria [*A prefix meaning multiplied by $10^4$*]
***MA1***.......... *Machine Accountant, First Class [Navy]*
**MA2**.......... Machine Accountant, Second Class [*Navy*]
**MA3**.......... Machine Accountant, Third Class [*Navy*]
**MAA**.......... Maastrichtial [*Paleontology*]
**MAA**.......... Maatschappijbelangen [*A publication*]
**MAA**.......... Macroaggregated Albumin [*Medicine*]
**MAA**.......... Madras [*India*] [*Airport symbol*] (OAG)
**MAA**.......... Magma Arizona Railroad Co. [*AAR code*]
**MAA**.......... Major Aircraft Accident (MCD)
**MAA**.......... Management Accounting [*A publication*]
**MAA**.......... Managing [*A publication*]
**MAA**.......... Manantiales [*Argentina*] [*Seismograph station code, US Geological Survey*] (SEIS)
**MAA**.......... Manufacturers Aircraft Association [*Supersedes AMA*] [*Defunct*] (EA)
**MAA**.......... Marina Association of America [*Defunct*] (EA)
**MAA**.......... Marineartillerieabteilung [*Naval Coast Artillery Battalion*] [*German military - World War II*]
**MA A**.......... Massachusetts Appeals Court Reports [*A publication*] (DLA)
**MAA**.......... Master of Applied Arts
**MAA**.......... Master-at-Arms [*Navy*]
**MAA**.......... Master Army Aviator
**MAA**.......... Material Access Area [*Nuclear energy*] (NRCH)
**MAA**.......... Mathematical Association of America (EA)
**MAA**.......... Maximum Authorized Altitude [*Aviation*]
**MAA**.......... Mecca Minerals Ltd. [*Vancouver Stock Exchange symbol*]
**MAA**.......... Mechanical Arm Assembly (NASA)
**MAA**.......... Mededeelingen. Koninklijke Nederlandsche Akademie van Wetenschappen te Amsterdam [*A publication*]
**MAA**.......... Mediaeval Academy of America (EA)
**MAA**.......... Medical Assistance for the Aged
**MAA**.......... Medium Antiaircraft Weapon (NATG)
**MAA**.......... Melanoma-Associated Antigen [*Oncology*]
**MAA**.......... Methacrylic Acid [*Organic chemistry*]
**MAA**.......... Methanearsonic Acid [*Organic chemistry*]
**MAA**.......... Mid-America Airways, Inc. [*Irving, TX*] [*FAA designator*] (FAAC)
**MAA**.......... Mission Area Analysis (MCD)
**MAA**.......... Mobilization Automation Appraisal (MCD)
**MAA**.......... Modeling Association of America [*Later, MAAI*]
**MAA**.......... Moderate Angle of Attack
**MAA**.......... Moped Association of America (EA)
**MAA**.......... Motel Association of America [*Later, National Innkeeping Association*]
**MAA**.......... Motor Agents' Association [*British*]
**MAA**.......... Municipal Arborist Association [*Later, MAUFS*] (EA)
**MAAA**........ Member of the American Academy of Actuaries
**MAAA**........ Memoirs. American Anthropological Association [*A publication*]
**MAAA**........ Metropolitan Area Apparel Association (EA)
**MAAAA**...... Mid-Am Antique Appraisers Association (EA)
**MAAB**........ Maintenance Air Abort [*Air Force*] (AFIT)
**MAAB**........ Materials Application Advisory Board [*NASA*] (NASA)
**MAABR**...... Maintenance Air Abort Rate [*Air Force*] (AFIT)
**MAAC**........ Maximum Allowable Actual Charge [*Medicare*]
**MAAC**........ Mid-Atlantic Area Council [*Regional power council*]
**MAAC**........ Mutual Assistance Advisory Committee
**MAACBA**... Middle Atlantic Association of Colleges of Business Administration
**MAACL**...... Multiple Affect Adjective Check List [*of Educational and Industrial Testing Service*] [*Psychology*]
**MAACP**...... Mediterranean Area Airlift Command Post (AFM)
**MAACS**...... Multi Address Asynchronous Communication System
**MAAF**........ Mediterranean Allied Air Force
**MAAF**........ Mediterranean Army Air Forces

**MAAF** ....... Michael Army Air Field (MCD)
**MAAF** ....... Museum Association of the American Frontier (EA)
**MAA-FDI** ... Museum of African Art - Frederick Douglass Institute [*Smithsonian Institution*] (EA)
**MAAFSc** ... Member of the Australian Academy of Forensic Science
**MAAG**....... Military Assistance Advisory Group [*Merged with US Military Assistance Command*]
**MAAH**....... Museum of African American History (EA)
**MAAH**....... Museum of Afro-American History (EA)
**MAAI** ....... Modeling Association of America International (EA)
**MAAL** ....... Monthly Adjustment Acceptance List [*Military*] (AFIT)
**MAAL** ....... Monumenti Antichi. Reale Accademia Nazionale dei Lincei [*A publication*]
**MAALOX** ... Magnesium-Aluminum Hydroxide [*Commercial antacid*]
**MAALT**..... Multiple Aircraft Approach and Landing Techniques (MCD)
**MAAM**...... Medium Antiaircraft Missile
**MAAN**....... Memorie. Reale Accademia di Archeologia, Lettere, e Belle Arti di Napoli [*A publication*]
**MAAN**....... Methyleneaminoacetonitrile [*Organic chemistry*]
**MAAN**....... Mutual Advertising Agency Network [*Grand Forks, ND*] (EA)
**Maandbl Landbouwvoorlichtingsdienst (Neth)** ... Maandblad voor de Landbouwvoorlichtingsdienst (Netherlands) [*A publication*]
**Maandbl Pieper** ... Maandblad de Pieper [*A publication*]
**Maandbl Vlaam Bieenb** ... Maandblad van de Vlaamse Bieenbond [*A publication*]
**Maandbl Vlaam Imkersb** ... Maandblad van de Vlaamse Imkersbond [*A publication*]
**Maandschr Bijent** ... Maandschrift voor Bijenteelt [*A publication*]
**Maandschr Kindergeneeskd** ... Maandschrift voor Kindergeneeskunde [*A publication*]
**MAANPI**... Mutual Aid Association of the New Polish Immigration (EA)
**MAAP** ....... Maintenance and Administration Panel [*Bell System*]
**MAAP** ....... Material Access Authorization Program [*Nuclear energy*] (NRCH)
**MAAP** ....... Milan Army Ammunition Plant (AABC)
**MAAR**....... MarCor Resorts, Inc. [*NASDAQ symbol*] (NQ)
**MAAR**....... Memoirs. American Academy at Rome [*A publication*]
**MAAR**....... Monthly Associate Administrator's Review [*NASA*] (NASA)
**MAARC** .... Magnetic Annular Arc (IEEE)
**MA Arch**.... Master of Arts in Architecture
**MAARM** ... Memory-Aided Antiradiation Missile (MCD)
**Ma'as**......... Ma'asroth (BJA)
**MAAS** ....... Manpower Allocation and Accounting Subsystem [*Air Force*] (AFM)
**MAAS** ....... Muhammad Ali Amateur Sports
**MAAS** ....... Multiple Array Avionics Subsystem
**MAASc**...... Member of the Australian Academy of Science
**MA(AsianStudies)** ... Master of Arts (Asian Studies)
**MAASL**..... Military Assistance Article and Service List (AFIT)
**MAASLA**.. Movimiento Argentino Antiimperialista de Solidaridad Latinoamericana
**Ma'asSh** .... Ma'aser Sheni (BJA)
**MAA Stud Math** ... MAA [*Mathematical Association of America*] Studies in Mathematics [*A publication*]
**MAAT** ....... MAC [*McDonnell Aircraft Corporation*] Acquisition and Attack Trainer (MCD)
**MAAT** ....... Management of Advanced Automation Technology Center [*Worcester Polytechnic Institute*] [*Research center*] (RCD)
**MAAT** ....... McCormick Affective Assessment Technique [*Teacher evaluation test*]
**MAAT** ....... Member of the Association of Accounting Technicians [*British*] (DCTA)
**MAATAG** ... Mission Area Analysis Test Advisory Group [*Army*]
**Maatalouden Tutkimuskeskus Maantutkimuslaitos Agrogeol Julk** ... Maatalouden Tutkimuskeskus. Maantutkimuslaitos. Agrogeologisia Julkaisuja [*A publication*]
**Maatalouden Tutkimuskeskus Maantutkimuslaitos Agrogeol Kart** ... Maatalouden Tutkimuskeskus. Maantutkimuslaitos. Agrogeologisia Karttoja [*A publication*]
**Maataloushal Aikakausk** ... Maataloushallinon Aikakauskirja [*A publication*]
**Maatalous Koetoim** ... Maatalous ja Koetoiminta [*A publication*]
**Maataloust Aikakausk** ... Maataloustieteelinen Aikakauskirja [*A publication*]
**Maataloustiet Aikak** ... Maataloustieteelinen Aikakauskirja [*A publication*]
**Maataloustieteelinen Aikak** ... Maataloustieteelinen Aikakauskirja [*A publication*]
**MAATC** .... Mobile Antiaircraft Training Center
**MAAU**....... Mexican-American Affairs Unit [*Office of Education*]
**MAAV**....... Maritime Archaeology Association of Victoria [*Australia*]
**MAAW**...... Medium Antitank Assault Weapon
**MAAWS**.... Middle Atlantic Association of Women Sailors
**MAB** .......... Maandblad voor Accountancy en Bedrijfshuishoudkunde [*A publication*]
**MAB** .......... Macroaddress Bus
**MAB** .......... Magazine Advertising Bureau [*of MPA*]
**MAB** .......... Magazine of Bank Administration [*A publication*]
**MAB** .......... Magnetic Amplifier Bridge
**MAB** .......... Mainly about Books [*A publication*]
**MAB** .......... Malfunction Analysis Branch [*NASA*]
**MAB** .......... Man and the Biosphere Program [*UNESCO*] [*Paris, France*]
**MAB** .......... Management Analysis Branch [*Vietnam*]
**MAB** .......... Manganese Alkaline Battery
**MAB** .......... Manhay [*Belgium*] [*Geomagnetic observatory code*]
**MAB** .......... Manual d'Archeologie Biblique [*A publication*] (BJA)
**MAB** .......... Maraba [*Brazil*] [*Airport symbol*] (OAG)
**MAB** .......... Marine Air Base
**MAB** .......... Marine Amphibious Brigade
**MAB** .......... Master Acquisition Bus [*Data processing*] (MCD)
**MAb**........... Masters Abstracts [*A publication*]
**MAB** .......... Materials Advisory Board [*Later, NMAB*] [*NAS-NRC*]
**MAB** .......... Materials Applications Board (MCD)
**MAB** .......... Mechanical Automation Breadboard (KSC)
**MAB** .......... Medical Advisory Board
**MAB** .......... Member, Advisory Board
**MAB** .......... Memoires. Academie Royale de Belgique [*A publication*]
**MAB** .......... Memorial Advisory Bureau [*British*] (CB)
**MAB** .......... Methylaminoazobenzene [*Organic chemistry*]
**MAB** .......... Metropolitan Asylums Board [*British*]
**MAB** .......... Mid-America Bancorp [*AMEX symbol*] (SPSG)
**MAB** .......... Millardair Ltd. [*Mississauga, ON*] [*FAA designator*] (FAAC)
**MAB** .......... Missile Activation Building [*NWA*]
**MAB** .......... Missile Assembly Building (MCD)
**MAB** .......... Mission Analysis Branch [*Manned Spacecraft Center*]
**MAB** .......... Mobile Assault Bridge [*Army*]
**MAb**........... Monoclonal Antibody [*Immunochemistry*]
**MAB** .......... Multibase Arithmetic Block (ADA)
**MAB** .......... Munitions Assignment Board [*Anglo-American*] [*World War II*]
**MAB** .......... Mutual Air Board [*Canada*] [*World War II*]
**MABA** ....... Meta-Aminobenzoic Acid [*Organic chemistry*]
**MABAC** .... Member of the Association of Business and Administrative Computing [*British*] (DBQ)
**MABCGT** ... Mutual Adjustment Bureau of Cloth and Garment Trades [*Inactive*] (EA)
**MABDG**.... Marine Aircraft Base Defense Group
**MABDW**... Marine Air Base Defense Wing
**MABE** ....... Master of Arts in Business Education
**MABE** ....... Member of the Association of Business Executives (DCTA)
**MABF**........ Master of Agricultural Business and Finance
**MABF**........ Mobile Assault Bridge/Ferry [*Army*] (RDA)
**MABFAI** ... Muenchener Beitraege zur Abwasser-, Fischerei-, und Flussbiologie [*A publication*]
**MABFEX**.. Marine Amphibious Brigade Field Exercise (NVT)
**MABL**........ Mass Addition Boundary Layer Program [*NASA*]
**M & ABL**... Montagu and Ayrton's Bankrupt Laws [*A publication*] (DLA)
**MABLE**..... Miniature Autonetics Baseline Equipment
**MABLEX**.. Marine Amphibious Brigade Landing Exercise (NVT)
**MABM**....... Multilayer Absorbing Bottom Layer
**MABNET** ... Global Network for Monitoring the Biosphere [*Marine science*] (MSC)
**MABO** ....... Marianas-Bonins Group
**MABOP** .... Mustargen [*Nitrogen mustard*], Adriamycin, Bleomycin, Oncovin [*Vincristine*], Prednisone [*Antineoplastic drug regimen*]
**MABP**........ Mean Arterial Blood Pressure [*Medicine*]
**MABPD**..... Military Assistance Basic Planning Document (CINC)
**MABRON** ... Marine Air Base Squadron
**MABS**........ Maltese-American Benevolent Society (EA)
**MABS**........ Marine Air Base Squadron
**MABS**........ Mixed Air Battle Simulation
**MABS**........ Monoclonal Antibodies, Inc. [*NASDAQ symbol*] (NQ)
**MABS**........ Moored Acoustic Buoy System [*Marine science*] (MSC)
**MABU** ....... Maschinengewehr-Eisenbeton-Unterstand [*Machine-Gun-Iron-Reinforced Concrete Emplacement*] [*German "pill box," battlefield redoubts*] [*World War I*]
**MAC** .......... Chief Machine Accountant [*Later, DPC*] [*Navy rating*]
**MAC** .......... Commercial Courier [*A publication*]
**MAC** .......... MAC [*Media Agencies Clients*]/Western Advertising [*A publication*]
**MAC** .......... Macabre [*A publication*]
**MAC** .......... Macadam (ADA)
**MAC** .......... Macalester College, Weyerhaeuser Library, St. Paul, MN [*OCLC symbol*] (OCLC)
**MAC** .......... MacAndrew [*Alcoholism scale*]
**Mac**............ Macassey's New Zealand Reports [*A publication*] (DLA)
**MAC** .......... Macau [*ANSI three-letter standard code*] (CNC)
**Mac**............ Macbeth [*Shakespearean work*]
**MAC** .......... Maccabees [*Old Testament book*] [*Roman Catholic canon*] (ROG)
**MAC** .......... MacConkey [*Agar*] [*Microbiology*]
**mac**............ Macedonian [*MARC language code*] [*Library of Congress*] (LCCP)
**MAC** .......... Macerare [*Macerate*] [*Pharmacy*]
**MAC** .......... Machine-Aided Cognition [*Computer project*] [*Massachusetts Institute of Technology*]
**MAC** .......... Mackerel [*Pimp*] [*Slang*] (DSUE)
**MAC** .......... Mackintosh (DSUE)
**Mac**............ Maclean's [*A publication*]
**Mac**............ Macmillan's Magazine [*A publication*]
**Mac**............ Macnaghten's English Chancery Reports [*A publication*] (DLA)

**MAC**......... Macon, GA [*Location identifier*] [*FAA*] (FAAL)
**MAC**......... Magistrates' Appeal Cases [*A publication*] (DLA)
**MAC**......... Magnetic Attitude Control
**MAC**......... Magnetic Automatic Calculator (DEN)
**MAC**......... Maintenance Advisory Committee [*NSIA*]
**MAC**......... Maintenance Allocation Chart [*Military*]
**MAC**......... Maintenance Analysis Center [*FAA*]
**MAC**......... Major Activity Center
**MAC**......... Major Air Command [*Later, MAJCOM*]
**MAC**......... Malignancy-Associated Changes [*Cancer*]
**MAC**......... Mammary Carcinoma [*Oncology*]
**MAC**......... Man and Computer (DIT)
**MAC**......... Management Accounting [*A publication*]
**MAC**......... Maneuver Analysis and Command
**MAC**......... Maneuver Area Command [*Army*]
**MAC**......... Manpower Advisory Committee (OICC)
**MAC**......... Manual Assistance Centre [*Australia*]
**MAC**......... Marine Affairs Council [*Marine science*] (MSC)
**MAC**......... Marine Amphibious Corps
**MAC**......... Maritime Advisory Committee [*Terminated, 1968*]
**MAC**......... Maritime Air Command [*Canada*] [*NATO*] (NATG)
**MAC**......... Mark West Springs [*California*] [*Seismograph station code, US Geological Survey*] (SEIS)
**MAC**......... Marker and Cell [*Computing technique*] [*NASA*]
**MAC**......... Mass Absorption Coefficient
**MAC**......... Massive Algebraic Computation [*Programming language*] [*1958*] [*Data processing*] (CSR)
**M Ac**......... Master of Accounting
**MAC**......... Material Availability Commitment (AAG)
**MAC**......... Materials Analysis Company
**MAC**......... Maximum Acid Concentration [*Clinical chemistry*]
**MAC**......... Maximum Admissible [*or Allowable*] Concentration
**MAC**......... Maximum Allowable Cost [*Medicare, Medicaid*]
**MAC**......... Maximum Atmospheric Concentration
**MAC**......... McLeod Aerating Cardiac
**MAC**......... McMaster University [*Hamilton, ON*] (DSUE)
**MAC**......... Mean Aerodynamic Center
**MAC**......... Mean Aerodynamic Chord
**MAC**......... Measurement and Analysis Center [*Telecommunications*] (TEL)
**MAC**......... Mechanical Advantage Changer
**MAC**......... Mechanical Analog Computer (DEN)
**MAC**......... Media Access Control [*Telecommunications*]
**MAC**......... Media Action Coalition (EA)
**Mac**......... Media, Agencies, Clients [*Later, Adweek*] [*A publication*]
**MAC**......... Medical Administrative Corps [*Army*] [*World War II*]
**MAC**......... Medical Advisory Committee [*IATA*] (DS)
**MAC**......... Medical Alert Center
**MAC**......... Mediterranean Air Command [*Military*]
**MAC**......... Medium Access Control
**MAC**......... Membrane Affinity Chromatography
**MAC**......... Membrane Applications Centre [*University of Bath*] [*British*] (CB)
**MAC**......... Membrane Attack Complex [*Biochemistry*]
**MAC**......... Memorias. Academia das Ciencias de Lisboa. Classe de Letras [*A publication*]
**MAC**......... Memory Access Controller
**MAC**......... Men after Christ Band [*R & B recording group*]
**MAC**......... Merchant Aircraft Carrier [*A ship carrying a cargo of oil or grain and provided with a flight deck for the operation of antisubmarine aircraft*] [*British*] [*World War II*]
**MAC**......... Mergers and Acquisitions [*A publication*]
**MAC**......... Message Authentication Code
**MAC**......... Metabolic and Analytical Chemistry
**MAC**......... Metacarpal Ash per Centimeter
**MAC**......... Metal Arc Cutting [*Welding*]
**MAC**......... Methotrexate, Actinomycin D, Cyclophosphamide [*Antineoplastic drug regimen*]
**MAC**......... Methyl Acetamido Cinnamate [*Organic chemistry*]
**MAC**......... Methyl Allyl Chloride [*Organic chemistry*]
**MAC**......... Michigan Apple Committee (EA)
**MAC**......... Microcomputer Applications Centre [*Australia*]
**MAC**......... Microcystic Adnexal Carcinoma [*Oncology*]
**MAC**......... Microfilm Aperture Card
**MAC**......... Microwave-Assisted Curing [*Chemical engineering*]
**MAC**......... Mid-American Conference [*College football*]
**MAC**......... Midarm Circumference
**MAC**......... Middle Atlantic Conference, East Riverdale MD [*STAC*]
**MAC**......... Midwest Archives Conference (EA)
**MAC**......... Military Aid to the Community [*British military*] (DMA)
**Mac**......... Military Aircraft Command [*Airline call sign*]
**MAC**......... Military Airlift Command [*Formerly, Military Air Transport Service*]
**MAC**......... Military/Allied Commission [*World War II*]
**MAC**......... Military Armistice Commission (KSC)
**MAC**......... Military Assistance Command (CINC)
**MAC**......... Mine Advisory Committee [*NAS-NRC*] (MCD)
**MAC**......... Mineralogical Association of Canada
**MAC**......... Mini-Accommodation Center [*In MAC-1, a low-cost, plastic sleeping module promoted by Texas businessman Charles McLaren*]
**MAC**......... Minimal Alveolar Concentration [*Anesthesiology*]
**MAC**......... Mining Association of Canada
**MAC**......... Missile Activation Circuit
**MAC**......... Missile Advisory Committee [*Pacific Missile Range*] (MUGU)
**MAC**......... Mission Assignment Code (NATG)
**MAC**......... Mitomycin C, Adriamycin, Cyclophosphamide [*Antineoplastic drug regimen*]
**MAC**......... Mitral Annular Calcification [*Cardiology*]
**MAC**......... MIUW [*Mobile Inshore Undersea Warfare*] Attack Craft [*Navy symbol*]
**MAC**......... Mixed Armistice Commission [*Arab-Israel borders*] (BJA)
**MAC**......... Mobile Inshore Undersea Warfare Attack Craft [*Navy*] (MCD)
**MAC**......... Model Airplane Club
**MAC**......... Model Algorithmic Control [*Chemical engineering*] [*Data processing*]
**MAC**......... Modern Arts Criticism [*A publication*]
**MAC**......... Modern Authors Checklist [*Publication series*]
**MAC**......... Monthly Availability Charge (BUR)
**MAC**......... Months after Contract Award
**MAC**......... Morning-After Call [*Sales*]
**MAC**......... Mosaic Resources Ltd. [*Vancouver Stock Exchange symbol*]
**MAC**......... Motion Analysis Camera
**MAC**......... Motor Accidents Cases [*A publication*] (APTA)
**MAC**......... Motor Ambulance Convoy
**MAC**......... MOUT [*Military Operations on Urbanized Terrain*] Assault Course (INF)
**MAC**......... Movimiento Amplio Colombiano [*Broad-Based Movement of Colombia*] [*Political party*] (PPW)
**MAC**......... Mudiad Amdyffyn Cymru [*Welsh Defense Movement*]
**MAC**......... Multiaction Computer
**MAC**......... Multiple Access Computer
**MAC**......... Multiple Access Control [*Data processing*] (DIT)
**MAC**......... Multiple Address Code
**MAC**......... Multiple Array Correlation (CAAL)
**MAC**......... Multiplexed Analog Component [*Satellite television*] [*British*]
**MAC**......... Multipurpose Arthritis Center [*Medical University of South Carolina*] [*Research center*]
**MAC**......... [*Robert B. Brigham*] Multipurpose Arthritis Center [*Brigham and Women's Hospital*] [*Research center*] (RCD)
**MAC**......... Municipal Assistance Corporation [*New York*] [*Also known as "Big Mac"*]
**MAC**......... Munitions Assignments Committee [*World War II*]
**MAC**......... Museums Association of Canada
**MAC**......... Musiciens Amateurs du Canada [*Canadian Amateur Musicians*] (EAIO)
**MAC**......... Mycobacterium Avium-Intracellulare Complex [*Bacteriology*]
**MACA**....... Mammoth Cave National Park
**MACA**....... Maritime Air Control Authority [*NATO*] (NATG)
**MAcA**....... Master of the Acupuncture Association [*British*] (DBQ)
**MACA**....... Master of Arts in Communication Arts
**MAcA**....... Member of the Acupuncture Association [*British*]
**MACA**....... Mexican-American Correctional Association (OICC)
**MACA**....... Military Airlift Clearance Authority (AABC)
**MACA**....... Mini-America's Cup Association (EA)
**MAC(A)**..... Munitions Assignments Committee (Air) [*World War II*]
**MACABRE** ... Material Ablation with Chemically Active Boundary Layers in Reentry [*NASA*]
**Mac Acta A** ... Macedoniae Acta Archaeologica [*A publication*]
**MACAF**..... Mediterranean Allied Coastal Air Forces
**MACAL**..... Military Airlift Command Airlift Operations Report
**Macalp Mon L** ... Macalpin on Money Lenders [*A publication*] (DLA)
**MACAM** ... Military Airlift Command Automated Management
**MACAP**..... Major Appliance Consumer Action Panel (EA)
**Mac A Pat Cas** ... MacArthur's Patent Cases [*District of Columbia*] [*A publication*] (DLA)
**MAC-API** ... Mordechai Anielewicz Circle of Americans for Progressive Israel (EA)
**MacAr**........ MacArthur's Patent Cases [*A publication*] (DLA)
**MacAr**........ MacArthur's Reports [*8-10 District of Columbia*] [*A publication*] (DLA)
**MacAr & M** ... MacArthur and Mackey's District of Columbia Supreme Court Reports [*A publication*] (DLA)
**MacAr & Mackey** ... MacArthur and Mackey's District of Columbia Supreme Court Reports [*A publication*] (DLA)
**Macaroni J** ... Macaroni Journal [*A publication*]
**MacAr Pat Cas** ... MacArthur's Patent Cases [*District of Columbia*] [*A publication*] (DLA)
**MACARS**.. Microfilm Aperture Card Automated Retrieval System
**MacArth**.... MacArthur's Patent Cases [*A publication*] (DLA)
**MacArth**.... MacArthur's Reports [*8-10 District of Columbia*] [*A publication*] (DLA)
**MacArth Ct Mar** ... MacArthur on Courts-Martial [*A publication*] (DLA)
**MacArth & M** ... MacArthur and Mackey's District of Columbia Supreme Court Reports [*A publication*] (DLA)
**MacArth & M (Dist Col)** ... MacArthur and Mackey's District of Columbia Supreme Court Reports [*A publication*] (DLA)
**MacArth Pat Cas** ... MacArthur's Patent Cases [*United States*] [*A publication*] (DLA)
**MacArthur** ... MacArthur's Patent Cases [*A publication*] (DLA)
**MacArthur** ... MacArthur's Reports [*8-10 District of Columbia*] [*A publication*] (DLA)

**MacArthur & M** ... MacArthur and Mackey's District of Columbia Supreme Court Reports [*A publication*] (DLA)
**MacArthur Pat Cas** ... MacArthur's Patent Cases [*United States*] [*A publication*] (DLA)
**Macas** ......... Macassey's New Zealand Reports [*A publication*] (DLA)
**MACAS**..... Magnetic Capability and Safety System (NVT)
**Macask Ex** ... Macaskie on Executors, Etc. [*A publication*] (DLA)
**Macaulay Hist Eng** ... Macaulay's History of England [*A publication*] (DLA)
**Macaulay Inst Soil Res Annu Rep** ... Macaulay Institute for Soil Research. Annual Report [*A publication*]
**Macaulay Inst Soil Res Collect Pap** ... Macaulay Institute for Soil Research. Collected Papers [*A publication*]
**MACB** ....... Missile Assembly Control Building
**MACBAB** ... Memorias. Real Academia de Ciencias y Artes de Barcelona [*A publication*]
**MACBASIC** ... Measurement and Control BASIC [*Programming language developed by Analog Devices*]
**Macc** .......... Maccabees [*Old Testament book*] [*Roman Catholic canon*]
**MACC** ....... Madison Academic Computing Center [*University of Wisconsin - Madison*] [*Information service or system*] [*Research center*]
**MACC** ....... Malaysian-American Chamber of Commerce [*Later, AAACC*]
**M Acc** ........ Master of Accountancy [*or Accounting*]
**MACC** ....... Methotrexate, Adriamycin, Cyclophosphamide, CCNU [*Lomustine*] [*Antineoplastic drug regimen*]
**MACC** ....... MidAmerican Communications Corp. [*Telecommunications service*] (TSSD)
**MACC** ....... Military Aid to Civil Community [*British*]
**MACC** ....... Ministerial Advisory Committee on Co-Operation [*Victoria, Australia*]
**MACC** ....... Mobility-Affect-Cooperation-Communication [*Psychiatry*]
**MACC** ....... Modular Alter and Compose Console [*Data processing*]
**MacCarthy** ... MacCarthy's Irish Land Cases [*A publication*] (DLA)
**Mac CC**...... MacGillivray's Copyright Cases [*1901-49*] [*A publication*] (DLA)
**Macc Cas** ... Maccala's Breach of Promise Cases [*A publication*] (DLA)
**Macch Motori Agr** ... Macchine e Motori Agricoli [*A publication*]
**Maccl** ......... Maccala's Reports [*Modern Reports, Part X*] [*1710-25*] [*A publication*] (DLA)
**Maccl Tr**.... Macclesfield's Trial (Impeachment) [*1725*] [*London*] [*A publication*] (DLA)
**Mac CM** .... Macomb on Courts-Martial [*A publication*] (DLA)
**M Acco**....... Master of Accounting
**M Accounting** ... Management Accounting [*A publication*]
**MACCS**..... Manufacturing Cost Collection System
**MACCS**..... Marine Air Command and Control System (NVT)
**M Accs**....... Master of Accounts
**MACCS**..... Molecular Access System [*Computer program*]
**MACCT**..... Multiple Assembly Cooling Cask Test [*Nuclear energy*] (NRCH)
**M ACCUR** ... Misce Accuratissime [*Mix Thoroughly*] [*Pharmacy*]
**MACD**....... MacDermid, Inc. [*NASDAQ symbol*] (NQ)
**MacD**......... MacDevitt's Irish Land Commissioner's Reports [*A publication*] (DLA)
**MACD**....... Metabolic Aspects of Cardiovascular Disease [*Elsevier Book Series*] [*A publication*]
**MACDA**.... Michigan Academician [*A publication*]
**MACDAC** ... Machine Communication with Digital Automatic Computer
**MACDAC** ... McDonnell Douglas Corporation (KSC)
**MACDATA** ... Materials and Components Development and Testing Association [*Paisley College of Technology*] [*United Kingdom*] (IRUK)
**MACDC** .... Military Assistance Command Director of Construction
**MacDermott Commission** ... Commission on the Isle Of Man Constitution. Report [*1959*] [*A publication*] (DLA)
**MacDev** ..... MacDevitt's Irish Land Cases [*1882-84*] [*A publication*] (DLA)
**Macd Jam** ... Macdougall's Jamaica Reports [*A publication*] (DLA)
**MACDS**..... Monitor and Control Display System (MCD)
**MACE** ....... Machine-Aided Composition and Editing
**MACE** ....... Maintenance Analysis Checkout Equipment
**MACE** ....... Management Applications in a Computer Environment (IEEE)
**MACE** ....... Managing Company Expansion [*Manpower Services Commission*] [*British*]
**MACE** ....... Marginal Absolute Certainty Equivalent [*Statistics*]
**MACE** ....... Master of Air Conditioning Engineering
**MACE** ....... Master of Arts in Civil Engineering
**MACE** ....... Mechanical Antenna Control Electronics (MCD)
**MACE** ....... Member of the Association of Conference Executives [*British*] (DBQ)
**MACE** ....... Member of the Australian College of Education
**MACE** ....... Methylchloroform Chloroacetophenone [*Riot-control gas*]
**MACE** ....... Mid-America Commodity Exchange [*Chicago, IL*]
**MACE** ....... Military Air Cargo Export [*Subsystem*]
**MACE** ....... Military Airlift Capability Estimator
**MACE** ....... Military Airlift Center, Europe (MCD)
**MACE** ....... Minority Advisory Committee on Energy [*Terminated, 1982*] (EGAO)
**Maced** ........ Macedonia
**MACED** .... Macedonian
**MACEJ** ..... Manitoba Association of Confluent Education. Journal [*A publication*]
**MAC Eng** .. Master of Air Conditioning Engineering
**MACER**..... Macerare [*Macerate*] [*Pharmacy*]
**MacF**.......... MacFarlane's Scotch Jury Court Reports [*1838-39*] [*A publication*] (DLA)
**MacF**.......... MacFarlane's Scotch Jury Trials [*A publication*] (DLA)
**MacFar**...... MacFarlane's Scotch Jury Court Reports [*1838-39*] [*A publication*] (DLA)
**MacFarl**..... MacFarlane's Scotch Jury Trials [*A publication*] (DLA)
**MacFarlane** ... MacFarlane's Scotch Jury Trials [*A publication*] (DLA)
**Macf Cop** ... Macfie on Copyright [*A publication*] (DLA)
**Macf Min**... Macfarland's Digest of Mining Cases [*A publication*] (DLA)
**MacF Pr**..... MacFarlane's Practice of the Court of Sessions [*A publication*] (DLA)
**Mac & G** .... Macnaghten and Gordon's English Chancery Reports [*A publication*] (DLA)
**MACG** ....... Maneuver Analysis and Command Group
**MACG** ....... Marine Air Control Group
**MACG** ....... Marshaling Area Control Group [*Military*] (AABC)
**MAC(G)** .... Munitions Assignments Committee (Ground) [*World War II*]
**MACGC** .... Equilink Corporation [*NASDAQ symbol*] (NQ)
**MacG CC**... MacGillivray's Copyright Cases [*1901-49*] [*A publication*] (DLA)
**MacGillivray & Parkington** ... MacGillivray and Parkington's Insurance Law [*6th ed.*] [*1975*] [*A publication*] (DLA)
**Mac & H** .... Cox, Macrae, and Hertslet's Reports, Crown Cases [*1847-58*] [*England*] [*A publication*] (DLA)
**MACH**....... Machabees [*Old Testament book*] [*Douay version*]
**MACH**....... Machine [*or Machinery*]
**Mach**.......... Machinery [*Later, Machinery and Production Engineering*] [*A publication*]
**MACH**....... Military Air Command Hunter [*In MACH 3, a video game by Mylstar Electronics*]
**MACH**....... Modular Automated Container Handling [*Shipping*] (DS)
**MACHA**.... Michigan Automated Clearing House Association
**MACHA**.... Mid-Atlantic Clearinghouse Association [*Maryland, Virginia, and Washington, DC*]
**MACHA**.... Midwest Automated Clearing House Association
**MACHA**.... Military Armistice Commission Headquarters Area (INF)
**Mach Agric Equip Rural** ... Machinisme Agricole et Equipement Rural [*France*] [*A publication*]
**Mach Agric Trop** ... Machinisme Agricole Tropical [*A publication*]
**Mach Agr Trop** ... Machinisme Agricole Tropical [*A publication*]
**MACHALT** ... Machinery Alteration
**Mach Build Ind** ... Machine Building Industry [*India*] [*A publication*]
**MACHDC** ... Machinability Data Center [*Computerized search services*] [*Metcut Research Associates, Inc.*]
**Mach Des** .. Machine Design [*A publication*]
**Mach Design** ... Machine Design [*A publication*]
**MA Chem** .. Master of Applied Chemistry
**Mach Equip Food Ind** ... Machinery and Equipment for Food Industry [*A publication*]
**MACHGR** ... Machine Group
**MA(ChildLit/Reading)** ... Master of Arts in Children's Literature and Reading
**MACHIMPEX** ... China National Machinery Import & Export Corp. [*People's Republic of China*] (IMH)
**Machine D** ... Machine Design [*A publication*]
**Machinery Prod Engng** ... Machinery and Production Engineering [*A publication*]
**Mach Korea** ... Machinery Korea [*A publication*]
**Mach Lloyd Int Rev Eng Equip** ... Machinery Lloyd. International Review of Engineering Equipment [*A publication*]
**Mach Market** ... Machinery Market [*A publication*]
**Mach Mod** ... Machine Moderne [*A publication*]
**MACHO**.... Machismo [*Spanish*] (DSUE)
**MACHO**.... Massive Compact Halo Object [*Astrophysics*]
**Macho** ........ Movimiento Anticomunista Hondureno [*Honduran Anti-Communist Movement*] [*Political party*] (PD)
**Mach Outil Fr** ... Machine Outil Francaise [*A publication*]
**Mach Prod E** ... Machinery and Production Engineering [*A publication*]
**Mach Prod Eng** ... Machinery and Production Engineering [*A publication*]
**Mach and Prod Eng** ... Machinery and Production Engineering [*A publication*]
**Mach & Prod Engng** ... Machinery and Production Engineering [*A publication*]
**m-AChr**...... Muscarinic Acetylcholine Receptor [*Biochemistry*]
**Mach Shop** ... Machine Shop [*A publication*]
**Mach Shop Eng Manuf** ... Machine Shop and Engineering Manufacture [*England*] [*A publication*]
**Mach and Tool** ... Machines and Tooling [*English Translation of Stanki i Instrument*] [*A publication*]
**Mach Tool** ... Machines and Tooling [*English Translation of Stanki i Instrument*] [*A publication*]
**Mach Tool Blue Book** ... Machine and Tool Blue Book [*A publication*]
**Mach Tool Eng** ... Machine Tool Engineering [*A publication*]
**Mach Tool Engl Transl** ... Machines and Tooling. English Translation [*A publication*]
**Mach Tool R** ... Machine Tool Review [*A publication*]
**MACHY**.... Machinery (ROG)
**Mac & I**...... Macrae and Hertslet's English Insolvency Cases [*1847-52*] [*A publication*] (DLA)
**MACI** ........ Member of the American Concrete Institute

**MACI** ........ Military Adaptation of Command [*or Commercial*] Items [*DoD*] (AABC)
**MACI** ........ Monitor, Access, and Control Interface (NASA)
**MAC II** ...... Mica and Chessy [*Acronym is name of interior decorating firm and is taken from first names of owners Mica Ertegun and Chessy Rayner*]
**MACII** ....... Missouri Aptitude and Career Information Inventory [*Vocational guidance test*]
**MACIMS** .. Military Airlift Command Integrated Management System
**MACIS** ...... Management and Contracts Information Service
**MACK** ....... Mack Trucks, Inc. [*NASDAQ symbol*] (NQ)
**MACK** ....... Mackenzie
**MAC(K)** ..... Military Armistice Commission (Korea) (AFM)
**Mack BL** .... Mackenzie on Bills of Lading [*A publication*] (DLA)
**Mack CL** .... Mackeldey on Modern Civil Law [*A publication*] (DLA)
**Mack Crim** ... Mackenzie's Treatise on Criminal Law [*4 eds.*] [*1678-1758*] [*Scotland*] [*A publication*] (DLA)
**Mack Cr L** ... Mackenzie's Treatise on Criminal Law [*4th ed.*] [*1678-1758*] [*Scotland*] [*A publication*] (DLA)
**Mack Ct Sess** ... Mackay. Court of Session Practice [*A publication*] (ILCA)
**Mackeld** ..... Mackeldey on Modern Civil Law [*A publication*] (DLA)
**Mackeld** ..... Mackeldey on Roman Law [*A publication*] (DLA)
**Mackeld Civil Law** ... Mackeldey on Modern Civil Law [*A publication*] (DLA)
**Mackeld Rom Law** ... Mackeldey on Roman Law [*A publication*] (DLA)
**Mackey** ...... Mackey's District of Columbia Reports [*12-20 District of Columbia*] [*A publication*] (DLA)
**Mack & F Jud A** ... Mackeson and Forbes' Judicature Acts [*A publication*] (DLA)
**Mack Inst** .. Mackenzie's Institutes of the Law of Scotland [*9 eds.*] [*1684-1758*] [*A publication*] (DLA)
**Mack Law of Prop** ... Mackay's Law of Property [*1882*] [*A publication*] (DLA)
**Mack Nat** ... Mackintosh's Law of Nature and Nations [*5th ed.*] [*1835*] [*A publication*] (DLA)
**Mack Obs** .. Mackenzie's Observations on Acts of Parliament [*1675, etc.*] [*Scotland*] [*A publication*] (DLA)
**Mack Rom Law** ... Mackenzie's Studies in Roman Law [*A publication*] (DLA)
**Macl** .......... Maclaren on Wills and Successions [*A publication*] (DLA)
**Macl** .......... Maclaurin's Scotch Criminal Decisions [*A publication*] (DLA)
**MACL** ....... Maximum Approximate Conditional Likelihood [*Statistics*]
**MACL** ....... Memoires. Academie d'Histoire de la Culture de Leningrad [*A publication*]
**MACL** ....... Memorias. Academia das Ciencias de Lisboa. Classe de Letras [*A publication*]
**MACL** ....... Mood Adjective Check List [*Psychometrics*]
**Macl Bank** ... Macleod's Theory and Practice of Banking [*A publication*] (DLA)
**MACLCL** .. Memorias. Academia das Ciencias de Lisboa. Classe de Letras [*A publication*]
**Maclean & R** ... Maclean and Robinson's Scotch Appeal Cases [*9 English Reprint*] [*A publication*] (DLA)
**Maclean & R (Sc)** ... Maclean and Robinson's Scotch Appeal Cases [*9 English Reprint*] [*A publication*] (DLA)
**MACLL** ..... Memorias. Academia das Ciencias de Lisboa. Classe de Letras [*A publication*]
**Macl Mag** .. Maclean's Magazine [*A publication*]
**Macl & R** ... Maclean and Robinson's Scotch Appeal Cases [*9 English Reprint*] [*A publication*] (DLA)
**Macl Rem Cas** ... Maclaurin's Remarkable Cases [*1670-1773*] [*Scotland*] [*A publication*] (DLA)
**Macl & Rob** ... Maclean and Robinson's Scotch Appeal Cases [*9 English Reprint*] [*A publication*] (DLA)
**Macl Sh** ..... Maclachlan on Merchant Shipping [*A publication*] (DLA)
**Macl Shipp** ... Maclachlan on Merchant Shipping [*A publication*] (DLA)
**Maclurean Lyc Contr** ... Maclurean Lyceum. Contributions [*A publication*]
**MACM** ...... Master Chief Machine Accountant [*Later, DPCM*] [*Navy rating*]
**MACM** ...... Military Aid to Civil Ministries [*British military*] (DMA)
**MA/CM** .... Milliamperes per Centimeter
**MACM** ...... Motorized Air Cycle Machine (MCD)
**MACMA** ... Military and Aerospace Connector Manufacturers Association (EA)
**MACMA** ... Mutual Aid Centre Managing Agency [*British*] (CB)
**MACMH** ... Altona Community Memorial Health Centre, Manitoba [*Library symbol*] [*National Library of Canada*] (NLC)
**Macmil** ....... Macmillan's Magazine [*A publication*]
**MACMIS** .. Maintenance and Construction Management Information System [*Data processing*]
**MACMIS** .. Major Army Command Management Information System
**MACMME** ... Ministerial Advisory Committee on Multicultural and Migrant Education [*Victoria, Australia*]
**MACMOL** ... Macromolecular
**MACMS** .... Miniature Arms Collectors/Makers Society (EA)
**Macn** .......... Macnaghten's Hindu Law Cases [*India*] [*A publication*] (DLA)
**Macn** .......... Macnaghten's Nizamut Adalat Cases [*1805-50*] [*Bengal, India*] [*A publication*] (DLA)
**Macn** .......... [*W. H.*] Macnaghten's Reports [*India*] [*A publication*] (DLA)
**Macn** .......... Macnaghten's Select Cases in Chancery Tempore King [*A publication*] (DLA)
**Macn** .......... Macnaghten's Select Cases, Sadr Diwani Adalat [*1791-1858*] [*Bengal, India*] [*A publication*] (DLA)
**MAC(N)** .... Munitions Assignments Committee (Navy) [*World War II*]
**Macn CM** .. Macnaghten on Courts-Martial [*A publication*] (DLA)
**Macn Cr Ev** ... Macnaghten's Criminal Evidence [*A publication*] (DLA)
**Macn El Hind L** ... Macnaghten's Elements of Hindu Law [*A publication*] (DLA)
**Macn Ev** ..... Macnally's Rules of Evidence on Pleas of the Crown [*A publication*] (DLA)
**Macn Fr** ..... [*Francis*] Macnaghten's Bengal Reports [*A publication*] (DLA)
**Macn & G** .. Macnaghten and Gordon's English Chancery Reports [*A publication*] (DLA)
**Macn & G (Eng)** ... Macnaghten and Gordon's English Chancery Reports [*A publication*] (DLA)
**MACNIMAATZ** ... MacArthur, Nimitz, and Spaatz [*Nickname for tripartite command in the Pacific of General of the Army Douglas MacArthur, Fleet Admiral Chester W. Nimitz, and Strategic Air Commander General Carl A. Spaatz*] [*World War II*]
**Macn NA Beng** ... Macnaghten's Nizamut Adalat Reports [*Bengal, India*] [*A publication*] (DLA)
**Macn Nul** ... Macnamara's Nullities and Irregularities in Law [*1842*] [*A publication*] (DLA)
**Macn SDA** ... Macnaghten's Select Cases, Sadr Diwani Adalat [*1791-1858*] [*Bengal, India*] [*A publication*] (DLA)
**Macn SDA Beng** ... [*W. H.*] Macnaghten's Sadr Diwani Adalat Reports [*India*] [*A publication*] (DLA)
**Macn Sel Cas** ... Select Cases in Chancery Tempore King, Edited by Macnaghten [*1724-33*] [*A publication*] (DLA)
**MACNYC** ... Men's Apparel Club of New York City (EA)
**Mac NZ** ..... Macassey's New Zealand Reports [*A publication*] (DLA)
**MACO** ....... Major Assembly Checkout [*NASA*] (NASA)
**MACO** ....... Marshaling Area Control Officer [*Military*] (AABC)
**MACOM** ... Major Army Command (AABC)
**Macomb CM** ... Macomb on Courts-Martial [*A publication*] (DLA)
**MA in Comm** ... Master of Arts in Communications
**MACON** .... Maintenance Console (MCD)
**MACON** .... Matrix Connector Punched Card Programmer [*Data processing*] (IEEE)
**MACONS** ... Mid-Atlantic Continental Shelf
**MACOP** .... Methotrexate, Ara-C, Cyclophosphamide, Oncovin [*Vincristine*], Prednisone [*Antineoplastic drug regimen*]
**MACOPS** ... Military Airlift Command Operational Phone System (AFM)
**MACOS** .... Man - A Course of Study [*Title of social-studies course*] [*National Science Foundation*]
**MACOS** .... Military Airlift Combat Operations Staff
**MACOV** ... Mechanized and Army Combat Operations Vietnam (AABC)
**MACP** ....... Michigan Association of Cherry Producers (EA)
**MACP** ....... Military Aid to the Civil Power [*British military*] (DMA)
**MACP** ....... Mission Analysis Computer Program
**Mac-Paps** .. Mackenzie-Papineau Battalion [*Canada*]
**Mac Pat Cas** ... Macrory's Patent Cases [*England*] [*A publication*] (DLA)
**Mac PC** ...... Macrory's Patent Cases [*England*] [*A publication*] (DLA)
**MACPCP** .. Member, Australian College of Private Consulting Psychologists
**Macph** ........ Macpherson, Lee, and Bell's Scotch Session Cases [*A publication*] (DLA)
**Macph** ........ Macpherson's Scotch Court of Session Cases [*1862-73*] [*A publication*] (DLA)
**Macph Inf** ... Macpherson on Infancy [*A publication*] (DLA)
**Macph Jud Com** ... Macpherson's Practice of the Judicial Committee of the Privy Council [*A publication*] (DLA)
**Macph L & B** ... Macpherson, Lee, and Bell [*Scotland*] [*A publication*] (DLA)
**Macph Pr C** ... Macpherson's Practice of the Judicial Committee of the Privy Council [*2nd ed.*] [*1873*] [*A publication*] (DLA)
**Macph Priv Counc** ... Macpherson's Privy Council Practice [*A publication*] (DLA)
**Macq** .......... Macqueen's Scotch Appeal Cases, House of Lords [*A publication*] (DLA)
**Macq D** ...... Macqueen's Debates on Life-Peerage Questions [*A publication*] (DLA)
**Macq Div** ... Macqueen's Marriage, Divorce, and Legitmacy [*2nd ed.*] [*1860*] [*A publication*] (DLA)
**Macq HL Cas** ... Macqueen's Scotch Appeal Cases, House of Lords [*A publication*] (DLA)
**Macq H & W** ... Macqueen's Rights and Liabilities of Husband and Wife [*4th ed.*] [*1905*] [*A publication*] (DLA)
**Macq Mar** ... Macqueen's Marriage, Divorce, and Legitimacy [*2nd ed.*] [*1860*] [*A publication*] (DLA)
**Macq Sc App Cas** ... Macqueen's Scotch Appeal Cases, House of Lords [*A publication*] (DLA)
**Mac R** ........ Macdougall's Jamaica Reports [*A publication*] (DLA)
**Mac R** ........ Macedonian Review [*A publication*]
**Mac R** ........ Maclean and Robinson's Scotch Appeal Cases [*1839*] [*A publication*] (DLA)
**Macr** .......... Macrobii [*of Lucian*] [*Classical studies*] (OCD)
**Macr** .......... Macrory's Patent Cases [*England*] [*A publication*] (DLA)
**MACR** ....... Member of the American College of Radiology
**MACR** ....... Methacrolein [*Also, MAL*] [*Organic chemistry*]
**MACR** ....... Minneapolis, Anoka & Cuyuna Range Railroad Co. [*AAR code*]
**MACR** ....... Missing Air Crew Report
**MACR** ....... Molecular Aspects of Cell Regulation [*Elsevier Book Series*] [*A publication*]

**MACR**....... Multiply, Accumulate, and Round
**Macr & H**... Macrae and Hertslet's English Insolvency Cases [*1847-52*] [*A publication*] (DLA)
**MACRI**...... Mercantile Atlantic Coastal Routing Instructions
**MACrimStudies** ... Master of Arts in Criminological Studies
**MACRIT**... Manpower Authorization Criteria [*Army*]
**MACRO**.... Merge and Correlate Recorded Output [*Data processing*] (NASA)
**Mac & Rob** ... Maclean and Robinson's Scotch Appeal Cases [*1839*] [*A publication*] (DLA)
**Macrob** ...... Macrobius [*Late fourth and early fifth century AD*] [*Classical studies*] (OCD)
**MACROL** ... Macro-Based Display Oriented Language [*Raytheon Co.*]
**Macromolec** ... Macromolecules [*A publication*]
**Macromol Phys** ... Macromolecular Physics [*A publication*]
**Macromol R** ... Macromolecular Reviews. Part D. Journal of Polymer Science [*A publication*]
**Macromol Rev** ... Macromolecular Reviews [*A publication*]
**Macromols** ... Macromolecules [*A publication*]
**Macr Pat Cas** ... Macrory's Patent Cases [*England*] [*A publication*] (DLA)
**Macr P Cas** ... Macrory's Patent Cases [*England*] [*A publication*] (DLA)
**MACRS**..... Modified Accelerated Cost Recovery System [*IRS*]
**MacS**.......... MacSweeney on Mines, Quarries, and Minerals [*5 eds.*] [*1884-1922*] [*A publication*] (DLA)
**MACS**........ Management & Computer Services, Inc. [*Information service or system*] (IID)
**MACS**........ Manned Air Combat Simulation (MCD)
**MACS**........ Marine Air Control Squadron
**MACS**........ Mass and Charge Spectroscopy
**MACS**........ Mastoid Air Cell System [*Anatomy*]
**MACS**........ McDonnell Automatic Checkout System [*McDonnell Douglas Corp.*]
**MACS**........ Medium-Altitude Communications Satellite
**MACS**........ Member of the American Chemical Society
**MACS**........ Microwave Attitude Control Sensor
**MACS**........ Military Aeronautical Communications Service
**MACS**........ Military Airlift Command Service (NATG)
**MACS**........ Missile Air-Conditioning System
**MACS**........ Mobile Acoustic Communications System
**MACS**........ Mobile Air Conditioning Society (EA)
**MACS**........ Monitoring and Control Station
**MACS**........ Multi-Access Computer Switch [*Telecommunications*] (TSSD)
**MACS**........ Multicenter AIDS [*Acquired Immune Deficiency Syndrome*] Cohort Study [*National Institutes of Health*]
**MACS**........ Multiple Access Communications System [*West German and Dutch*]
**MACS**........ Multiple Application Connector System
**MACS**........ Multiple-Technique Analytical Computer System
**MACS**........ Multiproject Automated Control System
**MACS**........ Multipurpose Arcade Combat Simulator [*Marksmanship training*] [*Army*] (INF)
**MACS**........ Senior Chief Machine Accountant [*Later, DPCS*] [*Navy rating*]
**MACSCO** ... Metropolitan Academic Consultants Sales Corporation
**MACSEA**.. Military Assistance Command, Southeast Asia
**MAC/SM** ... Maintenance Allocation Chart and System Maintenance (MCD)
**MACSOG** ... Military Assistance Command Studies and Observation Group (CINC)
**MACSQ**..... Marine Air Control Squadron
**MACSS** ..... Medium-Altitude Communications Satellite System
**MACSYMA** ... MAC [*Massive Algebraic Computation*] Symbolic Manipulator [*Programming language*] [*1969*] (CSR)
**MACT** ....... Master of Arts in College Teaching
**MACT** ....... Maximum Achievable [*or Available*] Control Technology [*Environmental chemistry*]
**MACTELNET** ... Military Airlift Command Teletype Network (AFM)
**MacTEP**.... Mac [*Apple's Mackintosh computer*] Terminal Emulation Program
**MACTIS** ... Marine and Coastal Technology Information Service [*United Nations*] (IID)
**MACTRAC** ... Military Airlift Command Traffic Reporting and Control System
**MACTU** .... Mines and Countermeasures Technical Unit [*Navy*]
**MACV** ....... Military Assistance Command, Vietnam
**MACV** ....... Multipurpose Airmobile Combat-Support Vehicle
**MACVFR**.. Make Altitude Changes Visual Flight Rules [*Aviation*] (FAAC)
**MACW**....... Missionary Association of Catholic Women (EA)
**MAC/WA** ... MAC [*Media Agencies Clients*]/Western Advertising [*A publication*]
**Mad**........... All India Reporter, Madras [*A publication*] (DLA)
**Mad**........... Indian Law Reports, Madras Series [*A publication*] (DLA)
**Mad**........... Indian Rulings, Madras Series [*A publication*] (DLA)
**MAD**.......... Machine Analysis Display
**MAD**.......... Machine ANSI Data
**Mad**........... Madagascar
**MAD**.......... Madam
**MAD**.......... Madang [*Papua New Guinea*] [*Seismograph station code, US Geological Survey*] (SEIS)
**Mad**........... Maddock's English Chancery Reports [*56 English Reprint*] [*1815-22*] [*A publication*] (DLA)
**Mad**........... Maddock's Reports [*9-18 Montana*] [*A publication*] (DLA)
**MAD**.......... Madison, CT [*Location identifier*] [*FAA*] (FAAL)
**Mad**........... Madras High Court Reports [*India*] [*A publication*] (DLA)
**MAD**.......... Madrid [*Spain*] (KSC)
**MAD**.......... Madrid [*Spain*] [*Airport symbol*] (OAG)
**MAD**.......... Magnetic Airborne Detector [*Navy*]
**MAD**.......... Magnetic Anomaly Detection [*or Detector*]
**MAD**.......... Magnetic Azimuth Detector (MCD)
**MAD**.......... Main Assembly Drawing
**MAD**.......... Maintenance Alert Directive [*Aviation*]
**MAD**.......... Maintenance Analysis Data [*or Diagram*] (MCD)
**MAD**.......... Maintenance, Assembly, and Disassembly
**MAD**.......... Management Analysis Division [*NASA*] (MCD)
**MAD**.......... Manhunter Assignment Device [*Data processing*]
**MAD**.......... Manufacturing Assembly Drawing
**MAD**.......... Maple Air Services Ltd. [*Maple, ON, Canada*] [*FAA designator*] (FAAC)
**MAD**.......... Marine Air [*or Aviation*] Detachment
**MAD**.......... Marine Air Detection (AFIT)
**MAD**.......... Mass Analyzer Detector
**MAD**.......... Master Accession Document [*Data processing*] (BUR)
**MAD**.......... Master Air Data [*Computer*]
**MAD**.......... Material Analysis Data
**MAD**.......... Material Assistance Designated [*Report*] (MCD)
**MAD**.......... Material Availability Date (CET)
**MAD**.......... Materials for the Assyrian Dictionary (BJA)
**MAD**.......... Materiel Acquisition and Delivery [*Military*]
**MAD**.......... Maximum Acceptable Deviation
**MAD**.......... Maximum Applicable Dose [*Environmental chemistry*]
**MAD**.......... Mean Absolute Deviation [*Statistics*]
**MAD**.......... MeCCNU [*Semustine*], Adriamycin [*Antineoplastic drug regimen*]
**MAD**.......... Median Absolute Deviation [*Statistics*]
**MAD**.......... Memoires. Academie des Sciences, des Arts, et des Belles-Lettres de Dijon [*A publication*]
**MAD**.......... Methylandrostenediol [*Methandriol*] [*Endocrinology*]
**MAD**.......... Michigan Algorithmic Decoder [*IBM Corp.*] [*University of Michigan*] [*Programming language*] [*1961*]
**MAD**.......... Mileage Accumulation Dynamometer
**MAD**.......... Militaerischer Abschirmdienst [*Counterintelligence*] [*Federal Republic of Germany*]
**MAD**.......... Mind-Altering Drug
**MAD**.......... Mine Assembly Depot [*Navy*]
**MAD**.......... Minimal Aural Dose
**MAD**.......... Minimum Absolute Deviation [*Statistics*]
**MAD**.......... Missile Assembly Data
**MA & D**..... Mission Analysis and Design
**MAD**.......... Mission Analysis Division [*NASA*] (KSC)
**MAD**.......... Mission Area Deficiency [*Army*]
**MAD**.......... Mixed Analog and Digital [*Telecommunications*] (TEL)
**MAD**.......... Model A Drivers (EA)
**MAD**.......... Motor Assembly and Disassembly
**MAD**.......... Multiple Access Device
**MAD**.......... Multiple-Aperture Device (MUGU)
**MAD**.......... Multiple Audio Distribution [*Communications*]
**MAD**.......... Multiple-Wavelength Anomalous Dispersion [*Crystallography*]
**MAD**.......... Multiply and Add
**MAD**.......... Music and Dance [*American Dance Festival project*]
**MAD**.......... Mutual Ability for Defense [*Pentagon defense policy*]
**MAD**.......... Mutual Assured Destruction [*Nuclear warfare*]
**MAD**.......... Myoadenylate Deaminase [*An enzyme*]
**MADA**....... Multiple Access Demand Assignment (MCD)
**MADA**....... Multiple Access - Discrete Address [*Navy tactical voice communication*]
**MADAEC** ... Military Application Division of the Atomic Energy Commission
**MADAG**.... Madagascar (ROG)
**Madagascar Dir Ind Mines Rapp Act Geol** ... Madagascar. Direction de l'Industrie et des Mines. Rapports d'Activite. Geologie [*A publication*]
**Madagascar Rev Geogr** ... Madagascar. Revue de Geographie [*A publication*]
**MADAIR**... Magnetic Anomaly Detection and Identification Ranging (MCD)
**MADAM**... Maintenance Diagnostic Assistance Module [*Military*] (CAAL)
**MADAM**... Manchester Automatic Digital Machine [*Manchester University*] [*British*] (DEN)
**MADAM**... Marine Air-Droppable Area Marker (MCD)
**MADAM**... Moderately Advanced Data Management [*Data processing*]
**MADAM**... Multipurpose Automatic Data Analysis Machine
**MADAP**.... Maastricht Automatic Data Processing and Display System [*Air traffic control*]
**MADAR**.... Malfunction Analysis, Detection, and Recording [*Data processing*]
**MADARS** ... Maintenance Analysis, Detection, and Reporting System [*Data processing*] (AFM)
**MADARS** ... Malfunction Analysis, Detection, and Recording Subsystem [*Data processing*]
**MADARTS** ... Malfunction Detection Analysis, Recording, and Training System
**Mad & B** .... Maddox and Bach's Reports [*19 Montana*] [*A publication*] (DLA)
**Mad Bar**..... Madox's Barona Anglia [*A publication*] (DLA)
**MADC**....... Machine-Assisted Detection and Classification (NVT)

**MADC**....... Multiplexer Analog-to-Digital Converter (MCD)
**MADCAP**... Mammoth Decimal Arithmetic Program [*NASA*] (KSC)
**Mad Ch Pr**... Maddock's English Chancery Practice [*3rd ed.*] [*1837*] [*A publication*] (DLA)
**MADCK**.... Marine Aide-de-Camp to the King [*British Admiralty*]
**Mad Co**...... Madras Code [*India*] [*A publication*] (DLA)
**MAD/CO**.. Mid-America Dance Company [*St. Louis, MO*]
**Madd**.......... Maddock's English Chancery Reports [*A publication*] (DLA)
**Madd**.......... Maddox's Reports [*9-18 Montana*] [*A publication*] (DLA)
**MADD**....... Module for Automatic Dock and Detumble [*Orbital rescue*] [*NASA*]
**MADD**....... Mothers Against Drunk Driving (EA)
**MADDAM**... Macromodule and Digital Differential Analyzer Machine [*Data processing*]
**Madd & B**.. Maddox and Bach's Reports [*19 Montana*] [*A publication*] (DLA)
**Madd Ch**.... Maddock's English Chancery Reports [*56 English Reprint*] [*1815-22*] [*A publication*] (DLA)
**Madd Ch (Eng)**... Maddock's English Chancery Reports [*56 English Reprint*] [*A publication*] (DLA)
**Madd Ch Pr**... Maddock's English Chancery Practice [*A publication*] (DLA)
**MADDDC**... Manufacturers of Aerial Devices and Digger-Derricks Council (EA)
**Madd & G**... Maddock and Geldart's English Chancery Reports [*A publication*] (DLA)
**Madd & Gel**... Maddock and Geldart's English Chancery Reports [*A publication*] (DLA)
**MADDIDA**... Magnetic Drum Digital Differential Analyzer
**MADDWU**... Mechanics' Assistants' and Dry Dock Workers' Union [*British*]
**MADE**....... Magnetic Device Evaluator [*Data processing*]
**MADE**....... Microalloy Diffused Electrode
**MADE**....... Minimum Airborne Digital Equipment
**MADE**....... Multichannel Analog-to-Digital Data Encoder
**Madem**....... Mademoiselle [*A publication*]
**Made in Mex**... Made in Mexico [*A publication*]
**Maden Tetkik Arama Enst Mecm**... Maden Tetkik ve Arama Enstitusu Mecmuasi [*A publication*]
**Maden Tetkik Arama Enst Yayin**... Maden Tetkik ve Arama Enstitusu Yayinlarindan [*A publication*]
**Maden Tetkik Arama Enst Yayinlarindan**... Maden Tetkik ve Arama Enstitusu Yayinlarindan [*Turkey*] [*A publication*]
**Maden Tetkik Arama Enst Yayin Seri A**... Maden Tetkik ve Arama Enstitusu Yayinlarindan. Seri A. Bildirigler [*A publication*]
**Maden Tetkik Arama Enst Yayin Seri B**... Maden Tetkik ve Arama Enstitusu Yayinlarindan. Seri B. Irdeller [*A publication*]
**Maden Tetkik Arama Enst Yayin Seri C**... Maden Tetkik ve Arama Enstitusu Yayinlarindan. Seri C. Monografiler [*A publication*]
**Maden Tetkik Arama Enst Yayin Seri D**... Maden Tetkik ve Arama Enstitusu Yayinlarindan. Seri D. Jeolojik Harta Materye-Leri [*A publication*]
**MADEPSQ**... Marine Air Depot Squadron
**MADERI**... Mexican-American Documentation and Educational Research Institute
**MADEX**.... Magnetic Anomaly Detection Exercise (NVT)
**Mad Exch**.. Madox's History of the Exchequer [*A publication*] (DLA)
**MADF**....... Maintenance Action Data Form [*Military*] (CAAL)
**Mad Fir Burg**... Madox's Firma Burgi [*A publication*] (DLA)
**Mad Form**... Madox's Formulare Anglicanum [*A publication*] (DLA)
**Mad Form Angl**... Madox's Formulare Anglicanum [*A publication*] (DLA)
**MADGE**.... Malaysian Air Defense Ground Environment [*RADAR*]
**MADGE**.... Microwave Aircraft Digital Guidance Equipment [*Helicopters*]
**Mad & Gel**... Maddock and Geldart's English Chancery Reports [*A publication*] (DLA)
**Mad HC**..... Madras High Court Reports [*India*] [*A publication*] (DLA)
**Mad Hist Exch**... Madox's History of the Exchequer [*A publication*] (DLA)
**Madh Pra**... All India Reporter, Madhya Pradesh [*A publication*] (DLA)
**Madhya Bharati J Univ Saugar Part 2 Sect B Nat Sci**... Madhya Bharati. Journal of the University of Saugar. Part 2. Section B. Natural Sciences [*A publication*]
**Madhya Bharati Pt 2 Sect A**... Madhya Bharati. Part 2. Section A. Physical Sciences [*A publication*]
**MADI**........ Master Data Index
**MADIS**...... Burda-MarketingInfoSystem [*Burda GmbH, Marketing Service Department*] [*Information service or system*] (IID)
**MADIS**...... Manual Aircraft Display Information System [*Military*] (CAAL)
**MADIS**...... Millivolt Analog-Digital Instrumentation System
**Mad Isls**..... Madeira Islands
**Madison Av**... Madison Avenue [*A publication*]
**Madison Ave**... Madison Avenue [*A publication*]
**MADIZ**..... Military Air Defense Identification Zone (MCD)
**M/ADJ**...... Manual Adjusting [*Automotive engineering*]
**Madjalah Inst Tek Bandung Proc**... Madjalah Institut Teknologi Bandung Proceedings [*Indonesia*] [*A publication*]
**Madjelis Ilmu Pengetahuan Indones Penerbitan**... Madjelis Ilmu Pengetahuan Indonesia Penerbitan [*A publication*]
**Madj Persat Dokt Gigi Indones**... Madjalah Persatuan Dokter Gigi Indonesia [*A publication*]
**Mad Jur**..... Madras Jurist [*India*] [*A publication*] (DLA)
**MADL**....... Microwave Acoustic Delay Line
**Mad Law Rep**... Madras Law Reporter [*India*] [*A publication*] (DLA)
**Mad LJ**...... Madras Law Journal [*A publication*]
**MADLR**.... Major Assembly Direct Labor Reporting (MCD)
**Mad L Rep**... Madras Law Reporter [*India*] [*A publication*] (DLA)
**Mad LT**...... Madras Law Times [*India*] [*A publication*] (DLA)
**Mad LW**.... Madras Law Weekly [*India*] [*A publication*] (DLA)
**MADM**...... Maintenance Automated Data Management
**MADM**...... Manchester Automatic Digital Machine [*Manchester University*] [*British*]
**M Adm**....... Master of Administration
**MADM**...... Medium Atomic Demolition Munition [*Military*] (AABC)
**MADMAN**... Magnetic Anomaly Detector Contact Man (NVT)
**M Adm E**... Master of Administrative Engineering
**MAdmin**.... Master of Administration
**M Admin**.... Master of Administrative Studies
**MAD-N**..... Mid-America Dance Network [*Kansas City, MO*]
**MADN**....... Mid-American Dance Network
**Madness**.... Madness Network News [*A publication*]
**MADNV**.... Mitteilungsblatt. Allgemeiner Deutsche Neuphilologenverband [*A publication*]
**MADO**....... Mulliken Approximation for Differential Overlap [*Physics*]
**MADOC**.... Medical Analysis of Days of Care [*Report*]
**Madoqua Ser I**... Madoqua. Series I [*A publication*]
**Madoqua Ser II**... Modoqua. Series II [*A publication*]
**Madox**........ Madox's Formulare Anglicanum [*A publication*] (DLA)
**Madox**........ Madox's History of the Exchequer [*A publication*] (DLA)
**MADP**....... Main Air Display Plot
**MADP**....... Major Acquisition Decision Point [*Military*] (MCD)
**MADP**....... Material Acquisition Decision Process [*Military*] (MCD)
**MADP**....... Mission Area Development Plan [*DoD*]
**MADPAC**... Materiel Deterioration Prevention and Control [*Program*] [*Army*] (RDA)
**Mad Papers**... James Madison's Papers [*A publication*] (DLA)
**Mad Q**....... Madison Quarterly [*A publication*]
**MADR**....... Madras [*India*] (ROG)
**Mad R**........ Madras Review [*A publication*]
**MADR**....... Madritum [*Madrid*] [*Imprint*] [*Latin*] (ROG)
**MADR**....... Materiel Acquisition Decision Review [*Army*]
**MADR**....... Microprogram Address Register
**MA(Drama)**... Master of Arts (Drama)
**Madras Agric J**... Madras Agricultural Journal [*A publication*]
**Madras Agr J**... Madras Agricultural Journal [*A publication*]
**Madras LJ**... Madras Law Journal [*A publication*]
**Madras LJ**... Madras Law Journal and Reports [*India*] [*A publication*] (DLA)
**Madras Med J**... Madras Medical Journal [*A publication*]
**Madras Vet Coll Annu**... Madras Veterinary College. Annual [*A publication*]
**Madras Vet J**... Madras Veterinary Journal [*A publication*]
**MADRE**.... Magnetic Drum Receiving Equipment
**MADRE**.... Manufacturing Data Retrieval System (NASA)
**MADRE**.... Martin Automatic Data-Reduction Equipment
**MADREC**... Malfunction Detection and Recording [*Checkout system for aircraft*] [*Air Force*]
**Mad Reg**.... Madden on Registration of Deeds [*A publication*] (DLA)
**Madrid Univ Fac Med Arch**... Madrid Universidad. Facultad de Medicina. Archivos [*A publication*]
**Madr Mitt**... Mitteilungen. Deutsches Archaeologische Institut. Abteilung Madrid [*A publication*]
**MADS**....... Machine-Aided Drafting System (IEEE)
**MADS**....... Macquarie Association of Disabled Students [*Australia*]
**MADS**....... Maintenance and Diagnosis System [*Military*] (CAAL)
**MADS**....... Mars Atmosphere Density Sensor
**MADS**....... Meteorological Airborne Data System
**MADS**....... Missile Attitude Determination System [*LASER device*] [*Air Force*]
**MADS**....... Mission Area Deficiency Statement [*Army*] (RDA)
**MADS**....... Mobile Air Defense System
**MADS**....... Mobile Airborne Defense Station Concept [*Air Force*]
**MADS**....... Modular Air Defense System (MCD)
**MADS**....... Modular Army Demonstration System (MCD)
**MADS**....... Modular Auxiliary Data Systems (NASA)
**Mad SDAR**... Madras Sadr Diwani Adalat Reports [*India*] [*A publication*] (DLA)
**Mad Sel Dec**... Madras Select Decrees [*A publication*] (DLA)
**Mad Ser**..... Indian Law Reports, Madras Series [*A publication*] (DLA)
**MADSPM**... Mobilization Against the Draft and Student Peace Mobilization [*An association*] (EA)
**MADT**....... Mean Administrative Delay Time
**MADT**....... Microalloy Diffused Transistor (MUGU)
**MADU**....... Methylaminodeoxyuridine [*Pharmacology*]
**MADVEC**... Magnetic Anomaly Detector Vectoring [*Military*] (CAAL)
**MADW**...... Military Air Defense Warning Network
**Mad WN**.... Madras Weekly Notes [*A publication*] (DLA)
**Mad WNCC**... Madras Weekly Notes, Criminal Cases [*India*] [*A publication*] (DLA)
**MADZAK**... Koninklijk Museum voor Midden-Afrika [*Tervuren, Belgie*]. Zoologische Documentatie [*A publication*]
**MAE**.......... Madera, CA [*Location identifier*] [*FAA*] (FAAL)
**MAE**.......... Maebashi [*Japan*] [*Seismograph station code, US Geological Survey*] (SEIS)
**Mae**............ Maestro [*Record label*] [*Belgium, etc.*]
**MAE**.......... Maintenance Engineer

**MAE** ......... Malignant Angioendotheliomatosis [*Oncology*]
**M Ae** ......... Master of Aeronautics
**MAE** ......... Master of Art Education
**MAE** ......... Master of Arts in Education
**MAE** ......... Matrix Arithmetic Expression
**MAE** ......... McDonnell Airborne Evaluator [*McDonnell Douglas Corp.*] (MCD)
**MAE** ......... Mean Absolute Error
**MAE** ......... Mean Area of Effectiveness (CINC)
**MAE** ......... Medical Air Evacuation
**MAE** ......... Medium Aevum [*A publication*]
**MAE** ......... (Methylamino)ethanol [*Organic chemistry*]
**MAE** ......... Miramar Energy Corp. [*Vancouver Stock Exchange symbol*]
**MAE** ......... Mission Accomplishment Estimate [*DoD*]
**MA & E** ..... Mission Analysis and Engineering [*NASA*]
**MAE** ......... Mobile Ammunition Evaluation
**MAE** ......... Motion Aftereffect
**MAE** ......... Mutual Assistance, Executive [*Military appropriation*] (NG)
**MAEB** ....... Material Application Evaluation Board [*NASA*] (MCD)
**MAEBR** ..... Management of Enlisted Bonus Recipients
**MAEC** ....... Master of Arts in Economics
**MAEC** ....... Minimum Adverse Effect Concentration [*Pollution technology*]
**MAEC** ....... Missile Attack Emergency Conference (MCD)
**MAECA** .... Modern Aspects of Electrochemistry [*A publication*]
**MAECDR** ... Marine Ecology. Pubblicazioni della Stazione Zoologica di Napoli. I [*A publication*]
**MAECO** .... NRA [*National Restaurant Association*] Multi-Unit Architects, Engineers, and Construction Officers (EA)
**MA (Econ)** ... Master of Arts in Economic and Social Studies [*University of Manchester*] [*British*]
**MA (Econ)** ... Master of Arts in Economic Studies [*Universities of Newcastle and Sheffield*] [*British*]
**MAECON** ... Mid-America Electronics Conference
**MA Ed** ....... Master of Arts in Education
**MAED** ....... Micro Area Electron Diffraction [*Surface analysis*]
**MAEE** ....... Marine Aircraft Experimental Establishment
**M Ae E** ....... Master of Aeronautical Engineering
**MAEE** ....... Mid-Atlantic Electrical Exhibition (ITD)
**M Ae Eng** ... Master of Aeronautical Engineering
**MAEL** ....... Marine Aircraft Experimental Laboratory [*British*]
**MAELU** .... Mutual Atomic Energy Liability Underwriters [*Chicago, IL*] (EA)
**MAEO** ....... Months after Exercise of Option
**MAEP** ....... Minimum AUTOLAND [*Automatic Landing*] Entry Point (NASA)
**MAEQA** .... Meetings on Atomic Energy [*A publication*]
**Maerisch-Schlesische Heimat** ... Maerisch-Schlesische Heimat. Vierteljahresschrift fuer Kultur und Wirtschaft [*A publication*]
**M Aero E** ... Master of Aeronautical Engineering
**M Aero Eng** ... Master of Aeronautical Engineering
**MAEROSPOPNSMGT** ... Masters Aerospace Operations Management [*Air Force*]
**MAERP** ..... Mutual Atomic Energy Reassurance Pool
**MAERU** .... Mobile Ammunition Evaluation and Reconditioning Unit
**Maes** .......... Maestoso [*Majestic*] [*Music*]
**MAES** ........ Maine Agriculture Experiment Station [*University of Maine at Orono*] [*Research center*] (RCD)
**M Ae S** ....... Master of Aeronautical Science
**MAES** ........ Medical Aid for El Salvador (EA)
**MAES** ........ Mexican-American Engineering Society (EA)
**MAES** ........ Michigan Agricultural Experiment Station [*Michigan State University*] [*Research center*] (RCD)
**M Ae Sc** ..... Master of Aeronautical Science
**MAESON** ... Marxist All-Ethiopian Socialist Movement [*Political party*] (PD)
**MAESTO** ... Maestoso [*Majestic*] [*Music*]
**MAESTRO** ... Machine-Assisted Educational System for Teaching by Remote Operation (IEEE)
**MAESTRO** ... Mission Analysis Evaluation and Space Trajectory Operations [*NASA*]
**MAET** ....... Microwave Amplifier Electron Tube
**MAET** ....... Missile Accident Emergency Team (AFM)
**MAETS** ..... Medical Air Evacuation Transport Squadron [*Army*] [*World War II*]
**MAETU** .... Medical Air Evacuation Transport Unit [*Australia*]
**MAEUDD** ... Meddelanden fran Avdelningen foer Ekologisk Botanik Lunds Universitet [*A publication*]
**MAev** ......... Medium Aevum [*A publication*]
**MAEW** ...... Men and Equipment Working (FAAC)
**MAF** ......... Front Militant Autonome [*Autonomous Militant Front*] [*French*] (PD)
**MAF** ......... Macrophage Activating Factor [*Biochemistry*]
**MAF** ......... Magnetic Anisotropy Field
**MAF** ......... Maintenance Action Form
**MAF** ......... Major Academic Field
**MAF** ......... Manpower Authorization File
**MAF** ......... Marine Air Facility
**MAF** ......... Marine Amphibious Force (AABC)
**MAF** ......... Marriage Adjustment Form [*Psychology*]
**MAF** ......... Master Appraisal File [*Real estate*]
**MAF** ......... Master Facility Tool (MCD)
**MAF** ......... Maximum Amplitude Filter
**MAF** ......... Medical Awareness Foundation [*Commercial firm*] (EA)
**MAF** ......... Michoud Assembly Facility [*NASA*] (MCD)
**MAF** ......... Midland/Odessa [*Texas*] [*Airport symbol*] (OAG)
**MAF** ......... Million Acre Feet [*Hydrology*]
**MAF** ......... Minimum Audible Field
**MAF** ......... Minister of Armed Forces (NATG)
**MAF** ......... Ministry of Agriculture and Fisheries [*British*]
**MAF** ......... Missile Assembly Facility
**MAF** ......... Mission Aviation Fellowship (EA)
**MAF** ......... Mixed Amine Fuel
**MAF** ......... Mobile Air Force (NATG)
**MAF** ......... Mobile Assault Ferry [*Army*]
**MAF** ......... Moisture and Ash Free
**MAF** ......... Morris Animal Foundation (EA)
**MAF** ......... Movement Aftereffect [*Optics*]
**MAF** ......... Multiple Access Facility [*Data processing*]
**MAFA** ....... Manchester Academy of Fine Arts [*England*]
**MAFA** ....... Middle Atlantic Fisheries Association (EA)
**MAFAC** ..... Marine Fisheries Advisory Committee [*Department of Commerce*] [*Washington, DC*] (EGAO)
**MAFAP** ..... Minimum Altitude over Facility on Final Approach Course [*Aviation*] (FAAC)
**MAFAS** ..... Marine Automated Flowcharting Analysis System
**MAFASA** .. Marine Amphibious Force Air Support Airfield (MCD)
**MAFB** ........ Malmstrom Air Force Base [*Montana*] (KSC)
**MAFB** ........ Mitchell Air Force Base
**MAFC** ........ Major Army Field Command (AABC)
**MAFC** ........ Mel Anderson Fan Club (EA)
**MAFC** ........ Mythadventures Fan Club (EA)
**MAFCA** ..... Model A Ford Club of America (EA)
**MAFCC** ..... Model A Ford Cabriolet Club (EA)
**MAFCO** .... Magnetic Field Code
**MAFD** ....... Minimum Acquisition Flux Density
**MAFE** ........ Maintenance of Air/FMF [*Fleet Marine Force*] Expeditionary Equipment (NG)
**MAFES** ..... Mississippi Agricultural and Forestry Experiment Station [*Mississippi State University*] [*Research center*] (RCD)
**MAFES Res Highlights Miss Agric For Exp Stn** ... MAFES Research Highlights. Mississippi Agricultural and Forestry Experiment Station [*A publication*]
**MAFF** ........ Ministry of Agriculture, Fisheries, and Food [*British*]
**MAFFC** ..... Munsters and the Addams Family Fan Club (EA)
**MAFFEX** .. Marine Amphibious Force Field Exercise [*Military*] (NVT)
**MAFFS** ..... Modular Airborne Fire Fighting System [*Air Force*]
**MA/FH** ..... Maintenance Actions per Flight Hour (MCD)
**MAFH** ....... Multicentric Angiofollicular (Lymph Node) Hyperplasia [*Oncology*]
**MAFI** ......... Medic Alert Foundation International [*Also known as Medic Alert*] (EA)
**MAFIA** ...... Marimba and Fife Inspectors Association [*Women's tongue-in-cheek organization*] [*Defunct*]
**MAFIA** ...... Morte alla Francia Italia Anelo [*Death to the French is Italy's Cry*], or Movimento Anti Francesi Italiano Azione [*Italian Action Movement Against the French*] [*When used in reference to the secret society often associated with organized crime, "Mafia" is from the Sicilian word for boldness or lawlessness*]
**MAFIS** ...... Mobile Automated Field Instrumentation System [*TRADOC*] (RDA)
**MAFL** ........ Manual of Air Force Law [*British*]
**MAFL** ........ Multiaperture Ferrite Logic
**MAFLA** ..... Mississippi, Alabama, and Florida [*Oil industry*]
**MAFLEX** .. Marine Amphibious Force Landing Exercise [*Military*] (NVT)
**MAFLIR** ... Modified Advanced Forward-Looking Infrared
**MAFOG** .... Mediterranean Area Fighter Operations Grid
**MAFOR** .... Marine Forecast [*Pronounced "mayfor"*]
**MAFP** ........ Military and Air Force Police [*British military*] (DMA)
**MAFR** ........ Marine Fisheries Review [*A publication*]
**MAFR** ........ Marriage and Family Review [*A publication*]
**MAFR** ........ Merged Accountability and Fund Reporting [*Air Force*] (AFM)
**MAfr** .......... Society of Missionaries of Africa (EAIO)
**MAFRC** ..... Middle Atlantic Fisheries Research Center [*National Oceanic and Atmospheric Administration*]
**MAFS** ........ Memoirs. American Folklore Society [*A publication*]
**MAFS** ........ Mobilization Air Force Specialty
**MAFSA9** ... Mitteilungen. Arbeitsgemeinschaft fuer Floristik in Schleswig-Holstein und Hamburg [*A publication*]
**MAFSC** ..... Mobilization Air Force Specialty Code
**MAFSI** ...... Marketing Agents for Food Service Industry (EA)
**MAFSS** ..... Multipoint Airfield Fuel Support System
**MAFV** ....... Mean Ambient Flow Vector [*Geology*]
**MAFVA** ..... Miniature Armoured Fighting Vehicle Association (EA)
**MAG** .......... Macrogenerator [*SEMIS*]
**MAG** .......... Madang [*Papua New Guinea*] [*Airport symbol*] (OAG)
**MAG** .......... Magadan [*USSR*] [*Seismograph station code, US Geological Survey*] (SEIS)
**mag** ............ Magahi [*MARC language code*] [*Library of Congress*] (LCCP)
**MAG** .......... Magazine (AFM)
**MAG** .......... Magazine Article Guide [*A publication*]

**MAG** ......... Magenta (ROG)
**MAG** ......... Maggie Mines [*Vancouver Stock Exchange symbol*]
**MAG** ......... Magistrate
**Mag** ......... [*The*] Magistrate [*London*] [*A publication*] (DLA)
**Mag** ......... [*The*] Magistrate [*Australia*] [*A publication*] (ILCA)
**Mag** ......... Magistrate and Municipal and Parochial Lawyer [*London*] [*A publication*] (DLA)
**MAG** ......... Magnesium [*Chemical symbol is Mg*]
**MAG** ......... Magnet Bank FSB [*AMEX symbol*] (SPSG)
**MAG** ......... MagneTek, Inc. [*NYSE symbol*] (SPSG)
**MAG** ......... Magnetic (AFM)
**MAG** ......... Magneto (KSC)
**MAG** ......... Magnetometry
**MAG** ......... Magnetron (CET)
**MAG** ......... Magnification
**MAG** ......... Magnitude (AFM)
**MAG** ......... Magnus [*Large*] [*Pharmacy*]
**Mag** ......... Magruder's Reports [*1, 2 Maryland*] [*A publication*] (DLA)
**MAG** ......... Magyar [*Language, etc.*] (ROG)
**MAG** ......... Management Assistance Group [*Washington, DC*] (EA)
**MAG** ......... Manager's Magazine [*A publication*]
**MAG** ......... Managing [*A publication*]
**MAG** ......... Marine Aircraft [*or Aviation*] Group
**MAG** ......... Maritime Air Group [*Canada*]
**MAG** ......... Marker-Adder Generator
**MAG** ......... Marketing Aids Group
**M Ag** ......... Master of Agriculture
**MAG** ......... Military Advisory Group
**MAG** ......... Minnesota Attorney General's Office, St. Paul, MN [*OCLC symbol*] (OCLC)
**MAG** ......... Mittelassyrisches Gesetz (BJA)
**MAG** ......... Monoammonium Glutamate [*Organic chemistry*]
**MAG** ......... Myelin-Associated Glycoprotein [*Biochemistry*]
**MAGA** ....... Magna International, Inc. [*Markham, ON*] [*NASDAQ symbol*] (NQ)
**MAGA** ....... Medium-Accuracy Gyro Assembly
**MAGA** ....... Member of the Australian Gas Association
**Magalog** ..... Magazine-Catalog [*Advertising*]
**MAGAMP** ... Magnetic Amplifier
**Mag Antiq** ... Magazine of Antiques [*A publication*]
**MAGARLM** ... Military Assistance Advisory Group, Army Branch, Logistics-Medical (CINC)
**Mag Art** ..... Magazine of Art [*A publication*]
**Mag of Art** ... Magazine of Art [*A publication*]
**Mag Asvanyolaj Foldgaz Kiserl Intez Kozl** ... Magyar Asvanyolaj-es Foldgaz Kiserleti Intezet Koezlemenyei [*A publication*]
**Magazin Ag** ... Magazine Age [*A publication*]
**MAGB** ....... Masectomy Association of Great Britain
**MAGB** ....... Microfilm Association of Great Britain
**Mag Bank Adm** ... Magazine of Bank Administration [*A publication*]
**Mag Belorv Arch Ideggyogy Sz** ... Magyar Belorvosi Archivum es Ideggyogyaszati Szemle [*A publication*]
**Mag Bihar Agr Coll** ... Magazine. Bihar Agricultural College [*A publication*]
**Mag Biol Kutatointez Munkai** ... Magyar Biologiai Kutatointezet Munkai [*A publication*]
**Mag Bldg** ... Magazine of Building [*A publication*]
**MAG BRIT** ... Magna Britannia [*Great Britain*] [*Latin*] (ROG)
**Mag Build Equip** ... Magazine of Building Equipment [*Japan*] [*A publication*]
**Mag of Business** ... Magazine of Business [*A publication*]
**MAGC** ....... Mathematical Applications Group, Inc. [*NASDAQ symbol*] (NQ)
**MAGCAP** ... Magazine Capacity [*Military*]
**Mag Cas** ..... Bittleston, Wise, and Parnell's Magistrates' Cases [*England*] [*A publication*] (DLA)
**Mag Cas** ..... Magisterial Cases [*England*] [*A publication*] (DLA)
**Mag Cas** ..... Magistrates' Cases [*Reprinted from Law Journal Reports*] [*1892-1910*] [*A publication*] (DLA)
**Mag Char** .. Magna Charta [*or Carta*] [*Great Charter*] [*Latin*] [*A publication*] (DLA)
**mag cit** ....... Magnesium Citrate [*Pharmacy*]
**Mag & Con** ... Magistrate and Constable [*A publication*] (DLA)
**MAGCON** ... Magnetized Concentration [*Lunar*]
**Mag Concrete Res** ... Magazine of Concrete Research [*A publication*]
**Mag Concr R** ... Magazine of Concrete Research [*A publication*]
**Mag Concr Res** ... Magazine of Concrete Research [*A publication*]
**Mag & Const** ... Magistrate and Constable [*A publication*] (DLA)
**Mag Ct** ....... Magistrates' Court (DLA)
**MAGD** ....... Magdalen College [*Oxford University*] (ROG)
**MAGD** ....... Magdalene College, Cambridge University [*England*] (ROG)
**MAGDA** .... Mechanisms of Ageing and Development [*A publication*]
**MAGDARR** ... Magnavox Doppler and Ranging RADAR (NG)
**Mag Datenverarb** ... Magazin fuer Datenverarbeitung [*A publication*]
**MAgDevEc** ... Master of Agricultural Development Economics (ADA)
**Mag Dig** ..... Magrath's South Carolina Digest [*A publication*] (DLA)
**MAGE** ....... Magma Energy, Inc. [*NASDAQ symbol*] (NQ)
**MAGE** ....... Mechanical Aerospace Ground Equipment (TEL)
**M Ag Ec** ...... Master of Agricultural Economics
**Mag & E Comp** ... Magnus and Estrin on Companies [*5th ed.*] [*1978*] [*A publication*] (DLA)
**M Ag Ed** .... Master of Agricultural Education
**MAGERT** ... Map and Geography Round Table [*American Library Association*]
**MAGES** ..... Magnitude Estimation Scaling (MCD)
**Mag Fantasy & Sci Fict** ... Magazine of Fantasy and Science Fiction [*A publication*]
**Mag Fil Sz** ... Magyar Filozofiai Szemle [*A publication*]
**MAGG** ....... Maggiore [*Major*] [*Music*]
**MAGG** ....... Modular Alphanumeric Graphics Generator (IEEE)
**MAGGE** .... Medium-Altitude Gravity Gradient Experiment
**MAGGI** ..... Million Ampere Generator [*British*] (DEN)
**MAGGS** .... Modular Advanced Graphics Generation System (IEEE)
**Mag Gyogyszeresztud Tarsasag Ert** ... Magyar Gyogyszeresztudomanyi Tarsasag Ertesitojc [*A publication*]
**Magh** ......... Maghreb (BJA)
**Mag of Hist** ... Magazine of History [*A publication*]
**Mag Hist** ... Magazine of History with Notes and Queries [*A publication*]
**Maghreb** .... Maghreb-Machrek [*A publication*]
**MAGI** ........ Mackenzie Art Gallery [*University of Regina*] [*Canada*] [*Research center*] (RCD)
**Mag I** ......... Magazine Index [*A publication*]
**MAGI** ........ Magna Group, Incorporated [*NASDAQ symbol*] (NQ)
**MAGI** ........ Maryland Automated Geographic Information System [*Maryland State Department of State Planning*] [*Information service or system*] (IID)
**MAGI** ........ Master Group Information System [*AT & T*]
**MAGI** ........ Military Gamma Irradiator
**MAGI** ........ Multiarray Gamma Irradiator
**MAGIC** ..... Machine-Aided Graphics for Illustration and Composition [*Bell Telephone*]
**MAGIC** ..... Machine for Automatic Graphics Interface to a Computer
**MAGIC** ..... Madison Avenue General Ideas Committee [*New York City*]
**MAGIC** ..... Magnetic and Germanium Integer Calculator (DEN)
**MAGIC** ..... Magnetic Immunochemistry [*Laboratory analysis*]
**MAGIC** ..... Marine Corps Air-Ground Intelligence Center (MCD)
**MAGIC** ..... Market Analysis Guide - Intercity Communications [*AT & T*]
**MAGIC** ..... Marketing and Advertising General Information Centre [*Datasolve Ltd.*] [*Great Britain*] [*Information service or system*]
**MAGIC** ..... Matrix Algebra General Interpretive Coding (IEEE)
**MAGIC** ..... Michigan Automatic General Integrated Computation (MCD)
**MAGIC** ..... Microprobe Analysis Generalized Intensity Corrections
**MAGIC** ..... Microprocessor Application of Graphic with Interactive Communication
**MAGIC** ..... [*American*] Military Advisory Group in China [*Post-World War II*]
**MAGIC** ..... Modern Analytical Generator of Improved Circuits [*Data processing*]
**MAGIC** ..... Modified Action Generated Input Control
**MAGIC** ..... Monodisperse Aerosol Generation Interface [*Physics*]
**MAGIC** ..... Motorola Automatically Generated Integrated Circuits
**MAGIC** ..... Multipurpose and Generalized Interface to COBOL [*Data processing*]
**MAGID** ..... Magnetic Intrusion Detector (NVT)
**MAGIE** ...... Midwest Agri Industries Expo [*Illinois Fertilizer and Chemical Association*] (TSPED)
**MAGIIC** .... Mobile Army Ground Imagery Interpretation Center (MCD)
**Mag Index** ... Magazine Index [*A publication*]
**Mag Ins** ...... Magen on Insurance [*A publication*] (DLA)
**MAGIS** ...... Magistrate
**MAGIS** ...... Marine Air Ground Intelligence System
**MAGIS** ...... Megawatt Air-to-Ground Illumination System (MCD)
**MAGIS** ...... Municipal Automated Geographic Information System [*District of Columbia Office of the Mayor*] [*Information service or system*] (IID)
**Magis & Const (PA)** ... Magistrate and Constable [*Pennsylvania*] [*A publication*] (DLA)
**Magis Ct** .... Magistrates' Court (DLA)
**Mag Istor** ... Magazin Istoric [*A publication*]
**MAGJB** ..... Magyar Allami Eoetvoes Lorand Geofizikai Intezet. Evi Jelentese [*A publication*]
**Mag Ke'm Foly** ... Magyar Kemiai Folyoira [*Hungarian Journal of Chemistry*] [*A publication*]
**Mag Kem Lapja** ... Magyar Kemikusok Lapja [*A publication*]
**Mag Kir Szolo Borgazd Kozp Kiserl Allomas Ampelol Intez Evk** ... Magyar Kir. Szolo es Borgazdasagi Kozponti Kiserleti Allomas (Ampelologiai Intezet) Evkonyve [*A publication*]
**Mag Kozlekedes Mely Vizepites** ... Magyar Kozlekedes. Mely es Vizepites [*A publication*]
**MAGL** ....... Material Acquisition Guidance Letter (MCD)
**MAGLAD** ... Marksmanship and Gunnery LASER Device (RDA)
**MAGLATCH** ... Magnetic Latch (MUGU)
**MAG-LEV** ... Magnetically-Levitated [*High-speed ground transportation*]
**Mag Litt** ..... Magazine Litteraire [*A publication*]
**MAGLOC** ... Magnetic Logic Computer
**Mag Lond (Roy Free Hosp) School Med Women** ... Magazine. London (Royal Free Hospital) School of Medicine for Women [*A publication*]
**Mag Macl** .. Magazine Maclean [*A publication*]
**Mag (MD)** ... Magruder's Reports [*1, 2 Maryland*] [*A publication*] (DLA)
**Mag Mern Epitesz Egylet Kozl** ... Magyar Mernok es Epitesz Egylet Koezloenye [*A publication*]

**Mag Min Health Saf MESA** ... Magazine of Mining Health and Safety. MESA [*Mining Enforcement and Safety Administration*] [*United States*] [*A publication*]
**MAGMOD** ... Magnetic Modulator
**Mag Mor** ... Magna Moralia [*of Aristotle*] [*Classical studies*] (OCD)
**Mag & M & PL** ... Magistrate and Municipal and Parochial Lawyer [*A publication*] (DLA)
**Mag Mun Par Law** ... Magistrate and Municipal and Parochial Lawyer [*A publication*] (DLA)
**MAGN**....... Magnetic (ROG)
**MAGN**....... Magnetics International, Inc. [*NASDAQ symbol*] (NQ)
**MAGN**....... Magnetron [*Electricity*]
**MAGN**....... Magnus [*Great*] [*Latin*] (ADA)
**MagN**....... Magyar Nyelvor [*A publication*]
**MAGN**....... Monoaminoguanidine Nitrate [*Organic chemistry*]
**Mag Nagpur Agr Coll** ... Magazine. Nagpur Agricultural College [*A publication*]
**Magna Rot Pip** ... Magnus Rotulus Pipae [*Great Roll of the Pipe*] [*Latin*] [*A publication*] (DLA)
**Mag Nat Hist** ... Magazine of Natural History [*A publication*]
**Mag N Entdeck Ges Naturk** ... Magazin fuer die Neuesten Entdeckungen in der Gesammten Naturkunde [*A publication*]
**Magnesium Mon Rev** ... Magnesium Monthly Review [*A publication*]
**Magnesium Rev Abstr** ... Magnesium Review and Abstracts [*A publication*]
**Magnes Lecture Ser** ... Magnes Lecture Series [*A publication*]
**Magnetohydrodyn** ... Magnetohydrodynamics [*A publication*]
**Mag Neuesten Erfahr Entdeckungen Berichtigungen Geb Pharm** ... Magazin fuer die Neuesten Erfahrungen. Entdeckungen und Berichtigungen im Gebiete der Pharmacie [*A publication*]
**Magn Gidrodin** ... Magnitnaya Gidrodinamika [*A publication*]
**Mag N H**.... Magazine of Natural History [*London*] [*A publication*]
**Magn Hydrodyn** ... Magnetohydrodynamics [*A publication*]
**magnif**........ Magnification
**Magnit Gidrodinamika** ... Akademija Nauk Latviiskoi SSR. Magnitnaja Gidrodinamika [*A publication*]
**Magnitogidrodin Metod Poluch Elektroenergii** ... Magnitogidrodinamicheskii Metod Polucheniya Elektroenergii [*A publication*]
**Magnitogidrodin Metod Preobraz Energ** ... Magnitogidrodinamicheskii Metod Preobrazovaniya Energii [*USSR*] [*A publication*]
**Magn Lett** ... Magnetism Letters [*A publication*]
**Magn Lovushki** ... Magnitnye Lovushki [*A publication*]
**Magn Magn Mater Dig** ... Magnetism and Magnetic Materials Digest [*A publication*]
**MAGNOX** ... Magnesium Oxide [*Magnesium-based alloy*]
**Magn Resonance Rev** ... Magnetic Resonance Review [*A publication*]
**Magn Reson Annu** ... Magnetic Resonance Annual [*A publication*]
**Magn Reson Imaging** ... Magnetic Resonance Imaging [*A publication*]
**Magn Reson Med** ... Magnetic Resonance in Medicine [*A publication*]
**Magn Reson Q** ... Magnetic Resonance Quarterly [*A publication*]
**Magn Reson Rev** ... Magnetic Resonance Review [*A publication*]
**Magn Soc India Newsl** ... Magnetics Society of India. Newsletter [*A publication*]
**Magn Soc India Trans** ... Magnetics Society of India. Transactions [*A publication*]
**Magon Inst Rech Agron Publ Ser Sci** ... Magon Institut de Recherches Agronomiques. Publication. Serie Scientifique [*A publication*]
**Magon Inst Rech Agron Publ Ser Tech** ... Magon Institut de Recherches Agronomiques. Publication. Serie Technique [*A publication*]
**MAGOX**.... Magnesium Oxide [*Acronym is trademark of Basic Chemicals*]
**MAGP**....... Microfibrillar-Associated Glycoprotein [*Biochemistry*]
**MAGp**........ Military Airlift Group [*Air Force*] (AFM)
**MAGPIE**... Machine Automatically Generating Production Inventory Evaluation [*Data processing*] (IEEE)
**MAGPIE**... Markov Game Planar Intercept-Evasion Package [*Data processing*]
**Mag Psz Sz** ... Magyar Pszichologiai Szemle [*A publication*]
**M Agr**........ Master of Agriculture
**MAgrDevEc** ... Master of Agricultural Development Economics
**M Agr E**..... Master of Agricultural Engineering
**M Agr Eng** ... Master of Agricultural Engineering
**M Agric**...... Master of Agriculture
**MAGROCV** ... Military Advisory Group, Government of the Republic of China, Vietnam
**Mag Rot**..... Magnus Rotulus [*Great Roll of the Exchequer*] [*Latin*] [*A publication*] (DLA)
**M Agr S**..... Master of Agricultural Science
**M Agr Sc**... Master of Agricultural Science
**MAgrSt**..... Master of Agricultural Studies (ADA)
**Magruder**... Magruder's Reports [*1, 2 Maryland*] [*A publication*] (DLA)
**MAGS**....... Magistrates (ROG)
**MAGS**....... Multiple Aminoglycosides [*Antibacterial agents*]
**MAGSAT**... Magnetic Field Satellite [*NASA*] (MCD)
**MAGSAT**... Magnetometer Satellite (NASA)
**MAgSc**....... Master of Agricultural Science (ADA)
**MAGSI**...... Minimum Altitude at Glide Slope Intersection Inbound [*Aviation*] (FAAC)
**Mag Soc Milit Med Sci** ... Magazine. Society of Military Medical Science [*A publication*]
**MAgSt**....... Master of Agricultural Studies
**Mag of Stand** ... Magazine of Standards [*A publication*]
**Mag Stand** ... Magazine of Standards [*A publication*]
**Mag Std**..... Magazine of Standards [*A publication*]
**MAGSTR**... Magistrate
**MAGTAF**... Marine Air-Ground Task Force (AFM)
**MAGTD**.... Magnitude
**MAGTF**..... Marine Air-Ground Task Force (NVT)
**MAG-THOR** ... Magnesium-Thorium [*Inorganic chemistry*]
**MAGTOP**... Management of Traffic Operations [*Federal Highway Administration*]
**MAGTRAC**... Magnetic Tracker (MUGU)
**Mag Traumatol Orthop Helyreallito Sebesz** ... Magyar Traumatologia, Orthopaedia, es Helyreallito-Sebeszet [*A publication*]
**Mag Tud Akad Agrartud Oszt Kozl** ... Magyar Tudomanyos Akademia. Agrartudomanyok Osztalyanak Koezlemenyei [*A publication*]
**Mag Tud Akad Biol Tud Oszt Kozl** ... Magyar Tudomanyos Akademia. Biologiai Tudomanyok Osztalyanak Koezlemenyei [*A publication*]
**Mag Tud Akad Kem Tud Oszt Kozl** ... Magyar Tudomanyos Akademia. Kemiai Tudomanyok Osztalyanak Koezlemenyei [*A publication*]
**Mag Tud Akad Kozp Fiz Kut Intez Kozl** ... Magyar Tudomanyos Akademia. Kozponti Fizikai Kutato Intezetenek Koezlemenyei [*A publication*]
**Mag Tud Akad Kozp Kem Intez Kozl** ... Magyar Tudomanyos Akademia. Kozponti Kemiai Kutato Intezetenek Koezlemenyei [*A publication*]
**Mag Tud Akad Mat Fiz Tud Oszt Kozl** ... Magyar Tudomanyos Akademia. Matematikai es Fizikai Tudomanyok Osztalyanak Koezlemenyei [*A publication*]
**Mag Tud Akad Musz Tud Oszt Kozl** ... Magyar Tudomanyos Akademia. Mueszaki Tudomanyok Osztalyanak Koezlemenyei [*A publication*]
**Mag Tud Akad 5 Otodik Orv Tud Oszt Kozl** ... Magyar Tudomanyos Akademia. 5 Otodik Orvosi Tudomanyok Osztalyanak Koezlemenyei [*A publication*]
**MAGW**...... Maximum Alternate Gross Weight
**MAGW**...... Mitteilungen. Anthropologische Gesellschaft in Wien [*A publication*]
**Mag Wall St** ... Magazine of Wall Street [*A publication*]
**Mag of Wall St** ... Magazine of Wall Street [*A publication*]
**Mag Wall Street** ... Magazine of Wall Street [*A publication*]
**MAG Wien** ... Mitteilungen. Anthropologische Gesellschaft in Wien [*A publication*]
**MagWJ**...... Magazin fuer die Wissenschaft des Judentums [*A publication*]
**Magy**.......... Magyar Muza [*Record label*] [*Hungary*]
**Magy Allami Eoetvoes Lorand Geofiz Intez Evi Jelentese** ... Magyar Allami Eoetvoes Lorand Geofizikai Intezet. Evi Jelentese [*A publication*]
**Magy Allatorv Lap** ... Magyar Allatorvosok Lapja [*A publication*]
**Magy Allatorv Lapja** ... Magyar Allatorvosok Lapja [*A publication*]
**Magy Allatorv Lap Kueloenszama** ... Magyar Allatorvosok Lapja Kueloenszama [*A publication*]
**Magy All Eotvos Lorand Geofiz Intez Evi Jel** ... Magyar Allami Eoetvoes Lorand Geofizikai Intezet. Evi Jelentese [*A publication*]
**Magy All Foldt Intez Evi Jel** ... Magyar Allami Foldtani Intezet. Evi Jelentese [*A publication*]
**Magy All Foldt Intez Evk** ... Magyar Allami Foldtani Intezet. Evkoenyve [*A publication*]
**Magy All Foldt Intez Modszertani Kozl** ... Magyar Allami Foldtani Intezet. Modszertani Koezlemenyek [*A publication*]
**Magy Alum** ... Magyar Aluminium [*A publication*]
**Magyar Filoz Szle** ... Magyar Filozofiai Szemle [*A publication*]
**Magyar Num Tars Ev** ... Magyar Numizmatikai Tarsulat Evkoenyve [*A publication*]
**Magyarorsz Allatvilaga** ... Magyarorszag Allatvilaga [*A publication*]
**Magyar Pszichol Szle** ... Magyar Pszichologiai Szemle [*A publication*]
**Magyar Textiltech** ... Magyar Textiltechnika [*A publication*]
**Magyar Tud Akad Filoz-Tort Oszt Kozlem** ... Magyar Tudomanyos Akademia. Filozofiai-Torteneti Osztalyanak Koezlemenyei [*A publication*]
**Magyar Tud Akad Mat Fiz Oszt Koezl** ... Magyar Tudomanyos Akademia. Matematikai es Fizikai Tudomanyok Osztalyanak Koezlemenyei [*A publication*]
**Magy Asvanyolaj-Foeldgazkiserl Intez Koezl** ... Magyar Asvanyolaj-es Foeldgazkiserleti Intezet Koezlemenyei [*A publication*]
**Magy Asvanyolaj Foldgaz Kiserl Intez Kiadv** ... Magyar Asvanyolaj-es Foldgaz Kiserleti Intezet Kiadvanyai [*Hungary*] [*A publication*]
**Magy Asvanyolaj Foldgaz Kiserl Intez Kozl** ... Magyar Asvanyolaj-es Foldgaz Kiserleti Intezet Koezlemenyei [*Hungary*] [*A publication*]
**Magy Belorv Arch** ... Magyar Belorvosi Archivum [*A publication*]
**Magy Biol Kutato Intezet Munkai** ... Magyar Biologiai Kutato Intezet Munkai [*A publication*]
**Magy Chem Folyoirat** ... Magyar Chemiai Folyoirat [*Hungary*] [*A publication*]
**Magy Epitoeipar** ... Magyar Epitoeipar [*A publication*]
**Magy Fiz Foly** ... Magyar Fizikai Folyoirat [*A publication*]
**Magy Geofiz** ... Magyar Geofizika [*A publication*]
**Magy Kem Fo** ... Magyar Kemiai Folyoirat [*A publication*]
**Magy Kem Foly** ... Magyar Kemiai Folyoirat [*A publication*]

**Magy Kem Folyoirat** ... Magyar Kemiai Folyoirat [*A publication*]
**Magy Kem Lapja** ... Magyar Kemikusok Lapja [*A publication*]
**Magy Koenyvszle** ... Magyar Koenyvszemle [*A publication*]
**Magy Koezl** ... Magyar Koezloeny [*A publication*]
**Magy Kult** ... Magyarorszag Kulturfloraja [*A publication*]
**Magy Kulturfloraja** ... Magyarorszag Kulturfloraja [*A publication*]
**Magy Mezoegazd** ... Magyar Mezoegazdasag [*A publication*]
**Magy Noeorv Lap** ... Magyar Noeorvosok Lapja [*A publication*]
**Magy Noeorv Lapja** ... Magyar Noeorvosok Lapja [*A publication*]
**Magy Onkol** ... Magyar Onkologia [*A publication*]
**Magy Orv Bibliogr** ... Magyar Orvosi Bibliografia [*A publication*]
**Magy Pszichol Szle** ... Magyar Pszichologiai Szemle [*A publication*]
**Magy Radiol** ... Magyar Radiologia [*A publication*]
**Magy Reumatol** ... Magyar Reumatologia [*A publication*]
**Magy Sebesz** ... Magyar Sebeszet [*A publication*]
**Magy Textiltech** ... Magyar Textiltechnika [*Hungary*] [*A publication*]
**Magy Traumatol Orthop** ... Magyar Traumatologia, Orthopaedia, es Helyreallito-Sebeszet [*A publication*]
**Magy Traumatol Orthop Helyreallito Sebesz** ... Magyar Traumatologia, Orthopaedia, es Helyreallito-Sebeszet [*A publication*]
**Magy Tud** .. Magyar Tudomany [*A publication*]
**Magy Tud Akad Agrartud Osztal Kozl** ... Magyar Tudomanyos Akademia. Agrartudomanyok Osztalyanak Koezlemenyei [*A publication*]
**Magy Tud Akad Biol Csoportjanak Kozlem (Budapest)** ... Magyar Tudomanyos Akademia. Biologiai Csoportjanak Koezlemenyei (Budapest) [*A publication*]
**Magy Tud Akad Biol Orv Tud Oszt Kozl** ... Magyar Tudomanyos Akademia. Biologiai es Orvosi Tudomanyok Osztalyanak Koezlemenyei [*A publication*]
**Magy Tud Akad Biol Tud Oszt Koezl** ... Magyar Tudomanyos Akademia. Biologiai Tudomanyok Osztalyanak Koezlemenyei [*A publication*]
**Magy Tud Akad Kem Tud Oszt Kozlem** ... Magyar Tudomanyos Akademia. Kemiai Tudomanyok Osztalyanak Koezlemenyei [*Hungary*] [*A publication*]
**Magy Tud Akad Mat Fiz Tud Oszt Kozlem** ... Magyar Tudomanyos Akademia. Matematikai es Fizikai Tudomanyok Osztalyanak Koezlemenyei [*Hungary*] [*A publication*]
**Magy Tud Akad Mat Kut Intez Kozlem** ... Magyar Tudomanyos Akademia. Matematikai Kutato Intezetenek Koezlemenyei [*Hungary*] [*A publication*]
**Magy Tud Akad Muesz Fiz Kut Intez Koezl** ... Magyar Tudomanyos Akademia. Mueszaki Fizikai Kutato Intezetenek Koezlemenyei [*A publication*]
**Magy Tud Akad Muszaki Tud Oszt Kozlem** ... Magyar Tudomanyos Akademia. Mueszaki Tudomanyok Osztalyanak Koezlemenyei [*Hungary*] [*A publication*]
**Magy Tud Akad Tihanyi Biol Kutatointez Evk** ... Magyar Tudomanyos Akademia. Tihanyi Biologiai Kutatointezet Evkoenyve [*A publication*]
**Magy Tud Akad Veszpremi Akad Bizottsaganak Ert** ... Magyar Tudomanyos Akademia. Veszpremi Akademiai Bizottsaganak Ertesitoje [*Hungary*] [*A publication*]
**Magy Tudom Akad Biol Osztal Kozl** ... Magyar Tudomanyos Akademia. Biologiai Osztalyanak Koezlemenyei [*A publication*]
**Magy Villamos Muevek Troeszt Koezl** ... Magyar Villamos Muevek Troeszt Koezlemenyei [*A publication*]
**Magz** .......... Magazine
**MAGZ** ....... Mitteilungen. Antiquarische Gesellschaft in Zurich [*A publication*]
**MAH** ......... Collection des Tablettes Cuneiformes du Musee d'Art et d'Histoire de Geneve (BJA)
**MAH** ......... Findlay, OH [*Location identifier*] [*FAA*] (FAAL)
**MAH** ......... Hampshire College, Amherst, MA [*Library symbol*] [*Library of Congress*] (LCLS)
**MAH** ......... Hanna [*M. A.*] Co. [*NYSE symbol*] (SPSG)
**MAH** ......... Magnesium Aspartate Hydrochloride [*Antihypertensive*]
**MAH** ......... Mahableshwar [*India*] [*Seismograph station code, US Geological Survey*] [*Closed*] (SEIS)
**MAH** ......... Mahogany (MSA)
**MAH** ......... Mahommedanism (ROG)
**MAH** ......... Mahon [*Spain*] [*Airport symbol*] (OAG)
**MAH** ......... Maleic Anhydride [*Also, MA*] [*Organic chemistry*]
**MAH** ......... Malignancy-Associated Hypercalcemia [*Oncology*]
**MAH** ......... Massachusetts Historical Society, Boston, MA [*OCLC symbol*] (OCLC)
**MAH** ......... Medical Abbreviations Handbook [*A publication*]
**MAH** ......... Melanges d'Archeologie et d'Histoire [*A publication*]
**MAH** ......... Metaal en Techniek. Vakblad voor de Metaalnijverheid [*A publication*]
**mAH** .......... Milliampere Hour
**MAHA** ....... Metropolitan Association of Handwriting Analysts (EA)
**MAHA** ....... Microangiopathic Hemolytic Anemia [*Medicine*]
**Maharaja Sayajirao Mem Lect** ... Maharaja Sayajirao Memorial Lectures [*A publication*]
**Maharashtra Coop Q** ... Maharashtra Cooperative Quarterly [*A publication*]
**Maharashtra LJ** ... Maharashtra Law Journal [*India*] [*A publication*] (DLA)
**Maharastra Coop Quart** ... Maharashtra Cooperative Quarterly [*A publication*]
**Mahatma Phule Agric Univ Res J** ... Mahatma Phule Agricultural University. Research Journal [*A publication*]
**MAHC** ....... Maximum Allowable Housing Cost [*Army*] (AABC)
**Mah & DRT** ... Mahaffy and Dodson's Road Traffic [*3rd ed.*] [*1961*] [*A publication*] (DLA)
**MAHE** ....... Master of Arts in Hebrew Education (BJA)
**MAHi** ........ Amherst Historical Society, Amherst, MA [*Library symbol*] [*Library of Congress*] (LCLS)
**MAHI** ........ Monarch Avalon, Incorporated [*NASDAQ symbol*] (NQ)
**MAHL** ....... Master of Hebrew Literature (BJA)
**Mah LJ** ....... Maharashtra Law Journal [*India*] [*A publication*] (DLA)
**Mah Med J** ... Maharashtra Medical Journal [*A publication*]
**MAHOG** ... Mahogany (DSUE)
**MA(Hons)** ... Master of Arts with Honours (ADA)
**MAHP** ....... Member of the Association of Hypnotists and Physiotherapists [*British*]
**MAHR** ....... Mid-America: An Historical Review [*A publication*]
**MAHS** ....... Mitteilungen der Auslandhochschule an der Universitaet Berlin [*A publication*]
**MAI** .......... M/A-Com, Inc. [*Formerly, Microwave Associates, Incorporated*] [*NYSE symbol*] (SPSG)
**MAI** .......... Machine-Aided Indexing (KSC)
**MAI** .......... Magister in Arte Ingeniaria [*Master of Engineering*]
**Mai** ........... Maine's Reports [*A publication*] (DLA)
**mai** ............ Maithili [*MARC language code*] [*Library of Congress*] (LCCP)
**MAI** .......... Maius [*May*] [*Latin*]
**MAI** .......... Maizuru [*Japan*] [*Seismograph station code, US Geological Survey*] [*Closed*] (SEIS)
**MAI** .......... Mantle Arm Index
**MAI** .......... Marianna, FL [*Location identifier*] [*FAA*] (FAAL)
**MAI** .......... Marriage Adjustment Inventory [*Psychology*]
**MAI** .......... Master of Fine Arts International [*British*]
**MAI** .......... Material Annex Item [*Military*]
**MAI** .......... Media Associates International [*An association*] (EA)
**MAI** .......... Medical Aid for Indochina [*An association*] (EA)
**MAI** .......... Member of the Anthropological Institute [*British*]
**MAI** .......... Member, Appraisal Institute [*Designation awarded by American Institute of Real Estate Appraisers of the National Association of Realtors*]
**MAI** .......... Memoires. Institut National de France. Academie des Inscriptions et Belles-Lettres [*A publication*]
**MAI** .......... Metropolitan Action Institute [*Formerly, SAI*] (EA)
**MAI** .......... Military Assistance Institute [*Air Force*]
**MAI** .......... Ministerium fuer Aussenhandel und Innerdeutschen Handel [*Ministry for Foreign Trade and Domestic German Trade*] [*See also MfAI*]
**MAI** .......... Mitteilungen des Deutschen Archaeologischen Instituts [*A publication*]
**MAI** .......... Moskovskij Archeologiceskij Institut [*A publication*]
**MAI** .......... Multiple Access Interface
**MAI** .......... Multiple Address Instruction
**MAI** .......... Mycobacterium Avium-Intracellulare [*Medicine*]
**MAIA** ........ Magnetic Antibody Immunoassay
**MAIA** ........ Member of the American Institute of Appraisers
**MAIAA** ..... Member of the American Institute of Aeronautics and Astronautics [*Formerly, MIAS*]
**Mai Anc L** ... Maine's Ancient Law [*A publication*] (DLA)
**MAIBL** ...... Midland & International Banks Limited [*British*]
**MAIC** ........ Member of the Australian Institute of Cartographers
**MAICE** ...... Member of the American Institute of Consulting Engineers
**MAIChE** .... Member of the American Institute of Chemical Engineers
**MAID** ........ Maidstone [*Municipal borough in England*]
**MAID** ........ Maintenance Automatic Integration Director [*Data processing*]
**MAID** ........ Manual Intervention and Display
**MAID** ........ Market Analysis and Information Database [*MAID Systems Ltd.*] [*Great Britain*] [*Information service or system*] (IID)
**MAID** ........ Master Area Interest Decks (MCD)
**MAID** ........ Merger Acquisition Improved Decision [*Data processing*]
**MAID** ........ Monroe Automatic Internal Diagnosis [*Data processing*]
**MAID/MILES** ... Magnetic Anti-Intrusion Detector/Magnetic Intrusion Line Sensor (MCD)
**MAIDS** ...... Machine-Aided Information and Dissemination Systems
**MAIDS** ...... Management Automated Information Display System (KSC)
**MAIDS** ...... Multipurpose Automatic Inspection and Diagnostic Systems [*Army*]
**MAIE** ........ Member of the British Association of Industrial Editors (DBQ)
**MAIEE** ...... Member of the American Institute of Electrical Engineers
**MAIEx** ...... Member of the Australian Institute of Export
**MAIF** ......... Major Analytical Instruments Facility [*Case Western Reserve University*] [*Research center*] (RCD)
**Mai Inst** ..... Maine's History of Institutions [*A publication*] (DLA)
**MAIL** ......... Mail Boxes, Etc. [*San Diego, CA*] [*NASDAQ symbol*] (NQ)
**MAILS** ...... Materiel Acquisition and Integrated Logistics Support
**MAILS** ...... Mid-America Interlibrary Services [*Library network*]
**MAILS** ...... Mississippi Automated Interlibrary Loan System [*Mississippi State Library Commission*] [*Information service or system*] (IID)
**MAIM** ....... Member of the Australian Institute of Management
**Maim** ......... Moses Maimonides [*Spanish Talmudist, 1135-1204*] (BJA)

**MAIME**..... Member of the American Institute of Mining and Metallurgical Engineers
**MAIME**..... Member of the Australian Institute of Mining Engineers
**MAIN**........ Maintenance (NASA)
**MAIN**........ Maritime Industries. Massachusetts Institute of Technology [*A publication*]
**MAIN**........ Material Automated Information System
**MAIN**........ Material Automated Inventory Network (MCD)
**MAIN**........ Medical Automation Intelligence [*System*]
**MAIN**........ Mid-America Interconnected Network [*Regional power council*]
**MAIN**........ Military Authorization Identification Number
**Main Curr M** ... Main Currents in Modern Thought [*A publication*]
**Maine**......... Maine Reports [*A publication*] (DLA)
**Maine Ag Dept B** ... Maine. Department of Agriculture. Quarterly Bulletin [*A publication*]
**Maine Ag Exp** ... Maine. Agricultural Experiment Station. Publications [*A publication*]
**Maine Agric Exp Stn Bull** ... Maine. Agricultural Experiment Station. Bulletin [*A publication*]
**Maine Agric Exp Stn Misc Publ** ... Maine. Agricultural Experiment Station. Miscellaneous Publication [*A publication*]
**Maine Agric Exp Stn Misc Rep** ... Maine. Agricultural Experiment Station. Miscellaneous Report [*A publication*]
**Maine Agric Exp Stn Official Inspect** ... Maine. Agricultural Experiment Station. Official Inspections [*A publication*]
**Maine Agric Exp Stn Off Inspect** ... Maine. Agricultural Experiment Station. Official Inspections [*A publication*]
**Maine Agric Exp Stn Tech Bull** ... Maine. Agricultural Experiment Station. Technical Bulletin [*A publication*]
**Maine Anc Law** ... Maine's Ancient Law [*A publication*] (DLA)
**Maine Basic Data Rep Ground Water Ser** ... Maine Basic-Data Reports. Ground-Water Series [*A publication*]
**Maine Farm Res** ... Maine Farm Research [*A publication*]
**Maine Field Nat** ... Maine Field Naturalist [*A publication*]
**Maine For Rev** ... Marine Forest Review [*A publication*]
**Maine Geol** ... Maine Geology [*A publication*]
**Maine Geol Surv Spec Econ Ser** ... Maine Geological Survey. Special Economic Series [*A publication*]
**Maine Geol Surv Spec Econ Stud Ser Bull** ... Maine. Geological Survey. Special Economic Studies Series. Bulletin [*A publication*]
**Maine Hist Soc Coll** ... Maine Historical Society. Collections [*A publication*]
**Maine Lib Assn Bul** ... Maine Library Association. Bulletin [*A publication*]
**Maine Life Agric Exp Stn Tech Bull** ... Maine. Life Sciences and Agricultural Experiment Station. Technical Bulletin [*A publication*]
**Maine Life Sci Agric Exp Stn Bull** ... Maine. Life Sciences and Agricultural Experiment Station. Bulletin [*A publication*]
**Maine Life Sci Agric Exp Stn Off Inspect** ... Maine. Life Sciences and Agricultural Experiment Station. Official Inspections [*A publication*]
**Maine Life Sci Agric Exp Stn Tech Bull** ... Maine. Life Sciences and Agricultural Experiment Station. Technical Bulletin [*A publication*]
**Maine L R** ... Maine Law Review [*A publication*]
**Maine L Rev** ... Maine Law Review [*A publication*]
**Maine PUR** ... Maine Public Utilities Commission Reports [*A publication*] (DLA)
**Maine R**.... Maine Reports [*A publication*] (DLA)
**Maine Rep** ... Maine Reports [*A publication*] (DLA)
**Maine Technol Exp Stn Univ Maine Pap** ... Maine. Technology Experiment Station. University of Maine. Paper [*A publication*]
**Maine Technology Expt Sta Bull Paper** ... Maine. Technology Experiment Station. Bulletin. Papers [*A publication*]
**Mainfraenk Jahrb** ... Mainfraenkisches Jahrbuch fuer Geschichte und Kunst [*A publication*]
**Mainfraenk Jb Gesch Kunst** ... Mainfraenkisches Jahrbuch fuer Geschichte und Kunst [*A publication*]
**Mainfr Jb**... Mainfraenkisches Jahrbuch fuer Geschichte und Kunst [*A publication*]
**Mainlobe**.... Major Investigation for Low-Frequency Ocean Bottom Loss Experiments [*Marine science*] (MSC)
**Main Rds** ... Main Roads [*A publication*]
**MA Inst Ung Ak** ... Mitteilungen. Archaeologisches Institut der Ungarischen Akademie der Wissenschaften [*A publication*]
**MAINT** ..... Maintain (FAAC)
**MAINT** ..... Maintenance (AFM)
**MA/INT**.... Maintenance Actions per Interval (MCD)
**MAINTCE** ... Maintenance (ROG)
**maintd**........ Maintained
**Maint Eng** ... Maintenance Engineering [*A publication*]
**Maint Eng (London)** ... Maintenance Engineering (London) [*A publication*]
**Maint Mgmt Internat** ... Maintenance Management International [*A publication*]
**MAINTNCE** ... Maintenance [*Freight*]
**MAINTRAIN** ... Maintenance and Training [*in complex equipment*]
**MAINTSUPPORTOFF** ... Maintenance Support Office [*Navy*]
**Mainzer Geowiss Mitt** ... Mainzer Geowissenschaftliche Mitteilungen [*A publication*]
**Mainz Z** ..... Mainzer Zeitschrift [*A publication*]
**MAIO** ........ Mashhad [*Iran*] [*Seismograph station code, US Geological Survey*] (SEIS)
**MAIP**......... Matrix Algebra Interpretive Program (IEEE)
**MAIP**......... Member of the Australian Institute of Physics
**Maipu Chile Estac Exp Agron Bol Tec** ... Maipu, Chile. Estacion Experimental Agronomica. Boletin Tecnico [*A publication*]
**MAIR** ........ Manufacturing and Inspection Record (KSC)
**MAIR** ........ Master of Arts in Industrial Relations
**MAIR** ........ Memorie. Classe di Scienze Morali, Storiche, e Filologiche. Accademia d'Italia (Roma) [*A publication*]
**MAIR** ........ Metro Airlines, Inc. [*NASDAQ symbol*] (NQ)
**MAIR** ........ Molecular Airborne Intercept RADAR
**MAIRMAR** ... Marine Air Depot, Miramar [*California*]
**MAIRS**...... Military Air Integrated Reporting System (MCD)
**MAIRU** ..... Mobile Aircraft Instrument Repair Unit
**MAIS**......... Maintenance Information System [*Military*] (NVT)
**MAIS**......... Mechanical Aids for the Individual Soldier [*Army*]
**MAIS**......... Mediterranean Association of International Schools (EA)
**MAIS**......... Microfilm Alpha Index System
**MAIS**......... Multicultural Australia Information System
**MAIS**......... Mycobacterium Avium-Intracellulare-Scrofulaceum [*Bacteriology*]
**MAISA**...... Middle Atlantic Intercollegiate Sailing Association
**MAISA**...... Multiple Analytical Isoelectrofocusing Scanning Apparatus
**MAISARC** ... Major Automated Information System Review Council [*Army*]
**MAISBP**.... Marine Invertebrates of Scandinavia [*A publication*]
**Mais D** ....... La Maison-Dieu [*A publication*]
**Mais Dieu** .. La Maison-Dieu [*A publication*]
**MAISRC** ... Major Automated Information Systems Review Council [*Army*]
**MAIT** ........ Maintenance Assistance and Instruction Team [*Army*] (AABC)
**Mait** ........... Maitland's Select Pleas of the Crown [*A publication*] (DLA)
**MAIT** ........ Matrix Analysis of Insider Threat [*Nuclear energy*] (NRCH)
**MAIT** ........ Member of the Australian Institute of Travel
**Mait Gl** ...... Maitland's Pleas of the Crown, County of Gloucester [*A publication*] (DLA)
**Maitland**.... Maitland's Manuscript Session Cases [*Scotland*] [*A publication*] (DLA)
**Maitland**.... Maitland's Pleas of the Crown [*1221*] [*England*] [*A publication*] (DLA)
**Maitland**.... Maitland's Select Pleas of the Crown [*A publication*] (DLA)
**MaitrePhon** ... Maitre Phonetique [*A publication*]
**Maize Genet Coop News Lett** ... Maize Genetics Cooperation. News Letter [*A publication*]
**MAJ** .......... Jones Library, Amherst, MA [*Library symbol*] [*Library of Congress*] (LCLS)
**MAJ** .......... Majestic Electronic Stores, Inc. [*Toronto Stock Exchange symbol*]
**MAJ** .......... Majolica [*Ceramics*] (ROG)
**MAJ** .......... Major [*Military*] (AABC)
**MAJ** .......... Majority (KSC)
**MAJ** .......... Majuro [*Marshall Islands*] [*Airport symbol*] (OAG)
**MAJ** .......... Maron [*Java*] [*Seismograph station code, US Geological Survey*] [*Closed*] (SEIS)
**MAJ** .......... Michael Anthony Jewelers, Inc. [*AMEX symbol*] (SPSG)
**MAJ** .......... Model Air Jet
**MAJAC**..... Maintenance Antijam Console [*Air Force*]
**Majalah Kedokt Surabaya** ... Majalah Kedokteran Surabaya [*A publication*]
**MAJBAC** .. Muelleria [*A publication*]
**Maj Batan** ... Majalah Batan [*A publication*]
**MAJC**........ Mount Aloysius Junior College [*Pennsylvania*]
**MAJC**........ Mutual Association of Journeymen Coopers [*A union*] [*British*]
**MAJCOM** ... Major Command [*Formerly, Major Air Command*] [*Military*]
**MAJCON** ... Major Air Command Controlled [*Units*]
**MAJCS** ...... Master of Arts in Jewish Communal Service (BJA)
**MAJCSSW** ... Master of Arts in Jewish Communal Studies and Social Work (BJA)
**Maj Daneshgah e Tehran Daneshkade ye Darusazi** ... Majallah. Daneshgah- e Tehran. Daneshkade- ye Darusazi [*A publication*]
**Maj Demog Indo** ... Majalah Demografi Indonesia [*A publication*]
**MAJE**........ Master of Arts in Jewish Education (BJA)
**MAJ GEN** ... Major General (AFM)
**MAJO** ....... Matsushiro [*Japan*] [*Seismograph station code, US Geological Survey*] (SEIS)
**Majority**..... Majority Report [*A publication*]
**Major Probl Clin Pediatr** ... Major Problems in Clinical Pediatrics [*A publication*]
**Major Probl Clin Surg** ... Major Problems in Clinical Surgery [*A publication*]
**Major Probl Intern Med** ... Major Problems in Internal Medicine [*A publication*]
**Major Probl Obstet Gynecol** ... Major Problems in Obstetrics and Gynecology [*A publication*]
**Major Probl Pathol** ... Major Problems in Pathology [*A publication*]
**MAJR**........ Major Realty Corp. [*NASDAQ symbol*] (NQ)
**MAJS**........ Master of Arts in Judaic Studies (BJA)
**MAJV**........ Major Video Corp. [*NASDAQ symbol*] (NQ)
**MAJX**........ Major Exploration, Inc. [*NASDAQ symbol*] (NQ)
**MAJY**........ Majority (ROG)
**MAK**.......... Makhachkala [*USSR*] [*Seismograph station code, US Geological Survey*] (SEIS)
**MAK**.......... Making
**MAK**.......... Makkoth (BJA)
**MAK**.......... Malakal [*Sudan*] [*Airport symbol*] (OAG)

**MAK**.......... Markway Resources Ltd. [*Vancouver Stock Exchange symbol*]
**MAK**.......... Maximale Arbeitsplatzkonzentration [*Maximum Workplace Concentration*] [*German*]
**MAK**.......... Medical Accessories Kit [*Apollo*] [*NASA*]
**MAK**.......... Methylated Albumin Kieselguhr [*Chromatography*]
**MAK**.......... Monopulse Antenna Kit
**MAKA**....... Major Karyotypic Abnormalities [*Medicine*]
**Maked Folkl** ... Makedonski Folklor [*A publication*]
**Maked Med Pregl** ... Makedonski Medicinski Pregled [*A publication*]
**Makedon Akad Nauk Umet Oddel Mat-Tehn Nauk Prilozi** ... Makedonska Akademija na Naukite i Umetnostite Oddelenie za Matematichki-Tehnichki Nauki. Prilozi [*A publication*]
**Makedon Akad Nauk Umet Oddel Prirod-Mat Nauk Prilozi** ... Makedonska Akademija na Naukite i Umetnostite Oddelenie za Prirodo-Matematicki Nauki Prilozi [*A publication*]
**Makedon Med Pregl** ... Makedonski Medicinski Pregled [*A publication*]
**Makerere LJ** ... Makerere Law Journal [*A publication*]
**Makerere Med J** ... Makerere Medical Journal [*A publication*]
**Mak F NY** ... Making Films in New York [*A publication*]
**Makhsh**..... Makhshirin (BJA)
**MAKIA**..... Maandschrift voor Kindergeneeskunde [*A publication*]
**Making Mus** ... Making Music [*A publication*]
**MAKL**....... Markel Corp. [*NASDAQ symbol*] (NQ)
**Mak LJ**...... Makerere Law Journal [*A publication*]
**Makr Ch**.... Makromolekulare Chemie [*A publication*]
**MAKRO**.... Management Analysis of Key Resource Operations [*Military*]
**Makrom Chem** ... Makromolekulare Chemie [*A publication*]
**Makromol Chem** ... Makromolekulare Chemie [*A publication*]
**Makromol Chem Rapid Commun** ... Makromolekulare Chemie. Rapid Communications [*A publication*]
**Makromol Chem Suppl** ... Makromolekulare Chemie. Supplement [*A publication*]
**Maks**.......... Makhshirin (BJA)
**Maksh**........ Makhshirin (BJA)
**MAKSUTSUB** ... Make Suitable Substitution
**MAKW**...... Mitteilungen. Altertumskommission fuer Westphalen [*A publication*]
**MAL**.......... Atti. Accademia Nazionale dei Lincei. Memorie. Classe di Scienze Morali, Storiche, e Filologiche [*A publication*]
**MAL**.......... Macroassembly Language [*Data processing*] (BUR)
**MAL**.......... Mad Art Lover
**MAL**.......... Magnetic Armature Loudspeaker
**MAL**.......... Maintain at Least [*Followed by altitude*] [*Aviation*] (FAAC)
**Mal**............ Malachi [*Old Testament book*]
**MAL**.......... Malachias [*Old testament book*] [*Douay version*]
**MAL**.......... Malaga [*Spain*] [*Seismograph station code, US Geological Survey*] (SEIS)
**MAL**.......... Malariology Technician [*Navy*]
**MAL**.......... Malaspina College Learning Resources Centre [*UTLAS symbol*]
**MAL**.......... Malate
**mal**............ Malayalam [*MARC language code*] [*Library of Congress*] (LCCP)
**MAL**.......... Malayan (AABC)
**MAL**.......... Malayan Airways Limited
**MAL**.......... Malaysian Air Lines
**Mal**............ Maleyl [*Biochemistry*]
**MAL**.......... Malfunction (KSC)
**MAL**.......... Malicious [*FBI standardized term*]
**MAL**.......... Malleable (MSA)
**mal**............ Malonate [*Organic chemistry*]
**MAL**.......... Malone College, Canton, OH [*OCLC symbol*] (OCLC)
**MAL**.......... Malone, NY [*Location identifier*] [*FAA*] (FAAL)
**MAL**.......... Man and LASER (MCD)
**MAL**.......... Mandated Airlines [*Australia*]
**MAL**.......... Manhattan Airlines [*Syracuse, NY*] [*FAA designator*] (FAAC)
**MAL**.......... Marco Resources [*Vancouver Stock Exchange symbol*]
**MAL**.......... Markenartikel. Zeitschrift fuer die Markenartikelindustrie [*A publication*]
**MAL**.......... Materiel Allowance List [*Military*]
**MAL**.......... Medullary Thick Ascending Limb [*Anatomy*]
**MAL**.......... Memory Access Logic
**MAL**.......... Mercury Arc Lamp
**MAL**.......... Meta Assembly Language
**MAL**.......... Methacrolein [*Also, MACR*] [*Organic chemistry*]
**MAL**.......... Midaxillary Line [*Medicine*]
**MAL**.......... Middle Assyrian Laws (BJA)
**MAL**.......... Miller Airlines [*Michigan*] (FAAC)
**MAL**.......... Mobile Airlock (MCD)
**MAL**.......... Modern American Law [*A publication*] (DLA)
**MAL**.......... Modern Austrian Literature [*A publication*]
**MAL**.......... Monumenti Antichi. Accademia Nazionale dei Lincei [*A publication*]
**MAL**.......... Multiairline [*Type of British pole line construction*]
**MAL**.......... Multiple Address Letter (NOAA)
**MALA**....... Manpower and Logistics Analysis (MCD)
**MAL-AAACE** ... Media and Adult Learning Section of the American Association for Adult and Continuing Education (EA)
**MALAC**..... Malacology
**Malacol Int J Malacol** ... Malacologia. International Journal of Malacology [*A publication*]
**Malacolog Soc London Proc** ... Malacological Society of London. Proceedings [*A publication*]
**Malacol Rev** ... Malacological Review [*A publication*]
**Malacol Soc Aust J** ... Malacological Society of Australia. Journal [*A publication*] (APTA)
**Malacol Soc L Pr** ... Malacological Society of London. Proceedings [*A publication*]
**MALAD**.... Maladjusted Child [*Social Work*] [*British*] (DSUE)
**Mala Econ R** ... Malayan Economic Review [*A publication*]
**Malagasy Rapp Annu Serv Geol** ... Malagasy. Rapport Annuel du Service Geologique [*A publication*]
**MALAGOC** ... Mutual Assistance of the Latin American Government Oil Companies [*See also ARPEL*] (EA)
**Malag Rep** ... Malagasy Republic
**Malahat Rev** ... Malahat Review [*A publication*]
**Malakol Abh (Dres)** ... Malakologische Abhandlungen (Dresden) [*A publication*]
**MaLAM**.... Medical Lobby for Appropriate Marketing [*Australia*]
**MalaR**........ Malahat Review [*A publication*]
**Malaria Internat Arch (Leipzig)** ... Malaria. International Archives (Leipzig) [*A publication*]
**Malaria (Roma)** ... Malaria e Malattie dei Paesi Caldi (Roma) [*A publication*]
**MALAS**..... Midwestern Association for Latin American Studies
**Malawian Geogr** ... Malawian Geographer [*A publication*]
**Malawi Annu Rep Dep Agric** ... Malawi. Annual Report of the Department of Agriculture [*A publication*]
**Malawi Dep Agric Fish Annu Rep Fish Part 2** ... Malawi. Department of Agriculture and Fisheries. Annual Report. Fisheries Research. Part 2 [*A publication*]
**Malawi For Res Inst Res Rec** ... Malawi Forest Research Institute. Research Record [*A publication*]
**Malawi Geol Surv Dep Bull** ... Malawi. Geological Survey Department. Bulletin [*A publication*]
**Malawi Geol Surv Dep Mem** ... Malawi. Geological Survey Department. Memoir [*A publication*]
**Malaya Dep Agric Bull** ... Malaya. Department of Agriculture. Bulletin [*A publication*]
**Malaya For Res Inst Res Pam** ... Malaya. Forest Research Institute. Research Pamphlet [*A publication*]
**Malaya Geol Surv Dep Mem** ... Malaya. Geological Survey Department. Memoir [*A publication*]
**Malay Agric J** ... Malayan Agricultural Journal [*A publication*]
**Malaya Law R** ... Malaya Law Review [*A publication*]
**Malaya LR** ... Malaya Law Review [*A publication*]
**Malaya L Rev** ... Malaya Law Review [*A publication*]
**Malayan Ag J** ... Malayan Agricultural Journal [*A publication*]
**Malayan Agric J** ... Malayan Agricultural Journal [*A publication*]
**Malayan Agr J** ... Malayan Agricultural Journal [*A publication*]
**Malayan Econ R** ... Malayan Economic Review [*A publication*]
**Malayan Lib J** ... Malayan Library Journal [*A publication*]
**Malayan LJ** ... Malayan Law Journal [*A publication*]
**Malay Dep Agric Bull** ... Malaya. Department of Agriculture. Bulletin [*A publication*]
**Malay For** ... Malayan Forester [*A publication*]
**Malay For Rec** ... Malayan Forest Records [*A publication*]
**Malay Nat J** ... Malayan Nature Journal [*A publication*]
**Malay Rep For Admin** ... Malay Report on Forest Administration [*A publication*]
**Malays Agric J** ... Malaysian Agricultural Journal [*A publication*]
**Malays Annu Rep Inst Med Res** ... Malaysia. Annual Report. Institute for Medical Research [*A publication*]
**Malays Appl Bio** ... Malaysian Applied Biology [*A publication*]
**Malays Borneo Reg Annu Rep Geol Surv** ... Malaysia. Borneo Region. Annual Report of the Geological Survey [*A publication*]
**Malays Div Agric Bull** ... Malaysia. Division of Agriculture. Bulletin [*A publication*]
**Malays For** ... Malaysian Forester [*A publication*]
**Malays For Res Inst Kepong Res Pam** ... Malaysia. Forest Research Institute. Kepong Research Pamphlet [*A publication*]
**Malays Geol Surv Annu Rep** ... Malaysia. Geological Survey. Annual Report [*A publication*]
**Malays Geol Surv Borneo Reg Bull** ... Malaysia. Geological Survey. Borneo Region. Bulletin [*A publication*]
**Malays Geol Surv Borneo Reg Mem** ... Malaysia. Geological Survey. Borneo Region. Memoir [*A publication*]
**Malays Geol Surv Borneo Reg Rep** ... Malaysia. Geological Survey. Borneo Region. Report [*A publication*]
**Malays Geol Surv Dist Mem** ... Malaysia. Geological Survey. District Memoir [*A publication*]
**Malays Geol Surv Map Bull** ... Malaysia. Geological Survey. Map Bulletin [*A publication*]
**Malays Geol Surv Rep** ... Malaysia. Geological Survey. Report [*A publication*]
**Malaysian Agric Res** ... Malaysian Agricultural Research [*A publication*]
**Malaysian Rubb Rev** ... Malaysian Rubber Review [*A publication*]
**Malays Inst Med Res Annu Rep** ... Malaysia Institute for Medical Research. Annual Report [*A publication*]
**Malays Inst Penylidikan Perubatan Lapuran Tahunan** ... Malaysia Institiut Penylidikan Perubatan Lapuran Tahunan [*A publication*]
**Malays J Pathol** ... Malaysian Journal of Pathology [*A publication*]
**Malays J Reprod Health** ... Malaysian Journal of Reproductive Health [*A publication*]

**Malays J Sci** ... Malaysian Journal of Science [*A publication*]
**Malays Minist Agric Co-Op Bull** ... Malaysia. Ministry of Agriculture and Co-Operatives. Bulletin [*A publication*]
**Malays Minist Agric Fish Bull** ... Malaysia. Ministry of Agriculture and Fisheries. Bulletin [*A publication*]
**Malays Minist Agric Lands Bull** ... Malaysia. Ministry of Agriculture and Lands. Bulletin [*A publication*]
**Malays Minist Agric Lands Tech Leafl** ... Malaysia. Ministry of Agriculture and Lands. Technical Leaflet [*A publication*]
**Malays Minist Agric Rural Dev Bull** ... Malaysia. Ministry of Agriculture and Rural Development. Bulletin [*A publication*]
**Malays Minist Agric Rural Dev Fish Bull** ... Malaysia. Ministry of Agriculture and Rural Development. Fisheries Bulletin [*A publication*]
**Malays Minist Agric Rural Dev Risalah Penerangan** ... Malaysia. Ministry of Agriculture and Rural Development. Risalah Penerangan [*A publication*]
**Malays Minist Agric Tech Leafl** ... Malaysia. Ministry of Agriculture. Technical Leaflet [*A publication*]
**Malays Minist Lands Mines Annu Rep Geol Surv Malays** ... Malaysia. Ministry of Lands and Mines. Annual Report of the Geological Survey of Malaysia [*A publication*]
**Malays Rep For Admin West Malaysia** ... Malaysia. Report on Forest Administration in West Malaysia [*Malaysia. Penyata Tahunan Perhutanan Di-Malaysia Barat Tahun*] [*A publication*]
**Malays Vet J** ... Malaysian Veterinary Journal [*A publication*]
**Malay Tin Rubber J** ... Malayan Tin and Rubber Journal [*A publication*]
**MALC** ....... Madison Area Library Council [*Library network*]
**MALC** ....... Mallard Coach Company, Inc. [*NASDAQ symbol*] (NQ)
**MALCAP**.. Maryland Library Center for Automated Processing [*Library network*]
**Mal Cardiovasc** ... Malattie Cardiovascolari [*A publication*]
**MALCM** ... Mercantile Adjuster and the Lawyer and Credit Man [*A publication*] (DLA)
**Malcolm Ethics** ... Malcolm's Legal and Judicial Ethics [*A publication*] (DLA)
**MALCS** ..... Mujeres Activas en Letras y Cambio Social (EA)
**MA(LD)**..... Master of Arts (Landscape Design), University of Manchester [*British*] (DBQ)
**MALD** ....... Master of Arts in Law and Diplomacy
**MALD** ....... Modular Analysis of Learning Difficulties (OICC)
**MALDEF**.. Mexican American Legal Defense and Educational Fund (EA)
**Mald Isls**.... Maldive Islands
**MALDT**..... Mean Administrative and Logistics Downtime [*Quality control*] (MCD)
**MALE**........ Multiaperture Logic Element
**Mal Econ R** ... Malayan Economic Review [*A publication*]
**Malerei u Zeichn** ... Malerei und Zeichnung [*A publication*] (OCD)
**MALF**........ Malfunction (KSC)
**MALF**........ Mobile Aerobee Launch Facility
**Malgache Repub Ann Geol Madagascar** ... Malgache Republique. Annales Geologiques de Madagascar [*A publication*]
**Malgache Repub Rapp Annu Serv Geol** ... Malgache Republique. Rapport Annuel. Service Geologique [*A publication*]
**MALGI**...... Micul Atlas Lingvistic al Graiurilor Istoromine [*A publication*]
**MALHC**.... Mensuario de Arte, Literatura, Historia, y Ciencia [*A publication*]
**Mal Hist**.... Malaysia in History [*A publication*]
**MALI**......... Material Annex Line Item [*Military*]
**MALI**......... Michigan Accident Location Index [*Michigan State Police*] [*Information service or system*] (IID)
**MALIB**...... Math Analysis Library (MCD)
**MA(LibSc)** ... Master of Arts (Library Science)
**malig** .......... Malignant [*Medicine*]
**MALIMET** ... Master List of Medical Indexing Terms
**MALinc** ..... Atti. Accademia Nazionale dei Lincei. Memorie. Classe di Scienze Morali, Storiche, e Filologiche [*A publication*]
**MALincei** .. Atti. Accademia Nazionale dei Lincei. Memorie. Classe di Scienze Morali, Storiche, e Filologiche [*A publication*]
**Mal Infez** ... Malattie da Infezione [*A publication*]
**MALIPR** ... Material Annex Line Item Progress Report [*Military*] (NG)
**MALL**........ AutoSpa AutoMalls, Inc. [*NASDAQ symbol*] (NQ)
**MALL**........ Malleable (KSC)
**MALL**........ Minnesota Association of Law Libraries [*Library network*]
**MALLAR**.. Manned Lunar Landing and Return [*NASA*]
**Mal Law M** ... Malynes' Ancient Law Merchant [*A publication*] (DLA)
**Mal Law R** ... Malaya Law Review [*A publication*]
**Mallee Hort Dig** ... Mallee Horticulture Digest [*A publication*] (APTA)
**Mallee Hortic Dig** ... Mallee Horticulture Digest [*A publication*] (APTA)
**Mall Ent** .... Mallory's Modern Entries [*A publication*] (DLA)
**Mal Lex Merc** ... Malynes' Lex Mercatoria [*3 eds.*] [*1622-36*] [*A publication*] (DLA)
**Mal LJ** ....... Malayan Law Journal [*A publication*]
**Mallory**...... Mallory's Irish Chancery Reports [*A publication*] (DLA)
**Mal L Rev** ... Malaya Law Review [*A publication*] (DLA)
**MALM** ...... Maryknoll Associate Lay Missioners (EA)
**MAL MISCH** ... Malicious Mischief [*Legal term*] (DLA)
**Malmohus Lans Hushallningssallsk Kvartallsskr** ... Malmoehus Laens Hushallningssaellskaps Kvartallsskrift [*A publication*]
**MALN** ....... Mallon Minerals Corp. [*Denver, CO*] [*NASDAQ symbol*] (NQ)
**MALN** ....... Mouvement Africain de Liberation Nationale [*African Movement for National Liberation*]
**MALODES** ... Modern Army Logistics Data Exchange System
**MALOF**..... Minimum Accepted Level of Fill [*Military*]
**Malone**....... Editor, 6, 9, and 10, Heiskell's Tennessee Reports [*A publication*] (DLA)
**MALOR** .... Mortar and Artillery Location RADAR (RDA)
**MALOS**..... Maintenance and Logistics Space [*System*]
**Mal Pharm J** ... Malayan Pharmaceutical Journal [*A publication*]
**Malpract Dig** ... Malpractice Digest [*A publication*]
**MAL PROS** ... Malicious Prosecution [*Legal term*] (DLA)
**Mal R**......... Malahat Review [*A publication*]
**MALR** ....... Malrite Communications Group, Inc. [*Cleveland, OH*] [*NASDAQ symbol*] (NQ)
**Mal Rub Dv** ... Malaysian Rubber Developments [*A publication*]
**Mal Rub R** ... Malaysian Rubber Review [*A publication*]
**MA in LS**... Master of Arts in Liberal Studies
**MALS**........ Master of Arts in Liberal Studies
**MALS**........ Master of Arts in Library Science
**MA in LS**... Master of Arts in Library Science
**MALS**........ Medium-Intensity Approach Lighting System [*Aviation*]
**MALS**........ Members of an Amalgamated Society [*Slang*] [*British*] (DSUE)
**MALSF** ..... Medium-Intensity Approach Lighting System with Sequenced Flashers [*Aviation*]
**MALSR**..... Medium-Intensity Approach Lighting System with Runway Alignment Indicator Lights [*Aviation*]
**MALT**........ Maltese (DSUE)
**MALT**........ Management Assistance, Incorporated Liquidating Trust [*New York, NY*] [*NASDAQ symbol*] (NQ)
**MALT**........ Military Adviser's Language Text
**MALT**........ Military Assistance Language Training
**MALT**........ Mnemonic Assembly Language Translator [*Data processing*] (IEEE)
**MALT**........ Monetary Allowance in Lieu of Transportation [*DoD*]
**MALTA**..... Middle Atlantic Lawn Tennis Association
**Malta Plan** ... Malta Guidelines for Progress Development Plan, 1980-1985 [*A publication*]
**M Altar**...... Musik und Altar [*A publication*]
**MALT Bulletin** ... Montana. Association of Language Teachers. Bulletin [*A publication*]
**Malt CM**.... Maltby on Courts-Martial [*A publication*] (DLA)
**Malting Brew Allied Processes** ... Malting, Brewing, and Allied Processes [*A publication*]
**Malt Res Inst Publ** ... Malt Research Institute. Publication [*A publication*]
**MALV** ....... Malva [*Mallow*] [*Pharmacy*] (ROG)
**Malynes**..... Malynes' Lex Mercatoria [*3 eds.*] [*1622-36*] [*A publication*] (DLA)
**MAm**.......... Amesbury Public Library, Amesbury, MA [*Library symbol*] [*Library of Congress*] (LCLS)
**M + Am**.... Compound Myopic Astigmatism [*Ophthalmology*]
**MAM**......... Joint II March-May Study [*Coastal Upwelling Ecosystems Analysis*] (MSC)
**MAM**......... Machinery Market [*A publication*]
**MAM**......... Madam (DSUE)
**MAM**......... Maintenance Assumes Monitor (FAAC)
**MAM**......... Mambajao [*Philippines*] [*Seismograph station code, US Geological Survey*] [*Closed*] (SEIS)
**MAM**......... Management and Administration Manual (NRCH)
**MAM**......... Management Analysis Memorandum [*DoD*] (MCD)
**MAM**......... Marquis Academic Media [*Publisher*]
**MAM**......... Master of Arts in Management
**MAM**......... Master Model (MCD)
**MAM**......... Matamoros [*Mexico*] [*Airport symbol*] (OAG)
**MAM**......... Materiel Acquisition Management Program [*Army*] (RDA)
**MAM**......... Medium-Altitude Missile (MCD)
**MAM**......... Medium Automotive Maintenance
**MAM**......... Memoires. Academie Malgache [*A publication*]
**MAM**......... Memory Allocation Manager
**MAM**......... Mercury Asset Management [*Commercial firm*] [*British*]
**MAM**......... Message Access Method [*Honeywell, Inc.*]
**MAM**......... Methylazoxymethanol Acetate [*Organic chemistry*]
**MAM**......... Mid-America Industries, Inc. [*AMEX symbol*] (SPSG)
**MAM**......... Military Air Movement
**MAM**......... Military Assistance Manual (AFM)
**MAM**......... Milliammeter
**MAM**......... Milliampere Minutes
**MAM**......... Missile Alarm Monitor
**MAM**......... Mission Air Ministries (EA)
**MAM**......... Mission Area Manager [*Army*]
**MAM**......... Monoacetylmorphine [*Organic chemistry*]
**MAM**......... Mot a Mot [*Word for Word*] [*French*]
**MAM**......... Multiapplication Monitor
**MAM**......... Multiple Access to Memory [*Data processing*] (IEEE)
**MAMA**...... [*The*] Mammatech Corp. [*NASDAQ symbol*] (NQ)
**MAMA**...... Management Accounting Maintenance Advertising, Inc.
**MAMA**...... Manual-Automatic Multipoint Apparatus (MCD)
**MAMA**...... Material Acquisition Management Application [*Suggested name for the Library of Congress computer system*]
**Ma de Ma**.. Matheus de Mathesillanis [*Flourished, 1381-1402*] [*Authority cited in pre-1607 legal work*] (DSA)
**MAMA**...... Middletown Air Materiel Area [*Air Force*]

**MAMA**...... Mobile Automated Metabolic Analyzer [*Aerospace*]
**MAMA**...... Monoammonium Methanearsonate
**MAMA**...... Monoclonal Antimalignant Antibody [*Immunochemistry*]
**MAMA**...... Monumenta Asiae Minoris Antiqua [*Manchester*] [*A publication*]
**MAMAD**... Manager Magazin [*West Germany*] [*A publication*]
**Ma de Math** ... Matheus de Mathesillanis [*Flourished, 1381-1402*] [*Authority cited in pre-1607 legal work*] (DSA)
**MAMB**...... Military Advisory Mission, Brazil
**MAMBO**... Mediterranean Association for Marine Biology and Oceanology [*ICSU*] (EAIO)
**MAMC**...... Altona Medical Centre Library, Manitoba [*Library symbol*] [*National Library of Canada*] (NLC)
**MAMC**...... Madigan Army Medical Center (AABC)
**MAMC**...... Midarm Muscle Circumference [*Myology*]
**MAME**...... Mawdsley Memoirs [*A publication*]
**MAME**...... Missile and Munitions Evaluation (MCD)
**MAME**...... Mobile America Corp. [*NASDAQ symbol*] (NQ)
**MA Mech**.. Master of Applied Mechanics
**MAMEE**... Meyer Ammunition Module - Emerson Electric
**MAmHi**..... Amesbury Historical Society, Amesbury, MA [*Library symbol*] [*Library of Congress*] (LCLS)
**M Am Hist** ... Magazine of American History [*A publication*]
**MAMI**....... Machine-Aided Manufacturing Information [*Data processing*]
**MAMI**....... Modified Alternate Mark Inversion [*Telecommunications*] (TEL)
**MAMI**....... Multiple Association Management Institute [*Later, IAMC*] (EA)
**MAMIDH** ... Marine Micropaleontology [*A publication*]
**MAMIE**..... Magnetic Amplification of Microwave Integrated Emissions (IEEE)
**MAMIE**..... Minimum Automatic Machine for Interpolation and Extrapolation
**M Am IMME** ... Member of the American Institute of Mining and Metallurgical Engineers
**Ma-Min**..... Milliampere-Minute
**MAML**...... Mid-American Lines, Inc. [*NASDAQ symbol*] (NQ)
**MAMLAN** ... Mammalia [*A publication*]
**Mamm**....... Mammalia. Morphologie, Biologie, Systematique des Mammiferes [*A publication*]
**MAMMA** ... Men Against the Maxi-Midi Atrocity [*Klosters, Switzerland, group opposing below-the-knee fashions introduced in 1970*]
**Mammal Inf** ... Mammalogical Informations [*A publication*]
**Mammal Rev** ... Mammal Review [*A publication*]
**Mamm Depicta** ... Mammalia Depicta [*A publication*]
**Mamm Depicta Beih Z Saeugetierkd** ... Mammalia Depicta. Beihefte zur Zeitschrift fuer Saeugetierkunde [*A publication*]
**Mamm Species** ... Mammalian Species [*A publication*]
**MAMNF**... Madre Mining Ltd. [*NASDAQ symbol*] (NQ)
**MAMOE**... Medical Administration and Miscellaneous Operating Expenses [*Veterans Administration*]
**MAMOS**... Marine Automatic Meteorological Observing Station [*Automatic system*]
**MAMOS**... Missouri Associated Migrant Opportunities Services (EA)
**MaMP**....... Maine State Planning Office, Augusta, ME [*Library symbol*] [*Library of Congress*] (LCLS)
**MAMP**...... Mainz Army Maintenance Plant (MCD)
**MAMP**...... Materiel Acquisition Management Plan
**MAMP**...... Michigan Army Missile Plant (MCD)
**MAMP**...... Mid-America Petroleum, Inc. [*NASDAQ symbol*] (NQ)
**MAMP**...... Mission Area Materiel Plan [*Army*]
**MAMRON** ... Marine Aircraft Maintenance Squadron
**MAMS**...... Maintenance Activity Management System [*Military*]
**MAMS**...... Maintenance Assist Modules (MCD)
**MAMS**...... Marine Mammal Science [*A publication*]
**MAMS**...... Marine Meteorological Services [*Marine science*] (MSC)
**MAMS**...... Materiel Acquisition Management System
**MAMS**...... Medical Administrative Management System
**MAMS**...... Member of the Association of Medical Secretaries, Practice Administrators, and Receptionists [*British*] (DBQ)
**MAMS**...... Military Aircraft Marshaling System
**MAMS**...... MIRCOM [*Missile Material Readiness Command*] Automated Microfilm System [*Army*] (IID)
**MAMS**...... Missile Altitude Measurement System
**MAMS**...... Missile Assembly and Maintenance Shop [*NASA*]
**MAMS**...... Modern Army Maintenance System
**MAMS**...... Multiple Access to Memory System [*Data processing*]
**M Am Soc CE** ... Member of the American Society of Civil Engineers
**MAMSS**.... Machine Augmented Manual Scheduling System (MCD)
**MAMT**...... Mean Active Maintenance Time (MCD)
**MAMTR**... Milliammeter
**MA (Mus)** ... Master of Arts in Music
**MAmW**...... Whittier Home Association, Amesbury, MA [*Library symbol*] [*Library of Congress*] (LCLS)
**MAN**......... Magnetic Automatic Navigation [*System*] (RDA)
**MAN**......... Mailorder Association of Nurserymen (EA)
**MAN**......... Mainly about Nature [*A publication*]
**MAN**......... Maintenance Alert Network [*RCA*]
**MAN**......... Manage [*A publication*]
**MAN**......... Management Focus [*A publication*]
**MAN**......... Manager [*or Managing*] (EY)
**Man**........... Mancando [*Dying Away*] [*Music*]
**MAN**......... Manchester [*England*] [*Airport symbol*] (OAG)
**MAN**......... Mandato de Accion y Unidad Nacional [*Mandate of Action and National Unity*] [*Bolivia*] [*Political party*] (PPW)
**man**........... Mandingo [*MARC language code*] [*Library of Congress*] (LCCP)
**MAN**......... Mane [*Morning*] [*Pharmacy*]
**MAN**......... Manege [*Horsemanship*] [*French*]
**MAN**......... Manhattan
**MAN**......... Manifest (AABC)
**MAN**......... Manila [*Philippines*] [*Later, MUT*] [*Geomagnetic observatory code*]
**MAN**......... Manila [*Philippines*]
**MAN**......... Manila [*Diliman*] [*Philippines*] [*Seismograph station code, US Geological Survey*] (SEIS)
**MAN**......... Manilla (ADA)
**MAN**......... Manipulus [*A Handful*] [*Pharmacy*]
**MAN**......... Manitoba [*Canadian province*]
**MAN**......... Manitoba Business [*A publication*]
**Man**........... Manitoba Law Reports [*Canada*] [*A publication*] (DLA)
**Man**........... Mankind [*A publication*]
**MAN**......... Mann Oil Resources, Inc. [*Vancouver Stock Exchange symbol*]
**Man**........... Manning's Reports [*1 Michigan*] [*A publication*] (DLA)
**Man**........... Manning's Reports, English Revision Court [*1832-35*] [*A publication*] (DLA)
**MAN**......... Mannion Air Charter, Inc. [*Ypsilanti, MI*] [*FAA designator*] (FAAC)
**Man**........... Mannose [*A sugar*]
**Man**........... Mannus. Zeitschrift fuer Vorgeschichte [*A publication*]
**MAN**......... Manpower PLC ADS [*NYSE symbol*] (SPSG)
**MAN**......... Mansfield State College, Mansfield, PA [*OCLC symbol*] (OCLC)
**Man**........... Manson's English Bankruptcy Cases [*A publication*] (DLA)
**MAN**......... Manual (KSC)
**MAN**......... Manuel Antonio Noriega [*Military commander and de facto ruler of Panama*]
**MAN**......... Manufacture
**Man**........... Manuscripta [*A publication*]
**MAN**......... Maschinenfabrik Augsburg-Nuernburg [*Manufacturer of diesel engines*]
**MAN**......... Meaningful Assistance in the Neighborhood [*of Legal Aid Bureau of George Washington University Law School*] (EA)
**MAN**......... Men's Antisexist Newsletter [*A publication*]
**MAN**......... Men's Association News [*A publication*] (APTA)
**MAN**......... Mensario. Arquivo Nacional. Ministerio da Justica. Arquivo Nacional. Divisao de Publicacoes [*A publication*]
**MAN**......... Metropolitan Area Network
**MAN**......... Microwave Aerospace Navigation
**MAN**......... Military Aviation Notice [*Air Force*]
**MAN**......... Molecular Anatomy
**MAN**......... Molesters Anonymous (EA)
**MAN**......... Mouvement pour une Alternative Non-Violente [*Movement for a Nonviolent Alternative*] [*France*] [*Political party*] (PPE)
**MAN**......... Movementu Antiyas Nobo [*New Antilles Movement*] [*Netherlands*] [*Political party*] (EAIO)
**MAN**......... University of Manitoba Library [*UTLAS symbol*]
**MANA**....... Manassas National Battlefield Park
**MANA**....... Manatron, Inc. [*Kalamazoo, MI*] [*NASDAQ symbol*] (NQ)
**MANA**....... Manufacturers Agents National Association (EA)
**MANA**....... Mexican American Women's National Association (EA)
**MANA**....... Midwives Alliance of North America (EA)
**MANA**....... Music Advisers' National Association [*British*]
**MANA**....... Musicians Against Nuclear Arms [*Defunct*] (EA)
**MANAAT** ... Man: A Monthly Record of Anthropological Science [*A publication*]
**Man Acts** ... Acts of Manitoba [*A publication*]
**MANADW** ... Manitoba Nature [*A publication*]
**Manag**........ Management [*A publication*]
**Manage Abstr** ... Management Abstracts [*A publication*]
**Manage Account** ... Management Accounting [*A publication*]
**Manage Advis** ... Management Adviser [*A publication*]
**Manage Controls** ... Management Controls [*A publication*]
**Manage Datamatics** ... Management Datamatics [*A publication*]
**Manage Decis** ... Management Decision [*A publication*]
**Manage Focus** ... Management Focus [*A publication*]
**Manage Gov** ... Management in Government [*A publication*]
**Manage e Inf** ... Management e Informatica [*A publication*]
**Manage Inf** ... Management Informatics [*A publication*]
**Manage Inf Syst Q** ... Management Information Systems Quarterly [*A publication*]
**Manage Int Rev** ... Management International Review [*A publication*]
**Management D** ... Management Digest [*A publication*] (APTA)
**Management Inf Serv** ... Management Information Services [*A publication*]
**Management NZ** ... Management. New Zealand Institute of Management [*A publication*]
**Management's Bibliog Data** ... Management's Bibliographic Data [*A publication*]
**Management Sci** ... Management Science [*A publication*]
**Management Servs** ... Management Services [*A publication*]

**Manage Objectives** ... Management by Objectives [*A publication*]
**Manage Plann** ... Managerial Planning [*A publication*]
**Manage Plng** ... Managerial Planning [*A publication*]
**Manage Rev** ... Management Review [*A publication*]
**Managerial Decis Econ** ... Managerial and Decision Economics [*England*] [*A publication*]
**Managerial and Decision Econ** ... Managerial and Decision Economics [*A publication*]
**Managerial Fin** ... Managerial Finance [*A publication*]
**Managerial Plan** ... Managerial Planning [*A publication*]
**Manage Sci** ... Management Science [*A publication*]
**Manage Serv** ... Management Services [*A publication*]
**Manage Serv Gov** ... Management Services in Government [*A publication*]
**Manage Today** ... Management Today [*A publication*]
**Manage World** ... Management World [*A publication*]
**Manag Int R** ... Management International Review [*A publication*]
**Manag Japan** ... Management Japan [*A publication*]
**Manag Objectives** ... Management by Objectives [*A publication*]
**Manag Sci** ... Management Science [*A publication*]
**Manag Sci A** ... Management Science. Series A. Theory [*A publication*]
**Manag Sci B** ... Management Science. Series B. Application [*A publication*]
**Manag Today** ... Management Today [*A publication*]
**MANAM**... Manual Amendment
**Man Bar News** ... Manitoba Bar News [*A publication*]
**Manb Coke** ... Manby's Abridgement of Coke's Reports [*A publication*] (DLA)
**Manb Fines** ... Manby on Fines [*A publication*] (DLA)
**Man B New** ... Manitoba Bar News [*A publication*]
**Man B News** ... Manitoba Bar News [*A publication*] (ILCA)
**MANC**....... Mancando [*Decreasing in Loudness*] [*Music*]
**MANCAN** ... Man-Carried Automatic Navigator (MCD)
**Man Cas** .... Manumission Cases in New Jersey, by Bloomfield [*A publication*] (DLA)
**MANCH**.... Manchester [*England*]
**Manch**........ Manchester Literary Club. Papers [*A publication*]
**Manch**........ Manchuria
**Man Chem** ... Manufacturing Chemist and Pharmaceutical and Fine Chemical Trade Journal [*A publication*]
**Manchester** ... Manchester School of Economic and Social Studies [*A publication*]
**Manchester Assoc Eng Trans** ... Manchester Association of Engineers. Transactions [*A publication*]
**Manchester G Soc Tr** ... Manchester Geological Society. Transactions [*A publication*]
**Manchester Lit Ph Soc Mem** ... Manchester Literary and Philosophical Society. Memoirs and Proceedings [*A publication*]
**Manchester Med Gaz** ... Manchester Medical Gazette [*England*] [*A publication*]
**Manchester M Soc Tr** ... Manchester Mining Society. Transactions [*A publication*]
**Manchester Sch Econ Soc Stud** ... Manchester School of Economic and Social Studies [*A publication*]
**Manchester Sch Ed Gazette** ... University of Manchester. School of Education. Gazette [*A publication*]
**Manchester School** ... Manchester School of Economic and Social Studies [*A publication*]
**Manch Guard** ... Manchester Guardian Weekly [*A publication*]
**Manch Lit Phil Soc Mem Proc** ... Manchester Literary and Philosophical Society. Memoirs and Proceedings [*A publication*]
**Manch Med Gaz** ... Manchester Medical Gazette [*A publication*]
**Manch Q**.... Manchester Quarterly [*A publication*]
**Manchr Rev** ... Manchester Review [*A publication*]
**Manch Univ Med Sch Gaz** ... Manchester University. Medical School. Gazette [*A publication*]
**MANCO**.... Mancando [*Decreasing in Loudness*] [*Music*]
**Man Couns** ... Manitoba Counsellor [*A publication*]
**MANCUN** ... Mancunium [*Signature of the Bishops of Manchester*] (ROG)
**Mand** ......... Mandaic (BJA)
**MAND**....... Mandamus [*We Command*] [*Latin*] (ADA)
**MAND**....... Mandatory (AABC)
**MAND**....... Mandible
**MAND**....... Mandolin [*Music*]
**MANDATE** ... Multiline Automatic Network Diagnostic and Transmission Equipment
**MANDEC** ... Maneuvering Decoy (MCD)
**Man Dem**... Mansel on Demurrer [*1828*] [*A publication*] (DLA)
**MANDFHAB** ... Male and Female Homosexual Association of Great Britain
**MANDO** ... Mancando [*Decreasing in Loudness*] [*Music*] (ROG)
**MANDS**.... Maintenance and Supply
**Mandschr Kindergeneeskd** ... Mandschrift voor Kindergeneeskunde [*A publication*]
**MANDSD** ... Mean and Standard Deviation
**Man Ed Res C Res B** ... Manitoba Educational Research Council. Research Bulletins [*A publication*]
**Manedsskr Prakt Laegegern** ... Manedsskrift foer Praktisk Laegegerning [*A publication*]
**Man El Cas** ... Manning's English Election Cases (Court of Revision) [*A publication*] (DLA)
**MANEX**.... Management Experten-Nachweis [*Management Experts Data Base*] [*Society for Business Information*] [*Information service or system*] (IID)
**Man Exch Pr** ... Manning's English Exchequer Practice [*A publication*] (DLA)
**MANF**....... Manifold (KSC)
**MANF**....... May, August, November, and February [*Denotes quarterly payments of interest or dividends in these months*] [*Business term*]
**Man Farm** ... Manual Farmaceutico [*A publication*]
**Manf Eng Trans** ... Manufacturing Engineering Transactions [*A publication*]
**MANFG**.... Manufacturing (ROG)
**MANFIST** ... Maneuver and Fire Support Team (MCD)
**Man For**..... Management Forum [*A publication*]
**MANFOR** ... Manpower Force Packaging [*Military*]
**MANFORCE** ... Manpower for a Clean Environment [*Water Pollution Control Federation*]
**MAN Forsch Planen Bauen** ... MAN [*Maschinenfabrik Augsburg-Nuernberg*] Forschen, Planen, Bauen [*A publication*]
**MANFR**.... Manufacturer
**MANFRD** ... Manufactured
**MANFRG** ... Manufacturing
**MANFST**.. Manifest
**MANG**....... Management
**Man & G**.... Manning and Granger's English Common Pleas Reports [*A publication*] (DLA)
**Manganese Dioxide Symp Proc** ... Manganese Dioxide Symposium. Proceedings [*A publication*]
**Manganese Lit Rev** ... Manganese Literature Review [*A publication*]
**Man Gaz**.... Manitoba Gazette [*A publication*] (DLA)
**MANGR**.... Manager
**Man Gr & S** ... Manning, Granger, and Scott's English Common Bench Reports, Old Series [*I-VIII*] [*A publication*] (DLA)
**MANGRSS** ... Manageress (ROG)
**Man G & S** ... Manning, Granger, and Scott's English Common Bench Reports, Old Series [*I-VIII*] [*A publication*] (DLA)
**MANGT**.... Management (ROG)
**Mangt Today** ... Management Today [*A publication*]
**Manhat**...... Manhattan [*A publication*]
**MANHC**.... Madras Army Native Hospital Corps [*British military*] (DMA)
**MAnHi**...... Andover Historical Society, Andover, MA [*Library symbol*] [*Library of Congress*] (LCLS)
**Man His Environ** ... Man and His Environment [*A publication*]
**MA-NHP**.. Massachusetts Natural Heritage Program [*Massachusetts State Division of Fisheries and Wildlife*] [*Information service or system*] (IID)
**MANI**........ Manifold [*Automotive engineering*]
**MANIAC**.. Mathematical Analyzer, Numerical Integrator and Computer
**MANIAC**.. Mechanical and Numerical Integrator and Computer (IEEE)
**MANIAJ**... Man in India [*A publication*]
**MANIF**...... Manifest
**manifest**..... Manifestation [*Medicine*]
**Mani LJ**..... Manitoba Law Journal [*A publication*]
**MAnimSc**.. Master of Animal Science, University of Liverpool [*British*] (DBQ)
**Man Ind**..... Man in India [*A publication*]
**Man Int Law** ... Manning's Commentaries on the Law of Nations [*A publication*] (DLA)
**Manip**........ All India Reporter, Manipur [*A publication*] (DLA)
**manip**......... Manipulation [*Medicine*]
**Manip**........ Manipulus [*A Handful*] [*Pharmacy*]
**MANIP**..... Manual Input [*Data processing*]
**MANIT**..... Manitoba [*Canadian province*]
**Manit CoOp** ... Manitoba Co-Operator [*A publication*]
**Manit Dep Mines Nat Resour Mines Branch Publ** ... Manitoba. Department of Mines and Natural Resources. Mines Branch. Publication [*A publication*]
**Manit Entomol** ... Manitoba Entomologist [*A publication*]
**Manit Med Rev** ... Manitoba Medical Review [*A publication*]
**Manit Nat**... Manitoba Nature [*A publication*]
**Manitoba**... Armour. Queen's Bench and County Court Reports Tempore Wood [*Manitoba*] [*A publication*] (DLA)
**Manitoba**... Manitoba Law Reports [*Canada*] [*A publication*] (DLA)
**Manitoba B**... Manitoba Business [*A publication*]
**Manitoba Dep Mines Natur Resour Mines Br Publ** ... Manitoba. Department of Mines and Natural Resources. Mines Branch. Publication [*A publication*]
**Manitoba Ent**... Manitoba Entomologist [*A publication*]
**Manitoba L (Can)** ... Manitoba Law Reports [*Canada*] [*A publication*] (DLA)
**Manitoba LJ** ... Manitoba Law Journal [*A publication*]
**MANIX**..... Machine Aids to Nike-X [*Army*] (AABC)
**Man J R Anthropol Inst** ... Man. Journal of the Royal Anthropological Institute [*A publication*]
**Mankind Monogr** ... Mankind Monographs [*A publication*]
**Mankind Q** ... Mankind Quarterly [*A publication*]
**MANL**....... Memorie. Accademia Nazionale dei Lincei [*A publication*]
**Man Lim**.... Mansel on Limitations [*1839*] [*A publication*] (DLA)
**Man L J**.... Manitoba Law Journal [*A publication*]
**Man LR**..... Manitoba Law Reports [*Canada*] [*A publication*] (DLA)
**Man LS Chron** ... Manchester Law Students' Chronicle [*A publication*] (DLA)
**Man LSJ**.... Manchester Law Students' Journal [*A publication*] (DLA)
**Man LSJ**.... Manitoba Law School. Journal [*A publication*]

**MANM**...... Methylated Albumin-Nitrocelluse Membrane [*Analytical biochemistry*]
**Man-Made T** ... Man-Made Textiles in India [*A publication*]
**Man Mag**... Manager Magazin [*A publication*]
**Man Math T** ... Manitoba Math Teacher [*A publication*]
**Man Med**... Man and Medicine [*A publication*]
**MANMED** ... Manual of the Medical Department [*Navy*]
**MANMEDDEPT** ... Manual of the Medical Department [*Navy*]
**Man MLJ** ... Manitoba Modern Language Journal [*A publication*]
**Man Mon Rec Anthropol Sci** ... Man: A Monthly Record of Anthropological Science [*A publication*]
**Man Mus Ed** ... Manitoba Music Educator [*A publication*]
**MANN** ...... Manna [*Pharmacy*] (ROG)
**Mann** ......... Manning's Digest of the Nisi Prius Reports [*England*] [*A publication*] (DLA)
**Mann** ......... Manning's English Court of Revision Reports [*A publication*] (DLA)
**Mann** ......... Manning's Reports [*1 Michigan*] [*A publication*] (DLA)
**MANN** ...... Mannlicher Rifle
**ManNac**..... N-Acetylmannosamine [*Biochemistry*]
**Man Nat** .... Man and Nature [*A publication*]
**Mann Bills** ... Manning on Bills and Notes [*A publication*] (DLA)
**Mann Com** ... Manning's Commentaries on the Law of Nations [*A publication*] (DLA)
**Mann EC**... Manning's Revision Cases [*1832-35*] [*A publication*] (DLA)
**Mannesmann Forschungsber** ... Mannesmann Forschungsberichte [*A publication*]
**Mann Ex Pr** ... Manning's English Exchequer Practice [*A publication*] (DLA)
**Mann & G (Eng)** ... Manning and Granger's English Common Pleas Reports [*A publication*] (DLA)
**Mann G & S** ... Manning, Granger, and Scott's English Common Bench Reports [*135-39 English Reprint*] [*1845-56*] [*A publication*] (DLA)
**Mann G & S (Eng)** ... Manning, Granger, and Scott's English Common Bench Reports, Old Series [*I-VIII*] [*A publication*] (DLA)
**Manning** .... Manning's Reports [*1 Michigan*] [*A publication*] (DLA)
**Manning** .... Manning's Unreported Cases [*Louisiana*] [*A publication*] (DLA)
**Manning LA** ... Manning's Unreported Cases [*Louisiana*] [*A publication*] (DLA)
**Manning's UC** ... Manning's Unreported Cases [*Louisiana*] [*A publication*] (DLA)
**Manning's Unrep Cases** ... Manning's Unreported Cases [*Louisiana*] [*A publication*] (DLA)
**Mann Nat** .. Manning's Commentaries on the Law of Nations [*A publication*] (DLA)
**Mann & R** .. Manning and Ryland's English King's Bench Reports [*1827-30*] [*A publication*] (DLA)
**Mann & R** .. Manning and Ryland's English Magistrates' Cases [*1827-30*] [*A publication*] (DLA)
**Mann & R (Eng)** ... Manning and Ryland's English King's Bench Reports [*1827-30*] [*A publication*] (DLA)
**Mann Unrep Cas** ... Manning's Unreported Cases [*Louisiana*] [*A publication*] (DLA)
**MANO** ...... Manometer
**MANOP**.... Manganese Nodule Program [*For sampling on ocean floor*]
**MANOP**.... Manual of Operations
**MANOVA** ... Multivariate Analysis of Variance [*Statistics*]
**MAnP**........ Phillips Academy, Andover, MA [*Library symbol*] [*Library of Congress*] (LCLS)
**MANPAD** ... Man-Portable Air Defense (AABC)
**MANPADS** ... Man-Portable Air Defense System (MCD)
**Manpower J** ... Manpower Journal [*A publication*]
**Manpower Unempl Res Afr** ... Manpower and Unemployment Research in Africa: A Newsletter [*A publication*]
**MAN PR** ... Mane Primo [*Early in the Morning*] [*Pharmacy*]
**MANPRINT** ... Manpower and Personnel Integration [*Military*] (RDA)
**MANPWR** ... Manpower (KSC)
**Man Q**........ Manchester Quarterly [*A publication*]
**MANR**....... Manager (ROG)
**ManR**......... Manchester Review [*A publication*]
**Man R**........ Manitoba Reports [*Maritime Law Book Co. Ltd.*] [*Information service or system*] [*A publication*] [*A publication*] (DLA)
**Man & R**.... Manning and Ryland's English King's Bench Reports [*1827-30*] [*A publication*] (DLA)
**Man & R**.... Manning and Ryland's English Magistrates' Cases [*1827-30*] [*A publication*] (DLA)
**Man Ray**.... Emmanuel Radnitsky [*American artist, 1890-1976*]
**MAN Res Eng Manuf** ... MAN [*Maschinenfabrik Augsburg-Nuernberg*] Research, Engineering, Manufacturing [*A publication*]
**Man Rev Stat** ... Manitoba Revised Statutes [*Canada*] [*A publication*] (DLA)
**MANRRDC** ... Manpower Resources Research and Development Center [*Army*] (RDA)
**Man RT Wood** ... Manitoba Reports Tempore Wood [*Canada*] [*A publication*] (DLA)
**Man & Ry** .. Manning and Ryland's English King's Bench Reports [*1827-30*] [*A publication*] (DLA)
**Man & Ry** .. Manning and Ryland's English Magistrates' Cases [*1827-30*] [*A publication*] (DLA)
**Man & Ry KB** ... Manning and Ryland's English King's Bench Reports [*1827-30*] [*A publication*] (ILCA)
**Man & Ry Mag** ... Manning and Ryland's English Magistrates' Cases [*1827-30*] [*A publication*] (DLA)
**Man & Ry Mag Cas** ... Manning and Ryland's English Magistrates' Cases [*1827-30*] [*A publication*] (DLA)
**Man & Ry MC** ... Manning and Ryland's English Magistrates' Cases [*1827-30*] [*A publication*] (DLA)
**Man & S**..... Manning and Scott's English Common Bench Reports, Old Series [*IX*] [*A publication*] (DLA)
**Mans**.......... Mansfield's Reports [*49-52 Arkansas*] [*A publication*] (DLA)
**MANS**....... Mansions
**Mans**.......... Manson's English Bankruptcy and Winding-Up Cases [*A publication*] (DLA)
**MANS**....... Map Analysis System [*Data processing*]
**Man & Sask Tax Rep (CCH)** ... Manitoba and Saskatchewan Tax Reporter (Commerce Clearing House) [*A publication*] (DLA)
**MANSAT** ... Manned Satellite
**Man & Sc**... Manning and Scott's English Common Bench Reports, Old Series [*IX*] [*A publication*] (DLA)
**Mans on C** ... Mansel on Costs [*A publication*] (DLA)
**Man Sci**...... Management Science [*A publication*]
**Man Sci Teach** ... Manitoba Science Teacher [*A publication*]
**Mans Dem** ... Mansel on Demurrer [*1828*] [*A publication*] (DLA)
**Mansf Dig** ... Mansfield's Digest of Statutes [*Arkansas*] [*A publication*] (DLA)
**MANSH**.... Manshead [*England*]
**Mans Lim** .. Mansel on Limitations [*1839*] [*A publication*] (DLA)
**Man Soc Sci T** ... Manitoba Social Science Teacher [*A publication*]
**Man/Soc/Tech** ... Man/Society/Technology [*A publication*]
**Manson**...... Manson's English Bankruptcy and Winding-Up Cases [*A publication*] (DLA)
**Manson Bankr Cas** ... Manson's English Bankruptcy and Winding-Up Cases [*A publication*] (DLA)
**Manson (Eng)** ... Manson's English Bankruptcy Cases [*A publication*] (DLA)
**Man Spectra** ... Manitoba Spectra [*A publication*]
**Man Stat**.... Manitoba Statutes [*Canada*] [*A publication*] (DLA)
**MANSWG** ... Manpower Systems Work Group
**MANT**....... [*The*] Manitowoc Co., Inc. [*NASDAQ symbol*] (NQ)
**M Ant** ........ Marcus Antoninus [*of Scriptores Historiae Augustae*] [*Classical studies*] (OCD)
**Man Teach** ... Manitoba Teacher [*A publication*]
**ManTech** ... ManTech Journal. US Army [*A publication*]
**MANTECH** ... Manufacturing Technology
**ManTech J** ... ManTech Journal. US Army [*A publication*]
**Man Text Ind Can** ... Manual of the Textile Industry of Canada [*A publication*]
**M Ant Fr**.... Memoires. Societe Nationale des Antiquaires de France [*A publication*]
**M Anthr G Wien** ... Mitteilungen. Anthropologische Gesellschaft in Wien [*A publication*]
**M Anthrop Ges Wien** ... Mitteilungen. Anthropologische Gesellschaft in Wien [*A publication*]
**MANTIS**... Manpack Tactical Intelligence System
**Mant Med** ... Mantova Medica [*A publication*]
**Man Tr**....... Manual Training Magazine [*Peoria, IL*] [*A publication*]
**MANTRAC** ... Manual Angle Tracking Capability
**MANTRAP** ... Management Training Program [*of Center for Research in Business and Economics, University of Houston*]
**Man T Wood** ... Manitoba Reports Tempore Wood [*Canada*] [*A publication*] (DLA)
**MANU** ...... Mozambique African National Union [*Later, FRELIMO*]
**Manual Arts Bul** ... Manual Arts Bulletin for Teachers in Secondary Schools [*A publication*] (APTA)
**Manual Calif Agr Exp Sta** ... Manual. California Agricultural Experiment Station [*A publication*]
**Manual Inst For (Chile)** ... Manual. Instituto Forestal (Santiago De Chile) [*A publication*]
**Manual Train** ... Manual Training Magazine [*A publication*]
**MANUF**.... Manufacturer [*or Manufacturing*] (ROG)
**Manufact** ... Manufacturer [*A publication*]
**Manufact Ind** ... Manufacturing Industry [*A publication*]
**Manufacturing Ind** ... Manufacturing Industries [*A publication*]
**Manufacturing Mgmt** ... Manufacturing and Management [*A publication*]
**Manuf Bul** ... Manufacturers' Bulletin [*A publication*] (APTA)
**Manuf Ch Ae** ... Manufacturing Chemist and Aerosol News [*A publication*]
**Manuf Chem** ... Manufacturing Chemist [*England*] [*A publication*]
**Manuf Chem** ... Manufacturing Chemist and Aerosol News [*A publication*]
**Manuf Chem Assoc Chem Saf Data Sheet** ... Manufacturing Chemists' Association. Chemical Safety Data Sheet [*A publication*]
**Manuf Chemist** ... Manufacturing Chemist [*A publication*]
**Manuf Confect** ... Manufacturing Confectioner [*A publication*]
**MANUFD** ... Manufactured (ROG)
**Manuf Eng** ... Manufacturing Engineering [*A publication*]
**Manuf Eng Manage** ... Manufacturing Engineering and Management [*Later, Manufacturing Engineering*] [*A publication*]
**Manuf Eng & Mgt** ... Manufacturing Engineering and Management [*Later, Manufacturing Engineering*] [*A publication*]
**MANUFG** ... Manufacturing (ADA)
**Manuf Ind** ... Manufacturing Industries [*A publication*] (APTA)
**Manuf & Management** ... Manufacturing and Management [*A publication*] (APTA)
**Manuf Milk Prod J** ... Manufactured Milk Products Journal [*A publication*]

**Manuf Mo** ... Manufacturers' Monthly [*A publication*] (APTA)
**Manuf Mon** ... Manufacturers' Monthly [*A publication*]
**Manuf Perfum** ... Manufacturing Perfumer [*A publication*]
**Manuf Rec** ... Manufacturers' Record [*A publication*]
**Manuf Technol Horiz** ... Manufacturing Technology Horizons [*A publication*]
**Manum Cas** ... Bloomfield's Manumission (or Negro) Cases [*New Jersey*] [*A publication*] (DLA)
**Manum Cases** ... Bloomfield's Manumission (or Negro) Cases [*New Jersey*] [*A publication*] (DLA)
**Man Univ Calif Agric Ext Serv** ... Manual. University of California. Agricultural Extension Service [*A publication*]
**Man Unr Cases** ... Manning's Unreported Cases [*Louisiana*] [*A publication*] (DLA)
**Man Unrep Cas** ... Manning's Unreported Cases [*Louisiana*] [*A publication*] (DLA)
**Man Unrep Cas (LA)** ... Manning's Unreported Cases [*Louisiana*] [*A publication*] (DLA)
**Manusc Math** ... Manuscripta Mathematica [*A publication*]
**Manuscr**..... Manuscripta [*A publication*]
**Manuscr Geod** ... Manuscripta Geodaetica [*A publication*]
**Manuscripta Math** ... Manuscripta Mathematica [*A publication*]
**Manuscr Rep McGill Univ (Montreal) Mar Sci Cent** ... Manuscript Report. McGill University (Montreal). Marine Sciences Centre [*A publication*]
**MANUV**.... Maneuvering (KSC)
**Manw**......... Manwood's Forest Laws [*1592, 1598, 1615*] [*A publication*] (DLA)
**Manw For Law** ... Manwood's Forest Laws [*1592, 1598, 1615*] [*A publication*] (DLA)
**Manwood** ... Manwood's Forest Laws [*1592, 1598, 1615*] [*A publication*] (DLA)
**MANX**....... Mannion Air Charter, Inc. [*Air carrier designation symbol*]
**Manx J Agr** ... Manx Journal of Agriculture [*A publication*]
**Manx J Agric** ... Manx Journal of Agriculture [*A publication*]
**MaNy**......... Magyar Nyelvor [*A publication*]
**MANZCP** ... Member of the Australian and New Zealand College of Psychiatrists
**MAO**.......... Magnetic Amplifier Output
**MAO**.......... Mailing Address Only [*Military*] (AABC)
**MAO**.......... Maintenance and Operation [*Army*] (AFIT)
**MAO**.......... Major Attack Option [*Military*] (MCD)
**MAO**.......... Manaus [*Brazil*] [*Airport symbol*] (OAG)
**MAO**.......... Manned Apollo Operations [*NASA*] (KSC)
**mao**............ Maori [*MARC language code*] [*Library of Congress*] (LCCP)
**MAO**.......... Marathon Office Supply, Inc. [*AMEX symbol*] (SPSG)
**MAO**.......... Marion, SC [*Location identifier*] [*FAA*] (FAAL)
**MAO**.......... Mars Aeronomy Orbiter (MCD)
**MAO**.......... Massive Attack Option (MCD)
**MAO**.......... Master of the Art of Obstetrics
**MAO**.......... Master of Art of Oratory
**MAO**.......... Material Adjustment Order (MCD)
**MAO**.......... Maximum [*or Minimum*] Acid Output [*Clinical chemistry*]
**MAO**.......... Military Assistance Officer [*Army*]
**MAO**.......... Monoamine Oxidase [*An enzyme*]
**MAO**.......... Movement to Arrest Oppressors (EA)
**MAO**.......... Muhammadan Anglo-Oriental
**MAOA**....... Meteorological Aspects of Ocean Affairs [*Marine science*] (MSC)
**MAOA**....... Meyers Aircraft Owners Association (EA)
**MAOB**....... Marine Observer [*A publication*]
**MAODP**.... Medic Alert Organ Donor Program (EA)
**MAOF**....... Mexican-American Opportunity Foundation (EA)
**MAoG**........ Mitteilungen. Altorientalische Gesellschaft [*Leipzig*] [*A publication*]
**MAOI**........ Monoamine Oxidase Inhibitor [*Biochemistry*]
**MAOP**....... Maximum Allowable Operating Pressure [*In pipelines*]
**Ma Opf & St** ... Mathematische Operationsforschung und Statistik [*A publication*]
**MAOS**....... Magnetic Amplifier Output Stage
**MAOS**....... Metal-Aluminum-Oxide Silicon (MSA)
**MAOS**....... Minimum Airfield Operating Surface [*Military*]
**MAOT**....... Master of Arts in Occupational Therapy
**MAOT**....... Maximum Allowable Operating Time (NASA)
**MAOT**....... Member, Association of Occupational Therapists [*British*]
**MAOT**....... Military Assistance Observer Team
**MAOT**....... Missile Auxiliary Output Tester
**MAOU**....... Member of the American Ornithologists' Union
**MAP**.......... Macro Arithmetic Processor [*Data processing*] (MDG)
**MAP**.......... Macroassembly Program [*Data processing*]
**MAP**.......... Madeira Abyssal Plain [*Geology*]
**MAP**.......... Maghreb-Arabe Presse [*Maghreb Arab Press Agency*] [*Morocco*]
**MAP**.......... Magnetic-Acoustic-Pressure (NVT)
**MAP**.......... Maine Public Service Co. [*AMEX symbol*] (SPSG)
**MAP**.......... Mainly about People [*A publication*]
**MA & P**...... Maintenance Analysis and Planning (NASA)
**MAP**.......... Maintenance Analysis Procedure [*Data processing*]
**MAP**.......... Maintenance Analysis Program [*NASA*] (KSC)
**MAP**.......... Maitre en Administration Publique [*Master of Public Administration*]
**Ma P**.......... Makedonski Pregled [*A publication*]
**map**............ Malayo-Polynesian [*MARC language code*] [*Library of Congress*] (LCCP)
**MAP**.......... Mamai [*Papua New Guinea*] [*Airport symbol*] (OAG)
**MAP**.......... Management Analysis [*or Assessment*] Program
**MAP**.......... Management Assistance for Profits
**MAP**.......... Management and Planning Committee [*Library of Congress*]
**MAP**.......... Manifold Absolute Pressure
**MAP**.......... Manifold Air Pressure
**MAP**.......... Manpower [*A publication*]
**MAP**.......... Manpower Absorption Plan [*Department of Labor*]
**MAP**.......... Manpower Analysis Paper
**MAP**.......... Manpower Assistance Project [*Department of Labor*]
**MAP**.......... Manufacturers' Assistance Program [*Michigan State Department of Commerce*] [*Lansing, MI*] [*Information service or system*] (IID)
**MAP**.......... Manufacturing Activity Projection
**MAP**.......... Manufacturing Automation Protocol [*Data communications standards*]
**MAP**.......... MAP [*Medical Assistance Programs*] International (EA)
**MAP**.......... Maples, MO [*Location identifier*] [*FAA*] (FAAL)
**MAP**.......... Mapping (MSA)
**MAP**.......... Marine Advisory Program [*Marine science*] (MSC)
**MAP**.......... Marketing Action Planner [*National Association of Printers and Lithographers*] [*A publication*]
**MAP**.......... Mars Atmosphere Probe
**MAP**.......... Master Activity Programming
**MAP**.......... Master Air Pilot
**MAP**.......... Material Acquisition Process [*or Program*] (MCD)
**MAP**.......... Materiel Acquisition Plan [*Army*]
**MAP**.......... Mathematical Analysis without Programming [*Data processing*]
**MAP**.......... Maximum A Posteriori [*Statistics*]
**MAP**.......... Maximum Average Price
**MAP**.......... Mean Aortic Pressure [*Medicine*]
**MAP**.......... Mean Arterial Pressure [*Medicine*]
**MAP**.......... Measure of Academic Progress [*Educational test*]
**MAP**.......... Measurement Assurance Program [*National Institute of Standards and Technology*]
**MAP**.......... Media Access Project (EA)
**MAP**.......... Media Analysis Project (EA)
**MAP**.......... Media and People [*Information service or system*] (IID)
**MAP**.......... Mediaeval Academy Publications [*A publication*]
**MAP**.......... Medical Aid Post
**MAP**.......... Medical Audit Program [*Computerized system of abstracted medical record information*]
**MAP**.......... Melphalan, Adriamycin, Prednisone [*Antineoplastic drug regimen*]
**MAP**.......... Memory Allocation and Protection
**MAP**.......... Mercapturic Acid Pathway [*Biochemistry*]
**MAP**.......... Mesenterial Arterial Pressure [*Medicine*]
**MAP**.......... Message Acceptance Pulse [*Aerospace communications*]
**MAP**.......... Meta-Aminophenol [*Organic chemistry*]
**MAP**.......... Meta-Aminopyrimethamine [*Biochemistry*]
**MAP**.......... Methionyl Aminopeptidase [*An enzyme*]
**MAP**.......... Methylacetoxyprogesterone [*Also, MPA*] [*Endocrinology*]
**MAP**.......... Methylacetylene Propadiene [*Organic chemistry*]
**MAP**.......... Methyl(acetylenyl)putrescine [*Biochemistry*]
**MAP**.......... Methyl(amino)propanediol [*Organic chemistry*]
**MAP**.......... Microelectronics Application Project [*British*] (DCTA)
**MAP**.......... Microprocessor Application Project [*In manufacturing industry*] [*Department of the Interior*]
**MAP**.......... Microprogrammed Array Processor
**MAP**.......... Microtubule-Associated Protein [*Cytology*]
**MAP**.......... Migrant Action Program (OICC)
**MAP**.......... Milestone Analysis Procedure
**MAP**.......... Military Assistance Program [*DoD*]
**MAP**.......... Military Association of Podiatrists [*Later, FSPMA*] (EA)
**MAP**.......... Military Audit Project
**MAP**.......... Military Awards Profile [*Information service or system*] (IID)
**MAP**.......... Miller Assessment for Preschoolers
**MAP**.......... Minimum Acceptable Performance [*Telecommunications*] (TEL)
**MAP**.......... Minimum Attack Parameter [*Military*]
**MAP**.......... Minimum Audible Pressure
**MAP**.......... Ministry of Aircraft Production [*British*]
**MAP**.......... Minorities Advancement Plan
**MAP**.......... Missed Approach Point [*Aviation*] (AFM)
**MAP**.......... Missed Approach Procedure [*Aviation*]
**MAP**.......... Missile Application Propulsion
**MAP**.......... Missile and Package Tester
**MAP**.......... Mission Application Program (NASA)
**MAP**.......... Mixed Aniline Point
**MAP**.......... Model and Program [*Data processing*]
**MAP**.......... Modified American Plan [*Travel*]
**MAP**.......... Modified Atmospheric Packaging [*Food industry*]
**MAP**.......... Modular Acoustic Panel
**MAP**.......... Modular Analysis Processor [*Applied Data Research, Inc.*]
**MAP**.......... Modular Application System [*Data processing*]
**MAP**.......... Modular Assembly Prosthesis [*Medicine*]
**MAP**.......... Monitoring Attitudes of the Public [*ACLI*]
**MAP**.......... Monoammonium Phosphate [*Inorganic chemistry*]

**MAP**......... Mothers of AIDS [*Acquired Immune Deficiency Syndrome*] Patients (EA)
**MAP**......... Mouse Antibody Production [*Test for virus*]
**MAP**......... Movement of the Assemblies of People [*Grenada*]
**MAP**......... Multi-Access Pointer (PCM)
**MAP**......... Multichannel Astrometric Photometer [*Astronomy*]
**MAP**......... Multicoverage Account Program [*Insurance*]
**MAP**......... Multicultural Australia Papers [*A publication*]
**MAP**......... Multiple Address Processing
**MAP**......... Multiple Aim Point [*ICBM*]
**MAP**......... Multiple Allocation Procedure [*PERT*]
**MAP**......... Multiple Array Processor
**MAP**......... Municipal Airport (MCD)
**MAP**......... Muscle Action Potential
**MAP**......... Museum Assessment Program [*National Foundation on the Arts and the Humanities*]
**MAP**......... Musical Aptitude Profile
**MAP**......... Mutual African Press Agency
**MAP**......... Mutual Assistance Pact
**MAP**......... Mutual Assistance Plan (NATG)
**MAP**......... Mutual Assistance Program
**MAP**......... National Oceanic and Atmospheric Administration [*Rockville, MD*] [*FAA designator*] (FAAC)
**MAPA**....... Mexican-American Political Association
**MAPA**....... Mooney Aircraft Pilots Association (EA)
**MAPAD**.... Military Assistance Program Address Directory
**MAPAG**.... Military Assistance Program Advisory Group
**MAPAI**...... Mifleget Po'alei Eretz-Yisrael (BJA)
**MAPAM**... Mifleget Po'alim Me'uhedet (BJA)
**MAPAR**..... Materials and Processes Acceptance Requirement
**MAPC**....... Migrating Action Potential Complex [*Electrophysiology*]
**MAPCC**..... Military Assistance Program Country Code (AFM)
**MAPCHE**... Mobile Automatic Programmed Checkout Equipment
**MAP/CIO**... Military Assistance Program/Common Item Order
**MAPCO**.... Mid-American Pipeline Company
**MAPD**....... Master Part Dimensioned (MCD)
**MAPDA**.... Mid-America Periodical Distributors Association
**MAPDFA**... Media-Advertising Partnership for a Drug-Free America [*Later, DFA*] (EA)
**MAPE**........ Maximum Absolute Percentage Error [*Statistics*]
**MAPE**........ Mean Absolute Percentage Error [*Statistics*]
**MAPE**........ Microcomputers and Primary Education
**MAPETT**.. Military Assistance Program Evaluation Team, Thailand (CINC)
**MAPEX**..... Mid-America Payment Exchange
**MAPEX**..... Military Articles Pacific Excesses (AFIT)
**MAPG**....... Maximum Available Power Gain (MSA)
**MAP-GA**... Military Assistance Program - Grant Aid
**MAPHILINDO**... Malaya-Philippines-Indonesia
**MAPI**......... Manufacturers Alliance for Productivity and Innovation (EA)
**MAPI**......... Millon Adolescent Personality Inventory [*Personality development test*] [*Psychology*]
**MAPICS**.... Manufacturing, Accounting, and Production Information Control System [*IBM Corp.*]
**MAPID**...... Machine-Aided Program for Preparation of Instruction Data
**MAPL**........ Manufacturing Assembly Parts List
**MAPL**........ Master Allowance Parts List [*Military*] (CAAL)
**MAPLA**..... Military Assistance Program Logistics Agency [*Merged with Defense Supply Agency*]
**Maple Syrup Dig**... Maple Syrup Digest [*A publication*]
**MAPLHGR**... Maximum Average Planar Linear Heat-Generation Rate [*Nuclear energy*] (NRCH)
**MAPMIS**.. Manpower and Personnel Management Information System [*Navy*]
**MAPMOPP**... Marine Pollution [*or Petroleum*] Monitoring Pilot Project [*Marine science*] (MSC)
**MAPNY**.... Maritime Association of the Port of New York [*Later, MAPONY/NJ*] (EA)
**MAPOLE**... Magnetic Dipole Spark Transmitter (NASA)
**MAPOM**... Military Assistance Program Owned Materiel (AFM)
**MAP/One**... Manufacturing Automation Protocol/One [*Local area network*] [*Industrial Networking, Inc.*]
**MAPONY**... Maritime Association of the Port of New York
**MAPONY/NJ**... Maritime Association of the Port of New York/New Jersey (EA)
**MAPORD**... Methodology Approach to Planning and Programming Air Force Operational Requirements, Research and Development (IEEE)
**MAPP**........ Manpower and Personnel Plan [*Army*] (AABC)
**MAPP**........ Manpower and Production Projections [*LIMRA*]
**MAPP**........ Masking Parameter Printout [*Data processing*]
**MAPP**........ MasterCard Automated Point-of-Sale Program
**MAPP**........ Mathematical Analysis of a Perception and Preference
**MAPP**........ Mid-Continent Area Power Pool [*Electric power*]
**MAPP**........ Mission Analysis and Performance Program
**MApp**......... Musical Appreciation [*Record label*]
**MAppPsych**... Master of Applied Psychology
**MAPPS**..... Management Association of Private Photogrammetric Surveyors (EA)
**MAppSc**.... Master of Applied Science
**MAppSc-BltEnvir**... Master of Applied Science - Built Environment
**MAppSc-MedPhys**... Master of Applied Science - Medical Physics
**MAPR**....... Manufacturing Aids Program Requirements (AAG)
**MAPRAT**... Maximum Power Ratio (IEEE)
**MAPRC**..... Mediterranean Allied Photographic Reconnaissance Command
**Map Read**.. Map Reader [*A publication*]
**MAPRES**.. Mini Air Passenger Reservation System
**MAPRIAL**... Mezhdunarodnaja Assotsiatsija Professorov Russkogo Jazyka i Literatury [*International Association of Teachers of Russian Language and Literature*] (EAIO)
**MAPROS**... Maintain Production Schedules
**MAPRP**..... Mesoscale Atmospheric Processes Research Program [*National Oceanic and Atmospheric Administration*]
**MAPS**........ Machine Automated Parts System (MCD)
**MAPS**........ Maintenance Analysis and Procedures System [*Data processing*]
**MAPS**........ Major Assembly Performance System (MCD)
**MAPS**........ Make-a-Picture Story [*Psychological testing*]
**MAPS**........ Management Accounting and Performance System
**MAPS**........ Management Analysis and Planning System
**MAPS**........ Management and Policy Studies Centre [*Canberra College of Advanced Education*] [*Australia*]
**MAPS**........ Manpower Analysis and Planning Society (EA)
**MAPS**........ Manpower Area Planning System [*Under CAMPS*]
**MAPS**........ Manpower and Production Survey [*LIMRA*]
**MAPS**........ Market-Auction Preferred Stock
**MAPS**........ Marketing, Advertising, and Promotions Solutions Exhibition [*British*] (ITD)
**MAPS**........ Master of Arts in Public Service
**MAPS**........ Measurement of Air [*or Atmospheric*] Pollution from Satellites
**MAPS**........ Medium Aevum. Philologische Studien [*A publication*]
**MAPS**........ Member of the Australian Psychological Society
**MAPS**........ Memoirs. American Philosophical Society [*A publication*]
**MAPS**........ Meteorological and Aeronautical Presentation Subsystem [*FAA*] (FAAC)
**MAPS**........ Methyl(deazaisoalloxazine)propanesulfonic Acid [*Organic chemistry*]
**MAPS**........ Metropolitan Air Post Society (EA)
**MAPS**........ Middle Atlantic Planetarium Society (EA)
**MAPS**........ Military Applications of Photovoltaic Systems
**MAPS**........ Miniature Air Pilot System
**MAPS**........ Minnesota Analysis and Planning System [*University of Minnesota*] [*Research center*] (RCD)
**MAPS**........ Missile Application Propulsion Study
**MAPS**........ Mobility Analysis Planning System (MCD)
**MAPS**........ Mobilization Asset Planning System [*Army*]
**MAPS**........ Modular Acoustic Processing System (MCD)
**MAPS**........ Modular Azimuth Position System [*Army*] (RDA)
**MAPS**........ Monetary and Payments System [*Committee*] [*American Bankers Association*]
**MAPS**........ Monitoring of Air Pollution by Satellites (KSC)
**MAPS**........ Monoclonal Antibody Purification System
**MAPS**........ Monopropellant Accessory Power Supply [*Aerospace*] (AAG)
**MAPS**........ Muhammad Ali Professional Sports [*Commercial firm*]
**MAPS**........ Multicolor Automatic Projection System (IEEE)
**MAPS**........ Multiple Address Processing System
**MAPS**........ Multiple Aim-Point System
**MAPS**........ Multiple Automated Printing Systems (MCD)
**MAPS**........ Multisatellite Attitude Program System [*NASA*]
**MAPS**........ Multitarget Automatic Plotting System
**MAPS**........ Multivariate Analysis, Participation, and Structure
**MAPS**........ Multivariate Analysis and Prediction of Schedules
**MAP3S**...... Multistate Atmospheric Power Production Pollution Study [*Department of Energy*]
**MAPSAC**.. Machine-Aided Planning, Scheduling, and Control
**MAPSAD**... Military Assistance Property Sales and Disposal (AFM)
**MAP/SAMSR**... Joint Army-Air Force Master Plan for the Satisfaction of Army Meteorological Support Requirements (MCD)
**MAPSAS**... Member of APSAS [*Association of Public Service Administrative Staff*] [*British*]
**MAPSE**..... Minimal APSE [*Ada Program Support Environment*] [*Data processing*]
**MAPSEP**... Mission Analysis Program for Solar Electric Propulsion [*Data processing*] [*NASA*]
**MAPSq**...... Mobile Aerial Port Squadron [*Air Force*]
**MAPT**........ Military Assistance Program Training (AFM)
**MAPT**........ Military Assistance Program Transfer (AFM)
**MAPT**........ More Advanced Petrol Tractors [*Germany*]
**MAPT**........ Mothers Are People Too (EA)
**MAPTAC**... Methacrylamidopropyltrimethylammonium Chloride [*Organic chemistry*]
**MAPTIS**.... Manpower Personnel and Training Information System [*Navy*]
**MAPU**....... Memory Allocation and Protection Unit (MSA)
**MAPU**....... Movimiento de Accion Popular Unida [*Unified Popular Action Movement*] [*Chile*] [*Political party*] (PD)
**MAPU**....... Multiple Address Processing Unit [*Military*] (AABC)
**MAPUC**.... Member of the Association for Promoting the Unity of Christendom [*British*]
**MAPUC**.... Modified Area Production Urgency Committee [*World War II*]
**MAPW**..... Medical Association for the Prevention of War [*Australia*]
**MAQ**......... Maandnotities Betreffende de Economische Toestand [*A publication*]
**MAQ**......... Maximum Acceptance Quantity

**MAQ**.......... Measures for Air Quality [*Program*] [*National Institute of Standards and Technology*]
**MAQ**.......... Monetary Allowance in Lieu of Quarters
**MAQR**....... Michigan Alumni Quarterly Review [*A publication*]
**Maquinas**... Maquinas & Metais [*A publication*]
**MAR**.......... At Sea [*Aviation code*] (FAAC)
**MAR**.......... Macroaddress Register
**MAR**.......... Magnetic Amplifier Relay
**MAR**.......... Maintainability Action Request (MCD)
**MAR**.......... Maintenance Analysis Report (MCD)
**MAR**.......... Maintenance and Refurbishment (MCD)
**MAR**.......... Maintenance and Repair
**MAR**.......... Major Assembly Release [*Military*] (AABC)
**MAR**.......... Malfunction Array RADAR
**MAR**.......... Managed Accounts Report [*A publication*] (ECON)
**MAR**.......... Management Analysis Report [*DoD*] (MCD)
**MAR**.......... Management Assessment Report (MCD)
**MAR**.......... Management Assessment Review (MCD)
**MAR**.......... Manistee & Repton R. R. [*AAR code*]
**MAR**.......... Mar-Gold Resources [*Vancouver Stock Exchange symbol*]
**Mar**........... Mar del Sur [*A publication*]
**MAR**.......... Maracaibo [*Venezuela*] [*Airport symbol*] (OAG)
**mar**............ Marathi [*MARC language code*] [*Library of Congress*] (LCCP)
**MAR**.......... Marcade Group, Inc. [*NYSE symbol*] (SPSG)
**MAR**.......... March (AFM)
**Mar**........... March's English King's Bench Reports [*1639-42*] [*A publication*] (DLA)
**MAR**.......... Marian Minerals [*Vancouver Stock Exchange symbol*]
**Mar**........... Marianum [*A publication*]
**MAR**.......... Marimba [*Music*]
**MAR**.......... Marine (MSA)
**Mar**........... Marion Laboratories, Inc.
**MAR**.......... Maritime
**MAR**.......... Maritime Administration Report [*Department of Commerce*]
**MAR**.......... Maritime Central Airways
**Mar**........... Marius [*of Plutarch*] [*Classical studies*] (OCD)
**MAR**.......... Market
**MAR**.......... Marketing [*A publication*]
**MAR**.......... Markeur. Marketing Magazine voor Universiteit en Bedrijfsleven [*A publication*]
**mar**............ Maroon [*Philately*]
**MAR**.......... Married
**MAR**.......... Marseilles [*France*] [*Seismograph station code, US Geological Survey*] [*Closed*] (SEIS)
**MAR**.......... Marshal (ROG)
**Mar**........... Marshall and Sevestre's Appeals [*1862-64*] [*Bengal, India*] [*A publication*] (DLA)
**Mar**........... Marshall's Circuit Court Reports [*United States*] [*A publication*] (DLA)
**Mar**........... Marshall's Reports [*Kentucky*] [*A publication*] (DLA)
**Mar**........... Marshall's Reports [*Ceylon*] [*A publication*] (DLA)
**Mar**........... Marshall's Reports [*Bengal*] [*A publication*] (DLA)
**MAR**.......... Martial [*Roman poet of the first century AD*] (ROG)
**Mar**........... Martin's Louisiana Reports [*A publication*] (DLA)
**Mar**........... Martin's North Carolina Reports [*1 North Carolina*] [*A publication*] (DLA)
**Mar**........... Marvel's Reports [*Delaware*] [*A publication*] (DLA)
**Mar**........... Mary (Queen of England) (DLA)
**MAR**.......... Mass Accumulation Rate [*Geology*]
**MAR**.......... Massachusetts College of Art, Boston, MA [*OCLC symbol*] (OCLC)
**M-Ar**.......... Massachusetts Secretary of State, Archives Division, Boston, MA [*Library symbol*] [*Library of Congress*] (LCLS)
**M Ar**.......... Master of Architecture
**MAR**.......... Master of Arts in Religion
**MAR**.......... Material Availability Report [*NASA*] (KSC)
**MAR**.......... Material Availability Request
**MAR**.......... Materialy po Archeologii Rossii [*A publication*]
**MAR**.......... Medication Administration Record [*Medicine*]
**MAR**.......... Memoires. Academie Roumaine [*A publication*]
**MAR**.......... Memory-Address Register [*Data processing*]
**MAR**.......... Microanalytical Reagent
**MAR**.......... Microprogram Address Register
**MAR**.......... Mid-Air Retrieval (MCD)
**MAR**.......... Mid-Atlantic Ridge [*of sea floor*]
**MAR**.......... Minimal Angle Resolution
**MAR**.......... Minimally Attended RADAR (MCD)
**MAR**.......... Minimum Acceptable Reliability
**MAR**.......... Mining Annual Review [*A publication*]
**MAR**.......... Mission Analysis Representative
**MAR**.......... Monoclonal Antibody Resistant [*Immunochemistry*]
**MAR**.......... Monumenta Artis Romanae [*A publication*]
**MAR**.......... Morocco [*ANSI three-letter standard code*] (CNC)
**MAR**.......... Movimento di Azione Rivoluzionaria [*Revolutionary Action Movement*] [*Italian*] (PD)
**MAR**.......... Movimiento de Accion Revolucionaria [*Revolutionary Action Movement*] [*Mexico*] (PD)
**MAR**.......... Multi-Adversity Resistance [*to root rot*] [*Plant pathology*]
**MAR**.......... Multifunction Array RADAR
**MAR**.......... Multiple Access Relay
**MAR**.......... Municipal Association Record [*A publication*]
**MAR**.......... Municipal Association Reports [*A publication*] (APTA)
**MAR**.......... Muscarinic Acetylcholine Receptor [*Biochemistry*]
**MaR**........... Myth and Ritual. Essays on the Myth and Ritual of the Hebrews in Relation to the Culture Pattern of the Ancient East [*A publication*] (BJA)
**MAR**.......... Mythology of All Races [*A publication*]
**MAR**.......... Revolutionary Action Movement [*Italy*]
**MAr**........... Robbins Public Library, Arlington, MA [*Library symbol*] [*Library of Congress*] (LCLS)
**MAR**.......... Tacoma, WA [*Location identifier*] [*FAA*] (FAAL)
**MARA**....... Majority Rule Association (EA)
**MARAAWEX**... Marine Antiair Warfare Exercise (NVT)
**MARAD**.... Maritime Administration [*Also, MA, MARITADMIN*] [*Department of Transportation*]
**MArAd**...... Master of Archive Administration, University of Liverpool [*British*] (DBQ)
**MARADVU**... Marine Advisory Unit
**MARAIRMED**... Maritime Air Forces Mediterranean [*NATO*] (NATG)
**MARAIRWING**... Marine Aircraft Wing
**MARALLWEAFITRARON**... Marine All Weather Fighter Training Squadron
**Marathwada Univ J Sci**... Marathwada University. Journal of Science [*A publication*]
**Marathwada Univ J Sci Sect A Phys Sci**... Marathwada University. Journal of Science. Section A. Physical Sciences [*A publication*]
**Marathwada Univ J Sci Sect B Biol Sci**... Marathwada University. Journal of Science. Section B. Biological Sciences [*A publication*]
**Mar Av**....... Marvin on General Average [*A publication*] (DLA)
**MARB**....... Marbled [*Edges or sides of cover*] [*Bookbinding*] (ROG)
**MARB**....... Materiel Acquisition Review Board [*Army*]
**MARB**....... Memoires. Academie Royale de Belgique [*A publication*]
**MARBA**.... Mid-America Regional Bargaining Association
**MARBAI**... Morris Arboretum. Bulletin [*A publication*]
**MARBARGE**... Maritime Maintenance Barge
**MARBASSCOL**... Marine Corps Basic School
**Mar Behav and Physiol**... Marine Behaviour and Physiology [*A publication*]
**Mar Behav Physiol**... Marine Behaviour and Physiology [*A publication*]
**Marb Geogr Schr**... Marburger Geographische Schriften [*A publication*]
**MARBI**...... Machine-Readable Form of Bibliographic Information [*American Library Association*]
**Mar Bills**.... Marius on Bills of Exchange [*A publication*] (DLA)
**Mar Biol**.... Marine Biology. International Journal of Life in Oceans and Coastal Waters [*A publication*]
**Mar Biol Assoc India J**... Marine Biological Association of India. Journal [*A publication*]
**Mar Biol (Berl)**... Marine Biology (Berlin) [*A publication*]
**Mar Biol Lett**... Marine Biology Letters [*A publication*]
**Mar Biol (NY)**... Marine Biology (New York) [*A publication*]
**Mar Biol (Vladivostok)**... Marine Biology (Vladivostok) [*A publication*]
**Mar BJ**...... Maryland Bar Journal [*A publication*]
**MARBKS**.. Marine Barracks
**MARBL**..... Memoires. Academie Royale de Belgique. Lettres [*A publication*]
**MARBO**.... Marianas-Bonins Command
**M Arb R**..... Magazin fuer Arbeitsrecht, Sozialpolitik, und Verwandte Gebiete [*A publication*]
**Mar Br**....... March's Brooke's New Cases [*1651*] [*England*] [*A publication*] (DLA)
**MARBRIG**... Marine Brigade
**Marb Winck Prog**... Marburger Winckelmann-Programm [*A publication*]
**Marb W Pr**... Marburger Winckelmann-Programm [*A publication*]
**MARC**....... Hruska Meat Animal Research Center [*Department of Agriculture*] (GRD)
**MARC**....... M/A/R/C, Inc. [*Irving, TX*] [*NASDAQ symbol*] (NQ)
**MARC**....... Machine-Readable Cards
**MARC**....... Machine-Readable Cataloging [*Library of Congress*]
**MARC**....... Manpower Authorization Request for Change [*Air Force*]
**MARC**....... Manpower Requirements Criteria [*Army*]
**MARC**....... Marcato [*Emphasized*] [*Music*]
**Marc**.......... Marcellus [*of Plutarch*] [*Classical studies*] (OCD)
**Marc**.......... Marcus [*of Scriptores Historiae Augustae*] [*Classical studies*] (OCD)
**MARC**....... Matador Automatic RADAR Command
**MARC**....... Material Accountability Recoverability Code
**MARC**....... Materiel Acquisition Resource Committee [*Military*]
**MARC**....... [*Roman L. Hruska*] Meat Animal Research Center [*Clay Center, NE*] [*Department of Agriculture*] (GRD)
**MARC**....... Media Action Research Center (EA)
**MARC**....... Methodist Archives and Research Centre [*John Rylands University Library of Manchester*] [*British*] (CB)
**MARC**....... Metropolitan Administration for Review and Comment [*Program using regional councils of government to serve as clearinghouses for Federal grants*]
**MARC**....... Micro-Analytical Research Centre [*Australia*]
**MARC**....... Micronesian Area Research Center [*University of Guam*] [*Research center*] (RCD)
**MARC**....... Mid-America Regional Council [*Information service or system*] (IID)
**MARC**....... Mining and Reclamation Council of America (EA)
**MARC**....... Minority Access to Research Careers [*Program*] [*Public Health Service*] [*Bethesda, MD*]

**MARC** ....... Missions Advanced Research and Communication Center (EA)
**MARC** ....... Model "A" Restorers Club (EA)
**MARC** ....... Monitoring and Assessment Research Centre [*Marine science*] (MSC)
**MARC** ....... Moore Automatic Remote Control
**MARC** ....... Mouvement d'Action pour la Resurrection du Congo [*Action Movement for the Resurrection of the Congo*] [*Zaire*] (PD)
**MARC** ....... Movimiento Agrario Revolucionario del Campesinado Boliviano [*Revolutionary Movement of Bolivian Indian Peasants*] [*Political party*] (PPW)
**MA(RCA)** ... Master of Arts, Royal College of Art (Photography) [*British*] (DBQ)
**MARCA** .... Mid-Continent Area Reliability Coordination Agreement [*Regional power council*]
**MARCAD** ... Marine Corps Aviation Cadet
**MARCAMP** ... Marine Corps Accrued Military Pay System (NG)
**MARCAN** ... Maneuvering Reentry Control and Ablation Studies
**MARCAS** .. Maneuvering Reentry Control and Ablation Studies (MCD)
**Mar Cas** ..... Maritime Cases, by Crockford and Cox [*1860-71*] [*A publication*] (DLA)
**MARCE** ..... Materiel Asset Redistribution Center Europe [*Military*]
**Marcell** ...... Pro Marcello [*of Cicero*] [*Classical studies*] (OCD)
**MARCEP** .. Maintainability and Reliability Cost-Effectiveness Program (IEEE)
**MARCH** .... Marchioness
**March** ........ March's English King's Bench and Common Pleas Reports [*A publication*] (DLA)
**March** ........ March's Translation of Brooke's New Cases, English King's Bench [*82 English Reprint*] [*A publication*] (DLA)
**M of Arch** .. Master of Architecture
**M Arch** ...... Master of Architecture
**MArch** ....... Medieval Archaeology [*A publication*]
**MARCH** .... Melt-Down Accident Response Characteristics [*Nuclear energy*] (NRCH)
**M3 Archaeol** ... M3 Archaeology [*England*] [*A publication*]
**M Arch in CP** ... Master of Architecture in City Planning
**M Arch Des** ... Master of Architectural Design
**March Dimes Birth Defects Found Birth Defects Orig Artic Ser** ... March of Dimes Birth Defects Foundation. Birth Defects Original Article Series [*A publication*]
**M Arch E** ... Master of Architectural Engineering
**Mar Chem** ... Marine Chemistry [*A publication*]
**Mar Chem (Neth)** ... Marine Chemistry (Netherlands) [*A publication*]
**M Arch Eng** ... Master of Architectural Engineering
**MArchivAdmin** ... Master of Archives Administration (ADA)
**March N** .... March's New Cases, English King's Bench and Common Pleas Reports [*A publication*] (DLA)
**March NC** ... March's New Cases, English King's Bench [*1639-42*] [*A publication*] (DLA)
**March NC** ... Translation of Brook's New Cases [*1515-58*] [*A publication*] (DLA)
**March NR** ... March's New Cases, English King's Bench [*1639-42*] [*A publication*] (DLA)
**MARCIA** ... Mathematical Analysis of Requirements for Career Information Appraisal
**MARCKS** .. Myristoylated Alanine-Rich C-Kinase Substrate [*Biochemistry*]
**Marc Mant** ... Marcus Mantua Benavidius [*Deceased, 1582*] [*Authority cited in pre-1607 legal work*] (DSA)
**MARCO** .... Machine Referenced and Coordinated Outline
**Mar Coat Conf Proc** ... Marine Coatings Conference. Proceedings [*A publication*]
**MARCOGAZ** ... Union of the Gas Industries of the Common Market Countries (EAIO)
**MARCOM** ... Maritime Command [*Canada, since 1964*]
**MARCOM** ... Microwave Airborne Communications Relay (IEEE)
**MARCOMNAVADGRU** ... Marine Corps Component Navy Advisory Group (CINC)
**MARCON** ... Mars Consortium
**MARCON** ... Micro Archives and Records Online [*Developed by AirS, Inc.*]
**MARCONFOR** ... Maritime Contingency Force [*NATO*] (NATG)
**MARCONFORLANT** ... Maritime Contingency Forces, Atlantic [*NATO*] (NATG)
**Marconi Instrum** ... Marconi Instrumentation [*A publication*]
**Marconi Rev** ... Marconi Review [*A publication*]
**MARCONP** ... Maritime Contingency Plans (NATG)
**Mar Conv** ... Marcy's Epitome of Conveyancing [*1881*] [*A publication*] (DLA)
**Mar Conv St** ... Marcy's Conveyancing Statutes [*5th ed.*] [*1893*] [*A publication*] (DLA)
**MARCOR** ... Marine Corps
**MARCORDISBOF** ... Marine Corps Disbursing Office
**MARCORESTRACEN** ... Marine Corps Reserve Training Center
**MARCORMAN** ... Marine Corps Manual
**MARCORPERSMAN** ... Marine Corps Personnel Manual
**MARCORPS** ... Marine Corps
**MARCORSUPDEP** ... Marine Corps Supply Depot
**MARCOT** ... Maritime Command Operational Team Training [*Canadian Navy*]
**Mar Crp G** ... Marine Corps Gazette [*A publication*]
**MARC-S** .... Machine-Readable Cataloguing - Serials (ADA)
**MARCS** ..... Melcom All Round Adaptive Consolidated Software [*Japan*]
**Marcus An** ... Marcus Antonius Blancus [*Deceased, 1548*] [*Authority cited in pre-1607 legal work*] (DSA)
**Marcus Anto** ... Marcus Antonius Blancus [*Deceased, 1548*] [*Authority cited in pre-1607 legal work*] (DSA)
**MARDAC** ... Manpower Research and Data Analysis Center [*DoD*] (NVT)
**MARDAN** ... Marine Differential Analyzer
**MARDATA** ... Maritime Data Network [*Lloyd's Maritime Data Network Ltd.*] [*Stamford, CT*] [*Database*]
**MARDEC** ... Malaysia Rubber Development Corporation (DS)
**MARDET** ... Marine Detachment
**Mar D Int** .. Maritime Defence. The Journal of International Naval Technology [*A publication*]
**MARDIS** ... Modernized Army Research and Development Information System
**MARDIV** ... Marine Division
**MARDO** .... Months after Receipt of Delivery Order (MCD)
**MARDS** ..... Medium Artillery Delivered Sensor [*Army*]
**MARE** ....... Major Accident Response Exercise (MCD)
**MARE** ....... Major Account Response Evaluation (MCD)
**MARE** ....... Maritime Engineering [*Canadian Navy*]
**MARE** ....... Months after Receipt of Equipment [*Navy*]
**MAREA** .... Member of the American Railway Engineering Association
**MAREA** .... Middle Leaf Area [*Botany*]
**MARECEBO** ... Manned Research on Celestial Bodies Committee [*International Academy of Astronautics*]
**Mar Ecol Prog Ser** ... Marine Ecology. Progress Series [*A publication*]
**Mar Ecol (Pubbl Stn Zool Napoli I)** ... Marine Ecology (Pubblicazioni Stazione Zoologica di Napoli. I) [*A publication*]
**MARECS** .. Maritime Communications Satellite
**MARED** .... Materiel Acquisition and Readiness Executive Development [*Program*] [*Army*] (RDA)
**MAREGSQ** ... Marine Air Regulating Squadron
**MAREMIC** ... Maintenance Repair and Minor Construction [*Program*] [*Air Force*]
**Mar Eng** ..... Marine Engineering [*Japan*] [*A publication*]
**Mar Eng** ..... Marine Engineering/Log [*A publication*]
**Mar Eng Cat** ... Marine Engineering/Log. Catalog and Buyer's Guide [*A publication*]
**Mar Eng/Log** ... Marine Engineering/Log [*A publication*]
**Mar Eng Nav Architect** ... Marine Engineer and Naval Architect [*A publication*]
**Mar Engng/Log** ... Marine Engineering/Log [*A publication*]
**Mar Eng Rev** ... Marine Engineers Review [*A publication*]
**Mar Engrs J** ... Marine Engineers Journal [*A publication*]
**Mar Engrs Rev** ... Marine Engineers Review [*A publication*]
**Mar Eng Yrb** ... Marine Engineering/Log. Yearbook and Maritime Review [*A publication*]
**MARENTS** ... Modified Advanced Research Environmental Test Satellite [*Air Force*]
**Mar Environ Res** ... Marine Environmental Research [*A publication*]
**MAREP** ..... Marine Environmental Prediction Task Group [*US government*] [*Terminated, 1969*]
**MARES** ..... Marine Corps Automated Readiness Evaluation System
**MARES/FORSTAT** ... Marine Corps Automated Readiness Evaluation System/Status of Forces
**MARESTNG** ... Marine Corps Reserve Training (NVT)
**MARF** ........ Master Availability Reference File [*Army Electronics Command*]
**Mar Fa** ....... Martinus de Fano [*Deceased circa 1275*] [*Authority cited in pre-1607 legal work*] (DSA)
**MARFAIR** ... Marine Fleet Air
**MARFAIRWEST** ... Marine Fleet Air, West Coast
**Mar Fan** ..... Martinus de Fano [*Deceased circa 1275*] [*Authority cited in pre-1607 legal work*] (DSA)
**MARFIREX** ... Marine Firing Exercise (NVT)
**Mar Fish Re** ... Marine Fisheries Review [*A publication*]
**MARFOR** ... Marine Forces [*Element of a Joint Task Force*]
**MARFS** ..... Multienvironment Active RF [*Radio Frequency*] Seeker
**MARG** ....... Margarine
**MARG** ....... Margin
**MARG** ....... Marine Amphibious Ready Group (MCD)
**MARG** ....... Market Analysis Report Generator [*Data processing*]
**MARG** ....... Mediterranean Amphibious Ready Group (MCD)
**MARGARFOR** ... Marine Garrison Force
**MARGE** .... Margarine (ADA)
**MARGEN** ... Management Report Generator [*Randolph Data Services, Inc.*] [*Software package*] [*Data processing*] (IEEE)
**Mar Geol** ... Marine Geology [*A publication*]
**Mar Geophys Res** ... Marine Geophysical Researches [*A publication*]
**Mar Geotech** ... Marine Geotechnology [*A publication*]
**Mar Geotechnol** ... Marine Geotechnology [*A publication*]
**MARGIE** ... Memory Analysis, Response Generation, and Interference in English
**MARGILSAREA** ... Marshalls-Gilberts Area
**MARGL** .... Marginal (ROG)
**MARHELILEX** ... Marine Helicopter Landing Exercise (NVT)
**Mar I** .......... March of India [*A publication*]
**MARI** ........ Marijuana Cigarette [*Slang*] (DSUE)

**Mari**.......... Marinus de Caramanico [*Flourished, 1269-85*] [*Authority cited in pre-1607 legal work*] (DSA)
**MARI**........ Medicare Administrative Reform Initiative [*Health Care Financing Administration*]
**MARI**........ Mercantile Atlantic Routing Instructions
**MARI**........ Microelectronics Applications Research Institute [*Newcastle-Upon-Tyne, England*]
**MARI**........ Motivator and Response Indicator
**Marian Libr Stud** ... Marian Library Studies [*A publication*]
**Marian Stds** ... Marian Studies [*A publication*]
**Maria Soci** ... Marianus Socinus [*Authority cited in pre-1607 legal work*] (DSA)
**MARIC**...... Marine Resources Information Center [*Massachusetts Institute of Technology*] (NOAA)
**Mari Gos Ped Inst Ucen Zap** ... Mariiskii Gosudarstvennyi Pedagogiceskii Institut. Ucenye Zapiski [*A publication*]
**Marijuana Rev** ... Marijuana Review [*A publication*] (DLA)
**Marina Ital** ... Marina Italiana [*A publication*]
**MARINE**... Management Analysis Reporting Information on the Naval Environment System (NG)
**Marine Bio** ... Marine Biology [*A publication*]
**Marine Biol Assn UK J** ... Marine Biological Association of the United Kingdom. Journal [*A publication*]
**Marine Ct R** ... Marine Court Reporter (McAdam's) [*New York*] [*A publication*] (DLA)
**Marine Eng** ... Marine Engineering [*A publication*]
**Marine Eng/Log** ... Marine Engineering/Log [*A publication*]
**Marine Fisheries R** ... Marine Fisheries Review [*A publication*]
**Marine Geotech** ... Marine Geotechnology [*A publication*]
**Marine Geotechnol** ... Marine Geotechnology [*A publication*]
**Marine March** ... Marine Marchande [*A publication*]
**Mariner Mir** ... Mariner's Mirror [*A publication*]
**Mariners Mir** ... Mariner's Mirror [*A publication*]
**Marine Tech Soc J** ... Marine Technology Society. Journal [*A publication*]
**MARINEX** ... Marine Express (AABC)
**Marin Frecc** ... Marinus Freccia [*Flourished, 16th century*] [*Authority cited in pre-1607 legal work*] (DSA)
**MARINTRARON** ... Marine Instrument Training Squadron
**Mar Invertebr Scand** ... Marine Invertebrates of Scandinavia [*A publication*]
**Mariol St** ... Mariologische Studien [*A publication*]
**Marion County Med Soc Bull** ... Marion County Medical Society. Bulletin [*Indiana*] [*A publication*]
**MARISAT** ... Maritime Satellite System [*COMSAT*]
**Marisia**...... Marisia Studii si Materiale Arheologice. Istorie. Etnografie [*A publication*]
**MARISP** ... Maritime Strike Plan
**MARIT**...... Maritime
**MARITA**... Maritime Airfield (NATG)
**MARITADMIN** ... Maritime Administration [*Also, MA, MARAD*] [*Department of Transportation*] (MUGU)
**MARITCOM** ... Maritime Commission
**Maritime Sediments Atlantic Geol** ... Maritime Sediments and Atlantic Geology [*A publication*]
**Maritimes L Rep (CCH)** ... Maritimes Law Reporter (Commerce Clearing House) [*A publication*] (DLA)
**Marit Policy & Manage** ... Maritime Policy and Management [*A publication*]
**Marit Sediments** ... Maritime Sediments [*Later, Maritime Sediments and Atlantic Geology*] [*A publication*]
**Marit Sediments Atl Geol** ... Maritime Sediments and Atlantic Geology [*A publication*]
**Marit Sediments & Atl Geol** ... Maritime Sediments and Atlantic Geology [*A publication*]
**MARITZ**... Maritzburg (ROG)
**Marius**....... Marius. Concerning Bills of Exchange [*4 eds.*] [*1651-84*] [*A publication*] (DLA)
**MARK**....... Maintenance and Reliability Kit [*Military*] (NVT)
**Mark**.......... Mark Twain Journal [*A publication*]
**Mark** Market
**MARK**....... MarkitStar, Inc. [*NASDAQ symbol*] (NQ)
**MARK**....... Mechanized Assignment and Record Keeping [*Database management system*]
**MARK**....... Mid-Atlantic Ridge Kane
**Mark Adjust Wood** ... Market Adjusted Wood. New Approaches in Forestry and Sawmills. Elmia Wood 81 [*A publication*]
**MARKAR** ... Mapping and Reconnaissance Ku-Band Airborne RADAR
**Mark Bull US Dep Agric** ... Marketing Bulletin. US Department of Agriculture [*A publication*]
**Mark Commun** ... Marketing Communications [*A publication*]
**Mark El**..... Markby's Elements of Law [*6th ed.*] [*1905*] [*A publication*] (DLA)
**Market Com** ... Marketing Communications [*A publication*]
**Market Eur** ... Market Research Europe [*A publication*]
**Marketing** ... Marketing Magazine [*A publication*]
**Marketing Res Rep USDA** ... Marketing Research Report. United States Department of Agriculture [*A publication*]
**Marketing Ser Agr Marketing Adv (India)** ... Marketing Series. Agricultural Marketing Adviser (India) [*A publication*]
**Market J**.... Marketing Journal [*A publication*]
**Market Research Soc J** ... Journal. Market Research Society [*A publication*]
**Market Rev** ... Market Review [*A publication*]
**Market Week** ... Adweek's Marketing Week [*A publication*]
**Markgr Jb** ... Markgraefler Jahrbuch [*A publication*]
**Mark Grow J** ... Market Grower's Journal [*A publication*]
**Markham R** ... Markham Review [*A publication*]
**Markham Rev** ... Markham Review [*A publication*]
**Mark Hung** ... Marketing in Hungary [*A publication*]
**Mark Media Decis** ... Marketing and Media Decisions [*A publication*]
**Mark Mix** ... Marketing Mix [*A publication*]
**Mark og Montre** ... Mark og Montre fra Sydvestjydske Museer [*A publication*]
**Mark News** ... Marketing News [*A publication*]
**MarkR**....... Markham Review [*A publication*]
**Mark Res Abstr** ... Market Research Abstracts [*A publication*]
**Mark Res Rep US Dep Agric** ... Marketing Research Report. United States Department of Agriculture [*A publication*]
**MARKS**..... Modern Army Record Keeping System (INF)
**MARKSIM** ... [*A*] Marketing Decision Simulation [*Game*]
**Marks & Sayre** ... Marks and Sayre's Reports [*108 Alabama*] [*A publication*] (DLA)
**Marks & Sayre's** ... Marks' and Sayre's Reports [*108 Alabama*] [*A publication*] (DLA)
**MARKSTRAT** ... Marketing Strategy [*Simulation package developed by Professors Jean-Claude Larreche and Hubert Gatignon*]
**Mark Twain** ... Mark Twain Journal [*A publication*]
**MARL**....... Marlboro [*Vermont*] [*Seismograph station code, US Geological Survey*] (SEIS)
**MARL**....... Master of Arts and Letters
**MARL**....... Mobile Acoustics Research Laboratory (MCD)
**Marl**........... Statute of Marlborough [*A publication*] (DSA)
**Mar LA**...... Martin's Louisiana Reports [*A publication*] (DLA)
**MARLAGS** ... Marine Life and Geochemical Studies [*Marine science*] (MSC)
**Mar de Lau** ... Martinus Caratti de Laude [*Flourished, 1438-45*] [*Authority cited in pre-1607 legal work*] (DSA)
**Mar Law**.... Maritime Lawyer [*A publication*]
**MARLB**..... Marlborough (ROG)
**Mar LC**...... Maritime Law Cases, by Crockford [*1860-71*] [*A publication*] (DLA)
**Mar L Cas (NS)** ... Maritime Law Cases (New Series), by Aspinall [*1870-1940*] [*A publication*] (DLA)
**Mar LC NS** ... Maritime Law Cases, New Series, by Aspinall [*1870-1940*] [*England*] [*A publication*] (DLA)
**Mar L and Com** ... Journal of Maritime Law and Commerce [*A publication*]
**Mar Leg Bib** ... Marvin's Legal Bibliography [*A publication*] (DLA)
**MARLEX**.. Marine Corps Reserve Landing Exercise (NVT)
**MARLIN**... Middle Atlantic Regional Information Network
**MARLIS** ... Multiaspect Relevance Linkage Information System
**Mar LJ**....... Maryland Law Journal and Real Estate Record [*A publication*] (DLA)
**Mar LR**...... Maritime Law Cases, First Series, by Crockford [*1860-71*] [*A publication*] (DLA)
**Mar LR**...... Maritime Law Cases, New Series, by Aspinall [*1870-1940*] [*A publication*] (DLA)
**Mar L Rec** ... Maryland Law Record [*A publication*] (DLA)
**Mar L Rev** ... Maryland Law Review [*A publication*]
**MARLSR**.. Manufacturers Association of Robes, Leisurewear, Shirts, and Rainwear [*Defunct*] (EA)
**Mar M**....... Marbacher Magazin [*A publication*]
**MARM**...... Middle Atlantic Regional Meeting [*of American Chemical Society*]
**MARM**...... Moving Average Rating Method [*Insurance*]
**Mar Mamm Sci** ... Marine Mammal Science [*A publication*]
**Mar Mant** ... Marcus Mantua Benavidius [*Deceased, 1582*] [*Authority cited in pre-1607 legal work*] (DSA)
**MARMAP** ... Marine Resources Monitoring, Assessment, and Prediction [*National Oceanic and Atmospheric Administration*]
**MARMDK** ... Marine Mining [*A publication*]
**Mar Mech E** ... Marine Mechanical Engineer
**Mar Med** ... Maroc Medical [*A publication*]
**MARMETS** ... Marine Meteorological Service
**Mar Micropaleontol** ... Marine Micropaleontology [*A publication*]
**Mar Min**.... Marine Mining [*A publication*]
**Mar Mining** ... Marine Mining [*A publication*]
**Mar Mirror** ... Mariner's Mirror [*A publication*]
**Mar Moore N** ... Marianne Moore Newsletter [*A publication*]
**Marm Par**.. Marmor Parium [*Classical studies*] (OCD)
**MARNAF** ... Marquardt Navair Fuel [*A boron slurry propellant for spacecraft*]
**Mar NC**..... March's New Cases, English King's Bench [*1639-42*] [*A publication*] (DLA)
**Mar NC**..... Martin's North Carolina Reports [*1 North Carolina*] [*A publication*] (DLA)
**MARNQ**.... Marion Corp. [*NASDAQ symbol*] (NQ)
**Mar N & Q** ... Maritime Notes and Queries [*1873-1900*] [*A publication*] (DLA)
**Mar NR**..... March's New Cases [*1639-42*] [*A publication*] (DLA)
**Mar NS**...... Martin's Louisiana Reports, New Series [*A publication*] (DLA)
**MARO**....... Maritime Air Radio Organization [*NATO*] (NATG)
**MARO**....... Marrow-Tech, Inc. [*NASDAQ symbol*] (NQ)
**Mar Obs**.... Marine Observer [*A publication*]
**Maroc Med** ... Maroc Medical [*A publication*]
**Maroc Serv Geol Notes Mem Serv Geol** ... Maroc. Service Geologique. Notes et Memoires du Service Geologique [*A publication*]

**MAROPS** ... Maritime Operations
**MArOr** ...... Monographs. Archiv Orientalni [*A publication*]
**MAROTS** ... Maritime Orbital Test Satellite
**MARP** ....... Manpower Allocation/Requirements Plan [*Navy*]
**MARP** ....... Marine Petroleum Trust [*NASDAQ symbol*] (NQ)
**MARP** ....... Mobilization Augmentee Revitalization Program [*Military*]
**MARP** ....... Months after Receipt of Problem [*Navy*] (NG)
**MARPAC** ... Headquarters, Department of the Pacific [*Marine Corps*]
**MARPAC** ... Maritime Command Pacific [*Canada, since 1964*]
**MARPDA** ... Mid-America Periodical Distributors Association (EA)
**MARPEP** .. Marine Physical Environmental Prediction
**Mar Pet Geol** ... Marine and Petroleum Geology [*A publication*]
**MARPIC** ... Marine Pollution Information Centre [*Marine Biological Association of the United Kingdom*] (IID)
**Marpie** ....... Middle-Aged Rural Professional [*Lifestyle classification*]
**MARPOL** ... International Convention for the Prevention of Pollution from Ships [*1973*]
**MARPOL** ... Maritime Pollution Convention [*1978*] (DS)
**Mar Policy** ... Marine Policy [*England*] [*A publication*]
**Mar Policy Manage** ... Marine Policy and Management [*England*] [*A publication*]
**Mar Pollut Bull** ... Marine Pollution Bulletin [*A publication*]
**Mar Pollut Res Titles** ... Marine Pollution Research Titles [*Plymouth*] [*A publication*]
**MARPOLMON** ... Sub-Group of Experts on Marine Pollution Monitoring [*Marine science*] (MSC)
**Mar Prov**.... Maritime Provinces Reports [*Canada*] [*A publication*] (DLA)
**MARPS**..... Mechanized Accounting Reserve Pay System
**Mar Psyiat Q** ... Maryland Psychiatric Quarterly [*A publication*]
**MARPT**..... Municipal Airport (FAAC)
**MARQ**....... Marquis [*or Marquess*]
**Marq LR**.... Marquette Law Review [*A publication*]
**Marq L Rev** ... Marquette Law Review [*A publication*]
**Marquette Busin R** ... Marquette Business Review [*A publication*]
**Marquette Bus R** ... Marquette Business Review [*A publication*]
**Marquette Bus Rev** ... Marquette Business Review [*A publication*] (DLA)
**Marquette Geologists Assoc Bull** ... Marquette Geologists Association. Bulletin [*A publication*]
**Marquette Law R** ... Marquette Law Review [*A publication*]
**Marquette L Rev** ... Marquette Law Review [*A publication*]
**MARQUIS** ... Master Remote Query Interface System [*Data processing*]
**Marr**........... Hay and Marriott's English Admiralty Reports [*A publication*] (DLA)
**Mar R** ........ Maritime Law Reports [*A publication*] (DLA)
**Marr**........... Marrack's European Assurance Cases [*England*] [*A publication*] (DLA)
**Marr**........... Marriage (DLA)
**MARR** ....... Maximum Annual Rate of Return [*Finance*]
**MARR** ....... Minimum Attractive Rate of Return [*Economics*]
**Marr Adm** ... Marriott's English Admiralty Reports [*A publication*] (DLA)
**MARRCS** .. Manpower Requirements and Resources Control System [*Navy*] (NVT)
**Mar Rd** ...... Marine-Rundschau [*A publication*]
**MARRD** .... Married (ROG)
**MARRDZ** ... Marine Research. Department of Agriculture and Fisheries for Scotland [*A publication*]
**MARRE**..... Manual RADAR Reconnaissance Exploitation (MCD)
**MARRE**..... Marriage (ROG)
**Mar Rec B** ... Martin's Recital Book [*A publication*] (DLA)
**Mar Reg**..... Mitchell's Maritime Register [*England*] [*A publication*] (DLA)
**MARRES** .. Manual RADAR Reconnaissance Exploitation System [*Air Force*]
**Mar Res Dep Agric Fish Scotl** ... Marine Research. Department of Agriculture and Fisheries for Scotland [*A publication*]
**Mar Res Indones** ... Marine Research in Indonesia [*A publication*]
**Mar Res Lab Educ Ser (St Petersburg FL)** ... Marine Research Laboratory. Educational Series (St. Petersburg, Florida) [*A publication*]
**Mar Res Lab Invest Rep (S-W Afr)** ... Marine Research Laboratory. Investigational Report (South-West Africa) [*A publication*]
**Mar Res Lab Prof Pap Ser (St Petersburg Florida)** ... Marine Research Laboratory. Professional Papers Series (St. Petersburg, Florida) [*A publication*]
**Mar Res Lab Spec Sci Rep (St Petersburg FL)** ... Marine Research Laboratory. Special Scientific Report (St. Petersburg, Florida) [*A publication*]
**Mar Res Lab Tech Ser (St Petersburg FL)** ... Marine Research Laboratory. Technical Series (St. Petersburg, Florida) [*A publication*]
**Mar Res Ser Scott Home Dep** ... Marine Research Series. Scottish Home Department [*A publication*]
**Marr Form** ... Marriott's Formulare Instrumentorum [*Admiralty Court*] [*1802*] [*A publication*] (DLA)
**Marriage**.... Marriage and Family Living [*A publication*]
**Marriage Fam Rev** ... Marriage and Family Review [*A publication*]
**MARRS**..... Mechanized Ammunition Recording and Reporting System
**MARR SETTL** ... Marriage Settlement [*Legal term*] (DLA)
**MARS**........ Machine-Aided Realization System
**MARS**........ Machine-Assisted Reference Section [*American Library Association*] [*Information service or system*] (IID)
**MARS**........ Machine-Assisted Reference Service [*St. Paul Public Library*] (OLDSS)
**MARS**........ Machine Automated Realty Service
**MARS**........ Machine Retrieval System
**MARS**........ Magnetic Airborne Recording System
**MARS**........ Maintenance Activities and Resources Simulation [*Data processing*]
**MARS**........ Maintenance Analysis and Recording Systems
**MARS**........ Maintenance Analysis Repair Set
**MARS**........ Maintenance Assistance and Repair System [*Military*]
**MARS**........ Man-Hour Accounting and Reporting System [*Military*] (MCD)
**MARS**........ Management Analysis Reporting System [*Data processing*]
**MARS**........ Management Reports and Statistics
**MARS**........ Manned Aerodynamic Reusable Spaceship
**MARS**........ Manned Astronautical Research Station [*Space laboratory*]
**MARS**........ Marconi Automatic Relay System (IEEE)
**MarS**.......... Marian Studies [*New York*] [*A publication*]
**MARS**........ Marine Account Reconciliation Service
**MARS**........ Marine Aircraft Repair Squadron
**MARS**........ Marine Reporting Station [*National Weather Service*]
**MARS**........ Maritime Surface and Subsurface [*Canadian Navy*]
**MARS**........ Market Analysis and Reference System [*Vancouver stock exchange computer system*] [*Canada*]
**Mars** .......... Marsden's Select Pleas in the Court of Admiralty [*Selden Society Publications, Vols. 6, 11*] [*A publication*] (DLA)
**MARS**........ Marsh Supermarkets, Inc. [*NASDAQ symbol*] (NQ)
**MARS**........ Martin Automatic Reporting System
**MARS**........ Master Attitude Reference System
**MARS**........ Material Action Reporting System (MCD)
**MARS**........ Material Response Study
**MARS**........ Materiel Acquisition Resource System [*Military*]
**MARS**........ Mathematics Anxiety Rating Scale [*Psychology*]
**MARS**........ Maximum Asset Return Strategy [*Allingham, Anderson, Roll & Ross*] [*British*] (ECON)
**MARS**........ Measuring Accuracy and Repeatability Study
**MARS**........ Mechanical Accessory Repair Shop (MCD)
**MARS**........ Media Alert and Response System [*Public relations project devised by Pharmaceutical Manufacturers Association*]
**MARS**........ Memory-Address Register Storage [*Data processing*]
**MARS**........ Meteorological Automatic Reporting Station [*Canada*]
**MARS**........ Midair Recovery [*or Retrieval*] System [*Rescue by helicopter*] [*Military*]
**MARS**........ Military Affiliated Radio System [*Amateur-operated radio stations*]
**MARS**........ Military Amphibious Reconnaissance System (RDA)
**MARS**........ Miniature Attitude Reference System
**MARS**........ Minimum-Altitude Release and Strafe (MCD)
**MARS**........ Mirror Advanced Reactor Study (MCD)
**MARS**........ Mission Maintenance and Reliability Simulation (MCD)
**MARS**........ Mobile Atlantic Range Stations [*Tracking stations*] (MUGU)
**MARS**........ Modular Airborne Recorder System (MCD)
**MARS**........ Modular Attack RADAR System (MCD)
**MARS**........ Monitor and Replenisher System
**MARS**........ Monitoring Accounting Reporting and Statistical System [*Aviation*]
**MARS**........ Monthly Aerial Reconnaissance Summary (MCD)
**MARS**........ Motorola Aerial Remote Sensing [*Flying laboratory*]
**MARS**........ Multiaperture Reluctance Switch [*Data storage unit*]
**MARS**........ Multiple Access Retrieval System [*Control Data Corp.*]
**MARS**........ Multiple Action Raid Simulation [*France*]
**MARS**........ Multiple Artillery Rocket System [*Army*]
**MARS**........ Multivariate Analysis, Retrieval, and Storage [*System*] [*NASA*]
**MARS**........ PTS Marketing and Advertising Reference Service [*Predicasts, Inc.*] [*Cleveland, OH*] [*Information service or system*] (IID)
**MARSA**..... Military Accepts Responsibility for Separation of Aircraft (AFM)
**Mars Adm** ... Marsden's English Admiralty [*A publication*] (DLA)
**Mar Sal**...... Marius Salomonius [*Deceased, 1557*] [*Authority cited in pre-1607 legal work*] (DSA)
**MARSAM** ... Multiple Airborne Reconnaissance Sensors Assessment Model (MCD)
**MARSAT** .. Maritime Satellite [*COMSAT*]
**MARSATS** ... Maritime Satellite System [*COMSAT*]
**MARSB2**... Maritime Sediments [*Later, Maritime Sediments and Atlantic Geology*] [*A publication*]
**M Ar Sc** ..... Master of Arts and Sciences
**Mars Chir** .. Marseille Chirurgical [*A publication*]
**Mar Sci Cent Manuscr Rep McGill Univ (Montreal)** ... Marine Sciences Centre. Manuscript Report. McGill University (Montreal) [*A publication*]
**Mar Sci Commun** ... Marine Science Communications [*A publication*]
**Mar Sci Cont Tab** ... Marine Science Contents Tables [*A publication*]
**Mar Sci Instrum** ... Marine Sciences Instrumentation [*A publication*]
**Mar Sci (NY)** ... Marine Science (New York) [*A publication*]
**Mar Sci Res Cent Spec Rep (Stony Brook)** ... Marine Sciences Research Center. Special Report (Stony Brook) [*A publication*]
**Mar Sci Res Cent (Stony Brook) Tech Rep** ... Marine Sciences Research Center (Stony Brook). Technical Report [*A publication*]
**Mars Coll**... Marsden's Collisions at Sea [*11th ed.*] [*1961*] [*A publication*] (DLA)
**MARSD4**... Marine Science [*New York*] [*A publication*]
**Marseille Med** ... Marseille Medical [*A publication*]

**Marsh** ........ Marshall and Sevestre's Appeals [*1862-64*] [*Bengal, India*] [*A publication*] (DLA)
**Marsh** ........ Marshall's Circuit Court Decisions [*United States*] [*A publication*] (DLA)
**Marsh** ........ Marshall's English Common Pleas Reports [*1814-16*] [*A publication*] (DLA)
**Marsh** ........ Marshall's High Court Reports [*Bengal*] [*A publication*] (DLA)
**Marsh** ........ Marshall's Reports [*Ceylon*] [*A publication*] (DLA)
**Marsh** ........ Marshall's Reports [*Kentucky*] [*A publication*] (DLA)
**Marsh** ........ Marshall's Reports [*4 Utah*] [*A publication*] (DLA)
**Marsh A K** ... [*A. K.*] Marshall's Kentucky Reports [*8-10 Kentucky*] [*A publication*] (DLA)
**Marshall** .... Marshall's Reports [*Bengal*] [*A publication*] (DLA)
**Marshall** .... Reports of Cases on Appeal [*Calcutta*] [*A publication*] (DLA)
**Marsh Beng** ... Marshall's Reports [*Bengal*] [*A publication*] (DLA)
**Marsh Calc** ... Marshall's Reports [*Calcutta*] [*A publication*] (DLA)
**Marsh Car** ... Marshall on Railways as Carriers [*A publication*] (DLA)
**Marsh Ceylon** ... Marshall's Ceylon Reports [*A publication*] (DLA)
**Marsh Costs** ... Marshall on the Law of Costs [*A publication*] (DLA)
**Marsh CP** .. Marshall's English Common Pleas Reports [*A publication*] (DLA)
**Marsh Dec** ... Marshall on the Federal Constitution [*A publication*] (DLA)
**Marsh Dec** ... Marshall's Circuit Court Decisions, by Brockenbrough [*United States*] [*A publication*] (DLA)
**Marsh (Eng)** ... Marshall's English Common Pleas Reports [*A publication*] (DLA)
**Marsh Ins** .. Marshall on Marine Insurance [*A publication*] (DLA)
**Marsh J J** .. [*J. J.*] Marshall's Kentucky Reports [*24-30 Kentucky*] [*A publication*] (DLA)
**Marsh (KY)** ... Marshall's Reports [*Kentucky*] [*A publication*] (DLA)
**MARSHL** ... Marshal (ROG)
**Marsh Op** .. Marshall's Constitutional Opinions [*A publication*] (DLA)
**Marsh Ry** ... Marshall on Railways as Carriers [*A publication*] (DLA)
**Marsh Ry** ... Marshall's Duties and Obligations of Railway Companies [*A publication*] (DLA)
**Mar Sill** ..... Martinus Sillimanus [*Flourished, 13th century*] [*Authority cited in pre-1607 legal work*] (DSA)
**MARSO** .... Marine Corps Shipping Order (NG)
**MA/RSO** ... Mobilization Augmentee/Reserve Supplement Officer [*Air Force*] (AFM)
**MARSTA** .. Marital Status [*Army*] (AABC)
**MARSTSIC** ... Marst on Sicca [*England*]
**Mar Stud San Pedro Bay Calif** ... Marine Studies of San Pedro Bay, California [*A publication*]
**MARSVC** .. [*Provide*] Services for Marine Training (NVT)
**MARSYAS** ... Marshall System for Aerospace Simulation [*Programming language*] [*1966-68*] (CSR)
**M of Art** ..... Magazine of Art [*Cassell's*] [*A publication*]
**MArt** .......... Magazine of Art [*A publication*]
**MART** ....... Maintenance Analysis Review Technique
**Mart** ........... Mart Magazine [*A publication*]
**Mart** ........... Martial [*Roman poet, 40-104AD*] [*Classical studies*] (OCD)
**Mart** ........... Martin's Louisiana Term Reports [*1809-30*] [*A publication*] (DLA)
**Mart** ........... Martin's North Carolina Reports [*1 North Carolina*] [*A publication*] (DLA)
**Mart** ........... Martinus Gosia [*Authority cited in pre-1607 legal work*] (DSA)
**MART** ....... Martius [*March*] [*Latin*]
**MART** ....... Martyr
**MART** ....... Marubeni Corp. [*NASDAQ symbol*] (NQ)
**MART** ....... Mean Active Repair Time (IEEE)
**MART** ....... Meaning and Art [*Elsevier Book Series*] [*A publication*]
**MART** ....... Mobile Automatic Radiation Tester
**MArt** .......... Mundus Artium [*A publication*]
**MARTAC** ... Martin Automatic Rapid Test and Control
**Mart Ark** ... Martin's Decisions in Equity [*Arkansas*] [*A publication*] (DLA)
**MARTC** ..... Marine Air Reserve Training Command
**MARTCOM** ... Marine Air Reserve Training Command
**Mart Cond LA** ... Martin's Condensed Louisiana Reports [*A publication*] (DLA)
**Mart Conv** ... Martin's Practice of Conveyancing [*A publication*] (DLA)
**MARTD** .... Marine Air Reserve Training Detachment
**Mart Dec** .... United States Decisions in Martin's North Carolina Reports [*A publication*] (DLA)
**MArte** ........ Musica y Arte [*A publication*]
**MARTEC** ... Martin Thin-Film Electronic Circuit
**Mar Technol** ... Marine Technology [*A publication*]
**Mar Technol Soc Annu Conf Prepr** ... Marine Technology Society. Annual Conference. Preprints [*A publication*]
**Mar Technol Soc Annu Conf Proc** ... Marine Technology Society. Annual Conference. Proceedings [*A publication*]
**Mar Technol Soc J** ... Marine Technology Society. Journal [*A publication*]
**Mar Tech S J** ... Marine Technology Society. Journal [*A publication*]
**MARTEL** .. Missile Antiradiation Television [*Military*] (CAAL)
**Mart Ex** ..... Martin on Executors [*A publication*] (DLA)
**Mart GA** .... Martin's Reports [*21-30 Georgia*] [*A publication*] (DLA)
**Marth W Ca** ... Martha Washington Cases [*A publication*] (DLA)
**MARTI** ...... Maneuverable Reentry Technology Investigation
**Martin** ........ Martin's Louisiana Reports [*A publication*] (DLA)
**Martin** ........ Martin's North Carolina Reports [*1 North Carolina*] [*A publication*] (DLA)
**Martin** ........ Martin's Reports [*21-30, 54-70 Georgia*] [*A publication*] (DLA)
**Martin Centre for Archtl & Urban Studies Trans** ... Martin Centre for Architectural and Urban Studies. Transactions [*A publication*]
**Martin Ctr Archit Urban Stud** ... Martin Centre for Architectural and Urban Studies. Transactions [*A publication*]
**Mart Ind** .... Martin's Reports [*54-70 Indiana*] [*A publication*] (DLA)
**Martin Dict** ... [*Edward*] Martin's English Dictionary [*A publication*] (DLA)
**MARTINI** ... Massive Analog Recording Technical Instrument for Nebulous Indications
**Martin Index** ... Martin's Index to Virginia Reports [*A publication*] (DLA)
**Martin (Lou) NS** ... Martin's Louisiana Reports, New Series [*A publication*] (DLA)
**Martin's Chy** ... Martin's Chancery Decisions [*Arkansas*] [*A publication*] (DLA)
**Martin's LA Rep** ... Martin's Louisiana Reports [*A publication*] (DLA)
**Martin's LA Rep NS** ... Martin's Louisiana Reports, New Series [*A publication*] (DLA)
**Martin's Louisiana R** ... Martin's Louisiana Reports [*A publication*] (DLA)
**Martin's NS** ... Martin's Louisiana Reports, New Series [*A publication*] (DLA)
**Martin's R NS** ... Martin's Louisiana Reports, New Series [*A publication*] (DLA)
**MartIs** ........ Martyrdom of Isaiah [*Pseudepigrapha*] (BJA)
**MartIsa** ...... Martyrdom of Isaiah [*Pseudepigrapha*] (BJA)
**MART J** .... Manitoba Association of Resource Teachers. Journal [*A publication*]
**Mart LA** ..... Martin's Louisiana Reports, Old and New Series [*A publication*] (DLA)
**Mart Laud** ... Martinus Caratti de Laude [*Flourished, 1438-45*] [*Authority cited in pre-1607 legal work*] (DSA)
**Mart Law Nat** ... Martens' Law of Nations [*A publication*] (DLA)
**Mart MC** .... Martin's Mining Cases [*Canada*] [*A publication*] (DLA)
**Mart NC** .... Martin's North Carolina Reports [*1 North Carolina*] [*A publication*] (DLA)
**Mart NS** .... Martin's Louisiana Reports, New Series [*A publication*] (DLA)
**Mart NS (LA)** ... Martin's Louisiana Reports, New Series [*A publication*] (DLA)
**MARTOS** ... Multiaccess Real-Time Operating System [*AEG Telefunken*] [*Federal Republic of Germany*]
**Mart OS (LA)** ... Martin's Louisiana Reports, Old Series [*A publication*] (DLA)
**MARTRA & REPLCOMS** ... Marine Training and Replacement Commands
**M Art (RCA)** ... Master of Art, Royal College of Art
**Mart Rep** ... Martin's Louisiana Reports [*A publication*] (DLA)
**Mart Rep NS** ... Martin's Louisiana Reports, New Series [*A publication*] (DLA)
**MarTropMed** ... Marches Tropicaux et Mediterraneens [*A publication*]
**MARTS** ..... Master RADAR Tracking Station
**MARTS** ..... Mobile Automatic Radio Telephone System (MCD)
**Mart USCC** ... Martin's Circuit Court Reports [*1 North Carolina*] [*A publication*] (DLA)
**Mart & Y** ... Martin and Yerger's Tennessee Reports [*8 Tennessee*] [*1825-28*] [*A publication*] (DLA)
**Mart & Yer** ... Martin and Yerger's Tennessee Reports [*8 Tennessee*] [*1825-28*] [*A publication*] (DLA)
**Mart & Yerg** ... Martin and Yerger's Tennessee Reports [*8 Tennessee*] [*1825-28*] [*A publication*] (DLA)
**Mart & Y (Tenn)** ... Martin and Yerger's Tennessee Reports [*8 Tennessee*] [*1825-28*] [*A publication*] (DLA)
**MARU** ....... Middle America Research Unit
**MARUNET** ... Maruzen Online Network [*Maruzen Co. Ltd.*] [*Japan*] [*Telecommunications*] (TSSD)
**MARUNITNG** ... Marine Unit Training (NVT)
**MARV** ....... Maneuverable AntiRADAR Vehicle (MCD)
**MARV** ....... Maneuverable Reentry Vehicle (AABC)
**MARV** ....... Marvelous (DSUE)
**Marv** .......... Marvel's Reports [*15-16 Delaware*] [*A publication*] (DLA)
**MARV** ....... Mobile Acoustic Recording Vehicle (MCD)
**Marv Av** ..... Marvin on General Average [*A publication*] (DLA)
**Marv (Del)** ... Marvel's Reports [*15-16 Delaware*] [*A publication*] (DLA)
**Marvel** ....... Marvel's Reports [*15-16 Delaware*] [*A publication*] (DLA)
**MARVEL** .. Mississippi Aerophysics Research Vehicle with Extended Latitude
**Marv Leg Bib** ... Marvin's Legal Bibliography [*A publication*] (DLA)
**Marv Wr & S** ... Marvin on Wreck and Salvage [*A publication*] (DLA)
**Mar Week** ... Marine Week [*A publication*]
**Mar Wr & S** ... Marvin on Wreck and Salvage [*A publication*] (DLA)
**MARX** ....... Mark Aero [*Air carrier designation symbol*]
**Marx Bl** ..... Marxistische Blaetter [*A publication*]
**Marxistische Bl** ... Marxistische Blaetter fuer Probleme der Gesellschaft, Wirtschaft, und Politik [*A publication*]
**Marxist Quar** ... Marxist Quarterly [*A publication*]
**Marx Td** .... Marxism Today [*A publication*]
**Mary** .......... Maryland Reports [*A publication*] (DLA)
**Mar & Yer** ... Martin and Yerger's Tennessee Reports [*8 Tennessee*] [*1825-28*] [*A publication*] (DLA)
**Maryland** ... Maryland Reports [*A publication*] (DLA)
**Maryland Ch Dec** ... Maryland Chancery Decisions [*A publication*] (DLA)

**Maryland Geol Survey County Geol Map** ... Maryland. Geological Survey. County Geologic Map [*A publication*]
**Maryland Geol Survey Rept Inv** ... Maryland. Geological Survey. Report of Investigations [*A publication*]
**Maryland L Rev** ... Maryland Law Review [*A publication*]
**Maryland MJ** ... Maryland State Medical Journal [*A publication*]
**Mary L Rev** ... Maryland Law Review [*A publication*]
**Maryl St Med J** ... Maryland State Medical Journal [*A publication*]
**Maryl St MJ** ... Maryland State Medical Journal [*A publication*]
**Mar Zool**.... Marine Zoologist [*A publication*]
**MAS** .......... Lithuanian Catholic Youth Association Ateitis (EA)
**MAS** .......... MacDonald Agricultural Services Ltd. [*British*]
**MAS** .......... Machine Accounting School
**MAS** .......... Macroassembler
**MAS** .......... Madang Air Services [*Australia*]
**MAS** .......... Magic Angle Spinning [*Spectroscopy*]
**MAS** .......... Magnesia-Alumina-Silicate [*Inorganic chemistry*]
**MAS** .......... Maintenance and Services (AFIT)
**MAS** .......... Maintenance and Supply (AFIT)
**MAS** .......... Malaysian Airline System
**MAS** .......... Management Accounting System
**MAS** .......... Management and Administrative Statistics (OICC)
**MAS** .......... Management Advisory Services
**MAS** .......... Management Appraisal Survey [*Test*]
**MAS** .......... Maneuvering Attack System (MCD)
**MAS** .......... Manifest Anxiety Scale [*Psychology*]
**MAS** .......... Manned Aerial Surveillance
**MAS** .......... Manual A1 Simplex [*Aviation*]
**MAS** .......... Manufacturing Advisory Service (DCTA)
**MAS** .......... Manufacturing Assembly Specification
**MAS** .......... Manus [*Papua New Guinea*] [*Airport symbol*] (OAG)
**MAS** .......... MAP [*Manufacturing Automation Protocol*]/One Applications Services [*Software*] [*Automotive engineering*]
**MAS** .......... Marine Acoustical Services
**MAS** .......... Marine Advisory Service [*See also NMAS*] [*National Oceanic and Atmospheric Administration*] [*Information service or system*] (IID)
**MAS** .......... Marine Archaeological Society [*Australia*]
**MAS** .......... Maritime Air Superiority (NVT)
**MAS** .......... Market Advisory Service [*British Overseas Trade Board*] (DS)
**MAS** .......... Mars Approach Sensor
**mas**............ Masai [*MARC language code*] [*Library of Congress*] (LCCP)
**MAS** .......... Masco Corp. [*NYSE symbol*] (SPSG)
**MAS** .......... Masculine
**MAS** .......... Mason [*or Masonry*] (ROG)
**MAS** .......... Mason Butte [*Idaho*] [*Seismograph station code, US Geological Survey*] [*Closed*] (SEIS)
**Mas**........... Mason's United States Circuit Court Reports [*A publication*] (DLA)
**Mas**........... Masorah (BJA)
**Mas**........... Massachusetts Reports [*A publication*] (DLA)
**MAS** .......... Massachusetts State Library, Boston, MA [*OCLC symbol*] (OCLC)
**Mas**........... Masseketh (BJA)
**MAS** .......... Master (DSUE)
**MAS** .......... Master of Accounting Science
**MAS** .......... Master Activation Schedule (AAG)
**MAS** .......... Master of Actuarial Science
**MAS** .......... Master of Administrative Studies (ADA)
**MAS** .......... Master Analysis Scheme [*Monitoring technique*]
**MAS** .......... Master of Applied Science
**MAS** .......... Master of Archival Studies
**MAS** .......... Material Activity Schedule
**MAS** .......... Material Availability Schedule
**MAS** .......... Mature Age Student (ADA)
**MAS** .......... McMaster University Library [*UTLAS symbol*]
**MAS** .......... Meconium Aspiration Syndrome [*Medicine*]
**MAS** .......... Medical Advisory Service [*British*]
**MAS** .......... Member of the Arundel Society [*British*]
**MAS** .......... Memory and Auxiliary Storage Subsystem [*Space Flight Operations Facility, NASA*]
**MAS** .......... Mercury Analyzer System [*Perkin-Elmer Co. instrument designation*]
**MAS** .......... Merged Area Schools (OICC)
**MAS** .......... Metal-Alumina-Silicon (IEEE)
**MAS** .......... Metal Anchor Slots [*Technical drawings*]
**MAS** .......... Metastable Atomic State
**MAS** .......... Methods of Air Sampling and Analysis [*Air Pollution Control Association*]
**MAS** .......... Methods and Standards (MCD)
**MAS** .......... Mezhdunarodnaya Assotsiatsiya Sudovladeltsev [*International Shipowners' Association*] (EAIO)
**MAS** .......... Micro Automation System
**MAS** .......... Microbeam Analysis Society (EA)
**MAS** .......... Midcourse Active System (MCD)
**MAS** .......... Military Agency for Standardization [*Brussels, Belgium*] [*NATO*]
**MAS** .......... Military Airlift Squadron [*Air Force*] (CINC)
**MAS** .......... Military Alert System (FAAC)
**MAS** .......... Military Assistance Sales (MCD)
**mAs**........... Milliampere-Second
**MAS** .......... Ministry of Aviation Supply [*British*]
**MAS** .......... Minnesota Academy of Science
**MAS** .......... Missile Alignment Set
**MAS** .......... Missile Assembly Site (NATG)
**MAS** .......... Missile Assigned Switch
**MAS** .......... Missile Auxiliaries System
**MAS** .......... MMICS Administration Subsystem (AFIT)
**MAS** .......... Model Assignment Sheet (MCD)
**MAS** .......... Modern Army Supply
**MAS** .......... Modern Army System
**MAS** .......... Modular Application Systems [*Martin Marietta Data Systems*]
**MAS** .......... Monaco Group, Inc. [*Toronto Stock Exchange symbol*]
**MAS** .......... Monetary Allowance in Lieu of Subsistence
**MAS** .......... Monitor and Alarm System (MCD)
**MAS** .......... Monoacetoxylscirpenol [*Organic toxin*]
**MAS** .......... Mount Angel Seminary [*Oregon*]
**MAS** .......... Movement Alarm System [*Gynecology*]
**MAS** .......... Movimiento al Socialismo [*Movement towards Socialism*] [*Venezuela*] [*Political party*] (PPW)
**MAS** .......... Movimiento al Socialismo [*Movement towards Socialism*] [*Argentina*] [*Political party*] (PPW)
**MAS** .......... Muenchener Aegyptologische Studien [*Berlin*] [*A publication*]
**MAS** .......... Muerte a los Secuestradores [*Death to Kidnappers*] [*Colombia*] (PD)
**MAS** .......... Multiaspect Signaling (IEEE)
**MAS** .......... Multiple Aim Structure (MCD)
**MAS** .......... Multiple Award Schedule [*Government contracting*]
**MAS** .......... Municipal Analysis Services, Inc. [*Information service or system*] (IID)
**MAS** .......... Mutually Assured Survival
**MAS** .......... Survey of Economic Conditions in Japan [*A publication*]
**MASA** ....... Mail Advertising Service Association International [*Bethesda, MD*]
**MASA** ....... Marine Accessories and Services Association [*Later, NAMPS*] (EA)
**MASA** ....... Medical Acronyms, Symbols & Abbreviations [*A publication*]
**MASA** ....... Merged Area Schools Administrators Association (OICC)
**MASA** ....... Military Accessories Service Association (EA)
**MASA** ....... Military Automotive Supply Agency
**MASA** ....... Mines' African Staff Association
**MASA** ....... Music and Arts Society of America (EA)
**MASAE**..... Member of the American Society of Agricultural Engineering
**MASAF**..... Mediterranean Allied Strategic Air Force
**MASAI**...... Mail Advertising Service Association International (EA)
**MASAL**..... Michigan Academy of Science, Arts, and Letters
**MASAP**..... Michigan Association of Single Adoptive Parents (EA)
**MASB**........ MASSBANK Corp. [*Reading, MA*] [*NASDAQ symbol*] (NQ)
**MA/SB**...... Motor Antisubmarine Boat [*Obsolete*] [*British*]
**MASC**........ Magazine Advertising Sales Club (EA)
**MASC**........ Magnetic Attitude Spin Coil
**MASC**........ Masculine
**MA Sc**........ Master of Applied Science
**MASC**........ Methylaluminum Sesquichloride [*Organic chemistry*]
**MASC**........ Microsoft Access Script Command [*Computer language*]
**MASC**........ Middletown Air Service Command [*Air Force*]
**MASC**........ Military Automotive Supply Center (MCD)
**MASC**........ Model to Evaluate Maintenance Support Concepts (MCD)
**MASC**........ Multiple Award Schedule Contract [*Government contracting*]
**MASCA**..... Museum Applied Science Center for Archeology [*University of Pennsylvania*]
**MASCA J** ... MASCA Journal. Museum Applied Science Center for Archaeology. University of Pennsylvania [*A publication*]
**MASCA Journal** ... Museum Applied Science Center for Archaeology. Journal [*A publication*]
**MASCAP**.. Museum Applied Science Center for Archaeology. Pamphlet [*A publication*]
**Mascar**....... [*Josephus*] Mascardus [*Deceased, 1588*] [*Authority cited in pre-1607 legal work*] (DSA)
**MASCAR**.. Museum Applied Science Center for Archaeology. Report [*A publication*]
**Mascard**..... [*Josephus*] Mascardus [*Deceased, 1588*] [*Authority cited in pre-1607 legal work*] (DSA)
**Mascard De Prob** ... Mascardus. De Probationibus [*A publication*] (DLA)
**MASCA Res Pap Sci Archaeol** ... MASCA [*Museum Applied Science Center for Archaeology*] Research Papers in Science and Archaeology [*A publication*]
**MASCDCS** ... Madison Avenue Sports Car Driving and Chowder Society (EA)
**MASCE**..... Member of the American Society of Civil Engineers
**Masch Elektrotech** ... Maschinenwelt Elektrotechnik [*A publication*]
**Maschinenbau Betr** ... Maschinenbau der Betrich [*A publication*]
**Maschintec** ... Maschinenbautechnik [*A publication*]
**Masch Werkzeung** ... Maschine und Werkzeung [*West Germany*] [*A publication*]
**MASCO** .... Mead Access Systems Company
**MASCO** .... Microprogrammed and Simulated Computer Organization
**MASCON** ... Mass Concentration [*of gravitational pull*]
**MASCOT** ... Manned Shuttle Comprehensive Optimization and Targeting [*NASA*]
**MASCOT** ... Meteorological Auxiliary Sea Current Observation Transmitter
**MASCOT** ... Military Air-Transportable Satellite Communications Terminal

**MASCOT** ... Modern Approach to Software Construction, Operation and Test [*Ministry of Defence*] [*British*]
**MASCOT** ... Modular Approach to System Construction Operation and Test (MCD)
**MASCOT** ... Motorola Automatic Sequential Computer Operated Tester
**MASCS** ..... Marriage Adjustment Sentence Completion Survey [*Psychology*]
**MASCU** ..... Marine Air Support Control Unit
**MASD** ....... Mobile Air and Space Defense [*Air Force*]
**MASDC** ..... Military Aircraft Storage and Disposition Center
**MASDR** ..... Measurement and Signature Data Requirements (MCD)
**MASE** ........ McDonnell Airborne Sidewinder Evaluator [*McDonnell Douglas Corp.*] (MCD)
**MASE** ........ Moore School Air Space Simulation Effort (MCD)
**MASEA** ..... Midwest Association of Student Employment Administrators [*Formerly, MAUSED*] (EA)
**MASEE** ..... Member of the Association of Supervisory and Executive Engineers [*British*] (DBQ)
**MASER** ..... Microwave [*or Molecular*] Amplification by Stimulated Emission of Radiation
**MASET** ..... Member of the Australian Society for Educational Technology
**MASEX** ..... Maritime Air Superiority Exercise (NVT)
**MASF** ........ Military Assistance Service Funded
**MASF** ........ Mobile Aeromedical Staging Facility
**MASFM** .... Maintenance and Supply Facility Management (AFIT)
**MAS/FS** ..... Mohawk Aerial Surveillance/Flight Simulator (MCD)
**MASG** ....... Marine Air Support Group
**MASG** ....... Missile Auxiliary Signal Generator
**MASG** ....... Monitor and Alarm Subsystem Group (MCD)
**MASGC** ..... Mississippi-Alabama Sea Grant Consortium [*Sea Grant College*] [*Research center*] (RCD)
**MASGP** ..... Military Airlift Support Group [*Air Force*]
**MASH** ....... Manned Antisubmarine Helicopter
**MASH** ....... Medical Aid for Sick Hippies [*Volunteer medical group*]
**MASH** ....... Melting-Assimilation-Storage-Homogenization [*Geology*]
**MASH** ....... Michigan Area Serial Holdings Consortium [*Library network*]
**MASH** ....... Mobile Army Surgical Hospital [*Acronym also used as title of a satirical film, 1970, and a TV series*]
**MASH** ....... Multiple Accelerated Summary Hearing [*Deportation of illegal aliens*] [*Immigration and Naturalization Service*]
**MASH** ....... Multiple Automated Sample Harvester [*for culture systems*]
**MASH** ....... Mutual Aid Self-Help Group
**MASHONLD** ... Mashonaland (ROG)
**Mash Tekhnol Pererab Polim** ... Mashiny i Tekhnologiya Pererabotki Polimerov [*A publication*]
**MASI** ......... Multilevel Academic Skills Inventory [*Educational test*]
**MASID** ...... Marine Science Division [*Instrument Society of America*] (MSC)
**MASINT** ... Measurement and Signature Intelligence (MCD)
**MASIS** ...... Management and Scientific Information System [*Air Force*]
**MASIS** ...... Maruzen Scientific Information Service Center [*Maruzen Co. Ltd.*] [*Japan*] [*Telecommunications*] (TSSD)
**MASIS** ...... Mercury Abort Sensing Instrumentation System [*NASA*] (AAG)
**MASJ** ........ Midcontinent American Studies. Journal [*A publication*]
**MASK** ........ Maneuvering and Seakeeping
**MASK** ........ Mobile Armored Strike Kommand [*Game*]
**MASK** ........ Multilevel Amplitude Shift Keying
**Maskin J** .... Maskinjournalen [*A publication*]
**Mask Koth** ... Maske und Kothurn [*A publication*]
**MAsl** .......... Ashland Public Library, Ashland, MA [*Library symbol*] [*Library of Congress*] (LCLS)
**MASL** ........ MA [*Military Assistance*] Articles and Services List [*DoD*]
**MASL** ........ Military Articles and Services List
**MASLIG** ... Association of Management Analysts in State and Local Government (EA)
**Maslob Zhir Delo** ... Masloboino Zhirovoe Delo [*A publication*]
**Maslob Zhirov Prom** ... Masloboino Zhirovaya Promyshlennost [*Later, Maslozhirovaya Promyshlennost*] [*A publication*]
**Maslob Zhir Promst** ... Masloboino Zhirovaya Promyshlennost [*Later, Maslozhirovaya Promyshlennost*] [*A publication*]
**Maslob Zir Prom** ... Masloboino Zirovaya Promyshlennost [*A publication*]
**Maslo Sapunena Promst** ... Maslo Sapunena Promyshlennost [*A publication*]
**Maslo Zhir Promst** ... Maslozhirovaya Promyshlennost [*Formerly, Masloboino Zhirovaya Promyshlennost*] [*A publication*]
**Masl Zhir Prom** ... Masloboino Zhirovaya Promyshlennost [*Later, Maslozhirovaya Promyshlennost*] [*A publication*]
**MASM** ...... Master of Arts in Sacred Music (BJA)
**MASM** ...... Meta-Assembler Language [*Sperry UNIVAC computer language*]
**MASM** ...... Military Assistance and Sales Manual (AFIT)
**MASM** ...... Motorized Antenna Switching Matrix
**MASMDP** ... Mississippi-Alabama Sea Grant Consortium. MASGP [*A publication*]
**MASME** .... Member of the American Society of Mechanical Engineers
**MASME** .... Member of the Australian Society for Music Education
**MAS/MILS** ... Minerals Availability System/Minerals Industry Location Subsystem [*Bureau of Mines*] [*Database*]
**MASMOD** ... Mass Model [*Computer program*]
**MASN** ....... Machine Accountant, Seaman [*Navy*]
**MASNC** .... Minerals Availability System [*Bureau of Mines*] [*Information service or system*] (IID)
**Mas NE Pr** ... Mason's New England Civil Practice [*A publication*] (DLA)
**MASNMR** ... Magic Angle Spinning Nuclear Magnetic Resonance [*Spectroscopy*]
**MASO** ....... Meijerbergs Arkiv foer Svensk Ordforskning [*A publication*]
**MASO** ....... Military Assistance Sales Order (CINC)
**MASO** ....... Munition Accountable Supply Officer [*Air Force*] (AFM)
**MA (Social Studies)** ... Master of Arts (Social Studies)
**MA(SocSci)** ... Master of Arts (Social Sciences), University of Glasgow [*British*] (DBQ)
**Mason** ........ Mason's United States Circuit Court Reports [*A publication*] (DLA)
**Mason CCR** ... Mason's United States Circuit Court Reports [*A publication*] (DLA)
**Mason Circt Ct R** ... Mason's United States Circuit Court Reports [*A publication*] (DLA)
**Mason R** .... Mason's United States Circuit Court Reports [*A publication*] (DLA)
**Mason's Code** ... Mason's United States Code, Annotated [*A publication*] (DLA)
**Mason's R** ... Mason's United States Circuit Court Reports [*A publication*] (DLA)
**Mason's Rep** ... Mason's United States Circuit Court Reports [*A publication*] (DLA)
**Mason US** ... Mason's United States Circuit Court Reports [*A publication*] (DLA)
**Mason US Circ Ct Rep** ... Mason's United States Circuit Court Reports [*A publication*] (DLA)
**Mason USR** ... Mason's United States Circuit Court Reports [*A publication*] (DLA)
**MASP** ........ Materialy po Arkheologii Severnogo Prichernomor'ia [*A publication*]
**MASP** ........ Modular Atmosphere Simulation Program [*NASA*] (KSC)
**MAS PIL** ... Massa Pilularum [*A Pill Mass*] [*Pharmacy*]
**MASPSq** ... Military Airlift Special Squadron [*Air Force*]
**MASPTSq** ... Military Airlift Support Squadron [*Air Force*]
**MASq** ........ Military Airlift Squadron [*Air Force*] (AFM)
**Mas R** ........ Massachusetts Reports [*A publication*] (DLA)
**MASR** ........ Multiple-Antenna Moving-Target Surveillance RADAR
**MASRC** ..... Mexican American Studies and Research Center [*University of Arizona*] [*Research center*] (RCD)
**Mas Rep** ..... Massachusetts Reports [*A publication*] (DLA)
**MASRT** ..... Marine Air Support RADAR Teams (IEEE)
**MASRU** .... Marine Air Support RADAR Unit [*DoD*]
**MASS** ........ Magic Angle Sample Spinning [*Spectroscopy*]
**MASS** ........ Manned Activity Scheduling System [*NASA*]
**MASS** ........ Marine Air Support Squadron
**MASS** ........ Massa [*A Mass*] [*Pharmacy*]
**MASS** ........ Massachusetts (AFM)
**Mass** .......... Massachusetts Reports [*A publication*]
**Mass** .......... Massachusetts Supreme Judicial Court Reports [*A publication*] (DLA)
**MASS** ........ Massage
**MA(SS)** ..... Master of Arts in Social Science (ADA)
**M As S** ...... Master of Association Science
**MASS** ........ Materials Acquisition Sub-System [*Data processing*]
**MASS** ........ Matrix Analysis Subsystem (MCD)
**MASS** ........ Mechanically Accelerated Sabot System [*Generation of high-density molecular beams*]
**MASS** ........ Membrane Affinity Separation System
**MASS** ........ Memorandum Accounts Statement System (DCTA)
**MASS** ........ Michigan Automatic Scanning System (IEEE)
**MAss** ......... Middle Assyrian [*Language, etc.*] (BJA)
**MASS** ........ Missile and Space Summary (MCD)
**MASS** ........ Missiles/Ammunition System Study
**MASS** ........ Modern Army Supply System
**MASS** ........ Modular Adaptive Signal Sorter
**MASS** ........ Monitor and Assembly System [*or Subsystem*] [*Data processing*] (BUR)
**MASS** ........ Multiple Access Sequential Selection [*Data processing*] (BUR)
**Massachusetts Stud Engl** ... Massachusetts Studies in English [*A publication*]
**Mass Acts** ... Acts and Resolves of Massachusetts [*A publication*] (DLA)
**Mass AD** .... Massachusetts Appellate Decisions [*A publication*] (DLA)
**Mass Admin Code** ... Code of Massachusetts Regulations [*A publication*] (DLA)
**Mass Admin Reg** ... Massachusetts Register [*A publication*] (DLA)
**Mass ADR** ... Massachusetts Appellate Division Reports [*A publication*] (DLA)
**Mass Adv Legis Serv** ... Massachusetts Advance Legislative Service [*Lawyers Co-Operative Publishing Co.*] [*A publication*] (DLA)
**Mass Adv Sh** ... Massachusetts Advance Sheets [*A publication*] (DLA)
**Mass Adv Sheets** ... Massachusetts Advance Sheets [*A publication*] (DLA)
**Mass Ag Exp** ... Massachusetts Agricultural Experiment Station. Publications [*A publication*]
**Mass Agric Exp Stn Bull** ... Massachusetts Agricultural Experiment Station. Bulletin [*A publication*]
**Mass Agric Exp Stn Control Ser Bull** ... Massachusetts Agricultural Experiment Station. Control Series. Bulletin [*A publication*]

**Mass Agric Exp Stn Ext Serv Publ** ... Massachusetts Agricultural Experiment Station. Extension Service Publication [*A publication*]
**Mass Agric Exp Stn Monogr Ser** ... Massachusetts Agricultural Experiment Station. Monograph Series [*A publication*]
**Mass Ann Laws** ... Annotated Laws of Massachusetts [*A publication*] (DLA)
**Mass Ann Laws (Law Co-Op)** ... Annotated Laws of Massachusetts (Lawyers' Co-Op) [*A publication*]
**Mass App Ct** ... Massachusetts Appeals Court Reports [*A publication*] (DLA)
**Mass App Ct Adv Sh** ... Massachusetts Appeals Court Advance Sheets [*A publication*] (DLA)
**Mass App Dec** ... Appellate Decisions (Massachusetts) [*A publication*]
**Mass App Dec** ... Massachusetts Appellate Decisions [*A publication*] (DLA)
**Mass App Div** ... Appellate Division Reports (Massachusetts) [*A publication*]
**Mass App Div** ... Massachusetts Appellate Division Reports [*A publication*] (DLA)
**Mass App Div Adv Sh** ... Appellate Division Advance Sheets (Massachusetts) [*A publication*]
**Mass App Rep** ... Massachusetts Appeals Court Reports [*A publication*] (DLA)
**MASSAR** .. Multimode Airborne Solid State Array RADAR
**Mass Basic Data Rep Ground Water Ser** ... Massachusetts Basic Data Report. Ground Water Series [*A publication*]
**Mass BC & A** ... Massachusetts Board of Conciliation and Arbitration Reports [*A publication*] (DLA)
**MASSBUS** ... Memory Bus [*Digital Equipment Corp.*]
**M As Sc** ..... Master of Association Science
**MASSCAL** ... Mass Casualties [*Military*] (AABC)
**Mass Cont Election Cushing S & J** ... Massachusetts Controverted Election Cases [*A publication*] (DLA)
**MASSDAR** ... Modular Analysis, Speedup, Sampling, and Data Reduction
**MASSDATA** ... Mark Sense Source Data Automation Test and Analysis (MCD)
**Mass Dent Soc J** ... Massachusetts Dental Society. Journal [*A publication*]
**Mass Dep Nat Resour Div Mar Fish Monogr Ser** ... Massachusetts Department of Natural Resources. Division of Marine Fisheries. Monographs Series [*A publication*]
**Mass DIA** ... Massachusetts. Department of Industrial Accidents. Bulletin [*A publication*] (DLA)
**Mass Div Mar Fish Tech Ser** ... Massachusetts. Division of Marine Fisheries. Technical Series [*A publication*]
**Mass Dr Com** ... Masse. Le Droit Commercial [*A publication*] (DLA)
**Mass EC L & R** ... Loring and Russell's Election Cases in Massachusetts [*A publication*] (DLA)
**Mass Elec Ca** ... Massachusetts Election Cases [*A publication*] (DLA)
**Mass Elec Cas** ... Massachusetts Election Cases [*A publication*] (DLA)
**Mass Election Cases** ... Loring and Russell's Election Cases in Massachusetts [*A publication*] (DLA)
**Mass Election Cases** ... Russell's Contested Election Cases [*Massachusetts*] [*A publication*] (DLA)
**Masses Ouvr** ... Masses Ouvrieres [*A publication*]
**Massey Agric Coll Dairyfarm Annu** ... Massey Agricultural College. Dairyfarming Annual [*A publication*]
**Massey Agric Coll Sheepfarm Annu** ... Massey Agricultural College. Sheepfarming Annual [*A publication*]
**Massey-Ferguson R** ... Massey-Ferguson Review [*A publication*] (APTA)
**Mass Fruit Grow Assoc Rep Annu Meet** ... Massachusetts Fruit Growers' Association. Report of the Annual Meeting [*A publication*]
**Mass Gen L** ... General Laws of the Commonwealth of Massachusetts [*A publication*]
**Mass Gen Laws** ... Massachusetts General Laws [*A publication*] (DLA)
**Mass Gen Laws Ann (West)** ... Massachusetts General Laws, Annotated (West) [*A publication*] (DLA)
**Mass Hist Soc Coll** ... Massachusetts Historical Society. Collections [*A publication*]
**Mass Hist Soc Proc** ... Massachusetts Historical Society. Proceedings [*A publication*]
**Mass Hlth J** ... Massachusetts Health Journal [*A publication*]
**Mass H R** .. Massachusetts House of Representatives [*A publication*]
**Mass Hydrol Data Rep** ... Massachusetts Hydrologic Data Report [*A publication*]
**Mass IAB** .. Massachusetts Industrial Accident Board Reports of Cases [*A publication*] (DLA)
**MASSIIS** .. Maintenance Analysis and Structural Integration Information System
**Mass Inst Tech Dep Civ Eng Hydrodyn Lab Rep** ... Massachusetts Institute of Technology. School of Engineering. Department of Civil Engineering. Hydrodynamics Laboratory. Report [*A publication*]
**Mass Inst Tech Dep Civ Eng Res Earth Phys Res Rep** ... Massachusetts Institute of Technology. School of Engineering. Department of Civil Engineering. Research in Earth Physics. Research Report [*A publication*]
**Mass Inst Tech Dep Civ Eng Soils Publ** ... Massachusetts Institute of Technology. School of Engineering. Department of Civil Engineering. Soils Publication [*A publication*]
**Mass Inst Tech Dep Nav Architect Mar Eng Rep** ... Massachusetts Institute of Technology. Department of Naval Architecture and Marine Engineering. Report [*A publication*]
**Mass Inst Tech Fluid Mech Lab Publ** ... Massachusetts Institute of Technology. Fluid Mechanics Laboratory. Publication [*A publication*]
**Mass Inst Technology Abs Theses** ... Massachusetts Institute of Technology. Abstracts of Theses [*A publication*]
**Mass Inst Technology and Woods Hole Oceanog Inst Paper** ... Massachusetts Institute of Technology and Woods Hole Oceanographic Institution. Papers [*A publication*]
**Mass Inst Technol Res Lab Electron Tech Rep** ... Massachusetts Institute of Technology. Research Laboratory of Electronics. Technical Report [*A publication*]
**Mass Inst Tech Res Lab Electron Tech Rep** ... Massachusetts Institute of Technology. Research Laboratory of Electronics. Technical Report [*A publication*]
**Mass Lib Assn Bul** ... Massachusetts Library Association. Bulletin [*A publication*]
**Mass L Q** ... Massachusetts Law Quarterly [*A publication*]
**Mass LR** .... Massachusetts Law Review [*A publication*]
**Mass LRC Dec** ... Massachusetts Labor Relations Commission Decisions [*A publication*] (DLA)
**Mass L Rev** ... Massachusetts Law Review [*A publication*]
**Mass M** ..... Massachusetts Magazine [*A publication*]
**Mass Med J** ... Massachusetts Medical Journal [*A publication*]
**Mass Med Newsl** ... Mass Media Newsletter [*A publication*]
**Mass Nurse** ... Massachusetts Nurse [*A publication*]
**Massoobmennye Protsessy Khim Tekhnol** ... Massoobmennye Protsessy Khimicheskoi Tekhnologii [*USSR*] [*A publication*]
**Mass Ouvr** ... Masses Ouvrieres [*A publication*]
**Mass Pil** ..... Massa Pilularum [*A Pill Mass*] [*Pharmacy*]
**Mass Prod** ... Mass Production [*A publication*]
**Mass Q** ...... Massachusetts Quarterly Review [*A publication*]
**MASSq** ...... Military Airlift Support Squadron [*Air Force*] (AFM)
**Mass R** ....... Massachusetts Reports [*A publication*] (DLA)
**Mass R** ....... Massachusetts Review [*A publication*]
**Mass Reg** ... Massachusetts Register [*A publication*]
**Mass Regs Code** ... Code of Massachusetts Regulations [*A publication*]
**Mass Rep** ... Massachusetts Reports [*A publication*] (DLA)
**Mass Rev** ... Massachusetts Review [*A publication*]
**Mass Spect Bull** ... Mass Spectrometry Bulletin [*A publication*]
**Mass Spectrom Bull** ... Mass Spectrometry Bulletin [*England*] [*A publication*]
**Mass Spectrom New Instrum Tech** ... Mass Spectrometry New Instruments and Techniques [*A publication*]
**Mass Spectrom Rev** ... Mass Spectrometry Reviews [*A publication*]
**Mass Spectrosc** ... Mass Spectroscopy [*A publication*]
**Mass St BC & A** ... Massachusetts State Board of Conciliation and Arbitration Reports [*A publication*] (DLA)
**Mass St Bd Educ** ... Massachusetts State Board of Education [*A publication*]
**Mass Stud E** ... Massachusetts Studies in English [*A publication*]
**Mass Supp** ... Supplement (Massachusetts) [*A publication*]
**MASST** ..... Major Ship Satellite Terminal
**MASST** ..... Major Shipboard SATCOM Terminal (MCD)
**MASSTER** ... Mobile Army Sensor System Test, Evaluation, and Review
**MASSTER** ... Modern Army Selected System Test, Evaluation, and Review
**Mass Transp** ... Mass Transportation [*A publication*]
**Mass Tribut** ... Massimario Tributario [*A publication*]
**Mass UCC Op** ... Massachusetts Unemployment Compensation Commission Opinions [*A publication*] (DLA)
**Mass UC Dig** ... Massachusetts Division of Unemployment Compensation Digest of Board of Review Decisions [*A publication*] (DLA)
**Mass UC Ops** ... Massachusetts Division of Unemployment Compensation Opinions [*A publication*] (DLA)
**Mass Univ Coll Food Nat Resour Agric Exp Stn Res Bull** ... Massachusetts University. College of Food and Natural Resources. Agricultural Experiment Station. Research Bulletin [*A publication*]
**Mass Univ Dep Geol Contrib** ... Massachusetts University. Department of Geology. Contribution [*A publication*]
**Mass Univ Dept Geology and Mineralogy Special Dept Pub** ... Massachusetts University. Department of Geology and Mineralogy. Special Department Publication [*A publication*]
**Mass WCC** ... Massachusetts Workmen's Compensation Cases [*A publication*] (DLA)
**MAST** ........ Magnetic Annular Shock Tube
**MAST** ........ Marine Stable Element
**MAST** ........ Market Structures and Trends on Italy [*Databank Ltd.*] [*British*] (ECON)
**MAST** ........ Master (ROG)
**Mast** ........... Master's Supreme Court Reports [*25-28 Canada*] [*A publication*] (DLA)
**MAST** ........ Mastoid [*Medicine*]
**MAST** ........ Memorie. Reale Accademia delle Scienze di Torino [*A publication*]
**MAST** ........ Michigan Alcoholism Screening Test
**MAST** ........ Midlevel Positions in Administrative, Staff, and Technical Services [*Civil Service Commission*]
**MAST** ........ Military Antishock Trousers [*Medicine*]
**MAST** ........ Military Assistance to Safety and Traffic [*Project*] [*Army*] (RDA)
**MAST** ........ Minimum Abbreviations of Serial Titles [*A publication*]
**MAST** ........ Missile Automatic Supply Technique
**MAST** ........ Mobile Assembly Sterilizer for Testing
**MAST** ........ Model Assembly Sterilizer for Testing [*NASA*]
**MAST** ........ Multilevel Academic Survey Test [*Educational test*]

**MAST**........ Multiple Applications Storage Tube
**MAST**........ Munitions Assistance and Standardization Team (MCD)
**MASTA**..... Medical Advisory Services for Travellers Abroad [*London School of Hygiene and Tropical Medicine*] [*Information service or system*] (IID)
**MastAcftCrmnBad** ... Master Aircraft Crewman Badge [*Military decoration*] (AABC)
**MASTARAV** ... Master Army Aviator (AABC)
**Mast AR Av Bad** ... Master Army Aviator Badge [*Military decoration*]
**MASTARS** ... Mechanical and Structural Testing and Referral Service [*National Institute of Standards and Technology*]
**Mast in Art** ... Masters in Art [*A publication*]
**Mast Div Bad** ... Master Diver Badge [*Military decoration*]
**Mast Draw** ... Master Drawings [*A publication*]
**Mas Teh Glas** ... Masinsko-Tehnicki Glasnik [*A publication*]
**Mast El**...... Masterman's Parliamentary Elections [*1880*] [*A publication*] (DLA)
**MASTER**.. Matching Available Student Time to Educational Resources [*Data processing*]
**MASTER**.. Miniaturized Sink-Rate Telemetering RADAR
**MASTER**.. Multiple Access Shared Time Executive Routine [*Control Data Corp.*] [*Data processing*]
**Master Bldr** ... Master Builder [*A publication*]
**Master Carriers NSW** ... Master Carriers of New South Wales [*A publication*] (APTA)
**Master Draw** ... Master Drawings [*A publication*]
**MASTER KEY** ... Managership of Soldier Training, Education, and Readiness with Knowledge and Excellence Year-Round [*Army*] (INF)
**Master Painter Aust** ... Master Painter of Australia [*A publication*]
**Master Plumber of SA** ... Master Plumber of South Australia [*A publication*] (APTA)
**Masters Abstr** ... Masters Abstracts [*A publication*]
**MASTICH** ... Mastiche [*Mastic*] [*Pharmacy*] (ROG)
**MASTIF**.... Multi-Axis Spin Test Inertia Facility [*Training device for astronauts*]
**MASTIR** ... Microfilmed Abstract System for Technical Information Retrieval [*Illinois Institute of Technology*] (IID)
**MAST J**..... Manitoba Association of School Trustees. Journal [*A publication*]
**Mast in Music** ... Masters in Music [*A publication*]
**MastPrchtBad** ... Master Parachutist Badge [*Military decoration*] (AABC)
**Mas Trakt St** ... Masino-Traktornaja Stancija [*A publication*]
**MASTS**..... Marine Associated Services Technology Systems Exposition [*Canada*] (ITD)
**MAstS**....... Member of the Astronomical Society
**MASTU**..... Mobile Antisubmarine Training Unit [*British*]
**MASU**....... Machined Surface
**MASU**....... Mesoamerican Archaeology Study Unit [*American Topical Association*] (EA)
**MASU**....... Metal Alloy Separation Unit
**MASU**....... Mobile Army Surgical Unit
**MASUA**..... Mid-America State Universities Association (EA)
**MASW**...... Master of Arts in Social Work
**MASWg**.... Military Airlift Support Wing [*Air Force*] (AFM)
**MASWSP** ... Manager, Antisubmarine Warfare Systems Project [*Navy*]
**MASWSPO** ... Manager, Antisubmarine Warfare Systems Project Office [*Navy*]
**MASWT**.... Mobile Antisubmarine Warfare Target (MCD)
**MASX**........ Masco Industries, Inc. [*NASDAQ symbol*] (NQ)
**MASY**........ Marketing Systems of America, Inc. [*NASDAQ symbol*] (NQ)
**Masya Indo** ... Masyarakat Indonesia [*A publication*]
**MASYDR** ... MRC [*Medical Research Council*] [*Great Britain*]. Laboratory Animals Centre. Symposia [*A publication*]
**MAT**.......... Machine-Assisted Translation
**MAT**.......... Machine Available Time [*Data processing*]
**MAT**.......... Maine Air Transport, Inc. [*Bangor, ME*] [*FAA designator*] (FAAC)
**MAT**.......... Maintenance Appraisal Team (MCD)
**MAT**.......... Mammary Ascites Tumor [*Oncology*]
**MAT**.......... Management Advisory Team (NRCH)
**MAT**.......... Manifold Air Temperature [*Automotive engineering*]
**MAT**.......... Manual Arts Therapist
**MA & T**..... Manufacturing Assembly and Test (MCD)
**MAT**.......... Marine Air Temperature [*Meteorology*]
**MAT**.......... Maritime, Aviation, and Transport Insurance (DLA)
**MAT**.......... Marketing Assistance Test
**Ma T**.......... Marxism Today [*A publication*]
**MAT**.......... Master Account Title [*Office of Management and Budget*]
**MAT**.......... Master of Arts in Teaching
**MA in T**..... Master of Arts in Teaching
**MAT**.......... Matachewan Consolidated Mines Ltd. [*Toronto Stock Exchange symbol*]
**MAT**.......... Matadi [*Zaire*] [*Airport symbol*] [*Obsolete*] (OAG)
**MAT**.......... Matching Abacus Test [*Parapsychology*]
**MAT**.......... Material (AFM)
**MAT**.......... Materiel [*Military*] (AFM)
**MAT**.......... Maternity
**MAT**.......... Mathematical Automata Theory
**MAT**.......... Matinee
**MAT**.......... Matins (ROG)
**MAT**.......... Matrix (MSA)
**Mat**............ Matrix [*A publication*]
**MAT**.......... Matsushiro [*Japan*] [*Seismograph station code, US Geological Survey*] (SEIS)
**MAT**.......... Mattel, Inc. [*NYSE symbol*] (SPSG)
**Mat**............ Mattheus de Mathesillanis [*Flourished, 1381-1402*] [*Authority cited in pre-1607 legal work*] (DSA)
**MAT**.......... Matthew [*New Testament book*]
**MAT**.......... Matured
**MAT**.......... Maturity
**MAT**.......... Matutinal (ADA)
**MAT**.......... Mean Annual Temperature [*Climatology*]
**MAT**.......... Measurement of Atmospheric Turbulence
**MAT**.......... Mechanical Aptitude Test
**MAT**.......... Mechanically Agitated Tank [*Engineering*]
**MAT**.......... Medium Artillery Tractor [*British military*] (DMA)
**MAT**.......... Medium Assault Transport (MCD)
**MAT**.......... Memorie. Reale Accademia delle Scienze di Torino [*A publication*]
**MAT**.......... Memory Access Table [*Data processing*]
**MAT**.......... Memory-Address Test
**MAT**.......... Meteorological Atmospheric Turbulence (MCD)
**MAT**.......... Methionine Adenosyltransferase [*An enzyme*]
**MAT**.......... Metropolitan Achievement Test
**MAT**.......... Metropolitan Area Trunk [*Telecommunications*] (TEL)
**MAT**.......... Microactivity Testing [*Catalysis technology*]
**MAT**.......... Microalloy Transistor
**MAT**.......... Microtray Agglutination Test [*Clinical chemistry*]
**MAT**.......... Microwave Antenna Tower
**MAT**.......... Military Air Transport
**MAT**.......... Military Aircraft Types
**MAT**.......... Miller Analogies Test [*Psychology*]
**MAT**.......... Mine Assembly Team [*Navy*] (NVT)
**MAT**.......... Minimal Aversion Threshold [*to noise*]
**MAT**.......... Minimum Allowable Threshold [*Chemistry*]
**MAT**.......... Missile Acceptance Team (AAG)
**MAT**.......... Missile Acceptance Test
**MAT**.......... Missile Adapter Tester
**MAT**.......... Missile Antitank
**MA and T**.. Missile Assembly and Test [*Building*] (NATG)
**MAT**.......... Mobile Aerial Target (AAG)
**MAT**.......... Mobile Arming Tower (KSC)
**MAT**.......... Mobile Assistance Team [*Federal disaster planning*]
**MAT**.......... Mobile Mine Assembly Team
**MAT**.......... Molecular Analysis Team
**MAT**.......... Monocyto-Angiotropin [*Biochemistry*]
**MAT**.......... Moscow Art Theater
**MAT**.......... Motivation Analysis Test [*Psychology*]
**MAT**.......... Motor Ambulance Trolley [*British*]
**MAT**.......... Moving Annual Total [*Statistics*] (DCTA)
**MAT**.......... Multiallelic Mating-Type Regulatory Gene
**MAT**.......... Multiple Access Test
**MAT**.......... Multiple Actuator Test (MCD)
**MAT**.......... Multiple Address Telegrams
**MAT**.......... Municipal Association of Tasmania [*Australia*]
**Mat A**......... Materialy Archeologiczne [*A publication*]
**MATA**....... Military Assistance Training Advisor
**MATA**....... Motorcycle and Allied Trades Association [*Later, MIC*] (EA)
**MATA**....... Musical Arena Theatres Association [*Later, PAMI*] (EA)
**Mat AB**...... Materialien aus der Arbeitsmarkt und Berufsforschung [*A publication*]
**MATACQ** ... Material Acquisition (NG)
**MATAF**..... Mediterranean Allied Tactical Air Force
**Mat Apl Comput** ... Matematica Aplicada e Computacional [*A publication*]
**Mat A Sev Pric** ... Materialy po Archeologii Severnogo Pricernomor'ja [*A publication*]
**MATB**....... Military Air Transport Board
**MATB**....... Missile Auxiliary Test Bench
**Mat Bilten** ... Matematicki Bilten [*A publication*]
**MATC**....... Maximum Acceptable Toxicant Concentration
**MATC**....... Military Air Transport Command (MUGU)
**MATC**....... Milwaukee Area Technical College (PCM)
**MATC**....... Missile Auxiliaries Test Console
**MATC**....... Mobilization Army Training Center
**MATC**....... Mountain Artillery Training Centre [*British military*] (DMA)
**MATCALS** ... Marine Air Traffic Control and Landing System [*Navy*]
**Mat Cas**...... Matematicky Casopis [*A publication*]
**Mat Casopis Sloven Akad Vied** ... Matematicky Casopis Slovenskej Akademie Vied [*A publication*]
**MATCAT** ... Material Category
**MATCH**.... Manpower and Talent Clearinghouse
**MATCH**.... Materials and Activities for Teachers and Children
**MATCH**.... Medium-Range Antisubmarine Torpedo Carrying Helicopter (NATG)
**MATCH**.... Multielement Assured Tracking Chopper
**Mat-Child Nurs J** ... Maternal-Child Nursing Journal [*A publication*]
**MATCO**.... Materials Analysis, Tracking, and Control [*Johnson Space Center data system*] [*NASA*] (NASA)
**MATCO**.... Military Air Traffic Coordinating Office [*or Officer*] [*Air Force*] (AFM)
**MATCOM** ... Materiel Command [*Army*] (AABC)

**MATCOMEUR** ... Materiel Command, Europe
**MATCON** ... Microwave Aerospace Terminal Control [*Air Force*]
**MATCONOFF** ... Material Control Officer (MCD)
**MatCo-Ord(N)** ... Material Co-Ordination Division (Naval) [*British*]
**MATCU** .... Marine Air Tactical [*later, Traffic*] Control Unit [*Marine Corps*]
**MATD** ....... Mine and Torpedo Detector [*SONAR*] [*Navy*]
**MATDA** .... Methylene-bis-(aminothiadiazole) [*Pesticide*]
**Mat Des** ..... Material and Design [*A publication*]
**MATDEV** ... Materiel Developer
**MATE** ....... Manually Aided Tracking Enhancement (MCD)
**MATE** ....... Marital Attitude Evaluation [*Psychology*]
**MATE** ....... Married Americans for Tax Equality
**MATE** ....... Master of Arts in the Teaching of English
**Mat E** ........ Materials Engineer
**MATE** ....... Matrix Automation through EMATS [*Military*] (MCD)
**MATE** ....... McDonnell Airborne Trainer and Evaluator [*McDonnell Douglas Corp.*] (MCD)
**MATE** ....... Measuring and Test Equipment (IEEE)
**MATE** ....... MICOM [*Missile Command*] Automated Test Equipment
**MATE** ....... Missile/Aircraft Test Equipment
**MATE** ....... Mission Analysis Technique for Experiments
**MATE** ....... Mobilization and Training Equipment (MCD)
**MATE** ....... Modular Automatic Test Equipment
**MATE** ....... Montana Agri-Trade Exposition [*Jerry Hanson and Associates, Inc.*] (TSPED)
**MATE** ....... Multiband Automatic Test Equipment
**MATE** ....... Multiple-Access Time-Division Experiment (IEEE)
**MATE** ....... Multiple Advanced Technique Evaluation [*Military*] (CAAL)
**MATE** ....... Multipurpose Automatic Test Equipment
**MATE** ....... Multisystem Automatic Test Equipment [*British*]
**MATEC**..... Maintenance Technician (NOAA)
**MA (T Ed)** ... Master of Arts in Teacher Education
**MAT-EF**.... Matrix Analogies Test - Expanded Form [*Intelligence test*]
**MATELO** ... Maritime Air Telecommunications Organization [*NATO*] (NATG)
**MATEM** ... Manual Templating Model (MCD)
**Matematika Period Sb Perevodov Inostran Statei** ... Matematika. Periodiceskii Sbornik Perevodov Inostrannyh Statei [*A publication*]
**Mat Engng** ... Materials Engineering [*A publication*]
**Mat Ensenanza** ... Matematicas y Ensenanza [*A publication*]
**Mat Ensenanza Univ** ... Matematica Ensenanza Universitaria [*Bogota*] [*A publication*]
**MATER**..... Material
**Mater Badaq Inst Gospod Wodnej** ... Materialy Badaqcze Instytut Gospodarki Wodnej [*A publication*]
**Mater Badaw Ser Gospod Wodna Ochr Wod** ... Materialy Badawcze. Seria. Gospodarka Wodna i Ochrona Wod [*A publication*]
**Mater Budow** ... Materialy Budowlane [*A publication*]
**Mater Chem** ... Materials Chemistry [*A publication*]
**Mater Chem and Phys** ... Materials Chemistry and Physics [*A publication*]
**Mater Compon Fossil Energy Appl** ... Materials and Components in Fossil Energy Applications [*A publication*]
**Mater Compon Newsl** ... Materials and Components Newsletter [*A publication*]
**Mater Constr (Bucharest)** ... Materiale de Constructs (Bucharest) [*A publication*]
**Mater Constr (Madrid)** ... Materiales de Construccion (Madrid) [*A publication*]
**Mater Constr Mater Struct** ... Materiaux et Constructions/Materials and Structures [*A publication*]
**Mater Constr (Paris)** ... Materiaux et Constructions (Paris) [*A publication*]
**Mater Des Eng** ... Materials in Design Engineering [*A publication*]
**Mater Des (Surrey)** ... Materials and Design (Surrey) [*A publication*]
**Mater Eng** ... Materials Engineering [*A publication*]
**Mater Eng (Cleveland)** ... Materials Engineering (Cleveland) [*A publication*]
**Mater Eng (Surrey)** ... Materials in Engineering (Surrey) [*A publication*]
**Mater Eval** ... Materials Evaluation [*A publication*]
**Mater Evaluation** ... Materials Evaluation [*A publication*]
**Mater Evol Fiziol** ... Materialy po Evolyutsionnoi Fiziologii [*A publication*]
**Mater Floryst Geobot** ... Materialy Florystyczne i Geobotaniczne [*A publication*]
**Mater Flow** ... Material Flow [*A publication*]
**Mater Genet Eksp Miner** ... Materialy po Geneticheskoi i Eksperimental'noi Mineralogii [*A publication*]
**Mater Geol Metallog Kol'sk Poluostrova** ... Materialy po Geologii i Metallogenii Kol'skogo Poluostrova [*A publication*]
**Mater Geol Polezn Iskop Buryat ASSR** ... Materialy po Geologii i Poleznym Iskopaemym Buryatskoi ASSR [*A publication*]
**Mater Geol Polezn Iskop Chit Obl** ... Materialy po Geologii i Poleznym Iskopaemym Chitinskoi Oblasti [*A publication*]
**Mater Geol Polezn Iskop Dal'nevost Kraya** ... Materialy po Geologii i Poleznym Iskopaemym Dal'nevostochnogo Kraya [*A publication*]
**Mater Geol Polezn Iskop Irkutsk Obl** ... Materialy po Geologii i Poleznym Iskopaemym Irkutskoi Oblasti [*A publication*]
**Mater Geol Polezn Iskop Krasnoyarsk Kraya** ... Materialy po Geologii i Poleznym Iskopaemym Krasnoyarskogo Kraya [*A publication*]
**Mater Geol Polezn Iskop Sev Vostoka Evr Chasti SSSR** ... Materialy po Geologii i Poleznym Iskopaemym Severo Vostoka Evropeiskoi Chasti SSSR [*A publication*]
**Mater Geol Polezn Iskop Sev Zapada RSFSR** ... Materialy po Geologii i Poleznym Iskopaemym Severo-Zapada RSFSR [*A publication*]
**Mater Geol Polezn Iskop Sev Zapada SSSR** ... Materialy po Geologii i Poleznym Iskopaemym Severo-Zapada SSSR [*A publication*]
**Mater Geol Polezn Iskop Tsentr Raionov Evr Chasti SSSR** ... Materialy po Geologii i Poleznym Iskopaemym Tsentral'nykh Raionov Evropeiskoi Chasti SSSR [*A publication*]
**Mater Geol Polezn Iskop Urala** ... Materialy po Geologii i Poleznym Iskopaemym Urala [*A publication*]
**Mater Geol Polezn Iskop Vost Sib** ... Materialy po Geologii i Poleznym Iskopaemym Vostochnoi Sibiri [*A publication*]
**Mater Geol Polezn Iskop Yakutsk ASSR** ... Materialy po Geologii i Poleznym Iskopaemym Yakutskoi ASSR [*A publication*]
**Mater Geol Polezn Iskop Yuzhn Kaz** ... Materialy po Geologii i Poleznym Iskopaemym Yuzhnogo Kazakhstana [*A publication*]
**Mater Geol Polezn Iskop Yuzhn Urala** ... Materialy po Geologii i Poleznym Iskopaemym Yuzhnogo Urala [*A publication*]
**Mater Geol Polezy Iskop Kaz** ... Materialy po Geologii i Poleznym Iskopaemym Kazakhstana [*A publication*]
**Mater Geol Suisse Geophys** ... Materiaux pour la Geologie de la Suisse. Geophysique [*A publication*]
**Mater Geol Tsentr Kaz** ... Materialy po Geologii Tsentral'nogo Kazakhstana [*A publication*]
**Mater Geol Tuvinskoi ASSR** ... Materialy po Geologii Tuvinskoi ASSR [*A publication*]
**Mater Geol Tyan Shanya** ... Materialy po Geologii Tyan-Shanya [*A publication*]
**Mater Geol Zapadno Sib Nizmennosti** ... Materialy po Geologii Zapadno Sibirskoi Nizmennosti [*A publication*]
**Mater Geol Zapadn Sib** ... Materialy po Geologii Zapadnoi Sibiri [*A publication*]
**Mater Handl Eng** ... Material Handling Engineering [*A publication*]
**Mater Handl Mgmt** ... Materials Handling and Management [*A publication*]
**Mater Handl News** ... Materials Handling News [*A publication*]
**Mater Handl & Storage** ... Materials Handling and Storage [*A publication*] (APTA)
**Materiale** ... Materiale si Cercetari Arheologice [*A publication*]
**Material H** ... Material Handling Engineering Package/Material Handling Interaction. Special Issue [*A publication*]
**Materialkd-Tech Reihe** ... Materialkundliche-Technische Reihe [*A publication*]
**Materialpruef** ... Materialpruefung [*A publication*]
**Materials Eng** ... Materials Engineering [*A publication*]
**Materials Eval** ... Materials Evaluation [*A publication*]
**Materialy Arch** ... Materialy Archeologiczne [*A publication*]
**Materialy Sem Kibernet** ... Materialy Seminara po Kibernetike [*A publication*]
**Mater Issled Pomoshch Proekt Stroit Karakum Kanala** ... Materialy Issledovanii v Pomoshch Proektirovaniyu i Stroitelstvu Karakumskogo Kanala [*A publication*]
**Mater Istor Zemled SSSR** ... Materialy po Istorii Zemledeliya SSSR [*A publication*]
**Mater Izuch Stavrop Kraya** ... Materialy po Izucheniyu Stavropol'skogo Kraya [*A publication*]
**Mater Izuch Zhen'shenya Drugikh Lek Sredstv Dal'nego Vostoka** ... Materialy k Izucheniyu Zhen'shenya i Drugikh Lekarstvennykh Sredstv Dal'nego Vostoka [*A publication*]
**Mater J SAMPE Quart** ... Materials Journal. SAMPE [*Society for the Advancement of Material and Process Engineering*] Quarterly [*A publication*]
**Mater Khar'k Otd Geogr Ova Ukr** ... Materialy Khar'kovskogo Otdela Geograficheskogo Obshchestva Ukrainy [*A publication*]
**Mater Kom Mineral Geochem Karpato Balk Geol Assoz** ... Materialien der Komission fuer Mineralogie und Geochemie. Karpato-Balkanische Geologische Assoziation [*A publication*]
**Mater Kom Mineral Geokhim Karpato Balk Geol Assots** ... Materialy Komissii Mineralogii i Geokhimii Karpato-Balkanskaya Geologicheskaya Assotsiatsiya [*A publication*]
**Mater Kompleksn Izuch Belogo Morya** ... Materialy po Kompleksnomu Izucheniyu Belogo Morya [*A publication*]
**Mater Konf Molodykh Biol Kirg** ... Materialy Konferentsii Molodykh Biologov Kirgizii [*A publication*]
**Mater Lett** ... Materials Letters [*A publication*]
**Mater Leve Geobot Suisse** ... Materiaux pour le Leve Geobotanique de la Suisse [*A publication*]
**Mater Manage J Rev** ... Material Management Journal and Review [*A publication*]
**Mater Maquinaria Metodos Constr** ... Materiales Maquinaria y Metodos para la Construccion [*A publication*]
**Mater Med Nordmark** ... Materia Medica Nordmark [*A publication*]
**Mater Med Pol** ... Material Medica Polona [*A publication*]
**Mater Met Konstr** ... Materialy po Metallicheskim Konstruktsiyam [*A publication*]
**Mater Metod Tekh Geologorazved Rab** ... Materialy po Metodike i Tekhnike Geologorazved Rabot [*A publication*]

**Mater Mineral Geokhim Petrogr Zabaik** ... Materialy po Mineralogii, Geokhimii, i Petrografii Zabaikal'ya [*A publication*]
**Mater Mineral Geokhim Petrogr Zabaikal'ya** ... Materialy po Mineralogii, Geokhimii, i Petrografii Zabaikal'ya [*A publication*]
**Mater Mineral Kol'sk Poluostrova** ... Materialy po Mineralogii Kol'skogo Poluostrova [*A publication*]
**Mater Mineral Petrogr Polezn Iskop Zapadn Sib** ... Materialy po Mineralogii, Petrografii, i Poleznym Iskopaemym Zapadnoi Sibiri [*A publication*]
**Mater Mol Res Div Newsl** ... Materials and Molecular Research Division. Newsletter [*United States*] [*A publication*]
**Maternal-Child Nurs J** ... Maternal-Child Nursing Journal [*A publication*]
**Mater Nauchn Konf Voronezh Skh Inst** ... Materialy Nauchnoi Konferentsii Voronezhskii Sel'skokhozyaistvennyi Institut [*A publication*]
**Mater Nauchno Tekh Konf Leningr Elektrotekh Inst Svyazi** ... Materialy Nauchno-Tekhnicheskoi Konferentsii Leningradskogo Elektrotekhnicheskogo Instituta Svyazi [*A publication*]
**Mater Nauc Konfer Aspir Azerb Pedag Inst Im Lenina** ... Materialy Naucnoi Konferencii Aspirantov Posvjascennoj Poluvekovomu Jubileju Azerbajdzanskogo Pedagogiceskogo Instituta Imeni V. I. Lenina [*A publication*]
**Matern Child Nurs J** ... Maternal-Child Nursing Journal [*A publication*]
**Matern Inf** ... Maternita ed Infanzia [*A publication*]
**Matern Infanc** ... Maternidade e Infancia [*A publication*]
**Mater Note Aust Aeronaut Res Lab** ... Australia. Aeronautical Research Laboratories. Materials Note [*A publication*] (APTA)
**Mater Nouv Tech Mond** ... Materiels Nouveaux et Techniques Mondiales [*A publication*]
**Mater Obmenu Opytom Nauchn Dostizh Med Promsti** ... Materialy po Obmenu Opytom i Nauchnymi Dostizheniyami v Meditsinskoi Promyshlennosti [*A publication*]
**Mater Ogniotrwale** ... Materialy Ogniotrwale [*Poland*] [*A publication*]
**Mater Org** ... Material und Organismen [*A publication*]
**Mater u Organ** ... Material und Organismen [*A publication*]
**Mater Org Beih** ... Materials und Organismen Beihefte [*A publication*]
**Mater Org (Berl)** ... Material und Organismen (Berlin) [*A publication*]
**Mater Perf** ... Materials Performance [*A publication*]
**Mater Perform** ... Materials Performance [*A publication*]
**Mater Performance** ... Materials Performance [*A publication*]
**Mater Plast (Bucharest)** ... Materiale Plastice (Bucharest) [*A publication*]
**Mater Plast Elastomeri** ... Materiale Plastice ed Elastomeri [*A publication*]
**Mater Plast Elastomeri Fibre Sint** ... Materiale Plastice, Elastomeri, Fibre Sintetice [*A publication*]
**Mater Polit Bildung** ... Materialien zur Politischen Bildung [*A publication*]
**Mater Poznaniyu Fauny Flory SSSR Otd Bot** ... Materialy k Poznaniyu Fauny i Flory SSSR Otdel Botanicheskii [*A publication*]
**Mater Poznaniyu Fauny Flory SSSR Otd Zool** ... Materialy k Poznaniyu Fauny i Flory SSSR Otdel Zoologicheskii [*A publication*]
**Mater Pr Antropol** ... Materialy i Prace Antropologiczne [*A publication*]
**Mater Process Technol** ... Materials and Process Technology [*A publication*]
**Mater Proizvod Silam Uzb** ... Materialy po Proizvoditel'nym Silam Uzbekistana [*A publication*]
**Mater Prot** ... Materials Protection [*Later, Materials Performance*] [*A publication*]
**Mater Prot Perform** ... Materials Protection and Performance [*Later, Materials Performance*] [*A publication*]
**Mater Prot Performance** ... Materials Protection and Performance [*Later, Materials Performance*] [*A publication*]
**Mater Pr Pol Akad Nauk Inst Geofiz** ... Materialy i Prace. Polska Akademia Nauk. Instytut Geofizyki [*A publication*]
**Materpruefengsamt Bauw Tech Hochsch Muenchen Ber** ... Materialpruefengsamt fuer das Bauwesen der Technischen Hochschule Muenchen. Bericht [*A publication*]
**Mater Pr Zakl Geofiz Pol Akad Nauk** ... Materialy i Prace. Zaklad Geofizyki Polska Akademia Nauk [*A publication*]
**Mater Rep Aust Aeronaut Res Lab** ... Australia. Aeronautical Research Laboratories. Materials Report [*A publication*] (APTA)
**Mater Rep Univ Mus Univ Tokyo** ... Material Reports. University Museum. University of Tokyo [*A publication*]
**Mater Res AECL** ... Materials Research in AECL [*Atomic Energy of Canada Limited*] [*A publication*]
**Mater Res Bull** ... Materials Research Bulletin [*A publication*]
**Mater Res Soc Symp Proc** ... Materials Research Society. Symposia. Proceedings [*A publication*]
**Mater Res Stand** ... Materials Research and Standards [*A publication*]
**Mater Res and Stand** ... Materials Research and Standards [*A publication*]
**Mater Sb Statni Vyzk Ustav Mater** ... Materialovy Sbornik Statni Vyzkumny Ustav Materialu [*A publication*]
**Mater Sci** ... Materials Science [*Poland*] [*A publication*]
**Mater Sci E** ... Materials Science and Engineering [*A publication*]
**Mater Sci and Eng** ... Material Science and Engineering [*A publication*]
**Mater Sci Eng** ... Materials Science and Engineering [*A publication*]
**Mater Sci Res** ... Materials Science Research [*A publication*]
**Mater Sci T** ... Materials Science and Technology [*A publication*]
**Mater Semin Kibern** ... Materialy Seminara po Kibernetike [*A publication*]
**Mater Soc** .. Materials and Society [*A publication*]
**Mater Stud Nauchn Ova Khar'k Politekh Inst** ... Materialy Studencheskogo Nauchnogo Obshchestva. Khar'kovskii Politekhnicheskii Institut [*A publication*]
**Mater Tech** ... Materiaux et Techniques [*A publication*]
**Mater Tech (Paris)** ... Materiaux et Techniques (Paris) [*A publication*]
**Mater Tekh Snabzhenie** ... Material'no Tekhnicheskoe Snabzhenie [*USSR*] [*A publication*]
**Mater Teknol (Sofia)** ... Materialoznavie i Tekhnologiya (Sofia) [*Bulgaria*] [*A publication*]
**Mater Teor Klin Med** ... Materialy Teoreticheskoi i Klinicheskoi Meditsiny [*A publication*]
**Mater Test** ... Materials Testing [*A publication*]
**Mater Tezisy VI Konf Khim Sel' Khoz** ... Materialy i Tezisy VI Konferentsii po Khimizatsii Sel'skogo Khozyaistva [*A publication*]
**Mater Ther** ... Materia Therapeutica [*A publication*]
**Mater Toksikol Radioakt Veshchestv** ... Materialy po Toksikologii Radioaktivnykh Veshchestv [*A publication*]
**Mater Tsentr Nauchno Issled Inst Bum Promsti** ... Materialy Tsentral'nogo Nauchno-Issledovatel'skogo Instituta Bumazhnoi Promyshlennosti [*A publication*]
**Mater Tsentr Nauchno Issled Inst Tekst Promsti** ... Materialy Tsentral'nogo Nauchno-Issledovatel'skogo Instituta Tekstil'noi Promyshlennosti [*A publication*]
**Mater Uch Merzlykh Zonakh Zemnoi Kory** ... Materialy k Ucheniyu o Merzlykh Zonakh Zemnoi Kory [*A publication*]
**Mater Vopr Prom Toksikol Klin Prof Bolezn** ... Materialy po Voprosam Promyshlennoi Toksikologii i Kliniki Professional'nykh Boleznei [*A publication*]
**Mater Vses Nauchno Issled Geol Inst** ... Materialy Vsesoyuznogo Nauchno-Issledovatel'skogo Geologicheskogo Instituta [*A publication*]
**Mater Vses Nauchno Issled Inst Bum Tsellyul Promsti** ... Materialy Vsesoyuznogo Nauchno-Issledovatel'skogo Instituta Bumazhnoi i Tsellyuloznoi Promyshlennosti [*A publication*]
**Mater Zachodniopomorskie Muz Pomorza Zachodniego** ... Materialy Zachodniopomorskie. Muzeum Pomorza Zachodniego [*A publication*]
MATES..... Medium Attack Tactical Employment School [*Military*] (CAAL)
MATES..... Mobilization and Training Equipment Site [*Military*] (AABC)
MA(TESOL) ... Master of Arts in Teaching English to Speakers of Other Languages
**Mat Eval**.... Materials Evaluation [*A publication*]
MATFA..... Meat and Allied Trade Federation of Australia
**Mat Fak Univ Kiril Metodij (Skopje) Godisen Zb** ... Matematicki Fakultet Univerzitetot Kiril i Metodij (Skopje). Godisen Zbornik [*A publication*]
MATFAP.. Metropolitan Area Transmission Facility Analysis Program [*AT & T*] [*Telecommunications*] (TEL)
**Mat Fiz** ...... Akademiya Nauk Ukrainskoi SSR. Institut Matematiki. Matematicheskaya Fizika [*A publication*]
**Mat Fiz i Funkcional Anal** ... Matematiceskaja Fizika i Funkcional'nyi Analiz [*A publication*]
**Mat Fiz List Ucenike Srednjih Sk** ... Matematicko Fizicki List za Ucenike Srednjih Skola [*A publication*]
**Mat-Fys Med** ... Matematisk-Fysiske Meddelelser. Kongelige Danske Videnskabernes Selskab [*A publication*]
**Mat-Fys Medd Danske Vid Selsk** ... Matematisk-Fysiske Meddelelser. Kongelige Danske Videnskabernes Selskab [*A publication*]
**Mat-Fys Medd Dan Vidensk Selsk** ... Matematisk-Fysiske Meddelelser. Kongelige Danske Videnskabernes Selskab [*A publication*]
**Mat Fyz Cas** ... Matematicko-Fyzikalny Casopis [*A publication*]
**Mat-Fyz Cas Slov Akad Vied** ... Matematicko-Fyzikalny Casopis. Slovenskej Akademie Vied [*Czechoslovakia*] [*A publication*]
Math .......... Adversus Mathematicos [*of Sextus Empiricus*] [*Classical studies*] (OCD)
MA(Th)..... Master of Arts in Theology
MATH....... Mathematics (EY)
MATH....... Mathematics Abstracts [*Fachinformationszentrum Karlsruhe GmbH*] [*Information service or system*]
Math .......... Matheus de Mathesillanis [*Flourished, 1381-1402*] [*Authority cited in pre-1607 legal work*] (DSA)
Math .......... Mathieu's Quebec Reports [*A publication*] (DLA)
MATH....... Mobile, Air-Transportable Hospital [*Military*]
**Math Agoge** ... Mathematike Agoge [*A publication*]
**Math Algorithms** ... Mathematical Algorithms [*A publication*]
**Math Ann** .. Mathematische Annalen [*A publication*]
**Math Annal** ... Mathematische Annalen [*A publication*]
**Math Anwendungen Phys Tech** ... Mathematik und Ihre Anwendungen in Physik und Technik [*A publication*]
**Math Appl** ... Mathematics and Its Applications [*A publication*]
**Math Appl Polit Sci** ... Mathematical Applications in Political Science [*A publication*]
**Math-Arbeitspapiere** ... Mathematik-Arbeitspapiere [*A publication*]
**Math Balk** ... Mathematica Balkanica [*A publication*]
**Math Biosci** ... Mathematical Biosciences [*A publication*]
**Math Cent Amsterdam Rekenafd** ... Mathematisch Centrum Amsterdam Rekenafdeling [*A publication*]
**Math Centre Tracts** ... Mathematical Centre. Tracts [*Amsterdam*] [*A publication*]
**Math Chronicle** ... Mathematical Chronicle [*A publication*]
**Math Colloq Univ Cape Town** ... Mathematics Colloquium. University of Cape Town [*A publication*]
**Math Comp** ... Mathematics of Computation [*A publication*]

**Math and Comp in Simulation** ... Mathematics and Computers in Simulation [*A publication*]
**Math of Comput** ... Mathematics of Computation [*A publication*]
**Math Comput** ... Mathematics of Computation [*A publication*]
**Math Comput Ed** ... Mathematics and Computer Education [*A publication*]
**Math and Comput Educ** ... Mathematics and Computer Education [*A publication*]
**Math Comput Simul** ... Mathematics and Computers in Simulation [*A publication*]
**Math Comput Simulation** ... Mathematics and Computers in Simulation [*A publication*]
**Math and Comput Simulation** ... Mathematics and Computers in Simulation [*A publication*]
**Math Concepts Methods Sci Engrg** ... Mathematical Concepts and Methods in Science and Engineering [*A publication*]
**Math Concepts and Methods in Sci and Engrg** ... Mathematical Concepts and Methods in Science and Engineering [*A publication*]
**Math D** ...... Doctor of Mathematics
**Math Dept Rep** ... Mathematics Department Report [*A publication*]
**MATHDI** .. Mathematical Didactics [*Fachinformationszentrum Energie, Physik, Mathematik GmbH*] [*Database*]
**Math Didaktik Unterrichtspraxis** ... Mathematik. Didaktik und Unterrichtspraxis [*A publication*]
**Mathe de Afflcti** ... Matthaeus de Afflictis [*Deceased, 1528*] [*Authority cited in pre-1607 legal work*] (DSA)
**Math Ed for Teaching** ... Mathematical Education for Teaching [*A publication*]
**Math Education** ... Mathematics Education [*A publication*]
**Math Educ Teach** ... Mathematical Education for Teaching [*A publication*]
**MA Theol** .. Master of Arts in Theology
**Math Forschungsber** ... Mathematische Forschungsberichte [*A publication*]
**Math Forum** ... Mathematical Forum [*A publication*]
**Math Gazette** ... Mathematical Gazette [*A publication*]
**Math Ingen Naturwiss Oekonom Landwirte** ... Mathematik fuer Ingenieure, Naturwissenschaftler, Oekonomen, und Landwirte [*A publication*]
**Math Ingen Naturwiss Okonom Sonstige Anwendungsorient Berufe** ... Mathematik fuer Ingenieure, Naturwissenschaftler, Oekonomen, und Sonstige Anwendungsorientierte Berufe [*A publication*]
**Math Ing Naturwiss Okon Landwirte** ... Mathematik fuer Ingenieure, Naturwissenschaftler, Oekonomen, und Landwirte [*A publication*]
**Math Intelligencer** ... Mathematical Intelligencer [*A publication*]
**Math Japon** ... Mathematica Japonicae [*A publication*]
**Math J Okayama Univ** ... Mathematical Journal. Okayama University [*A publication*]
**Math Kibernet Zogierth Sakith Gamokw** ... Mathematikuri Kibernetikis Zogierthi Sakithxis Gamokwewa [*A publication*]
**MATHL** ..... Mathematical
**MATHLAB** ... Mathematical Laboratory [*Programming language*] (CSR)
**Math Lecture Note Ser** ... Mathematics Lecture Note Series [*A publication*]
**Math Lecture Ser** ... Mathematics Lecture Series [*A publication*]
**Math Lehrb Monogr I** ... Mathematische Lehrbuecher und Monographien. I. Abteilung. Mathematische Lehrbuecher [*A publication*]
**Math Lehrbuecher Monogr I Abt Math Lehrbuecher** ... Mathematische Lehrbuecher und Monographien. I. Abteilung. Mathematische Lehrbuecher [*A publication*]
**Math Lehrbuecher Monogr II Abt Math Monogr** ... Mathematische Lehrbuecher und Monographien. II. Abteilung. Mathematische Monographien [*A publication*]
**Math Lehrer** ... Mathematik fuer Lehrer [*A publication*]
**Math Mag** ... Mathematics Magazine [*A publication*]
**Math Math Phys (Washington DC)** ... Mathematics and Mathematical Physics (Washington, DC) [*A publication*]
**Math Medley** ... Mathematical Medley [*A publication*]
**Math Methods Appl Sci** ... Mathematical Methods in the Applied Sciences [*A publication*]
**Math Methods Oper Res** ... Mathematical Methods of Operations Research [*A publication*]
**Math Miniaturen** ... Mathematische Miniaturen [*A publication*]
**Math Mo** ... Mathematical Monthly [*A publication*]
**Math Modelling** ... Mathematical Modelling [*A publication*]
**Math Monograph** ... Mathematische Monographien [*A publication*]
**MATHN**.... Mathematician (AFM)
**Math N** ...... Matthaeus Nerutius [*Flourished, 16th century*] [*Authority cited in pre-1607 legal work*] (DSA)
**Math Nachr** ... Mathematische Nachrichten [*A publication*]
**Math-Naturwiss Bibliothek** ... Mathematisch-Naturwissenschaftliche Bibliothek [*A publication*]
**Math-Naturwiss Taschenb** ... Mathematisch-Naturwissenschaftliche Taschenbuecher [*A publication*]
**Math Naturwiss Tech** ... Mathematik fuer Naturwissenschaft und Technik [*A publication*]
**Math Naturwiss Unterr** ... Mathematische und Naturwissenschaftliche Unterricht [*A publication*]
**Math Naturw Unterr** ... Mathematische und Naturwissenschaftliche Unterricht [*A publication*]
**Math Notae** ... Mathematicae Notae [*A publication*]
**Math Notes** ... Mathematical Notes [*A publication*]
**Math Notes Acad Sci (USSR)** ... Mathematical Notes. Academy of Sciences (USSR) [*A publication*]
**Math Numer Sin** ... Mathematica Numerica Sinica [*A publication*]
**Math Numer Sinica** ... Mathematica Numerica Sinica [*A publication*]
**Math Operationsforsch und Stat** ... Mathematische Operationsforschung und Statistik [*A publication*]
**Math Operationsforsch Stat** ... Mathematische Operationsforschung und Statistik [*A publication*]
**Math Operationsforsch Statist** ... Mathematische Operationsforschung und Statistik [*A publication*]
**Math Operationsforsch Statist Ser Optim** ... Mathematische Operationsforschung und Statistik. Series Optimization [*A publication*]
**Math Operationsforsch Statist Ser Optimization** ... Mathematische Operationsforschung und Statistik. Series Optimization [*A publication*]
**Math Operationsforsch Statist Ser Statist** ... Mathematische Operationsforschung und Statistik. Series Statistik [*A publication*]
**Math Operationsforsch und Stat Ser Optimiz** ... Mathematische Operationsforschung und Statistik. Series Optimization [*A publication*]
**Math Operationsforsch und Stat Ser Stat** ... Mathematische Operationsforschung und Statistik. Series Statistik [*A publication*]
**Math Oper Res** ... Mathematics of Operations Research [*A publication*]
**MATHP** .... Medium Artillery Terminal Homing Projectile
**Math Phys** ... Mathematik fuer Physiker [*A publication*]
**Math Phys Appl Math** ... Mathematical Physics and Applied Mathematics [*A publication*]
**Math Physiker** ... Mathematik fuer Physiker [*A publication*]
**Math Phys Monograph Ser** ... Mathematical Physics Monograph Series [*A publication*]
**Math Phys Monogr Ser** ... Mathematical Physics Monograph Series [*A publication*]
**Math-Phys Semesterber** ... Mathematisch-Physikalische Semesterberichte [*A publication*]
**Math Phys Stud** ... Mathematical Physics Studies [*A publication*]
**Math Pres Ev** ... Mathews on Presumptive Evidence [*A publication*] (DLA)
**Math Proc C** ... Mathematical Proceedings. Cambridge Philosophical Society [*A publication*]
**Math Proc Camb Philos Soc** ... Mathematical Proceedings. Cambridge Philosophical Society [*A publication*]
**Math Proc Cambridge Philos Soc** ... Mathematical Proceedings. Cambridge Philosophical Society [*A publication*]
**Math Proc Cambridge Phil Soc** ... Mathematical Proceedings. Cambridge Philosophical Society [*A publication*]
**Math Prog** ... Mathematical Programming [*A publication*]
**Math Progr** ... Mathematical Programming [*A publication*]
**Math Program** ... Mathematical Programming [*A publication*]
**Math Programming** ... Mathematical Programming [*A publication*]
**Math Programming Stud** ... Mathematical Programming Study [*A publication*]
**Math Program Stud** ... Mathematical Programming Studies [*A publication*]
**MathR** ....... Mathematical Reviews [*A publication*]
**Math Reihe** ... Mathematische Reihe [*A publication*]
**Math Rep College General Ed Kyushu Univ** ... Mathematical Reports. College of General Education. Kyushu University [*A publication*]
**Math Rep Kyushu Univ** ... Mathematical Reports. College of General Education. Kyushu University [*A publication*]
**Math Rep Toyama Univ** ... Toyama University. Mathematics Reports [*A publication*]
**Math Res** ... Mathematical Research [*A publication*]
**Math Research** ... Mathematical Research [*A publication*]
**Math Rev** ... Mathematical Reviews [*A publication*]
**Math Rev Sect** ... Mathematical Reviews Sections [*A publication*]
**MATHS** .... Mathematics
**Maths Bul** ... Mathematics Bulletin for Teachers in Secondary Schools [*A publication*] (APTA)
**Math Scand** ... Mathematica Scandinavica [*A publication*]
**Math in School** ... Mathematics in School [*A publication*]
**Math Schuelerbuecherei** ... Mathematische Schuelerbuecherei [*A publication*]
**Math Sci** .... Mathematical Sciences [*A publication*]
**Math Sci** .... Mathematical Scientist [*A publication*] (APTA)
**Math Sci Eng** ... Mathematics in Science and Engineering [*A publication*]
**Math Sci Engrg** ... Mathematics in Science and Engineering [*A publication*]
**Math Scientist** ... Mathematical Scientist [*A publication*] (APTA)
**Math Sci Hum** ... Mathematiques et Sciences Humaines [*A publication*]
**Math Sci Humaines** ... Centre de Mathematique Sociale. Ecole Pratique des Hautes Etudes. Mathematiques et Sciences Humaines [*A publication*]
**Math Sem** .. Mathematics Seminar [*Delhi*] [*A publication*]
**Math Semesterber** ... Mathematische Semesterberichte [*A publication*]
**Math Seminar** ... Mathematics Seminar [*A publication*]
**Math Sem Notes Kobe Univ** ... Mathematics Seminar. Notes. Kobe University [*A publication*]
**Math Sem Notes Kobe Univ Second Ed** ... Kobe University. Mathematics Seminar Notes. Second Edition [*A publication*]
**Math Ser**.... Mathematics Series [*A publication*]
**Math Slovaca** ... Mathematica Slovaca [*A publication*]
**Math Social Sci** ... Mathematical Social Sciences [*A publication*]

**Math Soc Sci** ... Mathematical Social Sciences [*A publication*]
**Math Spectrum** ... Mathematical Spectrum [*A publication*]
**Math Student** ... Mathematics Student [*A publication*]
**Math Surveys** ... Mathematical Surveys [*A publication*]
**Math Systems in Econom** ... Mathematical Systems in Economics [*A publication*]
**Math Systems Theory** ... Mathematical Systems Theory [*A publication*]
**Math Syst T** ... Mathematical Systems Theory [*A publication*]
**Math Teach** ... Mathematics Teacher [*A publication*]
**Math Teach** ... Mathematics Teaching [*A publication*]
**Math Teaching** ... Mathematics Teaching [*A publication*]
**Math Trans (Engl Transl)** ... Mathematical Transactions (English Translation of Matematicheskii Sbornik) [*A publication*]
**Math USSR Izv** ... Mathematics of the USSR. Izvestiya [*A publication*]
**Math USSR Sb** ... Mathematics of the USSR. Sbornik [*A publication*]
**Math Wirtschaftswiss** ... Mathematik fuer Wirtschaftswissenschaftler [*A publication*]
**Math Z**....... Mathematische Zeitschrift [*A publication*]
**MATIC**...... Multiple Area Technical Information Center
**MATICO**... Machine Applications to Technical Information Center Operations
**MATIF** ...... Marche a Terme des Instruments Financiers [*France's first financial futures market*]
**MATILDA** ... Microwave Analysis Threat Indication and Launch Direction Apparatus [*Military*]
**MATINSP** ... Material Inspection [*Navy*] (NVT)
**MatIRJa**.... Materialy i Issledovanija po Istorii Russkogo Jazyka [*A publication*]
**Mat Issled** ... Matematicheskie Issledovaniya [*A publication*]
**Mat Ist Muz (Bucuresti)** ... Materiale de Istorie si Muzeografie (Bucuresti) [*A publication*]
**Mat Kul't Tadzh** ... Material'naia Kul'tura Tadzhikistana [*A publication*]
**MATL**........ Material (KSC)
**MATL**........ Materiel [*Military*]
**MATL**........ Middle Atlantic
**MATLAB**.. Matrix Laboratory [*Data processing*]
**MATLAN** .. Matrix Language [*Data processing*] (IEEE)
**Mat Lapok** ... Matematikai Lapok [*A publication*]
**MATLAS**.. Melbourne Allied Tertiary Library Automation System [*Australia*]
**MATL REQ** ... Material Requisition
**Matls Sci**.... Materials Science [*A publication*]
**Mat L & T** ... Mathews on Landlord and Tenant [*A publication*] (DLA)
**Mat Metody Din Kosm App Akad Nauk SSSR Vychisl Tsentr** ... Matematicheskie Metody v Dinamike Kosmicheskikh Apparatov Akademiya Nauk SSSR Vychisislitel'nyi Tsentr [*USSR*] [*A publication*]
**Mat Metody i Fiz-Meh Polja** ... Akademija Nauk Ukrainskoi SSR L'vovskii Filial Matematiceskoi Fiziki Instituta Matematiki. Matematiceskie Metody i Fiziko-Mehaniceskie Polja [*A publication*]
**Mat Model Teor Elektr Tsepei** ... Matematicheskoe Modelirovanie i Teoriya Elektricheskikh Tsepei [*USSR*] [*A publication*]
**MATMOP** ... Materiel Management Optimization Program [*DoD*]
**MATMU**... Mobile Aircraft Torpedo Maintenance Unit
**Mat News Int** ... Materials News International [*A publication*]
**MATNO**.... Material Requested Is Not Available
**MATO**....... Military Air Traffic Operations [*British military*] (DMA)
**MATP**........ Masking Template [*Tool*] (AAG)
**MATP**........ Military Assistance Training Program (AABC)
**MATP**........ Missile Auxiliary Test Position
**Mat Par**...... Matthew Paris. Historia Minor [*A publication*] (DLA)
**Mat Paris**... Matthew Paris. Historia Minor [*A publication*] (DLA)
**Mat Part**.... Mathews on the Law of Partnership [*A publication*] (DLA)
**Mat-Phys Semesterber** ... Mathematisch-Physikalische Semesterberichte [*A publication*]
**Mat Plast**... Materiale Plastice [*A publication*]
**Mat Plast Elast** ... Materie Plastiche ed Elastomeri [*A publication*]
**MA-TPM** .. Maritime Administration Transport Planning Mobilization [*Federal emergency order*]
**Mat Por**...... Mathews on the Law of Portions [*A publication*] (DLA)
**Mat Probl Geofiz** ... Matematicheskie Problemy Geofiziki [*USSR*] [*A publication*]
**MATPS**..... Machine-Aided Technical Processing System [*Yale University Library*] [*New Haven, CT*] [*Data processing*]
**MATR**....... Management Access to Records
**MATR**....... Matriculate (ROG)
**MATR**....... Matron
**MATRAC** ... Military Air Traffic Control System
**MatRD**....... Materialy i Issledovanija po Russkoj Dialektologii [*A publication*]
**MATRD**.... Materiel Release Denial [*Army*] (AABC)
**MATRE**..... Material Requested
**MATRIC**... Matriculation
**MATRIS**... Manpower and Training Research Information System [*DoD*] [*Information service or system*] (IID)
**MATRIX**... Management Trial Exercise [*Career orientation simulation*]
**MATRIX**... Market Trend Index [*Associated Equipment Distributors program*]
**Matrix and Tensor Q** ... Matrix and Tensor Quarterly [*A publication*]
**Matrix Tensor Quart** ... Matrix and Tensor Quarterly [*London*] [*A publication*]
**Matrix Tensor Quart** ... Tensor Club of Great Britain. Matrix and Tensor Quarterly [*A publication*]
**MATRL**..... Matrimonial (ROG)
**Matrl Eng**.. Materials Engineering [*A publication*]
**Matrl Hand** ... Material Handling Engineering [*A publication*]
**Matrl Perf**... Materials Performance [*A publication*]
**MATRS**..... Miniature Airborne Telemetry Receiving Station
**Matr Tens Q** ... Matrix and Tensor Quarterly [*A publication*]
**MATS**........ Maintenance Analysis Task Sheet
**MATS**........ Maintenance Analysis Test Set
**MATS**........ Manual Versus Automatic Transmission Study (MCD)
**MATS**........ Matrimonial Matters [*Slang*] (DSUE)
**Mats**........... Matson's Reports [*22-24 Connecticut*] [*A publication*] (DLA)
**MATS**........ Mediterranean Air Transport Service
**MATS**........ Metropolitan Adelaide Transport Study [*Australia*]
**MATS**........ Military Air Transport Service [*Later, Military Airlift Command*]
**MATS**........ Missile Auxiliaries Test Set
**MATS**........ Mission Analysis and Trajectory Simulation (MCD)
**MATS**........ Mobile Automatic Telephone System [*Telecommunications*]
**MATS**........ Mobile Automatic Test Set (MCD)
**MATS**........ Model Aircraft Target System [*British military*] (DMA)
**MATS**........ Monitoring and Test Subsystem
**MATSA**..... Managerial, Administrative, Technical, and Supervisory Association [*British*] (DCTA)
**Mat Sb**....... Matematicheskie Sbornik [*A publication*]
**Mat Sb (NS)** ... Matematiceskii Sbornik (Novaja Serija) [*A publication*]
**Mat Sb (Tomsk)** ... Matematiceskii Sbornik (Tomsk) [*A publication*]
**MATSC**..... Middletown Air Technical Service Command [*Air Force*]
**Matscience Rep** ... Matscience Report [*Madras*] [*A publication*]
**MAT-SF**.... Matrix Analogies Test - Short Form [*Intelligence test*]
**Mat v Skole** ... Ministerstvo Prosvescenija RSSR Matematika v Skole [*A publication*]
**MatSl**......... Matica Slovenska [*A publication*]
**MATSO**..... Material Requested Being Supplied [*Military*]
**Matson**....... Matson's Reports [*22-24 Connecticut*] [*A publication*] (DLA)
**Mats Perf**... Materials Performance [*A publication*]
**MATSR**..... Military Air Transport Service [*later, Military Airlift Command*] Regulation
**Mats Reclam Wkly** ... Materials Reclamation Weekly [*A publication*]
**MATSS**..... Midwest Automated Technical Services Systems [*Information service or system*] (EISS)
**Mats Struct** ... Materials and Structures [*A publication*]
**Mat Star**.... Materialy Starozytne [*A publication*]
**Mat Stos**.... Matematyka Stosowana [*A publication*]
**Mat Stos 3** ... Roczniki Polskiego Towarzystwa Matematycznego. Seria III. Matematyka Stosowana [*A publication*]
**Matsushita Electr Works Tech Rep** ... Matsushita Electric Works. Technical Report [*A publication*]
**MAtt**.......... Attleboro Public Library, Attleboro, MA [*Library symbol*] [*Library of Congress*] (LCLS)
**Matt**........... Matthew [*New Testament book*]
**MATT**....... Matthews Studio Equipment Group [*NASDAQ symbol*] (NQ)
**MATT**....... Mobile Acoustic Torpedo Target (NG)
**Mat Testi Cl** ... Materiali e Discussioni per l'Analisi dei Testi Classici [*A publication*]
**Matth Com** ... Matthews' Guide to Commissioner in Chancery [*A publication*] (DLA)
**Matth Cr L** ... Matthews' Digest of Criminal Law [*A publication*] (DLA)
**Matthe de Affli** ... Matthaeus de Afflictis [*Deceased, 1528*] [*Authority cited in pre-1607 legal work*] (DSA)
**Matthews**... Matthews' Reports [*75 Virginia*] [*A publication*] (DLA)
**Matthews**... Matthews' Reports [*6-9 West Virginia*] [*A publication*] (DLA)
**Matth Exe** ... Matthews' Executors and Administrators [*2nd ed.*] [*1839*] [*A publication*] (DLA)
**Matth Gribal** ... Matthaeus Gribaldus [*Deceased, 1564*] [*Authority cited in pre-1607 legal work*] (DSA)
**Matth Part** ... Matthews on Partnership [*A publication*] (DLA)
**Matth Pr Ev** ... Matthews on Presumptive Evidence [*A publication*] (DLA)
**MATTS**..... Multiple Airborne Target Trajectory System
**MATU**....... Marine Air Traffic Unit
**MATUT**.... Matutinus [*In the Morning*] [*Pharmacy*]
**MATV**....... Master Antenna Television
**Mat Vesnik** ... Matematicki Vesnik [*A publication*]
**Mat Vesn Nova Ser** ... Matematichki Vesnik. Nova Seriya [*Yugoslavia*] [*A publication*]
**Mat Voprosy Upravlen Proizvodstvom** ... Moskovskii Gosudarstvennyi Universitet. Mehaniko-Matematiceskii Fakul'tet. Matematiceskii Voprosy Upravlenija Proizvodstvom [*A publication*]
**MATW**...... Metal Awning Type Window
**MATWAS** ... Marine Automatic Telephone Weather Answering Service [*Marine science*] (MSC)
**MATWING** ... Medium Attack Wing (NVT)
**MATYC J** ... MATYC [*Mathematics Association of Two-Year Colleges*] Journal [*A publication*]
**MATZ**....... Military Aerodrome Traffic Zone
**Mat Zachodnio-Pomorskie** ... Materialy Zachodnio-Pomorskie [*A publication*]

**Mat Zametki** ... Matematicheskie Zametki [*A publication*]
**MAU**.......... Maintenance Analysis Unit
**MAU**.......... Maintenance Augmenting Unit (NG)
**MAU**.......... Marine Advisory Unit [*Marine Corps*]
**MAU**.......... Marine Amphibious Unit (NVT)
**mau** ............ Massachusetts [*MARC country of publication code*] [*Library of Congress*] (LCCP)
**MAU**.......... Mathematical Advisory Unit [*Ministry of Transport*] [*British*]
**MAU**.......... Matua [*USSR*] [*Seismograph station code, US Geological Survey*] (SEIS)
**MAU**.......... Maupiti [*French Polynesia*] [*Airport symbol*] (OAG)
**Mau**............ Mauricius [*Authority cited in pre-1607 legal work*] (DSA)
**MAU**.......... Mauritius (ROG)
**Mau**............ [*Johannes*] Maurus [*Authority cited in pre-1607 legal work*] (DSA)
**MAU**.......... Media Access Unit [*Telecommunications*]
**MAU**.......... Medical Assistance Unit [*HEW*]
**MAU**.......... Medium Access Unit [*Data processing*] (BYTE)
**MAU**.......... Memory Access Unit
**mAU** .......... Milliabsorbance Unit [*Spectroscopy*]
**MAU**.......... Million Accounting Units (NASA)
**MAU**.......... Miscellaneous Armament Unit
**MAU**.......... Modern American Usage [*A publication*]
**MAU**.......... Mount Allison University [*New Brunswick, Canada*]
**MAU**.......... Multiattribute Utility (IEEE)
**MAU**.......... Multiple Access Unit
**MAUD**....... Ministry of Aircraft Uranium Development [*British*] [*World War II*]
**MAUD**....... Movimento Academico pela Uniao Democrata [*Academic Movement for Democratic Union*] [*Portugal*] [*Political party*] (PPE)
**MAUDE**.... Morse Automatic Decoder
**Maude & P** ... Maude and Pollock's Law of Merchant Shipping [*A publication*] (DLA)
**MAUDEP** ... Metropolitan Association of Urban Designers and Environmental Planners (EA)
**Maude & P Mer Shipp** ... Maude and Pollock's Law of Merchant Shipping [*A publication*] (DLA)
**Maude & P Shipp** ... Maude and Pollock's Law of Merchant Shipping [*A publication*] (DLA)
**Maud Ment Res** ... Maudsley on Mental Responsibility [*A publication*] (DLA)
**M Au E**...... Master of Automobile Engineering
**M Au Eng**.. Master of Automobile Engineering
**MAUF**....... Multiattribute Utility Function
**MAUFS**...... Municipal Arborists and Urban Foresters Society (EA)
**MAUG**....... MicroNet Apple User's Group [*CompuServe*] [*Database*]
**Maug Att** ... Maugham's Attorneys, Solicitors, and Agents [*1825*] [*A publication*] (DLA)
**Maug Att** ... Maugham's Statutes Relating to Attorneys, Etc. [*1839*] [*A publication*] (DLA)
**Maug Cr L** ... Maugham's Outlines of Criminal Law [*2nd ed.*] [*1842*] [*A publication*] (DLA)
**Maugh Lit Pr** ... Maugham's Literary Property [*1828*] [*A publication*] (DLA)
**Maugh RP** ... Maugham's Outlines of Real Property Law [*1842*] [*A publication*] (DLA)
**Maug Jur** ... Maugham's Outlines of the Jurisdiction [*1838*] [*A publication*] (DLA)
**Maug Law** ... Maugham's Outlines of Law [*1837*] [*A publication*] (DLA)
**MAUI**........ Maui Land & Pineapple Co., Inc. [*NASDAQ symbol*] (NQ)
**Maule & S** ... Maule and Selwyn's English King's Bench Reports [*A publication*] (DLA)
**MAULEX** ... Marine Amphibious Unit Landing Exercise (NVT)
**Maul & Sel** ... Maule and Selwyn's English King's Bench Reports [*A publication*] (DLA)
**MAULT** .... Manual or Automatic Ultrasonic Laboratory Test
**MAUOA**.... Music. American Guild of Organists [*A publication*]
**Mau & Pol Sh** ... Maude and Pollock's Law of Merchant Shipping [*A publication*] (DLA)
**Maur**.......... Mauretania [*A publication*]
**Maur**.......... Mauritania
**Maur**.......... Mauritius
**MA in Urb Pl** ... Master of Arts in Urban Planning
**Maur Dec**... Mauritius Decisions [*A publication*] (DLA)
**Maurit**........ Mauritania
**Mauritius Dep Agric Annu Rep** ... Mauritius. Department of Agriculture. Annual Report [*A publication*]
**Mauritius Dep Agric Bull** ... Mauritius. Department of Agriculture. Bulletin [*A publication*]
**Mauritius Inst Bull** ... Mauritius Institute. Bulletin [*A publication*]
**Mauritius Ministr Agric Nat Resour Annu Rep** ... Mauritius. Ministry of Agriculture and Natural Resources. Annual Report [*A publication*]
**Mauritius Sugar Cane Res Stn Annu Rep** ... Mauritius. Sugar Cane Research Station. Annual Report [*A publication*]
**Mauritius Sugar Ind Res Inst Annu Rep** ... Mauritius Sugar Industry Research Institute. Annual Report [*A publication*]
**Mauritius Sugar Ind Res Inst Bull** ... Mauritius Sugar Industry Research Institute. Bulletins [*A publication*]
**Mauritius Sugar Ind Res Inst Leafl** ... Mauritius Sugar Industry Research Institute. Leaflet [*A publication*]
**Mauritius Sugar Ind Res Inst Occas Pap** ... Mauritius Sugar Industry Research Institute. Occasional Paper [*A publication*]
**Mauritius Sugar Ind Res Inst Tech Circ** ... Mauritius Sugar Industry Research Institute. Technical Circular [*A publication*]
**MAUS**....... Mauser Rifle
**MAUS**....... Movimiento de Accion y Unidad Socialista [*Socialist Movement for Action and Unity*] [*Mexico*] [*Political party*] (PPW)
**MAUSB**..... Metals Australia [*Later, Metals Australasia*] [*A publication*]
**MAUSED** ... Midwest Association of University Student Employment Directors [*Later, MASEA*] (EA)
**Mau & Sel** ... Maule and Selwyn's English King's Bench Reports [*A publication*] (DLA)
**M Aus IMM** ... Member of the Australian Institute of Mining and Metallurgy
**MAUSS**...... Mouvement Anti-Utilitariste dans les Sciences Sociales [*Paris, France*] (EAIO)
**M Aust IM** ... Member of the Australian Institute of Mining and Metallurgy
**MAUTEL** ... Microminiaturized Autonetics Telemetry
**MauU**........ University of Mauritius, Reduit, Mauritius [*Library symbol*] [*Library of Congress*] (LCLS)
**MAUW**...... Modified Advanced Underwater Weapons (MCD)
**MAV**.......... Air Chaparral [*Reno, NV*] [*FAA designator*] (FAAC)
**MAV**.......... Macrosiphum avenae Virus
**MAV**.......... Madison Avenue [*A publication*]
**MAV**.......... Magyar Allamvasutak [*Hungarian State Railways*]
**MAV**.......... Maintenance Assistance Vehicle (MCD)
**MAV**.......... Maloelap [*Marshall Islands*] [*Airport symbol*] (OAG)
**MAV**.......... Manpower Authorization Voucher
**MAV**.......... Mars Ascent Vehicle [*NASA*]
**MAV**.......... Massive Resources Ltd. [*Vancouver Stock Exchange symbol*]
**MAV**.......... Maximum Allowable Variation [*Net weight labeling*]
**MAV**.......... Mean Absolute Value [*Statistics*]
**MAV**.......... MeCCNU [*Semustine*], Adriamycin, Vincristine [*Antineoplastic drug regimen*]
**MAV**.......... Military Aerospace Vehicle
**mA/V**......... Milliamperes per Volt (DEN)
**MAV**.......... Minimum Acceptable Value (MCD)
**MAV**.......... Motor Ambulance Van [*British*]
**MAV**.......... Myeloblastosis-Associated Virus
**MAVA**....... Moored Acoustic Vertical Array
**MAVAR**.... Modulating Amplifier Using Variable Resistance
**MAVCC**.... Mid-America Vocational Curriculum Consortium (OICC)
**MAVERICK** ... Manufacturers Assistance in Verifying, Identification in Cataloging
**MAVES**..... Manned Mars and Venus Exploration Studies
**MAVI**........ Microwave Automatic Vehicle Identification (MCD)
**MAVICA**... Magnetic Video Camera [*Sony Corp.*]
**MAVIN**..... Machine-Assisted Vendor Information Network
**MAVIN**..... Multiple Angle, Variable Interval, Nonorthogonal [*Magnetic resonance imaging*]
**MAVIS**...... McDonnell Douglas Automated Voice Information System (MCD)
**MAVIS**...... Mobile Armored Vehicle Indigo System [*Radio-controlled tank*]
**MAVPE**..... Metal Alkyl Vapor-Phase Epitaxy [*Semiconductor technology*]
**MAVR**....... Maverick Restaurant Corp. [*NASDAQ symbol*] (NQ)
**MAVS**....... Manned Aerial Vehicle for Surveillance (MCD)
**MAVWC**... Military Aircraft Voice Weather Code (NATG)
**MAW**......... Malden, MO [*Location identifier*] [*FAA*] (FAAL)
**MAW**......... Marine Air Wing
**MAW**......... Mawson [*Antarctica*] [*Seismograph station code, US Geological Survey*] (SEIS)
**MAW**......... Mawson [*Antarctica*] [*Geomagnetic observatory code*]
**MAW**......... Maximum Allowable Weight [*Military*] (INF)
**MAW**......... Mechanically Aimed Warhead
**MAW**......... Mededeelingen. Akademie van Wetenschappen [*A publication*]
**MAW**......... Medium Antiarmor Weapon (INF)
**MAW**......... Medium Antitank Weapon
**MAW**......... Medium Assault Weapon
**MAW**......... Military Airlift Wing [*Air Force*] (MCD)
**MAW**......... Minor Assist Work
**MAW**......... Mission Adaptive Wing (MCD)
**M & AW**.... Mountain and Arctic Warfare [*British military*] (DMA)
**MAW**......... Mythologies in the Ancient World [*A publication*]
**MAWB**....... Master Air Waybill [*Shipping*] (DS)
**MAWC**...... Marine Air West Coast
**MAWCS**..... Mobile Air Weapons Control System [*ESD*]
**MAWD**...... Mars Atmospheric Water Detection [*NASA*]
**MA/WD**.... Material Annex/Weapons Dictionary [*Military*]
**Mawdsley Mem** ... Mawdsley Memoirs [*A publication*]
**MAWEC** ... Maritime Aircraft Weather Code (NATG)
**MAWF**...... Movement Against War and Fascism [*Australia*]
**MAW & F** ... Movement Against War and Fascism [*Australia*]
**MAWg**....... Military Airlift Wing [*Air Force*] (AFM)
**MAWIA**..... Mexican American Workers Importation Act
**MAWL**..... Magnetic Aircraft Weapons Link
**MAWLOGS** ... Models of the [*US*] Army Worldwide Logistics System (AABC)
**MAWP**...... Marine Air Wing Pacific
**MAWS**...... Marine Air Warning Squadron
**MAWS**...... Modular Automated Weather System
**MAWTS**.... Marine Aviation Weapons and Tactics Squadron

**MAWTU**... Marine Air Weapons Training Unit (MCD)
**MAWU**...... Montserrat Allied Workers' Union (EY)
**MAX**.......... Madrid, Spain [*Spaceflight Tracking and Data Network*] [*NASA*]
**MAX**.......... Magic Answer Extractor [*Database*]
**max**............ Manx [*MARC language code*] [*Library of Congress*] (LCCP)
**MAX**.......... Maschinenmarkt [*A publication*]
**MAX**.......... Matam [*Senegal*] [*Airport symbol*] (OAG)
**MAX**.......... Maxilla [*Jawbone*]
**MAX**.......... Maxim (ROG)
**MAX**.......... Maximilian Numismatic and Historical Society (EA)
**Max**............ Maximinus [*of Scriptores Historiae Augustae*] [*Classical studies*] (OCD)
**MAX**.......... Maximum
**MAX**.......... Mercury Air Group [*AMEX symbol*] (SPSG)
**MAX**.......... Metropolitan Area Express [*Railway*] [*Portland, OR*] (ECON)
**MAX**.......... Minerex Resources Ltd. [*Vancouver Stock Exchange symbol*] [*Toronto Stock Exchange symbol*]
**MAX**.......... Modular Applications Executive [*Modular Computer Systems*]
**MAXC**....... Maxco, Inc. [*NASDAQ symbol*] (NQ)
**MAXCO**.... Maximum Dynamic Pressure (NASA)
**MAXCOM**... Modular Applications Executive for Communications [*Modular Computer Systems*]
**Max Dig**..... Maxwell's Nebraska Digest [*A publication*] (DLA)
**MAXE**....... Max & Erma's Restaurants, Inc. [*NASDAQ symbol*] (NQ)
**MAXG**....... Maximum Girth [*Pisciculture*]
**MAXI**........ Maxicare Health Plans, Inc. [*NASDAQ symbol*] (NQ)
**MAXID**..... Maximize Indefinite Delivery Contracts (AFM)
**Max Int Stat**... Maxwell on the Interpretation of Statutes [*A publication*] (DLA)
**MAXIT**...... Maximum Interference Threshold [*Telecommunications*] (TEL)
**Max LD**..... Maxwell's Law Dictionary [*A publication*] (DLA)
**MAXM**...... MAXAM Technologies, Inc. [*Landover, MD*] [*NASDAQ symbol*] (NQ)
**MAXMAR**... Maximum Mobile Army
**Max Mar L**... Maxwell's Marine Law [*A publication*] (DLA)
**MAXNOR**... Maximum Number of Runs (MCD)
**MAXPAR**... Maximum Pain Relief [*Medicine*]
**MAXPAX**... Maxwell House Coffee Package [*Vendor-machine system for Maxwell House coffee*]
**MAXPEN**... Maximum Penalty
**MAXPID**... Maximum Pain Intensity Difference [*Medicine*]
**Max-Planck-Ges Ber Mitt**... Max-Planck-Gesellschaft. Berichte und Mitteilungen [*A publication*]
**Max Planck Ges Foerd Wiss Projektgruppe Laserforsch Ber PLF**... Max-Planck-Gesellschaft zur Foerderung der Wissenschaften. Projektgruppe fuer Laserforschung. Bericht PLF [*A publication*]
**Max-Planck-Ges Jahrb**... Max-Planck-Gesellschaft. Jahrbuch [*A publication*]
**Max Planck Inst Kernphys Rep MPI H**... Max-Planck-Institut fuer Kernphysik. Report MPI H [*A publication*]
**Max-Planck-Inst Plasmaphys Presseinf**... Max-Planck-Institut fuer Plasmaphysik. Presseinformation [*A publication*]
**MAXSECON**... Maximum Security Communications
**MAXTOP**... Maximum Total Duration Penalty
**MAXTTR**... Maximum Time to Repair [*Navy*] (CAAL)
**MAXTWK**... Maximum Total Work Content
**Max Von Pettenkofer Inst Ber**... Max-Von-Pettenkofer-Institut. Berichte [*A publication*]
**Maxw Adv Gram**... [*W. H.*] Maxwell's Advanced Lessons in English Grammar [*A publication*] (DLA)
**Maxw Cr Proc**... Maxwell's Treatise on Criminal Procedure [*A publication*] (DLA)
**Maxwell**..... Irish Land Purchase Cases [*1904-11*] [*A publication*] (DLA)
**Maxwell**..... Maxwell on the Interpretation of Statutes [*A publication*] (DLA)
**Maxwell R**... Maxwell Review [*A publication*]
**Maxw Interp St**... Maxwell on the Interpretation of Statutes [*A publication*] (DLA)
**may**............ Malay [*MARC language code*] [*Library of Congress*] (LCCP)
**MAY**.......... Malye Karmakuly [*USSR*] [*Geomagnetic observatory code*]
**MAY**.......... Mangrove Cay [*Bahamas*] [*Airport symbol*] (OAG)
**MAY**.......... May Department Stores Co., Corporate Information Center, St. Louis, MO [*OCLC symbol*] (OCLC)
**MAY**.......... Mayfield [*Washington*] [*Seismograph station code, US Geological Survey*] [*Closed*] (SEIS)
**MAY**.......... Maynard Energy, Inc. [*Toronto Stock Exchange symbol*]
**May**............ [*Guillelmus*] Maynardi [*Authority cited in pre-1607 legal work*] (DSA)
**MAY**.......... Mayor (ROG)
**MAYA**....... Most Advanced, Yet Acceptable [*Industrial design*]
**May Act**..... Mayhew's Action at Law [*1828*] [*A publication*] (DLA)
**May Const Hist**... May's Constitutional History of England [*A publication*] (DLA)
**May Crim Law**... May's Criminal Law [*A publication*] (DLA)
**May Dam**... Mayne on the Law of Damages [*A publication*] (DLA)
**MAYF**........ Mayfair Industries, Inc. [*New York, NY*] [*NASDAQ symbol*] (NQ)
**May Fr Conv**... May's Fraudulent Conveyances [*3rd ed.*] [*1908*] [*A publication*] (DLA)
**May Ins**...... May on Insurance [*A publication*] (DLA)
**May Just**..... Mayo's Justice [*A publication*] (DLA)
**May LR**..... Mayurbhani Law Report [*India*] [*A publication*] (DLA)
**MAYM**...... Maymac Petroleum Corp. [*NASDAQ symbol*] (NQ)
**May Merg**... Mayhew on Merger [*1861*] [*A publication*] (DLA)
**Mayn**.......... Maynard's English Reports, Exchequer Memoranda of Edward I, and Year Books of Edward II [*A publication*] (DLA)
**Mayo Clin P**... Mayo Clinic. Proceedings [*A publication*]
**Mayo Clin Proc**... Mayo Clinic. Proceedings [*A publication*]
**Mayo Just**... Mayo's Justice [*A publication*] (DLA)
**Mayo & Moul**... Mayo and Moulton's Pension Laws [*A publication*] (DLA)
**May Parl**.... May's Parliamentary Practice [*A publication*] (ILCA)
**May Parl Law**... May's Parliamentary Law [*A publication*] (DLA)
**May Parl Pr**... May's Parliamentary Practice [*A publication*] (DLA)
**May PL**...... May's Parliamentary Practice [*A publication*] (DLA)
**MAYPOLE**... May Polarization Experiment [*RADAR storm sensing*]
**M & Ayr**..... Montagu and Ayrton's English Bankruptcy Reports [*1833-38*] [*A publication*] (DLA)
**MAYS**........ Mays [*J. W.*], Inc. [*Brooklyn, NY*] [*NASDAQ symbol*] (NQ)
**MAYW**...... Maywood & Sugar Creek [*AAR code*]
**MAZ**.......... Manager's Magazine [*A publication*]
**MAZ**.......... Mayaguez [*Puerto Rico*] [*Airport symbol*] (OAG)
**MAZ**.......... Mazatlan [*Mexico*] [*Seismograph station code, US Geological Survey*] (SEIS)
**Maz**............ Mazungumzo [*A publication*]
**MAZ**.......... Mazzite [*A zeolite*]
**MAZ**.......... Missed Approach Azimuth [*Aviation*]
**MAZ**.......... Mounting Azimuth [*Weaponry*] (INF)
**MAZ**.......... Personal. Mensch und Arbeit in Betrieb [*A publication*]
**MAZH**....... Missile Azimuth Heading [*Air Force*]
**MAZOAT**... Marine Zoologist [*A publication*]
**MB**............ All India Reporter, Madhya Bharat [*1950-57*] [*A publication*] (DLA)
**MB**............ Bachelor of Medicine [*Other than from Oxford*]
**mb-----**........ Black Sea and Area [*MARC geographic area code*] [*Library of Congress*] (LCCP)
**MB**............ Boston Public Library and Eastern Massachusetts Regional Public Library System, Boston, MA [*Library symbol*] [*Library of Congress*] (LCLS)
**MB**............ Maandblad voor het Boekhouden [*A publication*]
**MB**............ Machine Bolt [*Technical drawings*]
**MB**............ MacMillan Bloedel Ltd. [*Toronto Stock Exchange symbol*] [*Vancouver Stock Exchange symbol*]
**MB**............ Magazine of Building [*A publication*]
**MB**............ Magnetic Bearing [*Navigation*]
**MB**............ Magnetic Brake [*Industrial control*] (IEEE)
**MB**............ Mailbox (AAG)
**MB**............ Main Ballast
**MB**............ Main Base [*Air Force*] (AFM)
**MB**............ Main Battery [*Guns*]
**MB**............ Main Bus (MCD)
**MB**............ Maintenance Busy [*Telecommunications*] (TEL)
**M-B**............ Make-Break
**MB**............ Maldives International Airlines [*ICAO designator*] (FAAC)
**MB**............ Mallory Body [*Medicine*]
**MB**............ Management Baseline (NASA)
**MB**............ Manitoba [*Canadian province*] [*Postal code*]
**MB**............ March-Bender Factor [*Physiology*]
**MB**............ Mare Balticum [*A publication*]
**MB**............ Marine Barracks
**MB**............ Marine Base
**MB**............ Marine Board (EA)
**MB**............ Mark of the Beast [*Disparaging term for clerical waistcoats. So called because, when first worn by Protestant clergymen about 1830, they were said to indicate a Roman Catholic tendency*]
**MB**............ Marker Beacon [*Aviation*] (FAAC)
**MB**............ Marks Banco (ROG)
**MB**............ Marsh-Bender [*Factor*] [*Muscle tissue*]
**MB**............ Mass Balance
**M & B**........ Matched and Beaded
**MB**............ Material Balance
**MB**............ May & Baker Ltd. [*Great Britain*] [*Research code symbol*]
**MB**............ MBB-UV, MBB-UD [*Messerschmitt-Boelkow-Blohm*], und Pneuma-Technik [*Federal Republic of Germany*] [*ICAO aircraft manufacturer identifier*] (ICAO)
**MB**............ Mechanized Battalion [*Army*]
**MB**............ Medal of Bravery
**MB**............ Mediaevalia Bohemica [*A publication*]
**MB**............ Medial Bilateral (Neuron) [*Neuroanatomy*]
**MB**............ Median Bundle [*Botany*]
**MB**............ Medical Board
**MB**............ Medical Bulletin
**MB**............ Medicare Bureau [*Health Care Financing Administration - Social Security Administration*] (OICC)
**MB**............ Medicinae Baccalaureus [*Bachelor of Medicine*] [*Latin*]
**MB**............ Medium Bomber
**MB**............ Medium Bronze [*Numismatics*]
**MB**............ Megabar
**Mb**............ Megabase [*A unit of molecular size*]
**MB**............ MegaBIT [*Binary Digit*] [*Data processing*]

**MB** ........ Megabuck [*Defense industry colloquialism for one million dollars*] (AAG)
**Mb** ........ Megabyte [*Data storage capacity*] [*Data processing*]
**MB** ........ Melanges Baldensperger [*A publication*]
**MB** ........ Melbourne Bitter [*Brand of beer*] [*Initialism used by Australians as slang for "inebriated"*]
**MB** ........ Melt Back
**MB** ........ Memorandum Book (ROG)
**MB** ........ Memory Buffer [*Data processing*]
**MB** ........ Memory Bus
**MB** ........ Mercedes-Benz [*Automobile*]
**MB** ........ Merchant Bank
**MB** ........ Meridian & Bigbee Railroad Co. [*Later, MBRR*] [*AAR code*]
**MB** ........ Mesiobuccal [*Dentistry*]
**MB** ........ Message Business
**MB** ........ Messages of the Bible [*A publication*]
**MB** ........ Metabisulfite [*Inorganic chemistry*]
**MB** ........ Metal Box [*Commercial firm*] [*British*]
**MB** ........ Methyl Bromide [*Organic chemistry*]
**MB** ........ Methylene Blue [*Organic chemistry*]
**MB** ........ Metric Board (OICC)
**MB** ........ Metrication Board [*British*]
**MB** ........ Microbody
**MB** ........ Microelectronics Bibliography [*A publication*]
**MB** ........ Midbody
**MB** ........ Middle Babylonian [*Language, etc.*] (BJA)
**MB** ........ Middle of Bow [*Music*] (ROG)
**MB** ........ Middle Bronze Age (BJA)
**M & B** ........ Mild and Bitter [*Beer*]
**MB** ........ Militia Bureau [*Superseded in 1933 by National Guard Bureau*]
**mb** ........ Millibar [*Unit of pressure*]
**mb** ........ Millibarn [*Area of nuclear cross-section*]
**mb** ........ Millibyte [*Data processing*]
**MB** ........ Million Bytes [*Data processing*] (BUR)
**MB** ........ Milton Bradley Ltd. [*British*]
**MB** ........ Minimum Bid [*Philately*]
**MB** ........ Misce Bene [*Mix Well*] [*Pharmacy*]
**MB** ........ Miscellaneous Branch, Internal Revenue Bureau [*United States*] (DLA)
**MB** ........ Missile Body
**MB** ........ Missile Bomber
**MB** ........ Mission Bulletin [*A publication*]
**MB** ........ Mitteilungsblatt. Irgun Olej Merkas Europa [*Tel-Aviv*] [*A publication*]
**MB** ........ Mixed Bed [*Nuclear energy*] (NRCH)
**MB** ........ Mobile Base (DEN)
**MB** ........ Model Block (MSA)
**MB** ........ Module Balance [*Data processing*]
**MB** ........ Mohelbuch (BJA)
**MB** ........ Moisture Balance
**MB** ........ Molecular Biosystems, Inc. [*NYSE symbol*] (SPSG)
**MB** ........ Molybdenum [*Chemical element*] (ROG)
**m/b** ........ Mon Billet [*My Bill*] [*French*]
**M & B** ........ Montagu and Bligh's English Bankruptcy Reports [*1832-33*] [*A publication*] (DLA)
**MB** ........ Monthly Breakdown [*Used in atmospheric studies*]
**MB** ........ Monthly Bulletin of Decisions of the High Court of Uganda [*A publication*] (DLA)
**MB** ........ Montpelier & Barre Railroad Co. [*AAR code*]
**MB** ........ Mooring Buoy
**MB** ........ Morale Branch [*Military*]
**MB** ........ More Books [*A publication*]
**MB** ........ Morrell's English Bankruptcy Reports [*A publication*] (DLA)
**MB** ........ Mortar Board (EA)
**MB** ........ Motor Barge (ADA)
**MB** ........ Motor Boat
**MB** ........ Mountain Battery [*British military*] (DMA)
**MB** ........ Multiband (DEN)
**MB** ........ Municipal Bond
**MB** ........ Municipal Borough
**MB** ........ Munitions Board [*Abolished 1953, functions transferred to Department of Defense*]
**MB** ........ Musee Belge [*A publication*]
**MB** ........ Museum of Broadcasting
**MB** ........ Music for the Blind [*Defunct*] (EA)
**MB** ........ Musicae Baccalaureus [*Bachelor of Music*]
**MB** ........ Must Be [*Sold*] [*Classified advertising*]
**MB** ........ Myocardial Band [*Cardiology*]
**Mb** ........ Myoglobin [*Biochemistry, medicine*]
**MBA** ........ American Academy of Arts and Sciences, Boston, MA [*Library symbol*] [*Library of Congress*] (LCLS)
**MBA** ........ Europees Parlement. EP Nieuws [*A publication*]
**MBA** ........ Main Battle Area (AABC)
**MBA** ........ Make-or-Buy Authorization (AAG)
**MBA** ........ Makers of British Art [*A publication*]
**MBA** ........ Manufactured Buildings Association [*Inactive*] (EA)
**MBA** ........ Marching Bands of America (EA)
**MBA** ........ Marine Biological Association [*British*]
**MBA** ........ Master of the British Arts Association (DBQ)
**MBA** ........ Master of Business Administration
**MBA** ........ Material Balance Area [*Nuclear energy*]
**MBA** ........ Maximum Benefit Amount [*Unemployment insurance*]
**MBA** ........ MBA/Masters in Business Administration [*A publication*]
**MBA** ........ Merion Bluegrass Association (EA)
**MBA** ........ Methyl Benzyl Alcohol [*Organic chemistry*]
**MBA** ........ Methylbis(beta-chloroethyl)amine [*Nitrogen mustard*] [*Also, HN, NM*] [*Antineoplastic; war-gas base*]
**MBA** ........ Methylenebisacrylamide [*Organic chemistry*]
**MBA** ........ Microbiological Associates, Inc.
**MBA** ........ Migratory Bird Act
**MBA** ........ Military Base Agreement (CINC)
**MBA** ........ Military Benefit Association (EA)
**MBa** ........ Miniature Ball [*Horticulture*]
**MBA** ........ Minimum Burst Altitude (AABC)
**MBA** ........ Minor Basic Allergens [*Immunology*]
**MBA** ........ Mombasa [*Kenya*] [*Airport symbol*] (OAG)
**MBA** ........ Monument Builders of America [*Later, MBNA*]
**MBA** ........ Mortar Box Assembly
**MBA** ........ Mortgage Bankers Association of America [*Washington, DC*] (EA)
**MBA** ........ Motorized Bicycle Association [*Later, MAA*] (EA)
**MBA** ........ Mount Bingar [*Australia*] [*Seismograph station code, US Geological Survey*] [*Closed*] (SEIS)
**MBA** ........ Multibeam Antenna
**MBA** ........ Rural Municipality of Argyle Public Library, Baldur, Manitoba [*Library symbol*] [*National Library of Canada*] (NLC)
**MBAA** ........ Master Brewers Association of the Americas (EA)
**MBAA** ........ Messinian Benevolent Association "Aristomenis" (EA)
**MBAA** ........ Mini Bike Association of America (EA)
**MBAA** ........ Motel Brokers Association of America [*Later, AHMB*] (EA)
**MBAAS** ........ Master of Business Administration in Actuarial Science
**MBab** ........ Middle Babylonian [*Language, etc.*] (BJA)
**MBABS** ........ Synod Office, Diocese of Brandon, Anglican Church of Canada, Manitoba [*Library symbol*] [*National Library of Canada*] (NLC)
**MBAC** ........ Assiniboine Community College, Brandon, Manitoba [*Library symbol*] [*National Library of Canada*] (NLC)
**MBAC** ........ Marshall Booster Assembly Contractor (MCD)
**MBAC** ........ Member of the British Association of Chemists (DAS)
**MBACFM** ... American Board of Commissioners for Foreign Missions, Boston, MA [*Library symbol*] [*Library of Congress*] (LCLS)
**M-BACOD** ... Methotrexate (High-Dose) (with Citrovorum Factor Rescue), Bleomycin, Adriamycin, Cyclophosphamide, Oncovin [*Vincristine*], Dexamethasone [*Antineoplastic drug regimen*]
**M-BACOP** ... Myelosuppressive Bleomycin, Adriamycin, Cyclophosphamide, Oncovin [*Vincristine*], Prednisone [*Antineoplastic drug regimen*]
**MBAD** ........ Medical Badge
**MB Adm** ........ Master of Business Administration
**MBAG** ........ Modulated Bayard-Alpert Gauge
**MBAG** ........ Research Station, Agriculture Canada [*Station de Recherches, Agriculture Canada*] Brandon, Manitoba [*Library symbol*] [*National Library of Canada*] (NLC)
**MBAI** ........ Mosquito Biting Activity Index [*Canada*]
**MBAJ** ........ Magna Bibliotheca Anglo-Judaica (BJA)
**MBAK** ........ Merchants Savings Bank [*NASDAQ symbol*] (NQ)
**MBAM** ........ Main Beam Avoidance Maneuver
**MBAMT** ... Methyl(benzylideneamino)mercaptotriazole [*Reagent*]
**MBAN** ........ Metalbanc Corp. [*Miami, FL*] [*NASDAQ symbol*] (NQ)
**MBANA** ... Methods of Biochemical Analysis [*A publication*]
**M Bank Admin** ... Magazine of Bank Administration [*A publication*]
**mbar** ........ Millibar [*Unit of pressure*]
**MBAS** ........ Methylene Blue Active Substance [*Organic chemistry*]
**MBAS** ........ Mutual Benefit and Aid Society [*Later, WBF*] (EA)
**MBAS (Calcutta)** ... Monthly Bulletin. Asiatic Society (Calcutta) [*A publication*]
**MBASW** ........ Member of the British Association of Social Workers
**MBAt** ........ Boston Athenaeum, Boston, MA [*Library symbol*] [*Library of Congress*] (LCLS)
**MBAUK** ........ Marine Biological Association of the United Kingdom (ARC)
**MBAV** ........ Master Builders Association of Victoria [*Australia*]
**MBAWS** ........ Marine Base Air Warning System
**MBB** ........ Brandeis University, Waltham, MA [*OCLC symbol*] (OCLC)
**MBB** ........ Deutsche Bundesbank. Monatsberichte mit Statistischen Beiheften [*A publication*]
**MBB** ........ Make-before-Break
**MBB** ........ Marble Bar [*Australia*] [*Airport symbol*] (OAG)
**MBB** ........ Maurer, B. B., Chicago IL [*STAC*]
**MBB** ........ Messerschmitt-Boelkow-Blohm GmbH [*West German aircraft company*]
**MBB** ........ Miniature Brushless Blower
**MBB** ........ Mortgage-Backed Bonds
**MBBA** ........ Boston Bar Association, Boston, MA [*Library symbol*] [*Library of Congress*] (LCLS)
**MBBA** ........ (Methozybenzylidene)butylaniline [*Organic chemistry*]
**MBBA** ........ Military Benefit Base Amounts
**MbBAW** ........ Monatsbericht. Berliner Akademie der Wissenschaft [*A publication*]
**MBBI** ........ Babson College, Babson Park, MA [*Library symbol*] [*Library of Congress*] (LCLS)

**MBBL**........ Massachusetts Bureau of Library Extension, Boston, MA [*Library symbol*] [*Library of Congress*] (LCLS)
**MBBLS**..... Thousands of Barrels (MCD)
**MBbM**....... Massachusetts Maritime Academy, Buzzards Bay, MA [*Library symbol*] [*Library of Congress*] (LCLS)
**MBBR**........ Brokenhead River Regional Library, Beausejour, Manitoba [*Library symbol*] [*National Library of Canada*] (NLC)
**MBBS**........ Bostonian Society, Boston, MA [*Library symbol*] [*Library of Congress*] (LCLS)
**MBBSC**..... Bachelor of Medicine and Bachelor of Science [*British*] (ROG)
**MBBull**...... Bulletin Bibliographique. Musee Belge [*A publication*]
**MBB WF-Inf**... MBB [*Messerschmitt-Boelkow-Blohm*] WF-Information [*German Federal Republic*] [*A publication*]
**MBC**.......... American Congregational Association, Boston, MA [*Library symbol*] [*Library of Congress*] (LCLS)
**MBC**.......... Brandon University, Manitoba [*Library symbol*] [*National Library of Canada*] (NLC)
**MBC**.......... Mailbox Club [*Later, MCI*] (EA)
**MBC**.......... Main Beam Clutter
**MBC**.......... Malwa Bhil Corps [*British military*] (DMA)
**MBC**.......... Manhattan Bible College [*Kansas*]
**MBC**.......... Manhattan Bowery Corporation (EA)
**mbc**............ Manitoba [*MARC country of publication code*] [*Library of Congress*] (LCCP)
**MBC**.......... Manual Battery Control (AAG)
**MBC**.......... Marine Biomedical Center [*Duke University*] [*Research center*] (RCD)
**MBC**.......... Mary Baldwin College [*Virginia*]
**MBC**.......... Master of Beauty Culture
**MBC**.......... Master Bus Controller [*Data processing*]
**MBC**.......... Maximum Breathing Capacity
**MBC**.......... M'Bigou [*Gabon*] [*Airport symbol*] (OAG)
**MBC**.......... McLaughlin-Buick Club of Canada (EAIO)
**MBC**.......... Mediterranean Bombardment Code
**MBC**.......... Megabar Diamond Cell [*For high-pressure measurements*]
**MBC**.......... Memory Bus Controller
**MBC**.......... Mercantile Bank of Canada [*Toronto Stock Exchange symbol*] [*Vancouver Stock Exchange symbol*]
**MBC**.......... Metastatic Breast Cancer [*Medicine*]
**MBC**.......... Meteor Burst Communications [*Military*]
**MBC**.......... Methyl Benzimidazolecarbamate [*Organic chemistry*]
**MBC**.......... Metropolitan Borough Council [*British*]
**MBC**.......... Mewar Bhil Corps [*British military*] (DMA)
**MBC**.......... Mickelberry Corporation [*NYSE symbol*] (SPSG)
**MBC**.......... Military Budget Committee [*NATO*] (NATG)
**MBC**.......... Miniature Bayonet Cap
**MBC**.......... Miniaturized Ballistic Computer
**MBC**.......... Minimum Bactericidal Concentration
**MBC**.......... Minnesota Bible College [*Rochester*]
**MBC**.......... Modified Brequet Cruise [*SST*]
**MBC**.......... Monkees Buttonmania Club (EA)
**MBC**.......... Mononuclear Blood Cell [*Hematology*]
**MBC**.......... Morris Brown College [*Atlanta, GA*]
**MBC**.......... Morris Brown College, Atlanta, GA [*OCLC symbol*] (OCLC)
**MBC**.......... Mortar Ballistic Computer [*Formerly, MFCC*] [*Army*] (INF)
**MBC**.......... Mother and Baby Care [*Red Cross Nursing Services*]
**MBC**.......... Motorboat Crew [*British military*] (DMA)
**MBC**.......... Mould Bay [*Northwest Territories*] [*Seismograph station code, US Geological Survey*] (SEIS)
**MBC**.......... Mould Bay [*Northwest Territories*] [*Geomagnetic observatory code*]
**MBC**.......... Multiple Basic Channel
**MBC**.......... Multiple Burst Correcting
**MBCA**....... Archives, Brandon University, Manitoba [*Library symbol*] [*National Library of Canada*] (BIB)
**MBCA**....... Mechanical Bank Collectors of America (EA)
**MBCA**....... Mercedes-Benz Club of America (EA)
**MBCA**....... Merchant Bank of Central Africa Ltd.
**MBCA**....... Munitions Board Cataloging Agency
**MBCAM**... Commonwealth Air Training Plan Museum, Inc., Brandon, Manitoba [*Library symbol*] [*National Library of Canada*] (NLC)
**MBCC**....... Mail Boxes Coast to Coast, Inc. [*NASDAQ symbol*] (NQ)
**MBCC**....... Massachusetts Bay Community College [*Wellesley*]
**MBCC**....... McLaughlin-Buick Club of Canada (EA)
**MBCC**....... Migratory Bird Conservation Commission [*A federal government body*]
**MBCD**....... Modified Binary-Coded Decimal
**MBCG**....... Department of Geography, Brandon University, Manitoba [*Library symbol*] [*National Library of Canada*] (NLC)
**MBCHA**.... Master Builders, Construction, and Housing Association [*Australia*]
**MB-CHAA**... Master Builders, Construction, and Housing Association of Australia
**MBCK**....... Mallory Body Cytokeratin [*Medicine*]
**MBCM**...... Baccalaureus Medicinae, Chirurgiae Magister [*Bachelor of Medicine, Master of Surgery*]
**MBCM**...... New England Conservatory of Music, Boston, MA [*Library symbol*] [*Library of Congress*] (LCLS)
**MBCMA**... Metal Building Component Manufacturers' Association (EA)
**MBCMC**.... Milk Bottle Crate Manufacturers Council [*Defunct*] (EA)
**MBCo**........ Countway Library of Medicine, Boston, MA [*Library symbol*] [*Library of Congress*] (LCLS)
**MBCO**....... Member of the British College of Ophthalmic Opticians [*British*] (DBQ)
**MbCO**........ Myoglobin, Carboxy [*Biochemistry, medicine*]
**MBCS**........ Medium Bandwidth Compression System
**MBCS**........ Member of the British Computer Society (DCTA)
**MBCS**........ Meteor Burst Communication System
**MBCS**........ Motion Base Crew Station [*NASA*] (NASA)
**MBd**........... Bedford Free Public Library, Bedford, MA [*Library symbol*] [*Library of Congress*] (LCLS)
**MBD**.......... Episcopal Diocese of Massachusetts, Boston, MA [*Library symbol*] [*Library of Congress*] (LCLS)
**MBD**.......... Macroblock Design
**MBD**.......... Magnetic-Bubble Domain Device [*Data processing*] (IEEE)
**MBD**.......... Manual Burst Disable (AABC)
**MBD**.......... Marching Band Director [*A publication*]
**MBD**.......... Materials-by-Design [*Chemical engineering*]
**MBD**.......... Meander Belt Deposit [*Geology*]
**MBD**.......... Methotrexate, Bleomycin, Diamminedichloroplatinum [*Cisplatin*] [*Antineoplastic drug regimen*]
**MBD**.......... Methoxybenzylaminonitrobenzoxadiazole [*Fluorescent probe*] [*Biochemistry*]
**MBD**.......... Methylbutenedial [*Organic chemistry*]
**MBD**.......... Million Barrels Daily
**MBD**.......... Minimal Brain Damage [*or Dysfunction*]
**MBD**.......... Mission Baseline Description [*NASA*] (KSC)
**MBD**.......... Motor Belt Drive (MSA)
**MBDA**....... Metal Building Dealers Association [*Later, Systems Builders Association*] (EA)
**MBDA**....... Minority Business Development Agency [*Formerly, OMBE*] [*Department of Commerce*]
**MBDAACC**... Milling and Baking Division of American Association of Cereal Chemists (EA)
**MBdAF**...... United States Air Force, Cambridge Research Center, Bedford, MA [*Library symbol*] [*Library of Congress*] (LCLS)
**MBDC**....... Minority Business Development Center [*Minority Business Development Administration*]
**MBdD**........ Document Research Center, Bedford, MA [*Library symbol*] [*Library of Congress*] (LCLS)
**MBDET**..... Mobile Boarding Detachment [*Coast Guard*]
**MBDG**....... Marine Base Defense Group
**MBdgSc**..... Master of Building Science
**MBDio**....... Diocesan Library, Boston, MA [*Library symbol*] [*Library of Congress*] (LCLS)
**MBDL**....... Missile Battery Data Link (MCD)
**MBDL**....... Muenstersche Beitraege zur Deutschen Literatur [*A publication*]
**MBdM**....... Middlesex Community College, Bedford, MA [*Library symbol*] [*Library of Congress*] (LCLS)
**MBdMi**...... Mitre Corps., Bedford, MA [*Library symbol*] [*Library of Congress*] (LCLS)
**MBDP**....... Minority Bank Deposit Program [*Treasury Department*]
**MBDR**....... Make-or-Buy Data Record (KSC)
**MBdR**........ Raytheon Co., Missile Systems Division Library, Bedford, MA [*Library symbol*] [*Library of Congress*] (LCLS)
**MBDS**........ Modular Building Distribution System [*Telecommunications*] (TEL)
**MBdV**........ United States Veterans Administration Hospital, Bedford, MA [*Library symbol*] [*Library of Congress*] (LCLS)
**MBE**.......... Bethany Lutheran College, Mankato, MN [*OCLC symbol*] (OCLC)
**MBE**.......... Emerson College, Boston, MA [*Library symbol*] [*Library of Congress*] (LCLS)
**MBE**.......... Mail Boxes Etc. USA [*San Diego, CA*] [*Telecommunications*] (TSSD)
**MBE**.......... Management by Exception
**MBE**.......... Master of Business Economics
**MBE**.......... Master of Business Education
**MBE**.......... Member of the [*Order of the*] British Empire [*Facetious translation: "My Bloody Efforts"*]
**MBE**.......... Mennonite Board of Education (EA)
**MBE**.......... Minority Business Enterprise (MCD)
**MBE**.......... Missile-Borne Equipment
**MBE**.......... Molecular Beam Epitaxy [*Crystallography*]
**MBE**.......... Monbetsu [*Japan*] [*Airport symbol*] (OAG)
**MBE**.......... Monumenta Biblica et Ecclesiastica [*Rome*] [*A publication*] (BJA)
**MBE**.......... Moving Boundary Electrophoresis [*Analytical biochemistry*]
**MBE**.......... Multiple-Beam Experiment [*In MBE-4, a heavy-ion accelerator at the Lawrence Berkeley Laboratory*]
**MBE**.......... Multistate Bar Examination
**MBEA J**.... Mississippi Business Education Association. Journal [*A publication*]
**MBEA Today**... Michigan Business Education Association Today [*A publication*]
**MB Ed**....... Master of Business Education
**MBehaviouralSc**... Master of Behavioural Sciences (ADA)
**MBEI**......... Member of the Institute of Body Engineers [*British*] (DBQ)
**MBELDEF**... Minority Business Enterprise Legal Defense and Education Fund (EA)

**MBelm**....... Belmont Memorial Library, Belmont, MA [*Library symbol*] [*Library of Congress*] (LCLS)
**MBelmM**... McLean Hospital, Belmont, MA [*Library symbol*] [*Library of Congress*] (LCLS)
**M Bel R**...... Maandblad voor Belastingrecht [*A publication*]
**MBEmm**.... Emmanuel College, Boston, MA [*Library symbol*] [*Library of Congress*] (LCLS)
**MBENA**.... Medical and Biological Engineering [*Later, Medical and Biological Engineering and Computing*] [*A publication*]
**MBEnv**...... Master of the Built Environment (ADA)
**MBEPA**..... United States Environmental Protection Agency, Region I Library, Boston, MA [*Library symbol*] [*Library of Congress*] (LCLS)
**MBER**........ Member
**MBER**........ Molecular Beam Electric Resonance [*Physics*]
**M Berl Ges Anthrop**... Mitteilungen. Berliner Gesellschaft fuer Anthropologie, Ethnologie, und Urgeschichte [*A publication*]
**MBES**........ Member of the Bureau of Engineer Surveyors [*British*] (DBQ)
**MBES**........ Mezhdunarodnyi Bank Ekonomicheskovo Sotrudnichestva [*International Bank for Economic Co-Operation - IBEC*] [*Moscow, USSR*] (EAIO)
**MBev**......... Beverly Public Library, Beverly, MA [*Library symbol*] [*Library of Congress*] (LCLS)
**MBev-F**...... Beverly Farms Public Library, Beverly, MA [*Library symbol*] [*Library of Congress*] (LCLS)
**MBevHi**..... Beverly Historical Society, Beverly, MA [*Library symbol*] [*Library of Congress*] (LCLS)
**MBevN**...... North Shore Community College, Beverly, MA [*Library symbol*] [*Library of Congress*] (LCLS)
**MBevT**....... Beverly Times, Beverly, MA [*Library symbol*] [*Library of Congress*] (LCLS)
**MBF**.......... Main Boundary Fault [*Geophysics*]
**MBF**.......... Master Bibliographic File (ADA)
**MBF**.......... Materials Business File [*American Society for Metals, The Institute for Metals*] [*Information service or system*] (IID)
**MBF**.......... Military Banking Facility
**MBF**.......... Milk Bottlers Federation
**MBF**.......... Missile Beacon Filter
**MBF**.......... Molecular Beam Facility [*NASA*]
**MBF**.......... Myocardial Blood Flow [*Cardiology*]
**MBF**.......... Thousand Board Feet [*Lumber*]
**MBFA**........ Fellowes Athenaeum, Boston, MA [*Library symbol*] [*Library of Congress*] (LCLS)
**MBFC**........ Moe Bandy Fan Club (EA)
**MBFL**........ Mid-Bergen Federation of Public Libraries [*Library network*]
**MBFLD**..... Mitteilungsblatt. Bundesanstalt fuer Fleischforschung [*A publication*]
**MBFM**....... Massachusetts Grand Lodge, F & AM, Boston, MA [*Library symbol*] [*Library of Congress*] (LCLS)
**MBFo**........ Forsyth Dental Center, Boston, MA [*Library symbol*] [*Library of Congress*] (LCLS)
**MBFP**........ Manufacturing, Build, and Flow Plan (NASA)
**MBFR**........ Federal Reserve Bank of Boston, Boston, MA [*Library symbol*] [*Library of Congress*] (LCLS)
**MBFR**........ More Better for Russia [*Facetious translation of MBFR - Mutual and Balanced Force Reduction*]
**MBFR**........ Mutual and Balanced Force Reduction [*Proposed reduction of forces in central Europe by NATO and Warsaw Pact nations*]
**MBG**.......... Gardner Museum, Boston, MA [*Library symbol*] [*Library of Congress*] (LCLS)
**MBG**.......... Marburger Beitraege zur Germanistik [*A publication*]
**MBG**.......... Missouri Botanical Garden
**MBG**.......... Mobridge, SD [*Location identifier*] [*FAA*] (FAAL)
**MBGBA**.... Montana. Bureau of Mines and Geology. Bulletin [*A publication*]
**MBGE**....... Missile-Borne Guidance Equipment (AFM)
**MBGH**....... Library Services, Brandon General Hospital, Manitoba [*Library symbol*] [*National Library of Canada*] (NLC)
**MBG & H**.. Magna Brittannia, Gallia, et Hibernia [*Great Britain, France, and Ireland*] [*Latin*] (ROG)
**MBGi**......... Gillette Co., Boston R and D Laboratory, Boston, MA [*Library symbol*] [*Library of Congress*] (LCLS)
**MBGS**........ Missile-Borne Guidance Set (MCD)
**MBGSA**..... Montana. Bureau of Mines and Geology. Special Publication [*A publication*]
**MBGT**....... General Theological Library, Boston, MA [*Library symbol*] [*Library of Congress*] (LCLS)
**MBGT**....... Grand Turk [*Turks and Caicos Islands*] [*ICAO location identifier*] (ICLI)
**MBGTS**..... Missile-Borne Guidance Test Set (AABC)
**MBH**.......... Macquarie Broadcasting Holdings Ltd. [*Australia*]
**MBH**.......... Manual Bomb Hoist
**MBH**.......... Maryborough [*Australia*] [*Airport symbol*] (OAG)
**MBH**.......... Massachusetts Horticultural Society, Boston, MA [*Library symbol*] [*Library of Congress*] (LCLS)
**MBH**.......... Mediobasal Hypothalamus [*Brain anatomy*]
**MBH**.......... Minard, Bryant H., Pennsauken NJ [*STAC*]
**mbH**........... Mit Beschraenkter Haftung [*With Limited Liability*] [*German*]
**MBH**.......... Movimiento de Bases Hayistas [*Movement of Hayista Bases*] [*Peru*] [*Political party*] (PPW)
**MBH**.......... Thousands of BTU per Hour
**MBHA**....... Member of the British Hypnotherapy Association (DBQ)
**MBHC**....... Boissevain Health Centre, Manitoba [*Library symbol*] [*National Library of Canada*] (NLC)
**MBHE**....... Ministries to Blacks in Higher Education (EA)
**MBHH**...... Handel and Haydn Society, Boston, MA [*Library symbol*] [*Library of Congress*] (LCLS)
**MBHI**........ Member of the British Horological Institute (DBQ)
**MBHI**........ Millon Behavioral Health Inventory [*Personality development test*] [*Psychology*]
**MBHINST**... Member of the British Horological Institute (ROG)
**MBHM**...... Harvard Musical Association, Boston, MA [*Library symbol*] [*Library of Congress*] (LCLS)
**MBHoM**.... Houghton Mifflin Co., Boston, MA [*Library symbol*] [*Library of Congress*] (LCLS)
**MBHPFC**... [*The*] Monkees, Boyce and Hart Photo Fan Club (EA)
**MBI**........... Insurance Library Association of Boston, Boston, MA [*Library symbol*] [*Library of Congress*] (LCLS)
**MBI**........... Management by Initiative [*Management technique*]
**MBI**........... Marine Biomedical Institute [*University of Texas*] [*Research center*] (RCD)
**MBI**........... Maritime Bank of Israel (BJA)
**MBI**........... Maslach Burnout Inventory
**MBI**........... May Be Issued
**MBI**........... Mbeya [*Tanzania*] [*Airport symbol*] [*Obsolete*] (OAG)
**MBI**........... MBI. Medico-Biologic Information [*A publication*]
**MBI**........... MBIA, Inc. [*NYSE symbol*] (SPSG)
**MBI**........... Memory Bank Interface
**MBI**........... Menan Buttes [*Idaho*] [*Seismograph station code, US Geological Survey*] [*Closed*] (SEIS)
**MBI**........... Metal Belt Institute (EA)
**MBI**........... Michigan Biotechnology Institute [*Michigan State University*] [*Research center*] (RCD)
**MBI**........... Middle Bronze I [*Age*]
**MBI**........... Miscellaneous Babylonian Inscriptions [*A publication*] (BJA)
**MBI**........... Molecular Biosystems, Inc.
**MBI**........... Multibus Interface [*Data processing*] (MCD)
**MBIA**........ Malting Barley Improvement Association (EA)
**MBIA**........ Municipal Bond Insurance Association (EA)
**MBIAC**...... Missouri Basin Inter-Agency Committee
**MBIC**......... Michigan Bigfoot Information Center [*Later, MCBIC*] (EA)
**MBIC**......... Monmouth Biomedical Information Consortium [*Library network*]
**M Bi Ch**..... Master of Biological Chemistry
**MBID**........ Member of the British Institute of Interior Design (DBQ)
**M Bi E**....... Master of Biological Engineering
**MBIE**......... Member of the British Institute of Embalmers (DBQ)
**MBII**.......... Minority Business Information Institute [*New York, NY*] (EA)
**MBilC**........ Cabot Corp., Technical Information Center, Billerica, MA [*Library symbol*] [*Library of Congress*] (LCLS)
**M Bildung**... Musik und Bildung [*A publication*]
**MBilHi**...... Billerica Historical Society, Billerica, MA [*Library symbol*] [*Library of Congress*] (LCLS)
**MBIM**....... Member of the British Institute of Management [*Formerly, MIIA*]
**MBIO**........ Microprogrammable Block Input/Output
**MBIO**........ Moleculon, Inc. [*Cambridge, MA*] [*NASDAQ symbol*] (NQ)
**MBIOAJ**... Marine Biology [*Berlin*] [*A publication*]
**MBiomedE**... Master of Biomedical Engineering (ADA)
**M Biorad**.... Master of Bioradiology
**M Bi Phy**... Master of Biological Physics
**M Bi S**........ Master of Biological Sciences
**MBIS**......... Master of Business Information Systems
**MBIT**......... MegaBIT [*Binary Digit*] [*Data processing*] (MDG)
**MBIU**........ Multiplex Bus Interface Unit (MCD)
**MBJ**........... Michigan State Bar Journal [*A publication*]
**MBJ**........... Montego Bay [*Jamaica*] [*Airport symbol*] (OAG)
**MBJ**........... Multiple Blinking Jammer (MCD)
**MbJb**......... Mecklenburger Jahrbuch Schwerin [*A publication*]
**MBJT**........ Grand Turk [*Turks and Caicos Islands*] [*ICAO location identifier*] (ICLI)
**MBK**.......... Madchen-Bibel-Kreise [*Bible Reading Circles*] [*German*]
**MBK**.......... Medications and Bandage Kit (MCD)
**MBK**.......... Methyl Butyl Ketone [*Organic chemistry*]
**MBK**.......... Missing, Believed Killed (ADA)
**MBK**.......... Mitsubishi Bank Ltd. ADS [*NYSE symbol*] (SPSG)
**MBK**.......... Multibanc Financial Corp. [*Toronto Stock Exchange symbol*]
**MBK**.......... Multiple Beam Klystron
**MBK**.......... Schouw Vakblad voor Verwarming, Sanitair, en Keukenapparatuur [*A publication*]
**Mbl**........... Maandblad van de Centrale Raad van Beroep [*A publication*]
**MBL**.......... Manistee [*Michigan*] [*Airport symbol*] (OAG)
**MBL**.......... Marble Bar [*Australia*] [*Seismograph station code, US Geological Survey*] (SEIS)
**MBL**.......... Marine Biological Laboratory
**MBL**.......... Master Bidders List (NG)
**MBL**.......... Measured Blood Loss [*Physiology*]
**MBL**.......... Menstrual Blood Loss [*Medicine*]
**MBL**.......... Miniature Button Light

**MBL** ......... Minimal Bactericidal Level
**MBL** ......... Missile Baseline
**MBL** ......... Mobile (AFM)
**MBL** ......... Model Breakdown List
**MBL** ......... Modern British Literature [*A publication*]
**MBL** ......... Monterey Bay Area Cooperative Library System, Salinas, CA [*OCLC symbol*] (OCLC)
**MBL** ......... Multiples of Background Level [*Of environmental contaminants*]
**MBLA** ........ Methylbenzyllinoleic Acid [*Organic chemistry*]
**MBLA** ........ Mouse Specific Bone-Marrow-Derived Lymphocyte Antigen [*Immunology*]
**MBLA** ........ National Mercantile Bancorp [*NASDAQ symbol*] (NQ)
**Mbl Bdorg** ... Mededelingenblad Bedrijfsorganisatie [*A publication*]
**MBLC** ........ Lahey Clinic Foundation, Boston, MA [*Library symbol*] [*Library of Congress*] (LCLS)
**MBLC** ........ Microbore Liquid Chromatography
**MBldg** ....... Master of Building (ADA)
**MBldgSc** .... Master of Building Science (ADA)
**MBLE** ........ Mobile Gas Service Corp. [*NASDAQ symbol*] (NQ)
**MBLED** ..... Marine Biology Letters [*A publication*]
**MBLED7** ... Marine Biology Letters [*A publication*]
**Mbl Freiheitliche Wirtschaftspol** ... Monatsblaetter fuer Freiheitliche Wirtschaftspolitik [*A publication*]
**MBL (Mar Biol Lab) Lect Biol (Woods Hole)** ... MBL (Marine Biology Laboratory) Lectures in Biology (Woods Hole) [*A publication*]
**MBLPA3** ... Mediko-Biologichni Problemi [*A publication*]
**MBLR** ........ Madhya Bharat Law Reports [*India*] [*A publication*] (DLA)
**MBLS** ........ Microbiological Sciences, Inc. [*NASDAQ symbol*] (NQ)
**MBM** ......... Magnetic Bubble Memory [*Data processing*]
**MBM** ......... Malaysian Business [*A publication*]
**MBM** ......... Market Buy Market [*Information service or system*] (IID)
**MBM** ......... Master of Building Management (ADA)
**MBM** ......... Master of Business Management
**MBM** ......... Meat and Bone Meal
**MBM** ......... Metal-Barrier-Metal (IEEE)
**MBM** ......... Metal Bulletin Monthly [*A publication*]
**MBM** ......... Mineral Basal Medium [*Microbiology*]
**MBM** ......... Modern Black Men [*Johnson Publishing Co., Inc.*] [*A publication*]
**MBM** ......... Molecular Biology and Medicine [*A publication*]
**MBM** ......... Multibuoy Mooring [*Oil platform*]
**MBM** ......... Thousand Feet Board Measure [*Lumber*] (GPO)
**MBMA** ...... Metal Building Manufacturers Association (EA)
**MBMA** ...... Military Boot Manufacturers Association (EA)
**MBMC** ...... Middle Caicos [*Turks and Caicos Islands*] [*ICAO location identifier*] (ICLI)
**MBMetE** ... Metcalf & Eddy, Inc., Boston, MA [*Library symbol*] [*Library of Congress*] (LCLS)
**MBMF** ....... Multibeam Multifrequency (CAAL)
**MBMG** ...... Montana Bureau of Mines and Geology [*Montana College of Mineral Science and Technology*] [*Research center*] (RCD)
**MBMGH-T** ... Massachusetts General Hospital, Treadwell Library, Boston, MA [*Library symbol*] [*Library of Congress*] (LCLS)
**MBMH** ...... Brandon Mental Health Centre, Manitoba [*Library symbol*] [*National Library of Canada*] (NLC)
**MBMI** ....... Mean Body Mass Index
**MBMI** ....... Micro Bio-Medics, Incorporated [*Mount Vernon, NY*] [*NASDAQ symbol*] (NQ)
**MBMRF** .... Muenchener Beitraege zur Mediavistik und Renaissance-Forschung [*A publication*]
**MBMSA** .... Massachusetts College of Art, Boston, MA [*Library symbol*] [*Library of Congress*] (LCLS)
**MBMU** ...... Mobile Base Maintenance Unit
**MBMu** ....... Museum of Fine Arts, Boston, MA [*Library symbol*] [*Library of Congress*] (LCLS)
**MBMU** ...... University of Massachusetts, Boston, MA [*Library symbol*] [*Library of Congress*] (LCLS)
**MBN** .......... Boston Museum of Science, Boston, MA [*Library symbol*] [*Library of Congress*] (LCLS)
**MBN** .......... Metal Building News [*A publication*] (APTA)
**MBN** .......... Methylbenzylnitrosamine [*Organic chemistry*]
**MBN** .......... Metrobank NA [*AMEX symbol*] (SPSG)
**MBN** .......... Mixed Base Notation
**MBNA** ....... Mercedes Benz of North America
**MBNA** ....... Methyl(butyl)nitrosamine [*Organic chemistry*]
**MBNA** ....... Monument Builders of North America (EA)
**MBNAD** .... Marine Barracks, Naval Ammunition Depot
**MBNAS** .... Marine Barracks, Naval Air Station
**MBNC** ....... Mobile National Corporation [*Mobile, AL*] [*NASDAQ symbol*] (NQ)
**MBNC** ....... North Caicos [*Turks and Caicos Islands*] [*ICAO location identifier*] (ICLI)
**MBNECO** ... New England College of Optometry, Boston MA [*Library symbol*] [*Library of Congress*] (LCLS)
**MBNEH** .... New England Historic Genealogical Society, Boston, MA [*Library symbol*] [*Library of Congress*] (LCLS)
**MBNEL** ..... New England School of Law, Boston, MA [*Library symbol*] [*Library of Congress*] (LCLS)
**MBNEN** .... New England Nuclear Corp., Boston, MA [*Library symbol*] [*Library of Congress*] (LCLS)
**MBNMD** ... Marine Barracks, Naval Mine Depot
**MBNMHi** ... New England Methodist Historical Society, Inc., Boston, MA [*Library symbol*] [*Library of Congress*] (LCLS)
**MBNOA** .... Member of the British Naturopathic and Osteopathic Association
**MBNOB** .... Marine Barracks, Naval Operating Base
**MBNS** ....... Marine Barracks, Naval Station
**MBNU** ....... Northeastern University, Boston, MA [*Library symbol*] [*Library of Congress*] (LCLS)
**MBNU-L** ... Northeastern University, Law School, Boston, MA [*Library symbol*] [*Library of Congress*] (LCLS)
**MBNY** ....... Merchants Bank of New York [*NASDAQ symbol*] (NQ)
**MBNYD** .... Marine Barracks, Navy Yard
**MBO** .......... Maandblad voor Bedrijfsadministratie en Organisatie [*A publication*]
**MBO** .......... Madison, MS [*Location identifier*] [*FAA*] (FAAL)
**MBO** .......... Mamburao [*Philippines*] [*Airport symbol*] (OAG)
**MBO** .......... Management and Budget Office (MCD)
**MBO** .......... Management Buy-Out
**MBO** .......... Management by Objectives [*Management technique*] [*Facetious translations: "Management by Oblivion," and "Management by Others"*]
**MBO** .......... M'Bour [*Senegal*] [*Seismograph station code, US Geological Survey*] (SEIS)
**MBO** .......... M'Bour [*Senegal*] [*Geomagnetic observatory code*]
**MBO** .......... Meacham Bridge Oscillator [*Electronics*]
**MBO** .......... Mesiobucco-Occlusal [*Dentistry*]
**MBO** .......... Moist Burn Ointment [*Medicine*]
**MBO** .......... Monostable Blocking Oscillator [*Electronics*]
**MBO** .......... Motor Burnout (AABC)
**MBO** .......... Moving Base Operator
**$MbO_2$** ......... Myoglobin, Oxy [*Biochemistry, medicine*]
**MBOA** ....... Methoxybenzoxazolinone [*Biochemistry*]
**MBOC** ....... Minority Business Opportunity Committee [*Federal interagency group*]
**MBOCA** .... Methylenebis(ortho-chloroaniline) [*Also, MOCA*] [*Organic chemistry*]
**MBOH** ...... Minimum Break-Off Height
**MBOL** ....... Motor Burnout Locking (AABC)
**MBOM** ...... Boissevain and Morton Regional Library, Boissevain, Manitoba [*Library symbol*] [*National Library of Canada*] (NLC)
**MBOP** ....... Moniteur Bibliographique. Bulletin Officiel des Imprimes Publies en Pologne [*A publication*]
**MBOR** ....... Management by Objectives and Results [*Management technique*] (MCD)
**MBOT** ....... Mobot Corp. [*NASDAQ symbol*] (NQ)
**MBOU** ....... Member of the British Ornithologists Union (EY)
**MBOX** ....... MBI Business Centers, Inc. [*Rockville, MD*] [*NASDAQ symbol*] (NQ)
**MBP** .......... Major Basic Protein
**MBP** .......... Maltose-Binding Protein [*Biochemistry*]
**MBP** .......... Manhattan Bowery Project (EA)
**MBP** .......... Manpack Battery Pack
**MBP** .......... Massachusetts College of Pharmacy, Boston, MA [*Library symbol*] [*Library of Congress*] (LCLS)
**MBP** .......... Maximum Boiling Point
**MBP** .......... Mean Blood Pressure [*Medicine*]
**MBP** .......... Mean Brachial Artery Pressure [*Medicine*]
**MBP** .......... Mechanical Booster Pump
**MBP** .......... Mesiobuccopulpal [*Dentistry*]
**MBP** .......... Mid-Boiling Point
**MBP** .......... Muenchener Beitraege zur Papyrusforschung [*A publication*]
**MBP** .......... Myelin Basic Protein [*Neurology*]
**MBPA** ........ Marine Bancorp [*NASDAQ symbol*] (NQ)
**MBPA** ........ Master of Business and Public Administration
**MBPA** ........ Military Blood Program Agency (AABC)
**MBPAS** ..... Monthly Bulk Petroleum Accounting Summary [*Army*] (AABC)
**MBP-C** ...... Mannose-Binding Protein C [*Biochemistry*]
**MBPC** ....... Munitions Board Petroleum Committee
**MBPD** ....... Million Barrels per Day
**MBPDA** ..... Metropolitan Bag and Paper Distributors Association (EA)
**MB Pharm Bull** ... M and B Pharmaceutical Bulletin [*A publication*]
**MBPHAX** ... Marine Behaviour and Physiology [*A publication*]
**MBPI** ........ Pine Cay [*Turks and Caicos Islands*] [*ICAO location identifier*] (ICLI)
**MBPKN** .... Perry Normal School, Boston, MA [*Library symbol*] [*Library of Congress*] (LCLS)
**MBPM** ...... Master of Business and Public Management
**MBPO** ....... Military Blood Program Office (AABC)
**MBPRE** ..... Multitype Branching Process in a Random Environment [*Data processing*]
**MBPS** ....... Mechanical Booster Pump System
**MBPS** ....... MegaBITS [*Binary Digits*] per Second [*Transmission rate*] [*Data processing*]
**MBPS** ....... Million BITs [*Binary Digits*] per Second [*Data transmission speed*] [*Data processing*] (NASA)
**MBPT** ....... Many-Body Perturbation Theory [*Physics*]

**MBPV**........ Providenciales [*Turks and Caicos Islands*] [*ICAO location identifier*] (ICLI)
**MBPXL**..... MBPXL Corp. [*Formerly, Missouri Beef Packers - Kansas Beef Industries*]
**MBQ**.......... Mbarara [*Uganda*] [*Airport symbol*] (OAG)
**MBQ**.......... Modified Biquinary Code [*Data processing*]
**MBQ**.......... Montana Business Quarterly [*A publication*]
**MBR**.......... Belastingbeschouwingen. Onafhankelijk Maandblad voor Belastingrecht en Belastingpraktijk [*A publication*]
**MB en R**..... Maandblad voor Berechtiging en Reclassering van Volwassenen en Kinderen [*A publication*]
**MBR**.......... Maladapted Behavior Record [*Personality development test*] [*Psychology*]
**MBR**.......... Management by Results [*Management technique*]
**MBR**.......... Marker Beacon Receiver
**MBR**.......... Master Bedroom [*Real estate*]
**MBR**.......... Master Beneficiary Record [*Social Security Administration*]
**MBR**.......... Material Balance Report [*Nuclear energy*]
**MBR**.......... Maximum Base Rent
**MBR**.......... MBFC Mortgage Investments Corp. [*AMEX symbol*] (CTT)
**MBR**.......... Mechanical Bag Retriever [*Garbage collector*]
**MBR**.......... Mechanical Buffer Register [*Data processing*]
**MBR**.......... Member (AFM)
**MBR**.......... Membrane Bioreactor [*Chemical engineering*]
**MBR**.......... Membrane-Bound Ribosomes [*Cytology*]
**MBR**.......... Memory Base Register
**MBR**.......... Memory Buffer Register [*Data processing*]
**MBR**.......... Methylene Blue Reduced
**MBR**.......... Mission Briefing Room [*NASA*] (KSC)
**MBR**.......... Modified Bitumen, Reinforced
**MBR**.......... Montebello Resources Ltd. [*Vancouver Stock Exchange symbol*]
**MBR**.......... Motivation by Rotation
**MBR**.......... Moving Belt Radiator
**MBR**.......... Multibomb Rack
**MBR**.......... Multivariate Behavioral Research [*A publication*]
**MBr**........... Public Library of Brookline, Brookline, MA [*Library symbol*] [*Library of Congress*] (LCLS)
**MBRA**....... Marathon Boat Racers Association
**MBRA**....... Multibeam Radiometer Antenna
**MBradJ**..... Bradford Junior College [*Later, BC*], Bradford, MA [*Library symbol*] [*Library of Congress*] (LCLS)
**MBRDL**..... Medical Bioengineering Research and Development Laboratory [*Army*] (MCD)
**MBRE**........ Memory Buffer Register, Even [*Data processing*]
**MBRET**..... Middle Breton [*Language, etc.*]
**MBRF**........ Midbrain Reticular Formation [*Anatomy*]
**MBrHC**..... Hellenic College of Arts and Sciences and Holy Cross Greek Orthodox Theological School, Brookline, MA [*Library symbol*] [*Library of Congress*] (LCLS)
**MBridT**...... Bridgewater State College, Bridgewater, MA [*Library symbol*] [*Library of Congress*] (LCLS)
**M Brit IRE**... Member of the British Institution of Radio Engineers [*Later, MIERE*]
**M/BRK**...... Manual Brake [*Automotive engineering*]
**MBRL**........ Multiple Ballistic Rocket Launcher
**MBRMAO**... Multivariate Behavioral Research Monograph [*A publication*]
**MBRO**....... Memory Buffer Register, Odd [*Data processing*]
**MBrock**...... Brockton Public Library, Brockton, MA [*Library symbol*] [*Library of Congress*] (LCLS)
**MBrockV**... United States Veterans Administration Hospital, Brockton, MA [*Library symbol*] [*Library of Congress*] (LCLS)
**MBRR**....... Meridian & Bigbee Railroad Co. [*Formerly, MB*] [*AAR code*]
**MBRS**........ Miller Brothers Industries [*NASDAQ symbol*] (NQ)
**MBRS**........ Minority Biomedical Research Support Program [*Bethesda, MD*] [*National Institutes of Health*] (GRD)
**MBRT**........ Methylene Blue Reduction Time
**MBRUU**.... May Be Retained until Unserviceable
**MBRV**....... Maneuverable Ballistic Reentry Vehicle
**MBRWA**... Monthly Bulletin. International Railway Congress Association [*A publication*]
**MBS**........... Bethany Lutheran Theological Seminary, Mankato, MN [*OCLC symbol*] (OCLC)
**MBS**........... Magnetron Beam Switching
**MBS**........... Main "Bang" Suppressor
**MBS**........... Maleimidobenzoyl N-Hydroxysuccinimide [*Organic chemistry*]
**MBS**........... Manchester Business School [*England*]
**MBS**........... Master of Basic Science
**MBS**........... Master Bibliographic System (ADA)
**MBS**........... Medborgerlig Samling [*Citizens Rally*] [*Sweden*] [*Political party*] (PPE)
**MBS**........... Medicare Benefits Schedule [*Australia*]
**MBS**........... Mediterranean Base Section [*Army*] [*World War II*]
**MBS**........... Medium Bomber Strike (NATG)
**MB/S**......... MegaBITS [*Binary Digits*] per Second [*Transmission rate*] [*Data processing*]
**MBS**........... Member of the Bibliographical Society (ROG)
**MBS**........... Menorah Book Service (BJA)
**MBS**........... Methacrylate Butadiene Styrene [*Plastics technology*]
**MBS**........... Methionyl Bovine Somatotropin [*Biochemistry*]
**MBS**........... Methodist Boys' School
**MBS**........... Miniature Book Society (EA)
**MBS**........... Mission Budget Statement [*Army*]
**MBS**........... Monobutyl Sulfate [*Organic chemistry*]
**MBS**........... Monthly Bulletin of Statistics [*Israel*] [*A publication*]
**MBS**........... Monumental Brass Society (EA)
**MBS**........... Mortgage-Backed Securities Information Services [*The Bond Buyer, Inc.*] [*New York, NY*] [*Information service or system*] (IID)
**MBS**........... Mortgage-Backed Security Program [*Government National Mortgage Association*]
**MBS**........... Motion Base Simulator (MCD)
**MBS**........... Motor Bus Society (EA)
**MBS**........... Multiblade Slurry Saw [*Semiconductor technology*]
**MBS**........... Multiblock Synchronization Signal Unit [*Telecommunications*] (TEL)
**MBS**........... Multicore Bar Solder
**MBS**........... Multilingual Biblioservice of Alberta, Alberta Culture [*UTLAS symbol*]
**MBS**........... Multiple Batch Station [*Data processing*]
**MBS**........... Multiple Business System
**MBS**........... Mutual Broadcasting System
**MBS**........... Muzzle Bore Sight [*British military*] (DMA)
**MBS**........... Saginaw [*Michigan*] [*Airport symbol*] (OAG)
**MBS**........... Saginaw, MI [*Location identifier*] [*FAA*] (FAAL)
**MBS**........... Social Law Library, Boston, MA [*Library symbol*] [*Library of Congress*] (LCLS)
**MBSA**........ Maleylated Bovine Serum Albumin [*Biochemistry*]
**MBSA**........ Methylated Bovine Serum Albumin
**MBSA**........ Modular Building Standards Association (EA)
**MBSA**........ Munitions Board Standards Agency
**MBSB**........ Marine Barracks, Submarine Base
**MBSB**........ Mount Baker Bank [*Bellingham, WA*] [*NASDAQ symbol*] (NQ)
**MBSC**........ Boston State College, Boston, MA [*Library symbol*] [*Library of Congress*] (LCLS)
**MBSC**........ Major Bricklaying Sub-Contractors Association [*Australia*]
**MBSc**......... Master of Behavioural Science
**MB Sc**........ Master of Business Science
**MBSC**........ Modular Building Systems Council (EA)
**MBSC**........ South Caicos [*Turks and Caicos Islands*] [*ICAO location identifier*] (ICLI)
**MBSCSDD**... Master of Back Stabbin', Cork Screwin', and Dirty Dealin' [*Self-conferred degree held by Mordecai Jones in 1967 movie "The Flim-Flam Man"*]
**MBSI**......... Member of the Boot and Shoe Industry [*British*] (DAS)
**MBSI**......... Missile Battery Status Indicator
**MBSI**......... Musical Box Society, International (EA)
**MBSi**......... Simmons College, Boston, MA [*Library symbol*] [*Library of Congress*] (LCLS)
**MB-SL**....... British Museum - Sloan Herbarium [*London*]
**MBSL**........ Mouse Biochemical Specific Locus [*Test for mutagenesis*]
**MBSM**....... Maize Bushy Stunt Mycoplasm [*Plant pathology*]
**MBSM**....... Mexican Border Service Medal
**MBSOGB**... Musical Box Society of Great Britain
**MBSpnea**... Society for the Preservation of New England Antiquities, Boston, MA [*Library symbol*] [*Library of Congress*] (LCLS)
**MBSSM**.... Maxfield-Buchholz Scale of Social Maturity [*Psychology*]
**MBST**........ Motor Behavior Screening Test [*Physical education*]
**MBST**........ Multiple Beam Switching Tube
**MBSuf**....... Suffolk University, Boston, MA [*Library symbol*] [*Library of Congress*] (LCLS)
**MBSufC**..... Suffolk County Court House, Boston, MA [*Library symbol*] [*Library of Congress*] (LCLS)
**MBSX**........ MBS Textbook Exchange, Inc. [*NASDAQ symbol*] (NQ)
**MBSY**........ Salt Cay [*Turks and Caicos Islands*] [*ICAO location identifier*] (ICLI)
**MBT**.......... Main Ballast Tank
**MBT**.......... Main Battle Tank
**MBT**.......... Main Boundary Thrust [*Geology*]
**MBT**.......... Marble Bar - Town [*Australia*] [*Seismograph station code, US Geological Survey*] [*Closed*] (SEIS)
**MBT**.......... Marianna & Blountstown Railroad Co. [*AAR code*]
**MBT**.......... Masbate [*Philippines*] [*Airport symbol*] (OAG)
**MBT**.......... Mechanical Bathythermograph
**MBT**.......... Mercaptobenzothiazole [*Organic chemistry*]
**MBT**.......... Mercury Bombardment Thrustor
**MBT**.......... Metal-Base Transistor [*Electronics*] (IEEE)
**MBT**.......... Metal Bond Tape
**MBT**.......... Methylene Blue Test [*Analytical chemistry*]
**MBT**.......... Methylenebisthiocyanate [*Antimicrobial agent*]
**MBT**.......... Midblastula Stage [*Embryology*]
**MBT**.......... Minimum Best Torque
**MBT**.......... Mixed Bacterial Toxin
**MBT**.......... Mobile Boarding Team
**MBT**.......... Motor Burning Time
**MBT**.......... Murfreesboro, TN [*Location identifier*] [*FAA*] (FAAL)
**MBTA**....... Massachusetts Bay Transportation Authority [*Formerly, MTA*]
**MBTC**........ Mercedes-Benz Truck Company
**MBTCA**..... Miniature Bull Terrier Club of America (EA)
**MBTD/RP**... Main Battle Tank Distribution/Redistribution Plan (MCD)

**MBTFA**..... Methylbistrifluoroacetamide [*Organic chemistry*]
**MBTH**....... Methylbenzothiazolinone Hydrazone [*Organic chemistry*]
**MbThSt**..... Marburger Theologische Studien (BJA)
**MBTI**......... Boston Theological Institute, Learning Development Program, Boston, MA [*Library symbol*] [*Library of Congress*] (LCLS)
**MBTI**......... Manpower Business Training Institute
**MBTI**......... Myers-Briggs Type Indicator [*Psychology*]
**MBTI:AV**.. Myers-Briggs Type Indicator: Abbreviated Version [*Personality development test*] [*Psychology*]
**MBTS**........ Mercaptobenzothiazole Disulfide [*Organic chemistry*]
**MBTS**........ Meteorological Balloon Tracking System
**MBtS**......... Saint John's Seminary, Brighton, MA [*Library symbol*] [*Library of Congress*] (LCLS)
**MBtu**.......... Million British Thermal Units
**MBTWK**.... Multiple Beam Traveling Wave Klystron
**MBU**.......... Boston University, Boston, MA [*Library symbol*] [*Library of Congress*] (LCLS)
**MBU**.......... Boston University, School of Medicine, Boston, MA [*OCLC symbol*] (OCLC)
**MBU**.......... FAO [*Food and Agriculture Organization of the United Nations*] Monthly Bulletin of Statistics [*A publication*]
**MBU**.......... Hayward Map, CA [*Location identifier*] [*FAA*] (FAAL)
**MBU**.......... Mbambanakira [*Solomon Islands*] [*Airport symbol*] (OAG)
**MBU**.......... Memory Buffer Unit [*Data processing*]
**MBU**.......... MIRA [*Multifunctional Inertial Reference Assembly*] Basic Unit [*Air Force*] (MCD)
**MBU**.......... Mission Bricfing Unit
**MBU-E**...... Boston University, School of Education, Boston, MA [*Library symbol*] [*Library of Congress*] (LCLS)
**Mbuehne**.... Musikbuehne [*A publication*]
**MBUF**....... United Fruit Co., Boston, MA [*Library symbol*] [*Library of Congress*] (LCLS)
**MBuild**....... Master of Building (ADA)
**MBUK**....... Mercedes-Benz (United Kingdom)
**MBU-L**...... Boston University, School of Law, Boston, MA [*Library symbol*] [*Library of Congress*] (LCLS)
**M Bull (US Army Europe)**... Medical Bulletin (United States Army, Europe) [*A publication*]
**MBU-M**..... Boston University, School of Medicine, Boston, MA [*Library symbol*] [*Library of Congress*] (LCLS)
**MBUMR**... MIRA [*Multifunctional Inertial Reference Assembly*] Basic Unit Mounting Rack [*Air Force*] (MCD)
**MBurPRM**... P. R. Mallory & Co., Burlington, MA [*Library symbol*] [*Library of Congress*] (LCLS)
**MBus**......... Master of Business (ADA)
**MBus-Accy**... Master of Business - Accountancy
**MBusAd**.... Master of Business Administration (ADA)
**MBus-Comn**... Master of Business - Communication
**M Bus Ed**... Master of Business Education
**MBus-Mgt**... Master of Business - Management
**MBU-T**...... Boston University, School of Theology, Boston, MA [*Library symbol*] [*Library of Congress*] (LCLS)
**MBUUC**.... Minnesota Business Utility Users Council [*An association*] (TSSD)
**MBV**.......... Maandstatistiek van de Binnenlandse Handel en Dienstverlening [*A publication*]
**MBV**.......... Main Base Visit (NASA)
**MBV**.......... Mexican Border Veterans (EA)
**MBV**.......... Minimum Breakdown Voltage
**MBV**.......... United States Veterans Administration Hospital, Boston, MA [*Library symbol*] [*Library of Congress*] (LCLS)
**MBV-O**...... United States Veterans Administration, Outpatients Clinic, Boston, MA [*Library symbol*] [*Library of Congress*] (LCLS)
**MBVP**........ Mechanical Booster Vacuum Pump
**MBVPS**..... Mechanical Booster Vacuum Pump System
**MBVT**....... Merchants Banchares, Inc. [*Burlington, VT*] [*NASDAQ symbol*] (NQ)
**MBW**......... Mean Body Weight
**MBW**......... Medicine Bow, WY [*Location identifier*] [*FAA*] (FAAL)
**MBW**......... Medium Black and White [*Film*] (KSC)
**MBW**......... Metaalbewerking Werkplaatstechnisch Vakblad voor Nederland en Belgie [*A publication*]
**MBW**......... Metropolitan Board of Works [*British*]
**MBW**......... Microbiological Warfare
**MBW**......... Mount Baker [*Washington*] [*Seismograph station code, US Geological Survey*] (SEIS)
**MBW**......... Movement for a Better World (EA)
**MBW**......... Munitions Assignment Board (Washington) [*World War II*]
**MBW**......... Western Manitoba Regional Library, Brandon, Manitoba [*Library symbol*] [*National Library of Canada*] (NLC)
**MBWA**...... Management by Walking About [*or Wandering Around*] [*Facetious translation of MBO - Management by Objectives*]
**MBWO**...... Microwave Backward Wave Oscillator
**MBWS**....... Wheelock College, Boston, MA [*Library symbol*] [*Library of Congress*] (LCLS)
**MBX**.......... Maribor [*Yugoslavia*] [*Airport symbol*] (OAG)
**MBY**.......... Middleby Corp. [*AMEX symbol*] (SPSG)
**MBY**.......... Moberly, MO [*Location identifier*] [*FAA*] (FAAL)
**MBY & D**... Maintenance, Bureau of Yards and Docks [*Budget category*] [*Obsolete; see FEC*] [*Navy*]
**MBZ**.......... Menxel Bouzelfa [*Tunisia*] [*Seismograph station code, US Geological Survey*] (SEIS)
**MBZ**.......... Middle Border Zone [*Geology*]
**MC**............ Aermacchi SpA [*Italy*] [*ICAO aircraft manufacturer identifier*] (ICAO)
**MC**............ American Maritime Cases [*A publication*]
**MC**............ CAA Flying Unit [*United Kingdom*] [*ICAO designator*] (ICDA)
**MC**............ Cambridge Public Library, Cambridge, MA [*Library symbol*] [*Library of Congress*] (LCLS)
**MC**............ Consolata Missionary Sisters [*Roman Catholic religious order*]
**Mc**............ Maccabees [*Old Testament book*] [*Roman Catholic canon*]
**M-C**............ MacDonald-Cartier Highway [*Canada*]
**M/C**........... Machine (ROG)
**MC**............ Machine Cancellation [*Philately*]
**MC**............ Machine Console
**MC**............ Machinery Certificate [*Shipping*]
**MC**............ Magic Circle [*An association*] (EA)
**MC**............ Magister Chirurgiae [*Master of Surgery*]
**MC**............ Magistrates Cases [*Legal term*] [*British*]
**MC**............ Magistrates' Court [*Legal term*] [*Australia*]
**MC**............ Magnetic Card [*Word processing*]
**MC**............ Magnetic Clutch
**MC**............ Magnetic Core
**MC**............ Magnetic Course [*Navigation*]
**MC**............ Main Cabin
**M/C**........... Main Chamber [*NASA*] (KSC)
**MC**............ Main Channel
**MC**............ Main Chute (KSC)
**MC**............ Main Cock
**MC**............ Main Color [*Crocheting*]
**MC**............ Main Condenser [*Nuclear energy*] (NRCH)
**MC**............ Main Coolant (MSA)
**M/C**........... Maintenance and Calibration
**MC**............ Maintenance Center (MCD)
**M & C**........ Maintenance and Checkout (NASA)
**MC**............ Maintenance Command [*Obsolete*] [*Air Force*] [*British*]
**MC**............ Maintenance Console
**MC**............ Maintenance Cycle (MCD)
**MC**............ Major Component
**MC**............ Makers of Canada [*A publication*]
**MC**............ Malayan Cases [*1908-58*] [*A publication*] (DLA)
**MC**............ Management Contents [*Information Access Co.*] [*Information service or system*] (IID)
**M/C**........... Manchester (ROG)
**MC**............ Manganese Centre (EA)
**MC**............ Manhole Cover
**MC**............ Mantle Cavity
**MC**............ Mantle Collar
**MC**............ Manual Control
**M & C**........ Manufacturers and Contractors
**MC**............ Mapping Camera
**MC**............ Maps and Charts [*Interservice*] [*NATO*]
**MC**............ Mare Crisium [*Sea of Criscs*] [*Lunar area*]
**MC**............ Margin Call [*Banking, investments*]
**MC**............ Marginal Check [*Computer*]
**MC**............ Marginal Cost [*Business term*]
**M/C**........... Marginal Credit [*Business term*]
**MC**............ Marine Corps
**MC**............ Marine Craft [*British military*] (DMA)
**MC**............ Maritime Commission [*of Department of Commerce*] [*Merged with Federal Maritime Commission*]
**MC**............ Mark of the Craft [*Freemasonry*]
**MC**............ Mark Cross [*Initials often used as pattern on Mark Cross leather goods*]
**MC**............ Marked Capacity [*Freight cars*]
**MC**............ Market Capacity (ADA)
**MC**............ Marketing Center [*Veterans Administration*]
**MC**............ Marketing Communications [*A publication*]
**MC**............ Marmon Club (EA)
**MC**............ Marque de Commerce [*Trademark*]
**MC**............ Marriage Certificate
**MC**............ Married Couple (ADA)
**MC**............ Maryheart Crusaders (EA)
**MC**............ Mast Cell
**MC**............ Master of Ceremonies
**MC**............ Master of Chemistry
**MC**............ Master of Classics
**MC**............ Master Commandant
**MC**............ Master Commander [*Navy*] [*British*] (ROG)
**M of C**........ Master of Commerce
**MC**............ Master of Congress [*British*] (DAS)
**MC**............ Master Control
**MC**............ MasterCard [*Credit card*]
**MC**............ Mastercard International [*New York, NY*] (EA)
**MC**............ Matara Cases [*Ceylon*] [*A publication*] (DLA)
**MC**............ Material Code (MCD)
**MC**............ Material Control (AAG)
**MC**............ Materials Committee (MCD)

MC ........ Materiel Command [*Air Force*]
MC ........ Materiel Concept [*Army*]
M-in-C ........ Matron-in-Chief [*Navy*] [*British*]
MC ........ Matsushita Electric Industrial Co. Ltd. [*NYSE symbol*] (SPSG)
MC ........ Maury Center for Ocean Science [*Washington, DC*]
MC ........ Maximum Concentration
MC ........ Mayor's Court (DLA)
MC ........ McMurray Courier [*A publication*]
MC ........ Mechanical Council (EA)
MC ........ Medal Collector
MC ........ Media Coalition [*Later, MC/ACF*] (EA)
M & C ........ Media and Consumer [*A publication*]
MC ........ Medical Center
MC ........ Medical Certificate (ADA)
MC ........ Medical Chronicle [*Manchester*] [*A publication*]
MC ........ Medical Consultant [*Social Security Administration*] (OICC)
MC ........ Medical Corps [*Navy*]
MC ........ Medicine Cabinet (AAG)
M-C ........ Medico-Chirurgical
MC ........ Medium Capacity [*or Charge*] [*Bomb*]
MC ........ Medium Curing [*Asphalt grade*]
Mc ........ Megacurie
Mc ........ Megacycle
MC ........ Melamine Council [*Defunct*] (EA)
MC ........ Member of Congress
MC ........ Member of Council
MC ........ Memorandum Club (EA)
MC ........ Memorandum of Conditions
MC ........ Memorial Commission [*Federal body*]
MC ........ Memory Charts
M & C ........ Memory and Cognition [*A publication*]
MC ........ Memory Configuration [*Data processing*] (MCD)
MC ........ Memory Control [*Unit*] [*Data processing*]
MC ........ Mercado Comun [*Common Market*] [*Spanish*]
MC ........ Mercury Club (EA)
MC ........ Merkel Cell [*Anatomy*]
MC ........ Mesiocervical [*Dentistry*]
MC ........ Mess Call [*Military*]
MC ........ Message Center
MC ........ Message Change (MCD)
MC ........ Message Composer [*Communications, data processing*]
MC ........ MessageCheck (EA)
MC ........ Metacarpal [*or Metacarpus*] [*Anatomy*]
MC ........ Metal Carbide
MC ........ Metaling Clause [*Marine insurance*]
M/C ........ Metallic Currency (ROG)
MC ........ Meter-Candle
MC ........ Methacholine Challenge [*Medicine*]
MC ........ Methodist Chaplain
MC ........ Methyl Carbamate [*Organic chemistry*]
MC ........ Methylcellulose [*Organic chemistry*]
MC ........ Methylcholanthrene [*Also, MCA*] [*Organic chemistry*]
MC ........ Methylcystyosine [*Biochemistry*]
MC ........ Metric Carat [*200 milligrams*]
MC ........ Metropolitan Counties [*British*]
M/c ........ Mi Cuenta [*My Account, My Debit*] [*Business term*] [*Spanish*]
MC ........ Michigan Central Railroad [*Absorbed into Consolidated Rail Corp.*] [*AAR code*]
MC ........ Michigan Chemical Corp.
MC ........ Microcarrier [*Cell culture technology*]
MC ........ Microchromatographic
MC ........ Microcontrol
MC ........ Micronesia Coalition [*Inactive*] (EA)
MC ........ Midcourse
MC ........ Middle Chamber [*Freemasonry*]
MC ........ Miles on Course
MC ........ Military Characteristics
MC ........ Military College [*British*] (ROG)
MC ........ Military Committee [*NATO*]
MC ........ Military Computer (IEEE)
MC ........ Military Construction (AFM)
MC ........ Military Coordination [*British*]
MC ........ Military Cross [*British*] [*World War I nickname: Maconochie Cross*]
mC ........ Millicurie [*Also, mCi*]
MC ........ Millipore Corporation [*Bedford, MA*]
MC ........ Mine Clearance [*British military*] (DMA)
M-C ........ Mineralo-Corticoid [*Endocrinology*]
m/c ........ Minha Carta [*My Respects*] [*Portuguese*] [*Correspondence*]
m/c ........ Minha Conta [*My Regards*] [*Portuguese*] [*Correspondence*]
MC ........ Minimum Call [*Television studio on standby*]
MC ........ Mining Club (EA)
MC ........ Minor Construction (AFIT)
MC ........ Minorities in Cable (EA)
MC ........ Mirror Coil (MCD)
MC ........ Misionaras Clarisas [*Poor Clare Missionary Sisters*] [*Roman Catholic religious order*]
MC ........ Missile Checkout
MC ........ Missile Code (MUGU)
MC ........ Missile Command [*Army*]
MC ........ Missile Compartment
MC ........ Missile Container
MC ........ Missile Control
MC ........ Mission Capability [*NASA*] (NASA)
MC ........ Mission Completion (MCD)
MC ........ Mission Computer (MCD)
MC ........ Mission Continuation (MCD)
MC ........ Mission Control [*NASA*]
MC ........ Missionaries of Charity [*Roman Catholic women's religious order*]
MC ........ Missionary Catechists of the Sacred Hearts of Jesus and Mary [*Violetas*] [*Roman Catholic women's religious order*]
MC ........ Missionary Church (EA)
MC ........ Mitochondrial Complementation
MC ........ Mitomycin [*Also, M, MT*] [*Antineoplastic drug*]
MC ........ Mitral Valve Closure [*Cardiology*]
MC ........ Mixed Cell [*Lymphoma classification*]
MC ........ Mixed Condition [*Deltiology*]
MC ........ Mixed Cryoglobulinemia [*Medicine*]
MC ........ Mixing Chamber
M/C ........ Mixture Control [*Automobile fuel technology*]
MC ........ Mnemonic Code (AAG)
MC ........ Mobile Control (DEN)
MC ........ Mobile Crane (DCTA)
MC ........ Mode Change (CET)
MC ........ Mode Code
MC ........ Mode Counter
MC ........ Model Cities (OICC)
MC ........ Modular Computer
MC ........ Moisture Content [*Lumber*]
MC ........ Molded Components (IEEE)
MC ........ Momentary Contact [*Electronics*]
m/c ........ Mon Compte [*My Account*] [*French*] [*Business term*]
MC ........ Monaco [*ANSI two-letter standard code*] (CNC)
mc ........ Monaco [*MARC country of publication code*] [*Library of Congress*] (LCCP)
MC ........ Mondo Classico [*A publication*]
MC ........ Moneda Corriente [*Current Money*] [*Spanish*]
MC ........ Monetary Committee
MC ........ Monitor Call [*Data processing*] (IBMDP)
MC ........ Monitor and Control [*Data processing*] (BUR)
M & C ........ Monitor and Control Panel [*Data processing*] (NASA)
MC ........ Monkey Cells
MC ........ Monkey Complement [*Immunology*]
MC ........ Monocoupe Club (EA)
MC ........ Mononuclear Cell [*Clinical chemistry*] [*Also, MNC*]
MC ........ Monopolies Commission [*British*] (DCTA)
M & C ........ Montagu and Chitty's English Bankruptcy Reports [*1838-40*] [*A publication*] (DLA)
MC ........ Monte Carmelo [*A publication*]
MC ........ Montessori Center [*Education*]
MC ........ Monthly Criterion [*A publication*]
MC ........ Moore Theological College [*Australia*]
M & C ........ Morphine and Cocaine [*Mixture*] [*Slang*]
MC ........ Morse Code
MC ........ Morse Code - Barry Morse Fan Club (EA)
MC ........ Mortar Carrier [*British*]
MC ........ Mothercraft Certificate [*British*] (ADA)
MC ........ Motor Carrier
MC ........ Motor Chain
MC ........ Motor Coaches [*Public-performance tariff class*] [*British*]
MC ........ Motor Cortex [*Neuroanatomy*]
MC ........ Motorcycle
MC ........ Motorcycle Driver [*British military*] (DMA)
MC ........ Movement Control [*of troops*]
MC ........ Moving Coil [*Electronics*] (DEN)
MC ........ Muan Chon [*Mass Party*] [*Political party*]
MC ........ Mucous Cell
MC ........ Multichip [*Circuit*] [*Electronics*]
MC ........ Multichromatic
MC ........ Multiconfiguration [*Quantum mechanics*]
MC ........ Multiple Choice
MC ........ Multiple Contact
MC ........ Multiple Copy (FAAC)
MC ........ Munitions Command [*Later, Armaments Command*] [*Army*]
MC ........ Mushroom Caucus (EA)
MC ........ Myelocytomatosis [*Avian disease*]
M & C ........ Mylne and Craig's English Chancery Reports [*A publication*] (DLA)
MC ........ Myocarditis [*Medicine*]
MC ........ Submarine Chaser [*Navy symbol*]
MC ........ United States. Government Printing Office. Monthly Catalog of United States Government Publications [*A publication*]
M2C ........ Massachusetts Microelectronics Center [*Research center*] (RCD)
MC5 ........ Motor City Five [*Rock music group*]
MC's ........ Military Characteristics [*Technical specification document for nuclear bombs and warheads*]
MCA ........ Arthur D. Little, Inc., Cambridge, MA [*Library symbol*] [*Library of Congress*] (LCLS)
MCA ........ Magic Collectors' Association (EA)
MCA ........ Mail Control Authority (AFM)

**MCA**.......... Main Console Assembly [*NASA*] (KSC)
**MCA**.......... Maintenance Capability Audit [*Military*] (CAAL)
**MCA**.......... Major Coronary Arteries [*Cardiology*]
**MCA**.......... Malaysian Chinese Association [*Political party*] (PPW)
**MCA**.......... Management and Command Ashore (NVT)
**MCA**.......... Management Consultants Association [*British*] (DCTA)
**MCA**.......... Management Control Authority (NVT)
**MCA**.......... Manning Control Authority (MCD)
**MCA**.......... Manufacturers' Consumer Advertising
**MCA**.......... Manufacturing Change Analysis (MCD)
**MCA**.......... Manufacturing Chemists Association [*Later, CMA*] (EA)
**MCA**.......... Marine Corps Association (EA)
**MCA**.......... Maritime Control Area
**MCA**.......... Marky Cattle Association (EA)
**MCA**.......... Master Clock Assembly
**MCA**.......... Master of Commercial Arts
**MCA**.......... Master Community Antenna
**MCA**.......... Master Control Assembly [*NASA*] (NASA)
**MCA**.......... Mastiff Club of America (EA)
**MCA**.......... Material Control and Accountability (NRCH)
**MC & A**..... Material Control and Accounting [*Nuclear energy*] (NRCH)
**MCA**.......... Material Control Adjustment
**MCA**.......... Material Control Area (AAG)
**MCA**.......... Material Coordinating Agency
**MCA**.......... Maternity Center Association (EA)
**MCA**.......... Maximum Ceiling Absolute [*Aerospace*] (AAG)
**MCA**.......... Maximum Credible Accident [*Nuclear energy*] (NRCH)
**MCA**.......... Maximum Crossing Altitude (MCD)
**MCA**.......... MCA, Inc. [*NYSE symbol*] (SPSG)
**MCA**.......... McDonnell Douglas Automation Co., McAuto Campus Library, St. Louis, MO [*OCLC symbol*] (OCLC)
**MCA**.......... Mechanical Contractors Association of America
**MCA**.......... Mechanization Control Area (AAG)
**MCA**.......... Media Credit Association (EA)
**MCA**.......... Medical Correctional Association [*Defunct*] (EA)
**MCA**.......... Medical Council on Alcoholism [*British*]
**MCA**.......... Metal Construction Association (EA)
**MCA**.......... Methyl Cyanoacrylate [*Organic chemistry*]
**MCA**.......... Methylcholanthrene [*Also, MC*] [*Biochemistry*]
**MCA**.......... Metropolitan Club of America (EA)
**MCA**.......... Micro Channel Architecture [*Computer hardware*]
**MCA**.......... Microcentrifugal Analyzer [*Instrumentation*]
**MCA**.......... Microfilming Corporation of America [*Information service or system*] (IID)
**McA**.......... Microfilming Corporation of America, Glen Rock, NJ [*Library symbol*] [*Library of Congress*] (LCLS)
**MCA**.......... Microwave Communications Association (EA)
**MCA**.......... Microwave Control Assembly
**MCA**.......... Mid-Continental Airlines
**MCA**.......... Mid-West Compensation Association [*Superseded by ACA*] (EA)
**MCA**.......... Middle Cerebral Artery [*Anatomy*]
**MCA**.......... Midwest Commuter Airlines (FAAC)
**MCA**.......... Midwest Curling Association [*Defunct*] (EA)
**MCA**.......... Military Chaplains Association of the USA (EA)
**MCA**.......... Military Construction Appropriation [*or Authorization*] (AFM)
**MCA**.......... Military Construction Army (AFIT)
**MCA**.......... Military Coordinating Activity (MCD)
**MCA**.......... Millinery Credit Association [*Defunct*] (EA)
**MCA**.......... Minimum Crossing Altitude [*Aviation*]
**MCA**.......... Ministry of Civil Aviation [*Later, MTCA*] [*British*]
**MCA**.......... Missing Children of America (EA)
**MCA**.......... Mississippi Code, Annotated [*A publication*] (DLA)
**MCA**.......... Mistral Class Association (EA)
**MCA**.......... Model Cities Administration [*HUD*]
**MCA**.......... Modified Cost Approach Document [*Department of Housing and Urban Development*]
**MCA**.......... Mohair Council of America (EA)
**MCA**.......... Monetary Compensation Amount [*European Common Market*]
**MCA**.......... Monitoring and Control Assembly [*NASA*] (NASA)
**MCA**.......... Monochloroacetic Acid [*Also, MCAA*] [*Organic chemistry*]
**MCA**.......... Montana Code, Annotated [*A publication*] (DLA)
**MCA**.......... Motor Carriers Traffic Association Inc., Greensboro NC [*STAC*]
**MCA**.......... Motor Coach Australia
**MCA**.......... Motor Control Assembly (MCD)
**MCA**.......... Motor Cycle Industry Association of Great Britain (EAIO)
**MCA**.......... Movement Control Agency [*Army*]
**MCA**.......... Movers Conference of America
**MCA**.......... Multichannel Analyzer
**MCA**.......... Multiple Classification Analysis [*Aviation*]
**MCA**.......... Multiple Congenital Anomaly [*Syndrome*] [*Medicine*]
**MCA**.......... Multiprocessor Communications Adapter
**MCA**.......... Muse Air Corp. [*Dallas, TX*] [*FAA designator*] (FAAC)
**MCA**.......... Music Critics Association (EA)
**MCA**.......... Musicians Club of America (EA)
**MCA**.......... Mustang Club of America (EA)
**MCA**.......... Mutuelle Centrale d'Assurances [*France*] (EY)
**MCAA**........ Marine Corps Aviation Association (EA)
**MCAA**........ Mason Contractors Association of America (EA)
**MCAA**........ Master Concreters Association of Australia
**MCAA**........ Mechanical Contractors Association of America (EA)
**MCAA**........ Messenger Courier Association of America (EA)
**MCAA**........ Military Civil Affairs Administration [*Netherlands*] [*World War II*]
**MCAA**........ Monochloroacetic Acid [*Also, MCA*] [*Organic chemistry*]
**MCAAAC**... Medium Caliber Antiarmor Automatic Cannon
**MCAAC**.... Medium Caliber Antiarmor Automatic Cannon (MCD)
**MCAAF**..... Marine Corps Auxiliary Air Facility
**MCAAP**..... McAlester Army Ammunition Plant [*Oklahoma*] (AABC)
**MCAAS**..... Marine Corps Auxiliary Air Station
**MCAB**........ Marine Corps Air Base
**MCAB**........ Monoclonal Antibody [*Immunochemistry*]
**MCABM**.... Manner Common among Business Men
**MCAC**........ Machine Accessory [*Tool*] (AAG)
**MCAC**........ Military Common Area Control
**MC/ACF**... Media Coalition/Americans for Constitutional Freedom (EA)
**MCACO**.... Memoires. Commission des Antiquites de la Cote-D'Or [*A publication*]
**MCAD**........ Marine Corps Air Depot
**MCAD**........ Mechanical Computer-Aided Design
**MCAD**........ Military Contracts Administration Department
**MCAD**........ Minneapolis College of Art and Design
**McAdam Landl & T**... McAdam on Landlord and Tenant [*A publication*] (DLA)
**MCAE**........ Mechanical Computer-Aided Engineering
**MCAF**........ Marine Corps Air Facility
**MCAF**........ Marine Corps Air Field
**MCAF**........ Mediterranean Coastal Air Force Headquarters
**MCAF**........ Military Construction, Air Force
**MCAFB**...... McConnell Air Force Base [*Kansas*]
**MCAG**........ Mapping, Charting, and Geodesy [*Activity*] (MCD)
**MCAGCTC**... Marine Corps Air Ground Combat Training Center (MCD)
**MCAG/MGI**... Mapping, Charting, and Geodesy/Military Geography Information [*DoD*] (MCD)
**MCAIR**...... McDonnell Aircraft Co. [*Later, McDonnell Douglas Corp.*]
**McAl**.......... McAllister's United States Circuit Court Reports [*A publication*] (DLA)
**MCAL**........ [*The*] Merchant Bank of California [*Beverly Hills, CA*] [*NASDAQ symbol*] (NQ)
**MCALF**...... Marine Corps Auxiliary Landing Field
**McAll**.......... McAllister's United States Circuit Court Reports [*A publication*] (DLA)
**McAll (Cal)**... McAllister's United States Circuit Court Reports [*California*] [*A publication*] (DLA)
**McAllister US Circ Court R**... McAllister's United States Circuit Court Reports [*A publication*] (DLA)
**MCALS**..... Minnesota Computer-Aided Library System [*University of Minnesota*]
**McA L & Ten**... McAdam on Landlord and Tenant [*A publication*] (DLA)
**MCAM**...... Marine Corps Achievement Medal [*Military decoration*]
**MCAM**...... Member of the Communication, Advertising, and Marketing Education Foundation [*British*] (DBQ)
**McA Mar Ct**... McAdam's Marine Court Practice [*A publication*] (DLA)
**Mcan**.......... J. S. Canner & Co., Boston, MA [*Library symbol*] [*Library of Congress*] (LCLS)
**M Can L**...... Master of Canon Law
**MCAP**........ MET Capital Corp. [*NASDAQ symbol*] (NQ)
**MCAP**........ Military Construction Authorized Program
**MCAP**........ Minority Contractors Assistance Project [*Jamaica, NY*] (EA)
**MCAP**........ Multiple Channel Analysis Program
**MCAPI**...... Mid-Continent Association of the Pet Industry
**MCAR**........ Machine Check Analysis and Recording (BUR)
**MCAR**........ Machining Arbor [*Tool*] (AAG)
**McAr**.......... McArthur's District of Columbia Reports [*A publication*] (DLA)
**MCAR**........ Military Construction, Army Reserve (AABC)
**MCAR**........ Minnesota Code of Agency Rules [*A publication*]
**MCAR**........ Mixed Cell Agglutination Reaction [*Immunology*]
**MCar**.......... Monte Carmelo [*A publication*]
**M C Arh**..... Materiale si Cercetari Arheologice [*A publication*]
**MCARNG**... Military Construction, Army National Guard (AABC)
**MCARQUALS**... Marine Carrier Qualifications (NVT)
**McArth & M**... MacArthur and Mackey's District of Columbia Reports [*A publication*] (DLA)
**MCAS**........ Marine Corps Air Station
**MCASDZ**... Instituto Universitario Pedagogico de Caracas. Monografias Cientificas "Augusto Pi Suner" [*A publication*]
**MCAS(H)**... Marine Corps Air Station (Helicopter) (FAAC)
**MCASP**...... Multiple Constraint Alternative Selector Program [*Bell System*]
**MCAT**........ Maritime Central Analysis Team [*NATO*] (NATG)
**MCAT**........ Medical College Admission [*or Aptitude*] Test
**MCAT**........ Midwest Council on Airborne Television
**MCATA**..... Management Council of the American Trucking Association [*Defunct*] (EA)
**MCAU**........ Main Carrier Acquisition Unit (MCD)
**M CAUTE**... Misce Caute [*Mix Cautiously*] [*Pharmacy*]
**MCAUTO**... McDonnell Douglas Automation Co. [*Robotics*]
**MCAW**...... McCaw Cellular Communications, Inc. [*NASDAQ symbol*] (NQ)

**MCB** .......... Boyne Regional Library, Carman, Manitoba [*Library symbol*] [*National Library of Canada*] (NLC)
**MCB** .......... Maandschrift van het Centraal Bureau voor de Statistiek [*A publication*]
**MCB** .......... Main Control Board (NRCH)
**MCB** .......... Malaysian Cocoa Butter
**MCB** .......... Marine Construction Battalion
**MCB** .......... Marine Corps Base
**MCB** .......... Markings Center Brief (MCD)
**MCB** .......... Master Car Builder
**MCB** .......... Master of Clinical Biochemistry
**MCB** .......... Matheson, Coleman & Bell [*Commercial firm*]
**MCB** .......... MC Beverages [*Vancouver Stock Exchange symbol*]
**McB** .......... McBurney's [*Point*] [*Medicine*]
**MCB** .......... McComb, MS [*Location identifier*] [*FAA*] (FAAL)
**MCB** .......... Melanges Chinois et Bouddhiques [*A publication*]
**MCB** .......... Membranous Cytoplasmic Body
**MCB** .......... Message Control Block [*Data processing*] (CET)
**MCB** .......... Metal Corner Bead [*Technical drawings*]
**MCB** .......... Methodist College, Belfast [*Northern Ireland*]
**MCB** .......... Methylamino(chloro)benzophenone [*Organic chemistry*]
**MCB** .......... Miami City Ballet
**MC & B**...... Michigan Contractor & Builder [*A publication*]
**MCB** .......... Microcomputer Board
**MCB** .......... Millwork Cost Bureau [*Later, AWI*]
**MCB** .......... Miniature Circuit Breaker
**MCB** .......... Missouri Concert Ballet
**MCB** .......... Mobile Construction Battalion [*Navy*]
**MCB** .......... Module Control Block (KSC)
**MCB** .......... Molecular and Cellular Biology [*A publication*]
**MCB** .......... Monochlorinated Biphenyl [*Organic chemistry*]
**MCB** .......... Monochlorobenzene [*Organic chemistry*]
**MCB** .......... Moose Creek [*Alaska*] [*Seismograph station code, US Geological Survey*] [*Closed*] (SEIS)
**MCB** .......... Moscow Classical Ballet
**MCB** .......... Motor Cargo Boat
**MCB** .......... Motor Carriers Tariff Bureau Inc., Cleveland OH [*STAC*]
**MCB** .......... Myocardial Bridging [*Cardiology*]
**MCBA** ....... Master Car Builders' Association [*Later, CDOA*]
**MCBEB**..... Microbial Ecology [*A publication*]
**MCBETH** ... Military Computer Basic Environment for Test Handling
**MCBF**........ Mean Countdown Between Failures
**MCBF**........ Mean Cycles between Failures [*Quality control*]
**MCBIC**...... Michigan/Canadian Bigfoot Information Center (EA)
**M & C Bills** ... Miller and Collier on Bills of Sale [*A publication*] (DLA)
**MCBK** ....... Merchants Capital Corp. [*Formerly, MerchantsBank Boston*] [*NASDAQ symbol*] (SPSG)
**MCBM** ...... Marine Corps Brevet Medal
**MCBM** ...... Muscle Capillary Basement Membrane [*Medicine*]
**MCBN** ....... Mid-Coast Bancorp, Inc. [*NASDAQ symbol*] (NQ)
**MCBOMF** ... Mean Cycles between Operational Mission Failures [*Quality control*]
**MCBP**........ Mean Cycles between Premature Removals [*Quality control*] (MCD)
**MCBP**........ Melphalan, Cyclophosphamide, BCNU [*Carmustine*], Prednisone [*Antineoplastic drug regimen*]
**MCBP**........ Muscle Calcium Binding Parvalbumin [*Biochemistry*]
**MCBR** ....... Master Car Builders' Rules
**McBride**..... McBride's Reports [*1 Missouri*] [*A publication*] (DLA)
**McBride's**.. McBride's Magazine [*A publication*]
**MCBS**........ Micro Computer Business Services
**MCBS**........ Multicomponent Boot System [*Army*] (INF)
**MCBU** ....... Microconfined Bed Unit [*Chemical engineering*]
**MCBW** ...... Amalgamated Meat Cutters and Butcher Workmen of North America [*Later, UFCWIU*]
**MCC** .......... MacGillivray's Copyright Cases [*1901-49*] [*A publication*] (DLA)
**MCC** .......... Macquarie Commercial College [*Australia*]
**MCC** .......... Magdalene College, Cambridge University [*England*] (ROG)
**MCC** .......... Main Combustion Chamber (NASA)
**MCC** .......... Main Communications Center
**MCC** .......... Main Control Console [*Diving apparatus*]
**MCC** .......... Maintenance of Close Contact
**MCC** .......... Maintenance Control Center [*Telecommunications*] (AFM)
**MCC** .......... Major City Code [*IRS*]
**MCC** .......... Majority Congress Committee (EA)
**MCC** .......... Management Communication Consultants, Inc. [*Cincinnati, OH*] (TSSD)
**MCC** .......... Management Control Center [*Data processing*] (BUR)
**MCC** .......... Mandarin Capital Corp. [*Vancouver Stock Exchange symbol*]
**MCC** .......... Manhattan Chess Club (EA)
**MCC** .......... Manned Control Car [*Nuclear energy*]
**MCC** .......... Manual Combat Center [*Air Force*]
**MCC** .......... Manual Control Center [*Air Force*]
**MCC** .......... Map Collectors' Circle [*Defunct*] (EA)
**MCC** .......... Marine Corps Commandant
**MCC** .......... Maritime Coordination Center
**MCC** .......... Marked Cocontraction [*Medicine*]
**MCC** .......... Martin's Mining Cases [*British Columbia*] [*A publication*] (DLA)
**MCC** .......... Marylebone Cricket Club [*Governing body for cricket*]
**MCC** .......... Master Change Committee
**MCC** .......... Master Control Card [*IRS*]
**MCC** .......... Master Control Center (NATG)
**MCC** .......... Master Control Console
**MCC** .......... Matchbox Collectors Club (EA)
**MCC** .......... Material Category Code (MCD)
**MCC** .......... Material Characterization Center [*For nuclear wastes*]
**MCC** .......... Material Control Code
**MCC** .......... Maxwell Communication Corporation [*Formerly, BPCC*] [*British*]
**McC** .......... McCoy [*Antibodies*] [*Immunology*]
**MCC** .......... Mean Cell [*or Corpuscular*] Hemoglobin Concentration [*Hematology*]
**MC & C**...... Measurement, Command, and Control (NASA)
**MCC** .......... Mechanical Chemical Codes
**MCC** .......... Mechanically Compensated Crystal
**MCC** .......... Media Center for Children (EA)
**MCC** .......... Media Club of Canada [*Formerly, Canadian Women's Press Club*]
**MCC** .......... Media Commentary Council (EA)
**MCC** .......... Media Conversion Center [*Space Flight Operations Facility, NASA*]
**MCC** .......... Member of the County Council [*British*]
**MCC** .......... Mennonite Central Committee (EA)
**MCC** .......... Mercury Control Center
**MCC** .......... Mesoscale Convective Complex [*Meteorology*]
**MCC** .......... Mestek, Inc. [*NYSE symbol*] (SPSG)
**MCC** .......... Metacerebral Cell [*Neurobiology*]
**MCC** .......... Metrology and Calibration Center [*Army*] (MCD)
**MCC** .......... Metropolitan County Council [*British*]
**MCC** .......... Mica Creek [*British Columbia*] [*Seismograph station code, US Geological Survey*] [*Closed*] (SEIS)
**McC** .......... Micro Library Canisianum, Maastricht, Holland [*Library symbol*] [*Library of Congress*] (LCLS)
**MCC** .......... Microcrystalline Cellulose [*Organic chemistry*]
**MCC** .......... Microcrystalline Chitin
**MCC** .......... Microelectronics and Computer Technology Corporation
**MCC** .......... Midcourse Correction
**MCC** .......... Middlesex Community College [*Bedford, MA*]
**MCC** .......... Migrating Combustion Chamber [*Increases fuel efficiency*]
**MCC** .......... Military Climb Corridor [*Aviation*]
**MCC** .......... Military Colonization Company [*British ranch in the Calgary area of Canada*]
**MCC** .......... Military Communications Center, Inc. [*Minneapolis, MN*] (TSSD)
**MCC** .......... Military Comptrollership Course (MCD)
**MCC** .......... Military Cooperation Committee [*US-Canada*]
**MCC** .......... Military Coordinating Committee
**MCC** .......... Mini Car Club, USA (EA)
**MCC** .......... Miniature Center Cap
**MCC** .......... Miniaturized Cassegranian Concentration [*Instrumentation*]
**MCC** .......... Minimum Circumscribed Circle [*Manufacturing term*]
**MCC** .......... Mining Commissioner's Cases [*Canada*] [*A publication*] (DLA)
**MCC** .......... Ministerial Committee on Military Coordination [*British*] [*World War II*]
**MCC** .......... Miscellaneous Common Carrier
**MCC** .......... Missile Capability Console (MCD)
**MCC** .......... Missile Combat Crew (AAG)
**MCC** .......... Missile Command Coder (AAG)
**MCC** .......... Missile Compensating Control
**MCC** .......... Missile Control Center [*Air Force*]
**MCC** .......... Missile Control Console
**MCC** .......... Mission Control Center [*NASA*] (MCD)
**MCC** .......... Mississippi College, Law Library, Clinton, MS [*OCLC symbol*] (OCLC)
**MCC** .......... Mobile Command Center
**MCC** .......... Modified Close Control [*Air Force*]
**MCC** .......... Modified Continuous Cooking [*Pulp and paper technology*]
**MCC** .......... Modulation with Constant Control
**MCC** .......... Monitor Control Console (CAAL)
**MCC** .......... Monitored Command Code [*Marine Corps*]
**MCC** .......... Moody's English Crown Cases Reserved [*1824-44*] [*A publication*] (DLA)
**MCC** .......... Morgan Car Club (EA)
**MCC** .......... Motor Carrier Cases [*ICC*]
**MCC** .......... Motor Control Center
**MCC** .......... Motor Cycle Club [*British*]
**MCC** .......... Motorcycle Combination [*British*]
**MCC** .......... Movement Control Center [*Army*]
**MCC** .......... Multichannel Communications Controller
**MCC** .......... Multicomponent Circuits
**MCC** .......... Multiple-Chip Carrier [*Computer technology*]
**MCC** .......... Multiple Communications Control (BUR)
**MCC** .......... Multiple Computer Complex
**MCC** .......... Municipal Corporation's Chronicle [*Privately Printed*] [*A publication*] (DLA)
**MCC** .......... Munitions Carriers Conference (EA)
**MCC** .......... Muskegon Community College [*Michigan*]
**MCC** .......... Mutual Capital Certificate
**MCC** .......... Ontario Ministry of Culture and Communications (TSSD)

**MCC** .......... Royal Military College Certificate (Senior Department) [*British*] (ROG)
**MCC** .......... Sacramento, CA [*Location identifier*] [*FAA*] (FAAL)
**MCCA** ....... Conference of the Methodist Church in the Caribbean and the Americas (EAIO)
**MCCA** ....... Manufacturers Council on Color and Appearance [*Defunct*] (EA)
**MCCA** ....... Marche Commun Centramericain [*Central American Common Market - CACM*] [*French*]
**MCCA** ....... Media Conversion Computer Assembly [*Space Flight Operations Facility, NASA*]
**MCCA** ....... Medicare Catastrophic Coverage Act [*1988*]
**MCCA** ....... Mobile Communications Corporation of America [*NASDAQ symbol*] (NQ)
**MCCA** ....... Model Car Collectors Association (EA)
**MCCA** ....... Motor Car Collectors of America (EA)
**McCah** ....... McCahon's Kansas Reports [*1858-68*] [*A publication*] (DLA)
**McCahon** ... McCahon's Kansas Reports [*1858-68*] [*A publication*] (DLA)
**McCall Pr** .. McCall's Precedents [*A publication*] (DLA)
**McCanless** ... McCanless' Tennessee Reports [*A publication*] (DLA)
**McCann-E NR** ... McCann-Erickson, Inc. News Release [*A publication*]
**McCar** ........ McCarter's New Jersey Equity Reports [*A publication*] (DLA)
**McCart** ...... McCarter's New Jersey Equity Reports [*A publication*] (DLA)
**McCart** ...... McCarty's New York Civil Procedure Reports [*A publication*] (DLA)
**McCarter** ... McCarter's New Jersey Chancery Reports [*A publication*] (DLA)
**McCartney** ... McCarty's New York Civil Procedure Reports [*A publication*] (DLA)
**McCarty** ..... McCarty's New York Civil Procedure Reports [*A publication*] (DLA)
**McCarty Civ Proc** ... McCarty's New York Civil Procedure Reports [*A publication*] (DLA)
**MC Cas** ...... Municipal Corporation Cases, Annotated [*11 vols.*] [*A publication*] (DLA)
**MCCC** ....... Macomb County Community College [*Michigan*]
**MCCC** ....... Missile Combat Crew Commander
**MCCC** ....... Mission Control and Computing Center [*NASA*] (NASA)
**MCCCA** ..... Marine Corps Combat Correspondents Association (EA)
**McC Cl Ass** ... McCall's Clerk's Assistant [*A publication*] (DLA)
**MCCD** ....... Marine Corps Clothing Depot
**MCCD** ....... Mechanical Compatibility Control Drawing (MCD)
**MCCD** ....... Message Cryptographic Check Digits
**MCCDC** .... Marine Corps Combat Development Command [*Quantico, VA*] (GRD)
**MCC-DoD** ... Mission Control Center - Department of Defense [*NASA*] (NASA)
**MCCF** ........ Master Class Code File (MCD)
**McC F** ........ McCall's Forms [*A publication*] (DLA)
**M/CCFLS** ... Manitowoc Calumet Counties Library System [*Library network*]
**MCC-H** ...... Mission Control Center - Houston [*NASA*] (MCD)
**MCCHDC** ... Specialist Periodical Reports. Macromolecular Chemistry [*A publication*]
**MCCISWG** ... Military Command, Control, and Information Systems Working Group (NATG)
**McC Just** ... McCall's New York Justice [*A publication*] (DLA)
**MCC-K** ...... Mission Control Center - Cape Kennedy [*NASA*] (KSC)
**Mccl** ........... 10 Modern Reports, Macclesfield's Cases in Law and Equity [*1710-24*] [*A publication*] (DLA)
**MCCL** ........ Mason City & Clear Lake R. R. [*AAR code*]
**MCCL** ........ McClain Industries, Inc. [*NASDAQ symbol*] (NQ)
**McCl** .......... McClelland's English Exchequer Reports [*A publication*] (DLA)
**McCl** .......... McClure's Magazine [*New York*] [*A publication*]
**McClain Cr Law** ... McClain's Criminal Law [*A publication*] (DLA)
**McClain's Code** ... McClain's Annotated Code and Statutes [*Iowa*] [*A publication*] (DLA)
**McCl Dig** ... McClellan's Florida Digest [*A publication*] (DLA)
**McCle** ........ McClelland's English Exchequer Reports [*A publication*] (DLA)
**McClel** ....... McClelland's English Exchequer Reports [*A publication*] (DLA)
**McClel Dig** ... McClellan's Digest of Laws [*Florida*] [*A publication*] (DLA)
**McClell** ...... McClelland's English Exchequer Reports [*A publication*] (DLA)
**McClell & Y** ... McClelland and Younge's English Exchequer Reports [*1824-25*] [*A publication*] (DLA)
**McCl Ex** .... McClellan's Manual for Executors [*A publication*] (DLA)
**McCle & Yo** ... McClelland and Younge's English Exchequer Reports [*1824-25*] [*A publication*] (DLA)
**McCl IA Co** ... McClain's Iowa Code [*A publication*] (DLA)
**McCl Mal** .. McClelland on Civil Malpractice [*A publication*] (DLA)
**MCCLPHEI** ... Mass Conference of Chief Librarians of Public Higher Educational Institutions [*Library network*]
**McCl Pr** ..... McClellan's Probate Practice [*A publication*] (DLA)
**McClure** ..... McClure's Magazine [*New York*] [*A publication*]
**McClure's** .. McClure's Magazine [*A publication*]
**McCl & Y** ... McClelland and Younge's English Exchequer Reports [*1824-25*] [*A publication*] (DLA)
**MCCM** ...... Mexican Chamber of Commerce of US
**MCCN** ....... Midwest Curriculum Coordination Network (OICC)
**MCC-NASA** ... Mission Control Center - National Aeronautics and Space Administration (NASA)
**McCook** ..... McCook's Reports [*1 Ohio*] [*A publication*] (DLA)
**MCCOR** .... Motion Compensation - Coherent on Receive
**McCord** ...... McCord's South Carolina Law Reports [*1821-28*] [*A publication*] (DLA)
**McCord Ch** ... McCord's South Carolina Equity Reports [*1825-27*] [*A publication*] (DLA)
**McCord Eq** ... McCord's South Carolina Chancery Reports [*1825-27*] [*A publication*] (DLA)
**McCork** ...... McCorkle's Reports [*65 North Carolina*] [*A publication*] (DLA)
**McCorkle** ... McCorkle's Reports [*65 North Carolina*] [*A publication*] (DLA)
**MCCP** ........ Maintenance Console Control Panel
**MCCP** ........ Manufacturing Cost Control Program [*DoD*]
**MCCP** ........ Meta-Chlorophenylpiperazine [*Biochemistry*]
**MCCP** ........ Microwave Circuit Control Program [*Data processing*]
**MCCP** ........ Mission Control Computer Program [*NASA*]
**McCQ** ........ McCormick Quarterly [*A publication*]
**MCCR** ....... Master Change Compliance Record
**MCCR** ....... McCormick & Co., Inc. [*NASDAQ symbol*] (NQ)
**McCr** .......... McCrary's United States Circuit Court Reports [*A publication*] (DLA)
**MCCR** ....... Medical Committee for Civil Rights [*Defunct*] (EA)
**MCCR** ....... Memory Data Capture Cash and Credit Register [*Datacap Systems, Inc.*]
**MCCR** ....... Mission-Critical Computer Resource [*Data processing*]
**MCCR** ....... Molded Case Circuit Breaker
**McCrary** .... McCrary's United States Circuit Court Reports [*A publication*] (DLA)
**McCrary Elect** ... McCrary's American Law of Elections [*A publication*] (DLA)
**McCrary's Rep** ... McCrary's United States Circuit Court Reports [*A publication*] (DLA)
**McCr Elect** ... McCrary's American Law of Elections [*A publication*] (DLA)
**MCCRES** .. Marine Corps Combat Readiness Evaluation System
**MCCRTG** ... Marine Corps Combat Readiness Training Group
**MCCS** ........ Magistrates' Court Civil System [*Australia*]
**MCCS** ........ Master Calendar Control System [*New York City courts' speedup system*]
**MCCS** ........ Mechanized Calling Card Service [*Formerly, ABC*] [*Telecommunications*]
**MCCS** ........ Medco Containment Services, Inc. [*NASDAQ symbol*] (NQ)
**MCCS** ........ Military Committee in Chiefs of Staff Session [*NATO*] (NATG)
**MCCS** ........ Missile Critical Circuit Simulator
**MCCS** ........ Mission Control Center Simulation [*NASA*] (NASA)
**MCCSD** ..... Charles Stark Draper Laboratory, Inc., Technical Information Center, Cambridge, MA [*Library symbol*] [*Library of Congress*] (LCLS)
**MCCT** ....... Multistrip Cesium Contact Thrustor
**MCCTP** ..... Manpower and Community College Counselor Training Program (OICC)
**MCCU** ....... Mobile Coronary Care Unit [*Medicine*]
**MCCU** ....... Multiple Channel Control Unit
**MCCU** ....... Multiple Communications Control Unit [*Data processing*]
**McCul Dict** ... McCullough's Commercial Dictionary [*A publication*] (DLA)
**McCul Pol Econ** ... McCulloch's Political Economy [*A publication*] (DLA)
**MCCUSCUSRPG** ... Military Coordinating Committee, United States Element, Canada-United States Regional Planning Group (AABC)
**MCD** .......... Doctor of Comparative Medicine
**MCD** .......... Dynatech Research/Development Co., Cambridge, MA [*Library symbol*] [*Library of Congress*] (LCLS)
**MCD** .......... Magistrates' Court Decisions [*New Zealand*] [*A publication*] (DLA)
**MCD** .......... Magna Carta Dames, National Society (EA)
**MCD** .......... Magnetic Circular Dichroism
**MCD** .......... Magnetic Crack Definer [*Aviation*]
**MCD** .......... Malaria Control Detachment [*Army*] [*World War II*]
**MCD** .......... Manipulative Communications Deception [*Military*] (NVT)
**MCD** .......... Manual Control Device
**MCD** .......... Marginal Checking and Distribution
**MCD** .......... Maritime Commission Decisions
**MCD** .......... Marr, Cahalan & Dunn [*Law firm*]
**MCD** .......... Mast Cell Degranulating [*or Destroying*] Peptide [*Biochemistry*]
**MCD** .......... Master of Civic Design
**MCD** .......... Master Clerical Data [*Management system*]
**MCD** .......... Mathematics and Computer Division [*Supreme Headquarters Allied Powers Europe*] (NATG)
**MCD** .......... McDonald's Corp. [*NYSE symbol*] [*Toronto Stock Exchange symbol*] (SPSG)
**MCD** .......... McDonnell Douglas Corp.
**MCD** .......... Mean Cell [*or Corpuscular*] Diameter [*Hematology*]
**MCD** .......... Median Control Death
**MCD** .......... Medical Care Development, Inc. [*Augusta, ME*] (TSSD)
**MCD** .......... Medical Crew Director
**MCD** .......... Megawatt Cassegrain Diplexer

**MCD**......... Member of the College of Dentists [*British*]
**MCD**......... Memory Control Data
**MCD**......... Mercy College of Detroit [*Michigan*]
**MCD**......... Metacarpal Cortical Density [*Anatomy*]
**MCD**......... Metal-Covered Door [*Technical drawings*]
**MCD**......... Metals and Ceramics Division [*Air Force*]
**MCD**......... Microbial Coal Desulfurization
**MCD**......... Mid-Central District [*ATSC*]
**MCD**......... Military Contracts Department
**MCD**......... Military Coordination Detachment (NATG)
**mcD**......... Millicurie-Destroyed
**MCD**......... Mine Warfare and Clearance Diving [*Navy*] [*British*]
**MCD**......... Mines, Countermines, and Demolitions [*Military*] (RDA)
**MCD**......... Minimal Cerebral Dysfunction
**MCD**......... Minimal Change Disease [*Nephrology*]
**MCD**......... Minimum Cost Design (MCD)
**MCD**......... Minor Civil Division [*Bureau of Census*]
**MCD**......... Mission Control Directorate [*NASA*]
**MCD**......... Monitor Criteria Data [*Space Flight Operations Facility, NASA*]
**MCD**......... Months for Cyclical Dominance [*Economics*]
**MCD**......... Multiple Carboxylase Deficiency [*Medicine*]
**MCD**......... Multiple Concrete Duct [*Telecommunications*] (TEL)
**MCDA**....... Manpower and Career Development Agency
**MCDAA**.... Member of the Company Directors' Association of Australia
**MCDARS** ... Mechanized Cost Distribution and Reporting System (MCD)
**MCDAS**..... Metropolitan Cities Drug Association Secretaries (EA)
**MCDB**....... Master Code Database (MCD)
**MCDB**....... Minimum Cost Design Booster (KSC)
**MCDBSU** ... Master Control and Data Buffer Storage Unit
**MCDC**....... McDonnell Douglas Corporation
**MCDC**....... Mobilization Concepts Development Center [*Washington, DC*] [*DoD*] (MCD)
**MCDD**....... Monochlorodioxin [*Organic chemistry*]
**MCDE**....... Monochlorodimethyl Ether [*Organic chemistry*]
**MCDEC**.... Marine Corps Development and Education Command
**McDer Land L** ... McDermot's Irish Land Laws [*A publication*] (DLA)
**McDevitt**.... McDevitt's Irish Land Commissioner's Reports [*A publication*] (DLA)
**MCDF**....... Methyltrichlorodibenzofuran [*Organic chemistry*]
**MCDG**....... Monitor Criteria Data Set Generation Processor Assembly [*Space Flight Operations Facility, NASA*]
**MCDH**....... Master of Community Dental Health, University of Birmingham [*British*] (DBQ)
**MCDI**........ Minnesota Child Development Inventory [*Child development test*] [*Psychology*]
**MCDM**...... Multiple Criteria Decision Making
**McDon Jus** ... McDonald's Justice [*A publication*] (DLA)
**McDonnell** ... McDonnell's Sierra Leone Reports [*A publication*] (DLA)
**McDow Inst** ... McDowall's Institutes of the Law of Scotland [*A publication*] (DLA)
**MCDP**....... Microprogrammed Communication Data Processor (MCD)
**MCDP**....... Missionary Catechists of Divine Providence [*Roman Catholic women's religious order*]
**MCDR**....... Multichannel DIFAR [*Directional Frequency Analysis and Recording System*] Relay (NVT)
**MCDS**....... Maintenance Control and Display System [*NASA*] (NASA)
**MCDS**....... Multicommand Data System
**MCDS**....... Multifunction CRT [*Cathode-Ray Tube*] Display System (NASA)
**MCD/SLV** ... Minimum Cost Design/Space Launch Vehicle [*NASA*] (KSC)
**MCDSP**..... Master Combat Data System Plan [*Military*] (CAAL)
**MCDT**....... Mean Corrective Downtime [*Data processing*]
**MCDU**....... Multifunction CRT [*Cathode-Ray Tube*] Display Unit (NASA)
**MCDW**...... Monthly Climatic Data for the World [*A publication*]
**MCDY**....... Microdyne Corp. [*NASDAQ symbol*] (NQ)
**MCE**.......... Episcopal Divinity School, Cambridge, MA [*Library symbol*] [*Library of Congress*] (LCLS)
**MCE**.......... MacNeill Industrial, Inc. [*Vancouver Stock Exchange symbol*]
**MCE**.......... Maintenance Cleaning Equipment (MCD)
**MCE**.......... Management Centre/Europe
**MCE**.......... Mandatory Continuing Education
**MCE**.......... Manufacturing Cycle Effectiveness
**MCE**.......... Marginal Cost Efficiency [*Marketing*]
**MCE**.......... Maritime Commission, Emergency Ship
**MCE**.......... Master of Christian Education
**MCE**.......... Master of Civil Engineering
**MCE**.......... Maximum Capability Envelope
**MCE**.......... Mean Chance Expectation [*Parapsychology*]
**MCE**.......... Media Conversion Equipment [*Space Flight Operations Facility, NASA*]
**MCE**.......... Medical Care Evaluation
**MCE**.......... Memphis Cotton Exchange (EA)
**MCE**.......... Merced, CA [*Location identifier*] [*FAA*] (FAAL)
**McE**.......... Microcard Editions, Inc., Englewood, CO [*Library symbol*] [*Library of Congress*] (LCLS)
**MCE**.......... Microscopically Controlled Excision [*Medicine*]
**MCE**.......... Military Characteristics Equipment
**MCE**.......... Missile Compensating Equipment
**MCE**.......... Mission Control Equipment [*NASA*]
**MCE**.......... Mixed Cellulose Esters Membrane Filters
**MCE**.......... Mobile Command Element (NATG)
**MCE**.......... Modular Control Equipment [*DoD*]
**MCE**.......... Montgomery Cotton Exchange (EA)
**MCEAC**..... Marine Corps Emergency Actions Center
**MCEB**........ Marine Corps Equipment Board
**MCEB**........ Military Communications-Electronics Board [*DoD*] [*Washington, DC*]
**MCEC**....... Marine Corps Education Center
**MC Ed**....... Master of Commercial Education
**M Ce Eng**... Master of Cement Engineering
**MCEG**....... Management Company Entertainment, Inc. [*NASDAQ symbol*] (NQ)
**MCEI**......... Marketing Communications Executives International [*Dallas, TX*] (EA)
**MCEL**........ Machine Check Extended Logout
**McEM**....... Microfilming Executors & Methods Organization Ltd., Dublin, Ireland [*Library symbol*] [*Library of Congress*] (LCLS)
**MCE(Melb)** ... Master of Civil Engineering (Melbourne University)
**MCEMS**.... Marine Corps Environmentally Controlled Medical System (MCD)
**MCEN**....... Magic Circle Energy Corp. [*NASDAQ symbol*] (NQ)
**MCEN**....... Modified Current Expendable Launch Vehicle [*NASA*] (KSC)
**MC Eng**..... Master of Civil Engineering
**MCEP**....... Maneuver Criteria Evaluation Program [*Army*]
**MCEPEN** ... Midwest Continuing Education Professional Nurses (DHSM)
**MCER**....... Massachusetts Central [*AAR code*]
**MCERA**..... Mining and Chemical Engineering Review (Australia) [*A publication*]
**M Cer E**..... Master of Ceramic Engineering
**MCES**........ Main Condenser Evacuation System [*Nuclear energy*] (NRCH)
**MCES**........ Major City Earth Stations [*Telecommunications*] (TSSD)
**MCES**........ Multiple Cholesterol Emboli Syndrome [*Medicine*]
**MCESS**...... Marine Corps Expeditionary Shelter System (MCD)
**MCEU**....... Mobile Civil Emergency Unit
**MCEWG**... Multinational Communication-Electronics Working Group [*Formerly, SGCEC*] [*NATO*] (NATG)
**MCF**.......... Magnetic Confinement Fusion [*Physics*]
**MCF**.......... Magyar Communion of Friends (EA)
**MCF**.......... Maintenance and Checkout Facility [*NASA*] (KSC)
**MCF**.......... Maintenance Condemnation Factor (MCD)
**MCF**.......... Master Code File
**MCF**.......... Master Control File
**MCF**.......... Matched Crystal Filters
**MCF**.......... Maximal Contraction Force [*Myology*]
**MCF**.......... McFinley Red Lake Mines Ltd. [*Toronto Stock Exchange symbol*]
**MCF**.......... Medical Cybernetics Foundation (EA)
**MCF**.......... Medium Corpuscular Fragility [*Hematology*]
**MCF**.......... Merced County Free Library, Merced, CA [*OCLC symbol*] (OCLC)
**MCF**.......... Microcomplement Fixation [*Immunochemistry*]
**MCF**.......... Migrant Children's Fund [*Absorbed by NCEMC*]
**MCF**.......... Military Computer Family (MCD)
**M̄CF**.......... Million Cubic Feet
**MCF**.......... Mink Cell Focus-Inducing [*Virus*]
**MCF**.......... Mission Control Facility (MCD)
**MCF**.......... Mobile Calibration Facility
**MCF**.......... Mode Change Flag
**MCF**.......... Monolithic Crystal Filter
**MCF**.......... Mononuclear Cell Factor [*Cytology*]
**MCF**.......... Multichannel Fixed
**MCF**.......... Multiple Cassegrain Feed [*Deep Space Instrumentation Facility, NASA*]
**MCF**.......... Multiple Cost Factor
**MCF**.......... Mutual Coherence Function
**MCF**.......... Myocardial Contractile Force [*Cardiology*]
**MCF**.......... Tampa, FL [*Location identifier*] [*FAA*] (FAAL)
**MCF**.......... Taurus Municipal California Holdings [*NYSE symbol*] (SPSG)
**MCF**.......... Thousand Cubic Feet
**MCF-7**....... Michigan Cancer Foundation - Seventh Sample [*Strain of rapid-growing breast cancer cells used world-wide in cancer research*]
**MCFA**........ Medium-Chain Fatty Acids [*Organic chemistry*]
**MCFA**........ Monosegmented Continuous Flow Analysis [*Analytical chemistry*]
**McFar**........ McFarlane's Jury Court Reports [*Scotland*] [*A publication*] (DLA)
**MCFC**........ Mary Jo Cattlett Fan Club (EA)
**MCFC**........ Molten Carbonate Fuel Cell [*Energy source*]
**MCFC**........ Motley Crue Fan Club (EA)
**MCFD**....... Thousand Cubic Feet per Day
**MCFE**........ McFarland Energy, Inc. [*NASDAQ symbol*] (NQ)
**MCFH**....... Thousand Cubic Feet per Hour
**MCFIM**..... Microfilm
**MCFL**........ Master Civilian Facilities Listing [*DoD*]
**MCFLM**.... Microfilm (AAG)
**MCFO**....... Marine Corps Freight Office
**MCFP**........ Member of the College of Family Physicians [*British*]
**MCFS**........ Maneuver Control Functional Segment [*Army*] (RDA)
**MCFSA**..... Minority Caucus of Family Service America (EA)

**MCFSAA** .. Minorities Caucus of Family Service Association of America [*Later, MCFSA*] (EA)
**MCFSHE** .. Microfische
**MCG** .......... Macrophage Chemotactic Factor [*Immunochemistry*]
**MCG** .......... Magazine Cartoonists Guild [*Later, CG*] (EA)
**MCG** .......... Magnetic Compensator Group
**MCG** .......... Magneto Cumulative Generator (MCD)
**MCG** .......... Magnetocardiogram
**MCG** .......... Man Computer Graphics [*Data processing*] (MCD)
**MC & G** ..... Mapping, Charting, and Geodesy [*Air Force*] (AFM)
**MCG** .......... Marche. L'Hebdomadaire du Dirigeant [*A publication*]
**MCG** .......... McGill University, Graduate School of Library Science, Montreal, PQ, Canada [*OCLC symbol*] (OCLC)
**McG** .......... McGloin's Louisiana Court of Appeal Reports [*A publication*] (DLA)
**MCG** .......... McGrath [*Alaska*] [*Airport symbol*] (OAG)
**MCG** .......... McGrath, AK [*Location identifier*] [*FAA*] (FAAL)
**MCG** .......... Medical College of Georgia [*Augusta*]
**MCG** .......... Memory Character Generator
**MCG** .......... Metric Coordinating Group (MCD)
**MCG** .......... Michigan Energy Resources Co. [*NYSE symbol*] (SPSG)
**MCG** .......... Microgram [*One millionth of a gram*]
**MCG** .......... Microwave Command Guidance
**MCG** .......... Mid-Canada Gold & Copper [*Vancouver Stock Exchange symbol*]
**MCG** .......... Midbrain Central Gray [*Brain anatomy*]
**MCG** .......... Midcourse Guidance [*Navy*] (CAAL)
**MCG** .......... Millimeter Wave Contrast Guidance [*Munitions*] (MCD)
**MCG** .......... Minimally-Cleaned, Coal-Derived Gas
**MCG** .......... Mobile Command Guidance
**MCG** .......... Mobile Communications Group [*Air Force*] (MCD)
**MCG** .......... Monatshefte der Comenius-Gesellschaft [*A publication*]
**mCG** .......... Monkey Chorionic Gonadotrophin [*Endocrinology*]
**MCG** .......... Moving Coil Galvanometer [*Electronics*]
**MCGA** ........ Multicolor Graphics Adapter [*Computer technology*]
**MCGCM** ... Marine Corps Good Conduct Medal
**MCGF** ....... Myeloma Cell Growth Factor [*Biochemistry*]
**MCGFP** ..... Maraschino Cherry and Glace Fruit Processors (EA)
**McGill** ....... McGill's Manuscript Decisions, Scotch Court of Session [*A publication*] (DLA)
**McGill Dent Rev** ... McGill Dental Review [*A publication*]
**McGill J Educ** ... McGill Journal of Education [*A publication*]
**McGill L J** ... McGill Law Journal [*A publication*]
**McGill Univ Axel Heiberg Isl Res Rep Glaciol** ... McGill University. Axel Heiberg Island Research Reports. Glaciology [*A publication*]
**McGill Univ Mar Sci Cent Manuscr** ... McGill University. Marine Sciences Centre. Manuscript [*A publication*]
**McGill Univ (Montreal) Mar Sci Cent Manuscr Rep** ... McGill University (Montreal). Marine Sciences Centre. Manuscript Report [*A publication*]
**McGill Univ Peter Redpath Mus** ... McGill University [*Montreal*]. Peter Redpath Museum [*A publication*]
**McGl** .......... McGloin's Louisiana Courts of Appeal Reports [*A publication*] (DLA)
**McGl Al** ..... McGlashan. Aliment [*Scotland*] [*A publication*] (DLA)
**McG LJ** ..... McGill Law Journal [*A publication*]
**McGl (LA)** ... McGloin's Louisiana Courts of Appeal Reports [*A publication*] (DLA)
**McGloin** ..... McGloin's Louisiana Courts of Appeal Reports [*A publication*] (DLA)
**McGloin Rep (LA)** ... McGloin's Louisiana Courts of Appeal Reports [*A publication*] (DLA)
**McGl Sh** .... McGlashan's Sheriff Court Practice [*Scotland*] [*A publication*] (DLA)
**MC & G/MGI** ... Mapping, Charting, and Geodesy/Military Geography Information [*DoD*]
**MCGN** ....... Mixed Cryoglobulinemia-Associated Glomerulonephritis [*Medicine*]
**MCGP** ....... Member of the College of General Practitioners [*British*]
**MCGp** ....... Mobile Communications Group [*Air Force*] (AFM)
**MCGPPC** .. Manual on the Control of Government Property in the Possession of Contractors
**MCGR** ....... McGregor Corp. [*NASDAQ symbol*] (NQ)
**McGrath** .... McGrath's Mandamus Cases [*Michigan*] [*A publication*] (DLA)
**McGraw 2000** ... McGraw-Hill American Economy Prospects for Growth through 2000 [*A publication*]
**McGraw ESH** ... Annual McGraw-Hill Survey. Investment in Employee Safety and Health [*A publication*]
**McGraw Hill Med Health** ... McGraw-Hill's Medicine and Health [*Washington*] [*A publication*]
**McGraw Hill Wash Rep Med Health** ... McGraw-Hill's Washington Report on Medicine and Health [*A publication*]
**McGraw Ove** ... McGraw-Hill Overseas Operations of United States Industrial Companies [*A publication*]
**McGraw PE** ... McGraw-Hill Annual Survey of Business Plans for New Plants and Equipment [*A publication*]
**McGraw Pol** ... McGraw-Hill Annual Pollution Control Expenditures [*A publication*]
**McGraw RD** ... McGraw-Hill Annual Survey of Research and Development Expenditures [*A publication*]
**McGraw ST** ... McGraw-Hill Publications. US Business Outlook. Short Term [*A publication*]
**McGraw US** ... McGraw-Hill United States Business Outlook. Long Term [*A publication*]
**MCGS** ....... Microwave Command Guidance System [*RADC*]
**MCGW** ...... Maximum Certificated Gross Weight (MCD)
**MCH** .......... Churchill Public Library, Manitoba [*Library symbol*] [*National Library of Canada*] (NLC)
**MCH** .......... Machala [*Ecuador*] [*Airport symbol*] (OAG)
**MCH** .......... Machine-Check Handler [*Data processing*] (MCD)
**MCH** .......... Machynlleth [*Welsh depot code*]
**M Ch** .......... Magister Chirurgiae [*Master of Surgery*]
**MCH** .......... Mail Chute (AAG)
**MCH** .......... March
**MCH** .......... Masachapa [*Nicaragua*] [*Seismograph station code, US Geological Survey*] (SEIS)
**MCH** .......... Massachusetts Council for the Humanities [*Defunct*] (EA)
**MCH** .......... Maternal and Child Health Services [*Generic term*] (DHSM)
**MCH** .......... Mean Cell [*or Corpuscular*] Hemoglobin [*Hematology*]
**MCH** .......... MedChem Products, Inc. [*AMEX symbol*] (SPSG)
**MCH** .......... Melanin-Concentrating Hormone [*Endocrinology*]
**M-Ch** .......... Memory Channel
**MCH** .......... Methacholine [*A cholinergic*]
**MCH** .......... Methylcyclohexane [*Organic chemistry*]
**MCH** .......... Methylcyclohexenone [*Organic chemistry*]
**MCH** .......... Methylenecyclohexadiene [*Organic chemistry*]
**MCH** .......... Micham Explorations, Inc. [*Vancouver Stock Exchange symbol*]
**Mch** ............ Michigan Reports [*A publication*] (DLA)
**McH** ........... Microeditions Hachette, Paris, France [*Library symbol*] [*Library of Congress*] (LCLS)
**MCh** ........... Mikrasiatiki Chronika [*A publication*]
**mch** ............ Millicurie Hour
**MCH** .......... Mission Chapel [*Church of England*]
**MCHAC** ..... Memoires. Cercle Historique et Archeologique de Courtrai [*A publication*]
**MCHAN** .... Multichannel (AABC)
**MChB** ........ Boston College, Chestnut Hill, MA [*Library symbol*] [*Library of Congress*] (LCLS)
**MChB-WO** ... Boston College, Weston Observatory, Weston, MA [*Library symbol*] [*Library of Congress*] (LCLS)
**MCHC** ....... Mean Cell [*or Corpuscular*] Hemoglobin Concentration [*Hematology*]
**MCHC** ....... Mean Corpusculsar Hemoglobin Concentration [*Physiology*]
**MCHC** ....... Missing Children...Help Center (EA)
**MCHCL** .... Mechanically Cooled
**M Ch D** ...... Magister Chirurgiae Dentalis [*Master of Dental Surgery*]
**MCHE** ....... Eskimo Museum, Churchill, Manitoba [*Library symbol*] [*National Library of Canada*] (NLC)
**M Ch E** ...... Master of Chemical Engineering
**MCHEB** .... Mechanical and Chemical Engineering Transactions [*A publication*]
**MChelm** ..... Adams Library (Chelmsford Public Library), Chelmsford, MA [*Library symbol*] [*Library of Congress*] (LCLS)
**MChels** ...... Chelsea Public Library, Chelsea, MA [*Library symbol*] [*Library of Congress*] (LCLS)
**MChem** ...... Master of Chemistry (ADA)
**MChemA** ... Master in Chemical Analysis
**M Chem E** ... Master of Chemical Engineering
**MCHF** ....... Marine Corps Historical Foundation (EA)
**MCHFR** .... Minimum Critical Heat Flux Rates [*Nuclear energy*] (NRCH)
**MCHFR** .... Minimum Critical Heat Flux Ratio [*Nuclear energy*] (NRCH)
**MCHGD** .... Mott Center for Human Growth and Development (EA)
**MChi** .......... Chicopee Public Library, Chicopee, MA [*Library symbol*] [*Library of Congress*] (LCLS)
**MChiD** ....... Dow Jones & Co., Inc., Chicopee, MA [*Library symbol*] [*Library of Congress*] (LCLS)
**MChiL** ....... College of Our Lady of the Elms, Chicopee, MA [*Library symbol*] [*Library of Congress*] (LCLS)
**M Chir** ....... Magister Chirurgiae [*Master of Surgery*]
**M & Chit Bankr** ... Montagu and Chitty's English Bankruptcy Reports [*1838-40*] [*A publication*] (DLA)
**MCHM** ...... MacroChem Corp. [*Woburn, MA*] [*NASDAQ symbol*] (NQ)
**MCHMAS** ... Michaelmas [*Feast of St. Michael the Archangel, September 29*] (ROG)
**MCHMDI** ... Manufacturing Chemist [*A publication*]
**MCHN** ...... Machine
**MCHN** ...... Merchants National Corp. [*NASDAQ symbol*] (NQ)
**MCHND** ... Machined
**M Ch Orth** ... Master of Orthopaedic Surgery
**M Ch Otol** ... Master of Oto-Rhino-Laryngological Surgery
**MCHP** ....... (Methylcinnamylhydrazono)propionate [*Biochemistry*]
**MChP** ........ Pine Manor College, Chestnut Hill, MA [*Library symbol*] [*Library of Congress*] (LCLS)
**M'CHR** ...... Manchester [*County in England*] (ROG)
**MCHR** ....... Medical Committee for Human Rights [*Defunct*]
**M Chr Ed** ... Master of Christian Education
**MCHRF** .... Mechanically Refrigerated
**M Chr Lit** .. Magazine of Christian Literature [*A publication*]

**MChrom** .... Master of Chromatics [*British*]
**MCHRY** .... Machinery (MSA)
**MCHS** ....... Maternal and Child Health Service (EA)
**MChS** ....... Member of the Society of Chiropodists
**MCHS** ....... Micro Healthsystems, Inc. [*West Orange, NJ*] [*NASDAQ symbol*] (NQ)
**MCHSM** ... Mechanism
**MCHST**..... Machinist (MSA)
**MCHT** ....... Merchant
**M & Cht Bankr** ... Montagu and Chitty's English Bankruptcy Reports [*1838-40*] [*A publication*] (DLA)
**M'CHTR** ... Manchester [*County in England*] (ROG)
**MCHY**....... Machinery (ROG)
**Mchy fwd** ... Machinery Forward (DS)
**MCI** .......... Kansas City [*Missouri*] [*Airport symbol*] (OAG)
**MCI** .......... Kansas City, MO [*Location identifier*] [*FAA*] (FAAL)
**MCI** .......... Machine Check Interruption [*Data processing*] (BUR)
**MCI** .......... Major Capital Improvement [*Justification for rent increase*]
**MCI** .......... Malicious Call Identification [*Telecommunications*] (TEL)
**MCI** .......... Malleable Cast Iron
**MCI** .......... Managed Cost Improvement (NRCH)
**MCI** .......... Management Consultants International, Inc. [*Information service or system*] (IID)
**MCI** .......... Manual of Clinical Immunology [*A publication*]
**MCI** .......... Marine Corps Institute
**MCI** .......... Marketing Concepts, Incorporated [*New York, NY*] [*Telecommunications*] (TSSD)
**MCI** .......... MassMutual Corporate Investors [*NYSE symbol*] (SPSG)
**MCI** .......... Master Configuration Index (MCD)
**MCI** .......... Material Concept Investigation (MCD)
**MCI** .......... Materials Cost Index
**MCI** .......... Meal, Combat, Individual [*Military*] (AABC)
**MCI** .......... Mean Cardiac Index
**MCi**........... Megacurie
**MCI** .......... Member of the Credit Institute
**MCI** .......... Member of the Institute of Commerce [*British*] (DBQ)
**MCI** .......... Meridian Control Integrator
**MCI** .......... Mexican Coffee Institute (EA)
**McI** ........... Microfilm Center, Incorporated, Dallas, Texas [*Library symbol*] [*Library of Congress*] (LCLS)
**MCI** .......... Microwave Communications of America, Incorporated
**MCI** .......... Milk Can Institute [*Defunct*]
**mCi**........... Millicurie [*Also, mC*]
**MCI** .......... Minnesota Counseling Inventory [*Psychology*]
**MCI** .......... Mission Change Indicator [*Air Force*] (AFIT)
**MCI** .......... Mitsubishi Chemical Industries [*Japan*]
**MCI** .......... Monte Cassino [*Italy*] [*Seismograph station code, US Geological Survey*] [*Closed*] (SEIS)
**MCI** .......... Mottled Cast Iron
**MCIA** ........ Methyl Chloride Industry Association (EA)
**MCIA** ........ MicroComputer Investors Association [*Database producer*] (EA)
**MCIArb**..... Member of the Chartered Institute of Arbitrators [*Australia*]
**MCIBS** ...... Member of the Chartered Institution of Building Services [*British*] (DBQ)
**MCIC**......... Machine Check Interruption Code [*Data processing*]
**MCIC**......... MCI Communications Corp. [*NASDAQ symbol*] (NQ)
**MCIC**......... Medical Care Insurance Commission [*Canada*]
**MCIC**......... Member of the Chemical Institute of Canada
**MCIC**......... Metals and Ceramics Information Center [*DoD*] [*Battelle Memorial Institute*] [*Information service or system*] (IID)
**MCIC Rep** ... MCIC [*Metals and Ceramics Information Center*] Report [*A publication*]
**MCID** ........ Multipurpose Concealed Intrusion Detector [*Army*] (RDA)
**McIDAS**.... Man-Computer Interactive Data Access System
**MCIF**......... Member of the Canadian Institute of Forestry
**MCIM** ....... Member of the Canadian Institute of Mining
**MCIMM** ... Member of the Canadian Institute of Mining and Metallurgy
**McInc**......... Microcomfax, Incorporated, Camp Hill, PA [*Library symbol*] [*Library of Congress*] (LCLS)
**McIn & E Jud Pr** ... McIntyre and Evans' Judicature Practice [*A publication*] (DLA)
**McInt**......... McIntosh Music [*Record label*]
**MCIOB** ..... Member of the Chartered Institute of Building [*British*] (DBQ)
**MCIP**......... Mated Cast Iron Pair
**MCIR**......... MCR Capital, Inc. [*Toronto, ON*] [*NASDAQ symbol*] (NQ)
**MCIRA**...... Microelectronic Replacement Assembly (NG)
**MCIS**.......... Maintenance Control Information System (IEEE)
**MCIS**.......... Materials Compatibility in Sodium [*Nuclear energy*] (NRCH)
**MCIS**.......... Multichannel Initial System (MCD)
**MCIS**.......... Multiple Corridor Identification System [*Air Force*]
**MCIT**.......... Institute of Traditional Science, Cambridge, MA [*Library symbol*] [*Library of Congress*] (LCLS)
**MCIT**.......... Member of the Chartered Institute of Transport [*British*] (DCTA)
**MCIU** ........ Manipulator Controller Interface Unit (NASA)
**MCIU** ........ Master Control and Interface Unit [*NASA*] (NASA)
**MCIU** ........ Mission Control and Interface Unit [*NASA*] (NASA)
**MCJ**........... Maicao [*Colombia*] [*Airport symbol*] (OAG)
**MCJ**........... Master of Comparative Jurisprudence
**MCJ**........... Mensajero del Corazon de Jesus [*A publication*]
**MCJ**........... Michigan Civil Jurisprudence [*A publication*] (DLA)
**MCJ**........... Model Car Journal Association [*Publishing company*] (EA)
**MCJC**......... Maryknoll Center for Justice Concerns (EA)
**MCJC**......... Mason City Junior College [*Iowa*]
**MCJ News** ... Milton Centre of Japan. News [*A publication*]
**MCJR**......... Multichannel Jezebel [*Sonobuoy System*] Relay [*Military*] (NG)
**MCK**.......... Maintenance Check (FAAC)
**MCK**.......... Manson Creek Resources Ltd. [*Vancouver Stock Exchange symbol*]
**MCK**.......... Master Cook [*Navy*]
**MCK**.......... McCook [*Nebraska*] [*Airport symbol*] (OAG)
**MCK**.......... McCook, NE [*Location identifier*] [*FAA*] (FAAL)
**MCK**.......... McKesson Corp. [*NYSE symbol*] (SPSG)
**MCK**.......... McKinley [*Alaska*] [*Seismograph station code, US Geological Survey*] (SEIS)
**MCK**.......... Modification Change Kit
**MCKA** ....... Metal Cutting Knife Association (EA)
**MCKBA**..... Memoirs. College of Science. University of Kyoto. Series B [*A publication*]
**McK Consol Laws** ... McKinney's Consolidated Laws of New York [*A publication*] (DLA)
**MCKD**....... Multicystic Kidney Disease [*Medicine*]
**MCKEES** .. Marine Corps Key Experiences Evaluation System (MCD)
**McKelvey Ev** ... McKelvey on Evidence [*A publication*] (DLA)
**McKin Jus** ... McKinney's Justice [*A publication*] (DLA)
**McKin Phil Ev** ... McKinnon's Philosophy of Evidence [*A publication*] (DLA)
**McKinsey Q** ... McKinsey Quarterly [*A publication*]
**McKinsey Quart** ... McKinsey Quarterly [*A publication*]
**MCL**.......... Cebecoskoop [*A publication*]
**MCL**.......... Intervega - Movement for Compassionate Living the Vegan Way (EAIO)
**MCL**.......... Lesley College, Cambridge, MA [*Library symbol*] [*Library of Congress*] (LCLS)
**MCL**.......... Maintenance Checkoff List
**MCL**.......... Manufacturing Control Language [*Data processing*] (MCD)
**MCL**.......... Marine Corps League (EA)
**MCL**.......... Martin Classical Lectures [*A publication*]
**MCL**.......... Mass Change Log (MCD)
**MCL**.......... Master Change Log
**MCL**.......... Master of Civil Law
**MCL**.......... Master of Comparative Law
**MCL**.......... Master Component List (MCD)
**MCL**.......... Master Configuration List
**MCL**.......... Mathematics Computation Laboratory [*General Services Administration*]
**MCL**.......... Maximum Contaminant Level
**MCL**.......... McClellan Central Laboratory (MCD)
**M'Cl**........... McClelland's English Exchequer Reports [*A publication*] (DLA)
**McL**........... McLaren Micropublishing, Toronto, ON, Canada [*Library symbol*] [*Library of Congress*] (LCLS)
**Mc L** .......... McLean's United States Circuit Court Reports [*A publication*] (DLA)
**MCL**.......... McNeil River [*Alaska*] [*Seismograph station code, US Geological Survey*] (SEIS)
**MCL**.......... Medial Collateral Ligament [*Anatomy*]
**MCL**.......... Medial Cruciate Ligament [*Anatomy*]
**MCL**.......... Medical College of Ohio at Toledo, Toledo, OH [*OCLC symbol*] (OCLC)
**MCL**.......... Memory Control and Logging [*Hewlett-Packard Co.*]
**MCL**.......... Message Control Language [*Data processing*]
**MCL**.......... Metal Crystal Lattice
**MCL**.......... Microcomputer Center and Library [*Wisconsin State Department of Public Instruction*] [*Information service or system*] (IID)
**MCL**.......... Microprogram Control Logic [*Data processing*] (MDG)
**MCL**.......... Mid-Canada Line [*RADAR warning chain of fence across Canada; sometimes called the McGill Fence*]
**MCL**.......... Midclavicular Line [*Medicine*]
**MCL**.......... Midcostal Line [*Medicine*]
**MCL**.......... Mineral Constitution Laboratories [*Pennsylvania State University*] [*Research center*] (RCD)
**MCL**.......... Miniature Cartridge Light
**MCL**.......... Minimal Computer Load
**MCL**.......... Minority Carrier Lifetime [*Solar cell technology*]
**MCL**.......... Missile Continuity Loop (MCD)
**MCL**.......... Modified Chest Lead [*Medicine*]
**MCL**.......... Molten-Caustic-Leaching [*Coal technology*]
**M Cl**........... Mondo Classico [*A publication*]
**MCL**.......... Moore Corp. Ltd. [*NYSE symbol*] [*Toronto Stock Exchange symbol*] (SPSG)
**MCL**.......... Most Comfortable Loudness Test [*Audiometry*]
**MCL**.......... Moving Coil Loudspeaker [*Electronics*]
**MCL**.......... Multicolor LASER
**MCL**.......... Mushroom Canners League (EA)
**MCLA** ....... Marine Corps League Auxiliary (EA)
**MCLA** ....... Medical Contact Lens Association [*British*]
**MCLA** ....... Michigan Compiled Laws, Annotated [*A publication*] (DLA)
**MCLA** ....... Microcoded Communications Line Adapter

**MCLA** ....... Motor Carrier Lawyers Association (EA)
**MCLAMS** ... Measurement, Control, LEID [*Limit of Error of the Inventory Difference*], and MUF [*Material Unaccounted For*] Inventory Difference Simulation [*Nuclear energy*] (NRCH)
**McLar Tr** ... McLaren's Trusts in Scotland [*A publication*] (DLA)
**McLar W** ... McLaren's Law of Wills [*Scotland*] [*A publication*] (DLA)
**MCLB** ....... Modern and Classical Language Bulletin [*A publication*]
**MCLD** ....... Multicolor LASER Display
**MCLE** ....... Mandatory Continuing Legal Education [*Australia*]
**M'Cle** ....... M'Clelland's English Exchequer Reports [*148 English Reprint*] [*A publication*] (DLA)
**McLean** ...... McLean's United States Circuit Court Reports [*A publication*] (DLA)
**McLean Foram Lab Rept** ... McLean Foraminiferal Laboratory. Reports [*A publication*]
**McLean Hosp J** ... McLean Hospital Journal [*A publication*]
**McLean Paleont Lab Rept** ... McLean Paleontological Laboratory. Reports [*A publication*]
**McLean's CCR** ... McLean's United States Circuit Court Reports [*A publication*] (DLA)
**McLean's Rep** ... McLean's United States Circuit Court Reports [*A publication*] (DLA)
**M'Clel** ....... M'Clelland's English Exchequer Reports [*148 English Reprint*] [*A publication*] (DLA)
**M'Clel (Eng)** ... McClelland's English Exchequer Reports [*A publication*] (DLA)
**M'Clel & Y** ... M'Clelland and Younge's English Exchequer Reports [*148 English Reprint*] [*A publication*] (DLA)
**M'Clel & Y (Eng)** ... M'Clelland and Younge's English Exchequer Reports [*148 English Reprint*] [*A publication*] (DLA)
**M'Cle & Yo** ... M'Clelland and Younge's English Exchequer Reports [*148 English Reprint*] [*A publication*] (DLA)
**MCLFDC** .. Marine Corps Landing Force Development Center
**MCLG** ....... Major Caliber Lightweight Gun [*Navy*] (MCD)
**MCLG** ....... Maximum Contaminant Level Goal [*Environmental Protection Agency*]
**MCLI** ....... McLean Industries, Inc. [*NASDAQ symbol*] (NQ)
**MCLI** ....... Meiklejohn Civil Liberties Institute (EA)
**M Clin North America** ... Medical Clinics of North America [*A publication*]
**MClinPsych** ... Master of Clinical Psychology
**MClinPsychol** ... Master of Clinical Psychology (ADA)
**MClinSc** .... Master of Clinical Science (ADA)
**MCLJ** ....... Mifflin County Legal Journal [*Pennsylvania*] [*A publication*] (DLA)
**MCLK** ....... Master Clock
**MCLL** ....... Missile Compartment, Lower Level
**MCLN** ....... Mouvement Centrafricain de Liberation Nationale [*Central African Movement for National Liberation*] (PD)
**MCLO** ....... Medical Construction Liaison Office [*or Officer*] [*Air Force*] (AFM)
**MCLong** .... Longfellow House, Longfellow National Historic Site, Cambridge, MA [*Library symbol*] [*Library of Congress*] (LCLS)
**MCLORA** ... Marine Corps Level of Repair Analysis
**MCLOS** ..... Manual Command-to-Line-of-Sight [*Missile guidance system*] (INF)
**MCLP** ....... Military Committee Representative Liaison Paper to the International Staff [*North Atlantic Council*] (NATG)
**McL & R** .... McLean and Robinson's Scotch Appeal Cases [*1839*] [*A publication*] (DLA)
**MCLR** ....... Midwest Center for Labor Research (EA)
**MCLR** ....... Minimum Critical Leaching Rate
**MCLS** ....... Metropolitan Cooperative Library System [*Library network*]
**MCLS** ....... Monroe County Library System [*Library network*]
**MCLS** ....... Mucocutaneous Lymph Node Syndrome [*Medicine*]
**MCLSBLANT** ... Marine Corps Logistic Support Base, Atlantic (MCD)
**MCLSBPAC** ... Marine Corps Logistic Support Base, Pacific (MCD)
**MClSc** ....... Master of Clinical Science (ADA)
**MCLT** ....... Maximum Cruise Level Thrust (MCD)
**MCLWG** ... Major Caliber Lightweight Gun [*Navy*] (NG)
**M'Cl & Y** ... McClelland and Younge's English Exchequer Reports [*1824-25*] [*A publication*] (DLA)
**M'Cl & Yo** ... M'Clelland and Younge's English Exchequer Reports [*148 English Reprint*] [*A publication*] (DLA)
**MCM** ........ Circular Mils, Thousands
**MCM** ........ Cordi-Marian Missionary Sisters [*Roman Catholic religious order*]
**MCM** ........ Mac-Am Resources Corp. [*Vancouver Stock Exchange symbol*]
**MCM** ........ Machines for Coordinated Multiprocessing
**MCM** ........ Macon, MO [*Location identifier*] [*FAA*] (FAAL)
**MCM** ........ Magic Carpet Magazine [*A publication*]
**MCM** ........ Magnetic Core Memory [*Data processing*]
**MCM** ........ Maintenance Control Module [*Telecommunications*] (TEL)
**MCM** ........ Manned Circumlunar Mission
**MCM** ........ Mannes College of Music [*New York, NY*]
**MCM** ........ Manual of Clinical Microbiology [*A publication*]
**MCM** ........ Manual Communication Module [*Telecommunication device for the deaf*]
**MCM** ........ Manual for Courts-Martial
**MCM** ........ Marine Corps Manual
**MCM** ........ Marketing Communications [*A publication*]
**MCM** ........ Mass Control Module
**MCM** ........ Massachusetts Institute of Technology, Cambridge, MA [*Library symbol*] [*Library of Congress*] (LCLS)
**MCM** ........ Master of Church Music
**MCM** ........ Master Control Module
**MCM** ........ Materiel Change Management
**MCM** ........ McCarthy, Crisanti & Maffei, Inc. [*Information service or system*] (IID)
**MCM** ........ McMurdo Sound [*Antarctica*] [*Seismograph station code, US Geological Survey*] [*Closed*] (SEIS)
**MCM** ........ Medical Corps, Merchant Marine [*USNR officer designation*]
**MCM** ........ Mega Cisterna Magna [*Medicine*]
**MCM** ........ Megawatt Cassegrain Monopulse
**MCM** ........ Member of the College of Musicians [*British*]
**MCM** ........ Memory Control Module
**MCM** ........ Microcircuit Module
**McM** ........ Micromedia Ltd., Toronto, ON, Canada [*Library symbol*] [*Library of Congress*] (LCLS)
**MCM** ........ Military Characteristics Motor Vehicles
**MCM** ........ Military Committee Memorandum [*NATO*] (NATG)
**MCM** ........ Million Centimeters (MCD)
**MCM** ........ Mine Countermeasures (NG)
**MCM** ........ Minneapolis College of Music
**MCM** ........ Missile Carrying Missile (AAG)
**MCM** ........ Missile Control Module (NVT)
**MCM** ........ Mission Control Module
**MCM** ........ Mississippi College, Clinton, MS [*OCLC symbol*] (OCLC)
**MCM** ........ Monolithic Circuit Mask
**MCM** ........ Monte Carlo [*Monaco*] [*Airport symbol*] (OAG)
**MCM** ........ Monte Carlo Method [*Data processing*]
**MCM** ........ Moving Coil Microphone [*Electronics*]
**MCM** ........ Multichip Module [*Data processing*]
**MCM** ........ Multilayer Ceramic Multichip [*Electronics*]
**MCM** ........ Multinational Computer Models, Inc. [*Information service or system*] (IID)
**MCM** ........ Multiple Connected Motor
**MCM** ........ Multiple Contact Miscible [*Physical chemistry*]
**MCM** ........ Municipal Court of Montreal (DLA)
**MCM** ........ Music Clubs Magazine [*A publication*]
**MCM** ........ Thousand Circular Mils
**MCMA** ...... Machine Chain Manufacturers Association (EA)
**MCMA** ...... Metal Cookware Manufacturers Association [*Later, CMA*] (EA)
**McMas RR** ... McMaster's New York Railroad Laws [*A publication*] (DLA)
**McMaster Symp Iron Steelmaking Proc** ... McMaster University. Symposium on Iron and Steelmaking. Proceedings [*A publication*]
**MCMC** ...... Marine Corps Memorial Commission
**MCMC** ...... McM Corporation [*NASDAQ symbol*] (NQ)
**MCMC** ...... Medicine Cabinet Manufacturers Council (EA)
**MCMC** ...... Midwest Committee for Military Counseling (EA)
**McM Com Cas** ... McMaster's United States Commercial Cases [*A publication*] (DLA)
**McM Com Dec** ... McMaster's Commercial Decisions [*A publication*] (DLA)
**McMdL** ..... Micromedia Ltd., Toronto, ON, Canada [*Library symbol*] [*Library of Congress*] (LCLS)
**MCMES** .... Member of the Civil and Mechanical Engineering Society
**MCM-F** ..... Massachusetts Institute of Technology, University Film Study Center, Cambridge, MA [*Library symbol*] [*Library of Congress*] (LCLS)
**MCMFE** .... Membrane-Covered Mercury Film Electrode [*Electrochemistry*]
**MCMG** ...... Man-Carrying Motion Generator [*Space-flight simulation*]
**MCMG** ...... Military Committee Meteorological Group [*NATO*] (NATG)
**MCM-H** .... Massachusetts Institute of Technology, Francis Russell Hart Nautical Museum, Cambridge, MA [*Library symbol*] [*Library of Congress*] (LCLS)
**MCMHA** ... Metropolitan College Mental Health Association (EA)
**MCMI** ....... Malleable Chain Manufacturers Institute [*Later, American Chain Association*]
**MCMI** ....... Millon Clinical Multiaxial Inventory [*Psychology*]
**MCMI** ....... Minneapolis Center for Microbiological Investigations [*Public Health Service*] (GRD)
**MCMJ** ....... Michigan Mathematical Journal [*A publication*]
**MCM-L** ..... Massachusetts Institute of Technology, Lincoln Laboratory, Lexington, MA [*Library symbol*] [*Library of Congress*] (LCLS)
**MCML** ...... Missile Compartment, Middle Level
**MCMM** ..... Management Control - Material Management (IEEE)
**MCMN** ..... Motor Coils Manufacturing Co. [*NASDAQ symbol*] (NQ)
**MCMOPS** ... Mine Countermeasures Operations [*Military*] (NVT)
**MCMR** ...... Medical Corps, Merchant Marine, General Service [*USNR officer designation*]
**MC/MR** .... Minimum Change/Minimum Risk [*Mask design concept*] [*Army*] (INF)
**MCMS** ...... Medical Corps, Merchant Marine, Special Service [*USNR officer designation*]
**MCMS** ...... Midwest Center for Mass Spectrometry [*University of Nebraska - Lincoln*] [*Research center*] (RCD)
**M-CM-S** .... Mobility, Countermobility, and Survivability
**MCMS** ...... Multichannel Memory System [*Data processing*] (AAG)
**MCMS** ...... Multiple Countermeasure System

**MCMSM**... Modern Analytical and Computational Methods in Science and Mathematics [*Elsevier Book Series*] [*A publication*]
**MCMT**...... Main Currents in Modern Thought [*A publication*]
**MCMU**...... Mass Core Memory Unit (MCD)
**McMul**....... McMullan's South Carolina Law Reports [*A publication*] (DLA)
**McMul Eq** ... McMullan's South Carolina Equity Reports [*A publication*] (DLA)
**McMull Eq (SC)** ... McMullan's South Carolina Equity Reports [*A publication*] (DLA)
**McMull L (SC)** ... McMullan's South Carolina Law Reports [*A publication*] (DLA)
**MCMUS** ... Manual of Courts-Martial, United States
**MCMV** ...... Maize Chlorotic Mottle Virus
**MCMV** ...... Mine Countermeasures Vessel [*or Vehicle*] (NATG)
**MCMV** ...... Murine Cytomegalovirus
**MCN**.......... American Journal of Maternal Child Nursing [*A publication*]
**MCN**.......... Macon [*Georgia*] [*Airport symbol*] (OAG)
**MCN**.......... Maintenance Communications Net (MCD)
**MCN**.......... Maintenance Control Number
**MCN**.......... Management Change Notice (MCD)
**MCN**.......... Management Control Number [*Army*] (AABC)
**MCN**.......... Manual Control Number
**MCN**.......... Manufacturing Change Notice
**MCN**.......... Mapping Cylinder Neighborhood
**MCN**.......... Master Change Notice (KSC)
**MCN**.......... Master Control Number
**MCN**.......... Material Change Notice (MCD)
**MCN**.......... Material Complaint Notice
**MCN**.......... MCN Corp. [*Formerly, Michigan Consolidated Gas Co.*] [*NYSE symbol*] (SPSG)
**McN**.......... McNeil Laboratories, Inc. [*Research code symbol*]
**MCN**.......... McNeil Mantha, Inc. [*Toronto Stock Exchange symbol*]
**MCN**.......... Mercury [*Nevada*] [*Seismograph station code, US Geological Survey*] [*Closed*] (SEIS)
**MCN**.......... Michigan Consolidated Gas Co. [*NYSE symbol*] (SPSG)
**MCN**.......... Micrococcal Nuclease [*Also, MN*] [*An enzyme*]
**MCN**.......... Military Construction, Navy
**MCN**.......... Missing Children Network (EA)
**MCN**.......... Motor Cycle News [*A publication*]
**MCN**.......... Movimiento de Conciliacion Nacional [*National Conciliation Movement*] [*Dominican Republic*] [*Political party*] (PPW)
**MCN**.......... Museum Computer Network, Inc. [*American Association of Museums*] [*Research center*] (RCD)
**McNagh**..... Macnaghten's Select Cases in Chancery Tempore King [*A publication*] (DLA)
**McNal Ev** .. Macnally's Rules of Evidence [*A publication*] (DLA)
**MCNC**....... Carberry/North Cypress Library, Carberry, Manitoba [*Library symbol*] [*National Library of Canada*] (NLC)
**MCNC**....... Microelectronics Center of North Carolina [*Research center*] (RCD)
**MCNG**....... Military Construction, National Guard
**MCNJA**..... Maternal-Child Nursing Journal [*A publication*]
**McN-JR**..... McNeil Laboratories, Inc. [*Research code symbol*]
**MCNL** ....... Military Committee of National Liberation [*Mali*] [*Political party*] (PPW)
**McN R** ....... McNeese Review [*A publication*]
**MCNR**....... Military Construction, Naval Reserves
**MCNRF**..... Military Construction, Naval Reserve Facilities
**MCNRS**..... Meal Card Number Recording System (MCD)
**MCNY** ....... Museum of the City of New York
**MCNYA** .... Machinery [*Later, Machinery and Production Engineering*] [*A publication*]
**MCo**........... Concord Free Public Library, Concord, MA [*Library symbol*] [*Library of Congress*] (LCLS)
**MCO**.......... Magnetron Cutoff
**MCO**.......... MAI Systems Corp. [*NYSE symbol*] (SPSG)
**MCO**.......... Main Civilian Occupation
**MCO**.......... Maintenance Checkoff
**MCO**.......... Manual Change Order (MSA)
**MCO**.......... Marches Tropicaux et Mediterraneens [*A publication*]
**MCO**.......... Marine Corps Officer
**MCO**.......... Marine Corps Order
**MCO**.......... Massachusetts College of Optometry
**M Co** .......... Master of Cosmology
**MCO**.......... Mill Culls Out [*Lumber*]
**MCO**.......... Minneapolis Community College, Minneapolis, MN [*OCLC symbol*] (OCLC)
**MCO**.......... Miscellaneous Charges Order [*Business term*]
**MCO**.......... Missile Checkout (NG)
**MCO**.......... Missile Control Officer
**MCO**.......... Mission Control Operation [*NASA*]
**MCO**.......... Monaco [*ANSI three-letter standard code*] (CNC)
**MCO**.......... Movement Control Officer [*Army*]
**MCO**.......... Multiple Channel Oscilloscope
**MCO**.......... Orlando, FL [*Location identifier*] [*FAA*] (FAAL)
**MCO**.......... Orlando [*Florida*] International [*Airport symbol*] (OAG)
**MCOA**....... Mastiff Club of America (EA)
**MCOA**....... Music Center Opera Association [*Los Angeles*]
**MCOAG**.... Marine Corps Operations Analysis Group
**MCOAM**... Material Control Order Additional Material
**MCOFA** .... Machine Outil Francaise [*A publication*]
**M-COFT** ... Mobile Conduct of Fire Trainer [*Combat simulator*]
**MCOG**....... Member of the British College of Obstetricians and Gynaecologists (DAS)
**MCOGA**.... Mid-Continent Oil and Gas Association (EA)
**MCogSc**..... Master of Cognitive Science
**MCOHM** .. Military Community Oral Health Managers [*Army*]
**MCOLF**..... Marine Corps Outlying Landing Field
**MCollP**...... Member of the College of Preceptors [*British*] (DBQ)
**M Com**....... Master of Commerce
**MCOM**...... Mathematics of Computation (IEEE)
**MCOM**...... Medical Communications [*A publication*]
**MCOM**...... Midwest Communications Corp. [*NASDAQ symbol*] (NQ)
**MCom**........ Miscelanea Comillas [*A publication*]
**MCOM**...... Missile Command [*Army*] (MCD)
**M Com Adm** ... Master of Commercial Administration
**MComm**..... Master of Commerce (ADA)
**M Comm**.... Master of Commerce and Administration (ROG)
**MCOMM** ... Minimize Communications
**M Comm H** ... Master of Community Health
**M Comp L** ... Master of Comparative Law
**M Com Sc**.. Master of Commercial Science
**MCON**....... EMCON Associates [*NASDAQ symbol*] (NQ)
**MCON**....... Military Construction
**MConsE**..... Member of the Association of Consulting Engineers [*British*] (EY)
**MCOP**....... Major Command Orientation Program [*Air Force*] (AFM)
**MCOP**....... Marine Corps Ordnance Publication
**mCOP**........ Measured Colloidal Osmotic Pressure [*Clinical chemistry*]
**MCOP**....... Mission Control Operations Panel [*NASA*] (KSC)
**MCOP**....... Multiple Conductor, Oil-Resistant, Portable [*Cable*]
**MCOPB**..... Methods in Computational Physics [*A publication*]
**MCOPR** .... Major Command of Primary Responsibility [*Air Force*] (AFM)
**MCOR**....... Marine Corporation [*Springfield, IL*] [*NASDAQ symbol*] (NQ)
**MCOR**....... Methodist Committee for Overseas Relief [*Later, UMCOR*] (EA)
**MC/ORB**... Maritime Command Operational Research Branch [*Canada*]
**MC/ORD** .. Maritime Command Operational Research Division [*Canada*]
**M'Cord Eq (SC)** ... M'Cord's South Carolina Equity Reports [*A publication*] (DLA)
**M'Cord L (SC)** ... M'Cord's South Carolina Law Reports [*A publication*] (DLA)
**MCOS** ....... Macrose Industries Corp. [*NASDAQ symbol*] (NQ)
**MCOS** ....... Microprogrammable Computer Operating System
**MCoS**......... Military College of Science [*British military*] (DMA)
**MCOT**....... Missile Checkout Trailer
**MCOT**....... Missile Control Officer, Trainer (NG)
**MCOTEA** ... Marine Corps Operational Test and Evaluation Activity (CAAL)
**Mcoul**......... Millicoulomb
**MCouns(Ed)** ... Master of Counselling (Education) (ADA)
**MCOV**....... Main Chamber Oxidizer Valve [*NASA*] (KSC)
**MCOW**...... Medical College of Wisconsin
**MCoW**....... Wayside [*Minute Man National Historical Park*], Concord, MA [*Library symbol*] [*Library of Congress*] (LCLS)
**MCP**.......... Macapa [*Brazil*] [*Airport symbol*] (OAG)
**MCP**.......... Main Call Process [*Telecommunications*] (TEL)
**MCP**.......... Main Condensate Pump [*Navy*] (CAAL)
**MCP**.......... Main Coolant Pump (NVT)
**MCP**.......... Maintenance Control Panel [*Navy*] (CAAL)
**MCP**.......... Maintenance Control Point (NG)
**MCP**.......... Malawi Congress Party [*Nyasaland*] [*Political party*] (PPW)
**MCP**.......... Malayan Communist Party [*Political party*] (CINC)
**MCP**.......... Male Chauvinist Pig [*Feminist term*]
**MCP**.......... Management Control Plan
**MCP**.......... Manual Control Panel
**MCP**.......... Manufacturing Change Point
**MCP**.......... Marcana Petroleum Ltd. [*Vancouver Stock Exchange symbol*]
**MCP**.......... Marine Corps Capabilities Plan (MCD)
**MCP**.......... Martinique Communist Party [*Political party*]
**MCP**.......... Mary Cheney Library, Manchester, CT [*OCLC symbol*] (OCLC)
**MCP**.......... Massachusetts College of Pharmacy [*Boston*]
**MCP**.......... Massachusetts CPA [*Certified Public Accountant*] Review [*A publication*]
**MCP**.......... Master Change Proposal (KSC)
**M Cp**.......... Master of Chiropody
**MCP**.......... Master of City Planning
**MCP**.......... Master Computer Program [*NASA*] (KSC)
**MCP**.......... Master Control Program [*Burroughs Corp.*]
**MCP**.......... Materials Chemistry and Physics [*A publication*]
**MCP**.......... Materials Control Plan (NASA)
**MCP**.......... Materiel Command Procedure [*Military*]
**MCP**.......... Maximum Continuous Power
**MCP**.......... Measurements Control Procedure (KSC)
**MCP**.......... Medical College of Pennsylvania
**MCP**.......... Medical Continuation Pay [*Military*] (AABC)
**MCP**.......... MEECN Communication Plan (MCD)

**MCP** .......... Melphalan, Cyclophosphamide, Prednisone [*Antineoplastic drug regimen*]
**MCP** .......... Member of the College of Preceptors [*British*]
**MCP** .......... Member of the Colonial Parliament [*British*]
**MCP** .......... Memory-Centered Processing [*or Processor*] [*System*] [*Data processing*]
**MCP** .......... Message Control Program [*Data processing*]
**MCP** .......... Metacarpophalangeal [*Anatomy*]
**MCP** .......... Metal Case Profile [*Ammunition*]
**MCP** .......... Metal Casting Pattern (MSA)
**MCP** .......... Methyl-Accepting Chemotaxis Proteins [*Biochemistry*]
**MCP** .......... Methylchlorophenoxyacetic Acid [*Also, MCPA*] [*Herbicide*]
**McP** .......... Micro Photo Division, Bell & Howell Co., Wooster, OH [*Library symbol*] [*Library of Congress*] (LCLS)
**MCP** .......... Microchannel Plate [*Data processing*]
**MCP** .......... Microcrystalline Polymer [*Plastics technology*]
**MCP** .......... Microwave Coupled Plasma [*Spectroscopy*]
**MCP** .......... Military Construction Plan
**MCP** .......... Military Construction Program (AFIT)
**MCP** .......... Militia Career Program [*DoD*]
**MCP** .......... Mineral Commodity Profiles. US Bureau of Mines [*A publication*]
**MCP** .......... Missile Control Panel
**MCP** .......... Missile Control Point (NATG)
**MCP** .......... Mission Concept Paper (MCD)
**MCP** .......... Mission Control Programmer [*NASA*] (KSC)
**MCP** .......... Moca [*Puerto Rico*] [*Seismograph station code, US Geological Survey*] (SEIS)
**MCP** .......... Mode Control Panel
**MCP** .......... Model Cities Program
**MCP** .......... Monitoring and Control Panel (NASA)
**MCP** .......... Monocalcium Phosphate [*Inorganic chemistry*] [*Food additive*]
**MCP** .......... Monte Capellino [*Italy*] [*Later, ROB*] [*Geomagnetic observatory code*]
**MCP** .......... Mouvement Chretien pour la Paix [*Christian Movement for Peace - CMP*] [*Brussels, Belgium*] (EAIO)
**MCP** .......... Multicatalytic Proteinase [*An enzyme*]
**MCP** .......... Multichannel Communications Program (IEEE)
**MCP** .......... Multicomponent Plasma
**MCP** .......... Multiple-Chip Package
**MCP** .......... Multiple Comparison Procedure [*Statistics*]
**MCP** .......... Multiple Control Program [*Data processing*]
**MCP** .......... Mutation as Cellular Process
**MCP** .......... Polaroid Corp., Cambridge, MA [*Library symbol*] [*Library of Congress*] (LCLS)
**MCPA** ....... Member of the Canadian Psychological Association
**MCPA** ....... Member of the College of Pathologists Australasia
**MCPA** ....... Memory Clock Pulse Amplifier
**MCPA** ....... Methylchlorophenoxyacetic Acid [*Also, MCP*] [*Herbicide*]
**MCPA** ....... Methylenecyclopropylacetic Acid [*Organic chemistry*]
**McPA** ........ Microfilm Corporation of Pennsylvania, Pittsburgh, PA [*Library symbol*] [*Library of Congress*] (LCLS)
**MCPA** ....... Midwest College Placement Association
**MCPAAJ** .. Escuela Nacional de Agricultura [*Chapingo*]. Monografias [*A publication*]
**MCPAC**..... Military Construction Programs Advisory Committee (AFM)
**MCP Alum** ... Mineral Commodity Profiles. Aluminum [*A publication*]
**M & C Partidas** ... Moreau-Lislet and Carleton's Laws of Las Siete Partidas in Force in Louisiana [*A publication*] (DLA)
**MC Path** .... Member of the College of Pathologists [*British*]
**MCPBA**..... Meta-Chloroperoxybenzoic Acid [*Organic chemistry*]
**MCPC**........ Manipulator Controller Power Conditioner (MCD)
**MCPC**........ Musee Canadien de la Photographie Contemporaine [*Canadian Museum of Contemporary Photography - CMCP*]
**MCPC**........ Parks Canada [*Parcs Canada*] Churchill, Manitoba [*Library symbol*] [*National Library of Canada*] (NLC)
**MCP Chrom** ... Mineral Commodity Profiles. Chromium [*A publication*]
**MCP Clays** ... Mineral Commodity Profiles. Clays [*A publication*]
**MCP Cobalt** ... Mineral Commodity Profiles. Cobalt [*A publication*]
**MCP Columb** ... Mineral Commodity Profiles. Columbium [*A publication*]
**MCP Copper** ... Mineral Commodity Profiles. Copper [*A publication*]
**MCPD** ....... Marine Corps Procurement District
**MCPE**........ Modular Collective Protection Equipment (RDA)
**MCPER**...... Multiple Critical-Pole Equal-Ripple Rational (MCD)
**MCPESCF** ... Multiconfiguration Paired Excitation Self-Consistent Field [*Physics*]
**MCPG** ....... Media Conversion Program Generator
**MCPH** ....... Metacarpophalangeal [*Anatomy*]
**MCPH** ....... Ministry of Concern for Public Health (EA)
**McPherson** ... McPherson, Lee, and Bell's Scotch Session Cases [*A publication*] (DLA)
**MCPI**......... Medical Consumer Price Index (DHSM)
**MCP Iron** .. Mineral Commodity Profiles. Iron and Steel [*A publication*]
**MCP Iron O** ... Mineral Commodity Profiles. Iron Ore [*A publication*]
**MCPL**........ Magnetic Circularly Polarized Luminescence [*Spectroscopy*]
**MCPL**........ Members of Congress for Peace through Law [*An association*]
**MCPL**........ Multiple-Cue Probability Learning [*Psychology*]
**MCP Lead** ... Mineral Commodity Profiles. Lead [*A publication*]
**MCPM** ...... Member of the Confederation of Professional Management [*British*] (DBQ)
**MCP Mang** ... Mineral Commodity Profiles. Manganese [*A publication*]
**MCP Nickel** ... Mineral Commodity Profiles. Nickel [*A publication*]
**MCPO** ....... Master Chief Petty Officer [*Navy*]
**MCPO** ....... Military Committee Representative Communication to the Private Office of the NATO Secretary General (NATG)
**MCPOC** .... Master Chief Petty Officer of Command [*Navy*]
**MCPON**.... Master Chief Petty Officer of the Navy
**MCPP**........ Mecoprop [*Herbicide*]
**MCP Plat**... Mineral Commodity Profiles. Platinum Group Metals [*A publication*]
**MCP Potash** ... Mineral Commodity Profiles. Potash [*A publication*]
**MCPPR**..... Marine Corps Program Progress Report
**MCPQ** ....... Municipal Code of the Province of Quebec [*A publication*] (DLA)
**MCPR**........ Maximum Critical Power Ratio [*Nuclear energy*] (NRCH)
**MCPR**........ Minimum Critical Power Ratio [*Nuclear energy*] (NRCH)
**MCPS**........ Major Cost Proposal System (MCD)
**MCPS**........ Mechanical Copyright Protection Society [*British*]
**MCPS**........ Megachips per Second (MCD)
**MCPS**........ Megacycles per Second [*Megahertz*] [*See also MC/S, MCS, MH, MHz*]
**MCPS**........ Member of the Cambridge Philosophical Society (ROG)
**MCPS**........ Member of the College of Physicians and Surgeons [*British*]
**MCPS**........ Military Committee in Permanent Session [*NATO*] (NATG)
**MCPS**........ Mini Core Processing Subsystem (TEL)
**MCPS**........ Missouri Children's Picture Series [*Child development test*] [*Psychology*]
**MCP Silicn** ... Mineral Commodity Profiles. Silicon [*A publication*]
**MCP Silver** ... Mineral Commodity Profiles. Silver [*A publication*]
**MCP Soda A** ... Mineral Commodity Profiles. Soda Ash, Sodium Carbonate, and Sodium Sulfate [*A publication*]
**MCPT**........ Maritime Central Planning Team [*NATO*] (NATG)
**MCP Tantlm** ... Mineral Commodity Profiles. Tantalum [*A publication*]
**MCP Titanm** ... Mineral Commodity Profiles. Titanium [*A publication*]
**MCPU** ....... Multiple Central Processing Unit
**MCP Vandm** ... Mineral Commodity Profiles. Vanadium [*A publication*]
**MCP Zinc** ... Mineral Commodity Profiles. Zinc [*A publication*]
**MCQ**.......... Macquarie Island [*Australia*] [*Seismograph station code, US Geological Survey*] (SEIS)
**MCQ**.......... Macquarie Island [*Australia*] [*Geomagnetic observatory code*]
**Mcq**............ Macqueen's Scotch Appeal Cases, House of Lords [*A publication*] (DLA)
**MCQ**.......... Multiple Choice Questions (ADA)
**MCQA**....... McQuay, Inc. [*NASDAQ symbol*] (NQ)
**MCQP** ....... Milk Carton Quality Performing Council (EA)
**McQuillin Mun Corp** ... McQuillin on Municipal Corporations [*A publication*] (DLA)
**MCR** .......... Magistrates' Court Reports [*New Zealand*] [*A publication*] (DLA)
**MCR** .......... Magnetic Card Reader [*Data processing*]
**MCR** .......... Magnetic Character Reader [*Data processing*] (IEEE)
**MCR** .......... Magnetic Character Recognition [*Data processing*] (BUR)
**MCR** .......... Magnetic Confinement Reactor
**MCR** .......... Main Control Room (IEEE)
**MCR** .......... Maintenance Control Report
**MCR** .......... Management Coaching Relations Test
**MCR** .......... Manpower Control Report
**MCR** .......... Manual Change Request (MSA)
**MCR** .......... Manufacturing Change Request
**MCR** .......... Marine Corps Reserve
**MCR** .......... Mass Communications Review [*A publication*]
**MCR** .......... Master Change Record
**MCR** .......... Master Clock Receiver
**MCR** .......... Master of Comparative Religion
**MCR** .......... Master Control Record System (AABC)
**MCR** .......... Master Control Register
**MCR** .......... Master Control Relay [*Manufacturing term*]
**MCR** .......... Master Control Room (MCD)
**MCR** .......... Master Control Routine
**M Cr** .......... Master of Criminology
**MCR** .......... Matrimonial Causes Rules [*A publication*] (DLA)
**MCR** .......... Maximum Combat Readiness [*Military*]
**MCR** .......... Maximum Continuous Rating [*Also, MC(S)R*] [*Mechanical engineering*]
**MCR** .......... McCloud River Railroad Co. [*AAR code*]
**MCR** .......... MCO Resources, Inc. [*AMEX symbol*] (SPSG)
**MCR** .......... Medical Corps, General Service [*USNR officer designation*]
**MCR** .......... Mediterranean Communications Region [*Air Force*] (MCD)
**MCR** .......... Melbourne Critical Review [*University of Melbourne*] [*A publication*]
**MCR** .......... Memory Control Register
**MCR** .......... Mercer [*Alaska*] [*Seismograph station code, US Geological Survey*] [*Closed*] (SEIS)
**MCR** .......... Metabolic Clearance Rate
**MCR** .......... Methodists for Church Renewal
**MCR** .......... Metronome-Conditioned Relaxation
**MCR** .......... MFS Charter Income Trust [*NYSE symbol*] (SPSG)
**McR** .......... Micrecord Sales Corp., Chicago, IL [*Library symbol*] [*Library of Congress*] (LCLS)
**MCR** .......... Microcarbon Residue [*Petroleum analysis*]
**MCR** .......... Micrographic Catalog Retrieval
**MCR** .......... Micron Industries Ltd. [*Vancouver Stock Exchange symbol*]

**MCR** ......... Military Characteristics Requirement (MCD)
**MCR** ......... Military Command Region (MCD)
**MCR** ......... Military Compact Reactor
**MCR** ......... Missed Contact Rate (CAAL)
**MCR** ......... Missile Clock Receiver
**MCR** ......... Missile Computer Room
**MCR** ......... Mission Control Room [*Space Flight Operations Facility, NASA*]
**MCR** ......... Mission Control Routine [*NASA*]
**MCR** ......... Mobile Control Room (DEN)
**MCR** ......... Mobilization Contracting Requirement (AFIT)
**MCR** ......... Montreal Condensed Reports [*A publication*] (DLA)
**MCR** ......... Mother-Child Relationship [*Psychology*]
**MCR** ......... Multichannel Receiver
**MCR** ......... Multispectral Cloud Radiometer (MCD)
**MCr** ......... Museum Criticum [*A publication*]
**MCR** ......... Radcliffe College, Cambridge, MA [*Library symbol*] [*Library of Congress*] (LCLS)
**MCR** ......... University of Minnesota Technical College, Crookston, MN [*OCLC symbol*] (OCLC)
**MCRA** ....... Member of the College of Radiologists Australasia
**MCR-Ar** .... Radcliffe College, Archives, Cambridge, MA [*Library symbol*] [*Library of Congress*] (LCLS)
**MCRB** ....... Magnetic Compass Record Book
**MCRB** ....... Market Compilation and Research Bureau, Inc. [*North Hollywood, CA*] [*Information service or system*] (IID)
**MCRB** ....... Military Cost Review Board (MCD)
**MCRB** ....... Motor Carrier Rate Bureau
**MCRBIO**... Microbiology
**M Cr C**....... Madras Criminal Cases [*A publication*] (DLA)
**MCRC** ....... Marketing Communications Research Center [*Later, CMC*]
**McRC** ........ Microfilm Recording Company, Weston, ON, Canada [*Library symbol*] [*Library of Congress*] (LCLS)
**MCRD**....... Marine Corps Recruit Depot
**MCRD**....... Marine Corps Requirements Document (MCD)
**MCRD**....... Micro D, Inc. [*NASDAQ symbol*] (NQ)
**MCRDAC** ... Marine Corps Research, Development, and Acquisition Command [*Quantico, VA*] (GRD)
**MCRDEP** ... Marine Corps Recruit Depot
**MCRE** ....... Microenergy, Inc. [*Downers Grove, IL*] [*NASDAQ symbol*] (NQ)
**MCRE** ....... Mother-Child Relationship Evaluation [*Psychology*]
**MCREDA** ... Multivariate Experimental Clinical Research [*A publication*]
**MCREL**..... Mid-Continent Regional Educational Laboratory [*Aurora, CO*] [*Department of Education*]
**MCREP**..... Military Committee Representative [*to the North Atlantic Council*] (AABC)
**MCRFA**..... Microscope and Crystal Front [*A publication*]
**MCRH**....... Main Control Room Habitability [*Nuclear energy*] (NRCH)
**MCRHAC** ... Memoires. Cercle Royal Historique et Archeologique de Courtrai [*A publication*]
**MCRHS** .... Main Control Room Habitability System [*Nuclear energy*] (NRCH)
**MCRHS** .... Mid-Continent Railway Historical Society (EA)
**MCRI**......... Cambridge Research Institute, Inc., Cambridge, MA [*Library symbol*] [*Library of Congress*] (LCLS)
**MCRI**......... Marine Craft Radio Installation
**MCRI**......... Microcirculation Research Institute [*Texas A & M University*] [*Research center*] (RCD)
**MCRL**........ Mapping and Charting Research Laboratory [*Ohio State University*] (MCD)
**MCRL**........ Master Component Repair List
**MCRL**........ Master Cross-Reference List
**MCRL**........ Material Cross-Reference List (MCD)
**MCRML**.... Midcontinental Regional Medical Library Program [*University of Nebraska*] [*Library network*] (IID)
**MCRMLP** ... Midcontinental Regional Medical Library Program [*McGoogan Library of Medicine*] [*Information service or system*] (IID)
**MCRN** ....... Moscow City Relay Network
**MCR (NZ)** ... Magistrates' Court Reports (New Zealand) [*A publication*] (ILCA)
**MCRO** ....... Micro Mask, Inc. [*NASDAQ symbol*] (NQ)
**MCROA** ...... Marine Corps Reserve Officers Association (EA)
**MCROC** .... Marine Corps Recruit Option Center
**MCROSCPY** ... Microscopy
**MCRP**........ [*The*] Marine Corporation [*NASDAQ symbol*] (NQ)
**MCRP**........ Maritime Coal, Railway & Power Co. Ltd. [*AAR code*]
**MCRR** ....... Machine Check Recording and Recovery [*Data processing*]
**MCRR** ....... Marine Corps Reserve Ribbon
**MCRR** ....... [*The*] Monongahela Connecting Railroad Co. [*AAR code*]
**MCRRD** .... Marine Corps Reserve/Recruitment District
**MCRS**........ Maintenance Computing and Recording System
**MCRS**........ Marine Corps Recruiting Station
**MCRS**........ Micrographic Catalog Retrieval System
**MCRS**........ Micros Systems, Inc. [*NASDAQ symbol*] (NQ)
**MCR-S** ...... Radcliffe College, Schlesinger Library, Cambridge, MA [*Library symbol*] [*Library of Congress*] (LCLS)
**MCRSC** ..... Marine Corps Reserve Support Center
**MCRSS** ..... Marine Corps Recruiting Substation
**MCRT** ....... Multichannel Rotary Transformer [*Electronics*]
**MCRU** ....... Medical Care Research Unit [*University of Sheffield*] [*British*] (ECON)
**MCRV** ....... Manned Command/Reconnaissance Vehicle
**MCRWV** ... Microwave (AAG)
**MCRY** ....... Mercury Entertainment Corp. [*Los Angeles, CA*] [*NASDAQ symbol*] (NQ)
**MCS** .......... Harvard University, Monographic Cataloging Support Service, Cambridge, MA [*OCLC symbol*] (OCLC)
**MCS** .......... MacCartney Clan Society (EA)
**MCS** .......... Machine Cancel Society (EA)
**MCS** .......... Macmillan's Commercial Series [*A publication*]
**MCS** .......... Madras Civil Service [*British*]
**MCS** .......... Magnetic Coupling System (MCD)
**MCS** .......... Main Compution System
**MCS** .......... Maintenance and Checkout Station [*NASA*] (NASA)
**MCS** .......... Maintenance Control Section [*DCE*]
**MCS** .......... Maintenance Cost System (MCD)
**MCS** .......... Major Component Schedule (AAG)
**MCS** .......... Management Control System (MCD)
**MCS** .......... Manchester Cuneiform Studies [*A publication*]
**MCS** .......... Maneuver Control System [*Data processing*]
**MCS** .......... Manufacturing Control System
**MCS** .......... Mapping Camera System
**MCS** .......... Marco Island Airways, Inc. [*Opa Locka, FL*] [*FAA designator*] (FAAC)
**MCS** .......... Marcus Island [*Japan*] [*Seismograph station code, US Geological Survey*] (SEIS)
**MCS** .......... Marine Conservation Society [*British*]
**MCS** .......... Marine Cooks and Stewards Union
**MCS** .......... Marine Corps School [*Quantico, VA*]
**MCS** .......... Marine Corps Station
**MCS** .......... Marine Corps Supply Activity [*Obsolete*]
**MCS** .......... Maritime Communication Subsystem [*INTELSAT/INMARSAT*]
**MCS** .......... Mass Casualty Supplement [*Military*]
**MCS** .......... Master Circuit System
**MCS** .......... Master of Commercial Science
**MCS** .......... Master Composite Specification (MCD)
**MCS** .......... Master Control Station (NRCH)
**MCS** .......... Master Control System [*or Subsystem*]
**MCS** .......... Mathematical Code System
**MCS** .......... McChip Resources, Inc. [*Toronto Stock Exchange symbol*]
**MCS** .......... Mean Crew Size (MCD)
**MCS** .......... Measurements Calibration System (KSC)
**MCS** .......... Mechanical Control System [*Aviation*]
**MCS** .......... Mechanized Characteristics Screening
**MCS** .......... Medical Computer Services (IEEE)
**MCS** .......... Medical Consultant Staff [*Social Security Administration*] (OICC)
**MCS** .......... Medical Corps, Special Service [*USNR officer designation*]
**MCS** .......... Medium Close Shot [*Photography*] (ADA)
**MCS** .......... Megacycles per Second [*Megahertz*] [*See also MCPS, MH, MHz*]
**MCS** .......... Meridian Control Signal
**MCS** .......... Mesoscale Convective System [*Meteorology*]
**MCS** .......... Message Control System [*Burroughs Corp.*] [*Data processing*] (BUR)
**MCS** .......... Meter-Candle Second
**MCS** .......... Method of Constant Stimuli [*Psychophysics*]
**MCS** .......... Metropolitan Communications Squadron [*British military*] (DMA)
**MCS** .......... Microcomputer System
**McS** .......... Micromation Systems, Inc., Feasterville, PA [*Library symbol*] [*Library of Congress*] (LCLS)
**MCS** .......... Microprocessor Communications System (MCD)
**MCS** .......... Microwave Carrier Supply
**MCS** .......... Microwave Communication System
**MCS** .......... Milestone Car Society (EA)
**MCS** .......... Military Communications Stations
**MCS** .......... Miller Communications Systems Ltd. [*Telecommunications service*] (TSSD)
**MCS** .......... Mine Countermeasure Support [*Obsolete*] [*Military*]
**MCS** .......... Mine Countermeasures Ship [*Navy symbol*]
**MCS** .......... Minimum Chi-Square
**MCS** .......... Missile Calibration Station
**MCS** .......... Missile Checkout Set (AAG)
**MCS** .......... Missile Checkout Station
**MCS** .......... Missile Commit Sequence (AAG)
**MCS** .......... Missile Compensating System
**MCS** .......... Missile Control System
**MCS** .......... Mobile Checkout Station (AAG)
**MCS** .......... Mobile Communications System (MCD)
**MCS** .......... Model-Controlled System [*NASA*]
**MCS** .......... Modular Composition System [*Diskettes*]
**MCS** .......... Modular Computer System (IEEE)
**MCS** .......... Monitor and Control System [*Deep Space Instrumentation Facility, NASA*]
**MCS** .......... Monumenta Christiana Selecta [*A publication*]
**MCS** .......... Motor Circuit Switch
**MCS** .......... Movements Control Section [*British military*] (DMA)
**MCS** .......... Multichannel Scaling [*Mode*]

**MCS** ......... Multichannel Seismology [*Geophysics*]
**MCS** ......... Multidirectional Category System
**MCS** ......... Multiple Character Set (CMD)
**MCS** ......... Multiple Computer System
**MCS** ......... Multiple Console Support [*Fujitsu Ltd.*] [*Data processing*] (MCD)
**MCS** ......... Multiplexer Computer Systems (MCD)
**MCS** ......... Multiprogrammed Computer System (IEEE)
**MCS** ......... Multipurpose Communications and Signaling
**MCS** ......... Music Construction Set [*Computer program designed by Will Harvey and published by Electronic Arts*]
**MCS** ......... Residential Model Conservation Standard [*Pacific Northwest Electric Power and Conservation Planning Council*] [*Portland, OR*] (EGAO)
**MCSA**........ Marble Collectors Society of America (EA)
**MCSA**........ Marine Corps Supply Activity [*Obsolete*] (NVT)
**MCSA**........ Meritorious Civilian Service Award
**MCSA**........ Methuen's Commercial Series [*A publication*]
**MCSA**........ Metropolitan Church Schoolmasters' Association [*A union*] [*British*]
**MCSA**........ Microcomputer Software Association - of ADAPSO [*Association of Data Processing Service Organizations*] (EA)
**MCSA**........ Midwest Collegiate Sailing Association
**MCSA**........ Military Construction Supply Agency [*Later, Defense Construction Supply Center*]
**MCSA**........ Moscow, Camden & San Augustine Railroad [*AAR code*]
**MCSA**........ Multichannel Spectrum Analyzer [*Instrumentation*]
**MCSA**........ Smithsonian Institution, Astrophysical Observatory, Cambridge, MA [*Library symbol*] [*Library of Congress*] (LCLS)
**MCSAP**..... Motor Carrier Safety Assistance Program [*Department of Transportation*]
**MCSB**........ Morris County Savings Bank [*NASDAQ symbol*] (NQ)
**MCSB**........ Motor Carriers Service Bureau
**MCSC**........ Magdalen College School Cadets [*British military*] (DMA)
**MCSC**........ Marine Corps Supply Center
**MC Sc**........ Master of Commercial Science
**MCSC**........ Medical College of South Carolina
**MCSC**........ Model Codes Standardization Council [*Defunct*]
**MCSC**........ Movement Control Sub-Committee [*IATA*] (DS)
**MCSCF**..... Multiconfigurational Self-Consistent Field [*Chemical physics*]
**MCSD**........ Marine Corps Supply Depot (MUGU)
**MC Se**........ Master of Commercial Service
**MCSE**........ Minimum Critical Size of Ecosystem [*Project*]
**M-CSF**....... Macrophage-Colony Stimulating Factor [*Biochemistry*]
**MCSH**........ Maryville College of the Sacred Heart [*Missouri*]
**MCSI**......... Member of the Construction Surveyors' Institute [*British*] (DBQ)
**MCSL**........ Management Control Systems List [*DoD*]
**MCSL**........ Marine Corps Stock [*or Supply*] Lists
**MCSMAW**... Marine Corps Shoulder-Launched Multipurpose Assault Weapon (MCD)
**MCSP**........ Maintenance Control and Statistics Process [*Telecommunications*] (TEL)
**MCSP**........ Member of the Chartered Society of Physiotherapists [*British*]
**MCSP**........ Mission Completion Success Probability (MCD)
**MCSP**........ Multiple Conductor, Shielded, Pressure-Resistant [*Cable*]
**M & CSq**.... Mapping and Charting Squadron [*Air Force*]
**MC(S)R**..... Maximum Continuous (Service) Rating [*Also, MCR*] [*Mechanical engineering*]
**MCSR**........ Motor Carrier Safety Regulations [*Department of Transportation*]
**MCSS**........ Mechanical Circulatory Support System
**MCSS**........ Microscopic Camera Subsystem (KSC)
**MCSS**........ Military Clothing Sales Store
**MCSS**........ Military Communications Satellite System
**MCSS**........ Missile Checkout System Selector
**MCSS**........ Monitor and Control Subsystem [*Deep Space Instrumentation Facility, NASA*]
**MCSSG**..... Military Committee Special Study Group [*NATO*] (NATG)
**MCSSQT**.. Modified Combat System Ship Qualification Trial [*Navy*] (CAAL)
**MCSST**..... Multichannel Sea Surface Temperature [*Algorithms for oceanography*]
**MCST**........ Magnetic Card "Selectric" Typewriter [*IBM Corp.*]
**MCST**........ Member of the College of Speech Therapists [*British*]
**MCSTB**..... Motor Carriers Service Tariff Bureau
**MCSTSC**... Military Communications System Technical Standards Committee [*Army*] (AABC)
**MCSU**........ Management Consultation Services Unit [*LIMRA*]
**MCSU**........ Maximum Card Study Unit (EA)
**MCSW**........ Mining Club of the Southwest (EA)
**MCSW**........ Motor Circuit Switch (MSA)
**MCSWG**.... Multinational Command Systems Working Group (NATG)
**MCT**......... Magnetic Core Tape
**MCT**......... Magnetic Core Tester
**MCT**......... Main Central Thrust [*Geophysics*]
**MCT**......... Main Control Tank (MSA)
**MCT**......... Mainstream Corporation Tax
**MCT**......... Managed Change Technique [*Management*]
**MCT**......... MANPRINT [*Manpower and Personnel Integration*] Coordination Team [*Army*]
**MCT**......... Mass Culturing Technique [*Microbiology*]
**MCT**......... Master of Christian Training
**MCT**......... Mathematical Cuneiform Texts [*A publication*] (BJA)
**MCT**......... Maximum Climb Thrust (NASA)
**MCT**......... Maximum Continuous Thrust [*Aviation*]
**MCT**......... Maxwell Color Triangle
**MCT**......... Mean Cell [*or Corpuscular*] Thickness [*Hematology*]
**MCT**......... Mean Circulation Time [*Medicine*]
**MCT**......... Mean Corrective-Maintenance Time (MCD)
**MCT**......... Mechanical Comprehension Test
**MCT**......... Medium-Chain Triglyceride [*Biochemistry*]
**MCT**......... Medullary Cancer of the Thyroid [*Medicine*]
**MCT**......... Medullary Collecting Tubules [*Anatomy*]
**MCT**......... Memory Cycle Time [*Data processing*] (MCD)
**MCT**......... Mercury Cadmium Telluride [*Photodetector*]
**MCT**......... Message Control Task [*Data processing*]
**MCT**......... Meta-Chlorotoluene [*Organic chemistry*]
**MCT**......... Metrizamide Computed Tomography
**MCT**......... Microstat Development Corp. [*Vancouver Stock Exchange symbol*]
**MCT**......... Microwave Ceramic Triode
**MCT**......... Mid-Cycle Test [*Army training*] (INF)
**MCT**......... Military Command Technology (AAG)
**MCT**......... Minimum Competency Test [*Education*]
**MCT**......... Minimum Connecting Time [*Travel industry*]
**MCT**......... Minnesota Clerical Test
**MCT**......... Missile Compensating Tank
**MCT**......... Mission Control Table (MCD)
**MCT**......... Mobile Communication Terminal
**MCT**......... Mobile Contact Teams [*Military*] (AABC)
**MCT**......... Modified Clinical Technique [*Medicine*]
**MCT**......... Moment to Change Trim (DS)
**MCT**......... Mouse Colon Tumor [*Pathology*]
**MCT**......... Movable Core Transformer [*Nuclear energy*]
**MCT**......... Movement Control Team [*Air Force*] (AFM)
**MCT**......... Mucociliary Transport [*Physiology*]
**MCT**......... Multicell Test (MCD)
**MCT**......... Multiple Compressed Tablet [*Pharmacy*]
**MCT**......... Multistrip Cesium Thrustor
**MCT**......... Muscat [*Oman*] [*Airport symbol*] (OAG)
**MCT**......... United States Department of Transportation, Technical Information Center, Cambridge, MA [*Library symbol*] [*Library of Congress*] (LCLS)
**MCTA**....... Metropolitan Commuter Transportation Authority [*Greater New York City*] [*Later, Metropolitan Transportation Authority*]
**m/cta**......... Mi Cuenta [*My Account, My Debit*] [*Spanish*]
**MCTA**....... Motor Carriers Tariff Association
**MCTA**....... Motor Carriers Traffic Association
**MCTA**....... Multiple-Cycle Transient Analysis [*Chemistry*]
**MCTB**....... Motor Carriers Tariff Bureau (EA)
**MCTC**....... Maritime Cargo Transportation Conference [*of MTRB*]
**MCTC**....... Movimiento Campesino Tupaj Catari [*Bolivia*] [*Political party*] (PPW)
**MCTD**....... Medium Capacity Bomb with Temporary Delay Fuse [*British military*] (DMA)
**MCTD**....... Mixed Connective Tissue Disease [*Medicine*]
**m/cte**......... Mon Compte [*My Account*] [*French*] [*Business term*]
**MCTG**....... Model Change Training Guide
**MCTI**........ Metal Cutting Tool Institute (EA)
**MCTL**........ Mediterranean Contingency Target List (MCD)
**MCTL**........ Microtel Franchise & Development Corp. [*NASDAQ symbol*] (NQ)
**MCTL**........ Militarily Critical Technology List [*DoD*]
**MCTNS**..... Manportable Cannon Thermal Night Sight (MCD)
**MCTP**........ Missile Control Test Panel
**MCTR**....... Mackinac Transportation Co. [*AAR code*]
**MCTR**....... Message Center
**MCTRAP**.. Mechanized Customer Trouble Report Analysis Plan [*Telecommunications*] (TEL)
**MCTS**........ Master Central Timing System [*NASA*]
**MCTS**........ Motor Carriers Tariff Service (EA)
**MCTSA**..... Military Clothing and Textile Supply Agency [*Merged with Defense Supply Agency*] [*Army*]
**MCTSE**..... Marine Corps Test Support Element (MCD)
**MCTSSA**... Marine Corps Tactical Systems and Support Activity [*Camp Pendleton, CA*] (GRD)
**MCTT**........ Metal-Ceramic Transmitting Tube
**MCTT**........ Motion Control Technology, Inc. [*NASDAQ symbol*] (NQ)
**MCTV**....... Manhattan Cable TV, Inc. [*New York, NY*] [*Telecommunications*] (TSSD)
**MCU**......... Machine Control Unit
**MCU**......... Magma Copper Co. [*AMEX symbol*] (CTT)
**MCU**......... Maintenance Control Unit [*Data processing*]
**MCU**......... Major Crime Unit [*Elite police squad on television series "Crime Story"*]
**MCU**......... Malaria Control Unit [*Army*] [*World War II*]
**MCU**......... Manual Control Unit
**MCU**......... Marble Collectors Unlimited (EA)

**MCU**.......... Master Clock Unit
**MCU**.......... Master Control Unit
**MCU**.......... Maximum Care Unit [*Medicine*]
**MCU**.......... Medium Close Up [*A photograph or motion picture sequence taken from a relatively short distance*]
**MCU**.......... Memory Control Unit
**MCU**.......... Message Construction Unit
**MCU**.......... Microcomputer Control Unit
**MCU**.......... Microprocessor Control Unit
**MCU**.......... Microprogrammed Control Unit [*Navy*]
**mcU**........... Microunit
**MCU**.......... Miniature Command Unit
**MCU**.......... Mission Control Unit (MCD)
**MCU**.......... Modern Churchmen's Union [*British*]
**M & CU**..... Monitor and Control Unit [*Aerospace*] (AAG)
**MCU**.......... Monte Cristo Peak [*Utah*] [*Seismograph station code, US Geological Survey*] (SEIS)
**MCU**.......... Mosquito Conversion Unit [*British military*] (DMA)
**MCU**.......... Mountain Commando Units (CINC)
**MCU**.......... Multicoupler Unit [*Antenna*] [*Telecommunications*] (TEL)
**MCU**.......... Multiplexer Control Unit
**MCU**.......... Multiprocessor Communications Unit
**MCU**.......... Rochester, NY [*Location identifier*] [*FAA*] (FAAL)
**MCUB**....... Marine Corps Uniform Board [*Washington, DC*] (EGAO)
**MCUG**....... Military Computers Users Group
**MCUIS**...... Master Control and User Interface Software Subsystem [*Space Flight Operations Facility, NASA*]
**MCUL**....... Missile Compartment, Upper Level
**MCUMP**... Multidisciplinary Center for Urban and Minority Problems [*Florida State University*] [*Research center*] [*Defunct*] (RCD)
**MCurrSt**.... Master of Curriculum Studies
**MCurrStud**... Master of Curriculum Studies
**MCV**.......... Magnetic Cushion Vehicle (IEEE)
**MCV**.......... Maritime Commission, Victory Ship
**MCV**.......... Mean Cell [*or Corpuscular*] Volume [*Hematology*]
**MCV**.......... Mean Corpuscular Volume [*Physiology*]
**MCV**.......... Mechanised Combat Vehicle [*British military*] (DMA)
**MCV**.......... Medical Center of Virginia [*University of Virginia*]
**MCV**.......... Melanges. Casa de Velazquez [*A publication*]
**MCV**.......... Mercury [*Nevada*] [*Seismograph station code, US Geological Survey*] (SEIS)
**MCV**.......... Mesabi Community College, Virginia, MN [*OCLC symbol*] (OCLC)
**MCV**.......... Method of Composition Velocity [*Physical chemistry*]
**MCV**.......... Movable Closure Valve (NRCH)
**MCVD**....... Modified Chemical Vapor Deposition [*Telecommunications*]
**McVey Dig**... McVey's Ohio Digest [*A publication*] (DLA)
**MCVF**........ Multichannel Voice Frequency [*Telecommunications*]
**MCVFT**..... Multichannel Voice Frequency Telegraphy [*Telecommunications*] (TEL)
**MC-V(G)**... Medical Officers (Qualified for General Detail) [*USNR designation*]
**MCVG**....... Memory Character Vector Generator
**MCVP**....... Materials Control and Verification Program [*NASA*] (NASA)
**MCVQ Med Coll VA Q**... MCVQ. Medical College of Virginia. Quarterly [*A publication*]
**MC-V(S)**.... Medical Officers (Qualified for Specialist Duties) [*USNR designation*]
**MCW**......... Central Missouri State University, Warrensburg, MO [*OCLC symbol*] (OCLC)
**MCW**......... Mallinckrodt Chemical Works [*Later, Mallinckrodt, Inc.*]
**MCW**......... Mason City [*Iowa*] [*Airport symbol*] (OAG)
**MCW**......... Mason City, IA [*Location identifier*] [*FAA*] (FAAL)
**MC & W**.... Master Caution and Warning [*NASA*] (KSC)
**M and CW**... Maternity and Child Welfare [*Medicine*] [*British*]
**MCW**......... Medical Corps, Women's Reserve [*USNR officer designation*]
**MCW**......... Memory Card Writer [*Telecommunications*] (TEL)
**MCW**......... Metal Casement Window [*Technical drawings*]
**MCW**......... Metro-Cammell Weymaua Ltd. [*British*] (DCTA)
**MCW**......... Mills, Clarence W., Laurel MD [*STAC*]
**MCW**......... Modulated Continuous Wave [*Radio signal transmission*]
**MCW**......... Mount Constitution [*Washington*] [*Seismograph station code, US Geological Survey*] (SEIS)
**MCW**......... Weston School of Theology, Cambridge, MA [*Library symbol*] [*Library of Congress*] (LCLS)
**MCWA**...... Malaria Control in War Areas [*Later, Centers for Disease Control*]
**MCWA**...... Mid Continent Wildcatters Association [*Defunct*] (EA)
**MCWCS**.... Ministerial Conference of West and Central African States on Maritime Transportation [*See also CMEAOC*] [*Abidjan, Ivory Coast*] (EAIO)
**McWillie**.... McWillie's Reports [*73-76 Mississippi*] [*A publication*] (DLA)
**MCWM**..... Military Committee Working Memorandum (NATG)
**MCWR**...... Marine Corps Women's Reserve
**MCWU**...... Military Committee of Western European Union (NATG)
**MCX**.......... Marine Corps Exchange
**MCX**.......... MC Shipping [*AMEX symbol*] (SPSG)
**MCX**.......... Michelin Capital Ltd. [*Toronto Stock Exchange symbol*]
**MCX**.......... Minimum-Cost Expediting
**MCX**.......... Monticello, IN [*Location identifier*] [*FAA*] (FAAL)
**MCXO**....... Microprocessor-Controlled Crystal Oscillator [*Hughes Aircraft Co.*] (ECON)
**MCY**.......... Maroochydore [*Australia*] [*Airport symbol*] (OAG)
**MCY**.......... Mercury, NV [*Location identifier*] [*FAA*] (FAAL)
**MCY**.......... Mount Calvery Resources Ltd. [*Vancouver Stock Exchange symbol*]
**M/CYL**...... Master Cylinder [*Automotive engineering*]
**MCZ**.......... Maceio [*Brazil*] [*Airport symbol*] (OAG)
**MCZ**.......... Museum of Comparative Zoology [*Harvard University*] [*Research center*]
**MCZ**.......... Williamston, NC [*Location identifier*] [*FAA*] (FAAL)
**MCZAAZ**... Museum of Comparative Zoology [*Harvard University*]. Annual Report [*A publication*]
**MCZDO**.... Multicenter Zero Differential Overlap [*Physics*]
**MCZE**........ Minimum When Control Zone Effective [*Aviation*] (FAAC)
**MCZNE**.... Minimum When Control Zone Not Effective [*Aviation*] (FAAC)
**MD**............ Air Madagascar, Societe Nationale Malgache de Transports Aeriens [*Madagascar*] [*ICAO designator*] (FAAC)
**MD**............ Application for Writ of Mandamus Dismissed for Want of Jurisdiction [*Legal term*] (DLA)
**MD**............ Delalande [*France*] [*Research code symbol*]
**MD**............ La Maison-Dieu [*Paris*] [*A publication*] (BJA)
**m/d**............ Maande na Datum [*Months after Date*] [*Afrikaans*]
**MD**............ Machine Direction
**MD**............ Mackenzie Drift [*Canada*] [*A publication*]
**MD**............ Macular Degeneration [*Ophthalmology*]
**Md**............ Madinhae (BJA)
**MD**............ Madres de los Desamparados [*Mothers of the Helpless*] [*Roman Catholic religious order*]
**MD**............ Magnetic Deflection [*Cathode-ray tube*] (DEN)
**MD**............ Magnetic Disk [*Data processing*] (BUR)
**MD**............ Magnetic Drum
**M & D**........ Maidstone & District Motor Services Ltd. [*British*] (DCTA)
**MD**............ Main Droite [*With the Right Hand*] [*Music*]
**MD**............ Main Drum (CET)
**MD**............ Main Duct
**MD**............ Maintainability Demonstration (MCD)
**M/D**.......... Maintenance/Development [*Effort ratio*]
**MD**............ Maintenance Dose [*Medicine*]
**M-D**.......... Maiz Dulce [*Race of maize*]
**MD**............ Make Directory [*Data processing*]
**MD**............ Malate Dehydrogenase [*Also, MDH*] [*An enzyme*]
**MD**............ Male Treated with DOC [*Deoxycorticosterone*]
**M or D**....... Malfunction or Defect (FAAC)
**MD**............ Malfunction Detection (NASA)
**M/D**.......... Man Day
**MD**............ Management Data (MCD)
**MD**............ Management Directive
**MD**............ Managing Director
**MD**............ Manic-Depressive
**MD**............ Mano Destra [*With the Right Hand*] [*Music*]
**MD**............ Manu Dextra [*With the Right Hand*] [*Latin*]
**MD**............ Manual Data
**MD**............ Manual Direct (NASA)
**MD**............ Manual Disconnect (MCD)
**MD**............ Map Distance (ADA)
**MD**............ Marchand [*Merchant, Trader*] [*French*]
**MD**............ Marek's Disease [*Avian pathology*]
**MD**............ Marine Detachment
**MD**............ Market Day [*British*]
**MD**............ Marque Deposee [*Trademark*]
**MD**............ Married
**MD**............ Maryland [*Postal code*]
**MD**............ Maryland Reports [*A publication*] (DLA)
**Md**............ Maryland State Library, Annapolis, MD [*Library symbol*] [*Library of Congress*] (LCLS)
**MD**............ Master Diagram (MCD)
**MD**............ Master Dimension (NASA)
**MD**............ Master Directory [*NASA*] [*Information service or system*] (IID)
**MD**............ Master's Decisions (Patents) [*A publication*] (DLA)
**MD**............ Materiel Developer [*Army*]
**MD**............ Matrimonio Duxit [*Led into Matrimony*] [*Latin*] (ROG)
**MD**............ Maturity Date [*Banking*]
**MD**............ Maximum Degree Allowed to Fit
**MD**............ Maximum Design Meter
**MD**............ McDonnell Douglas Corp. [*NYSE symbol*] (SPSG)
**MD**............ MD: Medical Newsmagazine [*A publication*]
**MD**............ Mean Deviation
**MD**............ Measured Depth [*Diamonds*]
**MD**............ Measured Discard [*Nuclear energy*] (NRCH)
**MD**............ Measured Drilling [*Diamonds*]
**MD**............ Media Decisions [*A publication*]
**Md**............ Median
**MD**............ Medical Department [*Army*]
**MD**............ Medical Discharge [*from military service*]
**MD**............ Medicinae Doctor [*Doctor of Medicine*]
**M & D**........ Medicine and Duty [*Marked on a medical report and implying a suspicion of malingering*] [*Military*] [*British*]
**M/D**.......... Medicines/Drugs

**MD**............ Mediodorsal [*Anatomy*]
**MD**............ Medium Duty
**MD**............ Megadalton
**MD**............ Memorandum of Deposit [*Business term*]
**Md** ............ Mendelevium [*Chemical element*] [*Preferred form, but also see Mv*]
**MD**............ Mentally Deficient
**MD**............ Mentally Disabled (OICC)
**M & D**........ Mergers and Divestures
**MD**............ Mesiodistal [*Dentistry*]
**Md** ............ Mesoderm [*Botany*]
**MD**............ Mess Deck [*Naval*]
**MD**............ Message Data
**MD**............ Message-Dropping [*Military*]
**MD**............ Messages per Day
**MD**............ Metal Deactivator
**MD**............ Metal Dome [*Watchmaking*] (ROG)
**MD**............ Metals Disintegrating
**MD**............ Meteorology Department [*Navy*]
**M/D**.......... Meters per Day
**MD**............ Methyldichloroarsine [*Poison gas*]
**MD**............ Methyldopa [*Also, AMD*] [*Antihypertensive compound*]
**MD**............ Metropolitan District [*British*]
**MD**............ Microalloy Diffused
**MD**............ Microdot (KSC)
**MD**............ Microwave Desorber [*Instrumentation*]
**MD**............ Middle Deltoid [*Myology*]
**MD**............ Middle Distillate [*Fuel technology*]
**MD**............ Middle District (DLA)
**MD**............ Middle Door [*Theater*]
**MD**............ Middle Dutch [*Language, etc.*]
**MD**............ Mildly Diabetic
**MD**............ Military District [*USSR*] (NATG)
**mD** ............ Millidarcy
**MD**............ Millwall Dock [*British*]
**MD**............ Mine Depot [*Naval*]
**MD**............ Mine Disposal
**MD**............ Mini Disk [*Audio/video technology*]
**MD**............ Minimum Dosage [*Medicine*]
**M of D**........ Ministry of Defence [*British*]
**MD**............ Minute Difference
**MD**............ Miscellaneous Direct (MCD)
**MD**............ Miscellaneous Document
**MD**............ Missile Division (AAG)
**MD**............ Missile Driver
**MD**............ Mission Day
**MD**............ Mission Dependent
**MD**............ Mission Director [*NASA*] (KSC)
**MD**............ Mitral Disease [*Medicine*]
**MD**............ Mobile Depot [*Air Force*] (MCD)
**MD**............ Mode [*Grammar*] (ROG)
**MD**............ Moderate Dose [*Medicine*]
**MD**............ Moderately Differentiated
**MD**............ Modern Drama [*A publication*]
**MD**............ Modern Drummer [*A publication*]
**MD**............ Modified Design [*Cordite*] [*British military*] (DMA)
**MD**............ Modular Design
**M/D**.......... Modulator-Demodulator [*Telecommunications*] (CET)
**MD**............ Modulators [*JETDS nomenclature*] [*Military*] (CET)
**MD**............ Molecular Diameter
**MD**............ Molecular Dynamics
**MD**............ Money Down
**MD**............ Monitor Displays [*Data processing*] (BUR)
**MD**............ Monocular Deprivation [*Optics*]
**MD**............ Monroe Doctrine
**MD**............ Months after Date [*or Month's Date*] [*Business term*]
**MD**............ Mood [*Grammar*] (ROG)
**MD**............ More Dicto [*As Directed*] [*Pharmacy*]
**MD**............ Moroccan Dinar [*Monetary unit*]
**MD**............ Motor Direct
**MD**............ Motor Drive
**MD**............ Movement Directive
**MD**............ Multidimensional
**MD**............ Multidomain [*Grains in rocks*] [*Geophysics*]
**MD**............ Multinomial Distribution [*Statistics*]
**MD**............ Multiple Dialyzer [*Chemical analysis*]
**MD**............ Multiple Dissemination
**MD**............ Municipal Docks Railway of the Jacksonville Port Authority [*AAR code*]
**MD**............ Muscular Dystrophy [*Medicine*]
**MD**............ Musica Disciplina [*A publication*]
**MD**............ Musicae Doctor [*Doctor of Music*] (ROG)
**MD**............ Musical Director
**MD**............ Myocardial Disease [*Cardiology*]
**MD**............ Myotonic Dystrophy [*See also MyMD*] [*Medicine*]
**M³/D**......... Cubic Meters per Day
**MDA**.......... Dagbladpers [*A publication*]
**MDA**.......... Magen David Adom [*Israel's Red Cross Service*]
**MDA**.......... Magic Dealers Association [*Later, IMDA*]
**MDA**.......... Magnetic Deflection Amplifier
**MDA**.......... Main Distribution Assembly (NASA)
**MDA**.......... Maintainability Design Approach
**MDA**.......... Maintenance Data Analysis (MCD)
**MDA**.......... Maintenance Depot Assistance [*Air Force*] (AFM)
**MDA**.......... Maintenance Design Approach
**MDA**.......... Malondialdehyde [*Biochemistry*]
**MDA**.......... Manic-Depressive Association (EA)
**MDA**.......... MAPCO, Inc. [*NYSE symbol*] (SPSG)
**MDA**.......... Marketing and Distribution Abstracts [*A publication*]
**MDA**.......... Marking Device Association (EA)
**MD A**......... Maryland Appellate Reports [*A publication*] (DLA)
**MDA**.......... Master Design Award
**MDA**.......... Master Diversion Airfield (AIA)
**MDA**.......... Master of Dramatic Art
**MDA**.......... Master Drawings Association (EA)
**MDA**.......... Master Dyers Association (EA)
**MDA**.......... Material Disposal Authority
**MDA**.......... Maximum Demographic Appeal [*Objective of commercial television programming*]
**MDA**.......... Measurement, Decision, and Actuation [*Data processing*]
**MDA**.......... Mechanically Despun Antenna (KSC)
**MDA**.......... Mechanized Directory Assistance [*Telecommunications*] (TEL)
**MdA**.......... Melanges d'Archeologie Egyptienne et Assyrienne [*Paris*] [*A publication*]
**MDA**.......... Menthanediamine [*Organic chemistry*]
**MDA**.......... Mento-Dextra Anterior [*A fetal position*] [*Obstetrics*]
**MDA**.......... Metal Deactivator [*Fuel technology*]
**MDA**.......... Meteoroid Detector-Analyzer
**MDA**.......... Methyldopamine [*Biochemistry*]
**MDA**.......... Methylenedianiline [*Also, DAPM, DDM*] [*Organic chemistry*]
**MDA**.......... Methylenedioxyamphetamine [*Biochemistry*]
**MDA**.......... Microprocessor Development Aid
**MDA**.......... Middeck Assembly (MCD)
**MDA**.......... Military Damage Assessment
**MDA**.......... Minimum Descent Altitude [*Aviation*]
**MDA**.......... Minimum Detectable Activity [*Nuclear energy*] (NRCH)
**MDA**.......... Minimum Detectable Amount [*of radiation*] [*Analytical chemistry*]
**MDA**.......... Minnesota Department of Agriculture, St. Paul, MN [*OCLC symbol*] (OCLC)
**MDA**.......... Missilized Driver Assembly (MCD)
**MDA**.......... Mission Doctors Association (EA)
**MDA**.......... Mixed Distribution Analysis [*Mathematics*]
**MDA**.......... Mobile Depot Activities [*Air Force*]
**MDA**.......... Modern Professional Air [*Atlanta, GA*] [*FAA designator*] (FAAC)
**MDA**.......... Monochrome Display Adapter [*Computer technology*]
**MDA**.......... Monodehydroascorbate [*Biochemistry*]
**MDA**.......... Mothers for Decency in Action [*Group opposing sex education in schools*]
**MDA**.......... Motor Discriminative Acuity [*Psychology*]
**MDA**.......... Motor Drive Amplifier
**MDA**.......... Motorcycling Doctors Association (EA)
**MDA**.......... Mouvement pour la Democratie en Algerie [*Algeria*] [*Political party*] (MENA)
**MDA**.......... Multidimensional Access
**MDA**.......... Multidimensional Analysis (IEEE)
**MDA**.......... Multidimensional Array
**MDA**.......... Multiple Digit Absorbing [*Telecommunications*] (TEL)
**MDA**.......... Multiple Discriminant Analysis [*Statistics*]
**MDA**.......... Multiple Docking Adapter [*Apollo*] [*NASA*]
**MDA**.......... Muscular Dystrophy Association (EA)
**MDA**.......... Music Distributors Association (EA)
**MDA**.......... Mutual Defense Assistance
**MDA**.......... San Antonio, TX [*Location identifier*] [*FAA*] (FAAL)
**MdAA**........ Hall of Records Commission, Annapolis, MD [*Library symbol*] [*Library of Congress*] (LCLS)
**MDAA**....... Muscular Dystrophy Associations of America (EA)
**MDAA**....... Mutual Defense Assistance Act
**MdAAC**..... Public Library of Annapolis and Anne Arundel County, Annapolis, MD [*Library symbol*] [*Library of Congress*] (LCLS)
**MDaAr**...... Danvers Archival Center, Peabody Institute, Danvers, MA [*Library symbol*] [*Library of Congress*] (LCLS)
**MDAC**....... McDonnell Douglas Aircraft Corporation
**MDAC**....... Methyl(ciethylamino)coumarin [*Organic chemistry*]
**MDAC**....... Multiplying Digital-to-Analog Converter [*Data processing*] (IEEE)
**MDAC**....... Muscular Dystrophy Association of Canada
**MDAC**....... Mutual Defense Assistance, General Area of China
**MDAC**....... Mystery and Detection Annual [*A publication*]
**MD Acad Sci Bull** ... Maryland Academy of Sciences. Bulletin [*A publication*]
**MD Ac Sc Tr** ... Maryland Academy of Sciences. Transactions [*A publication*]
**MD Admin Code** ... Code of Maryland Regulations [*A publication*] (DLA)
**MdAEPA**... United States Environmental Protection Agency, Annapolis Field Office, Annapolis Science Center, Annapolis, MD [*Library symbol*] [*Library of Congress*] (LCLS)
**MDAERP** ... Medical Devices Adverse Experience Reporting Project
**MDAF** ....... Memoires. Delegation Archeologique Francaise [*A publication*] (BJA)
**MDAFWP** ... Motor-Driven Auxiliary Feedwater Pump (IEEE)

**MD Ag Exp** ... Maryland. Agricultural Experiment Station. Publications [*A publication*]
**MD Agric Exp Stn Bull** ... Maryland. Agricultural Experiment Station. Bulletin [*A publication*]
**MD Agric Exp Stn MP** ... Maryland. Agricultural Experiment Station. MP [*A publication*]
**MDAGT** .... Mutual Defense Assistance, Greece and Turkey
**MDAH** ...... M. D. Anderson Hospital and Tumor Institute [*Houston, TX*]
**MDAI** ........ Mitteilungen. Deutsches Archaeologische Institut [*A publication*]
**MDAI** ........ Multidisciplinary Accident Investigation [*National Accident Sampling System*]
**MDAIA** ..... Mitteilungen. Deutsches Archaeologische Institut. Abteilung Athens [*A publication*]
**MDAIK** ..... Mitteilungen. Deutsches Archaeologische Institut. Abteilung Kairo [*A publication*]
**MDAIKP** ... Mutual Defense Assistance, Iran, Republic of Korea, and Philippines
**MDAIM** .... Mitteilungen. Deutsches Archaeologische Institut. Abteilung Madrid [*A publication*]
**MDAIR** ..... Mitteilungen. Deutsches Archaeologische Institut. Abteilung Rome [*A publication*]
**MDAIS** ...... McDonnell Douglas Aerospace Information Services [*Formerly, MCATO*] (MCD)
**MDA J (Jefferson City)** ... MDA [*Missouri Dental Association*] Journal (Jefferson City, Missouri) [*A publication*]
**MD Ala** ...... United States District Court for the Middle District of Alabama (DLA)
**MDAM** ...... Majalle(H)-Ye Daneshkade(H)-Ye Adabiyyat-E Mashhad [*A publication*]
**MDAN** ....... Angelina, Cotui [*Dominican Republic*] [*ICAO location identifier*] (ICLI)
**MDan** ......... Meddelelser fra Dansklaererforeningen [*A publication*]
**MdAN** ........ United States Naval Academy, Annapolis, MD [*Library symbol*] [*Library of Congress*] (LCLS)
**MDANAA** ... Mutual Defense Assistance, North Atlantic Area
**MdANE** ..... United States Navy, Naval Ship Research and Development Laboratory, Annapolis, MD [*Library symbol*] [*Library of Congress*] (LCLS)
**MD Ann Code** ... Annotated Code of Maryland [*A publication*] (DLA)
**MDAP** ....... Machover Draw-A-Person Test [*Psychology*]
**MDAP** ....... Materiel Deployment/Acceptance Plan (MCD)
**MDAP** ....... Memoirs. Department of Archaeology in Pakistan [*A publication*]
**MDAP** ....... Mutual Defense Assistance Pact [*or Program*]
**MDaP** ........ Peabody Institute, Danvers, MA [*Library symbol*] [*Library of Congress*] (LCLS)
**MdApg** ....... United States Army, Technical Library, Aberdeen Proving Ground, Aberdeen, MD [*Library symbol*] [*Library of Congress*] (LCLS)
**MdApgC** .... United States Army, Chemical Systems Laboratory, Aberdeen Proving Ground, Aberdeen, MD [*Library symbol*] [*Library of Congress*] (LCLS)
**MdApgO** ... United States Army, Ordnance School, Aberdeen Proving Ground, Aberdeen, MD [*Library symbol*] [*Library of Congress*] (LCLS)
**MdApgOB** ... United States Army, Ordnance Board, Aberdeen Proving Ground, Aberdeen, MD [*Library symbol*] [*Library of Congress*] (LCLS)
**MdApgP** .... United States Army, Post Library, Aberdeen Proving Ground, Aberdeen, MD [*Library symbol*] [*Library of Congress*] (LCLS)
**MD App** ..... Maryland Appellate Reports [*A publication*] (DLA)
**MDAR** ....... Malfunction Detection Analysis and Recording [*NASA*] (KSC)
**MDAR** ....... Minimum Daily Adult Requirement
**MDARC** .... Medecine et Armees [*A publication*]
**MDarHi** ..... Old Dartmouth Historical Society, Dartmouth, MA [*Library symbol*] [*Library of Congress*] (LCLS)
**MDARS** ..... Military Damage Assessment Reporting System (MCD)
**MDAS** ....... Medical Data Acquisition System (KSC)
**MDAS** ....... Meteorological Data Acquisition System [*NASA*] (KSC)
**MDAS** ....... Miniature Data Acquisition System
**MDAS** ....... Mission Data Acquisition System [*NASA*] (NASA)
**MdAS** ........ Saint John's College, Annapolis, MD [*Library symbol*] [*Library of Congress*] (LCLS)
**Mdat** .......... Mandat [*Order*] [*Business term*] [*French*]
**MDA (Tehran)** ... Majalle(H)-Ye Daneshkade(H)-Ye Adabiyyat Va Olun-E Ensanie-Ye (Tehran) [*A publication*]
**MDAV** ....... Muscular Dystrophy Association of Victoria [*Australia*]
**MDB** .......... Bren Del Win Centennial Library, Deloraine, Manitoba [*Library symbol*] [*National Library of Canada*] (NLC)
**MDB** .......... Enoch Pratt Free Library, Baltimore, MD [*OCLC symbol*] (OCLC)
**MDB** .......... Master Database (MCD)
**MDB** .......... Master Distribution Box [*Missile system*] [*Army*]
**MDB** .......... MDI Mobile Data International, Inc. [*Toronto Stock Exchange symbol*] [*Vancouver Stock Exchange symbol*]
**MDB** .......... Memory-Data Bank
**MDB** .......... Mersey Dock Board [*British*] (DAS)
**MDB** .......... Message Database (MCD)
**MDB** .......... Metrology Data Bank [*GIDEP*]
**MDB** .......... Minimally Distinct Border [*Color perception*]
**MDB** .......... Mission Data Book [*NASA*] (NASA)
**MDB** .......... Mission Display Board Assembly [*Space Flight Operations Facility, NASA*]
**MDB** .......... Mitglied des Deutschen Bundestages [*Member of the German Federal Parliament*]
**MDB** .......... Movimento Democratico Brasileiro [*Brazilian Democratic Movement*] [*Political party*] (PPW)
**MDB** .......... Multilateral Development Bank
**MDB** .......... Multiple Drive Block
**MDB** .......... Multiplex Data Bus [*Data processing*] (MCD)
**MDB** .......... Mutual Defense Board [*US-Philippines*] (CINC)
**MdBAE** ..... United States Army, Corps of Engineers, Baltimore, MD [*Library symbol*] [*Library of Congress*] (LCLS)
**MdBaH** ...... Harford Community College, Bel Air, MD [*Library symbol*] [*Library of Congress*] (LCLS)
**MdBaHC** ... Harford County Library, Bel Air, MD [*Library symbol*] [*Library of Congress*] (LCLS)
**MdBAS** ...... Armco, Inc., Advanced Materials Division, Research Library, Baltimore, MD [*Library symbol*] [*Library of Congress*] (LCLS)
**MdBB** ........ Baltimore Bar Library, Baltimore, MD [*Library symbol*] [*Library of Congress*] (LCLS)
**MdBb** ......... United States Naval Training Center, Bainbridge, MD [*Library symbol*] [*Library of Congress*] (LCLS)
**MdBBC** ...... Baltimore Conference, Inc., United Methodist Historical Society, Baltimore, MD [*Library symbol*] [*Library of Congress*] (LCLS)
**MdBBJC** ... Community College of Baltimore, Baltimore, MD [*Library symbol*] [*Library of Congress*] (LCLS)
**MdBBO** ..... [*The*] Baltimore & Ohio Railroad Co., Employees' Library, Baltimore, MD [*Library symbol*] [*Library of Congress*] [*Obsolete*] (LCLS)
**MdBBR** ..... Bendix Corp., Baltimore, MD [*Library symbol*] [*Library of Congress*] (LCLS)
**MdBBS** ...... Bon Secours Medical Library, Baltimore, MD [*Library symbol*] [*Library of Congress*] (LCLS)
**MDBC** ....... Midland Bancorp [*NASDAQ symbol*] (NQ)
**MdBCC** ..... Catonsville Community College, Learning Resources Division, Baltimore, MD [*Library symbol*] [*Library of Congress*] (LCLS)
**MdBCH** ..... Baltimore City Court House, Baltimore, MD [*Library symbol*] [*Library of Congress*] (LCLS)
**MdBCIC** .... Counter Intelligence Center Corps School, Fort Holabird, Baltimore, MD [*Library symbol*] [*Library of Congress*] (LCLS)
**MdBCP** ...... Baltimore County Public Library, Towson, MD [*Library symbol*] [*Library of Congress*] (LCLS)
**MdBCPM** ... Chemical Pigment Co., Metals Division, Baltimore, MD [*Library symbol*] [*Library of Congress*] (LCLS)
**MdBCS** ...... Coppin State College, Baltimore, MD [*Library symbol*] [*Library of Congress*] (LCLS)
**MDBDF** .... March of Dimes Birth Defects Foundation (EA)
**MdBDH** ..... United States Department of Health and Human Services, Health Care Financing Administration, Office of Research Demonstrations and Statistics, Baltimore, MD [*Library symbol*] [*Library of Congress*] (LCLS)
**MdBE** ........ Enoch Pratt Free Library, Baltimore, MD [*Library symbol*] [*Library of Congress*] (LCLS)
**MdBeCA** .... Concepts Analysis Agency, Bethesda, MD [*Library symbol*] [*Library of Congress*] (LCLS)
**MdBeCI** ..... Congressional Information Service, Bethesda, MD [*Library symbol*] [*Library of Congress*] (LCLS)
**MdBEs** ....... Essex Community College, Baltimore, MD [*Library symbol*] [*Library of Congress*] (LCLS)
**MdBeU** ...... Uniform Services University of the Health Sciences, Bethesda, MD [*Library symbol*] [*Library of Congress*] (LCLS)
**MDBF** ....... Mean Distance between Failures [*Quality control*] (MCD)
**MdBFamP** ... Family Planning Training Institute, Baltimore, MD [*Library symbol*] [*Library of Congress*] (LCLS)
**MdBFH** ..... Fort Holabird Post Library, Baltimore, MD [*Library symbol*] [*Library of Congress*] (LCLS)
**MdBFM** .... Grand Lodge of Ancient Free and Accepted Masons of Maryland, Masonic Library, Baltimore, MD [*Library symbol*] [*Library of Congress*] (LCLS)
**MdBFr** ....... Friends Meeting, Stony Run, Baltimore, MD [*Library symbol*] [*Library of Congress*] (LCLS)
**MdBG** ........ Goucher College, Baltimore, MD [*Library symbol*] [*Library of Congress*] (LCLS)
**MdBGM-E** ... Martin Marietta Corp., Science and Technology Library, Baltimore, MD [*Library symbol*] [*Library of Congress*] (LCLS)
**MdBGM-N** ... Martin Marietta Corp., RIAS Library, Baltimore, MD [*Library symbol*] [*Library of Congress*] (LCLS)
**MdBH** ........ Baltimore City Hospitals, Doctors' Library, Baltimore, MD [*Library symbol*] [*Library of Congress*] (LCLS)
**MDBH** ....... Barahona [*Dominican Republic*] [*ICAO location identifier*] (ICLI)
**MdBHC** ..... Baltimore Hebrew College, Baltimore, MD [*Library symbol*] [*Library of Congress*] (LCLS)
**MDBI** ........ Mean Days between Injuries

**MdBJ**......... Johns Hopkins University, Baltimore, MD [*Library symbol*] [*Library of Congress*] (LCLS)
**MD BJ**....... Maryland Bar Journal [*A publication*]
**MdBJ-A**..... Johns Hopkins University, Applied Physics Laboratory, Silver Spring, MD [*Library symbol*] [*Library of Congress*] (LCLS)
**MdBJ-AIS** ... Johns Hopkins University, School of Advanced International Studies, Washington, DC [*Library symbol*] [*Library of Congress*] (LCLS)
**MdBJ-G** .... Johns Hopkins University, John Work Garrett Library, Baltimore, MD [*Library symbol*] [*Library of Congress*] (LCLS)
**MdBJ-H**.... Johns Hopkins University, School of Hygiene and Public Health, Maternal and Child Health-Population Dynamics Library, Baltimore, MD [*Library symbol*] [*Library of Congress*] (LCLS)
**MdBJ-P**..... Johns Hopkins University, George Peabody Library, Baltimore, MD [*Library symbol*] [*Library of Congress*] (LCLS)
**MdBJ-W** ... Johns Hopkins University, William H. Welch Medical Library, Baltimore, MD [*Library symbol*] [*Library of Congress*] (LCLS)
**MDBK**....... Madin-Darby Bovine Kidney [*Cell line*]
**MDBL** ....... Maintainability Data Baseline (MCD)
**MDBL** ....... Maintainability Design Baseline (MCD)
**MdBLH**..... Lutheran Hospital of Maryland, Baltimore, MD [*Library symbol*] [*Library of Congress*] (LCLS)
**MdBLN** ..... Loyola - Notre Dame Library, Inc., Baltimore, MD [*Library symbol*] [*Library of Congress*] (LCLS)
**MdBM**....... Medical and Chirurgical Faculty of the State of Maryland, Baltimore, MD [*Library symbol*] [*Library of Congress*] (LCLS)
**MDBM**...... MULTICS Data Base Manager
**MdBMA**.... Baltimore Museum of Art, Baltimore, MD [*Library symbol*] [*Library of Congress*] (LCLS)
**MdBMC**.... Morgan State College [*Later, Morgan State University*] Baltimore, MD [*Library symbol*] [*Library of Congress*] (LCLS)
**MdBMH**.... Mercy Hospital, McGlannan Memorial Library, Baltimore, MD [*Library symbol*] [*Library of Congress*] (LCLS)
**MdBMH-N** ... Mercy Hospital, School of Nursing, Baltimore, MD [*Library symbol*] [*Library of Congress*] (LCLS)
**MdBMI** ..... Maryland Institute, School of Fine and Applied Arts, Baltimore, MD [*Library symbol*] [*Library of Congress*] (LCLS)
**MdBMStA** ... Mount Saint Agnes College, Baltimore, MD [*Library symbol*] [*Library of Congress*] (LCLS)
**MdBNA**..... National Institute on Aging, Gerontology Research Center, Baltimore, MD [*Library symbol*] [*Library of Congress*] (LCLS)
**MdBo**......... Bowie State College, Bowie, MD [*Library symbol*] [*Library of Congress*] (LCLS)
**MdBOAS**.. United States Social Security Administration, Baltimore, MD [*Library symbol*] [*Library of Congress*] (LCLS)
**MdBP**........ Enoch Pratt Free Library, George Peabody Branch, Baltimore, MD [*Library symbol*] [*Library of Congress*] (LCLS)
**MDBP**....... Mechanically Deboned Broiler Product [*Food technology*]
**MdBPC**...... Peabody Conservatory of Music, Baltimore, MD [*Library symbol*] [*Library of Congress*] (LCLS)
**MdBPH**..... United States Public Health Service Hospital, Baltimore, MD [*Library symbol*] [*Library of Congress*] (LCLS)
**MdBPM**.... Peale Museum, Baltimore, MD [*Library symbol*] [*Library of Congress*] (LCLS)
**MdBR**........ Research Institute for Advanced Study, Baltimore, MD [*Library symbol*] [*Library of Congress*] (LCLS)
**MdBREC**... Engineering Society of Baltimore, Baltimore, MD [*Library symbol*] [*Library of Congress*] (LCLS)
**MdBS** ........ Saint Mary's Seminary and University, Baltimore, MD [*Library symbol*] [*Library of Congress*] (LCLS)
**MdBSAr**.... Sulpician Archives Baltimore, Baltimore, MD [*Library symbol*] [*Library of Congress*] (LCLS)
**MdBSet** ..... Seton Psychiatric Institute, Baltimore, MD [*Library symbol*] [*Library of Congress*] (LCLS)
**MdBSH**..... Sinai Hospital, Staff Library, Baltimore, MD [*Library symbol*] [*Library of Congress*] (LCLS)
**MdBS-P**..... Saint Mary's Seminary and University, Philosophy Library, Baltimore, MD [*Library symbol*] [*Library of Congress*] (LCLS)
**MdBSP**...... Sheppard-Pratt Hospital, Baltimore, MD [*Library symbol*] [*Library of Congress*] (LCLS)
**MdBSp** ...... Sunpapers Library, Baltimore, MD [*Library symbol*] [*Library of Congress*] (LCLS)
**MdBSt** ....... Saint Agnes Hospital, Baltimore, MD [*Library symbol*] [*Library of Congress*] (LCLS)
**MdBT** ........ Towson State University, Baltimore, MD [*Library symbol*] [*Library of Congress*] (LCLS)
**MdBU**........ University of Baltimore, Baltimore, MD [*Library symbol*] [*Library of Congress*] (LCLS)
**MdBU-L**.... University of Baltimore, Law Library, Baltimore, MD [*Library symbol*] [*Library of Congress*] (LCLS)
**MdBUM**.... Union Memorial Hospital, Finney Medical Library, Baltimore, MD [*Library symbol*] [*Library of Congress*] (LCLS)
**MD Bur Mines Ann Rept** ... Maryland. Bureau of Mines. Annual Report [*A publication*]
**MdBV**........ United States Veterans Administration Hospital, Baltimore, MD [*Library symbol*] [*Library of Congress*] (LCLS)
**MdBWA**.... Walters Art Gallery, Baltimore, MD [*Library symbol*] [*Library of Congress*] (LCLS)
**MdBWe**..... Westinghouse Defense and Space Center, Baltimore, MD [*Library symbol*] [*Library of Congress*] (LCLS)
**MdBWesE** ... Western Electric Co., Inc., Baltimore, MD [*Library symbol*] [*Library of Congress*] (LCLS)
**MDC**.......... Boston, MA [*Location identifier*] [*FAA*] (FAAL)
**MDC**.......... Dow Chemical Co., Library, Midland, MI [*OCLC symbol*] (OCLC)
**MDC**.......... Machinability Data Center [*Computerized search service*] [*Metcut Research Associates, Inc.*] (IID)
**MDC**.......... Machinery Diagnostic Consultant [*Software program*]
**MDC**.......... Main Display Console
**MDC**.......... Maintenance Data Center (MCD)
**MDC**.......... Maintenance Data Collection [*Military*] (AFM)
**MDC**.......... Maintenance Dependency Chart (IEEE)
**MDC**.......... Major Diagnostic Categories [*Medicine*]
**MDC**.......... Management Development Course (MCD)
**MDC**.......... Manhattan Drug Company
**MDC**.......... Manual Direction Center [*Air Force*] (AFM)
**MDC**.......... Master Data Center, Inc. [*Information service or system*] (IID)
**MDC**.......... Master Direction Center [*Air Force*]
**MDC**.......... Materials Dissemination Center [*Institute for Development of Educational Activities*]
**MDC**.......... Maximum Dependable Capacity [*Nuclear energy*] (NRCH)
**MDC**.......... McDonnell Douglas Corporation (MCD)
**MDC**.......... MDC Holdings, Inc. [*NYSE symbol*] (SPSG)
**MDC**.......... Mead Data Central, Inc. [*Dayton, OH*]
**MDC**.......... Mechanically Deboned Chicken [*Food technology*]
**MDC**.......... Medisch Contact [*A publication*]
**MDC**.......... Memory Disk Controller
**MDC**.......... Menado [*Indonesia*] [*Airport symbol*] (OAG)
**MDC**.......... Message Display Console (MCD)
**MDC**.......... Message Distribution Center (NATG)
**MDC**.......... Meteorological Data Collection
**MDC**.......... Metropolitan District Commission
**MDC**.......... Metropolitan District Council [*British*]
**MDC**.......... Mild Detonating Cord (MCD)
**MDC**.......... Million Dollar Contract [*File*] [*Military*]
**MDC**.......... Milwaukee-Downer College [*Later, Lawrence University*] [*Wisconsin*]
**MDC**.......... Mine Dispatch Control
**MDC**.......... Miniature Detonating Cord (MCD)
**MDC**.......... Minimobile Data Center [*Military*]
**MDC**.......... Minimum Detectable Concentration [*Analytical chemistry*]
**MDC**.......... Ministere des Communications [*Department of Communications*] [*Canada*]
**MDC**.......... Missile Development Center [*Air Force*]
**MDC**.......... Missile Direction Center
**MDC**.......... Mission Director Center [*NASA*] (KSC)
**MDC**.......... Mission Duty Cycle [*NASA*] (KSC)
**MDC**.......... Mobile Defence Corps [*British military*] (DMA)
**MDC**.......... Mobile Distress Call
**MDC**.......... Mongoloid Development Council [*Later, NADS*] (EA)
**MDC**.......... Montreal Diocesan College [*Quebec*]
**MDC**.......... Montreux Development [*Vancouver Stock Exchange symbol*]
**MDC**.......... More Developed Country
**MDC**.......... Mother's Day Council (EA)
**MDC**.......... Motor Direct-Connected
**MDC**.......... Mount Diablo [*California*] [*Seismograph station code, US Geological Survey*] (SEIS)
**MDC**.......... Movement Designator Code
**MDC**.......... Muller Data Corporation [*Information service or system*] (IID)
**MDC**.......... Multilayer Dielectric Coating
**MDC**.......... Multiple Delay Code (AFIT)
**MDC**.......... Multiple Device Controller
**MDC**.......... Multiple Drone Control (MCD)
**MDCA**....... Main Distribution Control Assembly (MCD)
**MDCA**....... Manufacturing Design Change Analysis
**MDCA**....... Mind Development and Control Association (EA)
**MdCam**...... Dorchester County Public Library, Cambridge, MD [*Library symbol*] [*Library of Congress*] (LCLS)
**MdCatSG**.. Spring Grove State Hospital, Catonsville, MD [*Library symbol*] [*Library of Congress*] (LCLS)
**MDCB**....... Moisture Detector Control Box
**MDCC**....... Master Data Control Console
**MdCe**......... Queen Anne's County Free Library, Centreville, MD [*Library symbol*] [*Library of Congress*] (LCLS)
**MDCEF**..... Medical-Dental Committee on Evaluation of Fluoridation [*Defunct*] (EA)
**MDCGC**.... Multidimensional Capillary Gas Chromatography
**MD Ch**....... Maryland Chancery Reports, by Johnson [*4 vols.*] [*A publication*] (DLA)
**MDCH**....... Middlesex, Duke of Cambridge's Hussars [*Military unit*] [*British*]
**MD Chan**... Maryland Chancery Decisions [*A publication*] (DLA)
**MD Chan Dec** ... Maryland Chancery Decisions [*A publication*] (DLA)

**MD Ch D**... Maryland Chancery Decisions [*A publication*] (DLA)
**MD Ch Dec** ... Maryland Chancery Decisions [*A publication*] (DLA)
**MdChW**..... Washington College, Chestertown, MD [*Library symbol*] [*Library of Congress*] (LCLS)
**MDCI** ........ Medical Action Industries, Inc. [*Farmingdale, NY*] [*NASDAQ symbol*] (NQ)
**MDCI** ........ Multidisciplinary Counterintelligence (MCD)
**MDCK** ....... Madin-Darby Canine Kidney [*Cell line*]
**MDCM**...... Medicinae Doctor Chirurgia Magister [*Doctor of Medicine and Master of Surgery*]
**MDCMA**... Melvil Dui Chowder and Marching Association [*Later, MDMCA*] (EA)
**MDCN**....... Medcan, Inc. [*NASDAQ symbol*] (NQ)
**MDCNAY** ... Medicina. Revista do Centro Academico Rocha Lima [*CARL*]. Hospital das Clinicas da Faculdade de Medicina de Ribeirao Preto. Universidade de Sao Paulo [*A publication*]
**MDCO**....... Consuelo, San Pedro De Macoris [*Dominican Republic*] [*ICAO location identifier*] (ICLI)
**MDCO**....... Marine Drilling Co. [*NASDAQ symbol*] (NQ)
**MdCoA** ...... Arctec, Inc., Columbia, MD [*Library symbol*] [*Library of Congress*] (LCLS)
**MD Code Ann** ... Annotated Code of Maryland [*A publication*] (DLA)
**MdCoG**...... W. R. Grace & Co., Research Library, Columbia, MD [*Library symbol*] [*Library of Congress*] (LCLS)
**MdCoH**...... Hittman Associates, Inc., Columbia, MD [*Library symbol*] [*Library of Congress*] (LCLS)
**MD Conserv** ... Maryland Conservationist [*A publication*]
**MD Const**.. Maryland Constitution [*A publication*] (DLA)
**MdCpM**..... United States Bureau of Mines, College Park Research Center, College Park, MD [*Library symbol*] [*Library of Congress*] (LCLS)
**MDCPZ**..... Monodesmethylchlorpromazine [*Biochemistry*]
**MDCR** ....... Cabo Rojo [*Dominican Republic*] [*ICAO location identifier*] (ICLI)
**MDCR** ....... Maintenance Data Collection Report (MCD)
**MDCR** ....... Medcross, Inc. [*NASDAQ symbol*] (NQ)
**MDCS** ....... Maintenance Data Collection System [*or Subsystem*] [*Navy*]
**MDCS** ....... Malfunction Display and Control System (MCD)
**MDCS** ....... Master Digital Command System
**MDCS** ....... Material Data Collection System [*NASA*] (KSC)
**MDCS** ....... Mission Data Collection Sheets (CINC)
**MDCS** ....... Mutual Defense Control Staff [*Department of State*]
**MDCS** ....... Santo Domingo [*Dominican Republic*] [*ICAO location identifier*] (ICLI)
**MDCSC**..... McDonnell Douglas Computer Systems Company [*Formerly, MICRODATA*] (MCD)
**MDC/SS** ... Multiple Drone Control Strike System (MCD)
**MD/CSU**... Motor Drive Cassette Support Unit
**MDCT** ....... Mechanical Draft Cooling Tower [*Nuclear energy*] (NRCH)
**MDCT** ....... Multidimensional Compensatory Task
**MdCu**......... Allegany County Library, Cumberland, MD [*Library symbol*] [*Library of Congress*] (LCLS)
**MDCU**....... Magnetic Disk Control Unit
**MDCU**....... Mobile Dynamic Checkout Unit (AAG)
**MdCuAC** ... Allegany Community College, Cumberland, MD [*Library symbol*] [*Library of Congress*] (LCLS)
**MdCvH**...... Crownsville State Hospital, Crownsville, MD [*Library symbol*] [*Library of Congress*] (LCLS)
**MDCZ** ....... Constanza [*Dominican Republic*] [*ICAO location identifier*] (ICLI)
**MdD** .......... Caroline County Public Library, Denton, MD [*Library symbol*] [*Library of Congress*] (LCLS)
**MDD**.......... Doctor of Dental Medicine
**MDD**.......... Madrid [*Spain*] [*Seismograph station code, US Geological Survey*] [*Closed*] (SEIS)
**MDD**.......... Magnetic Disk Drive
**MDD**.......... Maintenance Due Date (NVT)
**MDD**.......... Major Depressive Disorder [*Psychiatry*]
**MdD** .......... Mandaic Dictionary [*Oxford*] [*A publication*] (BJA)
**MDD**.......... Mate/Demate Device [*NASA*] (NASA)
**MDD**.......... McDonald & Co. Investments, Inc. [*NYSE symbol*] (SPSG)
**MDD**.......... Mean Daily Difference [*Medicine*]
**MDD**.......... Mean Daily Dose
**MdD** .......... Median Deviation [*Statistics*]
**MDD**.......... Median Droplet Diameter
**MDD**.......... Medical Devices, Diagnostics, and Instrumentation Reports: the Gray Sheet [*A publication*]
**MDD**.......... Meteorological Data Distribution
**MDD**.......... Middenstand [*A publication*]
**MDD**.......... Midland, TX [*Location identifier*] [*FAA*] (FAAL)
**MDD**.......... Milligrams per Square Decimeter per Day
**MDD**.......... Million-Dollar Deal
**MDD**.......... Million Dollar Directory [*Dun's Marketing Services*] [*Parsippany, NJ*] [*Database*]
**MDD**.......... Mission Data Display
**MD & D**..... Montagu, Deacon, and De Gex's English Bankruptcy Reports [*1840-44*] [*A publication*] (DLA)
**MDD**.......... Mouvement Democratique Dahomeen [*Dahomean Democratic Movement*] [*Political party*]
**MDD**.......... Multichannel Demultiplexer and Distributor
**MDD**.......... Multidimensional Database
**MDDA**....... Manic Depressive and Depressive Association [*Later, NDMDA*] (EA)
**MDDA**....... Mechanicsburg Defense Depot Activity [*AEC*]
**MDDC**....... Manhattan District Declassified Code [*AEC*]
**MDDCS** .... Memorial Dose Distribution Computation Service [*Memorial Sloan-Kettering Cancer Center*] [*Information service or system*] (IID)
**MDDD**....... Merrill-Demos DD Scale [*Drug abuse and delinquent behavior test*]
**MDDE**....... Maryland & Delaware Railroad Co. [*AAR code*]
**MD & DeG** ... Montagu, Deacon, and De Gex's English Bankruptcy Reports [*1840-44*] [*A publication*] (DLA)
**MD Dep Geol Mines Water Resour Bull** ... Maryland. Department of Geology. Mines and Water Resources Bulletin [*A publication*]
**MD Dept Geology Mines and Water Res Bull County Rept** ... Maryland. Department of Geology. Mines and Water Resources Bulletin. County Reports [*A publication*]
**MDDF** ....... Minimum Delay Data Format (MCD)
**MDDJ** ....... Dajabon [*Dominican Republic*] [*ICAO location identifier*] (ICLI)
**MDDPC** .... Methyl Dimethyldihydropyrancarboxylate [*Organic chemistry*]
**MDDS**....... Maintainability Design Data Sheets (MCD)
**MDDS**....... Material Directory Data Sheet (MCD)
**MDDX**....... Middlesex [*Region of London*]
**MDE**.......... Cincinnati, OH [*Location identifier*] [*FAA*] (FAAL)
**MDE**.......... Madame (ROG)
**MDE**.......... Magnetic Decision Element [*Data processing*] (BUR)
**MDE**.......... Major Defense Equipment (MCD)
**MDE**.......... Management Decision [*A publication*]
**MDE**.......... Matrix Difference Equation
**MDE**.......... Mechanical Design Environment
**MDE**.......... Medellin [*Colombia*] [*Airport symbol*] (OAG)
**MDE**.......... Meteoroid Detection Experiment (KSC)
**MDE**.......... Metina Development [*Vancouver Stock Exchange symbol*]
**MDE**.......... Military Damage Expectancy
**MDE**.......... Mindy Explorations Ltd. [*Vancouver Stock Exchange symbol*]
**MDE**.......... Minnesota State Department of Education, Professional Library, St. Paul, MN [*OCLC symbol*] (OCLC)
**MDE**.......... Missile Display Equipment
**MDE**.......... Mission Dependent Elements [*NASA*] (KSC)
**MDE**.......... Mission Dependent Equipment [*NASA*] (KSC)
**MDE**.......... Mission Dependent Experiment [*NASA*] (NASA)
**MDE**.......... Mission Display Equipment
**MDE**.......... Mobile District Engineer (AAG)
**MDE**.......... Mobile Telemetering Station [*ITU designation*] (DEN)
**MDE**.......... Modern Drug Encyclopedia [*A publication*]
**MDE**.......... Modular Design of Electronics (MCD)
**MDE**.......... Modular Display Electronics (MCD)
**MDE**.......... Mooring Dynamics Experiment [*Marine science*] (MSC)
**MdE**.......... Mount St. Mary's College, Emmitsburg, MD [*Library symbol*] [*Library of Congress*] (LCLS)
**MDE**.......... National Library of Medicine [*Source file*] [*UTLAS symbol*]
**MDEA** ....... Marketing and Distributive Education Association [*Later, MEA*] (EA)
**MDEA** ....... Methyldiethanolamine [*Organic chemistry*]
**MDEA** ....... Methylenedioxyethamphetamine [*Biochemistry*]
**MdEa**......... Talbot County Free Library, Easton, MD [*Library symbol*] [*Library of Congress*] (LCLS)
**MdEdgA**.... United States Army, Technical Library, Army Chemical Center, Edgewood, MD [*Library symbol*] [*Library of Congress*] (LCLS)
**MDedHi**.... Dedham Historical Society, Dedham, MA [*Library symbol*] [*Library of Congress*] (LCLS)
**MDE Digest** ... Marketing and Distributive Educators' Digest [*A publication*]
**MDee**......... Dickinson Library, Deerfield, MA [*Library symbol*] [*Library of Congress*] (LCLS)
**MDeeD**...... Deerfield Academy, Deerfield, MA [*Library symbol*] [*Library of Congress*] (LCLS)
**MDeeH**...... Historic Deerfield, Inc., Deerfield, MA [*Library symbol*] [*Library of Congress*] (LCLS)
**MDeeP**...... Pocumtuck Valley Memorial Association, Deerfield, MA [*Library symbol*] [*Library of Congress*] (LCLS)
**MDefStudies** ... Master of Defence Studies
**MDEFWP** ... Motor-Driven Emergency Feedwater Pump [*Nuclear energy*] (NRCH)
**MDEN**....... Enriquillo [*Dominican Republic*] [*ICAO location identifier*] (ICLI)
**MDEN**....... Males, Density Of [*Ecology*]
**MDENDET** ... Mobile Dental Detachment [*Coast Guard*]
**MD Energy Saver** ... Maryland Energy Saver [*A publication*]
**M Dent Sc** ... Master of Dental Science [*British*]
**MDEP** ....... Management Decision Package [*DoD*]
**MDERD**.... Monatsschrift fuer Deutsches Recht [*A publication*]
**M Des** ........ Master of Design
**MDES**........ Multiple Data Entry System
**M Des (RCA)** ... Master of Design, Royal College of Art
**MDET** ....... Militarized Digital Element Tester (MCD)
**MDEV** ....... Medical Devices, Inc. [*NASDAQ symbol*] (CTT)
**MDEX** ....... Medex, Inc. [*NASDAQ symbol*] (NQ)
**MDF** .......... Macrodefect Free [*Materials science*]

**MDF**.......... Magnetic Direction Finding [*Meteorology*]
**MDF**.......... Main Distributing Frame [*Bell System*]
**MDF**.......... Maintenance Depot Fabrication
**MDF**.......... Manipulator Deployment Facility (MCD)
**MDF**.......... Manipulator Development Facility [*NASA*] (NASA)
**MDF**.......... Manual Direction Finder [*Radio*]
**MDF**.......... Master Data File (AFIT)
**MDF**.......... Master Directory File [*Data processing*]
**MDF**.......... Master Document File [*Data processing*]
**MDF**.......... Mate/Demate Facility [*NASA*] (NASA)
**MDF**.......... Medium Density Fiberboard
**MDF**.......... Medium-Frequency Direction Finder [*or Finding*]
**MdF**.......... Mercure de France [*A publication*]
**MDF**.......... Metals Datafile [*Materials Information*] [*Information service or system*] (IID)
**MDF**.......... Metric Data Facility (MCD)
**MDF**.......... Micro-Dose-Focusing [*Electron microscopy*]
**MDF**.......... Microcomputer Development Facilities (IEEE)
**MDF**.......... Midland Doherty Financial Corp. [*Toronto Stock Exchange symbol*]
**MDF**.......... Mild Detonating Fuse
**MDF**.......... Mitteldeutsche Forschungen [*A publication*]
**MDF**.......... Mixed Dipterocarp Forest
**MDF**.......... Modify
**MDF**.......... Mooreland, OK [*Location identifier*] [*FAA*] (FAAL)
**MDF**.......... Multiband Direction Finder
**MdF**.......... Musees de France [*A publication*]
**MDF**.......... Myocardial Depressant Factor
**MDFC**....... Mason Dixon International Fan Club (EA)
**MDFC**....... Matt Dillon Fan Club (EA)
**MDFC**....... McDonnell Douglas Finance Corp. Ltd. [*British*]
**MdFdM**..... United States Army Medical Intelligence and Information Agency, Fort Detrick, MD [*Library symbol*] [*Library of Congress*] (LCLS)
**MdFhV**...... United States Veterans Administration Hospital, Fort Howard, MD [*Library symbol*] [*Library of Congress*] (LCLS)
**MD Fla**...... United States District Court for the Middle District of Florida (DLA)
**MDFLT**..... Multi-Directional Forklift Truck (MCD)
**MdFmA**..... United States Army, Fort George G. Meade Post Recreation Services Library, Fort George G. Meade, MD [*Library symbol*] [*Library of Congress*] (LCLS)
**MdFmN**..... National Security Agency, Fort George G. Meade, MD [*Library symbol*] [*Library of Congress*] (LCLS)
**MDFMR**... M-Day Force Materiel Requirement
**MDFNA**.... Maximum Density Fuming Nitric Acid
**MDFR**....... Make Descent From [*Aviation*] (FAAC)
**MdFreCR**.. Frederick Cancer Research Center, Frederick, MD [*Library symbol*] [*Library of Congress*] (LCLS)
**MdFreD**..... Fort Detrick Technical Library, Frederick, MD [*Library symbol*] [*Library of Congress*] (LCLS)
**MdFreFC**... Frederick Community College, Frederick, MD [*Library symbol*] [*Library of Congress*] (LCLS)
**MdFreH**..... Hood College, Frederick, MD [*Library symbol*] [*Library of Congress*] (LCLS)
**MdFreHi**... [*The*] Historical Society of Frederick County, Inc., Frederick, MD [*Library symbol*] [*Library of Congress*] (LCLS)
**MdFroS**..... Frostburg State College, Frostburg, MD [*Library symbol*] [*Library of Congress*] (LCLS)
**MDFRR**..... Mission Directors Flight Readiness Review [*NASA*] (KSC)
**MDFY**....... Modify (FAAC)
**MDG**.......... Madagascar [*ANSI three-letter standard code*] (CNC)
**MDG**.......... Madang [*Papua New Guinea*] [*Seismograph station code, US Geological Survey*] (SEIS)
**MDG**.......... Marina Development Group [*Commercial firm*] [*British*]
**MDG**.......... Medical Director-General [*Navy*] [*British*]
**MDG**.......... Metal Density Gauge
**MDG**.......... Metasystems Design Group, Inc. [*Arlington, VA*] [*Telecommunications service*] (TSSD)
**MDG**.......... Molecular Drag Gauge [*Instrumentation*]
**MDG**.......... Monatsschrift fuer das Deutsche Geistesleben [*A publication*]
**MDG**.......... Multiplier Decoder Gate [*Data processing*]
**MDG**.......... Multipurpose Display Group (MCD)
**MDG**.......... Valdosta, GA [*Location identifier*] [*FAA*] (FAAL)
**MDGA**....... Guerra [*Dominican Republic*] [*ICAO location identifier*] (ICLI)
**MD GA**...... United States District Court for the Middle District of Georgia (DLA)
**MDGC**....... Multidimensional Gas Chromatography
**MDGD**....... Mercury Doped Germanium Detector
**MD Geol Surv Basic Data Rep** ... Maryland. Geological Survey. Basic Data Report [*A publication*]
**MD Geol Surv Bull** ... Maryland. Geological Survey. Bulletin [*A publication*]
**MD Geol Surv Guideb** ... Maryland. Geological Survey. Guidebook [*A publication*]
**MD Geol Surv Inf Circ** ... Maryland. Geological Survey. Information Circular [*A publication*]
**MD Geol Surv Quadrangle Atlas** ... Maryland. Geological Survey. Quadrangle Atlas [*A publication*]
**MD Geol Surv Rep Invest** ... Maryland. Geological Survey. Report of Investigations [*A publication*]
**MDGF**....... Macrophage Derived Growth Factor [*Biochemistry*]
**MDGFA**.... Bulletin. Geological Society of Denmark [*A publication*]
**MDG(N)**.... Medical Director-General (Navy) [*British*]
**MDGNVO** ... Mitteilungen. Deutsche Gesellschaft fuer Natur- und Voelkerkunde Ostasiens [*A publication*]
**MD G S Sp Pub** ... Maryland. Geological Survey. Special Publication [*A publication*]
**MDGT**....... Midget (MSA)
**MDH**......... Carbondale [*Illinois*] [*Airport symbol*] (OAG)
**MDH**......... Carbondale/Murphysboro, IL [*Location identifier*] [*FAA*] (FAAL)
**MDH**......... Madison Holdings Ltd. [*Vancouver Stock Exchange symbol*]
**MDH**......... Magnetic Drum Head
**MDH**......... Malate Dehydrogenase [*Also, MD*] [*An enzyme*]
**MDH**......... Maneuver Director Headquarters [*Military*]
**MDH**......... Medullary Dorsal Horn [*Anatomy*]
**MDH**......... Month-Day-Hour [*Automotive manufacturing*]
**MdHag**...... Washington County Free Library, Hagerstown, MD [*Library symbol*] [*Library of Congress*] (LCLS)
**MDHBA**.... Medical-Dental-Hospital Bureaus of America (EA)
**MDHC**....... McDonnell Douglas Helicopter Company [*Formerly, HHI*] (MCD)
**MDHC**....... Mersey Docks and Harbour Company [*British*]
**MDHE**....... Herrera [*Dominican Republic*] [*ICAO location identifier*] (ICLI)
**MdHeH**..... Henryton State Hospital, Henryton, MD [*Library symbol*] [*Library of Congress*] (LCLS)
**MdHi**......... Maryland Historical Society, Baltimore, MD [*Library symbol*] [*Library of Congress*] (LCLS)
**MD His M** ... Maryland Historical Magazine [*A publication*]
**MD Hist**.... Maryland Historian [*A publication*]
**MD Hist M** ... Maryland Historical Magazine [*A publication*]
**MD Hist Mag** ... Maryland Historical Magazine [*A publication*]
**MD Hist Soc Fund-Publ** ... Maryland Historical Society. Fund-Publications [*A publication*]
**MDHJ**....... Methyl Dihydrojasmonate [*Organic chemistry*]
**MDHL**....... Modified Hodges-Lehmann Estimator [*Statistics*]
**MdHM**...... Maryland Historical Magazine [*A publication*]
**MDHR**...... Methyl Dihydroretinoate [*Biochemistry*]
**MDHR**...... Mini-Decay Heat Removal [*Nuclear energy*] (NRCH)
**MDHTSNAGEJTR** ... Movement of Dependents and Household Goods to Temporary Station[*s*] Not Authorized at Government Expense, Except as Prescribed in Joint Travel Regulations [*Army*] (AABC)
**MDHY**...... Higuey [*Dominican Republic*] [*ICAO location identifier*] (ICLI)
**MdHyD**..... De Sales Hall School of Theology, Hyattsville, MD [*Library symbol*] [*Library of Congress*] (LCLS)
**MdHyP**...... Prince George's County Memorial Library, Hyattsville, MD [*Library symbol*] [*Library of Congress*] (LCLS)
**MDI**........... Bemidji, MN [*Location identifier*] [*FAA*] (FAAL)
**MDI**........... Magnetic Direction Indicator
**MDI**........... Makurdi [*Nigeria*] [*Airport symbol*] (OAG)
**MDI**........... Management Development Institute (MCD)
**MDI**........... Manic Depression Interval [*Course*]
**MDI**........... Manic Depressive Illness
**MDI**........... Manual Data Input [*SAGE*]
**MDI**........... Market Decisions, Incorporated [*Information service or system*] (IID)
**MDI**........... Master of Didactics
**MDI**........... Master Direction Indicator
**MDI**........... Material Departmental Instruction
**MDI**........... Media Directions, Incorporated
**MDI**........... Memotec Data, Inc. [*Toronto Stock Exchange symbol*]
**MDI**........... Mental Development Index [*Bayley Scales of Infant Development*] [*Psychometrics*]
**MDI**........... Meridian Diagnostics, Inc.
**MDI**........... Metered Dose Inhaler [*Medicine*]
**MDI**........... Methane Diisocyanate [*Organic chemistry*]
**MDI**........... Methylenediphenyl Isocyanate [*Organic chemistry*]
**MDI**........... Microdosimetric Instrumentation
**MDI**........... Military Decision Items (AFIT)
**MDI**........... Mineral Deposit Inventory Database [*Ontario Geological Survey*] [*Information service or system*] [*Canada*] (CRD)
**MDI**........... Minimum Discrimination Information [*Statistics*]
**MDI**........... Miss-Distance Indicator [*Missiles*] (MUGU)
**MDI**........... Mission to the Deaf, International (EA)
**MDI**........... Mission Dependent Interface
**MDI**........... Mitteilungen. Deutsches Archaeologische Institut [*A publication*]
**MDI**........... Mobilization Day Increment [*Military*]
**MDI**........... Mobilization Day Index [*Military*] (NG)
**MDI**........... Monthly Debit Industrial [*Insurance*]
**MDI**........... Mouvement pour la Democratie et l'Independance [*Movement for Democracy and Independence*] [*Central Africa*] (PD)
**MDI**........... Multiple Display Indicator
**MDIA**........ Mitteilungen. Deutsches Institut fuer Aegyptische Altertumskunde (Kairo) [*A publication*]
**MDIBL**...... Mount Desert Island Biological Laboratory [*Salsbury Cove, ME*] [*Research center*]
**MDIC**........ Microwave Dielectric Integrated Circuit (IEEE)

**MDIC** ........ Multilateral Disarmament Information Centre [*British*]
**MDICP** ...... McDonnell Douglas Industrial Control Products (MCD)
**M DICT** ..... More Dicto [*As Directed*] [*Pharmacy*]
**M Dict** ........ Morison's Dictionary of Decisions, Scotch Court of Session [*1540-1808*] [*A publication*] (DLA)
**M Dict** ........ Morrison's Dictionary of Decisions, Scotch Court of Session [*A publication*] (DLA)
**M Did** ......... Master of Didactics
**M Di E** ........ Master of Diesel Engineering
**MDIE** ......... Mother-Daughter Ionosphere Experiment
**M Di Eng** ... Master of Diesel Engineering
**MDIF** ......... Manual Data Input Function [*Data processing*]
**MDIF & W** ... Maine Department of Inland Fisheries and Wildlife, Fishery Research Management Division [*Research center*] (RCD)
**MDIGB** ..... Mitteilungen. Deutsch-Israelitischer Gemeindebund [*A publication*]
**MDIIDI** ..... Medical Device and Diagnostic Industry [*A publication*]
**MDIK** ........ Mitteilungen. Deutsches Institut fuer Aegyptische Altertumskunde (Kairo) [*A publication*]
**MDIN** ........ Medalist Industries, Inc. [*NASDAQ symbol*] (NQ)
**MDIOME** ... Mitteilungsblatt. Irgun Olej Merkas Europa [*A publication*]
**M Dip** ........ Master of Diplomacy
**M-DIRT** .... Miss-Distance-Indicator Radioactive Tests [*Missiles*] (MUGU)
**MDIS** ......... Manual Data Input Section [*Data processing*]
**MDIS** ......... Manual Data Input System [*Data processing*]
**M Dis** ......... Marriage Dissolved
**MDISC** ....... McDonnell Douglas International Sales Corporation (MCD)
**M Disciplina** ... Musica Disciplina [*A publication*]
**MDISE** ....... Merchandise
**MDIU** ........ Manned Data Insertion Unit (KSC)
**MDIU** ........ Manual Data Input Unit [*Data processing*]
**M Div** ........ Master of Divinity
**MDJ** .......... Middle East Journal [*A publication*]
**MdJb** ......... Mitteldeutsches Jahrbuch [*A publication*]
**MdJC** ......... Maryland House of Corrections, Jessup, MD [*Library symbol*] [*Library of Congress*] (LCLS)
**MDJCS** ..... Memorandum by the Director, Joint Staff for the Joint Chiefs of Staff (MCD)
**Md J Int'l L & Trade** ... Maryland Journal of International Law and Trade [*A publication*] (DLA)
**MDJM** ...... Jainamosa [*Dominican Republic*] [*ICAO location identifier*] (ICLI)
**MDK** .......... Mbandaka [*Zaire*] [*Airport symbol*] (OAG)
**MDK** .......... Mechanical Disconnect Kit
**MDK** .......... Medicore, Inc. [*AMEX symbol*] (SPSG)
**MDKHD** ... Mukogawa Joshi Daigaku Kiyo. Yakugaku Hen [*A publication*]
**MDL** .......... Landbouwdocumentatie [*A publication*]
**MDL** .......... Macro Description Language [*Data processing*] (BUR)
**MDL** .......... Madill [*S.*] Ltd. [*Vancouver Stock Exchange symbol*]
**MDL** .......... Magnetic Delay Line
**MDL** .......... Magnetic Double Layer
**MDL** .......... Maintenance Diagnostic Logic [*Data processing*] (BUR)
**MDL** .......... Management Data List (AABC)
**MDL** .......... Manager's Discretionary Limit (DCTA)
**MDL** .......... Mandalay [*Burma*] [*Airport symbol*] (OAG)
**MDL** .......... Master Data Library [*NASA*]
**MDL** .......... Master of Divine Literature
**MDL** .......... Master Drawing List
**MDL** .......... Material Deviation List [*Military*]
**MDL** .......... Materialien zur Deutschen Literatur [*A publication*]
**MDL** .......... Mercury Delay Line
**MDL** .......... Microwave Delay Line
**MDL** .......... Microwave Development Laboratories
**MDL** .......... Middle (MSA)
**MDL** .......... Military Demarcation Line (CINC)
**MDL** .......... Mine Defense Laboratory [*Panama City, Florida*] [*Navy*]
**MDL** .......... Miniature Display Light
**MDL** .......... Minimum Detection Limit [*Chemistry*]
**MDL** .......... Model (ADA)
**MDL** .......... Modular Design Language [*Data processing*] (CSR)
**MDL** .......... Modular Dummy Load
**MDL** .......... Module (MSA)
**MDL** .......... Morris Dam Laboratory
**MDL** .......... Motor Distal Latency [*Medicine*]
**MDL** .......... Muddle [*A computer language*]
**MDL** .......... S Madill Limited [*Vancouver Stock Exchange symbol*]
**MDL** .......... University of Baltimore, Law Library, Baltimore, MD [*OCLC symbol*] (OCLC)
**MD LA** ...... United States District Court for the Middle District of Louisiana (DLA)
**MdLaD** ...... Divine Saviour Seminary, Lanham, MD [*Library symbol*] [*Library of Congress*] (LCLS)
**MdLapC** .... Charles County Community College, La Plata, MD [*Library symbol*] [*Library of Congress*] (LCLS)
**MD Law R** ... Maryland Law Review [*A publication*]
**MD Laws** ... Laws of Maryland [*A publication*] (DLA)
**MDLB** ....... Municipal Development and Loan Board [*Canada*]
**MDLC** ....... Materiel Development and Logistic Command [*Army - replaced Ordnance, Engineer, Signal, Chemical and Quartermaster Overall Commands*]
**MDLC** ....... Mutliple Data Link Controller
**MD LF** ....... Maryland Law Forum [*A publication*]
**MDLF** ........ Mobile Drydock Launch Facility
**MD Libr** .... Maryland Libraries [*A publication*]
**Md-LL** ....... Maryland State Law Library, Annapolis, MD [*Library symbol*] [*Library of Congress*] (LCLS)
**MDLLE** ..... Mademoiselle
**MDLLS** ..... Mediastinal Diffuse Large-Cell Lymphoma with Sclerosis [*Oncology*]
**MDLN** ....... Moduline International, Inc. [*NASDAQ symbol*] (NQ)
**MDLP** ....... Mobile Dryer Loan Program
**MdLP** ........ United States Department of the Interior, Patuxent Wildlife Research Center, Laurel, MD [*Library symbol*] [*Library of Congress*] (LCLS)
**MDLR** ....... La Romana [*Dominican Republic*] [*ICAO location identifier*] (ICLI)
**Md-LR** ....... Maryland Department of Legislative Reference, Baltimore, MD [*Library symbol*] [*Library of Congress*] (LCLS)
**MD LR** ...... Maryland Law Review [*A publication*]
**MDLRC** ..... Mental Disability Legal Resource Center [*Later, MPDLRSDB*] (EA)
**MD L Rec** .. Maryland Law Record [*Baltimore*] [*A publication*] (DLA)
**MD L Rep** ... Maryland Law Reporter [*Baltimore*] [*A publication*] (DLA)
**MD L Rev** ... Maryland Law Review [*A publication*]
**MDLS** ........ Marine Data Logger System
**MdLuW** ..... Maryland College for Women, Lutherville, MD [*Library symbol*] [*Library of Congress*] (LCLS)
**MDLX** ....... Military Demarkation Line Extended (MCD)
**MdLxp** ....... Lexington Park Library, Lexington Park, MD [*Library symbol*] [*Library of Congress*] (LCLS)
**MDM** ......... Magnetic Disc Memory
**MDM** ......... Magneto-Optical Display Memory
**MDM** ......... Maintenance Depot Material Control
**MDM** ......... Maize Dwarf Mosaic [*Viral disease of corn*]
**MDM** ......... Manipulator Deployment Mechanism (MCD)
**MDM** ......... Manpower Determination Model [*Military*]
**MDM** ......... Marking Diagram Master (MCD)
**MDM** ......... Marshall Drummond McCall, Inc. [*Toronto Stock Exchange symbol*]
**MDM** ......... Mass Democratic Movement [*Political coalition*] [*South Africa*]
**MDM** ......... Maternal Diabetes Mellitus [*Medicine*]
**MDM** ......... Maximum Design Meter (MSA)
**MDM** ......... Mechanically Deboned Meat [*Food technology*]
**MDM** ......... Mededelingenblad Bedrijfsorganisatie [*A publication*]
**MDM** ......... Medical Monitor (MCD)
**MDM** ......... Medium (AABC)
**MDM** ......... Medium-Depth Mine (MCD)
**MDM** ......... Metal-Dielectric-Metal [*Filter*]
**MDM** ......... Metal Disintegration Machining [*Nuclear energy*] (NRCH)
**MDM** ......... Methylenedioxymethamphetamine [*A hallucinogenic drug, also known as "Ecstasy," banned in 1985*] [*Also, MDMA*]
**MDM** ......... Mid-Diastolic Murmur [*Medicine*]
**MDM** ......... Midas Minerals, Inc. [*Toronto Stock Exchange symbol*]
**MDM** ......... Minor Determinant Mixture [*Medicine*]
**MDM** ......... Mobile Depot Maintenance [*Air Force*] (AFM)
**MDM** ......... Modified Diffusion Method (NRCH)
**MDM** ......... Monolithic Diode Matrix
**MDM** ......... Movement for a Democratic Military (EA)
**MDM** ......... Movimento Democratico de Mocambique [*Democratic Movement of Mozambique*]
**MDM** ......... Multiplexer/Demultiplexer (NASA)
**MDMA** ...... M-Day Materiel Assets (AFIT)
**MDMA** ...... Methylenedioxymethamphetamine [*A hallucinogenic drug, also known as "Ecstasy," banned in 1985*] [*Also, MDM*]
**MDMAF** ... Mekong Delta Mobile Afloat Force [*Vietnam*]
**MD Mag** .... Maryland Magazine [*A publication*]
**MDMC** ...... Monte Cristy [*Dominican Republic*] [*ICAO location identifier*] (ICLI)
**MDMCA** ... Melvil Dui Marching and Chowder Association (EA)
**MdMC-G** ... Montgomery College, Germantown Campus, Germantown, MD [*Library symbol*] [*Library of Congress*] (LCLS)
**MdMC-R** ... Montgomery College, Rockville Campus, Rockville, MD [*Library symbol*] [*Library of Congress*] (LCLS)
**MdMC-T** ... Montgomery College, Takoma Park Campus, Takoma Park, MD [*Library symbol*] [*Library of Congress*] (LCLS)
**mDMD** ...... Mouse Duchenne Muscular Dystrophy [*Medicine*]
**MDME** ...... Madame
**MD Med J** ... Maryland Medical Journal [*A publication*]
**Md-MH** ..... Maryland Department of Mental Hygiene, Baltimore, MD [*Library symbol*] [*Library of Congress*] (LCLS)
**MDMH** ..... Methylol Dimethylhydantoin [*Organic chemistry*]
**MDML** ...... Modified Maximum Likelihood [*Statistics*]
**MDMN** ..... Modified Posterior Mean [*Statistics*]
**MDMR** ...... M-Day Materiel Requirement (AFIT)
**MDMR** ...... M-Day Mobilization Requirement
**MDMS** ...... Marketing Data Management System [*British*]
**MDMS** ...... Microbiology Data Management System
**MDMS** ...... Miss-Distance Measuring System
**MDMS** ...... Moore Data Management Services [*Information service or system*] (IID)
**MDMV** ...... Maize Dwarf Mosaic Virus

**MdMwH**.... Mount Wilson State Hospital, Mount Wilson, MD [*Library symbol*] [*Library of Congress*] (LCLS)
**MDN** ......... Madison, IN [*Location identifier*] [*FAA*] (FAAL)
**MDN** ......... Maiden Race [*Horse racing*]
**MDN** ......... Managed Data Network
**MdN** .......... Mandibular Nerve [*Anatomy*]
**MDN** ......... Mark der Deutschen Notenbank [*Mark of the German Bank of Issue*] [*Later, M*]
**MDN** ......... Median (MSA)
**MDN** ......... Ministere de la Defense Nationale [*Department of National Defense*] [*Canada*]
**MDN** ......... Movimiento Democratico Nacionalista [*Nationalist Democratic Movement*] [*Guatemala*] [*Political party*]
**MDN** ......... Movimiento Democratico Nicaraguense [*Nicaraguan Democratic Movement*] [*Political party*] (PPW)
**MDNA**....... Machinery Dealers National Association (EA)
**MDNA**....... Maximum Density Nitric Acid
**MDNA**....... Mobilehome Dealers National Association (EA)
**MD Nat** ..... Maryland Naturalist [*A publication*]
**MD Naturalist** ... Maryland Naturalist [*A publication*]
**MDNB**....... Mean Daily Nitrogen Balance [*Medicine*]
**MDNB**....... Meta-Dinitrobenzene [*Organic chemistry*]
**MD/NC**..... Mechanical Drafting/Numerical Control (IEEE)
**MDNC**....... United States District Court for the Middle District of North Carolina (DLA)
**MDNIS** ..... Machinery Dealers' National Information System
**MDNKA**.... Miyazaki Daigaku Nogakubu. Kenkyu Hokoku [*A publication*]
**MDNMNA** ... Moorish Divine and National Movement in North America (EA)
**MDNP**....... Methyl Dinitropentanoate [*An explosive*]
**MDNPAR** ... Direccion General del Inventario Nacional Forestal. Publicacion [*A publication*]
**Md-NR** ...... Maryland State Department of Natural Resources, Annapolis, MD [*Library symbol*] [*Library of Congress*] (LCLS)
**MDNT**....... Midnight
**MD Nurse** ... Maryland Nurse [*A publication*]
**MDNX**....... Modern Air Transport [*Air carrier designation symbol*]
**MDO** ......... Marine Diesel Oil
**MdO** .......... Masorcten des Ostens (BJA)
**MDO** ......... Mechanized Desert Operations [*Military*] (MCD)
**MDO** ......... Medium Density Overlay [*Plywood*]
**MDO** ......... Membrane-Derived Oligosaccharide [*Biochemistry*]
**MDO** ......... Methylenedioxyphenyl [*Organic chemistry*]
**MDO** ......... Middleton Island, AK [*Location identifier*] [*FAA*] (FAAL)
**MDO** ......... Mitteilungen. Deutsche Orient-Gesellschaft zu Berlin [*A publication*]
**MDO** ......... Mobile District Office [*Army Corps of Engineers*]
**MDO** ......... Monthly Debit Ordinary [*Insurance*]
**MdO** .......... Ruth Enlow Library of Garrett County, Oakland, MD [*Library symbol*] [*Library of Congress*] (LCLS)
**M & DOD** ... Mission and Data Operations Directorate (MCD)
**MdOdN** ..... National Plastics Products Co., Odenton, MD [*Library symbol*] [*Library of Congress*] [*Obsolete*] (LCLS)
**MdOdS**...... Saran Yarn Co., Odenton, MD [*Library symbol*] [*Library of Congress*] [*Obsolete*] (LCLS)
**MDOF**....... Multiple Degree of Freedom [*Acoustics*]
**MDOG** ...... Mitteilungen. Deutsche Orient-Gesellschaft zu Berlin [*A publication*]
**MdOmR**..... Rosewood Center, Owing Mills, MD [*Library symbol*] [*Library of Congress*] (LCLS)
**MDOP**....... Malicious Destruction of Property
**MDOP**....... Maximum Design Operating Pressure [*NASA*]
**MDOPA** .... Methyldopamine [*Biochemistry*]
**MDOS**....... Motorola Disk Operating System
**MDOSIS** ... Management Data Online Status/Inquiry System (MCD)
**MDOT**....... Modular Digital Output Timer
**MDovC** ...... Chickering House, Dover, MA [*Library symbol*] [*Library of Congress*] (LCLS)
**MDovS** ...... Saint Stephen's College, Dover, MA [*Library symbol*] [*Library of Congress*] (LCLS)
**MDOW** ..... [*The*] Meadow Group, Inc. [*NASDAQ symbol*] (NQ)
**MDP** .......... Coppin State College, Parlett L. Moore Library, Baltimore, MD [*OCLC symbol*] (OCLC)
**MDP** .......... Ferrocarril Mexicano del Pacifico [*Mexican Pacific Railroad Co., Inc.*] [*AAR code*]
**MDP** .......... Magyar Dolgozok Partja [*Hungarian Workers' Party*] [*Political party*] (PPE)
**MDP** .......... Main Data Path
**MDP** .......... Maintainability Demonstration Plan (MCD)
**MDP** .......... Maintenance Data Program (MCD)
**MDP** .......... Maintenance Depot Production
**MDP** .......... Maintenance Display Panel (MCD)
**MDP** .......... Malfunction Detection Package
**MDP** .......... Malicious Destruction of Property
**MDP** .......... Management Development Programme [*British*] (DCTA)
**MDP** .......... Managing Director Posts [*British*] (DCTA)
**MDP** .......... Manpower Development Program [*Department of Labor*]
**MDP** .......... Master Decommissioning Plan [*Nuclear energy*] (NRCH)
**MDP** .......... Master Design Plan (MCD)
**MDP** .......... Master Display Panel (KSC)
**MDP** .......... Maximum Diastolic Potential [*Physiology*]
**MDP** .......... Mean Datum Plane
**MDP** .......... Mean Designation Point (CAAL)
**MDP** .......... Mechanically Deboned Poultry [*Food technology*]
**MDP** .......... Memoires. Delegation en Perse [*Paris*] [*A publication*]
**MDP** .......... Mento-Dextra Posterior [*A fetal position*] [*Obstetrics*]
**MDP** .......... Meredith Corp. [*NYSE symbol*] (SPSG)
**MDP** .......... Message Discrimination Process [*Telecommunications*] (TEL)
**MDP** .......... Meteorological Datum Plane
**MDP** .......... Methyldichlorophosphine [*Organic chemistry*]
**MDP** .......... Methylenediphosphonic Acid [*Organic chemistry*]
**MDP** .......... Milliyetci Demokrasi Partisi [*Nationalist Democracy Party*] [*Turkey*] [*Political party*] (EY)
**MDP** .......... Mindiptana [*Indonesia*] [*Airport symbol*] (OAG)
**MDP** .......... Minimum Discernible Pulse (MCD)
**MDP** .......... Mode Products, Inc. [*Vancouver Stock Exchange symbol*]
**MDP** .......... Moslem Democratic Party [*Philippines*] [*Political party*] (PPW)
**MDP** .......... Most Dispensable Program [*Television*]
**MDP** .......... Mouvement Democratique et Populaire [*Popular Democratic Movement*] [*Senegal*] [*Political party*] (PPW)
**MDP** .......... Movimento Democratico Portugues [*Portuguese Democratic Movement*] [*Political party*] (PPE)
**MDP** .......... Movimiento Democratico Peruano [*Peruvian Democratic Movement*] [*Political party*]
**MDP** .......... Movimiento Democratico Popular [*Popular Democratic Movement*] [*Chile*] [*Political party*] (PPW)
**MDP** .......... Movimiento Democratico Popular [*Popular Democratic Movement*] [*Ecuador*] [*Political party*] (PPW)
**MDP** .......... Muramyl Dipeptide [*Immunochemistry*]
**MDP** .......... Parkland Regional Library, Dauphin, Manitoba [*Library symbol*] [*National Library of Canada*] (NLC)
**MD PA** ...... United States District Court for the Middle District of Pennsylvania (DLA)
**MdPa** ......... United States Naval Air Station, Patuxent River, MD [*Library symbol*] [*Library of Congress*] (LCLS)
**MDPC** ....... Mount Diablo Peace Center (EA)
**MDPC** ....... Punta Cana [*Dominican Republic*] [*ICAO location identifier*] (ICLI)
**MDPF**........ Methoxy(diphenyl)furanone [*Organic chemistry*]
**MDPG**....... Magnetic Digital-Pulse Generator
**MD Pharm** ... Maryland Pharmacist [*A publication*]
**MDPI** ........ Media Products, Inc. [*NASDAQ symbol*] (NQ)
**MDPL** ....... Mouvement pour le Desarmement, la Paix, et la Liberte [*Movement for Disarmament, Peace, and Liberty*] (EAIO)
**MDPM**...... Maintenance Douglas Process Manual
**MDPM**...... Mechanically Deboned Poultry Meat [*Food technology*]
**MdPM** ....... University of Maryland, Eastern Shore, Princess Anne, MD [*Library symbol*] [*Library of Congress*] (LCLS)
**MDPN**....... Midshipman
**MD Poultryman** ... Maryland Poultryman [*A publication*]
**MDPP** ....... Puerto Plata/La Union [*Dominican Republic*] [*ICAO location identifier*] (ICLI)
**MDPPQ** .... Mouvement pour la Defense des Prisonniers Politiques du Quebec [*Movement for the Defense of Political Prisoners of Quebec*]
**MdPpV** ...... United States Veterans Administration Hospital, Perry Point, MD [*Library symbol*] [*Library of Congress*] (LCLS)
**MDPR** ....... Madrid Predict [*Orbit identification*]
**MDPR** ....... Manufacturing Development and Process Request (AAG)
**MDPS**........ Metric Data Processing System [*Air Force*]
**MDPS**........ Mission Data Preparation System [*Military*] (CAAL)
**MDPS**........ Mobilization and Deployment Planning System [*Army*]
**MDPTB**..... Medical Progress through Technology [*A publication*]
**MDPV** ....... Mitteilungen und Nachrichten. Deutscher Palaestina-Verein [*A publication*]
**MDQ** ......... Mar Del Plata [*Argentina*] [*Airport symbol*] (OAG)
**MDQ** ......... MDE Explorations [*Vancouver Stock Exchange symbol*]
**MDQ** ......... Minimum Detectable Quantity
**MDQS** ....... Management Data Query System [*Data processing*]
**MDR**.......... Madras [*India*] [*Seismograph station code, US Geological Survey*] (SEIS)
**MDR**.......... Magnetic Dipole Radiation
**MDR**.......... Magnetic Drum Recorder
**MDR**.......... Maintainability Demonstration Report (MCD)
**MDR**.......... Maintenance Data Report [*Army*] (AABC)
**MDR**.......... Maintenance Demand Rate (NASA)
**MDR**.......... Maintenance Design Requirement
**MDR**.......... Major Design Review (KSC)
**MDR**.......... Manual Data Room
**MDR**.......... Mark Document Reader [*Trademark*] [*Bell & Howell*]
**MDR**.......... Market Data Retrieval [*Westport, CT*] [*Information service or system*] (IID)
**MD R**......... Maryland Reports [*A publication*] (DLA)
**MDR**.......... Master Data Record (NG)
**MDR**.......... Master Discrepancy Report (AAG)
**MDR**.......... Material Deficiency Reports [*Program*]
**MDR**.......... McDermott International, Inc. [*NYSE symbol*] (SPSG)
**MDR**.......... MD Review [*Social Security Administration*] (OICC)
**MDR**.......... Mechanical Development Report (MCD)
**MDR**.......... Medfra, AK [*Location identifier*] [*FAA*] (FAAL)
**MDR**.......... Median Detection Range (NVT)

**MDR**.......... Memory-Data Register
**MDR**.......... Message Detail Recording [*Later, SMDR*] [*Telecommunications*]
**MDR**.......... Metropolitan District Railway [*London*]
**MDR**.......... Milestone Decision Review (MCD)
**MDR**.......... Minimum Daily Requirement [*of a vitamin, etc.*] [*Later, Recommended Daily Requirement*] [*FDA*]
**MDR**.......... Minor Discrepancy Repair [*NASA*] (KSC)
**MDR**.......... Missile Deviation Report (AAG)
**MDR**.......... Missing Data Report (NASA)
**MDR**.......... Mission Data Reduction
**MDR**.......... Mock-Up Discrepancy Report [*Aerospace*] (AAG)
**MDR**.......... Monthly Director's Review [*NASA*] (NASA)
**MDR**.......... Morphine-Dependent Rate
**MDR**.......... Morphology Dependent Resonance [*Physics*]
**MDR**.......... Motor-Driven Relay [*or Roter*]
**MDR**.......... Multichannel Data Recorder
**MDR**.......... Multidrug Resistance [*Medicine*]
**MDRA**....... Multidrug-Resistance Associated [*Genetics*]
**MDRAF**..... Mekong Delta Riverine Assault Force [*Vietnam*] (CINC)
**MDRC**....... Manual Data Relay Center (MCD)
**MDRC**....... Materiel Development and Readiness Command [*Formerly, AMC*] [*See also DARCOM*] [*Army*]
**MDRD**....... Mission Data Requirements Document [*NASA*] (KSC)
**MDRE**....... Mass Driver Reaction Engine [*Aerospace*]
**MD Reg**..... Maryland Register [*A publication*]
**MD Regs Code**... Code of Maryland Regulations [*A publication*]
**MD Rep**..... Maryland Reports [*A publication*] (DLA)
**MdRFD**..... United States Food and Drug Administration, Rockville, MD [*Library symbol*] [*Library of Congress*] (LCLS)
**MDRL**....... Mandrel [*Mechanical engineering*]
**MDRM**...... Mouvement Democratique de Renovation Malgache [*Democratic Movement Malagasy Restoration*]
**MdRMC**.... Montgomery County Department of Public Libraries, Rockville, MD [*Library symbol*] [*Library of Congress*] (LCLS)
**MdRNIO**... National Institute for Occupational Safety and Health, Rockville, MD [*Library symbol*] [*Library of Congress*] (LCLS)
**MDROC**.... Mission Design Requirements, Objectives, and Constraints
**MDROF**.... Managing Director of Royal Ordnance Factories [*British*] (RDA)
**MDRP**....... Mackenzie Delta Research Project [*Canada*] [*A publication*]
**MDRP**....... Migrant Dropout Reconnection Program [*Board of Cooperative Educational Services Geneseo Migrant Center*] (EA)
**MDRP**....... Movimiento Democratico Reformista Peruano [*Peruvian Democratic Reformist Movement*] [*Political party*] (PPW)
**MDRS**....... Management Data Reporting System (MCD)
**MDRS**....... Manufacturing Data Retrieval System (NASA)
**MDRS**....... Mission Data Retrieval System [*NASA*]
**MDRS**....... Mobilization Designation Reserve Section
**MDRS**....... Mylar Diaphragm Rupture System
**MDRSV**..... Maize Dwarf Ringspot Virus
**MDRT**....... Million Dollar Round Table [*Des Plaines, IL*] (EA)
**MDRTC**.... Diabetes Research and Training Center [*University of Michigan*] [*Research center*] (RCD)
**MDRUS**.... Miniature Donkey Registry of the United States (EA)
**MDRX**....... Medi-Rx America, Inc. [*Hauppauge, NY*] [*NASDAQ symbol*] (NQ)
**MDRY**....... Madison Railway Co., Inc. [*AAR code*]
**MDS**.......... Macintosh Development System [*Data processing*]
**MDS**.......... Madison [*Wisconsin*] [*Seismograph station code, US Geological Survey*] [*Closed*] (SEIS)
**MDS**.......... Madison Flying Service, Inc. [*Madison, IN*] [*FAA designator*] (FAAC)
**MDS**.......... Madison, SD [*Location identifier*] [*FAA*] (FAAL)
**Mds**........... Madrepores [*Quality of the bottom*] [*Nautical charts*]
**MDS**.......... Madrona Resources, Inc. [*Vancouver Stock Exchange symbol*]
**MDS**.......... Magnetic Detection of Submarines [*British military*] (DMA)
**MDS**.......... Magnetic Drum System
**MDS**.......... Mail Distribution Schedule [*Air Force*] (AFM)
**MDS**.......... Mail Distribution Scheme [*Army*]
**MDS**.......... Main Dressing Station
**MDS**.......... Maintenance Data System (MCD)
**MDS**.......... Maintenance Documentation System [*Bell System*]
**MDS**.......... Malfunction Detection System [*Gemini*] [*NASA*]
**MDS**.......... Management Data System (NASA)
**MDS**.......... Market Data System [*NYSE*]
**MDS**.......... Mass Digital Storage
**MDS**.......... Master Delivery Schedule (AAG)
**MDS**.......... Master of Dental Surgery
**MDS**.......... Master Development Schedule (KSC)
**MDS**.......... Master Dimension Specification (MSA)
**MDS**.......... Master Drum Sender
**MDS**.......... Mechanized Documentation System
**MDS**.......... Medical Documentation Service [*College of Physicians of Philadelphia*] [*Information service or system*] (IID)
**MDS**.......... Megawatt Demand Setter (NRCH)
**MDS**.......... Memoires Presentes par Divers Savants a l'Academie des Inscriptions et Belles-Lettres [*Paris*] [*A publication*]
**MDS**.......... Memory Disk System [*Data processing*] (IEEE)
**MDS**.......... Mennonite Disaster Service (EA)
**MDS**.......... Message Distribution Systems
**MDS**.......... Meteoroid Detection Satellite [*NASA*]
**MDS**.......... Meteorological Data System
**MDS**.......... "Micky the D" Show [*An association*] [*Later, MDS/MMFC*] (EA)
**MDS**.......... Microprocessor Development System [*Motorola, Inc.*]
**MDS**.......... Middle Caicos [*British West Indies*] [*Airport symbol*] (OAG)
**MDS**.......... Middle Distance Swimmer
**MDS**.......... Mine Detection Set
**MDS**.......... Minerals Data System [*Database*]
**MDS**.......... Minimum Data Set [*Data processing*]
**MDS**.......... Minimum Discernible Signal [*Radio*]
**MDS**.......... Minimum Discernible System (NASA)
**MDS**.......... Mission Design and Series [*Military*] (AFM)
**MDS**.......... Mission Development Simulator [*NASA*] (NASA)
**MDS**.......... Mobile Dental Services
**MDS**.......... Mobile Distribution System (AFM)
**MDS**.......... Model Designation and Series [*Military*] (AFIT)
**MDS**.......... Modern Data Systems (IEEE)
**MDS**.......... Modular Data System
**MDS**.......... Modular Distribution System
**MDS**.......... Modulate-Demodulate Subsystem
**MDS**.......... Molybdenum Disulfide [*Inorganic chemistry*]
**MDS**.......... Monitor Distribution System [*Television*]
**MDS**.......... Montant de Soutien [*Amount of Support*] [*A trade negotiating plan of EEC*]
**MDS**.......... Mouvement Democrate Socialiste [*Democratic Socialist Movement*] [*France*] [*Political party*] (PPW)
**MDS**.......... Mouvement des Democrates Socialistes [*Movement of Socialist Democrats*] [*Tunisia*] [*Political party*] (PPW)
**MDS**.......... Multidimensional Scaling [*Statistics*]
**MDS**.......... Multiple Dataset System
**MDS**.......... Multipoint Distribution Service [*Educational television*]
**MDS**.......... Multipoint Distribution System [*Line-of-sight relay system for electronic signals*]
**MDS**.......... Municipal Data Service [*International City Management Association*] [*Information service or system*] (IID)
**MDS**.......... Myelodysplasia [*Medicine*]
**MDS**.......... Myelodysplastic Syndrome [*Medicine*]
**MDS**.......... St. Mary's College of Maryland, St. Mary's City, MD [*OCLC symbol*] (OCLC)
**MDSAI**...... Memoires Presentes par Divers Savants a l'Academie des Inscriptions et Belles-Lettres [*Paris*] [*A publication*]
**MdSalS**...... Salisbury State College, Salisbury, MD [*Library symbol*] [*Library of Congress*] (LCLS)
**MdSalW**.... Wicomico County Free Library, Salisbury, MD [*Library symbol*] [*Library of Congress*] (LCLS)
**MDSC**....... Management Data Service Center
**MD Sc**....... Master of Dental Science [*British*]
**MDSC**....... Medical Self-Care [*A publication*]
**MDSC**....... Modular Digital Scan Converter (MCD)
**MDSCAD**... Medicina nei Secoli [*A publication*]
**MDSCC**..... Madrid Deep Space Communications Complex
**MDSD**....... Magnetic Disk Storage Device [*Data processing*]
**MDSD**....... Mate/Demate Stiff Leg Derrick (MCD)
**MDSD**....... Santo Domingo/De las Americas Internacional [*Dominican Republic*] [*ICAO location identifier*] (ICLI)
**MDSE**........ Merchandise (AFM)
**MDSF**........ Mass Data Storage Facility
**MDSF**........ Mouvement Democrate Socialiste de France [*Democratic Socialist Movement of France*] [*Political party*] (PPE)
**MDSG**........ Merchandising
**MDSI**......... Micro Display Systems, Incorporated [*Hastings, MN*] [*NASDAQ symbol*] (NQ)
**MDSI**......... San Isidro [*Dominican Republic*] [*ICAO location identifier*] (ICLI)
**MDSIA**...... MDS [*Multipoint Distribution System*] Industry Association [*Telecommunications*] (EA)
**MdSim**....... Howard County Library, Simpsonville, MD [*Library symbol*] [*Library of Congress*] (LCLS)
**MDSJ**........ San Juan [*Dominican Republic*] [*ICAO location identifier*] (ICLI)
**MDSJA**..... Medical Service Journal [*Canada*] [*A publication*]
**MDS/MMFC**... "Micky the D" Show/Metal Micky Fan Club (EA)
**MDSN**........ Madison Gas & Electric Co. [*NASDAQ symbol*] (NQ)
**MDSN**........ Maximum Dissolved Solids Nebulizer [*Product of Applied Research Laboratories*]
**MDSO**........ Medical and Dental Supply Office [*Military*]
**MDSO**........ Mentally Disordered Sex Offender
**MDSOR**.... Monthly Depot Space and Operating Report
**Md-SP**....... Maryland State Planning Commission, Baltimore, MD [*Library symbol*] [*Library of Congress*] (LCLS)
**MDSP**........ San Pedro De Macoris [*Dominican Republic*] [*ICAO location identifier*] (ICLI)
**MDSPR**..... Mode Suppressor (KSC)
**MDSS**........ Magnetic Drum Storage System
**MDSS**........ Maintenance Decision Support System
**MDSS**........ Mass Digital Storage System
**MDSS**........ McDonnell Douglas Support Services (MCD)

**MDSS**........ Meteorological Data Sounding System (IEEE)
**MDSS**........ Microprocessor Development Support System
**MDSS**........ Mission Data Support System [*NASA*] (KSC)
**MDSS**........ Multidimensional Switching System [*Instrumentation*]
**MdSsD** ...... Library of Dianetics and Scientology, Silver Spring, MD [*Library symbol*] [*Library of Congress*] (LCLS)
**MdSsFD**.... United States Food and Drug Administration, Bureau of Medical Services, Silver Spring, MD [*Library symbol*] [*Library of Congress*] (LCLS)
**MdSsGS**.... Church of Jesus Christ of Latter-Day Saints, Genealogical Society Library, Silver Spring Branch, Silver Spring, MD [*Library symbol*] [*Library of Congress*] (LCLS)
**MDSS-PCT** ... Multidimensional Switching System - Packed Column Trap [*Instrumentation*]
**MdSsV**....... Vitro Laboratories, Silver Spring Laboratory Library, Silver Spring, MD [*Library symbol*] [*Library of Congress*] (LCLS)
**MdSsW**...... Washington Theological Coalition, Silver Spring, MD [*Library symbol*] [*Library of Congress*] (LCLS)
**MdSsX**....... Xaverian College, Silver Spring, MD [*Library symbol*] [*Library of Congress*] (LCLS)
**MDST**........ MEDSTAT Systems, Inc. [*NASDAQ symbol*] (NQ)
**MDST**........ Santiago [*Dominican Republic*] [*ICAO location identifier*] (ICLI)
**MD State Med J** ... Maryland State Medical Journal [*A publication*]
**MdStm**....... St. Mary's College of Maryland, St. Mary's City, MD [*Library symbol*] [*Library of Congress*] (LCLS)
**MdSuFR**.... Washington National Records Center, General Services Administration, Suitland, MD [*Library symbol*] [*Library of Congress*] (LCLS)
**MDSV** ....... Manned Deep Space Vehicle
**MdSyH**...... Springfield State Hospital, Sykesville, MD [*Library symbol*] [*Library of Congress*] (LCLS)
**MDT**.......... Harrisburg [*Pennsylvania*] [*Airport symbol*] (OAG)
**MDT**.......... Maintenance Demand Time (MCD)
**MDT**.......... Maintenance Downtime (MCD)
**MDT**.......... Mandatory Date of Transportation [*Military*]
**MDT**.......... Mean Death Time
**MDT**.......... Mean Delay Time (CAAL)
**MDT**.......... Mean Detonating Time (NASA)
**MDT**.......... Mean Downtime [*Data processing*]
**MDT**.......... Measurement Descriptor Table (NASA)
**MDT**.......... Mechanically Deboned Turkey [*Food technology*]
**MDT**.......... Med-Tech Systems, Inc. [*Vancouver Stock Exchange symbol*]
**MDT**.......... Median Dorsal Tract [*Anatomy*]
**MDT**.......... Medtronic, Inc. [*NYSE symbol*] (SPSG)
**MDT**.......... Mento-Dextra Transversa [*A fetal position*] [*Obstetrics*]
**MDT**.......... Merchant Deposit Transmittal
**MDT**.......... Mercury Dynamic Test
**MDT**.......... Message Direction Table (MCD)
**MDT**.......... Message Display Terminal (MCD)
**MDT**.......... Middletown, PA [*Location identifier*] [*FAA*] (FAAL)
**MDT**.......... Minnesota Dance Theatre
**MDT**.......... Mobile Data Terminal (MCD)
**MDT**.......... Moderate (AFM)
**MDT**.......... Modular Display Tactical
**MDT**.......... Most Demands to Be Traded [*Baseball*]
**MDT**.......... Mountain Daylight Time
**MDT**.......... Multidimensional Tasking [*Honeywell, Inc.*]
**MDT**.......... Multidisciplinary Team
**MDT**.......... Mutual Defense Treaty
**MDTA**....... Manpower Development and Training Act [*1962*] [*Later, CETA*] [*Department of Labor*]
**MDTA**....... Megadata Corp. [*NASDAQ symbol*] (NQ)
**MDTA**....... Modulation, Demodulation, Terminal, and Associated Equipment
**MDTB**....... Milk Distribution Trade Board [*British*] (DAS)
**MDTC**....... MDT Corp. [*NASDAQ symbol*] (NQ)
**MD Tenn** ... United States District Court for the Middle District of Tennessee (DLA)
**MDTHA**.... Medicina Thoracalis [*A publication*]
**MDTI**........ Missile Director Train Indicator
**MDTM**...... Mechanically Deboned Turkey Meat [*Food technology*]
**MDTS**....... MegaBIT [*Binary Digit*] Digital Troposcatter Subsystem [*Communications*] (MCD)
**MDTS**....... Mobile Doppler Tracking Station
**MDTS**....... Modular Data Transaction System
**MDtShG**.... Mitteilungen. Deutsche Shakespeare-Gesellschaft [*A publication*]
**MDTU**....... Mobile Dockside Transfer Unit
**MdTW**....... Washington Missionary College, Tacoma Park, MD [*Library symbol*] [*Library of Congress*] [*Obsolete*] (LCLS)
**MDU** ......... Maintenance Data Unit (MCD)
**MDU** ......... Maintenance Diagnostic Unit
**mdu** ........... Maryland [*MARC country of publication code*] [*Library of Congress*] (LCCP)
**MDU** ......... Master Driver Unit
**MDU** ......... MDU Resources Group, Inc. [*NYSE symbol*] (SPSG)
**MDU** ......... Medical Defence Union [*Australia*]
**MDU** ......... Mendi [*Papua New Guinea*] [*Airport symbol*] (OAG)
**MDU** ......... Message Decoder Unit
**MDU** ......... Mid-North Resources [*Vancouver Stock Exchange symbol*]
**MDU** ......... Middle Dutch [*Language, etc.*]
**MDU** ......... Mine Disposal Unit
**MDU** ......... Mobile Demonstration Unit
**MDU** ......... Mobile Dynamic Unit (AAG)
**MDU** ......... Monatshefte fuer Deutschen Unterricht [*A publication*]
**MDU** ......... Moral Development Unit [*Prisoner reform program*]
**MDU** ......... Motion Detection Unit [*Nuclear energy*] (NRCH)
**MDU** ......... Multidimensional Unfolding [*Model*] [*Statistics*]
**MDU** ......... University of Maryland, Baltimore, Health Sciences Library, Baltimore, MD [*OCLC symbol*] (OCLC)
**MdU** .......... University of Maryland, College Park, MD [*Library symbol*] [*Library of Congress*] (LCLS)
**MdU-A** ...... University of Maryland, Art Library, College Park, MD [*Library symbol*] [*Library of Congress*] (LCLS)
**MdU-Ar**..... University of Maryland, Architecture Library, College Park, MD [*Library symbol*] [*Library of Congress*] (LCLS)
**MdU-BC**.... University of Maryland, Baltimore County Campus, Baltimore, MD [*Library symbol*] [*Library of Congress*] (LCLS)
**MdU-C** ...... University of Maryland, Chemistry Library, College Park, MD [*Library symbol*] [*Library of Congress*] (LCLS)
**MdU-E** ...... University of Maryland, Engineering and Physical Sciences Library, College Park, MD [*Library symbol*] [*Library of Congress*] (LCLS)
**MdU-H**...... University of Maryland, Health Sciences Library, Baltimore, MD [*Library symbol*] [*Library of Congress*] (LCLS)
**MDuHi**...... Duxbury Rural and Historical Society, Duxbury, MA [*Library symbol*] [*Library of Congress*] (LCLS)
**MdU-I**........ International Piano Archives at Maryland, University of Maryland, College Park, MD [*Library symbol*] [*Library of Congress*] (LCLS)
**MdU-L**....... University of Maryland, School of Law, Baltimore, MD [*Library symbol*] [*Library of Congress*] (LCLS)
**MDUO** ...... Myocardial Disease of Unknown Origin [*Cardiology*]
**MDUS**....... Medium Data Utilization Station [*Australia*] [*Telecommunications*] (TEL)
**MdU-U** ...... University of Maryland, Undergraduate Library, College Park, MD [*Library symbol*] [*Library of Congress*] (LCLS)
**MDV**.......... Baltimore, MD [*Location identifier*] [*FAA*] (FAAL)
**MDV**.......... Doctor of Veterinary Medicine
**MDV**.......... Maldives [*ANSI three-letter standard code*] (CNC)
**MDV**.......... Map and Data Viewer [*NASA*] (KSC)
**M & DV**..... Map and Data Viewer [*NASA*] (KSC)
**MDV**.......... Marek's Disease Virus
**MDV**.......... Master of Veterinary Medicine
**MDV**.......... Maxim Development Ltd. [*Vancouver Stock Exchange symbol*]
**MDV**.......... Medium-Dollar Value
**MDV**.......... Medouneu [*Gabon*] [*Airport symbol*] (OAG)
**MDV**.......... Middlebury [*Vermont*] [*Seismograph station code, US Geological Survey*] (SEIS)
**MDV**.......... Midivariant [*Genetics*]
**MDV**.......... Mine-Dispensing Vehicle [*Army*]
**MDV**.......... Minimum Detectable Velocity [*Physics*]
**MDV**.......... Mouvement Democratique Voltaique [*Upper Volta Democratic Movement*]
**MDV**.......... Mucosal Disease Virus
**MDV**.......... Multiple Dose Vial [*Pharmacy*]
**MDW**......... Chicago [*Illinois*] Midway [*Airport symbol*] (OAG)
**MDW**......... Delta Waterfowl Research Station, Manitoba [*Library symbol*] [*National Library of Canada*] (NLC)
**MDW**......... Fort Myer Library System and Fort McNair Post Library, Fort Myer, VA [*OCLC symbol*] (OCLC)
**MDW**......... Mars Departure Window [*Aerospace*]
**MdW**.......... Masoreten des Westens (BJA)
**MDW**......... Mass Destruction Weapons
**MDW**......... Meadow Mountain [*Vancouver Stock Exchange symbol*]
**MDW**......... Measured Daywork [*Payment system*]
**MDW**......... Midway [*Washington*] [*Seismograph station code, US Geological Survey*] (SEIS)
**MDW**......... Midway Airlines [*NYSE symbol*] (SPSG)
**MDW**......... Military Defence Works [*British*]
**MDW**......... Military District of Washington [*DC*]
**MDW**......... Mine Disposal Weapon (NATG)
**MDW**......... Minnesota, Dakota & Western Railway Co. [*AAR code*]
**MDW**......... Multidimensional Warfare [*Military*] (CAAL)
**MDW**......... Multipair Distribution Wire
**MDW**......... Multiple Drop Wire [*Telecommunications*] (TEL)
**MD WCC** .. Maryland Workmen's Compensation Cases [*A publication*] (DLA)
**MdWem**..... Carroll County Public Library, Westminster, MD [*Library symbol*] [*Library of Congress*] (LCLS)
**MdWemC** .. Western Maryland College, Westminster, MD [*Library symbol*] [*Library of Congress*] (LCLS)
**MDWF** ...... Midwife
**MDWFY** ... Midwifery
**MDWS** ...... Meadows (MCD)
**MDX**.......... Medical Data Exchange [*Commercial firm*] [*Los Altos, CA*]
**MDX**.......... Mercedes [*Argentina*] [*Airport symbol*] (OAG)
**MDX**.......... Merritech Development [*Vancouver Stock Exchange symbol*]
**MDX**.......... Middlesex [*County in England*]

**MDX**.......... University of Maryland, College of Library and Information Services, College Park, MD [*OCLC symbol*] (OCLC)
**MDXDCR**... Mode Transducer (KSC)
**MDXR**....... Medar, Inc. [*NASDAQ symbol*] (NQ)
**MDY**.......... Magnetic Deflection Yoke
**MDY**.......... Mid-Continent Airways [*Dallas, TX*] [*FAA designator*] (FAAC)
**MDY**.......... Middlebury College, Middlebury, VT [*OCLC symbol*] (OCLC)
**MDY**.......... Midland Gold Corp. [*Formerly, Midland Energy Corp.*] [*Vancouver Stock Exchange symbol*]
**MDY**.......... Midland Oil Co. [*NYSE symbol*] (SPSG)
**MDY**.......... Midway [*Midway Islands*] [*Seismograph station code, US Geological Survey*] [*Closed*] (SEIS)
**MDY**.......... Milieudefensie [*A publication*]
**MDY**.......... Month, Date, Year
**MDZ**.......... Maritime Defense Zone [*Program for drug interdiction*]
**MDZ**.......... MDC Corp. [*Toronto Stock Exchange symbol*]
**MDZ**.......... Medford, WI [*Location identifier*] [*FAA*] (FAAL)
**MDZ**.......... Mendoza [*Argentina*] [*Airport symbol*] (OAG)
**MDZ**.......... Mendoza [*Argentina*] [*Seismograph station code, US Geological Survey*] (SEIS)
**MDZ**.......... Missile Danger Zone (NVT)
**MDZ**.......... Modernize (FAAC)
**MDZN**....... Modernization (FAAC)
**Me**............. C. H. Boehringer Sohn, Ingelheim [*Germany*] [*Research code symbol*]
**me-----**........ Eurasia [*MARC geographic area code*] [*Library of Congress*] (LCCP)
**M/E**........... Machine (ROG)
**ME**............ Magic Eye (DEN)
**ME**............ Magnetoelastic
**ME**............ Magnitude Estimation
**ME**............ Main Engine (KSC)
**ME**............ Main Entry [*Library Science*] [*Online database field identifier*]
**ME**............ Maine [*Postal code*]
**ME**............ Maine Reports [*A publication*]
**Me**............. Maine State Library, Augusta, ME [*Library symbol*] [*Library of Congress*] (LCLS)
**ME**............ Maine Supreme Judicial Court Reports [*A publication*] (DLA)
**M & E**........ Maintenance and Equipment (NATG)
**ME**............ Maintenance Evaluation (MCD)
**ME**............ Maitre [*Barrister, Advocate*] [*French*] (ROG)
**ME**............ Majestic Eagles (EA)
**ME**............ Male Equivalents [*Entomology*]
**ME**............ "Malic" Enzyme
**ME**............ Malt Extract [*Microbiology*]
**ME**............ Man-Hours Earned
**ME**............ Management Engineering (KSC)
**ME**............ Managing Editor
**M & E**........ Maneuvers and Exercises (NATG)
**ME**............ Manpower Estimate (AAG)
**ME**............ Manson Evaluation [*Psychology*]
**ME**............ Manufacturing Engineering (MCD)
**ME**............ Marbled Edges [*Bookbinding*]
**ME**............ Marche de l'Europe [*March of Europe*] (EAIO)
**ME**............ Marine Engine
**ME**............ Marine Engineer
**ME**............ Marketing in Europe [*A publication*]
**ME**............ Marriage Encounter
**ME**............ Marriage Evaluation [*Marital relations test*]
**M-E**........... Martini-Enfield [*Rifle*]
**ME**............ Master of Education
**ME**............ Master of Elements
**ME**............ Master of Engineering
**ME**............ Master Equatorial
**M & E**........ Material and Equipment [*Nuclear energy*] (NRCH)
**ME**............ Math Error [*IRS*]
**ME**............ Maximum Effort
**ME**............ Maximum Energy
**ME**............ Meal
**Me**............. Meander [*A publication*]
**Me**............. Meaning [*A publication*]
**ME**............ Measuring Element
**ME**............ Mechanical Efficiency
**M/E**........... Mechanical/Electrical (AAG)
**M & E**........ Mechanical and Electrical Room (AAG)
**ME**............ Mechanical Engineer [*or Engineering*]
**ME**............ Medial Epicondyle [*Medicine*]
**Me**............. Median
**ME**............ Median Eminence [*of hypothalamus*] [*Anatomy*]
**ME**............ Medical Economics [*A publication*]
**ME**............ Medical Examiner
**ME**............ Medium Electroendosmosis [*Analytical biochemistry*]
**ME**............ Medium Energy
**Me**............. Me'ilah (BJA)
**Me**............. Melendus [*Flourished, 1188-1209*] [*Authority cited in pre-1607 legal work*] (DSA)
**ME**............ Memory Element [*Data processing*]
**ME**............ Mercaptoethanol [*Biochemistry*]
**ME**............ Message Element [*Telecommunications*] (TEL)
**ME**............ Messerschmitt AG [*Federal Republic of Germany*] [*ICAO aircraft manufacturer identifier*] (ICAO)
**ME**............ Metabolizable Energy
**ME**............ Metal Evaporated [*Videotape*]
**ME**............ Metalsmith [*Navy*]
**ME**............ Meters [*JETDS nomenclature*] [*Military*] (CET)
**ME**............ Methionine Enkephalin [*Biochemistry*]
**ME**............ Methodist
**ME**............ Methodist Episcopal
**ME**............ Methods Engineering (NG)
**ME**............ Methoxyethanol [*Organic chemistry*]
**Me**............. Methyl [*Organic chemistry*]
**ME**............ Metis Newsletter. Metis Association of the Northwest Territories [*Canada*] [*A publication*]
**ME**............ Microelectronic
**M-E**........... Microencapsulated
**ME**............ Micrometeoroid Explorer [*Satellite*]
**ME**............ Microsoft Editor [*Computer program*] (PCM)
**ME**............ Middle Ear
**ME**............ Middle East [*or Middle Eastern*]
**ME**............ Middle East Airlines - Air Liban [*Lebanon*] [*ICAO designator*] (FAAC)
**ME**............ Middle East Series [*Elsevier Book Series*] [*A publication*]
**ME**............ Middle English [*Language, etc.*]
**ME**............ Military Electronics (MCD)
**ME**............ Military Engineer
**ME**............ Mill Edge (ADA)
**ME**............ Milliequivalent [*or Milligram Equivalent*] [*Also, MEQ*]
**ME**............ Mining Engineer
**M of E**........ Ministry of Education [*British*]
**ME**............ Minneapolis Eastern Railway
**M of E**........ Minutes of Evidence
**ME**............ Miscellaneous Equipment (KSC)
**ME**............ Missile Electrician
**ME**............ Mission Envelope (AAG)
**ME**............ Mistress of English
**ME**............ Miter End [*Technical drawings*]
**ME**............ Mobility Equipment [*Military*] (AFM)
**ME**............ Modulation Efficiency
**ME**............ Molecular Electronics
**ME**............ Moneta Porcupine Mines, Inc. [*Toronto Stock Exchange symbol*]
**ME**............ Morristown & Erie Railroad Co. [*AAR code*]
**ME**............ Most Eminent [*Freemasonry*] (ROG)
**ME**............ Most Excellent [*In titles*]
**ME**............ Mouse Encephalitis
**ME**............ Mouvement Europeen [*European Movement*]
**ME**............ Movie Editor
**ME**............ Muhammadan Era
**ME**............ Multiengine
**ME**............ Municipal Engineering and Environmental Technology [*A publication*] [*British*]
**ME**............ Munitions Effectiveness
**M & E**........ Music and Effects [*Television*]
**ME**............ Musikerziehung [*A publication*]
**ME**............ Muzzle Energy
**M:E**........... Myeloid:Erythroid [*Ratio*] [*Hematology*]
**ME**............ Myoepithelium [*Cytology*]
**ME3**.......... Minority Engineering Education Effort [*Later, NACME*]
**MEA**.......... Accountantadviseur [*A publication*]
**MEA**.......... Macae [*Brazil*] [*Airport symbol*] (OAG)
**MEA**.......... Magnetic Engineering Associates, Inc.
**MEA**.......... Main Electronics Assembly (MCD)
**MEA**.......... Maine State Library, Augusta, ME [*OCLC symbol*] (OCLC)
**MEA**.......... Maintenance Engineering Analysis
**MEA**.......... Malt Extract Agar [*Culture media*]
**MEA**.......... Marine Engineering Artificer [*Navy rating*] [*British*]
**MEA**.......... Marine Engineers' Association [*A union*] [*British*]
**MEA**.......... Marine Environmental Activities [*Marine science*] (MSC)
**MEA**.......... Marketing Education Association (EA)
**MEA**.......... Master of Engineering Administration
**MEA**.......... Materials Experiment Assembly
**MEA**.......... [*The*] Mead Corp. [*NYSE symbol*] (SPSG)
**Mea**........... Meander [*A publication*]
**MEA**.......... Meanook [*Canada*] [*Geomagnetic observatory code*]
**MEA**.......... Measurements (NATG)
**MEA**.......... Meat Extract Agar [*Microbiology*]
**MEA**.......... Meath [*County in Ireland*] (ROG)
**MEA**.......... Medical Exhibitors Association [*Later, HCEA*] (EA)
**MEA**.......... Mercaptoethylamine [*Pharmacology*]
**MEA**.......... Metopon Ethnikis Adadimiourgias [*National Regeneration Front*] [*Greece*] [*Political party*] (PPE)
**MEA**.......... Metropolitan Economic Area
**MEA**.......... Metropolitan Electricity Authority [*Thailand*] (DS)
**MEA**.......... Middle East Airlines - Air Liban [*Lebanese*]
**MEA**.......... Middle Eastern Affairs [*A publication*]
**MEA**.......... Minimum Energy Absorbed
**MEA**.......... Minimum Enroute Altitude
**MEA**.......... Minister, External Affairs (CINC)
**MEA**.......... Ministry of External Affairs, Library Services Division [*UTLAS symbol*]

**MEA**.......... Missionary Evangelical Alliance [*See also AME*] [*Renens, Switzerland*] (EAIO)
**MEA**.......... Modular Engine Analyzer [*Automotive engineering*]
**MEA**.......... Monoethanolamine [*Organic chemistry*]
**MEA**.......... Monoethylamine [*Organic chemistry*]
**MEA**.......... Monteagle [*Australia*] [*Seismograph station code, US Geological Survey*] [*Closed*] (SEIS)
**MEA**.......... Multimode Error Analysis
**MEA**.......... Multiple Endocrine Abnormalities [*Medicine*]
**MEA**.......... Multiple Endocrine Adenomas [*Oncology*]
**MEA**.......... Music Editors Association (EA)
**MEAB**........ Maintenance Engineering Analysis Board
**MEAC**........ Mid-Eastern Athletic Conference
**MEACN**.... Maintenance Engineering Analyses Control Number [*DoD*]
**ME Acts**..... Acts, Resolves, and Constitutional Resolutions of the State of Maine [*A publication*] (DLA)
**MEAD**....... Maintenance Engineering Analysis Data
**MEAD**....... Memphis Army Depot (AABC)
**Mead Johnson Symp Perinat Dev Med** ... Mead Johnson Symposium on Perinatal and Developmental Medicine [*A publication*]
**MEADS**..... Maintenance Engineering Analysis Data System
**MEAF**........ Middle East Air Force [*British*]
**MEAFSA** .. Middle East/Southern Asia and Africa South of the Sahara [*Military*]
**MEAH**....... Miscelanea de Estudios Arabes y Hebraicos [*A publication*]
**MeAIB**....... (Methylamino)isobutyric Acid [*Biochemistry*]
**MEAL**........ Master Equipment Allowance [*or Authorization*] List [*Military*]
**MEAL**........ Media Expenditure Analysis Ltd. [*Database producer*]
**MEA(L)**...... Mission of Economic Affairs in London [*World War II*]
**MEAM**...... Advisory Committee for Mechanical Engineering and Applied Mechanics [*Washington, DC*] [*National Science Foundation*] [*Terminated, 1985*] (EGAO)
**MeAM**....... Augusta Mental Health Institute, Augusta, ME [*Library symbol*] [*Library of Congress*] (LCLS)
**MeAMH**.... Maine State Department of Human Services, Augusta, ME [*Library symbol*] [*Library of Congress*] (LCLS)
**MeAMM**... Maine State Museum, Augusta, ME [*Library symbol*] [*Library of Congress*] (LCLS)
**MEAN**....... Manganese-Enhanced Austenitic Nitrogen Steel
**MEAN**....... Microcomputer Education Application Network [*Commercial firm*] (EA)
**MEANINGEX** ... Meaning Extraction [*Programming language*] [*1971*] (CSR)
**Meanjin** ..... Meanjin Quarterly [*University of Melbourne*] [*A publication*]
**Meanjin Q** ... Meanjin Quarterly [*A publication*] (APTA)
**Means**........ Mean's Kansas Reports [*A publication*] (DLA)
**MEAP**........ Maintenance Engineering Analysis Program
**MEAP**........ Michigan Educational Assessment Program
**MEAP**........ Military Economic Advisory Panel (MCD)
**MEAPL**...... Manufacturing and Engineering Assembly Parts List [*File*]
**MEAPS**..... Method of Ensemble Average of Periodic Systems
**MEAR**....... Maintenance Engineering Analysis Record [*or Report*]
**MEAR**....... Maintenance Engineering Analysis Request [*NASA*] (NASA)
**Mears Just** ... Mears' Edition of Justinian and Gaius [*A publication*] (DLA)
**Meas**.......... Measure [*A publication*]
**MEAS**........ Measure (AABC)
**MEAS**........ Measurement (ROG)
**Meas & Autom News** ... Measurement and Automation News [*A publication*]
**Meas Contr** ... Measurement and Control [*A publication*]
**Meas and Control** ... Measurement and Control [*A publication*]
**Meas Control (1962-64)** ... Measurement and Control (1962-64) [*A publication*]
**Meas Eval G** ... Measurement and Evaluation in Guidance [*A publication*]
**Meas Focus** ... Measurement Focus [*A publication*]
**Meas Insp Technol** ... Measurement and Inspection Technology [*A publication*]
**Meas and Insp Technol** ... Measurement and Inspection Technology [*A publication*]
**Meas Instrum Rev** ... Measurement and Instrument Review [*England*] [*A publication*]
**Measmt Control** ... Measurement and Control [*A publication*]
**Measmt & Eval in Guid** ... Measurement and Evaluation in Guidance [*A publication*]
**Meas Tech** ... Measurement Techniques [*USSR*] [*A publication*]
**Meas Tech R** ... Measurement Techniques (USSR) [*A publication*]
**MEASURE** ... Metrology Automated System for Uniform Recall and Reporting [*Navy*]
**MEAT**....... Manpower Employment Assistance Training [*Act*] [*Pennsylvania*]
**MEAT**....... Multiedge Adaptive Tracker (MCD)
**Meat Facts** ... Meat Facts. A Statistical Summary about America's Largest Food Industry [*A publication*]
**Meat Ind**.... Meat Industry [*A publication*]
**Meat Ind Bul** ... Meat Industry Bulletin [*A publication*] (APTA)
**Meat Ind J** ... Meat Industry Journal [*A publication*] (APTA)
**Meat Ind J Q** ... Meat Industry Journal of Queensland [*A publication*] (APTA)
**Meat Marketing in Aust** ... Meat Marketing in Australia [*A publication*] (APTA)
**Meat Outlk** ... Meat Outlook [*A publication*]
**Meat Proc**.. Meat Processing [*A publication*]
**Meat Process** ... Meat Processing [*A publication*]
**Meat Prod & Exp** ... Meat Producer and Exporter [*A publication*] (APTA)
**Meat Res News Lett** ... Meat Research News Letter [*A publication*]
**Meat Sci**..... Meat Science [*A publication*]
**Meat Sci Inst Proc** ... Meat Science Institute. Proceedings [*A publication*]
**Meat Situat Outlook** ... Meat. Situation and Outlook [*A publication*]
**Meat Trades J Aust** ... Meat Trades Journal of Australia [*A publication*] (APTA)
**MeAu**......... Auburn Public Library, Auburn, ME [*Library symbol*] [*Library of Congress*] (LCLS)
**MeAU**........ University of Maine at Augusta, Augusta, ME [*Library symbol*] [*Library of Congress*] (LCLS)
**MEAV**....... Museum Education Association of Victoria [*Australia*]
**MEAVDO** ... Eidgenoessische Anstalt fuer das Forstliche Versuchswesen. Mitteilungen [*A publication*]
**Me B**.......... Bachelor of Metaphysics
**MEB**.......... Bangor Mental Health Institute, Bangor, ME [*OCLC symbol*] (OCLC)
**MeB**........... Bowdoin College, Brunswick, ME [*Library symbol*] [*Library of Congress*] (LCLS)
**MEB**.......... Main Electronics Box (NASA)
**MEB**.......... Maine Motor Rate Bureau, Portland ME [*STAC*]
**MEB**.......... Manufacturing Evaluation Board (MCD)
**MEB**.......... Marine Expeditionary Brigade
**MEB**.......... Master Electronics Board
**MEB**.......... Maxton, NC [*Location identifier*] [*FAA*] (FAAL)
**MEB**.......... Medial Efferent Bundle [*Neuroanatomy*]
**MEB**.......... Medical Board
**MEB**.......... Melbourne [*Australia*] [*Airport symbol*] (OAG)
**MEB**.......... Mercury Electron Bombardment
**MeB**........... Methylene Blue [*Organic chemistry*]
**MEB**.......... Midlands Electricity Board [*British*]
**MEB**.......... Military Early Bird
**MEB**.......... Missouri English Bulletin [*A publication*]
**MEB**.......... Moderate Environment Buoy [*Marine science*] (MSC)
**MeBa**......... Bangor Public Library, Bangor, ME [*Library symbol*] [*Library of Congress*] (LCLS)
**MEBA**....... Marine Engineers' Beneficial Association
**MeBaH**...... Husson College, Bangor, ME [*Library symbol*] [*Library of Congress*] (LCLS)
**MeBaHi**..... Bangor Historical Society, Bangor, ME [*Library symbol*] [*Library of Congress*] (LCLS)
**MeBarhJ** ... Jackson Laboratory, Bar Harbor, ME [*Library symbol*] [*Library of Congress*] (LCLS)
**MeBaT**....... Bangor Theological Seminary, Bangor, ME [*Library symbol*] [*Library of Congress*] (LCLS)
**MeBath**...... Patten Free Library, Bath, ME [*Library symbol*] [*Library of Congress*] (LCLS)
**MEBBAS** .. Mission Essential Bare Base Augmentation Sets [*Air Force*]
**ME Bd Agr An Rp** ... Maine. Board of Agriculture. Annual Report [*A publication*]
**MEBE**........ Middle East Basic Encyclopedia [*A publication*] (MCD)
**MEBEA**..... Medical Electronics and Biological Engineering [*A publication*]
**MEBFEX** .. Marine Expeditionary Brigade Field Exercise (NVT)
**MEBIEP**.... Monographs in Epidemiology and Biostatistics [*A publication*]
**MEBLEX** .. Marine Expeditionary Brigade Landing Exercise
**MEBO**....... Main Engine Burnout (NASA)
**MeBP**......... Pejepscot Historical Society, Brunswick, ME [*Library symbol*] [*Library of Congress*] (LCLS)
**Me-BPH**.... Maine State Library Service for the Blind and Physically Handicapped, Augusta, ME [*Library symbol*] [*Library of Congress*] (LCLS)
**MEBS**........ Marketing, Engineering, and Business Services [*Telecommunications*] (TEL)
**MEBS**........ Multicore Extruded Bar Solder
**MEBU**....... Maschinengewehr-Eisenbeton-Unterstand [*Machine-Gun-Iron-Concrete-Emplacement*] [*German "pill box," battlefield redoubts*] [*World War I*]
**MEBU**....... Mission Essential Backup (MCD)
**Mec**............ [*Lucius Volusius*] Maecianus [*Flourished, 2nd century*] [*Authority cited in pre-1607 legal work*] (DSA)
**MEC**.......... Main Engine Console (AAG)
**MEC**.......... Main Engine Controller [*NASA*] (NASA)
**MEC**.......... Main Engine Cutoff [*Aerospace*] (AAG)
**MEC**.......... Main Evaluation Center (NVT)
**MEC**.......... Maine Central Railroad Co. [*AAR code*]
**MEC**.......... Manta [*Ecuador*] [*Airport symbol*] (OAG)
**MEC**.......... Manual Emergency Controls [*Aerospace*] (KSC)
**MEC**.......... Manufacturing Engineering Council (EA)
**MEC**.......... Map Editing Console
**MEC**.......... Marginal Efficiency of Capital [*Economics*]
**MEC**.......... Marine Expeditionary Corps (NVT)
**MEC**.......... Maritime Electric Co. Ltd. [*Toronto Stock Exchange symbol*]
**MEC**.......... Market Economy Country
**M Ec**.......... Master of Economics
**MEC**.......... Master of Engineering Chemistry
**MEC**.......... Master Evaluation Center (MCD)
**MEC**.......... Master Event Controller [*NASA*] (NASA)
**MEC**.......... Maximum Endurable Concentration (NATG)
**MEC**.......... Mechernich [*Federal Republic of Germany*] [*Seismograph station code, US Geological Survey*] [*Closed*] (SEIS)

**MEC** .......... Meconium [*Gynecology*]
**MEC** .......... Medical Examination Centre [*British*] [*World War II*]
**MEC** .......... Member of Executive Council [*British*]
**MEC** .......... Mercado Comune Europeo [*European Common Market*] [*Spanish*] (DLA)
**MEC** .......... Merrimack Education Center [*Chelmsford, MA*] [*Information service or system*]
**MEC** .......... Meteorology Engineering Center [*Navy*] (MCD)
**MEC** .......... Methodist Episcopal Church
**MEC** .......... Microencapsulation [*Chemical engineering*]
**MEC** .......... Microwave Electronics Corporation
**MEC** .......... Middle East Centre [*University of Cambridge*] [*British*] (CB)
**MEC** .......... Middle East Command [*Military*]
**MEC** .......... Military Essentiality Class [*or Code*]
**MEC** .......... Minimum Effective Concentration [*Medicine*]
**MEC** .......... Minimum Essential Criteria (MCD)
**MEC** .......... Minimum Explosive Concentration [*Safety*]
**MEC** .......... Ministerio de Educacao e Cultura [*A publication*]
**MEC** .......... Missile Engagement Console [*Military*] (CAAL)
**MEC** .......... Missile Engagement Controller [*Military*] (CAAL)
**MEC** .......... Mission Events Controller [*NASA*] (MCD)
**MEC** .......... Mobility Equipment Command [*Later, TROSCOM*] [*Army*]
**MEC** .......... Molecular Exclusion Chromatography
**MEC** .......... Monethylcholine [*Biochemistry*]
**MEC** .......... Most Excellent Companion [*Freemasonry*] (ROG)
**MEC** .......... Movimiento Emergente de Concordia [*Emerging Movement for Harmony*] [*Guatemala*] [*Political party*] (PPW)
**MECA** ....... Main Engine Controller Assembly [*NASA*] (NASA)
**MECA** ....... Maintainable Electronics Component Assembly
**MECA** ....... Malfunctioned Equipment Corrective Action
**MECA** ....... Manufacturers of Emission Controls Association (EA)
**MECA** ....... Map Exercise Computer Assistance (MCD)
**MECA** ....... Mars: Evolution of Its Climate and Atmosphere [*Planetary science project*]
**MECA** ....... Medical Electronics Corporation of America [*NASDAQ symbol*] (NQ)
**MECA** ....... Medical Emergency Calling Aid (MCD)
**MECA** ....... Mercury Evaporation and Condensation Analysis [*NASA*]
**MECA** ....... Micro Education Corporation of America
**MECA** ....... Military Educators and Counselors Association (EA)
**MECA** ....... Molecular Emission Cavity Analysis [*Flame spectrophotometry*]
**MECA** ....... Multielement Centrifugal Aerowindow
**MECA** ....... Multielement Component Array
**Mecan Electrif Agr** ... Mecanizarea si Electrificarea Agriculturii [*A publication*]
**MECAP**..... Medical Examiners and Coroners Alert Program [*Consumer Product Safety Commission*]
**MECAR**..... Metropolitan Engineers Council on Air Resources
**MECAS**..... Middle East Center for Arab Studies
**MECAS**..... Multienergy Californium Assay System [*Nuclear energy*] (NRCH)
**MeCasM**.... Maine Maritime Academy, Castine, ME [*Library symbol*] [*Library of Congress*] (LCLS)
**MECC** ....... Micellar Electrokinetic Capillary Chromatography
**MECC** ....... Middle East Council of Churches (EA)
**MECC** ....... Miller Technology & Communications Corporation [*NASDAQ symbol*] (NQ)
**MECC** ....... Minnesota Educational Computing Corporation [*St. Paul, MN*] (CSR)
**MECCA**..... Master Electrical Common Connector Assembly (MCD)
**MECCA**..... Mechanized Catalog (IEEE)
**MECCA**..... Milwaukee Exposition and Convention Center and Arena
**MECCA**..... Missionary and Ecumenical Council of the Church Assembly [*Church of England*]
**MECCA**..... Modular Electron Column Control and Automation
**Mecc Agr** ... Meccanizzazione Agricola [*A publication*]
**MECCAS**.. Microbial Exchanges and Coupling in Coastal Atlantic Systems
**Mecc Ital**.... Meccanica Italiana [*A publication*]
**MeCCNU**.. Methyl(chloroethyl)cyclohexylnitrosourea [*Semustine*] [*Antineoplastic drug*]
**MECD** ....... Military Equipment Characteristics Document (RDA)
**MEcDev**..... Master of Economics of Development
**MECE**........ Master of Electrochemical Engineering
**MECE**........ Movement, Ethyl Chloride, and Elevation [*Medicine*]
**MECEA**..... Mutual Educational and Cultural Exchange Act of 1961
**MEC-ECR** ... Management Engineering Steering Committee for Embedded Computer Resources (MCD)
**Mec Elec**.... Mecanique Electricite [*A publication*]
**Mec Electr** ... Mecanique Electricite [*A publication*]
**MECF**........ Main Engine Computational Facilities [*NASA*] (NASA)
**MECF**........ Micks External Compression Fixator [*Instrumentation*]
**MECG**....... Material Electrocardiogram (MCD)
**MECH**....... Mechanic [*or Mechanics*] (AFM)
**Mech**.......... Mechanica [*of Aristotle*] [*Classical studies*] (OCD)
**MECH**....... Mechanism [*Automotive engineering*]
**MECH**....... Methodist Episcopal Church
**Mech Age D** ... Mechanisms of Ageing and Development [*A publication*]
**Mech Ageing Dev** ... Mechanisms of Ageing and Development [*A publication*]
**Mechanik**... Mechanik Miesiecznik Naukowo-Techniczny [*A publication*]
**Mech Autom Adm** ... Mechanizace Automatizace Administrativy [*A publication*]
**MECHBAD** ... Mechanic Badge
**MECHBAT** ... Mechanized Battalion [*Army*]
**Mech Chem Engng Trans Instn Engrs (Aust)** ... Mechanical and Chemical Engineering Transactions. Institution of Engineers (Australia) [*A publication*] (APTA)
**Mech Chem Eng Trans** ... Mechanical and Chemical Engineering Transactions [*Australia*] [*A publication*]
**Mech Chem Eng Trans Inst Eng (Aust)** ... Mechanical and Chemical Engineering Transactions. Institution of Engineers (Australia) [*A publication*] (APTA)
**Mech Compos Mater** ... Mechanics of Composite Materials [*A publication*]
**Mech Contract** ... Mechanical Contractor [*A publication*]
**Mech Corros Prop A Key Eng Mater** ... Mechanical and Corrosion Properties A. Key Engineering Materials [*A publication*]
**Mech Corros Prop B Single Cryst Prop** ... Mechanical and Corrosion Properties B. Single Crystal Properties [*A publication*]
**Mech Des**... Mechanical Design [*Japan*] [*A publication*]
**ME Ch E**.... Master of Electrochemical Engineering
**ME(Chem)** ... Master of Engineering (Chemical) (ADA)
**Mechem**..... Mechem on Agency [*A publication*] (DLA)
**Mechem**..... Mechem on Partnership [*A publication*] (DLA)
**Mechem Ag** ... Mechem on Agency [*A publication*] (DLA)
**Mechem Pub Off** ... Mechem on Public Offices and Officers [*A publication*] (DLA)
**Mech Eng** .. Mechanical Engineer
**Mech Eng** .. Mechanical Engineering [*A publication*]
**Mech Eng Bull** ... Mechanical Engineering Bulletin [*A publication*]
**Mech Eng News** ... Mechanical Engineering News [*A publication*]
**Mech Eng News (Washington DC)** ... Mechanical Engineering News (Washington, DC) [*A publication*]
**Mech Engng** ... Mechanical Engineering [*A publication*]
**Mech Engng Bull** ... Mechanical Engineering Bulletin [*A publication*]
**Mech Engng J** ... Mechanical Engineering Journal [*A publication*] (APTA)
**Mech Engng News** ... Mechanical Engineering News [*A publication*]
**MECHENGR** ... Mechanical Engineer
**Mech Eng Rep Aust Aeronaut Res Lab** ... Mechanical Engineering Report. Australia. Aeronautical Research Laboratories [*A publication*]
**Mech Eng Rep MP Natl Res Counc Can Div Mech Eng** ... Mechanical Engineering Report MP. National Research Council of Canada. Division of Mechanical Engineering [*A publication*]
**Mech Eng Sci Monogr** ... Mechanical Engineering Science Monograph. Institution of Mechanical Engineers [*London*] [*A publication*]
**Mech Eng Technol** ... Mechanical Engineering Technology [*England*] [*A publication*]
**Mech Eng Trans Inst Eng (Aust)** ... Mechanical Engineering Transactions. Institution of Engineers (Australia) [*A publication*]
**Mechenye Biol Atk Veshchestva** ... Mechenye Biologicheski Atkivnye Veshchestva [*A publication*]
**Mech of Fracture** ... Mechanics of Fracture [*A publication*]
**Mech Handl** ... Mechanical Handling [*A publication*]
**MECH I/C** ... Mechanic in Charge (DCTA)
**Mech Illus** ... Mechanix Illustrated [*A publication*]
**MECHINF** ... Mechanized Infantry [*Army*]
**MECH L**.... Mechanic's Lien [*Legal term*] (DLA)
**Mech Leafl GB Min Agr Fish Food** ... Mechanisation Leaflet. Great Britain Ministry of Agriculture, Fisheries, and Food [*A publication*]
**Mech Mach T** ... Mechanism and Machine Theory [*A publication*]
**Mech Mater** ... Mechanics of Materials [*A publication*]
**Mech Miesiecznik Nauk-Tech** ... Mechanik Miesiecznik Naukowo-Techniczny [*A publication*]
**Mech Mies Nauk Tech** ... Mechanik Miesiecznik Naukowo-Techniczny [*A publication*]
**Mech Mol Migr** ... Mechanisms of Molecular Migrations [*A publication*]
**MECHN**.... Mechanician [*Navy*] [*British*]
**MECHNL** ... Mechanical
**Mech Polim** ... Mechanika Polimerov [*A publication*]
**Mech Practice** ... Mechanics and Practice. Lixue Yu Shijian [*A publication*]
**Mech React Sulfur Comp** ... Mechanisms of Reactions of Sulfur Compounds [*A publication*]
**Mech React Sulfur Compd** ... Mechanisms of Reactions of Sulfur Compounds [*A publication*]
**Mech Res Comm** ... Mechanics Research Communications [*A publication*]
**Mech Res Commun** ... Mechanics Research Communications [*A publication*]
**Mech Roln** ... Mechanizacja Rolnictwa [*A publication*]
**Mech Sci**.... Mechanical Sciences [*A publication*]
**Mech Sci**.... Mechanical Sciences. Mashinovdeniye [*A publication*]
**MECHSFIL** ... Mechanized Sandbag Filler and Sealer (MCD)
**MECHSIM** ... Mechanical Simulation [*of a computer-based directory assistance system*]
**MECHSM** ... Mechanism
**Mech Solids** ... Mechanics of Solids [*A publication*]
**Mech Technol Budowy Masz (Bydgoszcz Pol)** ... Mechanika, Technologia Budowy Maszyn (Bydgoszcz, Poland) [*A publication*]
**Mech Teoret Stos** ... Polskie Towarzystwo Mechaniki Teoretycznej i Stosowana [*A publication*]

**Mech Teor i Stoso** ... Mechanika Teoretyczna i Stosowana [*A publication*]
**Mech Teor i Stosow** ... Mechanika Teoretyczna i Stosowana [*A publication*]
**MECHTRAM** ... Mechanization of Selected Transportation Movement
**Mech World Eng Rec** ... Mechanical World and Engineering Record [*England*] [*A publication*]
**MECI**......... Member of the Institute of Employment Consultants [*British*] (DBQ)
**MECI**......... Mission Essential Contingency Item [*Military*]
**MECL**......... Motorola Emitter-Coupled Logic (IEEE)
**MECM**...... Meridional Elementary Circulation Mechanism
**Mec-Mat-Elec** ... Mecanique- Materiaux- Electricite [*A publication*]
**Mec Mater Electr** ... Mecanique- Materiaux- Electricite [*A publication*]
**Mecmuasi Univ Fen Fak (Istanbul)** ... Mecmuasi Universite. Fen Fakulte (Istanbul) [*A publication*]
**MECO**....... Main Engine Cutoff [*Aerospace*]
**MECO**....... Manual Equipment Checkout (NG)
**MECO**....... Minerals Engineering Company [*NASDAQ symbol*] (NQ)
**MECOBO** ... Military Export Cargo Offering and Booking Office
**MECOM**... Middle East Command [*Military*]
**MECOM**... Middle East Electronic Communications Show and Conference [*Arabian Exhibition Management WLL*] [*Manama, Bahrain*] (TSPED)
**MECOM**... Mobility Equipment Command [*Later, TROSCOM*] [*Army*]
**MECOMSAG** ... Mobility Equipment Command Scientific Advisory Group (MCD)
**MEcon**....... Master of Economics
**Mecon J**..... Mecon Journal [*A publication*]
**MEconS**..... Master of Economic Science (ADA)
**MEconSt**.... Master of Economic Studies (ADA)
**MECP**........ Multielliptical Cavity Pump
**MECR**....... Maintenance Engineering Change Request (MCD)
**MEc(Reg Plan)** ... Master of Economics in Regional Planning (ADA)
**Mec Roches** ... Mecanique des Roches [*A publication*]
**MECS**........ Maximal Electroconvulsive Seizure [*Neurophysiology*]
**MECT**........ Mission Endurance Cycle Test
**MECU**....... Master Engine Control Unit
**MECU**....... Member of the English Church Union
**MECWB**.... Middle East Committee for the Welfare of the Blind (EA)
**MECY**....... Methotrexate, Cyclophosphamide [*Antineoplastic drug regimen*]
**MECZ**........ Mechanize (AAG)
**MED**......... Chicago, IL [*Location identifier*] [*FAA*] (FAAL)
**MED**......... Maine Department of Transportation, Augusta, ME [*OCLC symbol*] (OCLC)
**MED**......... Manhattan Engineer District [*Developed atomic bomb; dissolved, 1946*]
**MED**......... Manipulative Electronics Deception (MCD)
**MED**......... Manual Electron Device
**MED**......... Manual Entry Device
**MED**......... Marketing and Media Decisions [*A publication*]
**M Ed**......... Master of Education
**MED**......... Master of Elementary Didactics
**MED**......... Master of English Divinity
**MED**......... Mechanical Equipment Design
**MED**......... Medal [*Numismatics*]
**MED**......... Medallion Explorations Ltd. [*Vancouver Stock Exchange symbol*]
**MED**......... Medallist [*British*] (ROG)
**MED**......... Medan [*Sumatra*] [*Seismograph station code, US Geological Survey*] [*Closed*] (SEIS)
**Med**.......... Medea [*of Euripides*] [*Classical studies*] (OCD)
**MED**......... Media
**med**.......... Medial [*Medicine*]
**MED**......... Median (AFM)
**MED**......... Median Effective Dose [*Medicine*]
**MED**......... Median Erythrocyte Diameter [*Medicine*]
**Med**.......... Mediator [*Legal term*] (DLA)
**Med**.......... Medica [*A publication*]
**MED**......... Medical (AFM)
**MED**......... Medicamenta [*Medicaments*] [*Pharmacy*] (ROG)
**MED**......... Medication
**MED**......... Medicine (AABC)
**Med**.......... Medico [*A publication*]
**MED**......... Medieval
**MED**......... Medina [*Saudi Arabia*] [*Airport symbol*] (OAG)
**MED**......... MEDIQ, Inc. [*AMEX symbol*] (SPSG)
**MED**......... Meditation (ROG)
**MED**......... Mediterranean (AFM)
**MED**......... Mediterranean Engineer Division [*Army Engineers*]
**Med**.......... Mediterraneo [*A publication*]
**MED**......... Medium (AFM)
**MED**......... Message Entry Device
**MED**......... Microelectronic Device
**MED**......... Microwave Emission Detector [*Instrumentation*]
**MED**......... Middle English Dictionary [*A publication*]
**MED**......... Minimal Effective Dose [*Medicine*]
**MED**......... Minimal Erythema Dose [*Medicine*]
**MED**......... Minimum Engineering Development (MCD)
**MED**......... Mobile Energy Depot
**MED**......... Modular Evolutionary Development (MCD)
**MED**......... Molecular Electronic Device
**M Ed**......... Monde de l'Education [*A publication*]
**MED**......... Monitor Execution Dump [*Data processing*]
**MED**......... Multieffect Distillation [*Chemical engineering*]
**MEDA**....... Mennonite Economic Development Associates (EA)
**MEDA**....... (Mercaptoethyl)dimethylammonium Chloride [*Organic chemistry*]
**MEDA**....... Multiplex Electronic Doppler Analyzer
**MEDAB**.... Middle East Database (IID)
**Med Abstr** ... Medical Abstract Service [*A publication*]
**MEDAC**.... Medical Accounting [*and Billing Process*]
**MEDAC**.... Medical Electronic Data Aquisition and Control
**MEDAC**.... Military Electronic Data Advisory Committee [*NATO*] (NATG)
**MEDAC**.... Mouvement de l'Evolution Democratique de l'Afrique Centrale [*Central African Democratic Evolution Movement*]
**MEDAC**.... Multiple Endocrine Deficiency, Autoimmune-Candidiasis [*Syndrome*] [*Medicine*]
**Med Actual** ... Medicamentos de Actualidad [*A publication*]
**Med Actuelle** ... Medecine Actuelle [*A publication*]
**MEdAd**...... Master of Educational Administration (ADA)
**MEdAdm**... Master of Educational Administration (ADA)
**MEdAdmin** ... Master of Educational Administration
**MedAe**....... Medium Aevum [*A publication*]
**Med Aero**... Medecine Aeronautique [*A publication*]
**Med Aeronaut** ... Medecine Aeronautique [*A publication*]
**Med Aeronaut Spat Med Subaquat Hyperbare** ... Medecine Aeronautique et Spatiale, Medecine Subaquatique et Hyperbare [*A publication*]
**MedAev**..... Medium Aevum [*A publication*]
**Med Aff**...... Medical Affairs [*A publication*]
**Med Afr Noire** ... Medecine d'Afrique Noire [*A publication*]
**Med Aktuell** ... Medizin Aktuell [*A publication*]
**MEDAL**..... Medallion [*Automotive engineering*]
**MEDAL**..... Micromechanized Engineering Data for Automated Logistics
**MEDALSA** ... Mediterranean Algeria-Sahara Zone [*NATO*] (NATG)
**Med Ann DC** ... Medical Annals of the District of Columbia [*A publication*]
**Med Ann Distr Columbia** ... Medical Annals of the District of Columbia [*A publication*]
**Med Annu** ... Medical Annual [*England*] [*A publication*]
**Med Anthro** ... Medical Anthropology [*A publication*]
**Med Anthropol** ... Medical Anthropology [*A publication*]
**Med Anthropol Newsletter** ... Medical Anthropology Newsletter [*A publication*]
**Med Arb**..... Medicinsk Arbog [*A publication*]
**Med Arch**... Medicinskij Archiv [*A publication*]
**Med Arch**... Medieval Archaeology [*A publication*]
**Med Arh**.... Medicinski Arhiv [*A publication*]
**Med Arhiv**... Medicinski Arhiv [*A publication*]
**Med Arkh**.. Meditsinski Arkhiv [*Bulgaria*] [*A publication*]
**Med Armees**... Medecine et Armees [*A publication*]
**Med Art**..... Medical Art [*A publication*]
**Med Arts Sci** ... Medical Arts and Sciences [*A publication*]
**MEDAS**..... Medical Emergency Decisions Assistance System (MCD)
**MEDAS**..... Meteorological Data Acquisition System [*NASA*] (KSC)
**Med Aspects Hum Sex** ... Medical Aspects of Human Sexuality [*A publication*]
**Med Ass**..... Zeitschrift fuer Medizinstudenten und Assistenten [*A publication*]
**Med Assoc State Ala J** ... Medical Association of the State of Alabama. Journal [*A publication*]
**Med Audiovision** ... Medecine et Audiovision [*France*] [*A publication*]
**MEDAUG**... Medical Augmentation (MCD)
**Med Avh Univ Bergen** ... Medisinske Avhandlinger. Universitet i Bergen [*A publication*]
**MEDAX**.... Message Data Exchange Terminal (MCD)
**Med (B)**...... Medicina (Bogota) [*A publication*]
**MEDBAD**... Medical Badge
**Med Bio Eng** ... Medical and Biological Engineering [*Later, Medical and Biological Engineering and Computing*] [*A publication*]
**Med Bio Ill** ... Medical and Biological Illustration [*A publication*]
**Med Biol**.... Medecine et Biologie [*A publication*]
**Med Biol**.... Medical Biology [*A publication*]
**Med Biol Eng** ... Medical and Biological Engineering [*Later, Medical and Biological Engineering and Computing*] [*A publication*]
**Med and Biol Eng** ... Medical and Biological Engineering [*Later, Medical and Biological Engineering and Computing*] [*A publication*]
**Med Biol Eng Comput** ... Medical and Biological Engineering and Computing [*A publication*]
**Med and Biol Eng and Comput** ... Medical and Biological Engineering and Computing [*A publication*]
**Med Biol Engng** ... Medical and Biological Engineering [*Later, Medical and Biological Engineering and Computing*] [*A publication*]
**Med Biol (Helsinki)** ... Medical Biology (Helsinki) [*A publication*]
**Med Biol Illus** ... Medical and Biological Illustration [*A publication*]
**Med Biol Illustr** ... Medical Biology Illustrations [*A publication*]
**Med Biol Probl** ... Mediko-Biologichni Problemi [*A publication*]
**Med Biol (Tokyo)** ... Medicine and Biology (Tokyo) [*A publication*]
**Med Bl**....... Medizinische Blaetter [*A publication*]
**MEDBN**.... Medical Battalion [*Marine Corps*]
**MEDBO**.... Mediterranean Shipping Board [*World War II*]
**MEDBR**..... Medical Branch

**Med Bull Exxon Corp Affil Co** ... Medical Bulletin. Exxon Corporation and Affiliated Companies [*A publication*]
**Med Bull Fukuoka Univ** ... Medical Bulletin. Fukuoka University [*A publication*]
**Med Bull Istanbul Fac Med Istanbul Univ** ... Medical Bulletin. Istanbul Faculty of Medicine. Istanbul University [*A publication*]
**Med Bull Istanbul Med Fac** ... Medical Bulletin. Istanbul Medical Faculty [*A publication*]
**Med Bull Istanbul Med Fac Istanbul Univ** ... Medical Bulletin. Istanbul Medical Faculty. Istanbul University [*A publication*]
**Med Bull Istanbul Univ** ... Medical Bulletin. Istanbul University [*A publication*]
**Med Bull Natl Med Cent (Seoul)** ... Medical Bulletin. National Medical Center (Seoul) [*A publication*]
**Med Bull No Virginia** ... Medical Bulletin of Northern Virginia [*A publication*]
**Med Bull Providence Hosp (Southfield Mich)** ... Medical Bulletin. Providence Hospital (Southfield, Michigan) [*A publication*]
**Med Bull Stand Oil Co (NJ) Affil Co** ... Medical Bulletin. Standard Oil Company (New Jersey) and Affiliated Companies [*A publication*]
**Med Bull Univ Cincinnati** ... Medical Bulletin. University of Cincinnati [*A publication*]
**Med Bull (US Army)** ... Medical Bulletin (United States Army) [*A publication*]
**Med Bull US Army (Eur)** ... Medical Bulletin. US Army (Europe) [*A publication*]
**Med Bull Vet Adm** ... Medical Bulletin. Veterans Administration [*A publication*]
**Med Bydr**... Mediese Bydraes [*A publication*]
**Med Bydraes** ... Mediese Bydraes [*A publication*]
**MEDC** ....... Medical Care International, Inc. [*Dallas, TX*] [*NASDAQ symbol*] (NQ)
**MEDC** ....... Microelectronics Educational Development Centre [*Paisley College*] [*United Kingdom*] (CB)
**MEDC** ....... Moessbauer Effect Data Center [*University of North Carolina*] [*Information service or system*] (IID)
**MEDCAP** ... Medical Civic Action Patrol [*or Program*] [*Military*]
**Med Care**... Medical Care [*A publication*]
**Med Care Rev** ... Medical Care Review [*A publication*]
**MEDCASE** ... Medical Care Support Equipment (AABC)
**MEDCAT** ... Medical Civic Action Teams
**MEDCAT** ... Medium Altitude Clear-Air Turbulence (MCD)
**MEDCAT** ... Medium-Altitude Critical Atmospheric Turbulence (MCD)
**MEDCEN** ... Medical Center [*Army*] (AABC)
**MEDCENT** ... Central Mediterranean Area [*NATO*]
**Med Cent J Univ Mich** ... Medical Center Journal. University of Michigan [*A publication*]
**Med Chem (Leverkusen Ger)** ... Medizin und Chemie (Leverkusen, Germany) [*A publication*]
**Med Chem Ser Monogr** ... Medicinal Chemistry: A Series of Monographs [*A publication*]
**Med Chem Ser Rev** ... Medicinal Chemistry: A Series of Reviews [*A publication*]
**Med Chir Dig** ... Medecine et Chirurgie Digestives [*A publication*]
**Med Cir**...... Medicina y Cirugia [*A publication*]
**Med Cir Farm** ... Medicina, Cirugia, Farmacia [*A publication*]
**Med Cir Gu** ... Medicina y Cirugia de Guerra [*A publication*]
**Med Clin**.... Medicina Clinica [*A publication*]
**Med Clin NA** ... Medical Clinics of North America [*A publication*]
**Med Clin N Am** ... Medical Clinics of North America [*A publication*]
**Med Clin North Am** ... Medical Clinics of North America [*A publication*]
**Med Clin Sper** ... Medicina Clinica e Sperimentale [*A publication*]
**Med Colon (Madr)** ... Medicina Colonial (Madrid) [*A publication*]
**MEDCOM** ... Medical Command (MCD)
**MEDCOM** ... Mediterranean Communications [*Military*] (AFM)
**Med Commun** ... Medical Communications [*A publication*]
**MEDCOMP** ... Medical Early Direct Commissioning Program (MCD)
**Med and Comp** ... Medicine and Computer [*A publication*]
**Med Comp J** ... Medical Computer Journal [*A publication*]
**MEDCOMPLAN** ... Mediterranean Communications Plans [*NATO*] (NATG)
**MEDCON** ... Medical Contingency Report [*Air Force*]
**Med Cond** .. Medico Condotto [*A publication*]
**Med Condotto** ... Medico Condotto [*A publication*]
**Med Consult New Remedies** ... Medical Consultation and New Remedies [*A publication*]
**Med Cont**... Medicina Contemporanea [*A publication*]
**Med Contact** ... Medisch Contact [*Netherlands*] [*A publication*]
**Med Contemp** ... Medicina Contemporanea [*A publication*]
**Med Contemp (Lisbon)** ... Medicina Contemporanea (Lisbon) [*A publication*]
**Med Convers Bl** ... Medizinisches Conversationsblatt [*A publication*]
**MEDCOOP** ... Medical Continuity of Operations Plan [*Army*] (AABC)
**Med Cor-Bl Bayer Aerzte** ... Medizinisches Correspondenz-Blatt Bayerischer Aerzte [*A publication*]
**Med Cor-Bl Rhein u Westfael Aerzte** ... Medizinisches Correspondenz-Blatt Rheinischer und Westfaelischer Aerzte [*A publication*]
**Med Cor-Bl Wuerttemb Aerztl Landesver** ... Medizinisches Correspondenz-Blatt. Wuerttembergischer Aerztliche Landesverein [*A publication*]
**Med Cor-Bl Wuerttemb Aerztl Ver** ... Medizinisches Correspondenz-Blatt. Wuerttembergischer Aerztliche Verein [*A publication*]
**MEDCORE** ... Medical Resources Consortium of Central New Jersey [*Library network*]
**MEDCORPS** ... Medical Corps [*Air Force*]
**MEDCOS** ... Mediterranean Chiefs of Staff [*British*] [*World War II*]
**Med Counterpoint** ... Medical Counterpoint [*A publication*]
**Med Cult**.... Medicina e Cultura [*A publication*]
**Med Cut**..... Medicina Cutanea [*Later, Medicina Cutanea Ibero-Latino-Americana*] [*A publication*]
**Med Cutanea** ... Medicina Cutanea [*Later, Medicina Cutanea Ibero-Latino-Americana*] [*A publication*]
**Med Cutan Iber Lat Am** ... Medicina Cutanea Ibero-Latino-Americana [*A publication*]
**Med C Virg** ... Medical College of Virginia. Quarterly [*A publication*]
**Medd**.......... Meddaugh's Reports [*13 Michigan*] [*A publication*] (DLA)
**MEDDA**.... Mechanized Defense Decision Anticipation [*AFSC*]
**Medd Abo Akad Geol Mineral Inst** ... Meddelanden fran Abo Akademis Geologisk-Mineralogiska Institut [*A publication*]
**MEDDAC** ... Medical Department Activity [*Army*] (AABC)
**Medd Alnarpsinst Mejeriavd Statens Mejerifoers** ... Meddelande fran Alnarpsinstitutets Mejeriavdelning och Statens Mejerifoersoek [*A publication*]
**MEDDARS** ... Medical Display Analysis and Recording System
**Meddaugh** ... Meddaugh's Reports [*13 Michigan*] [*A publication*] (DLA)
**Medd Carlsberg Lab** ... Meddelelser fra Carlsberg Laboratorium [*A publication*]
**Medd Centralstyr Malmohus Lans Forsoks-Vaxtskyddsringar** ... Meddelande fran Centralstyrelsen foer Malmoehus Laens Foersoeksoch Vaxtskyddsringar [*A publication*]
**Medd Dan Fisk Havunders** ... Meddelelser fra Danmarks Fiskfri-og Havundersogelser [*A publication*]
**Medd Dan Geol Foren** ... Meddelelser fra Dansk Geologisk Forening [*A publication*]
**Medd Dansk Geol Forend** ... Meddelanden fra Dansk Geologiske Forendlingen [*A publication*]
**Med Decision Making** ... Medical Decision Making [*A publication*]
**Med Decis Making** ... Medical Decision Making [*A publication*]
**Meddel om Gronland** ... Meddelelser om Groenland [*A publication*]
**Meddel Komm Byggn** ... Meddelanden fran Statens Kommitte foer Byggnadsforskning [*A publication*]
**Meddel Lund** ... Meddelande fran Lunds Universitet Historiska Museum [*A publication*]
**Meddel Lund U Hist Mus** ... Meddelande fran Lunds Universitet Historiska Museum [*A publication*]
**Meddel Skogsfoers Anst** ... Meddelanden fran Statens Skogsfoersoeksanstalt [*A publication*]
**MED-DENT** ... Medical Dental Division [*Air Force*]
**Med Dent J** ... Medical/Dental Journal [*A publication*]
**Med Device & Diagn Ind** ... Medical Device and Diagnostic Industry [*A publication*]
**Med Devices Rep (CCH)** ... Medical Devices Reports (Commerce Clearing House) [*A publication*] (DLA)
**MEDDF** .... Master Engineering Drawing Data File System
**Medd Grafiska Forskningslab** ... Meddelande. Grafiska Forskningslaboratoriet [*A publication*]
**Medd Groenl** ... Meddelelser om Groenland [*A publication*]
**Medd Groenland** ... Meddelelser om Groenland [*A publication*]
**Medd Groenl Geosci** ... Meddelelser om Groenland. Geoscience [*A publication*]
**Medd Gronl** ... Meddelelser om Groenland [*A publication*]
**Medd Havsfiskelab Lysekil** ... Meddelande fran Havsfiskelaboratoriet Lysekil [*A publication*]
**MEdDHi** ... Dukes County Historical Society, Edgartown, MA [*Library symbol*] [*Library of Congress*] (LCLS)
**Med Dimensions** ... Medical Dimensions [*A publication*]
**Medd Inst Maltdrycksforsk** ... Meddelande fran Institutet foer Maltdrycksforskning [*A publication*]
**Med Dir Tuinb** ... Mededelingen. Directeur van de Tuinbouw [*A publication*]
**Medd Jordbrukste Inst** ... Meddelande-Jordbruksteknisk Institutet [*A publication*]
**Medd Kvismare Fagelstn** ... Meddelande fran Kvismare Fagelstation [*A publication*]
**Medd Lunds Geol Mineral Inst** ... Meddelanden fran Lunds Geologisk-Mineralogiska Institut [*A publication*]
**Medd Lunds Univ Hist Mus** ... Meddelande fran Lunds Universitet Historiska Museum [*A publication*]
**Meddn K Lantbrhogsk Lantbrfors Jordbrfors** ... Meddelanden fran Kungliga Lantbrukshogskolan och [*Statens*] Lantbruksforsok [*Statens*] Jordbruksforsok [*A publication*]
**Medd Nor Farm Selsk** ... Meddelelser fra Norsk Farmaceutisk Selskap [*A publication*]
**Medd Nor Inst Skogforsk** ... Meddelelser fra Norsk Institute foer Skogforskning [*A publication*]
**Medd Nor Myrselsk** ... Meddelelser fra det Norske Myrselskap [*A publication*]
**Medd Nor Sk** ... Meddelelser fra det Norske Skogforsoeksvesen [*A publication*]
**Medd Nor Skogforsoksves** ... Meddelelser fra det Norske Skogforsoeksvesen [*A publication*]

**Medd Norsk Tretekn Inst** ... Meddelelse Norsk Treteknisk Institutt [*A publication*]
**Meddn St Skogsforskinst (Stockholm)** ... Meddelanden fran Statens Skogsforskningsinstitut (Stockholm) [*A publication*]
**Meddn Sverig FroeodlFoerb** ... Meddelanden fran Sveriges Froeodlarefoerbund [*A publication*]
**MEDDOC** ... Medical Documentation Systems [*Eli Lilly & Co.*] [*Information service or system*] (IID)
**Med Dosw Mikrobiol** ... Medycyna Doswiadczalna i Mikrobiologia [*A publication*]
**Med Dosw Mikrobiol (Transl)** ... Medycyna Doswiadczalna i Mikrobiologia (Translation) [*A publication*]
**Med Dosw Spoleczna** ... Medycyna Doswiadczalna i Spoleczna [*A publication*]
**Medd Papirind Forskningsinst** ... Meddelelse fra Papirindustriens Forskningsinstitutt [*A publication*]
**MEDDPERSA** ... Medical Department Personnel Support Agency [*Army*] (MCD)
**Meddr Norske Myrselsk** ... Meddelelser fra det Norske Myrselskap [*A publication*]
**Meddr Norske Skogsfors Ves** ... Meddelelser fra det Norske Skogforsoeksvesen [*A publication*]
**MEDDS**..... Medical Data Specialist (AABC)
**Medd Statens Mejerifoers (Swed)** ... Meddelande fran Statens Mejerifoersoek (Sweden) [*A publication*]
**Medd Statens Planteavsforsog** ... Meddelelse Statens Planteavlsforsog [*A publication*]
**Medd Statens Skeppsprovningsanst** ... Meddelanden fran Statens Skeppsprovningsanstalt [*A publication*]
**Medd Statens Skogsforskningsinst** ... Meddelanden fran Statens Skogsforskningsinstitut [*A publication*]
**Medd Statens Skogsforskningsinst (Swed)** ... Meddelanden fran Statens Skogsforskningsinstitut (Sweden) [*A publication*]
**Medd Statens Viltunders** ... Meddelelser fra Statens Viltundersokelser [*Papers. Norwegian State Game Research Institute*] [*A publication*]
**Medd Statens Viltunders (Pap Norw State Game Res Inst)** ... Meddelelser fra Statens Viltundersokelser (Papers. Norwegian State Game Research Institute) [*A publication*]
**Medd Stat Forskningsanst Lantmannabyggnader** ... Meddelande fran Statens Forskningsanst Lantmannabyggnader [*A publication*]
**Medd Stift Rasforadl Skogstrad** ... Meddelanden fran Stiftelsen foer Rasforadling av Skogstrad [*A publication*]
**Medd Sven Mejeriernas Riksfoeren Produkttek Avd** ... Meddelande. Svenska Mejeriernas Riksfoerening. Produkttekniska Avdelningen [*A publication*]
**Medd Svenska Tek Vetenskapsakad Finl** ... Meddelande Svenska Tekniska Vetenskapsakademien i Finland [*A publication*]
**Medd Svenska Traforskn Inst (Trakem PappTekn)** ... Meddelanden fran Svenska Traforskningsinstitutet (Trakemi och Pappersteknik) [*A publication*]
**Medd Sven Textilforskningsinst** ... Meddelanden fran Svenska Textilforskningsinstitutet [*A publication*]
**Medd Sven Traskyddsinst** ... Meddelanden fran Svenska Traskyddsinstitutet [*A publication*]
**Medd Sver Kem Industrikontor** ... Meddelanden fran Sveriges Kemiska Industrikontor [*A publication*]
**Medd Vaextekol Inst Lund Univ** ... Meddelanden fran Vaextekologiska Institutionen Lunds Universitet [*A publication*]
**Medd Vestland Forstl Forsokssta** ... Meddelelser fra Vestlandets Forstlige Forsoeksstasjon [*A publication*]
**Medd Vestl Forstl Forsoeksstn** ... Meddelelser fra Vestlandets Forstlige Forsoeksstasjon [*A publication*]
**MEDDY**.... Mediterranean Eddy [*Oceanography*]
**MEDEA**.... Medecine [*A publication*]
**MEDEA**.... Multidiscipline Engineering Design, Evaluation, and Analysis (RDA)
**MEDEAST** ... Eastern Mediterranean Area [*NATO*] (NATG)
**Med Econ**... Medical Economics [*A publication*]
**Med Econ Surgeons** ... Medical Economics for Surgeons [*A publication*]
**Meded Alg Proefstn AVROS** ... Mededeelingen. Algemeen Proefstation der AVROS [*Algemeene Vereniging van Rubberplanters ter Oostkust van Sumatra*] [*A publication*]
**Meded Dir Tuinb** ... Mededelingen. Directeur van de Tuinbouw [*A publication*]
**Meded Fac Diergeneeskd Rijksuniv (Gent)** ... Mededelingen. Faculteit Diergeneeskunde Rijksuniversiteit (Gent) [*A publication*]
**Meded Fac Landbouwwet Rijksuniv (Gent)** ... Mededelingen. Faculteit Landbouwwetenschappen. Rijksuniversiteit (Gent) [*A publication*]
**Meded Fac LandWet (Gent)** ... Mededelingen. Faculteit Landbouwwetenschappen. Rijksuniversiteit (Gent) [*A publication*]
**Meded Geol Sticht** ... Mededelingen. Geologische Stichting [*A publication*]
**Meded Geol Sticht Nieuwe Ser (Neth)** ... Mededelingen. Geologische Stichting. Nieuwe Serie (Netherlands) [*A publication*]
**Meded Indones Inst Rubberonderz** ... Mededeelingen. Indonesisch Instituut voor Rubberonderzoek [*A publication*]
**Meded Ins Ratio Suikerprod** ... Mededelingen. Instituut voor Rationele Suikerproductie [*A publication*]
**Meded Inst Biol Scheik Onderz LandbGewass** ... Mededelingen. Instituut voor Biologisch en Scheikundig Onderzoek van Landbouwgewassen [*A publication*]
**Meded Inst Biol Scheik Onderz Landbougewassen (Wageningen)** ... Mededelingen. Instituut voor Biologisch en Scheikundig Onderzoek van Landbouwgewassen (Wageningen) [*A publication*]
**Meded Inst Graan Meel Brood TNO (Wageningen)** ... Mededeling. Instituut voor Graan. Meel en Brood TNO [*Toegepast Natuurwetenschappelijk Onderzoek*] (Wageningen) [*A publication*]
**Meded Inst Mod Veevoeding De Schothorst Hoogland Amersfoorst** ... Mededeling. Instituut voor Moderne Veevoeding "De Schothorst" te Hoogland bij Amersfoorst [*A publication*]
**Meded Inst Ration Suikerprod** ... Mededelingen. Instituut voor Rationele Suikerproductie [*A publication*]
**Meded Inst Rat Suik Prod** ... Mededelingen. Instituut voor Rationele Suikerproductie [*A publication*]
**Meded Inst Toegep Biol Onderz Nat** ... Mededelingen. Instituut voor Toegepast Biologisch Onderzoek in der Natuur [*A publication*]
**Meded K Acad Wet Lett en Schone Kunsten Belg** ... Mededelingen. Koninklijke Academie voor Wetenschappen. Letteren en Schone Kunsten van Belgie [*A publication*]
**Meded K Acad Wet Lett Schone Kunsten Belg Kl Wet** ... Mededelingen. Koninklijke Academie voor Wetenschappen. Letteren en Schone Kunsten van Belgie. Klasse der Wetenschappen [*A publication*]
**Meded Kon Nederl Ak Wetensch** ... Mededeelingen. Koninklijke Nederlandsche Akademie van Wetenschappen [*A publication*]
**Meded Kon Vl Ak Wetensch** ... Mededeelingen. Koninklijke Vlaamse Akademie van Wetenschappen [*A publication*]
**Meded K Vlaam Acad Wet Lett Schone Kunsten Belg Kl Wet** ... Mededelingen. Koninklijke Vlaamse Academie voor Wetenschappen. Letteren en Schone Kunsten van Belgie. Klasse der Wetenschappen [*A publication*]
**Meded Lab Houttechnol Rijkslandbouwhogesch (Gent)** ... Mededelingen. Laboratorium voor Houttechnologie. Rijkslandbouwhogeschool (Gent) [*A publication*]
**Meded Lab Physiol Chem Univ Amsterdam** ... Mededelingen. Laboratorium voor Physiologische Chemie. Universiteit van Amsterdam [*A publication*]
**Meded Lab Physiol Chem Univ Amsterdam Ned Inst Volksvoed** ... Mededelingen. Laboratorium voor Physiologische Chemie. Universiteit van Amsterdam et Nederlands Instituut voor Volksvoeding [*A publication*]
**Meded Lab Scheikd Onderz Buitenzorg** ... Mededeeling. Laboratorium voor Scheikundig Onderzoek te Buitenzorg [*A publication*]
**Meded LandbHogesch OpzoekStns Gent** ... Mededelingen. Landbouwhogeschool en Opzoekingsstations van de Staat te Gent [*A publication*]
**Meded Landbhogesch Wageningen** ... Mededelingen. Landbouwhogeschool te Wageningen [*A publication*]
**Meded Landbouwhogesch (Ghent)** ... Mededelingen. Landbouwhogeschool (Ghent) [*A publication*]
**Meded Landbouwhogesch Opzoekingssta (Ghent)** ... Mededelingen. Landbouwhogeschool en Opzoekingsstations (Ghent) [*A publication*]
**Meded Landbouwhogesch Opzoekingsstn Staat Gent** ... Mededelingen. Landbouwhogeschool en Opzoekingsstations van de Staat te Gent [*A publication*]
**Meded Landbouwhogesch Wageningen** ... Mededelingen. Landbouwhogeschool te Wageningen [*A publication*]
**Meded LandProefstn Suriname** ... Mededelingen. Landbouwproefstation in Suriname [*A publication*]
**Meded Lederinst TNO** ... Mededelingen. Lederinstituut TNO [*Toegepast Natuurwetenschappelijk Onderzoek*] [*A publication*]
**Meded L Vlaam Acad Wet Belg Kl Wet** ... Mededelingen. Koninklijke Vlaamse Academie voor Wetenschappen. Letteren en Schone Kunsten van Belgie. Klasse der Wetenschappen [*A publication*]
**Meded Nat Coop Aan- Verkoopver Landbouw Cen Bur** ... Mededelingen. Nationale Cooperatieve Aan- en Verkoopvereniging voor de Landbouw Central Bureau [*A publication*]
**Meded Ned Vacuumver** ... Mededelingenblad. Nederlandse Vacuumvereniging [*A publication*]
**Meded Ned Ver Koeltech** ... Mededelingen. Nederlande Vereniging voor Koeltechniek [*A publication*]
**Meded Proefstn Akker- en Weideb** ... Mededelingen. Proefstation voor de Akker- en Weidebouw [*A publication*]
**Meded Proefstn Groenteteelt Vollegrond Ned** ... Mededeling. Proefstation voor de Groenteteelt in de Vollegrond in Nederland [*A publication*]
**MEd(Ed/Psych)** ... Master of Education (Educational Psychology), University of Birmingham [*British*] (DBQ)
**Meded Rijksfac Landbouwwet Gent** ... Mededelingen. Rijksfaculteit Landbouwwetenschappen te Gent [*A publication*]
**Meded Rijks Geol Dienst** ... Mededelingen. Rijks Geologische Dienst [*A publication*]

**Meded Rijks Geol Dienst Nieuwe Ser (Neth)** ... Mededelingen. Rijks Geologische Dienst. Nieuwe Serie (Netherlands) [*A publication*]
**Meded Rijks Inst Pharm Ther Onderz** ... Mededelingen. Rijks Instituut voor Pharmaco-Therapeutisch Onderzoek [*A publication*]
**Meded Rijksproefstat Zaadcontr (Wageningen)** ... Mededeling. Rijksproefstation voor Zaadcontrole (Wageningen) [*A publication*]
**Meded Rom** ... Mededelingen van het Nederlands Historisch Instituut te Rome [*A publication*]
**Meded Rubber-Sticht (Delft)** ... Mededelingen. Rubber-Stichting (Delft) [*A publication*]
**Meded Stichting Nederl Graan-Cent** ... Mededeling. Stichting Nederlands Graan-Centrum [*A publication*]
**Meded Stichting Plantenveredeling (Wageningen)** ... Mededelingen. Stichting voor Plantenveredeling (Wageningen) [*A publication*]
**Med Educ**... Medical Education [*A publication*]
**Med Educ (Oxf)** ... Medical Education (Oxford) [*A publication*]
**Meded Veeartsenijsch Rijksuniv Gent** ... Mededelingen. Veeartsenijschool. Rijksuniversiteit te Gent [*A publication*]
**Meded Vezelinst TNO** ... Mededeling. Vezelinstituut TNO [*Toegepast Natuurwetenschappelijk Onderzoek*] [*A publication*]
**Meded Vlaam Chem Ver** ... Mededelingen. Vlaamse Chemische Vereniging [*A publication*]
**Meded Vl Topon Ver** ... Mededeelingen Uitgegeven. Vlaamse Toponymische Vereniging [*A publication*]
**Meded Zittingen K Acad Overzeese Wet (Brussels)** ... Mededelingen der Zittingen. Koninklijke Academie voor Overzeese Wetenschappen (Brussels) [*A publication*]
**Meded Zuid-Nederl Dial Centr** ... Mededeelingen. Zuid-Nederlandsche Dialect Centrale [*A publication*]
**Med Elec**.... Medical Electronics [*A publication*]
**Med Elec**.... Medical Electronics and Data [*A publication*]
**Med Electron** ... Medical Electronics [*A publication*]
**Med Electron Biol Eng** ... Medical Electronics and Biological Engineering [*A publication*]
**Med Electron Data** ... Medical Electronics and Data [*A publication*]
**Medelhavs Mus B** ... Medelhavsmuseet Bulletin [*Stockholm*] [*A publication*]
**MEDEMG** ... Medical Emergencies [*Computerized management course*]
**Med Era (St Louis)** ... Medical Era (St. Louis) [*A publication*]
**Med Ernaehr** ... Medizin und Ernaehrung [*A publication*]
**Med Esp**..... Medicina Espanola [*A publication*]
**Med Esporte** ... Medicina do Esporte [*A publication*]
**Med Essays and Obs (Edinb)** ... Medical Essays and Observations (Edinburgh) [*A publication*]
**MEDEVAC** ... Medical Evacuation Team [*Army*]
**MEDEVAL** ... Medical Evaluation [*Military*] (AABC)
**MEDEX**..... Medecin Extension [*Doctors' Aides, or Medics*] [*French*]
**Med Exp**.... Medicina Experimentalis [*A publication*]
**Med Exp Int J Exp Med** ... Medicina Experimentalis. International Journal of Experimental Medicine [*A publication*]
**MEDF** ....... Maximum Energy Distribution Function
**Med Fis Rehabil** ... Medicina Fisica y Rehabilitacion [*A publication*]
**MEDFLY**.. Mediterranean Fruit Fly
**Med Fr**....... Medecin de France [*A publication*]
**MEDG**....... Medco Group, Inc. [*New York, NY*] [*NASDAQ symbol*] (NQ)
**Med Geriatr** ... Medicina Geriatrica [*A publication*]
**Med Ges**..... Medizin und Gesellschaft [*A publication*]
**Med Glas**... Medicinski Glasnik [*A publication*]
**Med Group Manage** ... Medical Group Management [*A publication*]
**Med Group News** ... Medical Group News [*A publication*]
**Med Grundlagenforsch** ... Medizinische Grundlagenforschung [*A publication*]
**Med Gynaecol Androl Sociol** ... Medical Gynaecology, Andrology, and Sociology [*A publication*]
**Med Gynaecol Sociol** ... Medical Gynaecology and Sociology [*A publication*]
**MEDH**....... Maintainability Engineering Design Handbook
**Med Hist**.... Medical History [*A publication*]
**Med Hist Suppl** ... Medical History. Supplement [*A publication*]
**Med Hoje**... Medicina de Hoje [*A publication*]
**Med Hum**... Mediaevalia et Humanistica [*A publication*]
**Med et Hum** ... Mediaevalia et Humanistica [*A publication*]
**Med Hyg**.... Medecine et Hygiene [*A publication*]
**Med Hyg (Geneve)** ... Medecine et Hygiene (Geneve) [*A publication*]
**Med Hypnoanal** ... Medical Hypnoanalysis [*A publication*]
**Med Hypotheses** ... Medical Hypotheses [*A publication*]
**MEDI** ........ Marine Environmental Data Information Referral System [*UNESCO*] [*Paris, France*]
**MEDI** ........ Media Horizons, Inc. [*NASDAQ symbol*] (NQ)
**MEDI** ........ Medicine (DSUE)
**MEDI** ........ Moessbauer Effect Data Index
**MEDIA** ..... Magnavox Electronic Data Image Apparatus
**MEDIA** ..... Manufacturers Educational Drug Information Association
**Media**......... Mediafile [*A publication*]
**MEDIA** ..... Missile Era Data Integration Analysis
**MEDIA** ..... Move to End Deception in Advertising [*Student legal action organization*]
**Media, C & S** ... Media, Culture, and Society [*United Kingdom*] [*A publication*]
**Media Culture Soc** ... Media, Culture, and Society [*A publication*]
**Media Eco** ... Media Ecology Review [*A publication*]
**Media in Educ Dev** ... Media in Education and Development [*A publication*]
**Media Educ and Dev** ... Media in Education and Development [*A publication*]
**Mediaev Philos Pol** ... Mediaevalia Philosophica Polonorum [*A publication*]
**Mediaev St** ... Mediaeval Studies [*A publication*]
**Mediaev Stud** ... Mediaeval Studies [*A publication*]
**Media Ind N** ... Media Industry Newsletter [*A publication*]
**Media Inf Aust** ... Media Information Australia [*A publication*] (APTA)
**Media L Notes** ... Media Law Notes [*A publication*]
**Media L & P** ... Media Law and Practice [*A publication*] (DLA)
**Media L Rep BNA** ... Media Law Reporter. Bureau of National Affairs [*A publication*]
**Media Per**.. Media Perspektiven [*A publication*]
**Media Rep** ... Media Reporter [*United Kingdom*] [*A publication*]
**Media Rev Dig** ... Media Review Digest [*A publication*]
**Media Rpt** ... Media Report to Women [*A publication*]
**MEDIC**...... Mechanized Design and Integrated Control
**Medic**......... Medicamina Faciei [*of Ovid*] [*Classical studies*] (OCD)
**MEDICAID** ... Medical Aid [*Federal program providing financial assistance for medical expenses of individual needy citizens*]
**Medical**...... Medical Self-Care [*A publication*]
**Medical J Aust** ... Medical Journal of Australia [*A publication*] (APTA)
**Medicamenta (Ed Farm)** ... Medicamenta (Edicion para el Farmaceutico) [*A publication*]
**MEDICARE** ... Medical Care [*Federal program providing financial assistance for medical expenses of individual senior citizens*]
**Medic Educ Brief** ... Medical Education Briefing [*A publication*]
**Medic Educ Newsl** ... Medical Education Newsletter [*A publication*]
**MEDICO** .. Medical International Cooperation
**MEDICO** .. Model Experiment in Drug Indexing by Computer [*Rutgers University*]
**Medicolegal Dig** ... Medicolegal Digest [*A publication*]
**Medico Legal J** ... Medico-Legal Journal [*A publication*]
**Medico-Legal Soc Proc** ... Medico-Legal Society. Proceedings [*A publication*] (APTA)
**Medico-Legal Soc VIC Proc** ... Medico-Legal Society of Victoria. Proceedings [*A publication*] (APTA)
**Medicoleg Libr** ... Medicolegal Library [*A publication*]
**Medicoleg News** ... Medicolegal News [*A publication*]
**MEDICOM** ... Medical Communications
**MEDICOR** ... Centre for Offshore and Remote Medicine [*Memorial University of Newfoundland*] [*Research center*] (RCD)
**MEDICOS** ... Mediterranean Instructions to Convoys [*World War II*]
**Medico Vet (Torino)** ... Il Medico Veterinario (Torino) [*A publication*]
**MEDICS** ... Medical Information Computer System (NASA)
**MEDICS** ... Michael E. DeBakey International Cardiovascular Society [*Later, MEDISS*] (EA)
**Medien**....... Medien und Erziehung [*A publication*]
**MEDIEV**... Medieval
**Mediev A** ... Medieval Archaeology [*A publication*]
**Medieval Arch** ... Medieval Archaeology [*A publication*]
**Medieval Archaeol** ... Medieval Archaeology [*A publication*]
**Medieval Ceram** ... Medieval Ceramics [*A publication*]
**Mediev et Hum** ... Mediaevalia et Humanistica [*A publication*]
**MEDIF**...... Medical Information Form [*British*]
**MEDIHC**.. Military Experience Directed into Health Careers [*DoD/HEW project*]
**Med Imaging** ... Medical Imaging [*A publication*]
**MEDINET** ... Medical Information Network [*GTE Telenet Communications Corp.*] [*Telecommunications*]
**Med Inf**...... Medecine et Informatique [*A publication*]
**Med Inf**...... Medical Informatics [*A publication*]
**Med Infant** ... Medecine Infantile [*A publication*]
**Med Inf (Lond)** ... Medecine et Informatique (London) [*A publication*]
**MEDINFO** ... Medical Informatics
**Med Inform Statist** ... Medizinische Informatik und Statistik [*A publication*]
**MEDINSP** ... Medical Inspection [*Military*] (NVT)
**Med Instrum** ... Medical Instrumentation [*A publication*]
**Med Instrum (Arlington)** ... Medical Instrumentation (Arlington, VA) [*A publication*]
**MEDINT**... Medical Intelligence (MCD)
**Med Int**...... Medicine International [*Great Britain*] [*A publication*]
**Med Interna** ... Medicina Interna [*A publication*]
**Med Interna (Buchar)** ... Medicina Interna (Bucharest) [*A publication*]
**Med Interne** ... Medecine Interne [*A publication*]
**MEDIOC**.. Mediocris [*Middling*] [*Pharmacy*] (ROG)
**MEDIOL**... Mediolanum [*Milan*] [*Imprint*] (ROG)
**MEDIPHOR** ... Monitoring and Evaluation of Drug Interactions in a Pharmacy-Oriented Reporting System [*National Center for Health Services Research*] (DHSM)
**MEDIPP** ... Medical District Initiated Program Planning [*Veterans Administration*]
**MEDI-SOTA LIBR** ... Medi-Sota Library Consortium [*Library network*]
**MEDISS**.... Michael E. DeBakey International Surgical Society (EA)
**MEDISTAT** ... Banque de Donnees Socio-Economiques des Pays Mediterraneens [*Socioeconomic Data Bank on the Mediterranean Countries*] [*International Center for Advanced Mediterranean Agronomic Studies*] [*Information service or system*] (IID)
**Med Istraz** ... Medicinska Istrazivanja [*A publication*]
**Med Istraz Suppl** ... Medicinska Istrazivanja. Supplementum [*A publication*]
**MEDIT**...... Mediterranean
**Medit**......... Mediterraneo [*A publication*]

**MEDITEC** ... Dodumentation Medizinische Technik [*Medical Technology Documentation*] [*TechnicalInformation Center*] [*Federal Republic of Germany*] [*Information service or system*] (IID)
**Mediterr Med** ... Mediterranee Medicale [*A publication*]
**Meditsin Referat Zh** ... Meditsinskii Referatinynyi Zhurnal [*A publication*]
**MEDIUM** ... Missile Era Data Integration - Ultimate Method
**Medium Aev** ... Medium Aevum [*A publication*]
**Medizinhist J** ... Medizinhistorisches Journal [*A publication*]
**M Ed J**....... Music Educators Journal [*A publication*]
**MEDJA**..... Music Educators Journal [*A publication*]
**Med J Armed Forces (India)** ... Medical Journal. Armed Forces (India) [*A publication*]
**Med J Aust** ... Medical Journal of Australia [*A publication*]
**Med J Austral** ... Medical Journal of Australia [*A publication*]
**Med J Aust Supp** ... Medical Journal of Australia. Supplement [*A publication*] (APTA)
**Med J Chulalongkorn Hosp Med Sch (Bangkok)** ... Medical Journal. Chulalongkorn Hospital Medical School (Bangkok) [*A publication*]
**Med J Commun** ... Medical Journal for Communication [*A publication*]
**Med J (Engl Transl Lijec Vjesn)** ... Medical Journal (English Translation of Lijecnicki Vjesnik) [*A publication*]
**Med J Fraternity Mem Hosp** ... Medical Journal. Fraternity Memorial Hospital [*A publication*]
**Med J Han-Il Hosp** ... Medical Journal. Han-Il Hospital [*A publication*]
**Med J Hiroshima Prefect Hosp** ... Medical Journal. Hiroshima Prefectural Hospital [*A publication*]
**Med J Hiroshima Univ** ... Medical Journal. Hiroshima University [*Japan*] [*A publication*]
**Med J Kagoshima Univ** ... Medical Journal. Kagoshima University [*A publication*]
**Med J Kobe Univ** ... Medical Journal. Kobe University [*A publication*]
**Med J Malaya** ... Medical Journal of Malaya [*Later, Medical Journal of Malaysia*] [*A publication*]
**Med J Malays** ... Medical Journal of Malaysia [*A publication*]
**Med J Malaysia** ... Medical Journal of Malaysia [*A publication*]
**Med J Minami Osaka Hosp** ... Medical Journal. Minami Osaka Hospital [*Japan*] [*A publication*]
**Med J Mutual Aid Assoc** ... Medical Journal. Mutual Aid Association [*Japan*] [*A publication*]
**Med J Osaka Univ** ... Medical Journal. Osaka University [*A publication*]
**Med J Osaka Univ (Engl Ed)** ... Medical Journal. Osaka University (English Edition) [*A publication*]
**Med J Osaka Univ (Jpn Ed)** ... Medical Journal. Osaka University (Japanese Edition) [*A publication*]
**Med J Shinshu Univ** ... Medical Journal. Shinshu University [*A publication*]
**Med J South West** ... Medical Journal. South West [*A publication*]
**MED JUR** ... Medical Jurisprudence (ADA)
**Med J Zambia** ... Medical Journal of Zambia [*A publication*]
**Med Klin**.... Medizinische Klinik [*A publication*]
**Med Klin (Berlin)** ... Medizinische Klinik (Berlin) [*A publication*]
**Med Klin (Muenchen)** ... Medizinische Klinik (Muenchen) [*A publication*]
**MEDL** ....... Marconi Electronic Devices Ltd. [*British*] (IRUK)
**MEDL** ....... Materials Evaluation and Development Laboratory [*General Services Administration*]
**MEDL** ....... Medical
**Med (L)**...... Medicina (Lisbon) [*A publication*]
**Med Lab** .... Medizinische Laboratorium [*West Germany*] [*A publication*]
**Med Lab Observer** ... Medical Laboratory Observer [*A publication*]
**Med Laboratory Advisory** ... Medical Laboratory Advisory Service [*A publication*]
**Med Lab Sci** ... Medical Laboratory Sciences [*A publication*]
**Med Lab (Stuttg)** ... Medizinische Laboratorium (Stuttgart) [*A publication*]
**Med Lab Tec** ... Medical Laboratory Technology [*A publication*]
**Med Lab Technol** ... Medical Laboratory Technology [*A publication*]
**Med Lab World** ... Medical Laboratory World [*A publication*]
**MEDLARS** ... Medical Literature Analysis and Retrieval System [*National Library of Medicine*] [*Bethesda, MD*] [*Database*]
**Med Lav**..... Medicina del Lavoro [*A publication*]
**Med & Law** ... Medicine and Law [*A publication*]
**Med Law**.... Medicine and Law [*A publication*]
**Med-Legal J** ... Medico-Legal Journal [*A publication*] (DLA)
**Med-Legal Soc'y Trans** ... Medico-Legal Society. Transactions [*A publication*] (DLA)
**Med Leg Assicur** ... Medicina Legale e delle Assicurazioni [*A publication*]
**Med Leg Bull** ... Medico-Legal Bulletin [*A publication*]
**Med-Leg Criminol Rev** ... Medico-Legal and Criminological Review [*A publication*]
**Med Leg & Crim Rev** ... Medico-Legal and Criminological Review [*A publication*]
**Med Leg Dommage Corpor** ... Medecine Legale et Dommage Corporel [*A publication*]
**Med Leg J** ... Medico-Legal Journal [*A publication*]
**Med-Leg J (London)** ... Medico-Legal Journal (London) [*A publication*]
**Med-Leg J (NY)** ... Medico-Legal Journal (New York) [*A publication*]
**Med Leg N** ... Medico-Legal News [*A publication*]
**Med Leg Pap** ... Medico-Legal Papers [*A publication*] (DLA)
**Med Leg Soc Trans** ... Transactions. Medico-Legal Society [*A publication*] (ILCA)
**Med Leg Vic Proc** ... Medico-Legal Society of Victoria. Proceedings [*A publication*]
**Medlemsbl Dan Dyrlaegeforen** ... Medlemsblad foer den Danske Dyrlaegeforening [*A publication*]
**Medlemsbl Nor Veterinaerforen** ... Medlemsblad den Norske Veterinaerforening [*A publication*]
**Med Lett Drugs Ther** ... Medical Letter on Drugs and Therapeutics [*A publication*]
**MEDLI**...... Motoring Experience for the Disabled by Lions International [*British*]
**Med Liability Advisory** ... Medical Liability Advisory Service [*A publication*]
**Med Liab R** ... Medical Liability Reporter [*A publication*]
**Med Lib Assn Bul** ... Medical Library Association. Bulletin [*A publication*]
**Med Lib Assn Bull** ... Medical Library Association. Bulletin [*A publication*]
**Med Libr**.... Medical Libraries [*A publication*]
**MEDLINE** ... MEDLARS [*Medical Literature Analysis and Retrieval System*] On-Line [*National Library of Medicine*] [*Bibliographic database*]
**MEDList** ... Master Enumeration District List [*Bureau of Census*]
**Med LJ** ...... Medico-Legal Journal [*A publication*]
**Med LN** ..... Medico-Legal News [*A publication*] (DLA)
**MEDLOC** ... Mediterranean Location [*Navy*]
**Med L & P** ... Media Law and Practice [*1980*] [*A publication*] (DLA)
**Med LP**...... Medico-Legal Papers [*A publication*] (DLA)
**Med L & Pub Pol** ... Medicine, Law, and Public Policy [*A publication*] (DLA)
**M Ed LS**.... Master of Education in Library Science
**MEDM**...... Med-Mobile, Inc. [*Newark, NJ*] [*NASDAQ symbol*] (NQ)
**MEDMAL** ... Medical Malpractice Lawsuit Filings [*Medical Malpractice Verdicts, Settlements & Experts*] [*Information service or system*] (CRD)
**Med Malpract Cost Containment J** ... Medical Malpractice Cost Containment Journal [*A publication*]
**Med Market Media** ... Medical Marketing and Media [*A publication*]
**Med Mark Media** ... Medical Marketing and Media [*A publication*]
**Med Markt** ... Medical Marketing and Media [*A publication*]
**Med Markt Acta Medicotech** ... Medizinal-Markt/Acta Medicotechnica [*A publication*]
**MEd(Maths)** ... Master of Education (Mathematics)
**MEDMATS** ... Medical Matericl Management System [*Army*]
**MED Media Educ and Dev** ... MED. Media in Education and Development [*A publication*]
**Med Meetings** ... Medical Meetings [*A publication*]
**MEDMER** ... Medical Emergency Report [*Air Force*]
**Med Microbi** ... Medical Microbiology and Immunology [*A publication*]
**Med Microbiol Immunol** ... Medical Microbiology and Immunology [*A publication*]
**Med Midway** ... Medicine on the Midway [*A publication*]
**MEDMIS**.. Medical Management Information System [*Army*]
**Med Mkt** ... Medical Marketing and Media [*A publication*]
**Med Mod**... Medicina Moderna [*A publication*]
**Med Mod Can** ... Medecine Moderne du Canada [*A publication*]
**Med Mod (Paris)** ... Medecine Moderne (Paris) [*A publication*]
**Med Monatsschr** ... Medizinische Monatsschrift [*A publication*]
**Med Monatsschr Pharm** ... Medizinische Monatsschrift fuer Pharmazeuten [*A publication*]
**Med Monatssp** ... Medizinischer Monatsspiegel [*A publication*]
**Med Monde** ... Medecine dans le Monde [*A publication*]
**Med Morale** ... Medicina e Morale [*A publication*]
**Med Mysl Uzbekistana** ... Meditsinskaia Mysl Uzbekistana [*A publication*]
**Medna Esp** ... Medicina Espanola [*A publication*]
**Med Naturwiss Arch** ... Medizinisch-Naturwissenschaftliches Archiv [*A publication*]
**Med Ned Ver Int R** ... Mededelingen van de Nederlandse Vereniging voor Internationaal Recht [*A publication*]
**Med News** ... Medical News [*A publication*]
**MEDNOREAST** ... Northeast Mediterranean Area [*NATO*] (NATG)
**MEDNTPS** ... Mediterranean Near-Term Prepositioned Ship
**Med Nucl**... Medecine Nucleaire [*A publication*]
**Med Nucl Radiobiol Lat** ... Medicina Nucleare. Radiobiologica Latina [*A publication*]
**Med Nucl Radiobiol Lat Suppl** ... Medicina Nucleare. Radiobiologica Latina. Supplement [*Italy*] [*A publication*]
**Med Nutr**... Medecine et Nutrition [*A publication*]
**MEDO**....... Middle East Defense Organization (NATG)
**MEDO**....... Multipole Expansion of Diatomic Overlap [*Physics*]
**Med Obozr** ... Meditsinskoe Obozrienio Sprimona [*A publication*]
**MEDOC**.... Medical Documents [*Eccles Health Sciences Library - University of Utah*] [*Salt Lake City, UT*] [*Bibliographic database*]
**MEDOC**.... Mediterranean Oceanographic Project [*1969*]
**MEDOC**.... Western Mediterranean Area [*NATO*] (NATG)
**MEDOCHAN** ... Mary Ellen, Dorothy, Chuck, Ann [*Famous Canadian resort, named for the owners' children*]
**MEDOFCOM** ... Medical Officer-in-Command [*Military*]
**Med Officer** ... Medical Officer [*England*] [*A publication*]
**MEDOL** .... Medically Oriented Language
**Med Oncol Tumor Pharmacother** ... Medical Oncology and Tumor Pharmacotherapy [*A publication*]
**Med Opin Rev** ... Medical Opinion and Review [*A publication*]
**Med (P)**...... Medicina (Parma) [*A publication*]
**MEDP** ....... Medium Port

**Med Paedagog Jugendkd** ... Medizinische und Paedagogische Jugendkunde [*A publication*]
**Med Paises Calidos** ... Medicina de los Paises Calidos [*A publication*]
**Med Parazitol** ... Meditsinskaya Parazitologiya i Parazitarnye Bolezni [*A publication*]
**Med Parazitol Parazit Bolezni** ... Meditsinskaya Parazitologiya i Parazitarnye Bolezni [*A publication*]
**Med Pediatr Oncol** ... Medical and Pediatric Oncology [*A publication*]
**Med Pediatr Oncol Suppl** ... Medical and Pediatric Oncology. Supplement [*A publication*]
**Med Pharmacol Exp** ... Medicina et Pharmacologia Experimentalis [*A publication*]
**Med Pharmacol Exp Int J Exp Med** ... Medicina et Pharmacologia Experimentalis. International Journal of Experimental Medicine [*A publication*]
**Med and Phil Comment** ... Medical and Philosophical Commentaries [*A publication*]
**Med Phys**... Medical Physics [*A publication*]
**Med Phys Handb** ... Medical Physics Handbooks [*A publication*]
**Med Phys J** ... Medical and Physical Journal [*A publication*]
**Med Podmladak** ... Medicinski Podmladak [*A publication*]
**Med Post**.... Medical Post [*Canada*] [*A publication*]
**Med Pr**....... Medycyna Pracy [*A publication*]
**Med Prat**.... Medecine Praticienne [*A publication*]
**Med Prat (Napoli)** ... Medicina Pratica (Napoli) [*A publication*]
**Med Pregl**.. Medicinski Pregled [*A publication*]
**Med Press** ... Medical Press [*A publication*]
**Med Press and Circ** ... Medical Press and Circular [*A publication*]
**Med Prisma** ... Medizinische Prisma [*A publication*]
**Med Probl** ... Medicinski Problemi [*Bulgaria*] [*A publication*]
**Med Probl Performing Artists** ... Medical Problems of Performing Artists [*A publication*]
**Med Proc** ... Medical Proceedings [*A publication*]
**Med Prod Sales** ... Medical Products Sales [*A publication*]
**Med Prod Salesman** ... Medical Products Salesman [*A publication*]
**Med Prog Technol** ... Medical Progress through Technology [*A publication*]
**Med Prom-St SSSR** ... Meditsinskaya Promyshlennost SSSR [*A publication*]
**Med Pr Tech** ... Medical Progress through Technology [*A publication*]
**Med Psicosom** ... Medicina Psicosomatica [*A publication*]
**MEdPsych** ... Master of Educational Psychology (ADA)
**Med Q Indiana Univ Sch Med** ... Medical Quarterly. Indiana University. School of Medicine [*A publication*]
**MEDR**....... Medco Research, Inc. [*Los Angeles, CA*] [*NASDAQ symbol*] (NQ)
**Med R**........ Medioevo Romanzo [*A publication*]
**MedR**......... Mediterranean Review [*A publication*]
**Med Radiogr Photogr** ... Medical Radiography and Photography [*A publication*]
**Med Radiol** ... Meditsinskaya Radiologiya [*A publication*]
**Med Radiol (Mosk)** ... Meditsinskaia Radiologiia (Moskva) [*A publication*]
**Med Radiol (USSR)** ... Medical Radiology (USSR) [*A publication*]
**Med Razgledi** ... Medicinski Razgledi [*A publication*]
**Med Rec**..... Medical Record [*A publication*]
**Med Rec Ann** ... Medical Record and Annals [*A publication*]
**Med Rec Health Care Inf J** ... Medical Record and Health Care Information Journal [*A publication*]
**Med Rec Mississippi** ... Medical Record of Mississippi [*A publication*]
**Med Rec News** ... Medical Record News [*A publication*]
**Med Rec (NY)** ... Medical Record (New York) [*A publication*]
**MEDRED** ... Medical Unit Readiness Report [*Air Force*]
**Med Ref Serv Q** ... Medical Reference Services Quarterly [*A publication*]
**Med Ren** .... Mediaeval and Renaissance Studies [*A publication*]
**Med Rep Charles Univ Med Fac Hradec Kralove** ... Medical Reports. Charles University Medical Faculty at Hradec Kralove [*A publication*]
**Med Reposit** ... Medical Repository [*A publication*]
**Med Res Bull Repat Dept** ... Repatriation Department. Medical Research Bulletin [*Australia*] [*A publication*] (APTA)
**Med Res Cent (Nairobi) Annu Rep** ... Medical Research Centre (Nairobi). Annual Report [*A publication*]
**Med Res Counc (GB) Annu Rep** ... Medical Research Council (Great Britain). Annual Report [*A publication*]
**Med Res Counc (GB) Ind Health Res Board Rep** ... Medical Research Council (Great Britain). Industrial Health Research Board Report [*A publication*]
**Med Res Counc (GB) Lab Anim Cent Man Ser** ... Medical Research Council (Great Britain). Laboratory Animals Centre. Manual Series [*A publication*]
**Med Res Counc (GB) Lab Anim Cent Symp** ... Medical Research Council (Great Britain). Laboratory Animals Centre. Symposia [*A publication*]
**Med Res Counc (GB) Memo** ... Medical Research Council (Great Britain). Memorandum [*A publication*]
**Med Res Counc (GB) Monit Rep** ... Medical Research Council (Great Britain). Monitoring Report [*A publication*]
**Med Res Counc (GB) Spec Rep Ser** ... Medical Research Council (Great Britain). Special Report Series [*A publication*]
**Med Res Eng** ... Medical Research Engineering [*A publication*]
**Med Res Inst Tokyo Med Dent Univ Annu Rep** ... Medical Research Institute. Tokyo Medical and Dental University. Annual Report [*A publication*]
**Med Res Photosensit Dyes** ... Medical Researches for Photosensitizing Dyes [*A publication*]
**Med Res Proj** ... Medical Research Projects [*A publication*]
**Med Res Rev** ... Medicinal Research Reviews [*A publication*]
**Med Res Ser Monogr** ... Medicinal Research: A Series of Monographs [*A publication*]
**MEDRETES** ... Medical Readiness Training Exercises [*Army*]
**Med Rev (Belgr)** ... Medicinska Revija (Belgrade) [*A publication*]
**Med Rev CARL** ... Medicina. Revista do CARL [*Centro Academico Rocha Lima*] [*A publication*]
**Med Rev Cent Acad Rocha Lima (Sao Paulo)** ... Medicina. Revista do Centro Academico Rocha Lima [*CARL*] (Sao Paulo) [*A publication*]
**Med Rev Mex** ... Medicina Revista Mexicana [*A publication*]
**MEDREX** ... Medical Readiness Exercise (MCD)
**medRNA**.... Ribonucleic Acid, Mini-Exon-Derived [*Biochemistry, genetics*]
**MedRom**.... Medioevo Romanzo [*A publication*]
**MEDS**........ Marine Environmental Data Service [*Canada*] (NOAA)
**MEDS**........ Mechanized Embarkation Data System [*Military*] (NVT)
**MedS**......... Mediaeval Studies [*A publication*]
**MEDS**........ Medical Electronics and Data Society [*Later, MES*] (EA)
**MEDS**........ Medical Evaluation Data System (IEEE)
**MedS**......... Medical Socioeconomic Research Sources. American Medical Association [*A publication*]
**Meds**.......... Medications [*or Medicines*]
**Med (S)**...... Medizinische (Stuttgart) [*A publication*]
**MEDSAC** ... Medical Service Activity [*Army*] (AABC)
**MEDSARS** ... Maintenance Engineering Data Storage and Retrieval System (NG)
**Med Sc D**... Doctor of Medical Science [*or the Science of Medicine*]
**MEDSCH** ... Medical School (ADA)
**Medsche Klin (Muenchen)** ... Medizinische Klinik (Muenchen) [*A publication*]
**Medsche Mschr (Stuttg)** ... Medizinische Monatsschrift (Stuttgart) [*A publication*]
**Medsche Welt (Stuttg)** ... Medizinische Welt (Stuttgart) [*A publication*]
**Med Schl**... Medical School Rounds [*A publication*]
**MedSch(N)** ... Institute of Naval Medicine [*British*]
**Med Sci**...... Medical Science [*A publication*]
**Med Sci & L** ... Medicine, Science, and the Law [*A publication*]
**Med Sci Law** ... Medicine, Science, and the Law [*A publication*]
**Med and Sci Sport** ... Medicine and Science in Sports and Exercise [*A publication*]
**Med Sci Sports** ... Medicine and Science in Sports [*A publication*]
**Med Sci Sports Exerc** ... Medicine and Science in Sports and Exercise [*A publication*]
**Med Sci Spt** ... Medicine and Science in Sports [*A publication*]
**Med Segur Trab (Madr)** ... Medicina y Seguridad del Trabajo (Madrid) [*A publication*]
**Med Serv** ... Medical Service [*A publication*]
**MEDSERVC** ... Medical Service Corps [*Military*]
**Med Services J (Canada)** ... Medical Services Journal (Canada) [*A publication*]
**Med Serv J (Can)** ... Medical Service Journal (Canada) [*A publication*]
**MEDSERWRNT** ... Medical Service Warrant
**Med Sestra** ... Meditsinskaya Sestra [*A publication*]
**Medskaya Parazit** ... Meditsinskaya Parazitologiya i Parazitarnye Bolezni [*A publication*]
**MEDSOC** ... Medical Socioeconomic Research Sources. American Medical Association [*A publication*]
**Med Soc PA Tr** ... Medical Society of the State of Pennsylvania. Transactions [*A publication*]
**Med Soc (Turin)** ... Medicina Sociale (Turin) [*A publication*]
**MEDSOM** ... Medical Supply, Optical, and Maintenance [*Army*] (RDA)
**MEDSOUEAST** ... Southeast Mediterranean Area [*NATO*] (NATG)
**MEDSPECC** ... Medical Specialist Corps [*Military*]
**MEd(SpecEd)** ... Master of Education (Special Education)
**MEd(SpEd)** ... Master of Education in Special Education (ADA)
**Med Sper** ... Medicina Sperimentale [*A publication*]
**Med Sper Arch Ital** ... Medicina Sperimentale. Archivio Italiano [*A publication*]
**Med Sport** ... Medecine du Sport [*A publication*]
**Med Sport (Basel)** ... Medicine and Sport (Basel) [*A publication*]
**Med Sport (Berl)** ... Medizin und Sport (Berlin) [*A publication*]
**Med Sport (Berlin)** ... Medizin und Sport (Berlin) [*A publication*]
**Med Sport (Paris)** ... Medecine du Sport (Paris) [*A publication*]
**Med Sport Sci** ... Medicine and Sport Science [*A publication*]
**Med Sport (Turin)** ... Medicina dello Sport (Turin) [*A publication*]
**MEDSS**..... Multiple Echelon Direct Support System (MCD)
**MEdSt**...... Master of Educational Studies (ADA)
**Med St**....... Mediaeval Studies [*A publication*]
**MEDSTAR** ... Medical Staffing and Training to Augment Readiness (MCD)
**MEDSTOC** ... Medical Stock Control System [*Army*]
**Med Strucni Cas Zlh Podruznica Rijeka** ... Medicina Strucni Casopis Zlh Podruznica Rijeka [*A publication*]
**MEdStud** ... Master of Educational Studies
**MEDSUPDEP** ... Medical Supply Depot
**Med Surg** ... Medicine and Surgery [*A publication*]
**Med and Surg Monit** ... Medical and Surgical Monitor [*A publication*]
**MEDT**....... Mean Elapsed Downtime [*Data processing*] (MCD)
**MEDT**....... Medical 21 Corp. [*NASDAQ symbol*] (NQ)

**MEDT** ....... Military Equipment Delivery Team
**Med Teach** ... Medical Teacher [*A publication*]
**Med Tech**... Medizinische Technik [*West Germany*] [*A publication*]
**Med Tech Bull** ... Medical Technicians Bulletin [*A publication*]
**Med Technol Aust** ... Medical Technology in Australasia [*A publication*] (APTA)
**Med Technol Aust** ... Medical Technology in Australia [*A publication*]
**Med Technol Ser** ... Medical Technology Series [*A publication*]
**Med Tech Publ Co Int Rev Sci Biochem** ... Medical and Technical Publishing Company. International Review of Science. Biochemistry [*A publication*]
**Med Tekh** .. Meditsinskaya Tekhnika [*A publication*]
**Med Thorac** ... Medicina Thoracalis [*A publication*]
**Med Times** ... Medical Times [*A publication*]
**Med Times and Gaz (London)** ... Medical Times and Gazette (London) [*A publication*]
**Med Times (London)** ... Medical Times (London) [*A publication*]
**Med Times (NY)** ... Medical Times (New York) [*A publication*]
**Med Toxicol** ... Medical Toxicology [*A publication*]
**Med Tradic** ... Medicina Tradicionale [*A publication*]
**Med Treat (Tokyo)** ... Medical Treatment (Tokyo) [*A publication*]
**Med Trial Technique Q** ... Medical Trial Technique Quarterly [*A publication*]
**Med Trial Tech Q** ... Medical Trial Technique Quarterly [*A publication*]
**Med Trib**.... Medical Tribune [*A publication*]
**Med Trop**... Medecine Tropicale [*A publication*]
**Med Trop (Madr)** ... Medicina Tropical (Madrid) [*A publication*]
**Med Trop (Mars)** ... Medecine Tropicale (Marseilles) [*A publication*]
**Med Tr TQ** ... Medical Trial Technique Quarterly [*A publication*]
**M Educators J** ... Music Educators Journal [*A publication*]
**MEDUD2** ... Medical Education [*Oxford*] [*A publication*]
**Med Ultrasound** ... Medical Ultrasound [*A publication*]
**Med Univers** ... Medicina Universal [*A publication*]
**Medun Probl** ... Medunarodni Problemi [*A publication*]
**Med Unserer Zeit** ... Medizin in Unserer Zeit [*A publication*]
**MEDUSA** ... Multiple Element Directional Universally Steerable Antenna
**Med Utilization Rev** ... Medical Utilization Review [*A publication*]
**Med VBN** .. Mededelingen van het Verbond der Belgische Nijverheid [*A publication*]
**Med Versuche u Bemerk (Edinb)** ... Medizinischen Versuche und Bemerkungen (Edinburgh) [*A publication*]
**Med Vet Hell** ... Medecine Veterinaire Hellenique [*A publication*]
**Med Vet Que** ... Medecin Veterinaire du Quebec [*A publication*]
**Med Vjesnik** ... Medicinski Vjesnik [*A publication*]
**Med War**.... Medicine and War [*A publication*]
**Med Welt**... Medizinische Welt [*A publication*]
**Med Weter** ... Medycyna Weterynaryjna [*A publication*]
**Med World** ... Medical World News [*A publication*]
**Med World News** ... Medical World News [*A publication*]
**MEDX** ....... Medivix, Inc. [*NASDAQ symbol*] (NQ)
**MEDY** ....... Medical Dynamics, Inc. [*NASDAQ symbol*] (NQ)
**Medycyna Wet** ... Medycyna Weterynaryjna [*A publication*]
**Med Zh Uzb** ... Meditsinskii Zhurnal Uzbekistana [*A publication*]
**Med Ztg**..... Medizinische Zeitung [*A publication*]
**Med Ztg Russlands** ... Medizinische Zeitung. Russlands [*A publication*]
**MEE** .......... Maine Office of Energy Resources Library, Augusta, ME [*OCLC symbol*] (OCLC)
**MEE** .......... Maintenance Engineering Evaluation (MCD)
**MEE** .......... Mare [*Loyalty Islands*] [*Airport symbol*] (OAG)
**MEE** .......... Mass Energy Equivalent
**MEE** .......... Master of Electrical Engineering
**MEE** .......... Mechanical, Electrical, and Electronic (MCD)
**MEE** .......... Mechanical Evaluation Equipment
**MEE** .......... Meerut [*India*] [*Seismograph station code, US Geological Survey*] [*Closed*] (SEIS)
**MEE** .......... Methyl Ethyl Ether [*Organic chemistry*]
**MEE** .......... Middle Ear Effusion [*Medicine*]
**MEE** .......... Middle East Economist [*Cairo*] [*A publication*]
**MEE** .......... Middle East Executive Reports [*A publication*]
**MEE** .......... Military Essential Equipment (CINC)
**MEE** .......... Minimum Essential Equipment
**MEE** .......... Mission Essential Equipment [*NASA*] (KSC)
**MEE** .......... Muskogee, OK [*Location identifier*] [*FAA*] (FAAL)
**MEECN** .... Minimum Essential Emergency Communications Network [*Military*]
**ME Eco Hbk** ... Middle East Economic Handbook [*A publication*]
**MEED** ....... Microbial Ecology Evaluation Device [*NASA*] (KSC)
**MEED** ....... Middle East Economic Digest [*London*] [*A publication*]
**ME-EE** ...... Mechanical Engineer and Electrical Engineer [*Academic degree*]
**MEEF**........ Mobile Equipment Employment File [*Air Force*] (AFM)
**MEEL**........ Mission Equipment Essentiality List
**MeEl**.......... William Fogg Memorial Library, Eliot, ME [*Library symbol*] [*Library of Congress*] (LCLS)
**ME(Elec)**... Master of Engineering (Electrical) (ADA)
**ME Eng** ..... Master of Electrical Engineering
**MEEP**........ Management and Equipment Evaluation Program
**MEEP**........ Middle East Economic Papers [*A publication*]
**MEEPA**..... Methods of Experimental Physics [*A publication*]
**MEER**........ Mechanical/Electrical Equipment Room (MCD)
**Meerestech Mar Tech** ... Meerestechnik/Marine Technology [*A publication*]
**Meerestechnik Mar Technol** ... Meerestechnik/Marine Technology [*A publication*]
**MEERS**..... Maximum Effective Echo Ranging Speed (NVT)
**MEES**........ Middle East Economic Survey [*A publication*]
**MEES**........ Multipurpose Electromagnetic Environment Simulator (MCD)
**Mees & Ros** ... Meeson and Roscoe's English Exchequer Reports [*A publication*] (DLA)
**Mees & W** ... Meeson and Welsby's English Exchequer Reports [*A publication*] (DLA)
**Mees & Wels** ... Meeson and Welsby's English Exchequer Reports [*A publication*] (DLA)
**MEET**........ Minimum Essential Equipment for Training
**MEETA**..... Maximum Improvement in Electronics Effectiveness through Advanced Techniques
**MEETAT**.. Maximum Improvement in Electronics Effectiveness through Advanced Techniques
**Meeting Nw** ... Meeting News [*A publication*]
**Meet Place J R Ont Mus** ... Meeting Place Journal. Royal Ontario Museum [*A publication*]
**MEEV** ....... Maintenance and Electricity Equipment Vault (MCD)
**MEF** .......... Emerging Mexico Fund [*NYSE symbol*] (SPSG)
**MEF** .......... Maintenance Efficiency Factor
**MEF** .......... Major Equipment File (MCD)
**MEF** .......... Marine Expeditionary Force
**MEF** .......... Maximal Expiratory Flow [*Medicine*]
**MEF** .......... Mechanized Engineering File
**MEF** .......... Median Energy of Fission (NRCH)
**MEF** .......... Mediterranean Expeditionary Force [*British*] [*World War I*]
**MEF** .......... Mesopotamian Expeditionary Force [*British*]
**MEF** .......... Middle Ear Fluid
**MEF** .......... Middle East Forces [*British*]
**MEF** .......... Middle East Forum [*Lebanon*] (BJA)
**MEF** .......... Mideast File [*Tel-Aviv University*] [*Israel*] [*Information service or system*] (IID)
**MEF** .......... Migration Enhancement Factor [*Biochemistry*]
**MEF** .......... Minimum Essential Force (CINC)
**MEF** .......... Mortality Enhancing Factors [*Chemical and biological warfare*]
**MEF** .......... Mouse Embryo Fibroblast
**MEF** .......... Multiple Effect Flash [*Evaporator*] [*Seawater conversion system*]
**MEF** .......... Musicians Emergency Fund (EA)
**MEF** .......... Myocyte Enhancing Factor [*Genetics*]
**MEFA**........ Metal Etching and Fabricating Association [*Later, National Association of Name Plate Manufacturers*] (EA)
**MeFarGS**... Church of Jesus Christ of Latter-Day Saints, Genealogical Society Library, Augusta Branch, Farmingdale, ME [*Library symbol*] [*Library of Congress*] (LCLS)
**MeFarU**..... University of Maine at Farmington, Farmington, ME [*Library symbol*] [*Library of Congress*] (LCLS)
**MEFC**........ Maximum Economic Finding Cost
**MEFC**........ Mister Ed Fan Club (EA)
**MEFEX**..... Middle East Food and Equipment Exhibition [*Arabian Exhibition Management*] (TSPED)
**M-EFF**....... Myocardial Efficiency [*Cardiology*]
**MEFFEX**... Marine Expeditionary Force Field Exercise (NVT)
**MEFLEX**... Marine Expeditionary Force Landing Exercise (NVT)
**ME Fm Res** ... Maine Farm Research [*A publication*]
**MEFo**......... Middle East Focus [*A publication*]
**MEFO** ....... Miscelanea de Estudios Dedicados a Fernando Ortiz por Sus Discipulos [*A publication*]
**MEFPAK** .. Manpower and Equipment Force Packaging [*Military*]
**MEFR**........ Maximum Expiratory Flow Rate [*Medicine*]
**MEFR**........ Melanges d'Archeologie et d'Histoire. Ecole Francaise de Rome [*A publication*]
**MEFRA**..... Melanges. Ecole Francaise de Rome. Antiquite [*A publication*]
**MEFRM**.... Melanges. Ecole Francaise de Rome. Moyen Age. Temps Modernes [*A publication*]
**MeFtkU**..... University of Maine at Fort Kent, Fort Kent, ME [*Library symbol*] [*Library of Congress*] (LCLS)
**MEFTL** ..... Middle East Force Target List (MCD)
**MEFV**........ Maintenance Equipment Floor Valve (NRCH)
**MEG**.......... Madly Enthusiastic about Grapes
**MEG**.......... Magneto-Encephalogram
**MEG**.......... Magnetoencephalogram [*Medicine*]
**MEG**.......... Malange [*Angola*] [*Airport symbol*] (OAG)
**MEG**.......... Management Evaluation Group [*Department of State*]
**MEG**.......... Media General, Inc. [*AMEX symbol*] (SPSG)
**MEG**.......... Mega [*A prefix meaning multiplied by one million*] (AAG)
**Meg**............ Megakaryocyte [*Hematology*]
**Meg**............ Megiddo (BJA)
**MEG**.......... Megillah (BJA)
**MEG**.......... Megohm (AAG)
**Meg**............ Megone's Companies Acts Cases [*1888-90*] [*England*] [*A publication*] (DLA)
**MEG**.......... Message Entry Generator (NVT)
**MEG**.......... Message Expediting Group (IEEE)
**MEG**.......... Methyl(ethyl)glycine [*Biochemistry*]
**MEG**.......... Miniature Electrostatic Gyro
**MEG**.......... Multimedia Environmental Goals [*Environmental Protection Agency*]
**MEG**.......... NRA [*National Restaurant Association*] Marketing Executives Group [*Chicago, IL*] (EA)
**MEGA** ....... Military Evaluation of Geographic Areas

**MEGACE** ... Megestrol Acetate [*Antineoplastic drug*]
**Me-GAG**.... Methylglyoxalbis(guanylhydrazone) [*Mitoguazone*] [*Also, MGBG*] [*Antineoplastic drug*]
**MeGar** ....... Gardiner Public Library, Gardiner, ME [*Library symbol*] [*Library of Congress*] (LCLS)
**Megarry**..... Megarry's The Rent Acts [*A publication*] (DLA)
**MEGAS**..... Multienergy Gamma Assay System [*Nuclear energy*] (NRCH)
**MEGASTAR** ... Meaning of Energy Growth: An Assessment of Systems, Technologies, and Requirements [*NASA*]
**mEGF** ........ Mouse Epidermal Growth Factor
**mEGF-URO** ... Mouse Epidermal Growth Factor - Urogastrone [*Endocrinology*]
**MEGG**....... Merging [*Meteorology*] (FAAC)
**Megg Ass**... Meggison's Assets in Equity [*1832*] [*A publication*] (DLA)
**Meg-GPA** .. Megakaryocyte Growth-Promoting Activity [*Hematology*]
**MEGHP**.... Most Excellent Grand High Priest [*Freemasonry*]
**MEGI** ........ Megamation, Inc. [*NASDAQ symbol*] (NQ)
**MEGLF**..... Megaline Resources [*NASDAQ symbol*] (NQ)
**MEGLUMINE** ... N-Methylglucamine [*Organic chemistry*] [*USAN*]
**MEGM**...... Most Eminent Grand Master [*Freemasonry*] (ROG)
**MEGO**....... Megohm (MSA)
**MEGO**....... My Eyes Glaze Over [*An article, written about an important subject, that resists reader interest and has a soporific effect*] [*Journalistic slang*]
**Megone**...... Megone's Companies Acts Cases [*1888-90*] [*England*] [*A publication*] (DLA)
**MEGS**........ Male Electronic Genital Stimulator [*Developed by Biosonics, Inc.*]
**MEGS**........ Megasecond (AAG)
**MEGT** ....... Megatech Corp. [*NASDAQ symbol*] (NQ)
**MEGT** ....... Megaton [*Nuclear equivalent of one million tons of high explosive*] (AAG)
**MegTa'an**.. Megillat Ta'anit (BJA)
**MEGV** ....... Megavolt (AAG)
**MEGW**...... Megawatt [*Also, MW*]
**MEGWH**... Megawatt-Hour
**MEGX** ....... Monoethylglycine Xylidide [*Biochemistry*]
**MEH**.......... Maine State Department of Human Services, Augusta, ME [*OCLC symbol*] (OCLC)
**MEH**.......... Materials Handling News [*A publication*]
**MEH**.......... Meacham, OR [*Location identifier*] [*FAA*] (FAAL)
**MEH**.......... Mehamn [*Norway*] [*Airport symbol*] (OAG)
**MEH**.......... Multi-Engined Helicopter (MCD)
**Mehanika Period Sb Perevodov Inostran Statei** ... Mehanika. Periodiceskii Sbornik Perevodov Inostrannyh Statei [*A publication*]
**Mehanika Polimerov** ... Akademija Nauk Latviiskoi SSR. Institut Mehaniki Polimerov. Mehanika Polimerov [*A publication*]
**Meh Autom** ... Mehanizacija i Automatizacija [*A publication*]
**MEHBA**.... Meteorology and Hydrology [*A publication*]
**MEHDHQ** ... Medical Embarkment and Hospital Distribution Headquarters [*World War II*]
**MeHi** ......... Maine Historical Society, Portland, ME [*Library symbol*] [*Library of Congress*] (LCLS)
**ME His S**... Maine Historical Society. Collections [*A publication*]
**MEHP**....... Monoethylhexyl Phthalate [*Organic chemistry*]
**MEHQ**....... Monomethyl Ether of Hydroquinone [*Organic chemistry*]
**Mehran Univ Res J Eng and Technol** ... Mehran University. Research Journal of Engineering and Technology [*A publication*]
**Meh Tverd Tela** ... Mehanika Tverdogo Tela [*A publication*]
**MEHUA**.... Memoirs. Faculty of Engineering. Hokkaido University [*A publication*]
**MEHYA** .... Mental Hygiene [*A publication*]
**MEI** ........... Main Engine Ignition [*Aerospace*]
**MEI** ........... Maintenance Effectiveness Inspection (MCD)
**MEI** ........... Maintenance and Engineering Inspection
**MEI** ........... Maintenance Engineering Investigation [*DoD*]
**MEI** ........... Maintenance Evaluation Inspection (MCD)
**MEI** ........... Management Education Institute [*Arthur D. Little, Inc.*]
**MEI** ........... Management Effectiveness Inspection
**MEI** ........... Manpower Education Institute (EA)
**MEI** ........... Manual of Engineering Instructions
**MEI** ........... Marginal Efficiency of Investment
**MEI** ........... Marketing Economics Institute Ltd. [*New York, NY*]
**MeI** ........... Meconium Ileus [*Medicine*]
**MEI** ........... Media Info [*A publication*]
**MEI** ........... Medicare Economic Index
**MEI** ........... MEI Diversified, Inc. [*NYSE symbol*] (SPSG)
**Mei**............ Meiji Seika Kaisha Ltd. [*Japan*]
**MEI** ........... Meridian [*Mississippi*] [*Airport symbol*] (OAG)
**MEI** ........... Meridian, MS [*Location identifier*] [*FAA*] (FAAL)
**MEI** ........... Metals Engineering Institute (EA)
**MEI** ........... Middle East Information Service (BJA)
**MEI** ........... Middle East Institute (EA)
**MEI** ........... Military Engineering Item (MCD)
**MEI** ........... Minority Educational Institution
**MEI** ........... Mission Essential Item [*Army*]
**MEI** ........... Morpholinoethylisocyanide [*Organic chemistry*]
**MEI** ........... Myocardial Efficiency Index [*Cardiology*]
**MEIA** ........ Microparticle Enzyme Immunoassay
**MEIC**......... Member of the Engineering Institute of Canada
**MEIC**......... Middle East Intelligence Center [*World War II*]
**MEIC**......... Myanma Export-Import Corporation [*Burmese*] (GEA)
**Meid**........... Against Meidias [*of Demosthenes*] [*Classical studies*] (OCD)
**Meiden Rev (Int Ed)** ... Meiden Review (International Edition) [*A publication*]
**Meidensha Rev (Int Ed)** ... Meidensha Review [*later, Meiden Review*] (International Edition) [*A publication*]
**MEIDL**...... Manually Entered Identification Library (CAAL)
**MEIE**......... Microcomputer Electronic Information Exchange [*Institute for Computer Science and Technology*]
**MEIF**......... Mobile Equipment Information File [*Air Force*] (AFM)
**MEIFD**...... Minerva Ecologica, Idroclimatologica, Fisicosanitaria [*A publication*]
**MEIG** ........ Main Engine Ignition [*Aerospace*] (KSC)
**MEIGN** ..... Main Engine Ignition [*Aerospace*]
**Meigs** ......... Meigs' Tennessee Supreme Court Reports [*1838-39*] [*A publication*] (DLA)
**Meigs Dig** .. Meigs' Digest of Decisions of the Courts of Tennessee [*A publication*] (DLA)
**Meigs' R** .... Meigs' Tennessee Reports [*A publication*] (DLA)
**Meijeritiet Aikak** ... Meijeritieteellinen Aikakauskirja [*A publication*]
**Meijertiet Aikak Finn J Dairy Sci** ... Meijeritieteellinen Aikakauskirja/ Finnish Journal of Dairy Science [*A publication*]
**Me'il**.......... Me'ilah (BJA)
**MEIMN** .... Multiend Item Modification Notice [*NASA*] (KSC)
**MEIN** ........ Medium-Energy Intense Neutron
**MEINA** ..... Metal Industry [*A publication*]
**MEIR**......... Mideast Information Resource (BJA)
**MEIR**......... Ministere Federal de l'Expansion Industrielle Regionale [*Department of Regional Industrial Expansion - DRIE*] [*Canada*]
**MEIS** ......... Middle East Information Service (BJA)
**MEIS** ......... Military Entomology Information Service
**MEISA** ...... Minzoku Eisei [*A publication*]
**MEISR** ...... Minimum Essential Improvement in System Reliability (MCD)
**MEITAL** ... Medecine Interne [*Paris*] [*A publication*]
**MEITS** ...... Mission Effective Information Transmission System
**MEIU** ........ Main Engine Interface Unit (MCD)
**MEIU** ........ Middle East Interpretation Unit [*British*]
**MEIU** ........ Mobile Explosives Investigation Unit
**MEJ**........... Maine Criminal Justice Academy, Waterville, ME [*OCLC symbol*] (OCLC)
**MEJ**........... Marman Expansion Joint
**MEJ**........... Maximum Economic Justification
**MEJ**........... Meade, KS [*Location identifier*] [*FAA*] (FAAL)
**MEJ**........... Middle East Journal [*A publication*]
**MEJ**........... Movement for Economic Justice (EA)
**MEJ**........... Music Educators Journal [*A publication*]
**Mejeritek Medd** ... Mejeritekniska Meddelanden [*A publication*]
**MEJOAB** .. Lijecnicki Vjesnik [*English translation*] [*A publication*]
**MEK**.......... Maine State Library, Bookmobiles, Augusta, ME [*OCLC symbol*] (OCLC)
**MEK**.......... Meekatharra [*Australia*] [*Seismograph station code, US Geological Survey*] (SEIS)
**Mek**............ Mekhilta (BJA)
**MEK**.......... Melk [*A publication*]
**MEK**.......... Methyl Ethyl Ketone [*Organic chemistry*]
**MEKEA**..... Memoirs. Faculty of Science. Kyushu University. Series E. Biology [*A publication*]
**MeKh**......... Mekhilta (BJA)
**Mekhan Elektrif Sots Sel'Khoz** ... Mekhanizatsiya Elektrifikatsiya Sotsialisticheskogo Sel'skogo Khozyaistva [*A publication*]
**Mekh & Avtom Proiz** ... Mekhanizatsiya i Avtomatizatsiya Proizvodstva [*A publication*]
**Mekh i Avtom Proizvod** ... Mekhanizatsiya i Avtomatizatsiya Proizvodstva [*A publication*]
**Mekh Avtom Proizvod** ... Mekhanizatsiya i Avtomatizatsiya Proizvodstva [*A publication*]
**Mekh i Avtom Upr** ... Mekhanizahriya i Avtomahzatsiya Upravleniya [*A publication*]
**Mekh Avtom Upr** ... Mekhanizatsiya i Avtomatizatsiya Upravleniya [*A publication*]
**Mekh Deform Tverd Tel** ... Mekhanika Deformiruemykh Tverdykh Tel [*USSR*] [*A publication*]
**Mekh Elektrif Sel'sk Khoz** ... Mekhanizatsiia i Elektrifikatsiia Sel'skogo Khoziaistva [*A publication*]
**Mekh Khlopkovod** ... Mekhanizatsiya Khlopkovodstva [*A publication*]
**Mekh Kompozitnykh Mater** ... Mekhanika Kompozitnykh Materialov [*A publication*]
**Mekh Kompoz Mater** ... Mekhanika Kompozitnykh Materialov [*Latvian SSR*] [*A publication*]
**Mekh Nek Patol Protsessov** ... Mekhanizmy Nekotorykh Patologicheskikh Protsessov [*A publication*]
**Mekh Obrab Drev** ... Mekhanicheskaya Obrabotka. Drevesiny [*A publication*]
**Mekh Patol Protsessov** ... Mekhanizmy Patologicheskikh Protsessov [*A publication*]
**Mekh Polim** ... Mekhanika Polimerov [*A publication*]
**Mekh Razrusheniya Metal Nauk Ukr SSR Repub Mezhvedom Sb** ... Mekhanizm Razrusheniya Metallov Akademiya Nauk Ukrainskoi SSR Respublikanskii Mezhvedomstvennyi Sbornik [*A publication*]

**Mekh Silsk Hospod** ... Mekhanizatsiia Sil's'koho Hospodarstva [*A publication*]
**Mekh Tverd Tela** ... Akademiya Nauk Ukrainskoi SSR. Institut Prikladnoi Matematikii, Mekhaniki. Mekhanika Tverdogo Tela [*A publication*]
**Mekh Tverd Tela** ... Mekhanika Tverdogo Tela [*A publication*]
**Mekh Zhidk Gaza** ... Mekhanika Zhidkosti i Gaza [*USSR*] [*A publication*]
**MEKLA**..... Medizinische Klinik [*A publication*]
**MEKMA** ... Memoirs. Faculty of Engineering. Kumamoto University [*A publication*]
**MEKO**....... Methyl Ethyl Ketoxime [*Organic chemistry*]
**MEKOA**.... Metallurgiya i Koksokhimiya [*A publication*]
**MEKP**........ Methyl Ethyl Ketone Peroxide [*Organic chemistry*]
**MEKSA**..... Memoirs. Faculty of Engineering. Kyushu University [*A publication*]
**MEKYA**..... Memoirs. Faculty of Engineering. Kyoto University [*A publication*]
**MeL**........... Lewiston Public Library, Lewiston, ME [*Library symbol*] [*Library of Congress*] (LCLS)
**MEL**.......... Magnesium Elektron Ltd. [*British*] (IRUK)
**MEL**.......... Maintenance Expenditure Limit (MCD)
**MEL**.......... Maneuvering Element [*Military*] (AABC)
**MEL**.......... Many-Element LASER
**MEL**.......... Marchwood Engineering Laboratories [*British*] (IRUK)
**MEL**.......... Marine Engineering Laboratory [*Navy*]
**M El**.......... Master of Elements
**MEL**.......... Master of English Literature
**MEL**.......... Master Equipment List [*Military*] (NG)
**MEL**.......... Material Engineering Laboratory
**MEL**.......... Materials Evaluation Laboratory (MCD)
**MEL**.......... Maximum Expenditure Limit (MCD)
**MEL**.......... Maximum Exposure Limit [*Hazardous material control*]
**MEL**.......... Melamine
**Mel**............ Melanges [*A publication*]
**MEL**.......... Melanoma [*Oncology*]
**MEL**.......... Melbourne [*Australia*] [*Seismograph station code, US Geological Survey*] (SEIS)
**MEL**.......... Melbourne [*Australia*] [*Airport symbol*] (OAG)
**MEL**.......... Melbourne [*Australia*] [*Later, TOO*] [*Geomagnetic observatory code*]
**Mel**............ Melendus [*Flourished, 1188-1209*] [*Authority cited in pre-1607 legal work*] (DSA)
**MEL**.......... Mellis [*Of Honey*] [*Pharmacy*] (ROG)
**MEL**.......... Mellon Bank Corp. [*NYSE symbol*] (SPSG)
**MEL**.......... Melody
**MEL**.......... Melrose Resources Ltd. [*Vancouver Stock Exchange symbol*]
**MEL**.......... Metabolic Equivalent Level [*Medicine*]
**MEL**.......... Metal Bulletin [*A publication*]
**MEL**.......... Military Education Level (INF)
**MEL**.......... Minimum Earnings Level
**MEL**.......... Minimum Equipment List
**MEL**.......... Mistress of English Literature
**MEL**.......... Mobile Erector Launcher [*Military*]
**MEL**.......... Mouse Erythroleukemia
**MEL**.......... Multiengine Land [*Pilot rating*] (AIA)
**MEL**.......... Murine Erythroleukemia [*Oncology*]
**MEL**.......... Music Education League [*Defunct*] (EA)
**MEL**.......... Muzika Esperanto Ligo [*Esperantist Music League*] (EAIO)
**ME L**.......... University of Maine. Law Review [*A publication*] (DLA)
**MELA**........ Middle East Librarians' Association (EA)
**MELAA**..... Medicina del Lavoro [*A publication*]
**MELAB**..... Mechanical Engineering Laboratory [*NASA*] (KSC)
**MELABS**... Microwave Engineering Laboratories, Inc. (MCD)
**MELADG** ... Medicine and Law [*A publication*]
**MELAN** .... Melanesia (ROG)
**Melanesian Law J** ... Melanesian Law Journal [*A publication*]
**Melanesian LJ** ... Melanesian Law Journal [*A publication*]
**Melanges d'Arch** ... Melanges d'Archeologie et d'Histoire. Ecole Francaise de Rome [*A publication*] (OCD)
**Melanges Chamard** ... Melanges d'Histoire Litteraire de la Renaissance Offerts a Henri Chamard [*A publication*]
**Melanges Hoepffner** ... Melanges de Philologie Romane et de Litterature Medievale Offerts a Ernest Hoepffner [*A publication*]
**Melanges Roques** ... Melanges de Linguistique et de Litterature Romanes Offerts a Mario Roques [*A publication*]
**ME Laws** ... Laws of the State of Maine [*A publication*]
**MeLB**......... Bates College, Lewiston, ME [*Library symbol*] [*Library of Congress*] (LCLS)
**MELB**........ Melbourne [*Australia*] (ROG)
**MELBA**..... Multipurpose Extended Lift Blanket Assembly (IEEE)
**Melb Chamber of Commerce Yrbk** ... Melbourne Chamber of Commerce. Yearbook [*A publication*] (APTA)
**Melb City Mission Rec** ... Melbourne City Mission Record [*A publication*] (APTA)
**Melb Critical R** ... Melbourne Critical Review [*A publication*] (APTA)
**Melb Crit R** ... Melbourne Critical Review [*A publication*] (APTA)
**Mel (Beyrouth)** ... Melanges. Universite Saint Joseph (Beyrouth) [*A publication*]
**Melb Grad** ... Melbourne Graduate [*A publication*] (APTA)
**Melb Graduate** ... Melbourne Graduate [*A publication*] (APTA)
**Melb Hist J** ... Melbourne Historical Journal [*A publication*] (APTA)
**Melb Legacy Week Bul** ... Melbourne Legacy Week. Bulletin [*A publication*] (APTA)
**Melb Metro Board Works Monograph** ... Monograph. Melbourne and Metropolitan Board of Works [*A publication*] (APTA)
**Melb Mon Mag** ... Melbourne Monthly Magazine [*A publication*] (APTA)
**Melbourne Critical Rev** ... Melbourne Critical Review [*A publication*] (APTA)
**Melbourne Hist J** ... Melbourne Historical Journal [*A publication*] (APTA)
**Melbourne J Politics** ... Melbourne Journal of Politics [*A publication*]
**Melbourne Stud in Educ** ... Melbourne Studies in Education [*A publication*] (APTA)
**Melbourne ULR** ... Melbourne University. Law Review [*A publication*]
**Melbourne Univ Dep Civ Eng Transp Sect Bull** ... University of Melbourne. Department of Civil Engineering. Transport Section. Bulletin [*A publication*] (APTA)
**Melbourne Univ Dep Civ Eng Transp Sect Spec Rep** ... University of Melbourne. Department of Civil Engineering. Transport Section. Special Report [*A publication*] (APTA)
**Melbourne Univ Dep Mech Eng Hum Factors Group HF Rep** ... University of Melbourne. Department of Mechanical Engineering. Human Factors Group. HF Report [*A publication*] (APTA)
**Melbourne Univ Law Rev** ... Melbourne University. Law Review [*A publication*] (APTA)
**Melbourne Univ L Rev** ... Melbourne University. Law Review [*A publication*]
**Melb Rev** ... Melbourne Review [*A publication*] (APTA)
**Melb Rpt**.... Melbourne Report [*A publication*]
**MelbSS**...... Melbourne Slavonic Studies [*A publication*]
**Melb Stud Ed** ... Melbourne Studies in Education [*A publication*]
**Melb Stud Educ** ... Melbourne Studies in Education [*A publication*] (APTA)
**Melb Studies in Educ** ... Melbourne Studies in Education [*A publication*] (APTA)
**Melb UL Rev** ... Melbourne University. Law Review [*A publication*]
**Melb Univ Circ to Sch** ... Melbourne University. Circular to Schools [*A publication*] (APTA)
**Melb Univ Elect Engng Dep Rep** ... University of Melbourne. Department of Electrical Engineering. Report [*A publication*] (APTA)
**Melb Univ Gaz** ... Melbourne University. Gazette [*A publication*] (APTA)
**Melb Univ Law R** ... Melbourne University. Law Review [*A publication*] (APTA)
**Melb Univ Law Rev** ... Melbourne University. Law Review [*A publication*]
**Melb Univ LR** ... Melbourne University. Law Review [*A publication*]
**Melb Univ L Rev** ... Melbourne University. Law Review [*A publication*] (APTA)
**Melb Univ Mag** ... Melbourne University. Magazine [*A publication*] (APTA)
**Melb Univ Sch For Bull** ... University of Melbourne. School of Forestry. Bulletin [*A publication*] (APTA)
**Melb Walker** ... Melbourne Walker [*A publication*] (APTA)
**Melb Zool Gard Annu Rep** ... Melbourne Zoological Gardens. Annual Report [*A publication*]
**MELC**........ Melcombe [*England*]
**MELC**........ Mouse Erythroleukemia Cell
**Mel Casa Velazquez** ... Melanges. Casa de Velazquez [*A publication*]
**MELCO**..... Mitsubishi Electric Corp. [*Japan*]
**MELCOM** ... [*A*] computer series [*Mitsubishi Corp.*] [*Japan*]
**MELCOM** ... Middle East Libraries Committee
**MELCU**..... Multiple External Line Control Unit
**MeLDL**...... Methylated Low-Density Lipoprotein [*Biochemistry*]
**Meld Landbruksteknisk Inst** ... Melding-Landbruksteknisk Institut [*A publication*]
**Meld Meieriinst Nor Landbrukshogsk** ... Melding-Meieriinstituttet. Norges Landbrukshogskole [*A publication*]
**Meld Norg Landbrukshogsk** ... Meldinger fra Norges Landbrukshogskole [*A publication*]
**Meld Nor Landbrukshogsk** ... Meldinger fra Norges Landbrukshogskole [*A publication*]
**Meld Nor Landbrukshogsk Inst Blomsterdyrk Veksthusforsok** ... Melding-Norges Landbrukshogskole. Institutt foer Blomsterdyrking og Veksthusforsok [*A publication*]
**Meld St ForsGard Kvithamar** ... Melding Statens Forsoksgard Kvithamar [*A publication*]
**MELEC**..... Microelectronics (IEEE)
**ME Legis Serv** ... Maine Legislative Service [*A publication*] (DLA)
**Melekess Gos Ped Inst Ucen Zap** ... Melekesskii Gosudarstvennyi Pedagogiceskii Institut. Ucenye Zapiski [*A publication*]
**MELEM**.... Microelement (IEEE)
**MELF**........ Middle East Land Forces [*British*] (NATG)
**MELG**........ Middle East Liaison Group [*Military*] (AABC)
**MELI**.......... Master Equipment List Index [*Military*] (KSC)
**MELI**.......... Minimum Equipment List Index (NASA)
**Meliorace Prehl Lit Zemed Lesn Melior** ... Meliorace. Prehled Literatury Zemedelskych a Lesnickych Melioraci [*A publication*]
**Meliorat Acker- Pflanzenbau** ... Melioration Acker- und Pflanzenbau [*A publication*]
**Melior Ispol'z Osushennykh Zemel** ... Melioratsiya i Ispol'zovaniya Osushennykh Zemel [*A publication*]
**Melior Vodn Khoz** ... Melioratsiya Vodnoe Khozyaistva [*A publication*]
**MELIOS**... Miniature Eyesafe LASER Infrared Observation Set [*A rangefinder*]
**MELISS**.... Mitsubishi Electric Corp. Literature and Information Search Service

**Meliss Ellas** ... Melissokomike Ellas [*A publication*]
**MeliT**......... Melita Theologica. The Reviews of the Royal University Students' Theological Association [*La Valetta, Malta*] [*A publication*]
**MelitaT**...... Melita Theologica. The Reviews of the Royal University Students' Theological Association [*La Valetta, Malta*] [*A publication*]
**Melittologists' Bull** ... Melittologists' Bulletin [*A publication*]
**MELKONG** ... Mechanical Electric Kong [*Robot*]
**MELL**......... Mellis [*Of Honey*] [*Pharmacy*] (ROG)
**Melliand TextBer** ... Melliand Textilberichte [*A publication*]
**Melliand Textilber** ... Melliand Textilberichte International [*A publication*]
**Melliand Textilber Int** ... Melliand Textilberichte International [*A publication*]
**Mell Parl Pr** ... Mell's Parliamentary Practice [*A publication*] (DLA)
**Mell Textil** ... Melliand Textilberichte [*A publication*]
**MELM**...... Middle East Lutheran Ministry (EAIO)
**Mel Maker** ... Melody Maker [*A publication*]
**Mel Masp**.. Melanges Maspero [*A publication*] (OCD)
**M Elo**......... Master of Elocution
**MELO**....... Minimum Expected Loss [*Statistics*]
**Melos NeueZM** ... Melos. Neue Zeitschrift fuer Musik [*A publication*]
**MELP**........ Mid-European Law Project
**MelPHLJ**.. Melanges de Philosophie et de Litterature Juives [*Paris*] [*A publication*]
**Me-LR**....... Law and Legislative Reference Library, Augusta, ME [*Library symbol*] [*Library of Congress*] (LCLS)
**ME L Rev**.. Maine Law Review [*A publication*]
**Mel Rom**.... Melanges d'Archeologie et d'Histoire. Ecole Francaise de Rome [*A publication*]
**MELS**........ Molecularly Engineered Layered Structure
**MELSA**..... Metropolitan Library Service Agency [*Library network*]
**MelScR**...... Melanges de Science Religieuse [*A publication*]
**Melsheimer Entomol Ser** ... Melsheimer Entomological Series [*A publication*]
**Melsheimer Ent Ser** ... Melsheimer Entomological Series [*A publication*]
**MELSOR**.. Marx, Engels, Lenin, Stalin, October Revolution [*Given name popular in Russia after the Bolshevik Revolution*]
**Melsunger Med Pharm Mitt Wiss Prax** ... Melsunger Medizinisch Pharmazeutische Mitteilungen aus Wissenschaft und Praxis [*A publication*]
**Melsunger Med Pharm Mitt Wiss Prax Suppl** ... Melsunger Medizinisch Pharmazeutische Mitteilungen aus Wissenschaft und Praxis. Supplement [*A publication*]
**MELT**........ Melton Drilling & Exploration Co. [*NASDAQ symbol*] (NQ)
**MELT**........ Minimum Equipment Level for Training (MCD)
**Mel Univ St Joseph** ... Melanges. Universite Saint Joseph [*A publication*]
**MelUSJ**..... Melanges. Universite Saint Joseph [*A publication*]
**MELVA**..... Military Electronic Light Valve
**Melv Tr**...... Melvill's Trial (Impeachment) [*London*] [*A publication*] (DLA)
**Melyepitestud Sz** ... Melyepitestudomanyi Szemle [*A publication*]
**Mem**.......... De Memoria [*of Aristotle*] [*Classical studies*] (OCD)
**MEM**......... Magyar Elet Mozgalma [*Movement of Hungarian Life*] [*Political party*] (PPE)
**MEM**......... Maine State Museum, Augusta, ME [*OCLC symbol*] (OCLC)
**MEM**......... Marine Engineering Mechanic [*Navy rating*] [*British*]
**MEM**......... Mars Excursion Module
**Me M**......... Master of Metaphysics
**MeM**.......... Materiales en Marcha [*A publication*]
**MEM**......... Maximum Entropy Method [*Geomagnetism*] [*Data processing*]
**MEM**......... MEM Co., Inc. [*AMEX symbol*] (SPSG)
**MEM**......... Membach [*Belgium*] [*Seismograph station code, US Geological Survey*] (SEIS)
**MEM**......... Member (EY)
**MEM**......... Memento
**MEM**......... Memoir
**Mem**.......... Memorabilia [*of Xenophon*] [*Classical studies*] (OCD)
**MEM**......... Memorandum
**MEM**......... Memorial
**MEM**......... Memory (MSA)
**MEM**......... Memphis [*Tennessee*] [*Airport symbol*] (OAG)
**MEM**......... Mens en Maatschappij. Tijdschrift voor Sociale Wetenschappen [*A publication*]
**MeM**.......... Mens en Muziek [*A publication*]
**MEM**......... Meteoroid Exposure Module (MCD)
**MEM**......... Methoxyethoxymethyl [*Organic chemistry*]
**MEM**......... Mezoegazdasagi es Elelmezesuegyi Miniszterium [*Hungary*]
**MEM**......... Middle-Ear Muscle [*Anatomy*]
**MEM**......... Middle Eastern Monographs [*A publication*]
**MEM**......... Minimum Essential Medium [*Culture medium*]
**MEM**......... Missile Engagement Mechanism (MCD)
**MEM**......... Module Exchange Mechanism [*NASA*] (NASA)
**MEM**......... Molecular Exciton Microscopy
**MEM**......... Mondpaca Esperantista Movado [*Esperantist Movement for World Peace - EMWP*] [*Tours, France*] (EAIO)
**MEM**......... Most Efficient/Effective Method [*DoD*]
**MEM**......... Most Excellent Master [*Freemasonry*]
**MEM**......... Mount Emily Exploration Ltd. [*Vancouver Stock Exchange symbol*]
**MEM**......... Multienvironmental Electron Microscope
**MEMA**...... Marine Engine Manufacturers Association [*Formerly, OMMA*] (EA)
**MEMA**...... Microelectronic Modular Assembly
**MEMA**...... Middle-Ear Muscle Activity
**MEMA**...... Motor and Equipment Manufacturers Association (EA)
**MEMAC** ... Middle East Medical Advisory Committee [*World War II*]
**Mem Acad Chir** ... Memoires. Academie de Chirurgie [*France*] [*A publication*]
**Mem Acad Cienc Lisb Cl Cienc** ... Memorias. Academia das Ciencias de Lisboa. Classe de Ciencias [*A publication*]
**Mem Acad Cienc Zaragoza** ... Memorias. Academia de Ciencias de Zaragoza [*A publication*]
**Mem Acad Malgache** ... Memoires. Academie Malgache [*A publication*]
**Mem Acad Med (Paris)** ... Memoires. Academie de Medecine (Paris) [*A publication*]
**Mem Acad Mex Estud Num** ... Memorias. Academia Mexicana de Estudios Numismaticos [*A publication*]
**Mem Acad R Belg Cl Sci Collect 4o** ... Memoires. Academie Royale de Belgique. Classe des Sciences. Collection in Quarto [*A publication*]
**Mem Acad R Belg Cl Sci 4o Ser II** ... Memoires. Academie Royale de Belgique. Classe des Sciences. Collection in Quarto. Deuxieme Serie [*A publication*]
**Mem Acad R Med Belg** ... Memoires. Academie Royale de Medecine de Belgique [*A publication*]
**Mem Acad Roy Sci Lett Belg** ... Memoires. Academie Royale des Sciences, des Lettres, et des Beaux-Arts de Belgique [*A publication*]
**Mem Acad Roy Sci Outre-Mer (Brussels)** ... Memoires. Academie Royale des Sciences d'Outre-Mer (Brussels) [*A publication*]
**Mem Acad Sci** ... Memoires. Academie des Sciences. Institut de France [*A publication*]
**Mem Acad Sci Inscr B-Lett Toulouse** ... Memoires. Academie des Sciences, Inscriptions, et Belles-Lettres de Toulouse [*A publication*]
**Mem Acad Sci Inscriptions B L Toulouse** ... Memoires. Academie des Sciences, Inscriptions, et Belles-Lettres de Toulouse [*A publication*]
**Mem Acad Sci Inst Fr** ... Memoires. Academie des Sciences. Institut de France [*A publication*]
**Mem Acad Sci Toulouse** ... Memoires. Academie des Sciences, Inscriptions, et Belles-Lettres de Toulouse [*France*] [*A publication*]
**Mem Accad Sci Ist Bologna Cl Sci Fis** ... Memorie. Accademia delle Scienze. Istituto di Bologna. Classe di Scienze Fisiche [*A publication*]
**Mem Accad Sci Med Chir (Naples)** ... Memorie. Accademia di Scienze Mediche e Chirurgiche (Naples) [*A publication*]
**Mem Accad Sci Torino Cl Sci Fis Mat Nat** ... Memorie. Accademia delle Scienze di Torino. Classe di Scienze Fisiche, Matematiche, e Naturali [*A publication*]
**Mem Accad Sci Torino Cl Sci Fis Mat Nat Ser 4A** ... Memorie. Accademia delle Scienze di Torino. Classe di Scienze Fisiche, Matematiche, e Naturali. Serie 4A [*A publication*]
**Mem Accad Sci Torino Cl Sci Fis Mat Natur** ... Memorie. Accademia delle Scienze di Torino. Classe di Scienze Fisiche, Matematiche, e Naturali [*Turin*] [*A publication*]
**Mem Accad Sci Torino Cl Sci Fis Mat Natur 4** ... Memorie. Accademia delle Scienze di Torino. Classe di Scienze Fisiche, Matematiche, e Naturali. Serie 4 [*Turin*] [*A publication*]
**Mem Accad Sci Torino Cl Sci Fis Mat Natur 5** ... Accademia delle Scienze di Torino. Memorie. Classe di Scienze Fisiche, Matematiche, e Naturali. Serie 5 [*A publication*]
**Mem Acc Linc** ... Memorie. Atti della Accademia Nazionale dei Lincei. Classe de Scienze Morali, Storiche, e Filologiche [*A publication*]
**Mem Ac Inscr** ... Memoires Presentes par Divers Savants a l'Academie des Inscriptions et Belles Lettres [*A publication*]
**MeMacU** ... University of Maine at Machias, Machias, ME [*Library symbol*] [*Library of Congress*] (LCLS)
**Mem Akita Univ** ... Memoirs. Akita University [*A publication*]
**Mem Am Ac** ... Memoirs. American Academy in Rome [*A publication*]
**Mem Am Acad Arts Sci** ... Memoirs. American Academy of Arts and Sciences [*A publication*]
**Mem Am Assoc Pet Geol** ... Memoir. American Association of Petroleum Geologists [*A publication*]
**Mem Am Entomol Inst (Ann Arbor)** ... Memoirs. American Entomological Institute (Ann Arbor) [*A publication*]
**Mem Am Entomol Inst (Gainesville)** ... Memoirs. American Entomological Institute (Gainesville) [*A publication*]
**Mem Am Entomol Soc** ... Memoirs. American Entomological Society [*A publication*]
**Mem Amer Math Soc** ... Memoirs. American Mathematical Society [*A publication*]
**Mem Amer Philos Soc** ... Memoirs. American Philosophical Society [*A publication*]
**Mem Am Math** ... Memoirs. American Mathematical Society [*A publication*]
**Mem Am Philos Soc** ... Memoirs. American Philosophical Society [*A publication*]
**Mem Ant**.... Memoria Antiquitatis. Acta Musei Petrodavensis. Revista Muzeului Arheologic Piatra Neamt [*A publication*]
**Mem Antiq** ... Memoria Antiquitatis [*A publication*]
**Mem Artillerie Fr** ... Memorial de l'Artillerie Francaise [*A publication*]
**Mem Artillerie Fr Sci Tech Armement** ... Memorial de l'Artillerie Francaise. Sciences et Techniques de l'Armement [*A publication*]

**Mem Asoc Latinoam Prod Anim** ... Memoria. Asociacion Latinoamericana de Produccion Animal [*A publication*]
**Mem Assoc Int Hydrogeol** ... Memoires. Association Internationale des Hydrogeologues [*A publication*]
**Mem Assoc Int Hydrogeol Reunion Istanbul** ... Memoires. Association Internationale des Hydrogeologues. Reunion d'Istanbul [*A publication*]
**Mem Astron Soc India** ... Memoirs. Astronomical Society of India [*A publication*]
**MEMA/TTC** ... Motor and Equipment Manufacturers Association's Technical Training Council
**Mem Atti Cent Studi Ing Agrar** ... Memorie ed Atti. Centro di Studi per l'Ingegneria Agraria [*A publication*]
**Mem Aust Mus** ... Memoirs. Australian Museum [*A publication*] (APTA)
**MEMB** ...... Member
**MEMB** ...... Membranaceous Vellum [*Manuscripts*] (ROG)
**MEMB** ...... Membrane (MSA)
**MEMB** ...... Micro-Membranes, Inc. [*Newark, NJ*] [*NASDAQ symbol*] (NQ)
**Mem Barcel A** ... Memoria. Universidad de Barcelona. Instituto de Arqueologia y Prehistoria [*A publication*]
**MEMBBM** ... Methods in Membrane Biology [*A publication*]
**Mem Biol Mar Oceanogr** ... Memorie di Biologia Marina e di Oceanografia [*A publication*]
**MEMBIS** .. Member Budget Information System [*for House of Representatives*]
**MEMBLE** ... Memorable (ROG)
**Mem Bologna** ... Atti. Accademia delle Scienze. Istituto di Bologna. Memorie [*A publication*]
**Mem Boston Soc Nat Hist** ... Memoirs. Boston Society of Natural History [*A publication*]
**Mem Botan Surv S Afr** ... Memoirs. Botanical Survey of South Africa [*A publication*]
**Mem Bot Opname S-Afr** ... Memoirs. Botaniese Opname van Suid-Afrika [*A publication*]
**Mem Bot Surv S Afr** ... Memoir. Botanical Survey of South Africa [*A publication*]
**Membrane Biochem** ... Membrane Biochemistry [*A publication*]
**Membr Biochem** ... Membrane Biochemistry [*A publication*]
**Mem BRGM** ... Memoires. Bureau de Recherches Geologiques et Minieres [*France*] [*A publication*]
**Membr Proteins** ... Membrane Proteins [*A publication*]
**Mem Bur Rech Geol Minieres** ... Memoires. Bureau de Recherches Geologiques et Minieres [*France*] [*A publication*]
**MEMC** ...... Methoxyethylmercuric Chloride
**Mem Can Soc Pet Geol** ... Memoir. Canadian Society of Petroleum Geologists [*A publication*]
**Mem Cent Natl Rech Metall Sect Hainaut** ... Memoires. Centre National de Recherches Metallurgiques. Section du Hainaut [*A publication*]
**Mem Cent Nat Rech Metall Sect Hainaut** ... Memoires. Centre National de Recherches Metallurgiques. Section du Hainaut [*A publication*]
**Mem Chubu Electr Power Co Ltd** ... Memoirs. Chubu Electric Power Company Limited [*Japan*] [*A publication*]
**Mem Chubu Inst Technol** ... Memoirs. Chubu Institute of Technology [*A publication*]
**Mem Chubu Inst Technol A** ... Memoirs. Chubu Institute of Technology. Series A [*A publication*]
**Mem Chukyo Women's Coll Chukyo Women's J Coll** ... Memoirs. Chukyo Women's College. Chukyo Women's Junior College [*A publication*]
**Mem Cl Sci Acad R Belg Collect 8o** ... Memoires. Classe des Sciences. Academie Royale de Belgique. Collection in Octavo [*A publication*]
**Mem Cognit** ... Memory and Cognition [*A publication*]
**Mem Cognition** ... Memory and Cognition [*A publication*]
**Mem Coll Agric Ehime Univ** ... Memoirs. College of Agriculture. Ehime University [*A publication*]
**Mem Coll Agric Kyoto Univ** ... Memoirs. College of Agriculture. Kyoto University [*A publication*]
**Mem Coll Agric Kyoto Univ Agric Econ Ser** ... Memoirs. College of Agriculture. Kyoto University. Agricultural Economy Series [*A publication*]
**Mem Coll Agric Kyoto Univ Anim Sci Ser** ... Memoirs. College of Agriculture. Kyoto University. Animal Science Series [*A publication*]
**Mem Coll Agric Kyoto Univ Bot Ser** ... Memoirs. College of Agriculture. Kyoto University. Botanical Series [*A publication*]
**Mem Coll Agric Kyoto Univ Chem Ser** ... Memoirs. College of Agriculture. Kyoto University. Chemical Series [*A publication*]
**Mem Coll Agric Kyoto Univ Entomol Ser** ... Memoirs. College of Agriculture. Kyoto University. Entomological Series [*A publication*]
**Mem Coll Agric Kyoto Univ Fish Ser** ... Memoirs. College of Agriculture. Kyoto University. Fisheries Series [*A publication*]
**Mem Coll Agric Kyoto Univ Food Sci Technol Ser** ... Memoirs. College of Agriculture. Kyoto University. Food Science and Technology Series [*A publication*]
**Mem Coll Agric Kyoto Univ Genet Ser** ... Memoirs. College of Agriculture. Kyoto University. Genetical Series [*A publication*]
**Mem Coll Agric Kyoto Univ Hortic Ser** ... Memoirs. College of Agriculture. Kyoto University. Horticultural Series [*A publication*]
**Mem Coll Agric Kyoto Univ Phytopathol Ser** ... Memoirs. College of Agriculture. Kyoto University. Phytopathological Series [*A publication*]
**Mem Coll Agric Kyoto Univ Plant Breed Ser** ... Memoirs. College of Agriculture. Kyoto University. Plant Breeding Series [*A publication*]
**Mem Coll Agric Kyoto Univ Wood Sci Technol Ser** ... Memoirs. College of Agriculture. Kyoto University. Wood Science and Technology Series [*A publication*]
**Mem Coll Agric Natl Taiwan Univ** ... Memoirs. College of Agriculture. National Taiwan University [*A publication*]
**Mem Coll Agr Kyoto Univ** ... Memoirs. College of Agriculture. Kyoto University [*A publication*]
**Mem Coll Eng Kyoto Imp Univ** ... Memoirs. College of Engineering. Kyoto Imperial University [*A publication*]
**Mem Coll Eng Kyushu Imp Univ** ... Memoirs. College of Engineering. Kyushu Imperial University [*A publication*]
**Mem Coll Med Natl Taiwan Univ** ... Memoirs. College of Medicine. National Taiwan University [*A publication*]
**Mem Coll Sci Kyoto Imp Univ** ... Memoirs. College of Science. Kyoto Imperial University [*A publication*]
**Mem Coll Sci Univ Kyoto Ser A** ... Memoirs. College of Science. University of Kyoto. Series A [*A publication*]
**Mem Coll Sci Univ Kyoto Ser A Math** ... Memoirs. College of Science. University of Kyoto. Series A. Mathematics [*A publication*]
**Mem Coll Sci Univ Kyoto Ser B** ... Memoirs. College of Science. University of Kyoto. Series B [*Japan*] [*A publication*]
**Mem Coll Sci Univ Kyoto Ser B Geol Biol** ... Memoirs. College of Science. University of Kyoto. Series B. Geology and Biology [*A publication*]
**Mem Comun Inst Geol (Barcelona)** ... Memorias y Comunicaciones. Instituto Geologico (Barcelona) [*A publication*]
**MEMCON** ... Memorandum of Conversation
**Mem Conf Anu ATAC** ... Memoria. Conferencia Anual de la ATAC [*A publication*]
**Mem Cong Med Latino-Am (Buenos Aires)** ... Memoria. Congreso Medico Latino-Americano (Buenos Aires) [*A publication*]
**Mem Congr Nac Med Vet Zootec** ... Memorias. Congreso Nacional de Medicina Veterinaria y Zootecnia [*A publication*]
**Mem Conn Acad Arts Sci** ... Memoirs. Connecticut Academy of Arts and Sciences [*A publication*]
**Mem Cons Oceanogr Ibero Am** ... Memorias. Consejo Oceanografico Ibero-Americano [*A publication*]
**Mem Cornell Univ Agric Exper Station** ... Memoirs. Cornell University. Agricultural Experiment Station [*A publication*]
**Mem Cornell Univ Agric Exp Stn** ... Memoirs. Cornell University. Agricultural Experiment Station [*A publication*]
**Mem Cote D'Or** ... Memoires. Commission des Antiquites du Departement de la Cote-D'Or [*A publication*]
**Mem Creuse** ... Memoires. Societe des Sciences Naturelles et Archeologiques de la Creuse [*A publication*]
**Mem C R Soc R Can** ... Memoires et Comptes Rendus. Societe Royale du Canada [*A publication*]
**MEMDA** ... Memoranda (ROG)
**MEMDB** ... Medieval and Early Modern Data Bank [*Information service or system*] (EISS)
**Mem Def Acad** ... Memoirs. Defense Academy [*A publication*]
**Mem Def Acad (Jap)** ... Memoirs. Defense Academy (Japan) [*A publication*]
**Mem Def Acad Math Phys Chem Eng** ... Memoirs. Defense Academy. Mathematics, Physics, Chemistry, and Engineering [*A publication*]
**Mem Def Acad Math Phys Chem Eng (Yokosuka Jpn)** ... Memoirs. Defense Academy. Mathematics, Physics, Chemistry, and Engineering (Yokosuka, Japan) [*A publication*]
**Mem Defense Acad** ... Memoirs. Defense Academy. Mathematics, Physics, Chemistry, and Engineering [*Yokosuka*] [*A publication*]
**Mem Dep Agric India Bacteriol Ser** ... Memoirs. Department of Agriculture in India. Bacteriological Series [*A publication*]
**Mem Dep Agric India Bot Ser** ... Memoirs. Department of Agriculture in India. Botanical Series [*A publication*]
**Mem Dep Agric India Chem Ser** ... Memoirs. Department of Agriculture in India. Chemical Series [*A publication*]
**Mem Dep Agric India Entomol Ser** ... Memoirs. Department of Agriculture in India. Entomological Series [*A publication*]
**Mem Dep Mineral Univ Geneve** ... Memoire. Departement de Mineralogie. Universite de Geneve [*A publication*]
**MEMDUM** ... Memorandum (ROG)
**MEME** ...... Magnetic Environment Measuring Equipment (CAAL)
**MEME** ...... Multiple Entry Multiple Exit
**MEMEC**.... Memory and Electronic Components [*Commercial firm*] [*British*]
**ME(Mech)** ... Master of Engineering (Mechanical) (ADA)
**Mem Ecol Soc Aust** ... Memoirs. Ecological Society of Australia [*A publication*] (APTA)
**Mem Ehime Univ** ... Memoirs. Ehime University [*A publication*]
**Mem Ehime Univ Nat Sci Ser B (Biol)** ... Memoirs. Ehime University. Natural Science. Series B (Biology) [*A publication*]
**Mem Ehime Univ Nat Sci Ser C** ... Memoirs. Ehime University. Natural Science. Series C [*A publication*]
**Mem Ehime Univ Natur Sci Ser A** ... Memoirs. Ehime University. Natural Science. Series A [*A publication*]

**Mem Ehime Univ Sect 6 Agr** ... Memoirs. Ehime University. Section 6. Agriculture [*A publication*]
**Mem Ehime Univ Sect 6 (Agric)** ... Memoirs. Ehime University. Section 6 (Agriculture) [*A publication*]
**Mem Ehime Univ Sect 3 Eng** ... Memoirs. Ehime University. Section 3. Engineering [*Japan*] [*A publication*]
**Mem Ehime Univ Sect 3 Engrg** ... Memoirs. Ehime University. Section 3. Engineering [*A publication*]
**Mem Ehime Univ Sect 2 Nat Sci** ... Memoirs. Ehime University. Section 2. Natural Science [*A publication*]
**Mem Ehime Univ Sect 2 Ser C** ... Memoirs. Ehime University. Section 2. Natural Science. Series C. Chemistry [*A publication*]
**Mem Entomol Soc Can** ... Memoirs. Entomological Society of Canada [*A publication*]
**Mem Entomol Soc Que** ... Memoirs. Entomological Society of Quebec [*A publication*]
**Mem Entomol Soc South Afr** ... Memoirs. Entomological Society of Southern Africa [*A publication*]
**Mem Entomol Soc Sthn Afr** ... Memoirs. Entomological Society of Southern Africa [*A publication*]
**Mem Entomol Soc Wash** ... Memoirs. Entomological Society of Washington [*A publication*]
**Mem Ent S C** ... Memoirs. Entomological Society of Canada [*A publication*]
**Mem Ent Soc Can** ... Memoirs. Entomological Society of Canada [*A publication*]
**Mem Estud Mus Zool Univ Coimbra** ... Memorias e Estudos. Museu Zoologico. Universidade de Coimbra [*A publication*]
**MeMeth**..... Media and Methods [*A publication*]
**Mem Etud Sci Rev Metall** ... Memoires et Etudes Scientifiques de la Revue de Metallurgie [*A publication*]
**Mem Explic Cartes Geol Min Belg** ... Memoires pour Servir a l'Explication des Cartes Geologiques et Minieres de la Belgique [*A publication*]
**MEMFA**.... Metallurgia and Metal Forming [*A publication*]
**Mem Fac Agr Hokkaido U** ... Memoirs. Faculty of Agriculture. Hokkaido University [*A publication*]
**Mem Fac Agr Hokkaido Univ** ... Memoirs. Faculty of Agriculture. Hokkaido University [*A publication*]
**Mem Fac Agric Hokkaido Univ** ... Memoirs. Faculty of Agriculture. Hokkaido University [*A publication*]
**Mem Fac Agric Kagawa Univ** ... Memoirs. Faculty of Agriculture. Kagawa University [*A publication*]
**Mem Fac Agric Kagoshima Univ** ... Memoirs. Faculty of Agriculture. Kagoshima University [*A publication*]
**Mem Fac Agric Kinki Univ** ... Memoirs. Faculty of Agriculture. Kinki University [*A publication*]
**Mem Fac Agric Kochi Univ** ... Memoirs. Faculty of Agriculture. Kochi University [*A publication*]
**Mem Fac Agric Niigata Univ** ... Memoirs. Faculty of Agriculture. Niigata University [*A publication*]
**Mem Fac Agric Univ Miyazaki** ... Memoirs. Faculty of Agriculture. University of Miyazaki [*A publication*]
**Mem Fac Agr Kagawa Univ** ... Memoirs. Faculty of Agriculture. Kagawa University [*A publication*]
**Mem Fac Agr Kinki Univ** ... Memoirs. Faculty of Agriculture. Kinki University [*A publication*]
**Mem Fac Agr Univ Miyazaki** ... Memoirs. Faculty of Agriculture. University of Miyazaki [*A publication*]
**Mem Fac Ed Kumamoto Univ Natur Sci** ... Kumamoto University. Faculty of Education. Memoirs. Natural Science [*A publication*]
**Mem Fac Ed Kumamoto Univ Sect 1** ... Memoirs. Faculty of Education. Kumamoto University. Section 1 (Natural Science) [*A publication*]
**Mem Fac Ed Miyazaki Univ** ... Memoirs. Faculty of Education. Miyazaki University [*A publication*]
**Mem Fac Ed Shiga Univ Natur Sci** ... Shiga University. Faculty of Education. Memoirs. Natural Science [*A publication*]
**Mem Fac Ed Shimane Univ Natur Sci** ... Shimane University. Faculty of Education. Memoirs. Natural Science [*A publication*]
**Mem Fac Educ Akita Univ** ... Memoirs. Faculty of Education. Akita University [*A publication*]
**Mem Fac Educ Akita Univ Nat Sci** ... Memoirs. Faculty of Education. Akita University. Natural Science [*A publication*]
**Mem Fac Educ Kumamoto Univ** ... Memoirs. Faculty of Education. Kumamoto University [*A publication*]
**Mem Fac Educ Kumamoto Univ Nat Sci** ... Memoirs. Faculty of Education. Kumamoto University. Natural Science [*A publication*]
**Mem Fac Educ Kumamoto Univ Sect 1 (Nat Sci)** ... Memoirs. Faculty of Education. Kumamoto University. Section 1 (Natural Science) [*A publication*]
**Mem Fac Educ Mie Univ** ... Memoirs. Faculty of Education. Mie University [*A publication*]
**Mem Fac Educ Niigata Univ** ... Memoirs. Faculty of Education. Niigata University [*A publication*]
**Mem Fac Educ Shiga Univ Nat Sci** ... Memoirs. Faculty of Education. Shiga University. Natural Science [*A publication*]
**Mem Fac Educ Toyama Univ** ... Memoirs. Faculty of Education. Toyama University [*A publication*]
**Mem Fac Educ Yamanashi Univ** ... Memoirs. Faculty of Education. Yamanashi University [*Japan*] [*A publication*]
**Mem Fac Eng Fukui Univ** ... Memoirs. Faculty of Engineering. Fukui University [*Japan*] [*A publication*]
**Mem Fac Eng Hiroshima Univ** ... Memoirs. Faculty of Engineering. Hiroshima University [*A publication*]
**Mem Fac Eng Hokkaido Imp Univ** ... Memoirs. Faculty of Engineering. Hokkaido Imperial University [*A publication*]
**Mem Fac Eng Hokkaido Univ** ... Memoirs. Faculty of Engineering. Hokkaido University [*A publication*]
**Mem Fac Eng Hokkaido Univ (Sapporo Jpn)** ... Memoirs. Faculty of Engineering. Hokkaido University (Sapporo, Japan) [*A publication*]
**Mem Fac Eng Kobe Univ** ... Memoirs. Faculty of Engineering. Kobe University [*A publication*]
**Mem Fac Eng Kumamoto Univ** ... Memoirs. Faculty of Engineering. Kumamoto University [*A publication*]
**Mem Fac Eng Kyoto Univ** ... Memoirs. Faculty of Engineering. Kyoto University [*A publication*]
**Mem Fac Eng Kyushu Univ** ... Memoirs. Faculty of Engineering. Kyushu University [*A publication*]
**Mem Fac Eng Miyazaki Univ** ... Memoirs. Faculty of Engineering. Miyazaki University [*A publication*]
**Mem Fac Eng Nagoya Univ** ... Memoirs. Faculty of Engineering. Nagoya University [*A publication*]
**Mem Fac Eng Nagoya Univ** ... Memoirs. Nagoya University. Faculty of Engineering [*A publication*]
**Mem Fac Engng Kyoto Univ** ... Memoirs. Faculty of Engineering. Kyoto University [*A publication*]
**Mem Fac Engng Kyushu Univ** ... Memoirs. Faculty of Engineering. Kyushu University [*A publication*]
**Mem Fac Engng Nagoya Univ** ... Memoirs. Faculty of Engineering. Nagoya University [*A publication*]
**Mem Fac Eng Osaka City Univ** ... Memoirs. Faculty of Engineering. Osaka City University [*A publication*]
**Mem Fac Engrg Hiroshima Univ** ... Memoirs. Faculty of Engineering. Hiroshima University [*A publication*]
**Mem Fac Engrg Kyoto Univ** ... Memoirs. Faculty of Engineering. Kyoto University [*A publication*]
**Mem Fac Engrg Miyazaki Univ** ... Memoirs. Faculty of Engineering. Miyazaki University [*A publication*]
**Mem Fac Eng Tamagawa Univ** ... Memoirs. Faculty of Engineering. Tamagawa University [*A publication*]
**Mem Fac Eng Tehran Univ** ... Memoirs. Faculty of Engineering. Tehran University [*A publication*]
**Mem Fac Eng Yamaguchi Univ** ... Memoirs. Faculty of Engineering. Yamaguchi University [*Japan*] [*A publication*]
**Mem Fac Fish Hokkaido Univ** ... Memoirs. Faculty of Fisheries. Hokkaido University [*A publication*]
**Mem Fac Fish Kagoshima Univ** ... Memoirs. Faculty of Fisheries. Kagoshima University [*A publication*]
**Mem Fac Gen Ed Kumamoto Univ Natur Sci** ... Memoirs. Kumamoto University. Faculty of General Education. Natural Sciences [*A publication*]
**Mem Fac Gen Educ Hiroshima Univ** ... Memoirs. Faculty of General Education. Hiroshima University [*A publication*]
**Mem Fac Ind Arts Kyoto Tech Univ** ... Memoirs. Faculty of Industrial Arts. Kyoto Technical University. Science and Technology [*A publication*]
**Mem Fac Ind Arts Kyoto Tech Univ Sci and Technol** ... Memoirs. Faculty of Industrial Arts. Kyoto Technical University. Science and Technology [*A publication*]
**Mem Fac Indust Arts Kyoto Tech Univ Sci and Tech** ... Memoirs. Faculty of Industrial Arts. Kyoto Technical University. Science and Technology [*A publication*]
**Mem Fac Lib Arts Educ Miyazaki Univ** ... Memoirs. Faculty of Liberal Arts Education. Miyazaki University [*A publication*]
**Mem Fac Lib Arts Fukui Univ** ... Memoirs. Faculty of Liberal Arts. Fukui University [*A publication*]
**Mem Fac Liberal Arts Educ Yamanashi Univ** ... Memoirs. Faculty of Liberal Arts and Education. Yamanashi University [*Japan*] [*A publication*]
**Mem Fac Lit Sci Shimane Univ Nat Sci** ... Memoirs. Faculty of Literature and Science. Shimane University. Natural Sciences [*A publication*]
**Mem Fac Lit Sci Shimane Univ Natur Sci** ... Memoirs. Faculty of Literature and Science. Shimane University. Natural Sciences [*Matsue*] [*A publication*]
**Mem Fac Sci Eng Waseda Univ** ... Memoirs. Faculty of Science and Engineering. Waseda University [*A publication*]
**Mem Fac Sci Kochi Univ Ser A Math** ... Kochi University. Faculty of Science. Memoirs. Series A. Mathematics [*A publication*]
**Mem Fac Sci Kochi Univ Ser D Biol** ... Memoirs. Faculty of Science. Kochi University. Series D. Biology [*A publication*]
**Mem Fac Sci Kyoto Univ Ser Biol** ... Memoirs. Faculty of Science. Kyoto University. Series of Biology [*A publication*]
**Mem Fac Sci Kyoto Univ Ser Geol Mineral** ... Memoirs. Faculty of Science. Kyoto University. Series of Geology and Mineralogy [*A publication*]
**Mem Fac Sci Kyoto Univ Ser Phys Astrophys Geophys Chem** ... Memoirs. Faculty of Science. Kyoto University. Series of Physics, Astrophysics, Geophysics, and Chemistry [*A publication*]

**Mem Fac Sci Kyushu Univ** ... Memoirs. Faculty of Science. Kyushu University [*A publication*]
**Mem Fac Sci Kyushu Univ B** ... Memoirs. Faculty of Science. Kyushu University. Series B [*A publication*]
**Mem Fac Sci Kyushu Univ C** ... Memoirs. Faculty of Science. Kyushu University. Series C [*A publication*]
**Mem Fac Sci Kyushu Univ Ser A** ... Memoirs. Faculty of Science. Kyushu University. Series A. Mathematics [*A publication*]
**Mem Fac Sci Kyushu Univ Ser B** ... Memoirs. Faculty of Science. Kyushu University. Series B. Physics [*A publication*]
**Mem Fac Sci Kyushu Univ Ser C** ... Memoirs. Faculty of Science. Kyushu University. Series C. Chemistry [*A publication*]
**Mem Fac Sci Kyushu Univ Ser D** ... Memoirs. Faculty of Science. Kyushu University. Series D. Geology [*A publication*]
**Mem Fac Sci Kyushu Univ Ser D Geol** ... Memoirs. Faculty of Science. Kyushu University. Series D. Geology [*A publication*]
**Mem Fac Sci Kyushu Univ Ser E** ... Memoirs. Faculty of Science. Kyushu University. Series E. Biology [*A publication*]
**Mem Fac Sci Kyushu Univ Ser E Biol** ... Memoirs. Faculty of Science. Kyushu University. Series E. Biology [*A publication*]
**Mem Fac Sci Shimane Univ** ... Shimane University. Faculty of Science. Memoirs [*A publication*]
**Mem Fac Technol Kanazawa Univ** ... Memoirs. Faculty of Technology. Kanazawa University [*A publication*]
**Mem Fac Technol Tokyo Metrop Univ** ... Memoirs. Faculty of Technology. Tokyo Metropolitan University [*A publication*]
**Mem Fac Tech Tokyo Metropolitan Univ** ... Memoirs. Faculty of Technology. Tokyo Metropolitan University [*A publication*]
**Mem Gen Inst Geol Min Esp** ... Memoria General. Instituto Geologico y Minero de Espana [*A publication*]
**Mem Geol Soc Am** ... Memoir. Geological Society of America [*A publication*]
**Mem Geol Surv Can** ... Memoirs. Geological Survey of Canada [*A publication*]
**Mem Geol Surv GB Engl Wales Explan Sheet** ... Memoirs. Geological Survey of Great Britain. England and Wales Explanation Sheet [*A publication*]
**Mem Geol Surv GB (Scotl)** ... Memoirs. Geological Survey of Great Britain (Scotland) [*A publication*]
**Mem Geol Surv Gt Br** ... Memoirs. Geological Survey of Great Britain [*A publication*]
**Mem Geol Surv India** ... Memoirs. Geological Survey of India [*A publication*]
**Mem Geol Surv North Irel** ... Memoir. Geological Survey of Northern Ireland [*A publication*]
**Mem Geol Surv NSW** ... Memoirs. Geological Survey of New South Wales [*A publication*] (APTA)
**Mem Geol Surv of NSW** ... Memoirs. Geological Survey of New South Wales [*A publication*] (APTA)
**Mem Geol Surv of NSW Geol** ... Memoirs. Geological Survey of New South Wales. Department of Mines. Geology [*A publication*]
**Mem Geol Surv NSW Geol** ... New South Wales. Geological Survey. Memoirs. Geology [*A publication*] (APTA)
**Mem Geol Surv NSW Palaeontol** ... Memoirs. Geological Survey of New South Wales. Palaeontology [*A publication*]
**Mem Geol Surv Papua New Guinea** ... Memoirs. Geological Survey of Papua New Guinea [*A publication*]
**Mem Geol Surv S Afr** ... Memoirs. Geological Survey of South Africa [*A publication*]
**Mem Geol Surv South West Afr** ... Memoir. Geological Survey of South West Africa [*A publication*]
**Mem Geol Surv Vic** ... Memoirs. Geological Survey of Victoria [*A publication*] (APTA)
**Mem Geol Surv Vict** ... Memoirs. Geological Survey of Victoria [*A publication*]
**Mem Geol Surv West Aust** ... Memoirs. Geological Survey of Western Australia [*A publication*]
**Mem Geopaleontol Univ Ferrara** ... Memorie Geopaleontologiche. Universita di Ferrara [*A publication*]
**Mem Gifu Tech Coll** ... Memoirs. Gifu Technical College [*A publication*]
**Mem Hist Ant** ... Memorias de Historia Antigua. Universidad de Oviedo [*A publication*]
**Mem Hokkaido Inst Technol** ... Memoirs. Hokkaido Institute of Technology [*A publication*]
**Mem Hourglass Cruises** ... Memoirs. Hourglass Cruises [*A publication*]
**Mem Hyogo Univ Agric** ... Memoirs. Hyogo University of Agriculture [*A publication*]
**MEMI** ....... Master Equipment Management Index [*Air Force*] (AFM)
**MeMi**......... Millinocket Memorial Library, Millinocket, ME [*Library symbol*] [*Library of Congress*] (LCLS)
**Mem Indian Bot Soc** ... Memoirs. Indian Botanical Society [*A publication*]
**Mem Indian Mus** ... Memoirs. Indian Museum [*A publication*]
**Mem Inst** ... Memoires. Institut Francais d'Archeologie Orientale [*A publication*]
**Mem Inst Butantan** ... Memorias. Instituto Butantan [*A publication*]
**Mem Inst Butantan (Sao Paulo)** ... Memorias. Instituto Butantan (Sao Paulo) [*A publication*]
**Mem Inst Egypt** ... Memoires. Institut d'Egypte [*A publication*]
**Mem Inst Esp Oceanogr** ... Memorias. Instituto Espanol de Oceanografia [*A publication*]
**Mem Inst Geol Min Esp** ... Memorias. Instituto Geologico y Minero de Espana [*A publication*]
**Mem Inst Geol (Rom)** ... Memorii. Institutul Geologie (Romania) [*A publication*]
**Mem Inst Geol Univ Louv** ... Memoires. Institut Geologique. Universite de Louvain [*A publication*]
**Mem Inst High Speed Mech Tohoku Univ** ... Memoirs. Institute of High Speed Mechanics. Tohoku University [*Japan*] [*A publication*]
**Mem Inst Invest Cient Mocambique Ser A Cienc Biol** ... Memorias. Instituto de Investigacao Cientifica de Mocambique. Serie A. Ciencias Biologicas [*A publication*]
**Mem Inst Nat Fr** ... Memoires. Institut National de France [*A publication*]
**Mem Inst Oceanogr (Monaco)** ... Memoires. Institut Oceanographique (Monaco) [*A publication*]
**Mem Inst Oswaldo Cruz** ... Memorias. Instituto Oswaldo Cruz [*A publication*]
**Mem Inst Oswaldo Cruz (Rio De J)** ... Memorias. Instituto Oswaldo Cruz (Rio De Janeiro) [*A publication*]
**Mem Inst Protein Res Osaka Univ** ... Memoirs. Institute of Protein Research. Osaka University [*A publication*]
**Mem Inst Rech Sci Madagascar Ser A Biol Anim** ... Memoires. Institut de Recherche Scientifique de Madagascar. Serie A. Biologie Animale [*A publication*]
**Mem Inst Rech Sci Madagascar Ser B Biol Veg** ... Memoires. Institut de Recherche Scientifique de Madagascar. Serie B. Biologie Vegetale [*A publication*]
**Mem Inst Rech Sci Madagascar Ser F Oceanogr** ... Memoires. Institut de Recherche Scientifique de Madagascar. Serie F. Oceanographie [*A publication*]
**Mem Inst Sci Ind Res Osaka Univ** ... Memoirs. Institute of Scientific and Industrial Research. Osaka University [*A publication*]
**Mem Inst Sci Madagascar Ser B** ... Memoires. Institut de Recherche Scientifique de Madagascar. Serie B. Biologie [*A publication*]
**Mem Inst Sci Madagascar Ser D** ... Memoires. Institut de Recherche Scientifique de Madagascar. Serie D. Sciences de la Terre [*A publication*]
**Mem Int Assoc Hydrogeol** ... Memoirs. International Association of Hydrogeologists [*A publication*]
**Mem Int Soc Sugar Cane Technol** ... Memoirs. International Society of Sugar Cane Technologists [*A publication*]
**Mem Ist Geol Mineral Univ Padova** ... Memorie. Istituti di Geologia e Mineralogia. Universita di Padova [*A publication*]
**Mem Ist Ital Idrobiol** ... Memorie. Istituto Italiano di Idrobiologia [*A publication*]
**Mem Ist Ital Idrobiol Dott Marco De Marchi** ... Memorie. Istituto Italiano di Idrobiologia Dottore Marco De Marchi [*Italy*] [*A publication*]
**Mem Ist Ital Idrobiol Dott Marco De Marchi (Pallanza Italy)** ... Memorie. Istituto Italiano di Idrobiologia Dottore Marco De Marchi (Pallanza, Italy) [*A publication*]
**Mem Ist Ital Idrobiol Dott Marco Marchi** ... Memorie. Istituto Italiano di Idrobiologia Dottore Marco De Marchi [*A publication*]
**MEMISTOR** ... Memory Resistor (DEN)
**Mem Jornadas Agron** ... Memoria Jornadas Agronomicas [*A publication*]
**Mem Junta Invest Ultramar (Port)** ... Memorias. Junta de Investigacoes do Ultramar (Portugal) [*A publication*]
**Mem Junta Invest Ultramar Ser II** ... Memorias. Junta de Investigacoes do Ultramar. Serie II [*A publication*]
**Mem Junta Missoes Geogr Invest Ultramar (Port)** ... Memorias. Junta das Missoes Geograficas e de Investigacoes do Ultramar (Portugal) [*A publication*]
**Mem Kakioka Magn Obs** ... Memoirs. Kakioka Magnetic Observatory [*Japan*] [*A publication*]
**Mem Kanazawa Inst Technol** ... Memoirs. Kanazawa Institute of Technology [*A publication*]
**Mem Kitami Inst Tech** ... Memoirs. Kitami Institute of Technology [*A publication*]
**Mem Kobe Mar Obs (Kobe Jpn)** ... Memoirs. Kobe Marine Observatory (Kobe, Japan) [*A publication*]
**Mem Konan Univ Sci Ser** ... Memoirs. Konan University. Science Series [*A publication*]
**Mem Kyoto Tech Univ Sci Tech** ... Memoirs. Faculty of Industrial Arts. Kyoto Technical University. Science and Technology [*A publication*]
**Mem Kyushu Inst Technol Eng** ... Memoirs. Kyushu Institute of Technology. Engineering [*A publication*]
**MEML** ...... Master Equipment Management List [*Air Force*] (AFM)
**MEML** ...... Memorial (FAAC)
**MEML** ...... Molecular Engineering and Materials Laboratory [*MIT*] (MCD)
**MEMLACTV** ... Memorial Activities [*Military*] (AABC)
**Mem LJ** ..... Memphis Law Journal [*Tennessee*] [*A publication*] (DLA)
**Meml Meteorol Natl** ... Memorial de la Meteorologie Nationale [*A publication*]
**Mem Mat Inst Jorge Juan** ... Memorias de Matematica. Instituto Jorge Juan [*Madrid*] [*A publication*]
**Mem Meteorol Natl** ... Memorial de la Meteorologie Nationale [*A publication*]
**Mem Miner Resour Div (Tanzania)** ... Memoirs. Mineral Resources Division (Tanzania) [*A publication*]
**Mem Miner Resour Geol Surv Szechuan** ... Memoirs of Mineral Resources. Geological Survey of Szechuan [*A publication*]

**Mem Miyakonojo Tech Coll** ... Memoirs. Miyakonojo Technical College [*A publication*]
**Mem Muroran Inst Tech** ... Memoirs. Muroran Institute of Technology [*A publication*]
**Mem Muroran Inst Technol** ... Memoirs. Muroran Institute of Technology [*Japan*] [*A publication*]
**Mem Mus Civ Stor Nat Verona** ... Memorie. Museo Civico di Storia Naturale di Verona [*A publication*]
**Mem Mus Civ Stor Nat Verona IIA Ser Sez Sci Vita** ... Memorie. Museo Civico di Storia Naturale di Verona. IIA Serie. Sezione Scienze della Vita [*A publication*]
**Mem Mus Dr Alvaro De Castro** ... Memorias. Museu Dr. Alvaro De Castro [*A publication*]
**Mem Mus Hist Nat "Javier Prado"** ... Memorias. Museo de Historia Natural "Javier Prado" [*A publication*]
**Mem Mus Hist Nat (Paris) Ser C** ... Memoires. Museum National d'Histoire Naturelle (Paris). Serie C. Sciences de la Terre [*A publication*]
**Mem Mus Mar Ser Zool** ... Memorias. Museu do Mar. Serie Zoologica [*A publication*]
**Mem Mus Natl His Nat Ser C Sci Terre** ... Memoires. Museum National d'Histoire Naturelle. Serie C. Sciences de la Terre [*A publication*]
**Mem Mus Natl Hist Nat** ... Memoires. Museum National d'Histoire Naturelle [*A publication*]
**Mem Mus Natl Hist Nat Ser A (Paris)** ... Memoires. Museum National d'Histoire Naturelle. Serie A. Zoologie (Paris) [*A publication*]
**Mem Mus Natl Hist Nat Ser A Zool** ... Memoires. Museum National d'Histoire Naturelle. Serie A. Zoologie [*A publication*]
**Mem Mus Natl Hist Nat Ser B Bot** ... Memoires. Museum National d'Histoire Naturelle. Serie B. Botanique [*A publication*]
**Mem Mus Natl Hist Nat Ser C Geol** ... Memoires. Museum National d'Histoire Naturelle. Serie C. Geologie [*A publication*]
**Mem Mus Natl Hist Nat Ser C (Paris)** ... Memoires. Museum National d'Histoire Naturelle. Serie C. Sciences de la Terre (Paris) [*A publication*]
**Mem Mus Natl Hist Nat Ser D (Paris)** ... Memoires. Museum National d'Histoire Naturelle. Serie D. Sciences Physico-Chimiques (Paris) [*A publication*]
**Mem Mus Natn Hist Nat (Paris)** ... Memoires. Museum National d'Histoire Naturelle (Paris) [*A publication*]
**Mem Mus Stor Nat Venezia Tridentina** ... Memorie. Museo di Storia Naturale della Venezia Tridentina [*A publication*]
**Mem Mus Tridentino Sci Nat** ... Memorie. Museo Tridentino di Scienze Naturali [*A publication*]
**Mem Mus Victoria** ... Memoirs. Museum of Victoria [*A publication*]
**Mem Nap**... Memorie. Accademia di Archeologia, Lettere, e Belle Arti di Napoli [*A publication*]
**Mem Nas Mus Bloemfontein** ... Memoirs. Nasionale Museum Bloemfontein [*A publication*]
**Mem Nat Cult Res San-In Reg** ... Memoirs of Natural and Cultural Researches of the San-In Region [*A publication*]
**Mem Nat Defense Acad** ... Memoirs. National Defense Academy. Mathematics, Physics, Chemistry, and Engineering [*Yokosuka*] [*A publication*]
**Mem Natl Def Acad** ... Memoirs. National Defense Academy [*A publication*]
**Mem Natl Inst Polar Res Ser E Biol Med Sci** ... Memoirs. National Institute of Polar Research. Series E. Biology and Medical Science [*A publication*]
**Mem Natl Mus Vict** ... Memoirs. National Museum of Victoria [*A publication*] (APTA)
**Mem Natl Mus Victoria** ... Memoirs. National Museum of Victoria [*A publication*]
**Mem Natl Sci Mus (Tokyo)** ... Memoirs. National Science Museum (Tokyo) [*A publication*]
**Mem Nat Mus VIC** ... Memoirs. National Museum of Victoria [*A publication*] (APTA)
**Mem Natn Mus (Melb)** ... Memoirs. National Museum (Melbourne) [*A publication*]
**Mem Niihama Tech Coll** ... Memoirs. Niihama Technical College [*Japan*] [*A publication*]
**Mem Niihama Tech Coll Nat Sci** ... Memoirs. Niihama Technical College. Natural Sciences [*A publication*]
**Mem NM Bur Mines Miner Resour** ... Memoir. New Mexico Bureau of Mines and Mineral Resources [*A publication*]
**Mem Note Ist Geol Appl Univ Napoli** ... Memorie e Note. Istituto di Geologia Applicata. Universita di Napoli [*A publication*]
**Mem Notic Mus Miner Geol Univ Coimbra** ... Memorias e Noticias. Museu e Laboratorio Mineralogico e Geologico. Universidade de Coimbra [*A publication*]
**Mem Not Publ Mus Lab Miner Geol Univ Coimbra** ... Memorias e Noticias. Museu e Laboratorio Mineralogico e Geologico da Universidade de Coimbra [*A publication*]
**Mem NS Dep Mines** ... Memoirs. Nova Scotia Department of Mines [*A publication*]
**Mem Numer Math** ... Memoirs of Numerical Mathematics [*A publication*]
**Mem NY Agr Exp Sta** ... Memoir. New York Agricultural Experiment Station [*A publication*]
**Mem NY Bot Gard** ... Memoirs. New York Botanical Gardens [*A publication*]
**MEMO**...... Marine Environmental Management Office [*Marine science*] (MSC)
**MEMO**...... Medical Equipment Management Office [*Air Force*] (AFM)
**MEMO**...... Memorandum (AFM)
**MEMO**...... Middle East Money [*London-Beirut*] (BJA)
**MEMO**...... Mission Essential Maintenance Only (MCD)
**MEMO**...... Mission Essential Maintenance Operation (MCD)
**MEMO**...... Model for Evaluating Missile Observation
**MEMOA**... Medizinische Monatsschrift [*A publication*]
**MEMOCS** ... Mitsubishi Electric Corp. Multiterm Out-of-Context System
**Memo Div Chem Eng CSIRO** ... Memorandum. Division of Chemical Engineering. Commonwealth Scientific and Industrial Research Organisation [*A publication*] (APTA)
**Memo Div Chem Engng CSIRO** ... Memorandum. Division of Chemical Engineering. Commonwealth Scientific and Industrial Research Organisation [*A publication*] (APTA)
**Memo Fed Dept Agr Res (Nigeria)** ... Memorandum. Federal Department of Agricultural Research (Nigeria) [*A publication*]
**Mem Off Rech Sci Tech Outre-Mer** ... Memoires. Office de la Recherche Scientifique et Technique d'Outre-Mer [*A publication*]
**Mem Ofic Estud Espec Min Agr Dir Agr Pesca (Chile)** ... Memoria. Oficina de Estudios Especiales. Ministerio de Agricultura. Direccion de Agricultura y Pesca (Chile) [*A publication*]
**Memo Indian Tea Assoc Tocklai Exp Stn** ... Memorandum. Indian Tea Association. Tocklai Experimental Station [*A publication*]
**Memo Meat Res Inst** ... Memorandum. Meat Research Institute [*A publication*]
**Memo Med Res Counc** ... Memorandum. Medical Research Council [*London*] [*A publication*]
**Memo Mgmt** ... Memo to Management [*Australian Institute of Management, Queensland Division*] [*A publication*]
**Memo Nor Landbrukshogsk Inst Landbruksokom** ... Memorandum. Norges Landbrukshogskole Institutt foer Landbruksokonomi [*A publication*]
**Memorabilia Zool** ... Memorabilia Zoologica [*A publication*]
**MEMOREX** ... Memory Excellence [*Brand name*]
**Memorial Univ Newfoundland Occas Pap Biol** ... Memorial University of Newfoundland. Occasional Papers in Biology [*A publication*]
**Memorie Soc Ent Ital** ... Memorie. Societa Entomologica Italiana [*A publication*]
**Mem ORSTOM** ... Memoires. Office de la Recherche Scientifique et Technique d'Outre-Mer [*A publication*]
**MEMOS** ... Manufacturing Engineering Management Operations System (MCD)
**Mem Osaka Inst Technol Ser A Sci Technol** ... Memoirs. Osaka Institute of Technology. Series A. Science and Technology [*A publication*]
**Mem Osaka Inst Tech Ser A** ... Memoirs. Osaka Institute of Technology. Series A. Science and Technology [*A publication*]
**Mem Osaka Kyoiku Univ** ... Memoires. Osaka Kyoiku University [*A publication*]
**Mem Osaka Kyoiku Univ III Nat Sci Appl Sci** ... Memoirs. Osaka Kyoiku University. III. Natural Science and Applied Science [*A publication*]
**Mem Osaka Kyoiku Univ III Natur Sci Appl Sci** ... Memoirs. Osaka Kyoiku University. III. Natural Science and Applied Science [*A publication*]
**Mem Osaka Univ Lib Arts Educ B Natur Sci** ... Memoirs. Osaka University of Liberal Arts and Education. B. Natural Science [*A publication*]
**Memo Soc Fauna Flora Fenn** ... Memoranda Societatis pro Fauna et Flora Fennica [*A publication*]
**Memo Univ Coll Wales Dept Geogr** ... Memorandum. University College of Wales. Department of Geography [*A publication*]
**MEMP** ...... Maximization of Expected Maximum Profit [*Econometrics*]
**Mem Pac Coast Entomol Soc** ... Memoirs. Pacific Coast Entomological Society [*A publication*]
**Mem Palaeontol Ser Geol Surv (NSW)** ... Memoirs. Palaeontology Series. Geological Survey (New South Wales) [*A publication*]
**MEMPB**.... Moessbauer Effect Methodology. Proceedings of the Symposium [*A publication*]
**Memphis Bs** ... Memphis Business Journal [*A publication*]
**Memphis J Med Sc** ... Memphis Journal of the Medical Sciences [*A publication*]
**Memphis LJ** ... Memphis Law Journal [*Tennessee*] [*A publication*] (DLA)
**Memphis Med Month** ... Memphis Medical Monthly [*A publication*]
**Memphis Mid-South Med J** ... Memphis and Mid-South Medical Journal [*A publication*]
**Memphis State UL Rev** ... Memphis State University. Law Review [*A publication*]
**Memphis State Univ L Rev** ... Memphis State University. Law Review [*A publication*]
**Memphis St U L Rev** ... Memphis State University. Law Review [*A publication*]
**Memp LJ** ... Memphis Law Journal [*Tennessee*] [*A publication*] (DLA)
**Mem Pont Acc** ... Atti. Pontificia Accademia Romana di Archeologia. Memorie [*A publication*]
**Mem Poudres** ... Memorial des Poudres [*France*] [*A publication*]
**MEMPP**.... Morpholinoethylmethylphenylpyridazone [*An analgesic*]

**Mem Proc Manchester Lit Philos Soc** ... Memoirs and Proceedings. Manchester Literary and Philosophical Society [*A publication*]
MEMPT.... Memory Point
**Mem Publies Inst Prot Plant** ... Memoires Publies. Institut pour la Protection des Plantes [*A publication*]
**Mem Publ Soc Sci Arts Lett Hainaut** ... Memoires et Publications. Societe des Sciences, des Arts, et des Lettres du Hainaut [*A publication*]
MEMQ...... Married Enlisted Men's Quarters
**Mem Qd Mus** ... Memoirs. Queensland Museum [*A publication*] (APTA)
**Mem Queensl Mus** ... Memoirs. Queensland Museum [*A publication*]
ME (MR)... Medical Evidence (Medical Report or Record) (OICC)
MEMR...... Ramtron Australia Ltd. [*NASDAQ symbol*] (NQ)
MEMRA ... Mechanical Equipment Manufacturers Representatives Association (EA)
**Mem R Acad Cienc Artes Barc** ... Memorias. Real Academia de Ciencias y Artes de Barcelona [*A publication*]
**Mem R Acad Cienc Exactas Fis Nat Madrid** ... Memorias. Real Academia de Ciencias Exactas, Fisicas, y Naturales de Madrid [*A publication*]
**Mem R Acad Cienc Exactas Fis Nat Madrid Ser Cienc Exactas** ... Memorias. Real Academia de Ciencias Exactas, Fisicas, y Naturales de Madrid. Serie de Ciencias Exactas [*A publication*]
**Mem R Acad Cienc Exactas Fis Nat Madrid Ser Cienc Fis-Quim** ... Memorias. Real Academia de Ciencias Exactas, Fisicas, y Naturales de Madrid. Serie de Ciencias Fisico-Quimicas [*A publication*]
**Mem R Acad Cienc Exactas Fis Nat Madrid Ser Cienc Nat** ... Memorias. Real Academia de Ciencias Exactas, Fisicas, y Naturales de Madrid. Serie de Ciencias Naturales [*A publication*]
**Mem R Acad Cienc Exactas Fis Nat Madr Ser Cienc Nat** ... Memorias. Real Academia de Ciencias Exactas, Fisicas, y Naturales de Madrid. Serie de Ciencias Naturales [*A publication*]
**Mem R Accad Ital Cl Sci Fis Mat Nat** ... Memorie. Reale Accademia d'Italia. Classe di Scienze Fisiche, Matematiche, e Naturali [*A publication*]
**Mem R Accad Ital Cl Sci Fis Mat Nat Biol** ... Memorie. Reale Accademia d'Italia. Classe di Scienze Fisiche, Matematiche, e Naturali. Biologia [*A publication*]
**Mem R Accad Ital Cl Sci Fis Mat Nat Chim** ... Memorie. Reale Accademia d'Italia. Classe di Scienze Fisiche, Matematiche, e Naturali. Chimica [*A publication*]
**Mem R Accad Ital Cl Sci Fis Mat Nat Fis** ... Memorie. Reale Accademia d'Italia. Classe di Scienze Fisiche, Matematiche, e Naturali. Fisica [*A publication*]
**Mem R Accad Ital Cl Sci Fis Mat Nat Ing** ... Memorie. Reale Accademia d'Italia. Classe di Scienze Fisiche, Matematiche, e Naturali. Ingegneria [*A publication*]
**Mem R Accad Ital Cl Sci Fis Mat Nat Mat** ... Memorie. Reale Accademia d'Italia. Classe di Scienze Fisiche, Matematiche, e Naturali. Matematica [*A publication*]
**Mem R Accad Sci Ist Bologna Cl Sci Fis** ... Memorie. Reale Accademia delle Scienze. Istituto di Bologna. Classe di Scienze Fisiche [*A publication*]
**Mem R Accad Sci Lett Arti (Modena)** ... Memorie. Reale Accademia di Scienze, Lettere, ed Arti (Modena) [*A publication*]
**Mem Raman Res Inst** ... Memoirs. Raman Research Institute [*A publication*]
**Mem R Asiat Soc Bengal** ... Memoirs. Royal Asiatic Society of Bengal [*A publication*]
**Mem R Astron Soc** ... Memoirs. Royal Astronomical Society [*A publication*]
**Mem Real Acad Ci Art Barcelona** ... Memorias. Real Academia de Ciencias y Artes de Barcelona [*A publication*]
**Mem Real Acad Cienc Artes Barcelona** ... Memorias. Real Academia de Ciencias y Artes de Barcelona [*A publication*]
**Mem Real Acad Ci Exact Fis Natur Madrid** ... Memorias. Real Academia de Ciencias Exactas, Fisicas, y Naturales de Madrid. Serie de Ciencias Exactas [*A publication*]
**Mem Rend Accad Zel Acireale** ... Memorie e Rendiconti. Accademia di Scienze, Lettere, e Belle Arti degli Zelanti e dei Dafnici di Acireale [*A publication*]
**Mem Res Depart Toyo Bunko** ... Memoirs. Research Department. Toyo Bunko [*A publication*]
**Mem Res Inst Acoust Sci Osaka Univ** ... Memoirs. Research Institute of Acoustical Science. Osaka University [*A publication*]
**Mem Res Inst Food Sci Kyoto Univ** ... Memoirs. Research Institute for Food Science. Kyoto University [*A publication*]
**Mem Res Inst Sci and Eng Ritsumeikan Univ** ... Memoirs. Research Institute of Science and Engineering. Ritsumeikan University [*A publication*]
**Mem Res Inst Sci Eng Ritsumeikan Univ** ... Memoirs. Research Institute of Science and Engineering. Ritsumeikan University [*Kyoto, Japan*] [*A publication*]
**Mem Reun Tec Nac Mania** ... Memoria. Reunion Tecnica Nacional de Mania [*A publication*]
**Mem Rev Acad Nac Cienc** ... Memorias y Revista. Academia Nacional de Ciencias [*A publication*]
**Mem Rev Acad Nac Cienc "Antonio Alzate"** ... Memorias y Revista. Academia Nacional de Ciencias "Antonio Alzate" [*A publication*]
MEMS....... Micro Electro Mechanical Systems
MEMS....... Microbial Ecological Monitoring System [*Apollo*] [*NASA*]
MEMS....... Missile Equipment Maintenance Sets (MUGU)
MEMS....... Multieffect, Multistage
**Mem Sagami Inst Technol** ... Memoirs. Sagami Institute of Technology [*A publication*]
**Mem Sch Eng Okayama Univ** ... Memoirs. School of Engineering. Okayama University [*A publication*]
**Mem School Engrg Okayama Univ** ... Memoirs. School of Engineering. Okayama University [*A publication*]
**Mem School Sci Engrg Waseda Univ** ... Memoirs. School of Science and Engineering. Waseda University [*A publication*]
**Mem School Sci Eng Waseda Univ** ... Memoirs. School of Science and Engineering. Waseda University [*A publication*]
**Mem Sch Sci and Eng Waseda Univ** ... Memoirs. School of Science and Engineering. Waseda University [*A publication*]
**Mem Sch Sci Eng Waseda Univ** ... Memoirs. School of Science and Engineering. Waseda University [*A publication*]
**Mem Sci Rev Met** ... Memoires Scientifiques de la Revue de Metallurgie [*A publication*]
**Mem Sci Rev Metall** ... Memoires Scientifiques de la Revue de Metallurgie [*A publication*]
**Mems Comn Invest Paleont Prehist (Madr)** ... Memorias. Comision de Investigaciones Paleontologicas y Prehistoricas. Instituto Nacional de Ciencias Fisico-Naturales (Madrid) [*A publication*]
**Mem Semin Latino-Amer Irrig** ... Memoria. Seminario Latino-Americano de Irrigacion [*A publication*]
**Mem Ser Calcutta Math Soc** ... Memoir Series. Calcutta Mathematical Society [*A publication*]
**Mem Serv Carte Geol Alsace Lorraine** ... Memoires. Service de la Carte Geologique d'Alsace et de Lorraine [*A publication*]
**Mem Serv Chim Etat** ... Memorial des Services Chimiques de l'Etat [*A publication*]
**Mem Serv Geol Belg** ... Memoire. Service Geologique de Belgique [*A publication*]
**Mem Serv Geol Port** ... Memorias. Servicos Geologicos de Portugal [*A publication*]
**Mem Servir Explication Carte Geol Detaill Fr** ... Memoires pour Servir a l'Explication de la Carte Geologique Detaillee de la France [*A publication*]
**Mems Estud Mus Zool Univ Coimbra** ... Memorias e Estudos. Museu Zoologico. Universidade de Coimbra [*A publication*]
**Mems Inst Oswaldo Cruz** ... Memorias. Instituto Oswaldo Cruz [*A publication*]
**Mems Jta Invest Ultramar** ... Memorias. Junta de Investigacoes do Ultramar [*A publication*]
**Mem Soc AF** ... Memoires. Societe Nationale des Antiquaires de France [*A publication*]
**Mem Soc Agric Commer Sci Arts (Marne)** ... Memoires. Societe d'Agriculture, Commerce, Sciences, et Arts du Departement de la Marne (Chalons Sur Marne) [*A publication*]
**Mem Soc A Midi** ... Memoires. Societe Archeologique de Midi de la France [*A publication*]
**Mem Soc Ant Picardie** ... Memoires. Societe des Antiquaires de Picardie [*A publication*]
**Mem Soc Astron Ital** ... Memorie. Societa Astronomica Italiana [*A publication*]
**Mem Soc Astronom Ital NS** ... Memorie. Societa Astronomica Italiana. Nuova Serie [*A publication*]
**Mem Soc Belge Geol Paleontol Hydrol Ser 8** ... Memoires. Societe Belge de Geologie, de Paleontologie, et d'Hydrologie. Serie in Octavo [*A publication*]
**Mem Soc Bot Fr** ... Memoires. Societe Botanique de France [*A publication*]
**Mem Soc Broteriana** ... Memorias. Sociedade Broteriana [*A publication*]
**Mem Soc Centr Med Vet** ... Memoires. Societe Centrale de Medecine Veterinaire [*A publication*]
**Mem Soc Chalon** ... Memoires. Societe d'Histoire et d'Archeologie de Chalon-Sur-Saone [*A publication*]
**Mem Soc Cienc Nat (La Salle)** ... Memoria. Sociedad de Ciencias Naturales (La Salle) [*A publication*]
**Mem Soc Cient "Antonio Alzate"** ... Memorias. Sociedad Cientifica "Antonio Alzate" [*A publication*]
**Mem Soc Cubana Hist Nat "Felipe Poey"** ... Memorias. Sociedad Cubana de Historia Natural "Felipe Poey" [*A publication*]
**Mem Soc Endocrinol** ... Memoirs. Society for Endocrinology [*A publication*]
**Mem Soc Entomol Ital** ... Memorie. Societa Entomologica Italiana [*A publication*]
**Mem Soc Entomol Que** ... Memoires. Societe Entomologique du Quebec [*A publication*]
**Mem Soc Frib Sci Nat Bot** ... Memoires. Societe Fribourgeoise des Sciences Naturelles. Botanique [*A publication*]
**Mem Soc Frib Sci Nat Chim** ... Memoires. Societe Fribourgeoise des Sciences Naturelles. Chimie [*A publication*]
**Mem Soc Frib Sci Nat Geol Geogr** ... Memoires. Societe Fribourgeoise des Sciences Naturelles. Geologie et Geographie [*A publication*]
**Mem Soc Frib Sci Nat Math Phys** ... Memoires. Societe Fribourgeoise des Sciences Naturelles. Mathematique et Physique [*A publication*]
**Mem Soc Frib Sci Nat Physiol Hyg Bacteriol** ... Memoires. Societe Fribourgeoise des Sciences Naturelles. Physiologie, Hygiene, Bacteriologie [*A publication*]

**Mem Soc Frib Sci Nat Zool** ... Memoires. Societe Fribourgeoise des Sciences Naturelles. Zoologie [*A publication*]
**Mem Soc Geol Fr** ... Memoires. Societe Geologique de France [*A publication*]
**Mem Soc Geol Fr Nouv Ser** ... Memoires. Societe Geologique de France. Nouvelle Serie [*A publication*]
**Mem Soc Geol Ital** ... Memorie. Societa Geologica Italiana [*A publication*]
**Mem Soc Geol Mineral Bretagne** ... Memoires. Societe Geologique et Mineralogique de Bretagne [*A publication*]
**Mem Soc Helv Sci Nat** ... Memoires. Societe Helvetique des Sciences Naturelles [*A publication*]
**Mem Soc Hist Nat Afr Nord** ... Memoires. Societe d'Histoire Naturelle de l'Afrique du Nord [*A publication*]
**Mem Soc Hist Natur Afr Nord** ... Memoires. Societe d'Histoire Naturelle de l'Afrique du Nord [*A publication*]
**Mem Soc Ital Sci Nat Mus Civ Stor Nat Milano** ... Memorie. Societa Italiana di Scienze Naturali e Museo Civico di Storia Naturale di Milano [*A publication*]
**Mem Soc Math France NS** ... Memoire. Societe Mathematique de France. Nouvelle Serie [*A publication*]
**Mem Soc Natl Sci Nat Math Cherbg** ... Memoires. Societe Nationale des Sciences Naturelles et Mathematiques de Cherbourg [*A publication*]
**Mem Soc Neuchatel Sci Nat** ... Memoires. Societe Neuchateloise des Sciences Naturelles [*A publication*]
**Mem Soc R Belge Entomol** ... Memoires. Societe Royale Belge d'Entomologie [*A publication*]
**Mem Soc R Bot Belg** ... Memoires. Societe Royale de Botanique de Belgique [*A publication*]
**Mem Soc R Can** ... Memoires. Societe Royale du Canada [*A publication*]
**Mem Soc R Ent Belg** ... Memoires. Societe Royale Entomologique de Belgique [*A publication*]
**Mem Soc Roy Liege** ... Memorandum. Societe Royale de Liege [*A publication*]
**Mem Soc Roy Sci Liege Coll in-8o** ... Memoires. Societe Royale des Sciences de Liege. Collection in Octavo [*A publication*]
**Mem Soc R Sci Liege** ... Memoires. Societe Royale des Sciences de Liege [*A publication*]
**Mem Soc R Sci Liege Collect 8** ... Memoires. Societe Royale des Sciences de Liege. Collection in Octavo [*A publication*]
**Mem Soc R Sci Liege 4o** ... Memoires. Societe Royale des Sciences de Liege. Collection in Quarto [*A publication*]
**Mem Soc R Sci Liege 8o** ... Memoires. Societe Royale des Sciences de Liege. Collection in Octavo [*A publication*]
**Mem Soc R Sci Liege Vol Hors Ser** ... Memoires. Societe Royale des Sciences de Liege. Volume Hors Serie [*Belgium*] [*A publication*]
**Mem Soc Sci Nancy** ... Memoires. Societe des Sciences de Nancy [*A publication*]
**Mem Soc Sci Nat Phys Maroc Bot** ... Memoires. Societe des Sciences Naturelles et Physiques du Maroc. Botanique [*A publication*]
**Mem Soc Sci Nat Phys Maroc Zool** ... Memoires. Societe des Sciences Naturelles et Physiques du Maroc. Zoologie [*A publication*]
**Mem Soc Sci Phys Nat Bordeaux** ... Memoires. Societe des Sciences Physiques et Naturelles de Bordeaux [*A publication*]
**Mem Soc Vaudoise Sci Nat** ... Memoires. Societe Vaudoise des Sciences Naturelles [*A publication*]
**Mem Soc Zool Fr** ... Memoires. Societe Zoologique de France [*A publication*]
**Mem Soil Res Inst (Kumasi Ghana)** ... Memoir. Soil Research Institute (Kumasi, Ghana) [*A publication*]
**Mem South Calif Acad Sci** ... Memoirs. Southern California Academy of Sciences [*A publication*]
**Mem S R Met** ... Memoires Scientifiques de la Revue de Metallurgie [*A publication*]
**Mem St Bur Mines Miner Resour (New Mex)** ... Memoirs. State Bureau of Mines and Mineral Resources (New Mexico) [*A publication*]
**Mem St ULR** ... Memphis State University. Law Review [*A publication*]
**Mem St UL Rev** ... Memphis State University. Law Review [*A publication*] (DLA)
**Mem Suzuka Coll Technol** ... Memoirs. Suzuka College of Technology [*A publication*]
**Mem Tec Congr Latinoam Sider** ... Memoria Tecnica. Congreso Latinoamericano de Siderurgia [*A publication*]
**Mem Tokyo Univ Agr** ... Memoirs. Tokyo University of Agriculture [*A publication*]
**Mem Tokyo Univ Agric** ... Memoirs. Tokyo University of Agriculture [*A publication*]
**Mem Torrey Bot Club** ... Memoirs. Torrey Botanical Club [*A publication*]
**Mem Tottori Agric Coll** ... Memoirs. Tottori Agricultural College [*A publication*]
**Mem Trav Fac Cath** ... Memoires et Travaux. Facultes Catholiques de Lille [*A publication*]
**Mem Trav Soc Hydrot France** ... Memoires et Travaux. Societe Hydrotechnique de France [*A publication*]
**MEMU** ...... Manned Extravehicular Manipulating Unit (MCD)
**Mem Univ Calif** ... Memoirs. University of California [*A publication*]
**Mem Univ Lab Phys Chem Med Public Health Har Univ** ... Memoirs. University Laboratory of Physical Chemistry Related to Medicine and Public Health. Harvard University [*A publication*]
**MEMX** ...... Memory Sciences Corp. [*NASDAQ symbol*] (NQ)
**MEMY** ...... Memory (ROG)
**M En** .......... Master of English
**MEN** .......... Master Equipment Number [*Military*] (NG)
**MEN** .......... Meatworks Extension News [*A publication*] (APTA)
**Men** ........... Menaechmi [*of Plautus*] [*Classical studies*] (OCD)
**Men** ........... Menahot (BJA)
**Men** ........... Menander [*Fourth century BC*] [*Classical studies*] (OCD)
**men** ........... Mende [*MARC language code*] [*Library of Congress*] (LCCP)
**MEN** .......... Mendoza [*Argentina*] [*Seismograph station code, US Geological Survey*] [*Closed*] (SEIS)
**MEN** .......... Meno [*Slower*] [*Music*]
**Men** ........... [*Jacobus*] Menochius [*Deceased, 1607*] [*Authority cited in pre-1607 legal work*] (DSA)
**MEN** .......... Menology
**Men** ........... Menorah: Australian Journal of Jewish Studies [*A publication*] (APTA)
**MEN** .......... Men's Equality Now International (EA)
**Men** ........... Mensa [*Constellation*]
**MEN** .......... Mention
**Men** ........... Menzies' Cape Of Good Hope Reports [*1828-49*] [*A publication*] (DLA)
**MEN** .......... Mistozen Electronic Nebulizer
**MEN** .......... Multiple Endocrine Neoplasia [*Medicine*]
**MEN** .......... Multiple Event Network
**MEN** .......... MuniEnhanced Fund [*NYSE symbol*] (SPSG)
**MENA** ....... Middle East News Agency
**MENA** ....... Middle East and North Africa [*A publication*]
**MENA** ....... Mission Element Need Analysis (MCD)
**MENA** ....... Mitsubishi Engine North America, Inc.
**Menabo** ...... Menabo di Letteratura [*A publication*]
**MENC** ....... Music Educators National Conference (EA)
**MENCAP** ... Royal Society for Mentally Handicapped Children & Adults [*England*]
**Mence Lib** ... Mence's Law of Libel [*1824*] [*A publication*] (DLA)
**MEND** ....... Massive Economic Neighborhood Development [*New York City*]
**MEND** ....... Medical Education for National Defense
**MEND** ....... Mendelism
**MEND** ....... Metal Workers to Enforce Nuclear Disarmament [*Australia*]
**MEND** ....... Mothers Embracing Nuclear Disarmament [*An association*] (EA)
**Mendel Chem J** ... Mendeleev Chemistry Journal [*A publication*]
**Mendeleev Chem J** ... Mendeleev Chemistry Journal [*A publication*]
**Mendel Newsl** ... Mendel Newsletter [*A publication*]
**Men Dis LR** ... Mental Disability Law Reporter [*A publication*]
**Me Ne** ........ Meroitic Newsletter [*A publication*]
**Menemui Mat** ... Menemui Matematik [*Kuala Lumpur*] [*A publication*]
**MENEV** .... Menevensis [*Signature of the Bishops of St. David's*] [*British*] (ROG)
**MENEX** .... Maintenance Engineering Exchange
**Menex** ........ Menexemus [*of Plato*] [*Classical studies*] (OCD)
**M Eng** ........ Master of Engineering
**M Eng** ........ Master of English
**M Eng** ........ Mechanical Engineer
**M-ENG** ...... Multiengined
**M Eng & PA** ... Master in Engineering and Public Administration
**M Eng Sc** ... Master of Engineering Science
**MEngSt** ..... Master of Engineering Studies (ADA)
**M Engy Rev** ... Monthly Energy Review [*A publication*]
**MenJ** ......... Menorah Journal [*A publication*]
**Menken** ...... Menken's Civil Procedure Reports [*30 New York*] [*A publication*] (DLA)
**Menn** .......... Mennonite [*A publication*]
**Menn L** ...... Mennonite Life [*A publication*]
**Menn Life** .. Mennonite Life [*A publication*]
**Mennonite Q R** ... Mennonite Quarterly Review [*A publication*]
**Menn Q R** .. Mennonite Quarterly Review [*A publication*]
**Meno** .......... [*Jacobus*] Menochius [*Deceased, 1607*] [*Authority cited in pre-1607 legal work*] (DSA)
**MENO** ....... Menopause (DSUE)
**MENOA** .... Metano, Petrolio, e Nuove Energie [*A publication*]
**Menoch** ...... [*Jacobus*] Menochius [*Deceased, 1607*] [*Authority cited in pre-1607 legal work*] (DSA)
**Menorah J** ... Menorah Journal [*A publication*]
**Men Rel** ..... Menandri Reliquiae [*A publication*] (OCD)
**Men Retard** ... Mental Retardation [*A publication*]
**MENS** ....... Man-Environment Systems [*A publication*]
**Mens** ......... Mensa [*Constellation*]
**MENS** ....... Mensis [*Month*] [*Latin*]
**MENS** ....... Mensura [*By Measure*] [*Pharmacy*]
**MENS** ....... Middle East Neurosurgical Society (EAIO)
**MENS** ....... Mission Element Needs Statement (MCD)
**Mensaje Bol Inf Fed Iberoam Parques** ... Mensaje Boletin Informativo. Federacion Iberoamericana de Parques Zoologicos [*A publication*]
**Mensajero For** ... Mensajero Forestal [*A publication*]
**Mens Maatschap** ... Mens en Maatschappij [*A publication*]
**Mens en Mel** ... Mens en Melodie [*A publication*]
**Mens en Mij** ... Mens en Maatschappij [*A publication*]
**Mens Ond** ... Mens en Onderneming [*A publication*]
**MENSUR** ... Mensuration (ROG)
**M Ent** ......... Master of Entomology

**MENT**....... Mental
**MENT**....... Mentioned
**MENT**....... Mentor Graphics Corp. [*Beaverton, OR*] [*NASDAQ symbol*] (NQ)
**Mental Disab L Rep** ... Mental Disability Law Reporter [*A publication*]
**Mental Health in Aust** ... Mental Health in Australia [*A publication*] (APTA)
**Mental Hyg** ... Mental Hygiene [*A publication*]
**Mental & Physical Disab L Rep** ... Mental and Physical Disability Law Reporter [*A publication*] (DLA)
**Mental Reta** ... Mental Retardation [*A publication*]
**MENTD**.... Mentioned
**MENTH**.... Mentha [*Mint*] [*Pharmacy*] (ROG)
**Ment Health Aust** ... Mental Health in Australia [*A publication*] (APTA)
**Ment Health Program Rep** ... Mental Health Program Reports [*A publication*]
**Ment Health Res Inst Univ Mich Annu Rep** ... Mental Health Research Institute. University of Michigan. Annual Report [*A publication*]
**Ment Health Soc** ... Mental Health and Society [*A publication*]
**Ment Health Stat Note** ... Mental Health Statistical Note [*A publication*]
**Ment Hlth Aust** ... Mental Health in Australia [*A publication*]
**Ment Hlth Stat** ... Mental Health Statistics [*A publication*]
**Ment Hosp** ... Mental Hospitals [*A publication*]
**Ment Hyg** .. Mental Hygiene [*A publication*]
**Ment Hyg (Arlington VA)** ... Mental Hygiene (Arlington, Virginia) [*A publication*]
**MENTL**..... Mental
**MENTLY** ... Mentally
**MENTN**.... Mention (ROG)
**MENTOR** ... [*A*] programming language [*1963*] (CSR)
**Ment Ret**.... Mental Retardation [*A publication*]
**Ment Retard** ... Mental Retardation [*A publication*]
**Ment Retard Abstr** ... Mental Retardation Abstracts [*A publication*]
**Ment Retard Absts** ... Mental Retardation Abstracts [*A publication*]
**Ment Retard Dev Disabil** ... Mental Retardation and Developmental Disabilities [*A publication*]
**Ment Ret Bul** ... Mental Retardation Bulletin [*A publication*]
**MEnvS**....... Master of Environmental Science
**MEnvS**....... Master of Environmental Studies
**MEnvSc**..... Master of Environmental Science (ADA)
**MEnvSt** ..... Master of Environmental Studies (ADA)
**MEnvStud** ... Master of Environmental Studies (ADA)
**MEnvStudies** ... Master of Environmental Studies
**MeNwS**...... Saint Joseph's College, North Windham, ME [*Library symbol*] [*Library of Congress*] (LCLS)
**Menz**.......... Menzies' Cape Of Good Hope Reports [*1828-49*] [*A publication*] (DLA)
**MENZA** .... Methods in Enzymology [*A publication*]
**Menz Conv** ... Menzies' Conveyancing [*A publication*] (DLA)
**Menzies**...... Menzies' Cape Of Good Hope Reports [*1828-49*] [*A publication*] (DLA)
**MEO**.......... Jefferson City, MO [*Location identifier*] [*FAA*] (FAAL)
**MEO**.......... Maintenance Engineering Order [*NASA*] (KSC)
**MEO**.......... Major Engine Overhaul
**MEO**.......... Manned Earth Orbit
**MEO**.......... Manned Extravehicular Operation
**MEO**.......... Marine Engineer Officer [*British*]
**MEO**.......... Mass in Earth Orbit [*NASA*]
**MEO**.......... Mining Engineering Officer [*British military*] (DMA)
**MEO**.......... Montello Resources Ltd. [*Vancouver Stock Exchange symbol*]
**MEO**.......... Most Efficient/Effective Organization [*DoD*]
**MEOC**....... Methods of Elemento-Organic Chemistry [*Elsevier Book Series*] [*A publication*]
**MEOER** .... Member of the European Osteopathic Register
**MEOF** ....... Marine Environmental Observation and Forecasting (NOAA)
**MEOL**....... Mededeelingen Ex Oriente Lux [*A publication*]
**MEOL**....... Meridian Oil NL [*NASDAQ symbol*] (NQ)
**MEOM**...... Manned Earth Orbit Mission
**MEOOW**... Marine Engineer Officer of the Watch [*British*]
**MEOP** ....... Maximum Expected Operating Pressure
**MEOR**....... Microbial Enhanced Oil Recovery [*Petroleum technology*]
**MEOS** ....... Microsomal Ethanol-Oxidizing System [*Biochemistry*]
**MEOSAB** ... Missile Explosive Ordnance Safety Advisory Board [*Pacific Missile Range*] (MUGU)
**MEOTBF** .. Mean Engine Operating Time between Failures [*Quality control*]
**MEOV**....... Maximum Expected Operating Value [*FCC*]
**MEOW**...... Marine Engineer Officer's Writer [*British military*] (DMA)
**MEOW**...... [*The*] Moral Equivalent of War [*Phrase used by President Jimmy Carter to describe his energy bill*]
**MEOWS** ... Multimode Electro-Optical Weapon System
**MEP** .......... Magnetic Energy Product
**MEP** .......... Magyar Elet Partja [*Party of Hungarian Life*] [*Political party*] (PPE)
**MEP** .......... Mahajana Eksath Peramuna [*People's United Front*] [*Sri Lanka*] [*Political party*] (PPW)
**MEP** .......... Main Engine Propellant (MCD)
**MEP** .......... Main Entry Point (NASA)
**MEP** .......... Major Electronics Procurement
**MEP** .......... Major Extinction Position [*Polarizer-Analyzer*]
**MEP** .......... Management Engineering Program [*Air Force*] (AFM)
**MEP** .......... Management Evaluation Program (AAG)
**MEP** .......... Manual Entry Panel [*Military*] (CAAL)
**MEP** .......... Manuals of Engineering Practice [*ASCE*]
**MEP** .......... Manufacturing Engineering Plan
**MEP** .......... Mars Entry Probe
**MEP** .......... Master of Engineering Physics
**MEP** .......... Master Evaluation Plan [*Army*]
**MEP** .......... Maximum Escape Performance [*Ejection seat*] (MCD)
**MEP** .......... Maxwell Electronic Publishing [*Information service or system*] (IID)
**MEP** .......... May Energy Partners Ltd. [*AMEX symbol*] (SPSG)
**MEP** .......... Mean Effective Pressure
**MEP** .......... Medical Education Program [*Air Force*]
**MeP** ........... Mekedonski Pregled. Spisanie za Nauka. Literatura i Obsteostven Zivot [*A publication*]
**MEP** .......... Member of the European Parliament
**MEP** .......... MEP: Multicultural Education Papers [*A publication*] (APTA)
**MEP** .......... Meperidine [*Also, M*] [*An analgesic*]
**MEP** .......... Mersing [*Malaysia*] [*Airport symbol*] (OAG)
**MEP** .......... Methanol Environmental Performance [*Automotive engineering*]
**MEP** .......... Methods Engineering Program [*Navy*] (NVT)
**MEP** .......... Methyl Parathion [*Also, MP, MPN*] [*Pesticide*]
**MEP** .......... Methyl(ethyl)pyridine [*Organic chemistry*]
**MEP** .......... Microcircuit Emulation Program
**MEP** .......... Microelectronics Programme [*British*]
**MEP** .......... Midwest Express [*Appleton, WI*] [*FAA designator*] (FAAC)
**MEP** .......... Minimum Entry Point (MCD)
**MEP** .......... Minority Entrepreneurship Program [*Small Business Administration*]
**MEP** .......... Minuteman Education Program [*Air Force*] (AFM)
**MEP** .......... Mission Effects Projector [*Lunar exploration*]
**MEP** .......... Mission Equipment Package
**MEP** .......... Mobil Exploration & Producing Services, Inc., Dallas, TX [*OCLC symbol*] (OCLC)
**MEP** .......... Mobile Electric Power (NG)
**MEP** .......... Motor End Plate
**MEP** .......... Mouvement d'Ecologie Politique [*Ecology Political Movement*] [*France*] [*Political party*] (PPW)
**MEP** .......... Movimiento Electoral del Pueblo [*People's Electoral Movement*] [*Netherlands Antilles*] [*Political party*] (PPW)
**MEP** .......... Movimiento Electoral del Pueblo [*People's Electoral Movement*] [*Venezuela*] [*Political party*] (PPW)
**MEP** .......... Multielliptical Pump
**MEP** .......... Multimodality Evoked Potential [*Neurophysiology*]
**MEP** .......... Multiple-Exposure Photography
**MeP** ........... Portland Public Library, Portland, ME [*Library symbol*] [*Library of Congress*] (LCLS)
**MEP** .......... Societas Parisiensis Missionum ad Exteros [*Paris Foreign Missions Society*] [*Roman Catholic men's religious order*]
**MEPA**........ Master in Engineering and Public Administration
**MEPARC**.. Middle East Policy and Research Center (EA)
**MEPC**........ Marine Environment Protection Committee [*IMCO*] (MSC)
**MEPC**........ Miniature End Plate Current
**MEPCOM** ... Military Enlistment Processing Command [*DoD*]
**MEPED**..... Medium-Energy Proton and Electron Detector
**MEPF**........ Multiple Experiment Processing Furnace
**MEPGS**..... Mobile Electric Power Generator Set (MCD)
**MEPHISTO** ... Mephistopheles [*Foreman*] [*Slang*] [*British*] (DSUE)
**ME Phy** ..... Master of Engineering Physics
**MePM** ....... Maine Charitable Mechanic Association, Portland, ME [*Library symbol*] [*Library of Congress*] (LCLS)
**MEPM** ...... Medium-Term Energy Policy Model
**MePMC**..... Maine Medical Center, Portland, ME [*Library symbol*] [*Library of Congress*] (LCLS)
**MEPOL**..... Metropolitan Police Officers [*British*]
**MePosS** ..... United Society of Shakers, Shaker Library, Poland Spring, ME [*Library symbol*] [*Library of Congress*] (LCLS)
**MEPP**........ Middle East Peace Project (EA)
**MEPP**........ Miniature End Plate Potential
**MEPP**........ Mobile Electric Power Plant (NG)
**MePriU**...... University of Maine at Presque Isle, Presque Isle, ME [*Library symbol*] [*Library of Congress*] (LCLS)
**MEPROBAMATE** ... Methyl Propyltrimethylene Carbamate [*Tranquilizer*]
**MEPS**........ Means-End Problem-Solving Procedure [*or Test*] [*Psychology*]
**MEPS**........ Medium-Energy Particle Spectrometer (MCD)
**MEPS**........ Message Editing and Processing System (MCD)
**MEPS**........ Military Entrance and Processing Station
**MEPS**........ Modular Electrical Power Station
**MEPSA** ..... Middle East Peace and Stability Act [*1957*]
**MEPSCAT** ... Military Entrance Physical Strength Capacity Test (INF)
**MEPSDU** ... Module Experimental Process System Development Unit [*Photovoltaic energy systems*]
**MEPSI** ...... Mexico-Elmhurst Philatelic Society, International (EA)
**MEPSP** ..... Miniature Excitatory Postsynaptic Potential [*Neurophysiology*]
**MEPU** ....... Monofuel Emergency Power Unit
**MEQ**.......... Marine Environmental Quality [*Marine science*] (MSC)
**MEQ**.......... Married Enlisted Quarters
**MEQ**.......... Metal Bulletin Monthly [*A publication*]
**MEQ**.......... Milliequivalent [*or Milligram Equivalent*] [*Also, ME*]
**MEQA**....... Mechanized Equipment Assignment [*AT & T*]

**MEQ/L**...... Milliequivalent per Liter
**MER**.......... Madras European Regiment [*British military*] (DMA)
**MER**.......... Main Engine Room [*Navy*] (CAAL)
**MER**.......... Maine State Department of Environmental Protection and Department of Conservation, Augusta, ME [*OCLC symbol*] (OCLC)
**MER**.......... Maintenance Engineering Report (MCD)
**MER**.......... Malayan Economic Review [*A publication*]
**MER**.......... Manned Earth Reconnaissance [*Naval Air Electronic Systems Command project*]
**MER**.......... Manpower Evaluation Report [*Military*]
**MER**.......... Mass Energy Relationship
**MER**.......... Master Employee Record [*DoD*]
**MER**.......... Maximum Effective Range
**MER**.......... Maximum Efficient Rate [*Oil*]
**MER**.......... Maximum Energy Recovery [*Chemical engineering*]
**MER**.......... Mean Ejection Rate [*Medicine*]
**M & ER**...... Mechanical and Electrical Room (AAG)
**MER**.......... Mechanics, Electrical, and Radio (MCD)
**MER**.......... MER (Marine Engineers Review) [*United States*] [*A publication*]
**MER**.......... Mercantile
**MER**.......... Merced, CA [*Location identifier*] [*FAA*] (FAAL)
**Mer**............ Mercer Law Review [*A publication*]
**MER**.......... Merchandise (ADA)
**MER**.......... Merchant (AFM)
**MER**.......... Mercury (ADA)
**Mer**............ Mercury [*Record label*]
**Mer**............ Merian [*A publication*]
**MER**.......... Merida [*Mexico*] [*Seismograph station code, US Geological Survey*] (SEIS)
**MER**.......... Meridian (KSC)
**MER**.......... Meridional [*Geology*]
**Mer**............ Merivale's English Chancery Reports [*A publication*] (DLA)
**MER**.......... Merlinoite [*A zeolite*]
**MER**.......... Merrell-National Laboratories [*Research code symbol*]
**MER**.......... Merrill Lynch & Co., Inc. [*NYSE symbol*] (SPSG)
**MER**.......... Metal Etch Resist
**MER**.......... Metal Evaporated Resistor
**MER**.......... Methanol Extraction [*or Extruded*] Residue [*Immunology*]
**MER**.......... Middle East Record [*A publication*] (BJA)
**MER**.......... Midwest English Review [*A publication*]
**MER**.......... Minimum Energy Requirements
**MER**.......... Mission Evaluation Room [*NASA*] (NASA)
**MER**.......... Mitteleuropaeisches Reisebuero [*Middle European Travel Bureau*] [*German*]
**MER**.......... Monthly Energy Review [*Department of Energy*] [*Database*]
**MER**.......... Most Economical Rating
**MER**.......... Multielement RADAR
**MER**.......... Multiple Ejector Rack (NG)
**MER**.......... Museum Education Roundtable (EA)
**MERA**....... Maeventec Employers Rated Almanac [*Maeventec*] [*Information service or system*] (CRD)
**MERA**....... Medical Engineering Research Association [*Australia*]
**MERA**....... Molecular Electronics for RADAR Applications (IEEE)
**MERA**....... Mormons for ERA (EA)
**MERADCOM**... Mobility Equipment Research and Development Command [*Army*]
**MERADO**... Mechanical Engineering Research and Development Organisation
**MERALCO**... Manila Electric Railroad & Light Company [*Still known by acronym, although official name now Manila Electric Company*]
**MERALT**.. Meridian Altitude [*Navigation*]
**MERB**........ Merrill Bankshares Co. [*NASDAQ symbol*] (NQ)
**Merc**........... London Mercury [*A publication*]
**MERC**....... Meat Export Research Center [*Iowa State University*] [*Research center*] (RCD)
**MERC**....... Mercantile (ROG)
**Merc**........... Mercator [*of Plautus*] [*Classical studies*] (OCD)
**MERC**....... Mercedes [*Automobile*] (DSUE)
**MERC**....... [A] Mercenary
**MERC**....... Mercury
**Merc**........... Mercury [*Hobart*] [*A publication*] (APTA)
**MERC**....... Mercury Project [*NASA*] (KSC)
**MERC**....... Middle-Atlantic Educational and Research Center
**MERC**....... Middle East Resource Center [*Defunct*] (EA)
**MERC**....... Minority Economic Resource Center [*Howard University, Washington, DC*]
**MERC**....... Music Education Research Council (EA)
**Merc Ad & Law & Credit Man**... Mercantile Adjuster and Lawyer and Credit Man [*A publication*] (DLA)
**MERCASREP**... Merchant Ship Casualty Report [*Navy*] (NVT)
**MERCAST**... Merchant Ship Broadcast [*Navy*]
**MERCASUM**... Merchant Ship Casualty Summary [*Navy*] (NVT)
**Merc Cas**... Mercantile Cases [*A publication*] (DLA)
**MERCE**..... Mercedes [*Automobile*] (DSUE)
**Mercer**....... Mercer County Law Journal [*Pennsylvania*] [*A publication*] (DLA)
**Mercer Beasley L Rev**... Mercer Beasley Law Review [*A publication*] (DLA)
**Mercer BL Rev**... Mercer Beasley Law Review [*A publication*] (DLA)
**Mercer Dent Soc Newsl**... Mercer Dental Society. Newsletter [*A publication*]
**Mercer Law**... Mercer Law Review [*A publication*]
**Mercer Law Rev**... Mercer Law Review [*A publication*]
**Mercer L Rev**... Mercer Law Review [*A publication*]
**Mercersb**.... Mercersburg Review [*A publication*]
**Merc France**... Mercure de France [*A publication*]
**Merch**........ Merchandising [*A publication*]
**MERCH**.... Merchantable
**Merchand Vision**... Merchandising Vision [*A publication*]
**Merch Dict**... Merchants' Dictionary [*A publication*] (DLA)
**Merch Mo**... Merchandising Monthly [*A publication*]
**Merc (Hob)**... Mercury (Hobart) [*A publication*]
**MERCHT**... Merchant
**Merch W**.... Merchandising Week [*Later, Merchandising*] [*A publication*]
**Mercian Geol**... Mercian Geologist [*A publication*]
**Merck Agr Memo**... Merck Agricultural Memo [*A publication*]
**Merck Sharp Dohme Semin Rep**... Merck, Sharp, and Dohme. Seminar Report [*A publication*]
**Merc LJ**..... Mercantile Law Journal [*New York or Madras*] [*A publication*] (DLA)
**Merc LR**.... Mercer Law Review [*A publication*]
**Merc (Newspr) (Tas)**... Mercury Reports (Newspaper) (Tasmania) [*A publication*] (APTA)
**MERCO**.... Mercantile Communications [*Shipping*]
**MERCO**.... Merchant Ship Control [*Navy*]
**MERCOFORM**... Merchant Ship Communications Formatted (MCD)
**MERCON**... Universal Transversal Mercator Converter [*Computer program*]
**MERCOS**... Merchant Codes [*Shipping*]
**MERCPAC**... Mercury Enthusiast Restorer Custom Performance Auto Club (EA)
**Merc S Arch**... Mercury Series. Archaeological Survey of Canada. Papers [*A publication*]
**Merc S Ethn**... Mercury Series. Ethnology Division. Papers [*A publication*]
**Mercure**..... Mercure de France [*A publication*]
**MERCY**..... Medical Emergency Relief Care for Youth
**Mercy Med**... Mercy Medicine [*A publication*]
**MERDC**.... Mobility Equipment Research and Development Center [*Army*] (MCD)
**MERDD**.... Monthly Energy Review [*A publication*]
**MERDI**...... Montana Energy and Magneto-Hydrodynamics Research Institute [*Later, Montana Energy Research and Development Institute*] [*Research center*]
**MERDIFF**... Meridian Difference
**MERDL**..... Medical Equipment Research and Development Laboratory [*Army*]
**MEREA**..... Member of the American Electrical Railway Engineering Association
**Merentutkimuslaitoksen Julk**... Merentutkimuslaitoksen Julkaisu [*A publication*]
**MEREP**..... Merchant Ship Arrival and/or Departure Report (NATG)
**ME(Res)**.... Master of Engineering (Research)
**MERES**..... Matrix of Environmental Residuals for Energy Systems [*Computerized information system*]
**Meres Autom**... Meres es Automatika [*A publication*]
**Meres es Autom**... Meres es Automatika [*A publication*]
**Meresuegyi Koezl**... Meresuegyi Koezlemenyek [*A publication*]
**ME Rev Stat**... Maine Revised Statutes [*A publication*] (DLA)
**ME Rev Stat Ann**... Maine Revised Statutes, Annotated [*A publication*] (DLA)
**MERF**........ Melanges. Ecole Roumaine en France [*A publication*]
**Merg and Acq**... Mergers and Acquisitions [*A publication*]
**MERGE**..... Mechanized Retrieval for Greater Efficiency [*Data processing*]
**Merger & A I**... Mergers and Acquisitions Almanac and Index [*A publication*]
**Mergers**..... Mergers and Acquisitions [*A publication*]
**Mergers & Acquis**... Mergers and Acquisitions [*A publication*]
**Mergers Acquis**... Mergers and Acquisitions [*A publication*]
**MERGV**.... Martian Exploratory Rocket Glide Vehicle
**MERI**......... Mineral Exploration Research Institute [*See also IREM*] [*Canada*] [*Research center*] (RCD)
**MERI**......... Mining and Excavation Research Institute [*Research center*] (RCD)
**MERIC**...... Michigan Education Resources Information Center [*Michigan State Library*] [*Information service or system*] [*Defunct*] (IID)
**Meridn**....... Meridian [*A publication*]
**Merino Breed J**... Merino Breeders' Journal [*A publication*]
**MERINT**... Merchant Ship Intelligence (NVT)
**MERINTREP**... Merchant Ship Arrival and/or Departure Intermediate Report (NATG)
**MERIONS**... Merionethshire [*County in Wales*]
**MERIP**...... MERIP [*Middle East Research and Information Project*] Reports [*A publication*]
**MERIP**...... Middle East Research and Information Project (EA)
**MERIT**...... Method to Extend Research in Time [*National Institutes of Health*]
**MERIT**...... Michigan Educational Research Information Triad, Inc.
**MERIT**...... Monitor the Earth Rotation and Intercompare Techniques [*by means of radio telescope measurements*]
**Meriv**......... Merivale's English Chancery Reports [*A publication*] (DLA)
**Meriv (Eng)**... Merivale's English Chancery Reports [*A publication*] (DLA)

**MERJD**..... Moessbauer Effect Reference and Data Journal [*A publication*]
**Merkbl Angew Parasitenkd Schaedlingsbekaempf** ... Merkblaetter ueber Angewandte Parasitenkunde und Schaedlingsbekaempfung [*A publication*]
**Merkblatt Imker Verb Kleingaertner Siedler Kleintierz** ... Merkblatt. Imker des Verbandes der Kleingaertner, Siedler, und Kleintierzuechter [*A publication*]
**Merkbl Biol Bundesanst Land Forstwirtsch** ... Merkblatt. Biologische Bundesanstalt fuer Land und Forstwirtschaft [*A publication*]
**Merkbl Biol Bundesanst Land Forstwirtsch (Braunschweig)** ... Merkblatt. Biologische Bundesanstalt fuer Land und Forstwirtschaft (Braunschweig) [*A publication*]
**Merkbl Deutsch Landwirtsch Ges** ... Merkblatt. Deutsche Landwirtschafts-Gesellschaft [*A publication*]
**Merkbl Ver Zellst Chem** ... Merkblatt. Verein der Zellstoff- und Papier-Chemiker und -Ingenieure [*A publication*]
**MERL**........ Marine Ecosystem Research Laboratory [*University of Rhode Island*] [*Research center*]
**MERL**........ Materials Engineering Research Laboratory [*NASA*] (NASA)
**MERL**........ Materials Equipment Requirements List (NASA)
**MERL**........ Municipal Environmental Research Laboratory [*Environmental Protection Agency*] (GRD)
**MERLIN**... Machine Readable Library Information [*British Library*] [*Information service or system*] (IID)
**MERLIN**... Medium-Energy Reactor Light-Water Industrial Neutron [*British*] (DEN)
**MERLIN**... Multielement Radio-Linked Interferometer Network [*Astronomy*]
**Merlin Quest de Droit** ... Merlin's Questions de Droit qui se Presentent le Plus Frequemment dans les Tribunaux [*1819*] [*A publication*] (DLA)
**Merlin Repert** ... Merlin's Repertoire de Jurisprudence [*A publication*] (DLA)
**Mer LJ**....... Mercantile Law Journal [*Madras, India*] [*A publication*] (DLA)
**Merl Quest** ... Merlin's Questions de Droit [*A publication*] (DLA)
**Merl Repert** ... Merlin's Repertoire de Jurisprudence [*A publication*] (DLA)
**MERM**...... Material Evaluation Rocket Motor
**MERM**...... Multilateral Exchange Rate Model (ADA)
**MERMLS** ... Mid-Eastern Regional Medical Library Service [*Library network*]
**MERMUT** ... Mobile Electronic Robot Manipulator and Underwater Television (IEEE)
**Mernoekgeol Sz** ... Mernoekgeologiai Szemle [*A publication*]
**MERO**...... Mercom, Inc. [*NASDAQ symbol*] (NQ)
**Mer O-Mer** ... Mer-Outre-Mer [*A publication*]
**Merova Tech** ... Merova Technika [*A publication*]
**MerP**.......... Mercurio Peruano [*A publication*]
**MERPASS** ... Meridian Passage [*Navigation*]
**MERPL**..... Mission Essential Repair Parts List (MCD)
**MERRA**..... Middle East Relief and Rehabilitation Administration [*World War II*]
**Merr Att**..... Merrifield on Attorneys [*1830*] [*A publication*] (DLA)
**Merr Costs** ... Merrifield's Law of Costs [*A publication*] (DLA)
**MERRF**..... Myoclonic Epilepsy Associated with Ragged Red Fibres [*Medicine*]
**Merrill ML** ... Merrill Lynch Market Letter [*A publication*]
**Merrill-Palmer Q** ... Merrill-Palmer Quarterly [*A publication*]
**Merril-Pal** ... Merrill-Palmer Quarterly [*A publication*]
**Merrimack** ... Smith's New Hampshire Reports [*A publication*] (DLA)
**MERS**........ Medical Equipment Reporting System [*Veterans Administration*]
**MERS**........ Mobility Environmental Research Studies
**MERS**........ Most Economical Route Selection [*Also, ARS*] [*Bell System*] [*Telecommunications*]
**MERS**........ Movimiento de Estudiantes Revolucionarios Salvadorenos [*Revolutionary Movement of Salvadoran Students*] (PD)
**MERS**........ Multielement Radiometer System
**MERSAT**.. Meteorology and Earth Observation Satellite (NASA)
**MERSDW** ... Marine Environmental Research [*A publication*]
**MERSEX**.. Merchant Ship Code Systems [*NATO*] (NATG)
**Mersey Quart** ... Mersey Quarterly [*A publication*]
**MERSHIP** ... Merchant Ship [*Navy*] (NVT)
**MERSIGS** ... Merchant Signals [*Shipping*]
**Mer & St Corp** ... Merewether and Stephen's Municipal Corporations [*A publication*] (DLA)
**MERT**........ Maintenance Engineering Review Team [*Navy*] (NG)
**MERT**........ Merit Energy Corp. [*NASDAQ symbol*] (NQ)
**Mert**........... Merten's Law of Federal Income Taxation [*A publication*] (DLA)
**MERT**........ Merton College [*Oxford University*] (ROG)
**MERT**........ Milwaukee Electric Railway & Transport Co. [*AAR code*]
**MERTB**...... Mental Retardation [*A publication*]
**MER/TER**... Multiple Ejection Rack/Triple Ejection Rack (MCD)
**Mer (Tokyo) Bull Soc Fr Jpn Oceanogr** ... Mer (Tokyo). Bulletin de la Societe Franco-Japonaise d'Oceanographie [*A publication*]
**MERTS**...... Micropound Extended Range Thrust Stand [*NASA*]
**MERU**...... Milliearth Rate Unit [*NASA*] (KSC)
**MERX**....... Mercer Enterprises [*Air carrier designation symbol*]
**MERY**....... Merry Land & Investment Co., Inc. [*NASDAQ symbol*] (NQ)
**M Erz**......... Musikerziehung [*A publication*]
**MERZONE** ... Merchant Shipping Control Zone [*NATO*] (NATG)
**MES**.......... Maharashtra Ekikaran Samithi [*India*] [*Political party*] (PPW)
**MES**.......... Main Engine Start [*NASA*] (KSC)
**MES**.......... Main Equipment Supplier (NATG)
**MES**.......... Maine State Planning Office, Augusta, ME [*OCLC symbol*] (OCLC)
**MES**.......... Maintenance Electrolyte Solution [*Physiology*]
**MES**.......... Manned Exploration Site (MCD)
**MES**.......... Manual Entry System [*or Subsystem*] (IEEE)
**MES**.......... Manuals of Elementary Science [*A publication*]
**MES**.......... Mass Expulsion System (MCD)
**MES**.......... Master of Engineering Sciences
**MES**.......... Master of Engineering Studies
**MES**.......... Mated Elements [*or Events*] Simulator [*NASA*] (MCD)
**MES**.......... Maximal Electroshock [*Physiology*]
**MES**.......... Maximum Electroshock Seizure [*Medicine*]
**MES**.......... Medan [*Indonesia*] [*Airport symbol*] (OAG)
**MES**.......... Medical Economics [*A publication*]
**MES**.......... Medical Electronics Society (EA)
**MES**.......... Medium Energy Source Program [*Air Force*]
**MES**.......... Medsource Systems, Inc. [*Vancouver Stock Exchange symbol*]
**MES**.......... Melville Corp. [*Formerly, Melville Shoe Corp.*] [*NYSE symbol*] (SPSG)
**MES**.......... Mesaba Aviation [*Grand Rapids, MN*] [*FAA designator*] (FAAC)
**MES**.......... Mesozoic [*Period, era, or system*] [*Geology*]
**MES**.......... Message Entry System (MCD)
**MES**.......... Messina [*Italy*] [*Seismograph station code, US Geological Survey*] (SEIS)
**MES**.......... Mesylate [*Organic chemistry*]
**ME(S)**......... Methodist Episcopal, South
**MES**.......... Mexican Epigraphic Society (EA)
**MES**.......... Middle Eastern Studies [*A publication*]
**MES**.......... Military Engineer Services [*British*]
**MES**.......... Minerals Engineering Society [*British*]
**MES**.......... Miniature Edison Screw
**MES**.......... Minimum Efficiency Scale
**MES**.......... Missile Electrical Simulator
**MES**.......... Missile Engineering Station
**MES**.......... Mission Events Sequence (MCD)
**MES**.......... Moessbauer Emission Spectroscopy
**MES**.......... MOL [*Manned Orbiting Laboratory*] Environmental Shelter
**MES**.......... Monitoring Energy Systems
**MES**.......... More Effective Schools [*Program*] [*Defunct*]
**MES**.......... Morpholinoethanesulfonic Acid [*A buffer*]
**MES**.......... Motor End Support
**MES**.......... Movimento de Esquerda Socialista [*Movement of the Socialist Left*] [*Portugal*] [*Political party*] (PPE)
**MES**.......... Moving Earth Simulator (MCD)
**MES**.......... Multicultural Education Services [*Victoria, Australia*]
**MES**.......... Multiengine Sea [*Pilot rating*] (AIA)
**MES**.......... Multiple Endocrine Syndrome [*Endocrinology*]
**MES**.......... Myoelectric Signal
**MESA**........ Maintenance Engineering Support Analysis [*Military*] (CAAL)
**MesA**......... Maitre es Arts [*Master of Arts*] [*French*]
**MESA**........ Malaria Eradication Special Account
**MESA**........ Manned Environmental Systems Assessment [*NASA*]
**MESA**........ Marconi Espanola S.A. [*Spain*]
**MESA**........ Marine Ecosystems Analysis [*Pollution-monitoring project*]
**MESA**........ Marine Education Society of Australasia
**MESA**........ Maximum Entropy Spectrum Analysis
**MESA**........ Mechanics Educational Society of America (EA)
**MESA**........ Men to End Spouse Abuse (EA)
**MESA**........ Mesa Airlines, Inc. [*NASDAQ symbol*] (NQ)
**ME/SA**...... Middle East/Southern Asia
**MESA**........ Middle East Studies Association of North America (EA)
**MESA**........ Miniature Electrostatically Suspended Accelerometer (MCD)
**MESA**........ Minimum Essential Support Analysis (MCD)
**MESA**........ Mining Enforcement and Safety Administration [*Terminated, 1978; functions transferred to Mine Safety and Health Administration, Department of Labor*]
**MESA**........ Mobile Entertainments, Southern Area [*British military*] (DMA)
**MESA**........ Modularized Equipment Storage [*or Stowage*] Area [*or Assembly*] [*Apollo*] [*NASA*]
**MESA**........ Multiple Engagement Simulation Analyzer [*Military*]
**MESA**........ Music Editor, Scorer, and Arranger [*Computer program*] (PCM)
**MeSaco**...... Dyer Library, Saco, ME [*Library symbol*] [*Library of Congress*] (LCLS)
**MeSacoT** ... Thornton Academy, Saco, ME [*Library symbol*] [*Library of Congress*] (LCLS)
**MESA Mag Min Health Saf** ... MESA [*Mining Enforcement and Safety Administration*] Magazine of Mining Health and Safety [*United States*] [*A publication*]
**MESAN**..... Mouvement de l'Evolution Sociale de l'Afrique Noire [*Black African Social Evolution Movement*]
**MESA NY Bight Atlas Monogr** ... MESA [*Marine Ecosystems Analysis*] New York. Bight Atlas Monograph [*A publication*]
**MESAR**..... Multifunction Electric Scan Adaptive RADAR [*Military*] [*British*]

**MESBIC**.... Minority Enterprise Small Business Investment Company
**MESC**........ Marine Environmental Sciences Consortium [*Library network*]
**ME Sc**........ Master of Engineering Science
**MESC**........ Master Event Sequence Controller (KSC)
**MESC**........ Mescaline
**MESC**........ Middle East Service Command [*Army*] [*World War II*]
**MESC**........ Middle East Supply Center [*World War II*]
**MESC**........ Middle East Supply Council [*World War II*]
**MESC**........ Mission Events Sequence Controller [*NASA*] (KSC)
**MESCAK**.. Memoires. Societe Entomologique du Canada [*A publication*]
**Mes Controle Ind** ... Mesures et Controle Industriel [*A publication*]
**Mes Cope St** ... Mesopotamia. Copenhagen Studies in Assyriology [*A publication*]
**MESCPL**... Mess Corporal [*Marine Corps*]
**MESC(W)** ... Middle East Supply Committee (Washington) [*World War II*]
**MESD**........ Mesdames [*Plural of Mrs.*] [*France*]
**MESEDT**.. Marine Ecology. Progress Series [*A publication*]
**MeSepPM** ... Penobscot Marine Museum, Searsport, ME [*Library symbol*] [*Library of Congress*] (LCLS)
**MESF**........ Minimum Engineered Safety Features (NRCH)
**MESF**........ Mobile Earth Station Facility
**MESFET**... Metal-Semiconductor Field-Effect Transistor
**MESG**........ Maximum Experimental Safe Gap (IEEE)
**MESG**........ Mediterranean Shipping Group [*NATO*] (NATG)
**MESG**........ Microelectrostatic Gyro
**MESGA**..... Microelectrostatic Gyro-Accelerometer
**MeSH**........ Medical Subject Headings Vocabulary File [*National Library of Medicine*] [*Information service or system*] (CRD)
**MESH**....... Multiple Electronically Synopsing Hierarchy (RDA)
**MESH**....... Museum Exchange for System's Help [*National Museum of Natural History*] (IID)
**Mesic Prehl Met Pozor** ... Mesicni Prehled Meteorologickych Pozorovani [*A publication*]
**MESIM**..... Mission Essential Subsystem Inoperative Maintenance
**MeSk**........ Skowhegan Free Public Library, Skowhegan, ME [*Library symbol*] [*Library of Congress*] (LCLS)
**MESL**........ Membrane-Enveloped Soil Layer
**MESL**........ Merchants' Exchange of St. Louis (EA)
**MESL**........ Microwave Electronic Systems Limited
**MESL**........ Mission Essential Subsystems List (NVT)
**MESM**....... Multiechelon Supply Model (AABC)
**MESOP**..... Mesopotamia
**Mesopo**...... Mesopotamia. Rivista di Archeologia [*A publication*]
**Mesopot Agric** ... Mesopotamia Agriculture [*A publication*]
**Mesopotamia J Agric** ... Mesopotamia Journal of Agriculture [*A publication*]
**MESPBQ**.. Medizin und Sport [*Berlin*] [*A publication*]
**MESPOT**.. Mesopotamia (DSUE)
**MeSprN**..... Nasson College, Springvale, ME [*Library symbol*] [*Library of Congress*] (LCLS)
**MESq**......... Management Engineering Squadron [*Air Force*]
**Mes Reg Aut** ... Mesures, Regulation, Automatisme [*A publication*]
**Mes Regul Autom** ... Mesures, Regulation, Automatisme [*A publication*]
**Mes Regul Automat** ... Mesures, Regulation, Automatisme [*A publication*]
**MESRF**..... Middle East Special Requirement Fund
**MESS**........ Magnetic Emulsion Spectrometer
**MESS**........ Maximum Effective SONAR Speed (NVT)
**MESS**........ Mechanical Electronic Subassembly Simulator
**MESS**........ Messenger (MSA)
**Mess**......... Messenger [*A publication*]
**MESS**........ Messerschmitt [*German fighter aircraft*] (DSUE)
**MESS**........ Misalignment Estimation Software System (MCD)
**MESS**........ Mixed Evolutionarily Stable Strategy [*Breeding selection*]
**MESS**........ Monitor Event Simulation System (IEEE)
**MESSAGE** ... Modular Electronic Solid-State Aerospace Ground Equipment
**MESSCPL** ... Mess Corporal [*Marine Corps*]
**MESSE**...... Messuage (ROG)
**MESSER**... Messerschmitt [*German fighter aircraft*] (DSUE)
**Mess und Pruef** ... Messen und Pruefen [*A publication*]
**Mess Pruef** ... Messen und Pruefen [*A publication*]
**Mess Pruef Autom** ... Messen und Pruefen/Automatik [*A publication*]
**Mess Pruef Ver Autom** ... Messen und Pruefen Vereinigt mit Automatik [*A publication*]
**MESSR**..... Multispectrum Electronic Self-Scanning Radiometer (MCD)
**MESSRS**... Messieurs [*Plural of Mister*] [*French*]
**MESSSGT** ... Mess Sergeant [*Marine Corps*]
**Mess-Steuern-Regeln** ... Messen-Steuern-Regeln [*A publication*]
**Mess Steuern Regeln mit Automatisierungsprax** ... Messen, Steuern, Regeln mit Automatisierungspraxis [*A publication*]
**Mes-Steuern-Regeln** ... Messen-Steuern-Regeln [*A publication*]
**MEST**........ Maintenance Engineering Support Team (MCD)
**MEST**........ Ministere d'Etat, Sciences et Technologie [*Ministry of State for Science and Technology - MOSST*] [*Canada*]
**MEST**........ Missile Electrical System Test (NG)
**MESTA**..... Marine Ecosystem Study in Tropical Areas [*Marine science*] (MSC)
**MESTARABH** ... Miscelanea de Estudios Arabes y Hebraicos [*Granada*] [*A publication*]
**Mestn Promysl Chud Prom** ... Mestnaja Promyslennost' i Chudozestvennye Promysly [*A publication*]
**ME St Water Storage Comm An Rp** ... Maine State Water Storage Commission. Annual Report [*A publication*]
**MESU**....... Microelectronics Support Unit [*for the Microelectronics Education Programme*] [*British*]
**MESUCORA** ... Measurement, Control Regulation, and Automation (IEEE)
**MET**......... East Tennessee State University, Medical Library, Johnson City, TN [*OCLC symbol*] (OCLC)
**MET**......... Magic Eye Tube
**MET**......... Maintenance Engineering Technique
**MET**......... Management Engineering Team [*Air Force*] (AFM)
**MET**......... Manufacturer's Excise Tax
**MET**......... Master Events Timer (MCD)
**MET**......... Mean Elapsed Time (MCD)
**met**........... Measurement (DS)
**MET**......... Mechanical Engineering Technician
**MET**......... Medium Equipment Transporter (MCD)
**MET**......... Memphis [*Tennessee*] [*Seismograph station code, US Geological Survey*] (SEIS)
**MET**......... Metabolic Equivalent [*Medicine*]
**MET**......... Metal [*or Metallic*] (AAG)
**Met**........... Metall [*A publication*]
**MET**......... Metallurgical
**MET**......... Metalore Resources Ltd. [*Toronto Stock Exchange symbol*]
**Met**........... Metals Abstracts [*A publication*]
**Met**........... Metamorphoses [*of Ovid*] [*Classical studies*] (OCD)
**Met**........... Metamorphoses [*of Apuleius*] [*Classical studies*] (OCD)
**MET**......... Metaphor
**MET**......... Metaphysics
**MET**......... Metastasis [*Medicine*]
**MET**......... Metatarsus [*Flamenco dance term*]
**Met**........... Metcalfe's Reports [*58-61 Kentucky*] [*A publication*] (DLA)
**Met**........... Metcalf's Reports [*Massachusetts*] [*A publication*] (DLA)
**Met**........... Metcalf's Reports [*Rhode Island*] [*A publication*] (DLA)
**MET**......... Meteorological Office [*British*] (DSUE)
**MET**......... Meteorology (AFM)
**Met**........... Methionine [*Also, M*] [*An amino acid*]
**Met**........... Metroeconomica [*A publication*]
**MET**......... Metronome [*Music*]
**MET**......... Metropolis (ROG)
**MET**......... Metropolitan (AAG)
**MET**......... Metropolitan Electric Tramways [*British*] (ROG)
**MET**......... Metropolitan Music Hall [*London*] [*British*] (DSUE)
**MET**......... [*The*] Metropolitan Railway [*British*] (ROG)
**MET**......... Metropolitan Realty Corp. [*AMEX symbol*] (CTT)
**Met**........... Metropolitan Transit Authority [*Australia*]
**MET**......... Micro-Electronic Technology (ADA)
**MET**......... Midexpiratory Time [*Medicine*]
**MET**......... Midshipman Embarkation Team [*Navy*]
**MET**......... Minimum Energy Trajectory
**MET**......... Minimum Essentials Test [*Educational test*]
**MET**......... Minimum Exposure Time
**MET**......... Missile Escort Team [*Air Force*] (AFM)
**MET**......... Mission Elapsed Time [*NASA*] (KSC)
**MET**......... Mission Entry Time
**MET**......... Mission Environment Tape
**MET**......... Mission Event Timer [*NASA*] (KSC)
**MET**......... Mobile Engineering Team [*Navy*]
**MET**......... Mobile Equipment Transporter [*NASA*]
**MET**......... Modesto & Empire Traction Co. [*Formerly, METC*] [*AAR code*]
**MET**......... Modified Expansion Tube (IEEE)
**MET**......... Modular Equipment Transporter [*NASA*]
**MET**......... Molecular Electronic Technique
**MET**......... Mond Excavation at Thebes [*London*] [*A publication*] (BJA)
**MET**......... Monthly Energy Review [*A publication*]
**MET**......... Motorola Environmental Telemetry
**MET**......... Multi-Environment Trainer (MCD)
**MET**......... Multiemitter Transistor
**MET**......... Multiple Employer Trust [*Insurance*]
**META**....... Computer series [*Digital Scientific*]
**META**....... Maritime Education and Training Act of 1980
**META**....... Megachannel Extraterrestrial Array [*For receiving possible radio signals from non-earth civilizations*]
**Met A**......... Meteorologiske Annaler [*A publication*]
**META**....... Methods of Extracting Text Automatically [*Programming language*] [*General Electric Co.*] [*Data processing*] (IEEE)
**META**....... Metropolitan Educational Television Association [*Canada*]
**Metaalinst TNO Circ** ... Metaalinstituut TNO [*Nederlands Centrale Organisatie voor Toegepast-Natuurwetenschappelijk Onderzoek*]. Circulaire [*A publication*]
**Metaalinst TNO Publ** ... Metaalinstituut TNO [*Nederlands Centrale Organisatie voor Toegepast-Natuurwetenschappelijk Onderzoek*]. Publikatie [*A publication*]
**Metaal Tech** ... Metaal en Techniek [*A publication*]
**METAB**..... Metabolism
**MetAb**...... Metals Abstracts [*A publication*]
**METAB**..... Metalurgija [*Sisak, Yugoslavia*] [*A publication*]
**Metab Bone Dis Relat Res** ... Metabolic Bone Disease and Related Research [*A publication*]
**Metab Clin Exp** ... Metabolism - Clinical and Experimental [*A publication*]
**Metab Dis** ... Metabolism and Disease [*Japan*] [*A publication*]
**Met ABM**.. Metalurgia. ABM [*Associacao Brasileira de Metais*] [*A publication*]

**Metabolism** ... Metabolism - Clinical and Experimental [*A publication*]
**Metab Ophthalmol** ... Metabolic Ophthalmology [*A publication*]
**Metab Pediatr Ophthalmol** ... Metabolic and Pediatric Ophthalmology [*A publication*]
**Metab Pediatr Syst Ophthalmol** ... Metabolic, Pediatric, and Systemic Ophthalmology [*A publication*]
**Met Abstr** .. Metallurgical Abstracts [*A publication*]
**METAC**..... Medium Tactical Transport Aircraft [*Military*]
**METADEX** ... Metal Abstracts Index Data Base [*Bibliographic database*] [*British*] (IID)
**META J** .... Manitoba Elementary Teachers' Association. Journal [*A publication*]
**METAL**..... Metallurgy
**METAL**..... Militarily Significant Emergent Technologies Awareness List [*Proposed*] [*DoD*]
**Metal ABM** ... Metalurgia. ABM [*Associacao Brasileira de Metais*] [*A publication*]
**Metal Bul**... Metal Bulletin [*A publication*]
**Metal Bull Mon** ... Metal Bulletin Monthly [*A publication*]
**Metal Cons** ... Metal Construction [*A publication*]
**Metal Constr Br Weld J** ... Metal Construction and British Welding Journal [*Later, Metal Construction*] [*A publication*]
**Metal Electr** ... Metalurgia y Electricidad [*A publication*]
**Metal & Electr** ... Metalurgia y Electricidad [*A publication*]
**Metal Eng Q** ... Metals Engineering Quarterly [*A publication*]
**Metal Fin**... Metal Finishing [*A publication*]
**Metal Fing** ... Metal Finishing Guidebook and Directory [*A publication*]
**Metal Finish** ... Metal Finishing [*A publication*]
**Metal Form** ... Metal Forming [*A publication*]
**Metal Ind**... Metal Industry [*A publication*]
**Metall**........ Metallurgist [*A publication*]
**METALL** .. Metallurgy
**Metall Abstr** ... Metallurgical Abstracts [*A publication*]
**Metall Constr Mec** ... Metallurgie et la Construction Mecanique [*A publication*]
**Metall Eng IIT (Bombay)** ... Metallurgical Engineer. Indian Institute of Technology (Bombay) [*A publication*]
**Metallges Mitt Arbeitsbereich** ... Metallgesellschaft. Mitteilungen aus dem Arbeitsbereich [*A publication*]
**Metallges Period Rev** ... Metallgesellschaft. Periodic Review [*A publication*]
**Metallges Rev Act** ... Metallgesellschaft. Review of the Activities [*A publication*]
**Metallges Rev Activ** ... Metallgesellschaft AG [*Frankfurt/Main*]. Review of the Activities [*A publication*]
**Metall Gornorudn Promst** ... Metallurgicheskaya i Gornorudnaya Promyshlennost [*A publication*]
**Metall Ital** ... Metallurgia Italiana [*A publication*]
**Metall J** ..... Metallurgical Journal [*A publication*]
**Metall Khim Prom Kaz** ... Metallurgicheskaya i Khimicheskaya Promyshlennost Kazakhstana [*A publication*]
**Metall Koksokhim** ... Metallurgiya i Koksokhimiya [*A publication*]
**Metall Mater Technol** ... Metallurgist and Materials Technologist [*A publication*]
**Metall Met** ... Metallurgia and Metal Forming [*A publication*]
**Metall & Metal Form** ... Metallurgia and Metal Forming [*A publication*]
**Metall Metalloved Chist Met** ... Metallurgiya i Metallovedenic Chistykh Metallov [*A publication*]
**Metall Metalloved Chist Met Sb Nauchn Rab** ... Metallurgiya i Metallovedenie Chistykh Metallov Moskovskij Inzhenerno-Fizicheskij Institut Sbornik Nauchnykh Rabot [*A publication*]
**Metall Met Form** ... Metallurgia and Metal Forming [*A publication*]
**Metalloberfl** ... Metalloberflaeche-Angewandte Elektrochemie [*A publication*]
**Metalloberflaeche-Angew Elektrochem** ... Metalloberflaeche-Angewandte Elektrochemie [*A publication*]
**Metallofiz** .. Metallofizika [*A publication*]
**Metallog Geol Issled** ... Metallogenicheskie i Geologicheskie Issledovaniya [*A publication*]
**Metallogr Rev** ... Metallographic Review [*A publication*]
**Metalloved Sb Statei** ... Metallovedenie. Sbornik Statei [*A publication*]
**Metalloved Term Obrab** ... Metallovedenie i Termicheskaya Obrabotka [*A publication*]
**Metalloved i Term Obrab Met** ... Metallovedenie i Termicheskaya Obrabotka Metallov [*A publication*]
**Metalloved Term Obrab Met** ... Metallovedenie i Termicheskaya Obrabotka Metallov [*A publication*]
**Metallov i Term Obrab Metal** ... Metallovedenie i Termicheskaya Obrabotka Metallov [*A publication*]
**Metall Plant Technol** ... Metallurgical Plant and Technology [*West Germany*] [*A publication*]
**Metall-Reinig Vorbehandl** ... Metall-Reinigung und Vorbehandlung [*West Germany*] [*A publication*]
**Metall Rep Aeronaut Res Lab Aust** ... Australia. Aeronautical Research Laboratories. Metallurgy Report [*A publication*] (APTA)
**Metall Rep CRM** ... Metallurgical Reports. CRM [*Centre de Recherches Metallurgiques*] [*A publication*]
**Metall Rev** ... Metallurgical Reviews (Supplement to Metals and Materials) [*A publication*]
**Metall Rev MMIJ** ... Metallurgical Review. MMIJ [*Mining and Metallurgical Institute of Japan*] [*A publication*]
**Metall Soc Conf** ... Metallurgical Society. Conferences [*A publication*]
**Metall Soc Conf Proc** ... Metallurgical Society. Conferences. Proceedings [*A publication*]
**Metall Spec (Paris)** ... Metallurgie Speciale (Paris) [*A publication*]
**Metall T-A** ... Metallurgical Transactions. A. Physical Metallurgy and Materials Science [*A publication*]
**Metall T-B** ... Metallurgical Transactions. B. Process Metallurgy [*A publication*]
**Metall Tech Memo Aust Aeronaut Res Lab** ... Australia. Aeronautical Research Laboratories. Metallurgy Technical Memorandum [*A publication*] (APTA)
**Metall Topl** ... Mettallurgija i Toplivo [*A publication*]
**Metall Trans** ... Metallurgical Transactions [*A publication*]
**Metall Trans A** ... Metallurgical Transactions. A [*A publication*]
**Metall Trans B** ... Metallurgical Transactions. B [*A publication*]
**Metallurg**... Metallurgia [*Redhill*] [*A publication*]
**Metallwaren Ind Galvanotech** ... Metallwaren-Industrie und Galvanotechnik [*A publication*]
**Metallwirtsch** ... Metallwirtschaft, Metallwissenschaft, Metalltechnik [*A publication*]
**Metallwirtsch Metallwiss Metalltech** ... Metallwirtschaft, Metallwissenschaft, Metalltechnik [*A publication*]
**Metallwirtsch Wiss Tech** ... Metallwirtschaft, Metallwissenschaft, Metalltechnik [*East Germany*] [*A publication*]
**Metal Mod** ... Metalurgia Moderna [*A publication*]
**Metal Odlew** ... Metalurgia i Odlewnictwo [*A publication*]
**Metal Powder Ind Fed Stand** ... Metal Powder Industries Federation. MPIF Standard [*A publication*]
**33 Metal Prod** ... 33 Metal Producing [*A publication*]
**Metal Prog** ... Metal Progress [*A publication*]
**Metal Proszkow** ... Metalurgia Proszkow [*A publication*]
**Metals Abstr Index** ... Metals Abstracts Index [*A publication*]
**Metals Aust** ... Metals Australia [*Later, Metals Australasia*] [*A publication*] (APTA)
**Metal Sci** ... Metal Science [*A publication*]
**Metal Sci H** ... Metal Science and Heat Treatment [*A publication*]
**Metal Sci J** ... Metal Science Journal [*Later, Metal Science*] [*A publication*]
**Metals Eng Quart** ... Metals Engineering Quarterly [*A publication*]
**Metals Mater** ... Metals and Materials [*A publication*]
**Metals Mats** ... Metals and Materials [*A publication*]
**Metals Miner Int** ... Metals and Minerals International [*A publication*]
**Metals Soc Wld** ... Metals Society World [*A publication*]
**Metal Stamp** ... Metal Stamping [*A publication*]
**Metal Stat** ... Metal Statistics [*A publication*]
**Metals Tech** ... Metals Technology [*A publication*]
**Metal Trades J** ... Metal Trades Journal [*A publication*] (APTA)
**Metal Treat**... Metal Treating [*A publication*]
**Metalwork Econ** ... Metalworking Economics [*A publication*]
**Metalwork Interfaces** ... Metalworking Interfaces [*A publication*]
**Metalwork Manag** ... Metalworking Management [*A publication*]
**Metalwork Prod** ... Metalworking Production [*A publication*]
**Metalwrkg Prod** ... Metalworking Production [*A publication*]
**META M**... Metaphysical Magazine [*A publication*] (ROG)
**Met Anal Outlook** ... Metals Analysis and Outlook [*A publication*]
**Met Ann**..... Meteorologiske Annaler [*A publication*]
**Met Annu Conf Australas Inst Met** ... Metals. Annual Conference. Australasian Institute of Metals [*A publication*] (APTA)
**Metano Pet Nuove Energ** ... Metano, Petrolio, e Nuove Energie [*A publication*]
**METAPH** ... Metaphorical (ROG)
**Metaph** ...... Metaphysica [*of Aristotle*] [*Classical studies*] (OCD)
**METAPH** ... Metaphysical (ROG)
**METAPH** ... Metaphysics
**Metaphilos** ... Metaphilosophy [*A publication*]
**METAPLAN** ... Methods of Extracting Text Automatically Programming - Language [*General Electric Co.*] [*Data processing*] (IEEE)
**METAR**..... Aviation Routine Weather Report [*Aviation code*] (FAAC)
**METAS**..... Metastasize [*Medicine*]
**METASYMBOL** ... Metalanguage Symbol
**METATH** ... Metathesis
**Met Aust**.... Metals Australasia [*A publication*]
**Met Aust**.... Metals Australia [*Later, Metals Australasia*] [*A publication*] (APTA)
**Met Australas** ... Metals Australasia [*A publication*]
**Metaux (Corros-Ind)** ... Metaux (Corrosion-Industries) [*A publication*]
**Metaux Deform** ... Metaux Deformation [*A publication*]
**METB**........ Metal Base
**METB**........ Metropolitan Bancorp, Inc. [*NASDAQ symbol*] (NQ)
**METB**........ Metropolitan Borough
**Met Bull**..... Metal Bulletin [*A publication*]
**Met Bull (Loosdrecht Netherlands)** ... Metallic Bulletin (Loosdrecht, Netherlands) [*A publication*]
**Met Bull Mon** ... Metal Bulletin Monthly [*A publication*]
**Met Bur Bull** ... Bureau of Meteorology. Bulletin [*Australia*] [*A publication*] (APTA)
**Met Bur Met Study** ... Bureau of Meteorology. Meteorological Study [*Australia*] [*A publication*] (APTA)
**Met Bur Met Summ** ... Bureau of Meteorology. Meteorological Summary [*Australia*] [*A publication*] (APTA)
**Met Bur Proj Rep** ... Bureau of Meteorology. Project Report [*Australia*] [*A publication*] (APTA)

**Met Bur Working Paper** ... Bureau of Meteorology. Working Paper [*Australia*] [*A publication*] (APTA)
**METC**........ Metal Curb (AAG)
**METC**........ Metcalf & Eddy Companies, Inc. [*NASDAQ symbol*] (CTT)
**Metc**.......... Metcalfe's Reports [*58-61 Kentucky*] [*A publication*] (DLA)
**Metc**.......... Metcalf's Reports [*Massachusetts*] [*A publication*] (DLA)
**Metc**.......... Metcalf's Reports [*Rhode Island*] [*A publication*] (DLA)
**METC**........ Military Equipment Test Center (CAAL)
**METC**........ Modesto & Empire Traction Company [*Later, MET*] [*AAR code*]
**METC**........ Morgantown Energy Technology Center [*Department of Energy*] [*Morgantown, WV*] (GRD)
**METC**........ Mouse Embryo Tissue Culture
**METCA**..... Merchant Token Collectors Association (EA)
**METCAL**.. Metrology and Calibration [*Air Force*] (AFIT)
**Metc Cont**.. Metcalf on the Law of Contracts [*A publication*] (DLA)
**Metc KY** .... Metcalfe's Reports [*58-61 Kentucky*] [*A publication*] (DLA)
**Metc Mass** ... Metcalf's Reports [*Massachusetts*] [*A publication*] (DLA)
**METCO** .... Meteorological Coordination Officer (MUGU)
**METCO** .... Metropolitan Council for Educational Opportunity (EA)
**METCON** ... Metropolitan Intersection Control [*Victoria, Australia*]
**Met Const**.. Metal Construction [*A publication*]
**Met Constr** ... Metal Construction [*A publication*]
**Met Constr Br Weld J** ... Metal Construction and British Welding Journal [*Later, Metal Construction*] [*A publication*]
**Met Constr Mec** ... Metallurgie et la Construction Mecanique [*A publication*]
**Met (Corros-Ind)** ... Metaux (Corrosion-Industries) [*A publication*]
**Metc Yelv**... Metcalf's Edition of Yelverton [*A publication*] (DLA)
**METD** ....... Mean Effective Temperature Difference [*Refrigeration*]
**METD** ....... Metal Door
**METD** ....... Metastatic Disease [*Oncology*]
**Met Deform** ... Metaux Deformation [*A publication*]
**METDLGY** ... Methodology
**Met E**......... Metallurgical Engineer
**Mete**........... Meteorologica [*of Aristotle*] [*Classical studies*] (OCD)
**METE**........ Multiple ECM [*Electronic Countermeasures*] Threat Environment [*Military*] (CAAL)
**METEC**..... Meteoroid Technology [*Satellite*] [*NASA*]
**METEC**..... Meteorologist Technician (NOAA)
**Met Electr (Madrid)** ... Metalurgia y Electricidad (Madrid) [*A publication*]
**Met & Eng** ... Metal and Engineering [*A publication*] (APTA)
**Met Eng**..... Metals in Engineering [*Japan*] [*A publication*]
**Met Eng Q** ... Metals Engineering Quarterly [*A publication*]
**METEOR** ... Marine Environmental Testing and Electro-Optical Radiation (MCD)
**METEOR** ... Meteorological Satellite [*USSR*]
**METEOR** ... Meteorology
**Meteor Forschungsergeb Reihe A** ... Meteor Forschungsergebnisse. Reihe A. Allgemeines, Physik, und Chemie des Meeres [*A publication*]
**Meteor Forschungsergeb Reihe C** ... Meteor Forschungsergebnisse. Reihe C. Geologie und Geophysik [*A publication*]
**Meteor Forschungsergeb Reihe D Biol** ... Meteor Forschungsergebnisse. Reihe D. Biologie [*A publication*]
**Meteor Forschungsergen Reihe B** ... Meteor Forschungsergebnisse. Reihe B. Meteorologie und Aeronomie [*A publication*]
**Meteor & Geoastrophys Abstr** ... Meteorological and Geoastrophysical Abstracts [*A publication*]
**Meteor Gidrol Inf Byull** ... Meteorologiya i Gidrologiya. Informatsionnyi Byulleten [*A publication*]
**METEORIT** ... Meteoritical
**Meteorit Soc Contr** ... Meteoritical Society. Contributions [*A publication*]
**Meteor Klimat Gidrol** ... Meteorologija, Klimatologija, i Gidrologija [*A publication*]
**Meteor Mag** ... Meteorological Magazine [*A publication*]
**METEOROL** ... Meteorology
**Meteorol Abh Inst Meteorol Geophys Freie Univ (Berl)** ... Meteorologische Abhandlungen. Institut fuer Meteorologie und Geophysik. Freie Universitaet (Berlin) [*A publication*]
**Meteorol Abst and Biblio** ... Meteorological Abstracts and Bibliography [*A publication*]
**Meteorol Ann** ... Meteorologiske Annaler [*A publication*]
**Meteorol Dienst DDR Veroeff** ... Meteorologischer Dienst der Deutschen Demokratischen Republik. Veroeffentlichungen [*A publication*]
**Meteorol Geoastrophys Abstr** ... Meteorological and Geoastrophysical Abstracts [*A publication*]
**Meteorol Gidrol** ... Meteorologiya i Gidrologiya [*A publication*]
**Meteorol i Gidrol** ... Meteorologiya i Gidrologiya [*A publication*]
**Meteorol Gidrolog** ... Meteorologiya i Gidrologiya [*A publication*]
**Meteorol Hydrol** ... Meteorology and Hydrology [*United States*] [*A publication*]
**Meteorol Mag** ... Meteorological Magazine [*A publication*]
**Meteorol Monogr** ... Meteorological Monographs [*A publication*]
**Meteorol Rundsch** ... Meteorologische Rundschau [*A publication*]
**Meteorol Stud** ... Meteorological Study [*A publication*] (APTA)
**Meteorol Stud Meteorol Bur** ... Bureau of Meteorology. Meteorological Study [*Australia*] [*A publication*] (APTA)
**Meteorol Zpr** ... Meteorologicke Zpravy [*A publication*]
**Meteor Rund** ... Meteorologische Rundschau [*A publication*]
**METEOSAT** ... Meteorological Satellite [*European Space Agency*]
**METEPA** .. Tris(methylethylene)phosphoric Triamide [*Organic chemistry*]
**METF**........ Metal Flashing
**Met Fabr News** ... Metal Fabricating News [*A publication*]
**Met Finish** ... Metal Finishing [*A publication*]
**Met Finish Abstr** ... Metal Finishing Abstracts [*A publication*]
**Met Finish J** ... Metal Finishing Journal [*A publication*]
**Met Form**... Metal Forming [*England*] [*A publication*]
**Met Form Drop Forger** ... Metal Forming, Incorporating the Drop Forger [*A publication*]
**Met Forum** ... Metals Forum [*Australia*] [*A publication*]
**METG** ....... Metal Grill
**Met & GeoAb** ... Meteorological and Geoastrophysical Abstracts [*A publication*]
**Met Geoastrophys Abstr** ... Meteorological and Geoastrophysical Abstracts [*A publication*]
**MetH** ......... Mediaevalia et Humanistica [*A publication*]
**METH** ....... Methane (AAG)
**Meth** .......... Methedrine [*Stimulant*]
**METH**....... Methicillin [*An antibiotic*]
**METH**....... Method (ROG)
**METH**....... Methode Electronics, Inc. [*NASDAQ symbol*] (NQ)
**METH**....... Methodist
**METH**....... Methylated (ADA)
**METH**....... Methylated Spirit (DSUE)
**MetHb**....... Methemoglobin [*Biochemistry, medicine*]
**Meth Cancer Res** ... Methods in Cancer Research [*A publication*]
**MethCh** ..... Methodist Chaplain [*Navy*] [*British*]
**MeThCh** .... Methylthiocholine [*Biochemistry*]
**Meth Ch Ca** ... Report of Methodist Church Cases [*A publication*] (DLA)
**MeTHF** ..... Methyltetrahydrofolic Acid [*Biochemistry*]
**MethH** ...... Methodist History [*A publication*]
**METHIMAZOLE** ... Methylmercaptoimidazole [*Also, MMI*] [*Thyroid inhibitor*]
**Meth Inf Med** ... Methods of Information in Medicine [*A publication*]
**Meth M**...... Methodist Magazine [*A publication*]
**Meth Membrane Biol** ... Methods in Membrane Biology [*A publication*]
**Meth Mol Biol** ... Methods in Molecular Biology [*A publication*]
**Method Appraisal Phys Sci** ... Method and Appraisal in the Physical Sciences [*A publication*]
**Methoden Verfahren Math Phys** ... Methoden und Verfahren der Mathematischen Physik [*A publication*]
**Methodes Math Inform** ... Methodes Mathematiques de l'Informatique [*Paris*] [*A publication*]
**Methodes Phys Anal** ... Methodes Physiques d'Analyse [*Revue de Groupement pour l'Avancement des Methodes Spectrographiques*] [*A publication*]
**Method Inf Med** ... Methodik der Information in der Medizin [*A publication*]
**Methodist Hosp Dallas Med Staff Bull** ... Methodist Hospital of Dallas. Medical Staff. Bulletin [*A publication*]
**Methodol Dev Biochem** ... Methodological Developments in Biochemistry [*A publication*]
**Methodol Surv Biochem** ... Methodological Surveys in Biochemistry [*A publication*]
**Method Phys Anal** ... Methodes Physiques d'Analyse [*Revue de Groupement pour l'Avancement des Methodes Spectrographiques*] [*A publication*]
**Methods Achiev Exp Pathol** ... Methods and Achievements in Experimental Pathology [*A publication*]
**Methods Anim Exp** ... Methods of Animal Experimentation [*A publication*]
**Methods Biochem Anal** ... Methods of Biochemical Analysis [*A publication*]
**Methods Cancer Res** ... Methods in Cancer Research [*A publication*]
**Methods Carbohydr Chem** ... Methods in Carbohydrate Chemistry [*A publication*]
**Methods Cell Biol** ... Methods in Cell Biology [*A publication*]
**Method Sci** ... Methodology and Science [*A publication*]
**Methods Clin Pharmacol** ... Methods in Clinical Pharmacology [*A publication*]
**Methods Comput Phys** ... Methods in Computational Physics. Advances in Research and Applications [*A publication*]
**Methods Enzymol** ... Methods in Enzymology [*A publication*]
**Methods Exp Phys** ... Methods of Experimental Physics [*A publication*]
**Methods Find Exp Clin Pharmacol** ... Methods and Findings in Experimental and Clinical Pharmacology [*A publication*]
**Methods Free Radical Chem** ... Methods in Free Radical Chemistry [*A publication*]
**Methods Immunol Immunochem** ... Methods in Immunology and Immunochemistry [*A publication*]
**Methods Inf Med** ... Methods of Information in Medicine [*A publication*]
**Methods Inf Med (Suppl)** ... Methods of Information in Medicine (Supplement) [*A publication*]
**Methods Invest Diagn Endocrinol** ... Methods in Investigative and Diagnostic Endocrinology [*A publication*]
**Methods Med Res** ... Methods in Medical Research [*A publication*]
**Methods Membr Biol** ... Methods in Membrane Biology [*A publication*]
**Methods Mod Math Phys** ... Methods of Modern Mathematical Physics [*A publication*]
**Methods Mol Biol** ... Methods in Molecular Biology [*A publication*]
**Methods Mycoplasmol** ... Methods in Mycoplasmology [*A publication*]
**Methods Oper Res** ... Methods of Operations Research [*A publication*]
**Methods Pharmacol** ... Methods in Pharmacology [*A publication*]

**Methods Stereochem Anal** ... Methods in Stereochemical Analysis [*A publication*]
**Methods Subnucl Phys** ... Methods in Subnuclear Physics [*A publication*]
**Methods Virol** ... Methods in Virology [*A publication*]
**Meth Per Ind** ... Methodist Periodical Index [*A publication*]
**Meth Q** ...... Methodist Quarterly [*A publication*]
**Meth Q R**... Methodist Quarterly Review [*A publication*]
**Meth R**....... Methodist Review [*A publication*]
**METHS**..... Methylated Spirits (ADA)
**METI**......... Major Engineering Test Item (AAG)
**METI**......... Metis [*A publication*]
**METIA**...... Medical Times [*A publication*]
**METIMP**.. Meteorological Equipment Improvement Program (NG)
**Met Ind (China)** ... Metal Industries (China) [*A publication*]
**Met Ind (Johannesburg)** ... Metal Industries (Johannesburg) [*A publication*]
**Met Ind (London)** ... Metal Industry (London) [*A publication*]
**Met Inf Med** ... Methods of Information in Medicine [*A publication*]
**Met Ital**...... Metallurgia Italiana [*A publication*]
**Met Izv Akad Nauk SSSR** ... Metally Izvestiya Akademi Nauk SSSR [*A publication*]
**METJ** ........ Metal Jalousie
**Met J Univ Strathclyde Glasgow** ... Metallurgical Journal. University of Strathclyde, Glasgow [*A publication*]
**METK** ....... Memtek Corp. [*NASDAQ symbol*] (NQ)
**METL**........ Materials and Ecological Testing Laboratory [*Research center*] (RCD)
**METL**........ Metal
**METL**........ Mission Essential Task List [*Army*] (INF)
**Metl Bul M** ... Metal Bulletin Monthly [*A publication*]
**METLC**..... Metallic
**Met Leggeri Loro Appl** ... Metalli Leggeri e Loro Applicazioni [*A publication*]
**Met Life Stat Bull** ... Metropolitan Life Insurance Company. Statistical Bulletin [*A publication*]
**Metl Ind N** ... Metals Industry News [*A publication*]
**METLO**..... Metrological Equipment and Technical Liaison Officer [*Navy*] (NG)
**METM**...... Metal Mold
**MET M** ..... Metropolitan Magazine [*New York*] [*A publication*]
**MET/M**..... Missile Engine Technician/Mechanic (AAG)
**Met Mag (Lond)** ... Meteorological Magazine (London) [*A publication*]
**Met Mark Place Met Congr** ... Metals in the Market Place. Metals Congress [*A publication*] (APTA)
**Met Mark Rev** ... Metal Market Review [*A publication*]
**Met Mater** ... Metals and Materials [*A publication*]
**Met Mater Processes** ... Metals, Materials, and Processes [*A publication*]
**Met/Mater Today** ... Metals/Materials Today [*A publication*]
**METMD** ... Metamedicine [*A publication*]
**Met Miner Process** ... Metals and Minerals Processing [*South Africa*] [*A publication*]
**Met Miner Rev** ... Metals and Minerals Review [*India*] [*A publication*]
**Met Miner Rev (Calcutta)** ... Metals and Minerals Review (Calcutta) [*A publication*]
**Met Mus Bul** ... Metropolitan Museum of Art. Bulletin [*A publication*]
**Met Mus Bull** ... Metropolitan Museum of Art. Bulletin [*A publication*]
**Met Mus J** ... Metropolitan Museum. Journal [*A publication*]
**Met News (India)** ... Metal News (India) [*A publication*]
**Met Note Aust Aeronaut Res Lab** ... Australia. Aeronautical Research Laboratories. Metallurgy Note [*A publication*] (APTA)
**METO** ....... Maximum Engine Takeoff [*Power*] [*Air Force*]
**METO** ....... Maximum Except during Takeoff
**METO** ....... Meteorological Office [*or Officer*] [*Air Force*]
**METO** ....... Metro Cable Corp. [*NASDAQ symbol*] (NQ)
**METO** ....... Middle East Treaty Organization
**METOB** .... Meteorologist Observation (NOAA)
**Metod Mater Nauchn Soobshch** ... Metodicheskie Materialy i Nauchnye Soobshcheniya [*A publication*]
**Metodol Probl Nauki** ... Metodologiceskie Problemy Nauki [*A publication*]
**Metod Prepod Inostr Yazykov Vuze** ... Metodika Prepodavaniya Inostrannykh Yazykov v Vuze [*A publication*]
**Metod Prepod Khim** ... Metodika Prepodavaniya Khimii [*A publication*]
**Metod Prirucky Exp Bot** ... Metodicke Prirucky Experimentalni Botaniky [*A publication*]
**Metod Tekh Razved** ... Metodika i Tekhnika Razvedki [*A publication*]
**Metod Ukazaniya Geol S'emke Masshtaba 1:50000** ... Metodicheskie Ukazaniya po Geologicheskoi S'emke Masshtaba 1:50,000 [*A publication*]
**Metod Vopr Nauki** ... Metodologiceskie Voprosy Nauki [*A publication*]
**Metody Anal Khim Reakt Prep** ... Metody Analiza Khimicheskikh Reaktivov i Preparatov [*A publication*]
**Metody Anal Org Soedin Nefti Ikh Smesei Proizvodnykh** ... Metody Analiza Organicheskikh Soedinenii Nefti Ikh Smesei i Proizvodnykh [*A publication*]
**Metody Anal Org Soedin Neft Ikh Smesei Proizvodnykh** ... Metody Analiza Organicheskikh Soedinenii Nefti Ikh Smesei i Proizvodnykh [*USSR*] [*A publication*]
**Metody Anal Redkomet Miner Rud Gorn Porod** ... Metody Analiza Redkometal'nykh Mineralov Rud i Gornykh Porod [*A publication*]
**Metody Anal Veshchestv Osoboi Chist Monokrist** ... Metody Analiza Veshchestv Osoboi Chistoty i Monokristallov [*A publication*]
**Metody Diskret Analiz** ... Metody Diskretnogo Analiza [*Novosibirsk*] [*A publication*]
**Metody Ispyt Detalei Mash Prib** ... Metody Ispytanii Detalei Mashin i Priborov [*A publication*]
**Metody Issled Katal Katal Reakts** ... Metody Issledovaniya Katalizatorov i Kataliticheskikh Reaktsii [*USSR*] [*A publication*]
**Metody Issled Vinodel** ... Metody Issledovaniya v Vinodelii [*A publication*]
**Metody Izuch Veshchestv Sostava i Ikh Primen** ... Metody Izucheniya Veshchestvennogo Sostava i Ikh Primenenie [*A publication*]
**Metody Khim Anal Miner Syr'ya** ... Metody Khimicheskogo Analiza Mineral'nogo Syr'ya [*A publication*]
**Metody Opred Pestits Vode** ... Metody Opredeleniya Pestitsidov v Vode [*A publication*]
**Metody Paleogeogr Issled** ... Metody Paleogeograficheskikh Issledovanii [*A publication*]
**Metody Pochody Chem Technol** ... Metody a Pochody Chemicke Technologie [*A publication*]
**Metody Protsessy Khim Tekhnol** ... Metody i Protsessy Khimicheskoi Tekhnologii [*A publication*]
**Metody Razved Geofiz** ... Metody Razvedochnoi Geofiziki [*A publication*]
**Metody Rudn Geofiz** ... Metody Rudnoi Geofiziki [*A publication*]
**Metody Vychisl** ... Leningradskii Ordena Lenina Gosudarstvennyi Imeni A. A. Zhdanova Metody Vychislenii [*A publication*]
**Metody Vycisl** ... Metody Vycislenii [*A publication*]
**Metod Zavadeni Vysledku Vyzk Praxe** ... Metodiky pro Zavadeni Vysledku Vyzkumu do Praxe [*A publication*]
**Metod Zavad Vysled Vyzk Praxe** ... Metodiky pro Zavadeni Vysledku Vyzkumu do Praxe [*A publication*]
**METOF**..... Meteorological Office
**Met Off**...... Meteorological Office [*British*] (AIA)
**METOFOR** ... Methodology for Total Force Concept [*Military*]
**METON**.... Measured Tons Discharged or Loaded [*Shipping*]
**METON**.... Metonymy
**METOP**..... Maximum Expected Takeoff Power (AFM)
**Metopera** ... Metropolitan Opera Association (EA)
**MeToV** ...... United States Veterans Administration Center, Togus, ME [*Library symbol*] [*Library of Congress*] (LCLS)
**METOXI**... Military Effectiveness in a Toxin Environment (AABC)
**METP**........ Metal Partition
**METP**........ Metal Portion
**Met Phys** ... Metal Physics [*A publication*]
**Met Phys Semin** ... Metal Physics Seminar [*A publication*]
**Met Powder Rep** ... Metal Powder Report [*A publication*]
**33 Met Prod** ... 33 Metal Producing [*A publication*]
**Met Prog**.... Metal Progress [*A publication*]
**Met Prog Datab** ... Metal Progress Databook [*A publication*]
**Met Prop Counc Publ** ... Metal Properties Council. Publication [*A publication*]
**METR**........ Metal Roof
**METR**........ Meteorology (NG)
**Metr** ........... Metropolis [*A publication*]
**METR**........ Metropolitan
**MetR**.......... Metropolitan Railway [*British*]
**METR**........ Minimum Essential Training Requirements
**METRA**..... Metal RADAR
**Met Rdsch** ... Meteorologische Rundschau [*A publication*]
**Met Rec Electroplat** ... Metal Records and Electroplater [*A publication*]
**Met Reinig Vorbehandl Oberflaechentech Form** ... Metall-Reinigung, Vorbehandlung, Oberflaechentechnik, Formung [*A publication*]
**Met Rev (Suppl Metals Mater)** ... Metallurgical Reviews (Supplement to Metals and Materials) [*A publication*]
**METREX**.. Metropolitan Centrex [*Telephone network*]
**METRI**...... Military Essentiality through Readiness Indices
**METRIA**... Metropolitan Tree Improvement Alliance (EA)
**METRIC**... Multiechelon Technique for Recoverable Item Control (MCD)
**Metric Bul** ... Metric Bulletin [*A publication*]
**METRL**..... Meteorology (NG)
**METRL**..... Metrology Requirements List [*DoD*]
**Metr Mus J** ... Metropolitan Museum. Journal [*A publication*]
**METRO** .... Materiel Essential to Reconstitution Operations [*Air Force*] (AFM)
**METRO** .... Meteorological Equipment Terminal and Representative Observation (MCD)
**METRO** .... Meteorology
**Metro** ......... Metronome [*A publication*]
**METRO** .... Metropolitan
**METRO** .... Metropolitan [*Subway system*] (DSUE)
**METRO** .... Metropolitan Collegiate Athletic Conference (EA)
**METRO** .... Michigan Effectuation, Training, and Research Organization [*Computer-programmed simulation game*]
**METRO** .... New York Metropolitan Reference and Research Library Agency [*Brooklyn, NY*] [*Library network*]
**METROC** ... Meteorological Rocket
**Metroecon** ... Metroeconomica [*A publication*]
**Metrol**......... Metrologia [*A publication*]
**METROL** ... Metrology
**Metrol Apl** ... Metrologia Aplicata [*A publication*]
**Metrol Insp** ... Metrology and Inspection [*A publication*]
**METROMEX** ... Metropolitan Meteorological Experiment

**METROP** ... Metropolis (ADA)
**METROP** ... Metropolitan
**Metrop** ....... Metropolitan [*A publication*]
**Metrop Detroit Sci Rev** ... Metropolitan Detroit Science Review [*A publication*]
**Metrop Mus** ... Metropolitan Museum of Art. Bulletin [*A publication*]
**Metropolitan Life Stat Bul** ... Metropolitan Life Insurance Company. Statistical Bulletin [*A publication*]
**Metropolitan Life Statis Bul** ... Metropolitan Life Insurance Company. Statistical Bulletin [*A publication*]
**Metropolitan Toronto Bd Trade J** ... Metropolitan Toronto Board of Trade. Journal [*A publication*]
**Metropolitan Toronto Bus J** ... Metropolitan Toronto Business Journal [*A publication*]
**METRRA** ... Metal Re-Radiation RADAR [*Mine detection system*] [*Army*] (RDA)
**MetRS** ....... Methionyl-Transfer Ribonucleic Acid Synthetase [*An enzyme*]
**METS** ........ Maintainability Evaluation and Tracking System (MCD)
**METS** ........ Mechanized Export Traffic System [*Army*] (AABC)
**METS** ........ Met-Coil Systems Corp. [*Cedar Rapids, IA*] [*NASDAQ symbol*] (NQ)
**METS** ........ Metal Strip
**MET/S** ...... Missile Electrical Technician/Specialist (AAG)
**METS** ........ Missile Environmental Testing Study
**METS** ........ Mobile Engine Test Stand
**METS** ........ Modified Engineered Time Standards
**METS** ........ Modular Engine Test System (MCD)
**METS** ........ Modularized Equipment Transport System [*NASA*]
**METS** ........ Multiple Exposure Testing System [*Advertising analysis*]
**Metsanduse Tead Uurim Lab Metsandusl Uurim** ... Metsanduse Teadusliku Uurimise Laboratoorium. Metsanduslikud Uurimused [*A publication*]
**Metsantutkimuslaitoksen Julk** ... Metsantutkimuslaitoksen Julkaisuja [*A publication*]
**MET/SAT** ... Meteorological Satellite
**Metsatal Aikakausl** ... Metsataloudellinen Aikakauslehti [*A publication*]
**METSC** ..... Metal Science [*A publication*]
**Met Sci** ....... Metal Science [*A publication*]
**Met Sci and Heat Treat** ... Metal Science and Heat Treatment [*A publication*]
**Met Sci Heat Treat** ... Metal Science and Heat Treatment [*A publication*]
**Met Sci Heat Treat Met** ... Metal Science and Heat Treatment of Metals [*United States*] [*A publication*]
**Met Sci Heat Treat Met (Engl Transl)** ... Metal Science and Heat Treatment of Metals (English Translation) [*United States*] [*A publication*]
**Met Sci Heat Treat Met (USSR)** ... Metal Science and Heat Treatment of Metals (USSR) [*A publication*]
**Met Sci Heat Treat (USSR)** ... Metal Science and Heat Treatment (USSR) [*A publication*]
**Met Sci J** ... Metal Science Journal [*Later, Metal Science*] [*A publication*]
**Met Soc AIME Conf** ... Metallurgical Society. American Institute of Mining, Metallurgical, and Petroleum Engineers. Conferences [*A publication*]
**Met Soc AIME Inst Metals Div Spec Rep** ... Metallurgical Society. American Institute of Mining, Metallurgical, and Petroleum Engineers. Institute of Metals Division. Special Report [*A publication*]
**Met Soc AIME TMS Pap** ... Metallurgical Society. American Institute of Mining, Metallurgical, and Petroleum Engineers. TMS Papers [*A publication*]
**Met Soc World** ... Metals Society World [*A publication*]
**Met Stamp** ... Metal Stamping [*A publication*]
**Met Study Bur Met** ... Bureau of Meteorology. Meteorological Study [*Australia*] [*A publication*] (APTA)
**Met Summary Met Bur** ... Bureau of Meteorology. Meteorological Summary [*Australia*] [*A publication*] (APTA)
**METT** ........ Manned, Evasive Target Tank [*Army*]
**METT** ........ Mission, Enemy, Terrain and Weather, Troops and Firepower Available
**Met Tech Inf** ... Metokika a Technika Informaci [*A publication*]
**Met Technol** ... Metals Technology [*A publication*]
**Met Technol (Jpn)** ... Metals and Technology (Japan) [*A publication*]
**Met Technol (London)** ... Metals Technology. Institute of Metals (London) [*A publication*]
**METTM** .... Mission, Enemy, Terrain and Weather, Troops and Firepower Available, and Maneuver Space (MCD)
**Met Trans** ... Metallurgical Transactions [*A publication*]
**Met Treat** ... Metal Treating [*A publication*]
**Met Treat Drop Forg** ... Metal Treatment and Drop Forging [*England*] [*A publication*]
**Met Tr J** .... Metal Trades Journal [*A publication*]
**METT-T** .... Mission, Enemy, Terrain and Weather, Troops and Firepower Available and Time (INF)
**METU** ....... Marine Electronic Technical Unit (MUGU)
**METU** ....... Mobile Electronics Technical Unit
**METU** ....... Mobile Electronics Training Unit
**METU Faculty of Archre Occasional Paper Series** ... METU [*Middle East Technical University*] Faculty of Architecture. Occasional Paper Series [*A publication*]
**METU J Pure Appl Sci** ... Middle East Technical University. Journal of Pure and Applied Sciences [*A publication*]
**METU Studies Develop** ... Middle East Technical University. Studies in Development [*A publication*]
**METVC** ..... Main Engine Thrust Vector Control (MCD)
**METW** ...... Municipality of East Troy, Wisconsin [*AAR code*]
**Met Week** .. Metals Week [*A publication*]
**Metwork Prod** ... Metalworking Production [*A publication*]
**meu** ............ Maine [*MARC country of publication code*] [*Library of Congress*] (LCCP)
**MEU** .......... Marine Expeditionary Unit
**MEU** .......... Memory Expansion Unit
**MEU** .......... Message Encoder Unit
**MEU** .......... Methylumbelliferone [*Biochemistry*]
**MEU** .......... Multiplexer Encoder Unit
**MeU** .......... University of Maine, Orono, ME [*Library symbol*] [*Library of Congress*] (LCLS)
**MEU** .......... University of Maine, Orono, ME [*OCLC symbol*] (OCLC)
**MEUBAR** ... Ehime Daigaku Kiyo Shizenkagaku. B. Shirizu Seibutsugaku [*A publication*]
**MEUF** ....... Micellar-Enhanced Ultrafiltration [*Chemical engineering*]
**MEUG** ....... Major Energy Users' Group [*British*]
**MeU-G** ...... University of Maine at Portland/Gorham, Gorham, ME [*Library symbol*] [*Library of Congress*] (LCLS)
**MeU-L** ....... University of Maine, Law Library, Portland, ME [*Library symbol*] [*Library of Congress*] (LCLS)
**MEULEX** ... Marine Expeditionary Unit Landing Exercise (NVT)
**MeUmb** ...... Methylumbelliferyl [*Biochemistry*]
**Meunerie Franc** ... La Meunerie Francaise [*A publication*]
**MeU-P** ....... University of Maine at Portland/Gorham, Portland, ME [*Library symbol*] [*Library of Congress*] (LCLS)
**MEV** .......... Manned Entry Vehicle
**MEV** .......... Medical Evacuation Vehicle (MCD)
**MEV** .......... Mega [*or Million*] Electron Volts
**MEV** .......... Minden, NV [*Location identifier*] [*FAA*] (FAAL)
**MEvA** ........ Avco-Everett Research Laboratory, Everett, MA [*Library symbol*] [*Library of Congress*] (LCLS)
**M & Eval Guid** ... Measurement and Evaluation in Guidance [*A publication*]
**MEVE** ....... Mesa Verde National Park
**MEvP** ......... Parlin Memorial Library, Everett, MA [*Library symbol*] [*Library of Congress*] (LCLS)
**MEW** ......... Manitoba Department of Environment, Workplace Safety, and Health [*UTLAS symbol*]
**MEW** ......... Manufactures Empty Weight (MCD)
**MEW** ......... Marine Early Warning
**MEW** ......... Measure of Economic Welfare
**MEW** ......... Microwave Early Warning [*Radio*] [*Air Force*]
**MEW** ......... Middle East Watch [*An association*] (EA)
**MEW** ......... Ministry of Economic Warfare [*British*]
**MEW** ......... Missionaries of the Eternal Word [*Formerly, CFMA*] (EA)
**MEW** ......... Mobile Early Warning
**MEW** ......... Modern English Writers [*A publication*]
**MeW** .......... Waterville Public Library, Waterville, ME [*Library symbol*] [*Library of Congress*] (LCLS)
**MEWA** ...... Motor and Equipment Wholesalers Association [*Later, ASIA*]
**MEWA** ...... Multiple Employer Welfare Arrangement
**MeWC** ....... Colby College, Waterville, ME [*Library symbol*] [*Library of Congress*] (LCLS)
**MEWC** ...... Middle East Section of the War Cabinet [*British*] [*World War II*]
**MEWC** ...... Middle East War Council [*British military*] (DMA)
**MEWD** ...... Missile Electronic Warfare Division [*White Sands Missile Range*] (AAG)
**MeWe** ........ Wells Public Library, Wells, ME [*Library symbol*] [*Library of Congress*] (LCLS)
**MEWEA** ... Medizinische Welt [*A publication*]
**MeWebr** ..... Walker Memorial Library, Westbrook, ME [*Library symbol*] [*Library of Congress*] (LCLS)
**MEWG** ...... Maintenance Engineering Working Group [*NASA*] (NASA)
**MEWOA** ... Medical World [*A publication*]
**Mews** .......... Mews' Digest of English Case Law [*A publication*] (DLA)
**MEWS** ....... Microwave Electronic Warfare System
**MEWS** ....... Missile Early Warning Station (AFM)
**MEWS** ....... Missile Electronic Warfare System [*Army*]
**MEWS** ....... Mission Essential Weapon System [*Military*] (CAAL)
**MEWS** ....... Modular Electronic Warfare Simulator [*Navy*]
**Mews** .......... [*The*] Reports [*1893-95*] [*England*] [*A publication*] (DLA)
**Mews Dig** ... Mews' Digest of English Case Law [*A publication*] (DLA)
**MEWT** ...... Matrix Electrostatic Writing Technique
**MEWT** ...... Microelectronic Weld Tester
**MEWTA** ... Missile Electronic Warfare Technical Area [*White Sands Missile Range*] (AABC)
**MEX** .......... Mariner Explorations [*Vancouver Stock Exchange symbol*]
**MEX** .......... Marketing in Europe [*A publication*]
**M Ex** .......... Master of Expression
**MEx** ........... Mekhilta Exodus (BJA)
**MEX** .......... Memorex Corp., Memorex Technical Information Library, Santa Clara, CA [*OCLC symbol*] (OCLC)
**MEX** .......... Mexican (ROG)
**MEX** .......... Mexico [*ANSI three-letter standard code*] (CNC)
**MEX** .......... Mexico City [*Mexico*] [*Later, TEO*] [*Geomagnetic observatory code*]
**MEX** .......... Mexico City [*Mexico*] [*Airport symbol*] (OAG)

**MEX**.......... Military Engineering Experimental Establishment [*British*]
**MEX**.......... Military Exchange
**MEX**.......... Mobile Exercise
**MEX**.......... MODEM Executive [*Computer telecommunications program*]
**MEX**.......... "Temporary Rank" [*Army slang*]
**Mex Agr**..... Mexico Agricola [*A publication*]
**Mex Am R** ... Mexican-American Review [*Later, Mex-Am Review*] [*A publication*]
**MExB**........ Motor Explosive Boat [*British military*] (DMA)
**Mex Bosques** ... Mexico y Sus Bosques [*A publication*]
**Mex Com Dir Invest Recur Miner Bol** ... Mexico. Comite Directivo para la Investigacion de los Recursos Minerales. Boletin [*A publication*]
**Mex Cons Rec Nat No Ren Sem Int Anu Expl Geol Min Mem** ... Mexico. Consejo de Recursos Naturales No Renovables. Seminario Interno Anual sobre Exploracion Geologico-Minera. Memoria [*A publication*]
**Mex Cons Recur Nat No Renov Bol** ... Mexico. Consejo de Recursos Naturales No Renovables. Boletin [*A publication*]
**Mex Cons Recur Nat No Renov Publ** ... Mexico. Consejo de Recursos Naturales No Renovables. Publicacion [*A publication*]
**MEXE**........ Military Engineering Experimental Establishment [*British*]
**Mex Folkways** ... Mexican Folkways [*A publication*]
**Mex For**..... Mexico Forestal [*A publication*]
**Mexicn Rev** ... Mexican-American Review [*Later, Mex-Am Review*] [*A publication*]
**Mexico Anales Inst Biologia** ... Mexico. Anales del Instituto de Biologia [*A publication*]
**Mexico Com Fomento Min Bol** ... Mexico. Comision de Fomento Minero. Boletin [*A publication*]
**Mexico Consejo Rec Naturales No Renovables Bol Pub** ... Mexico. Consejo de Recursos Naturales No Renovables. Boletin. Publicaciones [*A publication*]
**Mexico Escuela Nac Cienc Biol Anales** ... Mexico. Escuela Nacional de Ciencias Biologicas. Anales [*A publication*]
**Mexico Inst Nac Inv Rec Minerales Bol** ... Mexico. Instituto Nacional para la Investigacion de Recursos Minerales. Boletin [*A publication*]
**Mexico Univ Nac Autonoma Inst Geografia Bol** ... Mexico. Universidad Nacional Autonoma. Instituto de Geografia. Boletin [*A publication*]
**Mexico Univ Nac Autonoma Inst Geologia Bol** ... Mexico. Universidad Nacional Autonoma. Instituto de Geologia. Boletin [*A publication*]
**Mex I G** ..... Mexico. Instituto Geologico [*A publication*]
**Mex Inst Nac Invest Recur Miner Bol** ... Mexico. Instituto Nacional para la Investigacion de Recursos Minerales. Boletin [*A publication*]
**Mex Min Fomento An** ... Mexico. Ministerio de Fomento. Anales [*A publication*]
**Mex M J**.... Mexican Mining Journal [*A publication*]
**MEXN**....... Mexican (FAAC)
**MexP**......... Mexican Pharmacopoeia [*A publication*]
**Mex Sec Fomento Bol** ... Mexico. Secretaria de Fomento. Boletin [*A publication*]
**Mex Secr Agric Ganad Of Estud Espec Foll Divul** ... Mexico. Secretaria de Agricultura y Ganaderia. Oficina de Estudios Especiales. Folleto de Divulgacion [*A publication*]
**Mex Secr Agric Ganad Of Estud Espec Foll Misc** ... Mexico. Secretaria de Agricultura y Ganaderia. Oficina de Estudios Especiales. Folleto Miscelaneo [*A publication*]
**Mex Secr Agric Ganad Of Estud Espec Foll Tec** ... Mexico. Secretaria de Agricultura y Ganaderia. Oficina de Estudios Especiales. Folleto Tecnico [*A publication*]
**MEXSVM** ... Mexican Service Medal
**MEXT**........ Maximal Exercise Testing
**Mex Univ Nac Auton Inst Geol Paleontol Mex** ... Mexico. Universidad Nacional Autonoma. Instituto de Geologia. Paleontologia Mexicana [*A publication*]
**Mex Univ Nac Auton Inst Geol Rev** ... Mexico. Universidad Nacional Autonoma. Instituto de Geologia. Revista [*A publication*]
**Mex Univ Nac Auton Inst Geol Ser Divulg** ... Mexico. Universidad Nacional Autonoma. Instituto de Geologia. Serie Divulgacion [*A publication*]
**MEY**.......... Mapleton, IA [*Location identifier*] [*FAA*] (FAAL)
**MEY**.......... Maximum Economic Yield [*Fishery management*] (MSC)
**MEY**.......... Meghauli [*Nepal*] [*Airport symbol*] (OAG)
**Meyer Des Inst Judiciares** ... Meyer's Des Institutiones Judiciares [*A publication*] (DLA)
**Meyler's Side Eff Drugs** ... Meyler's Side Effects of Drugs [*A publication*]
**MEYNA**.... Meyniana [*A publication*]
**MEYR**....... Meyer [*Fred*], Inc. [*Portland, OR*] [*NASDAQ symbol*] (NQ)
**MEZ**.......... Augusta Mental Health Institute, Augusta, ME [*OCLC symbol*] (OCLC)
**MEZ**.......... Mena, AR [*Location identifier*] [*FAA*] (FAAL)
**Mez**........... Mezuzah (BJA)
**MEZ**.......... Mezzo [*Moderate*] [*Music*]
**MEZ**.......... Mezzotinto [*Medium Tint, Half Tone*] [*Engraving*] (ROG)
**MEZ**.......... Missile Engagement Zone (NVT)
**MEZ**.......... Mittel Europaeische Zeit [*Central European Time*] [*German*]
**Mezdun Ezeg Polit Ekon** ... Mezdunarodnyj Ezegodnik. Politika i Ekonomika [*A publication*]
**Mezdun Zizn** ... Mezdunarodnaja Zizn [*A publication*]
**Mezhdunar Agroprom Zh** ... Mezhdunarodnyi Agropromyshlennyi Zhurnal [*A publication*]
**Mezhdunar Konf Fiz Vys Energ** ... Mezhdunarodnaya Konferentsiya po Fizike Vysokikh Energii [*A publication*]
**Mezhdunar Kongr Astronavt Dokl** ... Mezhdunarodnaya Kongress po Astronavtike Doklady [*A publication*]
**Mezhdunar Nauch Suvesh Kheterozisa** ... Mezhdunarodno Nauchno Suveshtanie po Kheterozisa [*A publication*]
**Mezhdunar Sel-Khoz Zh** ... Mezhdunarodnyi Sel'skokhozyaistvennyi Zhurnal [*A publication*]
**Mezhdunar Sel'skokhoz Zh** ... Mezhdunarodnyi Sel'skokhozyaistvennyi Zhurnal [*A publication*]
**Mezhdunar Selskostop Spis** ... Mezhdunarodno Selskostopansko Spisanie [*A publication*]
**Mezhdunar Simp Geterog Katal Tr** ... Mezhdunarodnyi Simpozium po Geterogennomu Katalizu Trudy [*A publication*]
**Mezhdunar S-Kh Zh** ... Mezhdunarodnyi Sel'skokhozyaistvennyi Zhurnal [*A publication*]
**Mezhduved Geofiz Kom** ... Mezhduvedomstvennyi Geofizicheskikh Komitet [*USSR*] [*A publication*]
**Mezhved Geofiz Kom Prezidiume Akad Nauk Ukr SSR Inf Byull** ... Mezhvedomstvennyi Geofizicheskii Komitet pri Prezidiume Akademii Nauk Ukrainskoi SSR Informatsionnyi Byulleten [*A publication*]
**Mezhvuzovskii Tematicheskii Sb-Yaroslavskii Gos Univ** ... Mezhvuzovskii Tematicheskii Sbornik-Yaroslavskii Gosudarstvennyi Universitet [*A publication*]
**Mezhvuz Sb Nauchn Tr Erevan Politekh Inst Ser 19** ... Mezhvuzovskii Sbornik Nauchnykh Trudov Erevanskii Politekhnicheskii Institut Seriya 19 Khimicheskaya Tekhnologiya [*A publication*]
**Mezhvuz Sb Tr Biol Kafedry Kirg Univ Ser Bot** ... Mezhvuzovskii Sbornik Trudov Biologicheskoi Kafedry Kirgizskogo Universiteta Seriya Botanicheskaya [*A publication*]
**Mezhvuz Temat Sb Leningr Inzh Stroit Inst** ... Mezhvuzovskii Tematicheskii Sbornik Leningradskii Inzhenerno Stroitel'nyi Institut [*A publication*]
**Mezhvuz Temat Sb Nauchn Tr Leningr Inzh Stroit Inst** ... Mezhvuzovskii Tematicheskii Sbornik Nauchnykh Trudov Leningradskii Inzhenerno Stroitel'nyi Institut [*A publication*]
**Mezhvuz Temat Sb Tr Leningr Inzh Stroit Inst** ... Mezhvuzovskii Tematicheskii Sbornik Trudov Leningradskii Inzhenerno Stroitel'nyi Institut [*A publication*]
**Mezhvuz Temat Sb Yarosl Gos Univ** ... Mezhvuzovskii Tematicheskii Sbornik Yaroslavskii Gosudarstvennyi Universitet [*A publication*]
**Mezin Vztahy** ... Mezinaradni Vztahy [*A publication*]
**Mezoegazd Kutat** ... Mezoegazdasagi Kutatasok [*A publication*]
**Mezogazd Gepesitesi Tanulmanyok Mezogazd Gepkiserl Intez** ... Mezoegazdasagi Gepesitesi Tanulmanyok A. Mezoegazdasag Gepkiserleti Intezet [*A publication*]
**Mezogazd Tech** ... Mezoegazdasagi Technika [*A publication*]
**Mezogazd Tud Kozl** ... Mezoegazdasagi Tudomanyos Koezlemenyek [*A publication*]
**Mezogazd Vilagirod** ... Mezoegazdasagi Vilagirodalom [*A publication*]
**Mezogazd Vilagirodalom** ... Mezoegazdasagi Vilagirodalom [*A publication*]
**MEZZ**........ Mezzanine (KSC)
**MEZZO** .... Mezzotint [*Printing*] (ROG)
**Mezzogiorn** ... Mezzogiorno d'Europa [*A publication*]
**Mezzogiorno d'Europa Q R** ... Mezzogiorno d'Europa. Quarterly Review [*A publication*]
**MF**............ Fall River Public Library, Fall River, MA [*Library symbol*] [*Library of Congress*] (LCLS)
**MF**............ Le Maitre Phonetique [*A publication*] (BJA)
**MF**............ Machine Finish [*Paper*]
**MF**............ Magazines for Friendship [*An association*] (EA)
**MF**............ Magnetic Field
**MF**............ Magnetic Focus [*of cathode-ray tube*] (DEN)
**MF**............ Magneto [*or Magnetic*] Field Generators [*JETDS Nomenclature*] [*Military*] (CET)
**MF**............ Magnetomotive Force (KSC)
**MF**............ Main Feed [*Technical drawings*]
**MF**............ Main Force [*Military*]
**MF**............ Maintenance Factor
**M/F**.......... Maintenance to Flight [*Ratio*]
**MF**............ Maintenance Float [*Military*]
**MF**............ Maintenance Fuel
**MF**............ Major Function (MCD)
**MF**............ Makedonski Folklor [*A publication*]
**MF**............ Malaysia Fund, Inc. [*NYSE symbol*] (SPSG)
**MF**............ Male to Female [*Ratio*]
**M & F**........ Male and Female [*Components, as of connecting devices*]
**MF**............ MAM Aviation Ltd. [*United Kingdom*] [*ICAO designator*] (ICDA)
**MF**............ Mantle Floor
**MF**............ Mare Feccunditatis [*Sea of Fertility*] [*Lunar area*]
**MF**............ Mark Forward [*Papers*] [*British*]
**M/F**.......... Marked For

MF ............ Martinus de Fano [*Deceased circa 1275*] [*Authority cited in pre-1607 legal work*] (DSA)
MF ............ Massora Finalis (BJA)
M/F ............ Master File
MF ............ Master of Finance
MF ............ Master of Forestry
MF ............ Master Frame
MF ............ Mastic Floor [*Technical drawings*]
MF ............ Matching Funds (OICC)
MF ............ Mate and Ferry [*NASA*] (NASA)
MF ............ Material Factor
M & F........ Materials and Facilities (MCD)
MF ............ Maurice-Farman [*British military*] (DMA)
mf ............ Mauritius [*MARC country of publication code*] [*Library of Congress*] (LCCP)
MF ............ Maximum Flowering Day [*Botany*]
MF ............ Measurement Facility [*Data processing*] (IBMDP)
MF ............ Meat Free [*Diet*]
MF ............ Mechanical Flap [*Aviation*]
MF ............ Meclofenamate [*Organic chemistry*]
MF ............ Medal of Freedom [*Military decoration*]
MF ............ Media Forum (EA)
MF ............ Medium Frequency [*Radio electronics*]
MF ............ Melamine-Formaldehyde [*Plastics technology*]
MF ............ Melomanes Francais [*Record label*] [*France*]
MF ............ Membrane Filter
MF ............ Merck Frosst Laboratories [*Canada*]
MF ............ Mercure de France [*A publication*]
MF ............ Merthiolate-Formaldehyde [*Solution*]
MF ............ Metal Factor [*Geophysical measurement*]
MF ............ Metallic Film
MF ............ Methyl Farnesoate [*Organic chemistry*]
MF ............ Methyl Formate [*Organic chemistry*]
MF ............ Methylfuran [*Organic chemistry*]
MF ............ Mezzo Forte [*Moderately Loud*] [*Music*] (ROG)
MF ............ Mi Favor [*My Favor*] [*Spanish*]
MF ............ Microfarad
MF ............ Microfiche [*Sheet microfilm*]
Mf ............ Microfilariae
MF ............ Microfilm
MF ............ Microfiltration
MF ............ Microform
MF ............ Microscopic Factor
MF ............ Middeck Forward (MCD)
MF ............ Middle Fork [*AAR code*]
MF ............ Midfuselage (NASA)
MF ............ Midwest Folklore [*A publication*]
MF ............ Mike Force [*Indigenous personnel trained and commanded jointly by US and Vietnamese forces, and used as a reaction and/or reinforcing unit*]
MF ............ Milk Foundation [*National Dairy Council*] (EA)
MF ............ Mill Finish
MF ............ Mill Fixture (MCD)
MF ............ Millard Filmore [*US president, 1800-1874*]
MF ............ Millifarad (GPO)
MF ............ Mind Freedom
MF ............ Minister [*or Ministry*] of Food [*British*]
M/F ............ Minorities/Females
MF ............ Miscellanea Francescana [*A publication*]
MF ............ Misiones Franciscanos [*A publication*]
MF ............ Missile Failure (AAG)
MF ............ Mitogenic Factor [*Cytology*]
MF ............ Mitomycin, Fluorouracil [*Antineoplastic drug regimen*]
MF ............ Mitotic Figure [*Genetics*]
MF ............ Mixed Flow (AAG)
MF ............ Modern Fiction
MF ............ Mole Fraction [*Chemistry*]
MF ............ Morningstar Foundation (EA)
MF ............ Mossy Fiber [*Neuroanatomy*]
M & F........ Mother and Father
MF ............ Mother Fooler [*Bowdlerized version*]
MF ............ Motor Field
MF ............ Motor Freight
MF ............ Multifrequency [*Telecommunications*]
MF ............ Multiplying Factor [*Microscopy*]
MF ............ Muscle Fiber
MF ............ Musicians Foundation (EA)
MF ............ Musikforschung [*A publication*]
MF ............ Mutual Fund [*Business term*]
M/F ............ My Favor (ADA)
MF ............ Mycosis Fungoides [*Dermatology*]
MF ............ Myelin Figure [*Medicine*]
MF ............ Myelinated Fiber [*Neuroanatomy*]
MF ............ Myofibrillar [*Anatomy*]
MF ............ Royal Munster Fusiliers [*Military unit*] (DMA)
MF ............ SAAB-Scania AB [*Sweden*] [*ICAO aircraft manufacturer identifier*] (ICAO)
MF ............ Spofa Ltd. [*Czechoslovakia*] [*Research code symbol*]
MFA .......... Mafia Islands [*Tanzania*] [*Airport symbol*] (OAG)
MFA .......... Malfunction Alert [*Data processing*] (BUR)
MFA .......... Malicious False Alarm [*Firefighting*]
MFA .......... Malta Fencible Artillery [*British*]
MFA .......... Manned Flight Awareness [*NASA*] (NASA)
MFA .......... Marconi-Franklin Antenna
M Fa .......... Martinus de Fano [*Deceased circa 1275*] [*Authority cited in pre-1607 legal work*] (DSA)
MFA .......... Master File Activities [*Data processing*]
MFA .......... Master of Fine Arts
MFA .......... Material Fielding Agreement [*Army*]
MFA .......... Menningar- og Fraedslusamband Althydu [*Workers' Educational Association*] [*Iceland*] (EY)
MFA .......... Men's Fashion Association of America (EA)
MFA .......... Mercantile Fleet Auxiliary [*British*]
MFA .......... Methyl Fluoracetate [*Organic chemistry*]
MFA .......... Miami, FL [*Location identifier*] [*FAA*] (FAAL)
MFA .......... Military Flying Area [*Canadian*]
MFA .......... Military Functions Appropriation (AABC)
MFA .......... Minister for Foreign Affairs [*British*]
MFA .......... Mitchell Field [*Alaska*] [*Seismograph station code, US Geological Survey*] [*Closed*] (SEIS)
MFA .......... Mobilization for Animals (EA)
MFA .......... Monofluoroacetate [*Organic chemistry*]
MFA .......... Movement for Federation of the Americas (EA)
MFA .......... Movimento das Forcas Armadas [*Armed Forces Movement*] [*Portugal*] [*Political party*] (PPE)
MFA .......... Multi-Fiber Arrangement [*International trade*]
MFA .......... Multifunction Antenna
MFA .......... Multifunctional Acrylate [*Organic chemistry*]
MFA .......... Multiple Filer Audit Program
MFA .......... Museum of Fine Arts [*Boston*] (BJA)
MFAA ....... Masters of Foxhounds Association of America [*Later, American Master of Foxhounds Association*] (EA)
MFA & A... Monuments, Fine Arts, and Archives [*SHAEF*] [*World War II*]
MfAb ........ Microfilm Abstracts [*A publication*]
MFAB........ Museum of Fine Arts, Boston
MFAB-F .... Mobile Floating Assault Bridge-Ferry [*Military*]
MFA Bull .. MFA Bulletin. Museum of Fine Arts [*Boston*] [*A publication*]
MFAC........ Magnetic Fusion Advisory Committee [*Department of Energy*] [*Washington, DC*]
MFAC........ Market Facts, Inc. [*NASDAQ symbol*] (NQ)
MFai .......... Millicent Library, Fairhaven, MA [*Library symbol*] [*Library of Congress*] (LCLS)
MFAIRWEST ... Marine Fleet Air, West Coast
MFal .......... Falmouth Public Library, Falmouth, MA [*Library symbol*] [*Library of Congress*] (LCLS)
MFalHi...... Falmouth Historical Society, Falmouth, MA [*Library symbol*] [*Library of Congress*] (LCLS)
MFAMW .. Modern Free and Accepted Masons of the World (EA)
MFAP........ Manned Flight Awareness Program [*NASA*] (KSC)
MFAR........ Modernized Fleet Accounting and Reporting
MFAR........ Multi-Function Array RADAR (MCD)
MFB .......... Bristol Community College, Fall River, MA [*Library symbol*] [*Library of Congress*] (LCLS)
MFB .......... Europese Investeringsbank. Mededelingen [*A publication*]
MFB .......... Medial Forebrain Bundle [*Medicine*]
MFB .......... Message from Base
MFB .......... Metallic Foreign Body
MFB .......... Metropolitan Fire Brigade [*British*]
MFB .......... MFB Mutual Insurance Co. [*from Manufacturers Mutual Fire Insurance Co., Firemen's Mutual Insurance Co., Blackstone Mutual Insurance Co.*]
MFB .......... Mill Fixture Base (MCD)
MFB .......... Mixed Functional Block (IEEE)
MFB .......... Moisture Free Basis
M F B.......... Monthly Film Bulletin [*A publication*]
MFB .......... Motional Feedback
MFB .......... Motor Freight Tariff Bureau, Springfield IL [*STAC*]
MFBAR..... Multifunction Band Airborne Radio
MFBB........ Mexican Food and Beverage Board (EA)
MFBF........ Mean Flights between Failures [*Military*] (CAAL)
MFBF........ Minimum Film Boiling Flux
MFBM....... Thousand Feet Board Measure [*Lumber*]
MFBMA.... Mitteilungen. Forstliche Bundes-Versuchsanstalt (Mariabrunn) [*A publication*]
MFBMP.... Project Manager, Fleet Ballistic Missile [*Navy*]
MFBP........ Main Feed Booster Pump (NVT)
MFBP........ Manufacturing Flow and Building Plan (NASA)
MFBZ........ Mutual Federal Savings Bank, a Stock Corp. [*NASDAQ symbol*] (NQ)
MFC .......... Magnesium Flat Cell
MFC .......... Magnetic Film Counter
MFC .......... Magnetic Tape Field Scan [*Data processing*]
MFC .......... Main Fuel Control (MCD)
MFC .......... Manual Frequency Control
MFC .......... Manufacturing Chemist, Incorporating Chemical Age [*A publication*]
MFC .......... Master File Copy [*Data processing*] (KSC)
MFC .......... Master Flow Controller [*Nuclear energy*] (NRCH)
MFC .......... Mastership in Food Control [*British*] (DBQ)
MFC .......... Median Femoral Condyle [*Anatomy*]
MFC .......... Medicated Face Conditioner [*Brand manufactured by Mennen*]
MFC .......... Merrell's Fan Club (EA)

**MFC** .......... Metropolitan Financial Corporation [*NYSE symbol*] (SPSG)
**MFC** .......... Microfilm Frame Card
**MFC** .......... Microfunctional Circuit
**MFC** .......... Military Frequency Changer
**MFC** .......... Minimal Flight Forecasting Charts [*Air Force*]
**MFC** .......... Mirinda's Friendship Club (EA)
**MFC** .......... Missile Fire Control (MCD)
**MFC** .......... Modern Foods Council [*Defunct*] (EA)
**MFC** .......... Mortar Fire Controller [*British*]
**MFC** .......... Mortgage Funding Corporation [*British*]
**MFC** .......... Motor Freight Controller [*National Accounting and Finance Council*] [*A publication*]
**MFC** .......... Movimiento Familiar Cristiano (EA)
**MFC** .......... Multifrequency Signaling, Compelled [*Telecommunications*] (TEL)
**MFC** .......... Multiple Flight Computer (NASA)
**MFC** .......... Multiple Flight Controller (NASA)
**MFC** .......... Municipal Financial Corp. [*Toronto Stock Exchange symbol*]
**MFCA**........ Master File Change Activity [*Data processing*] (MCD)
**MFCA**........ Miniature Figure Collectors of America (EA)
**MFCA**........ Mutlifunction Communications Adapter
**MFCAE**..... Masters of Foxhounds Club of America and England (EA)
**MFCBAC**.. Montana. Forest and Conservation Experiment Station. Bulletin [*A publication*]
**MFCC**........ Missile Fire Control Computer [*Military*] (CAAL)
**MFCC**........ Missile Flight Caution Corridor (AFM)
**MFCC**........ Mortar Fire Control Calculator [*Later, MBC*] [*Military*] (INF)
**MFCC**........ Mortar Fire Direction Center Data Calculator [*Army*]
**MFCF**........ Multinational Fuel Cycle Facility
**MFCG** ....... Mitteilungen und Forschungsbeitraege. Cusanus-Gesellschaft [*A publication*]
**MFCI**......... Molten Fuel Coolant Interaction [*Nuclear energy*] (NRCH)
**MFCI**......... Monterey Farming Corporation [*Santa Monica, CA*] [*NASDAQ symbol*] (NQ)
**MFCL**........ Master Fund Control List [*Air Force*] (AFM)
**MFCL**........ Memoire et Travaux Publies par les Facultes Catholiques de Lille [*A publication*]
**MFCM** ...... Member of the Faculty of Community Medicine [*British*]
**MFCM** ...... Multifunction Card Machine (BUR)
**MFCMA**.... Magnuson Fishery Conservation and Management Act [*1976*] [*Also, FCMA*]
**MFCNAE** ... Montana. Forest and Conservation Experiment Station. Note [*A publication*]
**MFCO** ....... Manual Fuel Cutoff (AAG)
**MFCO** ....... Melbourne Family Care Organisation [*Australia*]
**MFCO** ....... Microwave Filter Company, Inc. [*East Syracuse, NY*] [*NASDAQ symbol*] (NQ)
**MFCP**........ Multifunction Control/Panel (MCD)
**MFCS**........ Magnetic Field Calibration System
**MFCS**........ Manual Flight Control System [*NASA*]
**MFCS**........ Missile Fire Control System (NG)
**MFCSAT**... Montana. Forest and Conservation Experiment Station. Special Publication [*A publication*]
**MFCT**........ Major Fraction Thereof
**MFCU** ....... Multifunction Card Unit
**MFCusanusG** ... Mitteilungen und Forschungsbeitraege. Cusanus-Gesellschaft [*A publication*]
**MFCV**........ Modulating Flow Control Valve (MCD)
**MFD**.......... Canadian Department of Fisheries and Oceans, Marine Fish Division [*Research center*] (RCD)
**MFD**.......... Magic Foods, Inc. [*Vancouver Stock Exchange symbol*]
**MFD**.......... Magnetic Frequency Detector
**MFD**.......... Magnetofluiddynamic
**MFD**.......... Main Feed (MCD)
**MFD**.......... Malfunction Detection (NASA)
**MFD**.......... Mansfield [*Ohio*] [*Airport symbol*] (OAG)
**MFD**.......... Mansfield, OH [*Location identifier*] [*FAA*] (FAAL)
**MFD**.......... Manufactured
**MFD**.......... Master File Directory [*Data processing*]
**MFD**.......... Maximum Frequency Difference [*Statistics*]
**MFD**.......... Mechanical-Front-Drive [*Tractor*]
**MFD**.......... Memory-for-Designs [*Test*] [*Psychology*]
**MFD**.......... Metal Floor Deck [*Technical drawings*]
**MFD**.......... Microfarad
**MFD**.......... Midforceps Delivery [*Obstetrics*]
**MFD**.......... Military Forwarding Depot [*British military*] (DMA)
**MFD**.......... Millifarad (MCD)
**MFD**.......... Minimum Fatal Dose
**MFD**.......... Multifunction Display (MCD)
**MFD**.......... Multiple Family Dwelling [*Real estate*]
**MFD**.......... Multivariable Frequency Domain
**MFD**.......... Munford, Inc. [*NYSE symbol*] (SPSG)
**MFDC** ....... Morzen Mortar Fire Data Computer [*Military*] [*British*] (INF)
**MFDC** ....... Mouvement des Forces Democratiques de la Casamance [*Political party*] [*Senegal*]
**MF/DF**...... Medium-Frequency Direction Finder [*or Finding*] (NVT)
**MFDGAW** ... Communications. Faculte de Medecine Veterinaire. Universite de l'Etat Gand [*A publication*]
**MFDO**....... Member of the Faculty of Dispensing Opticians [*British*] (DBQ)
**MFDP**........ Maintenance Float Distribution Point [*Data processing*] (NATG)
**MFDP**........ Mississippi Freedom Democratic Party
**MFDSG**..... Multifunction Display Symbol Generator (MCD)
**MFDSUL**.. Multifunction Data Set Utility Language
**MFDT** ....... Memory-for-Designs Test [*Psychology*]
**MFDU** ....... Monatshefte fuer Deutschen Unterricht [*A publication*]
**MFE** .......... Machinery and Fixed Equipment [*British*]
**MFE** .......... Magnetic Field Energy
**MFE** .......... Magnetic Field Explorer [*NASA*]
**MFE** .......... Magnetic Fusion Energy
**MFE** .......... Maison de la Fondation Europeenne (EAIO)
**MFE** .......... Major Fleet Escort
**MFE** .......... Manual of Field Engineering [*British military*] (DMA)
**MFE** .......... Master of Forest Engineering
**MFE** .......... Mazingira. The World Forum for Environment and Development [*A publication*]
**MFE** .......... McAllen [*Texas*] [*Airport symbol*] (OAG)
**MFE** .......... McAllen, TX [*Location identifier*] [*FAA*] (FAAL)
**MFE** .......... Mercury Film Electrode [*Electrochemistry*]
**MFE** .......... Microabrasion Foil Experiment [*For cosmic dust retrieval*]
**MFE** .......... Mid-Frequency Executive (NASA)
**MFE** .......... Mischief Enterprises Ltd. [*Vancouver Stock Exchange symbol*]
**MFE** .......... Mouvement Federaliste Europeen [*European Federalist Movement*] [*France*]
**MFEA**........ Magnetic Fusion Engineering Act
**MFED** ....... Manned Flight Engineering Division [*NASA*]
**MFED** ....... Maury Federal Savings Bank [*Columbia, TN*] [*NASDAQ symbol*] (NQ)
**MFED** ....... Maximum Flat Envelope Delay
**MFed** ......... Miners' Federation of Great Britain (DAS)
**MFEHA** .... Memoirs. Faculty of Engineering. Hiroshima University [*A publication*]
**MFEIP** ...... Ministry of Food Education and Information Practice [*British*]
**MFEKA**..... Memoirs. Faculty of Engineering. Kobe University [*A publication*]
**MFEMA**.... Manufacturing Engineering and Management [*Later, Manufacturing Engineering*] [*A publication*]
**MFENAO** ... Montana. Forest and Conservation Experiment Station. Research Note [*A publication*]
**MFENET**.. Magnetic Fusion Energy Research Network [*Department of Energy*]
**MF Eng**...... Master of Forest Engineering
**MFES** ........ Major Fleet Escort Study [*Navy*] (CAAL)
**MFF**........... Flin Flon Public Library, Manitoba [*Library symbol*] [*National Library of Canada*] (NLC)
**MFF**........... Magnetic Flip-Flop [*Data processing*]
**MFF**........... Master Freight File
**MFF**........... Matching Familiar Figures [*Psychology*]
**MFF**........... Mezzo Fortissimo [*Rather Loud*] [*Music*] (ADA)
**MFF**........... Military Free Fall [*Parachute jump*] (MCD)
**MFF**........... Moanda [*Gabon*] [*Airport symbol*] (OAG)
**MFF**........... Munitions Filling Factory (ADA)
**MFF**........... St. Martin Du Fouilloux [*France*] [*Seismograph station code, US Geological Survey*] (SEIS)
**MFFC**........ Mayflower Financial Corporation [*NASDAQ symbol*] (NQ)
**MFFGH** .... Flin Flon General Hospital, Manitoba [*Library symbol*] [*National Library of Canada*] (NLC)
**MFFHB**..... Hudson Bay Mining & Smelting Co. Ltd., Flin Flon, Manitoba [*Library symbol*] [*National Library of Canada*] (NLC)
**MFFR**........ Modified Field Fire Range (MCD)
**MFFT**........ Matching Familiar Figures Test [*Education*]
**MFFT**........ Minimum Film Formation Temperature [*Coating technology*]
**MFG**.......... Major Functional Group [*NASA*] (KSC)
**MFG**.......... Manufacturing (AFM)
**MFG**.......... Message Flow Graph
**MFG**.......... Middle East Observer [*A publication*]
**MFG**.......... Milk Fat Globule
**MFG**.......... Molded Fiberglass
**MFG**.......... Munitions Family Group
**MFGA** ....... Master Furriers Guild of America (EA)
**MFGC** ....... Midwest Financial Group, Inc. [*NASDAQ symbol*] (NQ)
**Mfg Chem** ... Manufacturing Chemist [*A publication*]
**Mfg Chem Aerosol News** ... Manufacturing Chemist and Aerosol News [*A publication*]
**MFGEB**..... Manufacturing Engineering [*A publication*]
**Mfg Eng**..... Manufacturing Engineering [*A publication*]
**Mfg Eng Manage** ... Manufacturing Engineering and Management [*Later, Manufacturing Engineering*] [*A publication*]
**MFGI**......... Moore Financial Group, Incorporated [*NASDAQ symbol*] (NQ)
**MFGM** ...... Milk Fat Globule Membrane
**MFGR** ....... Metrobank Financial Group, Inc. [*NASDAQ symbol*] (NQ)
**Mfg Tech H** ... Manufacturing Technology Horizons [*A publication*]
**MFH**.......... Magnetic Film Handler (CMD)
**MFH**.......... Malignant Fibrous Histiocytoma [*Oncology*]
**MFH**.......... Markel Financial Holdings Ltd. [*Toronto Stock Exchange symbol*]
**MFH**.......... Master of Fox Hounds
**MFH**.......... Military Family Housing (AFM)

**MFH** .......... Mitteilungen. Institut fuer Handelsforschung. Universitaet zu Koeln [*A publication*]
**MFH** .......... Mobile Field Hospital
**MFHA** ....... Medal for Humane Action [*Berlin Airlift, 1948-9*] [*Military decoration*]
**MFHBF** ..... Mean Flight Hours between Failures [*Quality control*] (MCD)
**MFHBMA** ... Mean Flight Hours between Maintenance Actions [*Quality control*] (NVT)
**MFHBUMA** ... Mean Flight Hour between Unscheduled Maintenance Actions [*Quality control*] (MCD)
**MFHC** ....... Missile Flight Hazard Corridor (AFM)
**MFHFS** ..... Multifunction High-Frequency SONAR (MCD)
**MF Hom** .... Member of the Faculty of Homoeopathy [*British*]
**MFHR** ....... Media Fund for Human Rights (EA)
**MFi** ............ Fitchburg Public Library and Regional Center for Central Massachusetts, Regional Library System, Fitchburg, MA [*Library symbol*] [*Library of Congress*] (LCLS)
**MFI** ............ Magazines for Industry [*An association*]
**MFI** ............ Magnetic Field Indicator
**MFI** ............ Magnetic Field Intensity
**MFI** ............ Major Force Issues [*Army*] (AABC)
**MFI** ............ Managerial Finance [*A publication*]
**MFI** ............ Marketfax Infoservices Ltd. [*Vancouver Stock Exchange symbol*]
**MFI** ............ Marketing Freedom Index [*OPEC*] [*Business term*]
**MFI** ............ Marshfield [*Wisconsin*] [*Airport symbol*] (OAG)
**MFI** ............ Marshfield, WI [*Location identifier*] [*FAA*] (FAAL)
**MFI** ............ Melt-Flow Index [*of plastics*]
**MFI** ............ Metal Fabricating Institute (EA)
**MFI** ............ Midwest Folklore (Indiana University) [*A publication*]
**MFI** ............ Mobile Fuel Irradiator (IEEE)
**MFI** ............ Multiport Fuel Injection [*Automotive technology*]
**MFI** ............ Myofibril Fragmentation Index [*Food technology*]
**MFIC** ......... Military Flight Information Center
**MFIC** ......... Mutual Federation of Independent Cooperatives [*Later, Northeast Dairy Cooperative Federation*] (EA)
**MF-ICC** ..... Designation used on tariffs and schedules filed with Interstate Commerce Commission by carriers subject to Part II of Interstate Commerce Act
**MFID** ......... Multiple-Electrode Flame Ionization Detector
**MF-IFGR** .. Michael Fund (International Foundation for Genetic Research) (EA)
**MFin** .......... Master of Finance
**MFIP** ......... Microforms in Print [*Database*]
**MFIS** ......... Magnetic Field-Induced Superconductivity
**MFiT** ......... Fitchburg State College, Fitchburg, MA [*Library symbol*] [*Library of Congress*] (LCLS)
**MFIT** ......... Manual Fault Isolation Test
**MFITD** ...... Fukui Kogyo Daigaku Kenkyu Kiyo [*A publication*]
**MFIV** ......... Mainwater Feed Isolation Valve [*Nuclear energy*] (NRCH)
**MFIZA** ...... Metallofizika [*A publication*]
**MFJ** ........... Moala [*Fiji*] [*Airport symbol*] (OAG)
**MFJ** ........... Modified Final Judgment [*Telecommunications*]
**MFJ** ........... Municipal Finance Journal [*A publication*]
**MFJC** ......... Memorial Foundation for Jewish Culture (EA)
**MFJSA** ...... Mass Finishing Job Shops Association (EA)
**MFK** .......... Mafeking [*South Africa*] [*Airport symbol*] (OAG)
**MFK** .......... Mill Fixture Key [*Tool*]
**MFKCA** ..... Memoirs. Faculty of Science. Kyushu University. Series C [*Japan*] [*A publication*]
**MFKDA** .... Memoirs. Faculty of Science. Kyushu University. Series D. Geology [*A publication*]
**MFKLDH** ... Progress in Applied Microcirculation [*A publication*]
**MFKP** ........ Multifrequency Key Pulsing
**MFKPA** ..... Memoirs. Faculty of Science. Kyoto University. Series of Physics, Astrophysics, Geophysics, and Chemistry [*A publication*]
**MFKT** ........ Mobile Field Kitchen Trailer (MCD)
**MFL** ........... Magnetic Field Line
**MFL** ........... Main Feedwater Line [*Nuclear energy*] (NRCH)
**MFL** ........... Maintain Flight Level [*Aviation*]
**MFL** ........... Master of Family Life
**MFL** ........... Matrimonial and Family Law [*New York, NY*] [*A publication*]
**MFL** ........... Matrimonial and Family Life [*A publication*]
**MFL** ........... Maximum Foreseeable Loss [*Insurance*]
**MFL** ........... Methodists for Life (EA)
**MfL** ............ Microfile (Pty.) Ltd., Johannesburg, South Africa [*Library symbol*] [*Library of Congress*] (LCLS)
**MFL** ........... Missile Firing Laboratory (KSC)
**MFL** ........... Mobile Field Laboratory
**MFL** ........... Mobile Field Laundry [*Military*]
**MFL** ........... Modern Foreign Language
**MFL** ........... Motor Freight Line
**MFLA** ........ Midwest Federation of Library Associations
**MFLB** ........ Massachusetts Foreign Language Bulletin [*A publication*]
**MFLD** ........ Male-Female Longevity Difference
**MFLD** ........ Manifold (KSC)
**MFLD** ........ Message Field [*Data processing*]
**MFLOPS** ... Million Floating-Point Operations per Second [*Processing power units*] [*Data processing*]
**MFLP** ........ Multifile Linear Programming
**MFLR** ........ Mayflower Co-Operative Bank [*NASDAQ symbol*] (NQ)
**MFLRA** ..... Mededelingen. Faculteit Landbouwwetenschappen. Rijksuniversiteit (Gent) [*A publication*]
**MFLT** ........ Mean First Lesions Time [*Immunochemistry*]
**MFLX** ........ Mediflex Systems [*NASDAQ symbol*] (NQ)
**MFLZ** ........ Mejdunarodna Fondatzia Lyudmila Zhivkova [*Lyudmila Zhivkova International Foundation*] (EAIO)
**MFm** .......... Framingham Town Library, Framingham, MA [*Library symbol*] [*Library of Congress*] (LCLS)
**MFM** ......... Magnetic Field Monitor [*NASA*]
**MFM** ......... Magnetic Forming Machine
**MFM** ......... Magnetofluid Mechanic
**MFM** ......... Master File Maintenance [*Data processing*]
**MFM** ......... Master of Financial Management (ADA)
**MFM** ......... Maximally Flat Magnitude
**MFM** ......... Meals for Millions Foundation [*Later, MFM/FFH*] (EA)
**MFM** ......... MFC Mining Finance Corp. [*Toronto Stock Exchange symbol*] [*Vancouver Stock Exchange symbol*]
**MFM** ......... MFS Municipal Income Trust [*NYSE symbol*] (SPSG)
**MFM** ......... Micrometer Frequency Meter
**MFM** ......... Minced Fish Meat [*Food technology*]
**MFM** ......... Mine Firing Mechanism
**MFM** ......... Miniature Fluxgate Magnetometer
**MFM** ......... Minneapolis-St. Paul [*Minnesota*] [*Seismograph station code, US Geological Survey*] (SEIS)
**MFM** ......... Missile Farm Monitor [*Army*] (AABC)
**MFM** ......... Mississippi State University, Mississippi State, MS [*OCLC symbol*] (OCLC)
**MFM** ......... Modified Frequency Modulation [*Electronics*]
**MfM** .......... Monatshefte fuer Musikgeschichte [*A publication*]
**MFM** ......... Morrissey, Fernie & Michel Railway [*AAR code*]
**MFM** ......... Mouvement pour le Pouvoir Proletarien [*or aux Petits*] [*Movement for Proletarian Power*] [*Malagasy*] [*Political party*] (PPW)
**MFM** ......... Movable Fine Mesh
**MFM** ......... Multifunctional Monomer [*Organic chemistry*]
**MFM** ......... Multistage Frequency Multiplexer
**M2FM** ....... Modified Modified Frequency Modulation
**MFMA** ...... Maple Flooring Manufacturers Association (EA)
**MFMA** ...... Metal Findings Manufacturers Association (EA)
**MFMA** ...... Metal Framing Manufacturers Association (EA)
**MFMA** ...... Midwest Feed Manufacturers Association [*Later, AFMA*] (EA)
**MFMA** ...... Monolithic Ferrite Memory Array
**MFmcM** .... Marist College and Seminary, Framingham Center, MA [*Library symbol*] [*Library of Congress*] (LCLS)
**MFM/FFH** ... Meals for Millions/Freedom from Hunger Foundation (EA)
**MFMH** ...... Monofluoromethylhistidine [*Antineoplastic drug*]
**MFMI** ........ Men for Missions International (EA)
**MFM Mod Fototech** ... MFM. Moderne Fototechnik [*A publication*]
**MFMR** ...... Multifrequency Microwave Radiometer (MCD)
**MFmT** ....... Framingham State College, Framingham, MA [*Library symbol*] [*Library of Congress*] (LCLS)
**MFMT** ....... Microwave Frequency Modulation Transmitter
**MF/MWS** ... Male/Female - Married/Widow [*or Widower*]/Single
**MFN** .......... MDC Financial, Inc. [*Vancouver Stock Exchange symbol*]
**MFN** .......... Mercury Finance Co. [*NYSE symbol*] (SPSG)
**MFN** .......... Metal Fabricating News [*A publication*] (EAAP)
**MFN** .......... Milford Sound [*New Zealand*] [*Airport symbol*] (OAG)
**MFN** .......... Mitteilungen fuer Namenskunde [*Aachen*] [*A publication*]
**MFN** .......... Most-Favored-Nation [*Trading status*]
**MFNE** ........ Ministry of Finance and National Economy [*Saudi Arabia*] (ECON)
**MFNG** ....... Motion for a Finding of Not Guilty
**MFNS** ........ Millard Fillmore National Society (EA)
**MFNV** ....... Meddelelser fra Norsk Viltforskning [*A publication*]
**MFO** .......... Major Function Overlay (MCD)
**MFO** .......... Marine Fuel Oil
**MFO** .......... Master Frequency Oscillator (NG)
**MFO** .......... Material Fielding Operations (MCD)
**MFO** .......... MFS Income & Options Trust [*NYSE symbol*] (SPSG)
**MFO** .......... Military Forwarding Officer
**MFO** .......... Missile Field Office (AAG)
**MFO** .......... Missile Firing Order
**MFO** .......... Mixed-Function Oxidase [*Biochemistry*]
**MFO** .......... Multinational Force and Observers [*Eleven-nation peace-keeping force for the Sinai*]
**MFOA** ....... Municipal Finance Officers Association of US and Canada [*Later, GFOA*] (EA)
**MFOB** ....... Minimum Fuel on Board [*Aviation*] (FAAC)
**MFOC** ....... Military and Government Fiber Optics and Communications [*Conference*] (TSSD)
**MFOD** ....... Manned Flight Operations Directive [*NASA*] (KSC)
**MFOE** ....... Mixed-Function Oxidase Enzyme System
**MFOI** ........ Major Force Oriented Issue [*Military*] (AFM)
**MFON** ....... Missile Firing Order Normal [*Military*] (CAAL)
**MFOPP** ..... Missile Firing Order Patch Panel
**MFor** ......... Master of Forestry
**MForSc** ...... Master of Forest Science (ADA)
**M Forskning** ... Musik und Forskning [*A publication*]
**M Forum** .... Music Forum [*A publication*]

**MFOW**...... Pacific Coast Marine Firemen, Oilers, Watertenders, and Wipers Association
**MFP**........... Magnetic Field Perturbation
**MFP**........... Main Feed Power [*Nuclear energy*] (NRCH)
**MFP**........... Main Feed Pump (NVT)
**MFP**........... Main Feedwater Pump [*Nuclear energy*] (NRCH)
**MFP**........... Main Force Patrol [*In movie "Mad Max"*]
**MFP**........... Major Force Program [*Air Force*] (AFIT)
**MFP**........... Management Framework Plan
**MFP**........... Master File Program [*Data processing*]
**MFP**........... Matched Filter Performance
**MF & P**...... Materials Finishes and Processes (MCD)
**MFP**........... Materiel Fielding Plan
**MFP**........... Maximum Fluoride Protection [*Colgate-Palmolive Co.*]
**MFP**........... Maximum Freezing Point
**MFP**........... Mean Free Path
**MFP**........... Melphalan, Fluorouracil, Farlutal (Medroxyprogesterone acetate) [*Antineoplastic drug regimen*]
**MF(P)**........ Microfiche (Positive)
**MFP**........... Middle Free Path
**MFP**........... Minimal Flight Path
**MFP**........... Ministry of Fuel and Power [*British*]
**MFP**........... Mixed Fission Products [*Nuclear energy*]
**MFP**........... Moca [*Fernando Poo*] [*Equatorial Guinea*] [*Seismograph station code, US Geological Survey*] (SEIS)
**MFP**........... Molecular Free Path
**MFP**........... Monofluorophosphate [*Inorganic chemistry*]
**MFP**........... Monographs in Fetal Physiology [*Elsevier Book Series*] [*A publication*]
**MFP**........... Movement for a Free Philippines (EA)
**MFP**........... Multiform Printer
**MFP**........... Multifrequency Pulsing (MSA)
**MFP**........... Multifunction Peripheral [*Chip*] [*Data processing*]
**MFP**........... Multifunction Polis
**MFP**........... Myofascial Pain [*Medicine*]
**MFP Alum** ... Mineral Facts and Problems. Preprint. Aluminum [*A publication*]
**MFP Antim** ... Mineral Facts and Problems. Preprint. Antimony [*A publication*]
**MFP Arsenc** ... Mineral Facts and Problems. Preprint. Arsenic [*A publication*]
**MFP Asbsts** ... Mineral Facts and Problems. Preprint. Asbestos [*A publication*]
**MFPB**........ Mineral Fiber Products Bureau
**MFP Barite** ... Mineral Facts and Problems. Preprint. Barite [*A publication*]
**MFP Beryl** ... Mineral Facts and Problems. Preprint. Beryllium [*A publication*]
**MFP Bis** .... Mineral Facts and Problems. Preprint. Bismuth [*A publication*]
**MFP Boron** ... Mineral Facts and Problems. Preprint. Boron [*A publication*]
**MFP Bromin** ... Mineral Facts and Problems. Preprint. Bromine [*A publication*]
**MFPC**........ Multifunction Protocol Converter
**MFP Cadm** ... Mineral Facts and Problems. Preprint. Cadmium [*A publication*]
**MFP Clays** ... Mineral Facts and Problems. Preprint. Clays [*A publication*]
**MFP Columb** ... Mineral Facts and Problems. Preprint. Columbium [*A publication*]
**MFP Copper** ... Mineral Facts and Problems. Preprint. Copper [*A publication*]
**MFP C Stone** ... Mineral Facts and Problems. Preprint. Crushed Stone [*A publication*]
**MFPD**........ Modern Federal Practice Digest [*A publication*] (DLA)
**MFP Diamnd** ... Mineral Facts and Problems. Preprint. Diamond - Industrial [*A publication*]
**MFP Dime S** ... Mineral Facts and Problems. Preprint. Dimension Stone [*A publication*]
**MFP Feldsp** ... Mineral Facts and Problems. Preprint. Feldspar [*A publication*]
**MFPG**........ Mechanical Failures Prevention Group
**MFPG**........ Mixed Fission Products Generator [*Nuclear energy*]
**MFP Gallm** ... Mineral Facts and Problems. Preprint. Gallium [*A publication*]
**MFP Garnet** ... Mineral Facts and Problems. Preprint. Garnet [*A publication*]
**MFP Germnu** ... Mineral Facts and Problems. Preprint. Germanium [*A publication*]
**MFP Gold** ... Mineral Facts and Problems. Preprint. Gold [*A publication*]
**MFP Gypsum** ... Mineral Facts and Problems. Preprint. Gypsum [*A publication*]
**MFPh** ........ Member of the Faculty of Physiotherapists [*British*]
**MFPhys**..... Member of the Faculty of Physiatrists [*British*]
**MFP Indium** ... Mineral Facts and Problems. Preprint. Indium [*A publication*]
**MFP Iodine** ... Mineral Facts and Problems. Preprint. Iodine [*A publication*]
**MFP Iron O** ... Mineral Facts and Problems. Preprint. Iron Ore [*A publication*]
**MFP Lead** ... Mineral Facts and Problems. Preprint. Lead [*A publication*]
**MFP Magn** ... Mineral Facts and Problems. Preprint. Magnesium [*A publication*]
**MFP Mang** ... Mineral Facts and Problems. Preprint. Manganese [*A publication*]
**MFP Mica** ... Mineral Facts and Problems. Preprint. Mica [*A publication*]
**MFP Moly** ... Mineral Facts and Problems. Preprint. Molybdenum [*A publication*]
**MFP/MTP** ... Materiel Fielding Plan/Materiel Transfer Plan [*Army*] (RDA)
**MFPOF**..... Master Flight Plan on File [*Aviation*] (FAAC)
**MFP Peat** .. Mineral Facts and Problems. Preprint. Peat [*A publication*]
**MFP Perlit** ... Mineral Facts and Problems. Preprint. Perlite [*A publication*]
**MFP Prepnt** ... Mineral Facts and Problems. Preprints [*A publication*]
**MFP Quartz** ... Mineral Facts and Problems. Preprint. Quartz [*A publication*]
**MFP Rubid** ... Mineral Facts and Problems. Preprint. Rubidium [*A publication*]
**MFPS**........ Member of the Faculty of Physicians and Surgeons [*Glasgow*]
**MFPS**........ Mobile Field Photographic Section (NATG)
**MFPS**........ Modular Force Planning System (MCD)
**MFPSA**..... Monographies Francaises de Psychologie [*A publication*]
**MFP Salt**... Mineral Facts and Problems. Preprint. Salt [*A publication*]
**MFP Sand** ... Mineral Facts and Problems. Preprint. Sand and Gravel [*A publication*]
**MFP Sel** .... Mineral Facts and Problems. Preprint. Selenium [*A publication*]
**MFP Silicn** ... Mineral Facts and Problems. Preprint. Silicon [*A publication*]
**MFP Silver** ... Mineral Facts and Problems. Preprint. Silver [*A publication*]
**MFP Soda A** ... Mineral Facts and Problems. Preprint. Soda Ash and Sodium Sulfate [*A publication*]
**MFP Stront** ... Mineral Facts and Problems. Preprint. Strontium [*A publication*]
**MFP Sulfur** ... Mineral Facts and Problems. Preprint. Sulfur [*A publication*]
**MFPT**........ Main Feedwater Pump Turbine [*Nuclear energy*] (NRCH)
**MFPT**........ Mean First-Passage Time [*Biochemistry*]
**MFPTC**..... Main Feed Pump Turbine Condenser [*Nuclear energy*] (NRCH)
**MFP Tellur** ... Mineral Facts and Problems. Preprint. Tellurium [*A publication*]
**MFP Thorm** ... Mineral Facts and Problems. Preprint. Thorium [*A publication*]
**MFP Tin**.... Mineral Facts and Problems. Preprint. Tin [*A publication*]
**MFP Titanm** ... Mineral Facts and Problems. Preprint. Titanium [*A publication*]
**MFP Tungst** ... Mineral Facts and Problems. Preprint. Tungsten [*A publication*]
**MFPUL**..... Mississippi Forest Products Utilization Laboratory [*Mississippi State University*] [*Research center*] (RCD)
**MFP Vandm** ... Mineral Facts and Problems. Preprint. Vanadium [*A publication*]
**MFP Vermic** ... Mineral Facts and Problems. Preprint. Vermiculite [*A publication*]
**MFP Zinc**.. Mineral Facts and Problems. Preprint. Zinc [*A publication*]
**MFP Zirc**... Mineral Facts and Problems. Preprint. Zirconium and Hafnium [*A publication*]
**MFQ**.......... Maradi [*Niger*] [*Airport symbol*] (OAG)
**M'F R**......... MacFarlane's Scotch Jury Court Reports [*1838-39*] [*A publication*] (DLA)
**MFR** .......... Macfie Resources [*Vancouver Stock Exchange symbol*]
**MFR** .......... Mail File Requirement [*Code*] [*Data processing*]
**MFR** .......... Malfunction Rate
**MFR** .......... Maltese Folklore Review [*Balzan*] [*A publication*]
**MFR** .......... Manipulator Foot Restraint (NASA)
**MF & R**...... Manpower Forces and Readiness [*Military*]
**MFR** .......... Manufacture [*or Manufacturer*] (AFM)
**MFr**........... Mare Frigoris [*Sea of Cold*] [*Lunar area*]
**MFR** .......... Master Facility Register [*Nuclear energy*]
**MFR** .......... Maximum Flight Rate (NASA)
**MFR** .......... Medford [*Oregon*] [*Airport symbol*] (OAG)
**MFR** .......... Medford, OR [*Location identifier*] [*FAA*] (FAAL)
**MFr**........... Melomanes Francais [*Record label*] [*France*]
**MFR** .......... Melt-Flow Rate [*of plastics*]
**MFR** .......... Memorandum for Record [*Military*]
**MFr**........... Mercure de France [*A publication*]
**MfR**........... Microform Review, Inc., Weston, CT [*Library symbol*] [*Library of Congress*] (LCLS)
**MFR** .......... Middle French [*Language, etc.*]
**MFr**........... Miscellanea Francescana [*A publication*]
**MFR** .......... Missile Firing Range (AAG)
**MFR** .......... Model Form and Record
**MFR** .......... Multifrequency Receiver [*Telecommunications*]
**MFR** .......... Multifunction RADAR
**MFR** .......... Multifunctional Receiver (NASA)
**MFR** .......... Multifunctional Review (NASA)
**MFR** .......... Mutual Force Reductions
**M Fra**........ Moyen Francais [*A publication*]
**MFran**........ Ray Memorial Library, Franklin, MA [*Library symbol*] [*Library of Congress*] (LCLS)
**MFRC**........ Maritimes Forest Research Centre [*Research center*] (RCD)
**MfrChemAer** ... Manufacturing Chemist and Aerosol News [*A publication*]
**MFRD** ....... Medford Corp. [*NASDAQ symbol*] (NQ)
**MFRE**........ Manufacture (ADA)
**MFREA**..... Multiple Food Retailers Employers' Association [*British*]
**MFRF** ....... Mean-Family Replacement Factor
**MFRG** ....... Manufacturing
**MFRG** ....... Medical Functional Requirements Group (MCD)
**MFRI**......... Midwesco Filter Resources, Inc. [*NASDAQ symbol*] (NQ)

**MFRI**......... Migratory Fish Research Institute [*University of Maine*] [*Research center*] (RCD)
**MFRN**....... Manufacturers Number
**MFRP**........ Midwest Fuel Recovery Plant [*AEC*]
**MFRP**........ Multigrade Functional Rehabilitation Platform [*Medicine*]
**MFRPA**..... Maxey Flats Radioactive Protective Association (EA)
**MFRS**........ Master File Replacement System [*Data processing*]
**MFRS**........ Multifunction Receiver System
**MFRVA**..... Microform Review [*A publication*]
**MFS**........... Fleet Minesweeper (Steel-Hulled) [*Navy symbol*]
**MFS**........... Frostburg State College, Library, Frostburg, MD [*OCLC symbol*] (OCLC)
**MFS**........... Macintosh File System [*Data processing*]
**MF & S**...... Magazine Flooding and Sprinkling
**MFS**........... Magnetic Field Strength
**MFS**........... Magnetic Tape Field Search [*Data processing*]
**MFS**........... Malleable Founders' Society [*Later, Iron Castings Society - ICS*]
**MFS**........... Maltese Falcon Society (EA)
**MFS**........... Manned Flying System (MCD)
**MFS**........... Manufactures
**MFS**........... Manufacturing Systems [*A publication*]
**MFS**........... Marble Falls, TX [*Location identifier*] [*FAA*] (FAAL)
**MFS**........... Marine-Finish Slate (MSA)
**MFS**........... Master of Food Science
**MFS**........... Master of Foreign Service
**MFS**........... Master of Foreign Study
**MFS**........... Maxillofacial Surgery [*Medical specialty*] (DHSM)
**MFS**........... McCloud Flat South [*California*] [*Seismograph station code, US Geological Survey*] (SEIS)
**MFS**........... Medal Field Service [*Canada*]
**MFS**........... Meddelanden fran Strindbergssaellskapet [*A publication*]
**MFS**........... Mercury Feed System
**MFS**........... Message Format Service
**MfS**............ Microfilm Systems, Colorado Springs, CO [*Library symbol*] [*Library of Congress*] (LCLS)
**MFS**........... Microfuel Systems [*Vancouver Stock Exchange symbol*]
**MFS**........... Military Flight Service
**MfS**............ Ministerium fuer Staatssicherheit [*Ministry for State Security*] [*See also MISTAI, MSS*] [*German Democratic Republic*]
**MFS**........... Minnesota Follow-Up Study Rehabilitation Rating Scale
**MFS**........... Miraflores [*Colombia*] [*Airport symbol*] (OAG)
**MFS**........... Missile Firing Simulator (NATG)
**MFS**........... Missile Firing Station [*Army*]
**MFS**........... Missile Fuse Set Servo
**MFS**........... Missing from Shelf (ADA)
**MFS**........... Modern Fiction Studies [*A publication*]
**MFS**........... Modified Full Spray
**MFS**........... Modular Flexible Scheduling [*Education*]
**MFS**........... Multifunction Sensor (MCD)
**MFS**........... Multiple-Frequency Synthesizer
**MFS**........... Municipal Ferrous Scrap
**MFS**........... Mutual Friendly Society [*Australia*]
**MFS**........... National Mobilization for Survival (EA)
**MFSA**........ Metal Finishing Suppliers' Association (EA)
**MFSA**........ Methodist Federation for Social Action (EA)
**MFSB**........ Mother, Father, Sister, Brother [*Musical group*]
**MFSB**........ Pinnacle Bancorp, Inc. [*Formerly, MidFed Savings Bank*] [*NASDAQ symbol*] (NQ)
**MFSc**......... Master of Fisheries Science
**MFSC**........ Missile Flight Safety Center [*Pacific Missile Range*] (MUGU)
**MFSE**........ Main Fire Support Element (AABC)
**MFSF**........ Magazine of Fantasy and Science Fiction [*A publication*]
**MFSFU**..... Matt-Finish Structural Facing Units [*Technical drawings*]
**MFSG**........ Missile Firing Safety Group (MUGU)
**MFSK**........ Multiple-Frequency Shift Keying
**MFSL**........ Maryland Federal Bancorp, Inc. [*NASDAQ symbol*] (NQ)
**MFSO**........ Missile Flight Safety Officer
**MFSOA**..... Missile Flight Safety Officer Assistant (MUGU)
**MFSOC**..... Missile Flight Safety Officer Console (MUGU)
**MFSOP**..... Missile Flight Safety Operations Plan
**MFSR**........ Magnetic Film Strip Recorder
**MFSS**........ Medical Field Service School [*Army*]
**MFSS**........ Missile Flight Safety System (AAG)
**MFST**........ Manifest
**MFST**........ Mobile Fire Safety Team
**MFSU**........ Mobile Field Service Unit
**MFSV**........ Meddelelser fra Statens Viltundersokelser [*Papers. Norwegian State Game Research Institute*] [*A publication*]
**MFSW**....... Membrane-Filtered Sea Water
**MFT**.......... Drury Military Extension, Springfield, MO [*OCLC symbol*] (OCLC)
**MFT**.......... Magnetic Flow Transmitter
**MFT**.......... Mail for Tots (EA)
**MFT**.......... Mainframe Termination [*Telecommunications*] (TEL)
**MFT**.......... Major Fraction Thereof
**MFT**.......... Manufacturing Fit Test
**MFT**.......... Marconi Fast Tuning (MCD)
**MFT**.......... Marriage and Family Therapist [*Psychology*]
**MFT**.......... Master File Tax [*Code*] [*IRS*]
**MFT**.......... Master Fitness Trainer [*Army*] (INF)
**MFT**.......... Master of Foreign Trade
**MFT**.......... Materiel Field Test (MCD)
**MFT**.......... Materiel Fielding Team [*Army*] (RDA)
**MFT**.......... Mean Flight Time (KSC)
**MFT**.......... Mean Free Time
**MFT**.......... Mechanized Flame Thrower
**MFT**.......... Medical Field Service Technician [*Navy*]
**MFT**.......... Meson Field Theory
**MFT**.......... Metal Film Resistor
**MFT**.......... Metallic Facility Terminal [*Telecommunications*] (TEL)
**MFT**.......... MFS Multimarket Total Return [*NYSE symbol*] (SPSG)
**MFT**.......... Mine Fuse Train
**MFT**.......... Minimum Film-Forming Temperature [*Wax polishes*]
**MFT**.......... Ministry of Foreign Trade (IMH)
**M FT**......... Mistura Fiat [*Let a Mixture Be Made*] [*Pharmacy*]
**MFT**.......... Molecular Field Theory [*Physical chemistry*]
**MFT**.......... Morgan Financial Corp. [*Toronto Stock Exchange symbol*]
**MFT**.......... Motor Freight Tariff [*Business term*] (ADA)
**MFT**.......... Motor Freight Terminal
**MFT**.......... Multilingual Forestry Terminology
**MFT**.......... Multiprogramming with Fixed Number of Tasks [*Data processing*] (BUR)
**MFT**.......... Muscle Function Test
**MFTA**........ Managed Futures Trade Association (EA)
**MFTA**........ Multiduct Fuel Test Assembly [*Nuclear energy*] (NRCH)
**MFTAD**..... Master Flight Test Assignment Document (NASA)
**MFTB**........ Motor Freight Tariff Bureau
**MFTB**........ Myanma Foreign Trade Bank [*Burma*] (DS)
**MFTC**........ Metalworking Fair Trade Coalition [*Later, MTC*] (EA)
**MFTCom**... Member of the Faculty of Teachers in Commerce [*British*] (DBQ)
**MFTD**........ Mobile Field Training Detachment [*Military*] (AFM)
**MFTF**........ Mirror Fusion Test Facility [*For study of new energy source*]
**MFTF**........ Missionary Flight Training Foundation [*Defunct*]
**MFTGS**..... Midcourse Fix and Terminal Guidance System (MCD)
**MFTHBA**... Missouri Fox Trotting Horse Breed Association (EA)
**MFT L**....... Millifoot Lamberts (DEN)
**M FT M**..... Misce Fiat Mistura [*Mix to Make a Mixture*] [*Pharmacy*]
**MFTN**........ Metropolitan Federal Savings & Loan Association [*Nashville, TN*] [*NASDAQ symbol*] (NQ)
**MFTP**........ Modified Federal Test Procedure [*EPA engine test*]
**MFTRS**..... Magnetic Flight Test Recording System
**MFTS**........ Medial Femorotibial Space [*Anatomy*]
**MFT/S**...... Missile Facilities Technician/Specialist (AAG)
**MFTU**........ Macao Federation of Trade Unions
**MFTV**........ Mechanical Fit Test Vehicle
**MFU**.......... Magnetic Force Upset [*Metals*]
**MFU**.......... Marine Forecast Unit [*National Weather Service*]
**MFU**.......... Mfuwe [*Zambia*] [*Airport symbol*] (OAG)
**MFU**.......... Military Foul-Up [*Bowdlerized version*] (DSUE)
**MFU**.......... MIRA [*Multifunctional Inertial Reference Assembly*] Fighter Unit [*Air Force*] (MCD)
**MFU**.......... Myoclonus Families United (EA)
**MFU**.......... Pacific Coast Marine Firemen, Oilers, Watertenders, and Wipers Association [*Also known as Marine Firemen's Union*] (EA)
**MFUA**........ Medical Follow-Up Agency [*National Research Council*]
**MFUI**........ Mechanics Friendly Union Institution [*British*]
**MFUMR**... MIRA [*Multifunctional Inertial Reference Assembly*] Fighter Unit Mounting Rack [*Air Force*] (MCD)
**Mfurers Mon**... Manufacturers' Monthly [*A publication*]
**MFUW**...... Magnetic Force Upset Welding [*Metals*]
**MFV**.......... Magnetic Field Vector
**MFV**.......... Main Feedwater Valve [*Nuclear energy*] (NRCH)
**MFV**.......... Main Fuel Valve (KSC)
**MFV**.......... Maintenance Floor Valve (NRCH)
**MFV**.......... Mars Flyby Vehicle [*Aerospace*]
**MFV**.......... Melfa, VA [*Location identifier*] [*FAA*] (FAAL)
**MFV**.......... Methanol-Fueled Vehicle [*Automotive engineering*]
**MFV**.......... MFS Special Value Trust [*NYSE symbol*] (SPSG)
**MFV**.......... Microfilm Viewer
**MFV**.......... Military Flight Vehicles
**MFV**.......... Motor Fishing Vessel [*British military*] (DMA)
**MFVD**........ Maximum Forward Voltage Drop
**MFVFF**...... Meddelelser fra Vestlandets Forstlige Forsoeksstasjon [*A publication*]
**MFVP**........ Mauler Feasibility Validation Program
**MFVPT**..... Motor-Free Visual Perception Test
**mfVSG**....... Membrane Form of Variant Surface Glycoprotein [*Biochemistry*]
**MFW**......... Main Feedwater [*Nuclear energy*] (NRCH)
**MFW**......... Migrant Farm Worker (OICC)
**MFW**......... Milton-Freewater [*Oregon*] [*Seismograph station code, US Geological Survey*] (SEIS)
**MFW**......... Ms. Foundation for Women (EA)
**MFWC**...... Marine Fleet Air, West Coast
**MFWLB**.... Main Feedwater Line Break [*Nuclear energy*] (NRCH)
**MFWV**...... Main Feedwater Valve [*Nuclear energy*] (NRCH)
**MFX**.......... Mirror Fusion Experiment [*Nuclear energy*]
**MFY**.......... Mobilization for Youth
**MFY**.......... Music for Youth
**MFZ**.......... Mezzo Forzando [*Music*]

**MFZ** ........ Missile Firing Zone
**MG** ........ Geometric Mean [*Psychology*]
**MG** ........ Machine-Glazed [*Poster paper*]
**MG** ........ Machine Gun (MUGU)
**MG** ........ Machine Gunner [*British military*] (DMA)
**MG** ........ Machinery of Government [*British*]
**M & G** ........ Macnaghten and Gordon's English Chancery Reports [*A publication*] (DLA)
**MG** ........ Madagascar [*ANSI two-letter standard code*] (CNC)
**M & G** ........ Maddock and Geldart's English Chancery Reports [*1815-22*] [*A publication*] (DLA)
**mg** ........ Mafic Granulite [*Geology*]
**MG** ........ Magenta (ROG)
**MG** ........ Maggioni & C. [*Italy*] [*Research code symbol*]
**Mg** ........ Maghemite [*A mineral*]
**MG** ........ Magna International, Inc. [*Toronto Stock Exchange symbol*]
**Mg** ........ Magnesium [*Chemical element*]
**MG** ........ Magnetic Armature (MSA)
**MG** ........ Maharashtrawadi Gomantak [*India*] [*Political party*] (PPW)
**MG** ........ Main Gauche [*With the Left Hand*] [*Music*]
**MG** ........ Major General
**MG** ........ Make Good
**mg** ........ Malagasy Republic [*Madagascar*] [*MARC country of publication code*] [*Library of Congress*] (LCCP)
**MG** ........ Mammary Gland [*Anatomy*]
**MG** ........ Managerial Grid
**MG** ........ Manager's Guide
**MG** ........ Manchester Guardian [*A publication*]
**MG** ........ Mandaeische Grammatik [*A publication*]
**Mg** ........ Mangrove [*Maps and charts*]
**M & G** ........ Manning and Granger's English Common Pleas Reports [*A publication*] (DLA)
**MG** ........ Manual Group (NRCH)
**MG** ........ Manufacturing
**MG** ........ Maof Airlines [*Israel*] [*ICAO designator*] (ICDA)
**M & G** ........ Mapping and Geodesy [*Army*] (AABC)
**MG** ........ Marcus Gunn (Pupil) [*Ophthalmology*]
**MG** ........ Marginal (AAG)
**MG** ........ Marine Gunner
**MG** ........ Martinus Gosia [*Authority cited in pre-1607 legal work*] (DSA)
**MG** ........ Massorah Magna
**MG** ........ Master-General [*Military*] [*British*]
**MG** ........ Meaning (ROG)
**MG** ........ Media General Financial Services [*Information retrieval*]
**MG** ........ Medial Gastrocnemius [*Anatomy*]
**MG** ........ Medium Grain [*Lumber*]
**MG** ........ Megagram
**MG** ........ Melanesian Airlines Co. [*Pty.*] Ltd. [*Australia*] [*ICAO designator*] (FAAC)
**MG** ........ Membranous Glomerulopathy [*Nephrology*]
**MG** ........ Menopausal Gonadotropin [*Endocrinology*]
**MG** ........ Mesiogingival [*Dentistry*]
**MG** ........ Message Generator
**MG** ........ Metal Goods [*Department of Employment*] [*British*]
**MG** ........ Metallurgical Grade
**MG** ........ Meteorological Group [*Range Commanders Council*] [*White Sands Missile Range, NM*]
**MG** ........ Methods in Geomathematics [*Elsevier Book Series*] [*A publication*]
**MG** ........ Methyl Green [*A dye*]
**MG** ........ Methylene Glutamine
**MG** ........ Methylglucoside [*Organic chemistry*]
**MG** ........ Methylglyoxal [*Also, MGLY*] [*Organic chemistry*]
**MG** ........ MG Car Club (EA)
**MG** ........ Microwave Generator
**MG** ........ Middle Gimbal
**MG** ........ Migne Series. Graeca [*A publication*]
**M/G** ........ Miles per Gallon
**MG** ........ Military Government [*or Governor*]
**MG** ........ Mill Glazed [*Paper*]
**MG** ........ Millennium Guild (EA)
**mg** ........ Milligram
**MG** ........ Millwright Group (EA)
**MG** ........ Minnesota Groundswell (EA)
**MG** ........ Minority Group
**MG** ........ Miracle of Grace [*Pseudonym used by William Smith*]
**MG** ........ Misioneros de Guadalupe [*Missionaries of Guadalupe*] [*Mexico City, Mexico*] (EAIO)
**MG** ........ Missile Gas
**MG** ........ Missile Guidance
**MG** ........ Mixed Grain
**MG** ........ Mobile Generator (KSC)
**MG** ........ [*The*] Mobile & Gulf Railroad Co. [*Formerly, MGU*] [*AAR code*]
**MG** ........ Modified Guaranteed [*Securities trading*]
**MG** ........ Moeso-Gothic [*Language, etc.*] (ROG)
**MG** ........ Molodaya Gvardiya [*Moscow*] [*A publication*]
**MG** ........ Morning
**MG** ........ Morris Garage [*British automobile manufacturer; initialism used as name of sports car it produces*]
**MG** ........ Motion for Mandamus Granted [*Legal term*] (ILCA)
**MG** ........ Motor Generator
**MG** ........ Multigauge
**MG** ........ Muncie-Getrag [*Refers to an automotive transmission designed by Getrag, a West German company, and built by General Motors in Muncie, IN*]
**MG** ........ Myasthenia Gravis [*Medicine*]
**MG** ........ Myasthenia Gravis Foundation (EA)
**MG** ........ Myriagram [*Ten Thousand Grams*] (ROG)
**MG's** ........ Memphis Group [*In name of singing group "Booker T and the MG's"*]
**MGA** ........ Major-General in Charge of Administration [*British*]
**MGA** ........ Managing General Agent [*Insurance*]
**MGA** ........ Managua [*Nicaragua*] [*Airport symbol*] (OAG)
**MGA** ........ Master Gemology Association (EA)
**MGA** ........ Medium-Gain Antenna
**MGA** ........ Megaline Resources [*Vancouver Stock Exchange symbol*]
**MGA** ........ Melengestrol Acetate [*Endocrinology*]
**MGA** ........ Mercantile Gold [*Vancouver Stock Exchange symbol*]
**M & GA** ........ Meteorological and Geoastrophysical Abstracts [*American Meteorological Society*] [*Bibliographic database*] [*A publication*]
**MGA** ........ Meteorological and Geoastrophysical Abstracts [*American Meteorological Society*] [*Bibliographic database*] [*A publication*]
**MGA** ........ Middle Gimbal Angle (NASA)
**MGA** ........ Middle Gimbal Assembly (KSC)
**MGA** ........ Middle Gimbal Axis (KSC)
**MGA** ........ Milagra Ridge [*California*] [*Seismograph station code, US Geological Survey*] (SEIS)
**MGA** ........ Military Government Association
**MGA** ........ Mitteilungen. Gesamtarchiv der Deutschen Juden [*A publication*]
**MGA** ........ [*The*] Monongahela Railway Co. [*AAR code*]
**MGA** ........ Multiple Gas Analyzer
**MGA** ........ Mushroom Growers Association [*Commercial firm*] (EA)
**MGA** ........ Mushroom Growers Cooperative Association (EA)
**MGAA** ........ Medium-Gain Autotrack Antenna
**MGAA** ........ Miniature Golf Association of America (EA)
**MGAB** ........ Maintenance Ground Abort [*Air Force*] (AFIT)
**MGABR** ........ Maintenance Ground Abort Rate [*Air Force*] (AFIT)
**MGADJ** ........ Mitteilungen. Gesamtarchiv der Deutschen Juden [*A publication*]
**MGAGB** ........ Montana Geological Society. Annual Field Conference. Guidebook [*A publication*]
**MGAGES** ... Monografie di Genetica Agraria [*A publication*]
**MGAJA** ........ Magyar Allami Foldtani Intezet. Evi Jelentese [*A publication*]
**mgal** ........ Milligal [*Unit of acceleration*]
**MGAL/D** ... Million Gallons per Day
**MGaMW** ... Mount Wachusett Community College, Gardner, MA [*Library symbol*] [*Library of Congress*] (LCLS)
**MGAO** ........ Minority Graphic Arts Organization (EA)
**MGAP** ........ Magnetic Attitude Prediction
**MGAS** ........ Motor Gasoline [*Military*]
**MGAT** ........ Make Good a Track Of [*Followed by degrees*] [*Aviation*] (FAAC)
**MGATC** ........ Modern German Authors. Texts and Contexts [*A publication*]
**MGB** ........ Medium-Girder Bridge (RDA)
**MGB** ........ Motor Gunboat [*British*]
**MGB** ........ Mount Gambier [*Australia*] [*Airport symbol*] (OAG)
**MGB** ........ Muenchener Germanistische Beitraege [*A publication*]
**MGBC** ........ Maranatha Gospel Bottle Crusade [*Later, CEM*] (EA)
**MGBG** ........ Methylglyoxalbis(guanylhydrazone) [*Mitoguazone*] [*Also, Me-GAG*] [*Antineoplastic drug*]
**MGbl** ........ Muehlhauser Geschichtsblaetter [*A publication*]
**MGBN** ........ Bananera [*Guatemala*] [*ICAO location identifier*] (ICLI)
**MGC** ........ Machine-Gun Car [*or Carrier*] [*British*]
**MGC** ........ Machine-Gun Combination [*British*]
**MGC** ........ Machine-Gun Company [*or Corps*]
**MGC** ........ Machine Gun Corps [*British military*] (DMA)
**MGC** ........ Major Gain Control
**MGC** ........ Major General Commandant [*Marine Corps*]
**MGC** ........ Management Group Codes (MCD)
**MGC** ........ Manual Gain Control
**MGC** ........ Marriage Guidance Council [*British*]
**MGC** ........ Metallized Glass Coil
**MGC** ........ Methodist Girls Comradeship [*Australia*]
**MGC** ........ Michigan City [*Indiana*] [*Airport symbol*] (OAG)
**MGC** ........ Michigan City, IN [*Location identifier*] [*FAA*] (FAAL)
**MGC** ........ Midcourse Guidance and Control
**MGC** ........ Middle Georgia College [*Cochran*]
**MGC** ........ Minimal Glomerular Change [*Nephrology*]
**MGC** ........ Minimum Gelling Concentration [*Hematology*]
**MGC** ........ Missile Guidance Computer (MCD)
**MGC** ........ Missile Guidance and Control
**MGC** ........ Montgomery County Community College, Blue Bell, PA [*OCLC symbol*] (OCLC)
**MGC** ........ Morgan Grenfell Smallcap Fund, Inc. [*NYSE symbol*] (SPSG)
**MGC** ........ Movers Association of Greater Chicago, Chicago, IL [*STAC*]
**MGC** ........ Museums and Galleries Commission [*Government body*] [*British*]
**MGCA** ........ Men's Garden Clubs of America (EA)

**MGCA** ....... Mobile Ground-Controlled Approach [*Aviation*]
**MGCA** ....... Mushroom Growers Cooperative Association
**MGCB** ....... Coban [*Guatemala*] [*ICAO location identifier*] (ICLI)
**MGCC** ....... Medical Graphics Corporation [*NASDAQ symbol*] (NQ)
**MGCC** ....... Missile Guidance and Control Computer
**MGCC** ....... Mitsubishi Gas Chemical Company [*Japan*]
**MGCD** ....... MagnaCard, Inc. [*Lakeland, FL*] [*NASDAQ symbol*] (NQ)
**MGCD** ....... Maximum Gapless Coverage Distance (NG)
**MGCI** ....... Master Ground-Controller Interception RADAR (NATG)
**MGCO** ....... Mars Geoscience/Climatology Orbiter
**MGCO** ....... Medicare-Glaser Corporation [*NASDAQ symbol*] (NQ)
**Mg C Pop Cr** ... Monographs. Carolina Population Center [*A publication*]
**MGCR** ....... Carmelita [*Guatemala*] [*ICAO location identifier*] (ICLI)
**MGCR** ....... Maritime Gas-Cooled Reactor
**MGCR-CX** ... Maritime Gas-Cooled Reactor Critical Experiment
**MGCT** ....... Coatepeque [*Guatemala*] [*ICAO location identifier*] (ICLI)
**MGD** .......... Guardian [*A publication*]
**MGD** .......... Magadan [*USSR*] [*Later, FUR*] [*Geomagnetic observatory code*]
**MGD** .......... Magadan 1 [*USSR*] [*Seismograph station code, US Geological Survey*] (SEIS)
**MGD** .......... Magnetogasdynamic
**MGD** .......... Mean Gain Deviation (IEEE)
**MG/D** ........ Megagrams per Day
**MGD** .......... Mercury Germanium Detector
**MGD** .......... Miehle-Goss-Dexter [*Rockwell International Corp.*]
**MGD** .......... Military Geographic Documentation (AABC)
**mg/d** .......... Milligrams per Deciliter
**MGD** .......... Million Gallons per Day
**MGD** .......... Mixed Gonadal Dysgenesis [*Medicine*]
**MGD** .......... Murgold Resources, Inc. [*Toronto Stock Exchange symbol*]
**MGDF** ....... Modified Granular Diffusion Flame [*Propellant*]
**MGDSRCS Eng** ... Membership in General Dental Surgery, Royal College of Surgeons of England [*British*] (DBQ)
**MGDV** ....... Murgold Resources, Inc. [*NASDAQ symbol*] (NQ)
**MGE** .......... Evergreen Regional Library, Gimli, Manitoba [*Library symbol*] [*National Library of Canada*] (NLC)
**MGE** .......... Maintenance Ground Equipment [*Formerly, GSF*]
**MGE** .......... Marge Enterprises [*Vancouver Stock Exchange symbol*]
**MGE** .......... Marietta, GA [*Location identifier*] [*FAA*] (FAAL)
**MGE** .......... Message (ADA)
**MGE** .......... Milwaukee Grain Exchange [*Defunct*]
**MGE** .......... Minneapolis Grain Exchange (EA)
**MGE** .......... Missile Guidance Element
**M Ge E** ...... Master of Geological Engineering
**M Ge Eng** .. Master of Geological Engineering
**MGEK** ....... Mitteilungen. Gesellschaft zur Erforschung Judischer Kunstdenkmaeler [*A publication*]
**M & Gel** ..... Maddock and Geldart's English Chancery Reports [*1815-22*] [*A publication*] (DLA)
**MGEM** ...... Modern Gun Effectiveness Model (MCD)
**M GEN** ...... Major General
**MGEN** ....... Micro General Corp. [*NASDAQ symbol*] (NQ)
**MGenStud** ... Master of General Studies (ADA)
**MGEO** ....... Munson Geothermal, Inc. [*Fernley, NV*] [*NASDAQ symbol*] (NQ)
**M Geol E** ... Master of Geological Engineering
**MGES** ....... Esquipulas [*Guatemala*] [*ICAO location identifier*] (ICLI)
**MGES** ....... Maintenance Ground Equipment Section
**M Ges** ....... Musik und Gesellschaft [*A publication*]
**MGESA** ..... Mededelingen. Geologische Stichting. Nieuwe Serie [*A publication*]
**M Ges Salzb** ... Mitteilungen. Gesellschaft fuer Salzburger Landeskunde [*A publication*]
**MGEUS** .... Maintenance Ground Equipment Utilization Sheets
**Mgf** ............ Free Magnesium
**MGF** .......... Magnify (MSA)
**MGF** .......... Maringa [*Brazil*] [*Airport symbol*] (OAG)
**MGF** .......... Men's Guide to Fashion [*A publication*]
**MGF** .......... MFS Government Markets Income Trust [*NYSE symbol*] (SPSG)
**MGF** .......... Mobile Guerrilla Force [*Vietnam*]
**MGF** .......... Moment-Generating Function [*Mathematics*]
**MGF** .......... Motor-Generator Flywheel (MCD)
**MGF** .......... Myasthenia Gravis Foundation
**MGF** .......... Myoblast Growth Factor [*Biochemistry*]
**MGF** .......... Myxoma Growth Factor [*Biochemistry*]
**MGFC** ....... Mickey Gilley Fan Club (EA)
**MGFE** ....... Moment-Generating Function Estimator
**MGFEL** ..... Master Government-Furnished Equipment List (NVT)
**MGFG** ....... Magnifying
**MGFIAL** ... Annales. Instituti Geologici Publici Hungarici [*A publication*]
**MGFIB** ...... Morskie Gidrofizicheskie Issledovaniya [*A publication*]
**MGFL** ....... Flores [*Guatemala*] [*ICAO location identifier*] (ICLI)
**MGFO** ....... MGF Oil Corp. [*NASDAQ symbol*] (NQ)
**MGFS** ....... Media General Financial Services, Inc. [*Information service or system*] (IID)
**MGFZB** ..... Mein Gott, Fueg Es zum Besten [*My God, Order It for the Best*] [*German*] [*Motto of Sophie, consort of Georg Friedrich, Margrave of Brandenburg-Anspach (1563-1639)*]
**MGG** .......... Machine Gun Guards [*British military*] (DMA)
**MGG** .......... May-Gruenwald-Giemsa [*A stain*] [*Hematology*]
**MGG** .......... Mega Gold Resources Ltd. [*Vancouver Stock Exchange symbol*]
**MGG** .......... Memory Gate Generator [*Data processing*]
**MGG** .......... Methods in Geochemistry and Geophysics [*Elsevier Book Series*] [*A publication*]
**MGG** .......... MGG. Molecular and General Genetics [*A publication*]
**MGG** .......... MGM Grand, Inc. [*NYSE symbol*] (SPSG)
**MGG** .......... Missile Guidance Group
**MGG** .......... Mouse Gamma-Globulin
**MGG** .......... Musik in Geschichte und Gegenwart [*A publication*]
**MGGB** ....... Modular Guided Glide Bomb (MCD)
**MGGH** ...... Mitteilungen. Geographische Gesellschaft in Hamburg [*A publication*]
**MGG Mol Gen Genet** ... MGG. Molecular and General Genetics [*A publication*]
**MGGR** ....... Management Graphics, Inc. [*Downsview, ON*] [*NASDAQ symbol*] (NQ)
**MGGS** ....... Major General, General Staff
**MGGT** ....... Guatemala/La Aurora [*Guatemala*] [*ICAO location identifier*] (ICLI)
**MGGW** ...... Mitteilungen. Geographische Gesellschaft in Wien [*A publication*]
**MGH** ......... International Management [*A publication*]
**MGH** ......... Margate [*South Africa*] [*Airport symbol*] (OAG)
**MGH** ......... Massachusetts General Hospital, Treadwell Library, Boston, MA [*OCLC symbol*] (OCLC)
**mgh** ........... Milligram Hour [*Pharmacy*]
**MGH** ......... Monumenta Germaniae Historica [*A publication*]
**MGH** ......... Morden & Helwig Group, Inc. [*Toronto Stock Exchange symbol*]
**MGH** ......... Museum of Garden History [*London, England*]
**MGH News** ... Montreal General Hospital. News [*A publication*]
**MGHT** ....... Huehuetenango [*Guatemala*] [*ICAO location identifier*] (ICLI)
**MGI** ........... Gillam Municipal Library, Manitoba [*Library symbol*] [*National Library of Canada*] (NLC)
**MGI** ........... Macrophage and Granulocyte Inducer [*Biochemistry*]
**MGI** ........... Magnetics International Ltd. [*Toronto Stock Exchange symbol*]
**MGI** ........... Management Games Institute [*Raytheon Co.*]
**MGI** ........... Matagorda Island, TX [*Location identifier*] [*FAA*] (FAAL)
**MGI** ........... Mavtech Holdings, Inc. [*Toronto Stock Exchange symbol*]
**MGI** ........... Medial Giant Interneuron [*Neurobiology*]
**MGI** ........... Member of the Gas Institute [*British*]
**MGI** ........... Member of the Institute of Certificated Grocers [*British*]
**MGI** ........... Metal Grating Institute [*Defunct*]
**MGI** ........... MGI Properties [*NYSE symbol*] (SPSG)
**MGI** ........... Military Geographic Information [*or Intelligence*] (MCD)
**MGI** ........... Mobile Gamma Irradiator [*Nuclear energy*]
**MGI** ........... Multigraphic Interface [*XOR Systems*]
**MGIB** ........ Management and Graduate Item Bank [*Reasoning skills test*]
**MGIC** ........ Mortgage Guaranty Insurance Corporation [*Subsidiary of MGIC Investment Corp.*]
**MGID** ........ Military Geographic Information and Documentation (AABC)
**MGIN** ........ Margin (ROG)
**MGIN** ........ Mega Group, Incorporated [*NASDAQ symbol*] (NQ)
**MGITA2** .... Meteorologiya i Gidrologiya Informatsionnyi Byulleten [*A publication*]
**MGJ** .......... Monatsschrift fuer die Geschichte und Wissenschaft des Judentums [*A publication*]
**MGJ** .......... Montgomery, NY [*Location identifier*] [*FAA*] (FAAL)
**MGJF** ........ Mitteilungen. Gesellschaft fuer Juedische Familienforschung [*Berlin*] [*A publication*]
**MGJFF** ...... Mitteilungen. Gesellschaft fuer Juedische Familienforschung [*Berlin*] [*A publication*]
**MGJOAP** ... Market Grower's Journal [*A publication*]
**MGJV** ........ Mitteilungen. Gesellschaft fuer Juedische Volkskunde [*A publication*]
**MGK** .......... Michele Gold Mountain Ltd. [*Vancouver Stock Exchange symbol*]
**MGK** .......... Modern Greek [*Language, etc.*]
**MGKFA3** ... Hungarian Journal of Chemistry [*A publication*]
**MGkK** ........ Monatsschrift fuer Gottesdienst und Kirchliche Kunst [*Goettingen*] [*A publication*]
**MGl** ........... Gloucester Lyceum and Sawyer Free Public Library, Gloucester, MA [*Library symbol*] [*Library of Congress*] (LCLS)
**MGL** .......... Machine Gun LASER (MCD)
**MGL** .......... Magalia [*California*] [*Seismograph station code, US Geological Survey*] (SEIS)
**MGL** .......... Magnanimous Green Leprechaun
**MGL** .......... Marginal (MSA)
**MGL** .......... Matrix Generator Language [*Data processing*] (BUR)
**MGL** .......... Michigan General Corp. [*AMEX symbol*] (SPSG)
**MG/L** ........ Milligrams per Liter
**MGL** .......... Missouri Gravity Low [*Geology*]
**MGL** .......... Mogul
**MGL** .......... Mono Gold Mines, Inc. [*Vancouver Stock Exchange symbol*]
**MGL** .......... Monteagle, TN [*Location identifier*] [*FAA*] (FAAL)
**MGL** .......... Move-Grow-Learn [*Program for visual perception development*]
**MGLA** ....... Massachusetts General Laws Annotated [*A publication*]
**M GLAM** .. Mid Glamorgan [*County in Wales*]
**MGLD** ....... Marathon Gold Corp. [*NASDAQ symbol*] (NQ)

**MGLD**....... Mild General Learning Disability
**MGlHi**....... Cape Ann Historical Association, Gloucester, MA [*Library symbol*] [*Library of Congress*] (LCLS)
**MGLL**........ La Libertad [*Guatemala*] [*ICAO location identifier*] (ICLI)
**MGLL**........ McGill Manufacturing Co., Inc. [*NASDAQ symbol*] (NQ)
**MGLP**........ Methylglucose Lipopolysaccharide [*Biochemistry*]
**MGLY**....... Methylglyoxal [*Also, MG*] [*Organic chemistry*]
**MGM**......... Mailgram
**MGM**......... Master Group Multiplexer
**MGM**......... Mayer's Ganz Mispocheh [*Mayer's Whole Family*] [*A Yiddish nickname for Metro-Goldwyn-Mayer, it reflects the tendency of early studio chiefs to hire their relatives and friends*]
**MGM**......... Mechanics of Granular Materials
**MGM**......... Medical Group Missions of the Christian Medical and Dental Society (EA)
**MGM**......... Metro-Goldwyn-Mayer [*Record label*] [*USA, Great Britain, etc.*]
**MGM**......... MGM/UA [*Metro-Goldwyn-Mayer/United Artists*] Communications Co. [*NYSE symbol*] (SPSG)
**mgm**........... Milligram
**MGM**......... Miscellanea Giovanni Mercati [*Vatican City*] [*A publication*]
**MGM**......... Mobile-Launched Ground-Attack Missile
**MGM**......... Molecular and Genetic Medicine
**MGM**......... Montgomery [*Alabama*] [*Airport symbol*] (OAG)
**MGM**......... Morgain Minerals, Inc. [*Vancouver Stock Exchange symbol*]
**MG/M²**...... Megagrams per Square Meter
**MG/M³**...... Megagrams per Cubic Meter
**MGMA**...... Magma Power Co. [*NASDAQ symbol*] (NQ)
**MGMA**...... Medical Group Management Association (EA)
**MGMC**...... Multiple Gun Motor Carriage
**MGMD**...... Ministerial Group on the Misuse of Drugs [*British*]
**MGMG**...... MGM Grand, Inc. [*NASDAQ symbol*] (NQ)
**MGMIS**..... Medical Group Management Information Service [*Medical Group Management Association*] (DHSM)
**MGML**...... Malacatan [*Guatemala*] [*ICAO location identifier*] (ICLI)
**MGMM**..... Melchor De Mencos [*Guatemala*] [*ICAO location identifier*] (ICLI)
**MGMNT**... Management
**MGMPA**... Memorie. Istituti di Geologia e Mineralogia. Universita di Padova [*A publication*]
**MGMT**...... Make Good a Magnetic Track Of [*Followed by degrees*] [*Aviation*] (FAAC)
**MGMT**...... Management (KSC)
**MGMT**...... Medical Management Corp. [*NASDAQ symbol*] (NQ)
**Mgmt Acct**... Management Accounting [*A publication*]
**Mgmt Dec**... Management Decision [*A publication*]
**Mgmt Focus**... Management Focus [*A publication*]
**Mgmt Forum**... Management Forum [*A publication*]
**Mgmt in Govt**... Management in Government [*A publication*]
**Mgmt Prac**... Management Practice [*A publication*]
**Mgmt Printing**... Management in Printing [*A publication*]
**Mgmt Res News**... Management Research News [*A publication*]
**Mgmt Rev**.. Management Review [*A publication*]
**Mgmt Rev Dig**... Management Review and Digest [*A publication*]
**Mgmt Sci**... Management Science [*A publication*]
**Mgmt Serv**... Management Services [*A publication*]
**Mgmt Serv Govt**... Management Services in Government [*A publication*]
**Mgmt Today**... Management Today [*A publication*]
**Mgmt World**... Management World [*A publication*]
**MGMV**...... Molecular Genetics, Microbiology, and Virology [*USSR*] [*A publication*]
**MGN**......... Finish [*Amsterdam*] [*A publication*]
**MGN**......... Magneto [*Generator*]
**MGN**......... Margin [*Accounting*]
**MGN**......... Medial Geniculate Nucleus [*Medicine*]
**MGN**......... Membranous Glomerulonephritis [*Nephrology*]
**MGN**......... Mengen [*Turkey*] [*Seismograph station code, US Geological Survey*] (SEIS)
**M & GN**..... Midland and Great Northern Joint Line [*Railway*] [*British*] (ROG)
**MGN**......... Mirror Group Newspapers [*British*]
**MGN**......... Morgan Products Ltd. [*NYSE symbol*] (SPSG)
**MGN**......... Multigrounded Neutral [*Telecommunications*] (TEL)
**MGNC**....... MEDIAGENIC [*NASDAQ symbol*] (SPSG)
**MGNE**....... Magnetic Controls [*NASDAQ symbol*] (NQ)
**MGNES**.... Metal Goods Not Elsewhere Specified [*Department of Employment*] [*British*]
**MGNM**..... Mitteilungen. Germanisches Nationalmuseum [*A publication*]
**MGNSM**... Magnesium [*Chemical symbol is Mg*]
**MGNT**....... Migent Software, Inc. [*NASDAQ symbol*] (NQ)
**MGNTZD**... Magnetized
**MGNVO**.... Mitteilungen. Gesellschaft fuer Natur- und Voelkerkunde Ostasiens [*A publication*]
**MGO**......... Machine Gun Officer [*British military*] (DMA)
**MGO**......... Management by Goals and Objectives (MCD)
**MGO**......... Master General of the Ordnance [*Army*] [*British*]
**MGO**......... Master of Gynaecology and Obstetrics (ADA)
**MGO**......... Megagauss-Oersted [*Magnetic field strength*]
**MGO**......... Military Government Officer
**MGO**......... Million Gauss Oersted [*Unit of energy density*]
**MGO**......... Mortgage Insurance Co. of Canada [*Toronto Stock Exchange symbol*]
**MGOe**........ Megagauss-Oersted [*Also, MGO*] [*Magnetic field strength*]
**MGOKL**.... Mededeelingen. Geschied- en Oudheidkundige Kring voor Leuven en Omgeving [*A publication*]
**MGOKLeuven**... Mededeelingen. Geschied- en Oudheidkundige Kring voor Leuven en Omgeving [*A publication*]
**M & Gord**... Macnaghten and Gordon's English Chancery Reports [*A publication*] (DLA)
**M GOTH**... Moeso-Gothic [*Language, etc.*] (ROG)
**MGottesdienst**... Musik und Gottesdienst [*A publication*]
**MGP**.......... Application for Mandamus Granted in Part [*Legal term*] (DLA)
**MG(P)**....... Machinery of Government, Parliamentary Procedure [*British*]
**MGP**.......... Maguayo [*Puerto Rico*] [*Seismograph station code, US Geological Survey*] (SEIS)
**MGP**.......... Maintenance Ground Point
**MGP**.......... Manga [*Papua New Guinea*] [*Airport symbol*] (OAG)
**MGP**.......... Marginal Granulocyte Pool [*Hematology*]
**MGP**.......... Mary Glawgow Publications [*Publisher*] [*Great Britain*]
**MGP**.......... Merchants Group, Inc. [*AMEX symbol*] (SPSG)
**MGP**.......... Methyl Green Pyronine [*A stain*]
**MGP**.......... Methylglucose Polysaccharide [*Biochemistry*]
**MGP**.......... Morgan Gallup Poll [*Australia*]
**MGP**.......... Morrison-Grey Enterprises [*Vancouver Stock Exchange symbol*]
**MGP**.......... Mountain Gorilla Project (EA)
**MGP**.......... Mouvement Gaulliste Populaire [*Popular Gaullist Movement*] [*France*] [*Political party*] (PPW)
**MGP**.......... Mucous Glycoproteins [*Biochemistry*]
**MGP**.......... Multiple Goal Programming
**MGPB**....... Puerto Barrios [*Guatemala*] [*ICAO location identifier*] (ICLI)
**MGPC**....... Grandview Personal Care Home, Manitoba [*Library symbol*] [*National Library of Canada*] (NLC)
**MGPC**....... Malibu Grand Prix Corp. [*NASDAQ symbol*] (NQ)
**MGPCU**.... Missile Ground Power Control Unit (AAG)
**M-GPD**...... Million US Gallons per Day [*AEC, OSW*]
**MGPF**........ Multiprogram General-Purpose Facilities [*Oak Ridge National Laboratory*]
**MGPGA**.... Monatsblaetter. Gesellschaft fuer Pommersche Geschichte und Altertumskunde [*A publication*]
**MGPL**........ Marine Gene Probe Laboratory [*Dalhousie University*] [*Canada*]
**MGPNA**.... Metallurgicheskaya i Gornorudnaya Promyshlennost [*A publication*]
**MGPP**........ Poptun [*Guatemala*] [*ICAO location identifier*] (ICLI)
**MGPPL**..... Motor Glider Private Pilot's Licence [*British*] (AIA)
**MGQ**......... Management Science [*A publication*]
**MGQ**......... Mogadishu [*Somalia*] [*Airport symbol*] (OAG)
**MGQC**....... Quiche [*Guatemala*] [*ICAO location identifier*] (ICLI)
**MGQZ**....... Quezaltenango [*Guatemala*] [*ICAO location identifier*] (ICLI)
**MGR**.......... M. G. Ramachandran [*Indian film actor and political party leader*]
**MGR**.......... Machine Gun Regiment [*British military*] (DMA)
**MGR**.......... Manager (AFM)
**MGR**.......... Marrow Granulocyte Reserves [*Hematology*]
**MGR**.......... Medieval Greek [*Language, etc.*]
**MGR**.......... Merry-Go-Round Enterprises [*NYSE symbol*] (SPSG)
**MGR**.......... Metal Glaze Resistor
**MGR**.......... Method of Generated Responses [*Psychology*]
**M GR**......... Middle Greek [*Language, etc.*] (ROG)
**MGR**.......... Middlegate Resources, Inc. [*Vancouver Stock Exchange symbol*]
**MGR**.......... Miscellanea Greca e Romana [*A publication*]
**MGR**.......... Mobile-Launched Ground-Attack Rocket
**MGR**.......... Monsignor
**MGR**.......... Moraga Resources Ltd. [*Vancouver Stock Exchange symbol*]
**MGR**.......... Moultrie, GA [*Location identifier*] [*FAA*] (FAAL)
**MGR**.......... Moultrie/Thomasville [*Georgia*] [*Airport symbol*] (OAG)
**MGR**.......... Mouvement de la Gauche Reformatrice [*Movement of the Reformist Left*] [*France*] [*Political party*] (PPW)
**MGRA**....... Major-General, Royal Artillery [*Army*] [*British*]
**MGranbyS**... Saint Hyacinth College and Seminary, Granby, MA [*Library symbol*] [*Library of Congress*] (LCLS)
**MGRC**....... McGrath RentCorp [*NASDAQ symbol*] (NQ)
**MGRCAT**... Medicina Geriatrica [*A publication*]
**MGrefC**..... Greenfield Community College, Greenfield, MA [*Library symbol*] [*Library of Congress*] (LCLS)
**MGRESS**.. Manageress (ROG)
**MGRGT**.... Modular Gas-Cooled Reactor Gas Turbine [*Developed by MIT*] [*Nuclear energy*]
**MGRHS**.... May God Rest His Soul
**MGRI**........ Mobile Ground Radio Installation
**Mgrl Plan**.. Managerial Planning [*A publication*]
**MGRM**...... Major-General, Royal Marines [*British military*] (DMA)
**MGRM**...... Milligram (ROG)
**MGRO**...... MedPro Group, Inc. [*Minneapolis, MN*] [*NASDAQ symbol*] (NQ)
**MGRP**....... Minimum-Gradient Reaction Path [*Chemical kinetics*]
**MGRS**....... Ferrocarriles Nacionales de Mexico [*AAR code*]

MGrS......... Groton School, Groton, MA [*Library symbol*] [*Library of Congress*] (LCLS)
MGRS ....... Meter Gauge Rolling-Stock [*British*]
MGRS ....... Military Grid Reference System (AABC)
MGRT ....... Retalhuleu [*Guatemala*] [*ICAO location identifier*] (ICLI)
MGRW....... Matrix Generator and Report Writer [*Data processing*]
MGRY ....... Milgray Electronics, Inc. [*NASDAQ symbol*] (NQ)
MGS .......... MacGregor Sporting Goods, Inc. [*AMEX symbol*] (SPSG)
MGS .......... Machine Gun School [*British military*] (DMA)
MGS .......... Magellan Resources Corp. [*Vancouver Stock Exchange symbol*]
MGS .......... Mangaia [*Cook Islands*] [*Airport symbol*] (OAG)
MG & S...... Manning, Granger, and Scott's English Common Pleas Reports [*1845-56*] [*A publication*] (DLA)
MGS .......... Marine Geophysical Survey [*NOO*]
MGS .......... Master Gemology Society [*Defunct*] (EA)
MGS .......... Metal Gravel Stop
MGS .......... Metre-Gram-Second
MGS .......... Michigan Germanic Studies [*A publication*]
MGS .......... Microcomputer Graphic System
MGS .......... Middleton Gardens [*South Carolina*] [*Seismograph station code, US Geological Survey*] (SEIS)
MGS .......... Midwestern Gilbert and Sullivan Society (EA)
MGS .......... Military Government Section [*World War II*]
MGS .......... Missile Guidance Section [*or Set, or System*]
MGS .......... Mission Ground Station (MCD)
MGS .......... Mobile Ground System
MGS .......... Moment Gyro System
MGS .......... Motor Generator Set (CAAL)
MGSA ....... Melanoma Growth Stimulatory Activity [*Biochemistry*]
MGSA ....... Military General Supply Agency [*Merged with Defense General Supply Center*]
MGSA ....... Modern Greek Studies Association (EA)
MGSACU ... Geological Survey of Malaysia. Annual Report [*A publication*]
MGSC ....... Missile Guidance Set Control
MGSCD .... Martha Graham School of Contemporary Dance [*New York, NY*]
MGSDA .... Annual Statistical Summary. Michigan Geological Survey Division [*A publication*]
MGSE........ Maintenance Ground Support Equipment
MGSE........ Mechanical Ground Support Equipment
MGSE........ Missile Ground Support Equipment
MGSE........ Mobile Ground Support Equipment
MGSIUF... Marquis Giuseppe Scicluna International University Foundation (EA)
MGSJ ........ San Jose [*Guatemala*] [*ICAO location identifier*] (ICLI)
MGSL........ Minas Gerais. Suplemento Literario [*A publication*]
MGSLK..... Mitteilungen. Gesellschaft fuer Salzburger Landeskunde [*A publication*]
MGSM ...... San Marcos [*Guatemala*] [*ICAO location identifier*] (ICLI)
MGSMC.... Michigan. Geological Survey Division. Miscellany [*A publication*]
Mg Soc Anth ... Monographs on Social Anthropology [*A publication*]
MGST........ Military Geography Specialist Team
MGSVAN ... Geological Survey of Victoria. Memoir [*A publication*]
Mg S Wld .. Monograph Series in World Affairs. University of Denver [*A publication*]
MGT.......... Magenta Development Corp. [*Vancouver Stock Exchange symbol*]
MGT.......... Major Ground Test (NASA)
MGT.......... Management (AFM)
MGT.......... Master-Group Translator [*Telecommunications*] (TEL)
MGT.......... Megaton [*Nuclear equivalent of one million tons of high explosive*] (AAG)
MGT.......... Meteorological and Geoastrophysical Titles
MGT.......... Mobile [*Truck-Mounted*] Ground Terminal
MGT.......... Movie Going Time
Mgt Accounting ... Management Accounting [*A publication*]
Mgt Acct.... Management Accounting [*A publication*]
Mgt Adviser ... Management Adviser [*A publication*]
MGTANALYSO ... Management Analysis Officer [*Air Force*]
Mgt Controls ... Management Controls [*A publication*]
Mgt Decision ... Management Decision [*A publication*]
Mgt Educ & Dev ... Management, Education, and Development [*A publication*]
MGTENGR ... Management Engineer [*Air Force*]
Mgt Focus ... Management Focus [*A publication*]
Mgt in Govt ... Management in Government [*A publication*]
MGTI ........ Member of the Gymnastic Teachers' Institute [*British*] (ROG)
Mgt Info Service Rept ... Management Information Service Report [*A publication*]
Mgt Internat R ... Management International Review [*A publication*]
Mgt Int R... Management International Review [*A publication*]
Mgt Methods ... Management Methods [*A publication*]
MGTMTR ... Magnetometer
MGTO....... Mexican Government Tourism Office (EA)
MGTOA..... Magyar Tudomanyos Akademia. Kemiai Tudomanyok Osztalyanak Koezlemenyei [*A publication*]
Mgt Q ........ Management Quarterly [*A publication*]
Mgt R......... Management Review [*A publication*]
Mgt Rec ..... Management Record [*A publication*]
Mgt Sci ...... Management Science [*A publication*]
Mgt Ser...... Management Services [*A publication*]
Mgt Services ... Management Services [*A publication*]
Mgt Services in Govt ... Management Services in Government [*A publication*]
Mgt Today ... Management Today [*A publication*]
Mgt World ... Management World [*A publication*]
MGU ......... Main-Group Ureilite [*Meteorite component*]
MGU ......... MGM Resources Corp. [*Vancouver Stock Exchange symbol*]
MGU ......... Midcourse Guidance Unit [*Navy*] (CAAL)
MGU ......... Military Government Unit
MGU ......... [*The*] Mobile & Gulf Railroad Co. [*Later, MG*] [*AAR code*]
MGU ......... Moskovskiy Gosudarstvenniy Universitet [*Moscow State University*] [*USSR*] (MSC)
MGUN ...... Marine Gunner
MGV.......... Maandblad voor de Geestelijke Volksgezondheid [*A publication*]
MGV.......... Miniature Gate Valve
MGv........... Molodaia Gvardiia. Ezhemesiachnyi Literaturno-Khudozhestvennyi i Obshchestvenn-Politicheskii Zhurnal [*A publication*]
MGV.......... Monogram Oil & Gas, Inc. [*Vancouver Stock Exchange symbol*]
MGVC ....... Manual Governing Valve Control [*Nuclear energy*] (NRCH)
MGVT ....... Mated Ground Vibration Test (NASA)
MGVT ....... Montgomery [*Vermont*] [*Seismograph station code, US Geological Survey*] (SEIS)
MGW......... Magnesium Sulfate, Glycerine, and Water (Enema) [*Medicine*]
MGW......... Manchester Guardian Weekly [*A publication*]
MGW......... Mission Gross Weight
MGW......... Morgantown [*West Virginia*] [*Airport symbol*] (OAG)
MGW......... Morgantown, WV [*Location identifier*] [*FAA*] (FAAL)
MGWJ ...... Monatsschrift fuer die Geschichte und Wissenschaft des Judentums [*A publication*]
MGWR...... Midland Great Western Railway [*British*] (ROG)
MGWS ...... Modular Guided Weapon System (MCD)
MGX.......... Moabi [*Gabon*] [*Airport symbol*] (OAG)
MGY.......... Dayton, OH [*Location identifier*] [*FAA*] (FAAL)
MGY.......... Mega-Dyne Industrial Corp. [*Vancouver Stock Exchange symbol*]
MGYSGT ... Master Gunnery Sergeant [*Marine Corps*]
MGZ.......... Edelmetaal, Uurwerken, Edelstenen. Maandblad voor de Edelmetaalbranche, Uurwerkenbranche, Edelstenenbranche, en Diamantbranche [*A publication*]
MGZ.......... Management-Zeitschrift [*Switzerland*] [*A publication*]
MGZ.......... Maschinengewehr-Zieleinrichtung [*Machine-Gun Sighting Mechanism*] [*German military - World War II*]
MGZ.......... Mergui [*Burma*] [*Airport symbol*] (OAG)
MGZF ....... Maschinengewehr-Zielfernrohr [*Machine-Gun Telescopic Sight*] [*German military - World War II*]
MH ............ Air-Cushion Vehicle built by Mitsubishi [*Japan*] [*Usually used in combination with numerals*]
MH ............ [*A*] Grammar of Masoretic Hebrew [*A publication*] (BJA)
MH ............ Ha-Mo'atsah ha-Hakla'it (BJA)
MH ............ Harvard University, Cambridge, MA [*Library symbol*] [*Library of Congress*] (LCLS)
mh ............. Macao [*MARC country of publication code*] [*Library of Congress*] (LCCP)
MH ............ Magnetic Head [*or Heading*]
MH ............ Magnetite-Hematite [*Geology*]
MH ............ Mail Handler [*Data processing*]
MH ............ Main Hatch
MH ............ Maintenance Handbook
MH ............ Makkabi Hazair (BJA)
MH ............ Malaysian Airline System [*ICAO designator*] (FAAC)
MH ............ Malden Hospital [*Malden, MA*]
MH ............ Maleic Hydrazide [*Plant growth regulator*]
MH ............ Malignant Histiocytosis [*Medicine*]
MH ............ Malignant Hyperpyrexia [*Medicine*]
MH ............ Malignant Hyperthermia [*Medicine*]
MH ............ Malt House
MH ............ Mammotropic Hormone [*Endocrinology*]
MH ............ Man-Hour (MCD)
MH ............ Manhole (AAG)
MH ............ Manual Hold [*Telecommunications*]
MH ............ Mare Humorum [*Sea of Moisture*] [*Lunar area*]
MH ............ Marital History
MH ............ Marshall Islands [*ANSI two-letter standard code*] (CNC)
M-H............ Martini-Henry [*Rifle*]
MH ............ Masonic Hall (ROG)
MH ............ Master of Hamburgerology [*McDonald's Corp. Hamburger University*]
MH ............ Master Herbalist
MH ............ Master of the Horse [*British*] (ROG)
MH ............ Master of Horticulture
MH ............ Master Hosts [*An association*] [*Defunct*] (EA)
MH ............ Master of Hounds [*British*]
MH ............ Master of Humanics
MH ............ Master of the Hunt
MH ............ Master of Hygiene
MH ............ Materials Handling (NATG)
MH ............ Maximum Height [*Ballistics*]
MH ............ Mechanical Handling [*Describes type of produce; for example, MH-1 refers to a kind of tomato*]

**MH** ........ Medal of Honor [*Often erroneously called Congressional Medal of Honor*] [*Military decoration*]
**M & H** ........ Mediaevalia et Humanistica [*A publication*]
**MH** ........ Mediaevalia et Humanistica [*A publication*]
**MH** ........ Medical History
**MH** ........ Megahertz [*Megacycles per second*] [*See also MCPS, MCS, MC/S, MHZ*] (NATG)
**Mh** ........ Mehri (BJA)
**MH** ........ Melanophore Hormone [*Also, MSH*] [*Endocrinology*]
**MH** ........ Mended Hearts (EA)
**MH** ........ Menstrual History [*Medicine*]
**MH** ........ Mental Health
**MH** ........ Mental Hygiene [*A publication*]
**MH** ........ Merchants Haulage (DS)
**MH** ........ Mercurihematoporphyrin [*Pharmacology*]
**MH** ........ Meristem Height [*Botany*]
**MH** ........ MeSH Heading [*Online database field identifier*]
**MH** ........ Message Handler [*Data processing*]
**M/H** ........ Meters per Hour
**MH** ........ Methodist History [*A publication*]
**MH** ........ MHI Group, Inc. [*NYSE symbol*] (SPSG)
**MH** ........ Michigan History Magazine [*A publication*]
**MH** ........ Microhematuria [*Medicine*]
**MH** ........ Middlesex Hussars (Duke of Cambridge's) [*British military*] (DMA)
**M/H** ........ Miles per Hour [*Also, MPH*]
**MH** ........ Military History (AABC)
**MH** ........ Military Hospital (ADA)
**mH** ........ Millihenry (GPO)
**mH** ........ Millihour [*One-thousandth of an hour*] (AAG)
**MH** ........ Ministry of Health [*British*]
**M-H** ........ Minneapolis-Honeywell Regulator Co. [*Later, HON*]
**MH** ........ Minnesota History [*A publication*]
**MH** ........ Miscellaneous Hardware
**MH** ........ Mishnaic Hebrew [*Language, etc.*] (BJA)
**MH** ........ Missionalia Hispanica [*A publication*]
**MH** ........ Mitsubishi Heavy Industries Ltd. [*Japan*] [*ICAO aircraft manufacturer identifier*] (ICAO)
**MH** ........ Mobile High-Power [*Reactor*] [*Proposed*] (NRCH)
**MH** ........ Mobility Haiti (EA)
**MH** ........ Molting Hormone [*Endocrinology, entomology*]
**MH** ........ Monde Hebdomadaire [*A publication*]
**MH** ........ Most High [*Freemasonry*]
**MH** ........ Most Honorable
**MH** ........ Mount Hood Railway Co. [*AAR code*]
**M-H** ........ Mueller-Hinton [*Agar*] [*Microbiology*]
**MH** ........ Multihandicapped
**MH** ........ Murine Hepatitis
**M & H** ........ Murphy and Hurlstone's English Exchequer Reports [*1836-37*] [*A publication*] (DLA)
**MH** ........ Museum Helveticum [*A publication*]
**MH** ........ Music Hall [*Record label*]
**MH** ........ Musichandel [*A publication*]
**MH** ........ Muzzle Hatch
**MH2** ........ Mary Hartman, Mary Hartman [*Initialism is shortened form of television program title*] [*Also, $M^2H^2$*]
***$M^2H^2$*** ........ *Mary Hartman, Mary Hartman [Initialism is shortened form of television program title]* [*Also, MH2*]
**MHA** ........ Hamline University, St. Paul, MN [*OCLC symbol*] (OCLC)
**MH-A** ........ Harvard University, Arnold Arboretum, Cambridge, MA [*Library symbol*] [*Library of Congress*] (LCLS)
**MHa** ........ Haverhill Public Library, Haverhill, MA [*Library symbol*] [*Library of Congress*] (LCLS)
**MHA** ........ Machinery Haulers Association Agent, Saint Paul MN [*STAC*]
**MHA** ........ Madonna House Apostolate [*Combermere, ON*] (EAIO)
**MHA** ........ Mahdia [*Guyana*] [*Airport symbol*] (OAG)
**MHA** ........ Man-Hour Accounting (NVT)
**MHA** ........ Marine Historical Association [*Later, MSM*] (EA)
**MHA** ........ Master of Health Administration
**MHA** ........ Master of Hospital Administration
**M of HA** .... Matrons of Hospitals Association (ROG)
**MHA** ........ Maximum Hypothetical Accident [*Nuclear energy*] (IEEE)
**MHA** ........ Mean Horizontal Acceleration
**MHA** ........ Medal for Humane Action [*Berlin Airlift, 1948-9*] [*Military decoration*]
**MHA** ........ Member of House of Assembly [*British*]
**MHA** ........ Mennonite Health Association (EA)
**MHA** ........ Mental Health Abstracts [*Database*] [*IFI/Plenum Data Co.*] [*Information service or system*] (CRD)
**MHA** ........ Mental Health Administration [*Later, ADAMHA*]
**MHA** ........ Mental Health Association [*Later, NMHA*] (EA)
**MHA** ........ Methionine Hydroxy Analog [*Poultry feed*]
**MHA** ........ Microangiopathic Hemolytic Anemia [*Medicine*]
**MHA** ........ Minehunter, Auxiliary [*Navy symbol*] [*Obsolete*]
**MHA** ........ Minimum Holding Altitude [*Aviation*]
**MHA** ........ Mixed Hemadsorption Assay [*Clinical chemistry*]
**MHA** ........ Modified Handling Authorized [*Air Force*]
**MHA** ........ Mormon History Association (EA)
**MH-AA** ..... Harvard University, Afro-American Studies, Lamont Undergraduate Library, Cambridge, MA [*Library symbol*] [*Library of Congress*] (LCLS)
**MHAC** ........ Man-Hour Accounting Card
**MH-AH** ..... Harvard University, Andover-Harvard Theological Library, Cambridge, MA [*Library symbol*] [*Library of Congress*] (LCLS)
**MHAM** ..... Amapala [*Honduras*] [*ICAO location identifier*] (ICLI)
**MHaNE** ..... Northern Essex Community College, Haverhill, MA [*Library symbol*] [*Library of Congress*] (LCLS)
**MHansAF** ... United States Air Force Research Library, Hanscom Air Force Base, Hanscom, MA [*Library symbol*] [*Library of Congress*] (LCLS)
**MH-AO** ..... Harvard University, Oakes Ames Orchid Library, Cambridge, MA [*Library symbol*] [*Library of Congress*] (LCLS)
**MH-Ar** ....... Harvard University Archives, Cambridge, MA [*Library symbol*] [*Library of Congress*] (LCLS)
**MHAR** ....... Memoires. Section Historique. Academie Roumaine [*A publication*]
**MH-AS** ...... Harvard University, George R. Agassiz Station, Cambridge, MA [*Library symbol*] [*Library of Congress*] (LCLS)
**MHAS** ....... Mental Health Advocacy Service [*Australia*]
**MHathD** .... Danvers State Hospital, Hathorne, MA [*Library symbol*] [*Library of Congress*] (LCLS)
**MHA-TP** ... Microhemagglutination Assay Treponema Pallidum [*Immunochemistry*]
**MHAUS** .... Malignant Hyperthermia Association of the United States (EA)
**MHB** ........ Maintenance Handbook
**MHB** ........ Mary Hardin-Baylor College, Belton, TX [*OCLC symbol*] (OCLC)
**MHB** ........ Master Horizontal Bomber
**MHB** ........ Maximum Hospital Benefit [*Insurance*]
**MHb** ........ Medial Habenular [*Neuroanatomy*]
**MHB** ........ Mennonite Historical Bulletin [*A publication*]
**MHb** ........ Methemoglobin [*Biochemistry, medicine*]
**MHB** ........ Military History Branch [*USMACV*]
**MHB** ........ Mine-Hauling Bogie [*Mining engineering*]
**MHB** ........ Mueller-Hinton Broth [*Cell growth medium*]
**MHB** ........ Museum Ha'aretz Bulletin [*Tel Aviv*] [*A publication*]
**MHb** ........ Myohemoglobin [*Hematology*]
**MH-BA** ..... Harvard University, Graduate School of Business Administration, Boston, MA [*Library symbol*] [*Library of Congress*] (LCLS)
**MHBA** ....... Morgan Horse Breeders Association [*Defunct*] (EA)
**MH-BH** ..... Harvard University, Blue Hill Meteorological Observatory, Cambridge, MA [*Library symbol*] [*Library of Congress*] (LCLS)
**MHBK** ....... Mid-Hudson Savings Bank FSB [*Fishkill, NY*] [*NASDAQ symbol*] (NQ)
**MH-BL** ...... Harvard University, Biological Laboratories, Cambridge, MA [*Library symbol*] [*Library of Congress*] (LCLS)
**MH-BM** .... Harvard University, George David Birkhoff Mathematics Library, Cambridge, MA [*Library symbol*] [*Library of Congress*] (LCLS)
**MHBM** ...... Modern Heavy Ballistic Missile (ADA)
**MHBN** ...... Mothers' Home Business Network (EA)
**MH-BR** ...... Harvard University, Busch-Reisinger Museum of Germanic Culture, Cambridge, MA [*Library symbol*] [*Library of Congress*] (LCLS)
**MHBRI** ..... Mental Health Book Review Index [*A publication*]
**MH-BS** ...... Harvard University, Biochemical Sciences Tutorial Library, Cambridge, MA [*Library symbol*] [*Library of Congress*] (LCLS)
**MHBSS** ..... Modified Hank's Balanced Salt Solution [*Cell culture*]
**MH-C** ........ Harvard University, Chemistry Library, Cambridge, MA [*Library symbol*] [*Library of Congress*] (LCLS)
**MHC** ........ Historical Committee of the Mennonite Church (EA)
**MHC** ........ MAD [*Magnetic Anomaly Detector*] Hunting Circle (NVT)
**MHC** ........ Madras High Court Reports [*India*] [*A publication*] (DLA)
**MHC** ........ Major Histocompatibility Complex [*Immunology*]
**MHC** ........ Manufacturers Hanover Corporation [*NYSE symbol*] (SPSG)
**MHC** ........ Mars Hill College [*North Carolina*]
**MHC** ........ Mary Holmes College, West Point, MS [*OCLC symbol*] (OCLC)
**MHC** ........ Material Handling Crane [*Autocrane*] (MCD)
**MHC** ........ Mean Horizontal Candle [*Aerospace*]
**MHC** ........ Mechanical-Hydraulic Control [*Nuclear energy*] (NRCH)
**MHC** ........ Mental Health Course [*British*]
**MHC** ........ Mild Hydrocracking [*Petroleum technology*]
**MHC** ........ Minehunter, Coastal [*Navy symbol*]
**MHC** ........ Mobile Housing Carriers Conference Inc., Arlington VA [*STAC*]
**MHC** ........ Modern Healthcare [*A publication*]
**MHC** ........ Moisture Holding Capacity
**MHC** ........ Morgan Horse Club [*Later, American Morgan Horse Association*] (EA)
**MHC** ........ Morris Harvey College [*West Virginia*]
**MHC** ........ Mount Hamilton [*Lick Observatory*] [*California*] [*Seismograph station code, US Geological Survey*] (SEIS)
**MHC** ........ Mount Holyoke College [*South Hadley, MA*]
**MHC** ........ Myosin Heavy Chain [*Muscle biology*]
**MHCA** ....... Catacamas [*Honduras*] [*ICAO location identifier*] (ICLI)
**MHCC** ....... Mobile Housing Carriers Conference [*Defunct*] (EA)
**MHCC** ....... Multipak Heliax Coaxial Cable

**MH-CE**...... Harvard University, Commission on Extension Courses, Cambridge, MA [*Library symbol*] [*Library of Congress*] (LCLS)
**MHCG**....... Comayagua [*Honduras*] [*ICAO location identifier*] (ICLI)
**MHCH**....... Choluteca [*Honduras*] [*ICAO location identifier*] (ICLI)
**Mh Chem**... Monatshefte fuer Chemie und Verwandte Teile Anderer Wissenschaften [*A publication*]
**MH-CI**....... Harvard University, Center for International Affairs, Semitic Museum, Cambridge, MA [*Library symbol*] [*Library of Congress*] (LCLS)
**MHCI**........ Maione Companies, Incorporated [*NASDAQ symbol*] (NQ)
**MHCIMA**... Member of the Hotel, Catering, and Institutional Management Association [*British*] (DBQ)
**MH-CL**...... Harvard University, Career Reference Library, Cambridge, MA [*Library symbol*] [*Library of Congress*] (LCLS)
**MH-CM**.... Harvard University, Child Memorial and English Tutorial Library, Cambridge, MA [*Library symbol*] [*Library of Congress*] (LCLS)
**MHCO**...... Marquette & Huron Mountain Railroad Company, Inc. [*AAR code*]
**MHCO**...... Mine-Hunting Control Officer (NATG)
**MHCO**...... Moore-Handley, Inc. [*Birmingham, AL*] [*NASDAQ symbol*] (NQ)
**MHCOA**.... Motor, Hearse, and Car Owners Association (EA)
**MH-CP**...... Harvard University, Center for Population Studies, Boston, MA [*Library symbol*] [*Library of Congress*] (LCLS)
**MHCP**....... Mean Horizontal Candlepower
**MHCR**....... Madras High Court Reports [*India*] [*A publication*] (DLA)
**MH-CS**...... Harvard University, Godfrey Lowell Cabot Science Library, Cambridge, MA [*Library symbol*] [*Library of Congress*] (LCLS)
**MHCS**....... Mental Hygiene Consultation Service
**M/hct**......... Microhematocrit [*Clinical chemistry*]
**MHCT**....... Puerto Castilla [*Honduras*] [*ICAO location identifier*] (ICLI)
**MHCU**....... Mental Health Care Unit [*Medicine*]
**MHC & W**... Mississippi, Hill City & Western Railroad
**MHD**......... Maandstatistiek van de Buitenlandse Handel per Land [*A publication*]
**MHD**......... Magnetohydrodynamics [*Electric power*]
**MHD**......... Maintenance Hemodialysis [*Nephrology*]
**MHD**......... Mashhad [*Iran*] [*Airport symbol*] (OAG)
**MHD**......... Masthead (MSA)
**MHD**......... Mechanized Hebrew Dictionary [*A publication*] (BJA)
**MHD**......... Medical Holding Detachment
**MHD**......... Medium Hard Drawn (MSA)
**MHD**......... Mental Health Department [*Medicine*]
**MHD**......... Mental Health Digest
**MHD**......... Meter Heading Differential
**MHD**......... Military History Detachment
**MHD**......... Minimum Hamming Distance [*Data processing*]
**MHD**......... Minimum Hemolytic Dose
**MHD**......... Moving Head Disk [*Data processing*] (TEL)
**MHD**......... Multihead Disk (NASA)
**M & HDA**... Medical and Hospital Department, Army
**MHDC**....... Magnetohydrodynamic Conversion [*Nuclear energy*] (NRCH)
**MHDF**....... Medium- and High-Frequency Direction-Finding Station
**MHDG**...... Magnetic Heading (FAAC)
**MHDI**........ Morgan Horse Development Institute (EA)
**MHDNA**.... Mobile Home Dealers National Association [*Defunct*]
**MHDPA**.... Monohexadecylphosphoric Acid [*Organic chemistry*]
**MHDSRIP**... May His Departed Soul Rest in Peace (BJA)
**MHE**.......... Manufacturers Hanover Economic Report [*A publication*]
**MHE**.......... Master of Home Economics
**MHE**.......... Materials Handling Equipment [*Military*] (AFM)
**MHE**.......... Mechanical Handling Equipment (MCD)
**MHE**.......... Mental Health Enquiry [*Medical/computing registers*] [*British*]
**MHE**.......... Middle East Economic Survey [*A publication*]
**MHE**.......... Missile Handling Equipment
**MHE**.......... Mitchell [*South Dakota*] [*Airport symbol*] (OAG)
**MHE**.......... Mitchell, SD [*Location identifier*] [*FAA*] (FAAL)
**MHE**.......... Multiple Headspace Extraction [*Analytical chemistry*]
**MHE**.......... Munitions Handling Equipment (MCD)
**MHE**.......... Muzzle Hatch Electrical
**MH-EA**...... Harvard University, East Asian Research Center, Cambridge, MA [*Library symbol*] [*Library of Congress*] (LCLS)
**MHealthAdmin**... Master of Health Administration (ADA)
**MHEANA**... Masonic Homes Executives' Association of North America (EA)
**MH-EB**...... Harvard University, Oakes Ames Library of Economic Botany, Cambridge, MA [*Library symbol*] [*Library of Congress*] (LCLS)
**MHeb**........ Middle Hebrew [*Language, etc.*] (BJA)
**MHEC**....... Muzzle Hatch Electrical Control
**MH-Ed**...... Harvard University, Graduate School of Education, Cambridge, MA [*Library symbol*] [*Library of Congress*] (LCLS)
**MHED**....... Magnetic Head Corp. [*NASDAQ symbol*] (NQ)
**MHEDA**.... Material Handling Equipment Distributors Association (EA)
**MHE Ed**.... Master of Home Economics Education
**MHEF**....... Milton H. Erickson Foundation (EA)
**MH-ER**...... Harvard University, East Asian Studies Reading Room, Cambridge, MA [*Library symbol*] [*Library of Congress*] (LCLS)
**MH-ES**...... Harvard University, Center for European Studies, Cambridge, MA [*Library symbol*] [*Library of Congress*] (LCLS)
**MHETA J**... Manitoba Home Economics Teachers' Association. Journal [*A publication*]
**MHEX**....... Methohexital [*An anesthetic*]
**MH-F**......... Harvard University, Farlow Reference Library, Cambridge, MA [*Library symbol*] [*Library of Congress*] (LCLS)
**MHF**.......... Master History File
**MHF**.......... Materialy do Historii Filozofii Stredniowiecznej w Polsce [*A publication*]
**MHF**.......... Medium-High Frequency
**MHF**.......... Meridian House Foundation [*Later, MHI*]
**MHF**.......... Microsillon et Haute-Fidelite [*Record label*] [*France*]
**MHF**.......... Mixed Hydrazine Fuel
**MHF**.......... Monuments Historiques de la France [*A publication*]
**MHF**.......... Municipal High Income Fund, Inc. [*NYSE symbol*] (CTT)
**MHF**.......... Myosin Head Fragment [*Biochemistry*]
**MHF**.......... Smith Point, TX [*Location identifier*] [*FAA*] (FAAL)
**MH-FA**...... Harvard University, Fine Arts Library, Cambridge, MA [*Library symbol*] [*Library of Congress*] (LCLS)
**MHFA**....... Multiple Conductor, Heat and Flame Resistant, Armor [*Cable*]
**MHFB**....... Mental Health Film Board (EA)
**MHFC**....... Merle Haggard Fan Club (EA)
**MHFPR**..... Maximum Hypothetical Fission Product Release [*Nuclear energy*] (NRCH)
**MHFR**....... Maximum Hypothetical Fission Product Release [*Nuclear energy*] (NRCH)
**MHFR**....... Military Height-Finder RADAR Equipment (FAAC)
**MHFWPR**... Mental Health Fieldwork Performance Report [*Occupational therapy*]
**MH-G**........ Harvard University, Gray Herbarium, Cambridge, MA [*Library symbol*] [*Library of Congress*] (LCLS)
**MHG**......... Malartic Hygrade Gold Mines Ltd. [*AMEX symbol*] (SPSG)
**MHG**......... Mannheim [*West Germany*] [*Airport symbol*] (OAG)
**MHG**......... MDS Health Group Ltd. [*Toronto Stock Exchange symbol*]
**MHG**......... Middle High German [*Language, etc.*]
**MHG**......... Midrash ha-Gadol (BJA)
**MHG**......... Miniature Hydrogen Generator
**MHG**......... Mitteilungen. E. T. A. Hoffman-Gesellschaft [*A publication*]
**MHG**......... Modern High German [*Language, etc.*] (ROG)
**MH-GG**..... Harvard University, Committee on Experimental Geology and Geophysics, Hoffman Laboratory, Cambridge, MA [*Library symbol*] [*Library of Congress*] (LCLS)
**MH-GI**...... Harvard University, Hamilton A. R. Gibb Islamic Seminar, Cambridge, MA [*Library symbol*] [*Library of Congress*] (LCLS)
**MH-GM**.... Harvard University, Gordon McKay Library, Cambridge, MA [*Library symbol*] [*Library of Congress*] (LCLS)
**MH-GS**...... Harvard University, Geological Sciences Library, Cambridge, MA [*Library symbol*] [*Library of Congress*] (LCLS)
**MH-H**........ Harvard University, Houghton Library, Cambridge, MA [*Library symbol*] [*Library of Congress*] (LCLS)
**MHH**......... Mandala Holistic Health [*Inactive*] (EA)
**MH-H**........ Mare Humorum-Helmet [*Lunar area*]
**MHH**......... Marsh Harbour [*Bahamas*] [*Airport symbol*] (OAG)
**MH-HD**..... Harvard University, History Department Library, Cambridge, MA [*Library symbol*] [*Library of Congress*] (LCLS)
**MH-HF**..... Harvard University, Harvard Forest Library, Petersham, MA [*Library symbol*] [*Library of Congress*] (LCLS)
**MH-Hi**....... Harvard University, Hilles Library of Radcliffe College, Cambridge, MA [*Library symbol*] [*Library of Congress*] (LCLS)
**MHHI**....... Multihandicapped Hearing-Impaired
**MH-HJ**..... Harvard University, Arnold Arboretum, Horticultural Library, Jamaica Plain, MA [*Library symbol*] [*Library of Congress*] (LCLS)
**MH-HO**.... Harvard University, Lucien Howe Library of Ophthalmology, Boston, MA [*Library symbol*] [*Library of Congress*] (LCLS)
**MH-HP**..... Harvard University, Center for Analysis of Health Practices, Cambridge, MA [*Library symbol*] [*Library of Congress*] (LCLS)
**MH-HS**..... Harvard University, History of Science Library, Cambridge, MA [*Library symbol*] [*Library of Congress*] (LCLS)
**MHHS**....... Medal of Honor Historical Society (EA)
**MHHW**..... Mean Higher High Water [*Tides and currents*]
**MHHWS**... Mean Higher High-Water Springs [*Tides and currents*]
**MH-HY**..... Harvard University, Harvard-Yenching Library, Cambridge, MA [*Library symbol*] [*Library of Congress*] (LCLS)
**MHI**.......... Manufactured Housing Institute (EA)
**MHI**.......... Marine Hydrophysical Institute
**MHI**.......... Mashhad [*Iran*] [*Seismograph station code, US Geological Survey*] (SEIS)
**MHi**........... Massachusetts Historical Society, Boston, MA [*Library symbol*] [*Library of Congress*] (LCLS)
**MHI**.......... Material Handling Institute (EA)
**MHI**.......... Mental Health Institute (OICC)
**MHI**.......... Meridian House International (EA)

**MHI** Military History Institute [*Army*] (MCD)

**MHI** Mitsubishi Heavy Industries Ltd.

**MHI** Morgan Hydrocarbons, Inc. [*Toronto Stock Exchange symbol*]

**MHIA** Mitsubishi Heavy Industries America, Inc.

**MHIC** Islas Del Cisne O Santanilla [*Honduras*] [*ICAO location identifier*] (ICLI)

**MHID** Medical and Health Information Directory [*A publication*]

**MHIDAS** Major Hazard Incident Data Service [*Atomic Energy Authority*] [*Great Britain*] [*Information service or system*] (IID)

**M Hi E** Master of Highway Engineering

**M Hi Eng** Master of Highway Engineering

**MHIFC** Michael Harding International Fan Club (EA)

**MHIFM** Milton Helpern Institute of Forensic Medicine (EA)

**MHILC** Hampshire Inter-Library Center, Inc., Amherst, MA [*Library symbol*] [*Library of Congress*] [*Obsolete*] (LCLS)

**MHingM** Hingham Marine Museum, Hingham, MA [*Library symbol*] [*Library of Congress*] (LCLS)

**MHis** Mundo Hispanico [*A publication*]

**M of Hist** Magazine of History [*A publication*]

**M Hist Ver Pfalz** Mitteilungen des Historischen Vereins der Pfalz [*A publication*]

**MHJ** Malayan Historical Journal [*A publication*]

**MHJ** Medizin-Historisches Journal [*A publication*]

**MHJ** Melbourne Historical Journal [*A publication*] (APTA)

**MHJ** Microwave Hybrid Junction

**MHJ** Monumenta Hungariae Judaica [*A publication*]

**MHJU** Juticalpa [*Honduras*] [*ICAO location identifier*] (ICLI)

**MHK** Manhattan [*Kansas*] [*Seismograph station code, US Geological Survey*] (SEIS)

**MHK** Manhattan [*Kansas*] [*Airport symbol*] (OAG)

**MHK** Manhattan, KS [*Location identifier*] [*FAA*] (FAAL)

**MHK** Member of the House of Keys [*Isle Of Man*] [*British*]

**MHK** Military History of Korea

**MHK** Minimale Hemmkonzentration [*Minimum Inhibiting Concentration*] [*German*]

**MH-KG** Harvard University, Kennedy School of Government, Cambridge, MA [*Library symbol*] [*Library of Congress*] (LCLS)

**MH-KM** Harvard University, Kennedy Inter-Faculty Program in Medical Ethics, Cambridge, MA [*Library symbol*] [*Library of Congress*] (LCLS)

**MHKVLY** Mohawk Valley [*FAA*] (FAAC)

**MHL** Hamline University, School of Law, St. Paul, MN [*OCLC symbol*] (OCLC)

**MH-L** Harvard University, Law School, Cambridge, MA [*Library symbol*] [*Library of Congress*] (LCLS)

**M (HL)** House of Lords' Appeals, in Macpherson's Court of Sessions Cases, Third Series [*1862-73*] [*Scotland*] [*A publication*] (DLA)

**MHL** March Resources [*Vancouver Stock Exchange symbol*]

**MHL** Marshall Islands [*ANSI three-letter standard code*] (CNC)

**MHL** Marshall, MO [*Location identifier*] [*FAA*] (FAAL)

**MHL** Mast Hull Loop

**MHL** Master of Hebrew Letters (BJA)

**MHL** Master of Hebrew Literature

**MHL** Master of Humane Letters

**MHL** Metastable Helium Level

**MHL** Microprocessor Host Loader [*Electronics*]

**MHL** Minimum Helium Loss [*System*]

**MHL** Mitteilungen. Bundesstelle fuer Aussenhandelsinformation [*A publication*]

**MHL** Mitteilungen aus der Historischen Literatur [*A publication*]

**MHL** Modern Hebrew Literature [*A publication*]

**MHLC** La Ceiba/Goloson Internacional [*Honduras*] [*ICAO location identifier*] (ICLI)

**MHLC** Multidimensional Health Locus of Control [*Diagnostic scale*]

**MHLE** La Esperanza [*Honduras*] [*ICAO location identifier*] (ICLI)

**MH-Li** Harvard University, Linguistics Library, Cambridge, MA [*Library symbol*] [*Library of Congress*] (LCLS)

**MHLLDA** Mobile Home Landscapers and Landscape Designers Association (EA)

**MH-Lm** Harvard University, Lamont Undergraduate Library, Cambridge, MA [*Library symbol*] [*Library of Congress*] (LCLS)

**MHLM** San Pedro Sula/La Mesa Internacional [*Honduras*] [*ICAO location identifier*] (ICLI)

**MHLP** Mental Health Law Project (EA)

**MHLS** Metabolic Heat Load Simulator

**MHLS** Mid-Hudson Language Studies [*A publication*]

**MHLS** Mid-Hudson Library System [*Library network*]

**MHLTA** Men's Hat Linings and Trimmings Association [*Defunct*] (EA)

**MHLW** Mean Higher Low Water [*Tides and currents*]

**MHM** Maryland Historical Magazine [*A publication*]

**MHM** Michigan History Magazine [*A publication*]

**MHM** Mill Hill Missionaries [*Roman Catholic men's religious order*]

**MHM** Minchumina, AK [*Location identifier*] [*FAA*] (FAAL)

**MHM** Minimum Hardware Modification [*Aircraft landing*]

**MHM** Mount Hope Mineral Railroad Co. [*Absorbed into Consolidated Rail Corp.*] [*AAR code*]

**MHM** Muzzle Hatch Mechanical

**MHMA** Marcala [*Honduras*] [*ICAO location identifier*] (ICLI)

**MHMA** Mobile Home Manufacturers Association [*Later, Manufactured Housing Institute*]

**MHMC** Mental Health Materials Center (EA)

**MH-ME** Harvard University, Center for Middle Eastern Studies, Cambridge, MA [*Library symbol*] [*Library of Congress*] (LCLS)

**MH-MH** Harvard University, John Peabody Monks Library, Cambridge, MA [*Library symbol*] [*Library of Congress*] (LCLS)

**MH-ML** Harvard University, Ticknor Library of Modern Languages, Cambridge, MA [*Library symbol*] [*Library of Congress*] (LCLS)

**MHMS** Master of Human Movement Studies (ADA)

**MH-Mu** Harvard University, Music Library, Cambridge, MA [*Library symbol*] [*Library of Congress*] (LCLS)

**MHN** Manhattan Mineral [*Vancouver Stock Exchange symbol*]

**MHN** Mannitol Hexanitrate [*Organic chemistry*]

**MHN** McGraw-Hill News [*Database*] (IT)

**MHN** Mullen, NE [*Location identifier*] [*FAA*] (FAAL)

**MHNAMT** Methyl(hydroxylnaphthalamino)mercaptotriazole [*Organic chemistry*]

**MH-NE** Harvard University, Near Eastern Languages and Literatures Library, Cambridge, MA [*Library symbol*] [*Library of Congress*] (LCLS)

**MHNGS** Marble Hill Nuclear Generating Station (NRCH)

**MHNJ** Guanaja [*Honduras*] [*ICAO location identifier*] (ICLI)

**MH-NJ** Harvard University, Nieman Collection of Contemporary Journalism, Cambridge, MA [*Library symbol*] [*Library of Congress*] (LCLS)

**MHNPS** Marble Hill Nuclear Power Station (NRCH)

**MHNV** Nuevo Ocotepeque [*Honduras*] [*ICAO location identifier*] (ICLI)

**MH-O** Harvard University, Harvard College Observatory, Cambridge, MA [*Library symbol*] [*Library of Congress*] (LCLS)

**MHO** Maandblad voor het Handelsonderwijs [*A publication*]

**MHO** Manchester Resources Corp. [*Vancouver Stock Exchange symbol*]

**MHO** Mount Hopkins Observatory [*Later, FLWO*] [*Smithsonian Institution*] (GRD)

**mho** Reciprocal Ohm [*Unit of conductance*]

**MHOA** Olanchito [*Honduras*] [*ICAO location identifier*] (ICLI)

**M Ho Ec** Master of Household Economy

**MHOF** Mobile Home Owners Federation [*Superseded by NFMHO*] (EA)

**MHoly** Holyoke Public Library, Holyoke, MA [*Library symbol*] [*Library of Congress*] (LCLS)

**MHolyC** Holyoke Community College, Holyoke, MA [*Library symbol*] [*Library of Congress*] (LCLS)

**MHOM** Medical Homecare, Inc. [*NASDAQ symbol*] (NQ)

**M Hor** Master of Horticulture

**MHort(RHS)** National Diploma in Horticulture (Royal Horticultural Society) [*British*] (DBQ)

**MHortSc** Master of Horticultural Science

**MHOSA** Mental Hospitals [*A publication*]

**M Ho Sc** Master of Household Science

**MHP** Bedrijfskunde Tijdschrift voor Management [*A publication*]

**MH-P** Harvard University, Peabody Museum, Cambridge, MA [*Library symbol*] [*Library of Congress*] (LCLS)

**MHP** Maclean Hunter Ltd. [*Toronto Stock Exchange symbol*]

**MHP** Master of Health Planning (ADA)

**MHP** Materials Handling and Packaging [*A publication*] (APTA)

**MHP** McGraw-Hill, Inc. [*NYSE symbol*] (SPSG)

**MHP** Medium-High Pressure (MSA)

**MHP** Mental Health Project

**MHP** Mercurihydroxypropane [*Clinical chemistry*]

**MHP** Message Handling Processor

**MHP** Metabolic Heat Production [*Physiology*]

**MHP** Milli Hedef Partisi [*National Goal Party*] [*Turkish Cyprus*] [*Political party*] (PPE)

**MH-PA** Harvard University, Littauer Library of the Kennedy School of Government, Cambridge, MA [*Library symbol*] [*Library of Congress*] (LCLS)

**MHPA** Palmerola [*Honduras*] [*ICAO location identifier*] (ICLI)

**MH-PC** Harvard University, Palaeography Library, Cambridge, MA [*Library symbol*] [*Library of Congress*] (LCLS)

**MHPD** Masonite Hydropress Die (MSA)

**MHPE** Progreso [*Honduras*] [*ICAO location identifier*] (ICLI)

**MHPEd** Master of Health Personnel Education (ADA)

**MH PE & R** Master of Health, Physical Education, and Recreation

**MHPG** (Methoxyhydroxyphenyl)ethyleneglycol [*Also, MOPEG*] [*Organic chemistry*]

**MHPH** Man-Hours per Flying Hour [*Air Force*] (AFIT)

**MHPI** MHP Machines, Incorporated [*Cheektowaga, NY*] [*NASDAQ symbol*] (NQ)

**MH-PL** Harvard University, Milman Parry Collection of Oral Literature, Cambridge, MA [*Library symbol*] [*Library of Congress*] (LCLS)

**MHPL** Puerto Lempira [*Honduras*] [*ICAO location identifier*] (ICLI)

**MH-PO** Harvard University, Personnel Office Library, Cambridge, MA [*Library symbol*] [*Library of Congress*] (LCLS)

**MH-PP** Harvard University, Public Policy Program, Cambridge, MA [*Library symbol*] [*Library of Congress*] (LCLS)

**MH-PR**...... Harvard University, Physics Research Library, Cambridge, MA [*Library symbol*] [*Library of Congress*] (LCLS)
**MH-Ps**....... Harvard University, Psychology Research Library, Cambridge, MA [*Library symbol*] [*Library of Congress*] (LCLS)
**MHPU**....... Puerto Cortes [*Honduras*] [*ICAO location identifier*] (ICLI)
**MHQ**......... Mariehamn [*Finland*] [*Airport symbol*] (OAG)
**MHQ**......... Maritime Headquarters (NVT)
**MHQ**......... Military History Quarterly [*A publication*]
**MH-R**........ Harvard University, Russian Research Center, Cambridge, MA [*Library symbol*] [*Library of Congress*] (LCLS)
**MHR**......... Major Histocompatibility Region [*Immunology*]
**MHR**......... Man-Hour
**MHR**......... Maximum Heart Rate
**MHR**......... McGraw-Hill Ryerson Ltd. [*Toronto Stock Exchange symbol*]
**MHR**......... Measurement Handicap Rule [*Sailing*]
**MHR**......... Member of the House of Representatives
**MHR**......... Microwave Hologram RADAR
**MHR**......... Miniature Helium Refrigerator
**MHR**......... Missile Hazard Report (AFM)
**MHR**......... Missouri Historical Review [*A publication*]
**MHR**......... Mount Hamilton Road [*California*] [*Seismograph station code, US Geological Survey*] (SEIS)
**MHr**.......... Myohemerythrin [*Biochemistry*]
**MHR**......... Sacramento, CA [*Location identifier*] [*FAA*] (FAAL)
**MHR**......... United States Army Military History Institute, Carlisle Barracks, PA [*OCLC symbol*] (OCLC)
**MH-RA**..... Harvard University, Harvard Radio Astronomy Center, Fort Davis, TX [*Library symbol*] [*Library of Congress*] (LCLS)
**MHRA**....... Modern Humanities Research Association [*A publication*]
**MHRA**....... Modern Humanities Research Association, American Branch (EA)
**MHRA**....... Morab Horse Registry of America (EA)
**MHRA Bull**... Modern Humanities Research Association. Bulletin [*A publication*]
**MHRAC**.... Mine Health Research Advisory Committee [*National Institute for Occupational Safety and Health*] [*Morgantown, WV*] (EGAO)
**MHRADS**... Modern Humanities Research Association. Dissertation Series [*A publication*]
**MH-RB**...... Harvard University, Rubel Asiatic Research Bureau, Fogg Art Museum, Cambridge, MA [*Library symbol*] [*Library of Congress*] [*Obsolete*] (LCLS)
**MH-RC**..... Harvard University, Fred N. Robinson Celtic Seminar, Cambridge, MA [*Library symbol*] [*Library of Congress*] (LCLS)
**MHRev**...... Malahat Review [*A publication*]
**MHRI**........ Mental Health Research Institute [*University of Michigan*] [*Research center*]
**MHRKg**..... Monatshefte fuer Rheinische Kirchengeschichte [*A publication*]
**MHRM**...... Microcomputers in Human Resource Management [*Advanced Personnel Systems*] [*Information service or system*] (CRD)
**MH-RP**...... Harvard University, Robbins Library of Philosophy, Cambridge, MA [*Library symbol*] [*Library of Congress*] (LCLS)
**MHRS**....... Magnetic Heading Reference System
**MHRST**.... Medical and Health Related Sciences Thesaurus [*A publication*] (IEEE)
**MHRT**....... Mental Health Review Tribunal [*British*]
**MHRU**...... Ruinas De Copan [*Honduras*] [*ICAO location identifier*] (ICLI)
**MHRV**....... Movement for Human Rights in Vietnam (EA)
**MH-S**......... Harvard University, Statistics Library, Cambridge, MA [*Library symbol*] [*Library of Congress*] (LCLS)
**MHS**.......... Machined Hemispherical Shell
**MHS**.......... Magnetic Heading System (AAG)
**MHS**.......... Magnetomotive Hammer System
**MHS**.......... Maher, Inc. [*Toronto Stock Exchange symbol*]
**MHS**.......... Mail Handling System [*Data processing*]
**MHS**.......... Major Histocompatibility System [*Immunology*]
**MHS**.......... Malignant Hyperthermia Susceptible [*Medicine*]
**MHS**.......... Mammoth Hot Springs [*Wyoming*] [*Seismograph station code, US Geological Survey*] (SEIS)
**MHS**.......... Man-Hours per Sortie [*Air Force*] (AFIT)
**MHS**.......... Marine Hospital Service [*Public Health Service*]
**MHS**.......... Marriott Corp. [*NYSE symbol*] (SPSG)
**MHS**.......... Master Hotel Supplier [*Designation awarded by Educational Institute of the American Hotel and Motel Association*]
**MHS**.......... McMaster University Health Sciences Library [*UTLAS symbol*]
**MHS**.......... Measurement Handicapping System [*Yacht racing*]
**MHS**.......... Mechanical Handling System
**MHS**.......... Melanges d'Histoire Sociale [*A publication*]
**MHS**.......... Member of the Historical Society
**MHS**.......... Message Handling System [*Data processing*]
**MHS**.......... Methylhydrazine Sulfate [*Organic chemistry*]
**M/H/S**...... Miles per Hour per Second
**MHS**.......... Military Historical Society [*Defunct*] (EA)
**MHS**.......... Ministry of Home Security [*British*]
**MHS**.......... Minnesota Historical Society, St. Paul, MN [*OCLC symbol*] (OCLC)
**MHS**.......... Missile Hazard Space (AFM)
**MHS**.......... Moravian Historical Society (EA)
**MHS**.......... Moravian Historical Society. Transactions [*A publication*]
**MHS**.......... Mount Shasta, CA [*Location identifier*] [*FAA*] (FAAL)
**MHS**.......... Multiple Hospital System
**MHS**.......... Multiple Host Support
**MHS**.......... Musical Heritage Society [*Commercial firm*] (EA)
**MHS**.......... Sisters of the Most Holy Sacrament [*Roman Catholic religious order*]
**MHSB**....... Missouri Historical Society. Bulletin [*A publication*]
**MH-SC**...... Harvard University, Herbert Weir Smyth Classical Library, Cambridge, MA [*Library symbol*] [*Library of Congress*] (LCLS)
**MHSC**....... Manipulator Handset Controller (MCD)
**MHSC**....... Mental Health Study Center [*National Institute of Mental Health*] (GRD)
**MHSch**...... Monatsschrift fuer Hoehere Schulen [*A publication*]
**MHSCP**..... Mean Hemispherical Candlepower
**MH-SD**...... Harvard University, Graduate School of Design, Cambridge, MA [*Library symbol*] [*Library of Congress*] (LCLS)
**MHSDC**.... Multiple High-Speed Data Channel
**MH-SF**...... Harvard University, Schering Foundation Library, Boston, MA [*Library symbol*] [*Library of Congress*] (LCLS)
**MHSH**....... Mission Helpers of the Sacred Heart [*Roman Catholic women's religious order*]
**MH-SI**....... Harvard University, Program for Science and International Affairs Library, Cambridge, MA [*Library symbol*] [*Library of Congress*] (LCLS)
**MHSJ**........ Monumenta Historica Societatis Jesu [*A publication*]
**MH-SL**...... Harvard University, Sanskrit Library, Cambridge, MA [*Library symbol*] [*Library of Congress*] (LCLS)
**MHSLN**.... Midwest Health Science Library Network [*Library network*]
**MHSO**....... Masada, the Holocaust Survivors Organization (EA)
**MH-SP**...... Harvard University, Science and Public Police Program Library, Cambridge, MA [*Library symbol*] [*Library of Congress*] (LCLS)
**MHSP**....... San Pedro Sula [*Honduras*] [*ICAO location identifier*] (ICLI)
**MH-SR**...... Harvard University, Social Relations Library, Cambridge, MA [*Library symbol*] [*Library of Congress*] (LCLS)
**MHSR**....... Santa Rosa De Copan [*Honduras*] [*ICAO location identifier*] (ICLI)
**MHSS**....... Materials Handling Support System [*Military*] (AFM)
**MHSS**....... Mental Health Special Interest Section [*American Occupational Therapy Association*]
**MHSS(NI)**... Ministry of Health and Social Services (Northern Ireland)
**MHSSRI**... Michigan Health and Social Security Research Institute [*Detroit, MI*] [*Research center*] (RCD)
**MHSTB**..... Mental Handicap Staff Training Board [*British*]
**MHSV**....... Multipurpose High-Speed Vehicle (MCD)
**MHSZ**....... Santa Barbara [*Honduras*] [*ICAO location identifier*] (ICLI)
**MHT**.......... Maghemite, Inc. [*Vancouver Stock Exchange symbol*]
**MHT**.......... Manchester [*New Hampshire*] [*Airport symbol*] (OAG)
**MHT**.......... Manchester, NH [*Location identifier*] [*FAA*] (FAAL)
**MHT**.......... Manhattan [*Kansas*] [*Seismograph station code, US Geological Survey*] [*Closed*] (SEIS)
**MHT**.......... Manhattan Industries, Inc. [*NYSE symbol*] (SPSG)
**MHT**.......... Manufacturers Hanover Trust Co. [*of Manufacturers Hanover Corp.*] [*Nickname: "Manny Hanny"*]
**MHT**.......... Mean High Tide [*Tides and currents*]
**MHT**.......... Metalworking Production [*A publication*]
**MHT**.......... Methyl(hydroxyethyl)thiazole [*Organic chemistry*]
**MHT**.......... Meyer Hydraulic Theory
**MHT**.......... Mild Heat Treatment (IEEE)
**MHT**.......... Missile Handling Trailer (AAG)
**MHT**.......... Museum of History and Technology [*Smithsonian Institution*]
**MHTA**....... Molten High-Temperature Alloy
**MHTE**....... Tela [*Honduras*] [*ICAO location identifier*] (ICLI)
**MHTF**....... Manufactured Housing Task Force [*Inactive*] (EA)
**MHT Financ**... Manufacturers Hanover Trust Co. Financial Digest [*A publication*]
**MHTG**....... Marine Helicopter Training Group (NVT)
**MHTG**....... Tegucigalpa/Toncontin Internacional [*Honduras*] [*ICAO location identifier*] (ICLI)
**MHTGR**.... Modular High-Temperature Gas Reactor [*Nuclear energy*]
**Mh Tierheilk**... Monatshefte fuer Tierheilkunde [*A publication*]
**MHTJ**........ Trujillo [*Honduras*] [*ICAO location identifier*] (ICLI)
**MHTL**....... Motorola High-Threshold Logic
**MHTRA**.... Metal Science and Heat Treatment of Metals [*English Translation*] [*A publication*]
**MHTS**....... Main Heat Transport System [*Nuclear energy*] (NRCH)
**MHTTA**.... Member of the Highway and Traffic Technicians Association [*British*] (DBQ)
**MHTV**....... Manned Hypersonic Test Vehicle (MCD)
**MHU**......... Marketing in Hungary [*A publication*]
**M Hu**......... Master of Humanities
**MHU**......... Material Handling Unit (AFIT)
**MHUD**...... Monocular Heads-Up Display [*Aviation*]
**MHuGH**.... John H. Glenn High School, Huntington, NY [*Library symbol*] [*Library of Congress*] (LCLS)
**M Hum**...... Master of Humanities
**MHum**....... Mediaevalia et Humanistica [*A publication*]

**MH-UR**..... Harvard University, Ukrainian Research Institute Reference Library, Cambridge, MA [*Library symbol*] [*Library of Congress*] (LCLS)
**MHV**......... Magnetic Heart Vector [*Cardiology*]
**MHV**......... Manned Hypersonic Vehicle
**MHV**......... Mean Horizontal Velocity
**MHV**......... Miniature Homing Vehicle [*Missile*]
**MHV**......... Mojave, CA [*Location identifier*] [*FAA*] (FAAL)
**MHV**......... Mouse Hepatitis Virus
**MHV**......... Murine Hepatitis Virus
**MHVDF**.... Medium-, High-, and Very-High-Frequency Direction-Finding Station
**Mh VetMed** ... Monatshefte fuer Veterinaermedizin [*A publication*]
**MHVP**....... Mitteilungen des Historischen Vereins der Pfalz [*A publication*]
**MHVPS**..... Manual High-Voltage Power Supply
**MHW**........ Mean High Water [*Tides and currents*]
**MHW**........ Ministry of Health and Welfare [*Japan*]
**MHW**........ Morgan, H. W., Los Angeles CA [*STAC*]
**MHW**........ Multihundred Watt
**MH-WA**.... Harvard University, Charles Warren Center for Studies in American History, Cambridge, MA [*Library symbol*] [*Library of Congress*] (LCLS)
**MHWI**....... Mean High-Water Lunitidal Interval [*Tides and currents*]
**MHWLR**... Mobile Hostile Weapon Locating RADAR (NATG)
**MHWN**..... Mean High-Water Neap [*Tides and currents*]
**MHWS**...... Mean High-Water Springs [*Tides and currents*]
**MHX**........ Mine Hunter Experimental
**MHy**.......... Hyannis Public Library, Hyannis, MA [*Library symbol*] [*Library of Congress*] (LCLS)
**M Hy**......... Master of Hygiene
**MHY**......... Morehead [*Papua New Guinea*] [*Airport symbol*] (OAG)
**M Hyg**........ Master of Hygiene
**MHYPDB**... Medical Hypnoanalysis [*A publication*]
**MHyT**........ State Teachers' College, Hyannis, MA [*Library symbol*] [*Library of Congress*] [*Obsolete*] (LCLS)
**MH-Z**........ Harvard University, Museum of Comparative Zoology, Cambridge, MA [*Library symbol*] [*Library of Congress*] (LCLS)
**MHz**........... Megahertz [*Megacycles per Second*] [*See also MCPS, MCS, MC/S, MH*]
**MI**............. Lab. Miquel [*Spain*] [*Research code symbol*]
**MI**............. Mach Indicated
**MI**............. Machine Independent
**MI**............. Mackey International, Inc. [*USA*] [*ICAO designator*] (OAG)
**MI**............. Madras Infantry [*British*]
**MI**............. Magazine Index [*Information Access Corp.*] [*Information service or system*] (IID)
**MI**............. Maintenance Instruction (AAG)
**MI**............. Major Issue (MCD)
**MI**............. Major Item [*Military*]
**MI**............. Malachi [*Old Testament book*] (BJA)
**MI**............. Malleable Iron
**MI**............. Man in India [*A publication*]
**MI**............. Management Index [*A publication*]
**MI**............. Management Information (CAAL)
**MI**............. Management Intern
**M & I**......... Manpower and Immigration [*Canada*]
**MI**............. Manual Individual [*Nuclear energy*] (NRCH)
**MI**............. Manual Input [*Data processing*]
**MI**............. Manufacturing Index (MCD)
**MI**............. Manufacturing Industries [*Department of Employment*] [*British*]
**MI**............. Manufacturing Inspector (FAAC)
**MI**............. Manufacturing Instruction (MSA)
**MI**............. Marconi Industries [*General Electric Co.*] [*British*]
**MI**............. Mare Imbrium [*Sea of Showers*] [*Lunar area*]
**MI**............. Mare Island, California [*Site of naval base*]
**MI**............. Marginal Income [*Economics*]
**M & I**......... Marine & Industrial
**MI**............. Marine Insurance
**MI**............. Market Identifiers [*Dun's Marketing Services*] [*Database*]
**MI**............. Market Investigation [*Army*]
**MI**............. Marketing Insights [*A publication*]
**M & I**......... Marshall & Ilsley Bank
**MI**............. Marshall Industries [*NYSE symbol*] (SPSG)
**MI**............. Marshall Islands
**MI**............. Marubeni International Finance [*Trading company*] [*Japan*]
**MI**............. Master Index
**MI**............. Master Item (MSA)
**MI**............. Match Institute [*Defunct*] (EA)
**MI**............. Material Inspection [*Navy*]
**MI**............. Meat Inspection Division [*of ARS, Department of Agriculture*]
**MI**............. Mechanical Impedance
**M/I**........... Mechanical Impulse (KSC)
**MI**............. Meconium Ileus [*Medicine*]
**MI**............. Medical Illustrator
**MI**............. Medical Inspection
**MI**............. Medium Intensity (MSA)
**MI**............. Melanophore Index [*Biology*]
**MI**............. Mellon Institute [*Carnegie-Mellon University*] [*Research center*] (RCD)
**MI**............. Meloidogyne incognita [*A nematode*]
**MI**............. Memorial Inscription
**MI**............. Memory Interface
**MI**............. Mensa International [*London, England*] (EAIO)
**MI**............. Menstrual Induction [*Medicine*]
**MI**............. Mental Illness
**MI**............. (Mercaptoethyl)trimethylammonium Iodide [*Pharmacology*]
**MI**............. Merritt Island [*Florida*] [*NASA*] (KSC)
**MI**............. Mesha Inscription (BJA)
**MI**............. Mesioincisal [*Dentistry*]
**MI**............. Meso-Inositol [*or Myoinositol*] [*Organic chemistry*]
**MI**............. Metabolic Index
**MI**............. Metastases below the Head and Neck [*Oncology*]
**MI**............. Method Index [*British police term*]
**MI**............. Methylindole [*Organic chemistry*]
**M-I**........... Metro-International Program Services of New York (EA)
**Mi**............. Mica [*A mineral*]
**Mi**............. Micah [*Old Testament book*]
**MI**............. Michigan [*Postal code*]
**MI**............. Michigan Reports [*A publication*] (DLA)
**Mi**............. Michigan State Library, Lansing, MI [*Library symbol*] [*Library of Congress*] (LCLS)
**MI**............. Microinstruction [*Data processing*]
**MI**............. Micru International (EA)
**MI**............. Middle Initial
**MI**............. Middle Iron Age (BJA)
**MI**............. Migration Index [*Immunology*]
**MI**............. Migration Inhibition [*Cytology*]
**MI**............. Mil [*USSR*] [*ICAO aircraft manufacturer identifier*] (ICAO)
**MI**............. Mile
**MI**............. Military Institute
**MI**............. Military Intelligence [*Army*]
**MI**............. Military Internee
**MI**............. Military Item
**MI**............. Militia Mariae Immaculatae [*Militia of the Immaculate*] (EAIO)
**MI**............. Mill
**MI**............. Miller Integrator
**Mi**............. Mind [*A publication*]
**MI**............. Mineral Insulated [*Cable*] (NRCH)
**MI**............. Miniaturized Instrumentation (MCD)
**M/I**........... Minimum Impulse (KSC)
**M of I**........ Ministry of Information [*British*] [*World War II*]
**MI**............. Ministry of Information [*British*] [*World War II*]
**M & I**......... Minnesota & International Railway
**MI**............. Minor (ROG)
**MI**............. Minority Institution
**MI**............. Minority Interest [*Business term*]
**MI**............. Minute (ADA)
**Mi**............. Mishnah [*Basis of the Talmud*] (BJA)
**MI**............. Missed Interception [*Military*]
**MI**............. Missile (CINC)
**MI**............. Missile Industry (AAG)
**Mi**............. Missiology [*A publication*]
**MI**............. Mission Independent [*NASA*]
**MI**............. Mississippi [*Obsolete*] (ROG)
**MI**............. Missouri-Illinois Railroad Co. [*AAR code*]
**MI**............. Missouri School Music Magazine [*A publication*]
**Mi**............. Mitomycin C [*Also, MMC, MTC*] [*Antineoplastic drug*]
**MI**............. Mitotic Indices [*Cytology*]
**MI**............. Mitral Incompetence [*Cardiology*]
**MI**............. Mitral Insufficiency [*Cardiology*]
**MI**............. Mixed Income
**MI**............. Mobility Impairment (NVT)
**MI**............. Mobility International (EA)
**MI**............. Moderately Included [*Colored gemstone grade*]
**M & I**......... Modernization and Improvement (AABC)
**M & I**......... Modification and Installation (KSC)
**MI**............. Modification Instructions (KSC)
**M & I**......... Moisture and Impurities [*In fats*]
**MI**............. Moment of Inertia
**M of I**........ Moment of Inertia
**MI**............. Monetary Incentive
**MI**............. Money Stock [*British*] (DCTA)
**MI**............. Monitor Inspection (AFM)
**MI**............. Monitor International (ASF)
**MI**............. Monument Inscription [*Genealogy*]
**MI**............. Morphologic Index [*Volume of trunk divided by length of limbs*]
**MI**............. [*The*] Mortgage Index [*Hale Systems, Inc.*] [*Information service or system*] (CRD)
**MI**............. Motility Index [*Of intestine*] [*Gastroenterology*]
**MI**............. Mounted Infantry
**MI**............. Movement Instruction [*British military*] (DMA)
**M & I**......... Movements and Identification [*Military*] (AFM)
**MI**............. Murphy International Transport [*Commercial firm*] [*British*]
**MI**............. Muskies, Incorporated (EA)
**MI**............. Mutual Inductance
**MI**............. Mutual Interference
**MI**............. Myocardial Infarction [*Cardiology*]
**MI**............. Writ of Mandamus Will Issue [*Legal term*] (DLA)

**MiA**........... Alma Public Library, Alma, MI [*Library symbol*] [*Library of Congress*] (LCLS)
**MIA**........... [*An*] Introduction to the Apocrypha [*B. Metzger*] [*A publication*] (BJA)
**MIA**........... Manchester International Airport [*British*] (DS)
**MIA**........... Manila International Airport
**MIA**........... Marble Institute of America (EA)
**MIA**........... Master of Industrial Arts
**MIA**........... Master of International Affairs
**MIA**........... Materialy i Issledovanija po Arkheologii SSSR [*A publication*]
**MIA**........... Media Information Australia [*A publication*] (APTA)
**MIA**........... Medical Indemnity of America, Inc. (DHSM)
**MIA**........... Member of the Institute of Arbitrators [*British*]
**MIA**........... Metal Interface Amplifier
**MIA**........... Miami [*Florida*] [*Seismograph station code, US Geological Survey*] [*Closed*] (SEIS)
**MIA**........... Miami [*Florida*] [*Airport symbol*] (OAG)
**MIA**........... Miami University, Oxford, OH [*OCLC symbol*] (OCLC)
**MIA**........... Mica Industry Association (EA)
**MIA**........... Middle East Economic Digest [*A publication*]
**MIA**........... Military Inspection Agency (NATG)
**MIA**........... Military Intelligence Agency (MCD)
**MIA**........... Millinery Institute of America [*Later, MIB*] (EA)
**MIA**........... Minimum Instrument Altitude [*Aviation*] (AFM)
**MIA**........... Missile Intelligence Agency (AABC)
**MIA**........... Missing in Action [*Military*]
**MIA**........... Mission-Independent Area [*NASA*]
**MIA**........... Mitteilungen. Institut fuer Auslandsbeziehungen [*Stuttgart*] [*A publication*]
**MIA**........... Monoiodoacetic Acid [*Organic chemistry*]
**MIA**........... Moore's Indian Appeals [*A publication*] (DLA)
**MIA**........... "Mouse in Able" Program
**MIA**........... Multiplex Interface Adapter (NASA)
**MIA**........... Multiplexer Interface Adapter (NASA)
**MiAa**.......... Ann Arbor Public Library, Ann Arbor, MI [*Library symbol*] [*Library of Congress*] (LCLS)
**MIAA**........ Member of the Incorporated Association of Architects and Surveyors [*British*] (DBQ)
**MIAA**........ Member of the Institute of Affiliate Accountants (ADA)
**MIAA**........ Member of the Institute of Automobile Assessors [*British*]
**MIAA**........ Miniatures Industry Association of America (EA)
**MIAA**........ Mutual Insurance Advisory Association [*Defunct*] (EA)
**MiAaC**....... Concordia Lutheran College, Ann Arbor, MI [*Library symbol*] [*Library of Congress*] (LCLS)
**MiAaE**....... Environmental Research Institute of Michigan, Ann Arbor, MI [*Library symbol*] [*Library of Congress*] (LCLS)
**MiAaFL**..... Great Lakes Fisheries Laboratory, Ann Arbor, MI [*Library symbol*] [*Library of Congress*] (LCLS)
**MiAaK**....... KMS Fusion, Inc., Ann Arbor, MI [*Library symbol*] [*Library of Congress*] (LCLS)
**MiAaP**....... Parke, Davis & Co., Research Library, Ann Arbor, MI [*Library symbol*] [*Library of Congress*] (LCLS)
**MiAaW**...... Washtenaw County Library, Ann Arbor, MI [*Library symbol*] [*Library of Congress*] (LCLS)
**MiAaWC**... Washtenaw Community College, Ann Arbor, MI [*Library symbol*] [*Library of Congress*] (LCLS)
**MIAB**........ Modular Interchangeable Ambulance Body [*Military*] [*British*]
**MiAC**......... Alma College, Alma, MI [*Library symbol*] [*Library of Congress*] (LCLS)
**MIAC**........ Material Identification Accounting Code
**MIAC**........ Meat Industry Advisory Committee [*Australia*]
**MIAC**........ Minimum Automatic Computer (IEEE)
**MIACF**...... Meander Inverted Autocorrelated Function
**MIACS**...... Manufacturing Information and Control System
**MiAd**.......... Adrian Public Library, Adrian, MI [*Library symbol*] [*Library of Congress*] (LCLS)
**MiAdC**....... Adrian College, Adrian, MI [*Library symbol*] [*Library of Congress*] (LCLS)
**MiAdL**....... Lenawee County Library, Adrian, MI [*Library symbol*] [*Library of Congress*] (LCLS)
**MIADS**...... Map Information Assembly and Display System
**MIADS**...... Minot Air Defense Sector [*ADC*]
**MiAdS**....... Siena Heights College, Adrian, MI [*Library symbol*] [*Library of Congress*] (LCLS)
**MIAE**........ Member of the Institution of Automobile Engineers [*British*]
**MIAEA**...... Member of the Institute of Automotive Engineer Assessors [*British*] (DBQ)
**MI Ae E**..... Member of the Institute of Aeronautical Engineers [*British*]
**MIAEF**...... Missed Interception Due to Airborne Equipment Failure [*Air Force*]
**MIAeS**....... Member of the Institute of Aeronautical Sciences
**MIAFTR**... Motor Insurance Anti-Fraud and Theft Register [*Database*] [*British*]
**MIAG**........ Management Information and Analysis Group (MCD)
**MIAgrE**..... Member of the Institution of Agricultural Engineers [*British*]
**MIAH**........ Hamburg. Institut fuer Asienkunde. Mitteilungen [*A publication*]
**MIAHDA**... Mitteilungen aus dem Institut fuer Allgemeine Botanik [*Hamburg*] [*A publication*]
**MiAhO**...... Oakland Community College, Auburn Heights, MI [*Library symbol*] [*Library of Congress*] (LCLS)
**MIAK**........ Methyl Isoamyl Ketone [*Organic chemistry*]
**MIAKB**...... Myakkangaku [*A publication*]
**MiAlb**........ Albion Public Library, Albion, MI [*Library symbol*] [*Library of Congress*] (LCLS)
**MiAlbC**...... Albion College, Albion, MI [*Library symbol*] [*Library of Congress*] (LCLS)
**MiAlbW**.... Woodlands Library Cooperative, Albion, MI [*Library symbol*] [*Library of Congress*] (LCLS)
**MiAld**........ Helena Township Public Library, Alden, MI [*Library symbol*] [*Library of Congress*] (LCLS)
**MiAll**......... Allendale Township Library, Allendale, MI [*Library symbol*] [*Library of Congress*] (LCLS)
**MiAlle**........ Allegan Public Library, Allegan, MI [*Library symbol*] [*Library of Congress*] (LCLS)
**MiAllG**...... Grand Valley State College, Allendale, MI [*Library symbol*] [*Library of Congress*] (LCLS)
**MiAlmo**..... Henry Stephens Memorial Library, Almont, MI [*Library symbol*] [*Library of Congress*] (LCLS)
**MiAln**........ Alanson Public Library, Alanson, MI [*Library symbol*] [*Library of Congress*] (LCLS)
**MiAlp**........ Alpena County Library, Alpena, MI [*Library symbol*] [*Library of Congress*] (LCLS)
**MiAlpC**...... Alpena Community College, Alpena, MI [*Library symbol*] [*Library of Congress*] (LCLS)
**MIAM**....... Mid-Am, Inc. [*NASDAQ symbol*] (NQ)
**MIAMA**.... Member of the Incorporated Advertising Managers' Association [*British*] (DAS)
**MIAME**..... Member of the Institute of Automotive Mechanical Engineers (ADA)
**MIAMI**...... Microwave Ice Accretion Measurement Instrument (MCD)
**Miami Geol Soc Annu Field Trip (Guideb)**... Miami Geological Society. Annual Field Trip (Guidebook) [*A publication*]
**Miami Heral**... Miami Herald [*A publication*]
**Miami LQ**... Miami Law Quarterly [*A publication*] (DLA)
**Miami L Rev**... Miami Law Review [*Florida*] [*A publication*] (DLA)
**Miami Med**... Miami Medicine [*A publication*]
**Miami Revw**... Miami Review [*A publication*]
**Miami Univ Sch Marine Atmos Sci Annu Rep**... Miami University. School of Marine and Atmospheric Science. Annual Report [*A publication*]
**Miami Winter Symp**... Miami Winter Symposium [*A publication*]
**MIAMSI**... Movimiento Internacional de Apostolado en los Medios Sociales Independientes [*International Movement of Apostolate in the Independent Social Milieux*] [*Vatican City, Vatican City State*] (EAIO)
**MIAO**........ Master Index Assembly Outline [*Paper*]
**MiAp**......... Allen Park Public Library, Allen Park, MI [*Library symbol*] [*Library of Congress*] (LCLS)
**MIAP**......... Member of the Institution of Analysts and Programmers [*British*] (DBQ)
**MIAP**......... Military Incentive Analysis Program (MCD)
**MIAPD**...... Mid-Central Air Procurement District
**MiApDB**.... Detroit Baptist Divinity School, Allen Park, MI [*Library symbol*] [*Library of Congress*] (LCLS)
**MIAPL**...... Master Index of Allowable Parts Lists [*Navy*]
**MiApV**....... United States Veterans Administration Hospital, Allen Park, MI [*Library symbol*] [*Library of Congress*] (LCLS)
**M I Arch**.... Master of Interior Architecture
**M I Arch Eng**... Master of Interior Architectural Engineering
**MiArm**....... Armada Free Public Library, Armada, MI [*Library symbol*] [*Library of Congress*] (LCLS)
**MIARS**...... Maintenance Information Automated Retrieval System [*DoD*]
**MIAS**......... Major Item Automated System [*Army Materiel Command*] (AABC)
**MIAS**......... Marine Information and Advisory Service [*Institute of Oceanographic Sciences*] [*Databank*] [*British*] (IID)
**MIAS**......... Member of the Incorporated Association of Architects and Surveyors [*British*] (DBQ)
**MIAS**......... Member of the Institute of Aeronautical Science [*Later, MAIAA*]
**MIAS**......... Monroe Institute of Applied Sciences [*Later, TMI*] (EA)
**MIASA**...... Mineralogical Magazine and Journal of the Mineralogical Society (1876-1968) [*England*] [*A publication*]
**Miasn Ind SSSR**... Miasnaia Industriia SSSR [*A publication*]
**MIAT**........ Member of the Institute of Asphalt Technology [*British*] (DBQ)
**MiAt**.......... Montmorency County Public Library, Atlanta, MI [*Library symbol*] [*Library of Congress*] (LCLS)
**MIATCO**... Mid-America International Agri-Trade Council
**MiAth**........ Athens Township Library, Athens, MI [*Library symbol*] [*Library of Congress*] (LCLS)
**MiAu**.......... Augusta-Ross Township District Library (McKay Library), Augusta, MI [*Library symbol*] [*Library of Congress*] (LCLS)
**MIAX**........ McCulloch International Airlines [*Air carrier designation symbol*]
**MIB**........... Management Improvement Board (AAG)
**MIB**........... Management Information Base
**MIB**........... Manual Input Buffer [*Data processing*]
**MIB**........... Marine Index Bureau
**MIB**........... Marketing of Investments Board [*Finance*] [*British*]
**MIB**........... Master Instruction Book

**MIB** .......... Master Interconnect Board (MCD)
**MIB** .......... Mechanized Infantry Battalion (MCD)
**MIB** .......... Medical Impairment Bureau [*Insurance*]
**MIB** .......... Medical Information Bureau [*Databank*]
**MIB** .......... Men in Black [*UFO mythology*]
**MIB** .......... Mezhdunarodnyi Investitsionnyi Bank [*International Investment Bank - IIB*] [*Moscow, USSR*] (EAIO)
**MIB** .......... Michigan Intra-State Motor Tariff Bureau Inc., Lansing MI [*STAC*]
**MIB** .......... Microinstruction Bus [*Data processing*]
**MIB** .......... Military Intelligence Battalion (MCD)
**MIB** .......... Military Intelligence Board (MCD)
**MIB** .......... Millinery Information Bureau (EA)
**MIB** .......... Minimum Impulse BIT [*Binary Digit*] [*Data processing*] (MCD)
**MIB** .......... Minot, ND [*Location identifier*] [*FAA*] (FAAL)
**MIB** .......... Mint in the Box [*Doll collecting*]
**MIB** .......... Missionary Information Bureau
**MIB** .......... Motor Inspection Building
**MIB** .......... Motor Insurers' Bureau Limited [*British*] (ILCA)
**MIB** .......... Mouvement d'Insoumission Bretonne [*Breton Insubordination Movement*] [*France*] (PD)
**MIB** .......... Multibanc NT Financial Corp. [*Toronto Stock Exchange symbol*]
**MIB** .......... Multilayer Interconnection Board
**MIB** .......... Mustard Information Bureau (EA)
**MIB** .......... Mutual Inductance Bridge
**MiBa** .......... Bad Axe Public Library, Bad Axe, MI [*Library symbol*] [*Library of Congress*] (LCLS)
**MIBA** .......... Member of the Institute of British Architects (ROG)
**MIBA** .......... Metropolitan Intercollegiate Basketball Association (EA)
**MiBal** .......... Pathfinder Community Library, Baldwin, MI [*Library symbol*] [*Library of Congress*] (LCLS)
**MiBar** .......... Barryton Public Library, Barryton, MI [*Library symbol*] [*Library of Congress*] (LCLS)
**MiBar** .......... Burr Oak Township Library, Burr Oak, MI [*Library symbol*] [*Library of Congress*] (LCLS)
**MIBARS** ... Military Intelligence Battalion Aerial Reconnaissance and Support [*Army*] (AFM)
**MiBat** .......... Battle Creek Public School, Battle Creek, MI [*Library symbol*] [*Library of Congress*] (LCLS)
**MiBatC** ...... Battle Creek College, Battle Creek, MI [*Library symbol*] [*Library of Congress*] [*Obsolete*] (LCLS)
**MiBatK** ...... Kellogg Community College, Battle Creek, MI [*Library symbol*] [*Library of Congress*] (LCLS)
**MiBatV** ...... United States Veterans Administration Hospital, Battle Creek, MI [*Library symbol*] [*Library of Congress*] (LCLS)
**MiBatW** ..... Willard Public Library, Battle Creek, MI [*Library symbol*] [*Library of Congress*] (LCLS)
**MiBay** .......... Bay City Public Library, Bay City, MI [*Library symbol*] [*Library of Congress*] (LCLS)
**MiBayM** .... Bay Medical Center, Bay City, MI [*Library symbol*] [*Library of Congress*] (LCLS)
**MiBayS** ...... Bay County Library System, Bay City, MI [*Library symbol*] [*Library of Congress*] (LCLS)
**MiBayS-A** ... Bay County Library System, Auburn Branch Library, Auburn, MI [*Library symbol*] [*Library of Congress*] (LCLS)
**MiBayS-B** ... Bay County Library System, Broadway Branch Library, Bay City, MI [*Library symbol*] [*Library of Congress*] (LCLS)
**MiBayS-L** ... Bay County Library System, Linwood Branch Library, Linwood, MI [*Library symbol*] [*Library of Congress*] (LCLS)
**MiBayS-P** ... Bay County Library System, Pinconning Branch Library, Pinconning, MI [*Library symbol*] [*Library of Congress*] (LCLS)
**MiBayS-S** ... Bay County Library System, Sage Branch Library, Bay City, MI [*Library symbol*] [*Library of Congress*] (LCLS)
**MIBB** .......... Missouri & Illinois Bridge & Belt Railroad [*AAR code*] [*Terminated*]
**MIBC** .......... Methylisobutyl Carbinol [*Also, MIC*] [*Organic chemistry*]
**MIBCO** ..... Member of the Institution of Building Control Officers [*British*] (DBQ)
**MiBeiM** ..... Beaver Island Mormon Colony Library, St. James, Beaver Island, MI [*Library symbol*] [*Library of Congress*] [*Obsolete*] (LCLS)
**MiBel** .......... Bellevue Township Library, Bellevue, MI [*Library symbol*] [*Library of Congress*] (LCLS)
**MiBela** ....... Bellaire Public Library, Bellaire, MI [*Library symbol*] [*Library of Congress*] (LCLS)
**MiBen** .......... Benzonia Public Library, Benzonia, MI [*Library symbol*] [*Library of Congress*] (LCLS)
**MiBes** .......... Bessemer Public Library, Bessemer, MI [*Library symbol*] [*Library of Congress*] (LCLS)
**MiBeu** .......... Beulah Public Library, Beulah, MI [*Library symbol*] [*Library of Congress*] (LCLS)
**MIBF** .......... Member of the Institute of British Foundrymen
**MIBF** .......... Montreal International Book Fair
**MIBG** .......... Meta-Iodobenzylguanidine [*Biochemistry*]
**MiBhL** .......... Lake Michigan College, Benton Harbor, MI [*Library symbol*] [*Library of Congress*] (LCLS)
**MiBhW** ...... Whirlpool Corp., Technical Information Center, Benton Harbor, MI [*Library symbol*] [*Library of Congress*] (LCLS)
**MiBicr** ....... Thomas Fleschner Memorial Library, Birch Run, MI [*Library symbol*] [*Library of Congress*] (LCLS)
**MI Biol** ...... Member of the Institute of Biology [*British*] (EY)
**MiBir** .......... Baldwin Public Library, Birmingham, MI [*Library symbol*] [*Library of Congress*] (LCLS)
**MIBK** .......... Methyl Isobutyl Ketone [*Also, MIK*] [*Organic chemistry*]
**MiBla** .......... Rolland Township Library, Blanchard, MI [*Library symbol*] [*Library of Congress*] (LCLS)
**MiBloA** ...... Cranbrook Academy of Art, Bloomfield Hills, MI [*Library symbol*] [*Library of Congress*] (LCLS)
**MiBloC** ...... Cranbrook Institute of Science, Bloomfield Hills, MI [*Library symbol*] [*Library of Congress*] (LCLS)
**MiBloGS** ... Church of Jesus Christ of Latter-Day Saints, Genealogical Society Library, Bloomfield Hills Branch, Bloomfield Hills, MI [*Library symbol*] [*Library of Congress*] (LCLS)
**MIB Miner Ind Bull** ... MIB. Mineral Industries Bulletin [*United States*] [*A publication*]
**MIBNAU** .. Instituut voor Toegepast Biologisch Onderzoek in de Natuur [*Institute for Biological Field Research*]. Mededeling [*A publication*]
**MIBOC** ..... Marketing of Investments Board Organising Committee [*British*]
**MiBoy** .......... Boyne City Public Library, Boyne City, MI [*Library symbol*] [*Library of Congress*] (LCLS)
**MiBoyf** ....... Boyne Falls Public Library, Boyne Falls, MI [*Library symbol*] [*Library of Congress*] (LCLS)
**MIBPA** ...... Methyliminobispropylamine [*Organic chemistry*]
**Mi-BPH** ..... Michigan Department of Education, State Library Services, Blind and Physically Handicapped Library, Lansing, MI [*Library symbol*] [*Library of Congress*] (LCLS)
**MiBr** .......... Big Rapids Community Library, Big Rapids, MI [*Library symbol*] [*Library of Congress*] (LCLS)
**MiBrc** .......... Brown City Public Library, Brown City, MI [*Library symbol*] [*Library of Congress*] (LCLS)
**MiBre** .......... Howe Memorial Library, Breckenridge, MI [*Library symbol*] [*Library of Congress*] (LCLS)
**MiBrF** .......... Ferris State College, Big Rapids, MI [*Library symbol*] [*Library of Congress*] (LCLS)
**MiBrid** ....... Bridgeport Public Library, Bridgeport, MI [*Library symbol*] [*Library of Congress*] (LCLS)
**MiBridm** .... Bridgman Public Library, Bridgman, MI [*Library symbol*] [*Library of Congress*] (LCLS)
**MiBrig** ....... Brighton City Library, Brighton, MI [*Library symbol*] [*Library of Congress*] (LCLS)
**MIBritE** ..... Member of the Institute of British Engineers (EY)
**MIBritishE** ... Member of the Institute of British Engineers
**MIBS** .......... Master of International Business Studies
**MIBS** .......... Miami International Boat Show and Sailboat Show (ITD)
**MiBs** .......... Sparks Memorial Library, Berrien Springs, MI [*Library symbol*] [*Library of Congress*] (LCLS)
**MiBsA** ....... Andrews University, Berrien Springs, MI [*Library symbol*] [*Library of Congress*] (LCLS)
**MIBT** .......... Methyl Isatin-beta-thiosemicarbazone
**MiBu** .......... Taymouth Township Library, Burt, MI [*Library symbol*] [*Library of Congress*] (LCLS)
**MIBUB** ...... Mikrobiyoloji Bulteni [*A publication*]
**MIBUBI** .... Bulletin of Microbiology [*A publication*]
**MiBurl** ....... Burlington Township Library, Burlington, MI [*Library symbol*] [*Library of Congress*] (LCLS)
**MIBURN** .. Mississippi Burning [*Code name of FBI investigation*]
**MIC** .......... Congregatio Clericorum Regularium Marianorum sub titulo Immaculatae Conceptionis Beatae Mariae Virginis [*Marian Fathers*] [*Roman Catholic religious order*]
**MIC** .......... IEEE Medical Imaging Committee (EA)
**MIC** .......... Itasca Community College, Grand Rapids, MN [*OCLC symbol*] (OCLC)
**MIC** .......... Machinery Installation Certificate
**MIC** .......... Made in Canada [*Business term*]
**MIC** .......... Maintenance Identification Code [*Military*] (CAAL)
**MIC** .......... Maintenance Information Center [*Navy*] (NG)
**MIC** .......... Maintenance Information Chart [*DoD*]
**MIC** .......... Maintenance Inventory Center [*Air Force*] (AFIT)
**MIC** .......... Malaysian Indian Congress [*Political party*] (PPW)
**MIC** .......... Management Indicator Code (MCD)
**MIC** .......... Management & Industrial Consultants
**MIC** .......... Management Information Center
**MIC** .......... Management Information Corporation [*Cherry Hill, NJ*] [*Information service or system*] (IID)
**MIC** .......... Marine Information Centre [*Information service or system*] (EISS)
**MIC** .......... Market Impact Clearance
**MIC** .......... Marketing Intelligence Corporation [*Information service or system*] (IID)
**MIC** .......... Marketing International Corporation [*Washington, DC*] (TSSD)
**MIC** .......... Maruzen International Company, Inc. [*Information service or system*] (IID)
**MIC** .......... Masonry Industry Committee (EA)

**MIC** .......... Match Indicator Code (MCD)
**MIC** .......... Material Inventory Control
**MIC** .......... Materials Irradiation Chamber
**MIC** .......... Maternal and Infant Care [*Medicine*]
**MIC** .......... Maximum Inscribed Circle [*Manufacturing term*]
**MIC** .......... Meat Importers' Council [*Later, MICA*] (EA)
**MIC** .......... Mechanized Information Center [*Information service or system*]
**MIC** .......... Medical Industrial Complex
**MIC** .......... Medical Intensive Care
**MIC** .......... Medical Interfraternity Conference (EA)
**MIC** .......... Medium-Intensity Conflict [*Military*]
**MIC** .......... Medugorje Information Center (EA)
**MIC** .......... Mellon InvestData Corporation [*New York, NY*] [*Information service or system*] (IID)
**MIC** .......... Mellonics Information Center [*Information service or system*] (IID)
**MIC** .......... Memory Interface Connection [*Data processing*]
**MIC** .......... Merseyside Innovation Centre Ltd. [*British*] (CB)
**MIC** .......... Message Identification Code [*Data processing*] (BUR)
**MIC** .......... Meteorological Information Committee [*NATO*] (NATG)
**MIC** .......... Methyl Isocyanate [*Organic chemistry*]
**MIC** .......... Methylisobutyl Carbinol [*Also, MIBC*] [*Organic chemistry*]
**MIC** .......... Metro Industrial [*Vancouver Stock Exchange symbol*]
**MIC** .......... Metropolitan Industrial Court [*Victoria, Australia*]
**Mic** .......... Micah [*Old Testament book*]
**MIC** .......... Michigan Information Center [*Michigan State Department of Management and Budget*] [*Information service or system*] (IID)
**MIC** .......... Michigan Instructional Computer
**Mic** .......... Michigan Music Educator [*A publication*]
**MIC** .......... Michilla [*Chile*] [*Seismograph station code, US Geological Survey*] (SEIS)
**mic** .......... Micmac [*MARC language code*] [*Library of Congress*] (LCCP)
**MIC** .......... Microcomputer Index [*Information service or system*] (IID)
**MIC** .......... Microelectronic Integrated Circuit (MCD)
**MIC** .......... Micrometer [*A "mike"*]
**MIC** .......... Microphone (AABC)
**Mic** .......... Microscopium [*Constellation*]
**MIC** .......... Microscopy
**MIC** .......... Microwave Integrated Circuitry
**MIC** .......... Microwave Interference Coordination
**MIC** .......... Mid-Intensity Conflict [*Military*] (INF)
**MIC** .......... Middle Income Country [*Category of developing country*]
**M-IC** .......... Military-Industrial Complex
**MIC** .......... Military Information Center (EA)
**MIC** .......... Mineral Industries Census
**MIC** .......... Minimal [*or Minimum*] Inhibitory Concentration
**MIC** .......... Minimal Isorrheic Concentration [*Medicine*]
**MIC** .......... Minimum Ignition Current (IEEE)
**MIC** .......... Minimum Inhibitory Concentration [*Bactericidal characteristic*]
**MIC** .......... Minneapolis, MN [*Location identifier*] [*FAA*] (FAAL)
**MIC** .......... Missile Identification Code [*Military*] (CAAL)
**MIC** .......... Missing Interruption Checker (MCD)
**MIC** .......... Missionary Sisters of the Immaculate Conception [*Roman Catholic religious order*]
**MIC** .......... Mississippi Industrial College [*Holly Springs*]
**MIC** .......... Mobile Intensive Care [*Medicine*] (DHSM)
**MIC** .......... Modeling Identification and Control [*A publication*]
**MIC** .......... Monitoring, Identification, and Correlation
**MIC** .......... Monolithic Integrated Circuit
**MIC** .......... Morphology-Immunology-Cytogenetics [*Classification of Leukemias*]
**MIC** .......... Mortgage Insurance Company
**MIC** .......... Motorcycle Industry Council (EA)
**MIC** .......... Multimedia Interactive Control
**MIC** .......... Multinational Intelligence Cell (MCD)
**MIC** .......... Multiperil Insurance Conference
**MIC** .......... Music Industry Conference (EA)
**MIC** .......... Music Industry Council [*Later, Music Industry Conference*] (EA)
**MIC** .......... Mutual Improvement Class [*British railroad term*]
**MIC** .......... Mutual Interference Chart (IEEE)
**MiCa** .......... Indianfields Public Library, Caro, MI [*Library symbol*] [*Library of Congress*] (LCLS)
**MICA** .......... Macroinstruction Compiler Assembler [*Data processing*]
**MICA** .......... Meat Importers' Council of America (EA)
**MICA** .......... MicroAge, Inc. [*NASDAQ symbol*] (NQ)
**MICA** .......... Microwave Information Council of Australia
**MICA** .......... Mobile Industrial Caterers' Association (EA)
**MICA** .......... Mortgage Insurance Companies of America (EA)
**MiCac** .......... Rawson Memorial Library, Cass City, MI [*Library symbol*] [*Library of Congress*] (LCLS)
**MiCad** .......... Cadillac-Wexford Public Library, Cadillac, MI [*Library symbol*] [*Library of Congress*] (LCLS)
**MiCadM** .... Mid-Michigan Library League, Cadillac, MI [*Library symbol*] [*Library of Congress*] (LCLS)
**MiCadPS** ... Wexford Public Schools, Cadillac, MI [*Library symbol*] [*Library of Congress*] (LCLS)
**MICAF** ...... Measuring Improved Capability of Army Forces
**MiCal** .......... Calumet Public-School Library, Calumet, MI [*Library symbol*] [*Library of Congress*] (LCLS)
**MiCam** ....... Camden Township Library, Camden, MI [*Library symbol*] [*Library of Congress*] (LCLS)
**MICAM** .... Micro-Connection Assembly Method
**MICAM** .... Microammeter [*Electronics*]
**MICAP** ...... Measuring Improved Capability [*Army*]
**MICAP** ...... Mission Capability
**MICAP** ...... Mission Incapable, Awaiting Parts (MCD)
**MICAPS** .... Mine/Countermine Casualty Assessment Producing System (MCD)
**MICAS** ...... Military Intelligence Company, Aerial Surveillance (MCD)
**MiCassC** .... Cass County Library, Cassopolis, MI [*Library symbol*] [*Library of Congress*] (LCLS)
**MICB** .......... Meck Island Control Building [*Army*] (AABC)
**MICBM** ..... Mobile Intercontinental Ballistic Missile
**MiCc** .......... Carson City Public Library, Carson City, MI [*Library symbol*] [*Library of Congress*] (LCLS)
**MICC** .......... Malaysian International Chamber of Commerce (DS)
**MICC** .......... Metal Interconnect Cascade Cell [*Photovoltaic energy systems*]
**MICC** .......... Micron Corporation [*NASDAQ symbol*] (NQ)
**MICC** .......... Military Information Control Committee (CINC)
**MICC** .......... Mineral Insulated, Copper Covered [*Cable*]
**MICC** .......... Mortgage Insurance Company of Canada
**MICCC** ...... Monograph Series. International Council for Computer Communications [*Elsevier Book Series*] [*A publication*]
**MICCO** ..... Model Inner City Community Organization [*Washington, DC*]
**MICCS** ...... Minuteman Integrated Command and Control System [*Missiles*]
**Mic D** .......... Doctor of Microbiology
**MICDS** ...... Movable In-Core Detector System [*Nuclear energy*] (NRCH)
**MICE** .......... Material Transfer, Information Transfer, Control Transfer, Energy Transfer
**MICE** .......... Member of the Institution of Civil Engineers [*Formerly, AMICE*] [*British*]
**MICE** .......... Microelectronic Integrated Checkout Equipment
**MICE** .......... Money, Ideology, Compromise, Ego [*CIA acronym for possible explanations for spy defections*]
**MICE** .......... Mutual Insurance Council of Editors [*Later, PICA*] (EA)
**MiCe** .......... Nottawa Township Library, Centerville, MI [*Library symbol*] [*Library of Congress*] (LCLS)
**MiCeG** ....... Glen Oaks Community College, Centreville, MI [*Library symbol*] [*Library of Congress*] (LCLS)
**MICEI** ....... Member of the Institution of Civil Engineers of Ireland
**MICELEM** ... Microphone Element (IEEE)
**MiCen** ........ Leslie R. Foss Public Library, Center Line, MI [*Library symbol*] [*Library of Congress*] (LCLS)
**MiCenl** ....... Central Lake Township Library, Central Lake, MI [*Library symbol*] [*Library of Congress*] (LCLS)
**MiCES** ....... Microcomputer-Controlled Electroanalysis System [*Interactive Microwave*]
**MiCf** .......... Crystal Falls Community Library, Crystal Falls, MI [*Library symbol*] [*Library of Congress*] (LCLS)
**MICG** ........ Management Information Coordinating Group [*Navy*]
**MICG** ........ Mercury Iodide Crystal Growth
**MICH** ........ Michaelmas [*Feast of St. Michael the Archangel, September 29*]
**Mich** .......... Michaelmas Term [*British*] [*Legal term*] (DLA)
**MICH** ........ Michaels [*J.*], Inc. [*NASDAQ symbol*] (NQ)
**MICH** ........ Micheas [*Old Testament book*] [*Douay version*]
**MICH** ........ Michigan
**Mich** .......... Michigan Reports [*A publication*]
**Mich** .......... Michigan Supreme Court Reports [*A publication*] (DLA)
**MiCha** ........ Chase Public Library, Chase, MI [*Library symbol*] [*Library of Congress*] (LCLS)
**MichA** ........ Michigan Academician [*A publication*]
**Mich Acad** ... Michigan Academician [*A publication*]
**Mich Acad Sci Papers** ... Michigan Academy of Science, Arts, and Letters. Papers [*A publication*]
**Mich Ac Sc Rp An Rp** ... Michigan Academy of Science. Report. Annual Report [*A publication*]
**Mich Admin Code** ... Michigan Administrative Code [*A publication*] (DLA)
**Mich Adv** ... Michigan Reports Advanced Sheets [*A publication*] (DLA)
**Mich Ag Exp** ... Michigan. Agricultural Experiment Station. Publications [*A publication*]
**Mich Agric Exp Stn Annu Rep** ... Michigan. Agricultural Experiment Station. Annual Report [*A publication*]
**Mich Agric Exp Stn Mem** ... Michigan. Agricultural Experiment Station. Memoir [*A publication*]
**Mich Agric Exp Stn Q Bull** ... Michigan. Agricultural Experiment Station. Quarterly Bulletin [*A publication*]
**Mich Agric Exp Stn Spec Bull** ... Michigan. Agricultural Experiment Station. Special Bulletin [*A publication*]
**Mich Agric Exp Stn Tech Bull** ... Michigan. Agricultural Experiment Station. Technical Bulletin [*A publication*]
**Mich Alumni Quar Rev** ... Michigan Alumni Quarterly Review [*A publication*]
**Mich App** ... Michigan Appeals Reports [*A publication*]
**Mich App** ... Michigan Court of Appeals Reports [*A publication*] (DLA)
**MiChar** ...... Charlotte Public Library, Charlotte, MI [*Library symbol*] [*Library of Congress*] (LCLS)

**Mich Att'y Gen Biennial Rep** ... Biennial Report of the Attorney General of the State of Michigan [*A publication*] (DLA)
**Mich Audubon Newsl** ... Michigan Audubon Newsletter [*A publication*]
**Mich BJ**..... Michigan Bar Journal [*A publication*]
**Mich Bot**.... Michigan Botanist [*A publication*]
**Mich Bus R** ... Michigan Business Review [*A publication*]
**Mich Calidon** ... Michael Calidonius [*Flourished, 16th century*] [*Authority cited in pre-1607 legal work*] (DSA)
**Mich CCR** ... Michigan Circuit Court Reporter [*A publication*] (DLA)
**Mich Comp L Ann** ... Michigan Compiled Laws, Annotated [*A publication*] (DLA)
**Mich Comp Laws** ... Michigan Compiled Laws [*A publication*] (DLA)
**Mich Comp Laws Ann** ... Michigan Compiled Laws, Annotated [*A publication*] (DLA)
**Mich Comp Laws Ann (West)** ... Michigan Compiled Laws, Annotated (West) [*A publication*]
**Mich Corp Finance and Bus LJ** ... Michigan Corporate Finance and Business Law Journal [*A publication*]
**Mich Cr Ct Rep** ... Michigan Circuit Court Reporter [*A publication*] (DLA)
**Mich Ct Cl** ... Michigan Court of Claims Reports [*A publication*] (DLA)
**Mich Dent Assoc J** ... Michigan Dental Association. Journal [*A publication*]
**Mich Dep Conserv Game Div Rep** ... Michigan. Department of Conservation. Game Division Report [*A publication*]
**Mich Dep Conserv Geol Surv Div Water Invest** ... Michigan. Department of Conservation. Geological Survey Division. Water Investigation [*A publication*]
**MiChe**........ Cheboygan Area Public Library, Cheboygan, MI [*Library symbol*] [*Library of Congress*] (LCLS)
**Mich Ed J** ... Michigan Education Journal [*A publication*]
**MiChel**....... McKune Memorial Library, Chelsea, MI [*Library symbol*] [*Library of Congress*] (LCLS)
**MIChemE** ... Member of the Institution of Chemical Engineers [*British*] (EY)
**Mich Energy** ... Michigan Energy [*A publication*]
**Mich Ent**.... Michigan Entomologist [*A publication*]
**Mich Entomol** ... Michigan Entomologist [*A publication*]
**MiChes**...... Chesaning Public Library, Chesaning, MI [*Library symbol*] [*Library of Congress*] (LCLS)
**Mich Farm Econ** ... Michigan Farm Economics. Michigan State University. Cooperative Extension Service [*A publication*]
**Mich Geol Surv Bull** ... Michigan. Geological Survey. Bulletin [*A publication*]
**Mich Geol Surv Circ** ... Michigan. Geological Survey. Circular [*A publication*]
**Mich Geol Surv Div Misc** ... Michigan. Geological Survey Division. Miscellany [*A publication*]
**Mich Geol Surv Div Prog Rep** ... Michigan. Geological Survey Division. Progress Report [*A publication*]
**Mich Geol Surv Div Publ** ... Michigan. Geological Survey Division. Publication [*A publication*]
**Mich Geol Surv Div Water Invest** ... Michigan. Geological Survey Division. Water Investigation [*A publication*]
**Mich Geol Surv Rep Invest** ... Michigan. Geological Survey. Report of Investigation [*A publication*]
**Mich G S Rp** ... Michigan. Geological Survey. Michigan State Board of Geological Survey. Report [*A publication*]
**MichH**....... Michigan History Magazine [*A publication*]
**Mich His Col** ... Michigan Historical Commission. Collections [*A publication*]
**Mich His M** ... Michigan History Magazine [*A publication*]
**Mich Hist**.. Michigan History [*A publication*]
**Mich Hist Soc Coll** ... Michigan Pioneer and Historical Society Collections [*A publication*]
**Mich Hosp** ... Michigan Hospitals [*A publication*]
**Michie's GA Repts Ann** ... Georgia Reports, Annotated [*A publication*] (DLA)
**Michie's Jur** ... Michie's Jurisprudence of Virginia and West Virginia [*A publication*] (DLA)
**Michigan Bu** ... Michigan Business [*A publication*]
**Michigan Geol Survey Ann Statistical Summ** ... Michigan. Geological Survey Annual Statistical Summary [*A publication*]
**Michigan Geol Survey Rept Inv** ... Michigan. Geological Survey. Report of Investigation [*A publication*]
**Michigan Geol Survey Water Inv** ... Michigan. Geological Survey. Water Investigation [*A publication*]
**Michigan Med** ... Michigan Medicine [*A publication*]
**Michigan Univ Mus Paleontology Contr** ... Michigan University. Museum of Paleontology. Contributions [*A publication*]
**Michigan Univ Mus Zoology Occasional Paper** ... Michigan University. Museum of Zoology. Occasional Papers [*A publication*]
**Mich Jur**.... Michigan Jurisprudence [*A publication*] (DLA)
**Mich L**....... Michigan Lawyer [*A publication*] (DLA)
**Mich Law R** ... Michigan Law Review [*A publication*]
**Mich Law Rev** ... Michigan Law Review [*A publication*]
**Mich Legis Serv** ... Michigan Legislative Service [*A publication*] (DLA)
**Mich Leg News** ... Michigan Legal News [*A publication*] (DLA)
**Mich Libn** ... Michigan Librarian [*A publication*]
**Mich Lib News** ... Michigan Library News [*A publication*]
**Mich Librn** ... Michigan Librarian [*A publication*]
**Mich LJ**..... Michigan Law Journal [*A publication*] (DLA)
**Mich LR**.... Michigan Law Review [*A publication*]
**Mich L Rev** ... Michigan Law Review [*A publication*]
**Mich Math J** ... Michigan Mathematical Journal [*A publication*]
**Mich Med** ... Michigan Medicine [*A publication*]
**Mich Miner** ... Michigan Miner [*A publication*]
**Mich Munic R** ... Michigan Municipal Review [*A publication*]
**Mich Nat Resour Mag** ... Michigan Natural Resources Magazine [*A publication*]
**Mich Nisi Prius** ... Brown's Michigan Nisi Prius Reports [*A publication*] (DLA)
**Mich NP**.... Brown's Michigan Nisi Prius Reports [*A publication*] (DLA)
**Mich Nurse** ... Michigan Nurse [*A publication*]
**Mich Nurse Newsl** ... Michigan Nurse Newsletter [*A publication*]
**Michoacan Mex Com For Bol Ser Tec** ... Michoacan, Mexico. Comision Forestal. Boletin. Serie Tecnica [*A publication*]
**Mich Pub Acts** ... Public and Local Acts of the Legislature of the State of Michigan [*A publication*] (DLA)
**Mich PUC Ops** ... Michigan Public Utilities Commission Orders and Opinions [*A publication*] (DLA)
**MichQR**..... Michigan Quarterly Review [*A publication*]
**Mich Q Rev** ... Michigan Quarterly Review [*A publication*]
**Mich R**....... Michigan Reports [*A publication*] (DLA)
**Mich RC Dec** ... Michigan Railroad Commission Decisions [*A publication*] (DLA)
**Mich Reg** ... Michigan Register [*A publication*]
**MICHS**...... Michaelmas [*Feast of St. Michael the Archangel, September 29*]
**Mich SBA Jo** ... Michigan State Bar Association. Journal [*A publication*] (DLA)
**Mich S B J** ... Michigan State Bar Journal [*A publication*]
**Mich Sci Action Mich Agric Exp Stn** ... Michigan Science in Action. Michigan Agricultural Experiment Station [*A publication*]
**Mich Stat Ann** ... Michigan Statutes, Annotated [*A publication*] (DLA)
**Mich Stat Ann (Callaghan)** ... Michigan Statutes, Annotated (Callaghan) [*A publication*]
**Mich State Coll Vet** ... Michigan State College Veterinarian [*A publication*]
**Mich State Dent Assoc J** ... Michigan State Dental Association. Journal [*A publication*]
**Mich State Dent Soc Bull** ... Michigan State Dental Society. Bulletin [*A publication*]
**Mich State Dent Soc J** ... Michigan State Dental Society. Journal [*A publication*]
**Mich State Econ Rec** ... Michigan State Economic Record [*A publication*]
**Mich State Univ Agric Exp Stn Annu Rep** ... Michigan State University. Agricultural Experiment Station. Annual Report [*A publication*]
**Mich St BJ** ... Michigan State Bar Journal [*A publication*]
**Mich Supr Ct Rep** ... Michigan Reports [*A publication*] (DLA)
**Mich T**....... Michaelmas Term [*British*] [*Legal term*] (DLA)
**Mich Technol Univ Ford For Cent Res Notes** ... Michigan Technological University. Ford Forestry Center. Research Notes [*A publication*]
**Mich Univ Eng Res Inst Eng Res Bull** ... Michigan University. Engineering Research Institute. Engineering Research Bulletin [*A publication*]
**Mich Univ Inst Sci Technol Rep** ... Michigan University. Institute of Science and Technology. Report [*A publication*]
**Mich Univ Mus Zool Oc P** ... Michigan University. Museum of Zoology. Occasional Papers [*A publication*]
**MiChv**........ Charlevoix Public Library, Charlevoix, MI [*Library symbol*] [*Library of Congress*] (LCLS)
**Mich Vac**... Michaelmas Vacation [*British*] [*Legal term*] (DLA)
**Mich Water Res Comm Rept** ... Michigan Water Resources Commission. Report [*A publication*]
**Mich WCC** ... Michigan Industrial Accident Board, Workmen's Compensation Cases [*A publication*] (DLA)
**Mich YB Int'l Legal Stud** ... Michigan Yearbook of International Legal Studies [*A publication*]
**MICIS** ....... Material Information Control and Information System (MCD)
**MICIS** ....... Material Inventory Control and Inventory System (NASA)
**MICIS** ....... Microbial Culture Information Service [*Department of Trade and Industry*] [*Great Britain*] [*Information service or system*]
**MICK** ........ Manufacturers Item Correlation Key
**MICL**......... Missile In-Commission Level
**MiCla**......... Garfield Memorial Public Library, Clare, MI [*Library symbol*] [*Library of Congress*] (LCLS)
**MICLE**...... Institute of Continuing Legal Education, University of Michigan (DLA)
**MICLIC** .... Mine Clearing Line Charge [*Army*] (INF)
**MiClin** ....... Clinton Public Library, Clinton, MI [*Library symbol*] [*Library of Congress*] (LCLS)
**MICLO**...... Management Information Control Liaison Officers (MCD)
**MICM** ....... Associate Member of the Institute of Credit Management [*British*] (DBQ)
**MICM** ....... Monolithic Integrated Circuit Mask
**MIC Model Identif Control** ... MIC. Modeling, Identification, and Control [*Norway*] [*A publication*]
**MICMPTR** ... Microcomputer (MSA)
**MICNS**...... Modular Integrated Communications and Navigation System (RDA)
**MICO** ........ Management Information Systems Control Officer (MCD)
**MICO** ........ Member of the Institute of Careers Officers [*British*] (DBQ)
**MICO** ........ Midland Continental R. R. [*AAR code*] [*Obsolete*]
**MICOB** ..... Micron [*A publication*]
**MICOFT**... Mutual Insurance Committee on Federal Taxation (EA)

**MiCol**......... Coloma Public Library, Coloma, MI [*Library symbol*] [*Library of Congress*] (LCLS)
**MiCole**....... Coleman Area Library, Coleman, MI [*Library symbol*] [*Library of Congress*] (LCLS)
**Micol Ital**... Micologia Italiana [*A publication*]
**MiColo**....... Colon Township Library, Colon, MI [*Library symbol*] [*Library of Congress*] (LCLS)
**MiCom**....... Comstock Township Library, Comstock, MI [*Library symbol*] [*Library of Congress*] (LCLS)
**MICOM**.... Missile Command [*Army*] [*Redstone Arsenal, AL*]
**MICOMS**... Maintenance Information Concerning [*the repair and operation of*] Missile Systems
**MiCon**........ Constatine Township Library, Constatine, MI [*Library symbol*] [*Library of Congress*] (LCLS)
**MICON**..... Military Construction Program (MUGU)
**MICONEX**... Multinational Instrumentation Conference and Exposition [*China Instrument Society*] (TSPED)
**MiCoop**...... Coopersville District Library, Coopersville, MI [*Library symbol*] [*Library of Congress*] (LCLS)
**MI-COPICS**... Management Information for COPICS [*Communications Oriented Production Information and Control System*] Users [*IBM Corp.*]
**MICorrST**... Member of the Institute of Corrosion Science and Technology [*British*] (DBQ)
**MICP**......... Military Inventory Control Point (MCD)
**MICPAC**... Microelectronic Integrated Circuit Package (MCD)
**MICPAK**... Modular Integrated Circuit Package
**MIC PAN**... Mica Panis [*Crumb of Bread*] [*Pharmacy*]
**MICR**......... Magnetic Ink Character Recognition [*Banking*] [*Data processing*]
**MICR**......... Management Improvement and Cost Reduction Project Reporting System
**MICR**......... Microscope (MSA)
**Micr**........... Microscopium [*Constellation*]
**MICRAD**... Microwave Radiometry (MCD)
**MICRAM**... Microminiature Individual Components Reliable Assembled Modules
**MICRO**..... Microcomputer
**MICRO**..... Microelectronics Innovation and Computer Science Research Program [*University of California*] [*Research center*] (RCD)
**Micro**......... Microprocessing and Microprogramming [*A publication*]
**MICRO**..... Microprocessor
**micro**.......... Microscopic
**MICRO**..... Multiple Indexing and Console Retrieval Options [*Information retrieval*] [*Data processing*]
**MICROACE**... Microminiature Automatic Checkout Equipment
**Microb Drug Resist**... Microbial Drug Resistance [*A publication*]
**Microbeam Anal Soc Annu Conf Proc**... Microbeam Analysis Society. Annual Conference. Proceedings [*A publication*]
**Microb Ecol**... Microbial Ecology [*A publication*]
**Microb Genet Bull**... Microbial Genetics Bulletin [*A publication*]
**MICROBIOL**... Microbiological [*or Microbiology*]
**Microbiol Abstr**... Microbiological Abstracts [*A publication*]
**Microbiol Aliments Nutr**... Microbiologie, Aliments, Nutrition [*A publication*]
**Microbiol Esp**... Microbiologia Espanola [*A publication*]
**Microbiol Immunol**... Microbiology and Immunology [*Japan*] [*A publication*]
**Microbiolog**... Microbiology [*A publication*]
**Microbiology (Engl Transl Mikrobiologiya)**... Microbiology (English Translation of Mikrobiologiya) [*A publication*]
**Microbiol Parazitol Epidemiol**... Microbiologia, Parazitologia, Epidemiologia [*A publication*]
**Microbiol Parazitol Epidemiol (Buchar)**... Microbiologia, Parazitologia, Epidemiologia (Bucharest) [*A publication*]
**Microbiol Rev**... Microbiological Reviews [*A publication*]
**Microbiol Sci**... Microbiological Sciences [*A publication*]
**Microbios L**... Microbios Letters [*A publication*]
**Microbios Lett**... Microbios Letters [*A publication*]
**MICRO-C**... [*A*] programming language [*1977*] (CSR)
**Microchem J**... Microchemical Journal [*A publication*]
**Microchem J Symp Ser**... Microchemical Journal. Symposium Series [*A publication*]
**Microcirc Endothelium Lymphatics**... Microcirculation, Endothelium, and Lymphatics [*A publication*]
**Microcompu**... Microcomputing [*A publication*]
**Microcomput Printout**... Microcomputer Printout [*A publication*]
**Micro Decis**... Micro Decision [*A publication*]
**MICRODIS**... Microform Document of Information System (MCD)
**MICRO-DISC**... Microcomputer-Videodisc
**MICRODOC**... Council for Microphotography and Document Reproduction [*British*]
**Microelectron Eng**... Microelectronic Engineering [*A publication*]
**Microelectron J**... Microelectronics Journal [*A publication*]
**Microelectron and Reliab**... Microelectronics and Reliability [*A publication*]
**Microelectron Reliab**... Microelectronics and Reliability [*A publication*]
**Microel Rel**... Microelectronics and Reliability [*A publication*]
**Microfiche Fdn Newsl**... Microfiche Foundation. Newsletter [*A publication*]
**Microform R**... Microform Review [*A publication*]
**Microform Rev**... Microform Review [*A publication*]
**MICROG**.. Microgram [*One millionth of a gram*]
**Microgr Newsl**... Micrographics Newsletter [*A publication*]
**Micro-6502/6809 J**... Micro - The 6502/6809 Journal [*A publication*]
**Micro Jrl**.... Microwave Journal [*A publication*]
**MICROLAB**... Microfabrication Laboratory [*University of California, Berkeley*] [*Research center*] (RCD)
**Microlepid Palearct**... Microlepidoptera Palaearctica [*A publication*]
**MICROM**... Microinstruction Read-Only Memory [*Data processing*]
**MICROMIN**... Microminiature (IEEE)
**Micro Mktw**... Micro Marketworld [*A publication*]
**MICRON**.. Micronavigator [*Air Force*]
**Micronesica J Coll Guam**... Micronesica. Journal of the College of Guam [*A publication*]
**Micronesica J Univ Guam**... Micronesica. Journal of the University of Guam [*A publication*]
**Micron Microsc Acta**... Micron and Microscopica Acta [*A publication*]
**Microorg Infect Dis**... Microorganisms and Infectious Diseases [*A publication*]
**MICROPAC**... Micromodule Data Processor and Computer (IEEE)
**Micropaleon**... Micropaleontology [*A publication*]
**Micropaleontolog Spec Publ**... Micropaleontology. Special Publication [*A publication*]
**Micro Proc Annu Workshop Microprogram**... Micro Proceedings. Annual Workshop on Microprogramming [*A publication*]
**Microprocess and Microprogram**... Microprocessing and Microprogramming [*A publication*]
**Microprocess Microprogram**... Microprocessing and Microprogramming [*A publication*]
**Microprocess and Microsyst**... Microprocessors and Microsystems [*A publication*]
**Microprocessors Microsysts**... Microprocessors and Microsystems [*A publication*]
**Microprocess Software Q**... Microprocessor Software Quarterly [*A publication*]
**Microprocess Work**... Microprocessors at Work [*A publication*]
**MICROS**... Microscopy
**Microsc**...... Microscope [*A publication*]
**Microsc Act**... Microscopica Acta [*A publication*]
**Microsc Acta**... Microscopica Acta [*A publication*]
**Microsc Acta Suppl**... Microscopica Acta. Supplement [*A publication*]
**Microsc Cryst Front**... Microscope and Crystal Front [*England*] [*A publication*]
**Microsc Electron Biol Cel**... Microscopia Electronica y Biologia Celular [*A publication*]
**Microsc Handb**... Microscopy Handbooks [*A publication*]
**Microsc J Quekett Microsc Club**... Microscopy. Journal of the Quekett Microscopical Club [*A publication*]
**Microsc Soc Can Bull**... Microscopical Society of Canada. Bulletin [*A publication*]
**MICROSECS**... Microfilm Sequential Coding System [*Bell System*]
**MicroSIFT**... Microcomputer Software and Information for Teachers [*Northwest Regional Educational Laboratory*] [*Information service or system*] (IID)
**Microstruct Sci**... Microstructural Science [*A publication*]
**Micro Syst**... Micro Systems [*A publication*]
**Microsystm**... Microsystems [*A publication*]
**Microtec**..... Microtecnic [*A publication*]
**MICRO TR**... Microwave Tower [*Nautical charts*]
**Microvasc R**... Microvascular Research [*A publication*]
**Microvasc Res**... Microvascular Research [*A publication*]
**Microwave Energy Appl Newsl**... Microwave Energy Applications Newsletter [*A publication*]
**Microwave J**... Microwave Journal [*A publication*]
**Microwave Syst News**... Microwave Systems News [*A publication*]
**Microw Syst News**... Microwave Systems News [*A publication*]
**MICRS**...... Main Instrument Console and Readout Stations (NATG)
**MICRU**...... MICRU International (EA)
**MICS**......... Maintenance Inventory Control System [*Bell System*]
**MICS**......... Management Information and Control System [*Navy*]
**MICS**......... Management Integrated Control System
**MICS**......... Manned Interactive Control Stations (MCD)
**MICS**......... MICOM Systems, Inc. [*NASDAQ symbol*] (NQ)
**MICS**......... Microprocessor Inertia and Communication System
**MICS**......... Military Integrated Communications System (CINC)
**MICS**......... Mineral-Insulated Copper-Sheathed [*Cable*] (IEEE)
**MICS**......... Missile Inspection Completion Sheet (MCD)
**MICS**......... Multiplex Interior Communications (NG)
**MICSA**...... Maine Indian Claims Settlement Act [*1980*]
**MICTAR**... Minnesota Center for Twin and Adoption Research (ECON)
**MICU**........ Medical Intensive Care Unit [*Medicine*]
**MICU**........ Mobile Intensive Care Unit [*Medicine*]
**MICV**........ Mechanized Infantry Combat Vehicle [*Army*]
**MICV-FPW**... Mechanized Infantry Combat Vehicle - Firing Port Weapon (MCD)
**MICVS**...... Mechanized Infantry Combat Vehicle Systems [*Army*] (RDA)
**MiCw**......... Coldwater Public Library, Coldwater, MI [*Library symbol*] [*Library of Congress*] (LCLS)
**MICW**....... Member of the Institute of Clerks of Works of Great Britain, Inc. (DBQ)
**MiCwB**...... Branch County Library, Coldwater, MI [*Library symbol*] [*Library of Congress*] (LCLS)

**MiD** .......... Detroit Public Library, Detroit, MI [*Library symbol*] [*Library of Congress*] (LCLS)
**MID** .......... Magnetically Insulated Diode [*Physics*]
**MID** .......... Management Information Division [*Vietnam*]
**MID** .......... Manpower Information Division [*Navy*]
**MID** .......... Mare Island Division [*San Francisco Bay Naval Shipyard, Vallejo, CA*]
**MID** .......... Marginally Indigent Defendant
**MID** .......... Master of Industrial Design
**MID** .......... Meat Inspection Division [*of ARS, Department of Agriculture*]
**MID** .......... Median Infective Dose [*Bacteriology*]
**MID** .......... Mentioned in Dispatches (ADA)
**MID** .......... Merida [*Mexico*] [*Airport symbol*] (OAG)
**MID** .......... Mesioincisodistal [*Dentistry*]
**MID** .......... Message Input Description
**MID** .......... Message Input Device (AABC)
**MID** .......... Midbody (NASA)
**MID** .......... Midcon Oil & Gas Ltd. [*Toronto Stock Exchange symbol*]
**MID** .......... Middle (AFM)
**MID** .......... Middleton Island [*Alaska*] [*Seismograph station code, US Geological Survey*] (SEIS)
**Mid** .......... Middoth (BJA)
**MID** .......... Midland [*Topography*] (ROG)
**MID** .......... Midland Bank Review [*A publication*]
**MID** .......... MIDLNET [*Midwest Regional Library Network*], St. Louis, MO [*OCLC symbol*] (OCLC)
**MID** .......... Midnight
**Mid** .......... Midrash [*Interpretation of Old Testament writings*] (BJA)
**MID** .......... Midshipman [*Navy*]
**Mid** .......... Midstream [*A publication*]
**MID** .......... Midway Airlines, Inc. [*Chicago, IL*] [*FAA designator*] (FAAC)
**MID** .......... Midway Railroad Co. [*AAR code*]
**MID** .......... Midwifery (ROG)
**MID** .......... Military Intelligence Detachment (AABC)
**MID** .......... Military Intelligence Division [*War Department*] [*World War II*]
**MID** .......... Minimal Inhibiting Dose [*Medicine*]
**MID** .......... Minimum Infective Dose [*Bacteriology*]
**MID** .......... Ministerstvo Inostrannykh Del [*Ministry of Foreign Affairs*] [*USSR*]
**MID** .......... Missile Intelligence Directorate [*Army*] (AABC)
**MID** .......... Modified Ionization Detector (MCD)
**MID** .......... Mortgage Interest Differential
**MID** .......... Movimiento Independiente Democratico [*Independent Democratic Movement*] [*Panama*] [*Political party*] (PPW)
**MID** .......... Movimiento de Integracion Democratica [*Democratic Integration Movement*] [*Dominican Republic*] [*Political party*] (PPW)
**MID** .......... Multiple Infarct Dementia [*Neurology*]
**MID** .......... Multiple Ion Detection
**MID** .......... Munitions Inventions Department [*British military*] (DMA)
**MID** .......... Musically Intelligent Device [*Electronic musical instruments*]
**MiDA** .......... Detroit Institute of Arts, Detroit, MI [*Library symbol*] [*Library of Congress*] (LCLS)
**MIDA** .......... Major Items Data Agency [*Military*]
**MidA** .......... Mid-America: An Historical Review [*A publication*]
**MIDA** .......... Mid-American International Development Association [*Nigeria*]
**MIDAC** ..... Management Information for Decision and Control
**MIDAC** ..... Michigan [*University of*] Digital Automatic Computer
**MiDACI** ..... American Concrete Institute, Detroit, MI [*Library symbol*] [*Library of Congress*] (LCLS)
**MIDAD** ..... NIDA Research Monograph [*A publication*]
**MIDADE** .. Mouvement International d'Apostolat des Enfants [*International Movement of Apostolate of Children*] [*France*]
**MidAg** ........ Midrash Aggadah (BJA)
**MiDAIK** .... Mitteilungen. Deutsches Archaeologische Institut. Abteilung Kairo [*A publication*]
**Mid-Am** ..... Mid-America: An Historical Review [*A publication*]
**MIDAM** .... Midamerica Commodity Exchange (EA)
**MiDAMA** ... Automobile Manufacturers' Association, Inc., Detroit, MI [*Library symbol*] [*Library of Congress*] (LCLS)
**Mid-Am Hist** ... Mid-America: An Historical Review [*A publication*]
**Mid-Am Oil Gas Rep** ... Mid-America Oil and Gas Reporter [*A publication*]
**Mid Am Outlk** ... Mid-American Outlook [*A publication*]
**Mid-Am Spectrosc Symp Proc** ... Mid-America Spectroscopy Symposium. Proceedings [*A publication*]
**MIDAN** ..... Microprocessor Data Analyzer [*Instrumentation*]
**MIDAR** ..... Microwave Detection and Ranging
**MIDAR** ..... Motion Indicating RADAR (MCD)
**MID-ARK** ... Mid-Arkansas Regional Library [*Library network*]
**MIDARM** ... Microdynamic Angle and Rate Monitoring System
**MIDAS** ...... Management Integrated Data Accumulating System
**MIDAS** ...... Measurement Information Data Analysis System [*or Subsystem*] (IEEE)
**MIDAS** ...... Memory Implemented Data Acquisition Systems
**MIDAS** ...... Meteorological Information and Dose Acquisition System [*Nuclear energy*] (NRCH)
**MIDAS** ...... Meteorological Integrating Data Acquisition System [*Marine science*] (MSC)
**MIDAS** ...... Microcomputer-Interfaced Data Acquisition System [*Data processing*]
**MIDAS** ...... Microimaged Data Addition System [*CAPS Equipment Ltd.*]
**MIDAS** ...... Microprogrammable Integrated Data Acquisition System
**MIDAS** ...... Microprogramming Design Aided System [*RCA*]
**MIDAS** ...... Mine Detection and Avoidance System (MCD)
**MIDAS** ...... Miniature Data Acquisition System
**MIDAS** ...... Missile Defense Alarm [*or Alert*] System [*Air Force*]
**MIDAS** ...... Missile Detection and Alarm System [*Army*] (AABC)
**MIDAS** ...... Missile Detection and Surveillance (CAAL)
**MIDAS** ...... Missile Intercept Data Acquisition System
**MIDAS** ...... Modified Integration Digital Analog Simulator [*Data processing*] (MCD)
**MIDAS** ...... Modular Integrated Design Automated System
**MIDAS** ...... Modular Interactive Data Acquisition System [*National Institute of Standards and Technology*]
**MIDAS** ...... Modulator Isolation Diagnostic Analysis System (IEEE)
**MIDAS** ...... Monopoly Information and Data Analysis System
**MIDAS** ...... Multimode International Data Acquisition Service [*Australia*] [*Information service or system*] (IID)
**MIDAS** ...... Multioptional Interactive Display and Analytic System (MCD)
**MIDAS** ...... Multiple Index Data Access System [*Prime Computer, Inc.*]
**MIDAS** ...... Multiple Input Data Acquisition System [*Bell System*]
**MIDAS** ...... Multiple Integrated Document Assembly System [*Data processing*] (BYTE)
**MIDATA** ... Marconi Integrated Design and Test Automation [*Marconi Industries*] [*Telecommunications*] [*British*]
**Mid-Atl Ind Waste Conf Proc** ... Mid-Atlantic Industrial Waste Conference. Proceedings [*United States*] [*A publication*]
**MiDb** .......... Dearborn Public [*Henry Ford Centennial*] Library, Dearborn, MI [*Library symbol*] [*Library of Congress*] (LCLS)
**MiDB** .......... Detroit Bar Association, Detroit, MI [*Library symbol*] [*Library of Congress*] (LCLS)
**MiD-B** ....... Detroit Public Library, Burton Historical Collection, Detroit, MI [*Library symbol*] [*Library of Congress*] (LCLS)
**MiDbEI** ..... Edison Institute [*Henry Ford Museum and Greenfield Village*] Library, Dearborn, MI [*Library symbol*] [*Library of Congress*] (LCLS)
**MiDbF** ....... Ford Motor Co., Dearborn, MI [*Library symbol*] [*Library of Congress*] (LCLS)
**MiDbGS** .... Church of Jesus Christ of Latter-Day Saints, Genealogical Society Library, Dearborn Stake Branch, LDS Chapel, Dearborn, MI [*Library symbol*] [*Library of Congress*] (LCLS)
**MiDbHi** ..... Dearborn Historical Museum, Dearborn, MI [*Library symbol*] [*Library of Congress*] (LCLS)
**MiDbU** ...... University of Michigan, Dearborn Campus, Dearborn, MI [*Library symbol*] [*Library of Congress*] (LCLS)
**MiDC** ......... Detroit Chancery [*Catholic Church*] Archives, Detroit, MI [*Library symbol*] [*Library of Congress*] (LCLS)
**MIDC** ......... MidConn Bank [*Kensington, CT*] [*NASDAQ symbol*] (NQ)
**MIDC** ......... Movement for an Independent and Democratic Cuba (EA)
**MIDCD** ..... Modeling Identification and Control [*A publication*]
**MiDCh** ....... Children's Hospital of Michigan, Detroit, MI [*Library symbol*] [*Library of Congress*] (LCLS)
**MiDChryE** ... Chrysler Corp., Engineering Division, Detroit, MI [*Library symbol*] [*Library of Congress*] (LCLS)
**Midcon Conf Rec** ... Midcon Conference Record [*A publication*]
**Mid-Cont** ... Mid-Continent [*A publication*]
**Mid Cont Bk** ... Mid-Continent Banker [*A publication*]
**Midcontinent Am Studies Jour** ... Midcontinent American Studies. Journal [*A publication*]
**Mid-Cont Lepid Ser** ... Mid-Continent Lepidoptera Series [*A publication*]
**MIDCRU** .. Midshipman Cruise [*Navy*] (NVT)
**MIDDLE** ... Microprogram Design Description Language [*1977*] [*Data processing*] (CSR)
**Middlebury Hist Soc Papers and Pr** ... Middlebury [*Vermont*] Historical Society. Papers and Proceedings [*A publication*]
**Middle E** .... Middle East [*A publication*]
**Middle Eas** ... Middle East [*A publication*]
**Middle East Archtl Design** ... Middle East Architectural Design [*A publication*]
**Middle East Dent Oral Health** ... Middle East Dentistry and Oral Health [*A publication*]
**Middle East Econ Dig** ... Middle East Economic Digest [*A publication*]
**Middle East Electron** ... Middle East Electronics [*A publication*]
**Middle East Exec Repts** ... Middle East Executive Reports [*A publication*]
**Middle East J** ... Middle East Journal [*A publication*]
**Middle East J Anaesthesiol** ... Middle East Journal of Anaesthesiology [*A publication*]
**Middle East R** ... Middle East Review [*A publication*]
**Middle East Tech Univ J Pure Appl Sci** ... Middle East Technical University. Journal of Pure and Applied Sciences [*A publication*]
**Middle E Executive Rep** ... Middle East Executive Reports [*A publication*]
**Middle E J** ... Middle East Journal [*A publication*]
**Middle E Mg** ... Middle Eastern Monographs [*A publication*]
**Middle E St** ... Middle Eastern Studies [*A publication*]

**Middle States Assn Col & Sec Sch Proc** ... Middle States Association of Colleges and Secondary Schools. Proceedings [*A publication*]
**Middle States Council for Social Studies Proc** ... Middle States Council for the Social Studies. Proceedings [*A publication*]
**MiDDS**...... Duns Scotus College, Detroit, MI [*Library symbol*] [*Library of Congress*] (LCLS)
**MIDDX**..... Middlesex [*County in England*]
**Middx Sit**... Sittings for Middlesex at Nisi Prius [*A publication*] (DLA)
**MIDE**........ Methods in Investigative and Diagnostic Endocrinology [*Elsevier Book Series*] [*A publication*]
**MidEast**..... Middle East [*A publication*]
**Mid East E** ... Middle East and African Economist [*A publication*]
**Mid East Elect** ... Middle East Electricity [*A publication*]
**MIDEASTFOR** ... Middle East Force [*Military*] (AABC)
**Mid East J** ... Middle East Journal [*A publication*]
**Mid East J Anaesthesiol** ... Middle East Journal of Anaesthesiology [*A publication*]
**Mid East L Rev** ... Middle East Law Review [*A publication*] (DLA)
**MIDEAST MI LIB** ... Mideastern Michigan Library Cooperative [*Library network*]
**Mid East Stud** ... Middle Eastern Studies [*A publication*]
**MiDec**........ Van Buren County Library, Decatur, MI [*Library symbol*] [*Library of Congress*] (LCLS)
**MiDecD**..... Decatur Township Library, Webster Memorial Library Building, Decatur, MI [*Library symbol*] [*Library of Congress*] (LCLS)
**MiDeck**...... Deckerville Public Library, Deckerville, MI [*Library symbol*] [*Library of Congress*] (LCLS)
**MiDecV**..... Van Buren County Library, Webster Memorial Library Building, Decatur, MI [*Library symbol*] [*Library of Congress*] (LCLS)
**MiDEd**....... Detroit Edison Co., Detroit, MI [*Library symbol*] [*Library of Congress*] (LCLS)
**MIDEF**....... Microprocedure Definition
**MIDEFO**... Mission Debrief Forms (CINC)
**Mid E J**...... Middle East Journal [*A publication*]
**MiDelD**...... Delton District Library, Delton, MI [*Library symbol*] [*Library of Congress*] (LCLS)
**MIDEO**..... Melanges. Institut Dominicain d'Etudes Orientales [*A publication*]
**MIDES**...... Missile Detection System
**Mid E Stud** ... Middle Eastern Studies [*A publication*]
**Mid E Studies** ... Middle Eastern Studies [*A publication*]
**MiDet**........ De Tour Area School and Public Library, De Tour Village, MI [*Library symbol*] [*Library of Congress*] (LCLS)
**MiDew**....... De Witt Public Library, De Witt, MI [*Library symbol*] [*Library of Congress*] (LCLS)
**MiDex**........ Dexter District Library, Dexter, MI [*Library symbol*] [*Library of Congress*] (LCLS)
**MIDF**......... Major Item Data File (AABC)
**MIDF**......... Malaysian Industrial Development Finance (DS)
**MiDG**........ Gale Research Co., Detroit, MI [*Library symbol*] [*Library of Congress*] (LCLS)
**Mid G**......... Graduate Midwife
**MIDGA**..... Mitsubishi Denki Giho [*A publication*]
**MiDGH**..... Detroit General Hospital, Medical Library, Detroit, MI [*Library symbol*] [*Library of Congress*] (LCLS)
**MiDGM-L** ... General Motors World Headquarters, General Motors Law Library, Detroit, MI [*Library symbol*] [*Library of Congress*] (LCLS)
**MiDGrH**.... Grace Hospital, Detroit, MI [*Library symbol*] [*Library of Congress*] (LCLS)
**MIDH**........ Middletown & Hummelstown Railroad Co. [*AAR code*]
**MidHag**..... Midrash ha-Gadol (BJA)
**MiDHF**...... Henry Ford Hospital, Detroit, MI [*Library symbol*] [*Library of Congress*] (LCLS)
**MiDHH**..... Harper Hospital, Department of Libraries, Detroit, MI [*Library symbol*] [*Library of Congress*] (LCLS)
**MiDHi**....... Detroit Historical Society, Detroit, MI [*Library symbol*] [*Library of Congress*] (LCLS)
**MIDI**......... Minnesota Infant Development Inventory [*Child development test*] [*Psychology*]
**MIDI**......... Miss Distance Indicator (MCD)
**MIDI**......... Musical Instrument Digital Interface [*Port*] [*Socket on an electronic synthesizer that permits a direct computer connection*]
**MiDi**.......... Windsor Township Library, Dimondale, MI [*Library symbol*] [*Library of Congress*] (LCLS)
**MIDIA**....... Member of the Industrial Design Institute of Australia
**MIDIST**.... Mission Interministerielle de l'Information Scientifique et Technique [*Interministerial Mission for Scientific and Technical Information*] [*France*] [*Information service or system*] (IID)
**MiDIT**....... Detroit Institute of Technology, Detroit, MI [*Library symbol*] [*Library of Congress*] (LCLS)
**MIDIZ**....... Mid-Canada Identification Zone
**MidJob**...... Midrash Job (BJA)
**MidJonah**.. Midrash Jonah (BJA)
**MiDL**......... Michigan Library Consortium, Wayne State University, Detroit, MI [*Library symbol*] [*Library of Congress*] (LCLS)
**MIDL**........ Midland [*English dialect*] (ROG)
**MIDL**........ Midlantic Corp. [*NASDAQ symbol*] (NQ)
**Midland**..... Midland Monthly [*A publication*]
**Midland Bank R** ... Midland Bank Review [*A publication*]
**Midland Bank Rev** ... Midland Bank Review [*A publication*]
**Midland Hist** ... Midland History [*A publication*]
**Midland Sch** ... Midland Schools [*A publication*]
**MIDLAT**... Middle Latitude [*Navigation*]
**Midl Drug Pharm Rev** ... Midland Druggist and Pharmaceutical Review [*A publication*]
**MidLekTov** ... Midrash Lekah Tov (BJA)
**Midl Macromol Monogr** ... Midland Macromolecular Monographs [*A publication*]
**Midl Med Rev** ... Midland Medical Review [*A publication*]
**MIDLNET** ... Midwest Regional Library Network
**MiDM**....... Marygrove College, Detroit, MI [*Library symbol*] [*Library of Congress*] (LCLS)
**MidM**........ Midwest Monographs [*A publication*]
**MiDMC**..... Mercy College of Detroit, Detroit, MI [*Library symbol*] [*Library of Congress*] (LCLS)
**MiDMch**.... Mariners' Church, Detroit, MI [*Library symbol*] [*Library of Congress*] (LCLS)
**MID-MO**... Mid-Month [*Amount of pay to be received by payee on the 15th day of the month*] (AABC)
**MiDMP**..... Merrill-Palmer Institute, Detroit, MI [*Library symbol*] [*Library of Congress*] (LCLS)
**MIDMS**..... Machine Independent Data Management System [*Defense Intelligence Agency*] (MCD)
**MiDMtC** ... Mount Carmel Mercy Hospital, Medical Library, Detroit, MI [*Library symbol*] [*Library of Congress*] (LCLS)
**MIDN**........ Midnight (FAAC)
**MIDN**........ Midshipman [*Navy*]
**MiDo**.......... Dorr Township Library, Dorr, MI [*Library symbol*] [*Library of Congress*] (LCLS)
**MIDOC**..... Mildew-Induced Defacement of Organic Coatings
**MiDolb**...... Osceola Township Public and School Library, Dollar Bay, MI [*Library symbol*] [*Library of Congress*] (LCLS)
**MIDOP**..... Missile Doppler
**MIDOT**..... Multiple Interferometer Determination of Trajectories
**MiDow**....... Dowagiac Public Library, Dowagiac, MI [*Library symbol*] [*Library of Congress*] (LCLS)
**MIDP**........ Major Item Distribution Plan (AABC)
**MIDP**........ Microbiology and Infectious Diseases Program [*Bethesda, MD*] [*National Institute of Allergy and Infectious Diseases*] [*Department of Health and Human Services*] (GRD)
**MiDP**......... Providence Hospital, School of Nursing, Detroit, MI [*Library symbol*] [*Library of Congress*] (LCLS)
**MIDPAC**... US Army Forces, Middle Pacific [*Name commonly used for AFMIDPAC*] [*World War II*]
**MiDPD**...... Parke, Davis & Co., Detroit, MI [*Library symbol*] [*Library of Congress*] (LCLS)
**MIDPM**.... Member of the Institute of Data Processing Management [*British*] (DCTA)
**MidProv**..... Midrash Proverbs (BJA)
**MidPs**........ Midrash Tehillim [*or The Midrash on Psalms*] (BJA)
**MidQ**......... Midwest Quarterly [*A publication*]
**MIDR**........ Mandatory Incident and Defect Reporting (NATG)
**Midr**.......... Midrash [*Interpretation of Old Testament writings*] (BJA)
**MidR**......... Midwest Review [*A publication*]
**MID-RATS** ... Midnight Rations [*Navy*]
**MidrR**........ Midrash Rabbah (BJA)
**MidrSong**... Midrash to the Song of Songs (BJA)
**MiDry**........ Dryden Township Library, Dryden, MI [*Library symbol*] [*Library of Congress*] (LCLS)
**MIDS**......... Management Information and Data Systems (NVT)
**MIDS**......... Management Information Display System (MCD)
**MIDS**......... Marketing Information Data Systems, Inc. [*Information service or system*] (IID)
**MIDS**......... Mid-South Insurance Co. [*Fayetteville, NC*] [*NASDAQ symbol*] (NQ)
**MIDS**......... Miniature Integrated Data System (MCD)
**MIDS**......... Missile Ignition and Destruct Simulator
**MIDS**......... Movable Instrument Drive System [*Nuclear energy*] (NRCH)
**MIDS**......... Movement Information Distribution Station
**MIDS**......... Multifunctional Information Distribution System [*NATO*] (MCD)
**MIDS**......... Multimode Information Distribution System
**Midsag**....... Midsagittal [*Medicine*]
**MidSam**..... Midrash Samuel (BJA)
**Mid-S F**..... Mid-South Folklore [*A publication*]
**MiDSH**...... Sacred Heart Seminary, Detroit, MI [*Library symbol*] [*Library of Congress*] (LCLS)
**MIDSIM**... Maxwell International Development Simulation
**MiDSn**....... Sinai Hospital, Detroit, MI [*Library symbol*] [*Library of Congress*] (LCLS)
**Mid-South Q Bus R** ... Mid-South Quarterly Business Review [*A publication*]
**MIDSR**...... Midsummer (ROG)

**MIDTA** ..... Member of the International Dance Teachers' Association [*British*] (DBQ)
**MidTan**...... Midrash Tanna'im on Deuteronomy (BJA)
**Mid'Tehil**... Midrash Tehillim [*or The Midrash on Psalms*] (BJA)
**MIDTRARON** ... Midshipman Training Squadron [*Navy*] (NVT)
**MIDU**........ Malfunction Insertion and Display Unit [*Aviation*]
**MiDU** ........ University of Detroit, Detroit, MI [*Library symbol*] [*Library of Congress*] (LCLS)
**MiDU-C** .... University of Detroit, Colombiere Campus, Clarkston, MI [*Library symbol*] [*Library of Congress*] (LCLS)
**MiDU-D**.... University of Detroit, Dental Library, Detroit, MI [*Library symbol*] [*Library of Congress*] (LCLS)
**MiDU-L**..... University of Detroit, Law Library, Detroit, MI [*Library symbol*] [*Library of Congress*] (LCLS)
**MIDW**....... Midwestern (AFM)
**MIDW**....... Midwestern Companies [*NASDAQ symbol*] (NQ)
**MiDW** ....... Wayne State University, Detroit, MI [*Library symbol*] [*Library of Congress*] (LCLS)
**MiDWc**...... Wayne County Records, Court House, Wayne County, Detroit, MI [*Library symbol*] [*Library of Congress*] (LCLS)
**MiDWcC** ... Wayne County Community College, Detroit, MI [*Library symbol*] [*Library of Congress*] (LCLS)
**MIDWEEK** ... Manager Integrated Dictionary Week [*Manager Software Products*] (EA)
**Mid-West Bnk** ... Mid-Western Banker [*A publication*]
**Midwest Dent** ... Midwestern Dentist [*A publication*]
**Midwest Eng** ... Midwest Engineer [*A publication*]
**Midwest J** .. Midwest Journal [*A publication*]
**Midwest J Phil** ... Midwest Journal of Philosophy [*A publication*]
**Midwest Mus Conf Am Assoc Mus Q** ... Midwest Museums Conference. American Association of Museums. Quarterly [*A publication*]
**MIDWESTNAVFACENGCOM** ... Midwest Division Naval Facilities Engineering Command
**Midwest Q** ... Midwest Quarterly [*A publication*]
**Midwest R Publ Adm** ... Midwest Review of Public Administration [*A publication*]
**Midwest Stud Phil** ... Midwest Studies in Philosophy [*A publication*]
**Midwife Health Visit** ... Midwife and Health Visitor [*Later, Midwife, Health Visitor, and Community Nurse*] [*A publication*]
**Midwife Health Visit Community Nurse** ... Midwife, Health Visitor, and Community Nurse [*A publication*]
**Midwives Chron** ... Midwives Chronicle [*A publication*]
**Midw Jour Pol Sci** ... Midwest Journal of Political Science [*A publication*]
**MiDW-L**.... Wayne State University, Law Library, Detroit, MI [*Library symbol*] [*Library of Congress*] (LCLS)
**MiDW-M** .. Wayne State University, Medical Library, Detroit, MI [*Library symbol*] [*Library of Congress*] (LCLS)
**MiDW-Mi** ... Wayne State University, Miles Manuscript Collection, Detroit, MI [*Library symbol*] [*Library of Congress*] [*Obsolete*] (LCLS)
**MiDW-P**.... Wayne State University, School of Pharmacy, Detroit, MI [*Library symbol*] [*Library of Congress*] (LCLS)
**Midw Q**...... Midwest Quarterly [*A publication*]
**Midw Quar** ... Midwest Quarterly [*A publication*]
**MiDW-S**.... Wayne State University, Kresge-Hooker Science Library, Detroit, MI [*Library symbol*] [*Library of Congress*] (LCLS)
**Midw Stud P** ... Midwest Studies in Philosophy [*A publication*]
**MIDX** ........ Midwest Exploration, Inc. [*NASDAQ symbol*] (NQ)
**MiE**............ East Lansing Public Library, East Lansing, MI [*Library symbol*] [*Library of Congress*] (LCLS)
**MIE** .......... Magnetic Isotope Effect [*Physics*]
**MIE** .......... Magnetron Ion Etching [*Semiconductor technology*]
**MIE** .......... Major Items of Equipment
**MIE** .......... Maserati Information Exchange (EA)
**MIE** .......... Mass Inertia Excitation
**MIE** .......... Master of Industrial Engineering
**MIE** .......... Master of Irrigation Engineering
**MIE** .......... Member of the Institution of Engineers, Australia
**MIE** .......... Memoires. Institut d'Egypte [*A publication*]
**MIE** .......... Meteor Ionizing Efficiency
**Mi-E** .......... Michigan State Library, Escanaba Branch, Escanaba, MI [*Library symbol*] [*Library of Congress*] (LCLS)
**MIE** .......... Middle East and African Economist [*A publication*]
**MiE**............ Minimum Effect [*Pharmacology*]
**MIE** .......... Minimum Ignition Energy
**MIE** .......... Mission-Independent Equipment [*NASA*]
**MIE** .......... Muncie [*Indiana*] [*Airport symbol*] (OAG)
**MIE** .......... Muncie, IN [*Location identifier*] [*FAA*] (FAAL)
**MIEA** ........ Music Industry Educators Association (EA)
**MiEad**........ East Detroit Memorial Library, East Detroit, MI [*Library symbol*] [*Library of Congress*] (LCLS)
**MiEat**......... Eaton Rapids Public Library, Eaton Rapids, MI [*Library symbol*] [*Library of Congress*] (LCLS)
**MIE Aust**... Member of the Institution of Engineers, Australia
**MIEC**......... Branche Africaine du Mouvement International des Etudiants Catholiques [*African International Movement of Catholic Students - AIMCS*] (EAIO)
**MiEc** ......... Eau Claire District Library, Eau Claire, MI [*Library symbol*] [*Library of Congress*] (LCLS)
**MIEC**......... Military Intelligence Exchange Center (CINC)
**MIEC**......... Pax Romana, Mouvement International des Etudiants Catholiques [*Pax Romana, International Movement of Catholic Students - IMCS*] [*Paris, France*] (EAIO)
**MIED** ........ Member of the Institution of Engineering Designers [*British*] (DBQ)
**MIEE**......... Mechanical, Instrument, and Electrical Engineering [*Department of Employment*] [*British*]
**MIEE**......... Member of the Institution of Electrical Engineers [*Formerly, AMIEE*] [*British*] (EY)
**MIEEE**...... Member of the Institute of Electrical and Electronic Engineers
**MIEETAT** ... Major Improvements in Electronic Effectiveness through Advanced Technology (MCD)
**MIEF**......... Master Imagery Exchange Format (MCD)
**MIEI**.......... Member of the Institution of Engineering Inspection [*British*]
**MIE(Ind)**... Member of the Institution of Engineers, India
**MiElb**......... Elberta Public Library, Elberta, MI [*Library symbol*] [*Library of Congress*] (LCLS)
**MIEleclE**... Corporate Member of the Institution of Electrical and Electronics Incorporated Engineers [*British*] (DBQ)
**Miel Fr**....... Miel de France [*A publication*]
**MiElk** ........ Elk Rapids District Library, Elk Rapids, MI [*Library symbol*] [*Library of Congress*] (LCLS)
**MiEm**......... Glen Lake Community Library, Empire, MI [*Library symbol*] [*Library of Congress*] (LCLS)
**MIEM** ....... Master Member of the Institute of Executives and Managers [*British*] (DBQ)
**MiEM**........ Michigan State University, East Lansing, MI [*Library symbol*] [*Library of Congress*] (LCLS)
**Mie Med J** ... Mie Medical Journal [*A publication*]
**Mie Med J Suppl** ... Mie Medical Journal. Supplement [*A publication*]
**Mie Med Sci** ... Mie Medical Science [*Japan*] [*A publication*]
**MIENDE**... Minerals and the Environment [*A publication*]
**MI Eng** ...... Master of Industrial Engineering
**MIER**......... Management-Initiated Early Retirement (ADA)
**MiER** ......... Middle East Review [*A publication*]
**MIERE**...... Member of the Institution of Electronic and Radio Engineers [*Formerly, M Brit IRE*] [*British*]
**MIERS** ...... Modernized Imagery Exploitation and Reporting System (MCD)
**MIES** ......... Member of the Institution of Engineers and Shipbuilders, Scotland
**MiEsc** ........ Escanaba Public Library, Escanaba, MI [*Library symbol*] [*Library of Congress*] (LCLS)
**MiEscB**...... Bay De Noc Community College, Escanaba, MI [*Library symbol*] [*Library of Congress*] (LCLS)
**MiEv** .......... Evart Public Library, Evart, MI [*Library symbol*] [*Library of Congress*] (LCLS)
**MiEw** ......... McMillan Township Library, Ewen, MI [*Library symbol*] [*Library of Congress*] (LCLS)
**MI Ex** ........ Member of the Institute of Export [*British*]
**MIExE**....... Member of the Institute of Executive Engineers and Officers [*British*] (DBQ)
**MIEx(Grad)** ... Member of the Institute of Export [*British*] (DBQ)
**MIExpE**..... Member of the Institute of Explosives Engineers [*British*] (DBQ)
**MIF**............ Macrophage Inhibitory Factor [*Immunology*]
**MIF**............ Malfunction Investigations File (MCD)
**MIF**............ Manual Intervention Facility
**MIF**............ MARC [*Machine-Readable Cataloging*] International Format
**MIF**............ Marubeni International Finance [*Trading company*] [*Japan*]
**MIF**............ Master Index File
**MIF**............ Master Inventory File (AFIT)
**MIF**............ Master Item File (MCD)
**MIF**............ Maximal Inspiratory Flow [*Medicine*]
**MIF**............ Medina, OH [*Location identifier*] [*FAA*] (FAAL)
**MIF**............ Melanocyte-Inhibiting Factor [*Endocrinology*]
**MIF**............ Melanocyte-Stimulating-Hormone Release Inhibiting Factor [*Also, MRIF*] [*Endocrinology*]
**MIF**............ Membrane Immunofluorescence [*Analytical biochemistry*]
**MIF**............ Merthiolate-Iodine-Formaldehyde [*Technique*]
**MIF**............ Mesoderm-Inducing Factor [*Embryology*]
**MIF**............ Migration Inhibition [*or Inhibitory*] Factor [*Cytology*]
**MIF**............ Milk in First [*Tea-pouring procedure*]
**MIF**............ Milk Industry Foundation (EA)
**MIF**............ Miners' International Federation [*See also FIM*] [*Brussels, Belgium*] (EAIO)
**MIF**............ Missile-in-Flight
**MIF**............ Mobile Instrument Facility
**MIF**............ Monopulse Interference Filter
**MIF**............ Mortgage Indemnity Fund [*Veterans Administration*]
**MIF**............ Multisource Intelligence File (MCD)
**MIF**............ MuniInsured Fund [*AMEX symbol*] (SPSG)
**MIF**............ Myocardial Infarction [*Cardiology*] (DHSM)
**MIFA**......... Mitomycin C, Fluorouracil, Adriamycin [*Antineoplastic drug regimen*]
**MIFACS**.... Medical Institutions' Financial Accounting System
**MI-FA-MI** ... Misery, Famine, Misery [*Said to be "earth's song," in theory that all planets emit musical sounds governed by their paths around the sun*]

**MIFAO**...... Memoires Publies par les Membres de l'Institut Francais d'Archeologie Orientale du Caire [*A publication*]
**MIFAOC**... Memoires Publies par les Membres de l'Institut Francais d'Archeologie Orientale du Caire [*A publication*]
**MIFAS**...... Mechanized Integrated Financial Accounting System [*Department of State*]
**MIFASS**.... Marine Integrated Fire and Air Support System
**MiFaw**....... Farwell Public Library, Farwell, MI [*Library symbol*] [*Library of Congress*] (LCLS)
**MIFC**......... Madonna International Fan Club (EA)
**MIFC**......... Merthiolate-Iodine Formalin Concentration
**MIFD**......... Material Information Flow Device [*Military*] (AFM)
**MIFE**......... Minimum Independent Failure Element
**MiFg**.......... Fairgrove Township Library, Fairgrove, MI [*Library symbol*] [*Library of Congress*] (LCLS)
**MIFG**......... Shallow Fog (FAAC)
**MIFI**.......... MicroFrame, Incorporated [*Cranbury, NJ*] [*NASDAQ symbol*] (NQ)
**MIFI**.......... Missile In-Flight Indicator
**MiFil**.......... Fife Lake Public Library, Fife Lake, MI [*Library symbol*] [*Library of Congress*] (LCLS)
**MIFIR**....... Microwave Instantaneous Frequency Indication Receiver (MCD)
**MIFirE**...... Member of the Institution of Fire Engineers [*British*] (DCTA)
**MIFireE**..... Member of the Institution of Fire Engineers [*British*] (EY)
**MIFL**......... Master International Frequency List
**MiFli**.......... Flint Public Library, Flint, MI [*Library symbol*] [*Library of Congress*] (LCLS)
**MiFliACS**... AC Spark Plug Co., General Motors Corp., Flint, MI [*Library symbol*] [*Library of Congress*] (LCLS)
**MiFliC**....... University of Michigan at Flint, and Charles Stewart Mott Community College, Flint, MI [*Library symbol*] [*Library of Congress*] (LCLS)
**MiFliG**....... GMI Engineering and Management Institute, Flint, MI [*Library symbol*] [*Library of Congress*] (LCLS)
**MiFos**........ Watertown Township Library, Fostoria, MI [*Library symbol*] [*Library of Congress*] (LCLS)
**MiFow**........ Fowlerville Public Library, Fowlerville, MI [*Library symbol*] [*Library of Congress*] (LCLS)
**MIFR**......... Master International Frequency Register
**MIFR**......... Maximal Inspiratory Flow Rate [*Medicine*]
**MIFR**......... Multiband Infrared Filter Radiometer
**MiFra**......... Frankfort City Library, Frankfort, MI [*Library symbol*] [*Library of Congress*] (LCLS)
**MiFram**..... James E. Wickson Memorial Library, Frankenmuth, MI [*Library symbol*] [*Library of Congress*] (LCLS)
**MiFras**....... Fraser Public Library, Fraser, MI [*Library symbol*] [*Library of Congress*] (LCLS)
**MiFrem**...... Fremont Public Library, Fremont, MI [*Library symbol*] [*Library of Congress*] (LCLS)
**MIFRIFI**... Mittelfristige Finanzplanung [*Medium-Term Financial Planning*] [*German*]
**MIFS**......... Material Information Flow System [*Military*] (AFM)
**MIFS**......... Multiplex Interferometric Fourier Spectroscopy
**MIFSA**...... Missile In-Flight Safety Approval (MUGU)
**MIFT**......... Manchester International Freight Terminal [*British*] (DS)
**Mig**........... De Migratione Abrahami [*Philo*] (BJA)
**MIG**........... Magnetic Injection Gun (IEEE)
**MIG**........... Magnetized Ionized Gas
**MIG**........... Malaria Immune Globulin
**MIG**........... Management in Government [*A publication*]
**MIG**........... Management Information Guide [*Reference series*]
**MIG**........... Mars Investigation Group (EA)
**MIG**........... Measles Immune Globulin [*Immunology*]
**MIG**........... Medial Inferior Geniculate Artery [*Anatomy*]
**M-Ig**.......... Membrane Immunoglobulin [*Immunology*]
**MIG**........... Metal-Inert-Gas [*Underwater welding*]
**Mig**........... Mignon [*Horticulture*]
**MIG**........... Mikoyan and Gurevich [*Acronym used as designation for a Russian aircraft and is formed from the names of the aircraft's designers*]
**MIG**........... Military Intelligence Group (MCD)
**MIG**........... Military Intelligence Guide (MCD)
**MIG**........... Millington, TN [*Location identifier*] [*FAA*] (FAAL)
**MIG**........... Ming Mines Ltd. [*Vancouver Stock Exchange symbol*]
**MIG**........... Miniature Integrating Gyroscope
**MIG**........... Moody's Investment Grade
**MIG**........... Multilevel Interconnect Generator
**MIGA**........ Multilateral Investment Guarantee Agency [*World Bank*]
**MiGal**........ Galesburg Memorial Library, Galesburg, MI [*Library symbol*] [*Library of Congress*] (LCLS)
**MiGali**....... Galien Township Public Library, Galien, MI [*Library symbol*] [*Library of Congress*] (LCLS)
**MIGasE**..... Member of the Institution of Gas Engineers [*British*]
**MiGay**........ Gaylord-Otsego County Public Library, Gaylord, MI [*Library symbol*] [*Library of Congress*] (LCLS)
**MiGc**.......... Garden City Public Library, Garden City, MI [*Library symbol*] [*Library of Congress*] (LCLS)
**MIGD**........ Member of the Institute of Grocery Distribution [*British*] (DBQ)
**MIGeol**...... Member of the Institution of Geologists [*British*] (DBQ)
**MIGFW**..... Mitteilungen. Institut fuer Geschichtsforschung und Archivwissenschaft in Wien [*A publication*]
**MIgG**......... Monkey Immunoglobulin G [*Immunology*]
**MiGh**......... Loutit Library, Grand Haven, MI [*Library symbol*] [*Library of Congress*] (LCLS)
**MIGI**......... Meridian Insurance Group, Inc. [*NASDAQ symbol*] (NQ)
**MIGKA**..... Mineralogiya i Geokhimiya [*A publication*]
**MiGl**.......... Gladstone Public Library, Gladstone, MI [*Library symbol*] [*Library of Congress*] (LCLS)
**MiGlad**...... Gladwin County Library, Gladwin, MI [*Library symbol*] [*Library of Congress*] (LCLS)
**MiGlad-B**.. Gladwin County Library, Beaverton Branch Library, Beaverton, MI [*Library symbol*] [*Library of Congress*] (LCLS)
**MIGN**........ Michigan Northern Railway Co., Inc. [*AAR code*]
**Migne P G**... Patrologia Graeca (Migne) [*A publication*]
**Migne P L**... Patrologia Latina (Migne) [*A publication*]
**MiGp**......... Grosse Pointe Public Library, Grosse Pointe, MI [*Library symbol*] [*Library of Congress*] (LCLS)
**MiGr**.......... Grand Rapids Public Library, Grand Rapids, MI [*Library symbol*] [*Library of Congress*] (LCLS)
**MiGrA**....... Aquinas College, Grand Rapids, MI [*Library symbol*] [*Library of Congress*] (LCLS)
**Migraine Symp**... Migraine Symposium [*A publication*]
**MiGran**...... Grant Public Library, Grant, MI [*Library symbol*] [*Library of Congress*] (LCLS)
**MiGray**...... Crawford County Library, Grayling, MI [*Library symbol*] [*Library of Congress*] (LCLS)
**MiGrB**....... Grand Rapids Baptist College, Grand Rapids, MI [*Library symbol*] [*Library of Congress*] (LCLS)
**MiGrC**....... Calvin College and Seminary, Grand Rapids, MI [*Library symbol*] [*Library of Congress*] (LCLS)
**Migr Int**..... Migrations Internationales [*A publication*]
**MiGrJC**..... Grand Rapids Junior College, Grand Rapids, MI [*Library symbol*] [*Library of Congress*] (LCLS)
**MiGrl**......... Grand Ledge Public Library, Grand Ledge, MI [*Library symbol*] [*Library of Congress*] (LCLS)
**MiGrL**....... Grand Rapids Law Library, Grand Rapids, MI [*Library symbol*] [*Library of Congress*] (LCLS)
**Migr dans le Monde**... Migrations dans le Monde [*A publication*]
**MiGrMtM**... Mount Mercy Academy, Grand Rapids, MI [*Library symbol*] [*Library of Congress*] (LCLS)
**Migr Today**... Migration Today [*A publication*]
**MiGrW**...... Western Michigan Genealogical Society, Grand Rapids, MI [*Library symbol*] [*Library of Congress*] (LCLS)
**MIGS**......... Miniature Infrared Guidance Sensor
**MiGw**......... Forsythe Township Public Library, Gwinn, MI [*Library symbol*] [*Library of Congress*] (LCLS)
**MIH**........... Brownsville, TX [*Location identifier*] [*FAA*] (FAAL)
**MIH**........... Master of Industrial Health
**MIH**........... Member of the Institute of Housing [*British*] (DBQ)
**MIH**........... Member of the Institute of Hygiene [*British*]
**MIH**........... Miles in the Hour [*Rate of military march*]
**MIH**........... Missing Interruption Handler [*Data processing*] (IBMDP)
**MIH**........... Molecule-Induced Homolysis [*Chemistry*]
**MIH**........... Molt Inhibitory Hormone
**MIH**........... Multiplex Interface Handler
**MiHa**......... Hart Public Library, Hart, MI [*Library symbol*] [*Library of Congress*] (LCLS)
**MiHaf**........ Hartford Public Library, Hartford, MI [*Library symbol*] [*Library of Congress*] (LCLS)
**MiHal**........ Cromaine Library, Hartland, MI [*Library symbol*] [*Library of Congress*] (LCLS)
**MiHam**...... Hamtramck Public Library, Hamtramck, MI [*Library symbol*] [*Library of Congress*] (LCLS)
**MiHamb**.... Hamburg Township Library, Hamburg, MI [*Library symbol*] [*Library of Congress*] (LCLS)
**MiHan**....... Hancock Public-School Library, Hancock, MI [*Library symbol*] [*Library of Congress*] (LCLS)
**MiHanS**..... Suomi College, Hancock, MI [*Library symbol*] [*Library of Congress*] (LCLS)
**MiHars**...... Harrison Public Library, Harrison, MI [*Library symbol*] [*Library of Congress*] (LCLS)
**MiHarsM**.. Mid-Michigan Community College, Harrison, MI [*Library symbol*] [*Library of Congress*] (LCLS)
**MiHarv**..... Alcona County Library, Harrisville, MI [*Library symbol*] [*Library of Congress*] (LCLS)
**MiHas**........ Hastings Public Library, Hastings, MI [*Library symbol*] [*Library of Congress*] (LCLS)
**MiHb**......... Harbor Beach Public Library, Harbor Beach, MI [*Library symbol*] [*Library of Congress*] (LCLS)
**MIHC**........ M. I. Hummel Club (EA)
**Mi-HC**....... Michigan Historical Commission, State Archives Library, Lansing, MI [*Library symbol*] [*Library of Congress*] (LCLS)
**MiHe**......... Hesperia Public Library, Hesperia, MI [*Library symbol*] [*Library of Congress*] (LCLS)
**MIHE**........ Member of the Institute of Health Education [*British*]
**MIHEc**...... Member of the Institute of Home Economics [*British*] (DBQ)
**MiHem**...... Mary C. Rauchholz Memorial Library, Hemlock, MI [*Library symbol*] [*Library of Congress*] (LCLS)

**MiHil**......... Mitchell Public Library, Hillsdale, MI [*Library symbol*] [*Library of Congress*] (LCLS)
**MiHilC**...... Hillsdale College, Hillsdale, MI [*Library symbol*] [*Library of Congress*] (LCLS)
**MiHilm**...... Hillman Public Library, Hillman, MI [*Library symbol*] [*Library of Congress*] (LCLS)
**MiHl**.......... Houghton Lake Public Library, Houghton Lake, MI [*Library symbol*] [*Library of Congress*] (LCLS)
**MiHM**....... Michigan Technological University, Houghton, MI [*Library symbol*] [*Library of Congress*] (LCLS)
**MIHO**........ M/I Schottenstein Homes, Inc. [*Columbus, OH*] [*NASDAQ symbol*] (NQ)
**MiHol**........ Herrick Public Library, Holland, MI [*Library symbol*] [*Library of Congress*] (LCLS)
**MiHolH**..... Hope College, Holland, MI [*Library symbol*] [*Library of Congress*] (LCLS)
**MiHolW**.... Western Theological Seminary, Holland, MI [*Library symbol*] [*Library of Congress*] (LCLS)
**MiHom**...... Homer Public Library, Homer, MI [*Library symbol*] [*Library of Congress*] (LCLS)
**MiHow**....... Howell Carnegie Library, Howell, MI [*Library symbol*] [*Library of Congress*] (LCLS)
**MiHp**......... McGregor Public Library, Highland Park, MI [*Library symbol*] [*Library of Congress*] (LCLS)
**MiHP**......... Portage Lake District Library, Houghton, MI [*Library symbol*] [*Library of Congress*] (LCLS)
**MiHpDH**... Detroit Osteopathic Hospital, Highland Park, MI [*Library symbol*] [*Library of Congress*] (LCLS)
**MIHPED**... Microwave-Induced Helium Plasma Emission Detection (NATG)
**MIHT**........ Member of the Institution of Highways and Transportation [*British*] (DBQ)
**MiHu**......... Hudson Public Library, Hudson, MI [*Library symbol*] [*Library of Congress*] (LCLS)
**MiHudv**..... Hudsonville Public Library, Hudsonville, MI [*Library symbol*] [*Library of Congress*] (LCLS)
**MIHVE**..... Member of the Institution of Heating and Ventilating Engineers [*British*]
**MII**............ Caddo Mills, TX [*Location identifier*] [*FAA*] (FAAL)
**MII**............ Management Interest Inventory [*Test*]
**MII**............ Marilia [*Brazil*] [*Airport symbol*] (OAG)
**MI/I**.......... Microinches per Inch (KSC)
**MII**............ Military Intelligence Interpreter
**MII**............ Military Intelligence Interrogation
**MII**............ Mineral Information Institute (EA)
**MII**............ Minnesota Interlibrary Telecommunications Exchange, Minneapolis, MN [*OCLC symbol*] (OCLC)
**MII**............ Morton International, Inc. [*NYSE symbol*] (SPSG)
**MII**............ Motorists Information, Incorporated [*Defunct*] (EA)
**MIIA**.......... Medical Intelligence and Information Agency [*Formerly, MIO*] [*DoD*]
**MIIA**.......... Member of the Institute of Industrial Administration [*Later, MBIM*] [*British*]
**MIIA**.......... Merritt Island Industrial Area [*NASA*] (KSC)
**MIIA**.......... Mine Inspectors' Institute of America (EA)
**MIIC**.......... Pax Romana, Mouvement International des Intellectuels Catholiques [*Pax Romana, International Catholic Movement for Intellectual and Cultural Affairs - ICMICA*] [*Geneva, Switzerland*] (EAIO)
**MIICS**....... Master Item Identification Control System
**MIID**......... Media Institutes for Institute Directors
**MIIF**......... Master Item Intelligence File
**MIIGA**....... Mie Igaku [*A publication*]
**MIIL**.......... Master Item Identification List
**MIIM**........ Member of the Institution of Industrial Managers [*British*] (DCTA)
**MIIMA**...... Memorie. Istituto Italiano di Idrobiologia Dottore Marco De Marchi [*A publication*]
**MIIMD**...... Microbiology and Immunology [*A publication*]
**MI Inf Sc**... Member of the Institute of Information Scientists [*British*]
**MiInr**......... Indian River Public Library, Indian River, MI [*Library symbol*] [*Library of Congress*] (LCLS)
**MiIrmD**..... Dickinson County Library, Iron Mountain, MI [*Library symbol*] [*Library of Congress*] (LCLS)
**MiIrmD-N**... Dickinson County Library, Norway Branch, Norway, MI [*Library symbol*] [*Library of Congress*] (LCLS)
**MiIrmM**.... Mid-Peninsula Library Federation Headquarters, Iron Mountain, MI [*Library symbol*] [*Library of Congress*] (LCLS)
**MiIrmV**..... United States Veterans Administration Hospital, Iron Mountain, MI [*Library symbol*] [*Library of Congress*] (LCLS)
**MiIrr**.......... West Iron District Library, Iron River, MI [*Library symbol*] [*Library of Congress*] (LCLS)
**MiIrw**......... Ironwood Carnegie Library, Ironwood, MI [*Library symbol*] [*Library of Congress*] (LCLS)
**MiIs**........... Ishpeming Carnegie Library, Ishpeming, MI [*Library symbol*] [*Library of Congress*] (LCLS)
**MIIS**.......... Miscellaneous Inputs Information Subsystem [*Data processing*]
**MIISE**....... Member of the International Institute of Social Economics [*British*] (DBQ)
**MIISec**....... Member of the Institute of Industrial Security [*British*] (DBQ)
**MIIT**.......... Miles in Trail [*Aviation*] (FAAC)
**MiIt**............ Thompson Home Library, Ithaca, MI [*Library symbol*] [*Library of Congress*] (LCLS)
**MIJ**............ Dugway/Tooele, UT [*Location identifier*] [*FAA*] (FAAL)
**MIJ**............ Maatschappij [*Joint Stock Company*] [*Netherlands*]
**MIJ**............ Member of the Institution of Journalists
**MIJ**............ Metal Insulator Junction
**MIJ**............ Mili [*Marshall Islands*] [*Airport symbol*] (OAG)
**MiJa**.......... Jackson Public Library, Jackson, MI [*Library symbol*] [*Library of Congress*] (LCLS)
**MiJaC**........ Jackson County Library, Jackson, MI [*Library symbol*] [*Library of Congress*] (LCLS)
**MiJaCc**...... Jackson Community College, Jackson, MI [*Library symbol*] [*Library of Congress*] (LCLS)
**MiJam**....... Jamestown Township Library, Jamestown, MI [*Library symbol*] [*Library of Congress*] (LCLS)
**MIJARC**... Mouvement International de la Jeunesse Agricole et Rurale Catholique [*International Movement of Catholic Agricultural and Rural Youth - IMCARY*] [*Louvain, Belgium*] (EAIO)
**MiJen**........ Georgetown Township Library, Jenison, MI [*Library symbol*] [*Library of Congress*] (LCLS)
**MIJI**.......... Meaconing, Intrusion, Jamming, Interference [*Military*] (NVT)
**MIJO**......... Missile Joint Optimization
**MiK**............ Kalamazoo Public Library, Kalamazoo, MI [*Library symbol*] [*Library of Congress*] (LCLS)
**MIK**........... Methyl Isobutyl Ketone [*Also, MIBK*] [*Organic chemistry*]
**MIK**........... Mikkeli [*Finland*] [*Airport symbol*] (OAG)
**Mik**............ Mikva'ot (BJA)
**MIK**........... Minitrack [*Alaska*] [*Seismograph station code, US Geological Survey*] [*Closed*] (SEIS)
**MIK**........... More in the Kitchen [*Family dinner-table expression*]
**MiKa**.......... Kalkaska County Library, Kalkaska, MI [*Library symbol*] [*Library of Congress*] (LCLS)
**MIKA**......... Medical Imaging Centers of America, Inc. [*San Diego, CA*] [*NASDAQ symbol*] (NQ)
**MIKA**......... Minor Karyotypic Abnormalities [*Medicine*]
**MiKB**......... Borgess Hospital, Medical Library, Kalamazoo, MI [*Library symbol*] [*Library of Congress*] (LCLS)
**MiKC**......... Kalamazoo College, Kalamazoo, MI [*Library symbol*] [*Library of Congress*] (LCLS)
**MiKCS**....... Institute of Cistercian Studies, Western Michigan University, Kalamazoo, MI [*Library symbol*] [*Library of Congress*] (LCLS)
**MIKE**......... Mass-Analyzed Ion Kinetic Energy
**MIKE**......... Measurement of Instantaneous Kinetic Energy (IEEE)
**MIKE**......... Micro Interpreter for Knowledge Engineering [*Data processing*]
**MIKE**......... Microphone (CET)
**MIKER**...... Microbalance Inverted Knudsen Effusion Recoil
**MIKES**...... Mass-Analyzed Ion Kinetic Energy Spectrometry
**MikGed**..... Mikra'ot Gedolot (BJA)
**MiKin**........ Kingston Community Public Library, Kingston, MI [*Library symbol*] [*Library of Congress*] (LCLS)
**MiKins**....... Kingsley Public Library, Kingsley, MI [*Library symbol*] [*Library of Congress*] (LCLS)
**MIKK**........ Medjunarodni Institut za Kucnu Knjizevnost [*International Institute for Home Literature - IIHL*] [*Belgrade, Yugoslavia*] (EAIO)
**MIKKA**...... Metody Issledovaniya Katalizatorov i Kataliticheskikh Reaktsii [*A publication*]
**MiKL**......... Kalamazoo Library System, Kalamazoo, MI [*Library symbol*] [*Library of Congress*] (LCLS)
**MIKL**......... Michael Foods, Inc. [*NASDAQ symbol*] (NQ)
**Mikol Fitopat**... Mikologiya i Fitopatologiya [*A publication*]
**Mikol Fitopatol**... Mikologiya i Fitopatologiya [*A publication*]
**MiKPSc**..... Kalamazoo Public School District, Kalamazoo, MI [*Library symbol*] [*Library of Congress*] (LCLS)
**MIKR**........ Mikron Instrument Co., Inc. [*Wyckoff, NJ*] [*NASDAQ symbol*] (NQ)
**Mikrobiol**... Mikrobiologiya [*A publication*]
**Mikrobiol Prom Ref Sb**... Mikrobiologicheskaya Promyshlennost Referativnyi Sbornik [*A publication*]
**Mikrobiol Protsessy Pochvakh Mold**... Mikrobiologicheskie Protsessy v Pochvakh Moldavii [*A publication*]
**Mikrobiol Sint Sb Inf Mater**... Mikrobiologicheskii Sintez Sbornik Informatsii Materialov [*A publication*]
**Mikrobiol Zh**... Mikrobiologichnyi Zhurnal [*A publication*]
**Mikrobiol Zh (Kiev)**... Mikrobiolohichnyi Zhurnal (Kiev) [*A publication*]
**Mikrobiyol Bul**... Mikrobiyoloji Bulteni [*A publication*]
**Mikrobiyol Bul Suppl**... Mikrobiyoloji Bulteni. Supplement [*A publication*]
**Mikroch Act**... Mikrochimica Acta [*A publication*]
**Mikrochem Ver Mikrochim Acta**... Mikrochemie Vereinigt mit Mikrochimica Acta [*A publication*]
**Mikrochim Acta**... Mikrochimica Acta [*A publication*]
**Mikrochim Acta Suppl**... Mikrochimica Acta. Supplement [*A publication*]
**Mikrochim Ichnoanal Acta**... Mikrochimica et Ichnoanalytica Acta [*A publication*]
**Mikro Comp**... Mikrocomputer-Zeitschrift [*A publication*]
**Mikroehlektron**... Mikroehlektronika [*A publication*]

**Mikroelektronika Akad Nauk SSSR** ... Mikroelektronika Akademiya Nauk SSSR [*USSR*] [*A publication*]
**Mikroelem Med** ... Mikroelementy v Meditsine [*Ukrainian SSR*] [*A publication*]
**Mikroelem Pochvakh Sov Soyuza** ... Mikroelementy v Pochvakh Sovetskogo Soyuza [*A publication*]
**Mikroelem Prod Rast** ... Mikroelementy i Produktivnost' Rastenii [*A publication*]
**Mikroelem Sel'sk Khoz Med** ... Mikroelementy v Sel'skom Khozyaistve i Meditsine [*A publication*]
**Mikroelem Sib** ... Mikroelementy v Sibiri [*A publication*]
**Mikroelem Sib Inf Byull** ... Mikroelementy Sibiri Informatsionnyi Byulleten [*A publication*]
**Mikroelem Vost Sib Dal'nem Vostoke** ... Mikroelementy v Vostochnoi Sibiri i na Dal'nem Vostoke [*A publication*]
**Mikroelem Zhivotnovod Rastenievod** ... Mikroelementy v Zhivotnovodstve i Rastenievodstve [*A publication*]
**Mikro-Klein Comput** ... Mikro-Klein Computer [*A publication*]
**Mikroorg Rast Trudy Inst Mikrobiol Akad Nauk Latvii SSR** ... Mikroorganizmy i Rasteniya Trudy Instituta Mikrobiologii Akademii Nauk Latviiskoi SSR [*A publication*]
**Mikrowelin** ... Mikroweilen and Military Electronics [*A publication*]
**Mikrowellen Mag** ... Mikrowellen Magazin [*A publication*]
**Mikrozirk Forsch Klin** ... Mikrozirkulation in Forschung und Klinik [*A publication*]
**MiKUp** ...... Upjohn Co., Kalamazoo, MI [*Library symbol*] [*Library of Congress*] (LCLS)
**MiKV** ......... Kalamazoo Valley Community College, Kalamazoo, MI [*Library symbol*] [*Library of Congress*] (LCLS)
**Mikv** .......... Mikva'ot (BJA)
**MiKW** ........ Western Michigan University, Kalamazoo, MI [*Library symbol*] [*Library of Congress*] (LCLS)
**MiKWUp** ... W. E. Upjohn Institute for Employment Research, Kalamazoo, MI [*Library symbol*] [*Library of Congress*] (LCLS)
**miky** .......... Milky [*Philately*]
**MiL** ............ Lansing Public Library, Lansing, MI [*Library symbol*] [*Library of Congress*] (LCLS)
**MIL** .......... Magnetic Indicator Loop (NVT)
**MIL** .......... Malfunction Investigation Laboratory
**MIL** .......... Master Index List (MCD)
**MIL** .......... Master Instrumentation List
**MIL** .......... Master Item Identification List (AABC)
**MIL** .......... Member of the Institute of Linguists [*British*]
**MIL** .......... Memorie. Istituto Lombardo [*A publication*]
**MIL** .......... Merritt Island Tracking Station [*Florida*]
**Mi L** .......... Michigan Law Review [*A publication*]
**MIL** .......... Microimplementation Language [*Burroughs Corp.*]
**MIL** .......... Middle East [*A publication*]
**MIL** .......... Milan [*Italy*] [*Seismograph station code, US Geological Survey*] [*Closed*] (SEIS)
**MIL** .......... Milan [*Italy*] [*Airport symbol*] (OAG)
**MIL** .......... Mileage
**Mil** ............ Miles' Pennsylvania Reports [*A publication*] (DLA)
**MIL** .......... Military (EY)
**MIL** .......... Military Instrumentation List
**MIL** .......... Military Specification [*Followed by a single capital letter and numbers*] (IEEE)
**MIL** .......... Militia
**Mil** ............ Miller's Reports [*1-5 Louisiana*] [*A publication*] (DLA)
**Mil** ............ Miller's Reports [*3-18 Maryland*] [*A publication*] (DLA)
**mil** ............ Milli-Inch
**MIL** .......... Milliliter
**MIL** .......... Million
**MIL** .......... Millipore Corp. [*NYSE symbol*] (SPSG)
**Mil** ............ Mills' New York Surrogate's Court Reports [*A publication*] (DLA)
**Mil** ............ Mill's South Carolina Constitutional Reports [*A publication*] (DLA)
**MIL** .......... Milwaukee [*Wisconsin*]
**MIL** .......... Minnesota Instructional Language [*Data processing*] (CSR)
**MIL** .......... Module Interconnection Language
**MIL** .......... Mothers-in-Law Club International (EA)
**MIL** .......... Movimiento Iberico Libertario [*Spain*] [*Political party*]
**MIL** .......... Moving Inspection Lot
**MIL** .......... Office of Public Library and Interlibrary Cooperation, St. Paul, MN [*OCLC symbol*] (OCLC)
**Mil** ............ Pro Milone [*of Cicero*] [*Classical studies*] (OCD)
**Mi L** .......... University of Miami. Law Review [*A publication*]
**MILA** ......... Merritt Island Launch Area [*NASA*]
**MILA** ......... Milastar Corp. [*NASDAQ symbol*] (NQ)
**Mila** .......... Militia [*British military*] (DMA)
**MiLac** ........ Missaukee County Library, Lake City, MI [*Library symbol*] [*Library of Congress*] (LCLS)
**MILAD** ...... Military Advisor [*SEATO or ANZUS Council*] (CINC)
**MILADGOVT** ... Military Advisory Government
**MILADGRU** ... Military Advisory Group
**MILADREP** ... Military Advisors Representative (CINC)
**Mil Aff** ....... Military Affairs [*A publication*]
**Mil Affairs** ... Military Affairs [*A publication*]
**MiLai** ......... Laingsburg Public Library, Laingsburg, MI [*Library symbol*] [*Library of Congress*] (LCLS)
**MiLakv** ...... Cato Township Public Library, Lakeview, MI [*Library symbol*] [*Library of Congress*] (LCLS)
**MiLal** ......... Lake Linden-Hubbell Public School Library, Lake Linden, MI [*Library symbol*] [*Library of Congress*] (LCLS)
**MiLan** ........ L'Anse Township School and Public Library, L'Anse, MI [*Library symbol*] [*Library of Congress*] (LCLS)
**MILAN** ..... Missile, Infantry Light Antiarmor [*Antitank system*] (INF)
**MILAS** ...... Micrometer Low-Approach System
**MiLaw** ....... Lawton Public Library, Lawton, MI [*Library symbol*] [*Library of Congress*] (LCLS)
**MILBA** ...... Military Base Agreement (CINC)
**Milbank Mem** ... Milbank Memorial Fund. Quarterly [*A publication*]
**Milbank Mem Fund Annu Rep** ... Milbank Memorial Fund. Annual Report [*A publication*]
**Milbank Mem Fund Q** ... Milbank Memorial Fund. Quarterly [*A publication*]
**Milbank Meml Fund Q Health Soc** ... Milbank Memorial Fund. Quarterly. Health and Society [*A publication*]
**Milbank Memor Fund Quart** ... Milbank Memorial Fund. Quarterly [*A publication*]
**Milbank Q** ... Milbank Quarterly [*A publication*]
**Milb Mem Fund Q** ... Milbank Memorial Fund. Quarterly [*A publication*]
**MiLC** ......... Lansing Community College, Lansing, MI [*Library symbol*] [*Library of Congress*] (LCLS)
**MILC** ......... Metal Ion Liquid Chromatography
**MILC** ......... Midwest Interlibrary Center [*Later, CRL*]
**MILC** ......... Military Characteristics
**MILCAP** ... Military Civic Action Program
**MILCAP** ... Military Standard Contract Administration Procedures [*DoD*]
**MILCEST** ... Military Communications Electronic Systems Technology (MCD)
**Mil Chapl Rev** ... Military Chaplains' Review [*A publication*]
**Milchforsch-Milchprax** ... Milchforschung-Milchpraxis [*A publication*]
**Milch Prax Rindermast** ... Milch Praxis und Rindermast [*A publication*]
**Milchwirtsch Ber Bundesanst Wolfpassing Rotholz** ... Milchwirtschaftliche Berichte aus dem Bundesanstalten Wolfpassing und Rotholz [*A publication*]
**Milchwiss** .. Milchwissenschaft [*A publication*]
**Milchwissenschaft Milk Sci Int** ... Milchwissenschaft. Milk Science International [*A publication*]
**MILCOM** ... Military Committee Communication [*NATO*] (NATG)
**MILCOMP** ... Military Computer
**MILCOMSAT** ... Military Communications Satellite
**MILCON** .. Military Construction
**MILCON-DA** ... Military Construction, Defense Agencies
**MILCONF** ... Military Confinement
**MILCS** ...... Metropolitan Interlibrary Cooperative System [*New York Public Library*] [*Information service or system*]
**MILDAT** ... Military Damage Assessment Team (AABC)
**MILDDU** .. Military-Industry Logistics Data Development Unit
**MILDEC** ... Military Decision (NATG)
**MILDEPS** ... Military Departments (AABC)
**MILDEPT** ... Military Department
**MILDET** ... Military Detachment
**MILDIP** .... Military-Industry Logistics Data Interchange Procedures
**MILDIS** ..... Military-Industry Logistics Data Interchange System
**MiLe** .......... Leland Township Public Library, Leland, MI [*Library symbol*] [*Library of Congress*] (LCLS)
**MIL-E-CON** ... Military Electronic Conference
**Mil Electron/Countermeas** ... Military Electronics/Countermeasures [*A publication*]
**Mil Eng** ...... Military Engineer [*A publication*]
**MiLer** ......... LeRoy Public Library, LeRoy, MI [*Library symbol*] [*Library of Congress*] (LCLS)
**Miles** .......... Miles' District Court Reports [*1825-41*] [*Philadelphia, PA*] [*A publication*] (DLA)
**MILES** ...... Military Implications of LASER Employment by the Soviets
**MILES** ...... Multiple Integrated LASER Engagement Simulation [*or System*] [*Army*]
**Miles Int Symp Ser** ... Miles International Symposium Series [*A publication*]
**Miles (PA)** ... Miles' Pennsylvania Reports [*A publication*] (DLA)
**Miles R** ...... Miles' Pennsylvania Reports [*A publication*] (DLA)
**Miles Rep** .. Miles' Pennsylvania Reports [*A publication*] (DLA)
**Miles R & O** ... Miles' Rules and Orders [*A publication*] (DLA)
**Milestones Conn Agr Home Econ** ... Milestones in Connecticut Agricultural and Home Economics [*A publication*]
**MiLew** ........ Lewiston Public Library, Lewiston, MI [*Library symbol*] [*Library of Congress*] (LCLS)
**MiLex** ........ Moore Public Library, Lexington, MI [*Library symbol*] [*Library of Congress*] (LCLS)
**MILF** ......... Moro Islamic Liberation Front [*Political party*] [*Philippines*]
**Mil Fib Opt N** ... Military Fiber Optics News [*A publication*]
**MiLG** ......... Great Lakes Bible College, Lansing, MI [*Library symbol*] [*Library of Congress*] (LCLS)
**MILGP** ...... Military Group
**MiLGS** ....... Church of Jesus Christ of Latter-Day Saints, Genealogical Society Library, Lansing Branch, Stake Center, Lansing, MI [*Library symbol*] [*Library of Congress*] (LCLS)
**MIL-HDBK** ... Military Handbook
**Mil Hist J** ... Military History Journal [*A publication*]

**MIL-I**......... Military Specification on Interference (IEEE)
**MILI**.......... Multilevel Informal Language Inventory [*Test*]
**MILIC**....... Microwave Insular Line Integrated Circuit (IEEE)
**MILIC**....... Ministerial Libraries and Information Centers
**MILINREP** ... Military Incident Report (MCD)
**MILIRAD** ... Millimeter Wave RADAR Fuze (MCD)
**MiLit**......... Litchfield District Library, Litchfield, MI [*Library symbol*] [*Library of Congress*] (LCLS)
**MILIT**....... Military
**Militaergesch** ... Militaergeschichte [*A publication*]
**Militaerpol Dok** ... Militaerpolitik Dokumentation [*A publication*]
**Milit Aff**..... Military Affairs [*A publication*]
**Military Law R** ... Military Law Review [*A publication*]
**Military LJ** ... Military Law Journal [*A publication*] (DLA)
**Military M** ... Military Market Annual [*A publication*]
**Military R** ... Military Review [*A publication*]
**Milit Hist Tex Southwest** ... Military History of Texas and the Southwest [*A publication*]
**Milit LR**..... Military Law Review [*A publication*]
**Milit Med**.. Military Medicine [*A publication*]
**MILITRAN** ... Military in Transition Database [*Information service or system*] (IID)
**MiLivM**..... Madonna College, Livonia, MI [*Library symbol*] [*Library of Congress*] (LCLS)
**MiLivPS**.... Livonia Public Schools, Livonia, MI [*Library symbol*] [*Library of Congress*] (LCLS)
**Mil Jur Cas & Mat** ... Military Jurisprudence, Cases and Materials [*A publication*] (DLA)
**Milk Board J** ... Milk Board Journal [*A publication*]
**Milk Dlr**..... Milk Dealer [*A publication*]
**Milk Ind Found Conv Proc Lab Sect** ... Milk Industry Foundation. Convention Proceedings. Laboratory Section [*A publication*]
**Milk Ind Found Conv Proc Milk Supplies Sect** ... Milk Industry Foundation. Convention Proceedings. Milk Supplies Section [*A publication*]
**Milk Plant Mo** ... Milk Plant Monthly [*A publication*]
**Milk Plant Mon** ... Milk Plant Monthly [*A publication*]
**Milk Prod J** ... Milk Products Journal [*A publication*]
**Milk Sci Int** ... Milk Science International [*A publication*]
**Mill**........... Miller's Reports [*3-18 Maryland*] [*A publication*] (DLA)
**Mill**........... Miller's Reports [*1-5 Louisiana*] [*A publication*] (DLA)
**MILL**......... Millicom, Inc. [*NASDAQ symbol*] (NQ)
**MILL**......... Million
**Mill**........... Mills' New York Surrogate's Court Reports [*A publication*] (DLA)
**Mill**........... Mill's South Carolina Constitutional Reports [*A publication*] (DLA)
**Mill & C Bills** ... Miller and Collier on Bills of Sale [*A publication*] (DLA)
**Mill Civ L**.. Miller's Civil Law of England [*1825*] [*A publication*] (DLA)
**Mill Code**... Miller's Iowa Code [*A publication*] (DLA)
**Mill Const** ... Mill's South Carolina Constitutional Reports [*A publication*] (DLA)
**Mill Const (SC)** ... Mill's South Carolina Constitutional Reports [*A publication*] (DLA)
**Mill Dec**..... Miller's Circuit Court Decisions (Woolworth) [*United States*] [*A publication*] (DLA)
**Mill Dec**..... Miller's United States Supreme Court Decisions [*Condensed, Continuation of Curtis*] [*A publication*] (DLA)
**Mill El**....... Miller's Elements of the Law of Insurances [*A publication*] (DLA)
**Mill Eq M** ... Miller's Equitable Mortgages [*1844*] [*A publication*] (DLA)
**Miller**......... Miller's Reports [*1-5 Louisiana*] [*A publication*] (DLA)
**Miller**......... Miller's Reports [*3-18 Maryland*] [*A publication*] (DLA)
**Miller Const** ... Miller on the Constitution of the United States [*A publication*] (DLA)
**Miller's Code** ... Miller's Revised and Annotated Code [*Iowa*] [*A publication*] (DLA)
**Mill Fact**.... Mill and Factory [*A publication*]
**Mill & F Pr** ... Miller and Field's Federal Practice [*A publication*] (DLA)
**MILLIE**..... Maximum Interchange of the Latest Logistic Information Is Essential
**Millin**......... Petty Sessions Cases [*1875-98*] [*Ireland*] [*A publication*] (DLA)
**Milling**....... Milling and Baking News [*A publication*]
**Milling Feed Fert** ... Milling Feed and Fertiliser [*A publication*]
**Milling F & F** ... Milling Feed and Fertilizer [*A publication*]
**Milling S**.... Changing Face of Breadstuffs (Milling and Baking News. Special Edition) [*A publication*]
**Mill Ins**...... Miller's Elements of the Law of Insurances [*A publication*] (DLA)
**millisec**....... Millisecond
**Mill LA**...... Miller's Reports [*1-5 Louisiana*] [*A publication*] (DLA)
**Mill Log**..... Mill's Logic [*A publication*] (DLA)
**Mill MD**.... Miller's Reports [*3-18 Maryland*] [*A publication*] (DLA)
**MillN**......... Mill Newsletter [*A publication*]
**Mill News**.. Mill Newsletter [*A publication*]
**Mill Op**...... Miller's Circuit Court Decisions (Woolworth) [*United States*] [*A publication*] (DLA)
**Mill Part**.... Miller on Partition [*A publication*] (DLA)
**Mill Pl & Pr** ... Miller's Iowa Pleading and Practice [*A publication*] (DLA)
**Mil LR**....... Military Law Review [*A publication*]
**Mil L Rep**.. Military Law Reporter [*A publication*]
**Mil L Rev**... Military Law Review [*A publication*]
**Mills**.......... Mills' New York Surrogate's Court Reports [*A publication*] (DLA)
**Mills Ann St** ... Mills' Annotated Statutes [*Colorado*] [*A publication*] (DLA)
**Mills Em D** ... Mills on Eminent Domain [*A publication*] (DLA)
**Mills Em Dom** ... Mills on Eminent Domain [*A publication*] (DLA)
**Mills (NY)** ... Mills' New York Surrogate's Court Reports [*A publication*] (DLA)
**Mills' Surr Ct** ... Mills' New York Surrogate's Court Reports [*A publication*] (DLA)
**Mill & V Code** ... Milliken and Vertrees' Tennessee Code [*A publication*] (DLA)
**MIL-M**...... Military Manual (MCD)
**Mil Med**..... Military Medicine [*A publication*]
**MILMO**...... Military Motorcycle [*Army*] (INF)
**MILNET**... Military Network
**MILNRY**... Millinery
**MILO**........ Maryland Interlibrary Organization [*Information service or system*] (IID)
**MILO**........ Miami Valley Library Organization [*Library network*]
**MILO**........ Most Input for the Least Output [*Business term*]
**MILocoE**... Member of the Institution of Locomotive Engineers [*British*] (EY)
**MIL/OS**.... Military/Ordnance Specification (MCD)
**MILP**......... Mixed Integer Linear Program [*Statistics*]
**MILPAC**... Military Personnel Accounting Activity [*Army*] (AABC)
**MILPAS**.... Miscellaneous Information Listing Program Apollo Spacecraft [*NASA*] (KSC)
**MILPERCEN** ... Military Personnel Center [*Alexandria, VA*] [*Army*] (AABC)
**MILPERS** ... Military Personnel
**MILPERSINS** ... Military Personnel Information System
**MILPERSINST** ... Military Personnel Instructions (MCD)
**MILPERSIS** ... Military Personnel Information Subsystem (MCD)
**MILPHAP** ... Military Provincial Health Assistance Program (AABC)
**MILPO**...... Military Personnel Office (AABC)
**MILR**......... Maintenance Incident Log Report [*Navy*] (CAAL)
**MILR**......... Master of Industrial and Labor Relations
**MILREP**.... Military Representative (NATG)
**Mil Rep**...... Militia Reporter [*Boston*] [*A publication*] (DLA)
**Mil Rev**...... Military Review [*A publication*]
**MILRIS**..... Military Routing Identifier System
**MILS**......... Marine Integrated Logistics System
**MILS**......... Member of the Incorporated Law Society [*British*]
**MILS**......... Microcomputer Integrated Library System
**MILS**......... Microwave Instrument Landing System
**MILS**......... Military Standard Logistics System (MCD)
**MILS**......... Milliradians (KSC)
**MILS**......... Mineral Industry Location System [*Bureau of Mines*] [*Information service or system*] (IID)
**MILS**......... Missile Impact Locating [*or Location*] System
**MILSAT**.... Military Satellite
**MILSATCOM** ... Military Satellite Communications [*Systems*]
**MILSBILLS** ... Military Standard Billing System
**MILSCAP** ... Military Standard Contract Administration Procedures [*DoD*]
**Mil Sci Tech** ... Military Science and Technology [*A publication*]
**MILSIMDS** ... Military Standard Item Management Data System
**MILSIMS** ... Military Standard Inventory Management System
**MILSO**...... Military Standard Logistics Systems Office [*DoD*] (MCD)
**MILSPEC** ... Military Specification
**MILSPETS** ... Military Standard Petroleum System (MCD)
**MIL SPOT** ... Military Standard Procurement Operations Technique
**MILSPOT** ... Military Standard Purchase Operating Technique
**MILSPRED** ... Military Standard for Providing Research and Exploratory Development Data
**MILSTAAD** ... Military Standard Activity Address Directory
**MILSTAC** ... Military Staff Communication (NATG)
**MILSTAG** ... Military Standardization Agreement (CINC)
**MILSTAM** ... International Military Staff Memorandum [*NATO*] (NATG)
**MILSTAMP** ... Military Standard Transportation and Movement Procedure
**MILSTAN** ... Military Agency for Standardization [*NATO*]
**MILSTAR** ... Military Strategic and Tactical Relay System [*Satellite communications*]
**MILSTARAP** ... Military Standard Transportation Action Report and Accounting Procedures (MCD)
**MILSTD** ... Military Standard
**MILSTEP** ... Military Standard Evaluation Procedure
**MILSTEP** ... Military Supply and Transportation Evaluation Procedures (AFM)
**MILSTICC** ... Military Standard Item Characteristics Coding
**MILSTICCS** ... Military Standard Item Characteristics Coding Structure
**MILSTIICS** ... Military Standard Item Identification Coding System
**MILSTRAMP** ... Military Standard Transportation and Movement Procedure
**MILSTRAP** ... Military Standard Transaction Reporting and Accounting Procedures
**MILSTRIP** ... Military Standard Requisitioning and Issue Procedure
**Mil Surgeon** ... Military Surgeon [*A publication*]
**MILSVC**.... Military Services
**MILT**......... Milton [*England*]

**MILT**......... Miltope Group, Inc. [*NASDAQ symbol*] (NQ)
**MILT**......... Minister's Letter. Letter to Indian People on Current Issues. Minister of Indian Affairs and Northern Development [*A publication*]
**MILTA**...... Militaertechnik [*A publication*]
**MILTAG**... Military Technical Assistance Group
**MILTAM**.. Misrad Isre'eli Li-tevi'ot Mi-Germanyah (BJA)
**MiLTC**....... Thomas M. Cooley Law School, Lansing, MI [*Library symbol*] [*Library of Congress*] (LCLS)
**MILTELCOMM**... Military Telecommunications
**Milt Law R**... Military Law Review [*A publication*]
**Milton Keynes J Archaeol Hist**... Milton Keynes Journal of Archaeology and History [*A publication*]
**Milton N**.... Milton Newsletter [*A publication*]
**Milton Q**.... Milton Quarterly [*A publication*]
**Milton S**..... Milton Studies [*A publication*]
**Milton Stud**... Milton Studies [*A publication*]
**MILTOP**... Man-in-the-Loop Trajectory Optimization Program [*NASA*]
**MILTOSS**... Military Transportation of Small Shipments (NVT)
**Miltron**....... Miltronics [*A publication*]
**MiLud**........ Ludington Public Library, Ludington, MI [*Library symbol*] [*Library of Congress*] (LCLS)
**Mil & Vet C**... Military and Veterans Code [*A publication*] (DLA)
**MILW**........ Chicago, Milwaukee, St. Paul & Pacific Railroad Co. [*AAR code*]
**Milw**........... Milward's Irish Ecclesiastical Reports [*1819-43*] [*A publication*] (DLA)
**MILW**........ Milwaukee Insurance Group, Inc. [*Milwaukee, WI*] [*NASDAQ symbol*] (NQ)
**Milwau Jl**... Milwaukee Journal [*A publication*]
**Milwaukee Law**... Milwaukee Lawyer [*A publication*] (DLA)
**Milw BAG**... Milwaukee Bar Association. Gavel [*A publication*]
**Milw Ir Ecc Rep**... Milward's Irish Ecclesiastical Reports [*1819-43*] [*A publication*] (DLA)
**Milw Public Mus Contrib Biol Geol**... Milwaukee Public Museum. Contributions in Biology and Geology [*A publication*]
**Milw Public Mus Occas Pap Nat Hist**... Milwaukee Public Museum. Occasional Papers. Natural History [*A publication*]
**Milw Public Mus Publ Biol Geol**... Milwaukee Public Museum. Publications in Biology and Geology [*A publication*]
**Milw Public Mus Spec Publ Biol Geol**... Milwaukee Public Museum. Special Publications in Biology and Geology [*A publication*]
**MiLy**.......... Lyons Public Library, Lyons, MI [*Library symbol*] [*Library of Congress*] (LCLS)
**MIM**.......... Magnetic Interaction Mechanism
**MIM**.......... Maintenance Instructions Manual [*DoD*]
**MIM**.......... Marine Information Management [*Marine science*] (MSC)
**MIM**.......... Master of Industrial Management
**MIM**.......... Master of International Management
**MIM**.......... Member of the Institution of Metallurgists [*British*] (DBQ)
**MIM**.......... Merimbula [*Australia*] [*Airport symbol*] (OAG)
**MIM**.......... Message Input Module [*Telecommunications*] (TEL)
**MIM**.......... Metal Insulator Metal [*Light detector*]
**MIM**.......... Microion Mill
**MIM**.......... Mid Mountain Mining [*Vancouver Stock Exchange symbol*]
**MIM**.......... Military Iranian Mission [*World War II*]
**MIM**.......... Milo [*Maine*] [*Seismograph station code, US Geological Survey*] (SEIS)
**MIM**.......... Mimeographed (ADA)
**MIM**.......... Mindanao Independence Movement [*Philippines*] [*Political party*]
**MIM**.......... Mining and Industrial Magazine [*Manila*] [*A publication*]
**MIM**.......... Mining Magazine [*A publication*]
**MIM**.......... Minorities in Media (EA)
**MIM**.......... Missile Identification Module [*Military*] (CAAL)
**MIM**.......... Mobile-Launched Interceptor Missile
**MIM**.......... MODEM Interface Modules [*Data processing*]
**MIM**.......... Modified Index Method (IEEE)
**MIM**.......... Montagu Investments Management [*Commercial firm*] [*British*]
**MIM**.......... Morality in Media (EA)
**MIM**.......... Mouvement Independantiste Martiniquais [*Martinique Independence Movement*] [*Political party*] (PD)
**MIM**.......... Multilayer Interference Mirror [*Optical instrumentation*]
**MIM**.......... Multiple Ion Monitoring [*Mass spectrometry*]
**Mim**........... United States Internal Revenue Bureau, Commissioner's Mimeographed Published Opinions [*A publication*] (DLA)
**MIMA**....... Mineral Insulation Manufacturers Association (EA)
**MIMA**....... Minute Man National Historical Park
**MIMA**....... Modern Image Makers Association [*Australia*]
**MIMA**....... Music Industry Manufacturers Association [*Defunct*] (EA)
**MiMaci**...... Mackinac Island Public Library, Mackinac Island, MI [*Library symbol*] [*Library of Congress*] (LCLS)
**MiMack**..... Mackinaw City Public Library, Mackinaw City, MI [*Library symbol*] [*Library of Congress*] (LCLS)
**MIMAF**..... Musicians International Mutual Aid Fund
**MiMan**...... Manchester Township Library, Manchester, MI [*Library symbol*] [*Library of Congress*] (LCLS)
**MiManc**..... Mancelona Township Library, Mancelona, MI [*Library symbol*] [*Library of Congress*] (LCLS)
**MIManf**..... Member of the Institute of Manufacturing [*British*] (DBQ)
**MiMani**..... Manistee County Library, Manistee, MI [*Library symbol*] [*Library of Congress*] (LCLS)
**MiMant**..... Manton Public Library, Manton, MI [*Library symbol*] [*Library of Congress*] (LCLS)
**MiMar**....... M. Alice Chapin Memorial Library, Marion, MI [*Library symbol*] [*Library of Congress*] (LCLS)
**MiMarc**..... Marcellus Township Library, Marcellus, MI [*Library symbol*] [*Library of Congress*] (LCLS)
**MIMarE**.... Member of the Institute of Marine Engineers [*British*] (EY)
**MiMarl**...... Marlette Township Library, Marlette, MI [*Library symbol*] [*Library of Congress*] (LCLS)
**MiMarq**..... Peter White Public Library, Marquette, MI [*Library symbol*] [*Library of Congress*] (LCLS)
**MiMarqAS**... Marquette-Alger Intermediate School District, Learning Materials Center, Marquette, MI [*Library symbol*] [*Library of Congress*] (LCLS)
**MiMarqHi**... Marquette County Historical Society, John M. Longyear Memorial Library, Marquette, MI [*Library symbol*] [*Library of Congress*] (LCLS)
**MiMarqN**... Northern Michigan University, Marquette, MI [*Library symbol*] [*Library of Congress*] (LCLS)
**MiMarqS**... Superiorland Library Cooperative System, Marquette, MI [*Library symbol*] [*Library of Congress*] (LCLS)
**MiMars**..... Marshall Public Library, Marshall, MI [*Library symbol*] [*Library of Congress*] (LCLS)
**MiMary**..... Marysville Public Library, Marysville, MI [*Library symbol*] [*Library of Congress*] (LCLS)
**MiMas**....... Ingham County Library, Mason, MI [*Library symbol*] [*Library of Congress*] (LCLS)
**MIMAS**..... Magnetically Insulated Macroparticle Accelerator System
**MiMay**....... Mayville District Public Library, Mayville, MI [*Library symbol*] [*Library of Congress*] (LCLS)
**MIMBD**.... Montanaro d'Italia - Monti e Boschi [*A publication*]
**MIMBM**... Member of the Institute of Municipal Building Management [*British*] (DBQ)
**MIMC**....... Management Inventory on Managing Change [*Test*]
**MimC**......... Maxwell International Microforms Corporation, Fairview Park, Elmsford, NY [*Library symbol*] [*Library of Congress*] (LCLS)
**MIMC**....... Member of the Institute of Management Consultants
**MIMC**....... Microforms International Marketing Corporation [*Pergamon*]
**MIMC**....... Multivariable Internal Model Control [*Control engineering*]
**MIMCO**.... McGraw-Hill Information Management Co. [*Database producer*] (IID)
**MiMD**....... Dorsch Memorial Public Library, Monroe, MI [*Library symbol*] [*Library of Congress*] (LCLS)
**MIMD**....... Multiple Instruction Stream, Multiple Data Stream (MCD)
**MIME**....... Member of the Institute of Mining Engineers
**MIME**....... Member of the Institution of Mechanical Engineers [*Formerly, AMIMechE*] [*British*]
**MIME**....... Ministry of Information Middle East [*British*] [*World War II*]
**MiMe**......... Spies Public Library, Menominee, MI [*Library symbol*] [*Library of Congress*] (LCLS)
**MIMEA**..... Minerva Medica [*A publication*]
**MiMec**....... Morton Township Library, Mecosta, MI [*Library symbol*] [*Library of Congress*] (LCLS)
**MIMechE**... Member of the Institution of Mechanical Engineers [*Formerly, AMIMechE*] [*British*] (EY)
**MiMen**....... Mendon Township Library, Mendon, MI [*Library symbol*] [*Library of Congress*] (LCLS)
**MIMEO**.... Mimeographed (ADA)
**MIMEO**.... Multiple Input Memo Engineering Order (MCD)
**Mimeo AS Indiana Agr Exp Sta**... Mimeo AS. Indiana Agricultural Experiment Station [*A publication*]
**Mimeo AY Indiana Agr Exp Sta**... Mimeo AY. Indiana Agricultural Experiment Station [*A publication*]
**Mimeo Circ NS Dep Agric**... Mimeographed Circular Service. Nova Scotia Department of Agriculture and Marketing [*A publication*]
**Mimeo Circ Wyo Agric Exp Stn**... Mimeograph Circular. Wyoming Agricultural Experiment Station [*A publication*]
**Mimeo Co-Op Ext Serv Purdue Univ**... Mimeo. Co-Operative Extension Service. Purdue University [*A publication*]
**Mimeo EC Purdue Univ Coop Ext Serv**... Mimeo EC. Purdue University. Cooperative Extension Service [*A publication*]
**Mimeogr Bull A-E Ohio State Univ Dept Agr Econ Rural Sociol**... Mimeograph Bulletin A-E. Ohio State University. Department of Agricultural Economics and Rural Sociology [*A publication*]
**Mimeogr Circ Okla Agric Exp Stn**... Mimeograph Circular. Oklahoma Agricultural Experiment Station [*A publication*]
**Mimeogr Circ Univ RI Ext Serv Agr Home Econ**... Mimeograph Circular. University of Rhode Island. Extension Service in Agriculture and Home Economics [*A publication*]
**Mimeogr Circ Wyo Agr Exp Sta**... Mimeograph Circular. Wyoming Agricultural Experiment Station [*A publication*]
**Mimeogrd Publ Commonw Bur Past Fld Crops**... Mimeographed Publications. Commonwealth Bureau of Pastures and Field Crops [*A publication*]

**Mimeogr Publ Commonwealth Bur Pastures Field Crops** ... Mimeographed Publications. Commonwealth Bureau of Pastures and Field Crops [*A publication*]
**Mimeogr Publ Hawaii Univ Dept Hort** ... Mimeographed Publication. Hawaii University. Department of Horticulture [*A publication*]
**Mimeogr Rep Cambridge Univ Sch Agr Farm Econ Br** ... Mimeographed Report. Cambridge University. School of Agriculture. Farm Economics Branch [*A publication*]
**Mimeogr Ser Ark Agr Exp Sta** ... Mimeograph Series. Arkansas Agricultural Experiment Station [*A publication*]
**Mimeogr Ser Ark Agric Exp Stn** ... Mimeograph Series. Arkansas Agricultural Experiment Station [*A publication*]
**Mimeogr Ser GA Agr Exp Sta** ... Mimeograph Series. Georgia Agricultural Experiment Station [*A publication*]
**Mimeogr Ser GA Agric Exp Stn** ... Mimeograph Series. Georgia Agricultural Experiment Station [*A publication*]
**Mimeogr Ser Univ Arkansas Agric Exp Stn** ... Mimeograph Series. University of Arkansas. Agricultural Experiment Station [*A publication*]
**Mimeogr Ser Utah Agr Exp Sta** ... Mimeograph Series. Utah Agricultural Experiment Station [*A publication*]
**Mimeo ID Purdue Univ Dept Agr Ext** ... Mimeo ID. Purdue University. Department of Agricultural Extension [*A publication*]
**Mimeo Rep Fla Dep Agric Econ** ... Mimeo Report. Department of Agricultural Economics. Florida Agricultural Experiment Stations [*A publication*]
**Mimeo Rep Fla Everglades Exp Sta** ... Mimeo Report. Florida Everglades Experiment Station [*A publication*]
**MiMer** ....... Merrill District Library, Merrill, MI [*Library symbol*] [*Library of Congress*] (LCLS)
**MiMes** ....... Mesick Public Library, Mesick, MI [*Library symbol*] [*Library of Congress*] (LCLS)
**MIMEX** ..... Major Item Material Excess [*Air Force*] (AFIT)
**MIMF** ........ Member of the Institute of Metal Finishing [*British*] (DBQ)
**MIMGTechE** ... Member of the Institution of Mechanical Engineers and General Technician Engineers [*British*] (DBQ)
**MIMH** ....... Member of the Institute of Materials Handling [*British*] (DBQ)
**MIMI** ........ Member of the Institute of Motor Industry [*British*]
**MIMIC** ...... [*A*] programming language [*1965*] (CSR)
**MIMIC** ...... Measure and Inspection Masks for Integrated Circuits (MCD)
**MIMIC** ...... Microwave and Millimeter-Wave Monolithic Integrated Circuits Project [*DoD*]
**MIMIC/CUS** ... Michigan Metropolitan Information Center/Center for Urban Studies [*Wayne State University*] [*Information service or system*] (IID)
**MiMid** ....... Grace A. Dow Memorial [*Public*] Library, Midland, MI [*Library symbol*] [*Library of Congress*] (LCLS)
**MiMidD** .... Dow Chemical Co., Midland, MI [*Library symbol*] [*Library of Congress*] (LCLS)
**MiMidDC** ... Dow Corning Corp., Midland, MI [*Library symbol*] [*Library of Congress*] (LCLS)
**MiMidGS** ... Church of Jesus Christ of Latter-Day Saints, Genealogical Society Library, Midland Stake Branch, Midland, MI [*Library symbol*] [*Library of Congress*] (LCLS)
**MiMidN** .... Northwood Institute, Midland, MI [*Library symbol*] [*Library of Congress*] (LCLS)
**MiMil** ........ Milan Public Library, Milan, MI [*Library symbol*] [*Library of Congress*] (LCLS)
**MiMill** ....... Millington Township Library, Millington, MI [*Library symbol*] [*Library of Congress*] (LCLS)
**MIMinE** .... Member of the Institution of Mining Engineers [*British*] (EY)
**MiMio** ....... Oscoda County Public Library, Mio, MI [*Library symbol*] [*Library of Congress*] (LCLS)
**MIMIT** ...... Member of the Institute of Musical Instrument Technology [*British*] (DBQ)
**MIMJ** ........ Metal Insulator - Metal Junction
**MIMM** ...... Management Inventory on Modern Management [*Test*]
**MIMM** ...... Member of the Institute of Mining and Metallurgy [*British*] (EY)
**MIMMIS** .. Marine Corps Integrated Manpower Management Information System
**MIMMS** .... Marine Corps Integrated Maintenance Management System
**MIMN** ....... Micmac News [*A publication*]
**MIMNO** .... Mimeographed Notice (FAAC)
**MIMO** ....... Man In, Machine Out [*Data processing*]
**MIMO** ....... Modified Input - Modified Output [*Data processing*]
**MiMo** ......... Monroe County Library System, Monroe, MI [*Library symbol*] [*Library of Congress*] (LCLS)
**MIMO** ....... Multiple-Input/Multiple-Output [*Data processing*]
**MIMOLA** ... Machine Independent Microprogramming Language
**MiMor** ....... Stair Public Library, Morenci, MI [*Library symbol*] [*Library of Congress*] (LCLS)
**MiMory** ..... Morley-Stanwood Community Library, Morley, MI [*Library symbol*] [*Library of Congress*] (LCLS)
**MIMOSA** ... Mission Modes and Space Analysis (NASA)
**MIMP** ....... Magazine Industry Market Place [*A publication*]
**MIMR** ....... Magnetic Ink Mark Recognition
**MIMR** ....... May Institute of Medical Research
**MIMR** ....... Minimal Inhibitor Mole Ratio [*Biochemistry*]
**MIMS** ........ Major Item Management System (AABC)
**MIMS** ........ Material Information Management System (MCD)
**MIMS** ........ Medical Information Management System [*NASA*]
**MIMS** ........ Medical Inventory Management System
**MIMS** ........ Member of the Institute of Management Specialists [*British*] (DBQ)
**MIMS** ........ Metal Impact Monitoring System [*Nuclear energy*] (NRCH)
**MIMS** ........ Mineral Insulated, Metal Sheathed [*Cable*]
**MIMS** ........ Mitrol Industrial Management System [*Mitrol, Inc.*] [*Information service or system*] (IID)
**MIMS** ........ Modular Isodrive Memory Series
**MIMS** ........ Monthly Index of Medical Specialities [*A publication*] (APTA)
**MIMS** ........ Multi-Item Multisource (IEEE)
**MIMS** ........ Multiple Independently Maneuvering Submunitions (MCD)
**MI³MS** ...... Minolta Integrated Information and Image Management System [*Optical disc*] (IT)
**MIMSA** ..... Minerva Medica. Supplemento [*A publication*]
**MIMSq** ...... Missile Maintenance Squadron [*Air Force*] (AFM)
**MIMT** ....... Member of the Institute of Music Teachers (ADA)
**MiMtc** ........ Mount Clemens Public Library, Mount Clemens, MI [*Library symbol*] [*Library of Congress*] (LCLS)
**MiMtcM** .... Macomb County Library, Mount Clemens, MI [*Library symbol*] [*Library of Congress*] (LCLS)
**MiMtp** ....... Mount Pleasant Public Library, Mount Pleasant, MI [*Library symbol*] [*Library of Congress*] (LCLS)
**MiMtpC** .... Chippewa Library League, Mt. Pleasant, MI [*Library symbol*] [*Library of Congress*] (LCLS)
**MiMtpT** .... Central Michigan University, Mount Pleasant, MI [*Library symbol*] [*Library of Congress*] (LCLS)
**MiMu** ........ Hackley Public Library, Muskegon, MI [*Library symbol*] [*Library of Congress*] (LCLS)
**MiMuB** ...... Muskegon Business College, Muskegon, MI [*Library symbol*] [*Library of Congress*] (LCLS)
**MIMUG** .... Meetings Industry Microcomputer Users Group (EA)
**MiMul** ....... Mulliken District Library, Mulliken, MI [*Library symbol*] [*Library of Congress*] (LCLS)
**Mim Ulama** ... Mimbar Ulama [*Jakarta*] [*A publication*]
**MiMuM** .... Muskegon County Library, Muskegon, MI [*Library symbol*] [*Library of Congress*] (LCLS)
**MiMun** ...... Munising Public Library, Munising, MI [*Library symbol*] [*Library of Congress*] (LCLS)
**MIMunE** ... Member of the Institute of Municipal Engineers [*British*] (EY)
**MIMUSA** ... Matrix Iteration Method of Unfolding Spectra [*Data processing*]
**MIN** ........... Korte Berichten voor Milieu [*A publication*]
**MIN** ........... Marketing Information Network [*Information service or system*] (IID)
**MIN** ........... Master of Insurance
**MIN** ........... Media Industry Newsletter [*A publication*]
**MIN** ........... Meeting Individual Needs [*Educational publishing*]
**MIN** ........... Member Information Network [*for House of Representatives*]
**MIN** ........... Member of the Institute of Navigation [*British*]
**MIN** ........... MFS Intermediate Income SBI [*NYSE symbol*] (SPSG)
**Min** ........... Minaean [*or Minean*] (BJA)
**MIN** ........... Mineral [*California*] [*Seismograph station code, US Geological Survey*] (SEIS)
**MIN** ........... Mineral
**MIN** ........... Mineralogy
**Min** ........... Minerva [*A publication*]
**MIN** ........... Miniature
**MIN** ........... Minim
**MIN** ........... Minimum (AFM)
**MIN** ........... Mining
**MIN** ........... Minister [*or Ministry*]
**Min** ........... Minnesota Reports [*A publication*] (DLA)
**MIN** ........... Minor
**MIN** ........... Minority
**Min** ........... Minor's Alabama Reports [*A publication*] (DLA)
**MIN** ........... Minto Resources [*Vancouver Stock Exchange symbol*]
**MIN** ........... Minute (AFM)
**MIN** ........... Mobilization Identification Number [*Military*]
**MIN** ........... Molasses Information Network (EA)
**MIN** ........... Most in Need Population
**MIN** ........... Movimiento de Integracion Nacional [*National Integration Movement*] [*Ecuador*] [*Political party*] (PPW)
**MIN** ........... Movimiento de Integracion Nacional [*National Integration Movement*] [*Venezuela*] [*Political party*] (PPW)
**MIN** ........... Movimiento de Izquierda Nacional [*National Left-Wing Movement*] [*Bolivia*] [*Political party*] (PPW)
**MINA** ........ Member of the Institution of Naval Architects [*British*]
**MINA** ........ Monoisonitrosoacetone [*Biochemistry*]
**MINA** ........ Multiplexed Input NHRE [*National Hail Research Experiment*] Averager
**MINABB** ... Minimum Abbreviations [*of MAST*]
**MINAC** ..... Miniature Navigation Airborne Computer
**Min Act Dig** ... Mining Activity Digest [*A publication*]
**MINAGE** .. Minimum Seed-Bearing Age [*Botany*]
**Minamata Dis** ... Minamata Disease [*A publication*]
**Min Annu Rev** ... Mining Annual Review [*England*] [*A publication*]
**MiNas** ......... Putnam Public Library, Nashville, MI [*Library symbol*] [*Library of Congress*] (LCLS)
**Minas Gerais Braz Inst Agron Circ** ... Minas Gerais, Brazil. Instituto Agronomicao. Circular [*A publication*]

**MINAT** ..... Miniature
**MiNazC** ..... Nazareth College, Nazareth, MI [*Library symbol*] [*Library of Congress*] (LCLS)
**Min B** ......... Mining Bulletin [*A publication*]
**MiNb** ......... New Buffalo Public Library, New Buffalo, MI [*Library symbol*] [*Library of Congress*] (LCLS)
**MINBATFOR** ... Minecraft Battle Force, Pacific Fleet
**Min B/L** ..... Minimum Bill of Lading (DS)
**MINC** ........ Minicomputer
**Min Can** ..... Mining in Canada [*A publication*]
**MINCE** ...... Ministerio do Comercio Externo [*Ministry of Foreign Trade*] [*Portuguese*]
**MINCEX** ... Ministerio de Comercio Exterior [*Ministry of Foreign Trade*] [*Spanish*]
**Min Chem Engng Rev** ... Mining and Chemical Engineering Review [*A publication*] (APTA)
**Min Chem Eng Rev** ... Mining and Chemical Engineering Review [*Australia*] [*A publication*]
**Min Cong J** ... Mining Congress Journal [*A publication*]
**Min Congr J** ... Mining Congress Journal [*A publication*]
**MIND** ........ Magnetic Integrator Neuron Duplicator
**MIND** ........ Management Institute for National Development
**MIND** ........ Method in Natural Development [*Mental diet plan*]
**MIND** ........ Methods of Intellectual Development [*National Association of Manufacturers*]
**MInd** .......... Metting Index [*A publication*]
**MIND** ........ Mindscape, Inc. [*NASDAQ symbol*] (NQ)
**MIND** ........ Modular Interactive Network Designer
**MIND** ........ Multidisciplinary Institute for Neuropsychological Development (EA)
**MINDAC** .. Marine Inertial Navigation Data Assimilation Computer (IEEE)
**MINDAP** .. Microwave-Induced Nitrogen Discharge at Atmospheric Pressure [*Spectrometry*]
**MINDD** ..... Minimum Due Date per Order
**Min Dep Mag Univ Nottingham** ... Mining Department Magazine. University of Nottingham [*A publication*]
**Min Deposit** ... Mineralium Deposita [*A publication*]
**Min Dig** ..... Minot's Digest [*Massachusetts*] [*A publication*] (DLA)
**MINDIV** .... Mine Division [*Navy*]
**MINDO** ..... Modified Intermediate Neglect of Differential Overlap [*Quantum mechanics*]
**Mind Your Own Bus** ... Mind Your Own Business [*A publication*]
**MINE** ........ Microbial Information Network Europe [*EEC*]
**Min E** ......... Mineral Engineer
**Min E** ......... Mining Engineer
**MINE** ........ Minneapolis Eastern Railway Co. [*AAR code*]
**MINE** ........ Montana Information Network Exchange [*Library network*]
**MINEAC** ... Miniature Electronic Auto-Collimator
**MINEASYFAC** ... Mine Assembly Facilities
**MINEC** ...... Military Necessity
**MINECTRMEASSTA** ... Mine Countermeasure Station [*Military*]
**Mine Data Sheets Metallog Map 1:250000** ... Mine Data Sheets to Accompany Metallogenic Map 1:250,000 [*Sydney*] [*A publication*]
**MINEDEFLAB** ... Mine Defense Laboratory [*Navy*]
**Mine Dev Mon** ... Mine Development Monthly [*A publication*]
**MiNeg** ........ Negaunee Public Library, Negaunee, MI [*Library symbol*] [*Library of Congress*] (LCLS)
**Mine Inj Worktime Q** ... Mine Injuries and Worktime Quarterly [*A publication*]
**Min Electr Mech Eng** ... Mining, Electrical, and Mechanical Engineer [*England*] [*A publication*]
**Min Eng** ..... Mining Engineering [*A publication*]
**Min Eng (Colorado)** ... Mining Engineering (Colorado) [*A publication*]
**Min Eng (Harare)** ... Mining and Engineering (Harare) [*A publication*]
**Min Eng (Littleton Colo)** ... Mining Engineering (Littleton, Colorado) [*A publication*]
**Min Eng (Lond)** ... Mining Engineer (London) [*A publication*]
**Min Engng** ... Mining Engineering [*A publication*]
**Min Eng (NY)** ... Mining Engineering (New York) [*A publication*]
**Min Engr** ... Mining Engineer [*A publication*]
**Mine Pet Gaze** ... Mine, Petrol, si Gaze [*Romania*] [*A publication*]
**Mine Pet & Gaze (Bucharest)** ... Mine, Petrol, si Gaze (Bucharest) [*A publication*]
**Mine Pet Gaze (Bucharest)** ... Mine, Petrol, si Gaze (Bucharest) [*A publication*]
**Mine & Quarry Eng** ... Mine and Quarry Engineering [*A publication*]
**Mine Quarry Mech** ... Mine and Quarry Mechanisation [*A publication*] (APTA)
**Min Equip Int** ... Mining Equipment International [*A publication*]
**MINERAL** ... Mineralogy
**Mineral Abstr** ... Mineralogical Abstracts [*A publication*]
**Mineral Geokhim** ... Mineralogiya i Geokhimiya [*USSR*] [*A publication*]
**Mineral Industries Jour** ... Mineral Industries Journal [*A publication*]
**Mineral Issled** ... Mineralogicheskie Issledovaniya [*A publication*]
**Mineral J (Tokyo)** ... Mineralogical Journal (Tokyo) [*A publication*]
**Mineral Mag** ... Mineralogical Magazine [*A publication*]
**Mineral Mag J Mineral Soc (1876-1968)** ... Mineralogical Magazine and Journal of the Mineralogical Society (1876-1968) [*England*] [*A publication*]
**MINERALOG** ... Mineralogical
**Mineralog Abstr** ... Mineralogical Abstracts [*A publication*]
**Mineralog Mag** ... Mineralogical Magazine [*A publication*]
**Mineralog et Petrog Acta** ... Mineralogica et Petrographica Acta [*A publication*]
**Mineralog Soc America Spec Paper** ... Mineralogical Society of America. Special Paper [*A publication*]
**Mineralog Soc Utah Bull** ... Mineralogical Society of Utah. Bulletin [*A publication*]
**Mineral Petrogr Acta** ... Mineralogica et Petrographica Acta [*A publication*]
**Mineral Petrogr Mitt** ... Mineralogische und Petrographische Mitteilungen [*A publication*]
**Mineral Petrogr Mitt Tschermaks** ... Mineralogische und Petrographische Mitteilungen Tschermaks [*Austria*] [*A publication*]
**Mineral Plann** ... Mineral Planning [*A publication*]
**Mineral Pol** ... Mineralogia Polonica [*A publication*]
**Mineral Rec** ... Mineralogical Record [*A publication*]
**Mineral Sb (Lvov)** ... Mineralogicheskii Sbornik (Lvov) [*A publication*]
**Mineral Sb (L'vov Gos Univ)** ... Mineralogicheskiy Sbornik (L'vovskiy Gosudarstvennyy Universitet) [*A publication*]
**Mineral Sb (Sverdlovsk)** ... Mineralogicheskii Sbornik (Sverdlovsk) [*A publication*]
**Mineral Slovaca** ... Mineralia Slovaca [*A publication*]
**Mineral Soc Am Short Course Notes** ... Mineralogical Society of America. Short Course Notes [*A publication*]
**Mineral Soc Am Spec Pap** ... Mineralogical Society of America. Special Paper [*A publication*]
**Mineral Soc Bull** ... Mineralogical Society. Bulletin [*A publication*]
**Minerals Res CSIRO** ... Minerals Research in Commonwealth Scientific and Industrial Research Organisation [*A publication*]
**Mineral T N** ... Mineral Trade Notes [*A publication*]
**Mineral Zh** ... Mineralogicheskiy Zhurnal [*A publication*]
**Miner Assess Rep Inst Geol Sci** ... Mineral Assessment Report. Institute of Geological Sciences [*A publication*]
**Miner Brief Br Geol Surv** ... Mineral Brief. British Geological Survey [*A publication*]
**Miner Bull** ... Mineral Bulletin [*Canada*] [*A publication*]
**Miner Bull Energy Mines Resour Can** ... Mineral Bulletin. Energy, Mines, and Resources Canada [*A publication*]
**Miner Commod Profiles** ... Mineral Commodity Profiles [*A publication*]
**Miner Deposita** ... Mineralium Deposita [*A publication*]
**Miner Deposits** ... Mineral Deposits [*A publication*]
**Miner Deposits Circ Ontario Geol Surv** ... Mineral Deposits Circular. Ontario Geological Survey [*A publication*]
**Miner Dossier Miner Resour Consult Comm** ... Mineral Dossier. Mineral Resources Consultative Committee [*A publication*]
**Miner Dressing Notes** ... Mineral Dressing Notes [*A publication*]
**Miner Econ Ser (Indiana Geol Surv)** ... Mineral Economics Series (Indiana Geological Survey) [*A publication*]
**Miner Electrolyte Metab** ... Mineral and Electrolyte Metabolism [*Switzerland*] [*A publication*]
**Miner Energy Bull** ... Minerals and Energy Bulletin [*Australia*] [*A publication*]
**Miner Energy Resour** ... Mineral and Energy Resources [*United States*] [*A publication*]
**Miner Environ** ... Minerals and the Environment [*A publication*]
**Miner Fossiles** ... Mineraux et Fossiles [*A publication*]
**Miner Fossiles Guide Collect** ... Mineraux et Fossiles. Guide du Collectionneur [*A publication*]
**Mineria Metal (Madrid)** ... Mineria y Metalurgia (Madrid) [*A publication*]
**Mineria Met (Mexico City)** ... Mineria y Metalurgia (Mexico City) [*A publication*]
**Miner Ind** ... Mineral Industries [*United States*] [*A publication*]
**Miner Ind Bull** ... Mineral Industries Bulletin [*A publication*]
**Miner Ind NSW** ... Mineral Industry of New South Wales [*A publication*]
**Miner Ind Q South Aust** ... Mineral Industry Quarterly. South Australia [*A publication*]
**Miner Ind Res Lab Univ Alaska Rep** ... Mineral Industries Research Laboratory. University of Alaska. Report [*A publication*]
**Miner Ind Surv Sodium Compd** ... Mineral Industry Surveys. Sodium Compounds [*A publication*]
**Miner Ind (University Park PA)** ... Mineral Industries (University Park, Pennsylvania) [*A publication*]
**Miner Mag** ... Mineral Magazine and Journal. Mineralogical Society [*A publication*]
**Miner Mater** ... Minerals and Materials [*A publication*]
**Miner Metal** ... Mineracao, Metalurgia [*A publication*]
**Miner Metall Process** ... Minerals and Metallurgical Processing [*A publication*]
**Miner Met Rev** ... Minerals and Metals Review [*A publication*]
**Miner News Serv (Philipp)** ... Minerals News Service. Bureau of Mines (Philippines) [*A publication*]
**Miner Perspect US Bur Mines** ... Mineral Perspectives. United States Bureau of Mines [*A publication*]
**Miner Plann** ... Mineral Planning [*A publication*]
**Miner Policy Background Pap Miner Resour Branch (Ontario)** ... Mineral Policy Background Paper. Mineral Resources Branch (Ontario) [*A publication*]
**Miner Process** ... Minerals Processing [*A publication*]

**Miner Process Inf Note Warren Spring Lab** ... Mineral Processing Information Note. Warren Spring Laboratory [*A publication*]
**Miner Process Technol Rev** ... Mineral Processing and Technology Review [*A publication*]
**Miner Prod Abstr** ... Mineral Products Abstracts [*A publication*]
**Miner Rec**.. Mineralogical Record [*A publication*]
**Miner Reconnaissance Programme Rep Br Geol Surv** ... Mineral Reconnaissance Programme Report. British Geological Survey [*A publication*]
**Miner Reconnaissance Programme Rep Inst Geol Sci** ... Mineral Reconnaissance Programme Report. Institute of Geological Sciences [*A publication*]
**Miner Res CSIRO** ... Minerals Research in Commonwealth Scientific and Industrial Research Organisation [*A publication*] (APTA)
**Miner Res CSIRO (Aust)** ... Minerals Research in Commonwealth Scientific and Industrial Research Organisation (Australia) [*A publication*]
**Miner Res (Nagpur)** ... Mineral Research (Nagpur) [*A publication*]
**Miner Resour Bull (Geol Surv West Aust)** ... Mineral Resources Bulletin (Geological Survey of Western Australia) [*A publication*]
**Miner Resour Bull LA Geol Surv** ... Mineral Resources Bulletin. Louisiana Geological Survey [*A publication*]
**Miner Resour Bull Louisiana Geol Surv** ... Mineral Resources Bulletin. Louisiana Geological Survey [*A publication*]
**Miner Resour Bull (Saudi Arabia)** ... Mineral Resources Bulletin. Directorate General of Mineral Resources (Saudi Arabia) [*A publication*]
**Miner Resour Circ (Univ Tex Austin Bur Econ Geol)** ... Mineral Resource Circular (University of Texas at Austin. Bureau of Economic Geology) [*A publication*]
**Miner Resour Consult Comm Miner Dossier (GB)** ... Mineral Resources Consultative Committee. Mineral Dossier (Great Britain) [*A publication*]
**Miner Resour Geol Geophys Bur 1:250000 Geol Ser** ... Mineral Resources. Geology and Geophysics. Bureau of 1:250,000 Geological Series [*A publication*]
**Miner Resour Geol Surv NSW** ... New South Wales. Geological Survey. Mineral Resources [*A publication*] (APTA)
**Miner Resour Pam Geol Surv Guyana** ... Mineral Resources Pamphlet. Geological Survey of Guyana [*A publication*]
**Miner Resour Rep** ... Mineral Resources Report. Bureau of Mineral Resources. Geology and Geophysics [*A publication*] (APTA)
**Miner Resour Rep Commonw Geol Liaison Off** ... Mineral Resources Report. Commonwealth Geological Liaison Office [*A publication*]
**Miner Resour Rep Geol Surv Dep (Botswana)** ... Mineral Resources Report. Geological Survey Department (Botswana) [*A publication*]
**Miner Resour Rep Invest Saudi Arabia Dir Gen Miner Resour** ... Mineral Resources Report of Investigation. Saudi Arabia Directorate General of Mineral Resources [*A publication*]
**Miner Resour Rep PA Topogr Geol Surv** ... Mineral Resource Report. Pennsylvania Topographic and Geologic Survey [*A publication*]
**Miner Resour Res Dir Gen Miner Resour (Saudi Arabia)** ... Mineral Resources Research. Directorate General of Mineral Resources (Saudi Arabia) [*A publication*]
**Miner Resour Rev** ... Mineral Resources Review. Department of Mines. South Australia [*A publication*] (APTA)
**Miner Resour Rev Dep Mines S Aust** ... Mineral Resources Review. Department of Mines. South Australia [*A publication*]
**Miner Resour Rev South Aust Dep Mines** ... Mineral Resources Review. Department of Mines. South Australia [*A publication*] (APTA)
**Miner Resour Ser Rhod Geol Surv** ... Mineral Resources Series. Rhodesia Geological Survey [*A publication*]
**Miner Resour Ser WV Geol Econ Surv** ... Mineral Resources Series. West Virginia Geological and Economic Survey [*A publication*]
**Miner Resour Surv (NH Div Econ Dev)** ... Mineral Resources Survey (New Hampshire Division of Economic Development) [*A publication*]
**Miner Rocks** ... Minerals and Rocks [*A publication*]
**Miner Sci Eng** ... Minerals Science and Engineering [*A publication*]
**Miner Sci Eng (Johannesburg)** ... Minerals Science and Engineering (Johannesburg) [*A publication*]
**Miner Slovaca** ... Mineralia Slovaca [*A publication*]
**Miner Syr'e** ... Mineral'noe Syr'e [*A publication*]
**Miner Syr'e Ego Pererab** ... Mineral'noe Syr'e i Ego Pererabotka [*A publication*]
**Miner Syr'e Tsvetn Met** ... Mineral'noe Syr'e i Tsvetnye Metally [*A publication*]
**Miner Syr'e Vses Inst Miner Syr'ya** ... Mineral'noe Syr'e. Vsesoyuznyi Institut Mineral'nogo Syr'ya [*A publication*]
**Miner Syr'e Vses Nauchno Issled Inst Miner Syr'ya** ... Mineral'noe Syr'e. Vsesoyuznyi Nauchno-Issledovatel'skii Institut Mineral'nogo Syr'ya [*A publication*]
**Miner Trade Notes** ... Mineral Trade Notes [*A publication*]
**Miner Udobr Insektofungis** ... Mineral'nye Udobreniya i Insektofungisidy [*A publication*]
**Minerva Aerosp** ... Minerva Aerospaziale [*A publication*]
**Minerva Anestesiol** ... Minerva Anestesiologica [*A publication*]
**Minerva Bioepistemol** ... Minerva Bioepistemologica [*A publication*]
**Minerva Biol** ... Minerva Biologica [*A publication*]
**Minerva Cardioangiol** ... Minerva Cardioangiologica [*A publication*]
**Minerva Chir** ... Minerva Chirurgica [*A publication*]
**Minerva Dermatol** ... Minerva Dermatologica [*Italy*] [*A publication*]
**Minerva Diet** ... Minerva Dietologica [*A publication*]
**Minerva Dietol** ... Minerva Dietologica [*Later, Minerva Dietologica e Gastroenterologica*] [*A publication*]
**Minerva Dietol Gastroenterol** ... Minerva Dietologica e Gastroenterologica [*A publication*]
**Minerva Ecol Idroclimatol Fisicosanit** ... Minerva Ecologica, Idroclimatologica, Fisicosanitaria [*A publication*]
**Minerva Ecol Idroclimatol Fis Sanit** ... Minerva Ecologica, Idroclimatologica, Fisicosanitaria [*A publication*]
**Minerva Endocrinol** ... Minerva Endocrinologica [*A publication*]
**Minerva Farm** ... Minerva Farmaceutica [*A publication*]
**Minerva Fisiconucl** ... Minerva Fisiconucleare [*A publication*]
**Minerva Fisiconucl G Fis Sanit Prot Radiaz** ... Minerva Fisiconucleare. Giornale di Fisica, Sanitaria, e Protezione Contro le Radiazioni [*A publication*]
**Minerva Gastroenterol** ... Minerva Gastroenterologica [*A publication*]
**Minerva Ginecol** ... Minerva Ginecologica [*A publication*]
**Minerva Idroclimatol** ... Minerva Idroclimatologica [*Italy*] [*A publication*]
**Minerva Med** ... Minerva Medica [*A publication*]
**Minerva Med Eur Med** ... Minerva Medica. Europa Medica [*A publication*]
**Minerva Med Guiliana** ... Minerva Medica Guiliana [*A publication*]
**Minerva Med Rass Ipnosi Med Psicosom** ... Minerva Medica. Rassegna Ipnosi e Medicina Psicosomatica [*A publication*]
**Minerva Med Roma** ... Minerva Medica Roma [*A publication*]
**Minerva Med Sicil** ... Minerva Medica Siciliana [*A publication*]
**Minerva Med Suppl** ... Minerva Medica. Supplemento [*Italy*] [*A publication*]
**Minerva Nefrol** ... Minerva Nefrologica [*A publication*]
**Minerva Neurochir** ... Minerva Neurochirurgica [*A publication*]
**Minerva Nipiol** ... Minerva Nipiologica [*A publication*]
**Minerva Nucl** ... Minerva Nucleare [*Italy*] [*A publication*]
**Minerva Oftalmol** ... Minerva Oftalmologica [*Italy*] [*A publication*]
**Minerva ORL** ... Minerva Otorinolaringologica [*A publication*]
**Minerva Ortop** ... Minerva Ortopedica [*A publication*]
**Minerva Otorinolaringol** ... Minerva Otorinolaringologica [*A publication*]
**Minerva Ped** ... Minerva Pediatrica [*A publication*]
**Minerva Pediatr** ... Minerva Pediatrica [*A publication*]
**Minerva Pneumol** ... Minerva Pneumologica [*A publication*]
**Minerva Psichiatr** ... Minerva Psichiatrica [*A publication*]
**Minerva Psichiatr Psicol** ... Minerva Psichiatrica e Psicologica [*Later, Minerva Psichiatrica*] [*A publication*]
**Minerva Radiol** ... Minerva Radiologica [*A publication*]
**Minerva Radiol Fisioter Radio-Biol** ... Minerva Radiologica. Fisioterapica e Radio-Biologica [*Italy*] [*A publication*]
**Minerva Stomatol** ... Minerva Stomatologica [*A publication*]
**Minerva Urol** ... Minerva Urologica [*A publication*]
**Miner Waste Util Symp Proc** ... Mineral Waste Utilization Symposium. Proceedings [*A publication*]
**Miner Wealth Gujarat Dir Geol Min** ... Mineral Wealth. Gujarat Directorate of Geology and Mining [*A publication*]
**Miner YB 2** ... Minerals Yearbook. Volume 2. Area Reports, Domestic [*A publication*]
**Miner YB 3** ... Minerals Yearbook. Volume 3. Area Reports, International [*A publication*]
**Miner Yearb** ... Minerals Yearbook [*United States*] [*A publication*]
**Miner Yrbk** ... Minerals Yearbook. Volume 1. Metals and Minerals [*A publication*]
**Mine Safety & Health Rep BNA** ... Mine Safety and Health Reporter. Bureau of National Affairs [*A publication*]
**Mine Saf Health** ... Mine Safety and Health [*United States*] [*A publication*]
**Mines Dep Victoria Groundwater Invest Program Rep** ... Mines Department. Victoria Groundwater Investigation Program Report [*A publication*]
**Mines Geol Energie (Maroc)** ... Mines, Geologie, et Energie (Royaume du Maroc) [*A publication*]
**Mines Mag** ... Mines Magazine [*A publication*]
**Mines Met** ... Mines et Metallurgie [*A publication*]
**Mines Metall** ... Mines et Metallurgie [*A publication*]
**Mines Miner (Nagpur India)** ... Mines and Minerals (Nagpur, India) [*A publication*]
**Mines Miner (Scranton PA)** ... Mines and Minerals (Scranton, Pennsylvania) [*A publication*]
**Mines Prospects Map Ser Idaho Bur Mines Geol** ... Mines and Prospects Map Series. Idaho Bureau of Mines and Geology [*A publication*]
**Mines Year-End Rev Bur Mines (Philipp)** ... Mines Year-End Review. Bureau of Mines and Geo-Sciences (Philippines) [*A publication*]
**MINET**...... Medical Information Network [*GTE Telenet Communications Corp.*] [*Reston, VA*] [*Telecommunications*]
**MINET**...... Metropolitan Information Network
**MIN EV**..... Minutes of Evidence [*Legal term*] (DLA)
**MINEVDET** ... Mine Warfare Evaluation Detachment
**MiNew**....... Newaygo Carnegie Public Library, Newaygo, MI [*Library symbol*] [*Library of Congress*] (LCLS)
**MiNew-C**... Croton Public Library, Newaygo, MI [*Library symbol*] [*Library of Congress*] (LCLS)
**MINEX**..... Mine Warfare Exercise (NVT)

**MINEX** ..... Minelaying, Minesweeping, and Mine-Hunting Exercise [*NATO*] (NATG)
**MINF** ........ Minnesota Fabrics, Inc. [*NASDAQ symbol*] (NQ)
**Minfacts Minist Nat Resour (Ontario)** ... Minfacts. Ministry of Natural Resources (Ontario) [*A publication*]
**MINFDZ**... Medecine et Informatique [*A publication*]
**MINFDZ**... Medical Informatics [*A publication*]
**MINFLOT** ... Mine Flotilla [*Navy*]
**MING**........ Magnetic Induction Nuclear Gyroscope
**MIng**.......... Maitre en Ingenierie [*Master of Engineering*] [*French*]
**MING**........ Middle Class, Intelligent, Nice Girl [*Lifestyle classification*]
**Mingays Electrical W** ... Mingay's Electrical Weekly [*A publication*] (APTA)
**Min Geol**.... Mining Geology [*Japan*] [*A publication*]
**Min Geol J** ... Mining and Geological Journal [*A publication*] (APTA)
**Min & Geol J** ... Mining and Geological Journal [*A publication*] (APTA)
**Min Geol (Soc Min Geol Jap)** ... Mining Geology (Society of Mining Geologists of Japan) Journal [*A publication*]
**Min Geol Spec Issue (Tokyo)** ... Mining Geology (Society of Mining Geologists of Japan) Special Issue (Tokyo) [*A publication*]
**MINGSE**... Minimum Ground Support Equipment Concept (MCD)
**Ming Stud** ... Ming Studies [*A publication*]
**MiNhL**....... Lenox Township Library, New Haven, MI [*Library symbol*] [*Library of Congress*] (LCLS)
**MINI** ......... Miniature (KSC)
**MINI** ......... Minicomputer Industry National Interchange [*An association*] (EA)
**MINI** ......... Minimize Individually Negotiated Instruments (AFM)
**MINI** ......... Minimum (DSUE)
**MiNi** .......... Niles Community Library, Niles, MI [*Library symbol*] [*Library of Congress*] (LCLS)
**MINI** ......... Roger Brown Miniature Horse Farms, Inc. [*NASDAQ symbol*] (NQ)
**MINIACT** ... Minimum Acquisition Tracking System (MUGU)
**Mini Applic** ... Minicomputer Applications Analyzer [*A publication*]
**MINIAPS** ... Miniature Accessory Power Supply
**MINICATS** ... Miniaturization of Federal Catalog System Publications
**MINICOM** ... Minimum Communications
**Minicomput Rev** ... Minicomputer Review [*A publication*]
**MINICS**.... Minimal-Input Cataloguing System [*Loughborough University of Technology*]
**MINI-ELS** ... Mini-Emitter Location System (MCD)
**Miniluv** ...... Ministry of Love [*From George Orwell's novel, "1984"*]
**Mini-Micro** ... Mini-Micro Systems [*A publication*]
**Mini Micro S** ... Mini-Micro Systems Special Peripherals Digest. Fall, 1983 [*A publication*]
**Mini-Micro Syst** ... Mini-Micro Systems [*A publication*]
**MINI MUX** ... Miniaturized Multiplexes (MCD)
**Min Ind Q** ... Mineral Industry Quarterly [*A publication*]
**Min Ind Quebec** ... Mining Industry in Quebec [*A publication*]
**Min Ind Technol** ... Mining Industry Technology [*Taiwan*] [*A publication*]
**Mining Chem Engng Rev** ... Mining and Chemical Engineering Review [*A publication*]
**Mining & Chem Eng R** ... Mining and Chemical Engineering Review [*A publication*] (APTA)
**Mining Congr J** ... Mining Congress Journal [*A publication*]
**Mining Elec Mech Eng** ... Mining, Electrical, and Mechanical Engineer [*A publication*]
**Mining Eng (London)** ... Mining Engineer (London) [*A publication*]
**Mining Engng Rev** ... Mining and Engineering Review [*A publication*]
**Mining Eng (NY)** ... Mining Engineering (New York) [*A publication*]
**Mining Jrl** ... Mining Journal [*A publication*]
**Mining Mag** ... Mining Magazine [*A publication*]
**Mining Met Quart** ... Mining and Metallurgy. Quarterly [*A publication*]
**Mining Mg** ... Mining Magazine [*A publication*]
**Mining Miner Eng** ... Mining and Minerals Engineering [*A publication*]
**Mining R**.... Mining Review [*A publication*] (APTA)
**Mining Rev** ... Mining Annual Review [*A publication*]
**Mining Technol** ... Mining Technology [*A publication*]
**Min Inst**..... Minor's Institutes of Common and Statute Law [*A publication*] (DLA)
**MIN INVEST** ... Minimum Investment [*Finance*]
**Minipax**..... Ministry of Peace [*From George Orwell's novel, "1984"*]
**Miniplenty** ... Ministry of Plenty [*From George Orwell's novel, "1984"*]
**MINIRAD** ... Minimum Radiation (CAAL)
**MINIRAR** ... Minimum Radiation Requirements [*Missiles*] (IEEE)
**MINISID** .. Miniature Seismic Intrusion Detector [*DoD*]
**MINISINS** ... Miniature Ship Inertial Navigation System (MCD)
**Mini Soft**.... Mini-Micro Software [*A publication*]
**Minist Agric Aliment Ont Bull (Ed Fr)** ... Ministere de l'Agriculture et de l'Alimentation de l'Ontario. Bulletin (Edition Francaise) [*A publication*]
**Minist Agric Inst Colomb Agropecu Programa Nac Entomol** ... Ministerio de Agricultura. Instituto Colombiano Agropecuario. Programa Nacional de Entomologia [*A publication*]
**Minist Agric Mktg Guide** ... Marketing Guide. Ministry of Agriculture [*United Kingdom*] [*A publication*]
**Minist Agric Nat Resour Cent Agric Stn Res Rep (Guyana)** ... Ministry of Agriculture and Natural Resources. Central Agricultural Station. Research Report (Guyana) [*A publication*]
**Minist Agric Rural Dev Dep Bot Publ (Tehran)** ... Ministry of Agriculture and Rural Development. Department of Botany. Publication (Tehran) [*A publication*]
**Minist Cult Educ Fund Miguel Lillo Misc** ... Ministerio de Cultura y Educacion. Fundacion Miguel Lillo. Miscelanea [*A publication*]
**Minist Ganad Agric Cent Invest Agric Alberto Boerger Bol Tec** ... Ministerio de Ganaderia y Agricultura. Centro de Investigaciones Agricolas "Alberto Boerger." Boletim Tecnico [*A publication*]
**Minist Ind Commer Que Rapp Annu** ... Ministere de l'Industrie et du Commerce du Quebec. Rapport Annuel [*A publication*]
**Minist Justicia R (Venezuela)** ... Revista. Ministerio de Justicia (Venezuela) [*A publication*]
**Minist Mar Merc Mem** ... Ministero della Marina Mercantile. Memoria [*A publication*]
**MINI-SUBLAB** ... Miniature Submarine Laboratory
**Mini Sys** .... Mini-Micro Systems [*A publication*]
**MINIT**....... Minimum Interference Threshold [*Telecommunications*] (TEL)
**MINIT**....... Minutes in Trail [*Aviation*] (FAAC)
**MINITAB II** ... [*A*] programming language [*1970*] (CSR)
**MINITAS** ... Miniature True Airspeed Computer
**MINITEX** ... Minnesota Interlibrary Telecommunications Exchange [*Library cooperative*] [*Minnesota Higher Education Coordinating Board*] [*Minneapolis, MN*]
**MINITRACK** ... Minimum-Weight Tracking [*System*] (MUGU)
**Minitrue**..... Ministry of Truth [*From George Orwell's novel, "1984"*]
**Miniwatt Dig** ... Miniwatt Digest [*A publication*] (APTA)
**Miniwatt Tech Bull** ... Miniwatt Technical Bulletin [*A publication*] (APTA)
**Min J** ......... Mining Journal [*A publication*]
**Min J (Lond)** ... Mining Journal (London) [*A publication*]
**Min J (London)** ... Mining Journal (London) [*A publication*]
**MINL** ........ Minnetonka Corp. [*NASDAQ symbol*] (NQ)
**MINLANT** ... Mine Warfare Forces, Atlantic [*Navy*]
**MINLP**...... Mixed-Integer Nonlinear Program [*Data processing*]
**Min Mag**.... Mining Magazine [*A publication*]
**MIN MC** ... Minimum Material Condition [*Data processing*]
**Min & Met** ... Mining and Metallurgy [*A publication*]
**Min Metal** ... Mineracao, Metalurgia [*Brazil*] [*A publication*]
**Min Metal** ... Mineria y Metalurgia [*A publication*]
**Min Metall Q** ... Mining and Metallurgy. Quarterly [*A publication*]
**Min Metall Soc America Bull** ... Mining and Metallurgical Society of America. Bulletin [*A publication*]
**Min Metal Plast Electr** ... Mineria y Metalurgia, Plasticos y Electricidad [*A publication*]
**MINMETALS** ... National Minerals & Metals Import/Export Corp. [*People's Republic of China*] (IMH)
**Min Metal (Taipei)** ... Mining and Metallurgy (Taipei) [*A publication*]
**Min Met Rev** ... Minerals and Metals Review [*A publication*]
**Min Mex**.... Minero Mexicano [*A publication*]
**Min Miner Engng** ... Mining and Minerals Engineering [*A publication*]
**Min Mirror** ... Mining Mirror [*A publication*]
**Min & Mtrl** ... Minerals and Materials: A Monthly Survey [*A publication*]
**MINN**........ Minnesota (AFM)
**Minn** .......... Minnesota Supreme Court Reports [*A publication*] (DLA)
**Minn Acad Sci J** ... Minnesota Academy of Science. Journal [*A publication*]
**Minn Acad Sci Proc** ... Minnesota Academy of Science. Proceedings [*A publication*]
**Minn Ac N Sc B** ... Minnesota Academy of Natural Sciences. Bulletin [*A publication*]
**Minn Admin Reg** ... Minnesota State Register [*A publication*] (DLA)
**Minn Ag Exp** ... Minnesota. Agricultural Experiment Station. Publications [*A publication*]
**Minn Agric Economist** ... Minnesota Agricultural Economist [*A publication*]
**Minn Agric Exp Stn Bull** ... Minnesota. Agricultural Experiment Station. Bulletin [*A publication*]
**Minn Agric Exp Stn Misc Rep** ... Minnesota. Agricultural Experiment Station. Miscellaneous Report [*A publication*]
**Minn Agric Exp Stn Stn Bull** ... Minnesota. Agricultural Experiment Station. Station Bulletin [*A publication*]
**Minn Agric Exp Stn Tech Bull** ... Minnesota. Agricultural Experiment Station. Technical Bulletin [*A publication*]
**Minn Beekpr** ... Minnesota Beekeeper [*A publication*]
**Minn Bs Jl** ... Minnesota Business Journal [*A publication*]
**Minn Cities** ... Minnesota Cities [*A publication*]
**Minn Code Agency** ... Minnesota Code of Agency Rules [*A publication*] (DLA)
**Minn Code Ann** ... Minnesota Code, Annotated [*A publication*] (DLA)
**Minn Ct Rep** ... Minnesota Court Reporter [*A publication*] (DLA)
**Minn Dep Agric Annu Feed Bull** ... Minnesota. Department of Agriculture. Annual Feed Bulletin [*A publication*]
**Minn Dep Conserv Div Game Fish Sect Res Plann Invest Rep** ... Minnesota. Department of Conservation. Division of Game and Fish. Section on Research and Planning. Investigational Report [*A publication*]
**Minn Dep Conserv Tech Bull** ... Minnesota. Department of Conservation. Technical Bulletin [*A publication*]

**Minn Dep Nat Resour Div Fish Wildl Sect Wildl Wildl Res Q** ... Minnesota. Department of Natural Resources. Division of Fish and Wildlife. Section of Wildlife. Wildlife Research Quarterly [*A publication*]
**Minn Dep Nat Resour Div Game Fish Sect Tech Serv Invest Rep** ... Minnesota. Department of Natural Resources. Division of Game and Fish. Section of Technical Services. Investigational Report [*A publication*]
**Minn Dep Nat Resour Game Res Proj Q Prog Rep** ... Minnesota. Department of Natural Resources. Game Research Project. Quarterly Progress Report [*A publication*]
**Minn Dep Nat Resour Sect Fish Invest Rep** ... Minnesota. Department of Natural Resources. Section of Fisheries. Investigational Report [*A publication*]
**Minn Dept Conserv Div Waters Bull Tech Paper** ... Minnesota. Department of Conservation. Division of Waters. Bulletin. Technical Paper [*A publication*]
**Minn Div Waters Bull** ... Minnesota. Division of Waters. Bulletin [*A publication*]
**Minn DL & I Comp** ... Minnesota Department of Labor and Industries. Compilation of Court Decisions [*A publication*] (DLA)
**MINN DPW LIB** ... Minnesota Department of Public Welfare Library Consortium [*Library network*]
**Minneap Dist Dent J** ... Minneapolis District Dental Journal [*A publication*]
**Minneapolis Inst Bul** ... Minneapolis Institute of Arts. Bulletin [*A publication*]
**Minnesota Geol Survey Misc Map** ... Minnesota. Geological Survey. Miscellaneous Map [*A publication*]
**Minnesota Geol Survey Rept Inv** ... Minnesota. Geological Survey. Report of Investigations [*A publication*]
**Minnesota Geol Survey Spec Pub Ser** ... Minnesota. Geological Survey. Special Publication Series [*A publication*]
**Minnesota L Rev** ... Minnesota Law Review [*A publication*]
**Minnesota Med** ... Minnesota Medicine [*A publication*]
**Minnesota Min Dir** ... Minnesota Mining Directory [*A publication*]
**Minnesota Univ Water Resources Research Center Bull** ... University of Minnesota. Graduate School. Water Resources Research Center. Bulletin [*A publication*]
**Min Neurochir** ... Minerva Neurochirurgica [*A publication*]
**Min Newsletter** ... Mining Newsletter [*A publication*]
**Minn Farm & Home Sci** ... Minnesota Farm and Home Science [*A publication*]
**Minn Farm Home Sci** ... Minnesota Farm and Home Science [*A publication*]
**Minn Fish Game Invest Fish Ser** ... Minnesota Fish and Game Investigations. Fish Series [*A publication*]
**Minn Fish Invest** ... Minnesota Fisheries Investigations [*A publication*]
**Minn Fm Home Fact Sh Ent** ... Minnesota Farm and Home Science. Entomology Fact Sheet [*A publication*]
**Minn Forestry Res Note** ... Minnesota Forestry Research Notes [*A publication*]
**Minn For Notes** ... Minnesota Forestry Notes [*A publication*]
**Minn For Res Notes** ... Minnesota Forestry Research Notes [*A publication*]
**Minn Gen Laws** ... Minnesota General Laws [*A publication*] (DLA)
**Minn Geol Surv Bull** ... Minnesota. Geological Survey. Bulletin [*A publication*]
**Minn Geol Surv Rep Invest** ... Minnesota. Geological Survey. Report of Investigations [*A publication*]
**Minn Geol Surv Spec Publ Ser** ... Minnesota. Geological Survey. Special Publication Series [*A publication*]
**Minn (Gil)** ... Minnesota Reports (Gilfillan Edition) [*A publication*] (DLA)
**Minn (Gill)** ... Minnesota Reports (Gilfillan Edition) [*A publication*] (DLA)
**Minn G S** ... Minnesota. Geological and Natural History Survey [*A publication*]
**Minn H** ...... Minnesota History [*A publication*]
**Minn His** ... Minnesota History [*A publication*]
**Minn His B** ... Minnesota History. Bulletin [*A publication*]
**Minn His S** ... Minnesota Historical Society. Collections [*A publication*]
**Minn Hist** .. Minnesota History [*A publication*]
**Minn Hist B** ... Minnesota History. Bulletin [*A publication*]
**Minn History** ... Minnesota History [*A publication*]
**Minn Hist Soc Educ Bull** ... Minnesota Historical Society. Educational Bulletin [*A publication*]
**Minn Hort** ... Minnesota Horticulturist [*A publication*]
**Minn Hortic** ... Minnesota Horticulturist [*A publication*]
**Minn Inst Arts Bul** ... Minneapolis Institute of Arts. Bulletin [*A publication*]
**Minn Inst Bul** ... Minneapolis Institute of Arts. Bulletin [*A publication*]
**Minn J of Ed** ... Minnesota Journal of Education [*A publication*]
**Minn J Ed** ... Minnesota Journal of Education [*A publication*]
**Minn Jour Sci** ... Minnesota Journal of Science [*A publication*]
**Minn J Sci** ... Minnesota Journal of Science [*A publication*]
**Minn Law J** ... Minnesota Law Journal [*A publication*] (DLA)
**Minn Laws** ... Laws of Minnesota [*A publication*] (DLA)
**Minn Lib** .... Minnesota Libraries [*A publication*]
**Minn Libr** .. Minnesota Libraries [*A publication*]
**Minn LJ** ..... Minnesota Law Journal [*St. Paul*] [*A publication*] (DLA)
**Minn L R** ... Minnesota Language Review [*A publication*]
**Minn LR** .... Minnesota Law Review [*A publication*]
**Minn L Rev** ... Minnesota Law Review [*A publication*]
**Minn Med** ... Minnesota Medicine [*A publication*]
**Minn Munic** ... Minnesota Municipalities [*A publication*]
**Minn Nurs Accent** ... Minnesota Nursing Accent [*A publication*]
**Minn Off Iron Range Resour Rehabil Rep Inventory** ... Minnesota. Office of Iron Range Resources and Rehabilitation. Report of Inventory [*A publication*]
**MinnR** ........ Minnesota Review [*A publication*]
**Minn R** ....... Minnesota Rules [*A publication*]
**Minn Reg** ... Minnesota State Register [*A publication*]
**Minn Rep** ... Minnesota Reports [*A publication*] (DLA)
**Minn Reps** ... Minnesota Reports [*A publication*] (DLA)
**Minn Rev** ... Minnesota Review [*A publication*]
**Minn R & WCAT Div** ... Minnesota Railroad and Warehouse Commission. Auto Transportation Co. Division Reports [*A publication*] (DLA)
**Minn Sch Mines Exp Sta B** ... Minnesota School of Mines. Experiment Station. Bulletin [*A publication*]
**Minn Sci** .... Minnesota Science [*A publication*]
**Minn Sci Minn Agric Exp Stn** ... Minnesota Science. Minnesota Agricultural Experiment Station [*A publication*]
**Minn Sess Law Serv (West)** ... Minnesota Session Law Service (West) [*A publication*] (DLA)
**Minn Star** .. Minnesota Star and Tribune [*A publication*]
**Minn Stat** ... Minnesota Statutes [*A publication*]
**Minn Stat Ann** ... Minnesota Statutes, Annotated [*A publication*] (DLA)
**Minn Stat Ann (West)** ... Minnesota Statutes, Annotated (West) [*A publication*]
**Minn Stat Ann (West)** ... West's Minnesota Statutes, Annotated [*A publication*] (DLA)
**Minn St P B** ... Minneapolis-St. Paul City Business [*A publication*]
**Minn Symp Child Psychol** ... Minnesota Symposia on Child Psychology [*A publication*]
**Minn Univ Agric Ext Serv Ext Bull** ... Minnesota. University. Agricultural Extension Service. Extension Bulletin [*A publication*]
**Minn Univ Agric Ext Serv Ext Folder** ... Minnesota. University. Agricultural Extension Service. Extension Folder [*A publication*]
**Minn Univ Eng Exp Stn Bull** ... Minnesota. University. Engineering Experiment Station. Bulletin [*A publication*]
**Minn Univ Eng Exp Stn Tech Pap** ... Minnesota. University. Engineering Experiment Station. Technical Paper [*A publication*]
**Minn Univ Min Symp** ... Minnesota. University. Mining Symposium [*A publication*]
**Minn Univ Q B** ... Minnesota. University. Quarterly Bulletin [*A publication*]
**Minn Univ St Anthony Falls Hydraul Lab Proj Rep** ... Minnesota. University. St. Anthony Falls Hydraulic Laboratory. Project Report [*A publication*]
**Minn Univ St Anthony Falls Hydraul Lab Tech Pap** ... Minnesota. University. St. Anthony Falls Hydraulic Laboratory. Technical Paper [*A publication*]
**Minn Univ Water Resour Res Cent Bull** ... Minnesota. University. Water Resources Research Center. Bulletin [*A publication*]
**Minn WCD** ... Minnesota Workmen's Compensation Decisions [*A publication*] (DLA)
**Minoes Megbizh** ... Minoeseg es Megbizhatosag [*Hungary*] [*A publication*]
**MiNop** ....... Leelanau Township Library, Northport, MI [*Library symbol*] [*Library of Congress*] (LCLS)
**Minor** ......... Minor's Alabama Supreme Court Reports [*1820-26*] [*A publication*] (DLA)
**Minor** ......... Minor's Institutes [*A publication*] (DLA)
**Minor (Ala)** ... Minor's Alabama Reports [*A publication*] (DLA)
**Minor (Ala)** ... Minor's Institutes [*Alabama*] [*A publication*] (DLA)
**Minor Inst** ... Minor's Institutes of Common and Statute Law [*A publication*] (DLA)
**Minor Planet Circ** ... Minor Planet Circulars/Minor Planets and Comets [*A publication*]
**Minor's Alabama Rep** ... Minor's Alabama Reports [*A publication*] (DLA)
**Minor's Ala R** ... Minor's Alabama Reports [*A publication*] (DLA)
**Minor's Ala Rep** ... Minor's Alabama Reports [*A publication*] (DLA)
**Minor's R** ... Minor's Alabama Reports [*A publication*] (DLA)
**Minor's Rep** ... Minor's Alabama Reports [*A publication*] (DLA)
**MINOS** ..... Manual Intervention and Observation Simulator (AAG)
**MINOS** ..... Modular Input/Output System
**MINOX** ..... Minimum Oxidizer (KSC)
**MINPAC** ... Mine Warfare Forces, Pacific [*Navy*]
**Min Pediat** ... Minerva Pediatrica [*A publication*]
**MINPRI** ..... Metal and Mineral Prices [*Database*] [*Australia*]
**MINPROC** ... Mineral Processing Technology [*Canada Department of Energy, Mines, and Resources*] [*Information service or system*] (CRD)
**MINPRT** ... Minimum Processing Time per Operation
**MINQU** ..... Minimum Norm Quadratic Unbiased [*Statistics*]
**MINR** ........ Minimum R Factor [*Spectrometry*]
**Min R** ......... Mining Review [*A publication*] (APTA)
**Min R** ......... Minnesota Reports [*A publication*] (DLA)
**MINRA** ..... Miniature International Racing Association
**Min Record** ... Mining Record [*A publication*]
**Min Rep** ..... Minnesota Reports [*A publication*] (DLA)
**Min Res Bur Bull** ... Bureau of Mineral Resources. Bulletin [*Australia*] [*A publication*] (APTA)
**Min Res Bur Geol Map** ... Bureau of Mineral Resources. Geological Map [*Australia*] [*A publication*] (APTA)
**Min Res Bur 1:250000 Geol Ser** ... Bureau of Mineral Resources. 1:250,000 Geological Series [*Australia*] [*A publication*] (APTA)

**Min Res Bur Geophys Obs Rep** ... Bureau of Mineral Resources. Geophysical Observatory Report [*Australia*] [*A publication*] (APTA)
**Min Res Bur 1 Mile Geol Ser** ... Bureau of Mineral Resources. 1 Mile Geological Series [*Australia*] [*A publication*] (APTA)
**Min Res Bur Pamph** ... Bureau of Mineral Resources. Pamphlet [*Australia*] [*A publication*] (APTA)
**Min Res Bur Petrol Search Pub** ... Bureau of Mineral Resources. Petroleum Search Subsidy Acts. Publication [*Australia*] [*A publication*] (APTA)
**Min Res Bur Petrol Search Publ** ... Bureau of Mineral Resources. Petroleum Search Subsidy Acts. Publication [*Australia*] [*A publication*] (APTA)
**Min Res Bur Petrol Search Public** ... Bureau of Mineral Resources. Petroleum Search Subsidy Acts. Publication [*Australia*] [*A publication*] (APTA)
**Min Res Bur Rep** ... Bureau of Mineral Resources. Report [*Australia*] [*A publication*] (APTA)
**Min Res Bur Sum Rep** ... Bureau of Mineral Resources. Summary Report [*Australia*] [*A publication*] (APTA)
**Min Rev** ..... Mining Review [*A publication*] (APTA)
**Min Rev Adelaide** ... Mining Review. Adelaide (South Australia Department of Mines) [*A publication*] (APTA)
**MINRL** ...... Mineral
**MINRON** ... Mine Squadron [*Navy*]
**MINRTY** ... Minority
**MINS** ........ Mare Island Naval Shipyard [*Also, MINSY*] [*Later, MID*]
**MINS** ........ Miniature Inertial Navigation System
**MINS** ........ Minors in Need of Supervision [*Classification for delinquent children*]
**MINSD** ..... Minimum Planned Start Date per Operation
**MINSK** ...... [*A*] Russian digital computer [*Moscow University*]
**Minsk Gos Med Inst Sb Nauchn Rab** ... Minskii Gosudarstvennyi Meditsinskii Institut Sbornik Nauchnykh Rabot [*A publication*]
**MINSOP** ... Minimum Slack Time per Operation
**MINSQ** ..... Minimum Squares [*Mathematical statistics*]
**Min St** ........ Ministry Studies [*A publication*]
**MInstAEA** ... Member of the Institute of Automotive Engineer Assessors [*British*] (DBQ)
**M Inst AM** ... Member of the Institute of Administrative Management [*British*] (DCTA)
**MInstBB** .... Member of the Institute of British Bakers (DBQ)
**MInstBCA** ... Member of the Institute of Burial and Cremation Administration [*British*] (DBQ)
**MInstBE** .... Member of the Institution of British Engineers
**MInstBRM** ... Member of the Institute of Baths and Recreation Management [*British*] (DBQ)
**MInstBRMDip** ... Diploma Member of the Institute of Baths and Recreation Management [*British*] (DBQ)
**MInstBTM** ... Member of the Institute of Business and Technical Management [*British*] (DBQ)
**MInstCE** .... Member of the Institution of Civil Engineers [*Later, MICE*] [*British*] (EY)
**M Inst CM** ... Member of the Institute of Commercial Management [*British*] (DCTA)
**MInstE** ...... Member of the Institute of Energy [*British*] (DBQ)
**MInstE** ...... Member of the Institution of Engineers [*British*] (EY)
**MInstF** ...... Member of the Institute of Fuel [*British*]
**MInstFF** .... Member of the Institute of Freight Forwarders [*British*] (DBQ)
**MInstGasE** ... Member of the Institution of Gas Engineers [*British*] (EY)
**MInstHE** ... Member of the Institution of Highway Engineers [*British*]
**M Inst Jour** ... Member of the Institute of Journalists [*British*] (ROG)
**MInstM** ..... Member of the Institute of Marketing [*British*]
**MInstMC** .. Member of the Institute of Measurement and Control [*British*] (DBQ)
**MInstME** .. Member of the Institution of Mining Engineers [*British*]
**MInstMet** .. Member of the Institute of Metals [*British*]
**MInstMM** ... Member of the Institution of Mining and Metallurgy [*British*]
**MInstNA** ... Member of the Institution of Naval Architects [*British*] (EY)
**MInstNDT** ... Member of the British Institute of Non-Destructive Testing (DBQ)
**MInstP** ...... Member of the Institute of Physics (ADA)
**MInstPE** .... Member of the Institute of Petroleum Engineers (ADA)
**MInstPet** ... Member of the Institute of Petroleum [*British*] (EY)
**MInstPI** ..... Member of the Institute of Patentees and Inventors [*British*] (EY)
**M Inst PS** .. Member of the Institute of Purchasing and Supply [*British*] (DCTA)
**MInstR** ...... Member of the Institute of Refrigeration [*British*] (DBQ)
**MInstRA** ... Member of the Institute of Registered Architects [*British*]
**M Inst Rech Sci Mad** ... Memoires. Institut de Recherche Scientifique de Madagascar [*A publication*]
**MInstSMM** ... Member of the Institute of Sales and Marketing Management [*British*] (DBQ)
**MInstStructE** ... Member of the Institution of Structural Engineers (ADA)
**MInstT** ...... Member of the Institute of Technology [*British*] (EY)
**MInstT** ...... Member of the Institute of Transport [*British*]
**M Inst TA** ... Member of the Institute of Transport Administration [*British*] (DCTA)
**MInstW** ..... Member of the Institute of Welding [*British*]
**MInstWE** .. Member of the Institution of Water Engineers [*British*]
**Min Surv** .... Mining Survey [*Johannesburg*] [*A publication*]
**Min Surv (Johannesb)** ... Mining Survey (Johannesburg) [*A publication*]
**MINSY** ...... Mare Island Naval Shipyard [*Also, MINS*] [*Later, MID*]
**MINT** ........ [*The*] American Pacific Mint, Inc. [*NASDAQ symbol*] (NQ)
**MINT** ........ Bank of Montreal, Canadian Imperial Bank of Commerce, Bank of Nova Scotia, and Toronto-Dominion Bank
**MINT** ........ Major International Narcotics Traffickers [*Register*] [*Drug Enforcement Administration*]
**MINT** ........ Materiel Identification and New Item Control Technique [*AFLC*]
**MINT** ........ Minorities International Network for Trade (EA)
**MINT** ........ Municipal Insured National Trust
**MINTEC** ... Mining Technology Abstracts [*Canada Centre for Mineral and Energy Technology*] [*Information service or system*] (CRD)
**MINTECH** ... Ministry of Technology [*British*]
**Min Techn** ... Mineraloel-Technik [*A publication*]
**Min Technol** ... Mining Technology [*A publication*]
**MINTEK Res Dig** ... MINTEK [*Council for Mineral Technology*] Research Digest [*A publication*]
**MINTER** ... Ministerio do Interior [*Ministry of the Interior*] [*Information service or system*] (IID)
**MINTIE** .... Minimum Test Instrumentation Equipment
**MIntLaw** .... Master of International Law
**MINTR** ..... Miniature (MSA)
**MINTS** ...... Mutual Institutions National Transfer System, Inc. [*Banking*]
**MINTS** ...... Mutual Insurance National Transfer System, Inc.
**MINTWK** ... Minimum Total Work Content
**MINU** ........ Mobile Instrument Investigation Unit
**MINUA** ..... Minerva Nucleare [*A publication*]
**MINucE** ..... Member of the Institution of Nuclear Engineers [*British*]
**MI Nucl E** ... Member of the Institution of Nuclear Engineers [*British*]
**MINUET** ... Minimum Energy Trajectory Model [*Army*] (AABC)
**Minufiya J Agric Res** ... Minufiya Journal of Agricultural Research [*A publication*]
**MiNun** ....... Crockery Township Library, Nunica, MI [*Library symbol*] [*Library of Congress*] (LCLS)
**Minutes** ...... Minutes. Seminar in Ukrainian Studies [*A publication*]
**Minutes Annu Meet Natl Plant Board** ... Minutes. Annual Meeting. National Plant Board [*A publication*]
**Minutes Meet PA Electr Assoc Eng Sect** ... Minutes. Meeting. Pennsylvania Electric Association. Engineering Section [*A publication*]
**MINVS** ...... MIW Investors of Washington [*NASDAQ symbol*] (NQ)
**MINW** ....... Master Interface Network (MCD)
**Min Week** ... Mining Week [*South Africa*] [*A publication*]
**Min World** ... Mining World [*A publication*]
**MINX** ........ Minex Resources, Inc. [*NASDAQ symbol*] (NQ)
**MINX** ........ Multimedia Information Network Exchange [*Data processing*]
**MINY** ........ Mineralogy (ROG)
**MINY** ........ Miniscribe Corp. [*NASDAQ symbol*] (NQ)
**MINY** ........ Minority (ROG)
**Min Yearb (Denver)** ... Mining Yearbook (Denver) [*A publication*]
**Min Year Book** ... Mining Year Book [*United States*] [*A publication*]
**Min Zimbabwe** ... Mining in Zimbabwe [*A publication*]
**Minzokugaku** ... Minzokugaku-Kenkyu [*Japanese Journal of Ethnology*] [*A publication*]
**MIO** .......... Management Information Office [*or Officer*] [*Air Force*] (AFM)
**MIO** .......... Management Integration Office [*NASA*] (NASA)
**MIO** .......... Map Information Office [*US Geological Survey*]
**MIO** .......... Marine Inspection Office [*Coast Guard*]
**MIO** .......... Medical Intelligence Office [*Later, MIIA*] [*DoD*]
**MIO** .......... Meteoritic Impact Origin (AAG)
**MIO** .......... Metric Information Office [*National Institute of Standards and Technology*]
**MIO** .......... Miami, OK [*Location identifier*] [*FAA*] (FAAL)
**MIO** .......... Military Intelligence Officer [*British military*] (DMA)
**MIO** .......... Minimal Identifiable Odor
**MIO** .......... Mitteilungen des Instituts fuer Orientforschung [*A publication*]
**MIO** .......... Mobile Ionospheric Observatory [*Boston University*]
**MIO** .......... Mobile Issuing Office [*Navy*]
**MIO** .......... Movements Identification Officer [*Air Force*]
**MIO** .......... Movements Integration Office
**MIO** .......... Multi-Institutional Organization [*Generic term*] (DHSM)
**MIO** .......... Multiple Input/Output Stream [*Data processing*]
**MIO** .......... Musee Imperial Ottoman [*Istanbul*] [*A publication*]
**MIOB** ........ Member of the Institute of Building [*British*]
**MiOC** ......... Olivet College, Olivet, MI [*Library symbol*] [*Library of Congress*] (LCLS)
**MIOD** ........ Message Input-Output Devices (MCD)
**MIODAWB** ... Deutsche Akademie der Wissenschaften zu Berlin. Institut fuer Orientforschung. Mitteilungen [*A publication*]
**MIOEA** ..... Mineraloel [*A publication*]
**MI Oe G** .... Mitteilungen. Institut fuer Oesterreichische Geschichtsforschung [*A publication*]
**MIOF** ........ Mitteilungen. Institut fuer Orientforschung. Deutsche Akademie der Wissenschaften zu Berlin [*A publication*]
**MIOG** ........ Manual of Investigative and Operational Guidelines [*FBI*]
**MIOG** ........ Mitteilungen. Institut fuer Oesterreichische Geschichtsforschung [*A publication*]

**MIOGF** ..... Mitteilungen. Institut fuer Oesterreichische Geschichtsforschung [*A publication*]
**MIOK** ........ Magyar Izraelitak Orszagos Kepviselete (BJA)
**MiOlA** ....... Alumni Memorial Library, Orchard Lake, MI [*Library symbol*] [*Library of Congress*] (LCLS)
**MIONP** ..... Microwave-Induced Optical Nuclear Polarization [*Physics*]
**MiOnt** ........ Ontonagon Township Library, Ontonagon, MI [*Library symbol*] [*Library of Congress*] (LCLS)
**MIOP** ........ Member of the Institute of Osteopathy and Physiotherapy [*British*]
**MIOP** ........ Member of the Institute of Printing [*British*] (DBQ)
**MIOP** ........ Multiplexing Input-Output Processor [*Data processing*] (BUR)
**MIOR** ........ Miocene Resources, Inc. [*NASDAQ symbol*] (NQ)
**MI Or** ........ Mitteilungen. Institut fuer Orientforschung [*A publication*]
**MIOS** ........ Modular Input-Output System [*Telecommunications*] (TEL)
**MIOSH** ..... Member of the Institution of Occupational Safety and Health [*British*] (DCTA)
**MIOT** ........ Member of the Institute of Operating Theatre Technicians [*British*]
**MiOt** .......... Otsego District Public Library, Otsego, MI [*Library symbol*] [*Library of Congress*] (LCLS)
**MIOTA** ..... Minerva Otorinolaringologica [*A publication*]
**MiOv** ......... Ovid Public Library, Ovid, MI [*Library symbol*] [*Library of Congress*] (LCLS)
**MiOw** ......... Owosso Public Library, Owosso, MI [*Library symbol*] [*Library of Congress*] (LCLS)
**MiOwJW** ... John Wesley College, Owosso, MI [*Library symbol*] [*Library of Congress*] (LCLS)
**MIP** ........... Machine Instruction Processor [*Data processing*] (BUR)
**MIP** ........... Macrophage Inflammatory Protein [*Biochemistry*]
**MIP** ........... Main Instrument Panel (MCD)
**MIP** ........... Maintainer Instructional Package (MCD)
**MIP** ........... Maintenance Improvement Program
**MIP** ........... Maintenance Index Page
**MIP** ........... Malleable Iron Pipe
**MIP** ........... Management Implementation Plan (MCD)
**MIP** ........... Management Improvement Plan
**MIP** ........... Management Improvement Program [*Military*]
**MIP** ........... Management Incentive Program
**MIP** ........... Management Intern Program
**MIP** ........... Mandatory Inspection Point (KSC)
**MIP** ........... Manual Index Page [*SNMMMS*]
**MIP** ........... Manual Input Processing [*or Program*] [*Data processing*]
**MIP** ........... Manufacturers of Illumination Products (EA)
**MIP** ........... Marine Insurance Policy
**MIP** ........... Marketing Intelligence and Planning [*A publication*]
**MIP** ........... Master Improvement Program (AFIT)
**MIP** ........... Master Information Paper [*Military*] (CAAL)
**MIP** ........... Master Insurance Program
**MIP** ........... Material Improvement Plan [*or Program*] [*Aviation*]
**MIP** ........... Materiel Improvement Project [*Military*]
**MIP** ........... Matrix Inversion Program [*Data processing*] (BUR)
**MIP** ........... Maximum Inspiratory Pressure [*Medicine*]
**MIP** ........... Mean Indicated Pressure
**MIP** ........... Mechanized Infantry Program [*United States Army, Europe*] (MCD)
**MIP** ........... Medicaid Interim Payments
**MIP** ........... Member of the Institute of Plumbing [*British*] (DBQ)
**MIP** ........... Membrane-Intercalated Particles [*Cytology*]
**MIP** ........... Membrane Isolation Process [*Food technology*]
**MIP** ........... Merfin Hygienic [*Vancouver Stock Exchange symbol*]
**MIP** ........... Message Input Processor
**MIP** ........... Methodology Investigation Proposal (MCD)
**MIP** ........... Methods Improvement Program [*IBM Corp.*]
**MIP** ........... Microelectronic Integrated Processing [*Symposium*]
**MIP** ........... Microwave-Induced Plasma [*Spectrometry*]
**MIP** ........... Microwave Interference Protection
**MIP** ........... Military Improvement Program
**MIP** ........... Military Information Program
**MIP** ........... Military Interdepartmental Purchase
**MIP** ........... Million Instructions per Second
**MIP** ........... Milton, PA [*Location identifier*] [*FAA*] (FAAL)
**MIP** ........... Minimum Import Prices [*Economics*]
**MIP** ........... Minimum Impulse Pulse
**MIP** ........... Mint in Package [*Doll collecting*]
**MIP** ........... MIP Properties, Inc. [*AMEX symbol*] (SPSG)
**MIP** ........... Missile Impact Predictor [*Air Force*]
**MIP** ........... Missile Instrumentation Package [*Military*] (CAAL)
**MIP** ........... Missouri Institute of Psychiatry [*University of Missouri - Columbia*] [*Research center*] (RCD)
**MIP** ........... Missouri Institute of Psychiatry Library, St. Louis, MO [*OCLC symbol*] (OCLC)
**MIP** ........... Mixed Integer Programming [*Data processing*]
**MIP** ........... Model Implementation Plan
**MIP** ........... Model Improvements Program [*TRADOC*] (MCD)
**MIP** ........... Modest Improvement Program [*Military*] (NVT)
**MIP** ........... Modification Instruction Package (KSC)
**MIP** ........... Modulated Interframe Plan
**MIP** ........... Monthly Intelligence Production (MCD)
**MIP** ........... Monthly Investment Plan [*Stock exchange term*] (SPSG)
**MIP** ........... Mortgage Insurance Premium
**MIP** ........... Most Important Person
**MIP** ........... Motivation Indoctrination Program [*Military*]
**MIP** ........... Mouvement Independent Populaire [*Popular Independent Movement*] [*Luxembourg*] [*Political party*] (PPE)
**MIP** ........... Mouvement Islamique Progressiste [*Islamic Progressive Movement*] [*Tunisia*] [*Political party*] (PD)
**MIP** ........... Movimiento Independiente Peruano [*Peruvian Independent Movement*] [*Political party*]
**MIP** ........... Mycorrhiza Inoculum Potential [*Soil science*]
**MIP** ........... Myo-inositolphosphate [*Biochemistry*]
**MIPA** ......... Member of the Institute of Practitioners in Advertising [*British*]
**MIPA** ......... Member of the Institute of Public Administration (ADA)
**MIPA** ......... Methylisopropylaniline [*Organic chemistry*]
**MIPA** ......... Missile Procurement, Army (AABC)
**MIPA** ......... Monoisopropylamine [*Organic chemistry*]
**MiPa** .......... Port Austin Township Library, Port Austin, MI [*Library symbol*] [*Library of Congress*] (LCLS)
**MIP-AES** .. Microwave-Induced Plasma-Atomic Emission Spectroscopy
**MiPal** ......... Richmond Township Public Library, Palmer, MI [*Library symbol*] [*Library of Congress*] (LCLS)
**MiPar** ........ Parchment Community Library, Parchment, MI [*Library symbol*] [*Library of Congress*] (LCLS)
**MiPaw** ....... Paw Paw Public Library, Paw Paw, MI [*Library symbol*] [*Library of Congress*] (LCLS)
**MIPC** ......... Manifold Ignition Primary Charge
**MIPC** ......... Member of the Institute of Production Control [*British*] (DBQ)
**MIPC** ......... Metropolitan Information Processing Conference (MCD)
**MIPD** ........ Manufacturing Industry Products Division (MCD)
**MIPDC** ...... Management Improvement Program Design Committee [*Australia*]
**MIPE** ......... Magnetic Induction Plasma Engine
**MIPE** ......... Member of the Institution of Production Engineers [*British*] (DAS)
**MIPE** ......... Modular Information Processing Equipment
**MIPEA** ...... Minerva Pediatrica [*A publication*]
**MiPec** ........ Elk Township Library, Peck, MI [*Library symbol*] [*Library of Congress*] (LCLS)
**MiPel** ......... Pellston Public Library, Pellston, MI [*Library symbol*] [*Library of Congress*] (LCLS)
**MiPen** ........ Pentwater Township Library, Pentwater, MI [*Library symbol*] [*Library of Congress*] (LCLS)
**MiPet** ......... Petoskey Public Library, Petoskey, MI [*Library symbol*] [*Library of Congress*] (LCLS)
**MiPetN** ...... North Central Michigan College, Petoskey, MI [*Library symbol*] [*Library of Congress*] (LCLS)
**MIPEX** ...... Model Improvement Experiment (MCD)
**MIPG** ........ Master Index Pulse Generator
**MiPh** ......... Saint Clair County Library System, Port Huron, MI [*Library symbol*] [*Library of Congress*] (LCLS)
**MIPHE** ...... Member of the Institute of Public Health Engineers [*British*] (DBQ)
**MiPhS** ....... Saint Clair Community College, Port Huron, MI [*Library symbol*] [*Library of Congress*] (LCLS)
**MIPI** .......... Medicine in the Public Interest (EA)
**MIPI** .......... Member of the Institute of Professional Investigators [*British*] (DBQ)
**MiPi** .......... Pigeon District Library, Pigeon, MI [*Library symbol*] [*Library of Congress*] (LCLS)
**MIPIE** ....... Michigan Products Information Exchange [*Interchange Plus, Inc.*] [*Information service or system*] (IID)
**MiPin** ......... Pinckney Community Public Library, Pinckney, MI [*Library symbol*] [*Library of Congress*] (LCLS)
**MIPIR** ....... Missile Precision Instrumentation RADAR
**MIPIR** ....... Multimission Imagery Photographic Interpretation Report (MCD)
**MiPit** .......... Pittsford Township Library, Pittsford, MI [*Library symbol*] [*Library of Congress*] (LCLS)
**MiPl** ........... Charles A. Ransom Public Library, Plainwell, MI [*Library symbol*] [*Library of Congress*] (LCLS)
**MIPL** ......... Master Indentured Parts List
**MIPL** ......... Monthly Intelligence Production Listing (MCD)
**MIPlantE** .. Member of the Institution of Plant Engineers [*British*]
**MIPLOGS** ... Marine Integrated Personnel and Logistics Subsystem
**MiPlS** ........ State Technical Institute and Rehabilitation Center, Plainwell, MI [*Library symbol*] [*Library of Congress*] (LCLS)
**MiPlySJ** .... Saint John's Provincial Seminary, Plymouth, MI [*Library symbol*] [*Library of Congress*] (LCLS)
**MIPM** ....... Member of the Institute of Personnel Management [*British*]
**MIP/MA** ... Missile in Place/Missile Away
**MIPMS** ..... Microwave-Induced Plasma Mass Spectrometry
**MIPO** ........ Multiple Item Purchase Order (AAG)
**MiPon** ........ Pontiac Public Libraries, Pontiac, MI [*Library symbol*] [*Library of Congress*] (LCLS)
**MiPonO** ..... Oakland County Law Library, Clark J. Adams-Philip Pratt Library, Pontiac, MI [*Library symbol*] [*Library of Congress*] (LCLS)
**MiPonSJ** ... Saint Joseph Mercy Hospital, General Medical Library, Pontiac, MI [*Library symbol*] [*Library of Congress*] (LCLS)
**MiPor** ........ Portage Public Library, Portage, MI [*Library symbol*] [*Library of Congress*] (LCLS)
**MIPORN** .. Miami Pornography [*FBI undercover investigation, 1977-80*]

**MiPorPS**.... Portage Public Schools, Portage, MI [*Library symbol*] [*Library of Congress*] (LCLS)
**MiPot**......... Benton Township - Potterville District Library, Potterville, MI [*Library symbol*] [*Library of Congress*] (LCLS)
**MIPP**......... Maintainability Index Prediction Procedure
**MIPP**......... Milk Indemnity Payment Program
**MIPR**......... Manhattan Institute for Policy Research (EA)
**MIPR**......... Medical Intelligence Production Requirements (MCD)
**MIPR**......... Member of the Institute of Public Relations [*British*]
**MIPR**......... Military Interdepartmental Procurement [*or Purchase*] Request
**MIPR**......... Military Intergovernmental Purchase Request (NASA)
**MIPR**......... Monthly Interim Progress Report
**MIPRCS**.... Microprocessor (MSA)
**MIProdE** ... Member of the Institution of Production Engineers [*British*] (EY)
**MIPS**......... Magazine of Intelligent Personal Systems [*A publication*]
**MIPS**......... Management Information Progress Sheets (MCD)
**MIPS**......... Marine Integrated Personnel System (MCD)
**MIPS**......... Martinsreid Institute for Protein Sequence [*Database*] [*Max Planck Institute for Biochemistry*] [*Federal Republic of Germany*]
**MIPS**......... Member of the Phonographic Society [*British*] (ROG)
**MIPS**......... Membership Information Processing System [*AARP*]
**MIPS**......... Merritt Island Press Site [*NASA*] (NASA)
**MIPS**......... Microwave Pulse Storage System [*or Subsystem*] (MCD)
**MIPS**......... Military Information Processing System
**MIPS**......... Millions of Instructions per Second [*Facetious translations: "Meaningless Indication of Performance;" "Meaningless Instructions per Second;" "Meaningless Indicator of Processor Speed"*] [*Processing power units*] [*Data processing*]
**MIPS**......... Miniature Implantable Power System
**MIPS**......... Missile Impact Prediction System
**MIPS**......... Missile Information Processing System (MCD)
**MIPS**......... Modular Instrumentation Package System (MCD)
**MIPS**......... Modular Integrated Pallet System [*Tank monitoring*] [*Army*] (RDA)
**MIPS**......... Multiple Index Processing System (MCD)
**MiPs**.......... Sanilac Township Library, Port Sanilac, MI [*Library symbol*] [*Library of Congress*] (LCLS)
**MIPsiMed** ... Member of the Institute of Psionic Medicine [*British*]
**MIPSM**..... Member of the Institute of Purchasing and Supply Management (ADA)
**MIPSNY**... Metro-International Program Services of New York (EA)
**MIPTC**...... Men's International Professional Tennis Council (EA)
**MiPtl**......... Portland District Library, Portland, MI [*Library symbol*] [*Library of Congress*] (LCLS)
**MIQ**........... Maniwaki [*Quebec*] [*Seismograph station code, US Geological Survey*] (SEIS)
**MIQ**........... Member of the Institute of Quarrying [*British*] (DBQ)
**MIQ**........... Minimum Identifiable Quantity [*Analytical chemistry*]
**MIQ**........... Minnesota Importance Questionnaire [*Vocational test*]
**Miq**........... Miqva'ot [*or Miqwa'ot*] (BJA)
**MIQA**........ Member of the Institute of Quality Assurance [*British*] (DBQ)
**Mir**............ Horne's Mirror of Justice [*A publication*] (DLA)
**MIR**........... Magnetic Ink Read
**MIR**........... Main Immunogenic Region [*Immunology*]
**MIR**........... Maintenance Infusion Rate [*Medicine*]
**MIR**........... Malfunction Investigation Report [*NASA*] (KSC)
**MIR**........... Management Information Report
**MIR**........... Management International Review [*A publication*]
**M & IR**....... Manufacturing and Inspection Record (KSC)
**MIR**........... Master of Industrial Relations
**MIR**........... Master Inventory Record
**MIR**........... Material Inspection Report [*Navy*]
**MIR**........... Material Investigators Reactor [*NASA*]
**MIR**........... Maverick Interim Report
**MIR**........... Medical Incident Report
**MIR**........... Member of the Institute of Population Registration [*British*] (DBQ)
**MIR**........... Memory-Information Register [*Data processing*]
**MIR**........... Memory Input Register [*Data processing*]
**MIR**........... Method Improvement Request (MCD)
**MIR**........... Method of Integral Relations
**MIR**........... Microinstruction Register
**MIR**........... Mid-Infrared Spectrum [*Spectroscopy*]
**MIR**........... Middle East Executive Reports [*A publication*]
**MIR**........... Middle Irish [*Language, etc.*]
**MIR**........... Military Intelligence, Research [*World War II*]
**MIR**........... Mineta Resources Ltd. [*Vancouver Stock Exchange symbol*]
**MIR**........... Minimum Income Requirements (OICC)
**MIR**........... Minneapolis Industrial Railway Co. [*AAR code*]
**Mi R**.......... Minnesota Review [*A publication*]
**Mir**............ Miracle Science and Fantasy Stories [*A publication*]
**MIR**........... Mirny [*Antarctica*] [*Geomagnetic observatory code*]
**MIR**........... Mirny [*Antarctica*] [*Seismograph station code, US Geological Survey*] (SEIS)
**MIR**........... Mirror (KSC)
**MIR**........... Missile Identification Record
**MIR**........... Missile Intelligence Report
**MIR**........... Mission Inherent Reliability
**MIR**........... Model Incident Report [*Telecommunications*] (TEL)
**MIR**........... Monastir [*Tunisia*] [*Airport symbol*] (OAG)
**MIR**........... Mouvement pour l'Independance de la Reunion [*Movement for the Independence of Reunion*] [*Political party*] (PD)
**MIR**........... Mouvement International de la Reconciliation [*International Fellowship of Reconciliation*]
**MIR**........... Movimiento de Izquierda Revolucionaria [*Movement of the Revolutionary Left*] [*Bolivia*] [*Political party*] (PPW)
**MIR**........... Movimiento de Izquierda Revolucionario [*Movement of the Revolutionary Left*] [*Venezuela*] [*Political party*]
**MIR**........... Movimiento de Izquierda Revolucionario [*Movement of the Revolutionary Left*] [*Chile*] [*Political party*]
**MIR**........... Multiband Infrared Radiometer
**MIR**........... Multiple Internal Reflection [*Spectroscopy*]
**MIR**........... Multiple Isomorphous Replacement [*Crystallography*]
**MIR**........... Multiplex Intensity Rules
**MIR**........... Multitarget Instrumentation RADAR [*Military*] (CAAL)
**MIR**........... Music Information Retrieval [*Data processing*]
**MIR**........... Mutual Interference Report (MCD)
**MIRA**........ Miniature Infrared Alarm
**MIRA**........ Miramar Resources, Inc. [*NASDAQ symbol*] (NQ)
**MIRA**........ Monterey Institute for Research in Astronomy
**MIRA**........ Monthly Index of Russian Accessions [*Library of Congress*]
**MIRA**........ Motor Industry Research Association [*British*] (DCTA)
**MIRA**........ Movimiento de Independencia Revolutionaria en Armas [*Puerto Rican independence group*] [*Political party*]
**MIRA**........ Movimiento Independentista Armado [*Armed Pro-Independence Movement*] [*Puerto Rico*] [*Political party*] (PD)
**MIRA**........ Multifunctional Inertial Reference Assembly [*Air Force*] (MCD)
**MIRAC**...... Management Information Research Assistance Center (AABC)
**MIRACL**... Management Information Report Access without Computer Languages [*Data processing*] (IEEE)
**MIRACL**... Mid-Infrared Advanced Chemical LASER
**MIRACLE** ... Mokum Industrial Research Automatic Calculator for Laboratory and Engineering
**MIRACLE** ... Multidisciplinary Integrated Research Activities in Complex Laboratory Environments [*National Science Foundation*]
**MIRACODE** ... Microfilm Information Retrieval Access Code
**MIRADCOM** ... Missile Research and Development Command [*Army*]
**MIRADOR** ... Minefield Reconnaissance and Detector System [*Army*]
**MIRADS**... Management Information and Display System [*NASA*]
**MIRAGE**... Microelectronic Indicator for RADAR Ground Equipment (MCD)
**MIRAGE**... Moessbauer Isotopic Resonant Absorption of Gamma Emission [*Physics*]
**MIRAID**.... Maintenance Information Retrieval Aid
**MIRAID**.... Maritime Institute for Research and Industrial Development [*Washington, DC*] (EA)
**MIRAK**...... Minimum Rocket [*German*]
**MIRAN**..... Miniature Infrared Analyzer [*Spectrometer*]
**MIRAN**..... Missile Ranging
**MIRAS**...... Mortgage Interest Relief at Source [*British*] (DCTA)
**MIRAT**...... MILPERCEN Initial Recruiting and Training Plan (MCD)
**MIRB**......... Mutual Insurance Rating Bureau [*Defunct*] (EA)
**MIRBM**..... Medium Intermediate-Range Ballistic Missile (MCD)
**MIRC**......... Market Intelligence Research Company [*Palo Alto, CA*] (TSSD)
**MIRC**......... Michael-Initiated Ring Closure [*Organic chemistry*]
**MIRC**......... Missile-in-Range Computer (MCD)
**MiRc**.......... Reed City Public Library, Reed City, MI [*Library symbol*] [*Library of Congress*] (LCLS)
**MIRCEN**... Microbiological Resource Center [*UNESCO*]
**Mircen J Appl Microbiol Biotechnol** ... Mircen Journal of Applied Microbiology and Biotechnology [*A publication*]
**Mirch D & S** ... Mirchall's Doctor and Student [*A publication*] (DLA)
**MIRCOM** ... Missile Materiel Readiness Command [*Army*]
**MIRD**........ Materialy i Issledovanija po Russkoj Dialektologii [*A publication*]
**MIRD**........ Medical Internal Radiation Dose [*Committee*] [*Society of Nuclear Medicine*]
**MIRD**........ Minor Irregularities and Deficiencies
**MiRd**.......... Seville Township Library, Riverdale, MI [*Library symbol*] [*Library of Congress*] (LCLS)
**MIRDC**...... Metals Industry Research and Development Center [*Philippines*] (DS)
**MIRE**......... Member of the Institution of Radio Engineers [*British*] (EY)
**MIRE Aust** ... Member of the Institution of Radio Engineers, Australia
**MIRECC** ... Mental Illness Research, Education, and Clinical Center [*Department of Veterans Affairs*]
**MIRED**...... Microreciprocal Degrees
**Mireh Advow** ... Mirehouse on Advowsons [*1824*] [*A publication*] (DLA)
**Mireh Ti** .... Mirehouse on Tithes [*2nd ed.*] [*1822*] [*A publication*] (DLA)
**Mir Ek Mezd Otnos** ... Mirovaja Ekonomika i Mezdunarodnye Otnosenija [*A publication*]
**Mir Ekon Mezdun Otnos** ... Mirovaja Ekonomika i Mezdunarodnye Otnosenija [*A publication*]
**MiRem**....... Wheatland Township Library, Remus, MI [*Library symbol*] [*Library of Congress*] (LCLS)

**MiRep**........ Republic-Michigamme Public Library, Republic, MI [*Library symbol*] [*Library of Congress*] (LCLS)
**MIREQ**...... Minimum Requirements Specified
**MiRes**........ Reading Community Library, Reading, MI [*Library symbol*] [*Library of Congress*] (LCLS)
**MIRF**......... Major Item Removal Frequency [*Army Aviation Systems Command*]
**MIRF**......... Multiple Instantaneous Response File
**MIRF**......... Myopia International Research Foundation (EA)
**MIRFAC**... Mathematics in Recognizable Form Automatically Compiled [*Data processing*]
**MIRIAM**... Major Incident Room Index and Action Management [*Police computer*] [*British*]
**MiRic**......... Richmond Public Library, Richmond, MI [*Library symbol*] [*Library of Congress*] (LCLS)
**MiRicl**........ Richland Community Library, Richland, MI [*Library symbol*] [*Library of Congress*] (LCLS)
**MIRICLE**... Mirrored Ions Closed-Loop Electrons (MCD)
**MIRID**....... Miniature RADAR Illumination Detector (MCD)
**MIRINZ**.... Meat Industry Research Institute of New Zealand
**MIRIS**....... Modified Infrared Interferometer Spectrometer
**Mir Just**..... Horne's Mirror of Justice [*A publication*] (DLA)
**MIRL**......... Medium-Intensity Runway Lighting [*Aviation*] (FAAC)
**MIRL**......... Mineral Industry Research Laboratory
**MIRN**........ Movimento Independente da Reconstrucao Nacional [*Independent Movement of National Reconstruction*] [*Portugal*] (PPE)
**MIRNA8**... Koninklijk Belgisch Instituut voor Natuurwetenschappen. Verhandelingen [*A publication*]
**MIRN-PDP**... Movimento Independente de Reconstrucao Nacional - Partido da Derecha Portuguesa [*Independent Movement for National Reconstruction - Party of the Portuguese Right*] [*Political party*] (PPW)
**MiRochOU**... Oakland University, Rochester, MI [*Library symbol*] [*Library of Congress*] (LCLS)
**MiRog**........ Presque Isle County Library, Rogers City, MI [*Library symbol*] [*Library of Congress*] (LCLS)
**MiRom**....... Romeo District Library, Romeo, MI [*Library symbol*] [*Library of Congress*] (LCLS)
**MIROS**...... Modulation Inducing Retrodirective Optical System [*NASA*]
**MiRos**........ Roseville Public Library, Roseville, MI [*Library symbol*] [*Library of Congress*] (LCLS)
**MiRosc**...... Gerrish-Higgins School District Public Library, Roscommon, MI [*Library symbol*] [*Library of Congress*] (LCLS)
**MiRoscK**.... Kirtland Community College, Roscommon, MI [*Library symbol*] [*Library of Congress*] (LCLS)
**Mirovaya Ekon Mezhdunar Otnosheniya**... Mirovaya Ekonomikai i Mezhdunarodnye Otnosheniya [*USSR*] [*A publication*]
**MiRoy**........ Royal Oak Public Library, Royal Oak, MI [*Library symbol*] [*Library of Congress*] (LCLS)
**MiRoyWB**... William Beaumont Hospital, Royal Oak, MI [*Library symbol*] [*Library of Congress*] (LCLS)
**MIRP**......... Manipulated Information Rate Processor
**Mir Parl**..... Mirror of Parliament, London [*A publication*] (DLA)
**Mir Pat Off**... Mirror of the Patent Office [*Washington, DC*] [*A publication*] (DLA)
**MIR-Peru**.. Movimiento de Izquierda Revolucionaria [*Movement of the Revolutionary Left of Peru*] [*Political party*] (PPW)
**MIRPF**...... Micro Image Relative Position Formula [*Data processing*]
**MIRPL**...... Major Item Repair Parts List (NATG)
**MIRPS**...... Multiple Information Retrieval by Parallel Selection
**Mirr**........... Horne's Mirror of Justice [*A publication*] (DLA)
**MIRR**......... Material Inspection and Receiving Report [*Military*]
**MI & RR**.... Material Inspection and Receiving Report [*Military*] (KSC)
**MIRR**......... Mitsubishi Research Reactor [*Japan*]
**MIRRC**...... Motor Insurance Repair Research Centre [*British*] (CB)
**MIRROR**... Management Information Reporting and Review of Operational Resources System
**MIRROS**... Modulation Inducing Reactive Retrodirective Optical System [*NASA*]
**Mir Rybolovstvo**... Mirovoe Rybolovstvo [*A publication*]
**MIRS**......... Manpower Information Retrieval System (IEEE)
**MIRS**......... Military Intelligence Research Section [*Navy*]
**MIRS**......... MOTS [*Module Test Set*] Information Retrieval System
**MIRS**......... Multiple Internal Reflection Spectroscopy
**MiRsc**........ Ogemaw District Library, Rose City, MI [*Library symbol*] [*Library of Congress*] (LCLS)
**MIRSDQ**... MTP [*Medical & Technical Publishing Co.*] International Review of Science. Series One. Physiology [*A publication*]
**MIRSE**...... Member of the Institution of Railway Signal Engineers [*British*] (DBQ)
**MIRSE**...... Multipurpose Imaging Radiometer Spectrometer Equipment
**MIRSI**...... Monthly Inventory Report of Special Items
**MIRST**...... Multiple Infrared Scattered Light Recorder
**MIRT**......... Molecular Infrared Track (IEEE)
**MIRTAK**... Martin Infrared Tracker
**MIRTE**...... Member of the Institute of Road Transport Engineering [*British*] (DBQ)
**MiRud**........ Rudyard School Public Library, Rudyard, MI [*Library symbol*] [*Library of Congress*] (LCLS)
**MIRV**........ Mining Review [*A publication*]
**MIRV**........ Multiple Independently-Targetable Reentry Vehicle [*Military*]
**MIS**........... Maintenance Indicator System [*TACOM*] [*Army*] (RDA)
**MIS**........... Man in Space
**MIS**........... Management Information Science
**MIS**........... Management Information Service
**MIS**........... Management Information Specialist
**MIS**........... Management Information System [*Generic term*]
**MIS**........... Management Information Systems [*Corporation for Public Broadcasting*] [*Information service or system*] (IID)
**MIS**........... Management Information Systems Quarterly [*A publication*]
**MIS**........... Management Integrated System (TEL)
**MIS**........... Manifold Interest Schedule
**MIS**........... Manpower Information System (MCD)
**MIS**........... Manson Impact Structure [*Iowa*] [*Geology*]
**MIS**........... Manufacturing Information System [*Data processing*] (BUR)
**MIS**........... Marketing Information System
**MIS**........... Mary Immaculate Seminary [*Pennsylvania*]
**MIS**........... Master Implementation Schedule [*NATO Air Defense Ground Environment*] (NATG)
**MIS**........... Master Integrated Schedule (AAG)
**MIS**........... Master of International Service
**MIS**........... Material Inspection Service [*Navy*]
**MIS**........... Maturation-Inducing Substance [*Endocrinology*]
**MIS**........... Mechanical Impact System [*Aerospace*]
**MIS**........... Mechanical Interruption Summary [*FAA*]
**MIS**........... Mechanically Induced Stress [*Agriculture*]
**MIS**........... Median Iris Society (EA)
**MIS**........... Medical Information Science
**MIS**........... Member of the Institute of Statisticians [*Formerly, AIS*] [*British*]
**MIS**........... Member of the Institute of Surveyors (ADA)
**MIS**........... Metal Insulated Structure
**MIS**........... Metal-Insulator-Semiconductor (MCD)
**MIS**........... Metrology Information Service [*GIDEP*]
**MIS**........... Middle-East Intelligence Survey (BJA)
**MIS**........... Midstate Airlines, Inc. [*Marshfield, WI*] [*FAA designator*] (FAAC)
**MIS**........... Milieu Information Service (EA)
**MIS**........... Military Intelligence Services [*Army*]
**MIS**........... Military Intelligence Summary [*Defense Intelligence Agency*]
**MIS**........... Military Interim Specification [*Army*] (MCD)
**MIS**........... Mine Issuing Ship
**MIS**........... Mineral Information Section [*Natural Environment Research Council*] (IID)
**MIS**........... Minicube System, Inc., Carlisle PA [*STAC*]
**MIS**........... Miscarriage (DSUE)
**mis**............ Miscellaneous [*MARC language code*] [*Library of Congress*] (LCCP)
**MIS**........... Miscellaneous (NATG)
**MIS**........... Miserable (DSUE)
**MIS**........... Mishima [*Japan*] [*Seismograph station code, US Geological Survey*] (SEIS)
**MIS**........... Misima [*Papua New Guinea*] [*Airport symbol*] (OAG)
**Mis**............ Misopogon [*of Julian*] [*Classical studies*] (OCD)
**MIS**........... Misset's Pakblad [*A publication*]
**MIS**........... Missile
**MIS**........... Missile Interim Specification [*Army*]
**MIS**........... Missile Specification
**MIS**........... Missing (AABC)
**MIS**........... Mission College, Santa Clara, CA [*OCLC symbol*] (OCLC)
**MIS**........... Mission Information System [*or Subsystem*]
**MIS**........... Mississippi Music Educator [*A publication*]
**Mis**............ Mississippi Reports [*A publication*] (DLA)
**MIS**........... Missouri
**Mis**............ Missouri Reports [*A publication*] (DLA)
**MIS**........... Mistico [*Ship's rigging*] (ROG)
**MIS**........... Mobility Information Service [*British*]
**MIS**........... Modified in Situ [*Experimental technique for converting shale into oil*]
**MIS**........... Monte-Carlo Inelastic Scattering [*Code*] [*Data processing*] (NRCH)
**MIS**........... Moody Institute of Science (EA)
**MIS**........... Motor Inert Storage
**MIS**........... Muellerian Inhibiting Substance [*Biochemistry*] [*Embryology*]
**MIS**........... Myer Information Services [*Australia*]
**Mis**............ New York Miscellaneous Reports [*A publication*] (DLA)
**MIS**........... NRA [*National Restaurant Association*] Management Information Services [*Defunct*] (EA)
**MiS**............ Saginaw Public Libraries, Saginaw, MI [*Library symbol*] [*Library of Congress*] (LCLS)
**MISA**......... Maxwell International Subscription Agency
**MISA**......... Meat Industry Suppliers Association (EA)
**MISA**......... Military-Industrial Supply Agency
**MISAA**...... Middle Income Student Assistance Act [*1978*]
**MIS Abr**.... Mineral Industry Surveys. Abrasive Materials [*A publication*]
**MISAC**...... Member of the Incorporated Society of Advertisement Consultants [*British*] (DAS)
**Misaki Mar Biol Inst Kyoto Univ Spec Rep**... Misaki Marine Biological Institute. Kyoto University. Special Report [*A publication*]
**MiSal**......... Saline Public Library, Saline, MI [*Library symbol*] [*Library of Congress*] (LCLS)

**MIS Alum** ... Mineral Industry Surveys. Aluminum [*A publication*]
**MISAM**..... Multiple Index Sequential Access Method
**MiSan**........ Sandusky Public Library, Sandusky, MI [*Library symbol*] [*Library of Congress*] (LCLS)
**MIS Antim** ... Mineral Industry Surveys. Antimony [*A publication*]
**MISAR**...... Microfilm Information Storage and Retrieval (MCD)
**MISAR**...... Microprocessed Sensing and Automatic Regulation [*Engine control system*] [*Automotive industry*]
**MiSaS**........ Spring Arbor College, Spring Arbor, MI [*Library symbol*] [*Library of Congress*] (LCLS)
**MIS Asbsts** ... Mineral Industry Surveys. Asbestos [*A publication*]
**MIS Asphlt** ... Mineral Industry Surveys. Asphalt [*A publication*]
**MiSb**.......... Bingham Township Library, Suttons Bay, MI [*Library symbol*] [*Library of Congress*] (LCLS)
**MiS-B**........ Saginaw Public Libraries, Butman-Fish Library, Saginaw, MI [*Library symbol*] [*Library of Congress*] (LCLS)
**MIS Barite** ... Mineral Industry Surveys. Barite [*A publication*]
**MIS Baux**.. Mineral Industry Surveys. Bauxite [*A publication*]
**MIS Bauxit** ... Mineral Industry Surveys. Bauxite [*A publication*]
**MIS Beryl** ... Mineral Industry Surveys. Beryllium [*A publication*]
**MIS Bis** ..... Mineral Industry Surveys. Bismuth [*A publication*]
**MIS B Mica** ... Mineral Industry Surveys. Block and Film Mica [*A publication*]
**MIS Boron** ... Mineral Industry Surveys. Boron. Annual Advance Summary [*A publication*]
**MIS Bromin** ... Mineral Industry Surveys. Bromine [*A publication*]
**MISC**......... Malaysian International Shipping Corporation (DS)
**MiSc**.......... Mason County Library, Scottville, MI [*Library symbol*] [*Library of Congress*] (LCLS)
**MISC**......... Midland Southwest Corporation [*NASDAQ symbol*] (NQ)
**MISC**......... Miscarriage [*Medicine*]
**MISC**......... Miscellaneous (AFM)
**Misc**.......... Miscellaneous Reports [*New York*] [*A publication*] (DLA)
**MISC**......... Movement for an Independent Socialist Canada
**Misc**........... New York Miscellaneous Reports [*A publication*]
**MiS-C**........ Saginaw Public Libraries, Claytor Branch Library, Saginaw, MI [*Library symbol*] [*Library of Congress*] (LCLS)
**MIS Cadm** ... Mineral Industry Surveys. Cadmium [*A publication*]
**MiscAgost** ... Miscellanea Agostiniana [*Rome*] [*A publication*]
**MIS Calcm** ... Mineral Industry Surveys. Calcium and Calcium Compounds [*A publication*]
**Misc A Mataro** ... Miscellanies Arqueologiques sobre Mataro i el Maresme [*A publication*]
**MISCAP**.... Mission Capability Statement (MCD)
**MiscBarc** ... Miscellanea Barcinonensia [*A publication*]
**Misc Bav Mon** ... Miscellanea Bavarica Monacensia [*A publication*]
**MiscBibl**.... Miscellanea Biblica Edita a Pontificio Instituto Biblico ad Celebrandum Annum XXV ex quo Conditum est Institutum [*Rome*] [*A publication*]
**Misc Bryol Lichenol** ... Miscellanea Bryologica et Lichenologica [*A publication*]
**Misc Bull Botanic Gdn (Adelaide)** ... Botanic Gardens (Adelaide). Miscellaneous Bulletin [*A publication*] (APTA)
**Misc Bull Coun Agric Res (India)** ... Miscellaneous Bulletins. Council of Agricultural Research (India) [*A publication*]
**Misc Bull Div Market Econ Dep Agric NSW** ... Miscellaneous Bulletin. Division of Marketing and Economics. Department of Agriculture. New South Wales [*A publication*] (APTA)
**Misc Bull Ser Econ Serv Branch Dep Primary Ind** ... Miscellaneous Bulletin Series. Economic Services Branch. Department of Primary Industries [*A publication*]
**Misc Byz Mon** ... Miscellanea Byzantina Monacensia [*A publication*]
**Misc 2d** ...... Miscellaneous Reports, Second Series [*New York*] [*A publication*] (DLA)
**Misc 2d** ...... New York Miscellaneous Reports. Second Series [*A publication*]
**Misc Dec**.... Ohio Miscellaneous Decisions (Gottschall) [*1865-73*] [*A publication*] (DLA)
**Miscel**........ Miscellaneous Reports [*New York*] [*A publication*] (DLA)
**Miscelanea Mat** ... Miscelanea Matematica [*A publication*]
**MIS Cement** ... Mineral Industry Surveys. Cement [*A publication*]
**MISCEND** ... Miscendus [*To Be Mixed*] [*Pharmacy*]
**MIS Cesium** ... Mineral Industry Surveys. Cesium and Rubidium [*A publication*]
**MISCEX**.... Miscellaneous Exercise [*Military*] (NVT)
**Misc Ext Publ NC Univ Ext Serv** ... Miscellaneous Extension Publication. North Carolina University. Extension Service [*A publication*]
**Misc For Adm Nac Bosques (Argent)** ... Miscelaneas Forestales. Administracion Nacional de Bosques (Buenos Aires, Argentina) [*A publication*]
**Misc Fr** ...... Miscellanea Francescana [*A publication*]
**Misc Franc** ... Miscellanea Francescana [*A publication*]
**Misc Fund Miguel Lillo** ... Miscelanea. Fundacion Miguel Lillo [*A publication*]
**MIS Chrom** ... Mineral Industry Surveys. Chromium [*A publication*]
**MIS CI** ...... Mineral Industry Surveys. Copper Industry [*A publication*]
**Misc Inf Tokyo Univ For** ... Miscellaneous Information. Tokyo University Forests [*A publication*]
**Misc Invest Appl Sci Res Corp Thailand** ... Miscellaneous Investigation. Applied Scientific Research Corporation of Thailand [*A publication*]
**MISCL** ...... Miscellaneous
**MIS Clays** ... Mineral Industry Surveys. Clays [*A publication*]
**Misc Med** .. Miscellanea Mediaevalia [*A publication*]
**Misc Mon** .. Miscellanea Bavarica Monacensia [*A publication*]
**Misc Mus**... Miscellanea Musicologica [*A publication*]
**Misc Musicol** ... Miscellanea Musicologica [*A publication*]
**Misc (NY)** ... Miscellaneous Reports [*New York*] [*A publication*] (DLA)
**MISCO**...... McCall Information Systems Company
**MIS Cobalt** ... Mineral Industry Surveys. Cobalt [*A publication*]
**MIS Columb** ... Mineral Industry Surveys. Columbium and Tantalum [*A publication*]
**MISCON**... Misconduct
**MIS Copper** ... Mineral Industry Surveys. Copper [*A publication*]
**MIS Corund** ... Mineral Industry Surveys. Corundum [*A publication*]
**Misc Pap Exp For Taiwan Univ** ... Miscellaneous Papers. Experimental Forest. National Taiwan University [*A publication*]
**Misc Pap Gronl Geol Unders** ... Miscellaneous Papers. Gronlands Geologiske Undersogelse [*A publication*]
**Misc Pap Landbouwhogesch Wageningen** ... Miscellaneous Papers. Landbouwhogeschool Wageningen [*A publication*]
**Misc Pap Ont Div Mines** ... Miscellaneous Paper. Ontario Division of Mines [*A publication*]
**Misc Pap Ont Geol Surv** ... Miscellaneous Paper. Ontario Geological Survey [*A publication*]
**Misc Pap Oreg Dep Geol Miner Ind** ... Miscellaneous Paper. Oregon Department of Geology and Mineral Industries [*A publication*]
**Misc Pap Oreg State Coll Agr Exp Sta** ... Miscellaneous Paper. Oregon State College. Agricultural Experiment Station [*A publication*]
**Misc Pap Pac Southwest Forest Range Exp Sta US Forest Serv** ... Miscellaneous Paper. Pacific Southwest Forest and Range Experiment Station. US Forest Service [*A publication*]
**Misc Pap US Army Eng Waterw Exp Stn** ... Miscellaneous Paper. United States Army Engineers. Waterways Experiment Station [*A publication*]
**Misc Publ Agric Exp Stn Okla State Univ** ... Miscellaneous Publication. Agricultural Experiment Station. Oklahoma State University [*A publication*]
**Misc Publ Aust Entomol Soc** ... Miscellaneous Publication. Australian Entomological Society [*A publication*] (APTA)
**Misc Publ Aust Ent Soc** ... Miscellaneous Publication. Australian Entomological Society [*A publication*] (APTA)
**Misc Publ Entomol Soc Am** ... Miscellaneous Publications. Entomological Society of America [*A publication*]
**Misc Publ Genet Soc Can** ... Miscellaneous Publications. Genetics Society of Canada [*A publication*]
**Misc Publ Geol Surv India** ... Miscellaneous Publications. Geological Survey of India [*A publication*]
**Misc Publ Hawaii Univ Coop Ext Serv** ... Miscellaneous Publication. Hawaii University. Cooperative Extension Service [*A publication*]
**Misc Publ Hokkaido Natl Agric Exp Stn** ... Miscellaneous Publication. Hokkaido National Agricultural Experimentation Station [*A publication*]
**Misc Publ Land Resour Div Dir Overseas Surv** ... Miscellaneous Publication. Land Resources Division. Directorate of Overseas Surveys [*A publication*]
**Misc Publ Mus Zool Univ Mich** ... Miscellaneous Publications. Museum of Zoology. University of Michigan [*A publication*]
**Misc Publ Natl Inst Agric Sci Ser D Physiol Genet** ... Miscellaneous Publication. National Institute of Agricultural Sciences. Series D. Physiology and Genetics [*A publication*]
**Misc Publ Okla State Univ Agr Exp Sta** ... Miscellaneous Publication. Oklahoma State University. Agricultural Experiment Station [*A publication*]
**Misc Publ S Carol Ext Serv** ... Miscellaneous Publications. South Carolina Extension Service [*A publication*]
**Misc Publs Ent Soc Am** ... Miscellaneous Publications. Entomological Society of America [*A publication*]
**Misc Publs Forest Dep West Aust** ... Miscellaneous Publications. Forests Department. Western Australia [*A publication*] (APTA)
**Misc Publs Mus Zool Univ Mich** ... Miscellaneous Publications. Museum of Zoology. University of Michigan [*A publication*]
**Misc Publs Univ ME** ... Miscellaneous Publications. University of Maine [*A publication*]
**Misc Publs US Dep Agric** ... Miscellaneous Publications. United States Department of Agriculture [*A publication*]
**Misc Publs US Dep Agric Soil Conserv Serv** ... Miscellaneous Publications. United States Department of Agriculture. Soil Conservation Service [*A publication*]
**Misc Publ Tex Agr Exp Sta** ... Miscellaneous Publications. Texas Agricultural Experiment Station [*A publication*]
**Misc Publ Univ KY Co-Op Ext Serv Agr Home Econ HE** ... Miscellaneous Publication. University of Kentucky. Cooperative Extension Service. Agriculture and Home Economics. HE [*A publication*]
**Misc Publ Univ MD Agr Exp Sta** ... Miscellaneous Publication. University of Maryland. Agricultural Experiment Station [*A publication*]

**Misc Publ Univ NC State Coll Agr Eng Dept Agr Econ** ... Miscellaneous Publication. University of North Carolina. State College of Agriculture and Engineering. Department of Agricultural Economics [*A publication*]
**Misc Publ USDA** ... Miscellaneous Publication. United States Department of Agriculture [*A publication*]
**Misc Publ US Dep Agric** ... Miscellaneous Publication. United States Department of Agriculture [*A publication*]
**Misc Publ Wash State Univ Coll Agr Ext Serv** ... Miscellaneous Publication. Washington State University. College of Agriculture. Extension Service [*A publication*]
**Misc Publ W Va Univ Coll Agr Agr Ext Serv** ... Miscellaneous Publication. West Virginia University. College of Agriculture. Agricultural Extension Service [*A publication*]
**Misc Pub US Dep Agric** ... Miscellaneous Publication. United States Department of Agriculture [*A publication*]
**Misc Rep**.... Miscellaneous Reports [*New York*] [*A publication*] (DLA)
**Misc Rep Agric Exp Stn Univ Minn** ... Miscellaneous Report. Agricultural Experiment Station. University of Minnesota [*A publication*]
**Misc Rep (Arusha) Trop Pestic Res Inst** ... Miscellaneous Report (Arusha). Tropical Pesticides Research Institute [*A publication*]
**Misc Rep Lab Gov Chem (GB)** ... Miscellaneous Report. Laboratory of the Government Chemist (Great Britain) [*A publication*]
**Misc Rep Life Sci Agric Exp Stn Univ Maine** ... Miscellaneous Report. Life Sciences and Agriculture Experiment Station. University of Maine [*A publication*]
**Misc Rep Maine Agr Exp Sta** ... Miscellaneous Report. Maine Agricultural Experiment Station [*A publication*]
**Misc Rep Minn Agric Exp Stn** ... Miscellaneous Report. Minnesota Agricultural Experiment Station [*A publication*]
**Misc Rep Nebr Agr Exp Sta** ... Miscellaneous Report. Nebraska Agricultural Experiment Station [*A publication*]
**Misc Rep Ohio Div Geol Surv** ... Miscellaneous Report. Ohio Division of Geological Survey [*A publication*]
**Misc Reports** ... New York Miscellaneous Reports [*A publication*] (DLA)
**Misc Rep Res Inst Nat Resourc (Tokyo)** ... Miscellaneous Reports. Research Institute for Natural Resources (Tokyo) [*A publication*]
**Misc Rep Saskatchewan Energy Mines** ... Miscellaneous Report. Saskatchewan Energy and Mines [*A publication*]
**Misc Repts** ... New York Miscellaneous Reports [*A publication*] (DLA)
**Misc Rep Univ Minn Agr Exp Sta** ... Miscellaneous Report. University of Minnesota. Agricultural Experiment Station [*A publication*]
**Misc Rep Univ Minn Agric Exp Stn** ... Miscellaneous Report. University of Minnesota. Agricultural Experiment Station [*A publication*]
**Misc Rep Yamashina Inst Ornithol** ... Miscellaneous Reports. Yamashina Institute for Ornithology [*A publication*]
**Misc Rep Yamashina's Inst Ornithol Zool** ... Miscellaneous Reports. Yamashina's Institute for Ornithology and Zoology [*A publication*]
**MIS Cs** ...... Mineral Industry Surveys. Copper Sulfate [*A publication*]
**Misc Ser ND Geol Surv** ... Miscellaneous Series. North Dakota Geological Survey [*A publication*]
**Misc St L Crist Ant** ... Miscellanea di Studi di Letteratura Cristiana Antica [*A publication*]
**Misc Stor Lig** ... Miscellanea di Storia Ligure [*A publication*]
**Misc Univ Nac Tucuman Fac Agron Zootech** ... Miscelanea. Universidad Nacional de Tucuman. Facultad de Agronomia y Zootecnia [*A publication*]
**MiScW** ...... West Shore Community College, Scottville, MI [*Library symbol*] [*Library of Congress*] (LCLS)
**Misc Zool**... Miscelanea Zoologica [*A publication*]
**MISD**......... Management Information Systems Directorate [*Army Missile Command*] [*Redstone Arsenal, AL*]
**MISD**......... Misdemeanor [*FBI standardized term*]
**MISD**......... Multiple Instruction, Single Data [*Processor configuration*] (IEEE)
**MISDAS** ... Mechanical Impact System Design for Advanced Spacecraft (IEEE)
**MIS Diamnd** ... Mineral Industry Surveys. Diamond - Industrial [*A publication*]
**MIS Diato** ... Mineral Industry Surveys. Diatomite [*A publication*]
**MIS Dime S** ... Mineral Industry Surveys. Dimension Stone in 1982 [*A publication*]
**MISDMR** ... Misdemeanor (ROG)
**MISE**......... Mechanized Infantry in a Smoke Environment (MCD)
**MISE**......... Miniature Sample (AAG)
**MiSe**.......... Sebewaing Township Library, Sebewaing, MI [*Library symbol*] [*Library of Congress*] (LCLS)
**MISEA**...... Management Information Systems Economic Analysis
**MISEA**...... Meat Industry Supply and Equipment Association [*Later, MISA*] (EA)
**MISED**...... Machine Independent Systems Effectiveness Data System (MCD)
**MISEP**...... Mutual Information System on Employment Policies in Europe (EISS)
**MISER**...... Manned Interceptor SAGE Evaluation Routine (MCD)
**MISER**...... Media Insertion Schedule Evaluation Report [*Advertising*]
**MISER**...... Microwave Space Electronics Relay
**MISER**...... Minimum Size Executive Routines
**MISES**....... Merchandises (ROG)
**Mises Jour Cardiol** ... Mises a Jour Cardiologiques [*A publication*]
**Mises Jour Sci** ... Mises a Jour Scientifiques [*France*] [*A publication*]
**Mises Point Chim Anal Org Pharm Bromatol** ... Mises au Point de Chimie Analytique, Organique, Pharmaceutique, et Bromatologique [*A publication*]
**Mises Point Chim Anal Pure Appl Anal Bromatol** ... Mises au Point de Chimie Analytique, Pure, et Appliquee et d'Analyse Bromatologique [*A publication*]
**MIS Explsv** ... Mineral Industry Surveys. Explosives [*A publication*]
**MiSf**........... Southfield Public Library, Southfield, MI [*Library symbol*] [*Library of Congress*] (LCLS)
**MiSfB**........ Bendix Corp., Engineering Development Center, Bendix Center, Southfield, MI [*Library symbol*] [*Library of Congress*] (LCLS)
**MIS Feldsp** ... Mineral Industry Surveys. Feldspar and Related Minerals [*A publication*]
**MIS Ferro** ... Mineral Industry Surveys. Ferroalloys [*A publication*]
**MIS Ferros** ... Mineral Industry Surveys. Ferrosilicon [*A publication*]
**MISFET**.... Metal-Insulator-Semiconductor Field-Effect Transistor
**MiSfL**........ Lawrence Institute of Technology, Southfield, MI [*Library symbol*] [*Library of Congress*] (LCLS)
**MIS Fluor** ... Mineral Industry Surveys. Fluorspar in 1975 [*A publication*]
**MiSfM**....... Midrasha College of Jewish Studies, Southfield, MI [*Library symbol*] [*Library of Congress*] (LCLS)
**MIS F Mtls** ... Mineral Industry Surveys. Ferrous Metals Supply and Demand Data [*A publication*]
**Mis Fra**...... Miscellanea Francescana [*A publication*]
**MISFROR**... Multiple Investment Sinking Fund Rate of Return (ADA)
**MISG**......... Missing (FAAC)
**MIS Gallm** ... Mineral Industry Surveys. Gallium [*A publication*]
**MIS Garnet** ... Mineral Industry Surveys. Garnet [*A publication*]
**MISG-C**..... Maintenance Interservice Support Group Center (MCD)
**MIS Gem**... Mineral Industry Surveys. Gem Stones. Annual Advance Summary [*A publication*]
**MIS Gem St** ... Mineral Industry Surveys. Gem Stones [*A publication*]
**MIS Gold**... Mineral Industry Surveys. Gold and Silver [*A publication*]
**MIS Graph** .... Mineral Industry Surveys. Natural Graphite [*A publication*]
**MIS Grapht** ... Mineral Industry Surveys. Graphite [*A publication*]
**MIS Gyp Mn** ... Mineral Industry Surveys. Gypsum Mines and Calcining Plants [*A publication*]
**MIS Gypsum** ... Mineral Industry Surveys. Gypsum [*A publication*]
**Mish**........... Mishnah [*Basis of the Talmud*] (BJA)
**MiSh**.......... Shelby Public Library, Shelby, MI [*Library symbol*] [*Library of Congress*] (LCLS)
**MISHAP**... Missiles High-Speed Assembly Program
**MISHAP**... Much Increased Salary, Hardly Any Pension [*Lifestyle classification*]
**MiShep**...... Coe Township Library, Shepherd, MI [*Library symbol*] [*Library of Congress*] (LCLS)
**MiSHS** ...... Saginaw Health Sciences Library, Saginaw, MI [*Library symbol*] [*Library of Congress*] (LCLS)
**MISI**.......... Member of the Iron and Steel Institute [*British*]
**MISI**.......... Micro Imaging Systems, Incorporated [*New York, NY*] [*NASDAQ symbol*] (NQ)
**MISIA** ....... Memoirs. Institute of Scientific and Industrial Research. Osaka University [*A publication*]
**MISIAS**..... Management Information Systems Inventory and Analysis System [*Navy*]
**MIS/IL**...... Metal-Insulator-Semiconductor Inversion Layer [*Photovoltaic energy systems*]
**MISIM**...... Metal-Insulator-Semiconductor Insulator Metal (MCD)
**MIS(India)** ... Member of the Institution of Surveyors of India
**MIS Iodine** ... Mineral Industry Surveys. Iodine. Annual Advance Summary [*A publication*]
**MISIP**........ Management Information System Improvement Plan
**MISIP**........ Merck Infrared Spectral Interpretation Package [*For minicomputers*] [*Analytical chemistry*]
**MISIP**........ Minority Institutions Science Improvement Program [*National Science Foundation*]
**MIS Iron**.... Mineral Industry Surveys. Iron and Steel [*A publication*]
**MIS Iron O** ... Mineral Industry Surveys. Iron Ore [*A publication*]
**MIS Ir Ox** ... Mineral Industry Surveys. Iron Oxide Pigments [*A publication*]
**MIS I & S**.. Mineral Industry Surveys. Iron and Steel Scrap [*A publication*]
**MIS Kyan**.. Mineral Industry Surveys. Kyanite and Related Minerals [*A publication*]
**MISL**......... Major Indoor Soccer League (EA)
**MISL**......... Malfunction Investigation Support Laboratory [*NASA*] (KSC)
**MISL**......... Management Information System Laboratory
**MISL**......... Missile
**MiSl**........... South Lyon Public Library, South Lyon, MI [*Library symbol*] [*Library of Congress*] (LCLS)
**MIS LABS** ... Midwest Integrated Systems Laboratories, Inc. [*Watertown, WI*] (TSSD)
**MIS Lead**... Mineral Industry Surveys. Lead Industry [*A publication*]
**MIS Lead P** ... Mineral Industry Surveys. Lead Production [*A publication*]
**MIS Lime**.. Mineral Industry Surveys. Lime [*A publication*]
**MIS Lith**.... Mineral Industry Surveys. Lithium [*A publication*]
**MISLPA**.... Major Indoor Soccer League Players Association (EA)

**MISM**........ Member of the Institute of Supervisory Management [*British*] (DBQ)
**MISM**........ Metal-Insulator-Semiconductor Metal (MCD)
**MiSM**........ Michigan Lutheran Seminary, Saginaw, MI [*Library symbol*] [*Library of Congress*] (LCLS)
**MISMA**..... Major Item Supply Management Agency
**MISMA**..... Member of the Incorporated Sales Managers Association [*British*] (DAS)
**MISMAC**.. Missile and Munitions Materiel Center (MCD)
**MIS Magn** ... Mineral Industry Surveys. Magnesium and Magnesium Compounds [*A publication*]
**MIS Mang** ... Mineral Industry Surveys. Manganese [*A publication*]
**MISMD**..... Medical Illustration Service for Museum Design [*Armed Forces Institute of Pathology*] (RDA)
**MISMDS**.. Multiple Instruction Streams Multiple Data Steams
**MIS Mercry** ... Mineral Industry Surveys. Mercury [*A publication*]
**MIS Mercury** ... Mineral Industry Surveys. Mercury [*A publication*]
**MIS Mica**.. Mineral Industry Surveys. Mica [*A publication*]
**MISMO** .... Maintenance Interservice [*or Intersupport*] Management Office [*DARCOM*] (AFIT)
**MIS Moly** ... Mineral Industry Surveys. Molybdenum [*A publication*]
**Mis Mus** .... Mistress of Music
**MIS Nickel** ... Mineral Industry Surveys. Nickel [*A publication*]
**MIS Nitro** ... Mineral Industry Surveys. Nitrogen [*A publication*]
**MIS Nonfer** ... Mineral Industry Surveys. Nonferrous Metals [*A publication*]
**MIS Nonfl M** ... Mineral Industry Surveys. Raw Nonfuel Mineral Production [*A publication*]
**MISO** ........ Maintenance Interservice Office [*Air Force*] (AFIT)
**MISO** ........ Management Information Systems Office (AABC)
**MISO** ........ Materialy i Issledovanija Smolenskoj Oblasti [*A publication*]
**MISO** ........ Misonidazole [*Azomycin*] [*Oncology, Radiosensitizer*]
**MiSod**........ Sodus Township Library, Sodus, MI [*Library symbol*] [*Library of Congress*] (LCLS)
**MISP**......... Management Information System Plan
**MISP**......... Manned Interceptor Simulation Program
**MISP**......... Medical Information Systems Program [*Data processing*] (BUR)
**MISP**......... Microprocessor Industry Support Programme [*British*] (DCTA)
**MisP** .......... Miscellanea Phonetica [*A publication*]
**MISPC** ...... Mechanized Infantry Squad Proficiency Course [*Army*]
**MIS Peat** ... Mineral Industry Surveys. Advance Data on Peat [*A publication*]
**MIS Peat P** ... Mineral Industry Surveys. Peat Producers in the United States in 1980 [*A publication*]
**MIS Perlit** ... Mineral Industry Surveys. Perlite [*A publication*]
**MIS Phos R** ... Mineral Industry Surveys. Phosphate Rock [*A publication*]
**MiSpl**......... Warner Baird Library, Spring Lake, MI [*Library symbol*] [*Library of Congress*] (LCLS)
**MIS Plat**.... Mineral Industry Surveys. Platinum [*A publication*]
**MIS P Magn** ... Mineral Industry Surveys. Primary Magnesium [*A publication*]
**MIS Potash** ... Mineral Industry Surveys. Potash. Annual Advance Summary [*A publication*]
**MIS Pumice** ... Mineral Industry Surveys. Pumice and Volcanic Cinder [*A publication*]
**MIS-Q** ....... Maintenance Information System for Quality (MCD)
**MIS Qtly** ... Mineral Industry Surveys. Quarterly [*A publication*]
**MIS Quartz** ... Mineral Industry Surveys. Quartz Crystals [*A publication*]
**MISR**......... Major Item Status Report
**MISR**......... Matrix Ion Species Ratio [*Spectroscopy*]
**MISR**......... Minimum Industrial Sustaining Role (NG)
**Mis R** ......... Missionary Review of the World [*A publication*]
**Mis R** ......... Missouri Reports [*A publication*] (DLA)
**MISR**......... Modular Industrial Solar Retrofit Program [*Department of Energy*]
**MISRAN**... Missile Range
**MISRC** ...... Management Information Systems Research Center [*University of Minnesota*] [*Research center*] (RCD)
**MISRE** ...... Microwave Space Relay [*Electronics*]
**MISREP**.... Mission Report [*Air Force*] (AFM)
**Mis Rep** ..... Missouri Reports [*A publication*] (DLA)
**MIS Rhenm** ... Mineral Industry Surveys. Rhenium [*A publication*]
**MISS** ......... Major Item Special Study [*Army Aviation Systems Command*]
**MISS** ......... Man in Space Simulator
**MISS** ......... Man in Space Soonest
**MISS** ......... Management and Information System Staff [*United Nations Development Program*]
**MISS** ......... Mechanical Interruption Statistical Summary (IEEE)
**MISS** ......... Medical Information Science Section [*National Institutes of Health*] [*Information service or system*] (IID)
**MISS** ......... Microwave Imager Sensor Study (MCD)
**MISS** ......... Mid-Course Surveillance System (MCD)
**MISS** ......... Miniature SOFAR [*Sound Fixing and Ranging*] System
**MISS** ......... Minicomputer Interfacing Support System [*Data processing*]
**MISS** ......... Missile Intercept Simulation System
**Miss** .......... Missiology [*A publication*]
**MISS** ......... Mission [*NASA*] (KSC)
**miss**............ Missionary
**MISS** ......... Mississippi (AFM)
**Miss**........... Mississippi Reports [*A publication*]
**Miss** .......... Mississippi Supreme Court Reports [*A publication*] (DLA)
**MISS** ......... Mississippian [*Railway*] [*AAR code*]
**MISS** ......... Mississippian [*Period, era, or system*] [*Geology*]
**MISS** ......... Mobile Instrumentation Support System
**MISS** ......... Mobile Integrated Support System (MCD)
**MISS** ......... Multi-Item Single Source (IEEE)
**MISS** ......... Multiband Image Scanning System
**MiS-S** ........ Saginaw Public Libraries, South Jefferson Branch, Saginaw, MI [*Library symbol*] [*Library of Congress*] (LCLS)
**MiSs** .......... Sault Ste. Marie Carnegie Public Library, Sault Ste. Marie, MI [*Library symbol*] [*Library of Congress*] (LCLS)
**MISS** ......... Title for an unmarried woman; derived from "mistress."
**Miss Acad Sci J** ... Mississippi Academy of Sciences. Journal [*A publication*]
**Miss Acad Sci Jour** ... Mississippi Academy of Sciences. Journal [*A publication*]
**Miss Ag Exp** ... Mississippi. Agricultural Experiment Station. Publications [*A publication*]
**Miss Agr Exp Sta B** ... Mississippi. Agricultural Experiment Station. Bulletin [*A publication*]
**Miss Agric Exp Stn Annu Rep** ... Mississippi. Agricultural Experiment Station. Annual Report [*A publication*]
**Miss Agric Exp Stn Circ** ... Mississippi. Agricultural Experiment Station. Circular [*A publication*]
**Miss Agric Exp Stn Tech Bull** ... Mississippi. Agricultural Experiment Station. Technical Bulletin [*A publication*]
**Miss Agric For Exp Stn Annu Rep** ... Mississippi. Agricultural and Forestry Experiment Station. Annual Report [*A publication*]
**Miss Agric For Exp Stn Bull** ... Mississippi. Agricultural and Forestry Experiment Station. Bulletin [*A publication*]
**Miss Agric For Exp Stn Res Rep** ... Mississippi. Agricultural and Forestry Experiment Station. Research Report [*A publication*]
**Miss Agric For Exp Stn Tech Bull** ... Mississippi. Agricultural and Forestry Experiment Station. Technical Bulletin [*A publication*]
**MIS Salt** .... Mineral Industry Surveys. Salt [*A publication*]
**MIS Sand** .. Mineral Industry Surveys. Sand and Gravel [*A publication*]
**MiSsB**........ Baylis Public Library, Sault Ste. Marie, MI [*Library symbol*] [*Library of Congress*] (LCLS)
**Miss Board Water Comm Bull** ... Mississippi. Board of Water Commissioners. Bulletin [*A publication*]
**Miss Bus R** ... Mississippi Business Review [*A publication*]
**Miss CL Rev** ... Mississippi College. Law Review [*A publication*]
**Miss Code Ann** ... Mississippi Code, Annotated [*A publication*] (DLA)
**Miss Col LR** ... Mississippi College. Law Review [*A publication*]
**MISS-D**..... Minuteman Integrated Schedules Status and Data Systems [*Missiles*]
**Miss Dec**.... Mississippi Decisions [*A publication*] (DLA)
**Miss Dent Assoc J** ... Mississippi Dental Association. Journal [*A publication*]
**MIS Sel** ..... Mineral Industry Surveys. Selenium [*A publication*]
**Miss Farm Res** ... Mississippi Farm Research. Mississippi Agricultural Experiment Station [*A publication*]
**MissFR**...... Mississippi Folklore Register [*A publication*]
**Miss Geol** .. Mississippi Geology [*A publication*]
**Miss Geol Econ Topogr Surv Inf Ser MGS** ... Mississippi. Geological, Economic, and Topographical Survey. Information Series MGS [*A publication*]
**Miss Geol Surv Bull** ... Mississippi. Geological, Economic, and Topographical Survey. Bulletin [*A publication*]
**Miss G S B** ... Mississippi. Geological Survey. Bulletin [*A publication*]
**MissHisp**... Missionalia Hispanica [*A publication*]
**Miss His S** ... Mississippi Historical Society. Publications [*A publication*]
**Miss Hist Soc Publ** ... Mississippi Historical Society. Publications [*A publication*]
**MISSIL**..... Management Information System Symbolic Interpretive Language [*Data processing*] (MCD)
**MISSILEX** ... Missile Firing Exercise (NVT)
**MIS Silicn** ... Mineral Industry Surveys. Silicon [*A publication*]
**MISSIO**..... Internationales Katholisches Missionswerk [*Pontifical Mission Society*] [*Aachen, Federal Republic of Germany*] (EAIO)
**Missio**........ Missiology [*A publication*]
**MissionArchFrMem** ... Memoire. Mission Archeologique Francaise au Caire [*A publication*]
**Missionary R** ... Missionary Review [*A publication*] (APTA)
**Mission Hisp** ... Missionalia Hispanica [*Madrid*] [*A publication*]
**Mission Rev** ... Missionary Review [*A publication*] (APTA)
**Mississipi** .. Mississippi Business Journal [*A publication*]
**Mississippi Geol Econ and Topog Survey Bull** ... Mississippi. Geological, Economic, and Topographical Survey. Bulletin [*A publication*]
**Mississippi Med Rec** ... Mississippi Medical Record [*A publication*]
**Mississippi's Bus** ... Mississippi's Business [*A publication*]
**Mississippi Val J Busin Econ** ... Mississippi Valley Journal of Business and Economics [*A publication*]
**MiSsL**........ Lake Superior State College, Sault Ste. Marie, MI [*Library symbol*] [*Library of Congress*] (LCLS)
**MIS Slag** ... Mineral Industry Surveys. Slag, Iron, and Steel [*A publication*]
**Miss Law** ... Mississippi Lawyer [*A publication*] (DLA)
**Miss Law J** ... Mississippi Law Journal [*A publication*]
**Miss Law Rev** ... Mississippi Law Review [*A publication*] (DLA)
**Miss Laws** ... General Laws of Mississippi [*A publication*] (DLA)
**Miss Lawyer** ... Mississippi Lawyer [*A publication*] (DLA)
**Miss Lib News** ... Mississippi Library News [*A publication*]

**Miss L J**..... Mississippi Law Journal [*A publication*]
**Miss L Rev**... Mississippi Law Review [*A publication*] (DLA)
**Miss Med**.. Missouri Medicine [*A publication*]
**Misso**......... Missouri Reports [*A publication*] (DLA)
**MIS Sod C**... Mineral Industry Surveys. Sodium Compounds Annual [*A publication*]
**MIS Sodium**... Mineral Industry Surveys. Sodium Compounds [*A publication*]
**MISSOPH**... Man in Space Sophisticated (MUGU)
**Misso R**...... Missouri Reports [*A publication*] (DLA)
**Misso Rep**... Missouri Reports [*A publication*] (DLA)
**Missouri**..... Missouri Reports [*A publication*] (DLA)
**Missouri Bot Garden Annals**... Missouri Botanical Garden. Annals [*A publication*]
**Missouri Geol Survey and Water Resources Educ Ser**... Missouri. Geological Survey and Water Resources. Educational Series [*A publication*]
**Missouri Geol Survey and Water Resources Inf Circ**... Missouri. Geological Survey and Water Resources. Information Circular [*A publication*]
**Missouri Geol Survey and Water Resources Report**... Missouri. Geological Survey and Water Resources. Report [*A publication*]
**Missouri Geol Survey and Water Resources Rept Inv**... Missouri. Geological Survey and Water Resources. Report of Investigations [*A publication*]
**Missouri Geol Survey and Water Resources Spec Pub**... Missouri. Geological Survey and Water Resources. Special Publication [*A publication*]
**Missouri Law R**... Missouri Law Review [*A publication*]
**Missouri R**... Missouri Reports [*A publication*] (DLA)
**Missouri Rep**... Missouri Reports [*A publication*] (DLA)
**Missour Rep**... Missouri Reports [*A publication*] (DLA)
**MissQ**........ Mississippi Quarterly [*A publication*]
**Miss Quart**... Mississippi Quarterly [*A publication*]
**MISSR**...... Missioner (ROG)
**Miss R**....... Mississippi Reports [*A publication*] (DLA)
**Miss R**....... Mississippi Review [*A publication*]
**Miss R**....... Missouri Review [*A publication*]
**Miss RC**..... Mississippi Railroad Commission Reports [*A publication*] (DLA)
**Miss Rep**.... Mississippi Reports [*A publication*] (DLA)
**Miss RN**.... Mississippi RN [*A publication*]
**Miss & Roc**... Missiles and Rockets [*A publication*]
**Miss Rom**... Missale Romanum [*A publication*]
**Miss Serv W**... Missionary Service With
**Miss State Geol Surv Bull**... Mississippi State Geological Survey. Bulletin [*A publication*]
**Miss State Geol Survey Bull Circ**... Mississippi State Geological Survey. Bulletin. Circular [*A publication*]
**Miss State Univ Agr Expt Sta Tech Bull**... Mississippi State University. Agricultural Experiment Station. Technical Bulletin [*A publication*]
**Miss St Ca**... Morris' Mississippi State Cases [*1818-72*] [*A publication*] (DLA)
**Miss St Cas**... Morris' Mississippi State Cases [*1818-72*] [*A publication*] (DLA)
**MISST**....... Missile-Supersonic Transport
**MIS Stone**... Mineral Industry Surveys. Stone [*A publication*]
**MIS Stront**... Mineral Industry Surveys. Strontium [*A publication*]
**MIS Sulf U**... End Uses of Sulfur and Sulfuric Acid in 1982. Mineral Industry Survey [*A publication*]
**MIS Sulfur**... Mineral Industry Surveys. Sulfur [*A publication*]
**Miss Val Hist R**... Mississippi Valley Historical Review [*A publication*]
**Miss Val Hist Rev**... Mississippi Valley Historical Review. A Journal of American History [*A publication*]
**Miss V His R**... Mississippi Valley Historical Review [*A publication*]
**Miss V Med J**... Mississippi Valley Medical Journal [*A publication*]
**MISSY**...... Missionary
**MIST**......... Maximum Isothermal System Temperature [*Nuclear energy*] (NRCH)
**MIST**......... Medical Information System via Telephone [*University of Alabama*]
**MIST**......... Member of the Institute of Science Technology [*British*] (DBQ)
**MIST**......... Microbursts in Severe Thunderstorms
**MIST+**..... Microcomputer Information Support Tools [*2B Enterprises*] [*Washington, DC*] (TSSD)
**MIST**......... Minimum Structure Module
**MIST**......... Minor Isotopes Safeguards Techniques [*Nuclear energy*]
**MIST**......... Mistura [*Mixture*] [*Pharmacy*]
**MIST**......... Multi-Input Standard Tape
**MIST**......... Multiloop Integral System Test [*Nuclear energy*] (NRCH)
**MIS Talc**... Mineral Industry Surveys. Talc, Soapstone, and Pyrophyllite [*A publication*]
**MiStan**....... Stanton Public Library, Stanton, MI [*Library symbol*] [*Library of Congress*] (LCLS)
**MISTB**...... Transactions. Missouri Academy of Science [*A publication*]
**MISTC**...... Member of the Institute of Scientific and Technical Communicators [*British*] (DBQ)
**MISTC**...... Men's International Squash Tournament Council [*Cardiff, Wales*] (EAIO)
**MiStc**......... Saint Clair Shores Public Library, Saint Clair Shores, MI [*Library symbol*] [*Library of Congress*] (LCLS)
**MiStch**....... Saint Charles Public Library, Saint Charles, MI [*Library symbol*] [*Library of Congress*] (LCLS)
**MiSte**......... Lincoln Township Public Library, Stevensville, MI [*Library symbol*] [*Library of Congress*] (LCLS)
**MiStep**....... Menominee County Library, Stephenson, MI [*Library symbol*] [*Library of Congress*] (LCLS)
**MISTER**.... Mobile Integrated System Trainer, Evaluator, and Recorder [*Navy*]
**MiSth**......... Sterling Heights Public Library, Sterling Heights, MI [*Library symbol*] [*Library of Congress*] (LCLS)
**MiSthe**....... Richfield Township Public Library, St. Helen, MI [*Library symbol*] [*Library of Congress*] (LCLS)
**MiSti**.......... St. Ignace Public Library, St. Ignace, MI [*Library symbol*] [*Library of Congress*] (LCLS)
**MISTIC**..... Michigan State Integral Computer
**MISTIC**..... Missile System Target Illuminator Controlled (MCD)
**MISTIC**..... Model Interstate Scientific and Technical Information Clearinghouse
**MIS Tin**..... Mineral Industry Surveys. Tin [*A publication*]
**MISTIR**..... Multifunction Imaging Search/Track Infrared
**MIS Titanm**... Mineral Industry Surveys. Titanium [*A publication*]
**MiStjo**........ Bement Public Library, St. Johns, MI [*Library symbol*] [*Library of Congress*] (LCLS)
**MiStjW**...... Whirlpool Corp., Research Library, St. Joseph, MI [*Library symbol*] [*Library of Congress*] (LCLS)
**MiStlo**........ Theodore Austin Cutler Memorial Library, St. Louis, MI [*Library symbol*] [*Library of Congress*] (LCLS)
**MISTM**..... Member of the Institute of Sales Technology and Management [*British*] (DBQ)
**MISTR**...... Management of Items Subject to Repair [*Air Force*] (AFM)
**MISTRAL**... [*A*] programming language (CSR)
**MISTRAM**... Missile Trajectory Measurement [*Air Force*]
**MISTRANS**... Mistranslation (ADA)
**MIStructE**... Member of the Institution of Structural Engineers [*British*] (EY)
**MISTT**...... Midwest Interstate Sulfur Transformation and Transport [*Meteorology*]
**MiStu**......... Sturgis Public Library, Sturgis, MI [*Library symbol*] [*Library of Congress*] (LCLS)
**MIS Tungst**... Mineral Industry Surveys. Tungsten [*A publication*]
**MiSun**........ Sunfield District Library, Sunfield, MI [*Library symbol*] [*Library of Congress*] (LCLS)
**MISURA**... Miskito, Sumo, and Rama [*Nicaraguan Indian coalition*]
**MIS Uranm**... Mineral Industry Surveys. Uranium [*A publication*]
**MISURASATA**... Miskito, Sumo, and Rama [*Nicaraguan Indian coalition*]
**MiSV**......... United States Veterans Administration Hospital, Saginaw, MI [*Library symbol*] [*Library of Congress*] (LCLS)
**MIS Van**.... Mineral Industry Surveys. Vanadium [*A publication*]
**MIS Vandm**... Mineral Industry Surveys. Vanadium [*A publication*]
**MISVE**...... Management Information Systems for Vocational Education (OICC)
**MIS Vermic**... Mineral Industry Surveys. Vermiculite [*A publication*]
**MISW**........ Member of the Institute of Social Welfare [*British*] (DBQ)
**MiSW**........ White Pine Library System, Saginaw, MI [*Library symbol*] [*Library of Congress*] (LCLS)
**MiS-Z**........ Saginaw Public Libraries, Zauel Memorial Library, Saginaw, MI [*Library symbol*] [*Library of Congress*] (LCLS)
**MIS Zinc**... Mineral Industry Surveys. Zinc Industry [*A publication*]
**MIS Zinc O**... Mineral Industry Surveys. Zinc Oxide [*A publication*]
**MIS Zinc P**... Mineral Industry Surveys. Zinc Production [*A publication*]
**MIS Zirc**.... Mineral Industry Surveys. Zirconium and Hafnium [*A publication*]
**MIT**........... Macrotrends International [*Vancouver Stock Exchange symbol*]
**MIT**........... Male Impotence Test [*Psychology*]
**MIT**........... Market if Touched [*Stock exchange term*]
**MIT**........... Massachusetts Institute of Technology [*Facetious translation: "Made in Taiwan" because of large number of Asian-American students*]
**MIT**........... Massachusetts Investors Trust
**MIT**........... Master Instruction Tape [*Data processing*]
**MIT**........... Material Improvement Team (MCD)
**MIT**........... Medium Intertheater Transport (MCD)
**MIT**........... Mercury Integrated Test
**MIT**........... Mercury Ion Thruster
**MIT**........... Middle Italian [*Language, etc.*]
**MIT**........... Miles in Trail [*Aviation*] (FAAC)
**MIT**........... Military Intelligence Translator
**MIT**........... Milled in Transit [*Commodities*]
**MIT**........... Miller Air Transporters [*Jackson, MS*] [*FAA designator*] (FAAC)
**MIT**........... Milwaukee Institute of Technology [*Wisconsin*]
**MIT**........... Minimum Individual Training
**MIT**........... Miracidal Immobilization Test [*Parasitology*]
**MIT**........... Missouri-Illinois Traffic Service, East Saint Louis IL [*STAC*]
**Mit**............ Mitannian (BJA)
**MIT**........... Miter
**MIT**........... Mitigate
**MIT**........... Mito [*Japan*] [*Seismograph station code, US Geological Survey*] (SEIS)

**MIT** .......... Mitte [*Send*] [*Latin*]
**MIT** .......... Mobile Instructor Team (MCD)
**MIT** .......... Mobile Instructor Training [*Army*]
**MIT** .......... Modular Industrial Terminal
**MIT** .......... Modular Intelligent Terminal
**MIT** .......... Monoiodotyrosine [*Biochemistry*]
**MIT** .......... Motorist Inclusive Tour [*British*] (DCTA)
**MIT** .......... Multiple Incidence Technique [*Structure testing*]
**MIT** .......... Municipal Investment Trust
**MIT** .......... Shafter, CA [*Location identifier*] [*FAA*] (FAAL)
**MIT** .......... Society of Management Information Technology [*British*]
**MiT** .......... Traverse City Public Library, Traverse City, MI [*Library symbol*] [*Library of Congress*] (LCLS)
**MITA** ........ Member of the Industrial Transport Association [*British*]
**MITA** ........ Microcomputer Industry Trade Association
**MITA** ........ Minority Information Trade Annual [*A publication*]
**Mita J Econ** ... Mita Journal of Economics [*A publication*]
**MITAN** ..... Microwave Technology as Applied to Air Navigation (ADA)
**MITB** ........ Missile Interface Test Bench
**Mitb** .......... Mitbestimmung [*A publication*]
**Mitb Gespr** ... Mitbestimmungsgespraech [*A publication*]
**MiTc** .......... Iosco-Arenac Regional Library, Tawas City, MI [*Library symbol*] [*Library of Congress*] (LCLS)
**MITC** ......... Methylisothiocyanate [*Pesticide*]
**MITC** ......... Microfilm and Information Technology Center
**MiTc-A** ...... Iosco-Arenac Regional Library, AuGres Branch Library, AuGres, MI [*Library symbol*] [*Library of Congress*] (LCLS)
**MiTc-E** ...... Iosco-Arenac Regional Library, East Tawas Branch Library, East Tawas, MI [*Library symbol*] [*Library of Congress*] (LCLS)
**Mitch B & N** ... Mitchell on Bills, Notes, Etc. [*1829*] [*A publication*] (DLA)
**Mitchell's Mar Reg** ... Mitchell's Maritime Register [*England*] [*A publication*] (DLA)
**Mitch Mod Geog** ... Mitchell's Modern Geography [*A publication*] (DLA)
**Mitch MR** ... Mitchell's Maritime Register [*England*] [*A publication*] (DLA)
**Mit Ch Pl**... Mitford on Equity Pleading [*A publication*] (DLA)
**Mitchurin Beweg** ... Mitchurin Bewegung [*A publication*]
**MiTc-O** ...... Iosco-Arenac Regional Library, Oscoda Township Branch Library, Oscoda, MI [*Library symbol*] [*Library of Congress*] (LCLS)
**MiTc-P** ...... Iosco-Arenac Regional Library, Plainfield Township Branch Library, Hale, MI [*Library symbol*] [*Library of Congress*] (LCLS)
**MiTc-S** ...... Iosco-Arenac Regional Library, Standish Branch Library, Standish, MI [*Library symbol*] [*Library of Congress*] (LCLS)
**MiTc-T** ...... Iosco-Arenac Regional Library, Tawas City Branch Library, Tawas City, MI [*Library symbol*] [*Library of Congress*] (LCLS)
**MiTc-W** ..... Iosco-Arenac Regional Library, Whittemore Branch Library, Whittemore, MI [*Library symbol*] [*Library of Congress*] (LCLS)
**MITD** ........ Member of the Institute of Training and Development [*British*] (DBQ)
**MITDA** ..... Maryland Independent Truckers and Drivers Association [*Later, ITDA*] (EA)
**Mit Drunk** ... Mittermaier's Effect of Drunkenness on Criminal Responsibilty [*A publication*] (DLA)
**MITE** ......... Magnetic Insulation Test Experiment
**MITE** ......... Master Instrumentation Timing Equipment (CET)
**MITE** ......... Meetings and Incentive Travel Exposition [*Trade show*]
**MITE** ......... Microelectronic Integrated Test Equipment
**MITE** ......... Microelectronics Test and Evaluation [*Raytheon Co.*]
**MITE** ......... Miniaturized Integrated Telephone Equipment
**MITE** ......... Missile Integration Terminal Equipment [*Data processing*]
**MITE** ......... Multiple Input Terminal Equipment
**MiTe** .......... Tecumseh Public Library, Tecumseh, MI [*Library symbol*] [*Library of Congress*] (LCLS)
**MiTek** ........ Tekonsha Public Library, Tekonsha, MI [*Library symbol*] [*Library of Congress*] (LCLS)
**MITER** ...... Modular Installation of Telecommunications Equipment Racks (TEL)
**MITF** ......... Municipal Investment Trust Fund
**MITF** ......... Musser International Turfgrass Foundation (EA)
**Mitf Eq Pl** ... Mitford on Equity Pleading [*A publication*] (DLA)
**MIT Fluid Mech Lab Publ** ... Massachusetts Institute of Technology. Fluid Mechanics Laboratory. Publication [*A publication*]
**Mitf & Ty Eq Pl** ... Tyler's Edition of Mitford's Equity Pleading [*A publication*] (DLA)
**MITGS** ...... Marine Institute of Technology and Graduate Studies [*Baltimore*]
**MITH** ........ Marble-in-the-Hole [*Game used in psychometrics*]
**MiTho** ........ Betsie Valley District Library, Thompsonville, MI [*Library symbol*] [*Library of Congress*] (LCLS)
**MiThr** ........ Three Rivers Public Library, Three Rivers, MI [*Library symbol*] [*Library of Congress*] (LCLS)
**MIT Hydrodyn Lab Tech Rep** ... MIT [*Massachusetts Institute of Technology*] Hydrodynamics Laboratory. Technical Report [*A publication*]
**MITI** .......... Magnetic Information Technology [*NASDAQ symbol*] (NQ)
**MITI** .......... Ministry of International Trade and Industry [*Japan*]
**MITILAC** ... Massachusetts Institute of Technology Information Laboratory Automatic Coding
**Mit Insuf**.... Mitral Insufficiency [*Cardiology*]
**Mit J** .......... Mittellateinisches Jahrbuch [*A publication*]
**MITK** .......... Mitek Systems, Inc. [*NASDAQ symbol*] (NQ)
**MITKA** ....... Movimiento Indio Tupaj Katari [*Tupaj Katari Indian Movement*] [*Bolivia*] [*Political party*] (PPW)
**MITLA** ...... Microcircuit Technology in Logistics Applications [*Defense Logistics Agency*]
**MIT/LL**..... Massachusetts Institute of Technology/Lincoln Laboratory (AAG)
**MITM** ....... Management Inventory on Time Management [*Test*]
**MITM** ....... Military-Industry Technical Manual
**MITMA**..... Member of the Institute of Trade Mark Agents [*British*]
**MITMA**..... Military Traffic Management Agency [*Later, DTMS*]
**MIT (Mass Inst Technol) Press Res Monogr** ... MIT (Massachusetts Institute of Technology) Press. Research Monograph [*A publication*]
**MIT (Mass Inst Technol) Stud Am Polit Public Policy** ... MIT (Massachusetts Institute of Technology) Studies in American Politics and Public Policy [*A publication*]
**Mit MR**...... Mitchell's Maritime Register [*England*] [*A publication*] (ILCA)
**MITMS**..... Military-Industry Technical Manual Specifications
**MiTN**......... Northwestern Michigan College, Traverse City, MI [*Library symbol*] [*Library of Congress*] (LCLS)
**MIT/NSL** ... Massachusetts Institute of Technology/Naval Supersonic Laboratory (AAG)
**MITO** ........ Minimum Interval Takeoff
**MITOC** ..... Multiple Intercommunications Technical Operations Communications [*NASA*] (KSC)
**MITOCS**... Missile Technical Operations Communications System (MCD)
**MITOL**...... Machine-Independent Telemetry-Oriented Language [*Data processing*] (IEEE)
**MiTop**........ Topinabee Public Library, Topinabee, MI [*Library symbol*] [*Library of Congress*] (LCLS)
**MITP**......... Master Intern Training Plan [*Military*]
**MITP**......... Miniature Template [*Tool*]
**MiTP** ......... Peninsula Community Library, Traverse City, MI [*Library symbol*] [*Library of Congress*] (LCLS)
**MIT Press Res Monogr** ... MIT [*Massachusetts Institute of Technology*] Press. Research Monograph [*A publication*]
**MIT Press Ser Comput Sci** ... MIT [*Massachusetts Institute of Technology*] Press. Series in Computer Science [*A publication*]
**MIT Press Ser Signal Process Optim Control** ... MIT [*Massachusetts Institute of Technology*] Press. Series in Signal Processing. Optimization and Control [*A publication*]
**MITR**......... Massachusetts Institute of Technology Reactor
**MiTr** .......... Troy Public Library, Troy, MI [*Library symbol*] [*Library of Congress*] (LCLS)
**MIT Ralph M Parsons Lab Water Resour Hydrodyn Rep** ... Massachusetts Institute of Technology. School of Engineering. Ralph M. Parsons Laboratory for Water Resources and Hydrodynamics. Report [*A publication*]
**MitrArd** ..... Mitropolia Ardealului [*Sibiu, Rumania*] (BJA)
**MitrBan**..... Mitropolia Banatului [*Timisoara, Rumania*] (BJA)
**MITRE**...... Massachusetts Institute of Technology Research Establishment (NATG)
**MITRE**...... Miniature Individual Transmitter-Receiver Equipment (MCD)
**MitrMoldSuc** ... Mitropolia Moldovei si Sucevei [*Jassy, Rumania*] (BJA)
**MitrOlt**...... Mitropolia Olteniei [*A publication*]
**MITROPA** ... Mitteleuropa [*Central Europe*] [*German*]
**Mitrop Olteniei** ... Mitropolia Olteniei [*A publication*]
**MiTrWB**.... William Beaumont Hospital, Troy, MI [*Library symbol*] [*Library of Congress*] (LCLS)
**MITS** ......... Man-in-the-Sea Program [*Navy*]
**MITS** ......... Man in the Street [*The average man*] [*Usually "Mr. Mits"*] [*See also T C MITS*]
**MITS** ......... Management Information and Text System
**MITS** ......... Master's Intelligent Terminal System [*Software package*] [*Nippon Kokan*]
**MITS** ......... Michigan Information Transfer Source [*University of Michigan*] (IID)
**MITS** ......... Microfiche Image Transmission System (MCD)
**MITS** ......... Missile Ignition Test Simulator
**MITS** ......... Missile Interface Test Set
**MITS** ......... Missouri-Illinois Traffic Service
**MITS** ......... Mitsui & Co. Ltd. [*NASDAQ symbol*] (NQ)
**MITS** ......... Monthly International Terrorist Summary (MCD)
**MITSA** ...... Member of the Institute of Trading Standards Administration [*British*] (DBQ)
**MITSG** ...... Massachusetts Institute of Technology Sea Grant Program (NOAA)
**MIT/SL**..... Massachusetts Institute of Technology/Sloan Laboratory (AAG)
**MIT/SmL** ... Massachusetts Institute of Technology/Servomechanisms Laboratory (AAG)
**MIT/SpL**... Massachusetts Institute of Technology/Spectroscopy Laboratory (AAG)
**Mitsubishi Denki Lab Rep** ... Mitsubishi Denki Laboratory Reports [*A publication*]
**Mitsubishi Electr Adv** ... Mitsubishi Electric Advance [*A publication*]

**Mitsubishi Electr Eng** ... Mitsubishi Electric Engineer [*A publication*]
**Mitsubishi Heavy Ind Mitsubishi Tech Bull** ... Mitsubishi Heavy Industries. Mitsubishi Technical Bulletin [*A publication*]
**Mitsubishi Heavy Ind Tech Rev** ... Mitsubishi Heavy Industries Technical Review [*A publication*]
**Mitsubishi Plast Technol** ... Mitsubishi Plastics Technology [*Japan*] [*A publication*]
**Mitsubishi Steel Manuf Tech Rev** ... Mitsubishi Steel Manufacturing Technical Review [*A publication*]
**Mitsubishi Tech Bull** ... Mitsubishi Technical Bulletin [*A publication*]
**Mitsubishi Tech Rev** ... Mitsubishi Heavy Industries Technical Review [*A publication*]
**Mitsubishi Tech Rev** ... Mitsubishi Technical Review [*A publication*]
**Mitsui Tech Rev** ... Mitsui Technical Review [*A publication*]
**Mitsui Zosen Tech Rev** ... Mitsui Zosen Technical Review [*A publication*]
**MITT**......... Mitte [*Send*] [*Latin*]
**Mitt**........... Mitteilung [*Report*] [*German*] (BJA)
**Mitt Aarg Nat Ges** ... Mitteilungen der Aargauischen Naturforschenden Gesellschaft [*A publication*]
**Mitt (Agen)** ... Mitteilungen (Agen) [*A publication*]
**Mitt Agrarwiss Fak Mosonmagyarovar (Ung)** ... Mitteilungen. Agrarwissenschaftliche Fakultaet zu Mosonmagyarovar (Ungarn) [*A publication*]
**Mitt Agrarwiss Hochsch Mosonmagyarovar (Ung)** ... Mitteilungen. Agrarwissenschaftliche Hochschule zu Mosonmagyarovar (Ungarn) [*A publication*]
**Mitt Akad Wiss UdSSR** ... Mitteilungen. Akademie der Wissenschaften der UdSSR [*A publication*]
**Mitt Allg Pathol Pathol Anat** ... Mitteilungen ueber Allgemeine Pathologie und Pathologische Anatomie [*A publication*]
**Mitt Alpenl Geol Ver** ... Mitteilungen. Alpenlaendischer Geologische Verein [*A publication*]
**Mitt Anthrop Ges W** ... Mitteilungen. Anthropologische Gesellschaft in Wien [*A publication*]
**Mitt Anthropol Ges Wien** ... Mitteilungen. Anthropologische Gesellschaft in Wien [*A publication*]
**Mitt Arbeitsgem Florist Kartierung Bayerns** ... Mitteilungen. Arbeitsgemeinschaft zur Floristischen Kartierung Bayerns [*A publication*]
**Mitt Arbeitsgem Florist Schleswig-Holstein Hamburg** ... Mitteilungen. Arbeitsgemeinschaft fuer Floristik in Schleswig-Holstein und Hamburg [*A publication*]
**Mitt Arbeitsgem Geobot Schleswig-Holstein Hamburg** ... Mitteilungen. Arbeitsgemeinschaft Geobotanik in Schleswig-Holstein und Hamburg [*A publication*]
**Mitt Archaeol Inst Ung Akad Wiss** ... Mitteilungen. Archaeologisches Institut der Ungarischen Akademie der Wissenschaften [*A publication*]
**Mitt Astr Ges** ... Mitteilungen. Astronomische Gesellschaft [*A publication*]
**Mitt Astron Ges** ... Mitteilungen. Astronomische Gesellschaft [*German Federal Republic*] [*A publication*]
**MITTAT** ... Mittatur [*Let Be Sent*] [*Pharmacy*] (ROG)
**Mitt Bad Geol Landesanst** ... Mitteilungen. Badische Geologische Landesanstalt [*A publication*]
**Mitt Bad Landesver Naturkd Naturschutz (Freib Br)** ... Mitteilungen des Badischen Landesvereins fuer Naturkunde und Naturschutz EV (Freiburg Im Breisgau) [*A publication*]
**Mitt Basl Bot Ges** ... Mitteilungen der Basler Botanischen Gesellschaft [*A publication*]
**Mitt Bayer Landesanst Tier Grub Muenchen** ... Mitteilungen. Bayerische Landesanstalt fuer Tierzucht in Grub bei Muenchen [*A publication*]
**Mitt Bayer Landesanst Tierz Grub** ... Mitteilungen. Bayerische Landesanstalt fuer Tierzucht in Grub bei Muenchen [*A publication*]
**Mitt Bayer Staatssamml Palaeontol Hist Geol** ... Mitteilungen. Bayerische Staatssammlung fuer Palaeontologie und Historische Geologie [*A publication*]
**Mitt Berl Ges Anthropol** ... Mitteilungen. Berliner Gesellschaft fuer Anthropologie, Ethnologie, und Urgeschichte [*A publication*]
**Mitt B Fors** ... Mitteilungen. Bundesforschungsanstalt fuer Forst- und Holzwirtschaft [*A publication*]
**Mitt Biol Bund Anst Ld- u Forstw** ... Mitteilungen. Biologische Bundesanstalt fuer Land- und Forstwirtschaft [*A publication*]
**Mitt Biol Bundesanst Land- u Forstw** ... Mitteilungen. Biologische Bundesanstalt fuer Land- und Forstwirtschaft [*A publication*]
**Mitt Biol Bundesanst Land-Forstwirt (Berlin-Dahlem)** ... Mitteilungen. Biologische Bundesanstalt fuer Land- und Forstwirtschaft (Berlin-Dahlem) [*A publication*]
**Mitt Biol Bundesanst Land-Forstwirtsch (Berl-Dahlem)** ... Mitteilungen. Biologische Bundesanstalt fuer Land- und Forstwirtschaft (Berlin-Dahlem) [*A publication*]
**Mitt Bl Ber Zahn Ae** ... Mitteilungsblatt der Berliner Zahnaerzte [*A publication*]
**MittBl Chem Ges DDR** ... Mitteilungsblatt. Chemische Gesellschaft der Deutschen Demokratischen Republik [*A publication*]
**Mitt Bl Dt Gem Parad Fschg** ... Mitteilungsblatt der Deutschen Arbeitsgemeinschaft fuer Paradentose-Forschung [*A publication*]
**Mitt Bl DVW** ... Mitteilungsblatt. Deutscher Verein fuer Vermessungswesen [*A publication*]
**Mitt Bl Math Stat** ... Mitteilungsblatt fuer Mathematische Statistik [*A publication*]
**Mitt Bot Gart Mus Berl-Dahlem** ... Mitteilungen. Botanischer Garten und Museum Berlin-Dahlem [*A publication*]
**Mitt Bot Muenchen** ... Mitteilungen. Botanische Staatssammlung Muenchen [*A publication*]
**Mitt Bot Staatssamml Muench** ... Mitteilungen. Botanische Staatssammlung Muenchen [*A publication*]
**Mitt Brennstoffinst (Freiberg)** ... Mitteilungen. Brennstoffinstitut (Freiberg) [*A publication*]
**Mitt Bundesforschanst Forst- u Holzw** ... Mitteilungen. Bundesforschungsanstalt fuer Forst- und Holzwirtschaft [*A publication*]
**Mitt Bundesforsch (Reinbek/Hamburg)** ... Mitteilungen. Bundesforschungsanstalt fuer Forst- und Holzwirtschaft (Reinbek bei Hamburg) [*A publication*]
**Mitt Bundesforschungsanst Forst Holzwirtsch** ... Mitteilungen. Bundesforschungsanstalt fuer Forst- und Holzwirtschaft [*A publication*]
**Mitt Chem Forsch Inst Ind** ... Mitteilungen des Chemischen Forschungs-Instituts der Industrie [*A publication*]
**Mitt Chem Forschungsinst Wirtsch Oesterr** ... Mitteilungen. Chemisches Forschungsinstitut der Wirtschaft Oesterreichs [*A publication*]
**Mitt Dachpappen Ind** ... Mitteilungen aus der Dachpappen-Industrie [*A publication*]
**Mitt DDR**.. Mitteilungen. Wissenschaftlichen Bibliothekswesen der Deutschen Demokratischen Republik [*A publication*]
**Mitt Deut Landwirt Ges** ... Mitteilungen. Deutsche Landwirtschafts Gesellschaft [*A publication*]
**Mitt Deutschen Ges M Orients** ... Mitteilungen. Deutsche Gesellschaft fuer Musik des Orients [*A publication*]
**Mitt Direktor Osterr Nat Bank** ... Mitteilungen. Direktorium der Oesterreichischen National Bank [*A publication*]
**Mitt DLG**... Mitteilungen. Deutsche Landwirtschafts Gesellschaft [*A publication*]
**Mitt DOG** ... Mitteilungen der Deutschen Orient-Gesellschaft [*A publication*]
**Mitt Dt Ent Ges** ... Mitteilungen. Deutsche Entomologische Gesellschaft [*A publication*]
**Mitt Dt Germ Verb** ... Mitteilungen des Deutschen Germanisten-Verbandes [*A publication*]
**Mitt Dt LandsGes (Frankfurt/Main)** ... Mitteilungen. Deutsche Landwirtschafts Gesellschaft (Frankfurt/Main) [*A publication*]
**Mitt Dt Landw Ges** ... Mitteilungen. Deutsche Landwirtschafts Gesellschaft [*A publication*]
**Mitt Dt Orient Ges** ... Mitteilungen der Deutschen Orient-Gesellschaft zu Berlin [*A publication*]
**Mitt Dt Pharm Ges** ... Mitteilungen. Deutsche Pharmazeutische Gesellschaft [*A publication*]
**Mitt Dtsch Archaeol Inst Abt Kairo** ... Mitteilungen. Deutsches Archaeologische Institut. Abteilung Kairo [*A publication*]
**Mitt Dtsch Dendrol Ges** ... Mitteilungen. Deutsche Dendrologische Gesellschaft [*A publication*]
**Mitt Dtsche Ges Musik Orients** ... Mitteilungen. Deutsche Gesellschaft fuer Musik des Orients [*A publication*]
**Mitt Dtsch Entomol Ges** ... Mitteilungen. Deutsche Entomologische Gesellschaft [*A publication*]
**Mitt Dtsch Forschungsges Blechverarb Oberflaechenbehandl** ... Mitteilungen. Deutsche Forschungsgesellschaft fuer Blechverarbeitung und Oberflaechenbehandlung [*A publication*]
**Mitt Dtsch Forschungsinst Textilind Dresden** ... Mitteilungen. Deutsches Forschungsinstitut fuer Textilindustrie in Dresden [*A publication*]
**Mitt Dtsch Ges Holzforsch** ... Mitteilungen. Deutsche Gesellschaft fuer Holzforschung [*A publication*]
**Mitt Dtsch Landwirtsch Ges** ... Mitteilungen. Deutsche Landwirtschafts Gesellschaft [*A publication*]
**Mitt Dtsch Malakozool Ges** ... Mitteilungen der Deutschen Malakozoologischen Gesellschaft [*A publication*]
**Mitt Dtsch Pharm Ges** ... Mitteilungen. Deutsche Pharmazeutische Gesellschaft [*A publication*]
**Mitteilungsbl Abt Mineral Landesmus Joanneum** ... Mitteilungsblatt. Abteilung fuer Mineralogie am Landesmuseum Joanneum [*Austria*] [*A publication*]
**Mitteilungsbl Bundesanst Fleischforsch** ... Mitteilungsblatt. Bundesanstalt fuer Fleischforschung [*A publication*]
**Mitteilungsbl Chem Ges DDR** ... Mitteilungsblatt. Chemische Gesellschaft der Deutschen Demokratischen Republik [*East Germany*] [*A publication*]
**Mitteilungsbl Chem Ges Dtsch Demokr Repub Beih** ... Mitteilungsblatt. Chemische Gesellschaft der Deutschen Demokratischen Republik. Beiheft [*A publication*]
**Mitteilungsbl Dtsch Ges Sonnenenergie** ... Mitteilungsblatt. Deutsche Gesellschaft fuer Sonnenenergie [*West Germany*] [*A publication*]
**Mitteilungsbl Dtsch Keram Ges** ... Mitteilungsblatt. Deutsche Keramische Gesellschaft [*A publication*]

**Mitteilungsbl Fraunhofer-Ges** ... Mitteilungsblatt. Fraunhofer-Gesellschaft zur Foerderung der Angewandten Forschung EV [*A publication*]
**Mitteilungsbl Fraunhofer-Ges Foerd Angew Forsch** ... Mitteilungsblatt. Fraunhofer-Gesellschaft zur Foerderung der Angewandten Forschung EV [*A publication*]
**Mitteilungsbl GDCh Fachgruppe Lebensmittelchem Gerichtl Chem** ... Mitteilungsblatt. GDCh [*Gesellschaft Deutscher Chemiker*] Fachgruppe Lebensmittelchemie und Gerichtliche Chemie [*A publication*]
**Mitteilungsbl Jungen Gerberei Tech** ... Mitteilungsblaetter fuer den Jungen Gerberei-Techniker [*A publication*]
**Mitteilungsbl Strahlungsmessgeraete** ... Mitteilungsblaetter Strahlungsmessgeraete [*West Germany*] [*A publication*]
**Mitt Eisenhuettenmaenn Inst Tech Hochsch (Aachen)** ... Mitteilungen. Eisenhuettenmaennisches Institut der Technischen Hochschule (Aachen) [*A publication*]
**Mittellat Jb** ... Mittellateinisches Jahrbuch [*A publication*]
**Mitt Ent Ges (Basel)** ... Mitteilungen. Entomologische Gesellschaft (Basel) [*A publication*]
**Mitt Entomol Ges (Basel)** ... Mitteilungen. Entomologische Gesellschaft (Basel) [*A publication*]
**Mitt Entomol Ges BRD** ... Mitteilungen. Entomologische Gesellschaft in der Bundesrepublik Deutschland [*A publication*]
**Mitternb**..... Mitternachstbuecher [*A publication*]
**Mitt Florist-Soziol Arbeitsgem** ... Mitteilungen. Floristisch-Soziologische Arbeitsgemeinschaft [*A publication*]
**Mitt Flor Soz Arb** ... Mitteilungen. Floristisch-Soziologische Arbeitsgemeinschaft [*A publication*]
**Mitt Forsch Konstr Stahlbau** ... Mitteilungen ueber Forschung und Konstruktion in Stahlbau [*A publication*]
**Mitt Forschungsanst Gutehoffnungshuette Konzerns** ... Mitteilungen. Forschungsanstalten von Gutehoffnungshuette-Konzerns [*A publication*]
**Mitt Forschungsinst Ver Stahlwerke Ag (Dortmund)** ... Mitteilungen. Forschungsinstitut der Vereinigten Stahlwerke Aktiengesellschaft (Dortmund) [*A publication*]
**Mitt Forschungslab AGFA Gevaert AG (Leverkusen Muenchen)** ... Mitteilungen. Forschungslaboratorien der AGFA-Gevaert AG (Leverkusen-Muenchen) [*A publication*]
**Mitt Forschungslab AGFA (Leverkusen)** ... Mitteilungen. Forschungslaboratorium AGFA (Leverkusen) [*A publication*]
**Mitt Forstl Bundesversuchsanstalt (Mariabrunn)** ... Mitteilungen. Forstliche Bundes-Versuchsanstalt (Mariabrunn) [*Austria*] [*A publication*]
**Mitt Forstl Bundes-Versuchsanst (Mariabrunn)** ... Mitteilungen. Forstliche Bundes-Versuchsanstalt (Mariabrunn) [*A publication*]
**Mitt Forstl Bundes-Versuchsanst (Wien)** ... Mitteilungen. Forstliche Bundes-Versuchsanstalt (Wien) [*A publication*]
**Mitt Forstl VersAnst** ... Mitteilungen. Forstliche Bundes-Versuchsanstalt [*A publication*]
**Mitt Fr Geogr Ges** ... Mitteilungen der Fraenkischen Geographischen Gesellschaft [*A publication*]
**Mitt Geb Lebensmittelunters Hyg** ... Mitteilungen aus dem Gebiete der Lebensmitteluntersuchung und Hygiene [*A publication*]
**Mitt Geb Lebensmittelunters Hyg Trav Chim Aliment Hyg** ... Mitteilungen aus dem Gebiete der Lebensmitteluntersuchung und Hygiene. Travaux de Chimie Alimentaire et d'Hygiene [*A publication*]
**Mitt Geb Naturwiss Tech** ... Mitteilungen aus den Gebieten der Naturwissenschaft und Technik [*A publication*]
**Mitt Geodaet Inst Tech Univ Graz** ... Mitteilungen. Geodaetische Institut der Technischen Universitaet Graz [*A publication*]
**Mitt Geogr Ges Hamb** ... Mitteilungen. Geographische Gesellschaft in Hamburg [*A publication*]
**Mitt Geogr Ges Muenchen** ... Mitteilungen. Geographische Gesellschaft in Muenchen [*A publication*]
**Mitt Geol Ges Wien** ... Mitteilungen. Geologische Gesellschaft in Wien [*A publication*]
**Mitt Geol Inst Eidg Tech Hochsch Univ Zurich** ... Mitteilungen. Geologisches Institut der Eidgenoessischen Technischen Hochschule und der Universitaet Zuerich [*A publication*]
**Mitt Geol Palaeontol Inst Univ Hamburg** ... Mitteilungen. Geologisch-Palaeontologische Institut. Universitaet Hamburg [*A publication*]
**Mitt Geol Staatsinst Hamb** ... Mitteilungen. Geologisches Staatsinstitut in Hamburg [*A publication*]
**Mitt Germ Verb** ... Mitteilungen des Deutschen Germanisten-Verbandes [*A publication*]
**Mitt Ges Bayerische Mg** ... Mitteilungsblatt. Gesellschaft fuer Bayerische Musikgeschichte [*A publication*]
**Mitt Gesch Med Naturwiss Tech** ... Mitteilungen zur Geschichte der Medizin der Naturwissenschaften und Technik [*A publication*]
**Mitt Ges Erdk L** ... Mitteilungen der Gesellschaft fuer Erdkunde zu Leipzig [*A publication*]
**Mitt Ges Geol Bergbaustud Oesterr** ... Mitteilungen. Gesellschaft der Geologie- und Bergbaustudenten in Oesterreich [*A publication*]
**Mitt Ges Geol Bergbaustud Wien** ... Mitteilungen. Gesellschaft der Geologie- und Bergbaustudenten in Wien [*A publication*]
**Mitt Grenzgeb Med u Chir** ... Mitteilungen aus den Grenzgebieten der Medizin und Chirurgie [*A publication*]
**Mitt Grossforschungszentrum Chemieanlagen** ... Mitteilungen. Grossforschungszentrum Chemieanlagen [*A publication*]
**Mitt Hamb Staatskrankenanst** ... Mitteilungen. Hamburgische Staatskrankenanstalten [*A publication*]
**Mitt Hamb Zool Mus Inst** ... Mitteilungen. Hamburgisches Zoologische Museum und Institut [*A publication*]
**Mitt Hans Pfitzner Ges** ... Mitteilungen. Hans-Pfitzner-Gesellschaft [*A publication*]
**Mitt Hess Landesforstverw** ... Mitteilungen. Hessische Landesforstverwaltung [*A publication*]
**Mitt Hist Ver Pfalz** ... Mitteilungen des Historischen Vereins der Pfalz [*A publication*]
**Mitt Hoh Bundeslehr- u VersAnst Wein- Obst- u Gartenb** ... Mitteilungen der Hoeheren Bundeslehr- und Versuchsanstalten fuer Wein-, Obst-, und Gartenbau [*Klosterneuberg*] [*A publication*]
**Mitt Ind Forschungszent Chemieanlagen** ... Mitteilungen. Industrie-Forschungszentrum Chemieanlagen [*A publication*]
**Mitt Inst Aerodyn** ... Mitteilungen. Institut fuer Aerodynamik an der Eidgenoessischen Technischen Hochschule in Zuerich [*A publication*]
**Mitt Inst Allgemeine Bot (Hamb)** ... Mitteilungen aus dem Institut fuer Allgemeine Botanik (Hamburg) [*A publication*]
**Mitt Inst Angew Math** ... Mitteilungen aus dem Institut fuer Angewandte Mathematik [*A publication*]
**Mitt Inst Baustatik** ... Mitteilungen. Institut fuer Baustatik. Eidgenoessische Technische Hochschule in Zuerich [*A publication*]
**Mitt Inst Bautech** ... Mitteilungen. Institut fuer Bautechnik [*A publication*]
**Mitt Inst Colombo-Aleman Invest Cient "Punta De Betin"** ... Mitteilungen. Instituto Colombo-Aleman de Investigaciones Cientificas "Punta De Betin" [*A publication*]
**Mitt Inst Grundbau Bodenmech Eidg Tech Hochsch (Zurich)** ... Mitteilungen. Institut fuer Grundbau und Bodenmechanik. Eidgenoessische Technische Hochschule (Zuerich) [*A publication*]
**Mitt Inst Hydraul Gewaesserkd** ... Mitteilungen. Institut fuer Hydraulik und Gewaesserkunde. Technische Hochschule [*Muenchen*] [*A publication*]
**Mitt Inst Or F** ... Mitteilungen des Instituts fuer Orientforschung [*A publication*]
**Mitt Inst Orient F** ... Mitteilungen des Instituts fuer Orientforschung [*A publication*]
**Mitt Inst Orientforsch Dtsch Akad Wiss Berl** ... Mitteilungen. Institut fuer Orientforschung. Deutsche Akademie der Wissenschaften zu Berlin [*A publication*]
**Mitt Inst Textiltechnol Chemiefasern Rudolstadt** ... Mitteilungen. Institut fuer Textiltechnologie der Chemiefasern Rudolstadt [*A publication*]
**Mitt Inst Text Tech** ... Mitteilungen aus dem Institut fuer Textiltechnik [*A publication*]
**Mitt Inst Therm Turbomasch** ... Mitteilungen. Institut fuer Thermische Turbomaschinen. Eidgenoessische Technische Hochschule [*Zuerich*] [*A publication*]
**Mitt Int Moor-Torf-Ges** ... Mitteilungen. Internationale Moor- und Torf-Gesellschaft [*A publication*]
**Mitt Int Stiftung Mozarteum** ... Mitteilungen. Internationale Stiftung Mozarteum [*A publication*]
**Mitt Int Ver Saatgutpruef** ... Mitteilungen. Internationale Vereinigung fuer Saatgutpruefung [*A publication*]
**Mitt Int Ver Saatgutpruefung** ... Mitteilungen. Internationale Vereinigung fuer Saatgutpruefung [*A publication*]
**Mitt Int Ver Theor Angew Limnol** ... Mitteilungen. Internationale Vereinigung fuer Theoretische und Angewandte Limnologie [*A publication*]
**Mitt Josef Haas Ges** ... Mitteilungsblatt. Josef-Haas-Gesellschaft [*A publication*]
**Mitt (Kairo)** ... Mitteilungen. Deutsches Institut fuer Aegyptische Altertumskunde (Kairo) [*A publication*]
**Mitt Kaiser Wilhelm Inst Eisenforsch Duesseldorf** ... Mitteilungen. Kaiser-Wilhelm-Institut fuer Eisenforschung zu Duesseldorf [*A publication*]
**Mitt Kali Forsch Anst** ... Mitteilungen. Kali-Forschungs-Anstalt [*A publication*]
**Mitt K Anst Land-u Forstw** ... Mitteilungen. Kaiserliche Anstalt fuer Land- und Forstwirtschaft [*A publication*]
**Mitt Kinderaerz** ... Mitteilungen fuer Kinderaerzte [*A publication*]
**Mitt (Klosterneuburg)** ... Mitteilungen (Klosterneuburg) [*A publication*]
**Mitt Kohle Eisenforsch GmbH** ... Mitteilungen. Kohle- und Eisenforschung GmbH [*A publication*]
**Mitt Kraftwerksanlagenbau (DDR)** ... Mitteilungen. Kraftwerksanlagenbau (DDR) [*A publication*]
**Mitt Kunst** ... Mitteilungen des Kunsthistorischen Instituts in Florenz [*A publication*]
**Mitt Lab Geol Dienstes (DDR)** ... Mitteilungen. Laboratorien des Geologischen Dienstes (DDR) [*A publication*]
**Mitt Lab Preuss Geol Landesanst** ... Mitteilungen. Laboratorien der Preusseschen Geologischen Landesanstalt [*A publication*]
**Mitt Landbau Agric Bull** ... Mitteilungen fuer den Landbau. Agricultural Bulletin [*A publication*]

**Mitt Landesanst Tierz Grub** ... Mitteilungen. Landesanstalt fuer Tierzucht in Grub [*A publication*]
**Mitt Landw (Berl)** ... Mitteilungen fuer die Landwirtschaft (Berlin) [*A publication*]
**Mitt Landwirtsch** ... Mitteilungen fuer die Landwirtschaft [*A publication*]
**Mitt Landwirtsch Versuchsstellen (Ung) A** ... Mitteilungen. Landwirtschaftliche Versuchsstellen (Ungarn). A. Pflanzenbau [*A publication*]
**Mitt Landwirtsch Versuchsstellen (Ung) C** ... Mitteilungen. Landwirtschaftliche Versuchsstellen (Ungarn). C. Gartenbau [*A publication*]
**Mitt LMU** ... Mitteilungen aus dem Gebiete der Lebensmitteluntersuchung und Hygiene [*A publication*]
**Mitt Markscheidewes** ... Mitteilungen aus dem Markscheidewesen [*West Germany*] [*A publication*]
**Mitt Materialpruefungsanst Tech Hochsch (Darmstadt)** ... Mitteilungen. Materialpruefungsanstalt. Technische Hochschule (Darmstadt) [*A publication*]
**Mitt Math Ges (DDR)** ... Mitteilungen. Mathematische Gesellschaft (Deutsche Demokratische Republik) [*A publication*]
**Mitt Math Gesellsch (Hamburg)** ... Mitteilungen. Mathematische Gesellschaft (Hamburg) [*A publication*]
**Mitt Math Sem (Giessen)** ... Mitteilungen. Mathematisches Seminar (Giessen) [*A publication*]
**Mitt Max-Planck-Ges** ... Mitteilungen. Max-Planck-Gesellschaft [*A publication*]
**Mitt Max-Planck-Ges Foerd Wiss** ... Mitteilungen. Max-Planck-Gesellschaft zur Foerderung der Wissenschaften [*A publication*]
**Mitt Max-Planck-Inst Stroemungsforsch Aerodyn Versuchsanst** ... Mitteilungen. Max-Planck-Institut fuer Stroemungsforschung und der Aerodynamischen Versuchsanstalt [*A publication*]
**Mitt Max Reger Inst** ... Mitteilungen. Max Reger Institut [*A publication*]
**Mitt Med Fak Tok** ... Mitteilungen aus der Medizinischen Fakultaet der Kaiserlichen Japanischen Universitaet zu Tokio [*A publication*]
**Mitt Med Gesellsch Tokyo** ... Mitteilungen. Medizinische Gesellschaft zu Tokyo [*A publication*]
**Mitt Med Ges Tokyo** ... Mitteilungen. Medizinische Gesellschaft zu Tokyo [*A publication*]
**Mitt Mitglieder Tech Ueberwach-Ver (Bayern)** ... Mitteilungen fuer die Mitglieder des Technischen Ueberwachungs-Vereins (Bayern) [*A publication*]
**Mitt MPI Aeron** ... Mitteilungen. Max-Planck-Institut fuer Aeronomie [*A publication*]
**Mitt MPI Stroemungsforsch Aerodyn Versuchsanst** ... Mitteilungen. Max-Planck-Institut fuer Stroemungsforschung und der Aerodynamischen Versuchsanstalt [*A publication*]
**Mitt Muench Ent Ges** ... Mitteilungen. Muenchener Entomologische Gesellschaft [*A publication*]
**Mitt Muench Entomol Ges** ... Mitteilungen. Muenchener Entomologische Gesellschaft [*A publication*]
**Mitt Mus Voelkerk Hamburg** ... Mitteilungen. Museum fuer Voelkerkunde in Hamburg [*A publication*]
**Mitt Mus Voelkerk Leipzig** ... Mitteilungen. Museum fuer Voelkerkunde zu Leipzig [*A publication*]
**Mitt Na Kde** ... Mitteilungen fuer Namenkunde [*A publication*]
**Mitt Naturforsch Ges Bern** ... Mitteilungen. Naturforschende Gesellschaft in Bern [*A publication*]
**Mitt Naturwiss Ges Winterthur** ... Mitteilungen. Naturwissenschaftliche Gesellschaft in Winterthur [*A publication*]
**Mitt Naturwiss Mus Stadt Aschaffenburg** ... Mitteilungen. Naturwissenschaftliches Museum der Stadt Aschaffenburg [*A publication*]
**Mitt Naturwiss Ver Steiermark** ... Mitteilungen. Naturwissenschaftlicher Verein fuer Steiermark [*A publication*]
**Mitt Num Ges** ... Mitteilungen. Numismatische Gesellschaft [*A publication*]
**Mitt Obstbauversuchsring Alten Landes** ... Mitteilungen. Obstbauversuchsring des Alten Landes [*A publication*]
**Mitt ObstbVersAnst** ... Mitteilungen der Obstbauversuchsanstalt [*A publication*]
**Mitt ObstbVersuchsr Alten Landes** ... Mitteilungen. Obstbauversuchsring des Alten Landes [*A publication*]
**Mitt Obst Garten** ... Mitteilungen Obst und Garten [*A publication*]
**Mitt Oesterreich Ges Mw** ... Mitteilungen. Oesterreichische Gesellschaft fuer Musikwissenschaft [*A publication*]
**Mitt Oesterr Geol Ges** ... Mitteilungen. Oesterreichische Geologische Gesellschaft [*A publication*]
**Mitt Oesterr Ges Holzforsch** ... Mitteilungen. Oesterreichische Gesellschaft fuer Holzforschung [*A publication*]
**Mitt Oesterr Ges (Vienna)** ... Institut fuer Oesterreichische Geschichtsforschung. Mitteilungen (Vienna) [*A publication*]
**Mitt Oesterr Mineral Ges** ... Mitteilungen. Oesterreichische Mineralogische Gesellschaft [*A publication*]
**Mitt Oesterr Sanitaetsverwalt (Vienna)** ... Mitteilungen. Oesterreichische Sanitaetsverwaltung (Vienna) [*A publication*]
**Mitt Oest Geogr Ges** ... Mitteilungen der Oesterreichischen Geographischen Gesellschaft [*A publication*]
**Mitt O Geog** ... Mitteilungen. Oesterreichische Geographische Gesellschaft [*A publication*]
**Mitt Ost Bodenk Ges** ... Mitteilungen. Oesterreichische Bodenkundliche Gesellschaft [*A publication*]
**Mitt Osterreich Geol Ges** ... Mitteilungen der Oesterreichischen Geologischen Gesellschaft [*A publication*]
**Mitt Pollichia** ... Mitteilungen der Pollichia [*A publication*]
**Mitt Pollichia Pfaelz Ver Naturkd Naturschutz** ... Mitteilungen. Pollichia des Pfaelzischen Vereins fuer Naturkunde und Naturschutz [*A publication*]
**Mitt Praeh Kom** ... Mitteilungen der Praehistorischen Kommission der Kaiserlichen Akademie der Wissenschaften [*A publication*]
**Mitt Reichsamts Bodenforsch Zweigstelle Wien** ... Mitteilungen. Reichsamt Bodenforschung. Zweigstelle Wien [*A publication*]
**Mitt RG** ..... Mitteilungen der Raabe-Gesellschaft [*A publication*]
**Mitt Rheinische Mg** ... Mitteilungen. Arbeitsgemeinschaft fuer Rheinische Musikgeschichte [*A publication*]
**MITTS** ...... Minutes of Telecommunications Traffic [*Measure of voice, fax, and data transmission*]
**MITTS** ...... Mobile IGOR [*Intercept Ground Optical Recorder*] Tracking Telescope System [*Air Force*]
**MITT SANG ad UNC SALTEM** ... Mitte Sanguinem ad Uncias ____ Saltem [*Take Away ____ Ounces of Blood at Least*] [*Pharmacy*] (ROG)
**Mitt Schweiz Anst Forstl Versuchsw** ... Mitteilungen. Schweizerische Anstalt fuer das Forstliche Versuchswesen [*A publication*]
**Mitt Schweiz Anst Forstl Versuchswes** ... Mitteilungen. Schweizerische Anstalt fuer das Forstliche Versuchswesen [*A publication*]
**Mitt Schweiz Apoth Ver** ... Mitteilungen. Schweizerischer Apotheker-Verein [*A publication*]
**Mitt Schweiz Ent Ges** ... Mitteilungen. Schweizerische Entomologische Gesellschaft [*A publication*]
**Mitt Schweiz Entomol Ges** ... Mitteilungen. Schweizerische Entomologische Gesellschaft [*A publication*]
**Mitt Schweiz Entomol Ges Bull Soc Entomol Suisse** ... Mitteilungen. Schweizerische Entomologische Gesellschaft. Bulletin de la Societe Entomologique Suisse [*A publication*]
**Mitt Schweiz Fleckviehzuchtverb** ... Mitteilungen. Schweizerischer Fleckviehzuchtverband [*A publication*]
**Mitt Schweiz Landw** ... Mitteilungen fuer die Schweizerische Landwirtschaft [*A publication*]
**Mitt Schweiz Landwirt** ... Mitteilungen fuer die Schweizerische Landwirtschaft [*A publication*]
**Mitt Schweiz Landwirtsch** ... Mitteilungen fuer die Schweizerische Landwirtschaft [*A publication*]
**Mitt Schweiz Mf Ges** ... Mitteilungsblatt. Schweizerische Musikforschende Gesellschaft [*A publication*]
**Mitt Schw LW** ... Mitteilungen fuer die Schweizerische Landwirtschaft [*A publication*]
**Mitt SFV** ... Mitteilungen. Schweizerische Anstalt fuer das Forstliche Versuchswesen [*A publication*]
**Mitt Staatl Heimat Schlossmus Burgk/Saale** ... Mitteilungen. Staatliches Heimat und Schlossmuseum Burgk/Saale [*A publication*]
**Mitt Staatsinst Allg Bot (Hamb)** ... Mitteilungen. Staatsinstitut fuer Allgemeine Botanik (Hamburg) [*A publication*]
**Mitt Staatsinst Allg Bot (Hamburg)** ... Mitteilungen. Staatsinstitut fuer Allgemeine Botanik (Hamburg) [*A publication*]
**Mitt Steiermarkisches Landesmus (Graz) Mus Bergbau Geol Tec** ... Mitteilung-Steiermarkisches Landesmuseum (Graz). Museum fuer Bergbau, Geologie, und Technik [*A publication*]
**Mitt Stforstverw Bayerns** ... Mitteilungen. Staatsforstverwaltung Bayern [*A publication*]
**MITT TAL** ... Mitte Tales [*Send Such*] [*Pharmacy*]
**Mitt Tech Univ Braunschweig** ... Mitteilungen. Technische Universitaet Carolo-Wilhelmina zu Braunschweig [*A publication*]
**Mitt Tech Univ Carolo-Wilheimina** ... Mitteilungen. Technische Universitaet Carolo-Wilheimina [*West Germany*]
**Mitt Textilforsch Anst Krefeld** ... Mitteilungen. Textilforschungs-Anstalt Krefeld [*A publication*]
**Mitt Thurg Natf Ges** ... Mitteilungen der Thurgauischen Naturforschenden Gesellschaft [*A publication*]
**Mitt Tieraerztl Fak Reichsuniv Gent** ... Mitteilungen. Tieraerztliche Fakultaet der Reichsuniversitaet Gent [*A publication*]
**Mitt Tieraerztl Praxis Preuss Staate** ... Mitteilungen. Tieraerztliche Praxis im Preussischen Staate [*A publication*]
**Mitt Vaterl Gesch St Gall** ... Mitteilungen zur Vaterlaendischen Geschichte. Historischer Verein in St. Gallen [*A publication*]
**Mitt Ver Dtsch Emailfachl** ... Mitteilungen. Verein Deutscher Emailfachleute [*West Germany*] [*A publication*]
**Mitt Ver Dtsch Emailfachleute** ... Mitteilungen. Verein Deutscher Emailfachleute [*A publication*]
**Mitt Verein Schweiz Versicherungsmath** ... Vereinigung Schweizerischer Versicherungsmathematiker. Mitteilungen [*A publication*]
**Mitt Ver Forstl Standortskunde ForstpflZucht** ... Mitteilungen. Verein fuer Forstliche Standortskunde und Forstpflanzenzuechtung [*A publication*]
**Mitt Ver Gesch Nbg** ... Mitteilungen des Vereins fuer Geschichte der Stadt Nuernberg [*A publication*]
**Mitt Ver Grosskesselbesitzer** ... Mitteilungen. Vereinigung der Grosskesselbesitzer [*A publication*]
**Mitt Ver Grosskesselbetr** ... Mitteilungen. Vereinigung der Grosskesselbetreiber [*A publication*]

**Mitt Ver Metallwerke Ranshofen Berndorf** ... Mitteilungen. Vereinigte Metallwerke Ranshofen-Berndorf [*A publication*]
**Mitt Versuchsergeb Bundesanst Pflanzenbau Samenpruf Wien** ... Mitteilungen. Versuchsergebnissen der Bundesanstalt fuer Pflanzenbau und Samenpruefung in Wien [*A publication*]
**Mitt Versuchsstn Gaerungsgewerbe Wein** ... Mitteilungen. Versuchsstation fuer das Gaerungsgewerbe in Wien [*A publication*]
**Mitt Vers Wasserbau Hydrol Glaziologie** ... Mitteilungen. Versuchsanstalt fuer Wasserbau, Hydrologie, und Glaziologie [*A publication*]
**Mitt VGB (Tech Ver Grosskraftwerksbetr)** ... Mitteilungen. VGB (Technische Vereinigung der Grosskraftwerksbetreiber) [*German Federal Republic*] [*A publication*]
**Mitt VGN** .. Mitteilungen des Vereins fuer Geschichte der Stadt Nuernberg [*A publication*]
**Mitt VOB** .. Mitteilungen. Vereinigung Oesterreichischer Bibliothek [*A publication*]
**Mitt VWF** ... Verband der Wissenschaftler an Forschungsinstituten. Mitteilungen [*A publication*]
**Mitt Wasserbau** ... Mitteilungen aus dem Gebiete des Wasserbaues und der Grundbauforschung [*A publication*]
**Mitt WWI** ... Mitteilungen des Wirtschaftswissenschaftlichen Instituts der Gewerkschaften [*A publication*]
**Mitt Zentr Soz Arbeitsgemeinsch** ... Mitteilungsblatt. Zentrale Sozialistische Arbeitsgemeinschaft [*A publication*]
**Mitt Zool Mus Berl** ... Mitteilungen. Zoologisches Museum in Berlin [*A publication*]
**MiTu** .......... Tustin Public Library, Tustin, MI [*Library symbol*] [*Library of Congress*] (LCLS)
**MIU** .......... Maharishi International University [*Fairfield, IA*]
**MIU** .......... Maharishi International University, Fairfield, IA [*OCLC symbol*] (OCLC)
**MIU** .......... Maiduguri [*Nigeria*] [*Airport symbol*] (OAG)
**MIU** .......... Malfunction Insertion Unit [*Aviation*]
**MIU** .......... Message Interface Unit (CAAL)
**MIU** .......... Methylisourea [*Organic chemistry*]
**miu** .......... Michigan [*MARC country of publication code*] [*Library of Congress*] (LCCP)
**MIU** .......... Microalgae International Union (EA)
**mIU** .......... Milli-International Unit
**MIU** .......... Missile Interface Unit
**MIU** .......... Mobile Inspection Unit [*Military*] (AFM)
**MIU** .......... Moisture, Insolubles, and Unsaponifiables [*Fat analysis*]
**MIU** .......... Motor Impeller Unit
**MIU** .......... Multiplex Interface Unit (NASA)
**MIU** .......... Multistation Interface Unit [*Data processing*]
**MiU** .......... University of Michigan, Ann Arbor, MI [*Library symbol*] [*Library of Congress*] (LCLS)
**MiU-A** .......... University of Michigan, Asia Library, Ann Arbor, MI [*Library symbol*] [*Library of Congress*] (LCLS)
**MiUb** .......... Sleeper Public Library, Ubly, MI [*Library symbol*] [*Library of Congress*] (LCLS)
**MiU-BA** .......... University of Michigan, Graduate School of Business Administration, Ann Arbor, MI [*Library symbol*] [*Library of Congress*] (LCLS)
**MiU-C** .......... University of Michigan, William L. Clements Library, Ann Arbor, MI [*Library symbol*] [*Library of Congress*] (LCLS)
**MiUcD** .......... Delta College, University Center, MI [*Library symbol*] [*Library of Congress*] (LCLS)
**MiUcS** .......... Saginaw Valley College, University Center, MI [*Library symbol*] [*Library of Congress*] (LCLS)
**MiU-G** .......... University of Michigan, Bureau of Government Library, Ann Arbor, MI [*Library symbol*] [*Library of Congress*] (LCLS)
**MiU-H** .......... University of Michigan, Michigan Historical Collection, Ann Arbor, MI [*Library symbol*] [*Library of Congress*] (LCLS)
**MiU-Ho** .......... University of Michigan, Avery and Julie Hopwood Room, Ann Arbor, MI [*Library symbol*] [*Library of Congress*] (LCLS)
**MiU-L** .......... University of Michigan, Law Library, Ann Arbor, MI [*Library symbol*] [*Library of Congress*] (LCLS)
**MiU-M** .......... University of Michigan, Medical Center, Ann Arbor, MI [*Library symbol*] [*Library of Congress*] (LCLS)
**MiUnv** .......... Columbia Township Library, Unionville, MI [*Library symbol*] [*Library of Congress*] (LCLS)
**MiU-RE** .......... University of Michigan, Center for Research on Economic Development, Ann Arbor, MI [*Library symbol*] [*Library of Congress*] (LCLS)
**MIUS** .......... Modular Integrated Utility System [*HUD*]
**MIUSA** .......... Mobility International USA (EA)
**MiU-T** .......... University of Michigan, Transportation Library, Ann Arbor, MI [*Library symbol*] [*Library of Congress*] (LCLS)
**MiUt** .......... Utica Public Library, Utica, MI [*Library symbol*] [*Library of Congress*] (LCLS)
**MIUTC** .......... Military Intelligence Unit Training Center (AABC)
**MiUtS** .......... Shelby Township Library, Utica, MI [*Library symbol*] [*Library of Congress*] (LCLS)
**MIUW** .......... Mobile Inshore Undersea Warfare [*Navy*] (NG)
**MIUWS** .......... Mobile Inshore Undersea Warfare Surveillance [*Navy*] (NVT)
**MIUWSU** ... Mobile Inshore Undersea Warfare Surveillance Unit [*Navy*] (CINC)
**MIV** .......... Main Instrumentation Van [*NASA*]
**MIV** .......... MassMutual Income Investors, Inc. [*NYSE symbol*] (SPSG)
**MIV** .......... Materialy po i Zuceniju Vostoka [*A publication*]
**MIV** .......... MICC Investments Ltd. [*Toronto Stock Exchange symbol*]
**MIV** .......... Millville, NJ [*Location identifier*] [*FAA*] (FAAL)
**MIV** .......... Mobile Instrumentation Van (KSC)
**MIV** .......... Moving Ion Voltmeter
**MiVa** .......... Bullard-Sanford Public Library, Vassar, MI [*Library symbol*] [*Library of Congress*] (LCLS)
**MIVA-America** ... Missionary Vehicle Association of America (EA)
**MIVAC** .......... Microwave Vacuum [*Dryer*] (MCD)
**MIVC** .......... Magnetically Induced Velocity Charge [*Southwest Research Institute*]
**MiVer** .......... Vermontville Public Library, Vermontville, MI [*Library symbol*] [*Library of Congress*] (LCLS)
**MiVes** .......... Vestaburg Public Library, Vestaburg, MI [*Library symbol*] [*Library of Congress*] (LCLS)
**MiVi** .......... Vicksburg Community Library, Vicksburg, MI [*Library symbol*] [*Library of Congress*] (LCLS)
**MIW** .......... Marshalltown, IA [*Location identifier*] [*FAA*] (FAAL)
**MIW** .......... Microinstruction Word
**MIW** .......... Mine Warfare (NVT)
**MIWAC** .......... Marine and Inland Waters Advisory Committee [*Australian Environment Council*]
**MiWaC** .......... Wayne County Federated Library System, Wayne, MI [*Library symbol*] [*Library of Congress*] (LCLS)
**MiWaC-B** ... Wayne County Federated Library System, Department for the Blind and Physically Handicapped, Wayne, MI [*Library symbol*] [*Library of Congress*] (LCLS)
**MiWak** .......... Wakefield Public Library, Wakefield, MI [*Library symbol*] [*Library of Congress*] (LCLS)
**MiWal** .......... Melrose Township Public Library, Walloon Lake, MI [*Library symbol*] [*Library of Congress*] (LCLS)
**MiWald** .......... Waldron District Library, Waldron, MI [*Library symbol*] [*Library of Congress*] (LCLS)
**MiWalv** .......... Walkerville Public Library, Walkerville, MI [*Library symbol*] [*Library of Congress*] (LCLS)
**MiWar** .......... Warren Public Library, Warren, MI [*Library symbol*] [*Library of Congress*] (LCLS)
**MiWarBH** ... Bi-County Community Hospital, Warren, MI [*Library symbol*] [*Library of Congress*] (LCLS)
**MiWarGMR** ... General Motors Corp., Research Laboratories Division, Warren, MI [*Library symbol*] [*Library of Congress*] (LCLS)
**MiWarGMR-E** ... General Motors Corp., Engineering Staff Library, Warren, MI [*Library symbol*] [*Library of Congress*] (LCLS)
**MiWarM** ... Macomb County Community College, Warren, MI [*Library symbol*] [*Library of Congress*] (LCLS)
**MiWatv** .......... Watervliet Public Library, Watervliet, MI [*Library symbol*] [*Library of Congress*] (LCLS)
**MIWE** .......... Member of the Institution of Water Engineers [*British*] (EY)
**MiWe** .......... West Branch Public Library, West Branch, MI [*Library symbol*] [*Library of Congress*] (LCLS)
**MiWeld** .......... Gladys MacArthur Memorial Library, Weidman, MI [*Library symbol*] [*Library of Congress*] (LCLS)
**MiWh** .......... White Pigeon Township Library, White Pigeon, MI [*Library symbol*] [*Library of Congress*] (LCLS)
**MiWhc** .......... E. Jack Sharpe Public Library, White Cloud, MI [*Library symbol*] [*Library of Congress*] (LCLS)
**MIWHR** .......... Melpomene Institute for Women's Health Research (EA)
**MIWHTE** ... Member of the Institution of Works and Highways Technician Engineers [*British*] (DBQ)
**Miwi Ber** .......... Milchwissenschaftliche Berichte [*A publication*]
**MiWin** .......... Fremont Township Library, Winn, MI [*Library symbol*] [*Library of Congress*] (LCLS)
**MIWM** .......... Member of the Institution of Works Managers [*British*]
**MIWMA** ... Member of the Institute of Weights and Measures Administration [*British*]
**MiWol** .......... Wolverine Community Library, Wolverine, MI [*Library symbol*] [*Library of Congress*] (LCLS)
**MiWp** .......... Carp Lake Township Library, White Pine, MI [*Library symbol*] [*Library of Congress*] (LCLS)
**MIWPC** .......... Member of the Institute of Water Pollution Control [*British*]
**MIWPD** .......... Mid-Atlantic Industrial Waste Conference. Proceedings [*A publication*]
**MIWS** .......... Multipurpose Individual Weapon System (MCD)
**MIWSP** .......... Member of the Institute of Work Study Practitioners [*British*]
**MIWT** .......... Member of the Institute of Wireless Technology [*British*]
**MiWy** .......... Bacon Memorial Public Library, Wyandotte, MI [*Library symbol*] [*Library of Congress*] (LCLS)
**MIX** .......... Magnetic Ionization Experiment
**MIX** .......... McGraw-Hill Information Exchange for Educators
**MIX** .......... Member Information Exchange [*American Society for Training and Development - ASTD*] [*Alexandria, VA*] [*Information service or system*] (IID)
**MIX** .......... Methylisobutylxanthine [*Also, IBMX*] [*Biochemistry*]
**MIX** .......... Metropolis, IL [*Location identifier*] [*FAA*] (FAAL)
**MIX** .......... Mix Canyon Road [*California*] [*Seismograph station code, US Geological Survey*] (SEIS)
**MIX** .......... Mixture (KSC)
**MIXS** .......... Morehouse Industries, Inc. [*NASDAQ symbol*] (NQ)
**MIXT** .......... Mixtura [*Mixture*] [*Pharmacy*]
**MIXX** .......... Medical Innovations, Inc. [*NASDAQ symbol*] (NQ)

**MIY** .......... Miyako [*Japan*] [*Seismograph station code, US Geological Survey*] (SEIS)
**MIY** .......... Montgomeryshire Imperial Yeomanry [*British military*] (DMA)
**MiY** .......... Ypsilanti Area Public Library, Ypsilanti, MI [*Library symbol*] [*Library of Congress*] (LCLS)
**Miyagi Prefect Inst Public Health. Annu Rep** ... Miyagi Prefectural Institute of Public Health. Annual Report [*A publication*]
**MiYCC** ...... Cleary College, Ypsilanti, MI [*Library symbol*] [*Library of Congress*] (LCLS)
**MiYEM** ..... Eastern Michigan University, Ypsilanti, MI [*Library symbol*] [*Library of Congress*] (LCLS)
**MIZ** .......... Journal. Arab Maritime Transport Academy [*A publication*]
**MIZ** .......... Marginal Ice Zone [*Oceanography*]
**Miz** .......... Mizrachi [*or Mizrahi*] (BJA)
**MIZ** .......... Mizusawa [*Japan*] [*Geomagnetic observatory code*]
**MIZ** .......... Mizusawa [*Japan*] [*Seismograph station code, US Geological Survey*] (SEIS)
**MiZ** .......... Zeeland Public Library, Zeeland, MI [*Library symbol*] [*Library of Congress*] (LCLS)
**MIZEX** ...... Marginal Ice Zone Experiment [*Oceanography*]
**MIZL** ........ Mizel Petro Resources, Inc. [*NASDAQ symbol*] (NQ)
**MIZPAC** ... Marginal Sea Ice Zone Pacific [*Marine science*] (MSC)
**MJ** .......... Le Monde Juif [*A publication*]
**MJ** .......... Madras Jurist [*India*] [*A publication*] (DLA)
**MJ** .......... Major Subject Descriptor [*Online database field identifier*]
**MJ** .......... Makedonski Jazik [*A publication*]
**MJ** .......... Makerere Journal [*A publication*]
**MJ** .......... Manufacturers' Junction Railway Co. [*AAR code*]
**MJ** .......... Marijuana
**MJ** .......... Marine Jet
**MJ** .......... Master of Journalism
**MJ** .......... Master of Jurisprudence
**MJ** .......... Mastic Joint [*Technical drawings*]
**MJ** .......... Mead Johnson & Co. [*Research code symbol*]
**MJ** .......... Mechanical Joint (NASA)
**MJ** .......... Megajoule
**MJ** .......... Menorah Journal [*A publication*]
**MJ** .......... Michael Joseph [*Commercial firm*] [*British*]
**MJ** .......... Microturbo [*France*] [*ICAO aircraft manufacturer identifier*] (ICAO)
**MJ** .......... Midwest Journal [*A publication*]
**MJ** .......... Military Judge (AFM)
**MJ** .......... Military Justice Reporter (West) [*A publication*] (DLA)
**MJ** .......... Milwaukee Journal [*A newspaper*]
**MJ** .......... Mining Journal [*A publication*]
**MJ** .......... Minister van Justitie [*A publication*]
**MJ** .......... Mittellateinisches Jahrbuch [*A publication*]
**mj** .......... Montserrat [*MARC country of publication code*] [*Library of Congress*] (LCCP)
**MJ** .......... Moudjahik [*A publication*]
**MJ** .......... Municipal Journal [*A publication*]
**MJ** .......... Museum Journal [*A publication*]
**MJ** .......... Music Journal [*A publication*]
**MJ** .......... Servisair Ltd. [*Great Britain*] [*ICAO designator*] (FAAC)
**M³/J** ........ Cubic Meters per Joule
**MJA** .......... Manja [*Madagascar*] [*Airport symbol*] (OAG)
**MJA** .......... Medical Journal of Australia [*A publication*] (APTA)
**MJA** .......... Midstates Jeepster Association (EA)
**MJAA** ........ Messianic Jewish Alliance of America (EA)
**MJAGDE** ... Mesopotamia Journal of Agriculture [*A publication*]
**MJAO** ........ Mediterranean Joint Air Orders
**MJASA** ..... Mysore Journal of Agricultural Sciences [*A publication*]
**Mjasn Ind** .. Mjasnaja Industrija SSSR [*A publication*]
**MJAUA** ..... Medical Journal of Australia [*A publication*]
**MJ Australia** ... Medical Journal of Australia [*A publication*]
**M Jb** .......... Mainfraenkisches Jahrbuch fuer Geschichte und Kunst [*A publication*]
**MJB** .......... Master Jet Base [*Navy*] (NVT)
**MJB** .......... Mejit [*Marshall Islands*] [*Airport symbol*] (OAG)
**MJB** .......... Mindener Jahrbuch [*A publication*]
**MJB** .......... Missile Junction Box
**MJB** .......... Moore Jig Borer
**MJB** .......... Muenchener Jahrbuch der Bildenden Kunst [*A publication*]
**MJBK** ........ Muenchener Jahrbuch der Bildenden Kunst [*A publication*]
**MJC** .......... Junior College District, Kansas City, MO [*OCLC symbol*] (OCLC)
**MJC** .......... Majestic Contractors Ltd. [*Toronto Stock Exchange symbol*]
**MJC** .......... Man [*Ivory Coast*] [*Airport symbol*] (OAG)
**MJC** .......... Manitoba Journal of Counselling [*A publication*]
**MJC** .......... Marshalltown Junior College [*Iowa*]
**MJC** .......... Medieval Jewish Chronicles [*A publication*] (BJA)
**MJC** .......... Mercy Junior College [*Missouri*] [*Closed, 1971*]
**MJC** .......... Miami-Jacobs College [*Ohio*]
**MJC** .......... Midway Junior College [*Kentucky*]
**MJC** .......... Military Junior College (AABC)
**MJC** .......... Moberly Junior College [*Missouri*]
**MJC** .......... Modesto Junior College [*California*]
**MJC** .......... Montgomery Junior College [*Maryland*]
**MJC** .......... Morse Junior College [*Connecticut*]
**MJC** .......... Morton Junior College [*Later, Morton College*] [*Cicero, IL*]
**MJC** .......... Muscatine Junior College [*Iowa*]
**MJCA** ........ Midbody Jettison Control Assembly (NASA)
**MJCS** ........ Memorandum for the Joint Chiefs of Staff (MCD)
**MJD** .......... Doctor of Medical Jurisprudence
**MJD** .......... Modified Julian Date [*Astronomy*] (TEL)
**MJD** .......... Mohenjo Daro [*Pakistan*] [*Airport symbol*] (OAG)
**MJDQ** ........ Minnesota Job Description Questionnaire [*Research test*]
**MJDSA** ..... Mukogawa Joshi Daigaku Kiyo. Shizenkagakuhen [*A publication*]
**MJELQ** ..... Majestic Electro Industries [*NASDAQ symbol*] (NQ)
**M Jeu** ........ Musique en Jeu [*A publication*]
**MJF** .......... Greenville, TX [*Location identifier*] [*FAA*] (FAAL)
**MJF** .......... Multiple Juxtapositional Fixedness [*Tongue-in-cheek description of unusually strong bonding between metal ions and some ligands*]
**MJG** .......... Moore Jig Grinder
**MJGA** ........ Manufacturing Jewelers Golf Association (EA)
**MJGA** ........ Midwest Job Galvanizers Association [*Defunct*] (EA)
**MJGK** ........ Mainfraenkisches Jahrbuch fuer Geschichte und Kunst [*A publication*]
**MJH** .......... Michigan Jewish History [*A publication*]
**MJI** .......... Masters and Johnson Institute [*St. Louis, MO*] [*Formerly, Reproductive Biology Research Foundation*] [*Research center*]
**MJI** .......... Member of the Journalists Institute
**MJIE** ........ Member of the Junior Institute of Engineers [*British*]
**MJIMB** ..... Major Problems in Internal Medicine [*A publication*]
**MJJ** .......... Materialy po Jafeticeskomu Jazykoznaniju [*A publication*]
**MJL** .......... Marketing Journal [*A publication*]
**MJL** .......... Meyer, Jr., L. Agnew, Washington DC [*STAC*]
**MJL** .......... Mouila [*Gabon*] [*Airport symbol*] (OAG)
**MJL** .......... Murray's Jat Lancers [*British military*] (DMA)
**MJLF** ........ Midwestern Journal of Language and Folklore [*A publication*]
**MJM** .......... Man-Job Match [*Military*]
**MJM** .......... Mbuji-Mayi [*Zaire*] [*Airport symbol*] (OAG)
**MJMA** ........ Mechanical Jack Manufacturers Association (EA)
**MJMI** ........ Messianic Jewish Movement International (EA)
**MJMJ** ........ Missionaries of Jesus, Mary, and Joseph [*Roman Catholic women's religious order*]
**MJMLAI** .. Medical Journal of Malaysia [*A publication*]
**MJN** .......... Majunga [*Madagascar*] [*Airport symbol*] (OAG)
**MJN** .......... Muenchener Juedische Nachrichten [*A publication*]
**MJO** .......... Mariner Jupiter Orbit [*NASA*]
**MJO** .......... Owens Technical College, Learning Resource Media Center, Toledo, OH [*OCLC symbol*] (OCLC)
**MJP** .......... Jackson Metropolitan Library System, Jackson, MS [*OCLC symbol*] (OCLC)
**MJP** .......... Management Japan [*A publication*]
**MJP** .......... Master of Jewish Pedagogy
**MJP** .......... Mount John Pukaki [*New Zealand*] [*Seismograph station code, US Geological Survey*] (SEIS)
**MJPS** ........ Midwest Journal of Political Science [*A publication*]
**MJPS** ........ Mouvement des Jeunesses Progressistes Soudanaises [*Sudanese Progressive Youth Movement*] [*Mali*]
**MJQ** .......... Jackson, MN [*Location identifier*] [*FAA*] (FAAL)
**MJQ** .......... Modern Jazz Quartet [*Musical group*]
**MJR** .......... Maintenance Job Request
**Mjr** .......... Major [*Record label*]
**MJR** .......... Major Group, Inc. [*NYSE symbol*] (SPSG)
**MJR** .......... Management Job Review [*LIMRA*]
**MJR** .......... Missouri Journal of Research in Music Education [*A publication*]
**MJS** .......... Manipulator Jettison System [*or Subsystem*] (MCD)
**MJS** .......... Mariner Jupiter-Saturn [*NASA*]
**MJS** .......... Master of Japanese Studies (ADA)
**MJS** .......... Master of Juridical Science (DLA)
**MJS** .......... Member of the Japan Society
**MJS** .......... Movimiento Juvenil Salesiano [*Salesian Youth Movement - SYM*] (EAIO)
**MJSA** ........ Manufacturing Jewelers Sales Association
**MJSA** ........ Manufacturing Jewelers and Silversmiths of America (EA)
**MJSA** ........ Mouvement des Jeunesses Socialistes Africaines [*African Socialist Youth Movement*]
**MJSD** ........ March, June, September, and December [*Denotes quarterly payments of interest or dividends in these months*] [*Business term*]
**MJSFA** ...... Mises a Jour Scientifiques [*A publication*]
**MJSG** ........ Medem Jewish Socialist Group (EA)
**MJT** .......... Majorteck Industries [*Vancouver Stock Exchange symbol*]
**MJT** .......... Materials Joining Tool
**MJT** .......... Multijet Transport
**MJT** .......... Mytilene [*Greece*] [*Airport symbol*] (OAG)
**MJTA** ........ McDonald's Junior Tennis Australia
**MJTG** ........ Malayan Journal of Tropical Geography [*A publication*]
**MJTOA** ..... Mineralogical Journal (Tokyo) [*A publication*]
**MJU** .......... Jackson State University, Jackson, MS [*OCLC symbol*] (OCLC)
**MJU** .......... Mamuju [*Indonesia*] [*Airport symbol*] (OAG)
**MJU** .......... Mariner Jupiter-Uranus [*Mission*] [*NASA*]
**MJu** .......... Medica Judaica [*A publication*] (BJA)
**MJU** .......... Multijunction Unit [*Data processing*] (BUR)

**MJudaica**... Musica Judaica [*A publication*]
**MJugend**.... Musikalische Jugend [*A publication*]
**MJULAO** ... Communications. Instituti Forestalis Fenniae [*A publication*]
**MJUPG**..... Movimiento da Juventude da Uniao Popular da Guine [*Youth Movement of Guinean People's Union*]
**MJUPS** ..... Mouvement des Jeunes de l'Union Progressiste Senegalaise [*Youth Movement of the Senegalese Progressive Movement*]
**MJur**......... Master of Jurisprudence
**MJV**.......... Mitteilungen. Gesellschaft fuer Juedische Volkskunde [*A publication*]
**MJV**.......... Mitteilungen zur Juedischen Volkskunde [*A publication*]
**MJV**.......... Murcia [*Spain*] [*Airport symbol*] (OAG)
**MJW** ......... Madison Junction [*Wyoming*] [*Seismograph station code, US Geological Survey*] [*Closed*] (SEIS)
**MJWG** ...... MANPRINT [*Manpower and Personnel Integration*] Joint Working Group [*Army*]
**MJX**.......... Toms River, NJ [*Location identifier*] [*FAA*] (FAAL)
**MJY**.......... Majesty Resources [*Vancouver Stock Exchange symbol*]
**MJZ**.......... Mount John [*New Zealand*] [*Seismograph station code, US Geological Survey*] (SEIS)
**MK**............ Air Mauritius [*ICAO designator*] (FAAC)
**MK**............ Mackenzie Times [*A publication*]
**MK**............ Magic Kingdom [*Walt Disney World*]
**MK**............ Magyar Koenyvszemle [*A publication*]
**MK**............ Manual Clock [*Data processing*] (MDG)
**Mk** ............ Mark [*New Testament book*]
**MK**............ Mark (KSC)
**MK**............ Mark [*Ammunition*] (NATG)
**MK**............ Mark Controls Corp. [*NYSE symbol*] (SPSG)
**MK**............ Markka [*Monetary unit*] [*Finland*] (GPO)
**MK**............ Marschkolonne [*March Column*] [*German military - World War II*]
**MK**............ Mask [*Data processing*]
**MK**............ Master Key [*Locks*] (ADA)
**MK**............ Mebyon Kernow [*Sons of Cornwall*] [*National liberation party*] [*Political party*]
**MK**............ Mededelingen van het Kadaster [*A publication*]
**MK**............ Medizinische Klinik [*A publication*]
**MK**............ Member of Knesset (BJA)
**MK**............ Menaquinone [*Vitamin K*] [*Also, MQ*] [*Biochemistry*]
**MK**............ Merck & Co., Inc. [*Research code symbol*]
**MK**............ Metarrithmistikon Komma [*Reformist Party*] [*Greece*] [*Political party*] (PPE)
**MK**............ Microphone (MDG)
**MK**............ Middle Kingdom [*Egyptology*] (ROG)
**MK**............ Miesiecznik Koscielny [*A publication*]
**mK**............ Millikelvin
**MK**............ Minzokugaku-Kenkyu [*Japanese Journal of Ethnology*] [*A publication*]
**MK**............ Miscellaneous Kits [*JETDS nomenclature*] [*Military*] (CET)
**MK**............ Mit Kappe [*With Cap*] [*German military - World War II*]
**MK**............ Mit Kern [*With Core*] [*German military - World War II*]
**MK**............ Modification Kit (AAG)
**MK**............ Mo'ed Katan (BJA)
**MK**............ Monk
**MK**............ Monkey Kidney
**M-K** .......... Morrison-Knudsen Co., Inc. [*Boise, ID*] (TSSD)
**MK**............ Morse Key (DEN)
**MK**............ Moskovskij Kraeved [*A publication*]
**MK**............ Multiple Kill [*Aerospace*]
**mk** ............ Muscat and Oman [*Oman*] [*MARC country of publication code*] [*Library of Congress*] (LCCP)
**M & K** ....... Mylne and Keen's English Chancery Reports [*A publication*] (DLA)
**MK**............ Mysl Karaimska [*A publication*]
**MKA**.......... Machine Knife Association (EA)
**MKA**.......... Makaopuhi [*Hawaii*] [*Seismograph station code, US Geological Survey*] (SEIS)
**MKA**.......... Marine-Kuestenartillerie [*Naval Coast Artillery*] [*German military - World War II*]
**MKA**.......... Master Kennel Association [*Commercial firm*] (EA)
**MKA**.......... Miller, SD [*Location identifier*] [*FAA*] (FAAL)
**Mk Aerztl Fortb** ... Monatskurse fuer die Aerztliche Fortbildung [*A publication*]
**MKAI** ........ Majallat Kulliyat al-Adab, al-Iskandariyyah [*A publication*]
**MKAI** ........ Molokai Ranch Ltd. [*NASDAQ symbol*] (NQ)
**MKARAH** ... Mitteilungen der Hoeheren Bundeslehr- und Versuchsanstalten fuer Wein-, Obst-, und Gartenbau [*Klosterneuburg*]. Serie A. Rebe und Wein [*A publication*]
**MKAS**........ Meyer-Kendall Assessment Survey [*Interpersonal skills and attitudes test*]
**MKASA**..... Mikrochimica Acta. Supplement [*A publication*]
**MKAW**...... Mededeelingen. Koninklijke Nederlandsche Akademie van Wetenschappen. Afdeling Letterkunde [*A publication*]
**MKAWA**... Mededelingen. Koninklijke Academie voor Wetenschappen. Letteren en Schone Kunsten van Belgie. Klasse der Wetenschappen [*A publication*]
**MKB** .......... Megakaryoblast [*Hematology*]
**MKB** .......... Mekambo [*Gabon*] [*Airport symbol*] (OAG)
**MKBF**........ Mean Kilometers between Failures
**MKBOAD** ... Mitteilungen der Hoeheren Bundeslehr- und Versuchsanstalten fuer Wein- und Obstbau [*Klosterneuburg*]. Serie B. Obst und Garten [*A publication*]
**MKBWU** ... Machine Knife and Bayonet Workers' Union [*British*]
**MKC**.......... Kansas City [*Missouri*] [*Airport symbol*] (OAG)
**MKC**.......... Magic Kingdom Club [*Walt Disney Productions*]
**MKC**.......... Marion Merrell Dow [*NYSE symbol*] (SPSG)
**MKC**.......... Mark Resources, Inc. [*Toronto Stock Exchange symbol*]
**MKC**.......... McKeesport Connecting Railroad Co. [*AAR code*]
**MKC**.......... Moncks Corner [*South Carolina*] [*Seismograph station code, US Geological Survey*] [*Closed*] (SEIS)
**MKC**.......... University of Health Sciences, Kansas City, MO [*OCLC symbol*] (OCLC)
**MKCO**....... Kamenstein [*M.*], Inc. [*White Plains, NY*] [*NASDAQ symbol*] (NQ)
**MKCT** ....... Make Check Turn [*Aviation*] (FAAC)
**MKD**.......... Handelspartner. Nederlands Duitse Handelscourant [*A publication*]
**MKD**.......... Marked (MSA)
**MKDIR** ..... Make Directory [*Data processing*]
**MKDKA** .... Muroran Kogyo Daigaku Kenkyu Hokoku [*A publication*]
**MKE**.......... Market Research Europe [*A publication*]
**MKE**.......... Michaels Stores, Inc. [*AMEX symbol*] (SPSG)
**MKE**.......... Milwaukee [*Wisconsin*] [*Airport symbol*] (OAG)
**MKE**.......... Molecular Kinetic Energy
**MKEMA** ... Mikroelementy v Meditsine [*A publication*]
**MKEY** ....... Mast/Keystone, Inc. [*Davenport, IA*] [*NASDAQ symbol*] (NQ)
**MKF** .......... Mackenzie Financial Corp. [*Toronto Stock Exchange symbol*]
**MKG**.......... Magnetocardiogram
**MKG**.......... Making
**MKG**.......... Maurer Kunst Geselle [*Fellowcraft*] [*German*] [*Freemasonry*]
**M-KG**........ Meter-Kilogram (KSC)
**MKG**.......... Munson, K. G., Weyers Cave VA [*STAC*]
**Mkg** .......... Musikerziehung [*A publication*]
**MKG**.......... Muskegon [*Michigan*] [*Airport symbol*] (OAG)
**MKG**.......... Muskegon, MI [*Location identifier*] [*FAA*] (FAAL)
**M³/KG**....... Cubic Meters per Kilogram
**MKgP** ........ Posse School, Inc., Kendal Green, MA [*Library symbol*] [*Library of Congress*] [*Obsolete*] (LCLS)
**MKGS** ....... Markings
**MKH** ......... Mauna Kea [*Hawaii*] [*Seismograph station code, US Geological Survey*] (SEIS)
**MKH** ......... Million of Kilowatt Hours (MCD)
**MKH** ......... Mokhotlong [*Lesotho*] [*Airport symbol*] (OAG)
**MKH** ......... Multiple Key Hashing
**MKI** .......... M-Corp Inc. [*Formerly, Mike's Submarines*] [*Toronto Stock Exchange symbol*]
**MKIMP**..... Mirovoe Khoziaistvo i Mirovaia Politika [*A publication*]
**M Kirche**.... Musik und Kirche [*A publication*]
**MKJ**.......... Makoua [*Congo*] [*Airport symbol*] (OAG)
**MKJK**........ Kingston [*Jamaica*] [*ICAO location identifier*] (ICLI)
**MKJM**....... Montego Bay [*Jamaica*] [*ICAO location identifier*] (ICLI)
**MKJP**........ Kingston/Norman Manley International [*Jamaica*] [*ICAO location identifier*] (ICLI)
**MKJS**........ Montego Bay/Sangster International [*Jamaica*] [*ICAO location identifier*] (ICLI)
**MKK**.......... Kaunakakai, HI [*Location identifier*] [*FAA*] (FAAL)
**MKK**.......... Mal Kwa Kul [*Speech and Language*] [*A publication*]
**MKK**.......... Mobelkultur. Fachzeitschrift fuer die Mobelwirtschaft [*A publication*]
**MKK**.......... Molokai/Kaunakakai [*Hawaii*] [*Airport symbol*] (OAG)
**MKK**.......... Morgan, Keenan, Kellman [*System*] [*Astronomy*]
**MKKZ**....... Muenchener Katholische Kirchenzeitung fuer das Erzbistum Muenchen und Freising [*A publication*]
**MKL**.......... Jackson [*Tennessee*] [*Airport symbol*] (OAG)
**MKL**.......... Jackson, TN [*Location identifier*] [*FAA*] (FAAL)
**MKL**.......... Lakeland Regional Library, Killarney, Manitoba [*Library symbol*] [*National Library of Canada*] (NLC)
**MKL**.......... Maskali [*Djibouti*] [*Seismograph station code, US Geological Survey*] (SEIS)
**MKL**.......... Mededelingen. Koninklijke Nederlandse Academie van Wetenschappen. Afdeling Letterkunde [*Elsevier Book Series*] [*A publication*]
**M Kl**.......... Medizinische Klinik [*A publication*]
**MKL**.......... Megakaryocytic Leukemia [*Hematology*]
**MKM**......... Kansas City, MO [*Location identifier*] [*FAA*] (FAAL)
**MKM**......... Marksman [*Marine Corps*]
**MKM**......... Mink Minerals Resources, Inc. [*Vancouver Stock Exchange symbol*]
**MKM**......... Mukah [*Malaysia*] [*Airport symbol*] (OAG)
**MKM**......... Myopic Keratomileusis [*Ophthalmology*]
**MKMA**....... Machine Knife Manufacturers Association (EA)
**MkmQualBad** ... Marksman Qualification Badge [*Military decoration*] (AABC)
**MKN**.......... Malekolon [*Papua New Guinea*] [*Airport symbol*] (OAG)
**MKN**.......... Northeast Missouri State University, Kirksville, MO [*OCLC symbol*] (OCLC)
**MKNA**....... Mededeelingen. Koninklijke Nederlandsche Akademie van Wetenschappen. Afdeling Letterkunde [*A publication*]

**MKNAL**.... Mededeelingen. Koninklijke Nederlandsche Akademie van Wetenschappen. Afdeling Letterkunde [*A publication*]
**MKNAWL**... Mededeelingen. Koninklijke Nederlandsche Akademie van Wetenschappen. Afdeling Letterkunde [*A publication*]
**MKNL**........ Multnomah Kennel Club [*NASDAQ symbol*] (NQ)
**MKO**.......... Machinery Korea [*A publication*]
**MKO**.......... Mikado Resources Ltd. [*Vancouver Stock Exchange symbol*]
**MKO**.......... Modification Kit Order
**MKO**.......... Muskogee, OK [*Location identifier*] [*FAA*] (FAAL)
**MKOH**........ Mededeelingen. Kunst- en Oudheidkundigen Kring van Herenthals [*A publication*]
**MKOR**....... McCormick Capital, Inc. [*Chicago, IL*] [*NASDAQ symbol*] (NQ)
**MKOUA**.... Memoirs. Konan University. Science Series [*A publication*]
**MKP**.......... Magyar Kommunista Part [*Hungarian Communist Party*] [*Political party*] (PPE)
**MKP**.......... Makemo [*French Polynesia*] [*Airport symbol*] (OAG)
**MKP**.......... McKeesport, PA [*Location identifier*] [*FAA*] (FAAL)
**MkP**........... Mikropress GmbH, Bonn, Germany [*Library symbol*] [*Library of Congress*] (LCLS)
**MKQ**.......... Merauke [*Indonesia*] [*Airport symbol*] (OAG)
**MKQCP**.... Member of the King's and Queen's College of Physicians [*Ireland*]
**MKQUA4**... Mankind Quarterly [*A publication*]
**MKR**.......... Glasgow, MT [*Location identifier*] [*FAA*] (FAAL)
**MKR**.......... Maker
**MKR**.......... Marker [*Beacon*]
**MKR**.......... Meekatharra [*Australia*] [*Airport symbol*] (OAG)
**MKR**.......... Militair Keuringsreglement [*A publication*]
**mKRB**........ Modified Krebs-Ringer Bicarbonate [*Solution*]
**MKR Schriften**... MKR [*Mitteldeutscher Kulturrat*] Schriften [*A publication*]
**MKS**.......... Makassar [*Celebes*] [*Seismograph station code, US Geological Survey*] (SEIS)
**MKS**.......... Marketing Science [*A publication*]
**MKS**.......... Marks & Spencer Canada, Inc. [*Toronto Stock Exchange symbol*]
**MKS**.......... Marksman [*Marine Corps*]
**MKS**.......... Maul- und Klauenseuche [*Hoof-and-Mouth Disease*] [*German*]
**MKS**.......... Mekane [*Ethiopia*] [*Airport symbol*] (OAG)
**MKS**.......... Meter-Kilogram-Second [*System of units*]
**MKS**.......... Microwave Keying Switch
**MKS**.......... Mon-Khmer Studies [*A publication*]
**MKS**.......... Moncks Corner, SC [*Location identifier*] [*FAA*] (FAAL)
**MKSA**........ Meter-Kilogram-Second-Ampere [*System of units*]
**MKSS**........ Microwave Keying Switching Station
**MKSTNG**... Marksmanship Training (NVT)
**MKT**.......... Mankato [*Minnesota*] [*Airport symbol*] (OAG)
**MKT**.......... Mankato, MN [*Location identifier*] [*FAA*] (FAAL)
**MKT**.......... Market
**MKT**.......... Marketing Times [*A publication*]
**MKT**.......... Mathematische Keilschrifttexte [*A publication*]
**MKT**.......... Missouri-Kansas-Texas Railroad Co. [*AAR code*]
**MKT**.......... Mobile Kitchen Trailer [*Military*] (INF)
**MKT**.......... Mu Kappa Tau (EA)
**MKTA**....... Makita Electric Works Ltd. [*NASDAQ symbol*] (NQ)
**MKTG**....... Marketing [*A publication*]
**MKTG**....... Marketing
**Mktg Dec**... Marketing and Media Decisions [*A publication*]
**Mktg Dec S**... Marketing and Media Decisions. Special Seasonal Edition [*A publication*]
**Mktg Demonst Leafl Minist Agric**... Marketing Demonstration Leaflet. Ministry of Agriculture and Fisheries [*United Kingdom*] [*A publication*]
**Mktg and DE Today**... Marketing and Distributive Education Today [*A publication*]
**Mktg Educator's N**... Marketing Educator's News [*A publication*]
**Mktg Eur**... Marketing in Europe [*A publication*]
**Mktg Hung**... Marketing in Hungary [*A publication*]
**Mktg Leafl Minist Agric**... Marketing Leaflet. Ministry of Agriculture and Fisheries [*United Kingdom*] [*A publication*]
**Mktg News**... Marketing News [*A publication*]
**Mktg Revw**... Marketing Review [*A publication*]
**Mktg Times**... Marketing Times [*A publication*]
**Mktg (UK)**... Marketing (United Kingdom) [*A publication*]
**Mktg Ungarn**... Marketing in Ungarn [*A publication*]
**Mktg Week**... Marketing Week [*A publication*]
**MKTI**........ Mission Kit Technical Instruction (NASA)
**MKTI**........ Morrison-Knudsen Technologies, Incorporated [*Boise, ID*] [*Telecommunications*] (TSSD)
**Mkt Inform Guide**... [*The*] Marketing Information Guide [*A publication*]
**MKTLH**.... Tri-Lake Health Centre, Killarney, Manitoba [*Library symbol*] [*National Library of Canada*] (NLC)
**Mkt & Media Decisions**... Marketing and Media Decisions [*A publication*]
**MKTNG**.... Marketing
**MKTP**....... Mark Template [*Tool*]
**MKTT**....... Missouri-Kansas-Texas Railroad Co. (of Texas) [*AAR code*]
**MKTU**....... Marksmanship Training Unit (AABC)
**MKTW**...... Marketing Week [*A publication*]
**MKU**.......... Makokou [*Gabon*] [*Airport symbol*] (OAG)
**MKU**.......... Mary Kathleen Uranium Ltd. [*Australia*] (NRCH)
**MKU**.......... Mock-Up
**MKUBA**.... Memoirs. College of Agriculture. Kyoto University [*A publication*]
**M Ku Hist Florenz**... Mitteilungen des Kunsthistorischen Instituts in Florenz [*A publication*]
**MKUP**....... Makeup
**MKV**.......... Marksville, LA [*Location identifier*] [*FAA*] (FAAL)
**MKV**.......... Miniature Kill Vehicle [*Military*] (SDI)
**MKVAB**.... Mededeelingen. Koninklijke Vlaamse Akademie van Wetenschappen, Letteren en Schone Kunsten v Belgie [*A publication*]
**MKW**......... Magnetokinetic Wave
**MKW**......... Manokwari [*Indonesia*] [*Airport symbol*] (OAG)
**MKW**......... Mikawa [*Japan*] [*Seismograph station code, US Geological Survey*] (SEIS)
**MKW**......... Military Knight of Windsor [*British*]
**MKW**......... Munitionskraftwagen [*Ammunition Truck*] [*German military - World War II*]
**MKY**.......... Mackay [*Australia*] [*Airport symbol*] (OAG)
**MKY**.......... Makeyevka [*USSR*] [*Seismograph station code, US Geological Survey*] [*Closed*] (SEIS)
**MKY**.......... Marco Island, FL [*Location identifier*] [*FAA*] (FAAL)
**MKYFC**..... Mike and Kathy Yager Fan Club [*Later, MYFC*] (EA)
**MKZ**.......... Los Angeles, CA [*Location identifier*] [*FAA*] (FAAL)
**MKZ**.......... Malacca [*Malaysia*] [*Airport symbol*] (OAG)
**ML**............. Avioligure [*Italy*] [*ICAO designator*] (FAAC)
**ML**............. Land Mobile Station [*ITU designation*] (NATG)
**ML**............. Licentiate in Medicine
**ML**............. Licentiate in Midwifery
**ML**............. Machine Language [*Data processing*]
**ML**............. Madras Lancers [*British military*] (DMA)
**ML**............. Magic Lantern Society of the United States and Canada (EA)
**ML**............. Magnetogasdynamics Laboratory [*MIT*] (MCD)
**ML**............. Mail
**ML**............. Main Line [*Business term*]
**ML**............. Main Lobe (IEEE)
**ML**............. Mainland (MUGU)
**ML**............. Maintenance Laboratory (MUGU)
**M/L**.......... Maintenance Loop (MCD)
**ML**............. Major League [*Baseball*]
**ML**............. Major Lobe (MSA)
**ML**............. Malachi [*Old Testament book*]
**ML**............. Mali [*ANSI two-letter standard code*] (CNC)
**ml**.............. Mali [*MARC country of publication code*] [*Library of Congress*] (LCCP)
**ML**............. Malignant Lymphoma [*Oncology*]
**ML**............. Management Level
**ML**............. Management List
**M and L**..... Management and Logistics [*NATO*] (NATG)
**ML**............. Mandibular Line [*Jaw anatomy*]
**ML**............. Mantle Length
**ML**............. Mantle Lip
**ML**............. Manual Loader (AAG)
**ML**............. Manufacturing License (NRCH)
**ML**............. Maple Leaf Gardens Ltd. [*Toronto Stock Exchange symbol*]
**ML**............. March for Life (EA)
**ML**............. Mark-Up Language [*Data processing*]
**Ml**............. Marl [*Quality of the bottom*] [*Nautical charts*]
**M-L**.......... Martin-Lewis [*Medium*] [*Microbiology*]
**ML**............. Martin Marietta Corp. [*NYSE symbol*] (SPSG)
**M/L**.......... Mass to Luminosity [*Ratio*] [*Astronomy*]
**ML**............. Master of Laws
**ML**............. Master of Letters
**ML**............. Master of Literature
**M & L**........ Matched and Lost [*Business term*]
**ML**............. Mater Lectionis (BJA)
**ML**............. Material List (MSA)
**ML**............. Maule Aircraft Corp. [*ICAO aircraft manufacturer identifier*] (ICAO)
**ML**............. Maurer Lehrling [*Entered Apprentice*] [*German*] [*Freemasonry*]
**ML**............. Maximum Likelihood [*Statistics*]
**ML**............. Mean Level
**ML**............. Medial Lemniscus [*Neuroanatomy*]
**ML**............. Medical Letter (EA)
**ML**............. Medieval Latin [*Language, etc.*]
**ML**............. Medium Lorry [*British*]
**ML**............. Megaliter
**ML**............. Mein Lieber [*My Dear*] [*German*]
**ML**............. Memory Location [*Data processing*]
**ML**............. Mennonite Life [*A publication*]
**ML**............. Mere Loge [*Mother Lodge*] [*French*] [*Freemasonry*]
**ML**............. Mesiolingual [*Dentistry*]
**ML**............. Metabolic Loss [*Physiology*]
**M-L**.......... Metallic-Longitudinal (IEEE)
**ML**............. Meteorological Devices [*JETDS nomenclature*] [*Military*] (CET)
**ML**............. Methods of Limits (IEEE)
**ML**............. Mexican League [*Baseball*]
**ML**............. Microprogramming Language
**ML**............. Microwave Laboratory [*Stanford University*] (MCD)
**ML**............. Middeck Left (MCD)

**ML**.......... Middle Latin [*Language, etc.*]
**ML**.......... Middle Lobe [*Of lung*]
**ML**.......... Midline
**ML**.......... Migne Series [*Latina*] [*A publication*] (BJA)
**ML**.......... Military Law
**ML**.......... Military Liaison
**ML**.......... Military Payroll Money List
**ML**.......... Mill
**mL**.......... Millilambert
**mL**.......... Milliliter
**ML**.......... Minelayer [*or Minelaying*]
**ML**.......... Mineral Lease (ADA)
**ML**.......... Minerva Library [*A publication*]
**ML**.......... Minilab
**ML**.......... Mining and Logging [*Tires*]
**ML**.......... Missile Launcher
**ML**.......... Missile Layout
**M/L**.......... Missile-Lift [*Aerospace*] (AAG)
**ML**.......... Missile Liner
**ML**.......... Mission Life [*Aerospace*]
**ML**.......... Mission Load (AABC)
**ML**.......... Mixed Lengths
**Ml**.......... Mladost [*A publication*]
**ML**.......... Mobile Launcher [*NASA*] (KSC)
**ML**.......... Mobile Low-Power [*Reactor*] (NRCH)
**ML**.......... Moderately Long [*Botany*]
**ML**.......... Modern Languages [*A publication*]
**ML**.......... Modern Liturgy [*A publication*]
**ML**.......... Mold Line [*Technical drawings*]
**ML**.......... Molder [*Navy rating*]
**ML**.......... Molecular Layer [*of the hippocampus*] [*Neurology*]
**ML**.......... Monarchist League [*Defunct*] (EA)
**ML**.......... Moneda Legal [*Legal Tender*] [*Spanish*] [*Business term*]
**ML**.......... Money List
**M/L**.......... Monocyte-Lymphocyte [*Ratio*] [*Clinical chemistry*]
**ML**.......... Monolayer [*Physical chemistry*]
**ML**.......... Monolithic
**ML**.......... Monthly Letter EMG [*A publication*]
**ML**.......... Morocco Lined [*Covers*] [*Bookbinding*] (ROG)
**ML**.......... Motor Launch
**ML**.......... Mountain Leader [*British military*] (DMA)
**ML**.......... Mouse Laminin
**ML**.......... Mouse Lysozyme [*Biochemistry*]
**ML**.......... Mucolipidosis [*Medicine*]
**ML**.......... Mucrones Length [*Of Crustacea*]
**ML**.......... Multilayer [*Pharmacy*]
**ML**.......... Multiple-Line [*Insurance*]
**ML**.......... Multiple Location [*Insurance*]
**ML**.......... Multiple-Locus [*Light flashes*]
**ML**.......... Munitions List
**ML**.......... Music and Letters [*A publication*]
**M & L**.......... Music and Letters [*A publication*]
**ML**.......... Music Library Records [*Record label*]
**ML**.......... Muslim League [*Political party*] [*Bangladesh*] (FEA)
**ML**.......... Mutual Inductance [*Symbol*] (DEN)
**ML**.......... Muzzle-Loading
**ML**.......... Myelogenous Leukemia [*Oncology*]
**ML**.......... Myrialiter [*Unit of measurement*] (ROG)
**ML**.......... Small Minesweeper [*Navy symbol*]
**ML**.......... Statute Miles (FAAC)
**ML1**.......... Molder, First Class [*Navy rating*]
**ML2**.......... Molder, Second Class [*Navy rating*]
**ML3**.......... Molder, Third Class [*Navy rating*]
**MLA**.......... Auxiliary Motor Launches (NATG)
**MLA**.......... Forty-Mile Air [*Tok, AK*] [*FAA designator*] (FAAC)
**MLA**.......... Magnetic Lens Assembly
**MLA**.......... Maine Lobstermen's Association (EA)
**mla**.......... Malagasy [*MARC language code*] [*Library of Congress*] (LCCP)
**MLA**.......... Malaspina [*Alaska*] [*Seismograph station code, US Geological Survey*] (SEIS)
**MLA**.......... Malta [*Airport symbol*] (OAG)
**MLA**.......... Maneuver Load Alleviation [*Aviation*]
**MLA**.......... Manpack Loop Antenna
**M & LA**.......... Manpower and Logistics Analysis
**MLA**.......... Marine Librarians Association (EA)
**MLA**.......... Maritime Law Association of the US (EA)
**MLA**.......... Marlat Resources Ltd. [*Vancouver Stock Exchange symbol*]
**MLA**.......... Master of Landscape Architecture
**MLA**.......... Matching Logic and Adder
**MLA**.......... MDM [*Manipulator Deployment Mechanism*] Launch Aft [*NASA*]
**MLA**.......... Mean Line of Advance [*Military*] (NVT)
**MLA**.......... Mechanical Lubricator Association
**MLA**.......... Medial Left Abdomen [*Injection site*]
**MLA**.......... Medical Library Association (EA)
**MLA**.......... Member of the Legislative Assembly
**MLA**.......... Member of the Library Association [*British*] (ROG)
**MLA**.......... Mento-Laeval Anterior [*A fetal position*] [*Obstetrics*]
**MLA**.......... Merritt Island Tracking Station [*Florida*]
**MLA**.......... Mesiolabial [*Dentistry*]
**MLA**.......... Metal Lath Association [*Later, ML/SFA*] (EA)
**MLA**.......... Metrolina Library Association [*Library network*]
**MLA**.......... Microprocessor Language Assembler [*Data processing*]
**MLA**.......... Microwave Linear Accelerator
**MLA**.......... Midland Co. [*AMEX symbol*] (SPSG)
**MLA**.......... Minimal Lactose-Arabinose [*Culture medium*]
**MLA**.......... Mistress of Liberal Arts
**MLA**.......... Mixed Lead Alkyl [*Organic chemistry*]
**MLA**.......... MLA [*Modern Language Association of America*] International Bibliography of Books and Articles on the Modern Languages and Literature [*Database*] [*A publication*]
**MLA**.......... Modern Language Abstracts [*A publication*]
**MLA**.......... Modern Language Association of America (EA)
**MLA**.......... Monochrome Lens Assembly (MCD)
**MLA**.......... Motor Launch, Auxiliary [*NATO*]
**MLA**.......... Multi-Housing Laundry Association (EA)
**MLA**.......... Multilinear Array [*In earth scanning*]
**MLA**.......... MultiLink Advanced [*Local area network*] [*The Software Link, Inc.*]
**MLA**.......... Multiplex Line Adapter
**MLA**.......... Music Library Association (EA)
**MLA**.......... Muzzle Loaders' Association of Great Britain
**MLAA**.......... Master Locksmiths Association of Australasia Ltd.
**MLAA**.......... Medical Library Assistance Act [*1965*]
**MLAANZ Newsletter**... Maritime Law Association of Australia and New Zealand. Newsletter [*A publication*] (APTA)
**MLAB**.......... Modeling Laboratory [*Programming language*] [*1970*] (CSR)
**MLAB**.......... Monitor Technologies, Inc. [*Formerly, Monitor Laboratories*] [*NASDAQ symbol*] (NQ)
**M Labor R**... Monthly Labor Review [*A publication*]
**M Lab R**.......... Monthly Labor Review [*A publication*]
**Mlad Misl**... Mladezka Misl [*A publication*]
**MLAF**.......... Missile Loading Alignment Fixture
**MLAI**.......... Mesiolabioincisal [*Dentistry*]
**MLA Int Bibl**... Modern Language Association of America. International Bibliography [*A publication*]
**Ml Airbase**... Military Airbase [*A publication*]
**Ml Airport**... Military Airports [*A publication*]
**M La L**.......... Master of Latin Letters
**MLAMH**.......... Mona Lisas and Mad Hatters (EA)
**MLAN**.......... Midland Resources [*NASDAQ symbol*] (NQ)
**MLAN**.......... Music Library Association. Notes [*A publication*]
**MLANA**.......... Melkite Laymen's Association of North America (EA)
**MLanc**.......... Lancaster Town Library, Lancaster, MA [*Library symbol*] [*Library of Congress*] (LCLS)
**M Lang**.......... Modern Languages [*A publication*]
**MLAP**.......... Mean Left Atrial Pressure [*Cardiology*]
**MLaP**.......... Mesiolabiopulpal [*Dentistry*]
**MLAP**.......... Migrant Legal Action Program (EA)
**MLAP**.......... Muslim League Assembly Party [*Political party*] [*Pakistan*] (FEA)
**MLAPU**.......... Marxist-Leninist Armed Propaganda Unit [*Turkey*]
**MLA Q**.......... Missouri Library Association. Quarterly [*A publication*]
**MLAR**.......... Mill Arbor
**ML Arch**.......... Master of Landscape Architecture
**MLASES**.......... Molasses [*Freight*]
**MLA-SMHL**... Medical Library Association, Section on Mental Health Libraries (EA)
**MLAT**.......... Mean Latitude
**MLAT**.......... Modern Language Aptitude Test [*Military*] (AFM)
**MlatJb**.......... Mittellateinisches Jahrbuch [*A publication*]
**MLAUK**.......... Member of the Library Association, United Kingdom (ROG)
**M'Laur**.......... M'Laurin's Scotch Judiciary Cases [*1774*] [*A publication*] (DLA)
**M Lauriacum**... Mitteilungen des Museumsvereins "Lauriacum" [*Enns*] [*A publication*]
**MLaw**.......... Lawrence Free Public Library, Lawrence, MA [*Library symbol*] [*Library of Congress*] (LCLS)
**MLB**.......... Major League Baseball
**MLB**.......... Malabar [*Java*] [*Seismograph station code, US Geological Survey*] [*Closed*] (SEIS)
**MLB**.......... Manufacturing Load Boards (MCD)
**MLB**.......... Maritime Labor Board [*Terminated, 1942*]
**MLB**.......... Maritime Law Book Key Number Data Base [*Maritime Law Book Company Ltd.*] [*Canada*] [*Information service or system*] (CRD)
**MLB**.......... Medallion Books Ltd. [*Vancouver Stock Exchange symbol*]
**MLB**.......... Melbourne [*Florida*] [*Airport symbol*] (OAG)
**MLB**.......... Metallic Link Belt (AABC)
**MLB**.......... Metropolitan Toronto Library Board, Systems Unit [*UTLAS symbol*]
**MLB**.......... Middle Linebacker [*Football*]
**MLB**.......... Mobile Logistics Support Base (NVT)
**MLB**.......... Monaural Loudness Balance [*Audiology*]
**MLB**.......... Motor Lifeboat
**MLB**.......... Multilayer Board
**MLB**.......... Suesswarenmarkt. Fachzeitschrift fuer Markt, Marketing, und Merchandising von Suesswaren [*A publication*]
**Ml Balance**... Military Balance [*A publication*]
**MLBM**.......... Modern Large Ballistic Missile
**MLBPA**.......... Mailing List Brokers Professional Association [*Defunct*] (EA)

**MLBPA**..... Major League Baseball Players Association (EA)
**MLBR**........ Medium Low-BIT [*Binary Digit*] Rate [*Data processing*]
**MLBU**....... Mobile Laundry and Bath Unit [*Military*] [*British*]
**MLC**.......... Machine Level Control [*Data processing*]
**MLC**.......... Madras Light Cavalry [*British military*] (DMA)
**MLC**.......... Magnetic Ledger Card (CMD)
**MLC**.......... Main Lobe Clutter
**MLC**.......... Major Landing Craft
**MLC**.......... Major Legislation of Congress [*Data processing system*] [*Congressional Research Service*]
**MLC**.......... Major Line Component [*of NOAA*] (NOAA)
**MLC**.......... Management Level Chart [*Military*] (AFIT)
**MLC**.......... Management Level Code [*Military*] (AFIT)
**ML-C**......... Management List - Consolidated
**MLC**.......... Maneuver Load Control [*Aviation*]
**MLC**.......... Manhattan National Corporation [*NYSE symbol*] (SPSG)
**MLC**.......... Manufacturers Life Capital Corp., Inc. [*Toronto Stock Exchange symbol*]
**MLC**.......... Manzanita Lake [*California*] [*Seismograph station code, US Geological Survey*] (SEIS)
**MLC**.......... Maple Leaf Club (EA)
**MLC**.......... Master Labor Contract (AABC)
**MLC**.......... McAlester [*Oklahoma*] [*Airport symbol*] (OAG)
**MLC**.......... McAlester, OK [*Location identifier*] [*FAA*] (FAAL)
**MLC**.......... Meat and Livestock Commission [*British*] (ARC)
**MLC**.......... Medical Liability Commission [*Defunct*] (EA)
**MLC**.......... Medical Library Center (DIT)
**MLC**.......... Member of the Legislative Council
**MLC**.......... Memphis Library Council [*Library network*]
**MLC**.......... Mesh Level Control
**MLC**.......... Metropolitan Toronto Library Board, Cataloguing Department [*UTLAS symbol*]
**MLC**.......... Micellar Liquid Chromatography
**MLC**.......... Michigan Library Consortium [*Lansing, MI*] [*Library network*]
**MLC**.......... Microelectric Logic Circuit
**MLC**.......... Microprogram Location Counter
**MLC**.......... Midlife Conversion
**MLC**.......... Miles College, Birmingham, AL [*OCLC symbol*] (OCLC)
**MLC**.......... Military Landing Craft
**MLC**.......... Military Liaison Committee [*Energy Research and Development Administration*]
**MLC**.......... Military Load Class (RDA)
**MLC**.......... Minimum Lethal Concentration
**MLC**.......... Mississippi State Library Commission [*Information service or system*] (IID)
**MLC**.......... Mixed Leukocyte Culture [*Hematology*]
**MLC**.......... Mixed Lymphocyte Culture [*Hematology*]
**MLC**.......... Mobile Launch Center
**MLC**.......... Mobile Launcher Computer [*NASA*] (NASA)
**MLC**.......... Modern Language Caucus [*of New University Conference*]
**MLC**.......... MOL [*Manned Orbiting Laboratory*] Launch Complex (MCD)
**MLC**.......... Molder, Chief [*Navy rating*]
**MLC**.......... Monarchist League of Canada (EAIO)
**MLC**.......... Morphine-Like Compound [*Immunology*]
**MLC**.......... Motor Launch, Cabin
**MLC**.......... Motor Load Control
**MLC**.......... Multilayer Ceramic [*Materials technology*]
**MLC**.......... Multilayer Circuit
**MLC**.......... Multilens Camera
**MLC**.......... Multiline Control (BUR)
**MLC**.......... Multiplanar Link Chain
**MLC**.......... Municipal Leasing Corporation
**MLC**.......... Myosin Light Chain [*Muscle biology*]
**MLC**.......... Myth, Legend, Custom in the Old Testament [*A publication*] (BJA)
**MLCAEC**.. Military Liaison Committee to the Atomic Energy Commission (IEEE)
**MLCB**........ Missile Launch Control Blockhouse
**MLCB**........ Moored Limited Capability Buoy [*Marine science*] (MSC)
**MLCB**........ Multilayer Circuit Board
**ML/CB-CC**... Malignant Lymphoma/Centroblastic-Centrocytic [*Oncology*]
**ML/CC**...... Malignant Lymphoma/Centrocytic [*Oncology*]
**MLCC**........ Mined Land Conservation Conference [*Later, BCR*]
**MLCC**........ Multilayer Ceramic Capacitor [*Electronics*]
**MLCG**....... Missile Launcher Control Group
**MLCH**....... Major Logistical Control Headquarters (MCD)
**MLCIM**..... Marquette League for Catholic Indian Missions (EA)
**MLCK**....... Myosin Light Chain Kinase [*An enzyme*]
**MLCM**...... Molder, Master Chief [*Navy rating*]
**MLCNY**.... Medical Library Center of New York [*Information service or system*] (IID)
**MLCOM**... Member of the London College of Osteopathic Medicine [*British*] (DBQ)
**MLCP**........ Mobile Land Command Post (AABC)
**MLCP**........ Multiline Communications Processor
**MLCR**........ Medical Laboratory Contract Reports [*Army*] (MCD)
**MLCS**........ Molder, Senior Chief [*Navy rating*]
**MLCT**........ Metal-to-Ligand Charge Transfer [*Physical chemistry*]
**MLCU**....... Mill Cutter [*Tool*]
**MLD**.......... Legislative Reference Library - Minnesota Document Collection, St. Paul, MN [*OCLC symbol*] (OCLC)
**MLD**.......... Maandstatistiek van de Landbouw [*A publication*]
**MLD**.......... Machine Language Debugger [*National Computer Sharing Service*]
**MLD**.......... Main Line of Defense
**MLD**.......... Malad City, ID [*Location identifier*] [*FAA*] (FAAL)
**MLD**.......... Malden [*Missouri*] [*Seismograph station code, US Geological Survey*] [*Closed*] (SEIS)
**MLD**.......... Marginally Learning Disabled
**MLD**.......... Masking Level Difference [*Hearing*]
**MLD**.......... Master of Landscape Design
**MLD**.......... Master Layout Duplicate (MSA)
**MLD**.......... Maximum Likelihood Detection (MCD)
**MLD**.......... Mean Low-Water Datum [*Nuclear energy*] (NRCH)
**MLD**.......... Median Lethal Dose [*Also, $LD_{50}$ Lethal for 50%*] [*Medicine*]
**MLD**.......... Metachromatic Leukodystrophy [*Medicine*]
**MLD**.......... Middle Landing
**MLD**.......... Midland [*AAR code*]
**MLD**.......... Minimal Lesion Disease
**MLD**.......... Minimum Lethal Dose
**MLD**.......... Minimum Line of Detection [*Air Force*]
**MLD**.......... Missile Launch Detector (MCD)
**MLD**.......... Mitteilungen des Medizinischen Literatur-Dienstes [*A publication*]
**MLD**.......... Mixed Layer Depth (MCD)
**MLD**.......... Molded (KSC)
**MLD**.......... Molding [*Technical drawings*]
**MLD**.......... Mouvement pour la Liberation de Djibouti [*Movement for the Liberation of Djibouti*] (PD)
**MLDAS**..... Meteorological and Lighting Data Acquisition System [*NASA*] (KSC)
**MLDB**....... Regional Library, Lac Du Bonnet, Manitoba [*Library symbol*] [*National Library of Canada*] (NLC)
**MLDC**....... Miner's Legal Defense Committee (EA)
**ML Des**...... Master of Landscape Design
**MLDG**....... Molding (KSC)
**ML Dig & R**... Monthly Law Digest and Reporter [*Canada*] [*A publication*] (DLA)
**MLDL**....... Mooring Line Data Line [*Environmental buoy cable*]
**MLDMA**... Melody Maker [*A publication*]
**MLDR**....... Molder (ADA)
**MLDS**........ Motor Launch, Double Shelter
**MLDT**....... Mean Logistic Delay Time [*Military*] (CAAL)
**MLDT**....... Mean Logistic Down Time
**MLDU**....... Marriage Law Defence Union [*British*]
**MLE**.......... Magazine Lee-Enfield [*British military*] (DMA)
**MLE**.......... Male [*Maldives*] [*Airport symbol*] (OAG)
**MLE**.......... Manned Lunar Exploration [*NASA*] (AAG)
**MLE**.......... Martin Lawrence Limited Editions [*NYSE symbol*] (SPSG)
**MLE**.......... Maryland Law Encyclopedia [*A publication*] (DLA)
**MLE**.......... Master of Land Economy
**MLE**.......... Maximum Likelihood Estimate [*or Estimator*] [*Statistics*]
**MLE**.......... Maximum Loss Expectancy [*Insurance*]
**MLE**.......... Medium Local Exchange [*Telecommunications*] (TEL)
**MLE**.......... Microprocessor Language Editor [*Data processing*]
**MLE**.......... Mile
**MLE**.......... Mileto [*Italy*] [*Seismograph station code, US Geological Survey*] [*Closed*] (SEIS)
**MLE**.......... Missile Launch Envelope
**MLE**.......... Module Resources, Inc. [*Vancouver Stock Exchange symbol*]
**MLE**.......... Molecular Layer Epitaxy [*Coating technology*]
**MLE**.......... Muconate Lactonizing Enzyme
**MLE**.......... Myocardial Lactate Extraction [*Clinical chemistry*]
**MLE**.......... Omaha, NE [*Location identifier*] [*FAA*] (FAAL)
**MLEA**........ Multiple-Line Exclusive Agent [*Insurance*]
**M'Lean's R**... McLean's United States Circuit Court Reports [*A publication*] (DLA)
**MLEGB**..... Metallurgical Engineer. Indian Institute of Technology (Bombay) [*A publication*]
**MLenB**....... Berkshire Christian College, Lenox, MA [*Library symbol*] [*Library of Congress*] (LCLS)
**ML Eng**...... Master of Landscape Engineering
**Ml Eng**....... Military Engineer [*A publication*]
**MLeo**......... Leominster Public Library, Leominster, MA [*Library symbol*] [*Library of Congress*] (LCLS)
**MLEP**........ Manned Lunar Exploration Program [*NASA*] (KSC)
**MLEP**........ Minority Legislative Education Program
**MLEP**........ Multipurpose Long Endurance Plane
**MLES**........ Multiple-Line Encryption System (AABC)
**MLetters**.... Music and Letters [*A publication*]
**MLEV**........ Manned Lifting Entry Vehicle (MCD)
**MLex**......... Cary Memorial Library, Lexington, MA [*Library symbol*] [*Library of Congress*] (LCLS)
**MLexHi**..... Lexington Historical Society, Lexington, MA [*Library symbol*] [*Library of Congress*] (LCLS)
**MLexK**...... Kennecott Copper Corp., Ledgemont Laboratory, Lexington, MA [*Library symbol*] [*Library of Congress*] (LCLS)
**MLexM**..... Museum of Our National Heritage, Lexington, MA [*Library symbol*] [*Library of Congress*] (LCLS)
**MLexSC**.... Scottish Rite of Freemasonry, Northern Jurisdiction USA, Supreme Council Library, Lexington, MA [*Library symbol*] [*Library of Congress*] (LCLS)

**MLF**.......... Fast Motor Launches (NATG)
**MLF**.......... Luthi Aviation, Inc. [*Fargo, ND*] [*FAA designator*] (FAAC)
**MLF**.......... Maintenance Level Function
**MLF**.......... Male Liberation Foundation (EA)
**MLF**.......... Maximum Load Factor
**MLF**.......... MDM [*Manipulator Deployment Mechanism*] Launch Forward [*NASA*]
**MLF**.......... Media Language and Format (CET)
**MLF**.......... Medial Longitudinal Fasciculus [*Medicine*]
**MLF**.......... Medical Liberation Front (EA)
**M/LF**......... Medium/Low Frequency (NATG)
**MLF**.......... Microlog Fiche Service from Micromedia [*A publication*]
**MLF**.......... Milford [*Ohio*] [*Seismograph station code, US Geological Survey*] (SEIS)
**MLF**.......... Milford, UT [*Location identifier*] [*FAA*] (FAAL)
**MLF**.......... Mobile Land Force (NATG)
**MLF**.......... Mobile Launcher Facility [*NASA*] (KSC)
**MLF**.......... Modern Language Forum [*A publication*]
**MLF**.......... Modersmalslararnas Forening. Arsskrift [*A publication*]
**MLF**.......... MOL [*Manned Orbiting Laboratory*] Launch Facilities (MCD)
**MLF**.......... Motor Launch, Fast [*NATO*]
**MLF**.......... Multilateral Force [*NATO*] (MCD)
**MLFA**........ Fireman Apprentice, Molder, Striker [*Navy rating*]
**MLFA**........ Maine Lobster Fishermen's Association (EA)
**MLFA**........ Modersmalslararnas Forening. Arsskrift [*A publication*]
**MLFAT**..... MOL [*Manned Orbiting Laboratory*] Launch Facilities Acceptance Team (MCD)
**MLFC**........ Michele Lee Fan Club (EA)
**MLFC**........ Michigan Library Film Circuit [*Library network*]
**MLFC**........ Mike Lunsford Fan Club (EA)
**MLFN**........ Fireman, Molder, Striker [*Navy rating*]
**MLFX**........ Mill Fixture [*Tool*]
**MLG**.......... Mailing
**MLG**.......... Main Landing Gear
**MLG**.......... Malang [*Indonesia*] [*Airport symbol*] (OAG)
**MLG**.......... Metalgesellschaft Canada Investment [*Toronto Stock Exchange symbol*]
**MLG**.......... Middle Low German [*Language, etc.*]
**MLG**.......... Milling [*Freight*]
**MLG**.......... Mission Liaison Group [*Military*]
**MLG**.......... Mitteilungen aus der Livlandischen Geschichte [*A publication*]
**MLG**.......... Multiple Line Group [*Radiation*]
**MLGCV**..... Movement for the Liberation of Portuguese Guinea and the Cape Verde Islands
**MLGM**...... Mother Lode Gold Mines Consolidated [*NASDAQ symbol*] (NQ)
**MLGP**........ Movimento de Libertacao da Guine Portuguesa [*Movement for the Liberation of Portuguese Guinea*]
**MLGS**........ Microwave Landing Guidance System [*FAA*]
**MLGW**...... Maximum Landing Gross Weight
**MLH**.......... Mauna Loa [*Hawaii*] [*Seismograph station code, US Geological Survey*] (SEIS)
**MLH**.......... Medium Lift Helicopter (MCD)
**MLH**.......... Merlin Resources Ltd. [*Vancouver Stock Exchange symbol*]
**MLH**.......... Mulhouse/Basel [*France*] [*Airport symbol*] (OAG)
**MLHGR**.... Maximum Linear Heat Generation Ratio (NRCH)
**MLHR**....... Miller [*Herman*], Inc. [*NASDAQ symbol*] (NQ)
**MLHW**...... Mean Lower High Water [*Tides and currents*]
**MLI**........... Machine Language Instruction
**MLI**........... Magnetic Level Indicator
**MLI**........... Maislin Industries Ltd. [*Toronto Stock Exchange symbol*]
**MLI**........... Malad Range [*Idaho*] [*Seismograph station code, US Geological Survey*] (SEIS)
**MLI**........... Mali [*ANSI three-letter standard code*] (CNC)
**MLI**........... Maltese Light Infantry [*British military*] (DMA)
**MLI**........... Marine Light Infantry [*Navy*] [*British*] (ROG)
**MLI**........... Marker Light Indicator
**MLI**........... Master Listing Index
**MLI**........... Master of Literary Interpretation
**MLI**........... Mean Linear Intercept
**MLI**........... Mesiolinguoincisal [*Dentistry*]
**MLI**........... Metropolitan Life Insurance Company. Statistical Bulletin [*A publication*]
**MLI**........... Minimum Line of Interception [*Air Force*]
**MLI**........... Mixed Lymphocyte Interaction [*Immunology*]
**MLI**........... Moline [*Illinois*] [*Airport symbol*] (OAG)
**MLI**........... Moline, IL [*Location identifier*] [*FAA*] (FAAL)
**MLI**........... Mollie Gibson Mines [*Vancouver Stock Exchange symbol*]
**MLI**........... Multilayer Insulation
**MLI**........... Multiple Link Interface [*Data processing*]
**MLI**........... Munitions List Item (MCD)
**MLIA**......... Multiplex Loop Interface Adapter
**MLib**.......... Master of Librarianship
**MLIFC**....... Mark Lindsay International Fan Club [*Defunct*] (EA)
**MLIFC**....... Michelle Lynn International Fan Club (EA)
**MLIHB**...... Mitteilungen des Landwirtschaftlichen Instituts der Hochschule fuer Bodenkultur [*A publication*]
**MLIM**........ Matrix Log-In Memory
**MLing**........ Master of Languages [*British*] (DBQ)
**M Ling**....... Modeles Linguistiques [*A publication*]
**Ml Intel**...... Military Intelligence [*A publication*]
**MLIRB**...... Multi-Line Insurance Rating Bureau [*Later, ISO*]
**MLIS**......... Master of Library and Information Science
**MLIS**......... Measurement Laboratory Information Service [*Battelle Memorial Institute*]
**MLIS**......... Micropolis Corp. [*NASDAQ symbol*] (NQ)
**MLIS**......... Molecular LASER Isotope Separation
**MLIS**......... Multiple Level Indexing Scheme [*Data processing*]
**MLISB**...... Medical Instrumentation [*Arlington, VA*] [*A publication*]
**MLISP**....... Meta LISP [*List Processor*] [*Programming language*] [*Data processing*] (CSR)
**M Lit**.......... Master of Letters
**M Lit**.......... Master of Literature
**MLit**........... Miesiecznik Literacki [*A publication*]
**MLitI**......... Inforonics Inc., Littleton, MA [*Library symbol*] [*Library of Congress*] (LCLS)
**MLitSt**....... Master of Literary Studies (ADA)
**M Litt**......... Master of Letters
**MLitt**.......... Master of Literature
**ML IV**......... Mucolipidosis IV [*A genetic disease*]
**MLJ**........... Madras Law Journal [*A publication*]
**MLJ**........... Makerere Law Journal [*A publication*]
**MLJ**........... Malayan Law Journal [*A publication*]
**MLJ**........... Manitoba Law Journal [*A publication*]
**MLJ**........... Memphis Law Journal [*A publication*] (DLA)
**MLJ**........... Milledgeville, GA [*Location identifier*] [*FAA*] (FAAL)
**MLJ**........... Mississippi Law Journal [*A publication*]
**MLJ**........... Modern Language Journal [*A publication*]
**MLJ Supp**... Malayan Law Journal. Supplement [*A publication*]
**MLK**.......... Malta, MT [*Location identifier*] [*FAA*] (FAAL)
**MLK**.......... Matlack Systems [*AMEX symbol*] (CTT)
**MLK**.......... Milford [*Kansas*] [*Seismograph station code, US Geological Survey*] (SEIS)
**MLKCNSC**... Martin Luther King, Jr., Center for Nonviolent Social Change (EA)
**MLKCSC**.. Martin Luther King, Jr., Center for Social Change [*Later, MLKCNSC*] (EA)
**MLKIII**...... Martin Luther King III
**MLL**.......... Macmillan, Inc. [*Formerly, CRW*] [*NYSE symbol*] (SPSG)
**MLL**.......... Mandella Resources Ltd. [*Vancouver Stock Exchange symbol*]
**MLL**.......... Manned Lunar Landing [*NASA*]
**MLL**.......... Marshall [*Alaska*] [*Airport symbol*] (OAG)
**MLL**.......... Marshall, AK [*Location identifier*] [*FAA*] (FAAL)
**MLL**.......... Master of Latin Literature
**MLL**.......... Master of Law Librarianship (ILCA)
**MLL**.......... Master Lines Layout (MSA)
**MLL**.......... Maynard Listener Library (EA)
**MLL**.......... MDM [*Manipulator Deployment Mechanism*] Launch Left [*NASA*]
**MLL**.......... Mean Lesion Length [*Pathology*]
**MLL**.......... Mistress of Liberal Learning
**MLL**.......... University of Minnesota, Law Library, Minneapolis, MN [*OCLC symbol*] (OCLC)
**ML/LB**...... Malignant Lymphoma/Lymphoblastic [*Oncology*]
**MLLCC**..... Millcrest Products [*NASDAQ symbol*] (NQ)
**MLLE**........ Mademoiselle [*Miss*] [*French*] (EY)
**Mlle**........... Mademoiselle [*A publication*]
**MLLE**........ Medium Large Local Exchange [*Telecommunications*] (TEL)
**ML Libr**..... Master of Law Librarianship
**MLLP**........ Manned Lunar Landing Program [*NASA*]
**ML/LPC**.... Malignant Lymphoma/Lymphoplasmacytoid [*Oncology*]
**MLLW**....... Mean Lower Low Water [*Tides and currents*]
**MLLWS**.... Mean Lower Low-Water Springs [*Tides and currents*]
**MLM**......... Magazine Lee-Metford [*British military*] (DMA)
**MLM**......... Mailing-List Manager [*Type of database*]
**MLM**......... Massive Liver Metastasis [*Oncology*]
**MLM**......... Master of Landscape Management
**MLM**......... Maximum Likelihood Method [*Statistics*]
**MLM**......... Mesa Lucera [*New Mexico*] [*Seismograph station code, US Geological Survey*] (SEIS)
**MLM**......... Metall Mining Corp. [*Toronto Stock Exchange symbol*]
**MLM**......... Microbial Load Monitor (MCD)
**MLM**......... Military Liaison Mission [*German Democratic Republic*]
**MLM**......... Mixed Level Matrix
**MLM**......... Moody Literature Ministries (EA)
**MLM**......... Morelia [*Mexico*] [*Airport symbol*] (OAG)
**MLM**......... Mound Laboratory, Miamisburg [*AEC*] (MCD)
**MLM**......... Multilayer Metalization (IEEE)
**MLM**......... Multilevel Marketing
**MLM**......... Multipurpose Lightweight Missile
**MLM**......... Multnomah Literature Ministries [*Publisher*] [*Portland, OR*]
**MLMA**...... Metal Ladder Manufacturers Association (EA)
**MLMA**...... Metal Lath Manufacturers Association [*Later, ML/SFA*]
**MLMA**...... Multilevel Multiaccess
**MLMC**...... Multi-Local Media Corp. [*NASDAQ symbol*] (NQ)
**MLMIA**..... Multi-Level Marketing International Association [*Irvine, CA*] (EA)
**MLML**....... Moss Landing Marine Laboratories [*San Jose State University*] [*Research center*] (RCD)
**MLMN**...... Mal-i-Mic News. Metis and Non-Statute Indians in New Brunswick [*Canada*] [*A publication*]
**MLMS**....... Member of the London Mathematical Society

**MLMS** ....... Multipurpose Lightweight Missile System
**MLMTT** .... Marxism-Leninism-Mao Tse-Tung Thought [*Ideologies guiding the New People's Army, a guerrilla movement in the Philippines*]
**MLN** .......... Management List - Navy (NVT)
**MLN** .......... Melilla [*Spain*] [*Airport symbol*] (OAG)
**MLN** .......... Metropolitan Library Network [*Library network*]
**MLN** .......... Mid-Lateral Nerve
**MLN** .......... Milan Resources & Development [*Vancouver Stock Exchange symbol*]
**MLN** .......... Minuteman Library Network [*Information service or system*] (IT)
**MLN** .......... Modern Language Notes [*A publication*]
**MLN** .......... Mouvement de Liberation Nationale [*National Liberation Movement*] [*Upper Volta*] [*Banned, 1974*] [*Political party*]
**MLN** .......... Movimiento de Liberacion Nacional [*National Liberation Movement*] [*Guatemala*] [*Political party*] (PPW)
**MLN** .......... Movimiento de Liberacion Nacional [*National Liberation Movement*] [*Uruguay*] [*Political party*]
**MLN** .......... Multiple Length Number
**MLN** .......... Mulungwishi [*Zaire*] [*Seismograph station code, US Geological Survey*] (SEIS)
**MLN Bull** .. MLN [*Minnesota League for Nursing*] Bulletin [*A publication*]
**MLNC** ....... Missouri Library Network Corporation [*Information service or system*] (IID)
**MLND** ....... Miller Industries, Inc. [*NASDAQ symbol*] (NQ)
**M L New** .... Malcolm Lowry Newsletter [*A publication*]
**MLNIS** ...... Modified Atlantic Naval Intelligence Summary (MCD)
**mLNRc** ...... Mouse Lymph Node Homing Receptor
**MLNS** ........ Ministry of Labour and National Service [*British*] [*World War II*]
**MLNS** ........ Mucocutaneous Lymph Node Syndrome [*Medicine*]
**MLNSBP** .. Mammalian Species [*A publication*]
**MLO** .......... M. L. Cass Petroleum [*Vancouver Stock Exchange symbol*]
**MLO** .......... Main Lube Oil [*System*] (NRCH)
**MLO** .......... Manipulative Learning Operation [*in laboratory work*]
**MLO** .......... Manned Lunar Orbiter [*NASA*]
**MLO** .......... Marxisten-Leninisten Oesterreichs [*Marxists-Leninists of Austria*] [*Political party*] (PPE)
**MLO** .......... Master Layout Original (MSA)
**MLO** .......... Mauna Loa Observatory [*Hawaii*] [*National Weather Service*]
**MLO** .......... Mechanized Letter Office (DCTA)
**MLO** .......... Medical Laboratory Observer [*A publication*]
**MLO** .......... Medical Liaison Officer [*Australia*]
**MLO** .......... Mesiolinguo-Occlusal [*Dentistry*]
**MLO** .......... Military Landing Officer
**MLO** .......... Military Liaison Officer [*British*]
**MLO** .......... Milos [*Greece*] [*Airport symbol*] (OAG)
**MLO** .......... Missile Launch Officer (AAG)
**MLO** .......... Missile Lift-Off (AAG)
**MLO** .......... Movement Liaison Officer (NATG)
**MLO** .......... Mycoplasma-Like Organisms [*Microbiology*]
**Mlody Tech** ... Mlody Technik [*Poland*] [*A publication*]
**MLOG** ....... Microlog Corp. [*NASDAQ symbol*] (NQ)
**MLon** ......... Richard Salter Storrs Library, Longmeadow, MA [*Library symbol*] [*Library of Congress*] (LCLS)
**MLonHi** ..... Longmeadow Historical Society, Longmeadow, MA [*Library symbol*] [*Library of Congress*] (LCLS)
**MLOR** ........ Maintenance/Logistics Observer Report
**MLOSA** ..... Mededelingen. Landbouwhogeschool en Opzoekingsstations van de Staat te Gent [*A publication*]
**MLow** ......... Lowell City Library, Lowell, MA [*Library symbol*] [*Library of Congress*] (LCLS)
**MLowT** ...... Lowell Technological Institute, Lowell, MA [*Library symbol*] [*Library of Congress*] [*Obsolete*] (LCLS)
**MLowTC** ... Lowell State College, Lowell, MA [*Library symbol*] [*Library of Congress*] [*Obsolete*] (LCLS)
**MLowU** ..... University of Lowell, Lowell, MA [*Library symbol*] [*Library of Congress*] (LCLS)
**MLowU-N** ... University of Lowell - North Campus, Alumni/Lydon Memorial Library, Lowell, MA [*Library symbol*] [*Library of Congress*] (LCLS)
**MLP** .......... Machine Language Program [*Data processing*]
**MLP** .......... Major Late Promoter [*Genetics*]
**MLP** .......... Major Late Promotor [*Biochemistry*]
**MLP** .......... Malabang [*Philippines*] [*Airport symbol*] (OAG)
**MLP** .......... Malaspina [*Alaska*] [*Seismograph station code, US Geological Survey*] (SEIS)
**MLP** .......... Malfunction-Linked People
**MLP** .......... Malta Labor Party [*Political party*] (PPW)
**MLP** .......... Master Limited Partnership
**MLP** .......... Master Logistics Plan (AABC)
**MLP** .......... Mauritius Labor Party [*Political party*] (PPW)
**MLP** .......... Maximum Likelihood Program
**MLP** .......... Mentoleva Posterior [*A fetal position*] [*Obstetrics*]
**MLP** .......... Mesa Limited Partnership [*NYSE symbol*] (SPSG)
**MLP** .......... Mesiolinguopulpal [*Dentistry*]
**MLP** .......... Metal Lath and Plaster [*Technical drawings*]
**MLP** .......... Michigan Law and Practice [*A publication*] (DLA)
**MLP** .......... Microsomal Lipoprotein [*Immunochemistry*]
**MLP** .......... Millipore Corp., Bedford, MA [*OCLC symbol*] (OCLC)
**MLP** .......... Minimum Latency Programming
**MLP** .......... Mirror Landing Procedures (MCD)
**MLP** .......... Mobile Launcher Platform [*NASA*] (NASA)
**MLP** .......... Modified Longest Path
**MLP** .......... Monthly List of Publications [*A publication*] (APTA)
**MLP** .......... Mortgage Loan Partnership [*Investment term*]
**MLP** .......... Movimiento de Liberacion Proletaria [*Mexico*] [*Political party*]
**MLP** .......... Movimiento de Liberacion del Pueblo [*People's Liberation Movement*] [*El Salvador*] [*Political party*] (PD)
**MLP** .......... Mullan Pass, ID [*Location identifier*] [*FAA*] (FAAL)
**MLP** .......... Multi-Step Products [*Toronto Stock Exchange symbol*]
**MLP** .......... Multilevel Precedence
**MLP** .......... Multilevel Procedure (MCD)
**MLP** .......... Multilevel Programmer
**MLP** .......... Multiple Line Printing (CMD)
**MLPA** ........ Modified Link Pack Area (MCD)
**MLPC** ........ Management-Labor Policy Committee
**MLPC** ........ Mouvement de Liberation du Peuple Centrafricain [*Movement for the Liberation of the Central African People*] (PD)
**MLPC** ........ Multilayer Printed Circuit
**MLPCB** ..... Machine Language Printed Circuit Boards [*Data processing*] (IEEE)
**MLPD** ....... Maximum Likelihood Predictive Density [*Statistics*]
**MLPED** ..... Mobile Launcher Pedestal [*NASA*] (NASA)
**MLPF** ........ Miniature Low Pass Filter
**MLPFS** ...... Merrill Lynch, Pierce, Fenner & Smith [*of Merrill Lynch & Co., Inc.*] [*Stockbrokers*] [*Wall Street slang name: "Thundering Herd"*]
**MLPNPP** .. Mobile Low-Power Nuclear Power Plant
**MLPP** ........ Multilevel Precedence and Preemption [*Telecommunications*] (TEL)
**MLPS** ........ Multilingual Publishing Software
**MLPSA** ..... Monthly List of Publications of South Australian Interest Received in the State Library of South Australia [*A publication*] (APTA)
**MLP USA** ... Marxist-Leninist Party of the USA (EA)
**MLPWB** .... Multilayer Printed-Wiring Board (IEEE)
**MLQ** .......... Malabar Law Quarterly [*A publication*] (DLA)
**MLQ** .......... Malalaua [*Papua New Guinea*] [*Airport symbol*] (OAG)
**MLQ** .......... Modern Language Quarterly [*A publication*]
**MLR** .......... Leaf Rapids Public Library, Manitoba [*Library symbol*] [*National Library of Canada*] (NLC)
**MLR** .......... Magnetic Latching Relay (MCD)
**MLR** .......... Main Line of Resistance
**M/LR** ......... Maintenance Loop Recorder (MCD)
**MLR** .......... Malayan Law Reports [*1950-54*] [*A publication*] (DLA)
**MLR** .......... Manitoba Law Reports [*Canada*] [*A publication*] (DLA)
**MLR** .......... Marginal Lending Rate [*Finance*]
**MLR** .......... Marine Life Resources [*Program*]
**MLR** .......... Maryland Law Record [*A publication*] (DLA)
**MLR** .......... Master-Locating RADAR (AABC)
**MLR** .......... Matched Logistic Regression [*Statistics*]
**MLR** .......... Mauritius Law Reporter [*A publication*] (DLA)
**MLR** .......... MDM [*Manipulator Deployment Mechanism*] Launch Right [*NASA*]
**MLR** .......... Mechanized Line Records [*Later, LMOS*] [*Bell System*]
**MLR** .......... Memory Lockout Register [*Data processing*]
**MLR** .......... Meston Lake Resources, Inc. [*Toronto Stock Exchange symbol*] [*Vancouver Stock Exchange symbol*]
**MLR** .......... Middle Latency Response [*Medicine*]
**MLR** .......... Millersburg, OH [*Location identifier*] [*FAA*] (FAAL)
**MLR** .......... Minimum Latency Routine
**MLR** .......... Minimum Lending Rate
**MLR** .......... Minnesota Legislative Reference Library, St. Paul, MN [*OCLC symbol*] (OCLC)
**MLR** .......... Missile Launch Response [*Navy*] (CAAL)
**MLR** .......... Mixed Lymphocyte [*or Leukocyte*] Reaction [*or Response*] [*Immunology*]
**MlR** ............ Mladinska Revija [*A publication*]
**MLR** .......... Modern Language Review [*A publication*]
**MLR** .......... Modern Law Review [*A publication*]
**MLR** .......... Monodisperse Latex Reactor
**MLR** .......... Monotone Likelihood Ratio [*Statistics*]
**MLR** .......... Monthly Labor Review [*A publication*]
**MLR** .......... Monthly Letter Report
**MLR** .......... Montreal Law Reports [*A publication*] (DLA)
**MLR** .......... Mortar Locating RADAR (MCD)
**MLR** .......... Multilayer Resist [*Lithography*]
**MLR** .......... Multiple Linear Regression [*Mathematics*]
**MLR** .......... Multiple Location Risk [*Insurance*]
**MLR** .......... Multiply and Round
**MLR** .......... Muntele Rosu [*Romania*] [*Seismograph station code, US Geological Survey*] (SEIS)
**MLR** .......... Muzzle-Loading Rifle
**MLRA** ....... Major Land Resource Area [*USDA topographic characterization*]
**MLRA** ....... Marriage Law Reform Association [*British*]
**MLRA** ....... Multivariate Linear Regression Analysis [*Advertising marketing*]
**MLRB** ........ Master Logistics Review Board (AAG)

**MLRB**........ Mutual Loss Research Bureau [*Later, Property Loss Research Bureau*] (EA)
**MLRC**........ Mallon Resources Corp. [*NASDAQ symbol*] (CTT)
**MLRC**........ Master Logistics Review Committee (AAG)
**MLRC**........ Minor League Research Committee (EA)
**MLRC**........ Multilevel Rail Car
**MLRCA**..... Mini Lop Rabbit Club of America (EA)
**MLR CS**.... Montreal Law Reports, Superior Court [*Canada*] [*A publication*] (DLA)
**Ml Rev**....... Military Review [*A publication*]
**MLRG**....... Marine Life Research Group [*Scripps Institution of Oceanography*]
**MLRG**....... Muzzle-Loading Rifled Gun
**MLRP**........ Marine Corps Long-Range Plans
**MLRP**........ Marine Life Research Program
**MLRQB**..... Montreal Law Reports, Queen's Bench [*A publication*] (DLA)
**MLRS**........ Manual Launch - RADAR Search
**MLRS**........ Monodisperse Latex Reactor System
**MLRS**........ Multiple Launch Rocket System [*DoD*] (MCD)
**MLRSC**..... Montreal Law Reports, Superior Court [*Canada*] [*A publication*] (DLA)
**MLRS-TGW**... Multiple Launch Rocket System Terminally Guided Warhead
**MLS**........... Mac Library System [*Computer Advanced Software Products - CASPR*] [*Cupertino, CA*] [*Information service or system*] (IID)
**MLS**........... Machine Literature Searching [*Data processing*] (DIT)
**MLS**........... Maintenance Loading Sheet (MCD)
**MLS**........... Mall Airways, Inc. [*Albany, NY*] [*FAA designator*] (FAAC)
**MLS**........... Manistique & Lake Superior R. R. [*AAR code*]
**MLS**........... Manned Lunar Surface [*NASA*]
**MLS**........... Master Laboratory Station
**MLS**........... Master of Librarianship
**MLS**........... Master of Library Science
**MLS**........... Master of Library Studies
**MLS**........... Maxwell Library Systems [*Information service or system*] (IID)
**MLS**........... Mechanical Limit Stop
**MLS**........... Mechanical Limit Switch
**MLS**........... Median Longitudinal Section
**MLS**........... Medium Life Span
**MLS**........... Medium Long Shot [*A photograph or motion picture sequence taken from a relatively great distance*]
**MLS**........... Metal Slitting
**MLS**........... Metropolitan Libraries Section [*Public Library Association*]
**MLS**........... Microwave Landing System [*Aviation*]
**MLS**........... Microwave Limb Sounder
**MLS**........... Microwave Line Stretcher
**MLS**........... Miles City [*Montana*] [*Airport symbol*] (OAG)
**MLS**........... Miles City, MT [*Location identifier*] [*FAA*] (FAAL)
**MLS**........... Military Labor Service
**ML/S**......... Milliliters per Second
**MLS**........... Mills (MCD)
**MLS**........... Miniature Linguistic Systems
**MLS**........... Minimum Launch Speed [*British military*] (DMA)
**MLS**........... Minimum Legal Size [*Pisciculture*]
**MLS**........... Minor Lymphocyte Stimulating [*Genetics*]
**MLS**........... Missile-Launching System (NG)
**MLS**........... Missile Lift System (AAG)
**MLS**........... Missile Location System (IEEE)
**MLS**........... Mississippi County Library System, Blytheville, AR [*OCLC symbol*] [*Inactive*] (OCLC)
**MLS**........... MLS: Marketing Library Services [*A publication*]
**MLS**........... Mobile Library Service [*British*]
**MLS**........... Mobile Logistic Support (CINC)
**MLS**........... Modern Language Studies [*A publication*]
**MLS**........... MOL [*Manned Orbiting Laboratory*] Launch Site (MCD)
**MLS**........... Moskovskij Letopisnyj Svod Konca [*A publication*]
**MLS**........... Moulis [*France*] [*Seismograph station code, US Geological Survey*] (SEIS)
**MLS**........... Movimento per le Liberta Statuarie [*Movement for Statutory Liberty*] [*Sanmarinese*] (PPE)
**MLS**........... Movimiento de Liberacion Sebta [*Ceuta Liberation Movement*] [*Spain*] (PD)
**MLS**........... Multilanguage System [*Data processing*] (IEEE)
**MLS**........... Multilayered Structure [*Botany*]
**MLS**........... Multilevel Security (MCD)
**MLS**........... Multinational Business [*A publication*]
**MLS**........... Multiparameter Light Scattering [*Physics*]
**MLS**........... Multiple Listing Service [*Real estate*]
**MLS**........... Music Learning System [*Trademark*]
**MLSA**........ Ministry of Labour Staff Association [*British*]
**MLSB**........ Major League Scouting Bureau [*Baseball*]
**MLSB**........ Member of the London School Board
**ML Sc**........ Master of Library Science
**MLSC**........ Member of the London Society of Compositors
**MLSC**........ Micronesian Legal Services Corporation (EA)
**MLSE**........ Mechanical Launch Support Equipment [*NASA*] (KSC)
**MLSF**........ Mobile Logistic Support Forces (MCD)
**ML/SFA**.... Metal Lath/Steel Framing Association Division of National Association of Architectural Metal Manufactureres (EA)
**MLSG**........ Mobile Logistics Support Group (NVT)
**MLSI**......... Multilevel Large-Scale Integration
**MLSJ**......... Macquarie Law Students Journal [*A publication*]
**MLSK**........ Master Lock, Skeleton Key
**MLSO**........ Mode-Locked Surface-Acoustic Wave Oscillator [*Telecommunications*] (TEL)
**MLSP**........ Multiple-Link Satellite Program
**MLSR**........ Molder, Ship Repair [*Navy rating*]
**MLSRC**..... Molder, Ship Repair, Cupola Tender [*Navy rating*]
**MLSRF**..... Molder, Ship Repair, Foundryman [*Navy rating*]
**MLSRM**.... Molder, Ship Repair, Molder [*Navy rating*]
**MLSS**........ Mechanized Letter Sorting System [*Hong Kong Post Office*]
**MLSS**........ Military and Federal Specifications and Standards [*Information Handling Services*] [*Information service or system*] (CRD)
**MLSS**........ Mixed-Liquor Suspended Solid [*Water pollution*]
**MLSSA**..... Marine Life Society of South Australia
**MLST**........ Merrill Language Screening Test [*Educational test*]
**MLST**........ Milstead [*AAR code*]
**MLSTP**..... Movimento de Libertacao de Sao Tome e Principe [*Movement for the Liberation of Sao Tome and Principe*] [*Portugal*] (PPW)
**MLT**.......... Madras Law Times [*India*] [*A publication*] (DLA)
**MLT**.......... Magnetic Levitation Transportation
**MLT**.......... Magnetic Local Time
**MLT**.......... Malaysia Industrial Digest [*A publication*]
**MLT**.......... Malta [*ANSI three-letter standard code*] (CNC)
**mlt**............ Maltese [*MARC language code*] [*Library of Congress*] (LCCP)
**MLT**.......... Manned Lunar Test [*NASA*] (KSC)
**MLT**.......... Manufacturing Lead Time
**MLT**.......... Mass Loaded Transducer
**MLT**.......... Master of Law and Taxation
**MLT**.......... Master Library Tape [*Data processing*]
**MLT**.......... Maximum Lethal Time [*of radiation exposure*] (DEN)
**MLT**.......... Mean Length per Turn
**MLT**.......... Mean Life Time (NATG)
**MLT**.......... Mean Logistical Time (IEEE)
**MLT**.......... Mean Low Tide [*Tides and currents*]
**MLT**.......... Mechanized Line Testing [*Telecommunications*] (TEL)
**MLT**.......... Mechanized Loop Testing (MCD)
**MLT**.......... Median Lethal Time [*of radiation exposure*]
**MLT**.......... Medical Laboratory Technician [*or Technologist*]
**MLT**.......... Medium Level Tripod [*British military*] (DMA)
**MLT**.......... Melatonin
**MLT**.......... Microlayer Transistor
**MLT**.......... Millinocket, ME [*Location identifier*] [*FAA*] (FAAL)
**MLT**.......... Misallat [*Egypt*] [*Geomagnetic observatory code*]
**MLT**.......... Mitel Corp. [*NYSE symbol*] [*Toronto Stock Exchange symbol*] (SPSG)
**MLT**.......... Mixing-Length Theory [*Physics of convection*] [*Chemical engineering*]
**MLT**.......... Mobile Laboratory Table
**MLT**.......... Mobile Launch Tower
**MLT**.......... Muexins-Length Theory
**MLTA**........ Multiple Line Terminal Adapter [*Data processing*] (BUR)
**MLT-AD**.... Medical Laboratory Technology-Associate Degree
**MLTC**........ Mixed Lymphocyte-Tumor Culture [*Immunology*]
**MLTC**........ Multi-Tech Corporation [*NASDAQ symbol*] (NQ)
**ML Tech**.... Military Technology [*A publication*]
**MLTF**........ Major Late Transcription Factor [*Genetics*]
**MLTF**........ Military Law Task Force (EA)
**MLTF**........ Multibank Financial Corp. [*NASDAQ symbol*] (NQ)
**MLTG**........ Melting
**MLTG**........ Missile Launch Tube Group
**MLTI**......... Mixed Lymphocyte-Tumor [*Cell*] Interaction [*Immunology*]
**ML/TL**...... Mucrones Length to Total Body Length Ratio [*Of Crustacea*]
**MLTLVL**... Melting Level [*Meteorology*] (FAAC)
**MLTMS**.... Multileg Tanker Mooring System (MCD)
**MLTP**........ Ministers Leadership Training Program [*Defunct*] (EA)
**MLTPL**..... Multiplane
**MLTSL**..... Multiple Sail [*Navy*] (NVT)
**MLTU**........ Missile Loop Test Unit
**MLTY**........ Military (MDG)
**MLU**.......... Major League Umpires Association
**MLU**.......... Malka Resources Ltd. [*Vancouver Stock Exchange symbol*]
**MLU**.......... Mean Length of Utterance [*Linguistics*]
**MLU**.......... Memory Loading Unit [*of FADAC*] [*Military*]
**MLU**.......... Memory Logic Unit [*Data processing*]
**MLU**.......... Miscellaneous Live Unit [*Military*] (AFM)
**MLU**.......... Mobile Laundry Unit
**MLU**.......... Mobile Living Unit [*Mobile home*]
**MLU**.......... Monroe [*Louisiana*] [*Airport symbol*] (OAG)
**MLU**.......... Monroe, LA [*Location identifier*] [*FAA*] (FAAL)
**MLU**.......... Multiple Logical Unit
**MLUA**........ Major League Umpires Association (EA)
**MLURI**...... Macaulay Land Use Research Institute, Aberdeen [*United Kingdom*] (IRUK)
**ML/USA**... Mailing List User and Supplier Association [*Lake Worth, FL*] (EA)
**MLV**.......... Bedrijfsontwikkeling; Maandblad voor Agrarische Produktie, Verwerking, en Afzet [*A publication*]

**MLV**.......... Main LOX [*Liquid Oxygen*] Valve [*NASA*] (KSC)
**MLV**.......... Malvaux [*France*] [*Seismograph station code, US Geological Survey*] (SEIS)
**MLV**.......... Matrix Light Valve
**MLV**.......... Maximum Lung Volume [*Physiology*]
**MLV**.......... McDonnell Launch Vehicle [*McDonnell Douglas Corp.*] (MCD)
**MLV**.......... Medium Launch Vehicle
**MLV**.......... Membrane Light Valve [*Optics*]
**MLV**.......... Moloney Leukemia Virus [*Also, MLV(M)*]
**MLV**.......... Multilamellar Large Vesicle [*Pharmacy*] [*Biochemistry*]
**MLV**.......... Multilaminar Phospholipid Vesicle [*Immunology*]
**MLV**.......... Murine Leukemia Virus [*Also, MuLV*]
**MLV(A)**..... Murine Leukemia Virus (Abelson)
**MLVBA**..... Metallverarbeitung [*A publication*]
**MLV(M)**.... Murine Leukemia Virus (Moloney)
**MLVP**........ Manned Lunar Vehicle Program [*NASA*] (AAG)
**MLVPS**..... Manual Low-Voltage Power Supply
**MLV(R)**..... Murine Leukemia Virus (Rauscher)
**MLVS**........ Mededelingen mit de Leidse Verzameling van Spijkerschrift Inscripties [*A publication*]
**MLVS**........ Mill Vise
**MLVS**........ Multilevel Voltage Select (MCD)
**MLVSS**..... Mixed-Liquor Volatile Suspended Solids [*Chemical engineering*]
**MLV/T**...... Tribus. Veroeffentlichungen des Linden-Museums. Museum fuer Laender- und Voelkerkunde [*A publication*]
**MLW**......... Madras Law Weekly [*India*] [*A publication*] (DLA)
**MLW**......... Maximum Landing Weight [*Aviation*]
**MLW**......... Mean Low Water [*Tides and currents*]
**MLW**......... Milwaukee [*Wisconsin*] [*Seismograph station code, US Geological Survey*] [*Closed*] (SEIS)
**MLW**......... Monrovia [*Liberia*] [*Airport symbol*] (OAG)
**MLW**......... Mountain Life and Work [*A publication*]
**MLWI**........ Mean Low-Water Lunitidal Interval [*Tides and currents*]
**MLWMS**... Miscellaneous Liquid Waste Management System (NRCH)
**MLWN**...... Mean Low-Water Neap [*Tides and currents*]
**MLWS**....... Mean Low-Water Spring [*Tides and currents*]
**MLWS**....... Miniature LASER Weapon Simulator (MCD)
**MLWS**....... Minimum Level Water Stand (NATG)
**MLX**.......... Malatya [*Turkey*] [*Airport symbol*] (OAG)
**MLX**.......... Mauna Loa 2 [*Hawaii*] [*Seismograph station code, US Geological Survey*] (SEIS)
**MLX**.......... Merritt Island, Florida [*Spaceflight Tracking and Data Network*] [*NASA*]
**MLXX**........ MLX Corp. [*Troy, MI*] [*NASDAQ symbol*] (NQ)
**MLy**........... Lynn Public Library, Lynn, MA [*Library symbol*] [*Library of Congress*] (LCLS)
**MLY**.......... Manley Hot Springs [*Alaska*] [*Airport symbol*] (OAG)
**MLY**.......... Manley Hot Springs, AK [*Location identifier*] [*FAA*] (FAAL)
**MLY**.......... Moly Mite Resources [*Vancouver Stock Exchange symbol*]
**MLY**.......... Multiply (MDG)
**MlyKA**....... Arkib Negara [*National Archives of Malaysia*], Federal Government Building, Kuala Lumpur, Malaysia [*Library symbol*] [*Library of Congress*] (LCLS)
**MlyKU**....... University of Malaya, Kuala Lumpur, Malaysia [*Library symbol*] [*Library of Congress*] (LCLS)
**Mlyn L**....... Mlynarske Listy [*A publication*]
**Mlyn Pek Prum Tech Skladovani Obili**... Mlynsko-Pekarensky Prumysl a Technika Skladovani Obili [*A publication*]
**Mlyn Pol**.... Mlynarz Polski [*A publication*]
**Mlynsko-Pekar Prum Tech Sklad Obili**... Mlynsko-Pekarensky Prumysl a Technika Skladovani Obili [*A publication*]
**MlyPS**........ Universiti Sains Malaysia (University of Science, Malaysia), Minden, Penang, Malaysia [*Library symbol*] [*Library of Congress*] (LCLS)
**MLZ**.......... Melo [*Uruguay*] [*Airport symbol*] (OAG)
**MM**........... Maal og Minne [*A publication*]
**MM**........... Machine-Made Snow [*Skiing*]
**MM**........... Machinery
**MM**........... Machinist's Mate [*Navy rating*]
**MM**........... Maclean's Magazine [*A publication*]
**MM**........... Made Merchantable
**MM**........... Madrider Mitteilungen [*A publication*]
**MM**........... Maelzel's Metronome [*Music*]
**MM**........... Magister Melendus [*Flourished, 1188-1209*] [*Authority cited in pre-1607 legal work*] (DSA)
**MM**........... Main Memory
**MM**........... Main Module (NASA)
**MM**........... Maintenance Manual
**M of M**...... Maintenance of Membership [*Labor unions*]
**MM**........... Maintenance Monitor
**MM**........... Maitland Mercury [*A publication*] (APTA)
**MM**........... Majesties
**MM**........... Major Medical [*Insurance*]
**MM**........... Major Mode (KSC)
**M & M**...... Make and Mend
**MM**........... Malignant Melanoma [*Oncology*]
**mm**............ Malta [*MARC country of publication code*] [*Library of Congress*] (LCCP)
**MM**........... Man-Month (AFM)
**MM**........... Management Manual (KSC)
**M & M**...... Manchester & Milford Railway [*Wales*]
**MM**........... Manmade [*Diamonds*]
**MM**........... Manual Maximal Displacement [*Sports medicine*]
**MM**........... Manual Morse (MCD)
**MM**........... Manufacturers' Monthly [*A publication*] (APTA)
**MM**........... Manufacturing Management
**MM**........... Manufacturing Manual (AAG)
**MM**........... Marilyn Monroe [*American motion picture star, 1926-1962*]
**MM**........... Marine Midland Banks, Inc. [*NYSE symbol*] (SPSG)
**MM**........... Mariner Mars Project [*NASA*]
**MM**........... Mariner's Mirror [*A publication*]
**MM**........... Maritime Mobile
**MM**........... Mark Mason (ROG)
**MM**........... Mark Master [*Freemasonry*]
**MM**........... Martha Movement (EA)
**M & M**...... Martha and the Muffins [*Musical group*]
**M-M**.......... Martin Marietta Corp.
**MM**........... Martyres [*Martyrs*]
**MM**........... Maryknoll Missioners [*Catholic Foreign Mission Society*] [*Roman Catholic religious order*]
**MM**........... Mass Memory (NASA)
**MM**........... Massachusetts Music News [*A publication*]
**MM**........... Masses and Mainstream [*A publication*]
**MM**........... Massorah Magna [*or Massora Magna*] (BJA)
**MM**........... Master of Management
**MM**........... Master Mason [*Freemasonry*]
**MM**........... Master Mechanic
**MM**........... Master of Medicine
**MM**........... Master Monitor
**MM**........... Master of Music
**MM**........... Masters
**MM**........... Materia Medica (ROG)
**M & M**...... Materials and Maintenance (NASA)
**MM**........... Materials Management [*Nuclear energy*]
**MM**........... Matcrials Mcasurement (IEEE)
**MM**........... Math Model (KSC)
**MM**........... Matrimonium [*Matrimony*] [*Latin*]
**M/M**.......... Maximum and Minimum (KSC)
**MM**........... Measure for Measure [*Shakespearean work*]
**MM**........... Med Mera [*And So Forth*] [*Latin*] (ILCA)
**MM**........... Medal for Merit [*Military decoration*]
**MM**........... Medial Meniscus [*Anatomy*]
**MM**........... Median Method [*Mathematics*]
**MM**........... Medical Man (ROG)
**mm-----**...... Mediterranean Sea and Area [*MARC geographic area code*] [*Library of Congress*] (LCCP)
**MM**........... Medium Maintenance
**MM**........... Megamega [*A prefix meaning multiplied by one trillion*] (DEN)
**MM**........... Megameter
**MM**........... Melaveh Malka (BJA)
**MM**........... Melody Maker [*A publication*]
**MM**........... Membranes [*Leaves of parchment*] (ROG)
**MM**........... Memory Module (MCD)
**MM**........... Memory Multiplexer [*Data processing*] (MDG)
**MM**........... Mercantile Marine
**MM**........... Merchant Marine
**M & M**...... Merchants and Manufacturers Association (EA)
**MM**........... Messageries Maritimes [*Forwarding agents*] [*French*]
**MM**........... Messieurs [*Plural of Mister*] [*French*]
**MM**........... Metal Manufacture [*Department of Employment*] [*British*]
**M & M**...... Metals and Minerals Research Services [*British*]
**MM**........... Methyl Methacrylate [*Also, MMA*] [*Organic chemistry*]
**MM**........... Methylmalonyl-CoA Mutase [*An enzyme*]
**MM**........... Metronome Mark (ROG)
**MM**........... Microfilm
**MM**........... Micromanipulator [*Instrumentation*]
**MM**........... Micromodule (AAG)
**MM**........... Midcourse Mode [*Navy*] (CAAL)
**MM**........... Middle Marker [*in an instrument landing system*]
**MM**........... Middle Minoan [*Archaeology*] (BJA)
**MM**........... Military Medal [*British*] [*World War I nickname: Maconochie Medal*]
**MM**........... Military Medicine
**M & M**...... Milk and Molasses [*Enema*] [*Medicine*]
**MM**........... Milla Wa-Milla (BJA)
**mm**............ Millimeter [*Metric*]
**mM**........... Millimole [*Mass*]
**MM**........... Minelayer Fleet [*Navy symbol*] [*Obsolete*]
**MM**........... Minimal Medium [*Microbiology*]
**M/M**.......... Minimum/Maximum
**MM**........... Mining Magazine [*A publication*]
**MM**........... Minister of Munitions [*British*] [*World War II*]
**MM**........... Ministry of Mines [*British*] (DAS)
**MM**........... Mint Mark [*Numismatics*]
**MM**........... Minuteman [*Missile*] (AABC)
**MM**........... Miscellaneous Man [*A publication*]
**Mm**........... Misch Metal [*A commercial mixture of rare earth metals*]
**MM**........... Mismated [*Merchandising slang*]
**MM**........... Missile Master [*Fire direction and coordination system*]
**MM**........... Missile Minder (MCD)

MM........... Missile Motion
MM........... Mission Manager (NASA)
MM........... Mission Module
MM........... Mission Monitor (MCD)
M/M......... Mister or Mrs. [*In addresses*] [*Correspondence*]
MM........... Mistress of Music
MM........... Mitochondrial Myopathy [*Medicine*]
MM........... Mitteilungen. Internationale Stiftung Mozarteum [*A publication*]
MM........... Modern Motor [*A publication*]
MM........... Modern Music [*A publication*]
MM........... Modification or Maintenance [*Aircraft*]
MM........... Modified Mercalli [*Scale measuring earthquake intensity*] [*Seismology*]
MM........... Mois Maconnique [*Masonic Month*] [*French*] [*Freemasonry*]
MM........... Molecular Mechanics [*Physical chemistry*]
MM........... Money Market [*Investment term*]
M & M....... Montagu and MacArthur's English Bankruptcy Reports [*A publication*] (DLA)
MM........... Monthly Meetings [*Quakers*]
MM........... Monuments et Memoires Publies par l'Academie des Inscriptions et Belles-Lettres [*A publication*]
M & M....... Moody and Malkin's English Nisi Prius Reports [*A publication*] (DLA)
MM........... Moody Monthly [*A publication*]
MM........... Moral Majority [*An association*] (EA)
MM........... Morality in Media (EA)
MM........... Moslem Mosque (EA)
MM........... Mothers Matter [*Commercial firm*] (EA)
MM........... Motor Magnet
MM........... Motor Maintenance [*Army*]
MM........... Motor Maintenance Aptitude Area [*Army*]
MM........... Motor Mechanic [*British military*] (DMA)
MM........... Mouse Myoblast [*Cell line*]
MM........... Moving Magnet [*Stereo equipment*]
MM........... Mozambique Metical [*Monetary unit*] (IMH)
MM........... Much Married [*Slang*]
MM........... Mucous Membrane
MM........... Muenchener Museum [*A publication*]
MM........... Multi-Media (OICC)
MM........... Multimeter
MM........... Multiple Myeloma [*Medicine*]
MM........... Munitions Maintenance (MCD)
MM........... Muscles [*Medicine*]
MM........... Museum Media [*A publication*]
MM........... Music and Musicians [*A publication*]
MM........... Musical Majority [*Inactive*] (EA)
MM........... Mutatis Mutandis [*With the Necessary Changes*] [*Latin*]
MM........... Myeloid Metaplasia [*Medicine*]
MM........... Myelomeningocele [*Medicine*]
MM........... Myriameters [*Metric system*] (ROG)
MM........... Sociedad Aeronautica de Medellin [*Colombia*] [*ICAO designator*] (FAAC)
MM........... Xaverian Missionary Society of Mary, Inc. [*Roman Catholic women's religious order*]
MM1.......... Machinist's Mate, First Class [*Navy rating*]
MM2.......... Machinist's Mate, Second Class [*Navy rating*]
$MM^2$.......... Square Millimeter
$MM^3$.......... Cubic Millimeter
MM3.......... Machinist's Mate, Third Class [*Navy rating*]
M & M's .... Mass and Meals [*Refers to nuns who appear only at these activities*]
MMA......... Average Male Mass
MMA......... MacRobertson Miller Airline Services [*Australia*]
MMA......... Magnetotactic Multicellular Aggregate [*Microbiology*]
MMA......... Malmo [*Sweden*] [*Airport symbol*] (OAG)
MMA......... Management Accounting [*A publication*]
MMA......... Management and Marketing Abstracts [*PIRA*] [*Bibliographic database*] [*British*]
MMA......... Manual Metal Arc [*Welding*]
MMA......... Marine Mammal Act [*1972*] (MSC)
MMA......... Marine Maritime Academy
MMA......... Marine Motor Association (ROG)
MMA......... Married Man's Allowance [*Taxes*] [*British*]
MMA......... Massachusetts Maritime Academy [*Buzzards Bay*]
MMA......... Massachusetts Maritime Academy, Captain C. H. Hurley Library, Buzzards Bay, MA [*OCLC symbol*] (OCLC)
MMA......... Massachusetts Military Academy
MMA......... Master of Management and Administration, Cranfield Institute of Technology [*British*] (DBQ)
MMA......... Master of Municipal Administration
MMA......... Master of Musical Arts
MMA......... Masters of Medicine [*A publication*]
MMA......... Material Manufacturing Authorization (AAG)
MMA......... Materials Marketing Associates [*Hartford, CT*] (EA)
MMA......... Maymac Petroleum Corp. [*Vancouver Stock Exchange symbol*]
MMA......... Mazda Motors of America
MMA......... Medical Management of America, Inc. [*AMEX symbol*] (CTT)
MMA......... Medical Materiel Account [*Military*] (AABC)
MMA......... Memory-to-Memory Adapter [*Data processing*]
MMA......... Merchandise Marks Act (ROG)
MMA......... Merchants and Manufacturers Association
MMA......... Merrill's Marauders Association (EA)
MMA......... Methyl Methacrylate [*Also, MM*] [*Organic chemistry*]
MMA......... Methylmalonic Acid [*Organic chemistry*]
MMA......... Methylmalonic Acidemia [*Medicine*]
MMA......... Metropolitan Magazine Association [*Later, Magazine Publishers Association*] (EA)
MMA......... Metropolitan Museum of Art [*New York*] (BJA)
MMA......... Microminiature Mixer Amplifier
MMA......... Middle Meningeal Artery [*Neuroanatomy*]
MMA......... Military Medical Academy [*Armed forces medical college*]
MMA......... Minelayer Auxiliary Ship [*Navy symbol*] [*Obsolete*]
MMA......... Mirror Manufacturers Association
MMA......... Miscellanea Musicologica [*A publication*]
MMA......... Missile Maintenance Area (AAG)
MMA......... Mitomycin A [*Antineoplastic drug*]
MMA......... Modified Motorcycle Association
MMA......... Monographs on Mediterranean Antiquity [*A publication*]
MMA......... Monomethyl Arsonic Acid [*Organic chemistry*]
MMA......... Monomethylamine [*Organic chemistry*]
MMA......... Monorail Manufacturers Association (EA)
MMA......... Monovalent Metal Azide [*Inorganic chemistry*]
M & M'A ... Montagu and MacArthur's English Bankruptcy Reports [*A publication*] (DLA)
MMA......... Motoring in Miniature Association (EA)
MMA......... Motorsports Marketing Association [*Langhorne, PA*] [*Defunct*] (EA)
MMA......... Multifunction Microwave Aperture
MMA......... Multiple Module Access
MMA......... Multiplexed Matrix Array
MMA......... Mummy Mountain [*Arizona*] [*Seismograph station code, US Geological Survey*] [*Closed*] (SEIS)
MMA......... Music Masters' Association [*British*]
$M^3$/(M A).. Cubic Meters per Meter Year
$M^3$/($M^2$ A) ... Cubic Meters per Square Meter Year
MMAA...... Acapulco/General Juan N. Alvarez Internacional [*Mexico*] [*ICAO location identifier*] (ICLI)
MMAA...... Merchandise Mart Apparel Association [*Defunct*]
MMAA...... Monomethylarsonic Acid [*Organic chemistry*]
MMAC...... Material Management Aggregation Code (MCD)
MMAC...... Medical Materiel Advice Code [*Military*] (AFM)
MMAC...... Multiple Model Adaptive Control [*Flight control*]
MMACS..... Maintenance Management and Control System (MCD)
MMAD...... Macallat al-Macma al-Limi al-Arabi Dimasq [*A publication*]
MMAD...... Mass-Median Aerodynamic Diameter [*of particles*]
MMADA... Modern Materials. Advances in Development and Applications [*A publication*]
MM Adm... Master of Municipal Administration
M Ma E..... Master of Marine Engineering
M Ma Eng ... Master of Marine Engineering
MMAF...... Memoires. Mission Archeologique Francaise au Caire [*Paris*] [*A publication*]
MMAFC.... Memoires. Mission Archeologique Francaise au Caire [*Paris*] [*A publication*]
MMAI....... Monuments et Memoires Publies par l'Academie des Inscriptions et Belles-Lettres [*A publication*]
MMal........ Malden Public Library, Malden, MA [*Library symbol*] [*Library of Congress*] (LCLS)
MMam....... Marstons Mills Public Library, Marstons Mills, MA [*Library symbol*] [*Library of Congress*] (LCLS)
MMAN...... Aeropuerto del Norte [*Mexico*] [*ICAO location identifier*] (ICLI)
MMAN...... Minute Man of America [*NASDAQ symbol*] (NQ)
MManHi... Manchester Historical Society, Manchester, MA [*Library symbol*] [*Library of Congress*] (LCLS)
MMAP...... Memorias. Museos Arqueologicos Provinciales [*Madrid*] [*A publication*]
MMAR...... Main Memory Address Register
MMar........ Marlborough Public Library, Marlborough, MA [*Library symbol*] [*Library of Congress*] (LCLS)
M-MARP.. Mobilization Manpower Allocations/Requirements Plan [*Military*]
MMarsW... Historic Winslow House, Marshfield, MA [*Library symbol*] [*Library of Congress*] (LCLS)
MMAS...... Aguascalientes [*Mexico*] [*ICAO location identifier*] (ICLI)
MMAS...... Master of Military Art and Science (MCD)
MMAS...... Material Management Accountability System (NASA)
MmAS....... Minerva Mikrofilm A/S, Hellerup, Denmark [*Library symbol*] [*Library of Congress*] (LCLS)
MMASA ... Modern Machine Shop [*A publication*]
MMat........ Free Public Library, Mattapoisett, MA [*Library symbol*] [*Library of Congress*] (LCLS)
MMAT...... Mobile Mine Assembly Team (NG)
MMath...... Master of Mathematics
MMAU...... Master Multiattribute Utility (IEEE)
MMB......... MacMillan Bloedel, Inc. [*NYSE symbol*] (SPSG)
MMB......... Master Menu Board [*Military*]
MMB......... Memanbetsu [*Japan*] [*Airport symbol*] (OAG)
MMB......... Memanbetsu [*Japan*] [*Geomagnetic observatory code*]
MMB......... Membrane [*Medicine*]

**MMB**......... Mercedarian Missionaries of Berriz [*Also, OMerc*] [*Roman Catholic women's religious order*]
**MMB**......... Method of Mass Balance [*Physical chemistry*]
**MMB**......... Methylmercury Bromide [*Organic chemistry*]
**MMB**......... Midwest Motor Carriers Bureau, Inc., Oklahoma City OK [*STAC*]
**MMB**......... Milk Marketing Board for England and Wales
**MMB**......... Million Barrels
**MMB**......... Mixer Manufacturers Bureau [*Defunct*] (EA)
**MMB**......... Monumenta Musicae Belgicae [*A publication*]
**MMB**......... Muenzen- und Medaillensammler Berichte aus allen Gebieten der Geld-, Muenzen-, und Medaillenkunde [*A publication*]
**MMBAT**... Main Missile Battery
**MMB/D**.... Million Barrels per Day
**MMBEMD**... Mean Miles between Essential Maintenance Demand [*Quality control*]
**MMBF**....... Mean Miles between Failures [*Quality control*]
**MMBL**...... MacMillan Bloedel Ltd. [*Vancouver, BC*] [*NASDAQ symbol*] (NQ)
**MMBMF**... Mean Miles between Mission Failures [*Quality control*] (MCD)
**MMBOMF**... Mean Miles between Operational Mission Failures [*Quality control*] (MCD)
**MMBP**...... Military Medical Benefits Property (AABC)
**MMBR**...... Mean Miles between Removals [*Quality control*] (MCD)
**MMBSF**.... Mean Miles between System Failures [*Quality control*] (MCD)
**MMBTU**... Million British Thermal Units (MENA)
**MMBUMA**... Mean Miles between Unscheduled Maintenance Actions [*Quality control*] (MCD)
**MMC**......... Machinist's Mate, Chief [*Navy rating*]
**MMC**......... Magnesium Methyl Carbonate [*Organic chemistry*]
**MMC**......... Maintenance Management Center
**MMC**......... Maintenance Management Course [*Army*]
**MMC**......... Man-Machine Communication [*Data processing*]
**MMC**......... Man Marketing Council [*New York City*]
**MMC**......... Manufacturing Methods Committee
**MMC**......... Marine Mammal Commission [*Marine science*] (MSC)
**MMC**......... Marsh & McLennan Companies, Inc. [*NYSE symbol*] (SPSG)
**MMC**......... Martin Marietta Corporation (KSC)
**MMC**......... Martin's Reports of Mining Cases [*Canada*] [*A publication*] (DLA)
**MMC**......... Mary Morstan's Companions [*An association*]
**MMC**......... Marymount Manhattan College [*New York, NY*]
**MMC**......... Massachusetts Microelectronics Center [*Research center*] (RCD)
**MMC**......... Matched Memory Cycle [*Data processing*]
**MMC**......... Materiel Management Center [*Military*] (AABC)
**MMC**......... Materiel Management Code [*Military*] (AFM)
**MMC**......... Maximum Material Condition
**MMC**......... Maximum Metal Concept
**MMC**......... Maximum Metal Condition (IEEE)
**MMC**......... Maximum Miscibility Composition [*Physical chemistry*]
**MMC**......... Mazda Motor Corporation
**MMC**......... Memory Management Controller (IEEE)
**MMC**......... Merchant Marine Council [*Coast Guard*]
**MMC**......... Metabolic Measurement Cart [*Beckman Instruments, Inc.*]
**MMC**......... Metal-Matrix Composite
**MMC**......... Metropolitan Motor Carriers Conference Inc., Dover NJ [*STAC*]
**MMC**......... Micronesian Minerals [*Vancouver Stock Exchange symbol*]
**MMC**......... Midcourse Measurement Correction
**MMC**......... Middle Cape [*Alaska*] [*Seismograph station code, US Geological Survey*] (SEIS)
**MMC**......... Migrating Myoelectric Complexes [*Electrophysiology*]
**MMC**......... Millsaps College, Jackson, MS [*OCLC symbol*] (OCLC)
**MMC**......... Minelayer, Coastal [*Navy symbol*] [*Obsolete*]
**MMC**......... Minicar and Microcar Club (EA)
**MMC**......... Miscellanea Musicologica [*A publication*]
**MMC**......... Missile Maintenance Crew (AFM)
**MMC**......... Missile Measurements Center
**MMC**......... Missile Motion Computer
**MMC**......... Mission Management Center [*NASA*] (NASA)
**MMC**......... Mission Monitoring Center [*Army*]
**MMC**......... Mitomycin C [*Mutamycin*] [*Also, Mi, MTC*] [*Antineoplastic drug*]
**MMC**......... Mitsubishi Motors Corporation
**MMC**......... Money Management Council [*British*]
**MMC**......... Money Market Certificate [*Investment term*]
**MMC**......... Monopolies and Mergers Commission [*British*]
**MMC**......... Mortar Motor Carrier
**MMC**......... Mount Marty College [*South Dakota*]
**MMC**......... Mount Mary College [*Wisconsin*]
**MMC**......... Mount Mercy College [*Iowa; Pennsylvania*]
**MMC**......... Mucosal Mast Cell [*Medicine*]
**MMC**......... Multiport Memory Controller
**MMCA**...... Cananea [*Mexico*] [*ICAO location identifier*] (ICLI)
**MMCA**...... Materials Management Council of Australia
**MMCA**...... Methyl Monochloroacetate [*Organic chemistry*]
**MMCA**...... Midbody Motor Control Assembly (NASA)
**MMCA**...... Minor Military Construction, Army
**M & McA**.. Montagu and MacArthur's English Bankruptcy Reports [*A publication*] (DLA)
**M McA**...... Montague and McArthur's English Bankruptcy Reports [*A publication*] (DLA)
**MM Cas**.... Martin's Reports of Mining Cases [*Canada*] [*A publication*] (DLA)
**MMCB**...... Cuernavaca [*Mexico*] [*ICAO location identifier*] (ICLI)
**MMCB**...... Midwest Motor Carriers Bureau, Inc.
**MMCBE**.... Machinist's Mate, Construction Battalion, Equipment Operator [*Navy rating*]
**MMCC**...... Ciudad Acuna [*Mexico*] [*ICAO location identifier*] (ICLI)
**MMCC**...... Manhattan Miniature Camera Club (EA)
**MMCC**...... Mid-Century Mercury Car Club (EA)
**MMCD**...... Master Monitor Criteria Data File
**MMCE**...... Ciudad Del Carmen [*Mexico*] [*ICAO location identifier*] (ICLI)
**MMCF**...... Million Cubic Feet
**MMCFD**... Million Cubic Feet a Day
**MMCG**...... Nuevo Casas Grandes [*Mexico*] [*ICAO location identifier*] (ICLI)
**MMCH**...... Chilpancingo [*Mexico*] [*ICAO location identifier*] (ICLI)
**MMCI**....... Mopar Muscle Club International (EA)
**MMCIAC**... Metal Matrix Composites Information Analysis Center [*DoD*] [*Information service or system*] (IID)
**MMCL**...... Culiacan [*Mexico*] [*ICAO location identifier*] (ICLI)
**MMCL**...... Major Missile Component List
**MMCL**...... Master Measurement and Control List (MCD)
**MMCM**..... Chetumal [*Mexico*] [*ICAO location identifier*] (ICLI)
**MMCM**..... Machinist's Mate, Master Chief [*Navy rating*]
**MMCMP**.. Mobilization, Military and Civilian Manpower Program (AABC)
**MMCN**...... Ciudad Obregon [*Mexico*] [*ICAO location identifier*] (ICLI)
**MMCNA**... Moto Morini Club of North America (EA)
**MMCO**...... Merelin Mining Co. [*NASDAQ symbol*] (NQ)
**MMCP**...... Campeche [*Mexico*] [*ICAO location identifier*] (ICLI)
**M/MCRP**... AUTODIN Memory/Memory Control Replacement Program (MCD)
**MMCS**...... Ciudad Juarez/Abraham Gonzalez Internacional [*Mexico*] [*ICAO location identifier*] (ICLI)
**MMCS**...... Machinist's Mate, Senior Chief [*Navy rating*]
**MMCS**...... Mass Memory Control Subsystem (TEL)
**MMCS**...... Minimum Modified Chi-Squared [*Statistics*]
**MMCS**...... Missile and Munitions Center and School [*Army*] (RDA)
**MMCS**...... Modernization Management and Control System [*Social Security Administration*]
**MMCS**...... Multiple-Mission Command System [*NASA*]
**MMCT**...... Maritime Mobile Coastal Telegraphy
**MMCT**...... Mobile Maintenance Contact Team (MCD)
**MMCU**...... Chihuahua/Internacional [*Mexico*] [*ICAO location identifier*] (ICLI)
**MMCV**...... Ciudad Victoria [*Mexico*] [*ICAO location identifier*] (ICLI)
**MMCY**...... Celaya [*Mexico*] [*ICAO location identifier*] (ICLI)
**MMCZ**...... Cozumel/Internacional [*Mexico*] [*ICAO location identifier*] (ICLI)
**MMD**......... Maintenance Management Division [*Army*] (INF)
**MMD**......... Manual of the Medical Department [*Navy*]
**MMD**......... Mass Median Diameter
**MMD**......... Master Makeup and Display
**MMD**......... Master Monitor Display
**MMD**......... Material, Maintenance, and Distribution (MCD)
**MMD**......... Materiel Management Decision [*Military*]
**MMD**......... Materiel Management Division [*Army*]
**MMD**......... Maximum Mixing Depths [*Meteorology*]
**MMD**......... Mean Mass Density
**MMD**......... Mean Mass Diameter
**MMD**......... Mean Measure of Divergence [*Statistics*]
**MMD**......... Mean Missile [*or Mission*] Duration (KSC)
**MMD**......... Merchant Marine Detail
**MMD**......... Microwave Mixer Diode
**MMD**......... Minami Daito Jima [*Volcano Islands*] [*Airport symbol*] (OAG)
**MMD**......... Minelayer, Fast [*Navy symbol*]
**MMD**......... Missile Miss Distance [*Military*] (CAAL)
**MMD**......... Mission Management and Dissemination (MCD)
**MMD**......... Mobile Servicing Center, Maintenance Department [*Canada*]
**MMD**......... Molecular Mass Distribution [*Organic chemistry*]
**MMD**......... Money Market Directories, Inc. [*Also, an information service or system*] (IID)
**MMD**......... Moore Medical Corp. [*AMEX symbol*] (SPSG)
**MMD**......... Movement for Multi-Party Democracy [*Zambia*] [*Political party*] (ECON)
**MMD**......... Moving Map Display
**MMD**......... MSFC [*Marshall Space Flight Center*] Management Directive [*NASA*]
**MMD**......... Multimode Display
**$M^3$/(M D)**.. Cubic Meters per Meter Day
**$M^3$/($M^2$ D)**... Cubic Meters per Square Meter Day
**MMDA**...... Mass Merchandising Distributors' Association (EA)
**MMDA**...... (Methoxy)methylenedioxyamphetamine [*A hallucinogen*]
**MMDA**...... Money Market Deposit Account [*Investment term*]
**MMDB**...... Mass Memory Database (NASA)
**MMDB**...... Master Measurement Database (NASA)
**MMDC**...... Manual Master Direction Center
**MMDC**...... Master Message Display Console (MCD)

**MMDC**...... Mount Misalignment Data Collection Routine
**MMDF**...... Mission Model Data File [*NASA*] (NASA)
**MMDL**...... Microminiature Delay Line
**MMDM**..... Ciudad Mante [*Mexico*] [*ICAO location identifier*] (ICLI)
**MMDO** ..... Durango [*Mexico*] [*ICAO location identifier*] (ICLI)
**MMDPB7** ... Mammalia Depicta [*A publication*]
**MMDS**...... Maintenance Management Data System [*Military*] (CAAL)
**MMDS**...... Martin Marietta Data Systems
**MMDS**...... Multichannel Multipoint Distribution Service [*Broadcasting term*]
**MME**......... Machinist's Mate, Engineman [*Navy rating*]
**MME**......... Madame [*Mrs.*] [*French*] (EY)
**MME**......... Master of Mechanical Engineering
**M Me**......... Master of Metaphysics
**MME**......... Master of Mining Engineering
**MME**......... Master of Music Education
**MME**......... Material Military Establishment [*Formerly, OSRD*] (MCD)
**MME**......... Maximum Maintenance Effort [*Military*] (AFM)
**MMe**......... Medford Public Library, Medford, MA [*Library symbol*] [*Library of Congress*] (LCLS)
**MME**......... Mediterranean Medical Entente (EAIO)
**MME**......... Methylmethacrylate [*Organic chemistry*]
**MME**......... Micrometeoric Erosion (AAG)
**MME**......... Million Market Edition [*US News and World Report*]
**MME**......... Minimum Mean Estimate
**MME**......... Missile Maintenance Equipment (AABC)
**MME**......... Tees-Side [*England*] [*Airport symbol*] (OAG)
**MMEC**...... Machinery Maintenance Engineering Center (AFIT)
**MMEC**...... Machinery-Metals Export Club [*Later, International Industrial Marketing Club*] (EA)
**MMEC**...... Migrating Myoelectric Complex [*Physiology*]
**M Mech E** ... Master of Mechanical Engineering
**MMECT**.... Multiple-Monitored Electroconvulsive Therapy [*Schizophrenia*]
**MMED**...... Mass Median Equivalent Diameter [*of airborne particles*]
**M Med**....... Master of Medicine
**MM Ed**...... Master of Music Education
**MMED**...... Multimedia, Inc. [*NASDAQ symbol*] (NQ)
**MMEDA**... Military Medicine [*A publication*]
**MMEDDC** ... Man and Medicine [*A publication*]
**M Medii Aevi** ... Musica Medii Aevi [*A publication*]
**M Med Sc** ... Master of Medical Science
**MMEF**...... Maximal Midexpiratory Flow [*Also, MMF*] [*Medicine*]
**MMEFR**.... Maximal Midexpiratory Flow Rate [*Medicine*]
**MMel**......... Melrose Public Library, Melrose, MA [*Library symbol*] [*Library of Congress*] (LCLS)
**MM Eng**.... Master of Mechanical Engineering
**MMEP**...... Marine Mammal Events Program (EA)
**MMEP**...... Minuteman Education Program [*Air Force*] (AFM)
**MMEP**...... Multiple Modality Evoked Potential [*Neurophysiology*]
**MMEP**...... Tepic [*Mexico*] [*ICAO location identifier*] (ICLI)
**MMERD**... MER (Marine Engineers Review) [*A publication*]
**MMER Rep Dep Mech Eng Monash Univ** ... MMER Report. Department of Mechanical Engineering. Monash University [*A publication*] (APTA)
**MMES**....... Ensenada [*Mexico*] [*ICAO location identifier*] (ICLI)
**MMES**....... Master Material Erection Schedule [*Shipbuilding*] (NG)
**MMES**....... Mesdames [*Plural of Mrs.*] [*French*]
**MMES**....... MSFC [*Marshall Space Flight Center*] Mated Element Systems [*NASA*] (NASA)
**MMES**....... Southwestern Manitoba Regional Library, Melita, Manitoba [*Library symbol*] [*National Library of Canada*] (NLC)
**M Met**........ Master of Metallurgy
**MMeT**....... Tufts University, Medford, MA [*Library symbol*] [*Library of Congress*] (LCLS)
**M Met E**.... Master of Metallurgical Engineering
**MMetEng** ... Master of Metallurgy and Engineering, University of Sheffield [*British*] (DBQ)
**MMeT-EP** ... Tufts University, Eliot Pearson Department of Child Study, Medford, MA [*Library symbol*] [*Library of Congress*] (LCLS)
**MMeT-F** ... Tufts University, Fletcher School of Law and Diplomacy, Medford, MA [*Library symbol*] [*Library of Congress*] (LCLS)
**MMeT-Hi** ... Tufts University, Universalist Historical Society, Medford, MA [*Library symbol*] [*Library of Congress*] (LCLS)
**MMeT-M** ... Tufts University, Medical and Dental School, Boston, MA [*Library symbol*] [*Library of Congress*] (LCLS)
**M Met Soc Am B** ... Mining and Metallurgical Society of America. Bulletin [*A publication*]
**MMEX**...... Map Maneuver Exercise (MCD)
**MMEX**...... Mexico [*Mexico*] [*ICAO location identifier*] (ICLI)
**MMF**......... ACM Managed Multi-Market Trust, Inc. [*NYSE symbol*] (SPSG)
**MMF**......... Fleet Minelayer [*Navy symbol*]
**mmf**........... Magnetomotive Force
**MMF**......... Mamfe [*Cameroon*] [*Airport symbol*] (OAG)
**MMF**......... Maritime Life Assurance Co. [*Toronto Stock Exchange symbol*]
**MMF**......... Maximum Midexpiratory Flow [*Also, MMEF*] [*Medicine*]
**MMF**......... Medunarodni Monetarni Fond [*International Monetary Fund*] [*Yugoslavian*]
**MMF**......... Member of the Medical Faculty
**MM & F**..... Merchant Marine and Fisheries Committee [*Congressional committee*] (MSC)
**MMF**......... Microelectronics Manufacturing Facility [*Philco-Ford Corp.*] (MCD)
**MMF**......... Micromation Microfilm
**MMF**......... Micromembrane Filter
**MMF**......... Micromicrofarad (MUGU)
**MMF**......... Minelayer, Fleet [*Navy symbol*] [*Obsolete*]
**MMF**......... Mobile Magnetic Field
**MMF**......... Mobility Maintenance Facility (NVT)
**MMF**......... Module Maintenance Facility
**MMF**......... Money Market Fund [*Investment term*]
**MMF**......... Moravian Music Foundation (EA)
**MMF**......... Mutual Musicians Foundation (EA)
**MMF**......... National Association of Master Mechanics and Foremen of Naval Shore Establishments
**MMFA**...... Fireman Apprentice, Machinist's Mate, Striker [*Navy rating*]
**MMFC**...... Michael Murphy Fan Club (EA)
**MMFC-MF** ... Marilyn Monroe Fan Club - Marilyn Forever (EA)
**MMFD**...... Micromicrofarad (GPO)
**MMFN**...... Fireman, Machinist's Mate, Striker [*Navy rating*]
**MMFN**...... Manitoba Metis Federation News [*Canada*] [*A publication*]
**MMFO**...... Maintenance Management Field Office [*Military*] (MCD)
**MMFO**...... Material Management Field Office
**MMFPA**.... Man-Made Fiber Producers Association [*Later, MMFPAI*] (EA)
**MMFPAI**.. Man-Made Fiber Producers Association, Inc. (EA)
**MMFPB**.... Mill Mutual Fire Prevention Bureau [*Chicago, IL*] (EA)
**MMFQ**...... Milbank Memorial Fund. Quarterly. Health and Society [*A publication*]
**MMFR**...... Maximum Midexpiratory Flow Rate [*Physiology*]
**MMFS**....... Manufacturing Messaging Format Standards [*Automotive engineering*]
**MMFSBQ** ... Museo Civico di Storia Naturale di Verona. Memorie. Fuori Serie [*A publication*]
**MMFV**...... Manned Mars Flyby Vehicle [*Aerospace*]
**MMG**......... Machinist's Mate, Industrial Gas Generating Mechanic [*Navy rating*]
**MMG**......... MacMillan Gold [*Vancouver Stock Exchange symbol*]
**MMG**......... Magdalena Milpas Altas [*Gautemala*] [*Seismograph station code, US Geological Survey*] (SEIS)
**MMG**......... Manager Magazin [*A publication*]
**MMG**......... Mean Maternal Glucose [*Clinical chemistry*]
**MMG**......... Mechanomyography [*Medicine*]
**MMG**......... Medium Machine Gun
**M Mg**......... Monatshefte fuer Musikgeschichte [*A publication*]
**MMG**......... Motor Machine Gun Corps [*British military*] (DMA)
**MMG**......... Motor-Motor Generator [*Nuclear energy*] (NRCH)
**MMG**......... Mount Magnet [*Australia*] [*Airport symbol*] (OAG)
**MMG**......... Movie Makers Guild (EA)
**MMGB**...... Motor Machine Gun Battalion [*British military*] (DMA)
**MMGI**....... Member of the Mining, Geological, and Metallurgical Institute of India
**MMGL**...... Guadalajara/Miguel Hidalgo Y Costilla Internacional [*Mexico*] [*ICAO location identifier*] (ICLI)
**MMGM**..... Guaymas/General Jose Maria Yanez Internacional [*Mexico*] [*ICAO location identifier*] (ICLI)
**MMGS**...... Melbourne Monographs in Germanic Studies [*A publication*]
**MMGS**...... Motor Machine Gun Service [*British military*] (DMA)
**MMGT**...... Guanajuato [*Mexico*] [*ICAO location identifier*] (ICLI)
**MMH**........ Macromicromodular Hyperplasia [*Medicine*]
**MMH**........ Maintenance Man-Hours (NG)
**MMH**........ Mammoth Lakes [*California*] [*Airport symbol*] (OAG)
**MMH**........ Mammoth Lakes, CA [*Location identifier*] [*FAA*] (FAAL)
**MMH**........ Maplex Management & Holdings Ltd. [*Toronto Stock Exchange symbol*]
**MMH**........ Monmouth Airlines [*Farmingdale, NJ*] [*FAA designator*] (FAAC)
**MMH**........ Monomethylhydrazine [*Organic chemistry*]
**MMH**........ Montana: The Magazine of Western History [*A publication*]
**MMH**........ Multimode Hydrophone [*Military*] (CAAL)
**MMHA**..... Metropolitan Mutual Housing Association [*Defunct*] (EA)
**MMHC**...... Tehuacan [*Mexico*] [*ICAO location identifier*] (ICLI)
**MMH/FH** ... Maintenance Man-Hours per Flight Hours
**mmHg**........ Millimeters of Mercury [*A measurement of pressure*] (KSC)
**MMhHi**...... Marblehead Historical Society, Marblehead, MA [*Library symbol*] [*Library of Congress*] (LCLS)
**MMHi**....... Milton Historical Society, Milton, MA [*Library symbol*] [*Library of Congress*] (LCLS)
**MMHIO**.... Midwest Migrant Health Information Office (EA)
**MMH/MA** ... Mean Manhours per Maintenance Action
**MMHO**..... Hermosillo/Internacional [*Mexico*] [*ICAO location identifier*] (ICLI)
**MMH/OH** ... Maintenance Man-Hours per Operating Hours (MCD)
**MMHQ**..... Meta-Methoxyhydroquinone [*Organic chemistry*]
**MMHR**...... Maintenance Man-Hours
**MMHR/FH** ... Maintenance Man-Hours per Flight Hours (MCD)
**MMH/S**.... Maintenance Man-Hours per Sortie [*Aerospace*] (MCD)
**MMHS**..... Mechanized Materials Handling System [*Air Force*]
**MMI**.......... Athens, TN [*Location identifier*] [*FAA*] (FAAL)

**MMI**.......... Macrophage Migration Inhibition [*Cytology*]
**MMI**.......... Maintenance Management International [*A publication*]
**MMI**.......... Major Market Index
**MMI**.......... Man-Machine Interface
**MMI**.......... Management and Maintenance Inspection (NVT)
**MMI**.......... Management of Motives Index [*Test*]
**MMI**.......... Manpower Management Information
**MMI**.......... Manufacturing Message Interface [*Data communications standards*]
**MMI**.......... Materials Management Institute
**MMI**.......... Mature Market Institute [*An association*] (EA)
**MMI**.......... Mean Motility Index [*For intestine*]
**MMI**.......... Mechanized Manufacturing Information
**MMI**.......... Medical Microbiology and Immunology [*A publication*]
**MMI**.......... Medicus Mundi Internationalis [*International Organization for Cooperation in Health Care - IOCHC*] [*Nijmegen, Netherlands*] (EAIO)
**MMI**.......... Methylmercaptoimidazole [*Also, METHIMAZOLE*] [*Thyroid inhibitor*]
**MMI**.......... Michigan Molecular Institute, Inc. [*Formerly, Midland Macromolecular Institute*] [*Research center*] (RCD)
**MMI**.......... Micromagnetic Industries
**MMI**.......... Middle Management Institute [*Special Libraries Association*]
**MMI**.......... Midland Macromolecular Institute [*Midland, MI*]
**MMI**.......... Mild [*or Minimal*] Memory Impairment [*Medicine*]
**MMI**.......... Minnesota Mining & Manufacturing Co., St. Paul, MN [*OCLC symbol*] (OCLC)
**MMI**.......... Mode-Media Interaction (MCD)
**MMI**.......... Modified Mercalli Intensity [*Earthquake magnitude*] [*Seismology*]
**MMI**.......... Money Management Institute [*Commercial firm*] (EA)
**MMI**.......... Monolithic Memories, Incorporated [*Data processing*]
**MMI**.......... Montana Myotis Leukoencephalitis [*Virus*]
**MMI**.......... MSFC [*Marshall Space Flight Center*] Management Instruction [*NASA*]
**MMIA**....... Colima [*Mexico*] [*ICAO location identifier*] (ICLI)
**MMIA**....... Medical Malpractice Insurance Association
**MMIA**....... Military Mission to the Italian Army [*World War II*]
**MMIB**....... Man-Machine Integration Branch [*Ames Research Center*] [*NASA*]
**M Mic**........ Master of Microbiology
**MMIC**....... Millimeter/Microwave Integrated Circuit
**MMIC**....... Monolithic Memories, Incorporated [*NASDAQ symbol*] (NQ)
**MMIC**....... Monolithic Microwave Integrated Circuit
**MMICS**..... Maintenance Management Information and Control System
**MMID**....... Merida [*Mexico*] [*ICAO location identifier*] (ICLI)
**M Mi E**...... Master of Mining Engineering
**MMIF**........ Mutual Mortgage Insurance Fund [*Federal Housing Administration*]
**MMIFC**..... Marilyn Monroe International Fan Club (EA)
**MMII**........ Mass Marketing Insurance Institute (EA)
**MMII**........ Matrix Medica, Inc. [*NASDAQ symbol*] (NQ)
**MMII**........ Multimedia Individualized Instruction [*Army*]
**MMIIP**...... Multimedia Individualized Instructional Package [*Army*]
**MMilt**........ Milton Public Library, Milton, MA [*Library symbol*] [*Library of Congress*] (LCLS)
**MMiltC**..... Curry College, Milton, MA [*Library symbol*] [*Library of Congress*] (LCLS)
**MMIM**...... Isla Mujeres [*Mexico*] [*ICAO location identifier*] (ICLI)
**MMIM**...... MMI Medical, Inc. [*Pomona, CA*] [*NASDAQ symbol*] (NQ)
**MMIN**....... Midnite Mines, Inc. [*NASDAQ symbol*] (NQ)
**M$^3$/MIN**.... Cubic Meters per Minute
**M Minima**... Musica Minima [*A publication*]
**MMIO**....... Saltillo [*Mexico*] [*ICAO location identifier*] (ICLI)
**MMIP**....... Maintenance Management Improvement Program (MCD)
**MMIP**....... Manual of Meat Inspection Procedures [*of the USDA*]
**MMIRC**..... Mind-Machine Interaction Research Center [*University of Florida*] [*Research center*] (RCD)
**MMIS**........ Maintenance Management Information System [*Military*] (AFM)
**MMIS**........ Medicaid Management Information System [*HEW*]
**MMIS**........ Multinational Meetings Information Services BV [*Netherlands*] [*Information service or system*] (IID)
**MMIS**........ Municipal Management Information System [*Civil Defense*]
**M Misc**...... Midwestern Miscellany [*A publication*]
**MMIT**........ Iztepec [*Mexico*] [*ICAO location identifier*] (ICLI)
**MMIT**........ Man-Machine Interrogation Technique
**MMIU**....... Multiport Memory Interface Unit
**MMJ**......... Matsumoto [*Japan*] [*Airport symbol*] (OAG)
**MMJ**......... Pittsburgh, PA [*Location identifier*] [*FAA*] (FAAL)
**MMJA**....... Jalapa [*Mexico*] [*ICAO location identifier*] (ICLI)
**MMJC**....... Meridian Municipal Junior College [*Mississippi*]
**MMJ MD Med J**... MMJ. Maryland Medical Journal [*A publication*]
**MMK**......... Loparskaya [*Formerly, Murmansk*] [*USSR*] [*Geomagnetic observatory code*]
**MMK**......... Maison Master Keyed [*Locks*] (ADA)
**MMK**......... Material Mark
**MMK**......... Materialy Mongol'skoj Kommissii [*A publication*]
**MMK**......... Meriden, CT [*Location identifier*] [*FAA*] (FAAL)
**MMK**......... Mideast Markets [*A publication*]
**MMK**......... Murmansk [*USSR*] [*Airport symbol*] (OAG)
**MMKR**...... Middle Marker [*in an instrument landing system*]
**MML**......... Maintenance Management Level [*Military*]
**MML**......... Man-Machine Language [*Data processing*] (TEL)
**MML**......... Manual of Military Law [*British*]
**MML**......... Marshall [*Minnesota*] [*Airport symbol*] (OAG)
**MML**......... Marshall, MN [*Location identifier*] [*FAA*] (FAAL)
**MML**......... Master Measurements List (NASA)
**MML**......... Master of Modern Languages
**MML**......... McKinley Memorial Library, Niles, OH [*OCLC symbol*] (OCLC)
**MML**......... Menika Mining Ltd. [*Vancouver Stock Exchange symbol*]
**MML**......... Metal-Metal Laminate
**MML**......... Micromedia Limited [*ACCORD*] [*UTLAS symbol*]
**mM/L**........ Millimole/Liter [*Chemistry*]
**MML**......... Mote Marine Laboratory (NOAA)
**MML**......... Motor Movement Latency
**MML**......... Multimaterial Laminate
**MMLA**...... Majallat Majma al-Lughah al-Arabiyah [*Cairo*] [*A publication*]
**MMLA**...... Military Mission of Liaison Administration [*World War II*]
**MMLC**...... Lazaro Cardenas [*Mexico*] [*ICAO location identifier*] (ICLI)
**MMLE**...... Modified Maximum Likelihood Estimates [*Statistics*]
**MMLEC**.... Munitions Management and Labour Efficiency Committee [*British*] [*World War II*]
**MMLES**.... Map-Matching Location - Estimation System [*Aviation*]
**MMLI**....... Majallat al-Majma al-Limi al-Iraqi [*A publication*]
**MMLL**....... Michigan Regional Libraries Film Program at Cadillac [*Library network*]
**MMLM**..... Los Mochis [*Mexico*] [*ICAO location identifier*] (ICLI)
**MMLME**.. Mediterranean, Mediterranean Littoral, and/or Middle East (AABC)
**MMLMP**... Materialy po Matematiceskoj Lingvistike i Masinnomu Perevodu [*A publication*]
**MMLO**...... Leon [*Mexico*] [*ICAO location identifier*] (ICLI)
**MMLP**....... La Paz/General Manuel Marquez de Leon Internacional [*Mexico*] [*ICAO location identifier*] (ICLI)
**MMLRAI**... Mammal Review [*A publication*]
**MMLS**....... Military Microwave Landing System (MCD)
**M-M-L-S**... Model-Modes-Loads-Stresses (NASA)
**MMLT**...... Loreto [*Mexico*] [*ICAO location identifier*] (ICLI)
**MMM**........ Maine Maritime Academy, Castine, ME [*OCLC symbol*] (OCLC)
**MMM**........ Maintenance Man-Minute
**MMM**........ Maintenance Management Manual
**MMM**........ Maintenance and Material Management [*Navy*]
**MMM**........ Manned Mars Mission [*NASA*]
**MMM**........ Mark Master Mason [*Freemasonry*]
**MMM**........ Mars Mission Module
**MMM**........ Mass Media Ministries [*An association*]
**MMM**........ Material Maintenance Management (MCD)
**MM & M**... Material Manual and Memorandum (AAG)
**MMM**........ McAdam Resources, Inc. [*Toronto Stock Exchange symbol*]
**MMM**........ Measuring Monitoring Module (KSC)
**MMM**........ Medical Marketing and Media [*A publication*]
**MMM**........ Medical Materiel Manager [*Military*] (AABC)
**MMM**........ Medical Missionaries of Mary [*Roman Catholic women's religious order*]
**MMM**........ Melanges Malraux Miscellany [*A publication*]
**MMM**........ Member of the Order of Military Merit
**MMM**........ Middlemount [*Australia*] [*Airport symbol*] (OAG)
**MMM**........ Militia Mea Multiplex [*Pseudonym used by William Tooke*]
**MMM**........ Minnesota Mining & Manufacturing Co. [*Also known as 3M Co.*] [*NYSE symbol*] (SPSG)
**MMM**........ Modern Music Masters Society
**MMM**........ Money Market Monitor [*Financial Products Group*] [*Information service or system*] (IID)
**MMM**........ Monomethylmetoxuron [*Organic chemistry*]
**MMM**........ Mormon Mesa, NV [*Location identifier*] [*FAA*] (FAAL)
**MMM**........ Mouvement Militant Mauricien [*Mauritian Militant Movement*] [*Political party*] (PPW)
**MMM**........ Mouvement Mondial des Meres [*World Movement of Mothers - WMM*] [*Paris, France*] (EAIO)
**MMM**........ Multigrid Modulator Multiplier
**MMM**........ Multimission Module [*Aerospace*]
**MMM**........ Multimode Mode Matrix (MCD)
**MMM**........ Myelofibrosis and Myeloid Metaplasia [*Hematology*]
**MMMA**..... Matamoros Internacional [*Mexico*] [*ICAO location identifier*] (ICLI)
**MMMC**..... Medical Materiel Management Center [*Military*] (AABC)
**MMMC**..... Milking Machine Manufacturers Council (EA)
**MMMD**..... Merida/Lic. Manuel Crecencio Rejon Internacional [*Mexico*] [*ICAO location identifier*] (ICLI)
**MMMEP**.. Military Manpower Management Evaluation Project (NG)
**MMMF**..... Man-Made Mineral Fiber
**MMMF**..... Money Market Mutual Fund [*Investment term*]
**MMMF**..... Multinational Mixed Manned Force (NATG)
**MMMFS**... Money Market Mutual Fund Shares [*Investment term*]
**MMMI**...... Masters Merchandise Mart [*NASDAQ symbol*] (NQ)
**MMMI**...... Meat Machinery Manufacturers Institute (EA)
**MMMIS**.... Maintenance and Material Management Information System
**MMML**..... Mexicali/General Rodolfo Sanchez Taboada Internacional [*Mexico*] [*ICAO location identifier*] (ICLI)

**MMMM**.... Connect to Stations [*Communications*] (FAAC)
**MMMM**.... Morelia [*Mexico*] [*ICAO location identifier*] (ICLI)
**MMMN** .... [*The*] Memorial of Moses on Mount Nebo [*A publication*] (BJA)
**MMMOEI** ... Monographs of Marine Mollusca [*A publication*]
**MMMOS**.. Mobile Micrometeorological Observation System
**MMMPC**.. Maintenance and Material Management Project Center [*Navy*]
**MMMR**..... Medical Material Mission Reserve [*Military*] (AABC)
**MMMS**..... Maintenance and Material Management System (KSC)
**MMMS**..... Minerals, Metals, and Materials Society (EA)
**MMMSM** ... Millenaire Monastique du Mont Saint-Michel [*A publication*]
**MM & M Soc of Am** ... Member of the Mining and Metallurgical Society of America
**MMMSP**... Mouvement Militant Mauricien Socialiste Progressiste [*Mauritius Militant Socialist Progressive Movement*] (PPW)
**MMMT**..... Malignant Mixed Muellerian Tumor [*Oncology*]
**MMMT**..... Minatitlan [*Mexico*] [*ICAO location identifier*] (ICLI)
**MMMTF**... Mobilization Materiel Management Task Force
**MMMV**..... Monclova [*Mexico*] [*ICAO location identifier*] (ICLI)
**MMMX**..... Mexico/Lic. Benito Juarez Internacional [*Mexico*] [*ICAO location identifier*] (ICLI)
**MMMY**..... Monterrey/General Mariano Escobedo Internacional [*Mexico*] [*ICAO location identifier*] (ICLI)
**MMMZ**..... Mazatlan/General Rafael Buelna [*Mexico*] [*ICAO location identifier*] (ICLI)
**MMN** ........ Marathon Minerals [*Vancouver Stock Exchange symbol*]
**MMN** ........ Marianne Moore Newsletter [*A publication*]
**MMN** ........ Medial Muscle Motoneuron [*Neuroanatomy*]
**MMN** ........ Miami, FL [*Location identifier*] [*FAA*] (FAAL)
**MMN** ........ Mitteilungen zur Geschichte der Medizin und der Naturwissenschaft [*A publication*]
**MMN** ........ Modified Melin-Norkram's Agar [*Microbiology*]
**MMNA**...... Moto Morini Club of North America (EA)
**MMNAFWB** ... Master's Men of the National Association of Free Will Baptists (EA)
**MMNCAH** ... Memoires. Museum National d'Histoire Naturelle. Serie C. Sciences de la Terre [*A publication*]
**MMNG** ..... Nogales/Internacional [*Mexico*] [*ICAO location identifier*] (ICLI)
**MMNIC** .... Main Mediterranean Naval Intelligence Center [*Navy*]
**MMNL**...... Nuevo Laredo [*Mexico*] [*ICAO location identifier*] (ICLI)
**MMNPAM** ... Manitoba. Department of Mines and Natural Resources. Mines Branch. Publication [*A publication*]
**MMNRW** ... Manitoba. Department of Mines, Natural Resources, and Environment. Wildlife Research MS Reports [*Canada*] [*A publication*]
**MMNT**...... Momentum, Inc. [*NASDAQ symbol*] (NQ)
**MMNU** ..... Nautla [*Mexico*] [*ICAO location identifier*] (ICLI)
**MMO** ........ Main Meteorological Office
**MMO** ........ Maio [*Cape Verde Islands*] [*Airport symbol*] (OAG)
**MMO** ........ Marseilles, IL [*Location identifier*] [*FAA*] (FAAL)
**MMO** ........ Medio Mundo [*Nicaragua*] [*Seismograph station code, US Geological Survey*] (SEIS)
**MMO** ........ Mercantile Marine Office [*or Officer*] [*British*]
**MMO** ........ Micrographics Management Officer (MCD)
**MMO** ........ MIPR [*Military Interdepartmental Purchase Request*] Management Office (AFIT)
**MMO** ........ MMT Resources [*Vancouver Stock Exchange symbol*]
**MMO** ........ Monarch Machine Tool Co. [*NYSE symbol*] (SPSG)
**MMO** ........ Music Minus One [*Recording label*]
**MMOA**...... Mobile Modular Office Association (EA)
**MMOAG**... Research Station, Agriculture Canada [*Station de Recherches, Agriculture Canada*] Morden, Manitoba [*Library symbol*] [*National Library of Canada*] (NLC)
**MMOB**...... Military Money Order Branch (AFM)
**MMOBCD** ... Millions of Octane-Barrels per Calendar Day [*Petroleum industry*]
**MMOD** ..... Micromodule (IEEE)
**MMODE**... Mirror Mode (MCD)
**MMOECB** ... Maintenance Mode Operational Equipment Checkout Box (MCD)
**MMOG** ..... Merchant Marine Officers Guild [*Defunct*] (EA)
**mmol** .......... Millimole [*Mass*]
**MMOS**...... Message Multiplexer Operating System
**MMOS**...... Mobile Micrometeorological Observation System (KSC)
**MMOS**...... Multimode Optical Sensor (NASA)
**MMOSD**... Molybdenum Mosaic [*A publication*]
**MMOU** ..... Multilateral Memorandum of Understanding
**MMOW** .... Morden-Winkler Regional Library, Morden, Manitoba [*Library symbol*] [*National Library of Canada*] (NLC)
**MMOW** .... South Central Regional Library, Morden, Manitoba [*Library symbol*] [*National Library of Canada*] (NLC)
**MMOX**...... Oaxaca [*Mexico*] [*ICAO location identifier*] (ICLI)
**MMP**......... International Organization of Masters, Mates, and Pilots (EA)
**MMP**......... M & M Porcupine Gold Mines [*Vancouver Stock Exchange symbol*]
**MMP**......... Machined Metal Part
**MMP**......... Magyar Megujulas Partja [*Party of Hungarian Renewal*] [*Political party*] (PPE)
**MMP**......... Maintenance Management Plan
**MMP**......... Maintenance Message Process [*Telecommunications*] (TEL)
**MMP**......... Maintenance Monitor Panel (MCD)
**MMP**......... Manufacturing Methods Procedure (MCD)
**MMP**......... Marian Movement of Priests (EA)
**MMP**......... Maritime Mobile Phone
**MMP**......... Mashonaland Mounted Police [*British military*] (DMA)
**MMP**......... Master Mobilization Plan [*DoD*]
**MMP**......... Matabeleland Mounted Police [*British military*] (DMA)
**MMP**......... Merchant Marine Personnel Division [*Coast Guard*]
**MMP**......... Methadone Maintenance Program
**MMP**......... Microform Market Place [*A publication*]
**MMP**......... Microprogrammable Multiprocessor (MCD)
**MMP**......... Military Mounted Police
**MMP**......... Minimum Miscibility Pressure [*Physical chemistry*]
**MMP**......... Missile Mode Panel (MCD)
**mmp** .......... Mixed Melting Point [*Chemistry*]
**MMP**......... Modernization Management Plan
**MMP**......... Modes in Math Project [*National Science Foundation*]
**MMP**......... Momentum Management Program [*NASA*] (KSC)
**MMP**......... Mompos [*Colombia*] [*Airport symbol*] (OAG)
**MMP**......... Money Market Preferred Stock [*Investment term*]
**MMP**......... Mount Mary [*New Zealand*] [*Seismograph station code, US Geological Survey*] (SEIS)
**MMP**......... Multiplexed Message Processor
**MMPA**...... Magnetic Materials Producers Association (EA)
**MMPA**...... Marine Mammals Protection Act [*1972*]
**MMPA**...... Poza Rica [*Mexico*] [*ICAO location identifier*] (ICLI)
**MMPAS**.... Mobilization Manpower Policy Analysis [*Military*]
**MMPB**...... Manpower Management Planning Board
**MMPB**...... Puebla [*Mexico*] [*ICAO location identifier*] (ICLI)
**MMPC**...... Maritime Mobile Phone Coastal
**MMPC**...... Mobilization Material Procurement Capability
**MMPC**...... Pachuca [*Mexico*] [*ICAO location identifier*] (ICLI)
**MMPD**...... Methoxy-Meta-Phenylenediamine [*Organic chemistry*]
**MMPD**...... Money Manager Profile Diskettes [*Investment Management Institute*] [*Information service or system*] (IID)
**MMPDABC** ... Medical Materiel Program for Defense Against Biological and Chemical Agents [*Army*] (AABC)
**MMPDC**... Maritime Mobile Phone Distress and Calling
**MMPDS**... Methoxy-Meta-Phenylenediamine Sulfate [*Organic chemistry*]
**MMPE**...... Punta Penasco [*Mexico*] [*ICAO location identifier*] (ICLI)
**MMPF**...... Master Military Pay File (AABC)
**MMPF**...... Microgravity and Materials Processing Facility
**MMPG**...... Piedras Negras [*Mexico*] [*ICAO location identifier*] (ICLI)
**MMPI**....... Marquest Medical Products, Incorporated [*NASDAQ symbol*] (NQ)
**MMPI**....... Minnesota Multiphasic Personality Inventory [*Psychology*]
**MMPI**....... Montgomery Medical and Psychological Institute (EA)
**MMPJAE** ... Manufactured Milk Products Journal [*A publication*]
**MMPN**...... Uruapan [*Mexico*] [*ICAO location identifier*] (ICLI)
**MMPNC**... Medical Materiel Program for Nuclear Casualties [*Army*] (AABC)
**MMPP**...... Mechanized Market Programming Procedures [*Data processing*] (TEL)
**mmpp** ......... Millimeters Partial Pressure
**MMPR**...... Methylmercaptopurine Ribose [*Biochemistry*]
**MMPR**...... Missile Manufacturer's Planning Report
**MMPR**...... Puerto Vallarta/Lic. Gustavo Dias Ordaz Internacional [*Mexico*] [*ICAO location identifier*] (ICLI)
**MMPS**...... MEECN Message Processing System [*Military*]
**MMPS**...... Puerto Escondido [*Mexico*] [*ICAO location identifier*] (ICLI)
**MMPSE**.... Multiuse Mission Payload Support Equipment (MCD)
**MMPT** ...... Man-Machine Partnership Translation [*Telecommunications*] (IEEE)
**MMPT** ...... Monitored and Modulated Periodontal Therapeutics [*Dentistry*]
**MMPU**...... Memory Manager and Protect Unit (IEEE)
**MMPVS**.... Modified Military Pay Voucher System (AABC)
**MMQ** ........ Management Quarterly [*A publication*]
**MMQ** ........ Metalectrovisie [*A publication*]
**MMQ** ........ Minimum Manufacturing Quality
**MMQT**...... Queretaro [*Mexico*] [*ICAO location identifier*] (ICLI)
**MMQUB**... Mining and Metallurgy. Quarterly [*English Translation*] [*A publication*]
**MMR**......... Austin, TX [*Location identifier*] [*FAA*] (FAAL)
**MMR**......... Mach Meter Reading (MCD)
**MMR**......... Machinist's Mate, Refrigeration [*Navy rating*]
**MMR**......... Magnetically-Modulated Microwave Reflection [*Spectrometer*]
**MMR**......... Main Memory Register
**MMR**......... Maine State Department of Marine Resources, West Boothbay Harbor, ME [*OCLC symbol*] (OCLC)
**MMR**......... Maintenance Management Review (MCD)
**MMR**......... Management Milestone Records [*Navy*] (NG)
**MMR**......... Mass Miniature Radiography
**MMR**......... Master Microfiche Record
**MMR**......... Materiel Management Review [*DoD*]
**MMR**......... Maternal Mortality Rate [*Gynecology*]
**MMR**......... Measles-Mumps-Rubella [*Immunology*]
**MMR**......... Miniature Micropower Resistor
**MMR**......... Minimum Marginal Return

**MMR**......... Minnedosa Regional Library, Minnedosa, Manitoba [*Library symbol*] [*National Library of Canada*] (NLC)
**MMR**......... Missed Message Rate (CAAL)
**MMR**......... Mitchell's Maritime Register [*England*] [*A publication*] (DLA)
**MMR**......... Mixed Municipal Refuse
**MMR**......... Mobilization Materiel Requirement [*Military*]
**MMR**......... Modular Multiband Radiometer
**MMR**......... Monomethylolrutin [*Organic chemistry*]
**MMR**......... Monroe Mendelsohn Research, Inc. [*Information service or system*] (IID)
**MMR**......... Monthly Musical Record [*A publication*]
**MMR**......... Monumental Maintenance Requirements (MCD)
**MMR**......... Moore McCormack Resources, Inc. [*Formerly, Moore & McCormack Lines, Inc.*] [*NYSE symbol*] (SPSG)
**MMR**......... Morris Minor Registry (EA)
**MMR**......... Motorized Microfilm Reader
**MMR**......... Multimode RADAR
**MMR**......... Multimode Receiver
**MMR**......... Multiple Match Resolver
**MMR**......... Mustang Motorcycle Registry (EA)
**MMRA**...... Mobilization Materiel Requirement Adjustment [*Military*] (NG)
**MMRB**...... Maintenance Management Review Board (MCD)
**MMRB**...... Materiel Management Review Board (AFIT)
**MMRB**...... MOS [*Military Occupational Specialty*] Medical Retention Board [*Army*]
**MMRBM**.. Mobile Medium-Range Ballistic Missile [*Air Force*]
**MMRC**...... Materials and Mechanics Research Center [*Army*] (MCD)
**MMRC**...... Mountain Meadow Research Center [*Colorado State University*] [*Research center*] (RCD)
**M-MRCP**.. Multi-Management Resolution Control Processor
**MMRD**...... Materials and Molecular Research Division [*Lawrence Berkeley Laboratory*] [*Research center*] (RCD)
**MMRD**...... Miniature Multipurpose RADIAC Device (MCD)
**MMRE**...... Materials Methods Research and Engineering (MCD)
**MMRH**...... MMR Holding Corp. [*NASDAQ symbol*] (NQ)
**MMRI**....... Mississippi Mineral Resources Institute [*University of Mississippi*] [*Research center*] (RCD)
**MMRI**....... Multi-Media Reviews Index [*A publication*]
**MMRIM**... Mat Molding Reaction Injection Molding [*Plastics technology*]
**MMR Miner Met Rev**... MMR. Minerals and Metals Review [*India*] [*A publication*]
**MMRP**...... Marine Corps Midrange Objectives Plan (MCD)
**MMRP**...... Minerals and Materials Research Programs [*North Carolina State University*] [*Research center*] (RCD)
**MMRP**...... Missile Master Replacement Program
**MMRR**...... Military Manpower Requirements Report (MCD)
**MMRRI**..... Utah Mining and Minerals Resources Research Institute [*University of Utah*] [*Research center*] (RCD)
**MMR & S**... Military Medical Research and Services Program (CINC)
**MMRSA**.... Methods in Medical Research [*A publication*]
**MMRT**...... Mini Mart Corp. [*NASDAQ symbol*] (NQ)
**MMRX**...... Medi-Mail, Inc. [*NASDAQ symbol*] (NQ)
**MMRX**...... Reynosa/General Lucio Blanco Internacional [*Mexico*] [*ICAO location identifier*] (ICLI)
**MMS**......... British vessel corresponding to US YMS
**MMS**......... Macbride Museum Society (EA)
**MMS**......... Machinist's Mate, Shop Mechanic [*Navy rating*]
**MMS**......... Macmillan's Manuals for Students [*A publication*]
**MMS**......... Magnetic Minesweeping (MSA)
**MMS**......... Maintenance Management Software
**MMS**......... Man-Machine System (MCD)
**MMS**......... Manpower Management Staff [*NATO*] (NATG)
**MMS**......... Manpower Management System [*Marine Corps*]
**MMS**......... Manufacturing Message Specification [*or Standard*] [*Data processing*]
**MMS**......... Manufacturing Monitoring System [*Data processing*] (IBMDP)
**MMS**......... Marks, MS [*Location identifier*] [*FAA*] (FAAL)
**MMS**......... Mass Memory Store [*Data processing*] (IEEE)
**MMS**......... Mast Mounted Sight
**MMS**......... Master of Management Studies
**MMS**......... Master of Mechanical Science
**MMS**......... Master of Medical Science
**MMS**......... Matam [*Senegal*] [*Seismograph station code, US Geological Survey*] [*Closed*] (SEIS)
**MMS**......... Maternity and Maternity Services [*British*]
**MMS**......... Medical Mission Sisters (EA)
**M Ms**......... Medizinische Monatsschrift [*A publication*]
**MMS**......... Member of the Institute of Management Services [*British*] (DBQ)
**MMS**......... Memory Management System
**MMS**......... Merchant Marine Safety
**MMS**......... Metabolic Monitoring System
**MMS**......... Metacaine Methanesulfonate [*Local anesthetic*]
**MMS**......... Metastable Metal Surface [*Catalyst science*]
**MMS**......... Meteorological Measuring System
**MMS**......... Methodist Missionary Society [*British*]
**MMS**......... Methyl Methanesulfonate [*Experimental mutagen*]
**MMS**......... Metropolitan Museum. Studies [*A publication*]
**MMS**......... Mexican Meteorological Service (NOAA)
**MMS**......... Michigan Multispectral Scanner
**MMS**......... Microfiche Management System
**MMS**......... Micromembrane Suppressor [*Ion chromatography*]
**MMS**......... Mid Maine Savings Bank [*AMEX symbol*] (SPSG)
**MMS**......... Middle Meningeal System [*Neuroanatomy*]
**MMS**......... Military Message Service [*British military*] (DMA)
**MM/S**........ Millimeters per Second
**MMS**......... Minerals Management Service [*Department of the Interior*] [*Washington, DC*]
**MMS**......... Mini-Mental State [*Psychometric testing*]
**MMS**......... Missile Mix Study [*NAVAIR*] (NG)
**MMS**......... Missile Monitor System [*Army*]
**MMS**......... Mission Modular Spacecraft (MCD)
**MMS**......... Mississippi County Community College Library, Blytheville, AR [*OCLC symbol*] (OCLC)
**MMS**......... Mobile Monitoring Station
**MMS**......... Modular Measuring System
**MMS**......... Modular Modeling System
**MMS**......... Modular Multiband Scanner (MCD)
**MMS**......... Modular Multimission Spacecraft [*NASA*]
**MMS**......... Modular Multispectral Scanner
**MMS**......... Money Management System
**MMS**......... Money Market Services, Inc. [*Belmont, CA*] [*Database producer*]
**MMS**......... Moravian Missionary Society
**MMS**......... Motor Minesweeper
**MMS**......... Muenstersche Mittelalter-Schriften [*A publication*]
**MMS**......... Multimedia System
**MMS**......... Multimission Modular Spacecraft [*NASA*] (NASA)
**MMS**......... Multimission Ship [*DoD*]
**MMS**......... Multimode Seeker (MCD)
**MMS**......... Multiplex Modulation System
**MMS**......... Munitions Maintenance Squadron [*Air Force*]
**MMS**......... Munitions Maintenance and Storage
**MMS**......... Musical Masterpiece Society [*Record label*] [*USA, Europe*]
**MMS**......... Myeloma Morphology Score [*Oncology*]
**$M^3/(M^2 S)$**... Cubic Meters per Square Meter Second
**MMSA**...... Manual Molder Shielded Arc
**MMSA**...... Master of Midwifery, Society of Apothecaries
**MMSA**...... Materials and Methods Standards Association (EA)
**MMSA**...... Medical Mycological Society of the Americas (EA)
**MMSA**...... Mercantile Marine Service Association [*British*]
**MMSA**...... Methods and Materials Standards Association (EA)
**MMSA**...... Military Medical Supply Agency [*Later, Defense Medical Supply Center*]
**MMSA**...... Mining and Metallurgical Society of America (EA)
**MMSA**...... Mitsubishi Motor Sales of America, Inc.
**MMSA**...... Multiple-Mission Support Area [*Space Flight Operations Facility, NASA*]
**MM & SC**... Major Mission and Support Category
**MM Sc**....... Master of Mechanical Science
**MM Sc**....... Master of Medical Science
**MMSC**...... Mediterranean Marine Sorting Center
**MMSC**...... Minnesota Metropolitan State College
**MMSC**...... Multimode SONAR Console
**MMSCEC**... Marine Mammal Science [*A publication*]
**MMSCFD**... Million Standard Cubic Feet per Day
**M Msch W**... Mitteilungen aus dem Markscheidewesen [*A publication*]
**MMSCV**.... Manned Military System Capability Vehicle
**MMSD**...... Mixed Motor and Sensory Deficits [*Neurology*]
**MMSD**...... San Jose Del Cabo [*Mexico*] [*ICAO location identifier*] (ICLI)
**MMSE**....... Mini-Mental State Examination [*Psychometrics*]
**MMSE**....... Minimum Mean Squared Error
**MMSE**....... Mission Module Simulation Equipment (MCD)
**MMSE**....... Multiple-Mission Support Equipment [*NASA*]
**MMSJ**....... Medical Mobilization for Soviet Jewry (EA)
**MMSL**....... Microgravity Materials Science Laboratory [*NASA*]
**MMSM**..... Santa Lucia [*Mexico*] [*ICAO location identifier*] (ICLI)
**MMSP**....... San Luis Potosi [*Mexico*] [*ICAO location identifier*] (ICLI)
**MMSQ**...... Munitions Maintenance Squadron [*Air Force*]
**MMSR**...... Machinist's Mate, Ship Repair [*Navy rating*]
**MMSR**...... Master Materiel Support Record
**MMSR**...... Monthly Materiel Status Report
**MMSR**...... Multiple-Mission Support Recording [*NASA*]
**MMSRE**.... Machinist's Mate, Ship Repair, Engine Operator [*Navy rating*]
**MMSRI**..... Machinist's Mate, Ship Repair, Instrument Maker [*Navy rating*]
**MMSRO**... Machinist's Mate, Ship Repair, Outside Machinist [*Navy rating*]
**MMSRS**.... Machinist's Mate, Ship Repair, Inside Machinist [*Navy rating*]
**MMSS**....... Manned Maneuverable Space System
**MMSS**....... Manual Mode Space Simulator
**MMSS**....... Marine Meteorological Services System [*WMO*] (MSC)
**MMSS**....... Massachusettensis Medicinae Societatis Socius [*Fellow of the Massachusetts Medical Society*]
**MMSS**....... Mast Mounted Sight System (MCD)
**MMSS**....... Measurement Specialties, Inc. [*Wayne, NJ*] [*NASDAQ symbol*] (NQ)
**MMSS**....... Missile Motion Subsystem
**MMSS**....... Multimodule Space Station [*NASA*] (KSC)
**MMST**....... MedMaster Systems, Inc. [*Logan, UT*] [*NASDAQ symbol*] (NQ)

**MM St**....... Mitteilungsblatt fuer Mathematische Statistik und Ihre Anwendungsgebiete [*A publication*]
**MMST**....... Multimode Storage Tube
**MMSW**..... International Union of Mine, Mill, and Smelter Workers [*Later, USWA*]
**MMT**......... Alpha-Methyl-m-tyrosine [*Pharmacology*]
**MMT**......... Columbia, SC [*Location identifier*] [*FAA*] (FAAL)
**MMT**......... Macmillan's Manuals for Teachers [*A publication*]
**MMT**......... Main Mantle Thrust [*Geology*]
**MMT**......... Management Technology [*A publication*]
**MMT**......... Manual Muscle Test
**MM & T**.... Manufacturing Methods and Technology [*Program*] [*Army Materiel Command*] (RDA)
**MMT**......... Marine Minerals Technology [*National Oceanic and Atmospheric Administration*]
**MMT**......... Maritime Mobile Telegraph
**MMT**......... Mass Memory Test (NASA)
**MMT**......... Master of Medical Technology
**MMT**......... Math Model Test (MCD)
**MMT**......... Merchant Marine Technical Division [*Coast Guard*]
**MMT**......... Metal Mount
**MMT**......... Methylcyclopentadienylmanganese Tricarbonyl [*Organic chemistry*]
**MMT**......... MFS Multimarket Income [*NYSE symbol*] (SPSG)
**MMT**......... Military Mail Terminal (AFM)
**MMT**......... Million Metric Tons (IMH)
**MMT**......... Mini Mobile Target [*Military*] (CAAL)
**MMT**......... Missile Maintenance Technician (AABC)
**MMT**......... Missile Mate Test
**MMT**......... Mobile Maintenance Team (MCD)
**MMT**......... Modernization Management Team [*Military*] (CAAL)
**mmt**............ Monomethoxytrityl [*As substituent on nucleoside*] [*Biochemistry*]
**MMT**......... Monthly Mean Temperature [*Meteorology*]
**MMT**......... Monument Resources [*Vancouver Stock Exchange symbol*]
**mMT**......... Mouse Metallothionein [*Biochemistry*]
**MMT**......... Muenchner Mode-Tage [*Federal Republic of Germany*] (TSPED)
**MMT**......... Multimode Tonotron
**MMT**......... Multiple-Mirror Telescope [*Mount Hopkins, AZ*] [*Jointly operated by Smithsonian Institution and the University of Arizona*] [*Astronomy*]
**MMT**......... Multiple-Mission Telemetry [*NASA*]
**MMT**......... Murine Metallothionein [*Biochemistry*]
**MMTA**...... Mercantile Marine Trawlermen's Association [*A union*] [*British*]
**MMTA**...... Minor Metals Traders' Association [*British*]
**MMTA**...... Tlaxcala [*Mexico*] [*ICAO location identifier*] (ICLI)
**MMTB**...... Tuxtla Gutierrez [*Mexico*] [*ICAO location identifier*] (ICLI)
**MMTC**...... Marine Minerals Technology Center [*National Oceanic and Atmospheric Administration*]
**MMTC**...... Maritime Mobile Telegraphy Calling
**MMTC**...... Materiel Management Training Center [*Military*]
**MMTC**...... Metro Manila Transit Corporation [*Philippines*] (DS)
**MMTC**...... Mouvement Mondial des Travailleurs Chretiens [*World Movement of Christian Workers - WMCW*] [*Brussels, Belgium*] (EAIO)
**MMTC**...... Torreon [*Mexico*] [*ICAO location identifier*] (ICLI)
**MMTD**...... Multimode Tonotron Display
**MMTDC**... Maritime Mobile Telegraph Distress and Calling
**MMTF**....... Military Manpower Task Force
**MMTG**...... Tuxtla Gutierrez [*Mexico*] [*ICAO location identifier*] (ICLI)
**MMTGS**.... Murray Mortgage Investors SBI [*NASDAQ symbol*] (NQ)
**MMTJ**....... Tijuana/General Abelardo L. Rodriguez Internacional [*Mexico*] [*ICAO location identifier*] (ICLI)
**MMTL**....... Tulancingo [*Mexico*] [*ICAO location identifier*] (ICLI)
**MMT/M**... Missile Maintenance Technician/Mechanic (AAG)
**MMTM**..... Multimedia Training Material
**MMTM**..... Tampico/General Francisco Javier Mina Internacional [*Mexico*] [*ICAO location identifier*] (ICLI)
**MMTN**...... Tamuin [*Mexico*] [*ICAO location identifier*] (ICLI)
**MMTO**...... Multiple Mirror Telescope Observatory [*Research center*] (RCD)
**MMTO**...... Toluca [*Mexico*] [*ICAO location identifier*] (ICLI)
**MMTP**...... Methyl(methylthio)phenol [*Organic chemistry*]
**MMTP**...... Tapachula [*Mexico*] [*ICAO location identifier*] (ICLI)
**MMTQ**...... Tequesquitengo [*Mexico*] [*ICAO location identifier*] (ICLI)
**MMTR**...... Mean-Maintenance-Man-Hours to Repair (MCD)
**MMTR**...... Military Manpower Training Report (MCD)
**M/MTRG**... Main Metering [*Automotive engineering*]
**MMTS**....... Multiple-Mission Telemetry System [*NASA*]
**MMTSF**.... Million Metric Tons of Standard Fuel
**MMTT**...... Multimechanical Thermal Treatment
**MMTTU**... Modular Magnetic Tape Transport Units (MCD)
**MMTV**...... Mouse Mammary Tumor Virus
**MMTX**...... Tuxpan [*Mexico*] [*ICAO location identifier*] (ICLI)
**MMTY**...... Monterrey [*Mexico*] [*ICAO location identifier*] (ICLI)
**MMU**........ Main Memory Unit
**MMU**........ Manned Maneuvering Unit [*Aerospace*]
**MMU**........ Mass Memory Unit
**MMU**........ Medical Maintenance Unit [*Army*] [*World War II*]
**MMU**........ Memory Management Unit [*Computer chip*]
**MMU**........ Metered Message Unit [*Telecommunications*] (TEL)
**MMU**........ Midcourse Maneuvering Unit [*Aerospace*] (MCD)
**MMU**........ Midcourse Measurement Unit [*Aerospace*] (KSC)
**MMU**........ Millimass Unit (DEN)
**MMU**........ Missile Motion Unit
**MMU**........ Mobile Monitoring Unit
**MMU**........ Modular Maneuvering Unit [*Aerospace*]
**MMU**........ Morristown, NJ [*Location identifier*] [*FAA*] (FAAL)
**MMU**........ Multimessage Unit [*Telecommunications*] (TEL)
**MMU**........ University of Missouri, Columbia, Health Sciences Library, Columbia, MO [*OCLC symbol*] (OCLC)
**MMUC**...... Midwest Medical Union Catalog
**M'Mul Ch SC**... M'Mullan's South Carolina Equity Reports [*1840-42*] [*A publication*] (DLA)
**M'Mul LSC**... M'Mullan's South Carolina Law Reports [*1840-42*] [*A publication*] (DLA)
**MMUN**..... Cancun [*Mexico*] [*ICAO location identifier*] (ICLI)
**M Mus**....... Master of Music
**M Mus Ed**... Master of Music Education
**M Mus Lauriacum**... Mitteilungen des Museumsvereins "Lauriacum" [*Enns*] [*A publication*]
**M Mus (Mus Ed)**... Master of Music in Music Education
**M Mus (Mus Lit)**... Master of Music in Music Literature
**M Mus (PSM)**... Master of Music in Public School Music
**M Mus (RCM)**... Master of Music, Royal College of Music
**M Mus (W Inst)**... Master of Music in Wind Instruments
**MMV**......... Maize Mosaic Virus
**MMV**......... Mast Mount Visionics (MCD)
**MMV**......... Maubois, Mocquot, and Vassal [*Cheesemaking*]
**MMV**......... McMinnville, OR [*Location identifier*] [*FAA*] (FAAL)
**MMV**......... Monostable Multivibrator
**MMVA**...... Villahermosa [*Mexico*] [*ICAO location identifier*] (ICLI)
**MMVIEB**... Memoirs. Museum of Victoria [*A publication*]
**MMVR**...... Veracruz/General Heriberto Jara [*Mexico*] [*ICAO location identifier*] (ICLI)
**MMVS**...... Mast Mount Visionics System (MCD)
**MMW**........ Mean Maximum Weight
**MMW**........ Miami, OK [*Location identifier*] [*FAA*] (FAAL)
**MMW**........ Millimeter Wave
**MMW**........ Muenchener Medizinische Wochenschrift [*A publication*]
**MMW**........ Multimegawatt (SDI)
**MMWCS**... Multimission Weapons Control System
**MMWE**..... Millimeter Wave Experiment
**MMWG**..... Military Mobilization Working Group
**MMWOA**... Muenchener Medizinische Wochenschrift [*A publication*]
**MMWOAU**... Muenchener Medizinische Wochenschrift [*A publication*]
**MMWR**..... Morbidity and Mortality Weekly Report [*Information service or system*] [*A publication*]
**MMWR CDC Surveill Summ**... MMWR [*Morbidity and Mortality Weekly Report*] - CDC [*Center for Disease Control*] Surveillance Summaries [*A publication*]
**MMWR Surveill Summ**... MMWR [*Morbidity and Mortality Weekly Report*] Surveillance Summaries [*A publication*]
**MMX**......... Mastergroup Multiplex [*AT & T*]
**MMX**......... Memory Multiplexer [*Data processing*]
**MMY**......... Many, LA [*Location identifier*] [*FAA*] (FAAL)
**MMY**......... Mental Measurements Yearbook [*Psychology*] [*A publication*]
**MMY**......... Military Man-Years (AABC)
**MMY**......... Miyakojima [*Japan*] [*Airport symbol*] (OAG)
**MMYD**...... Mental Measurements Yearbook Database [*University of Nebraska, Lincoln*] [*Database*]
**MMZ**......... Maimana [*Afghanistan*] [*Airport symbol*] [*Obsolete*] (OAG)
**MMZC**...... Zacatecas [*Mexico*] [*ICAO location identifier*] (ICLI)
**MMZH**...... Zihuatanejo [*Mexico*] [*ICAO location identifier*] (ICLI)
**MMZM**..... Zamora [*Mexico*] [*ICAO location identifier*] (ICLI)
**MMZO**...... Manzanillo [*Mexico*] [*ICAO location identifier*] (ICLI)
**MMZP**...... Zapopan [*Mexico*] [*ICAO location identifier*] (ICLI)
**MMZT**...... Mazatlan [*Mexico*] [*ICAO location identifier*] (ICLI)
**MM Zt**....... Militaer-Musikerzeitung [*A publication*]
**MN**........... Commercial Air Services [*Pty.*] Ltd. [*South Africa*] [*ICAO designator*] (FAAC)
**MN**........... Machinery Numeral [*Marine insurance*] (DS)
**MN**........... Madeleine Mines Ltd. [*Toronto Stock Exchange symbol*]
**MN**........... Magnetic North
**MN**........... Main (AAG)
**MN**........... Main Network [*Telecommunications*] (TEL)
**MN**........... Making of the Nations [*A publication*]
**MN**........... Malawi News [*A publication*]
**MN**........... Management Network (MCD)
**MN**........... Manchester Evening News [*A publication*]
**M et N**....... Mane et Nocte [*Morning and Night*] [*Pharmacy*]
**Mn**............ Manganese [*Chemical element*]
**MN**........... Manpower, Inc. [*NYSE symbol*] (SPSG)
**MN**........... Mantle Nerve
**MN**........... Manual
**MN**........... Manx Airlines Ltd.
**MN**........... Mare Nectaris [*Sea of Nectar*] [*Lunar area*]
**MN**........... Master Navigator [*Air Force*]
**MN**........... Master of Nursing
**MN**........... Material Number

**MN** ........... Materiel Needs [*Army*]
**MN** ........... Maxim Nordenfelt Gun
**M & N**........ May and November [*Denotes semiannual payments of interest or dividends in these months*] [*Business term*]
**Mn** ............ Mean Range [*Difference in height between mean high water and mean low water*] [*Tides and currents*]
**MN** ........... Mecanorma [*Graphic artist products*] [*British*]
**MN** ........... Media Network (EA)
**MN** ........... Median Nerve [*Anatomy*]
**M & N**........ Medical and Nursing [*Red Cross Disaster Services*]
**MN** ........... Meganewton
**MN** ........... Meniere's Network [*An association*] (EA)
**MN** ........... Meningopneumonitis [*Medicine*]
**MN** ........... Merchant Navy
**m-N** ........... Meter-Newton
**MN** ........... Michigan [*Obsolete*] (ROG)
**MN** ........... Micrococcal Nuclease [*Also, MCN*] [*An enzyme*]
**MN** ........... Microneutralization [*Chemistry*]
**MN** ........... Midnight
**MN** ........... Migrating Neuron [*Neuroanatomy*]
**mN** ............ Millinormal [*One one-thousandth of normal*]
**MN** ........... Mineman [*Navy rating*]
**MN** ........... Minnesota [*Postal code*]
**Mn** ............ Minnesota State Law Library, St. Paul, MN [*Library symbol*] [*Library of Congress*] (LCLS)
**MN** ........... Minor Subject Descriptor [*Online database field identifier*]
**MN** ........... Miscellanea Numismatica [*A publication*]
**MN** ........... Mnemonic
**Mn** ............ Mnemosyne [*A publication*]
**Mn** ............ Modern [*Linguistics*]
**M/N**.......... Moneda Nacional [*National Money*] [*Spanish*]
**MN** ........... Mongolia [*ANSI two-letter standard code*] (CNC)
**MN** ........... Mononuclear [*Hematology*]
**MN** ........... Month Name (BJA)
**MN** ........... Monumenta Nipponica [*A publication*]
**MN** ........... Moon (ROG)
**MN** ........... Moreh Nebukhim [*Maimonides*] (BJA)
**M & N**........ Morning and Night [*Medicine*]
**MN** ........... Moscow News [*A publication*]
**MN** ........... Motor Neuron [*Anatomy*]
**MN** ........... Multinodular [*or Multinodulate*] [*Medicine*]
**MN** ........... Museum News [*A publication*]
**MN** ........... Mutato Nomine [*The Name Being Changed*] [*Latin*]
**MN** ........... Myoneural [*Medicine*]
**MN1** .......... Mineman, First Class [*Navy rating*]
**MN2** .......... Mineman, Second Class [*Navy rating*]
**MN3** .......... Mineman, Third Class [*Navy rating*]
**MNA**.......... Augsburg College, Minneapolis, MN [*OCLC symbol*] (OCLC)
**M Na**.......... Master of Navigation
**MNA**.......... Master of Nursing Administration
**MN(A)**....... Material Need (Abbreviated) (MCD)
**MNA**.......... Maximum Noise Area
**MNA**.......... Medizinisch-Naturwissenschaftliches Archiv [*A publication*]
**MNA**.......... Melanguane [*Indonesia*] [*Airport symbol*] (OAG)
**MNA**.......... Melinga Resources Ltd. [*Vancouver Stock Exchange symbol*]
**MNA**.......... Member of the National Assembly [*British*]
**MNA**.......... Meta-Nitroaniline [*Organic chemistry*]
**MNA**.......... Methoxynaphthylamine [*Organic chemistry*]
**MNA**.......... Methylnitroaniline [*Organic chemistry*]
**MNA**.......... Mina [*Nevada*] [*Seismograph station code, US Geological Survey*] (SEIS)
**MNA**.......... Missing, Not Enemy Action
**M & NA**..... Missouri & North Arkansas Railroad [*Nickname: May Never Arrive*]
**MNA**.......... Mouvement d'Action Politique et Sociale [*Political and Social Action Movement*] [*Switzerland*] [*Political party*] (PPW)
**MNA**.......... Mouvement National Algerien [*National Algerian Movement*]
**MNA**.......... Multinetwork Area [*Term used in TV ratings*]
**MNA**.......... Multishare Network Architecture [*Mitsubishi Corp.*] (BUR)
**MNA,B,C**.. Main Bus A,B, or C (NASA)
**MNAC**........ Maine National Corporation [*NASDAQ symbol*] (NQ)
**Mn-Ad** ....... Minnesota State Department of Administration, Budget Library, St. Paul, MN [*Library symbol*] [*Library of Congress*] (LCLS)
**MNAEA**.... Member of the National Association of Estate Agents [*British*] (DBQ)
**Mn-Ag** ....... Minnesota Department of Agriculture, St. Paul, MN [*Library symbol*] [*Library of Congress*] (LCLS)
**MnAlb** ....... Albert Lea Public Library, Albert Lea, MN [*Library symbol*] [*Library of Congress*] (LCLS)
**MN & ALOA** ... Merchant Navy and Air Line Officers' Association [*A union*] [*British*] (DS)
**MNAM**...... Military North African Mission [*World War II*]
**MNam** ....... Nantucket Athenaeum, Nantucket, MA [*Library symbol*] [*Library of Congress*] (LCLS)
**MnAnA**...... Anoka-Ramsey Community College, Anoka, MN [*Library symbol*] [*Library of Congress*] (LCLS)
**MnAnGS** ... Anoka County Genealogical Society, Anoka, MN [*Library symbol*] [*Library of Congress*] (LCLS)
**MnAnHi** .... Anoka County Historical Society, Anoka, MN [*Library symbol*] [*Library of Congress*] (LCLS)
**MNanHi**.... Nantucket Historical Association, Nantucket, MA [*Library symbol*] [*Library of Congress*] (LCLS)
**MNanMM** ... Nantucket Maria Mitchell Association, Nantucket, MA [*Library symbol*] [*Library of Congress*] (LCLS)
**MnAnVT** ... Anoka Area Vocational Technical Institute, Anoka, MN [*Library symbol*] [*Library of Congress*] (LCLS)
**MNanW** .... Nantucket Whaling Museum, Nantucket, MA [*Library symbol*] [*Library of Congress*] (LCLS)
**MNAO** ...... Mobile Naval Airfield Organization
**MNAOA**.... Merchant Navy and Air Line Officers' Association [*A union*] [*British*] (DCTA)
**MN Arch** ... Master of Naval Architecture
**MNAS** ....... Member of the National Academy of Sciences
**MNASTD** ... Multicultural Network of the American Society for Training and Development (EA)
**MNAT**....... NoNAT Capital Corp. [*Kansas City, MO*] [*NASDAQ symbol*] (NQ)
**MNatQ** ...... United States Quartermaster Research and Development Center, Natick, MA [*Library symbol*] [*Library of Congress*] (LCLS)
**MNatRes**... Master of Natural Resources (ADA)
**MnAu**......... Austin Public Library, Austin, MN [*Library symbol*] [*Library of Congress*] (LCLS)
**MNAU** ...... Mobile Naval Airfield Unit
**MnAuH** ..... Hormel Institute, University of Minnesota, Austin, MN [*Library symbol*] [*Library of Congress*] (LCLS)
**MnAuPS**.... Austin Public Schools Media, Austin, MN [*Library symbol*] [*Library of Congress*] (LCLS)
**MnAuS** ...... Austin State Junior College, Austin, MN [*Library symbol*] [*Library of Congress*] (LCLS)
**MnAuV**...... Austin Vocational Technical Institute, Austin, MN [*Library symbol*] [*Library of Congress*] (LCLS)
**MnAvZ** ...... Minnesota Zoological Garden, Apple Valley, MN [*Library symbol*] [*Library of Congress*] (LCLS)
**MNAWL**... Mededeelingen. Koninklijke Nederlandsche Akademie van Wetenschappen. Afdeling Letterkunde [*A publication*]
**MNB**.......... Bemidji State University, Bemidji, MN [*OCLC symbol*] (OCLC)
**MNB**.......... Maverick Naturalite Beef Corp. [*Vancouver Stock Exchange symbol*]
**MNB**.......... Median Neuroblast [*Cytology*]
**MNB**.......... Mint No Box [*Doll collecting*]
**MNB**.......... Moanda [*Zaire*] [*Airport symbol*] (OAG)
**MNB**.......... Mobile Naval Base [*British military*] (DMA)
**MNB**.......... Moscow Narodny Bank Ltd. [*USSR*]
**MNB**.......... Multinozzle Base
**MNB**.......... Texte de Louvre [*Paris*]: Monuments de Ninive et de Babylone [*A publication*] (BJA)
**MNBA**....... Minimum Normal Burst Altitude
**MNBA**....... Mono-normal-butylamine [*Organic chemistry*]
**M/NBA**..... Multi/National Business Association (EA)
**MNBC**....... Miners National Bancorp, Inc. [*NASDAQ symbol*] (NQ)
**MNBDF** .... Meta-Nitrobenzenediazonium Tetrafluoroborate [*Organic chemistry*]
**MNBDO**.... Mobile Naval Base Defence Organization [*British*] [*World War II*]
**MNBedf**..... New Bedford Free Public Library, New Bedford, MA [*Library symbol*] [*Library of Congress*] (LCLS)
**MNBedfHi** ... Old Dartmouth Historical Society, New Bedford Whaling Museum, New Bedford, MA [*Library symbol*] [*Library of Congress*] (LCLS)
**MnBemS**.... Bemidji State College [*Later, Bemidji State University*], Bemidji, MN [*Library symbol*] [*Library of Congress*] (LCLS)
**MNBL** ....... Bluefields [*Nicaragua*] [*ICAO location identifier*] (ICLI)
**MN Bl**....... Mathematisch-Naturwissenschaftliche Blaetter [*A publication*]
**MNBLE**..... Modified Nearly Best Linear Estimator [*Statistics*]
**MNBR** ....... Los Brasiles/Carlos Ulloa [*Nicaragua*] [*ICAO location identifier*] (ICLI)
**MnBrC**....... Brainerd Community College, Brainerd, MN [*Library symbol*] [*Library of Congress*] (LCLS)
**MnBulR**..... Range Geneaological Society, Buhl, MN [*Library symbol*] [*Library of Congress*] (LCLS)
**MNBZ** ....... Bonanza [*Nicaragua*] [*ICAO location identifier*] (ICLI)
**MNC**.......... Concordia College, St. Paul, MN [*OCLC symbol*] (OCLC)
**MNC**.......... Magnocellular Neurosecretory Cells
**MNC**.......... Major NATO Command [*or Commander*] (NATG)
**MNC**.......... Mental Nurses' Cooperation (ROG)
**MNC**.......... Microcomputer Numerical Control (MCD)
**MNC**.......... Mineman, Chief [*Navy rating*]
**Mn-C** ......... Minnesota State Department of Corrections, St. Paul, MN [*Library symbol*] [*Library of Congress*] (LCLS)
**MNC**.......... MIT Freightlines Ltd. [*Toronto, ON, Canada*] [*FAA designator*] (FAAC)
**MNC**.......... MNC Financial, Inc. [*NYSE symbol*] (CTT)
**MNC**.......... Moncalieri [*Italy*] [*Seismograph station code, US Geological Survey*] [*Closed*] (SEIS)
**MNC**.......... Monica Resources [*Vancouver Stock Exchange symbol*]
**MNC**.......... Mononucleated Cell [*Clinical chemistry*] [*Also, MC*]
**MNC**.......... Mouvement National du Congo-Lumumba [*Congo National Movement-Lumumba*] [*Zaire*] (PD)

**MNC**.......... Mouvement National Congolais [*Congolese National Movement*]
**MNC**.......... Multinational Corporation
**MNC**.......... Multiplicative Noise Compensator [*Telecommunications*] (TEL)
**MNC**.......... Nederlands College voor Belastingconsulenten. Nationale Associatie van Accountantsadministratieconsulenten, Nederlandse Vereniging van Boekhoudbureaux en Administratiekantoren. Mededelingenblad [*A publication*]
**MNC**.......... Shelton, WA [*Location identifier*] [*FAA*] (FAAL)
**MnCaE**...... East Central Regional Library, Cambridge, MN [*Library symbol*] [*Library of Congress*] (LCLS)
**MNCBAY**... Comunicaciones Botanicas. Museo de Historia Natural de Montevideo [*A publication*]
**MNCDN**.... Mededeelingen. Nijmeegse Centrale voor Dialecten Naamkunde [*A publication*]
**MnCh**......... Carver County Library, Chaska, MN [*Library symbol*] [*Library of Congress*] (LCLS)
**MNCH**...... Chinandega/German Pomares [*Nicaragua*] [*ICAO location identifier*] (ICLI)
**MnChil**...... Iron Range Research Library, Chisholm, MN [*Library symbol*] [*Library of Congress*] (LCLS)
**MNCI**........ Corn Island [*Nicaragua*] [*ICAO location identifier*] (ICLI)
**MNCI**........ Neepawa Collegiate Institute, Manitoba [*Library symbol*] [*National Library of Canada*] (NLC)
**MNCIS**...... Management Numerical Control Information System (MCD)
**MNC-K**...... Mouvement National Congolais - Kalonji [*Congolese National Movement*] [*Kalonji Wing*]
**MnCl**.......... Cloquet Public Library, Cloquet, MN [*Library symbol*] [*Library of Congress*] (LCLS)
**MNC-L**...... Mouvement National Congolais - Lumumba [*Congolese National Movement*] [*Lumumba Wing*]
**MNCM**...... Mineman, Master Chief [*Navy rating*]
**MNCMPTR**... Minicomputer (MSA)
**MNCO**....... Michigan National Corporation [*NASDAQ symbol*] (NQ)
**MNCPPC**... Maryland-National Capital Park and Planning Commission
**MnCr**......... Polk County Library, Crookston, MN [*Library symbol*] [*Library of Congress*] (LCLS)
**MnCrpM**... Mercy Medical Center, Coon Rapids, MN [*Library symbol*] [*Library of Congress*] (LCLS)
**MnCrU**...... University of Minnesota Technical College, Crookston, MN [*Library symbol*] [*Library of Congress*] (LCLS)
**MNCR/V**... Vinculos. Revista de Antropologia. Museo Nacional de Costa Rica [*A publication*]
**MNCS**....... Mineman, Senior Chief [*Navy rating*]
**MNCS**....... Multipoint Network-Control System
**MnCS**........ St. John's University, Collegeville, MN [*Library symbol*] [*Library of Congress*] (LCLS)
**MNCV**....... Motor Nerve Conduction Velocity [*Medicine*]
**MND**......... Mandalay [*Burma*] [*Seismograph station code, US Geological Survey*] [*Closed*] (SEIS)
**MND**......... Marlin Developments [*Vancouver Stock Exchange symbol*]
**MND**......... Martin Nuclear Division [*AEC*] (MCD)
**MND**......... Medial Nuclear Division [*Cytology*]
**MND**......... Mendenhall, AK [*Location identifier*] [*FAA*] (FAAL)
**MND**......... Midsummer Night's Dream [*Shakespearean work*]
**MND**......... Minimum Necrosing Dose
**MND**......... Minister of National Defence [*Canada*]
**MND**......... Ministry of National Defence [*British*] (MCD)
**MND**......... Ministry of National Development [*Singapore*] (DS)
**MND**......... Minor Neurological Dysfunction
**MND**......... Mitchell Energy & Development Corp. [*AMEX symbol*] (SPSG)
**MND**......... Monde [*A publication*]
**MND**......... Motor Neuron Disease [*Medicine*]
**MND**......... Mound
**MND**......... Movimento Nacional Democratico [*National Democratic Movement*] [*Portugal*] [*Political party*] (PPE)
**MND**......... University of Minnesota-Duluth, Duluth, MN [*OCLC symbol*] (OCLC)
**MNDA**....... Missionary Sisters of Notre Dame des Anges [*Roman Catholic religious order*]
**MNDO**....... Merchant Navy Discipline Organisation [*British*] (DS)
**MNDO**....... Modified Neglect of Differential Overlap [*Quantum mechanics*]
**MNDP**....... Bibliotheque Pere Champagne [*Pere Champagne Library*], Notre-Dame-De-Lourdes, Manitoba [*Library symbol*] [*National Library of Canada*] (BIB)
**MNDPV**.... Mitteilungen und Nachrichten. Deutscher Palaestina-Verein [*A publication*]
**MNDTH**... Minimum Depth (NOAA)
**MNDTS**.... Member of the Non-Destructive Testing Society of Great Britain
**MnDu**........ Duluth Public Library, Duluth, MN [*Library symbol*] [*Library of Congress*] (LCLS)
**MnDuEPA**... United States Environmental Protection Agency, National Water Quality Laboratory, Duluth, MN [*Library symbol*] [*Library of Congress*] (LCLS)
**MnDuM**.... Miller-Dawn Hospital and Medical Center, Duluth, MN [*Library symbol*] [*Library of Congress*] (LCLS)
**MnDuStL**.. Saint Luke's Hospital, Duluth, MN [*Library symbol*] [*Library of Congress*] (LCLS)
**MnDuStM**... Saint Mary's Hospital, Duluth, MN [*Library symbol*] [*Library of Congress*] (LCLS)
**MnDuStS**.. College of Saint Scholastica, Duluth, MN [*Library symbol*] [*Library of Congress*] (LCLS)
**MnDuU**..... University of Minnesota, Duluth, MN [*Library symbol*] [*Library of Congress*] (LCLS)
**MNE**.......... College of St. Catherine, St. Paul, MN [*OCLC symbol*] (OCLC)
**Mne**........... Marine [*British military*] (DMA)
**MNE**.......... Master of Naval Engineering
**MNE**.......... Master of Nuclear Engineering
**MNE**.......... Merchant Navy Establishment [*British*] (DS)
**MNE**.......... Methylallyl Nitrophenyl Ether [*Organic chemistry*]
**MNE**.......... Methylnorepinephrine [*Also, Normetanephrine*] [*Biochemistry*]
**MNE**.......... Minden, LA [*Location identifier*] [*FAA*] (FAAL)
**MNE**.......... Mineo [*Sicily*] [*Seismograph station code, US Geological Survey*] [*Closed*] (SEIS)
**MNE**.......... Minimum Number of Elements
**Mn-E**.......... Minnesota State Department of Education, St. Paul, MN [*Library symbol*] [*Library of Congress*] (LCLS)
**MNE**.......... Modern English [*Language, etc.*]
**MNE**.......... Multinational Enterprise
**MNe**.......... Newburyport Public Library, Newburyport, MA [*Library symbol*] [*Library of Congress*] (LCLS)
**MNEA**....... Merchant Navy Establishment Administration [*British*] (DS)
**MNECP**..... Mobile National Emergency Command Post [*Air Force*]
**MN Ed**...... Master of Nursing Education
**MN ED**..... Material Need Engineering Development (MCD)
**MnEdS**...... Southdale-Hennepin Area Library, Edina, MN [*Library symbol*] [*Library of Congress*] (LCLS)
**MNEE**....... Mission Nonessential Equipment [*NASA*] (KSC)
**MNeeS**....... GTE-Sylvania, Electric Systems Group, Needham, MA [*Library symbol*] [*Library of Congress*] (LCLS)
**MNeHi**...... Newburyport Historical Society, Newburyport, MA [*Library symbol*] [*Library of Congress*] (LCLS)
**MnElyV**..... Vermillion Community College, Ely, MN [*Library symbol*] [*Library of Congress*] (LCLS)
**MNEMA9**... Manitoba Entomologist [*A publication*]
**Mnemos**..... Mnemosyne [*A publication*] (OCD)
**Mnemosyne**... Mnemosyne. Bibliotheca Classica Batava [*A publication*]
**MN Eng**..... Master of Naval Engineering
**MNES**....... Mine Safety Appliances Co. [*NASDAQ symbol*] (NQ)
**MNET**....... Mission and Data Operations Directorate Network (MCD)
**MNEV**....... Musica Nostra et Vostra, National Corp. of America (EA)
**MnF**........... Buckham Memorial Library, Faribault, MN [*Library symbol*] [*Library of Congress*] (LCLS)
**MNF**.......... College of St. Benedict, St. Joseph, MN [*OCLC symbol*] (OCLC)
**MNF**.......... Forbes Library, Northampton, MA [*Library symbol*] [*Library of Congress*] (LCLS)
**MNF**.......... Mana [*Fiji*] [*Airport symbol*] (OAG)
**MNF**.......... Manitou Reef Resources [*Vancouver Stock Exchange symbol*]
**MNF**.......... Millers' National Federation (EA)
**MNF**.......... Mizo National Front [*India*] (PD)
**MNF**.......... Morehead & North Fork R. R. [*AAR code*]
**MNF**.......... Mountain View, MO [*Location identifier*] [*FAA*] (FAAL)
**MNF**.......... Multilateral Nuclear Force
**MNF**.......... Multinational Force [*Eleven-nation peace-keeping force for the Sinai*]
**MNF**.......... Multisystem Networking Facility
**MNF**.......... Textilia [*A publication*]
**MnFa**......... Martin County Library, Fairmont, MN [*Library symbol*] [*Library of Congress*] (LCLS)
**MNFE**....... Missile Not Fully Equipped (AAG)
**MnFf**.......... Fergus Falls Public Library, Fergus Falls, MN [*Library symbol*] [*Library of Congress*] (LCLS)
**MNFF**........ Magyar Nemzeti Fueggetlensegi Front [*Hungarian National Independence Front*]
**MnFfC**....... Fergus Falls Community College, Fergus Falls, MN [*Library symbol*] [*Library of Congress*] (LCLS)
**MnFfH**....... Lake Region Hospital, Fergus Falls, MN [*Library symbol*] [*Library of Congress*] (LCLS)
**MnFfL**....... Lutheran Brethren Schools, Fergus Falls, MN [*Library symbol*] [*Library of Congress*] (LCLS)
**MNFI**........ Michigan Natural Features Inventory [*Michigan State Department of Natural Resources*] [*Information service or system*] (IID)
**MNFLD**.... Manifold (KSC)
**MNFP**....... Magyar Nemzeti Fueggetlensegi Part [*Hungarian National Independence Party*] [*Political party*] (PPE)
**MNFP**....... Multinational Fighter Program [*Air Force*]
**MNFRM**... Main Frame
**MnFrUH**... Unity Hospital, Fridley, MN [*Library symbol*] [*Library of Congress*] (LCLS)
**M Nfr VH**... Mitteilungen. Nordfriesischer Verein fuer Heimatkunde [*A publication*]
**MNFS**........ Meddelelser fra Norsk Forening foer Sprog-Videnskap [*A publication*]
**MnFS**......... Seabury Divinity School, Faribault, MN [*Library symbol*] [*Library of Congress*] (LCLS)
**MNFSA**..... Meddelelser fra Norsk Farmaceutisk Selskap [*A publication*]

**MNFT** ....... Monfort of Colorado, Inc. [*NASDAQ symbol*] (NQ)
**MNG** ........ Gustavus Adolphus College, St. Peter, MN [*OCLC symbol*] (OCLC)
**MNG** ........ Managing (MSA)
**MNG** ........ Mangahao [*New Zealand*] [*Seismograph station code, US Geological Survey*] (SEIS)
**MNG** ........ Maningrida [*Australia*] [*Airport symbol*] [*Obsolete*] (OAG)
**mng** ........ Meaning
**MNG** ........ Microwave Negative Grid
**MNG** ........ Mongolia [*ANSI three-letter standard code*] (CNC)
**MNG** ........ Morning
**MNG** ........ Mourning (ROG)
**MNGBA** .... Mitteilungen. Naturforschende Gesellschaft in Bern [*A publication*]
**MNGMD** .. Management [*A publication*]
**MNGMT** ... Management (ADA)
**Mngmt Dec** ... Management Decision [*A publication*]
**MNGP** ...... Monticello Nuclear Generating Plant (NRCH)
**MNGR** ...... Manager
**MNGR** ...... Monsignor
**MnGrI** ...... Itasca Community College, Grand Rapids, MN [*Library symbol*] [*Library of Congress*] (LCLS)
**MNGS** ...... Manitoba Geographical Series [*Canada*] [*A publication*]
**Mngt** ........ Management
**MnGvH** ..... Golden Valley Health Center, Golden Valley, MN [*Library symbol*] [*Library of Congress*] (LCLS)
**MNH** ........ Magnum Resources [*Vancouver Stock Exchange symbol*]
**MNH** ........ Makers of National History [*A publication*]
**MNH** ........ Manufactured Homes, Inc. [*AMEX symbol*] (SPSG)
**MnH** ........ Minnesota History [*A publication*]
**Mn-H** ........ Minnesota State Department of Health, St. Paul, MN [*Library symbol*] [*Library of Congress*] (LCLS)
**MNH** ........ Mint Never Hinged [*Philately*]
**MNH** ........ Munchen [*Federal Republic of Germany*] [*Later, FUR*] [*Geomagnetic observatory code*]
**MNH** ........ Munich [*Federal Republic of Germany*] [*Seismograph station code, US Geological Survey*] [*Closed*] (SEIS)
**MNH** ........ Museum of Natural History [*Smithsonian Institution*]
**MNH** ........ University of Minnesota-Duluth, Health Science Library, Duluth, MN [*OCLC symbol*] (OCLC)
**MnHi** ........ Minnesota Historical Society, St. Paul, MN [*Library symbol*] [*Library of Congress*] (LCLS)
**MnHib** ...... Hibbing Public Library, Hibbing, MN [*Library symbol*] [*Library of Congress*] (LCLS)
**MnHibC** .... Hibbing Community College, Hibbing, MN [*Library symbol*] [*Library of Congress*] (LCLS)
**MNHIR** ..... Mededeelingen. Nederlandsch-Historisch Institut le Rome [*A publication*]
**MNHLA** .... Musicians National Hot Line Association (EA)
**M-NHSS** ... Modified New Haven Schizophrenic Scale
**Mn-Hw** ..... Minnesota State Department of Transportation, St. Paul, MN [*Library symbol*] [*Library of Congress*] (LCLS)
**MNI** .......... Mach Number Indicated (MCD)
**MNI** .......... Madras Native Infantry [*British*]
**MNI** .......... Manado [*Celebes*] [*Seismograph station code, US Geological Survey*] (SEIS)
**MNI** .......... Manning, SC [*Location identifier*] [*FAA*] (FAAL)
**MNI** .......... McClatchy Newspapers, Inc. [*NYSE symbol*] (SPSG)
**MNI** .......... Member of the Nautical Institute [*British*]
**MNI** .......... Meridian Technologies, Inc. [*Toronto Stock Exchange symbol*]
**MNI** .......... Minimum Number of Individuals [*Statistics*]
**MNI** .......... Ministry of National Insurance [*British*]
**MNI** .......... Modern Asia [*A publication*]
**MNI** .......... Montserrat [*Airport symbol*] (OAG)
**MNI** .......... Movimiento Nacionalista de Izquierda [*Bolivia*] (PPW)
**MNI** .......... Winona State University, Winona, MN [*OCLC symbol*] (OCLC)
**MNIB** ........ Marketing and National Importing Board [*Grenadian*] (GEA)
**MnIf** ......... International Falls Public Library, International Falls, MN [*Library symbol*] [*Library of Congress*] (LCLS)
**MnIfBC** ..... Boise Cascade Corp., Research Library, International Falls, MN [*Library symbol*] [*Library of Congress*] (LCLS)
**MnIfRC** ..... Rainy River Community College, International Falls, MN [*Library symbol*] [*Library of Congress*] (LCLS)
**MnIgS** ....... Inver Hills State Junior College, Inver Grove Heights, MN [*Library symbol*] [*Library of Congress*] (LCLS)
**MNIH** ........ Member of the National Institute of Hardware [*British*] (DBQ)
**MNIMH** .... Member of the National Institute of Medical Herbalists [*British*]
**MNI Microcomput News Int** ... MNI. Microcomputer News International [*A publication*]
**MNip** ........ Monumenta Nipponica [*A publication*]
**MNIR** ........ Mededeelingen. Nederlandsch-Historisch Institut le Rome [*A publication*]
**MNJ** .......... Mananjary [*Madagascar*] [*Airport symbol*] (OAG)
**MNJ** .......... Microelectronic Noise Jammer
**MNJ** .......... Middletown & New Jersey Railway Co., Inc. [*AAR code*]
**MNJ** .......... Mining Journal [*A publication*]
**MNJ** .......... Movimiento Nacionalista Justicialista [*Justicialist Nationalist Movement - JNM*] [*Argentina*] (PPW)
**MNJ** .......... Myoneural Junction [*Medicine*]
**MNJ** .......... St. John's University, Collegeville, MN [*OCLC symbol*] (OCLC)
**MNJTS** ..... Mouvement National des Jeunes Travailleurs du Senegal [*National Movement of Young Workers of Senegal*]
**MNK** ......... Bethel College, Learning Resources Center, St. Paul, MN [*OCLC symbol*] (OCLC)
**MNK** ......... Maiana [*Kiribati*] [*Airport symbol*] (OAG)
**MNK** ......... Pleshenitzi [*Formerly, Minsk*] [*USSR*] [*Geomagnetic observatory code*]
**MNK** ......... Rochester, MN [*Location identifier*] [*FAA*] (FAAL)
**MNKA** ....... Minimum Number of Animals Known Alive [*Ecology*]
**MNKMA5** ... Mankind Monographs [*A publication*]
**MNKP** ....... Materialy po Nacional'no - Kolonial'nym Problemam [*A publication*]
**MNL** .......... Mangla [*New Mirpur*] [*Pakistan*] [*Seismograph station code, US Geological Survey*] (SEIS)
**MNL** .......... Manila [*Philippines*] [*Airport symbol*] (OAG)
**MNL** .......... Manual (MSA)
**MNL** .......... Marine Navigating Light
**MNL** .......... McConnell Peel Resources [*Vancouver Stock Exchange symbol*]
**MNL** .......... Medical Nutrition Laboratory [*Army*]
**MNL** .......... Mesenteric Node Lymphocyte
**MNL** .......... Minnesota National Laboratory
**MNL** .......... Molecular Neurobiology Laboratory [*Salk Institute for Biological Studies*]
**MNL** .......... Mononuclear Leukocyte [*Hematology*]
**MNL** .......... Montgomery County-Norristown Public Library, Norristown, PA [*OCLC symbol*] (OCLC)
**MNL** .......... Movement for National Liberation [*Barbados*] [*Political party*] (PPW)
**MNL** .......... Multinomial Logit [*Statistics*]
**MNL** .......... National Liberation Movement [*Guatemala*] [*Political party*] (PD)
**MNL** .......... Valdez, AK [*Location identifier*] [*FAA*] (FAAL)
**MNLAB9** .. Arquivos. Museu Bocage [*A publication*]
**MnLaiL** ..... Lake Itasca Forestry and Biological Station, Lake Itasca, MN [*Library symbol*] [*Library of Congress*] (LCLS)
**MNLCA** .... Methylnorlaudanosolinecarboxylic Acid [*Biochemistry*]
**MNLD** ....... Mainland (FAAC)
**Mn-Leg** ...... Minnesota State Legislative Library, St. Paul, MN [*Library symbol*] [*Library of Congress*] (LCLS)
**MnLeW** ..... Washington County Library, Lake Elmo, MN [*Library symbol*] [*Library of Congress*] (LCLS)
**MNLF** ....... Malayan National Liberation Front [*Singapore*] [*Political party*] (PD)
**MNLF** ....... Moro National Liberation Front [*Philippines*] [*Political party*] (PD)
**MNLN** ....... Leon/Fanor Urroz [*Nicaragua*] [*ICAO location identifier*] (ICLI)
**MN LR** ...... Minnesota Law Review [*A publication*]
**MNLS** ........ Marine Navigating Light System
**MnLsG** ...... Green Giant Corp., Le Sueur, MN [*Library symbol*] [*Library of Congress*] (LCLS)
**MNLY** ....... Mainly (FAAC)
**MNM** ........ Mankato State University, Mankato, MN [*OCLC symbol*] (OCLC)
**MNM** ........ Menominee [*Michigan*] [*Airport symbol*] (OAG)
**MNM** ........ Military Necessity Modification
**MNM** ........ Minimum
**MNM** ........ Minneapolis [*Minnesota*] [*Seismograph station code, US Geological Survey*] (SEIS)
**MnM** ........ Minneapolis Public Library and Information Center, Minneapolis, MN [*Library symbol*] [*Library of Congress*] (LCLS)
**MNM** ........ Museum of New Mexico [*Research center*] (RCD)
**MnMA** ....... Augsburg College and Seminary, Minneapolis, MN [*Library symbol*] [*Library of Congress*] (LCLS)
**MnMAb** ..... Abbott-Northwestern Hospitals, Inc., Minneapolis, MN [*Library symbol*] [*Library of Congress*] (LCLS)
**MnMAC** .... Anoka County Library, Minneapolis, MN [*Library symbol*] [*Library of Congress*] (LCLS)
**MnMAM** ... American Medical Systems, Inc., Minneapolis, MN [*Library symbol*] [*Library of Congress*] (LCLS)
**MnManBC** ... Bethany Lutheran College, Mankato, MN [*Library symbol*] [*Library of Congress*] (LCLS)
**MnManBS** ... Bethany Lutheran Theological Seminary, Mankato, MN [*Library symbol*] [*Library of Congress*] (LCLS)
**MnManM** ... Minnesota Valley Regional Library, Mankato, MN [*Library symbol*] [*Library of Congress*] (LCLS)
**MnManS** ... Mankato State College [*Later, Mankato State University*], Mankato, MN [*Library symbol*] [*Library of Congress*] (LCLS)
**MnManTD** ... Traverse des Sioux Library System, Mankato, MN [*Library symbol*] [*Library of Congress*] (LCLS)
**MNMANY** ... Men's Neckwear Manufacturers Association of New York [*Defunct*] (EA)
**MnMAR** .... American Rehabilitation Foundation Minneapolis, MN [*Library symbol*] [*Library of Congress*] (LCLS)
**MnMar** ...... Marshall-Lyon County Library, Marshall, MN [*Library symbol*] [*Library of Congress*] (LCLS)

**MnMarS**.... Southwest Minnesota State College, Marshall, MN [*Library symbol*] [*Library of Congress*] (LCLS)
**MnMBL** .... Bakken Library of Electricity in Life, Minneapolis, MN [*Library symbol*] [*Library of Congress*] (LCLS)
**MNMC**...... Medical Network for Missing Children (EA)
**MNMCA**... Memoires. Societe Nationale des Sciences Naturelles et Mathematiques de Cherbourg [*A publication*]
**MnMCA**.... Minneapolis College of Art and Design, Minneapolis, MN [*Library symbol*] [*Library of Congress*] (LCLS)
**MnMCC**.... Minneapolis Community College, Minneapolis, MN [*Library symbol*] [*Library of Congress*] (LCLS)
**MnMF**....... Fairview Hospital, Minneapolis, MN [*Library symbol*] [*Library of Congress*] (LCLS)
**MnMFL**..... Association of Free Lutheran Congregation and Seminary Headquarters, Minneapolis, MN [*Library symbol*] [*Library of Congress*] (LCLS)
**MnMG**....... Golden Valley Lutheran College, Minneapolis, MN [*Library symbol*] [*Library of Congress*] (LCLS)
**MNMG** ..... Managua/Augusto Cesar Sandino [*Nicaragua*] [*ICAO location identifier*] (ICLI)
**MnMGM**... General Mills, Inc., Minneapolis, MN [*Library symbol*] [*Library of Congress*] (LCLS)
**MnMGS**.... Church of Jesus Christ of Latter-Day Saints, Genealogical Society Library, Minneapolis Branch, Minneapolis, MN [*Library symbol*] [*Library of Congress*] (LCLS)
**MnMH**...... Hennepin County Medical Society, Minneapolis, MN [*Library symbol*] [*Library of Congress*] (LCLS)
**MnMHCL**... Hennepin County Library, Minneapolis, MN [*Library symbol*] [*Library of Congress*] (LCLS)
**MnMHen**.. Henkel Corp., Minneapolis, MN [*Library symbol*] [*Library of Congress*] (LCLS)
**MnMHH**... Hennepin County General Hospital, Minneapolis, MN [*Library symbol*] [*Library of Congress*] (LCLS)
**MnMHLL**... Hennepin County Law Library, Minneapolis, MN [*Library symbol*] [*Library of Congress*] (LCLS)
**MnMI**........ Interlutheran Theological Seminary and Bible School, Minneapolis, MN [*Library symbol*] [*Library of Congress*] (LCLS)
**MNMIA**.... Men's Neckwear Manufacturers Institute of America (EA)
**MnMIn**...... Interstudy, Minneapolis, MN [*Library symbol*] [*Library of Congress*] (LCLS)
**MnMK**....... Kenny Rehabilitation Institute, Minneapolis, MN [*Library symbol*] [*Library of Congress*] (LCLS)
**MnMLD**.... Lutheran Deaconess Hospital, Minneapolis, MN [*Library symbol*] [*Library of Congress*] (LCLS)
**MnMMC**... Metropolitan State Community College, Minneapolis, MN [*Library symbol*] [*Library of Congress*] (LCLS)
**MnMMe**.... Medtronic, Inc., Minneapolis, MN [*Library symbol*] [*Library of Congress*] (LCLS)
**MnMMeH**... Methodist Hospital, Minneapolis, MN [*Library symbol*] [*Library of Congress*] (LCLS)
**MnMMet**... Metropolitan Medical Center, Medical Library, Minneapolis, MN [*Library symbol*] [*Library of Congress*] (LCLS)
**MnMMet-H**... Metropolitan Medical Center, Hospital Services Library, Minneapolis, MN [*Library symbol*] [*Library of Congress*] (LCLS)
**MnMMetS**... Metropolitan State Junior College, Minneapolis, MN [*Library symbol*] [*Library of Congress*] (LCLS)
**MnMMH**.. Minneapolis-Honeywell Regulator Co., Minneapolis, MN [*Library symbol*] [*Library of Congress*] (LCLS)
**MnMMSC**... MTS Systems Corporation, Minneapolis, MN [*Library symbol*] [*Library of Congress*] (LCLS)
**MnMMtS**... Mount Sinai Hospital, Minneapolis, MN [*Library symbol*] [*Library of Congress*] (LCLS)
**MnMN**...... Normandale Community College, Minneapolis, MN [*Library symbol*] [*Library of Congress*] (LCLS)
**MnMNC**.... North Central Bible College, Minneapolis, MN [*Library symbol*] [*Library of Congress*] (LCLS)
**MnMNH**... North Memorial Hospital, Minneapolis, MN [*Library symbol*] [*Library of Congress*] (LCLS)
**MnMNHe**... North Hennepin Community College, Minneapolis, MN [*Library symbol*] [*Library of Congress*] (LCLS)
**MnMohC**... Concordia College, Moorhead, MN [*Library symbol*] [*Library of Congress*] (LCLS)
**MnMohL**... Lake Agassiz Regional Library, Moorhead, MN [*Library symbol*] [*Library of Congress*] (LCLS)
**MnMohPS**... Moorhead Public Schools System, Moorhead, MN [*Library symbol*] [*Library of Congress*] (LCLS)
**MnMohS**... Moorhead State College, Moorhead, MN [*Library symbol*] [*Library of Congress*] (LCLS)
**MnMoU**..... University of Minnesota, Morris, MN [*Library symbol*] [*Library of Congress*] (LCLS)
**MnMov**...... Chippewa County Library System, Montevideo, MN [*Library symbol*] [*Library of Congress*] (LCLS)
**MnMS**....... Saint Louis Park Medical Center, Minneapolis, MN [*Library symbol*] [*Library of Congress*] (LCLS)
**MnMSMC**... Saint Mary's Junior College, Minneapolis, MN [*Library symbol*] [*Library of Congress*] (LCLS)
**MnMSMH**... Saint Mary's Hospital, Minneapolis, MN [*Library symbol*] [*Library of Congress*] (LCLS)
**MNMT**...... Monument [*Board on Geographic Names*]
**MnMULS**... University of Minnesota Union List of Serials, Minneapolis, MN [*Library symbol*] [*Library of Congress*] (LCLS)
**MnMVA**.... United States Veterans Administration Hospital, Minneapolis, MN [*Library symbol*] [*Library of Congress*] (LCLS)
**MNN**......... Carleton College, Northfield, MN [*OCLC symbol*] (OCLC)
**MNN**......... Madness Network News (EA)
**MNN**......... Marion, OH [*Location identifier*] [*FAA*] (FAAL)
**MNN**......... Minneapolis [*Minnesota*] [*Seismograph station code, US Geological Survey*] (SEIS)
**Mn-N**......... Minnesota State Department of Natural Resources, St. Paul, MN [*Library symbol*] [*Library of Congress*] (LCLS)
**MNN**......... Monenco Ltd. [*Toronto Stock Exchange symbol*]
**MNN**......... Muenchener Neueste Nachrichten [*A publication*]
**MNNA**...... Manitoba Nature [*Canada*] [*A publication*]
**MnNbU**..... United Theological Seminary of the Twin Cities, New Brighton, MN [*Library symbol*] [*Library of Congress*] (LCLS)
**MnNC**........ Carleton College, Northfield, MN [*Library symbol*] [*Library of Congress*] (LCLS)
**MnNeuL**.... Doctor Martin Luther College, New Ulm, MN [*Library symbol*] [*Library of Congress*] (LCLS)
**MNNG**...... Methylnitronitrosoguanidine [*Biochemistry*]
**MnNHi**...... Norwegian-American Historical Association, Northfield, MN [*Library symbol*] [*Library of Congress*] (LCLS)
**MNNMBL**... Museo Nacional de Historia Natural. Noticiario Mensual [*Santiago, Chile*] [*A publication*]
**MnNmT**..... Mankato Area Vocational-Technical Institute, North Mankato, MN [*Library symbol*] [*Library of Congress*] (LCLS)
**MnNS**........ Saint Olaf College, Northfield, MN [*Library symbol*] [*Library of Congress*] (LCLS)
**MNNTB8**.. Man and Nature [*A publication*]
**MNO**......... Maddona Resources Corp. [*Vancouver Stock Exchange symbol*]
**mno**........... Manobo [*MARC language code*] [*Library of Congress*] (LCCP)
**MNO**......... Manono [*Zaire*] [*Airport symbol*] (OAG)
**MNO**......... Meubelecho [*A publication*]
**MnO**.......... Owatonna Free Public Library, Owatonna, MN [*Library symbol*] [*Library of Congress*] (LCLS)
**MNO**......... Refugio, TX [*Location identifier*] [*FAA*] (FAAL)
**MNO**......... Saint Olaf College, Northfield, MN [*OCLC symbol*] (OCLC)
**MNoadT**.... North Adams State College, North Adams, MA [*Library symbol*] [*Library of Congress*] (LCLS)
**MNoanM**... Merrimack College, North Andover, MA [*Library symbol*] [*Library of Congress*] (LCLS)
**MNoanMV**... Merrimack Valley Textile Museum, North Andover, MA [*Library symbol*] [*Library of Congress*] (LCLS)
**MNodS**...... Southeastern Massachusetts University, North Dartmouth, MA [*Library symbol*] [*Library of Congress*] (LCLS)
**MNoeS**...... Stonehill College, North Easton, MA [*Library symbol*] [*Library of Congress*] (LCLS)
**MNOMU**.. Mobile Nuclear Ordnance Maintenance Unit (MCD)
**MNOPF**.... Merchant Navy Officers' Pension Fund [*British*] (DS)
**MNORM**... Missile Not Operationally Ready - Maintenance [*Air Force*]
**MNORP**.... Missile Not Operationally Ready - Parts [*Air Force*]
**MNOS**....... Metal-Nitride-Oxide Silicon [*or Semiconductor*]
**MNOSFET**... Metal-Nitride-Oxide-Semiconductor Field-Effect Transistor
**M Not R Ast**... Monthly Notices. Royal Astronomical Society [*A publication*]
**MNoW**....... Wheaton College, Norton, MA [*Library symbol*] [*Library of Congress*] (LCLS)
**MNP**.......... Marine National Park [*Australia*]
**MNP**.......... Maximum Negative Pressure [*Nuclear energy*] (NRCH)
**MNP**.......... Meta-Nitrophenol [*Organic chemistry*]
**MNP**.......... Microcomputer Networking Protocol
**MNP**.......... Midnapore (1979) Resources, Inc. [*Vancouver Stock Exchange symbol*]
**Mn-P**.......... Minnesota State Department of Planning, St. Paul, MN [*Library symbol*] [*Library of Congress*] (LCLS)
**MNP**.......... Monde Nouveau-Paru [*A publication*]
**MNP**.......... Movimiento Nacionalista Popular [*Popular Nationalist Movement*] [*Chile*] [*Political party*] (PD)
**MNP**.......... Multinomial Probit [*Statistics*]
**MNP**.......... Northern Mariana Islands [*ANSI three-letter standard code*] (CNC)
**MNP**.......... University of Minnesota, St. Paul, MN [*OCLC symbol*] (OCLC)
**MNPA**....... Mono-normal-propylamine [*Organic chemistry*]
**MNPAAS**... Morfologia Normala si Patologica [*Bucharest*] [*A publication*]
**MNPC**....... Puerto Cabezas [*Nicaragua*] [*ICAO location identifier*] (ICLI)
**MNPD**....... Missile and Nuclear Programming Data (AABC)
**MNPI**........ Microcom, Inc. [*NASDAQ symbol*] (NQ)
**MNPL**....... Machinists Non-Partisan Political League (EA)
**MNPO**....... Median Preoptic Area [*Brain anatomy*]
**MNPO**....... Mobile Navy Post Office
**MNPP**....... Midland Nuclear Power Plant (NRCH)
**MN-PPL**.... Machinists Non-Partisan Political League (EA)
**MnPr**......... Kitchigami Regional Library, Pine River, MN [*Library symbol*] [*Library of Congress*] (LCLS)
**MNPS**........ Millstone Nuclear Power Station (NRCH)
**MNPS**........ Movimiento Nazionale Pan-Somalo [*Pan-Somali National Movement*] [*Political party*]
**MNPT**....... Meta-Nitro-para-toluidine [*Organic chemistry*]
**MNPWR**... Manpower (AFM)
**MNPZ**....... Mononitrosopiperazine [*Biochemistry*]

**MNQ** ......... Manicouagan [*Quebec*] [*Seismograph station code, US Geological Survey*] (SEIS)
**MNQ** ......... Methylnaphthoquinone [*Organic chemistry*]
**MNQ** ......... Monto [*Australia*] [*Airport symbol*] (OAG)
**MNQ** ......... Montoro Resources [*Vancouver Stock Exchange symbol*]
**MNQ** ......... University of Minnesota, Waseca, Waseca, MN [*OCLC symbol*] (OCLC)
**MNR** ......... James J. Hill Reference Library, St. Paul, MN [*OCLC symbol*] (OCLC)
**MNR** ......... Maintenance/Nonconformance Record (MCD)
**MNR** ......... Manor (MCD)
**MNR** ......... Manor Care, Inc. [*NYSE symbol*] (SPSG)
**MNR** ......... Massive Nuclear Retaliation (AAG)
**MNR** ......... McMaster Nuclear Reactor [*Canada*]
**MNR** ......... McNellen Resources, Inc. [*Vancouver Stock Exchange symbol*] [*Toronto Stock Exchange symbol*]
**MNR** ......... Mean Neap [*Tide*] Rise [*Tides and currents*]
**MNR** ......... Mines Road [*California*] [*Seismograph station code, US Geological Survey*] (SEIS)
**MNR** ......... Minimum Noise Routes
**MNR** ......... Ministry of National Resources [*Philippines*] (DS)
**MNR** ......... Mongu [*Zambia*] [*Airport symbol*] (OAG)
**MNR** ......... Morphine-Naive Rats
**MNr** ......... Morrill Memorial Library, Norwood, MA [*Library symbol*] [*Library of Congress*] (LCLS)
**MNR** ......... Mouvement Nationaliste Revolutionnaire [*Revolutionary Nationalist Movement*] [*France*] [*Political party*] (PD)
**MNR** ......... Movimiento Nacional Reformista [*National Reformist Movement*] [*Honduras*] [*Political party*]
**MNR** ......... Movimiento Nacional Revolucionario [*National Revolutionary Movement*] [*El Salvador*] [*Political party*] (PPW)
**MNR** ......... Movimiento Nacionalista Revolucionario [*National Revolutionary Movement*] [*Bolivia*] [*Political party*] (PPW)
**MNR** ......... Movimiento Nacionalista Revolucionario Julio [*Revolutionary Nationalist Movement (Julio)*] [*Bolivia*] [*Political party*] (PPW)
**MNR** ......... Mozambique National Resistance Movement
**MnR** ......... Rochester Public Library, Rochester, MN [*Library symbol*] [*Library of Congress*] (LCLS)
**MNRAA** .... Monthly Notices. Royal Astronomical Society [*A publication*]
**MNRC** ....... Minorco [*Formerly, Minerals & Resources Corp. Ltd.*] [*NASDAQ symbol*] (NQ)
**MNRCS** ..... Median Normalized RADAR Cross Section
**MNRH** ...... Movimiento Nacionalista Revolucionario Historico [*Historic Revolutionary Nationalist Movement*] [*Bolivia*] [*Political party*] (PPW)
**MNRL** ....... Mineral (MSA)
**MNRL** ....... Mineral Development, Inc. [*NASDAQ symbol*] (NQ)
**MNRLD** .... Mineraloel [*A publication*]
**MNRLSM** ... Manitoba. Department of Natural Resources. Library Service Manuscripts [*Canada*] [*A publication*]
**MnRM** ....... Mayo Clinic, Rochester, MN [*Library symbol*] [*Library of Congress*] (LCLS)
**MnRMeH** ... Rochester Methodist Hospital, Rochester, MN [*Library symbol*] [*Library of Congress*] (LCLS)
**MnRoN** ...... Northwestern College, Roseville, MN [*Library symbol*] [*Library of Congress*] (LCLS)
**MnRoP** ...... Minnesota State Pollution Control Agency, Roseville, MN [*Library symbol*] [*Library of Congress*] (LCLS)
**MNRP** ....... Movimiento Nacionalista Revolucionario del Pueblo [*Nationalist Revolutionary People's Movement*] [*Bolivia*] [*Political party*] (PPW)
**MNRPM** ... Malay Nationalist Revolutionary Party of Malaya [*Partai Kebangsaan Melayu Revolusioner Malaya*] [*Political party*] (PPW)
**MnRPS** ...... Rochester Public Schools, Rochester, MN [*Library symbol*] [*Library of Congress*] (LCLS)
**MnRR** ........ Rochester State Junior College, Rochester, MN [*Library symbol*] [*Library of Congress*] (LCLS)
**MNRS** ....... Mobile Neutron Radiographic System
**MnRS** ........ Southeastern Libraries Cooperating [*SELCO*], Rochester Public Library, Rochester, MN [*Library symbol*] [*Library of Congress*] (LCLS)
**MnRStM** ... Saint Mary's Hospital, Rochester, MN [*Library symbol*] [*Library of Congress*] (LCLS)
**MNRT** ....... Monmouth Real Estate Investment Trust [*NASDAQ symbol*] (NQ)
**MNRTA** .... Mental Retardation [*A publication*]
**MNRU** ....... Modulated Noise Reference Unit [*Telecommunications*] (TEL)
**MnRw** ........ Red Wing Public Library, Red Wing, MN [*Library symbol*] [*Library of Congress*] (LCLS)
**MNS** .......... College of Saint Scholastica Library, Duluth, MN [*OCLC symbol*] (OCLC)
**MNS** .......... [*The*] MacNeal-Schwendler Corp. [*AMEX symbol*] (SPSG)
**MNS** .......... Mansa [*Zambia*] [*Airport symbol*] (OAG)
**MNS** .......... Martin's Louisiana Reports, New Series [*A publication*] (DLA)
**MNS** .......... Master of Nursing Science
**MNS** .......... Master of Nutritional Science
**MNS** .......... Maturity News Service
**MNS** .......... McGuire Nuclear Station (NRCH)
**MNS** .......... Member of the Numismatical Society [*British*]
**MNS** .......... Meta-Nitride Semiconductor (MCD)
**MNS** .......... Microband National System, Inc. [*New York, NY*] [*Telecommunications*] (TSSD)
**MNS** .......... Microneurography Society (EA)
**MNS** .......... Mine Neutralization System [*Military*] (CAAL)
**MNS** .......... Mines
**MNS** .......... Ministry of National Service [*British*] [*World War I*]
**MNS** .......... Minneapolis, Northfield & Southern Railway [*AAR code*]
**MNS** .......... Molded Nylon Screw
**MNS** .......... Movement for a New Society (EA)
**MNS** .......... Movimiento Nacional de Salvacion [*National Movement of Salvation*] [*Dominican Republic*] [*Political party*] (PPW)
**MnS** ........... St. Paul Public Library, St. Paul, MN [*Library symbol*] [*Library of Congress*] (LCLS)
**MNS** .......... Smith College, Northampton, MA [*Library symbol*] [*Library of Congress*] (LCLS)
**MNSA** ....... Seaman Apprentice, Mineman, Striker [*Navy rating*]
**MnSAG** ..... Minnesota Attorney General's Office, St. Paul, MN [*Library symbol*] [*Library of Congress*] (LCLS)
**MNSaS** ...... Swift River Valley Historical Society, New Salem, MA [*Library symbol*] [*Library of Congress*] (LCLS)
**MnSB** ........ Bethel College, St. Paul, MN [*Library symbol*] [*Library of Congress*] (LCLS)
**MNSBC** ...... Minnesota North Stars Booster Club (EA)
**MnSBH** ..... Bethesda Lutheran Hospital, St. Paul, MN [*Library symbol*] [*Library of Congress*] (LCLS)
**MNSC** ....... Main Network Switching Center [*Telecommunications*] (TEL)
**MN Sc** ........ Master of Nursing Science
**MNSC** ....... San Carlos/San Juan [*Nicaragua*] [*ICAO location identifier*] (ICLI)
**MnSc** ......... Sauk Centre Public Library, Sauk Centre, MN [*Library symbol*] [*Library of Congress*] (LCLS)
**MnSCC** ...... Concordia College, St. Paul, MN [*Library symbol*] [*Library of Congress*] (LCLS)
**MnSCH** ..... Children's Hospital, St. Paul, MN [*Library symbol*] [*Library of Congress*] (LCLS)
**MnScL** ....... Sinclair Lewis Foundation, Sauk Centre, MN [*Library symbol*] [*Library of Congress*] (LCLS)
**MnSEA** ...... Minnesota Energy Agency, St. Paul, MN [*Library symbol*] [*Library of Congress*] (LCLS)
**MNSF** ........ Monoclonal-Nonspecific Suppressor Factor [*Immunology*]
**MnSG** ........ Gillette State Hospital for Crippled Children, St. Paul, MN [*Library symbol*] [*Library of Congress*] (LCLS)
**MnSGC** ..... Minnesota Governor's Commission on Crime Prevention and Control, St. Paul, MN [*Library symbol*] [*Library of Congress*] (LCLS)
**MnSGH** ..... Group Health, Inc., St. Paul, MN [*Library symbol*] [*Library of Congress*] (LCLS)
**MnSH** ........ Hamline University, St. Paul, MN [*Library symbol*] [*Library of Congress*] (LCLS)
**MnSH-L** .... Hamline University, School of Law, St. Paul, MN [*Library symbol*] [*Library of Congress*] (LCLS)
**MnShS** ....... Scott County Library, Shakopee, MN [*Library symbol*] [*Library of Congress*] (LCLS)
**MNSI** ........ Siuna [*Nicaragua*] [*ICAO location identifier*] (ICLI)
**MnSJ** ......... James J. Hill Reference Library, St. Paul, MN [*Library symbol*] [*Library of Congress*] (LCLS)
**MNSKA** .... Meddelelser fra det Norske Skogforsoeksvesen [*A publication*]
**MnSL** ......... Luther Theological Seminary, St. Paul, MN [*Library symbol*] [*Library of Congress*] [*Obsolete*] (LCLS)
**MnSLN** ..... Luther-Northwestern Seminary, St. Paul, MN [*Library symbol*] [*Library of Congress*] (LCLS)
**MnSM** ........ Macalester College, St. Paul, MN [*Library symbol*] [*Library of Congress*] (LCLS)
**MnSMMfg** ... Minnesota Mining & Manufacturing Co., Technical Library, St. Paul, MN [*Library symbol*] [*Library of Congress*] [*Obsolete*] (LCLS)
**MnSMN** .... Mounds-Midway School of Nursing, St. Paul, MN [*Library symbol*] [*Library of Congress*] (LCLS)
**MnSN** ........ Northwestern Lutheran Theological Seminary, St. Paul, MN [*Library symbol*] [*Library of Congress*] [*Obsolete*] (LCLS)
**MNSN** ....... Seaman, Mineman, Striker [*Navy rating*]
**MnSOD** ..... Manganese Superoxide Dismutase
**MnSOEO** .. Minnesota Office of Economic Opportunity, St. Paul, MN [*Library symbol*] [*Library of Congress*] (LCLS)
**MNSPBL** .. Medecine du Sport [*Paris*] [*A publication*]
**MnSRC** ...... Ramsey County Public Library, St. Paul, MN [*Library symbol*] [*Library of Congress*] (LCLS)
**MnSRM** .... Ramsey County Medical Society, St. Paul, MN [*Library symbol*] [*Library of Congress*] (LCLS)
**MNSS** ........ Modified Need Satisfaction Schedule
**MnSS** ......... St. Paul Seminary, St. Paul, MN [*Library symbol*] [*Library of Congress*] (LCLS)
**MNS-S** ...... Smith College, Sophia Smith Collection, Northampton, MA [*Library symbol*] [*Library of Congress*] (LCLS)
**MnSSC** ...... College of St. Catherine, St. Paul, MN [*Library symbol*] [*Library of Congress*] (LCLS)
**MnSSJ** ....... St. John's Hospital, St. Paul, MN [*Library symbol*] [*Library of Congress*] (LCLS)

**MnSSJos**... St. Joseph's Hospital, St. Paul, MN [*Library symbol*] [*Library of Congress*] (LCLS)
**MnSSP**...... St. Paul Ramsey Hospital, St. Paul, MN [*Library symbol*] [*Library of Congress*] (LCLS)
**MnSSpU**.... Sperry UNIVAC, St. Paul, MN [*Library symbol*] [*Library of Congress*] (LCLS)
**MnSST**...... College of St. Thomas, St. Paul, MN [*Library symbol*] [*Library of Congress*] (LCLS)
**MNST**....... Minstar, Inc. [*NASDAQ symbol*] (NQ)
**MNSTB**..... Monostable (MSA)
**MNSTBMV**... Monostable Multivibrator (MSA)
**MnStbSP**... Saint Paul Bible College, Saint Bonifacius, MN [*Library symbol*] [*Library of Congress*] (LCLS)
**MnStclG**.... Great River Regional Library, St. Cloud, MN [*Library symbol*] [*Library of Congress*] (LCLS)
**MnStclS**..... St. Cloud State University, St. Cloud, MN [*Library symbol*] [*Library of Congress*] (LCLS)
**MnStclV**.... United States Veterans Administration Hospital, St. Cloud, MN [*Library symbol*] [*Library of Congress*] (LCLS)
**MnStj**......... Watonwan County Library, St. James, MN [*Library symbol*] [*Library of Congress*] (LCLS)
**MnStjoS**.... College of St. Benedict, St. Joseph, MN [*Library symbol*] [*Library of Congress*] (LCLS)
**MnSTM**.... 3M Co., 201 Technical Library, St. Paul, MN [*Library symbol*] [*Library of Congress*] (LCLS)
**MnSTM-A**... 3M Co., 251 Library, St. Paul, MN [*Library symbol*] [*Library of Congress*] (LCLS)
**MnSTM-B**... 3M Co., Business Information Service, St. Paul, MN [*Library symbol*] [*Library of Congress*] (LCLS)
**MnSTM-E**... Three M (3M) Co., Engineering Information Services, St. Paul, MN [*Library symbol*] [*Library of Congress*] (LCLS)
**MnSTM-G**... 3M Co., 235 Library, St. Paul, MN [*Library symbol*] [*Library of Congress*] (LCLS)
**MnSTM-H**... 3M Co., Health Care Library, St. Paul, MN [*Library symbol*] [*Library of Congress*] (LCLS)
**MnSTM-M**... 3M Co., 236 Library, St. Paul, MN [*Library symbol*] [*Library of Congress*] (LCLS)
**MnSTM-P**... 3M Co., 209 Library, St. Paul, MN [*Library symbol*] [*Library of Congress*] (LCLS)
**MnSTM-T**... 3M Co., 230 Library, St. Paul, MN [*Library symbol*] [*Library of Congress*] (LCLS)
**MnStpeG**... Gustavus Adolphus College, St. Peter, MN [*Library symbol*] [*Library of Congress*] (LCLS)
**MnSU**........ University of Minnesota, St. Paul, MN [*Library symbol*] [*Library of Congress*] (LCLS)
**MnSU-Bc**.. University of Minnesota, Biochemistry Library, St. Paul, MN [*Library symbol*] [*Library of Congress*] (LCLS)
**MnSU-Et**... University of Minnesota, Entomology Library, St. Paul, MN [*Library symbol*] [*Library of Congress*] (LCLS)
**MnSU-F**.... University of Minnesota, Forestry Library, St. Paul, MN [*Library symbol*] [*Library of Congress*] (LCLS)
**MnSUH**..... United Hospitals, Inc., St. Paul, MN [*Library symbol*] [*Library of Congress*] (LCLS)
**MnSU-PP**... University of Minnesota, Plant Pathology Library, St. Paul, MN [*Library symbol*] [*Library of Congress*] (LCLS)
**MnSUSF**... United States Forest Service, North Central Forest Experiment Station, St. Paul, MN [*Library symbol*] [*Library of Congress*] (LCLS)
**MnSU-V**.... University of Minnesota, Veterinary Medicine Library, St. Paul, MN [*Library symbol*] [*Library of Congress*] (LCLS)
**MNSV**....... Meddelelser fra Norsk Forening foer Sprog-Videnskap [*A publication*]
**MnSWM**... William Mitchell College of Law, St. Paul, MN [*Library symbol*] [*Library of Congress*] (LCLS)
**MNT**.......... College of St. Thomas, St. Paul, MN [*OCLC symbol*] (OCLC)
**Mn-T**.......... Minnesota State Department of Taxation, St. Paul, MN [*Library symbol*] [*Library of Congress*] (LCLS)
**MNT**.......... Minto [*Alaska*] [*Airport symbol*] (OAG)
**MNT**.......... Minute [*Angle*]
**MNT**.......... Modern Network Theory [*Electrical engineering computer*]
**MNT**.......... Moffatt New Testament Commentary [*A publication*] (BJA)
**MNT**.......... Monitor
**MNT**.......... Mononitrotoluene [*Organic chemistry*]
**MNT**.......... Montedison SpA [*NYSE symbol*] (SPSG)
**MNT**.......... Montoro Gold, Inc. [*Vancouver Stock Exchange symbol*]
**MNT**.......... Montreal [*Quebec*] [*Seismograph station code, US Geological Survey*] (SEIS)
**MNT**.......... Mount (KSC)
**MNt**........... Newton Free Library, Newton, MA [*Library symbol*] [*Library of Congress*] (LCLS)
**MNTB**....... Medial Nucleus of Trapezoid Body [*Neuroanatomy*]
**MNTB**....... Merchant Navy Training Board [*British*] (DS)
**MNTC**....... Mexican National Tourist Council (FA)
**MNTC**....... Moffatt New Testament Commentary [*A publication*] (BJA)
**MNtcA**....... Andover Newton Theological School, Newton Center, MA [*Library symbol*] [*Library of Congress*] (LCLS)
**MnTcFW**... United States Fish and Wildlife Service, Science Reference Library, Twin Cities, MN [*Library symbol*] [*Library of Congress*] (LCLS)
**MnTcM**..... United States Bureau of Mines, Twin Cities, MN [*Library symbol*] [*Library of Congress*] (LCLS)
**MNTG**....... Mounting
**MNTHZ**.... Methylnitrosothiazolidine [*Organic chemistry*]
**MNTJ**........ Montejas Energy Resources, Inc. [*NASDAQ symbol*] (NQ)
**MNTK**....... Mezhotraslevoi Naucho-Tekhni-Cheskii Kompleks [*Interdisciplinary Scientific-Technological Complex*] [*Russian*]
**MNTK**....... Movimiento Nacional Tupaj Katari [*Bolivia*] [*Political party*] (PPW)
**MNTL**....... Manufacturers National Corp. [*NASDAQ symbol*] (NQ)
**Mntl Pt**...... Mental Patients Liberation/Therapy [*A publication*]
**MNTMP**... Minimum Temperature (NOAA)
**MNTN**....... Maintain
**MNTN**....... Mountain
**MnTN**........ Northland State Junior College, Thief River Falls, MN [*Library symbol*] [*Library of Congress*] (LCLS)
**Mntn Life**... Mountain Life and Work [*A publication*]
**MnTNR**..... Northwest Regional Library, Thief River Falls, MN [*Library symbol*] [*Library of Congress*] (LCLS)
**MnTPPS**... Manganese Tetraphenylporphine Sulfonate [*Organic chemistry*]
**MNTR**....... Mentor Corp. [*NASDAQ symbol*] (NQ)
**MNTR**....... Monitor (MDG)
**MNTS**....... Medial Nucleus Tractus Solitarius [*Neuroanatomy*]
**MNtS**......... Swedenborg School of Religion, Newton, MA [*Library symbol*] [*Library of Congress*] (LCLS)
**MNtSH**..... Newton College of the Sacred Heart [*Later, Newton College*], Newton, MA [*Library symbol*] [*Library of Congress*] (LCLS)
**MNTV**....... Mercury Network Test Vehicle (MUGU)
**MNTX**....... Minntech Corp. [*Minneapolis, MN*] [*NASDAQ symbol*] (NQ)
**MNu**.......... Mare Nubium [*Sea of Clouds*] [*Lunar area*]
**MNU**......... Methylnitrosourea [*Also, NMU*] [*Organic chemistry*]
**MNU**......... Middle Name Unknown (MCD)
**MNU**......... Milford North [*Utah*] [*Seismograph station code, US Geological Survey*] (SEIS)
**mnu**............ Minnesota [*MARC country of publication code*] [*Library of Congress*] (LCCP)
**MNU**......... Moulmein [*Burma*] [*Airport symbol*] (OAG)
**MNU**......... Mundee Mines Ltd. [*Vancouver Stock Exchange symbol*]
**Mnu**........... Mundo Nuevo [*A publication*]
**MnU**.......... University of Minnesota, Minneapolis, MN [*Library symbol*] [*Library of Congress*] (LCLS)
**MNU**......... University of Minnesota, Minneapolis, MN [*OCLC symbol*] (OCLC)
**MnU-Ar**..... University of Minnesota, Archives, Minneapolis, MN [*Library symbol*] [*Library of Congress*] (LCLS)
**MnU-B**...... University of Minnesota, Biomedical Library, Minneapolis, MN [*Library symbol*] [*Library of Congress*] (LCLS)
**MnU-Fb**..... University of Minnesota, Freshwater Biological Institute, Navarre, MN [*Library symbol*] [*Library of Congress*] (LCLS)
**MNUGD6**... Memorias e Noticias Publicacoes. Museu e Laboratorio Mineralogico e Geologico. Universidade de Coimbra [*A publication*]
**MnU-IA**..... University of Minnesota, Immigration History Research Center, St. Paul, MN [*Library symbol*] [*Library of Congress*] (LCLS)
**MnU-K**...... University of Minnesota, Kerlan Children's Books Collection, Minneapolis, MN [*Library symbol*] [*Library of Congress*] (LCLS)
**MnU-L**....... University of Minnesota, Law Library, Minneapolis, MN [*Library symbol*] [*Library of Congress*] (LCLS)
**MnU-MS**... University of Minnesota, Manuscript Collection, Minneapolis, MN [*Library symbol*] [*Library of Congress*] (LCLS)
**MnU-Ph**.... University of Minnesota, Pharmacy Library, Minneapolis, MN [*Library symbol*] [*Library of Congress*] (LCLS)
**MNUR**....... Mouvement National pour l'Union et la Reconciliation au Zaire [*National Movement for Union and Reconciliation in Zaire*] [*Political party*] (PD)
**MnU-Rb**.... University of Minnesota, Rare Book Division, Minneapolis, MN [*Library symbol*] [*Library of Congress*] (LCLS)
**MnU-SW**... University of Minnesota, Social Welfare History Archives Center, St. Paul, MN [*Library symbol*] [*Library of Congress*] (LCLS)
**MNV**.......... Madisonville, TN [*Location identifier*] [*FAA*] (FAAL)
**MNV**.......... Marginal Net Value
**MNV**.......... Mina [*Nevada*] [*Seismograph station code, US Geological Survey*] (SEIS)
**MNV**.......... Mine-Neutralization Vehicle [*Military*] (MCD)
**Mn-V**......... Minnesota State Vocational Rehabilitation Library, St. Paul, MN [*Library symbol*] [*Library of Congress*] (LCLS)
**MNV**.......... Modular Nuclear Vehicle
**MNV**.......... Southwest State University, Marshall, MN [*OCLC symbol*] (OCLC)
**MNV**.......... United States Veterans Administration Hospital, Northampton, MA [*Library symbol*] [*Library of Congress*] (LCLS)
**MnV**........... Virginia Public Library, Virginia, MN [*Library symbol*] [*Library of Congress*] (LCLS)
**MnVA**........ Arrowhead Library System, Virginia, MN [*Library symbol*] [*Library of Congress*] (LCLS)
**MNVAD**.... Mededelingenblad. Nederlandse Vacuumvereniging [*A publication*]

**MnVM**....... Mesabi Community College, Virginia, MN [*Library symbol*] [*Library of Congress*] (LCLS)
**MNVM**...... Million Nighttime Vehicle Mile
**MNVR**....... Maneuver (KSC)
**MNW**........ Marketing News [*A publication*]
**M & NW**.... Minnesota & Northwestern Railroad
**Mn-W**........ Minnesota State Department of Public Welfare, St. Paul, MN [*Library symbol*] [*Library of Congress*] (LCLS)
**MNW**........ Moneywise Resources [*Vancouver Stock Exchange symbol*]
**MNW**........ Monowai [*New Zealand*] [*Seismograph station code, US Geological Survey*] (SEIS)
**MNW**........ Northwest Missouri State University, Maryville, MO [*OCLC symbol*] (OCLC)
**MnWas**...... Le Sueur-Waseca Regional Library, Waseca, MN [*Library symbol*] [*Library of Congress*] (LCLS)
**MnWasU**... University of Minnesota Technical College, Waseca, MN [*Library symbol*] [*Library of Congress*] (LCLS)
**MnWayC**... Cargill Instructional Center, Wayzata, MN [*Library symbol*] [*Library of Congress*] (LCLS)
**MnWblL**.... Lakewood Community College, White Bear Lake, MN [*Library symbol*] [*Library of Congress*] (LCLS)
**MnWilRL**.. Crow River Regional Library, Willmar, MN [*Library symbol*] [*Library of Congress*] (LCLS)
**MnWilS**..... Willmar State Junior College, Willmar, MN [*Library symbol*] [*Library of Congress*] (LCLS)
**MnWino**.... Winona Public Library, Winona, MN [*Library symbol*] [*Library of Congress*] (LCLS)
**MnWinoCT**... College of Saint Teresa, Winona, MN [*Library symbol*] [*Library of Congress*] (LCLS)
**MnWinoS**.. Winona State College [*Later, Winona State University*], Winona, MN [*Library symbol*] [*Library of Congress*] (LCLS)
**MnWinoSM**... Saint Mary's College, Winona, MN [*Library symbol*] [*Library of Congress*] (LCLS)
**MnWoN**..... Nobles County Library, Worthington, MN [*Library symbol*] [*Library of Congress*] (LCLS)
**MnWoP**..... Plum Creek Library System, Worthington, MN [*Library symbol*] [*Library of Congress*] (LCLS)
**MnWoS**..... Worthington State Junior College [*Later, Worthington Community College*], Worthington, MN [*Library symbol*] [*Library of Congress*] (LCLS)
**MnWspD**... Dakota County Library, West St. Paul, MN [*Library symbol*] [*Library of Congress*] (LCLS)
**MNX**.......... University of Minnesota, Morris, Morris, MN [*OCLC symbol*] (OCLC)
**MNXI**........ MNX, Incorporated [*St. Joseph, MO*] [*NASDAQ symbol*] (NQ)
**MNy**.......... Magyar Nyelvjarasok [*A publication*]
**MNY**.......... Messager de New York [*A publication*]
**MNY**.......... Mono Island [*Solomon Islands*] [*Airport symbol*] (OAG)
**MNY**.......... Monteynard [*France*] [*Seismograph station code, US Geological Survey*] (SEIS)
**MNY**.......... Saint Mary's College, Winona, MN [*OCLC symbol*] (OCLC)
**MNY**.......... Taurus Municipal New York Holdings [*NYSE symbol*] (SPSG)
**MNyj**......... Magyar Nyelvjarasok [*A publication*]
**MNZ**.......... College of Saint Teresa, Winona, MN [*OCLC symbol*] (OCLC)
**MNZ**.......... Manassas [*Virginia*] [*Airport symbol*] (OAG)
**MNZ**.......... Manzanillo [*Mexico*] [*Seismograph station code, US Geological Survey*] (SEIS)
**MO**............ Abbott Laboratories [*Research code symbol*]
**MO**............ Air Mindanao Corp. [*Philippines*] [*ICAO designator*] (FAAC)
**MO**............ Macau [*ANSI two-letter standard code*] (CNC)
**MO**............ Machine Operation (AFM)
**M & O**........ Machinery and Optics
**MO**............ Magneto-Optic Storage [*Data processing*]
**MO**............ Mail Order [*Business term*]
**MO**............ Maintenance Officer (MCD)
**MO**............ Maintenance and Operating [*Factor*] (NG)
**M/O**........... Maintenance to Operation [*Ratio*]
**M & O**........ Maintenance and Operation (MCD)
**M/O**........... Maintenance/Organization (MCD)
**M & O**........ Maintenance and Overhaul
**MO**............ Major Objective (KSC)
**MO**............ Make Offer
**MO**............ Making Objects [*Research test*] [*Psychology*]
**MO**............ Management Office
**MO**............ Management Order (NOAA)
**M & O**........ Management and Organization
**M/O**........... Manned and Operational (MUGU)
**MO**............ Manned Orbiter (MCD)
**M & O**........ Manpower and Organization [*Military*]
**MO**............ Manual Orientation (MCD)
**MO**............ Manual Output
**MO**............ Manually Operated
**MO**............ Manufacturer's Output
**MO**............ Manufacturing Order (NASA)
**MO**............ Manufacturing Outline
**MO**............ Mark Off
**MO**............ Mars Orbiter [*NASA*] (KSC)
**MO**............ Masonry Opening [*Technical drawings*]
**MO**............ Mass Observation
**MO**............ Master of Obstetrics
**MO**............ Master of Oratory
**MO**............ Master Oscillator [*Radio*]
**MO**............ Master of Osteopathy
**M & O**........ Materials and Others
**MO**............ Mature Outlook (EA)
**MO**............ Medical Officer [*Military*]
**MO**............ Medium Oocyte
**MO**............ Memory Operation
**MO**............ Memory Output [*Data processing*]
**MO**............ Mesio-Occlusal [*Dentistry*]
**MO**............ Mesityl Oxide [*Also, MSO*] [*Organic chemistry*]
**MO**............ Meteorological Office [*British*]
**MO**............ Meteorology Officer (MUGU)
**MO**............ Method of Operation
**MO**............ Methoxime [*Organic chemistry*]
**MO**............ Micro-Opaque
**MO**............ Micro-Osmometer
**mO**............ Mid-Oxygen [*Beta-alumina crystallography*]
**MO**............ Middeck Overhead (MCD)
**MO**............ Military Operations [*British military*] (DMA)
**MO**............ Military Orders Issued by the President as Commander in Chief of the Armed Forces [*A publication*] (DLA)
**MO**............ Mineral Oil
**MO**............ Mineral Order [*Defense Minerals Exploration Administration*] [*Department of the Interior*] [*A publication*] (DLA)
**MO**............ Ministerstvo Oborony [*Ministry of Defense*] [*USSR*]
**MO**............ Minute Output [*Of heart*]
**MO**............ Miscellanea Orientalia [*A publication*]
**MO**............ Miscellaneous Operation (MUGU)
**MO**............ Missile Officer (AAG)
**MO**............ Mission Operations [*NASA*]
**MO**............ Mission Oriented
**MO**............ Missionerskoe Obozrienie [*A publication*]
**MO**............ Missouri [*Postal code*] (AFM)
**MO**............ Missouri Reports [*A publication*]
**Mo**............ Missouri State Library, Jefferson City, MO [*Library symbol*] [*Library of Congress*] (LCLS)
**MO**............ Missouri Supreme Court Reports [*1821-1956*] [*A publication*] (DLA)
**MO**............ Mitral Valve Opening [*Cardiology*]
**MO**............ Mixed Oxide (NRCH)
**M & O**........ Mobile & Ohio Railroad
**MO**............ Mobile Station [*Air Force*]
**Mo**............ Mode [*Statistics*]
**MO**............ Moderato [*Moderate Speed*] [*Music*] (ADA)
**MO**............ Moderator
**MO**............ Modern Orthodox (BJA)
**Mo**............ Modern Reports [*England*] [*A publication*] (DLA)
**MO**............ Modification Order (AFIT)
**MO**............ Modulate Open [*Nuclear energy*] (NRCH)
**MO**............ Modus Operandi [*Police term for distinctive techniques used by criminals*]
**MO**............ Mohawk Airlines, Inc. [*Obsolete*]
**MO**............ Molded [*Construction*]
**MO**............ Molecular Orbital [*Atomic physics*]
**Mo**............ Molybdenum [*Chemical element*]
**MO**............ Moment (DSUE)
**MO**............ Monaco [*IYRU nationality code*] (IYR)
**Mo**............ Monaldus [*Flourished, 13th century*] [*Authority cited in pre-1607 legal work*] (DSA)
**Mo**............ Monat [*A publication*]
**MO**............ Monatshefte [*A publication*]
**MO**............ Monde Oriental [*A publication*]
**Mo**............ Money [*A publication*]
**MO**............ Money Order
**MO**............ Monitor Output
**MO**............ Monooxygenase [*An enzyme*]
**MO**............ Month (AFM)
**MO**............ Monthly Order [*Navy*]
**MO**............ Mooney Aircraft, Inc. [*ICAO aircraft manufacturer identifier*] (ICAO)
**Mo**............ [*J. B.*] Moore's English Common Pleas Reports [*A publication*] (DLA)
**Mo**............ [*Sir Francis*] Moore's English King's Bench Reports [*A publication*] (DLA)
**Mo**............ Moore's English Privy Council Reports [*1836-62*] [*A publication*] (DLA)
**Mo**............ Moore's Indian Appeals [*A publication*] (DLA)
**MO**............ Moravian
**MO**............ Morning
**MO**............ Morse Code Light [*or Fog Signal*] [*Navigation signal*]
**Mo**............ Moskva [*A publication*]
**MO**............ Mother
**MO**............ Motion for Mandamus Overruled [*Legal term*] (DLA)
**MO**............ Motor Operated (MSA)
**MO**............ Moustache (DSUE)
**MO**............ Mouth
**MO**............ Move (NASA)
**MO**............ Movement Orders
**MO**............ Movimento Operaio [*A publication*]

**MO** ........... Multi-Option (MCD)
**MO** ........... Municipal Offices (ROG)
**MO** ........... Murphy Oil Co. Ltd. [*Toronto Stock Exchange symbol*]
**MO** ........... Musical Opinion [*A publication*]
**MO** ........... Mustered Out [*of military service*]
**MO** ........... Philip Morris Companies, Inc. [*NYSE symbol*] (SPSG)
**$MO_2$** ........... Mixed Oxides
**MOA**.......... Made on Assembly
**MOA**.......... Make on Arrival (NASA)
**MOA**.......... Management Operations Audit [*Navy*] (NG)
**MOA**.......... Manual-Off-Automatic (KSC)
**MOA**.......... Marine Officer's Attendant [*British military*] (DMA)
**MOA**.......... Matrix Output Amplifier
**MOA**.......... McDonald's Operators' Association (EA)
**MOA**.......... Medium Observation Aircraft
**MOA**.......... Memorandum of Agreement
**MOA**.......... Method of Accomplishment (AFIT)
**MOA**.......... Method of Adjustment [*Aviation*]
**MOA**.......... Methods of Administration [*Department of Education*] (OICC)
**MOA**.......... Military Assistance Program Order Amendment (AFM)
**MOA**.......... Military Operations Area (FAAC)
**MOA**.......... Ministry of Agriculture [*Philippines*] (DS)
**MOA**.......... Ministry of Aviation [*British*]
**MOA**.......... Minute-of-Angle (NASA)
**MOA**.......... Misr Overseas Airways [*Egypt*]
**MOA**.......... Missile Optical Alignment
**MOA**.......... Missouri Botanical Garden, St. Louis, MO [*OCLC symbol*] (OCLC)
**MOA**.......... Moa [*Cuba*] [*Airport symbol*] (OAG)
**MOA**.......... Modern Operating Agreement [*Labor negotiations*]
**MOA**.......... Molln [*Austria*] [*Seismograph station code, US Geological Survey*] (SEIS)
**MOA**.......... Mountain Lake Resources, Inc. [*Vancouver Stock Exchange symbol*]
**MOA**.......... Municipal Officers' Association (ROG)
**MOA**.......... Music Operators of America [*Later, AMOA*] (EA)
**MOAA**......... Mail Order Association of America (EA)
**MoAB**........ Monoclonal Antibody [*Immunochemistry*]
**MO Acad Sci Occas Pap** ... Missouri Academy of Science. Occasional Paper [*A publication*]
**MO Admin Code** ... Missouri Code of State Regulations [*A publication*] (DLA)
**MO Admin Reg** ... Missouri Register [*A publication*] (DLA)
**MOADS**.... Montgomery Air Defense Sector [*of SAGE*] (MUGU)
**MO Ag Bd** ... Missouri State Board of Agriculture. Publications [*A publication*]
**MO Ag Exp** ... Missouri. Agricultural Experiment Station. Publications [*A publication*]
**MO Agric Exp Stn Bull** ... Missouri. Agricultural Experiment Station. Bulletin [*A publication*]
**MO Agric Exp Stn Res Bull** ... Missouri. Agricultural Experiment Station. Research Bulletin [*A publication*]
**MO Agric Exp Stn Spec Rep** ... Missouri. Agricultural Experiment Station. Special Report [*A publication*]
**Moak**.......... Moak's English Reports [*A publication*] (DLA)
**Moak (Eng)** ... Moak's English Reports [*A publication*] (DLA)
**Moak Eng Rep** ... Moak's English Reports [*A publication*] (DLA)
**Moak Und** ... Moak's Edition of Underhill on Torts [*A publication*] (DLA)
**Moak Underh Torts** ... Moak's Edition of Underhill on Torts [*A publication*] (DLA)
**Moak Van S Pl** ... Moak's Edition of Van Santvoord's Equity Pleading [*A publication*] (DLA)
**MOALC**.... Mobile Air Logistics Center [*Air Force*]
**MOAMA**... Mobile Air Materiel Area
**MO Ann Stat (Vernon)** ... Vernon's Annotated Missouri Statutes [*A publication*] (DLA)
**MO Ap**....... Missouri Appeal Reports [*A publication*] (DLA)
**MO App**..... Missouri Appeal Reports [*A publication*] (DLA)
**MO Appeals** ... Missouri Appeal Reports [*A publication*] (DLA)
**MO App (KC)** ... Missouri Appeal Reports [*Kansas City*] [*A publication*] (DLA)
**MO App Rep** ... Missouri Appeal Reports [*A publication*] (DLA)
**MO Apps**... Missouri Appeal Reports [*A publication*] (DLA)
**MO App (St L)** ... Missouri Appeal Reports [*St. Louis*] [*A publication*] (DLA)
**MO AR**...... Missouri Appellate Reporter [*A publication*] (DLA)
**MOARS**.... Mobilization Assignment Reserve Section [*Military*]
**MOAT**....... Missile on Aircraft Test
**MOATL**.... Modal Acoustic Transmission Loss (MCD)
**Mo Aust Dem R** ... Monthly Australian Demographic Review [*A publication*] (APTA)
**MOB**.......... Main Operating Base
**M & OB**..... Maintenance and Operations Branch [*BUPERS*]
**MOB**.......... Make or Buy [*Economics*]
**MOB**.......... Man-Overboard
**MOB**.......... Menlo Park [*California*] [*Seismograph station code, US Geological Survey*] (SEIS)
**MOB**.......... Ministry of Budget [*Philippines*] (DS)
**MOB**.......... Missile Order of Battle (AFM)
**MOB**.......... Mobil Corp. [*NYSE symbol*] [*Toronto Stock Exchange symbol*] (SPSG)
**MOB**.......... Mobile [*Alabama*] [*Airport symbol*]
**MOB**.......... Mobile (NATG)
**MOB**.......... Mobilization [*or Mobilize*] (AFM)
**Mob**........... Mobley's Contested Election Cases, United States House of Representatives [*1882-89*] [*A publication*] (DLA)
**MOB**.......... Mock-Up Board [*Navy*] (AFIT)
**MoB**.......... Monde de la Bible [*A publication*]
**MOB**.......... Money-Order Business
**MOB**.......... Mortgage Banking [*A publication*]
**MOB**.......... Municipals over Bonds [*Investment term*]
**MOB**.......... Mustargen [*Nitrogen mustard*], Oncovin [*Vincristine*], Bleomycin [*Antineoplastic drug regimen*]
**MOB**.......... Southwest Baptist College, Bolivar, MO [*OCLC symbol*] (OCLC)
**MOBA**....... Military Operations in Built-Up Areas
**MOBAC**.... Monterey Bay Area Cooperative Library System [*Library network*]
**MO Bar J**.. Missouri Bar. Journal [*A publication*]
**MOBAS**..... Model Basin
**MOBAT**.... Mobile Battalion Antitank Gun [*British military*] (DMA)
**MOBCOM** ... Mobile Communications
**MOBCON** ... Mobilization Construction Plan [*Military*] (NVT)
**MOBDES** ... Mobilization Designation [*or Designee*]
**MOBDIC** ... Mobile Digital Computer
**MOBED**.... Mobile Education Demonstration
**MOBEU**.... Mobile Emergency Unit (NOAA)
**MOBEX**.... Mobile Excursion (MCD)
**MOBEX**.... Mobile Exploration [*NASA*]
**MOBEX**.... Mobility Test Exercise [*Military*]
**MO B G**..... Missouri Bureau of Geology and Mines [*A publication*]
**MOBIDA**.. Mobile Data Acquisition System (MCD)
**MOBIDAC** ... Mobile Data Acquisition System
**MOBIDIC** ... Mobile Digital Computer [*Sylvania Electric Products Co.*]
**MOB-III**.... Mitomycin C, Oncovin [*Vincristine*], Bleomycin, Cisplatin [*Antineoplastic drug regimen*]
**MOBIL**...... Mobility
**Mobil Country J** ... Mobil Country Journal [*A publication*] (APTA)
**MOBILESAT** ... Mobile Satellite Corp. [*King Of Prussia, PA*] [*Telecommunications*] (TSSD)
**Mobil Ph N** ... Mobile Phone News [*A publication*]
**Mobil Rev**.. Mobil Review [*A publication*] (APTA)
**MOBIS**...... Management-Oriented Budget Information System
**MO B J**...... Missouri Bar. Journal [*A publication*]
**MOBL**....... Macro-Oriented Business Language [*Data processing*]
**MOBL**....... Main Operating Base LASER
**Mobl**.......... Mobley's Contested Election Cases, United States House of Representatives [*1882-89*] [*A publication*] (DLA)
**MOBMAN** ... Mobilization Manpower Planning System [*DoD*]
**MOBMDR** ... Mobilization Master Data Record [*Army*]
**MOBOL**.... Mohawk Business-Oriented Language [*Mohawk Data Systems*]
**MoBolS**...... Southwest Baptist College, Bolivar, MO [*Library symbol*] [*Library of Congress*] (LCLS)
**MOBOT**.... Mobile Remote-Controlled Robot
**MOBOT**.... Modular Robot
**MO Bot Gard Ann** ... Missouri Botanical Garden. Annals [*A publication*]
**MO Bot Gard Bull** ... Missouri Botanical Garden. Bulletin [*A publication*]
**MOBPERSACS** ... Mobilization Personnel Structure and Composition System [*DoD*]
**MoBr** ......... Brentwood Public Library, Brentwood, MO [*Library symbol*] [*Library of Congress*] (LCLS)
**MOBRASOP** ... Mobilization Requirements in Support of the Army Strategic Objectives Plan
**MOBS**....... Mobile Hospitals [*Military slang*]
**MOBS**....... Multiple-Orbit Bombardment System
**MOBSSL-UAF** ... Merritt and Miller's Own Block Structured Simulation Language, Unpronounceable Acronym For [*1969*] [*Data processing*] (CSR)
**MOBSSq**... Mobility Support Squadron [*Air Force*]
**MOBTB**..... Mobilization Troop Basis [*Army*] (AABC)
**MOBTDA** ... Mobilization Table of Distribution and Allowances [*Military*] (AABC)
**MOBTR**.... Mobile Trainer
**MOBU**....... Mobilization Base Units
**MOBULA** ... Model Building Language [*Programming language*] (IEEE)
**MOBYC**.... My Own Bloody Yacht Club [*Founded in England; registered with Lloyds of London*]
**MOC**.......... Bedrijfshuishouding. Magazine voor Interne en Civiele Diensten [*A publication*]
**MOC**.......... Magnetic Optic Converter
**MOC**.......... Maintenance Operations Center [*Military*]
**MOC**.......... Management of Change
**MOC**.......... Manual Operations Control
**MOC**.......... Marcos Owners Club [*Formerly, Marcos Club*] (EA)
**MOC**.......... Marine Operation Center [*NASA*] (NASA)
**MOC**.......... Marlin Owners' Club (EA)
**MOC**.......... Master Operational Computer [*or Controller*]
**MOC**.......... Master Operations Center
**MOC**.......... Master Operations Console
**MOC**.......... Master Operations Control
**MOC**.......... Master Ordnance Configuration File [*Navy*]
**MOC**.......... Mathematical Operations Computer

**MOC**.......... Maximum Oxygen Consumption
**MOC**.......... Memorandum of Conditions
**MOC**.......... Memory Operating Characteristic [*Data processing*] (IEEE)
**MOC**.......... Merland Explorations Ltd. [*Toronto Stock Exchange symbol*]
**MOC**.......... Messerschmitt Owners Club (EA)
**MOC**.......... Method of Characteristics [*Equilibrium flow*]
**MOC**.......... Metropolitan Owners' Club [*Woking, Surrey, England*] (EAIO)
**MOC**.......... Military Occupation Code (MCD)
**MOC**.......... Military Order of the Carabao (EA)
**MOC**.......... Minimal Oxygen Consumption
**MOC**.......... Minimum Operational Characteristics
**MOC**.......... Ministry of Communications (CINC)
**MOC**.......... Missile Operation Center [*Air Force*]
**MOC**.......... Mission Operation Computer
**MOC**.......... Mission Operations Complex [*NASA*] (KSC)
**MOC**.......... Mobile Oil Cooler
**M & OC**..... Monitor and Operations Control System [*Space Flight Operations Facility, NASA*]
**MOC**.......... Montes Claros [*Brazil*] [*Airport symbol*] (OAG)
**MOC**.......... Morris College, Sumter, SC [*OCLC symbol*] [*Inactive*] (OCLC)
**MOC**.......... Mustang Owners Club (EA)
**MOC**.......... Myanma Oil Corporation [*Burma*] (DS)
**MOC**.......... Supreme Pup Tent, Military Order of the Cootie (EA)
**MOCA**....... Methotrexate, Oncovin [*Vincristine*], Cyclophosphamide, Adriamycin [*Antineoplastic drug regimen*]
**MOCA**....... Methylenebis(ortho-chloroaniline) [*Also, MBOCA*] [*Organic chemistry*]
**MOCA**....... Minimum Obstruction Clearance Altitude [*Aviation*]
**MOCA**....... Mitsubishi Owner's Club of America
**MOCA**....... Montezuma Castle National Monument
**MOCA**....... Museum of Contemporary Art [*Los Angeles*]
**MOCAM**... Mobile Checkout and Maintenance (AAG)
**Mocambique Missao Combate Tripanossomiases Annu Rep** ... Mocambique Missao de Combate as Tripanossomiases. Annual Report [*A publication*]
**MOCAN**.... Motor Can
**MoCanC** .... Culver-Stockton College, Canton, MO [*Library symbol*] [*Library of Congress*] (LCLS)
**MOCAS** .... Mechanization of Contract Administration Service (MCD)
**MOCC**....... MG Octagon Car Club [*Formerly, Octagon Car Club*] (EA)
**MOCCA**.... Methylprednisolone, Oncovin [*Vincristine*], CCNU [*Lomustine*], Cyclophosphamide, Alkeran [*Melphalan*] [*Antineoplastic drug regimen*]
**Moccasin Tel** ... Moccasin Telegraph [*A publication*]
**MOccThy**.. Master of Occupational Therapy (ADA)
**MOCF** ....... Maintenance Operations Control File (MCD)
**MOCF** ....... Mission Operations Computational Facilities [*NASA*] (NASA)
**MoCg**......... Cape Girardeau Public Library, Cape Girardeau, MO [*Library symbol*] [*Library of Congress*] (LCLS)
**MoCgS**....... Southeast Missouri State University, Cape Girardeau, MO [*Library symbol*] [*Library of Congress*] (LCLS)
**MOCI** ........ Mound City Group National Monument
**MOCI** ........ Mustang Owners Club International (EA)
**MOCIC** ..... Molecular Orbital Constraint of Interaction Coordinates [*Atomic physics*]
**MOCL** ....... Metz Owners Club Library (EA)
**MoClS** ....... Saint Louis Junior College, Clayton, MO [*Library symbol*] [*Library of Congress*] [*Obsolete*] (LCLS)
**MOCM**...... Missile Out of Commission for Maintenance (MUGU)
**MOCNA**.... Metropolitan Owners Club of North America (EA)
**MOCNESS** ... Multiple Opening-Closing Net and Environmental Sensing System [*For collecting marine samples*]
**MOCO**....... Machinery Overhaul Company
**MOCO**....... Missile Operations Control Officer (AAG)
**MOCO**....... Modern Controls, Inc. [*NASDAQ symbol*] (NQ)
**MoCoC** ...... Christian College, Columbia, MO [*Library symbol*] [*Library of Congress*] (LCLS)
**MO Code Regs** ... Missouri Code of State Regulations [*A publication*]
**MOCODES** ... Mobile Coastal Defense System (MCD)
**MoCoGS**.... Church of Jesus Christ of Latter-Day Saints, Genealogical Society Library, Columbia Missouri Branch, Columbia, MO [*Library symbol*] [*Library of Congress*] (LCLS)
**MOCOM**... Mobility Command [*AMC*]
**MOCON** ... Mobile Repair Parts Container
**MoConA**.... Conception Abbey and Seminary, Conception, MO [*Library symbol*] [*Library of Congress*] (LCLS)
**MO Conserv** ... Missouri Conservationist [*A publication*]
**MoCoS**....... Stephens College, Columbia, MO [*Library symbol*] [*Library of Congress*] (LCLS)
**MoCoV** ...... Harry S Truman Memorial Veterans Hospital, Columbia, MO [*Library symbol*] [*Library of Congress*] (LCLS)
**MOCP** ....... Missile Out of Commission for Parts (AFM)
**MOCR**....... Metz Owners Club Register (EA)
**MOCR**....... Mission Operations Control Room
**MOCR**....... Moores Creek National Military Park
**MOCRA** .... Molecular Crystals [*A publication*]
**MOCS** ....... Master Operations Control System (KSC)
**MOCS** ....... Military Order of Columbia's Shield (EA)
**MOCS** ....... Multichannel Ocean Color Sensor [*NASA*]
**MoCStP**..... Saint Paul's College, Concordia, MO [*Library symbol*] [*Library of Congress*] (LCLS)
**MOCSW** ... Monitor and Operations Control Software Subsystem [*Space Flight Operations Facility, NASA*]
**MOCT** ....... Mean Overhaul Cycle Time [*Quality control*] (MCD)
**MOCT** ....... Moccasin Telegraph [*A publication*]
**MOCV**....... Manual Oxygen Control Valve (NASA)
**MO-CVD**... Metal-Organic Chemical Vapor Deposition [*Also, MO-VPE, OM-CVD, OM-VPE*] [*Semiconductor technology*]
**MOD** ......... Drury College, Springfield, MO [*OCLC symbol*] (OCLC)
**MOD** ......... Magnetic Optical Display
**MOD** ......... Magneto-Optical Disc [*Digital audio technology*]
**MOD** ......... Mail-Order Delivery
**MOD** ......... Mail Order Department [*Business term*]
**MOD** ......... Manager on Duty
**MOD** ......... Manned Orbital Development Station [*See also MODS, MOSS, MTSS*] [*Air Force/NASA*]
**MOD** ......... Manpower and Organization Division [*Air Force*]
**MOD** ......... Mapping of Disease
**MOD** ......... March on Drugs [*An association*]
**MOD** ......... Maturity Onset Diabetes [*Medicine*]
**MOD** ......... Medical Officer of the Day [*Military*]
**MOD** ......... Medicine, Osteopathy, and Dentistry [*HEW program*]
**MOD** ......... Mesial, Occlusal, and Distal [*Describes location of openings in a carious tooth*] [*Dentistry*]
**MOD** ......... Message Output Description [*Data processing*]
**MOD** ......... Metallo-Organic Deposition [*Materials technology*]
**MOD** ......... Microfilm-Output Device
**MOD** ......... Microwave Oscillating Diode (MCD)
**MOD** ......... Military Obligation Designator
**MOD** ......... Military Orbital Development System [*See also MODS, MOSS, MTSS*] [*Air Force/NASA*]
**MOD** ......... Ministry of Defence [*British*]
**MOD** ......... Ministry of Overseas Development [*British*] (ILCA)
**MOD** ......... Miscellaneous Obligation Document
**MOD** ......... Mission Objectives Document (MCD)
**MOD** ......... Mission Operations Director [*NASA*] (KSC)
**MOD** ......... Mobile Obstacle Detachment (MCD)
**MOD** ......... Mobility Opportunity and Development
**MOD** ......... Modal (Verb) [*Linguistics*]
**MOD** ......... Modatech Systems, Inc. [*Vancouver Stock Exchange symbol*]
**MOD** ......... Model (KSC)
**MOD** ......... Moderate [*Used to qualify icing, turbulence, interference, or static reports*] [*Aviation*] (FAAC)
**MOD** ......... Moderate [*or Moderator*] (AABC)
**MOD** ......... Moderato [*Moderate Speed*] [*Music*]
**MOD** ......... Modern
**Mod**............ Modern Reports [*England*] [*A publication*] (DLA)
**MOD** ......... Modesto [*California*] [*Airport symbol*] (OAG)
**MOD** ......... Modification [*or Modify*] (AFM)
**MOD** ......... Modifier [*Linguistics*]
**MOD** ......... Modiim [*Israel*] [*Later, AMT*] [*Geomagnetic observatory code*]
**MOD** ......... Modular Observation Device (RDA)
**MOD** ......... Modulation [*Telecommunications*] (KSC)
**MOD** ......... Modulator (CET)
**MOD** ......... Modulator-Demodulator [*Telecommunications*] (MCD)
**MOD** ......... Module [*or Modular or Modulation*] (KSC)
**MOD** ......... Modulus
**MOD** ......... Money-Order Department
**MOD** ......... Month of Detachment
**MOD** ......... Motor-Operated Disconnect [*Nuclear energy*] (NRCH)
**MOD** ......... Moving Domain Memories [*Data processing*] (MDG)
**Mod**............ Style's English King's Bench Reports [*1646-55*] [*A publication*] (DLA)
**MOD10** ..... Modulus 10 Check Digit [*Data processing*]
**MODA**....... Ministry of Defense and Aviation (MCD)
**Mod A** ........ Modern Age [*A publication*]
**MODA**....... Motion Detector and Alarm [*Army*]
**MODABUND** ... Mosquito Data Bank of the University of Notre Dame
**MODAC**.... Mountain System Digital Automatic Computer
**MODACS** ... Modular Data Acquisition and Control System [*or Subsystem*] [*Modular Computing Systems, Inc.*]
**MOD(AD)** ... Ministry of Defence (Army Department) [*British*]
**Mod Age** .... Modern Age [*A publication*]
**Mod Aging Res** ... Modern Aging Research [*A publication*]
**MODAL**.... [*A*] programming language [*1973*] (CSR)
**Mod Am Law** ... Modern American Law [*A publication*] (DLA)
**MODAP**.... Modified Apollo [*NASA*] (MCD)
**MODAP**.... Multiple Operational Data Acquisition Program [*Data processing*]
**MODAPS** ... Maintenance and Operational Data Presentation Study (AAG)
**MODAPS** ... Modal Data Acquisition and Processing System
**MODAPTS** ... Modular Arrangement of Predetermined Time Standards
**MODART** ... Methods of Defeating Advanced RADAR Threats (NASA)
**Mod Arts News** ... Modern Arts News [*A publication*] (APTA)
**MODAS** .... Multidirectional Osmotic Drug Absorption System [*Medicine*]
**Mod Asian S** ... Modern Asian Studies [*A publication*]
**Mod Asian Stud** ... Modern Asian Studies [*A publication*]
**MODASM** ... Modular Air-to-Surface Missile (MCD)
**Mod Aspects Electrochem** ... Modern Aspects of Electrochemistry [*A publication*]
**Mod Aspects Neurosurg** ... Modern Aspects of Neurosurgery [*A publication*]

**Mod Aspects Vitreous State** ... Modern Aspects of the Vitreous State [*A publication*]
**Mod As Stud** ... Modern Asian Studies [*London*] [*A publication*]
**Mod Ath and Coach** ... Modern Athlete and Coach [*A publication*]
**Mod Athl Coach** ... Modern Athlete and Coach [*A publication*]
**MODATS** ... Mohawk Data Transmission System (MCD)
**Mod Aust L** ... Modern Austrian Literature [*A publication*]
**Mod Austrian Lit** ... Modern Austrian Literature [*A publication*]
**MODB**....... Military Occupational Data Bank [*Later, AOSP*] (AABC)
**Mod B**........ Modern Boating [*A publication*] (APTA)
**Mod Beekeep** ... Modern Beekeeping [*A publication*]
**Mod Biol**.... Modern Biology [*A publication*]
**Mod Brew**.. Modern Brewer [*A publication*]
**Mod Brew Age** ... Modern Brewery Age [*A publication*]
**Mod Brew M** ... Modern Brewery Age. Magazine Section [*A publication*]
**Mod Bus Law** ... Modern Business Law [*A publication*]
**Mod Ca per Far** ... 6 and 7 Modern Reports [*1702-45*] [*A publication*] (DLA)
**Mod Ca L & Eq** ... 8 and 9 Modern Reports [*88 English Reprint*] [*1721-55*] [*A publication*] (DLA)
**Mod Camera Mag** ... Modern Camera Magazine [*A publication*]
**MODCAR** ... Modified Owners and Drivers Corporation for the Advancement of Racing (EA)
**Mod Cas**.... Modern Cases [*6 Modern Reports*] [*1702-45*] [*A publication*] (DLA)
**Mod Cas per Far** ... Modern Cases Tempore Holt, by Farresley [*7 Modern Reports*] [*A publication*] (DLA)
**Mod Cas L & Eq** ... Modern Cases at Law and Equity [*8, 9 Modern Reports*] [*1721-55*] [*A publication*] (DLA)
**Mod Cast** ... Modern Castings [*A publication*]
**Mod Cast Am Foundryman** ... Modern Casting and American Foundryman [*A publication*]
**Mod Cas T Holt** ... Modern Cases Tempore Holt, by Farresley [*7 Modern Reports*] [*A publication*] (DLA)
**Mod Ca T Holt** ... 7 Modern Reports [*1702-45*] [*A publication*] (DLA)
**Mod C Cardi** ... Modern Concepts of Cardiovascular Disease [*A publication*]
**Mod Cell Biol** ... Modern Cell Biology [*A publication*]
**Mod Ch**...... Modern Churchman [*A publication*]
**Mod Chem** ... Modern Chemistry [*Japan*] [*A publication*]
**Mod China** ... Modern China [*A publication*]
**Mod China Stud** ... Modern China Studies [*A publication*]
**Mod Chin Lit Newsl** ... Modern Chinese Literature Newsletter [*Berkeley*] [*A publication*]
**ModChm**.... Modern Churchman [*A publication*]
**Mod Clin**.... Modern Clinics [*Japan*] [*A publication*]
**MODCOM** ... Modular Computer System
**MOD CON** ... Modern Convenience (DSUE)
**Mod Concepts Cardiovasc Dis** ... Modern Concepts of Cardiovascular Disease [*A publication*]
**Mod Concr** ... Modern Concrete [*A publication*]
**MODCPS** ... Multiple Output Direct Current Power Supply
**MODD**...... Military Order of Devil Dogs (EA)
**ModD**......... Modern Drama [*A publication*]
**Mod Dairy** ... Modern Dairy [*A publication*]
**Mod Data**... Modern Data [*A publication*]
**Mod Dev Powder Metall** ... Modern Development in Powder Metallurgy [*A publication*]
**MODDF**.... Military Order, Devil Dog Fleas (EA)
**MOD DICT** ... In the Manner Directed [*Abbreviation from the Latin*] [*Pharmacy*] (ROG)
**ModDr**....... Modern Drama [*A publication*]
**Mod Drama** ... Modern Drama [*A publication*]
**Mod Drugs** ... Modern Drugs [*A publication*]
**MODE**....... Management of Objectives with Dollars through Employees [*Department of Agriculture*]
**MODE**....... Merchant Oriented Data Entry
**MODE**....... Methoxy(O-desmethyl)encainide [*Biochemistry*]
**MODE**....... Mid-Ocean Dynamics Experiment [*National Science Foundation*]
**Mode**.......... Modern Office and Data Equipment [*A publication*] (APTA)
**MODE**....... Monitor Data Equipment
**MO Dec**..... Missouri Decisions [*A publication*] (DLA)
**Mod Ed**...... Modern Education [*A publication*]
**Model Biol Med Resp Mezhved Sb** ... Modelirovanie v Biologii i Meditsine Respublikanskii Mezhvedomstvennyi Sbornik [*A publication*]
**Model Bus Corp Act Anno 2d** ... American Bar Association Model Business Corporation Act, Annotated, Second Series [*A publication*] (DLA)
**Model Business Corp Act** ... American Bar Association Model Business Corporation Act, Annotated [*A publication*] (DLA)
**Model Eng** ... Model Engineer [*A publication*]
**Model Identif Control** ... Modeling Identification and Control [*Norway*] [*A publication*]
**Modelirovanie Ekonom Processov** ... Otdelenie Ekonomiceskoi Kivernetiki Ekonomiceskogo Fakul'teta Moskovogo Gosudarstvennogo Universiteta Imeni M. V. Lomonosova. Modelirovanie Ekonomiceskih Processov [*A publication*]
**Model Land Dev Code** ... American Law Institute Model Land Development Code [*A publication*] (DLA)
**Model Simul Proc Annu Pittsburgh Conf** ... Modeling and Simulation. Proceedings. Annual Pittsburgh Conference [*A publication*]
**Models Lab Rep Dep Archit Sci Syd Univ** ... Models Laboratory Reports. Department of Architectural Science. University of Sydney [*A publication*] (APTA)
**MODEM**... Modulate/Demodulate [*or Modulation/Demodulation or Modulator-Demodulator*] [*Data processing*]
**Mod (Eng)** ... English King's Bench Modern Reports [*86-88 English Reprint*] [*A publication*] (DLA)
**Mod Eng**.... Modern Engineer [*A publication*]
**MOD ENT** ... Modern Entries [*Legal term*] (DLA)
**MO Dent J** ... Missouri Dental Journal [*A publication*]
**MO Dep Conserv Terr Ser** ... Missouri. Department of Conservation. Terrestrial Series [*A publication*]
**Modern Boating** ... Modern Boating and Seacraft [*A publication*]
**Modern Drum** ... Modern Drummer [*A publication*]
**Moderne Lehrtexte Wirtschaftwiss** ... Moderne Lehrtexte. Wirtschaftswissenschaften [*Cologne*] [*A publication*]
**Moderne Math Elem Darstellung** ... Moderne Mathematik in Elementarer Darstellung [*A publication*]
**Modern Lit** ... Modern Liturgy [*A publication*]
**Modern LR** ... Modern Law Review [*A publication*]
**Modern L Rev** ... Modern Law Review [*A publication*]
**Modern O**.. Modern Occasions [*A publication*]
**Modern Plastics Int** ... Modern Plastics International [*A publication*]
**Modern P S** ... Modern Poetry Studies [*A publication*]
**Modern Railw** ... Modern Railways [*A publication*]
**Modern Vocational Trends Career Mon** ... Modern Vocational Trends. Career Monographs [*A publication*]
**Modes**........ [*Herennius*] Modestinus [*Flourished, 3rd century*] [*Authority cited in pre-1607 legal work*] (DSA)
**MODEST** ... Missile Optical Destruction Technique
**Modesti**...... [*Herennius*] Modestinus [*Flourished, 3rd century*] [*Authority cited in pre-1607 legal work*] (DSA)
**Modest Pistor** ... Modestinus Pistoris [*Deceased, 1565*] [*Authority cited in pre-1607 legal work*] (DSA)
**MODET**.... Mortar Detection
**MODEX**.... Mobilization Deployment Exercise (MCD)
**MODF**....... Modify (AAG)
**Mod Farmer** ... Modern Farmer [*A publication*]
**Mod Farming** ... Modern Farming [*A publication*]
**Mod Farming Cent Afr** ... Modern Farming in Central Africa [*A publication*]
**MODFET** ... Modulation-Doped Field-Effect Transistor [*Solid-state physics*]
**Mod Fict St** ... Modern Fiction Studies [*A publication*]
**Mod Fict Stud** ... Modern Fiction Studies [*A publication*]
**MODFLIR** ... Modular Forward-Looking Infrared Seeker
**MODFN**.... Modification (AAG)
**MODFR**.... Modifier (AAG)
**Mod'g**........ Modifying [*Legal term*] (DLA)
**Mod Geol**... Modern Geology [*A publication*]
**MODHATR** ... Modified Hatrack [*Cyclone forecasting*] [*Navy*]
**Mod Health** ... Modern Healthcare [*A publication*]
**Mod Healthcare** ... Modern Healthcare [*A publication*]
**Mod Heb Lit** ... Modern Hebrew Literature [*A publication*]
**Mod Holzverarb** ... Moderne Holzverarbeitung [*A publication*]
**Mod Hosp** ... Modern Hospital [*A publication*]
**MODI**........ Major Oversea Depot and Installation Method [*Army*]
**MODI**........ Modified Distribution
**MODI**........ Modine Manufacturing Co. [*Racine, WI*] [*NASDAQ symbol*] (NQ)
**MODI**........ Modular Optical Digital Interface
**MODICON** ... Modular-Dispersed-Control
**MODIF**..... Modification (KSC)
**Modif Polim Mater** ... Modifikatsiya Polimernykh Materialov [*Latvian SSR*] [*A publication*]
**MODIG**..... Modular Digital Image Generation [*Data processing*]
**MODIGSI** ... Modular Digital Simulation (MCD)
**MODILS**... Modular Instrument Landing System
**MODIM**.... MOTS [*Module Test Set*] Design Information Memorandum
**Mod Ind**..... Modern Industry [*A publication*]
**Mod Ind Energy** ... Modern Industrial Energy [*United States*] [*A publication*]
**Mod Int**...... Brown's Modus Intrandi [*A publication*] (DLA)
**Mod Int Dr** ... Modern International Drama [*A publication*]
**Modio**......... MODEM and Radio [*Telecommunications*]
**MOD/IRAN** ... Modification/Inspection and Repair as Necessary
**MODIS**..... Mode Shape Display [*Module*]
**MODISCO** ... Mechanization of Defense Industrial Security Clearance Office [*DoD*]
**Mod Jud**..... Modern Judaism [*A publication*]
**Mod Judaism** ... Modern Judaism [*A publication*]
**Mod Kemi**.. Modern Kemi [*A publication*]
**Mod Knit**.... Modern Knitting Management [*A publication*]
**ModLA**...... Modern Language Association, New York, NY [*Library symbol*] [*Library of Congress*] (LCLS)
**Mod Lan**.... Modern Language Notes [*A publication*]
**Mod Lang**.. Modern Languages [*A publication*]
**Mod Lang Assn Pub** ... Modern Language Association of America. Publications [*A publication*]
**Mod Lang Forum** ... Modern Language Forum [*A publication*]
**Mod Lang J** ... Modern Language Journal [*A publication*]
**Mod Lang N** ... Modern Language Notes [*A publication*]
**Mod Lang Q** ... Modern Language Quarterly [*A publication*]
**Mod Lang R** ... Modern Language Review [*A publication*]

**Mod Lang Rev** ... Modern Language Review [*A publication*]
**Mod Lang St** ... Modern Language Studies [*A publication*]
**Mod Law R** ... Modern Law Review [*A publication*]
**Mod Law Soc** ... Modern Law and Society [*A publication*]
**Mod Libn** ... Modern Librarian [*A publication*]
**Mod Lit** ...... Modern Liturgy [*A publication*]
**Mod Lithography** ... Modern Lithography [*A publication*]
**MODLOC** ... Modified Location
**MODLOG 77** ... Modernization of Logistics 1977 [*Army*]
**Mod LR** ..... Modern Law Review [*A publication*]
**Mod L Rev** ... Modern Law Review [*A publication*]
**Mod L & Soc'y** ... Modern Law and Society [*A publication*] (DLA)
**MODM** ..... Magneto-Optical Display Memory
**MODM** ..... Major Oversea Depot Method [*Army*]
**MODM** ..... Manned One-Day Mission [*NASA*]
**Mod M** ....... Modern Motor [*A publication*] (APTA)
**Mod Mach Shop** ... Modern Machine Shop [*A publication*]
**Mod Mater** ... Modern Materials [*A publication*]
**Mod Mater Adv Dev Appl** ... Modern Materials. Advances in Development and Applications [*A publication*]
**Mod Mater Handl** ... Modern Materials Handling [*A publication*]
**Mod Mat H** ... Modern Materials Handling [*A publication*]
**Mod Med** ... Modern Medicine [*A publication*]
**Mod Med** ... Moderne Medizin [*A publication*]
**Mod Med Asia** ... Modern Medicine of Asia [*A publication*]
**Mod Med Aust** ... Modern Medicine of Australia [*A publication*]
**Mod Med (Chicago)** ... Modern Medicine (Chicago) [*A publication*]
**Mod Med (Jpn)** ... Modern Medicine (Japan) [*A publication*]
**Mod Med (Minneapolis)** ... Modern Medicine (Minneapolis) [*A publication*]
**Mod Met** .... Modern Metals [*A publication*]
**Mod Metals** ... Modern Metals [*A publication*]
**Mod Met Finish** ... Modern Metal Finishing [*A publication*]
**Mod Method Plant Anal New Ser** ... Modern Methods of Plant Analysis. New Series [*A publication*]
**Mod Methods Pharmacol** ... Modern Methods in Pharmacology [*A publication*]
**Mod Mfg** .... Modern Manufacturing [*A publication*]
**Mod Miller** ... Modern Miller [*A publication*]
**Mod Miller Bakers News** ... Modern Miller and Bakers News [*A publication*]
**Mod Min** .... Modern Mining [*A publication*]
**Mod Motor** ... Modern Motor [*A publication*] (APTA)
**Mod Mus** ... Modern Music [*A publication*]
**Mod Music** ... Modern Music [*A publication*]
**MOD(N)** .... Ministry of Defence (Navy) [*British*]
**MoDNM** .... Morpholinodaunomycin [*Also, MRD*] [*Antineoplastic drug*]
**Mod Nurs Home** ... Modern Nursing Home [*A publication*]
**Mod Nutr** ... Modern Nutrition [*A publication*]
**MODO** ...... Moderato [*Moderate Speed*] [*Music*] (ROG)
**Mod Off** ..... Modern Office Procedures [*A publication*]
**Mod Off** ..... Modern Office Technology [*A publication*]
**Mod Off and Data Manage** ... Modern Office and Data Management [*A publication*]
**Mod Off Dat Man** ... Modern Office and Data Management [*A publication*]
**Mod Office Data Mgmt** ... Modern Office and Data Management [*A publication*]
**Mod Off Proc** ... Modern Office Procedures [*A publication*]
**Mod Off Proced** ... Modern Office Procedures [*A publication*]
**Mod Off Procedures** ... Modern Office Procedures [*A publication*]
**MODOP** .... Mobil Oil Direct Oxidation Process [*Gas desulfurization process*]
**MODOR** ... Molecularized Doppler RADAR
**MODP** ....... Modern Programming Practice
**MODPAC** ... Modular Restraint, Recovery, and Survival Package
**Mod Packag** ... Modern Packaging [*A publication*]
**Mod Paint** ... Modern Paint and Coatings [*A publication*]
**MOD(PE)** ... Ministry of Defence (Procurement Executive) [*British*]
**Mod Perspect Psychiatry** ... Modern Perspectives in Psychiatry [*A publication*]
**Mod Pharm** ... Modern Pharmacology [*A publication*]
**Mod Phil** .... Modern Philology [*A publication*]
**Mod Philol** ... Modern Philology [*A publication*]
**Mod Phot** ... Modern Photography [*A publication*]
**Mod Photogr** ... Modern Photography [*A publication*]
**Mod Phys Monogr Ser** ... Modern Physics Monograph Series [*A publication*]
**Mod Pkg** .... Modern Packaging [*A publication*]
**Mod Pkg En** ... Modern Packaging Encyclopedia and Buyer's Guide Issue [*A publication*]
**Mod Plas** ... Modern Plastics [*A publication*]
**Mod Plast** .. Modern Plastics [*A publication*]
**Mod Plastics** ... Modern Plastics [*A publication*]
**Mod Plast Int** ... Modern Plastics International [*A publication*]
**Mod Plst Int** ... Modern Plastics International [*A publication*]
**Mod Poetry Stud** ... Modern Poetry Studies [*A publication*]
**Mod Poet St** ... Modern Poetry Studies [*A publication*]
**MODPOT** ... Model Potential [*Physics*]
**Mod Power and Eng** ... Modern Power and Engineering [*A publication*]
**Mod Power Eng** ... Modern Power and Engineering [*A publication*]
**Mod Power Syst** ... Modern Power Systems [*A publication*]
**Mod Pract Comm** ... Modern Practice Commentator [*A publication*] (DLA)
**MOD PRAESCRIPT** ... Modo Praescripto [*In the Manner Prescribed*] [*Pharmacy*]
**MOD PRESCR** ... Modo Praescripto [*In the Manner Prescribed*] [*Pharmacy*] (ROG)
**Mod Probl Ophthalmol** ... Modern Problems in Ophthalmology [*A publication*]
**Mod Probl Paediatr** ... Modern Problems in Paediatrics [*A publication*]
**Mod Probl Paediatr** ... Moderne Probleme der Paediatrie [*Switzerland*] [*A publication*]
**Mod Probl Pharmacopsychiatry** ... Modern Problems of Pharmacopsychiatry [*A publication*]
**Mod Prob Ophth** ... Modern Problems in Ophthalmology [*A publication*]
**Mod Psychoanal** ... Modern Psychoanalysis [*A publication*]
**Mod Quart Misc** ... Modern Quarterly Miscellany [*A publication*]
**Mod Quart Res SE A** ... Modern Quarterly Research in Southeast Asia [*Rotterdam*] [*A publication*]
**Mod R** ........ Modern Review [*A publication*]
**MODR** ....... Monodetail Drawing (MSA)
**Mod Railw** ... Modern Railways [*A publication*]
**Mod R (Calcutta)** ... Modern Review (Calcutta) [*A publication*]
**Mod Refrig** ... Modern Refrigeration [*A publication*]
**Mod Refrig Air Cond** ... Modern Refrigeration and Air Conditioning [*A publication*]
**Mod Refrig Air Control News** ... Modern Refrigeration and Air Control News [*A publication*]
**MODREFTRA** ... Modified Refresher Training [*Navy*] (NVT)
**Mod Rep** .... Modern Reports [*England*] [*A publication*] (DLA)
**Mod Rep** .... Style's English King's Bench Reports [*1646-55*] [*A publication*] (DLA)
**ModRev** ..... Modern Review [*A publication*]
**Mod Roentgen-Fotogr** ... Moderne Roentgen-Fotografie [*A publication*]
**Mod Rr** ...... Modern Railroads [*A publication*]
**MODS** ....... Major Operations Data System (NVT)
**MODS** ....... Manned Orbital Development Station [*See also MOD, MOSS, MTSS*] [*Air Force/NASA*]
**MODS** ....... Manpower Operations Data System [*Employment and Training Administration*] [*Department of Labor*]
**MODS** ....... Medically Oriented Data System (MCD)
**MODS** ....... Medium Ocean Data Station
**MODS** ....... Military Orbital Development System [*See also MOD, MOSS, MTSS*] [*Air Force/NASA*]
**MODS** ....... Missile Offense/Defense System
**MODS** ....... Mission Operations Design Support
**MODS** ....... Models (MCD)
**MODS** ....... Moderations [*First public Oxford examination*] (ROG)
**MODS** ....... Modular Oriented Direct Support (MCD)
**MODSC** .... Magnetooptically Detected Spin Conversion [*Physics*]
**Mod Sch** ..... Modern Schoolman [*A publication*]
**Mod Schoolm** ... Modern Schoolman [*A publication*]
**Mod Solid State Phys Simon Fraser Univ Lect** ... Modern Solid State Physics. Simon Fraser University. Lectures [*A publication*]
**Mod Sp** ...... Moderne Sprachen [*A publication*]
**Mod St Lit** ... Modernist Studies. Literature and Culture, 1920-1940 [*A publication*]
**Mod Stud** ... Modernist Studies [*A publication*]
**Mod Stud Assoc Yearb** ... Modern Studies Association Yearbook [*A publication*]
**Mod Sugar Plant** ... Modern Sugar Planter [*A publication*]
**Modszertani Kozl Mag All Foldt Intez** ... Modszertani Kozlemenyek. Magyar Allami Foldtani Intezet [*A publication*]
**Mod Teach** ... Modern Teaching [*A publication*] (APTA)
**MODTEPS** ... Modular Toxic Environment Protective Suit [*NASA*]
**Mod Tex B** ... Modern Textile Business [*A publication*]
**Mod Text** ... Modern Textiles Magazine [*A publication*]
**Mod Textil** ... Modern Textiles [*A publication*]
**Mod Text Mag** ... Modern Textiles Magazine [*A publication*]
**Mod Theor Chem** ... Modern Theoretical Chemistry [*A publication*]
**Mod Tire Dealer** ... Modern Tire Dealer [*A publication*]
**MODTO** .... Moderato [*Moderate Speed*] [*Music*]
**Mod Tramway** ... Modern Tramway [*A publication*]
**Mod Treat** ... Modern Treatment [*A publication*]
**Mod Trends Anaesth** ... Modern Trends in Anaesthesia [*A publication*]
**Mod Trends Cardiol** ... Modern Trends in Cardiology [*A publication*]
**Mod Trends Dermatol** ... Modern Trends in Dermatology [*A publication*]
**Mod Trends Drug Depend Alcohol** ... Modern Trends in Drug Dependence and Alcoholism [*A publication*]
**Mod Trends Endocrinol** ... Modern Trends in Endocrinology [*A publication*]
**Mod Trends Gastroenterol** ... Modern Trends in Gastroenterology [*A publication*]
**Mod Trends Hum Reprod Physiol** ... Modern Trends in Human Reproductive Physiology [*A publication*]
**Mod Trends Immunol** ... Modern Trends in Immunology [*A publication*]
**Mod Trends Med Virol** ... Modern Trends in Medical Virology [*A publication*]
**Mod Trends Neurol** ... Modern Trends in Neurology [*A publication*]
**Mod Trends Orthop** ... Modern Trends in Orthopaedics [*A publication*]
**Mod Trends Pharmacol Ther** ... Modern Trends in Pharmacology and Therapeutics [*A publication*]
**Mod Trends Plast Surg** ... Modern Trends in Plastic Surgery [*A publication*]
**Mod Trends Psychosom Med** ... Modern Trends in Psychosomatic Medicine [*A publication*]
**Mod Trends Radiother** ... Modern Trends in Radiotherapy [*A publication*]
**Mod Trends Rheumatol** ... Modern Trends in Rheumatology [*A publication*]

**Mod Trends Ser Psychosom Med** ... Modern Trends Series. Psychosomatic Medicine [*A publication*]
**Mod Trends Surg** ... Modern Trends in Surgery [*A publication*]
**MODU** ...... Mobile Offshore Drilling Unit
**MODULA** ... Modular Programming Language (CSR)
**MODULAB** ... Modular Clinical Laboratory [*Military*] (CAAL)
**Modular I St** ... Modular Instruction in Statistics [*A publication*]
**Mod Un**...... Modern Unionist [*A publication*]
**Mod Unfallverhuet** ... Moderne Unfallverhuetung [*A publication*]
**Mod Unionist** ... Modern Unionist [*A publication*]
**Mod Vet Pract** ... Modern Veterinary Practice [*A publication*]
**Mod World** ... Modern World [*A publication*]
**MODX**....... Modulaire Industries [*San Francisco, CA*] [*NASDAQ symbol*] (NQ)
**MODY**....... Maturity-on-Death Diabetes in the Young [*Medicine*]
**Mod Ytbehandling** ... Modern Ytbehandling [*A publication*]
**MOE**.......... Evangel College, Springfield, MO [*OCLC symbol*] (OCLC)
**MOE**.......... Maintenance of Effort [*Medicare Act*]
**MOE**.......... Major Organizational Entity (MCD)
**MOE**.......... Mars Orbit Ejection (MCD)
**MOE**.......... Master of Oral English
**MOE**.......... Measure of Effectiveness
**MOE**.......... Ministry of Education [*British*] (DAS)
**MOE**.......... Ministry of Energy [*Philippines*] (DS)
**MOE**.......... Ministry of Environment [*Canada*]
**MOE**.......... Mission-Oriented Equipment
**MOE**.......... Modulus of Elasticity [*Mechanics*]
**MOE**.......... Molecular Endocrinology [*Elsevier Book Series*] [*A publication*]
**MOE**.......... Moli Energy Ltd. [*Toronto Stock Exchange symbol*] [*Vancouver Stock Exchange symbol*]
**MOE**.......... Momeik [*Burma*] [*Airport symbol*] (OAG)
**MOE**.......... Ontario Ministry of Education, Information Centre, Research Branch [*UTLAS symbol*]
**MOE**.......... Telemetering Mobile Station [*ITU designation*]
**MOED**....... Molecular Orbital Energy Diagram
**MOED**....... Morristown-Edison National Park Service Group
**MOEDA**.... Measures of Effectiveness, Development, and Application (MCD)
**MOEIG**..... Mitteilungen. Oesterreichisches Institut fuer Geschichtsforschung [*A publication*]
**MOEMDJ** ... Motivation and Emotion [*A publication*]
**M Oe Num Ges** ... Mitteilungen der Oesterreichischen Numismatischen Gesellschaft [*A publication*]
**MOEP**....... Meteorological and Oceanographic Equipment Program (NG)
**MOERO**.... Medium Orbiting Earth Resources Observatory (IEEE)
**Moessbauer Eff Methodol** ... Moessbauer Effect Methodology [*A publication*]
**Moessbauer Eff Methodol Proc Symp** ... Moessbauer Effect Methodology. Proceedings of the Symposium [*A publication*]
**MOETLO** ... Meteorological and Oceanographic Equipment Technical Liaison Officer
**M Oe Ur Frueh Gesch** ... Mitteilungen der Oesterreichischen Arbeitgemeinschaft fuer Ur- und Fruehgeschichte [*A publication*]
**MoExGS**.... Excelsior Springs Genealogical Society, Excelsior Springs, MO [*Library symbol*] [*Library of Congress*] (LCLS)
**MOF**.......... Fontbonne College, St. Louis, MO [*OCLC symbol*] (OCLC)
**MOF**.......... Manned Orbital Flight [*NASA*] (NASA)
**MOF**.......... Marine Oxidation/Fermentation
**MOF**.......... Maumere [*Indonesia*] [*Airport symbol*] (OAG)
**MOF**.......... Maximum Observed Frequency [*Radio*]
**MOF**.......... Maximum Operating Frequency
**MOF**.......... MeCCNU [*Semustine*], Oncovin [*Vincristine*], Fluorouracil [*Antineoplastic drug regimen*]
**MOF**.......... Metal-Oxide Film
**MOF**.......... Michoud Operations Facility [*NASA*] (AAG)
**MOF**.......... Ministry of Finance [*Philippines*] (DS)
**MOF**.......... Ministry of Food [*British*]
**MOF**.......... Mission Operations Facility [*NASA*] (KSC)
**MOF**.......... Moffat Communications Ltd. [*Toronto Stock Exchange symbol*]
**Mo (F)**........ [*Sir Francis*] Moore's English King's Bench Reports [*A publication*] (DLA)
**MOF**.......... Multi-Option Facility
**MOF**.......... Multioption Fuze (MCD)
**MOF**.......... Multiple Organ Failure [*Medicine*]
**MOFAB** .... Mobile Floating Assault Bridge-Ferry [*Military*] (MCD)
**MOFACS**.. Multiorder Feedback and Compensation Synthesis
**MOFAP**..... Ministry of Fuel and Power [*British*]
**MOFAST**.. Mechanization of Freight and Shipping Terminal [*DoD*]
**MoFC**......... Central Methodist College, Fayette, MO [*Library symbol*] [*Library of Congress*] (LCLS)
**MOFC** ....... Michael O'Leary Fan Club (EA)
**MOFERT** ... Ministry of Foreign Economic Relations and Trade [*People's Republic of China*]
**MOFF**........ Multiple Options Funding Facility [*Euronotes*]
**MoFlM** ...... Mark Twain Shrine, Mark Twain State Park, Florida, MO [*Library symbol*] [*Library of Congress*] (LCLS)
**MoFloSS** ... Saint Stanislaus Seminary, Florissant, MO [*Library symbol*] [*Library of Congress*] (LCLS)
**MOF-STREP** ... MeCCNU [*Semustine*], Oncovin [*Vincristine*], Fluorouracil, Streptozotocin [*Antineoplastic drug regimen*]
**MoFuWC**... Westminster College, Fulton, MO [*Library symbol*] [*Library of Congress*] (LCLS)
**MOFW**...... Military Order of Foreign Wars of the United States (EA)
**MOG**......... Assemblies of God Graduate School, Springfield, MO [*OCLC symbol*] (OCLC)
**MOG**......... Mannville Oil & Gas Ltd. [*Toronto Stock Exchange symbol*]
**MO & G**..... Master of Obstetrics and Gynaecology
**MOG**......... Material Ordering Guide [*Shipbuilding*]
**MOG**......... Material Other than Grape [*Wine making*]
**MOG**......... Metropolitan Opera Guild (EA)
**MOG**......... Milicias Obreras Guatemaltecas [*Guatemalan Workers' Militia*] (PD)
**MOG**......... Mogadishu [*Somalia*] [*Seismograph station code, US Geological Survey*] [*Closed*] (SEIS)
**MOG**......... Monghsat [*Burma*] [*Airport symbol*] (OAG)
**MOG**......... Montague, CA [*Location identifier*] [*FAA*] (FAAL)
**MOG**......... Moog, Inc. [*AMEX symbol*] (SPSG)
**MOG**......... Municipal Officers' Guild (ROG)
**MOGA**....... Management of Officer Grade Authorization (MCD)
**MOGA**....... Microwave and Optical Generation and Amplification (MCD)
**MOGA**....... Mitteilungen. Oesterreichische Gesellschaft fuer Anthropologie, Ethnologie, und Praehistorie [*A publication*]
**MOGA**....... Montana Outfitters and Guides Association (EA)
**MOGAS**.... Motor Gasoline [*Military*]
**MOGC**....... McCormick Oil & Gas Partnership [*NASDAQ symbol*] (NQ)
**MO Geol Surv Rep Invest** ... Missouri. Geological Survey. Report of Investigations [*A publication*]
**MO Geol Surv Water Resour Inf Circ** ... Missouri. Geological Survey and Water Resources. Information Circular [*A publication*]
**MO Geol Surv Water Resour Inform Circ** ... Missouri. Geological Survey and Water Resources. Information Circular [*A publication*]
**MO Geol Surv Water Resour Misc Publ** ... Missouri. Geological Survey and Water Resources. Miscellaneous Publication [*A publication*]
**MO Geol Surv Water Resour Rep** ... Missouri. Geological Survey and Water Resources. Report [*A publication*]
**MO Geol Surv Water Resour Rep Invest** ... Missouri. Geological Survey and Water Resources. Report of Investigations [*A publication*]
**MO Geol Surv Water Resour Spec Publ** ... Missouri. Geological Survey and Water Resources. Special Publication [*A publication*]
**MO Geol Surv Water Resour Water Resour Rep** ... Missouri. Geological Survey and Water Resources. Water Resources Report [*A publication*]
**MOGI**........ Minden Oil & Gas, Incorporated [*NASDAQ symbol*] (NQ)
**MOGMS**... Meddelelser om Groenland. Man and Society [*A publication*]
**MOGN**...... MGI PHARMA, Inc. [*NASDAQ symbol*] (NQ)
**MOGO**...... Monogram Oil & Gas, Inc. [*NASDAQ symbol*] (NQ)
**MOGR**....... Meddelelser om Groenland [*A publication*]
**MOGR**....... Moderate or Greater (FAAC)
**MO G S MO Bur G Mines** ... Missouri. Geological Survey. Missouri Bureau of Geology and Mines [*A publication*]
**Moguyde**.... Mouvement Guyanais de Decolonisation [*Guiana Decolonization Movement*] [*France*] [*Political party*] (PPW)
**MoH**......... Hannibal Free Public Library, Hannibal, MO [*Library symbol*] [*Library of Congress*] (LCLS)
**MOH**......... Hydrological and Meteorological Mobile Station [*ITU designation*]
**MOH**......... Magazine of Horror [*A publication*]
**MOH**......... Master of Otter Hounds
**MOH**......... Maximum Operating Hours (MCD)
**MOH**......... Medal of Honor [*Often erroneously called Congressional Medal of Honor*] [*Military decoration*]
**MOH**......... Medical Officer of Health [*British*]
**MOH**......... Ministry of Health [*British*]
**MOH**......... Moche Resources, Inc. [*Vancouver Stock Exchange symbol*]
**MOH**......... Mohasco Corp. [*NYSE symbol*] (SPSG)
**moh**.......... Mohawk [*MARC language code*] [*Library of Congress*] (LCCP)
**MOH**......... Mohawk Airlines, Inc. [*Obsolete*]
**Moh**.......... [*Johannes*] Mohedanus [*Deceased circa 1550*] [*Authority cited in pre-1607 legal work*] (DSA)
**MoH**......... Monatshefte [*A publication*]
**MOH**......... Museum of Holography [*New York City*]
**MOH**......... New York, NY [*Location identifier*] [*FAA*] (FAAL)
**MOH**......... St. Louis Priory School, St. Louis, MO [*OCLC symbol*] (OCLC)
**MOHAM**.. Mohammedan (ROG)
**MoHarC**.... Cass County Public Library, Harrisonville, MO [*Library symbol*] [*Library of Congress*] (LCLS)
**MOHAT**.... Modular Handling and Transport
**MOHATS** ... Mobile Overland Hauling and Transport System [*Air Force*]
**Mohed**........ [*Johannes*] Mohedanus [*Deceased circa 1550*] [*Authority cited in pre-1607 legal work*] (DSA)
**MoHi**......... Missouri State Historical Society, Columbia, MO [*Library symbol*] [*Library of Congress*] (LCLS)
**MO His Col** ... Missouri Historical Society. Collections [*A publication*]
**MO His R** ... Missouri Historical Review [*A publication*]
**MO Hist Rev** ... Missouri Historical Review [*A publication*]
**MO Hist Soc Bull** ... Missouri Historical Society. Bulletin [*A publication*]
**MOH(LHA)** ... Medical Officer of Health (Local Health Authority) [*British*]

**MoHM** ...... Mark Twain Museum, Hannibal, MO [*Library symbol*] [*Library of Congress*] (LCLS)
**MOHO** ...... Mohorovicic Discontinuity [*Geology*]
**MOHOA** ... Modern Hospital [*A publication*]
**MOHOLE** ... [*A*] deep hole exploratory project [*MOHO derived from last name of Andrija Mohorovicic, Yugoslav seismologist who proposed the project*]
**MOHS** ....... Master of Occupational Health and Safety
**MOHSLG** ... Health Sciences Library [*Library network*]
**MoHu** ........ Huntsville Public Library, Huntsville, MO [*Library symbol*] [*Library of Congress*] (LCLS)
**MOI** .......... Main-d'Oeuvre Indigene [*Indigenous Manpower*] [*Congo - Leopoldville*]
**MOI** .......... Maintenance Operating Instruction [*Air Force Logistics Command*]
**MOI** .......... Mars Orbit [*or Orbital*] Insertion [*Aerospace*]
**MOI** .......... Maximum Obtainable Irradiance
**MOI** .......... Memorandum of Interest (MCD)
**MOI** .......... Message of Operational Intent (NVT)
**MOI** .......... Methods of Instruction
**MOI** .......... Military Occupational Information (AABC)
**MOI** .......... Military Operations and Intelligence
**MOI** .......... Minimum Operating Inventory [*Business term*]
**MOI** .......... Ministry of Information [*British*] [*World War II*]
**MOI** .......... Ministry of Irrigation [*Sudan*]
**MOI** .......... Mitiaro [*Cook Islands*] [*Airport symbol*] (OAG)
**MOI** .......... Molco Industries [*Vancouver Stock Exchange symbol*]
**MOI** .......... Moment of Inertia
**MOI** .......... Monaco Oceanographic Institute
**MOI** .......... Moniteur du Commerce International [*A publication*]
**MOI** .......... Mouvement Ouvrier International (BJA)
**MOI** .......... Multiplicity of Infection
**MOI** .......... William Jewell College, Liberty, MO [*OCLC symbol*] (OCLC)
**Mo IA** ........ Moore's Indian Appeals [*A publication*] (DLA)
**MOIC** ........ Medical Officer-in-Charge [*Military*]
**MOIC** ........ Military Oceanographic Information Center (NATG)
**MOIDE** ..... Military Occupational Information Data Bank
**MOIED** ..... Modern Industrial Energy [*A publication*]
**MOIG** ........ Master of Occupational Information and Guidance
**MOIG** ........ Mitteilungen. Oesterreichisches Institut fuer Geschichtsforschung [*A publication*]
**MOIGF** ..... Mitteilungen. Oesterreichisches Institut fuer Geschichtsforschung [*A publication*]
**MOIL** ........ Maynard Oil Co. [*NASDAQ symbol*] (NQ)
**MOIL** ........ Motor Oil
**Mo Illust** .... Monthly Illustrator [*A publication*]
**MoIM** ........ Mid-Continent Public Library Service, Independence, MO [*Library symbol*] [*Library of Congress*] (LCLS)
**MoIMC** ..... Independence Medical Center, Independence, MO [*Library symbol*] [*Library of Congress*] (LCLS)
**MOIP** ........ Mandatory Oil Import Program
**MOIP** ........ Missile on Internal Power
**MOIPI** ....... Multi-Purpose Offshore Industrial Port Islands (NOAA)
**MOIR** ........ Movimiento Obrero Independiente Revolucionario [*Independent Revolutionary Workers' Movement*] [*Colombia*] [*Political party*] (PPW)
**MOIR** ........ Movimiento Obrero Izquierdista Revolucionario [*Colombia*] [*Political party*] (PPW)
**MoIRC** ....... Reorganized Church of Jesus Christ of Latter-Day Saints, Independence, MO [*Library symbol*] [*Library of Congress*] (LCLS)
**Moir Cap Pun** ... Moir on Capital Punishment [*A publication*] (DLA)
**Moirs Aust Investments** ... Moir's Australian Investments [*A publication*] (APTA)
**MoIS** .......... Independence Sanitarium and Hospital, Independence, MO [*Library symbol*] [*Library of Congress*] (LCLS)
**MOIS** ........ Michigan Occupational Information System [*Michigan State Department of Education*] [*Lansing*] [*Information service or system*] (IID)
**MOIS** ........ Mission Operations Intercommunication System [*NASA*]
**Mois Chim Electrochim** ... Mois Chimique et Electrochimique [*A publication*]
**Mois Econ et Fin** ... Mois Economique et Financier [*A publication*]
**Mois Minier Metall** ... Mois Minier et Metallurgique [*A publication*]
**Mois Sci Ind** ... Mois Scientifique et Industriel [*A publication*]
**MOIST** ....... Macro Output System [*NASA*] (KSC)
**Moist Fert** ... Moisture and Fertility. American Potash Institute [*A publication*]
**MOISTR** ... Moisture
**MoIT** ......... Harry S Truman Library, Independence, MO [*Library symbol*] [*Library of Congress*] (LCLS)
**MOIV** ........ Mechanically Operated Inlet Valve (ADA)
**MOJ** .......... Material on Job Date [*Telecommunications*] (TEL)
**MOJ** .......... Metering over Junction [*Network administration*] [*Telecommunications*] (TEL)
**Mo J** .......... Modern Judaism [*A publication*]
**MOJA** ....... Movement for Justice in Africa [*Liberia*] [*Political party*] (PPW)
**MOJA-G** ... Movement for Justice in Africa-Gambia [*Political party*]
**Mo J Australian-American Assoc** ... Australian-American Association. Monthly Journal [*Sydney*] [*A publication*] (APTA)
**Mo J B** ....... [*J. B.*] Moore's English Common Pleas Reports [*A publication*] (DLA)
**MoJc** .......... Thomas Jefferson Library System, Jefferson City, MO [*Library symbol*] [*Library of Congress*] (LCLS)
**MoJcL** ....... Lincoln University, Jefferson City, MO [*Library symbol*] [*Library of Congress*] (LCLS)
**MoJo** .......... Joplin Public Library, Joplin, MO [*Library symbol*] [*Library of Congress*] (LCLS)
**MOJOD** .... Mother Jones [*A publication*]
**MoJoM** ...... Missouri Southern State College, Joplin, MO [*Library symbol*] [*Library of Congress*] (LCLS)
**MO J Res Mus Ed** ... Missouri Journal of Research in Music Education [*A publication*]
**Mo Jur** ....... Monthly Jurist [*A publication*] (DLA)
**MoK** .......... Kansas City Public Library, Kansas City, MO [*Library symbol*] [*Library of Congress*] (LCLS)
**MOK** .......... Mokapu [*Hawaii*] [*Seismograph station code, US Geological Survey*] (SEIS)
**MOK** .......... Oesterreichisches Institut fuer Wirtschaft Forschung. Monatsberichte [*A publication*]
**MoKA** ........ American Nurses' Association, Kansas City, MO [*Library symbol*] [*Library of Congress*] (LCLS)
**MoKAI** ...... Kansas City Arts Institute, Kansas City, MO [*Library symbol*] [*Library of Congress*] (LCLS)
**MoKAv** ..... Avila College, Kansas City, MO [*Library symbol*] [*Library of Congress*] (LCLS)
**MoKB** ........ Bar Library Association of Kansas City, Kansas City, MO [*Library symbol*] [*Library of Congress*] (LCLS)
**MoKBa** ...... Barstow School, Kansas City, MO [*Library symbol*] [*Library of Congress*] (LCLS)
**MoKBen** .... Bendix Corp., Technical Information Center, Kansas City, MO [*Library symbol*] [*Library of Congress*] (LCLS)
**MoKBH** ..... Baptist Memorial Hospital, Kansas City, MO [*Library symbol*] [*Library of Congress*] (LCLS)
**MoKBM** .... Burns and McDonnell Engineering Co., Kansas City, MO [*Library symbol*] [*Library of Congress*] (LCLS)
**MoKBV** ..... Black & Veatch Consulting Engineers, Central Library, Kansas City, MO [*Library symbol*] [*Library of Congress*] (LCLS)
**MoKCH** ..... Children's Mercy Hospital, Kansas City, MO [*Library symbol*] [*Library of Congress*] (LCLS)
**MoKChe** .... Chemagro, Kansas City, MO [*Library symbol*] [*Library of Congress*] (LCLS)
**MoKCO** ..... Kansas City College of Osteopathic Medicine, Kansas City, MO [*Library symbol*] [*Library of Congress*] (LCLS)
**MoKCoH** ... Jackson County Public Hospital, Kansas City, MO [*Library symbol*] [*Library of Congress*] (LCLS)
**MOKE** ....... Magneto-Optic Kerr Effect
**MoKEP** ...... United States Environmental Protection Agency, Kansas City, MO [*Library symbol*] [*Library of Congress*] (LCLS)
**MoKF** ........ Farmland Industries Inc., Communications Services, Kansas City, MO [*Library symbol*] [*Library of Congress*] (LCLS)
**MoKFR** ...... Federal Reserve Bank of Kansas City, Kansas City, MO [*Library symbol*] [*Library of Congress*] (LCLS)
**MOKG** ....... Morgan, Olmstead, Kennedy & Gardner Corp. [*Los Angeles, CA*] [*NASDAQ symbol*] (NQ)
**MoKGH** ..... Kansas City General Hospital, Kansas City, MO [*Library symbol*] [*Library of Congress*] (LCLS)
**MoKGS** ...... Church of Jesus Christ of Latter-Day Saints, Genealogical Society Library, Kansas City Branch, Kansas City, MO [*Library symbol*] [*Library of Congress*] (LCLS)
**MoKHA** ..... Kansas City Area Hospital Association, Kansas City, MO [*Library symbol*] [*Library of Congress*] (LCLS)
**MOKIA** ..... Monatsschrift fuer Kinderheilkunde [*A publication*]
**MoKiCO** .... Kirksville College of Osteopathy and Surgery, Kirksville, MO [*Library symbol*] [*Library of Congress*] (LCLS)
**MoKiU** ....... Northeast Missouri State University, Kirksville, MO [*Library symbol*] [*Library of Congress*] (LCLS)
**MoKJ** ......... Jackson County Medical Society, Kansas City, MO [*Library symbol*] [*Library of Congress*] (LCLS)
**MoKKM** .... Martin Luther King Memorial Hospital, Kansas City, MO [*Library symbol*] [*Library of Congress*] (LCLS)
**MoKL** ........ Linda Hall Library, Kansas City, MO [*Library symbol*] [*Library of Congress*] (LCLS)
**MoKLH** ..... Lakeside Hospital, Kansas City, MO [*Library symbol*] [*Library of Congress*] (LCLS)
**MoKLo** ...... Loretto in Kansas City, Kansas City, MO [*Library symbol*] [*Library of Congress*] (LCLS)
**MoKMB** .... Midwestern Baptist Theological Seminary, Kansas City, MO [*Library symbol*] [*Library of Congress*] (LCLS)
**MoKMC** .... Midwest College of Medical Assistants, Kansas City, MO [*Library symbol*] [*Library of Congress*] (LCLS)
**MoKMI** .... Missouri Institute of Technology, Kansas City, MO [*Library symbol*] [*Library of Congress*] (LCLS)
**MoKML** .... Marion Laboratories, Inc., Kansas City, MO [*Library symbol*] [*Library of Congress*] (LCLS)
**MoKMM** ... Menorah Medical Center, Kansas City, MO [*Library symbol*] [*Library of Congress*] (LCLS)
**MoKMR** .... Midwest Research Institute, Kansas City, MO [*Library symbol*] [*Library of Congress*] (LCLS)
**MoKMW** ... Maple Woods Community College, Kansas City, MO [*Library symbol*] [*Library of Congress*] (LCLS)

**MoKN**........ Nazarene Theological Seminary, Kansas City, MO [*Library symbol*] [*Library of Congress*] (LCLS)
**MoKNE**..... Newman Ecumenical Seminary, Kansas City, MO [*Library symbol*] [*Library of Congress*] (LCLS)
**MoKNG**..... Nelson Art Gallery, Art Reference Library, Kansas City, MO [*Library symbol*] [*Library of Congress*] (LCLS)
**MoKNT**..... Saint Paul School of Theology, Kansas City, MO [*Library symbol*] [*Library of Congress*] (LCLS)
**MOKOAI**.. Moskovskii Kolkhoznik [*A publication*]
**MoKP**........ Penn Valley Junior College, Kansas City, MO [*Library symbol*] [*Library of Congress*] (LCLS)
**MoKPC**...... Pembroke County Day School, Kansas City, MO [*Library symbol*] [*Library of Congress*] (LCLS)
**MoKPh**...... Park Hill North Junior High School, Kansas City, MO [*Library symbol*] [*Library of Congress*] (LCLS)
**MoKR**........ Rockhurst College, Kansas City, MO [*Library symbol*] [*Library of Congress*] (LCLS)
**MoKRes**..... Research Hospital and Medical Center, Kansas City, MO [*Library symbol*] [*Library of Congress*] (LCLS)
**MoKRh**...... Rockhurst High School, Kansas City, MO [*Library symbol*] [*Library of Congress*] (LCLS)
**MoKSH**..... Sunset Hill School, Kansas City, MO [*Library symbol*] [*Library of Congress*] (LCLS)
**Mokslas Tech** ... Mokslas ir Technika [*A publication*]
**Mokslo Darb Vilniaus Valstybinis Pedagog Inst** ... Mokslo Darbai. Vilniaus Valstybinis Pedagoginis Institutas [*A publication*]
**MoKStJ**..... Saint Joseph's Hospital, Kansas City, MO [*Library symbol*] [*Library of Congress*] (LCLS)
**MoKStL**..... Saint Luke's Hospital of Kansas City, Kansas City, MO [*Library symbol*] [*Library of Congress*] (LCLS)
**MoKStM**... Saint Mary's Hospital, Kansas City, MO [*Library symbol*] [*Library of Congress*] (LCLS)
**MoKStT**..... Saint Theresa's Academy, Kansas City, MO [*Library symbol*] [*Library of Congress*] (LCLS)
**MoKT**........ Teachers College of Kansas City, Kansas City, MO [*Library symbol*] [*Library of Congress*] [*Obsolete*] (LCLS)
**MoKTrL**.... Trinity Lutheran Hospital, Kansas City, MO [*Library symbol*] [*Library of Congress*] (LCLS)
**MoKU**........ University of Missouri at Kansas City, Kansas City, MO [*Library symbol*] [*Library of Congress*] (LCLS)
**MoKU-D**... University of Missouri at Kansas City, Dental School, Kansas City, MO [*Library symbol*] [*Library of Congress*] (LCLS)
**MoKU-I**..... University of Missouri at Kansas City, Instructional Materials Center, Kansas City, MO [*Library symbol*] [*Library of Congress*] (LCLS)
**MoKU-M**... University of Missouri at Kansas City, Medical Library, Kansas City, MO [*Library symbol*] [*Library of Congress*] (LCLS)
**MoKU-Mus**... University of Missouri at Kansas City, Music Conservatory, Kansas City, MO [*Library symbol*] [*Library of Congress*] (LCLS)
**Mokuzai Gakkai Shi/J Jap Wood Res Soc** ... Mokuzai Gakkai Shi/Journal. Japan Wood Research Society [*A publication*]
**MoKVA**..... United States Veterans Administration Hospital, Kansas City, MO [*Library symbol*] [*Library of Congress*] (LCLS)
**MoKW**....... Western Missouri Mental Health Center, Kansas City, MO [*Library symbol*] [*Library of Congress*] (LCLS)
**MOL**.......... Machine-Oriented Language [*Programming language*]
**MOL**.......... Manned Orbiting Laboratory [*NASA*]
**MOL**.......... Master of Oriental Languages
**MOL**.......... Master of Oriental Learning
**MOL**.......... Maximum Operating Level
**MOL**.......... Maximum Output Level
**MOL**.......... Metallo-Organic LASER
**MOL**.......... Method of Lines [*Mathematics*]
**MOL**.......... Ministry of Labour [*Later, DE*] [*British*]
**MO L**......... Missouri Law Review [*A publication*]
**MOL**.......... Missouri State Library, Jefferson City, MO [*OCLC symbol*] (OCLC)
**mol**............ Moldavian [*MARC language code*] [*Library of Congress*] (LCCP)
**MOL**.......... Molde [*Norway*] [*Airport symbol*] (OAG)
**mol**............ Mole [*Amount of substance*] [*SI unit*]
**MOL**.......... Molecular Layer
**MOL**.......... Molecule [*or Molecular*] (AAG)
**MOL**.......... Molenaar Weekblad voor de Graanverwerkende Industrie en Veevoederindustrie [*A publication*]
**MOL**.......... Molesting [*FBI standardized term*]
**MOL**.......... Moliere [*Pseudonym of French actor and dramatist Jean Baptiste Poquelin, 1622-1673*] (ROG)
**Mol**............ [*Carolus*] Molinaeus [*Deceased, 1566*] [*Authority cited in pre-1607 legal work*] (DSA)
**Mol**............ Molloy's De Jure Maritimo [*A publication*] (DLA)
**Mol**............ Molloy's Irish Chancery Reports [*1827-31*] [*A publication*] (DLA)
**MOL**.......... Molodezhnaya [*USSR*] [*Geomagnetic observatory code*]
**MOL**.......... Molson Companies Ltd. [*Toronto Stock Exchange symbol*] [*Vancouver Stock Exchange symbol*]
**MOL**.......... Montebello, VA [*Location identifier*] [*FAA*] (FAAL)
**M-O-L**....... My Old Lady [*Wife*] [*Slang*]
**MOL**.......... Universite de Moncton, Law Library [*UTLAS symbol*]
**MOLA**....... Midwest Open Land Association (EA)
**MOLAA**.... Monatsschrift fuer Ohrenheilkunde und Laryngo-Rhinologie [*A publication*]
**MOLAB**.... Mobile Laboratory [*NASA*]
**Mo Labor R** ... Monthly Labor Review [*A publication*]
**Mo Labor Rev** ... Monthly Labor Review [*A publication*]
**Mo Lab Rev** ... Monthly Labor Review [*A publication*]
**Mol Aspects Cell Regul** ... Molecular Aspects of Cellular Regulation [*A publication*]
**Mol Aspects Med** ... Molecular Aspects of Medicine [*A publication*]
**Mo Law Rep** ... Monthly Law Reporter [*A publication*] (DLA)
**MO Laws**... Laws of Missouri [*A publication*] (DLA)
**MOLB**....... Majestic Circle, Military Order of Lady Bugs of USA (EA)
**Mol Basis Microb Pathog** ... Molecular Basis of Microbial Pathogenicity. Report of the Molecular Basis of the Ineffective Process, Berlin, 1979 [*A publication*]
**Mol Biochem Parasitol** ... Molecular and Biochemical Parasitology [*A publication*]
**Mol Biol**..... Molecular Biology [*A publication*]
**Mol Biol**..... Molekulyarnaya Biologiya [*A publication*]
**Mol Biol Biochem Biophys** ... Molecular Biology, Biochemistry, and Biophysics [*A publication*]
**Mol Biol Engl Transl Mol Biol (Mosc)** ... Molecular Biology. English Translation of Molekulyarnaya Biologiya (Moscow) [*A publication*]
**Mol Biol Evol** ... Molecular Biology and Evolution [*A publication*]
**Mol Biol Int Ser Monogr Textb** ... Molecular Biology; an International Series of Monographs and Textbooks [*A publication*]
**Mol Biol (Kiev)** ... Molekulyarnaya Biologiya (Kiev) [*A publication*]
**Mol Biol Mamm Gene Appar** ... Molecular Biology of the Mammalian Genetic Apparatus [*A publication*]
**Mol Biol Med** ... Molecular Biology and Medicine [*A publication*]
**Mol Biol & Med** ... Molecular Biology and Medicine [*A publication*]
**Mol Biol (Mosc)** ... Molekulyarnaya Biologiya (Moscow) [*A publication*]
**Mol Biol Rep** ... Molecular Biology Reports [*A publication*]
**Mol Biol Rp** ... Molecular Biology Reports [*A publication*]
**Mol Brain Res** ... Molecular Brain Research [*A publication*]
**Mo Lbr R**... Monthly Labor Review [*A publication*]
**MOLC**....... Multiple Operational Launch Complex (MUGU)
**MOLCAB** ... Mobile Landing Craft Advanced Base
**Mol Carcinog** ... Molecular Carcinogenesis [*A publication*]
**Mol C Bioch** ... Molecular and Cellular Biochemistry [*A publication*]
**Mol Cell Biochem** ... Molecular and Cellular Biochemistry [*A publication*]
**Mol Cell Biol** ... Molecular and Cellular Biology [*A publication*]
**Mol Cell Endocr** ... Molecular and Cellular Endocrinology [*A publication*]
**Mol Cell Endocrinol** ... Molecular and Cellular Endocrinology [*A publication*]
**Mol C Endoc** ... Molecular and Cellular Endocrinology [*A publication*]
**Mol Cryst**... Molecular Crystals [*A publication*]
**Mol Cryst Liq Cryst** ... Molecular Crystals and Liquid Crystals [*A publication*]
**Mol Cryst and Liq Cryst** ... Molecular Crystals and Liquid Crystals [*A publication*]
**Mol Cryst and Liq Cryst Lett** ... Molecular Crystals and Liquid Crystals. Letters [*A publication*]
**Mol Cryst Liq Cryst Lett** ... Molecular Crystals and Liquid Crystals. Letters [*A publication*]
**Mol Cryst and Liq Cryst Suppl Ser** ... Molecular Crystals and Liquid Crystals. Supplement Series [*A publication*]
**MOLD**....... Model of Light Diode
**Mol De Jure Mar** ... Molloy's De Jure Maritimo et Navali [*A publication*] (DLA)
**MOLDS**.... Management On-Line Data System [*University of Syracuse*]
**MOLDS**.... Modernization of Land Data Systems [*North American Institute for the Modernization of Land Data Systems*] [*Falls Church, VA*]
**MOLDS**.... Multiple Online Debugging System [*Data processing*] (IEEE)
**MOLE**....... FlowMole Corp. [*NASDAQ symbol*] (NQ)
**MOLE**....... Molecular Optics LASER Examiner [*Spectrometry*]
**MOLEC**..... Molecular
**Molec Biol** ... Molecular Biology [*A publication*]
**Molec Cryst** ... Molecular Crystals and Liquid Crystals [*A publication*]
**MOLECOM** ... Molecularized Digital Computer
**Molec Pharm** ... Molecular Pharmacology [*A publication*]
**Molec Phys** ... Molecular Physics [*A publication*]
**Molecular Phys** ... Molecular Physics [*A publication*]
**MoLeeH**.... Lee's Summit Hospital, Lee's Summit, MO [*Library symbol*] [*Library of Congress*] (LCLS)
**MoLeeL**..... Longview Community College, Lee's Summit, MO [*Library symbol*] [*Library of Congress*] (LCLS)
**MoLeeU**..... Unity School Library, Lee's Summit, MO [*Library symbol*] [*Library of Congress*] (LCLS)
**Mo Leg Exam** ... Monthly Legal Examiner [*New York*] [*A publication*] (DLA)
**MO Legis Serv** ... Missouri Legislative Service [*A publication*]
**MO Legis Serv (Vernon)** ... Missouri Legislative Service (Vernon) [*A publication*] (DLA)
**MOLETRONICS** ... Molecular Electronics
**MOLEVATOR** ... Motor Elevator [*Mechanical lifting stand for arc lamps*]
**MOLEX**.... Molecular Executive [*Graphic substructure chemical search system*]
**Mol Fiz Biofiz Vodn Sist** ... Molekulyarnaya Fizika i Biofizika Vodnykh Sistem [*A publication*]

**Mol Fiz Biofiz Vod Sis** ... Molekulyarnaya Fizika i Biofizika Vodnykh Sistem [*A publication*]
**MOLGEN** ... Molecular Genetics [*Program*] [*Data processing*]
**Mol Genet Mikrobiol Virusol** ... Molekulyarnaya Genetika, Mikrobiologiya, i Virusologiya [*A publication*]
**Mol Gen Genet** ... Molecular and General Genetics [*A publication*]
**Mol G Genet** ... Molecular and General Genetics [*A publication*]
**MO Lib Assn Newsl** ... Missouri Library Association. Newsletter [*A publication*]
**MO Lib Assn Q** ... Missouri Library Association. Quarterly [*A publication*]
**MO Libr Ass Q** ... Missouri Library Association. Quarterly [*A publication*]
**Mol Immunol** ... Molecular Immunology [*A publication*]
**Molin** ......... [*Carolus*] Molinaeus [*Deceased, 1566*] [*Authority cited in pre-1607 legal work*] (DSA)
**Molini Ital** ... Molini d'Italia [*A publication*]
**MOLINK** .. Moscow/Washington Emergency Communications Link (MCD)
**Molirena** .... Movimiento Liberal Republicano Nacionalista [*Nationalist Liberal Republican Movement*] [*Panama*] [*Political party*] (PPW)
**MoLiWJ** .... William Jewell College, Liberty, MO [*Library symbol*] [*Library of Congress*] (LCLS)
**MOLJA** ..... Modern Language Journal [*A publication*]
**Mol JM** ..... Molloy's De Jure Maritimo et Navali [*A publication*] (DLA)
**Molk Kaeserei Ztg** ... Molkerei- und Kaeserei- Zeitung [*A publication*]
**Molk Ztg (Berlin)** ... Molkerei-Zeitung (Berlin) [*A publication*]
**Molk Ztg (Hildesheim Ger)** ... Molkerei-Zeitung (Hildesheim, Germany) [*A publication*]
**Molk Ztg Welt Milch** ... Molkerei-Zeitung Welt der Milch [*West Germany*] [*A publication*]
**MOLL** ....... Metallo-Organic Liquid LASER
**Moll** ........... Moller Organ Co. [*Record label*]
**MOLL** ....... Mollis [*Soft*] [*Pharmacy*]
**Moll** ........... Molloy's De Jure Maritimo [*A publication*] (DLA)
**Moll** ........... Molloy's Irish Chancery Reports [*1827-31*] [*A publication*] (DLA)
**MOLLI** ...... Micro OnLine Library Information [*Nichols Advanced Technologies, Inc.*]
**MOLLUS** ... Military Order of the Loyal Legion of the United States (EA)
**MOL/M³** ... Moles per Cubic Meter
**Mo L Mag** ... Monthly Law Magazine [*London*] [*A publication*] (DLA)
**Mol Med** .... Molecular Medicine [*A publication*]
**Mol Microbiol** ... Molecular Microbiology [*A publication*]
**MOLNS** .... Ministry of Labour and National Service [*World War II*] [*British*] (DAS)
**MOLO** ....... Mideastern Ohio Library Organization [*Library network*]
**MOLOC** .... Ministry of Labour Occupational Classification [*Later, CODOT*] [*British*]
**Moloch Myas Zhivotnovod** ... Molochnoe i Myasnoe Zhivotnovodstvo [*A publication*]
**Molochn Myasn Skotovod (Moscow)** ... Molochnoe i Myasnoe Skotovodstvo (Moscow) [*A publication*]
**Molochno Masloden Promst** ... Molochno-Maslodel'naya Promyshlennost [*A publication*]
**Molochno Myasn Skotovod (Kiev)** ... Molochnoe i Myasnoe Skotovodstvo (Kiev) [*A publication*]
**Molochn Prom-St** ... Molochnaya Promyshlennost [*A publication*]
**Molodoi Nauchn Rab Estestv Nauki** ... Molodoi Nauchnyi Rabotnik. Estestvennye Nauki [*A publication*]
**Mol Pharmacol** ... Molecular Pharmacology [*A publication*]
**Mol Photoch** ... Molecular Photochemistry [*A publication*]
**Mol Photochem** ... Molecular Photochemistry [*A publication*]
**Mol Phys** ... Molecular Physics [*A publication*]
**Mol Physiol** ... Molecular Physiology [*A publication*]
**Mol Plant Microbe Interact** ... Molecular Plant-Microbe Interactions [*A publication*]
**MO LR** ...... Missouri Law Review [*A publication*]
**MO L Rev** ... Missouri Law Review [*A publication*]
**MOLS** ....... Magnetic-Operated Limit Switch
**MOLS** ....... Mirror Optional Landing System [*Aviation*] (NG)
**MOLS** ....... Mobile Object Location System
**MOLS** ....... Multiple Object Location System [*Army*]
**MOLS** ....... Mutually Orthogonal Latin Square
**MOLSINK** ... Molecular Sink of Outer Space [*Vacuum testing chamber for spacecraft systems*]
**Mol Spectros** ... Molecular Spectroscopy [*A publication*]
**Mol Spectrosc Mod Res** ... Molecular Spectroscopy. Modern Research [*A publication*]
**Mol Spektrosk** ... Molekulyarnaya Spektroskopiya [*A publication*]
**Mol Struct Diffr Methods** ... Molecular Structure by Diffraction Methods [*A publication*]
**Mol Struct Dimensions Ser A** ... Molecular Structures and Dimensions. Series A [*A publication*]
**MOLT** ....... Molten
**Molten Met** ... Molten Metal [*A publication*]
**MOLTOL** ... Manned Orbiting Laboratory Test-Oriented Language [*NASA*] (MCD)
**MOL WT** .. Molecular Weight [*Also, M, MW*]
**MOLX** ....... Molex, Inc. [*NASDAQ symbol*] (NQ)
**MOLY** ....... Molecular Analysis [*by a computer graphics system*] [*Chemistry*]
**Moly** ........... Molyneaux's Reports. English Courts, Tempore Car. I [*A publication*] (DLA)
**MOLY** ....... Mouse Lymphoma Cells [*Oncology*]
**Molysulfide Newslett** ... Molysulfide Newsletter [*United States*] [*A publication*]
**MOM** ........ Macro Observation Module [*Microscopy*]
**MOM** ........ Maintenance Operations Management (MCD)
**MOM** ........ Manned Orbiting Mission [*NASA*]
**MOM** ........ Measure of Merit (MCD)
**MOM** ........ Men's Own Movement [*Australia*]
**MOM** ........ Message Output Module [*Telecommunications*] (TEL)
**MOM** ........ Metal-Oxide Metal (MCD)
**MOM** ........ Methods of Moderation [*An association*] (EA)
**MOM** ........ Micromation Online Microfilmer
**MOM** ........ Middle of the Month
**MOM** ........ Military Official Mail (AABC)
**MOM** ........ Military Ordinary Mail (AABC)
**MOM** ........ Military Overseas Mail [*An association*] (EA)
**MOM** ........ Milk of Magnesia
**MOM** ........ Minutes of Meeting
**MOM** ........ Missile Operations Manager (MUGU)
**MOM** ........ Missionary Sisters of Our Lady of Mercy [*Roman Catholic religious order*]
**MOM** ........ Mobelmarkt. Fachzeitschrift fuer die Mobelwirtschaft [*A publication*]
**MOM** ........ Modern Office [*A publication*]
**MOM** ........ Modified Operational Missile
**MOM** ........ Momentary (MSA)
**MOM** ........ Momentum
**MOM** ........ Momote [*Admiralty Islands*] [*Seismograph station code, US Geological Survey*] (SEIS)
**MOM** ........ Mother's Restaurants Ltd. [*Toronto Stock Exchange symbol*]
**M-O-M** ..... My Old Man [*Husband*] [*Slang*]
**MOM's** ...... Multiples over the Median [*Statistics*]
**MOMA** ...... Madagasikara Otronin'ny Malagasy [*Formerly, MONIMA*] [*Madagascar Led by Malagasy*]
**MOMA** ...... Methoxyhydroxymandelic Acid [*Organic chemistry*]
**MOMA** ...... Museum of Modern Art [*New York*]
**MOMAC** ... Monkey Mountain Advisory Center [*Military*] (CINC)
**MOMAG** ... Mobile Mine Assembly Group [*Military*] (CAAL)
**MoManW** ... Laura Ingalls Wilder - Rose Wilder Lane Home and Museum, Mansfield, MO [*Library symbol*] [*Library of Congress*] (LCLS)
**MOMAR** ... Modern Mobile Army [*Military*]
**MoMaryU** ... Northwest Missouri State University, Maryville, MO [*Library symbol*] [*Library of Congress*] (LCLS)
**MOMAT** ... Mobile Mine Assembly Team
**MOMAU** .. Mobile Mine Assembly Unit (NVT)
**MOMB** ...... Mombasa [*Island near Kenya*] (ROG)
**MOMBE** ... Metallo-Organic Molecular Beam Epitaxy [*Solid state physics*]
**MOMC** ...... Mount McKinley National Park
**MOMCOMS** ... Man-on-the-Move Communications
**MOMEA** ... Montpellier Medical [*A publication*]
**MO Med** .... Missouri Medicine [*A publication*]
**MoMex** ...... Mexico-Audrain County Library, Mexico, MO [*Library symbol*] [*Library of Congress*] (LCLS)
**MOMI** ....... Museum of the Moving Image [*London*] (ECON)
**Mo Micro J** ... Monthly Microscopical Journal [*A publication*]
**MOMIMTS** ... Military and Orchestral Musical Instrument Makers' Trade Society [*A union*] [*British*] (DCTA)
**MOML** ...... Moslem Meal [*Airline notation*] (ADA)
**MoMM** ...... Missouri Valley College, Marshall, MO [*Library symbol*] [*Library of Congress*] (LCLS)
**MOMM** .... Motor Machinist's Mate [*Navy rating*]
**MOMMSR** ... Motor Machinist's Mate, Ship Repair [*Navy rating*]
**MOMP** ...... Major Outer Membrane Protein [*Biochemistry*]
**MOMP** ...... Michigan Ordnance Missile Plant [*Army*]
**MOMP** ...... Mid-Ocean Meeting Place
**MOMP** ...... Mustargen [*Nitrogen mustard*], Oncovin [*Vincristine*], Methotrexate, Prednisone [*Antineoplastic drug regimen*]
**MOMR** ...... Ministry of Oil and Mineral Resources [*Yemen Arab Republic*] (ECON)
**MOMS** ...... Measure of Mission Success [*Military*] (CAAL)
**MOMS** ...... Mervardesskatt [*Value-Added Tax*] [*Sweden*]
**MOMS** ...... Meteorological and Oceanographic Measurements System [*Chevron Oil Co.*]
**MOMS** ...... Meteorological Optic Measuring System (MCD)
**MOMS** ...... Missile Operate Mode Simulator
**MOMS** ...... Modular Optoelectronic Multispectral Scanner (MCD)
**MOMS** ...... Mothers of Men in Service [*World War II*]
**MOMS** ...... Mothers for Moral Stability [*Group opposing sex education in schools*]
**MOMS** ...... Multimegabit Operation Multiplexer System
**MOMS** ...... Multiple Orbit - Multiple Satellite
**MoMSV** ..... Moloney Mouse Sarcoma Virus
**MoMuLV** .. Moloney Murine Leukemia Virus [*Also, MLV*]
**Mo Mus Rec** ... Monthly Musical Record [*A publication*]
**MOM/WOW** ... Men Our Masters/Women Our Wonders [*Antifeminist group*] (EA)
**MON** ......... Above Mountains [*Aviation*] (FAAC)
**MON** ......... Member of the Order of the Niger [*Nigeria*]

**MON** ......... Memorandum of Negotiation (MCD)
**MON** ......... Ministerstvo Oborony Narodowej [*A publication*]
**MON** ......... Missouri Valley College, Marshall, MO [*OCLC symbol*] [*Inactive*] (OCLC)
**MON** ......... Mixed Oxides of Nitrogen
**MON** ......... Monaco [*Monaco*] [*Seismograph station code, US Geological Survey*] (SEIS)
**MON** ......... Monaghan [*County in Republic of Ireland*] (ROG)
**Mon**........... Monaghan's Unreported Cases (Pennsylvania Superior Court) [*A publication*] (DLA)
**Mon**........... Monarch [*Record label*] [*Great Britain*]
**MON** ......... Monarch Capital Corp. [*NYSE symbol*] (SPSG)
**MON** ......... Monarch Investments Ltd. [*Toronto Stock Exchange symbol*]
**Mon**........... Monash University [*Australia*]
**MON** ......... Monastery
**MON** ......... Monday (AFM)
**MON** ......... Monetary (AFM)
**MON** ......... Money [*A publication*]
**mon** ........... Mongol [*MARC language code*] [*Library of Congress*] (LCCP)
**MON** ......... Mongolian (AABC)
**Mon**........... [*The*] Monist [*A publication*]
**Mon**........... Moniteur Belge [*A publication*] (ILCA)
**MON** ......... Monitor [*Navy ship symbol*]
**MON** ......... Monitor (DEN)
**mon** ........... Monitor/Contractor [*MARC relator code*] [*Library of Congress*] (LCCP)
**MON** ......... Monmouthshire [*County in Wales*]
**Mon**........... Monoceros [*Constellation*]
**MON** ......... Monoclinic [*Crystallography*]
**Mon**........... Monoclonal Antibodies, Inc.
**MON** ......... Monocyte [*Hematology*]
**MON** ......... Monogram [*Numismatics*]
**mon** ........... Monograph (BJA)
**Mon**........... [*T. B.*] Monroe's Kentucky Reports [*17-23, 40-57 Kentucky*] [*A publication*] (DLA)
**MON** ......... Montana
**Mon**........... Montana Reports [*A publication*] (DLA)
**Mon**........... Montana Supreme Court Reports [*A publication*] (DLA)
**MON** ......... Month
**MON** ......... Monticello, AR [*Location identifier*] [*FAA*] (FAAL)
**MON** ......... Monument (AAG)
**MON** ......... Monument Still Exists [*Genealogy*] (ROG)
**MON** ......... Motor Octane Number [*Fuel technology*]
**MON** ......... Mount Cook [*New Zealand*] [*Airport symbol*] (OAG)
**MoN**........... Mountain Name (BJA)
**MoN**........... North Kansas City Public Library, North Kansas City, MO [*Library symbol*] [*Library of Congress*] (LCLS)
**MON** ......... Universite de Moncton, Bibliotheque [*UTLAS symbol*]
**MONA** ...... Modular Navigation [*Aviation*]
**Mona**.......... Monaghan's Reports [*147-165 Pennsylvania*] [*A publication*] (DLA)
**MONA** ...... Monitor Assembly [*Ground Communications Facility, NASA*]
**MONAB**.... Mobile Naval Advanced Base [*British military*] (DMA)
**MONAB**.... Mobile Noise Analysis Barge
**MONAB**.... Mobile Operating Naval Air Base
**Monaco Mus Anthropol Prehist Bull** ... Monaco. Musee d'Anthropologie Prehistorique. Bulletin [*A publication*]
**MonAeg**..... Monumenta Aegyptiaca [*Brussels*] [*A publication*]
**Monag**........ Monaghan's Reports [*147-165 Pennsylvania*] [*A publication*] (DLA)
**MONAGH** ... Monaghan [*County in Republic of Ireland*] (ROG)
**Monaghan** ... Monaghan's Reports [*147-165 Pennsylvania*] [*A publication*] (DLA)
**Monaghan (PA)** ... Monaghan's Reports [*147-165 Pennsylvania*] [*A publication*] (DLA)
**MONAGN** ... Monaghan [*County in Republic of Ireland*]
**MONAL**.... Mobile Nondestructive Assay Laboratory [*AEC*]
**MonAL** ...... Monumenti Antichi Pubblicati dell'Accademia dei Lincei [*A publication*]
**Mon Analyt Bull Inter-Afr Bur Soils** ... Monthly Analytical Bulletin. Inter-African Bureau for Soils [*A publication*]
**Mon Anc** .... Monumentum Ancyranum [*Classical studies*] (OCD)
**Mon Angl**... Monasticon Anglicanum [*A publication*] (DLA)
**Mon Ant**..... Monumenti Antichi [*A publication*]
**Monash LR** ... Monash University. Law Review [*A publication*] (APTA)
**Monash UL Rev** ... Monash University. Law Review [*A publication*]
**Monash Univ Gaz** ... Monash University. Gazette [*A publication*] (APTA)
**Monash Univ Law Rev** ... Monash University. Law Review [*A publication*]
**Monash Univ L Rev** ... Monash University. Law Review [*A publication*] (APTA)
**Monat** ........ Monatshefte; a Journal Devoted to the Study of German Language and Literature [*A publication*]
**Monat f Deut Unt** ... Monatshefte fuer Deutschen Unterricht [*A publication*]
**Monatsber Deut Akad Wiss Berlin** ... Monatsberichte. Deutsche Akademie der Wissenschaften zu Berlin [*A publication*]
**Monatsber Dtsch Akad Wiss Berl** ... Monatsberichte. Deutsche Akademie der Wissenschaften zu Berlin [*A publication*]
**Monatsber Dtschen Bundesbank** ... Monatsberichte. Deutsche Bundesbank [*A publication*]
**Monatsber Int Altersforsch Altersbekaempf** ... Monatsberichte fuer Internationale Altersforschung und Altersbekaempfung [*A publication*]
**Monatsber Oesterr Inst Wirtsch-Forsch** ... Monatsberichte. Oesterreichisches Institut fuer Wirtschaftsforschung [*A publication*]
**Monats Chem** ... Monatshefte fuer Chemie [*A publication*]
**Monatschr Geburtsh u Gynak** ... Monatsschrift fuer Geburtshilfe und Gynaekologie [*A publication*]
**Monatschr Ornithol Vivarienkd Ausg B** ... Monatsschrift fuer Ornithologie und Vivarienkunde. Ausgabe B. Aquarien und Terrarien [*East Germany*] [*A publication*]
**Monatschr Psychiat u Neurol** ... Monatsschrift fuer Psychiatrie und Neurologie [*A publication*]
**Monatsh Chem** ... Monatshefte fuer Chemie [*A publication*]
**Monatsh Chem Verw Teile Anderer Wiss** ... Monatshefte fuer Chemie und Verwandte Teile Anderer Wissenschaften [*A publication*]
**Monatshefte** ... Monatshefte fuer Deutschen Unterricht. Deutsche Sprache und Literatur [*A publication*]
**Monatsh Math** ... Monatshefte fuer Mathematik [*Vienna*] [*A publication*]
**Monatsh Math Phys** ... Monatshefte fuer Mathematik und Physik [*Austria*] [*A publication*]
**Monatsh Naturwiss Unterr Aller Schulgattungen Natur Sch** ... Monatshefte fuer den Naturwissenschaftlichen Unterricht Aller Schulgattungen und Natur und Schule [*A publication*]
**Monatsh Prakt Dermat** ... Monatshefte fuer Praktische Dermatologie [*A publication*]
**Monatsh Prakt Tierh** ... Monatshefte fuer Praktische Tierheilkunde [*A publication*]
**Monatsh Seide Kunstseide Zellwolle** ... Monatshefte fuer Seide und Kunstseide. Zellwolle [*A publication*]
**Monatsh Tierheilkd** ... Monatshefte fuer Tierheilkunde [*A publication*]
**Monatsh Vet** ... Monatshefte fuer Veterinaermedizin [*A publication*]
**Monatsh Veterinaermed** ... Monatshefte fuer Veterinaermedizin [*A publication*]
**Monatsh Veterinarmed** ... Monatshefte fuer Veterinaermedizin [*A publication*]
**Monats Kind** ... Monatsschrift fuer Kinderheilkunde [*A publication*]
**Monatskurse Aerztl Fortbild** ... Monatskurse fuer die Aerztliche Fortbildung [*A publication*]
**Monats Math** ... Monatshefte fuer Mathematik [*A publication*]
**Monatsschr Brau** ... Monatsschrift fuer Brauerei [*A publication*]
**Monatsschr Brauerei** ... Monatsschrift fuer Brauerei [*A publication*]
**Monatsschr Dtsch Recht** ... Monatsschrift fuer Deutsches Recht [*A publication*]
**Monatsschr Geburshilfe Gynaekol** ... Monatsschrift fuer Geburtshilfe und Gynaekologie [*A publication*]
**Monatsschr Kinderheilkd** ... Monatsschrift fuer Kinderheilkunde [*A publication*]
**Monatsschr Krebsbekaempf** ... Monatsschrift fuer Krebsbekaempfung [*A publication*]
**Monatsschr Lungenkr Tuberk-Bekaempf** ... Monatsschrift fuer Lungenkrankheiten und Tuberkulose-Bekaempfung [*A publication*]
**Monatsschr Ohrenheilkd Laryngo-Rhinol** ... Monatsschrift fuer Ohrenheilkunde und Laryngo-Rhinologie [*A publication*]
**Monatsschr Ornithol Vivarienkd Ausg B Aquarien Terrarien** ... Monatsschrift fuer Ornithologie und Vivarienkunde. Ausgabe B. Aquarien und Terrarien [*A publication*]
**Monatsschr Psychiatr Neurol** ... Monatsschrift fuer Psychiatrie und Neurologie [*A publication*]
**Monatsschr Text Ind** ... Monatsschrift fuer Textil-Industrie [*A publication*]
**Monatsschr Unfallheikd Versicher-Versorg Verkehrsmed** ... Monatsschrift fuer Unfallheilkunde. Versicherungs-, Versorgungs-, und Verkehrsmedizin [*A publication*]
**Monatsschr Unfallheilkd** ... Monatsschrift fuer Unfallheilkunde [*A publication*]
**Monatsschr Unfallheilkd Versicher Versorg Verkehrsmed** ... Monatsschrift fuer Unfallheilkunde. Versicherungs-, Versorgungs-, und Verkehrsmedizin [*A publication*]
**Monats Unfa** ... Monatsschrift fuer Unfallheilkunde [*A publication*]
**MONBA**.... Monatsschrift fuer Brauerei [*A publication*]
**Mon Bull Agric Intell Plant Dis** ... Monthly Bulletin of Agricultural Intelligence and Plant Disease [*A publication*]
**Mon Bull Agric Sci Pract** ... Monthly Bulletin of Agricultural Science and Practice [*A publication*]
**Mon Bull Am Bakers Assoc** ... Monthly Bulletin. American Bakers Association [*A publication*]
**Mon Bull Can Inst Min Metall** ... Monthly Bulletin. Canadian Institute of Mining and Metallurgy [*A publication*]
**Mon Bull Can Min Inst** ... Monthly Bulletin. Canadian Mining Institute [*A publication*]
**Mon Bull Ceram Ind** ... Monthly Bulletin for the Ceramic Industry [*A publication*]
**Mon Bull Coffee Board Kenya** ... Monthly Bulletin. Coffee Board of Kenya [*A publication*]
**Mon Bull Int Railw Congr Assoc** ... Monthly Bulletin. International Railway Congress Association [*A publication*]
**Mon Bull Int Railw Congr Assoc (Engl Ed)** ... Monthly Bulletin. International Railway Congress Association (English Edition) [*A publication*]

**Mon Bull Int Ry Congr Ass Cybern Electron Ry** ... Monthly Bulletin. International Railway Congress Association. Cybernetics and Electronics of the Railways [*A publication*]
**Mon Bull Minist Health Public Health Lab** ... Monthly Bulletin. Ministry of Health and the Public Health Laboratory [*A publication*]
**Mon Bull Minist Health Public Health Lab Serv** ... Monthly Bulletin. Ministry of Health and the Public Health Laboratory Service [*England*] [*A publication*]
**Mon Bull Minst Mines Hydrocarbons (Caracas)** ... Monthly Bulletin. Ministry of Mines and Hydrocarbons (Caracas) [*A publication*]
**MONC**....... Metropolitan Opera National Council
**Mon Cat US Gov Publications** ... Monthly Catalog of United States Government Publications [*A publication*]
**Mon Checkl State Publ** ... Monthly Checklist of State Publications [*United States*] [*A publication*]
**Monc Inn** ... Moncrieff's Liability of Innkeepers [*1874*] [*A publication*] (DLA)
**Mon Corresp Befoerd Erd Himmelskunde** ... Monatliche Correspondenz zur Befoerderung der Erd und Himmelskunde [*East Germany*] [*A publication*]
**MOND**...... Monday (ROG)
**Monda Ling-Prob** ... Monda Lingvo-Problemo [*A publication*]
**Monde Alpin Rhod** ... Monde Alpin et Rhodanien [*A publication*]
**Monde Apic** ... Monde Apicole [*A publication*]
**Monde Dent** ... Monde Dentaire [*A publication*]
**Monde de l'Educ** ... Monde de l'Education [*A publication*]
**Monde Med (Paris)** ... Monde Medical (Paris) [*A publication*]
**Monde Miner** ... Monde et les Mineraux [*A publication*]
**Monde Mod** ... Monde Moderne [*A publication*]
**Monde Plant** ... Monde des Plantes [*A publication*]
**Mondes Asiat** ... Mondes Asiatiques [*A publication*]
**Mondes Dev** ... Mondes en Developpement [*Paris*] [*A publication*]
**Mondes en Develop** ... Mondes en Developpement [*A publication*]
**MON/DIR** ... Mission Monitoring Direction
**Mond Nickel Bull** ... Mond Nickel Bulletin [*A publication*]
**Mondo Agric** ... Mondo Agricolo [*A publication*]
**Mondo Econ** ... Mondo Economico [*A publication*]
**Mondo Fin** ... Mondo Finanziario [*A publication*]
**Mondo Odontostomatol** ... Mondo Odontostomatologico [*A publication*]
**Mondo Ortod** ... Mondo Ortodontico [*A publication*]
**Mondo Sotterraneo Pubbl Nuova Ser** ... Mondo Sotterraneo. Circolo Speleologico e Idrologico Friulano. Pubblicazione. Nuova Serie [*A publication*]
**Mondo Tess** ... Mondo Tessile [*A publication*]
**MONE**....... Monetary Resources [*NASDAQ symbol*] (NQ)
**MONECA** ... Motor Network Calculator
**Mon Econ Lett** ... Monthly Economic Letter [*United States*] [*A publication*]
**Moneda y Cred** ... Moneda y Credito [*A publication*]
**Mon Energy Rev** ... Monthly Energy Review [*A publication*]
**MONES**.... Molecular Nonthermal Excitation Spectrometry
**MONET**.... Monetary
**Moneta e Cred** ... Moneta e Credito [*A publication*]
**MONEVAL** ... Monthly Evaluation Report [*Military*]
**MONEX**.... Monsoon Experiment [*Also, MONSOONEX*]
**MonF**......... Monde Francais [*A publication*]
**MONG**...... Mitteilungen. Oesterreichische Numismatische Gesellschaft [*A publication*]
**MONG**...... Mongolian [*Language, etc.*]
**MONG**...... Mongrel (DSUE)
**MONG**...... Moning [*Tea trade*] (ROG)
**Mongrafias Inst Eduardo Torroja Constr Cem** ... Monografias. Instituto Eduardo Torroja de la Construccion y del Cemento [*A publication*]
**Mong Stud** ... Mongolian Studies [*A publication*]
**MoNHI**...... Missouri Natural Heritage Inventory [*Missouri State Department of Conservation*] [*Information service or system*] (IID)
**MONIMA** ... Mouvement National pour l'Independance de Madagascar [*National Movement for the Independence of Madagascar*] [*Political party*] (PPW)
**Mon Ist**...... Monumenti Inediti Pubblicati dell'Istituto di Corrispondenza Archeologica [*A publication*]
**Monit**......... Moniteur Belge [*A publication*]
**Monit Belge** ... Moniteur Belge [*A publication*]
**Monit Ceram Verrerie J Ceram Chaufournier Reunis** ... Moniteur de la Ceramique et de la Verrerie et Journal du Ceramiste et de Chaufournier Reunis [*A publication*]
**Moniteur Commer Internat** ... Moniteur du Commerce International [*A publication*]
**Monit Farm Ter** ... Monitor de la Farmacia y de la Terapeutica [*A publication*]
**Monit Hop** ... Moniteur des Hopitaux [*A publication*]
**Monit Hyg Salubr Publique** ... Moniteur d'Hygiene et de Salubrite Publique [*A publication*]
**Monit Maille** ... Moniteur de la Maille [*A publication*]
**Monitore Zool Ital Monogr** ... Monitore Zoologico Italiano [*Italian Journal of Zoology*]. Monografia [*A publication*]
**Monitor Proc Inst Radio Electron Eng (Aust)** ... Monitor. Proceedings. Institution of Radio and Electronics Engineers (Australia) [*A publication*]
**Monit Ostet-Ginecol** ... Monitore Ostetrico-Ginecologico [*A publication*]
**Monit Ostet-Ginecol Endocrinol Metab** ... Monitore Ostetrico-Ginecologico di Endocrinologia e del Metabolismo [*A publication*]
**Monit Papet Belge** ... Moniteur de la Papeterie Belge [*A publication*]
**Monit Papet Fr** ... Moniteur de la Papeterie Francaise [*A publication*]
**Monit Peint** ... Moniteur de la Peinture [*A publication*]
**Monit Pet Roman** ... Monitorul Petrolului Roman [*A publication*]
**Monit Photogr** ... Moniteur de la Photographie [*A publication*]
**Monit Prod Chim** ... Moniteur des Produits Chimiques [*A publication*]
**Monit Prof Electr Electron** ... Moniteur Professionnel de l'Electricite et Electronique [*France*] [*A publication*]
**Monit Tec**.. Monitore Tecnico [*A publication*]
**Monit Tein Apprets Impress Tissus** ... Moniteur de la Teinture des Apprets et de l'Impression des Tissus [*A publication*]
**Monit Trav Publics Batim** ... Moniteur des Travaux Publics et du Batiment [*France*] [*A publication*]
**Monit Zool Ital** ... Monitore Zoologico Italiano [*Italian Journal of Zoology*] [*A publication*]
**Monit Zool Ital/Ital J Zool New Ser** ... Monitore Zoologico Italiano/Italian Journal of Zoology. New Series [*A publication*]
**Monit Zool Ital/Ital J Zool New Ser Suppl** ... Monitore Zoologico Italiano/ Italian Journal of Zoology. New Series. Supplement [*A publication*]
**Monit Zool Ital Monogr** ... Monitore Zoologico Italiano [*Italian Journal of Zoology*]. Monografia [*A publication*]
**Monit Zool Ital Suppl** ... Monitore Zoologico Italiano [*Italian Journal of Zoology*]. Supplemento [*A publication*]
**Mon J Inst Ind Sci Univ Tokyo** ... Monthly Journal. Institute of Industrial Science. University of Tokyo [*A publication*]
**Mon Labor Rev** ... Monthly Labor Review [*A publication*]
**Mon Lab Re** ... Monthly Labor Review [*A publication*]
**Mon Law Mag** ... Monthly Law Magazine [*London*] [*A publication*] (DLA)
**Mon Law Rep** ... Monthly Law Reporter [*A publication*] (DLA)
**Mon Leg R (PA)** ... Monroe Legal Reporter [*Pennsylvania*] [*A publication*] (DLA)
**Mon L R**..... Monash University. Law Review [*A publication*]
**Mon L Rev** ... Monash University. Law Review [*A publication*] (APTA)
**Mon L Rev** ... Montana Law Review [*A publication*]
**Mon Memor Paint Res Stn (Taddington)** ... Monthly Memorandum. Paint Research Station (Taddington) [*A publication*]
**Mon Meth** ... Monahan's Method of the Law [*1878*] [*A publication*] (DLA)
**MoNMH** ... North Kansas City Memorial Hospital, North Kansas City, MO [*Library symbol*] [*Library of Congress*] (LCLS)
**Monmouth Ant** ... Monmouthshire Antiquary [*A publication*]
**Monmouth County Med Soc Newsletter** ... Monmouth County Medical Society. Newsletter [*A publication*]
**Monmouthshire Ant** ... Monmouthshire Antiquary. Proceedings. Monmouthshire and Caerleon Antiquarian Society [*A publication*]
**Monmouthshire Antiq** ... Monmouthshire Antiquary [*A publication*]
**MONMS**... Monmouthshire [*County in Wales*]
**Mon Nipp**.. Monumenta Nipponica [*A publication*]
**Mon Not**.... Moniteur du Notariat et de l'Enregistrement. Journal de Legislation et de Jurisprudence [*A publication*]
**Mon Not Astron Soc S Afr** ... Monthly Notes. Astronomical Society of Southern Africa [*A publication*]
**Mon Notes Astron Soc South Afr** ... Monthly Notes. Astronomical Society of Southern Africa [*A publication*]
**Mon Not R Astron Soc** ... Monthly Notices. Royal Astronomical Society [*England*] [*A publication*]
**MONO**...... Monaural (KSC)
**Mono**.......... Monoceros [*Constellation*]
**MONO**...... Monochrome (DSUE)
**mono**........... Monocyte [*Hematology*]
**Mono**.......... Monogram [*Record label*]
**MONO**...... Mononucleosis [*Medicine*]
**MONO**...... Monophonic
**MONO**...... Monotype (ADA)
**MONOB** ... Mobile Noise Barge
**MONOC** ... Monocoque (MSA)
**MONOCL** ... Monoclinic
**MONOG**... Monograph
**Monogr Acad Nat Sci Phila** ... Monographs. Academy of Natural Sciences of Philadelphia [*A publication*]
**Monograf Inst Mat** ... Monografias. Instituto de Matematicas [*Mexico City*] [*A publication*]
**Monograf Mat** ... Monografie Matematyczne [*A publication*]
**Monograf Math** ... Monografias de Matematica [*Rio De Janeiro*] [*A publication*]
**Monograf Mat Pura Apl** ... Monografias de Matematicas Pura e Aplicada [*Campinas*] [*A publication*]
**Monograf Psych** ... Monografie Psychologiczne [*A publication*]
**Monogr Allergy** ... Monographs in Allergy [*A publication*]
**Monogr Am Assoc Ment Defic** ... Monographs. American Association on Mental Deficiency [*A publication*]
**Monogr Amer Phytopathol Soc** ... Monograph. American Phytopathological Society [*A publication*]
**Monogr Am Soc Agron** ... Monographs. American Society of Agronomy [*A publication*]
**Monogr Anaesthesiol** ... Monographs in Anaesthesiology [*A publication*]
**Monogr Angew Entomol** ... Monographien zur Angewandten Entomologie [*A publication*]

**Monogr Ann Radiol** ... Monographies des Annales de Radiologie [*A publication*]
**Monogr Annu Soc Fr Biol Clin** ... Monographie Annuelle. Societe Francaise de Biologie Clinique [*A publication*]
**Monograph Enseign Math** ... Monographies de l'Enseignement Mathematique [*Geneva*] [*A publication*]
**Monographiae Biol** ... Monographiae Biologicae [*A publication*]
**Monograph Linguist Math** ... Monographies de Linguistique Mathematique [*A publication*]
**Monograph Math** ... Monographies de Mathematique [*A publication*]
**Monograph Modernen Math** ... Monographien zur Modernen Mathematik [*A publication*]
**Monograph Sci Maison Franco-Japon** ... Monographies Scientifiques de la Maison Franco-Japonaise [*A publication*]
**Monograph Ser Utah St Univ** ... Monograph Series. Utah State University [*A publication*]
**Monographs Population Biol** ... Monographs in Population Biology [*A publication*]
**Monographs Stud Math** ... Monographs and Studies in Mathematics [*A publication*]
**Monographs Surveys Water Res Engrg** ... Monographs and Surveys in Water Resource Engineering [*A publication*]
**Monographs Textbooks Mech Solids Fluids Mech Anal** ... Monographs and Textbooks on Mechanics of Solids and Fluids. Mechanics Analysis [*A publication*]
**Monographs Textbooks Mech Solids Fluids Mech Continua** ... Monographs and Textbooks on Mechanics of Solids and Fluids. Mechanics of Continua [*A publication*]
**Monographs Textbooks Mech Solids Fluids Mech Dynam Systems** ... Monographs and Textbooks on Mechanics of Solids and Fluids. Mechanics of Dynamical Systems [*A publication*]
**Monographs Textbooks Mech Solids Fluids Mech Genesis Method** ... Monographs and Textbooks on Mechanics of Solids and Fluids. Mechanics of Genesis and Method [*A publication*]
**Monographs Textbooks Mech Solids Fluids Mech Plastic Solids** ... Monographs and Textbooks on Mechanics of Solids and Fluids. Mechanics of Plastic Solids [*A publication*]
**Monographs Textbooks Pure Appl Math** ... Monographs and Textbooks in Pure and Applied Mathematics [*A publication*]
**Monograph Wissenschaftstheorie Grundlagenforsch** ... Monographien zur Wissenschaftstheorie und Grundlagenforschung [*A publication*]
**Monogr Atheroscler** ... Monographs on Atherosclerosis [*A publication*]
**Monogr Biol** ... Monographiae Biologicae [*A publication*]
**Monogr BIPM** ... Monographie. BIPM [*Bureau International des Poids et Mesures*] [*A publication*]
**Monogr Bot** ... Monographiae Botanicae [*A publication*]
**Monogr Clin Cytol** ... Monographs in Clinical Cytology [*A publication*]
**Monogr Clin Neurol Neurosurg** ... Monographs on Clinical Neurology and Neurosurgery [*A publication*]
**Monogr Dev Biol** ... Monographs in Developmental Biology [*A publication*]
**Monogr Dev Pediatr** ... Monographs in Developmental Pediatrics [*A publication*]
**Monogr Drugs** ... Monographs on Drugs [*A publication*]
**Monogr Endocrinol** ... Monographs on Endocrinology [*A publication*]
**Monogr Epidemiol Biostat** ... Monographs in Epidemiology and Biostatistics [*A publication*]
**Monogr Fauny Pol** ... Monografie Fauny Polski [*A publication*]
**Monogr Geol Surv Alabama** ... Monograph. Geological Survey of Alabama [*A publication*]
**Monogr Gesamtgeb Neurol Psychiatr** ... Monographien. Gesamtgebiete der Neurologie und Psychiatrie [*A publication*]
**Monogr Gesamtgeb Psychiatr (Berlin)** ... Monographien. Gesamtgebiete der Psychiatrie. Psychiatry Series (Berlin) [*A publication*]
**Monogr Giovanni Lorenzini Found** ... Monographs. Giovanni Lorenzini Foundation [*A publication*]
**Monogr Groupe Etude Main** ... Monographies. Groupe d'Etude de la Main [*A publication*]
**Monogr Hum Genet** ... Monographs in Human Genetics [*A publication*]
**Monogr Hunter Valley Res Fdn** ... Monograph. Hunter Valley Research Foundation [*A publication*] (APTA)
**Monogr Hunter Valley Res Found** ... Monograph. Hunter Valley Research Foundation [*A publication*] (APTA)
**Monogr INIA** ... Monografias. INIA [*Instituto Nacional de Investigaciones Agrarias*] [*A publication*]
**Monogr Inst Butantan (Sao Paulo)** ... Monografias. Instituto Butantan (Sao Paulo) [*A publication*]
**Monogr Inst Oswaldo Cruz (Rio De J)** ... Monografias. Instituto Oswaldo Cruz (Rio De Janeiro) [*A publication*]
**Monogr Kans Agric Exp Stn** ... Monograph. Kansas Agricultural Experiment Station [*A publication*]
**Monogr Mar Mollusca** ... Monographs of Marine Mollusca [*A publication*]
**Monogr Mat** ... Monografie Matematyczne [*A publication*]
**Monogr Med Sci** ... Monographies Medicales et Scientifiques [*A publication*]
**Monogr Memo Natl Res Inst Mach Des (Bechovice Czech)** ... Monographs and Memoranda. National Research Institute for Machine Design (Bechovice, Czechoslovakia) [*A publication*]
**Monogr Mod Chem** ... Monographs in Modern Chemistry [*A publication*]
**Monogr Natl Bur Stand (US)** ... Monograph. National Bureau of Standards (United States) [*A publication*]
**Monogr Ned Entomol Ver** ... Monografieen van de Nederlandse Entomologische Vereniging [*A publication*]
**Monogr Neoplast Dis Various Sites** ... Monographs on Neoplastic Disease at Various Sites [*Scotland*] [*A publication*]
**Monogr Neural Sci** ... Monographs in Neural Sciences [*A publication*]
**Monogr Nucl Med Biol** ... Monographs on Nuclear Medicine and Biology [*A publication*]
**Monogr Nucl Med Biol Ser** ... Monographs on Nuclear Medicine and Biology Series [*A publication*]
**Monogr Oceanogr Methodol** ... Monographs on Oceanographic Methodology [*A publication*]
**Monogr Ophthalmol** ... Monographs in Ophthalmology [*A publication*]
**Monogr Oral Sci** ... Monographs in Oral Science [*A publication*]
**Monogr Paediatr** ... Monographs in Paediatrics [*A publication*]
**Monogr Parazytol** ... Monografie Parazytologiczne [*A publication*]
**Monogr Pathol** ... Monographs in Pathology [*A publication*]
**Monogr Percy Fitzpatrick Inst Afr Ornithol** ... Monographs. Percy Fitzpatrick Institute of African Ornithology [*A publication*]
**Monogr Pharmacol Physiol** ... Monographs in Pharmacology and Physiology [*A publication*]
**Monogr Physiol Causale** ... Monographie de Physiologie Causale [*A publication*]
**Monogr Physiol Soc** ... Monographs. Physiological Society [*A publication*]
**Monogr Physiol Soc Phila** ... Monographs. Physiological Society of Philadelphia [*A publication*]
**Monogr Physiol Soc Philadelphia** ... Monographs. Physiological Society of Philadelphia [*A publication*]
**Monogr Physiol Veg** ... Monographies de Physiologie Vegetale [*A publication*]
**Monogr Plast** ... Monographs on Plastics [*A publication*]
**Monogr Popul Biol** ... Monographs in Population Biology [*A publication*]
**Monogr Primatol** ... Monographs in Primatology [*A publication*]
**Monogr Psychiatr Clin Helsinki Univ Cent Hosp** ... Monographs. Psychiatric Clinic. Helsinki University Central Hospital [*A publication*]
**Monogr Psychiatr Fenn** ... Monographs of Psychiatria Fennica [*A publication*]
**Monogr Quekett Microsc Club** ... Monographs. Quekett Microscopical Club [*A publication*]
**Monogr Radiol** ... Monographies de Radiologie [*A publication*]
**Monogr Rutgers Cent Alcohol Stud** ... Monographs. Rutgers Center of Alcohol Studies [*A publication*]
**Monogr Semicond Phys** ... Monographs in Semiconductor Physics [*A publication*]
**Monogr Ser Australas Inst Min Metall** ... Monograph Series. Australasian Institute of Mining and Metallurgy [*A publication*]
**Monogr Ser Inst Bot Acad Sin** ... Monograph Series. Institute of Botany. Academia Sinica [*A publication*]
**Monogr Ser Miner Deposits** ... Monograph Series on Mineral Deposits [*A publication*]
**Monogr Ser Res Inst Appl Electr Hokkaido Univ** ... Monograph Series. Research Institute of Applied Electricity. Hokkaido University [*A publication*]
**Monogr Soc Res Child Dev** ... Monographs. Society for Research in Child Development [*A publication*]
**Monogr Srpska Akad Nauka** ... Monografii Srpska Akademija Nauka [*A publication*]
**Monogr Surg Sc** ... Monographs in the Surgical Sciences [*A publication*]
**Monogr Surg Sci** ... Monographs in the Surgical Sciences [*United States*] [*A publication*]
**Monogr Teach** ... Monographs for Teachers [*A publication*]
**Monogr Tea Prod Ceylon** ... Monographs on Tea Production in Ceylon [*A publication*]
**Monogr Textb Mater Sci** ... Monographs and Textbooks in Material Science [*A publication*]
**Monogr Textb Mech Solids Fluids Mech Anal** ... Monographs and Textbooks on Mechanics of Solids and Fluids. Mechanics Analysis [*A publication*]
**Monogr Textb Mech Solids Fluids Mech Elast Stab** ... Monographs and Textbooks on Mechanics of Solids and Fluids. Mechanics of Elastic Stability [*A publication*]
**Monogr Textb Mech Solids Fluids Mech Surf Struct** ... Monographs and Textbooks on Mechanics of Solids and Fluids. Mechanics of Surface Structures [*A publication*]
**Monogr Theor Appl Genet** ... Monographs on Theoretical and Applied Genetics [*A publication*]
**Monogr Virol** ... Monographs in Virology [*A publication*]
**Monogr West Found Vertebr Zool** ... Monographs. Western Foundation of Vertebrate Zoology [*A publication*]
**MONOK** ... Monitor Resumed Normal Operation [*Aviation communications*]
**Monokrist Stsintill Org Lyuminofory** ... Monokristally. Stsintillyatory i Organicheskie Lyuminofory [*A publication*]
**Monokrist Tekh** ... Monokristally i Tekhnika [*A publication*]
**MONOS**.... Monitor Out of Service [*Aviation communications*]
**Mo Notes** ... Monthly Notes. Australian School of Pacific Administration [*A publication*] (APTA)
**Mon Paediat** ... Monographs in Paediatrics [*A publication*]
**Mon Piot**.... Monuments et Memoires Publies par l'Academie des Inscriptions et Belles-Lettres. Fondation Piot [*A publication*]
**Mon Rep Can Miner Ind** ... Monthly Report. Canadian Mineral Industry [*A publication*]

**Mon Rep Civ Eng Res Inst Hokkaido Dev Bur** ... Monthly Report. Civil Engineering Research Institute of Hokkaido. Development Bureau [*Japan*] [*A publication*]
**Mon Rev** .... Monthly Review [*A publication*]
**Mon Rev Am Electroplat Soc** ... Monthly Review. American Electroplaters' Society [*A publication*]
**Mon Rev Fed Reserve Bank Kans City** ... Monthly Review. Federal Reserve Bank of Kansas City [*A publication*]
**Monro** ........ Acta Cancellariae [*England*] [*A publication*] (DLA)
**Monro AC** ... Monro's Acta Cancellariae [*1545-1625*] [*A publication*] (DLA)
**Monroe** ...... Monroe Legal Reporter [*Pennsylvania*] [*A publication*] (DLA)
**Monroe LR** ... Monroe Legal Reporter [*Pennsylvania*] [*A publication*] (DLA)
MONS....... Monastery
MONS....... Monmouthshire [*County in Wales*]
MONS....... Monsieur [*In France this form is considered contemptuous*] [*Preferred form is M*]
**Monsanto R** ... Monsanto Review [*A publication*] (APTA)
**Monsanto Tech Rev** ... Monsanto Technical Review [*A publication*]
MONSEE ... Monitoring of the Sun Earth Environment [*International Council of Scientific Unions*] (MCD)
MONSIG .. Monsignor [*Lord, Sir*] [*French*]
MONSOONEX ... Monsoon Experiment [*Also, MONEX*]
**Mon S Res C** ... Monographs. Society for Research in Child Development [*A publication*]
**Mon Stud** ... Monastic Studies [*A publication*]
**Mont** .......... Montagu's English Bankruptcy Reports [*A publication*] (DLA)
MONT....... [*Michel Eyquem De*] Montaigne [*French essayist, 1533-1592*] (ROG)
MONT....... Montana (AFM)
**Mont** .......... Montana: The Magazine of Western History [*A publication*]
**Mont** .......... Montana Reports [*A publication*]
**Mont** .......... Montana Supreme Court Reports [*A publication*] (DLA)
MONT....... Montgomeryshire [*County in Wales*]
**Mont** .......... Montilla [*Record label*] [*USA, Spain, etc.*]
MONT....... Montmorillonite [*Mineralogy*]
**Mont** .......... Montriou's Bengal Reports [*A publication*] (DLA)
**Mont & A** ... Montagu and Ayrton's English Bankruptcy Reports [*1833-38*] [*A publication*] (DLA)
**Mont Acad Sci Proc** ... Montana Academy of Sciences. Proceedings [*A publication*]
**Mont Admin R** ... Administrative Rules of Montana [*A publication*] (DLA)
**Mont Admin Reg** ... Montana Administrative Register [*A publication*] (DLA)
**Mont Ag Exp** ... Montana. Agricultural Experiment Station. Publications [*A publication*]
**Mont Agric Exp Stn Bull** ... Montana. Agricultural Experiment Station. Bulletin [*A publication*]
**Mont Agric Exp Stn Circ** ... Montana. Agricultural Experiment Station. Circular [*A publication*]
**MonTal** ...... Monumenta Talmudica (BJA)
**Montana Acad Sci Proc** ... Montana Academy of Sciences. Proceedings [*A publication*]
**Montana Bur Mines and Geology Bull** ... Montana. Bureau of Mines and Geology. Bulletin [*A publication*]
**Montana Bur Mines and Geology Spec Pub** ... Montana. Bureau of Mines and Geology. Special Publication [*A publication*]
**Montana Lib** ... Montana Libraries [*A publication*]
**Montana Lib Q** ... Montana Library Quarterly [*A publication*]
**Montana L Rev** ... Montana Law Review [*A publication*]
**Montanaro Ital-Monti Boschi** ... Montanaro d'Italia - Monti e Boschi [*Italy*] [*A publication*]
**Montan-Rundsch** ... Montan-Rundschau [*Austria*] [*A publication*]
**Montan-Ztg** ... Montan-Zeitung [*Austria*] [*A publication*]
**Mont & Ayr** ... Montagu and Ayrton's English Bankruptcy Reports [*1833-38*] [*A publication*] (DLA)
**Mont & Ayr Bankr** ... Montagu and Ayrton's English Bankruptcy Reports [*1833-38*] [*A publication*] (DLA)
**Mont & Ayr Bankr (Eng)** ... Montagu and Ayrton's English Bankruptcy Reports [*1833-38*] [*A publication*] (DLA)
**Mont & Ayr BL** ... Montagu and Ayrton's Bankrupt Laws [*A publication*] (DLA)
**Montazhn Rab Stroit** ... Montazhnye Raboty v Stroitel'stve [*A publication*]
**Montazhn Spet Rab Stroit** ... Montazhnye i Spetsial'nye Raboty v Stroitel'stve [*A publication*]
**Mont & B** ... Montagu and Bligh's English Bankruptcy Reports [*1832-33*] [*A publication*] (DLA)
**Mon T B**..... T. B. Monroe's Kentucky Reports [*17-23 Kentucky*] [*A publication*] (DLA)
**Mont Bankr (Eng)** ... Montagu's English Bankruptcy Reports [*A publication*] (DLA)
**Mont Bank Rep** ... Montagu's English Bankruptcy Reports [*A publication*] (DLA)
**Mont & B Bankr** ... Montagu and Bligh's English Bankruptcy Reports [*1832-33*] [*A publication*] (DLA)
**Mont & B Bankr (Eng)** ... Montagu and Bligh's English Bankruptcy Reports [*1832-33*] [*A publication*] (DLA)
**Mont BC**.... Montagu's English Bankruptcy Reports [*A publication*] (DLA)
**Mont Bk L** ... Montagu's Bankrupt Law [*4th ed.*] [*1827*] [*A publication*] (DLA)
**Mont & Bl** ... Montagu and Bligh's English Bankruptcy Reports [*1832-33*] [*A publication*] (DLA)
**Mont Bur Mines Geol Bull** ... Montana. Bureau of Mines and Geology. Bulletin [*A publication*]
**Mont Bur Mines Geol Mem** ... Montana. Bureau of Mines and Geology. Memoir [*A publication*]
**Mont Bur Mines Geol Misc Contrib** ... Montana. Bureau of Mines and Geology. Miscellaneous Contributions [*A publication*]
**Mont Bur Mines Geol Spec Publ** ... Montana. Bureau of Mines and Geology. Special Publication [*A publication*]
**Mont Bus Q** ... Montana Business Quarterly [*A publication*]
**Mont & C**... Montagu and Chitty's English Bankruptcy Reports [*1838-40*] [*A publication*] (DLA)
**Mont Cas**... Montriou's Cases in Hindoo Law [*A publication*] (DLA)
**Mont & C Bankr** ... Montagu and Chitty's English Bankruptcy Reports [*1838-40*] [*A publication*] (DLA)
**Mont & C Bankr (Eng)** ... Montagu and Chitty's English Bankruptcy Reports [*1838-40*] [*A publication*] (DLA)
**Mont & Ch** ... Montagu and Chitty's English Bankruptcy Reports [*1838-40*] [*A publication*] (DLA)
**Mont & Chitt** ... Montagu and Chitty's English Bankruptcy Reports [*1838-40*] [*A publication*] (DLA)
**Mont Code Ann** ... Montana Code, Annotated [*A publication*] (DLA)
**Mont Co LR** ... Montgomery County Law Reporter [*A publication*]
**Mont Co L Rep** ... Montgomery County Law Reporter [*A publication*]
**Mont Comp** ... Montagu on Composition [*1823*] [*A publication*] (DLA)
**Mont Cond Rep** ... Montreal Condensed Reports [*A publication*] (DLA)
**Mont D & DeG** ... Montagu, Deacon, and De Gex's English Bankruptcy Reports [*1840-44*] [*A publication*] (DLA)
**Mont Dig** ... Montagu's Digest of Pleadings in Equity [*A publication*] (DLA)
**Mon Tech Rev** ... Monthly Technical Review [*A publication*]
**Mont Ed**..... Montana Education [*A publication*]
**Monten** ...... Montenegro
**Mont Eq Pl** ... Montagu's Digest of Pleadings in Equity [*A publication*] (DLA)
**Montesq**..... Montesquieu's Esprit des Lois [*Spirit of Laws*] [*A publication*] (DLA)
**Montesq Esprit des Lois** ... Montesquieu's Esprit des Lois [*Spirit of Laws*] [*A publication*] (DLA)
**Mont Fish Game Dep Tech Bull** ... Montana. Fish and Game Department. Technical Bulletin [*A publication*]
**Mont For Conserv Exp Stn Bull** ... Montana. Forest and Conservation Experiment Station. Bulletin [*A publication*]
**Mont For Conserv Exp Stn Lubrecht Ser** ... Montana. Forest and Conservation Experiment Station. Lubrecht Series [*A publication*]
**Mont For Conserv Exp Stn Note** ... Montana. Forest and Conservation Experiment Station. Note [*A publication*]
**Mont For Conserv Exp Stn Res Note** ... Montana. Forest and Conservation Experiment Station. Research Note [*A publication*]
**Mont For Conserv Exp Stn Spec Publ** ... Montana. Forest and Conservation Experiment Station. Special Publication [*A publication*]
**Mont For Conserv Exp Stn Study Rep** ... Montana. Forest and Conservation Experiment Station. Study Report [*A publication*]
**Mont Forest Ind News** ... Montana Forest Industry News [*A publication*]
**Montfort** .... Montfort. Vierteljahresschrift fuer Geschichte und Gegenwartskunde Vorarlbergs [*A publication*]
**Mont G** ...... Montana Gothic [*A publication*]
**Montg** ........ Montgomery County Law Reporter [*A publication*]
MONTG.... Montgomeryshire [*County in Wales*]
**Montg Co**... Montgomery County Law Reporter [*A publication*]
**Montg Co Law Rep'r** ... Montgomery County Law Reporter [*A publication*]
**Montg Co LR** ... Montgomery County Law Reporter [*A publication*]
**Mont'g Co L Rep** ... Montgomery County Law Reporter [*A publication*]
**Montg Co L Rep'r** ... Montgomery County Law Reporter [*A publication*]
**Montg Co LR (PA)** ... Montgomery County Law Reporter (Pennsylvania) [*A publication*]
**Mont Geol Soc Annu Field Conf Guideb** ... Montana Geological Society. Annual Field Conference. Guidebook [*A publication*]
**Mont'g L Rep** ... Montgomery County Law Reporter [*A publication*]
MONTGOM ... Montgomeryshire [*County in Wales*]
**Montgomeryshire Collect** ... Montgomeryshire Collections [*A publication*]
**Montg (PA)** ... Montgomery County Law Reporter (Pennsylvania) [*A publication*]
**Month Dig Tax Articles** ... Monthly Digest of Tax Articles [*A publication*] (DLA)
**Mont His S** ... Montana Historical Society. Contributions [*A publication*]
**Month JL**... Monthly Journal of Law [*A publication*] (DLA)
**Month Jur** ... Monthly Jurist [*Bloomington, IL*] [*A publication*] (DLA)
**Month Lab Rev** ... Monthly Labor Review [*A publication*]
**Month Law Bul** ... Monthly Law Bulletin [*New York*] [*A publication*] (DLA)
**Month Law Rep** ... Law Reporter [*Boston*] [*A publication*] (DLA)
**Month L Bull (NY)** ... Monthly Law Bulletin (New York) [*A publication*] (DLA)
**Month Leg Ex** ... Monthly Legal Examiner [*New York*] [*A publication*] (DLA)
**Month Leg Exam** ... Monthly Legal Examiner [*New York*] [*A publication*] (DLA)
**Month Leg Exam (NY)** ... Monthly Legal Examiner (New York) [*A publication*] (DLA)
**Month LJ**... Monthly Journal of Law [*Washington*] [*A publication*] (DLA)
**Month LM** ... Monthly Law Magazine [*London*] [*A publication*] (DLA)
**Month L Rep** ... Monthly Law Reporter [*Boston*] [*A publication*] (DLA)

**Month L Rep** ... Monthly Law Reports [*Canada*] [*A publication*] (DLA)
**Month L Rev** ... Monthly Law Review [*A publication*] (DLA)
**Monthly Am J G** ... Monthly American Journal of Geology and Natural Science [*A publication*]
**Monthly Catalog US Govt Publ** ... Monthly Catalog of United States Government Publications [*A publication*]
**Monthly Cat US Govt Pub** ... Monthly Catalog of United States Government Publications [*A publication*]
**Monthly Crop Rep** ... Monthly Crop Report [*A publication*]
**Monthly F Bull** ... Monthly Film Bulletin [*London*] [*A publication*]
**Monthly Labor R** ... Monthly Labor Review [*A publication*]
**Monthly Labor Rev** ... Monthly Labor Review [*A publication*]
**Monthly Lab Rev** ... Monthly Labor Review [*A publication*] (DLA)
**Monthly L Bul** ... New York Monthly Law Bulletin [*A publication*] (DLA)
**Monthly Notices Roy Astronom Soc** ... Monthly Notices. Royal Astronomical Society [*A publication*]
**Monthly R** ... Monthly Review [*A publication*]
**Monthly Statist Rev** ... Monthly Statistical Review [*England*] [*A publication*]
**Monthly Vital Stat Rep** ... Monthly Vital Statistics Report [*United States*] [*A publication*]
**Monthly Weather Rev** ... Monthly Weather Review [*A publication*]
**Month West Jur** ... Monthly Western Jurist [*A publication*] (DLA)
**Mon Times** ... Monetary Times [*A publication*]
**Mont Ind**.... Monthly Index to Reporters [*A publication*] (DLA)
**Mont Inst**... Montriou's Institutes of Jurisprudence [*A publication*] (DLA)
**Mont Instal** ... Montajes e Instalaciones [*A publication*]
**Mont Law** .. Montana Lawyer [*A publication*] (DLA)
**Mont Law Re** ... Montana Law Review [*A publication*]
**Mont Laws** ... Laws of Montana [*A publication*] (DLA)
**Mont Leg News** ... Montreal Legal News [*A publication*] (DLA)
**Mont Liens** ... Montagu on Liens [*A publication*] (DLA)
**Mont LR**.... Montana Law Review [*A publication*]
**Mont LR**.... Montreal Law Reports, Queen's Bench [*A publication*] (DLA)
**Mont LR**.... Montreal Law Reports, Superior Court [*A publication*] (DLA)
**Mont L Rev** ... Montana Law Review [*A publication*]
**Mont LRQB** ... Montreal Law Reports, Queen's Bench [*A publication*] (DLA)
**Mont LRSC** ... Montreal Law Reports, Superior Court [*A publication*] (DLA)
**Mont & M** ... Montagu and MacArthur's English Bankruptcy Reports [*A publication*] (DLA)
**Mont & MacA** ... Montagu and MacArthur's English Bankruptcy Reports [*A publication*] (DLA)
**Mont Mag Hist** ... Montana: The Magazine of Western History [*A publication*]
**Mont & M Bankr (Eng)** ... Mantagu and MacArthur's English Bankruptcy Reports [*1826-30*] [*A publication*] (DLA)
**Mont Merc Law** ... Montefiore's Synopsis of Mercantile Law [*A publication*] (DLA)
**Mont Part** .. Montagu's Digest of the Law of Partnership [*A publication*] (DLA)
**Montpellier Med** ... Montpellier Medical [*France*] [*A publication*]
**Montpel Med** ... Montpellier Medical [*A publication*]
**MONTR**.... Monitor (FAAC)
**Montr**......... Montemora [*A publication*]
**MONTR**.... Montreal [*Canada*]
**Montr**......... Montriou's Bengal Reports [*A publication*] (DLA)
**Montr**......... Montriou's Supplement to Morton's Reports [*A publication*] (DLA)
**Montr Cond Rep** ... Montreal Condensed Reports [*A publication*] (DLA)
**Montreal LQB (Can)** ... Montreal Law Reports, Queen's Bench [*Canada*] [*A publication*] (DLA)
**Montreal LRQB** ... Montreal Law Reports, Queen's Bench [*Canada*] [*A publication*] (DLA)
**Montreal LRSC** ... Montreal Law Reports, Superior Court [*Canada*] [*A publication*] (DLA)
**Montreal LSC (Can)** ... Montreal Law Reports, Superior Court [*Canada*] [*A publication*] (DLA)
**Montreal Med J** ... Montreal Medical Journal [*A publication*]
**Montreal Pharm J** ... Montreal Pharmaceutical Journal [*A publication*]
**Montreal Univ Service Biogeographie Bull** ... Montreal Universite. Service de Biogeographie. Bulletin [*A publication*]
**Mont Rep**... Montriou's Reports, Supreme Court [*1846*] [*Bengal, India*] [*A publication*] (DLA)
**Mont Rev Code Ann** ... Montana Revised Code, Annotated [*A publication*] (DLA)
**MONTRG** ... Monitoring (AABC)
**Montr Leg N** ... Montreal Legal News [*A publication*] (DLA)
**Montr QB** .. Montreal Law Reports, Queen's Bench [*A publication*] (DLA)
**Montr Super** ... Montreal Law Reports, Superior Court [*A publication*] (DLA)
**Mont Rural Electr News** ... Montana Rural Electric News [*A publication*]
**MONTSAME** ... Mongolyn Tsahilgaan Medeeniy Agentlag [*Press agency*] [*Mongolia*]
**Mont SO**.... Montagu. Set-Off [*2nd ed.*] [*1828*] [*A publication*] (DLA)
**Mont Sp L** ... Montesquieu's Spirit of Laws [*A publication*] (DLA)
**Mont State Coll Eng Exp Stn Bull** ... Montana State College. Engineering Experiment Station. Bulletin [*A publication*]
**Mont Super** ... Montreal Law Reports, Superior Court [*A publication*] (DLA)
**MONT TER** ... Montana Territory
**Mont Univ B** ... Montana University. Bulletin [*A publication*]
**Mont Wool Grow** ... Montana Wool Grower [*A publication*]
**MONU**...... Monumental Corp. [*NASDAQ symbol*] (NQ)
**MONU**...... Monumentum. International Council of Monuments and Sites [*A publication*]
**Mon ULR** .. Monash University. Law Review [*A publication*]
**Monumenta Nip** ... Monumenta Nipponica [*A publication*]
**Monuments Piot** ... Academie des Inscriptions et Belles-Lettres. Fondation Eugene Piot. Monuments et Memoires [*Paris*] [*A publication*]
**Monum Nippon** ... Monumenta Nipponica [*A publication*]
**MO Nurse** ... Missouri Nurse [*A publication*]
**MoNvC**...... Cottey College, Nevada, MO [*Library symbol*] [*Library of Congress*] (LCLS)
**Mon Vital Stat Rep** ... Monthly Vital Statistics Report [*US*] [*A publication*]
**Mon Weather Rev** ... Monthly Weather Review [*A publication*]
**Mon WJ**..... Monthly Western Jurist [*A publication*] (DLA)
**MONY**....... Mutual of New York [*Insurance company*]
**Mon Zoll**.... Monumenta Zollerana [*A publication*]
**MOO**......... Management Operations Officer [*Social Security Administration*]
**MOO**......... Milkbottles Only Organization (EA)
**MOO**......... Missile Operations Officer [*NASA*] (KSC)
**MOO**......... Money-Order Office
**Moo**........... Moody's English Crown Cases [*168, 169 English Reprint*] [*A publication*] (DLA)
**MOO**......... Moomba [*Australia*] [*Airport symbol*] [*Obsolete*] (OAG)
**MOO**......... Moongold Resources [*Vancouver Stock Exchange symbol*]
**Moo**........... [*J. B.*] Moore's English Common Pleas Reports [*A publication*] (DLA)
**Moo**........... [*Sir Francis*] Moore's English King's Bench Reports [*A publication*] (DLA)
**Moo**........... [*E. F.*] Moore's Privy Council Cases [*12-15 English Reprint*] [*1836-62*] [*A publication*] (DLA)
**MOO**......... Moorlands [*Tasmania*] [*Seismograph station code, US Geological Survey*] (SEIS)
**MOO**......... School of the Ozarks, Point Lookout, MO [*OCLC symbol*] (OCLC)
**Moo A**........ Moore's Reports [*Bosanquet and Puller*] [*England*] [*A publication*] (DLA)
**Moo CC**..... Moody's English Crown Cases Reserved [*1824-44*] [*A publication*] (DLA)
**Moo CP**...... Moore's English Common Pleas Reports [*A publication*] (DLA)
**Moo Cr C**... Moody's English Crown Cases Reserved [*1824-44*] [*A publication*] (DLA)
**MOO C of S** ... Management Office, Office, Chief of Staff
**MOOD**...... Moodus Savings Bank [*NASDAQ symbol*] (NQ)
**Mood**.......... Moody's English Crown Cases Reserved [*1824-44*] [*A publication*] (DLA)
**Mood CC** ... Moody's English Crown Cases Reserved [*1824-44*] [*A publication*] (DLA)
**Mood & M** ... Moody and Malkin's English Nisi Prius Reports [*A publication*] (DLA)
**Mood & Malk** ... Moody and Malkin's English Nisi Prius Reports [*A publication*] (DLA)
**Mood & R** .. Moody and Robinson's English Nisi Prius Reports [*A publication*] (DLA)
**Mood & Rob** ... Moody and Robinson's English Nisi Prius Reports [*A publication*] (DLA)
**Moody**........ Moody's English Crown Cases [*168, 169 English Reprint*] [*A publication*] (DLA)
**Moody**........ Moody's Magazine [*A publication*]
**Moody CC (Eng)** ... Moody's English Crown Cases [*168, 169 English Reprint*] [*A publication*] (DLA)
**Moody Cr C** ... Moody's English Crown Cases [*168, 169 English Reprint*] [*A publication*] (DLA)
**Moody Cr Cas** ... Moody's English Crown Cases [*168, 169 English Reprint*] [*A publication*] (DLA)
**Moody & M** ... Moody and Malkin's English Nisi Prius Reports [*A publication*] (DLA)
**Moody M**... Moody Monthly [*A publication*]
**Moody & M (Eng)** ... Moody and Malkin's English Nisi Prius Reports [*A publication*] (DLA)
**Moody & R** ... Moody and Robinson's English Nisi Prius Reports [*A publication*] (DLA)
**Moody & R (Eng)** ... Moody and Robinson's English Nisi Prius Reports [*A publication*] (DLA)
**Moody's Inv Serv** ... Moody's Investors Service [*A publication*]
**Moo F**........ [*Sir Francis*] Moore's English King's Bench Reports [*A publication*] (DLA)
**Moo GC**..... Moore's Gorham Case, English Privy Council [*A publication*] (DLA)
**Moo Ind App** ... Moore's Reports, Privy Council, Indian Appeals [*1836-72*] [*A publication*] (DLA)
**Moo KB**..... [*Sir Francis*] Moore's English King's Bench Reports [*A publication*] (DLA)
**Moo & M**... Moody and Malkin's English Nisi Prius Reports [*A publication*] (DLA)
**Moo & Mal** ... Moody and Malkin's English Nisi Prius Reports [*A publication*] (DLA)
**Moon**.......... 13th Moon [*A publication*]
**MOON**...... Meeting Our Operational Needs

**Moon**.......... Moon's Reports [*133-144 Indiana*] [*6-14 Indiana Appeals*] [*A publication*] (DLA)
**Moo NS**..... [*E. F.*] Moore's Privy Council Cases, New Series [*15-17 English Reprint*] [*1862-73*] [*A publication*] (DLA)
**Moons L T**... Moons and Lion Tailes [*A publication*]
**MOOP**....... Missile Out of Order for Parts (MCD)
**Moo & P**..... Moore and Payne's English Common Pleas Reports [*A publication*] (DLA)
**Moo & Pay**... Moore and Payne's English Common Pleas Reports [*A publication*] (DLA)
**Moo PC**...... Moore's English Privy Council Cases, Old and New Series [*A publication*] (DLA)
**Moo PCC**... Moore's English Privy Council Cases [*A publication*] (DLA)
**Moo PC Cas NS**... Moore's English Privy Council Cases, New Series [*A publication*] (DLA)
**Moo PCC NS**... Moore's English Privy Council Cases, New Series [*A publication*] (DLA)
**Moo PC (NS)**... Moore's English Privy Council Cases, New Series [*A publication*] (DLA)
**Moor**.......... English King's Bench Reports, by Sir Francis Moore [*1512-1621*] [*A publication*] (DLA)
**Moo & R**.... Moody and Robinson's English Nisi Prius Reports [*A publication*] (DLA)
**Moore**........ Moore's English Common Pleas Reports [*A publication*] (DLA)
**Moore**........ [*Sir Francis*] Moore's English King's Bench Reports [*A publication*] (DLA)
**Moore**........ Moore's English Privy Council Reports [*A publication*] (DLA)
**Moore**........ Moore's Reports [*Alabama*] [*A publication*] (DLA)
**Moore**........ Moore's Reports [*Texas*] [*A publication*] (DLA)
**Moore**........ Moore's Reports [*Arkansas*] [*A publication*] (DLA)
**Moore A**..... Moore's Reports [*Bosanquet and Puller*] [*England*] [*A publication*] (DLA)
**Moore Abs**... Moore's Abstracts of Title [*6th ed.*] [*1925*] [*A publication*] (DLA)
**Moore CP**.. Moore's English Common Pleas Reports [*A publication*] (DLA)
**Moore Cr Law**... Moore's Criminal Law and Procedure [*A publication*] (DLA)
**Moore EI**... Moore's East Indian Appeals [*A publication*] (DLA)
**Moore Fed Practice**... Moore's Federal Practice [*A publication*] (DLA)
**Moore GC**... Moore's Gorham Case, English Privy Council [*A publication*] (DLA)
**Moore Ind App**... Moore's Indian Appeals [*A publication*] (DLA)
**Moore Ind App (Eng)**... Moore's Indian Appeals [*England*] [*A publication*] (DLA)
**Moore Indian App**... Moore's Indian Appeals [*England*] [*A publication*] (DLA)
**Moore Int L**... Moore's Digest of International Law [*A publication*] (DLA)
**Moore KB**.. [*Sir Francis*] Moore's English King's Bench Reports [*A publication*] (DLA)
**Moore KB (Eng)**... [*Sir Francis*] Moore's English King's Bench Reports [*A publication*] (DLA)
**Moore & P**... Moore and Payne's English Common Pleas Reports [*A publication*] (DLA)
**Moore PC**.. Moore's English Privy Council Reports [*A publication*] (DLA)
**Moore PCC**... Moore's English Privy Council Cases [*A publication*] (DLA)
**Moore PCC (Eng)**... Moore's English Privy Council Cases [*A publication*] (DLA)
**Moore PCC NS**... Moore's English Privy Council Cases, New Series [*A publication*] (DLA)
**Moore PCC NS (Eng)**... Moore's English Privy Council Cases, New Series [*A publication*] (DLA)
**Moore PC NS**... Moore's English Privy Council Reports, New Series [*A publication*] (DLA)
**Moore & P (Eng)**... Moore and Payne's English Common Pleas Reports [*A publication*] (DLA)
**Moore Presby Dig**... Moore's Presbyterian Digest [*A publication*] (DLA)
**Moore QB**... Moore's English Queen's Bench Reports [*A publication*] (DLA)
**Moore & S**... Moore and Scott's English Common Pleas Reports [*1831-34*] [*A publication*] (DLA)
**Moore & S (Eng)**... Moore and Scott's English Common Pleas Reports [*1831-34*] [*A publication*] (DLA)
**Moore & W**... Moore and Walker's Reports [*22-24 Texas*] [*A publication*] (DLA)
**Moore & Walker**... Moore and Walker's Reports [*22-24 Texas*] [*A publication*] (DLA)
**Moorg Wal S**... Moorgate and Wall Street [*A publication*]
**MOORNG**... Mooring [*Freight*]
**Moo & Rob**... Moody and Robinson's English Nisi Prius Reports [*A publication*] (DLA)
**MOOS**....... Modular Ocean Observation System [*Marine science*] (MSC)
**Moo & S**..... Moore and Scott's English Common Pleas Reports [*1831-34*] [*A publication*] (DLA)
**MoOs**......... Saint Clair County Library, Osceola, MO [*Library symbol*] [*Library of Congress*] (LCLS)
**Moo & Sc**... Moore and Scott's English Common Pleas Reports [*1831-34*] [*A publication*] (DLA)
**MOOSE**.... Man [*or Manual*] Orbital Operations Safety Equipment [*Space life raft*] [*NASA*]
**MOOSE**.... Man Out of Space Easiest
**MOOSE**.... Move Out of Saigon Expeditiously [*Army project, Vietnam*]
**MOOSEMUSS**... Maneuver, Objective, Offensive, Surprise, Economy of Force, Mass, Unity of Command, Simplicity, Security [*Basic principles of war*] [*See also MOSS MOUSE*]
**Moo Sep Rep**... Moore's Separate Report of Westerton Versus Liddell [*A publication*] (DLA)
**MOOSSE**... Manned Orbital Oceanographic Survey System Experiment
**MOOT**....... Move Out of Town [*Reduction of troop concentrations in cities*] [*Military*]
**Moot Ct Bull**... University of Illinois. Moot Court Bulletin [*A publication*] (DLA)
**Moo Tr**....... Moore's Divorce Trials [*A publication*] (DLA)
**MOOW**..... Medical Officer of the Watch
**MOP**.......... Magnetized Orange Pipe [*Minesweeping device*] [*Navy*]
**MOP**.......... Maintenance Operating Procedure (MCD)
**MOP**.......... Maintenance Outline Procedure [*Nuclear energy*] (NRCH)
**MOP**.......... Major Overhaul Program [*Navy*]
**MOP**.......... Manned Orbital Platform
**MOP**.......... Manner of Performance [*Officer rating*]
**MOP**.......... Manual Operations Panel
**MOP**.......... Manual Override Panel (AAG)
**MOP**.......... Manufacturers Output Policy [*Insurance*]
**MOP**.......... Manuscript on Paper
**MOP**.......... Margin of Profit [*Accounting*]
**MOP**.......... Mary's Own Paper [*A publication*] (APTA)
**MOP**.......... Master Operating Panel (CAAL)
**MOP**.......... Matrix Operations Programming
**MOP**.......... Measures of Performance (MCD)
**MOP**.......... Medical Outpatient
**MOP**.......... Member of Parliament [*British*]
**MOP**.......... Memorandum of Policy
**MOP**.......... Memory Organization Packet [*Artificial intelligence*]
**MOP**.......... Message Output Processing
**MOP**.......... Methoxypsoralen [*Also, MP*] [*Pharmacology*]
**MOP**.......... Migrant Opportunity Program [*Department of Labor*]
**MOP**.......... Minimum Ordered Partition
**MOP**.......... Ministry of Pensions [*British*]
**MOP**.......... Ministry of Power [*British*]
**MOP**.......... Ministry of Production [*British*]
**MOP**.......... Mission Operations Plan (MCD)
**MOP**.......... Mobility Operating Procedure [*Military*] (AFM)
**MOP**.......... Mode of Operation
**MOP**.......... Model Operational Plan
**MOP**.......... Modern Office Procedures [*A publication*]
**MOP**.......... Modern Plastics International [*A publication*]
**MOP**.......... Modular Operating Procedure (MUGU)
**MOP**.......... Modulation on the Pulse (NG)
**MOP**.......... Monarch Peak [*California*] [*Seismograph station code, US Geological Survey*] (SEIS)
**Mo & P**....... Moore and Payne's English Common Pleas Reports [*A publication*] (DLA)
**MOP**.......... Mother-of-Pearl
**MOP**.......... Mount Pleasant, MI [*Location identifier*] [*FAA*] (FAAL)
**MOP**.......... Mouvement pour l'Ordre et la Paix [*Movement for Order and Peace*] [*New Caledonia*] [*Political party*] (PD)
**MOP**.......... Mouvement Ouvriers-Paysans [*Workers' and Peasants' Movement*] [*Haiti*] (PD)
**MOP**.......... Multiple Online Programming [*Data processing*] (DIT)
**MOP**.......... Muriate of Potash [*Fertilizer*]
**MOP**.......... Mustard, Onions, Pickles [*Restaurant slang*]
**MOP**.......... Mustargen [*Nitrogen mustard*], Oncovin [*Vincristine*], Prednisone [*Antineoplastic drug regimen*]
**MOP**.......... Mustargen [*Nitrogen mustard*], Oncovin [*Vincristine*], Procarbazine [*Antineoplastic drug regimen*]
**MOP**.......... Mustering-Out Pay [*Military*]
**MOP**.......... St. Louis College of Pharmacy, St. Louis, MO [*OCLC symbol*] (OCLC)
**MOPA**....... Master Oscillator Power Amplifier [*Radio*]
**MOPA**....... Methoxyphenylacetic Acid [*Herbicide*]
**MOPA**....... Methoxypropylamine [*Organic chemistry*]
**MOPA**....... Modus Operandi - Personal Appearance [*FBI computer procedure*]
**MOPAC**.... Methoxyhydroxyphenylacetic Acid [*Organic chemistry*]
**MOPAC**.... Missouri Pacific Railroad Co.
**MOPAC**.... Mixed Oligonucleotide Primed Amplification of cDNA [*Biochemistry*]
**MOPAR**.... Master Oscillator Power Amplifier RADAR
**MoParkC**... Park College, Parkville, MO [*Library symbol*] [*Library of Congress*] (LCLS)
**MOPB**....... Manually Operated Plotting Board
**MOP-BAP**... Mustargen [*Nitrogen mustard*], Oncovin [*Vincristine*], Procarbazine, Bleomycin, Adriamycin, Prednisone [*Antineoplastic drug regimen*]
**Mo PC**......... Moore's English Privy Council Reports [*A publication*] (DLA)
**MOPC**....... Mouse Plasmocytoma [*Cell line*]
**MOPCOM**... Matrix Operations Programming Combination of Estimates
**MOPE**....... Method of Personnel Evaluation
**MOPE**....... Multiple Object Parameter Estimation
**MOPED**.... Motor/Pedal [*Motorized bicycle*]
**MOPEG**.... (Methoxyhydroxyphenyl)ethyleneglycol [*Also, MHPG*] [*Organic chemistry*]

**MoPeS**....... Saint Mary's Seminary, Perryville, MO [*Library symbol*] [*Library of Congress*] (LCLS)
**MOPET**..... Methoxyhydroxyphenylethanol [*Organic chemistry*]
**MOPF**....... Missile Onloading Prism Fixture
**MOPF**....... Mobile Optical Propagation Facility
**MOPGC**.... Malaysian Oil Palm Growers' Council (DS)
**MOPH**....... Military Order of the Purple Heart of the United States of America (EA)
**MOPI**........ Maximum Rate Output Initiator (NASA)
**MOPIC**...... Motion Picture [*Army*] (AABC)
**MOPIMS**... Mathematical, Optical, and Philosophical Instrument Makers' Society [*A union*] [*British*]
**M Opinion**... Musical Opinion [*A publication*]
**MOPIX**...... Motion Pictures
**MOPLD**.... Moon and the Planets [*A publication*]
**MoPlS**........ School of the Ozarks, Point Lookout, MO [*Library symbol*] [*Library of Congress*] (LCLS)
**MOPMS**.... Modular Pack Mine System (RDA)
**MOPN**....... Methoxypropionitrile [*Organic chemistry*]
**MoPobT**..... Three Rivers Community College, Poplar Bluff, MO [*Library symbol*] [*Library of Congress*] (LCLS)
**MoPobV**.... United States Veterans Administration Hospital, Medical Library, Poplar Bluff, MO [*Library symbol*] [*Library of Congress*] (LCLS)
**MOPOCO**... Movimiento Popular Colorado [*Colorado Popular Movement*] [*Paraguay*] (PD)
**MOPP**....... Mission-Oriented Protection Posture [*Army*] (AABC)
**MOPP**....... Modular Operating Procedure (MUGU)
**MOPP**....... Mustargen hydrochloride, Oncovin [*Vincristine*], Procarbazine, Prednisone [*Antineoplastic drug regimen*]
**MOPP**....... Mustargen [*Nitrogen mustard*], Oncovin [*Vincristine*], Procarbazine, Prednisone [*Antineoplastic drug regimen*]
**MOPP/ABV**... Mustargen [*Nitrogen mustard*], Oncovin [*Vincristine*], Procarbazine, Prednisone, Adriamycin, Bleomycin, Vinblastine [*Antineoplastic drug regimen*]
**MOPP-BLEO**... Mustargen [*Nitrogen mustard*], Oncovin [*Vincristine*], Procarbazine, Prednisone, Bleomycin [*Antineoplastic drug regimen*]
**MOPPCPF**... Mustargen [*Nitrogen mustard*], Oncovin [*Vincristine*], Procarbazine, Prednisone (for Patients with Compromised Pulmonary Function) [*Antineoplastic drug regimen*]
**MOPPE**..... Modified Operational Propulsion Plan Examination [*Navy*] (NVT)
**MOPPHDB**... Mustargen [*Nitrogen mustard*], Oncovin [*Vincristine*], Procarbazine, Prednisone, High-Dose Bleomycin [*Antineoplastic drug regimen*]
**MOPPLDB**... Mustargen [*Nitrogen mustard*], Oncovin [*Vincristine*], Procarbazine, Prednisone, Low-Dose Bleomycin [*Antineoplastic drug regimen*]
**MOPR**....... Manner of Performing Rating
**MOPR**....... Mission Operations Planning Review [*NASA*] (NASA)
**MOPR**....... Mission Operations Planning Room (MCD)
**MOPR**....... Mop Rack
**MOPr**........ Mustargen [*Nitrogen mustard*], Oncovin [*Vincristine*], Prednisone [*Antineoplastic drug regimen*]
**MOPr**........ Mustargen [*Nitrogen mustard*], Oncovin [*Vincristine*], Procarbazine [*Antineoplastic drug regimen*]
**Mo Prec**..... Moile's Precedents [*A publication*] (DLA)
**MOPS**....... Mail-Order Protection Scheme [*British*]
**MOPS**....... Man-Operated Propulsion System
**MOPS**....... Maneuver Operations Program System [*NASA*]
**MOPS**....... Marine Oil Pickup Service [*Marine science*] (MSC)
**MOPS**....... Maritime Officer Production Study [*Canadian Navy*]
**MOPS**....... Mechanized Outdoor Planning System
**MOPS**....... Microwave Optical-Photoselection Microscopy
**MOPS**....... Military Operation Phone System
**MOPS**....... Million Operations per Second [*Processing power units*] [*Data processing*]
**MOPS**....... Missile Operations
**MOPS**....... Missile Operations Paging [*or Phone*] System [*NASA*]
**MOPS**....... Mission Operations Planning System [*NASA*] (KSC)
**MOPS**....... Morpholinopropanesulfonic Acid [*A buffer*]
**MOPS**....... Multispectral Opium Poppy Sensor System
**MO PSC**.... Missouri Public Service Commission Reports [*A publication*] (DLA)
**MO PSC (NS)**... Missouri Public Service Commission Reports (New Series) [*A publication*] (DLA)
**MO PSCR**... Missouri Public Service Commission Reports [*A publication*] (DLA)
**M Opt**........ Master of Optometry
**MOPT**....... Mean One Way Propagation Time [*Telecommunications*] (TEL)
**MOPTAR**... Multiobject Phase Tracking and Ranging [*FAA*]
**MOPTE**..... Measure of Potential Training Effectiveness [*Army*]
**MOptom**.... Master of Optometry (ADA)
**MOPTS**..... Mobile Photographic Tracking Station (IEEE)
**MO PUR**... Missouri Public Utility Reports [*A publication*] (DLA)
**MOPV**....... Monovalent Oral Polio Vaccine [*Immunology*]
**MOQ**......... Fort Stewart (Hinesville), GA [*Location identifier*] [*FAA*] (FAAL)
**MOQ**......... Lindenwood College, St. Charles, MO [*OCLC symbol*] (OCLC)
**MOQ**......... Married Officer Quarters
**MOQ**......... Minimum Order Quantity (MCD)
**MOQ**......... Morocco Explorations [*Vancouver Stock Exchange symbol*]
**MOQ**......... Morondava [*Madagascar*] [*Airport symbol*] (OAG)
**MOR**......... Magneto-Optical Rotation
**MOR**......... Management Operating Ratios (NG)
**MOR**......... Mandatory Occurrence Reporting
**MOR**......... Manufacturing Operation Record (NASA)
**MOR**......... Market Opinion Research, Inc. [*Information service or system*] (IID)
**MOR**......... Mars Orbital Rendezvous
**M Or**......... Master of Oratory
**MOR**......... Mathematics of Operations Research [*A publication*]
**MOR**......... Medical Officer Report [*Navy*] (NG)
**MOR**......... Memory Output Register [*Data processing*]
**MOR**......... Merchandising and Operating Results
**MOR**......... Mid-Oceanic Ridge
**MOR**......... Middle of the Road [*Broadcasting*]
**MOR**......... Military Operations Research
**MOR**......... Mining and Oil Review [*A publication*] (APTA)
**MOR**......... Missile Operationally Ready [*Air Force*]
**MOR**......... Missions Operations Report [*NASA*] (KSC)
**MO R**......... Missouri Reports [*A publication*] (DLA)
**MOR**......... Modulus of Rupture [*Mechanics*]
**M Or**......... Monde Oriental [*A publication*]
**MOR**......... Monthly Operating Report (IEEE)
**Mo R**......... Monthly Review [*A publication*]
**Mo & R**...... Moody and Robinson's English Nisi Prius Reports [*A publication*] (DLA)
**MOR**......... Moral (ROG)
**Mor**........... Moralia [*of Plutarch*] [*Classical studies*] (OCD)
**MOR**......... Moravian College, Bethlehem, PA [*OCLC symbol*] (OCLC)
**MOR**......... Moray [*County in Scotland*] (ROG)
**MOR**......... Mordenite [*A zeolite*]
**MOR**......... Morendo [*Gradually Softer*] [*Music*]
**MOR**......... Morgan Keegan & Co., Inc. [*NYSE symbol*] (SPSG)
**MOR**......... Morgan, M. B., Glen Burnie MD [*STAC*]
**MOR**......... Morgan Owners Register (EA)
**MOR**......... Mori [*Japan*] [*Seismograph station code, US Geological Survey*] [*Closed*] (SEIS)
**Mor**........... Morison's Dictionary of Decisions, Scotch Court of Session [*1540-1808*] [*A publication*] (DLA)
**MOR**......... Morning Star Resources [*Vancouver Stock Exchange symbol*]
**MOR**......... Morocco
**MOR**......... Morocco Leather [*Bookbinding*] (ROG)
**MOR**......... Morphine [*A narcotic*]
**MOR**......... Morpholine [*Organic chemistry*]
**Mor**........... Morris' Reports [*Jamaica*] [*A publication*] (ILCA)
**MOR**......... Morristown, TN [*Location identifier*] [*FAA*] (FAAL)
**MOR**......... Mortality Odds Ratio
**MOR**......... Mortar
**MORA**....... Mandibular Orthopedic Repositioning Appliance [*Dentistry*]
**MORA**....... Moraga Corp. [*NASDAQ symbol*] (NQ)
**MORA**....... Mount Rainier National Park
**MORAB**.... Morgan and Arabian [*Type of horse developed from these two breeds*] [*Acronym is also said to stand for "Muscular, Outstanding, Refined, Athletic, Beautiful," the horse's distinguishing characteristics*]
**Mora Ferenc Muz Ev**... Mora Ferenc Muzeum Evkoenyve [*A publication*]
**MORAL**.... Massachusetts Organization for the Repeal of Abortion Laws
**Moral Ed**.... Moral Education [*A publication*]
**MORASS**.. Modern Ramjet System Synthesis (MCD)
**Moravian Mus**... Moravian Music Foundation. Bulletin [*A publication*]
**Moravian Mus**... Moravian Music Journal [*A publication*]
**Morav Num Zpr**... Moravske Numismaticke Zpravy [*A publication*]
**Moravske Num Zpravy**... Moravske Numismaticke Zpravy [*A publication*]
**Morav Th S Bul**... Moravian Theological Seminary. Bulletin [*A publication*]
**MORB**....... Mid-Ocean Ridge Basalt [*Geology*]
**Morbidity Mortality Wkly Rep US Dep Hlth Educ Welf**... Morbidity and Mortality Weekly Report. United States Department of Health, Education, and Welfare [*A publication*]
**Morbid Mortal Weekly Rep**... Morbidity and Mortality Weekly Report [*A publication*]
**MORBREPT**... Morbidity Report
**MORBTGREPT**... Morbidity Telegraphic Report
**MORC**....... Medical Officers' Reserve Corps
**MORC**....... Midget Ocean Racing Class [*or Club*]
**Mor & Carl**... Moreau-Lislet and Carleton's Laws of Las Siete Partidas in Force in Louisiana [*A publication*] (DLA)
**Mor Chy Acts**... Morgan's Chancery Acts and Orders [*6th ed.*] [*1885*] [*A publication*] (DLA)
**Mor Comp**... Morris on Compensations [*A publication*] (DLA)
**Mor Corp**... Morawetz on Private Corporations [*A publication*] (DLA)
**MORD**....... Medical Operations Requirements Document (MCD)
**MORD**....... Military Operations Research Department
**MORD**....... Ministry of Revolutionary Development [*Vietnam*]
**MORD**....... Mission Operations Requirements Document [*NASA*] (NASA)
**Mor Dic**..... Morison's Dictionary of Decisions, Scotch Court of Session [*1540-1808*] [*A publication*] (DLA)
**Mor Dict**.... Morison's Dictionary of Decisions, Scotch Court of Session [*1540-1808*] [*A publication*] (DLA)

**MOR DICT** ... Moro Dicto [*As Directed*] [*Pharmacy*]
**Mor Dig** ..... Morley's Digest of the Indian Reports [*A publication*] (DLA)
**Mor Dig** ..... Morrison's New Hampshire Digest [*A publication*] (DLA)
**Mor Dil** ...... Morris on Dilapidations [*2nd ed.*] [*1871*] [*A publication*] (DLA)
**MORDS** .... Manned Orbital Research and Development System
**MORDT** .... Mobilization Operational Readiness Deployment Test [*DoD*]
**MORE** ....... Microbial Oil Recovery Enhancement [*Petroleum technology*]
**MORE** ....... Military Officer Record Examination
**MORE** ....... Minority Officer Recruitment Effort
**MORE** ....... Money, Opportunity, Responsibility, and Equality [*Of organization "MORE for Women"*]
**MORE** ....... Multioptical Reconnaissance Equipment [*Military*] (CAAL)
**Mor Eas** ..... Morris on the Law of Easements [*A publication*] (DLA)
**Moreau & Carleton's Partidas** ... Moreau-Lislet and Carleton's Laws of Las Siete Partidas in Force in Louisiana [*A publication*] (DLA)
**MORE DICT** ... More Dicto [*As Directed*] [*Pharmacy*] (ROG)
**MO Reg** ..... Missouri Register [*A publication*]
**MOREL** .... Michigan-Ohio Regional Educational Laboratory
**More Lect** .. More's Lectures on the Law of Scotland [*A publication*] (DLA)
**Mo Rel M** .. Monthly Religious Magazine [*A publication*]
**MORENA** ... Movimiento de Renovacion Nacional [*National Renewal Movement*] [*Venezuela*] [*Political party*] (PPW)
**MO Rep** ..... Missouri Reports [*A publication*] (DLA)
**MOREP** .... Monthly Report
**MOREPS** .. Monitor Station Reports
**Mor E & RD Law** ... Morice's English and Roman Dutch Law [*A publication*] (DLA)
**MORES** ..... Minerals, Oils, and Resources Shares Fund [*British*]
**MORE SOL** ... More Solito [*In the Usual Way*] [*Pharmacy*] (ROG)
**MOREST** .. Mobile Arresting Gear [*Navy*]
**More St** ...... More's Notes on Stair's Institutes of Scotland [*A publication*] (DLA)
**MORET** .... Moreton [*England*]
**Mo Rev** ...... Monthly Review [*A publication*]
**Mo Review** ... Monthly Review [*A publication*]
**MO Rev Stat** ... Missouri Revised Statutes [*A publication*] (DLA)
**Morey Out Rom Law** ... Morey's Outlines of Roman Law [*A publication*] (DLA)
**MORF** ....... Manned Orbital Research Facility [*NASA*] (MCD)
**MORF** ....... Mor-Flo Industries, Inc. [*NASDAQ symbol*] (NQ)
**MORFA** .... Morskoi Flot [*A publication*]
**Morfog Regener** ... Morfogenez i Regeneratsiya [*A publication*]
**Morfol Norm si Pat** ... Morfologia Normala si Patologica [*A publication*]
**Morfol Norm Patol (Buchar)** ... Morfologia Normala si Patologica (Bucharest) [*A publication*]
**Morfol Osn Mikrotsirk (Moscow)** ... Morfologicheskie Osnovy Mikrotsirkulyatsii (Moscow) [*A publication*]
**Morfol Reakt Izmen Perifer Nervn Sist Usloviyakh Eksp** ... Morfologiya Reaktivnykh Izmenenii Perifericheskoi Nervnoi Sistemy v Usloviyakh Eksperimenta [*A publication*]
**Morg** .......... Morgan's Chancery Acts and Orders [*6th ed.*] [*1885*] [*A publication*] (DLA)
**Morgan** ...... Morgan's Digest [*Ceylon*] [*A publication*] (DLA)
**Morgan Gty** ... Morgan Guaranty Survey [*A publication*]
**Morgan LM** ... Morgan's Legal Miscellany [*Ceylon*] [*A publication*] (DLA)
**Morg Ch** .... Morgan's Chancery Acts and Orders [*6th ed.*] [*1885*] [*A publication*] (DLA)
**Morg & Ch Jud Acts** ... Morgan and Chute on the Judicature Acts [*A publication*] (DLA)
**Morg Lit** .... Morgan on the Law of Literature [*A publication*] (DLA)
**Morg Tar** ... Morgan on the United States Tariff [*A publication*] (DLA)
**Morg & WLJ** ... Morgan and Williams' Law Journal [*London*] [*A publication*] (DLA)
**Mor Hors** ... Morrell on the Law of Horses [*A publication*] (DLA)
**MORI** ........ Market and Opinion Research International [*Polling organization*]
**Mor IA** ....... Morris' Iowa Reports [*1839-46*] [*A publication*] (DLA)
**MoRih** ........ Richmond Heights Memorial Library, Richmond Heights, MO [*Library symbol*] [*Library of Congress*] (LCLS)
**MORITZER** ... Mortar Howitzer (NATG)
**MORL** ....... Manned Orbital [*or Orbiting*] Research Laboratory [*NASA*]
**MORL** ....... Morlan International, Inc. [*Philadelphia, PA*] [*NASDAQ symbol*] (NQ)
**Morl Dig** .... Morley's East Indian Digest [*A publication*] (DLA)
**Mor M** ....... Master Mortician
**MoRM** ....... University of Missouri at Rolla, Rolla, MO [*Library symbol*] [*Library of Congress*] (LCLS)
**Mor Min Rep** ... Morrison's Mining Reports [*A publication*] (DLA)
**Mor Miss** ... Morris' Reports [*Mississippi*] [*A publication*] (DLA)
**MORN** ....... Morning
**Morn Watch** ... Morning Watch [*A publication*]
**MORO** ...... Morocco Leather [*Bookbinding*] (ROG)
**Morocco Serv Geol Notes Mem** ... Morocco. Service Geologique. Notes et Memoires [*A publication*]
**MORP** ....... Medical and Occupational Radiation Program [*HEW*]
**MORP** ....... Meteorite Observation and Recovery Project [*Canada*]
**MORP** ....... Moore Products Co. [*NASDAQ symbol*] (NQ)
**MORPH** .... Morphology
**Morph Jb** ... Morphologisches Jahrbuch [*A publication*]
**MORPHOL** ... Morphology
**Morphol Embryol** ... Morphologie et Embryologie [*Romania*] [*A publication*]
**Morphol Embryol (Bucur)** ... Morphologie et Embryologie (Bucurest) [*A publication*]
**Morphol Igazsagugyi Orv Sz** ... Morphologiai es Igazsagugyi Orvosi Szemle [*A publication*]
**Morphol Jahrb** ... Morphologisches Jahrbuch [*A publication*]
**Morphol Med** ... Morphologia Medica [*A publication*]
**MORPHS** ... Minicomputer-Operated Retrieval (Partially Heuristic) System [*Data processing*]
**Mor Pr** ....... Morehead's Practice [*A publication*] (DLA)
**Mor Priv Corp** ... Morawetz on Private Corporations [*A publication*] (DLA)
**MORPS** ..... Maritime Other Ranks Production Study [*Canadian Navy*]
**MorR** ......... Bibliotheque Generale et Archives, Rabat, Morocco [*Library symbol*] [*Library of Congress*] (LCLS)
**Morr** .......... Morrell's English Bankruptcy Reports [*A publication*] (DLA)
**Morr** .......... Morris' Iowa Reports [*1839-46*] [*A publication*] (DLA)
**Morr** .......... Morris' Jamaica Reports [*A publication*] (DLA)
**Morr** .......... Morris' Reports [*Oregon*] [*A publication*] (DLA)
**Morr** .......... Morris' Reports [*California*] [*A publication*] (DLA)
**Morr** .......... Morris' Reports [*Bombay, India*] [*A publication*] (DLA)
**MORR** ....... Morrison, Inc. [*NASDAQ symbol*] (NQ)
**MORR** ....... Morristown National Historical Park
**Morr Bankr Cas** ... Morrell's English Bankruptcy Cases [*A publication*] (DLA)
**Morr BC** .... Morrell's English Bankruptcy Reports [*A publication*] (DLA)
**Morr Bomb** ... Morris' Reports [*Bombay, India*] [*A publication*] (DLA)
**Morr Cal** .... Morris' Reports [*California*] [*A publication*] (DLA)
**Morr Dict** ... Morrison's Dictionary of Decisions, Scotch Court of Session [*A publication*] (DLA)
**Morr Dig** .... Morrison's Digest of Mining Decisions [*A publication*] (DLA)
**Morr Dig** .... Morrison's New Hampshire Digest [*A publication*] (DLA)
**Morrell Bankr Cas** ... Morrell's English Bankruptcy Cases [*A publication*] (DLA)
**Morrell BC** ... Morrell's English Bankruptcy Cases [*A publication*] (DLA)
**Morrell (Eng)** ... Morrell's English Bankruptcy Cases [*A publication*] (DLA)
**Mor Rep** ..... Morris' Law of Replevin [*A publication*] (DLA)
**Morris** ........ Morris' Iowa Reports [*1839-46*] [*A publication*] (DLA)
**Morris** ........ Morris' Jamaica Reports [*A publication*] (DLA)
**Morris** ........ Morris' Reports [*Mississippi*] [*A publication*] (DLA)
**Morris** ........ Morris' Reports [*Bombay, India*] [*A publication*] (DLA)
**Morris** ........ Morris' Reports [*California*] [*A publication*] (DLA)
**Morris** ........ Morris' Reports [*Oregon*] [*A publication*] (DLA)
**Morris** ........ Morrissett's Reports [*80, 98 Alabama*] [*A publication*] (DLA)
**Morris Arbor Bull** ... Morris Arboretum. Bulletin [*A publication*]
**Morris & Har** ... Morris and Harrington's Reports [*Bombay, India*] [*A publication*] (DLA)
**Morris (IA)** ... Morris' Iowa Reports [*1839-46*] [*A publication*] (DLA)
**Morris (Iowa)** ... Morris' Iowa Reports [*1839-46*] [*A publication*] (DLA)
**Morrison Min Rep** ... Morrison's Mining Reports [*United States*] [*A publication*] (DLA)
**Morris R** .... Morris' Jamaica Reports [*A publication*] (DLA)
**Morris Repl** ... Morris on Replevin [*A publication*] (DLA)
**Morris St Cas** ... Morris' Mississippi State Cases [*1818-72*] [*A publication*] (DLA)
**Morr Jam** ... Morris' Jamaica Reports [*A publication*] (DLA)
**Morr Mines** ... Morrison's Digest of Mining Decisions [*A publication*] (DLA)
**Morr Min R** ... Morrison's Mining Reports [*United States*] [*A publication*] (DLA)
**Morr Min Rep** ... Morrison's Mining Reports [*A publication*] (DLA)
**Morr Miss** ... Morris' Reports [*Mississippi*] [*A publication*] (DLA)
**Morr MR** ... Morrison's Mining Reports [*United States*] [*A publication*] (DLA)
**Morr Repl** .. Morris' Law of Replevin [*A publication*] (DLA)
**Morr St Cas** ... Morris' Mississippi State Cases [*1818-72*] [*A publication*] (DLA)
**Morr Trans** ... Morrison's Transcript of United State Supreme Court Decisions [*A publication*] (DLA)
**Mor Ry Com** ... Morris on Railway Compensations [*A publication*] (DLA)
**MORS** ....... Military Operations Research Society (EA)
**MORS** ....... Military Operations Research Symposia (MCD)
**MORS** ....... Multi-Outlet Reservoir Study [*Department of the Interior*] (GRD)
**M Or Sc** ..... Master of the Science of Oratory
**MORSEAFRON** ... Moroccan Sea Frontier [*Navy*] [*World War II*]
**Morse Arb** ... Morse on the Law of Arbitration and Award [*A publication*] (DLA)
**Morse Banks** ... Morse on the Law of Banks and Banking [*A publication*] (DLA)
**Morse Bk** ... Morse on the Law of Banks and Banking [*A publication*] (DLA)
**Morse Exch Rep** ... Morse's Exchequer Reports [*Canada*] [*A publication*] (DLA)
**Morse Tr** .... Morse's Famous Trials [*A publication*] (DLA)
**Morsk Fl** .... Morskoi Flot [*A publication*]
**Morsk Flot** ... Morskoi Flot [*A publication*]
**Morsk Gidrofiz Issled** ... Morskie Gidrofizicheskie Issledovaniya [*A publication*]
**Morski Inst Rybacki Pr Ser A** ... Morski Instytut Rybacki. Prace. Seria A. Oceanografia i Biologia Rybacka [*A publication*]
**Morsk Sb** ... Morskoi Sbornik [*A publication*]
**MORSL** ..... Mobilization Reserve Stockage List [*Army*] (AABC)

**MOR SOL** ... More Solito [*In the Usual Way*] [*Pharmacy*]
**Mor St Ca** .. Morris' Mississippi State Cases [*1818-72*] [*A publication*] (DLA)
**Mor St Cas** ... Morris' Mississippi State Cases [*1818-72*] [*A publication*] (DLA)
**Mor Supp** ... Morison's Dictionary of Decisions, Scotch Court of Session, Supplement [*1620-1768*] [*A publication*] (DLA)
**Mor Syn** ..... Morison's Synopsis, Scotch Session Cases [*1808-16*] [*A publication*] (DLA)
**MORT** ....... Management Oversight and Risk Tree (NASA)
**MORT** ....... Master Operational Recording Tape [*SAGE*]
**MORT** ....... Missile Operation [*or Ordnance*] Readiness Test [*or Testing*]
**MORT** ....... Morse Taper
**mort** ........... Mortality
**MORT** ....... Mortar (AABC)
**MORT** ....... Mortgage (ADA)
**MORT** ....... Mortuary (ADA)
**Mort Banker** ... Mortgage Banker [*A publication*]
**Mort Banking** ... Mortgage Banking [*A publication*]
**MORTG** .... Mortgage
**Mortg Bank** ... Mortgage Banking [*A publication*]
**Mortg Bnkr** ... Mortgage Banker [*A publication*]
**Morton** ....... Morton's Reports, Calcutta Superior Court [*India*] [*A publication*] (DLA)
**Mor Tran** ... Morrison's Transcript of United States Supreme Court Decisions [*A publication*] (DLA)
**MORTREP** ... Mortar Bombing Report
**Mort Vend** ... Morton's Vendors and Purchasers [*1837*] [*A publication*] (DLA)
**MORU** ....... Mount Rushmore National Memorial
**MORV** ....... Mobile Overpass Roadway-Repair Vehicle
**MORW** ...... II Morrow, Inc. [*Salem, OR*] [*NASDAQ symbol*] (NQ)
**Mor Wills** .. Morrell on the Law of Wills [*A publication*] (DLA)
**Mos** ........... De Vita Mosis [*Philo*] (BJA)
**MOS** .......... Major Operating System [*Army*] (AABC)
**MOS** .......... Man-on-the-Street Interview [*Journalism*]
**MOS** .......... Management Operating System
**MOS** .......... Management Orientation School [*LIMRA*]
**MOS** .......... Manned Orbital Station (AAG)
**MOS** .......... Manual Override Switch
**MOS** .......... Manufacturing Operating System [*IBM Corp.*]
**MOS** .......... Manufacturing Operations Survey (MCD)
**MOS** .......... Margin of Safety [*Business term*]
**MOS** .......... Marine Observation Satellite [*Japan*]
**MOS** .......... Maritime Operational Intelligence Summary (MCD)
**MOS** .......... Marking of Overseas Shipments
**MOS** .......... Master Operating System [*Sperry UNIVAC*]
**MOS** .......... Material Ordering Schedule
**MOS** .......... Mathematical Off-Print Service [*American Mathematical Society*]
**MOS** .......... Mean Opinion Score
**MOS** .......... Measure of Suitability (CAAL)
**MOS** .......... Mechanical Oblique Sketcher
**MOS** .......... Memory Operating Software [*Data processing*]
**MOS** .......... Memory-Oriented System
**MOS** .......... Mercantile Open Stock
**MOS** .......... Mesa Offshore Trust UBI [*NYSE symbol*] (SPSG)
**MOS** .......... Metal-Oxide Semiconductor
**MOS** .......... Metal-Oxide-Silicon [*Integrated circuit*] [*Electronics*]
**MOS** .......... Metal Oxide on a Substrate (MCD)
**MOS** .......... Methods in Organic Synthesis [*A publication*]
**MOS** .......... Microprogram Operating System
**MOS** .......... Military Occupational Specialty [*Army*]
**MOS** .......... Military Occupational Specification Serial Number [*British*] [*World War II*]
**MOS** .......... Military Overseas Supply [*British*]
**MOS** .......... Ministry of State [*British*]
**MOS** .......... Ministry of Supply [*Also, MS*] [*British*]
**MOS** .......... Minus Optical Sound [*Film industry*]
**MOS** .......... Missile Operations Station
**MOS** .......... Missile on Stand
**MOS** .......... Mission Operations Strategy [*NASA*]
**MOS** .......... Mission Operations System [*NASA*]
**MOS** .......... Mit Out Sound [*i.e., "without sound"*] [*Film industry*]
**MOS** .......... Model Output Statistics [*Meteorology*]
**MOS** .......... Modular Operating System (BUR)
**MOS** .......... Months
**Mo & S** ....... Moore and Scott's English Common Pleas Reports [*1831-34*] [*A publication*] (DLA)
**MOS** .......... Morton Air Services Ltd.
**MOS** .......... Mosaic
**MOS** .......... Moscow [*USSR*] [*Geomagnetic observatory code*]
**MOS** .......... Moscow [*USSR*] [*Seismograph station code, US Geological Survey*] (SEIS)
**Mos** ........... Moseley's English Chancery Reports [*25 English Reprint*] [*A publication*] (DLA)
**Mos** ........... Mosella [*of Ausonius*] [*Classical studies*] (OCD)
**MOS** .......... Moses Point, AK [*Location identifier*] [*FAA*] (FAAL)
**MOS** .......... Mosport Park Corp. [*Vancouver Stock Exchange symbol*]
**mos** ........... Mossi [*MARC language code*] [*Library of Congress*] (LCCP)
**MOS** .......... Multiprogramming Operating System
**MoS** .......... St. Louis Public Library, St. Louis, MO [*Library symbol*] [*Library of Congress*] (LCLS)
**MOS** .......... Springfield-Greene County Library, Springfield, MO [*OCLC symbol*] (OCLC)
**MOSA** ....... Medical Officers of Schools Associations [*British*]
**MOSA** ....... Method of Standard Addition [*Statistics*]
**MOSA** ....... Mitteilungen. Oesterreichisches Staatsarchiv [*A publication*]
**MoSAB** ...... Anheuser-Busch, Inc., St. Louis, MO [*Library symbol*] [*Library of Congress*] (LCLS)
**MOSAIC** ... Macro Operation Symbolic Assembler and Information Compiler [*Data processing*] (IEEE)
**MOSAIC** ... Metal-Oxide-Semiconductor Advanced Integrated Circuit [*Electronics*] (IEEE)
**MOSAIC** ... Ministry of Supply Automatic Integrator and Computer [*British*] (DEN)
**MOSAIC** ... Mobile System for Accurate ICBM Control (MCD)
**Mosaic J Molybdenum Metall** ... Mosaic. Journal of Molybdenum Metallurgy [*A publication*]
**MOSAR** .... Modulation Scan Array RADAR [*or Receiver*]
**MoSavHi** ... Andrew County Historical Society, Savannah, MO [*Library symbol*] [*Library of Congress*] (LCLS)
**MOSAW** ... Medium Operating Speed Automatic Weapon [*Military*]
**MOSB** ....... Military Order of the Stars and Bars (EA)
**MoSB** ......... Missouri Botanical Garden, St. Louis, MO [*Library symbol*] [*Library of Congress*] (LCLS)
**MOSC** ....... Management Orientation Study Course [*LIMRA*]
**MOSC** ....... Manned Orbital Systems Concepts [*NASA*]
**MOSC** ....... Military Occupational Specialty Code (AABC)
**MOSC** ....... Military Oil Subcommittee [*of North African Economic Board*] [*World War II*]
**Mo & Sc** ..... Moore and Scott's English Common Pleas Reports [*1831-34*] [*A publication*] (DLA)
**MoSCC** ...... St. Louis Community College, Instructional Resource Technical Services, St. Louis, MO [*Library symbol*] [*Library of Congress*] (LCLS)
**MOSCEQ** ... Moscosoa [*A publication*]
**MoSCEx** .... Christ Seminary-Seminex, St. Louis, MO [*Library symbol*] [*Library of Congress*] (LCLS)
**MoSCH** ..... Concordia Historical Institute, St. Louis, MO [*Library symbol*] [*Library of Congress*] (LCLS)
**MOSCH** .... Moschus [*Musk*] [*Pharmacology*] (ROG)
**MO Sch Mines Metall Bull Tech Ser** ... Missouri School of Mines and Metallurgy. Bulletin. Technical Series [*A publication*]
**Moschr** ....... Monatsschrift [*A publication*]
**MoSCo** ....... St. Louis County Library, St. Louis, MO [*Library symbol*] [*Library of Congress*] (LCLS)
**Mos Cont** ... Moseley's Contraband of War [*1861*] [*A publication*] (DLA)
**Moscow Nar** ... Press Bulletin. Moscow Narodny Bank Ltd. [*A publication*]
**Moscow Narodny Bank Q R** ... Moscow Narodny Bank. Quarterly Review [*A publication*]
**Moscow Univ Biol Sci Bull (Engl Transl)** ... Moscow University. Biological Sciences Bulletin (English Translation) [*A publication*]
**Moscow Univ Bull Ser 3** ... Moscow University. Bulletin. Series 3. Physics and Astronomy [*A publication*]
**Moscow Univ Comput Math and Cybern** ... Moscow University. Computational Mathematics and Cybernetics [*A publication*]
**Moscow Univ Geol Bull (Engl Transl)** ... Moscow University. Geology Bulletin (English Translation) [*A publication*]
**Moscow Univ Math Bull** ... Moscow University. Mathematics Bulletin [*A publication*]
**Moscow Univ Math Bull (Engl Transl)** ... Moscow University. Mathematics Bulletin (English Translation) [*A publication*]
**Moscow Univ Mech Bull** ... Moscow University. Mechanics Bulletin [*English Translation of Vestnik Moskovskogo Universiteta. Mekhanika*] [*A publication*]
**Moscow Univ Mech Bull (Engl Transl)** ... Moscow University. Mechanics Bulletin (English Translation of Vestnik Moskovskogo Universiteta. Mekhanika) [*A publication*]
**Moscow Univ Phys Bull** ... Moscow University. Physics Bulletin [*A publication*]
**Moscow Univ Soil Sci Bull (Engl Transl)** ... Moscow University. Soil Science Bulletin (English Translation) [*A publication*]
**MoSCP** ...... St. Louis College of Pharmacy, St. Louis, MO [*Library symbol*] [*Library of Congress*] (LCLS)
**MoSCRR** ... Center for Reformation Research, St. Louis, MO [*Library symbol*] [*Library of Congress*] (LCLS)
**MoSCS** ...... Concordia Seminary, St. Louis, MO [*Library symbol*] [*Library of Congress*] (LCLS)
**MoSCT** ...... Covenant Theological Seminary, St. Louis, MO [*Library symbol*] [*Library of Congress*] (LCLS)
**Mosc Univ Biol Sci Bull** ... Moscow University. Biological Sciences Bulletin [*A publication*]
**Mosc Univ Biol Sci Bull (Engl Transl Vestn Mosk Univ Biol)** ... Moscow University. Biological Sciences Bulletin (English Translation of Vestnik. Moskovskogo Universiteta. Biologiya) [*A publication*]
**Mosc Univ Chem Bull** ... Moscow University. Chemistry Bulletin [*A publication*]
**Mosc Univ Comput Math Cybern** ... Moscow University. Computational Mathematics and Cybernetics [*A publication*]

**Mosc Univ Geol Bull** ... Moscow University. Geology Bulletin [*A publication*]
**Mosc Univ Math Bull** ... Moscow University. Mathematics Bulletin [*A publication*]
**Mosc Univ Mech Bull** ... Moscow University. Mechanics Bulletin [*A publication*]
**Mosc Univ Phys Bull** ... Moscow University. Physics Bulletin [*A publication*]
**Mosc Univ Soil Sci Bull** ... Moscow University. Soil Science Bulletin [*A publication*]
**MoSDM** .... United States Air Force, Defense Mapping Agency Aerospace Center, St. Louis, MO [*Library symbol*] [*Library of Congress*] (LCLS)
**MOSE** ....... [*The*] Moseley Holding Corp. [*NASDAQ symbol*] (NQ)
**MoSe**.......... Sedalia Public Library, Sedalia, MO [*Library symbol*] [*Library of Congress*] (LCLS)
**MoSE**......... United States Army, Corps of Engineers, District Library St. Louis, St. Louis, MO [*Library symbol*] [*Library of Congress*] (LCLS)
**MOSEL**..... Molten-Salt Epithermal Reactor
**Moseley** ..... Moseley's English Chancery Reports [*25 English Reprint*] [*A publication*] (DLA)
**Mos El L**.... Moseley's Elementary Law [*2nd ed.*] [*1878*] [*A publication*] (DLA)
**Mosely (Eng)** ... Moseley's English Chancery Reports [*25 English Reprint*] [*A publication*] (DLA)
**Moser ML** ... Hans Joachim Moser Musik-Lexikon [*A publication*]
**MOSES**..... Manned Open Sea Experiment Station (NOAA)
**MOSES**..... Manufacturing Operations Short Event Scheduling
**MOSES**..... Motor-Operated Sled Ejection System (MCD)
**MOSES**..... Movable Search System (MCD)
**MOSES**..... Multioccupant Sealed Environment Simulator
**MoSF**......... Fontbonne College, St. Louis, MO [*Library symbol*] [*Library of Congress*] (LCLS)
**MOSFET** .. Metal-Oxide-Semiconductor [*or Silicon*] Field-Effect Transistor
**MoSFi**........ Eugene Field House, St. Louis, MO [*Library symbol*] [*Library of Congress*] (LCLS)
**MoSFRR** ... Foundation for Reformation Research, St. Louis, MO [*Library symbol*] [*Library of Congress*] [*Obsolete*] (LCLS)
**MoSGS**...... Church of Jesus Christ of Latter-Day Saints, Genealogical Society Library, St. Louis Branch, St. Louis, MO [*Library symbol*] [*Library of Congress*] (LCLS)
**Mosh**.......... Moshav [*or Moshava*] (BJA)
**MoSHi**....... Missouri Historical Society, St. Louis, MO [*Library symbol*] [*Library of Congress*] (LCLS)
**MoSHT** ..... Harris Teachers College, St. Louis, MO [*Library symbol*] [*Library of Congress*] (LCLS)
**MOSI** ........ Mosinee Paper Corp. [*NASDAQ symbol*] (NQ)
**MoSIG**....... International Graduate School, St. Louis, MO [*Library symbol*] [*Library of Congress*] (LCLS)
**MoSIO**....... International Library, Archives, and Museum of Optometry, St. Louis, MO [*Library symbol*] [*Library of Congress*] (LCLS)
**MoSIP** ....... Missouri Institute of Psychiatry, St. Louis, MO [*Library symbol*] [*Library of Congress*] (LCLS)
**Mosk Fiz Tekh Inst Tr Ser Obshch Mol Fiz** ... Moskovskii Fiziko-Tekhnicheskii Institut. Trudy. Seriya "Obshchaya i Molekulyarnaya Fizika" [*A publication*]
**Mosk Inst Nar Khoz Sverdl Fil Sb Nauchn Tr** ... Moskovskii Institut Narodnogo Khozyaistva. Sverdlovskii Filial. Sbornik Nauchnykh Trudov [*A publication*]
**Mosk Inst Stali Sb** ... Moskovskii Institut Stali. Sbornik [*A publication*]
**Mosk Inst Tonkoi Khim Tekhnol Tr** ... Moskovskii Institut Tonkoi Khimicheskoi Tekhnologii. Trudy [*A publication*]
**Mosk Kolkhozn** ... Moskovskii Kolkhoznik [*A publication*]
**Mosk Nauchno Issled Inst Gig Im F F Erismana Sb Nauchn Tr** ... Moskovskii Nauchno-Issledovatel'skii Institut Gigieny Imeni F. F. Erismana. Sbornik Nauchnykh Trudov [*A publication*]
**Moskov Aviacion Inst Ordzonikidze Trudy** ... Moskovskii Ordena Lenina Aviacionnyi Institut Imeni Sergo Ordzonikidze. Trudy [*A publication*]
**Moskov Gos Ped Inst Ucen Zap** ... Moskovskii Gosudarstvennyi Pedagogiceskii Institut Imeni V. I. Lenina. Ucenye Zapiski [*A publication*]
**Moskov Gos Univ Soobsc Gos Astronom Inst Sternberg** ... Moskovskii Gosudarstvennyi Universitet Imeni M. V. Lomonosova. Soobscenija Gosudarstvennogo Astronomiceskogo Instituta Imeni P. K. Sternberga [*A publication*]
**Moskov Gos Univ Soobshch Gos Astronom Inst Sternberga** ... Moskovskii Gosudarstvennyi Universitet Imeni M. V. Lomonosova. Soobshcheniya Gosudarstvennogo Astronomicheskogo Instituta Imeni P. K. Sternberga [*A publication*]
**Moskov Gos Univ Trudy Gos Astronom Inst Sternberg** ... Moskovskii Gosudarstvennyi Universitet Imeni M. V. Lomonosova. Trudy Gosudarstvennogo Astronomiceskogo Instituta Imeni P. K. Sternberga [*A publication*]
**Moskov Gos Zaocn Ped Inst Sb Naucn Trudov** ... Moskovskii Gosudarstvennyi Zaocnyi Pedagogiceskii Institut. Sbornik Naucnyh Trudov [*A publication*]
**Moskov Inst Elektron Masinostroenija-Trudy MIEM** ... Moskovskii Institut Elektronnogo Masinostroenija. Trudy MIEM [*A publication*]
**Moskov Inst Inz Zeleznodoroz Transporta Trudy** ... Moskovskii Institut Inzenerov Zeleznodoroznogo Transporta. Trudy [*A publication*]
**Moskov Inz-Stroitel Inst Sb Trudov** ... Moskovskii Inzenerno-Stroitelskii Institut Imeni V. V. Kuibyseva. Sbornik Trudov [*A publication*]
**Moskov Lesotehn Inst Naucn Trudy** ... Moskovskii Lesotehniceskii Institut. Naucnye Trudy [*A publication*]
**Moskov Oblast Ped Inst Ucen Zap** ... Moskovskii Oblastnoi Pedagogiceskii Institut. Ucenye Zapiski [*A publication*]
**Moskov Obshch Ispytateley Prirody Byull Otdel Geol** ... Byulleten' Moskovskogo Obshchestva Ispytateley Prirody Otdel Geologicheskiy [*A publication*]
**Mosk O-Vo Ispyt Prir Byull Otd Geol** ... Moskovskoye Obshchestvo Ispytateley Prirody. Byulleten. Otdel Geologicheskiy [*A publication*]
**Mosk Univ Vestn Ser 6 Biol Pochvoved** ... Moskovskiy Universitet. Vestnik. Seriya 6. Biologiya. Pochvovedeniye [*A publication*]
**Mosk Univ Vestn Ser Geogr** ... Moskovskiy Universitet. Vestnik. Seriya Geografii [*A publication*]
**MoSL**......... Law Library Association of St. Louis, St. Louis, MO [*Library symbol*] [*Library of Congress*] (LCLS)
**Moslem W** ... Moslem World [*A publication*]
**MOSLS**..... Military Occupational Specialty Level System
**MOS/LSI** ... Metal Oxide Silicon/Large Scale Integration [*Electronics*]
**MOSM**...... Metal-Oxide Semimetal (IEEE)
**mOsm**......... Milliosmol [*or Milliosmole*] [*Chemistry*]
**MOSM**...... Mission Operations System Manager [*NASA*]
**MoSM** ....... St. Louis Mercantile Library Association, St. Louis, MO [*Library symbol*] [*Library of Congress*] (LCLS)
**MoSMa** ..... Maryville College, St. Louis, MO [*Library symbol*] [*Library of Congress*] (LCLS)
**MoSMal** .... Mallinckrodt Chemical Works [*Later, Mallinckrodt, Inc.*], St. Louis, MO [*Library symbol*] [*Library of Congress*] (LCLS)
**Mos Man**... Moses on the Law of Mandamus [*A publication*] (DLA)
**MoSMc**...... McDonnell Douglas Corp., Corporate Library, St. Louis, MO [*Library symbol*] [*Library of Congress*] (LCLS)
**MoSMcA**... McDonnell Douglas Automation Co., St. Louis, MO [*Library symbol*] [*Library of Congress*] (LCLS)
**MoSMed**.... St. Louis Medical Society, St. Louis, MO [*Library symbol*] [*Library of Congress*] (LCLS)
**MoSMon** ... Monsanto Chemical Co., St. Louis, MO [*Library symbol*] [*Library of Congress*] (LCLS)
**MOSNAG** ... Mossine Nagant Rifle
**Mosonmagy Agrartud Foisk Kozl** ... Mosonmagyarovari Agrartudomanyi Foiskola Kozlemenyei [*A publication*]
**Mosonmagyarovari Agrartud Foiskola Kozl** ... Mosonmagyarovari Agrartudomanyi Foiskola Kozlemenyei [*A publication*]
**Mosonmagyarovari Mezogazdasagtud Kar Kozl** ... Mosonmagyarovari Mezogazdasagtudomanyi Kar Kozlemenyei [*A publication*]
**MOSP** ....... Master Ordnance Systems Pattern File [*Navy*]
**MoSp** ......... Public Libraries of Springfield and Greene County, Springfield, MO [*Library symbol*] [*Library of Congress*] (LCLS)
**MoSpA** ...... Assemblies of God Graduate School, Springfield, MO [*Library symbol*] [*Library of Congress*] (LCLS)
**MoSpBB**.... Baptist Bible College, Springfield, MO [*Library symbol*] [*Library of Congress*] (LCLS)
**MoSpCB**.... Central Bible College, Springfield, MO [*Library symbol*] [*Library of Congress*] (LCLS)
**MoSpD** ...... Drury College, Springfield, MO [*Library symbol*] [*Library of Congress*] (LCLS)
**MoSPD**...... St. Louis Post-Dispatch, St. Louis, MO [*Library symbol*] [*Library of Congress*] (LCLS)
**MoSpE**....... Evangel College, Springfield, MO [*Library symbol*] [*Library of Congress*] (LCLS)
**MO Speleology** ... Missouri Speleology [*A publication*]
**MOSPF** ..... Mosport Park Corp. [*NASDAQ symbol*] (NQ)
**MOSPO** .... Mobile Satellite Photometric Observatory [*NASA*] (NASA)
**MOSPOR** ... Movement for the Struggle for Political Rights [*Uganda*] (PD)
**MoSPS** ...... St. Louis Priory School, St. Louis, MO [*Library symbol*] [*Library of Congress*] (LCLS)
**MoSpS**...... Southwest Missouri State College, Springfield, MO [*Library symbol*] [*Library of Congress*] (LCLS)
**MOSQAU** ... Mosquito News [*A publication*]
**Mosq Control Res Annu Rep** ... Mosquito Control Research. Annual Report [*A publication*]
**Mosq News** ... Mosquito News [*A publication*]
**Mosq Syst** ... Mosquito Systematics [*A publication*]
**Mosq Syst News Lett** ... Mosquito Systematics News Letter [*A publication*]
**Mosquito Ne** ... Mosquito News [*A publication*]
**MoSR**......... City Art Museum of St. Louis, St. Louis, MO [*Library symbol*] [*Library of Congress*] (LCLS)
**MOSRD** .... Motor Machinist's Mate, Ship Repair, Diesel Engineering Mechanic [*Navy rating*]
**MOSRG** .... Motor Machinist's Mate, Ship Repair, Gasoline Engine Mechanic [*Navy rating*]
**MOSS**........ Maintenance-Operations Support Set (AFM)
**MOSS**........ Manned Orbital Space Station [*or System*] [*See also MOD, MODS, MTSS*] [*Air Force/NASA*]

**MOSS**........ Market-Oriented, Sector-Selective [*or Specific*] [*Trade negotiations between United States and Japan*]
**MOSS**........ Market Oversight Surveillance System
**MOSS**........ Middle-Aged, Overstressed, Semiaffluent Suburbanite [*Lifestyle classification*]
**MOSS**........ Military Orbital Space System [*See also MOD, MODS, MTSS*] [*Air Force/NASA*]
**MOSS**........ Military Overseas Shelter Survey [*Civil Defense*]
**MOSS**........ Mobile Submarine Simulator (NVT)
**MOSS**........ Mobility Support Set [*or System*] [*for aircraft*] (MCD)
**MOSS**........ Monitor Output Signal Strength
**MOSS**........ Mothers of Sons in Service [*World War II*]
**MOSS**........ Mutually Owned Society for Songwriters
**MOSSA**..... Northern Rhodesia Mine Officials and Salaried Staff Association
**MoSSJ**....... St. John Cantius Seminary, St. Louis, MO [*Library symbol*] [*Library of Congress*] (LCLS)
**MOSS MOUSE** ... Maneuver, Objective, Security, Surprise, Mass, Offensive, Unity of Command, Simplicity, Economy of Force [*Basic principles of war*] [*See also MOOSEMUSS*] (MCD)
**MOSSRS**... Management Order Ship Status Reporting System (MCD)
**MOSST**..... Ministry of State for Science and Technology [*Canada*]
**MOST**....... Management Operation System Technique
**MOST**....... Manned Orbital Solar Telescope
**MOST**....... Metal-Oxide-Semiconductor Transistor
**MOST**....... Mission Oriented System Tape [*Military*] (CAAL)
**MOST**....... Mobile Optical Surveillance Tracker
**MOST**....... Mobile SONAR Technology [*Marine science*] (MSC)
**MOST**....... Molonglo Observatory Synthesis Telescope
**MOST**....... Motorcycle Operator Skill Test
**MOST**....... Multipulse Observation Sizing Technique [*Southwest Research Institute*]
**MOSTA**..... Midwest Old Settlers and Threshers Association (EA)
**MOSTAB** ... Modular Stability [*Derivative program*]
**MO St Ann** ... Missouri Statutes, Annotated [*A publication*] (DLA)
**MoStc**........ St. Charles City-County Library, St. Charles, MO [*Library symbol*] [*Library of Congress*] (LCLS)
**MoStcL**...... Lindenwood College, St. Charles, MO [*Library symbol*] [*Library of Congress*] (LCLS)
**Mostell**....... Mostellaria [*of Plautus*] [*Classical studies*] (OCD)
**M Ostens**... Musik des Ostens [*A publication*]
**MOstf**........ Marburger Ostforschungen [*A publication*]
**MoStgA**..... Sainte Genevieve Archives, Sainte Genevieve County Court, Ste. Genevieve, MO [*Library symbol*] [*Library of Congress*] (LCLS)
**MoStj**......... St. Joseph Public Library, St. Joseph, MO [*Library symbol*] [*Library of Congress*] (LCLS)
**MoStjM**..... Methodist Medical Center, St. Joseph, MO [*Library symbol*] [*Library of Congress*] (LCLS)
**MoStjMW** ... Missouri Western State College, St. Joseph, MO [*Library symbol*] [*Library of Congress*] (LCLS)
**MoStjS**....... St. Joseph State Hospital, St. Joseph, MO [*Library symbol*] [*Library of Congress*] (LCLS)
**MOSTL**..... Metal-Oxide-Semiconductor Transistor Logic (CET)
**Mostra Int Ind Conserve Aliment Congr** ... Mostra Internazionale delle Industrie per le Conserve Alimentari. Congressi [*A publication*]
**MOST/TDIS** ... Mobile SONAR Technology/Technical Document Information System [*Marine science*] (MSC)
**MOSU**....... Mobile Ordnance Service Unit
**MoSU**........ St. Louis University, St. Louis, MO [*Library symbol*] [*Library of Congress*] (LCLS)
**MoSU-C**.... St. Louis University, School of Commerce and Finance, St. Louis, MO [*Library symbol*] [*Library of Congress*] (LCLS)
**MoSU-D**.... St. Louis University, School of Divinity, St. Louis, MO [*Library symbol*] [*Library of Congress*] (LCLS)
**MoSUE**...... Union Electric Co., St. Louis, MO [*Library symbol*] [*Library of Congress*] (LCLS)
**MoSU-L**.... St. Louis University, School of Law, St. Louis, MO [*Library symbol*] [*Library of Congress*] (LCLS)
**MoSU-M**... St. Louis University, School of Medicine, St. Louis, MO [*Library symbol*] [*Library of Congress*] (LCLS)
**Mo Summary Aust Cond** ... Monthly Summary of Australian Conditions [*A publication*] (APTA)
**MoSU-P**.... St. Louis University, School of Philosophy, St. Louis, MO [*Library symbol*] [*Library of Congress*] (LCLS)
**MoSV**........ Catholic Central Union of America, St. Louis, MO [*Library symbol*] [*Library of Congress*] (LCLS)
**MOSVA**.... Mitteilungen. Oesterreichische Sanitaetsverwaltung [*A publication*]
**MoSVA**...... United States Veterans Administration Hospital, St. Louis, MO [*Library symbol*] [*Library of Congress*] (LCLS)
**MoSW**....... Washington University, St. Louis, MO [*Library symbol*] [*Library of Congress*] (LCLS)
**MoSW-D**... Washington University, School of Dentistry, St. Louis, MO [*Library symbol*] [*Library of Congress*] (LCLS)
**MoSW-F**.... Washington University, School of Fine Arts, St. Louis, MO [*Library symbol*] [*Library of Congress*] (LCLS)
**MoSW-L**.... Washington University, School of Law, St. Louis, MO [*Library symbol*] [*Library of Congress*] (LCLS)
**MoSW-M**.. Washington University, Medical School, St. Louis, MO [*Library symbol*] [*Library of Congress*] (LCLS)
**MOSZ**....... Massive Offshore Surf Zone
**MOT**......... Manned Orbital Telescope [*NASA*]
**MOT**......... Manufacturing Operation and Tooling
**MOT**......... [*The*] March of Time [*Radio and motion picture series*]
**MOT**......... Marine Oil Transportation [*AAR code*]
**MOT**......... Mark on Top (NVT)
**MOT**......... Master Operability Test (CAAL)
**MOT**......... Maximum Operating Time (NG)
**MOT**......... McDonald Observatory [*Texas*] [*Seismograph station code, US Geological Survey*] (SEIS)
**MOT**......... Mean Operating Time
**MOT**......... Mechanical Operability Test
**MOT**......... Medial Olfactory Tract [*Anatomy*]
**MOT**......... Member of Our Tribe [*Jewish slang*]
**MOT**......... Military Ocean Terminal (AABC)
**MOT**......... Ministry of Tourism [*Philippines*] (DS)
**MOT**......... Ministry of Transport [*British or Canadian*]
**MOT**......... Minot [*North Dakota*] [*Airport symbol*] (OAG)
**MOT**......... Missile Operability Test (MCD)
**MOT**......... Molecular-Orbital Theory [*Physical chemistry*]
**MOT**......... Monalta Resources, Inc. [*Vancouver Stock Exchange symbol*]
**MOT**......... Month of Travel [*Military*]
**MOT**......... Motion
**MOT**......... Motor (AAG)
**MOT**......... Motor Operating Time
**MOT**......... Motorized
**MOT**......... Motorola, Inc. [*NYSE symbol*] (SPSG)
**MOT**......... Mouse Operating Table [*Research instrumentation*]
**MOT**......... Murine Ovarian Teratocarcinoma [*Animal pathology*]
**MOT**......... Tarkio College, Tarkio, MO [*OCLC symbol*] (OCLC)
**MOTA**....... Materials Open-Test Assembly [*Nuclear energy*] (NRCH)
**MOTA**....... Michigan Ohio Telecommunications Association (TSSD)
**MOTA**....... Mid-Ocean Target Array (AAG)
**MOTA**....... Museum of Temporary Art [*Washington, DC*]
**MoTaC**...... Tarkio College, Tarkio, MO [*Library symbol*] [*Library of Congress*] (LCLS)
**MOTACC** ... Manufacturers of Telescoping and Articulating Cranes Council (EA)
**MOTAR**.... Modular Thermal Analyzer Routine [*Data processing*]
**MOTARDES** ... Moving Target Detection System (IEEE)
**MOTARDIV** ... Mobile Target Division [*Mine Force*] [*Navy*]
**MOTARDS** ... Moving Target Detection System
**Mo Tax Features** ... Monthly Tax Features [*A publication*]
**MOTBA**.... Military Ocean Terminal, Bay Area [*Oakland, CA*] (AABC)
**Mot Boat**.... Motor Boat [*A publication*]
**Mot Boat Yacht** ... Motor Boat and Yachting [*A publication*]
**MOTBY**.... Military Ocean Terminal, Bayonne (AABC)
**MOTC**....... Ministry of Transport and Communications [*Philippines*] (DS)
**MOTC**....... Montreal Tramways [*AAR code*]
**MOTCP**..... Ministry of Town and Country Planning [*British*] (DAS)
**Mot Cycle**.. Motor Cycle [*A publication*]
**MOT & E**... Multinational Operational Test and Evaluation
**MOTEL**..... Motor Hotel
**MOTESZ**.. Magyar Orvostudomanyi Tarsasagok Szovetsege [*Federation of Hungarian Medical Societies*] (EAIO)
**MOTF**....... Manganese Oxide Thin Film
**MOTG**....... Marine Operational Training Group
**MOTG**....... Morally Obliged to Go [*British*] [*Slang*]
**Moth Earth** ... Mother Earth News [*A publication*]
**Mother J**.... Mother Jones [*A publication*]
**Moth Jones** ... Mother Jones [*A publication*]
**Moths Am North Mex** ... Moths of America, North of Mexico [*A publication*]
**Motion Pict Tech Bull** ... Motion Picture Technical Bulletin [*A publication*]
**MOTIS**...... Missile on Stand Timing Simulator (MCD)
**Motiv Emotion** ... Motivation and Emotion [*A publication*]
**MOTKI**..... Military Ocean Terminal, King's Bay (AABC)
**MOTNAC** ... Manual of Tumor Nomenclature [*Medicine*] (DHSM)
**MOTNE**.... Meteorological Operational Telecommunications Network Europe
**Motn Life**... Mountain Life and Work [*A publication*]
**MOTO**....... Moto Photo, Inc. [*NASDAQ symbol*] (NQ)
**MOTOGAS** ... Motor Gasoline [*Military*]
**MOTOR**.... Mobile Oriented Triangulation of Reentry
**Motor B**..... Motor Boating [*A publication*]
**Motor B & S** ... Motor Boating and Sailing [*A publication*]
**Motor Bus** ... Motor Business [*A publication*]
**MOTOREDE** ... Movement to Restore Decency [*Group opposing sex education in schools*]
**MotorIntnl** ... Motor Report International [*A publication*]
**Motoris Agr** ... Motorisation Agricole [*A publication*]
**Motor M**.... Motor Manual [*A publication*] (APTA)
**Motorola Tech Dev** ... Motorola Technical Developments [*A publication*]
**Motorola Tech Disclosure Bull** ... Motorola Technical Disclosure Bulletin [*A publication*]
**Motor Serv (Chicago)** ... Motor Service (Chicago) [*A publication*]
**Motor T**..... Motor Trend [*A publication*]
**Motortech Z** ... Motortechnische Zeitschrift [*A publication*]
**Motor Trade J** ... Motor Trade Journal [*A publication*] (APTA)
**Motor Transp** ... Motor Transport [*A publication*]

**MOTP**....... Manufacturing or Testing Process (KSC)
**MOTP**....... Medical Officer Training Plan [*Canada*]
**MOTPICT**... Motion Picture
**MoTr**......... Grundy County-Jewett Norris Library, Trenton, MO [*Library symbol*] [*Library of Congress*] (LCLS)
**MOTR**....... Motor Club of America [*NASDAQ symbol*] (NQ)
**Mo Trade & Shipping R**... Monthly Trade and Shipping Review [*A publication*] (APTA)
**MOTS**....... Mend Our Tongues Society (EA)
**MOTS**....... Metal Oxide Threshold Switches (MCD)
**MOTS**....... Minitrack Optical Tracking Station [*or System*] [*NASA*]
**MOTS**....... Missile Operability Test Station (MCD)
**MOTS**....... Mobile Optical Tracking System
**MOTS**....... Module Test Set
**Mot Ship**.... Motor Ship [*A publication*]
**Mot Sk**....... Motor Skills. Theory into Practice [*A publication*]
**MOTSU**...... Military Ocean Terminal, Sunny Point (AABC)
**MOTT**....... Mycobacteria Other Than Tubercle Bacilli
**Mot Trader**... Motor Trader [*A publication*] (APTA)
**MOTU**....... Mobile Operational Training Unit (MCD)
**MOTU**....... Mobile Optical Tracking Unit (MCD)
**MOTU**....... Mobile Ordnance Technical Unit [*Military*] (CAAL)
**MOTU**....... Mobile Technical Unit (NG)
**MOU**......... Memorandum of Understanding
**mou**............ Missouri [*MARC country of publication code*] [*Library of Congress*] (LCCP)
**MOU**......... Motor Business [*A publication*]
**MOU**......... Mountain Village [*Alaska*] [*Airport symbol*] (OAG)
**Mou**............ Mouse [*Data processing*] (PCM)
**MOU**......... Southwest Missouri State University, Springfield, MO [*OCLC symbol*] (OCLC)
**MoU**........... University of Missouri, Columbia, MO [*Library symbol*] [*Library of Congress*] (LCLS)
**MoU-D**...... University of Missouri, School of Dentistry, Kansas City, MO [*Library symbol*] [*Library of Congress*] (LCLS)
**MOUG**...... Map Online Users Group (EA)
**Moult Ch**... Moulton's New York Chancery Practice [*A publication*] (DLA)
**Moult Ch P**... Moulton's New York Chancery Practice [*A publication*] (DLA)
**MoU-M**..... University of Missouri, Medical Library, Kansas City, MO [*Library symbol*] [*Library of Congress*] (LCLS)
**MO Univ Eng Exp Stn Eng Repr Ser**... Missouri University. Engineering Experiment Station. Engineering Reprint Series [*A publication*]
**MO Univ Sch Mines Metall Bull Gen Ser**... Missouri University. School of Mines and Metallurgy. Bulletin. General Series [*A publication*]
**Mountain Geol**... Mountain Geologist [*A publication*]
**Mount Plains Libr Q**... Mountain Plains Library Association. Quarterly [*A publication*]
**MOUS**....... Multiple Occurrences of Unexplained Symptoms [*Medicine*]
**MO U Sch Mines & Met Bul Tech Ser**... University of Missouri. School of Mines and Metallurgy. Bulletin. Technical Series [*A publication*]
**MOUSE**.... Minimum Orbital Unmanned Satellite of the Earth
**MoU-St**...... University of Missouri at St. Louis, St. Louis, MO [*Library symbol*] [*Library of Congress*] (LCLS)
**MOUT**....... Military Operations on Urbanized Terrain (MCD)
**MOUTH**... Modular Output Unit for Talking to Humans
**Mouth**......... Mouth of the Dragon [*A publication*]
**Mo Utopia**... Modern Utopia [*A publication*]
**MOUTRE**... Mission Oriented Unit Training by Echelon [*Military*] (INF)
**MoU-V**...... University of Missouri, Veterinary Medicine Library, Columbia, MO [*Library symbol*] [*Library of Congress*] (LCLS)
**Mouvement Soc**... Mouvement Social [*A publication*]
**Mouvement Synd Mond**... Mouvement Syndical Mondial [*A publication*]
**Mouv Soc**... Mouvement Social [*A publication*]
**MOV**.......... Main Oxidizer Valve (KSC)
**MOV**.......... Manned Orbiting Vehicle [*NASA*]
**MOV**.......... Manuscript on Vellum
**MOV**.......... Mass of Vehicle
**MOV**.......... Materiel Obligation Validation (AFIT)
**MOV**.......... Metal-Oxide Varistor
**MOV**.......... Military-Owned Vehicle
**MOV**.......... Monclova, MX [*Location identifier*] [*FAA*] (FAAL)
**MOV**.......... Monument Valley, UT [*Location identifier*] [*FAA*] (FAAL)
**MOV**.......... Moranbah [*Australia*] [*Airport symbol*] (OAG)
**MOV**.......... Morovis [*Puerto Rico*] [*Seismograph station code, US Geological Survey*] (SEIS)
**MOV**.......... Moshassuck Valley Railroad Co. [*AAR code*]
**MOV**.......... Motor-Operated Valve (NRCH)
**MOV**.......... Movable [*Technical drawings*]
**MOV**.......... Movement (AABC)
**Mov**............ Movoznavstvo [*A publication*]
**MOV**.......... Stephens College, Columbia, MO [*OCLC symbol*] (OCLC)
**MOVB**....... Mitteilungen. Oesterreichischer Verein fuer Bibliothekwesen [*A publication*]
**MOVBW**... Mitteilungen. Oesterreichischer Verein fuer Bibliothekwesen [*A publication*]
**MOVCO**.... Movement Control Organisation [*British military*] (DMA)
**MOVDHHG**... Movement of Dependents and Household Goods in Advance of Permanent Change of Station Orders is Authorized [*Army*] (AABC)
**MOVE**....... Manage Old Vehicles Easily [*Performance Data Services, Inc.*] [*Software*]
**MOVE**....... Management of Value Engineering
**MOVE**....... Peregrine Entertainment Ltd. [*NASDAQ symbol*] (NQ)
**MOVECAP**... Movement Capabilities [*Military*] (CINC)
**MOVEM**... Movement Overseas Verification of Enlisted Members [*Army*] (AABC)
**MOVEREP**... Movement Report [*Military*] (NATG)
**Movietone**.. Movietone News [*A publication*]
**Movietone N**... Movietone News [*A publication*]
**Mov Im**...... Moving Image [*A publication*]
**MOVIMS**... Motor Vehicle Information Management System [*Bell System*]
**MOVLAS**... Manually Operated Visual Landing Aid System (NG)
**Mov M**....... Movie Maker [*A publication*]
**MOVMT**... Movement
**MOV Nachr**... MOV [*Marine-Offizier-Vereinigung*] Nachrichten [*A publication*]
**Mov Operaio Soc**... Movimento Operaio e Socialista [*A publication*]
**MOVORD**... Movement Order [*Military*] (NVT)
**MOVP**....... Military-Owned Vehicle Plan (AFM)
**MO-VPE**.... Metal-Organic Vapor Phase Epitaxy [*Also, MO-CVD, OM-CVD, OM-VPE*] [*Semiconductor technology*]
**MOVPER**... Supreme Council, Mystic Order Veiled Prophets of Enchanted Realm (EA)
**MOVREP**... Movement Report [*Military*] (NVT)
**MOVS**....... Military-Owned Vehicle Service (AABC)
**MOVSUM**... [*Daily*] Movement Summary [*Navy*] (NVT)
**MOVT**....... Movement [*Music*] (ROG)
**MOVY**....... New Star Entertainment, Inc. [*Beverly Hills, CA*] [*NASDAQ symbol*] (NQ)
**MOW**........ Meals on Wheels
**MOW**........ Ministry of Works [*British*] (MCD)
**MOW**........ Mission Operation Wing [*NASA*] (KSC)
**MOW**........ Montana Western Railway [*AAR code*]
**MOW**........ Moscow [*USSR*] [*Airport symbol*] (OAG)
**MOW**........ Movie of the Week [*Television programming*]
**MOW**........ Westminster College, Fulton, MO [*OCLC symbol*] (OCLC)
**MOWAM**... Mobile Water Mine (MCD)
**MoWarbT**... Central Missouri State University, Warrensburg, MO [*Library symbol*] [*Library of Congress*] (LCLS)
**MoWarbTR**... Trails Regional Library, Johnson County-Lafayette County Library, Warrensburg, MO [*Library symbol*] [*Library of Congress*] (LCLS)
**MOWASP**... Mechanization of Warehousing and Shipment Procedures [*or Processing*] [*Defense Supply Agency*]
**MOWB**...... Ministry of Works and Buildings [*British*]
**MOWBC**... Winnipeg Bible College, Otterburne, Manitoba [*Library symbol*] [*National Library of Canada*] (NLC)
**MoWgK**..... Saint Louis Roman Catholic Theological [*Kenrick*] Seminary, Webster Groves, MO [*Library symbol*] [*Library of Congress*] (LCLS)
**MoWgT**..... Eden Theological Seminary, Webster Groves, MO [*Library symbol*] [*Library of Congress*] (LCLS)
**MoWgW**.... Webster College, Webster Groves, MO [*Library symbol*] [*Library of Congress*] (LCLS)
**MoWitt**...... Mobile Window Thermal Test Facility [*Berkeley, CA*] [*Lawrence Berkeley Laboratory*] [*Department of Energy*] (GRD)
**Mo W Jur**.. Monthly Western Jurist [*A publication*] (DLA)
**MOWS**...... Manned Orbital Weapon Station [*or System*]
**Mow St**....... Mowbray's Styles of Deeds [*A publication*] (DLA)
**MOWT**...... Ministry of War Transport [*Terminated, 1956*] [*British*]
**MOWW**..... Military Order of the World Wars (EA)
**MOX**.......... Mixed Oxide [*Fuel*]
**MOX**.......... Morris, MN [*Location identifier*] [*FAA*] (FAAL)
**MOX**.......... Moxa [*German Democratic Republic*] [*Seismograph station code, US Geological Survey*] (SEIS)
**MOX**.......... Moxalactam [*An antibiotic*]
**MOXA**....... Moxa Energy Corp. [*NASDAQ symbol*] (NQ)
**MOXE**....... Moxie Industries, Inc. [*NASDAQ symbol*] (NQ)
**MOXIE**..... Men Organized to X-press Indignant Exasperation [*Seattle group opposing below-the-knee fashions introduced in 1970*]
**MOXY**....... Model X-Y [*AEC computer code*]
**MOY**.......... Mahogany Minerals [*Vancouver Stock Exchange symbol*]
**MOY**.......... Mondy [*USSR*] [*Seismograph station code, US Geological Survey*] (SEIS)
**MOY**.......... Money
**MOY**.......... Salt Lake City, UT [*Location identifier*] [*FAA*] (FAAL)
**Moyle**......... Moyle's Criminal Circulars [*India*] [*A publication*] (DLA)
**Moyle**......... Moyle's Entries [*1658*] [*England*] [*A publication*] (DLA)
**MOZ**.......... Missouri Southern State College, Library, Joplin, MO [*OCLC symbol*] (OCLC)
**MOZ**.......... Moorea Island [*French Polynesia*] [*Airport symbol*] (OAG)
**MOZ**.......... Mozambique [*ANSI three-letter standard code*] (CNC)
**Moz**............ [*Petrus Nicolaus*] Mozzius [*Flourished, 16th century*] [*Authority cited in pre-1607 legal work*] (DSA)

**Mozambique Serv Geol Minas Ser Geol Minas Mem Commun Bol** ... Mozambique. Servicos de Geologia e Minas. Serie de Geologia e Minas. Memorias e Communicacoes. Boletim [*A publication*]
**MozartJb** ... Mozart-Jahrbuch [*A publication*]
**Moz Jb** ....... Mozart-Jahrbuch [*A publication*]
**MOZL** ....... Military Order of the Zouave Legion of the United States (EA)
**Mozley & W** ... Mozley and Whiteley's Law Dictionary [*A publication*] (DLA)
**Mozley & Whiteley** ... Mozley and Whiteley's Law Dictionary [*A publication*] (DLA)
**MOZLUS** ... Military Order of the Zouave Legion of the US (EA)
**Moz & W** ... Mozley and Whiteley's Law Dictionary [*A publication*] (DLA)
**MP** ............ All India Reporter, Madhya Pradesh [*A publication*] (DLA)
**Mp** ............ Import [*Economics*]
**MP** ............ Machine Pressed
**MP** ............ Maciej Poleski [*Pen name of Polish author, Czeslaw Bielecki*]
**MP** ............ Mackenzie Pilot [*Canada*] [*A publication*]
**MP** ............ Macroprocessor
**MP** ............ Madonna Plan (EA)
**MP** ............ Magnetic Particle
**MP** ............ Magnetic Pressure (NVT)
**MP** ............ Magnetopause [*In a magnetic field*]
**M/P** ............ Mail Payment [*Banking*]
**M/P** ............ Main Parachute (MCD)
**MP** ............ Main Phase (IEEE)
**MP** ............ Mains Propres [*Personal Delivery*] [*French*]
**MP** ............ Maintainability Plan
**MP** ............ Maintenance Panel (AAG)
**MP** ............ Maintenance Period
**MP** ............ Maintenance Plan
**MP** ............ Maintenance Point
**MP** ............ Maintenance Prints
**MP** ............ Maintenance Procedure (MCD)
**MP** ............ Maintenance Program
**MP** ............ Maitre Phonetique [*A publication*]
**MP** ............ Major Program (CAAL)
**MP** ............ Mallinckrodt, Inc. [*Research code symbol*]
**MP** ............ Management Package (NASA)
**MP** ............ Management Plan
**M-P** ............ Mandat-Poste [*Money Order*] [*French*]
**MP** ............ Manifold Pressure
**MP** ............ Manpower
**MP** ............ Manpower and Personnel (MCD)
**MP** ............ Mansfield Park [*Novel by Jane Austen*]
**MP** ............ Manu Propria [*In documents, after king's signature*] [*Italian*]
**MP** ............ Manual Proportional [*Attitude control system of Mercury spacecraft*]
**MP** ............ Manual Pulser
**MP** ............ Manufacturing Process
**MP** ............ Marginal Physical Product [*Economics*]
**MP** ............ Marginal Product
**MP** ............ Marine Police
**MP** ............ Marine Pollution
**MP** ............ Marine Provost [*British military*] (DMA)
**MP** ............ Maritime Patrol (NATG)
**MP** ............ Maritime Polar Air Mass
**MP** ............ Maritime Policy [*British*] (ROG)
**MP** ............ Market Price [*Business term*]
**MP** ............ Marshall's Posse (EA)
**MP** ............ Martainair Holland NV [*ICAO designator*] (FAAC)
**MP** ............ Masinnyj Perevod Trudy Instituta Tocnoj Mechaniki i Vycislitel Hoj Techniki Akademiy Nauk SSR [*A publication*]
**MP** ............ Mass Properties (MCD)
**MP** ............ Massa Pilularum [*A Pill Mass*] [*Pharmacy*] (ROG)
**MP** ............ Massorah Parva [*or Massora Parva*] (BJA)
**MP** ............ Master of Painting
**MP** ............ Master Pointer [*Data processing*] (BYTE)
**MP** ............ Match Problems [*Research test*] [*Psychology*]
**MP** ............ Material Pass (AAG)
**M & P** ........ Material and Process
**MP** ............ Mathematical Programming [*Data processing*]
**MP** ............ Matthew Pelosi [*Designer's mark when appearing on US coins*]
**MP** ............ Maturity Phase
**MP** ............ Maxillary Process
**MP** ............ Maximum Flowering Period [*Botany*]
**M/P** ............ Maximum Performance [*Automotive engineering*]
**MP** ............ McIntyre Mines Ltd. [*Formerly, McIntyre Porcupine Mines Ltd.*] [*NYSE symbol*] [*Toronto Stock Exchange symbol*] (SPSG)
**MP** ............ Measurement Pipette
**MP** ............ Measuring Point (NASA)
**MP** ............ Mechanical Paper
**MP** ............ Mechanical Part
**MP** ............ Mechanical Printer
**MP** ............ Media Processor [*Data processing*] (BUR)
**MP** ............ Media Project (EA)
**MP** ............ Medial Pallium [*Neuroanatomy*]
**MP** ............ Medical Payment [*Insurance*]
**MP** ............ Medical Press and Circular [*A publication*]
**MP** ............ Medium Pressure
**MP** ............ Meeting Point [*Military*]
**MP** ............ Melchor Developments Ltd. [*Toronto Stock Exchange symbol*]
**MP** ............ Melphalan, Prednisone [*Antineoplastic drug regimen*]
**MP** ............ Melting Point
**MP** ............ Melting Pot
**MP** ............ Member of Parliament [*British*]
**MP** ............ Member of Police
**M/P** ............ Memorandum of Partnership [*Business term*]
**MP** ............ Menstrual Period [*Medicine*]
**MP** ............ Mental Process [*Work-factor system*]
**MP** ............ Mentum Posterior [*In reference to the chin*]
**MP** ............ Mercaptopurine [*Purinethol*] [*Also, M, P*] [*Antineoplastic drug*]
**MP** ............ Meridional Part [*Navigation*]
**MP** ............ Mesiopulpal [*Dentistry*]
**MP** ............ Metacarpophalangeal [*Anatomy*]
**M-P** ............ Metal or Plastic (AAG)
**MP** ............ Metal-Powder [*Videotape*]
**MP** ............ Metatarsophalangeal [*Anatomy*]
**MP** ............ Meteorology Panel (MCD)
**MP** ............ Methodist Protestant
**MP** ............ Methods and Phenomena [*Elsevier Book Series*] [*A publication*]
**MP** ............ Methoxypsoralen [*Also, MOP*] [*Pharmacology*]
**MP** ............ Methyl Palmoxirate [*Organic chemistry*]
**MP** ............ Methyl Parathion [*Also, MEP, MPN*] [*Pesticide*]
**MP** ............ Methylprednisolone [*Endocrinology*]
**MP** ............ Methylpurine [*Organic chemistry*]
**MP** ............ Metropolitan Police
**MP** ............ Mexican Peso [*Monetary unit*]
**MP** ............ Mezzo Piano [*Moderately Soft*] [*Music*]
**m/p** ............ Mi Pagare [*My Promissory Note*] [*Business term*] [*Spanish*]
**MP** ............ Michoud Plant [*NASA*] (MCD)
**M(P)** ........... Microfilm (Positive)
**MP** ............ Microprint
**MP** ............ Microprocessor [*Instrumentation*]
**MP** ............ Microprogram
**MP** ............ Mid-Phase
**MP** ............ Middle Point
**MP** ............ Midland Plant [*Nuclear energy*] (NRCH)
**MP** ............ Midline Precursor [*Cytology*]
**MP** ............ Mile-Post
**MP** ............ Military Pay (AFM)
**MP** ............ Military Police [*Army*]
**MP** ............ Military Prohibitionist [*Slang*]
**MP** ............ Military Property (MCD)
**M/P** ............ Milk/Plasma [*Ratio*] [*Physiology*]
**MP** ............ Millia Passuum [*1,000 Paces; the Roman mile*]
**MP** ............ [*The*] Mini Page [*A newspaper supplement*]
**MP** ............ Minimum Phase (IEEE)
**MP** ............ Minimum Premium [*Insurance*]
**MP** ............ Minister Plenipotentiary
**MP** ............ Minuteman Platform
**MP** ............ Minutes Played [*Hockey*]
**MP** ............ Miscellaneous Paper [*or Publication*]
**MP** ............ Missile Platform
**MP** ............ Missile Positioning
**MP** ............ Missing Perforation [*Philately*]
**MP** ............ Missing Person
**MP** ............ Mission Payload (MCD)
**MP** ............ Mission Planner (MCD)
**MP** ............ Mission Profile (MCD)
**MP** ............ Missouri Pacific Railroad Co. [*AAR code*]
**MP** ............ Mistress of Philosophy
**MP** ............ Mixed Pattern
**MP** ............ Mixed Population
**MP** ............ Mobilization Plan
**MP** ............ Modern Packaging [*A publication*]
**MP** ............ Modern Philology [*A publication*]
**MP** ............ Modo Praescripto [*In the Manner Prescribed*] [*Pharmacy*]
**MP** ............ Modus Ponens [*Rule of inference*] [*Logic*] [*Latin*]
**MP** ............ Monetary Policy
**mp** ............ Mongolia [*MARC country of publication code*] [*Library of Congress*] (LCCP)
**MP** ............ Monitor Panel
**MP** ............ Monitor Printer (CET)
**MP** ............ [*The*] Month in Parliament [*A publication*] [*British*]
**M/P** ............ Months after Payment [*Business term*]
**MP** ............ Monumentum Posuit [*Erected a Monument*] [*Latin*]
**M & P** ........ Moore and Payne's English Common Pleas Reports [*A publication*] (DLA)
**MP** ............ Mooring Pipe [*or Post*] (ADA)
**M/P** ............ Morjumiid-Pterocephalid Boundary [*Paleogeologic boundary*]
**MP** ............ Mortgage-Participation Certificate [*Investment term*]
**MP** ............ Mortgage Payment in Full
**MP** ............ Motherland Party [*Anatavan Partisi*] [*Turkey*] [*Political party*] (PPW)
**MP** ............ Motion Picture Production [*Navy*]
**MP** ............ Motor Potential
**MP** ............ Mounted Police

**MP**............ Mouvement Populaire [*Popular Movement*] [*Morocco*] [*Political party*] (PPW)
**MP**............ Movement Protein [*Cytology*]
**MP**............ Mucopeptide [*Biochemistry*]
**MP**............ Mucopolysaccharide [*Also, MPS*] [*Clinical chemistry*]
**MP**............ Multiparous [*Obstetrics*]
**MP**............ Multiperil [*Insurance*]
**MP**............ Multiple Processor [*or Multiprocessing*] [*Data processing*] (BUR)
**MP**............ Multiplier Phototube
**MP**............ Multipole
**MP**............ Multipurpose
**MP**............ Municipal Police
**M/P**............ Muscle Plasma [*Ratio*]
**MP**............ My Pal [*Slang*]
**MP**............ Mycoplasma Pneumonia [*Medicine*]
**MP**............ Northern Mariana Islands [*ANSI two-letter standard code*] (CNC)
**MP**............ Pinawa Public Library, Manitoba [*Library symbol*] [*National Library of Canada*] (NLC)
**MPA**............ American Review of Public Administration [*A publication*]
**MPA**............ Magazine Publishers of America [*New York, NY*] [*Database producer*] (IID)
**MPA**............ Main Propulsion Assistant
**MPA**............ Main Pulmonary Artery [*Anatomy*]
**MPA**............ Man-Powered Aircraft
**MPA**............ Management Professionals Association [*Madras, India*] (EA)
**MPA**............ Manpower and Personnel Administration [*Military*] [*British*]
**MPA**............ Maritime Patrol Aircraft (NATG)
**MPA**............ Marketing and Promotion Association [*British*]
**MPA**............ Maryland & Pennsylvania Railroad Co. [*AAR code*]
**M Pa**............ Master of Painting
**MPA**............ Master Personnel Administration
**MPA**............ Master Printers of America (EA)
**MPA**............ Master of Professional Accountancy [*or Accounting*]
**MPA**............ Master of Professional Arts
**MPA**............ Master Project Assignment (MCD)
**MPA**............ Master of Public Administration
**MPA**............ Master of Public Affairs
**MPA**............ Mechanical Packing Association [*Later, Fluid Sealing Association*] (EA)
**MPA**............ Medical Procurement Agency
**MPA**............ Medroxyprogesterone Acetate [*Also, MAP*] [*Endocrinology*]
**MPa**............ Megapascal
**MPA**............ Mercaptopropionic Acid [*Organic chemistry*]
**MPA**............ Metal Powder Association [*Later, MPIF*]
**MPA**............ Methacrylate Producers Association (EA)
**MPA**............ Methoxypropylamine [*Organic chemistry*]
**MPA**............ Methylphosphoric Acid [*Organic chemistry*]
**MPA**............ Michigan CPA [*Certified Public Accountant*] [*A publication*]
**MPA**............ Microwave Power Amplifier
**MPA**............ Mid Pacific Airlines, Inc. [*Honolulu, HI*] [*FAA designator*] (FAAC)
**MPA**............ Midwestern Psychological Association (MCD)
**MPA**............ Military Pay Account
**MPA**............ Military Pay and Allowance
**MPA**............ Military Pay Area (AFM)
**MPA**............ Military Personnel Appropriation (AFM)
**MPA**............ Military Personnel, Army
**MPA**............ Military Police Association [*Defunct*] (EA)
**MPA**............ Military Proposal and Analysis
**mPa**............ Millipascal [*Unit of pressure*]
**MPA**............ Miniature Photocell Activator
**MPA**............ Miniature Piston Actuator (MCD)
**MPA**............ Missile Procurement, Army (AABC)
**MPA**............ Mission Performance Assessment [*NASA*] (KSC)
**MPA**............ Mission Phase Analysis
**MPA**............ Mission Profile Analysis
**MPA**............ Missionary Pilots Association [*Defunct*] (EA)
**MPA**............ Mobile Press Association (EA)
**MPA**............ Models and Photographers of America (EA)
**MPA**............ Modern Poetry Association (EA)
**MPA**............ Modification Proposal and Analysis (MCD)
**MPA**............ Molybdeophosphoric Acid [*Inorganic chemistry*]
**MPA**............ Moose Pass [*Alaska*] [*Seismograph station code, US Geological Survey*] (SEIS)
**MPA**............ Mortar Package Assembly
**MPA**............ Motion Picture Alliance
**MPA**............ Multiplant Action [*Nuclear energy*] (NRCH)
**MPA**............ Multiple Parameter Analysis
**MPA**............ Multiple-Period Average (IEEE)
**MPA**............ Multiple Peripheral Adapter
**MPA**............ Multiprecision Arithmetic
**MPA**............ Museum Publications of America
**MPA**............ Music Publishers' Association of the United States (EA)
**MPA**............ Mycophenolic Acid [*Biochemistry*]
**MPA**............ Nampa, ID [*Location identifier*] [*FAA*] (FAAL)
**MPAA**........ Motion Picture Association of America (EA)
**MPAB**........ Military Petroleum Advisory Board
**MPAC**........ Impact Systems, Inc. [*NASDAQ symbol*] (NQ)
**MPAC**........ Military Pay and Allowance Committee (AFM)
**MPACS**..... Management Planning and Control System [*IBM Corp.*]
**MPAD**....... Manpower Personnel Assignment Document (AFM)
**MPAD**....... Maximum Permissible Accumulated Dose [*of radiation*] (ADA)
**M Pad**........ Memorie. Reale Accademia di Scienze, Lettere, ed Arti di Padova [*A publication*]
**MPAD**....... Menlo Park Applications Development [*IBM Corp.*]
**MPAD**....... Mission Planning and Analysis Division [*NASA*]
**MP Adm**.... Master of Public Administration
**MPAI**......... Maximum Permissible Annual Intake [*Radiation*] (NRCH)
**MPAI**......... Mid Pacific Air Corp. [*NASDAQ symbol*] (NQ)
**MPAIAC**... Movimiento para la Autodeterminacion y Independencia del Archipielago Canario [*Movement for the Self-Determination and Independence of the Canary Archipelago*] [*Canary Islands*] [*Spanish*] (PD)
**MPAJA**..... Malayan People's Anti-Japanese Army [*World War II*]
**MPAJU**..... Malayan People's Anti-Japanese Union [*World War II*]
**MPAM**...... Maritime Polar Air Mass (MSA)
**MPAMA**... Milk Products Advertising-Merchandising Association (EA)
**MPAP**....... Mean Pulmonary Artery Pressure [*Cardiology*]
**MPAPS**..... Motivation and Potential for Adoptive Parenthood Scale [*Psychology*]
**MPAR**....... Maintenance Program Analysis Report
**MPAR**....... Microprogram Address Register
**MP Arkansas Univ Coop Ext** ... MP - University of Arkansas. Cooperative Extension Service [*A publication*]
**MPAS**........ Maritime Patrol Airship Study
**MPAS**........ Maryland Parent Attitude Survey [*Psychology*]
**MPASS**..... Modular Processing and Support System
**MPast**........ Master in Pastoral Studies
**MPAT**........ Multipurpose All-Terrain Vehicle
**MPATI**...... Midwest Program for Airborne Television Instruction [*Defunct*]
**MPB**.......... Berkshire Athenaeum, Pittsfield, MA [*Library symbol*] [*Library of Congress*] (LCLS)
**MPB**.......... Machine-Pressed Bales
**MPB**.......... Magnetic Particle Brake
**MPB**.......... Maine Potato Board (EA)
**MPB**.......... Maintenance Parts Breakdown (KSC)
**MPB**.......... Male-Pattern Baldness
**MPB**.......... Master of Physical Biology
**MPB**.......... Material Performance Branch [*Air Force*]
**MPB**.......... Materials Properties Branch [*Army*] (RDA)
**MPB**.......... Matrix Program Board
**MPB**.......... Mechanically Processed Beef [*Food technology*]
**MPB**.......... Merit Promotion Bulletin [*Military*]
**MPB**.......... Metropolitan Circuits, Inc. [*AMEX symbol*] (SPSG)
**MPB**.......... Miami [*Florida*] Public Seaplane Base [*Airport symbol*] (OAG)
**MPB**.......... Miniature Precision Bearing, Inc.
**MPB**.......... Missing Persons Bureau
**MPB**.......... Montpelier & Barre Railroad Co. [*Later, MB*] [*AAR code*]
**MPB**.......... Motorized Pontoon Bridge (MCD)
**MPB**.......... Mouvement Progressiste de Burundi [*Progressive Movement of Burundi*]
**MPB**.......... Multilayer Printed Board
**MPB**.......... Munitions Packaging Branch [*Picatinny Arsenal*] [*Army*] (RDA)
**MPB**.......... Musica Popular Brasileira [*Pop music*]
**MPBA**........ Machine Printers' Beneficial Association [*Later, MPEA*]
**MPBB**........ Maximum Permissible Body Burden [*Radiation*]
**MPBB**........ Methyl(phenyl)(butyl)barbituric (Acid) [*Biochemistry*]
**MPBC**........ Berkshire Community College, Pittsfield, MA [*Library symbol*] [*Library of Congress*] (LCLS)
**MPBDS**..... Material Properties Bibliographic Data System [*Purdue University*] [*Database*]
**MPBE**........ Molten Plutonium Burn-Up Experiment [*Nuclear energy*] (IEEE)
**MPBL**........ Berkshire Law Library Association, Pittsfield, MA [*Library symbol*] [*Library of Congress*] (LCLS)
**MP Bl**........ Muensterisches Pastoralblatt [*A publication*]
**MP Bl**........ Musikpaedagogische Blaetter [*A publication*]
**MPBME**.... Munitions Production Base Modernization, Expansion (RDA)
**MPBN**........ Military Police Battalion
**MPBO**........ Bocas Del Toro [*Panama*] [*ICAO location identifier*] (ICLI)
**MPBP**........ Mechanically Processed Beef Product [*Food technology*]
**MPBP**........ Metal Polishers, Buffers, Platers, and Allied Workers International Union (EA)
**MPBR**........ Multipunch Bar
**MPBS**........ Medical Pocket-Book Series [*A publication*]
**MPBS**........ Multipurpose Bayonet System [*Army*] (INF)
**MPBW**....... Ministry of Public Building and Works [*Later, DOE*] [*British*]
**MPC**.......... Machine Punch Card
**MPC**.......... Magnetic Particle Clutch
**MPC**.......... Maharashtra Prajatantra Congress [*India*] [*Political party*] (PPW)
**MPC**.......... Maharashtra Progressive Congress [*India*] [*Political party*] (PPW)
**MPC**.......... Maidstone Paper Converters [*Commercial firm*] [*British*]
**MPC**.......... Maine Potato Council [*Later, MPB*] (EA)
**MPC**.......... Maintenance Parts Catalog
**MP & C**...... Maintenance Planning and Control (MCD)

**MPC** .......... Maintenance Policy Council [*DoD*] [*Washington, DC*]
**MPC** .......... Maintenance Priority Code
**MPC** .......... Maintenance Procedure Chart
**MPC** .......... Mandatory Product Control
**MPC** .......... Manpower and Personnel Council [*DoD*]
**MPC** .......... Manpower Planning Council
**MPC** .......... Manpower Priorities Committee
**MPC** .......... Manual Pointing Controller (MCD)
**MPC** .......... Manufacturing Plan Change
**MPC** .......... Manufacturing, Planning, and Control
**MPC** .......... Marco Polo Club (EA)
**MPC** .......... Marginal Propensity to Consume [*Economics*]
**MPC** .......... Marine Protein Concentrate [*See also FPC*] (MSC)
**MPC** .......... Marker Pulse Conversion [*Telecommunications*] (TEL)
**MPC** .......... Market Performance Committee [*of NYSE*]
**MPC** .......... Master Parts Card
**MPC** .......... Master Phasing Chart (MCD)
**MPC** .......... Master Program Chart (MCD)
**MPC** .......... Materials Preparation Center [*Ames, IA*] [*Ames Laboratory*] [*Department of Energy*] (GRD)
**MPC** .......... Materials Processing Center [*Massachusetts Institute of Technology*] [*Research center*] (RCD)
**MPC** .......... Materials Properties Council (EA)
**MPC** .......... Materiel Program Code [*Air Force*] (AFM)
**MPC** .......... Maximum Permissible Concentration [*Later, RCG*] [*Radiation*]
**MPC** .......... Mechanical Positioning Control
**MPC** .......... Mechanized Production Control
**MPC** .......... Medical Press and Circular [*A publication*]
**MPC** .......... Megaparsec
**MPC** .......... Member of Parliament of Canada
**MPC** .......... Member Pickwick Club [*From "The Pickwick Papers" by Charles Dickens*]
**MPC** .......... Membrane Protein Complex [*Cytology*]
**MPC** .......... Memory Protection Check (MCD)
**MPC** .......... Meperidine, Promethazine, and Chlorpromazine [*Drug regime*]
**MPC** .......... Merleau-Ponty Circle (EA)
**MPC** .......... Message Processing Center
**MPC** .......... Metal Pi Complexes [*Elsevier Book Series*] [*A publication*]
**MPc** .......... Metallophthalocyanine [*Organic chemistry*]
**MPC** .......... Meteorological Prediction Center (KSC)
**MPC** .......... Metromedia Producers Corporation [*Secaucus, NJ*]
**MPC** .......... Microcircuit Power Converter
**MPC** .......... Microparticle Concentration [*Analytical chemistry*]
**MPC** .......... Microprogram Control
**MPC** .......... Micropurulent Cervicitis [*Medicine*]
**MPC** .......... Midbody Pyro Controller (NASA)
**MPC** .......... Midwest Parentcraft Center (EA)
**MPC** .......... Military Payment Certificate
**MPC** .......... Military Personnel Center (AFM)
**MPC** .......... Military Pioneer Corps [*British*]
**MPC** .......... Military Police Corps
**MPC** .......... Military Postal Clerk (AFM)
**MPC** .......... Military Property Custodian (AFIT)
**Mpc** .......... Million Parsecs [*Interstellar space measure*]
**MPC** .......... Miniature Protector Connector [*Telecommunications*] (TEL)
**MPC** .......... Minimal Flight Planning Charts [*Air Force*]
**MPC** .......... Minimum Protozoacidal Concentration
**MPC** .......... Minor Planet Center [*Smithsonian Institution*]
**MPC** .......... Mission Planning Center (MCD)
**MPC** .......... Mission Profile Course (MCD)
**MPC** .......... Mississippi Library Commission, Jackson, MS [*OCLC symbol*] (OCLC)
**MPC** .......... Mitsubishi Petrochemical Company [*Tokyo, Japan*]
**MPC** .......... Mobile Processing Center (MCD)
**MPC** .......... Mode and Power Control [*Aviation*]
**MPC** .......... Model Predictive Control [*Chemical engineering*]
**MPC** .......... Modular Peripheral Interface Converter
**MPC** .......... Monagas Pipeline Crude [*Petrochemical engineering*]
**MPC** .......... Monterey Peninsula College [*California*]
**MPC** .......... Montreal Presbyterian College
**MPC** .......... Moore's English Privy Council Cases [*A publication*] (DLA)
**MPC** .......... Morphine Positive Control [*Epidemiology*]
**MPC** .......... Motion Picture Camera (MCD)
**MPC** .......... Motion Picture Control Panel (MSA)
**MPC** .......... Mouse Myeloma Cell [*Cell biology*]
**MPC** .......... Mouvement Patriotique Congolais [*Congo Patriotic Movement*] [*Political party*]
**MPC** .......... Movable Platform Configuration
**MPC** .......... Multi-Party Conference [*Namibia*] [*Political party*] (PPW)
**MPC** .......... Multipath Core
**MPC** .......... Multiple Process Chart
**MPC** .......... Multiple-Profile Configuration (MCD)
**MPC** .......... Multiple-Purpose Communications (NG)
**MPC** .......... Multiprocessor Computer
**MPC** .......... Multiprogram Control [*Data processing*]
**MPC** .......... Multipurpose Center
**MPC** .......... Multipurpose Computer (CMD)
**MPC** .......... Multispectral Photographic Camera (KSC)
**MPCA** ....... Magnetic Powder Core Association (EA)
**MPCA** ....... Markham Prayer Card Apostolate (EA)
**MPCA** ....... Melanin-Producing Cell Autoantibody [*Endocrinology*]
**MPCA** ....... Miniature Pinscher Club of America (EA)
**MPCABS** .. Michigan Project for Computer-Assisted Biblical Studies [*University of Michigan*] [*Information service or system*] (IID)
**MPCAG** .... Military Parts Control Advisory Group [*DoD*]
**MPCB** ........ Minuteman Parts Control Board [*Missiles*]
**MPCB** ........ Multilayer Printed Circuit Board
**MPCC** ........ Manufacturing Planning Change Coordination (MCD)
**MPCC** ........ Material Purchase Contracts Control
**MPCC** ........ Multiprocessor Computer Complex
**MPCC** ........ Multiprotocol Communications Controller
**MPCCC** ...... Metropolitan Post Card Collectors Club (EA)
**MPCD** ....... Manufacturing Process Control Document (KSC)
**MPCD** ....... Minimum Perceptible Color Difference
**MPCD** ....... Mouvement Populaire Constitutionnel Democratique [*Popular Democratic Constitutional Movement*] [*Morocco*] [*Political party*] (PPW)
**MPCD** ....... Multipurpose Color Display
**MPCE** ........ Music Publishers Contact Employees
**MPCF** ........ Campo De Francia/Enrique A. Jimenez [*Panama*] [*ICAO location identifier*] (ICLI)
**MPCFP** ..... Canadian Food Products Development Center, Portage La Prairie, Manitoba [*Library symbol*] [*National Library of Canada*] (NLC)
**MPCH** ....... Changuinola/Cap. Manuel Nino [*Panama*] [*ICAO location identifier*] (ICLI)
**MPCH** ....... Methodist Protestant Church
**MPCI** ......... Mandatory Product Control Items (MCD)
**MPCI** ......... Military Police Criminal Investigation
**MPCI** ......... Multiport Programmable Communications Interface
**MPCID** ....... Military Police Criminal Investigation Detachment
**MPCL** ........ Monolithical Peltier Cooled LASER (MCD)
**MPCL** ........ Mooney Problem Check List [*Psychology*]
**MPCLP** ...... Mental Patient Civil Liberties Project (EA)
**MPCM** ....... Microprogram Control Memory
**MPCO** ....... Colon [*Panama*] [*ICAO location identifier*] (ICLI)
**MPCO** ....... Military Police Commanding Officer (MCD)
**MPCO** ....... Military Police Company
**MPCP** ....... Mid-Peninsula Conversion Project [*Later, CEC*] (EA)
**MP/CP** ..... Military Personnel/Civilian Personnel
**MPCP** ....... Missile Power Control Panel (AAG)
**MPCPC** ..... Mathematical Proceedings. Cambridge Philosophical Society [*A publication*]
**MPCR** ....... Memorandum Program Change Request [*Military*] (CAAL)
**MPCRI** ...... Mercantile Pacific Coastal Routing Instructions
**MPCS** ........ Machinery, Plant Control System [*Navy*]
**MPCS** ........ Manual Propositional Control System (AAG)
**MPCS** ........ Multiparty Connection Subsystem [*Telecommunications*] (TEL)
**MPCS** ........ Multiprocessing Control System [*Data processing*]
**MPCSOT** .. Machinery, Plant Control System Operator Trainer [*Navy*]
**MPCSW** .... Multipurpose Close Support Weapon [*Military*] (AABC)
**MPCU** ....... Maximum Permissible Concentration of Unidentified Radionuclides in Water
**MPD** .......... m-Phenylenediamine [*Also, MPDA*] [*Organic chemistry*]
**MPD** .......... Magnetoplasmadynamic
**MPD** .......... Main DC [*Direct Current*] Power Distributor Assembly (MCD)
**MPD** .......... Main Pancreatic Duct [*Anatomy*]
**MPD** .......... Maintenance Policy Document [*Deep Space Instrumentation Facility, NASA*]
**MPD** .......... Management Policy and Directives
**MPD** .......... Map Pictorial Display
**MPD** .......... Marlborough Productions Ltd. [*Vancouver Stock Exchange symbol*]
**M Pd** .......... Master of Pedagogy
**MPD** .......... Materials Physics Division [*Air Force*]
**MPD** .......... Materials Proximity Detector
**MPD** .......... Maximum Packing Depth (NG)
**MPD** .......... Maximum Permissible Dose [*Radiation*]
**MPD** .......... Mean Phenetic Distance
**MPD** .......... Mean Photon Flux Density
**MPD** .......... Mean Population Doubling [*Cytology*]
**MPD** .......... Medical Pay Date
**MPD** .......... Membrane Polarographic Detector [*Instrumentation*]
**MPD** .......... Methane Phophonyl Dichloride [*Nerve gas intermediate*] [*Organic chemistry*]
**MPD** .......... Methylpentanediol [*Organic chemistry*]
**MPD** .......... Methylphosphonic Diamide [*Flame retardant*] [*Organic chemistry*]
**MPD** .......... Metropolitan Police District [*London*]
**MPD** .......... Microwave Plasma Detector [*Instrumentation*]
**MPD** .......... Midwest Presenters Directory [*Information service or system*] (EISS)
**MPD** .......... Military Pay Division, Finance Center, US Army
**MPD** .......... Military Position Description
**MPD** .......... Military Priority Date
**MPD** .......... Military Prisons Department [*British military*] (DMA)
**MPD** .......... Minimum Permissible Dose
**MPD** .......... Minimum Premarket [*Health and Safety*] Data [*OEEC*]
**MPD** .......... Minnesota Percepto-Diagnostic Test

**MPD** ........ Missile Purchase Description [*Army*]
**MPD** ........ Modification Program Directive (AFIT)
**MPD** ........ Monographs in Psychobiology and Disease [*Elsevier Book Series*] [*A publication*]
**MPD** ........ Movimiento Popular Democratico [*Popular Democratic Movement*] [*Ecuador*] [*Political party*] (PPW)
**MPD** ........ Movimiento Popular Dominicano [*Dominican Popular Movement*] [*Dominican Republic*] [*Political party*] (PPW)
**MPD** ........ Multiperson Prisoner's Dilemma [*Statistics*]
**MPD** ........ Multiphoton Dissociation [*Physical chemistry*]
**MPD** ........ Multiple Personality Disorder
**MPD** ........ Multipurpose Diffractometer
**MPD** ........ Multipurpose Display (MCD)
**MPD** ........ Myofascial Pain Dysfunction [*Neurology*]
**MP2D** ........ Multipart, Two Dimensional
**MPDA** ........ David/Enrique Malek [*Panama*] [*ICAO location identifier*] (ICLI)
**MPDA** ........ m-Phenylenediamine [*Also, MPD*] [*Organic chemistry*]
**MPDA** ........ Monitor-Printer-Diskette Adapter
**MPDC** ........ Mechanical Properties Data Center [*Defense Logistics Agency*] [*Information service or system*]
**MPDC** ........ Missile Prelaunch Data Computer (MCD)
**MPDD** ........ Meteorological Penetration Detection Development
**MPDES** ..... Microprocessor Data Extraction System [*Military*] (CAAL)
**MPDFA** ..... Master Photo Dealers' and Finishers' Association [*Later, PMA*] (EA)
**MPDI** ........ Marine Products Development Irradiator
**MPDI** ........ Memory Protection Devices, Incorporated [*Plainview, NY*] [*NASDAQ symbol*] (NQ)
**MPDI** ........ Multipunch Die
**MPDLRSDB** ... Commission on the Mentally Disabled [*Formerly, Mental and Physical Disability Legal Research Services and Data Bases*] (EA)
**MPDM** ...... Maintenance Planning Data Manual (MUGU)
**MPDP** ....... Manpower Development Program [*Department of Labor*]
**MPDS** ........ Mechanical Provisioning Data System
**MPDS** ........ Message Processing and Distributing System [*Navy*] (NVT)
**MPDS** ........ Mission Planning Debriefing Station (MCD)
**MPDT** ....... Mean Preventive Downtime [*Data processing*]
**MPDT** ....... Minnesota Percepto-Diagnostic Test [*Psychology*]
**MPE** .......... Manual Plot Entry (MCD)
**MPE** .......... Master of Physical Education
**M & PE** ...... Materials and Process Engineering (MCD)
**MPE** .......... Mathematical and Physical Sciences and Engineering (IEEE)
**MPE** .......... Maximum Permissible Exposure [*Radiation*]
**MPE** .......... Maximum Possible Error
**MPE** .......... Meat Promotion Executive [*British*]
**MPE** .......... Mechanized Production of Electronics
**MPE** .......... Meeting Planners Expo (ITD)
**MPE** .......... Memory Parity Error
**MPE** .......... Metaphenoxylene [*Analytical chemistry*]
**MPE** .......... Methidiumpropyl Ethylenediaminetetraacetic Acid [*Analytical biochemistry*]
**MPE** .......... Minimum Perceptible Erythema [*Dermatology*]
**MPE** .......... Minimum Potential Energy [*Fission*]
**MPE** .......... Missile Positioning Equipment (KSC)
**MPE** .......... Mission-Peculiar Equipment
**MPE** .......... Mission and Performance Envelope
**MPE** .......... Monthly Project Evaluation
**MPE** .......... Moving Paper Electrophoresis
**MPE** .......... Multipion Exchange
**MPE** .......... Multiple Phase Ejector
**MPE** .......... Multiprogramming Executive [*Hewlett-Packard Co.*]
**MPEA** ........ Machine Printers and Engravers Association of the United States (EA)
**MPEA** ........ Meat and Poultry Export Association
**MPEA** ........ Mouvement Populaire d'Evolution Africaine [*African People's Evolution Movement*]
**MPEAA** ..... Motion Picture Export Association of America (EA)
**MPeaHi** ..... Peabody Historical Society, Peabody, MA [*Library symbol*] [*Library of Congress*] (LCLS)
**MPeaI** ........ Peabody Institute, Peabody, MA [*Library symbol*] [*Library of Congress*] (LCLS)
**MPECC** ..... Multiprocessor Experimental Computer Complex
**MPEd** ........ Master of Physical Education
**MPEDA** ..... Marine Products Export Development Authority [*Indian*] (ASF)
**M Pe E** ....... Master of Petroleum Engineering
**MPEEA** ..... Moniteur Professionnel de l'Electricite et Electronique [*A publication*]
**M Pe Eng** ... Master of Petroleum Engineering
**MPEG** ....... Methoxypolyethylene Glycol [*Organic chemistry*]
**MPEG** ....... Military Police Escort Guard
**MPEL** ........ Maximum Permissible Exposure Levels [*Radiation*]
**MPEP** ....... Manual of Patent Examining Procedures
**MPEP** ....... Metalworking Processes and Equipment Program
**MPER** ........ Material-in-Process Engineering Request
**MPERR** ..... Master Personnel Record
**MPES** ........ Mass Properties Engineering Section
**MPES** ........ Maximum Performance Ejection Seat [*Navy*]
**MPESA7** ... Mar y Pesca [*A publication*]
**MPESS** ...... Mission-Peculiar Experiment Support Structure (NASA)
**MPET** ........ Magellan Petroleum Corp. [*NASDAQ symbol*] (NQ)
**MPETA J** ... Manitoba Physical Education Teachers' Association. Journal [*A publication*]
**MP Ex** ....... Modern Practice of the Exchequer [*A publication*] (DLA)
**MPF** .......... Machine Parts Fabrication
**MPF** .......... Master Parts File (MCD)
**MPF** .......... Materials Processing Facility [*NASA*] (KSC)
**MPF** .......... Maturation-Promoting Factor [*Cytology*]
**MPF** .......... Mean Power Frequency [*of myoelectric signals*]
**MPF** .......... Median and Paired Fins [*Ichthyology*]
**MPF** .......... Medical Passport Foundation [*Inactive*] (EA)
**MPF** .......... Metal Parts Furnace (MCD)
**MPF** .......... Methodist Peace Fellowship (EA)
**MPF** .......... Metropolitan Police Force [*Scotland Yard*] [*London, England*]
**MPF** .......... Mexico Pilgrims Foundation (EA)
**MPF** .......... Micellar Polymer Flooding [*Petroleum technology*]
**MPF** .......... Million Pair Feet [*Telecommunications*] (TEL)
**MPF** .......... Missile Pressure Fuel (AAG)
**MPF** .......... Mission Planning Forecast
**MPF** .......... Mizrachi Palestine Fund (EA)
**MPF** .......... Multiple Primary Feed [*Deep Space Instrumentation Facility, NASA*]
**MPF** .......... Multipurpose Food [*Refers to a specific combination of ingredients used in a food relief program*]
**MPF** .......... Multispectral Photographic Facility
**MPF** .......... Murine Pathogen Free [*Rats or mice*]
**MPF** .......... Religious Teachers, Filippini [*Roman Catholic women's religious order*]
**MPFASAF** ... Military Police Functional Automation System for the Army in the Field (MCD)
**MPFC** ........ Mamas and the Papas Fan Club (EA)
**MPFC** ........ Mobile Petrol Filling Centre [*British military*] (DMA)
**MPFC** ........ Morgan Plus Four Club (EA)
**MPFC** ........ Multipurpose Fire Control System
**MPFE** ........ Motion Picture Film Editors [*Defunct*] (EA)
**MPFEE8** ... Psychiatria Fennica Monografiasarja [*A publication*]
**MPFP** ........ Melt-Processible Fluoropolymers [*Plastics technology*]
**MPFS** ........ Fuerte Sherman [*Panama*] [*ICAO location identifier*] (ICLI)
**MPFS** ........ MACRIT [*Manpower Authorization Criteria*] Planning Factors Study [*Army*]
**MPFS** ........ Microwave Position-Fixing System (NOAA)
**MPFS** ........ Multiple Primary Feed System [*Deep Space Instrumentation Facility, NASA*]
**MPG** .......... General Electric Co., Pittsfield, MA [*Library symbol*] [*Library of Congress*] (LCLS)
**MPG** .......... Georgetown University, Medical Library Processing Center, Washington, DC [*OCLC symbol*] (OCLC)
**MPG** .......... Magazine Promotion Group [*Defunct*] (EA)
**MPG** .......... Magnetopneumogram [*Medicine*]
**MPG** .......... Manhattan Publishing Group (EA)
**MPG** .......... Master Planning Grant [*FAA*] (FAAC)
**MPG** .......... Matched Power Gain
**MPG** .......... Max-Planck-Gesellschaft [*West German research organization*]
**MPG** .......... McArthur, OH [*Location identifier*] [*FAA*] (FAAL)
**MPG** .......... Micrograms per Gram
**MPG** .......... Microwave Pulse Generator
**MPG** .......... Miles per Gallon
**MPG** .......... Military Products Group
**MPG** .......... Miniature Precision Gyrocompass (IEEE)
**MPG** .......... Mobile Protected Gun [*Army*] (RDA)
**MPG** .......... Molecular Presentation Graphics [*Software program*]
**MPG** .......... MPG Investment Corp. Ltd. [*Toronto Stock Exchange symbol*] [*Vancouver Stock Exchange symbol*]
**MPG** .......... Multipoint Grounding (NASA)
**MPG** .......... Patrologia Graeca [*J. P. Migne*] [*Paris*] [*A publication*] (BJA)
**MPGF** ........ Male Pronucleus Growth Factor [*Biochemistry*]
**MPGHM** ... Mobile Payload Ground Handling Mechanism (MCD)
**MPGI** ........ Mouvement Populaire pour la Guadeloupe Independante [*Popular Movement for Independent Guadeloupe*] (PD)
**MPG (Max-Planck-Ges) Spiegel Aktuel Inf** ... MPG (Max-Planck-Gesellschaft) Spiegel. Aktuelle Informationen [*West Germany*] [*A publication*]
**MPGN** ....... Membranoproliferative Glomerulonephritis [*Nephrology*]
**MPG Presseinf** ... MPG [*Max-Planck-Gesellschaft*] Presseinformation [*A publication*]
**MPGS** ........ Microprogram Generating System
**MPGS** ........ Mobile Protected Gun System [*Army*] (MCD)
**MPG Spiegel Aktuelle Inf** ... MPG [*Max-Planck-Gesellschaft*] Spiegel. Aktuelle Informationen [*A publication*]
**MPH** .......... Maintenance Parts Handbook
**MPh** .......... Maitre Phonetique [*A publication*]
**M Ph** .......... Master of Philosophy
**MPH** .......... Master of Physical Education and Health
**MPH** .......... Master of Public Health
**MPH** .......... McGregor Point, HI [*Location identifier*] [*FAA*] (FAAL)
**MPH** .......... Melphalan [*Also, A, L-PAM, M, MPL*] [*Antineoplastic drug*]
**MPH** .......... Mentally and Physically Handicapped (OICC)
**MPH** .......... Micro-Phonics Technology International Corp. [*Vancouver Stock Exchange symbol*]

**MPH** .......... Miles per Hour [*Also, M/H*]
**M Ph** .......... Mistress of Philosophy
**MPh** .......... Modern Philology [*A publication*]
**MPH** .......... Multiple Probe Head [*Laboratory technology*]
**MPh** .......... Museum. Maanblad voor Philologie en Geschiedenis [*A publication*]
**MPHAE6** .. Medical Physics Handbooks [*A publication*]
**M Phar** ....... Master of Pharmacy
**M Phar C** ... Master of Pharmaceutical Chemistry
**M Pharm** ... Master of Pharmacy
**M Ph C** ...... Master of Pharmaceutical Chemistry
**MPHE** ....... Master of Public Health Engineering
**MPHE** ....... Material and Personnel Handling Equipment (NASA)
**MPH Ed** .... Master of Public Health Education
**MPH Eng** .. Master of Public Health Engineering
**M Phil** ........ Master of Philosophy
**M Phil** ........ Modern Philology [*A publication*]
**MPhL** ........ Museum Philologum Londiniense [*A publication*]
**MPHN** ....... Master of Public Health Nursing
**MPHO** ....... Howard Air Force Base [*Panama*] [*ICAO location identifier*] (ICLI)
**M Pho** ........ Master of Photography
**MPHO** ....... Medphone Corp. [*NASDAQ symbol*] (NQ)
**MPhon** ....... Maitre Phonetique [*A publication*]
**M Photo** ..... Modern Photography [*A publication*]
**MPhP** ........ Mediaevalia Philosophica Polonorum [*A publication*]
**MPHPS** ...... Miles per Hour per Second
**MPHR** ....... Maximum Predicted Heart Rate [*Cardiology*]
**M Ph S** ....... Master of Physical Science
**M Ph Sc** ..... Master of Physical Science
**MPHTM** ... Master of Public Health and Tropical Medicine
**MPhty** ....... Master of Physiotherapy [*British*] (ADA)
**M Phy** ........ Master of Physics
**M Phys A** ... Member of the Physiotherapists' Association [*British*]
**MPI** .......... Magnetic Particle Inspection
**MPI** .......... Magnetic Press, Inc. [*Information service or system*] (EISS)
**MPI** .......... Malaria Philatelists International (EA)
**MPI** .......... Mamitupo [*Panama*] [*Airport symbol*] (OAG)
**MPI** .......... Man-Portable Illuminator
**MPI** .......... Manitoba Properties, Inc. [*Toronto Stock Exchange symbol*] [*Vancouver Stock Exchange symbol*]
**MPI** .......... Mannosephosphate Isomerase [*An enzyme*]
**MPI** .......... Manufacturing Process Instructions
**MPI** .......... Marginal Propensity to Invest [*Economics*]
**MPI** .......... Marriage-Personality Inventory [*Psychology*]
**MPI** .......... Martin Processing, Incorporated [*AMEX symbol*] (SPSG)
**MPI** .......... Mass Psychogenic Illness
**MPI** .......... Matter of Public Importance (ADA)
**MPI** .......... Maudsley Personality Inventory [*Psychology*]
**MPI** .......... Max-Planck-Institut fuer Astronomie [*Max Planck Institute for Astronomy*] [*Federal Republic of Germany*]
**MPI** .......... Maximal Permitted Intake [*Medicine*]
**MPI** .......... Maximum Point of Impulse
**MPI** .......... Mean Point of Impact [*Air Force*]
**MPI** .......... Meeting Planners International (EA)
**MPI** .......... Message Pattern Indicator
**MPI** .......... Message Processing Interactive (MCD)
**MPI** .......... Metal Powder Industries Federation
**MPI** .......... Microprocessor Interface
**MPI** .......... Milestone Properties [*NYSE symbol*] (SPSG)
**MPI** .......... Militaerpsykologiska Institutet [*A publication*]
**MPI** .......... Military Police Investigator [*or Investigation*] (AABC)
**MPI** .......... Military Procurement Instruction
**MPI** .......... Minneapolis Public Library and Information Center, Minneapolis, MN [*OCLC symbol*] (OCLC)
**MPI** .......... Minnesota Preschool Inventory [*Child development test*]
**MPI** .......... Missile Periodic Inspection (AAG)
**MPI** .......... Missing Persons International (EA)
**MPI** .......... Mission Payload Integration (MCD)
**MPI** .......... Molded Plastic Insulation
**MPI** .......... Molecular Parameter Index
**MPI** .......... Monographs of the Peshitta Institute [*A publication*] (BJA)
**MPI** .......... Monsoon Pollen Index [*Paleoceanography*]
**MPI** .......... Morris Pratt Institute Association (EA)
**MPI** .......... Movimiento pro Independencia de Puerto Rico (EA)
**MPI** .......... Multiphase Ionization [*Chemical physics*]
**MPI** .......... Multiphasic Personality Inventory
**MPI** .......... Multiphoton Ionization [*Spectrometry*]
**MPI** .......... Multiple Protocol Interface [*Data processing*]
**MPI** .......... Multipoint-Electronic Fuel Injection [*Automotive engineering*]
**MPI** .......... Myocardial Perfusion Imaging [*Cardiology*]
**MPIA** ........ Master in Political and Institutional Administration
**MPIA** ........ Max-Planck-Institut fuer Astronomie [*Max Planck Institute for Astronomy*] [*Federal Republic of Germany*]
**MPIB** ........ Malaysian Pineapple Industry Board (DS)
**MPIC** ........ Message Processing Interrupt Count
**MPIC** ........ Mobile Phase Ion Chromatography
**MPIC** ........ Motion Picture Industry Controllers (EA)
**MPIC** ........ Motion Picture Industry Council (EA)
**MPIC** ........ Motion Picture Institute of Canada
**MPIF** ........ Metal Powder Industries Federation (EA)
**MPIIN** ....... Modification Procurement Instrument Identification Number [*NASA*] (NASA)
**MPiKL** ....... Masinnyj Perevod i Prikladnaja Lingvistika [*A publication*]
**MPIM** ....... Multipurpose Individual Munition [*Weapon*]
**MPI (McKee Pedersen Instrum) Appl Notes** ... MPI (McKee-Pedersen Instruments) Applications Notes [*A publication*]
**MPIO** ........ Mission and Payload Integration Office [*NASA*]
**MPIP** ........ Machine Parts Inspection Plans (MCD)
**MPIP** ........ Maintenance Posture Improvement Program (MCD)
**MPIP** ........ Meat and Poultry Inspection Program [*Department of Agriculture*]
**MPIPEM** .. Memoires Publies. Institut pour la Protection des Plantes [*A publication*]
**MPIR** ........ Missile Precision Instrumentation RADAR (MSA)
**MPIRO** ...... Multiple Peril Insurance Rating Organization [*Later, Multiperil Insurance Conference*]
**MP & IS** .... Material Process and Inspection Specification (AAG)
**MPJ** .......... Metacarpophalangeal Joint [*Anatomy*]
**MPJ** .......... Morrilton, AR [*Location identifier*] [*FAA*] (FAAL)
**MPJ** .......... Mouvement Panafricain de la Jeunesse [*Pan-African Youth Movement - PYM*] [*Algeria*]
**MPJE** ........ Jaque [*Panama*] [*ICAO location identifier*] (ICLI)
**MP-JFI** ...... Managerial and Professional Job Functions Inventory [*Test*]
**MPK** .......... Maintenance Parts Kit (MSA)
**mpk** .......... Manpack
**MPK** .......... Martis Peak [*California*] [*Seismograph station code, US Geological Survey*] (SEIS)
**MPK** .......... Microphone Probe Kit
**MPK** .......... Mitteilungen der Praehistorischen Kommission der Oesterreichischen Akademie der Wissenschaften [*A publication*]
**MPL** .......... Magnesium Pemoline [*Pharmacology*]
**MPL** .......... Maintenance Parts Lists
**MPL** .......... Man Position Locator
**MPL** .......... Managerial Planning [*A publication*]
**MPL** .......... Mandatory Parts List [*DoD*]
**MPL** .......... Manipulator Positioning Latches (MCD)
**MPL** .......... Manufacturing Parts List (AAG)
**MPL** .......... Maple Technology Limited [*Vancouver Stock Exchange symbol*]
**MPL** .......... Marine Physical Laboratory [*Research center*] (RCD)
**MPL** .......... Marine Physics Laboratory [*Scripps*]
**MPL** .......... Mars Probe Lander [*Aerospace*]
**MPL** .......... Master Parts List
**MPL** .......... Master of Patent Law
**MPL** .......... Master of Polite Literature
**MPL** .......... Mavis, Paul A., South Bend IN [*STAC*]
**MPL** .......... Maxillofacial Prosthesis Laboratory [*WRAMC*] (RDA)
**MPL** .......... Maximum Penalized-Likelihood [*Statistics*]
**MPL** .......... Maximum Permissible Level [*Radiation*] (DEN)
**MPL** .......... Maximum Possible Loss [*Insurance*]
**MPL** .......... Maximum Probable Loss [*Insurance*]
**MPL** .......... Maximum Procurement Level (AFIT)
**MPL** .......... Mechanical Parts List (NASA)
**MPL** .......... Mechanical Properties Loop [*Nuclear energy*] (NRCH)
**MPL** .......... Melphalan [*Also, A, L-PAM, M, MPH*] [*Antineoplastic drug*]
**MPL** .......... Message Processing Language [*Burroughs Corp.*]
**MPL** .......... Metals Processing Laboratory [*MIT*] (MCD)
**MPL** .......... Metering Pumps Limited
**MPL** .......... Microprocessor [*or Motorola's*] Programming Language [*1975*] [*Data processing*] (CSR)
**MPL** .......... Mine Planter (NATG)
**MPL** .......... Minimum Power Level (KSC)
**MPL** .......... Minnesota Power & Light Co. [*NYSE symbol*] (SPSG)
**MPL** .......... Mission Planning Laboratory [*NASA*] (KSC)
**MPL** .......... Mistress of Polite Literature
**MPL** .......... Monessen Public Library, Monessen, PA [*OCLC symbol*] (OCLC)
**MPL** .......... Monkey Placental Lactogen
**MPL** .......... Monophosphoryl Lipid [*Biochemistry*]
**MPL** .......... Montpellier [*France*] [*Airport symbol*] (OAG)
**MPL** .......... Motion Picture Laboratories [*Commercial firm*]
**MPL** .......... Motivated Productivity Level [*Quality control*]
**MPL** .......... Mouvement Politique Lulua [*Lulua Political Movement*] [*Political party*]
**MPL** .......... Movimento Politica dei Lavoratori [*Workers' Political Movement*] [*Italy*] [*Political party*] (PPE)
**MPL** .......... Muenchener Papiere zur Linguistik [*A publication*]
**MPL** .......... Multiple Payload Launcher
**MPL** .......... Multischedule Private Line
**MPL** .......... Musician, Player, and Listener [*A publication*]
**MPL** .......... Patrologia Latina [*J. P. Migne*] [*Paris*] [*A publication*] (BJA)
**MPl** ........... Plymouth Public Library, Plymouth, MA [*Library symbol*] [*Library of Congress*] (LCLS)
**MPlA** ........ Antiquarian House, Plymouth, MA [*Library symbol*] [*Library of Congress*] (LCLS)
**MPLA** ........ Malayan People's Liberation Army
**MPLA** ........ Monophosphoryl Lipid A [*Biochemistry*]
**MPLA** ........ Movimento Popular de Libertacao de Angola [*Popular Movement for the Liberation of Angola*] [*Political party*]
**MPlanStud** ... Master of Planning Studies

**MPLA-PT** ... Movimento Popular de Libertacao de Angola - Partido do Trabalho [*Popular Movement for the Liberation of Angola - Party of Labor*] [*Political party*] (PPW)
**MPLB** ........ Balboa/Albrook [*Panama*] [*ICAO location identifier*] (ICLI)
**MPLB** ........ Maximum Permissible Lung Burden [*Industrial hygiene*]
**MPLC** ........ Medium-Pressure Liquid Chromatography
**MPLC** ........ Mid-Peninsula Library Cooperative [*Library network*]
**MPLC** ........ Movimento Popular de Libertacao de Cabinda [*Popular Movement for the Liberation of Cabinda*] [*Angola*] [*Political party*] (PD)
**MPLE** ........ Multipurpose Long Endurance [*Aircraft*]
**MPLJ** ........ Melanges de Philosophie et de Litterature Juives [*A publication*]
**MPLL** ........ Malayan People's Liberation League
**MPLMB** .... Modifikatsiya Polimernykh Materialov [*A publication*]
**MPLN** ........ Maintenance Planning [*Database*] (NASA)
**MPLO** ........ Military Postal Liaison Office
**MPLP** ........ La Palma [*Panama*] [*ICAO location identifier*] (ICLI)
**MPLP** ........ Mental Patients Liberation Projects
**MPlP** ........ Plimoth Plantation, Inc., Plymouth, MA [*Library symbol*] [*Library of Congress*] (LCLS)
**MPLP** ........ Portage Plains Regional Library, Portage La Prairie, Manitoba [*Library symbol*] [*National Library of Canada*] (NLC)
**MPLPDC** .. MDC Library, Manitoba Developmental Centre, Portage La Prairie [*Library symbol*] [*National Library of Canada*] (BIB)
**MPLPM** .... Manitoba School, Portage La Prairie, Manitoba [*Library symbol*] [*National Library of Canada*] (NLC)
**MPlPS** ....... Pilgrim Society, Plymouth, MA [*Library symbol*] [*Library of Congress*] (LCLS)
**MPLR** ........ Medium Power Loop Range
**MPLR** ........ Municipal and Planning Law Reports [*A publication*]
**MPLS** ........ Maximal Principle Least Squares
**MPLSS** ...... Marketing of Public Library Services Section [*Public Library Association*]
**MPLU** ........ Most Probable Library User
**MPLX** ........ Mediplex Group [*NASDAQ symbol*] (NQ)
**MPLX** ........ Multiplexer
**MPLXR** ..... Multiplexer
**MPM** ......... Magnetic Phase Modulator
**MPM** ......... Main Propulsion Motor
**MPM** ......... Maintenance Planning Manual (NG)
**MPM** ......... Maintenance Program Management [*Military*] (AABC)
**MPM** ......... Major Program Memorandum [*Military*]
**MPM** ......... Major Project Manager
**MPM** ......... Malignant Papillary Mesothelioma [*Medicine*]
**MPM** ......... Manipulator Positioning Mechanism (NASA)
**MPM** ......... Manpower Planning Model
**MPM** ......... Manufacture Procedure Manual (KSC)
**MPM** ......... Maputo [*Mozambique*] [*Airport symbol*] (OAG)
**MPM** ......... Marginal Propensity to Import [*Economics*]
**MPM** ......... Master of Psychological Management
**MPM** ......... Master of Psychological Medicine (ADA)
**MPM** ......... Master of Public Management
**MPM** ......... Maximum Permitted Mileage [*Airlines*]
**MPM** ......... Message Processing Modules (MCD)
**MPM** ......... Metal-Plastic Metal [*Automotive engineering*]
**MPM** ......... Meters per Minute
**MPM** ......... Metra-Potential Method [*Graph theory*]
**MPM** ......... Microprogram Memory
**MPM** ......... Microscope-Photometer
**MPM** ......... Microwave Power Meter
**MPM** ......... Miles per Minute
**MPM** ......... Milestone Planning Meeting (MCD)
**MPM** ......... Miniaturized Pointing Mount [*Spacelab*] [*NASA*]
**MPM** ......... Missile Power Monitor (AAG)
**MPM** ......... Monocycle Position Modulation
**MPM** ......... Mouse Peritoneal Macrophages
**MPM** ......... Mouvement Populaire Mahorais [*Mayotte People's Movement*] [*Comoros*] [*Political party*] (PPW)
**MPM** ......... Moving Presentation Mode
**MP/M** ....... Multiprocessing Monitor Control Program [*Data processing*]
**MPM** ......... Multiprogramming Monitor
**MPM** ......... Multipurpose Meal
**MPM** ......... Multipurpose Missile (MCD)
**MPMA** ...... Master of Public Management and Administration
**MPMA** ...... Methylphorbol Myristate Acetate [*Organic chemistry*]
**MPMA** ...... Montford Point Marine Association (EA)
**MP & MAC** ... Marine Petroleum and Minerals Advisory Committee [*National Oceanic and Atmospheric Administration*] [*Terminated, 1976*] (NOAA)
**MPMC** ...... Military Personnel, Marine Corps
**MP MD Agric Exp Stn** ... MP. Maryland Agricultural Experiment Station [*A publication*]
**MPMG** ...... Marine Pollution Management Group [*British*]
**MPMG** ...... Panama/Paitilla, Marco A. Gelabert [*Panama*] [*ICAO location identifier*] (ICLI)
**MPMH** ...... Mean Preventive Maintenance Hours
**MPMI** ....... Magazine and Paperback Marketing Institute (EA)
**MPMIC** ..... Mechanical Properties of Materials Information Center (MCD)
**MPMIS** ..... Military Police Management Information System
**MPML** ....... Mid-Pacific Marine Laboratory (MSC)
**MPML** ....... Montana Precision Mining Ltd. [*NASDAQ symbol*] (NQ)
**MPMMG** .. Marine Pollution Monitoring Management Group (ASF)
**MPMP** ....... Mass Properties Management Plan (NASA)
**MPMP** ....... (Methylpiperidyl)methylphenothiazine [*Sedative*]
**MPMP** ....... Modification Program Management Plan (MCD)
**MPMPR** .... Metropolitan Police Missing Persons Register [*British*]
**MPMRP** .... Master Petroleum Material Requirements Plan (MCD)
**MPMS** ....... Mattress and Palliasse Makers' Society [*A union*] [*British*]
**MPMS** ....... Missile Performance Measuring System (MCD)
**MPMS** ....... Multiple-Pressure Measuring System
**MPMSE** .... Multiuse Payload and Mission Support Equipment (MCD)
**MPMT** ...... Mean Preventive Maintenance Time (MCD)
**MPMT** ...... Mellon Participating Mortgage Trust, Series 85/10 [*NASDAQ symbol*] (NQ)
**MPMT** ...... Multiple Primary Malignant Tumor [*Oncology*]
**MPMTA** .... Tschermaks Mineralogische und Petrographische Mitteilungen [*A publication*]
**MPMUL** ... Military Production Master Urgency List
**MPMV** ...... Mason-Pfizer Monkey Virus
**MPN** .......... Manufacturers Part Number (MCD)
**MPN** .......... Manufacturer's Productivity Network [*Hewlett-Packard Co.*]
**MPN** .......... Mean Probable Number (MCD)
**MPN** .......... Medial Preoptic Nucleus [*Brain anatomy*]
**MPN** .......... Methyl Parathion [*Also, MEP, MP*] [*Pesticide*]
**MPN** .......... Military Pay, Navy [*An appropriation*]
**MPN** .......... Military Personnel, Navy
**MPN** .......... Mobile Pulse RADAR Navigational Aid (FAAC)
**MPN** .......... Monongahela Power Co. [*AMEX symbol*] (SPSG)
**MPN** .......... Most Probable Number
**MPNA** ....... Midwest Professional Needlework Association [*Later, APNRA*] (EA)
**MPNBAZ** ... Marine Pollution Bulletin [*A publication*]
**MPNC** ....... Mouvement pour le Progres National Congolais [*Movement for National Congolese Progress*]
**MPNDS** ..... Material Properties Numerical Data System [*Purdue University*] [*Database*]
**MPNF** ....... Manpower-Needs Forecasting (MCD)
**MPNI** ........ Ministry of Pensions and National Insurance [*Later, MSS*] [*British*]
**MPNST** ..... Malignant Peripheral Nerve Sheath Tumor
**MPO** .......... Macedonian Patriotic Organization of US and Canada (EA)
**MPO** .......... Major Program Objective (MCD)
**MPO** .......... Managers, Proprietors, and Officials
**MPO** .......... Manufacturing Production Order (NRCH)
**MPO** .......... Maputo [*Mozambique*] [*Geomagnetic observatory code*]
**MPO** .......... Marine Policy. The International Journal of Ocean Affairs [*A publication*]
**MPO** .......... Maximum Power Output
**MPO** .......... Medial Preoptic [*Brain anatomy*]
**MPO** .......... Member of the Post Office [*British*]
**MPO** .......... Memory Printout [*Data processing*]
**MPO** .......... Memory Protect Override
**MPO** .......... Metropolitan Police Office [*Familiarly called "Scotland Yard" from its site at New Scotland Yard*] [*British*]
**MPO** .......... Military Pay Order
**MPO** .......... Military Permit Office [*or Officer*]
**MPO** .......... Military Personnel Office
**MPO** .......... Military Planning Office [*SEATO*] (CINC)
**MPO** .......... Military Post Office
**MPO** .......... Misconduct Policy Officer [*National Institutes of Health*]
**MPO** .......... Missile Processing Operation (MCD)
**MPO** .......... Mobile Post Office
**MPO** .......... Motion Picture Operator
**MPO** .......... Mount Pocono, PA [*Location identifier*] [*FAA*] (FAAL)
**MPO** .......... Mustering Petty Officer
**MPO** .......... Myeloperoxidase [*An enzyme*]
**MPO** .......... Withholding Tax [*Indonesia*] (IMH)
**MPOA** ....... Medial Preoptic Area [*Medicine*]
**MPOA** ....... Puerto Obaldia [*Panama*] [*ICAO location identifier*] (ICLI)
**MPOAH** .... Medial Preoptic-Anterior Hypothalamic [*Brain anatomy*]
**MPOBA** .... Monographs in Population Biology [*A publication*]
**MPOD** ....... Mean Planned Outage Duration [*Electronics*] (IEEE)
**MPOI** ........ Master Program of Instruction [*Army*] (AABC)
**MPOIS** ...... Military Police Operations and Information System [*Army*] (MCD)
**MPolAdmin** ... Master of Policy and Administration
**MPolEcon** ... Master of Political Economy [*British*] (ADA)
**MPOLL** ...... Military Post Office Location List (AFM)
**MPolLaw** ... Master of Policy and Law
**MPologne** .. Musique en Pologne [*A publication*]
**M Pol Sc** .... Master of Political Science
**MPOM** ...... Maintenance Program Operations Management [*Military*] (AABC)
**MPOR** ....... Maintenance Plant at Ober Ramstadt [*Army*] (MCD)
**MPOS** ....... Mobile Post Office Society (EA)
**MPOS** ....... Multipurpose Optimization System [*Data processing*]
**MPOTB** ..... Modern Problems in Ophthalmology [*A publication*]
**MPOUA** .... Memorial des Poudres [*A publication*]
**MPP** .......... Mailer's Postmark Permit
**MPP** .......... Maintainability Program Plan

**MPP** .......... Major Program Proposal (AAG)
**MPP** .......... Manipur People's Party [*India*] [*Political party*] (PPW)
**M & PP** ...... Manitou & Pike's Peak Railway
**MPP** .......... Martens Polarization Photometer [*Physics*]
**MPP** .......... Massively Parallel Processor [*Image processing*]
**MPP** .......... Master Patch Panel [*Air Force*] (MCD)
**MPP** .......... Master Program Plan (NG)
**MPP** .......... Master of Public Policy
**MPP** .......... Material Processing Procedure (NASA)
**M & PP** ...... Materials and Plant Protection [*Nuclear energy*] (NRCH)
**MPP** .......... Materiel Performance Package [*Military*] (AFM)
**MPP** .......... Maximum Positive Pressure [*Nuclear energy*] (NRCH)
**MPP** .......... Mediaevalia Philosophica Polonorum [*A publication*]
**MPP** .......... Medical Personnel Pool
**MPP** .......... Medical Properties [*AMEX symbol*] (SPSG)
**MPP** .......... Melphalan, Prednisone, Procarbazine [*Antineoplastic drug regimen*]
**MPP** .......... Member of Provincial Parliament [*British*]
**MPP** .......... Merit Promotion Plan [*or Program*] [*NASA*] (NASA)
**MPP** .......... Message Processing Program [*Data processing*]
**MPP** .......... Meta Postprocessor [*Software program*] [*Symbolic Control, Inc.*]
**MPP** .......... Methyl(phenyl)pyridine [*Biochemistry*]
**MPP** .......... Methylpiperazine [*Organic chemistry*]
**MPP** .......... Microfilm Printer/Plotter
**MPP** .......... Microprogrammable Processor (MCD)
**MPP** .......... Miles per Pound [*NASA*] (KSC)
**MPP** .......... Military Pay Procedures
**MPP** .......... Minimum Premium Plans [*Insurance*]
**MPP** .......... Miscellaneous Personal Property [*Legal term*] (DLA)
**MPP** .......... Missile Power Panel (AAG)
**MPP** .......... Mitochondrial Processing Peptidase [*Biochemistry*]
**MPP** .......... Modern Programming Practice
**MPP** .......... Mongol People's Party [*Political party*] [*Mongolia*] (FEA)
**MPP** .......... Monodisperse Polymer Particle
**MPP** .......... Most Probable Position [*Navigation*]
**MPP** .......... Mothers in Prison Projects (EA)
**MPP** .......... Motion Picture Pioneers (EA)
**MPP** .......... Motion Picture Projector (MSA)
**MPP** .......... Mount Pasian [*Philippines*] [*Seismograph station code, US Geological Survey*] (SEIS)
**MPP** .......... Mulatupo [*Panama*] [*Airport symbol*] (OAG)
**MPP** .......... Multiple Particle Plasma
**MPP** .......... Multiple Payload Program [*Military*]
**MPPA** ........ Metal Powder Producers Association (EA)
**MPPA** ........ Music Publishers' Protective Association [*Later, NMPA*] (EA)
**MPPAA** ..... Moderne Probleme der Paediatrie [*A publication*]
**MPPAEC** .. Medical Problems of Performing Artists [*A publication*]
**MPPB** ........ Methyl(phenyl)(propyl)barbituric (Acid) [*Biochemistry*]
**MPPC** ........ Mailer's Postmark Permit Club (EA)
**MPPC** ........ Master Program Phasing Chart (MCD)
**MPPC** ........ Medical Personnel (Priority) Committee [*World War II*]
**MPPC** ........ Military Pay Procedure Committee
**MPPC** ........ Panama [*Panama*] [*ICAO location identifier*] (ICLI)
**MPPCF** ..... Million Particles per Cubic Foot [*in air*]
**MPPD** ....... Maximum Probable Property Damage [*Hazard analysis*]
**MPPH** ....... Motion Picture Phonographic Unit
**MPPHA** .... Multiparameter Pulse Height Analyzer
**MP i PL** ..... Masinnyj Perevod i Prikladnaja Lingvistika [*A publication*]
**MPPL** ........ Multipunch Plate
**MPPL** ........ Multipurpose Processing Language [*Data processing*] (IEEE)
**MPPL** ........ Multipurpose Programming Language
**MPPM** ....... Master of Public and Private Management
**MPPM** ....... Military Personnel Procurement Manual
**MPPM** ....... Mission Prediction and Performance Module [*Aerospace*]
**MPPO** ....... Modified Polyphenylene Oxide [*Plastics technology*]
**MPPP** ........ Mechanically Processed Pork Product [*Food technology*]
**MPPP** ........ Methyl(phenyl)(propionoxy)piperidine [*Organic chemistry*]
**MPPR** ........ Mobilization Production Planning Requirements [*Military*]
**MPPR** ........ Modification Program Progress Report (AFIT)
**MPPR** ........ Monthly Production Progress Reports (MCD)
**MPPRB** ..... Materiel Procurement Priorities Review Board [*Army*] (AABC)
**MPPRC** ..... Materiel Procurement Priorities Review Committee [*Army*] (RDA)
**MPPS** ........ Master Production Planning Schedule [*Air Force*] (AFIT)
**MPPS** ........ Master Program Planning Schedule
**MPPS** ........ Medicare Prospective Payment System
**MPPS** ........ Moroccan Party of Progress and Socialism [*Political party*]
**MPPS** ........ Multipurpose (AABC)
**MPPSE** ..... Multipurpose Payload Support Equipment (NASA)
**MPPT** ........ Maximum Power Point Tracking [*Power system*]
**MPPT** ........ Methylprednisolone Pulse Therapy [*Medicine*]
**MPPT** ........ Moller-Plesset Perturbation Theory [*Physical chemistry*]
**MPPWCOM** ... Military Police Prisoner of War Command (AABC)
**MPQ** .......... McGill Pain Questionnaire [*Dentistry*]
**MPQ** .......... Multidimensional Personality Questionnaire [*Personality development test*] [*Psychology*]
**MPR** .......... Machined Part Requisition (MCD)
**MPR** .......... Maintainability Problem Report (NASA)
**MPR** .......... Maintenance Personnel Roster
**MPR** .......... Management Program Review [*NASA*] (NASA)
**MPR** .......... Mane Primo [*Early in the Morning*] [*Pharmacy*] (ROG)
**MPR** .......... Manpower (AABC)
**MPR** .......... Manufacturing Parts Record (KSC)
**MPR** .......... Manufacturing Planning Review (MCD)
**MPR** .......... Mariposa Resources, Inc. [*Vancouver Stock Exchange symbol*]
**MPR** .......... Maritime Provinces Reports [*Canada*] [*A publication*] (DLA)
**MPR** .......... Marrow Production Rate [*Hematology*]
**MPR** .......... Master Power Regulator
**MPR** .......... Material Purchase Requisition
**MPR** .......... Materials and Process Requirement [*Navy*]
**MPR** .......... Maximum Potential Representation (MUGU)
**MPR** .......... Maximum Practical Rate [*Aviation*]
**MPR** .......... Mayaguez [*Puerto Rico*] [*Seismograph station code, US Geological Survey*] (SEIS)
**MPR** .......... McPherson, KS [*Location identifier*] [*FAA*] (FAAL)
**MPR** .......... Mechanical Pressure Regulator (NRCH)
**MPR** .......... Medium Power RADAR (NATG)
**MPR** .......... Mercaptopurine Ribonucleoside [*Antineoplastic drug*]
**MPR** .......... Mercury Plunger Relay
**MPR** .......... Mervyn Peake Review [*A publication*]
**MPR** .......... Message Processing Region [*IBM Corp.*]
**MPR** .......... Met-Pro Corp. [*AMEX symbol*] (SPSG)
**MPR** .......... Military Pay Record
**MPR** .......... Military Personnel Record (AFM)
**MPR** .......... Mine Production Report
**MPR** .......... Mock-Up Purchase Request [*NASA*] (NASA)
**MPR** .......... Mongolian Peoples Republic (CINC)
**MPR** .......... Monoclonal Antibody Production Rate
**MPR** .......... Monopulse RADAR (MSA)
**MPR** .......... Monthly Progress Report
**MPR** .......... Monthly Project Report
**MPR** .......... Mouvement Populaire de la Revolution [*Popular Revolutionary Movement*] [*Zaire*] (PD)
**MPR** .......... Mouvement Populaire Revolutionnaire [*Popular Revolutionary Movement*] [*Tunisia*] [*Political party*] (PD)
**MPR** .......... Movimento Popolare Rivoluzionario [*Popular Revolutionary Movement*] [*Italy*] [*Political party*] (PD)
**MPR** .......... Muenchener Beitraege zur Papyrusforschung und Antiken Rechtsgeschichte [*A publication*]
**MPR** .......... Multipurpose Recorder
**MPR** .......... Music Power Rating
**MPRA** ....... Military Police Regimental Association (EA)
**MPRC** ........ Maryland Psychiatric Research Center [*University of Maryland*] [*Research center*] (RCD)
**MPRC** ........ Medical Program Review Committee [*DoD*] [*Washington, DC*] (EGAO)
**MPRC** ........ Military Personnel Records Center (MCD)
**MPRC** ........ Motion Picture Research Council
**MPRC** ........ Multipurpose Range Complex [*Army*] (INF)
**MPRC-H** ... Multipurpose Range Complex - Heavy [*Army*]
**MPRC-L** .... Multipurpose Range Complex - Light [*Army*]
**MPRE** ........ Medium Power Reactor Experiment
**MPRESS** ... Medium Pressure
**mPRF** ........ Median Pontine Reticular Formation [*Neurophysiology*]
**MPRF** ........ Medium Pulse Recurrence Frequency (MCD)
**MPRF** ........ Motion Picture Relief Fund [*Later, MPTF*] (EA)
**M Pr Gph** ... Master in Professional Geophysics
**MPRH** ....... Rio Hato [*Panama*] [*ICAO location identifier*] (ICLI)
**M Pr Hist Kom (Wien)** ... Mitteilungen der Praehistorischen Kommission der Oesterreichischen Akademie der Wissenschaften (Wien) [*A publication*]
**MPRI** ......... Member of the Plastics and Rubber Institute [*British*] (DBQ)
**MPRI** ......... Merchant Pacific Routing Instructions [*Shipping*]
**MPRI** ......... Mount Prat [*Italy*] [*Seismograph station code, US Geological Survey*] (SEIS)
**MPRI** ......... Multiphoton Resonance Ionization [*Spectrometry*]
**MPRIA** ...... Member of the Public Relations Institute of Australia
**MPRJ** ........ Military Personnel Records Jacket [*Army*] (AABC)
**MPRL** ........ Manpower and Personnel Research Laboratory [*Army Research Institute for the Behavioral and Social Sciences*] (RDA)
**MPRL** ........ Master Parts Reference List
**MPRL** ........ Military Physics Research Laboratory [*University of Texas*] (MCD)
**M Pr M** ...... Master of Preventive Medicine
**MPR Met Powder Rep** ... MPR. Metal Powder Report [*A publication*]
**MPRO** ........ Machine Processing Section [*National Security Agency*]
**MPRO** ........ MicroPro International Corp. [*San Rafael, CA*] [*NASDAQ symbol*] (NQ)
**MProcEng** ... Master of Process Engineering, University of Sheffield [*British*] (DBQ)
**M Prof Acc** ... Master of Professional Accountancy
**MPROM** ... Mask Programmed Read-Only Memory [*Data processing*]
**MPRP** ........ Mercaptopurine Ribonucleotide [*Antineoplastic drug*]
**MPRP** ........ Mongolian People's Revolutionary Party [*Mongol Ardyn Khuv'sgalt Nam*] [*Political party*] (PPW)
**MPRP** ........ Moslem People's Republican Party [*Iran*] [*Political party*] (PPW)
**MPRS** ........ Microform Personnel Records System (NVT)
**MPRSA** ..... Marine Protection, Research, and Sanctuaries Act [*1972*]
**M Pr T** ....... Monatsschrift fuer Praktische Tierheilkunde [*A publication*]
**MPRT** ........ Multipurpose Rail Transport (NRCH)

**MPRT/R** ... Missile Pneudraulic Repair Technician/Repairman (AAG)
**MPS** .......... Magazine Printers Section (EA)
**MPS** .......... Magnetic Pole Strength
**MPS** .......... Mail Preference Service [*Direct Mail Advertising Association*]
**MPS** .......... Main Power Switch
**MPS** .......... Main Propulsion System [*or Subsystem*] [*NASA*] (KSC)
**MPS** .......... Maintenance Performance System [*DoD*]
**MPS** .......... Maintenance Problem Summary
**MPS** .......... Management Policy Statement
**MPS** .......... Managerial Philosophies Scale [*Test*]
**MPS** .......... Manpower System (NRCH)
**MPS** .......... Manual Phase Shifter
**MPS** .......... Manufacturing Process Specification (AAG)
**MPS** .......... Marbled Paper Sides [*Bookbinding*]
**MPS** .......... Marginal Propensity to Save [*Economics*]
**MPS** .......... Marine Polymetalic Sulfide
**MPS** .......... Marine Prepositioned Ships Program
**MPS** .......... Maritime Postmark Society [*Later, USCS*] (EA)
**MPS** .......... Maritime Prepositioning Ship (MCD)
**MPS** .......... Marriage Prediction Schedule [*Psychology*]
**MPS** .......... Master of Personnel Services
**MPS** .......... Master Planning Schedule (MCD)
**MPS** .......... Master Production Schedule
**MPS** .......... Master of Professional Studies in Human Relations
**MPS** .......... Master Program Schedule (NASA)
**MPS** .......... Master Project Summary [*Civil Defense*]
**M Ps** .......... Master of Psychology
**MPS** .......... Material Planning Study
**MPS** .......... Material Processing Specification (NASA)
**MPS** .......... Material Processing System
**MPS** .......... Materials Processing in Space
**MPS** .......... Materiel Planning Study [*Army*]
**MPS** .......... Mathematical Programming Society [*Voorburg, Netherlands*] (EAIO)
**MPS** .......... Mathematical Programming Studies [*Elsevier Book Series*] [*A publication*]
**MPS** .......... Mathematical Programming System [*Data processing*]
**MPS** .......... Mechanical Phase Shifter
**MPS** .......... Mechanical Power Systems
**MPS** .......... Median Period of Survival
**MPS** .......... MegaBITS [*Binary Digits*] per Second [*Transmission rate*] [*Data proccssing*] (MCD)
**MPS** .......... Member of the Pharmaceutical Society [*British*]
**MPS** .......... Member of the Philological Society [*British*]
**MPS** .......... Member of the Physical Society [*British*]
**MPS** .......... Memory Processor Switch
**MPS** .......... Mercury Procedures Simulator [*NASA*]
**MPS** .......... Merit Pay System (MCD)
**MPS** .......... Mervyn Peake Society (EA)
**MPS** .......... Message Processing System (NVT)
**MPS** .......... Meters per Second
**MPS** .......... Methodist Philatelic Society (EA)
**MPS** .......... Microbial Profile System [*Microbiology*]
**MPS** .......... Microphone Power Supply
**MPS** .......... Microprocessor Series [*or System*] (MDG)
**MPS** .......... Microwave Phase Shifter
**MPS** .......... Microwave Pressure Sounder (MCD)
**MPS** .......... Microwave Pulse Source
**MPS** .......... Miles per Second
**MPS** .......... Military Planning Staff (CINC)
**MPS** .......... Military Postal Service (AFM)
**MPS** .......... Military Production Specifications
**MPS** .......... Minimum Piecework Standard [*British*]
**MPS** .......... Minimum Property Standards [*FHA*]
**MPS** .......... Minister of Public Security [*British*]
**MPS** .......... Miss Porter's School [*Farmington, CT*]
**MPS** .......... Mission Parcels Society [*British*]
**MPS** .......... Mission Preparation Sheet
**MPS** .......... Mission Profile Simulator [*NASA*]
**MPS** .......... Modern Poetry Studies [*A publication*]
**MPS** .......... Modular Power System (MCD)
**MPS** .......... Molecular Photoemission Spectroscopy
**MPS** .......... Mononuclear Phagocyte System [*Hematology*]
**MPS** .......... Mont Pelerin Society (EA)
**MPS** .......... Motion Picture Service [*Department of Agriculture*]
**MPS** .......... Motor Pump System (MCD)
**MPS** .......... Mount Pleasant [*Texas*] [*Airport symbol*] [*Obsolete*] (OAG)
**MPS** .......... Mouvement Populaire Senegalais [*Senegalese Popular Movement*] [*Political party*]
**MPS** .......... Movement-Produced Stimuli
**MPS** .......... MPS [*Mucopolysaccharidoses*] Society (EA)
**MPS** .......... Mucopolysaccharide [*Also, MP*] [*Clinical chemistry*]
**MPS** .......... Mucopolysaccharidosis [*Medicine*]
**MPS** .......... Multiparticle Spectrometer [*Brookhaven National Laboratory*]
**MPS** .......... Multiphasic Screening [*Medicine*]
**MPS** .......... Multiple Protective Structure [*Missile bases*]
**MPS** .......... Multiple Vertical Protective Shelter [*for missiles*]
**MPS** .......... Multiprocessing System [*Data processing*]
**MPS** .......... Multiprogramming System [*Data processing*]
**MPS** .......... Multipurpose Ship (AABC)
**MPS** .......... Muzzle Position Sensor (MCD)
**MPS** .......... Myeloma Progression Score [*Oncology*]
**MPS** .......... Society for Mucopolysaccharide Diseases (EA)
**MPSA** ........ Master of Public School Art
**MPSA** ........ Metropolitan Pharmaceutical Secretaries Association (EA)
**MPSA** ........ Military Petroleum Supply Agency [*Later, Defense Petroleum Supply Center*]
**MPSA** ........ Santiago [*Panama*] [*ICAO location identifier*] (ICLI)
**MPSB** ........ MPS Bancorp [*NASDAQ symbol*] (NQ)
**MPSC** ........ Marianas Political Status Commission
**MPSC** ........ Material Planning Schedule and Control [*Division of Inspection Offices, Navy*]
**MPSC** ........ Military Personnel Security Committee
**MPSC** ........ Military Provost Staff Corps [*British*]
**MPSC** ........ Movimiento Popular Socialcristiano [*Christian Social Popular Movement*] [*El Salvador*] [*Political party*] (PD)
**MPSCL** ..... Mathematical Programming System Control Language [*1974*] [*Data processing*] (CSR)
**MPSE** ........ Motion Picture Sound Editors (EA)
**MPSE** ........ Multipurpose Payload Support Equipment (MCD)
**MPSG** ........ Marketing Programs and Services Group, Inc. [*Gaithersburg, MD*] [*Information service or system*] [*Telecommunications*] (TSSD)
**MPSG** ........ MPSI Systems, Inc. [*NASDAQ symbol*] (NQ)
**M & P Sh** ... Maude and Pollock's Law of Merchant Shipping [*A publication*] (DLA)
**MPSH** ....... Mean Pressure Suction Head (AAG)
**MPS-HHSA** ... Master of Professional Studies-Hospital and Health Services Administration
**MPSI** ......... Message Processing Systems, Incorporated [*Charlotte, NC*] [*Telecommunications service*] (TSSD)
**MPSI** ......... Meyers Parking System, Incorporated [*NASDAQ symbol*] (NQ)
**MPSIG** ...... Monty Python Special Interest Group (EA)
**MPSK** ........ Multiple Phase Shift Keying [*Data processing*] (TEL)
**MPSM** ....... Master Problem Status Manual
**MPSM** ....... Master of Public School Music
**MPSM** ....... MODEM Pooling Service Module [*Telecommunications*]
**MPSM** ....... Multipurpose Submunition (RDA)
**MPSN** ....... Microwave Pulse Shaping Network
**M Ps N** ...... Monatsschrift fuer Psychiatrie und Neurologie [*A publication*]
**MPSNY** ..... Montserrat Progressive Society of New York (EA)
**MPSOA** ..... Preprint Series. Institute of Mathematics. University of Oslo [*A publication*]
**MP SOV GR COM** ... Most Puissant Sovereign Grand Commander [*United States*] [*Freemasonry*] (ROG)
**MPSP** ........ Mathematical Problem-Solving Project [*National Science Foundation*]
**MPSP** ........ Military Personnel Security Program
**MPSR** ........ Mission Profile Storage and Retrieval [*NASA*] (NASA)
**MPSR** ........ Multipurpose Support Room (MCD)
**MPSRT** ..... Matched-Pairs Signed-Rank Test [*Statistics*]
**MPSS** ........ Main Parachute Support Structure (NASA)
**MPSS** ........ Mission Payload System Segment
**MPSS** ........ Multipurpose Sampling System
**MPSSA** ..... Meditsinskaya Promyshlennost SSSR [*A publication*]
**M Ps Sc** ..... Master of Physic Sciences
**MPSSP** ...... Modern Problems in Solid State Physics [*Elsevier Book Series*] [*A publication*]
**MPST** ........ Minimum Performance Standard Test [*Military*] (CAAL)
**M Ps Th** ..... Master of Psycho-Therapy
**MPSTWG** ... Mission Planning System Test Working Group [*Military*] (CAAL)
**MPSU** ........ Missile Pressure Status Unit (AAG)
**MPSV** ........ Myeloproliferative Sarcoma Virus
**MPSX** ........ Mathematical Programming System Extended [*IBM Corp.*] [*Data processing*]
**MPsych** ...... Master of Psychology
**MPsychApp** ... Master of Applied Psychology (ADA)
**MPsych(Clin)** ... Master of Psychology (Clinical)
**MPsych(Ed)** ... Master of Psychology (Education)
**MPsychMed** ... Master of Psychological Medicine, University of Liverpool [*British*] (DBQ)
**MPsychol** ... Master of Psychology
**M Psy Med** ... Master of Psychological Medicine
**MPSZA** ..... Magyar Pszichologiai Szemle [*A publication*]
**MPT** .......... Alpha-Methyl-p-tyrosine [*Also, AMPT*] [*Pharmacology*]
**MPT** .......... Magnetic Particle Testing [*Nuclear energy*] (NRCH)
**MPT** .......... Main Propulsion Test [*NASA*] (NASA)
**MPT** .......... Male Pipe Thread (MSA)
**MPT** .......... Maneuver Planning Table [*NASA*]
**MPT** .......... Manpower, Personnel, and Training
**MPT** .......... Marginal Propensity to Tax [*Economics*]
**MPT** .......... Maryland Public Television [*Owings Mills*] [*Information service or system*] [*Telecommunications*] (TSSD)
**MPT** .......... Matupit Island [*New Britain*] [*Seismograph station code, US Geological Survey*] (SEIS)
**MPT** .......... Mean Preventive Maintenance Time (MCD)
**MPT** .......... Mean Pulse Time
**MPT** .......... Mechanical Power Transmission
**M PT** .......... Melting Point (ROG)
**MPT** .......... Memory Processing Time

**MPT** .......... Mercury Procedures Trainer
**MPT** .......... Metal-Phthalocyanine Tetramine [*Organic chemistry*]
**MPT** .......... Methyl-para-Tyrosine [*Biochemistry*]
**MPT** .......... Michigan Picture Test [*Psychology*]
**MPT** .......... Microprogramming Technique
**MPT** .......... Military Potential Test (AABC)
**MPT** .......... Minimum Pressurization Temperature [*Nuclear energy*] (NRCH)
**MPT** .......... Minimum Process Time
**MPT** .......... Ministry of Posts and Telecommunications [*Japan*] (ECON)
**MPT** .......... Missile Preflight Tester
**MPT** .......... Missile Procedure Trainer
**MPT** .......... Mission Planning Table [*NASA*] (KSC)
**MPT** .......... Mission Planning Terminal (MCD)
**MPT** .......... Mixed Parotid Gland Tumor [*Oncology*]
**MPT** .......... Modern Portfolio Theory [*Finance*]
**MPT** .......... MOS [*Military Occupational Specialty*] Proficiency Training [*DoD*]
**MPT** .......... Motional Pickup Transducer (MCD)
**MPT** .......... Mouvement Populaire Tchadien [*Chadian Popular Movement*] [*Political party*]
**MPT** .......... Mouvement Populaire Togolais [*Togolese Popular Movement*] [*Political party*]
**MPT** .......... Multilateral Preparatory Talks (NATG)
**MPT** .......... Multiple Pure Tone [*Sound*]
**MPT** .......... Multiple-Purpose Telescope
**MPTA**........ Main Propulsion Test Article [*NASA*]
**MPTA**........ Manpower, Personnel, and Training Analysis
**MPTA**........ Mechanical Power Transmission Association (EA)
**MPTAO** .... Military Personnel and Transportation Assistance Office (MCD)
**MPTB**........ Multisolid Pneumatic Transport Bed [*Chemical engineering*]
**MPTCA**..... Motion Picture and Television Credit Association (EA)
**MPTCMA** ... Motion Picture and Television Credit Managers Association [*Later, MPTCA*] (EA)
**MPTE**........ Multipurpose Test Equipment
**MPTEDA** ... Mechanical Power Transmission Equipment Distributors Association [*Later, Power Transmission Distributors Association*] (EA)
**MPTF**........ Main Propulsion Test Facility [*NASA*] (NASA)
**MPTF**........ Mission Planning Task Force (KSC)
**MPTF**........ Motion Picture and Television Fund (EA)
**MP & TF** ... Motion Picture and Television Fund
**MPTF**........ Music Performance Trust Funds (EA)
**MPTH**........ Methylphenothiazine [*Organic chemistry*]
**MPTh**........ Monatsschrift fuer Pastoraltheologie [*Goettingen*] [*A publication*]
**MPTHDI**... Monographs in Ophthalmology [*A publication*]
**MPTMH**... Major Peace Treaties of Modern History, 1648-1967 [*A publication*] (DLA)
**MPTO** ....... Methods and Procedures Technical Orders
**MPTO** ....... Tocumen/General Omar Torrijos H. [*Panama*] [*ICAO location identifier*] (ICLI)
**MPTP**........ Main Propulsion Test Program (MCD)
**MPTP**........ Materials Processing. Theory and Practices [*Elsevier Book Series*] [*A publication*]
**MPTP**........ Methyl(phenyl)tetrahydropyridine [*Organic chemistry*]
**MPTP**........ Music Preference Test of Personality [*Psychology*]
**MPTR**........ Mobile Position Tracking RADAR
**MPTR**........ Multipurpose Training Range [*Army*]
**MPTS**........ Manpower, Personnel, Training, and Safety [*Army*]
**MPTS**........ Manpower, Personnel, and Training Support [*Military*] (CAAL)
**MPTS**........ Metal Parts (AABC)
**MPTS**........ Mobile Photographic Tracking Station
**MPTS**........ Multipurpose Tool Set (MCD)
**MP(TSWG)** ... Military Police Tripartite Standing Working Group (AABC)
**MPTUS**...... Marble Polishers' Trade Union Society [*British*]
**MPTWT**.... Medium Power Traveling Wave Tube
**MPU**.......... Main Power Unit
**MPU**.......... Main Propulsion Unit
**MPU**.......... Major Projects Unit [*Victoria, Australia*]
**MPU**.......... Malayan Planning Unit [*World War II*]
**MPU**.......... Manpack Unit (MCD)
**MPU**.......... Mapua [*Papua New Guinea*] [*Airport symbol*] [*Obsolete*] (OAG)
**MPU**.......... Medical Practitioners' Union [*Later, Medical Practitioners' Section - MPS*] [*British*] (DCTA)
**MPU**.......... Memory Protection Unit
**MPU**.......... Message Picking-Up
**MPU**.......... Microprocessor Unit [*CPU of microcomputer*] [*Data processing*]
**MPU**.......... MIDI [*Musical Instrument Digital Interface*] Processing Unit [*Computer technology*]
**MPU**.......... Miniature Portable Unit
**MPU**.......... Minutes per Unit
**MPU**.......... Mixing and Pumping Unit [*Bulk explosives*] (MCD)
**MPU**.......... Monitor Printing Unit [*Data processing*]
**MPU**.......... Motor Pressurization Unit
**MPU**.......... Motorola Processor Unit
**M Pub Adm** ... Master of Public Administration
**MPubLaw** ... Master of Public Law
**MPubPol** ... Master of Public Policy
**MPUL** ....... Military Production Urgencies List (NG)
**MPUS**........ Military Production Urgencies System
**MPV** .......... Magistrae Piae Venerini [*Religious Venerini Sisters*] [*Roman Catholic religious order*]
**MPV** .......... Magnetic Polarization Vector
**MPV** .......... Man-Powered Vehicle
**MPV** .......... Mass Mutual Participating Investors [*NYSE symbol*] (CTT)
**MPV** .......... Mean Platelet Volume [*Hematology*]
**MPV** .......... Meerwein-Ponndorf-Verley [*Organic chemistry*]
**MPV** .......... Methane-Powered Vehicle
**MPV** .......... Military Pay Voucher
**MPV** .......... Montpelier [*Vermont*] [*Airport symbol*] (OAG)
**MPV** .......... Mountain Province [*Vancouver Stock Exchange symbol*]
**MPV** .......... Multipurpose Passenger Vehicle
**MPV** .......... Multipurpose Vehicle [*Automotive engineering*]
**MPVA** ....... Main Propellant Valve Actuator (MCD)
**MPVA** ....... Maintain a Position VFR [*Visual Flight Rules*] and Advise [*Aviation*] (FAAC)
**MP/VAP** ... Maritime Patrol/Reconnaissance Attack Aircraft (NATG)
**MPVO**....... Mestnaia Protivovozdushnaia Oborona [*Local Anti-Air Defense*] [*USSR*]
**MPVR** ....... El Porvenir [*Panama*] [*ICAO location identifier*] (ICLI)
**MPVSCS**... Military Pay Voucher Summary and Certification Sheet
**MPVT**........ Montpelier [*Vermont*] [*Seismograph station code, US Geological Survey*] (SEIS)
**MPW** ......... Ministry of Public Works [*Vietnam*]
**MPW** ......... Modified Plane Wave (IEEE)
**MPW** ......... Whiteshell Nuclear Research Establishment, Atomic Energy of Canada [*Etablissement de Recherche Nucleaire Whiteshell, L'Energie Atomique du Canada*] Pinawa, Manitoba [*Library symbol*] [*National Library of Canada*] (NLC)
**MPWB** ...... Multilayer Printed-Wiring Board
**MPWC** ...... Michigan Pure Water Council (EA)
**MPWD** ...... Machine-Prepared Wiring Data [*Telecommunications*] (TEL)
**MPWG** ...... Minuteman Parts Working Group [*Missiles*]
**MPWH**...... Ministry of Public Works and Highways [*Philippines*] (DS)
**MPWS**....... Mobile Protected Weapon System (RDA)
**MPWSEX** ... West Virginia University. Agriculture and Forestry Experiment Station. Miscellaneous Publication [*A publication*]
**MPWU** ...... Movement for Political World Union [*Blommenslyst, Fyn, Denmark*] (EA)
**MPX** .......... Microprocessor Exchange [*Data processing*]
**MPX** .......... Multiplex [*or Multiplexer*] [*Telecommunications*]
**MPX** .......... Multiprogramming Executive [*Data processing*]
**MPXR**........ Multiplexer
**MPY** .......... Milli-Inches per Year [*Corrosion technology*]
**MPY** .......... Multiple Problem Youth
**MPY** .......... Multiply (MDG)
**MPZ** .......... Modified Protamine Zinc [*Insulin*]
**MPZ** .......... Mount Pleasant, IA [*Location identifier*] [*FAA*] (FAAL)
**MPZL**........ Panama [*Panama*] [*ICAO location identifier*] (ICLI)
**MQ** ............ Management Quarterly Magazine [*A publication*] (EAAP)
**MQ** ............ MARC [*Machine-Readable Cataloging*] Quebecois [*Source file*] [*UTLAS symbol*]
**MQ** ............ Marketing Quota
**mq** ............. Martinique [*MARC country of publication code*] [*Library of Congress*] (LCCP)
**MQ** ............ Martinique [*ANSI two-letter standard code*] (CNC)
**MQ** ............ Massachusetts Law Quarterly [*A publication*]
**MQ** ............ Menaquinone [*Vitamin K*] [*Also, MK*] [*Biochemistry*]
**MQ** ............ Merit Quotient
**MQ** ............ Metol-Quinol [*Developer*] [*Photography*] (ROG)
**MQ** ............ Midwest Quarterly [*A publication*]
**MQ** ............ Milton Quarterly [*A publication*]
**MQ** ............ Mining and Quarrying [*Department of Employment*] [*British*]
**MQ** ............ Modern Quarterly [*A publication*]
**MQ** ............ Mo'ed Qatan [*or Qattan*] (BJA)
**MQ** ............ Mothering Quotient
**MQ** ............ Multiplier Quotient [*Data processing*]
**MQ** ............ Musical Quarterly [*A publication*]
**MQ** ............ Societa Aerea Mediterranea [*Italy*] [*ICAO designator*] (FAAC)
**MQ** ............ Thomas Crane Public Library, Quincy, MA [*Library symbol*] [*Library of Congress*] (LCLS)
**MQA**.......... Adams Mansion, Quincy, MA [*Library symbol*] [*Library of Congress*] (LCLS)
**MQA**.......... Manual of Qualification for Advancement
**MQA**.......... Manuel des Questions Actuelles [*A publication*]
**MQA**.......... Manufacturing Quality Assurance
**MQA**.......... Murrayaquinone-A [*Biochemistry*]
**MQAD**........ Materials Quality Assurance Directorate [*Ministry of Defence*] [*British*]
**MQB**.......... Macomb, IL [*Location identifier*] [*FAA*] (FAAL)
**MQCL**........ Master Quality Characteristic List (MCD)
**MQD** ......... Manhattan, KS [*Location identifier*] [*FAA*] (FAAL)
**MQD** ......... Milner. Questions de Droit [*A publication*] (DLA)
**MQD** ......... Monolithic Quad Device
**MQE**.......... Message Queue Element [*Data processing*]
**MQELA** .... Mecanique Electricite [*A publication*]
**MQF**.......... Mobile Quarantine Facility [*NASA*]

**MQG** ......... General Dynamics, Quincy Shipbuilding Division, Quincy, MA [*Library symbol*] [*Library of Congress*] (LCLS)
**MQG** ......... Mitteilungen. Rheinisch-Westfaelisches Institut fuer Wirtschaftsforschung [*A publication*]
**MQHi** ........ Quincy Historical Society, Quincy, MA [*Library symbol*] [*Library of Congress*] (LCLS)
**MQI** .......... Macquarie Island [*Australia*] [*Seismograph station code, US Geological Survey*] [*Closed*] (SEIS)
**MQI** .......... Manteo, NC [*Location identifier*] [*FAA*] (FAAL)
**MQIL** ........ Miniature Quartz Incandescent Lamp
**MQJ** .......... Indianapolis, IN [*Location identifier*] [*FAA*] (FAAL)
**MQK** .......... Youngstown, OH [*Location identifier*] [*FAA*] (FAAL)
**Mq L** .......... Marquette Law Review [*A publication*]
**MQL** .......... Mildura [*Australia*] [*Airport symbol*] (OAG)
**MQL** .......... Miniature Quartz Lamp
**Mq LR** ....... Marquette Law Review [*A publication*]
**MQM** ........ Message Queue Manager [*Data processing*] (MCD)
**MQM** ........ Mohajir Qami Movement [*Pakistan*] [*Political party*]
**MQM** ........ Monida, MT [*Location identifier*] [*FAA*] (FAAL)
**MQM** ........ University of New Mexico, Medical Center Library, Albuquerque, NM [*OCLC symbol*] (OCLC)
**MQN** ......... Magnetic Quantum Number [*Atomic physics*]
**MQO** ......... Marksmanship Qualification Order [*Marine Corps*]
**MQO** ......... Mosquito Creek Gold Mining [*Vancouver Stock Exchange symbol*]
**MQP** .......... Military Qualification Program (NG)
**MQP** .......... Mineral Wells, TX [*Location identifier*] [*FAA*] (FAAL)
**MQP** .......... Motor Qualification Program (NG)
**MQR** .......... Mennonite Quarterly Review [*A publication*]
**MQR** .......... Michigan Quarterly Review [*A publication*]
**MQR** .......... Miscellaneous Quote Request (MCD)
**MQR** .......... Multiplier Quotient Register [*Data processing*]
**MQRYA** .... Mine and Quarry [*A publication*]
**MQS** .......... Coatesville, PA [*Location identifier*] [*FAA*] (FAAL)
**MQS** .......... Maintenance Quality Specialist (MCD)
**MQS** .......... Master of Quantitative Systems
**MQS** .......... Military Qualification Standard
**MQS** .......... Motion to Quash Subpoena (NRCH)
**MQS** .......... Mustique [*Windward Islands*] [*Airport symbol*] (OAG)
**MQSS** ......... Mary Queen of Scots Society (EAIO)
**MQT** .......... Macquest Resources Ltd. [*Toronto Stock Exchange symbol*]
**MQT** .......... Macroscopic Quantum Tunneling [*Quantum mechanics*]
**MQT** .......... Marquette [*Michigan*] [*Airport symbol*] (OAG)
**MQT** .......... Military Qualification Test (NG)
**MQT** .......... Mission Qualification Training
**MQT** .......... Model Qualification Test
**MQT** .......... Motor Qualification Test (NG)
**MQU** ......... Beckley, WV [*Location identifier*] [*FAA*] (FAAL)
**MQU** ......... Makus Resources, Inc. [*Vancouver Stock Exchange symbol*]
**MQU** ......... Management Quarterly [*A publication*]
**MQU** ......... Mariquita [*Colombia*] [*Airport symbol*] (OAG)
**MQU** ......... Media Quality Unit [*Communications*]
**MQU** ......... Multinational Business [*A publication*]
**MQU** ......... Multiplier Quotient Unit [*Data processing*]
**MQW** ......... McRae, GA [*Location identifier*] [*FAA*] (FAAL)
**MQW** ......... Multiple Quantum Well [*Switch for an optical computer*]
**MQX** .......... Makale [*Ethiopia*] [*Airport symbol*] (OAG)
**MQY** .......... Smyrna, TN [*Location identifier*] [*FAA*] (FAAL)
**MR** ............. Air Mauritanie [*Mauritania*] [*ICAO designator*] (ICDA)
**MR** ............. Application for Writ of Mandamus Refused [*Legal term*] (DLA)
**MR** ............. Machine Records
**MR** ............. Machine Rifle
**MR** ............. Machinery Repairman [*Navy rating*]
**M & R** ........ Maclean and Robinson's Scotch Appeal Cases [*1839*] [*A publication*] (DLA)
**MR** ............. Macrophage Rich
**MR** ............. Magister [*Master*] [*Latin*] (ROG)
**MR** ............. Magnetic Recorder (DEN)
**MR** ............. Magnetic Resonance
**MR** ............. Magnitude of Rotation
**MR** ............. Maintainability Report
**MR** ............. Maintenance Ratio (MCD)
**M & R** ........ Maintenance and Refurbishment (NASA)
**M & R** ........ Maintenance and Repair
**MR** ............. Maintenance Review
**MR** ............. Mainzer Reihe [*A publication*]
**MR** ............. Management Requirements (MCD)
**MR** ............. Management Reserve (MCD)
**MR** ............. Manitoba Law Reports [*Canada*] [*A publication*] (DLA)
**M & R** ........ Manning and Ryland's English King's Bench Reports [*1827-30*] [*A publication*] (DLA)
**MR** ............. Manpower Requirements
**MR** ............. Manual Removal [*Medicine*]
**MR** ............. Manufacturer's Representative
**MR** ............. Manufacturing Requisition
**MR** ............. Map Reading
**MR** ............. Map Reference
**MR** ............. Marble (AAG)
**MR** ............. Marca Registrada [*Registered Trademark*] [*Spanish*]
**MR** ............. March [*A publication*]
**MR** ............. March
**MR** ............. Marche Romane [*A publication*]
**MR** ............. Marginal Return [*Army*] (AABC)
**MR** ............. Marginal Revenue [*Economics*]
**MR** ............. Marine-Rundschau [*A publication*]
**MR** ............. Maritime Reconnaissance (NATG)
**MR** ............. Maritime Regiment
**MR** ............. Marketing Research Division [*of AMS, Department of Agriculture*]
**MR** ............. Mask Register
**MR** ............. Massachusetts Review [*A publication*]
**MR** ............. Master [*British military*] (DMA)
**MR** ............. Master Reset (MCD)
**MR** ............. Master of the Rolls
**MR** ............. Material Request [*or Requisition*] (MCD)
**MR** ............. Material Review [*Aviation*] (AAG)
**MR** ............. Materiel Readiness [*Army*]
**MR** ............. Mate's Receipt
**MR** ............. Mathematical Reviews [*A publication*]
**MR** ............. Mauritania [*ANSI two-letter standard code*] (CNC)
**MR** ............. Mauritius Decisions [*A publication*] (DLA)
**MR** ............. Mauritius Reports [*A publication*] (DLA)
**MR** ............. Maximal Response
**MR** ............. May Repeat [*Medicine*]
**MR** ............. Mean Radius (MCD)
**Mr** ............. Meander [*A publication*]
**MR** ............. Measles, Rubella [*Immunology*]
**M & R** ........ Measure and Record
**MR** ............. Mechanical Restraint [*for mental patients*] [*British*]
**M & R** ........ Mediaeval and Renaissance Studies [*A publication*]
**MR** ............. Medial Rectus [*Eye anatomy*]
**MR** ............. Medical Record
**MR** ............. Medical Rectus [*Muscle*] [*Anatomy*]
**MR** ............. Medical Report
**MR** ............. Medium Range
**MR** ............. Medium-Range Planes [*Navy*]
**MR** ............. Medium Resolution
**MR** ............. Memorandum Receipt [*Military*] (MUGU)
**MR** ............. Memorandum for Record [*Military*] (AFM)
**MR** ............. Memorandum Report
**MR** ............. Memory Read [*Data processing*]
**MR** ............. Memory Reclaimer
**MR** ............. Memory Register [*Data processing*]
**MR** ............. Mental Retardation
**MR** ............. Mercury-Redstone [*NASA*]
**MR** ............. Message Register (AAG)
**MR** ............. Message Repeat
**MR** ............. Metabolic Rate
**MR** ............. Meter
**MR** ............. Methacholine Response [*Medicine*]
**MR** ............. Methyl Red [*A dye*]
**MR** ............. Methyl Reductase [*An enzyme*]
**MR** ............. Metropolitan Railway [*British*]
**MR** ............. Mi Remesa [*My Remittance*] [*Spanish*] [*Business term*]
**MR** ............. Michael Resources Ltd. [*Vancouver Stock Exchange symbol*]
**MR** ............. Microform Review [*A publication*]
**MR** ............. Microminiature Relay
**MR** ............. Microplate Reader [*Data processing*]
**MR** ............. Middle Repetitive [*Genetics*]
**MR** ............. [*The*] Middlesex Regiment [*British*]
**MR** ............. Midland Railway [*British*]
**MR** ............. Midrib [*Botany*]
**MR** ............. Military Readiness
**MR** ............. Military Region [*Viet Cong term*]
**MR** ............. Military Regulation
**MR** ............. Military Representative (NATG)
**MR** ............. Military Requirement
**M/R** ........... Military Reserve (CINC)
**MR** ............. Military Review (MCD)
**MR** ............. Militia Reserve [*British military*] (DMA)
**MR** ............. Mill Run [*Unselected lot of a manufactured product*]
**MR** ............. Milliradian (DEN)
**MR** ............. Millirem (DEN)
**mr** ............. Milliroentgen
**MR** ............. Milrinone [*Biochemistry*]
**M & R** ........ Milton and the Romantics [*A publication*]
**MR** ............. Mine-Run
**MR** ............. Mineral Rubber
**MR** ............. Mineralo-Corticoid Receptor [*Endocrinology*]
**MR** ............. Mini Registry (EA)
**MR** ............. Minimum Required
**MR** ............. Mining Reports, Edited by R. S. Morrison [*Chicago*] [*A publication*] (DLA)
**MR** ............. Minister-Residentiary [*Diplomacy*]
**MR** ............. Ministry of Reconstruction [*British*] [*World War I*]
**MR** ............. Minnesota Review [*A publication*]
**MR** ............. Minor Repair (MCD)
**MR** ............. Miscellaneous Report
**MR** ............. Missale Romanum [*A publication*]
**MR** ............. Missile RADAR [*Military*] (CAAL)
**MR** ............. Missile Receiver

MR ............ Missile Reference
MR ............ Missile Rounds (MCD)
M/R ............ Missiles and Rockets [*A publication*]
MR ............ Mission Radius (MCD)
MR ............ Mission Ready [*Aircraft*]
MR ............ Mission Reliability
MR ............ Mission Report [*NASA*]
MR ............ Missionarius Rector [*Missionary Rector*] [*Latin*]
MR ............ Missionswissenschaft und Religionswissenschaft [*A publication*]
MR ............ Mister
MR ............ Mistura [*Mixture*] [*Pharmacy*] (ROG)
MR ............ Mitochondriarich [*Cytology*]
MR ............ Mitral Regurgitation [*Cardiology*]
MR ............ Mittleres Reich in Aegypten [*A publication*] (BJA)
MR ............ Mixture Ratio (KSC)
MR ............ Mladinska Revija [*A publication*]
Mr ............ Mobile Revertant [*Bacteriology*]
MR ............ Mobility Required [*Civil Service*]
MR ............ Mobilization Regulation [*Army*]
MR ............ MODEM Ready [*Data processing*]
MR ............ Moderately Resistant [*Plant pathology*]
MR ............ [*The*] Modern Reader's Bible (1907) [*A publication*] (BJA)
MR ............ Modern Review [*A publication*]
MR ............ Modification Request [*or Requirement*]
M-R ............ Modification and Restriction [*of DNA*] [*Biochemistry, genetics*]
MR ............ Modular Redundancy
MR ............ Modulation Response
MR ............ Moisture Resistant (IEEE)
MR ............ Molar Refraction
MR ............ Molecular Replacement [*Crystallography*]
MR ............ Moment of Resistance
MR ............ Mondcivitan Republic (EAIO)
MR ............ Monitor Recorder
MR ............ Montana Law Review [*A publication*]
MR ............ Monthly Report
MR ............ Monthly Review
MR ............ Monthly Review [*A publication*]
M & R ............ Moody and Robinson's English Nisi Prius Reports [*1830-44*] [*A publication*] (DLA)
MR ............ Morgan's Foods [*AMEX symbol*] (SPSG)
MR ............ Morning Report [*Army*]
mr ............ Morocco [*MARC country of publication code*] [*Library of Congress*] (LCCP)
MR ............ Morris Register [*An association*] (EAIO)
MR ............ Mortality Rates
MR ............ Motivation Research
MR ............ Motor Reduction
MR ............ Multi-Mirror Reflector [*Lamp*]
MR ............ Multiple Requesting [*IBM Corp.*]
MR ............ Multiplier Register
MR ............ Municipal Reform [*or Reformer*]
MR ............ Muscle Relaxant
MR ............ Music Records [*Record label*]
MR ............ Music Review [*A publication*]
Mr ............ Musikrevy [*A publication*]
MR ............ Muster Report
MR ............ Mutual Responsibility [*Movement within Anglican Communion to make its mission more efficacious*]
MR ............ Mycorrhizal Roots [*Botany*]
MR ............ Radiolocation Mobile Station [*ITU designation*]
MR ............ Reading Public Library, Reading, MA [*Library symbol*] [*Library of Congress*] (LCLS)
mr----- ............ Red Sea and Area [*MARC geographic area code*] [*Library of Congress*] (LCCP)
MR ............ Societe Nationale Air Mauritanie [*ICAO designator*] (FAAC)
MR1 ............ Machinery Repairman, First Class [*Navy rating*]
MR2 ............ Machinery Repairman, Second Class [*Navy rating*]
MR3 ............ Machinery Repairman, Third Class [*Navy rating*]
MR 13 ............ Movimiento Revolucionario 13 de Noviembre [*Guatemala*]
MRA ............ Golden Myra Resources, Inc. [*Toronto Stock Exchange symbol*]
MRA ............ Machine Readable Archives Division [*Public Archives of Canada*] [*Information service or system*] (IID)
MRA ............ Machine Records Activity
MRA ............ Mainzer Romanistische Arbeiten [*A publication*]
M & RA ............ Manpower and Reserve Affairs
MRA ............ Manufacturers Representatives of America (EA)
MRA ............ Maritime Royal Artillery [*British military*] (DMA)
MR & A ............ Market Research and Analysis
MRA ............ Marketing Research Association [*Chicago, IL*] (EA)
MRA ............ Masonic Relief Association of USA and Canada (EA)
MRA ............ Materials Review Area (AAG)
MRA ............ Maximum Rendezvous Altitude
MRA ............ Mean Right Atrial [*Cardiology*]
MRA ............ Mechanical Readiness Assessment (NASA)
MRA ............ Medial Right Abdomen [*Injection site*]
MRA ............ Medical Record Administrator
MRA ............ Medium-Powered Radio Range (Adcock)
MRA ............ Men's Rights Association (EA)
MRA ............ Menswear Retailers of America (EA)
MRA ............ Mental Retardation Abstracts [*A publication*]
MRA ............ Messtechnik, Regelungstechnik, Automatik [*Hoppenstedt Wirtschaftsdatenbank GmbH*] [*Federal Republic of Germany*] [*Information service or system*] (CRD)
MRA ............ Metropolitan Regional Abattoir [*Australia*]
MRA ............ Microgravity Research Associates
MRA ............ Midwest Resources Association [*Defunct*]
MRA ............ Minimum Reception Altitude [*Aviation*]
MRA ............ Minimum Reserve Authorization
MRA ............ Minimum Resolvable Angle
MRA ............ Missile RADAR Altimeter (MCD)
MRA ............ Misurata [*Libya*] [*Airport symbol*] (OAG)
MRA ............ Mixed Refrigerant Autocascade [*Cryogenic system*]
MRA ............ Model Reporting Area [*for Blindness Statistics*] [*HEW*]
MRA ............ Moral Re-Armament (EA)
MRA ............ Motorcycle Retailers of America [*Later, NMRA*] (EA)
MRA ............ Motorcycle Riders' Association [*Australia*]
MRA ............ Mountain Rescue Association (EA)
MRA ............ Multiple Recording Accelerometer
MRA ............ Multiple Resource Area Nomination [*National Register of Historic Places*]
MRA ............ Mycelium Radius Atrovirens [*A fungus*]
MRA ............ Rapid City Regional Library, Manitoba [*Library symbol*] [*National Library of Canada*] (NLC)
MRAA ............ Marine Retailers Association of America (EA)
MRAA ............ Mental Retardation Association of America (EA)
MRAALS ............ Marine Corps Remote Area Approach and Landing System (MCD)
MRAAM ............ Medium-Range Air-to-Air Missile (MCD)
MRAC ............ Manifold-Regulator Accumulator Charging [*Formerly, NCP*] (AAG)
MRAC ............ Measurement Research Advisory Committee [*Australia*]
MRAC ............ Member of the Royal Agricultural College [*British*]
MRAC ............ Meter-Reading Access Circuit [*Bell Laboratories*]
MRAC ............ Microamerica, Inc. [*NASDAQ symbol*] (CTT)
MRACP ............ Member of Royal Australasian College of Physicians
MRACS ............ Member of the Royal Australasian College of Surgeons
MRAD ............ Mass Random Access Disk [*Data processing*]
M Rad ............ Master of Radiology
MRAD ............ Milliradians (KSC)
MRadA ............ Member of the Radionic Association [*British*]
M Rad (D) ............ Master of Radiology (Radiodiagnosis)
MRADS ............ Mass Random Access Data Storage [*Data processing*]
M Rad (T) ............ Master of Radiology (Radiotherapy)
M Ra E ............ Master of Radio Engineering
M Ra Eng ............ Master of Radio Engineering
MRAeS ............ Member of the Royal Aeronautical Society [*British*] (ADA)
MRAF ............ Marshal of the Royal Air Force [*British*]
M-RAG ............ Moderately Repressive Authoritarian Government
MRAIC ............ Member of the Royal Architectural Institute of Canada
MRAJ ............ Aranjuez [*Costa Rica*] [*ICAO location identifier*] (ICLI)
MRaK ............ Myth, Ritual, and Kingship. Essays on the Theory and Practice of Kingship in the Ancient Near East and in Israel [*A publication*] (BJA)
MRAL ............ Alajuela [*Costa Rica*] [*ICAO location identifier*] (ICLI)
MRA & L ............ Manpower, Reserve Affairs and Logistics (MCD)
MRAL ............ Materiel Readiness Authorization List [*Military*]
MRAL ............ Memorie. Reale Accademia Nazionale dei Lincei [*A publication*]
MRAM ............ Amubri [*Costa Rica*] [*ICAO location identifier*] (ICLI)
MRAM ............ Member of the Royal Academy of Music [*British*]
MRAO ............ Mobilization Reserve Acquisition Objective [*Military*]
MRAP ............ Marginal Revenue/Average Physical Product [*Economics*]
MRAP ............ Mean Right Atrial Pressure [*Cardiology*]
MRAP ............ Mouvement Contre le Racisme et pour l'Amitie Entre les Peuples [*Movement Against Racism and for Friendship between People*] (EAIO)
MRAP ............ Movimiento de Resistencia Armada Puertorriquena [*Puerto Rican Armed Resistance Movement*] [*Political party*] (PD)
MRAPCON ............ Mobile RADAR Approach Control (AFM)
MRAR ............ Atirro [*Costa Rica*] [*ICAO location identifier*] (ICLI)
MRAS ............ Management Resources Accounting System
MRAS ............ Manpower Resources Accounting System [*Air Force*]
MRAS ............ Member of the Royal Academy of Science [*British*]
MRAS ............ Member of the Royal Asiatic Society [*British*]
MRASB ............ Member of the Royal Asiatic Society of Bengal
MRASE ............ Member of the Royal Agricultural Society of England
MRASM ............ Medium-Range Air-to-Surface Missile (MCD)
MRAT ............ Altamira De San Carlos [*Costa Rica*] [*ICAO location identifier*] (ICLI)
MRATCAB ............ Murray River and Tributaries - Current Awareness Bulletin [*A publication*] (APTA)
MRATE ............ Money Market Rates [*I. P. Sharp Associates*] [*Canada*] [*Information service or system*] (CRD)
MRAZBN ............ Musee Royal de l'Afrique Centrale [*Tervuren, Belgique*]. Annales. Serie in Octavo. Sciences Zoologiques [*A publication*]
MRB ............ Magnetic Recording Boresight [*or Borescope*]
MRB ............ Magnetospheric Radio Burst
MRB ............ Maintenance Review Board (MCD)

**MRB** ......... Malaysian Rubber Bureau (EA)
**MRB** ......... Marble [*Technical drawings*]
**MRB** ......... Marble Base (AAG)
**MRB** ......... Martinsburg, WV [*Location identifier*] [*FAA*] (FAAL)
**MRB** ......... Master Reference Buoy [*Navy*] (NVT)
**MRB** ......... Material Review Board [*Aviation*] (MCD)
**MRB** ......... Metals Reserve Board [*of the Reconstruction Finance Corp.*]
**MRB** ......... Mileage Rationing Board [*World War II*]
**MRB** ......... Mission Review Board [*NASA*]
**MRB** ......... Mister Build Industry, Inc. [*Vancouver Stock Exchange symbol*]
**MRB** ......... Mobile Riverine Base [*Navy*]
**MRB** ......... Modification Requirements Board [*NASA*] (KSC)
**MRB** ......... Modification Review Board (AFM)
**MRB** ......... Motor Rescue Boat
**MRB** ......... Motor Truck Rate Bureau Inc., Columbia SC [*STAC*]
**MRB** ......... Motorized Rifle Battalion [*USSR*] (INF)
**MRB** ......... Multi-Role Bomber [*Program*] [*DoD*]
**MRB** ......... Mutual Reinsurance Bureau (EA)
**MRBA** ....... Buenos Aires [*Costa Rica*] [*ICAO location identifier*] (ICLI)
**MRBA** ....... Merchants Bancorp, Inc. [*NASDAQ symbol*] (NQ)
**MRBB** ....... Babilonia [*Costa Rica*] [*ICAO location identifier*] (ICLI)
**MRBC** ....... Barra Del Colorado [*Costa Rica*] [*ICAO location identifier*] (ICLI)
**MRBC** ....... Missouri River Basin Commission
**MRBC** ....... Molded Rubber Blended Cover
**MRBC** ....... Monkey Red Blood Cells
**MRBCMA** ... Mean Rounds between Corrective Maintenance Actions [*Quality control*] (MCD)
**MR-BD** ...... Mercury-Redstone Booster Development [*Spacecraft*] [*NASA*]
**MRBDT** ..... Mitteilungen des Reichsbunds Deutscher Technik [*A publication*]
**MRBF** ........ Mean Renal Blood Flow [*Nephrology*]
**MRBF** ........ Mean Rounds between Failures [*Military*] (CAAL)
**MRBIR** ...... Municipal Registered Bond Interest Record [*Standard & Poor's Corp.*] [*Information service or system*] (CRD)
**MRBK** ....... Mercantile Bankshares Corp. [*NASDAQ symbol*] (NQ)
**MRBL** ........ Marble Financial Corp. [*Rutland, VT*] [*NASDAQ symbol*] (NQ)
**MRBM** ...... Bremen [*Costa Rica*] [*ICAO location identifier*] (ICLI)
**MRBM** ...... Medium [*or Mid*]-Range Ballistic Missile
**MRBN** ....... Bataan [*Costa Rica*] [*ICAO location identifier*] (ICLI)
**MRBNA** .... Member of the Royal British Nursing Association (ROG)
**MRBO** ....... Boca Naranjo [*Costa Rica*] [*ICAO location identifier*] (ICLI)
**MRBOAS** ... Marine Biology [*New York*] [*A publication*]
**MRBOMF** ... Mean Rounds between Operational Mission Failures [*Quality control*] (MCD)
**MRBP** ........ Barra De Parismina [*Costa Rica*] [*ICAO location identifier*] (ICLI)
**MRBP** ........ Missouri River Basin Project
**MRBS** ........ Mean Rounds between Stoppages [*Quality control*] (MCD)
**MRBS** ........ Modified Road Brigade Slice (MCD)
**MRBT** ........ Barra De Tortuguero [*Costa Rica*] [*ICAO location identifier*] (ICLI)
**MRBT** ........ Multirod Burst Test [*Nuclear energy*] (NRCH)
**MRC** .......... Columbia/Mt. Pleasant, TN [*Location identifier*] [*FAA*] (FAAL)
**MRC** .......... Graduate Center for Materials Research [*University of Missouri - Rolla*] [*Research center*] (RCD)
**MRC** .......... Interdepartmental Committee on Manpower Requirements [*British*] [*World War II*]
**MRC** .......... Machine-Readable Code
**MRC** .......... Machinery Repairman, Chief [*Navy rating*]
**MRC** .......... Magnetic Rectifier Control
**MRC** .......... Magnetic Research Corporation (MCD)
**MRC** .......... Maintenance and Repair Cycle
**MRC** .......... Maintenance Requirement Card
**MRC** .......... Major Readiness Command (MCD)
**MRC** .......... Major Retail Center
**MRC** .......... Management Research Center [*University of Wisconsin - Milwaukee*] [*Research center*] (RCD)
**MRC** .......... Management Research Corporation [*Shelbyville, IN*] [*Information service or system*] (IID)
**MRC** .......... Manitoba Research Council [*Research center*] (RCD)
**MRC** .......... Marietta College, Marietta, OH [*OCLC symbol*] (OCLC)
**MRC** .......... Marine Research Committee
**MRC** .......... Marine Resources Council
**MRC** .......... Market Research Council
**MRC** .......... Master of Rehabilitation Counseling
**MRC** .......... Master Requirements Code
**MRC** .......... Material Redistribution Center
**MRC** .......... Materials Research Center [*Northwestern University*] [*Research center*] (RCD)
**MRC** .......... Materials Research Center [*Lehigh University*] [*Research center*] (RCD)
**MRC** .......... Materials Research Corporation
**MRC** .......... Materials Review Crib (AAG)
**MRC** .......... Materiel Readiness Command [*Military*]
**MRC** .......... Materiel Release Confirmation [*Army*] (AABC)
**MRC** .......... Mathematics Research Center (MCD)
**MRC** .......... Maximum Reverse Current
**MRC** .......... Measurement Requirements Committee [*NASA*] (NASA)
**MRC** .......... Measurement Research Center [*University of Iowa*]
**MRC** .......... Medical Research Council [*United Kingdom*] [*Research center*] (IRC)
**MRC** .......... Medical Reserve Corps
**MRC** .......... Memorial Research Center [*University of Tennessee*] [*Research center*] (RCD)
**MRC** .......... Memory Request Controller
**MRC** .......... Men's Resource Center (EA)
**MRC** .......... Metals Reserve Company [*World War II*]
**MRC** .......... Meteorological Research Committee [*British*]
**MRC** .......... Methylrosaniline Chloride [*Also, GV*] [*A dye*]
**MRC** .......... Metrics Research Corporation [*Information service or system*] (IID)
**MRC** .......... Midwestern Relay Company [*Milwaukee, WI*] [*Telecommunications*] (TSSD)
**MRC** .......... Military Reform Caucus (EA)
**MRC** .......... Military Region Command (MCD)
**MRC** .......... Military Representatives Committee [*NATO*] (NATG)
**MRC** .......... Military Reunions Council (EA)
**MRC** .......... Military Revolutionary Council (CINC)
**MRC** .......... Milton Roy Company [*NYSE symbol*] (SPSG)
**MRC** .......... Minorco Canada Ltd. [*Toronto Stock Exchange symbol*]
**MRC** .......... Mission Requirements Change [*NASA*] (KSC)
**MRC** .......... Mississippi River Commission [*Army*] [*Vicksburg, MS*]
**MRC** .......... Model Railway Club [*British*]
**MRC** .......... Montrose [*Colorado*] [*Seismograph station code, US Geological Survey*] [*Closed*] (SEIS)
**MRC** .......... Moon's RADAR Coordinates
**MRC** .......... Morning Readiness Check
**MRC** .......... Motorized Rifle Company (INF)
**MRC** .......... Movement Report Center [*Military*]
**MRC** .......... Multiple Register Counter (IEEE)
**MRC** .......... Multiple Regression/Correlation [*Statistical analysis*]
**MRCA** ....... Canas [*Costa Rica*] [*ICAO location identifier*] (ICLI)
**MRCA** ....... Most Recent Common Ancestor
**MRCA** ....... Multirole Combat Aircraft
**MRCAS** ..... Monetary Ration Credit Allowance System [*Military*] (AFM)
**MRCAT** ..... Miniature Radio-Controlled Aerial Target (MCD)
**MRCC** ....... Coto 47 [*Costa Rica*] [*ICAO location identifier*] (ICLI)
**MRCC** ....... Mark Controls Corp. [*NASDAQ symbol*] (NQ)
**MRCC** ....... Material Review Central Control [*Aviation*] (MCD)
**MRCC** ....... Member of the Royal College of Chemistry [*British*]
**MRCC** ....... Mercury Recovery Control Center
**MRCC** ....... Molded Rubber Coupling Cushion
**MRCC** ....... Movement Report Control Center [*Military*]
**MRCCC** ..... Medical Research Council, Collaborative Centre [*British*] (CB)
**MRCD** ....... Caledonia [*Costa Rica*] [*ICAO location identifier*] (ICLI)
**MRCE** ....... Carate [*Costa Rica*] [*ICAO location identifier*] (ICLI)
**MRCE** ....... Marginal Relative Certainty Effect [*Statistics*]
**MRCF** ........ Mayo Biotechnology Research Computer Facility [*Mayo Clinic*] [*Research center*] (RCD)
**MRCF** ........ Module Repair Calibration Facility
**MRCGP** ..... Member of the Royal College of General Practitioners [*British*]
**MRCH** ....... Chacarita [*Costa Rica*] [*ICAO location identifier*] (ICLI)
**MRCHB** ..... Marine Chemistry [*A publication*]
**MRCHBD** ... Marine Chemistry [*A publication*]
**MRCI** ......... Ciruelas [*Costa Rica*] [*ICAO location identifier*] (ICLI)
**MRCI** ......... Marci International Imports, Inc. [*NASDAQ symbol*] (NQ)
**MRCI** ......... Mine Readiness/Certification Inspection (MCD)
**MRCL** ......... Mercurial
**MRCLBP** .. Marcellia [*A publication*]
**MRCM** ...... Machinery Repairman, Master Chief [*Navy rating*]
**MRCM** ...... Marcom Telecommunications, Inc. [*NASDAQ symbol*] (NQ)
**MRC (Med Res Counc) (GB) Lab Anim Cent Symp** ... MRC (Medical Research Council) (Great Britain). Laboratory Animals Centre. Symposia [*A publication*]
**MRCO** ....... Manufacturing Research Corp. of Ontario [*Research center*] [*Canada*] (RCD)
**MRCO** ....... Member of the Royal College of Organists [*British*]
**MRCO** ....... Meridian National Corporation [*Toledo, OH*] [*NASDAQ symbol*] (NQ)
**MRCOD** .... Mechanics Research Communications [*A publication*]
**MRCOG** .... Member of the Royal College of Obstetricians and Gynaecologists [*British*]
**MRCP** ........ Member of the Royal College of Physicians [*British*]
**MRCP** ........ Member of the Royal College of Preceptors [*British*]
**MRCP** ........ Microfilm Research Centers Project (EA)
**MRCP** ........ Mobile RADAR Control Post
**MRCPA** ..... Member of the Royal College of Pathologists of Australia
**MRCPA** ..... Mobilization Reserve Components Program of the Army (AABC)
**MRC Path** ... Member of the Royal College of Pathologists [*British*]
**MRCPE** ..... Member of the Royal College of Physicians, Edinburgh
**MRCPEd** ... Member of the Royal College of Physicians of Edinburgh
**MRCP Edin** ... Member of the Royal College of Physicians of Edinburgh
**MRCPGlas** ... Member of the Royal College of Physicians of Glasgow
**MRCP Glasg** ... Member of the Royal College of Physicians of Glasgow
**MRCPI** ...... Member of the Royal College of Physicians of Ireland
**MRCP Irel** ... Member of the Royal College of Physicians of Ireland
**MRC Psych** ... Member of the Royal College of Psychiatrists [*British*]

**MRCP UK** ... Member of the Royal Colleges of Physicians of the United Kingdom
**MRCR** ....... Carrillo [*Costa Rica*] [*ICAO location identifier*] (ICLI)
**MRCR** ....... Measurement Requirement Change Request [*NASA*] (KSC)
**MRCRR**..... Machine-Readable Collections Reading Room [*Library of Congress*] (IT)
**MRCS**........ Machinery Repairman, Senior Chief [*Navy rating*]
**MRCS**........ [*The*] Marcus Corp. [*NASDAQ symbol*] (NQ)
**MRCS**........ Mechanoreceptor Cueing Subsystem (MCD)
**MRCS**........ Medium Resolution Camera System (MCD)
**MRCS**........ Member of the Royal College of Surgeons [*British*]
**MRCS**........ Missile Range Calibration Satellite (MCD)
**MRCS**........ Multiple Report Creation System
**MRCSA**..... Medical Research Council. Special Report Series [*A publication*]
**MRCSE**..... Member of the Royal College of Surgeons, Edinburgh
**MRCSI**...... Member of the Royal College of Surgeons, Ireland (ROG)
**MRCV**....... Cabo Velas [*Costa Rica*] [*ICAO location identifier*] (ICLI)
**MRCV**....... Mixture Ratio Control Valve (KSC)
**MRCVS**..... Member of the Royal College of Veterinary Surgeons [*British*] (EY)
**MRCY**....... Mercury General Corp. [*Los Angeles, CA*] [*NASDAQ symbol*] (NQ)
**MRCYA**.... Mercury [*A publication*]
**MRCZ**....... Carrizal [*Costa Rica*] [*ICAO location identifier*] (ICLI)
**MR & D**..... Management Review and Digest [*A publication*]
**MRD**.......... Mandatory Retirement Date [*Army*] (AABC)
**MRD**.......... Manual Ringdown [*Telecommunications*] (TEL)
**MRD**.......... Maritime Research Department [*An association*] [*Inactive*] (EA)
**MRD**.......... Marketing Requirement Document
**MRD**.......... Master Requirements Directory [*Military*] (AFM)
**MR & D**..... Material Redistribution and Disposal
**MRD**.......... Material Requirements Deck (AAG)
**MRD**.......... Material Requirements Drawing (MCD)
**MRD**.......... Material Review Disposition [*Aviation*]
**MRD**.......... Materiel Redistribution Division [*Army*] (AFIT)
**MRD**.......... Materiel Release Denial [*Military*] (AABC)
**MRD**.......... Materiel Requirements Document [*Army*]
**MRD**.......... Media Review Digest [*A publication*]
**MRD**.......... Medical Research Division
**MRD**.......... Melcor Developments Ltd. [*Toronto Stock Exchange symbol*]
**MRD**.......... Memoirs. Research Department. Toyo Bunko [*A publication*]
**MRD**.......... Memory Raster Display [*Data processing*]
**MRD**.......... Merida [*Venezuela*] [*Airport symbol*] (OAG)
**MRD**.......... Meridian Air Cargo, Inc. [*Meridian, MS*] [*FAA designator*] (FAAC)
**MRD**.......... Metal Rolling Door [*Technical drawings*]
**MRD**.......... Metal Roof Deck [*Technical drawings*]
**MRD**.......... Milestone Review Documentation [*Army*]
**MRD**.......... Military Reference Data
**MRD**.......... Military Requirements Determination
**mrd**............ Millirutherford
**MRD**.......... Minimal Residual Disease [*Medicine*]
**MRD**.......... Minimum Reacting Dose
**MRD**.......... Mission Requirements Document [*NASA*] (KSC)
**MRD**.......... Mississippi River Division [*Army Corps of Engineers*]
**MRD**.......... Missouri River Division [*Army Corps of Engineers*]
**MRD**.......... Mobil Research & Development Corp., Engineering Information Center, Princeton, NJ [*OCLC symbol*] (OCLC)
**MRD**.......... Monostable Relay Driver
**MRD**.......... Morpholinodaunorubicin [*Also, MoDNM*] [*Antineoplastic drug*]
**MRD**.......... Motor Receiving Dolly
**MRD**.......... Motorized Rifle Division [*USSR*] (NATG)
**MRD**.......... Movement for the Restoration of Democracy [*Nepal*] [*Political party*]
**MRD**.......... Movement for the Restoration of Democracy [*Pakistan*] [*Political party*] (PD)
**MRD**.......... Multireference Double Excitation [*Physics*]
**MRD**.......... Russell and District Regional Library, Russell, Manitoba [*Library symbol*] [*National Library of Canada*] (NLC)
**MRDA**....... Maintenance Requirement Development Activity [*Military*] (CAAL)
**MR & DA**.. Material Redistribution and Disposal Administration
**MRDA**....... Media Research Directors Association (EA)
**MRDC**....... Medical Research and Development Command [*Army*] [*Frederick, MD*]
**MRDC**....... Military Requirement and Development Committee (NATG)
**MRDC**....... Military Research and Development Center [*US-Thailand*]
**MRDC**....... Missile Research and Development Command [*Army*] (MCD)
**MRDC**....... Module RADAR Display Console
**MRDD**....... Don Diego [*Costa Rica*] [*ICAO location identifier*] (ICLI)
**MRDD**....... Mental Retardation and Developmental Disabilities [*National Institutes of Health*]
**MR/DD**..... Mentally Retarded and Developmentally Disabled
**MRDDD8**... Mental Retardation and Developmental Disabilities [*A publication*]
**MRDE**....... Mining Research and Development Establishment [*National Coal Board*] [*British*]
**MRDEC**..... Missile Research Development and Engineering Center [*Formerly, Army Missile Laboratory*] (RDA)
**M & RDET**... Maintenance and Repair Detachment
**MRDF**....... Machine-Readable Data Files
**MRDF**....... Marine Resources Development Foundation
**MRDF**....... Maritime Radio Direction Finding
**MRDF**....... Metals Research and Development Foundation [*Defunct*] (EA)
**MRDFS**..... Man-Portable Radio Direction-Finding System
**MRDG**....... Manufacturing Research and Design Group [*McMaster University*] [*Canada*] [*Research center*] (RCD)
**MRDIS**...... Message Reproduction and Distribution System [*Military*] (CAAL)
**MRDL**....... Mean Reciprocal Detection Latency
**MRDL**....... Missouri River Division Laboratory [*Army Corps of Engineers*]
**MRDN**....... Meridian Bancorp, Inc. [*NASDAQ symbol*] (NQ)
**MRDN**....... Mouvement Revolutionnaire pour la Democratie Nouvelle [*Revolutionary Movement for New Democracy*] [*Senegal*] (PD)
**MRDO**....... Dieciocho [*Costa Rica*] [*ICAO location identifier*] (ICLI)
**MRDOS**.... Mapped Real-Time Disk Operating System [*Data processing*] (MDG)
**MRDR**....... Material Receipt Discrepancy Record
**MRDR**....... Material Review Disposition Record (NASA)
**MRDS**....... MARC [*Machine-Readable Cataloging*] Records Distribution Service [*National Library of Canada*] (IID)
**MRDS**....... Member of the Royal Drawing Society [*British*] (ROG)
**MRDS**....... Message Reproduction and Distribution System [*Military*] (MCD)
**MRDS**....... Mineral Resources Data System [*US Geological Survey*] [*Information service or system*] (IID)
**MRDS**....... Modular Responsive Defense System
**MRDS**....... Molded Rubber Duct System
**MRDTB**..... Memoirs. Research Department. Toyo Bunko [*A publication*]
**MRDTI**...... Metal Roof Deck Technical Institute [*Later, Steel Deck Institute*] (EA)
**MRE**.......... Management Review [*A publication*]
**MRE**.......... Mara Lodges [*Kenya*] [*Airport symbol*] (OAG)
**MRE**.......... Maritime Radio Executive [*British*]
**M Re**.......... Master of Religion
**MRE**.......... Master of Religious Education
**MRE**.......... Materiel Readiness Expediter [*Army*]
**MRE**.......... Matter (ROG)
**MRE**.......... Maximal Relative Error [*Mathematical statistics*]
**MRE**.......... Meal, Ready-to-Eat [*Army rations designation, replaces C-rations*]
**MRE**.......... Mean Radial Error
**MRE**.......... Melissa Resources, Inc. [*Vancouver Stock Exchange symbol*]
**MRE**.......... Metal Regulatory Element [*Genetics*]
**MRE**.......... Metal-Responsive Element [*Genetics*]
**MRE**.......... Microbiological Research Establishment [*British*]
**MRE**.......... Microrocket Engine
**MRE**.......... Mid-Range Estimate
**MRE**.......... Militia Royal Engineers [*British military*] (DMA)
**MRE**.......... Mobil Research & Development Corp., Paulsboro, NJ [*OCLC symbol*] (OCLC)
**MRE**.......... Modern Ramjet Engine (MCD)
**M & RE**...... Money and Real Estate [*Newspaper section*] (ADA)
**MRE**.......... Monographies Reine Elisabeth [*Brussels*] [*A publication*]
**MRE**.......... Movimiento Revolucionario Espartaco [*Bolivia*] [*Political party*] (PPW)
**MRE**.......... Multiple-Response Enable (IEEE)
**MREA**....... Estero Azul [*Costa Rica*] [*ICAO location identifier*] (ICLI)
**MREAC**..... Mon Repos Est au Ciel [*My Rest Is in Heaven*] [*French*] [*Motto of Ludwig Philipp, Count of the Palatinate of Simmern (1602-1654)*]
**MREC**....... El Carmen [*Costa Rica*] [*ICAO location identifier*] (ICLI)
**MREC**....... Miracle Recreation Equipment Company [*NASDAQ symbol*] (NQ)
**MR Ed**....... Master of Religious Education
**MRED**....... Mountain Research and Development [*A publication*]
**MREDA**.... Marine Resources and Engineering Development Act [*1966*] (MSC)
**M Re E**....... Master of Refrigeration Engineering
**M Re Eng**... Master of Refrigeration Engineering
**MRegSc**..... Master of Regional Science (ADA)
**MReh**......... Blanding Free Public Library, Rehoboth, MA [*Library symbol*] [*Library of Congress*] (LCLS)
**MREHIS**... Member of the Royal Environmental Health Institute of Scotland (DBQ)
**MREI**......... Marriage Role Expectation Inventory [*Psychology*]
**M-REIT**..... Mutual Real Estate Investment Trust
**MRELB**..... Malaysian Rubber Exchange and Licensing Board (DS)
**mrem**.......... Millirem
**MREM**...... Milliroentgen Equivalent Man [*Radiation measurement*]
**mrem/h**..... Millirem per Hour (DS)
**MREmpS**... Member of the Royal Empire Society [*British*]
**Mr Eng/Log**... Marine Engineering/Log [*A publication*]
**M Reporter**... Mining Reporter [*A publication*]
**MRER**....... El Ron Ron [*Costa Rica*] [*ICAO location identifier*] (ICLI)
**MRERB**..... Marine Engineers Review [*A publication*]

**MRERF**..... Manufacturers Representatives Educational Research Foundation [*Rolling Meadows, IL*] (EA)
**MRES**........ Material Requirements Estimation System [*Navy*]
**MRES**........ Member of the Royal Entomological Society [*British*] (ROG)
**MRES**........ Military Requirements Estimation System
**MRES**........ Missouri Research Laboratories, Inc. [*NASDAQ symbol*] (NQ)
**MRET**........ Esterillos [*Costa Rica*] [*ICAO location identifier*] (ICLI)
**M Ret**......... Master of Retailing
**MRET**........ Meret, Inc. [*Columbus, OH*] [*NASDAQ symbol*] (NQ)
**MRev**......... Mediterranean Review [*A publication*]
**M REV**....... Most Reverend
**MRev**......... Revere Public Library, Revere, MA [*Library symbol*] [*Library of Congress*] (LCLS)
**MRF**.......... Maintenance and Refurbishment Facility [*NASA*] (KSC)
**MRF**.......... Maintenance Repair Facility
**MRF**.......... Maintenance Repair Frequency
**MRF**.......... Maintenance Replacement Factor (NG)
**MRF**.......... Maintenance Responsibility File (MCD)
**MRF**.......... Manager Magazin [*A publication*]
**MRF**.......... Mankind Research Foundation (EA)
**MRF**.......... Marble Floor (AAG)
**MRF**.......... Marfa, TX [*Location identifier*] [*FAA*] (FAAL)
**MRF**.......... Marine Recreational Fishing [*Marine science*] (MSC)
**MRF**.......... Markov Random Field [*Mathematics*]
**MRF**.......... Materials Recovery Facility [*for recycling of glass, plastics, etc.*]
**MRF**.......... Maximum Retarding Force (NASA)
**MRF**.......... Measurements/Stimuli Request Form [*NASA*] (NASA)
**MRF**.......... Megawatt Receiver Filter
**MRF**.......... Melanocyte-Stimulating Hormone Releasing Factor [*Endocrinology*]
**MRF**.......... Mental Retardation Facility
**MRF**.......... Merfin Resources Ltd. [*Vancouver Stock Exchange symbol*]
**MRF**.......... Mesencephalic [*or Midbrain*] Reticular Formation [*Anatomy*]
**MRF**.......... Message Refusal [*Telecommunications*] (TEL)
**MRF**.......... Metal Regulatory Factor [*Genetics*]
**MRF**.......... Meteorological Rocket Facility
**MRF**.......... Milestone Reference File [*Military*] (CAAL)
**MRF**.......... Military Reconnaissance Force [*British military*] (DMA)
**MRF**.......... Miraflores [*Peru*] [*Seismograph station code, US Geological Survey*] (SEIS)
**MRF**.......... Mission Readiness Flying
**MRF**.......... Mission Reliability Factor [*Military*] (AABC)
**MRF**.......... Mitral Regurgitant Flow [*Medicine*]
**MRF**.......... Mobile Riverine Force [*Navy*] (NVT)
**MRF**.......... Muellerian Repressor Factor [*Embryology*]
**MRF**.......... Multipath Reduction Factor [*Electronics*]
**MRF**.......... Music Research Foundation
**MRF**.......... Myopia Research Foundation [*Later, MIRF*]
**MRFA**........ Fireman Apprentice, Machinery Repairman, Striker [*Navy rating*]
**MRFAC**..... Manufacturers Radio Frequency Advisory Committee (EA)
**MRFD**........ Finca Delicias [*Costa Rica*] [*ICAO location identifier*] (ICLI)
**MRFDK**..... Mechanical Remote Fuze Disassembly Kit [*Military*] (CAAL)
**MRFI**......... Finca 10 (Nuevo Palmar Sur) [*Costa Rica*] [*ICAO location identifier*] (ICLI)
**MRFI**......... Mutually Responsible Facilitation Inventory [*Personality development test*] [*Psychology*]
**MRFIT**...... Multiple Risk Factor Intervention Trial [*Cardiology*]
**MRFL**........ Flamengo [*Costa Rica*] [*ICAO location identifier*] (ICLI)
**MRFL**........ Master Radio Frequency List (NATG)
**MRFN**....... Fireman, Machinery Repairman, Striker [*Navy rating*]
**MRFO**........ Macmillan Ring-Free Oil Co. [*NASDAQ symbol*] (NQ)
**MRFP**........ Finca La Promesa [*Costa Rica*] [*ICAO location identifier*] (ICLI)
**MRFR**........ Mobilization Reserve for Retention [*Military*]
**MRFS**........ Finca 63 [*Costa Rica*] [*ICAO location identifier*] (ICLI)
**MRFS**........ Mid-Range Force Study [*DoD*]
**MRFT**........ Missile Ready for Test (MCD)
**MRFT**........ Modified Rapid Fermentation Test
**MRFU**....... Multiple Rocket Firing Unit
**MRFV**........ Maize Rayado Fino Virus
**MRFWA4**... Malaysia. Report on Forest Administration in West Malaysia [*Malaysia. Penyata Tahunan Perhutanan Di-Malaysia Barat Tahun*] [*A publication*]
**MRFY**........ MRFY Corp. [*NASDAQ symbol*] (NQ)
**MRG**.......... Magnetic Radiation Generator
**MRG**.......... Main Repair Group [*British military*] (DMA)
**MRG**.......... Management Research Groups [*British*]
**MRG**.......... Mandatory Resource Group (MCD)
**MRG**.......... Manridge Explorations Ltd. [*Toronto Stock Exchange symbol*]
**MRG**.......... Master of Religious Guidance
**MRG**.......... Material Review Group [*Aviation*]
**MRG**.......... Medium Range
**MRG**.......... Merge [*Data processing*]
**MRG**.......... Methane Rich Gas
**MRG**.......... Militaerregierungsgesetz [*A publication*]
**MRG**.......... Minority Rights Group (EAIO)
**MRG**.......... Mission Rules Guidelines [*NASA*] (KSC)
**MRG**.......... Mitteilungen der Raabe-Gesellschaft [*A publication*]
**MRG**.......... Modelling Research Group [*University of Southern California*] [*Research center*] (RCD)
**MRG**.......... Mooring (MSA)
**MRG**.......... Morgantown [*West Virginia*] [*Seismograph station code, US Geological Survey*] (SEIS)
**MRG**.......... Mouvement des Radicaux de Gauche [*Left Radical Movement*] [*France*] [*Political party*] (PPE)
**MRG**.......... Mouvement des Radicaux de Gauche [*Left Radical Movement*] [*Reunion*] [*Political party*] (PPW)
**MRG**.......... Movement Requirements Generator
**MRGA**....... Garza [*Costa Rica*] [*ICAO location identifier*] (ICLI)
**MRGA**....... Manhattan Ryegrass Growers Association (EA)
**MRGB**....... Mittelrheinische Geschichtsblaetter [*A publication*]
**MRGC**....... Mister Gasket Company [*NASDAQ symbol*] (NQ)
**MRGF**....... Golfito [*Costa Rica*] [*ICAO location identifier*] (ICLI)
**MRGGAT**... Morgagni [*A publication*]
**MRGITF**... Machine-Readable Government Information Task Force [*Government Documents Round Table*] [*American Library Association*]
**MRGL**....... Marginal (FAAC)
**MRGO**....... Margo Nursery Farms, Inc. [*NASDAQ symbol*] (NQ)
**MR-GO**..... Mississippi River-Gulf Outlet
**MRGP**....... Guapiles [*Costa Rica*] [*ICAO location identifier*] (ICLI)
**MRGR**....... Mean Relative Growth Rate [*Physiology*]
**MRGR**....... Morgro Chemical Co. [*NASDAQ symbol*] (NQ)
**MRGRAS**... Musee Royal de l'Afrique Centrale [*Tervuren, Belgique*]. Rapport Annuel. Departement de Geologie et de Mineralogie [*A publication*]
**MRGS**....... Member of the Royal Geographical Society [*British*]
**MRGT**....... Guatuso [*Costa Rica*] [*ICAO location identifier*] (ICLI)
**MRGTAY**... Marine Geotechnology [*A publication*]
**MRGU**....... Guanacaste [*Costa Rica*] [*ICAO location identifier*] (ICLI)
**MRGX**....... Margaux, Inc. [*NASDAQ symbol*] (NQ)
**MRH**......... Beaufort, NC [*Location identifier*] [*FAA*] (FAAL)
**MRH**......... Hinds Junior College, Raymond, MS [*OCLC symbol*] (OCLC)
**MRH**......... Magnetic Recording Head
**MRH**......... Mango Resources [*Vancouver Stock Exchange symbol*]
**MRH**......... Master of Russian History
**MRH**......... Mechanical Recording Head
**MRH**......... Melanocyte-Releasing Hormone [*Endocrinology*]
**MRH**......... Mild Resid Hydrocracking [*M. W. Kellogg Co. process*]
**mr/h**......... Milliroentgens per Hour (DS)
**MRH**......... Mission-Related Hardware
**MRH**......... Mobile Remote Handler
**MRH**......... Rossburn District Hospital, Rossburn, Manitoba [*Library symbol*] [*National Library of Canada*] (NLC)
**MRHA**....... Mannose-Resistant Hemagglutination
**MRHD**...... Mounted Ration Heating Device [*Army*] (INF)
**MRHG**....... Hacienda Rancho Grande [*Costa Rica*] [*ICAO location identifier*] (ICLI)
**MRHJ**....... Hacienda Jaco (Harbor Land) [*Costa Rica*] [*ICAO location identifier*] (ICLI)
**mrhm**.......... Milliroentgens per Hour at One Meter
**MRHO**...... Hacienda Rio Cuarto [*Costa Rica*] [*ICAO location identifier*] (ICLI)
**MRHP**....... Hacienda Platanar [*Costa Rica*] [*ICAO location identifier*] (ICLI)
**mr/hr**......... Milliroentgens per Hour
**MRHS**....... Hacienda La Suerte [*Costa Rica*] [*ICAO location identifier*] (ICLI)
**MRHS**....... Materiel Request History and Status
**MRHS**....... Member of the Royal Historical Society [*British*] (ROG)
**MRHS**....... Midwest Railway Historical Society (EA)
**MRHV**....... Maintain Runway Heading for Vector [*Aviation*] (FAAC)
**MRI**........... Anchorage, AK [*Location identifier*] [*FAA*] (FAAL)
**MRI**........... Information Dynamics Corp., Reading, MA [*Library symbol*] [*Library of Congress*] (LCLS)
**MRI**........... Maandstatistiek van de Brijzen [*A publication*]
**MRI**........... Machine Records Installation [*Military*]
**MRI**........... Magnetic Resonance Imaging [*Medicine*]
**MRI**........... Malt Research Institute [*Later, NMRI*]
**MRI**........... Manufacturing Run-In
**MRI**........... Marine Research Institute
**MRI**........... Marital Roles Inventory [*Psychology*]
**MRI**........... Mass Retailing Institute [*Formerly, Mass Merchandising Research Institute*] [*Later, NMRI*]
**MRI**........... Material Receiving Instruction [*Bechtel*] [*Nuclear energy*] (NRCH)
**MRI**........... Material Review Item [*Aviation*]
**MRI**........... Mauritius Island [*Mascarene Islands*] [*Seismograph station code, US Geological Survey*] [*Closed*] (SEIS)
**MRI**........... Mauritius Island [*Mascarene Islands*] [*Later, PLS*] [*Geomagnetic observatory code*]
**MRI**........... McRae Industries, Inc. [*AMEX symbol*] (SPSG)
**MRI**........... Mean Rise Interval [*Tides and currents*]
**MRI**........... Measurement Requirements and Interface (MCD)
**MRI**........... Meat Research Institute [*British*]
**MRI**........... Mediamark Research, Incorporated [*Database producer and database*] [*Information service or system*] (IID)
**MRI**........... Medical Research Institute [*Florida Institute of Technology*] [*Research center*] (RCD)
**MRI**........... Medium-Range Interceptor
**MRI**........... Member of the Royal Institution [*British*]

**MRI** .......... Memory Reference Instruction
**MRI** .......... Mental Research Institute (EA)
**MRI** .......... Microwave Research Institute [*Polytechnic Institute of Brooklyn*] (MCD)
**MRI** .......... Midwest Research Institute
**MRI** .......... MILSTRIP [*Military Standard Requisitioning and Issue Procedure*] Routing Identifier (AFM)
**MRI** .......... Mineral Resources Institute [*University of Alabama*] [*Research center*] (RCD)
**MRI** .......... Mineral Resources International Ltd. [*Toronto Stock Exchange symbol*]
**MRI** .......... Minority Research Institution [*Program*] [*National Science Foundation*]
**MRI** .......... Miscellaneous RADAR Input
**MRI** .......... Missile Range Index
**MRI** .......... Moderate Renal Insufficiency [*Medicine*]
**MRI** .......... Monopulse Resolution Improvement
**MRI** .......... Multiple RADAR Interrogator (MUGU)
**MRIA** ........ Magnetic Recording Industry Association [*Later, Electronic Industries Association*] (EA)
**MRIA** ........ Member of the Royal Irish Academy (EY)
**MRIA** ........ Model Railroad Industry Association (EA)
**MRIAI** ....... Member of the Royal Institute of the Architects of Ireland
**MRIBA** ...... Member of the Royal Institute of British Architects (ROG)
**MRIC** ........ Mandatory Recovery Items Code (MCD)
**M-RIC** ....... Manpower Resource Identification Code [*Military*]
**MRIC** ........ Member of the Royal Institute of Chemistry [*British*]
**MRIC** ........ Morning Report Indicator Code [*Army*] (AABC)
**MRIC** ........ Revolutionary Movement of the Christian Left [*Ecuador*] [*Political party*] (PPW)
**MRICC** ...... Missile and Rockets Inventory Control Center [*Army*]
**MRICD** ...... Medical Research Institute of Chemical Defense (RDA)
**MRICS** ...... Member of the Royal Institution of Chartered Surveyors [*British*]
**MRIF** ........ Melanocyte-Stimulating-Hormone Release Inhibiting Factor [*Also, MIF*] [*Endocrinology*]
**MRIL** ........ Mandatory Recovery Items List (MCD)
**MRIL** ........ Master Repairable Item List
**MRIN** ........ Member of the Royal Institute of Navigation [*British*] (DBQ)
**MRINA** ...... Member of the Royal Institution of Naval Architects [*British*]
**MRINAQ** .. Marine Research in Indonesia [*A publication*]
**MR INC** ..... Men's Rights, Incorporated (EA)
**MRINCS** ... Multidisciplinary Research [*A publication*]
**MRINDO** ... Modified Rydberg Intermediate Neglect of Differential Overlap [*Physics*]
**MRIO** ........ Multiregional Input-Output
**MRIP** ........ Australian Marine Research in Progress [*Database*]
**MRIP** ........ Imperio [*Costa Rica*] [*ICAO location identifier*] (ICLI)
**MRIP** ........ Management Review and Improvement Program [*Department of Labor*]
**MRIP** ........ Prairie Crocus Regional Library, Rivers, Manitoba [*Library symbol*] [*National Library of Canada*] (NLC)
**MRIPA** ...... Member of the Royal Institute of Public Administration (ADA)
**MRIPHH** .. Member of the Royal Institute of Public Health and Hygiene [*British*]
**MRIPWC** .. Member of the Royal Institute of Painters in Water Colours [*British*] (ROG)
**MRIR** ........ Medium-Resolution Infrared Radiometer [*NASA*]
**MRIRBM** ... Medium-Range and Intermediate-Range Ballistic Missile (MCD)
**MRIS** ........ Maritime Research Information Service [*National Academy of Sciences*]
**MRIS** ........ Market Research Information System [*Bell System*]
**MRIS** ........ Marshall & Isley Corp. [*NASDAQ symbol*] (NQ)
**MRIS** ........ Material Readiness Index System [*Military*]
**MRIS** ........ Medical Research Information System [*Veterans Administration*]
**MRIS** ........ Mobile Range Instrumentation System
**MRIS** ........ Modernization Resource Information Submission [*Army*] (RDA)
**MRISAN** ... Maintenance Requirement Interim Support Asset Notice (MCD)
**MRI Technical Report Series** ... Mineral Resources Institute. Technical Report Series [*A publication*]
**MRIW** ........ Mitteilungen des Rumaenischen Instituts an der Universitaet Wien [*A publication*]
**MRJ** .......... Microwave Rotary Joint
**MRJ** .......... Mineral Point, WI [*Location identifier*] [*FAA*] (FAAL)
**MRJ** .......... Miniature Revolving Joint
**MRJE** ........ Multileaving Remote Job Entry [*IBM Corp.*]
**MRK** .......... Marco Island [*Florida*] [*Airport symbol*] (OAG)
**MRK** .......... Mark
**MRK** .......... Marketing. Zeitschrift fuer Forschung und Praxis [*A publication*]
**MRK** .......... Merck & Co., Inc. [*NYSE symbol*] (SPSG)
**MRK** .......... Merrimack College, McQuade Library, North Andover, MA [*OCLC symbol*] (OCLC)
**MRK** .......... Millrock Development Corp. [*Vancouver Stock Exchange symbol*]
**MRK** .......... Morioka [*Japan*] [*Seismograph station code, US Geological Survey*] (SEIS)
**MRK** .......... Myth, Ritual, and Kingship [*A publication*] (BJA)
**MRK** .......... Rayville, LA [*Location identifier*] [*FAA*] (FAAL)
**MRKD** ....... Marked [*Data processing*] (MDG)
**MRKTD** .... Marktforschung [*A publication*]
**MRL** .......... Machine Representation Language
**MRL** .......... Maintenance Repair Level (MCD)
**MRL** .......... Maintenance Requirements List (MCD)
**MRL** .......... Manipulator Retention Latch [*or Lock*] (NASA)
**MRL** .......... Manufacturing Reference Line
**MRL** .......... Manufacturing Research Laboratory
**MRL** .......... Maritime Rear Link (MCD)
**MRL** .......... Marketing Research Library
**MRL** .......... Martel Oil & Gas [*Vancouver Stock Exchange symbol*]
**MRL** .......... Master Repair List (AFIT)
**MRL** .......... Master Report List
**MRL** .......... Materials Research Laboratories [*National Science Foundation*] [*Research center*]
**MRL** .......... Materiel Requirements List [*Military*]
**MRL** .......... Maximum Recording Level
**MRL** .......... Meaning-Representation Language [*Data processing*]
**MRL** .......... Meat Research Laboratory [*Australia*]
**MRL** .......... Medical Record Librarian
**MRL** .......... Medical Research Laboratory [*Navy and Air Force*] (MCD)
**MRL** .......... Medium-Powered Radio Range [*Loop radiators*]
**MRL** .......... Merrell-National Laboratories [*Research code symbol*]
**MRL** .......... Minerals Research Laboratory (MCD)
**MRL** .......... Minimal Response Level [*Audiometry*]
**MRL** .......... Minimum Residue Level
**MRL** .......... Missionary Research Library (EA)
**MRL** .......... Mobile Replenishment List (AFIT)
**MRL** .......... Monthly Retail Trade. Current Business Report [*A publication*]
**MRL** .......... Motor Refrigeration Lighter (ADA)
**MRL** .......... Movimiento Revolucionario Liberal [*Colombian political party*]
**MRL** .......... Multiple Rocket Launcher
**MRL** .......... Multiple Ruby LASER
**MRL** .......... Multipoint Recorder/Logger
**MRL** .......... Mutation Research Letters [*A publication*]
**MRLA** ........ La Paquita [*Costa Rica*] [*ICAO location identifier*] (ICLI)
**MRLAA2** ... Marine Research Laboratory. Investigational Report [*South-West Africa*] [*A publication*]
**MRLAB** ..... Mededelingen. Rijksfaculteit Landbouwwetenschappen te Gent (Belgium) [*A publication*]
**MRLB** ........ Liberia/Tomas Guardia Internacional [*Costa Rica*] [*ICAO location identifier*] (ICLI)
**MRLC** ........ Los Chiles [*Costa Rica*] [*ICAO location identifier*] (ICLI)
**MRLE** ........ Laurel [*Costa Rica*] [*ICAO location identifier*] (ICLI)
**MRLF** ........ La Flor [*Costa Rica*] [*ICAO location identifier*] (ICLI)
**MRLF** ........ Monthly Report on the Labor Force (OICC)
**MRLG** ........ La Garroba [*Costa Rica*] [*ICAO location identifier*] (ICLI)
**MRLI** ......... La Ligia [*Costa Rica*] [*ICAO location identifier*] (ICLI)
**MRLL** ........ Las Lomas [*Costa Rica*] [*ICAO location identifier*] (ICLI)
**MRLL** ........ Merrill Corp. [*St. Paul, MN*] [*NASDAQ symbol*] (NQ)
**MRLM** ....... Limon/Limon Internacional [*Costa Rica*] [*ICAO location identifier*] (ICLI)
**MRLN** ........ Marlin Oil Co. [*NASDAQ symbol*] (NQ)
**MRLOGAEUR** ... Minimum Required Logistics Augmentation Europe (MCD)
**MRLPC** ..... Mouvement de Regroupement et de Liberation du Peuple Congolais [*Movement for the Regroupment and Liberation of the Congolese People*]
**MRLR** ........ La Roca [*Costa Rica*] [*ICAO location identifier*] (ICLI)
**MRLT** ........ Las Trancas [*Costa Rica*] [*ICAO location identifier*] (ICLI)
**MRLTAP** .. Murrelet [*A publication*]
**MRLU** ........ La Maruca [*Costa Rica*] [*ICAO location identifier*] (ICLI)
**MRLV** ........ La Cueva [*Costa Rica*] [*ICAO location identifier*] (ICLI)
**MRLY** ........ La Yolanda [*Costa Rica*] [*ICAO location identifier*] (ICLI)
**MRM** ......... Mail Readership Measurement
**MRM** ......... Maintenance, Reporting, and Management [*Military*] (MCD)
**MRM** ......... Maintenance Returns Monitor (FAAC)
**MRM** ......... Management Responsibility Matrix
**MRM** ......... Management Review Meeting (AFIT)
**MRM** ......... Manari [*Papua New Guinea*] [*Airport symbol*] (OAG)
**MRM** ......... Mechanically Removed Meat
**MRM** ......... Medical Repair Technician [*Navy*]
**MRM** ......... Medium-Range Missile (MCD)
**MRM** ......... Merrimac Industries [*AMEX symbol*] (SPSG)
**MRM** ......... Metabolic Rate Monitor [*Trademark*]
**MRM** ......... Michelson Rotating Mirror
**MRM** ......... Miles of Relative Movement [*Navigation*]
**MRM** ......... Movimento da Resistencia de Mozambique [*Mozambique Resistance Movement*]
**MRM** ......... Multiple Reaction Monitoring [*Chemistry*]
**MRM** ......... Music for the Rights of Man (EA)
**MRMA** ....... Montealto [*Costa Rica*] [*ICAO location identifier*] (ICLI)
**M & RMC** ... Manning and Ryland's English Magistrates' Cases [*1827-30*] [*A publication*] (DLA)
**MRMC** ....... Medical Research Modernization Committee (EA)
**MRMC** ....... Murcielago [*Costa Rica*] [*ICAO location identifier*] (ICLI)
**MR Miss Agr Exp Sta** ... MR. Mississippi Agricultural Experiment Station [*A publication*]

**MRMJ**....... Mojica [*Costa Rica*] [*ICAO location identifier*] (ICLI)
**MRMK**....... Merrimack Bancorp, Inc. [*NASDAQ symbol*] (NQ)
**MRML**....... Medium-Range Missile Launcher
**MRML**....... Montelimar O Los Sitios [*Costa Rica*] [*ICAO location identifier*] (ICLI)
**MRMO**....... Mobilization Reserve Materiel Objective [*Army*]
**MRMO-A**... Mobilization Reserve Materiel Objective - Acquisition [*Army*] (AFIT)
**MRMP**....... Marginal Revenue/Marginal Physical Product [*Economics*]
**MRMPO**... Mobilization Reserve Materiel Procurement Objective [*Army*]
**MRMR**....... Mobilization Reserve Materiel Requirement [*Army*]
**MRMS**....... MARC [*Machine-Readable Cataloging*] Record Management System
**MRMS**....... Metabolic Rate Measuring System
**MRMS**....... Monetary Ration Management System [*Military*] (AFM)
**MRMT**....... Memory Metals, Inc. [*Stamford, CT*] [*NASDAQ symbol*] (NQ)
**MRMU**....... Mobile Radiological Measuring Unit
**MRMU**....... Mobile Remote Manipulating Unit [*Air Force*]
**MRN**.......... Marion [*South Africa*] [*Geomagnetic observatory code*]
**MRN**.......... Maritime Radionavigation
**MRN**.......... Median Raphe Nucleus [*Medicine*]
**MRN**.......... Medium-Round Nose [*Diamond drilling*]
**MRN**.......... Mental Retardation Nursing Certificate [*Australia*]
**MRN**.......... Meteorological Rocket Network [*NASA*]
**MRN**.......... Minimum Rejection Number
**MRN**.......... Moran Resources Corp. [*Vancouver Stock Exchange symbol*]
**MRN**.......... Morganton, NC [*Location identifier*] [*FAA*] (FAAL)
**MRN**.......... Morning (ROG)
**MRN**.......... Morrison-Knudsen Co., Inc. [*NYSE symbol*] (SPSG)
**MRN**.......... Movimiento de Renovacion Nacional [*Movement for National Renovation*] [*Colombia*] [*Political party*] (PPW)
**mRNA**........ Ribonucleic Acid, Messenger [*Biochemistry, genetics*]
**MRNC**....... Marina Limited Partnership [*Noblesville, IN*] [*NASDAQ symbol*] (NQ)
**MRNC**....... Nicoya [*Costa Rica*] [*ICAO location identifier*] (ICLI)
**MRND**....... Maintenance Required Not Developed (MSA)
**MRND**....... Mouvement Revolutionnaire National pour le Developpement [*National Revolutionary Movement for Development*] [*Rwanda*] [*Political party*] (PPW)
**MRNG**....... Morning
**MRNJ**....... Naranjo (Seveers) [*Costa Rica*] [*ICAO location identifier*] (ICLI)
**MRNL**....... Medical Research and Nutrition Laboratory [*Army*] (MCD)
**MRNO**....... Morino, Inc. [*NASDAQ symbol*] (SPSG)
**mRNP**........ Ribonucleoprotein, Messenger [*Biochemistry*]
**MRNPF**...... Member, Royal Nurses Pension Fund [*British*] (ROG)
**MRNS**....... Modular Reusable Nuclear Shuttle
**MRNS**....... Nosara [*Costa Rica*] [*ICAO location identifier*] (ICLI)
**MRO**.......... Maintenance, Repair, and Operation
**MRO**.......... Maintenance, Repair, and Overhaul
**MRO**.......... Management Review Officer
**MRO**.......... Manufacturing Rework Order
**MRo**.......... Marche Romane [*A publication*]
**MRO**.......... Masterton [*New Zealand*] [*Airport symbol*] (OAG)
**MRO**.......... Materiel Readiness Officer (MCD)
**MRO**.......... Materiel Release Order [*Air Force*]
**MRO**.......... Mechanized RADAR Observer
**MRO**.......... Medical Records Officer [*Australia*]
**MRO**.......... Medical Regulating Office [*or Officer*] [*Army*] (AABC)
**MRO**.......... Medical Research Organization [*Generic term*]
**MRO**.......... Member of the Register of Osteopaths [*British*]
**MRO**.......... Meridor Resources Ltd. [*Vancouver Stock Exchange symbol*]
**MRO**.......... Message Releasing Officer
**MRO**.......... Message Review Officer (MCD)
**MRO**.......... Mid-Range Objectives
**MRO**.......... Military Release Orders
**MRO**.......... Motor Routing Order
**MRO**.......... Movement Report Office [*Military*]
**MRO**.......... Muscle Receptor Organ [*Neurophysiology*]
**MRO**.......... Rossburn Regional Library, Manitoba [*Library symbol*] [*National Library of Canada*] (NLC)
**MROA**....... Magnetic Raman Optical Activity [*Spectrometry*]
**M & Rob**.... Maclean and Robinson's Scotch Appeal Cases [*1839*] [*A publication*] (DLA)
**M & Rob**.... Moody and Robinson's English Nisi Prius Reports [*A publication*] (DLA)
**MROC**....... Mobile Range Operation Center (NVT)
**MROC**....... San Jose/Juan Santamaria Internacional [*Costa Rica*] [*ICAO location identifier*] (ICLI)
**MROD**....... Medical Research and Operations Directorate [*NASA*] (KSC)
**MROF**....... Maintenance, Repair, and Operation of Facility (KSC)
**MROL**....... Minimum Resolvable Object Length
**MROM**....... Macro Read-Only Memory [*Data processing*]
**MRom**....... Marche Romane [*A publication*]
**MROM**....... Masked Read-Only Memory [*Data processing*]
**MRoxH**...... Hebrew Teachers College, Roxbury, MA [*Library symbol*] [*Library of Congress*] (LCLS)
**MRP**.......... American Review of Public Administration [*A publication*]
**MRP**.......... Application for Writ of Mandamus Refused in Part [*Legal term*] (DLA)
**MRp**.......... Carnegie Library, Rockport, MA [*Library symbol*] [*Library of Congress*] (LCLS)
**MRP**.......... Maintenance Rally Point [*Military*] (INF)
**MRP**.......... Maintenance Real Property (NVT)
**MRP**.......... Malfunction Reporting Program [*Navy*]
**MRP**.......... Manned Reusable Payload
**MRP**.......... Manned Rotating Platform
**MRP**.......... Manual Reporting Post (NATG)
**MRP**.......... Manufacturing Requirements Planning [*Purchasing computer program*] (PCM)
**MRP**.......... Manufacturing Resource Planning [*Data processing*]
**MRP**.......... Marginal Revenue Product [*Economics*]
**MRP**.......... Markov Renewal Program
**MRP**.......... Marla [*Australia*] [*Airport symbol*] (OAG)
**MRP**.......... Mass Resolving Power [*Physics*]
**MRP**.......... Master of Regional Planning
**MRP**.......... Master Restationing Plan [*DoD*]
**MRP**.......... Material Reliability Program [*Military*] (AFIT)
**MRP**.......... Material Requirements Planning [*Pronounced "merp"*]
**MRP**.......... Material Reserve Planning
**MRP**.......... Materiel Returns Program [*Military*] (AFIT)
**MRP**.......... Mathematics Resources Project [*National Science Foundation*]
**MRP**.......... Maximum Rated Power
**MRP**.......... Maximum Resolving Power
**MRP**.......... Maximum Retail Price [*British*]
**MRP**.......... Medical Record Practitioner [*Medicare*] (DHSM)
**MRP**.......... Medical Reimbursement Plan
**MRP**.......... Merapi [*Java*] [*Seismograph station code, US Geological Survey*] [*Closed*] (SEIS)
**MRP**.......... Message Routing Process [*Telecommunications*] (TEL)
**MRP**.......... Meteorological Reporting Point [*Air Traffic Service*] (FAAC)
**MRP**.......... Mid-Range Plan [*1969-70*] [*Military*]
**MRP**.......... Militarism Resource Project (EA)
**MRP**.......... Military Rated Power (NG)
**MRP**.......... Military Representatives of Associated Pacific Powers [*World War II*]
**MRP**.......... Military Requirements Plan (NATG)
**MRP**.......... Minimum Reaction Posture (NVT)
**MRP**.......... Miscellaneous Relay Panel (MCD)
**MRP**.......... Mission Resource Partnership LP [*AMEX symbol*] (SPSG)
**MRP**.......... Mitochondrial RNA [*Ribonucleic Acid*] Processing [*Cytology*]
**MRP**.......... Mobile Repair Party (MCD)
**MRP**.......... Modern Religious Problems [*A publication*]
**MRP**.......... Molybdate-Reactive Phosphorus [*Analytical chemistry*]
**MRP**.......... Monthly Report of Progress
**MRP**.......... Morley Library, Painesville, OH [*OCLC symbol*] (OCLC)
**MRP**.......... Morrison Petroleums Ltd. [*Toronto Stock Exchange symbol*]
**MRP**.......... Motor Racing Publications [*Publisher*] [*Great Britain*]
**MRP**.......... Mouvement Republicain Populaire [*Popular Republican Movement*] [*France*] [*Political party*] (PPE)
**MRP**.......... Movimiento Republicano Progresista [*Progressive Republican Movement*] [*Venezuela*] [*Political party*]
**MRP**.......... Movimiento Revolucionario del Pueblo - Ixim [*People's Revolutionary Movement - Ixim*] [*Guatemala*] [*Political party*] (PD)
**MRP**.......... Multiplex Recording Photography
**MRP**.......... Reston and District Regional Library, Reston, Manitoba [*Library symbol*] [*National Library of Canada*] (NLC)
**MRPA**....... Modified Random Phase Approximation
**MRPA**....... Punta Burica [*Costa Rica*] [*ICAO location identifier*] (ICLI)
**MRPARABAD**... Master Parachutist Badge [*Military decoration*]
**MRPB**....... Playa Blanca [*Costa Rica*] [*ICAO location identifier*] (ICLI)
**MRPC**....... Mercury Rankine Power Conversion [*Nuclear energy*]
**MRPC**....... Mouvement de Regroupement des Populations Congolaises [*Movement for the Regroupment of the Congolese People*] [*Political party*]
**MRPC**....... Paso Canoas [*Costa Rica*] [*ICAO location identifier*] (ICLI)
**MRPD**....... Pandora [*Costa Rica*] [*ICAO location identifier*] (ICLI)
**MRPE**....... Palo Verde [*Costa Rica*] [*ICAO location identifier*] (ICLI)
**MRPF**....... Maintenance of Real Property Facilities (AABC)
**MRPG**....... Potrero Grande [*Costa Rica*] [*ICAO location identifier*] (ICLI)
**MRPI**........ Paissa [*Costa Rica*] [*ICAO location identifier*] (ICLI)
**MRPJ**....... Puerto Jimenez [*Costa Rica*] [*ICAO location identifier*] (ICLI)
**MRPL**....... Material Requirements Planning List [*Navy*]
**MRPL**....... Portalon [*Costa Rica*] [*ICAO location identifier*] (ICLI)
**MRPM**...... Material Research and Production Methods (MCD)
**MRPM**...... Palmar Sur [*Costa Rica*] [*ICAO location identifier*] (ICLI)
**MRPN**....... Pelon Nuevo [*Costa Rica*] [*ICAO location identifier*] (ICLI)
**MRPP**....... Mortgage Rate Protection Program [*Canada*]
**MRPP**....... Movimento Reorganizativo do Partido do Proletariado [*Portugal*] [*Political party*]
**MRPR**....... Parrita [*Costa Rica*] [*ICAO location identifier*] (ICLI)
**MRPRA**..... Malaysian Rubber Producers' Research Association [*Research center*] [*British*] (IRC)
**MRPS**....... Matricularum Regni Poloniae Summaria [*A publication*]
**MRPS**....... Paissa [*Costa Rica*] [*ICAO location identifier*] (ICLI)
**MRPV**....... San Jose/Tobias Bolanos Internacional [*Costa Rica*] [*ICAO location identifier*] (ICLI)
**MRQ**.......... Marinduque [*Philippines*] [*Airport symbol*] (OAG)
**MRQ**.......... Maximum Release Quantity [*DoD*]

**MRQP**....... Quepos (La Managua) [*Costa Rica*] [*ICAO location identifier*] (ICLI)
**MRR**.......... Macara [*Ecuador*] [*Airport symbol*] (OAG)
**MRR**.......... Machine-Readable Record (MCD)
**MRR**.......... Mad River Review [*A publication*]
**MRR**.......... [*The*] Magistrates of the Roman Republic [*A publication*] (OCD)
**MRR**.......... Maintenance, Repairs, and Replacements [*Military*]
**MRR**.......... Maintenance, Replacement, Removal (AFIT)
**MRR**.......... Mandatory Removal Roster [*Army*]
**MRR**.......... Manistee Railroad
**MRR**.......... Market Research Great Britain [*A publication*]
**MRR**.......... Marrow Release Rate [*Hematology*]
**MRR**.......... Master Record Repository (MCD)
**MRR**.......... Material Receiving [*Inspection*] Report [*Nuclear energy*] (NRCH)
**MRR**.......... Material Rejection Report
**MRR**.......... Material Reliability Report (MCD)
**MRR**.......... Material Review Record [*or Reports*] [*Aviation*] (MCD)
**MRR**.......... Material Review Request
**MRR**.......... Materiel Readiness Report [*Army*] (AABC)
**MRR**.......... Maximal Relaxation Rate [*Medicine*]
**MRR**.......... Maximum Rate of Rise [*Biometrics*]
**MRR**.......... Mechanical Reliability Report [*FAA*]
**MRR**.......... Mechanical Research Report
**MRR**.......... Medical Research Reactor
**MRR**.......... Medium-Range RADAR (NG)
**MRR**.......... Medium-Range Recovery
**MRR**.......... Metal Removal Rate
**MRR**.......... Microelectronic Radio Receiver
**MRR**.......... Microfilm Reader Recorder
**MRR**.......... Milestone Readiness Review [*NASA*] (KSC)
**MRR**.......... Military Renegotiation Regulation
**MRR**.......... Miniature Reed Relay
**MRR**.......... Minimum Rediscount Rate
**MRR**.......... Minimum Reporting Requirement [*NASA*] (KSC)
**MRR**.......... Minimum Risk Route (MCD)
**MRR**.......... Mission Reconfiguration Request (MCD)
**MRR**.......... Molecular Rotational Resonance
**MRR**.......... Monthly Review Report
**MRR**.......... Motorized Rifle Regiment [*USSR*] (INF)
**MRR**.......... Multiple Response Resolver
**MRR**.......... Multirole RADAR
**MRR**.......... Muroran [*Japan*] [*Seismograph station code, US Geological Survey*] (SEIS)
**MRRB**....... Maintenance Requirements Review Board [*Military*] (AFIT)
**MRRB**....... Materiel Release Review Board [*Military*]
**MRRB**....... Materiel Requirements Review Board [*Military*] (AFIT)
**MRRC**....... Materiel Requirements Review Committee [*Military*]
**MRRC**....... Mechanical Reliability Research Center
**MRRC**....... Mental Retardation Research Center [*University of California, Los Angeles*] [*Research center*] (RCD)
**MRRC**....... Ralph L. Smith Mental Retardation Research Center [*University of Kansas*] [*Research center*] (RCD)
**MRREDD**... Medicinal Research Reviews [*A publication*]
**MRRF**........ Monitor Research and Recovery Foundation
**MRRF**........ Rio Frio O Progreso [*Costa Rica*] [*ICAO location identifier*] (ICLI)
**MRRI**........ Marine Resources Research Institute [*South Carolina Wildlife and Marine Resources Department*] [*Research center*] (RCD)
**MRRL**........ Materiel Repair Requirement List [*Military*] (AFIT)
**MRRL**........ Metabolism and Radiation Research Laboratory [*North Dakota State University*] [*Research center*] (RCD)
**MRRM**....... Rancho Del Mar [*Costa Rica*] [*ICAO location identifier*] (ICLI)
**MRRN**........ Rancho Nuevo [*Costa Rica*] [*ICAO location identifier*] (ICLI)
**MRRP**........ Maintenance and Repair of Real Property [*Military*]
**MRRP**........ Motorways, Roads, and Road Programmes [*British*]
**MRRS**........ Magnetic Reed Rotary Switch
**MRRS**........ Materiel Readiness Reporting System [*Army*]
**MRRS**........ Mobile Rail Repair Shop (MCD)
**MRRS**........ Multiple Railroad System
**MRRT**........ Maintenance Requirements Review Team (MUGU)
**MRRTS**..... Manitoba. Department of Renewable Resources and Transportation Services. Research Branch. Reports [*Canada*] [*A publication*]
**MRRVB**..... Meteornoe Rasprostranenie Radiovoln [*A publication*]
**MRRX**........ Roxana Farms [*Costa Rica*] [*ICAO location identifier*] (ICLI)
**MRS**.......... Maars [*Alaska*] [*Seismograph station code, US Geological Survey*] (SEIS)
**MRS**.......... Mado Robin Society (EA)
**MRS**.......... Magnetic Reed Switch
**MRS**.......... Magnetic Resonance Spectrum
**MRS**.......... Maintenance, Repair, and Service
**MRS**.......... Maintenance Reporting System [*Army*]
**MRS**.......... Maintenance Requirement Substantiated (MSA)
**MRS**.......... Malfunction Reporting System [*Boeing*]
**MRS**.......... Management Relations Survey [*Test*]
**MRS**.......... Management Reporting System
**MRS**.......... Management Review System (NASA)
**MRS**.......... Manipulator Repair Shop (NRCH)
**MRS**.......... Manned Reconnaissance Satellite [*Air Force*]
**MRS**.......... Manufacturers Railway Co. [*AAR code*]
**MRS**.......... Marches (ROG)
**MRS**.......... Marginal Rate of Substitution [*Economics*]
**MRS**.......... Mariah Resources Ltd. [*Vancouver Stock Exchange symbol*]
**MRS**.......... Market Research Society [*British*]
**MRS**.......... Marseille [*France*] [*Airport symbol*] (OAG)
**MRS**.......... Mastectomy Rehabilitation Service [*Australia*]
**MRS**.......... Master Repair Schedule [*Air Force*] (AFM)
**MRS**.......... Material Request [*or Requirement*] Summary
**MRS**.......... Material Returned to Store [*NASA*] (KSC)
**MRS**.......... Material Routing Slip
**MRS**.......... Materials Research Society (EA)
**MRS**.......... Materials Research Society. Symposia. Proceedings [*Elsevier Book Series*] [*A publication*]
**MRS**.......... Materiel Repair System [*Air Force*] (AFM)
**MRS**.......... Media Resource Service [*Scientists' Institute for Public Information*] [*Information service or system*] (IID)
**M & RS**...... Mediaeval and Renaissance Studies [*A publication*]
**MRS**.......... Mediaeval and Renaissance Studies [*A publication*]
**MRS**.......... Medical Receiving Station
**MRS**.......... Medical Research Society [*British*]
**MRS**.......... Medium Range Search
**MRS**.......... Medium-Range SONAR (NVT)
**MRS**.......... Memo Routing Slip
**MRS**.......... Metals Removal System [*Petroleum refining*]
**MRS**.......... Michigan Romance Studies [*A publication*]
**MRS**.......... Microfilm Replacement System [*Data processing*]
**MRS**.......... Migration and Refugee Services (EA)
**MRS**.......... Military Railway Service [*Army*]
**MRS**.......... Military Retirement System
**MRS**.......... Mini-Reconstruction System (MCD)
**MRS**.......... Minimum Radial Separation [*Manufacturing term*]
**MRS**.......... Missile Reentry Systems (AFIT)
**MRS**.......... Mission de Ras Shamra [*A publication*] (BJA)
**MRS**.......... Mission-Related Software
**MRS**.......... Mixed Reproductive Strategy [*Avian biology*]
**MRS**.......... Mobilization Requirement Study
**MRS**.......... Mobilization Reserve Stocks [*Army*]
**MRS**.......... Modification Record Sheet [*NASA*] (KSC)
**MRS**.......... Monitored Retrievable Storage [*of nuclear waste*]
**MRS**.......... Monorail System
**MRS**.......... Moore-Rott-Sears [*Theory*]
**MRS**.......... Morse Shoe, Inc. [*NYSE symbol*] (SPSG)
**MRS**.......... Mothers Return to School
**MRS**.......... Motor Rotation Stand
**MRS**.......... Mouvement Republicain Senegalais [*Senegalese Republican Movement*] [*Political party*] (PPW)
**MRS**.......... Movement and Reinforcement Study (MCD)
**MRS**.......... Movement Report Sheet [*Military*]
**MRS**.......... Multilateral RADAR Strike System [*Air Force*] (MCD)
**MRS**.......... Multilateral RADAR Surveillance System [*Air Force*] (MCD)
**MRS**.......... Multipurpose Research System
**MRS**.......... Muzzle Reference System (MCD)
**MRS**.......... Title for a married woman; originally an abbreviation for "mistress." Pronounced "missus"
**MRS3**........ Multilateral RADAR Surveillance/Strike System [*Air Force*]
**MRSA**........ Machinery Repairman, Seaman Apprentice [*Navy rating*]
**MRSA**........ Maine Revised Statutes, Annotated [*A publication*] (DLA)
**MRSA**........ Mandatory RADAR Service Area
**MRSA**........ Materiel Readiness Support Activity [*Army*] (RDA)
**MRSA**........ Materiel Readiness Support Agency [*Navy*]
**MRSA**........ Member of the Royal Society of Arts [*British*]
**MRSA**........ Methicillin-Resistant Staphylococcus Aureus [*Antimicrobial therapy*]
**MRSA**........ Microwave Radiometer, Scatterometer, and Altimeter (MCD)
**MRSA**........ Military RADAR Service Area [*Aviation*] (AIA)
**MRSA**........ San Alberto [*Costa Rica*] [*ICAO location identifier*] (ICLI)
**MR San A**... Member of the Royal Sanitary Association of Scotland
**MRSB**........ Material Requirements for Stock Balance
**MRSB**........ San Cristobal [*Costa Rica*] [*ICAO location identifier*] (ICLI)
**Mr SBA**..... Maryland State Bar Association, Report [*A publication*] (DLA)
**MRSC**........ Maritime Rescue Sub-Center [*Canada*]
**MRSc**......... Master of Rural Science [*British*] (ADA)
**MRSC**........ Member of the Royal Society of Canada
**MRSC**........ Member of the Royal Society of Chemistry [*British*] (DBQ)
**MRSC**........ Metal Resources Corp. [*NASDAQ symbol*] (NQ)
**MRSC**........ Mississippi Remote Sensing Center [*Mississippi State University*] [*Research center*] (RCD)
**MRSC**........ Santa Cruz [*Costa Rica*] [*ICAO location identifier*] (ICLI)
**MRSD**........ Maximum Rated Standard Deviation [*Statistics*]
**MRSD**........ Mission Requirements on System Design [*NASA*]
**MRSG**........ Santa Clara De Guapiles [*Costa Rica*] [*ICAO location identifier*] (ICLI)
**MRSH**........ Marsh (ADA)
**MRSH**........ Member of the Royal Society of Health [*British*]
**MRSH**........ Shiroles [*Costa Rica*] [*ICAO location identifier*] (ICLI)
**MRSHAO**... Marine Research Series. Scottish Home Department [*A publication*]
**MRSI**......... Maintenance Repair Spares Instruction (MCD)

**MRSI**......... Maintenance and Repair Support Items
**MRSI**......... Member of the Royal Sanitary Institute [*British*] (ROG)
**MRSI**......... Missouri River Services, Inc. [*NASDAQ symbol*] (NQ)
**MRSI**......... Mobilization Requirements, Secondary Items
**MRSI**......... San Isidro De El General [*Costa Rica*] [*ICAO location identifier*] (ICLI)
**MRSJ**......... San Jose [*Costa Rica*] [*ICAO location identifier*] (ICLI)
**MRSJ**......... United Church of Christ Ministers for Racial and Social Justice (EA)
**MRSL**......... Member of the Royal Society of Literature [*British*]
**MRSLA2**... Memoires. Societe Royale des Sciences de Liege. Collection in Octavo [*A publication*]
**MRSM**...... Mississippi River Suspended Matter
**MRSM**...... Santa Marta [*Costa Rica*] [*ICAO location identifier*] (ICLI)
**MRSN**....... Machinery Repairman, Seaman [*Navy rating*]
**MRSN**....... Sirena [*Costa Rica*] [*ICAO location identifier*] (ICLI)
**MRSO**....... Mobilization Reserve Stockage Objective [*Army*]
**MRSO**....... Santa Maria De Guacimo [*Costa Rica*] [*ICAO location identifier*] (ICLI)
**MRSP**........ Multifunction RADAR Signal Processor (MCD)
**MRSP**........ San Pedro [*Costa Rica*] [*ICAO location identifier*] (ICLI)
**MRSPD**..... Materials Research Society. Symposia. Proceedings [*A publication*]
**MRSPWC**... Member of the Royal Society of Painters in Water Colours [*British*]
**MRSQ**....... Medical Reference Services Quarterly [*A publication*]
**MR-SR**...... Material Review - Ships Record (MCD)
**MRSR**........ Samara [*Costa Rica*] [*ICAO location identifier*] (ICLI)
**MRSS**........ Main and Reheat Steam System [*Nuclear energy*] (NRCH)
**MRSS**........ Master Remote Slave Station (MCD)
**MRSS**........ San Joaquin de Abangares [*Costa Rica*] [*ICAO location identifier*] (ICLI)
**MRST**........ Member of the Royal Society of Teachers [*British*]
**MRST**........ San Agustin [*Costa Rica*] [*ICAO location identifier*] (ICLI)
**MRSV**........ Maneuverable Recoverable Space Vehicle
**MRSV**........ Military Railway Service Veterans (EA)
**MRSV**........ San Vito De Jaba [*Costa Rica*] [*ICAO location identifier*] (ICLI)
**MRSW**...... Member of the Royal Society of Scottish Painters and Watercolours [*British*] (DAS)
**MRSX**........ Sixaola [*Costa Rica*] [*ICAO location identifier*] (ICLI)
**MRT**.......... Machine-Readable Tapes [*Data processing*]
**MRT**.......... Maintainability Review Team [*Navy*] (NG)
**MRT**.......... Major Role Therapy [*Schizophrenia*]
**MRT**.......... Marble Threshold (AAG)
**MRT**.......... Marietta Resources [*Vancouver Stock Exchange symbol*]
**MRT**.......... Marysville, OH [*Location identifier*] [*FAA*] (FAAL)
**MRT**.......... Mass Rapid Transport [*British*]
**MRT**.......... Material Review Tag [*Aviation*] (MCD)
**MRT**.......... Mauritania [*ANSI three-letter standard code*] (CNC)
**MRT**.......... Maximum Rated Thrust (MCD)
**MRT**.......... Maze-Running Time [*Psychology*]
**MRT**.......... Mean Radiant Temperature
**MRT**.......... Mean Radiative-Transfer [*Meteorology*]
**MRT**.......... Mean Ready Time (MCD)
**MRT**.......... Mean Repair Time
**MRT**.......... Mean Residence Time [*Kinetics*]
**MRT**.......... Mean Retention Time [*Physiology*]
**MRT**.......... Medium-Range Typhon [*Missile*] (NG)
**MRT**.......... Meridional Ray Trace
**Mrt**............ Merit [*Record label*]
**MRT**.......... Metropolitan Readiness Test
**MRT**.......... Mildew-Resistant Thread
**MRT**.......... Milestones Reporting Techniques
**MRT**.......... Militair Rechtelijk Tijdschrift [*A publication*]
**MRT**.......... Military Rated Thrust (NG)
**MRT**.......... Miniature Receiver Terminal
**MRT**.......... Minimum Resolvable Temperature (MCD)
**MRT**.......... Missile Round Trainer (MCD)
**MRT**.......... Missile Round Transporter (MCD)
**MR & T**...... Mississippi River and Tributaries [*Flood-control project*]
**MRT**.......... Mobile RADAR Target
**MRT**.......... Modified Rhyme Test
**MRT**.......... Mortgage & Realty Trust [*NYSE symbol*] (SPSG)
**MRT**.......... Movimento Revolucionario Tiradentes [*Revolutionary Tiradentes Movement*] [*Brazil*] [*Political party*] (PD)
**MRT**.......... Murotomisaki [*Japan*] [*Seismograph station code, US Geological Survey*] (SEIS)
**MRT**.......... Muscle Response Test
**MRT**.......... Reformed Theological Seminary, Jackson, MS [*OCLC symbol*] (OCLC)
**MRTA**....... Marietta Corp. [*Cortland, NY*] [*NASDAQ symbol*] (NQ)
**MRTA**....... Marketing Research Trade Association [*Later, MRA*] (EA)
**MRTA**....... Tamarindo de Bagaces [*Costa Rica*] [*ICAO location identifier*] (ICLI)
**MRTB**....... Ticaban [*Costa Rica*] [*ICAO location identifier*] (ICLI)
**MRTC**....... Marine Corps Reserve Training Center
**MRTC**....... Military Real-Time Computer (AAG)
**MRTC**....... Multiple Real-Time Commands (NASA)
**MRTE**....... Master of Radio and Television Engineering
**MRT Eng**... Master of Radio and Television Engineering
**MRTFB**..... Major Range and Test Facility Base [*Military*] (CAAL)
**MRTG**....... Taboga [*Costa Rica*] [*ICAO location identifier*] (ICLI)
**MRTI**......... Multirole Thermal Imager [*Defense electronics*]
**MRTK**....... Maritek Corp. [*NASDAQ symbol*] (NQ)
**MRTK**....... Movimiento Revolucionario Tupaj Katari [*Tupaj Katari Revolutionary Movement*] [*Bolivia*] [*Political party*] (PPW)
**MRTM**...... Maritime (FAAC)
**MRTM**...... Tamarindo de Santa Cruz [*Costa Rica*] [*ICAO location identifier*] (ICLI)
**MRTMBB**... Maritimes [*A publication*]
**MRTN**....... Marten Transport Ltd. [*Mondovi, WI*] [*NASDAQ symbol*] (NQ)
**MRTP**........ Military Reliable Tube Program
**MRTPI**...... Member of the Royal Town Planning Institute [*British*]
**MRTR**....... Tambor [*Costa Rica*] [*ICAO location identifier*] (ICLI)
**MRTS**........ Marginal Rate of Technical Substitution [*Ecology*]
**MRTS**........ Master RADAR Tracking Station
**MRTS**........ Meteorological Real-Time System [*Data processing*] (KSC)
**MRTS**........ Multi-Media Remote Teaching System [*AT & T Co., Illinois Institute of Technology*]
**MRTT**........ Modular Record Traffic Terminal [*Formerly, COED*] [*Army*] (MCD)
**MRTU**....... Multiplex Remote Terminal Unit (MCD)
**MRU**.......... Machine Records Unit [*Data processing*]
**MRU**.......... Mano River Union [*See also UFM*] (EAIO)
**MRU**.......... Maritime Reconnaissance Unit [*British military*] (DMA)
**MRU**.......... Mass Radiography Unit
**MRU**.......... Material Recovery Unit
**MRU**.......... Mauritius [*Airport symbol*] (OAG)
**MRU**.......... Message Retransmission Unit
**MRU**.......... Microfilm Recording Unit
**MRU**.......... Microwave Relay Unit
**MRU**.......... Minimal Reproductive Units [*Bacteriology*]
**MRU**.......... Minimum Replacement Unit
**MRU**.......... Mobile Radio Unit [*Air Force*]
**MRU**.......... Mobile Refrigeration Unit (KSC)
**MRU**.......... Mobile Remote Unit [*From computer game "Hacker II"*]
**MRU**.......... Much Regret, I Am Unable
**MRU**.......... Multifunction Reference Unit (MCD)
**MRUASTAS**... Medium-Range Unmanned Aerial Surveillance and Target Acquisition System (NATG)
**M Ru E**....... Master of Rural Engineering
**M Ru Eng**.. Master of Rural Engineering
**MRUP**....... Upala [*Costa Rica*] [*ICAO location identifier*] (ICLI)
**MRurSc**..... Master of Rural Science [*British*] (ADA)
**MRUSI**...... Member of the Royal United Service Institution [*British*]
**MRV**.......... Maneuvering Reentry Vehicle
**MRV**.......... Mark V Petroleums & Mines [*Vancouver Stock Exchange symbol*]
**Mr V**.......... Metallreinigung Vorbehandlung, Oberflaechentechnik, Formung [*A publication*]
**MRV**.......... Mex-Am Review [*A publication*]
**MRV**.......... Middlesex Rifle Volunteers [*Military*] [*British*] (ROG)
**MRV**.......... Mineral Nyye Vody [*USSR*] [*Airport symbol*] (OAG)
**MRV**.......... Minute Respiratory Volume
**MRV**.......... Mixed Respiratory Vaccine
**MRV**.......... Mouvement de Regroupement Voltaique [*Upper Volta Regroupment Movement*] [*Political party*]
**MRV**.......... Multiple Reentry Vehicle [*Military*]
**MRVC**....... Member of the Royal Veterinary College [*British*]
**MRVI**........ Monte Reale Valcellina [*Italy*] [*Seismograph station code, US Geological Survey*] (SEIS)
**MRVLP**..... Maneuvering Reentry Vehicle for Low-Level Penetration (MCD)
**MRVNAN**... RIVON [*Rijksinstituut voor Veldbiologische Onderzoek ten Behoeve van het Natuurbehoud*] Jaarverslag [*A publication*]
**MRVO**....... Militaerregierungsverordnung [*A publication*]
**MRVP**....... Mean Right Ventricular Pressure [*Cardiology*]
**MRVP**....... Methyl-Red, Voges-Proskauer [*Medium*] [*Bacteriology*]
**MRVTB**..... Maximally Restrictive Verifiable Test Ban [*For nuclear bombs*]
**MRW**......... Morale, Recreation, and Welfare [*Military*] (AFM)
**MRW**......... Morioka [*Japan*] [*Airport symbol*] (OAG)
**MRWC**...... Multiple Read-Write Compute
**MRWKA**.... Marine Week [*A publication*]
**MRX**.......... Mobil Oil Corp., Toxicology Division, Information Center, Princeton, NJ [*OCLC symbol*] (OCLC)
**MRX**.......... National Bank of Ethiopia. Quarterly Bulletin. New Series [*A publication*]
**MRX**.......... Riverside, CA [*Location identifier*] [*FAA*] (FAAL)
**MRY**.......... Marilyn Resources [*Vancouver Stock Exchange symbol*]
**MRY**.......... Mary [*USSR*] [*Seismograph station code, US Geological Survey*] [*Closed*] (SEIS)
**MRY**.......... Mercury Airways, Inc. [*Melrose Park, IL*] [*FAA designator*] (FAAC)
**MRY**.......... Monterey [*California*] [*Airport symbol*] (OAG)
**MRYAA**.... Memoirs. Royal Astronomical Society [*A publication*]
**MRYIBO**... Miscellaneous Reports. Yamashina Institute for Ornithology and Zoology [*A publication*]
**MRZ**.......... Moree [*Australia*] [*Airport symbol*] (OAG)

**MRZ**.......... Syracuse, NY [*Location identifier*] [*FAA*] (FAAL)
**MRZGA**.... Metody Razvedochnoi Geofiziki [*A publication*]
**MRZP**........ Zapotal De Guanacaste [*Costa Rica*] [*ICAO location identifier*] (ICLI)
**M & S**........ Bureau of Medicine and Surgery [*Navy*]
**MS**............ Egypt Air [*ICAO designator*] (FAAC)
**MS**............ IEEE Magnetics Society (EA)
**MS**............ Maandblad N. Samson. Gewijd aan de Belangen der Gemeenteadministratie [*A publication*]
**MS**............ Ma'aser Sheni (BJA)
**MS**............ Machine Screw
**MS**............ Machine Selection (IEEE)
**MS**............ Machine Steel
**MS**............ Machinery Survey [*Shipping*]
**MS**............ Macro Society (EA)
**MS**............ Macromodular System [*Data processing*] (IEEE)
**MS**............ Magnetic South
**MS**............ Magnetic Stirrer [*Biotechnology*]
**MS**............ Magnetic Storage [*Data processing*]
**MS**............ Magnetostriction
**MS**............ Mail Steamer
**M/S**.......... Mail Stop
**MS**............ Mail on Sunday [*A publication*]
**MS**............ Main Sequence [*Astronomy*]
**MS**............ Main Steam (NRCH)
**MS**............ Main Storage
**MS**............ Main Switch
**M/S**.......... Mainstage [*NASA*] (KSC)
**MS**............ Maintenance and Service
**MS**............ Maintenance Standard
**MS**............ Maintenance Superintendent [*Military*] (AFIT)
**M & S**........ Maintenance and Supply
**MS +**........ Maintenance Support Positive
**MS**............ Major Subject [*Military*]
**MS**............ Majority Stockholder
**MS**............ Maladjustment Score [*Psychology*]
**MS**............ Male Servant
**MS**............ Malone Society (EA)
**MS**............ Mammal Society (EAIO)
**MS**............ Management Science [*Data processing*] (BUR)
**MS**............ Management Services (KSC)
**MS**............ Management System (OICC)
**MS**............ Manchester School of Economic and Social Studies [*A publication*]
**M & S**........ Manning and Scott's English Common Bench Reports [*IX*] [*A publication*] (DLA)
**MS**............ Mano Sinistra [*With the Left Hand*] [*Music*]
**M/S**.......... Manslaughter
**MS**............ Manual Sequential (NRCH)
**MS**............ Manual Supplement
**MS**............ Manual System (DCTA)
**MS**............ Manufacturing Specification (AAG)
**MS**............ Manufacturing Standard
**MS**............ Manufacturing Status (AAG)
**MS**............ Manufacturing Support
**MS**............ Manuscript Reports [*A publication*] (DLA)
**MS**............ Manuscript Society (EA)
**MS**............ Manuscriptum [*Manuscript*] [*Latin*]
**MS**............ Mar del Sur [*A publication*]
**M & S**........ March and September [*Denotes semiannual payments of interest or dividends in these months*] [*Business term*]
**MS**............ Mare Serenitatis [*Sea of Serenity*] [*Lunar area*]
**MS**............ Margin of Safety [*Engineering*]
**MS**............ Marijuana Smoke
**MS**............ Marital Status
**MS**............ Mark Sensing (MSA)
**M & S**........ Marks & Spencer [*English department store chain*]
**MS**............ Marquandia Society (EA)
**MS**............ Marshall Steel Ltd. [*Toronto Stock Exchange symbol*]
**MS**............ Mass Spectrography
**MS**............ Mass Spectrometry
**MS**............ Mass Storage [*Data processing*]
**MS**............ Master Scheduler (CMD)
**MS**............ Master of Science [*Facetious translation "More of the Same"*]
**MS**............ Master Sequencer (AAG)
**MS**............ Master Sergeant
**MS**............ Master of Surgery
**MS**............ Master Switch
**MS**............ Master Synchronizer (CET)
**MS**............ Matched Set [*Philately*]
**MS**............ Material Specifications
**MS**............ Material Support
**MS**............ Materials Science
**M & S**........ Materials and Services [*NASA*] (KSC)
**M & S**........ Materials and Structures (SDI)
**MS**............ Mathis Society (EA)
**MS**............ Mating Sequence and Control (NASA)
**M & S**........ Maule and Selwyn's English King's Bench Reports [*A publication*] (DLA)
**MS**............ Mauritius
**MS**............ Maximum Stress
**M & S**........ McClelland & Stewart [*Canadian publisher*]
**MS**............ Mean Square
**MS**............ Measured Service Pricing [*Telecommunications*] (TEL)
**M/S**.......... Measurement Stimuli (NASA)
**MS**............ Measuring Set
**MS**............ Measuring System
**MS**............ Mechanical Seal
**MS**............ Mechanized Scheduling [*Telecommunications*] (TEL)
**M/S**.......... Media/Scope [*A publication*]
**MS**............ Media-Service GmbH [*Database producer*] (IID)
**M & S**........ Media and Status [*Code*] [*DoD*]
**MS**............ Mediaeval Studies [*A publication*]
**MS**............ Medial Septum [*Anatomy*]
**MS**............ Medical Services [*Navy*] [*British*]
**MS**............ Medical Staff [*British military*] (DMA)
**MS**............ Medical Supplies [*Military*]
**MS**............ Medical Survey [*Navy*]
**MS**............ Medicine and Surgery [*Navy*] (IEEE)
**MS**............ Medium Setting [*Asphalt grade*]
**MS**............ Medium Shot [*Refers to distance from which a photograph or motion picture sequence is taken*]
**MS**............ Medium Steel
**MS**............ Meeting Series [*Online database field identifier*]
**MS**............ Meeting of Signatories [*INTELSAT*]
**MS**............ Mega Society (EA)
**MS**............ Megasporocyte [*Botany*]
**MS**............ Melanges Syriens Offerts a Monsieur Rene Dussaud [*A publication*]
**MS**............ Melville Society (EA)
**M/S**.......... Member State (DCTA)
**M/S**.......... Memorandum Slip [*for informal interoffice communications*]
**MS**............ Memoriae Sacrum [*Sacred to the Memory Of*] [*Latin*]
**MS**............ Memorias Succintas. Kahal Kados [*Amsterdam*] [*A publication*]
**MS**............ Memory System
**MS**............ Men of the Stones (EA)
**MS**............ Mencken Society (EA)
**MS**............ Mental Status [*Psychology*]
**MS**............ Merchant Shipping
**MS**............ Mercury-Scout [*Spacecraft*] [*NASA*]
**MS**............ Merit System (OICC)
**MS**............ Mesa [*Type of transistor*] (MDG)
**MS**............ Mestome Sheath [*Botany*]
**Ms**............ Mesyl [*Organic chemistry*]
**MS**............ Metal Stamping
**MS**............ [*The*] Metallurgical Society [*Later, TMS*]
**MS**............ Metals Society [*Later, IOM*] (EAIO)
**MS**............ Meteoritical Society (EA)
**MS**............ Meteoroid Shield (KSC)
**M/S**.......... Meters per Second
**MS**............ Methionine Synthase [*An enzyme*]
**MS**............ Method of Sale
**M & S**........ Methods and Standards
**MS**............ Metric System
**MS**............ Mezzo Soprano [*Music*] (ROG)
**MS**............ Microcirculatory Society (EA)
**MS**............ Microprogram Storage [*Data processing*] (MDG)
**MS**............ Microscopic System
**MS**............ Microsoft [*Software manufacturer*]
**MS**............ Microsphere
**MS**............ Microstructural Science [*Elsevier Book Series*] [*A publication*]
**MS**............ Microwave Spectrum
**MS**............ Mid-Shot
**MS**............ Midnight Sun. Igloolik [*A publication*]
**MS**............ Mild Steel
**MS**............ Milestone (KSC)
**MS**............ Military Science (AABC)
**MS**............ Military Secretary [*British*]
**MS**............ Military Service
**MS**............ Military Service Act [*British*]
**MS**............ Military Specification (AAG)
**MS**............ Military Staff [*British military*] (DMA)
**MS**............ Military Standard
**MS**............ Military Survivors (EA)
**MS**............ Millennium Society (EA)
**ms**............ Millisecond
**mS**............ Millisiemens
**M & S**........ Milwaukee & Superior Railroad
**MS**............ Minesweeper [*or Minesweeping*]
**MS**............ Minister of State [*British*]
**MS**............ Ministry of Shipping [*British*]
**MS**............ Ministry of Supply [*Also, MOS*] [*British*]
**M/S**.......... Minor Support (KSC)
**MS**............ Minority Stockholder
**MS**............ Mint State
**MS**............ Minus
**MS**............ Minutes (AAG)
**MS**............ Miscellaneous
**MS**............ Miscellaneous Services [*Department of Employment*] [*British*]
**MS**............ Miss or Mrs. [*Pronounced "Miz"*]
**MS**............ Missile Station (AAG)

**MS** ........ Missile System
**MS** ........ Mission Simulator
**MS** ........ Mission Specialist (MCD)
**MS** ........ Mission Station (MCD)
**MS** ........ Mission Support
**MS** ........ Missionaries of Our Lady of LaSalette [*Roman Catholic religious order*]
**MS** ........ Missionary Sisters of Our Lady of Africa [*White Sisters*] [*Roman Catholic religious order*]
**MS** ........ Missionary Society [*British*]
**MS** ........ Missions to Seamen (EA)
**MS** ........ Mississippi [*Postal code*]
**Ms** ........ Mississippi State Library, Jackson, MS [*Library symbol*] [*Library of Congress*] (LCLS)
**MS** ........ Mitral Stenosis [*Cardiology*]
**M-S** ........ Mitte-Seite [*Stereo*] (IEEE)
**MS** ........ Mitteilungen aus dem Gebiete der Statistik [*A publication*]
**MS** ........ Mittelsatz [*Middle Movement*] [*Music*]
**MS** ........ Mobile Searchlight [*British*]
**MS** ........ Mobile Service [*Telecommunications*] (TEL)
**MS** ........ Mobile Surgery [*British*]
**MS** ........ Mobilization Station [*DoD*]
**MS** ........ Modal Sensation [*Psychology*]
**MS** ........ Modal Sensitivity [*Medicine*]
**M & S** ........ Model and Series (AAG)
**MS** ........ Model Station
**MS** ........ Moderately Susceptible [*Plant pathology*]
**MS** ........ Modern Science [*A publication*]
**MS** ........ Moderna Sprak [*A publication*]
**MS** ........ Modulation Sensitivity
**MS** ........ Molar Degree of Substitution [*Organic chemistry*]
**MS** ........ Molar Solution [*Dentistry*]
**MS** ........ Monde Slave [*A publication*]
**MS** ........ Money Supply
**MS** ........ Mongolian Spot [*Medicine*]
**MS** ........ Monitor Station
**MS** ........ Monorail Society (EA)
**MS** ........ Months after Sight [*or Month's Sight*] [*Business term*]
**MS** ........ Montserrat [*ANSI two-letter standard code*] (CNC)
**MS** ........ Monumenta Serica [*A publication*]
**M & S** ........ Moore and Scott's English Common Pleas Reports [*1831-34*] [*A publication*] (DLA)
**MS** ........ More Significant [*Statistics*]
**MS** ........ Morgan Stanley Group, Inc. [*NYSE symbol*] (SPSG)
**MS** ........ Morphine Sulfate [*Narcotic*]
**MS** ........ Most Significant
**MS** ........ Motile Sperm
**MS** ........ Motion Sensitivity (KSC)
**MS** ........ Motor Ship
**MS** ........ Motor Supports
**MS** ........ Mouvement Sociologique [*A publication*]
**Ms** ........ Ms Magazine [*A publication*]
**MS** ........ MS. Manuscript [*Los Angeles*] [*A publication*]
**MS** ........ Multiple Sclerosis [*Medicine*]
**MS** ........ Multiple Section (MSA)
**MS** ........ Multistring (NASA)
**MS** ........ Murashige-Skoog [*Medium*] [*Botany*]
**MS** ........ Muscle Shortening [*Medicine*]
**MS** ........ Muscle Strength
**MS** ........ Musculactive Substance [*Medicine*]
**MS** ........ Musculoskeletal [*Medicine*]
**MS** ........ Music Survey [*A publication*]
**Ms** ........ Mussels [*Quality of the bottom*] [*Nautical charts*]
**MS** ........ Mustard Seed (EA)
**MS** ........ Muttersprache [*A publication*]
**M S** ........ Muzikal'niy Sovremennik [*A publication*]
**MS** ........ Mycoplasma Synoviae [*A pathogen*]
**MS** ........ Mythopoeic Society (EA)
**MS** ........ Ship Station [*ITU designation*] (CET)
**MS** ........ Somerset Library [*Bibliotheque Somerset*], Manitoba [*Library symbol*] [*National Library of Canada*] (BIB)
**MS** ........ Springfield City Library, Springfield, MA [*Library symbol*] [*Library of Congress*] (LCLS)
**M/0/0/S** ........ Minutes Zero Zero Seconds [*Aerospace*] (AAG)
**M1S** ........ Matte One Side [*Aluminum*]
**MS-2** ........ Mare Serenitatis [*Sea of Serenity*] [*Lunar area*]
**M2S** ........ Matte Two Sides [*Aluminum*]
**M/S²** ........ Meters per Second Squared
**M²/S** ........ Square Meters per Second
**M³/S** ........ Cubic Meters per Second
**MS-3** ........ Military Staffing Standards System
**MS3** ........ Munitions Support Structure Study [*Army*]
**MS3** ........ Munitions System Support Structure
**MSA** ........ Magazine Shippers Association
**MSA** ........ Mahri, Suqutri, and Shahri (BJA)
**MSA** ........ Main Store Allocator
**MSA** ........ Malaysia-Singapore Airlines
**MSA** ........ Management Science Associates, Inc. [*Information service or system*] (IID)
**MSA** ........ Management System Analysis
**MSA** ........ Mandusa Resources Ltd. [*Vancouver Stock Exchange symbol*]
**MSA** ........ Marigold Society of America (EA)
**MSA** ........ Marine Science Activities [*Program*] [*Coast Guard*]
**MSA** ........ Mariological Society of America (EA)
**MSA** ........ Marker Signal Attenuation
**MSA** ........ Market Science Associates, Inc. [*Information service or system*] (IID)
**MSA** ........ Marlowe Society of America (EA)
**MSA** ........ Marquetry Society of America (EA)
**MSA** ........ Masonic Service Association of the United States (EA)
**MSA** ........ Mass-Separating Agent [*Chemical engineering*]
**MSA** ........ Mass Storage Adapter
**MSA** ........ Massachusetts School of Art
**MSA** ........ Master of Science in Accountancy
**MSA** ........ Master of Science in Agriculture
**MSA** ........ Master of Science and Arts
**MSA** ........ Master of Scientific Agriculture
**MSA** ........ Material Service Area (NASA)
**MSA** ........ Material Stores Area (KSC)
**MSA** ........ Material Surveillance Assembly [*Nuclear energy*] (NRCH)
**MSA** ........ Mean Spherical Approximation [*Physical chemistry*]
**MSA** ........ Mechanical Signature Analysis
**MSA** ........ Media Studies Association [*British*]
**MSA** ........ Medical Services Account
**MSA** ........ Medical Services Administration [*HEW*]
**MSA** ........ Medical Services Adviser [*Australia*]
**MSA** ........ Medusa Corp. [*NYSE symbol*] (CTT)
**MSA** ........ Member of the Society of Apothecaries [*British*]
**MSA** ........ Member of the Society of Architects [*British*] (DAS)
**MSA** ........ Member of the Society of Arts [*British*]
**MSA** ........ Membrane-Stabilizing Activity [*Cardiology*]
**MSA** ........ Merchant Shipping Act
**MSA** ........ Mercury Singapore Airlines
**MSA** ........ Mermaid Series [*A publication*]
**MSA** ........ Mesa Public Library, Mesa, AZ [*OCLC symbol*] (OCLC)
**MSA** ........ Metaphysical Society of America (EA)
**MSA** ........ Meteorological Support Activity [*Army Electronics Command*]
**MSA** ........ Methanesulfonic Acid [*Organic chemistry*]
**MSA** ........ Method of Standard Additions
**MSA** ........ Methyltrimethylsilylacetamide [*Organic chemistry*]
**MSA** ........ Metropolitan Service Area [*Telecommunications*] (TSSD)
**MSA** ........ Metropolitan Statistical Area [*Census Bureau*]
**MSA** ........ Microcomputer Software Association (EA)
**MSA** ........ Microgravity Science and Applications
**MSA** ........ Microsomal Antibody
**MSA** ........ Middle States Association of Colleges and Schools (EA)
**MSA** ........ Middle Stone Age [*Anthropology*]
**MSA** ........ Military Service Act [*British*] (DMA)
**MSA** ........ Military Subsistence Agency [*Merged with Defense Supply Agency*]
**MSA** ........ Milton Society of America (EA)
**MSA** ........ Mine Safety Appliance
**MSA** ........ Mineralogical Society of America (EA)
**MSA** ........ Minesweeper, Auxiliary [*Navy symbol*] [*Obsolete*]
**MSA** ........ Minimum Safe Altitude [*Aviation*]
**MSA** ........ Minimum Sector Altitudes [*Aviation*] (FAAC)
**MSA** ........ Minimum Surface Area (KSC)
**MSA** ........ Minnesota Statutes, Annotated [*A publication*] (DLA)
**MSA** ........ Misce Secundum Artem [*Mix Pharmaceutically*] [*Latin*]
**MSA** ........ Missile Support Activity (MCD)
**MSA** ........ Missile System Availability (MCD)
**MSA** ........ Mission Services Association (EA)
**MSA** ........ Mission Support Area [*NASA*]
**MSA** ........ Missionary Sisters of the Assumption [*Roman Catholic religious order*]
**MSA** ........ Mobile Subscriber Access (MCD)
**MSA** ........ Monitor and Switching Assembly
**MSA** ........ Morale Support Activities [*Military*] (AABC)
**MSA** ........ Most Seriously Affected [*Food-deficient nations*]
**MSA** ........ Mount Pleasant, TX [*Location identifier*] [*FAA*] (FAAL)
**MSA** ........ Mount San Antonio [*New Mexico*] [*Seismograph station code, US Geological Survey*] (SEIS)
**MSA** ........ Mouvement Socialiste Africain [*African Socialist Movement*] [*Congo - Brazzaville*] [*Political party*]
**MSA** ........ Mouvement Souverainete Association [*Canada*] (PPW)
**MSA** ........ Multichannel Signal Averager [*Data processing*]
**MSA** ........ Multiple System Atrophy [*Medicine*]
**MSA** ........ Multiplication Stimulating Activity [*Cytochemistry*]
**MSA** ........ Multisubsystem Adapter [*Sperry UNIVAC*]
**MSA** ........ Museum Store Association (EA)
**MSA** ........ Muslim Students' Association of the US and Canada (EA)
**MSA** ........ Mutual Security Act [*1954*]
**MSA** ........ Mutual Security Agency [*Functions transferred to Foreign Operations Administration, 1953*]
**MSA** ........ Mycological Society of America (EA)
**MSa** ........ Salem Public Library, Salem, MA [*Library symbol*] [*Library of Congress*] (LCLS)
**MSA** ........ Vakblad voor de Handel in Aardappelen, Groenten, en Fruit [*A publication*]
**MSAA** ........ Moderately Severe Aplastic Anemia [*Hematology*]
**MSAA** ........ Multiple-Sclerosis-Associated Agent [*A virus*]
**MSAAB** ........ Military Services Ammunition Allocation Board (AABC)

**MSAAEQ** ... American Group Psychotherapy Association. Monograph Series [*A publication*]
**MSAAP**..... Mississippi Army Ammunition Plant (AABC)
**MsAb**......... Evans Memorial Library, Aberdeen, MS [*Library symbol*] [*Library of Congress*] (LCLS)
**MS/AB**...... Massenet Society/American Branch (EA)
**MSAc**......... Master of Science in Accounting
**MSAC**........ Missile System Analyst Console (AAG)
**MSAC**........ Moore School of Automatic Computers [*University of Pennsylvania*]
**MSAC**........ Mount Saint Agnes College [*Maryland*] [*Merged with Loyola College*]
**MSAC**........ Murray State Agricultural College [*Oklahoma*]
**MSAC**........ Sonsonate/Acajutla [*El Salvador*] [*ICAO location identifier*] (ICLI)
**MS/Accy** ... Master of Science in Accountancy
**MSACHA** ... Mid-South Automated Clearing House Association
**M Sacra** ..... Musica Sacra [*A publication*]
**M Sacrae Ministerium** ... Musicae Sacrae Ministerium [*A publication*]
**MSAD** ....... Materials Summary Acceptance Document (MCD)
**MSAD** ....... Multisatellite Attitude Determination [*NASA*]
**MSaE**......... Essex Institute, Salem, MA [*Library symbol*] [*Library of Congress*] (LCLS)
**MSAE**........ Master of Science in Aeronautical Engineering
**MS in AE**... Master of Science in Aeronautical Engineering
**MSAE**........ Member of the Society of Automotive Engineers
**MSAE-A**.... Member of the Society of Automotive Engineers - Australasia
**MS in Aero E** ... Master of Science in Aeronautical Engineering
**MSAF**........ Memoires. Societe Nationale des Antiquaires de France [*A publication*]
**MSafetySc** ... Master of Safety Science
**MSAFP** ..... Maternal Serum Alpha Fetoprotein [*Clinical chemistry*]
**MSAFV** ..... Mitteilungen der Schweizerischen Anstalt fuer das Forstliche Versuchswesen [*A publication*]
**MS (Ag)**..... Master of Science in Agriculture
**MS in Ag** ... Master of Science in Agriculture
**MSAGD9** .. Maritime Sediments and Atlantic Geology [*A publication*]
**MS in Ag E** ... Master of Science in Agricultural Education
**MS (Ag E)** ... Master of Science in Agricultural Engineering
**MS in Ag Ec** ... Master of Science in Agricultural Economics
**MS Agr**....... Master of Science in Agriculture
**MS in Agr** ... Master of Science in Agriculture
**MS in Agr Ed** ... Master of Science in Agricultural Education
**MSAI**......... American International College, Springfield, MA [*Library symbol*] [*Library of Congress*] (LCLS)
**MSAI**......... Management Science America, Incorporated [*NASDAQ symbol*] (NQ)
**MSAICE** ... Member of the South African Institution of Civil Engineers
**MSAInstMM** ... Member of the South African Institute of Mining and Metallugy
**MsAM**....... Alcorn Agricultural and Mechanical College, Lorman, MS [*Library symbol*] [*Library of Congress*] (LCLS)
**MSAM** ...... Marsam Pharmaceuticals, Inc. [*NASDAQ symbol*] (NQ)
**MSAM** ...... Master of Science in Applied Mechanics
**M-SAM** ..... Medium Surface-to-Air Missile [*Army*]
**MSAM** ...... Memoires. Societe des Antiquaires de la Morinie [*A publication*]
**MSAM** ...... Mobile Surface-to-Air Missile
**MSAM** ...... Morgan Stanley Asset Management [*Commercial firm*]
**MSAM** ...... Morpholinomethyl Salicyclamide [*Analgesic compound*]
**MSAM** ...... Multi-Indexed Sequential Access Method [*Data processing*]
**MSAMP**.... Master Ship Acquisition Milestone Plan
**MSAMS**.... Mobile Surface-to-Air Missile System (MCD)
**M San** ....... Master of Sanitation
**MS in AN** .. Master of Science in Agricultural Engineering
**MSanHi**.... Sandwich Historical Society, Sandwich, MA [*Library symbol*] [*Library of Congress*] (LCLS)
**MSANS**..... Multiple Small-Angle Neutron Scattering [*Surface analysis*]
**M San Sc** ... Master of Sanitary Science
**MSAO** ....... Medical Services Accountable Officer
**MSAO** ....... Memoires. Societe des Antiquaires de l'Ouest [*A publication*]
**MSAO** ....... Morale Support Activities Office
**MSAP**........ Master Space Allocation Plan (MCD)
**MSAP**........ Mean Systemic Arterial Pressure [*Cardiology*]
**MSAP**........ Memoires. Societe des Antiquaires de Picardie [*A publication*]
**MSAP**........ Military Security Assistance Projection [*Military*]
**MSAP**........ Multisatellite Attitude Prediction [*NASA*]
**MSaP**......... Peabody Museum of Salem, Salem, MA [*Library symbol*] [*Library of Congress*] (LCLS)
**MSAPD2**... MIT [*Massachusetts Institute of Technology*] Studies in American Politics and Public Policy [*A publication*]
**MSAR**........ Memoires. Societe Archeologique Imperiale Russe [*A publication*]
**MSAR**........ Mines Safety Appliance Research (IEEE)
**Ms-Ar** ....... Mississippi Department of Archives and History, Jackson, MS [*Library symbol*] [*Library of Congress*] (LCLS)
**MSARC**..... Marine Systems Acquisition Review Council (MCD)
**MS Arch** .... Master of Science in Architecture
**MSARLRP** ... McGill Sub-Arctic Research Laboratory. Research Paper [*A publication*]
**MSAS**........ Mandel Social Adjustment Scale [*Psychology*]
**MSAS**........ Marine Sciences Affairs Staff [*A publication*]
**MSAS**........ Minnesota School Attitude Survey [*Educational test*]
**MSAS**........ Modal Suppression Augmentation System [*Aerospace*]
**M Sa Sc** ..... Master of Sacred Sciences
**MSAT**........ Minnesota Scholastic Aptitude Test
**MSaT**......... Salem State College, Salem, MA [*Library symbol*] [*Library of Congress*] (LCLS)
**MSATA**..... Motorcycle, Scooter, and Allied Trades Association [*Later, MIC*]
**MSATA**..... Societa Astronomica Italiana. Memorie [*A publication*]
**MSAU** ....... Multistation Access Unit [*Telecommunications*] (TSSD)
**MS in Aud & Sp** ... Master of Science in Audiology and Speech
**MSAUSC**.. Muslim Students' Association of the United States and Canada (EA)
**MSAutE** .... Member of the Society of Automobile Engineers [*British*]
**MSAVAH** ... Institut Suisse de Recherches Forestieres. Memoires [*A publication*]
**MSAW** ...... Minimum Safe Altitude Warning [*Aviation*]
**MSAWS**.... Mobile Surface-to-Air Weapon System (MCD)
**MsB** .......... Biloxi Public Library, Biloxi, MS [*Library symbol*] [*Library of Congress*] (LCLS)
**MSB**.......... Iola, KS [*Location identifier*] [*FAA*] (FAAL)
**MSB**.......... Magnetic Susceptibility Bridge
**MSB**.......... Main Steamline Break [*Nuclear energy*] (NRCH)
**MSB**.......... Main Support Base [*Air Force*] (AFM)
**MSB**.......... Main Switchboard
**MSB**.......... Maintenance Standard Book
**MSB**.......... Male Sexual Biomass [*Botany*]
**MSB**.......... Manpower Services Branch [*Military*] (MCD)
**MSB**.......... Maritime Safety Board [*Japan*] (CINC)
**MSB**.......... Maritime Subsidy Board [*Maritime Administration*] [*Department of Commerce*]
**MSB**.......... Martin's Scarlet Blue [*Histologic stain*]
**MSB**.......... Mass Spectrometry Bulletin [*Mass Spectrometry Data Centre*] [*Bibliographic database*] [*British*]
**Ms B** .......... Master of Bacteriology
**MSB**.......... Master of Science in Business
**MSB**.......... Material Support Branch [*NASA*] (KSC)
**MSB**.......... Mediterranean Shipping Board [*World War II*]
**MSB**.......... Member of the School Board [*British*] (ROG)
**MSB**.......... Memory Storage Buffer [*Data processing*] (CAAL)
**MSB**.......... Mesabi Trust Certificates SBI [*NYSE symbol*] (SPSG)
**MSB**.......... Methylstyrylbenzene [*Fluorescent compound*]
**MSB**.......... Metropolitan Separate School Board [*UTLAS symbol*]
**MSB**.......... Michael Stanley Band [*Musical group*]
**MSB**.......... Military Security Board
**MSB**.......... Military Service Branch [*World War I*] [*Canada*]
**MSB**.......... Minesweeping Boat [*Navy symbol*]
**MSB**.......... Missile Storage Building (NATG)
**MSB**.......... Mission Simulator Building (MCD)
**MSB**.......... Mongolia Society. Bulletin [*A publication*]
**MSB**.......... Mongolian Studies. Journal of the Mongolia Society [*A publication*]
**MSB**.......... Montadale Sheep Breeders Association (EA)
**MSB**.......... Montclair Bancorp, Inc. [*NASDAQ symbol*] (NQ)
**MSB**.......... Most Significant BIT [*Binary Digit*] [*Data processing*]
**MSB**.......... Motor Surfboat
**MSB**.......... Multi-Step Industries [*Vancouver Stock Exchange symbol*]
**MSB**.......... Multnomah School of the Bible [*Oregon*]
**MSB**.......... Municipal Securities Board [*Approved by Congress May 22, 1975*] [*Securities and Exchange Commission*]
**MSB**.......... Museum of Southwestern Biology [*University of New Mexico*] [*Research center*] (RCD)
**MSB**.......... Music Sound Books [*Record label*]
**MSB**.......... Mutual Savings Bank
**MS in BA**... Master of Science in Business Administration
**MSBA**........ Master of Science in Business Administration
**MSBA**........ Military School Band Association (EA)
**MsBB**......... Beauvoir, the Jefferson Davis Shrine, Biloxi, MS [*Library symbol*] [*Library of Congress*] (LCLS)
**MSBC**........ Master of Science in Building Construction
**MSBC**........ Mid-State Bancorp [*NASDAQ symbol*] (NQ)
**MSBC**........ Steinbach Bible College, Manitoba [*Library symbol*] [*National Library of Canada*] (BIB)
**MSBCD2**... Marine Studies of San Pedro Bay, California [*A publication*]
**MSB-COD** ... Minority Small Business-Capital Ownership Development Program [*Small Business Administration*]
**MSBE**........ Molten-Salt Breeder Experiment [*Nuclear energy*]
**MsBel** ........ Humphreys County Library, Belzoni, MS [*Library symbol*] [*Library of Congress*] (LCLS)
**MSBF**........ Mean Sorties between Flights (MCD)
**MSBG-A** ... Masalah Bangunan [*A publication*]
**MSBIA**...... Member of Spa Bath Industry of Australia
**MSBIDK**... Methodological Surveys in Biochemistry [*A publication*]
**MSBK**........ Medford Savings Bank [*Medford, MA*] [*NASDAQ symbol*] (NQ)
**MSBL**........ Member of the School Board, London [*Defunct*] [*British*] (ROG)
**MSBLA**..... Mouse Specific B Lymphocyte Antigen [*Immunology*]
**MSBLS**...... Microwave Scanning Beam Landing Station [*or System*] [*NASA*] (NASA)

**MS in Bl Sc** ... Master of Science in Biological Sciences
**MSBLS-GS** ... Microwave Scanning Beam Landing System Ground Station [*NASA*] (NASA)
**MsBm** ........ Blue Mountain College, Blue Mountain, MS [*Library symbol*] [*Library of Congress*] (LCLS)
**MSBMRS** ... Marine Sciences Branch. Manuscript Report Series. Canada Department of Energy, Mines, and Resources [*A publication*]
**MSBO** ....... Mooring and Salvage Officer [*Navy*] [*British*]
**Ms-BPH** .... Mississippi Library Commission, Services for the Handicapped, Jackson, MS [*Library symbol*] [*Library of Congress*] (LCLS)
**MsBr** .......... Lincoln-Lawrence-Franklin Regional Library, Brookhaven, MS [*Library symbol*] [*Library of Congress*] (LCLS)
**MSBR** ........ Maximum Storage Bus Rate
**MSBR** ........ Military Strength Balance Report (AFM)
**MSBR** ........ Molten-Salt Breeder Reactor
**MSbrA** ....... American Optical Corp., Southbridge, MA [*Library symbol*] [*Library of Congress*] (LCLS)
**MsBs** .......... City-County Memorial Library, Bay St. Louis, MS [*Library symbol*] [*Library of Congress*] (LCLS)
**MSBS** ........ Minimum Social Behavior Scale [*Psychology*]
**MsBsNA** .... National Aeronautics and Space Administration, NASA/NSTL Research Library, NSTL Station, Bay St. Louis, MS [*Library symbol*] [*Library of Congress*] (LCLS)
**MsBsS** ....... Divine Word Seminary, Bay St. Louis, MS [*Library symbol*] [*Library of Congress*] (LCLS)
**MSBT** ......... Missionary Servants of the Most Blessed Trinity [*Roman Catholic women's religious order*]
**MSBTA** ..... Memoires. Academie des Sciences, Inscriptions, et Belles-Lettres de Toulouse [*A publication*]
**MSBTh** ...... Member of the Society of Health and Beauty Therapists [*British*] (DBQ)
**MS Bus** ....... Master of Science in Business
**MSBVW** .... Magnetostatic Backward Volume Wave [*Telecommunications*] (TEL)
**MSBY** ........ Most Significant Byte [*Data processing*]
**MSC** .......... Chief Mess Management Specialist [*Formerly, CSC, CST, SDC*] [*Navy rating*]
**MSC** .......... College de St.-Boniface, Manitoba [*Library symbol*] [*National Library of Canada*] (NLC)
**MSC** .......... Congregation of the Sisters Marianites of Holy Cross [*Roman Catholic religious order*]
**MSC** .......... [*The*] MacNeal-Schwendler Corp.
**MSC** .......... Macro Selection Compiler [*Data processing*] (BUR)
**MSC** .......... Madras Staff Corps [*British*]
**MSC** .......... Magnetic Surface Current
**MSC** .......... Magnetically Settable Counter
**MSC** .......... Maharashtra Socialist Congress [*India*] [*Political party*] (PPW)
**MSC** .......... Main Storage Control [*Data processing*] (BUR)
**MSC** .......... Maine Sardine Council (EA)
**MSC** .......... Maintenance Support Center (MCD)
**MSC** .......... Maisach [*Federal Republic of Germany*] [*Geomagnetic observatory code*]
**MSC** .......... Major Subcontract (MCD)
**MSC** .......... Major Subordinate Command [*Military*]
**MSC** .......... Management Science [*A publication*]
**MSC** .......... Management Services Contractor [*INTELSAT*]
**MSC** .......... Manchester Ship Canal
**MSC** .......... Mandatum sine Clausula [*Authority without Restriction*] [*Latin*]
**MSC** .......... Mankato State College [*Later, Mankato State University*] [*Minnesota*]
**MSC** .......... Manned Spacecraft Center [*Later, Johnson Space Center*] [*NASA*]
**MSC** .......... Manpower Services Commission [*British*]
**MSC** .......... Maple Syrup Council (EA)
**MSC** .......... Marine Safety Council [*Coast Guard*]
**MSC** .......... Marine Science Center [*Oregon State University*] [*Research center*] (RCD)
**MSC** .......... Marine Science Council [*Marine science*] (MSC)
**MSC** .......... Marital Status Code [*IRS*]
**MSC** .......... Maritime Service Committee [*New York, NY*] (EA)
**MSC** .......... Marketing Services Conference [*LIMRA*]
**MS & C** ...... Marley, Scrooge, and Cratchit [*Accounting agency*]
**MSC** .......... Marquise [*Marchioness*] [*French*] (ROG)
**MSC** .......... Maryland State College [*Merged with University of Maryland*]
**MSC** .......... Mass Storage Control [*Data processing*] (BUR)
**M Sc** .......... Master of Science
**MS in C** ...... Master of Science in Commerce
**MSC** .......... Master Sequence Controller (NASA)
**MSC** .......... Master Status Chart
**MSC** .......... Material Sciences Corporation [*AMEX symbol*] (SPSG)
**MSC** .......... Material Source Code
**MSC** .......... Materials Science Center [*Cornell University*]
**MSC** .......... Materials Service Center [*NASA*] (NASA)
**MSC** .......... Materiel Screening Code [*DoD*] (AFIT)
**MSC** .......... Materiel Status Committee [*Military*] (AABC)
**MSC** .......... Materiel Support Center (MCD)
**MSC** .......... Materiel Support Command (MCD)
**MSC** .......... Medical Service Commission [*Canada*]
**MSC** .......... Medical Service Corps [*Military*]
**MSC** .......... Medical Social Coordinator
**MSC** .......... Medical Specialist Corps [*Military*]
**MSC** .......... Medical Staff Corps [*British*]
**MSC** .......... Mediterranean Society of Chemotherapy (EAIO)
**MSC** .......... Mediterranean Sub-Commission [*Silva Mediterranea*] [*FAO*]
**MSC** .......... Memory Storage Control [*Data processing*]
**MSC** .......... Memphis Service Center [*IRS*]
**MSC** .......... Mesa [*Arizona*] [*Airport symbol*] [*Obsolete*] (OAG)
**MSC** .......... Mesitylenesulfonyl Chloride [*Biochemistry*]
**MSC** .......... Message Sequence Chart [*Telecommunications*] (TEL)
**MSC** .......... Message Switching Center [*Telecommunications*]
**MSC** .......... Message Switching Computer [*Telecommunications*] (TEL)
**MSC** .......... Message Switching Concentration
**MSC** .......... Metal Shielded Cabinet
**MSC** .......... Methane Sulfonyl Chloride [*Organic chemistry*]
**MSC** .......... Metric System - Conversion (NATG)
**MSC** .......... Metropolitan State College [*Denver, CO*]
**MSC** .......... Micronesia Support Committee [*Later, MC*] (EA)
**MSC** .......... Microscale Cloud [*Module*] [*Air Force*]
**MSC** .......... Midwestern Simulation Council
**MSC** .......... Migent Software [*Vancouver Stock Exchange symbol*]
**MSC** .......... Mile of Standard Cable
**MSC** .......... Milestone Schedule Charts (MCD)
**MSC** .......... Military Scout Car [*British*]
**MSC** .......... Military Sealift Command [*Formerly, MSTS, NTS*] [*Navy*] (NOAA)
**MSC** .......... Military Staff Committee [*United Nations*] (DLA)
**MSC** .......... Military Studies Center (EA)
**MSC** .......... Milliwatts per Square Centimeter
**MSC** .......... Minesweeper, Coastal [*Nonmagnetic*] [*Navy symbol*]
**MSC** .......... Minor Suma Corporation [*Kansas City, MO*] (TSSD)
**MSC** .......... Mirror Sign Convention
**MSC** .......... Mirror Streak Camera
**MSC** .......... Miscellaneous (ADA)
**MSC** .......... Missile Sequence Charts (AAG)
**MSC** .......... Missile and Space Council [*Defunct*] (AAG)
**M & SC** ...... Missile and Space Council [*Defunct*] (EA)
**MSC** .......... Missile System Checkout (AAG)
**MSC** .......... Missionarii Sacratissimi Cordis [*Missionaries of the Most Sacred Heart*] [*Roman Catholic men's religious order*]
**MSC** .......... Missionarii Sancti Caroli [*Missionaries of St. Charles*] [*Roman Catholic men's religious order*]
**MSC** .......... Missionary Sisters of the Most Sacred Heart of Jesus [*Roman Catholic religious order*]
**MSC** .......... Missionary Sisters of the Sacred Heart [*Cabrini Sisters*] [*Roman Catholic religious order*]
**MSC** .......... Mississippi Central R. R. [*AAR code*]
**Ms-C** .......... Mississippi Library Commission, Jackson, MS [*Library symbol*] [*Library of Congress*] (LCLS)
**MSC** .......... Mississippi Southern College
**MSC** .......... Mobile Servicing Center [*Canada*]
**MSC** .......... Mode Selector Controller (MCD)
**MSC** .......... Moding Sequencing and Control (MCD)
**MSC** .......... Montana State College (MCD)
**M & Sc** ....... Moore and Scott's English Common Pleas Reports [*1831-34*] [*A publication*] (DLA)
**MSC** .......... Moorhead State College [*Minnesota*]
**MSC** .......... Morgan State College [*Later, Morgan State University*] [*Baltimore, MD*]
**MSC** .......... Most Significant Character [*Data processing*] (MDG)
**MSC** .......... Motor Speed Control
**MSC** .......... Motor Starting Contractor
**MSC** .......... Motor Submersible Canoe [*British Marines' Special Forces*] [*World War II*]
**MSC** .......... Moved, Seconded, and Carried
**MSC** .......... Multiple Scan Correlator
**MSC** .......... Multiple Spindle Chucker
**MSC** .......... Multiple Systems Coupling [*Data processing*]
**MSC** .......... Multipotential Stem Cells [*Hematology*]
**MSC** .......... Multisensor Correlator (CAAL)
**MSC** .......... Multiservice Center
**MSC** .......... Multistrip Coupler [*Telecommunications*] (TEL)
**MSC** .......... Multisystem Coupling [*Data processing*]
**MSC** .......... Murray State College [*Later, MSU*] [*Kentucky*]
**MSC** .......... Museum Support Center [*Smithsonian Institution*]
**M Sc** .......... Musik in der Schule [*A publication*]
**MSC** .......... Muskingum College, New Concord, OH [*OCLC symbol*] (OCLC)
**Msc** ............ New York Miscellaneous Reports [*A publication*] (DLA)
**MSC** .......... Springfield College, Springfield, MA [*Library symbol*] [*Library of Congress*] (LCLS)
**MsCa** ......... Canton Public Library, Canton, MS [*Library symbol*] [*Library of Congress*] (LCLS)
**MScA** ......... Maitre es Sciences Appliquees [*Master of Applied Science*] [*French*]
**MSCA** ........ Make or Subcontract Authorization (AAG)
**MSCA** ........ McCarthy Scales of Children's Abilities [*Education*]
**MSCA** ........ Microwave Switch Control Assembly
**MSCA** ........ Military Support to Civil Authorities (AABC)
**MSCA** ........ Missile Site Construction Agency [*Army*]

**msca**........... Missing Cargo (DS)
**MSCA**........ Mixed Spectrum Critical Assembly [*Nuclear energy*]
**MSCA**........ MS Carriers, Inc. [*Memphis, TN*] [*NASDAQ symbol*] (NQ)
**MSc(Acoustics)** ... Master of Science (Acoustics) (ADA)
**MSc(Ag)**.... Master of Science (Agriculture)
**M Sc in Agr Eng** ... Master of Science in Agricultural Engineering
**M Sc in Agr Ex** ... Master of Science in Agricultural Extension
**MScAgri**.... Master of Science in Agriculture
**MSc(Agric)** ... Master of Science in Agriculture
**MSc(AgricE)** ... Master of Science (Agricultural Economics) (ADA)
**MSc(AgricEc)** ... Master of Science (Agricultural Economics) (ADA)
**MSCAJC**... Martin Steinberg Center of the American Jewish Congress (EA)
**MsCaM**..... Madison County Library, Canton, MS [*Library symbol*] [*Library of Congress*] (LCLS)
**MScan**....... Mediaeval Scandinavia [*A publication*]
**MSc(Appl)** ... Master of Science (Applied) (ADA)
**MsCar**........ Leake County Library, Carthage, MS [*Library symbol*] [*Library of Congress*] (LCLS)
**MSc(Arch)** ... Master of Science (Architecture)
**MSc(Arch)(Cons)** ... Master of Science (Architectural) (Conservation)
**M Sc (Architecture)** ... Master of Science in Architecture
**MSCB**........ Missile Site Control Building (AABC)
**MS in C & BA** ... Master of Science in Commercial and Business Administration
**MsCba**....... Shelby Memorial Library, Columbia, MS [*Library symbol*] [*Library of Congress*] (LCLS)
**MSc(Biotech)** ... Master of Science (Biotechnology) (ADA)
**MSc(BuildServ)** ... Master of Science (Building Services) (ADA)
**MSCC**........ Major Subcontract Change Coordination (MCD)
**MSCC**........ Manned Space Flight Control Center [*Air Force*]
**MSCC**........ Master Simulator Control Console (MCD)
**MSCC**........ Microsemi Corporation [*NASDAQ symbol*] (NQ)
**MSCC**........ Missile Site Control Center (MCD)
**MSCC**........ Morgan Sports Car Club (EA)
**M Sc CE**.... Master of Science in Chromo-Electronic Science
**MScCE**....... Master of Science in Civil Engineering [*British*] (ADA)
**MSc(Cer)**... Master of Science in Ceramics (ADA)
**MScChemTech** ... Master of Science in Chemical Technology [*British*] (ADA)
**MScCom**.... Master in Commercial Sciences
**M Sc D**....... Doctor of Medical Science
**M Sc D**....... Doctor of the Science of Medicine
**MScD**........ Magister Scientia Dentalis [*Master of Dental Science*] [*British*]
**MScD**........ Master of Dental Science
**MSCD**........ Military Support of Civil Defense (AABC)
**Msc 2d**....... New York Miscellaneous Reports, Second Series [*A publication*] (DLA)
**MSCDA**..... Monographs. Society for Research in Child Development [*A publication*]
**MSCDC**..... Missouri State Census Data Center [*Information service or system*] (EISS)
**MSc(Dent)** ... Master of Science in Dentistry
**MSCDEX**.. MS-DOS, CD-ROM Extension [*Data processing*]
**MSCE**........ Main Storage Control Element [*Data processing*] (IEEE)
**MS in CE**... Master of Science in Civil Engineering
**MSCE**........ Master of Science in Civil Engineering
**M Sc (Econ)** ... Master of Science in Economics
**M Sc Ed**..... Master of Science in Education
**M Sc EE**..... Master of Science in Electrical Engineering
**MSc(Elec)** ... Master of Science in Electronics [*British*] (ADA)
**M Sc (Elec Eng)** ... Master of Science in Electrical Engineering
**M Scene**..... Music Scene [*A publication*]
**M Sc (Eng)** ... Master of Science (Engineering)
**MSc(Engg)** ... Master of Science (Engineering)
**MS in Cer**.. Master of Science in Ceramics
**MS in Cer E** ... Master of Science in Ceramic Engineering
**MS (Cer E)** ... Master of Science in Ceramic Engineering
**MS in Cer Tech** ... Master of Science in Ceramic Technology
**MScF**......... Master of the Science of Forestry [*or Master of Science in Forestry*]
**MSCF**........ Millions of Standard Cubic Feet (AAG)
**MSCF**........ Multisource Correlation Facility (MCD)
**MSCFAM** ... Royal Canadian Army Museum, Canadian Forces Base, Shilo, Manitoba [*Library symbol*] [*National Library of Canada*] (NLC)
**M Sc (For)** ... Master of Science in Forestry
**MS in Ch** ... Master of Science in Chemistry
**MSCH**....... Mode Switch Chassis
**MSch**......... Modern Schoolman [*A publication*]
**MsCh**......... Tallahatchie County Library, Charleston, MS [*Library symbol*] [*Library of Congress*] (LCLS)
**M Schallplatte** ... Musica Schallplatte [*A publication*]
**MS in Ch E** ... Master of Science in Chemical Engineering
**MSChE**....... Master of Science in Chemical Engineering
**MS in Ch Eng** ... Master of Science in Chemical Engineering
**M Sch Mus** ... Master of School Music
**MSc(HomeScience)** ... Master of Science (Home Science)
**MSc(Hort)** ... Master of Science in Horticulture [*British*] (ADA)
**Mschr Wien Tieraerztl** ... Monatsschrift Wiener Tieraerztliche [*A publication*]
**MSCI**......... Master Ships Configuration Index (MCD)
**MSCI**......... Medical Services Committee of Inquiry [*Australia*]
**MSCI**......... Mediterranean Secret Convoy Instructions [*World War II*]
**MSCI**......... Missile Status Control Indicator [*Military*] (CAAL)
**M/SCI**....... Mission/Safety Critical Item [*NASA*] (NASA)
**MSCI**......... Molten Steel Coolant Interaction (NRCH)
**MSCI**......... Morgan Stanley Capital International
**M Science**.. Mining Science [*A publication*]
**M Sci Mil**.. Master of Military Science
**MSC(IndDes)** ... Master of Science (Industrial Design) (ADA)
**M Sci Rel**... Melanges de Science Religieuse [*A publication*]
**MSCIS**....... Master of Science in Computer Information Systems
**MScitHi**..... Scituate Historical Society, Scituate, MA [*Library symbol*] [*Library of Congress*] (LCLS)
**MSCJA-AJC** ... Martin Steinberg Center for Jewish Artists - American Jewish Congress (EA)
**MSCKC**..... Measurement of Self Concept in Kindergarten Children [*Psychology*]
**M Sc L**....... Master of the Science of Law
**MSCL**........ Master Ships Configuration List (MCD)
**MSCL**........ Mississippi State Chemical Laboratory [*Mississippi State University*] [*Research center*] (RCD)
**MsCld**........ Carnegie Public Library, Clarksdale, MS [*Library symbol*] [*Library of Congress*] (LCLS)
**MsCle**........ Bolivar County Library, Cleveland, MS [*Library symbol*] [*Library of Congress*] (LCLS)
**MsCleD**..... Delta State College, Cleveland, MS [*Library symbol*] [*Library of Congress*] (LCLS)
**MsCleP**...... Presbyterian Church Library, Cleveland, MS [*Library symbol*] [*Library of Congress*] (LCLS)
**MsCliBHi** ... Mississippi Baptist Historical Society, Clinton, MS [*Library symbol*] [*Library of Congress*] (LCLS)
**MsCliM**..... Mississippi College, Clinton, MS [*Library symbol*] [*Library of Congress*] (LCLS)
**M Sc (Lond)** ... Master of Science, London
**MSCM**...... Master Chief Mess Management Specialist [*Navy rating*] [*Formerly, SDCM*]
**M Sc M**...... Master of the Science of Medicine
**MSCM**...... MOSCOM Corp. [*East Rochester, NY*] [*NASDAQ symbol*] (NQ)
**M Sc in ME** ... Master of Science in Mechanical Engineering
**M Sc (Mech Eng)** ... Master of Science in Mechanical Engineering
**M Sc Med** ... Master of Medical Science
**MSc(Med)** ... Master of Science (Medical)
**MScMed**.... Master of Science in Medicine [*British*] (ADA)
**M Sc Met**... Master of Science in Metallurgy
**MSc(Min)** ... Master of Science in Mining [*British*] (ADA)
**MScN**........ Master of Science in Nursing
**MSc(NatResMgt)** ... Master of Science in Natural Resources Management
**MSc(Nutr)** ... Master of Science in Nutrition [*British*] (ADA)
**MSCNY**..... Marine Society of the City of New York (EA)
**MSCO**....... Manned Spacecraft Operations [*NASA*] (KSC)
**MSCO**....... Manual Sustainer Cutoff [*NASA*] (KSC)
**MSCO**....... Masstor Systems Corporation [*NASDAQ symbol*] (NQ)
**M Sc O**...... Master of the Science of Oratory
**MSC(O)**..... Minesweeper, Coastal (Old) [*Navy symbol*]
**MSCOA**.... Metallurgical Society. Conferences [*A publication*]
**MsCol**........ Lowndes County Library System, Columbus, MS [*Library symbol*] [*Library of Congress*] (LCLS)
**MsColS**...... Mississippi State College for Women, Columbus, MS [*Library symbol*] [*Library of Congress*] (LCLS)
**MS in Con** ... Master of Science in Conservation
**MS Cons**.... Master of Science in Conservation
**MScOptom** ... Master of Science in Optometry (ADA)
**MsCor**........ Northeast Regional Library, Corinth, MS [*Library symbol*] [*Library of Congress*] (LCLS)
**M Sc (Ost)** ... Master of Science in Osteopathy
**MSCOTSG** ... Medical Service Corps, Office of the Surgeon General
**M & Scott**.. Moore and Scott's English Common Pleas Reports [*1831-34*] [*A publication*] (DLA)
**MSCP**........ Master of Science in Community Planning
**MSCP**........ Mean Spherical Candlepower
**MSCP**........ Member of the Society of Certified Professionals [*British*] (DBQ)
**MScPhm**.... Master of Science in Pharmacy (ADA)
**MSCPR**..... Mixed-Suspension, Classified-Product Removal [*Crystallizer*] [*Chemical engineering*]
**M Sc Press** ... Mining and Scientific Press [*A publication*]
**MSCR**........ Machine Screw
**MSCR**........ Measurement/Stimuli Change Request (MCD)
**MSCR/A** ... Major Subcontract Change Request/Approval (MCD)
**MScRel**...... Melanges de Science Religieuse [*Lille*] [*A publication*]
**MS in CRP** ... Master of Science in City and Regional Planning
**MsCs**......... Crystal Springs Library, Crystal Springs, MS [*Library symbol*] [*Library of Congress*] (LCLS)
**MSCS**........ Management Scheduling and Control System [*Telecommunications*] (TEL)
**MSCS**........ Mankato State College [*later Mankato State University*] Studies [*A publication*]
**MSCS**........ Manual SHORAD [*Short Range Air Defense*] Control System (RDA)
**MSCS**........ Master of Science in Computer Science
**MSCS**........ Merchant Ship Control Service [*Navy*]

**MSCS**........ Miner Sentence Completion Scale [*Psychology*]
**MSCS**........ Multiservice Communications Systems (RDA)
**MSCS**........ Senior Chief Mess Management Specialist [*Formerly, CSCS, SDCS*] [*Navy rating*]
**M Sc (Social Sciences)**... Master of Science in the Social Sciences
**M Sc (Soc Sci)**... Master of Science (Social Science)
**MScSt**........ Master of Scientific Studies (ADA)
**MSCT**........ Malignant Small Cell Tumor [*Oncology*]
**MSCT**........ Marine Science Contents Tables [*A publication*]
**MSCT**........ Member of the Society of Cardiological Technicians [*British*]
**M Sc Tech**... Master of Science in Technology
**M Sc Tech**... Master of Technical Science
**MSCTR**..... Message Center (FAAC)
**MSCU**....... Modular Store Control Unit
**MSC(UN)**... Military Staff Committee of the United Nations
**MSCV**........ Connecticut Valley Historical Museum, Springfield, MA [*Library symbol*] [*Library of Congress*] (LCLS)
**MSCVAN**... [*An*] MSC [*Military Sealift Command*] Leased/Controlled Seavan or Milvan
**MSCW**....... Marked Stack Control Word
**MSCW**....... Mississippi State College for Women [*Columbus*]
**MSCX**........ Members Service Corp. [*NASDAQ symbol*] (NQ)
**MSD**.......... Doctor of Medical Science
**Ms D**.......... Doctor of Metaphysics
**MsD**........... Holmes County Library, Durant, MS [*Library symbol*] [*Library of Congress*] (LCLS)
**MSD**.......... Magnetic Storage Drum [*Data processing*]
**MSD**.......... Major Seismic Disturbance
**MSD**.......... Management Services Department [*British*] (DCTA)
**MSD**.......... Mansfield, LA [*Location identifier*] [*FAA*] (FAAL)
**MSD**.......... Manual SHORAD [*Short Range Air Defense*] Control System [*Army*]
**MsD**........... Manuscript Decisions [*Commissioner of Patents*] [*United States*] [*A publication*] (DLA)
**MsD**........... Manuscript Decisions [*Comptroller General*] [*United States*] [*A publication*] (DLA)
**MSD**.......... Marine Sanitation Device
**MSD**.......... Marine Sciences Directorate [*Canada*] (MSC)
**MSD**.......... Maritime-Self-Defense
**MSD**.......... Mass Selector Detector [*Gas chromatography*]
**MSD**.......... Mass Sensor Demonstration
**MSD**.......... Mass Storage Device [*Data processing*]
**MSD**.......... Master Resources & Developments Ltd. [*Vancouver Stock Exchange symbol*]
**MSD**.......... Master of Science in Dentistry
**MSD**.......... Master of Scientific Didactics
**MSD**.......... Master Standard Data
**MSD**.......... Master Surgeon Dentist
**MSD**.......... Material Safety Data
**MSD**.......... Material Support Data (MCD)
**MSD**.......... Materials and Structures Division [*NASA*]
**MSD**.......... McNaney Spectroelectric Device
**MSD**.......... Mean Solar Day
**MSD**.......... Mean Square Deviation
**MSD**.......... Mean Square Difference
**MSD**.......... Mean-Square Displacement [*Statistical graphing*]
**MSD**.......... Mechanical Setting Device
**MSD**.......... Merck, Sharp & Dohme [*Later, Merck & Co., Inc.*]
**MSD**.......... Merck, Sharp & Dohme [*Later, Merck & Co., Inc.*] Research Laboratory, West Point, PA [*OCLC symbol*] (OCLC)
**MSD**.......... Metal Sensor Detection
**MSD**.......... Metering Suction Differential (NG)
**MSD**.......... Method of Steepest Descent
**MSD**.......... Microdata Software Development (MCD)
**MSD**.......... Military Sales Department
**MSD**.......... Military Store Department [*British military*] (DMA)
**MSD**.......... Military Support Division [*of Materiel Testing Directorate*] (RDA)
**MSD**.......... Minesweeper, Drone [*Navy symbol*]
**MSD**.......... Minimal Steric Difference [*Organic chemistry*]
**MSD**.......... Minimum Safe Distance (AABC)
**MSD**.......... Misce, Signa, Da [*Mix, Write (the Directions), and Give (to the Patient)*] [*Pharmacy*] (ROG)
**MSD**.......... Missile Support Days (AAG)
**MSD**.......... Missile Systems Development (AAG)
**MSD**.......... Missiles and Space Division [*NASA*] (KSC)
**MSD**.......... MODEM Sharing Device
**MSD**.......... Molecular Size Distribution [*Chemistry*]
**MSD**.......... Molecular Structures and Dimensions [*A publication*]
**MSD**.......... Molten Salt Destruction [*Incineration process*]
**MSD**.......... Monorail and Suspension Device [*British*]
**MSD**.......... Morale Support Detachment [*Army*]
**MSD**.......... Most Significant Digit [*Data processing*]
**MSD**.......... Motor Storage Dolly
**MSD**.......... Mount Pleasant [*Utah*] [*Airport symbol*] (OAG)
**MSD**.......... Movimento Social Democrata [*Social Democrat Movement*] [*Portugal*] [*Political party*] (PPE)
**MSD**.......... Moving Scene Display
**MSD**.......... Multifrequency Signal Detector [*Telecommunications*]
**MSD**.......... Multiple Spark Discharge [*Autotronic Controls Corp.*] [*Automotive engineering*]
**MSD**.......... Multisensor Display
**MSD**.......... Multisensory Disorder
**MSDB**........ Main Storage Database
**MSDC**....... Maintenance Signal Data Converter (MCD)
**MSDC**....... Manual Slave Direction Center [*RADAR site*]
**MSDC**....... Mass Spectrometry Data Centre [*Royal Society of Chemistry*] (IID)
**MSDC**....... Microwave Spectra Data Center [*National Institute of Standards and Technology*]
**MSDC**....... Molten Salts Data Center [*Rensselaer Polytechnic Institute*] [*National Institute of Standards and Technology*] [*Research center*] (IID)
**MSDC News**... MSDC (Medical Society of the District of Columbia) News [*A publication*]
**MSde**......... Tilton Library, South Deerfield, MA [*Library symbol*] [*Library of Congress*] (LCLS)
**MSDEF**..... Missile System Development and Evaluation Facility (MCD)
**MS Dent**.... Master of Science in Dentistry
**MSDEQ**.... Mothers' Sensory Developmental Expectation Questionnaire [*Occupational therapy*]
**MS in Derm**... Master of Science in Dermatology
**MS Des**...... Master of Science in Design
**MSDF**........ Maritime Self-Defense Force [*Japan*]
**MSDF**........ Maritime Staff Defense Force (CINC)
**MSDG**....... Multiple Sensor Display Group (MCD)
**MS Di**........ Master of Scientific Didactics
**MSDI**......... Mayonnaise and Salad Dressings Institute [*Later, Association for Dressings and Sauces*] (EA)
**MS Diss**..... Manuscript Dissertation [*A publication*]
**MSDL**........ Magnetostrictive Delay Line
**MSDM**...... Medium-Speed DynaBIT [*Binary Digit*] Memory [*Data processing*]
**MSDNA**.... Multicopy Single-Stranded Deoxyribonucleic Acid [*Biochemistry, genetics*]
**MSDO**....... Management Systems Development Office
**MS-DOS**... Microsoft Disk Operating System [*IBM Corp.*] [*Data processing*]
**MSDP**........ Missile Site Data Processor (AABC)
**MSDPS**..... Missile Site Data Processing System (AABC)
**MSDPSS**... Missile Site Data Processing Subsystem (AABC)
**MSDR**....... Maintenance Signal Data Recorder (MCD)
**MSDR**....... Master Sensor Data Record [*For spacecraft*]
**MSDR**....... Materials Science Double Rack
**MSDRS**..... Maintenance Signal Data Recording Set [*or System*] (MCD)
**MSDS**........ Magnetic Storage Drum System [*Data processing*]
**MSDS**........ Material Safety Data Sheets [*Occupational Health Services, Inc.*] [*Information service or system*]
**MSDS**........ Message Switching Data Service
**MSDS**........ Missile Static Development Site (AAG)
**MSDS**........ Missile System Development Stand (AAG)
**MSDS**........ Multisolvent Delivery System
**MSDS**........ Multispectral Scanner and Data System
**MSDT**........ Maintenance Strategy Diagraming Technique (IEEE)
**MS in Dt**.... Master of Science in Dietetics
**MSDT**........ Mean Supply Downtime (CAAL)
**MSDT**........ Meshless Storage Display Tube
**MSE**........... Maandblad voor Sociaal Economiese. Wetenschappen [*A publication*]
**MSE**........... Magnetic Strain Energy
**MSE**........... Maintenance Support Equipment [*Deep Space Instrumentation Facility, NASA*]
**MSE**........... Major Source of Employment
**MSE**........... Manufacturing Systems Engineering
**MSE**........... Marshall Energy Ltd. [*Vancouver Stock Exchange symbol*]
**MSE**........... Mass Storage Editor [*Data processing*] (MCD)
**MSE**........... Massachusetts Studies in English [*A publication*]
**MSE**........... Master of Sanitary Engineering
**MSE**........... Master of Science in Chemical Engineering
**MSE**........... Master of Science in Education
**MS in E**...... Master of Science in Education
**MSE**........... Master of Science in Engineering
**MS in E**...... Master of Science in Engineering
**MSE**........... Master of Systems Engineering
**MS & E**...... Materials Science and Engineering
**MSE**........... Materiel Status Evaluation [*Army*] (AABC)
**MSE**........... Mathematical Studies in Economics and Statistics in the USSR and Eastern Europe [*A publication*]
**MSE**........... Mean Square Error [*Statistics*]
**MSE**........... Measuring and Stimuli Equipment (NASA)
**MSE**........... Mechanical Support Equipment (KSC)
**MSE**........... Medical Support Equipment (NASA)
**MSE**........... Member of the Society of Engineers [*British*]
**MSE**........... Merck, Sharp & Dohme [*Later, Merck & Co., Inc.*] Research Laboratory, Rahway, NJ [*OCLC symbol*] (OCLC)
**MSE**........... Merit Students Encyclopedia [*A publication*]
**MSE**........... Mesa Aviation Services, Inc. [*Farmington, NM*] [*FAA designator*] (FAAC)
**MSE**........... Metaphloem Sieve Element [*Botany*]
**MSE**........... Mid-Song Element [*Ornithology*]
**MSE**........... Midwest Stock Exchange [*Chicago, IL*] (EA)
**MSE**........... Military Specification Exception (RDA)

**MSE**.......... Military Standard Engines
**MSE**.......... Milk-Sensitive Enteropathy [*Medicine*]
**MSE**.......... Milwaukee School of Engineering [*Wisconsin*]
**MSE**.......... Missile Support Element (AABC)
**MSE**.......... Missile Support Equipment
**MSE**.......... Mission Staff Engineer (MCD)
**MSE**.......... Mission Support Element (MCD)
**MSE**.......... Mississippi Export Railroad Co. [*AAR code*]
**MSE**.......... Mobile Subscriber Equipment [*Military*]
**MSE**.......... Modern Ship Equivalent
**MSE**.......... Multiple Simultaneous Engagement (MCD)
**MSE**.......... Muscle-Specific Enhancer [*Genetics*]
**M Se A**....... Master of Secretarial Arts
**MSEA**........ Medical Society Executives Association [*Later, AAMSE*] (EA)
**MSEC**........ Maintenance Support Equipment Center
**MSEC**........ Master of Science in the Economic Aspects of Chemistry
**MSEC**........ Master Separation Events Controller (MCD)
**MSEC**........ Memoires. Societe d'Emulation de Cambrai [*A publication*]
**msec**.......... Millisecond
**MS Ed**........ Master of Sanitary Education
**MS in Ed**.... Master of Science in Education
**MS Ed**........ Master of Science in Education
**MSED**........ Minimum Signal Element Duration [*Telecommunications*] (TEL)
**MSED**........ Ministry of State for Economic Development [*Canada*]
**MSED**........ Mobile Source Enforcement Division [*Environmental Protection Agency*]
**MS in EE**... Master of Science in Electrical Engineering
**MSEE**........ Master of Science in Electrical Engineering
**MSEE**........ Mean Square Error Efficiency [*Statistics*]
**MSE (Elec)**... Master of Science in Engineering - Electrical
**MSEF**........ Missile System Evaluation Flight (MUGU)
**MSEG**........ Memory-Segment [*Data processing*]
**MSEG**........ Missile Systems Evaluation Group (CINC)
**MSEI**......... Mean Square Error Inefficiency [*Statistics*]
**MSEL**......... Lord Selkirk Regional School, Selkirk, Manitoba [*Library symbol*] [*National Library of Canada*] (NLC)
**MSEL**......... Master Scenario Events List (MCD)
**MSEL**......... Master of Science and English Literature
**MSEL**......... Merisel, Inc. [*NASDAQ symbol*] (SPSG)
**MSEL**......... Mullen Scales of Early Learning [*Child development test*] [*Psychology*]
**MSEL**......... Selkirk Community Library, Manitoba [*Library symbol*] [*National Library of Canada*] (NLC)
**MS Elect E**... Master of Science in Electrical Engineering
**MS in EM**... Master of Science in Engineering Mechanics
**MSEM**........ Master of Science in Engineering Mechanics
**MS in EM**... Master of Science in Engineering of Mines
**MSEM**........ Mission Status and Evaluation Module
**MS in E Mgt**... Master of Science in Engineering Management
**MSEMH**... Selkirk Mental Health Centre, Manitoba [*Library symbol*] [*National Library of Canada*] (NLC)
**MS/EMI**... Mission Sequence/Electromagnetic Interference
**MSEMPR**... Missile Support Equipment Manufacturers Planning Reports (MCD)
**MS Eng**...... Master of Sanitary Engineering
**MS Eng**...... Master of Science in Engineering
**MS Ent**...... Master of Science in Entomology
**MSEO**........ Marine Services Engineer Officer [*Navy*] [*British*]
**MSEP**........ Maintenance Standardization Evaluation Program [*Air Force*] (AFM)
**MS in EP**... Master of Science in Engineering Physics
**MSEP**........ Mercury Scientific Experiment Panel
**MSEP**........ Military Standard Evaluation Program
**MSEPN**..... School of Psychiatric Nursing, Selkirk, Manitoba [*Library symbol*] [*National Library of Canada*] (NLC)
**MSEPS**...... Modular Space Electrical Power Station
**M/SEQ**...... Master Sequencer
**MSER**........ Management System Evaluation Review (NG)
**MSER**........ Mean Systolic Ejection Rate [*Cardiology*]
**MSER**........ Memoires. Societe d'Emulation de Roubaix [*A publication*]
**MSer**.......... Monumenta Serica [*A publication*]
**MSER**........ Multiple Stores Ejection Rack [*For munitions*] (MCD)
**MSERD**..... Ministry of State for Economic and Regional Development [*Canada*]
**MSERT**..... Member of the Society of Electronic and Radio Technicians [*British*] (DBQ)
**MSES**........ Marine Scientific Equipment Service [*British*]
**MS in ES**... Master of Science in Engineering Science [*or Sciences*]
**MSES**........ Medical School Environmental Stress
**MSES**........ Mobile Status Entry System
**M Se Sc**..... Master of Secretarial Science
**M Se St**...... Master of Secretarial Studies
**MSET**........ Maintenance Standardization and Evaluation Team (MCD)
**MSEUE**..... Mouvement Socialiste pour les Etats Unis d'Europe
**MSEWA**.... Memoirs. School of Science and Engineering. Waseda University [*A publication*]
**M S Ex**....... Melville Society. Extracts [*A publication*]
**MSEX**........ Middlesex Water Co. [*NASDAQ symbol*] (NQ)
**MSF**.......... Congregatio Missionariorum a Sancta Familia [*Congregation of the Missionaries of the Holy Family*] [*Roman Catholic men's religious order*]
**MSF**.......... Macrophage Spreading Factor [*Hematology*]
**MSF**.......... Maintenance Source File (MCD)
**MSF**.......... Manned Space Flight [*NASA*] (KSC)
**MSF**.......... Manufacturing Science Finance [*A union*] [*British*]
**MSF**.......... Mark Sense Form (MCD)
**MSF**.......... Market Support Fund [*Australia*]
**MSF**.......... Marvel Science Fiction [*A publication*]
**MSF**.......... Mass Storage Facility [*Data processing*] (IBMDP)
**MSF**.......... Master of Science in Finance
**MSF**.......... Master of the Science of Forestry
**MSF**.......... Master Source File [*Data processing*] (BUR)
**MSF**.......... Maximum Shear Force
**MSF**.......... Medecins sans Frontieres [*Doctors without Borders - DWB*] (EAIO)
**MSF**.......... Medium Standard Frequency (DEN)
**MSF**.......... Memorie Storiche Forogiuliesi [*A publication*]
**MSF**.......... Merit Shop Foundation [*Washington, DC*] (EA)
**MSF**.......... Metal Space-Frame (MCD)
**MSF**.......... MetaScience Foundation (EA)
**MSF**.......... Metastasis-Stimulating Factor [*Immunosuppressant*]
**MSF**.......... Methanesulfonyl Fluoride [*Organic chemistry*]
**MSF**.......... Migration Stimulating Factor [*Cytology*]
**MSF**.......... Military Support Fund (MCD)
**MSF**.......... Mind Science Foundation (EA)
**MSF**.......... Minesweeper, Fleet [*Steel hull*] [*Navy symbol*]
**MSF**.......... Minimum Sustaining Field [*Atomic reactor*]
**MSF**.......... Mission Simulator Facility
**MSF**.......... Mobile Striking Force [*Military*]
**MSF**.......... Mobility Support Forces [*Military*]
**MSF**.......... Moisture Seekers Foundation [*Later, Sjogren's Syndrome Foundation - SSF*] (EA)
**MSF**.......... Monoecious Sex Form
**MSF**.......... Month-Second-Foot [*Measurement*]
**MSF**.......... Morale Support Funds (MCD)
**MSF**.......... Moroccan Sea Frontier [*Navy*] [*World War II*]
**MSF**.......... Motorcycle Safety Foundation (EA)
**MSF**.......... Mott Scattering Formula [*Physics*]
**MSF**.......... Multiaxial Stress Field
**MSF**.......... Multistage Flash [*Desalination method*]
**MSF**.......... Muscle Shock Factor
**MsFa**.......... Jefferson County Library, Fayette, MS [*Library symbol*] [*Library of Congress*] (LCLS)
**MSFB**........ Multi-Solids Fluidized Bed [*Chemical engineering*]
**MSFC**........ Mark Slade Fan Club (EA)
**MSFC**........ Marshall Space Flight Center [*Also known as GCMSC*] [*NASA*]
**MSFC**........ McCarver Sisters Fan Club (EA)
**MSFC**........ Minnesota Stargazer's Fan Club [*Later, MNSBC*] (EA)
**MSFC**........ Morale Support Fund Council [*Military*] (AABC)
**MSFC**........ Mountain States Financial Corporation [*NASDAQ symbol*] (NQ)
**MSFC**........ Mutual Society of the French Community (EA)
**MSFDPS**... Manned Space Flight Data Processing System [*NASA*]
**MSFEB**..... Manned Space Flight Experiments Board [*NASA*] (KSC)
**MSFFF**...... Memoranda Societatis pro Fauna et Flora Fennica [*A publication*]
**MSFH**........ Manned Space Flight Headquarters [*NASA*]
**MSFL**........ Metodologia delle Scienze e Filosofia del Linguaggio [*A publication*]
**MSFLV**..... Manned Space Flight and Launch Vehicles [*Panel*]
**MSFM**........ Master of Science in Forest Management
**MSFN**........ Manned Space Flight Network [*NASA*]
**MSFNOC**... Manned Space Flight Network Operations Center [*NASA*] (KSC)
**MSFO**........ Manned Space Flight Operations [*NASA*] (KSC)
**MSFO**........ Memoires. Societe Finno-Ougrienne [*A publication*]
**MS in For**.. Master of Science in Forestry
**MS For**...... Master of Science in Forestry
**MSForogiuliesi**... Memorie Storiche Forogiuliesi [*A publication*]
**MSFOu**...... Memoires. Societe Finno-Ougrienne [*A publication*]
**MSFP**........ Manned Space Flight Program [*NASA*] (KSC)
**MSFP**........ Migrant and Seasonal Farmworkers Program [*Title III*] (OICC)
**MSFRSP**... Male Sterile-Facilitated Recurrent Selection Population [*Plant breeding*]
**MSFS**........ Main Steam and Feed Water System (IEEE)
**MSFS**........ Manned Space Flight Subcommittee [*NASA*] (AAG)
**MSFS**........ Missionaries of St. Francis of Sales [*Roman Catholic religious order*]
**MSFSG**..... Manned Space Flight Support Group (MCD)
**MSFSRD**... Manned Space Flight Support Requirements Documentation [*NASA*]
**MSFT**........ Microsoft Corp. [*Redmond, WA*] [*NASDAQ symbol*] (NQ)
**MSFU**........ Merchant Service Fighter Unit [*Air Force*] [*British*]
**MSFVW**.... Magnetostatic Forward Volume Wave [*Telecommunications*] (TEL)
**MSFW**....... Migrant and Seasonal Farmworkers
**MSFX**........ Master Fixture
**MSG**.......... [*The*] Imperial Merchant Service Guild [*British*]
**MSG**.......... Madison Square Garden Network [*Cable-television system*]

**MSG** ......... Maintenance Steering Group (MCD)
**MSG** ......... Manufacturers Standard Gauge
**MSG** ......... Mapper Sweep Generator
**MSG** ......... Marine Security Guard
**MSG** ......... Mascot Gold Mines Ltd. [*Toronto Stock Exchange symbol*] [*Vancouver Stock Exchange symbol*]
**MSG** ......... Master Sergeant [*Army*] (AABC)
**MSG** ......... Mechanical Subsystem Group [*NASA*] (NASA)
**MSG** ......... Message (AFM)
**MSG** ......... Microcomputer Support Group
**MSG** ......... Microwave Signal Generator
**MSG** ......... Ministry of Solicitor General [*Canada*]
**MSG** ......... Ministry of the Solicitor General Library [*UTLAS symbol*]
**MSG** ......... Miscellaneous Simulation Generator
**MSG** ......... Missile Systems Group [*of General Motors Corp.*]
**MSG** ......... Missing [*Military*]
**MSG** ......... Mission Support Groups (MCD)
**MSG** ......... Mitteilungen. Sonzino-Gesellschaft [*A publication*]
**MSG** ......... Mobile Support Group [*Military*] (NVT)
**MSG** ......... Modular Steam Generator (NRCH)
**MSG** ......... Moessingen [*Federal Republic of Germany*] [*Seismograph station code, US Geological Survey*] (SEIS)
**MSG** ......... Monosodium Glutamate [*Pharmacology*] [*Food additive*]
**MsG** ......... William Alexander Percy Memorial Library, Greenville, MS [*Library symbol*] [*Library of Congress*] (LCLS)
**MSGA** ....... Master Gauge
**MSGB** ....... Manorial Society of Great Britain (EAIO)
**MSGB** ....... Muslim Society in Great Britain
**MSGBI** ...... Mineralogical Society of Great Britain and Ireland [*London, England*] (EAIO)
**MSGCEN** ... Message Center
**MS in GE** ... Master of Science in General Engineering
**MSGFM** .... Message Form (MUGU)
**MSGFOK** ... Mitteilungen. Schweizerische Gesellschaft der Freunde Ostasiatischer Kultur [*A publication*]
**MSGG** ....... Message Generator (MSA)
**MSGL** ....... Multishot Grenade Launcher (RDA)
**MSGM** ...... Master of Science in Government Management
**MSG Mgt** .. Master of Science in Game Management
**MSGO** ....... Mediterranean Secret General Orders
**MsGoH** ...... Holmes Junior College, Goodman, MS [*Library symbol*] [*Library of Congress*] (LCLS)
**MSGP** ....... Mobile Support Group [*Military*]
**MS in Gp Engr** ... Master of Science in Geophysical Engineering
**MSGR** ....... Messenger (AFM)
**MSGR** ....... Mobile Support Group [*Military*]
**MSGR** ....... Monseigneur
**MSGR** ....... Monsignor
**MsGren** ...... Grenada County Library, Grenada, MS [*Library symbol*] [*Library of Congress*] (LCLS)
**MSGSB** ..... Gijutsu Shiryo. Mitsubishi Sekiyu Kabushiki Kaisha [*A publication*]
**MS in GSM** ... Master of Science in General Science and Mathematics
**MSGT** ........ Master Sergeant
**MsGu** ......... Gulfport-Carnegie-Harrison County Library, Gulfport, MS [*Library symbol*] [*Library of Congress*] (LCLS)
**MSGV** ....... Mitteilungen. Schlesische Gesellschaft fuer Volkskunde [*A publication*]
**MsGW** ....... Washington County Library System, Greenville, MS [*Library symbol*] [*Library of Congress*] (LCLS)
**MSGWA** ... Military and Sporting Gun Workers' Association [*A union*] [*British*]
**MsGwL** ...... Greenwood-Leflore Public Library, Greenwood, MS [*Library symbol*] [*Library of Congress*] (LCLS)
**MSG/WTG** ... Message Waiting (MDG)
**MSh** .......... Ma'aser Sheni (BJA)
**MSH** .......... [*US*] Marshals Service, Department of Justice [*Washington, DC*] [*FAA designator*] (FAAC)
**MSH** .......... Mashhad [*Iran*] [*Seismograph station code, US Geological Survey*] [*Closed*] (SEIS)
**MSH** .......... Master of Staghounds
**MSH** .......... Mauler Seeker Head
**MSH** .......... Medical Self-Help [*Defunct*]
**MSH** .......... Melanocyte-Stimulating Hormone [*Also, MH*] [*Endocrinology*]
**MSH** .......... Men of the Sacred Hearts (EA)
**MSH** .......... Metastable Helium (MCD)
**MSH** .......... Metropolitan Cooperative Library System, Pasadena, CA [*OCLC symbol*] (OCLC)
**MSH** .......... Minesweeper Hunter Vessel
**MSH** .......... Mishibishu Resources [*Vancouver Stock Exchange symbol*]
**MSH** .......... Missionaries of the Sacred Heart [*Roman Catholic men's religious order*]
**Ms-H** ......... Mississippi State Board of Health, Jackson, MS [*Library symbol*] [*Library of Congress*] (LCLS)
**MsHa** ......... Hattiesburg Public Library, Hattiesburg, MS [*Library symbol*] [*Library of Congress*] (LCLS)
**MSHA** ....... Master of Science in Hospital Administration
**MSHA** ....... Mine Safety and Health Administration [*Department of Labor*]
**MSha** ......... Sharon Public Library, Sharon, MA [*Library symbol*] [*Library of Congress*] (LCLS)
**MSHAA** .... Member of the Society of Hearing Aid Audiologists [*British*] (DBQ)
**MSHAA** .... Morocco Spotted Horse Association of America [*Defunct*] (EA)
**MShaK** ...... Kendall Whaling Museum, Sharon, MA [*Library symbol*] [*Library of Congress*] (LCLS)
**MsHaU** ...... University of Southern Mississippi, Hattiesburg, MS [*Library symbol*] [*Library of Congress*] (LCLS)
**MsHaW** ..... William Carey College, Hattiesburg, MS [*Library symbol*] [*Library of Congress*] (LCLS)
**MSHB** ....... Minimum Safe Height of Burst [*Military*]
**MSHDI** ..... Memoires. Societe pour l'Histoire du Droit et des Institutions des Anciens Pays Bourguignons, Comtois, et Romands [*A publication*]
**MsHe** ......... First Regional Library, Hernando, MS [*Library symbol*] [*Library of Congress*] (LCLS)
**MSHE** ....... Master of Science in Home Economics
**MS in HE** .. Master of Science in Home Economics
**MSHE** ....... Master of Science in Hydraulic Engineering
**MSH Ec** ..... Master of Science in Home Economics
**MS in H Ec** ... Master of Science in Home Economics
**MSHG** ....... Meshing
**MShM** ....... Mount Holyoke College, South Hadley, MA [*Library symbol*] [*Library of Congress*] (LCLS)
**MS Hort** .... Master of Science in Horticulture
**MsHos** ....... Marshall County Library, Holly Springs, MS [*Library symbol*] [*Library of Congress*] (LCLS)
**MsHosR** .... Rust College, Holly Springs, MS [*Library symbol*] [*Library of Congress*] (LCLS)
**MsHou** ....... Houston Carnegie Public Library, Houston, MS [*Library symbol*] [*Library of Congress*] (LCLS)
**MSHP** ....... Maintain System History Program [*IBM Corp.*]
**MSH & Ph Ed** ... Master of Science in Health and Physical Education
**MS in HR** .. Master of Science in Human Relations
**MSHR** ....... [*The*] Mischer Corp. [*NASDAQ symbol*] (NQ)
**MSHR** ....... Missionary Sisters of Our Lady of the Holy Rosary [*Blackrock, County Dublin, Republic of Ireland*] (EAIO)
**MS Hyg** ..... Master of Science in Hygiene
**MsHz** ......... Copiah-Jefferson Regional Library, Hazelhurst, MS [*Library symbol*] [*Library of Congress*] (LCLS)
**MSI** ........... Maintenance Significant Items (NASA)
**MSI** ........... Maintenance Support Index
**MSI** ........... Manned Satellite Inspector
**MSI** ........... Marine Science Institute [*University of California, Santa Barbara*] [*Research center*] (RCD)
**MSI** ........... Marital Satisfaction Inventory [*Psychology*]
**MSI** ........... Marketing Science Institute [*Cambridge, MA*] (EA)
**MSI** ........... Master of Science in Insurance
**MSI** ........... Mathematical Sciences Institute [*Cornell University*] [*Research center*] (RCD)
**MSI** ........... Maximum Speed Indicator
**MSI** ........... Maxwell Scientific International [*Inc.*]
**MSI** ........... Mean Spleen Index
**MSI** ........... Medical Seminars International (EA)
**MSI** ........... Medium-Scale Integration [*Circuit packaging*]
**MSI** ........... Member of the Sanitary Institute [*British*] (ROG)
**MSI** ........... Member of the Surveyors' Institution [*British*] (ROG)
**MSI** ........... Messina ING [*Istituto Nazionale Geodetico*] [*Sicily*] [*Seismograph station code, US Geological Survey*] (SEIS)
**MSI** ........... Microwave Services International, Inc. [*Denville, NJ*] [*Telecommunications*] (TSSD)
**MSI** ........... Military Static Inverter
**MSI** ........... Minesweeper, Inshore [*Navy symbol*]
**MSI** ........... Missile Status Indicator
**MSI** ........... Mission Success Indicator (MCD)
**MSI** ........... Moderate Scale Integration [*Electronics*]
**MSI** ........... Molecular Surface Ionization
**MSI** ........... Moody Street Irregulars [*A publication*]
**MSI** ........... Moon Sphere of Influence (KSC)
**MSI** ........... Mother Symptom Inventory [*Psychology*]
**MSI** ........... Motor Skills Inventory [*Sensorimotor skills test*]
**MSI** ........... Movimento Sociale Italiano [*Italian Social Movement*] [*Political party*] (PPE)
**MSI** ........... MSI Data Corp. [*AMEX symbol*] (SPSG)
**MSI** ........... Multicomm Sciences International, Inc. [*Denville, NJ*] (TSSD)
**MSI** ........... Multiple Spark Igniter
**MSI** ........... Multisensor Imagery
**MSI** ........... Multisystem Involvement [*Medicine*]
**MSI** ........... Museum of Science and Industry [*Chicago, IL*]
**MSI** ........... Museum Services Institute [*Department of Education*] (OICC)
**MSI** ........... Second Independence Movement [*Ecuador*] [*Political party*] (PPW)
**MSIA** ......... Master of Science in Industrial Administration
**MSIA** ......... Member of the Society of Industrial Artists [*British*]
**MSIA** ......... Multispectral Image Analyzer (MCD)
**MSIAD** ...... Member of the Society of Industrial Artists and Designers [*British*] (DBQ)
**MsIbM** ...... Mississippi Valley State College, Itta Bena, MS [*Library symbol*] [*Library of Congress*] (LCLS)
**MSIC** ......... Missile and Space Intelligence Center [*DoD*]
**MSID** ......... Mass Spectrometric Isotope Dilution

**MS in ID**.... Master of Science in Industrial Design
**MSID**......... Measurement Stimulation Identification (MCD)
**MSID**......... Medium-Scale Integration Device [*Circuit packaging*]
**MS in IE**.... Master of Science in Industrial Engineering
**MSIE**......... Master of Science in Industrial Engineering
**MSIE**......... MSI Electronics, Inc. [*NASDAQ symbol*] (NQ)
**M et Sig**..... Misce et Signa [*Mix and Label*] [*Pharmacy*]
**MSIGM**..... Macintosh Special Interest Group of Mensa (EA)
**MSII**......... Medicine Shoppe International, Inc. [*NASDAQ symbol*] (NQ)
**MSIIP**........ Missile System Installation Interrupted for Parts (NVT)
**MSIM**........ Master of Science in Industrial Management
**MS in IM**... Master of Science in Industrial Management
**MSIMD**..... Multiple Single Instruction, Multiple Data (MCD)
**MsIn**......... Henry M. Seymour Library, Indianola, MS [*Library symbol*] [*Library of Congress*] (LCLS)
**MS Ind E**... Master of Science in Industrial Engineering
**MS in Ind Ed**... Master of Science in Industrial Education
**MSINZ**...... Member of the Surveyors' Institute of New Zealand
**MSIO**......... Mass Storage Input-Output [*Data processing*] (IEEE)
**MSIP**......... Multinational Staged Improvement Program (MCD)
**MSIR**......... Machine Survey and Installation Report
**MSIR**......... Master of Social and Industrial Relations
**MSIR**......... Master Stock Item Record
**MSIS**......... Main Steam Isolation Signal [*Nuclear energy*] (NRCH)
**MSIS**......... Manned Satellite Inspection System
**MSIS**......... Marine Safety Information System [*Coast Guard*] (MSC)
**MSIS**......... Mask Shop Information System [*Bell Laboratories*]
**MSIS**......... Mass Spectral Information System
**MSIS**......... Master of Science in Computer-Based Information Systems
**MSIS**......... Multistate Information System [*Patient records*]
**MSISL**....... Moore School Information Systems Laboratory
**Ms IT**......... Manuscript, Inner Temple [*A publication*] (DLA)
**MSIT**......... Member of the Society of Instrument Technology [*British*]
**MSIV**......... Main Steam Isolation Valve [*Nuclear energy*] (NRCH)
**MSIVLCS**... Main Steam Isolation Valve Leakage Control System [*Nuclear energy*] (NRCH)
**MSIX**......... Mining Services International Corp. [*NASDAQ symbol*] (NQ)
**MSIZ**......... Microsize, Inc. [*Salt Lake City, UT*] [*NASDAQ symbol*] (NQ)
**MsJ**........... Jackson Municipal Library, Jackson, MS [*Library symbol*] [*Library of Congress*] (LCLS)
**MSJ**........... Machine Screw Jack
**MSJ**........... Master of Science in Journalism
**MSJ**........... Misawa [*Japan*] [*Airport symbol*] (OAG)
**MSJ**........... Mission San Jose [*California*] [*Seismograph station code, US Geological Survey*] (SEIS)
**MSJ**........... Multiple Subsonic Jet
**MsJB**......... Belhaven College, Jackson, MS [*Library symbol*] [*Library of Congress*] (LCLS)
**MSJMAZ**... Mount Sinai Journal of Medicine [*A publication*]
**MsJMC**..... Millsaps College, Jackson, MS [*Library symbol*] [*Library of Congress*] (LCLS)
**MsJPED**.... Episcopal Diocese of Mississippi, Jackson, MS [*Library symbol*] [*Library of Congress*] (LCLS)
**MsJRD**...... Research and Development Center Library, Jackson, MS [*Library symbol*] [*Library of Congress*] (LCLS)
**MsJRT**...... Reformed Theological Seminary, Jackson, MS [*Library symbol*] [*Library of Congress*] (LCLS)
**MsJS**......... Jackson State College [*Later, Jackson State University*], Jackson, MS [*Library symbol*] [*Library of Congress*] (LCLS)
**MsJV**......... United States Veterans Administration Hospital, Jackson, MS [*Library symbol*] [*Library of Congress*] (LCLS)
**MsJW**......... Wesley Biblical Seminary, Jackson, MS [*Library symbol*] [*Library of Congress*] (LCLS)
**MSK**.......... Magyar Statisztikai Kozlemenyek [*Hungary*]
**MSK**.......... Manual Select Keyboard [*Data processing*] (KSC)
**MSK**.......... Medvedev, Sponheuer, Karnick [*Earthquake intensity scale*]
**MsK**........... Mid-Mississippi Regional Library, Kosciusko, MS [*Library symbol*] [*Library of Congress*] (LCLS)
**MSK**.......... Minimum Shift Keying
**MSK**.......... Misaki [*Japan*] [*Seismograph station code, US Geological Survey*] [*Closed*] (SEIS)
**MSK**.......... Mission Support Kit
**MSK**.......... Mitteilungen. Stadtarchiv von Koeln [*A publication*]
**MSK**.......... Mobility Support Kit
**MSKC**........ Memorial Sloan-Kettering Cancer Center [*Research center*] (RCD)
**MSKCC**..... Memorial Sloan-Kettering Cancer Center [*New York*]
**MSKEDJ**... Japanese Journal of Michurin Biology [*A publication*]
**MsL**........... Laurel Library Association, Laurel, MS [*Library symbol*] [*Library of Congress*] (LCLS)
**MSL**........... Machine Specification Language
**MSL**........... Magnetic Surfaces Laboratory
**MSL**........... Main Sea Level (AAG)
**MSL**........... Main Steam Line [*Nuclear energy*] (NRCH)
**MSL**........... Maintenance Supply Liaison [*Air Force*] (AFM)
**MSL**........... Management Selection Limited
**MSL**........... Management Systems Laboratories [*Virginia Polytechnic Institute and State University*] [*Research center*] (RCD)
**MSL**........... Manchester School of Economic and Social Studies [*A publication*]
**MSL**........... Manpower Source Listing (MCD)
**MSL**........... Marine Systems Laboratory [*Smithsonian Institution*]
**MSL**........... Master of Sacred Literature
**MSL**........... Master Save List [*Military*] (AFIT)
**MSL**........... Master Scheduling Letter
**MSL**........... Master of Science in Language
**MSL**........... Master of Science in Linguistics
**MSL**........... Master Support List (MCD)
**MSL**........... Masterseal [*Record label*]
**MSL**........... Materialien zum Sumerischen Lexikon. B. Landsberger. Patrologiae Cursus Completus. Series Latina [*A publication*] (BJA)
**MSL**........... Materials and Structures Laboratory [*Texas A & M University*] [*Research center*] (RCD)
**MSL**........... Maximum Service Life [*or Limit*] (AAG)
**MSL**........... Maximum Stillwater Level [*Nuclear energy*] (NRCH)
**MSL**........... Mean Sea Level
**MSL**........... Measurement Standards Laboratory
**MSL**........... Measurement System Laboratory (MCD)
**MSL**........... Mechanical Systems Laboratory [*NASA*] (NASA)
**MSL**........... Memoires. Societe Linguistique de Paris [*A publication*]
**MSL**........... Mercury Savings & Loan Association [*NYSE symbol*] (SPSG)
**MSL**........... Message Switched Line (MCD)
**MSL**........... Meteorological Satellite Laboratory
**MSL**........... Methuen's Standard Library [*A publication*]
**MSL**........... Microstar Software Limited [*Nepean, ON*] [*Telecommunications*] (TSSD)
**MSL**........... Midsternal Line
**MSL**........... Military Shipping Label
**MSL**........... Military Side Loader [*Air transport*] [*British*]
**MSL**........... Military Support List (MCD)
**MSL**........... Minesweeping Launch [*Navy ship symbol*]
**MSL**........... Minimum Size Limit [*Pisciculture*]
**MSL**........... Minnesota State Law Library, St. Paul, MN [*OCLC symbol*] (OCLC)
**MSL**........... Miscellanea di Storia Ligure [*A publication*]
**MSL**........... Missile (AFM)
**MSL**........... Missile Sea Level
**MSL**........... Molecular Spectroscopy Laboratory [*Fisk University*] [*Research center*] (RCD)
**MSL**........... Mouvement des Sociaux-Liberaux [*Movement of Social Liberals*] [*France*] [*Political party*] (PPW)
**MSL**........... Multiple Stinger Launcher
**MSL**........... Municipal Savings & Loan Corp. [*Toronto Stock Exchange symbol*]
**MSL**........... Muscle Shoals [*Alabama*] [*Airport symbol*] (OAG)
**MSL**........... Snow Lake Community Library, Manitoba [*Library symbol*] [*National Library of Canada*] (NLC)
**MSlA**......... Atlantic Union College, South Lancaster, MA [*Library symbol*] [*Library of Congress*] (LCLS)
**MSLA**........ Main Steam Line Accident [*Nuclear energy*] (NRCH)
**MSLA**........ Metropolitan Financial Savings & Loan Association [*Dallas, TX*] [*NASDAQ symbol*] (NQ)
**MSLA**........ Missionary Sisters of Our Lady of the Angels [*Lennoxville, PQ*] (EAIO)
**MSLA**........ Mouse Specific Lymphocyte Antigen [*Immunology*]
**MSLAET**... Member of the Society of Licensed Aircraft Engineers and Technologists [*British*] (DBQ)
**MSLAVA J**... Manitoba School Library Audio-Visual Association. Journal [*A publication*]
**MsLb**......... Long Beach Public Library, Long Beach, MS [*Library symbol*] [*Library of Congress*] (LCLS)
**MSLB**........ Main Steam Line Break [*Nuclear energy*] (NRCH)
**MSLBA**..... Muscle Biology [*A publication*]
**MsLbU**...... University of Southern Mississippi, Gulf Park, Richard G. Cox Library, Long Beach, MS [*Library symbol*] [*Library of Congress*] (LCLS)
**MSLC**........ Minnesota Short Lines Company [*AAR code*]
**MSLC**........ Miscellanea di Studi di Letteratura Cristiana Antica [*A publication*]
**MSLC**........ Missile Sites Labor Commission [*A federal government body*] [*Abolished 1967; functions transferred to Federal Mediation and Conciliation Service*]
**MSLC**........ Modernist Studies. Literature and Culture, 1920-1940 [*A publication*]
**MSLCOMD**... Missile Command [*Army*]
**MSLD**........ Mass Spectrometer Leak Detector (NRCH)
**MsLE**......... Lauren Rogers Library and Museum of Art, Laurel, MS [*Library symbol*] [*Library of Congress*] (LCLS)
**MSLF**........ Mountain States Legal Foundation (EA)
**MSLFM**.... Massenet Society and Lovers of French Music [*Later, MSAB*] (EA)
**MSLG**........ Maintenance Support Logistics Group [*Military*] (CAAL)
**Ms LI**......... Manuscript, Lincoln's Inn [*A publication*] (DLA)
**MsLi**.......... Microfilm Services Ltd., Auckland, New Zealand [*Library symbol*] [*Library of Congress*] (LCLS)
**MSLIR**...... Master of Science in Labor and Industrial Relations
**MS Litt**...... Master of Sacred Letters
**MSLIVSS**... Main Steam Line Isolation Valve Sealings System [*Nuclear energy*] (NRCH)
**MS LJ**........ Mississippi Law Journal [*A publication*]

MSLL........ Monograph Series on Languages and Linguistics. Georgetown University [*A publication*]
MSLMAINTSq ... Missile Maintenance Squadron [*Air Force*]
MSLN........ Mari Sandoz Library Network [*Library network*]
MSLO........ Master Layout
MSLO........ Medical Service Liaison Officer [*Air Force*]
MSLOB..... Mineralia Slovaca [*A publication*]
MSLOUG ... Medium-Sized Libraries/OCLC [*Online Computer Library Center*] Users Group
MSLP........ Memoires. Societe Linguistique de Paris [*A publication*]
MSLP........ San Salvador/El Salvador Internacional [*El Salvador*] [*ICAO location identifier*] (ICLI)
MS & LR ... Manchester, Sheffield & Lincolnshire Railway [*Later, Great Central*] [*British*] (ROG)
MSLR........ Manchester, Sheffield & Lincolnshire Railway [*Later, Great Central*] [*British*]
MSLS........ Maneuverable Satellite Landing System (MUGU)
MSLS........ Master of Science in Law and Society (DLA)
MSLS........ Master of Science in Library Science
MS in LS ... Master of Science in Library Science
MSLSc....... Master of Science in Library Science
MSLT........ Multiple Sleep Latency Test
MSLund..... Meddelanden fran Seminarierna foer Slaviska Sprak, Jamforande Sprakforskning och Finsk-Ugriska Sprak vis Lunds Universitet [*A publication*]
MSLWARNINGSq ... Missile Warning Squadron [*Air Force*]
MSLY........ Mostly (MSA)
MSM......... Major System Mode (CAAL)
MSM......... Manhattan School of Music
MSM......... Manned Support Module [*NASA*] (NASA)
MSM......... Manufacturing Standards Manual
MSM......... Marine Safety Manual [*Coast Guard*] [*A publication*] (DLA)
MSM......... Mars Surface Module (MCD)
MSM......... Mass Scatterable Mine (RDA)
MSM......... Master of Medical Science
MSM......... Master of Sacred Music
MSM......... Master Scheduling Manager
MSM......... Master of Science in Management
MSM......... Master of Science in Music
MSM......... Master Slave Manipulator [*Nuclear energy*]
MSM......... Materials Science Monographs [*Elsevier Book Series*] [*A publication*]
MSM......... Mauritian Socialist Movement [*Political party*]
MSM......... Mechanically Separated Meat [*Food technology*]
MSM......... Medium Minesweeper (NATG)
MSM......... Memoires. Societe d'Agriculture, Commerce, Sciences, et Arts du Departement de la Marne [*A publication*]
MSM......... Memory Storage Module
MSM......... Mercury Specialist Management [*Commercial firm*] [*British*]
MsM......... Meridian Public Library, Meridian, MS [*Library symbol*] [*Library of Congress*] (LCLS)
MSM......... Meritorious Service Medal [*Military decoration*]
MSM......... Messman
MSM......... Metal-Semiconductor-Metal (IEEE)
MSM......... Methyl Sulfonylmethane [*Biochemistry*]
MSM......... Millimeter and Submillimeter Conference (MCD)
MSM......... Minesweeper, River [*Navy symbol*] [*Obsolete*]
MSM......... Mission Simulation Model
MSM......... Missouri School of Mines
MSM......... Modified Source Multiplication (NRCH)
MSM......... Montana School of Mines
MSM......... Morehouse School of Medicine [*Atlanta, GA*]
MSM......... Motorized Switching Matrix
MSM......... Mott's Holdings, Inc. [*AMEX symbol*] (SPSG)
MSM......... Mount St. Mary's College, Emmitsburg, MD [*OCLC symbol*] (OCLC)
MSM......... Mouvement Social Mohutu [*Mohutu Social Movement*]
MSM......... Mouvement Solidaire Muluba [*Muluba Solidarity Movement*] [*Political party*]
MsM......... Ms Magazine [*A publication*]
MSM......... Mystic Seaport Museum (EA)
MSM......... Thousand Feet Surface Measure [*Lumber*]
MSMA...... Mail Systems Management Association [*New York, NY*] (EA)
MSMA...... Major Symphony Managers Association (EA)
MSMA...... Margarine and Shortening Manufacturers Association (EAIO)
MSMA...... Medical-Surgical Manufacturers Association [*Later, HIMA*]
MSMA...... Meteorological Services to Marine Activities [*WMO*] (MSC)
MSMA...... Metropolitan Symphony Managers Association (EA)
MSMA...... Monosodium Methyl Arsonate [*Herbicide*]
MsMac...... Noxubee County Library, Macon, MS [*Library symbol*] [*Library of Congress*] (LCLS)
MsMar...... Quitman County Library, Marks, MS [*Library symbol*] [*Library of Congress*] (LCLS)
MSMarne ... Memoires. Societe d'Agriculture, Commerce, Sciences, et Arts du Departement de la Marne [*A publication*]
MSMC...... Master Schedule and Milestone Chart (MCD)
MSMC...... Masterkey. Southwest Museum (Los Angeles, California) [*A publication*]
MSMC...... Member of the Spectacle Makers Company [*British*] (ROG)
MSMC...... Military Subsistence Market Center (MUGU)
MsMc........ Pike-Amite Library System, McComb, MS [*Library symbol*] [*Library of Congress*] (LCLS)
MSMCDN ... Medical Research Council (Great Britain). Laboratory Animals Centre. Manual Series [*A publication*]
MSMD...... Madras Subordinate Medical Department [*British military*] (DMA)
MSMD...... Mesa Medical, Inc. [*Wheat Ridge, CO*] [*NASDAQ symbol*] (NQ)
MSMDA ... Mutual Sewing Machine Dealers Association (EA)
MSME....... Master of Science in Mechanical Engineering
MS in ME ... Master of Science in Mechanical Engineering
MS in Mech ... Master of Science in Engineering Mechanics
MS Mech E ... Master of Science in Mechanical Engineering
MS in Med ... Master of Science in Medicine
MS in Met ... Master of Science in Metallurgy
MS Met E ... Master of Science in Metallurgical Engineering
MS in Met E ... Master of Science in Metallurgical Engineering
MSMF....... Maintenance Support Management File (MCD)
MsMFM.... Masonic Library, Meridian, MS [*Library symbol*] [*Library of Congress*] (LCLS)
MSMG...... Missionary Sisters of the Mother of God [*Roman Catholic religious order*]
MS Mgt E ... Master of Science in Management Engineering
MSMHD... Medecine Aeronautique et Spatiale, Medecine Subaquatique et Hyperbare [*A publication*]
MSMIA..... Medical and Sports Music Institute of America (EA)
MS/MIS.... Master of Science/Management Information Systems
MSML....... Minesweeping Motorlaunch [*Navy*]
MSMLCS ... Mass Service Mainline Cable Systems
MsMM...... Meridian Junior College, Meridian, MS [*Library symbol*] [*Library of Congress*] (LCLS)
MSMND... South African Medical Equipment News [*A publication*]
MsMo........ Lawrence County Public Library, Monticello, MS [*Library symbol*] [*Library of Congress*] (LCLS)
MSMP....... Master Sensitized Material Print (MSA)
MSMP....... Multispectral Measurements Program (MCD)
MSMPR.... Mixed-Suspension, Mixed-Product Removal [*Crystallizer*] [*Chemical engineering*]
MSMR...... Missouri School of Mines Reactor
MSMS....... Machine Strap Makers' Society [*A union*] [*British*]
MS/MS..... Mass Spectrometry/Mass Spectrometry
MS/MS..... Materials Science and Manufacturing in Space [*Program*] [*NASA*]
MSMS....... Max Steiner Memorial Society (EA)
MSMS....... Membership Section for Multihospital Systems [*Later, HCS*] (EA)
MSMS....... Meteorological Systems Management Section
MSMS....... MSM Systems, Inc. [*NASDAQ symbol*] (NQ)
MSMS....... Mutual Security Military Sales
MS-MS...... Tandem Mass Spectroscopy
MSMSD.... Mechanics of Materials [*A publication*]
MSMSP.... Project Manager, Surface Missile Systems [*Navy*]
MsMStA ... Saint Aloysius Academy, Meridian, MS [*Library symbol*] [*Library of Congress*] (LCLS)
MS MT...... Manuscript, Middle Temple [*A publication*] (DLA)
MSMT....... Measurement (KSC)
MSMTH ... Metalsmith [*Navy*]
MsMU....... Mississippi State University, Meridian Branch, Meridian, MS [*Library symbol*] [*Library of Congress*] (LCLS)
MSMU...... Mobile Spectrum Monitoring Unit
MS in Mus ... Master of Science in Music
MS in Mus Ed ... Master of Science in Music Education
MSMV...... Monostable Multivibrator
MSMW..... Magnetically Suspended Momentum Wheel
MSN.......... Madison [*Wisconsin*] [*Airport symbol*] (OAG)
MSN.......... Manned Space Network [*NASA*] (MCD)
MS in N..... Master of Science in Nursing
MSN.......... Master of Science in Nursing
MSN.......... Master Serial Number (AAG)
MSN.......... Material Supply Notice (AAG)
MSN.......... Message Sequence Number (CAAL)
MSN.......... Microwave Systems News [*A publication*]
MSN.......... Military Serial Number
MSN.......... Military Service Number
MSN.......... Mission (AFM)
MSN.......... Mobil Showcase Network [*Television*]
MSN.......... Modern Satellite Network [*Cable-television system*]
MSN.......... Monthly Science News [*A publication*]
MSN.......... Morrison Minerals Ltd. [*Toronto Stock Exchange symbol*]
MSN.......... Music, Sport, News [*Radio broadcasting format*]
MsN.......... Public Library of Natchez and Adams County, Natchez, MS [*Library symbol*] [*Library of Congress*] (LCLS)
MsNa........ Jennie Belle Stephens Smith Library, New Albany, MS [*Library symbol*] [*Library of Congress*] (LCLS)
MSNA....... Mission Accomplished [*Military*] (AABC)
MSNAF..... Memoires. Societe Nationale des Antiquaires de France [*A publication*]
MSNAP..... Merchant Ship Naval Augmentation Program [*Navy*]
MSNAP..... Microwave Steerable Null Antenna Processor (MCD)
MS in NE .. Master of Science in Nursing Education

**MsNe** ......... Newton Public Library, Newton, MS [*Library symbol*] [*Library of Congress*] (LCLS)
**MsNeC** ...... Clarke Memorial College, Newton, MS [*Library symbol*] [*Library of Congress*] (LCLS)
**MS in N Ed** ... Master of Science in Nursing Education
**MSNF**......... Milk Solids - Not Fat [*Food industry*]
**MSNF**......... Multisystem Networking Facility [*Data processing*]
**MSNGR** .... Messenger (ADA)
**MSNH**........ Memoires. Societe Neophilologique de Helsinki [*A publication*]
**MSNHP** .... Mississippi Natural Heritage Program [*Mississippi State Department of Wildlife Conservation*] [*Jackson, MS*] [*Information service or system*] (IID)
**MSNI** ........ (Mesitylenesulfonyl)nitroimidazole [*Organic chemistry*]
**MS & NI**.... Michigan Southern & Northern Indiana Railroad
**MSN Microwave Syst News** ... MSN. Microwave Systems News [*A publication*]
**MS in Nr Ed** ... Master of Science in Nursing Education
**MSNRY**..... Masonry (MSA)
**MS in NT** .. Master of Science in Nuclear Technology
**MSNT** ....... (Mesitylenesulfonyl)nitrotriazolide [*Biochemistry*]
**MS in Nucl E** ... Master of Science in Nuclear Engineering
**MSNY** ....... Massena [*New York*] [*Seismograph station code, US Geological Survey*] (SEIS)
**MSNY** ....... Mattachine Society of New York [*Defunct*] (EA)
**MSO**.......... Main Signal Office [*British*]
**MSO**.......... Maintenance Standard Order
**MSO**.......... Maintenance Support Office [*Navy*]
**MSO**.......... Management Science Office
**MSO**.......... Management Systems Office [*NASA*]
**MSO**.......... Manned Solar Observatory (MCD)
**MSO**.......... Manned Spacecraft Operations [*NASA*] (KSC)
**MSO**.......... Manufacturing Sequence Outline (MCD)
**MSO**.......... Marine Safety Office (MCD)
**MSO**.......... Marine Staff Officers (EA)
**MSO**.......... Marketing Services Officer [*Insurance*]
**MSO**.......... Mars Surface Operation
**MSO**.......... Mass Spectrometer Outgasing (KSC)
**MSO**.......... Master of the Science of Oratory
**M So** .......... Master of Sociology
**MSO**.......... Material Sales Order
**MSO**.......... Materiel Status Office (MCD)
**MSO**.......... Medial Superior Olive [*Brain anatomy*]
**MSO**.......... Member of the Society of Osteopaths [*British*]
**MSO**.......... Mesityl Oxide [*Organic chemistry*] [*Also, MO*]
**MSO**.......... Methionine Sulfoxime [*Biochemistry*]
**MSO**.......... Military Satellite Organization
**MSO**.......... Military Service Obligation (AFM)
**MSO**.......... Military Supply Officer (AFM)
**MSO**.......... Minesweeper, Ocean [*Nonmagnetic*] [*Navy symbol*]
**MSO**.......... Missabe Southern Railroad
**MSO**.......... Missile Safety Officer (AFM)
**MSO**.......... Missoula [*Montana*] [*Airport symbol*] (OAG)
**MSO**.......... Missoula [*Montana*] [*Seismograph station code, US Geological Survey*] (SEIS)
**MSO**.......... Mixed Services Organisation [*British Armed Services*]
**MSO**.......... Mobile Switching Office [*Bell System*]
**MSO**.......... Model for Spare Optimization (MCD)
**MSO**.......... Morale Support Officer [*Military*] (AABC)
**MSO**.......... Moss Resources Ltd. [*Vancouver Stock Exchange symbol*]
**MSO**.......... Mouvement Socialiste Occitan [*Occitanian Socialist Movement*] [*France*] [*Political party*] (PPE)
**MSO**.......... Multiple System Operator [*Cable television*]
**MSo** ........... Public Library of the City of Somerville, Somerville, MA [*Library symbol*] [*Library of Congress*] (LCLS)
**MSOA** ....... Military Studies and Operational Analysis (ADA)
**MSOB** ....... Manned Spacecraft Operations Building [*NASA*] (KSC)
**MSOB** ....... Master of Science in Organizational Behavior
**MSOC** ....... Marine Systems Operational Compiler
**MSOC** ....... Maritime Sector Operations Center [*NATO*] (NATG)
**MSoc**.......... Master of Sociology (ADA)
**MSocAdmin** ... Master of Social Administration
**MSOCC**..... Multisatellite Operations Control Center [*NASA*]
**M Soc E** ..... Member of the Society of Engineers [*British*]
**M Soc NS J** ... Mining Society of Nova Scotia. Journal [*A publication*]
**MSocSc**...... Master of Social Sciences
**MSocSci** .... Master of Social Sciences
**MSocStud** ... Master of Social Studies (ADA)
**MSocWk** ... Master of Social Work
**MSOD** ....... Military Service Obligation Date (AFM)
**MSOE** ....... Milwaukee School of Engineering [*Wisconsin*]
**MSOE** ....... Multiband Spectral Observation Equipment
**MSOF**........ Multi Soft, Inc. [*NASDAQ symbol*] (NQ)
**MSOG** ....... Glenwood and Souris Regional Library, Souris, Manitoba [*Library symbol*] [*National Library of Canada*] (NLC)
**MSohG** ...... Gordon-Conwell Theological Seminary Library, South Hamilton, MA [*Library symbol*] [*Library of Congress*] (LCLS)
**MSOIN** ..... Minor Subcontractor or IDWA [*Interdivisional Work Authorization*] Notification [*NASA*] (NASA)
**MSOINST** ... Maintenance Support Office Instructions [*Navy*]
**Mson**.......... Maison [*House, Firm*] [*Business term*] [*French*]
**MSON**........ Microsonics Corp. [*NASDAQ symbol*] (NQ)
**MSonHi**..... South Natick Historical, Natural History, and Library Society, South Natick, MA [*Library symbol*] [*Library of Congress*] (LCLS)
**MSOP** ....... Measurement System Operating Procedure (NG)
**MSOP** ....... Mezzo Soprano [*Music*]
**MSOP** ....... Mutual Security Objectives Plan (CINC)
**M Sopr**....... Mezzo Soprano [*Music*]
**MSOR** ....... Maximum System Operational Range
**MS Orn Hort** ... Master of Science in Ornamental Horticulture
**MSORS**..... Mechanized Sales Office Record System [*Telecommunications*] (TEL)
**MSOS**........ Mass Storage Operating System [*Control Data Corp.*] [*Data processing*] (NVT)
**MSOS**........ Mitteilungen. Seminar fuer Orientalische Sprachen zu Berlin [*A publication*]
**M So Sc** ..... Master of Social Science
**MSOSD**...... Mathematical Social Sciences [*A publication*]
**M So Se** ..... Master of Social Service
**M So W**..... Master of Social Work
**MSOW** ...... Modular Standoff Weapon [*Ballistic missile*]
**MsP** ........... Jackson County - Pascagoula City Library, Pascagoula, MS [*Library symbol*] [*Library of Congress*] (LCLS)
**MSP**........... Magnetic Scalar Potential
**MSP**........... Maintenance Service Plan
**MSP**........... Maintenance Support Plan [*or Program*] [*Army*]
**MSP**........... Maintenance Surveillance Procedure (IEEE)
**MSP**........... Manager Support Programs (MCD)
**MSP**........... Maritime Shore Patrol
**MSP**........... Market Stabilization Price [*Department of Agriculture*]
**MSP**........... Mass Storage Processor [*Honeywell, Inc.*]
**MSP**........... Master of Science in Pharmacy
**MSP**........... Master Shuttle Verification Plan (MCD)
**MSP**........... Master Simulator Program (NVT)
**M Sp** .......... Master of Speech
**MSP**........... Material Support Plan [*or Program*]
**MSP**........... Maximum Sound Pressure
**MSP**........... Mededelingen Spinozahuis [*A publication*] (BJA)
**MSP**........... Medical Specialist
**MSP**........... Medium-Speed Printer (AABC)
**MSP**........... Medium Stressed Platform
**MSP**........... Metal Splash Pan (AAG)
**MSP**........... Microspectrophotometry
**MSP**........... Military Space Program (AAG)
**MSP**........... Millisecond Pulsar [*Astronomy*]
**MSP**........... Miniature Series of Painters [*A publication*]
**MSP**........... Minimum Sustaining Power
**MSP**........... Minneapolis-St. Paul [*Minnesota*] [*Airport symbol*]
**MSP**........... Miscellaneous Small Parts
**MSP**........... Missile Setting Panel [*Military*] (CAAL)
**MSP**........... Missile Simulator Plug
**MSP**........... Missile Support Plan
**MSP**........... Mission Scientifique en Perse (BJA)
**MSP**........... Mission Support Plan (MCD)
**MSP**........... Mobile Support Package (MCD)
**MSP**........... Moderata Samlingspartiet [*Moderate Unity Party*] [*Sweden*] [*Political party*] (PPE)
**MSP**........... Modular System Programs [*IBM Corp.*]
**MSP**........... Monosodium Orthophosphate [*Inorganic chemistry*]
**MSP**........... Mosaic Sensor Program (MCD)
**MSP**........... Most Significant Position (CMD)
**MSP**........... Mount St. Thomas [*Philippines*] [*Seismograph station code, US Geological Survey*] (SEIS)
**MSP**........... Movimento Socialista Popular [*Popular Socialist Movement*] [*Portugal*] [*Political party*] (PPE)
**MSP**........... Multisensor Processor (CAAL)
**MSp** ........... Muttersprache [*A publication*]
**MSP**........... Mutual Security Program
**MSP**........... Mutual Support Program
**MSPA**........ Maine Sardine Packers Association (EA)
**MSPA**........ Marin Self-Publishers Association (EA)
**MS in PA**... Master of Science in Public Administration
**MSPA**........ Member, Society of Pension Actuaries [*Designation awarded by American Society of Pension Actuaries*]
**MSPA**........ Missinipe Achimowin. Churchill River Information [*A publication*]
**MSPA**........ Modified Sodium Polyacrylate [*Organic chemistry*]
**MSPAIRS** ... Missinipe Achimowin. Interim Report Supplement [*A publication*]
**MSPB**........ Medical Specialist Preference Blank
**MSPB**........ Merit Systems Protection Board [*Formerly, Civil Service Commission*]
**MSPC**........ Medical Specialist Corps [*Military*]
**MSPC**........ MOPAR Scat Pack Club (EA)
**MSPC**........ Multivariate Statistical Process Control
**MSPCL** ..... Lower Fort Garry National Historic Park, Parks Canada [*Parc Historique National Lower Fort Garry, Parcs Canada*] Selkirk, Manitoba [*Library symbol*] [*National Library of Canada*] (NLC)
**MSPCP** ..... Mobile Source Pollution Control Program [*Environmental Protection Agency*]

**MSPD**........ Master of Social Planning and Development (ADA)
**MSPD**........ Maximum Speed
**MSPD**........ Mulheres Portuguesas Social-Domocratas [*An association*] (EAIO)
**MSPE**........ Maintenance Safety and Protection Equipment (AFIT)
**MSPE**........ Master Plate [*Tool*] (AAG)
**MS in PE**... Master of Science in Petroleum Engineering
**MS in PE**... Master of Science in Physical Education
**MSPE**........ Master of Science in Physical Education
**MS in P Ed**... Master of Science in Physical Education
**MsPeM**...... Mississippi Gulf Coast Junior College, Perkinston, MS [*Library symbol*] [*Library of Congress*] (LCLS)
**MSpeSJ**..... Saint Joseph's Abbey, Spencer, MA [*Library symbol*] [*Library of Congress*] (LCLS)
**MS in Pet E**... Master of Science in Petroleum Engineering
**MSPF**........ Multispectral Photographic Facility
**MSPG**........ Materiel Support Planning Guidance [*Military*] (AABC)
**MSPGN**..... Mesangial Proliferative Glomerulonephritis [*Nephrology*]
**MSPH**....... Master of Science in Poultry Husbandry
**MS in PH**.. Master of Science in Public Health
**MSPH**....... Master of Science in Public Health
**MsPh**........ Neshoba County Library, Philadelphia, MS [*Library symbol*] [*Library of Congress*] (LCLS)
**MS in Phar**... Master of Science in Pharmacy
**MSPHE**..... Master of Science in Public Health Engineering
**MSPH Ed**... Master of Science in Public Health Education
**MS in Phy**... Master of Science in Physics
**MsPi**.......... Crosby Memorial Library, Picayune, MS [*Library symbol*] [*Library of Congress*] (LCLS)
**MSPI**.......... Modified Ship Plan Index
**MSPIR**...... Master of Science in Personnel and Industrial Relations
**MSPLT**..... Master Source Program Library Tape [*Data processing*] (BUR)
**MsPMF**..... United States Department of Commerce, National Marine Fisheries Service, Pascagoula, MS [*Library symbol*] [*Library of Congress*] (LCLS)
**MSPO**....... Mercury Support Planning Office (MUGU)
**MSPO**....... Military Support Planning Officer [*Civil Defense*]
**MSPO**....... Mission System Project Office [*Military*] (CAAL)
**MsPog**....... Harriette Person Memorial Library, Port Gibson, MS [*Library symbol*] [*Library of Congress*] (LCLS)
**MsPon**....... Dixie Regional Library, Pontotoc, MS [*Library symbol*] [*Library of Congress*] (LCLS)
**MsPop**....... Poplarville Public Library, Poplarville, MS [*Library symbol*] [*Library of Congress*] (LCLS)
**MSPP**........ Maharastra Sahitya Parisad Patrika [*A publication*]
**MSPP**........ Michigan Screening Profile of Parenting [*Psychology*]
**MsPr**.......... Jefferson Davis County Library, Prentiss, MS [*Library symbol*] [*Library of Congress*] (LCLS)
**MSPR**........ Master Spares Positioning Resolver [*Data processing*]
**MSPR**........ Medical System Program Review [*Army*] (RDA)
**MSPR**........ Model State Packaging Regulation [*National Institute of Standards and Technology*]
**MSpr**.......... Moderna Sprak [*A publication*]
**MSprak**..... Moderna Sprak [*A publication*]
**MSPRB**..... Meteorological Satellite Program Review Board [*NOAA and NASA*]
**MS in PRE**... Master of Science in Petroleum Refining Engineering
**MSPRS**...... Multispectral Photographic Reconnaissance (MCD)
**MSPS**........ Mega Symbols per Second (MCD)
**MSpS**......... Misioneros del Espiritu Santo [*Missionaries of the Holy Spirit*] [*Mexico City, Mexico*] (EAIO)
**MSPS**........ Modular Space Power Station
**MSPS**........ Multisource Processing System (MCD)
**MSPS**........ Myocardial Stress Perfusion Scintigram [*Medicine*]
**MS in PSM**... Master of Science in Public School Music
**MSpThy**.... Master of Speech Therapy (ADA)
**MS in Py Sc**... Master of Science in Poultry Science
**Msq**........... Masque [*Record label*]
**MSQ**.......... Minnesota Satisfaction Questionnaire
**MSQ**.......... Minsk [*USSR*] [*Airport symbol*] (OAG)
**MSQ**.......... Mosquito Construction Gold [*Vancouver Stock Exchange symbol*]
**MSQSAK**.. Mosquito Systematics [*A publication*]
**MSQT**....... Missile Ship Qualification Test [*Navy*] (NVT)
**MSQT**....... Modified Ship Qualification Test
**MsR**.......... Capital Area Regional Library, Raymond, MS [*Library symbol*] [*Library of Congress*] (LCLS)
**MSR**.......... Industrie- und Handelsrevue [*A publication*]
**MSR**.......... Machine Stress Rated
**MSR**.......... Magnetic Shift Register
**MSR**.......... Magnetic Storage Ring [*Data processing*]
**MSR**.......... Main Supply Road [*or Route*]
**MSR**.......... Malone Society. Reprints [*A publication*]
**MSR**.......... Management Systems Representative (MCD)
**MSR**.......... Manufacturing Specification Request (AAG)
**MSR**.......... Mark Sense Reading
**MSR**.......... Mark Sheet Reader [*Data processing*] (BUR)
**MSR**.......... Market Share Reporter [*A publication*]
**MSR**.......... Marketing Service Representative
**MSR**.......... Marketing Support Representative
**MSR**.......... Mass Storage Resident [*Data processing*] (IEEE)
**MS (R)**....... Master of Science in Research
**MSR**.......... Material Status Report [*AEC*]
**MSR**.......... Maximum Steam Rate [*Nuclear energy*] (NRCH)
**MSR**.......... McDonnell Simulator Recorder [*McDonnell Douglas Corp.*] (MCD)
**MSR**.......... Mean Spring Rise [*Tides and currents*]
**MSR**.......... Mechanized Storage and Retrieval [*Data processing*]
**MSR**.......... Melanges de Science Religieuse [*A publication*]
**MSR**.......... Member of the Society of Radiographers [*British*]
**MSR**.......... Membrane-Spanning Region [*Cytology*]
**MSR**.......... Merchant Ship Reactor [*Navy*]
**MS & R**...... Merchant Shipbuilding and Repairs
**MSR**.......... Message Has Been Misrouted [*Communications*]
**MSR**.......... Metal Seal Ring
**MSR**.......... Metalsmith, Ship Repair [*Navy*]
**MSR**.......... Meteorological Sounding Rocket
**MSR**.......... Micro Support Resource Corp. [*Atlanta, GA*]
**MSR**.......... Midwest Sunbeam Registry (EA)
**MSR**.......... Milestone Status Report [*Military*] (AFIT)
**MSR**.......... Mine Smelter and Refinery Databank [*Commodities Research Unit Ltd.*] [*Information service or system*] (CRD)
**MSR**.......... Mineral-Surface Roof [*Technical drawings*]
**MSR**.......... Minesweeper, Patrol [*Navy symbol*] [*Obsolete*]
**MSR**.......... Missile Scoring Reliability (MCD)
**MSR**.......... Missile Site RADAR [*Army*] (MCD)
**MSR**.......... Missile Site Range
**MSR**.......... Mission Success Ratio [*Military*] (CAAL)
**MSR**.......... Mission Support Recording [*Deep Space Instrumentation Facility, NASA*]
**MSR**.......... Mission Support Room [*NASA*] (KSC)
**MSR**.......... Mobile Satellite Reports [*Telecommunications service*] [*A publication*] (TSSD)
**MSR**.......... Mobile Sea Range (NVT)
**MSR**.......... Modification Status Report (KSC)
**MSR**.......... Module Support Rack (NASA)
**MSR**.......... Moisture Separator Reheater (NRCH)
**MSR**.......... Molten-Salt Reactor
**MSR**.......... Monthly Status Report [*Navy*]
**MSR**.......... Montserrat [*ANSI three-letter standard code*] (CNC)
**MSR**.......... Movimiento Socialista Revolucionario [*Revolutionary Socialist Movement*] [*Panama*] [*Political party*] (PPW)
**MSR**.......... MSR Exploration Ltd. [*AMEX symbol*] [*Toronto Stock Exchange symbol*] (SPSG)
**MSR**.......... Multicomet Sample Return [*Space science*]
**MSR**.......... Multijunction Semiconductor Rectifier
**MSR**.......... Multispeed Repeater
**MSR**.......... Munster [*West Germany*] [*Airport symbol*] (OAG)
**MSR**.......... St. Louis Art Museum, St. Louis, MO [*OCLC symbol*] (OCLC)
**MSRA**........ Middle States Regatta Association (EA)
**MSRA**........ Midwest Ski Representatives Association (EA)
**MS in Rad**... Master of Science in Radiology
**MSR/ASR**... Main Supply Route/Alternative Supply Route (MCD)
**MSRB**........ Margaret Sanger Research Bureau [*Defunct*] (EA)
**MSRB**........ Metalsmith, Ship Repair, Blacksmith [*Navy*]
**MSRB**........ Municipal Securities Rulemaking Board [*Securities and Exchange Commission*]
**MSRC**........ Marine Sciences Research Center [*State University of New York at Stony Brook*] [*Research center*] (RCD)
**MSRC**........ Materiel Studies Review Committee [*Army*]
**MSRC**........ Medical and Surgical Relief Committee [*Defunct*] (EA)
**MSRC**........ Memoires. Societe Royale du Canada [*A publication*]
**MSRC**........ Metalsmith, Ship Repair, Coppersmith [*Navy*]
**MSRD**........ Mean Square Relative Displacement [*Spectra*]
**MSRD**........ Mobile Servicing and Repair Detachment [*Military*] [*British*]
**MSRE**........ Master of Science in Real Estate and Urban Affairs
**MSRE**........ Molten Salt Reactor Experiment
**MSRE**........ Moon Signal Rejection Equipment (AFM)
**MS in Rec**.. Master of Science in Recreation
**MS in Ret**.. Master of Science in Retailing
**MSRF**........ Metalsmith, Ship Repair, Forger-Anglesmith [*Navy*]
**MSRF**........ Microwave Space Research Facility
**MSRFT**..... Minesweeper Refresher Training [*Navy*] (NVT)
**MSRG**....... Member of the Society of Remedial Gymnasts [*British*]
**MSRG**....... Moated Sites Research Group (EA)
**MSRG**....... Modular Shift Register Generator
**MsRH**........ Hinds Junior College, Raymond, MS [*Library symbol*] [*Library of Congress*] (LCLS)
**MsRi**.......... Pine Forest Regional Library, Richton, MS [*Library symbol*] [*Library of Congress*] (LCLS)
**MSRIS**...... Molten-Salt Reactor Information System
**MSRK**........ Mathias-Soave-Redlich-Kwong [*Equation of state*]
**MSRL**........ Marine Sciences Research Laboratory [*Canada*] (MSC)
**MSRL**........ Mobile Secondary Reference Laboratory
**MSRM**....... Main Steam Radiation Monitor (IEEE)
**MSR Mess Steuern Regeln**... MSR. Messen, Steuern, Regeln [*A publication*]
**MSRN**........ Mountain Safety Research Newsletter [*A publication*]
**MSRNW**.... North-West Regional Library, Swan River, Manitoba [*Library symbol*] [*National Library of Canada*] (NLC)
**MSRO**....... Missile System Requirements Outline (MCD)
**MSRP**........ Management Sciences Research Project [*University of California*] (MCD)

**MSRP**........ Manufacturer's Suggested Retail Price
**MSRP**........ Massive Selective Retaliatory Power (NATG)
**MSRP**........ Meteorological Sounding Rocket Program [*NASA*]
**MSRP**........ Missile, Space and Range Pioneers (EA)
**MSRP**........ Mission Support Real Property [*NASA*] (KSC)
**MSRPP**..... Multidimensional Scale for Rating Psychiatric Patients
**MSR (R)**.... Member of the Society of Radiographers (Radiography) [*British*]
**MSRR**........ MidSouth Corp. [*NASDAQ symbol*] (NQ)
**MSRR**........ Mission and System Requirements Review [*NASA*]
**MSRS**........ Main Steam Radiation System (IEEE)
**MSRS**........ Materiel System Requirements Specification [*Military*]
**MSRS**........ Medical Socioeconomic Research Sources [*A publication*]
**MSRS**........ Metalsmith, Ship Repair, Sheet Metal Worker [*Navy*]
**MSRS**........ Meteoroid Shield Release System (MCD)
**MSRS**........ Military Spending Research Services, Inc. [*Information service or system*] (EISS)
**MSRS**........ Missile Strike Reporting System
**MSRSIM**... Missile Site RADAR Simulation [*Missile system evaluation*] (RDA)
**MSRT**........ Mean Supply Response Time
**MSR (T)**.... Member of the Society of Radiographers (Radiotherapy) [*British*]
**MSRT**........ Missile System Readiness Test (IEEE)
**MSRT**........ Mobile Subscriber Radio Terminal [*Army*]
**MSRTE**..... Misroute
**MSRT J**..... MSRT [*Michigan Society for Respiratory Therapy*] Journal [*A publication*]
**MS-RTP**.... Micelle-Stabilized Room-Temperature Phosphorescence
**MSRV**........ Main Steam Relief Valve [*Nuclear energy*] (NRCH)
**MSRY**........ Masonry
**MSS**........... Magnetic Storm Satellite [*Air Force/NASA*]
**MSS**........... Main Steam System [*Nuclear energy*] (NRCH)
**MSS**........... Main Support Structure (NRCH)
**MSS**........... Maintenance Standards Study (MCD)
**MSS**........... Maintenance Status System (MCD)
**MSS**........... Maintenance Support Schedule [*Air Force*] (AFM)
**MSS**........... Make Suitable Substitution
**MSS**........... Management Science Systems (IEEE)
**MSS**........... Management Statistics Subsystem (TEL)
**MSS**........... Management Summary Sheets (MCD)
**MSS**........... Management Supplier Selection (AAG)
**MSS**........... Management Support Staff [*Social Security Administration*]
**MSS**........... Management Systems Study (MCD)
**MSS**........... Manned Space Station [*NASA*]
**MSS**........... Manual Safety Switch
**MSS**........... Manufacturers Standardization Society of the Valve and Fittings Industry (EA)
**MSS**........... Manuscript, Signed
**MSS**........... Manuscripta [*Manuscripts*] [*Latin*]
**MSS**........... Manuscripts
**MSS**........... Manuscripts [*A publication*]
**MSS**........... MAP [*Manufacturing Automation Protocol*]/One System Software [*Industrial Networking, Inc.*]
**M & SS**...... Mapping and Survey System (KSC)
**MSS**........... Marine Safety Services [*British*] (DCTA)
**MSS**........... Maritime Support Service
**MSS**........... Marvel Science Stories [*A publication*]
**MSS**........... Mary Stuart Society of America (EA)
**MSS**........... Mass Storage System [*Data processing*]
**MSS**........... Massage
**MSS**........... Massena [*New York*] [*Airport symbol*] (OAG)
**MSS**........... Master of Sanitary Science
**MSS**........... Master of Social Science
**MSS**........... Master of Social Service
**MSS**........... Master of Social Studies
**MSS**........... Master Surveillance Station [*Air Force*]
**MSS**........... Master Switching Station (MCD)
**MSS**........... Master System Schedule (MCD)
**MSS**........... Mastergroup Surveillance System [*AT & T*]
**MSS**........... Mayo Smith Society (EA)
**MSS**........... Mechanical Support System (MCD)
**MSS**........... Mechanically Separated Spleen [*Food technology*]
**MSS**........... Medical Service School [*Air Force*] (AFM)
**MSS**........... Medium Survey Ship [*Marine science*] (MSC)
**MSS**........... Member of the Statistical Society [*British*] (ROG)
**MSS**........... Men's Social Services [*Salvation Army*]
**MSS**........... Mental Status Schedule [*Psychology*]
**MSS**........... Message Support Subsystem (MCD)
**MSS**........... Message Switching Station [*Telecommunications*] (CET)
**MSS**........... Messtetten [*Federal Republic of Germany*] [*Seismograph station code, US Geological Survey*] (SEIS)
**MSS**........... Metal Spring Seal
**MSS**........... Meteorological Satellite Section
**MSS**........... Meter Stamp Society (EA)
**MSS**........... Methylprednisolone Sodium Succinate [*Antirheumatoid compound*]
**MSS**........... Mexican-Spanish Speaking (OICC)
**MSS**........... Microwave Switching Station
**MSS**........... Midcourse Surveillance System (MCD)
**MSS**........... Military Security Service [*RVNAF*]
**MSS**........... Military Supply Standards [*DoD*] (MCD)
**MSS**........... Minesweeper, Special [*Device*] [*Navy symbol*]
**MSS**........... Miniature Signaling System [*Railway term*] (DCTA)
**MSS**........... Miniature Stepping Switch
**MSS**........... Ministry of Social Security [*British*]
**MSS**........... Minnesota Satisfactoriness Scale [*Job performance test*]
**MSS**........... Missile Select Switch
**MSS**........... Missile Stabilization System
**MSS**........... Missile Station Select
**MSS**........... Missile Subsystem
**MSS**........... Mission Simulator System
**MSS**........... Mission Specialist Station [*NASA*] (NASA)
**MSS**........... Mission Status Summary (MCD)
**MSS**........... Mission Support Site [*Army*]
**MSS**........... Mississauga Public Library [*UTLAS symbol*]
**MSS**........... Mixed Spectrum Superheater [*Nuclear energy*]
**MSS**........... Mobile Satellite Service
**MSS**........... Mobile Service Structure (KSC)
**MSS**........... Mobile Servicing System [*For space station*]
**MSS**........... Mobility Subsystem (KSC)
**MSS**........... Mode Selection Switch (KSC)
**MSS**........... Mode Sickness Susceptibility (KSC)
**MSS**........... Model Skin Surface [*Artificial skin*]
**MSS**........... Modelling and Simulation Studies [*Marine science*] (MSC)
**MSS**........... Modern Satellite Systems, Inc. [*Whitehouse Station, NJ*] [*Telecommunications*] (TSSD)
**MSS**........... Modified Scram System [*Nuclear energy*] (NRCH)
**MSS**........... Modular Space Station
**MSS**........... Moored Surveillance System [*To detect and destroy enemy submarines*] [*Navy*]
**MSS**........... Motion Sickness Susceptibility (MCD)
**MSS**........... Movement Shorthand Society [*Later, Center for Sutton Movement Writing*] (EA)
**MSS**........... Mucus-Stimulating Substance
**MSS**........... Muenchener Studien zur Sprachwissenschaft [*A publication*]
**MSS**........... Multibeam Steering System
**MSS**........... Multiple Sclerosis Society [*British*]
**MSS**........... Multiple Steady States [*Chemical engineering*]
**MSS**........... Multispectral Scanner [*or Sensor*]
**MSS**........... Muscular Subaortic Stenosis [*Cardiology*]
**MSS**........... Music Story Series [*A publication*]
**MSS**........... Special Minesweeper [*Navy symbol*]
**MSSA**........ Maintenance Supply Services Agency (NATG)
**MSSA**........ Manchester Scales of Social Adaptation [*Psychology*]
**MSSA**........ Military Selective Service Act (OICC)
**MSSA**........ Military Subsistence Supply Agency [*Later, Defense Subsistence Supply Center*]
**MSsA**......... Missionaries of the Holy Apostles [*Roman Catholic men's religious order*]
**MSSA**........ Missionary Servants of St. Anthony [*Roman Catholic women's religious order*]
**MSSanE**.... Master of Science in Sanitary Engineering
**MSSB**........ Mid-State Federal Savings Bank [*NASDAQ symbol*] (NQ)
**MSSC**........ Management System for Support Contracts [*Social Security Administration*]
**MSSC**........ Mass Storage System Communicator [*Data processing*] (IBMDP)
**MSSC**........ Mass Storage System Control [*Data processing*] (BUR)
**MS Sc**........ Master of Sanitary Science
**MS Sc**........ Master of Social Science
**MSSc**......... Master of Surgical Science, University of Dundee [*British*] (DBQ)
**MSSC**........ Medium SEAL [*Sea, Air, and Land*] Support Craft [*Navy symbol*]
**MSSC**........ Military Standard and Specification Committee
**MSSC**........ Military Store Staff Corps [*British military*] (DMA)
**MSSC**........ Missionary Society of St. Columban (EAIO)
**MSSCC**..... Military Space Surveillance Control Center (MUGU)
**MSSCC**..... Missionarii a Sacris Cordibus Jesus et Mariae [*Missionaries of the Sacred Hearts of Jesus and Mary*] [*Roman Catholic men's religious order*]
**MSSCC**..... Multicolor Spin-Scan Cloudcover Camera
**MSSCD**..... Microstructural Science [*A publication*]
**MSSCE**..... Mixed Spectrum Superheater Critical Experiment [*Nuclear energy*]
**MSSCEK**... Medicine and Sport Science [*A publication*]
**MSSCS**...... Manned Space Station Communications System [*NASA*]
**MSSD**........ Model Secondary School for the Deaf (EA)
**MSSE**........ Master of Science in Sanitary Engineering
**MSSE**........ Missile System Support Equipment
**MSS/EC**.... Missile System Supervisor/Engagement Controller [*Military*] (CAAL)
**MSSG**........ Message
**MSS & H**... Master of Science in Speech and Hearing
**MSSH**........ Springfield Hospital, Medical Center Library, Springfield, MA [*Library symbol*] [*Library of Congress*] (LCLS)
**MSSJ**......... Missionary Servants of St. Joseph [*Roman Catholic women's religious order*]
**MSSJ**......... Multiple Subsonic Jet
**MSSL**........ Management Systems Summary List
**MSSL**........ Missile System Stockage List (AFIT)

**MSSLA** ..... Missili [*A publication*]
**MSSM** ....... Mars Spinning Support Module [*NASA*] (KSC)
**MSSM** ....... Missionary Sisters of the Society of Mary [*Rome, Italy*] (EAIO)
**MsSM** ........ Mississippi State University, State College, MS [*Library symbol*] [*Library of Congress*] (LCLS)
**MSSMS** .... Munitions Section of Strategic Missile Squadron (AAG)
**MSSN** ........ Mission
**MSSO** ........ Mount Stromlo and Siding Springs Observatories [*Australia*]
**MSSP** ........ International Association of Marble, Slate and Stone Polishers, Rubbers and Sawyers, Tile and Marble Setters' Helpers, and Marble Mosaic and Terrazzo Workers' Helpers [*Later, Tile, Marble, Terrazzo Finishers, Shopworkers, and Granite Cutters International Union*] (EA)
**MS in Sp** .... Master of Science in Speech
**MSSP** ........ Miscellaneous Small Special Projects (AAG)
**MSSp** ......... Mission Sisters of the Holy Spirit [*Roman Catholic religious order*]
**MSSP** ........ Model Seafood Surveillance Project [*National Marine Fisheries Service*]
**MSSPA** ..... Missionary Society of St. Paul the Apostle (EA)
**M & SSq** .... Maintenance and Supply Squadron [*Air Force*]
**MSSR** ........ Mars Soil [*or Surface*] Sample Return
**MSSR** ........ Medical Society for the Study of Radiesthesia (EA)
**MSSR** ........ Mixed Spectrum Superheat Reactor
**MSSR** ........ Mobility, Survivability, Sizing Recommendations (MCD)
**MSSS** ........ Main Steam Supply System [*Nuclear energy*] (NRCH)
**MSSS** ........ Maintenance Supply Services System (NATG)
**MSSS** ........ Manned Space Station Simulator [*NASA*] (MUGU)
**MSSS** ........ Manned Static Space Simulator
**MSSS** ........ Manuscripts, Signed
**MSSS** ........ Mass Spectral Search System [*National Bureau of Standards, Environmental Protection Agency, and National Institutes of Health*] [*Database*]
**MS in SS** ... Master of Science in Sanitary Science
**MSSS** ........ Master of Science in Social Science
**MS in SS** ... Master of Science in Social Service
**MSSS** ........ Missionary Sisters of the Most Blessed Sacrament [*Roman Catholic religious order*]
**MSSS** ........ Mobile Spectrum Search System
**MSSS** ........ Multiple-Start Systematic Sampling [*Statistics*]
**MSSS** ........ San Salvador/Ilopango Internacional [*El Salvador*] [*ICAO location identifier*] (ICLI)
**MSSSM-MMS** ... Missionary Sisters of the Society of Saint Mary - Marist Missionary Sisters (EA)
**MSSSO** ..... Mount Stromlo and Siding Springs Observatories [*Australia*]
**MSSST** ...... Meeting Street School Screening Test [*Used to detect learning disabilities*]
**MSSSW** .... Mass Spectral Search System-Wiley [*Cornell University*] [*Database*]
**MSST** ........ Jamco Ltd. [*Formerly, Mister Steak*] [*NASDAQ symbol*] (SPSG)
**MSST** ........ Manufacturing Standards and Specifications for Textbooks
**MSST** ........ Master of Science in Science Teaching
**MSST** ........ Mean Sea Surface Temperature
**MSST** ........ Meldesammelstelle [*Message Center*] [*German military - World War II*]
**MSST** ........ Member of the Society of Surveying Technicians [*British*] (DBQ)
**MSST** ........ Ministry of State for Science and Technology [*Canada*]
**MSST** ........ Missionary Servants of the Most Holy Trinity [*Roman Catholic men's religious order*]
**MsSt** .......... Oktibbeha County Library System, Starkville, MS [*Library symbol*] [*Library of Congress*] (LCLS)
**MSST** ........ Springfield Technical Community College, Springfield, MA [*Library symbol*] [*Library of Congress*] (LCLS)
**MSSTC** ..... Mobile Service Structure Test Conductor (KSC)
**MSSU** ........ Meteorology on Stamps Study Unit [*American Topical Association*] (EA)
**MSSU** ........ Midstream Specimen of Urine [*Medicine*]
**MsSu** ......... Sunflower County Library, Sunflower, MS [*Library symbol*] [*Library of Congress*] (LCLS)
**MSSV** ........ Maximum Safe Sampling Volume [*Analytical chemistry*]
**MSSVD** ..... Medical Society for the Study of Venereal Diseases [*Leeds, England*] (EAIO)
**MSSVFI** .... Manufacturers Standardization Society of the Valve and Fittings Industry (EA)
**MSSW** ....... Magnetostatic Surface Wave [*Telecommunications*] (TEL)
**MSSW** ....... Master of Science in Social Work
**MS in SW** ... Master of Science in Social Work
**MSSYBF** ... Specialist Periodical Reports. Mass Spectrometry [*A publication*]
**MST** ........... Association of Maximum Service Telecasters (EA)
**MsT** ........... Lee-Itawamba Regional Library, Tupelo, MS [*Library symbol*] [*Library of Congress*] (LCLS)
**MST** ........... Maastricht [*Netherlands*] [*Airport symbol*] (OAG)
**MST** ........... Machine Shock Test
**MST** ........... Machine Steel
**MST** ........... Machinery Safety Tag
**MST** ........... Magnetostrictive Transducer
**MST** ........... Maintenance Standard Tests [*Military*]
**MST** ........... Maintenance Support Team (MCD)
**MST** ........... Management Survey Team (AAG)
**MST** ........... Mass Spectrometer Tube
**MST** ........... Mass Storage Task [*Data processing*] (NOAA)
**MST** ........... Master (MCD)
**MST** ........... Master of Sacred Theology
**MST** ........... Master of Science in Taxation
**MST** ........... Master of Science in Teaching
**M St** ........... Master of Statistics
**MSt** ........... Master of Studies, University of Oxford [*British*] (DBQ)
**MST** ........... Master of Teaching
**MST** ........... Maximum Service Telecasters
**MST** ........... Maximum Summer Temperature [*Climatology*]
**MST** ........... Mean Selected Temperature
**MST** ........... Mean Solar Time
**MST** ........... Mean Survival Time
**MST** ........... Mean Swell Time [*Botulism test*] [*Food analysis*]
**MST** ........... Measurement
**MST** ........... Measurement Status Table (NASA)
**MST** ........... Median Survival Time
**MST** ........... Medium-Scale Technology
**MST** ........... Medium STOL [*Short Takeoff and Landing*] Transport [*Aircraft*]
**MST** ........... Memotron Storage Tube
**MST** ........... Mercantile Stores Co., Inc. [*NYSE symbol*] (SPSG)
**MST** ........... Mercury System Test [*NASA*]
**MST** ........... Message Status Table (MCD)
**MST** ........... Microsecond Trip
**MST** ........... Microwave Satellite Technologies, Inc. [*Wellington, NJ*] (TSSD)
**MST** ........... Middle East Transport [*A publication*]
**MST** ........... Midsummer Time
**MST** ........... Military Science Training
**MST** ........... Military Shipping Tag
**MST** ........... Minimal Spanning Tree [*Data processing*]
**MST** ........... Minimum Spawning Time [*Pisciculture*]
**MST** ........... Ministarstvo Spoljne Trgovine [*Ministry of Foreign Trade*] [*Yugoslavian*]
**MST** ........... Ministry, Society, and Theology [*A publication*] (APTA)
**MST** ........... Missile Surveillance Technology (MCD)
**MST** ........... Missile System Test
**MST** ........... Mission Support Team (MCD)
**MST** ........... Mistral Resources Ltd. [*Vancouver Stock Exchange symbol*]
**MSt** ........... Mitteldeutsche Studien [*A publication*]
**MST** ........... Mobile Service Tower [*Aerospace*]
**MST** ........... Mobile Strike Team
**MST** ........... Mobile Support Team (NVT)
**MST** ........... Modal Survey Test (MCD)
**MST** ........... Module Service Tool (NASA)
**MSt** ........... Monastic Studies [*A publication*]
**MST** ........... Monolithic Systems Technology
**M St** ........... More's Notes on Stair's Institutes of Scotland [*A publication*] (ILCA)
**MST** ........... Mostar [*Yugoslavia*] [*Seismograph station code, US Geological Survey*] [*Closed*] (SEIS)
**MST** ........... Mountain Standard Time
**MST** ........... Multimode Storage Tube
**MST** ........... Multisystem Test [*Military*]
**MST** ........... Mustang Aviation, Inc. [*Dallas, TX*] [*FAA designator*] (FAAC)
**MST** ........... Mutual Security Treaty (MCD)
**MST** ........... St. Cloud State University, St. Cloud, MN [*OCLC symbol*] (OCLC)
**MSTA** ........ Manufacturers Surgical Trade Association [*Later, HIMA*] (EA)
**MSTA** ........ Master Tape (AAG)
**MSTA** ........ Member of the Swimming Teachers' Association [*British*] (DBQ)
**MSTA** ........ Mumps Skin Test Antigen [*Clinical chemistry*]
**MSTAN** ..... Modal Stamen Number per Flower [*Botany*]
**MStat** ........ Master of Statistics
**MSTB** ........ Mission Simulator and Training Building
**MSTC** ........ Management Systems Training Council [*British*]
**MSTC** ........ Manned Spacecraft Test Center [*NASA*] (KSC)
**MSTC** ........ Manufacturing Systems and Technology Center [*Baltimore, MD*] [*Westinghouse Electric Corp.*]
**MSTC** ........ Maryland State Teachers College
**MSTC** ........ Massachusetts State Teachers College
**MSTC** ........ Mastic
**MSTC** ........ Microwave Sensitivity Time Control [*Circuit*]
**MSTC** ........ Midwest Securities Trust Company
**MSTCS(GB)** ... Member of the Society of Thoracic and Cardiovascular Surgeons (Great Britain)
**MSTD** ........ Master Steward [*Marine Corps*]
**M St E** ........ Master of Structural Engineering
**MST & E** .... Multiservice Test and Evaluation [*Military*]
**MSTE** ........ Steinbach Public Library, Manitoba [*Library symbol*] [*National Library of Canada*] (NLC)
**MS (T Ed)** ... Master of Science in Teacher Education
**MSTEL** ..... Member of the Society of Telegraph Engineers, London [*British*] (ROG)
**M St Eng** .... Master of Structural Engineering
**M-STEP** .... Multi-State Teacher Education Project
**MSTFA** ..... (Methyl)trimethylsilyltrifluoroacetamide [*Organic chemistry*]

**MSTG**........ Marine Sciences and Technologies Grants [*Australia*]
**MSTG**........ Mass Storage Task Group [*CODASYL*]
**MSTG**........ Material Safety Task Group [*Air Force*] (AFM)
**MSTGA**..... Library Allard, St. Georges, Manitoba [*Library symbol*] [*National Library of Canada*] (BIB)
**MSTGP**..... Material Safety Task Group [*Air Force*]
**MSTh**........ Mesothorium [*Radioelement*]
**MsTI**.......... Itawamba Junior College, Tupelo Campus, Tupelo, MS [*Library symbol*] [*Library of Congress*] (LCLS)
**MS in T & I**... Master of Science in Trade and Industrial Education
**MSTI**......... Medical Sterilization, Incorporated [*NASDAQ symbol*] (NQ)
**M ST J**....... Ordinary Member of the Order of St. John of Jerusalem
**MSTJ**......... Public Library, St. James-Assiniboia, Manitoba [*Library symbol*] [*National Library of Canada*] (NLC)
**MSTL**......... Military Subvention Type Lorry [*British*]
**MSTL**......... Minneapolis & St. Louis Railway Co. [*Later, MSL Industries, Inc.*] [*AAR code*]
**MSTLAB**... Materials and Science Toxicology Laboratory [*University of Tennessee*] [*Research center*] (RCD)
**MSTM**....... Mennonite Village Museum, Steinbach, Manitoba [*Library symbol*] [*National Library of Canada*] (NLC)
**MStoc**........ Stockbridge Library Association, Stockbridge, MA [*Library symbol*] [*Library of Congress*] (LCLS)
**MStocA**..... Austen Riggs Center, Inc., Stockbridge, MA [*Library symbol*] [*Library of Congress*] (LCLS)
**MSTOL**..... Medium-Slow Takeoff and Landing
**MSTOS**..... South Interlake Regional Library, Stonewall, Manitoba [*Library symbol*] [*National Library of Canada*] (NLC)
**MsToT**....... Tougaloo College, Tougaloo, MS [*Library symbol*] [*Library of Congress*] (LCLS)
**MStp**.......... Maize Stripe [*Plant pathology*]
**MSTP**......... Master Template
**MSTP**......... Medical Scientist Training Program [*National Institutes of Health*]
**M & StP**..... Milwaukee & St. Paul Railway
**MStP & A**... Minneapolis, St. Paul & Ashland Railway
**MSTPHC**.. Multistop Time-to-Pulse Height Converter [*NASA*]
**MSTPJ**...... Jolys Regional Library, St. Pierre, Manitoba [*Library symbol*] [*National Library of Canada*] (NLC)
**MSTP & SSM**... Minneapolis, St. Paul & Sault Ste. Marie Railway Co.
**MStpV**....... Maize Stripe Virus
**MSTR**........ [*The*] Massena Terminal Railroad Co. [*AAR code*]
**MSTR**........ Master
**MSTR**........ Masters Energy Corp. [*NASDAQ symbol*] (NQ)
**MSTR**........ Moisture (FAAC)
**MSTR**........ Multivariable Self-Tuning Regulator [*Control technology*]
**MSTR**........ Ste-Rose Regional Library, Manitoba [*Library symbol*] [*National Library of Canada*] (NLC)
**MS in Trans E**... Master of Science in Transportation Engineering
**MSTRE**...... Moisture (MSA)
**MSTS**........ McDonnell Scrap Tool System [*McDonnell Douglas Corp.*] (MCD)
**MSTS**........ Military Sea Transportation Service [*Later, MSC*] [*Navy*]
**MSTS**........ Missile Simulator Test Set (MCD)
**MSTS**........ Missile Static Test Site [*Air Force*]
**MSTS**........ Missile Subsystem Test Set [*Military*] (CAAL)
**MSTS**........ Multisubscriber Time-Sharing Systems [*Computer system*]
**MSTSFE**.... Military Sea Transport Service, Far East
**MSTSO**..... Military Sea Transportation Service Office [*Obsolete*]
**MSTU**........ Military Sea Transport Union
**MStud**....... Milton Studies [*A publication*]
**MStuO**....... Old Sturbridge Village Library, Sturbridge, MA [*Library symbol*] [*Library of Congress*] (LCLS)
**MSTV**........ Manned Supersonic Test Vehicle (MCD)
**MSTV**........ Master-Scale Television
**MsTy**......... Walthall County Library, Tylertown, MS [*Library symbol*] [*Library of Congress*] (LCLS)
**MSu**........... Goodnow Library, Sudbury, MA [*Library symbol*] [*Library of Congress*] (LCLS)
**MSU**.......... Main Storage Unit [*Data processing*]
**MSU**.......... Maintenance Signal Unit [*Telecommunications*] (TEL)
**MSU**.......... Maintenance and Status Unit [*Telecommunications*] (TEL)
**MSU**.......... Malaria Survey Unit [*Army*] [*World War II*]
**MSU**.......... Management Signal Unit [*Telecommunications*] (TEL)
**MSU**.......... Management Support Unit
**MSU**.......... Management Systems Unit
**MSU**.......... Marysvale [*Utah*] [*Seismograph station code, US Geological Survey*] (SEIS)
**MSU**.......... Maseru [*Lesotho*] [*Airport symbol*] (OAG)
**MSU**.......... Masonic Study Unit [*American Topical Association*] (EA)
**MSU**.......... Mass Storage Unit [*Data processing*] (NASA)
**MSU**.......... Material Salvage Unit
**MSU**.......... Mathematical Study Unit [*American Topical Association*] (EA)
**MSU**.......... Measuring Stimuli Units (NASA)
**MSU**.......... Medical Service Unit [*Air Force*] (AFM)
**MSU**.......... Medical Subjects Unit [*American Topical Association*] (EA)
**MSU**.......... Memory Service Unit [*Data processing*]
**MSU**.......... Memphis State University [*Tennessee*]
**MSU**.......... Message Switching Unit
**MSU**.......... Meteorology on Stamps Study Unit [*American Topical Association*] (EA)
**MSU**.......... Michigan State University [*East Lansing*]
**MSU**.......... Microwave Sounding Unit [*Telecommunications*] (TEL)
**MSU**.......... Middle South Utilities, Inc. [*Later, ETR*] [*NYSE symbol*] (SPSG)
**MSU**.......... Midstream Specimen of Urine [*Medicine*]
**MSU**.......... Mill Sawyers' Union [*British*]
**msu**............ Mississippi [*MARC country of publication code*] [*Library of Congress*] (LCCP)
**MSU**.......... Mitteilungen. Septuaginta Unternehmen [*Berlin/Goettingen*] [*A publication*]
**MSU**.......... Mobile Signals Unit [*British military*] (DMA)
**MSU**.......... Mode Selector Unit
**MSU**.......... MODEM-Sharing Unit [*Telecommunications*] (TSSD)
**MSU**.......... Monosodium Urate [*Organic chemistry*]
**MSU**.......... Montana State University [*Bozeman*]
**MSU**.......... Morgan State University, Baltimore, MD [*OCLC symbol*] (OCLC)
**MSU**.......... MSU [*Michigan State University*] Business Topics [*A publication*]
**MSU**.......... Multiblock Synchronization Signal Unit [*Telecommunications*] (TEL)
**MSU**.......... Multiple Signal Unit [*Telecommunications*] (TEL)
**MSU**.......... Murray State University [*Kentucky*]
**MSU**.......... Skyway Aviation, Inc. [*Fort Leonard Wood, MO*] [*FAA designator*] (FAAC)
**MsU**........... University of Mississippi, University, MS [*Library symbol*] [*Library of Congress*] (LCLS)
**MSU Business Topics**... Michigan State University Business Topics [*A publication*] (DLA)
**MSU Bus To**... MSU [*Michigan State University*] Business Topics [*A publication*]
**MSU Bus Top**... MSU [*Michigan State University*] Business Topics [*A publication*]
**MSU Bus Topics**... MSU [*Michigan State University*] Business Topics [*A publication*]
**MSUCLE**.. Missouri State University Continuing Legal Education (DLA)
**MSUD**....... Maple Sugar [*or Syrup*] Urine Disease [*Medicine*]
**MSUDC**.... Michigan State University Discrete Computer
**MSUL**........ Medical Schools of the University of London (DAS)
**MsU-L**....... University of Mississippi, Law School, University, MS [*Library symbol*] [*Library of Congress*] (LCLS)
**MSUM**...... Mission Society for United Methodists (EA)
**MsU-M**...... University of Mississippi, Medical Center, Jackson, MS [*Library symbol*] [*Library of Congress*] (LCLS)
**MSU (Mich State Univ) Bus Topics**... MSU (Michigan State University) Business Topics [*A publication*]
**MsU-P**....... University of Mississippi, School of Pharmacy, University, MS [*Library symbol*] [*Library of Congress*] (LCLS)
**M Sur**......... Master of Surgery
**MSurv**........ Master of Surveying
**MSurvSc**.... Master of Surveying Science
**MSUS**........ Mouvement Socialiste d'Union Senegalaise [*Senegalese Socialist Movement*] [*Political party*]
**MSUSM**.... Medical Society of the United States and Mexico (EA)
**MSUS/PALS**... Minnesota State Universities System Project for Automated Library Systems [*Mankato State University Library*] [*Mankato, MN*] [*Information service or system*]
**MSuSR**...... Sperry Rand Research Center, Sudbury, MA [*Library symbol*] [*Library of Congress*] (LCLS)
**MSV**.......... Catskills/Sullivan County [*New York*] [*Airport symbol*] [*Obsolete*] (OAG)
**MSV**.......... Maandstatistiek Verkeer en Vervoer [*A publication*]
**MSV**.......... Magnetically Supported Vehicle
**MSV**.......... Maintenance Support Vessel
**MSV**.......... Maize Streak Virus
**MSV**.......... Manned Space Vehicle [*NASA*] (AAG)
**MSV**.......... Martian Surface Vehicle
**MSV**.......... Mass Stimulated Vehicles (MCD)
**MSV**.......... Mass Storage Volume
**MSV**.......... Maximal Sustained Level of Ventilation [*Medicine*]
**MSV**.......... Mean Square Velocity
**MSV**.......... Mean Square Voltage (NRCH)
**mSv**........... Millisievert [*Radiation dose*]
**MSV**.......... Miniature Solenoid Valve
**MSV**.......... Miscellanea Storica della Valdelsa [*A publication*]
**MSV**.......... Missionary Sisters of Verona [*Roman Catholic religious order*]
**MSV**.......... Mississippi & Skuna Valley Railroad Co. [*AAR code*]
**MSV**.......... Mobile Surface Vehicle (AAG)
**MSV**.......... Molecular Solution Volume
**MSV**.......... Molinia Streak Virus
**MSV**.......... Monitored Sine Vibration [*Test*] (MCD)
**MSV**.......... Monticello, NY [*Location identifier*] [*FAA*] (FAAL)
**MSV**.......... Mouse Sarcoma Virus
**MSV**.......... Multifunctional Service Vessel [*Off-shore drilling technology*]
**MSV**.......... Multipurpose Support Vessel [*Offshore drilling*]
**MSV**.......... Murine Sarcoma Virus
**MSV**.......... Musica sul Velluto (EAIO)
**MsV**........... Vicksburg Public Library, Vicksburg, MS [*Library symbol*] [*Library of Congress*] (LCLS)

**MSVC**........ Mass Storage Volume Control [*Data processing*] (BUR)
**MSVC**........ Mount St. Vincent College [*New York*]
**MSVCS**..... Missile Sight Video Camera Systems (MCD)
**MSVD**....... Missile and Space Vehicle Department [*NASA*] (KSC)
**MsVE**........ United States Army, Corps of Engineers, Waterways Experiment Station, Vicksburg, MS [*Library symbol*] [*Library of Congress*] (LCLS)
**MSV(M)**.... Murine Sarcoma Virus (Moloney)
**MsVO**........ Old Court House Museum Library, Vicksburg, MS [*Library symbol*] [*Library of Congress*] (LCLS)
**MSVP**........ Master Shuttle Verification Plan (MCD)
**MSVR**........ Mandatory Securities Valuation Reserve [*National Association of Insurance Commissioners*]
**MSW**......... Machine Status Word [*Data processing*]
**MSW**......... Macht Sich Wichtig (BJA)
**MSW**......... Magnetostatic Waves [*Telecommunications*] (TEL)
**MS & W**..... Maintenance Shop and Warehouse (NRCH)
**MSW**......... Massawa [*Ethiopia*] [*Airport symbol*] (OAG)
**MSW**......... Master of Social Welfare
**MSW**......... Master of Social Work
**MSW**......... Master Switch
**MSW**......... Mean Sea Water
**MSW**......... Mean Shallow Water
**MSW**......... Medical Social Worker [*British*]
**MSW**......... Meters of Seawater [*Deep-sea diving*]
**MSW**......... MI Software Co. [*Vancouver Stock Exchange symbol*]
**MSW**......... Microswitch (KSC)
**MSW**......... Microwave Spectrometer (TEL)
**MSW**......... Mikheyev-Smirnov-Wolfenstein Theory [*Oscillation effect*] [*Particle physics*]
**MSW**......... Mission West Properties [*AMEX symbol*] (SPSG)
**MSW**......... Multiple Shrapnel Wounds
**MSW**......... Municipal Solid Waste
**MSW**......... Western Massachusetts Regional Public Library System, Springfield, MA [*Library symbol*] [*Library of Congress*] (LCLS)
**MSWAP**.... Master of Social Welfare and Administration Planning
**MSWD**...... Mean Square Weighted Deviation [*Statistics*]
**MSWD**...... Multisystem Weapon Delivery [*Air Force*]
**MSWFA**.... Messwerte [*A publication*]
**MSWG**...... Manpower Systems Work Group
**MsWJ**....... Jefferson College, Washington, MS [*Library symbol*] [*Library of Congress*] [*Obsolete*] (LCLS)
**MSWJ**....... Midland and South Western Junction Railway [*British*]
**MsWov**...... Wilkinson County Library System, Woodville, MS [*Library symbol*] [*Library of Congress*] (LCLS)
**MsWp**........ Tombigbee Regional Library, West Point, MS [*Library symbol*] [*Library of Congress*] (LCLS)
**MsWpCt**.... Court House Library, West Point, MS [*Library symbol*] [*Library of Congress*] (LCLS)
**MsWpMH**... Mary Holmes College, West Point, MS [*Library symbol*] [*Library of Congress*] (LCLS)
**MsWv**........ Water Valley Public Library, Water Valley, MS [*Library symbol*] [*Library of Congress*] (LCLS)
**MSX**.......... Minesweeper, Experimental [*Navy symbol*]
**MSX**.......... Mossendjo [*Congo*] [*Airport symbol*] (OAG)
**MSX**.......... Multinucleate Nature, Spherical Shape, Unknown History
**MS3-X**....... Munitions System Support Structure - Extended [*Army*]
**MSY**.......... Maximum Sustainable Yield
**MSY**.......... Minimum Sustainable Yield [*Pisciculture*]
**MSY**.......... New Orleans [*Louisiana*] [*Airport symbol*]
**MsY**........... Yazoo-Sharkey Library System, Yazoo City, MS [*Library symbol*] [*Library of Congress*] (LCLS)
**MSYNAB**... Mosquito Systematics News Letter [*A publication*]
**MSYNC**..... Master Synchronization [*Telecommunications*] (TEL)
**MSYNC**..... Master Synchronizer (MSA)
**MSYS**........ Medical Technology Systems, Inc. [*NASDAQ symbol*] (NQ)
**M Sy Th**..... Master of Systematic Theology
**MSZ**.......... Massive Surf Zone
**MSZ**.......... Milford Sound [*New Zealand*] [*Seismograph station code, US Geological Survey*] (SEIS)
**MSZ**.......... Mossamedes [*Angola*] [*Airport symbol*] (OAG)
**MSzA**......... Mainzer Studien zur Amerikanistik [*A publication*]
**MSZDP**..... Magyar Szocial Demokrata Part [*Hungarian Social Democratic Party*] [*Political party*] (PPE)
**MSZMP**.... Magyar Szocialista Munkaspart [*Hungarian Socialist Workers' Party*] [*Political party*] (PPE)
**MSZS**........ Muenchener Studien zur Sprachwissenschaft [*A publication*]
**MT**............ Core Melt Through [*Nuclear energy*] (IEEE)
**MT**............ Empty [*Slang*]
**MT**............ Flame Tight
**MT**............ Internacia Asocio Monda Turismo [*International Association for World Tourism*] (EAIO)
**MT**............ Internal Revenue Bureau Miscellaneous Tax Ruling [*United States*] [*A publication*] (DLA)
**MT**............ Machine Tool
**MT**............ Machine Tool Technology Program [*Association of Independent Colleges and Schools specialization code*]
**MT**............ Machine Translation [*Data processing*]
**MT**............ Machine Translation [*A publication*]
**MT**............ Magnetic
**MT**............ Magnetic Particle Testing [*Nuclear energy*] (IEEE)
**MT**............ Magnetic Tape
**MT**............ Magnetic Tube
**mt**............. Magnetite [*CIPW classification*] [*Geology*]
**MT**............ Magnetotelluric [*Geological surveying*]
**MT**............ Mail Transfer
**MT**............ Mail Tray (AAG)
**MT**............ Main Telescope
**MT**............ Maintenance Technician (MUGU)
**M & T**........ Maintenance and Test (AAG)
**MT**............ Maintenance Time
**MT**............ Maintenance Trailer
**MT**............ Malaria Therapy [*British*]
**MT**............ Malignant Teratoma [*Oncology*]
**MT**............ Malta [*IYRU nationality code*] [*ANSI two-letter standard code*] (CNC)
**MT**............ Malta Air Charter Co. Ltd. [*ICAO designator*] (FAAC)
**MT**............ Mammary Tumor [*Medicine*]
**MT**............ Mammilothalamic Tract [*Anatomy*]
**MT**............ Management Today [*A publication*]
**MT**............ Mandated Territory
**MT**............ Mantle Tentacle
**MT**............ Manual Test
**M/T**........... Manual Transmission [*Automotive engineering*]
**MT**............ Manufacturing Technology (RDA)
**MT**............ Mare Tranquillitatis [*Sea of Tranquility*] [*Lunar area*]
**MT**............ Maritime Tropical Air Mass
**MT**............ Market Town [*Geographical division*] [*British*]
**MT**............ Marvel Tales [*A publication*]
**MT**............ Marxism Today [*A publication*]
**MT**............ Masking Template (MCD)
**MT**............ Masoretic Text [*of the Bible*] [*Hebrew tradition*]
**MT**............ Master Teacher (ADA)
**MT**............ Master of Teaching
**MT**............ Master Timer
**MT**............ Master Tool (NASA)
**MT**............ Mat
**MT**............ Matematisk Tidsskrift [*A publication*]
**MT**............ Material Transfer (NRCH)
**MT**............ Materials Test (IEEE)
**Mt**............. Matthew [*New Testament book*]
**MT**............ Maximal Therapy [*Medicine*]
**MT**............ Maximum Torque
**MT**............ Mean Tide [*Tides and currents*]
**MT**............ Mean Time
**MT**............ Measured Time
**MT**............ Measurement Ton (MUGU)
**MT**............ Mechanical Technician (KSC)
**MT**............ Mechanical Test (MCD)
**MT**............ Mechanical Time [*Fuse*] (AABC)
**MT**............ Mechanical Traction [*British military*] (DMA)
**MT**............ Mechanical Translation [*Data processing*]
**MT**............ Mechanical Translation [*A publication*]
**MT**............ Mechanical Transport
**MT**............ Mediaeval Towns [*A publication*]
**MT**............ Medial Triceps Brachii [*Medicine*]
**MT**............ MediaTel [*Database*] [*British*]
**MT**............ Medical Technician [*British military*] (DMA)
**MT**............ Medical Technologist
**MT**............ Medical Times and Gazette [*London*] [*A publication*]
**MT**............ Meditrust SBI [*NYSE symbol*] (SPSG)
**MT**............ Medium Truck [*British*]
**mt**............. Meerestechnik [*A publication*]
**MT**............ Megaton [*Nuclear equivalent of one million tons of high explosive*] (AFM)
**MT**............ Megatron (CET)
**MT**............ Melt Through [*Nuclear energy*] (NRCH)
**MT**............ Membrana Tympani [*Anatomy*]
**MT**............ Mesenteric Traction [*Medicine*]
**MT**............ Mesotocin [*Endocrinology*]
**MT**............ Metal Threshold (AAG)
**MT**............ Metallothionein [*Biochemistry*]
**MT**............ Metatarsal [*Anatomy*]
**MT**............ Meteor Construzioni Aeronautiche & Elettroniche SpA [*Italy*] [*ICAO aircraft manufacturer identifier*] (ICAO)
**MT**............ Meter (MCD)
**MT**............ Methoxytryptamine [*Biochemistry*]
**MT**............ Methoxytyramine [*Biochemistry*]
**MT**............ Methyltryptophan [*Biochemistry*]
**MT**............ Methyltyrosine [*Biochemistry*]
**MT**............ Metric Ton [*1,000 kilograms*]
**MT**............ Michaelmas Term [*British*] [*Legal term*] (ROG)
**MT**............ Microptic Theodolite
**MT**............ Microthrombus [*Hematology*]
**MT**............ Microtome [*Instrumentation*]
**MT**............ Microtubule [*Cytology*]
**MT**............ Microwave Thermograph [*Medical instrumentation*]
**MT**............ Middle Temple [*London*] [*One of the Inns of Court*]
**MT**............ Middle Temporal [*Anatomy*]
**MT**............ Middle Temporal Lobe [*of the brain*]
**MT**............ Midrash Tanna'im (BJA)

**MT** ............ Midship Deep Tank
**MT** ............ Might
**MT** ............ Migratory Trout
**MT** ............ Military Tanker [*British*]
**MT** ............ Military Technician
**MT** ............ Military Tractor [*British*]
**MT** ............ Military Train [*British military*] (DMA)
**MT** ............ Military Training
**MT** ............ Military Transport
**mT** ............ Millitesla
**MT** ............ Minimum Temperature (DS)
**MT** ............ Minimum Transfer (DCTA)
**MT** ............ Ministry of Transport [*Later, DOE*] [*British*]
**MT** ............ Mishneh Torah [*Maimonides*] (BJA)
**MT** ............ Missile Technician [*Navy rating*]
**MT** ............ Missile Test
**MT** ............ Missile Tilt
**MT** ............ Mission Time (MCD)
**MT** ............ Mission Trajectory (MCD)
**MT** ............ Mitomycin [*Also, M, MC*] [*Antineoplastic drug*]
**MT** ............ Mitral [*Valve*] [*Cardiology*]
**MT** ............ Mo Time [*An association*] (EA)
**MT** ............ Mobile Traveler [*Recreational vehicle*]
**MT** ............ Moccasin Telegraph. Fort Chipewyan [*A publication*]
**MT** ............ Mode Transducer
**MT** ............ Modified Tape Armor [*Telecommunications*] (TEL)
**MT** ............ Modus Tolens [*Rule of inference*] [*Logic*] [*Latin*]
**MT** ............ Montana [*Postal code*]
**MT** ............ Montana Reports [*A publication*] (DLA)
**Mt** ............ Montana State Library, Helena, MT [*Library symbol*] [*Library of Congress*] (LCLS)
**Mt** ............ Montant [*Amount*] [*Business term*] [*French*]
**MT** ............ More Than
**MT** ............ Motor Driver [*British military*] (DMA)
**MT** ............ Motor Tanker
**MT** ............ Motor Threshold [*Medicine*]
**MT** ............ Motor Transport [*Military*]
**MT** ............ Mount [*Maps and charts*] (KSC)
**MT** ............ Mountain [*Board on Geographic Names*]
**MT** ............ Mountain Time
**MT** ............ Mounted [*Technical drawings*]
**MT** ............ Mountings [*JETDS nomenclature*] [*Military*] (CET)
**MT** ............ Movement Time [*Physical education*]
**M and T** ..... Movements and Transports (NATG)
**MT** ............ MTC Electronic [*Vancouver Stock Exchange symbol*]
**MT** ............ Muertos Trough [*Geology*]
**MT** ............ Multiple Transfer
**MT** ............ Multitasking
**MT** ............ Museum Tusculanum [*A publication*]
**MT** ............ Music Theory Spectrum [*A publication*]
**MT** ............ Music Therapist [*or Therapy*]
**MT** ............ Musical Times [*A publication*]
**MT** ............ MUX [*Multiplex*] Terminal (MCD)
**Mt** ............ Mycobacterium Tuberculosis [*Bacteriology*]
**MT** ............ Myelotomography [*Medicine*]
**MT** ............ Transcona Public Library, Manitoba [*Library symbol*] [*National Library of Canada*] (NLC)
**MT1** .......... Missile Technician, First Class [*Navy rating*]
**MT2** .......... Missile Technician, Second Class [*Navy rating*]
**MT3** .......... Missile Technician, Third Class [*Navy rating*]
**MTA** .......... MAC [*Military Airlift Command*] Transportation Authorization (AFM)
**MTA** .......... Mack Trucks Australia
**MTA** .......... Magnetic Tape Accessory [*General Electric Co.*]
**MTA** .......... Magyar Tudomanyos Akademia. Nyelv-es Irodalomtudomanyi Osztalyanak. Koezlemenyei [*A publication*]
**MTA** .......... Maintenance Task Analysis
**MTA** .......... Major Test Article (NASA)
**MTA** .......... Major Training Area [*Army*]
**MTA** .......... Management Transactions Audit [*Test*]
**MTA** .......... Manual Target Acquisition (MCD)
**MTA** .......... Marionette Theate of Australia
**MTA** .......... Maritime Training Association (EA)
**MTA** .......... Mark Twain Association (EA)
**MTA** .......... Mass Thermal Analysis (MCD)
**MTA** .......... Master Timer Assembly
**MTA** .......... Materials Engineering [*A publication*]
**MTA** .......... Materials Testing Activity (MCD)
**MTA** .......... Materiel Transfer Agreement [*DoD*]
**MTA** .......... Media Technology Associates Ltd. [*Bethesda, MD*] [*Telecommunications service*] (TSSD)
**MTA** .......... Medical and Technical Assistant
**MTA** .......... Melamine Tableware Association (EA)
**MTA** .......... Message Terminal Area (MCD)
**MTA** .......... Meta Communications Group, Inc. [*Toronto Stock Exchange symbol*]
**MTA** .......... MetaTechnologies Associates [*Oakland, CA*] [*Telecommunications service*] (TSSD)
**MTA** .......... Methods-Time Analysis [*Industrial engineering*]
**MTA** .......... Methylthionadenosine [*Biochemistry*]
**MTA** .......... Metropolitan Transit Authority [*Later, MBTA*] [*Initialism also title of folk song about Boston's transit system*]
**MTA** .......... Metropolitan Transportation Authority [*Greater New York City*]
**MTA** .......... Metropolitan Travel Agents [*Inactive*] (EA)
**MTA** .......... Mid-West Truckers Association (EA)
**MTA** .......... Midterm Availability
**MTA** .......... Military Testing Association (MCD)
**MTA** .......... Military Training Airspace (NATG)
**MTA** .......... Military Transportation Authorization [*Air Force*]
**MTA** .......... Miniature Truck Association (EA)
**MTA** .......... Minimum Terms Agreement
**MTA** .......... Minimum Terrain-Clearance Altitude [*Aviation*]
**MTA** .......... Minor Task Authorization [*Navy*]
**MTA** .......... Missile Tube Air
**MTA** .......... Mississippi Test Area [*Aerospace*] (AAG)
**MTA** .......... Mobile Training Assistance (CINC)
**MTA** .......... Mobility Test Article [*Lunar-surface rover*] [*NASA*]
**MTA** .......... Monopulse Tracking Antenna
**MTA** .......... Motion-Time Analysis
**MTA** .......... Motorhome Travelers Association (EA)
**MTA** .......... Mount Allison University Library [*UTLAS symbol*]
**MTA** .......... Mount Auburn Hospital, Cambridge, MA [*OCLC symbol*] (OCLC)
**MTA** .......... Movimiento Teresiano de Apostolado [*Teresian Apostolic Movement - TAM*] [*Rome, Italy*] (EAIO)
**MTA** .......... Multiple-Terminal Access [*Data processing*] (IBMDP)
**MTA** .......... Multiterminal Adapter (IEEE)
**MTA** .......... Multitumor Antibody [*Clinical chemistry*]
**MTA** .......... Municipal Treasurers Association of the United States and Canada
**MTA** .......... Museum Trustee Association (EA)
**MTA** .......... Musical Theatres Association
**MTa** .......... Taunton Public Library, Taunton, MA [*Library symbol*] [*Library of Congress*] (LCLS)
**MTA 4** ....... Medical Technician, Acting, 4th Class [*British military*] (DMA)
**MTAA** ....... Mopar Trans-Am Association [*Commercial firm*] (EA)
**MTaB** ........ Bristol County Law Library, Taunton, MA [*Library symbol*] [*Library of Congress*] (LCLS)
**MTAB** ....... Marginal Terrain Assault Bridge [*Military*] (RDA)
**MTAB** ....... Military Technical Acceptance Board (MCD)
**MTAC** ....... Mailers Technical Advisory Committee (EA)
**MTAC** ....... Mathematical Tables and Other Aids to Computation
**MTACCS** .. Marine Tactical Command and Control System (MCD)
**MTACLS** .. Marine Tactical Air Control and Landing System
**MTAD** ....... N-methyl-triazolinedione
**MTADS** ..... Marine Corps Tactical Data System (AFIT)
**MT & AETF** ... Missile Tilt and Azimuth Error Test Fixture
**MTAF** ....... Mediterranean Tactical Air Force Headquarters
**MTAG** ....... Manufacturing Technology Advisory Group [*DoD*] (RDA)
**MTaHi** ...... Old Colony Historical Society, Taunton, MA [*Library symbol*] [*Library of Congress*] (LCLS)
**MTAI** ........ Meal Tickets Authorized and Issued [*Army*] (AABC)
**MTAI** ........ Member of the Institute of Travel Agents [*British*]
**MTAI** ........ Minnesota Teacher Attitude Inventory
**MTAIF** ...... Member of the Australian Institute of Fund Raising
**MTAJ** ....... MTA [*Motor Traders Association of New South Wales*] Official Journal [*A publication*] (APTA)
**MTAK** ....... Magyar Tudomanyos Akademia Konyvtara [*Hungarian Academy of Sciences Library*] [*Budapest*] [*Information service or system*] (IID)
**MTAK** ....... Magyar Tudomanyos Akademia. Nyelv-es Irodalomtudomanyi Osztalyanak. Koezlemenyej [*A publication*]
**mTAL** ........ Medullary Thick Ascending Limb [*Anatomy*]
**MTAL** ........ Metallurgical Industries, Inc. [*NASDAQ symbol*] (NQ)
**MTAM** ....... Maritime Tropical Air Mass (MSA)
**MTANSW** ... Music Teachers Association of New South Wales [*Australia*]
**MTAP** ........ Management Technical Applications Plan (MCD)
**MTAR** ....... Manual Terrain Avoidance RADAR
**MTAR** ....... Moving Target Acquisition RADAR (MCD)
**MT(ASCP)** ... Registered Medical Technologist (American Society of Clinical Pathologists)
**MTAT** ....... Mean Turn-Around Time [*Quality control*]
**MTatD** ...... Materialy po Tatarskoj Dialektologii [*A publication*]
**MTA US & C** ... Municipal Treasurers Association of the US and Canada (EA)
**MTB** .......... Main Terminal Board
**MTB** .......... Maintenance Time Budget
**MTB** .......... Maintenance of True Bearing
**MTB** .......... Malaysian Tin Bureau (EA)
**MTB** .......... Marine Test Boat
**MTB** .......... Materials Testing Branch [*Kennedy Space Center*]
**MTB** .......... Materials Transportation Bureau [*Department of Transportation*]
**MTB** .......... Mechanical Time Base
**MTB** .......... Medium Tank Battalion
**MTB** .......... Message to Base
**MTB** .......... Methantheline [*or Methanthine*] Bromide [*Pharmacology*]
**MTB** .......... Methoxy(trifluoromethyl)butyrophenone [*Biochemistry*]
**MTB** .......... Methylthymol Blue [*An indicator*] [*Chemistry*]
**MTB** .......... Modified Tyrode's Buffer [*Clinical chemistry*]

**MTB** .......... Module Test Bed [*Military*] (CAAL)
**MTB** .......... Monte Libano [*Colombia*] [*Airport symbol*] (OAG)
**MTB** .......... Monterey, CA [*Location identifier*] [*FAA*] (FAAL)
**MTB** .......... (Morpholinylthio)benzothiazole [*Organic chemistry*]
**MTB** .......... Motor Tariff Bureau, Charleston WV [*STAC*]
**MTB** .......... Motor Torpedo Boat
**MTB** .......... Multichannel Triple Bridge
**MTB** .......... Seaplane Bomber [*Russian symbol*]
**MTB** .......... Tokyo. Toyo Bunko [*Oriental Library*]. Research Department. Memoirs [*A publication*]
**MTBA** ....... Machine Tool Builders' Association
**MTBA** ....... Methyl-tert-butylaniline [*Organic chemistry*]
**MTBAMA** ... Mean Time between Any Maintenance Actions [*Quality control*] (MCD)
**MTBASIC** ... Multitasking BASIC [*Data processing*]
**MTBC**......... MetroBanc, Federal Savings Bank [*Grand Rapids, MI*] [*NASDAQ symbol*] (NQ)
**MtBC**......... Montana State University at Bozeman, Bozeman, MT [*Library symbol*] [*Library of Congress*] (LCLS)
**MTBCF**..... Mean Time between Confirmed Failures [*Quality control*]
**MTBCF**..... Mission Time between Critical Failures
**MTBCME** ... Mean Time between Corrective Maintenance Events [*Quality control*] (CAAL)
**MTBCMI**.. Mean Time between Corrective Maintenance Interrupts [*Quality control*] (CAAL)
**MTBD** ....... Mean Time between Degradations [*Quality control*] [*Telecommunications*] (TEL)
**MTBD** ....... Mean Time between Demands [*Quality control*] (MCD)
**MTBD** ....... Mean Time between Discrepancies [*Quality control*]
**MTBD** ....... Methyl(triazabicyclo)decene [*Organic chemistry*]
**MTBDE**..... Mean Time between Downing Events [*Quality control*]
**MTBE**........ Mean Time between Errors [*Quality control*]
**MTBE**........ Mean Time between Events [*Quality control*]
**MTBE**........ Methyl Tertiary Butyl Ether [*Fuel additive*]
**MTBEMA** ... Mean Time between Essential Maintenance Actions [*Quality control*]
**MTBERA**.. Mean Time between Essential Replacement Actions [*Quality control*]
**MTBETF**... Methyl Tertiary Butyl Ether Task Force (EA)
**MTBF**........ Mean Time between [*or before*] Failures [*Quality control*]
**MTBFA**..... Mean Time between False Alarms [*Quality control*] (AABC)
**MTBFC**..... Mean Time between Flight Cancellations [*Quality control*]
**MTBFEC**... Motor Truck, Bus, and Fire Engine Club (EA)
**MTBFL**..... Mean Time between Function Loss [*Quality control*]
**MTBFRO** ... Mean Time between Failures Requiring Overhaul [*Quality control*]
**MTBHA**.... Mark Twain Boyhood Home Associates (EA)
**MTBHQ**.... Mono-Tertiarybutylhydroquinone [*Also, TBHQ*] [*Organic chemistry*]
**MTBI**......... Mean Time between Interrupts [*Quality control*]
**MtBil** ......... Billings Public Library, Billings, MT [*Library symbol*] [*Library of Congress*] (LCLS)
**MtBilB**....... Bureau of Land Management, Billings, MT [*Library symbol*] [*Library of Congress*] (LCLS)
**MtBilE**....... Eastern Montana College, Billings, MT [*Library symbol*] [*Library of Congress*] (LCLS)
**MtBilFW**... United States Fish and Wildlife, Billings, MT [*Library symbol*] [*Library of Congress*] (LCLS)
**MtBilGS**.... Church of Jesus Christ of Latter-Day Saints, Genealogical Society Library, Billings Branch, Billings, MT [*Library symbol*] [*Library of Congress*] (LCLS)
**MtBilR**....... Rocky Mountain College, Billings, MT [*Library symbol*] [*Library of Congress*] (LCLS)
**MtBilSV**.... Saint Vincents Hospital, Billings, MT [*Library symbol*] [*Library of Congress*] (LCLS)
**MTBM**...... Mean Time between Maintenance [*Quality control*] (AFM)
**MTBMA**... Mean Time between Maintenance Actions [*Quality control*]
**MTBMCF**... Mean Time between Mission Critical Failure [*Quality control*]
**MTBME**.... Mean Time between Malfunction Events [*Quality control*] (CAAL)
**MTBN**....... Motor Transportation Battalion [*Military*]
**MTBO**....... Mean Time between Outages [*Quality control*] [*Telecommunications*] (TEL)
**MTBO**....... Mean Time between Overhauls [*Quality control*] (MCD)
**MTBO**....... Minimum Time before Overhaul [*Quality control*]
**MTBOMF**... Mean Time between Operational Mission Failures [*Quality control*] (MCD)
**MTBR**........ Mean Time between Removal [*or Repair or Replacement*] [*Quality control*]
**MTBRDR**... Mean Time between Removal for Depot Repair [*Quality control*] (MCD)
**MTBRON**... Motor Torpedo Boat Squadron [*Navy*]
**MTBS**........ Mean Time between Service [*Quality control*] (MCD)
**MTBS**........ Methuen's Text-Books of Science [*A publication*]
**MTBS**........ Metro Bancshares, Inc. [*NASDAQ symbol*] (CTT)
**MTBSD**..... Mean Time between Supply Demands [*Quality control*] (MCD)
**MTBSF**..... Mean Time between Software Failures [*Quality control*] (CAAL)
**MTBSF**..... Mean Time between System Failures [*Quality control*]
**MTBSHF**.. Mean Time between System Hardware Failures [*Quality control*] (MCD)
**MTBSOF**.. Mean Time between System Operational Failures [*Quality control*] (MCD)
**MTBSP**..... Mobilization Troop Basic Stationing Plan (MCD)
**MTBSTC**... Motor Torpedo Boat Squadrons Training Center [*Melville, RI*] [*Navy*]
**MTBT**........ Miniature Thermal Bar Torch [*Army*] (RDA)
**MtBu**.......... Butte Free Public Library, Butte, MT [*Library symbol*] [*Library of Congress*] (LCLS)
**MtBuE**....... Montana Energy Research and Development Institute, Butte, MT [*Library symbol*] [*Library of Congress*] (LCLS)
**MtBULM**.. Union List of Montana Serials, Bozeman, MT [*Library symbol*] [*Library of Congress*] (LCLS)
**MtBuM**...... Montana College of Mineral Science and Technology, Butte, MT [*Library symbol*] [*Library of Congress*] (LCLS)
**MTBUMA** ... Mean Time between Unscheduled Maintenance Actions [*Quality control*]
**MTBUR**.... Mean Time between Unscheduled Removals [*or Replacements*] [*Quality control*]
**MTC**.......... Carroll College, Library, Helena, MT [*OCLC symbol*] (OCLC)
**MTC**.......... Machine Tool Control
**MTC**.......... Machine Trim Compensator (AAG)
**MTC**.......... Magnetic Tape Cassette [*Data processing*]
**MTC**.......... Magnetic Tape Channel [*Data processing*]
**MTC**.......... Magnetic Tape Control [*Data processing*]
**MTC**.......... Main Trunk Circuit [*World Meteorological Organization*] [*Telecommunications*] (TEL)
**MTC**.......... Maintenance Task Cycle
**MTC**.......... Maintenance Time Constraint (IEEE)
**MTC**.......... Majestic Resources [*Vancouver Stock Exchange symbol*]
**MTC**.......... Make Today Count (EA)
**MTC**.......... Maneuver Training Command [*Army*] (AABC)
**MTC**.......... Manhattan Theater Club
**MTC**.......... Manual Traffic Control (MCD)
**MTC**.......... Manufacturing Technology Centre of New Brunswick [*Research center*] (RCD)
**MTC**.......... Marcus Tullius Cicero [*Roman orator and author, 106-43 BC*]
**MTC**.......... Maritime Transport Committee [*OECD*] (DS)
**MTC**.......... Mass Transfer Coefficient
**MTC**.......... Master Tape Control
**MTC**.......... Master of Textile Chemistry
**MTC**.......... Master Thrust Control [*or Controller*] [*NASA*] (NASA)
**MTC**.......... Master Training Concept [*Problem solving*]
**MTC**.......... Material Testing Center
**MTC**.......... Materiel Testing Command [*Merged with Weapons and Mobility Command*] [*Army*]
**MTC**.......... Maximum Toxic Concentration [*Medicine*]
**MTC**.......... Maximum Track Capacity
**MTC**.......... Mechanical Torpedo Countermeasure [*Military*] (CAAL)
**MTC**.......... Mechanical Transport Corps
**MTC**.......... Medical Test Cabinet
**MTC**.......... Medical Training Center [*Later, Academy of Health Sciences*] [*Army*]
**MTC**.......... Medium Terminal Complexes (MCD)
**MTC**.......... Medullary Thyroid Carcinoma [*Medicine*]
**MTC**.......... Meet the Composer (EA)
**MTC**.......... Memory Test Computer [*SAGE*]
**MTC**.......... Message Table of Contents (MCD)
**MTC**.......... Message Transmission Controller
**MTC**.......... Meteorological Training Center
**Mtc**............ Methylthiocarbamoyl [*Biochemistry*]
**MTC**.......... Metocurine [*A muscle relaxant*]
**MTC**.......... Microelectronics Technology Centre [*Australia*]
**MTC**.......... MIDI [*Musical Instrument Digital Interface*] Time Code
**MTC**.......... Military Tactical Computer (MCD)
**MTC**.......... Military Training Cadets [*A boys' World War II organization*]
**MTC**.......... Military Transportation Command
**MTC**.......... Military Transportation Committee [*NATO*] (NATG)
**MTC**.......... Missile Technician, Chief [*Navy rating*]
**MTC**.......... Missile Test Center
**MTC**.......... Missile Transfer Car
**MTC**.......... Missile Tube Control
**MTC**.......... Mission and Test Computer
**MTC**.......... Mission and Traffic Control
**MTC**.......... Mitomycin C [*Mutamycin*] [*Also, Mi, MMC*] [*Antineoplastic drug*]
**MTC**.......... Mitsui Toatsu Chemicals, Inc. [*Japan*]
**MTC**.......... Mobile Target Carrier
**MTC**.......... Moderator Temperature Coefficient (NRCH)
**MTC**.......... Monsanto Company [*NYSE symbol*] (SPSG)
**MTC**.......... Morgan Territory [*California*] [*Seismograph station code, US Geological Survey*] (SEIS)
**MTC**.......... Morse Telegraph Club (EA)
**MTC**.......... Motor Transport Corps [*Military*]
**MTC**.......... Mount Clemens, MI [*Location identifier*] [*FAA*] (FAAL)
**MTC**.......... MOUT [*Military Operations on Urbanized Terrain*] Training Complex [*Army*] (INF)
**MTC**.......... Mouvement Traditionaliste Congolais [*Congolese Traditionalist Movement*]
**MTC**.......... Moving Target Carrier (MCD)

**MTC** .......... Multicomm Telecommunications Corporation [*Formerly, Mutual Satellite Services*]
**MTC** .......... Multiple Tube Counts
**MTC** .......... Multistate Tax Commission (EA)
**MTC** .......... Mystic Terminal Company [*AAR code*]
**MTC** .......... Ontario Ministry of Transportation and Communications [*Canada*] (TSSD)
**MTC** .......... Ontario Ministry of Transportation and Communications [*UTLAS symbol*]
**MTCA** ....... Cayes [*Haiti*] [*ICAO location identifier*] (ICLI)
**MTCA** ....... Magazine. Texas Commission on Alcoholism [*A publication*]
**MTCA** ....... Methyltetrahydrocarbolinecarboxylic Acid [*Organic chemistry*]
**MTCA** ....... Military Terminal Control Area
**MTCA** ....... Minimum Terrain-Clearance Altitude [*Aviation*]
**MTCA** ....... Ministry of Transport and Civil Aviation [*Later, MT*] [*British*] (MCD)
**MTCA** ....... Monitor and Test Control Area [*NASA*] (NASA)
**MTCA** ....... Multiple-Terminal Communication Adapter [*Data processing*]
**MTCACS** .. Marine Corps Tactical Command and Control System (MCD)
**MTCC** ....... Magnetic Technologies Corporation [*NASDAQ symbol*] (NQ)
**MTCC** ....... Master Timing and Control Circuit
**MTCC** ....... Military Air Transport Service [*later, Military Airlift Command*] Transport Control Center
**MTCC** ....... Modular Tactical Communications Center
**MTCD** ....... Microvolume Thermal Conductivity Detector [*Instrumentation*]
**MTCE**........ Maintenance [*Telecommunications*] (TEL)
**MTCE**........ Million Tons of Coal Equivalent [*A comparative unit of energy content widely used in the oil industry*]
**MT & CE**... Missile Test and Checkout Equipment
**MTCF**........ Mean Time to Catastrophic Failure [*Quality control*]
**MTCF**........ Missile Tube Comparator Fixture
**MtCG**......... Glacier County Library, Cut Bank, MT [*Library symbol*] [*Library of Congress*] (LCLS)
**MTCH**....... Cap Haitien Internacional [*Haiti*] [*ICAO location identifier*] (ICLI)
**MT Ch** ....... Master of Textile Chemistry
**MTCH**....... Mining Technology Clearing House [*British*] [*Information service or system*] (IID)
**MTCH**....... MTech Corp. [*Irving, TX*] [*NASDAQ symbol*] (NQ)
**MTCI**......... Magnetic Tape Control Interface (MCD)
**MTCI**......... Management Technologies, Inc. [*NASDAQ symbol*] (NQ)
**MTCL**........ First National Bank Corp. [*NASDAQ symbol*] (NQ)
**MTCL**........ Motorcycle
**MTCM** ...... Missile Technician, Master Chief [*Navy rating*]
**MTCO** ....... Macon Terminal Company [*AAR code*]
**MTCOECD** ... Maritime Transport Committee of the OECD [*Paris, France*] (EAIO)
**MTCP**........ Master of Town and Country Planning (ADA)
**MTCP**........ Ministry of Town and Country Planning [*British*]
**MTCPCI** ... Marine Technology Society. Annual Conference. Preprints [*A publication*]
**MTCR** ....... Missile Technology Control Regime [*US, Canada, Britain, France, West Germany, Japan*]
**MTCS**........ Meteor Trail Communications System
**MTCS**........ Minimal Terminal Communications System (NVT)
**MTCS**........ Minimum Teleprocessing Commmunications System
**MTCS**........ Missile Technician, Senior Chief [*Navy rating*]
**MTCU** ....... Magnetic Tape Control Unit [*Data processing*]
**MTCV** ....... Main Turbine Control Valve (IEEE)
**MTCW** ...... Major 20th-Century Writers [*A publication*]
**MTD**.......... Magnetic Tape Disk (MCD)
**MTD**.......... Main Technical Directorate (RDA)
**MTD**.......... Maintenance Task Demand File (MCD)
**MTD**.......... Maintenance Technology Development
**MTD**.......... Maintenance Training Department
**MTD**.......... Management Decision [*A publication*]
**MTD**.......... Manager, Traffic Department
**MTD**.......... Manager, Transportation Department
**MTD**.......... Manufacturing Technology Development (RDA)
**MTD**.......... Manufacturing Technology Directorate [*Army*] (RDA)
**MTD**.......... Manufacturing Technology Division [*Air Force*]
**MTD**.......... Maritime Trades Department, AFL-CIO [*American Federation of Labor and Congress of Industrial Organizations*] (EA)
**MTD**.......... Market Trends Digest [*A publication*]
**MTD**.......... Mass Tape Duplicator/Verifier [*Data processing*] (MCD)
**MTD**.......... Master Tape Data
**MTD**.......... Master of Textile Dyeing
**MTD**.......... Master Time Display
**MTD**.......... Master Tracking Data [*NASA*]
**MTD**.......... Master of Transport Design
**MTD**.......... Materiel Testing Directorate [*Army*] (RDA)
**MTD**.......... Maximum Tolerated Dose [*Medicine*]
**MTD**.......... Mean Temperature Difference
**MTD**.......... Mean Therapeutic Dose [*Medicine*]
**MTD**.......... Mean Tolerated Dose [*Medicine*]
**MTD**.......... Mean Tubular Diameter
**MTD**.......... Mechanical Road Transport Driver [*British military*] (DMA)
**MTD**.......... Meta-Toluenediamine [*Organic chemistry*]
**MTD**.......... Metacarpal Total Density [*Anatomy*]
**MTD**.......... Metal Trades Department, AFL-CIO [*American Federation of Labor and Congress of Industrial Organizations*] (EA)
**MTD**.......... Methyltriazolinedione [*Organic chemistry*]
**MTD**.......... Microwave Target Designator
**MTD**.......... Midwife Teacher's Diploma [*British*]
**MTD**.......... Military Test Directorate [*Program*] [*Army*] (RDA)
**MTD**.......... Minimal Toxic Dose (IEEE)
**MTD**.......... Mintel International Development Corp. [*Vancouver Stock Exchange symbol*]
**MTD**.......... Mitte Tales Doses [*Send Such Doses*] [*Pharmacy*]
**MTD**.......... Mobile Target Division [*Mine Force*] [*Navy*]
**MTD**.......... Mobile Training Detachment
**MTD**.......... Mobilization Table of Distribution [*Military*]
**MTD**.......... Mount Darwin [*Rhodesia*] [*Seismograph station code, US Geological Survey*] (SEIS)
**MTD**.......... Mounted
**MTD**.......... Moving Target Detector [*RADAR*]
**MTD**.......... Multiple Target Deception (MCD)
**MTD**.......... Multiple Target Discrimination (MCD)
**MTD**.......... Multiple Tile Duct [*Telecommunications*] (TEL)
**MTDA**....... Methyl Trimethylsilyl Dimethylketene Acetal [*Organic chemistry*]
**MTDA**....... Modification Table of Distribution and Allowances [*Army*] (AABC)
**MTDC**....... Modified Total Direct Costs [*Economics*]
**MTDDA**.... Minnesota Test for Differential Diagnosis of Aphasia [*Psychology*]
**MTDE**....... Maritime Tactical Data Exchange (NATG)
**MTDE**....... Modern Technology Demonstration Engine
**MT Des**...... Master of Textile Design
**MTDF**....... Master Tracking Data File [*NASA*]
**MTDFA**..... Metal Treatment and Drop Forging [*A publication*]
**MtDiGS**..... Church of Jesus Christ of Latter-Day Saints, Genealogical Society Library, Butte Stake Branch, Dillon Chapel, Dillon, MT [*Library symbol*] [*Library of Congress*] (LCLS)
**MtDiW**...... Western Montana College, Dillon, MT [*Library symbol*] [*Library of Congress*] (LCLS)
**MTDL**....... Multiple Tap Delay Line
**mtDNA**...... Deoxyribonucleic Acid, Mitochondrial [*Biochemistry, genetics*]
**MTDP**....... Medium Term Defense Plan (NATG)
**MTDP**....... Medium Term Development Plan [*Economics*] (FEA)
**MTDS**........ Manufacturing Test Data System (IEEE)
**MTDS**........ Marine Tactical Data System
**MTDS**........ Marine Toebreak Data System (NG)
**MTDS**........ Metallurgical and Thermochemical Data Service [*Department of Trade and Industry*] [*Information service or system*] (IID)
**MTDS**........ Missile Trajectory Data System (MUGU)
**MTDSK**..... Magnetic Tape Disk [*Data processing*] (NASA)
**MTDYA**.... Modern Trends in Dermatology [*A publication*]
**MTE**.......... Magnetosphere-Thermosphere Explorer [*NASA*]
**MTE**.......... Maintenance Test Equipment (MCD)
**MTE**.......... Maintenance Training Equipment (MCD)
**MTE**.......... Manteigas [*Portugal*] [*Seismograph station code, US Geological Survey*] (SEIS)
**MTE**.......... Master of Textile Engineering
**MTE**.......... Maximum Temperature Engine
**MTE**.......... Maximum Tracking Error
**M & TE**...... Measurement and Test Equipment (KSC)
**MTE**.......... Member of the Telegraph Engineers [*British*] (ROG)
**MTE**.......... Merit Technologies Ltd. [*Vancouver Stock Exchange symbol*]
**mte**............ Metal-Engraver [*MARC relator code*] [*Library of Congress*] (LCCP)
**MTE**.......... Microwave Test Equipment
**MTE**.......... Missile Test Engineer (MUGU)
**MTE**.......... Mitre Corp., Bedford Operations Library, Bedford, MA [*OCLC symbol*] (OCLC)
**MTE**.......... Mobile Telephone Exchange [*Nordic Mobile Telephone*]
**MTE**.......... Modern Technology Engine
**MTE**.......... Module Table Entry [*Data processing*] (BYTE)
**MTE**.......... Multiple Terminal Emulator
**MTE**.......... Multipurpose Test Equipment
**MTE**.......... Multisystem Test Equipment [*Military*]
**MTEA**....... Minimum Target Elevation Angle (MCD)
**MTEAA**..... (Methylthio)ethyl Acetoacetate [*Organic chemistry*]
**MTEC**........ Machine Technology, Inc. [*NASDAQ symbol*] (NQ)
**MTEC**........ Maintenance Test Equipment Catalog (MCD)
**MTec**......... Metric Tons Energy Consumption
**M Tech**...... Master of Technology
**MTEE**........ Maintenance Test Equipment, Electrical (NASA)
**MTEE**........ Mission Time Extreme Environment [*NASA*] (KSC)
**MTEEC**..... Maintenance Test Equipment, Electronic (NASA)
**MTEF**........ Maintenance Test Equipment, Fluid (NASA)
**MTEG**....... Port-Au-Prince [*Haiti*] [*ICAO location identifier*] (ICLI)
**MTEK**....... Monitek Technologies, Inc. [*NASDAQ symbol*] (NQ)
**MTEL**........ Manning Table and Equipment List
**MTEL**........ Materiel [*Military*] (FAAC)
**MTEL**........ MCS Telecommunications, Inc. [*NASDAQ symbol*] (NQ)
**MTEL**........ Methyltriethyllead [*Organic chemistry*]
**MTEM**...... Maintenance Test Equipment Module (MCD)
**MTEM**...... Mechanical Maintenance Test Equipment (NASA)

**MT Eng** ..... Master of Textile Engineering
**MTEO** ....... Maintenance Test Equipment, Optical (NASA)
**M'TER** ....... Manchester [*City in England*] (ROG)
**MTER** ........ Multitest Evaluation Report [*Nuclear energy*] (NRCH)
**MTES** ........ Metastable Transfer Emission Spectroscopy
**MTET** ........ Maximal Treadmill Exercise Test
**MTEWS/AD** ... Mobile Tactical Early Warning System for Air Defense [*NATO*]
**MTF** .......... Fairbanks, AK [*Location identifier*] [*FAA*] (FAAL)
**MTF** .......... Machine Tool Forum
**MTF** .......... Maintenance Test Flight (MCD)
**MTF** .......... Mean Time to Failure [*Quality control*]
**MTF** .......... Mechanical Time Fuze
**MTF** .......... Medical Treatment Facility (AABC)
**MTF** .......... Megawatt Transmitter Filter
**MTF** .......... Men's Tie Foundation [*Later, NAA*] (EA)
**MTF** .......... Metastable Time of Flight
**MTF** .......... Meteorological Task Force (MCD)
**MTF** .......... Microwave Test Facility
**MTF** .......... Military Treatment Facility [*DoD*]
**MTF** .......... Mississippi Test Facility [*Later, NSTL*] [*NASA*]
**MTF** .......... Mizan Teferi [*Ethiopia*] [*Airport symbol*] [*Obsolete*] (OAG)
**MTF** .......... Mock-Up Test Facility (MCD)
**MTF** .......... Modulation Transfer Function [*Resolution measure*]
**MTF** .......... Multiple Tube Fermentation
**MTF** .......... Multitarget Frequency
**MTFA** ........ Modulation Transfer Function Analyzer
**MTFC** ........ Masters Track and Field Committee (EA)
**MTFCA** ..... Model "T" Ford Club of America (EA)
**MTFCI** ...... Model T Ford Club International (EA)
**MTFD** ....... Minimum Tracking Flux Density
**MTFE** ....... Mercury Thin Film Electrode [*Electrochemistry*]
**MTFEX** ..... Mountain Field Exercise [*Military*] (NVT)
**MTFF** ........ Mean Time to First Failure [*Quality control*] (AAG)
**MtFhV** ....... United States Veterans Administration Center, Fort Harrison, MT [*Library symbol*] [*Library of Congress*] (LCLS)
**MTFL** ........ Man-Tended Free-Flying Laboratory [*European Space Agency*]
**MTFL** ........ Mean Time to Fault Locate [*Quality control*] (CAAL)
**MTFMPP** ... Meta-Trifluoromethylphenylpiperazine [*Biochemistry*]
**MTFO** ....... Modular Training Field Option (NASA)
**MTFP** ....... Marema Tlou Freedom Party [*Lesotho*]
**MTFR** ........ Metal Furring [*Technical drawings*]
**MTFR** ........ [*The*] Minnesota Transfer Railway Co. [*AAR code*]
**MTFS** ........ Marine Terminal Fuel Separator (MCD)
**MTFS** ........ Medium-Term Financial Strategy
**MTFTS** ..... Marine Terminal Fuel Tankage System (MCD)
**MtG** ........... Glendive Public Library, Glendive, MT [*Library symbol*] [*Library of Congress*] (LCLS)
**MTG** .......... Main Traffic Group [*Telecommunications*] (TEL)
**MTG** .......... Main Turbogenerator
**MTG** .......... Medical Times and Gazette [*London*] [*A publication*]
**MTG** .......... Meeting (AFM)
**MTG** .......... Melt-Textured Growth [*Chemistry*]
**MTG** .......... Methanol-to-Gasoline [*Process*] [*Mobil Oil Corp.*]
**MTG** .......... Methoxytriglycol [*Organic chemistry*]
**MTG** .......... Methyl Tetradecylglycidate [*Biochemistry*]
**MTG** .......... (Methyl)thiogalactoside [*Biochemistry*]
**MTG** .......... MGI Properties [*Formerly, Mortgage Growth Investors*] [*AMEX symbol*] (SPSG)
**MTG** .......... Montague Island [*Alaska*] [*Seismograph station code, US Geological Survey*] (SEIS)
**MTG** .......... Mortgage [*Finance*] (SPSG)
**MTG** .......... Motor-Torque Generator
**MtG** ........... Mount Gravatt College of Advanced Education [*Australia*]
**MTG** .......... Mounting
**MTG** .......... Multiple-Trigger Generator
**MTG** .......... Multipurpose Target Generator
**MTGAS** ..... Mechanical Transport Gasoline [*Military*] [*British*]
**MTGC** ....... Mounting Center (MSA)
**MTGCF** ..... Mobile Transportation Ground Command Facility (MCD)
**MtGD** ........ Dawson College, Glendive, MT [*Library symbol*] [*Library of Congress*] (LCLS)
**MTGD** ....... Mortgaged (ROG)
**MTGE** ....... Mortgage
**MTGEE** ..... Mortgagee
**Mt Geol** ...... Mountain Geologist [*A publication*]
**MTGF** ........ Mouse Transforming Growth Factor [*Biochemistry*]
**MtGl** .......... Glasgow City-County Library, Glasgow, MT [*Library symbol*] [*Library of Congress*] (LCLS)
**MTGOR** .... Mortgagor
**MTGP** ....... Monitor Table Generator Program (MCD)
**MtGr** .......... Great Falls Public Library, Great Falls, MT [*Library symbol*] [*Library of Congress*] (LCLS)
**MTGRB** ..... Metallographic Review [*A publication*]
**MtGrCE** .... College of Great Falls, Great Falls, MT [*Library symbol*] [*Library of Congress*] (LCLS)
**MtGrCH** .... Columbus Hospital, Health Sciences Library, Great Falls, MT [*Library symbol*] [*Library of Congress*] (LCLS)
**MtGrGS** .... Church of Jesus Christ of Latter-Day Saints, Genealogical Society Library, Great Falls Branch, Great Falls, MT [*Library symbol*] [*Library of Congress*] (LCLS)
**Mt Grow** .... Mountaineer Grower [*A publication*]
**MTGS** ........ Metal-to-Glass Seal
**MTGS** ........ Midcourse and Terminal Guidance System [*NASA*]
**MTGSA** ..... Mitteilungen aus dem Arbeitsbereich. Metallgesellschaft AG [*A publication*]
**MTGU** ....... Australian Master Tax Guide Updater [*A publication*]
**MTGW** ...... Maximum Total Gross Weight (MCD)
**MTG/WESS** ... Main Tank Gunfire/Weapon Effects Signature Simulator (MCD)
**MtH** ........... Helena Public Library, Helena, MT [*Library symbol*] [*Library of Congress*] (LCLS)
**MTH** .......... Magnetic Tape Handler [*Data processing*]
**MTH** .......... Marathon [*Florida*] [*Airport symbol*] (OAG)
**MTH** .......... Massachusetts Institute of Technology [*Cambridge, MA*] [*FAA designator*] (FAAC)
**M Th** .......... Master of Theology
**MTH** .......... Meath [*County in Ireland*] (ROG)
**MTH** .......... Methylthiohydantoin [*Organic chemistry*]
**MTH** .......... Microptic Theodolite
**MTH** .......... Mithramycin (Aureolic acid, mithracin) [*Antineoplastic drug*]
**MTH** .......... Month
**MTH** .......... Mount Holyoke College, South Hadley, MA [*OCLC symbol*] (OCLC)
**MTH** .......... Mount Hood Railway Co. [*Later, MH*] [*AAR code*]
**Mth** ............ Mouth [*Maps and charts*]
**MTH** .......... Thompson Public Library, Manitoba [*Library symbol*] [*National Library of Canada*] (NLC)
**MtHamRL** ... United States National Institute of Health, Rocky Mountain Laboratory Library, Hamilton, MT [*Library symbol*] [*Library of Congress*] (LCLS)
**MtHar** ........ Big Horn County Public Library, Hardin, MT [*Library symbol*] [*Library of Congress*] (LCLS)
**MTHB** ....... Mark Twain Home Board (EA)
**MTHBD** .... Motherboard (MSA)
**MtHC** ........ Carroll College, Helena, MT [*Library symbol*] [*Library of Congress*] (LCLS)
**MTHD** ....... Method (MSA)
**M Theol** ..... Master of Theology
**Mtherapie** ... Musiktherapie [*A publication*]
**MTHF** ....... Methyltetrahydrofolate [*or Methyltetrahydrofolic*] [*Biochemistry*]
**MTHF** ....... Methyltetrahydrofuran [*Organic chemistry*]
**MThGH** .... Metallothionein-Human Growth Hormone [*Endocrinology*]
**MtHGS** ...... Church of Jesus Christ of Latter-Day Saints, Genealogical Society Library, Helena Branch, Helena, MT [*Library symbol*] [*Library of Congress*] (LCLS)
**MTHHF** .... Methyltetrahydrohomofolate [*Biochemistry*]
**MtHi** .......... Montana Historical Society, Helena, MT [*Library symbol*] [*Library of Congress*] (LCLS)
**Mthly** ......... Monthly (DLA)
**Mthly Bull Constr Indices (Bldg Civil Engng)** ... Monthly Bulletin of Construction Indices (Building and Civil Engineering) [*A publication*]
**Mthly Dig Transp News** ... Monthly Digest of Transport News [*A publication*]
**Mthly Lab R** ... Monthly Labor Review [*A publication*]
**Mthly Publ Opin Surv** ... Monthly Public Opinion Surveys [*A publication*]
**Mthly R** ..... Monthly Review [*A publication*]
**MTHM** ...... Million Tons Heavy Metal
**MThPast** ... Maitre en Theologie Pastorale [*Master in Pastoral Theology*] [*French*]
**MTHR** ....... Merthyr [*Cardiff*] [*Welsh depot code*]
**MTHR** ....... Mother
**MTHRD** .... Male Threaded
**MThS** ........ Muenchener Theologische Studien [*A publication*]
**MtHS** ......... Shodair Children's Hospital, Helena, MT [*Library symbol*] [*Library of Congress*] (LCLS)
**MtHSP** ...... Saint Peter's Community Hospital, Helena, MT [*Library symbol*] [*Library of Congress*] (LCLS)
**MTHWL** ... Motherwell [*Scotland*]
**M Th Z** ...... Muenchener Theologische Zeitschrift [*A publication*]
**MTI** ........... Machine Tools Industry (MCD)
**MTI** ........... Maeventec Travel Information [*Maeventec*] [*Information service or system*] (CRD)
**MTI** ........... Magyar Tavirati Iroda [*Press agency*] [*Hungary*]
**MTI** ........... Main Tank Injection
**MTI** ........... Manitoba Technical Institute [*Canada*]
**MTI** ........... Manpower Training Institute
**MTI** ........... Marketing and Training Institute (EA)
**MTI** ........... Material Thickness Indicator
**MTI** ........... Materials Technology Institute of the Chemical Process Industries (EA)
**MTI** ........... Mechanical Technology, Inc.
**MTI** ........... Mechanical Tolerance Index [*Food technology*]
**MTI** ........... Media Technology International [*British*]
**MTI** ........... Metal Treating Institute (EA)
**MTI** ........... Methylthioinosine [*Biochemistry*]
**MTI** ........... Methyltransferase I [*An enzyme*]
**MTI** ........... Military Training Instructor (AFM)
**MTI** ........... Minimum Time Interval [*Medicine*]
**MTI** ........... Missile Training Installation (NATG)

**MTI** ........... Mobile Training Institute [*Klamath Falls, OR*] [*Telecommunications service*] (TSSD)
**MTI** ........... Modern Telecommunications, Incorporated [*New York, NY*] (TSSD)
**MTI** ........... Morton Thiokol, Inc. [*Later, TKC*] [*NYSE symbol*] (SPSG)
**MTI** ........... Mosteiros [*Cape Verde Islands*] [*Airport symbol*] (OAG)
**MTI** ........... Mouvement de la Tendance Islamique [*Islamic Trend Movement*] [*Tunisia*] (PD)
**MTI** ........... Moving Target Indicator
**MTIAA**...... Metalurgiya [*Sofia, Bulgaria*] [*A publication*]
**MTIAC**...... Manufacturing Technology Information Analysis Center [*DoD*] [*Information service or system*] (IID)
**MTIB**......... Malaysian Timber Industry Board (DS)
**MTIC**......... Malaysia Tourist Information Center (EA)
**MTIC**......... Moving Target Indicator Coherent (IEEE)
**MTICFAR** ... Moving Target Indicator Constant False Alarm Rate (CET)
**MTIE**......... Microthrust Ion Engine
**MTIF**......... Maritime Technical Information Facility [*Maritime Administration*] [*Database producer*] (IID)
**MTIF**......... Master Tailored Interest File [*Navy*] (NG)
**MTIK**......... Miller Building Systems, Inc. [*NASDAQ symbol*] (NQ)
**MTIK**......... Missile Test Installation Kit
**MTIK**......... Moving Target Indicator Kit
**M Times** .... Musical Times [*A publication*]
**MTIRA**...... Machine Tool Industry Research Association [*British*]
**M Tire Dealr** ... Modern Tire Dealer [*A publication*]
**MTIS**......... Maintenance Task Information System (NG)
**MTIS**......... Material Turned into Stores
**MTIS**......... Mean Time in Shop [*Quality control*] (MCD)
**MTIS**......... MTI Systems Corp. [*NASDAQ symbol*] (NQ)
**MTIX**......... Mechanical Technology, Inc. [*NASDAQ symbol*] (NQ)
**MTJ**........... Mark Twain Journal [*A publication*]
**MTJ**........... Mesifta Tifereth Jerusalem (BJA)
**MTJ**........... Missile Track Jamming [*Military*] (CAAL)
**MTJ**........... Montrose [*Colorado*] [*Airport symbol*] (OAG)
**MTJ**........... Mount Tsukuba [*Japan*] [*Seismograph station code, US Geological Survey*] (SEIS)
**MTJA**........ Jacmel [*Haiti*] [*ICAO location identifier*] (ICLI)
**MTJE**......... Jeremie [*Haiti*] [*ICAO location identifier*] (ICLI)
**MTK**.......... Camp Ripley/Little Falls, MN [*Location identifier*] [*FAA*] (FAAL)
**MtK** ........... Flathead County Free Library, Kalispell, MT [*Library symbol*] [*Library of Congress*] (LCLS)
**MTK**.......... Makin [*Kiribati*] [*Airport symbol*] (OAG)
**MTK**.......... Mechanical Time Keeping (NASA)
**MTK**.......... Medium Tank
**MTK**.......... Mintek Resources [*Vancouver Stock Exchange symbol*]
**MTK**.......... Mitaka [*Japan*] [*Seismograph station code, US Geological Survey*] [*Closed*] (SEIS)
**MtKF**......... Flathead Valley Community College, Kalispell, MT [*Library symbol*] [*Library of Congress*] (LCLS)
**MtKGS**...... Church of Jesus Christ of Latter-Day Saints, Genealogical Society Library, Kalispell Branch, Kalispell, MT [*Library symbol*] [*Library of Congress*] (LCLS)
**MtKH**........ Kalispell Regional Hospital, Kalispell, MT [*Library symbol*] [*Library of Congress*] (LCLS)
**MTL**.......... Main Transfer Line (MCD)
**MTL**.......... Maitland [*Australia*] [*Airport symbol*] (OAG)
**MTL**.......... Manufacturing and Technology Laboratory
**MTL**.......... Master Tape Loading
**MTL**.......... Matched Transmission Line
**MTL**.......... Material (KSC)
**MTL**.......... Materials Research Corp. [*AMEX symbol*] (SPSG)
**MTL**.......... Materials Technology Laboratory [*Army*] [*Watertown, MA*] (RDA)
**MTL**.......... Materials Test Loop [*Nuclear energy*] (NRCH)
**MTL**.......... Mean Tide Level [*Tides and currents*]
**MTL**.......... Medial Temporal Lobe [*Brain anatomy*]
**MTL**.......... Median Tolerance Limit [*Toxicity*]
**MTL**.......... Medium Term Loan (DCTA)
**MTL**.......... Merged-Transistor Logic
**MTL**.......... Metal (AAG)
**MTL**.......... Minimum Time Limit
**MTL**.......... Mobilization Training Loss [*Military*]
**MTL**.......... Mobiltherm Light (NRCH)
**Mt-L**.......... Montana State Law Library, Helena, MT [*Library symbol*] [*Library of Congress*] (LCLS)
**MTL**.......... Motivation and Training Laboratory [*Army*] (RDA)
**MTL**.......... Mount Taylor [*New Mexico*] [*Seismograph station code, US Geological Survey*] (SEIS)
**MTLA**........ Micropublishers' Trade List Annual [*A publication*]
**MTLC**........ Metalclad Corp. [*NASDAQ symbol*] (NQ)
**MTLC**........ Metallic (MSA)
**MTLD**........ Mouvement pour le Triomphe des Libertes Democratiques [*Movement for the Triumph of Democratic Liberties*] [*Algerian*]
**MtLe**.......... Lewistown City Library, Lewistown, MT [*Library symbol*] [*Library of Congress*] (LCLS)
**Mtlg**........... Mitteilung [*Report*] [*German*] (BJA)
**MTLGA**..... Metallurgie [*A publication*]
**MTLI**......... Marine Transport Lines, Incorporated [*NASDAQ symbol*] (NQ)
**MTLP**........ Master Tape Loading Program
**MTLP**........ Metabolic Toxemia of Late Pregnancy [*Medicine*]
**MTLP**........ Monitor Table Listing Program (NASA)
**MTLR**........ Moving Target Locating RADAR (AABC)
**MTLS**........ Munitions Transfer [*or Transporter*] and Loading System (MCD)
**M-TLX**...... Mitsubishi Transfer-Line Heat Exchanger
**MTLZ**........ Metallize (MSA)
**MTM**......... Journal of Methods-Time Measurement [*A publication*]
**MTM**......... Maintenance Test Module
**MTM**......... Management Team [*A publication*]
**MTM**......... Manpower Tradeoff Methodology [*Military*]
**MTM**......... Marches Tropicaux et Mediterraneens [*A publication*]
**MTM**......... Mark-to-Market [*Securities*]
**MTM**......... Mark Twain Memorial (EA)
**MTM**......... Marketing Times [*A publication*]
**MTM**......... Marlborough Technical Management [*British*]
**MTM**......... Mary Tyler Moore [*Actress after whom film studio MTM Enterprises is named*]
**MTM**......... Matsumoto [*Japan*] [*Seismograph station code, US Geological Survey*] (SEIS)
**MTM**......... Mean Time Measurement
**MTM**......... Mechanical Road Transport Mechanic [*British military*] (DMA)
**MTM**......... Mechanical Test Model
**MTM**......... Methods-Time Measurement [*Industrial engineering*]
**MTM**......... Metlakatla [*Alaska*] [*Airport symbol*] (OAG)
**MTM**......... Metlakatla, AK [*Location identifier*] [*FAA*] (FAAL)
**MTM**......... Michelin Tire Monitor [*System*] [*Automotive engineering*]
**MTM**......... Million Ton Miles
**MTM**......... Million Train Miles
**MTM**......... Mobile Transfer Method (AAG)
**MTM**......... Modified Thayer-Martin [*Medium*] [*Microbiology*]
**MTM**......... Modular Torque Motor
**MTM**......... Moving Terrain Model
**MTM**......... Mt. Grant Mines Ltd. [*Vancouver Stock Exchange symbol*]
**MTM**......... MTM [*Methods-Time Measurement*] Association for Standards and Research (EA)
**MTM**......... MTM Productions, Inc. [*Named for actress Mary Tyler Moore*]
**MTM**......... Multiple Threat Modulation [*Military*] (CAAL)
**MTM's**....... Magnetic Tape Transmissions (CET)
**MTMA**...... Military Terminal Major Aerodromes (NATG)
**MTMA**...... Military Traffic Management Agency [*Later, DTMS*]
**MTMASR** ... MTM [*Methods-Time Measurement*] Association for Standards and Research [*Later, MTM*] (EA)
**MTMC**...... (Methylthio)-meta-Cresol [*Organic chemistry*]
**MtMc**......... Miles City Public Library, Miles City, MT [*Library symbol*] [*Library of Congress*] (LCLS)
**MTMC**...... Military Traffic Management Command [*DoD*]
**MtMcC**...... Miles Community College, Miles City, MT [*Library symbol*] [*Library of Congress*] (LCLS)
**MTMCEA** ... Military Traffic Management Command, Eastern Area [*Bayonne, NJ*]
**MTMCTEA** ... Military Traffic Management Command Transportation Engineering Agency (AABC)
**MTMCTTU** ... Military Traffic Management Command Transportation Terminal Unit (AABC)
**MTMCWA** ... Military Traffic Management Command, Western Area [*Oakland, CA*]
**MT/MF**..... Magnetic Tape to Microfilm
**MtMis**........ Missoula Public and Missoula County Free Library, Missoula, MT [*Library symbol*] [*Library of Congress*] (LCLS)
**MtMisGS**.. Church of Jesus Christ of Latter-Day Saints, Genealogical Society Library, Missoula Branch, Missoula, MT [*Library symbol*] [*Library of Congress*] (LCLS)
**MtMisSP**... Saint Patrick Hospital, Missoula, MT [*Library symbol*] [*Library of Congress*] (LCLS)
**MtMisW**.... Western Montana Clinic, Missoula, MT [*Library symbol*] [*Library of Congress*] (LCLS)
**MTML**...... Metromail Corp. [*Lincoln, NE*] [*NASDAQ symbol*] (NQ)
**MTMR**...... Military Traffic Management Regulation
**MTMS**....... Metal-to-Metal Seal
**MTMS**....... Military Traffic Management Service (MCD)
**MTMS**....... Mobilization Training Management System [*DoD*]
**MTMTS**.... Military Traffic Management and Terminal Service [*Later, MTMC*] [*Army*]
**MTN**.......... Baltimore, MD [*Location identifier*] [*FAA*] (FAAL)
**MTN**.......... Manton [*Australia*] [*Seismograph station code, US Geological Survey*] (SEIS)
**MTN**.......... Medium-Term Note [*Finance*]
**MTN**.......... Mirtone International, Inc. [*Toronto Stock Exchange symbol*]
**MTN**.......... Mizlou Television Network
**MTN**.......... Mobil Producing TX & NM, Inc., Houston, TX [*OCLC symbol*] (OCLC)
**MTN**.......... Motion (MSA)
**MTN**.......... Mountain
**MTN**.......... Mountain Medical Equipment, Inc. [*AMEX symbol*] (SPSG)
**MTN**.......... Multilateral Trade Negotiations

**MTNA**....... Montana Naturals International, Inc. [*NASDAQ symbol*] (NQ)
**MTNA**....... Music Teachers National Association (EA)
**MTND**....... Mercury Tube Nutation Damper
**MTNFC**...... Mel Tillis National Fan Club (EA)
**MTNG**....... Mandated Territory of New Guinea [*Australia*]
**MTNHP**.... Montana Natural Heritage Program [*Helena, MT*] [*Information service or system*] (IID)
**MTNI**........ Mirtone International, Inc. [*Downsview, ON*] [*NASDAQ symbol*] (NQ)
**MTNR**....... Mountaineer Bankshares of West Virginia [*Martinsburg, WV*] [*NASDAQ symbol*] (NQ)
**MTNS**....... Metal-Thick Oxide-Nitride-Silicon
**MTO**.......... Magnetic Tape Operator (MCD)
**MTO**.......... Maintenance Technology Office [*Air Force Logistics Command*]
**MTO**.......... Management Today [*A publication*]
**MTO**.......... Master Timing Oscillator (MCD)
**MTO**.......... Mattoon [*Illinois*] [*Airport symbol*] (OAG)
**MTO**.......... Maximum Time Out (MCD)
**MTO**.......... Medical Transport Officer [*Navy*]
**MTO**.......... Mediterranean Theater of Operations, United States Army [*Shortened form of MTOUSA*] [*World War II*]
**MTO**.......... Message Terminal Operation [*Military*] (CAAL)
**MTO**.......... Methanol-to-Olefin [*Process*]
**MTO**.......... Mission, Task, Objective
**MTO**.......... Mississippi Test Operations [*NASA*]
**MTO**.......... Modification Task Outline (KSC)
**MTO**.......... Motor Transport Officer [*Military*]
**MTO**.......... Mouvement Togolais pour la Democratie [*Togolese Movement for Democracy*] [*Political party*] (PD)
**MTO**.......... Movement Transfer Order (MCD)
**MTO**.......... Multimodal Transport Operator
**MTOB**....... Manned Test Operations Board [*NASA*]
**MTOC**....... Microtubular Organizing Complex [*Physiology*]
**MTOC**....... Microtubule Organizing Center [*Cytology*]
**MTOC**....... Mitotic Organizing Center [*Cytology*]
**MTOE**....... Million Tons of Oil Equivalent
**MTOE**....... Modification Table of Organization and Equipment [*Army*] (AABC)
**MTOGW**... Maximum Takeoff Gross Weight [*Aviation*] (MCD)
**MTOK**....... Microphonics Technology Corp. [*Auburn, WA*] [*NASDAQ symbol*] (NQ)
**M i TOM**... Metallovedenie i Termiceskaja Obrabotka Metallov [*A publication*]
**MTON**....... Measurement Ton
**Mtone News**... Movietone News [*A publication*]
**MTONS**.... Metal-Thick Oxide-Nitride-Silicon (MSA)
**MTOP**...... Molecular Total Overlap Population (IEEE)
**MTOR**....... Meritor Savings Bank [*Philadelphia, PA*] [*NASDAQ symbol*] (NQ)
**MTORQ**.... Maximum Torque
**MTOS**....... Magnetic Tape Operations System [*Data processing*] (NRCH)
**MTOS**....... Major Trauma Outcome Study [*American College of Surgeons Committee on Trauma*]
**MTOS**....... Metal-Thick Oxide-Silicon
**MTOUSA**... Mediterranean Theater of Operations, United States Army [*Sometimes shortened to MTO*] [*World War II*]
**MTOW**...... Maximum Takeoff Weight [*Aviation*] (MCD)
**MTP**.......... Island Helicopter, Inc. [*Long Island, NY*] [*FAA designator*] (FAAC)
**MTP**.......... Maintenance Test Package (MCD)
**MTP**.......... Manufacturing Technical Procedure [*NASA*] (NASA)
**MTP**.......... Manufacturing Technology Program [*Aviation Systems Command*] (RDA)
**MTP**.......... Manufacturing Technology Projects [*Manufacturing Technology Information Analysis Center*] [*Information service or system*] (CRD)
**MTP**.......... Manufacturing Test Procedure
**M & TP**...... Manufacturing and Testing Process (KSC)
**MTP**.......... Master Test Plan (KSC)
**MTP**.......... Master of Town and Country Planning
**MTP**.......... Master of Town Planning
**MTP**.......... Master Transportation Plan (AAG)
**MTP**.......... Materiel Test Procedure [*Army*]
**MTP**.......... Materiel Transfer Plan [*Army*]
**MTP**.......... Maximum Tire Pressure (ADA)
**MTP**.......... Mechanical Thermal Pulse (IEEE)
**MTP**.......... Message Transmission Part [*Telecommunications*] (TEL)
**MTP**.......... Metatarsophalangeal [*Anatomy*]
**MTP**.......... (Methylthio)phenol [*Organic chemistry*]
**MTP**.......... Microtubule Protein [*Cytology*]
**MTP**.......... Military Type Property
**MTP**.......... Miniature Trimmer Potentiometer
**MTP**.......... Missile Transfer Panel (AAG)
**MTP**.......... Missile Tube Pressurization
**MTP**.......... Mission Tailored Product
**MTP**.......... Mission Test Plan (KSC)
**MTP**.......... Mission Training Plan [*Military*] (INF)
**MTP**.......... Mobilization Training Program [*Military*]
**MTP**.......... Mobilization Troop Program [*Army*]
**MTP**.......... Montana Power Co. [*NYSE symbol*] (SPSG)
**MTP**.......... Montauk Point [*New York*] [*Airport symbol*] [*Obsolete*] (OAG)
**MTP**.......... Monte Pirata [*Puerto Rico*] [*Seismograph station code, US Geological Survey*] (SEIS)
**MTP**.......... Multiple-Task Performance
**MTP**.......... [*The*] Pas Public Library, Manitoba [*Library symbol*] [*National Library of Canada*] (NLC)
**MTPA**........ Master Textile Printers Association (EA)
**MTPA**........ (Methoxy)trifluoromethylphenylacetic Acid [*Organic chemistry*]
**MTPC**........ Metal Tube Packaging Council of North America [*Later, TCNA*] (EA)
**MTPCNA**... Metal Tube Packaging Council of North America [*Later, TCNA*]
**MTPF**........ Maximum Total Peaking Factor [*Nuclear energy*] (NRCH)
**MTPH**....... Maximum Temperature of Previous Heating [*Archaeology*]
**MTPI**......... Member of the Town Planning Institute [*British*]
**MTP Int Rev Sci Biochem**... MTP [*Medical & Technical Publishing Co.*] International Review of Science. Biochemistry [*A publication*]
**MTPK**........ Keewatin Community College, The Pas, Manitoba [*Library symbol*] [*National Library of Canada*] (NLC)
**Mt Plains Lib Assn Q**... Mountain Plains Library Association. Quarterly [*A publication*]
**MTP (Med Tech Publ Co) Int Rev Sci Ser One Physiol**... MTP (Medical and Technical Publishing Company) International Review of Science. Series One. Physiology [*A publication*]
**MTPP**........ Material Test Procedure Pamphlet
**MTPP**........ Missile-to-Target Patch Panel
**MTPP**........ Port-Au-Prince/Internacional [*Haiti*] [*ICAO location identifier*] (ICLI)
**MTPS**........ Magnetic Tape Programming System [*Data processing*] (IEEE)
**MTPT**........ Minimal Total Processing Time (IEEE)
**MTPU**....... Missile Tank Pressurization Unit (AAG)
**MTPUG**.... Pascal/MT Users Group [*Defunct*] (EA)
**MTPX**........ Port-De-Paix [*Haiti*] [*ICAO location identifier*] (ICLI)
**MTPY**........ Millions of Tons per Year [*of solids, e.g., coal*]
**MTQ**.......... Greenville, MS [*Location identifier*] [*FAA*] (FAAL)
**MTQ**.......... Mark Twain Quarterly [*A publication*]
**MTQ**.......... Martinique [*ANSI three-letter standard code*] (CNC)
**MTQ**.......... Methaqualone [*or Methyltolylquinazolone, or Metolquizolone*] [*Sedative*]
**MTQ**.......... Mitchell [*Australia*] [*Airport symbol*] (OAG)
**MTQ**.......... Mount Allard Resources [*Vancouver Stock Exchange symbol*]
**MTR**.......... Magic-Tone Records [*Record label*]
**MTR**.......... Magnetic Tape Recorder
**MTR**.......... Major Trouble Report (MCD)
**MTR**.......... Marginal Rate of Tax
**MTR**.......... Mass Transit Railway (DS)
**MTR**.......... Material Transfer Recorder [*LASER*] [*Army*]
**MTR**.......... Materials Testing Reactor
**MTR**.......... Materials Testing Report
**MTR**.......... Maximum Tracking Range
**MTR**.......... Mean Time to Removal [*or Repair or Replacement*] [*Quality control*]
**MTR**.......... Meinicke Turbidity Reaction [*Obsolete test for syphilis*]
**MTR**.......... Mental Treatment Rules [*British*]
**MTR**.......... Mesa Royalty Trust UBI [*NYSE symbol*] (SPSG)
**MTR**.......... Meter [*or Metering*] (AAG)
**MTR**.......... Methylthioribose [*Biochemistry*]
**MTR**.......... Metroflight, Inc. [*Houston, TX*] [*FAA designator*] (FAAC)
**Mtr**............ Metronome [*Record label*] [*Scandinavia, Germany, etc.*]
**MTR**.......... Military Temperature Range
**MTR**.......... Military Training Route Program (FAAC)
**MTR**.......... Minimum Time Rate
**MTR**.......... Missile Track [*or Tracking*] RADAR [*Air Force*]
**MTR**.......... MITRE Corp., Library Department, McLean, VA [*OCLC symbol*] (OCLC)
**MTR**.......... Mitsubishi Bank Review [*A publication*]
**MTR**.......... Mobile Tracking Range [*Military*] (CAAL)
**MTR**.......... Modification Traceability Record (MCD)
**MTR**.......... Monitor [*Data processing*] (BUR)
**MTR**.......... Monopulse Tracking Receiver
**MTR**.......... Monteria [*Colombia*] [*Airport symbol*] (OAG)
**MTR**.......... Monterrey [*California*] [*Seismograph station code, US Geological Survey*] (SEIS)
**MTR**.......... Montour Railroad Co. [*AAR code*]
**MTR**.......... Motor (AABC)
**MTR**.......... Moving Target Reactor
**MTR**.......... Multiple Thermocouple Reference
**MTR**.......... Multiple Track RADAR
**MTR**.......... Multiple Tracking Range
**MTR**.......... Mutual Resources [*Vancouver Stock Exchange symbol*]
**MTR**.......... Universite de Montreal, Bibliotheque [*UTLAS symbol*]
**M/TRANS**... Manual Transmission [*Automotive engineering*]
**MTRB**........ Maritime Transportation Research Board [*National Research Council*]
**MTRB**........ Motor Truck Rate Bureau
**MTRC**........ Mercantile Bancorporation, Inc. [*NASDAQ symbol*] (NQ)
**MTRCL**..... Motorcycle (AABC)

**MTRDN**.... Motor-Driven
**MTRE**........ Magnetic Tape Recorder End
**MTRE**........ Missile Test and Readiness Equipment
**MT REVD** ... Most Reverend (ROG)
**MTRF**........ Mark Twain Research Foundation (EA)
**MTRF**........ Master Training File [*Data processing*]
**MTRG**....... Metering (MSA)
**MTRI**......... Missile Test Range Instrumentation
**MTRK**....... Minitrack (KSC)
**MTRL**........ Material (FAAC)
**MTRM**...... Moniterm Corp. [*Minnetonka, MN*] [*NASDAQ symbol*] (NQ)
**mtRNA**...... Ribonucleic Acid, Mitochondrial [*Biochemistry, genetics*]
**MTRO**....... Metro-Tel Corp. [*NASDAQ symbol*] (NQ)
**MTR OP**.... Motor Operated [*Freight*]
**MTRP**........ Machine Tool Retrofit Program
**MTRP**........ Master of Town and Regional Planning [*British*] (ADA)
**MTRS**........ Magnetic Tape Recorder Set
**MTRS**........ Magnetic Tape Recorder Start
**MTRS**........ Magnetic Tape Reformatting System [*Hewlett-Packard Co.*]
**MTRS**........ Mattress (MSA)
**MT Rulings** ... Miscellaneous Tax Rulings [*Australia*] [*A publication*]
**MTRX**....... Matrix Science Corp. [*NASDAQ symbol*] (NQ)
**MTRY**....... Momentary (FAAC)
**MTS**........... Machine-Tractor Stations
**MTS**........... Magnetic Tape Station [*Data processing*] (CET)
**MTS**........... Magnetic Tape System [*Data processing*]
**MTS**........... Main Trunk System [*Telecommunications*] (TEL)
**MTS**........... Maintenance Training Set (MCD)
**MTS**........... Maintenance Transmittal Sheet
**MTS**........... Manitoba Telephone System [*Telecommunications service*] (TSSD)
**MTS**........... Manned Teller System
**MTS**........... Manpower Training Services
**MTS**........... Manual Testing System [*Sports medicine*]
**MTS**........... Manufacturing Technology Section [*Navy*]
**MTS**........... Manzini [*Swaziland*] [*Airport symbol*] (OAG)
**MTS**........... Mardan Test Set
**MTS**........... Marine Technology Series [*Elsevier Book Series*] [*A publication*]
**MTS**........... Marine Technology Society (EA)
**MTS**........... Maritime Tactical Schools (MCD)
**MTS**........... Mark Twain Society [*Defunct*] (EA)
**MTS**........... Marketing Technical Services
**MTS**........... Marketing and Transportation Situation [*Series*] [*A publication*]
**MTS**........... MARS [*Military Affiliate Radio System*] Technical Service (CET)
**MTS**........... Maschinen-Traktoren-Station [*Machine-Tractor-Stations*] [*German*]
**MTS**........... Mashinno-Traktornye-Stantsii [*Machine-Tractor-Stations*] [*Russian*]
**MTS**........... Mass Termination System [*Data processing*] (IEEE)
**MTS**........... Master Test Station
**MTS**........... Master Timing System
**MTS**........... Material Test Specification (MSA)
**MTS**........... Matsue [*Japan*] [*Seismograph station code, US Geological Survey*] (SEIS)
**MTS**........... Medical Testing Systems [*Commercial firm*]
**MTS**........... Member of the Technical Staff [*A generic term*]
**MTS**........... Memory Test System
**MTS**........... Meridian Telecommunication Services [*Indianapolis, IN*] (TSSD)
**MTS**........... Message Telecommunications Service
**MTS**........... Message Toll Service [*Communications*]
**MTS**........... Message Traffic Study
**MTS**........... Message Transmission Subsystem [*Telecommunications*] (TEL)
**MTS**........... Meteoroid Technology Satellite [*NASA*]
**MTS**........... Methods-Time Study [*Industrial engineering*]
**MTS**........... Methyltrichlorosilane [*Organic chemistry*]
**MTS**........... Metric Time System (NASA)
**MTS**........... Michigan Terminal System [*Data processing*]
**MTS**........... Microtubule-Stabilizing Solution [*Cytology*]
**MTS**........... Microwave Test Set (MCD)
**MTS**........... Military Test Satellite
**MTS**........... Military Training Standard (AFM)
**MTS**........... Missile Test Set
**MTS**........... Missile Test Stand
**MTS**........... Missile Test Station
**MTS**........... Missile Tracking Station [*DoD*]
**MTS**........... Missile Tracking System (IEEE)
**MTS**........... Missile Training Squadron
**MTS**........... Missile Tube Supply
**MTS**........... Missions to Seamen [*British*]
**MTS**........... Mississippi Test Site [*Aerospace*] (AAG)
**MTS**........... Mobile Telephone Service
**MTS**........... Mobile Terminal System [*IBM Corp.*]
**MTS**........... Mobile Tracking Station [*NASA*]
**MTS**........... Mobile Training Set (AFM)
**MTS**........... Module Test Set (MCD)
**MTS**........... Module Tracking System (NRCH)
**MTS**........... Montgomery Street Income Securities, Inc. [*NYSE symbol*] (SPSG)
**MTS**........... Monthly Treasury Statement [*Government*] (AFM)
**MTS**........... Most Thrilling Science Ever Told [*A publication*]
**MTS**........... Motion-Time Standards [*Industrial engineering*]
**MTS**........... Motor-Operated Transfer Switch
**MTS**........... Motor Tariff Service
**MTS**........... Mountains [*Board on Geographic Names*]
**MTS**........... Moving Target Screen (MCD)
**MTS**........... Moving Target Simulator (RDA)
**MTS**........... Moving Time Series
**MTS**........... Multichannel Television Sound [*or Stereo*]
**MTS**........... Multiple Target Screen
**MTS**........... Multiple Time Scale
**MTS**........... Muscle Testing System [*Myology*]
**MTS**........... State Law Library of Montana, Helena, MT [*OCLC symbol*] (OCLC)
**MTSA**......... Seaman Apprentice, Missile Technician, Striker [*Navy rating*]
**MTSC**......... Magnetic Tape "Selectric" Composer [*IBM Corp.*]
**MTSC**......... MTS Systems Corporation [*NASDAQ symbol*] (NQ)
**MTSD**......... Military Transmission Systems Department [*NORAD*]
**MTSE**......... Magnetic Trap Stability Experiment (IEEE)
**MT & SE**... Maintenance Test and Support Equipment
**MTSGT**..... Master Technical Sergeant [*Marine Corps*]
**MTSGT(C)** ... Master Technical Sergeant (Commissary) [*Marine Corps*]
**MTSHB5**... Morioka Tabako Shikenjo Hokoku [*A publication*]
**Mt Sinai J** ... Mount Sinai Journal of Medicine [*A publication*]
**Mt Sinai J Med** ... Mount Sinai Journal of Medicine [*A publication*]
**MTSJBB**... Marine Technology Society. Journal [*A publication*]
**MTSN**....... Seaman, Missile Technician, Striker [*Navy rating*]
**MTSO**....... Mobile Telephone Switching Office [*Telecommunications*]
**MTSP**....... Maintenance Test Support Package [*Army*]
**MTSPS**...... Multiple Transducer Seismic Profiling System
**MTSQ**....... Mechanical Time, Superquick [*Fuse*] [*Weaponry*]
**MTSR**........ Mean Time to Service Restoral [*Quality control*] [*Telecommunications*] (TEL)
**MTSR**........ Mid-Term Status Reports
**MTSR**........ Mountain States Resources Corp. [*NASDAQ symbol*] (NQ)
**MTSS**........ Magnetic Tape Storage System
**MTSS**........ Manned Test Space System [*See also MOD, MODS, MOSS*] [*Air Force/NASA*]
**MTSS**........ Military Test Space Station [*See also MOD, MODS, MOSS*] [*Air Force/NASA*]
**MTST**........ Magnetic Tape "Selectric" Typewriter [*IBM Corp.*]
**Mt States Miner Age** ... Mountain States Mineral Age [*A publication*]
**MTSU**....... Magnetic Tape Search Unit [*Data processing*]
**MTSU**....... Middle Tennessee State University
**MTS/VO**... Motor Transportation Supervisor/Vehicle Operator (AAG)
**MTT**.......... Magnetic Tape Terminal [*Data processing*]
**MTT**.......... Magnetic Tape Transport [*Data processing*] (IEEE)
**MTT**.......... Maintenance Training Team (MCD)
**MTT**.......... Mammillothalamic Tract [*Neuroanatomy*]
**MTT**.......... Maritime Telegraph & Telephone Co. Ltd. [*Toronto Stock Exchange symbol*]
**MTT**.......... Master of Textile Technology
**MTT**.......... Material Testing Technology (MCD)
**MTT**.......... Maximum Touch Temperature (MCD)
**MTT**.......... Mean Transit Time
**MTT**.......... Medium Tactical Transport [*Army*]
**MTT**.......... Medium Tactical Truck [*Army*] (RDA)
**MTT**.......... Methyl(thio)tetrazole [*Biochemistry*]
**MTT**.......... Metropolitan Edison Co. [*NYSE symbol*] (SPSG)
**MTT**.......... Mi-Tsiyon Tetse Torah [*Tel Aviv*] (BJA)
**MTT**.......... Microwave Theory and Technique (MCD)
**MTT**.......... Military Training Team (MCD)
**MTT**.......... Minatitlan [*Mexico*] [*Airport symbol*] (OAG)
**MTT**.......... Missionary Tech Team (EA)
**MTT**.......... Mobile Training Team
**MTT**.......... Mobile Travel Team (MCD)
**MTT**.......... Monetta Fire Tower [*South Carolina*] [*Seismograph station code, US Geological Survey*] (SEIS)
**MTT**.......... Multiple Target Tracker
**MTT**.......... Munitions Transfer Truck (MCD)
**MTTA**....... Mean Time to Accomplish [*Quality control*] (NASA)
**MTTA**....... Multi-Tenant Telecommunications Association (EA)
**MTTB**........ Mean Time to Bench [*Repair*] [*Quality control*]
**MTTC**........ Mean Time to Change Parts [*Quality control*] (MCD)
**MTTC**........ Mechanised Transport Training Corps [*British military*] (DMA)
**MTTD**....... Mean Time to Detect [*Quality control*] (MCD)
**MTTD**....... Mean Time to Diagnosis [*Quality control*] (BUR)
**MTTE**........ Magnetic Tape Terminal Equipment [*Data processing*] (CET)
**MTTE**........ Mean Time to Exchange [*Quality control*] (MCD)
**MTTEA**..... Marine Towing and Transportation Employers Association (EA)
**MTTF**........ Mean Time to Failure [*Quality control*]
**MTTFF**..... Mean Time to First Failure [*Quality control*]
**MTTHS**..... Modern Transport Technical and Historical Society [*Later, SFCH*] (EA)
**MTTI**......... Mean Time to Inspect [*Quality control*] (CAAL)
**MTTI**......... Modified Tension Time Index [*Cardiology*]

**MTTKA**...... Meteoritika [*A publication*]
**MTTL**........ Mobile Telecommunications Technologies Corp. [*NASDAQ symbol*] (CTT)
**MTTM**...... Magnetic Tape and Telemetry (MCD)
**MTTM**...... Mean Time to Maintain [*Quality control*] (CMD)
**MTTMA**... Memoirs. Faculty of Technology. Tokyo Metropolitan University [*A publication*]
**MTTN**....... Multi-Tranche Tap Note [*Finance*] [*British*]
**MTTO**....... Minuetto [*Slow Air*] [*Music*] (ROG)
**MTTP**....... Materials Testing and Technology Program
**MTTPO**..... Mean Time to Planned Outage (IEEE)
**MTTQ**....... Medical Trial Technique Quarterly [*A publication*]
**MTTR**........ Mean Time to Removal [*Quality control*]
**MTTR**........ Mean Time to Repair [*Quality control*] (CAAL)
**MTTR**........ Mean Time to Replacement [*Quality control*]
**MTTR**........ Mean Time to Restore [*Quality control*] (IEEE)
**MTTR**........ Missile Target Tracking RADAR (MCD)
**MTTRF**..... Mission Time to Restore Function
**MTTRS**..... Mean Time to Restore Software [*Quality control*] (CAAL)
**MTTRS**..... Mean Time to Restore System [*Quality control*]
**MTTS**........ IEEE Microwave Theory and Techniques Society (EA)
**MTTS**........ Marine Terminal Tankage System (MCD)
**MTTS**........ Mean Time to Service [*Quality control*]
**MTTS**........ Mobile Target Tracking System
**MTTS**........ Multitask Terminal System
**MTTU**....... Modular Timing Terminal Unit
**MTTUO**.... Mean Time to Unplanned Outage (IEEE)
**MTTW**...... Mean Time to Wait for Parts [*Quality control*] (MCD)
**MTU**.......... Magnetic Tape Unit [*Data processing*]
**MTU**.......... Maintenance Training Unit
**MTU**.......... Master Terminal Unit [*Instrumentation*]
**MTU**.......... Master Time Unit
**MTU**.......... Methylthiouracil [*Pharmacology*]
**MTU**.......... Metric Ton Unit
**MTU**.......... Metric Tons of Uranium
**MTU**.......... Metric Units (FAAC)
**MTU**.......... Michigan Technological University [*Houghton*]
**MTU**.......... MIRA [*Multifunctional Inertial Reference Assembly*] Transport Unit [*Air Force*] (MCD)
**MTU**.......... Missile Tracking Unit (MCD)
**MTU**.......... Missile Training Unit [*Air Force*]
**MTU**.......... Mist Therapy Unit [*Medicine*]
**MTU**.......... Mobile Technical Unit (MCD)
**MTU**.......... Mobile Test Unit [*Army*] (RDA)
**MTU**.......... Mobile Training Unit
**MTU**.......... Module Test Unit [*Nuclear energy*] (NRCH)
**mtu**............ Montana [*MARC country of publication code*] [*Library of Congress*] (LCCP)
**MTU**.......... Montreal Trustco, Inc. [*Toronto Stock Exchange symbol*]
**MTU**.......... Mosquito Training Unit [*British military*] (DMA)
**MTU**.......... Muenchener Texte und Untersuchungen zur Deutschen Literatur des Mittelalters [*A publication*]
**MTU**.......... Multiplexer and Terminal Unit
**MTU**.......... Multiterminal Unit (TEL)
**MTU**.......... Myton, UT [*Location identifier*] [*FAA*] (FAAL)
**MtU**........... University of Montana at Missoula, Missoula, MT [*Library symbol*] [*Library of Congress*] (LCLS)
**MTUDLM**... Muenchener Texte und Untersuchungen zur Deutschen Literatur des Mittelalters [*A publication*]
**MtU-L**....... University of Montana at Missoula, Law School, Missoula, MT [*Library symbol*] [*Library of Congress*] (LCLS)
**MTUMR**... MIRA [*Multifunctional Inertial Reference Assembly*] Transport Unit Mounting Rack [*Air Force*] (MCD)
**MTUOP**.... Mobile Training Units Out for Parts
**MTV**.......... Conference des Ministres Europeens du Travail [*Conference of European Ministers of Labour*] (EAIO)
**MTV**.......... Mammary Tumor Virus
**MTV**.......... Management Television [*Air Force*] (AFM)
**MTV**.......... Maneuvering Technology Vehicle
**MTV**.......... Marginal Terrain Vehicle
**MTV**.......... Martinsville, VA [*Location identifier*] [*FAA*] (FAAL)
**M TV**......... Master of Television
**MTV**.......... Mean Transformed Value
**MTV**.......... Missile Test Vehicle
**MTV**.......... Missile Training Vehicle
**MTV**.......... Mota Lava [*Vanuatu*] [*Airport symbol*] (OAG)
**MTV**.......... Motor Torpedo Vessel [*British*]
**MTV**.......... Motor Transport Volunteers [*Military unit*] [*British*]
**MTV**.......... Mount Tassie [*Australia*] [*Seismograph station code, US Geological Survey*] [*Closed*] (SEIS)
**MTV**.......... Mountain Valley Air Service, Inc. [*Vancouver, WA*] [*FAA designator*] (FAAC)
**MTV**.......... Multicultural Television (ADA)
**MTV**.......... Munition Test Vehicle
**MTV**.......... Munitions Tow Vehicle (MCD)
**MTV**.......... Music Television [*Warner Amex Satellite Entertainment Co.*] [*Cable-television system*]
**MTV**.......... Mutatur Terminatio Versiculi [*The Termination of the Little Verse Is Changed*]
**MTVAL**..... Master Tape Validation
**MTVC**....... Manned [*or Manual*] Thrust Vector Control (MCD)
**MTVP**........ Moving Target Video Processor
**MTVS**........ Mission Test and Video System
**MTVU**....... Module Thruster Valve Unit
**MTW**......... Machine Tool Wire
**MTW**......... Main Trawl Winch
**MTW**......... Manitowoc [*Wisconsin*] [*Airport symbol*] (OAG)
**MTW**......... Marinette, Tomahawk & Western Railroad Co. [*AAR code*]
**MTW**......... Maximum Taxi Weight [*Aviation*]
**MTW**......... Military Transport Wagon [*British*]
**MTW**......... Mission to the World (EA)
**MTW**......... Mobile Training Wing [*Air Force*]
**MTW**......... Mountain Waves [*Aviation*] (FAAC)
**MTW**......... Music Treasures of the World [*Record label*]
**MTWA**...... Maximum Total Weight Authorized [*Aviation*] (AIA)
**MTWC**...... Morgan Three-Wheeler Club (EA)
**MTWF**....... Metal Thru-Wall Flashing [*Technical drawings*]
**MTWN**...... Mark Twain Bancshares, Inc. [*NASDAQ symbol*] (NQ)
**MTWO**...... Melamine Chemicals, Inc. [*NASDAQ symbol*] (NQ)
**MTWOA**... Metalworking [*A publication*]
**MTWS**....... Manual Track While Scan
**MTWX**...... Mechanized Teletypewriter Exchange (TEL)
**MTX**.......... Fairbanks [*Alaska*] Metro Field [*Airport symbol*] [*Obsolete*] (OAG)
**MTX**.......... Manual Transaxle
**MTX**.......... Master of Taxation
**MTX**.......... Metex Corp. [*AMEX symbol*] (SPSG)
**MTX**.......... Methotrexate [*Antineoplastic drug*]
**MTX**.......... Microwave TOKAMAK [*Toroidal Kamera Magnetic*] Experiment [*Plasma physics*]
**MTX**.......... Military Traffic Expediting Service (AABC)
**MTX**.......... Morrell Tank Line [*AAR code*]
**MTX-CF**.... Methotrexate with Citrovorum Factor Rescue [*Antineoplastic drug regimen*]
**MTXI**......... MTX International, Inc. [*NASDAQ symbol*] (NQ)
**MTY**.......... Empty
**MTY**.......... Marlton Technologies [*AMEX symbol*] (SPSG)
**MTY**.......... Matsuyama [*Japan*] [*Seismograph station code, US Geological Survey*] (SEIS)
**MTY**.......... Maturity [*Business term*]
**MTY**.......... Mekhon ha-Tekanim ha-Yisre'eli (BJA)
**MTY**.......... Million Tons per Year
**MTY**.......... Monterrey [*Mexico*] [*Airport symbol*] (OAG)
**MTY**.......... MTM. Journal of Methods Time Measurement [*A publication*]
**MTYR**........ McIntyre Mines Ltd. [*NASDAQ symbol*] (NQ)
**MTZ**.......... Mass Transfer Zone [*Chemical engineering*]
**MTZ**.......... Montezuma [*Chile*] [*Seismograph station code, US Geological Survey*] [*Closed*] (SEIS)
**MTZ**.......... Motorized (AAG)
**MTZ**.......... Motortechnische Zeitschrift [*Stuttgart*] [*A publication*]
**MTZ**.......... Muenchener Theologische Zeitschrift [*A publication*]
**MTZ**.......... Tuskegee, AL [*Location identifier*] [*FAA*] (FAAL)
**MTZM**........ Martinez & Murphy, Inc. [*NASDAQ symbol*] (NQ)
**MTZ Motortech Z**... MTZ. Motortechnische Zeitschrift [*A publication*]
**MU**............ Akaflieg Muenchen [*Federal Republic of Germany*] Mitsubishi Heavy Industries [*Japan*] [*ICAO aircraft manufacturer identifier*] (ICAO)
**MU**............ Machine Unit
**MU**............ Mail Unit (KSC)
**MU**............ Maintenance Unit [*Military*]
**MU**............ Makeup (NRCH)
**MU**............ Maneuvering Unit (KSC)
**MU**............ Marginal Utility [*Economics*]
**MU**............ Markup
**MU**............ Mass Units
**MU**............ Master Unit (NASA)
**mu**.............. Mauritania [*MARC country of publication code*] [*Library of Congress*] (LCCP)
**MU**............ Mauritius [*ANSI two-letter standard code*] (CNC)
**MU**............ Measurement Unit
**MU**............ Memory Unit [*Data processing*] (MCD)
**MU**............ Mental Units of Growth [*Psychology*]
**MU**............ Message Unit [*Telecommunications*]
**MU**............ Methylene Unit
**MU**............ Methylumbelliferone [*Biochemistry*]
**MU**............ Methylurea [*Organic chemistry*]
**MU**............ Micron Technology, Inc. [*NYSE symbol*] (SPSG)
**M & U**........ Middletown & Unionville Railroad [*Nickname: Miserable and Useless*]
**Mu**.............. Millimicron (AAG)
**MU**............ Mobile Unit
**MU**............ Mock-Up (AAG)
**MU**............ Monetary Unit (ADA)
**M/U**........... Monitor Unit [*Telecommunications*] (TEL)
**MU**............ Montevideo Units [*Of uterine activity*]
**MU**............ Mothers' Union [*Episcopalian*]
**MU**............ Motor Union
**MU**............ Motor Unit
**MU**............ Mouse Unit [*With reference to radium emanations*]
**MU**............ Mueller Cell [*Eye anatomy*]
**MU**............ Muk Air Taxi [*Denmark*] [*ICAO designator*] (FAAC)
**Mu**.............. Mulino [*A publication*]

**MU** ........... Multidestination [*Carrier*]
**MU** ........... Multiple Unit
**MU** ........... Multiplexing Unit
**MU** ........... Munitions Command [*Later, Armaments Command*] [*Army*] (MCD)
**MU** ........... Music Program [*Association of Independent Colleges and Schools specialization code*]
**MU** ........... Musical Union [*Oberlin College*] [*Ohio*]
**MU** ........... Musician [*Navy rating*]
**MU** ........... Musicians' Union [*British*] (DCTA)
**MU** ........... Muster [*Business term*] (DCTA)
**Mu**............ Mutator [*A bacteriophage*]
**Mu**............ Muttersprache. Zeitschrift zur Pflege und Erforschung der Deutschen Sprache [*A publication*]
**MU** ........... University of Massachusetts, Amherst, MA [*Library symbol*] [*Library of Congress*] (LCLS)
**MU1** .......... Musician, First Class [*Navy rating*]
**MU2** .......... Musician, Second Class [*Navy rating*]
**MU3** .......... Musician, Third Class [*Navy rating*]
**MUA**.......... Mail Users' Association [*British*]
**MUA**.......... Manned Undersea [*or Underwater*] Activity [*Marine science*]
**MUA**.......... Materials Usage Agreement (NASA)
**MUA**.......... Maui Air, Inc. [*Kahulu Maui, HI*] [*FAA designator*] (FAAC)
**MUA**.......... Maximum Usable Altitude [*Aviation*]
**MUA**.......... Memorandum of Understanding and Agreement
**MUA**.......... Metallurgistes Unis d'Amerique [*United Steelworkers of America - USWA*]
**MUA**.......... Ministry of State for Urban Affairs [*Canada*]
**MUA**.......... Mixed Underachievers [*Education*]
**MUA**.......... Multiple Unit Activity [*Neurophysiology*]
**MUA**.......... Munda [*Solomon Islands*] [*Airport symbol*] (OAG)
**MUAA**....... Major Unit Assembly Area (MCD)
**MUAC**....... Mid Upper Arm Circumference [*Anatomy*]
**MUACS**..... Manpower Utilization and Control System
**MUAG**....... Central Agramonte [*Cuba*] [*ICAO location identifier*] (ICLI)
**MU/AG**..... Mid-Upper [*Turret*] Air Gunner [*British military*] (DMA)
**MUAP**....... Motor Unit Action Potential [*Physiology*]
**MUAT**....... Antilla [*Cuba*] [*ICAO location identifier*] (ICLI)
**MUAT**....... Mobile Underwater Acoustic Unit (NATG)
**MUB**.......... Maun [*Botswana*] [*Airport symbol*] (OAG)
**MUB**.......... Melanges. Universite Saint Joseph (Beyrouth) [*A publication*]
**MUB**.......... University of Maryland, Baltimore County Campus, Catonsville, MD [*OCLC symbol*] (OCLC)
**MUBA**....... Baracoa/Oriente [*Cuba*] [*ICAO location identifier*] (ICLI)
**MUBBDD** ... Moscow University. Biological Sciences Bulletin [*A publication*]
**MUBE**....... El Caribe [*Cuba*] [*ICAO location identifier*] (ICLI)
**MUBI**....... Cayo Mambi [*Cuba*] [*ICAO location identifier*] (ICLI)
**MUBIS**....... Multiple Beam Interval Scanner
**MUBO**....... Batabano [*Cuba*] [*ICAO location identifier*] (ICLI)
**MUBY**....... Bayamo [*Cuba*] [*ICAO location identifier*] (ICLI)
**MUC**.......... Maximum Urinary Concentration [*Medicine*]
**MUC**.......... Meritorious Unit Citation [*Military decoration*]
**MUC**.......... Meritorious Unit Commendation [*Military decoration*] (AFM)
**MUC**.......... Mount Union College [*Alliance, OH*]
**MUC**.......... Mucilaginous (ROG)
**MUC**.......... Mucosal Ulcerative Colitis [*Medicine*]
**MUC**.......... Multicoupler
**MUC**.......... Munich [*West Germany*] [*Airport symbol*] (OAG)
**MUC**.......... Musician, Chief [*Navy rating*]
**MUCA**....... Ciego De Avila [*Cuba*] [*ICAO location identifier*] (ICLI)
**MUCB**....... Caibarien [*Cuba*] [*ICAO location identifier*] (ICLI)
**MUCC**....... Cunagua [*Cuba*] [*ICAO location identifier*] (ICLI)
**MUCC**....... Michigan United Conservation Clubs
**MUCF**....... Cienfuegos [*Cuba*] [*ICAO location identifier*] (ICLI)
**Much D & S** ... Muchall's Doctor and Student [*A publication*] (DLA)
**MUCIA**..... Midwest Universities Consortium for International Activities [*University of Indiana*]
**MUCILAG** ... Mucilaginous (ROG)
**MUCL**....... Cayo Largo Del Sur [*Cuba*] [*ICAO location identifier*] (ICLI)
**MUCM**...... Camaguey/Ignacio Agramonte [*Cuba*] [*ICAO location identifier*] (ICLI)
**MUCM**...... Musician, Master Chief [*Navy rating*]
**MUCN**....... Ciego De Avila Norte [*Cuba*] [*ICAO location identifier*] (ICLI)
**MUCO**....... Colon [*Cuba*] [*ICAO location identifier*] (ICLI)
**MUCO**....... Materiel Utilization Control Office (AFIT)
**MUCOM**... Munitions Command [*Later, Armaments Command*] [*Army*]
**Mu Corp Ca** ... Municipal Corporation Cases [*United States*] [*A publication*] (DLA)
**Mu Corp Cir** ... Municipal Corporation Circular [*England*] [*A publication*] (DLA)
**MUCS**....... Central Noel Fernandez [*Cuba*] [*ICAO location identifier*] (ICLI)
**MUCS**....... Musician, Senior Chief [*Navy rating*]
**MUCU**....... Santiago De Cuba/Antonio Maceo [*Cuba*] [*ICAO location identifier*] (ICLI)
**MUCUSA** ... Missionary Union of the Clergy in the United States of America [*Later, PMUPR*] (EA)
**MUCV**....... Las Clavellinas [*Cuba*] [*ICAO location identifier*] (ICLI)
**MUCY**....... Cayajabo [*Cuba*] [*ICAO location identifier*] (ICLI)
**MUD**.......... Macromind Utility Disk
**MUD**.......... Memory Unit Drum [*Data processing*]
**MUD**.......... Middle, Up, Down [*in game of bridge*]
**MUD**.......... Mouvement Union Democratique [*Democratic Union Movement*] [*Monaco*] [*Political party*] (PPE)
**MUD**.......... Multi-User Dungeon [*Computer game*]
**MUDAR**.... Mulheres por um Desenvoluimento Alternativo [*Development Alternatives with Women for a New Era - DAWN*] [*Rio De Janeiro, Brazil*] (EAIO)
**MUDET**.... Militarized Universal Digital Element Tester (MCD)
**MUDL**....... Microwave Ultrasonic Delay Line
**MUDPAC** ... Melbourne University Dual-Package Analog Computer [*Australia*] (ADA)
**MUDR**....... Multidetail Drawing (MSA)
**MUDS**....... Multiple Usage Data Sheet (MCD)
**Mudst**......... Mudstone Soil [*Agronomy*]
**MUDWNT** ... Makeup Demineralizer Waste Neutralizer Tank (IEEE)
**MUE**.......... Kamuela [*Hawaii*] [*Airport symbol*] (OAG)
**MUE**.......... Meritorious Unit Emblem [*Military decoration*]
**MUEHA**.... Muehle [*A publication*]
**Muehle Mischfuttertech** ... Muehle und Mischfuttertechnik [*A publication*]
**Mue Jb**....... Muenchner Jahrbuch der Bildenden Kunst [*A publication*]
**MUEL**....... Mueller [*Paul*] Co. [*NASDAQ symbol*] (NQ)
**MUELC**..... Mundo Electronico [*A publication*]
**Muench Beit Abwasser-Fisch- Flussbiol** ... Muenchener Beitraege zur Abwasser-, Fischerei-, und Flussbiologie [*A publication*]
**Muench Beitr** ... Muenchener Beitraege zur Romanischen und Englischen Philologie [*A publication*]
**Muench Beitr Abwasser Fisch Flussbiol** ... Muenchener Beitraege zur Abwasser-, Fischerei-, und Flussbiologie [*West Germany*] [*A publication*]
**Muenchen Med Wchnschr** ... Muenchener Medizinische Wochenschrift [*A publication*]
**Muench Geogr Abh** ... Muenchener Geographische Abhandlungen [*A publication*]
**Muench Jahr Bild Kunst** ... Muenchener Jahrbuch der Bildenden Kunst [*A publication*]
**Muench Med Wochenschr** ... Muenchener Medizinische Wochenschrift [*A publication*]
**Muench Med Wschr** ... Muenchener Medizinische Wochenschrift [*A publication*]
**Muenchner Beitr Abwasser Fisch Flussbiol** ... Muenchener Beitraege zur Abwasser-, Fischerei-, und Flussbiologie [*A publication*]
**Muench St Spr Wiss** ... Muenchener Studien zur Sprachwissenschaft [*A publication*]
**Muench Tieraerztl Wochenschr** ... Muenchener Tieraerztliche Wochenschrift [*A publication*]
**Muenster Forsch Geol Palaeontol** ... Muenstersche Forschungen zur Geologie und Palaeontologie [*A publication*]
**Muenstersche Forsch Geol Palaeontol** ... Muenstersche Forschungen zur Geologie und Palaeontologie [*A publication*]
**Muenstersche N Z** ... Muenstersche Numismatische Zeitung [*A publication*]
**Mueszaki Terv** ... Mueszaki Tervezes [*A publication*]
**Mueszeruegyi Merestech Koezl** ... Mueszeruegyi es Merestechnikai Koezlemenyek [*Hungary*] [*A publication*]
**Muesz Koezl Lang Gepgyar Muesz Gazd Tajek** ... Mueszaki Koezlemenyek. Lang Gepgyar Mueszaki es Gazdasagi Tajekoztatoja [*Hungary*] [*A publication*]
**Muesz Tud** ... Mueszaki Tudomany [*Hungary*] [*A publication*]
**MUF**.......... Makeup Feed [*Boiler*]
**MUF**.......... Material Unaccounted For [*Nuclear energy*]
**MUF**.......... Maximum Usable Frequency [*Signal transmission*]
**MUF**.......... Muffler
**MUF**.......... Muting [*Indonesia*] [*Airport symbol*] (OAG)
**MUFC**....... Central Amancio Rodriguez [*Cuba*] [*ICAO location identifier*] (ICLI)
**MUFD**....... Makeup Feed [*Boiler*]
**MUFL**....... Florida [*Cuba*] [*ICAO location identifier*] (ICLI)
**MUFLNG** ... Mouvement pour l'Unification des Forces de Liberation de la Guadeloupe [*Movement for the Unification of National Liberation Forces of Guadeloupe*] [*Political party*] (PD)
**MUFM**...... Mouvement Universal pour une Federation Mondiale [*World Association of World Federalists - WAWF*] [*Netherlands*]
**MUFOB**.... Metempirical UFO [*Unidentified Flying Object*] Bulletin [*A publication*]
**MUFON**.... Mutual UFO [*Unidentified Flying Object*] Network (EA)
**MUFT**....... Multigroup Fourier Transform [*Code*] [*Nuclear energy*] (NRCH)
**MUFTI**...... Minimum Use of Force Tactical Intervention [*British police*]
**MUG**.......... Manning Unit Group [*Air Force*] (AFM)
**MUG**.......... Marcive Users Group [*Library network*]
**MUG**.......... Maximum Usable Gain [*Bell System*]
**MUG**.......... Methylumbelliferylglucuronide [*Biochemistry*]
**MUG**.......... Ministry of Useless Gestures [*Organization to increase number of voters*] [*British*]
**MUG**.......... Mitosis with Unreplicated Genome [*Cytology*]
**MUG**.......... Mulege [*Mexico*] [*Airport symbol*] [*Obsolete*] (OAG)
**MUG**.......... Multiset Users Group (EA)
**MUG**.......... MUMPS [*Massachusetts General Hospital Utility Multiprogramming System*] Users' Group (EA)
**MUG**.......... Murgor Resources, Inc. [*Vancouver Stock Exchange symbol*]
**MuG**........... Musik und Gesellschaft [*A publication*]

**MUGA**....... Multiple-Gated Acquisition [*Nuclear medicine*]
**MU Gazette** ... Melbourne University. Gazette [*A publication*] (APTA)
**MUGB**....... Methylumbelliferyl Guanidinobenzoate [*Biochemistry*]
**MUGM**...... Guantanamo, US Naval Air Base [*Cuba*] [*ICAO location identifier*] (ICLI)
**MUGN** ...... Giron [*Cuba*] [*ICAO location identifier*] (ICLI)
**MUGSE** .... Multimission-Unique Ground Support Equipment (MCD)
**MUGT**....... Guantanamo [*Cuba*] [*ICAO location identifier*] (ICLI)
**MUH** ........ Memorial University of Newfoundland, Health Sciences Library [*UTLAS symbol*]
**Muh** .......... Muhasebe [*Accounting, Accountancy*] [*Turkish*]
**MUHA** ...... Habana/Jose Marti [*Cuba*] [*ICAO location identifier*] (ICLI)
**MUHG** ...... Holguin [*Cuba*] [*ICAO location identifier*] (ICLI)
**MUHLA2** ... Muehlenzeitung [*A publication*]
**Muhle Mischfuttertech** ... Muehle und Mischfuttertechnik [*A publication*]
**MUI**.......... Fort Indiantown Gap (Annville), PA [*Location identifier*] [*FAA*] (FAAL)
**MUI**.......... Machine Utilization Index [*Data processing*]
**MUI**.......... Mashhad University [*Iran*] [*Seismograph station code, US Geological Survey*] (SEIS)
**MUI**.......... Mass Unbalance Input [*Data processing*]
**MUI**.......... Mode-Independent Unnumbered Information
**MUI**.......... Monsoonal Upwelling Index [*Paleoceanography*]
**MUI**.......... Movement for the Unity of the Left [*Ecuador*] [*Political party*] (PPW)
**MuI**.......... Music Index [*A publication*]
**MUIG**........ Minicomputer Users Interest Group [*Later, Mini/Micro Special Interest Group*] (EA)
**Muir Gai**.... Muirhea's Institutes of Gaius [*A publication*] (DLA)
**Muirhead Tech** ... Muirhead Technique [*A publication*]
**Muirh Lib P** ... Muirhead Library of Philosophy [*A publication*]
**MUIS**......... Isabella [*Cuba*] [*ICAO location identifier*] (ICLI)
**MUJ** ......... Mui [*Ethiopia*] [*Airport symbol*] (OAG)
**MUJA** ....... Majana [*Cuba*] [*ICAO location identifier*] (ICLI)
**MUJSAX**.. Marathwada University. Journal of Science. Section A. Physical Sciences [*A publication*]
**MUJSBY**... Marathwada University. Journal of Science. Section B. Biological Sciences [*A publication*]
**MUK**.......... Alamogordo, NM [*Location identifier*] [*FAA*] (FAAL)
**MuK**.......... Maske und Kothurn [*A publication*]
**MUK**.......... Mauke [*Cook Islands*] [*Airport symbol*] (OAG)
**MUK**.......... Mukerian [*India*] [*Seismograph station code, US Geological Survey*] [*Closed*] (SEIS)
**MUK**.......... Wirtschaftlichkeit [*A publication*]
**Mukomol'-Elevator Prom** ... Mukomol'no-Elevatornaya Promyshlennost' [*A publication*]
**Mukomolno Elevat Kombikormovaya Promst** ... Mukomol'no Elevatornaya i Kombikormovaya Promyshlennost [*A publication*]
**Mukomolno Elevat Promst** ... Mukomol'no-Elevatornaya Promyshlennost' [*A publication*]
**MUL**.......... Manned Underwater Laboratories [*Marine science*] (MSC)
**MUL**.......... Manufacturing under Licence [*British*] (DS)
**MUL**.......... Master Urgency List [*Navy*]
**MUL**.......... Mobile-Moored Undersea Laboratory
**MUL**.......... Moultrie, GA [*Location identifier*] [*FAA*] (FAAL)
**MUL**.......... Mullan [*Idaho*] [*Seismograph station code, US Geological Survey*] (SEIS)
**MUL**.......... MULS [*Minnesota Union List of Serials*], Minneapolis, MN [*OCLC symbol*] (OCLC)
**mul** ........... Multilingual [*MARC language code*] [*Library of Congress*] (LCCP)
**MUL**.......... Multiplexer
**MUL**.......... Multiply (MDG)
**MuL**.......... Music and Letters [*A publication*]
**MULA**....... Monash University Law Alumni [*Australia*]
**MULASSS** ... Multiple LASER Source Signature Simulator (MCD)
**MU Law R** ... Melbourne University. Law Review [*A publication*] (APTA)
**MULB** ....... Habana [*Cuba*] [*ICAO location identifier*] (ICLI)
**MULDEM** ... Multiplexer/Demultiplexer [*Bell Laboratories*]
**MULDEX** ... Multipoint Cross-Reference Index
**MULE**....... Manned-Unmanned Lunar Explorer
**MULE**....... Modular Universal LASER Equipment (MCD)
**MULE**....... Multiple Use Linear Engergizer [*Automotive engineering*]
**MULH**....... Habana [*Cuba*] [*ICAO location identifier*] (ICLI)
**Mu LJ**........ Municipal Law Journal [*A publication*] (DLA)
**MULL** ....... Modern Uses of Logic in Law
**MULL** ....... Mullion [*Technical drawings*]
**Mullard Tech Commun** ... Mullard Technical Communications [*A publication*]
**MULM**...... La Coloma [*Cuba*] [*ICAO location identifier*] (ICLI)
**MULO**...... Multipurpose Lightweight Overboot [*Army*]
**MULR**....... Malayan Union Law Reports [*1946-47*] [*A publication*] (ILCA)
**MULR**....... Melbourne University. Law Review [*A publication*]
**MULR**....... Muller
**MULRA6**.. Muellerei [*A publication*]
**MULS**........ Minnesota Union List of Serials [*A publication*]
**MULS**........ Signed Multiplication [*Data processing*]
**MULSP**..... Missouri Union List of Serial Publications [*St. Louis Public Library*] [*Missouri*] [*Information service or system*] (IID)
**MULT** ....... Multi Solutions, Inc. [*NASDAQ symbol*] (NQ)
**MULT** ....... Multiple
**MULT** ....... Multiply (NASA)
**MULTA** .... Multiple-Use Land Alliance (EA)
**MULTEWS** ... Multiple Electronics Warfare Surveillance [*DoD*]
**MULTEWS** ... Multitarget Electronic Warfare System
**MULTH**.... Multilith
**multi**.......... Multicolored [*Philately*]
**MULTI**...... Multiplexer
**MULTICAP** ... Australian Society for Multiply Handicapped Children
**MULTICS** ... Multiplexed Information and Computing Service [*Honeywell, Inc.*]
**Multicult**.... Multiculturalism [*A publication*]
**Multicult Ed** ... Multicultural Education [*A publication*]
**Multicult Ed J** ... Multicultural Education Journal [*A publication*]
**Multidisciplinary Res** ... Multidisciplinary Research [*A publication*]
**Multidiscip Res** ... Multidisciplinary Research [*A publication*]
**Multinational Bus** ... Multinational Business [*A publication*]
**Multinatl**.... Multinational Monitor [*A publication*]
**Multinatl Monit** ... Multinational Monitor [*A publication*]
**multip**......... Multiparous [*Obstetrics*]
**Multi Scler Abstr** ... Multiple Sclerosis Abstracts [*A publication*]
**Multivar Behav Res** ... Multivariate Behavioral Research [*A publication*]
**Multivar Behav Res Monogr** ... Multivariate Behavioral Research Monograph [*A publication*]
**Multiv Be R** ... Multivariate Behavioral Research [*A publication*]
**multivits**..... Multivitamins [*Pharmacy*]
**Mult Mon**.. Multinational Monitor [*A publication*]
**MULTOTS** ... Multiple Units Link 11 Test and Operational Training System [*Navy*] (NVT)
**MULTR**..... Multimeter (AAG)
**MULTR**..... Multiplier
**MULU**....... Unsigned Multiplication [*Data processing*]
**MuLV**........ Murine Leukemia Virus [*Also, MLV*]
**Mum**.......... Chrysanthemum [*Horticulture*]
**MUM**........ Maximum Useful Magnification (MCD)
**MUM**........ Melbourne University. Magazine [*A publication*] (APTA)
**MUM**........ Method of Unweighted Means [*Statistics*]
**MUM**........ Methodology for Unmanned Manufacture [*Robotics project*] [*Japan*]
**MUM**........ Multiple Unit Message [*Telecommunications*] (IEEE)
**MUM**........ Multiuse Manuscript
**MUM**........ Multiuser Monitor
**MUM**........ Mumias [*Kenya*] [*Airport symbol*] [*Obsolete*] (OAG)
**MUM**........ Music Ministry [*A publication*]
**MUM**........ University of Mississippi, University, MS [*OCLC symbol*] (OCLC)
**MUMA**...... Punta De Maisi [*Cuba*] [*ICAO location identifier*] (ICLI)
**MUMAD**... Museum Angkatan Darat [*Indonesia*]
**MUMC**...... Melbourne University Mountaineering Club [*Australia*]
**MUMEB**... Music Clubs Magazine [*A publication*]
**MUMED9** ... Museum Memoir [*Salisbury*] [*A publication*]
**MUMEEA** ... Mundo Medico [*A publication*]
**Mumf**......... Mumford's Jamaica Reports [*A publication*] (DLA)
**MUMG**...... Managua [*Cuba*] [*ICAO location identifier*] (ICLI)
**MUMH**..... Matahambre [*Cuba*] [*ICAO location identifier*] (ICLI)
**MUMI**....... Manzanillo [*Cuba*] [*ICAO location identifier*] (ICLI)
**MUMJ**...... Mayajigua [*Cuba*] [*ICAO location identifier*] (ICLI)
**Mum Jam**.. Mumford's Jamaica Reports [*A publication*] (DLA)
**MUMMERS** ... Manned-Unmanned Environmental Research Station (MSC)
**MUMMS**.. Marine Corps Unified Materiel Management System
**Mummy**..... Mature Upwardly Mobile Mommy [*Lifestyle classification*]
**MUMO**..... Moa [*Cuba*] [*ICAO location identifier*] (ICLI)
**MUMP**...... Marshall - University of Michigan Probe [*Rocket flight*]
**MUMPS**.... Massachusetts General Hospital Utility Multiprogramming System [*Programming language*]
**MUMS**...... Mobile Utility Module System (IEEE)
**MUMS**...... Multiple Unguided Mine System (MCD)
**MUMS**...... Multiple-Use MARC [*Machine-Readable Cataloging*] System [*Online retrieval system*] [*Information service or system*] [*Library of Congress*]
**MUMSCMR** ... McGill University [*Montreal*]. Marine Sciences Centre. Manuscript Report [*A publication*]
**MUMT**...... Matanzas [*Cuba*] [*ICAO location identifier*] (ICLI)
**MuMTV**.... Murine Mammary Tumor Virus
**MUMUA**... Music and Musicians [*A publication*]
**MUMZ**...... Manzanillo [*Cuba*] [*ICAO location identifier*] (ICLI)
**MUN**......... Maturin [*Venezuela*] [*Airport symbol*] (OAG)
**MUN**......... Memorial University of Newfoundland [*Marine science*] (MSC)
**MUN**......... Memorial University of Newfoundland Library [*UTLAS symbol*]
**MUN**......... Mundaring [*Australia*] [*Seismograph station code, US Geological Survey*] (SEIS)
**Mun**........... Munford's Reports [*15-20 Virginia*] [*A publication*] (DLA)
**MUN**......... Municipal
**Mun**........... Municipal Law Reporter [*A publication*] (DLA)
**MUN**......... Munitions (AFM)
**Mun**........... Munitions Appeals Reports [*England*] [*A publication*] (DLA)
**MUN**......... Munsingwear, Inc. [*NYSE symbol*] (SPSG)
**MUN**......... Munz Northern Airlines [*Nome, AK*] [*FAA designator*] (FAAC)

**MUN** ......... Musical Newsletter [*A publication*]
**MUNA** ...... La Cubana [*Cuba*] [*ICAO location identifier*] (ICLI)
**MUNAF**.... Movimento de Unidade Nacional Antifacista [*National United Antifascist Movement*] [*Portugal*] [*Political party*] (PPE)
**Mun App**.... Munitions Appeals Reports [*England*] [*A publication*] (DLA)
**Mun App Rep** ... Munitions Appeals Reports [*England*] [*A publication*] (DLA)
**Mun App Sc** ... Munitions of War Acts, Appeal Reports [*1916-20*] [*Scotland*] [*A publication*] (DLA)
**Mun Att'y** .. Municipal Attorney [*A publication*]
**MUNB**....... San Nicolas De Bari [*Cuba*] [*ICAO location identifier*] (ICLI)
**MUNBG**.... Munitions Building [*Obsolete*] [*Washington, DC*]
**MUNC**....... Munitions Command [*Later, Armaments Command*] [*Army*]
**MUNC**....... Nicaro [*Cuba*] [*ICAO location identifier*] (ICLI)
**Munca Sanit** ... Munca Sanitara [*A publication*]
**MunchThZ** ... Muenchener Theologische Zeitschrift [*Munich*] [*A publication*]
**Mun Corp Cas** ... Municipal Corporation Cases [*A publication*] (DLA)
**Mun Ct**....... Municipal Court (DLA)
**Mun Ct App Dist Col** ... Municipal Court of Appeals for the District of Columbia (DLA)
**Mund** ......... De Mundo [*of Aristotle*] [*Classical studies*] (OCD)
**MUND** ...... Model Urban Neighborhood Demonstration
**Mund** ......... Mundus Artium [*A publication*]
**Mundo Apic** ... Mundo Apicola [*A publication*]
**Mundo Electron** ... Mundo Electronico [*A publication*]
**Mundo Text Argent** ... Mundo Textil Argentino [*A publication*]
**MundusA**... Mundus Artium [*A publication*]
**Mundus Art** ... Mundus Artium [*A publication*]
**Mundy** ....... Abstracts of Star Chamber Proceedings [*1550-58*] [*A publication*] (DLA)
**MUNE**....... Multiple Negative [*Circuit*] (AAG)
**Mun & El Cas** ... Municipal and Election Cases [*India*] [*A publication*] (DLA)
**Munf**.......... Munford's Reports [*15-20 Virginia*] [*A publication*] (DLA)
**MUNFA** .... Moderne Unfallverhuetung [*A publication*]
**MUNFLA** ... Memorial University of Newfoundland Folklore and Language Archive [*Research center*] [*Canada*] (RCD)
**Munf (VA)** ... Munford's Reports [*15-20 Virginia*] [*A publication*] (DLA)
**MUNG** ...... Mush until No Good [*Describes destruction of computer software*]
**MUNG** ...... Nueva Gerona [*Cuba*] [*ICAO location identifier*] (ICLI)
**Munger Africana Lib Notes** ... Munger Africana Library Notes [*A publication*]
**Mung Pay** .. Munger on Application of Payments [*A publication*] (DLA)
**MUNI**........ Municipal (AFM)
**MUNI**........ Municipal Development Corp. [*New York, NY*] [*NASDAQ symbol*] (NQ)
**Munibe**....... Munibe. Sociedad de Ciencias Naturales Aranzadi [*San Sebastian*] [*A publication*]
**MUNIC** ..... Municipal
**Munic Adm Eng** ... Municipal Administration and Engineering [*A publication*]
**Munic Aff** .. Municipal Affairs [*A publication*]
**Munic Bldg Mgmt** ... Municipal Building Management [*A publication*]
**Munic & Co Eng** ... Municipal and County Engineering [*A publication*]
**Munic Cty Eng** ... Municipal and County Engineering [*A publication*]
**Munic Eng** ... Municipal Engineer [*A publication*]
**Munic Eng Aust** ... Municipal Engineering in Australia [*A publication*] (APTA)
**Munic Eng in Aust** ... Municipal Engineering in Australia [*A publication*] (APTA)
**Munic Eng (Indianapolis)** ... Municipal Engineering (Indianapolis) [*A publication*]
**Munic Eng J** ... Municipal Engineers Journal [*A publication*]
**Munic Eng (London)** ... Municipal Engineering (London) [*A publication*]
**Munic Engng** ... Municipal Engineering [*A publication*]
**Munic Engr** ... Municipal Engineer [*A publication*]
**Munic J**...... Municipal Journal [*A publication*]
**Munic J Eng** ... Municipal Journal and Engineer [*A publication*]
**Munic J Public Works** ... Municipal Journal and Public Works [*A publication*]
**Munic LR (PA)** ... Municipal Law Reporter [*Pennsylvania*] [*A publication*] (DLA)
**Munic Mirror** ... Municipal Mirror and Queensland Shire Record [*A publication*] (APTA)
**Munic News** ... Municipal News [*A publication*]
**Munic News Water Works** ... Municipal News and Water Works [*A publication*]
**Munic & PL** ... Municipal and Parish Law Cases [*England*] [*A publication*] (DLA)
**Munic and Public Services J** ... Municipal and Public Services Journal [*A publication*]
**Munic Ref Lib Notes** ... New York City Public Library. Municipal Reference Library. Notes [*A publication*]
**Munic Ref & Res Center Notes** ... New York City Municipal Reference and Research Center. Notes [*A publication*]
**Munic Rev** ... Municipal Review [*A publication*]
**Munic & Road Board Gaz** ... Municipal and Road Board Gazette [*A publication*] (APTA)
**Munic & Road Board Gazette** ... Municipal and Road Board Gazette [*A publication*] (APTA)
**Munic Sanit** ... Municipal Sanitation [*A publication*]
**Munic Util** ... Municipal Utilities [*A publication*]
**Munic Util Mag** ... Municipal Utilities Magazine [*A publication*]
**Muni Fin J** ... Municipal Finance Journal [*A publication*]
**MUNIMT** ... Muniment (ROG)
**MUNIREP** ... Munitions Report [*Worldwide report of location and status of air munitions*] [*Military*]
**MUniv** ....... Master of the University
**Munkaved Munka Uezemeue** ... Munkavedelem. Munka-es Uezemegeszseguegy [*A publication*]
**Munk Emp Liab** ... Munkman's Employer's Liability at Common Law [*8th ed.*] [*1975*] [*A publication*] (DLA)
**Mun L Ct Dec** ... Municipal Law Court Decisions [*A publication*]
**Mun LJ**........ Municipal Law Journal [*A publication*] (DLA)
**Mun LR** ..... Municipal Law Reporter [*Pennsylvania*] [*A publication*] (DLA)
**Mun LR** ..... Municipal Law Reports [*1903-13*] [*Scotland*] [*A publication*] (DLA)
**Mun L Rep** ... Chrostwaite's Pennsylvania Municipal Law Reporter [*A publication*] (DLA)
**MUNOPB** ... Memorial University of Newfoundland. Occasional Papers in Biology [*A publication*]
**Mun Ord Rev** ... Municipal Ordinance Review [*A publication*]
**Mun Plan L Rep** ... Municipal and Planning Law Reports [*A publication*]
**Mun Rep**.... Municipal Reports [*Canada*] [*A publication*] (DLA)
**MUNSDM** ... Marathwada University. Journal of Science [*A publication*]
**Munsey**...... Munsey's Magazine [*A publication*]
**MUNSS**..... Munition Support Squadron
**Mun Tort Lib** ... Municipal, School, and State Tort Liability [*A publication*] (DLA)
**MUNU** ...... Central Brasil [*Cuba*] [*ICAO location identifier*] (ICLI)
**MUO** ......... Maximum Undistorted Output
**MUO** ......... Mountain Home, ID [*Location identifier*] [*FAA*] (FAAL)
**MUO** ......... Municipal University of Omaha [*Later, University of Nebraska at Omaha*]
**MUO** ......... Mutual of Omaha Interest Shares, Inc. [*NYSE symbol*] (SPSG)
**MUO** ......... Myocardiopathy of Unknown Origin [*Cardiology*]
**MUOD** ...... Mean Unplanned Outage Duration (IEEE)
**MU Oddfellows Mag** ... Manchester Unity Oddfellows' Magazine [*A publication*] (APTA)
**MUON** ...... Mu-Meson [*An elementary particle*]
**MUOX**....... Musk-Ox [*A publication*]
**MUOXD**.... Musk-Ox [*A publication*]
**MU & P** ..... Makeup and Purification [*Nuclear energy*] (NRCH)
**MUP**.......... Manchester University Press [*Manchester, England*]
**MUP**.......... Master of Urban Planning
**MUP**.......... Molded Urea Plastics
**MUP**.......... Motor Unit Potential
**MUP**.......... Mouvement de l'Unite Populaire [*Popular Unity Movement*] [*Tunisia*] [*Political party*] (PD)
**MUPA** ....... Punta Alegre [*Cuba*] [*ICAO location identifier*] (ICLI)
**MUPAS**..... Melbourne University Programme in Antarctic Studies [*Australia*]
**MUPB** ....... Baracoa Playa/Habana [*Cuba*] [*ICAO location identifier*] (ICLI)
**MUPEJARS** ... Multiple Peanut-Butter Jars [*Unconventional musical instrument used in performance by the "Music for Homemade Instruments" ensemble*]
**MUPID** ..... Multiple Universally Programmable Intelligent Decoder [*Telecommunications*] (TSSD)
**MUPL** ....... Military Urgency Planning List (NG)
**MUPL** ....... Mock-Up Planning
**MUPL** ....... Pilon [*Cuba*] [*ICAO location identifier*] (ICLI)
**MUPO**....... Maximum Undistorted Power Output
**MUPO**....... Multiple Positive [*Circuit*] (AAG)
**MUPPATS** ... Multiparticle Position- and Time- Sensitive Detector
**MUPPET** .. Marionette and Puppet
**Muppie**....... Mennonite Urban Professional [*Lifestyle classification*]
**Muppie**....... Middle-Aged Urban Pinhead [*Lifestyle classification*]
**Muppie**....... Middle-Aged Urban Professional [*Lifestyle classification*]
**Muppy** ....... Male Urban Professional [*Lifestyle classification*]
**MUPR** ....... Pinar Del Rio [*Cuba*] [*ICAO location identifier*] (ICLI)
**MUPROF** ... Multiple Projected Fibonacci [*Microwave circuit*]
**MUPS**........ Central Guatemala [*Cuba*] [*ICAO location identifier*] (ICLI)
**MUPS**........ Manpower Utilisation and Payment Structure [*Imperial Chemical Industries*] [*British*]
**MUPS**........ Mechanized Unit Property System [*Telecommunications*] (TEL)
**MUPS**........ Minimum Universal Pension System [*Proposed to reform pension coverage*]
**MUPS**........ Multiple Utility Peripheral System [*Data processing*]
**MUPT** ....... Patria [*Cuba*] [*ICAO location identifier*] (ICLI)
**MuPV** ........ Murine Polyomavirus [*Medicine*]
**MUR**.......... Al-Mustansiriya University. Review [*Baghdad*] [*A publication*]
**MUR**.......... Management Update and Retrieval System (NRCH)
**MUR**.......... Manpower Utilization Report (MCD)
**MUR**.......... Marudi [*Malaysia*] [*Airport symbol*] (OAG)
**MUR**.......... Melbourne University Rifles [*Australia*]
**MUR**.......... Mock-Up Reactor [*NASA*]
**MUR**.......... Montana Utilities Reports [*A publication*] (DLA)
**Mur**........... Muramic Acid [*Also, MurA*] [*Biochemistry*]
**MUR**.......... Murder [*FBI standardized term*]

**MUR**......... Murgab [*USSR*] [*Seismograph station code, US Geological Survey*] [*Closed*] (SEIS)
**Mur**........... Murlyn [*Record label*]
**Mur**........... Murphey's Reports [*5-7 North Carolina*] [*A publication*] (DLA)
**MUR**......... Murphy Oil Corp. [*NYSE symbol*] (SPSG)
**Mur**........... Murray's Ceylon Reports [*A publication*] (DLA)
**Mur**........... Murray's Jury Court Cases [*1815-30*] [*Scotland*] [*A publication*] (DLA)
**Mur**........... Murray's Reports [*New South Wales*] [*A publication*] (APTA)
**MUR**......... Mustang Resources, Inc. [*Vancouver Stock Exchange symbol*]
**Mur**........... Pro Murena [*of Cicero*] [*Classical studies*] (OCD)
**MUR**......... Radio Relay Message Unit [*Telecommunications*] (TEL)
**MURA**....... Midwestern Universities Research Association
**MurA**......... Muramic Acid [*Also, Mur*] [*Biochemistry*]
**Murat Antiq Med Aevi** ... Muratori's Antiquitates Medii Aevi [*A publication*] (DLA)
**MURB**....... Multiple Unit Residential Building [*Canada*]
**MUrbDes(Arch)** ... Master of Urban Design
**MURC**....... Measurable Undesirable Respiratory Contaminants [*Pollution index*] [*Superseded by PSI*]
**MURD**....... Murder (ROG)
**Murd Epit**.. Murdoch's Epitome Canada [*A publication*] (DLA)
**MUREAV** ... Mutation Research. Section on Environmental Mutagenesis and Related Subjects [*A publication*]
**Murex Rev** ... Murex Review [*A publication*]
**MURF**....... Material Utilization Reference File [*Military*]
**MURFAAM** ... Mutual Reduction of Forces and Armaments and Associated Measures
**MURFAAMCE** ... Mutual Reduction of Forces and Armaments and Associated Measures in Central Europe
**Murfree Off Bonds** ... Murfree on Official Bonds [*A publication*] (DLA)
**MURG**....... Machine Utilization Report Generator
**Mur & H**.... Murphy and Hurlstone's English Exchequer Reports [*1836-37*] [*A publication*] (DLA)
**Mur & Hurl** ... Murphy and Hurlstone's English Exchequer Reports [*1836-37*] [*A publication*] (DLA)
**MURI**....... Mild Upper Respiratory Illness [*Virus*] [*Obsolete usage*]
**MURL**....... Mock-Up Release
**Murm Olenevodcheskaya Opytn Stn Sb Nauchn Rab** ... Murmanskaya Olenevodcheskaya Opytnaya Stantsiya. Sbornik Nauchnykh Rabot [*A publication*]
**Muromsk Gos Ped Inst Ucen Zap** ... Muromskii Gosudarstvennyi Pedagogiceskii Institut. Ucenye Zapiski [*A publication*]
**MURP**....... Manned Upperstage Reusable Payload
**MURP**....... Master of Urban and Regional Planning
**Murph**........ Murphey's Reports [*5-7 North Carolina*] [*A publication*] (DLA)
**Murp & H**.. Murphy and Hurlstone's English Exchequer Reports [*1836-37*] [*A publication*] (ILCA)
**Murph & H** ... Murphy and Hurlstone's English Exchequer Reports [*1836-37*] [*A publication*] (DLA)
**Murph (NC)** ... Murphey's Reports [*5-7 North Carolina*] [*A publication*] (DLA)
**Murr**.......... Murray's Ceylon Reports [*A publication*] (DLA)
**Murr**.......... Murray's Jury Court Cases [*1815-30*] [*Scotland*] [*A publication*] (DLA)
**Murr**.......... Murray's Laws and Acts of Parliament [*Scotland*] [*A publication*] (DLA)
**Murr**.......... Murray's Reports [*New South Wales*] [*A publication*] (APTA)
**MURR**....... University of Missouri Research Reactor
**Murray**....... Murray's Magazine [*A publication*]
**Murray**....... Murray's Scotch Jury Court Reports [*A publication*] (DLA)
**Murray (Ceylon)** ... Murray's Ceylon Reports [*A publication*] (DLA)
**Murray (Scot)** ... Murray's Scotch Jury Trials [*A publication*] (DLA)
**Murray's Eng Dict** ... Murray's English Dictionary [*A publication*] (DLA)
**Murray VA** ... Murray Valley Annual [*A publication*] (APTA)
**Murr Over Cas** ... Murray's Overruled Cases [*A publication*] (DLA)
**MURS**....... Mouvement Universel de la Responsabilite Scientifique [*Universal Movement for Scientific Responsibility - UMSR*] (EAIO)
**MURS**....... Mursley [*England*]
**MURT**....... Murrelet [*A publication*]
**Mur Tab Cas** ... Murray's Table of United States Cases [*A publication*] (DLA)
**Mur Us**...... Murray's History of Usury [*A publication*] (DLA)
**Mur US Ct** ... Murray's Proceedings in the United States Courts [*A publication*] (DLA)
**MUS**......... Magnetic Unloading System
**MUS**......... Maintenance Utilization Sheet
**MUS**......... Manned Underwater Station
**MUS**......... Mass Unbalance Spin
**MUS**......... Master of Urban Studies (ADA)
**MUS**......... Mauritius [*ANSI three-letter standard code*] (CNC)
**MUS**......... Methylumbelliferone Sulfate [*Biochemistry*]
**MUS**......... Monetary Unit Sampling (ADA)
**MUS**......... Multinational Services [*A publication*]
**MUS**......... Multiprogramming Utility System [*Regnecentralen*] [*Denmark*]
**MUS**......... Multiutility System (MCD)
**Mus**........... Musca [*Constellation*]
**MUS**......... Muschocho Explorations Ltd. [*Toronto Stock Exchange symbol*]
**MUS**......... Muscimol [*Biochemistry*]
**Mus**........... Museon. Revue d'Etudes Orientales [*A publication*]
**MUS**......... Museum
**Mus**........... Museum of Foreign Literature [*Littell's*] [*A publication*]
**Mus**........... Museum. Maanblad voor Philologie en Geschiedenis [*A publication*]
**MUS**......... Music
**MUS**......... Music Now [*A publication*]
**MUS**......... Muskinabad [*USSR*] [*Seismograph station code, US Geological Survey*] [*Closed*] (SEIS)
**mus**............ Muskogee [*MARC language code*] [*Library of Congress*] (LCCP)
**Mus**........... Muslim
**MUS**......... University of Southern Mississippi, Hattiesburg, MS [*OCLC symbol*] (OCLC)
**MUSA**....... Manufacturing USA [*A publication*]
**MUSA**....... Multiple Unit Steerable Antenna [*Electronics*]
**MUSA**....... San Antonio De Los Banos [*Cuba*] [*ICAO location identifier*] (ICLI)
**MUSA**....... Seaman Apprentice, Musician, Striker [*Navy rating*]
**Mus Academy Jl** ... Music Academy. Journal [*A publication*]
**Mus AD**..... Doctor of Musical Arts
**Mus Afr**..... Museum Africum [*A publication*]
**Mus Am**..... Musical America [*A publication*]
**Mus Anal**... Musical Analysis [*A publication*]
**Mus Antropol Etnogr** ... Museo di Antropologia ed Etnografia [*A publication*]
**MUSAP**..... Multisatellite Augmentation Program [*NASA*]
**MUSARC** ... Major United States Army Reserve Command (AABC)
**Mus y Artes** ... Boletin de Musica y Artes Visuales [*A publication*]
**Mus & Artists** ... Music and Artists [*A publication*]
**MUSB**....... Mobile Unit Support Base (AAG)
**MusB**......... Musee Belge [*A publication*]
**Mus B**........ Musicae Baccalaureus [*Bachelor of Music*]
**Mus Bac**..... Musicae Baccalaureus [*Bachelor of Music*]
**Mus Bach**... Musicae Baccalaureus [*Bachelor of Music*]
**MUSBDU** ... Moscow University. Soil Science Bulletin [*A publication*]
**Mus Belge** ... Musee Belge [*A publication*] (OCD)
**Mus u Bild** ... Musik und Bildung [*A publication*]
**MUSC**....... Medical University of South Carolina
**MUSC**....... Memphis Union Station Company [*AAR code*]
**Musc**......... Musca [*Constellation*]
**MUSC**....... Muscarine [*Alkaloid*]
**MUSC**....... Muscles [*or Muscular*]
**MUSC**....... Santa Clara [*Cuba*] [*ICAO location identifier*] (ICLI)
**Muscan**...... Musicanada [*English Edition*] [*A publication*]
**MU Sci R**... Melbourne University. Science Review [*A publication*] (APTA)
**Mus Civ Stor Nat Verona Mem Fuori Ser** ... Museo Civico di Storia Naturale di Verona. Memorie. Fuori Serie [*A publication*]
**MUSCLE**.. Millions of Unusual Small Creatures Lurking Everywhere [*Toy by Mattel, Inc.*]
**Muscle Biol** ... Muscle Biology [*A publication*]
**Mus Clubs Mag** ... Music Clubs Magazine [*A publication*]
**Mus Comp Zool (Harv Univ) Annu Rep** ... Museum of Comparative Zoology (Harvard University). Annual Report [*A publication*]
**Mus Comp Zool Mem** ... Museum of Comparative Zoology [*Harvard University*]. Memoirs [*A publication*]
**Mus Cour**.... Musical Courier [*A publication*]
**Mus Crit**.... Museum Criticum [*A publication*]
**Mus D**........ Musicae Doctor [*Doctor of Music*]
**Mus & Dance** ... Music and Dance [*A publication*]
**Mus Dealer** ... Music Dealer [*A publication*]
**Mus Denmark** ... Musical Denmark [*A publication*]
**Mus Dev**.... Muscular Development [*A publication*]
**Mus Disc**.... Musica Disciplina [*A publication*]
**Mus Doc**.... Musicae Doctor [*Doctor of Music*]
**MUSE**....... Medical Use of Simulation Electronics
**MUSE**....... Microcomputer Users in Education
**MUSE**....... MIDI [*Musical Instrument Digital Interface*] Users Sequencer/ Editor [*Roland International Corp.*]
**MUSE**....... Mobile Utilities Support Equipment [*Navy*] (NG)
**MUSE**....... Monitor of Ultraviolet Solar Energy
**MUSE**....... Multimedia User Environment [*Data processing*]
**MUSE**....... Multiple Sub-Nyquist Subsampling Encoding [*Digital recording system introduced 1984*]
**MUSE**....... Musicians United for Safe Energy (EA)
**MUSE**....... Musicians United to Stop Exclusion (EA)
**MUSE**....... Mustang Resources Corp. [*NASDAQ symbol*] (NQ)
**Mus in Ed**.. Music in Education [*A publication*]
**Mus Ed B**... Bachelor of Music Education
**Mus Ed D**.. Doctor of Music Education
**Mus Ed J**... Music Educators Journal [*A publication*]
**Mus Ed M**... Master of Music Education
**Mus Educ J**... Music Educators Journal [*A publication*]
**Musee Guimet Annales Bibl d'Etud** ... Musee Guimet. Annales. Bibliotheque d'Etudes [*A publication*]
**Musee Guimet Annales Bibl de Vulg** ... Musee Guimet. Annales. Bibliotheque de Vulgarisation [*A publication*]

**Musee Nat Homme Centre Canad Et Culture Trad** ... Musee National de l'Homme. Centre Canadien d'Etudes sur la Culture Traditionnelle [*A publication*]
**Museo Nac de Hist Nat de Buenos Aires Anales** ... Museo Nacional de Historia Natural de Buenos Aires. Anales [*A publication*]
**Museum Comp Zool Memoirs** ... Harvard University. Museum of Comparative Zoology. Memoirs [*A publication*]
**Museum d'Hist Nat de Lyon Archives** ... Museum d'Histoire Naturelle de Lyon. Archives [*A publication*]
**Museums Jnl** ... Museums Journal [*A publication*]
**Museum Stud** ... Museum Studies [*A publication*]
**Museum UNESCO** ... Museum. A Quarterly Review Published by UNESCO [*A publication*]
**Mus Events** ... Musical Events [*A publication*]
**MUSF**........ Habana/Santa Fe [*Cuba*] [*ICAO location identifier*] (ICLI)
**Mus Felipe Poey Acad Cienc Cuba Trab Divulg** ... Museo "Felipe Poey." Academia de Ciencias de Cuba. Trabajos de Divulgacion [*A publication*]
**Mus Forum** ... Music Forum [*A publication*]
**MUSG**....... Sagua La Grande [*Cuba*] [*ICAO location identifier*] (ICLI)
**Mus Gal It** ... Musei e Gallerie d'Italia [*A publication*]
**Mus Geneve** ... Musees de Geneve [*A publication*]
**Mus u Ges** ... Musik und Gesellschaft [*A publication*]
**Mus u Gottesd** ... Musik und Gottesdienst [*A publication*]
**Mus G Paed** ... Musicae Graduatus Paedagogus [*Graduate Teacher in Music*]
**Mus Guimet Ann Bibl Etudes** ... Musee Guimet. Annales. Bibliotheque d'Etudes [*A publication*]
**Mus Guimet Ann Bibl Vulg** ... Musee Guimet. Annales. Bibliotheque de Vulgarisation [*A publication*]
**MusH**......... Music Hall [*Record label*] [*Argentina*]
**MUSHA**.... Music Trades [*A publication*]
**Mus Haaretz** ... Museum Ha'aretz [*Tel-Aviv*] Yearbook [*A publication*]
**Mus Ha'aretz Bull** ... Museum Ha'aretz Bulletin [*Tel Aviv*] [*A publication*]
**Mus Helv** ... Museum Helveticum [*A publication*]
**Mus High Educ** ... Music in Higher Education [*A publication*]
**Mus Hist Nat Grigore Antipa Trav** ... Museum d'Histoire Naturelle Grigore Antipa. Travaux [*A publication*]
**Mus Hist Nat Lyon Nouv Arch** ... Museum d'Histoire Naturelle de Lyon. Nouvelles Archives [*A publication*]
**Mus Hist Nat Lyon Nouv Arch Suppl** ... Museum d'Histoire Naturelle de Lyon. Nouvelles Archives. Supplement [*A publication*]
**Mus Hist Nat Mars Bull** ... Museum d'Histoire Naturelle de Marseille. Bulletin [*A publication*]
**Mus at Home** ... Music at Home [*A publication*]
**Mushroom Sci** ... Mushroom Science [*A publication*]
**MUSI**......... Mexico-United States Institute (EA)
**Mus I** ......... Music Index [*A publication*]
**MUSIC**...... Mass Unity Sounding in Concert [*Duke Ellington definition of music*]
**MUSIC**...... McGill University System for Interactive Computing
**MUSIC**...... Multiple System Intelligent Controller [*Data processing*]
**MUSICAM** ... Masking Pattern Universal Sub-Band Integrated Coding and Multiplexing [*Broadcasting*]
**Music Am** .. Music America [*A publication*]
**Music Artic Guide** ... Music Article Guide [*A publication*]
**Music Disci** ... Musica Disciplina [*A publication*]
**Music in Ed** ... Music in Education [*A publication*]
**Music Ed Jnl** ... Music Educators Journal [*A publication*]
**Music Educ** ... Music Educators Journal [*A publication*]
**MusicI**........ Music Index [*A publication*]
**Music Ind**... Music Index [*A publication*]
**Music J** ...... Music Journal [*A publication*]
**Music Lett** ... Music and Letters [*A publication*]
**Music Lib Assn Notes** ... Music Library Association. Notes [*A publication*]
**Music Libr Ass Notes** ... Music Library Association. Notes [*A publication*]
**Music Man** ... Music and Man [*A publication*]
**Musicol** ...... Musicology [*A publication*]
**Musicol Slovaca** ... Musicologica Slovaca [*A publication*]
**MUSICOMP** ... Music Composition
**Music Quart** ... Musical Quarterly [*A publication*]
**Music R** ..... Music Review [*A publication*]
**Music Rev** ... Music Review [*A publication*]
**Music (SMA)** ... Music (Schools of Music Association) [*A publication*]
**Music Teach** ... Music and the Teacher [*A publication*] (APTA)
**Music Time** ... Musical Times [*A publication*]
**Music Trad** ... Music Trades [*A publication*]
**Musikforsch** ... Musikforschung [*A publication*]
**MUSIL**...... Multiprogramming Utility System Interpretive Language [*Regnecentralen*] [*Denmark*]
**Musil S** ...... Musil Studien [*A publication*]
**Mus Industry** ... Music Industry [*A publication*]
**Mus Int** ...... Musik International - Instrumentenbau-Zeitschrift [*A publication*]
**MUSIP**...... Marquette University. Slavic Institute. Papers [*A publication*]
**MUSJ**........ Melanges. Universite Saint Joseph [*A publication*]
**Mus J**......... Museums Journal [*A publication*]
**Mus J**......... Music Journal [*A publication*]
**MUSJ**........ San Julian (Escuela de Aviacion) [*Cuba*] [*ICAO location identifier*] (ICLI)
**Mus Jazz**.... Musica Jazz [*A publication*]
**Mus Jeu**..... Musique en Jeu [*A publication*]
**Mus Jl**........ Music Journal [*A publication*]
**Mus Judaica** ... Musica Judaica [*A publication*]
**MUSKA** .... Music in Education [*A publication*]
**Mus u Kir**... Musik und Kirche [*A publication*]
**Mus Koeln** ... Museen in Koeln. Bulletin [*A publication*]
**MUSL**........ Marconi Underwater Systems Ltd. [*British*]
**MUSL**........ Multiple Stinger Launcher
**MusL**......... Music and Letters [*A publication*]
**MUSL**........ Musician's Library [*A publication*]
**MUSL**........ Muslin (ROG)
**MUSL**........ Santa Lucia [*Cuba*] [*ICAO location identifier*] (ICLI)
**MUSLE**..... Modified Universal Soil Loss Equation [*Agricultural Research Service*]
**Mus Leader** ... Musical Leader [*A publication*]
**Mus and Let** ... Music and Letters [*A publication*]
**Mus & Lett** ... Music and Letters [*A publication*]
**Mus Lib Assn Notes** ... Music Library Association. Notes [*A publication*]
**Muslim W** ... Muslim World [*A publication*]
**Muslim Wld** ... Muslim World [*A publication*]
**Muslim Wrld** ... Muslim World [*A publication*]
**Mus Lit**...... Music and Liturgy [*A publication*]
**Mus et Lit**.. Musique et Liturgie [*A publication*]
**MUSLO** .... Morocco-United States Liaison Office (AFM)
**MuslW**....... Muslim World [*A publication*]
**MUSM** ...... Muscocho Explorations Ltd. [*NASDAQ symbol*] (NQ)
**Mus M** ....... Musicae Magister [*Master of Music*]
**Mus Mag** ... Music Magazine [*A publication*]
**Mus Mak**... Music Maker [*A publication*] (APTA)
**MusMComp** ... Master of Music Composition, University of Manchester [*British*] (DBQ)
**Mus Mem (Salisbury)** ... Museum Memoir (Salisbury) [*A publication*]
**Mus Midden-Afr Ann Reeks in 8O Geol Wet** ... Museum voor Midden-Afrika. Annalen. Reeks in Octavo. Geologische Wetenschappen [*A publication*]
**Mus Min**.... Music Ministry [*A publication*]
**Mus Mod Art Bul** ... New York City Museum of Modern Art. Bulletin [*A publication*]
**MusMPerf** ... Master of Music Performance, University of Manchester [*British*] (DBQ)
**Mus & Mus** ... Music and Musicians [*A publication*]
**Mus N** ........ Museum News [*A publication*]
**Musn**.......... Musician [*British military*] (DMA)
**MUSN**....... Seaman, Musician, Striker [*Navy rating*]
**MUSN**....... Siguanea, Isla De La Juventud [*Cuba*] [*ICAO location identifier*] (ICLI)
**Mus Nac Hist Nat Bol (Santiago)** ... Museo Nacional de Historia Natural. Boletin (Santiago) [*A publication*]
**Mus Nac Hist Nat Bol (Santiago De Chile)** ... Museo Nacional de Historia Natural. Boletin (Santiago De Chile) [*A publication*]
**Mus Nac Hist Nat Notic Mens (Santiago)** ... Museo Nacional de Historia Natural. Noticiario Mensual (Santiago) [*Chile*] [*A publication*]
**Mus Nac Hist Nat Not Mens (Santiago)** ... Museo Nacional de Historia Natural. Noticiario Mensual (Santiago) [*Chile*] [*A publication*]
**Mus Nac Hist Nat (Santiago De Chile) Publ Ocas** ... Museo Nacional de Historia Natural (Santiago De Chile). Publicacion Ocasional [*A publication*]
**Mus Nac Hist Natur Buenos Aires An** ... Museo Nacional de Historia Natural de Buenos Aires. Anales [*A publication*]
**Mus Nac Mex An** ... Museo Nacional de Mexico. Anales [*A publication*]
**Mus Nac Pubs Avulas** ... Museu Nacional. Publicacoes Avulsas [*A publication*]
**Mus Nat Homme Publ Ethnol** ... Musee National de l'Homme. Publications d'Ethnologie [*A publication*]
**Mus Nat Homme Public Archeol** ... Musee National de l'Homme. Publications d'Archeologie [*A publication*]
**Mus Natl Hist Nat Bull** ... Museum National d'Histoire Naturelle. Bulletin [*A publication*]
**Mus Natl Hist Nat Mem Ser A (Paris)** ... Museum National d'Histoire Naturelle. Memoires. Serie A. Zoologie (Paris) [*A publication*]
**Mus Natl Hist Nat Not Syst** ... Museum National d'Histoire Naturelle. Notulae Systematicae [*A publication*]
**Mus Natl Hist Nat (Paris) Mem Ser C** ... Museum National d'Histoire Naturelle. Memoires. Serie C. Sciences de la Terre (Paris) [*A publication*]
**Mus Natl Histoire Nat Bull** ... Museum National d'Histoire Naturelle. Bulletin [*A publication*]
**Mus Natl Hung Ann Hist-Nat** ... Museum Nationale Hungaricum. Annales Historico-Naturales [*A publication*]
**Mus Natnl Hist Nat (Paris) Mem Ser C** ... Museum National d'Histoire Naturelle. Memoires. Serie C (Paris) [*A publication*]
**Mus News** ... Music News [*A publication*]
**Mus News** ... Musical Newsletter [*A publication*]
**Mus News Prague** ... Music News from Prague [*A publication*]
**Mus North Ariz Bull** ... Museum of Northern Arizona. Bulletin [*A publication*]
**Mus North Ariz Res Cent (Flagstaff) Annu Rep** ... Museum of Northern Arizona and Research Center (Flagstaff). Annual Report [*A publication*]

**Mus Not Am Num Soc** ... Museum Notes. American Numismatic Society [*A publication*]
**Mus Oggi** ... Musica d'Oggi. Rassegna di Vita e di Cultura Musicale [*A publication*]
**Mus d'Oggi** ... Musica d'Oggi. Rassegna di Vita e di Cultura Musicale [*A publication*]
**Mus Op** ...... Musical Opinion [*A publication*]
**Mus Paleontol Pap Paleontol** ... Museum of Paleontology. Papers on Paleontology [*A publication*]
**Mus Parade** ... Music Parade [*A publication*]
**Mus Para Emilio Goeldi Publ Avulsas** ... Museu Paraense Emilio Goeldi. Publicacoes Avulsas [*A publication*]
**Mus Par E Goeldi Pub Avulsas** ... Museu Paraense Emilio Goeldi. Publicacoes Avulsas [*A publication*]
**Mus P & L** ... Musician, Player, and Listener [*A publication*]
**Mus Pontevedra** ... Museo de Pontevedra [*A publication*]
**Mus Q** ........ Musical Quarterly [*A publication*]
**Mus Qu** ...... Musical Quarterly [*A publication*]
**Mus R** ........ Music Review [*A publication*]
**MUSR** ....... Simon Reyes [*Cuba*] [*ICAO location identifier*] (ICLI)
**Mus R Afr Centr (Tervuren Belg) Rapp Annu Dep Geol Mineral** ... Musee Royal de l'Afrique Centrale (Tervuren, Belgique). Rapport Annuel du Departement de Geologie et de Mineralogie [*A publication*]
**Mus R Afr Cent (Tervuren Belg) Ann Ser Octavo Sci Geol** ... Musee Royal de l'Afrique Centrale (Tervuren, Belgique). Annales. Serie in Octavo. Sciences Geologiques [*A publication*]
**Mus R Afr Cent (Tervuren Belg) Ann Ser Octavo Sci Zool** ... Musee Royal de l'Afrique Centrale (Tervuren, Belgique). Annales. Serie in Octavo. Sciences Zoologiques [*A publication*]
**Mus R Afr Cent (Tervuren Belg) Doc Zool** ... Musee Royal de l'Afrique Centrale (Tervuren, Belgique). Documentation Zoologique [*A publication*]
**Mus R Afr Cent (Tervuren Belg) Do Zool** ... Musee Royal de l'Afrique Centrale (Tervuren, Belgique). Documentation Zoologique [*A publication*]
**Mus Reg Sci Nat Boll** ... Museo Regionale di Scienze Naturali. Bollettino [*A publication*]
**Mus Rev** ..... Music Review [*A publication*]
**Mus R d'Hist Nat Belgique B** ... Musee Royal d'Histoire Naturelle de Belgique. Bulletin [*A publication*]
**Mus Roy Afr Cent Dep Geol Mineral Rap Ann** ... Musee Royal de l'Afrique Centrale. Departement de Geologie et de Mineralogie. Rapport Annuel [*A publication*]
**MUSRP** ..... McGill University Savanna Research Project (MCD)
**MUSS** ........ Missile Unit Support System
**MUSS** ........ Module Utility Support Structure (NASA)
**MusS** ......... Musees Suisses [*A publication*]
**MUSS** ........ Musical Series [*A publication*]
**MUSS** ........ Sancti Spiritus [*Cuba*] [*ICAO location identifier*] (ICLI)
**Mus Sacra** ... Musica Sacra [*A publication*]
**Mus Scene** ... Music Scene [*A publication*]
**Mus Schall** ... Musica Schallplatte. Zeitschrift fuer Schallplattenfreunde [*A publication*]
**Mus in Schule** ... Musik in der Schule [*A publication*]
**Mus Slovaca** ... Musicologica Slovaca [*A publication*]
**Mus Stor Nat Ven Tridentia Studi Trentini Sci Nat** ... Museo di Storia Naturale della Venezia Tridentina. Studi Trentini di Scienze Naturali [*Italy*] [*A publication*]
**Mus Stud** ... Museum Studies. Art Institute of Chicago [*A publication*]
**Mus Superv J** ... Music Supervisors Journal [*A publication*]
**Mus Survey** ... Music Survey [*A publication*]
**MUS & T** ... Manned Undersea Science and Technology [*Marine science*] (MSC)
**MUST** ....... Manned Undersea Station
**MUST** ....... Manpower Utilization System and Techniques [*Department of State*]
**MUST** ....... Maximum Utilization of Skills and Training [*Civil Service Commission*]
**MUST** ....... Medical Unit Self-Contained Transportable [*Field hospital*] [*Army*]
**MUST** ....... Mobile Underwater Surveillance Team (MCD)
**MUST** ....... Mobile Unit Sanitation Trailer
**Mus T** ........ Musical Times [*A publication*]
**MUST** ....... Mustang Co., Inc. [*NASDAQ symbol*] (NQ)
**MUSTARD** ... Multiunit Space Transport and Recovery Device (MCD)
**Mus Tcr** ..... Music Teacher and Piano Student [*A publication*]
**Mus Teach Nat Assn Proc** ... Music Teachers National Association. Proceedings [*A publication*]
**Mus Teyler Archiv** ... Musee Teyler. Archives [*A publication*]
**Mus Theory Spectrum** ... Music Theory Spectrum [*A publication*]
**Mus Times** ... Musical Times [*A publication*]
**Mus Today Nl** ... Music Today Newsletter [*A publication*]
**MUSTRAC** ... Multiple-Simultaneous-Target Steerable Telemetry Tracking System [*Navy*]
**Mus Trade Rev** ... Music Trade Review [*A publication*]
**Mus Trades** ... Music Trades [*A publication*]
**Mus Tusc** ... Museum Tusculanum [*Kobenhavn*] [*A publication*]
**Mus USA** ... Music USA. Review of the Music Industry and Amateur Music Participation [*A publication*]
**Mus West** .. Music of the West Magazine [*A publication*]
**MUSYA** .... Multiple-Use Sustained-Yield Act of 1960
**Musz Elet** ... Muszaki Elet [*A publication*]
**Muszerugyi Merestech Kozl** ... Muszerugyi es Merestechnikai Kozlemenyek [*Hungary*] [*A publication*]
**Musz Tud** ... Muszaki Tudomany [*A publication*]
**Mut** ........... De Mutatione Nominum [*Philo*] (BJA)
**MUT** .......... Makeup Tank [*Nuclear energy*] (NRCH)
**MUT** .......... Mean Up Time [*NASA*] (KSC)
**MUT** .......... Mercury Unit Test
**MUT** .......... Mock-Up Template
**MUT** .......... Module under Test
**MUT** .......... Multinational Resources [*Vancouver Stock Exchange symbol*]
**MUT** .......... Muntinlupa [*Philippines*] [*Geomagnetic observatory code*]
**MUT** .......... Muscatine, IA [*Location identifier*] [*FAA*] (FAAL)
**MUT** .......... Mutilated
**Mut** ........... Muttersprache [*A publication*]
**MUT** .......... Mutual (ADA)
**Mut** ........... Mutukisna's Ceylon Reports [*A publication*] (DLA)
**MUTA** ....... Multiple Unit Training Assembly [*Army*] (AABC)
**MUTACI** ... Mutuelle des Autochtones de la Cote d'Ivoire [*Mutual Association of the Natives of the Ivory Coast*]
**Mutat Res** .. Mutation Research [*A publication*]
**Mutat Res Genet Toxicol Test** ... Mutation Research; Genetic Toxicology Testing [*A publication*]
**Mutat Res Int J Mutagen Chromosome Breakage Relat Subj** ... Mutation Research. International Journal on Mutagenesis, Chromosome Breakage, and Related Subjects [*A publication*]
**Mutat Res Sect Environ Mutagenesis Relat Subj** ... Mutation Research. Section on Environmental Mutagenesis and Related Subjects [*A publication*]
**Mutat Res Sect Environ Mutagen Relat Subj** ... Mutation Research Section on Environmental Mutagenesis and Related Subjects [*A publication*]
**MUTD** ....... Trinidad [*Cuba*] [*ICAO location identifier*] (ICLI)
**MUTE** ....... Multiple Unit for Transmission Elimination [*Military*] (CAAL)
**Mutech Chem Eng J** ... Mutech Chemical Engineering Journal [*A publication*]
**MUTED** .... Muszaki Tervezes [*A publication*]
**Mut Funds Guide CCH** ... Mutual Funds Guide. Commerce Clearing House [*A publication*]
**MUTI** ........ Manati [*Cuba*] [*ICAO location identifier*] (ICLI)
**Mutisia Acta Bot Colomb** ... Mutisia. Acta Botanica Colombiana [*A publication*]
**MUTL** ....... Mutual (ROG)
**MUTO** ....... Mutual Oil of America [*NASDAQ symbol*] (NQ)
**MUTRS** ..... Mutual Real Estate Investment Trust [*NASDAQ symbol*] (NQ)
**MUTS** ....... Manual Unit Test Set
**MUTS** ....... Multiple Target Simulation (MCD)
**MUTS** ....... Mutual Savings Life Insurance [*NASDAQ symbol*] (NQ)
**MUTSA** ..... Music Teacher [*A publication*]
**MUTSAF** .. Acta Botanica Colombiana [*A publication*]
**MUTT** ....... Military Utility Tactical Truck
**MUTT** ....... Mobile Utility Transfer Tank [*To collect used oils*]
**MUTTS** ..... Multiple Unit Terminal Test Set (MCD)
**MUTU** ....... Mutual Federal Savings & Loan Association [*Elkin, NC*] [*NASDAQ symbol*] (NQ)
**Mutukisna** ... Mutukisna's Ceylon Reports [*A publication*] (DLA)
**MUU** ......... Mount Union, PA [*Location identifier*] [*FAA*] (FAAL)
**MUU** ......... University of Missouri, Columbia, Columbia, MO [*OCLC symbol*] (OCLC)
**MUUJA** .... Musart [*A publication*]
**MUV** .......... Mechanized Utility Vehicle (MCD)
**MUV** .......... Middle Ultraviolet
**MUV** .......... Mobile Underwater Vehicle
**MUV** .......... Philadelphia, PA [*Location identifier*] [*FAA*] (FAAL)
**MUVA** ....... Central Primero De Enero [*Cuba*] [*ICAO location identifier*] (ICLI)
**Muves Ertes** ... Mueveszettoerteneti Ertesitoe [*A publication*]
**MUVR** ....... Varadero [*Cuba*] [*ICAO location identifier*] (ICLI)
**MUVT** ....... Las Tunas [*Cuba*] [*ICAO location identifier*] (ICLI)
**MUW** ......... Mascara [*Algeria*] [*Airport symbol*] (OAG)
**MUW** ......... Music Wire
**MUW** ......... University of Mississippi, School of Law Library, University, MS [*OCLC symbol*] (OCLC)
**MUWO** ..... Muir Woods National Monument
**MUWS** ..... Manned Underwater Station
**MUWU** ..... Mouse Uterine Weight Unit [*Gynecology*]
**MUX** .......... Multan [*Pakistan*] [*Airport symbol*] (OAG)
**MUX** .......... Multiplex [*or Multiplexer*] [*Telecommunications*]
**MUX** .......... Musto Explorations Ltd. [*Toronto Stock Exchange symbol*]
**MUXART** ... Multiplexed Asynchronous Receiver/Transmitter (MCD)
**MUX/DEMUX** ... Multiplexer and Demultiplexer
**MUXER** .... Multiplexer
**MUXES** .... Multiplexes [*or Multiplexers*] [*Telecommunications*]
**MUXMOD** ... Multiplex Modulation
**MUX/PRI/SEC** ... Multiplexer/Priority/Second
**MUXV** ....... Musto Explorations Ltd. [*Vancouver, BC*] [*NASDAQ symbol*] (NQ)
**MUY** .......... Management International Review [*A publication*]
**MUY** .......... Toolik, AK [*Location identifier*] [*FAA*] (FAAL)

**MUZ** Musoma [*Tanzania*] [*Airport symbol*] (OAG)
**Muz** Muzeon [*A publication*]
**Muza** Muza and Other Labels [*Record label*] [*Poland*]
**MUZAK** Music and Kodak [*Terms combined to coin brand name for canned music*]
**Muz F** Muzykal'naya Fol'kloristika [*A publication*]
**MUZG** Zaragoza [*Cuba*] [*ICAO location identifier*] (ICLI)
**MUZH** Muzzle Hatch
**Muzikol Zbornik** Muzikoloski Zbornik [*A publication*]
**Muz Istor Munic Bucur** Muzeul de Istorie al Municipiului Bucuresti [*A publication*]
**Muz Nat** Muzeul National [*A publication*]
**Muz Pam Kul** Muzei i Pametnizi na Kulturata [*A publication*]
**Muz Pam Kult** Muzei i Pametnizi na Kulturata [*A publication*]
**Muz Pitesti** Muzeul din Pitesti. Studii si Comunicari. Istorie-Stiintele Naturii [*A publication*]
**Muz Stiint Naturii Bacau Stud Comun** Muzeul de Stiintele Naturii Bacau Studii si Comunicari [*A publication*]
**Muz Vlastivedna Prace** Muzejni a Vlastivedna Prace [*A publication*]
**Muz Zbornik** Muzikoloski Zbornik - Musicological Annual [*A publication*]
**MV** Airlines of Western Australia [*Australia*] [*ICAO designator*] (ICDA)
**M/V** Magnetic Variation (MCD)
**MV** Mahzor Vitry [*A publication*] (BJA)
**MV** Main Verb [*Linguistics*]
**MV** Majority-Vote Technique [*Parapsychology*]
**MV** Maldives [*ANSI two-letter standard code*] (CNC)
**MV** Manned Vehicle
**MV** Manpower Voucher [*Army*] (AABC)
**MV** Mantle Vessel
**MV** Manual Valve (MCD)
**MV** Manufacturing Verification (NASA)
**MV** Mare Vaporum [*Sea of Vapor*] [*Lunar area*]
**MV** Mariner Venus Project [*NASA*]
**MV** Market Value
**MV** Mauve [*Philately*] (ROG)
**MV** McFaddin Ventures, Inc. [*AMEX symbol*] (SPSG)
**MV** Mean Value
**MV** Mean Variation
**MV** Measles Virus
**MV** Measured Value
**M and V** Meat-and-Vegetable [*A canned ration*] [*Military*]
**MV** Mechanical Ventilation [*Medicine*]
**MV** Medial Vestibular Nucleus [*Neuroanatomy*]
**MV** Medicus Veterinarius [*Veterinary Physician*]
**MV** Medium Voltage
**MV** Medium Volume
**MV** Megavolt
**Mv** Mendelevium [*Chemical element*] [*Symbol is Md*]
**MV** Mentor Exploration & Development Co. Ltd. [*Toronto Stock Exchange symbol*]
**M of V** [*The*] Merchant of Venice [*Shakespearean work*]
**MV** Merchant Vessel
**MV** Mercury Vapor
**MV** Methyl Violet [*A dye*]
**MV** Methyl Viologen [*Organic chemistry*]
**MV** Mezza Voce [*Half the Power of the Voice*] [*Music*]
**MV** Microvilli [*Cytology*]
**MV** Midland Valley R. R. [*AAR code*]
**MV** Military Vigilance (NATG)
**MV** Million Volts
**mV** Millivolt
**MV** Minority Voices [*A publication*]
**MV** Minute Ventilation [*Medicine*]
**MV** Minute Volume [*Medicine*]
**MV** Mitral Valve [*Cardiology*]
**MV** Mixed Venous [*Blood*]
**MV** Modern Varieties [*Agriculture*]
**MV** Modus Vivendi [*Way of Living*] [*Latin*]
**MV** Molar Volume [*Chemistry*]
**MV** Money Velocity [*Economics*]
**MV** Montevideo [*City in Uruguay*] (ROG)
**MV** Motor Vessel
**MV** Motor Volunteers [*British military*] (DMA)
**MV** Motorized Valve (KSC)
**MV** Move [*Telecommunications*] (TEL)
**MV** Multivibrator
**MV** Multivitamins [*Nutrition*]
**MV** Music of the Vatican [*Record label*] [*France*]
**MV** Musica Viva (ADA)
**MV** Muzzle Velocity [*Ballistics*]
**MV** Mycoplasmatales Virus
**MVA** Machine Vision Association [*Later, MVA/SME*] (EA)
**MVA** Machinists Vise Association [*Later, HTI*] (EA)
**MVA** Main Valve Actuator (NASA)
**MVA** Manufacturing Value Added
**MVA** Marginal Value Analysis (MCD)
**MVA** Mean Vertical Acceleration
**MVA** Megavolt-Ampere
**MvA** Memorie van Antwoord [*A publication*]
**MVA** Mercury Volatilizing Activity
**MVA** Merrimack Valley College Library, Manchester, NH [*OCLC symbol*] (OCLC)
**MVA** Mevalonic Acid [*Organic chemistry*]
**MVA** Million Volt Amperes
**MVA** Mina, NV [*Location identifier*] [*FAA*] (FAAL)
**MVA** Minimum Vector Altitude (FAAC)
**MVA** Minnova, Inc. [*Toronto Stock Exchange symbol*] (SPSG)
**MVA** Mississippi Valley Airways, Inc. [*LaCrosse, WI*] [*FAA designator*] (FAAC)
**MVA** Missouri Valley Authority
**MVA** Mitral Valve Area [*Cardiology*]
**MVA** Modern Volunteer Army
**MVA** Monovinylacetylene [*Organic chemistry*]
**MVA** Motor Vehicle Accident [*Medicine*] (AFM)
**MVA** Motor Vehicle Assembly [*Military*] [*World War II*]
**MVA** Music Video Association (EA)
**MVA** Myvatn [*Iceland*] [*Airport symbol*] [*Obsolete*] (OAG)
**MVAA** Mitteilungen. Verein zur Abwehr des Antisemitismus [*A publication*]
**MVAeG** Mitteilungen. Vorderasiatisch-Aegyptische Gesellschaft [*A publication*]
**MVAG** Mitteilungen. Vorderasiatisch-Aegyptische Gesellschaft [*A publication*]
**MVAI** Mississippi Valley Airways, Incorporated [*NASDAQ symbol*] (NQ)
**MvA II** Memorie van Antwoord aan de Tweede Kamer [*A publication*]
**MVal** Market Value [*Insurance*]
**MVAL** Mississippi Valley Gas Co. [*NASDAQ symbol*] (NQ)
**MVAP** Modern Volunteer Army Program (AABC)
**MVAR** Megavar
**MVARH** Megavar-Hour
**MVAS** Multipurpose Ventricular Actuating System (NASA)
**MVAS** Murray Valley Air Service [*Australia*]
**MVA/SME** Machine Vision Association [*Society of Manufacturing Engineers*] (EA)
**MVAT** Metacyclic Variant Antigen Type [*Immunology*]
**MVAU** Maximum Volt-Ampere Utilization [*Electronics*]
**MVB** Jahrbuch der Absatz- und Verbrauchsforschung [*A publication*]
**MvB** Maandblad voor Belastingrecht [*A publication*]
**MVB** Martin Van Buren [*US president, 1782-1862*]
**MVB** Mechanical Vacuum Booster
**MVB** Mississippi Valley Motor Freight Bureau, Saint Louis MO [*STAC*]
**MVB** Motor V-Belt
**MVB** Motor Vessel Boat
**MVB** Multivesicular Body
**MVB** Multivibrator
**MVB** Mvengue [*Gabon*] [*Airport symbol*] (OAG)
**MV/BA** Baessler-Archiv. Museen fuer Voelkerkunde [*A publication*]
**MVBC** Mission-Valley Bancorp [*NASDAQ symbol*] (NQ)
**MVBD** Multiple V-Belt Drive
**MVBI** Mitteilungen. Verband Ehemaliger Breslauer und Schlesier in Israel [*Tel Aviv*] [*A publication*]
**MVBL** Movable (MSA)
**MVBR** Multivibrator
**MVBRAV** Multivariate Behavioral Research [*A publication*]
**MVC** Manual Volume Control
**MVC** Maryville College, St. Louis, MO [*OCLC symbol*] (OCLC)
**MVC** Master Vellum Center [*Jet Propulsion Laboratory, NASA*]
**MVC** Master Volume Control (NASA)
**MVC** Maui Volcanic Complex [*Geology*]
**MVC** Maximal Voluntary Contraction
**MVC** Mechanical Vapor Compressor [*Engineering*]
**MVC** Micro Ventures Ltd. [*Vancouver Stock Exchange symbol*]
**MVC** Mississippi Vocational College
**MVC** Missouri Valley College
**MVC** Missouri Valley Conference [*Sports*]
**MVC** Monroeville, AL [*Location identifier*] [*FAA*] (FAAL)
**MVC** Motor Volunteer Corps [*British military*] (DMA)
**MVC** Multiple Variate Counter (IEEE)
**MVCC** Military Vehicle Collectors Club [*Later, MVPA*] (EA)
**MVCDGS** Motor Vehicles and Components Development Grants Scheme [*Australia*]
**MVCU** Multivariable Control Unit [*Data processing*]
**MVD** Doctor of Veterinary Medicine
**MVD** Map and Visual Display
**MVD** Minimum-Variance Deconvolution (MCD)
**MVD** Montevideo [*Uruguay*] [*Airport symbol*] (OAG)
**MVD** Motor Vehicle Department (DLA)
**MVD** Motor Vehicle Distributing [*Military*]
**MVD** Motor Vehicle Driver Selection Battery [*Army*]
**MVDA** Motor Vehicle Dealers Act
**MVDA** Multivariate Variance and Discriminant Analysis [*Mathematics*]
**MVDF** Medium- and Very-High-Frequency Direction-Finding Station
**MVDFC** Mamie Van Doren Fan Club (EA)
**MVD-MGB** Ministerstvo Vnutrennikh Del-Ministerstvo Gosudarstvennoe Bezopasnosti [*Later, KGB*]
**MVDr** Medicus Veterinarius Doctor [*Doctor of Veterinary Medicine*]
**MVDS** Modular Video Data System [*Sperry UNIVAC*]

**MVE** .......... Maple Valley Explorations Ltd. [*Vancouver Stock Exchange symbol*]
**MVE** .......... Mauve [*Philately*] (ROG)
**MVE** .......... Methyl Vinyl Ether [*Organic chemistry*]
**MVE** .......... Mitral Valve Echogram [*Cardiology*]
**MVE** .......... Mobile Vocational Evaluation [*Vocational guidance test*]
**MVE** .......... Montevideo, MN [*Location identifier*] [*FAA*] (FAAL)
**MVE** .......... Multivariate Exponential Distribution [*Statistics*]
**MVE** .......... Murray Valley Encephalitis [*Virus*]
**MVE** .......... Virden-Elkhorn Regional Library, Virden, Manitoba [*Library symbol*] [*National Library of Canada*] (NLC)
**MV Ed** ....... Master of Vocational Education
**MVEE** ........ Military Vehicles and Engineering Establishment [*British*]
**MVEJDP** .. Malaysian Veterinary Journal [*A publication*]
**MVEL** ........ Motor Vehicle Emission Laboratory [*Environmental Protection Agency*]
**MVEMJSUNP** ... My Very Excellent Mother Just Served Us Nine Pies [*Mnemonic guide to the nine planets: Mercury, Venus, Earth, Mars, Jupiter, Saturn, Uranus, Neptune, Pluto*]
**MVEOL** .... Mededeelingen en Verhandelingen Ex Oriente Lux [*A publication*]
**MVEQDC** ... Medecin Veterinaire du Quebec [*A publication*]
**MVetClinStud** ... Master of Veterinary Clinical Studies
**MVetSc** ...... Master of Veterinary Science [*British*] (ADA)
**MVF** .......... Manned Vertical Flight (MCD)
**MVF** .......... Missile Verification Firing
**MVF** .......... MuniVest Fund, Inc. [*AMEX symbol*] (SPSG)
**MVFC** ........ Mack Vickery Fan Club (EA)
**MVFC** ........ Mr. V Fan Club (EA)
**MVFR** ........ Maintain Visual Flight Rules [*Aviation*] (FAAC)
**MVFV** ........ Manned Venus Flyby Vehicle
**MVG** .......... Mengenverbrauchsguttern [*Mass Consumption Goods*] [*German*]
**MVG** .......... Minven Gold Corp. [*Toronto Stock Exchange symbol*]
**MVG** .......... Minven Gold Corp. [*Vancouver Stock Exchange symbol*]
**MVG** .......... MinVen Gold Corp. [*AMEX symbol*] (SPSG)
**MVG** .......... Most Valuable Girl
**MVG** .......... Moving
**MVG** .......... Mycoplasmatales Virus [*from*] Goat
**MVGAFr** ... Mitteilungen. Verein fuer Geschichte und Altertumskunde in Frankfurt-Am-Main [*A publication*]
**MVGDB** .... Mitteilungen. Verein fuer Geschichte der Deutschen in Boehmen [*A publication*]
**MVGGA** .... Mitteilungen. Versuchsstation fuer das Gaerungsgewerbe in Wien (Austria) [*A publication*]
**MVGKA** .... Mitteilungen. Vereinigung der Grosskesselbesitzer [*A publication*]
**MVGKB** .... Mitteilungen. VGB [*Technische Vereinigung der Grosskraftwerksbetreiber*] [*A publication*]
**MVGOW** ... Mitteilungen. Verein fuer Geschichte von Ost- und West Preussen [*A publication*]
**MVGSN** .... Mitteilungen. Verein fuer Geschichte der Stadt Nuernberg [*A publication*]
**MVGVT** .... Mated Vertical Ground Vibration Test [*NASA*] (NASA)
**MvH** .......... Magazijn van Handelsrecht [*A publication*]
**MVH** .......... Mohave Gold, Inc. [*Vancouver Stock Exchange symbol*]
**MVH** .......... Mountain View [*Hawaii*] [*Seismograph station code, US Geological Survey*] (SEIS)
**MVH** .......... Munzautomat Mainz [*A publication*]
**MVh** .......... Vineyard Haven Public Library, Vineyard Haven, MA [*Library symbol*] [*Library of Congress*] (LCLS)
**MVHD** ...... Hospital District Number 10, Virden, Manitoba [*Library symbol*] [*National Library of Canada*] (NLC)
**MVHG** ...... Mitteilungen. Verein der Freunde des Humanistischen Gymnasiums [*A publication*]
**MVHR** ....... Mississippi Valley Historical Review [*A publication*]
**MVI** .......... Maandblad der Vereniging van Inspecteurs van Financien [*A publication*]
**MVI** .......... Macrotrends Ventures, Inc. [*Vancouver Stock Exchange symbol*]
**MVI** .......... Medium Value Item (NATG)
**MVI** .......... Merchant Vessel Inspection Division [*Coast Guard*]
**MVI** .......... Mercury Vapor Isolator
**MVI** .......... Metal Ventilator Institute (EA)
**MV/I** .......... Millivolt to Current [*Converter*] [*Nuclear energy*] (NRCH)
**MVI** .......... Minami Daito Jima [*Volcano Islands*] [*Seismograph station code, US Geological Survey*] (SEIS)
**MVI** .......... Miniature Variable Inductor
**MVI** .......... Motor Vehicle Inspection
**MVIC** ........ Machine Vision International Corporation [*Ann Arbor, MI*] [*NASDAQ symbol*] (NQ)
**MVII** .......... Minnesota Vocational Interest Inventory
**MVIJC** ...... Motor Vehicle Industry Joint Council [*British*] (DCTA)
**MVIS** ......... Maximum Voluntary Isometric Strength
**MVJ** .......... Mandeville [*Jamaica*] [*Airport symbol*] [*Obsolete*] (OAG)
**MVJC** ........ Mount Vernon Junior College [*Washington, DC*]
**MVK** .......... Methyl Vinyl Ketone [*Organic chemistry*]
**MVK** .......... Mulka [*Australia*] [*Airport symbol*] [*Obsolete*] (OAG)
**MVKAUO** ... Mitteilungen. Verein fuer Kunst und Altertum in Ulm und Oberschwaben Ulm [*A publication*]
**MVL** .......... Maandschrift voor Liturgie [*A publication*]
**MVL** .......... Man-Vehicle Laboratory [*Massachusetts Institute of Technology*] [*Research center*] (RCD)
**MVL** .......... Manville Corp. [*NYSE symbol*] (CTT)
**MVL** .......... Marley Vehicle Leasing [*Commercial firm*] [*British*]
**MVL** .......... Mercury Vapor Lamp
**MVL** .......... Monografieen over Vlaamse Letterkunde [*A publication*]
**MVL** .......... Morrisville, VT [*Location identifier*] [*FAA*] (FAAL)
**MVL** .......... Mountain Valley Library System, Sacramento, CA [*OCLC symbol*] (OCLC)
**MVL** .......... Mycoplasmatales Virus [*from*] Acholeplasma laidlawii
**MVL** .......... Mylan Ventures Ltd. [*Vancouver Stock Exchange symbol*]
**MVLA** ....... Mount Vernon Ladies' Association of the Union (EA)
**MVLCA** ..... Mededelingen. Vlaamse Chemische Vereniging [*A publication*]
**MVLS** ........ Magic Valley Regional Library System [*Library network*]
**MVLS** ........ Mandibular Vestibulolingual Sulcoplasty [*Surgery*]
**MVLU** ....... Minimum Variance Linear Unbiased [*Statistics*]
**MVM** ......... Mariner Venus-Mercury Project [*NASA*]
**MVM** ......... Master of Veterinary Medicine
**MVM** ......... Medium-Voltage Mode
**MVM** ......... Million Vehicle Miles
**mV/m** ........ Millivolts per Meter (DEN)
**MVM** ......... Minimum Virtual Memory
**MVM** ......... Minute Virus of Mice
**MVM** ......... Multivolume Monographs
**MVMA** ...... Motor Vehicle Manufacturers Association of the United States (EA)
**MVMC** ...... Motor Vehicle Maintenance Course
**MVMF** ...... Ministerstvo Voenno-Morskogo Flota [*Ministry of the Navy*] [*1950-53; merged into the MO*] [*USSR*]
**MVMFB** .... Mississippi Valley Motor Freight Bureau
**MVMT** ...... Movement (AFM)
**MVN** ......... Magna Ventures Ltd. [*Vancouver Stock Exchange symbol*]
**MVN** ......... Mededeelingen. Vereniging Naamkunde te Leuven en Commissie Naamkunde te Amsterdam [*A publication*]
**MVN** ......... Median Ventricular Nerve [*Medicine*]
**MVN** ......... Mount Vernon [*Illinois*] [*Airport symbol*] (OAG)
**MVNAG** .... Mitteilungen. Verein fuer Nassauische Altertumskunde und Geschichts-Forschung [*A publication*]
**MVNLA** .... Mededeelingen. Vereniging Naamkunde te Leuven en Commissie Naamkunde te Amsterdam [*A publication*]
**MVO** .......... Maximum Venous Outflow [*Medicine*]
**MVO** .......... Member of the Royal Victorian Order [*British*]
**MVO** .......... Military Vehicles Operation [*of General Motors Corp.*]
**MVO** .......... MMC Video One Canada Ltd. [*Toronto Stock Exchange symbol*] [*Vancouver Stock Exchange symbol*]
**MVO** .......... Money Value Only (AFIT)
**MVP** .......... Magnetic Vector Potential
**MVP** .......... Maintenance Verification Plan
**MVP** .......... Manpower Validation Program
**MVP** .......... Master Verification Plan (MCD)
**MVP** .......... Mechanical Vacuum Pump
**MVP** .......... Methyl-Violet Paper (MSA)
**MVP** .......... Minimum Viable Population [*Demographics*]
**MVP** .......... Minority Vendors Program
**MVP** .......... Mitral Valve Prolapse [*Cardiology*]
**MVP** .......... Mitu [*Colombia*] [*Airport symbol*] (OAG)
**MV & P** ...... Morton's Vendors and Purchasers [*1837*] [*A publication*] (DLA)
**MVP** .......... Most Valuable Player [*Athletics*] [*Facetious translation: "Most Volatile Player"*]
**MVP** .......... Most Valuable Princess [*Princess Diana*] [*British*] [*Slang*]
**MVP** .......... Mountain View Public Library, Mountain View, CA [*OCLC symbol*] (OCLC)
**MVP** .......... Multivalue Program [*Data processing*]
**MVP** .......... MVP Capital Corp. [*Toronto Stock Exchange symbol*]
**MVPA** ....... Military Vehicle Preservation Association (EA)
**MVP Ber** ... MVP [*Max-Von-Pettenkofer-Institut*] Berichte [*A publication*]
**MVPhW** .... Mitteilungen. Verein Klassischer Philologen in Wien [*A publication*]
**MVPP** ........ Mustargen [*Nitrogen mustard*], Vinblastine, Procarbazine, Prednisone [*Antineoplastic drug regimen*]
**MVPS** ........ Manually Variable Phase Shifter
**MVPS** ........ Mechanical Vacuum Pump System
**MVPS** ........ Medicare Volume Performance Standard
**MVPS** ........ Mitral Valve Prolapse Syndrome [*Cardiology*]
**MVPS** ........ Multiple Vertical Protective Shelter [*for missiles*] (MCD)
**MVPT** ........ Motor-Free Visual Perception Test
**MVPTG** ..... Medial Vascularized Patellar Tendon Graft [*Sports medicine*]
**MVQ** .......... Malvern, AR [*Location identifier*] [*FAA*] (FAAL)
**MVR** .......... Malabar Volunteer Rifles [*British military*] (DMA)
**MVR** .......... Maneuver (AABC)
**MVR** .......... Maroua [*Cameroon*] [*Airport symbol*] (OAG)
**MVR** .......... Mean Value Reference [*Mathematics*]
**MVR** .......... Mechanical Vapor Recompression [*For evaporators*]
**MVR** .......... Missing Volume Report
**MVR** .......... Mitral Valve Replacement [*Cardiology*]
**mvr** ........... Moldavian Soviet Socialist Republic [*MARC country of publication code*] [*Library of Congress*] (LCCP)
**MVR** .......... Mondavi Resources Ltd. [*Vancouver Stock Exchange symbol*]
**MVR** .......... Motor Vehicle Report
**MVR** .......... Motor Vehicle Reports [*A publication*]

**MVR** ......... Mussoorie Volunteer Rifles [*British military*] (DMA)
**MVRA** ....... Metropolitan Visiting and Relief Association [*British*]
**MVRG** ....... Medieval Village Research Group (EA)
**MVRI** ........ Mixed Vaccine, Respiratory Infection [*Medicine*]
**MVRS** ........ Mechanical Vapor Recovery System [*Engineering*]
**MVRS** ........ Mystic Valley Railway Society (EA)
**MVS** .......... Magnetic Voltage Stabilizer
**MVS** .......... Master of Veterinary Studies
**MVS** .......... Master of Veterinary Surgery
**MVS** .......... Mechanical Vibration System
**MVS** .......... Megastar Ventures [*Vancouver Stock Exchange symbol*]
**MVS** .......... Mennonite Voluntary Service
**MVS** .......... Middle Valve Select (MCD)
**MVS** .......... Millersville State College, Millersville, PA [*OCLC symbol*] (OCLC)
**MVS** .......... Minimum Visual Signal
**MVS** .......... Ministerstvo Vooruzhennykh Sil [*Ministry of the Armed Forces*] [*1946-50; superseded by VM, MVMF*] [*USSR*]
**MVS** .......... Missile Velocity Servo
**MVS** .......... Mission Video System [*NASA*]
**MVS** .......... Mobile Video Services Ltd. [*Washington, DC*] [*Telecommunications*] (TSSD)
**MVS** .......... Modular 8mm Video System [*Eastman Kodak Co.*]
**MVS** .......... Modularized Vehicle Stimulation [*Program*]
**MVS** .......... Movie Star, Inc. [*AMEX symbol*] (SPSG)
**MVS** .......... Multiple Vibration System
**MVS** .......... Multiple Virtual Storage [*IBM Corp.*] [*Data processing*]
**MVS** .......... Multiple Virtual System [*Data processing*]
**MVS** .......... Multivariable Storage [*Data processing*]
**MVSB** ........ Motor Vehicle Storage Building
**MV Sc** ........ Master of Veterinary Science
**MVSL** ........ Mouse Visible Specific Locus [*Test for mutagenesis*]
**MVSMA** .... Mechanical Vibrating Screen Manufacturers Association [*Later, Vibrating Screen Manufacturers Association*] (EA)
**MVSP** ........ Maintain Visual Separation [*Aviation*]
**MVSR** ........ Monthly Vital Statistics Report [*A publication*] (DHSM)
**MVSS** ........ Motor Vehicle Safety Standard
**MVSS** ........ Motor Vehicle Storage Shed [*Army*] (AABC)
**MVSSE** ..... Multiple Virtual Storage System Extension
**MVSt** ......... Master of Veterinary Studies (ADA)
**MVST** ........ Multivest Corp. [*Great Neck, NY*] [*NASDAQ symbol*] (NQ)
**MVSZGA** ... Mein Vertrauen Steht zu Gott Allein [*My Trust Is in God Alone*] [*German*] [*Motto of Johann Adolf II, Duke of Saxony-Weissenfels (1649-97)*]
**MVT** .......... Malfunction Verification Test (MCD)
**MVT** .......... Marginal Value Theorem [*Mathematical model developed by Dr. Eric Charnov*]
**MVT** .......... Market-Value Transmission [*Pricing concept*]
**MVT** .......... Mataiva [*French Polynesia*] [*Airport symbol*] (OAG)
**MVT** .......... Miscellaneous Vector Table
**MVT** .......... Mission Verification Test [*NASA*] (NASA)
**MVT** .......... Mississippi Valley Type [*Ore deposits*] [*Geology*]
**MVT** .......... Moisture Vapor Transmission Rate
**MVT** .......... Monte Vettore [*Italy*] [*Seismograph station code, US Geological Survey*] (SEIS)
**MVT** .......... Mount Vernon Terminal [*AAR code*]
**MVT** .......... Movement (MSA)
**MVT** .......... Multinational Volunteer Teams
**MVT** .......... Multiprogramming with a Variable Number of Tasks [*IBM Corp.*] [*Control program*] [*Data processing*]
**MVTR** ....... Moisture Vapor Transmission Rate
**MVU** .......... Minimum Variance Unbiased [*Statistics*]
**MVU** .......... Musgrave [*Australia*] [*Airport symbol*] [*Obsolete*] (OAG)
**MVUE** ....... Man/Vehicular User Equipment
**MVUE** ....... Minimum Variance Unbiased Estimate [*Statistics*]
**MVULE** ..... Minimum Variance Unbiased Linear Estimator [*Statistics*]
**MVV** .......... Dibevo [*A publication*]
**MVV** .......... Maximum Voluntary Ventilation
**MVV** .......... Mean Vertical Velocity
**MVVPP** ..... Mustargen [*Nitrogen mustard*], Vincristine, Vinblastine, Procarbazine, Prednisone [*Antineoplastic drug regimen*]
**MVW** ......... Missile Viewing Window
**MVW** ......... Mount Vernon [*Washington*] [*Airport symbol*] (OAG)
**MVW** ......... Mud Volcano [*Wyoming*] [*Seismograph station code, US Geological Survey*] (SEIS)
**MVW** ......... Uitvaartwezen [*A publication*]
**MVW/AV** ... Archiv fuer Voelkerkunde Museum fuer Voelkerkunde in Wien und von Verein Freunde der Voelkerkunde [*A publication*]
**MVWDU** ... Missile Viewing Window Deicing Unit
**MVX** .......... Media Videotex [*Vancouver Stock Exchange symbol*]
**MVX** .......... Minvoul [*Gabon*] [*Airport symbol*] (OAG)
**MVY** .......... Martha's Vineyard [*Massachusetts*] [*Airport symbol*] (OAG)
**MVZ** .......... Museum of Vertebrate Zoology [*University of California, Berkeley*]
**MVZADA** ... Mitteilungen. Verein zur Abwehr des Antisemitismus [*A publication*]
**MVZG** ....... Mein Verlangen zu Gott [*My Desires (I Give) to God*] [*German*] [*Motto of Anna Marie, Margravine of Brandenburg (1609-80)*]
**M of W** ....... Maintenance of Way [*Railroading*]
**mw** ............. Malawi [*MARC country of publication code*] [*Library of Congress*] (LCCP)
**MW** ............ Malawi [*ANSI two-letter standard code*] (CNC)
**MW** ............ Man Watchers (EA)
**MW** ............ Man-Week (NASA)
**MW** ............ Management World [*Administrative Management Society*] [*A publication*]
**MW** ............ Manual Word
**MW** ............ Manufacturing Week (MCD)
**MW** ............ Marginal Wage [*Economics*]
**MW** ............ Marginal Wings [*Botany*]
**MW** ............ Master of Wine [*Bestowed by the Worshipful Company of Vintners, one of the ancient guilds in the City of London*]
**M/W** .......... Mate With (MCD)
**MW** ............ Matthews & Wright Group [*AMEX symbol*] (SPSG)
**MW** ............ Maya Airways [*Great Britain*] [*ICAO designator*] (FAAC)
**MW** ............ Media Watch [*An association*] (EA)
**MW** ............ Medium Wall
**MW** ............ Medium Wave Band
**M & W** ....... Meeson and Welsby's English Exchequer Reports [*A publication*] (DLA)
**MW** ............ Megawatt [*Also, MEGW*]
**MW** ............ Memory Write [*Data processing*]
**M-W** .......... Merriam-Webster [*Publisher*]
**MW** ............ Message Waiting
**MW** ............ Metachrondral Wave [*Physiology*]
**MW** ............ Metalworker [*British military*] (DMA)
**M/W** .......... Methanol/Water
**MW** ............ Microwave
**MW** ............ Middle Way. Buddhist Society [*A publication*]
**MW** ............ Middle Welsh [*Language, etc.*]
**MW** ............ Midwing [*Aviation*] (AIA)
**MW** ............ Migratory Worker (OICC)
**mW** ............ Milliwatt
**MW** ............ Mine Warfare
**MW** ............ Mine Warning (NATG)
**MW** ............ Ministry of Works [*British*]
**MW** ............ Mixed Widths
**MW** ............ Mobile Workshop [*British*]
**MW** ............ Moewe Flugzeugbau, Heini Dittmar [*Federal Republic of Germany*] [*ICAO aircraft manufacturer identifier*] (ICAO)
**MW** ............ Molecular Weight [*Also, M, MOL WT*]
**MW** ............ Money Wages [*Economics*]
**MW** ............ Most Worshipful [*Freemasonry*]
**MW** ............ Most Worthy
**MW** ............ Motor Wagon [*British*]
**MW** ............ Multiple Wounds
**MW** ............ Multipurpose Weapon (MCD)
**MW** ............ Music Weekly Magazine [*British*] [*A publication*]
**MW** ............ Music Wire
**MW** ............ Muslim World [*A publication*]
**Mw** ............ Weighted Mean [*Psychology*]
**MW** ............ Winnipeg Centennial Library, Manitoba [*Library symbol*] [*National Library of Canada*] (NLC)
**MW** ............ Worcester Public Library and Central Massachusetts Regional Library System Headquarters, Worcester, MA [*Library symbol*] [*Library of Congress*] (LCLS)
**MWA** ......... American Antiquarian Society, Worcester, MA [*Library symbol*] [*Library of Congress*] (LCLS)
**MWA** ......... Manitoba Department of Agriculture, Winnipeg, Manitoba [*Library symbol*] [*National Library of Canada*] (NLC)
**MWA** ......... Manufacturing Work Authority
**MWA** ......... Marion [*Illinois*] [*Airport symbol*] (OAG)
**MWA** ......... Mayflower Warehousemen's Association (EA)
**MWA** ......... Media Women's Association
**MWA** ......... Men's Wear [*A publication*]
**MWA** ......... Meteorological Watch Advisory
**MWA** ......... Mineral Workings Act [*Town planning*] [*British*]
**MWA** ......... Modern Woodmen of America (EA)
**MWA** ......... Momentum-Wheel Assembly
**MWA** ......... Movers' & Warehousemen's Association of America Inc., Washington DC [*STAC*]
**MWA** ......... Munitions of War Act [*British*]
**MWA** ......... Mystery Writers of America (EA)
**MW/AA** .... Missile Warning/Attack Assessment (MCD)
**MWAA** ...... Movers' and Warehousemen's Association of America [*Defunct*] (EA)
**M & WAA** ... Movers' and Warehousemen's Association of America [*Defunct*]
**M & W Abr** ... Marshall and Wood's Abridgment [*A publication*] (DLA)
**MWAC** ...... Air Command Headquarters, Canadian Forces Base, Westwin, Manitoba [*Library symbol*] [*National Library of Canada*] (NLC)
**MWAC** ...... Assumption College, Worcester, MA [*Library symbol*] [*Library of Congress*] (LCLS)
**MWAC** ...... Midwest Archeological Center [*National Park Service*] (GRD)
**MWAD** ...... Alcohol and Drug Education Service, Winnipeg, Manitoba [*Library symbol*] [*National Library of Canada*] (NLC)
**MWAF** ...... Alcoholism Foundation of Manitoba, Winnipeg, Manitoba [*Library symbol*] [*National Library of Canada*] (NLC)

**MWAG**...... Research Station, Agriculture Canada [*Station de Recherches, Agriculture Canada*] Winnipeg, Manitoba [*Library symbol*] [*National Library of Canada*] (NLC)
**MWal**......... Waltham Public Library, Waltham MA [*Library symbol*] [*Library of Congress*] (LCLS)
**MWalA**...... American Jewish Historical Society, Waltham, MA [*Library symbol*] [*Library of Congress*] (LCLS)
**MWalAF** ... African Studies Association, Brandeis University, Waltham, MA [*Library symbol*] [*Library of Congress*] (LCLS)
**MWalB**...... Brandeis University, Waltham, MA [*Library symbol*] [*Library of Congress*] (LCLS)
**MWalBe**.... Bentley College, Waltham, MA [*Library symbol*] [*Library of Congress*] (LCLS)
**MWalFAR** ... Federal Archives and Records Center, General Services Administration, Waltham, MA [*Library symbol*] [*Library of Congress*] (LCLS)
**MWalG**...... General Telephone & Electronics Laboratories, Inc., Waltham Research Center Library, Waltham, MA [*Library symbol*] [*Library of Congress*] (LCLS)
**MWalK**...... John F. Kennedy Library, Waltham, MA [*Library symbol*] [*Library of Congress*] (LCLS)
**MWalMT** ... Mobil Tyco Solar Energy Corp., Waltham, MA [*Library symbol*] [*Library of Congress*] (LCLS)
**MWAMA** ... Administration Branch, Manitoba Department of Municipal Affairs, Winnipeg, Manitoba [*Library symbol*] [*National Library of Canada*] (NLC)
**MWAMT**.. Aikins, MacAulay, and Thorvaldson Law Firm, Winnipeg, Manitoba [*Library symbol*] [*National Library of Canada*] (NLC)
**MWARA**... Major World Air Route Area
**MWARN**... Manitoba Association of Registered Nurses, Winnipeg, Manitoba [*Library symbol*] [*National Library of Canada*] (NLC)
**MWARS**.... Synod Office, Diocese of Rupert's Land, Anglican Church of Canada, Winnipeg, Manitoba [*Library symbol*] [*National Library of Canada*] (NLC)
**MWAS** ...... Arthritis Society, Winnipeg, Manitoba [*Library symbol*] [*National Library of Canada*] (NLC)
**MWASD** ... Assiniboine South School Division No. 3, Winnipeg, Manitoba [*Library symbol*] [*National Library of Canada*] (NLC)
**MWat** ........ Watertown Free Public Library, Watertown, MA [*Library symbol*] [*Library of Congress*] (LCLS)
**MWatM** .... Massachusetts Bay Community College, Watertown, MA [*Library symbol*] [*Library of Congress*] (LCLS)
**MWatP**...... Perkins School for the Blind, Watertown, MA [*Library symbol*] [*Library of Congress*] (LCLS)
**MWatP-BPH** ... Regional Library for the Blind and Physically Handicapped, Perkins School for the Blind, Watertown, MA [*Library symbol*] [*Library of Congress*] (LCLS)
**MWAV**...... Microwave Laboratories, Inc. [*Raleigh, NC*] [*NASDAQ symbol*] (NQ)
**MWAVE**... Microwave
**MWAX**...... Mountain West Airline [*Air carrier designation symbol*]
**M-Way** ...... Motorway [*British*]
**MWayR**..... Raytheon Co., Wayland, MA [*Library symbol*] [*Library of Congress*] (LCLS)
**MWB**......... Master Work Book (NASA)
**MWB**......... Maxwell-Wien Bridge [*Electronics*]
**MWB**......... Metropolitan Water Board [*British*]
**MWB**......... Middlewest Motor Freight Bureau, Kansas City MO [*STAC*]
**MWB**......... Ministry of Works and Buildings [*British*]
**MWB**......... Motor Whale Boat
**MWB**......... Multilayer Wiring Board
**MWBA**...... Bristol Aerospace Ltd., Winnipeg, Manitoba [*Library symbol*] [*National Library of Canada*] (NLC)
**MWBAS**.... Mail Will Be Addressed to Show
**MWBC**...... Technical Library, Boeing of Canada Ltd., Winnipeg, Manitoba [*Library symbol*] [*National Library of Canada*] (NLC)
**MWBe**....... Becker Junior College, Worcester, MA [*Library symbol*] [*Library of Congress*] (LCLS)
**MWBH**...... Bethel Hospital, Winkler, Manitoba [*Library symbol*] [*National Library of Canada*] (NLC)
**MWBM**..... Bethania Mennonite Personal Care Home, Winnipeg, Manitoba [*Library symbol*] [*National Library of Canada*] (NLC)
**MWbriM**... Massasoit Community College, West Bridgewater, MA [*Library symbol*] [*Library of Congress*] (LCLS)
**MWBWA**.. Mededelingen. Koninklijke Vlaamse Academie voor Wetenschappen. Letteren en Schone Kunsten van Belgie. Klasse der Wetenschappen [*A publication*]
**MWC**......... Clark University, Worcester, MA [*Library symbol*] [*Library of Congress*] (LCLS)
**MWC**......... Mad World Campaign [*An association*] (EA)
**MWC**......... Magnetoionic Wave Component
**MWC**......... Mary Washington College [*University of Virginia*]
**MWC**......... Maxwell Communication Corp. [*Toronto Stock Exchange symbol*]
**MWC**......... Miltonvale Wesleyan College [*Kansas*]
**MWC**......... Milwaukee, WI [*Location identifier*] [*FAA*] (FAAL)
**MWC**......... Minister for [*or Ministry of*] War Communications [*British*] [*World War II*]
**MWC**......... Missile Weapons Control (MCD)
**MWC**......... Monod-Wyman-Changeux [*Model*] [*Enzymology*]
**MWC**......... Mount Wilson [*California*] [*Seismograph station code, US Geological Survey*] (SEIS)
**MWC**......... Moving-Withdrawal Chromatography
**MWC**......... Multiple Water Connector (KSC)
**MWC**......... Music and Record Library, Canadian Broadcasting Corp. [*Musicotheque et Discotheque, Societe Radio-Canada*] Winnipeg, Manitoba [*Library symbol*] [*National Library of Canada*] (NLC)
**MWCA**...... Monetary Working Capital Adjustment [*British*]
**MWCA**...... Monterey Wine Country Association (EA)
**M & W Cas** ... Mining and Water Cases, Annotated [*United States*] [*A publication*] (DLA)
**MWCB**...... Cayman Brac/Gerrard Smith [*Cayman Islands*] [*ICAO location identifier*] (ICLI)
**MWCC**...... Mineral Water Co. of Canada (ECON)
**MWCCA**... Manitoba Department of Consumer and Corporate Affairs, Winnipeg, Manitoba [*Library symbol*] [*Obsolete*] [*National Library of Canada*] (NLC)
**MWCCI**..... Manitoba Consumer's Bureau, Winnipeg, Manitoba [*Library symbol*] [*National Library of Canada*] (NLC)
**MWCCIR** ... Central Region Information Resources Center, Canada Department of Communications [*Centre de Documentation Region du Centre, Ministere des Communications*] Winnipeg, Manitoba [*Library symbol*] [*National Library of Canada*] (NLC)
**MWC/CS**.. Mechanized Wire Centering/Cross Section [*AT & T*] [*Telecommunications*] (TEL)
**MWCE**...... Controlled Environments Ltd., Winnipeg, Manitoba [*Library symbol*] [*National Library of Canada*] (NLC)
**MWCE**...... Millimeter Wave Communications Experiment
**MWCF** ...... Canadian Forces Aerospace and Navigation School, Canadian Forces Base Winnipeg, Westwin, Manitoba [*Library symbol*] [*National Library of Canada*] (NLC)
**MWCG**...... Grand Cayman [*Cayman Islands*] [*ICAO location identifier*] (ICLI)
**MWCH**...... Concordia Hospital, Winnipeg, Manitoba [*Library symbol*] [*National Library of Canada*] (NLC)
**MWCH**...... Monchik-Weber Corporation [*NASDAQ symbol*] (NQ)
**MWCHA**... Charles Howard & Associates, Winnipeg, Manitoba [*Library symbol*] [*National Library of Canada*] (NLC)
**MWCHD**... Charleswood Public Library, Winnipeg, Manitoba [*Library symbol*] [*National Library of Canada*] (NLC)
**MWCI** ....... Canertech, Inc., Winnipeg, Manitoba [*Library symbol*] [*National Library of Canada*] (NLC)
**MWCL**...... Little Cayman/Boddenfield [*Cayman Islands*] [*ICAO location identifier*] (ICLI)
**MWCL**...... Worcester County Law Library Association, Worcester, MA [*Library symbol*] [*Library of Congress*] (LCLS)
**MWCM**..... Canadian Mennonite Bible College, Winnipeg, Manitoba [*Library symbol*] [*National Library of Canada*] (NLC)
**MWCMS**... Centre for Mennonite Brethren Studies in Canada, Winnipeg, Manitoba [*Library symbol*] [*National Library of Canada*] (NLC)
**MWCO**...... Molecular Weight Cutoff [*Chemistry*]
**MWCR**...... Georgetown/Owen Roberts International [*Cayman Islands*] [*ICAO location identifier*] (ICLI)
**MWCR**...... Mercury-Wetted Contact Relay
**MWCS**....... Marine Wing Communication Squadron
**MWCS**....... Mental Welfare Commission for Scotland
**MWCS**....... Midwest Cable & Satellite, Inc. [*Minneapolis, MN*] [*Telecommunications*] (TSSD)
**MWCS**....... Millimeter Wave Contrast Seeker (MCD)
**MWCS**....... Missile Weapons Control System (MCD)
**MWCS**....... Mobile Weapons Control System
**MWCSJ** .... Minimum Wage Coalition to Save Jobs (EA)
**MWCT** ...... Manitoba Cancer Treatment and Research Foundation, Winnipeg, Manitoba [*Library symbol*] [*National Library of Canada*] (NLC)
**MWCU**...... Credit Union Central of Manitoba, Winnipeg, Manitoba [*Library symbol*] [*National Library of Canada*] (NLC)
**MWCWB**.. Canadian Wheat Board [*Commission Canadienne du Ble*] Winnipeg, Manitoba [*Library symbol*] [*National Library of Canada*] (NLC)
**MWD**......... Measurement while Drilling
**MWD**......... Megawatt-Day
**MWD**......... Megaword
**MWD**......... Metalworking Digest [*A publication*]
**MWD**......... Metering Water Dispenser [*Apollo*] [*NASA*]
**MWD**......... Meters Water Depth
**MWD**......... Metropolitan Water District
**MWD**......... Millimeter Wave Device
**MWD**......... Molecular Weight Distribution
**MWD**......... Moving Window Display (MCD)
**MWD**......... Rochester, NY [*Location identifier*] [*FAA*] (FAAL)
**MWDCA**... Midwest Decoy Collectors Association (EA)
**MWDDEA** ... Mutual Weapons Development Data Exchange Agreement [*NATO*]
**MWDDEP** ... Mutual Weapons Development Data Exchange Procedures [*NATO*]

**MWDI**....... Master Water Data Index [*US Geological Survey*] [*Information service or system*] (CRD)
**MWDL**...... Deer Lodge Hospital, Winnipeg, Manitoba [*Library symbol*] [*National Library of Canada*] (NLC)
**MWD/MTU** ... Megawatt-Days per Metric Ton of Uranium
**MWDP**...... Mutual Weapons Development Program [*NATO*]
**MWDRR**... Manitoba Department of Renewable Resources, Winnipeg, Manitoba [*Library symbol*] [*National Library of Canada*] (NLC)
**MWDS**...... Missile Warning and Display System [*or Subsystem*] (MCD)
**MWD/T**.... Megawatt-Days per Ton
**MWDT**...... Mutual Weapons Development Team [*Military*]
**MWDU**...... Ducks Unlimited, Winnipeg, Manitoba [*Library symbol*] [*National Library of Canada*] (NLC)
**MWE**......... Manitoba Department of Education, Winnipeg, Manitoba [*Library symbol*] [*National Library of Canada*] (NLC)
**MWe**.......... Megawatts of Electric Power
**MWE**......... Merowe [*Sudan*] [*Airport symbol*] (OAG)
**MWE**......... Midwest Energy Co. [*NYSE symbol*] (SPSG)
**MWE**......... Millimeter Wave Experiment
**MWeA**....... Westfield Athenaeum, Westfield, MA [*Library symbol*] [*Library of Congress*] (LCLS)
**MWEAE**... Central Region Headquarters, Atmospheric Environment Service, Environment Canada [*Quartier-General de la Region Centrale, Service de l'Environnement Atmospherique, Environnement Canada*] Winnipeg, Manitoba [*Library symbol*] [*National Library of Canada*] (NLC)
**M Weather R**... Monthly Weather Review [*A publication*]
**M Weath Rev**... Monthly Weather Review [*A publication*]
**MWebaC**... Cape Cod Community College, West Barnstable, MA [*Library symbol*] [*Library of Congress*] (LCLS)
**MWECW**.. Canadian Wildlife Service, Environment Canada [*Service Canadien de la Faune, Environnement Canada*] Winnipeg, Manitoba [*Library symbol*] [*National Library of Canada*] (NLC)
**MWEE**...... Mechanised Warfare Experimental Establishment [*British military*] (DMA)
**MWEEP**.... Environmental Protection Service, Environment Canada [*Service de la Protection de l'Environnement, Environnement Canada*] Winnipeg, Manitoba [*Library symbol*] [*National Library of Canada*] (NLC)
**MWelC**...... Wellesley College, Wellesley, MA [*Library symbol*] [*Library of Congress*] (LCLS)
**MWelD**...... Dana Hall School Library, Wellesley, MA [*Library symbol*] [*Library of Congress*] (LCLS)
**MWeldI**..... Member of the Welding Institute [*British*] (DBQ)
**MWEM**..... Manitoba Environmental Management Division, Winnipeg, Manitoba [*Library symbol*] [*National Library of Canada*] (NLC)
**MWEM**..... Mine Warfare Evaluation Model
**MWEMM**... Manitoba Energy and Mines, Winnipeg, Manitoba [*Library symbol*] [*National Library of Canada*] (NLC)
**MWenhG**... Gordon College, Wenham, MA [*Library symbol*] [*Library of Congress*] (LCLS)
**MWenhHi**... Wenham Historical Society and Museum, Wenham, MA [*Library symbol*] [*Library of Congress*] (LCLS)
**MWERA**... Mechanical World and Engineering Record [*A publication*]
**MWES**....... Member of the Women's Engineering Society [*British*] (DBQ)
**MWESM**... Special Materials Services, Manitoba Department of Education, Winnipeg, Manitoba [*Library symbol*] [*National Library of Canada*] (NLC)
**M West Hist**... Magazine of Western History [*A publication*]
**MWestonGS**... Church of Jesus Christ of Latter-Day Saints, Genealogical Society Library, Boston Branch, Weston, MA [*Library symbol*] [*Library of Congress*] (LCLS)
**MWestonR**... Regis College, Weston, MA [*Library symbol*] [*Library of Congress*] (LCLS)
**MWeT**....... Westfield State College, Westfield, MA [*Library symbol*] [*Library of Congress*] (LCLS)
**MWEWSH**... Manitoba Department of Environment, Workplace Safety and Health, Winnipeg, Manitoba [*Library symbol*] [*National Library of Canada*] (NLC)
**MWeyAA**.. Abigail Adams Historical Society, Weymouth, MA [*Library symbol*] [*Library of Congress*] (LCLS)
**MWF**......... Make-a-Wish Foundation [*Later, MWFA*] (EA)
**MWF**......... Marine General Workers' Federation
**MWF**......... Medical Women's Federation [*British*] (DAS)
**MWFA**....... Make-a-Wish Foundation of America (EA)
**MWFC**...... Mary Wilson Fan Club (EA)
**MWFD**...... Fred Douglas Lodge Nursing Home, Winnipeg, Manitoba [*Library symbol*] [*National Library of Canada*] (NLC)
**MWFG**...... Fort Garry Public Library, Winnipeg, Manitoba [*Library symbol*] [*National Library of Canada*] (NLC)
**MWFI**........ Manitoba Department of Finance, Winnipeg, Manitoba [*Library symbol*] [*National Library of Canada*] (NLC)
**MWFM**...... Microwave Window Failure Mechanism
**MWfo**........ J. V. Fletcher Library, Westford, MA [*Library symbol*] [*Library of Congress*] (LCLS)
**MWFOPS**... Mine Warfare Operations (NVT)
**MWFP**....... Winnipeg Free Press Co. Ltd., Manitoba [*Library symbol*] [*National Library of Canada*] (NLC)
**MWFRS**.... Manitoba Department of Fitness, Recreation and Sport, Winnipeg, Manitoba [*Library symbol*] [*National Library of Canada*] (NLC)
**MWFS**....... Marine Wing Facilities Squadron
**MWFS**....... Maritime Warfare School [*Canadian Navy*]
**MWFSD**.... Frontier School Division, Winnipeg, Manitoba [*Library symbol*] [*National Library of Canada*] (NLC)
**MWFW**..... Freshwater Institue, Fisheries and Oceans Canada [*Institut des Eaux Douces, Peches et Oceans Canada*] Winnipeg, Manitoba [*Library symbol*] [*National Library of Canada*] (NLC)
**MWG**......... Maintenance Analyzer Working Group (MCD)
**MWG**......... Meteorological Working Group
**MWG**......... Muenster-Westfalen [*Federal Republic of Germany*] [*Seismograph station code, US Geological Survey*] (SEIS)
**MWG**......... Music Wire Gauge
**MWGBP**... Guertin Brothers Paint Library, Winnipeg, Manitoba [*Library symbol*] [*National Library of Canada*] (NLC)
**MWGC**...... Midwestern Governors Conference
**MWGCP**... Most Worthy Grand Chief Patriarch
**MWGH**..... Grace Hospital, Winnipeg, Manitoba [*Library symbol*] [*National Library of Canada*] (NLC)
**MWGHA**.. Gunn Hoffer & Associates Law Firm, Winnipeg, Manitoba [*Library symbol*] [*National Library of Canada*] (NLC)
**MWGM**..... Most Worshipful [*or Worthy*] Grand Master [*Freemasonry*]
**MWGP**...... Midwest Grain Products, Inc. [*NASDAQ symbol*] (CTT)
**MWGR**...... Canadian Grain Commission, Agriculture Canada [*Commission Canadienne des Grains, Agriculture Canada*] Winnipeg, Manitoba [*Library symbol*] [*National Library of Canada*] (NLC)
**MWGW**..... Great West Life Assurance Co., Winnipeg, Manitoba [*Library symbol*] [*National Library of Canada*] (NLC)
**MWH**........ College of the Holy Cross, Worcester, MA [*Library symbol*] [*Library of Congress*] (LCLS)
**MWH**........ Manitoba Hydro, Winnipeg, Manitoba [*Library symbol*] [*National Library of Canada*] (NLC)
**MWh**......... Megawatt-Hour (MCD)
**MW(H)**...... Megawatts (Heat) (IEEE)
**MWH**........ Milliwatt Hour
**M & WH**.... Missile and Warhead Magazines
**MWH**........ Model Wave Height
**MWH**........ Mokuaweoweo [*Hawaii*] [*Seismograph station code, US Geological Survey*] (SEIS)
**MWH**........ Moses Lake [*Washington*] [*Airport symbol*] (OAG)
**MWHB**...... Hudson's Bay House, Winnipeg, Manitoba [*Library symbol*] [*National Library of Canada*] (NLC)
**MWhB**....... Marine Biological Laboratory, Woods Hole, MA [*Library symbol*] [*Library of Congress*] (LCLS)
**MWHG**..... Marine Wing Headquarters Group
**MWHGL**... Multiple Wheel Heavy Gear Loading [*Aviation*]
**MWHi**....... Worcester Historical Society, Worcester, MA [*Library symbol*] [*Library of Congress*] (LCLS)
**MWhN**...... United States National Marine Fisheries Service, Northeast Fisheries Center, Woods Hole, MA [*Library symbol*] [*Library of Congress*] (LCLS)
**MWHO**..... Manitoba Health Organizations, Winnipeg, Manitoba [*Library symbol*] [*National Library of Canada*] (NLC)
**MWHP**...... Information Resources Center, Manitoba Health, Winnipeg, Manitoba [*Library symbol*] [*National Library of Canada*] (NLC)
**MWHR**...... Henderson Regional Library, Winnipeg, Manitoba [*Library symbol*] [*National Library of Canada*] (NLC)
**MWHS**...... Library Services, Health Sciences Centre, Winnipeg, Manitoba [*Library symbol*] [*National Library of Canada*] (NLC)
**MWHS**...... Marine Wing Headquarters Squadron (NVT)
**MWHS**...... Modified Warhead Section (MCD)
**MWHSC**... Manitoba Health Services Commission, Winnipeg, Manitoba [*Library symbol*] [*National Library of Canada*] (NLC)
**MWHT**...... Miscellaneous Waste Holdup Tank [*Nuclear energy*] (NRCH)
**MWI**.......... Insurance Institute of Winnipeg, Manitoba [*Library symbol*] [*National Library of Canada*] (NLC)
**MWI**.......... Malawi [*ANSI three-letter standard code*] (CNC)
**MWI**.......... Mantle Width Index
**MWI**.......... Many Worlds Interpretation [*Term coined by authors John Barrow and Frank Tipler in their book, "The Anthropic Cosmological Principle"*]
**MWI**.......... Master Weavers Institute (EA)
**MWI**.......... Measured Workload Index [*Aviation*]
**MWI**.......... Message-Waiting Indicator
**MWI**.......... Missionary Women International (EA)
**MWI**.......... Montserrat [*Montserrat*] [*Seismograph station code, US Geological Survey*] (SEIS)
**MWI**.......... Motor-Ways Inc., Des Moines IA [*STAC*]
**MWIA**....... Medical Women's International Association [*See also AIFM*] [*Cologne, Federal Republic of Germany*] (EAIO)
**MWIAP**..... Prairie Regional Office, Parks Canada [*Bureau Regional des Pres, Parcs Canada*] Winnipeg, Manitoba [*Library symbol*] [*National Library of Canada*] (NLC)

**MWIC** ....... Manitoba Department of Economic Development, Winnipeg, Manitoba [*Library symbol*] [*National Library of Canada*] (NLC)
**MWiCA** ..... Sterling and Francine Clark Art Institute, Williamstown, MA [*Library symbol*] [*Library of Congress*] (LCLS)
**MWIDE** .... IDE Engineering Co., Winnipeg, Manitoba [*Library symbol*] [*National Library of Canada*] (NLC)
**MWIE** ....... Indus Electronic, Winnipeg, Manitoba [*Library symbol*] [*National Library of Canada*] (NLC)
**MWIF** ........ Ivan Franko Museum & Library, Winnipeg, Manitoba [*Library symbol*] [*National Library of Canada*] (NLC)
**MWIN** ....... Indian and Northern Affairs Canada [*Affaires Indiennes et du Nord Canada*], Winnipeg, Manitoba [*Library symbol*] [*National Library of Canada*] (BIB)
**MWIR** ....... Midwave Infrared Sensor (MCD)
**MWIS** ........ National Network of Minority Women in Science (EA)
**MWiW** ....... Williams College, Williamstown, MA [*Library symbol*] [*Library of Congress*] (LCLS)
**MWiW-C** ... Williams College, Chapin Library, Williamstown, MA [*Library symbol*] [*Library of Congress*] (LCLS)
**MWJ** ......... Canada Department of Justice [*Ministere de la Justice*] Winnipeg, Manitoba [*Library symbol*] [*National Library of Canada*] (NLC)
**MWJ** ......... Magazin fuer die Wissenschaft des Judentums [*A publication*]
**MWJ** ......... Matthews Ridge [*Guyana*] [*Airport symbol*] (OAG)
**MWJC** ....... Marjorie Webster Junior College [*Washington, DC*]
**MWJHS** .... Jewish Historical Society of Western Canada, Winnipeg, Manitoba [*Library symbol*] [*National Library of Canada*] (NLC)
**MWJP** ....... Jewish Public Library, Winnipeg, Manitoba [*Library symbol*] [*National Library of Canada*] (NLC)
**MWK** ......... Kelvin High School, Winnipeg, Manitoba [*Library symbol*] [*National Library of Canada*] (NLC)
**MWK** ......... Mill Work [*Technical drawings*]
**MWK** ......... Mount Airy, NC [*Location identifier*] [*FAA*] (FAAL)
**MWL** ......... Law Society of Manitoba, Winnipeg, Manitoba [*Library symbol*] [*National Library of Canada*] (NLC)
**MWL** ......... Malawi Women's League
**MWL** ......... Management World [*A publication*]
**MWL** ......... Mean Water Level
**MWL** ......... Meteoric Water Line [*Geology*]
**MWL** ......... Milled-Wood Lignin
**mWL** ......... Milliwatt Logic
**MWL** ......... Mineral Wells, TX [*Location identifier*] [*FAA*] (FAAL)
**MWL** ......... Minimum Wage Laws (OICC)
**MWL** ......... Motor Water Lighter (ADA)
**MWL** ......... Muslim World League (BJA)
**M & W Law Dic** ... Mozley and Whiteley's Law Dictionary [*A publication*] (ILCA)
**MWLCC** .... Lutheran Council in Canada, Winnipeg, Manitoba [*Library symbol*] [*National Library of Canada*] (NLC)
**MWLD** ...... Man Worn LASER Detector [*Assembly*] (MCD)
**MWLDA** ... Maine Wholesale Lobster Dealers Association [*Defunct*] (EA)
**MWLG** ...... Midwest Women's Legal Group (EA)
**MWLMV** .. Maize White Line Mosaic Virus
**MWLR** ...... Labour Research Library, Manitoba Department of Labour and Manpower, Winnipeg, Manitoba [*Library symbol*] [*National Library of Canada*] (NLC)
**MWLS** ....... Faculty of Law, University of Manitoba, Winnipeg, Manitoba [*Library symbol*] [*National Library of Canada*] (NLC)
**MWM** ........ Maxwell-Wagner Mechanism [*Physics*]
**MWM** ........ Medical Library, University of Manitoba, Winnipeg, Manitoba [*Library symbol*] [*National Library of Canada*] (NLC)
**MWM** ........ Millimeter Wave Mixer
**MWM** ........ Minskoff, Wiseman, Minskoff [*Program for the development of language abilities*]
**MWM** ........ Mode-Woche-Muenchen [*Munich Fashion Week - International Fashion Fair*] [*Federal Republic of Germany*] (TSPED)
**MWM** ........ Moments with Meredith - Meredith Baxter-Birney Fan Club (EA)
**MWM** ........ Morfee Wheel Manufacturing [*Vancouver Stock Exchange symbol*]
**MWM** ........ Windom, MN [*Location identifier*] [*FAA*] (FAAL)
**MWM** ........ Worcester Art Museum, Worcester, MA [*Library symbol*] [*Library of Congress*] (LCLS)
**MWMA** ..... Manitoba Department of Municipal Affairs, Winnipeg, Manitoba [*Library symbol*] [*National Library of Canada*] (NLC)
**MWMBC** .. Mennonite Brethren Bible College, Winnipeg, Manitoba [*Library symbol*] [*National Library of Canada*] (NLC)
**MWMCA** .. Michigan Women for Medical Control of Abortion (EA)
**MWME** ..... Maclaren Engineering, Winnipeg, Manitoba [*Library symbol*] [*National Library of Canada*] (NLC)
**MWMFB** ... Middlewest Motor Freight Bureau
**MWMG** ..... Misericordia General Hospital, Winnipeg, Manitoba [*Library symbol*] [*National Library of Canada*] (NLC)
**MWMH** .... Winnipeg Municipal Hospital, Manitoba [*Library symbol*] [*National Library of Canada*] (NLC)
**MWMHC** ... Mennonite Heritage Centre, Winnipeg, Manitoba [*Library symbol*] [*National Library of Canada*] (NLC)
**MWMM** .... Manitoba Museum of Man & Nature, Winnipeg, Manitoba [*Library symbol*] [*National Library of Canada*] (NLC)
**MWMMP** ... Meadowood Manor Personal Care Home, Winnipeg, Manitoba [*Library symbol*] [*National Library of Canada*] (NLC)
**MWMP** ..... City of Winnipeg Metro Planning Division, Manitoba [*Library symbol*] [*National Library of Canada*] (NLC)
**MWMPE** .. Manitoba Pool Elevators Library, Winnipeg, Manitoba [*Library symbol*] [*National Library of Canada*] (NLC)
**MWMRC** .. Manitoba Research Council, Winnipeg, Manitoba [*Library symbol*] [*National Library of Canada*] (NLC)
**MWMTC** .. Manitoba Theater Center, Winnipeg, Manitoba [*Library symbol*] [*National Library of Canada*] (NLC)
**MWMTS** ... Manitoba Teachers Socity, Winnipeg, Manitoba [*Library symbol*] [*National Library of Canada*] (NLC)
**MWMU** ..... University of Massachusetts, Medical Center, Worcester, MA [*Library symbol*] [*Library of Congress*] (LCLS)
**MWn** .......... GAR Memorial Library, West Newbury, MA [*Library symbol*] [*Library of Congress*] (LCLS)
**MWN** ........ Gordon College, Wenham, MA [*OCLC symbol*] [*Inactive*] (OCLC)
**MWN** ........ Madras Weekly Notes [*India*] [*A publication*] (DLA)
**MWN** ........ Medical World News [*A publication*]
**MWN** ........ Mount Washington, NH [*Location identifier*] [*FAA*] (FAAL)
**MWNCC** ... Madras Weekly Notes, Criminal Cases [*India*] [*A publication*] (DLA)
**MWNLN** ... Mid-West Nigeria Legal Notice [*A publication*] (DLA)
**MWO** ........ Maintenance Work Order
**MWO** ........ Manufacturing Work Order
**MWO** ........ Master Warrant Officer [*Canadian Forces, since 1964*]
**MWO** ........ Master Work Order (AAG)
**MWO** ........ Mental Welfare Officer [*British*]
**MWO** ........ Meteorological Watch Office (FAAC)
**MWO** ........ Middletown, OH [*Location identifier*] [*FAA*] (FAAL)
**MWO** ........ Millimeter Wave Observatory [*University of Texas at Austin*] [*Research center*] (RCD)
**MWO** ........ Millimeter Wavelength Oscillator
**MWO** ........ Modification Work Order
**MWO** ........ Rev. Peres Oblats, Winnipeg, Manitoba [*Library symbol*] [*National Library of Canada*] (NLC)
**MWo** .......... Woburn Public Library, Woburn, MA [*Library symbol*] [*Library of Congress*] (LCLS)
**MWOA** ...... Mizrachi Women's Organization of America [*Later, AMW*] (EA)
**MWOC** ...... Mothers without Custody (EA)
**MWOFP** .... Modification Work Order Fielding Plan
**MWOGA2** ... Montana Wool Grower [*A publication*]
**MWollE** ..... Eastern Nazarene College, Wollaston, MA [*Library symbol*] [*Library of Congress*] (LCLS)
**M World** .... Mining World [*A publication*]
**MWOT** ...... Master Warrant Officer Training [*DoD*]
**MWP** ......... Legislative Library of Manitoba, Winnipeg, Manitoba [*Library symbol*] [*National Library of Canada*] (NLC)
**MWP** ......... Malta Workers Party [*Political party*] (PPE)
**MWP** ......... Maneuvering Work Platform [*NASA*]
**MWP** ......... Master of Welfare Policy
**MWP** ......... Maximum Working Pressure
**MWP** ......... Mechanical Wood Pulp [*Paper*]
**MWP** ......... Membrane Waterproofing
**MWP** ......... Metabolic Waste Production
**MWP** ......... Mexican Water Plan [*Land use*]
**MWP** ......... Millimeter Wave Propagation
**MWP** ......... Ministry of Works and Planning [*British*]
**MWP** ......... Missile Warning Position (MCD)
**MWP** ......... Most Worthy Patriarch
**MWP** ......... Worcester Polytechnic Institute, Worcester, MA [*Library symbol*] [*Library of Congress*] (LCLS)
**MWPA** ...... Married Women's Property Act [*1882*] [*British*] (AIA)
**MWPA** ...... Provincial Archives of Manitoba, Winnipeg, Manitoba [*Library symbol*] [*National Library of Canada*] (NLC)
**MWPC** ...... Multiple Wire Proportional Counter
**MWPCPA** ... Archaeology Subsection Office, Prairie Region Library, Parks Canada [*Recherches Archeologiques, Bibliotheque de la Region des Pres, Parcs Canada*] Winnipeg, Manitoba [*Library symbol*] [*National Library of Canada*] (NLC)
**MWPCPH** ... Historic Resources Conservation Subsection Office, Prairie Region Library, Parks Canada [*Ressources et Conservation Historiques, Bibliotheque de la Region des Pres, Parcs Canada*] Winnipeg, Manitoba [*Library symbol*] [*National Library of Canada*] (NLC)
**MWPCR** .... Riding Mountain National Park, Parks Canada [*Parc National Riding Mountain, Parcs Canada*] Wasagaming, Manitoba [*Library symbol*] [*National Library of Canada*] (NLC)
**MWPI** ........ Munson-Williams-Proctor Institute [*Utica, NY*]
**MWPL** ....... Montreal Working Papers in Linguistics [*A publication*]
**MWPL** ....... Public Library Services, Manitoba Department of Culture, Heritage and Recreation, Winnipeg, Manitoba [*Library symbol*] [*National Library of Canada*] (NLC)
**MWPNR** ... Park Management Library, Manitoba Department of Natural Resources, Winnipeg, Manitoba [*Library symbol*] [*National Library of Canada*] (NLC)
**MWPO** ...... Mine Warfare Project Office [*Naval Material Command*]

**MWPPH** ... Provincial Public Health Nursing Services, Winnipeg, Manitoba [*Library symbol*] [*National Library of Canada*] (NLC)
**MWPR** ...... Monthly Work Package Report [*NASA*] (NASA)
**MWPS** ....... Manitoba Probation Services, Winnipeg, Manitoba [*Library symbol*] [*National Library of Canada*] (NLC)
**MWPS** ....... Multimeter Wave Power Source
**MWQ** ......... Magwe [*Burma*] [*Airport symbol*] (OAG)
**MWQ** ......... Midwest Quarterly [*A publication*]
**MWQ** ......... Quinsigamond Community College, Worcester, MA [*Library symbol*] [*Library of Congress*] (LCLS)
**MWQCG** ... Media and Information Services, Quadraplegic Communications Group, Inc., Winnipeg, Manitoba [*Library symbol*] [*National Library of Canada*] (NLC)
**MWR** ......... Maintenance Work Request [*or Requirement*]
**MWR** ......... Man-Worn Receiver (MCD)
**mwr** ........... Marwari [*MARC language code*] [*Library of Congress*] (LCCP)
**MWR** ......... Mean Width Ratio
**MWR** ......... Metal Whisker Reinforcement
**MWR** ......... Method of Weighted Residual
**MWR** ......... Midwest Resources [*NYSE symbol*] (SPSG)
**MWR** ......... Mine Watching RADAR (NATG)
**MWR** ......... Monthly Wholesale Trade [*A publication*]
**MWR** ......... Morale, Welfare, and Recreation [*DoD*]
**MWR** ......... Mountain-West Resources [*Vancouver Stock Exchange symbol*]
**MWR** ......... Muncie & Western Railroad Co. [*AAR code*]
**MWR** ......... Royal Winnipeg Ballet, Manitoba [*Library symbol*] [*National Library of Canada*] (NLC)
**MWRA** ...... Morale, Welfare, and Recreation Activity [*DoD*] (AFIT)
**MWRC** ...... Maintain Well to Right of Course [*Aviation*] (FAAC)
**MWRC** ...... Mount Washington Railway Company [*AAR code*]
**MWRC** ...... RCMP [*Royal Canadian Mounted Police*] Crime Laboratory, Winnipeg, Manitoba [*Library symbol*] [*National Library of Canada*] (NLC)
**MWRCC** ... Roman Catholic Chancery Office, Winnipeg, Manitoba [*Library symbol*] [*National Library of Canada*] (NLC)
**MWroxV** ... United States Veterans Administration Hospital, West Roxbury, MA [*Library symbol*] [*Library of Congress*] (LCLS)
**MWRR** ...... Learning Resources Centre, Red River Community College, Winnipeg, Manitoba [*Library symbol*] [*National Library of Canada*] (NLC)
**MWRRC** ... Montana Water Resources Research Center [*Montana State University, University ofMontana, and Montana College of Mineral Science and Technology*] [*Research center*] (RCD)
**MWRRL**.... Library Technician Program, Red River Community College, Winnipeg, Manitoba, LS [*National Library of Canada*] (NLC)
**MWRS** ...... Richardson Securities of Canada, Winnipeg, Manitoba [*Library symbol*] [*National Library of Canada*] (NLC)
**MWRT** ...... Mobile Wing Reconnaissance Technical [*Squadron*]
**MWS** ......... Major Weapon System [*Manager*] (MCD)
**MWS** ......... Management Work Station (BUR)
**MWS** ......... Marine Weather Service (NOAA)
**MWS** ......... Mawashi [*Ryukyu Islands*] [*Seismograph station code, US Geological Survey*] [*Closed*] (SEIS)
**MWS** ......... Maximum Wind Speed
**MWS** ......... Medium Wide Shot [*Photography*]
**MWS** ......... Megawatt Waveguide Switch
**MWS** ......... Member of the Wernerian Society [*British*] (ROG)
**MWS** ......... Microwave Scatterometer [*Telecommunications*] (TEL)
**MWS** ......... Microwave Station
**MWS** ......... Microwave Wind Spectrometer
**MWS** ......... Missile Warning Squadron
**MWS** ......... Missile Weapon System [*Military*] (CAAL)
**MWS** ......... Missouri Western State College, St. Joseph, MO [*OCLC symbol*] (OCLC)
**MWS** ......... Mobile Weapon System
**MWS** ......... Most Wise Sovereign [*Freemasonry*]
**MWS** ......... Most Worshipful Scribe [*Freemasonry*] (ROG)
**MWS** ......... Mount Wilson, CA [*Location identifier*] [*FAA*] (FAAL)
**MWS** ......... Multiwork Station
**MWSA** ...... St. Andrew's College, Winnipeg, Manitoba [*Library symbol*] [*National Library of Canada*] (NLC)
**MWSAC**.... St. Amant Center, Winnipeg, Manitoba [*Library symbol*] [*National Library of Canada*] (NLC)
**MWSACB** ... Salvation Army Catherine Booth Bible College, Winnipeg, Manitoba [*Library symbol*] [*National Library of Canada*] (BIB)
**MWSB**....... Mountain West Savings Bank [*NASDAQ symbol*] (NQ)
**MWSB**....... Saint Boniface Public Library, Winnipeg, Manitoba [*Library symbol*] [*National Library of Canada*] (NLC)
**MWSBM**... Saint Boniface General Hospital Medical Library, Winnipeg, Manitoba [*Library symbol*] [*National Library of Canada*] (NLC)
**MWSBN** ... Saint Boniface General Hospital School of Nursing Library, Winnipeg, Manitoba [*Library symbol*] [*National Library of Canada*] (NLC)
**MWSC**....... American Men and Women of Science [*Database*] [*R. R. Bowker Co.*] [*Information service or system*] (CRD)
**MWSC**....... Midwestern Simulation Council
**MWSC**....... Society for Manitobans with Disabilities, Inc., Winnipeg, Manitoba [*Library symbol*] [*National Library of Canada*] (NLC)
**MWSCS** .... Midwestern Signal Corps School
**MWSD** ...... Teachers' Library and Resource Centre, Winnipeg School Division No. 1, Manitoba [*Library symbol*] [*National Library of Canada*] (NLC)
**MWSG** ...... Marine Wing Support Group (NVT)
**MWSGR**.... Marine Wing Staff Ground (MCD)
**MWSH** ...... Worcester State Hospital, Worcester, MA [*Library symbol*] [*Library of Congress*] (LCLS)
**MWSJ** ....... St. John's College, Winnipeg, Manitoba [*Library symbol*] [*National Library of Canada*] (NLC)
**MWSM** ..... Stony Mountain Institution Library, Winnipeg, Manitoba [*Library symbol*] [*National Library of Canada*] (NLC)
**MWSOGH** ... Educational Services, Seven Oaks General Hospital, Winnipeg, Manitoba [*Library symbol*] [*National Library of Canada*] (NLC)
**MWSP**....... St. Paul's College, Winnipeg, Manitoba [*Library symbol*] [*National Library of Canada*] (NLC)
**MWSPA**.... Spiece Associates, Winnipeg, Manitoba [*Library symbol*] [*National Library of Canada*] (NLC)
**MWSPC**.... Social Planning Council of Winnipeg, Manitoba [*Library symbol*] [*National Library of Canada*] (NLC)
**MWSR** ...... Magnetic Wire Shift Register
**MWSS**....... Manitoba Regional Library, Secretary of State Canada [*Bibliotheque Regionale du Manitoba, Secretariat d'Etat*], Winnipeg, Manitoba [*Library symbol*] [*National Library of Canada*] (NLC)
**MWSS**....... Metropolitan Waterworks and Sewerage System [*Philippines*] (DS)
**MWST**....... Mean Weighted Skin Temperature
**MWST**....... Miscellaneous Waste Storage Tank [*Nuclear energy*] (NRCH)
**MWST**....... Missile Warning System Test (MCD)
**MWSV** ...... St. Vital Public Library, Winnipeg, Manitoba [*Library symbol*] [*National Library of Canada*] (NLC)
**MWT** ......... Makeup Water Treatment (IEEE)
**MWT** ......... Master of Wood Technology
**MWT** ......... Mean Water Temperature
**MWT** ......... Megawatt Thermal [*Nuclear energy*] (NRCH)
**MWT** ......... Millimeter Wave Tube
**MWT** ......... Ministry of War Transport [*Terminated, 1956*] [*British*]
**MWT** ......... Moolawatana [*Australia*] [*Airport symbol*] [*Obsolete*] (OAG)
**Mwt**........... Thermal Megawatt [*Also, TMW*]
**MWT** ......... Winnipeg Tribune, Manitoba [*Library symbol*] [*National Library of Canada*] (NLC)
**MWTA** ...... Airworthiness Library, Central Region, Transport Canada [*Bibliotheque de la Navigabilite Aerienne, Region Centrale, Transports Canada*], Winnipeg, Manitoba [*Library symbol*] [*National Library of Canada*] (NLC)
**MWTC** ...... Ministry of War Time Communications [*British*] [*World War II*]
**MWTC** ...... Teshmount Consultants, Winnipeg, Manitoba [*Library symbol*] [*National Library of Canada*] (NLC)
**MWTCR**.... Central Regional Library, Transport Canada [*Bibliotheque Regionale du Centre, Transports Canada*], Winnipeg, Manitoba [*Library symbol*] [*National Library of Canada*] (NLC)
**MWTCS**.... Modernized Weather Teletypewriter Communication System (FAAC)
**MWTE** ...... Interdisciplinary Engineering, Winnipeg, Manitoba [*Library symbol*] [*National Library of Canada*] (NLC)
**MWTE** ...... Modern Weapons Training Exercises (MCD)
**MW(th)**...... Megawatts (Thermal)
**MWTR** ...... Monthly Wholesale Trade Report [*A publication*]
**MWTS**....... Manitoba Telephone System, Winnipeg, Manitoba [*Library symbol*] [*National Library of Canada*] (NLC)
**MWTU** ...... Marble Workers' Trade Union [*British*]
**MWU**......... Maccabi World Union [*Ramat Gan, Israel*] (EAIO)
**MWU**......... Mercer University, Southern School of Pharmacy, Atlanta, GA [*OCLC symbol*] (OCLC)
**MWU**......... Mine Workers Union [*South Africa*] (IMH)
**MWU**......... Modified Wohlgemuth Unit [*Of hydrolytic enzyme activity*]
**MWU**......... Mussau [*Papua New Guinea*] [*Airport symbol*] (OAG)
**MWU**......... University of Manitoba, Winnipeg, Manitoba [*Library symbol*] [*National Library of Canada*] (NLC)
**MWUA**....... Ukrainian Academy of Arts and Science, Winnipeg, Manitoba [*Library symbol*] [*National Library of Canada*] (NLC)
**MWUAF** ... Architecture and Fine Arts Library, University of Manitoba, Winnipeg, Manitoba [*Library symbol*] [*National Library of Canada*] (NLC)
**MWUC** ...... University of Winnipeg, Manitoba [*Library symbol*] [*National Library of Canada*] (NLC)
**MWUCE** ... Ukrainian Cultural and Educational Centre, Winnipeg, Manitoba [*Library symbol*] [*National Library of Canada*] (NLC)
**MWUD**...... Dental Library, University of Manitoba, Winnipeg, Manitoba [*Library symbol*] [*National Library of Canada*] (NLC)
**MWUG**...... Department of Geography, University of Manitoba, Winnipeg, Manitoba [*Library symbol*] [*National Library of Canada*] (NLC)

**MWUGG**... United Grain Growers, Winnipeg, Manitoba [*Library symbol*] [*National Library of Canada*] (NLC)
**MWUM**..... Map and Atlas Collection, University of Manitoba, Winnipeg, Manitoba [*Library symbol*] [*National Library of Canada*] (NLC)
**MWUML**.. Underwood McLellan Ltd., Winnipeg, Manitoba [*Library symbol*] [*National Library of Canada*] (NLC)
**MWUSA**... Minute Women of the United States of America (EA)
**MWV**......... Maximum Working Voltage [*Electronics*]
**MWV**......... Mexican War Veteran
**MWV**......... Milkweed Virus
**MWV**......... Motor Tariff Bureau of West Virginia, Charleston WV [*STAC*]
**MWVGH**... Victoria General Hospital, Winnipeg, Manitoba [*Library symbol*] [*National Library of Canada*] (NLC)
**MWVS**...... Branch Library, Manitoba Veterinarian Services, Winnipeg, Manitoba [*Library symbol*] [*National Library of Canada*] (NLC)
**MWW**........ Majestic Wine Warehouses [*Commercial firm*] [*British*]
**MWW**........ Manual Wire Wrap
**MWW**........ Mark's Work Wearhouse Ltd. [*Toronto Stock Exchange symbol*]
**MWW**........ Marquis Who's Who [*Marquis Who's Who, Inc.*] [*Information service or system*] [*A publication*]
**MWW**........ Metall. Internationale Zeitschrift fuer Technik und Wirtschaft [*A publication*]
**MWW**........ Municipal Wastewater
**MWW**........ William Ave. Branch, Winnipeg Public Library, Manitoba [*Library symbol*] [*National Library of Canada*] (NLC)
**MWW**........ Worcester State College, Worcester, MA [*Library symbol*] [*Library of Congress*] (LCLS)
**MWWA**..... Metropolitan Water Works Authority [*Thailand*] (DS)
**MWWA**..... Winnipeg Art Gallery, Manitoba [*Library symbol*] [*National Library of Canada*] (NLC)
**MWWC**..... Military Weather Warning Center (NOAA)
**MWWC**..... Winnipeg Clinic, Manitoba [*Library symbol*] [*National Library of Canada*] (NLC)
**MWWF**..... Manual Wire Wrap Fixture
**MWWII**..... Mothers of World War II
**MWWK**..... West Kildonan Public Library, Winnipeg, Manitoba [*Library symbol*] [*National Library of Canada*] (NLC)
**MWWLW**... W. L. Wardrop & Associates, Winnipeg, Manitoba [*Library symbol*] [*National Library of Canada*] (NLC)
**MWWR**..... Water Resources Division, Manitoba Department of Natural Resources, Winnipeg, Manitoba [*Library symbol*] [*National Library of Canada*] (NLC)
**MWWSH**.. Manitoba Workplace Safety and Health Division, Winnipeg, Manitoba [*Library symbol*] [*National Library of Canada*] (NLC)
**MWWU**..... Marine Wing Weapon Unit
**MWWV**..... Movement of Working Women and Volunteers [*Tel Aviv, Israel*] (EAIO)
**MWX**......... Montpelier, VT [*Location identifier*] [*FAA*] (FAAL)
**MWY**......... Miranda Downs [*Australia*] [*Airport symbol*] [*Obsolete*] (OAG)
**MWZ**......... Mwanza [*Tanzania*] [*Airport symbol*] (OAG)
**MX**............ Compania Mexicana de Aviacion [*ICAO designator*] (OAG)
**MX**............ Matrix (BUR)
**Mx**............ Maxwell [*Unit of magnetic flux*] [*Also, abWb*]
**MX**............ Measurex Corp. [*NYSE symbol*] (SPSG)
**MX**............ Mexican L & P Co. Ltd. [*Toronto Stock Exchange symbol*]
**MX**............ Mexicana [*Airline*] (DS)
**mx**............ Mexico [*IYRU nationality code*] [*MARC country of publication code*] [*Library of Congress*] (LCCP)
**MX**............ Mexico [*ANSI two-letter standard code*] (CNC)
**M & X**........ Microscope and X-Ray Inspection
**MX**............ Middlesex [*Region of London*]
**MX**............ Missile, Experimental
**MX**............ Mix
**MX**............ Mixed Type of Ice Formation [*White and Clear*] [*Aviation code*] (FAAC)
**MX**............ Multiple Address
**MX**............ Multiplex [*or Multiplexer*]
**MX**............ Murexide [*An indicator*] [*Chemistry*]
**M-18-X**....... Movimiento 18 de Octubre de Accion Revolucionaria Astra [*Astra 18th October Movement of Revolutionary Action*] [*Ecuador*] [*Political party*] (PD)
**MXA**.......... Manila, AR [*Location identifier*] [*FAA*] (FAAL)
**MXA**.......... Mobile Exercise Area [*Military*] (NVT)
**MXAL**........ Mercury Xenon Arc Lamp
**MXB**.......... Masamba [*Indonesia*] [*Airport symbol*] (OAG)
**MXC**.......... MATEC Corp. [*AMEX symbol*] (SPSG)
**MXC**.......... Maxon Computer Systems, Inc. [*Toronto Stock Exchange symbol*]
**MXC**.......... Monticello [*Utah*] [*Airport symbol*] (OAG)
**MXC**.......... Multiplexer Channel [*Data processing*]
**MXC**.......... University of Cincinnati, Medical Center, Cincinnati, OH [*OCLC symbol*] (OCLC)
**MxChGS**... Church of Jesus Christ of Latter-Day Saints, Genealogical Society Library, Colonia Juarez Branch, Chihuahua, Mexico [*Library symbol*] [*Library of Congress*] (LCLS)
**MXD**.......... Mixed
**MXD**.......... Multiple Transmitter Duplicator
**MXDA**........ Meta-Xylenediamine [*Organic chemistry*]
**MXD CL**.... Mixed Carload [*Freight*]
**MXDCR**.... Mode Transducer (MSA)
**MXDTH**.... Maximum Depth (NOAA)
**MXE**.......... Mexico Equity & Income Fund [*NYSE symbol*] (SPSG)
**MXE**.......... Modena, PA [*Location identifier*] [*FAA*] (FAAL)
**MXF**.......... [*The*] Mexico Fund, Inc. [*NYSE symbol*] (SPSG)
**MXF**.......... Montgomery, AL [*Location identifier*] [*FAA*] (FAAL)
**MXFL**........ Mixed Flow
**MXG**.......... Mixing (MSA)
**MxGuBF**... Biblioteca Benjamin Franklin, Guadalajara, Mexico [*Library symbol*] [*Library of Congress*] (LCLS)
**MXIC**......... MX Information Center [*Defunct*] (EA)
**MXIM**........ Maxim Integrated Products, Inc. [*NASDAQ symbol*] (NQ)
**MXK**.......... Camp Springs, MD [*Location identifier*] [*FAA*] (FAAL)
**MXK**.......... Multiple-Frequency X- and K-Band
**MXL**.......... Mexicali [*Mexico*] [*Airport symbol*] (OAG)
**MXLU**........ Malcolm X Liberation University
**MXM**.......... Maximum (ADA)
**MXM**.......... MAXXAM, Inc. [*AMEX symbol*] (SPSG)
**MXM**.......... Morombe [*Madagascar*] [*Airport symbol*] (OAG)
**MxMBF**.... Biblioteca Benjamin Franklin, Mexico City, Mexico [*Library symbol*] [*Library of Congress*] (LCLS)
**MxMBN**.... Biblioteca Nacional de Mexico, Mexico City, Mexico [*Library symbol*] [*Library of Congress*] (LCLS)
**MxMC**....... Centro de Investigacion y de Estudios Avanzados, Instituto Politecnico Nacional, Mexico City, Mexico [*Library symbol*] [*Library of Congress*] (LCLS)
**MxMCM**... Colegio de Mexico, Mexico, Mexico City, Mexico [*Library symbol*] [*Library of Congress*] (LCLS)
**MxMGS**.... Church of Jesus Christ of Latter-Day Saints, Genealogical Society Library, Mexico City Branch, Mexico City, Mexico [*Library symbol*] [*Library of Congress*] (LCLS)
**MxMI**........ Universidad Iberoamericana, Mexico [*Library symbol*] [*Library of Congress*] (LCLS)
**MxMoT**..... Instituto Tecnologico y de Estudios Superiores de Monterrey, Monterrey, Mexico [*Library symbol*] [*Library of Congress*] (LCLS)
**MxN**.......... Maxillary Nerve [*Neuroanatomy*]
**MXN**.......... Morlaix [*France*] [*Airport symbol*] (OAG)
**MX-NM**.... Matrix - National Module
**MXO**.......... Monticello, IA [*Location identifier*] [*FAA*] (FAAL)
**MXP**.......... MaxPharma, Inc. [*AMEX symbol*] (SPSG)
**MXP**.......... Milan [*Italy*] Malpensa Airport [*Airport symbol*] (OAG)
**MXPST**..... Maximum Possible Storm (NOAA)
**MXQ**.......... Modular X-Ray Quantometer
**MXQ**.......... Wilmington, OH [*Location identifier*] [*FAA*] (FAAL)
**MXR**.......... Mask Index Register
**MXR**.......... Mass X-Ray
**MXR**.......... Mixer (MSA)
**MXR**.......... Raton, NM [*Location identifier*] [*FAA*] (FAAL)
**MXRAN**.... Maximum Rainfall (NOAA)
**M-X/RES**.. M-X [*Missile*] Renewable Energy System
**MXRV**....... Middlesex Rifle Volunteers [*Military*] [*British*] (DMA)
**MXS**.......... Max Minerals, Inc. [*Vancouver Stock Exchange symbol*]
**MXS**.......... Maxus Energy Corp. [*NYSE symbol*] (SPSG)
**MXT**.......... Chicago, IL [*Location identifier*] [*FAA*] (FAAL)
**MXT**.......... Maintirano [*Madagascar*] [*Airport symbol*] (OAG)
**MXT**.......... Message Exchange Terminal
**MXT**.......... Mixture
**MXTMP**.... Maximum Temperature (NOAA)
**MXTR**....... Maxtor Corp. [*San Jose, CA*] [*NASDAQ symbol*] (NQ)
**MXU**.......... Mullewa [*Australia*] [*Airport symbol*] [*Obsolete*] (OAG)
**MXU**.......... Multiplexer Unit [*Telecommunications*]
**MxU**.......... Universidad Nacional Autonoma de Mexico, Mexico City, Mexico [*Library symbol*] [*Library of Congress*] (LCLS)
**MXVRC**..... Middlesex Volunteer Rifle Corps [*British military*] (DMA)
**MXW**.......... Maxwell, CA [*Location identifier*] [*FAA*] (FAAL)
**MXWL**....... Maxwell Laboratories, Inc. [*NASDAQ symbol*] (NQ)
**MXWND**... Maximum Wind (NOAA)
**MXX**.......... International Murex Technologies [*AMEX symbol*] (SPSG)
**MXX**.......... Mora [*Sweden*] [*Airport symbol*] (OAG)
**MXXM**....... MAXAXAM Corp. [*South Portland, ME*] [*NASDAQ symbol*] (NQ)
**MXXX**....... Mars Stores, Inc. [*NASDAQ symbol*] (NQ)
**MXY**.......... McCarthy [*Alaska*] [*Airport symbol*] (OAG)
**MXY**.......... McCarthy, AK [*Location identifier*] [*FAA*] (FAAL)
**MY**............ Air Mali [*ICAO designator*] (FAAC)
**My**............ All India Reporter, Mysore Series [*A publication*] (ILCA)
**MY**............ Mahzor Yanai (BJA)
**MY**............ Malaysia [*IYRU nationality code*] [*ANSI two-letter standard code*] (CNC)
**my**............ Malaysia [*MARC country of publication code*] [*Library of Congress*] (LCCP)
**MY**............ Man-Year (AFM)
**M/Y**........... Marshaling Yards [*Military*]
**M & Y**........ Martin and Yerger's Tennessee Reports [*8 Tennessee*] [*1825-28*] [*A publication*] (DLA)
**MY**............ May [*A publication*]
**MY**............ May

**my** ............ Mayer [*A unit of heat capacity*]
**MY** ............ Mean Yield [*Agriculture*]
**MY** ............ Miller-Yoder Language Comprehension Test
**MY** ............ Million Years
**MY** ............ Montgomeryshire Yeomanry [*British military*] (DMA)
**MY** ............ Motor Yacht
**MY** ............ Muddy [*Track condition*] [*Thoroughbred racing*]
**MY** ............ Myopia
**MY** ............ Myria [*A prefix meaning multiplied by* $10^4$]
***MYA*** ............ *Million Years Ago*
***MYA*** ............ *Moruya [Australia] [Airport symbol]* (OAG)
**MYAB** ....... Clarence Bain, Andros Island [*Bahamas*] [*ICAO location identifier*] (ICLI)
**MYAF** ....... Andros Town, Andros Island [*Bahamas*] [*ICAO location identifier*] (ICLI)
**MYAG** ....... Gorda Cay, Abaco Island [*Bahamas*] [*ICAO location identifier*] (ICLI)
**MYAK** ....... Congo Town, Andros Island [*Bahamas*] [*ICAO location identifier*] (ICLI)
**MYAM** ...... Marsh Harbour, Abaco Island [*Bahamas*] [*ICAO location identifier*] (ICLI)
**MYAN** ....... San Andros, Andros Island [*Bahamas*] [*ICAO location identifier*] (ICLI)
**MYAO** ....... Moores Island, Abaco Island [*Bahamas*] [*ICAO location identifier*] (ICLI)
**MYAP** ....... Spring Point [*Bahamas*] [*ICAO location identifier*] (ICLI)
**MYAPP** ..... Main Yankee Atomic Power Plant (NRCH)
**MYAS** ....... Sandy Point, Abaco Island [*Bahamas*] [*ICAO location identifier*] (ICLI)
**Myasn Ind SSSR** ... Myasnaya Industriya SSSR [*A publication*]
**Myasn Molochn Promst SSSR** ... Myasnaya i Molochnaya Promyshlennost SSSR [*A publication*]
**MYAT** ....... Treasure Cay, Abaco Island [*Bahamas*] [*ICAO location identifier*] (ICLI)
**MYAW** ...... Walker Cay, Abaco Island [*Bahamas*] [*ICAO location identifier*] (ICLI)
**MYB** .......... Mayoumba [*Gabon*] [*Airport symbol*] (OAG)
**MYBC** ....... Chub Cay, Berry Island [*Bahamas*] [*ICAO location identifier*] (ICLI)
**MYBG** ....... Bullocks Harbour/Great Harbour Cay, Berry Island [*Bahamas*] [*ICAO location identifier*] (ICLI)
**MYBO** ....... Ocean Cay, Bimini Island [*Bahamas*] [*ICAO location identifier*] (ICLI)
**MYBP** ........ Million Years before Present [*Geology*]
**MYBS** ........ Alice Town/South Bimini, Bimini Island [*Bahamas*] [*ICAO location identifier*] (ICLI)
**MYBT** ........ Cistern Cay, Berry Island [*Bahamas*] [*ICAO location identifier*] (ICLI)
**MYBW** ...... Big Whale Cay, Berry Island [*Bahamas*] [*ICAO location identifier*] (ICLI)
**MYBX** ....... Little Whale Cay, Berry Island [*Bahamas*] [*ICAO location identifier*] (ICLI)
**MYC** .......... Malartic Hygrade Gold Mines Ltd. [*Vancouver Stock Exchange symbol*]
**MYC** .......... Maracay [*Venezuela*] [*Airport symbol*] (OAG)
**MYC** .......... Middlesex Yeomanry Cavalry [*British military*] (DMA)
**MYC** .......... Montgomeryshire Yeomanry Cavalry [*British military*] (DMA)
**MYC** .......... Multiyear Contract
**My & C** ...... Mylne and Craig's English Chancery Reports [*A publication*] (DLA)
**MYCA** ....... Arthur's Town, Eleuthera Island [*Bahamas*] [*ICAO location identifier*] (ICLI)
**MYCB** ....... New Bight, Cat Island [*Bahamas*] [*ICAO location identifier*] (ICLI)
**MYCGA** .... Memory and Cognition [*A publication*]
**MYCH** ....... Hawks Nest Creek/Hawks Nest, Cat Island [*Bahamas*] [*ICAO location identifier*] (ICLI)
**MYCI** ......... Colonel Hill, Crooked Island [*Bahamas*] [*ICAO location identifier*] (ICLI)
**MYCI** ......... Mirrer Yeshiva Central Institute (EA)
**MYCO** ....... Mycobacterium
**MYCO** ....... Mycogen Corp. [*NASDAQ symbol*] (NQ)
**Mycol** ......... Mycologia [*A publication*]
**MYCOL** .... Mycology
**Mycol Abstr** ... Mycological Abstracts [*A publication*]
**Mycol Helv** ... Mycologia Helvetica [*A publication*]
**Mycol Mem** ... Mycologia Memoir [*A publication*]
**Mycol Pap Commonw Mycol Inst** ... Mycological Papers. Commonwealth Mycological Institute [*A publication*]
**Mycol Res** ... Mycological Research [*A publication*]
**Mycopath Mycol Appl** ... Mycopathologia et Mycologia Applicata [*A publication*]
**Mycopathol Mycol Appl** ... Mycopathologia et Mycologia Applicata [*A publication*]
**Mycopathol Mycol Appl Suppl Iconogr Mycol** ... Mycopathologia et Mycologia Applicata. Supplementum Iconographia Mycologica [*A publication*]
**Mycopatholo** ... Mycopathologia [*A publication*]
**MYCOS** ..... My Compact Operating System [*Toshiba*]
**MYCP** ........ Pittsdown, Crooked Island [*Bahamas*] [*ICAO location identifier*] (ICLI)
**My & Cr** ..... Mylne and Craig's English Chancery Reports [*A publication*] (DLA)
**MYCS** ........ Cay Sal [*Bahamas*] [*ICAO location identifier*] (ICLI)
**MYCX** ....... Cutlass Bay, Cat Island [*Bahamas*] [*ICAO location identifier*] (ICLI)
**MYD** .......... Malindi [*Kenya*] [*Airport symbol*] (OAG)
**MYD** .......... Miyadu [*Japan*] [*Seismograph station code, US Geological Survey*] [*Closed*] (SEIS)
**MYDIS** ...... [*Reference*] My Dispatch [*Military*]
**MYDW** ...... Multiple Yield Defense Weapon
**MYE** .......... Mary Ellen Resources Ltd. [*Vancouver Stock Exchange symbol*]
**MYE** .......... Miyake Jima [*Japan*] [*Airport symbol*] (OAG)
**MYE** .......... Myers Industries, Inc. [*AMEX symbol*] (SPSG)
**MYEAA** .... Minerals Yearbook [*A publication*]
**MYEC** ....... Cape Eleuthera, Eleuthera Island [*Bahamas*] [*ICAO location identifier*] (ICLI)
**MYEG** ....... George Town, Exuma Island [*Bahamas*] [*ICAO location identifier*] (ICLI)
**MYEH** ....... North Eleuthera, Eleuthera Island [*Bahamas*] [*ICAO location identifier*] (ICLI)
**MYEL** ........ Myelin [*or Myelinated*] [*Medicine*]
**MYEL** ........ Myelocyte [*Hematology*]
**MYEL** ........ Staniel Cay, Exuma Island [*Bahamas*] [*ICAO location identifier*] (ICLI)
**myelo** .......... Myelocyte [*Hematology*]
**MYEM** ...... Governor's Harbour, Eleuthera Island [*Bahamas*] [*ICAO location identifier*] (ICLI)
**MYEN** ....... Norman's Cay, Exuma Island [*Bahamas*] [*ICAO location identifier*] (ICLI)
**MYER** ....... Rock Sound/International, Eleuthera Island [*Bahamas*] [*ICAO location identifier*] (ICLI)
**Myer Dig** ... Myer's Texas Digest [*A publication*] (DLA)
**Myer Fed Dec** ... Myer's Federal Decisions [*A publication*] (DLA)
**M and Yerger's Rep** ... Martin and Yerger's Tennessee Reports [*8 Tennessee*] [*1825-28*] [*A publication*] (DLA)
**Myer's Fed Dec** ... Myer's Federal Decisions [*United States*] [*A publication*] (DLA)
**MYES** ........ Lee Stocking Island, Exuma Island [*Bahamas*] [*ICAO location identifier*] (ICLI)
**MYEY** ....... Hog Cay, Exuma Island [*Bahamas*] [*ICAO location identifier*] (ICLI)
**MYF** .......... Methodist Youth Fellowship
**MYF** .......... San Diego [*California*] Montgomery Field [*Airport symbol*] [*Obsolete*] (OAG)
**MYFR** ........ Mayfair Super Markets, Inc. [*NASDAQ symbol*] (NQ)
**MYG** .......... Food Analysis [*A publication*]
**MYG** .......... Massachusetts Institute of Technology, Cambridge, MA [*OCLC symbol*] (OCLC)
**MYG** .......... Matka [*Yugoslavia*] [*Seismograph station code, US Geological Survey*] (SEIS)
**MYG** .......... Mayaguana [*Bahamas*] [*Airport symbol*] (OAG)
**MYG** .......... Maytag Corp. [*NYSE symbol*] (SPSG)
**MYG** .......... Myasthenia Gravis [*Medicine*]
**MYG** .......... Myriagram [*Ten Thousand Grams*]
**MYGD** ....... Deep Water Cay, Grand Bahama Island [*Bahamas*] [*ICAO location identifier*] (ICLI)
**MYGF** ....... Freeport/International, Grand Bahama Island [*Bahamas*] [*ICAO location identifier*] (ICLI)
**MYGM** ...... Grand Bahama Auxiliary Air Force Base, Grand Bahama Island [*Bahamas*] [*ICAO location identifier*] (ICLI)
**MYGW** ...... West End, Grand Bahama Island [*Bahamas*] [*ICAO location identifier*] (ICLI)
**MYH** .......... Milieuhygiene [*A publication*]
**MYHEED** ... Mycologia Helvetica [*A publication*]
**MY I** .......... First Multiyear Contract [*Military*] (RDA)
**MYI** .......... Magical Youths International (EA)
**MYI** .......... Metallic Yarns Institute [*Defunct*]
**MYIG** ........ Matthew Town, Great Inagua Island [*Bahamas*] [*ICAO location identifier*] (ICLI)
**MY II** ......... Second Multiyear Contract [*Military*] (RDA)
**MYIM** ....... Mylar Insulation Material
**MYJ** .......... Matsuyama [*Japan*] [*Airport symbol*] (OAG)
**MYK** .......... May Creek [*Alaska*] [*Airport symbol*] (OAG)
**MYK** .......... May Creek, AK [*Location identifier*] [*FAA*] (FAAL)
**MYK** .......... Metrovisie [*A publication*]
**MYK** .......... Miyakojima [*Ryukyu Islands*] [*Seismograph station code, US Geological Survey*] (SEIS)
**My & K** ...... Mylne and Keen's English Chancery Reports [*A publication*] (DLA)
**Mykol Sb** ... Mykologicky Sbornik [*A publication*]
**Mykol Zentbl** ... Mykologisches Zentralblatt [*A publication*]
**Mykrobiol Zh** ... Mykrobiolchichniyi Zhurnal [*A publication*]
**MYL** .......... McCall, ID [*Location identifier*] [*FAA*] (FAAL)
**MYL** .......... Monthly Labor Review [*A publication*]
**MYL** .......... Mylan Laboratories, Inc. [*NYSE symbol*] (SPSG)
**MYL** .......... Myrialiter [*Unit of measurement*]
**Myl & C** ..... Mylne and Craig's English Chancery Reports [*A publication*] (DLA)
**Myl & C (Eng)** ... Mylne and Craig's English Chancery Reports [*A publication*] (DLA)

**Myl & Cr**.... Mylne and Craig's English Chancery Reports [*A publication*] (DLA)
**MYLD**....... Deadman's Cay, Long Island [*Bahamas*] [*ICAO location identifier*] (ICLI)
**My LJ**........ Mysore Law Journal [*India*] [*A publication*] (DLA)
**Myl & K**..... Mylne and Keen's English Chancery Reports [*A publication*] (DLA)
**Myl & K (Eng)** ... Mylne and Keen's English Chancery Reports [*A publication*] (DLA)
**Mylne & K** ... Mylne and Keen's English Chancery Reports [*A publication*] (DLA)
**MYLR**........ Diamond Roads, Long Island [*Bahamas*] [*ICAO location identifier*] (ICLI)
**MYLS**........ Mid-York Library System [*Library network*]
**MYLS**........ Stella Maris, Long Island [*Bahamas*] [*ICAO location identifier*] (ICLI)
**MYLTR**..... [*Reference*] My Letter [*Military*]
**MYLX**...... Mylex Corp. [*Miami, FL*] [*NASDAQ symbol*] (NQ)
**MYM**......... Marley Mines Ltd. [*Vancouver Stock Exchange symbol*]
**MYM**......... Monkey Mountain [*Guyana*] [*Airport symbol*] (OAG)
**MYM**......... MONY Real Estate Investors [*Formerly, MONY Mortgage Investors*] [*NYSE symbol*] (SPSG)
**MYM**......... Myriameter
**MyMD**....... Myotonic Muscular Dystrophy [*See also MD*] [*Medicine*]
**MYMGM** ... [*Reference*] My Mailgram [*Military*]
**MYMM**..... Mayaguana Auxiliary Air Force Base, Mayaguana Island [*Bahamas*] [*ICAO location identifier*] (ICLI)
**MYMS** ...... Mothers of Young Mongoloids [*Later, PODSC*] (EA)
**MYMSG** .... [*Reference*] My Message [*Military*]
**MYN**.......... Mareb [*Yemen Arab Republic*] [*Airport symbol*] [*Obsolete*] (OAG)
**myn** ............ Mayan [*MARC language code*] [*Library of Congress*] (LCCP)
**MYN**.......... Mayan Energy, Inc. [*Vancouver Stock Exchange symbol*]
**MYNA**....... Nassau [*Bahamas*] [*ICAO location identifier*] (ICLI)
**MYNN**....... Nassau/International, New Providence Island [*Bahamas*] [*ICAO location identifier*] (ICLI)
**Mynsing**..... [*Joachim*] Mynsinger [*Deceased, 1588*] [*Authority cited in pre-1607 legal work*] (DSA)
**MYO**.......... Murray Ohio Manufacturing Co. [*NYSE symbol*] (SPSG)
**MYOB**....... Mind Your Own Business [*Slang*]
**MYOBB** .... Mind Your Own Business, Buster [*Slang*]
**MYOGA**.... Materialy Ogniotrwale [*A publication*]
**Myonj-Ji Univ J Nat Sci** ... Myonj-Ji University. Journal of Natural Science [*A publication*]
**MYOT**....... Myo-Tech Corp. [*NASDAQ symbol*] (NQ)
**Myotis Mitteilungsbl Fledermauskundler** ... Myotis Mitteilungsblatt fuer Fledermauskundler [*A publication*]
**MY/P**......... Mean Yield/Plants [*Agriculture*]
**MYP**.......... Multiyear Procurement [*DoD*]
**MYP Alum** ... Minerals Yearbook. Preprint. Aluminum [*A publication*]
**MYP A M** ... Minerals Yearbook. Preprint. Abrasive Materials [*A publication*]
**MYP Antim** ... Minerals Yearbook. Preprint. Antimony [*A publication*]
**MYP Asbsts** ... Minerals Yearbook. Preprint. Asbestos [*A publication*]
**MYP Barite** ... Minerals Yearbook. Preprint. Barite [*A publication*]
**MYP Bauxit** ... Minerals Yearbook. Preprint. Bauxite [*A publication*]
**MYP Beryl** ... Minerals Yearbook. Preprint. Beryllium [*A publication*]
**MYP Bis**.... Minerals Yearbook. Preprint. Bismuth [*A publication*]
**MYP Boron** ... Minerals Yearbook. Preprint. Boron [*A publication*]
**MYP Bromin** ... Minerals Yearbook. Preprint. Bromine [*A publication*]
**MYP Cadm** ... Minerals Yearbook. Preprint. Cadmium [*A publication*]
**MYP Calcm** ... Minerals Yearbook. Preprint. Calcium and Calcium Compounds [*A publication*]
**MYP Cement** ... Minerals Yearbook. Preprint. Cement [*A publication*]
**MYP Chrom** ... Minerals Yearbook. Preprint. Chromium [*A publication*]
**MYP Clays** ... Minerals Yearbook. Preprint. Clays [*A publication*]
**MYP Cobalt** ... Minerals Yearbook. Preprint. Cobalt [*A publication*]
**MYP Columb** ... Minerals Yearbook. Preprint. Columbium and Tantalum [*A publication*]
**MYP Copper** ... Minerals Yearbook. Preprint. Copper [*A publication*]
**MYP C Stone** ... Minerals Yearbook. Preprint. Crushed Stone [*A publication*]
**MYP Diato** ... Minerals Yearbook. Preprint. Diatomite [*A publication*]
**MYP Dime S** ... Minerals Yearbook. Preprint. Dimension Stone [*A publication*]
**MYP Felsp** ... Minerals Yearbook. Preprint. Feldspar, Nepheline, Syenite, and Aplite [*A publication*]
**MYP Ferro** ... Minerals Yearbook. Preprint. Ferroalloys [*A publication*]
**MYP Fluor** ... Minerals Yearbook. Preprint. Fluorspar [*A publication*]
**MYP Gallm** ... Minerals Yearbook. Preprint. Gallium [*A publication*]
**MYP Gem St** ... Minerals Yearbook. Preprint. Gem Stones [*A publication*]
**MYP Gold** ... Minerals Yearbook. Preprint. Gold [*A publication*]
**MYP Grapht** ... Minerals Yearbook. Preprint. Graphite [*A publication*]
**MYP Gypsum** ... Minerals Yearbook. Preprint. Gypsum [*A publication*]
**MYP Helium** ... Minerals Yearbook. Preprint. Helium [*A publication*]
**MYP Iodine** ... Minerals Yearbook. Preprint. Iodine [*A publication*]
**MYP Iron** .. Minerals Yearbook. Preprint. Iron and Steel [*A publication*]
**MYP Iron O** ... Minerals Yearbook. Preprint. Iron Ore [*A publication*]
**MYP Iron S S** ... Minerals Yearbook. Preprint. Iron and Steel Slag [*A publication*]
**MYP Ir Ox** ... Minerals Yearbook. Preprint. Iron Oxide Pigments [*A publication*]
**MYP I & S S** ... Minerals Yearbook. Preprint. Iron and Steel Scrap [*A publication*]
**MYP Kyan** ... Minerals Yearbook. Preprint. Kyanite and Related Materials [*A publication*]
**MYP Lead** ... Minerals Yearbook. Preprint. Lead [*A publication*]
**MYP Lime** ... Minerals Yearbook. Preprint. Lime [*A publication*]
**MYP Lith** .. Minerals Yearbook. Preprint. Lithium [*A publication*]
**MYP Magn C** ... Minerals Yearbook. Preprint. Magnesium Compounds [*A publication*]
**MYP Mercry** ... Minerals Yearbook. Preprint. Mercury [*A publication*]
**MYP Mica** ... Minerals Yearbook. Preprint. Mica [*A publication*]
**MYP Mining** ... Minerals Yearbook. Preprint. Mining and Quarrying Trends in the Metal and Nonmetal Industries [*A publication*]
**MYP M N Mtl** ... Minerals Yearbook. Preprint. Minor Nonmetals [*A publication*]
**MYP Moly** ... Minerals Yearbook. Preprint. Molybdenum [*A publication*]
**MYP Nitro** ... Minerals Yearbook. Preprint. Nitrogen [*A publication*]
**MYP Nonfl M** ... Minerals Yearbook. Preprint. Nonfuel Minerals Survey Methods [*A publication*]
**MYPO**....... Multiyear Procurement Objective [*DoD*]
**MYP O Mtl** ... Minerals Yearbook. Preprint. Other Metals [*A publication*]
**MYP O Nmtl** ... Minerals Yearbook. Preprint. Other Nonmetals [*A publication*]
**MYP Peat** ... Minerals Yearbook. Preprint. Peat [*A publication*]
**MYP Phos R** ... Minerals Yearbook. Preprint. Phosphate Rock [*A publication*]
**MYP Platnm** ... Minerals Yearbook. Preprint. Platinum - Group Metals [*A publication*]
**MYP Potash** ... Minerals Yearbook. Preprint. Potash [*A publication*]
**MYP Prod** ... Minerals Yearbook. Preprint. Products [*A publication*]
**MYP Pumic** ... Minerals Yearbook. Preprint. Pumice and Volcanic Cinder [*A publication*]
**MYP Pumice** ... Minerals Yearbook. Preprint. Pumice and Pumicite [*A publication*]
**MYP Rev** ... Minerals Yearbook. Preprint. Review of the Mineral Industry [*A publication*]
**MYP Rhenm** ... Minerals Yearbook. Preprint. Rhenium [*A publication*]
**MYP Salt**... Minerals Yearbook. Preprint. Salt [*A publication*]
**MYP Sand** ... Minerals Yearbook. Preprint. Sand and Gravel [*A publication*]
**MYP Silver** ... Minerals Yearbook. Preprint. Silver [*A publication*]
**MYP Slag**.. Minerals Yearbook. Preprint. Slag - Iron and Steel [*A publication*]
**MYP Sodium** ... Minerals Yearbook. Preprint. Sodium and Sodium Compounds [*A publication*]
**MYP State** ... Minerals Yearbook. Preprint. Area Reports. Individual States [*A publication*]
**MYP Stat S** ... Minerals Yearbook. Preprint. Statistical Summary [*A publication*]
**MYP Stone** ... Minerals Yearbook. Preprint. Stone [*A publication*]
**MYP Sulfur** ... Minerals Yearbook. Preprint. Sulfur and Pyrites [*A publication*]
**MYP Talc**.. Minerals Yearbook. Preprint. Talc, Soapstone, and Pyrophyllite [*A publication*]
**MYP Terr** ... Minerals Yearbook. Preprint. Territorial Mineral Industry of Puerto Rico, Virgin Islands, and Pacific Islands [*A publication*]
**MYP Thorm** ... Minerals Yearbook. Preprint. Thorium [*A publication*]
**MYP Tin**.... Minerals Yearbook. Preprint. Tin [*A publication*]
**MYP Titanm** ... Minerals Yearbook. Preprint. Titanium [*A publication*]
**MYP Tungst** ... Minerals Yearbook. Preprint. Tungsten [*A publication*]
**MYP Vandm** ... Minerals Yearbook. Preprint. Vanadium [*A publication*]
**MYP Vermic** ... Minerals Yearbook. Preprint. Vermiculite [*A publication*]
**MYP Wld Min** ... Minerals Yearbook. Preprint. Minerals in the World Economy [*A publication*]
**MYP Zinc** ... Minerals Yearbook. Preprint. Zinc [*A publication*]
**MYP Zirc** .. Minerals Yearbook. Preprint. Zirconium and Hafnium [*A publication*]
**MYQ**.......... Windsor Locks, CT [*Location identifier*] [*FAA*] (FAAL)
**M & YR** ..... Martin and Yerger's Tennessee Reports [*8 Tennessee*] [*1825-28*] [*A publication*] (DLA)
**MYR**.......... Maximum Yield Research [*Agricultural technology*]
**m/yr** ........... Milli-Inches per Year [*Corrosion technology*]
**MYR**.......... Million Years [*Also, MY*]
**MYR**.......... [*The*] Myers [*L. E.*] Co. Group [*NYSE symbol*] (SPSG)
**Myr** ........... Myrick's California Probate Court Reports [*1872-79*] [*A publication*] (DLA)
**myr** ............ Myrtle [*Philately*]
**MYR**.......... Myrtle Beach [*South Carolina*] Myrtle Air Force Base [*Airport symbol*] (OAG)
**MYRA** ....... Multiyear Rescheduling Agreement [*Banking*]
**MYRAA** .... Model Yacht Racing Association of America (EA)
**MYRAD** .... [*Reference*] My Radio [*Military*]
**Myr Cal Prob** ... Myrick's California Probate Court Reports [*1872-79*] [*A publication*] (DLA)
**MYRD**....... Duncan Town, Exuma Island [*Bahamas*] [*ICAO location identifier*] (ICLI)
**Myrick (Cal)** ... Myrick's California Probate Court Reports [*1872-79*] [*A publication*] (DLA)
**Myrick Prob (Cal)** ... Myrick's California Probate Court Reports [*1872-79*] [*A publication*] (DLA)

**Myrick's Prob Rep** ... Myrick's California Probate Court Reports [*1872-79*] [*A publication*] (DLA)
**MYRP**........ Port Nelson, Exuma Island [*Bahamas*] [*ICAO location identifier*] (ICLI)
**Myr Prob** ... Myrick's California Probate Court Reports [*1872-79*] [*A publication*] (DLA)
**Myr Prob Rep** ... Myrick's California Probate Court Reports [*1872-79*] [*A publication*] (DLA)
**Mys**............ All India Reporter, Mysore [*A publication*] (DLA)
**MYS** .......... Malaysia [*ANSI three-letter standard code*] (CNC)
**MYS** .......... Man-Year-Space [*Army*] (AABC)
**MYS** .......... Myasthenic Syndrome [*Neurology*]
**MYS** .......... Mystery Mountain Minerals [*Vancouver Stock Exchange symbol*]
**MYS** .......... Mystic, KY [*Location identifier*] [*FAA*] (FAAL)
**MYS** .......... Mystic Marinelife Aquarium, New London, CT [*OCLC symbol*] (OCLC)
**Mys Ch Ct** ... Mysore Chief Court Reports [*India*] [*A publication*] (DLA)
**MYSER**..... [*Reference*] My Serial [*Military*]
**Mys HCR** .. Mysore High Court Reports [*India*] [*A publication*] (DLA)
**Mys LJ** ...... Mysore Law Journal [*India*] [*A publication*] (DLA)
**Mys LR**...... Mysore Law Reports [*India*] [*A publication*] (DLA)
**MYSM** ...... Cockburn Town, San Salvador Island [*Bahamas*] [*ICAO location identifier*] (ICLI)
**Mysore**....... Mysore Law Reports [*India*] [*A publication*] (DLA)
**Mysore Agric J** ... Mysore Agricultural Journal [*A publication*]
**Mysore Agr J** ... Mysore Agricultural Journal [*A publication*]
**Mysore Dep Mines Geol Geol Stud** ... Mysore. Department of Mines and Geology. Geological Studies [*A publication*]
**Mysore Econ R** ... Mysore Economic Review [*A publication*]
**Mysore J Agric Sci** ... Mysore Journal of Agricultural Sciences [*A publication*]
**Mysore LJ** ... Mysore Law Journal [*India*] [*A publication*] (DLA)
**Mysore Or** ... Mysore Orientalist [*A publication*]
**MYSPDLTR** ... [*Reference*] My Speedletter [*Military*]
**Mys R (R)**.. Mysore Reports (Reprint) [*1878-1923*] [*India*] [*A publication*] (DLA)
**MYST**........ Mystery
**Mys WN**.... Mysore Weekly Notes [*1891-92*] [*India*] [*A publication*] (DLA)
**MYT** .......... Myitkyina [*Burma*] [*Airport symbol*] (OAG)
**MYT** .......... Mysterious Traveler Mystery Reader [*A publication*]
**MYT** .......... Mytec Technology, Inc. [*Vancouver Stock Exchange symbol*]
**MYT** .......... Mythology
**MYTA** ....... Maintainability Task Analyses (NASA)
**MYTAB**..... Myristyltrimethylammonium Bromide [*Organic chemistry*]
**MYTEL**...... [*Reference*] My Telegram [*Military*]
**MYTH**....... Mythology
**MythosP**.... Mythos Papers [*A publication*]
**Myth Vat** ... Mythographi Vaticani [*A publication*] (OCD)
**MYU**......... Mekoryuk [*Alaska*] [*Airport symbol*] (OAG)
**MYV**.......... Maandstatistiek van de Industrie [*A publication*]
**MYV**.......... Marysville, CA [*Location identifier*] [*FAA*] (FAAL)
**MYVAL**..... Maintainability Evaluation (NASA)
**MYW**......... Mtwara [*Tanzania*] [*Airport symbol*] (OAG)
**MYW**......... Multiple Yield Weapon
**MYX**.......... Marion, VA [*Location identifier*] [*FAA*] (FAAL)
**MYX**.......... Menyamya [*Papua New Guinea*] [*Airport symbol*] (OAG)
**MYXO**........ Myxomatosis (DSUE)
**MYY**.......... Miri [*Malaysia*] [*Airport symbol*] (OAG)
**MYY**.......... Philadelphia, PA [*Location identifier*] [*FAA*] (FAAL)
**MYZ**.......... Marysville, KS [*Location identifier*] [*FAA*] (FAAL)
**MYZ**.......... Mix. Ijzerwaren, Doe het Zelf [*A publication*]
**MYZ**.......... Miyazaki [*Japan*] [*Seismograph station code, US Geological Survey*] (SEIS)
**MZ**............. Mainzer Zeitschrift [*A publication*]
**MZ**............. Mangels Zahlung [*For Non-Payment*] [*Business term*] [*German*]
**MZ**............. Mantle Zone
**MZ**............. Marginal Zone [*Neurology*]
**m-z** ............. Mass to Charge Ratio
**MZ**............. Merpati Nusantara PT [*Indonesia*] [*ICAO designator*] (FAAC)
**Mz**............. Methoxyphenylazobenzyloxycarbonyl [*Biochemistry*]
**MZ**............. Mezzo [*Moderate*] [*Music*] (ROG)
**MZ**............. Midzone Phenomenon [*Immunology*]
**MZ**............. Miesiecznik Zydowski (BJA)
**MZ**............. Monozygotic [*Genetics*]
**MZ**............. Mozambique [*ANSI two-letter standard code*] (CNC)
**mz**............... Mozambique [*MARC country of publication code*] [*Library of Congress*] (LCCP)
**MZ**............. Muzikoloski Zbornik - Musicological Annual [*A publication*]
**MZA** .......... Mariazell [*Austria*] [*Seismograph station code, US Geological Survey*] (SEIS)
**MZA** .......... Monozygotic Twins Reared Apart [*Genetics*]
**MZB** .......... San Diego, CA [*Location identifier*] [*FAA*] (FAAL)
**MZBZ**........ Belize/International [*Belize*] [*ICAO location identifier*] (ICLI)
**MZC** .......... Mitzic [*Gabon*] [*Airport symbol*] (OAG)
**MZF** .......... Manganese Zinc Ferrite
**MZF** .......... Mazirat [*France*] [*Seismograph station code, US Geological Survey*] (SEIS)
**MZFR**........ Mehrzweck Forschungs [*Reactor*] [*West Germany*] (NRCH)
**MZFW**....... Maximum Zero Fuel Weight [*Aviation*] (MCD)
**MZG**.......... Makung [*Taiwan*] [*Airport symbol*] (OAG)
**MZI** ........... Mopti [*Mali*] [*Airport symbol*] (OAG)
**MZISA**...... Monitore Zoologico Italiano [*Italian Journal of Zoology*]. Supplemento [*A publication*]
**M Zizn** ....... Muzikal'naja Zizn [*A publication*]
**MZJ**........... Marana, AZ [*Location identifier*] [*FAA*] (FAAL)
**MZK**.......... Marakei [*Kiribati*] [*Airport symbol*] (OAG)
**MZL** .......... Manizales [*Colombia*] [*Airport symbol*] (OAG)
**MZL** .......... Muzzle (MSA)
**MZLU** ....... Mizlou Communications Co., Inc. [*NASDAQ symbol*] (NQ)
**MZM**.......... Metz [*France*] [*Airport symbol*] (OAG)
**MZN**.......... Maruzen Co. Ltd. [*UTLAS symbol*]
**MZN**.......... Mount Vernon Nazarene College, Mount Vernon, OH [*OCLC symbol*] (OCLC)
**MZO**.......... Manzanillo [*Cuba*] [*Airport symbol*] (OAG)
**MZO**.......... Mazie Landing [*Oklahoma*] [*Seismograph station code, US Geological Survey*] (SEIS)
**MZOA**....... Masada of the Zionist Organization of America (EA)
**MZOHDT** ... Miscellanea Zoologica Hungarica [*A publication*]
**MZOODG** ... Miscellanea Zoologica [*A publication*]
**MZP** .......... Meta-Azidopyrimethamine [*Biochemistry*]
**MZR**.......... Mazar-I-Sharif [*Afghanistan*] [*Airport symbol*] (OAG)
**MZR**.......... Monroe, LA [*Location identifier*] [*FAA*] (FAAL)
**MZRKF**..... Mackenzie Energy Corp. [*NASDAQ symbol*] (NQ)
**MZS** .......... Spokane, WA [*Location identifier*] [*FAA*] (FAAL)
**MZ Sc**........ Master of Zoological Science
**MZSCS** ..... Martinek-Zaichkowsky Self-Concept Scale for Children [*Child development test*]
**MZSH** ....... Missionary Zelatrices of the Sacred Heart [*Roman Catholic women's religious order*]
**MZsL**......... Magyar Zsido Lexikon [*A publication*] (BJA)
**MZT** .......... Mazatlan [*Mexico*] [*Airport symbol*] (OAG)
**MZT** .......... Monozygotic Twins Reared Together [*Genetics*]
**MZV** .......... Magyar Zsidok Vilagszovetsege [*World Federation of Hungarian Jews*] (EAIO)
**MZV** .......... Moline, IL [*Location identifier*] [*FAA*] (FAAL)
**MZWMA**.. Molkerei-Zeitung Welt der Milch [*A publication*]
**MZX** .......... Augusta, GA [*Location identifier*] [*FAA*] (FAAL)
**MZY** .......... Mazzei Flying Service, Inc. [*Fresno, CA*] [*FAA designator*] (FAAC)
**MZZ** .......... Marion, IN [*Location identifier*] [*FAA*] (FAAL)

# N

N ............... All India Reporter, Nagpur Series [*A publication*] (ILCA)
n ............... Amino [*As substituent on nucleoside*] [*Biochemistry*]
n ............... Amount of Substance [*Molecular quantity*] [*Symbol*] [*IUPAC*]
N ............... Avogadro Number [*Number of molecules in one gram-molecular weight of a substance*]
N ............... Cementex [*Research code symbol*]
N ............... Clearance Not Delivered [*Aviation*] (FAAC)
N ............... Digestum Novum [*A publication*] [*Authority cited in pre-1607 legal work*] (DSA)
N ............... Dr. Karl Thomae GmbH [*Germany*] [*Research code symbol*]
N ............... Dumb [*Auxiliary craft suffix*] [*British*] [*Navy*]
N ............... Educational Premises [*Public-performance tariff class*] [*British*]
N ............... Electron N-Type Semiconductor Material
N ............... Employment [*Economics*]
N ............... Flying Boat [*Russian aircraft symbol*]
n ............... Footnote (DLA)
N ............... H. Lundbeck [*Denmark*] [*Research code symbol*]
N ............... Haploid Number [*Genetics*]
N ............... INCO Ltd. [*Formerly, International Nickel Co. of Canada Ltd.*] [*NYSE symbol*] [*Toronto Stock Exchange symbol*] (SPSG)
n ............... [*An*] Indefinite Quantity [*Mathematics*] (ROG)
N ............... Knight [*Chess*]
N ............... Magnetic Flux [*Symbol*] (ROG)
N ............... Nail
N ............... Name
N ............... Nan [*Phonetic alphabet*] [*World War II*] (DSUE)
n ............... Nano [*A prefix meaning divided by one billion*] [*SI symbol*]
N ............... Naringenin [*Organic chemistry*]
N ............... Naris [*Nostril*] [*Pharmacy*]
N ............... Narrow
N ............... Nasal
N ............... Nation [*A publication*]
N ............... National [*Screw threads*]
N ............... National League [*Baseball*]
N ............... Nationalist (ROG)
N ............... Nationalist Party [*British*]
N ............... Native [*Ecology*]
N ............... Natural Division [*Geography*]
N ............... Natus [*Birth*] [*Latin*]
N ............... Nautical
N ............... Naval [*British military*] (DMA)
N ............... Navigation
N ............... Navigational Aids [*JETDS nomenclature*]
N ............... Navy
N ............... Nay [*Vote*]
N ............... Near the Nut (or Heel) of the Bow [*Music*] (ROG)
N ............... Necrotic
N ............... Need [*Psychology*]
n ............... Negative [*Crystal*]
N ............... Negro
N ............... Neisseria [*Medicine*]
N ............... Nematocyst [*Zoology*]
N ............... Neophilologus [*A publication*]
N ............... Neper [*A unit on a natural logarithmic scale*] (DEN)
N ............... Nephew
N ............... Nepos [*Grandson*] [*Latin*]
N ............... Nervus [*Nerve*] [*Anatomy*]
N ............... Nested [*Freight*]
N ............... Nesting [*Ornithology*]
N ............... Net
n ............... Netto [*Net*] [*Business term*] [*German*]
N ............... Neuraminidase [*An enzyme*]
N ............... Neurogenic Element
N ............... Neurology
N ............... Neuter
N ............... Neutral
n ............... Neutron [*A nuclear particle*]
N ............... Neutrophil [*Hematology*]
N ............... New [*Stock exchange term*] (SPSG)
N ............... New Persian
N ............... New York State Library, Albany, NY [*Library symbol*] [*Library of Congress*] (LCLS)
N ............... New York Stock Exchange [*New York, NY*]
N ............... Newfoundland Standard Time [*Aviation*] (FAAC)
N ............... News
N ............... Newspaper
N ............... Newton [*Symbol*] [*SI unit of force*]
N ............... Nicolaus Furiosus [*Flourished, 12th century*] [*Authority cited in pre-1607 legal work*] (DSA)
N ............... Nicotinamide [*Also, NAA*] [*Vitamin*]
N ............... Niece (ADA)
N ............... Nifedipine [*Pharmacology*]
N ............... Night [*Broadcasting term*]
N ............... Night [*Approach and landing charts*] [*Aviation*]
N ............... Night Fighter [*When suffix to plane designation*] [*Navy*]
N ............... Night Game [*Baseball*]
N ............... Nitrogen [*Chemical element*]
N ............... No
N ............... No Uniform [*For schoolgirls*] [*British*]
N ............... Nocte [*At Night*] [*Pharmacy*]
N ............... Nodal [*Oncology*]
N ............... Node [*Lymphatic*] [*Anatomy*]
N ............... Noise [*Broadcasting*]
N ............... Nomen [*Name*] [*Latin*]
N ............... Nominal [*Stock exchange term*] (SPSG)
N ............... Nominally Labeled [*Compound, with radioisotope*]
N ............... Nominative
N ............... None
N ............... Nonmalignant [*Of tumors*] [*Medicine*]
N ............... Nonne [*Globulin test*]
N ............... Noon
N ............... Norein [*Geology*]
N ............... Norland Potato
N ............... Normal
n ............... Normal [*Of molecular structure*] [*Chemistry*]
N ............... Normal [*Solute concentration*] [*Chemistry*]
N ............... Normal Depth [*Earthquakes*]
N ............... Normal Horsepower
N ............... Norse [*Language, etc.*]
N ............... Norske Veritas [*Norwegian ship classification society*] (ROG)
N ............... North [*or Northern*]
n------......... North America [*MARC geographic area code*] [*Library of Congress*] (LCCP)
N ............... Northeastern Reporter [*Commonly cited NW*] [*A publication*] (DLA)
N ............... Northern Ireland Law Reports [*A publication*] (DLA)
N ............... Northgate Exploration Ltd. [*Gold producer*] [*Canada*]
N ............... Northwestern Reporter [*Commonly cited NE*] [*A publication*] (DLA)
N ............... Norway [*IYRU nationality code*]
N ............... Noster [*Our*] [*Latin*]
N ............... Note
n/ ............... Notre [*Our*] [*Business term*] [*French*]
N ............... Noun
N ............... Novellae [*Novels*] [*New Constitutions of Justinian*] [*A publication*] (DLA)
N ............... Novelty [*Insulation*]
N ............... November [*Phonetic alphabet*] [*International*] (DSUE)
N ............... November
N ............... November [*A publication*]
N ............... Novice Slope [*Skiing*]
N ............... Nuclear
N ............... Nuclear Propelled [*When following vessel classification, as CAG(N)*] [*Navy*]
N ............... [*A*] Nucleoside [*One-letter symbol; see Nuc*]
N ............... Nucleus [*Of a cell*] [*Biology*]
n ............... Nucleus [*Psychology*]
N ............... Nucleus (of Syllable) [*Linguistics*]
N ............... Nullity [*Divorce cases*] [*British*] (ROG)
N ............... Number
N ............... Number of Molecules [*Symbol*] [*IUPAC*]

N ... Numeric
N ... Nun
N ... Nun [*Buoy*]
N ... Nunnery
N ... Nupta [*Married*] [*Latin*]
N ... Nurse (ADA)
N ... Nuts [*Phonetic alphabet*] [*Royal Navy*] [*World War I*] [*Pre-World War II*] (DSUE)
N ... Nylon (AAG)
N ... Nymph [*Entomology*]
N ... Nystatin [*Antifungal antibiotic*]
**n** ... Principal Quantum Number [*Atomic physics*] (DEN)
N ... Probe [*Missile vehicle type symbol*]
**n** ... Refractive Index [*Symbol*] [*Physics*]
N ... Rockwell International Corp. [*ICAO aircraft manufacturer identifier*] (ICAO)
N ... Sound in Air [*JETDS nomenclature*]
N ... South African Law Reports, Natal Province Division [*1910-46*] [*A publication*] (DLA)
N ... Special Test, Permanent [*Aircraft classification letter*]
N ... Stauffer Chemical Co. [*Research code symbol*]
N ... Tilt Correction
N ... United States [*Aircraft nationality and registration mark*] (FAAC)
**2N** ... Diploid Number [*Genetics*]
**5N** ... Nigeria [*Aircraft nationality and registration mark*] (FAAC)
**9N** ... Nepal [*Aircraft nationality and registration mark*] (FAAC)
**N/30** ... Net in Thirty Days
**N (Bomb)** ... Neutron Bomb
**NA** ... De Natura Animalium [*of Aelianus*] [*Classical studies*] (OCD)
**NA** ... Nachrichten-Aufklaerung [*Signal intelligence*] [*German military - World War II*]
**NA** ... Nachrichtenabteilung [*Signal battalion*] [*German military - World War II*]
**NA** ... NAFEC [*National Aviation Facilities Experimental Center*] (FAAC)
**Na** ... Nahum [*Old Testament book*]
**NA** ... Nailable [*Technical drawings*]
**Na** ... Naira [*Monetary unit*] [*Nigeria*]
**N/A** ... Name and Address
**NA** ... Names [*A publication*]
**NA** ... Namibia [*ANSI two-letter standard code*] (CNC)
**nA** ... Nanoampere
**NA** ... Naphthalene Dicarboxylic Acid
**NA** ... Naphthylacetamide [*Organic chemistry*]
**NA** ... Naphthylamine [*Organic chemistry*]
**NA** ... Napoleonic Association [*Enfield, Middlesex, England*] (EAIO)
**NA** ... Narcotics Anonymous (EA)
**NA** ... Narrow Angle
**NA** ... Nash Papyrus (BJA)
**Na** ... [*Guillelmus*] Naso [*Flourished, 1220-34*] [*Authority cited in pre-1607 legal work*] (DSA)
**N & A** ... Nation and Athenaeum [*A publication*]
**NA** ... Nation and Athenaeum [*A publication*]
**NA** ... National Academician
**NA** ... National Academy (ROG)
**NA** ... National Acme [*Thread*]
**NA** ... National Airlines, Inc. [*ICAO designator*]
**NA** ... National Airport [*Under control of BAA*] [*British*]
**NA** ... National Alliance (EA)
**NA** ... National Ambucs (EA)
**NA** ... [*The*] National Archives [*of the United States*]
**NA** ... National Army
**NA** ... National Assistance [*British*]
**NA** ... National Association [*National Bank*]
**NA** ... National Bank of Canada [*Toronto Stock Exchange symbol*] [*Vancouver Stock Exchange symbol*]
**NA** ... Nationale Aktion fuer Volk und Heimat [*National Action for People and Homeland*] [*Switzerland*] [*Political party*] (PPE)
**Na** ... Natrium [*Sodium*] [*Chemical element*]
**NA** ... Natural Axis
**NA** ... Naturally Aspirated [*Diesel engines*]
**Na** ... Nature [*London*] [*A publication*]
**NA** ... Nautical Almanac
**N & A** ... Nautical & Aviation Publishing Co.
**NA** ... Naval Academy
**NA** ... Naval Accounts [*British*]
**NA** ... Naval Air Systems Command Manual
**NA** ... Naval Aircraft
**NA** ... Naval Airman [*Navy rating*] [*British*]
**NA** ... Naval Architect
**NA** ... Naval Assistant [*Navy rating*] [*British*]
**NA** ... Naval Attache [*Diplomacy*]
**NA** ... Naval Auxiliary
**NA** ... Naval Aviator
**NA** ... Navion Aircraft Co. [*ICAO aircraft manufacturer identifier*] (ICAO)
**NA** ... Nederlandsch Archievenblad [*A publication*]
**NA** ... Needle Aspiration [*Surgery*]
**NA** ... Needs Assessment (OICC)
**NA** ... Nelson Associates [*Also, an information service or system*] (IID)
**NA** ... Neo-Assyrian [*or New Assyrian*] [*Language, etc.*] (BJA)
**NA** ... Net Assessment Organization [*Navy*]
**NA** ... Net Assets [*Banking*]
**na** ... Netherlands Antilles [*MARC country of publication code*] [*Library of Congress*] (LCCP)
**NA** ... Network Adapter (MCD)
**NA** ... Neues Archiv der Gesellschaft fuer Aeltere Deutsche Geschichtskunde [*A publication*]
**NA** ... Neuraminidase Activity [*An enzyme*]
**NA** ... Neuropathology [*Medicine*] (DHSM)
**NA** ... Neutestamentliche Abhandlungen [*A publication*]
**NA** ... Neutral Axis
**NA** ... Neutralizing Antibody [*Immunochemistry*]
**NA** ... New Account
**NA** ... New Adelphi [*A publication*]
**NA** ... New African [*A publication*]
**NA** ... New Age [*Later, LR*] [*An association*] (EA)
**NA** ... New Alternative Party [*Venezuela*]
**NA** ... New Associations [*Later, NAP*] [*A publication*]
**NA** ... News Agencies [*A publication*]
**NA** ... Newsletter Association (EA)
**NA** ... Newton Abbot [*British depot code*]
**NA** ... Next Action (NASA)
**NA** ... Next Assembly
**NA** ... Ney-Allen [*Astronomy*]
**NA** ... Nicotinic Acid [*Biochemistry*]
**NA** ... Night Alarm [*Telecommunications*] (TEL)
**NA** ... Nitrobenzene Association [*Defunct*] (EA)
**NA** ... Nizamut Adalat Reports [*India*] [*A publication*] (DLA)
**NA** ... No Access [*Telecommunications*] (TEL)
**NA** ... No Account [*Banking*]
**N/A** ... No Action
**N/A** ... No Advice [*Business term*]
**NA** ... No Assets (AFIT)
**NA** ... Noctes Atticae [*of Gellius*] [*Classical studies*] (OCD)
**NA** ... Nomina Anatomica [*System of anatomical terminology*]
**NA** ... Non Allocatur [*Legal*] [*Latin*] (ROG)
**N/A** ... Nonacceptance [*Business term*]
**NA** ... Nonacquiescence [*Legal term*] (DLA)
**NA** ... Nonactivated
**NA** ... Nonalcoholic
**NA** ... Nonattendance
**NA** ... Nora Alice [*DoD satellite*]
**NA** ... Noradrenaline [*Also known as NE: Norepinephrine*] [*Biochemistry*]
**NA** ... Normal Adult
**NA** ... North Africa
**NA** ... North America
**NA** ... North American Archaeologist [*A publication*]
**NA** ... North Atlantic Industries
**NA** ... Northanger Abbey [*Novel by Jane Austen*]
**NA** ... Nostra Aetate [*Declaration on the Relationship of the Church to the Non-Christian Religions*] [*Vatican II document*]
**NA** ... Nostro Account [*Our Account*] [*An account maintained by a bank with a bank in a foreign country*]
**N/A** ... Not Above
**N/A** ... Not Affected (AAG)
**NA** ... Not And [*Logical operator*] [*Data processing*]
**NA** ... Not Applicable
**NA** ... Not Appropriated
**NA** ... Not Assigned
**NA** ... Not Authorized
**NA** ... Not Available
**NA** ... Note d'Archivio per la Storia Musicale [*A publication*]
**NA** ... Notes Africaines [*A publication*]
**NA** ... Nozzle Assembly
**NA** ... Nucleic Acid [*Biochemistry*]
**NA** ... Nucleus Accumbens [*Neuroanatomy*]
**NA** ... Nucleus Ambiguus [*Neuroanatomy*]
**NA** ... Numerical Analysis [*Data processing*] (BUR)
**NA** ... Numerical Aperture [*Microscopy*]
**NA** ... Nuova Antologia [*A publication*]
**NA** ... Nuovi Argomenti [*A publication*]
**NA** ... Nurse's Aide
**NA** ... Nurses Almanac
**NA** ... Nursing Assistant
**NA** ... Nursing Auxiliary [*British*]
**NA** ... Nurturant-Authoritative [*Psychotherapy*]
**NA** ... Nutrient Agar [*Microbiology*]
**NA** ... Office of Noise Abatement [*FAA*] (FAAC)
**NA** ... Organon, Inc. [*Research code symbol*]
**N4A** ... National Association of Academic Advisors for Athletics (EA)
**N4A** ... National Association of Area Agencies on Aging [*Also, NAAAA*] (EA)
**NAA** ... Naalehu [*Hawaii*] [*Seismograph station code, US Geological Survey*] [*Closed*] (SEIS)
**NAA** ... Nanny Academy of America [*Commercial firm*] (EA)
**NAA** ... Naphthylacetic [*or Napthaleneacetic*] Acid [*Organic chemistry*]
**NAA** ... Narody Azii i Afriki [*A publication*]

**NAA**.......... Narrabri [*Australia*] [*Airport symbol*] (OAG)
**NAA**.......... Narrow-Angle Acquisition
**NAA**.......... National Academy of Arbitrators (EA)
**NAA**.......... National Academy of Astrology (EA)
**NAA**.......... National Aeronautic Association of the USA (EA)
**NAA**.......... National Aeronautics and Space Administration, Washington, DC [*OCLC symbol*] (OCLC)
**NAA**.......... National Aerosol Association (EA)
**NAA**.......... National Aftermarket Audit Co.
**NAA**.......... National Alumni Association (EA)
**NAA**.......... National Apartment Association (EA)
**NAA**.......... National Arborist Association (EA)
**NAA**.......... National Archery Association of the United States (EA)
**NAA**.......... National Ash Association (EA)
**NAA**.......... National Association of Accountants [*Montvale, NJ*] (EA)
**NAA**.......... National Auctioneers Association (EA)
**NAA**.......... Natural Areas Association (EA)
**NAA**.......... Naval Air Arm [*British*]
**NAA**.......... Naval Airship Association (EA)
**NAA**.......... Naval Attache for Air
**NAA**.......... Neckwear Association of America (EA)
**NAA**.......... Network Analysis Area [*Space Flight Operations Facility, NASA*]
**NAA**.......... Neutral Amino Acid [*Biochemistry*]
**NAA**.......... Neutron Activation Analysis
**NAA**.......... New Art Association (EA)
**NAA**.......... Newsletter Association of America (EA)
**NAA**.......... Nicotinic Acid Amide [*Also, N*]
**NAA**.......... Nigerian-American Alliance (EA)
**NAA**.......... No Apparent Abnormalities [*Medicine*]
**NAA**.......... Nocturnal Acid Accumulation [*Botany*]
**NAA**.......... Nord Africa Aviazione
**NAA**.......... North American Aviation, Inc. [*Later, Rockwell International Corp.*]
**NAA**.......... North Atlantic Assembly
**NAA**.......... Northeast Atlantic Airlines, Inc. [*Somers, CT*] [*FAA designator*] (FAAC)
**NAA**.......... Northern Attack Area
**NAA**.......... Norway-America Association (EA)
**NAA**.......... Not Always Afloat [*Shipping*]
**NAA**.......... Notices d'Archeologie Armoricaine [*A publication*]
**NAA**.......... Numismatic Association of Australia
**NAAA**........ National Agricultural Aviation Association (EA)
**NAAA**........ National Alarm Association of America (EA)
**NAAA**........ National Alliance of Athletic Associations [*Defunct*] (EA)
**NAAA**........ National Association of Arab Americans (EA)
**NAAA**........ National Auto Auction Association [*Lincoln, NE*] (EA)
**NAAAA**..... National Association for the Advancement of Aardvarks in America (EA)
**NAAAA**..... National Association of Area Agencies on Aging [*Also, N4A*] (EA)
**NAAACC**.. National Association of Antique Automobile Clubs of Canada
**NAAACPA** ... National Association of Asian American Certified Public Accountants (EA)
**NAAAID**... National Association of Americans of Asian Indian Descent (EA)
**NAAAP**..... National Association of Asian-American Professionals (EA)
**NAAAP**..... North American Association of Alcoholism Programs [*Later, ADPA*] (EA)
**NAAAS**..... National Association for Applied Arts and Sciences (EA)
**NAAASL**... National Association of African American Students of Law (EA)
**NAAB**........ National Architectural Accrediting Board (EA)
**NAAB**........ National Archival Appraisal Board [*Canada*]
**NAAB**........ National Association of Animal Breeders (EA)
**NAABA**...... National Association for the Advancement of the Black Aged (EA)
**NAABAVE** ... National Association for the Advancement of Black Americans in Vocational Education (EA)
**NAABC**...... National Association American Business Clubs [*High Point, NC*]
**NAABCV**... National Association American Balloon Corps Veterans (EA)
**NAABI**...... National Association of Alcoholic Beverage Importers [*Later, NABI*] (EA)
**NAABSA**... Not Always Afloat but Safe Aground [*Shipping*]
**NAA Bul**..... National Association of Accountants. Bulletin [*A publication*]
**NAAC**........ National Adoption Assistance Center (EA)
**NAAC**........ National Association for Ambulatory Care (EA)
**NAAC**........ National Association of Avon Collectors (EA)
**NAAC**........ Navy Aeroballistics Advisory Committee (MCD)
**NAAC**........ North American Adoption Congress (EA)
**NAACC**..... National Association for American Composers and Conductors (EA)
**NAACC**..... National Association of Angling and Casting Clubs [*Later, ACA*]
**NAACLS**... National Accrediting Agency for Clinical Laboratory Sciences (EA)
**NAACO**..... National Association of American Community Organizations (EA)
**NAACOG** ... NAACOG: the Organization for Obstetric, Gynecologic, and Neonatal Nurses [*Formerly, Nurses Association of the American College of Obstetricians and Gynecologists*] (EA)
**NAACP**..... National Association for the Advancement of Colored People (EA)
**NAACP**..... Neoplasia, Allergy, Addison's Disease, Collagen Disease, and Parasites [*Medicine*]
**NAACS**...... National Association of Accredited Cosmetology Schools (EA)
**NAACS**...... National Association of Aircraft and Communications Suppliers (EA)
**NAACSS**... National Association for the Accreditation of Colleges and Secondary Schools (EA)
**NAACSW** ... North American Association of Christians in Social Work [*Later, NACSW*] (EA)
**NAACT**..... National Association of Assessors and Collectors of Taxes [*A union*] [*British*]
**NAAD**........ National Association of Aluminum Distributors (EA)
**NAAD**........ Navajo Army Depot [*Arizona*] (AABC)
**NAAD**........ Nicotinic Acid Adenine Dinucleotide [*Biochemistry*]
**NAAD**........ North American Association for the Diaconate (EA)
**NAADAA** ... National Antique and Art Dealers Association of America (EA)
**NAADAC**.. National Association of Alcoholism and Drug Abuse Counselors (EA)
**NAADC**..... National Association of Art and Design Companies (EA)
**NAADC**..... North American Air Defense Command (AAG)
**NAADS**..... New Army Authorization Documents System (AABC)
**NAADS**..... New Army Automatic Data System
**NAAE**........ National Association of Aeronautical Examiners (EA)
**NAAE**........ National Association of Afro-American Educators
**NAAE**........ National Association of Agriculture Employees (EA)
**NAAE**........ Nordic Association for Adult Education (EAIO)
**NAAE**........ North American Academy of Ecumenists (EA)
**NAAF**........ National Alopecia Areata Foundation (EA)
**NAAF**........ Naval Auxiliary Air Facility
**NAAF**........ New Amino Acid Formula [*Nutrition*]
**NAAF**........ North African Air Force [*World War II*]
**NAAFA**..... National Association to Advance Fat Acceptance (EA)
**NAAFI**....... Navy, Army, and Air Force Institutes [*Responsible for clubs, canteens, and provision of some items for messing of British armed forces*]
**NAAFW**.... National Association of Air Forces Women
**NAAG**........ N-Acetylaspartylglutamic Acid [*Biochemistry*]
**NAAG**........ National Association of Attorneys General (EA)
**NAAG**........ NATO Army Advisory Group (NATG)
**NAAG**........ NATO Army Armaments Group (AABC)
**NAAG**........ Nordic Association of Applied Geophysics (EA)
**NAAG**........ North African Adjutant General [*World War II*]
**NAAGA**..... North African Adjutant General, Analysis and Control Division [*World War II*]
**NAAGC**..... North African Adjutant General, Casualty Branch [*World War II*]
**NAAGE**..... North African Adjutant General, Personnel Division [*World War II*]
**NAAGG**..... North African Adjutant General, Executive Division [*World War II*]
**NAAGO**..... North African Adjutant General, Operations Division [*World War II*]
**NAAGP**..... North African Adjutant General, Postal Division [*World War II*]
**NAAGS**..... North African Adjutant General, Statistical Division [*World War II*]
**NAAHE**..... National Association for the Advancement of Humane Education [*LA NAHEE*] (EA)
**NAAHP**..... National Association of Advisors for the Health Professions (EA)
**NAAHSC**.. North American Association of Hunter Safety Coordinators
**NAAI**......... National Alliance of Arts and Industry
**NAAI**......... National Association of Accountants in Insolvencies (EA)
**NAA-ICIF** ... North American Association of the ICIF [*International Cooperative Insurance Federation*] [*Detroit, MI*] (EA)
**NAAIS**....... National Aircraft Accident Investigation School [*FAA*]
**NAAIS**....... North American Association of Inventory Services [*Greensboro, NC*] (EA)
**NAAJHHA** ... North American Association of Jewish Homes and Housing for the Aging (EA)
**NAAJS**....... National Academy for Adult Jewish Studies (EA)
**NAAL**......... National Alliance for Animal Legislation (EA)
**NAAL**......... North American Academy of Liturgy (EA)
**NAAL**......... North American Aerodynamic Laboratory [*Wind tunnel*] (NASA)
**NAALAS**... Northern Australian Aboriginal Legal Aid Service
**NAALBWV** ... National Association for the Advancement of Leboyer's Birth Without Violence (EA)
**NAALC**..... National Afro-American Labor Council [*Later, NALC*]
**NAALS**...... Navigational Aids and Landing Systems (MCD)
**NAAM**....... National Association of Anvil Makers [*A union*] [*British*]
**NAAM**....... North American Aliyah Movement (EA)
**NAAMA**.... National Agricultural Advertising and Marketing Association [*Later, NAMA*]

**NAAMACC** ... National Association for the Accreditation of Martial Arts Colleges and Curriculum (EA)
**NAAMIC** .. National Association of Automotive Mutual Insurance Companies [*Later, American Insurers Highway Safety Alliance*] (EA)
**NAAMM**... National Association of Architectural Metal Manufacturers (EA)
**NAAMM**... North American Academy of Musculoskeletal Medicine (EA)
**NAAN**........ National Advertising Agency Network [*New York, NY*] (EA)
**NAAN**........ Nuclear Arms Alert Network [*Inactive*] (EA)
**NAANACM** ... National Association for the Advancement of Native American Composers and Musicians
**NA Anarch** ... North American Anarchist [*A publication*]
**NAANBW** ... National Amalgamated Association of Nut and Bolt Workers [*A union*] [*British*]
**NAAND**..... North American Association for the Diaconate (EA)
**NAANGHT** ... National Association of Air National Guard Health Technicians (EA)
**NAAO**........ National Association of Amateur Oarsmen [*Later, USRA*] (EA)
**NAAO**........ National Association of Artists' Organizations (EA)
**NAAO**........ National Association of Assessing Officers [*Later, IAAO*]
**NAAO**........ Navy Area Audit Office [*London*]
**NAAO**........ North American Automotive Operations [*Ford Motor Co.*]
**NAAOJ** ..... National Association for the Advancement of Orthodox Judaism (EA)
**NAAOP**..... National Association for the Advancement of Older People (EA)
**NAAP**........ N-Acetylaminophenazone [*Organic chemistry*]
**NAAP**........ National Association for Accreditation in Psychoanalysis (EA)
**NAAP**........ National Association of Activity Professionals (EA)
**NAAP**........ National Association of Advertising Publishers [*Later, AFCP*] (EA)
**NAAP**........ National Association of Apnea Professionals (EA)
**NAAP**........ Newport Army Ammunition Plant (AABC)
**NAAPABAC** ... National Association for the Advancement of Psychoanalysis and the American Boards for Accreditation and Certification (EA)
**NAAPAE**... National Association for Asian and Pacific American Education (EA)
**NAAPHE** .. National Association for the Advancement of Private Higher Education [*Later, United Student Association*] (EA)
**NAAPI**....... National Association of Accountants for the Public Interest [*Later, API*] (EA)
**NAAPM** .... National Association for the Advancement of Perry Mason (EA)
**NAAPPB**... National Association of Amusement Parks, Pools, and Beaches [*Later, IAAPA*]
**NAAQS**..... National Ambient Air Quality Standards [*Environmental Protection Agency*]
**Naar Elec**... Naar on Suffrage and Elections [*A publication*] (DLA)
**NAARMC** ... National Association of Auto Racing Memorabilia Collectors (EA)
**NAARPR**... National Alliance Against Racist and Political Repression (EA)
**NAARS**...... National Automated Accounting Research System [*American Institute of Certified Public Accountants*] [*Database*] [*Information service or system*] (IID)
**NAAS**........ National Academy of American Scholars (EA)
**NAAS**........ National Agricultural Advisory Service [*Later, ADAS*] [*British*]
**NAAS**........ National Anorexic Aid Society (EA)
**NAAS**........ National Association of Academies of Science (EA)
**NAAS**........ National Association of Art Services [*Later, NAADC*] (EA)
**NAAS**........ National Aviation Assistance
**NAAS**........ Naval Area Audit Service
**NAAS**........ Naval Auxiliary Air Station
**NAAS**........ Navy Aircraft Accounting System
**NAAS**........ Newsletter. Association for Asian Studies [*A publication*]
**NAAS**........ Nordic Association for American Studies (EAIO)
**NAAS**........ North American Apiotherapy Society (EA)
**NAAS Advis Pap** ... National Agricultural Advisory Service. Advisory Papers [*England*] [*A publication*]
**NAASC**...... Northwest African Air Service Command [*World War II*]
**NAASER**... National Association of American School Employees and Retirees (EA)
**NAASERLDC** ... National Association of American School Employees and Retirees Legal Defense Counsel (EA)
**NAASFEP** ... National Association of Administrators of State and Federal Education Programs (EA)
**NAASL**...... North American Academy of the Spanish Language (EA)
**NAASLANT** ... Navy Auxiliary Air Stations, Atlantic
**NAASMWB** ... National Amalgamated Association of Sheet Metal Workers and Blaziers [*A union*] [*British*]
**NAASPAC** ... Navy Auxiliary Air Stations, Pacific
**NAASPL**... North American Association of State and Provincial Lotteries (EA)
**NAAS Prog Rep** ... National Agricultural Advisory Service. Progress Report [*England*] [*A publication*]
**NAAS Q Rev** ... NAAS [*National Agricultural Advisory Service*] Quarterly Review [*England*] [*A publication*]
**NAAS Quart Rev** ... NAAS [*National Agricultural Advisory Service*] Quarterly Review [*England*] [*A publication*]
**NAASR**...... National Association for Armenian Studies and Research (EA)
**NAASR**...... North American Association for the Study of Jean-Jacques Rousseau (EA)
**NAASS**...... North American Association of Summer Sessions (EA)
**NAATA** ..... National Asian American Telecommunications Association (EA)
**NAATC** ..... Naval Air Advanced Training Command
**NAATP**...... National Association of Alcoholism Treatment Programs (EA)
**NAATPWB** ... National Amalgamated Association of Tin Plate Workers and Blaziers [*A union*] [*British*]
**NAATS**...... National Association of Air Traffic Specialists (EA)
**NAATS**...... National Association of Auto Trim Shops (EA)
**NAATTFO** ... National Association of Alcohol and Tobacco Tax Field Officers
**NAAUTC** .. National Amateur Athletic Union Taekwondo Committee [*Later, NAAUTUUSA*] (EA)
**NAAUTUUSA** ... National AAU [*Amateur Athletic Union*] Taekwondo Union of the United States of America [*Formerly, NAAUTC*] (EA)
**NAAV**........ National Alliance Against Violence (EA)
**NAAV**........ National Association of Atomic Veterans (EA)
**NAAV**........ North American Association of Ventriloquists (EA)
**NAAW**....... National Association of Accordion Wholesalers [*Defunct*] (EA)
**NAAWFS** ... Naval Air All Weather Flight Squadron
**NAAWP**.... National Association for the Advancement of White People (EA)
**NAAWS** .... NORAD Automatic Attack Warning System (TEL)
**NAAWS** .... North American Association of Wardens and Superintendents (EA)
**NAAWT**.... National Action Against War Toys [*Australia*]
**NAAWUL** ... National Agricultural and Allied Workers' Union of Liberia (IMH)
**Nab** ........... Nabatean (BJA)
**NAB**........... National Acoustics Board (MUGU)
**NAB**........... National Advisory Body [*British*]
**NAB**........... National Aircraft Beacon
**NAB**........... National Alliance of Business [*Washington, DC*] (EA)
**NAB**........... National Associated Businessmen [*Defunct*] (EA)
**NAB**........... National Association of Bioengineers [*Defunct*] (EA)
**NAB**........... National Association of Boards of Examiners for Nursing Home Administrators (EA)
**NAB**........... National Association of Broadcasters (EA)
**NAB**........... National Australia Bank ADS [*NYSE symbol*] (SPSG)
**NAB**........... Nation's Business [*A publication*]
**NAB**........... Naval Advanced Base
**NAB**........... Naval Air Base
**NAB**........... Naval Amphibious Base
**NAB**........... Navigational Aid to Bombing [*Air Force*]
**NAB**........... Nederlandsch Archievenblad [*A publication*]
**NAB**........... Needle Aspiration Biopsy [*Surgery*]
**NAb** ........... Neues Abendland [*A publication*]
**NAB**........... New American Bible
**NAB**........... News Agency of Burma
**NAB**........... Newspaper Advertising Bureau [*New York, NY*] (EA)
**NAB**........... Nickel Alkaline Battery
**NAB**........... Nigeria-Arab Bank Ltd.
**NAB**........... None of the Above
**NAB**........... North American Biologicals, Inc.
**NAB**........... Not Above [*Aviation*]
**NAB**........... Nuclear Air Burst
**NAB**........... Nuclear Assembly Building
**NAB**........... Nut and Bolt
**NABA**........ National Alliance of Black Americans
**NABA**........ National Amateur Basketball Association (EA)
**NABA**........ National Association of Black Accountants [*Washington, DC*] (EA)
**NABA**........ National Association of Breweriana Advertising (EA)
**NABA**........ Naval Amphibious Base Annex
**NABA**........ North American Ballet Association (EA)
**NABA**........ North American Benefit Association [*Port Huron, MI*] (EA)
**NABAC** ..... National Association for Bank Auditors and Comptrollers [*Later, BAI*] (EA)
**NABATRA** ... Naval Air Basic Training Center
**NABB**........ National Association of Barber Boards (EA)
**NABB**........ National Association for Better Broadcasting (EA)
**NABB**........ National Association of Business Brokers (EA)
**NABBA** ..... North American Brass Band Association (EA)
**NABBEA**... National Association of Boards of Barbers Examiners of America [*Later, NABB*] (EA)
**NABBS**...... National Association of Bench and Bar Spouses (EA)
**NABC**........ National Association of Basketball Coaches of the United States (EA)
**NABC**........ National Association of Boys' Clubs [*British*]
**NABC**........ North American Blueberry Council (EA)
**NABCA** ..... National Alcoholic Beverage Control Association (EA)
**NABCA** ..... National Association for Bank Cost Analysis (EA)
**NABCA** ..... National Association for Bank Cost and Management Accounting (EA)
**NABCA** ..... National Association of Black Catholic Administrators (EA)
**NAB$2CC** ... National Association of Bicentennial $2 Cancellation Collectors (EA)

**NABCE**...... National Association of Black Consulting Engineers (EA)
**NABCJ**...... National Association of Blacks in Criminal Justice (EA)
**NABCM**.... National Association of Baby Carriage Manufacturers (EA)
**NABCM**.... National Association of Brattice Cloth Manufacturers (EA)
**NABCO**..... National Alliance of Breast Cancer Organizations (EA)
**NABCO**..... National Association of Black County Officials (EA)
**NABCO**..... Nippon Air Brake Company Ltd. [*Tokyo, Japan*]
**NABD**........ National Association of Bank Directors [*Later, ASBD*] (EA)
**NABD**........ National Association of Brick Distributors (EA)
**NABD**........ Naval Advanced Base Depot
**NABDC**..... National Association of Blueprint and Diazotype Coaters [*Later, ARMM*]
**NABDCC**.. North American Band Directors Coordinating Committee (EA)
**NABE**........ National Association of Bar Executives (EA)
**NABE**........ National Association for Bilingual Education (EA)
**NABE**........ National Association of Biological Engineering
**NABE**........ National Association of Boards of Education (EA)
**NABE**........ National Association of Book Editors [*Defunct*] (EA)
**NABE**........ National Association of Business Economists (EA)
**NABE**........ Nuclear Air Burst Effect
**NABEA**..... North American Bicycle Exhibitor Association (EA)
**NABER**...... National Association of Business and Educational Radio (EA)
**NABESS**.... National Association of Business Education State Supervisors [*Stillwater, OK*] (EA)
**NABET**...... National Association Broadcast Employees and Technicians (EA)
**NABF**........ National Alliance of Black Feminists (EA)
**NABF**........ National Amateur Baseball Federation (EA)
**NABF**........ North American Baptist Fellowship (EA)
**NABF**........ North American Boxing Federation (EA)
**NABG**........ National Association of Blacks within Government (EA)
**NABGG**..... National Association of Black Geologists and Geophysicists (EA)
**NABHP**..... National Association of Black Hospitality Professionals (EA)
**NABI**......... National Association of Beverage Importers (EA)
**NABI**......... National Association of Biblical Instructors [*Later, American Academy of Religion*] (EA)
**NABIC**....... National Alcoholic Beverages Industries Council [*Australia*]
**NABIM**..... National Association of Band Instrument Manufacturers (EA)
**NABIS**....... National Association of Business and Industrial Saleswomen [*Denver, CO*] (EA)
**NABIS**....... National Biological Survey
**NABISCO**... National Biscuit Company [*Acronym now used as company name*]
**NABJ**......... National Association of Black Journalists (EA)
**NAB-JOBS**... National Alliance of Business - Job Opportunities in the Business Sector (OICC)
**NABK**........ National Asset Bank [*NASDAQ symbol*] (NQ)
**NABL**........ National Association of Bond Lawyers (EA)
**NABL**........ National Association of Builders' Labourers [*A union*] [*British*]
**NABLT**...... National Association of Business Law Teachers [*Later, NBLC*] (EA)
**NABM**....... National Association of Bedding Manufacturers [*Later, ISPA*] (EA)
**NABM**....... National Association of Black Manufacturers (EA)
**NABM**....... National Association of Blouse Manufacturers (EA)
**NABM**....... National Association of Boat Manufacturers (EA)
**NABM**....... National Association of Boating Magazines [*Defunct*] (EA)
**NABM**....... National Association of Book Manufacturers (EA)
**NABM**....... National Association of British Manufacturers
**NABM**....... National Association of Building Manufacturers [*Later, HMC*] (EA)
**NABMA**.... National Association of British Market Authorities
**NABMCC**... National Association of Black and Minority Chambers of Commerce [*Later, NBCC*] (EA)
**NABMO**.... NATO Bullpup Management Office [*Missiles*] (NATG)
**NABMP**.... National Association of Black Media Producers
**NABO**....... National Alliance of Black Organizations (EA)
**NABOB**..... National Association of Black Owned Broadcasters (EA)
**NABOM**.... National Association of Building Owners and Managers [*Later, BOMA*] (EA)
**NABP**........ National Association of Black Professors (EA)
**NABP**........ National Association of Boards of Pharmacy (EA)
**NABPAC**... National Association of Business Political Action Committees (EA)
**NABPARS**... Navy Automatic Broadcasting, Processing, and Routing System (NG)
**NABPLEX**... National Association of Boards of Pharmacy Licensure Examination
**NABPO**..... NATO Bullpup Production Organization [*Missiles*] (NATG)
**NABPR**...... National Association of Baptist Professors of Religion (EA)
**NABR**........ National Association of Baby Sitter Registries [*Later, NASR*] (EA)
**NABR**........ National Association of Basketball Referees (EA)
**NABR**........ National Association for BioMedical Research (EA)
**NABR**........ Natural Bridges National Monument
**NABREP**... National Association of Black Real Estate Professionals (EA)
**NABRTI**.... National Association of Bar-Related Title Insurers [*San Diego, CA*] (EA)
**NABS**......... National Advertising Benevolent Society [*British*]
**NABS**......... National Alliance of Blind Students (EA)
**NABS**......... National Association of Bank Servicers (EA)
**NABS**......... National Association of Barber Schools [*Later, NABSS*] (EA)
**NABS**......... National Association of Black Students (EA)
**NABS**......... National Association of Business Services [*Baldwin, NY*] (EA)
**NABS**......... National Association of Buying Services (EA)
**NABS**......... North American Benthological Society (EA)
**NABS**......... North American Blue-Bird Society (EA)
**NABS**......... Nuclear-Armed Bombardment Satellite [*Study*] [*Air Force*] (AAG)
**NABSC**...... National Association of Building Service Contractors [*Later, BSCA*]
**NABSCAN**... National Advertised Brands Scanning Reports [*Research project*]
**NABSE**...... National Alliance of Black School Educators (EA)
**NABSP**...... National Association of Blue Shield Plans [*Later, BCBSA*] (EA)
**NABSS**...... National Association of Barber Styling Schools (EA)
**NABSTP**... Navy Adult Basic Skills Training Program (NVT)
**NABSW**..... National Association of Black Social Workers (EA)
**NABT**........ National Association of Bankruptcy Trustees (EA)
**NABT**........ National Association of Biology Teachers (EA)
**NABT**........ National Association of Blind Teachers (EA)
**NABTA**..... National Association of Business Travel Agents (EA)
**NABTC**...... National Associated Building Trades Council [*A union*] [*British*]
**NABTC**...... Naval Air Base Training Command
**NABTE**...... National Association for Business Teacher Education [*Reston, VA*] (EA)
**NABTE Rev**... NABTE [*National Association for Business Teacher Education*] Review [*A publication*]
**NABTS**...... National Alliance Building Trades Society [*A union*] [*British*]
**NABTTI**.... National Association of Business Teacher-Training Institutions
**NABU**........ Naval Advanced Base Unit
**NABU**........ Nonadjusting Ball-Up [*A hopeless state of confusion*] [*Military slang*]
**NABUG**..... National Association of Broadcast Unions and Guilds (EA)
**NABV**........ National Association for Black Veterans (EA)
**NABVICU**... National Association of Blind and Visually Impaired Computer Users (EA)
**NABW**....... National Association of Bank Women [*Chicago, IL*] (EA)
**NABWA**.... National Association of Black Women Attorneys (EA)
**NABWE**.... National Association of Black Women Entrepreneurs [*Detroit, MI*] (EA)
**NABWMT**... National Association of Black and White Men Together: A Gay Multiracial Organization for All People (EA)
**NABWS**..... National Amalgamated Brass Workers' Society [*A union*] [*British*]
**NAC**.......... Management Accounting [*A publication*]
**NAC**.......... N-Acetyl-L-Cysteine [*Biochemistry*]
**NAC**.......... Nacelle [*Aviation*]
**Nac**............ Nacion [*A publication*]
**NAC**.......... Naples Alcofuel Club [*Defunct*] (EA)
**NAC**.......... National Academy of Conciliators (EA)
**NAC**.......... National Access Center (EA)
**NAC**.......... National Accreditation Council for Agencies Serving the Blind and Visually Handicapped (EA)
**NAC**.......... National Achievement Clubs (EA)
**NAC**.......... National Adoption Center [*Information service or system*] (EISS)
**NAC**.......... National Advertising Campaign [*Army*]
**NAC**.......... National Advisory Committee
**NAC**.......... National Advisory Council
**NAC**.......... National Aero Club (EA)
**NAC**.......... National Aeronautical Corporation
**NAC**.......... National Agency Check [*Security clearance*]
**NAC**.......... National Agricultural Centre [*British*] (CB)
**NAC**.......... National Air Carrier Association (MCD)
**NAC**.......... National Air Communications [*British*]
**NAC**.......... National Alumni Council of the United Negro College Fund (EA)
**NAC**.......... National Anglers' Council [*British*]
**NAC**.......... National Arts Centre [*Canada*]
**NAC**.......... National Arts Club (EA)
**NAC**.......... National Asbestos Council (EA)
**NAC**.......... National Association of Cemeteries [*Later, ACA*] (EA)
**NAC**.......... National Association of College Wind and Percussion Instructors. Journal [*A publication*]
**NAC**.......... National Association of Composers, USA (EA)
**NAC**.......... National Association of Concessionaires (EA)
**NAC**.......... National Association of Coopers [*A union*] [*British*]
**NAC**.......... National Association of Coroners (EA)
**NAC**.......... National Association of Counties
**NAC**.......... National Asthma Center [*Later, NJCIRM*]
**NAC**.......... National Audiovisual Center [*General Services Administration*]
**NAC**.......... National Aviation Club (EA)
**NAC**.......... National Aviation Corporation
**NAC**.......... Native American Church (ECON)
**NAC**.......... Native Appeal Courts [*South Africa*] [*A publication*] (DLA)
**NAC**.......... Natural Area Council (EA)
**NAC**.......... Naval Academy

**NAC**.......... Naval Air Center
**NAC**.......... Naval Air Command [*British*]
**NAC**.......... Naval Aircraftman [*British*]
**NAC**.......... Naval Avionics Center (MCD)
**NAC**.......... Navy Advanced Concept (CAAL)
**NAC**.......... Negative Air Cushion [*Aviation*] [*Air Force*]
**NAC**.......... Neighbourhood Advice Council
**NAC**.......... Neo-American Church (EA)
**NAC**.......... Network Access Center [*Telecommunications*]
**NAC**.......... Network Access Controller
**NAC**.......... Network Advisory Committee [*to Library of Congress and Council on Library Resources*]
**NAC**.......... Network Analysis Center [*Contel, Inc.*] [*Telecommunications service*] (TSSD)
**NAC**.......... Nipple Areolar Complex [*Oncology*]
**NAC**.......... Nitrogen Mustard [*Mustargen*], Adriamycin, CCNU [*Lomustine*] [*Antineoplastic drug regimen*]
**NAC**.......... No Additional Charge
**NAC**.......... No Apparent Change (MCD)
**NAC**.......... Noise Advisory Council [*British*]
**NAC**.......... Nonairline Carrier [*Aerospace*]
**NAC**.......... Nordic Academic Council (EA)
**NAC**.......... Nordic Actors' Council (EAIO)
**NAC**.......... Nordic Association for Campanology (EA)
**NAC**.......... Normal Approach Course [*Navy*] (NVT)
**NAC**.......... North American Collectors (EA)
**NAC**.......... North Atlantic Coast
**NAC**.......... North Atlantic Council
**NAC**.......... North Atlantic Shipping Conference (DS)
**NAC**.......... Northeast Air Command
**NAC**.......... Northern Air Cargo, Inc. [*Anchorage, AK*] [*FAA designator*] (FAAC)
**NAC**.......... Nozzle Area Control
**NAC**.......... Numismatica e Antichita Classiche [*A publication*]
**NAC**.......... US Catholic Bishops' National Advisory Council (EA)
**NACA**........ National Academy of Code Administration (EA)
**NACA**........ National Acoustical Contractors Association [*Later, CISCA*] (EA)
**NACA**........ National Advisory Committee for Aeronautics [*Functions transferred to NASA, 1958*]
**NACA**........ National Agricultural Chemicals Association (EA)
**NACA**........ National Air Carrier Association (EA)
**NACA**........ National Animal Control Association (EA)
**NACA**........ National Armored Car Association (EA)
**NACA**........ National Association for Campus Activities (EA)
**NACA**........ National Association of Catastrophe Adjusters [*Comfort, TX*] (EA)
**NACA**........ National Association of Cellular Agents (EA)
**NACA**........ National Association of Christians in the Arts (EA)
**NACA**........ National Association of Cost Accountants [*Later, NAA*]
**NACA**........ National Advisory of County Administrators (EA)
**NACA**........ National Association for Court Administration (EA)
**NACA**........ National Association of Cuban Architects (in Exile) (EA)
**NACA**........ National Autosound Challenge Association [*Later, IASCA*] (EA)
**NACA**........ Naval Aviation Cadet Act of 1942
**NACA**........ Netherlands-America Community Association (EA)
**NACA**........ North American Center on Adoption (EA)
**NACA**........ North American College of Acupuncture
**NACA**........ North American Corriente Association (EA)
**NACA**........ North American Currach Association (EA)
**NACAA**..... National Assembly of Community Arts Agencies (EA)
**NACAA**..... National Association of Community Action Agencies (EA)
**NACAA**..... National Association of Consumer Agency Administrators (EA)
**NACAA**..... National Association of County Agricultural Agents (EA)
**NACAB**..... National Accreditation Council for Agencies Serving the Blind and Visually Handicapped [*New York, NY*]
**NACAC**..... National Association of Catholic Alumni Clubs [*Later, CACI*] (EA)
**NACAC**..... National Association of College Admission Counselors (EA)
**NACAC**..... North African Antiaircraft Section [*World War II*]
**NACAC**..... North American Council on Adoptable Children (EA)
**NACADA**.. National Academic Advising Association (EA)
**NACAE**..... National Advisory Council on Adult Education [*Washington, DC*]
**NACAF**...... Northwest African Coastal Air Force [*World War II*]
**NACAL**..... Navy Air Cooperation and Liaison Committee
**NACAP**..... National Association of Co-Op Advertising Professionals [*Upper Saddle River, NJ*] (EA)
**NACARM**... Northwest America Civil Air Routes Manual
**NACAS**...... National Association of College Auxiliary Services (EA)
**NACAT**..... National Association of College Automotive Teachers (EA)
**NACATS**... North American Clear Air Turbulence Tracking System [*Aviation*]
**NACAWM-USA**... National Association of Cuban Women and Men of the United States (EA)
**NACAW-USA**... National Association of Cuban-American Women of the USA (EA)
**NACB**........ Native American Community Board (EA)
**NACB**........ Navy and Army Canteen Board [*British military*] (DMA)
**NACBA**..... National Association of Church Business Administration (EA)
**NACBFAA**... National Association of Customs Brokers and Forwarders Association of America
**NACBO**..... National Association of Cosmetic Boutique Owners (EA)
**NACBS**...... National Affiliation of Concerned Business Students [*Defunct*] (EA)
**NACBS**...... National Association and Council of Business Schools
**NACBS**...... North American Conference on British Studies (EA)
**NacC**.......... Nacional (Caracas) [*A publication*]
**NACC**........ National Advisory Cancer Council
**NACC**........ National Agency Check Center (AFM)
**NACC**........ National Air Conservation Commission (EA)
**NACC**........ National Alliance of Czech Catholics (EA)
**NACC**........ National Association of Catholic Chaplains (EA)
**NACC**........ National Association of Childbearing Centers (EA)
**NACC**........ National Association of Collegiate Commissioners [*Later, CCA*] (EA)
**NACC**........ National Association for Core Curriculum (EA)
**NACC**........ National Association of Counsel for Children (EA)
**NACC**........ National Automatic Controls Conference
**NACC**........ Naval Academy Computer Center
**NACC**........ Norwegian American Chamber of Commerce
**NAC (C)**..... Selected Decisions of the Native Appeal Court (Central Division) [*1948-51*] [*South Africa*] [*A publication*] (DLA)
**NACCA**..... National Association of Claimants' Counsel of America [*Also known as NACCA Bar Association*] [*Later, ATLA*]
**NACCA**..... National Association of Consumer Credit Administrators (EA)
**NACCA**..... National Association of County 4-H Club Agents [*Later, NAE4-HA*] (EA)
**NACCA**..... National Association of County Civil Attorneys (EA)
**NACCA**..... National Association for Creative Children and Adults (EA)
**NACCALJ**... National Association of Claimants' Compensation Attorneys. Law Journal [*A publication*] (DLA)
**NACCAM**... National Coordinating Committee for Aviation Meteorology
**NACCAS**... National Accrediting Commission of Cosmetology Arts and Sciences (EA)
**NACCB**..... National Association of Computer Consultant Businesses (EA)
**NACCC**..... National Association of Citizens Crime Commissions (EA)
**NACCC**..... National Association of Congregational Christian Churches [*Later, CCCNA*] (EA)
**NACCCA**... National Association of Civilian Conservation Corps Alumni (EA)
**NACCCAN**... National Centre for Christian Communities and Networks [*Westhill College*] [*British*] (CB)
**NACCDD**.. National Association of County Community Development Directors (EA)
**NACCE**..... National Advisory Council on Continuing Education (OICC)
**NACCES**... National Advisory Committee on the Commonwealth Employment Service [*Australia*]
**NACCM**.... National Association for Child Care Management [*Defunct*] (EA)
**NACCME**... National Advisory and Coordinating Committee on Multicultural Education [*Australia*]
**NAC (C & O)**... Reports of the Decisions of the Native Appeal Courts, Cape Province and the Orange Free State [*South Africa*] [*A publication*] (ILCA)
**NACCRT**... North America Coordinating Center for Responsible Tourism (EA)
**NACCW**.... National Advisory Centre on Careers for Women [*British*] (CB)
**NACD**........ National Alliance of Cleaning Distributors [*Commercial firm*] (EA)
**NACD**........ National Association for Cave Diving [*Inactive*]
**NACD**........ National Association of Chemical Distributors (EA)
**NACD**........ National Association for Community Development [*Defunct*] (EA)
**NACD**........ National Association of Conservation Districts (EA)
**NACD**........ National Association of Container Distributors (EA)
**NACD**........ National Association of Corporate Directors [*Washington, DC*] (EA)
**NACDA**..... National Arts and Cultural Development Act of 1964
**NACDA**..... National Association of Collegiate Directors of Athletics (EA)
**NACDAC**.. National Association for City Drug and Alcohol Coordination (EA)
**NACDAP**.. National Advisory Council for Drug Abuse Prevention [*Terminated, 1975*] (EGAO)
**NACDC**..... National Association of Career Development Consultants (EA)
**NACDD**..... National Advisory Council on Services and Facilities for the Developmentally Disabled [*Terminated, 1978*] [*HEW*] (EGAO)
**NACDE**..... National Association for Child Development and Education [*Later, NACCM*] (EA)
**NACDFB**... National Association of Canada Dry Franchise Bottlers (EA)
**NACDFLM**... National Association of Catholic Diocesan Family Life Ministers [*Later, NACFLM*] (EA)
**NACDL**..... National Association of Criminal Defense Lawyers (EA)
**NACDLF**... National Association of Community Development Loan Funds (EA)
**NACDPA**.. National Association of County Data Processing Administrators (EA)

**NACDR**..... National Association of College Deans and Registrars [*Later, NACDRAO*] (EA)
**NACDRAO** ... National Association of College Deans, Registrars, and Admissions Officers (EA)
**NACDS**..... National Association of Chain Drug Stores (EA)
**NACDS**..... North American Clinical Dermatologic Society (EA)
**NACE**........ National Advisory Committee for Electronics
**NACE**........ National Association for Career Education (EA)
**NACE**........ National Association of Catering Executives (EA)
**NACE**........ National Association of Childbirth Education (EA)
**NACE**........ National Association of Corrosion Engineers (EA)
**NACE**........ National Association of County Engineers (EA)
**NACE**........ National Autobody Congress and Exposition [*Precision Planning and Sales, Inc.*] (TSPED)
**NACE**........ Native Americans for a Clean Environment (EA)
**NACE**........ Neutral Atmospheric Composition Experiment [*Geophysics*]
**NACE**........ NMCSSC [*National Military Command System Support Center*] Automated Control Executive
**NACE**........ North American Cycle Exhibitor Association (EA)
**NACEBE**... National Association of Classroom Educators in Business Education [*Cambridge City, IN*] (EA)
**NACEC**..... National Association of Charitable Estate Counselors (EA)
**NACEC**..... North American Committee of Enamel Creators (EA)
**NACECE**... National Advisory Council on Extension and Continuing Education
**NACED**..... National Advisory Committee on the Education of the Deaf [*Terminated, 1973*] [*HEW*] (EGAO)
**NACED**..... National Advisory Council on the Employment of the Disabled [*British*]
**NACEDC**.. National Advisory Council on Education of Disadvantaged Children (OICC)
**NAC/EDP**... National Advisory Council on Education Professions Development [*HEW*] (EGAO)
**NACEEO**.. National Advisory Council on Equality of Educational Opportunity [*Terminated, 1979*] [*HEW*] (EGAO)
**NACEHC**.. National Accreditation Council for Environmental Health Curricula (EA)
**NACEIC**.... National Advisory Council on Education for Industry and Commerce (MCD)
**NACEL**...... Navy Air Crew Equipment Laboratory [*Philadelphia, PA*]
**NACEO**..... National Advisory Council on Economic Opportunity (EA)
**NACEPD**... National Advisory Council on Education Professions Development [*Terminated, 1976*] [*HEW*] (OICC)
**NACERI**.... National Advisory Council for Educational Research and Improvement [*Washington, DC*] [*Department of Education*] (GRD)
**NACES**...... National Advisory Committee on Extension Services [*Australia*]
**NACES**...... National Association of Credential Evaluation Services (EA)
**NACES**...... Navy Aircrew Common Ejection Seat [*British*]
**NACETA**... National Association of County Employment and Training Administrators [*Later, NACTEP*] (EA)
**NACF**........ National Art-Collectors' Fund [*British*]
**NACF**........ Navy Air Combat Fighter (MCD)
**NACFA**...... North American Clun Forest Association (EA)
**NACFE**...... National Association of Certified Fraud Examiners (EA)
**NACFFA**... National Advisory Committee for the Flammable Fabrics Act
**NACFL**...... National Advisory Committee on Farm Labor [*Defunct*] (EA)
**NACFLM**... National Association of Catholic Family Life Ministers (EA)
**NACFR**...... National Association of Casual Furniture Retailers (EA)
**NACFT**...... National Academy of Counselors and Family Therapists (EA)
**NACG**........ National Association of County Governments (OICC)
**NACG**........ North African Commanding General [*World War II*]
**NACGC**..... National Association of Collegiate Gymnastics Coaches (Men) (EA)
**NACGC**..... National Association of Colored Girls Clubs [*Later, NAGC*] (EA)
**NACGG**..... North American Commercial Gladiolus Growers [*Later, CGD-NAGC*] (EA)
**NACGM**.... National Association of Chewing Gum Manufacturers (EA)
**NACH**........ National Academy of Clinicians and Holistic Health (EA)
**NACH**........ National Association of Clergy Hypnotherapists (EA)
**NACH**........ National Association of Coal Haulers [*Defunct*] (EA)
**NACH**........ National Association for the Craniofacially Handicapped (EA)
**nAch**........... Need for Achievement
**NACHA**...... National Automated Clearing House Association [*Washington, DC*] (EA)
**Nachb**......... Nachbarn [*A publication*]
**NACHC**..... National Advisory Committee on Handicapped Children [*Terminated, 1973*] [*HEW*] (EGAO)
**NACHC**..... National Association of Community Health Centers (EA)
**Nach Elek**.. Nachrichtentechnik-Elektronik [*A publication*]
**Nach Elktr** ... Nachrichten-Elektronik und Telematik [*A publication*]
**NACHES**... Association of Jewish Family, Children's Agency Professionals (EA)
**NACHFA**.. National Association of County Health Facility Administrators (EA)
**NACHM**.... Nachmittags [*Afternoon*] [*German*]
**NACHO**..... National Association of County Health Officials (EA)
**NACHP**..... North African Chaplain's Section [*World War II*]
**NAChR**...... Nicotinic Acetylcholine Receptor [*Immunology*]
**Nachr Aerztl Miss** ... Nachrichten aus der Aerztlichen Mission [*A publication*]
**Nachr Akad Wiss Goettingen** ... Nachrichten. Akademie der Wissenschaften zu Goettingen [*A publication*]
**Nachr Akad Wiss Goettingen Math-Phys Kl II** ... Nachrichten. Akademie der Wissenschaften zu Goettingen. II. Mathematisch-Physikalische Klasse [*A publication*]
**Nachr Akad Wiss Goett Philologisch-Hist Kl** ... Nachrichten. Akademie der Wissenschaften zu Goettingen. Philologisch-Historische Klasse [*A publication*]
**Nachr Akad Wiss UdSSR** ... Nachrichten. Akademie der Wissenschaften der UdSSR [*A publication*]
**Nachr Ak Goett** ... Nachrichten. Akademie der Wissenschaften in Goettingen [*A publication*]
**Nachr Arb Gem Ges Wes** ... Nachrichten der Arbeitsgemeinschaft fuer das Gesundheitswesen [*A publication*]
**Nachr Bl Bay Ent** ... Nachrichtenblatt der Bayerischen Entomologen [*A publication*]
**NachrBl Bayer Ent** ... Nachrichtenblatt der Bayerischen Entomologen [*A publication*]
**Nachrbl Dt Pflschutzdienst (Berl)** ... Nachrichtenblatt. Deutscher Pflanzenschutzdienst (Berlin) [*A publication*]
**NachrBl Dt PflSchutzdienst (Berlin)** ... Nachrichtenblatt. Deutschen Pflanzenschutzdienst (Berlin) [*A publication*]
**Nachrbl Dt Pflschutzdienst (Stuttg)** ... Nachrichtenblatt. Deutschen Pflanzenschutzdienst (Stuttgart) [*A publication*]
**NachrBl Dt PflSchutzdienst (Stuttgart)** ... Nachrichtenblatt. Deutschen Pflanzenschutzdienst (Stuttgart) [*A publication*]
**Nachrbl Dtsch Pflschdienst (Berlin)** ... Nachrichtenblatt. Deutschen Pflanzenschutzdienst (Berlin) [*A publication*]
**Nachrbl Dtsch Pflschdienst (Braunschweig)** ... Nachrichtenblatt. Deutschen Pflanzenschutzdienst (Braunschweig) [*A publication*]
**NachrBl PflSchutzdienst DDR** ... Nachrichtenblatt fuer den Pflanzenschutzdienst in der DDR [*A publication*]
**Nachr Chem Tech** ... Nachrichten aus Chemie und Technik [*Later, Nachrichten aus Chemie, Technik, und Laboratorium*] [*A publication*]
**Nachr Chem Tech Lab** ... Nachrichten aus Chemie, Technik, und Laboratorium [*Formerly, Nachrichten aus Chemie und Technik*] [*A publication*]
**Nachr fuer Dok** ... Nachrichten fuer Dokumentation [*A publication*]
**Nachr Dok** ... Nachrichten fuer Dokumentation [*A publication*]
**Nachr Dokum** ... Nachrichten fuer Dokumentation [*A publication*]
**Nachr Dtsch Geol Ges** ... Nachrichten. Deutsche Geologische Gesellschaft [*A publication*]
**Nachr Elektron** ... Nachrichten-Elektronik [*A publication*]
**Nachr Elektron and Telematik** ... Nachrichten-Elektronik und Telematik [*A publication*]
**Nachr Ges N Vk Ostas** ... Nachrichten der Gesellschaft fuer Natur und Voelkerkunde Ostasiens [*A publication*]
**Nachr Ges Wiss Goettingen Math Phys Kl** ... Nachrichten. Gesellschaft der Wissenschaften zu Goettingen. Mathematisch-Physikalische Klasse [*A publication*]
**Nachr Ges Wiss Goettingen Math-Phys Kl Fachgruppe 2** ... Nachrichten. Gesellschaft der Wissenschaften zu Goettingen. Mathematisch-Physikalische Klasse. Fachgruppe 2. Physik, Astronomie, Geophysik, Technik [*West Germany*] [*A publication*]
**Nachr Ges Wiss Goettingen Math Phys Kl Fachgruppe 3** ... Nachrichten. Gesellschaft der Wissenschaften zu Goettingen. Mathematisch-Physikalische Klasse. Fachgruppe 3. Chemie, Einschliesslich Physikalische Chemie [*A publication*]
**Nachr Ges Wiss Goettingen Math Phys Kl Fachgruppe 4** ... Nachrichten. Gesellschaft der Wissenschaften zu Goettingen. Mathematisch-Physikalische Klasse. Fachgruppe 4. Geologie und Mineralogie [*A publication*]
**Nachr Ges Wiss Goettingen Math Phys Kl Fachgruppe 6** ... Nachrichten. Gesellschaft der Wissenschaften zu Goettingen. Mathematisch-Physikalische Klasse. Fachgruppe 6. Biologie [*A publication*]
**Nachr Ges Wiss Goetting Math Phys Kl Fachgruppe 1** ... Nachrichten. Gesellschaft der Wissenschaften zu Goettingen. Mathematisch-Physikalische Klasse. Fachgruppe 1. Mathematik [*A publication*]
**Nachr Giessen** ... Nachrichten der Giessener Hochschulgesellschaft [*A publication*]
**NACHRI** ... National Association of Children's Hospitals and Related Institutions (EA)
**Nachrichtenbl Deut Pflanzenschutzdienst (Berlin)** ... Nachrichtenblatt. Deutscher Pflanzenschutzdienst (Berlin) [*A publication*]
**Nachrichtenbl Deut Pflanzenschutzdienst (Stuttgart)** ... Nachrichtenblatt. Deutschen Pflanzenschutzdienst (Stuttgart) [*A publication*]
**Nachrichtenbl Dtsch Ges Gesch Med Naturwiss Tech** ... Nachrichtenblatt. Deutsche Gesellschaft fuer Geschichte der Medizin. Naturwissenschaft und Technik [*A publication*]
**Nachrichtenbl Dtsch Pflanzenschutzdienst (Berlin)** ... Nachrichtenblatt. Deutschen Pflanzenschutzdienst (Berlin) [*A publication*]
**Nachrichtenbl Dtsch Pflanzenschutzdienst (Braunschw)** ... Nachrichtenblatt des Deutschen Pflanzenschutzdienstes (Braunschweig) [*A publication*]

**Nachrichtenbl Dtsch Pflanzenschutzdienstes (Braunschweig)** ... Nachrichtenblatt. Deutschen Pflanzenschutzdienst (Braunschweig) [*A publication*]
**Nachrichtenbl Pflanzenschutz DDR** ... Nachrichtenblatt fuer den Pflanzenschutzdienst in der DDR [*A publication*]
**Nachrichtenbl Pflanzenschutzdienst DDR** ... Nachrichtenblatt fuer den Pflanzenschutzdienst in der DDR [*A publication*]
**Nachrichtenbl Photogr Handwerk** ... Nachrichtenblatt fuer das Photographen Handwerk [*A publication*]
**Nachrichtentech-Elektron** ... Nachrichtentechnik-Elektronik [*A publication*]
**Nachrichtentech Elektronik** ... Nachrichtentechnik-Elektronik [*A publication*]
**Nachrichtentech Fachber** ... Nachrichtentechnische Fachberichte [*West Germany*] [*A publication*]
**Nachrichtentech Fachber Beih NTZ** ... Nachrichtentechnische Fachberichte. Beihefte der Nachrichtentechnische Zeitschrift [*A publication*]
**Nachrichtentech Z** ... Nachrichtentechnische Zeitung [*A publication*]
**NACHRK** .. North American Coalition for Human Rights in Korea (EA)
**Nachr Kgl Ges WG** ... Nachrichten der Koeniglichen Gesellschaft der Wissenschaften zu Goettingen [*A publication*]
**Nachr Naturwiss Mus Stadt (Aschaffenburg)** ... Nachrichten. Naturwissenschaftliches Museum der Stadt (Aschaffenburg) [*A publication*]
**Nachr Naturw Mus (Aschaffenb)** ... Nachrichten. Naturwissenschaftliches Museum der Stadt (Aschaffenburg) [*A publication*]
**Nachr Niedersachs Urgesch** ... Nachrichten aus Niedersachsens Urgeschichte [*A publication*]
**Nachr/Nouv/Notiz** ... Nachrichten/Nouvelles/Notizie [*A publication*]
**Nachr RVA** ... Nachrichten des Reichsversicherungsamts [*A publication*]
**Nachrtech Z** ... Nachrichtentechnische Zeitschrift [*A publication*]
**Nachr Telefonbau & Normalzeit** ... Nachrichten der Telefonbau und Normalzeit [*A publication*]
**Nachr Trop Med (Tiflis)** ... Nachrichten der Tropischen Medizin (Tiflis) [*A publication*]
**Nachr Verein Schweizer Bibl** ... Nachrichten. Vereinigung Schweizerischer Bibliothekare [*A publication*]
**Nachr Z** ...... Nachrichtentechnische Zeitschrift [*A publication*]
**NACHSA** .. National Association of County Human Services Administrators (EA)
**NACHVRO** ... National Air Conditioning, Heating, Ventilating, and Refrigeration Officials (EA)
**Nach Zeit** ... Nachrichtentechnische Zeitschrift [*A publication*]
**NACI** ......... National Agency Check and Written Inquiries
**NACI** ......... National Association for the Cottage Industry (EA)
**NACIA** ...... National Association of Crop Insurance Agents [*Anoka, MN*] (EA)
**NACIE** ....... National Advisory Council on Indian Education (OICC)
**NACIFO** .... National Association of Church and Institutional Financing Organizations [*Atlanta, GA*] (EA)
**NACIME** ... North American Committee for IME [*Institut Medical Evangelique*] [*Defunct*] (EA)
**NACIO** ...... National Association of County Information Officers (EA)
**NACIO** ...... Naval Air Combat Information Office [*or Officer*]
**NACIP** ....... Navy Assessment and Control of Installation Pollutants
**NACIS** ....... National Credit Information Service [*TRW, Inc.*] [*Long Beach, CA*] [*Credit-information databank*] (IID)
**NACIS** ....... Naval Air Combat Information School
**NACIS** ....... Navy Air Control and Identification System
**NACIS** ....... Networking Analytical and Computing Information Systems [*National Aeronautics and Space Administration*]
**NACIS** ....... North American Cartographic Information Society (EA)
**NACISO** .... NATO Communications and Information Systems Organization (EAIO)
**NACJ** ......... National Association of Costume Jewelers [*Defunct*] (EA)
**NACJP** ....... National Association of Criminal Justice Planners (EA)
**NACK** ........ Negative Acknowledgment [*Telecommunications*]
**NACK** ........ Nonacknowledgment Character [*Data processing*]
**NACL** ........ National Advisory Commission on Libraries
**NACL** ........ National Association for Community Leadership (EA)
**NACL** ........ Navy/ARPA [*Advanced Research Projects Agency*] Chemical LASER (MCD)
**NACL** ........ Nippon Aviatronics Corporation Limited [*Japan*]
**NACLA** ..... North American Congress on Latin America (EA)
**NACLEO** ... National Association of Coin Laundry Equipment Operators (EA)
**NACLIS** .... National Advisory Council for Library and Information Services [*Proposed*] [*Australia*]
**NACLIS** .... National Commission on Libraries and Information Science [*Washington, DC*]
**NACLM** .... North African Claims Section [*World War II*]
**NACLO** ..... National Association of Canoe Liveries and Outfitters (EA)
**NACLO** ..... National Association of Community Leadership Organizations [*Later, National Association for Community Leadership*] (EA)
**NACLS** ...... National Association of Commission Lumber Salesmen
**NACLS** ...... North Alabama Cooperative Library System [*Library network*]
**NACLSO** ... National Assembly of Chief Livestock Sanitary Officials [*Later, United States Animal Health Association*] (EA)
**NACM** ....... National Association of Chain Manufacturers (EA)
**NACM** ....... National Association for Court Management (EA)
**NACM** ....... National Association of Credit Management [*New York, NY*] (EA)
**NACMA** .... National Armored Cable Manufacturers Association (EA)
**NACMB** .... National Association of Certified Mortgage Bankers [*Later, NSREF*] (EA)
**NACMC** .... National Association of Christian Marriage Counselors [*Inactive*] (EA)
**NACMC** .... National Association for Church Management Consultants (EA)
**NACME** .... National Action Council for Minorities in Engineering (EA)
**NACMEMS** ... National Association of Continuing Medical Education Meetings and Seminars (EA)
**NACMIS** ... Navy Automated Civilian Management Information System
**NACMO** .... National Association of Competitive Mounted Orienteering (EA)
**NACN** ........ Native Canadian [*A publication*]
**NACN** ........ Newspaper Advertising Co-Op Network (EA)
**NAC (NE)** ... Decisions of the Native Appeal Court (North Eastern Division) [*South Africa*] [*A publication*] (ILCA)
**NACNE** ..... National Advisory Council on Nutrition Education [*British*]
**NAC News Pestic Rev** ... NAC [*National Agriculture Chemicals Association*] News and Pesticide Review [*United States*] [*A publication*]
**NAC (N & T)** ... Decisions of the Native Appeal and Divorce Court (Transvaal and Natal) [*South Africa*] [*A publication*] (ILCA)
**NAC & O** ... Cape and Orange Free State Native Appeal Court, Selected Decisions [*A publication*] (DLA)
**NACO** ........ National Advisory Committee on Oceanography [*Marine science*] (MSC)
**NACO** ........ National Association of Condominium Owners
**NACO** ........ National Association of Consumer Organizations
**NACO** ........ National Association of Cooperative Officials [*A union*] [*British*] (DCTA)
**NACo** ......... National Association of Counties (EA)
**NACO** ........ National Coordinated Cataloging Operations [*Library science*]
**NACO** ........ Navy Coolant [*Gunpowder*]
**NACO** ........ Night Alarm Cutoff (AAG)
**NACOA** ..... If Not Available Your Command, Obtain Accounting Data from Administrative Command [*Army*] (AABC)
**NACOA** ..... National Advisory Committee on Oceans and Atmosphere [*Marine science*] (MSC)
**NACOA** ..... National Association for Children of Alcoholics (EA)
**NACODS** .. National Association of Colliery Overmen, Deputies, and Shotfirers [*A union*] [*British*] (DCTA)
**NACOI** ...... National Association of Canadians of Origins in India
**NACOL** ..... National Advisory Commission on Libraries
**NACOM** .... National Communications [*System*]
**NACOM** .... Northern Area Command
**NACON** ..... Newspaper Advertising Co-Op Network [*Arlington Heights, IL*] (EA)
**NACOPRW** ... National Conference of Puerto Rican Women (EA)
**NACOR** ..... National Advisory Committee on Radiation
**NaCOR** ...... National Center on Occupational Readjustment (EA)
**NACORE** .. National Association of Corporate Real Estate Executives (EA)
**NACORF** ... National Association of Counties Research Foundation
**NACOS** ..... National Communications Schedule
**NACOS** ..... NATO Courier Service (NATG)
**NACOS** ..... North African Chief of Staff [*World War II*]
**NACOSH** .. National Advisory Committee on Occupational Safety and Health
**NACOSH** .. National Advisory Committee on Scouting for the Handicapped (EA)
**NACP** ........ National Association of County Planners (EA)
**NACP** ........ NORAD/CONAD Airborne Command Post
**NACPA** ..... National Association of Church Personnel Administrators (EA)
**NACPA** ..... National Association of County and Prosecuting Attorneys [*Later, NDAA*]
**NACPD** ..... National Association of County Planning Directors [*Later, NACP*] (EA)
**NACPDCG** ... National Association of Catholic Publishers and Dealers in Church Goods (EA)
**NACPR** ...... National Association of Corporate and Professional Recruiters (EA)
**NACPRO** .. National Association of County Park and Recreation Officials (EA)
**NACPU** ..... National Amalgamated Coal Porters' Union [*British*]
**NACPUISCW** ... National Amalgamated Coal Porters' Union of Inland and Seaborne Coal Workers [*British*]
**NACR** ........ National Advisory Committee on Radiation
**NACRC** ..... National Association of County Recorders and Clerks (EA)
**NACRCD** .. National Advisory Council on Rural Civil Defense
**NACRF** ...... National Association of Counties Research Foundation (OICC)
**NACRMR** ... National Advisory Committee on Rhesus Monkey Requirements
**NACRO** ...... National Association for the Care and Resettlement of Offenders [*British*]
**NACRS** ...... North African Censorship Section, US [*World War II*]
**NACR (SR)** ... Native Appeal Court Reports (Southern Rhodesia) [*A publication*] (ILCA)
**NACRT** ..... National Association of Canadian Race Tracks

**NACRU**..... North American Committee for Reconciliation in Ulster (EA)
**NACS**........ National Association of Carpet Specialists [*Defunct*]
**NACS**........ National Association for Check Safekeeping [*Washington, DC*] (EA)
**NACS**........ National Association for Chicano Studies (EA)
**NACS**........ National Association of Christian Schools [*Defunct*] (EA)
**NACS**........ National Association of Christian Singles (EA)
**NACS**........ National Association of Civic Secretaries (EA)
**NACS**........ National Association of College Stores (EA)
**NACS**........ National Association of Computer Stores [*Later, IVCI*] (EA)
**NACS**........ National Association of Concession Services (EA)
**NACS**........ National Association of Convenience Stores (EA)
**NACS**........ National Association of Cosmetology Schools (EA)
**NACS**........ Natural Areas of Canadian Significance [*NPPAC*]
**NACS**........ Neurologic and Adaptive Capacity Scoring [*System*]
**NACS**........ North American Communications Corp. [*Hector, MN*] [*NASDAQ symbol*] (NQ)
**NACS**........ North Atlantic Current System [*Oceanography*]
**NACS**........ Northern Area Communications System (MCD)
**NACS**........ Nucleic Acid Chromatography System
**NAC (S)**..... Selected Decisions of the Native Appeal Court (Southern Division) [*South Africa*] [*A publication*] (ILCA)
**NACSA**...... National Advisory Committee on Safety in Agriculture
**NACSA**...... National Association of Casualty and Surety Agents [*Bethesda, MD*] (EA)
**NACSA**...... National Association for Corporate Speaker Activities (EA)
**NACSA**...... North American Computer Service Association (EA)
**NACSAA**... National Advisory Council for South Asian Affairs (EA)
**NACSAP**... National Alliance Concerned with School-Age Parents [*Defunct*] (EA)
**NACSARS**... National Association of Companion Sitter Agencies and Referral Services [*Later, PCA*] (EA)
**NACSB**...... Naval Aviation Cadet Selection Board
**NACSC**...... National Association of Cold Storage Contractors (EA)
**NACSCAOM**... National Accreditation Commission for Schools and Colleges of Acupuncture and Oriental Medicine (EA)
**NACSCS**... National Advisory Council on Supplementary Centers and Services
**NACSDA**... National Association of Commissioners, Secretaries, and Directors of Agriculture [*Later, NASDA*] (EA)
**NACSDC**... North American Conference of Separated and Divorced Catholics (EA)
**NACSE**...... National Association of Casualty and Surety Executives [*New York, NY*] (EA)
**NACSE**...... National Association of Civil Service Employees (EA)
**NACSIC**.... National Association of Cold Storage Insulation Contractors (EA)
**NACSIM**.... NATO Communications Security Information (NATG)
**NACSM**.... National Association of Catalog Showroom Merchandisers (EA)
**NACSPMR**... National Association of Coordinators of State Programs for the Mentally Retarded [*Later, National Association of State Mental Retardation Program Directors*] (EA)
**NACST**...... National Association of Catholic School Teachers (EA)
**NACSW**..... North American Association of Christians in Social Work (EA)
**NACT**........ NASA Activities [*A publication*]
**NACT**........ National Alliance of Cardiovascular Technologists (EA)
**NACT**........ National Association of Consumers and Travelers (EA)
**NACT**........ National Association of Corporate Treasurers [*Washington, DC*] (EA)
**NACT**........ National Automatic Controller for Testing (MUGU)
**NACTA**..... National Association of Colleges and Teachers of Agriculture (EA)
**NACTAC**... Navy Antenna Computer Tracking and Command
**NACTA J Natl Assoc Coll Teach Agric**... NACTA Journal. National Association of Colleges and Teachers of Agriculture [*A publication*]
**NACTEFL**... National Advisory Council on the Teaching of English as a Foreign Language (EA)
**NACTEP**... National Association of County Training and Employment Professionals [*Washington, DC*] (EA)
**NACTFO**... National Association of County Treasurers and Finance Officers (EA)
**NAC (T & N)**... Reports of the Decisions of the Native Appeal Courts (Transvaal and Natal) [*South Africa*] [*A publication*] (ILCA)
**NACTP**...... National Association of Computerized Tax Processors (EA)
**NACTU**..... Night Attack Combat Training Unit [*Navy*]
**NACU**........ National Association of Colleges and Universities
**NACUA**..... National Association of College and University Administrators [*Superseded by NEA Higher Education Council*] (EA)
**NACUA**..... National Association of College and University Attorneys (EA)
**NACUBO**... National Association of College and University Business Officers [*Washington, DC*] (EA)
**NACUC**..... National Association of College and University Chaplains and Directors of Religious Life (EA)
**NACUFS**... National Association of College and University Food Services (EA)
**NACUP**..... National Association of Credit Union Presidents (EA)
**NACUSA**... National Association of Composers, USA (EA)
**NACUSS**... National Association of College and University Summer Sessions [*Later, NAASS*]
**NACUTCD**... National Advisory Committee on Uniform Traffic Control Devices [*Terminated, 1979*] [*Department of Transportation*] (EGAO)
**NACUTSO**... National Association of College and University Traffic and Security Officers (EA)
**NACV**........ National Association of Concerned Veterans (EA)
**NACVCB**... National Association of Crime Victim Compensation Boards (EA)
**NACVE**..... National Advisory Council on Vocational Education
**NA-CVR**.... National Association for Crime Victims Rights (EA)
**NACW**....... National Association of College Women [*Later, NAUW*] (EA)
**NACW**....... National Association of Commissions for Women (EA)
**NACWC**.... National Association of Colored Women's Clubs (EA)
**NACWD**.... National Association of County Welfare Directors [*Later, NACHSA*] (EA)
**NACWEP**... National Advisory Council on Women's Educational Programs (OICC)
**NACWIS**... Navy Controlled Waste Information System
**NACWPI**... NACWPI [*National Association of College Wind and Percussion Instructors*] Journal [*A publication*]
**NACWPI**... National Association of College Wind and Percussion Instructors (EA)
**NACWRR**... National Advisory Committee on Water Resources Research [*Canada*]
**NACWS**..... North African Chemical Warfare Section [*World War II*]
**NACX**........ Northern Air Cargo, Inc. [*Air carrier designation symbol*]
**NAd**.......... Addison Public Library, Addison, NY [*Library symbol*] [*Library of Congress*] (LCLS)
**NAD**.......... Naphthaleneacetamide [*Herbicide*]
**NAD**.......... National Academy of Design (EA)
**NAD**.......... National Advertising Division [*of the Council of Better Business Bureaus*]
**NAD**.......... National Armaments Director (NATG)
**NAD**.......... National Association of the Deaf (EA)
**NAD**.......... NATO Air Doctrine (NATG)
**NAd**.......... Naval Adviser [*British*]
**NAD**.......... Naval Air Defense (NATG)
**NAD**.......... Naval Air Depot
**NAD**.......... Naval Air Detachment (MCD)
**NAD**.......... Naval Air Detail
**NAD**.......... Naval Air Development Center
**NAD**.......... Naval Air Development Center, Warminster, PA [*OCLC symbol*] (OCLC)
**NAD**.......... Naval Air Division [*British*]
**NAD**.......... Naval Ammunition Depot [*Charleston, SC*]
**NAD**.......... Naval Armament Depot [*British*]
**NAD**.......... Network Access Device
**NAD**.......... New Antigenic Determinant [*Immunochemistry*]
**NAD**.......... Nicotinamide-Adenine Dinucleotide [*Preferred form, but also see ARPPRN, DPN, NADH*] [*Biochemistry*]
**NAD**.......... Night Air Defence [*British*] [*World War II*]
**Nad**.......... Nitrosamide [*Biochemistry*]
**NAD**.......... No Abnormality Detected [*Medicine*]
**NAD**.......... No-Acid Descaling (IEEE)
**NAD**.......... No Acute Distress [*Medicine*]
**NAD**.......... No Apparent Defect [*Shipping*]
**NAD**.......... No Apparent Distress [*Medicine*]
**NAD**.......... No Appreciable Disease [*Medicine*]
**NAD**.......... Noise Amplitude Distribution
**NAD**.......... Nordiska Namden for Alkohol- och Drogforskning [*Nordic Council for Alcohol and Drug Research - NCADR*] (EAIO)
**NAD**.......... Normal Axis Deviation [*Medicine*]
**NAD**.......... North American Aero Dynasty [*Vancouver Stock Exchange symbol*]
**NAD**.......... North American Datum
**NAD**.......... North Atlantic Division [*Army Engineers*]
**NAD**.......... Not on Active Duty
**NAD**.......... Nothing Abnormal Discovered [*Medicine*]
**NAD**.......... Nuclear Accident Dosimetry
**NADA**........ N-Acetyldopamine [*Biochemistry*]
**NADA**........ National Art Dealers Association [*Later, ADA*] (EA)
**NADA**........ National Association of Dealers in Antiques (EA)
**NADA**........ National Association of Dental Assistants (EA)
**NADA**........ National Association for Disabled Athletes (EA)
**NADA**........ National Association of Drama Advisers [*British*]
**NADA**........ National Automobile Dealers Association [*McLean, VA*] (EA)
**NADA**........ Native Affairs Department. Annual [*A publication*]
**NADA**........ Network of Alcohol and Other Drugs Agencies [*Australia*]
**NADA**........ New Animal Drug Application [*Food and Drug Administration*]
**NADAC**..... National Damage Assessment Center
**NADAC**..... Naval ASW [*Antisubmarine Warfare*] Data Center (NVT)
**NADAC**..... Pacific Command, North Vietnam Air Defense Analysis and Coordinating Group (CINC)
**NADAF**..... National Association of Decorative Architectural Finishes (EA)
**NADAG**..... National Association of Diocesan Altar Guilds of the Protestant Episcopal Church (EA)
**NADAP**..... National Association on Drug Abuse Problems (EA)

**NADAR**..... No After Duty Action Required [*Military*]
**NADAR**..... North American Data Airborne Recorder
**NADase**..... Nicotinamide-Adenine Dinucleotide Glycohydrolase [*Also, DPNase*] [*An enzyme*]
**NADASO**.. National Association of Design and Art Service Organizations (EA)
**NADASO**.. National Association Drug and Allied Sales Organizations [*Wyncote, PA*] (EA)
**NADB**........ National Air Data Branch [*Environmental Protection Agency*] [*Information service or system*] (IID)
**NADB**........ National Audience Data Bank [*Newspaper Marketing Bureau*] [*Information service or system*] (CRD)
**NADBR**..... National Association for the Deaf, Blind, and Rubella [*British*]
**NADC**........ National Advisory Drug Committee [*HEW*]
**NADC**........ National Animal Disease Center [*Ames, IA*] [*Department of Agriculture*] [*Research center*] (GRD)
**NADC**........ National Anti-Drug Coalition (EA)
**NADC**........ National Anti-Dumping Committee (EA)
**NADC**........ National Association of Demolition Contractors (EA)
**NADC**........ National Association of Dredging Contractors (EA)
**NADC**........ NATO Air Defense Committee
**NADC**........ NATO Defense College [*Also, NADEFCOL, NDC*]
**NADC**........ Naval Aide-de-Camp [*British military*] (DMA)
**NADC**........ Naval Air Development Center [*Also, NADEVCEN, NAVAIRDEVCEN*] [*Warminster, PA*]
**NADC**........ Naval Ammunition Depot, Concord [*California*]
**NADC**........ Northern Australia Development Conference
**NADCA**..... National Animal Damage Control Association (EA)
**NADCA**..... North American Draft Cross Association (EA)
**NADC-AC** ... Naval Air Development Center - Aerospace Crew Equipment Department
**NADC-AE** ... Naval Air Development Center - Aero-Electronic Technology Department
**NADC-AI**.. Naval Air Development Center - Aeronautical Instruments Laboratory
**NADC-AM** ... Naval Air Development Center - Aero-Mechanics Department
**NADC-AP** ... Naval Air Development Center - Aeronautical Photographic Experimental Laboratory
**NADC-AR** ... Naval Air Development Center - Aviation Armament Laboratory
**NADC-ASW** ... Naval Air Development Center - Antisubmarine Warfare Laboratory
**NADC-AW** ... Naval Air Development Center - Air Warfare Research Department
**NADC-AWG** ... Naval Air Development Center - Acoustical Working Group
**NADC-CS** ... Naval Air Development Center - Crew Systems Department
**NADC-ED** ... Naval Air Development Center - Engineering Development Laboratory
**NADC-EL** ... Naval Air Development Center - Aeronautical Electronic and Electrical Laboratory
**NADC-LS** ... Naval Air Development Center - Life Sciences and Bio-Equipment Group
**NADC-ML** ... Naval Air Development Center - Aviation Medical Acceleration Laboratory
**NADC-MR** ... Naval Air Development Center - Aerospace Medical Research Department
**NADCO**..... National Association of Development Companies (EA)
**NAD-CO** ... Naval Ammunition Depot, Concord [*California*]
**NA & D C & O** ... Selection of Cases Decided in the Native Appeal and Divorce Court, Cape and Orange Free State [*A publication*] (DLA)
**NAD-CR**.... Naval Ammunition Depot, Crane [*Indiana*]
**NADC-SD** ... Naval Air Development Center - Systems Analysis and Engineering Department
**NADC-ST** ... Naval Air Development Center - Aero Structures Department
**NADC-SY** ... Naval Air Development Center - Systems Project Department
**NADC-WR** ... Naval Air Development Center - Air Warfare Research Department
**NADD**........ National Association of Diemakers and Diecutters [*Formerly, DDA*] (EA)
**NADD**........ National Association of Disco Disc Jockeys [*Defunct*] (EA)
**NADD**........ National Association of Distributors and Dealers of Structural Clay Products [*Later, NABD*] (EA)
**NADDC**..... National Association of Developmental Disabilities Councils (EA)
**NADDM**.... National Association of Daytime Dress Manufacturers [*Defunct*]
**NADE**........ National Association for Design Education [*British*]
**NADE**........ National Association for Developmental Education (EA)
**NADE**........ National Association of Disability Examiners (EA)
**NADE**........ National Association of Document Examiners (EA)
**NADEC**..... Navy Decision Center
**NADEC**..... Navy Development Center (CAAL)
**NADEE**..... National Association of Divisional Executives for Education [*British*]
**NADEEC**... NATO Air Defense Electronic Environment Committee
**NADEFCOL** ... NATO Defense College [*Also, NADC, NDC*] [*Rome, Italy*]
**NADEM**.... National Association of Dairy Equipment Manufacturers [*Later, DFISA*] (EA)
**NADEO**..... National Association of Diocesan Ecumenical Officers (EA)
**NADEP**..... National Association of Disability Evaluating Professionals [*Later, IHC*] (EA)
**NADEPA**... National Democratic Party [*Solomon Islands*] [*Political party*] (PPW)
**NADET**..... National Association of Distributive Education Teachers
**NADEVCEN** ... Naval Air Development Center [*Also, NADC, NAVAIRDEVCEN*]
**NADEX**..... NATO Data Exchange (NATG)
**Nadezn i Kontrol'kacestva** ... Nadeznost i Kontrol'kacestva [*A publication*]
**NADF**........ National Addison's Disease Foundation (EA)
**NADF**........ National Arbor Day Foundation (EA)
**NADFA**..... North American Deer Farmers Association (EA)
**NADFAS**... [*The*] National Association of Decorative and Fine Arts Societies [*British*]
**NADFD**..... National Association of Decorative Fabric Distributors (EA)
**NADFPM** ... National Association of Domestic and Farm Pump Manufacturers [*Later, WSC*]
**NADGA**..... Nagoya Kogyo Daigaku Gakuho [*A publication*]
**NADGE**..... NATO Air Defense Ground Environment
**NADGE**..... NATO Air Defense Ground Equipment
**NADGECO** ... NATO Air Defense Ground Environment Consortium
**NADGEMO** ... NATO Air Defense Ground Environment Management Organization (NATG)
**NADH**........ Naval Ammunition Depot, Hawaii
**NADH**........ Nicotinamide-Adenine Dinucleotide (Reduced) [*See also NAD*] [*Biochemistry*]
**NADHCI**... North American District Heating and Cooling Institute (EA)
**NADI**......... National Association of Display Industries [*New York, NY*] (EA)
**NADI**......... Naval Ammunition Depot, Indiana
**NADIE**...... National Association for Drama in Education [*Australia*]
**NADIN**...... National Airspace Data Interchange Network (FAAC)
**NADIP**...... Navy Display Improvement Program
**NADIS**....... National Aerometric Data Information System [*Environmental Protection Agency*]
**NADKA**..... Nagasaki Daigaku Suisan-Gakubu Kenkyu Hokoku [*A publication*]
**NADL**........ National Animal Disease Laboratory [*Iowa*]
**NADL**........ National Association of Dental Laboratories (EA)
**NADL**........ Navy Authorized Data List (NG)
**NADLCC**... National Association of Defense Lawyers in Criminal Cases [*Later, NACDL*] (EA)
**NADL J**..... NADL [*National Association of Dental Laboratories*] Journal [*A publication*]
**NADM**....... National Association of Discount Merchants [*Defunct*] (EA)
**NADM**....... National Association of Doll Manufacturers [*Later, NADSTM*] (EA)
**NADM**....... Naval Administration
**NADMC**.... Naval Air Development and Material Center
**NADMR**.... National Association of Diversified Manufacturers Representatives [*Later, NAGMR*] (EA)
**NADMW**... National Association of Direct Mail Writers
**NADO**....... National Association of Development Organizations (EA)
**NADO**....... Navy Accounts Disbursing Office
**NADOA**..... National Association of Division Order Analysts (EA)
**NADOI**...... National Association of Dog Obedience Instructors (EA)
**NADOP**..... North American Defense Operation Plan [*NORAD*]
**NADP**........ National Acid Deposition Program [*Air pollution*]
**NADP**........ National Association of Desktop Publishers (EA)
**NADP**........ National Atmospheric Deposition Program [*Department of Agriculture*]
**NADP**........ NAVAIR Advanced Development Plan (MCD)
**NADP**........ Nicotinamide-Adenine Dinucleotide Phosphate [*Preferred form, but see also TPN*] [*Biochemistry*]
**NADPB**..... North Atlantic Defense Production Board (NATG)
**NADPH**..... Nicotinamide-Adenine Dinucleotide Phosphate (Reduced) [*Preferred form, but see also TPNH*] [*Biochemistry*]
**NADREPS** ... National Armaments Directors Representatives
**NADS**........ National Armament Directors [*NATO*]
**NADS**........ National Association Diaper Services (EA)
**NADS**........ National Association for Down Syndrome (EA)
**NADS**........ Naval Air Development Station
**NADS**........ Newsletter. American Dialect Society [*A publication*]
**NADS**........ North American Dostoevsky Society (EA)
**NADS**........ North Atlantic Defense System
**NADSA**..... National Association of Dramatic and Speech Arts (EA)
**NADSC**..... National Association of Direct Selling Companies [*Later, DSA*] (EA)
**NADSP**...... National Association of Dental Service Plans [*Insurance*] (DHSM)
**NADSTM** ... National Association of Doll and Stuffed Toy Manufacturers (EA)
**NADT**........ National Association for Drama Therapy (EA)
**NA & DT & N** ... Transvaal and Natal Native Appeal and Divorce Court Decisions [*A publication*] (DLA)
**NADU**....... Naval Air Development Unit (MUGU)
**NADU**....... Naval Aircraft Delivery Unit
**NADUG**.... North American Datamanager Users Group (EA)
**NADUS**..... National Association of Doctors in the United States (EA)
**NADUSM** ... National Association of Deputy United States Marshals (EA)
**NADW**....... North Atlantic Deep Water [*Oceanography*]

**NADWAGNS** ... National Association of Deans of Women and Advisors to Girls in Negro Schools [*Defunct*] (EA)
**NADWARN** ... Natural Disaster Warning
**NADWAS** ... Natural Disaster Warning Survey (NOAA)
**NADWAS** ... North American Dr. Who Appreciation Society (EA)
**NAE** .......... Nake [*Tuamotu Archipelago*] [*Seismograph station code, US Geological Survey*] (SEIS)
**NAE** .......... National Academy of Education
**NAE** .......... National Academy of Engineering [*Washington, DC*] (GRD)
**NAE** .......... National Administrative Expenses (NATG)
**NAE** .......... National Adoption Exchange (EA)
**NAE** .......... National Aeronautical Establishment [*Research center*] [*Canada*] (IRC)
**NAE** .......... National Association of Evangelicals (EA)
**NAE** .......... Navy Acquisition Executive (MCD)
**NAE** .......... New Age Encyclopedia [*A publication*]
**NAE** .......... No American Equivalent [*Language*]
**NAE** .......... Noise Acoustic Emitter [*Military*] (CAAL)
**NAE** .......... Nursery Association Executives [*Later, NAENA*] (EA)
**NAEA** ........ National Aerospace Education Association [*Formerly, NAEC*] [*Defunct*]
**NAEA** ........ National Art Education Association (EA)
**NAEA** ........ National Artists Equity Association (EA)
**NAEA** ........ National Association of Enrolled Agents (EA)
**NAEA** ........ National Association of Extension 4-H Agents (EA)
**NAEA** ........ Newspaper Advertising Executives Association [*Later, INAME*] (EA)
**NAE-ASEB** ... National Academy of Engineering Aeronautics and Space Engineering Board
**NAEB** ........ National Association of Educational Broadcasters [*Formerly, Association of College and University Broadcasting Stations (1934)*] (EA)
**NAEB** ........ National Association of Educational Buyers [*Woodbury, NY*] (EA)
**NAEB** ........ Naval Aviation Evaluation Board
**NAEB** ........ North African Economic Board [*World War II*]
**NAEBJ** ...... National Association of Educational Broadcasters. Journal [*A publication*]
**NAEBM** .... National Association of Engine and Boat Manufacturers [*Later, NMMA*] (EA)
**NAEC** ........ National Advisory Eye Council
**NAEC** ........ National Aerospace Education Council [*Later, NAEA*] (EA)
**NAEC** ........ National Association for Educational Computing (EA)
**NAEC** ........ National Association of Electric Companies [*Later, EEI*] (EA)
**NAEC** ........ National Association of Elevator Contractors (EA)
**NAEC** ........ National Association of Engineering Companies (EA)
**NAEC** ........ National Association Executives Club (EA)
**NAEC** ........ Naval Air Engineering Center [*Closed*]
**NAEC** ........ Northern Agricultural Energy Center
**NAECA** ..... National Appliance Energy Conservation Act [*1987*]
**NAECOE** .. National Academy of Engineering Committee on Ocean Engineering
**NAECON** ... National Aerospace Electronics Conference [*IEEE*] (MCD)
**NAEd** ........ National Academy of Education (EA)
**NAED** ........ National Association of Electrical Distributors (EA)
**NAEDA** ..... National American Eskimo Dog Association (EA)
**NAEDA** ..... North American Equipment Dealers Association (EA)
**NAEE** ........ North American Association for Environmental Education (EA)
**NAEEO** ..... National Association for Equal Educational Opportunities (EA)
**NAEF** ........ Naval Air Engineering Facility (MCD)
**NAEFA** ...... North American Economics and Finance Association (EA)
**NAEFTA** ... National Association of Enrolled Federal Tax Accountants (EA)
**NAEGA** ..... North American Export Grain Association (EA)
**NAEH** ....... National Alliance to End Homelessness (EA)
**NAE4-HA** ... National Association of Extension 4-H Agents (EA)
**NAEHCA** .. National Association of Employers on Health Care Alternatives (EA)
**NAEHE** ..... National Association of Extension Home Economists (EA)
**NAEHMO** ... National Association of Employers on Health Maintenance Organizations [*Later, NAEHCA*] (EA)
**Naehr** ......... Naehrung. Chemie, Biochemie, Mikrobiologie, Technologie [*A publication*]
**NAEIC** ....... Nevada Applied Ecology Information Center [*Department of Energy*] (IID)
**NAEIR** ....... National Association for the Exchange of Industrial Resources (EA)
**NAEKM** .... National Association of Electronic Keyboard Manufacturers (EA)
**NAEL** ........ Naval Air Engineering Laboratory (MCD)
**NAELA** ...... National Academy of Elder Law Attorneys (EA)
**NAELC** ...... National Architect-Engineer Liaison Commission [*Defunct*] (EA)
**NAELSI** .... Naval Air Electronics Shipboard Installation
**NAEM** ....... National Association of Exposition Managers (EA)
**NAEMB** .... National Academy of Engineering Marine Board
**NAEMSP** .. National Association of Emergency Medical Service Physicians (EA)
**NAEMT** .... National Association of Emergency Medical Technicians (EA)
**NAEN** ........ National Association of Educational Negotiators (EA)
**NAENA** ..... Nursery Association Executives of North America (EA)
**NAE-NEPP** ... National Academy of Engineering Navy Environmental Protection Program Study Group
**NAENG** ..... North African Engineer Section [*World War II*]
**NAEO** ........ National Activity Education Organization (EA)
**NAEO** ........ National Association of Extradition Officials (EA)
**NAEOM** .... National Association of Electronic Organ Manufacturers
**NAEOP** ..... National Association of Educational Office Personnel (EA)
**NAEP** ........ National Assessment of Educational Progress, The Nation's Report Card (EA)
**NAEP** ........ National Association of Environmental Professionals (EA)
**NAEPC** ...... National Association of Estate Planning Councils (EA)
**NAEPIRS** ... National Assessment of Educational Progress Information Retrieval System [*National Institute of Education*] [*Database*]
**NAEPS** ...... National Academy of Economics and Political Science (EA)
**NAER** ........ National Association of Executive Recruiters (EA)
**NAERC** ..... North American Electric Reliability Council (EA)
**NAERI** ....... National Agricultural Economic Research Inventory [*A publication*] (APTA)
**Naeringsforskning Suppl** ... Naeringsforskning. Supplement [*A publication*]
**NAES** ......... National Association of Ecumenical Staff (EA)
**NAES** ......... National Association of Educational Secretaries [*Later, NAEOP*] (EA)
**NAES** ......... National Association of Episcopal Schools (EA)
**NAES** ......... National Association for Ethnic Studies (EA)
**NAES** ......... National Association of Executive Secretaries (EA)
**NAES** ......... Native American Educational Service [*Later, NAESC*] (EA)
**NAES** ......... Naval Air Experimental Station
**NAES** ......... Nevada Agricultural Experiment Station [*University of Nevada - Reno*] [*Research center*] (RCD)
**NAES** ......... North African Army Exchange Service [*World War II*]
**NAESA** ...... National Association of Elevator Safety Authorities (EA)
**NAESA** ...... North American Economic Studies Association (EA)
**NAESC** ...... National Association of Energy Service Companies (EA)
**NAESC** ...... Native American Educational Services College (EA)
**NAESCO** ... National Association of Energy Service Companies (EA)
**NAESDI** .... NATO [*North Atlantic Treaty Organization*] ASI [*Advanced Science Institutes*] Series. Series E. Applied Sciences [*A publication*]
**NAESP** ...... National Association of Elementary School Principals (EA)
**NAESU** ..... Naval Aviation Engineering Service Unit [*Philadelphia, PA*]
**NAET** ........ National Association of Educational Technicians [*British*]
**NAETV** ..... National Association for Educational Television [*Defunct*]
**NAEW** ....... NATO Airborne Early Warning
**NAEWTF** ... NATO Aircrew Electronic Warfare Tactics Facility (NATG)
**NAEYC** ..... National Association for the Education of Young Children (EA)
**NAF** ........... Guilder [*Florin*] [*Monetary unit*] [*Netherlands Antilles*]
**NAF** ........... NAFCO Financial Group, Inc. [*Later, BFL*] [*NYSE symbol*] (SPSG)
**NAF** ........... Nafimidone [*Biochemistry*]
**NAF** ........... Name and Address File [*IRS*]
**NAF** ........... National Abortion Federation (EA)
**NAF** ........... National Aging Foundation (EA)
**NAF** ........... National Amputation Foundation (EA)
**NAF** ........... National Analytical Facility [*National Oceanic and Atmospheric Administration*]
**NAF** ........... National Angling Federation [*British*]
**NAF** ........... National Arts Foundation (EA)
**NAF** ........... National Ataxia Foundation (EA)
**NAF** ........... National Aviation Forum
**NAF** ........... National Forum. Phi Kappa Phi Journal [*A publication*]
**NAF** ........... Naval Air Facility
**NAF** ........... Naval Air Force
**NAF** ........... Naval Aircraft Factory
**NAF** ........... Naval Avionics Facility [*Later, NAC*] [*Indianapolis, IN*]
**NAF** ........... Nernst Approximation Formula [*Physics*]
**NAF** ........... Netherland-America Foundation [*Later, Netherlands-America Community Association*] (EA)
**NAF** ........... Network Access Facility
**NAF** ........... New African [*A publication*]
**NAF** ........... New Age Federation (EA)
**NAF** ........... No Abnormal Findings [*Medicine*]
**NAF** ........... Nonappropriated Fund [*or Funds*]
**NAF** ........... Nordisk Anaestesiologisk Forening [*Scandinavian Society of Anaesthesiologists - SSA*] (EA)
**NAF** ........... North American Federation of Third Order Franciscans (EA)
**NAF** ........... North American Fire [*Vancouver Stock Exchange symbol*]
**NAF** ........... North Anatolian Fault [*Turkey*] [*Geology*]
**NAF** ........... North West Atlantic Fisheries, Memorial University [*UTLAS symbol*]
**NAF** ........... Northern Attack Force [*Navy*]
**NAF** ........... Nouvelle Action Francaise [*New French Action*] [*Political party*] (PPE)
**NAF** ........... Numbered Air Force (AFM)
**NAFA** ........ National Air Filtration Association (EA)
**NAFA** ........ National Aircraft Finance Association (EA)
**NAFA** ........ National American Farmers Association (EA)
**NAFA** ........ National Association to Aid Fat Americans [*Bellrose, NY*]

**NAFA**........ National Association of Fine Arts (EA)
**NAFA**........ National Association of Fleet Administrators [*Iselin, NJ*] (EA)
**NAFA**........ National Automotive Fleet Administration Ltd. [*Australia*]
**NAFA**........ Net Acquisition of Financial Assets (ADA)
**NAFA**........ Nonappropriated Fund Activity (CINC)
**NAFA**........ North American Falconers Association (EA)
**NAFA**........ North American Farm Alliance (EA)
**NAFA**........ Northwest Atlantic Fisheries Act of 1950
**NAFAC**...... National Association for Ambulatory Care [*Formerly, NAFEC*] (EA)
**NAFAD**..... National Association of Fashion and Accessory Designers (EA)
**NAFAG**..... NATO Air Force Advisory Group (NATG)
**NAFAG**..... NATO Air Force Armaments Group
**NAFAPAC**... National Association for Association Political Action Committees (EA)
**NAFAX**...... National Facsimile Network [*National Weather Service*]
**NAFB**........ National Association of Farm Broadcasters (EA)
**NAFB**........ National Association of Franchised Businessmen [*Defunct*] (EA)
**NAFB**........ Norton Air Force Base [*California*]
**NAFBO**..... National Association for Business Organizations [*Baltimore, MD*] (EA)
**NAFBRAT**... National Association for Better Radio and Television [*Later, NABB*] (EA)
**NAFC**........ Nash-Finch Company [*NASDAQ symbol*] (NQ)
**NAFC**........ National Accounting and Finance Council [*Alexandria, VA*] (EA)
**NAFC**........ National Anthropological Film Center [*Smithsonian Institution*] (GRD)
**NAFC**........ National Association of Fan Clubs (EA)
**NAFC**........ National Association of Financial Consultants (EA)
**NAFC**........ National Association of Food Chains [*Later, FMI*] (EA)
**NAFC**........ National Association of Friendship Centres [*Canada*]
**NAFC**........ Naval Air Ferry Command [*World War II*]
**NAFC**........ Navy Accounting and Finance Center
**NAFC**........ North American Fishing Club (EA)
**NAFC**........ North American Forestry Commission [*UN Food and Agriculture Organization*]
**NAFC**........ North American Forum on the Catechumenate (EA)
**NAFC**........ Northern Attack Force Commander [*Navy*]
**NAFCA**...... North American Family Campers Association (EA)
**NAFCD**..... National Association of Floor Covering Distributors (EA)
**NAFCE**...... National Association of Federal Career Employees [*Defunct*] (EA)
**NAFCI**....... National Association of Floor Covering Installers [*Later, AIDS International*] (EA)
**NAFCO**..... National Association of Franchise Companies (EA)
**NAFCO**..... National Floor Products Company, Inc.
**NAFCR**...... National Association of Foster Care Reviewers (EA)
**NAFCU**..... National Association of Federal Credit Unions (EA)
**NAFD**........ National Association of Flour Distributors (EA)
**NAFD**........ New America Fund [*NASDAQ symbol*] (NQ)
**NAFDC**..... National Association for Family Day Care (EA)
**NAFDI**....... National Foundation for Depressive Illness (EA)
**NAFE**........ National Association for Female Executives [*New York, NY*] (EA)
**NAFE**........ National Association for Film in Education [*British*]
**NAFE**........ National Association of Forensic Economists (EA)
**NAFE**........ National Association for Free Enterprise [*Washington, DC*] (EA)
**NAFE**........ Non-Advanced Further Education [*British*]
**NAFEC**...... National Association of Farmer Elected Committeemen (EA)
**NAFEC**...... National Association of Freestanding Emergency Centers [*Later, NAAC*] (EA)
**NAFEC**...... National Aviation Facilities Experimental Center [*of FAA*] [*Atlantic City, NJ*]
**NAFED**..... National Association of Fire Equipment Distributors (EA)
**NAFEM**..... National Association of Food Equipment Manufacturers (EA)
**NAFEMS**.. National Agency for Finite Element Methods and Standards [*British*] (IRUK)
**NAFEO**..... National Association for Equal Opportunity in Higher Education (EA)
**NAFEX**...... North American Fruit Explorers (EA)
**NAFF**........ National Association for Freedom [*British*]
**nAff**........... Need for Affection
**NAFFP**...... National Association of Frozen Food Packers [*Later, AFFI*] (EA)
**NAFFS**...... National Association of Fruits, Flavors, and Syrups (EA)
**NAFGDA**.. National Auto and Flat Glass Dealers Association [*Later, NGA*]
**NAFI**......... National Association of Fire Investigators (EA)
**NAFI**......... National Association of Flight Instructors (EA)
**NAFI**......... National Association of Forest Industries [*Australia*]
**NAFI**......... Naval Air Fighting Instructions
**NAFI**......... Naval Avionics Facility, Indianapolis [*Later, NAC*]
**NAFI**......... Nonappropriated Fund Instrumentalities [*DoD*] (MCD)
**NAFI**......... Northern Air Freight, Incorporated [*NASDAQ symbol*] (NQ)
**NAFIC**....... National Association of Fraternal Insurance Counsellors [*Sheboygan, WI*] (EA)
**NAFIN**...... North African Finance Section [*World War II*]
**NAFIPS**..... North American Fuzzy Information Processing Society (EA)
**NAFIS**....... National Association of Federally Impacted Schools (EA)
**NAFIS**....... Naval Forces Intelligence Study (MCD)
**NAFIS**....... Navigational Aid Flight Inspection System (AFM)
**NAFISS**..... Nonappropriated Funds Information Standard System [*Army*]
**NAFL**......... National Alliance for Family Life [*Later, NACFT*] (EA)
**NAFLANT**... Naval Air Facilities, Atlantic
**NAFLFD**... National Association of Federally Licensed Firearms Dealers (EA)
**NAFLI**....... Natural Flight Indication (MCD)
**NAFLI**....... Natural Flight Instrument System
**NAFM**....... National Association of Fan Manufacturers [*Later, AMCA*]
**NAFM**....... National Association of Flag Manufacturers
**NAFM**....... National Association of Furniture Manufacturers [*Later, AFMA*] (EA)
**NAFMAB**... National Armed Forces Museum Advisory Board [*Smithsonian Institution*]
**NAFMB**..... National Association of FM [*Frequency Modulation*] Broadcasters [*Later, NRBA*] (EA)
**NAFMG**.... National Association of Foreign Medical Graduates [*Later, ACIP*]
**NAFMIS**... Nonappropriated Funds Management Information System
**NAFMOW**... National Action Forum for Midlife and Older Women (EA)
**NAFMW**... National Action for Former Military Wives (EA)
**NAFO**........ National Association of Farmworker Organizations [*Defunct*] (EA)
**NAFO**........ Northwest Atlantic Fisheries Organization (EA)
**NAFOW**.... National Action Forum for Older Women [*Later, NAFMOW*] (EA)
**NAFPA**...... National Alcohol Fuels Producers Association (EA)
**NAFPA**...... National Association of Federal Education Program Administrators (EA)
**NAFPAC**... Naval Air Facilities, Pacific
**NAFPB**...... National Association of Freight Payment Banks [*Pittsburgh, PA*] (EA)
**NAFPC**...... National Academy for Fire Prevention and Control [*of FEMA*]
**NAFPP**...... National Accelerated Food Production Project [*Agency for International Development*]
**NAFPP**...... National Association of Fresh Produce Processors (EA)
**NAFPU**...... North American Friends of Palestinian Universities (EA)
**N Afr**.......... North Africa
**NAfr**........... Notes Africaines [*A publication*]
**NAFRC**...... National Association of Fiscally Responsible Cities [*Defunct*] (EA)
**NAFRD**..... National Association of Fleet Resale Dealers [*Los Angeles, CA*] (EA)
**NAFRF**...... Navy Alternate Fuel Reference File [*Battelle Memorial Institute*] [*Information service or system*] [*Defunct*] (IID)
**NAFRTM**... National Association of Farm and Ranch Trailer Manufacturers (EA)
**NAFS**......... Naval Air Fighter School
**NAFS**......... Newark Air Force Station [*Ohio*]
**NAFSA**...... National Association of Fire Science and Administration [*Defunct*] (EA)
**NAFSA**...... National Association for Foreign Student Affairs (EA)
**NAFSA**...... No American Flag Shipping Available
**NAFSLAC**... National Association of Federations of Syrian and Lebanese American Clubs (EA)
**NAFSONW**... Nonappropriated Fund Statement of Operations and Net Worth
**NAFSWMA**... National Association of Flood and Storm Water Management Agencies (EA)
**NAFT**........ Natural Adjuvant Factor Toxoid [*Medicine*]
**NAFT**........ Network for Analysis of Fireball Trajectories (EA)
**NAFTA**...... National Amalgamated Furnishing Trades Association [*A union*] [*British*]
**NAFTA**...... National Association of Futures Trading Advisors (EA)
**NAFTA**...... North Atlantic Free Trade Area
**NAFTAT**... National Association for the Advancement of Time (EA)
**NAFTC**...... National Association of Freight Transportation Consultants (EA)
**NAFTF**...... National Association of Finishers of Textile Fabrics [*Later, ATMI*] (EA)
**NAFTRAC**... National Foreign Trade Council (EA)
**NAFTZ**...... National Association of Foreign-Trade Zones [*Washington, DC*] (EA)
**NAFV**........ National Association of Federal Veterinarians (EA)
**NAFW**....... National Association of Future Women [*Later, NAFWIC*] (EA)
**NAFWA**.... North American Flowerbulb Wholesalers Association (EA)
**NAFWIC**... National Association for Women in Careers (EA)
**Nag**............ All India Reporter, Nagpur [*A publication*] (DLA)
**NAG**.......... Goddard Space Flight Center, Greenbelt, MD [*OCLC symbol*] (OCLC)
**Nag**............ Indian Law Reports, Nagpur Series [*A publication*] (DLA)
**Nag**............ Indian Rulings, Nagpur Series [*A publication*] (DLA)
**NAG**.......... N-Acetylglucosamine [*Biochemistry*]
**NAG**.......... N-Acetylglucosaminidase [*An enzyme*]
**NAG**.......... Nachrichten der Akademie der Wissenschaften in Goettingen. Philologisch-Historische Klasse [*A publication*] (BJA)
**NAG**.......... Nagoya [*Japan*] [*Seismograph station code, US Geological Survey*] (SEIS)
**NAG**.......... Nagpur [*India*] [*Airport symbol*] (OAG)

**NAG**.......... Narrow Angle Glaucoma [*Medicine*]
**NAG**.......... National Academy of Geosciences (EA)
**NAG**.......... National Acquisitions Group [*Libraries*] [*British*]
**NAG**.......... National Action Group [*Antibusing organization*]
**NAG**.......... National Advisory Group, Convenience Stores/Petroleum Companies (EA)
**NAG**.......... National Air-Racing Group (EA)
**NAG**.......... National Association of Gagwriters (EA)
**NAG**.......... National Association of Gardeners [*Later, PGMS*] (EA)
**NAG**.......... National Association of Goldsmiths [*British*]
**NAG**.......... Naval Advisory Group
**NAG**.......... Naval Analysis Group (MCD)
**NAG**.......... Naval Applications Group
**NAG**.......... Navy Astronautics Group (MUGU)
**NAG**.......... Negro Actors Guild of America (EA)
**NAG**.......... NERVA [*Nuclear Engine for Rocket Vehicle Application*] Advisory Group [*NASA*] (KSC)
**NAG**.......... Networking Advisory Group [*Library of Congress*]
**NA f G**........ Neues Archiv der Gesellschaft fuer Aeltere Deutsche Geschichtskunde [*A publication*]
**NAG**.......... Neues Archiv der Gesellschaft fuer Aeltere Deutsche Geschichtskunde [*A publication*]
**N-Ag**.......... Neutralization Antigenic Site [*Immunogenetics*]
**Nag**............ No-Acronym Sort of Guy [*Lifestyle classification*] [*Term coined by William F. Doescher, publisher of "D & B Reports"*]
**NAG**.......... Nonagglutinable [*or Nonagglutinating*] [*Immunochemistry*]
**NAG**.......... Nor-Acme Gold Mines Ltd. [*Toronto Stock Exchange symbol*]
**NAG**.......... Northern Army Group (NATG)
**NAG**.......... Nova Scotia Agricultural College Library [*UTLAS symbol*]
**NAG**.......... Numerical [*formerly, Nottingham*] Algorithms Group
**NAGA**........ National Advertising Golf Association (EA)
**NAGA**........ National Amputee Golf Association (EA)
**NAGA**........ North American Gamebird Association (EA)
**NAGA**........ North American Ginseng Association (EA)
**NAGADGK** ... Neues Archiv der Gesellschaft fuer Aeltere Deutsche Geschichtskunde [*A publication*]
**NAGAP**..... National Association of Gay Alcoholism Professionals [*Later, NALGAP*] (EA)
**NAGARA**.. National Association of Government Archives and Records Administrators (EA)
**NAGARD** ... NATO Advisory Group for Aeronautical Research and Development
**Nagasaki Igakkai Zasshi Suppl** ... Nagasaki Igakkai Zasshi. Supplement [*Japan*] [*A publication*]
**Nagasaki Med J** ... Nagasaki Medical Journal [*A publication*]
**NAGBA**..... National Gas Bulletin [*A publication*]
**NAGBM**.... National Association of Golf Ball Manufacturers (EA)
**NAGB & SPA** ... North American Game Breeders and Shooting Preserve Association [*Later, NAGA*] (EA)
**NAGC**........ National Association for Gifted Children (EA)
**NAGC**........ National Association of Girls Clubs (EA)
**NAGC**........ National Association of Government Communicators (EA)
**NAGC**........ Naval Armed Guard Center
**NAGC**........ Navy Astronautics Group Conference [*Navy*]
**NAGC**........ North American Gladiolus Council (EA)
**NAGCD**..... National Association of Glass Container Distributors [*Later, NACD*] (EA)
**NAGCM**.... National Association of Golf Club Manufacturers (EA)
**NAGCO**..... Naval Air Ground Center
**NAGCP**..... National Association of Greeting Card Publishers [*Later, GCA*] (EA)
**NAGCR**..... North American Guild of Change Ringers (EA)
**NAGDA**..... Nara Gakugei Daigaku Kiyo [*A publication*]
**NAGDCA**.. National Association of Government Deferred Compensation Administrators (EA)
**NAGDM**.... National Association of Garage Door Manufacturers (EA)
**NAGE**........ National Association of Government Employees (EA)
**NAGE**........ NATO Air Defense Group Environment (AABC)
**NagHammSt** ... Nag Hammadi Studies [*A publication*] (BJA)
**NAGHSR**.. National Association of Governors' Highway Safety Representatives (EA)
**NAGI**......... National Association of Government Inspectors [*Later, National Association of Government Inspectors and Quality Assurance Personnel*] (EA)
**Nag Ig Zass** ... Nagasaki Igakkai Zasshi [*A publication*]
**NAGIM**..... North American Gunnery Instruction Monitor
**NAGI/QAP** ... National Association of Government Inspectors and Quality Assurance Personnel (EA)
**Nag J Med Sci** ... Nagoya Journal of Medical Science [*A publication*]
**Nag LJ**....... Nagpur Law Journal [*India*] [*A publication*] (DLA)
**Nag LN**...... Nagpur Law Notes [*India*] [*A publication*] (DLA)
**NAGLO**..... National Association of Governmental Labor Officials (EA)
**Nag LR**...... Nagpur Law Reports [*India*] [*A publication*] (DLA)
**NAGM**....... National Association of Glove Manufacturers (EA)
**NAGM**....... National Association of Glue Manufacturers [*Defunct*] (EA)
**NAGMA**.... College of Agriculture (Nagpur). Magazine [*A publication*]
**Nag Math J** ... Nagoya Mathematical Journal [*A publication*]
**NAGMR**.... National Association of General Merchandise Representatives [*Chicago, IL*] (EA)
**NagoKR**..... Nagoya Daigaku Bungakubu Kenkyu Ronshu [*Journal of the Faculty of Literature. Nagoya University*] [*A publication*]
**Nagoya J Med Sci** ... Nagoya Journal of Medical Science [*A publication*]
**Nagoya Math J** ... Nagoya Mathematical Journal [*A publication*]
**Nagoya Med J** ... Nagoya Medical Journal [*A publication*]
**Nagoya Univ Dep Earth Sci Collect Pap Earth Sci** ... Nagoya University. Department of Earth Sciences. Collected Papers on Earth Sciences [*A publication*]
**Nagoya Univ Inst Plasma Phys Annu Rev** ... Nagoya University. Institute of Plasma Physics. Annual Review [*A publication*]
**Nagoya Univ Jour Earth Sci** ... Nagoya University. Journal of Earth Sciences [*A publication*]
**NAGPA**..... National Association of General Practitioners of Australia
**NAGPTDU** ... National Action Group for the Prevention and Treatment of Decubitus Ulcers (EA)
**Nagpur Agric Coll Mag** ... Nagpur Agricultural College. Magazine [*A publication*]
**Nagpur Univ J** ... Nagpur University. Journal [*A publication*]
**NAGR**........ National Geographic Research [*A publication*]
**NAGRA**..... National Association of Gambling Regulatory Agencies (EA)
**NAGS**........ National Association of Government Secretaries [*Defunct*]
**NAGS**........ Naval Air Gunners School
**NAGSC**..... National Association of Government Service Contractors [*Washington, DC*] (EA)
**NAGSCT**... National Association of Guidance Supervisors and Counselor Trainers
**NAGSHKP** ... Neues Archiv fuer die Geschichte der Stadt Heidelberg und der Kurpfalz [*A publication*]
**NAGSHRP** ... Neues Archiv fuer die Geschichte der Stadt Heidelberg und der Rheinischen Pfalz [*A publication*]
**NAGT**........ National Association of Geology Teachers (EA)
**NAGTC**..... North American Gasoline Tax Conference (EA)
**Nag UCL Mag** ... Nagpur University. College of Law. Magazine [*1933-34*] [*India*] [*A publication*] (DLA)
**NAGVG**..... National Association Greenhouse Vegetable Growers (EA)
**NAGWS**..... National Association for Girls and Women in Sport (EA)
**NAGZA**..... Nagasaki Igakkai Zasshi [*A publication*]
**NAH**.......... Naha [*Ryukyu Islands*] [*Seismograph station code, US Geological Survey*] (SEIS)
**NAH**.......... Naha [*Indonesia*] [*Airport symbol*] (OAG)
**nah**............ Nahuatlan [*MARC language code*] [*Library of Congress*] (LCCP)
**Nah**............ Nahum [*Old Testament book*]
**NAH**.......... National Autism Hotline (EA)
**NAH**.......... Night Adoration in the Home (EA)
**NAH**.......... No-Antihalation Film
**NAH**.......... Nordic Association of Hairdressers (EAIO)
**NAH**.......... Nordic Association for the Handicapped (EA)
**NAH**.......... Nordic Association for Hydrology (EA)
**NAH**.......... Not at Home
**NAHA**....... National Association of Handwriting Analysts
**NAHA**....... National Association of Hotel Accountants [*Later, International Association of Hospitality Accountants*] (EA)
**NAHA**....... North American Highway Association
**NAHA**....... Norwegian-American Historical Association (EA)
**NAHAD**.... National Association of Hose and Accessories Distributors (EA)
**NAHAL**..... Noar Halutzi Lohem [*Pioneering Fighting Youth*] [*Israel*]
**NAHAM**... National Association of Hospital Admitting Managers (EA)
**NAHAWA** ... North American Heating and Airconditioning Wholesalers Association
**NAHB**........ National Alliance of Homebased Businesswomen [*Midland Park, NJ*] (EA)
**NAHB**........ National Association of Home Builders of the United States (EA)
**NAHB**........ National Association of Homes for Boys [*Later, NFCCE*]
**NAHBB**..... National Association of Home Based Businesses [*Baltimore, MD*] (EA)
**NAHBE**..... Naval Academy Heat Balanced Engine [*Pronounced "knobby"*]
**NAHB/RC** ... NAHB Remodelers Council (EA)
**NAHC**........ National Advisory Health Council
**NAHC**........ National Anti-Hunger Coalition (EA)
**NAHC**........ National Association for Home Care (EA)
**NAHC**........ National Association of Homes for Children (EA)
**NAHC**........ National Association of Housing Cooperatives (EA)
**NAHC**........ North American Hunting Club (EA)
**NAHCR**..... National Association of Healthcare Recruitment (EA)
**NAHCS**..... National Association of Health Career Schools (EA)
**NAHCSP**... National Association of Hospital Central Service Personnel [*Later, IAHCSM*] (EA)
**NAHD**....... National Association of Hillel Directors [*Later, IAHD*] (EA)
**NAHD**....... National Association for Hospital Development (EA)
**NAHD**....... National Association for Human Development (EA)
**NAHDDM** ... National Association of House and Daytime Dress Manufacturers (EA)
**NAHDO**.... National Association of Health Data Organizations (EA)
**NAHDSA**.. National Association of Hebrew Day School Administrators (EA)
**NAHE**........ National Alliance for Hydroelectric Energy (EA)
**NAHE**........ National Association for Holocaust Education (EA)
**NAHE**........ National Association for Humanities Education (EA)
**NAHEE**...... National Association for Humane and Environmental Education (EA)

**NAHES** ..... National Association of Home Economics Supervisors [*Later, NASSVHE*] (EA)
**NAHFAGIF** ... National Archives and Historical Foundation of the American GI Forum (EA)
**NAHG** ....... National Association of Humanistic Gerontology (EA)
**NAHHA** .... National Association of Home Health Agencies [*Later, NAHC*] (EA)
**NAHHH** .... National Association of Hospital Hospitality Houses (EA)
**NAHHIC** ... National Association of House to House Installment Companies [*Later, NAIC*] (EA)
**NAHI** ......... National Athletic Health Institute (EA)
**NAHICUS** ... Nuclear Attack Hazards in the Continental United States
**NAHID3** .... Instituto Nacional para la Conservacion de la Naturaleza. Naturalia Hispanica [*A publication*]
**NAHIS** ...... National Arts and Handicapped Information Service (EA)
**NA Hisp** ..... Noticiario Arqueologico Hispanico [*A publication*]
**NAHJ** ........ National Association of Hispanic Journalists (EA)
**NAHL** ........ North American Hockey League
**NAHL** ........ North American Holding Corp. [*East Hartford, CT*] [*NASDAQ symbol*] (NQ)
**NAHM** ...... National Association of Home Manufacturers [*Later, HMC*] (EA)
**NAHM** ...... National Association of Hosiery Manufacturers (EA)
**NAHMA** ... National Association of Hotel and Motel Accountants [*Later, International Association of Hospitality Accountants*]
**NAHN** ....... National Association of Hispanic Nurses (EA)
**NAHNS** .... National Association of the Holy Name Society (EA)
**NAHO** ....... National Aboriginal Health Organisation [*Australia*]
**NAHP** ........ National Association of Hispanic Publications (EA)
**NAHP** ........ National Association of Horseradish Packers (EA)
**NAHPA** ..... National Association of Hospital Purchasing Agents [*Later, NAHPMM*] (EA)
**NAHPM** .... National Association of Hospital Purchasing Management [*Later, NAHPMM*] (EA)
**NAHPMM** ... National Association of Hospital Purchasing Materials Management (EA)
**NAHPS** ..... North American Habitat Preservation Society (EA)
**NAHQAO** ... Nebraska. University. College of Agriculture and Home Economics. Quarterly [*A publication*]
**NAHRMP** ... National Association of Hotel and Restaurant Meat Purveyors [*Later, NAMP*] (EA)
**NAHRO** .... National Association of Housing and Redevelopment Officials (EA)
**NAHRW** ... National Association of Human Rights Workers (EA)
**NAHS** ........ National Association of Horological Schools (EA)
**NAHS** ........ North American Heather Society (EA)
**NAHSA** ..... National Association for Hearing and Speech Action (EA)
**NAHSA** ..... North American Horticultural Supply Association (EA)
**NAHSE** ..... National Association of Health Services Executives (EA)
**NAHST** ..... National Association of Human Services Technologies (EA)
**NAHT** ........ National Association of Head Teachers [*British*]
**NAHU** ....... NAHU, an Association of Bull Users [*Formerly, North American Honeywell Users Association*] (EA)
**NAHU** ....... National Association of Health Underwriters [*Washington, DC*] (EA)
**NAHUC** .... National Association of Health Unit Clerks-Coordinators (EA)
**NAHW** ...... National Association of Hardwood Wholesalers [*Defunct*]
**NAHWMUMC** ... National Association of Health and Welfare Ministries of the United Methodist Church [*Later, United Methodist Association of Health and Welfare Ministries - UMA*] (EA)
**NAHWW** .. National Association of Home and Workshop Writers (EA)
**NAI** ............ Annai [*Guyana*] [*Airport symbol*] (OAG)
**NAI** ............ Nairobi [*Kenya*] [*Seismograph station code, US Geological Survey*] (SEIS)
**NAI** ............ Nairobi [*Kenya*] [*Geomagnetic observatory code*]
**NAI** ............ Named Areas of Interest [*Army intelligence matrix*] (INF)
**NAI** ............ National Agricultural Institute [*Later, ACA*] (EA)
**NAI** ............ National Apple Institute [*Later, IAI*] (EA)
**NAI** ............ National Association of Interpretation (EA)
**NAI** ............ Negro Airmen International (EA)
**NAI** ............ Net Annual Inflow [*Pensions*]
**NAI** ............ Netherlands Arbitration Institute (ILCA)
**NAI** ............ New Acronyms and Initialisms [*Later, NAIA*] [*A publication*]
**NAI** ............ New Alchemy Institute (EA)
**NAI** ............ No Action Indicated
**NAI** ............ No-Address Instruction (AAG)
**NAI** ............ No Airborne Intercept [*Fighter aircraft lacking airborne intercept RADAR*]
**NAI** ............ Nonaccidental Injury
**nai** ............ North American Indian [*MARC language code*] [*Library of Congress*] (LCCP)
**NAI** ............ Northern Alberta Institute of Technology [*UTLAS symbol*]
**NAI** ............ Northrop Aeronautical Institute [*Later, Northrop University*]
**NAI** ............ Northrop Aircraft, Incorporated (MCD)
**NAI** ............ N'shei Agudath Israel (BJA)
**NAIA** ......... National Association of Industrial Artists [*Later, IG*]
**NAIA** ......... National Association of Insurance Agents [*Later, IIAA*] (EA)
**NAIA** ......... National Association of Intercollegiate Athletics (EA)
**NAIA** ......... New Acronyms, Initialisms, and Abbreviations [*Formerly, NAI*] [*A publication*]
**NAIA** ......... North American Indian Association (EA)
**NAIB** ......... National Association of Independent Business [*Defunct*]
**NAIB** ......... National Association of Insurance Brokers [*Washington, DC*] (EA)
**NAIC** ......... National Adoption Information Clearinghouse (EA)
**NAIC** ......... National Advice and Information Centre for Outdoor Education [*Doncaster Metropolitan Institute of Higher Education*] [*British*] (CB)
**NAIC** ......... National AIDS [*Acquired Immune Deficiency Syndrome*] Information Clearinghouse [*Information service or system*] (EISS)
**NAIC** ......... National Association of Installment Companies [*New York, NY*] (EA)
**NAIC** ......... National Association of Insurance Commissioners [*Kansas City, MO*] (EA)
**NAIC** ......... National Association of Intercollegiate Commissioners (EA)
**NAIC** ......... National Association of Investment Companies (EA)
**NAIC** ......... National Association of Investors Corporation (EA)
**NAIC** ......... National Astronomy and Ionosphere Center [*Ithaca, NY*] [*National Science Foundation*]
**NAIC** ......... Nuclear Accident and Incident Control [*Army*] (AABC)
**NAICA** ...... National American Indian Cattlemen's Association (EA)
**NAICC** ....... National Alliance of Independent Crop Consultants (EA)
**NAICC** ....... National Association of Independent Computer Companies
**NAICC** ....... Nuclear Accident and Incident Control Center [*Army*] (AABC)
**NAICCA** .... National American Indian Court Clerks Association (EA)
**NAICJA** .... National American Indian Court Judges Association (EA)
**NAICO** ...... Nuclear Accident and Incident Control Officer [*Army*] (AABC)
**NAICOM/MIS** ... Navy Integrated Command Management Information System
**NAICP** ....... Nuclear Accident and Incident Control Plan [*Army*]
**NAICU** ...... National Association of Independent Colleges and Universities (EA)
**NAICV** ...... National Association of Ice Cream Vendors (EA)
**NAID** ......... National Associates for Informed Depressives [*Defunct*] (EA)
**NAID** ......... National Association of Installation Developers (EA)
**NAID** ......... National Association of Interior Designers (EA)
**NAIDST** .... National AIDS Trust [*British*]
**NAIEA** ...... National Association of Inspectors and Educational Advisers [*British*]
**NAIEC** ....... National Association for Industry-Education Cooperation [*Buffalo, NY*] (EA)
**NAIEHS** .... National Association of Importers and Exporters of Hides and Skins [*Later, USHSLA*] (EA)
**NAIEM** ..... National Association of Insect Electrocutor Manufacturers (EA)
**NAIES** ....... National Adoption Information Exchange System [*Formerly, ARENA*] (EA)
**NAIES** ....... National Association of Interdisciplinary Ethnic Studies (EA)
**NAIF** .......... National Association for Irish Freedom (EA)
**NAIF** .......... Nordiska Akademiska Idrottsforbund [*Scandinavian Federation for University Sport*] (EA)
**NAIF** .......... NOTAM Already in File (FAAC)
**NAIFA** ....... National Association of Independent Fee Appraisers (EA)
**NAIFR** ....... National Association of Independent Food Retailers [*Defunct*] (EA)
**NAIG** ......... National Insurance Group [*NASDAQ symbol*] (NQ)
**NAIG** ......... Nippon Atomic Industry Group [*Japan*]
**NAIGA** ...... Nagoya Igaku [*A publication*]
**NAIG AR** ... NAIG [*Nippon Atomic Industry Group*] Annual Review [*A publication*]
**NAIHC** ...... National American Indian Housing Council (EA)
**NAII** .......... National Association of Ice Industries [*Later, PIA*]
**NAII** .......... National Association of Independent Insurers [*Des Plaines, IL*] (EA)
**NAIIA** ........ National Association of Independent Insurance Adjusters [*Chicago, IL*] (EA)
**NAIIU** ....... Not Authorized If Issued Under [*Army*]
**NAIJ** .......... National Association for Irish Justice [*Superseded by National Association for Irish Freedom*] (EA)
**NAIKAB** .... Internal Medicine [*A publication*]
**Naika Hok** ... Naika Hokan [*A publication*]
**NAIL** ......... National Association for Independent Living (EA)
**NAIL** ......... National Association of Independent Lubes (EA)
**NAIL** ......... National Association of Independent Lumbermen [*Defunct*] (EA)
**NAIL** ......... Neurotics Anonymous International Liaison (EA)
**NAILBA** .... National Association of Independent Life Brokerage Agencies [*Washington, DC*] (EA)
**NAILD** ...... National Association of Independent Lighting Distributors (EA)
**NAILM** ..... National Association of Institutional Laundry Managers [*Later, National Association of Institutional Linen Management*] (EA)
**NAILM** ..... National Association of Institutional Linen Management (EA)
**NAILS** ....... National Automated Immigration Lookout System [*Immigration and Naturalization Service*]
**NAILS** ....... Naval Aviation Integrated Logistic Support Task Force (NG)
**NAILSC** .... Naval Aviation Integrated Logistic Support Center (MCD)
**NAILSS** ..... National Aboriginal and Islander Legal Service Secretariat [*Australia*]

**NAILTE**.... National Association of Instructional Leaders in Technical Education (EA)
**NAIM**........ NAIM [*North American Indian Mission*] Ministries (EA)
**NAIMA**..... North American Indian Museums Association (EA)
**NAIMD**..... National Association of Independent Music Dealers [*Defunct*] (EA)
**NAIME**..... National Association of Independent Maritime Educators (EA)
**NAIMSAL**... National Anti-Imperialist Movement in Solidarity with African Liberation (EA)
**NAIOP**...... National Association of Industrial and Office Parks (EA)
**NAIOP**...... Navigational Aid Inoperative for Parts
**NAIP**......... National Assault on Illiteracy Program (EA)
**NAIP**......... National Association of Independent Publishers (EA)
**NAIP**......... National Association of Industrial Parks [*Later, NAIOP*]
**NAIP**......... National Association of Insured Persons (EA)
**NAIPTS**.... National Amalgamated Iron Plate Trade Society [*A union*] [*British*]
**NAIR**......... Narrow Absorption Infrared
**NAIR**......... National Association of Independent Resurfacers (EA)
**NAIR**......... Network Action Item Report (MCD)
**NAIRD**...... National Association of Independent Record Distributors and Manufacturers (EA)
**NAIRDM**.. National Association of Independent Record Distributors and Manufacturers (EA)
**NAIRE**....... National Association of Internal Revenue Employees [*Later, NTEU*] (EA)
**NAIREC**.... Nimbus Arctic Ice Reconnaissance [*Canadian project*]
**NAIRO**...... National Association of Intergroup Relations Officials [*Later, NAHRW*] (EA)
**Nairobi J Med**... Nairobi Journal of Medicine [*A publication*]
**NAIRS**....... National Athletic Injury/Illness Reporting System [*Pennsylvania State University*] [*Defunct*]
**NAIRS**....... Navy Aircraft and Readiness System
**NAIRU**...... Naval Air Intelligence Reserve Units
**NAIRU**...... Non-Accelerating-Inflation Rate of Unemployment
**NAIS**.......... National Aquaculture Information System (NOAA)
**NAIS**.......... National Association of Independent Schools (EA)
**NAIS**.......... National Association of Investigative Specialists (EA)
**NAIS**.......... Navy Attitudinal Information System (NVT)
**NAIS**.......... Night Attack Interdiction System
**NAISC**....... National American Indian Safety Council (EA)
**NAISEO**.... National Association of Inspectors of Schools and Educational Organisers [*British*]
**NAIT**......... National Association of Industrial Technology (EA)
**NAIT**......... Naval Air Intermediate Training
**NAIT**......... North American Islamic Trust (EA)
**NAIT**......... Northern Alberta Institute of Technology [*Edmonton, AB*]
**NAITC**....... National Arts Industry Training Committee [*Australia*]
**NAIT(C)**.... Naval Air Intermediate Training (Command)
**NAITE**....... National Association of Industrial Teacher Educators [*Later, NAITTE*] (EA)
**NAITF**....... Naval Air Intercept Training Facility (MUGU)
**NAITP**....... National Association of Income Tax Preparers (EA)
**NAITPD**.... National Association of Independent Television Producers and Distributors [*Defunct*] (EA)
**NAITTE**.... National Association of Industrial and Technical Teacher Educators (EA)
**NAIW**........ National Association of Insurance Women (International) [*Tulsa, OK*] (EA)
**NAIWA**..... North American Indian Women's Association (EA)
**NAJ**........... Napierville Junction Railway Co. [*Later, NJ*] [*AAR code*]
**NAJ**........... National Academy of Jazz (EA)
**NAJ**........... National Aeronautics and Space Administration, Johnson Space Center, Houston, TX [*OCLC symbol*] (OCLC)
**NAJ**........... National Association for Justice
**NAJA**........ National Association of Jewelry Appraisers (EA)
**NAJA**........ National Association of Junior Auxiliaries (EA)
**NAJA**........ North American Judges Association [*Later, AJA*]
**NAJAFRA**... National Jazz Fraternity
**NAJAG**...... North African Judge Advocate General's Section [*World War II*]
**NAJCA**...... National Association of Juvenile Correctional Agencies (EA)
**NAJCW**..... National Association of Jewish Center Workers [*Later, AJCW*] (EA)
**NAJD**........ National Association of Journalism Directors [*Later, JEA*] (EA)
**NAJD/MBAP**... National Association of JD/MBA [*Juris Doctor/Master of Business Administration*] Professionals [*New York, NY*] (EA)
**NAJE**......... National Association of Jazz Educators [*Later, IAJE*] (EA)
**NAJEM**..... North African Joint Economic Mission [*World War II*]
**NAJF**......... National Association of Jai Alai Frontons (EA)
**NAJFCHP**... National Association of Jewish Family, Children's, and Health Professionals (EA)
**NAJHA**..... National Association of Jewish Homes for the Aged [*Later, NAAJHHA*] (EA)
**NAJLA**...... North American Junior Limousin Association (EA)
**NA Jl Expl Agric**... New Zealand Journal of Experimental Agriculture [*A publication*]
**NAJMDP**... North American Journal of Fisheries Management [*A publication*]
**NAJN**........ North American Journal of Numismatics [*A publication*]
**NAJRC**...... North African Joint Rearmament Committee [*World War II*]
**NAJSA**...... North American Jewish Students Appeal (EA)
**NAJSN**...... North American Jewish Students' Network (EA)
**NAJU**........ Nordic Association of Journalists' Unions (EA)
**NAJVS**...... National Association of Jewish Vocational Services (EA)
**NAJYC**...... North American Jewish Youth Council (EA)
**NAK**........... Nakhichevan [*USSR*] [*Seismograph station code, US Geological Survey*] [*Closed*] (SEIS)
**NAk**........... Narodopisne Aktuality [*A publication*]
**NAK**........... Navik Air, Inc. [*Rochester, NY*] [*FAA designator*] (FAAC)
**NAK**........... Negative Acknowledge [*or Acknowledgment*] [*Data communication*]
**NAK**........... Network Acknowledgment
**NAK**........... Nothing Adverse Known (ADA)
**Na K-ATPase**... Adenosine Triphosphatase (Na, K-Activated) [*An enzyme*]
**NAKBA**..... National Association to Keep and Bear Arms (EA)
**NAkG**........ Nachrichten. Akademie der Wissenschaften zu Goettingen [*A publication*]
**NAKG**........ Nederlandsch Archief voor Kerkgeschiedenis [*A publication*]
**nakl**........... Bill of Lading, Waybill, Invoice
**NAKN**........ National Anti-Klan Network (EA)
**NAKOSTA**... Natural Convection in the Stationary Condition [*Computer program*]
**NAKS**........ North American Kant Society (EA)
**NAl**........... Albany Public Library, Albany, NY [*Library symbol*] [*Library of Congress*] (LCLS)
**NAL**........... N-Acetyllactopamine [*Biochemistry*]
**NAL**........... Naloxone [*A drug*]
**NAL**........... Name, Address, and Legal File [*Real estate*]
**NAL**........... National Accelerator Laboratory [*AEC*]
**NAL**........... National Aeronautical Laboratory (MCD)
**NAL**........... National Agricultural Library [*Department of Agriculture*] [*Beltsville, MD*]
**NAL**........... National Air [*Marston Mills, MA*] [*FAA designator*] (FAAC)
**NAL**........... National Assistance League (EA)
**NAL**........... National Association of Laity (EA)
**NAL**........... National Association of Landowners (EA)
**NAL**........... National Astronomical League
**NAL**........... Naval Aeronautical Laboratory
**NAL**........... New Aalesund [*Norway*] [*Geomagnetic observatory code*]
**NAL**........... New American Library [*Publisher*]
**NAL**........... New Assembly Language
**NAL**........... Newalta Corp. [*Toronto Stock Exchange symbol*]
**NAL**........... Newspapers in Australian Libraries [*A publication*] (APTA)
**NAL**........... Norwegian America Line
**NAL**........... Numerical Analysis Laboratory (MCD)
**NAlA**......... Albany Medical College, Albany, NY [*Library symbol*] [*Library of Congress*] (LCLS)
**NALA**........ National Academy of Literary Arts (EA)
**NALA**........ National Affiliation for Literacy Advance (EA)
**NALA**........ National Agricultural Limestone Association [*Later, National Limestone Institute*]
**NALA**........ National Association of Language Advisers [*British*]
**NALA**........ National Association of Legal Assistants (EA)
**NALA**........ Native Library Advocate [*Ottawa, Canada*] [*A publication*]
**NALAA**...... National Assembly of Local Arts Agencies (EA)
**NALAM**.... National Association of Livestock Auction Markets
**NAlb**.......... Shelter Rock Public Library, Albertson, NY [*Library symbol*] [*Library of Congress*] (LCLS)
**NALBA**...... North American Log Builders Association (EA)
**NAlBC**....... Albany Business College, Albany, NY [*Library symbol*] [*Library of Congress*] (LCLS)
**NAlbH**....... Human Resources Center, Albertson, NY [*Library symbol*] [*Library of Congress*] (LCLS)
**NAlbi**......... Swan Library, Albion, NY [*Library symbol*] [*Library of Congress*] (LCLS)
**NAlbiH**...... Arnold Gregory Memorial Hospital, Albion, NY [*Library symbol*] [*Library of Congress*] (LCLS)
**NALC**........ National Afro-American Labor Council (EA)
**NALC**........ National Association of Letter Carriers of the USA (EA)
**NALC**........ National Association of Life Companies [*Washington, DC*] (EA)
**NALC**........ National Association of Litho Clubs (EA)
**NALC**........ National Association of Local Councils [*British*]
**NALC**........ Naval Aviation Logistics Center (NVT)
**NALC**........ Navy Ammunition Logistics Code
**NALC**........ New Age Learning Center (EA)
**NALCC**...... National Automatic Laundry and Cleaning Council (EA)
**NALCDVE**... National Association of Large City Directors of Vocational Education (EA)
**NAlCI**........ Center for International Studies, Albany, NY [*Library symbol*] [*Library of Congress*] (LCLS)
**NALCM**.... National Association of Lace Curtain Manufacturers [*Defunct*]
**NALCO**..... Naval Air Logistics Control Office
**NALCO**..... Newfoundland & Labrador Corporation
**NALCOEURREP**... Naval Air Logistics Control Office European Representative
**NALCOLANT**... Naval Air Logistics Control Office Atlantic
**NALCOMIS**... Naval Aviation Logistics Command Management Information System (MCD)

**NALCON**.. Navy Laboratory Computer Network
**NALCOPAC** ... Naval Air Logistics Control Office Pacific
**NALCOPACREP** ... Naval Air Logistics Control Office Pacific Representative
**NALCOREP** ... Naval Air Logistics Control Office Representative
**NAlCSR**..... College of Saint Rose, Albany, NY [*Library symbol*] [*Library of Congress*] (LCLS)
**NAlD** ......... Dudley Observatory, Albany, NY [*Library symbol*] [*Library of Congress*] (LCLS)
**NALDA**..... Naval Aviation Logistics Data Analysis (NVT)
**NALDEF**... Native American Legal Defense and Education Foundation (EA)
**NAlDH**...... New York State Department of Health, Division of Laboratories and Research, Albany, NY [*Library symbol*] [*Library of Congress*] (LCLS)
**NAlDS**....... New York State Department of State, Community Affairs Library, Albany, NY [*Library symbol*] [*Library of Congress*] (LCLS)
**NALECOM** ... National Law Enforcement Telecommunications System
**NALED** ..... National Association of Limited Edition Dealers (EA)
**NAleNH** .... E. J. Noble Hospital, Medical Library, Alexandria Bay, NY [*Library symbol*] [*Library of Congress*] (LCLS)
**NALEO** ..... National Association of Latino Elected and Appointed Officials (EA)
**NAlf**........... Alfred University, Alfred, NY [*Library symbol*] [*Library of Congress*] (LCLS)
**NALF**......... National Agricultural Legal Fund (EA)
**NALF**......... Naval Auxiliary Landing Field (NG)
**NALF**......... Negro American Literature Forum [*A publication*]
**NALF**......... North American Limousin Foundation (EA)
**NALF**......... North American Loon Fund (EA)
**NAlfC** ........ State University of New York, College of Ceramics at Alfred University, Alfred, NY [*Library symbol*] [*Library of Congress*] (LCLS)
**NALFMA** ... National Association of Law Firm Marketing Administrators (EA)
**NAlf-ST**..... Alfred University, School of Theology, Alfred, NY [*Library symbol*] [*Library of Congress*] [*Obsolete*] (LCLS)
**NAlfUA** ..... State University of New York, Agricultural and Technical College at Alfred, Alfred, NY [*Library symbol*] [*Library of Congress*] (LCLS)
**NALG** ........ National Association of Left-Handed Golfers (EA)
**NALGAP**... National Association of Lesbian/Gay Alcoholism Professionals (EA)
**NALGHW** ... National Association of Local Governments on Hazardous Wastes (EA)
**NALGM**.... National Association of Lawn and Garden Manufacturers [*Inactive*] (EA)
**NALGM**.... National Association of Leather Glove Manufacturers [*Later, NAGM*]
**NALGO**..... National and Local Government Officers' Association [*British*]
**NAlGS**....... United States Geological Survey, Water Resources Services, New York District, Albany, NY [*Library symbol*] [*Library of Congress*] (LCLS)
**NAlH**......... Hospital Educational and Research Fund, Inc., Albany, NY [*Library symbol*] [*Library of Congress*] (LCLS)
**NALHC**...... North American Log Homes Council (EA)
**NALHI**...... National Authority for the Ladies Handbag Industry (EA)
**NALHM**.... National Association of Licensed House Managers [*Pronounced "nalem"*] [*A union*] [*British*] (DCTA)
**NAlI**........... Albany Institute of History of Art, Albany, NY [*Library symbol*] [*Library of Congress*] (LCLS)
**NALI** ......... National Agricultural Limestone Institute [*Later, National Limestone Institute*]
**NALI** ......... National Association of Legal Investigators (EA)
**NALI** ......... North Atlantic Lobster Institute (EA)
**NAlJ** .......... Junior College of Albany, Albany, NY [*Library symbol*] [*Library of Congress*] (LCLS)
**NALJS** ...... Nordic Atomic Libraries Joint Secretariat [*Information service or system*] (IID)
**NALLA**...... National Long-Lines Agency (NATG)
**NALLD** ..... National Association of Learning Laboratory Directors [*Later, IALL*]
**NALLDJ** ... National Association of Language Laboratory Directors. Journal [*A publication*]
**NALLO** ..... National Association of License Law Officials [*Later, NARELLO*] (EA)
**NAlLS** ....... Albany Law School, Albany, NY [*Library symbol*] [*Library of Congress*] (LCLS)
**NAlM** ........ Maria College, Albany, NY [*Library symbol*] [*Library of Congress*] (LCLS)
**NALM**....... National Association for Lay Ministry (EA)
**NALMCO** ... International Association of Lighting Management Companies (EA)
**NALMCO** ... National Association of Lighting Maintenance Contractors (EA)
**NAlMem**.... Memorial Hospital, Medical Library, Albany, NY [*Library symbol*] [*Library of Congress*] (LCLS)
**NAlMH**..... New York State Department of Mental Hygiene, Mental Hygiene Research Library, Albany, NY [*Library symbol*] [*Library of Congress*] (LCLS)
**NALMS**..... North American Lake Management Society (EA)
**NAlMV**...... New York State Department of Motor Vehicles, Research Library, Albany, NY [*Library symbol*] [*Library of Congress*] (LCLS)
**NALN**........ National Agricultural Libraries Network [*National Agricultural Library*]
**NALN**........ Native Authority Legal Notice [*Northern Nigeria*] [*A publication*] (DLA)
**NALN**........ North African Liaison Section [*World War II*]
**NALNET**... NASA Library Network [*NASA*] [*Washington, DC*] [*Library network*] (MCD)
**NALO**........ Naval Air Liaison Officer
**NALOH**..... National Association Legions of Honor (EA)
**NALOP**..... NATO Letter of Promulgation
**NALOXONE** ... N-Allylnoroxymorphone [*Narcotic antagonist*]
**NAlP**.......... Albany College of Pharmacy, Albany, NY [*Library symbol*] [*Library of Congress*] (LCLS)
**NALP** ......... National Association for Law Placement (EA)
**NALPA**...... National American Legion Press Association (EA)
**NALPM**..... National Association of Lithographic Plate Manufacturers (EA)
**NALPN** ..... National Association of Licensed Practical Nurses (EA)
**NALR** ........ National Association of Lighting Representatives (EA)
**NALS**......... National Advisory Logistics Staff (NATG)
**NALS**......... National Association of Laboratory Suppliers [*Inactive*] (EA)
**NALS**......... National Association of Legal Secretaries (International) [*Tulsa, OK*] (EA)
**NALS**......... National Association of Lumber Salesmen (EA)
**NALS**......... North American Lily Society (EA)
**NAlS** .......... Saint Peter's Hospital, Albany, NY [*Library symbol*] [*Library of Congress*] (LCLS)
**NALSA**...... Native American Law Students Association (EA)
**NALSAS** ... National Association for Legal Support of Alternative Schools (EA)
**NALSDJ** ... NATO [*North Atlantic Treaty Organization*] ASI [*Advanced Science Institutes*] Series. Series A. Life Sciences [*A publication*]
**NALSF** ...... National ALS [*Amyotrophic Lateral Sclerosis*] Foundation (EA)
**NALSI** ....... National Association of Life Science Industries (EA)
**NAlSS**........ New York State Department of Social Sciences, Social Services and Statistics Library, Albany, NY [*Library symbol*] [*Library of Congress*] (LCLS)
**Nal St P** ..... Nalton's Collection of State Papers [*A publication*] (DLA)
**NAlSU**....... State University of New York, Union List of Serials, Albany, NY [*Library symbol*] [*Library of Congress*] (LCLS)
**NALSVHE** ... National Association of Local Supervisors of Vocational Home Economics (EA)
**NALT** ........ Naltrexone [*A drug*]
**NALT** ........ National Association of the Legitimate Theatre [*Defunct*] (EA)
**NAltL**......... La Salette Seminary, Altamont, NY [*Library symbol*] [*Library of Congress*] (LCLS)
**NALTS**...... National Advertising Lead Tracking System [*Navy*] (NVT)
**NALU**........ National Association of Life Underwriters [*Washington, DC*] (EA)
**NAlU** ......... State University of New York at Albany, Albany, NY [*Library symbol*] [*Library of Congress*] (LCLS)
**NALUAS**... North American Life Union Assurance Society (EA)
**NAlU-F**...... State University of New York at Albany, Filmdex, Albany, NY [*Library symbol*] [*Library of Congress*] (LCLS)
**NAlUHL** ... Upper Hudson Library Federation, Albany, NY [*Library symbol*] [*Library of Congress*] (LCLS)
**NAlU-L** ..... State University of New York at Albany Library School, Albany, NY [*Library symbol*] [*Library of Congress*] (LCLS)
**NAlULS** .... New York State Union List of Serials, Albany, NY [*Library symbol*] [*Library of Congress*] (LCLS)
**NAlU-PA**... State University of New York at Albany, Graduate School of Public Affairs, Albany, NY [*Library symbol*] [*Library of Congress*] (LCLS)
**NALUS**...... National Association of Leagues, Umpires, and Scorers (EA)
**NAlVA**....... United States Veterans Administration Hospital, Albany, NY [*Library symbol*] [*Library of Congress*] (LCLS)
**NAM**.......... N-(Acridinyl)maleimide [*Organic chemistry*]
**NAM**.......... Namangan [*USSR*] [*Seismograph station code, US Geological Survey*] [*Closed*] (SEIS)
**NAM**.......... Named
**NAM**.......... Namibia [*ANSI three-letter standard code*] (CNC)
**NAM**.......... Namlea [*Indonesia*] [*Airport symbol*] (OAG)
**NAM**.......... National Account Management [*Bell System*]
**NAM**.......... National Air Museum [*of the Smithsonian Institution*] [*Later, NASM*]
**NAM**.......... National Apple Month (EA)
**NAM**.......... National Army Museum [*British military*] (DMA)
**NAM**.......... National Association of Manufacturers (EA)
**NAM**.......... Natural Actomyosins [*Biochemistry*]
**NAM**.......... Nautical Air Miles
**NAM**.......... Naval Air Mechanic [*British military*] (DMA)
**NAM**.......... Naval Aircraft Modification
**NAM**.......... Naval Aviation Museum [*Pensacola, FL*]
**NAM**.......... Navy Achievement Medal [*Military decoration*]

**NAM**.......... Network Access Machine [*National Institute of Standards and Technology*] [*Data processing*]
**NAM**.......... Network Access Method [*Control Data Corp.*] [*Telecommunications*] (TEL)
**NAM**.......... Network Analysis Model
**NAM**.......... New America Movement (EA)
**NAM**.......... Newspaper Association Managers (EA)
**NAM**.......... NOAA [*National Oceanic and Atmospheric Administration*] Accounting Manual (NOAA)
**NAM**.......... Nonaligned Movement
**NAM**.......... North America
**NAM**.......... North American Metals Corp. [*Vancouver Stock Exchange symbol*]
**NAM**.......... Norwegian American Museum Corp. (EA)
**NAM**.......... Nurses Against Misrepresentation (EA)
**NAM**.......... State University of New York at Albany, Albany, NY [*OCLC symbol*] (OCLC)
**Nam**........... Vietnam
**NAma**......... Amagansett Free Library, Amagansett, NY [*Library symbol*] [*Library of Congress*] (LCLS)
**NAMA**....... National Account Marketing Association (EA)
**NAMA**....... National Agri-Marketing Association (EA)
**NAMA**....... National Assistance Management Association [*Washington, DC*] (EA)
**NAMA**....... National Association of Master Appraisers (EA)
**NAMA**....... National Automatic Merchandising Association [*Chicago, IL*] (EA)
**NAMA**....... National Automotive Muffler Association [*Defunct*] (EA)
**NAMA**....... Naval Aeronautical Material Area (NG)
**NAMA**....... North American Manx Association (EA)
**NAMA**....... North American Mycological Association (EA)
**NAMAB**.... National Air Museum Advisory Board (MUGU)
**NAMAC**.... National Alliance of Media Arts Centers (EA)
**NAMAC**.... National Amateur Missile Analysis Center
**NAMAC**.... National Association of Men's Apparel Clubs [*Later, NAMBAC, Bureau of Wholesale Sales Representatives*]
**NAMAC**.... National Association of Merger and Acquisition Consultants (EA)
**NAMAD**.... National Association of Minority Automobile Dealers [*Detroit, MI*] (EA)
**NAMAE**.... Northern Air Materiel Area, Europe [*Army*]
**NAmaHi**.... Amagansett Historical Association, Amagansett, NY [*Library symbol*] [*Library of Congress*] (LCLS)
**NAMAP**.... Northern Air Materiel Area, Pacific [*Army*]
**NAMAPUS** ... Naval Assistant to the Military Aide to the President of the United States
**NAMAR**.... North American Mustang Association and Registry (EA)
**NAMAS**.... National Measurement Accreditation Service [*United Kingdom*] [*Research center*] (IRC)
**NAMAST** ... System of National Accounts and System of Material Product Balances [*United Nations Statistical Office*] [*Information service or system*] (CRD)
**NAMATCEN** ... Naval Air Material Center [*Also, NAMC, NAVAIRMATCEN*]
**NAMATE** ... Naval Air Material Command
**NAMB**....... National Association of Media Brokers (EA)
**NAMB**....... National Association of Mortgage Brokers [*Washington, DC*] (EA)
**NAMB**....... Naval Academy Midshipmen Branch
**NAMB**....... Naval Amphibious Base
**NAMBAC** ... National Association of Men's and Boys' Apparel Clubs [*Later, Bureau of Wholesale Sales Representatives*] (EA)
**N Am Bird Bander** ... North American Bird Bander [*A publication*]
**NAMBLA** ... North American Man-Boy Love Association
**NAMBO**.... National Association of Motor Bus Owners [*Later, ABA*] (EA)
**NAMC**....... National Air Material Center (KSC)
**NAMC**....... National Association of Management Consultants (EA)
**NAMC**....... National Association of Minority Contractors (EA)
**NAMC**....... Naval Aerospace Medical Center
**NAMC**....... Naval Air Material Center [*Also, NAMATCEN, NAVAIRMATCEN*]
**NAMC**....... Naval Air Materiel Command
**NAMC**....... North American National Corporation [*NASDAQ symbol*] (NQ)
**NAMC**....... North Atlantic Military Committee
**NAMC**....... Notiziario Archeologico del Ministero delle Colonie [*A publication*]
**NAMCA**.... National Association for Middle Class Americans (EA)
**NAMC-AEL** ... Naval Air Material Center - Aeronautical Engine Laboratory
**NAMC-AIL** ... Naval Air Material Center - Aeronautical Instruments Laboratory [*Philadelphia, PA*]
**NAMC-AML** ... Naval Air Material Center - Aeronautical Materials Laboratory
**NAMC-APEL** ... Naval Air Material Center - Aeronautical Photographic Experimental Laboratory
**NAMCAR** ... North America/Caribbean (AIA)
**NAMC-ARRL** ... Naval Air Material Center - Aeronautical Radio and RADAR Laboratory
**NAMC-ASL** ... Naval Air Material Center - Aeronautical Structures Laboratory
**NAMCC**.... National Association of Mutual Casualty Companies (EA)
**NAMCF**.... National Association of Minority CPA [*Certified Public Accounting*] Firms
**NAMCO**.... Air-Cushion Vehicle built by Nakamura Seisakusho [*Japan*] [*Usually used in combination with numerals*]
**NAMCPAF** ... National Association of Minority Certified Public Accounting Firms (EA)
**NAMCS**.... National Ambulatory Medical Care Survey [*National Center for Health Statistics*]
**NAMCU**.... National Association of Minority Consultants and Urbanologists [*Defunct*] (EA)
**NAMCW**... National Association of Maternal and Child Welfare [*British*]
**NAMD**....... National Association of Marble Dealers [*Later, MIA*] (EA)
**NAMD**....... National Association of Marine Dealers
**NAMD**....... National Association of Market Developers [*New York, NY*] (EA)
**NAMD**....... National Association of Membership Directors of Chambers of Commerce [*Defunct*] (EA)
**NAMD**....... Naval Ammunition Depot [*Charleston, SC*]
**NAMD**....... Newsletter of the Army Medical Department
**NAMDA**.... North American Medical/Dental Association (EA)
**NAMDB**.... National Association of Medical-Dental Bureaus [*Later, MDHBA*]
**NAMDDU** ... Naval Air Mine Defense Development Unit (MUGU)
**NAMDEX** ... Name Index
**NAMDI**..... National Marine Data Inventory
**NAMDRA** ... National American Motors Drivers and Racers Association (EA)
**NAMDT**.... National Association of Milliners, Dressmakers, and Tailors (EA)
**NAME**....... National Association of Management/Marketing Educators [*Inactive*] (EA)
**NAME**....... National Association of Media Educators (EA)
**NAME**....... National Association of Medical Examiners (EA)
**NAME**....... National Association of Miniature Enthusiasts (EA)
**NAME**....... National Association for Minority Education
**NAME**....... National Association of Minority Entrepreneurs (EA)
**NAME**....... National Association for Multiracial Education [*British*]
**NAME**....... North American Monogrammers and Embroiderers (EA)
**NAMEC**.... National Association of Marine Engineers of Canada
**NAMED**.... North African Medical Section [*World War II*]
**NAMEPA** ... National Association of Minority Engineering Program Administrators (EA)
**NAmerR**.... North American Review [*A publication*]
**NAMES**..... National Association of Medical Equipment Suppliers (EA)
**NAMESAKES** ... Naval Aviators Must Energetically Sell Aviation to Keep Effective Strength
**NAMESU** ... National Association of Music Executives in State Universities (EA)
**NAMET**.... Naval Mathematics and English Test [*British military*] (DMA)
**NAMF**....... National Association of Metal Finishers (EA)
**N Am Fauna** ... North American Fauna [*A publication*]
**NAMFAX** ... National and Aviation Meteorological Facsimile Network [*National Weather Service*]
**NAMFC**.... North Atlantic Mediterranean Freight Conference (EA)
**NAMFI**...... NATO Missile Firing Installation
**N Am Flora** ... North American Flora [*A publication*]
**N Am Flora Ser II** ... North American Flora. Series II [*A publication*]
**NAMFREL** ... National Citizens' Movement for Free Elections [*Philippines*] [*Political party*]
**NAMFSM** ... National Association of Meat and Food Seasoning Manufacturers [*Later, NSMA*] (EA)
**NAMG**....... Narrow-Angle Mars Gate [*NASA*]
**NAMG**....... National Association of Mining Groups (EA)
**NAMG**....... North American Group Ltd. [*Chicago, IL*] [*NASDAQ symbol*] (NQ)
**NAMGAR** ... North American MGA [*Morris Garage Automobile*] Register (EA)
**NAMH**...... National Association for Mental Health (EA)
**NAMHA**... North American Morab Horse Association (EA)
**NAMHH**... National Association of Methodist Hospitals and Homes
**NAMHI**..... National Association for the Mentally Handicapped of Ireland (EAIO)
**NAmi**......... Amityville Public Library, Amityville, NY [*Library symbol*] [*Library of Congress*] (LCLS)
**NAMI**........ National Alliance for the Mentally Ill (EA)
**NAMI**........ Naval Aerospace Medical Institute
**NAMIA**..... National Association of Mutual Insurance Agents [*Later, PIA*] (EA)
**Namibia N** ... Namibia News [*A publication*]
**NAMIC**..... National Association of Mutual Insurance Companies [*Indianapolis, IN*] (EA)
**NAMID**..... National Moving Image Database [*American Film Institute*] [*Information service or system*] (IID)
**NAmiGH**... Brunswick General Hospital, Amityville, NY [*Library symbol*] [*Library of Congress*] (LCLS)
**NAMILCOM** ... North Atlantic Military Committee
**NAMILPO** ... NATO Military Posture (AABC)
**NAMIM**.... National Association of Musical Instrument Mechanics (EA)
**NAMIS**...... Nitride-Barrier Avalanche Injection Missile (MCD)
**NAmiSH**.... South Oaks Hospital, Amityville, NY [*Library symbol*] [*Library of Congress*] (LCLS)

**NAMISTESTCEN** ... Naval Air Missile Test Center
**N Am J Fish Manage** ... North American Journal of Fisheries Management [*A publication*]
**NAML** ....... National Applied Mathematics Laboratory [*National Institute of Standards and Technology*] (MCD)
**NAML** ....... Naval Aircraft Materials Laboratory (MCD)
**NAML Dig** ... National Association of Manufacturers Law Digest [*A publication*] (DLA)
**NAMLM** ... National Association for Multi-Level Marketing (EA)
**NAMLNC** ... National Association of Medical Legal Nurse Consultants (EA)
**NAMM** ...... National Association of Margarine Manufacturers (EA)
**NAMM** ...... National Association of Mass Merchandisers (EA)
**NAMM** ...... National Association of Mirror Manufacturers (EA)
**NAMM** ...... National Association of Music Merchants (EA)
**NAMM** ...... North African Military Mission [*World War II*]
**NAMMA** ... NATO Multi-Role Combat Aircraft Development and Production Management Agency
**NAMMD** ... National Association of Marinas and Marine Dealers (EA)
**NAMMIS** ... Navy Aviation Maintenance and Material Support System (NG)
**NAMMM** ... National Association of Musical Merchandise Manufacturers [*Later, GAMA*] (EA)
**NAMMOS** ... Navy Manpower Mobilization System
**NAMMR** ... National Association for Milk Marketing Reform [*Later, NIDA*] (EA)
**NAMMR** ... North American Mini Moke Registry (EA)
**NAMMS** ... Navy Aviation Maintenance and Material Support System
**NAMMW** ... National Association of Musical Merchandise Wholesalers [*Later, MDA*] (EA)
**NAMNPM** ... National Association of Metal Name Plate Manufacturers
**NAMO** ...... National Agricultural Marketing Officials [*Richmond, VA*] (EA)
**NAMO** ...... National Association of Manufacturing Opticians (EA)
**NAMO** ...... National Association of Multifamily Owners
**NAMO** ...... Naval Aircraft Maintenance Orders
**NAMOA** .... National Association of Miscellaneous Ornamental and Architectural Products Contractors (EA)
**NAMOA9** ... Natura Mosana [*A publication*]
**NA Monthly** ... North Australian Monthly [*A publication*] (APTA)
**NAMORB** ... North Atlantic Mid-Ocean-Ridge Basalt [*Geology*]
**NAMOS** .... National Art Museum of Sport (EA)
**NAMP** ....... National Alliance of Mental Patients [*Later, NAPS*] (EA)
**NAMP** ....... National Association of Magazine Publishers [*Later, Magazine Publishers Association*]
**NAMP** ....... National Association of Marble Producers (EA)
**NAMP** ....... National Association of Mature People (EA)
**NAMP** ....... National Association of Meal Programs (EA)
**NAMP** ....... National Association of Meat Purveyors (EA)
**NAMP** ....... National Association of Midwifery Practitioners [*Defunct*] (EA)
**NAMP** ....... NATO Annual Manpower Plan (NATG)
**NAMP** ....... Naval Aviation Maintenance Program (MCD)
**NAMP** ....... Nonaccounting Majors Program
**NAMPA** .... NATO Maritime Patrol Aircraft Agency (NATG)
**NAMPBG** ... National Association of Manufacturers of Pressed and Blown Glassware [*Defunct*] (EA)
**NAMPI** ..... National Association of Missing Persons Investigators (EA)
**NAMPPF** .. Nautical Air Miles per Pound of Fuel (AAG)
**NAMPS** ..... National Association of Marine Products and Services (EA)
**NAMPS** ..... Navy Manpower Planning System (NVT)
**NAMPW** ... National Association of Meat Processors and Wholesalers (EA)
**N Am R** ...... North American Review [*A publication*]
**NAMRA** .... North American Mini-Champ Racing Association (EA)
**NAMRAD** ... Non-Atomic Military Research and Development [*Subcommittee*]
**NAMRC** .... North American Marten Rabbit Club (EA)
**N Am Rev** .. North American Review [*A publication*]
**NAMRI/SME** ... North American Manufacturing Research Institution of SME [*Society of Manufacturing Engineers*] (EA)
**NAMRL** .... Naval Aerospace Medical Research Laboratory
**NAMRP** .... National Apostolate with Mentally Retarded Persons (EA)
**NAMRU** .... Navy Medical Research Unit [*World War II*]
**NAms** ......... Amsterdam Free Library, Amsterdam, NY [*Library symbol*] [*Library of Congress*] (LCLS)
**NAMS** ....... NAMSCO Corp. [*NASDAQ symbol*] (NQ)
**NAMS** ....... National Ambient Air Monitoring Station [*or System*] [*Environmental Protection Agency*]
**NAMS** ....... National Association of Marine Services (EA)
**NAMS** ....... National Association of Marine Surveyors (EA)
**NAMS** ....... National Association of Municipal Securities Dealers
**NAMS** ....... North American Membrane Society (EA)
**NAMS** ....... North American Menopause Society (EA)
**NAMS** ....... Nouvelles Archives des Missions Scientifiques et Litteraires [*A publication*]
**NAMS** ....... Nurses and Army Medical Specialists
**NAMSA** .... NATO Maintenance and Supply Agency (AABC)
**NAMSA** .... North American Multihull Sailing Association (EA)
**NAMSB** ..... National Association of Men's Sportswear Buyers (EA)
**NAMSB** ..... National Association of Mutual Savings Banks (EA)
**NAMSC** .... North American Maple Syrup Council (EA)
**NAMSCO** ... National Association of MDS [*Multipoint Distribution System*] Service Companies [*Later, MDSIA*] (EA)
**NAMSDIC** ... National Arthritis and Musculoskeletal and Skin Diseases Information Clearinghouse [*Later, NAMSIC*] (EA)
**NAMSE** ..... National Association of Minority Students and Educators in Higher Education (EA)
**NAMSIC** ... National Arthritis and Musculoskeletal and Skin Diseases Information Clearinghouse (EA)
**NAmsM** ..... Mohasco Corp., Corporate Planning Library, Amsterdam, NY [*Library symbol*] [*Library of Congress*] (LCLS)
**NAMSO** .... NATO Maintenance and Supply Organization [*Formerly, NATO Maintenance Supply Service Agency*] [*Luxembourg*]
**NAMSO** .... Navy Maintenance Support Office
**NAMSOINST** ... Navy Maintenance Support Office Instruction (MCD)
**NAMSP** ..... National Association of Mail Service Pharmacies [*Later, AMCPA*] (EA)
**NAMSRC** ... National AM Stereophonic Radio Committee
**NAMSS** ..... National Association Medical Staff Services (EA)
**NAMT** ....... National Association for Music Therapy (EA)
**NAMT** ....... Naval Air Maintenance Trainer (MUGU)
**NAMT** ....... Naval Aircraft Mobile Trainer
**NAMTA** .... National Art Materials Trade Association (EA)
**NAMTAC** ... National Association of Management and Technical Assistance Centers [*Washington, DC*] (EA)
**NAMTC** .... Naval Air Missile Test Center
**NAMTD** .... Naval Air Maintenance Training Detachment
**NAMTD** .... Naval Air Maintenance Training Devices
**NAMTG** .... Naval Air Maintenance Training Group (MCD)
**NAMTM** ... Naval Air Mobile Training Maintenance
**NAMTRA** ... Naval Air Maintenance Training
**NAMTRADET** ... Naval Air Maintenance Training Detachment (MCD)
**NAMTRAGRU** ... Naval Air Maintenance Training Group (MCD)
**NAMU** ...... Naval Aircraft Material Utility
**NAMU** ...... Naval Aircraft Modification Unit
**NAMV** ....... North American Metals Corp. [*NASDAQ symbol*] (NQ)
**N Am Vet** ... North American Veterinarian [*A publication*]
**NAMW** ...... National Association of Media Women (EA)
**NAMW** ...... National Association of Military Widows (EA)
**NAMW** ...... National Association of Ministers' Wives [*Later, NAMWMW*] (EA)
**NAMWB** ... National Association of Minority Women in Business [*Kansas City, MO*] (EA)
**NAMWMW** ... National Association of Ministers' Wives and Ministers' Widows (EA)
**NAMZ** ....... Neue Allgemeine Missions-Zeitschrift [*A publication*] (BJA)
**NAN** .......... N-Acetylneuraminic Acid [*Also, AcNeu, NANA*] [*Biochemistry*]
**NAN** .......... Nachrichten fuer Dokumentation. Zeitschrift fuer Information und Dokumentation [*A publication*]
**NAN** .......... Nadi [*Fiji*] [*Airport symbol*] (OAG)
**NAN** .......... Nanking [*Republic of China*] [*Seismograph station code, US Geological Survey*] (SEIS)
**NAN** .......... Nantucket Industries, Inc. [*AMEX symbol*] (SPSG)
**NAN** .......... Nassauische Annalen [*A publication*]
**NAN** .......... National Academy of Needlearts (EA)
**NAN** .......... National Academy of Neuropsychology (EA)
**NAN** .......... National AIDS [*Acquired Immune Deficiency Syndrome*] Network (EA)
**NAN** .......... National Association of Neighborhoods (EA)
**NAN** .......... Network Application Node
**NAN** .......... Neues Archiv fuer Niedersachsen [*A publication*]
**NAN** .......... Nisi Aliter Notetur [*Unless Otherwise Noted*] [*Latin*]
**Nan** ............ Nitrosamine [*Biochemistry*]
**NAN** .......... No Action Necessary [*Military*] (CINC)
**NAN** .......... North American Nippon Technologies Corp. [*Vancouver Stock Exchange symbol*]
**NAN** .......... North Atlantic Network (EA)
**NaN** ........... Not a Number [*Computer programming*] (BYTE)
**NANA** ........ N-Acetylneuraminic Acid [*Also, AcNeu, NAN*] [*Biochemistry*]
**NANA** ........ National Advertising Newspaper Association [*Later, SNA*] (EA)
**NANA** ........ National Association of Nail Artists [*Later, NANAA*] (EA)
**NANA** ........ North American Newspaper Alliance
**NANA** ........ North American Normande Association (EA)
**NANA** ........ Northwest Alaska Native Association [*Later, MA*]
**NANAA** ..... National Aesthetician and Nail Artist Association [*Formerly, NANA*] [*Absorbed by WINBA*] (EA)
**NANAC** ..... National Aircraft Noise Abatement Council [*Defunct*] (EA)
**NANASP** ... National Association of Nutrition and Aging Services Programs (EA)
**NAnB** ......... Bard College, Annandale-On-Hudson, NY [*Library symbol*] [*Library of Congress*] (LCLS)
**NANB** ........ Non-A, Non-B [*Virology*]
**NANBA** ..... North American National Broadcasters Association (EA)
**NANBH** .... Non-A, Non-B Hepatitis [*Medicine*]
**NANBPWC** ... National Association of Negro Business and Professional Women's Clubs [*Washington, DC*] (EA)
**NANBV** ..... Non-A, Non-B Hepatic Virus
**NANC** ........ National Association of New Careerists (EA)

**NANCB**..... National Association of Negotiated Commissioned Brokers [*Inactive*] (EA)
**NANCF**..... North Atlantic Naval Coastal Frontier
**NANCI**...... New Aeronautical and Nautical Chart Investigations (NOAA)
**NANCO**...... National Association of Noise Control Officials (EA)
**NANCRFUG**... North American NCR [*National Cash Register Co.*] Financial Users Group (EA)
**NAND**....... Naval Ammunition and Net Depot
**NAND**....... Not And [*Logical operator*] [*Data processing*]
**NANDA**..... North American Nursing Diagnosis Association (EA)
**NANE**........ National Association for Nursery Education [*Later, NAEYC*] (EA)
**NANEAP**.. North Africa, Near East, Asia, and Pacific Region [*Program of ACTION, an independent government agency*]
**NANED**..... Neuropathology and Applied Neurobiology [*A publication*]
**NANEP**..... Navy Air Navigation Electronic Project
**NANEWS**... Naval Aviation News
**NANFA**..... North American Native Fishes Association (EA)
**NANFAC**.. Naval Air Navigation Facility Advisory Committee
**NAng**.......... Angelica Free Library, Angelica, NY [*Library symbol*] [*Library of Congress*] (LCLS)
**NANHC**.... National Association of Neighborhood Health Centers [*Later, NACHC*] (EA)
**NANI**......... National Academy of Nannies, Incorporated (EA)
**Nankai Univ Res Lab Appl Chem Rep**... Nankai University. Research Laboratory of Applied Chemistry. Reports [*A publication*]
**NA/NLP**.... National Association of Neuro-Linguistic Programming (EA)
**NANM**...... N-Allylnormetazocine [*Biochemistry*]
**NANM**...... N-Allylnormorphine [*Narcotic antagonist*]
**NANM**...... National Association of Negro Musicians (EA)
**NANNP**..... Nordic Association of Non-Commercial Phonogram Producers (EA)
**N Ann Sc Nat (Bologna)**... Nuovi Annali delle Scienze Naturali (Bologna) [*A publication*]
**NANO**....... Nanometrics, Inc. [*Sunnyvale, CA*] [*NASDAQ symbol*] (NQ)
**NANOVA**... Nonorthogonal Analysis of Variance (ADA)
**NANP**........ National Association of Naturopathic Physicians (EA)
**NANPE**..... National Association of Newspaper Purchasing Executives [*Later, NPMA*] (EA)
**NANPMA**... North American Nutrition and Preventive Medicine Association (EA)
**NANR**........ National Association of Nurse Recruiters [*Later, NAHCR*] (EA)
**NANS**........ National Association for Neighborhood Schools (EA)
**NANS**........ National Catholic News Service (EA)
**NANS**........ Naval Air Navigation School
**NANS**........ North American Nietzsche Society (EA)
**NANS**........ North Atlantic and Neighboring Seas (NOAA)
**Nansei Reg Fish Res Lab Bull**... Nansei Regional Fisheries Research Laboratory. Bulletin [*Japan*] [*A publication*]
**NAnt**.......... Nuova Antologia di Scienze, Lettere, ed Arti [*A publication*]
**Nanta Math**... Nanta Mathematica [*A publication*]
**NANTDDDC**... National Association of Negro Tailors, Designers, Dressmakers, and Dry Cleaners (EA)
**NANTIS News Bull**... Nottingham and Nottinghamshire Technical Information Service. News Bulletin [*A publication*]
**NANTS**..... National Association of Naval Technical Supervisors (EA)
**NANU**....... National Association of NIDS [*National Investor Data Service*] Users (EA)
**NANWEP**... Navy Numerical Weather Prediction [*Computer system*] [*Control Data Corp.*]
**NANWEP**... Navy Numerical Weather Problems [*Group*]
**NANWR**.... North American Network of Women Runners (EA)
**Nanyang Univ J Part III**... Nanyang University. Journal. Part III. Natural Sciences [*A publication*]
**NAO**.......... Charleston, SC [*Location identifier*] [*FAA*] (FAAL)
**NAO**.......... National Academy of Opticianry (EA)
**NAO**.......... National Audit Office [*British*] (ECON)
**NAO**.......... Naval Aviation Observer [*Obsolete*]
**NAO**.......... Norsar Array Site 01A00 [*Norway*] [*Seismograph station code, US Geological Survey*] (SEIS)
**NAO**.......... Nurse Aide/Orderly (OICC)
**NAOA**........ National Apartment Owners Association [*Later, NAA*] (EA)
**NAOA**........ National Association of Older Americans [*Later, Heartline/ National Association of Older Americans*] (EA)
**NAOB**........ Naval Aviation Observer Bombardier (MUGU)
**NAOBMISB**... National Association of Operative Boiler Makers and Iron Ship Builders [*A union*] [*British*]
**NAOC**........ National Antique Oldsmobile Club (EA)
**NAOC**........ Naval Aviation Observer Controller (MUGU)
**NAOC**........ Naval Aviation Officer Candidate
**NAOCJ**..... National Association of Operative Carpenters and Joiners [*A union*] [*British*]
**NAOE**........ National Association for Outdoor Education [*British*]
**NAOEJ**...... National Association of Oil Equipment Jobbers [*Later, PEI*] (EA)
**NAOGE**..... National Association of Government Engineers [*Defunct*] (EA)
**NAOGTC**.. North American Opel GT [*Gran Turismo*] Club (EA)
**NAOHSM**... National Association of Oil Heating Service Managers (EA)
**NAOI**........ Naval Aviation Observer Intercept (MUGU)
**NAOIG**...... North African Inspector General's Section [*World War II*]
**Na Okika O Hawaii Hawaii Orchid J**... Na Okika O Hawaii/Hawaii Orchid Journal [*A publication*]
**NAOL**......... National Association of Orchestra Leaders (EA)
**NAON**........ National Association of Orthopaedic Nurses (EA)
**NAON**........ Naval Aviation Observer Navigator (MUGU)
**NAOO**........ National Association of Optometrists and Opticians (EA)
**NAOODA**... North American Offshore One-Design Association (EA)
**NAOP**........ National Alliance for Optional Parenthood [*Formerly, NON*]
**NAOP**........ National Association for Olmsted Parks (EA)
**NAOP**........ National Association of Operative Plasterers
**NAOP**........ National Association of Operative Plumbers [*A union*] [*British*]
**NAOP**........ Nonadditive Operational Project [*Military*]
**NAOPL**..... National Association of Operative Plasterers' Labourers [*A union*] [*British*]
**NAOR**........ Natural Organics Corp. [*Los Angeles, CA*] [*NASDAQ symbol*] (NQ)
**NAOR**........ Naval Aviation Observer RADAR (MUGU)
**NAORD**..... North African Ordnance Section [*World War II*]
**NAORPB**.. North Atlantic Ocean Regional Planning Board [*NATO*] (NATG)
**NAORPG**.. North Atlantic Ocean Regional Planning Group [*NATO*] (NATG)
**NAORTS**... Naval Aviation Ordnance Test Station
**NAOS**........ NASA Aircrew Oxygen System
**NAOS**........ North Atlantic Ocean Station [*WMO*]
**NAOSMM**... National Association of Scientific Material Managers (EA)
**NAOSP**..... North Atlantic Ocean Stations Program (MUGU)
**NAOSW**.... National Association of Oncology Social Workers (EA)
**NAOT**........ National Association of Organ Teachers [*Later, IAOT*]
**NAOT**........ National Association of Orthopaedic Technologists (EA)
**NAOT**........ Naval Air Operational Training
**NAOTB**..... National Association of Off-Track Betting (EA)
**NAOTC**..... National Association of OTC [*Over-the-Counter*] Companies [*Later, APTC*] (EA)
**NAOTC**..... National Association of Timetable Collectors (EA)
**NAOTC**..... Naval Air Operational Training Command
**NAOTS**..... Naval Aviation Ordnance Test Station
**NAOWES**... National Association of Older Worker Employment Services [*Washington, DC*] (EA)
**NAP**........... Armed Proletarian Nuclei [*Italy*]
**NAP**........... Bangladesh National Awami Party [*Political party*] (PPW)
**NAP**........... Napa Resources, Inc. [*Vancouver Stock Exchange symbol*]
**NAP**........... Napay [*USSR*] [*Seismograph station code, US Geological Survey*] [*Closed*] (SEIS)
**NAP**........... Napier Air Service, Inc. [*Dothan, AL*] [*FAA designator*] (FAAC)
**NAP**........... Naples [*Italy*] [*Airport symbol*] (OAG)
**NAP**........... Napoleon [*or Napoleonic*]
**NAP**........... Napoleonic Age Philatelists (EA)
**NAP**........... [*The*] Narragansett Pier Railroad Co., Inc. [*AAR code*]
**NAP**........... National Action Party [*Turkey*] [*Political party*] (PD)
**NAP**........... National Advertising Program
**NAP**........... National Appeals Panel [*Australia*]
**NAP**........... National Apprenticeship Program [*Bureau of Apprenticeship and Training*] [*Department of Labor*]
**NAP**........... National Archives Publication
**NAP**........... National Association of Parliamentarians (EA)
**NAP**........... National Association of Planners [*Defunct*] (EA)
**NAP**........... National Association of Postmasters of the United States
**NAP**........... National Association of the Professions (EA)
**NAP**........... National Association of Publishers [*Defunct*] (EA)
**NAP**........... National Awami Party [*Pakistan*] [*Political party*] (PD)
**NAP**........... National Awami Party-Bashani [*Political party*] [*Bangladesh*] (FEA)
**NAP**........... Nationalist Action Party [*Political party*]
**NAP**........... Native American Program (OICC)
**NAP**........... Naval Air Plan (CAAL)
**NAP**........... Naval Air Priorities
**NAP**........... Naval Auxiliary Patrol [*British military*] (DMA)
**NAP**........... Naval Aviation Pilot
**NAP**........... Naval Aviation Plan (NVT)
**NAP**........... Navigation Analysis Program [*NASA*] (NASA)
**NAP**........... Neighborhood Action Program [*New York City*] (EA)
**NAP**........... Network Access Pricing [*Telecommunications*] (TEL)
**NAP**........... Network Access Protocol
**NAP**........... Neutrophil Activating Protein
**NAP**........... Neutrophil Alkaline Phosphatase [*An enzyme*]
**NAP**........... New Associations and Projects [*Formerly, NA*] [*A publication*]
**NAP**........... Night Attack Program [*Military*]
**NAP**........... Noise Abatement Procedure (AAG)
**NAP**........... Noise Analysis Program
**NAP**........... Nomina Anatomica Parisiensia [*Medicine*]
**NAP**........... Nonacquisition Project [*Military*] (CAAL)
**NAP**........... Nonagency Purchase
**NAP**........... Nonaggression Pact
**NAP**........... Nonnuclear Armament Plan (MCD)
**NAP**........... Normalized Abundance Pattern [*Geochemistry*]
**NAP**........... Not A Priori
**NAP**........... Not at Present
**NAP**........... Nuclear-Active Particles [*Astrophysics*]
**NAP**........... Nuclear Auxiliary Power

**NAP** .......... Nuclei Armati Proletari [*Armed Proletarian Nuclei*] [*Italian*] (PD)
**NAP** .......... Nucleic Acid Phosphorus [*Biochemistry*]
**NAP** .......... Nucleoacidic Protein [*Cytochemistry*]
**NAPA** ........ N-Acetyl-p-aminophenol [*Organic chemistry*]
**NAPA** ........ N-Acetylprocainamide [*Cardiac depressant*]
**NAPA** ........ National Academy of Public Administration (EA)
**NAPA** ........ National Agricultural Plastics Association [*Later, ASP*] (EA)
**NAPA** ........ National Agricultural Press Association (EA)
**NAPA** ........ National Amateur Press Association (EA)
**NAPA** ........ National Asphalt Pavement Association (EA)
**NAPA** ........ National Association of the Partners of the Alliance [*Later, Partners of the Americas*] (EA)
**NAPA** ........ National Association of Performing Artists
**NAPA** ........ National Association of Polish Americans
**NAPA** ........ National Association for the Practice of Anthropology (EA)
**NAPA** ........ National Association of Pro America (EA)
**NAPA** ........ National Association of Purchasing Agents [*Later, NAPM*] (EA)
**NAPA** ........ National Automotive Parts Association (EA)
**NAPA** ........ National Police Officers Association of America
**NAPA** ........ Native American Press Association (EA)
**NAPA** ........ Network Against Psychiatric Assault (EA)
**NAPA** ........ North American Photonics Association (EA)
**NAPA** ........ North American Pizza Association [*Defunct*]
**NAPA** ........ North Atlantic Ports Association (EA)
**NAPAC** ..... National Arson Prevention and Action Coalition (EA)
**NAPAC** ..... National Association of Paper and Advertising Collectors (EA)
**NAPAC** ..... National Association for Professional Associations and Corporations (EA)
**NAPAC** ..... National Program for Acquisitions and Cataloging [*Library of Congress*]
**NAPAEO** .. National Association of Principal Agricultural Education Officers [*British*]
**NAPAF** ...... National Association of Private Art Foundations (EA)
**NAPALM** ... Naphthenic and Palmitic Acids [*Major constituents of flame thrower*]
**NAPALM** ... National ADP [*Automatic Data Processing*] Program for AMC [*Army Materiel Command*] Logistics Management
**NAPALSA** ... National Asian Pacific American Law Student Association (EA)
**NAPAMA** ... National Association of Performing Arts Managers and Agents (EA)
**NAPAMS** ... Navy Automated Pilot Aptitude Measurement System
**NAPAN** ..... National Association for the Prevention of Addiction to Narcotics [*Later, NADAP*]
**NAPAP** ...... National Acid Precipitation Assessment Program [*Council on Environmental Quality*] [*Washington, DC*]
**NAPAP** ...... Noyaux Armes pour l'Autonomie Populaire [*Armed Cells for Popular Autonomy*] [*France*] (PD)
**NAPARE** ... National Association for Perinatal Addiction Research and Education (EA)
**NAPAS** ...... National Association of Protection and Advocacy Systems (EA)
**NAPATMO** ... NATO Patriot Management Office
**NAPAVHEE** ... National Association of Postsecondary and Adult Vocational Home Economics Educators (EA)
**NAPB** ........ National Association of Professional Bureaucrats [*Later, INATAPROBU*]
**NAPBC** ...... Native American Public Broadcasting Consortium (EA)
**NAPBFC** ... National Association of Pat Boone Fan Clubs (EA)
**NAPBIRT** ... National Association of Professional Band Instrument Repair Technicians (EA)
**NAPBL** ...... National Association of Professional Baseball Leagues (EA)
**NAPBTA** ... National American Pit Bull Terrier Association (EA)
**NAPC** ........ National Air Pollution Control (KSC)
**NAPC** ........ National Alliance of Preservation Commissions (EA)
**NAPC** ........ National Assault Prevention Center (EA)
**NAPC** ........ National Association of Pastoral Counselors (EA)
**NAPC** ........ National Association of Personnel Consultants [*Defunct*] (EA)
**NAPC** ........ National Association of Pet Cemeteries [*Later, IAPC*]
**NAPC** ........ National Association of Plumbing Contractors [*Later, NAPHCC*]
**NAPC** ........ National Association of Precancel Collectors (EA)
**NAPC** ........ Naval Air Propulsion Center [*Trenton, NJ*]
**NAPCA** ..... National Air Pollution Control Administration [*Obsolete*]
**NAPCA** ..... National Association of Pension Consultants and Administrators [*Atlanta, GA*] (EA)
**NAPCA** ..... National Association of Pipe Coating Applicators (EA)
**NAPCA** ..... National Association of Professional Contracts Administrators [*Later, NCMA*] (EA)
**NAPCA** ..... National Automatic Pistol Collectors Association (EA)
**NAPCA** ..... North American Poultry Cooperative Association (EA)
**NAPCAE** ... National Association for Public Continuing and Adult Education (EA)
**NAPCAN** .. National Association for the Prevention of Child Abuse and Neglect [*Australia*]
**NAPCE** ...... National Association of Professors of Christian Education (EA)
**NAPCMM-ELCA** ... Native American Program Commission for Multicultural Ministries of ELCA [*Evangelical Lutheran Church in America*] (EA)
**NAPCOR** .. National Association for Plastic Container Recovery (EA)
**NAPCR** ...... National Association for Puerto Rican Civil Rights
**NAPCRG** ... North American Primary Care Research Group (EA)
**NAPCRO** .. National Association of Police Community Relations Officers (EA)
**NAPCU** ..... Northwest Association of Private Colleges and Universities [*Library network*] (EA)
**NAPCWA** ... National Association of Public Child Welfare Administrators (EA)
**NAPD** ........ National Association of Plastics Distributors (EA)
**NAPD** ........ National Association of Precollege Directors (EA)
**NAPDA** ..... North American Professional Driver's Association (EA)
**NAPDEA** ... North American Professional Driver Education Association (EA)
**NAPE** ........ National Alliance of Postal Employees [*Later, NAPFE*]
**NAPE** ........ National Association of Port Employers [*British*]
**NAPE** ........ National Association of Power Engineers (EA)
**NAPE** ........ National Association of Private Enterprise [*Fort Worth, TX*] (EA)
**NAPE** ........ National Association of Professional Educators (EA)
**NAPE** ........ National Association of Professional Engravers (EA)
**NAPE** ........ National Properties Corp. [*NASDAQ symbol*] (NQ)
**NAPE** ........ Nuclear Attack Preparedness Evaluation
**NAPEC** ...... Naval Ammunition Production Engineering Center
**NAPECW** ... National Association for Physical Education of College Women [*Later, NAPEHE*] (EA)
**NAPEDNC** ... National Association of Political Ex-Deportees of the Nazi Camps [*Italy*] [*Political party*] (EAIO)
**NAPEHE** .. National Association for Physical Education in Higher Education (EA)
**NAPEM** .... National Association of Public Exposition Managers [*Later, HGSEI*] (EA)
**NAPENA** .. National Association of Public Employer Negotiators and Administrators [*Later, NAPPENA*] (EA)
**NAPEP** ...... National Association of Planners, Estimators, and Progressmen (EA)
**NAPET** ...... National Association of Photo Equipment Technicians (EA)
**NAPEX** ...... National Philatelic Exhibition
**NAPF** ......... National Association of Petroleum Funds [*British*]
**NAPF** ......... National Association of Plastic Fabricators (EA)
**NAPF** ......... Naval Aviation Publication Facility
**NAPF** ......... Nuclear Age Peace Foundation (EA)
**NAPFA** ...... National Association of Personal Financial Advisors (EA)
**NAPFE** ...... National Alliance of Postal and Federal Employees (EA)
**NAPFM** ..... National Association of Packaged Fuel Manufacturers [*Defunct*] (EA)
**NAPFR** ...... National Association of Professional Fund Raisers (EA)
**NAPG** ........ National Association of Professional Gardeners [*Later, PGMS*]
**NAP(G)** ..... Naval Aviation Pilot (Glider)
**NAPGCW** ... National Association of Plasters, Granolithic, and Cement Workers [*A union*] [*British*]
**NAPH** ........ Naphtha (ADA)
**NAPH** ........ National Association of the Physically Handicapped (EA)
**NAPH** ........ National Association of Professors of Hebrew (EA)
**NAPH** ........ National Association of Public Hospitals (EA)
**NAPHA** ..... National Amusement Park Historical Association (EA)
**NAPhA** ...... North American Photonics Association (EA)
**NAPHCC** .. National Association of Plumbing-Heating-Cooling Contractors [*Formerly, NAPC*] (EA)
**NAPHT** ..... National Association of Patients on Hemodialysis and Transplantation [*Later, AAKP*] (EA)
**NAPI** ......... National Appaloosa Pony (EA)
**NAPI** ......... National Association of the Pet Industry [*Inactive*] (EA)
**NAPIA** ....... National Association of Public Insurance Adjusters [*Baltimore, MD*] (EA)
**NAPIAP** .... National Agricultural Pesticide Impact Assessment Program [*Department of Agriculture*]
**NAPIC** ....... National Association of Private Industry Councils [*Washington, DC*] (EA)
**NAPIL** ....... National Association for Public Interest Law (EA)
**NAPIM** ..... National Association of Printing Ink Manufacturers (EA)
**NAPL** ........ National Association of Police Laboratories (EA)
**NAPL** ........ National Association of Printers and Lithographers (EA)
**NAPL** ........ Nonaqueous Phase Liquid [*Chemistry*]
**Naples Sta Zool Pubbl** ... Naples. Stazione Zoologica. Pubblicazioni [*A publication*]
**NAP-LP** ..... National Association of Para-Legals Personnel (EA)
**NAPLPS** .... North American Presentation Level Protocol Syntax [*Computer display system*] [*Pronounced "naplips"*]
**NAPM** ....... National Academy of Popular Music (EA)
**NAPM** ....... National Association of Paper Merchants [*British*]
**NAPM** ....... National Association of Pattern Manufacturers [*LA PPTBA*] (EA)
**NAPM** ....... National Association of Pharmaceutical Manufacturers (EA)
**NAPM** ....... National Association of Photographic Manufacturers (EA)
**NAPM** ....... National Association of Punch Manufacturers (EA)
**NAPM** ....... National Association of Purchasing Management (EA)
**NAP-M** ...... National Awami Party-Muzaffar [*Political party*] [*Bangladesh*] (FEA)
**NAPMA** .... NATO AEWC [*Airborne Early Warning and Control*] Program Management Agency

**NAPMDAC** ... National Air Pollution Manpower Development Advisory Committee [*HEW*] [*Terminated, 1976*] (EGAO)
**NAPMG**.... North African Provost Marshal General [*World War II*]
**NAPMM**... National Association of Produce Market Managers [*Hartford, CT*] (EA)
**NAPMO**.... NATO Airborne Early Warning and Control Programme Management Organization [*Brunssum, Netherlands*]
**NAPN**........ National Association of Physician Nurses (EA)
**NAPN**........ Native American Policy Network (EA)
**NAPN**........ Native Authority Public Notice [*Nigeria*] [*A publication*] (ILCA)
**NAPN**........ North American Poetry Network (EA)
**NAPNAP**... National Association of Pediatric Nurse Associates and Practitioners (EA)
**NAPNES**... National Association for Practical Nurse Education and Service (EA)
**NAPNM**.... National Association of Pipe Nipple Manufacturers (EA)
**Nap Nobil**.. Napoli Nobilissima [*A publication*]
**NAPNOC**.. Neighborhood Arts Program National Organizing Committee (EA)
**NAPNSC**... National Association of Private, Nontraditional Schools and Colleges (EA)
**NAPNW**.... Nurses Alliance for the Prevention of Nuclear War (EA)
**NAPO**........ NASA Pasadena Office
**NAPO**........ National Association of Pizza Operators [*Commercial firm*] (EA)
**NAPO**........ National Association of Police Organizations (EA)
**NAPO**........ National Association of Pool Owners
**NAPO**........ National Association of Professional Organizers (EA)
**NAPO**........ National Association of Property Owners (EA)
**NAPO**........ NATO Airborne Early Warning Program Office (NATG)
**NAPO**........ Naval Air Priorities Office
**NAPO**........ New Afrikan People's Organization (EA)
**NAPO**........ United National Association of Post Office Craftsmen [*Later, APWU*]
**NAPOCOR** ... National Power Corporation [*Philippines*] (DS)
**NAPOG**..... Naval Airborne Project Press Operations Group [*Hickam AFB, HI*]
**NAPOLI**.... National Politics [*Behavioral science game*]
**NAPOMHWMGL** ... National Association of Post Office Mail Handlers, Watchmen, Messengers, and Group Leaders [*Later, NPOMHWMGL*] (EA)
**NAPP**........ National Association of Play Publishers
**NAPP**........ National Association of Priest Pilots (EA)
**NAPP**........ National Association of Printing Purchasers [*Defunct*] (EA)
**NAPP**........ National Association of Private Process Servers (EA)
**NAPP**........ Native American Publishing Program [*of Harper & Row, Publishers, Inc.*]
**NAPP**........ Naval Aviation Preparatory Program
**NAPP**........ Neighborhood Adult Participation Project
**NAPP**........ Net Aerial Primary Productivity [*Forestry*]
**NAPPA**...... National Association of Physical Plant Administrators of Universities and Colleges [*Later, Association of Physical Plant Administrators of Universities and Colleges*] (EA)
**NAPPA**...... National Association of Pupil Personnel Administrators [*Later, NAPSA*] (EA)
**NAPPB**...... National Association of Professional Print Buyers (EA)
**NAPPC**...... National Association of Party Plan Companies [*Defunct*] (EA)
**NAPPENA** ... National Association of Public and Private Employer Negotiators and Administrators (EA)
**NAPPF**...... North American Power Petroleums, Inc. [*NASDAQ symbol*] (NQ)
**NAPPH**..... National Association of Private Psychiatric Hospitals (EA)
**Nappie**....... Neuilly, Auteil, and Passy [*Elegant Paris neighborhoods; the term, Nappie, is used as a nickname for French Yuppies*]
**Nappies**...... New Age Professional People in Esoteric Studies [*Lifestyle classification*]
**NAPPO**..... National Association of Plant Patent Owners (EA)
**Nap Pres**.... Napier. Prescription [*A publication*] (ILCA)
**NAPPS**...... National Association for the Preservation and Perpetuation of Storytelling (EA)
**NAPPS**...... National Association of Private Placement Syndicators [*Later, California Investment Real Estate Forum*] (EA)
**NAPPS**...... National Association of Professional Process Servers (EA)
**NAPR**........ NASA Procurement Regulation
**NAPR**........ National Association of Park Rangers (EA)
**NAPR**........ National Association for Pastoral Renewal [*Defunct*] (EA)
**NAPR**........ National Association of Physician Recruiters (EA)
**NAPR**........ National Association of Publishers' Representatives (EA)
**NAPR**........ NATO Armaments Planning Review (NATG)
**NAPRA**..... National Association of Progressive Radio Announcers (EA)
**NAPRA**..... New Age Publishing and Retailing Alliance (EA)
**NAPRALERT** ... Natural Products Alert [*University of Illinois at Chicago*] [*Information service or system*] (IID)
**NAPRCR**... National Association for Puerto Rican Civil Rights (EA)
**NAPRE**..... National Association Practical Refrigerating Engineers [*Later, RETA*] (EA)
**Napred Pcel** ... Napredno Pcelarstvo [*A publication*]
**NAPRFMR** ... National Association of Private Residential Facilities for the Mentally Retarded (EA)
**NAPRW**.... Northwest African Photographic Reconnaissance Wing [*World War II*]
**NAPS**......... National Association of Pet Sitters (EA)
**NAPS**......... National Association of Postal Supervisors (EA)
**NAPS**......... National Association for Professional Saleswomen (EA)
**NAPS**......... National Association of Psychiatric Survivors (EA)
**NAPS**......... National Auxiliary Publications Service [*American Society for Information Science*]
**NAPS**......... Naval Academy Preparatory School
**NAPS**......... Night Aerial Photographic System
**NAPS**......... Nimbus Automatic Programming System (IEEE)
**NAPS**......... Nonspecific Air Pollution Syndrome
**NAPS**......... North American Patristic Society (EA)
**NAPS**......... North American Precis Syndicate
**NAPS**......... North Anna Power Station [*Virginia*] [*Nuclear energy*] (NRCH)
**NAPS**......... Northern Australian Photo Survey
**NAPSA**...... National Appliance Parts Suppliers Association (EA)
**NAPSA**...... National Association of Pupil Services Administrators (EA)
**NAPSAA**... National Association of Public School Adult Administrators [*Later, NAPSAE*]
**NAPSAC**... International Association of Parents and Professionals for Safe Alternatives in Childbirth [*Association retains acronym of its former name*] (EA)
**NAPSAC**... Naval Atomic Planning, Support, and Capabilities Report (NG)
**NAPSAE**... National Association for Public School Adult Educators [*Later, NAPCAE*] (EA)
**NAPSAP**... Naval Airship Program for Sizing and Performance (MCD)
**NAPSEC**... National Association of Private Schools for Exceptional Children (EA)
**NAPSG**...... National Association of Principals of Schools for Girls (EA)
**NAPSIC**.... North American Power Systems Interconnection Committee [*US and Canada*] [*Electric power*]
**NAPSIS**..... Navy Air Pollution Source Information System
**NAPSLO**... National Association of Professional Surplus Lines Offices (EA)
**NAPSOE**... National Association of Public Service Organization Executives (EA)
**NAPSS**...... National Association of Professional Secretarial Services [*Later, PASS*] (EA)
**NAPSS**...... Numerical Analysis Problem Solving System
**NAPSV**...... National Association of Private Security Vaults (EA)
**Napt**.......... Napton's Reports [*4 Missouri*] [*A publication*] (DLA)
**NAPT**........ National Action on Public Transport [*Australia*]
**NAPT**........ National Association of Physical Therapists (EA)
**NAPT**........ National Association for Poetry Therapy (EA)
**NAPT**........ National Association for Pupil Transportation (EA)
**NAPT**........ Naval Air Primary Training
**NAPT**........ Nordic Association of Plumbers and Tinsmiths (EAIO)
**NAPTC**...... Naval Air Primary Training Command
**NAPTC**...... Naval Air Propulsion Test Center [*Later, NAPC*]
**NAPTCA**... National Alliance for the Prevention and Treatment of Child Abuse (EA)
**NAPTC-AED** ... Naval Air Propulsion Test Center - Aeronautical Engine Department
**NAPTC-ATD** ... Naval Air Propulsion Test Center - Aeronautical Turbine Department
**NAPTCC**... National Association of Psychiatric Treatment Centers for Children (EA)
**NAPTC-OP** ... Naval Air Propulsion Test Center - Operations and Plant Engineering Department
**NAPTC-PE** ... Naval Air Propulsion Test Center - Propulsion Technology and Project Engineering Department
**NAPTCRO** ... Naval Air Primary Training Command Regional Office
**NAPTDC**... National Association of Professional Truck Driving Champions (EA)
**NAPTIC**.... National Air Pollution Technical Information Center [*of National Air Pollution Control Administration*] [*Also, APTIC*] (DIT)
**NAPT J**..... NAPT [*National Association of Physical Therapists*] Journal [*A publication*]
**Napton**....... Napton's Reports [*4 Missouri*] [*A publication*] (DLA)
**NAPTR**...... National Association of Property Tax Representatives [*Defunct*] (EA)
**NAPTS**...... National Association of Public Television Stations [*Later, APB*] (EA)
**NAPU**........ National Association of Professional Upholsterers (EA)
**NAPU**........ Nuclear Auxiliary Power Unit
**NAPUBFAC** ... Naval Air Publication Facility (MCD)
**NAPUS**...... National Association of Postmasters of the United States (EA)
**NAPUS**...... Nuclear Auxiliary Power Unit System
**NAPVI**....... National Association for Parents of the Visually Impaired (EA)
**NAPVO**..... National Association of Passenger Vessel Owners (EA)
**NAPW**....... National Association of Personnel Workers (EA)
**NAPWA**.... National Association of People with AIDS [*Acquired Immune Deficiency Syndrome*] (EA)
**NAPWDA** ... North American Police Work Dog Association (EA)
**NAPWPT** ... National Association of Professional Word Processing Technicians [*Philadelphia, PA*] (EA)
**NAQ**.......... Narssarssuaq [*Denmark*] [*Geomagnetic observatory code*]

**NAQAP**..... National Association of Quality Assurance Professionals (EA)
**NAQF**........ North Atlantic Quality Figure
**N de Aqi**..... Nicholas de Aquila [*Flourished, 1197-1217*] [*Authority cited in pre-1607 legal work*] (DSA)
**NAQMC**.... North African Quartermaster Section [*World War II*]
**NAQP**........ National Association of Quick Printers (EA)
**NAQUADAT** ... National Water Quality Data Bank [*Environment Canada*] [*Information service or system*] (IID)
**NAR**.......... Air Continental, Inc. [*Elyria, OH*] [*FAA designator*] (FAAC)
**NAR**.......... Nagase Analbuminemia Rat
**NAR**.......... Nara [*Japan*] [*Seismograph station code, US Geological Survey*] (SEIS)
**NAR**.......... Narcotic (ROG)
**NAR**.......... Nare [*Colombia*] [*Airport symbol*] (OAG)
**NAR**.......... Narration [*Films, television, etc.*]
**NAR**.......... Narrow (AAG)
**NaR**.......... Nasa Rec [*Paris*] [*A publication*]
**NAR**.......... Nasal Airway Resistance [*Medicine*]
**NAR**.......... National Archives and Records Service, Washington, DC [*OCLC symbol*] (OCLC)
**NAR**.......... National Association of Realtors (EA)
**NAR**.......... National Association of Rocketry (EA)
**NAR**.......... Naval Air Reserve
**NAR**.......... Naval Auxiliary Reserve
**NAR**.......... Naval Research and Development
**NAR**.......... Navy Ammunition Reclassification
**NAR**.......... Net Advertising Revenue [*Television*] [*British*]
**NAR**.......... Net Assimilation Rate [*Botany*]
**NAR**.......... New American Review [*Later, American Review*] [*A publication*]
**NAR**.......... No Action [*or Answer*] Required (NVT)
**NAR**.......... Noise-Adding Radiometer
**NAR**.......... Nordic Association for Rehabilitation (EAIO)
**NAR**.......... Nordiska Akademiker Radet [*Nordic Academic Council - NAC*] (EA)
**NAR**.......... North American Review [*A publication*]
**NAR**.......... North American Rockwell Corp. [*Later, Rockwell International Corp.*] (MCD)
**NAR**.......... North American Route [*Aviation*]
**NAR**.......... North Australia Railway
**NAR**.......... Northern Alberta Railways Co. [*AAR code*]
**NAR**.......... Nose Alone Reference [*Aviation*] (MCD)
**NAR**.......... Not According to Routine
**NAR**.......... Notice of Ammunition Reclassification [*Navy*] (NG)
**NAR**.......... Nuclear Acoustic Resonance
**NAR**.......... Nuclear Androgen Receptor [*Endocrinology*]
**NAR**.......... Nuclear Assessment Routine (MCD)
**NAR**.......... Nuclei Armati Rivoluzionari [*Armed Revolutionary Nuclei*] [*Italian*] (PD)
**NAR**.......... Numerical Analysis Research (MCD)
**NAr**.......... Nuovi Argomenti [*A publication*]
**NAR**.......... Nutrition Abstracts and Reviews [*Information service or system*] [*A publication*]
**NARA**........ Narcotics Addict Rehabilitation Act [*1966*]
**NARA**........ National Alliance for Rural Action (EA)
**NARA**........ National Archives and Records Administration [*Independent government agency*] [*Formerly, NARS*]
**NARA**........ National Association of Recovered Alcoholics (EA)
**NARA**........ National Association of Rehabilitation Agencies (EA)
**NARA**........ National Association of Republican Attorneys (EA)
**NARA**........ National Association of Review Appraisers (EA)
**NARA**........ Naval Aircraft Restorers Association (EA)
**NARA**........ North American Radio Archives (EA)
**NARA**........ North American Radon Association (EA)
**NARA**........ North American Regional Alliance of IATA [*International Amateur Theatre Association*] (EA)
**NARAA**..... National Association of Recruitment Advertising Agencies [*Defunct*] (EA)
**NARAD**..... Naval Air Research and Development (MUGU)
**NARADCOM** ... Natick Research and Development Command [*Army*]
**NARAL**..... National Abortion Rights Action League (EA)
**NARAL**..... Net Advertising Revenue after Levy [*Television*] [*British*]
**NARA/MU** ... National Association of Review Appraisers and Mortgage Underwriters (EA)
**NARANEXOS** ... Name, Rate, Service Number, and Expiration of Obligated Service [*Navy*]
**NARANO** ... Name, Rate, and Service Number [*Navy*]
**NARAS**...... National Academy of Recording Arts and Sciences (EA)
**NARASO** .. Nevada Association Race and Sports Book Operators (EA)
**NARASPO** ... Navy Regional Airspace Officer (MUGU)
**NARAT**..... NATO Request for Air Transport Support [*Military*]
**NARATE**... Navy Automatic RADAR Test Equipment (KSC)
**NARAVA** .. National Archives and Records Administration Volunteer Association (EA)
**NARB**........ Narcotic Addict Rehabilitation Branch [*National Institute of Mental Health*]
**NARB**........ National Advertising Review Board [*New York, NY*] (EA)
**NARB**........ National Assembly of Religious Brothers (EA)
**NARB**........ National Association of Referees in Bankruptcy [*Later, National Conference of Bankruptcy Judges*] (EA)
**NARB**........ National Association for Regional Ballet [*Later, RDA*]
**NARB**........ National Association of Retired Bankers [*Later, RBA*] (EA)
**NARB**........ Nonazeotropic Refrigerant Blend
**NARBA**..... North American Regional Broadcasting Agreement [*To minimize interference between AM stations*]
**NARBC**..... National Angora Rabbit Breeders Club (EA)
**NARBL**...... Net Advertising Revenue before Levy [*Television*] [*British*]
**NARBW**.... National Association of Railway Business Women (EA)
**NARC**........ Narcotics [*FBI standardized term*]
**NARC**........ National Amateur Retriever Club (EA)
**NARC**........ National Army Revolutionary Committee [*or Council*] [*Laos*] (CINC)
**NARC**........ National Association of Regional Councils (EA)
**NARC**........ National Association for Retarded Citizens [*Later, ARC*] (EA)
**NARC**........ Nonautomatic Relay Center (AABC)
**NARC**........ North American Riders Club (EA)
**NARC**........ North American Rockwell Corporation [*Later, Rockwell International Corp.*] (MCD)
**NARCA**..... National Antidrug Reorganization and Coordination Act
**NARCE**..... National Association of Retired Civil Employees [*Later, NARFE*] (EA)
**NARCF**...... National Association of Retail Clothiers and Furnishers [*Later, MRA*] (EA)
**NARCL**...... Nuclear Accident Response Capability Listing (MCD)
**NARCO**..... Narcotics Commission [*United Nations*]
**NARCO**..... National Aeronautical Corporation (MCD)
**NARCOG** ... Narcotics Coordination Group [*CIA*]
**NARCOM** ... Narration, Commentary [*Motion pictures*]
**NARCOM** ... North Atlantic Relay Communication Satellite
**Nar Conv**.... Nares' Penal Convictions [*1815*] [*A publication*] (DLA)
**NAR CORP** ... North American Rockwell Corp. [*Later, Rockwell International Corp.*]
**Narcotics L Bull** ... Narcotics Law Bulletin [*A publication*] (DLA)
**NARCUP** .. National Association for Retired Credit Union People (EA)
**NArd**.......... Ardsley Public Library, Ardsley, NY [*Library symbol*] [*Library of Congress*] (LCLS)
**NARD**........ National Association of Retail Druggists (EA)
**NARD**........ National Association of Rudimental Drummers [*Defunct*]
**NARDA**..... National Association of Retail Dealers of America (EA)
**NARDAC** .. Navy Regional Data Automation Center
**NARDELOG** ... Navy Rapid Delivery Logistics (AFIT)
**NARDIC**.... Navy Research and Development Information Center
**NARDIS**.... Navy Automated Research and Development Information System [*Later, NAVWUIS*]
**NARDIV** ... Naval Air Reserve Divisions
**NARDV**.... National Association Rainbow Division Veterans (EA)
**NARE**........ National Association for Remedial Education [*British*]
**NARE**........ Norwegian Antarctic Research Expedition
**NAREA**..... National Association of Real Estate Appraisers (EA)
**NAREB**...... National Association of Real Estate Boards [*Later, National Association of Realtors*] (EA)
**NAREB**...... National Association of Real Estate Brokers
**NAREB**...... Nature and Resources [*France*] [*A publication*]
**NAREBB**... National Association of Real Estate Buyer Brokers (EA)
**NAREC**..... National Association of Real Estate Companies (EA)
**NAREC**..... Naval Research Electronic Computer
**NAREE**...... National Association of Real Estate Editors (EA)
**NAREIF**.... National Association of Real Estate Investment Funds [*Later, NAREIT*] (EA)
**NAREIT**.... National Association of Real Estate Investment Trusts (EA)
**NARELLO** ... National Association of Real Estate License Law Officials (EA)
**NAREMCO** ... National Records Management Council (EA)
**NARETPA** ... National Agricultural Research, Extension, and Teaching Policy Act of 1977
**NaRev**........ Nassau Review [*A publication*]
**NARF**........ National Association of Rehabilitation Facilities (EA)
**NARF**........ Native American Rights Fund (EA)
**NARF**........ Naval Aerospace Research Facility
**NARF**........ Naval Air Reserve Force
**NARF**........ Naval Air Rework Facility
**NARF**........ Navy Arctic Research Facility
**NARF**........ Nuclear Aerospace Research Facility (IEEE)
**NARFE**...... National Association of Retired Federal Employees (EA)
**NARG**........ Northern Areas Regional Group [*Australia*]
**N Arg**........ Nuovi Argomenti [*A publication*]
**NARGUS** .. National Association of Retail Grocers of the United States [*Later, NGA*] (EA)
**NARHA**..... North American Riding for the Handicapped Association (EA)
**NARHA**..... Nucleic Acids Research [*A publication*]
**NARHC**..... National Association of River and Harbor Contractors [*Later, NADC*] (EA)
**NARHS**..... National Auto Racing Historical Society (EA)
**NARI**......... National Alliance for Reduction of Imprisonment [*Defunct*] (EA)
**NARI**......... National Association of Recycling Industries [*Later, ISRI*] (EA)
**NARI**......... National Association of Rehabilitation Instructors (EA)
**NARI**......... National Association of the Remodeling Industry (EA)
**NARI**......... National Association of Residents and Interns (EA)
**NARI**......... Native American Research Institute (EA)
**NARI**......... Nuclear Aerospace Research Institute [*Air Force*]

**NARIC**....... National Rehabilitation Information Center (EA)
**NARICM**... National Association of Retail Ice Cream Manufacturers [*Later, NICYRA*] (EA)
**NARISCO** ... North American Rockwell Information Systems Company
**Narisi Istor Prirodoznav i Tekhn** ... Narisi z Istorii Prirodoznavstva i Tekhniki [*A publication*]
**Narisi Istor Prirodozn Tekh** ... Narisi z Istorii Prirodoznavstva i Tekhniki [*USSR*] [*A publication*]
**NARIST**.... Naristillae [*Nasal Drops*] [*Pharmacy*]
**Nar Khoz Sov Latv** ... Narodnoe Khozyaistvo Sovetskoi Latvii [*A publication*]
**Nar Khoz Uzb** ... Narodnoe Khozyaistvo Uzbekistana [*A publication*]
**NARKOMVNUDEL** ... Narodnyi Komissariat Vnutrennikh Del [*People's Commissariat of Internal Affairs (1917-1946)*] [*Also known as NKVD*] [*Soviet secret police organization*]
**NARL**......... Naval Arctic Research Laboratory
**NARM**....... National Association of Recording Merchandisers (EA)
**NARM**....... National Association of Relay Manufacturers (EA)
**NARM**....... National Association of Restaurant Managers [*Scottsdale, AZ*] (EA)
**NARM**....... Naturally Occurring or Accelerator-Produced Radioactive Material
**NARM**....... Naval Resource Model (MCD)
**NARMC**.... National Association of Regional Media Centers (EA)
**NARMC**.... Naval Aerospace and Regional Medical Center [*Bureau of Medicine*]
**NARMFD** ... National Association of Retail Meat and Food Dealers
**NARMH**.... National Association for Rural Mental Health (EA)
**NARMIC**... National Action/Research on the Military Industrial Complex (EA)
**NArmN**...... North Castle Library, Armonk, NY [*Library symbol*] [*Library of Congress*] (LCLS)
**NARMU**.... Naval Air Reserve Maintenance Units
**Nar Muz (Prague) Cas Oddil Prirodoved** ... Narodni Muzeum. Casopis. Oddil Prirodovedny (Prague) [*A publication*]
**NARN**........ National Association of Registered Nurses (EA)
**NARO**........ National Association of Recycling Operations [*Australia*]
**NARO**........ National Association of Reimbursement Officers [*Washington, DC*] (EA)
**NARO**........ National Association of Royalty Owners (EA)
**NAROCTESTSTA** ... Naval Air Rocket Test Station
**Narod Azii Afriki** ... Narody Azii i Afriki [*A publication*]
**Narod Khoz Uzbek** ... Narodnoe Khozyaistvo Uzbekistana [*A publication*]
**Narody AA** ... Narody Azii i Afriki [*Moscow*] [*A publication*]
**Narody Azii Afr** ... Narody Azii i Afriki [*A publication*]
**NARP**........ National Association of Railroad Passengers (EA)
**NARP**........ National Association for Registered Plans (EA)
**NARP**........ New Australian Republican Party [*Political party*]
**NARP**........ Nonaqueous Reversed Phase [*Chromatography*]
**NARPA**..... National Air Rifle and Pistol Association [*British*]
**NARPA**..... National Association for Rights Protection and Advocacy (EA)
**NARPD**..... National Association for the Relief of Paget's Disease [*British*]
**NARPPS**... National Association of Rehabilitation Professionals in the Private Sector (EA)
**NARPV**..... National Association for Remotely Piloted Vehicles (MCD)
**NARR**........ Narragansett Capital [*NASDAQ symbol*] (NQ)
**NARR**........ Narrator
**Narrag Reg** ... Narragansett Historical Register [*A publication*]
**NARRD**..... National Association of Record Retailer Dealers [*Defunct*] (EA)
**Narr Mod**... Narrationes Modernae [*Style's English King's Bench Reports*] [*1646-55*] [*A publication*] (DLA)
**NARS**........ Narrative Accomplishment Reporting System [*Department of Agriculture*] [*Information service or system*] (IID)
**NARS**........ National Acupuncture Research Society (EA)
**NARS**........ National Annual Report Service [*NYSE*]
**NARS**........ National Archives and Records Service [*of GSA*] [*Washington, DC*] [*Later, NARA*]
**NARS**........ National Association of Radiation Survivors (EA)
**NARS**........ National Association of Radiotelephone Systems [*Later, Telocator Network of America*] (EA)
**NARS**........ National Association of Rail Shippers (EA)
**NARS**........ National Association of Refunders and Shoppers [*Defunct*] (EA)
**NARS**........ National Association of Rehabilitation Secretaries (EA)
**NARS**........ Naval Air Rescue Service (MUGU)
**NARS**........ New Atlantean Research Society [*Defunct*] (EA)
**NARS**........ Nonaffiliated Reserve Section
**NARS**........ North Atlantic Radio System
**NARS**........ Northampton Activity Rating Scale [*Psychology*]
**NARSA**...... National Automotive Radiator Service Association (EA)
**NARSAB**... National Association of Rail Shippers Advisory Boards (EA)
**NARSAD**... National Alliance for Research on Schizophrenia and the Depressions (EA)
**NARSC**...... National Association of Reinforcing Steel Contractors (EA)
**NARSLL**... National Association to Reform State Liquor Laws [*Later, National Association to Reform State Drinking Ages*] [*Defunct*] (EA)
**Na Rs Rev**.. Naval Research Reviews [*A publication*]
**NARST**...... National Association for Research in Science Teaching (EA)
**NARSTC**... Naval Air Rescue Training Command
**NARSUP**... Navy Acquisition Regulations Supplement
**NARSVA**... National Archives and Record Service Volunteer Association [*Later, NARAVA*] (EA)
**NARSVPD** ... National Association of Retired Senior Volunteer Program Directors (EA)
**NART**........ National Association of Recreation Therapists [*Later, NTRS*] (EA)
**NART**........ New Adult Reading Test
**NARTA**..... North American Restaurant and Tavern Alliance (EA)
**NARTB**...... National Association of Radio and Television Broadcasters [*Later, NAB*]
**NARTC**..... National Association of Railroad Trial Counsel (EA)
**NARTC**..... Naval Air Research Training Command
**NARTC**..... Naval Air Rocket Test Center (MUGU)
**NARTC**..... North America Regional Test Center (NATG)
**NARTE**...... National Association of Radio and Telecommunications Engineers (EA)
**NARTEL**... North Atlantic Radio Telephone Committee
**NARTRANS** ... North American Rockwell Training and Services [*Obsolete*]
**NARTS**...... National Association of Reporter Training Schools [*Defunct*] (EA)
**NARTS**...... National Association of Resale and Thrift Shops (EA)
**NARTS**...... Naval Aeronautics Test Station
**NARTS**...... Naval Air Rocket Test Station
**NARTU**..... Naval Air Reserve Training Unit
**Nar Tvor ta Etnogr** ... Narodna Tvorcist' ta Etnografija [*A publication*]
**NARU**........ Naval Air Reserve Unit (NVT)
**NARUC**..... National Association of Regulatory Utility Commissioners (EA)
**NARUS**..... Navy Aircraft Resources Utilization Study
**NARVRE**... National Association of Retired and Veteran Railroad Employees (EA)
**NARW**....... National Assembly of Religious Women (EA)
**NARW**....... National Association of Refrigerated Warehouses [*Later, IARW*] (EA)
**NARWA**.... Nordic Agricultural Research Workers Association (EA)
**Nar Zdrav**.. Narodno Zdravlje [*A publication*]
**Nar Zdravlje** ... Narodno Zdravlje [*Yugoslavia*] [*A publication*]
**NAS**........... N-Acetylserotonin [*Biochemistry*]
**NAS**........... Narrow-Angle Sensor
**NAS**........... Nasal
**NAS**........... Nasangga [*Fiji*] [*Seismograph station code, US Geological Survey*] (SEIS)
**Nas**............. [*Guillelmus*] Naso [*Flourished, 1220-34*] [*Authority cited in pre-1607 legal work*] (DSA)
**NAS**........... Nassau [*Bahamas*] [*Airport symbol*] (OAG)
**NAS**........... Nasta International [*AMEX symbol*] (SPSG)
**NAS**........... National Academy of Sciences [*Washington, DC*]
**NAS**........... National Academy of Songwriters (EA)
**NAS**........... National Academy of Sports (EA)
**NAS**........... National Advocates Society (EA)
**NAS**........... National Aerospace Standards (MCD)
**NAS**........... National Aircraft Standards
**NAS**........... National Airspace System [*NASA*]
**NAS**........... National Alliance for Salvation [*Political party*] [*Sudan*] (MENA)
**NAS**........... National Aquarium Society (EA)
**NAS**........... National Aquatic School [*Red Cross*]
**NAS**........... National Art School [*Australia*]
**NAS**........... National Association of Sanitarians [*Later, NEHA*] (EA)
**NAS**........... National Association of Scholars (EA)
**NAS**........... National Association of Schoolmasters [*British*]
**NAS**........... National Association of Specialized Carriers, Marietta GA [*STAC*]
**NAS**........... National Association of Stevedores (EA)
**NAS**........... National Association of Supervisors [*Later, Federal Managers Association*] (EA)
**NAS**........... National Astrological Society [*Defunct*] (EA)
**NAS**........... National Audubon Society (EA)
**NAS**........... National Autistic Society [*British*]
**NAS**........... National Aviation System [*FAA*]
**NAS**........... National Avionics Society (EA)
**NAS**........... National Seastar [*Vancouver Stock Exchange symbol*]
**NAS**........... Natuursteen [*A publication*]
**NAS**........... Naval Air Service
**NAS**........... Naval Air Station
**NAS**........... Naval Air Systems Command, Washington, DC [*OCLC symbol*] (OCLC)
**NAS**........... Navigation Avoidance System (KSC)
**NAS**........... Network Access Switch [*Telecommunications*] (MCD)
**NAS**........... Newsreel Access Systems, Inc. [*Also, an information service or system*] (IID)
**NAS**........... No Added Salt [*Medicine*]
**NAS**........... Nocturnal Adoration Society (EA)
**NAS**........... Noise Abatement Society [*British*]
**NAS**........... Nonavailability Statement [*Military*]
**NAS**........... Nonlinear Antenna System
**NAS**........... NORAD Alert System (MCD)
**NAS**........... Nord Amerikanischer Sangerbund (EA)
**NAS**........... Normalized Alignment Score
**NAS**........... North American Shale [*Geology*]
**NAS**........... North American Supply [*World War II*]

**NAS**.......... Norwegian-American Studies [*A publication*]
**NAS**.......... Notizie degli Archivi di Stato [*A publication*]
**NAS**.......... Nozzle Actuating System [*Aerospace*] (MCD)
**NAS**.......... Numerical Aerodynamic Simulation [*NASA supercomputer system*]
**NAS**.......... Numerical Analysis Subroutines [*Data processing*] (BUR)
**NAS**.......... Numerical and Atmospheric Sciences Network [*NASA*]
**NAS**.......... Nursery Association Secretaries [*Later, Nursery Association Executives*] (EA)
**NAS**.......... Nursing Auxiliary Service [*British*]
**NASA**........ National Acoustical Suppliers Association [*Defunct*] (EA)
**NASA**........ National Advertising Sales Association (EA)
**NASA**........ National Aeronautics and Space Act of 1958
**NASA**........ National Aeronautics and Space Administration [*Washington, DC*]
**NASA**........ National Aerospace Services Association [*Defunct*] (MCD)
**NASA**........ National Appliance Service Association (EA)
**NASA**........ National Association of School Affiliates (EA)
**NASA**........ National Association of Schools of Art (EA)
**NASA**........ National Association of Securities Administrators
**NASA**........ National Association of Shippers' Agents [*Washington, DC*] (EA)
**NASA**........ National Association of State Archeologists (EA)
**NASA**........ National Association of Synagogue Administrators (EA)
**NASA**........ National Automobile Salesmen's Association
**NASA**........ Newspaper Advertising Sales Association (EA)
**NASA**........ North American Savings Association [*Grandview, MO*] [*NASDAQ symbol*] (NQ)
**NASA**........ North American Saxophone Alliance (EA)
**NASA**........ North American Securities Administrators Association [*Also, NASAA*] (EA)
**NASA**........ North American Shippers Association (EA)
**NASA**........ North American Singers Association (EA)
**NASA**........ North American Swiss Alliance (EA)
**NASA**........ North Atlantic Seafood Association (EA)
**NASA**........ North Atlantic Shippers Association (DS)
**NASAA**..... National Assembly of State Arts Agencies (EA)
**NASAA**..... National Association of State Approval Agencies (EA)
**NASAA**..... National Association of Student Activity Advisers (EA)
**NASAA**..... North American Securities Administrators Association [*Topeka, KS*] (EA)
**NASAB**...... National Association of Shippers Advisory Boards (EA)
**NASABCA**... National Aeronautics and Space Administration Board of Contract Appeals
**NASABW**... Noticias Agricolas. Servicio Shell para el Agricultor [*A publication*]
**NASA Conf Publ**... NASA [*National Aeronautics and Space Administration*] Conference Publication [*A publication*]
**NASA Contract Rep**... NASA [*National Aeronautics and Space Administration*] Contractor Report [*A publication*]
**NASACT**... National Association of State Auditors, Comptrollers, and Treasurers (EA)
**NASACU**... National Association of State Approved Colleges and Universities (EA)
**NASAD**..... National Association of Schools of Art and Design (EA)
**NASAD**..... National Association of Sport Aircraft Designers (EA)
**NASADAD**... National Association of State Alcohol and Drug Abuse Directors (EA)
**NASAE**...... National Association of Supervisors of Agricultural Education (EA)
**NASAF**...... Northwest African Strategic Air Force [*British military*] (DMA)
**NASAGA**.. North American Simulation and Gaming Association (EA)
**NASAHOE**... National Association of Supervisors and Administrators of Health Occupations Education (EA)
**NASAKOM**... Nasional, Agama, Kommunist [*Indonesian President Sukarno's policy of unity among National, Religious, and Communist forces*]
**NASA-KSC**... National Aeronautics and Space Administration - Kennedy Space Center
**NASAL**...... National Association of Single Adult Leaders (EA)
**NASAMECU**... Natura Sanat, Medicus Curat [*Nature Heals, the Doctor Cures*] [*Title of collected talks by Dr. Georg Groddeck, published in 1913*]
**NASA Memo**... NASA [*National Aeronautics and Space Administration*] Memorandum [*A publication*]
**NASA-MSC**... National Aeronautics and Space Administration - Manned Spacecraft Center
**NASAO**..... National Association of State Aviation Officials (EA)
**NASAOCARE**... National Association of State Aviation Officials Center for Aviation Research and Education (EA)
**NASAP**...... Network Analysis for Systems Applications Program [*Computer program*] [*NASA*]
**NASAP**...... Nonproliferation Alternative Systems Assessment Program [*Nuclear energy*] (NRCH)
**NASAP**...... North American Society of Adlerian Psychology (EA)
**NASAP**...... Nuclear Alternative System Assessment Program
**NASAPR**... National Aeronautics and Space Administration Procurement Regulations
**NASAPRD**... National Aeronautics and Space Administration Procurement Regulations Directive
**NASAR**...... National Association for Search and Rescue (EA)
**NASA/RECON**... National Aeronautics and Space Administration Remote Console
**NASA Ref Publ**... NASA [*National Aeronautics and Space Administration*] Reference Publication [*A publication*]
**NASA Rep Ed**... NASA [*National Aeronautics and Space Administration*] Report to Educators [*A publication*]
**NASARR**... North American Search and Range RADAR [*Military*]
**NASASP**... National Association State Agencies for Surplus Property (EA)
**NASA Spec Publ**... NASA [*National Aeronautics and Space Administration*] Special Publications [*A publication*]
**NASASPS**... National Association of State Administrators and Supervisors of Private Schools (EA)
**NASA/STIF**... National Aeronautics and Space Administration/Scientific and Technical Information Facility
**NASATE**... National Association of Substance Abuse Trainers and Educators (EA)
**NASA Tech Brief**... NASA [*National Aeronautics and Space Administration*] Technical Briefs [*A publication*]
**NASA Tech Briefs**... NASA [*National Aeronautics and Space Administration*] Technical Briefs [*A publication*]
**NASA Tech Memo**... NASA [*National Aeronautics and Space Administration*] Technical Memorandum [*A publication*]
**NASA Tech Note**... NASA [*National Aeronautics and Space Administration*] Technical Note [*A publication*]
**NASA Tech Pap**... NASA [*National Aeronautics and Space Administration*] Technical Paper [*A publication*]
**NASA Tech Rep**... NASA [*National Aeronautics and Space Administration*] Technical Report [*A publication*]
**NASA Tech Transl**... NASA [*National Aeronautics and Space Administration*] Technical Translation [*A publication*]
**NASA-TR**... NASA Tank Reactor
**NASB**......... Nancy Ann Story Book [*Doll collecting*]
**NASB**......... National Animal Serum Bank [*Australia*]
**NASB**......... National Association of School Boards (OICC)
**NASB**......... National Association of Spanish Broadcasters (EA)
**NASB**......... Navigational Aid Support Base
**NASB**......... New American Standard Bible [*A publication*] (BJA)
**NASBA**...... National Association of State Boards of Accountancy [*New York, NY*] (EA)
**NASBA**...... National Automobile Safety Belt Association [*British*]
**NASBCO**... National Association of School Bus Contract Operators [*Later, NSTA*] (EA)
**NASBE**...... National Association of State Boards of Education (EA)
**NASBE**...... National Association of Supervisors of Business Education [*Fort Lauderdale, FL*] (EA)
**NASBERM**... Naval Air Station, Bermuda
**NASBIC**.... National Association of Small Business Investment Companies [*Washington, DC*] (EA)
**NASBLA**... National Association of State Boating Law Administrators (EA)
**NASBO**..... National Association of State Budget Officers (EA)
**NASBO**..... North African Shipping Board [*World War II*]
**NASBOE**... National Association of Supervisors of Business and Office Education [*Later, NASBE*]
**NASBP**...... National Association of Surety Bond Producers [*Bethesda, MD*] (EA)
**NASC**........ National Aeronautics and Space Council [*Terminated, 1973*]
**NASC**........ National Aircraft Standards Committee
**NASC**........ National Alliance for Safer Cities (EA)
**NASC**........ National Alliance of Senior Citizens (EA)
**NASC**........ National Aloe Science Council [*Later, IASC*] (EA)
**NASC**........ National Amalgamated Society of Coopers [*A union*] [*British*]
**NASC**........ National Aquatic Sports Camps (EA)
**NASC**........ National Association of School Counselors [*Defunct*] (EA)
**NASC**........ National Association of Service Contractors [*Defunct*] (EA)
**NASC**........ National Association of Solar Contractors (EA)
**NASC**........ National Association of Specialized Carriers (EA)
**NASC**........ National Association of Student Councils (EA)
**NASC**........ National Athletic Steering Committee (EA)
**NASC**........ NATO Supply Center
**NASC**........ Naval Air Systems Command
**NASC**........ Naval Aircraft Standards Committee (AFIT)
**NASC**........ Navy Aviation Safety Center (MUGU)
**NASC**........ North America Supply Council
**NASC**........ North American Shale Composite [*Geology*]
**NASC**........ Northwest Association of Schools and Colleges (EA)
**NASCA**...... NASA [*National Aeronautics and Space Administration*] Technical Note [*A publication*]
**NASCA**...... National Association of State Cable Agencies (EA)
**NASCA**...... North American Swing Club Association (EA)
**NASCAR**... National Association for Stock Car Auto Racing (EA)
**NASCAS**... National Academy of Sciences Committee on Atmospheric Science
**NASCAT**... National Association of Securities and Commercial Law Attorneys (EA)
**NASCCD**... National Association of State Catholic Conference Directors (EA)
**NASCCEN**... Naval Air Systems Command Representative, Central
**NAS-CD**.... National Academy of Sciences - Chemistry Division
**NASCD**..... National Association for Sickle Cell Disease (EA)

**NASCD** ..... National Association of Soil Conservation Districts [*Later, National Association of Conservation Districts*]
**NASCDD** .. National Association of State Civil Defense Directors [*Later, NEMA*] (EA)
**NASCL** ...... North American Student Cooperative League
**NASCLANT** ... Naval Air Systems Command Representative, Atlantic
**NASCO** ..... National Academy of Sciences Committee on Oceanography
**NASCO** ..... National Association of Smaller Communities (EA)
**NASCO** ..... National Association of State Charity Officials (EA)
**NASCO** ..... National Scientific Committee on Oceanography [*Marine science*] (MSC)
**NASCO** ..... North American Students of Cooperation (EA)
**NASCO** ..... North Atlantic Salmon Conservation Organization [*Edinburgh, Scotland*] (EAIO)
**NASCOE**... National Association of ASCS [*Agricultural Stabilization and Conservation Service*] County Office Employees (EA)
**NASCOM** ... NASA Communications Network
**NASCOM** ... National Airspace Communications System
**NASCOM** ... Naval Air Systems Command (MCD)
**NASCOP**... NASA Communications Operating Procedures (MCD)
**NAS/COW** ... National Academy of Sciences/Committee on Water [*Marine science*] (MSC)
**NASCP**...... National Association of Sports for Cerebral Palsy [*Later, USCPAA*] (EA)
**NASCP**...... North American Society for Corporate Planning [*Later, PF*] (EA)
**NASCPA**... North American Study Center for Polish Affairs (EA)
**NASCPAC** ... Naval Air Systems Command Representative, Pacific
**NASCPD**... National Association of Senior Companion Project Directors (EA)
**NASCPNCLA** ... Naval Air Systems Command Representative, Naval Air Training Command, Pensacola [*Florida*]
**NASCRIST** ... Naval Air Station Corpus Christi
**NASCRL**... Naval Air Systems Command Representative, Atlantic
**NASCS**...... National Association of Shoe Chain Stores [*Later, FDRA*] (EA)
**NASCSP**.... National Association for State Community Service Programs (EA)
**NASCUMC** ... National Association of Schools and Colleges of the United Methodist Church (EA)
**NASCUS**... National Association of State Credit Union Supervisors (EA)
**NASD**........ National Association of Schools of Dance (EA)
**NASD**........ National Association of Schools of Design [*Later, NASA*]
**NASD**........ National Association of Securities Dealers [*Washington, DC*] (EA)
**NASD**........ National Association of Selective Distributors (EA)
**NASD**........ National Association of Service Dealers (EA)
**NASD**........ Naval Air [*or Aviation*] Supply Depot
**NASDA** ..... National Association of Sign and Display Advertisers [*Defunct*]
**NASDA** ..... National Association of State Departments of Agriculture (EA)
**NASDA** ..... National Association of State Development Agencies (EA)
**NASDA** ..... North American South Devon Association (EA)
**NASDAD**.. National Association of Seventh-Day Adventist Dentists (EA)
**NASDAGS** ... National Association of State Directors of Administration and General Service (EA)
**NASDAPC** ... National Association of State Drug Abuse Program Coordinators [*Later, NASADAD*] (EA)
**NASDAQ**.. National Association of Securities Dealers Automated Quotations [*Over-the-counter stock quotations*] [*Bunker Ramo Corp.*] [*Trumbell, CT*] [*Information service or system*]
**NASDCD**.. National Association of State Directors of Child Development
**NASDDP**... National Association of State Directors for Disaster Preparedness [*Later, NEMA*] (EA)
**NASDI**....... National Association of Selective Distributors (EA)
**NASDIEGO** ... Naval Air Station San Diego
**NASDIM**... National Association of Securities Dealers and Investment Managers [*Securities and Investment Board*] [*British*]
**NASD J** ..... Journal. National Association for Staff Development in Further and Higher Education [*A publication*]
**NASDLET** ... National Association of State Directors of Law Enforcement Training
**NASDM** .... National Association of Special Delivery Messengers [*Later, APWU*] [*AFL-CIO*] (EA)
**NASDME** ... National Association of State Directors of Migrant Education (EA)
**NASDS**...... National Amalgamated Stevedores' and Dockers' Society [*A union*] [*British*]
**NASDS**...... National Association of Scuba Diving Schools [*Commercial firm*] [*Later, CA*] (EA)
**NASDS**...... Naval Aviation Supply Distribution System (AFIT)
**NASDS**...... North American Sheep Dog Society (EA)
**NASDSE**... National Association of State Directors of Special Education [*Database producer*] (EA)
**NASDSSE** ... National Association of State Directors and Supervisors of Secondary Education [*Later, NASSDSE*] (EA)
**NASDT**...... Naval Aviators' Speech Discrimination Test
**NASDT**...... North American Society for Dialysis and Transplantation (EA)
**NASDTEC** ... National Association of State Directors of Teacher Education and Certification (EA)
**NASDVA**... National Association of State Directors of Veterans Affairs (EA)
**NASDVE**... National Association of State Directors of Vocational Education (EA)
**NASE**......... National Academy of School Executives [*of American Association of School Administrators*]
**NASE**......... National Academy of Stationary Engineers [*British*] (DAS)
**NASE**......... National Association for the Self-Employed [*Fort Worth, TX*] (EA)
**NASE**......... National Association of Steel Exporters [*Defunct*] (EA)
**NASE**......... Nonacoustic Submarine Effects (NVT)
**NASEA**...... National Association of Student Employment Administrators (EA)
**NASEA**...... Native American Science Education Association [*Defunct*] (EA)
**NASEAB**... Naval Air Systems Effectiveness Advisory Board
**NASEAN**... National Association for State Enrolled Assistant Nurses
**NASECODE** ... Numerical Analysis of Semiconductor Devices and Integrated Circuits [*Data processing*]
**NASEDC**... NATO [*North Atlantic Treaty Organization*] Advanced Study Institutes Series. Series E. Applied Science [*A publication*]
**NASEDIO** ... National Association of State Education Department Information Officers (EA)
**NASEES**.... National Association for Soviet and East European Studies [*British*]
**NASEM**..... National Association of Satellite Equipment Manufacturers (EA)
**NASEMP**.. National Association of State Educational Media Professionals (EA)
**NASEMSD** ... National Association of State EMS Directors (EA)
**NASEPA**... National Association of State Environmental Programs Agencies [*Marine science*] (MSC)
**NAS/ESB** ... National Academy of Sciences/Environmental Studies Board [*Marine science*] (MSC)
**NASF**......... National American Studies Faculty [*Defunct*] (EA)
**NASF**......... National Arts Stabilization Fund (EA)
**NASF**......... National Association of State Foresters (EA)
**NASF**......... North American Soccer Foundation [*Inactive*] (EA)
**NASF**......... Numerical Aerodynamic Simulation Facility
**NASFA**...... National Association of State Facilities Administrators (EA)
**NASFAA**... National Association of Student Financial Aid Administrators (EA)
**NASFCA**... National Automatic Sprinkler and Fire Control Association (EA)
**NASFCB**... National Association of Specialty Food and Confection Brokers (EA)
**NASFM**..... National Association of Store Fixture Manufacturers (EA)
**NASFT**...... National Association for the Specialty Food Trade (EA)
**NASG**........ National Alliance for Spiritual Growth (EA)
**NASGA** ..... Neues Archiv fuer Sacchsische Geschichte und Altertumskunde [*A publication*]
**NASGA** ..... North American Strawberry Growers Association (EA)
**NASGAK**... Neues Archiv fuer Saechsische Geschichte und Altertumskunde [*A publication*]
**NASGC** ..... National Association of Small Government Contractors (EA)
**NASGEJ** ... NATO [*North Atlantic Treaty Organization*] ASI [*Advanced Science Institutes*] Series. Series G. Ecological Sciences [*A publication*]
**NAS/GRB** ... National Academy of Sciences/Geophysical Research Board [*Marine science*] (MSC)
**NASGS**...... North African Secretary General Staff [*World War II*]
**NASGTMO** ... Naval Air Station Guantanamo
**NASGW** .... National Association of Sporting Goods Wholesalers (EA)
**NASH**........ Nahariya to Ashkelon [*Proposed name for possible "super-city" formed by the urban sprawl between these two*] [*Israel*]
**NASHA** ..... National Association for Speech and Hearing Action (EA)
**NASHAC**.. National Association for Safety and Health in the Arts and Crafts (EA)
**NASHAW** ... National Association for Statewide Health and Welfare (EA)
**NASHC** ..... National All States Hobby Club (EA)
**NASHOC**.. North American Student Humanist Organizing Committee (EA)
**Nash Pl**...... Nash's Ohio Pleading and Practice [*A publication*] (DLA)
**NASHRD**.. National Association of State Human Resource Directors (EA)
**NASIC**....... Northeast Academic Science Information Center
**NASID**....... National Association of the Sixth Infantry Division (EA)
**NASIG**....... North African Signal Section [*World War II*]
**NASIG**....... North American Serials Group (EA)
**NASILP**..... National Association of Self-Instructional Language Programs (EA)
**NASIMD**... National Association of the Sixth Infantry/Motorized Division [*Later, NASID*] (EA)
**Nas Inst** ..... Nasmith's Institutes of English Private Law [*1873*] [*A publication*] (DLA)
**Nas Inst Priv** ... Nasmith's Institutes of English Private Law [*1873*] [*A publication*] (DLA)
**Nas Inst Pub** ... Nasmith's Institutes of English Public Law [*1873*] [*A publication*] (DLA)
**NASIS** ....... NASA Aerospace Safety Information System
**NASIS** ....... National Association for State Information Systems (EA)
**NASIS** ....... NATO Subject Indicator System (NATG)

**NASISS**..... National Association of Sailing Instructors and Sailing Schools (EA)
**NASJA**...... North American Ski Journalists Association (EA)
**NASJAX**... Naval Air Station Jacksonville
**NASL**......... National Association of State Lotteries (EA)
**NASL**......... Naval Applied Science Laboratory
**NASL**......... North American Soccer League (EA)
**NA 1SL**...... Naval Assistant to the First Sea Lord [*British military*] (DMA)
**NASLAKE**... Naval Air Station Lakehurst
**NASLI**....... National Association for Senior Living Industries (EA)
**NASLPA**... North American Soccer League Players Association (EA)
**NASLR**...... National Association of State Land Reclamationists (EA)
**NASLS**...... National Association of Small Loan Supervisors (EA)
**NASM**....... National Air and Space Museum [*Smithsonian Institution*] [*Formerly, NAM*]
**NASM**....... National Association of Sandwich Manufacturers (EA)
**NASM**....... National Association of Schools of Music (EA)
**NASM**....... National Association of Schools of Music. Proceedings [*A publication*]
**NASM**....... National Association of Service Managers (EA)
**NASM**....... National Association of Service Merchandising (EA)
**NASM**....... National Association of State Militia (EA)
**NASM**....... National Association of Surrogate Mothers (EA)
**NASM**....... Naval Aviation School of Medicine
**NASMA**.... Parti Nasionalis Malaysia [*Political party*] [*Malaysia*] (FEA)
**NASMAC**... Naval Air Software Management Advisory Committee (MCD)
**NASMBCM**... National Association of Sanitary Milk Bottle Closure Manufacturers [*Defunct*] (EA)
**NASMD**.... National Association of School Music Dealers (EA)
**NASMD**.... National Association of Sewing Machine Dealers [*Defunct*] (EA)
**NASMD**.... National Association of Sewing Machine Distributors [*Defunct*] (EA)
**NASMD**.... National Association of Sheet Music Dealers [*Later, NAMM*] (EA)
**NASMD**.... Northamerican Association of Sheet Metal Distributors [*Later, division of NHAW*] (EA)
**NASMHPD**... National Association of State Mental Health Program Directors (EA)
**NASMI**...... National Association of Secondary Material Industries [*Later, NARI*] (EA)
**NAS(MISC)**... North American Supply Committee, Miscellaneous [*World War II*]
**NASMO**.... NATO Starfighter Management Office
**NASMP**..... National Association of Sales and Marketing Professionals [*Inactive*] (EA)
**Nas Mus Bloemfontein Jaarversl**... Nasionale Museum Bloemfontein Jaarverslag [*A publication*]
**NASMV**.... National Association on Standard Medical Vocabulary (EA)
**NASN**........ National Air Sampling Network [*Public Health Service*]
**NASN**........ National Air Surveillance Network [*Environmental Protection Agency*]
**NASN**........ National Association of School Nurses (EA)
**NAS/NAE**... National Academy of Sciences/National Academy of Engineering [*Marine science*] (MSC)
**NASNI**...... Naval Air Station North Island
**NAS-NRC**... National Academy of Sciences - National Research Council (EA)
**NAS-NRC D Chem Chem Technol Annu Rep**... National Academy of Sciences - National Research Council. Division of Chemistry and Chemical Technology. Annual Report [*A publication*]
**NAS-NRC Div Chem Chem Technol Annu Rep**... National Academy of Sciences - National Research Council. Division of Chemistry and Chemical Technology. Annual Report [*A publication*]
**NAS-NRC Nucl Sci Ser Rep**... National Academy of Sciences - National Research Council. Nuclear Sciences Series. Report [*A publication*]
**NAS-NRC Publ**... National Academy of Sciences - National Research Council. Publication [*A publication*]
**NASNSA**... National Association of Special Needs State Administrators (EA)
**NASO**........ Natchez & Southern Railway Co. [*AAR code*] [*Terminated*]
**NASO**........ National Adult School Organisation [*British*]
**NASO**........ National Association of Sports Officials (EA)
**NASO**........ National Astrological Society [*Defunct*] (EA)
**NASO**........ National Astronomical Space Observatory
**NASO**........ Naval Aviation Supply Office
**NASO**........ Nonacoustic Sensor Operator [*Military*] (CAAL)
**NAS/OAB**... National Academy of Sciences/Ocean Affairs Board [*Marine science*] (MSC)
**NASOC**..... North American Singer Owners Club (EA)
**NASOH**..... North American Society for Oceanic History (EA)
**NA So Rhod**... Southern Rhodesia Native Appeal Court Reports [*A publication*] (DLA)
**NASORLO**... National Association of State Outdoor Recreation Liaison Officers (EA)
**NAS/OSB**... National Academy of Sciences/Ocean Sciences Board [*Marine science*] (MSC)
**NASP**......... National Aerospace Plane Program [*NASA, DoD*]
**NASP**......... National Airport System Plans [*Department of Transportation*]
**NASP**......... National Alternative Schools Program
**NASP**......... National Association of School Psychologists (EA)
**NASP**......... National Association of Schools and Publishers (EA)
**NASP**......... National Association of Securities Professionals (EA)
**NASP**......... National Association of Single Persons (EA)
**NASP**......... National Association for the Southern Poor (EA)
**NASP**......... National Atmospheric Sciences Program
**NASP**......... National Aviation System Plan [*A publication*]
**NASP**......... Negro, Anglo-Saxon Protestant
**NASPA**...... National Association of Student Personnel Administrators (EA)
**NaSPA**....... National Systems Programmers Association (EA)
**NASPA**...... North American Soccer Players Association [*Later, NASLPA*] (EA)
**NASPAA**... National Association of Schools of Public Affairs and Administration (EA)
**NASPA J**... NASPA [*National Association of Student Personnel Administrators*] Journal [*A publication*]
**NASPD**...... National Association of State Park Directors (EA)
**NASPD**...... National Association of Steel Pipe Distributors (EA)
**NASPE**...... National Association for Sport and Physical Education (EA)
**NASPE**...... National Association of State Personnel Executives (EA)
**NASPE**...... North American Society of Pacing and Electrophysiology (EA)
**NASPENSA**... Naval Air Station Pensacola
**NASPG**...... North American Society for Pediatric Gastroenterology [*Later, NASPGN*] (EA)
**NASPGN**... North American Society for Pediatric Gastroenterology and Nutrition (EA)
**NASPHV**... National Association of State Public Health Veterinarians (EA)
**NASPM**..... National Association of Slipper and Playshoe Manufacturers (EA)
**NASPO**..... National Airspace System Program Office [*FAA*] (MCD)
**NASPO**..... National Alliance of Statewide Preservation Organizations (EA)
**NASPO**..... National Association of State Purchasing Officials (EA)
**NASPO**..... NATO Starfighter Production Organization
**NASPR**...... NASA Procurement Regulation (KSC)
**NASPRFMR**... National Association of Superintendents of Public Residential Facilities for the Mentally Retarded
**NASPSM**.. National Association of Shirt, Pajama, and Sportswear Manufacturers [*Later, AAMA*]
**NASPSPA**... North American Society for the Psychology of Sport and Physical Activity (EA)
**NASPSPA Newsl**... NASPSPA [*North American Society for Psychology of Sport and Physical Activity*] Newsletter [*A publication*]
**NASQAN**.. National Stream Quality Accounting Network [*Department of the Interior*]
**NASQUON**... Naval Air Station Quonset Point
**NASR**........ National Annual Symposium on Reliability [*IEEE*] (MCD)
**NASR**........ National Association of Sitter Registries [*Defunct*] (EA)
**NASR**........ National Association of Solvent Recyclers (EA)
**NASR**........ National Association of Swine Records (EA)
**NASR**........ Norwegian-American Studies and Records [*A publication*]
**NASRA**...... National Academy of Sciences - National Research Council. Publication [*United States*] [*A publication*]
**NASRA**...... National Association of State Retirement Administrators (EA)
**NASRC**...... National Association of State Racing Commissioners [*Later, ARCI*] (EA)
**NASRC**...... North American Salmon Research Center [*Later, Atlantic Salmon Research Institute*] [*Canada*] [*Research center*] (RCD)
**NASRC**...... North Atlantic Salmon Research Center [*Marine science*] (MSC)
**NASRN**..... National Association of State Radio Networks (EA)
**NASRO**..... National Association of Shooting Range Owners (EA)
**NASRP**...... National Association of Special and Reserve Police [*Defunct*]
**NASRP**...... National Association of State Recreation Planners (EA)
**NASRPM**... National Association of State River Program Managers (EA)
**NASRR**...... North American Search and Range RADAR [*Military*]
**NASRWCBL**... National Amalgamated Society of Railway Wagon and Carriage Builders and Lifters [*A union*] [*British*]
**NASS**......... Nassau (ROG)
**NASS**......... National Accident Sampling System [*Washington, DC*] [*National Highway Traffic Safety Administration*]
**NASS**......... National Agricultural Statistics Service [*Department of Agriculture*] [*Information service or system*] (IID)
**NASS**......... National Alliance for Safe Schools (EA)
**NASS**......... National Alliance of Supermarket Shoppers (EA)
**NASS**......... National Association of Saw Shops (EA)
**NASS**......... National Association of Secretarial Services [*St. Petersburg, FL*] (EA)
**NASS**......... National Association of Secretaries of State (EA)
**NASS**......... National Association of Specialized Schools [*Defunct*] (EA)
**NASS**......... National Association of Suggestion Systems (EA)
**NASS**......... National Association of Summer Sessions [*Later, NAASS*]
**NASS**......... Naval Air Signal School
**NASS**......... Network Access Switching Subsystem [*Telecommunications*] (MCD)
**NASS**......... North African Special Service Section [*World War II*]
**NASS**......... North American Shagya-Arabian Society (EA)

**NASS**......... North American Spine Society (EA)
**NASS**......... North American Super Sports (EA)
**NAS(S)**...... North American Supply Committee, Scientific Subcommittee [*World War II*]
**NASSA**....... National Aerospace Services Association [*Defunct*] (EA)
**NASSAM**... National Association for the Self-Supporting Active Ministry (EA)
**Nass Ann**... Nassauische Annalen [*A publication*]
**Nassauischer Ver Naturk Jb**... Nassauischer Verein fuer Naturkunde. Jahrbuecher [*A publication*]
**Nassau L**.... Nassau Lawyer [*A publication*]
**NASSB**...... National Association of Supervisors of State Banks [*Later, CSBS*] (EA)
**NASSC**...... National Alliance on Shaping Safer Cities [*Later, NASC*] (EA)
**NASSCO**... National Association of Sewer Service Companies (EA)
**NASSCO**... National Steel & Shipbuilding Company
**NASSD**...... National Association of School Security Directors (EA)
**NASSDC**... National Social Science Documentation Centre [*Information service or system*] (IID)
**NASSDE**... National Association of State Supervisors of Distributive Education (EA)
**NASSDK**... NATO [*North Atlantic Treaty Organization*] Advanced Study Institutes Series. Series A. Life Sciences [*A publication*]
**NASSDOC**... National Social Science Documentation Centre [*Information service or system*] (IID)
**NASSDSE**... National Association of State Supervisors and Directors of Secondary Education (EA)
**NAS/SEC**... National Academy of Sciences' Site Evaluation Committee
**NASSH**..... North American Society for Sport History (EA)
**NASSHE**... National Association of State Supervisors of Home Economics [*Later, NASSVHE*]
**NASSL**...... National Association of Spanish Speaking Librarians (EA)
**NASS & LS**... National Association of State Savings and Loan Supervisors [*Later, ACSSS*] (EA)
**NASSM**..... National Association of Scissors and Shears Manufacturers (EA)
**NASSM**..... National Association of State Supervisors of Music (EA)
**NASSM**..... North American Society for Sport Management (EA)
**NASSP**...... National Association of Secondary School Principals (EA)
**NASSP**...... North American Society for Social Philosophy (EA)
**NASSP-B**.. National Association of Secondary-School Principals. Bulletin [*A publication*]
**NASSP Bull**... NASSP [*National Association of Secondary School Principals*] Bulletin [*A publication*]
**NASSPE**.... National Alliance of Spanish-Speaking People for Equality (EA)
**NASSS**...... North American Society for the Sociology of Sport (EA)
**NASSSA**.... National Association of State Social Security Administrators [*Later, NCSSSA*] (EA)
**NASSTA**... National Association of Secretaries of State Teachers Associations [*Later, NCSEA*] (EA)
**NASSTIE**... National Association of State Supervisors of Trade and Industrial Education (EA)
**NASSTRAC**... National Small Shipments Traffic Conference [*Acronym now used as official name of association*] (EA)
**NASSVHE**... National Association of State Supervisors of Vocational Home Economics (EA)
**NAST**......... National Association of Schools of Theatre (EA)
**NAST**......... National Association of State Treasurers (EA)
**NAST**......... Native Art Studies Association of Canada. Newsletter [*A publication*]
**NAST**......... Nuclear Accident Support Team [*Canada*]
**NASTA**...... National Association of State Text Book Administrators (EA)
**NASTAR**... National Standard Race [*Skiing*]
**NASTAT**... North American Society of Teachers of the Alexander Technique (EA)
**NASTBD**... National Association of State Text Book Directors [*Later, NASTA*] (EA)
**NASTD**...... National Association of State Telecommunications Directors (EA)
**NASTD**...... National Association of State and Territorial Apprenticeship Directors [*Bureau of Apprenticeship and Training*] [*Department of Labor*]
**NASTEMP**... National Association of State Educational Media Professionals (EA)
**NASTI**....... Next Assembly Support Table Index [*Aerospace*] (MCD)
**NASTOCK**... North American Stock Market [*I. P. Sharp Associates*] [*Canada*] [*Information service or system*]
**NASTPHV**... National Association of State and Territorial Public Health Veterinarians [*Later, NASPHV*] (EA)
**NASTRAN**... NASA Structural Analysis [*Computer program*]
**NAS/TRB**... National Academy of Sciences/Transportation Board [*Marine science*] (MSC)
**Na Stroikakh Ross**... Na Stroikakh Rossii [*A publication*]
**NASTS**...... National Association for Science, Technology, and Society (EA)
**NASTT**...... North American Society for Trenchless Technology (EA)
**NASU**........ National Adult School Union [*British*] (DAS)
**NASU**........ National Association of State Universities [*Later, NASULGC*]
**NASU**........ Navy Air Support Unit
**NASU**........ Navy Underwater Sound Laboratory (MUGU)
**NASU**........ North American Singers Union (EA)
**NASUA**..... National Association of State Units on Aging (EA)
**NASUCA**... National Association of State Utility Consumer Advocates (EA)
**NASULGC**... National Association of State Universities and Land-Grant Colleges (EA)
**NASUP**...... National Association on Service to Unmarried Parents (EA)
**NASUTRA**... National Sugar Trading Co. [*Philippines*] (DS)
**NAS-UWT**... National Association of Schoolmasters - Union of Women Teachers [*British*]
**NASV**........ National Academy of Sports Vision (EA)
**Nas Versnellersentrum Nuus**... Nasionale Versnellersentrum Nuus [*A publication*]
**NASVG**..... Nordic Association for Study and Vocational Guidance [*See also NRSY*] (EAIO)
**NASVH**..... National Association of State Veterans Homes (EA)
**NASW**....... National Association of Science Writers (EA)
**NASW**....... National Association of Social Workers (EA)
**NASW**....... North American Slope Water [*Oceanography*] (MSC)
**NASWA**.... North American Shortwave Association (EA)
**NASWF**..... Naval Air Special Weapons Facility
**NASWHP**... National Association of Sheltered Workshops and Homebound Programs [*Later, NARF*] (EA)
**NASWS**..... National Aeronautics and Space Administration White Sands [*Proving ground*]
**NASWSO**... National Association of Soft Water Service Operators [*Later, WQA*]
**NAT**.......... Information Content Natural Unit [*Information theory*]
**NAT**.......... N-Acetyltransferase [*An enzyme*]
**NAT**.......... N-Acetyltryptophan [*Biochemistry*]
**NAT**.......... NASA Apollo Trajectory (KSC)
**NAT**.......... NASA STI [*Scientific and Technical Information*] Facility, BWI [*Baltimore-Washington International*] Airport, MD [*OCLC symbol*] (OCLC)
**NAT**.......... Natal
**NAT**.......... Natal [*Brazil*] [*Airport symbol*] (OAG)
**NAT**.......... Natal [*Brazil*] [*Seismograph station code, US Geological Survey*] (SEIS)
**Nat**............ Nation [*A publication*]
**NAT**.......... National
**NAT**.......... National Academy of Teaching (EA)
**NAT**.......... National Agency for Tourism
**NAT**.......... National Arbitration Tribunal [*British*]
**NAT**.......... National Association of Teachers of Singing. Bulletin [*A publication*]
**NAT**.......... National Association of Toolmakers [*A union*] [*British*]
**NAT**.......... National Drug Co. [*Research code symbol*]
**Nat**............ National Party [*Australia*] [*Political party*]
**NAT**.......... National Transport, Inc.
**NAT**.......... Nationality (AAG)
**NAT**.......... Native (AAG)
**NAT**.......... Nativity [*Church calendars*] (ROG)
**NAT**.......... Natrolite [*A zeolite*]
**NAT**.......... Natural (AAG)
**Nat**............ Naturalist [*A publication*]
**Nat**............ Naturalized [*Botany*]
**Nat**............ Nature [*or Naturalist*]
**NAT**.......... Natus [*Birth*] [*Latin*]
**NAT**.......... Naval Air Technical Services Facility (MUGU)
**NAT**.......... Naval Air Training
**NAT**.......... Network Analysis Team
**NAT**.......... New Age Thinking
**NAT**.......... Nitric Acid Trihydrate [*Inorganic chemistry*]
**NAT**.......... No Action Taken
**NAT**.......... Non-Verbal Ability Tests [*Intelligence test*]
**NAT**.......... Normal Allowed Time (IEEE)
**NAT**.......... North African Theater [*World War II*]
**NAT**.......... North Atlantic Regional Area [*Aviation*]
**NAT**.......... North Atlantic Treaty
**NAT**.......... Not ARTS [*Automated RADAR Terminal System*] Tracked (FAAC)
**NATA**........ N-Acetyltyramine [*Biochemistry*]
**NATA**........ Narcotic Addict Treatment Act of 1974
**NATA**........ National Air Transportation Association (EA)
**NATA**........ National Airfreight Trucking Alliance (EA)
**NATA**........ National Association of Tax Accountants [*Defunct*] (EA)
**NATA**........ National Association of Tax Administrators (EA)
**NATA**........ National Association of Teachers' Agencies (EA)
**NATA**........ National Association of Temple Administrators (EA)
**NATA**........ National Association of Transportation Advertising [*Later, Transit Advertising Association*]
**NATA**........ National Athletic Trainers Association (EA)
**NATA**........ National Automobile Transporters Association [*Detroit, MI*] (EA)
**NATA**........ National Automotive Trade Association
**NATA**........ National Aviation Trades Association
**Nat A**......... Nationalmuseets Arbeidsmark [*A publication*]
**NATA**........ Natural Alternatives, Inc. [*NASDAQ symbol*] (NQ)
**NATA**........ North American Tasar Association (EA)
**NATA**........ North American Telecommunications Association (EA)
**NATA**........ North American Telephone Association (EA)

**NATA**........ North American Trakehner Association (EA)
**NATA**........ North American Travel Association (EA)
**NATA**........ North Atlantic Treaty Alliance
**Nat Acad Sci Biog Mem** ... National Academy of Sciences. Biographical Memoirs [*A publication*]
**Nat Acad Sci Nat Res Counc Publ** ... National Academy of Sciences - National Research Council. Publication [*A publication*]
**Nat Acad Sci Proc** ... National Academy of Sciences. Proceedings [*A publication*]
**NATAD**..... National Association of Textile and Apparel Distributors [*Defunct*] (EA)
**NATAF**...... Northwest African Tactical Air Force [*World War II*]
**Nat Agr**...... Nation's Agriculture [*A publication*]
**Natal Inst Eng J** ... Natal Institute of Engineers. Journal [*A publication*]
**Natal LJ**..... Natal Law Journal [*South Africa*] [*A publication*] (DLA)
**Natal LM**.... Natal Law Magazine [*South Africa*] [*A publication*] (DLA)
**Natal LQ**.... Natal Law Quarterly [*South Africa*] [*A publication*] (DLA)
**Natal LR**.... Natal Law Reports [*South Africa*] [*A publication*] (DLA)
**Natal Mus Ann** ... Natal Museum. Annals [*A publication*]
**Natal UL Rev** ... Natal University. Law Review [*A publication*]
**Natal Univ Law Rev** ... Natal University. Law Review [*A publication*]
**Nat Am**...... Native Americans [*A publication*]
**Nat Appl Sci Bull** ... Natural and Applied Science Bulletin [*A publication*]
**NATAPROBU** ... National Association of Professional Bureaucrats [*Later, INATAPROBU*]
**Nat Areas J** ... Natural Areas Journal [*A publication*]
**Nat Art Ed Assn Yrbk** ... National Art Education Association. Yearbook [*A publication*]
**Nat Arthritis N** ... National Arthritis News [*A publication*]
**NATAS**...... National Academy of Television Arts and Sciences (EA)
**NATAS**...... National Appropriate Technology Assistance Service [*Butte, MT*] [*Department of Energy*] (GRD)
**NATAS**...... North American Thermal Analysis Society (EA)
**Nat Assn Deans Women J** ... National Association of Deans of Women. Journal [*A publication*]
**Nat Assn Sec-Sch Prin Bul** ... National Association of Secondary-School Principals. Bulletin [*A publication*]
**Nat Assn State Univs Trans & Proc** ... National Association of State Universities. Transactions and Proceedings [*A publication*]
**Nat Assn Stud Council Yrbk** ... National Association of Student Councils. Yearbook [*A publication*]
**Nat Assoc of Inspectors and Ednl Advisers J** ... National Association of Inspectors and Educational Advisers. Journal [*A publication*]
**NATaT**...... National Association of Towns and Townships (EA)
**NATAW**.... National Association of Textile and Apparel Wholesalers [*Later, NATAD*] (EA)
**NATB**........ National Automobile Theft Bureau (EA)
**NATB**........ Naval Air Training Base
**NATB**........ Naval Training Bulletin
**NAtB**.......... Nitrosoanatabine [*Organic chemistry*]
**NATB**........ Nonreading Aptitude Test Battery [*US Employment Service*] [*Department of Labor*]
**Nat Bank Austsia M Summ** ... National Bank of Australasia. Monthly Summary of Australian Conditions [*A publication*] (APTA)
**Nat Bank Egypt Econ Bul** ... National Bank of Egypt. Economic Bulletin [*A publication*]
**Nat Bank Ethiopia Q Bul ns** ... National Bank of Ethiopia. Quarterly Bulletin. New Series [*A publication*]
**Nat Banking R** ... National Banking Review [*A publication*]
**Nat Bank Reg** ... National Bankruptcy Register Reports [*United States*] [*A publication*] (DLA)
**Nat Bankr Law** ... National Bankruptcy Law [*A publication*] (DLA)
**Nat Bankr N & R** ... National Bankruptcy News and Reports [*A publication*] (DLA)
**Nat Bankr R** ... National Bankruptcy Register [*United States*] [*A publication*] (DLA)
**Nat Bankr Reg** ... National Bankruptcy Register [*United States*] [*A publication*] (DLA)
**Nat Bankr Rep** ... National Bankruptcy Register Reports [*United States*] [*A publication*] (DLA)
**Nat Bank Yugoslavia Q Bul** ... National Bank of Yugoslavia. Quarterly Bulletin [*A publication*]
**Nat Bar Bull** ... National Bar Bulletin [*A publication*]
**Nat Bar J** ... National Bar Journal [*A publication*] (DLA)
**NATBASES** ... Naval Air Training Bases
**Nat B Belg** ... National Bank of Belgium. Report [*A publication*]
**Nat BC**....... National Bank Cases [*United States*] [*A publication*] (DLA)
**Nat Bee Krs Dig** ... National Bee Keepers Digest [*A publication*]
**Nat Belg**..... Naturalistes Belges [*A publication*]
**NATBF**...... Northwest African Tactical Bomber Force [*World War II*]
**Nat Biol**...... Natura. Seria Biologie [*A publication*]
**Nat BJ**........ National Bar Journal [*A publication*] (DLA)
**Nat Bk (Aus)** ... National Bank. Monthly Summary (Australia) [*A publication*]
**Nat Bldgs Organisation Jnl** ... National Buildings Organisation. Journal [*A publication*]
**Nat Bldr**..... National Builder [*A publication*]
**Nat Bottlers' Gaz** ... National Bottlers' Gazette [*A publication*]
**Nat BR**....... National Bankruptcy Register [*United States*] [*A publication*] (DLA)
**Nat Brev**..... Fitzherbert's Natura Brevium [*A publication*] (DLA)
**Nat Bsns Ed Q** ... National Business Education Association. Quarterly [*A publication*]
**Nat Bsns Ed Yrbk** ... National Business Education Association. Yearbook [*A publication*]
**Nat Bsns Woman** ... National Business Woman [*A publication*]
**Nat Builder** ... National Builder [*A publication*]
**Nat Bur Stand Appl Math Ser** ... National Bureau of Standards. Applied Mathematics Series [*A publication*]
**Nat Bur Standards TNB** ... National Bureau of Standards. Technical News Bulletin [*A publication*]
**Nat Bur Stand Bldg Sci Ser** ... National Bureau of Standards. Building Science Series [*A publication*]
**Nat Bur Stand Handb** ... National Bureau of Standards. Handbook [*A publication*]
**Nat Bur Stand Misc Pubs** ... National Bureau of Standards. Miscellaneous Publications [*A publication*]
**Nat Bur Stand Monogr** ... National Bureau of Standards. Monographs [*A publication*]
**Nat Bur Stand Spec Publ** ... National Bureau of Standards. Special Publication [*A publication*]
**Nat Bur Stand Tech News Bull** ... National Bureau of Standards. Technical News Bulletin [*A publication*]
**Nat Bur Stand Tech Note** ... National Bureau of Standards. Technical Note [*A publication*]
**Nat Bus Educ Yrbk** ... National Business Education Association. Yearbook [*A publication*]
**Nat Butter & Cheese J** ... National Butter and Cheese Journal [*A publication*]
**Nat Butter J** ... National Butter Journal [*A publication*]
**NAtC**.......... Columbia-Greene Community College, Athens, NY [*Library symbol*] [*Library of Congress*] (LCLS)
**NATC**........ NaTec Resources, Inc. [*NASDAQ symbol*] (NQ)
**NATC**........ National Air Transportation Conferences [*Later, NATA*]
**NATC**........ National Alcohol Tax Coalition (EA)
**NATC**........ National Association of Taurine Clubs
**NATC**........ National Association of Tax Consultors (EA)
**NATC**........ National Association of Telemarketing Consultants [*Defunct*] [*Provo, UT*] (EA)
**NATC**........ Naval Air Test Center
**NATC**........ Naval Air Training Center
**NATC**........ Naval Air Training Command (CAAL)
**NATC**........ Nordic Amateur Theatre Council (EAIO)
**NATC**........ Nordic Automobile Technical Committee (EAIO)
**NATC**........ North Atlantic Treaty Council (NATG)
**NATC**........ Northwest African Training Command [*World War II*]
**NATCA**...... National Air Traffic Controllers Association (EA)
**NATCA**...... National Association of Trial Court Administrators (EA)
**Nat Cambs** ... Nature in Cambridgeshire [*A publication*]
**Nat Can**...... Nature Canada [*A publication*]
**Nat Canada** ... Nature Canada [*A publication*]
**Nat Cancer Inst J** ... National Cancer Institute. Journal [*A publication*]
**Nat Cancer Inst Monogr** ... National Cancer Institute. Monographs [*A publication*]
**Nat Can I M** ... National Cancer Institute. Monographs [*A publication*]
**Nat Can (Ottawa)** ... Nature Canada (Ottawa) [*A publication*]
**Nat Can (Quebec)** ... Naturaliste Canadien (Quebec) [*A publication*]
**NATCAS**... Navigation, Air Traffic Control and Collision Avoidance System (FAAC)
**Nat Cath Ed Assn Bul** ... National Catholic Educational Association. Bulletin [*A publication*]
**Nat Cath Ed Assn Proc** ... National Catholic Educational Association. Proceedings [*A publication*]
**Nat Cath Rep** ... National Catholic Reporter [*A publication*]
**NATCC**..... National Air Transport Coordinating Committee [*Later, ADC*] (FAAC)
**NATCC**..... Northwest African Troop Carrier Command [*World War II*]
**NATCEM** ... National Cemetery
**Nat Cheese J** ... National Cheese Journal [*A publication*]
**Nat Child Labor Com Proc** ... National Child Labor Committee. Proceedings [*A publication*]
**Nat Christ Coun R** ... National Christian Council. Review [*Mysore City*] [*A publication*]
**Nat Cities**... Nation's Cities [*A publication*]
**Nat Civic R** ... National Civic Review [*A publication*]
**Nat Civic Rev** ... National Civic Review [*A publication*]
**Nat Civ Rev** ... National Civic Review [*A publication*]
**NATCO**..... National Association of Transit Consumer Organizations (EA)
**NATCO**..... National Automatic Tool Company
**NATCO**..... National Coordinator [*Marine science*] (MSC)
**NATCO**..... Navy Air Traffic Coordinating Officer
**NATCO**..... North American Transplant Coordinators Organization (EA)
**NATCO**..... Northern Advanced Technologies Corp. [*Research center*] (RCD)
**NATCO**..... Nuclear Auditing and Testing Company
**Nat Coffee** ... National Coffee Drinking Survey [*A publication*]
**NATCOL**... Natural Food Colours Association [*Basel, Switzerland*] (EAIO)
**NATCOM** ... National Communications Center [*FAA*] (FAAC)
**NATCOM** ... National Communications Symposium [*IEEE*]
**NATCOM** ... National Conference on Communications (MCD)

**NATCOM** ... NATO Communication (NATG)
**Nat Comm Teach Ed & Prof Stand Off Rep** ... National Commission on Teacher Education and Professional Standards. Official Report [*A publication*]
**Nat Conf City Govt** ... National Conference for Good City Government. Proceedings [*A publication*]
**Nat Conf Publ Inst Eng Aust** ... National Conference Publication. Institution of Engineers of Australia [*A publication*] (APTA)
**Nat Conf Publs Instn Engrs Aust** ... National Conference Publications. Institution of Engineers of Australia [*A publication*] (APTA)
**Nat Conf Soc Work** ... National Conference of Social Work. Proceedings [*A publication*]
**Nat Conserv Branch Transvaal Bull** ... Nature Conservation Branch. Transvaal Bulletin [*A publication*]
**Nat Conserv News** ... Nature Conservancy News [*United States*] [*A publication*]
**Nat Corp Rep** ... National Corporation Reporter [*A publication*]
**Nat Council O** ... National Council Outlook [*A publication*]
**Nat Council Social Stud Yrbk** ... National Council for the Social Studies. Yearbook [*A publication*]
**Nat Council Teach Math Yrbk** ... National Council of Teachers of Mathematics. Yearbook [*A publication*]
**NATCS**...... National Air Traffic Control Service (IEEE)
**NATCS**...... National Air Traffic Control System (NATG)
**Nat D**......... De Natura Deorum [*of Cicero*] [*Classical studies*] (OCD)
**NATD**........ National Association of Telecommunications Dealers (EA)
**NATD**........ National Association of Test Directors (EA)
**NATD**........ National Association of Tobacco Distributors (EA)
**NATDEFSM** ... National Defense Service Medal [*Military decoration*]
**Nat Development** ... National Development [*A publication*] (APTA)
**Nat Dev Q** ... National Development Quarterly [*A publication*]
**NATDS**...... National Association of Truck Driving Schools (EA)
**NATDS**...... Naval Air Tactical Data System (MCD)
**NATE**........ National Association for Teachers of Electronics [*Defunct*] (EA)
**NATE**........ National Association of Teachers of English
**NATE**........ National Association of Temple Educators (EA)
**NATE**........ Neutral Atmosphere Temperature Experiment
**NATEBE**... National Association of Teacher Educators for Business Education [*DeKalb, IL*] (EA)
**NATEBOE** ... National Association of Teacher Educators for Business and Office Education [*Later, NATEBE*] (EA)
**NATEC**...... Naval Air Training and Experimental Command
**NATECHTRACEN** ... Naval Air Technical Training Center
**NATECHTRAU** ... Naval Air Technical Training Unit
**NATECOM** ... Naval Airship Training and Experimentation Command
**Nat Ed Assn Proc** ... National Education Association. Addresses and Proceedings [*A publication*]
**Nat Ed Assn Res Bul** ... National Education Association. Research Bulletin [*A publication*]
**Nat Educ Assn J** ... National Education Association. Journal [*A publication*]
**NATEF**...... National Automotive Technicians Education Foundation (EA)
**NATEL**...... Nortronics Automatic Test Equipment Language [*Data processing*]
**Nat Elec Mfr Ass Stand Publ** ... National Electrical Manufacturers Association. Standards Publication [*A publication*]
**Nat El Prin** ... National Elementary Principal [*A publication*]
**NAtenea**..... Nueva Atenea [*Chile*] [*A publication*]
**Nat Eng**...... National Engineer [*A publication*]
**Nat Eng Lab Rep** ... National Engineering Laboratory. Report [*A publication*]
**Nat Environ Res Counc Inst Terr Ecol Annu Rep** ... Natural Environment Research Council. Institute of Terrestrial Ecology. Annual Report [*A publication*]
**Nat Environ Res Counc News J** ... Natural Environment Research Council. News Journal [*A publication*]
**NATES**...... National Analysis of Trends in Emergency Systems [*Canada*] (MSC)
**NATESA**... National Association of Television and Electronic Servicers of America [*Absorbed by NESSDA*] (EA)
**NATESTCEN** ... Naval Air Test Center
**NATEVHE** ... National Association of Teacher Educators for Vocational Home Economics (EA)
**NATEX**...... National Stock Exchange [*Dissolved, 1975*]
**Nat F**.......... National Forum [*A publication*]
**NATF**........ Naval Air Test Facility
**NATF**........ New Arrivals Task Force (MCD)
**NATFB**...... National Archives Trust Fund Board
**NATFC**...... North American Toyah Fan Club (EA)
**NATFHE**... National Association of Teachers in Further and Higher Education [*British*]
**Nat Fmrs Un Annu Conf** ... National Farmers' Union. Annual Conference [*A publication*] (APTA)
**Nat Forum** ... National Forum [*A publication*]
**Nat Found March Dimes Birth Defects Orig Artic Ser** ... National Foundation. March of Dimes. Birth Defects Original Article Series [*A publication*]
**NATF-SI** ... Naval Air Test Facility - Ship Installations
**NATG**........ [*The*] National Guardian Corp. [*Greenwich, CT*] [*NASDAQ symbol*] (NQ)
**NATGA**..... Natuurwetenschappelijk Tijdschrift (Ghent) [*A publication*]
**Nat Gall SA Bull** ... National Gallery of South Australia. Bulletin [*A publication*] (APTA)
**Nat Gall VIC A Bull** ... National Gallery of Victoria. Annual Bulletin [*A publication*] (APTA)
**Nat Gal Rep** ... National Gallery of Art. Report [*A publication*]
**Nat Gas**...... Natural Gas [*A publication*]
**Nat Gas A**.. Natural Gas Annual, 1983 [*A publication*]
**Nat Gas As Am Pr** ... Natural Gas Association of America. Proceedings [*A publication*]
**Nat Gas Bul** ... National Gas Bulletin [*A publication*] (APTA)
**Nat Gas Bull** ... National Gas Bulletin [*A publication*] (APTA)
**Nat Gas/Fuel Forecast Ser A** ... Natural Gas/Fuel Forecast. Series A. Geographic [*United States*] [*A publication*]
**Nat Gas/Fuel Forecast Ser B** ... Natural Gas/Fuel Forecast. Series B. Industrial [*United States*] [*A publication*]
**Nat Gas Gasoline J** ... Natural Gas and Gasoline Journal [*A publication*]
**Nat Gas Ind** ... Natural Gas Industry [*A publication*]
**Nat Gas Mag** ... Natural Gas Magazine [*A publication*]
**Nat Geog**.... National Geographic Magazine [*A publication*]
**Nat Geog J Ind** ... National Geographical Journal of India [*Varanasi*] [*A publication*]
**Nat Geog M** ... National Geographic Magazine [*A publication*]
**Nat Geog R** ... National Geographic Research [*A publication*]
**Nat Geog Soc Nat Geog Mon** ... National Geographic Society. National Geographic Monographs [*A publication*]
**Nat Geog World** ... National Geographic World [*A publication*]
**NATH**........ Nathan's Famous, Inc. [*NASDAQ symbol*] (NQ)
**Nathan**....... Nathan's Common Law of South Africa [*A publication*] (DLA)
**NATHE**..... National Associations of Teachers of Home Economics [*British*]
**Nat Health Serv Inf Bul** ... National Health Services Information Bulletin [*A publication*] (APTA)
**Nat Heimat** ... Natur und Heimat [*A publication*]
**Nat Herb NSW Contrib** ... National Herbarium of New South Wales. Contributions [*A publication*] (APTA)
**Nat Hisp**.... Naturalia Hispanica [*A publication*]
**Nat Hist**..... Natural History [*A publication*]
**Nat Hist Bull Siam Soc** ... Natural History Bulletin. Siam Society [*A publication*]
**Nat Hist Mag** ... Natural History Magazine [*A publication*]
**Nat Hist Misc (Chic)** ... Natural History Miscellanae (Chicago) [*A publication*]
**Nat Hist Mus Los Ang Cty Contrib Sci** ... Natural History Museum of Los Angeles County. Contributions in Science [*A publication*]
**Nat Hist Mus Los Ang Cty Sci Bull** ... Natural History Museum of Los Angeles County. Science Bulletin [*A publication*]
**Nat Hist Mus Los Ang Cty Sci Ser** ... Natural History Museum of Los Angeles County. Science Series [*A publication*]
**Nat Hist Mus Los Angeles Cty Sci Bull** ... Natural History Museum of Los Angeles County. Science Bulletin [*A publication*]
**Nat Hist Natl Parks Hung** ... Natural History of the National Parks of Hungary [*A publication*]
**Nat Hist (NY)** ... Natural History (New York) [*A publication*]
**Nat Hist Rennell Isl Br Solomon Isl** ... Natural History of Rennell Island, British Solomon Islands [*A publication*]
**Nat Hort M** ... National Horticultural Magazine [*A publication*]
**Nat Hosp** ... National Hospital [*A publication*] (APTA)
**Nat Hospital** ... National Hospital [*A publication*] (APTA)
**Nat I Anim** ... National Institute of Animal Health. Quarterly [*A publication*]
**NATIE**....... National Association for Trade and Industrial Education (EA)
**NATII**........ National Association of Trade and Industrial Instructors (EA)
**Nat Immun Cell Growth Regul** ... Natural Immunity and Cell Growth Regulation [*A publication*]
**NATINADS** ... NATO Integrated Air Defense System (NATG)
**Nat Inc Tax Mag** ... National Income Tax Magazine [*A publication*] (DLA)
**Nat Inst Arch Ed Bul** ... National Institute for Architectural Education. Bulletin [*A publication*]
**Nat Inst B Pr Pr N S** ... National Institution for the Promotion of Science. Bulletin of the Proceedings. Proceedings. New Series [*A publication*]
**Nat Inst Econ R** ... National Institute Economic Review [*A publication*]
**Nat Inst Econ Rev** ... National Institute Economic Review [*A publication*]
**Nat Inst Educ Res B** ... National Institute for Educational Research. Bulletin [*Tokyo*] [*A publication*]
**Nat Inst Soc Sci** ... National Institute of Social Sciences. Proceedings [*A publication*]
**National Inst Health Bull US Pub Health Serv** ... National Institute of Health. Bulletin. United States Public Health Service [*A publication*]
**Nation and Ath** ... Nation and Athenaeum [*A publication*]
**Nation Athen** ... Nation and Athenaeum [*A publication*]
**Nation (Lond)** ... Nation and Athenaeum (London) [*A publication*]
**Nation Rev** ... Nation Review [*A publication*] (APTA)
**Nation's Ag** ... Nation's Agriculture [*A publication*]
**Nation's Agric** ... Nation's Agriculture [*A publication*]
**Nation's Bus** ... Nation's Business [*A publication*]
**Nation's Sch** ... Nation's Schools [*A publication*]
**NATIP**....... Navy Technical Information Program
**NATIS**....... National Information Systems [*Later, GIP*] [*UNESCO*]
**NATIS**....... Naval Air Training Information System
**NATIS**....... North Atlantic Treaty Information Service (NATG)
**NATIV**....... Nativity

**NATIV**....... North American Test Instrument Vehicle [*Air Force test rocket*]
**Native Sch Bul** ... Native School Bulletin [*A publication*] (APTA)
**Nat J** .......... National Journal [*A publication*]
**Nat J Crim Def** ... National Journal of Criminal Defense [*A publication*]
**Nat J Criminal Defense** ... National Journal of Criminal Defense [*A publication*]
**Nat J Leg Ed** ... National Journal of Legal Education [*A publication*] (DLA)
**Nat Jutl**...... Natura Jutlandica [*A publication*]
**Nat Jutlandica** ... Natur Jutlandica [*A publication*]
**NATL** ........ National (AAG)
**NATL** ........ National Agricultural Transportation League (EA)
**NATL** ........ Naval Aeronautical Turbine Laboratory
**NATL** ........ North Atlantic Industries, Inc. [*NASDAQ symbol*] (NQ)
**NATLA**...... Nauchnye Trudy Leningradskaya Lesotekhnicheskaya Akademiya Imeni S. M. Kirova [*A publication*]
**Natl Acad Med Sci (India) Ann** ... National Academy of Medical Sciences (India). Annals [*A publication*]
**Natl Acad Sci Biog Mem Proc** ... National Academy of Sciences. Biographical Memoirs. Proceedings [*A publication*]
**Natl Acad Sci Comm Polar Res Rep US Antarc Res Act Rep SCAR** ... National Academy of Sciences. Committee on Polar Research. Report of United States Antarctic Research Activities. Report to SCAR [*Scientific Committee on Antarctic Research*] [*A publication*]
**Natl Acad Sci (India) Annu Number** ... National Academy of Sciences (India). Annual Number [*A publication*]
**Natl Acad Sci Lett** ... National Academy of Science and Letters [*India*] [*A publication*]
**Natl Acad Sci Lett (India)** ... National Academy of Science. Letters (India) [*A publication*]
**Natl Acad Sci Natl Research Council Pub** ... National Academy of Sciences - National Research Council. Publication [*A publication*]
**Natl Acad Sci Proc** ... National Academy of Sciences. Proceedings [*A publication*]
**Natl Acad Sci Pub** ... National Academy of Sciences. Publication [*A publication*]
**Natl Acad Sci USA Biogr Mem** ... National Academy of Sciences of the United States of America. Biographical Memoirs [*A publication*]
**Natl Accel Cent News** ... National Accelator Centre. News [*South Africa*] [*A publication*]
**Natl Advis Comm Aeronaut Annu Rep** ... National Advisory Committee for Aeronautics. Annual Report [*A publication*]
**Natl Advis Comm Aeronaut Rep** ... National Advisory Committee for Aeronautics. Reports [*A publication*]
**Natl Advis Comm Aeronaut Tech Notes** ... National Advisory Committee for Aeronautics. Technical Notes [*A publication*]
**Natl Advisory Comm Research Geol Sci** ... National Advisory Committee on Research in the Geological Sciences [*A publication*]
**Natl Aeronaut Establ Mech Eng Rep MS (Can)** ... National Aeronautical Establishment. Mechanical Engineering Report MS (Canada) [*A publication*]
**Natl Aerosp Electron Conf Proc** ... National Aerospace Electronics Conference. Proceedings [*United States*] [*A publication*]
**Natl Air Pollut Control Adm (US) Publ AP Ser** ... National Air Pollution Control Administration (United States). Publication. AP Series [*A publication*]
**Natl Air Pollut Control Adm (US) Publ APTD Ser** ... National Air Pollution Control Administration (United States). Publication. APTD [*Air Pollution Technical Data*] Series [*A publication*]
**Natl Am Miller** ... National and American Miller [*A publication*]
**Nat Lamp**... National Lampoon [*A publication*]
**Nat Land**.... Natur und Land [*A publication*]
**Nat Landschaft** ... Natur und Landschaft [*A publication*]
**Nat Landschap** ... Natuur en Landschap Tijdschrift van de Contact Commissie voor Natuur- en Landschapsebescherming [*A publication*]
**N Atlantic Reg Bus L Rev** ... North Atlantic Regional Business Law Review [*A publication*] (DLA)
**NATLAS**... National Testing Laboratory Accreditation Scheme [*Military*] [*British*]
**Natl Assn Sec-Schl Princ** ... National Association of Secondary-School Principals. Bulletin [*A publication*]
**Natl Assoc Margarine Manuf Bull** ... National Association of Margarine Manufacturers. Bulletin [*A publication*]
**Nat Law Guild Q** ... National Lawyers Guild Quarterly [*A publication*] (DLA)
**Natl Biomed Sci Instrum Symp Proc** ... National Biomedical Sciences Instrumentation Symposium. Proceedings [*A publication*]
**Natl Bitum Concr Assoc Qual Improv Program Publ** ... National Bituminous Concrete Association. Quality Improvement Program. Publication [*A publication*]
**Natl Board Examiner** ... National Board Examiner [*United States*] [*A publication*]
**Natl Board Fire Underwrit Res Rep** ... National Board of Fire Underwriters. Research Report [*A publication*]
**Natl Board Fire Underwrit Tech Surv** ... National Board of Fire Underwriters. Technical Survey [*A publication*]
**Natl Bot Gard (Lucknow) Annu Rep** ... National Botanic Gardens (Lucknow). Annual Report [*A publication*]
**Natl Bur Stand (US) Circ** ... National Bureau of Standards (United States). Circular [*A publication*]
**Natl Bur Stand (US) Handb** ... National Bureau of Standards (United States). Handbook [*A publication*]
**Natl Bur Stand (US) Monogr** ... National Bureau of Standards (United States). Monograph [*A publication*]
**Natl Bur Stand (US) Spec Publ** ... National Bureau of Standards (United States). Special Publication [*A publication*]
**Natl Bur Stand (US) Tech News Bull** ... National Bureau of Standards (United States). Technical News Bulletin [*A publication*]
**Natl Bur Stand (US) Tech Note** ... National Bureau of Standards (United States). Technical Note [*A publication*]
**Natl Bus Educ Yrbk** ... National Business Education Association. Yearbook [*A publication*]
**Natl Bus Woman** ... National Business Woman [*A publication*]
**Natl Butter Cheese J** ... National Butter and Cheese Journal [*A publication*]
**Natl Butter J** ... National Butter Journal [*A publication*]
**Natl Cactus Succulent J** ... National Cactus and Succulent Journal [*A publication*]
**Natl Cancer Conf Proc** ... National Cancer Conference. Proceedings [*A publication*]
**Natl Cancer Inst Carcinog Tech Rep Ser (US)** ... National Cancer Institute. Carcinogenesis Technical Report Series (United States) [*A publication*]
**Natl Cancer Inst Monogr** ... National Cancer Institute. Monographs [*A publication*]
**Natl Cancer Inst Res Rep** ... National Cancer Institute. Research Report [*A publication*]
**Natl Canners' Assoc Res Lab Bull** ... National Canners' Association. Research Laboratory. Bulletin [*A publication*]
**Natl Canners' Assoc Res Lab Circ** ... National Canners' Association. Research Laboratory. Circular [*United States*] [*A publication*]
**Natl Cheese J** ... National Cheese Journal [*United States*] [*A publication*]
**Natl Chem Pet Instrum Symp** ... National Chemical and Petroleum Instrumentation Symposium [*A publication*]
**Natl Civic Rev** ... National Civic Review [*A publication*]
**Natl Civ Rev** ... National Civic Review [*A publication*] (ILCA)
**Natl Clay Prod Quarrying** ... National Clay Products and Quarrying [*A publication*] (APTA)
**Natl Cleaner Dyer** ... National Cleaner and Dyer [*United States*] [*A publication*]
**Natl Clgh Poison Control Cent Bull** ... National Clearinghouse for Poison Control Centers. Bulletin [*A publication*]
**Natl Comput Conf** ... National Computer Conference [*United States*] [*A publication*]
**Natl Conf Dent Public Relat** ... National Conference on Dental Public Relations [*US*] [*A publication*]
**Natl Conf Earth Sci Pap (Alberta Univ)** ... National Conference on Earth Science. Papers (Alberta University) [*A publication*]
**Natl Conf Individ Onsite Wastewater Syst Proc** ... National Conference for Individual Onsite Wastewater Systems. Proceedings [*A publication*]
**Natl Conf Publ Inst Eng Aust** ... National Conference Publications. Institution of Engineers of Australia [*A publication*] (APTA)
**Natl Coop Highw Res Program Rep** ... National Cooperative Highway Research Program. Report [*A publication*]
**Natl Coop Highw Res Program Synth Highw Pract** ... National Cooperative Highway Research Program. Synthesis of Highway Practice [*A publication*]
**Natl Council Social Stud Yrbk** ... National Council for the Social Studies. Yearbook [*A publication*]
**Natl Council Teach Math Yrbk** ... National Council of Teachers of Mathematics. Yearbook [*A publication*]
**Natl Counc Radiat Prot Meas Annu Meet** ... National Council on Radiation Protection and Measurements. Annual Meeting [*A publication*]
**Natl Counc Res Dev Rep NCRD (Isr)** ... National Council for Research and Development. Report NCRD (Israel) [*A publication*]
**Natl Cycling** ... National Cycling [*A publication*] (APTA)
**Natl Dairy Res Inst (Karnal) Annu Rep** ... National Dairy Research Institute (Karnal). Annual Report [*A publication*]
**Natl Def**..... National Defense [*A publication*]
**Natl Def Med J (Tokyo)** ... National Defense Medical Journal (Tokyo) [*A publication*]
**Natl Dent Assoc J** ... National Dental Association. Journal [*US*] [*A publication*]
**Natl Dent Health Conf** ... National Dental Health Conference [*US*] [*A publication*]
**Natl Dev**..... National Development [*Australia*] [*A publication*]
**Natl Dist Heat Assoc Off Proc** ... National District Heating Association. Official Proceedings [*A publication*]
**Natl Drug**... National Druggist [*A publication*]
**Natl Eclectic Med Q** ... National Eclectic Medical Quarterly [*A publication*]
**Natl Eco**..... National Institute Economic Review [*A publication*]
**Natl Educ**.... National Education [*A publication*]
**Natl Electron Rev** ... National Electronics Review [*A publication*]
**Natl El Prin** ... National Elementary Principal [*A publication*]
**Natl Eng**..... National Engineer [*A publication*]
**Natl Eng Lab Rep (GB)** ... National Engineering Laboratory. Report (Great Britain) [*A publication*]
**Nat LF** ....... Natural Law Forum [*A publication*]

**Natl Fert Dev Cent Bull Y (US)** ... National Fertilizer Development Center. Bulletin Y (United States) [*A publication*]
**Natl Fert Rev** ... National Fertilizer Review [*A publication*]
**Natl Fire Codes** ... National Fire Codes [*United States*] [*A publication*]
**Natl Fisherman** ... National Fisherman [*A publication*]
**Natl Food Rev** ... National Food Review [*A publication*]
**Natl Forum Hosp Health Aff** ... National Forum on Hospital and Health Affairs [*US*] [*A publication*]
**Natl Found Cancer Res Cancer Res Assoc Symp** ... National Foundation for Cancer Research. Cancer Research Association Symposia [*A publication*]
**Natl Found March Dimes Birth Defects Orig Artic Ser** ... National Foundation. March of Dimes. Birth Defects Original Article Series [*A publication*]
**Natl Fuels Lubr Mtg** ... National Fuels and Lubricants Meeting [*A publication*]
**Natl Gas Bull** ... National Gas Bulletin [*A publication*] (APTA)
**Natl Gas Bull (Melbourne)** ... National Gas Bulletin (Melbourne) [*A publication*]
**Natl Geographic Mag** ... National Geographic Magazine [*A publication*]
**Natl Geogr Mag** ... National Geographic Magazine [*A publication*]
**Natl Geogr Res** ... National Geographic Research [*A publication*]
**Natl Geogr Soc Res Rep** ... National Geographic Society. Research Reports [*A publication*]
**Natl Geol Surv China Spec Rep** ... National Geological Survey of China. Special Report [*A publication*]
**Natl Geophys Res Inst (Hyderabad India) Bull** ... National Geophysical Research Institute (Hyderabad, India). Bulletin [*A publication*]
**Natl Glass** ... National Glass Budget [*A publication*]
**Natl Glass Budget** ... National Glass Budget [*United States*] [*A publication*]
**Natl Ground Water Qual Symp Proc** ... National Ground Water Quality Symposium. Proceedings [*A publication*]
**Nat L Guild Q** ... National Lawyers Guild Quarterly [*A publication*] (DLA)
**Natl Health Insur Jt Comm Med Res Comm (GB) Spec Rep Ser** ... National Health Insurance Joint Committee. Medical Research Committee (Great Britain). Special Report Series [*A publication*]
**Natl Health Insur Rep** ... National Health Insurance Reports [*United States*] [*A publication*]
**Natl Health Med Res Counc (Canberra) Med Res** ... National Health and Medical Research Council (Canberra). Medical Research [*A publication*]
**Natl Health Med Res Counc (Canberra) Med Res Proj** ... National Health and Medical Research Council (Canberra). Medical Research Projects [*A publication*]
**Natl Health Med Res Counc (Canberra) Rep** ... National Health and Medical Research Council (Canberra). Report [*A publication*]
**Natl Hortic Mag** ... National Horticultural Magazine [*A publication*]
**Natl Hosp Health Care** ... National Hospital Health Care [*A publication*]
**NatLib**........ National Liberal Party [*Australia*] [*Political party*]
**Natl I Eco**... National Institute Economic Review [*A publication*]
**Nat Life Southeast Asia** ... Nature and Life in Southeast Asia [*A publication*]
**Nat Lime Ass Bull** ... National Lime Association. Bulletin [*A publication*]
**Nat'l Income Tax Mag** ... National Income Tax Magazine [*A publication*] (DLA)
**Natl Ind Res Inst (Seoul) Rev** ... National Industrial Research Institute (Seoul). Review [*A publication*]
**Natl Inst Agric Bot (Camb) Rep Acc** ... National Institute of Agricultural Botany (Cambridge). Report and Accounts [*A publication*]
**Natl Inst Anim Health Q** ... National Institute of Animal Health. Quarterly [*A publication*]
**Natl Inst Anim Health Q (Yatabe)** ... National Institute of Animal Health. Quarterly (Yatabe) [*A publication*]
**Natl Inst Drug Abuse Res Monogr Ser** ... National Institute on Drug Abuse. Research Monograph Series [*A publication*]
**Natl Inst Econ R** ... National Institute Economic Review [*A publication*]
**Natl Inst Econ Rev** ... National Institute Economic Review [*A publication*]
**Natl Inst Genet (Mishima) Annu Rep** ... National Institute of Genetics (Mishima). Annual Report [*A publication*]
**Natl Inst Health Consensus Dev Conf Summ** ... National Institutes of Health. Consensus Development Conference. Summaries [*US*] [*A publication*]
**Natl Inst Metall Repub S Afr Rep** ... National Institute for Metallurgy. Republic of South Africa. Report [*A publication*]
**Natl Inst Nutr Annu Rep** ... National Institute of Nutrition. Annual Report [*A publication*]
**Natl Inst Polar Res Mem Ser C Earth Sci** ... National Institute of Polar Research. Memoirs. Series C. Earth Sciences [*A publication*]
**Natl Inst Polar Res Mem Spec Issue** ... National Institute of Polar Research. Memoirs. Special Issue [*A publication*]
**Natl Inst Polar Res (Tokyo) Antarct Geol Map Ser** ... National Institute of Polar Research (Tokyo). Antarctic Geological Map Series [*A publication*]
**Natl Inst Res Dairy Rep (Engl)** ... National Institute for Research in Dairying. Report (England) [*A publication*]
**Natl Inst Res Nucl Sci (GB) Rep** ... National Institute for Research in Nuclear Science (Great Britain). Report [*A publication*]
**Natl Inst Water Supply (Neth) Q Rep** ... National Institute for Water Supply (Netherlands). Quarterly Report [*A publication*]
**Nat Lith**..... National Lithographer [*A publication*]
**Nat LJ**........ Natal Law Journal [*South Africa*] [*A publication*] (DLA)
**Natl J**......... National Journal [*United States*] [*A publication*]
**Natl J Crim Def** ... National Journal of Criminal Defense [*A publication*]
**Natl Jt Comm Fert Appl Proc Annu Meet** ... National Joint Committee on Fertilizer Application. Proceedings of the Annual Meeting [*A publication*]
**Nat'l Law Guild Prac** ... National Lawyers Guild. Practitioner [*A publication*]
**Nat'l Legal Mag** ... National Legal Magazine [*A publication*] (DLA)
**Natl Libr Wales J** ... National Library of Wales. Journal [*A publication*]
**Natl Lithogr** ... National Lithographer [*A publication*]
**Nat'l LJ**..... National Law Journal [*A publication*]
**Natl Lucht Ruimtevaartlab Rapp** ... Nationaal Lucht- en Ruimtevaartlaboratorium. Rapport [*A publication*]
**Natl Lucht Ruimtevaartlab Versl Verh** ... Nationaal Lucht- en Ruimtevaartlaboratorium. Verslagen en Verhandelingen [*A publication*]
**Nat LM**...... Natal Law Magazine [*South Africa*] [*A publication*] (DLA)
**Natl M**....... National Magazine [*A publication*]
**Nat'l M (Bost)** ... National Magazine (Boston) [*A publication*]
**Natl Meas Lab Tech Pap (Aust)** ... National Measurement Laboratory. Technical Paper (Australia) [*A publication*]
**Natl Meas Lab Tech Pap CSIRO Aust** ... Australia. Commonwealth Scientific and Industrial Research Organisation. National Measurement Laboratory. Technical Paper [*A publication*] (APTA)
**Natl Med Care Utilization and Expenditure Survey** ... National Medical Care Utilization and Expenditure Survey [*United States*] [*A publication*]
**Natl Med J China (Peking)** ... National Medical Journal of China (Peking) [*A publication*]
**Natl Miller** ... National Miller [*United States*] [*A publication*]
**Natl Miller Am Miller** ... National Miller and American Miller [*A publication*]
**Nat'l Mun Rev** ... National Municipal Review [*A publication*]
**Natl Mus Bloemfontein Annu Rep** ... National Museum Bloemfontein. Annual Report [*A publication*]
**Natl Mus Bloemfontein Res Mem** ... National Museum Bloemfontein. Researches Memoir [*A publication*]
**Natl Mus Can Bull** ... National Museum of Canada. Bulletin [*A publication*]
**Natl Mus Can Nat Hist Pap** ... National Museum of Canada. Natural History Papers [*A publication*]
**Natl Mus Korea Art Mag** ... National Museum of Korea. Art Magazine [*Republic of Korea*] [*A publication*]
**Natl Mus Nat Sci (Ottawa) Publ Biol Oceanogr** ... National Museum of Natural Sciences (Ottawa). Publications in Biological Oceanography [*A publication*]
**Natl Mus Nat Sci (Ottawa) Publ Bot** ... National Museum of Natural Sciences (Ottawa). Publications in Botany [*A publication*]
**Natl Mus Nat Sci (Ottawa) Publ Nat Sci** ... National Museum of Natural Sciences (Ottawa). Publications in Natural Sciences [*A publication*]
**Natl Mus Nat Sci (Ottawa) Publ Palaeontol** ... National Museum of Natural Sciences (Ottawa). Publications in Palaeontology [*A publication*]
**Natl Mus Nat Sci (Ottawa) Publ Zool** ... National Museum of Natural Sciences (Ottawa). Publications in Zoology [*A publication*]
**Natl Mus NZ Misc Ser** ... National Museum of New Zealand. Miscellaneous Series [*A publication*]
**Natl Mus NZ Rec** ... National Museum of New Zealand. Records [*A publication*]
**Natl Mus Victoria Mem** ... National Museum of Victoria. Memoirs [*A publication*]
**Natl Nosocomial Infect Study** ... National Nosocomial Infections Study [*A publication*]
**Natl Observer** ... National Observer [*A publication*]
**Natl Oceanic Atmos Adm (US) Circ** ... National Oceanic and Atmospheric Administration (United States). Circular [*A publication*]
**Natl Oceanic Atmos Adm (US) Fish Bull** ... National Oceanic and Atmospheric Administration (United States). Fishery Bulletin [*A publication*]
**Natl Oceanic Atmos Adm (US) Spec Sci Rep Fish** ... National Oceanic and Atmospheric Administration (United States). Special Scientific Report. Fisheries [*A publication*]
**Natl Paint Bull** ... National Paint Bulletin [*A publication*]
**Natl Painters Mag** ... National Painters Magazine [*A publication*]
**Natl Paint Varn Lacquer Assoc Abstr Rev** ... National Paint, Varnish, and Lacquer Association. Abstract Review [*A publication*]
**Natl Parks** ... National Parks Magazine [*Formerly, National Parks and Conservation Magazine*] [*A publication*]
**Natl Parks Conserv Mag** ... National Parks and Conservation Magazine [*Later, National Parks Magazine*] [*A publication*]
**Natl Parks Mag** ... National Parks Magazine [*Formerly, National Parks and Conservation Magazine*] [*A publication*]
**Natl Pet News** ... National Petroleum News [*United States*] [*A publication*]
**Natl Pet Refin Assoc Tech Publ** ... National Petroleum Refiners Association. Technical Publication [*United States*] [*A publication*]
**Natl Pet Refiners Assoc Pap** ... National Petroleum Refiners Association. Papers [*A publication*]
**Natl Pet Refiners Assoc Tech Publ** ... National Petroleum Refiners Association. Technical Publication [*A publication*]

**Natl Petroleum Bibliography** ... National Petroleum Bibliography [*A publication*]
**Natl Phys Lab Notes Appl Sci (UK)** ... National Physical Laboratory. Notes on Applied Science (United Kingdom) [*A publication*]
**Natl Phys Lab Rep** ... National Physical Laboratory. Reports [*United Kingdom*] [*A publication*]
**Natl Phys Lab (UK) Div Chem Stand Rep** ... National Physical Laboratory (United Kingdom). Division of Chemical Standards. Report [*A publication*]
**Natl Phys Lab (UK) Proc Symp** ... National Physical Laboratory (United Kingdom). Proceedings of a Symposium [*A publication*]
**Natl Phys Lab (UK) Rep** ... National Physical Laboratory (United Kingdom). Report [*A publication*]
**Natl Phys Lab (UK) Symp** ... National Physical Laboratory (United Kingdom). Symposium [*A publication*]
**Natl Prior**... Setting National Priorities. The 19-- Budget [*United States*] [*A publication*]
**Natl Prov** ... National Provisioner [*A publication*]
**Nat'l Pub Empl Rep** ... National Public Employment Reporter [*A publication*] (DLA)
**Natl Pub Empl Rep Lab Rel Press** ... National Public Employment Reporter. Labor Relations Press [*A publication*]
**Nat LQ**....... Natal Law Quarterly [*South Africa*] [*A publication*] (DLA)
**Nat LR**....... Natal Law Reports [*South Africa*] [*A publication*] (ILCA)
**Natl Racq**... National Racquetball [*United States*] [*A publication*]
**Natl Ready Mixed Concr Assoc Publ** ... National Ready Mixed Concrete Association. Publication [*A publication*]
**Natl Real Estate Investor** ... National Real Estate Investor [*A publication*]
**Nat L Rec**... National Law Record [*A publication*] (DLA)
**Nat L Rep**.. National Law Reporter [*A publication*] (DLA)
**Natl Rep Sys** ... National Reporter System (DLA)
**Natl Res Cent Disaster Prev Rep** ... National Research Center for Disaster Prevention. Report [*A publication*]
**Natl Res Counc Build Res Advis Board Tech Rep** ... National Research Council. Building Research Advisory Board. Technical Report [*A publication*]
**Natl Res Counc Can Aeronaut Rep** ... National Research Council of Canada. Aeronautical Report [*A publication*]
**Natl Res Counc Can Assoc Comm Sci Criter Environ Qual Publ** ... National Research Council of Canada. Associate Committee on Scientific Criteria for Environmental Quality. Publication [*A publication*]
**Natl Res Counc Can Bull** ... National Research Council of Canada. Bulletin [*A publication*]
**Natl Res Counc Can Div Build Res Fire Study** ... National Research Council of Canada. Division of Building Research. Fire Study [*A publication*]
**Natl Res Counc Can Div Build Res Tech Pap** ... National Research Council of Canada. Division of Building Research. Technical Paper [*A publication*]
**Natl Res Counc Can Div Mech Eng Energy** ... National Research Council of Canada. Division of Mechanical Engineering. Energy [*A publication*]
**Natl Res Counc Can Div Mech Eng Energy Newsl** ... National Research Council of Canada. Division of Mechanical Engineering. Energy Newsletter [*A publication*]
**Natl Res Counc Can Div Mech Eng Lab Tech Rep** ... National Research Council of Canada. Division of Mechanical Engineering. Laboratory Technical Report [*A publication*]
**Natl Res Counc Can Div Mech Eng Mech Eng Rep** ... National Research Council of Canada. Division of Mechanical Engineering. Mechanical Engineering Report [*A publication*]
**Natl Res Counc Can Div Mech Eng Mech Eng Rep MP** ... National Research Council of Canada. Division of Mechanical Engineering. Mechanical Engineering Report. Series MP [*A publication*]
**Natl Res Counc Can Div Mech Eng Mech Eng Rep MS** ... National Research Council of Canada. Division of Mechanical Engineering. Mechanical Engineering Report MS [*A publication*]
**Natl Res Counc Can Div Mech Eng Q Bull** ... National Research Council of Canada. Division of Mechanical Engineering. Quarterly Bulletin [*A publication*]
**Natl Res Counc Can Div Mech Gen Newsl** ... National Research Council of Canada. Division of Mechanical Engineering. General Newsletter [*A publication*]
**Natl Res Counc Can Environ Secr Publ** ... National Research Council of Canada. Environmental Secretariat. Publication [*A publication*]
**Natl Res Counc Can Mech Eng Rep MP** ... National Research Council of Canada. Mechanical Engineering Report. Series MP [*A publication*]
**Natl Res Counc Can Rep** ... National Research Council of Canada. Report [*A publication*]
**Natl Res Counc Curr Issues Stud (US)** ... National Research Council. Current Issues and Studies (United States) [*A publication*]
**Natl Res Counc Philipp Bull** ... National Research Council of the Philippines. Bulletin [*A publication*]
**Natl Res Counc Rev** ... National Research Council. Review [*A publication*]
**Natl Res Inst Occup Dis S Afr Med Res Counc Annu Rep** ... National Research Institute for Occupational Diseases. South African Medical Research Council. Annual Report [*A publication*]
**Nat L Rev**... National Law Review [*A publication*] (DLA)
**Natl Rev**..... National Review [*A publication*]
**Natl Rural Letter Carrier** ... National Rural Letter Carrier [*A publication*]
**Natl Saf**...... National Safety [*A publication*]
**Natl Saf Congr Trans** ... National Safety Congress. Occupational Health Nursing Section. Transactions [*A publication*]
**Natl Saf News** ... National Safety News [*A publication*]
**Natl SAMPE Symp Exhib Proc** ... National SAMPE [*Society for the Advancement of Material and Process Engineering*] Symposium and Exhibition. Proceedings [*A publication*]
**Natl SAMPE Tech Conf** ... National SAMPE [*Society for the Advancement of Material and Process Engineering*] Technical Conference [*A publication*]
**Natl Sand Gravel Assoc NSGA Circ** ... National Sand and Gravel Association. NSGA Circular [*A publication*]
**Nat'l School L Rptr** ... National School Law Reporter [*A publication*] (DLA)
**Natl Sci Counc Mon** ... National Science Council. Monthly [*Taiwan*] [*A publication*]
**Natl Sci Counc Proc Part 2 (Taiwan)** ... National Science Council. Proceedings. Part 2. Biological, Medical, and Agricultural Sciences (Taiwan) [*A publication*]
**Natl Sci Counc (Taipei) Proc Part 1 Nat Math Sci** ... National Science Council (Taipei). Proceedings. Part 1. Natural and Mathematical Sciences [*A publication*]
**Natl Sci Found Annu Rep** ... National Science Foundation. Annual Report [*A publication*]
**Natl Sci Found NSF** ... National Science Foundation. NSF [*A publication*]
**Natl Sci Found Res Appl Natl Needs Rep NSF/RA (US)** ... National Science Foundation. Research Applied to National Needs. Report NSF/RA (US) [*A publication*]
**Natl Sci Found Sci Manpower Bull** ... National Science Foundation. Scientific Manpower Bulletin [*A publication*]
**Natl Sci Mus Bull Ser C (Tokyo)** ... National Science Museum. Bulletin. Series C. Geology (Tokyo) [*A publication*]
**Natl Sci Mus (Tokyo) Bull Ser C Geol Paleontol** ... National Science Museum (Tokyo). Bulletin. Series C. Geology and Paleontology [*A publication*]
**Natl Sci Mus (Tokyo) Mem** ... National Science Museum (Tokyo). Memoirs [*A publication*]
**Natl Sfty News** ... National Safety News [*United States*] [*A publication*]
**Natl Shade Tree Conf Proc** ... National Shade Tree Conference. Proceedings [*A publication*]
**Natl Soc Clean Air Annu Conf Proc** ... National Society for Clean Air. Annual Conference. Proceedings [*A publication*]
**Natl Soc Stud Educ Yrbk** ... National Society for the Study of Education. Yearbook [*A publication*]
**Natl Speleol Soc Bull** ... National Speleological Society. Bulletin [*A publication*]
**Natl Speleol Soc Occasional Paper** ... National Speleological Society. Occasional Paper [*A publication*]
**Natl Stand Lab Tech Pap CSIRO Aust** ... Australia. Commonwealth Scientific and Industrial Research Organisation. National Standards Laboratory. Technical Paper [*A publication*] (APTA)
**Natl Stand Ref Data Ser Natl Bur Stand** ... National Standard Reference Data Series. National Bureau of Standards [*A publication*]
**Natl Stand Ref Data Ser NBS** ... National Standard Reference Data Series. US National Bureau of Standards [*A publication*]
**Natl Stand Ref Data Ser US Natl Bur Stand** ... National Standard Reference Data Series. United States National Bureau of Standards [*A publication*]
**Natl Stand Ref Data Syst LBL** ... National Standard Reference Data System. Lawrence Berkeley Laboratory. University of California [*A publication*]
**Natl Swed Build Res Doc** ... National Swedish Building Research. Document [*Statens Institut foer Byggnadsforskning*] [*A publication*]
**Natl Sym**.... National Symphony Program Notes [*A publication*]
**Natl Tax J** ... National Tax Journal [*United States*] [*A publication*]
**Natl Tech Inf Serv Search** ... National Technical Information Service Search [*United States*] [*A publication*]
**Natl Tech Rep** ... National Technical Report [*A publication*]
**Natl Tech Rep (Matsushita Electr Ind C Osaka)** ... National Technical Report (Matsushita Electric Industrial Co., Osaka) [*A publication*]
**Natl Toxicol Program Tech Rep Ser** ... National Toxicology Program. Technical Report Series [*A publication*]
**Nat Lucht Ruimtevaartlab** ... National Lucht- en Ruimtevaartlaboratorium [*A publication*]
**Nat Lucht-Ruimtevaartlab Verslagen en Verhandel** ... Nationaal Lucht- en Ruimtevaartlaboratorium. Verslagen en Verhandelingen [*A publication*]
**Natl Underwrit (Life Health)** ... National Underwriter (Life and Health Insurance Edition) [*A publication*]
**Natl Underwrit (Life Health Insur Ed)** ... National Underwriter (Life and Health Insurance Edition) [*A publication*]
**Natl Univ Peiping Coll Agric Res Bull** ... National University of Peiping. College of Agriculture. Research Bulletin [*A publication*]
**Natl Veg Res Stn Annu Rep (Wellsbourne)** ... National Vegetable Research Station. Annual Report (Wellsbourne) [*A publication*]
**Natl Vitam Found Annu Rep** ... National Vitamin Foundation. Annual Report [*A publication*]
**Natl Vitam Found Nutr Symp Ser** ... National Vitamin Foundation. Nutrition Symposium Series [*United States*] [*A publication*]

**Natl Vitamin Found Annu Rep** ... National Vitamin Foundation. Annual Report [*A publication*]
**Natl Waste News** ... National Waste News [*United States*] [*A publication*]
**Natl Westminster Bank Q Rev** ... National Westminster Bank. Quarterly Review [*England*] [*A publication*]
**Natl Wildl** ... National Wildlife [*A publication*]
**Natl Wool Grow** ... National Wool Grower [*A publication*]
**Nat M** ........ National Magazine [*A publication*]
**NATMA** .... NASA [*National Aeronautics and Space Administration*] Technical Memorandum [*A publication*]
**NATMA** .... National Award and Trophy Manufacturers Association (EA)
**NATMAC** ... National Air Traffic Management Advisory Committee [*British*]
**Nat Mag** ..... National Magazine [*A publication*]
**Nat Malays** ... Nature Malaysiana [*A publication*]
**Nat Malgache** ... Naturaliste Malgache [*A publication*]
**Nat Map Bull** ... National Mapping Bulletin [*A publication*] (APTA)
**NATMC** .... National Advanced Technology Management Conference
**Nat Mensch** ... Natuur en Mensch [*A publication*]
**NATMH** .... National Association of Teachers of the Mentally Handicapped [*British*]
**NATMILCOMSYS** ... National Military Command System
**Nat Monspel** ... Naturalia Monspeliensia [*A publication*]
**Nat Monspeliensia Ser Bot** ... Naturalia Monspeliensia. Serie Botanique [*A publication*]
**Nat Monspel Ser Bot** ... Naturalia Monspeliensia. Serie Botanique [*A publication*]
**Nat Mosana** ... Natura Mosana [*A publication*]
**Nat Mosana Suppl B Bot** ... Natura Mosana. Supplement B. Botanique [*A publication*]
**Nat Mosana Suppl CD Zool** ... Natura Mosana. Supplement CD. Zoologie [*A publication*]
**Nat Munic R** ... National Municipal Review [*A publication*]
**Nat Munic Rev** ... National Municipal Review [*A publication*]
**Nat Mun Rev** ... National Municipal Review [*A publication*]
**Nat Mus** ..... Natur und Museum [*A publication*]
**Nat Mus Council Bul** ... National Music Council. Bulletin [*A publication*]
**Nat Mus Senckenb Naturforsch Ges** ... Natur und Museum. Senckenbergische Naturforschende Gesellschaft [*A publication*]
**Nat Mus VIC Mem** ... National Museum of Victoria. Memoirs [*A publication*] (APTA)
**NA T & N** .. Selected Decisions of the Native Appeal Court, Transvaal and Natal [*A publication*] (DLA)
**NATNAV** .. North Atlantic Navigation
**NATNAVMEDCEN** ... National Naval Medical Center [*Bethesda, MD*]
**Natn Bank Mon Sum** ... National Bank. Monthly Summary [*A publication*]
**Natn Bank Mon Sum Aust Cond** ... National Bank of Australasia. Monthly Summary of Australian Conditions [*A publication*]
**Natn Bldr** ... National Builder [*A publication*]
**Nat New Biol** ... Nature: New Biology [*A publication*]
**NATNews** ... NATNews. National Association of Theatre Nurses [*A publication*]
**Natn Farmer** ... National Farmer [*A publication*]
**Natn Geogr Mag** ... National Geographic Magazine [*A publication*]
**Natn Hosp** ... National Hospital [*A publication*]
**Natn Jewish Mon** ... National Jewish Monthly [*A publication*]
**Natn Parks J** ... National Parks Journal [*A publication*]
**Natn Rehab Digest** ... National Rehabilitation Digest [*A publication*]
**Natn Res Progm Agric Res Serv** ... National Research Program. Agricultural Research Service [*A publication*]
**Natns Bus** .. Nation's Business [*A publication*]
**Natns Restr** ... Nation's Restaurant News [*A publication*]
**Natn Symp Hydrol** ... National Symposium on Hydrology [*A publication*] (APTA)
**Natn Times** ... National Times [*A publication*] (APTA)
**Natn Times Mag** ... National Times Magazine [*A publication*]
**NATO** ........ Narrow-Angle Target of Opportunity [*Photography*] [*NASA*]
**NATO** ........ National Association of Taxicab Owners [*Later, ITA*] (EA)
**NATO** ........ National Association of Telephone Operators [*A union*] [*British*]
**NATO** ........ National Association of Theatre Owners (EA)
**NATO** ........ National Association of Trailer Owners (EA)
**NATO** ........ National Association of Travel Organizations [*Later, TIA*] (EA)
**NATO** ........ North African Theater of Operations [*World War II*]
**NATO** ........ North Atlantic Treaty Organization [*Facetious translation: "No Action, Talk Only"*] [*Brussels, Belgium*]
**NATO 16** ... NATO's Sixteen Nations. North Atlantic Treaty Organization [*A publication*]
**NATOA** ..... National Association of Telecommunications Officers and Advisors (EA)
**NATO Adv Study Inst Ser B** ... NATO [*North Atlantic Treaty Organization*] Advanced Study Institutes. Series B. Physics [*A publication*]
**NATO Adv Study Inst Ser B Physics** ... NATO [*North Atlantic Treaty Organization*] Advanced Study Institutes. Series B. Physics [*A publication*]
**NATO Adv Study Inst Ser C** ... NATO [*North Atlantic Treaty Organization*] Advanced Study Institutes. Series C. Mathematical and Physical Sciences [*A publication*]
**NATO Adv Study Inst Ser D** ... NATO [*North Atlantic Treaty Organization*] Advanced Study Institutes. Series D. Behavioural and Social Sciences [*A publication*]
**NATO Adv Study Inst Ser E** ... NATO [*North Atlantic Treaty Organization*] Advanced Study Institutes. Series E. Applied Sciences [*A publication*]
**NATO Adv Study Inst Ser Ser A Life Sci** ... NATO [*North Atlantic Treaty Organization*] Advanced Study Institutes Series. Series A. Life Sciences [*A publication*]
**NATO Adv Study Inst Ser Ser E Appl Sci** ... NATO [*North Atlantic Treaty Organization*] Advanced Study Institutes Series. Series E. Applied Science [*A publication*]
**NATO-AGARD** ... North Atlantic Treaty Organization - Advisory Group for Aeronautical Research and Development
**NATO ASI (Adv Sci Inst) Ser Ser A Life Sci** ... NATO [*North Atlantic Treaty Organization*] ASI (Advanced Science Institutes) Series. Series A. Life Sciences [*A publication*]
**NATO ASI (Adv Sci Inst) Ser Ser E Appl Sci** ... NATO [*North Atlantic Treaty Organization*] ASI (Advanced Science Institutes) Series. Series E. Applied Sciences [*A publication*]
**NATO ASI (Adv Sci Inst) Ser Ser G Ecol Sci** ... NATO [*North Atlantic Treaty Organization*] ASI (Advanced Science Institutes) Series. Series G. Ecological Sciences [*A publication*]
**NATO/CCMS Air Pollut** ... NATO/CCMS [*North Atlantic Treaty Organization/Committee on the Challenges of Modern Society*] Air Pollution [*A publication*]
**NATO Comm Challenges Mod Soc Air Pollut** ... NATO [*North Atlantic Treaty Organization*]/Committee on the Challenges of Modern Society. Air Pollution [*A publication*]
**NATOELLA** ... North Atlantic Treaty Organization - European Long Lines Agency
**NAT-OJT** ... National On-the-Job Training Program [*Department of Labor*]
**Nat -Okon Tss** ... Nationalokonomisk Tidsskrift [*A publication*]
**NATO-LRSS** ... North Atlantic Treaty Organization - Long-Range Scientific Studies
**NATOMILOCGRP** ... North Atlantic Treaty Organization - Military Oceanography Group (NATG)
**NATOPS** ... Naval Air Training and Operating Procedures Standardization (MCD)
**NATO-RDPP** ... North Atlantic Treaty Organization - Multilateral Research and Development Production Program
**NATOSAT** ... North Atlantic Treaty Organization Satellite
**NATO-SC** ... North Atlantic Treaty Organization Science Committee
**NATO's Fift Nations** ... NATO's [*North Atlantic Treaty Organization*] Fifteen Nations [*A publication*]
**NATOUSA** ... North African Theater of Operations, United States Army [*World War II*]
**NATO War P** ... NATO [*North Atlantic Treaty Organization*] and the Warsaw Pact Force Comparisons [*A publication*]
**NATP** ........ National Association of Tax Practitioners (EA)
**Nat P** .......... Nationalities Papers [*A publication*]
**NATPA** ...... North America Taiwanese Professors' Association (EA)
**NAT PAC** ... National PAC [*Political Action Committee*] (EA)
**Nat Pal Mus B** ... National Palace Museum. Bulletin [*Taipai*] [*A publication*]
**Nat Parent-Teach** ... National Parent-Teacher [*A publication*]
**Nat Parks** ... National Parks Magazine [*Formerly, National Parks and Conservation Magazine*] [*A publication*]
**Nat Parks & Con Mag** ... National Parks and Conservation Magazine [*Later, National Parks Magazine*] [*A publication*]
**NATPE** ...... NATPE [*National Association of Television Program Executives*] International (EA)
**Nat Pet N** ... National Petroleum News [*A publication*]
**Nat Petrol Refiners Ass Tech Papers** ... National Petroleum Refiners Association. Technical Papers [*A publication*]
**Nat Philos** ... Natural Philosopher [*A publication*]
**Nat Phys Lab (Gt Brit) Notes Appl Sci** ... National Physical Laboratory (Great Britain). Department of Scientific and Industrial Research. Notes on Applied Science [*A publication*]
**Nat Phys Lab UK Collect Res** ... National Physical Laboratory (United Kingdom). Collected Researches [*A publication*]
**NATPN** ..... North African Transportation Section [*World War II*]
**Nat Poult Impr Plan Rep US Dept Agric Sci Educ Admin** ... National Poultry Improvement Plan. Report. United States Department of Agriculture. Science and Education Administration [*A publication*]
**Nat Probation Assn Yrbk** ... National Probation and Parole Association. Yearbook [*A publication*]
**Nat Prod Rep** ... Natural Product Reports [*A publication*]
**Nat Public Accountant** ... National Public Accountant [*A publication*]
**Nat Q** ......... National Quarterly Review [*A publication*]
**Nat Q Rev** .. National Quarterly Review [*A publication*]
**NATR** ........ Natchez Trace Parkway [*National Park Service designation*]
**Nat R** .......... Nation Review [*A publication*] (APTA)
**NATR** ........ National Representative [*Red Cross*]
**Nat R** .......... National Review [*A publication*]
**NATR** ........ Natrium [*Sodium*] [*Pharmacy*]
**NATR** ........ Natural Resources
**NATR** ........ Nature's Sunshine Products, Inc. [*NASDAQ symbol*] (NQ)
**NATR** ........ No Additional Traffic Reported [*Aviation*]
**NATR** ........ Nordischer Amator Theater Rat [*Nordic Amateur Theatre Council - NATC*] (EAIO)

**NATRA** ..... National Association of Television and Radio Artists [*Inactive*]
**NATRA** ..... Nature [*A publication*]
**NATRA** ..... Naval Air Training Command (AFIT)
**Nat Racq** .... National Racquetball [*A publication*]
**NATRAP**... Narrow-Band Transmission of RADAR Pictures (MCD)
**NATRC** ..... North American Trail Ride Conference (EA)
**Nat Real Estate Invest** ... National Real Estate Investor [*A publication*]
**Nat Real Estate Investor** ... National Real Estate Investor [*A publication*]
**Nat Reg** ...... National Register, Edited by Mead [*1816*] [*A publication*] (DLA)
**Nat Rep** ...... National Republic [*A publication*]
**Nat Rept Syst** ... National Reporter System (DLA)
**Nat Res Counc Bldg Res Adv Bd Tech Rep** ... National Research Council. Building Research Advisory Board. Technical Report [*A publication*]
**Nat Res Counc Can Aeronaut Rep** ... National Research Council of Canada. Aeronautical Report [*A publication*]
**Nat Res Counc Can Annu Rep** ... National Research Council of Canada. Annual Report [*A publication*]
**Nat Res Counc Can Ass Comm Geod Geophys Proc Hydrol Symp** ... National Research Council of Canada. Associate Committee on Geodesy and Geophysics. Proceedings of Hydrology Symposium [*A publication*]
**Nat Res Counc Can Ass Comm Geotech Res Tech Memo** ... National Research Council of Canada. Associate Committee on Geotechnical Research. Technical Memorandum [*A publication*]
**Nat Res Counc Can Div Bldg Res Bibliogr** ... National Research Council of Canada. Division of Building Research. Bibliography [*A publication*]
**Nat Res Counc Can Div Mech Eng Mech Eng Rep** ... National Research Council of Canada. Division of Mechanical Engineering. Mechanical Engineering Report [*A publication*]
**Nat Res Counc Can Mech Eng Rep ME** ... National Research Council of Canada. Mechanical Engineering Report. ME [*A publication*]
**Nat Res Counc Can Unsteady Aerodyn Lab Lab Tech Rep** ... National Research Council of Canada. Unsteady Aerodynamics Laboratory. Laboratory Technical Report [*A publication*]
**Nat Res Counc Comm Probl Drug Depend Proc Annu Sci Meet (US)** ... National Research Council. Committee of Problems of Drug Dependence. Proceedings. Annual Scientific Meeting (United States) [*A publication*]
**Nat Res Counc Conf Elec Insul Annu Rep** ... National Research Council. Conference on Electrical Insulation. Annual Report [*A publication*]
**Nat Res Council Can Div Mech Engng Gen** ... National Research Council of Canada. Division of Mechanical Engineering. General Newsletter [*A publication*]
**Nat Res Counc Nat Acad Sci Rep** ... [*US*] Research Council. National Academy of Sciences. Reports [*A publication*]
**Nat Res J** ... Natural Resources Journal [*A publication*]
**Nat Res Law** ... Natural Resources Law [*A publication*]
**Nat Res Lawyer** ... Natural Resources Lawyer [*A publication*]
**Nat Resour** ... Nature and Resources [*A publication*]
**Nat Resources J** ... Natural Resources Journal [*A publication*]
**Nat Resources Jour** ... Natural Resources Journal [*A publication*]
**Nat Resources Law** ... Natural Resources Lawyer [*A publication*]
**Nat Resources L Newsl** ... Natural Resources Law Newsletter [*A publication*]
**Nat Resour Earth Sci** ... Natural Resources and Earth Sciences. Abstract Newsletter [*A publication*]
**Nat Resour Forum** ... Natural Resources Forum [*A publication*]
**Nat Resour Forum Libr** ... Natural Resources Forum Library [*A publication*]
**Nat Resour Lawyer** ... Natural Resources Lawyer [*A publication*]
**Nat Resour Res (Paris)** ... Natural Resources Research (Paris) [*A publication*]
**Nat Rev** ...... Nation Review [*A publication*] (APTA)
**Nat Rev** ...... National Review [*A publication*]
**NATRFD**... National Association of Television-Radio Farm Directors [*Later, NAFB*] (EA)
**NATRI** ....... National Association of Treasurers of Religious Institutes (EA)
**NATRI** ....... Navy Training Requirements Information
**NATRON** ... National Cash Register Electronic Data Processing System (MCD)
**NAT-RPG** ... North Atlantic Treaty Regional Planning Group (NATG)
**Nat Rubber** ... Natural Rubber News [*A publication*]
**Nat Rubb News** ... Natural Rubber News [*A publication*]
**NATS** ......... National Activity to Test Software
**NATS** ......... National Air Traffic Services [*British*]
**NATS** ......... National Association of Teachers of Singing (EA)
**NATS** ......... National Association of Teachers of Singing. Bulletin [*A publication*]
**NATS** ......... National Association of Temporary Services [*Alexandria, VA*] (EA)
**NATS** ......... National Association of Textile Supervisors (EA)
**NATS** ......... National Securities Corp. [*NASDAQ symbol*] (NQ)
**NATS** ......... Naval Air Transport Service
**NATS** ......... Needlework and Accessories Trade Show (ITD)
**NATS** ......... New Aircraft Tool System [*Army*]
**NATS** ......... Noise Abatement Test System [*FAA*] (FAAC)
**NATS** ......... Nordisk Avisteknisk Samarbetsnamnd [*Nordic Joint Technical Press Board*] (EAIO)
**NATS** ......... North American Truffling Society (EA)
**NATSA** ...... National Associated Truck Stops and Associates (EA)
**NATSAA**... NATO Air Traffic Service Advisory Agency (NATG)
**Nat Safety News** ... National Safety News [*A publication*]
**Nat Saf News** ... National Safety News [*A publication*]
**Nat Sand Gravel Ass NSGA Circ** ... National Sand and Gravel Association. NSGA Circular [*A publication*]
**Nat Savings and Loan League J** ... National Savings and Loan League. Journal [*A publication*]
**NATS Bul** ... NATS [*National Association of Teachers of Singing*] Bulletin [*A publication*]
**NATS Bull** ... National Association of Teachers of Singing. Bulletin [*A publication*]
**NATSC** ...... National Association of Training School Chaplains (EA)
**NATSC** ...... National Association of Trap and Skeet Clubs (EA)
**Nat Sc As Staten Island Pr** ... Natural Science Association of Staten Island. Proceedings [*A publication*]
**Nat Sch** ...... Nation's Schools [*A publication*]
**Nat Schedule Rates** ... National Schedule of Rates [*A publication*]
**Nat Sci** ....... Natural Science [*A publication*]
**Nat Sci Bull Univ Amoy** ... Natural Science Bulletin. University of Amoy [*A publication*]
**Nat Sci Prog** ... Nature. Science Progress [*A publication*]
**Nat Sci Rep Ochanomizu Univ** ... Natural Science Report. Ochanomizu University [*A publication*]
**Nat Sci Res Nat Sci Inst Chosun Univ** ... Natural Science Research. Natural Science Institute. Chosun University [*A publication*]
**Nat Sculp R** ... National Sculpture Review [*A publication*]
**Nat Sculpt** ... National Sculpture Review [*A publication*]
**NATSECM** ... National Security Medal
**Nat Sec R**... National Security Record [*A publication*]
**Nat Seedsman** ... National Seedsman [*A publication*]
**Nat Semi** .... National Semiconductor Corp.
**NATSF** ...... Naval Air Technical Services Facility (MCD)
**NATSFERRY** ... Naval Air Transport Service, Ferry Command [*World War II*]
**Nat Sicil** ..... Naturalista Siciliano [*A publication*]
**NATSJA** ... National Association of Training School and Juvenile Agencies [*Later, NAJCA*] (EA)
**NATSLANT** ... Naval Air Transport Service, Atlantic Wing [*World War II*]
**NATSO** ..... National Association of Truck Stop Operators (EA)
**Nat Soc Med Res Bull** ... National Society for Medical Research. Bulletin [*United States*] [*A publication*]
**Nat Soc Study Ed Yrbk** ... National Society for the Study of Education. Yearbook [*A publication*]
**NATSOPA** ... National Society of Operative Printers and Assistants [*British*]
**NATSPAC** ... Naval Air Transport Service, Pacific Wing [*World War II*]
**NAT-STD** ... NATO STANAG International Standards
**Nat Stock & F** ... National Stockman and Farmer [*A publication*]
**Nat Study**.... Nature Study [*A publication*]
**NATSU** ..... Naval Air Technical Services Unit (NVT)
**NATSYN**... Natural and Synthetic [*Type of long-wearing rubber, which is actually wholly synthetic*]
**NATT** ........ National Association of Towns and Township Officials (EA)
**Nat T** .......... National Times [*A publication*] (APTA)
**Natt** ............ [*Marcus Antonius*] Natta [*Flourished, 16th century*] [*Authority cited in pre-1607 legal work*] (DSA)
**NATT** ........ Naval Air Technical Training
**NATT** ........ North Atlantic Technology, Inc. [*NASDAQ symbol*] (NQ)
**NAtt** ........... Stevens Memorial Library, Attica, NY [*Library symbol*] [*Library of Congress*] (LCLS)
**NATTA** ..... Network of Alternative Technology and Technology Assessment (EAIO)
**NATTA** ..... North American Trackless Trolley Association (EA)
**Nat Tax J**... National Tax Journal [*A publication*]
**Nat Tax Mag** ... National Tax Magazine [*A publication*] (DLA)
**NATTC** ...... Naval Air Technical Training Center
**Nat Tech** .... Natur und Technik [*A publication*]
**Nat Tech** .... Natuur en Techniek [*A publication*]
**Nat Tech Rep** ... National Technical Report [*Matsushita Electric Industrial Co., Osaka*] [*A publication*]
**Nat Times** .. National Times [*A publication*] (APTA)
**NATTKE**... National Association of Theatrical, Television, and Kine Employees [*A union*] [*British*] (DCTA)
**Nat T Mag** ... National Times Magazine [*A publication*] (APTA)
**Nat Trust** ... National Trust [*A publication*]
**Nat Trust Aust Bull** ... National Trust of Australia. Bulletin [*A publication*] (APTA)
**Nat Trust Bul** ... National Trust Bulletin [*A publication*] (APTA)
**Nat Trust Studies** ... National Trust Studies [*A publication*]
**NATTS** ...... National Association of Trade and Technical Schools (EA)
**NATTS** ...... Naval Air Turbine Test Station
**NATTS** ...... North American Transvestite/Transsexual Society (EA)
**NATTS-ATL** ... Naval Air Turbine Test Station - Aeronautical Turbine Laboratory
**NATTU** ..... Naval Air Technical Training Unit
**NATU** ........ Natura Energy Corp. [*NASDAQ symbol*] (NQ)
**NATU** ........ Naval Aircraft Torpedo Unit
**NATUA** ..... Nature [*A publication*]
**Nat UL Rev** ... Natal University. Law Review [*A publication*]
**Nat UL Rev** ... National University. Law Review [*1921-31*] [*A publication*] (DLA)

**Nat Underw** ... National Underwriter [*A publication*]
**Nat Underw (Fire Ed)** ... National Underwriter (Fire and Casualty Insurance Edition) [*A publication*]
**Nat Underw (Life)** ... National Underwriter (Life and Health Insurance Edition) [*A publication*]
**Nat Underw (Life Ed)** ... National Underwriter (Life and Health Insurance Edition) [*A publication*]
**Nat Underw (Prop Ed)** ... National Underwriter (Property and Casualty Insurance Edition) [*A publication*]
**Nat Underw (Property Ed)** ... National Underwriter (Property and Casualty Insurance Edition) [*A publication*]
**Natural Food Fmg** ... Natural Food and Farming [*A publication*]
**Natural Gard** ... Natural Gardening [*A publication*]
**Natural Gas Ind** ... Natural Gas for Industry [*A publication*]
**Natural Hi** ... Natural History [*A publication*]
**Naturalia Monspel Ser Bot** ... Naturalia Monspeliensia. Serie Botanique [*A publication*]
**Naturaliste Can** ... Naturaliste Canadien [*A publication*]
**Natural L F** ... Natural Law Forum [*A publication*]
**Natural Resources J** ... Natural Resources Journal [*A publication*]
**Natural Resources Jnl** ... Natural Resources Journal [*A publication*]
**Natural Resources Law** ... Natural Resources Lawyer [*A publication*]
**Natural Resources Lawy** ... Natural Resources Lawyer [*A publication*]
NATURBTESTSTA ... Naval Air Turbine Test Station
**Naturegp Ocean Guide Books** ... Naturegraph Ocean Guide Books [*A publication*]
**Naturegr Ocean Guide Books** ... Naturegraph Ocean Guide Books [*A publication*]
**Nature and Life SE Asia** ... Nature and Life in Southeast Asia [*A publication*]
**Nature (London) New Biol** ... Nature (London). New Biology [*A publication*]
**Nature (London) Phys Sci** ... Nature (London). Physical Science [*A publication*]
**Nature Mag** ... Nature Magazine [*A publication*]
**Nature New Biol** ... Nature: New Biology [*A publication*]
**Naturens Verd** ... Naturens Verden [*A publication*]
**Nature: Phys Sci** ... Nature: Physical Science [*A publication*]
**Nature and Sci Ed R** ... Nature and Science Education Review [*A publication*]
**Nature Syst** ... Nature and System [*A publication*]
**Naturf Gesell Basel Verh** ... Naturforschende Gesellschaft in Basel. Verhandlungen [*A publication*]
**Naturf Gesell Bern Mitt Neue Folge** ... Naturforschende Gesellschaft in Bern. Mitteilungen. Neue Folge [*A publication*]
**Naturf Gesell Zurich Vierteljahrsschr** ... Naturforschende Gesellschaft in Zuerich. Vierteljahresschrift [*A publication*]
**Naturforsch Ges Basel Verh** ... Naturforschende Gesellschaft in Basel. Verhandlungen [*A publication*]
**Naturforsch Ges Freib im Breisgau Ber** ... Naturforschende Gesellschaft zu Freiburg im Breisgau. Berichte [*A publication*]
**Naturforsch Ges Zuerich Vierteljahrsschr** ... Naturforschende Gesellschaft in Zuerich. Vierteljahrsschrift [*A publication*]
**Natur Hist** ... Natural History [*A publication*]
**Naturhist Ges Hannover Ber** ... Naturhistorische Gesellschaft zu Hannover. Bericht [*A publication*]
**Naturhist Mus (Bern) Jahrb** ... Naturhistorisches Museum (Bern). Jahrbuch [*A publication*]
**Naturhist Mus Stadt Bern Jahrb** ... Naturhistorisches Museum der Stadt Bern. Jahrbuch [*A publication*]
**Naturhist Mus Wien Ann** ... Naturhistorisches Museum in Wien. Annalen [*A publication*]
**Naturhist Mus Wien Veroeff Neue Folge** ... Naturhistorisches Museum in Wien. Veroeffentlichungen. Neue Folge [*A publication*]
**Naturh-Med Ver Heidelberg Verh** ... Naturhistorisch-Medicinischer Verein zu Heidelberg. Verhandlungen [*A publication*]
**Naturh Ver Preus Rheinl Verh** ... Naturhistorischer Verein der Preussischen Rheinlande und Westphalens. Verhandlungen [*A publication*]
**Naturh Ver Preus Rheinl Verh (Niederrhein Ges Bonn) Szb** ... Naturhistorischer Verein der Preussischen Rheinlande. Verhandlungen (Niederrheinische Gesellschaft fuer Naturund Heilkunde in Bonn). Sitzungsberichte [*A publication*]
**Naturk Jb Stadt Linz** ... Naturkundliches Jahrbuch der Stadt Linz [*A publication*]
**Natur Landsch** ... Natur und Landschaft [*A publication*]
**Natur u Mus** ... Natur und Museum [*A publication*]
**Natur Mus (Arhus)** ... Natur og Museum (Arhus) [*A publication*]
**Natur Mus (Frankf)** ... Natur und Museum (Frankfurt) [*A publication*]
**Natur Res J** ... Natural Resources Journal [*A publication*]
**Natur Res L** ... Natural Resources Lawyer [*A publication*]
**Natur Resou** ... Natural Resources Lawyer [*A publication*]
**Natur Resources Forum** ... Natural Resources Forum [*A publication*]
**Natur Resources J** ... Natural Resources Journal [*A publication*]
**Natursch Naturp** ... Naturschutz- und Naturparke [*A publication*]
**Natur Sci Rep Ochanomizu Univ** ... Natural Science Report. Ochanomizu University [*A publication*]
**Natur u Volk** ... Natur und Volk [*A publication*]
**Naturw Abh** ... Naturwissenschaftliche Abhandlungen [*A publication*]
**Naturwiss**... Naturwissenschaften [*A publication*]
**Naturwissen** ... Naturwissenschaften [*A publication*]
**Naturwissenschaft Med** ... Naturwissenschaft und Medizin [*A publication*]
**Naturwiss Fak Muenich Univ Inaug-Diss** ... Naturwissenschaftliche Fakultaet Muenich Universitaet. Inaugural-Dissertation [*A publication*]
**Naturwiss Med** ... Naturwissenschaft und Medizin [*A publication*]
**Naturwiss Monatsh Biol Chem Geogr Geol Unterr** ... Naturwissenschaftliche Monatshefte fuer den Biologischen, Chemischen, Geographischen, und Geologischen Unterricht [*A publication*]
**Naturwiss Rundsch** ... Naturwissenschaftliche Rundschau [*A publication*]
**Naturwiss Umsch Chem Ztg** ... Naturwissenschaftliche Umschau der Chemiker-Zeitung [*A publication*]
**Naturwiss Unterr Phys/Chem** ... Naturwissenschaften im Unterricht (Teil) Physik/Chemie [*West Germany*] [*A publication*]
**Naturwiss Unterr Phys Chem Biol** ... Naturwissenschaften im Unterricht. Physik/Chemie/Biologie [*A publication*]
**Naturwiss Verein (Darmst) Ber** ... Naturwissenschaftlicher Verein (Darmstadt). Bericht [*A publication*]
**Naturwiss Ver Schleswig-Holstein Schr** ... Naturwissenschaftlicher Verein fuer Schleswig-Holstein. Schriften [*A publication*]
**Naturwiss Z Forst Landwirtsch** ... Naturwissenschaftliche Zeitschrift fuer Forst- und Landwirtschaft [*A publication*]
**Naturw Rdsch** ... Naturwissenschaftliche Rundschau [*A publication*]
**Naturw Rdsch (Stuttg)** ... Naturwissenschaftliche Rundschau (Stuttgart) [*A publication*]
**Naturw Ver (Halle) Jber** ... Naturwissenschaftlicher Verein (Halle). Jahresberichte [*A publication*]
**Naturw Ver Neuvorpommern und Ruegen in Greifswald Mitt** ... Naturwissenschaftlicher Verein fuer Neuvorpommern und Ruegen in Greifswald. Mitteilungen [*A publication*]
**Naturw Ver Steiermark Mitt** ... Naturwissenschaftlicher Verein fuer Steiermark. Mitteilungen [*A publication*]
**Naturw Wchnschr** ... Naturwissenschaftliche Wochenschrift [*A publication*]
**Naturw Wochensch** ... Naturwissenschaftliche Wochenschrift [*A publication*]
**Naturw Z Forst u Landw** ... Naturwissenschaftliche Zeitschrift fuer Forst- und Landwirtschaft [*A publication*]
**Naturw Z Land-u Forstw** ... Naturwissenschaftliche Zeitschrift fuer Land- und Forstwirtschaft [*A publication*]
NATUS ..... Naturalized United States Citizen
NATUS ..... US message dealing with NATO subject matter (NATG)
NATUSA... North African Theater, United States Army [*World War II*]
**Natuurhist Maandbl** ... Natuurhistorisch Maandblad [*A publication*]
**Natuurh Maandbl** ... Natuurhistorisch Maandblad [*A publication*]
**Natuurkd Voordr** ... Natuurkundige Voordrachten [*A publication*]
**Natuurk Tijdschr Ned-Indie** ... Natuurkundig Tijdschrift voor Nederlandsch-Indie [*A publication*]
**Natuurwet Studiekring Suriname Ned Antillen Uitg** ... Natuurwetenschappelijke Studiekring voor Suriname en de Nederlandse Antillen. Uitgaven [*A publication*]
**Natuurwet Tijdschr** ... Natuurwetenschappelijk Tijdschrift [*A publication*]
**Natuurwet Tijdschr Ned Indie** ... Natuurwetenschappelijk Tijdschrift voor Nederlandsch-Indie [*A publication*]
**Natuurwet Werkgroep Nederlandse Antillen Uitgaven** ... Natuurwetenschappelijke Werkgroep Nederlandse Antillen Uitgaven [*A publication*]
NATVA ..... National All Terrain Vehicle Association (EA)
NATVAS... National Academy of Television Arts and Sciences (EA)
**Nat Verden** ... Naturens Verden [*A publication*]
**Nat Vivante** ... Nature Vivante [*A publication*]
**Nat Volk (Frankf)** ... Natur und Volk (Frankfurt) [*A publication*]
**Natv Self**.... Native Self-Sufficiency [*A publication*]
NATW ....... National Association of Texaco Wholesalers (EA)
NATW ....... National Association of Town Watch (EA)
NATWA .... National Auto and Truck Wreckers Association [*Later, ADRA*] (EA)
NATwA ..... North American Tiddlywinks Association (EA)
**Nat Wales** ... Nature in Wales [*A publication*]
**Nat W Bank** ... National Westminster Bank. Quarterly Review [*A publication*]
NatWest..... National Westminster [*Bank*]
**Nat West Bank Q Rev** ... National Westminster Bank. Quarterly Review [*A publication*]
**Nat Westminster Bank Q R** ... National Westminster Bank. Quarterly Review [*A publication*]
**Nat Wetlands Newsletter** ... National Wetlands Newsletter [*A publication*]
NATWF..... North American Tug of War Federation (EA)
**Nat Wildlife** ... National Wildlife [*A publication*]
NATWJ..... National Alliance of Third World Journalists (EA)
NATWP .... Naval Air Transport Wing, Pacific
NaTY ......... Sodium Hydrogen Phosphate-Tryptone-Yeast Extract [*Growth medium*] [*Microbiology*]
NAU .......... Confederation Nordique des Cadres, Techniciens, et Autres Responsables [*Nordic Confederation of Supervisors, Technicians, and Other Managers*] (EAIO)
NAU .......... Nalcus Resources [*Vancouver Stock Exchange symbol*]
NAU .......... Napuka [*Marquesas Islands*] [*Airport symbol*] (OAG)
NAU .......... Narcotics Assistance Unit [*Department of State*]
NAU .......... Naval Administrative Unit
NAU .......... Network Access Unit [*Telecommunications*]
NAU .......... Network Address Unit [*Data processing*] (BUR)
NAU .......... Noise Augmentation Unit [*Military*] (CAAL)

**NAU**.......... Nordic Confederation of Supervisors, Technicians, and Other Managers [*Formerly, Nordic Union of Foremen*] (EA)
**NAu**............ Seymour Library, Auburn, NY [*Library symbol*] [*Library of Congress*] (LCLS)
**NAUA**........ National Automobile Underwriters Association [*Later, ISO*] (EA)
**NAUB**........ National Association of Urban Bankers (EA)
**NAuC**......... Cayuga County Community College, Auburn, NY [*Library symbol*] [*Library of Congress*] (LCLS)
**Nauc Bjulletin Leningrad** ... Naucnyj Bjulletin Leningradskogo Gosud. Universiteta [*A publication*]
**Nauc Dokl Vyss Skoly Filos Nauki** ... Naucnye Doklady Vyssej Skoly Filosofskie Nauki [*A publication*]
**Nauc Dokl Vyss Skoly Nauc Kommunizma** ... Naucnye Doklady Vyssej Skoly Naucnyj Kommunizma [*A publication*]
**Nauch Dokl Vysshei Shkoly Biol Nauk** ... Nauchnye Doklady Vysshei Shkoly Biologicheskie Nauki [*A publication*]
**Nauch Konf Yadern Meteor (Obninsk)** ... Nauchnaya Konferentsiya po Yadernoi Meteorologii (Obninsk) [*A publication*]
**Nauchn Byull Leningr Gos Univ** ... Nauchnye Byulleten Leningradskogo Gosudarstvennogo Universiteta [*A publication*]
**Nauchn Byull Vses Nauchno Issled Inst Khlopku** ... Nauchni Byulleten Vsesoyuznogo Nauchno Issledovatel'skogo Instituta po Khlopku [*A publication*]
**Nauchn Dokl Vyssh Shk Biol Nauki** ... Nauchnye Doklady Vysshei Shkoly Biologicheskie Nauki [*A publication*]
**Nauchn Dokl Vyssh Shk Elektromekh Avtom** ... Nauchnye Doklady Vysshei Shkoly Elektromekhanika i Avtomatika [*A publication*]
**Nauchn Dokl Vyssh Shk Energ** ... Nauchnye Doklady Vysshei Shkoly Energetika [*A publication*]
**Nauchn Dokl Vyssh Shk Fiz Mat Nauki** ... Nauchnye Doklady Vysshei Shkoly Fiziko-Matematicheskie Nauki [*A publication*]
**Nauchn Dokl Vyssh Shk Geol Geogr Nauki** ... Nauchnye Doklady Vysshei Shkoly Geologo-Geograficheskie Nauki [*A publication*]
**Nauchn Dokl Vyssh Shk Gorn Delo** ... Nauchnye Doklady Vysshei Shkoly Gornoe Delo [*A publication*]
**Nauchn Dokl Vyssh Shk Khim Khim Tekhnol** ... Nauchnye Doklady Vysshei Shkoly Khimiya i Khimicheskaya Tekhnologiya [*USSR*] [*A publication*]
**Nauchn Dokl Vyssh Shk Lesoinzh Delo** ... Nauchnye Doklady Vysshei Shkoly Lesoinzhenernoe Delo [*A publication*]
**Nauchn Dokl Vyssh Shk Mashinostr Priborostr** ... Nauchnye Doklady Vysshei Shkoly Mashinostroenie i Priborostroenie [*A publication*]
**Nauchn Dokl Vyssh Shk Metall** ... Nauchnye Doklady Vysshei Shkoly Metallurgiya [*A publication*]
**Nauchn Dokl Vyssh Shk Radiotekh Elektron** ... Nauchnye Doklady Vysshei Shkoly Radiotekhnika i Elektronika [*A publication*]
**Nauchn Dokl Vyssh Shk Stroit** ... Nauchnye Doklady Vysshei Shkoly Stroitel'stvo [*A publication*]
**Nauchn Ezheg Chernovits Univ** ... Nauchnyi Ezhegodnik Chernovitskogo Universiteta [*A publication*]
**Nauchn Ezheg Chernovits Univ Biol Fak Chernovtsy** ... Nauchnye Ezhegodnik Chernovitskogo Universiteta Biologicheskii Fakul'tet Chernovtsy [*A publication*]
**Nauchn Ezheg Odess Gos Univ Biol Fak** ... Nauchnyi Ezhegodnik Odesskii Gosudarstvennyi Universitet Biologicheskii Fakul'tet [*A publication*]
**Nauchn Ezheg Odess Gos Univ Khim Fak** ... Nauchnyi Ezhegodnik Odesskii Gosudarstvennyi Universitet Khimicheskii Fakul'tet [*A publication*]
**Nauchn Ezheg Odess Univ** ... Nauchnyi Ezhegodnik Odesskogo Universiteta [*A publication*]
**Nauchn Issled Klin Lab** ... Nauchnye Issledovaniva v Klinikakh I V Laboratoriyakh [*A publication*]
**Nauchni Tr Inst Pochv Izsled** ... Nauchni Trudove. Instituta za Pochveni Izsledvaniya [*A publication*]
**Nauchni Tr Inst Spets Usuvursh Lek** ... Nauchni Trudove. Institut za Spetsializatsiya i Usuvurshenstvuvane na Lekarite [*A publication*]
**Nauchni Tr Nauchnoizsled Inst Durzh Kontrol Lek Sredstva** ... Nauchni Trudove. Nauchnoizsledovatelski Institut za Durzhaven Kontrol na Lekarstvenite Sredstva [*A publication*]
**Nauchni Tr Nauchnoizsled Inst Konservna Promst (Plovdiv)** ... Nauchni Trudove. Nauchnoizsledovatelski Institut po Konservna Promishlenost (Plovdiv) [*A publication*]
**Nauchni Tr Nauchnoizsled Inst Okhr Tr Prof Zabol** ... Nauchni Trudove. Nauchnoizsledovatelskiya Instituta po Okhrana na Truda i Profesionalnite Zabolyavaniya [*A publication*]
**Nauchni Tr Nauchnoizsled Inst Pediatr** ... Nauchni Trudove. Nauchnoizsledovatelskiya Institut po Pediatriya [*A publication*]
**Nauchni Tr Nauchnoizsled Inst Radiobiol Radiats Khig** ... Nauchni Trudove. Nauchnoizsledovatelski Institut po Radiobiologiya i Radiatsionna Khigiena [*A publication*]
**Nauchni Tr Nauchnoizsled Inst Vinar Pivovar Promst (Sofia)** ... Nauchni Trudove. Nauchnoizsledovatelski Institut po Vinarska i Pivovarna Promishlenost (Sofia) [*A publication*]
**Nauchni Tr Plovdivski Univ Mat Fiz Khim Biol** ... Nauchni Trudove. Plovdivski Universitet. Matematika, Fizika, Khimiya, Biologiya [*Bulgaria*] [*A publication*]
**Nauchni Tr Selskostop Akad (Sofia) Ser Rastenievud** ... Nauchni Trudove. Selskostopanska Akademiya "Georgi Dimitrov" (Sofia) Seriya. Rastenievudstvo [*A publication*]
**Nauchni Tr Tsentr Nauchnoizsled Inst Tekhnol Mashinostr** ... Nauchni Trudove. Tsentralniya Nauchnoizsledovatelski Institut po Tekhnologiya na Mashinostroineto [*A publication*]
**Nauchni Trud Minist Zemed Gorite** ... Nauchni Trudove. Ministerstvo na Zemedelieto i Gorite [*A publication*]
**Nauchni Trudove Ser Gorsko Stop** ... Nauchni Trudove. Seriia Gorsko Stopanstvo [*A publication*]
**Nauchni Trud Vissh Lesotekh Inst** ... Nauchni Trudove. Vissh Lesotekhnicheski Institut [*A publication*]
**Nauchni Trud Vissh Selskostop Inst "Vasil Kolarov"** ... Nauchni Trudove. Vissh Selskostopanski Institut "Vasil Kolarov" [*A publication*]
**Nauchni Tr Vissh Inst Khranit Vkusova Promst (Plovdiv)** ... Nauchni Trudove. Vissh Institut po Khranitelna i Vkusova Promishlenost (Plovdiv) [*A publication*]
**Nauchni Tr Vissh Lesotekh Inst (Sofia)** ... Nauchni Trudove. Vissh Lesotekhnicheski Institut (Sofia) [*Bulgaria*] [*A publication*]
**Nauchni Tr Vissh Lesotekh Inst (Sofia) Ser Gorsko Stop** ... Nauchni Trudove. Vissh Lesotekhnicheski Institut (Sofia). Seriya Gorsko Stopanstvo [*A publication*]
**Nauchni Tr Vissh Lesotekh Inst (Sofia) Ser Mekh Tekhnol Durv** ... Nauchni Trudove. Vissh Lesotekhnicheski Institut (Sofia). Seriya Mekhanichna Tekhnologiya na Durvesinata [*Bulgaria*] [*A publication*]
**Nauchni Tr Vissh Lesotekh Inst (Sofia) Ser Ozelenyavane** ... Nauchni Trudove. Vissh Lesotekhnicheski Institut (Sofia). Seriya Ozelenyavane [*A publication*]
**Nauchni Tr Vissh Med Inst (Sofia)** ... Nauchni Trudove na Visshiya Meditsinski Institut (Sofia) [*A publication*]
**Nauchni Tr Vissh Med Inst (Varna)** ... Nauchni Trudove na Visshiya Meditsinski Institut (Varna) [*A publication*]
**Nauchni Tr Vissh Pedagog Inst (Plovdiv) Mat Fiz Khim Biol** ... Nauchni Trudove. Vissh Pedagogicheski Institut (Plovdiv). Matematika, Fizika, Khimiya, Biologiya [*A publication*]
**Nauchni Tr Vissh Selskostop Inst (Plovdiv)** ... Nauchni Trudove. Vissh Selskostopanski Institut "Vasil Kolarov" (Plovdiv) [*A publication*]
**Nauchni Tr Vissh Selskostop Inst (Sofia) Agron Fak** ... Nauchni Trudove. Vissh Selskostopanski Institut "Georgi Dimitrov" (Sofia). Agronomicheski Fakultet [*A publication*]
**Nauchni Tr Vissh Selskostop Inst Sofia Agron Fak Rastenievyd** ... Nauchni Trudove. Vissh Selskostopanski Institut (Sofia). Agronomicheski Fakultet. Seriya Rastenievydstvo [*A publication*]
**Nauchni Tr Vissh Selskostop Inst (Sofia) Zootekh Fak** ... Nauchni Trudove. Vissh Selskostopanski Institut "Georgi Dimitrov" (Sofia). Zootekhnicheski Fakultet [*A publication*]
**Nauchni Tr Vissh Veterinarnomed Inst (Sofia)** ... Nauchni Trudove. Vissh Veterinarnomeditsinski Institut "Prof. Dr. G. Pavlov" (Sofia) [*A publication*]
**Nauchno Agron Zh** ... Nauchno Agronomicheskii Zhurnal [*A publication*]
**Nauchno Inf Byull Nauchno Issled Otd Kiev Ind Inst** ... Nauchno-Informatsionnyi Byulleten Nauchno-Issledovatel'skogo Otdeleniya Kievskogo Industrial'nogo Instituta [*A publication*]
**Nauchno-Issled Inst Epidemio Mikrobiol Tr (Sofia)** ... Nauchno-Issledovatel'skii Institut Epidemiologii i Mikrobiologii Trudy (Sofia) [*A publication*]
**Nauchno Issled Inst Geol Arktiki Tr** ... Nauchno-Issledovatel'skiy Institut Geologii Arktiki Trudy [*A publication*]
**Nauchno Issled Kozhno Venerol Inst Sb Nauchn Tr (Minsk)** ... Nauchno-Issledovatel'skii Kozhno-Venerologicheskii Institut. Sbornik Nauchnykh Trudov (Minsk) [*A publication*]
**Nauchno-Issled Lab Geol Zarubezh Stran Tr** ... Nauchno-Issledovatel'skaya Laboratoriya Geologii Zarubezhnykh Stran Trudy [*A publication*]
**Nauchno-Issled Rab Vses Nauchno Issled Inst Torf Promsti** ... Nauchno-Issledovatel'skie Raboty Vsesoyuznogog Nauchno-Issledovatel'skogo Instituta Torfyanoi Promyshlennosti [*A publication*]
**Nauchno-Issled Tr Ivanov Tekst Inst** ... Nauchno-Issledovatel'skie Trudy Ivanovskii Tekstil'nye Institut [*A publication*]
**Nauchno-Issled Tr Kalinin Nauchno-Issled Inst Tekst Promsti** ... Nauchno-Issledovatel'skie Trudy Kalininskii Nauchno-Issledovatel'skii Institut Tekstil'noi Promyshlennosti [*A publication*]
**Nauchno-Issled Tr Latv Nauchno-Issled Inst Legk Promsti** ... Nauchno-Issledovatel'skie Trudy Latviiskii Nauchno-Issledovatel'skii Institut Legkoi Promyshlennosti [*A publication*]
**Nauchno-Issled Tr Litov Nauchno-Issled Inst Tekst Promsti** ... Nauchno-Issledovatel'skie Trudy Litovskii Nauchno-Issledovatel'skii Institut Tekstil'noi Promyshlennosti [*A publication*]
**Nauchno-Issled Tr Mosk Tekst Inst** ... Nauchno-Issledovatel'skie Trudy Moskovskii Tekstil'nyi Institut [*A publication*]

**Nauchno-Issled Tr Tsentr Inst Nauchno-Tekh Inf Legk Promsti** ... Nauchno-Issledovatel'skie Trudy Tsentral'nyi Institut Nauchno-Tekhnicheskoi Informatsii Legkoi Promyshlennosti [*A publication*]
**Nauchno-Issled Tr Tsentr Nauchno-Issled Inst Sherst Promsti** ... Nauchno-Issledovatel'skie Trudy Tsentral'nyi Nauchno-Issledovatel'skii Institut Sherstyanoi Promyshlennosti [*A publication*]
**Nauchno-Issled Tr Vses Nauchno-Issled Inst Mekhovoi Promsti** ... Nauchno-Issledovatel'skie Trudy Vsesoyuznyi Nauchno-Issledovatel'skii Institut Mekhovoi Promyshlennosti [*A publication*]
**Nauchnoizsled Inst Epidemiol Mikrobiol Tr** ... Nauchnoizsledovatelski Institut po Epidemiologiya i Mikrobiologiya. Trudove [*A publication*]
**Nauchnoizsled Inst Okeanogr Ribno Stop Varna Izv** ... Nauchnoizsledovatelski Institut po Okeanografiya i Ribno Stopanstvo. Varna. Izvestiya [*A publication*]
**Nauchnoizsled Inst Okhr Tr Prof Zabol Tr** ... Nauchnoizsledovatelski Institut po Okhrana na Truda i Profesionalnite Zabolyavaniya. Trudove [*A publication*]
**Nauchnoizsled Inst Stroit Mater Tr (Sofia)** ... Nauchnoizsledovatelski Institut po Stroitelni Materiali Trudove (Sofia) [*A publication*]
**Nauchnoizsled Inst Tsvetna Metal (Plovdiv) God** ... Nauchnoizsledovatelski Institut po Tsvetna Metalurgiya (Plovdiv). Godishnik [*A publication*]
**Nauchnoizsled Tr Inst Tekst Promost (Sofia)** ... Nauchnoizsledovatelski Trudove na Instituta po Tekstilna Promishlenost (Sofia) [*A publication*]
**Nauchno-Prakt Inf Tsentr Aptechn Nauchno-Issled Inst** ... Nauchno-Prakticheskaya Informatsiya. Tsentral'nyi Aptechnyi Nauchno-Issledovatel'skii Institut [*A publication*]
**Nauchn Osn Tekhnol Obrab Vody** ... Nauchnye Osnovy Tekhnologii Obrabotki Vody [*A publication*]
**Nauchno Tekh Biul Vses Nauchno Issled Inst Mekh Sel'sk Khoz** ... Nauchno-Tekhnicheskii Biulleten. Vsesoiuznyi Nauchno-Issledovatel'skii Institut Mekhanizatsii Sel'skogo Khoziaistva [*A publication*]
**Nauchno-Tekh Byull Agron Fiz** ... Nauchno-Tekhnicheskii Byulleten' po Agronomicheskoi Fizike [*A publication*]
**Nauchno-Tekh Byull Nauchno-Issled Inst Mekh Rybn Promsti** ... Nauchno-Tekhnicheskii Byulleten Nauchno-Issledovatel'skogo Instituta Mekhanizatsii Rybnoi Promyshlennosti [*A publication*]
**Nauchno-Tekh Byull Nauchno-Issled Inst Teploenerg Priborostr** ... Nauchno-Tekhnicheskii Byulleten Nauchno-Issledovatel'skii Institut Teploenergeticheskogo Priborostroeniya [*A publication*]
**Nauchno-Tekh Byull Tsentr Genet Lab** ... Nauchno-Tekhnicheskii Byulleten' Tsentral'noi Geneticheskoi Laboratorii [*A publication*]
**Nauchno-Tekh Byull Vses Nauchno-Issled Inst Khlopkovod** ... Nauchno-Tekhnicheskii Byulleten. Vsesoyuznyi Nauchno-Issledovatel'skii Institut Khlopkovodstva [*A publication*]
**Nauchno-Tekh Byull Vses Sel-Genet Inst** ... Nauchno-Tekhnicheskii Byulleten' Vsesoyuznogo Selektsionno-Geneticheskogo Instituta [*A publication*]
**Nauchno-Tekh Inf** ... Nauchno-Tekhnicheskaya Informatsiya [*A publication*]
**Nauchno-Tekh Inf Byull Leningr Politekh Inst** ... Nauchno-Tekhnicheskii Informatsionnyi Byulleten Leningradskogo Politekhnicheskogo Instituta [*USSR*] [*A publication*]
**Nauchno-Tekh Inf Byull Nauchn Inst Udobr Insektofungits** ... Nauchno-Tekhnicheskii Informatsionnyi Byulleten Nauchnogo Instituta po Udobreniyam i Insektofungitsidam [*A publication*]
**Nauchno-Tekh Inf Litov Nauchno-Issled Vet Inst** ... Nauchno-Tekhnicheskaya Informatsiya Litovskii Nauchno-Issledovatel'skii Veterinarnyi Institut [*A publication*]
**Nauchno-Tekh Inf Ser 1** ... Nauchno-Tekhnicheskaya Informatsiya. Seriya 1. Organizatsiya i Metodika Informatsionnoi Raboty [*A publication*]
**Nauchno-Tekh Inf Ser 2** ... Nauchno-Tekhnicheskaya Informatsiya. Seriya 2. Informatsionnye Protsessy i Sistemy [*A publication*]
**Nauchno-Tekh Inf (Sofia)** ... Nauchno-Tekhnicheskaya Informatsiya (Sofia) [*A publication*]
**Nauchno-Tekh Obz Ser Geol Razved Gaz Gazokondens Mestorozhd** ... Nauchno-Tekhnicheskii Obzor. Seriya. Geologiya, Razvedka Gazovykh, i Bazokondensatnykh Mestorozhdenii [*A publication*]
**Nauchno-Tekh Obz Ser Pererab Gaza Gazov Kondens** ... Nauchno-Tekhnicheskii Obzor. Seriya. Pererabotka Gaza i Gazovogo Kondensata [*A publication*]
**Nauchno-Tekh O-va SSSR** ... Nauchno-Tekhnicheskie Obshchestva SSSR [*USSR*] [*A publication*]
**Nauchno-Tekh Probl Goreniya Vzryva** ... Nauchno-Tekhnicheskie Problemy Goreniya i Vzryva [*A publication*]
**Nauchno Tekh Ref Sb Ser Fosfornaya Promst** ... Nauchno-Tekhnicheskii Referativnyi Sbornik. Seriya Fosfornaya Promyshlennost [*A publication*]
**Nauchno-Tekh Sb Dobyche Nefti** ... Nauchno-Tekhnicheskii Sbornik po Dobyche Nefti [*A publication*]
**Nauchno-Tekh Sb Geol Razrab Transp Ispolz Prir Gaza** ... Nauchno-Tekhnicheskii Sbornik po Geologii, Razrabotke, Transportu, i Ispol'zovaniyu Prirodnogo Gaza [*A publication*]
**Nauchno-Temat Sb Ufim Neft Inst** ... Nauchno-Tematicheskii Sbornik. Ufimskii Neftyanoi Institut [*A publication*]
**Nauchn i Prikl Fotogr i Kinematogr** ... Zhurnal Nauchnoi i Prikladnoi Fotografii i Kinematografii [*A publication*]
**Nauchn Rab Inst Okhr Tr Vses Tsentr Sov Prof Soyuz** ... Nauchnye Raboty Institutov Okhrany Truda Vsesoyuznogo Tsentral'nogo Soveta Professional'nykh Soyuzov [*A publication*]
**Nauchn Rab Inst Okhr Tr Vses Tsentr Sov Prof Soyuzov** ... Nauchnye Raboty Institutov Okhrany Truda Vsesoyuznogo Tsentral'nogo Soveta Professional'nykh Soyuzov [*A publication*]
**Nauchn Rab Stud Mosk Farm Inst** ... Nauchnye Raboty Studentov Moskovskogo Farmatsevticheskogo Instituta [*A publication*]
**Nauchn Rab Stud Mosk Gorn Inst** ... Nauchnye Raboty Studentov Moskovskogo Gornogo Instituta [*A publication*]
**Nauchn Rab Stud Mosk Med Stomatol Inst** ... Nauchnye Raboty Studentov Moskovskogo Meditsinskogo Stomatologicheskogo Instituta [*A publication*]
**Nauchn Rab Stud Novocherk Politekh Inst** ... Nauchnye Raboty Studentov Novocherkasskii Politekhnicheskii Institut [*A publication*]
**Nauchn Rab Stud Sverdl Gorn Inst** ... Nauchnye Raboty Studentov Sverdlovskii Gornyi Institut [*A publication*]
**Nauchn Rab Vrach Mord SSSR** ... Nauchnye Raboty Vrachei Mordovskoi SSSR [*A publication*]
**Nauchn Soobshch Arm Nauchno Issled Inst Stroit Mater Sooruzh** ... Nauchnye Soobshcheniya Armyanskii Nauchno-Issledovatel'skii Institut Stroitel'nykh Materialov i Sooruzhenii [*A publication*]
**Nauchn Soobshch Gos Vses Nauchno Issled Inst Tsem Prom-Sti** ... Nauchnye Soobshcheniya Gosudarstvennyi Vsesoyuznyi Nauchno-Issledovatel'skii Institut Tsementnoi Promyshlennosti [*USSR*] [*A publication*]
**Nauchn Soobshch Inst Fiziol Akad Nauk SSSR** ... Nauchnye Soobshcheniya Instituta Fiziologii Akademii Nauk SSSR [*A publication*]
**Nauchn Soobshch Inst Gorn Dela Im A A Skochinskogo** ... Nauchnye Soobshcheniya Institut Gornogo Dela Imeni A. A. Skochinskogo [*USSR*] [*A publication*]
**Nauchn Soobshch Inst Gorn Dela (Moscow)** ... Nauchnye Soobshcheniya Institut Gornogo Dela (Moscow) [*A publication*]
**Nauchn Soobshch Vses Nauchno Issled Inst Tsem Promsti** ... Nauchnye Soobshcheniya Vsesoyuznyi Nauchno-Issledovatel'skii Institut Tsementnoi Promyshlennosti [*A publication*]
**Nauchn Soobshch Yakutsk Fil Akad Nauk SSSR** ... Nauchnye Soobshcheniya. Yakutskii Filial Akademiya Nauk SSSR [*A publication*]
**Nauchn Tr Akad Kommunal'n Khoz** ... Nauchnye Trudy Akademii Kommunal'nogo Khozyaistva [*A publication*]
**Nauchn Tr Aspir Odess Skh Inst** ... Nauchnye Trudy Aspirantov Odesskii Sel'skokhozyaistvennyi Institut [*A publication*]
**Nauchn Tr Aspir Ordinatorov Pervogo Mosk Med Inst** ... Nauchnye Trudy Aspirantov i Ordinatorov Pervogo Moskovskogo Meditsinskogo Instituta [*A publication*]
**Nauchn Tr Bashk Gos Med Inst** ... Nauchnye Trudy Bashkirskogo Gosudarstvennogo Meditsinskogo Instituta [*A publication*]
**Nauchn Tr Bashk Med Inst** ... Nauchnye Trudy Bashkirskogo Meditsinskogo Instituta [*A publication*]
**Nauchn Tr Bukhar Gos Pedagog Inst** ... Nauchnye Trudy Bukharskii Gosudarstvennyi Pedagogicheskii Institut [*A publication*]
**Nauchn Tr Bykovskoi Bakhchevoi Opytn Stn** ... Nauchnye Trudy Bykovskoi Bakhchevoi Opytnai Stantsii [*A publication*]
**Nauchn Tr Chelyab Obl Klin Bol'n** ... Nauchnye Trudy Chelyabinskoi Oblastnoi Klinicheskoi Bol'nitsy [*A publication*]
**Nauchn Tr Dnepropetr Metall Inst** ... Nauchnye Trudy Dnepropetrovskii Metallorgicheskii Institut [*A publication*]
**Nauchn Tr Donskoi Zon Nauchno Issled Inst Sel'sk Khoz** ... Nauchnye Trudy Donskoi Zonal'nyi Nauchno-Issledovatel'skii Institut Sel'skogo Khozyaistva [*A publication*]
**Nauchn Tr Erevan Gos Univ Ser Geol Nauk** ... Nauchnye Trudy Erevanskii Gosudarstvennyi Universitet Seriya Geologicheskikh Nauk [*A publication*]
**Nauchn Tr Erevan Gos Univ Ser Khim Nauk** ... Nauchnye Trudy Erevanskii Gosudarstvennyi Universitet Seriya Khimicheskikh Nauk [*A publication*]
**Nauchn Tr Gos Nauchno-Issled Proektn Inst Redkomet Prom-Sti** ... Nauchnye Trudy Gosudarstvennyi Nauchno-Issledovatel'skii i Proektnyi Institut Redkometallicheskoi Promyshlennosti [*USSR*] [*A publication*]
**Nauchn Tr Gruz Skh Inst** ... Nauchnye Trudy Gruzinskii Sel'skokhozyaistvennyi Institut [*A publication*]
**Nauchn Tr Inst Avtom** ... Nauchnye Trudy Instituta Avtomatiki [*Ukrainian SSR*] [*A publication*]
**Nauchn Tr Inst Chern Metall (Dnepropetrovsk)** ... Nauchnye Trudy Institut Chernoi Metallurgii (Dnepropetrovsk) [*A publication*]
**Nauchn Tr Inst Entomol Fitopatol** ... Nauchnye Trudy Instituta Entomologii i Fitopatologii [*A publication*]

**Nauchn Tr Inst Entomol Fitopatol Akad Nauk Ukr SSR** ... Nauchnye Trudy Instituta Entomologii i Fitopatologii Akademii Nauk Ukrainskoi SSR [*A publication*]
**Nauchn Tr Inst Fiziol Rast Agrokhim Akad Nauk Ukr SSR** ... Nauchnye Trudy Institut Fiziologii Rastenii i Agrokhimii. Akademiya Nauk Ukrainskoi SSR [*A publication*]
**Nauchn Tr Inst Mineral Resur (Ukrainian SSR)** ... Nauchnye Trudy Instituta Mineral'nykh Resursov (Ukrainian SSR) [*A publication*]
**Nauchn Tr Irkutsk Gos Med Inst** ... Nauchnye Trudy Irkutskii Gosudarstvennyi Meditsinskii Institut [*A publication*]
**Nauchn Tr Irkutsk Gos Nauchno Issled Inst Redk Met** ... Nauchnye Trudy Irkutskii Gosudarstvennyi Nauchno-Issledovatel'skii Institut Redkikh Metallov [*A publication*]
**Nauchn Tr Irkutsk Gos Nauchno Issled Inst Redk Tsvetn Met** ... Nauchnye Trudy Irkutskii Gosudarstvennyi Nauchno-Issledovatel'skii Institut Redkikh i Tsvetnykh Metallov [*A publication*]
**Nauchn Tr Irkutsk Med Inst** ... Nauchnye Trudy Irkutskii Meditsinskii Institut [*A publication*]
**Nauchn Tr Kamenets Podol'sk Skh Inst** ... Nauchnye Trudy Kamenets Podol'skii Sel'skokhozyaistvennyi Institut [*A publication*]
**Nauchn Tr Karagand Fil Inst Obogashch Tverd Goryuch Iskop** ... Nauchnye Trudy Karagandinskii Filial Instituta Obogashcheniya Tverdykh Goryuchikh Iskopaemykh [*USSR*] [*A publication*]
**Nauchn Tr Karagand Nauchno Issled Ugol'n Inst** ... Nauchnye Trudy Karagandinskii Nauchno-Issledovatel'skii Ugol'nyi Institut [*A publication*]
**Nauchn Tr Kazan Med Inst** ... Nauchnye Trudy Kazanskogo Meditsinskogo Instituta [*A publication*]
**Nauchn Tr Khark Gorn Inst** ... Nauchnye Trudy Khar'kovskii Gornyi Institut [*A publication*]
**Nauchn Tr Khar'k Inst Inzh Kommunal'n Stroit** ... Nauchnye Trudy Khar'kovskii Institut Inzhenerov Kommunal'nogo Stroitel'stva [*A publication*]
**Nauchn Tr Khar'k S-Kh Inst** ... Nauchnye Trudy Khar'kovskogo Sel'skokhozyaistvennogo Instituta [*A publication*]
**Nauchn Tr Kirg Med Inst** ... Nauchnye Trudy Kirgizskogo Meditsinskogo Instituta [*A publication*]
**Nauchn Tr Krasnodar God Pedagog Inst** ... Nauchnye Trudy Krasnodarskogo Gosudarstvennogo Pedagogicheskogo Instituta [*A publication*]
**Nauchn Tr Krasnodar Nauchno Issled Inst Sel'sk Khoz** ... Nauchnye Trudy Krasnodarskogo Nauchno-Issledovatel'skogo Instituta Sel'skogo Khozyaistva [*A publication*]
**Nauchn Tr Krasnodar Nauchno Issled Vet Stn** ... Nauchnye Trudy Krasnodarskoi Nauchno-Issledovat'skoi Veterinarnoi Stantsii [*A publication*]
**Nauchn Tr Krym Gos Med Inst** ... Nauchnye Trudy Krymskii Gosudarstvennyi Meditsinskii Institut [*A publication*]
**Nauchn Tr Kuban Gos Med Inst** ... Nauchnye Trudy Kubanskogo Gosudarstvennogo Meditsinskogo Instituta [*A publication*]
**Nauchn Tr Kuban Gos Univ** ... Nauchnye Trudy Kubanskii Gosudarstvennyi Universitet [*A publication*]
**Nauchn Tr Kurgan S-Kh Inst** ... Nauchnye Trudy Kurganskogo Sel'skokhozyaistvennogo Instituta [*A publication*]
**Nauchn Tr Kursk Gos Pedagog Inst** ... Nauchnye Trudy Kurskij Gosudarstvennyj Pedagogicheskij Institut [*A publication*]
**Nauchn Tr Kursk Gos Skh Optn Stn** ... Nauchnye Trudy Kurskoi Gosudarstvennoi Sel'skokhozyaistvennoi Opytnoi Stantsii [*A publication*]
**Nauchn Tr Kursk Gos Skh Opytn Stn** ... Nauchnye Trudy Kurskoi Gosudarstvennoi Sel'skokhozyaistvennoi Opytnoi Stantsii [*A publication*]
**Nauchn Tr Kursk Politekh Inst** ... Nauchnye Trudy Kurskii Politekhnicheskii Institut [*USSR*] [*A publication*]
**Nauchn Tr Kursk Selkh Inst** ... Nauchnye Trudy Kurskogo Sel'skokhozyaistvennogo Instituta [*A publication*]
**Nauchn Tr Leningr Gorn Inst Nov Issled Khim Metall Obogashch** ... Nauchnye Trudy Leningradskii Gornyi Institut Novye Issledovaniya v Khimii, Metallurgii, i Obogashchenii [*A publication*]
**Nauchn Tr Leningr Gos Inst Usoversh Vrachei** ... Nauchnye Trudy Leningradskogo Gosudarstvennogo Instituta Usovershenstvovaniya Vrachei [*A publication*]
**Nauchn Tr Leningr Inst Tochn Mekh Opt** ... Nauchnye Trudy Leningradskii Institut Tochnoi Mekhaniki i Optiki [*A publication*]
**Nauchn Tr Leningr Inst Usoversh Vrachei Im S M Kirova** ... Nauchnye Trudy Leningradskogo Instituta Usovershenstvovaniya Vrachei Imeni S. M. Kirova [*A publication*]
**Nauchn Tr Leningr Inzh Stroit Inst** ... Nauchnye Trudy Leningradskii Inzhenerno-Stroitel'nyi Institut [*A publication*]
**Nauchn Tr Leningr Lesotekh Akad** ... Nauchnye Trudy Leningradskoi Lesotekhnicheskoi Akademii [*A publication*]
**Nauchn Tr Leningr Nauchno Issled Inst Pereliv Krovi** ... Nauchnye Trudy Leningradskii Nauchno-Issledovatel'skii Institut Perelivaniya Krovi [*A publication*]
**Nauchn Tr Leningr Tekhnol Inst Im Lensoveta** ... Nauchnye Trudy Leningradskogo Tekhnologicheskogo Instituta Imeni Lensoveta [*A publication*]
**Nauchn Tr Lesokhoz Fak Ukr Skh Akad** ... Nauchnye Trudy Lesokhozyaistevennogo Fakul'teka Ukrainskoi Sel'skokhozyaistvennoi Akademii [*A publication*]
**Nauchn Tr Litov S-Kh Akad** ... Nauchnye Trudy Litovskoi Sel'skokhozyaistvennoi Akademii [*A publication*]
**Nauchn Tr L'vov Lesotekh Inst** ... Nauchnye Trudy L'vovskogo Lesotekhnicheskogo Instituta [*A publication*]
**Nauchn Tr L'vov Zoovet Inst** ... Nauchnye Trudy L'vovskii Zooveterinarnyi Institut [*A publication*]
**Nauchn Tr Melitopol'skoi Opytn Stn Sadovod** ... Nauchnye Trudy Melitopol'skoi Opytnoi Stantsii Sadovodstva [*A publication*]
**Nauchn Tr Melitop Opytn Stn Sadovod** ... Nauchnye Trudy Melitopol'skoi Opytnoi Stantsii Sadovodstva [*A publication*]
**Nauchn Tr Mosk Gor Klin Bol'n N 52** ... Nauchnye Trudy Moskovskoi Gorodskoi Kliniceskci Bol'nitsy N 52 [*A publication*]
**Nauchn Tr Mosk Gorn Inst** ... Nauchnye Trudy Moskovskogo Gornogo Instituta [*USSR*] [*A publication*]
**Nauchn Tr Mosk Inst Radioelektron Gorn Elektromekh** ... Nauchnye Trudy Moskovskii Institut Radioelektroniki i Gornoi Elektromekhaniki [*A publication*]
**Nauchn Tr Mosk Inzh Ekon Inst** ... Nauchnye Trudy Moskovskogo Inzhenerno-Ekonomicheskogo Instituta [*USSR*] [*A publication*]
**Nauchn Tr Mosk Lesotekh Inst** ... Nauchnye Trudy Moskovskogo Lesotekhnicheskogo Instituta [*A publication*]
**Nauchn Tr Mosk Nauchno-Issled Inst Vaktsin Syvorot** ... Nauchnye Trudy Moskovskogo Nauchno-Issledovatel'skogo Instituta Vaktsin i Syvorotok [*A publication*]
**Nauchn Tr Mosk Poligr Inst** ... Nauchnye Trudy Moskovskii Poligraficheskii Institut [*A publication*]
**Nauchn Tr Mosk Tekhnol Inst Legk Promsti** ... Nauchnye Trudy Moskovskogo Tekhnologicheskogo Instituta Legkoi Promyshlennosti [*A publication*]
**Nauchn Tr Nauchno Issled Gornometall Inst (Yerevan)** ... Nauchnye Trudy Nauchno-Issledovatelskii Gornometallurgicheskii Institut (Yerevan) [*A publication*]
**Nauchn Tr Nauchno-Issled Inst Gorn Sadovod Tsvetovod** ... Nauchnye Trudy Nauchno-Issledovatel'skogo Instituta Gornogo Sadovodstva i Tsvetovodstva [*A publication*]
**Nauchn Tr Nauchno-Issled Inst Kartofel'n Khoz** ... Nauchnye Trudy Nauchno-Issledovatel'skii Institut Kartofel'nogo Khoziaistva [*A publication*]
**Nauchn Tr Nauchno-Issled Inst Pediatr** ... Nauchnye Trudy Nauchno-Issledovatel'skogo Instituta po Pediatrii [*A publication*]
**Nauchn Tr Nauchno-Issled Inst Pushnogo Zverovod Krolikovod** ... Nauchnye Trudy Nauchno-Issledovatel'skii Institut Pushnogo Zverovodstva i Krolikovodstva [*A publication*]
**Nauchn Tr Nauchno-Issled Inst Radiol Radiats Gig** ... Nauchnye Trudy Nauchno-Issledovatel'skii Institut Radiologii i Radiatsionnoi Gigieny [*Bulgaria*] [*A publication*]
**Nauchn Tr Nauchno Issled Inst Sel'sk Khoz Yugo Vostoka** ... Nauchnye Trudy Nauchno-Issledovatel'skii Institut Sel'skogo Khozyaistva Yugo-Vostoka [*A publication*]
**Nauchn Tr Nauchno-Issled Inst S-Kh Yugo-Vost** ... Nauchnye Trudy Nauchno-Issledovatel'skogo Instituta Sel'skokhozyaistva Yugo-Vostoka [*A publication*]
**Nauchn Tr Nauchno Issled Vet Inst (Minsk)** ... Nauchnye Trudy Nauchno-Issledovatel'skogo Veterinarnogo Instituta (Minsk) [*A publication*]
**Nauchn Tr Novosib Med Inst** ... Nauchnye Trudy Novosibirskogo Meditsinskogo Instituta [*A publication*]
**Nauchn Tr Novosib Nauchno Issled Vet Stn** ... Nauchnye Trudy Novosibirskoi Nauchno-Issledovatel'skoi Veterinarnoi Stantsii [*A publication*]
**Nauchn Tr Obninskii Otd Geogr Ova SSSR** ... Nauchnye Trudy Obninskii Otdel Geograficheskogo Obshchestva SSSR [*A publication*]
**Nauchn Tr Obogashch Briket Uglei** ... Nauchnye Trudy po Obogashcheniyu i Briketirovaniyu Uglei [*USSR*] [*A publication*]
**Nauchn Tr Omsk Med Inst** ... Nauchnye Trudy Omskii Meditsinskii Institut [*A publication*]
**Nauchn Tr Omsk S-Kh Inst** ... Nauchnye Trudy Omskogo Sel'skokhozyaistvennogo Instituta [*A publication*]
**Nauchn Tr Omsk Vet Inst** ... Nauchnye Trudy Omskogo Veterinarnogo Instituta [*A publication*]
**Nauchn Tr Orlov Ob Skh Opytn Stn** ... Nauchnye Trudy Orlovskaya Oblastnaya Sel'skokhozyaistvennaya Opytnaya Stantsiya [*A publication*]
**Nauchn Tr Permsk Farm Inst** ... Nauchnye Trudy Permskogo Farmatsevticheskogo Instituta [*A publication*]
**Nauchn Tr Permsk Nauchno Issled Ugoln Inst** ... Nauchnye Trudy Permskii Nauchno Issledovatel'skii Ugol'nye Institut [*A publication*]
**Nauchn Tr Permsk Politekh Inst** ... Nauchnye Trudy Permskii Politekhnicheskii Institut [*USSR*] [*A publication*]
**Nauchn Tr Poltav Skh Inst** ... Nauchnye Trudy Poltavskii Sel'skokhozyaistvennyi Institut [*A publication*]
**Nauchn Tr Primorsk S-Kh Inst** ... Nauchnye Trudy Primorskogo Sel'skokhozyaistvennogo Instituta [*A publication*]
**Nauchn Tr Ptitsevod Nauchno-Issled Inst Ptitsevod** ... Nauchnye Trudy Ptitsevodstvo Nauchno-Issledovatel'skii Institut Ptitsevodstva [*A publication*]

**Nauchn Tr Rizh Nauchno Issled Inst Travmatol Ortop** ... Nauchnye Trudy Rizhskii Nauchno-Issledovatel'skii Institut Travmatologii i Ortopedii [*A publication*]
**Nauchn Tr Rostov Na Donu Inzh Stroit Inst** ... Nauchnye Trudy Rostovskii-Na-Donu Inzhenerno-Stroitel'nyi Institut [*A publication*]
**Nauchn Tr Ryazan Med Inst** ... Nauchnye Trudy Ryazanskii Meditsinskii Institut [*A publication*]
**Nauchn Tr Samark Gos Univ** ... Nauchnye Trudy Samarkandskogo Gosudarstvennogo Universiteta [*A publication*]
**Nauchn Tr Samark Koop Inst Tsentrosoyuza** ... Nauchnye Trudy Samarkandskogo Kooperativnogo Instituta Tsentrosoyuza [*A publication*]
**Nauchn Tr Samark Med Inst** ... Nauchnye Trudy Samarkandskogo Meditsinskogo Instituta [*A publication*]
**Nauchn Tr Samark Skh Inst** ... Nauchnye Trudy Samarkandskii Sel'skokhozyaistvennyi Institut [*A publication*]
**Nauchn Tr Samark Univ** ... Nauchnye Trudy Samarkandskogo Universiteta [*A publication*]
**Nauchn Tr Sarat Politekh Inst** ... Nauchnye Trudy Saratovskii Politekhnicheskii Institut [*A publication*]
**Nauchn Tr Sev-Zapadn Nauchno-Issled Inst Sel'sk Khoz** ... Nauchnye Trudy Severo-Zapadnogo Nauchno-Issledovatel'skogo Instituta Sel'skogo Khozyaistva [*A publication*]
**Nauchn Tr Sib Gos Nauchno Issled Proekt Inst Tsvet Metall** ... Nauchnye Trudy Sibirskii Gosudarstvennyi Nauchno-Issledovatel'skii i Proektnyi Institut Tsvetnoi Metallurgii [*USSR*] [*A publication*]
**Nauchn Tr Sib Gos Nauchno Issled Proektn Inst Tsvetn Metall** ... Nauchnye Trudy Sibirskii Gosudarstvennyi Nauchno-Issledovatel'skii i Proektnyi Institut Tsvetnoi Metallurgii [*A publication*]
**Nauchn Tr Sib Nauchno Issled Inst Selsk Khoz** ... Nauchnye Trudy Sibirskii Nauchno Issledovatel'skii Institut Sel'skogo Khozyaistva [*A publication*]
**Nauchn Tr S'kh Inst (Sofia) Agron Fak Ser Obshch Zemled** ... Nauchnye Trudy. Sel'skokhozyaistvennyi Institut (Sofia). Agronomicheskii Fakul'tet. Seriya Obshchee Zemledelie [*A publication*]
**Nauchn Tr Stavrop S-Kh Inst** ... Nauchnye Trudy Stavropol'skogo Sel'skokhozyaistvennogo Instituta [*A publication*]
**Nauchn Tr Stud Gruz Skh Inst** ... Nauchnye Trudy Studentov Gruzinskii Sel'skokhozyaistvennyi Institut [*A publication*]
**Nauchn Tr Stud Gruz Ssk Inst** ... Nauchnye Trudy Studentov Gruzinskogo Sel'skokhozyaistvennogo Instituta [*A publication*]
**Nauchn Tr Sverdl Gos Pedagog Inst** ... Nauchnye Trudy Sverdlovskii Gosudarstvennyi Pedagogicheskii Institut [*A publication*]
**Nauchn Tr Tashk Gos Univ Im V I Lenina** ... Nauchnye Trudy Tashkentskii Gosudarstvennyi Universitet Imeni V. I. Lenina [*USSR*] [*A publication*]
**Nauchn Tr Tashk Tekst Inst** ... Nauchnye Trudy Tashkentskogo Tekstil'nogo Instituta [*A publication*]
**Nauchn Tr Tsentr Inst Usoversh Vrachei** ... Nauchnye Trudy Tsentral'nogo Instituta Usovershenstovaniya Vrachei [*A publication*]
**Nauchn Tr Tsentr Nauchno Issled Inst Mekh Obrab Drev** ... Nauchnye Trudy Tsentral'nyi Nauchno Issledovatel'skii Institut Mekhanicheskoi Obrabotki Drevesiny [*A publication*]
**Nauchn Tr Tsentr Nauchno-Issled Inst Olovyannoi Promsti** ... Nauchnye Trudy Tsentral'nyi Nauchno-Issledovatel'skii Institut Olovyannoi Promyshlennosti [*A publication*]
**Nauchn Tr Tsentr Nauchno Issled Inst Tsellyul Bum Promsti** ... Nauchnye Trudy Tsentral'nyi Nauchno-Issledovatel'skii Institut Tsellyuloznoi i Bumazhnoi Promyshlennosti [*A publication*]
**Nauchn Tr Tul Gorn Inst** ... Nauchnye Trudy Tul'skogo Gornogo Instituta [*A publication*]
**Nauchn Tr Tul Gos Pedagog Inst** ... Nauchnye Trudy Tulskogo Gosudarstvennogo Pedagogicheskogo Instituta [*A publication*]
**Nauchn Tr Tyumen Skh Inst** ... Nauchnye Trudy Tyumenskogo Sel'skokhozyaistvennogo Instituta [*A publication*]
**Nauchn Tr Uch Prakt Vrachei Uzb** ... Nauchnye Trudy Uchenykh i Prakticheskikh Vrachei Uzbekistana [*A publication*]
**Nauchn Tr Ukr Inst Eksp Vet** ... Nauchnye Trudy Ukrainskii Instituta Eksperimental'noi Veterinarii [*A publication*]
**Nauchn Tr Ukr Inst Gidrotekh Melior** ... Nauchnye Trudy Ukrainskogo Instituta Gidrotekhniki i Melioratsii [*A publication*]
**Nauchn Tr Ukr Nauchno Issled Inst Eksp Vet** ... Nauchnye Trudy Ukrainskii Nauchno-Issledovatel'skii Institut Eksperimental'noi Veterinarii [*A publication*]
**Nauchn Tr Ukr Nauchno Issled Inst Fiziol Rast** ... Nauchnye Trudy Ukrainskii Nauchno-Issledovatel'skii Institut Fiziologii Rastenii [*A publication*]
**Nauchn Tr Ukr Nauchno Issled Inst Gig Tr Profzabol** ... Nauchnye Trudy Ukrainskii Nauchno-Issledovatel'skii Institut Gigieny Truda i Profzabolevanii [*A publication*]
**Nauchn Tr Ukr Nauchno Issled Inst Lesn Khoz Agrolesomelior** ... Nauchnye Trudy Ukrainskii Nauchno-Issledovatel'skogo. Instituta Lesnogo Khozyaistva i Agrolesomelioratsii [*A publication*]
**Nauchn Tr Ukr Nauchno Issled Inst Mekh Obrab Drev** ... Nauchnye Trudy Ukrainskii Nauchno-Issledovatel'skii Institut Mekhanicheskoi Obrabotki Drevesiny [*A publication*]
**Nauchn Tr Ukr Nauchno Issled Inst Pochvoved** ... Nauchnye Trudy Ukrainskii Nauchno-Issledovatel'skii Institut Pochvovedeniya [*A publication*]
**Nauchn Tr Ukr Nauchno-Issled Inst Rastenievod Sel Genet** ... Nauchnye Trudy Ukrainskogo Nauchno-Issledovatel'skogo Instituta Rastenievodstva Selestsii i Genetiki [*A publication*]
**Nauchn Tr Ukr Nauchno Issled Inst Sadovod** ... Nauchnye Trudy Ukrainskii Nauchno-Issledovatel'skii Institut Sadovodstva [*A publication*]
**Nauchn Tr Ukr Nauchno Issled Inst Ugleobogashch** ... Nauchnye Trudy Ukrainskogo Nauchno-Issledovatel'skogo Instituta Ugleobogashcheniya [*A publication*]
**Nauchn Tr Ukr Nauchno Issled Inst Vinograd Vinodel** ... Nauchnye Trudy Ukrainskogo Nauchno-Issledovatel'skogo Instituta Vinogradarstva i Vinodeliya [*A publication*]
**Nauchn Tr Ukr Nauchno Issled Inst Zashch Rast** ... Nauchnye Trudy Ukrainskii Nauchno-Issledovatel'skii Institut Zashchity Rastenii [*A publication*]
**Nauchn Tr Ukr Nauchno-Issled Stn Vinograd Osvo Peskov** ... Nauchnye Trudy Ukrainskoi Nauchno-Issledovatel'skoi Stantsii Vinogradarstva i Osvoeniya Peskov [*A publication*]
**Nauchn Tr Ukr Skh Akad** ... Nauchnye Trudy Ukrainskaya Sel'skokhozyaistvennaya Akademiya [*A publication*]
**Nauchn Tr Uzb Skh Inst** ... Nauchnye Trudy Uzbekskogo Sel'skokhozyaistvennogo Instituta [*A publication*]
**Nauchn Tr Vopr Pererab Kach Uglei** ... Nauchnye Trudy Voprosam Pererabotki i Kachestva Uglei [*A publication*]
**Nauchn Tr Voronezh Inzh Stroit Inst** ... Nauchnye Trudy Voronezhskii Inzhenerno-Stroitel'nyi Institut [*A publication*]
**Nauchn Tr Voronezh Lesotekh Inst** ... Nauchnye Trudy Voronezhskogo Lesotekhnicheskogo Instituta [*A publication*]
**Nauchn Tr Vrachei Magnitogorsk** ... Nauchnye Trudy Vrachei Magnitogorsk [*A publication*]
**Nauchn Tr Vses Nauchno Issled Inst Podzemn Gazif Uglei** ... Nauchnye Trudy Vsesoyuznyi Nauchno-Issledovatel'skii Institut Podzemnoi Gazifikatsii Uglei [*A publication*]
**Nauchn Tr Vses Nauchno Issled Inst Sazhevoi Promsti** ... Nauchnye Trudy Vsesoyuznyi Nauchno-Issledovatel'skii Institut Sazhevoi Promyshlennosti [*A publication*]
**Nauchn Tr Vses Nauchno Issled Inst Zernobobovykh Kult** ... Nauchnye Trudy Vsesoyuznyi Nauchno-Issledovatel'skii Institut Zernobobovykh Kul'tur [*A publication*]
**Nauchn Tr Vses Sel Genet Inst** ... Nauchnye Trudy Vsesoyuznogo Selektsionno Geneticheskogo Instituta [*A publication*]
**Nauchn Tr Vses Zaochn Mashinostroit Inst** ... Nauchnye Trudy Vsesoyuznyi Zaochnyi Mashinostroitel'nyi Institut [*USSR*] [*A publication*]
**Nauchn Tr Vyssh Uchebn Zaved Lit SSR Biol** ... Nauchnye Trudy Vysshykh Uchebnykh Zavedenii Litovskoi SSR Biologiya [*A publication*]
**Nauchn Tr Vyssh Uchebn Zaved Lit SSR Med (Vilnius)** ... Nauchnye Trudy Vysshykh Uchebnykh Zavedenii Litovskoi SSR Meditsina (Vilnius) [*A publication*]
**Nauchn Tr Vyssh Uchebn Zaved Lit SSR Ultrazvuk** ... Nauchnye Trudy Vysshikh Uchebnykh Zavedenii Litovskoi SSR Ultrazvuk [*A publication*]
**Nauchn Tr Vyssh Uchebn Zaved Lit SSR Vibrotekh** ... Nauchnye Trudy Vysshikh Uchebnykh Zavedenii Litovskoi SSR Vibrotekhnika [*A publication*]
**Nauchn Tr Zhitomir Skh Inst** ... Nauchnye Trudy Zhitomirskii Sel'skokhozyaistvennyi Institut [*A publication*]
**Nauchn Tr Zootekhnol Fak Zoovet Inst** ... Nauchnye Trudy Zootekhnologicheskogo Fakulteta Zooveterinarnogo Instituta [*A publication*]
**Nauchn Tr Zootekhnologicheskogo Inst** ... Nauchnye Trudy Zootekhnologicheskogo Instituta [*A publication*]
**Nauchnye Zap Dnepropetr Gos Univ** ... Nauchnye Zapiski Dnepropetrovskogo Gosudarstvennogo Universiteta [*A publication*]
**Nauchn Zap Belotserk Skh Inst** ... Nauchnye Zapiski Belotserkovskogo Sel'skokhozyaistvennogo Instituta [*A publication*]
**Nauchn Zap Chernovits Gos Med Inst** ... Nauchnye Zapiski Chernovitskii Gosudarstvennyi Meditsinskii Institut [*A publication*]
**Nauchn Zap Dnepropetr Gos Univ** ... Nauchnye Zapiski Dnepropetrovskogo Gosudarstvennogo Universiteta [*A publication*]
**Nauchn Zap Donetsk Inst Sov Torg** ... Nauchnye Zapiski Donetskogo Instituta Sovetskoi Torgovli [*A publication*]
**Nauchn Zap Gos Eksp Inst Sakh Promsti** ... Nauchnye Zapiski Gosudarstvennogo Eksperimentnogo Instituta Sakharnoi Promyshlennosti [*A publication*]
**Nauchn Zap Gos Nauchno-Issled Proektn Inst Ugol'n Prom-Sti** ... Nauchnye Zapiski Gosudarstvennyi Nauchno-Issledovatel'skii i Proektnyi Institut Ugol'noi Promyshlennosti [*USSR*] [*A publication*]
**Nauchn Zap Khar'k Aviats Inst** ... Nauchnye Zapiski Khar'kovskogo Aviatsionnogo Instituta [*A publication*]
**Nauchn Zap Khar'k Inst Mekh Elektrif Sel'sk Khoz** ... Nauchnye Zapiski Khar'kovskii Institut Mekhanizatsii i Elektrifikatsii Sel'skogo Khozyaistva [*A publication*]

**Nauchn Zap Khar'k Inst Mekh Sel'sk Khoz** ... Nauchnye Zapiski Khar'kovskii Institut Mekhanizatsii Sel'skogo Khozyaistva [*A publication*]
**Nauchn Zap Khar'k Inst Mekh Sots Sel'sk Khoz** ... Nauchnye Zapiski Khar'kovskii Institut Mekhanizatsii Sotsialisticheskogo Sel'skogo Khozyaistva [*A publication*]
**Nauchn Zap Khar'k Poligr Inst** ... Nauchnye Zapiski Khar'kovskii Poligraficheskii Institut [*A publication*]
**Nauchn Zap Kherson Skh Inst Im A D Tsiurupy** ... Nauchnye Zapiski Khersonskogo Sel'skokhozyaistvennogo Instituta Imeni A. D. Tsiurupy [*A publication*]
**Nauchn Zap Lugansk Skh Inst** ... Nauchnye Zapiski Luganskogo Sel'skokhozyaistvennogo Instituta [*A publication*]
**Nauchn Zap Lvov Politekh Inst** ... Nauchnye Zapiski L'vovskogo Politekhnicheskogo Instituta [*A publication*]
**Nauchn Zap L'vov Skh Inst** ... Nauchnye Zapiski L'vovskogo Sel'skokhozyaistvennogo Instituta [*A publication*]
**Nauchn Zap L'vov Torg Ekon Inst** ... Nauchnye Zapiski L'vovskogo Torgovo Ekonomicheskogo Instituta [*A publication*]
**Nauchn Zap Mosk Gidromelior Inst** ... Nauchnye Zapiski Moskovskii Gidromeliorativnyi Institut [*A publication*]
**Nauchn Zap Odess Politekh Inst** ... Nauchnye Zapiski Odesskii Politekhnicheskii Institut [*A publication*]
**Nauchn Zap Sakh Promsti** ... Nauchnye Zapiski po Sakhnarnoi Promyshlennosti [*A publication*]
**Nauchn Zap Sakh Promsti Agron Vyp** ... Nauchnye Zapiski po Sakharnoi Promyshlennost Agronomicheskii Vypusk [*A publication*]
**Nauchn Zap Sakh Promsti Tekhnol Vyp** ... Nauchnye Zapiski po Sakharnoi Promyshlennosti Tekhnologicheskii Vypusk [*A publication*]
**Nauchn Zap Ukr Poligr Inst** ... Nauchnye Zapiski Ukrainskii Poligraficheskii Institut [*A publication*]
**Nauchn Zap Uzhgorod Gos Univ** ... Nauchnye Zapiski Uzhgorodskogo Gosudarstvennogo Universiteta [*A publication*]
**Nauchn Zap Voronezh Lesokhim Inst** ... Nauchnye Zapiski Voronezhskogo Lesokhimicheskogo Instituta [*A publication*]
**Nauchn Zap Voronezh Lesotekh Inst** ... Nauchnye Zapiski Voronezhskogo Lesotekhnicheskogo Instituta [*A publication*]
**Nauchn Zap Voronezh Otd Geogr Ova SSSR** ... Nauchnye Zapiski Voronezhskogo Otdela Geograficheskogo Obshchestva SSSR [*A publication*]
**Nauchn Zap Voronezh Otd Vses Bot Ova** ... Nauchnye Zapiski Voronezhskogo Otdeleniya Vsesoyuznogo Botanicheskogo Obshchestva [*A publication*]
**Nauchn Zap Voroshilovgr Skh Inst** ... Nauchnye Zapiski Voroshilovgradskogo Sel'skokhozyaistvennogo Instituta [*A publication*]
**Nauch Soobshch Inst Fiziol Pavlov** ... Nauchnye Soobshcheniya Institut Fiziologii Imeni I. P. Pavlova [*A publication*]
**Nauch-Tekh Inf** ... Nauchno-Tekhnicheskaya Informatsiya [*A publication*]
**Nauch Tr Dobrudzhan Selskostop Nauchnoizsled Inst** ... Nauchni Trudove na Dobrudzhanskiya Selskostopanski Nauchnoizsledovatelski Institut [*A publication*]
**Nauch Tr Poltav Nauch-Issled Inst Svinovod** ... Nauchnye Trudy Poltavskii Nauchno-Issledovatel'skii Institut Svinovodstva [*A publication*]
**Nauch Trudy** ... Nauchnye Trudy [*A publication*]
**Nauch Trudy Altaisk Nauchno-Issled Inst Sel Khoz** ... Nauchnye Trudy Altaiskogo Nauchno-Issledovatel'skogo Instituta Sel'skogo Khozyaistva [*A publication*]
**Nauch Trudy Kuibyshev Gos Pedagog Inst Zhivot Povolzh'ya** ... Nauchnye Trudy Kuibyshevskii Gosudarstvennyi Pedagogicheskii Institut Zhivotnye Povolzh'ya [*A publication*]
**Nauch Trudy Kuibyshevskii Gos Ped Inst** ... Nauchnye Trudy Kuibyshevskii Gosudarstvennyi Pedagogicheskii Institut Imeni V. V. Kuibysheva [*A publication*]
**Nauch Trudy Nauchno-Issled Inst Pchel** ... Nauchnye Trudy Nauchno-Issledovatel'skii Institut Pchelovodstva [*A publication*]
**Nauch Trudy Stavropol Sek'Khoz Inst** ... Nauchnye Trudy Stavropol'skogo Sel'Skokhozyaistvennogo Instituta [*A publication*]
**Nauch Trudy Ukr Nauchno-Issled Inst Les Khoz Agrolesomelior** ... Nauchnye Trudy Ukrainskogo Nauchno-Issledovatel'skogo Instituta Lesnogo Khozyaistva i Agrolesomelioratsii [*A publication*]
**Nauch Trudy Ukr Nauchno-Issled Inst Pochv** ... Nauchnye Trudy Ukrainskogo Nauchno-Issledovatel'skogo Instituta Pochvovedeniya [*A publication*]
**Nauch Trudy Ukr Sel'Khoz Akad** ... Nauchnye Trudy Ukrainskoi Sel'Skokhozyaistvennoi Akademii [*A publication*]
**Nauch Trudy Voronezh Sel'Khoz Inst** ... Nauchnye Trudy Voronezhskii Sel'skokhozyaistvennyi [*A publication*]
**Nauch Tr Veselopodol Opyt-Selek Sta** ... Nauchnye Trudy Veselopodolyanskoi Opytno-Selektsionnoi Stantsii [*A publication*]
**Nauch Tr Vissh Selskostop Inst "Georgi Dimitrov" Agron Fak** ... Nauchni Trudove. Vissh Selskostopanski Institut "Georgi Dimitrov." Agronomicheski Fakultet [*A publication*]
**Nauch Tr Vissh Selskostop Inst "Georgi Dimitrov" Zootekh Fak** ... Nauchni Trudove. Vissh Selskostopanski Institut "Georgi Dimitrov" (Sofia). Zootekhnicheski Fakultet [*A publication*]
**Nauch Tr Vissh Selskostop Inst "Vasil Kolarov"** ... Nauchni Trudove. Vissh Selskostopanski Institut "Vasil Kolarov" [*A publication*]
**Naucno-Teh Pregl** ... Naucno-Tehnicki Pregled [*A publication*]
**Naucn Tr Mosk Nauchno-Issled Inst Vaktsin Syvorotok** ... Nauchnye Trudy Moskovskogo Nauchno-Issledovatel'skogo Instituta Vaktsin i Syvorotok [*A publication*]
**Nauc Trud Lesoteh Inst (Ser Gorsko Stop)** ... Naucni Trudove Vissh Lesotehniceski Institut (Serija Gorsko Stopanstvo) [*A publication*]
**Nauc Trud Lesoteh Inst (Ser Meh Tehn Darv)** ... Naucnye Trudove Vissh Lesotehniceski Institut (Serija Mehanicna Tehnologija na Darvesinata) [*A publication*]
**Nauc Trudy Kursk Pedag Inst** ... Naucnye Trudy Kurskogo Pedagogiceskogo Instituta [*A publication*]
**Nauc Trudy Leningr Lesoteh Akad** ... Naucnye Trudy Leningradskaja Ordena Lenina Lesotehniceskja Akademija Imeni S. M. Kirova [*A publication*]
**Nauc Trudy (Novosib Gos Pedag Inst)** ... Naucnye Trudy (Novosibirskij Gosudarstvennyj Pedagogiceskij Institut) [*A publication*]
**Nauc Trudy Novosib Pedag Inst** ... Naucnye Trudy Novosibirskogo Pedagogiceskogo Instituta [*A publication*]
**Nauc Trudy Saratov Politehn Inst** ... Naucnye Trudy Saratovskogo Politehniceskogo Instituta [*A publication*]
**Nauc Trudy Sverdlovsk Pedag Inst** ... Naucnye Trudy Sverdlovskogo Pedagogiceskogo Instituta [*A publication*]
**Nauc Trudy Sverdlovsk Pedag Inst Sociol Probl** ... Naucnye Trudy Sverdlovskogo Pedagogiceskogo Instituta. Sociologiceskogo Problemi [*A publication*]
**Nauc Trudy (Taskent Pedag Inst)** ... Naucnye Trudy (Taskentskij Pedagogiceskij Institut) [*A publication*]
**Nauc Trudy Taskent Univ** ... Naucnye Trudy Taskentskogo Universiteta [*A publication*]
**Nauc Trudy Tjumensk Univ** ... Naucnye Trudy Tjumenskogo Universiteta [*A publication*]
**Nauc Trudy Vyss Uceb Zaved Litov SSR** ... Naucnye Trudy Vyssyh Ucebnyh Zavedennij Litovskoj SSR [*A publication*]
**Nauc Upravl Obsc** ... Naucnye Upravlenie Obscestva [*A publication*]
**NAUE**........ New and Unused Equipment (MCD)
**NAUF**........ Name and Address Update File [*IRS*]
**NAUFMA** ... National Association of Urban Flood Management Agencies [*Later, NAFSWMA*] (EA)
**NAUFOF** .. North American UFO Federation [*Defunct*] (EA)
**NAUG** ....... National AppleWorks Users Group (EA)
**NAUG** ....... Naugles, Inc. [*NASDAQ symbol*] (NQ)
**Nauheimer Fortbild-Lehrgaenge** ... Nauheimer Fortbildungs-Lehrgaenge [*A publication*]
**NAUHF**..... Northern Area Ultrahigh Frequency Radio System [*Green Pine*] (MCD)
**NAuHi**....... Cayuga County Historical Society, Auburn, NY [*Library symbol*] [*Library of Congress*] (LCLS)
**NAUI**......... National Association of Underwater Instructors (EA)
**NAUI News** ... NAUI (National Association of Underwater Instructors) News [*A publication*]
**NAUJA** ..... Nagpur University. Journal [*A publication*]
**Nauka Pered Opyt Sel'Khoz** ... Nauka i Peredovoi Opyt v Sel'skom Khozyaistve [*A publication*]
**Nauka Peredovoi Opyt Sel'sk Khoz** ... Nauka i Peredovoi Opyt v Sel'skom Khozyaistve [*A publication*]
**Nauka Pol** ... Nauka Polska [*A publication*]
**Nauka Proizvod (Tiflis)** ... Nauka Proizvodstvu (Tiflis) [*A publication*]
**Nauka Skh Proizvod** ... Nauka Sel'skokhozyaistvennomu Proizvodstvu [*A publication*]
**Nauka Tekh Gor Khoz** ... Nauka i Tekhnika v Gorodskom Khozyaistve [*A publication*]
**Nauka Tekh (Leningrad)** ... Nauka i Tekhnika (Leningrad) [*A publication*]
**Nauka Zhivotnovod** ... Nauka Zhivotnovodstvu [*A publication*]
**Nauk & Inf** ... Naukovedenie i Informatika [*A publication*]
**Nauk Pr Aspir Ukr Akad Sil's'kogospod Nauk** ... Naukovi Pratsi Aspirantiv Ukrains'ka Akademiya Sil's'kogospodars'kikh Nauk [*A publication*]
**Nauk Pratsi Ukr Sil-Hospod Akad** ... Naukovi Pratsi Ukrayins'ka Sil's'kohospodars'ka Akademiya [*A publication*]
**Nauk Pr Inst Entomol Fitopatol Akad Nauk Ukr RSR** ... Naukovi Pratsi Institut Entomologii ta Fitopatologii Akademii Nauk Ukrains'koi RSR [*A publication*]
**Nauk Pr Inst Livarnogo Virobnitstva Akad Nauk Ukr RSR** ... Naukovi Pratsi Institutu Livarnogo Virobnitstva Akademiya Nauk Ukrains'koi RSR [*A publication*]
**Nauk Pr Kamenets Podol'sk Sil's'kogospod Inst** ... Naukovi Pratsi Kamenets-Podol'skii Sil's'kogospodars'kii Institut [*A publication*]
**Nauk Pr Khark Sil's'kogospod Inst** ... Naukovi Pratsi Kharkivs'kii Sil's'kogospodars'kii Institut [*A publication*]
**Nauk Pr L'viv Sil's'kogospod Inst** ... Naukovi Pratsi L'vivs'kii Sil's'kogospodars'kii Institut [*A publication*]
**Nauk Pr L'viv Zootekh Vet Inst** ... Naukovi Pratsi L'vivs'kii Zootekhnichno-Veterinarnii Institut [*A publication*]
**Nauk Pr L'viv Zoovet Inst** ... Naukovi Pratsi L'vivs'kii Zooveterinarnii Institut [*A publication*]
**Nauk Pr Nauchn Tr Derzh Sil's'kohospod Dosl Stn** ... Naukovi Pratsi Nauchnye Trudy Derzhavna Sil's'kohospodars'ka Doslidna Stantsiya [*A publication*]
**Nauk Pr Poltav Sil's'kogospod Inst** ... Naukovi Pratsi Poltavs'kogo Sil's'kogospodars'skogo Institutu [*A publication*]

**Nauk Pr Sums'ka Derzh Sil's'kogospod Dosl Stn** ... Naukovi Pratsi. Sums'ka Derzhavna Sil's'kogospodars'ka Doslidna Stantsiya [*A publication*]
**Nauk Pr Ukr Inst Eksp Vet** ... Naukovi Pratsi Ukrains'kii Institut Eksperimental'noi Veterinarii [*A publication*]
**Nauk Pr Ukr Nauk Dosl Inst Eksp Vet** ... Naukovi Pratsi Ukrains'kii Naukovo-Doslidnii Institut Eksperimental'noi Veterinarii [*A publication*]
**Nauk Pr Ukr Nauk Dosl Inst Fiziol Rosl** ... Naukovi Pratsi Ukrains'kii Naukovo-Doslidnii Institut Fiziologii Roslin [*A publication*]
**Nauk Pr Ukr Nauk Dosl Inst Sadivn** ... Naukovi Pratsi Ukrains'kii Naukovo-Doslidnii Institut Sadivnitstva [*A publication*]
**Nauk Pr Ukr Nauk Dosl Inst Zakhistu Rosl** ... Naukovi Pratsi Ukrains'kii Naukovo-Doslidnii Institut Zakhistu Roslin [*A publication*]
**Nauk Pr Ukr Nauk Dosl Inst Zemlerob** ... Naukovi Pratsi Ukrainskii Naukovo-Doslidnoi Institut Zemlerobstva [*A publication*]
**Nauk Pr Ukr Sil'kohospod Akad** ... Naukovi Pratse Ukrayins'ka Sil's'kohospodars'ka Akademiya [*A publication*]
**Nauk Pr Vet Fak L'viv Zoovet Inst** ... Naukovi Pratsi Veterinarnogo Fakul'tetu L'vivs'kii Zooveterinarnii Institut [*A publication*]
**Nauk Pr Vet Fak Ukr Sil's'kohospod Akad** ... Naukovi Pratsi Veterynarnoho Fakul'tetu Ukrayins'koyi Sil's'kohospodars'koyi Akademii [*A publication*]
**Nauk Pr Volyn Derzh Sil's'kohospod Doslid Sta** ... Naukovi Pratsi Volyns'ka Derzhavna Sil's'kohospodars'ka Doslidna Stantsiya [*A publication*]
**Nauk Pr Zhytomyr Sil's'kohospod Inst** ... Naukovi Pratsi Zhytomyrs'koho Sil's'kohospodars'koho Instytutu [*A publication*]
**Nauk Pr Zootekh Fak Kamenets Podol'sk Sil's'kogospod Inst** ... Naukovi Pratsi Zootekhnichnogo Fakul'tetu Kamenets-Podol'skii Sil's'kogospodars'kii Institut [*A publication*]
**Nauk Shchorichnik Kiiv Derzh Univ Im T G Shevchenka** ... Naukovii Shchorichnik. Kiivs'kii Derzhavnii Universitet Imeni T. G. Shevchenka [*A publication*]
**Nauk-Tekh Visn** ... Naukovo-Tekhnichnii Visnik [*A publication*]
**Nauk Za L'viv Derzh Pedagog Inst** ... Naukovi Zapysky L'vivs'koho Derzhavnoho Pedagogichnoho Instytutu [*A publication*]
**Nauk Zap Cherk Derzh Pedagog Inst** ... Naukovi Zapysky Cherkas'koho Derzhavnoho Pedagogichnoho Instytutu [*A publication*]
**Nauk Zap Dnepropetr Derzh Univ** ... Naukovi Zapiski Dnepropetrovs'kii Derzhavnii Universitet [*A publication*]
**Nauk Zap Ivano Frankivs'kii Derzh Med Inst** ... Naukovi Zapiski Ivano-Frankivs'kii Derzhavnii Medichnii Institut [*A publication*]
**Nauk Zap Kherson Derzh Pedagog Inst** ... Naukovi Zapiski Khersons'kogo Derzhavnogo Pedagogichnogo Instituta [*A publication*]
**Nauk Zap Kiiv Derzh Univ** ... Naukovi Zapiski Kiivs'kii Derzhavnii Universitet [*A publication*]
**Nauk Zap Kiiv Derzh Univ Pr Bot Sadu** ... Naukovi Zapiski Kiivs'kii Derzhavnii Universitet Pratsi Botanichnogo Sadu [*A publication*]
**Nauk Zap Krivoriz Derzh Pedagog Inst** ... Naukovi Zapiski Krivoriz'kogo Derzhavnogo Pedagogichnogo Instituta [*A publication*]
**Nauk Zap L'viv Derzh Pedagog Inst** ... Naukovi Zapysky L'vivs'koho Derzhavnoho Pedagogichnoho Instytutu [*A publication*]
**Nauk Zap L'viv Derzh Univ Ser Biol** ... Naukovi Zapiski L'vivs'kii Derzhavnii Universitet Seriya Biologichna [*A publication*]
**Nauk Zap L'viv Derzh Univ Ser Fiz Mat** ... Naukovi Zapiski L'vivs'kii Derzhavnii Universitet Seriya Fiziko-Matematichna [*A publication*]
**Nauk Zap L'viv Derzh Univ Ser Geol** ... Naukovi Zapiski L'vivs'kii Derzhavnii Universitet Seriya Geologichna [*A publication*]
**Nauk Zap L'viv Torg Ekon Inst** ... Naukovi Zapiski L'vivs'kogo Torgovo-Ekonomichnogo Institutu [*A publication*]
**Nauk Zap Nizhin Derzh Pedagog Inst** ... Naukovi Zapiski Nizhins'kii Derzhavnii Pedagogichnii Institut [*A publication*]
**Nauk Zap Nizhyns'koho Derzh Pedagog Inst** ... Naukovi Zapysky Nizhyns'koho Derzhavnoho Pedagogichnoho Institutu [*A publication*]
**Nauk Zap Odes Biol Stn Akad Nauk Ukr RSR** ... Naukovi Zapiski Odes'koi Biologichnoi Stantsii Akademiya Nauk Ukrains'koi RSR [*A publication*]
**Nauk Zap Odes Derzh Pedagog Inst** ... Naukovi Zapiski Odes'kii Derzhavnii Pedagogichnii Institut [*A publication*]
**Nauk Zap Odes Politekh Inst** ... Naukovi Zapiski Odes'kii Politekhnichnii Institut [*A publication*]
**Nauk Zap Stanisl Derzh Med Inst** ... Naukovi Zapiski Stanislavs'kii Derzhavnii Medichnii Institut [*A publication*]
**Nauk Zap Sumskogo Derzh Pedagog Inst** ... Naukovi Zapiski Sumskogo Derzhavnego Pedagogicheskogo Instituta [*A publication*]
**Nauk Zap Ukr Biokhem Inst** ... Naukovi Zapiski Ukrains'kogo Biokhemichnogo Instituta [*A publication*]
**Nauk Zap Ukr Poligr Inst** ... Naukovi Zapiski Ukrains'kii Poligrafichnii Institut [*A publication*]
**Nauk Zap Ukr Tekh Gospod Inst (Munich)** ... Naukovi Zapiski Ukrains'kii Tekhnichno-Gospodars'kii Institut (Munich) [*A publication*]
**Nauk Zap Uzhgorod Derzh Univ** ... Naukovi Zapiski Uzhgorods'kogo Derzhavnogo Universitetu [*A publication*]
**Nauk Zap Uzhorod Derzh Univ** ... Naukovi Zapysky Uzhorods'koho Derzhavnoho Universytetu [*A publication*]
**NAUL**........ Netherland-America University League [*Defunct*] (EA)
**NAULAS**... North American Union Life Assurance Society [*Chicago, IL*] (EA)
**NAUM** ...... National Association of Uniform Manufacturers [*Later, NAUMD*] (EA)
**NAUMD** ... National Association of Uniform Manufacturers and Distributors (EA)
**NAuMH** .... Auburn Memorial Hospital, Learning Resources Center, Auburn, NY [*Library symbol*] [*Library of Congress*] (LCLS)
**NAUN** ....... Nearest Active Upstream Neighbor [*Data processing*]
**Naunyn Schmied Arch Pharmacol** ... Naunyn Schmiedeberg's Archives of Pharmacology [*A publication*]
**Naunyn-Schmiedebergs Arch Exp Pathol Pharmakol** ... Naunyn-Schmiedebergs Archiv fuer Experimentelle Pathologie und Pharmakologie [*A publication*]
**Naunyn-Schmiedebergs Arch Exp Path Pharmak** ... Naunyn-Schmiedebergs Archiv fuer Experimentelle Pathologie und Pharmakologie [*A publication*]
**Naunyn-Schmiedebergs Arch Pharmacol** ... Naunyn-Schmiedeberg's Archives of Pharmacology [*A publication*]
**Naunyn-Schmiedebergs Arch Pharmakol** ... Naunyn-Schmiedebergs Archiv fuer Pharmakologie [*Formerly, Naunyn-Schmiedebergs Archiv fuer Pharmakologie und Experimentelle Pathologie*] [*A publication*]
**Naunyn-Schmiedebergs Arch Pharmakol Exp Pathol** ... Naunyn-Schmiedebergs Archiv fuer Pharmakologie und Experimentelle Pathologie [*Later, Naunyn-Schmiedebergs Archiv fuer Pharmakologie*] [*A publication*]
**NAUP**........ National Association of Unemployed Persons (EA)
**NAUPA**..... National Amalgamated Union of Shop Assistants [*A union*] [*British*]
**NAUPA**..... National Association of Unclaimed Property Administrators (EA)
**NAURI**...... Nonaccelerating-Unemployment Rate of Inflation [*Economics*]
**NAurW**...... Wells College, Aurora, NY [*Library symbol*] [*Library of Congress*] (LCLS)
**NAUS**........ National Aerospace Utilization System (NOAA)
**NAUS**........ National Association for Uniformed Services (EA)
**NAuS**......... Seward House, Auburn, NY [*Library symbol*] [*Library of Congress*] (LCLS)
**NAUSAWC** ... National Amalgamated Union of Shop Assistants, Warehousemen, and Clerks [*A union*] [*British*]
**N Aust M**... North Australian Monthly [*A publication*] (APTA)
**NAuT**......... Auburn Theological Seminary, Auburn, NY [*Library symbol*] [*Library of Congress*] [*Obsolete*] (LCLS)
**NAUT**........ Nautical (AAG)
**Naut**........... Nautilus [*Madrid*] [*A publication*]
**Nau Tekh Inf Ser 1** ... Nauchno-Tekhnicheskaya Informatsiya. Seriya 1. Organizatsiya i Metodika Informatsionnoi Raboty [*A publication*]
**Nau-T Inf 1** ... Nauchno-Tekhnicheskaya Informatsiya. Seriya 1. Organizatsiya i Metodika Informatsionnye Raboty [*A publication*]
**Nau-T Inf 2** ... Nauchno-Tekhnicheskaya Informatsiya. Seriya 2. Informatsionnye Protessy i Sistemy [*A publication*]
**Naut M**...... Nautical Magazine [*A publication*]
**NAUTO**..... Nautophone
**NAUTS**..... Nautical Miles (ROG)
**NAUTT**..... National Association of Unions in the Textile Trade [*British*] (DCTA)
**NAUW**....... National Association of University Women (EA)
**NAUWS**.... Naval Advanced Undersea Weapons School
**NAV**.......... Narrows [*Virginia*] [*Seismograph station code, US Geological Survey*] (SEIS)
**NAV**.......... National American Veterans
**NAV**.......... National Association of Videographers [*Defunct*] (EA)
**nav**............. Navajo [*MARC language code*] [*Library of Congress*] (LCCP)
**NAV**.......... Naval (MSA)
**NAV**.......... Naval Artillery Volunteers [*British*] (ROG)
**NAV**.......... Navigate (AAG)
**NAV**.......... Navigator (DSUE)
**NAV**.......... Navistar International Corp. [*NYSE symbol*] (SPSG)
**Nav**............ Navorscher [*A publication*]
**NAV**.......... Navy (AAG)
**NAV**.......... Net Annual Value [*Business term*] (ADA)
**NAV**.......... Net Asset Value
**NAV**.......... Next Generation Advanced Vehicle [*Nippon Steel Corp.*]
**NAV**.......... Nonalcoholic Volunteers
**NAV**.......... North American Ventures, Inc. [*Vancouver Stock Exchange symbol*]
**NAV**.......... Nuovo Archivio Veneto [*A publication*]
**NAV**.......... Nurserymen's Association of Victoria [*Australia*]
**NAV**.......... Visual Navigation (MCD)
**NAVA**........ National Association for Veterinary Acupuncture (EA)
**NAVA**........ National Association of Veterinary Assistants [*Defunct*] (EA)
**NAVA**........ National Association of Visual Arts [*Australia*]
**NAVA**........ National Audio-Visual Association [*Later, ICIA*] (EA)
**NAVA**........ Navajo National Monument

**NAVA**........ North American Vexillological Association (EA)
**NAVAC**...... National Audiovisual Aids Centre [*British*]
**NAVACAD** ... Naval Academy
**NAVACO**.. Navigation Action Cutout Switchboard
**NAVACT**... All Navy Activities [*A dispatch to all activities in an area*]
**NAVAD**..... Naval Administrator At [*Place*]
**NAVADCOM** ... Naval Administrative Command
**NAVADGP** ... Naval Advisory Group
**NAVADGRU** ... Naval Advisory Group (CINC)
**NAVADGRU** ... Navy Administrative Group
**NAV-ADMIN** ... Navigation-Administration [*Inquiry program*] (AFIT)
**NAVADMINO** ... Navy Administrative Office [*or Officer*]
**NAVADMINU** ... Naval Administration Unit (MUGU)
**NAVADUNIT** ... Naval Administrative Unit
**NAVADVUSEAWPNSCOL** ... Naval Advanced Undersea Weapons School (MUGU)
**NAVAE**..... National Association for Vietnamese American Education (EA)
**NAVAER**... Navy Aeronautics
**NAVAEROMEDCEN** ... Naval Aeronautical Medical Center
**NAVAERORECOV** ... Naval Aerospace Recovery Facility
**NAVAERORECOVFAC** ... Naval Aerospace Recovery Facility
**NAVAEROSPMEDINST** ... Naval Aerospace Medical Institute
**NAVAGLOBE** ... Long-Distance Navigation System, Global [*Air Force*]
**NAVAID** ... Navigation Aid
**NAVAIDE** ... Naval Aide
**NAVAIR**.... Naval Air Systems Command
**NAVAIRANDACT** ... Naval Air Research and Development Activities (MUGU)
**NAVAIRDEVCEN** ... Naval Air Development Center [*Also, NADC, NADEVCEN*] (MUGU)
**NAVAIRDEVU** ... Naval Air Development Unit (MUGU)
**NAVAIRECONTECHSUPCEN** ... Naval Air Reconnaissance Technical Support Center
**NAVAIRENGCEN** ... Naval Air Engineering Center [*Closed*]
**NAVAIRENGRFAC** ... Naval Air Engineering Facility (MUGU)
**NAVAIREWORKF** ... Naval Air Rework Facility
**NAVAIREWORKFAC** ... Naval Air Rework Facility
**NAVAIRFAC** ... Naval Air Facility
**NAVAIRINST** ... Naval Air Systems Command Instruction
**NAVAIRINTO** ... Naval Air Intelligence Office (MUGU)
**NAVAIRLANT** ... Naval Air Force, Atlantic Fleet
**NAVAIRMATCEN** ... Naval Air Material Center [*Also, NAMATCEN, NAMC*] (MUGU)
**NAVAIRMINDEFDEVU** ... Naval Air Mine Defense Development Unit (MUGU)
**NAVAIRPAC** ... Naval Air Force, Pacific Fleet
**NAVAIRPROPCEN** ... Naval Air Propulsion Center (GRD)
**NAVAIRPROPTESTCEN** ... Naval Air Propeller Test Center
**NAVAIRRES** ... Naval Air Reserve
**NAVAIRSUPPU** ... Naval Air Support Unit
**NAVAIRSYSCO** ... Naval Air Systems Command (MCD)
**NAVAIRSYSCOM** ... Naval Air Systems Command
**NAVAIRSYSCOMHQ** ... Naval Air Systems Command Headquarters
**NAVAIRSYSCOMREP** ... Naval Air Systems Command Representative
**NAVAIRSYSCOMREPAC** ... Naval Air Systems Command Representative, Pacific
**NAVAIRSYSCOMREPCENT** ... Naval Air Systems Command Representative, Central
**NAVAIRSYSCOMREPLANT** ... Naval Air Systems Command Representative, Atlantic
**NAVAIRSYSCOMREP PNCLA** ... Naval Air Systems Command Representative, Naval Air Training Command, Pensacola [*Florida*]
**NAVAIRTECHSERVFAC** ... Naval Air Technical Services Facility (MUGU)
**NAVAIRTESTCEN** ... Naval Air Test Center (MUGU)
**NAVAIRTESTCENT** ... Naval Air Test Center (GRD)
**NAVAIRTESTFAC** ... Naval Air Test Facility (MUGU)
**NAVAIRTORPU** ... Naval Aircraft Torpedo Unit (MUGU)
**NAVAIRTRACEN** ... Naval Air Training Center
**NAVAIRTURBTESTSTA** ... Naval Air Turbine Test Station (MUGU)
**Naval Eng J** ... Naval Engineers' Journal [*A publication*]
**Naval Engrs J** ... American Society of Naval Engineers. Journal [*A publication*]
**Naval F**...... Naval Forces [*A publication*]
**NAVALOT** ... Allotment Division [*Navy*]
**Naval Res Logist Quart** ... Naval Research Logistics. Quarterly [*A publication*]
**Naval Res Log Quart** ... Naval Research Logistics. Quarterly [*A publication*]
**Naval Stores R** ... Naval Stores Review [*A publication*]
**Naval Stores Rev** ... Naval Stores Review [*A publication*]
**NAVALT**... Navy Alterations
**Naval War College R** ... Naval War College. Review [*A publication*]
**NAVAMDEP** ... Naval Ammunition Depot [*Charleston, SC*]
**NAVANTRA** ... Naval Air Advanced Training Center
**NAVANTRACOM** ... Naval Air Advanced Training Command
**NAVAP**..... National Association of VA [*Veterans Administration*] Physicians (EA)
**NAVAPI**.... North American Voltage and Phase Indicator (IEEE)
**NAVAR**..... Navigation RADAR
**NAVARA**.. Navy Appellate Review Activity
**Nav Arch**.... Naval Architect [*Academic degree*]
**Nav Archit** ... Naval Architect [*A publication*]
**NAVAREAAUDSVC** ... Naval Area Audit Service
**NAVARHO** ... Navigation and Radio Homing [*Aviation*]
**NAVARMDEP** ... Superintendent [*or Officer*] in Charge Naval Armament and/or Ammunition Depot At [*Place*]
**NAVASCOPE** ... Airborne RADARscope Used in NAVAR [*Air Force*]
**NAVASCREEN** ... Navigation RADAR Screen [*Air Force*]
**NAVASTROGRU** ... Navy Astronautics Group (MUGU)
**NAVASWDATACEN** ... Navy Antisubmarine Warfare Data Center
**NAVAUD** ... Navy Auditor
**NAVAUDSVC** ... Director, Naval Audit Service
**NAVAUTH** ... Naval Authority
**NAVAVIONICFAC** ... Naval Avionics Facility [*Later, NAC*] (MUGU)
**NAVAVNLOGCEN** ... Naval Aviation Logistics Center (NVT)
**NAVAVNSAFECEN** ... Naval Aviation Safety Center
**NAVAVNSCOLCOM** ... Naval Aviation School Command
**NAVAVNWEPSFAC** ... Naval Aviation Weapons Facilities
**Nav Av Nws** ... Naval Aviation News [*A publication*]
**NAVBALTAP** ... Allied Naval Forces, Baltic Approaches [*NATO*] (NATG)
**NAVBASE** ... Naval Base
**NAVBASELANT** ... Naval Bases Atlantic
**NAVBASEPAC** ... Naval Bases Pacific
**NAVBEACHGRU** ... Naval Beach Group (CINC)
**NAVBIOLAB** ... Naval Biological Laboratory (MUGU)
**NAVBM**.... Navy Ballistic Missile
**NAVBMC** ... Navy Ballistic Missile Committee
**NAVBOILAB** ... Navy Boiler Laboratory
**NAVC**........ Naval Aviation Cadet
**NAVCAD**.. Naval Aviation Cadet
**NAVCALS** ... Naval Communication Area Local Station (NVT)
**NAVCAMS** ... Naval Communication Area Master Station (NVT)
**NAVCARGOHANBN** ... Naval Cargo Handling Battalion
**NAVCAT**... Naval Career Appraisal Team (MUGU)
**NAVCBCEN** ... Naval Construction Battalion Center
**NAVCC**..... Naval Communications Center (MCD)
**NAVCENFRACO** ... Navy Central Freight Control Office
**NAVCENT** ... Allied Naval Forces, Central Europe [*NATO*]
**NAVCG**..... Coast Guard Publication [*Formerly, NCG*]
**NAVCHAPGRU** ... Navy Cargo Handling and Port Group (NVT)
**NAVCJ**...... National Association on Volunteers in Criminal Justice [*Later, IAJV*] (EA)
**NAVCLODEP** ... Naval Clothing Depot
**NAVCLOTEXTRSCHU** ... Navy Clothing and Textile Research Unit
**NAVCM**.... Navigation Countermeasures and Deception
**NAVCMD** ... Navigation Command (MCD)
**NAVCOM** ... Naval Communications [*System*]
**NAVCOMCOM** ... Naval Communications Command
**NAVCOMM** ... Naval Communications [*System*]
**NAVCOMMAREA** ... Naval Communications Area (NVT)
**NAVCOMMCOM** ... Naval Communications Command
**NAVCOMMFAC** ... Naval Communications Facility (NVT)
**NAVCOMMIS** ... Naval Communications Command Management Information System (MCD)
**NAVCOMMSTA** ... Naval Communication Station
**NAVCOMMSYS** ... Naval Communication System (MUGU)
**NAVCOMMTRACEN** ... Naval Communications Training Center (MUGU)
**NAVCOMMU** ... Naval Communication Unit
**NAVCOMPARS** ... Naval Communications Processing and Routing System (MCD)
**NAVCOMPT** ... Office of the Comptroller of the Navy
**NAVCOMPTINST** ... Office of the Comptroller of the Navy Instruction
**NAVCOMPTMAN** ... Naval Comptroller Manual
**NAVCOMSYSTORE** ... Navy Commissary Store
**NAVCOMU** ... Naval Communications Unit
**NAVCON** ... Naval Countermeasures (CINC)
**NAVCON** ... Navigation Control Systems (RDA)
**Nav Const**.. Naval Constructor [*Academic degree*]
**NAVCONTRACEN** ... Naval Construction Training Center
**NAVCONVHOSP** ... Naval Convalescent Hospital
**NAVCOSSACT** ... Naval Command Systems Support Activity
**NAVCRUITAREA** ... Navy Recruiting Area
**NAVCRUITSTA** ... Navy Recruiting Station
**NAVCSG**... National Archives Volunteers Constitution Study Group (EA)
**NAVCURSERV** ... Naval Courier Service
**NAVCURSERVHQ** ... Naval Courier Service Headquarters
**NAVD**........ National Association of Video Distributors (EA)
**NAVDAB**.. Navy Ocean Experimental Acoustic Data Bank (MSC)
**NAVDAC**.. Naval Data Automation Command (MCD)
**NAVDAC**.. Navigation Data Assimilation Computer
**NAVDAD**.. Navigationally-Derived Air Data (MCD)
**NAVDAMCONTRACEN** ... Navy Damage Control Training Center
**NAVDAR**.. Naval Defense Acquisition Regulations (MCD)
**NAVDEGSTALANT/PAC** ... Naval Degaussing Station, Atlantic/Pacific
**NAVDENCEN** ... Naval Dental Center
**NAVDENCLINIC** ... Naval Dental Clinic
**NAVDENSCOL** ... Naval Dental School
**NAVDENTECHSCOL** ... Naval Dental Technicians School
**NAVDEP**... Naval Deputy [*NATO*] (NATG)

**NAVDEPCENT** ... Naval Deputy to Commander-in-Chief, Allied Forces, Central Europe [*NATO*] (NATG)
**NAVDEPT** ... Navy Department
**NAVDES**... Navy Design Selection List
**NAVDESCOL** ... Naval Destroyer School (NVT)
**NAVDESSCOL** ... Naval Destroyer School
**NAVDET** .. Naval Detachment
**NAVDEVTRACEN** ... Navy Development Training Center
**NAVDI** ...... National Association for Ventilator Dependent Individuals (EA)
**NAVDIS**.... Naval District
**NAVDISCBAR** ... Naval Disciplinary Barracks
**NAVDISCOM** ... Navy Disciplinary Command
**NAVDISEAVECTORCONCEN** ... Navy Disease Vector Control Center
**NAVDISP** ... Naval Dispensary
**NAVDIST** ... Naval District
**NAVDOC** ... Navy Department Orientation Course (NG)
**NAVDOCKS** ... Bureau of Yards and Docks Publications [*Obsolete*] [*Navy*]
**NAVDOCSP** ... Bureau of Yards and Docks Publications [*Obsolete*] [*Navy*]
**Nav E** ......... Naval Engineer [*Academic degree*]
**NAVEA** ..... National Adult Vocational Education Association (EA)
**NAVEDTRA** ... Naval Education and Training Command (MCD)
**NAVELECSYSCOM** ... Naval Electronics Systems Command
**NAVELECSYSCOMCENLANTDIV** ... Naval Electronics Systems Command, Central Atlantic Division
**NAVELECSYSCOMHQ** ... Naval Electronics Systems Command Headquarters
**NAVELECSYSCOMNEDIV** ... Naval Electronics Systems Command, Northeast Division
**NAVELECSYSCOMSEDIV** ... Naval Electronics Systems Command, Southeast Division
**NAVELECSYSCOMWESTDIV** ... Naval Electronics Systems Command, Western Division
**NAVELEX** ... Naval Electronics Systems Command
**NAVELEXINST** ... Naval Electronics Systems Command Instruction
**Nav Eng J** .. Naval Engineers' Journal [*A publication*]
**NAVENGRXSTA** ... Naval Engineering Experiment Station
**NAVENVPREDRSCHFAC** ... Naval Environmental Prediction Research Facility (MCD)
**NAVEODFAC** ... Naval Explosive Ordnance Disposal Facility
**NAVESNP** ... National Association of Vocational Education Special Needs Personnel (EA)
**NAVEU** ..... [*US*] Naval Forces, European Waters
**NAVEUR** .. [*US*] Naval Forces, Europe (MCD)
**NAVEX** ..... Navigation Exercise [*Navy*] (NVT)
**NAVEXAM** ... Naval Examining Board
**NAVEXAMCEN** ... Navy Examination Center
**NAVEXHIBCEN** ... Naval Exhibit Center
**NAVEXOS** ... Executive Office of the Secretary [*Navy*]
**NAVF** ........ Naval Avionics Facility [*Later, NAC*] (AFIT)
**NAVF** ........ Norges Allmennvitenskapelige Forskningsrad [*Norwegian Research Council for Science and the Humanities*] [*Information service or system*] (IID)
**NAVFAC**... Naval Facilities Engineering Command [*Formerly, Bureau of Yards and Docks*]
**NAVFAC**... Naval Facility
**NAVFACDM** ... Naval Facilities Engineering Command Design Manuals
**NAVFACENG** ... Naval Facilities Engineering Command (CAAL)
**NAVFACENGCOM** ... Naval Facilities Engineering Command [*Formerly, Bureau of Yards and Docks*]
**NAVFACENGCOMHQ** ... Naval Facilities Engineering Command Headquarters
**NAVFACENSYSCOM** ... Naval Facilities Engineering Systems Command
**NAVFACINST** ... Naval Facilities Engineering Command Instructions
**NAVFACLANT/PAC** ... Naval Facilities Atlantic/Pacific
**NAVFACP** ... Naval Facilities Engineering Command Publications
**NAVFAC-TP-AD** ... Naval Facilities Engineering Command Technical Publications - Administration
**NAVFAC-TP-MO** ... Naval Facilities Engineering Command Technical Publications - Maintenance Operation
**NAVFAC-TP-PL** ... Naval Facilities Engineering Command Technical Publications - Planning
**NAVFAC-TP-PU** ... Naval Facilities Engineering Command Technical Publications - Public Utilities
**NAVFAMALWACT** ... Navy Family Allowance Activity
**NAVFE**...... [*US*] Naval Forces, Far East
**NAVFEC**... Naval Facilities Engineering Command [*Formerly, Bureau of Yards and Docks*]
**NAVFINCEN** ... Navy Finance Center
**NAVFINOFF** ... Navy Finance Office
**NAVFLDOPINTO** ... Naval Field Operational Intelligence Office
**NAVFLDOPSUPPGRU** ... Naval Field Operations Support Group
**NAVFLIGHTPREPSCOL** ... Naval Flight Preparatory School
**NAVFOR** .. [*US*] Naval Forces
**NAVFOREU** ... [*US*] Naval Forces, Europe [*Later, NAVEU*]
**NAVFORGER** ... [*US*] Naval Forces, Germany
**NAVFORJAP** ... [*US*] Naval Forces, Japan
**NAVFORKOR** ... [*US*] Naval Forces, Korea
**NAVFORNORAD** ... [*US*] Naval Forces, North American Air Defense Command (MUGU)
**NAVFORSTAT** ... Naval Force Status Report (NVT)
**NAVFORV** ... [*US*] Naval Forces, Vietnam (CINC)
**NAVFROF** ... Navy Freight Office
**NAVFUELDEP** ... Naval Fuel Depot
**NAVFUELSUPO** ... Naval Fuel Supply Office
**NAVG**........ [*The*] Navigators Group, Inc. [*New York, NY*] [*NASDAQ symbol*] (NQ)
**NAVGEN**.. Navy General Publications
**NAVGMSCHOL** ... Navy Guided Missile School
**NAVGMU** ... Navy Guided Missile Unit
**NAVGP**..... Naval Advisory Group
**NAVGRU** ... Naval Group
**NAVGSUP** ... Navigational Guidance Support (NVT)
**NAVGUN** ... Naval Gun Factory [*Later, NWF*]
**NAVH** ....... National Association for Visually Handicapped (EA)
**NAVHET**.. National Association of Vocational Home Economics Teachers (EA)
**NAVHISTDISPLAYCEN** ... Navy Historical Display Center
**NAVHLTHRSCHC** ... Naval Health Research Center
**NAVHOME** ... Naval Home [*Philadelphia, PA*]
**NAVHOSP** ... Naval Hospital
**NAVHOSPCORPSCOL** ... Naval Hospital Corps School
**NAVHOUSINGACT** ... Naval Housing Activity
**NAVHT**..... National Association of Vocational Homemakers Teachers [*Later, National Association of Vocational Home Economics Teachers*] (EA)
**NAVI** ......... North American Ventures, Inc. [*NASDAQ symbol*] (NQ)
**NAVIC** ...... Navy Information Center (MCD)
**NAVICERT** ... Navigation Certificate [*Paper issued by British government to merchant vessel, certifying that cargo was non-contraband, that is, not consigned to Germany*] [*World War II*]
**NAVID** ...... Navigation Aid (NASA)
**NAVIG** ...... Navigation
**Navig**.......... Navigation [*A publication*] (APTA)
**NAVIGA** ... World Organization for Modelship Building and Modelship Sport (EAIO)
**Navig Int**.... Navigation Interieure [*A publication*]
**NAVILCO** ... Navy International Logistics Control Office (MCD)
**NAVINSGEN** ... Naval Inspector General
**NAVINTCOM** ... Naval Intelligence Command
**NAVINTCOMINST** ... Naval Intelligence Command Instructions
**NAVINTCOMM** ... Naval Intelligence Command
**NAVINTEL** ... Naval Intelligence
**NAVINVSERVHQ** ... Naval Investigative Service Headquarters (NVT)
**NAVINVSERVO** ... Naval Investigative Service Office
**NAVION**... North American Aviation, Inc. [*Later, Rockwell International Corp.*] [*Acronym also used to refer to light aircraft of World War II*]
**NAVJAC**... North American Vane Jump Angle Computer
**NAVJAG**... Judge Advocate General's Office Publications [*Navy*]
**NAVJAP**... [*US*] Naval Forces, Japan
**NAVJIT**.... Naval Jet Instrument Trainer
**NAVJUSTSCOL** ... Naval Justice School
**Navl Eng J** ... Naval Engineers' Journal [*A publication*]
**NAVLIS**.... Navy Logistics Information System
**NAVLO**..... Naval Liaison Officer
**NAVLOGSIP** ... Navy Logistic Support Improvement Plan (NG)
**Nav M**........ Naval Magazine [*A publication*]
**NAVMACS** ... Naval Modular Automated Communications System (NVT)
**NAVMAG** ... Naval Magazine [*A publication*]
**NAVMAIRCOMCON** ... Naval and Maritime Air Communications-Electronics Conference [*NATO*] (NATG)
**NAVMAP** ... Navy Missile Analysis Program (MCD)
**NAVMAR** ... [*US*] Naval Forces, Marianas
**NAVMARCORESTRACEN** ... Navy and Marine Corps Reserve Training Center
**NAVMARJUDACT** ... Navy-Marine Corps Judiciary Activity
**NAVMAT** ... Naval Material Command [*Formerly, NMSE*] (MCD)
**NAVMATCOM** ... Naval Material Command [*Formerly, NMSE*]
**NAVMATCOMSUPPACT** ... Naval Material Command Support Activity
**NAVMATINST** ... Naval Material Command Instruction
**NAVMATMOCON** ... Navy Material Movement Control Plan
**NAVMC**.... Navy-Marine Corps
**NAVMED** ... Naval Aerospace Medical Institute (MCD)
**NAVMED** ... [*US*] Naval Forces, Mediterranean [*Formerly, NAVNAW*]
**NAVMED** ... Naval Medicine
**NAVMEDATASERVCEN** ... Naval Medical Data Service Center
**NAVMEDIS** ... Navy Medical Information System
**NAVMEDRSCHINST** ... Naval Medical Research Institute
**NAVMEDRSCHU** ... Naval Medical Research Unit
**NAVMEDSCOL** ... Naval Medical School
**NAVMGTSYSCEN** ... Naval Management Systems Center (MCD)
**NAVMILPERSCOM** ... Naval Military Personnel Command (MCD)
**NAVMINCOMEASTA** ... Navy Mine Countermeasures Station
**NAVMINDEFLAB** ... Navy Mine Defense Laboratory [*Later, NCSC*]
**NAVMINDEP** ... Naval Mine Depot
**NAVMINENGRFAC** ... Naval Mine Engineering Facility
**NAVMINWARTRACEN** ... Naval Mine Warfare Training Center
**NAVMIRO** ... Naval Material Industrial Resources Office
**NAVMIS**... Naval Mission
**NAVMISCEN** ... Naval Missile Center [*Point Mugu, CA*] (MCD)
**NAVMISFAC** ... Naval Missile Facility [*Also, NMF*] (MUGU)

**NAVMMAC** ... Navy Manpower and Material Analysis Center (NVT)
**NAVMMACLANT** ... Navy Manpower and Material Analysis Center, Atlantic
**NAVMMACPAC** ... Navy Manpower and Material Analysis Center, Pacific
**NAVMOBCONSTBN** ... Navy Mobile Construction Battalion
**NAVMTO** ... Navy Material Transportation Office
**NAVMTO** ... Navy Movement and Transportation Office
**NAVMUTAID** ... Navy Mutual Aid
**NAVN** ........ Naval Aviation News
**NAVNAW** ... [*US*] Naval Forces, Northwest African Waters [*Later, NAVMED*]
**NAVNET** .. Navigation Network (NVT)
**NAVNETDEP** ... Naval Net Depot
**NAVNON** ... Allied Naval Forces, North Norway [*NATO*] (NATG)
**NAVNORSOLS** ... [*US*] Naval Forces, Northern Solomons [*World War II*]
**NAVNORTH** ... Allied Naval Forces, Northern Europe [*NATO*]
**NAVNUPWRTRAU** ... Naval Nuclear Power Training Unit (MCD)
**NAVNUPWRU** ... Naval Nuclear Power Unit
**NAVNZ**..... [*US*] Naval Forces, New Zealand [*World War II*]
**NAVO**........ National Association of Volvo Owners [*Defunct*] (EA)
**NAVOBS**... Naval Observatory (MUGU)
**NAVOBSY** ... Naval Observatory [*Navy*]
**NAVOBSYFLAGSTAFFSTA** ... Naval Observatory Flagstaff [*Arizona*] Station
**NAVOCEANDISTO** ... Naval Oceanographic District Office
**NAVOCEANO** ... Naval Oceanographic Office [*Also known as NOO; formerly, HO, NHO, USNHO*] [*Bay St. Louis, MS*]
**NAVOCFORMED** ... Naval On-Call Force, Mediterranean [*NATO*] (NATG)
**NAVOCS**... Naval Officer Candidate School
**NAVOPFAC** ... Naval Operating Facility
**NAVOPNET** ... Naval Operations Network (CINC)
**NAVOPSUPPGRULANT** ... Naval Operations Support Group, Atlantic
**NAVOPSUPPGRUPAC** ... Naval Operations Support Group, Pacific
**NAVORD** ... Naval Ordnance (MUGU)
**NAVORD** ... Naval Ordnance Systems Command [*Later, Naval Sea Systems Command*]
**NAVORDCH** ... Naval Ordnance Chart (MCD)
**NAVORDFAC** ... Naval Ordnance Facility
**NAVORDINST** ... Naval Ordnance Systems Command Instruction
**NAVORDMISTESTFAC** ... Naval Ordnance Missile Test Facility
**NAVORDSTA** ... Naval Ordnance Station
**NAVORD-SWOP** ... Naval Ordnance Systems Command, Special Weapons Ordnance Publication
**NAVORDSYSCO** ... Naval Ordnance Systems Command [*Later, Naval Sea Systems Command*] (MCD)
**NAVORDSYSCOM** ... Naval Ordnance Systems Command [*Later, Naval Sea Systems Command*]
**NAVORDSYSCOMHQ** ... Naval Ordnance Systems Command Headquarters
**NAVORDSYSSUPPO** ... Naval Ordnance Systems Support Office
**NAVORDTECHREP** ... Naval Ordnance Technical Representative (MCD)
**NAVORDTESTU** ... Naval Ordnance Test Unit
**NAVORDU** ... Naval Ordnance Unit
**NAVOROUS** ... Naval Order of the United States [*Later, NOUS*] [*An association*] (EA)
**Navorsinge Nas Mus (Bloemfontein)** ... Navorsinge van die Nasionale Museum (Bloemfontein) [*A publication*]
**Navors Nas Mus (Bloemfontein)** ... Navorsinge van die Nasionale Museum (Bloemfontein) [*A publication*]
**NAVP**........ National Association of Vision Professionals (EA)
**NAVPA**...... National Association of Veterans Program Administrators (EA)
**NAVPAOEASCO** ... Naval Public Affairs Office, East Coast
**NAVPAOMWEST** ... Naval Public Affairs Office, Midwest
**NAVPAOWESCO** ... Naval Public Affairs Office, West Coast
**NAVPC**...... National Association of Vision Program Consultants [*Later, NAVP*] (EA)
**NAVPECO** ... Naval Production Equipment Control Office
**NAVPEP**... Navy Program Evaluation Procedures
**NAVPERS** ... Bureau of Naval Personnel [*Also, BNP, BUPERS*]
**NAVPERSCEN** ... Naval Personnel Center
**NAVPERSINST** ... Bureau of Naval Personnel Instruction
**NAVPERS-PRD** ... Bureau of Naval Personnel - Personnel Research Division
**NAVPERSPROGSUPPACT** ... Naval Personnel Program Support Activity
**NAVPERSRANDLAB** ... Navy Personnel Research and Development Laboratory
**NAVPERSREACT** ... Naval Personnel Research Activity
**NAVPERSRSCHACT** ... Naval Personnel Research Activity
**NAVPETOFF** ... Navy Petroleum Office
**NAVPETRES** ... Naval Petroleum Reserves
**NAVPETRESO** ... Naval Petroleum Reserves Office
**NAVPGCOL** ... Navy Postgraduate College
**NAVPGSCOL** ... Naval Postgraduate School
**NAVPHIBASE** ... Naval Amphibious Base (MUGU)
**NAVPHIBASELANT** ... Naval Amphibious Base Atlantic
**NAVPHIBSCOL** ... Naval Amphibious School (NVT)
**NAVPHIL** ... [*US*] Naval Forces, Philippines
**NAVPHOTOCEN** ... Naval Photographic Center
**NAVPLANTREP** ... Naval Plant Representative Office [*or Officer*] (MCD)
**NAVPLANTREPO** ... Naval Plant Representative Office [*or Officer*]
**NAVPO**..... National Association of Van Pool Operators [*Later, Association of Commuter Transportation*] (EA)
**NAVPOOL** ... Navigation Parameter Common Pool (NASA)
**NAVPORCO** ... Naval Port Control Office [*or Officer*]
**NAVPORCOF** ... Naval Port Control Office [*or Officer*]
**NAVPOSTGRADSCOL** ... Naval Postgraduate School
**NAVPOWFAC** ... Naval Powder Factory
**NAVPREFLIGHTSCOL** ... Naval Preflight School
**NAVPRIS** ... Naval Prison
**NAVPRO** .. Naval Plant Representative Office [*or Officer*]
**NAVPROV** ... Naval Proving Ground [*Dahlgren, VA*]
**NAVPUB**... Navy Publications and Printing Service
**NAVPUBFORMCEN** ... Naval Publications and Forms Center (MCD)
**NAVPUBINST** ... Navy Publications and Printing Service Instruction
**NAVPUBPRINTO** ... Navy Publications and Printing Office
**NAVPUBPRINTSERVO** ... Navy Publications and Printing Service Office
**NAVPUBSCONBD** ... Navy Department Publications Control Board
**NAVPUBWKSCEN** ... Navy Public Works Center
**NAVPUR** .. Navy Purchasing Office
**NAVPURO** ... Navy Purchasing Office
**NAVPVNTMEDU** ... Navy Preventive Medicine Unit
**NAVRADCON** ... Naval Radiological Control
**NAVRADLDEFLAB** ... Navy Radiological Defense Laboratory
**NAVRADSTA** ... Naval Radio Station
**NAVRDSATCOMMGRU** ... Naval Research and Development Satellite Communications Group (MUGU)
**NAVRECONTECHSUPPCEN** ... Naval Reconnaissance and Technical Support Center
**NAVRECSTA** ... Naval Receiving Station (NVT)
**NAVREGFINCEN** ... Navy Regional Finance Center
**NAVREGS** ... Navy Regulations
**NAVREL**... Navy Relief Society
**NAVREP**... Navy Representative [*to the Federal Aviation Administration*] (FAAC)
**NAVREPFAC** ... Naval Repair Facility (MCD)
**NAVRES**... Naval Reserve
**Nav Reserv** ... Naval Reservist [*A publication*]
**NAVRESLAB** ... Naval Research Laboratory [*ONR*]
**Nav Res Log** ... Naval Research Logistics. Quarterly [*A publication*]
**Nav Res Logistics Q** ... Naval Research Logistics. Quarterly [*A publication*]
**Nav Res Logist Q** ... Naval Research Logistics. Quarterly [*A publication*]
**NAVRESMANPOWERCEN** ... Naval Reserve Manpower Center
**NAVRESMIDSCOL** ... Naval Reserve Midshipmen's School
**Nav Res Rev** ... Naval Research Reviews [*A publication*]
**NAVRESSO** ... Navy Resale and Services Support Office
**NAVRESTRACEN** ... Naval Reserve Training Center
**NAVRESTRACOM** ... Naval Reserve Training Command
**NAVRESTRAFAC** ... Naval Reserve Training Facility
**NAVRETRAINCOM** ... Naval Retraining Command
**NAVROUTE** ... Navy Routing Office
**NAVRSCHLAB** ... Naval Research Laboratory [*ONR*]
**NAVRYUKYUS** ... [*US*] Naval Forces, Ryukyus [*World War II*]
**NAVS** ........ National Anti-Vivisection Society (EA)
**NAVS** ........ National Association of Variety Stores [*Inactive*] (EA)
**NAVS** ........ Navigation System
**NAVS** ........ North American Vegetarian Society (EA)
**NAVSAFECEN** ... Naval Safety Center
**NAVSANDA** ... Bureau of Supplies and Accounts [*Later, NSUPSC*] [*Navy*]
**NAVSAT**... Navigational Satellite [*NASA*]
**NAVSCAP** ... Allied Naval Forces, Scandinavian Approaches [*NATO*] (NATG)
**NAVSCIENTECHINTCEN** ... Naval Scientific and Technical Intelligence Center
**NAVSCOLCOM** ... Naval Schools Command
**NAVSCOLCOM NORVA** ... Naval Schools Command, Norfolk, Virginia
**NAVSCOLCONST** ... Naval Schools Construction
**NAVSCOLMINWARFARE** ... Naval Mine Warfare School
**NAVSCSCOL** ... Naval Supply Corps School
**NAVSEA**... Naval Avionics Support Equipment Appraisal (NG)
**NAVSEA**... Naval Sea [*formerly, Ship*] Systems Command (MCD)
**NAVSEACARCOR** ... Navy Sea Cargo Coordinator (NVT)
**NAVSEC** ... Naval Ship Engineering Center
**NAVSECENGRFAC** ... Naval Security Engineering Facility
**NAVSECGRU** ... Naval Security Group
**NAVSECGRUACT** ... Navy Security Group Activity
**NAVSECGRUDET** ... Naval Security Group Detachment
**NAVSECGRUHQ** ... Navy Security Group Headquarters
**NAVSECINST** ... Naval Ship Engineering Center Instruction
**NAVSECNORDIV** ... Naval Ship Engineering Center, Norfolk Division
**NAVSECPHILA** ... Naval Ship Engineering Center, Philadelphia Division
**NAVSECPHILADIV** ... Naval Ship Engineering Center, Philadelphia Division
**NAVSECSTA** ... Naval Security Station
**NAVSEEACT** ... Naval Shore Electronics Engineering Activity
**NAVSEEC** ... Naval Electronics Systems Command Headquarters
**NAVSEG**... Navigation Satellite Executive Steering Group
**NAVSERVSCOLCOM** ... Naval Service School Command
**NAVSEX**... Naval Standing Exercises (NATG)
**NAVSHIP** ... Naval Ship Systems Command [*Later, NAVSEA, NSSC*]
**NAVSHIPENGCEN** ... Naval Ship Engineering Center
**NAVSHIPENGSUPPACT** ... Naval Ship Engineering Support Activity

**NAVSHIPLO** ... Navy Shipbuilding Office
**NAVSHIPMISYSENGSTA** ... Naval Ship Missile System Engineering Station
**NAVSHIPREPFAC** ... Naval Ship Repair Facility
**NAVSHIPS** ... Naval Ship Systems Command [*Later, NAVSEA, NSSC*]
**NAVSHIPSA** ... Navy Shipbuilding Scheduling Activity
**NAVSHIPSINST** ... Naval Ship Systems Command Instruction
**NAVSHIPSO** ... Navy Shipbuilding Scheduling Office
**NAVSHIPSYSCOM** ... Naval Ship Systems Command [*Later, NAVSEA, NSSC*]
**NAVSHIPSYSCOMHQ** ... Naval Ship Systems Command Headquarters
**NAVSHIPYD** ... Naval Shipyard
**NAVSMO** ... Navigation Satellite Management Office
**NAVSO** ..... Naval Supply Office
**NAVSO** ..... Navy, Secretary's Office
**NAVSO** ..... Navy Staff Offices
**NAVSOUTH** ... Allied Naval Forces, Southern Europe [*NATO*] (NATG)
**NAVSPASUR** ... Naval Space Surveillance [*Center or System*]
**NAVSPECWARGP** ... Naval Special Warfare Group (AABC)
**NAVSPECWARGRU** ... Naval Special Warfare Group (NVT)
**NAVSSES** ... Naval Ship Systems Engineering Station
**NAVSTA**... Naval Station
**NAVSTALANT** ... Naval Stations Atlantic
**NAVSTAPAC** ... Naval Stations Pacific
**NAVSTAR** ... Navigation Satellite Tracking and Ranging [*Later, GPS*] [*Air Force*]
**NAVSTAR** ... Navy Study of Transport Aircraft Requirements
**NAVSTAR-GPS** ... Navigation Satellite Tracking and Ranging Global Positioning System [*Air Force*] (MCD)
**NAVSTIC** ... Naval Scientific and Technical Intelligence Center
**NAVSTRIP** ... Navy Standard Requisitioning and Issuing Procedure
**NAVSUBBASE** ... Naval Submarine Base
**NAVSUBMEDCEN** ... Naval Submarine Medical Center
**NAVSUBSCOL** ... Naval Submarine School
**NAVSUP** ... Naval Supply Systems Command [*Formerly, Bureau of Supplies and Accounts*] (MCD)
**NAVSUPACT** ... Naval Support Activity (NVT)
**NAVSUPCEN** ... Naval Supply Center
**NAVSUPFORANT** ... Naval Support Forces, Antarctica
**NAVSUPGRU** ... Naval Support Group (NVT)
**NAVSUPINST** ... Naval Supply Systems Command Instruction
**NAVSUPMIS** ... Navy Supply Management Information System
**NAVSUPPACT** ... Naval Supply Activity
**NAVSUPPFOR** ... Naval Support Force
**NAVSUPPFORANTARCTIC** ... Naval Support Forces, Antarctic
**NAVSUPRANDFA** ... Naval Supply Research and Development Facility
**NAVSUPSYSCOM** ... Naval Supply Systems Command [*Formerly, Bureau of Supplies and Accounts*]
**NAVSUPSYSCOMHQ** ... Naval Supply System Command Headquarters
**NAVSURMISYS** ... Naval Surface Missile Systems (MCD)
**NAVSWC** ... Naval Surface Weapons Center [*Later, NSWC*] (CAAL)
**NAVSWOP** ... Naval Special Weapons Ordnance Publication
**NAVSYD**... Naval Shipyard
**NAVTA** ..... National Automatic Vendors' Trade Association (EA)
**NAVTAC**... Tactical Navigation System
**NAVTACDOCACT** ... Navy Tactical Doctrine Activity
**NAVTACSTANS** ... Naval Tactical Standards (MCD)
**NAVTACSUPPACT** ... Navy Tactical Support Activity (NVT)
**NAVTAG** .. Naval Tactical Game
**NAVTAG** .. Navy Tactical Action Game
**NAVTEC**... National Association of Vocational-Technical Education Communicators (EA)
**NAVTECHJAP** ... Naval Technical Mission to Japan
**NAVTECHREP** ... Naval Technical Representative
**NAVTECHTRACEN** ... Naval Air Technical Training Center
**NAVTECMISEU** ... Naval Technical Mission in Europe
**NAVTELCOM** ... Naval Telecommunications Command
**NAVTNG** .. Navigator Training [*Air Force*]
**NAVTNGSq** ... Navigator Training Squadron [*Air Force*]
**NAVTORPSTA** ... Naval Torpedo Station
**NAVTRA**... Naval Training Command
**NAVTRACOM** ... Naval Training Command
**NAVTRADEV** ... Naval Training Device Center
**NAVTRADEVCEN** ... Naval Training Device Center
**NAVTRADISTCEN** ... Naval Training and Distribution Center
**NAVTRAEQUIPC** ... Naval Training Equipment Center
**NAVTRAEQUIPCEN** ... Naval Training Equipment Center
**NAVTRAFSAT** ... Navigational/Traffic-Control Satellite (MCD)
**NAVTRAIDSCEN** ... Naval Training Aids Center
**Nav Train Bull** ... Naval Training Bulletin [*A publication*]
**NAVTRAINST** ... Naval Training Support Command Instruction (MCD)
**NAVTRANSAIR** ... [*For*] Naval Transport Aircraft Class Travel, Priority Is Hereby Certified
**NAVTRANSCO** ... Naval Transportation Coordinating Office
**NAVTRAPUBCEN** ... Naval Training Publications Center (MCD)
**NAVTRASCOL** ... Naval Training School
**NAVTRASTA** ... Naval Training Station
**NAVUSEARANDCEN** ... Naval Undersea Research and Development Center (MCD)
**NAVUSEARESDEVCEN** ... Naval Undersea Research and Development Center
**NAVUSEAWARCEN** ... Naval Undersea Warfare Center
**NAVUWSES** ... Naval Underwater Systems Engineering Center
**NAVUWSOUNDLAB** ... Naval Underwater Sound Laboratory [*Later, NUSC*]
**NAVWAG** ... Naval Warfare Analysis Group
**NAVWARCOL** ... Naval War College
**Nav War Col Rev** ... Naval War College. Review [*A publication*]
**Nav War C Rev** ... Naval War College. Review [*A publication*] (DLA)
**NAVWASS** ... Navigation and Weapon-Aiming Subsystem (MCD)
**NAVWEARSCHFA** ... Navy Weather Research Facility
**NAVWEASERV** ... Naval Weather Service Command
**NAVWEPS** ... Bureau of Naval Weapons [*Obsolete*]
**NAVWESA** ... Naval Weapons Engineering Support Activity
**NAVWESPAC** ... [*US*] Naval Forces, Western Pacific
**NAVWESS** ... National Aviation Weather System Study (NOAA)
**NAVWPNCEN** ... Naval Weapons Center (MCD)
**NAVWPNEVALFAC** ... Naval Weapons Evaluation Facility
**NAVWPNLAB** ... Naval Weapons Laboratory [*Later, NSWC*]
**NAVWPNQUALASSURO** ... Naval Weapons Quality Assurance Office [*Washington, DC*]
**NAVWPNSCEN** ... Naval Weapons Center
**NAVWPNSERVO** ... Naval Weapons Services Office [*Also, NWSO, WEPSO*]
**NAVWPNSTA** ... Naval Weapons Station (MCD)
**NAVWPNSYSANALO** ... Naval Weapons Systems Analysis Office
**NAVWUIS** ... Navy Work Unit Information Service (IID)
**NAVXDIVINGU** ... Navy Experimental Diving Unit
**Navy Dep RAN Rep** ... Department of the Navy. RAN [*Royal Australian Navy*] Reports [*A publication*] (APTA)
**NAVYEO** .. Navigator's Yeoman [*British military*] (DMA)
**Navy Intnl** ... Navy International [*A publication*]
**Navy League J** ... Navy League Journal [*A publication*] (APTA)
**Navy News** ... Navy News and Undersea Technology [*A publication*]
**Navy Rec Soc Publ** ... Navy Records Society. Publications [*A publication*]
**Navy Tech F S** ... Navy Technology Transfer Fact Sheet [*A publication*]
**NAW** .......... Narathiwat [*Thailand*] [*Airport symbol*] (OAG)
**NAW** .......... National Agricultural Workers Union
**NAW** .......... National Association of Wholesaler-Distributors [*Washington, DC*] (EA)
**NAW** .......... Negative Afterwave [*Microelectrode recording*]
**N/AW** ........ Night/Adverse Weather Evaluator (IEEE)
**NAW** .......... Non-All-Weather (CINC)
**NAW** .......... North African Waters
**NAW** .......... Northwest African Waters
**NAWA** ....... National Academy of Western Art (EA)
**NAWA** ....... National Apple Week Association [*Later, NAM*] (EA)
**NAWA** ....... National Association of Women Artists (EA)
**NAWA** ....... North American Warmblood Association (EA)
**NAWAC** .... National Weather Analysis Center [*Air Force, Navy*]
**NAWAF** .... Navy with Air Force
**NAWAPA** ... North American Water and Power Alliance
**NAWAR** .... Navy with Army
**NAWARCOL** ... Naval War College (MUGU)
**NAWAS** .... National Warning System [*Civil Defense*]
**NAWB** ....... National Association of Wine Bottlers [*Later, NWA*] (EA)
**NAWBO** .... National Association of Women Business Owners [*Chicago, IL*] (EA)
**NAWC** ....... National Art Workers Community [*Later, FCA*] (EA)
**NAWC** ....... National Association of Water Companies (EA)
**NAWC** ....... National Association for Women in Careers [*Later, NAFWIC*] (EA)
**NAWC** ....... National Association of Women's Centers (EA)
**NAWC** ....... Naval War College
**NAWCAS** ... National Association of Women's and Children's Apparel Salesmen [*Later, Bureau of Wholesale Sales Representatives*] (EA)
**NAWCC** .... National Association of Watch and Clock Collectors (EA)
**NAWCC** .... National Association of Women in Chambers of Commerce (EA)
**NAWCH** .... National Association for the Welfare of Children in Hospital [*British*]
**NAWCJ** ..... National Association of Women in Criminal Justice (EA)
**NAWCM** ... National Association of Wiping Cloth Manufacturers [*Later, IAWCM*] (EA)
**NAWD** ....... Notice of Award
**NAWDA** .... North American Working Dog Association (EA)
**NAWDAC** ... National Association for Women Deans, Administrators, and Counselors (EA)
**NAWDAC Journal** ... National Association for Women Deans, Administrators, and Counselors. Journal [*A publication*]
**NAWDC** .... National Association of Waste Disposal Contractors [*British*] (DCTA)
**NAWDC** .... National Association of Women Deans and Counselors [*Later, NAWDAC*] (EA)
**NAWDEX** ... National Water Data Exchange [*United States Geological Survey*] [*Reston, VA*] [*Information service or system*]
**NAWE** ....... Nahama & Weagent Energy Co. [*NASDAQ symbol*] (NQ)
**NAWF** ....... North American Wildlife Foundation (EA)
**NAWF** ....... North American Wolf Society (EA)

**NAWFA** .... North Atlantic Westbound Freight Association (DS)
**NAWFC** .... National Association of Wholesale Fur Cleaners
**NAWFC** .... National Association of Women Federal Contractors [*Later, NAWGC*] (EA)
**NAWG** ....... Nachrichten. Akademie der Wissenschaften zu Goettingen. Philologisch-Historische Klasse [*A publication*]
**NAWG** ....... National Association of Wheat Growers (EA)
**NAWGA** .... National-American Wholesale Grocers' Association (EA)
**NAWGC** .... National Association of Women Government Contractors (EA)
**NAWGF** .... National Association of Wheat Growers Foundation (EA)
**NAWGott** .. Nachrichten. Akademie der Wissenschaften zu Goettingen [*A publication*]
**NAWH** ...... National Association of Women in Horticulture (EA)
**NAWHSL** ... National Association of Women Highway Safety Leaders (EA)
**NAWiC** ...... National Association for Women in Careers [*Later, NAFWIC*] (EA)
**NAWIC** ..... National Association of Women in Construction (EA)
**NAWID** ..... National Association of Water Institute Directors (EA)
**NAWID** ..... National Association of Writing Instrument Distributors (EA)
**NAWJ** ....... National Association of Women Judges (EA)
**NAWL** ....... National Association of Women Lawyers (EA)
**NAWLA** .... North American Wholesale Lumber Association (EA)
**NAWM** ...... National Association of Wool Manufacturers [*Later, American Textile Manufacturers Institute*] (EA)
**NAWM** ...... Naval Air Weapons Meet (MUGU)
**NAWMD** ... National Association of Waste Material Dealers [*Later, NARI*]
**NAWMP** ... National Association of Waste Material Producers [*Inactive*] (EA)
**NAWP** ....... National Anti-Waste Programme [*British*] (DCTA)
**NAWP** ....... National Association for Widowed People [*Later, IAWP*] (EA)
**NAWPA** .... North American Water and Power Alliance
**NAWPB** .... National Association of Wholesale Pie Bakers (EA)
**NAWPB** .... National Association of Wine Producers and Bottlers [*Later, NWA*] (EA)
**NAWPC** .... National Aircraft War Production Council [*World War II*]
**NAWPF** ..... North American Wildlife Park Foundation (EA)
**NAWPS** ..... National Association of Word Processing Specialists [*Later, WPS*] (EA)
**NAWR** ....... National Assembly of Women Religious (EA)
**NAWRSRF** ... New Age World Religious and Scientific Research Foundation (EA)
**NAWS** ....... National Aviation Weather System
**NAWS** ....... NORAD Attack Warning System (MCD)
**NAWS** ....... North African War Shipping [*World War II*]
**NAWS** ....... North American Wolf Society (EA)
**NAWSS** ..... North American Wilderness Survival School
**NAWTPD** ... Naval All Weather Testing Program Detachment
**NAWTS** ..... National Association of World Trade Secretaries [*Later, AWTCE*] (EA)
**NAWU** ....... National Agricultural Workers Union (EA)
**NAWU** ....... National Asphalt Workers' Union [*A union*] [*British*]
**NAWW** ....... National Association of Wheat Weavers (EA)
**NAWWO** ... National Association of Woolen and Worsted Overseers [*Later, NATS*] (EA)
**NAX** .......... Ewa, HI [*Location identifier*] [*FAA*] (FAAL)
**NAX** .......... New Arcadia Explorations [*Vancouver Stock Exchange symbol*]
**NAXSTA** ... Naval Air Experimental Station
**NAY** .......... New Alster Energy [*Vancouver Stock Exchange symbol*]
**NAYA** ........ North American Yngling Association (EA)
**NAYGTA** .. North American Youth Glider Training Association
**NAYO** ........ National Association of Youth Orchestras (EAIO)
**NAYPIC** .... National Association of Young People in Care [*British*]
**NAYRE** ..... National Association for Year-Round Education (EA)
**NAYRU** ..... North American Yacht Racing Union (EA)
**NAYSI** ....... North American Youth Sport Institute (EA)
**NAYW** ....... National Association for Young Writers (EA)
**Naz** ............ Nazir (BJA)
**NAZ** .......... Neueste Auslaendische Zeitschriften [*A publication*]
**NAZ** .......... Norddeutsche Allgemeine Zeitung [*A publication*]
**NAZ** .......... Normal Analytical Zone [*Chemistry*]
**NAZI** ......... Nationalsozialistische Deutsche Arbeiterpartei [*National Socialist German Workers' Party, 1919-45*] [*Political party*]
**NB** ............. Brooklyn Public Library, Brooklyn, NY [*Library symbol*] [*Library of Congress*] (LCLS)
**NB** ............. Nabonidus and Belshazzar (BJA)
**NB** ............. Nachrichtenblatt. Deutscher Verein vom Heiligen Lande [*A publication*]
**NB** ............. Namm och Bygd [*A publication*]
**NB** ............. Narodna Banka [*National Bank*] [*Yugoslavian*]
**NB** ............. Narrow Beam (NATG)
**NB** ............. Narrowband
**NB** ............. National Board
**NB** ............. Naval Base
**NB** ............. Navigation Base (NASA)
**NB** ............. Navy Band
**NB** ............. Neath and Brecon Railway [*Wales*]
**Nb** ............. Nebraska State Library, Lincoln, NE [*Library symbol*] [*Library of Congress*] (LCLS)
**NB** ............. Negative Binomial Distribution [*Statistics*]
**NB** ............. Nemzeti Bank [*National Bank*] [*Hungarian*]
**NB** ............. Neo-Babylonian [*or New Babylonian*] (BJA)
**NB** ............. Network Booter [*Data processing*] (BYTE)
**NB** ............. Neues Beginnen. Zeitschrift der Arbeiterwohlfahrt [*A publication*]
**NB** ............. Neuroblast [*Cytology*]
**NB** ............. Neurometric Test Battery [*Neurometrics*]
**NB** ............. New Benloe's Reports, English King's Bench [*1531-1628*] [*A publication*] (DLA)
**NB** ............. New Boiler
**NB** ............. New Bottom [*On ships*]
**NB** ............. New Brunswick [*Canadian province*] [*Postal code*]
**NB** ............. New Brunswick Reports [*A publication*] (DLA)
**NB** ............. New Business
**NB** ............. Newborn
**NB** ............. Next Brochure
**NB** ............. Niels Bohr. Collected Works [*Elsevier Book Series*] [*A publication*]
**NB** ............. Nimbus [*Cloud*] [*Meteorology*]
**Nb** ............. Niobium [*See Cb*] [*Chemical element*]
**NB** ............. Nitrobenzene [*Organic chemistry*]
**NB** ............. Nitrogen Base (NASA)
**NB** ............. No Ball [*Cricket*]
**NB** ............. No Bias [*Relay*] [*Electronics*]
**NB** ............. No Bid [*or Bidders*]
**NB** ............. Noise Blanker
**N/B** ............ Noise Power/Bandwidth
**NB** ............. Nominal Bore [*Tubing*]
**NB** ............. Nonbattle [*Army*] (AABC)
**NB** ............. Nonbusiness [*IRS*]
**NB** ............. Nordiska Batradet [*Nordic Boat Council*] (EAIO)
**NB** ............. North Borneo (ADA)
**NB** ............. North Britain [*i.e., Scotland*]
**NB** ............. Northampton & Bath Railroad Co. [*AAR code*]
**NB** ............. Northbound
**NB** ............. Not a Bean [*Penniless*] [*Facetious translation of NB, Nota Bene (Note Well)*] (DSUE)
**NB** ............. Not Bent [*Freight*]
**NB** ............. Not Blind [*Experimental conditions*]
**NB** ............. Nota Bene [*Note Well*] [*Latin*]
**NB** ............. Nuclear Blank (NRCH)
**NB** ............. Nuclear Boiler (NRCH)
**NB** ............. Nucleus Basalis [*Brain anatomy*]
**NB** ............. Nulla Bona [*No Goods*] [*Latin*] [*Legal term*] (DLA)
**Nb** ............. Numbers [*Old Testament book*] (BJA)
**NB** ............. Sterling Airways Ltd. [*Sweden*] [*ICAO designator*] (FAAC)
**NB2** ........... Norsar Array Site 02B00 [*Norway*] [*Seismograph station code, US Geological Survey*] (SEIS)
**NB3** ........... Norsar Array Site 03B00 [*Norway*] [*Seismograph station code, US Geological Survey*] (SEIS)
**NB4** ........... Norsar Array Site 04B00 [*Norway*] [*Seismograph station code, US Geological Survey*] (SEIS)
**NB5** ........... Norsar Array Site 05B00 [*Norway*] [*Seismograph station code, US Geological Survey*] (SEIS)
**NBA** ........... Amateur Astronomers Association, Brooklyn, NY [*Library symbol*] [*Library of Congress*] (LCLS)
**NBa** ........... Davenport Library, Bath, NY [*Library symbol*] [*Library of Congress*] (LCLS)
**NBA** ........... N-Bromoacetamide [*Organic chemistry*]
**NBA** ........... N-Butylamine [*Organic chemistry*]
**NBA** ........... Narrow-Beam Adapter
**NBA** ........... Narrowband Allocation
**NBA** ........... Narrowband Analyzer
**NBA** ........... National Ballet of America
**NBA** ........... National Band Association (EA)
**NBA** ........... National Bank Act of 1863
**NBA** ........... National Bank. Monthly Summary [*Melbourne*] [*A publication*]
**NBA** ........... National Bankers Association [*Washington, DC*] (EA)
**NBA** ........... National Bankruptcy Act [*1898*]
**NBA** ........... National Bar Association (EA)
**NBA** ........... National Basketball Association (EA)
**NBA** ........... National Beefmaster Association (EA)
**NBA** ........... National Benevolent Association of the Christian Church [*Disciples of Christ*] (EA)
**NBA** ........... National Biographical Association (EA)
**NBA** ........... National Boat Association (EA)
**NBA** ........... National Book Awards [*Discontinued*]
**NBA** ........... National Bowling Association (EA)
**NBA** ........... National Boxing Association of America [*Later, WBA*]
**NBA** ........... National Braille Association (EA)
**NBA** ........... National Broiler Association [*Later, NBC*]
**NBA** ........... National Buffalo Association (EA)
**NBA** ........... National Building Agency [*British*]
**NBA** ........... National Business Association (EA)
**NBA** ........... National Butterfly Association (EA)
**NBA** ........... National Button Association
**NBA** ........... Net Book Agreement [*British*]
**NBA** ........... Net Building Area (ADA)
**NBA** ........... Nickel-Base Alloy
**NBA** ........... North British Academy

**NBAA**........ National Business Aircraft Association (EA)
**NBab**.......... Babylon Public Library, Babylon, NY [*Library symbol*] [*Library of Congress*] (LCLS)
**NBAB**........ Biological Station, Fisheries and Oceans Canada [*Station de Biologie, Peches et Oceans Canada*] St. Andrews, New Brunswick [*Library symbol*] [*National Library of Canada*] (NLC)
**NBab**.......... Neo-Babylonian [*or New Babylonian*] (BJA)
**NBAC**........ National Black Alcoholism Council (EA)
**NBAC**........ Nuovo Bulletino di Archeologia Cristiana [*A publication*]
**NBACCH**.. Charlotte County Historical Society, Inc., St. Andrews, New Brunswick [*Library symbol*] [*National Library of Canada*] (NLC)
**NB Acts**..... Acts of New Brunswick [*A publication*]
**NBAD**........ N-beta-Alanyldopamine [*Biochemistry*]
**NBAD**........ National Bank of Abu Dhabi
**NBAD**........ Naval Bases Air Defense
**NBADA**..... National Barrel and Drum Association [*Later, NABADA - The Association of Container Reconditioners*] (EA)
**NBAF**........ National Blonde d'Aquitaine Foundation (EA)
**NBAGLE**... National Black Alliance for Graduate Level Education (EA)
**NBAJ**......... National Buffalo Association Juniors [*Defunct*] (EA)
**NBAK**........ National Bancorp of Alaska, Inc. [*NASDAQ symbol*] (NQ)
**NBald**......... Baldwin Public Library, Baldwin, NY [*Library symbol*] [*Library of Congress*] (LCLS)
**NBaldBE**... Brookside Elementary School, Baldwin, NY [*Library symbol*] [*Library of Congress*] (LCLS)
**NBaldCE**... Collidge Elementary School, Baldwin, NY [*Library symbol*] [*Library of Congress*] (LCLS)
**NBaldHE**... Harbor Elementary School, Baldwin, NY [*Library symbol*] [*Library of Congress*] (LCLS)
**NBaldHJ**... Harbor Junior High School, Baldwin, NY [*Library symbol*] [*Library of Congress*] (LCLS)
**NBaldLE**... Lenox Elementary School, Baldwin, NY [*Library symbol*] [*Library of Congress*] (LCLS)
**NBaldME**.. Meadow Elementary School, Baldwin, NY [*Library symbol*] [*Library of Congress*] (LCLS)
**NBaldMiE**... Milburn Elementary School, Baldwin, NY [*Library symbol*] [*Library of Congress*] (LCLS)
**NbaldPE**.... Plaza Elementary School, Baldwin, NY [*Library symbol*] [*Library of Congress*] (LCLS)
**NBaldPrE**... Prospect Elementary School, Baldwin, NY [*Library symbol*] [*Library of Congress*] (LCLS)
**NBaldSE**.... Shubert Elementary School, Baldwin, NY [*Library symbol*] [*Library of Congress*] (LCLS)
**NBaldSH**... Baldwin Senior High School, Baldwin, NY [*Library symbol*] [*Library of Congress*] (LCLS)
**NBaldStE**.. Steele Elementary School, Baldwin, NY [*Library symbol*] [*Library of Congress*] (LCLS)
**NBAO**........ New Brunswick Area Office [*Later, NBL*] [*AEC*]
**NBar**.......... Barker Free Library, Barker, NY [*Library symbol*] [*Library of Congress*] (LCLS)
**nbar**........... Nanobar
**NBAS**......... Neonatal Behavioural Assessment Scale [*Developed by Brazelton*]
**NBat**.......... Richmond Memorial Library, Batavia, NY [*Library symbol*] [*Library of Congress*] (LCLS)
**NBatC**........ Genesee Community College, Batavia, NY [*Library symbol*] [*Library of Congress*] (LCLS)
**NBatGH**.... Genesee Memorial Hospital, Batavia, NY [*Library symbol*] [*Library of Congress*] (LCLS)
**NBatHHi**... Holland Purchase Historical Society, Batavia, NY [*Library symbol*] [*Library of Congress*] (LCLS)
**NBatStJ**..... Saint Jerome Hospital, Medical Library, Batavia, NY [*Library symbol*] [*Library of Congress*] (LCLS)
**NBatV**........ United States Veterans Administration Hospital, Library Service, Batavia, NY [*Library symbol*] [*Library of Congress*] (LCLS)
**NBAU**........ No Business as Usual (EA)
**NBaVA**...... United States Veterans Administration Hospital, Bath, NY [*Library symbol*] [*Library of Congress*] (LCLS)
**NBAW**....... Notable Black American Women [*A publication*]
**NBAWADU**... National Black Anti-War Anti-Draft Union (EA)
**N Bay Ms**... Niederbayerische Monatsschrift [*A publication*]
**NBayv**........ Bayville Free Library, Bayville, NY [*Library symbol*] [*Library of Congress*] (LCLS)
**NbB**............ Beatrice Public Library, Beatrice, NE [*Library symbol*] [*Library of Congress*] (LCLS)
**NBB**........... Brooklyn Museum, Brooklyn, NY [*Library symbol*] [*Library of Congress*] (LCLS)
**NBB**........... Central Bank of Libya. Economic Bulletin [*A publication*]
**NBB**........... Narrowband Beam [*Physics*]
**NBB**........... NBB Bancorp [*Formerly, New Bedford Institution for Savings*] [*NYSE symbol*] (SPSG)
**NBB**........... Neue Beitraege zur Bausparmathematik [*A publication*]
**NBB**........... New Bedford Institution for Savings [*NYSE symbol*] (SPSG)
**NBB**........... Norsk Bibliografisk Bibliotek [*A publication*]
**NB & BA**.... National Bed-and-Breakfast Association (EA)
**NBBB**........ National Better Business Bureau [*Later, CBBB*] (EA)
**NBBC**........ Bibliotheque Medicale, Hopital Regional Chaleur [*Medical Library, Chaleur Regional Hospital*] Bathurst, New Brunswick [*Library symbol*] [*National Library of Canada*] (NLC)
**NBBCC**...... College Communautaire du New Brunswick, Bathurst, New Brunswick [*Library symbol*] [*National Library of Canada*] (NLC)
**NBBDA**..... National Burlap Bag Dealers Association [*Later, Textile Bag and Packaging Association*] (EA)
**NbBe**.......... Bellevue Public Library, Bellevue, NE [*Library symbol*] [*Library of Congress*] (LCLS)
**NBB-E**....... Brooklyn Museum, Wilbour Library of Egyptology, Brooklyn, NY [*Library symbol*] [*Library of Congress*] (LCLS)
**NBBI**.......... National Blue Books, Incorporated [*Canoga Park, CA*] [*Publisher*]
**NBBI**.......... Nederlands Bureau voor Bibliotheekwezen en Informatieverzorging [*Netherlands Organization for Libraries and Information Services*] [*Information service or system*] (IID)
**NBBL**......... National Bath, Bed, and Linen Association (EA)
**NBB & L**.... National Bath, Bed, and Linen Show (ITD)
**NbBla**......... Blair Public Library, Blair, NE [*Library symbol*] [*Library of Congress*] (LCLS)
**NBBLA**...... National Bath, Bed, and Linen Association [*Later, NBBL*] (EA)
**NbBlaD**...... Dana College, Blair, NE [*Library symbol*] [*Library of Congress*] (LCLS)
**NBBLC**...... National Black on Black Love Campaign (EA)
**NBBMA**.... National Beauty and Barber Manufacturers Association [*Later, ABA*] (EA)
**NBBMAN**... Neurobiology [*Copenhagen*] [*A publication*]
**NBBMK**.... Mussee de Kent, Bouctouche, New Brunswick [*Library symbol*] [*National Library of Canada*] (NLC)
**NBBN**........ Nepisiguit Centennial Public Library, Bathurst, New Brunswick [*Library symbol*] [*National Library of Canada*] (NLC)
**Nb-BPH**..... Nebraska Library Commission, Library for Blind and Physically Handicapped, Lincoln, NE [*Library symbol*] [*Library of Congress*] (LCLS)
**NBBPVI**.... National Board of Boiler and Pressure Vessel Inspectors (EA)
**NbBro**........ Broken Bow Carnegie Library, Broken Bow, NE [*Library symbol*] [*Library of Congress*] (LCLS)
**NBBWM**... Central New Brunswick Woodmen's Museum, Boiestown, New Brunswick [*Library symbol*] [*National Library of Canada*] (NLC)
**NBC**........... Beaufort, SC [*Location identifier*] [*FAA*] (FAAL)
**NBC**........... Brooklyn College, Brooklyn, NY [*Library symbol*] [*Library of Congress*] (LCLS)
**NBC**........... Concordia College, Seward, NE [*OCLC symbol*] (OCLC)
**NBC**........... Cook [*N. B.*] Corp. Ltd. [*Toronto Stock Exchange symbol*] [*Vancouver Stock Exchange symbol*]
**NBC**........... Narrowband Conducted (IEEE)
**NBC**........... National Ballet of Cuba
**NBC**........... National Baseball Congress (EA)
**NBC**........... National Battlefields Commission [*See also CCBN*]
**NBC**........... National Beagle Club (EA)
**NBC**........... National Beef Congress
**NBC**........... National Bibliographic Control
**NBC**........... National Board for Certification in Dental Laboratory Technology (EA)
**NBC**........... National Book Committee [*Defunct*]
**NBC**........... National Book Council [*Later, NBL*] [*United Kingdom*]
**NBC**........... National Bowling Council (EA)
**NBC**........... National Boxing Council [*British*]
**NBC**........... National Braille Club [*Later, NBA*] (EA)
**NBC**........... National Broadcasting Company, Inc. [*New York, NY*]
**NBC**........... National Broiler Council (EA)
**NBC**........... National Broom Council [*Later, NBMC*] (EA)
**NBC**........... National Building Code
**NBC**........... National Bus Company [*British*]
**NBC**........... National Business College [*Australia*]
**NBC**........... Natural Background Clutter
**NBC**........... Natural Birth Control
**NBC**........... Navy Beach Commando
**NBC**........... Neumann Boundary Conditions
**NBC**........... Newcastle Business College [*Australia*]
**NBC**........... Newfoundland Base Command [*Army*] [*World War II*]
**NBC**........... Nies Babylonian Collection [*Yale University*] (BJA)
**NBC**........... Nigerian Broadcasting Corporation
**NBC**........... Noise Balancing Circuit (DEN)
**NBC**........... Nonbattle Casualty (NVT)
**NBC**........... Nordic Boat Council (EA)
**NBC**........... Nostalgia Book Club
**NBC**........... Nuclear, Biological, and Chemical [*Warfare*]
**NBC**........... Number Base Conversion
**NBCA**........ Campbellton Centennial Public Library, New Brunswick [*Library symbol*] [*National Library of Canada*] (NLC)
**NBCA**........ National Beagle Club of America (EA)
**NBCA**........ National Bituminous Concrete Association [*Later, NAPA*] (EA)
**NBCA**........ National Business Circulation Association (EA)

**NBCAC** ..... Chaleur Library Region, Campbellton, New Brunswick [*Library symbol*] [*National Library of Canada*] (NLC)
**NBCAM** .... Campobello Public Library, New Brunswick [*Library symbol*] [*National Library of Canada*] (BIB)
**NBCAP**...... National Beacon Code Allocation Plan (FAAC)
**NBCBP**...... Bibliotheque Publique Mgr. Paquet, Caraquet, New Brunswick [*Library symbol*] [*National Library of Canada*] (NLC)
**NBCC** ........ National Baby Care Council [*Defunct*] (EA)
**NBCC** ........ National Banc of Commerce Company [*Charlestown, WV*] [*NASDAQ symbol*] (NQ)
**NBCC** ........ National Beauty Career Center (EA)
**NBCC** ........ National Bidders Control Center
**NBCC** ........ National Bituminous Coal Commission [*Functions transferred to Department of the Interior, 1939*]
**NBCC** ........ National Black Chamber of Commerce (EA)
**NBCC** ........ National Board for Certified Counselors (EA)
**NBCC** ........ National Book Critics Circle (EA)
**NBCC** ........ National Budget and Consultation Committee [*Defunct*] (EA)
**NBCC** ........ National Building Code of Canada
**NBCC** ........ National Bureau for Co-Operation in Child Care [*British*]
**NBCC** ........ National Business Career Center (EA)
**NBCC** ........ Netherlands British Chamber of Commerce (DS)
**NBCC** ........ Nigerian British Chamber of Commerce [*London*] (DCTA)
**NBCC** ........ Nuclear, Biological, Chemical, Conventional [*Warfare*]
**NBCCA** ..... National Business Council for Consumer Affairs [*Terminated, 1974*] [*Department of Commerce*] (EGAO)
**NBCCC**...... Miramichi Campus, New Brunswick Community College [*Campus Miramichi, College Communautaire du Nouveau-Brunswick*], Chatham, New Brunswick [*Library symbol*] [*National Library of Canada*] (NLC)
**NBCCC**...... National Black Catholic Clergy Caucus (EA)
**NBC-CDTP** ... National Board for Certification - Certified Dental Technician Program (EA)
**NBCD**........ Natural Binary-Coded Decimal
**NBCD**........ Negate BCD [*Binary-Coded Decimal*] Number [*Data processing*]
**NBCD**........ Nuclear, Biological, and Chemical Defense (NATG)
**NBCDCE**... Nuclear, Biological, and Chemical Defense Control Element [*Military*]
**NBCDI** ...... National Black Child Development Institute (EA)
**NBCDL**...... National Board for Certification of Dental Laboratories [*Later, CDL*] (EA)
**NBCDX** ..... Nuclear, Biological, and Chemical Defense Exercise [*NATO*] (NATG)
**NBCE** ........ Nuclear, Biological, and Chemical Element
**NbCen**........ Hards Memorial Library, Central City, NE [*Library symbol*] [*Library of Congress*] (LCLS)
**NbCenC** ..... Nebraska Central College, Central City, NE [*Library symbol*] [*Library of Congress*] [*Obsolete*] (LCLS)
**NBCFAE** ... National Black Coalition of Federal Aviation Employees (EA)
**NBCGT** ..... National Business Consortium for the Gifted and Talented (EA)
**NbCh** ......... Chadron Public Library, Chadron, NE [*Library symbol*] [*Library of Congress*] (LCLS)
**NBCH**......... Historical Society Nicolas Denys, Societe Historique Nicolas Denys, Caraquet, New Brunswick [*Library symbol*] [*National Library of Canada*] (NLC)
**NBCHD**..... Health Sciences Library, Hotel-Dieu Hospital, Chatham, New Brunswick [*Library symbol*] [*National Library of Canada*] (BIB)
**NBCHR**..... Bibliotheque de la Sante, Centre Hospitalier Restigouche, Campbellton, New Brunswick [*Library symbol*] [*National Library of Canada*] (BIB)
**NbChS**....... Chadron State College, Chadron, NE [*Library symbol*] [*Library of Congress*] (LCLS)
**NBCI** ......... Nigerian Bank for Commerce and Industry
**NBCIA**....... National Blue Crab Industry Association (EA)
**NBCL**......... National Beauty Culturists' League (EA)
**NBC/LEO** ... National Black Caucus of Local Elected Officials (EA)
**NBCM**....... Miramichi Natural History Society, Chatham, New Brunswick [*Library symbol*] [*National Library of Canada*] (NLC)
**NBCMA** .... Mussee Acadien, Caraquet, New Brunswick [*Library symbol*] [*National Library of Canada*] (NLC)
**NBCMu** ..... Brooklyn Children's Museum, Brooklyn, NY [*Library symbol*] [*Library of Congress*] (LCLS)
**NbCo**.......... Columbus Public Library, Columbus, NE [*Library symbol*] [*Library of Congress*] (LCLS)
**NbCoC** ....... Platte Technical Community College, Columbus, NE [*Library symbol*] [*Library of Congress*] (LCLS)
**NBCP**......... Brooklyn College of Pharmacy, Brooklyn, NY [*Library symbol*] [*Library of Congress*] (LCLS)
**NBCP**......... National Bladder Cancer Project [*National Cancer Institute*]
**NBCPC**...... National Board for Cardiovascular and Pulmonary Credentialing [*Later, Cardiovascular Credentialing International - CCI*] (EA)
**NbCr** .......... Crete Public Library, Crete, NE [*Library symbol*] [*Library of Congress*] (LCLS)
**NbCrD** ....... Doane College, Crete, NE [*Library symbol*] [*Library of Congress*] (LCLS)
**NBCRS**...... Nuclear-Biological-Chemical Reconnaissance System [*Military*]
**NBCS**......... National Black Communicators Society (EA)
**NBCS**......... St. Thomas University, Fredericton, New Brunswick [*Library symbol*] [*National Library of Canada*] (NLC)
**NBCSA**...... National Black Catholic Seminarians Association (EA)
**NBCSDA**... National Broom Corn and Supply Dealers Association (EA)
**NBCSH** ..... La Societe Historique de Clair, Inc., New Brunswick [*Library symbol*] [*National Library of Canada*] (NLC)
**NBCSI** ....... National Board of the Coat and Suit Industry [*Defunct*] (EA)
**NBCSL**....... National Black Caucus of State Legislators (EA)
**NBCT** ........ National Bancshares Corp. of Texas [*NASDAQ symbol*] (NQ)
**NBCU**........ National Bureau of Casualty Underwriters [*Later, ISO*] (EA)
**NBC USA** ... National Baptist Convention, USA (EA)
**NBCV**........ Narrowband Coherent Video (IEEE)
**NBCVHA**.. Le Village Historique Acadien, Caraquet, New Brunswick [*Library symbol*] [*National Library of Canada*] (NLC)
**NBCW**....... National Bird Cage Week
**NBCW**....... National Board of Catholic Women [*British*]
**NBCWRS**.. Nuclear, Biological, and Chemical Warning and Reporting System
**NBD**........... Doane College, Crete, NE [*OCLC symbol*] (OCLC)
**NBD**........... Narrowband Detector
**NBD**........... NBD Bancorp., Inc. [*NYSE symbol*] (SPSG)
**NBD**........... Negative Binomial Distribution [*Statistics*]
**NBD**........... Neurogenic Bladder Dysfunction [*Medicine*]
**NBD**........... Neutral Beam Divider
**NBD**........... Nitrobenzoxadiazole [*Organic chemistry*]
**NBD**........... Norbornadiene [*Organic chemistry*]
**NB 2d**......... New Brunswick Reports, Second Series [*A publication*] (DLA)
**NBDA**........ National Barrel and Drum Association
**NBDA**........ National Bicycle Dealers Association (EA)
**NBDB**........ National Bibliographic Database [*Australia*]
**NBDC**........ National Blood Data Center [*American Blood Commission*] [*Information service or system*] (IID)
**NBDC**........ National Bomb Data Center
**NBDCA**..... National Baptist Deacons Convention of America (EA)
**NBDE**........ National Bureau of Document Examiners (EA)
**NBDEA**..... National Beverage Dispensing Equipment Association (EA)
**NB Dep Nat Resour Miner Resour Branch Rep Invest** ... New Brunswick. Department of Natural Resources. Mineral Resources Branch. Report of Investigation [*A publication*]
**NB Dep Nat Resour Miner Resour Branch Top Rep** ... New Brunswick. Department of Natural Resources. Mineral Resources Branch. Topical Report [*A publication*]
**NB Dep Nat Resour Repr** ... New Brunswick. Department of Natural Resources. Reprint [*A publication*]
**NBDF** ........ Narrow Band Device - Fix
**NBDF** ........ Narrowband Dicke-Fix [*Electronics*] (CET)
**NBDFB**...... Nitrobenzenediazonium Tetrafluoroborate [*Organic chemistry*]
**NBDFX**...... Narrowband Dicke-Fix [*Electronics*] (MSA)
**NBDKH**..... Keillor House Museum, Dorchester, New Brunswick [*Library symbol*] [*National Library of Canada*] (NLC)
**NBDL**........ Narrowband Data Line
**NBDL**........ Naval Biodynamics Laboratory (GRD)
**NBDM**....... Miramichi Salmon Museum, Inc., Doaktown, New Brunswick [*Library symbol*] [*National Library of Canada*] (NLC)
**NBDMO**.... N-Bromo(dimethyl)oxazolidinone [*Organic chemistry*]
**NBD-PS**..... Nitrobenzoxadiazole Phosphatidylserine [*Biochemistry*]
**NBDRRM** ... Restigouche Regional Museum, Dalhousie, New Brunswick [*Library symbol*] [*National Library of Canada*] (NLC)
**NBDS** ........ Nuclear Burst Detection Systems (MCD)
**NBE**........... Dallas, TX [*Location identifier*] [*FAA*] (FAAL)
**NbE**............ Exeter Public Library, Exeter, NE [*Library symbol*] [*Library of Congress*] (LCLS)
**NBE**........... National Bank of Egypt. Economic Bulletin [*A publication*]
**NBE**........... Neutron Binding Energy
**NBE**........... Newbery Corp. [*Formerly, Newbery Energy Corp.*] [*AMEX symbol*] (SPSG)
**NBE**........... Newburyport Birders' Exchange (EA)
**NBE**........... Nominal Band Edge
**NBE**........... Normal Binocular Experience [*Ophthalmology*]
**NbE**............ North by East
**NBE**........... Nova Beaucage Mines Ltd. [*Toronto Stock Exchange symbol*]
**NBE**........... Nuclear Binding Energy
**NBEA**........ National Ballroom and Entertainment Association (EA)
**NBEA**........ National Black Evangelical Association (EA)
**NBEA**........ National Broadcast Editorial Association (EA)
**NBEA**........ National Business Education Association [*Reston, VA*] (EA)
**NBEA Y**..... National Business Education Association. Yearbook [*A publication*]
**NBEBR**...... Bibliotheque Regionale du Haut Saint-Jean, Edmundston, New Brunswick [*Library symbol*] [*National Library of Canada*] (NLC)
**NBEC** ........ National Business and Education Council (OICC)
**NBECC**...... New Brunswick Community College, Edmundston, New Brunswick [*Library symbol*] [*National Library of Canada*] (NLC)
**NBed**.......... Bedford Free Library, Bedford, NY [*Library symbol*] [*Library of Congress*] (LCLS)
**NBEDC** ..... National Black Economic Development Conference
**NBedh**........ Bedford Hills Free Library, Bedford Hills, NY [*Library symbol*] [*Library of Congress*] (LCLS)

**NBEET**...... National Board of Employment, Education, and Training [*Australia*]
**NBEF**......... National Bowhunter Education Foundation (EA)
**NBel**.......... Bellport Memorial Library, Bellport, NY [*Library symbol*] [*Library of Congress*] (LCLS)
**NBEL**......... National Beryllia Corp. [*NASDAQ symbol*] (NQ)
**NBelf**.......... Belfast Public Library, Belfast, NY [*Library symbol*] [*Library of Congress*] (LCLS)
**NBelL**........ Long Island Library Resources Council, Inc., Bellport, NY [*Library symbol*] [*Library of Congress*] (LCLS)
**NBellm**....... Bellmore Memorial Library, Bellmore, NY [*Library symbol*] [*Library of Congress*] (LCLS)
**NBelS**........ Suffolk Cooperative Library System, Bellport, NY [*Library symbol*] [*Library of Congress*] (LCLS)
**NBEMM**... Musee de Madawaska, Edmundston, New Brunswick [*Library symbol*] [*National Library of Canada*] (NLC)
**N Ben**......... New Benloe's Reports, English King's Bench [*1531-1628*] [*A publication*] (DLA)
**N Benl**........ New Benloe's Reports, English King's Bench [*1531-1628*] [*A publication*] (DLA)
**NBEO**........ National Board of Examiners in Optometry (EA)
**NBEOPS**... National Board of Examiners for Osteopathic Physicians and Surgeons [*Later, NBOME*] (EA)
**NB Eq**........ New Brunswick Equity Reports [*A publication*] (DLA)
**NB Eq Ca**... New Brunswick Equity Cases [*A publication*] (DLA)
**NB Eq R**..... New Brunswick Equity Reports [*A publication*] (DLA)
**NB Eq Rep**... New Brunswick Equity Reports [*A publication*] (DLA)
**NBER**........ National Bureau of Economic Research (EA)
**NBER**........ National Bureau of Engineering Registration
**NBERA**....... National Bicentennial Ethnic-Racial Alliance
**NBerG**........ Gillam-Grant Community Center Library, Bergen, NY [*Library symbol*] [*Library of Congress*] (LCLS)
**NBER Gen S**... National Bureau of Economic Research. General Studies [*A publication*]
**NBernN**..... Bernardsville News, Bernardsville, NJ [*Library symbol*] [*Library of Congress*] (LCLS)
**NBER Oc P**... National Bureau of Economic Research. Occasional Papers [*A publication*]
**NBerR**........ Bergen Reading Center, Bergen, NY [*Library symbol*] [*Library of Congress*] (LCLS)
**NBES**......... National Business Equipment Survey [*British*]
**NBESLM**.. Centre Universitaire Saint-Louis Maillet, Edmundston, New Brunswick [*Library symbol*] [*National Library of Canada*] (NLC)
**NBet**........... Bethpage Public Library, Bethpage, NY [*Library symbol*] [*Library of Congress*] (LCLS)
**NBetCaE**... Campagne Elementary School, Bethpage, NY [*Library symbol*] [*Library of Congress*] (LCLS)
**NBetCE**..... Central Elementary School, Bethpage, NY [*Library symbol*] [*Library of Congress*] (LCLS)
**NBETF**...... Neutral-Beam Engineering Test Facility [*Terminated*] [*Lawrence Berkeley Laboratory*] [*Department of Energy*] (GRD)
**NBetG**........ Grumman Aerospace Corp., Bethpage, NY [*Library symbol*] [*Library of Congress*] (LCLS)
**NBetH**....... Mid-Island Hospital, Bethpage, NY [*Library symbol*] [*Library of Congress*] (LCLS)
**NBethKJ**.... John F. Kennedy Junior High School, Bethpage, NY [*Library symbol*] [*Library of Congress*] (LCLS)
**NBethSH**... Bethpage Senior High School, Bethpage, NY [*Library symbol*] [*Library of Congress*] (LCLS)
**NBetKE**..... Kramer Elementary School, Bethpage, NY [*Library symbol*] [*Library of Congress*] (LCLS)
**NBF**........... Brooklyn Friends School, New York, NY [*Library symbol*] [*Library of Congress*] (LCLS)
**NBF**........... Narrowband Filter
**NBF**........... National Birman Fanciers (EA)
**NBF**........... National Boating Federation (EA)
**NBF**........... National Burn Federation (EA)
**NBF**........... Neutral Buoyancy Facility [*Navy*] (MCD)
**NBF**........... New Biotechnology Firm
**NBF**........... New Business Funds (MCD)
**NBF**........... Nordisk Barnkirurgisk Forening [*Scandinavian Association of Paediatric Surgeons - SAPS*] (EAIO)
**NBF**........... North Bergen Federation of Public Libraries [*Library network*]
**NBF**........... Northbay Financial [*AMEX symbol*] (SPSG)
**NBF**........... Northwest AHEC [*Area Health Education Center*] - Bowman Gray School of Medicine, Taylorsville, NC [*OCLC symbol*] (OCLC)
**NBF**........... Nucleotide Binding Fold [*Genetics*]
**NBFA**........ National Baseball Fan Association (EA)
**NBFA**........ National Business Forms Association [*Alexandria, VA*] (EA)
**NBFA**........ New Business Fund Authorization (MCD)
**NBFA**........ Provincial Archives of New-Brunswick [*Archives Provinciales du Nouveau-Brunswick*] Fredericton, New Brunswick [*Library symbol*] [*National Library of Canada*] (NLC)
**NBFAA**...... National Burglar and Fire Alarm Association (EA)
**NBFAFA**... Archives, Diocese of Fredericton, Anglican Church of Canada, New Brunswick [*Library symbol*] [*National Library of Canada*] (NLC)
**NBFAG**...... Research Station, Agriculture Canada [*Station de Recherches, Agriculture Canada*] Fredericton, New Brunswick [*Library symbol*] [*National Library of Canada*] (NLC)
**NBFB**......... Beaverbrook Collection, New Brunswick Archives, Fredericton, New Brunswick [*Library symbol*] [*National Library of Canada*] (NLC)
**NbFb**.......... Fairbury Public Library, Fairbury, NE [*Library symbol*] [*Library of Congress*] (LCLS)
**NbFbC**....... Southeast Community College, Fairbury, NE [*Library symbol*] [*Library of Congress*] (LCLS)
**NBFBS**...... New Brunswick Barristers Society, Fredericton, New Brunswick [*Library symbol*] [*National Library of Canada*] (NLC)
**NbFC**......... Central Lutheran Theological Seminary, Fremont, NE [*Library symbol*] [*Library of Congress*] (LCLS)
**NBFC**......... New Brunswick Library Service, Fredericton, New Brunswick [*Library symbol*] [*National Library of Canada*] (NLC)
**NbFc**.......... Woods Memorial Library, Falls City, NE [*Library symbol*] [*Library of Congress*] (LCLS)
**NBFDEC**... Dr. Everett Chalmers Hospital, Fredericton, New Brunswick [*Library symbol*] [*National Library of Canada*] (NLC)
**NBFE**......... Maritimes Forest Research Centre, Environment Canada [*Centre de Recherches Forestieres des Maritimes, Environnement Canada*] Fredericton, New Brunswick [*Library symbol*] [*National Library of Canada*] (NLC)
**NBFED**...... New Brunswick Department of Education, Fredericton, New Brunswick [*Library symbol*] [*National Library of Canada*] (NLC)
**NBFFO**...... National Board of Fur Farm Organizations (EA)
**NBFHR**..... New Brunswick Department of Historical Resources, Fredericton, New Brunswick [*Library symbol*] [*National Library of Canada*] (NLC)
**NBFI**.......... Non-Bank Financial Intermediary (ADA)
**NBFJS**....... Sunbury West Historical Society, Fredericton Junction, New Brunswick [*Library symbol*] [*National Library of Canada*] (NLC)
**NBFJWO**.. National Bureau of Federated Jewish Women's Organizations (EA)
**NBFKL**...... Kings Landing Historical Settlement, Fredericton, New Brunswick [*Library symbol*] [*National Library of Canada*] (NLC)
**NBFL**......... Legislative Library [*Bibliotheque Legislative*] Fredericton, New Brunswick [*Library symbol*] [*National Library of Canada*] (NLC)
**NBFLM**..... Photogrammetry Branch, New Brunswick Department of Lands and Mines, Fredericton, New Brunswick [*Library symbol*] [*National Library of Canada*] (NLC)
**NBFM**....... Narrowband Frequency Modulation [*Radio*]
**NBFMM**... Medley Memorial Library, Christ Church Cathedral, Fredericton, New Brunswick [*Library symbol*] [*National Library of Canada*] (NLC)
**NBFNR**..... New Brunswick Department of Natural Resources and Energy, Fredericton, New Brunswick [*Library symbol*] [*National Library of Canada*] (NLC)
**NBFO**........ National Black Feminist Organization
**NBFP**......... New Brunswick Power, Fredericton, New Brunswick [*Library symbol*] [*National Library of Canada*] (NLC)
**NBFPO**...... Premier's Office, Province of New Brunswick, Fredericton, New Brunswick [*Library symbol*] [*National Library of Canada*] (NLC)
**NbFr**.......... Fremont Public Library, Fremont, NE [*Library symbol*] [*Library of Congress*] (LCLS)
**NbFrM**...... Midland Lutheran College, Fremont, NE [*Library symbol*] [*Library of Congress*] (LCLS)
**NBFRP**...... New Brunswick Research and Productivity Council, Fredericton, New Brunswick [*Library symbol*] [*National Library of Canada*] (NLC)
**NBFS**......... Societe d'Histoire de la Riviere Saint Jean, Fredericton, New Brunswick [*Library symbol*] [*National Library of Canada*] (BIB)
**NBFSS**....... New Brunswick Department of Social Services, Fredericton, New Brunswick [*Library symbol*] [*National Library of Canada*] (NLC)
**NBFT**......... Bureau de Traduction, Gouvernement du Nouveau-Brunswick [*Translation Bureau, Governement of New Brunswick*] Fredericton, New Brunswick [*Library symbol*] [*National Library of Canada*] (NLC)
**NBFTR**...... New Brunswick Department of Transportation, Fredericton, New Brunswick [*Library symbol*] [*National Library of Canada*] (NLC)
**NBFU**........ National Board of Fire Underwriters [*Later, AIA*] (EA)
**NBFU**........ University of New Brunswick, Fredericton, New Brunswick [*Library symbol*] [*National Library of Canada*] (NLC)
**NBFUA**..... Archives and Special Collections Department, University of New Brunswick, Fredericton, New Brunswick [*Library symbol*] [*National Library of Canada*] (NLC)
**NBFUE**...... Engineering Library, University of New Brunswick, Fredericton [*Library symbol*] [*National Library of Canada*] (BIB)
**NBFUL**...... Law Library, University of New Brunswick, Fredericton, New Brunswick [*Library symbol*] [*National Library of Canada*] (NLC)

**NBFUM** .... Map Room, Government Documents Department, University of New Brunswick, Fredericton, New Brunswick [*Library symbol*] [*National Library of Canada*] (NLC)
**NBFY** ......... York-Sunbury Historical Society, Fredericton, New Brunswick [*Library symbol*] [*National Library of Canada*] (NLC)
**NBFYR** ...... York Regional Library, Fredericton, New Brunswick [*Library symbol*] [*National Library of Canada*] (NLC)
**NBFYRC** ... New Brunswick Department of Youth, Recreation and Cultural Resources, Fredericton, New Brunswick [*Library symbol*] [*National Library of Canada*] (NLC)
**NBG** .......... Bowman Gray School of Medicine, Winston-Salem, NC [*OCLC symbol*] (OCLC)
**NBG** .......... Brooklyn Botanic Garden, Brooklyn, NY [*Library symbol*] [*Library of Congress*] (LCLS)
**NbG** .......... Grand Island Public Library, Grand Island, NE [*Library symbol*] [*Library of Congress*] (LCLS)
**NBG** .......... National Bank of Greece
**NBG** .......... Naval Beach Group (NVT)
**NBG** .......... New Orleans, LA [*Location identifier*] [*FAA*] (FAAL)
**NBG** .......... Nieuwe Vertaling Nederlands Bijbelgenootschap [*A publication*] (BJA)
**NBG** .......... No Blasted Good [*Slang*]
**NBG** .......... No Bloody Good [*British slang*]
**NBG** .......... Nuclear Beta Gauge
**NBGACF** ... Canadian Forces Base, Gagetown, New Brunswick [*Library symbol*] [*National Library of Canada*] (NLC)
**NBGFCC** ... New Brunswick Community College, Grand Falls, New Brunswick [*Library symbol*] [*National Library of Canada*] (NLC)
**NBGFH** ..... Grand Falls Historical Society, New Brunswick [*Library symbol*] [*National Library of Canada*] (NLC)
**Nbg Forsch** ... Nuernberger Forschungen [*A publication*]
**NBGG** ....... Grand Manan Historical Society, Grand Harbour, Grand Manan Island, New Brunswick [*Library symbol*] [*National Library of Canada*] (NLC)
**NBGMM** ... Grand Manan Museum, Grand Harbour, Grand Manan Island, New Brunswick, [*Library symbol*] [*National Library of Canada*] (NLC)
**NBGPL** ...... Nederlandsche Bijdragen op het Gebied van Germaansche Philologie en Linguistiek [*A publication*]
**NBGQA** ..... National Building Granite Quarries Association (EA)
**NBGS** ........ New Bedford Glass Society (EA)
**NBGSA** ...... Nippon Butsuri Gakkaishi [*A publication*]
**NBH** .......... Hastings College, Hastings, NE [*OCLC symbol*] (OCLC)
**NbH** .......... Hastings Public Library, Hastings, NE [*Library symbol*] [*Library of Congress*] (LCLS)
**NBH** .......... National Bank of Hungary
**NBH** .......... National Bellas Hess [*Inc.*] [*Commercial firm*]
**NBH** .......... Network Busy Hour [*Telecommunications*] (TEL)
**NBH** .......... North Bay [*Hawaii*] [*Seismograph station code, US Geological Survey*] [*Closed*] (SEIS)
**NBHA** ........ National Bicentennial Hospitality Alliance [*American Revolution Bicentennial Administration*]
**NBHA** ........ National Builders' Hardware Association [*Later, DHI*] (EA)
**NbHC** ........ Hastings College, Hastings, NE [*Library symbol*] [*Library of Congress*] (LCLS)
**NBHCA** ..... Albert County Historical Society, Inc., Hopewell Cape, New Brunswick [*Library symbol*] [*National Library of Canada*] (NLC)
**NBHCA** ..... National Belgian Hare Club of America [*Defunct*] (EA)
**NbHCC** ...... Central Technical Community College, Hastings, NE [*Library symbol*] [*Library of Congress*] (LCLS)
**NbHCro** ..... Crosier Fathers' Library, Hastings, NE [*Library symbol*] [*Library of Congress*] (LCLS)
**NbHi** ......... Nebraska State Historical Society, Lincoln, NE [*Library symbol*] [*Library of Congress*] (LCLS)
**NB His S** .... New Brunswick Historical Society. Collections [*A publication*]
**NbHo** ......... Holdrege-Phelps County Library, Holdrege, NE [*Library symbol*] [*Library of Congress*] (LCLS)
**NBHPA** ..... National Black Health Planners Association (EA)
**NBHPB** ..... Neuroscience and Behavioral Physiology [*A publication*]
**NBHS** ........ National Bureau for Handicapped Students [*British*] (CB)
**NBi** ............ Binghamton Public Library, Binghamton, NY [*Library symbol*] [*Library of Congress*] (LCLS)
**NBI** ............ Nabisco Brands, Incorporated [*Toronto Stock Exchange symbol*]
**NBI** ............ Nathaniel Branden Institute
**NBI** ............ National BankAmericard, Incorporated [*Later, Visa USA, Inc.*]
**NBI** ............ NBI, Inc. [*NYSE symbol*] (SPSG)
**NBI** ............ Neue Berliner Illustrierte [*A publication*]
**NBI** ............ Neutral Beam Injection (MCD)
**NBI** ............ No Bone Injury [*Medicine*]
**NBI** ............ Nonbattle Injuries
**NBI** ............ Northern Business Information, Inc. [*New York, NY*] [*Information service or system*] (TSSD)
**NBI** ............ Nothing but Initials [*Initialism is name of commercial word processor firm*]
**NBI** ............ Nuclear Burst Indicator (NATG)
**NBIA** ......... National Business Incubation Association [*Carlisle, PA*] (EA)
**NBiBT** ....... Broome Technical Community College, Binghamton, NY [*Library symbol*] [*Library of Congress*] (LCLS)
**NBIC** ......... National Business Information Center [*Dun & Bradstreet*]
**NBIC** ......... News from Behind the Iron Curtain [*A publication*]
**NBIC** ......... Northeast Bancorp, Incorporated [*NASDAQ symbol*] (NQ)
**NBIE** .......... National Burn Information Exchange [*Information service or system*] (CRD)
**NBiF** .......... Four County Library System, Binghamton, NY [*Library symbol*] [*Library of Congress*] (LCLS)
**NBiL** .......... Our Lady of Lourdes Hospital, Binghamton, NY [*Library symbol*] [*Library of Congress*] (LCLS)
**NBIO** ......... North American Biologicals, Inc. [*NASDAQ symbol*] (NQ)
**NBIP** .......... National Biomonitoring Inventory Program [*Department of Energy*] (MSC)
**NBiSC** ........ New York State Supreme Court Law Library, Binghamton, NY [*Library symbol*] [*Library of Congress*] (LCLS)
**NBiSEG** ..... New York State Electric & Gas Corp., Binghamton, NY [*Library symbol*] [*Library of Congress*] (LCLS)
**NBiSL** ........ Singer Co., Link Division, Binghamton, NY [*Library symbol*] [*Library of Congress*] (LCLS)
**NBISS** ....... National Building Industry Specification System [*Australia*]
**NBiSU** ....... State University of New York at Binghamton, Binghamton, NY [*Library symbol*] [*Library of Congress*] (LCLS)
**NBIT** .......... New Bedford Institute of Technology [*Massachusetts*]
**NBJ** ........... Kingsbrook Jewish Medical Center, Brooklyn, NY [*Library symbol*] [*Library of Congress*] (LCLS)
**NBJ** ........... National Bar Journal [*A publication*] (DLA)
**NBJ** ........... Noord Brabant [*A publication*]
**NB Jb** ......... Neues Beethoven Jahrbuch [*A publication*]
**NbK** ........... Kearney Public Library, Kearney, NE [*Library symbol*] [*Library of Congress*] (LCLS)
**NBK** .......... Kingsborough Community College of the City University of New York, Brooklyn, NY [*Library symbol*] [*Library of Congress*] (LCLS)
**NBK** .......... Nabu Network Corp. [*Toronto Stock Exchange symbol*]
**NBK** .......... National Bank of Kuwait
**NBK** .......... Nebelkerze [*Smoke-Candle*] [*German military - World War II*]
**NBK** .......... Nordisk Bilteknisk Kommitte [*Nordic Automobile Technical Committee - NATC*] (EAIO)
**NBKC** ........ New England Bancorp, Inc. [*NASDAQ symbol*] (NQ)
**NbKi** .......... Kimball Public Library, Kimball, NE [*Library symbol*] [*Library of Congress*] (LCLS)
**N Bkpt R** .... National Bankruptcy Register Reports [*United States*] [*A publication*] (DLA)
**N Bkpt Reg** ... National Bankruptcy Register Reports [*United States*] [*A publication*] (DLA)
**N Bk R** ....... National Bankruptcy Register Reports [*United States*] [*A publication*] (DLA)
**NbKS** ......... Kearney State College, Kearney, NE [*Library symbol*] [*Library of Congress*] (LCLS)
**NBL** ........... Brooklyn Law School, Brooklyn, NY [*Library symbol*] [*Library of Congress*] (LCLS)
**NbL** ............ Lincoln City Libraries, Lincoln, NE [*Library symbol*] [*Library of Congress*] (LCLS)
**NBL** ........... National Bicycle League (EA)
**NBL** ........... National Book League [*Formerly, NBC*]
**NBL** ........... National Business League [*Washington, DC*] (EA)
**NBL** ........... Naval Biosciences Laboratory [*Research center*]
**NBL** ........... Navy Basic Logistic [*Plan*]
**Nb L** ........... Nebraska Law Review [*A publication*]
**NBL** ........... Nebraska Library Commission, Lincoln, NE [*OCLC symbol*] (OCLC)
**NBL** ........... Neue Badener Landeszeitung [*A publication*]
**NBL** ........... Neue Beitraege zur Literaturwissenschaft [*A publication*]
**NBL** ........... New Brunswick Laboratory [*Formerly, NBAO*] [*Department of Energy*] [*Argonne, IL*]
**NBL** ........... Night Bombardment - Long Distance [*Air Force*]
**NBL** ........... No Berth List [*Shipping*] (DS)
**NBL** ........... Noble Affiliates, Inc. [*NYSE symbol*] (SPSG)
**NBL** ........... Norbaska Mines Limited [*Toronto Stock Exchange symbol*]
**nbl** ............. Normoblast [*Hematology*]
**NBL** ........... Not Bloody Likely [*British slang*]
**NBL** ........... Nuclear Bomb Line (CINC)
**NBla** .......... Blauvelt Free Library, Blauvelt, NY [*Library symbol*] [*Library of Congress*] (LCLS)
**NBLA** ........ National Businesswomen's Leadership Association [*Shawnee Mission, KS*] (EA)
**NBlaD** ........ Dominican College, Blauvelt, NY [*Library symbol*] [*Library of Congress*] (LCLS)
**NBLB** ......... Nebraska Law Bulletin [*A publication*] (DLA)
**NBLC** ......... National Business Law Council [*Formerly, NABLT*] (EA)
**Nb-LC** ........ Nebraska Public Library Commission, Lincoln, NE [*Library symbol*] [*Library of Congress*] (LCLS)
**NBLCC** ...... National Black Lay Catholic Caucus (EA)
**NBLD** ........ Narrowband Linear Detector (MCD)
**NBLE** ......... Nearly Best Linear Estimator [*Statistics*]
**NBLiCH** ..... Long Island College Hospital, Brooklyn, NY [*Library symbol*] [*Library of Congress*] (LCLS)
**NBLiHi** ...... Long Island Historical Society, Brooklyn, NY [*Library symbol*] [*Library of Congress*] (LCLS)
**NBLiU** ....... Long Island University, Brooklyn, NY [*Library symbol*] [*Library of Congress*] (LCLS)

**NbLNP**...... United States Department of the Interior, National Park Service, Midwest Archaeological Center, Lincoln, NE [*Library symbol*] [*Library of Congress*] (LCLS)
**NbLo**.......... Loup City Township Library, Loup City, NE [*Library symbol*] [*Library of Congress*] (LCLS)
**NBLP**......... National Bureau for Lathing and Plastering [*Later, International Institute for Lath and Plaster*] (EA)
**NBLR**........ National Black Leadership Roundtable (EA)
**Nb LR**........ Nebraska Law Review [*A publication*]
**Nb-LR**........ Nebraska Legislative Council, Reference Library, Lincoln, NE [*Library symbol*] [*Library of Congress*] (LCLS)
**NBLR**........ North Borneo Law Reports [*A publication*] (DLA)
**NBLSA**...... National/Black Law Student Association (EA)
**NbLSc**........ Southeast Community College, Lincoln, NE [*Library symbol*] [*Library of Congress*] (LCLS)
**N Bl Sch H Sch W**... Nachrichtenblatt fuer das Schleswig-Holsteinische Schulwesen [*A publication*]
**NBLU**........ Naucnyj Bjulletin Leningradskogo Universiteta [*A publication*]
**NbLU**......... Union College, Lincoln, NE [*Library symbol*] [*Library of Congress*] (LCLS)
**NbLVA**...... United States Veterans Administration Hospital, Lincoln, NE [*Library symbol*] [*Library of Congress*] (LCLS)
**NbLW**........ Nebraska Wesleyan University, Lincoln, NE [*Library symbol*] [*Library of Congress*] (LCLS)
**NB Lwss**.... Neue Beitraege zur Literaturwissenschaft [*A publication*]
**NBm**........... Briarcliff Manor Public Library, Briarcliff Manor, NY [*Library symbol*] [*Library of Congress*] (LCLS)
**NbM**.......... McCook Public Library, McCook, NE [*Library symbol*] [*Library of Congress*] (LCLS)
**NBM**.......... Medical Research Library of Brooklyn, Brooklyn, NY [*Library symbol*] [*Library of Congress*] (LCLS)
**NBM**.......... National Building Museum (EA)
**NBM**.......... National Bureau of Metrology
**NBM**.......... Navy Basic Modernization [*Plan*]
**NBM**.......... Nitro-Form Bind Medium [*Analytical biochemistry*]
**NBM**.......... Nonbook Materials (ADA)
**NBM**.......... Nothing by Mouth
**NBM**.......... Nuclear Ballistic Missile
**NBM**.......... Nucleus Basalis Magnocellularis [*Cytology*]
**nbM**.......... Nucleus Basalis of Meynert [*Brain anatomy*]
**NBMAIA**... National Broom Manufacturers and Allied Industries Association [*Later, NBMC*] (EA)
**NBmB**........ Briarcliff College, Briarcliff Manor, NY [*Library symbol*] [*Library of Congress*] (LCLS)
**NBMB**....... National Bus Military Bureau (EA)
**NBMBAA**... National Black MBA [*Master of Business Administration*] Association [*Chicago, IL*] (EA)
**NbMC**........ McCook Community College, McCook, NE [*Library symbol*] [*Library of Congress*] (LCLS)
**NBMC**....... National Bar Mitzvah Club [*Later, AZYF*] (EA)
**NBMC**....... National Black Media Coalition (EA)
**NBMC**....... National Black Music Caucus - of the Music Educators National Conference (EA)
**NBMC**....... National Broom and Mop Council [*Defunct*]
**NBMC**....... National Businessmen's Council [*Defunct*] (EA)
**NBMCM**... Minto Coal Museum, New Brunswick [*Library symbol*] [*National Library of Canada*] (NLC)
**NBMDA**.... National Building Material Distributors Association (EA)
**NBMDR**.... National Bone Marrow Donor Registry (EA)
**NBME**....... Medgar Evers College of the City University of New York, Brooklyn, NY [*Library symbol*] [*Library of Congress*] (LCLS)
**NBME**....... National Board of Medical Examiners (EA)
**NBMG**....... Navigational Bombing and Missile Guidance (MCD)
**NBMGS**.... Navigational Bombing and Missile Guidance System (AAG)
**NBMHD**... Hopital Docteur Georges - L. Dumont [*Docteur Georges - L. Dumont Hospital*] Moncton, New Brunswick [*Library symbol*] [*National Library of Canada*] (NLC)
**NbMi**......... Milford Public Library, Milford, NE [*Library symbol*] [*Library of Congress*] (LCLS)
**NB Miner Resour Branch Inf Circ**... New Brunswick. Mineral Resources Branch. Information Circular [*A publication*]
**NB Miner Resour Branch Rep Invest**... New Brunswick. Mineral Resources Branch. Report of Investigations [*A publication*]
**NB Miner Resour Branch Top Rep**... New Brunswick. Mineral Resources Branch. Topical Report [*A publication*]
**NbMiS**....... Southeast Community College, Milford, NE [*Library symbol*] [*Library of Congress*] (LCLS)
**NBmK**........ King's College, Briarcliff Manor, NY [*Library symbol*] [*Library of Congress*] (LCLS)
**NBmlA**....... Adirondack Historical Association Museum Library, Blue Mountain Lake, NY [*Library symbol*] [*Library of Congress*] (LCLS)
**NBMMH**... Health Sciences Library, The Moncton Hospital, New Brunswick [*Library symbol*] [*National Library of Canada*] (NLC)
**NBMOA**.... National Black McDonald's Operators Association (EA)
**NBMOAL**... Atlantic Lottery Corporation [*Societe des Loteries de l'Atlantique*], Moncton, New Brunswick [*Library symbol*] [*National Library of Canada*] (NLC)
**NBMOCC**... New Brunswick Community College, Moncton, New Brunswick [*Library symbol*] [*National Library of Canada*] (NLC)
**NBMOF**.... Fisheries and Oceans Canada [*Peches et Oceans Canada*] Moncton, New Brunswick [*Library symbol*] [*National Library of Canada*] (NLC)
**NBMOLM**... Lutz Mountain Heritage Foundation, Inc., Moncton, New Brunswick [*Library symbol*] [*National Library of Canada*] (NLC)
**NBMOM**... Moncton Museum, New Brunswick [*Library symbol*] [*National Library of Canada*] (NLC)
**NBMORE**... Canada Department of Regional Industrial Expansion [*Ministere de l'Expansion Industrielle Regionale*] Moncton, New Brunswick [*Library symbol*] [*National Library of Canada*] (NLC)
**NBMOTA**... Airworthiness Library, Atlantic Region, Transport Canada [*Bibliotheque de la Navigabilite Aerienne, Region de l'Atlantique, Transports Canada*], Moncton, New Brunswick [*Library symbol*] [*National Library of Canada*] (NLC)
**NBMOTAR**... Atlantic Regional Library, Transport Canada [*Bibliotheque Regionale de l'Atlantique, Transports Canada*], Moncton, New Brunswick [*Library symbol*] [*National Library of Canada*] (NLC)
**NBMOU**.... Universite de Moncton, New Brunswick [*Library symbol*] [*National Library of Canada*] (NLC)
**NBMOUA**... Archives Acadiennes, Universite de Moncton, New Brunswick [*Library symbol*] [*National Library of Canada*] (NLC)
**NBMOUD**... Bibliotheque de Droit, Universite de Moncton, New Brunswick [*Library symbol*] [*National Library of Canada*] (NLC)
**NBMOW**... Albert-Westmorland-Kent Regional Library, Moncton, New Brunswick [*Library symbol*] [*National Library of Canada*] (NLC)
**NBMR**....... NATO Basic Military Requirements (AABC)
**NBMR**....... Northern Bengal Mounted Rifles [*British military*] (DMA)
**NBMS**....... National Bulk Mail System [*Postal Service*]
**NBMT**....... NATO Basic Military Techniques (NATG)
**NB Mus Monogr Ser**... New Brunswick Museum. Monographic Series [*A publication*]
**Nbn**........... Nabonidus (BJA)
**NBN**........... Narrowband Network
**NBN**........... Narrowband Noise
**NBN**........... National Bank of Nigeria Ltd.
**NBN**........... National Bibliography Number
**NBN**........... National Black Network [*A radio network*]
**NBN**........... National Book Number [*British*]
**NBN**........... Nationality Broadcasting Network [*Cable-television system*]
**NBN**........... Network for Better Nutrition (EA)
**NBN**........... Neubabylonisches Namenbuch zu den Geschaeftsurkunden [*A publication*] (BJA)
**NBN**........... Newborn Nursery [*Medicine*]
**NBN**........... Nixdorf Broadband Network [*Communications*] [*British*]
**NBN**........... Old Manse Library, Newcastle, New Brunswick [*Library symbol*] [*National Library of Canada*] (NLC)
**NBNA**........ National Bank of North America [*New York*]
**NBNA**........ National Black Nurses Association (EA)
**NBNAM**.... Archives of the Miramichi Historical Society, Newcastle, New Brunswick [*Library symbol*] [*National Library of Canada*] (NLC)
**NBNA Newsl**... National Black Nurses Association. Newsletter [*A publication*]
**NbNb**......... Neubabylonisches Namenbuch zu den Geschaeftsurkunden [*A publication*] (BJA)
**NbNc**.......... Nebraska City Public Library, Nebraska City, NE [*Library symbol*] [*Library of Congress*] (LCLS)
**NBNC**........ New York City Community College of the City University of New York, Brooklyn, NY [*Library symbol*] [*Library of Congress*] (LCLS)
**NBNC**........ Noted but Not Corrected (MCD)
**NBND**........ Northbound (FAAC)
**NBNDH**.... New Denmark Historical Museum, New Brunswick [*Library symbol*] [*National Library of Canada*] (NLC)
**NbNf**.......... Norfolk Public Library, Norfolk, NE [*Library symbol*] [*Library of Congress*] (LCLS)
**NbNfN**....... Northeast Technical Community College, Norfork, NE [*Library symbol*] [*Library of Congress*] (LCLS)
**NBNM**....... Health Sciences Library, Miramichi Hospital, Newcastle, New Brunswick [*Library symbol*] [*National Library of Canada*] (NLC)
**NbNp**......... North Platte Public Library, North Platte, NE [*Library symbol*] [*Library of Congress*] (LCLS)
**NbNpM**..... Mid-Plains Community College, North Platte, NE [*Library symbol*] [*Library of Congress*] (LCLS)
**NBNR**........ National Bankruptcy News and Reports [*A publication*] (DLA)
**NBN Rep**... National Bankruptcy News and Reports [*A publication*] (DLA)
**NBNZAK**.. Notas Biologicas. Facultad de Ciencias Exactas, Fisicas, y Naturales. Universidad Nacional del Nordeste. Corrientes Zoologia [*A publication*]
**NBO**........... Boekblad [*A publication*]
**NBo**........... Bolivar Free Library, Bolivar, NY [*Library symbol*] [*Library of Congress*] (LCLS)
**NBO**........... Nairobi [*Kenya*] [*Airport symbol*] (OAG)

**NBO** .......... Navy Bureau of Ordnance [*Obsolete*]
**NBO** .......... Network Buildout (IEEE)
**NBO** .......... Nordiska Kooperativa och Allmannyttiga Bostadsforetags Organisation [*Organization of Cooperative and Non-Profit Making Housing Enterprises in the Nordic Countries*] (EAIO)
**NBO** .......... Normal-Branch Oscillation [*Astronomy*]
**NBO** .......... Norsar Array Site 01B00 [*Norway*] [*Seismograph station code, US Geological Survey*] (SEIS)
**NbO** .......... Omaha Public Library, Omaha, NE [*Library symbol*] [*Library of Congress*] (LCLS)
**NBO** .......... Omaha Public Library, Omaha, NE [*OCLC symbol*] (OCLC)
**NBO** .......... Organization of Cooperative and Non-Profit-Making Housing Enterprises in the Nordic Countries (EAIO)
**NBO** .......... Oromocto Public Library, New Brunswick [*Library symbol*] [*National Library of Canada*] (NLC)
**NBOA** ........ National Ballroom Operators Association [*Later, National Ballroom and Entertainment Association*]
**NBOA** ........ National Business Owners Association (EA)
**NbOB** ......... Boys Town Center for the Study of Youth Development, Omaha, NE [*Library symbol*] [*Library of Congress*] (LCLS)
**NbOC** ........ Creighton University, Omaha, NE [*Library symbol*] [*Library of Congress*] (LCLS)
**NBOC** ........ Network Building Out Capacitor [*Telecommunications*] (TEL)
**NBOC** ........ Newman Communications Corp. [*Albuquerque, NM*] [*NASDAQ symbol*] (NQ)
**NbOC-A** .... Creighton University, Alumni Library, Omaha, NE [*Library symbol*] [*Library of Congress*] (LCLS)
**NbOC-D** .... Creighton University, School of Dentistry, Omaha, NE [*Library symbol*] [*Library of Congress*] (LCLS)
**NbOC-H** .... Creighton University, Health Sciences Library, Omaha, NE [*Library symbol*] [*Library of Congress*] (LCLS)
**NbOC-L** ..... Creighton University, School of Law, Omaha, NE [*Library symbol*] [*Library of Congress*] (LCLS)
**NbOC-M** ... Creighton University, School of Medicine and School of Pharmacy, Omaha, NE [*Library symbol*] [*Library of Congress*] (LCLS)
**NbOD** ........ Duchesne College, Omaha, NE [*Library symbol*] [*Library of Congress*] (LCLS)
**NbOg** ......... Goodall City Library, Ogallala, NE [*Library symbol*] [*Library of Congress*] (LCLS)
**NbOGS** ...... Church of Jesus Christ of Latter-Day Saints, Genealogical Society Library, Omaha Branch, Omaha, NE [*Library symbol*] [*Library of Congress*] (LCLS)
**NBoh** ......... Connetquot Public Library, Bohemia, NY [*Library symbol*] [*Library of Congress*] (LCLS)
**NBohCH** .... Connetquot High School, Bohemia, NY [*Library symbol*] [*Library of Congress*] (LCLS)
**NbOJ** ......... Joslyn Art Museum, Omaha, NE [*Library symbol*] [*Library of Congress*] (LCLS)
**NbOMC** ..... Metropolitan Technical Community College, Omaha, NE [*Library symbol*] [*Library of Congress*] (LCLS)
**NBOME** .... National Board of Osteopathic Medical Examiners (EA)
**NbONPS** ... United States National Park Service, Midwest Regional Office, Omaha, NE [*Library symbol*] [*Library of Congress*] (LCLS)
**NbOP** ......... Presbyterian Theological Seminary, Omaha, NE [*Library symbol*] [*Library of Congress*] (LCLS)
**NBOR** ........ Network Building Out Resistor [*Telecommunications*] (TEL)
**NBOR** ........ Nucleus of Basal Optic Root [*Neuroanatomy*]
**NbOsc** ........ Osceola Public Library, Osceola, NE [*Library symbol*] [*Library of Congress*] (LCLS)
**NbOU** ........ University of Nebraska at Omaha, Omaha, NE [*Library symbol*] [*Library of Congress*] (LCLS)
**NbOV** ........ United States Veterans Administration Hospital, Omaha, NE [*Library symbol*] [*Library of Congress*] (LCLS)
**NBp** ............ Bayport-Blue Point Public Library, Blue Point, NY [*Library symbol*] [*Library of Congress*] (LCLS)
**NBP** ........... Name Binding Protocol [*Data processing*]
**NBP** ........... National Booster Program (AAG)
**NBP** ........... National Braille Press (EA)
**NBP** ........... National Business Publications [*Later, ABP*] (EA)
**NBP** ........... Needs-Based Payment [*Job Training and Partnership Act*] (OICC)
**NBP** ........... Neutral Bitter Principle [*Pharmacy*]
**NBP** ........... New Birth Party [*Political party*] [*Cyprus*]
**NBP** ........... (Nitrobenzyl)pyridine [*Organic chemistry*]
**NBP** ........... Normal Boiling Point
**NBP** ........... Nucleic Acid Binding Protein [*Biochemistry*]
**NBP** ........... Peru State College Library, Peru, NE [*OCLC symbol*] (OCLC)
**NBP** ........... Pratt Institute, Brooklyn, NY [*Library symbol*] [*Library of Congress*] (LCLS)
**NBP** ........... Wonen. Vakblad voor de Woninginrichting [*A publication*]
**NBPA** ........ National Back Pain Association (EAIO)
**NBPA** ........ National Bark Producers Association (EA)
**NBPA** ........ National Basketball Players Association (EA)
**NBPA** ........ National Beverage Packaging Association (EA)
**NBPA** ........ National Black People's Assembly (EA)
**NBPA** ........ National Black Police Association (EA)
**NBPA** ........ National Building Products Association [*Defunct*] (EA)
**NBPA** ........ Navy Board for Production Awards
**NBPA** ........ Northeastern Bancorp [*NASDAQ symbol*] (NQ)
**NBPASV** ... Southern Victoria Historical Society, Perth-Andover, New Brunswick [*Library symbol*] [*National Library of Canada*] (NLC)
**NBPB** ......... National Biotechnology Policy Board
**NBPC** ......... National Black Political Convention [*1972*]
**NBPC** ......... National Black Programming Consortium (EA)
**NBPC** ......... National Border Patrol Council (EA)
**NBPDW** .... National Brotherhood of Packinghouse and Dairy Workers [*Formerly, NBPW*] (EA)
**NBPE** ......... National Board of Podiatry Examiners
**NBPE** ......... National Board of Polygraph Examiners [*Later, APA*] (EA)
**NbPerS** ...... Peru State College, Peru, NE [*Library symbol*] [*Library of Congress*] (LCLS)
**NBPHA** ..... N-Benzoyl(phenyl)hydroxylamine [*Organic chemistry*]
**NBPI** .......... National Board for Prices and Incomes [*British*]
**NBPIW** ...... National Brotherhood of Packinghouse and Industrial Workers (EA)
**NbPl** .......... Plattsmouth Public Library, Plattsmouth, NE [*Library symbol*] [*Library of Congress*] (LCLS)
**NBPM** ....... Narrowband Phase Modulation (MCD)
**NBPME** ..... National Board of Podiatric Medical Examiners (EA)
**NBPNPA** ... National Board of Pediatric Nurse Practitioners and Associates [*Later, NCBPNP/N*] (EA)
**NBPO** ........ NATO Bullpup Production Organization [*Missiles*] (NATG)
**NBPol** ........ Polytechnic Institute of New York, Brooklyn, NY [*Library symbol*] [*Library of Congress*] (LCLS)
**NBPol-G** .... Polytechnic Institute of New York, Long Island Graduate Center, Farmingdale, NY [*Library symbol*] [*Library of Congress*] (LCLS)
**NBPP** ......... National Black Political Party
**NBPRP** ...... National Board for the Promotion of Rifle Practice (EA)
**NBPTE** ...... National Board of Physical Therapy Examiners (EA)
**NBPTS** ...... National Board for Professional Teaching Standards (EA)
**NBPW** ....... National Brotherhood of Packinghouse Workers [*Later, NBPDW*]
**NBQ** .......... Nitro(benzothiazolo)quinolinium Perchlorate [*Antineoplastic drug*]
**NBR** .......... Nabors Industries, Inc. [*AMEX symbol*] (SPSG)
**NBR** .......... Narrowband Radiated (IEEE)
**NBR** .......... National Bankruptcy Register Reports [*United States*] [*A publication*] (DLA)
**NBR** .......... National Board of Review of Motion Pictures
**NBR** .......... National Buildings Record [*British*]
**NBR** .......... National Business Review [*New Zealand*] [*A publication*]
**NBR** .......... Nederlandsche Bank NV. Kwartaalbericht [*A publication*]
**NBR** .......... Neighborhood Business Revitalization [*Program*]
**NBR** .......... New Beginnings Resources [*Vancouver Stock Exchange symbol*]
**NBR** .......... New Boston Review [*A publication*]
**NBR** .......... New Brunswick Reports [*Maritime Law Book Co. Ltd.*] [*Canada*] [*Information service or system*] [*A publication*] (CRD)
**NBR** .......... [*The*] Nightly Business Reports [*Television program*]
**NBR** .......... Nitrile-Butadiene Rubber
**NBR** .......... Nonborrowed Reserve [*Banking*]
**NBR** .......... Nonbreathing
**NBR** .......... North British Railway
**NBR** .......... Nuclear Boiler Rated (NRCH)
**NBR** .......... Null Balance Recorder
**NBR** .......... Number (KSC)
**NBR** .......... Number of Bids Received [*DoD*]
**NBR** .......... Nursing Boards Review [*Course*] [*American Journal of Nursing*]
**NBRA** ........ National Brain Research Association (EA)
**NbRal** ......... Ralston Public Library, Ralston, NE [*Library symbol*] [*Library of Congress*] (LCLS)
**NBR All** ..... Allen's New Brunswick Reports [*Canada*] [*A publication*] (DLA)
**NBR Ber** .... Berton's New Brunswick Reports [*A publication*] (DLA)
**NBRC** ........ National Black Republican Council (EA)
**NBRC** ........ National Board for Respiratory Care (EA)
**NBRCA** ..... Atlantic Institution, Correctional Service Canada [*Etablissement Atlantique, Service Correctionnel Canada*], Renous, New Brunswick [*Library symbol*] [*National Library of Canada*] (BIB)
**NBR Carl** ... Carleton's New Brunswick Reports [*A publication*] (DLA)
**NBR Chip** .. Chipman's New Brunswick Reports [*1825-35*] [*A publication*] (DLA)
**NbRcW** ...... Willa Cather Pioneer Memorial, Red Cloud, NE [*Library symbol*] [*Library of Congress*] (LCLS)
**NBR 2d** ...... New Brunswick Reports, Second Series [*A publication*] (DLA)
**NBre** .......... Brewster Public Library, Brewster, NY [*Library symbol*] [*Library of Congress*] (LCLS)
**NBREH** ..... L'Eglise Historique St-Henri-De-Barachois, Robichaud, New Brunswick [*Library symbol*] [*National Library of Canada*] (NLC)
**NBren** ........ Brentwood Public Library, Brentwood, NY [*Library symbol*] [*Library of Congress*] (LCLS)

**NBrenIMC** ... District Instructional Media Center, Brentwood, NY [*Library symbol*] [*Library of Congress*] (LCLS)
**NBrenSJ**.... Saint Joseph's College, Brentwood, NY [*Library symbol*] [*Library of Congress*] (LCLS)
**NB Rep**...... New Brunswick Reports [*A publication*] (DLA)
**NB Rev Stat** ... New Brunswick Revised Statutes [*Canada*] [*A publication*] (DLA)
**NBRF**......... National Biomedical Research Foundation [*Georgetown University*] [*Research center*]
**NBRG**......... National Basic Reference Graphic (MCD)
**NBR Han**... Hannay's New Brunswick Reports [*12, 13 New Brunswick*] [*A publication*] (DLA)
**NBRHD**..... Neighborhood (FAAC)
**NBri**........... Bay Shore-Brightwaters Public Library, Brightwaters, NY [*Library symbol*] [*Library of Congress*] (LCLS)
**NBrih**......... Hampton Library, Bridgehampton, NY [*Library symbol*] [*Library of Congress*] (LCLS)
**NBR Kerr**... Kerr's New Brunswick Reports [*A publication*] (DLA)
**NBRL**......... Naval Biomedical Research Laboratory
**NBRL**......... Naval Blood Research Laboratory [*Bureau of Medicine*]
**NBRMP**..... National Board of Review of Motion Pictures (EA)
**NBRN**......... Nestart Library, Richibucto, New Brunswick [*Library symbol*] [*National Library of Canada*] (NLC)
**NBrockU** ... State University of New York, College at Brockport, Brockport, NY [*Library symbol*] [*Library of Congress*] (LCLS)
**NBron**......... Bronxville Public Library, Bronxville, NY [*Library symbol*] [*Library of Congress*] (LCLS)
**NBronC**...... Concordia College, Bronxville, NY [*Library symbol*] [*Library of Congress*] (LCLS)
**NBronSL**... Sarah Lawrence College, Bronxville, NY [*Library symbol*] [*Library of Congress*] (LCLS)
**NBroo**......... Brookhaven Free Library, Brookhaven, NY [*Library symbol*] [*Library of Congress*] (LCLS)
**NBrooHS**... Bellport Senior High School, Brookhaven, NY [*Library symbol*] [*Library of Congress*] (LCLS)
**NBRP & B** ... Pugsley and Burbridge's New Brunswick Reports [*A publication*] (DLA)
**NBRPC**...... New Brunswick Research and Productivity Council
**NBRP & T** ... Pugsley and Trueman's New Brunswick Reports [*A publication*] (DLA)
**NBR Pug**.... Pugsley's New Brunswick Reports [*A publication*] (DLA)
**NBR Pugs**.. Pugsley's New Brunswick Reports [*1876-93*] [*Canada*] [*A publication*] (DLA)
**NBRSA**...... National Bench Rest Shooters Association (EA)
**NBRT**......... National Board for Respiratory Therapy [*Formerly, ARIT*] [*Later, NBRC*] (EA)
**NBR Tru**.... Trueman's New Brunswick Reports [*A publication*] (DLA)
**N Bruns**...... New Brunswick Reports [*A publication*] (DLA)
**NbRVt**........ Neubabylonische Rechts- und Verwaltungstexte [*A publication*] (BJA)
**NbRVu**....... Neubabylonische Rechts- und Verwaltungsurkunden Uebersetzt und Erlaeutert [*A publication*] (BJA)
**NBS**........... Bureau of Ships Publications [*Obsolete*] [*Navy*]
**NBS**........... Kekaha, Kauai, HI [*Location identifier*] [*FAA*] (FAAL)
**NBS**........... N-Bromosuccinimide [*Organic chemistry*]
**NBS**........... Narrowband Search (MCD)
**NBS**........... National Australia Bank. Monthly Summary [*A publication*] (ADA)
**NBS**........... National Bank Monthly Summary [*Australia*] [*A publication*]
**NBS**........... National Book Sale [*British*]
**NBS**........... National Bookkeepers' Society (EA)
**NBS**........... National Bridal Service (EA)
**NBS**........... National Broadcasting Service [*of New Zealand*]
**NBS**........... National Broadcasting System
**NBS**........... National Brotherhood of Skiers (EA)
**NBS**........... National Bureau of Standards [*Department of Commerce*] [*Later, NIST*]
**NBS**........... National Bureau of Standards, Gaithersburg, MD [*OCLC symbol*] (OCLC)
**NBS**........... National Business Systems, Inc. [*Toronto Stock Exchange symbol*]
**NBS**........... National Button Society (EA)
**NBS**........... Natural Black Slate (MSA)
**NBS**........... Navigational Bombing System [*British military*] (DMA)
**NBS**........... NBS [*National Bureau of Standards*] Update [*A publication*]
**NBS**........... Needs-Based Staffing (ADA)
**NBS**........... Neighborhood Bible Studies (EA)
**NBS**........... Netherland Benevolent Society of New York [*Later, Netherlands-America Community Association*] (EA)
**NBS**........... Neurobehavioral Scale
**NBS**........... Neutral Buoyancy Simulator [*Navy*] (MCD)
**NBS**........... New British Standard [*Imperial wire gauge*]
**NBS**........... New Brunswick Scientific Co., Inc.
**NBS**........... Night Bombardment - Short Distance [*Air Force*]
**NBS**........... No Bacteria Seen [*Clinical microbiology*]
**NBS**........... Nonbaseline Software Library (MCD)
**NBS**........... Nordiska Byggforskningsorgans Samarbetsgrupp [*Nordic Building Research Cooperation Group*] (EAIO)
**NBS**........... Normandy Base Section [*World War II*]
**NBS**........... Numeric Backspace Character [*Data processing*]
**NBS**........... Numismatic Bibliomania Society (EA)
**NBS**........... Saint John Regional Library, New Brunswick [*Library symbol*] [*National Library of Canada*] (NLC)
**NbS**............ Scottsbluff Public Library, Scottsbluff, NE [*Library symbol*] [*Library of Congress*] (LCLS)
**NBSA**......... National Bakery Suppliers Association (EA)
**NBSAB**...... Fort Beausejour Museum, Sackville, New Brunswick [*Library symbol*] [*National Library of Canada*] (NLC)
**NBSAC**...... National Boating Safety Advisory Council [*Department of Transportation*] [*Washington, DC*] (EGAO)
**NBSACW** ... Canadian Wildlife Service, Environment Canada [*Service Canadien de la Faune, Environnement Canada*] Sackville, New Brunswick [*Library symbol*] [*National Library of Canada*] (NLC)
**NBSAE**...... Norwegian-British-Swedish Antarctic Expedition [*1949-52*]
**NBSAM**..... Mount Allison University, Sackville, New Brunswick [*Library symbol*] [*National Library of Canada*] (NLC)
**NBSARM** ... Ross Memorial Library, St. Andrews, New Brunswick [*Library symbol*] [*National Library of Canada*] (BIB)
**NBSBL**...... National Bureau of Standards Boulder Laboratories
**NBS Build Sci Ser** ... National Bureau of Standards. Building Science Series [*United States*] [*A publication*]
**NBSC**......... Health Sciences Library, Centracare Saint John, Inc., New Brunswick [*Library symbol*] [*National Library of Canada*] (NLC)
**NBSC**......... National Black Sisters' Conference (EA)
**NBSC**......... New Brunswick Scientific Company, Inc. [*NASDAQ symbol*] (NQ)
**NBSCA**...... National Beauty Salon Chain Association [*Later, ICSA*] (EA)
**NBSCCST** ... National Bureau of Standards Center for Computer Sciences and Technology (DIT)
**NBSCM**..... Centre Marin, Shippagan, New Brunswick [*Library symbol*] [*National Library of Canada*] (NLC)
**NBSCU**...... Centre Universitaire de Shippagan, New Brunswick [*Library symbol*] [*National Library of Canada*] (NLC)
**NBSD**........ Night Bombardment - Short Distance [*Air Force*] (IEEE)
**NBSDI**....... National Brands Soft Drinks Institute (EA)
**NBsdQ**....... Queensborough Community College of the City University of New York, Bayside, NY [*Library symbol*] [*Library of Congress*] (LCLS)
**NbSe**.......... Seward Public Library, Seward, NE [*Library symbol*] [*Library of Congress*] (LCLS)
**NbSeT**........ Concordia Teachers College, Seward, NE [*Library symbol*] [*Library of Congress*] (LCLS)
**NBSF**......... Nitrobenzenesulfonyl Fluoride [*Organic chemistry*]
**NBSFS**....... National Bureau of Standards Frequency Standard (IEEE)
**NbSHS**...... Hiram Scott College, Scottsbluff, NE [*Library symbol*] [*Library of Congress*] [*Obsolete*] (LCLS)
**NBSI**.......... National Business Systems, Incorporated [*Mississauga, ON*] [*NASDAQ symbol*] (NQ)
**NbSi**........... Sidney Public Library, Sidney, NE [*Library symbol*] [*Library of Congress*] (LCLS)
**NBSIR**....... National Bureau of Standards Interagency Reports
**NBSLD**...... National Bureau of Standards Load Determination [*Computer program*]
**NBSM**....... New Brunswick Museum, Saint John, New Brunswick [*Library symbol*] [*National Library of Canada*] (NLC)
**NBSMA**..... National Boot and Shoe Manufacturers' Association [*Later, FIA*]
**NBSMA**..... National Bureau of Standards. Monographs [*A publication*]
**NBS Monogr** ... National Bureau of Standards. Monographs [*A publication*]
**NbSN**......... Nebraska Western College, Scottsbluff, NE [*Library symbol*] [*Library of Congress*] (LCLS)
**NBSQH**..... Quaco Historical and Library Society, St. Martins, New Brunswick [*Library symbol*] [*National Library of Canada*] (NLC)
**NBSR**......... National Bureau of Standards Reactor
**NBSRH**..... Health Sciences Library, Saint John Regional Hospital [*Bibliotheque des Sciences de la Sante, Hopital Regional de Saint-Jean*], New Brunswick [*Library symbol*] [*National Library of Canada*] (NLC)
**NBSS**......... National Bank Surveillance System
**NBSS**......... Naval Beach Signal Section
**NBsSH**...... Southside Hospital, Bay Shore, NY [*Library symbol*] [*Library of Congress*] (LCLS)
**NBS Spec Publ** ... National Bureau of Standards. Special Publication [*A publication*]
**NBSSSC**.... St. Croix Public Library, St. Stephen, New Brunswick [*Library symbol*] [*National Library of Canada*] (NLC)
**NBST**......... Narrowband Subscriber Terminal (CET)
**NBST**......... [*The*] New Braunfels & Servtex Railroad, Inc. [*AAR code*]
**NbSt**.......... Nimbostratus [*Cloud*] [*Meteorology*] (AIA)
**NBSTAC**... St. Andrews Campus, New Brunswick Community College [*Library symbol*] [*National Library of Canada*] (BIB)
**NBS/TAD** ... National Bureau of Standards/Technical Analysis Division (NOAA)
**NB Stat**...... New Brunswick Statutes [*Canada*] [*A publication*] (DLA)
**NBS Tech News Bull** ... National Bureau of Standards. Technical News Bulletin [*A publication*]
**NBStF**........ Saint Francis College, Brooklyn, NY [*Library symbol*] [*Library of Congress*] (LCLS)

**NBSTIM** ... Le Musee de St-Isidore, Inc., New Brunswick [*Library symbol*] [*National Library of Canada*] (NLC)
**NBStJC** ..... Saint Joseph's College, Brooklyn, NY [*Library symbol*] [*Library of Congress*] (LCLS)
**NBS TN** ..... United States Department of Commerce. National Bureau of Standards. Technical Notes [*A publication*]
**NbSu** .......... Superior Carnegie Library, Superior, NE [*Library symbol*] [*Library of Congress*] (LCLS)
**NBSU** ........ University of New Brunswick, Saint John, New Brunswick [*Library symbol*] [*National Library of Canada*] (NLC)
**NBSUH** ..... Kings County Historical Society, Sussex, New Brunswick [*Library symbol*] [*National Library of Canada*] (NLC)
**NBSUS** ...... Sussex Public Library, New Brunswick [*Library symbol*] [*National Library of Canada*] (NLC)
**NBSV** ......... Narrowband Secure Voice System [*Army*] (CAAL)
**NBSVS** ...... Narrowband Secure Voice System [*Army*] (MCD)
**NBSVS** ...... Saint John Vocational School, New Brunswick [*Library symbol*] [*National Library of Canada*] (NLC)
**NBT** ........... Brunswick, ME [*Location identifier*] [*FAA*] (FAAL)
**NBT** ........... Narrow-Beam Transducer [*National Ocean Survey*]
**NBT** ........... Navigator Bombardier Training [*Air Force*] (AFM)
**NBT** ........... Nederlands Bosbouw Tijdschrift Orgaan voor Bosbouw en Landschapsbouw [*A publication*]
**NBT** ........... Netherlands Board of Tourism (EA)
**NBT** ........... Networks for Biotechnology
**NBT** ........... Neues Berner Taschenbuch [*A publication*]
**NBT** ........... Neutral Buoyancy Trainer [*Navy*] (MCD)
**NBT** ........... New Brunswick Telephone Co. Ltd. [*Toronto Stock Exchange symbol*]
**NBT** ........... Nimbus Beacon Transmitter
**NBT** ........... Nitroblue Tetrazolium [*A stain*] [*Hematology*]
**NBT** ........... Null-Balance Transmissometer (IEEE)
**NBTA** ........ National Baton Twirling Association (EA)
**NBTA** ........ National Board of Trial Advocacy (EA)
**NBTA** ........ National Bus Traffic Association (EA)
**NBTA** ........ National Business Travel Association (EA)
**NBTC** ........ National Building Technology Centre [*Australia*]
**NBTC** ........ New Brands and Their Companies [*Formerly, NTN*] [*A publication*]
**NBTC** ........ New Brunswick Teachers College
**NBT-DF** .... Nitroblue Tetrazolium Diformazan [*A stain*] [*Hematology*]
**NBTDR** ..... Narrowband Time Domain Reflectometry (MCD)
**NBTE** ........ Nonbacterial Thrombotic Endocarditis [*Cardiology*]
**NbTe** .......... Tekamah Carnegie Public Library, Tekamah, NE [*Library symbol*] [*Library of Congress*] (LCLS)
**NBTF** ......... National Building Trades Federation [*A union*] [*British*]
**NBTH** ......... Bibliotheque Medicale, Hotel-Dieu Saint-Joseph-De-Tracadie, New Brunswick [*Library symbol*] [*National Library of Canada*] (BIB)
**NBTL** ......... National Battery Test Laboratory [*Department of Energy*]
**NBTL** ......... Naval Boiler and Turbine Laboratory
**NBTM** ....... Le Musee Historique de Tracadie, New Brunswick [*Library symbol*] [*National Library of Canada*] (NLC)
**NBTNF** ...... Newborn, Term, Normal, Female [*Obstetrics*]
**NBTNM** .... Newborn, Term, Normal, Male [*Obstetrics*]
**NBTR** ........ Narrowband Tape Recorder
**NBTS** ......... National Blood Transfusion Service
**NBTS** ......... New Brunswick Theological Seminary [*New Jersey*]
**NBTS** ......... Northern Baptist Theological Seminary [*Lombard, IL*]
**NBTT** ........ Net Barter Terms of Trade
**NBTY** ........ Nature's Bounty, Inc. [*NASDAQ symbol*] (NQ)
**NBu** ........... Buffalo and Erie County Public Library, Buffalo, NY [*Library symbol*] [*Library of Congress*] (LCLS)
**NBU** ........... Glenview, IL [*Location identifier*] [*FAA*] (FAAL)
**NBU** ........... NBU Mines Ltd. [*Toronto Stock Exchange symbol*]
**nbu** ............ Nebraska [*MARC country of publication code*] [*Library of Congress*] (LCCP)
**NBU** ........... New Better than Used [*Statistics*]
**NBU** ........... Nordiska Bankmannaunionen [*Confederation of Nordic Bank Employees' Unions*] (EA)
**NbU** ........... University of Nebraska, Lincoln, NE [*Library symbol*] [*Library of Congress*] (LCLS)
**NBU** ........... University of Nebraska at Omaha, Omaha, NE [*OCLC symbol*] (OCLC)
**NBuA** ......... Allied Corp., Specialty Chemicals Division, Buffalo, NY [*Library symbol*] [*Library of Congress*] (LCLS)
**NbU-A** ....... University of Nebraska, Agriculture Library, Lincoln, NE [*Library symbol*] [*Library of Congress*] (LCLS)
**NBuAA** ...... Acres American, Inc., Buffalo, NY [*Library symbol*] [*Library of Congress*] (LCLS)
**NBuAK** ...... Albright-Knox Art Gallery Library, Buffalo Fine Arts Academy, Buffalo, NY [*Library symbol*] [*Library of Congress*] (LCLS)
**NBuAn** ....... Andco, Inc., Buffalo, NY [*Library symbol*] [*Library of Congress*] (LCLS)
**NBuB** ......... Buffalo Society of Natural Sciences, Buffalo Museum of Science, Buffalo, NY [*Library symbol*] [*Library of Congress*] (LCLS)
**NBuBA** ...... Bell Aerosystems Co., Buffalo, NY [*Library symbol*] [*Library of Congress*] (LCLS)
**NBuBLH** ... Bry-Lin Hospital, Buffalo, NY [*Library symbol*] [*Library of Congress*] (LCLS)
**NBuBO** ...... Buffalo Organization for Social and Technological Innovation, Inc. (BOSTI), Buffalo, NY [*Library symbol*] [*Library of Congress*] (LCLS)
**NBuC** ......... State University of New York, College at Buffalo, Buffalo, NY [*Library symbol*] [*Library of Congress*] (LCLS)
**NBuCA** ...... Cornell Aeronautical Laboratory, Buffalo, NY [*Library symbol*] [*Library of Congress*] (LCLS)
**NBuCC** ...... Canisius College, Buffalo, NY [*Library symbol*] [*Library of Congress*] (LCLS)
**NBuCEC** .... CECOS International, Buffalo, NY [*Library symbol*] [*Library of Congress*] (LCLS)
**NBuCH** ...... Children's Hospital, Buffalo, NY [*Library symbol*] [*Library of Congress*] (LCLS)
**NBuCo** ....... Buffalo Color Corp., Buffalo, NY [*Library symbol*] [*Library of Congress*] (LCLS)
**NBuD** ......... D'Youville College, Buffalo, NY [*Library symbol*] [*Library of Congress*] (LCLS)
**NBuDa** ....... Daemen College, Buffalo, NY [*Library symbol*] [*Library of Congress*] (LCLS)
**NBuDD** ...... DeLancey Divinity School, Buffalo, NY [*Library symbol*] [*Library of Congress*] [*Obsolete*] (LCLS)
**NBuDY** ...... E. I. Du Pont de Nemours & Co., Yerkes Research Laboratory, Buffalo, NY [*Library symbol*] [*Library of Congress*] (LCLS)
**NBUE** ........ New Better than Used in Expectation [*Statistics*]
**NBuEC** ...... Erie Community College-North, Buffalo, NY [*Library symbol*] [*Library of Congress*] (LCLS)
**NBuEC-C** .. Erie Community College-North, City Campus, Buffalo, NY [*Library symbol*] [*Library of Congress*] (LCLS)
**NBuEC-U** .. Erie Community College-North, Urban Center, Buffalo, NY [*Library symbol*] [*Library of Congress*] (LCLS)
**NBuEE** ...... Ecology and Environment, Inc., Buffalo, NY [*Library symbol*] [*Library of Congress*] (LCLS)
**NBuEMH** ... Edward J. Meyer Memorial Hospital Medical Library, Buffalo, NY [*Library symbol*] [*Library of Congress*] (LCLS)
**NBuF** ......... Falcon Research & Development, Inc., Buffalo, NY [*Library symbol*] [*Library of Congress*] (LCLS)
**NBUF** ........ National Black United Front (EA)
**NBUF** ........ National Black United Fund (EA)
**NBuG** ......... Grosvenor Reference Division, Buffalo and Erie County Public Library, Buffalo, NY [*Library symbol*] [*Library of Congress*] (LCLS)
**NBuGC** ...... Graphic Controls Corp., Buffalo, NY [*Library symbol*] [*Library of Congress*] (LCLS)
**NBuGH** ..... Buffalo General Hospital, Buffalo, NY [*Library symbol*] [*Library of Congress*] (LCLS)
**NBuGH-N** ... Buffalo General Hospital, School of Nursing, Buffalo, NY [*Library symbol*] [*Library of Congress*] (LCLS)
**NBuHi** ....... Buffalo and Erie County Historical Society, Buffalo, NY [*Library symbol*] [*Library of Congress*] (LCLS)
**NBuHSA** ... Health Systems Agency of Western New York, Inc., Buffalo, NY [*Library symbol*] [*Library of Congress*] (LCLS)
**NbU-L** ....... University of Nebraska, College of Law, Lincoln, NE [*Library symbol*] [*Library of Congress*] (LCLS)
**NBuLH** ...... Lafayette General Hospital, Buffalo, NY [*Library symbol*] [*Library of Congress*] (LCLS)
**NBuM** ........ Medaille College, Buffalo, NY [*Library symbol*] [*Library of Congress*] (LCLS)
**NbU-M** ...... University of Nebraska, College of Medicine, Omaha, NE [*Library symbol*] [*Library of Congress*] (LCLS)
**NBuMM** .... Marine Midland Services Corp., Technical Information Center, Buffalo, NY [*Library symbol*] [*Library of Congress*] (LCLS)
**NBuPC** ....... Buffalo Psychiatric Center, Buffalo, NY [*Library symbol*] [*Library of Congress*] (LCLS)
**NBuPL** ....... Pennwalt Corp., Lucidol Division, Buffalo, NY [*Library symbol*] [*Library of Congress*] (LCLS)
**NBuRH** ...... Rosary Hill College, Buffalo, NY [*Library symbol*] [*Library of Congress*] [*Obsolete*] (LCLS)
**NBUSA** ..... United States Army, Fort Hamilton Post Library, Fort Hamilton, Brooklyn, NY [*Library symbol*] [*Library of Congress*] (LCLS)
**NBuSCA** .... SCA Chemical Services, Inc., Buffalo, NY [*Library symbol*] [*Library of Congress*] (LCLS)
**NBuSCH** ... Sisters of Charity Hospital, Buffalo, NY [*Library symbol*] [*Library of Congress*] (LCLS)
**NBuSK** ....... Spencer Kellogg Division, Textron, Inc., Buffalo, NY [*Library symbol*] [*Library of Congress*] (LCLS)
**NBuSMH** .. Sheehan Memorial Emergency Hospital, Buffalo, NY [*Library symbol*] [*Library of Congress*] (LCLS)
**NBuSR** ....... Sierra Research Corp., Buffalo, NY [*Library symbol*] [*Library of Congress*] (LCLS)
**NBuStM** .... Saint Mary's School for the Deaf, Buffalo, NY [*Library symbol*] [*Library of Congress*] (LCLS)
**NBuTC** ...... Trocaire College, Buffalo, NY [*Library symbol*] [*Library of Congress*] (LCLS)
**NBuU** ......... State University of New York at Buffalo, Buffalo, NY [*Library symbol*] [*Library of Congress*] (LCLS)

**NBuU-A**..... State University of New York at Buffalo, Art Library, Buffalo, NY [*Library symbol*] [*Library of Congress*] (LCLS)
**NBuU-AR** ... State University of New York at Buffalo, Archives, Buffalo, NY [*Library symbol*] [*Library of Congress*] (LCLS)
**NBuU-BA** ... State University of New York at Buffalo, Bell Annex, Buffalo, NY [*Library symbol*] [*Library of Congress*] (LCLS)
**NBuU-BS** .. State University of New York at Buffalo, Bell Science Library, Buffalo, NY [*Library symbol*] [*Library of Congress*] (LCLS)
**NBuU-C**..... State University of New York at Buffalo, Chemistry Library, Buffalo, NY [*Library symbol*] [*Library of Congress*] (LCLS)
**NBuU-D** .... State University of New York at Buffalo, Documents Library, Buffalo, NY [*Library symbol*] [*Library of Congress*] (LCLS)
**NBuU-E**..... State University of New York at Buffalo, Educational Opportunity Center, Buffalo, NY [*Library symbol*] [*Library of Congress*] (LCLS)
**NBuU-H** .... State University of New York at Buffalo, Health Sciences Library, Buffalo, NY [*Library symbol*] [*Library of Congress*] (LCLS)
**NBuU-HA** ... State University of New York at Buffalo, Harriman Library, Buffalo, NY [*Library symbol*] [*Library of Congress*] (LCLS)
**NBuU-L**..... State University of New York at Buffalo, Law Library, Buffalo, NY [*Library symbol*] [*Library of Congress*] (LCLS)
**NBuU-LL** .. State University of New York at Buffalo, Library Literature Library, Buffalo, NY [*Library symbol*] [*Library of Congress*] (LCLS)
**NBuU-LS** .. State University of New York at Buffalo, Library Science Library, Buffalo, NY [*Library symbol*] [*Library of Congress*] (LCLS)
**NBuU-Mu** ... State University of New York at Buffalo, Music Library, Buffalo, NY [*Library symbol*] [*Library of Congress*] (LCLS)
**NBuU-P**..... State University of New York at Buffalo, Physics Library, Buffalo, NY [*Library symbol*] [*Library of Congress*] (LCLS)
**NBuU-PO** ... State University of New York at Buffalo, Poetry Library, Buffalo, NY [*Library symbol*] [*Library of Congress*] (LCLS)
**NBuU-R**..... State University of New York at Buffalo, Reference, Buffalo, NY [*Library symbol*] [*Library of Congress*] (LCLS)
**NBuU-RL** .. State University of New York at Buffalo, Ridge Lea, Buffalo, NY [*Library symbol*] [*Library of Congress*] (LCLS)
**NBuU-RP** .. State University of New York at Buffalo, Roswell Park Memorial Institute, Buffalo, NY [*Library symbol*] [*Library of Congress*] (LCLS)
**NBuU-SE** .. State University of New York at Buffalo, Science and Engineering Library, Buffalo, NY [*Library symbol*] [*Library of Congress*] (LCLS)
**NBuVA** ...... United States Veterans Administration Hospital, Buffalo, NY [*Library symbol*] [*Library of Congress*] (LCLS)
**NBuVM** ..... Villa Maria College of Buffalo, Buffalo, NY [*Library symbol*] [*Library of Congress*] (LCLS)
**NBuVNA** ... Visiting Nursing Association of Buffalo, Buffalo, NY [*Library symbol*] [*Library of Congress*] (LCLS)
**NBuW**........ Worthington Compressor & Engine International, Buffalo, NY [*Library symbol*] [*Library of Congress*] (LCLS)
**NBuWeP**.... Westwood Pharmaceuticals, Inc., Buffalo, NY [*Library symbol*] [*Library of Congress*] (LCLS)
**NBUWH** ... Carleton County Historical Society, Upper Woodstock, New Brunswick [*Library symbol*] [*National Library of Canada*] (NLC)
**NBuWNED** ... WNED-TV, Buffalo, NY [*Library symbol*] [*Library of Congress*] (LCLS)
**NBV**.......... Net Book Value (TEL)
**NbV**............ Valentine Public Library, Valentine, NE [*Library symbol*] [*Library of Congress*] (LCLS)
**NBVA**........ National Bulk Vendors Association (EA)
**NBVA**........ United States Veterans Administration Hospital, Brooklyn, NY [*Library symbol*] [*Library of Congress*] (LCLS)
**NBV Ad**..... New Brunswick Vice Admiralty Reports [*A publication*] (DLA)
**NBVA-O**.... United States Veterans Administration Hospital, Outpatient Clinic, Brooklyn, NY [*Library symbol*] [*Library of Congress*] (LCLS)
**NBVCXO** .. Narrowband Voltage-Controlled Crystal Oscillator
**NBVF**......... National Burn Victim Foundation (EA)
**NBVO**........ National Black Veterans Organization [*Defunct*] (EA)
**NBW**.......... L. P. Fisher Public Library, Woodstock, New Brunswick [*Library symbol*] [*National Library of Canada*] (NLC)
**NBW**.......... NABW [*National Association of Bank Women*] Journal [*A publication*]
**NBW**.......... National Barristers' Wives [*Later, NABBS*] (EA)
**NBW**.......... Natural Bandwidths [*Spectroscopy*]
**NBW**.......... Nebraska Wesleyan University, Lincoln, NE [*OCLC symbol*] (OCLC)
**NBW**.......... Neue Betriebswirtschaft [*A publication*]
**NBW**.......... Nieuw Burgerlijk Wetboek [*A publication*]
**NBW**.......... Noise Bandwidth
**NBW**.......... Normal Birth Weight
**NbW**.......... North by West
**NBWA**....... National Beer Wholesalers' Association (EA)
**NBWA**....... National Blacksmiths and Welders Association (EA)
**NBWA**....... National Buddhist Women's Associations (EA)
**NbWayS**.... Wayne State College, Wayne, NE [*Library symbol*] [*Library of Congress*] (LCLS)
**NBWH**....... Carleton Memorial Hospital, Woodstock, New Brunswick [*Library symbol*] [*National Library of Canada*] (BIB)
**NBWHP**.... National Black Women's Health Project (EA)
**NbWi**......... Dvoracek Memorial Library, Wilber, NE [*Library symbol*] [*Library of Congress*] (LCLS)
**NBWPLC** .. National Black Women's Political Leadership Caucus (EA)
**NBWROP** ... Naval Bureau of Weapons Reserve Ordnance Plant
**NBWTAU** ... National British Women's Total Abstinence Union (EAIO)
**NBWV**....... Victoria-Carleton Courthouse, Woodstock, New Brunswick [*Library symbol*] [*National Library of Canada*] (NLC)
**NBWY**....... York Regional Library, Headquarters No. 2, Woodstock, New Brunswick [*Library symbol*] [*National Library of Canada*] (NLC)
**NBX**........... Nabire [*Indonesia*] [*Airport symbol*] (OAG)
**NBY**........... Nearest Besselian Year
**NBY**........... Nutrient Broth Yeast [*Microbiology*]
**NbY**........... York Public Library, York, NE [*Library symbol*] [*Library of Congress*] (LCLS)
**NbYC**......... York College, York, NE [*Library symbol*] [*Library of Congress*] (LCLS)
**NBYLC**...... National Black Youth Leadership Council (EA)
**NBysSH**.... Bay Shore Senior High School, Bay Shore, NY [*Library symbol*] [*Library of Congress*] (LCLS)
**NBZ**........... New Braunfelser Zeitung [*A publication*]
**nc-----**......... Central America [*MARC geographic area code*] [*Library of Congress*] (LCCP)
**NC**............. Chloropicrin Stannic Chloride [*Inorganic chemistry*]
**NC**............. [*The*] Item Requested Is Classified in the Interest of National Security and Is Therefore Exempt from Public Disclosure [*Supply action error code*] [*Army*]
**NC**............. La Nouvelle Clio [*Brussels*] [*A publication*] (BJA)
**NC**............. NACCO Industries, Inc. [*NYSE symbol*] (SPSG)
**NC**............. Name Control [*IRS*]
**nc**............... Nanocurie
**NC**............. Narrow Coverage
**NC**............. Narrowband Communicative Services [*Telecommunications*]
**NC**............. Nashville, Chattanooga & St. Louis [*Louisville & Nashville Railroad Co.*] [*AAR code*]
**NC**............. Natal Carabiniers [*British military*] (DMA)
**NC**............. National Catholic News Service
**NC**............. National Churches [*A publication*]
**NC**............. National Coarse [*Thread*]
**NC**............. National Colonialist Party [*Australia*] [*Political party*]
**NC**............. National Cooperatives [*An association*] [*Later, UNICO*]
**NC**............. Native Cavalry [*British military*] (DMA)
**NC**............. NATO Center (NATG)
**NC**............. NATO Confidential (NATG)
**NC**............. Natural Cytotoxic [*Cells*] [*Immunochemistry*]
**NC**............. Nature Conservancy [*NERC*] [*British*]
**NC**............. Naval Cadet [*British*] (ROG)
**NC**............. Naval Correspondence
**NC**............. Navigation Computer
**NC**............. Navigation Console
**NC**............. Navy Component
**NC**............. Navy Cross
**NC**............. Neanderthal Conservative [*Slang*]
**NC**............. Nearly Commensurate Model [*Physics*]
**NC**............. Necrosis
**Nc**............. Negative Wave in Children [*Neurophysiology*]
**NC**............. Neighborhood Coalition (EA)
**NC**............. Nerve Center [*An association*] (EA)
**NC**............. Nerve Conduction
**NC**............. Net Capital [*Business term*]
**NC**............. Net Charter [*Business term*] (DS)
**NC**............. Net Control (MCD)
**NC**............. Net Cost
**NC**............. Netilmicin-Clindamycin [*Antibiotic combination*]
**NC**............. Network Card [*British Rail*]
**NC**............. Network Congestion [*Telecommunications*] (TEL)
**NC**............. Network Connect
**NC**............. Network Controller
**NC**............. Network Countdown
**NC**............. Neural Crest [*Anatomy*]
**NC**............. Neurologic Check [*Medicine*]
**NC**............. Neutral Current [*Physics*]
**NC**............. Neutralizing Capacitance [*or Coil*] (DEN)
**NC**............. Neutron Controller [*Nuclear energy*] (NRCH)
**N/C**........... New Account (ROG)
**NC**............. New Caledonia [*ANSI two-letter standard code*] (CNC)
**NC**............. New Canada Press
**NC**............. New Cases (Bingham's New Cases) in Common Pleas [*1834-40*] [*A publication*] (DLA)
**NC**............. New Cavendish Books [*Publisher*] [*British*]
**N/C**........... New Charter [*Navigation*]
**NC**............. New Church (ROG)

**NC**............. New Construction [*Navy*]
**NC**............. New Consultants [*A publication*]
**NC**............. New Criterion [*A publication*]
**NC**............. New Crop
**NC**............. Neylan Conference (EA)
**NC**............. Nickel Clad
**NC**............. Night Coach [*Airline designation*]
**N-C**............. Nightingale-Conant [*Audio publisher*]
**NC**............. Nineteenth Century and After [*A publication*]
**NC**............. Nineteenth Century Music [*A publication*]
**NC**............. Nippon Club (EA)
**NC**............. Nitrocellulose [*Organic chemistry*]
**NC**............. No Change
**NC**............. No Charge
**NC**............. No Circuits
**NC**............. No Coil (MSA)
**NC**............. No Collaterals [*Medicine*]
**NC**............. No Comment (NASA)
**N/C**............. No Complaints [*Medicine*]
**NC**............. No Connection [*Valve pins*] [*Technical drawings*] [*Radio*]
**NC**............. No Contact
**NC**............. No Contest [*Sports*]
**NC**............. No Cost (AAG)
**NC**............. Noise Correlation (MSA)
**NC**............. Noise Criterion
**NC**............. Nominating Committee [*American Occupational Therapy Association*]
**NC**............. Non-Continuous Liner [*Shipping*] (DS)
**NC**............. Non-Curling [*Photographic film*] (ROG)
**NC**............. Noncallable Bond [*Investment term*]
**NC**............. Noncollectable
**NC**............. Noncommercial [*Rate*] [*Value of the English pound*]
**NC**............. Noncomplex (MCD)
**NC**............. Nonconforming
**NC**............. Nonconformist [*Indicating religious preference*] [*Military*] [*British*]
**NC**............. Noncontributory [*Medicine*]
**NC**............. Nonlinear Capacitance
**NC**............. Nordic Council
**NC**............. NORDLEK Council (EAIO)
**NC**............. Normal Children
**NC**............. Normal Control
**NC**............. Normal Copy [*Oncology*]
**NC**............. Normally Closed [*Switch*]
**NC**............. Norman Conquest [*of England, 1066*]
**NC**............. North Carolina [*Postal code*]
**NC**............. North Carolina Railroad
**NC**............. North Carolina Reports [*A publication*] (DLA)
**Nc**............. North Carolina State Library, Raleigh, NC [*Library symbol*] [*Library of Congress*] (LCLS)
**NC**............. North Carolina Supreme Court Reports [*A publication*] (DLA)
**NC**............. North Central Airlines, Inc. [*ICAO designator*] (OAG)
**NC**............. North Coast (ADA)
**NC**............. North Country (ROG)
**NC**............. Northcor Resources Ltd. [*Vancouver Stock Exchange symbol*]
**NC**............. Northern Command
**NC**............. Northern Consolidated Airlines, Inc.
**NC**............. Northrop Corporation (KSC)
**NC**............. Norwegian Club (EA)
**NC**............. Nose Cone [*Aviation*] (AFM)
**NC**............. Not Carried
**NC**............. Not Coded (MCD)
**NC**............. Not Connected [*Electronics*] (DEN)
**NC**............. Not Controlled [*Experimental conditions*]
**N/C**............. Not Critical (NASA)
**NC**............. Notes of Cases [*Australian Jurist*] [*A publication*] (DLA)
**NC**............. Notes of Cases, English Ecclesiastical and Maritime Courts [*1841-50*] [*A publication*] (DLA)
**NC**............. Notes of Cases at Madras (Strange) [*A publication*] (DLA)
**n/c**............. Notre Compte [*Our Account*] [*French*]
**NC**............. Nouvelle Critique [*A publication*]
**NC**............. Nuclear Capability
**NC**............. Nuclear Congress
**NC**............. Nucleus of Ciliated Cell
**NC**............. Nuestra Cuenta [*Our Account*] [*Business term*] [*Spanish*]
**NC**............. "Nuff Ced" [*Enough Said*] [*Slang*]
**NC**............. Numerical Control [*Data processing*]
**NC**............. Numismatic Chronicle [*A publication*]
**NC**............. Numismatic Chronicle and Journal. Numismatic Society [*A publication*]
**NC**............. Nuova Corrente [*A publication*]
**NC**............. Nurse Corps [*Military*]
**NC**............. Sagrada Biblia [*1944*] [*Eloino Nacar Fuster and Alberto Colunga*] (BJA)
**NC**............. Sandoz Pharmaceuticals [*Research code symbol*]
**nc**............. Sodium Carbonate [*CIPW classification*] [*Geology*]
**NC**............. Warner-Lambert Pharmaceutical Co. [*Research code symbol*]
**NC3**........... Norsar Array Site 03C00 [*Norway*] [*Seismograph station code, US Geological Survey*] (SEIS)
**NC5**........... Norsar Array Site 05C00 [*Norway*] [*Seismograph station code, US Geological Survey*] (SEIS)
**NC-17**........ No Children under 17 Admitted [*Movie rating*]
**NCa**........... Canton Free Library, Canton, NY [*Library symbol*] [*Library of Congress*] (LCLS)
**NCA**........... College of New Caledonia Library [*UTLAS symbol*]
**NCA**........... Jacksonville, NC [*Location identifier*] [*FAA*] (FAAL)
**NCA**........... N-Carboxy Anhydride [*Organic chemistry*]
**NCA**........... N-Chloroethylnorapomorphine [*Organic chemistry, biochemistry*]
**NCA**........... NAIG [*Nippon Atomic Industry Group*] Critical Assembly [*Nuclear reactor*] [*Japan*]
**NCA**........... National Camping Association (EA)
**NCA**........... National Candle Association (EA)
**NCA**........... National Canners Association [*Later, NFPA*] (EA)
**NCA**........... National Capital Award
**NCA**........... National Carousel Association (EA)
**NCA**........... National Cashmere Association [*Defunct*] (EA)
**NCA**........... National Caterers Association [*Later, ICA*] (EA)
**NCA**........... National Cathedral Association (EA)
**NCA**........... National Cattlemens Association (EA)
**NCA**........... National Caves Association (EA)
**NCA**........... National Ceramic Association [*Later, ICA*] (EA)
**NCA**........... National Certificate of Agriculture [*British*]
**NCA**........... National Certification Agency for Medical Lab Personnel (EA)
**NCA**........... National Chaplain's Association (EA)
**NCA**........... National Charcoal Association
**NCA**........... National Chastity Association (EA)
**NCA**........... National Cheerleaders Association (EA)
**NCA**........... National Chiropractic Association [*Formed by a merger of Universal Chiropratic Association and American Chiropratic Association*] [*Later, American Chiropractic Association*]
**NCA**........... National Christian Association (EA)
**NCA**........... National Civic Association
**NCA**........... National Club Association (EA)
**NCA**........... National Coal Association (EA)
**NCA**........... National Coffee Association of the United States of America (EA)
**NCA**........... National Color-Bred Association (EA)
**NCA**........... National Command Authorities
**NCA**........... National Commission on Accrediting [*Later, COPA*] (EA)
**NCA**........... National Communication Agencies (NATG)
**NCA**........... National Communications Association (EA)
**NCA**........... National Composition Association [*Later, NCPA*] (EA)
**NCA**........... National Computer Association (EA)
**NCA**........... National Concilio of America (EA)
**NCA**........... National Confectioners Association of the United States (EA)
**NCA**........... National Conference of Artists (EA)
**NCA**........... National Congressional Analysis Corp. (IID)
**NCA**........... National Constables Association (EA)
**NCA**........... National Constructors Association (EA)
**NCA**........... National Contesters Association (EA)
**NCA**........... National Contingency Account (OICC)
**NCA**........... National Cosmetology Association (EA)
**NCA**........... National Costumers Association (EA)
**NCA**........... National Council on the Aging [*Washington, DC*]
**NCA**........... National Council on Alcoholism [*Later, NCADD*] (EA)
**NCA**........... National Council on the Arts [*of NFAH*]
**NCA**........... National Coursing Association [*Later, NGA*] (EA)
**NCA**........... National Cranberry Association
**NCA**........... National Creameries Association [*Later, NMPF*] (EA)
**NCA**........... National Cricket Association [*British*]
**NCA**........... National Crime Authority [*Australia*]
**NCA**........... Naval Center for Cost Analysis
**NCA**........... Naval Command Assistant
**NCA**........... Naval Communications Annex
**NCA**........... Navy Contract Administrator
**NCA**........... NCA Minerals [*Vancouver Stock Exchange symbol*]
**NCA**........... Network Career Advancement Institute [*Telecommunications service*] (TSSD)
**NCA**........... Neurocirculatory Asthenia [*Medicine*]
**NCA**........... Neutrophil Chemotactic Activity [*Clinical chemistry*]
**NCA**........... New Communities Administration [*HUD*]
**NC of A**...... Newfoundland Club of America (EA)
**NCA**........... Newfoundland Club of America (EA)
**NCA**........... Nickel-Copper Alloy (MSA)
**NCA**........... Nippon Cargo Airlines [*Japan*]
**NCA**........... No Copies Available (ADA)
**NCA**........... No Coupons Attached (DLA)
**NCA**........... Noise Control Association (EA)
**NCA**........... Noncombat Aircraft [*Military*] (MCD)
**NCA**........... Noncontractual Authorization
**NCA**........... Nonorganic Ceramic Adhesive
**NCA**........... Nonspecific Cross-Reacting Antigen [*Immunology*]
**NCA**........... Nor-Cal Aviation, Inc. [*Redding, CA*] [*FAA designator*] (FAAC)
**NCA**........... North Caicos [*British West Indies*] [*Airport symbol*] (OAG)
**NCA**........... North Carolina Court of Appeals Reports [*A publication*] (DLA)
**NCA**........... North Central Association of Colleges and Secondary Schools [*Later, NCACS*]

**NCA**.......... North Central Bible College, Minneapolis, MN [*OCLC symbol*] (OCLC)
**NCA**.......... North Coast Airlines [*Australia*]
**NCA**.......... Northern Communications Area [*Military*]
**NCA**.......... Northern Consolidated Airlines, Inc.
**NCA**.......... Northwest Computing Association
**NCA**.......... Nuclear and Chemical Agency [*Army*]
**NCA**.......... Nurse Consultants Association (EA)
**NCA**.......... Nuveen California Municipal Fund [*NYSE symbol*] (SPSG)
**NcA**.......... Pack Memorial Public Library, Asheville, NC [*Library symbol*] [*Library of Congress*] (LCLS)
**NCAA**........ National Center on Arts and the Aging (EA)
**NCAA**........ National Center for Audio Tapes Archive (EA)
**NCAA**........ National Change of Address Association [*Commercial firm*] [*New York, NY*] (EA)
**NCAA**........ National Collegiate Athletic Association (EA)
**NCAA**........ National Credit Adjustment Association [*New York, NY*] (EA)
**NCAA**........ Naval Civilian Administrators Association [*Later, NCMA*] (EA)
**NCAA**........ Nonnuclear Consumable Annual Analysis (MCD)
**NCAAA**..... National Center of Afro-American Artists
**NCAAA**..... National Council of Affiliated Advertising Agencies [*Later, First Network of Affiliated Advertising Agencies*] (EA)
**NcAAB**...... Asheville-Buncombe Technical Institute, Asheville, NC [*Library symbol*] [*Library of Congress*] (LCLS)
**NCAAC**..... National Consumer Affairs Advisory Council [*Australia*]
**NCAADA**.. National Community Action Agency Directors Association [*Formerly, NCAAEDA*] [*Later, NACAA*] (EA)
**NCAADACCB**... National Commission on Accreditation of Alcoholism and Drug Abuse Counselor Credentialing Bodies (EA)
**NCAAE**..... National Council of Administrators of Adult Education (EA)
**NCAAEDA**... National Community Action Agency Executive Directors Association (EA)
**NcAAP**...... Amcel Propulsion Co., Asheville, NC [*Library symbol*] [*Library of Congress*] (LCLS)
**NCAAP**..... National Coalition for Adequate Alcoholism Programs [*Defunct*] (EA)
**NCAB**........ National Association of Citizen Advice Bureaux [*British*]
**NCAB**........ National Cancer Advisory Board
**NCAB**........ National Collegiate Athletic Bureau [*Later, NCSS*] (EA)
**NCAB**........ National Committee for Amateur Baseball [*Later, USBF*]
**NCAB**........ National Cyclopaedia of American Biography [*A publication*]
**NCAB**........ Navy Contract Adjustment Board
**NCABHP**.. National Center for the Advancement of Blacks in the Health Professions (EA)
**NcAbMR**... North Carolina Marine Resources Center, Bogue Banks Library, Atlantic Beach, NC [*Library symbol*] [*Library of Congress*] (LCLS)
**NCAC**........ National Catholic Action Coalition [*Defunct*] (EA)
**NCAC**........ National Christian Action Coalition [*Defunct*] (EA)
**NCAC**........ National Clean Air Coalition (EA)
**NCAC**........ National Coalition Against Censorship (EA)
**NCAC**........ National Consumer Advisory Council
**NCAC**........ National Council of Acoustical Consultants (EA)
**NCAC**........ National Council Against Conscription [*World War I*] [*Great Britain*]
**NCAC**........ NCA Corporation [*NASDAQ symbol*] (NQ)
**NCAC**........ Nordic Customs Administrative Council (EA)
**NCAC**........ Northern Combat Area Command [*Burma*]
**NCACC**..... National Conference of Appellate Court Clerks (EA)
**NCACME**... National Center for Adult, Continuing, and Manpower Education [*Office of Education*]
**NCACP**...... National Campaign for the Abolition of Capital Punishment [*Founded in 1955*] [*British*]
**NCACPS**... National Coalition to Abolish Corporal Punishment in Schools (EA)
**NCACS**...... National Coalition of Alternative Community Schools (EA)
**NCACS**...... North Central Association of Colleges and Schools (EA)
**NCAD**........ New Cumberland Army Depot [*Pennsylvania*] (AABC)
**NCAD**........ Notice of Cancellation at Anniversary Date [*Insurance*] (DCTA)
**NCADD**..... National Commission Against Drunk Driving (EA)
**NCADD**..... National Council on Alcoholism and Drug Dependence (EA)
**NCADH**..... National Committee Against Discrimination in Housing (EA)
**NCADI**...... National Clearinghouse for Alcohol and Drug Information [*US Public Health Service*] [*Information service or system*] (IID)
**NC Admin Code**... North Carolina Administrative Code [*A publication*] (DLA)
**NCADP**..... National Coalition Against the Death Penalty (EA)
**NCADV**..... National Coalition Against Domestic Violence (EA)
**NC Adv Legis**... Advance Legislative Service to the General Statutes of North Carolina [*A publication*]
**NC Adv Legis Serv**... North Carolina Advance Legislative Service (Michie) [*A publication*] (DLA)
**NCAE**........ National Center for Alcohol Education [*National Institutes of Health*]
**NCAE**........ National Center for Audio Experimentation [*Defunct*] (EA)
**NCAE**........ National College of Agricultural Engineering [*British*] (ARC)
**NCAE**........ National Conference on Airborne Electronics (MCD)
**NCAE**........ National Council of Agricultural Employers (EA)
**NCAEE**...... National Committee on Art Education for the Elderly (EA)
**NCAEF**...... National Ceramic Association Educational Foundation (EA)
**NCAEG**..... National Confederation of American Ethnic Groups (EA)
**NCAEI**....... National Conference on the Application of Electrical Insulation
**NCAF**........ National Committee Against Fluoridation [*Absorbed by National Health Federation - NHF*] (EA)
**NCAF**........ National Community Action Foundation (EA)
**NCAFP**...... National Committee on American Foreign Policy (EA)
**NCAG**........ National Council on the Arts and Government (EA)
**NC Ag Exp**... North Carolina. Agricultural Experiment Station. Publications [*A publication*]
**NC Agric Exp Stn Bull**... North Carolina. Agricultural Experiment Station. Bulletin [*A publication*]
**NC Agric Exp Stn Tech Bull**... North Carolina. Agricultural Experiment Station. Technical Bulletin [*A publication*]
**NC Agric Ext Serv Ext Circ**... North Carolina. Agricultural Extension Service. Extension Circular [*A publication*]
**NC Agric Ext Serv Ext Folder**... North Carolina. Agricultural Extension Service. Extension Folder [*A publication*]
**NC Agric Ext Serv Leafl**... North Carolina. Agricultural Extension Service. Leaflet [*A publication*]
**NC Agric Res Serv Bull**... North Carolina. Agricultural Research Service. Bulletin [*A publication*]
**NC Agric Res Serv Tech Bull**... North Carolina. Agricultural Research Service. Technical Bulletin [*A publication*]
**NC Agr Statist**... North Carolina Agricultural Statistics [*A publication*]
**NcAh**.......... Ahoskie Public Library, Ahoskie, NC [*Library symbol*] [*Library of Congress*] (LCLS)
**NCAH**........ National Committee, Arts for the Handicapped [*Later, VSA*] (EA)
**NCAHCP**.. National Council on Alternative Health Care Policy (EA)
**NcAHE**...... Mountain Area Health Education Center, Health Sciences Library, Asheville, NC [*Library symbol*] [*Library of Congress*] (LCLS)
**NCAHE**..... National Commission on Allied Health Education [*American Occupational Therapy Association*]
**NCAHF**..... National Council Against Health Fraud (EA)
**NcAHH**..... Highland Hospital, Medical Library, Asheville, NC [*Library symbol*] [*Library of Congress*] (LCLS)
**NcAhRC**.... Roanoke-Chowan Technical Institute, Ahoskie, NC [*Library symbol*] [*Library of Congress*] (LCLS)
**NCAHRN**... National Central American Health Rights Network (EA)
**NCAHUAC**... National Committee to Abolish the House Un-American Activities Committee [*Later, NCARL*] (EA)
**NCAI**......... Aitutaki [*Cook Islands*] [*ICAO location identifier*] (ICLI)
**NCAI**......... National Clearinghouse for Alcohol Information [*National Institutes of Health*] [*Rockville, MD*]
**NCAI**......... National Congress of American Indians (EA)
**NCAI**......... National Council of American Importers [*Later, AAEI*] (EA)
**NCAIAE**.... National Center for American Indian Alternative Education (EA)
**NCAIC**....... Nuclear Chemical Accident Incident Control (MCD)
**NCAIE**....... National Center for American Indian Education [*Later, NCAIAE*] (EA)
**NCAIE**....... National Council of the Arts in Education [*Later, ACAE*] (EA)
**NCAIL**....... National Council Against Illegal Liquor [*Defunct*] (EA)
**NCAIP**....... National Consumer Affairs Internship Program (EA)
**NCAIR**....... National Center for Automated Information Retrieval (IID)
**NCAJ**......... National Center for Administrative Justice [*Formerly, CAJ*] (EA)
**NCA/JCS**... National Command Authorities and Joint Chiefs of Staff
**NCAJL**...... National Council on Art in Jewish Life (EA)
**NCALAC**... National Customs Agents Licensing Advisory Committee [*Australia*]
**NcAlb**......... Albemarle-Stanly County Public Library, Albemarle, NC [*Library symbol*] [*Library of Congress*] (LCLS)
**NcAlbS**...... Stanly Technical Institute, Albemarle, NC [*Library symbol*] [*Library of Congress*] (LCLS)
**NCALHBCU**... National Consortium of Arts and Letters for Historically Black Colleges and Universities (EA)
**NCALI**....... National Clearinghouse for Alcohol Information [*National Institutes of Health*] (IID)
**NCALL**...... National Council on Agricultural Life and Labor Research Fund (EA)
**NcAlP**........ Pamlico Technical Institute, Alliance, NC [*Library symbol*] [*Library of Congress*] (LCLS)
**NCalv**......... Baiting Hollow Free Library, Calverton, NY [*Library symbol*] [*Library of Congress*] (LCLS)
**NCAM**....... National Center for Advanced Materials [*Later, Berkeley Center for Advanced Materials*]
**NCAM**....... Network Communication Access Method
**N-CAM**...... Neural Cell Adhesion Molecule [*Biochemistry*]
**NCAMI**..... National Committee Against Mental Illness (EA)
**NCAMP**.... National Coalition Against the Misuses of Pesticides (EA)
**NCAMR**.... Nordic Council for Arctic Medical Research (EA)
**NCAN**........ Incan Superior Ltd. [*AAR code*]
**NCAN**........ National Citizens Action Network (EA)
**NCAN**........ National Coalition of American Nuns (EA)
**NCAN**........ National Committee for Amnesty Now (EA)

**NCaN**......... North Country Reference and Research Resources Council, Canton, NY [*Library symbol*] [*Library of Congress*] (LCLS)
**NcAnA**....... Anson Technical Institute, Ansonville, NC [*Library symbol*] [*Library of Congress*] (LCLS)
**NCanC**....... Community College of the Finger Lakes, Canandaigua, NY [*Library symbol*] [*Library of Congress*] (LCLS)
**NcANCC**... United States National Oceanic and Atmospheric Administration, National Climatic Center, Ashville, NC [*Library symbol*] [*Library of Congress*] (LCLS)
**NcAnd**........ Andrews Carnegie Library, Andrews, NC [*Library symbol*] [*Library of Congress*] (LCLS)
**NCanHi**..... Ontario County Historical Society, Canandaigua, NY [*Library symbol*] [*Library of Congress*] (LCLS)
**NCaNNH**.. Northern New York Health Information Cooperative, Canton, NY [*Library symbol*] [*Library of Congress*] (LCLS)
**NCanV**....... United States Veterans Administration Hospital, Canandaigua, NY [*Library symbol*] [*Library of Congress*] (LCLS)
**NCAO**........ National Coalition of Aboriginal Organisations [*Australia*]
**NCAO**........ Naval Civil Affairs Officer [*World War II*]
**NCAOS**..... National Coalition of Aboriginal Organisations Secretariat [*Australia*]
**N-CAP**....... National Coalition Against Pornography (EA)
**NCAP**........ Neighborhood Community Action Program
**NCAP**........ Nematic Curvilinear Aligned Phase [*Emulsion film used in windows*] [*Taliq Corp.*]
**NCAP**........ New Car Assessment Program [*Automobile testing*]
**NCAP**........ Night Combat Air Patrol [*Military*]
**NCAP**........ Nonlinear Circuit Analysis Program (MCD)
**NCAP**........ Nordic Council for Animal Protection (EA)
**NCAP**........ Nucleotide Column Affinity for Purification [*Biochemical analysis*]
**N-CAP**....... Nurses Coalition for Action in Politics
**NCAPC**...... National Center for Air Pollution Control [*Obsolete*] [*Public Health Service*]
**NCAPO**..... National Council of Adoptive Parents Organizations [*Absorbed by NACAC*]
**NC App**...... North Carolina Court of Appeals Reports [*A publication*] (DLA)
**NCAPS**...... Naval Control and Protection of Shipping (NVT)
**NCapV**....... United States Veterans Administration Hospital, Medical Library, Castle Point, NY [*Library symbol*] [*Library of Congress*] (LCLS)
**NCAR**........ National Center for Association Resources (EA)
**NCAR**........ National Center for Atmospheric Research [*Boulder, CO*] [*National Science Foundation*] (GRD)
**NCAR**........ National Conference on the Advancement of Research (EA)
**NCAR**........ Nonconformance and Corrective Action Reporting System [*NASA*] (KSC)
**N Car**......... North Carolina (DLA)
**N Car**......... North Carolina Reports [*A publication*] (DLA)
**Nc-Ar**......... North Carolina State Department of Archives and History, Raleigh, NC [*Library symbol*] [*Library of Congress*] (LCLS)
**NCARAI**.... Navy Center for Applied Research in Artificial Intelligence [*Washington, DC*] (GRD)
**NCARB**..... National Council of Architectural Registration Boards (EA)
**NCaRC**...... North Country Reference and Research Resources Council, Canton, NY [*Library symbol*] [*Library of Congress*] [*Obsolete*] (LCLS)
**N Car Central LJ**... North Carolina Central Law Journal [*A publication*]
**NCARF**...... National Committee for Amish Religious Freedom (EA)
**NCarF**....... North Carolina Folklore [*A publication*]
**NCARL**...... National Committee Against Repressive Legislation (EA)
**N Car Law Rep**... Carolina Law Repository (Reprint) [*North Carolina*] [*A publication*] (DLA)
**NCARMD**... National Commission on Arthritis and Related Musculoskeletal Disease
**N Carol Dent Gaz**... North Carolina Dental Gazette [*A publication*]
**N Carolina Cases**... North Carolina Reports [*A publication*] (DLA)
**N Carolina Lib**... North Carolina Libraries [*A publication*]
**NCARP**...... Collegiate Association for Research of Principle (EA)
**NCAR Q**.... National Center for Atmospheric Research. Quarterly [*A publication*]
**N Car Rep**... North Carolina Reports [*A publication*] (DLA)
**NCAS**........ National Coalition of Advocates for Students (EA)
**NCAS**........ National Coalition Against Surrogacy (EA)
**NCAS**........ National Collegiate Association for Secretaries [*Defunct*] (EA)
**N of Cas**..... Notes of Cases, English Ecclesiastical and Maritime Courts [*1841-50*] [*A publication*] (DLA)
**N of Cas**..... Notes of Cases at Madras (Strange) [*A publication*] (DLA)
**NcA-S**........ Pack Memorial Public Library, Sondley Reference Library, Asheville, NC [*Library symbol*] [*Library of Congress*] (LCLS)
**NCaS**......... Saint Lawrence University, Canton, NY [*Library symbol*] [*Library of Congress*] (LCLS)
**NCASA**...... National Coalition Against Sexual Assault (EA)
**NCASAA**.... National Court Appointed Special Advocates Association (EA)
**NcAsbC**..... Randolph Public Library, Asheboro, NC [*Library symbol*] [*Library of Congress*] (LCLS)
**NcAsbR**..... Randolph Technical Institute, Asheboro, NC [*Library symbol*] [*Library of Congress*] (LCLS)
**NCASC**...... National Council of Acupuncture Schools and Colleges (EA)
**NCASC**...... Nordic Council for Adult Studies in Church [*See also NKS*] (EAIO)
**NCASEPS**... North Central Alaskan Seasonal Earned Premium Scale [*Aviation*] (AIA)
**NCASF**...... National Council of American-Soviet Friendship (EA)
**NCASI**....... National Council of the Paper Industry for Air and Stream Improvement (EA)
**NCASI Atm Poll Tech Bull**... National Council of the Paper Industry for Air and Stream Improvement. Atmospheric Pollution Technical Bulletin [*A publication*]
**NCASI Monthly Bull**... National Council of the Paper Industry for Air and Stream Improvement. Monthly Bulletin [*A publication*]
**NCASI Regul Rev**... National Council of the Paper Industry for Air and Stream Improvement. Regulatory Review [*A publication*]
**NCASI Tech Bull**... National Council of the Paper Industry for Air and Stream Improvement. Technical Bulletin [*A publication*]
**NCASI Tech Bull Atmos Qual Improv Tech Bull**... National Council of the Paper Industry for Air and Stream Improvement. Technical Bulletin. Atmospheric Quality Improvement. Technical Bulletin [*A publication*]
**NCASI Tech Rev**... National Council of the Paper Industry for Air and Stream Improvement. Technical Review [*A publication*]
**NCAT**........ Atiu [*Cook Islands*] [*ICAO location identifier*] (ICLI)
**NCAT**........ National Center for Appropriate Technology (EA)
**NCAT**........ National Center for Audiotape [*Later, NCATA*] (EA)
**NCAT**........ National Centre for Alternative Technology [*British*]
**NCAT**........ National Program for Clear Air Turbulence [*Air Force*]
**NCAT**........ Naval College Aptitude Test (NVT)
**NCATA**..... National Center for Audiotape Archive (EA)
**NCATA**..... National Coalition of Arts Therapy Associations (EA)
**NCATB**...... National Congress of Animal Trainers and Breeders (EA)
**NCATE**...... National Council for Accreditation of Teacher Education (EA)
**NCATH**..... National Campaign Against Toxic Hazards (EA)
**NCathW**.... New Catholic World [*A publication*]
**NcAu**.......... Sallie H. Jenkins Memorial Public Library, Aulander, NC [*Library symbol*] [*Library of Congress*] (LCLS)
**NcAU**......... University of North Carolina at Asheville, Asheville, NC [*Library symbol*] [*Library of Congress*] (LCLS)
**NCaUA**...... State University of New York, Agricultural and Technical College, Canton, NY [*Library symbol*] [*Library of Congress*] (LCLS)
**NcAV**......... United States Veterans Administration, Hospital Library Service, Asheville, NC [*Library symbol*] [*Library of Congress*] (LCLS)
**NCAVAE**... National Committee for Audio-Visual Aids in Education [*British*]
**NCAVC**..... National Center for the Analysis of Violent Crime [*Quantico, VA*] [*Department of Justice*] (GRD)
**NCAWA**.... National Coinamatic Auto Wash Association [*Later, ICA/NCC*]
**NCAWE**.... National Council of Administrative Women in Education (EA)
**NCAWP**.... National Council for Alternative Work Patterns (EA)
**NCAWRR**... National Committee Against War, Racism, and Repression
**NCAYR**..... National Chaplains Association for Youth Rehabilitation [*Defunct*]
**NCazC**....... Cazenovia College, Cazenovia, NY [*Library symbol*] [*Library of Congress*] (LCLS)
**NCB**........... Barber-Scotia College, Concord, NC [*OCLC symbol*] (OCLC)
**NCB**........... National Cargo Bureau (EA)
**NCB**........... National Central Bureau [*INTERPOL term*]
**NCB**........... National Children's Bureau [*British*]
**NCB**........... National Classification Board [*American Trucking Association*]
**NCB**........... National Coal Board [*British*]
**NCB**........... National Codification Bureau [*NATO*] (NATG)
**NCB**........... National Collection of Industrial Bacteria [*British*]
**NCB**........... National Commercial Bank [*Saudi Arabia*]
**NCB**........... National Computer Board [*Singapore*] (DS)
**NCB**........... National Conservation Bureau [*Defunct*]
**NCB**........... Naval Communications Board
**NCB**........... Naval Construction Battalion
**NC & B**...... Naval Courts and Boards
**NCB**........... Navy Comptroller Budget (NG)
**NCB**........... NCNB Corp. [*NYSE symbol*] (SPSG)
**NCB**........... Nederlandse Credietbank NV [*Financial institution*] [*Netherlands*] (EY)
**NCB**........... Net Clearing Balance [*Finance*]
**NCB**........... Netherlands Convention Bureau (EA)
**NCB**........... Network Control Block
**NCB**........... New Century Bible [*A publication*] (BJA)
**NCB**........... New Comprehensive Biochemistry [*Elsevier Book Series*] [*A publication*]
**NCB**........... New Crime Buffer
**NCB**........... Nickel-Cadmium Battery
**NCB**........... Nippon Credit Bank [*Japan*]
**NCB**........... No Claim Bonus [*Insurance*] (ADA)
**NCB**........... Noncallable Bond [*Investment term*]
**NCB**........... North China Block [*Geology*]
**NCB**........... Northwest Cherry Briners (EA)

**NcBa**.......... Mitchell County Library, Bakersville, NC [*Library symbol*] [*Library of Congress*] (LCLS)
**NCBA**........ National Candy Brokers Association (EA)
**NCBA**........ National Catholic Bandmasters' Association (EA)
**NCBA**........ National Caucus and Center on Black Aged (EA)
**NCBA**........ National Chinchilla Breeders of America [*Later, ECBC*] (EA)
**NCBA**........ National Color-Bred Association (EA)
**NCBA**........ National Commodity and Barter Association (EA)
**NCBA**........ National Cooperative Business Association (EA)
**NCBA**........ National Council on Black Aging (EA)
**NcBaneL**.... Lees-McRae College, Banner Elk, NC [*Library symbol*] [*Library of Congress*] (LCLS)
**NCBBC**...... National Council of Bible Believing Churches [*Later, CBBC*] (EA)
**NcBc**.......... Marianna Black Library, Bryson City, NC [*Library symbol*] [*Library of Congress*] (LCLS)
**NCBC**........ National Commerce Bancorporation [*NASDAQ symbol*] (NQ)
**NCBC**........ National Committee for the Berne Convention (EA)
**NCBC**........ Naval Construction Battalion Center
**NCBC**........ New Century Bible Commentary [*A publication*]
**NCBC**........ North Carolina Biotechnology Center [*Research center*] (RCD)
**NcBcF**........ Fontana Regional Library, Bryson City, NC [*Library symbol*] [*Library of Congress*] (LCLS)
**NCBCS**...... National Conference of States on Building Codes and Standards (OICC)
**NcBe**.......... Belmont Abbey College, Belmont, NC [*Library symbol*] [*Library of Congress*] (LCLS)
**NCBE**........ National Clearinghouse for Bilingual Education [*Wheaton, MD*]
**NCBE**........ National Conference of Bar Examiners (EA)
**NCBE**........ National Conference of Bar Executives [*Later, NABE*] (EA)
**NCBE**........ National Council for Better Education (EA)
**NcBea**........ Cateret County Public Library, Beaufort, NC [*Library symbol*] [*Library of Congress*] (LCLS)
**NCBEA**...... National Catholic Business Education Association [*Emporia, KS*] (EA)
**NcBeaAE**... United States Marine Fisheries Service, Southeast Fisheries Center, Beaufort Laboratory, Beaufort, NC [*Library symbol*] [*Library of Congress*] (LCLS)
**NCBEC**...... National Center for Business and Economic Communication [*American University*] [*Research center*] (RCD)
**NCBEL**...... [*The*] New Cambridge Bibliography of English Literature [*A publication*]
**NcBeSH**..... Sacred Heart College, McCarthy Library, Belmont, NC [*Library symbol*] [*Library of Congress*] (LCLS)
**NcBesL**...... Lithium Corp. of America, Ellestad Research Library, Bessemer City, NC [*Library symbol*] [*Library of Congress*] (LCLS)
**NCBF**......... National Conference of Bar Foundations (EA)
**NCBFAA**... National Customs Brokers and Forwarders Association of America [*New York, NY*] (EA)
**NCBFE**...... National Center for a Barrier Free Environment (EA)
**NCBG**........ National Coalition of Black Gays (EA)
**ncbh--**........ British Honduras [*MARC geographic area code*] [*Library of Congress*] (LCCP)
**NCBH**........ National Coalition to Ban Handguns [*Later, CSGV*] (EA)
**NCBHC**..... National Committee on Black and Hispanic Concerns (EA)
**NCBI**......... National Center for Biotechnology Information (EISS)
**NCBI**......... National Cotton Batting Institute (EA)
**NCBIAE**.... National Council of BIA [*Bureau of Indian Affairs*] Educators (EA)
**NCBJ**......... National Conference of Bankruptcy Judges (EA)
**NCBJS**...... National Council of Beth Jacob Schools [*Later, FCBJS*] (EA)
**NcBl**........... Bridger Memorial Public Library, Bladenboro, NC [*Library symbol*] [*Library of Congress*] (LCLS)
**NCBL**......... National Conference of Black Lawyers (EA)
**NCBL**......... Natural Convection Boiling Loops
**NCBLG**...... National Coalition of Black Lesbians and Gays (EA)
**NcBlm**........ Black Mountain Public Library, Black Mountain, NC [*Library symbol*] [*Library of Congress*] (LCLS)
**NCBLRDC**... National Coalition of Black Lung and Respiratory Disease Clinics (EA)
**NcBlv**......... Phillip Leff Memorial Library, Beulaville, NC [*Library symbol*] [*Library of Congress*] (LCLS)
**NCBM**....... National City Bancorporation [*NASDAQ symbol*] (NQ)
**NCBM**....... National Conference of Black Mayors (EA)
**NCBM**....... National Council on Business Mail (EA)
**NCBMP**..... National Coalition of Black Meeting Planners (EA)
**NCBMP**..... National Council of Building Material Producers [*A union*] [*British*]
**NcBo**.......... Watauga County Library, Boone, NC [*Library symbol*] [*Library of Congress*] (LCLS)
**NcBoA**....... Appalachian State University, Boone, NC [*Library symbol*] [*Library of Congress*] (LCLS)
**NCBOR**..... No Claim Bonus on Renewal [*Insurance*] (AIA)
**NCBP**.......... National Conference of Bar Presidents (EA)
**NCBPD**...... National Consortium for Black Professional Development (EA)
**Nc-BPH**..... North Carolina Library for the Blind and Physically Handicapped, Raleigh, NC [*Library symbol*] [*Library of Congress*] (LCLS)
**NCBPNP/N**... National Certification Board of Pediatric Nurse Practitioners and Nurses (EA)
**NCBR**........ National Center for Bilingual Research [*National Institute of Education*] [*Research center*] (RCD)
**NCBR**........ National Community Banks, Inc. [*NASDAQ symbol*] (NQ)
**NCBR**........ Near Commercial Breeder Reactor [*Also, PLBR*]
**NcBre**......... Transylvania County Library, Brevard, NC [*Library symbol*] [*Library of Congress*] (LCLS)
**NcBreC**...... Brevard College, Brevard, NC [*Library symbol*] [*Library of Congress*] (LCLS)
**NCBS**......... National Cage Bird Show (EA)
**NCBS**......... National Council for Black Studies (EA)
**NCBSA**...... National Candy Brokers and Salesmen's Association [*Later, NCBA*] (EA)
**NcBsG**....... Gardner-Webb College, Boiling Springs, NC [*Library symbol*] [*Library of Congress*] (LCLS)
**NCBT**........ Nashville City Bank & Trust Co. [*NASDAQ symbol*] (NQ)
**NCBTA**...... Nordic Cooperative of Brick and Tilemakers' Associations [*Stockholm, Sweden*] (EAIO)
**NcBuC**....... Campbell College, Buies Creek, NC [*Library symbol*] [*Library of Congress*] (LCLS)
**NcBur**......... Central North Carolina Regional Library, Burlington, NC [*Library symbol*] [*Library of Congress*] (LCLS)
**NcBurgP**.... Pender County Library, Burgaw, NC [*Library symbol*] [*Library of Congress*] (LCLS)
**NcBurT**...... Technical Institute of Alamance, Burlington, NC [*Library symbol*] [*Library of Congress*] (LCLS)
**NcBurWE**.. Western Electric Co., Technical Library, Burlington, NC [*Library symbol*] [*Library of Congress*] (LCLS)
**NcButM**..... Murdoch Center, School Library, Butner, NC [*Library symbol*] [*Library of Congress*] (LCLS)
**NcBv**.......... Yancey County Public Library, Burnsville, NC [*Library symbol*] [*Library of Congress*] (LCLS)
**NCBVA**..... National Concrete Burial Vault Association (EA)
**NCBVP**...... National Coalition on Black Voter Participation (EA)
**NCBW**....... National Cage Bird Week Association [*Defunct*] (EA)
**NCBWA**.... National Collegiate Baseball Writers Association (EA)
**NcBy**.......... Palmico County Library, Bayboro, NC [*Library symbol*] [*Library of Congress*] (LCLS)
**NCC**........... Chadron State College, Chadron, NE [*OCLC symbol*] (OCLC)
**NCC**........... NAACOG [*Nurses Association of the American College of Obstetricians and Gynecologists*] Certification Corporation (EA)
**NCC**........... NASA Class Code (NASA)
**NCC**........... National Cambridge Collectors (EA)
**NCC**........... National Cancer Center (EA)
**NCC**........... National Capital Commission [*Canada*]
**NCC**........... National Capon Council [*Defunct*] (EA)
**NCC**........... National Carbon Company (MCD)
**NCC**........... National Career Center (EA)
**NCC**........... National Carwash Council [*Later, ICA*] (EA)
**NCC**........... National Castings Council [*Defunct*] (EA)
**NCC**........... National Chile Center [*Formerly, NCCSC*] (EA)
**NCC**........... National Citizens Coalition [*Canada*]
**NCC**........... National Citizens Committee. Bulletin [*A publication*]
**NCC**........... National City Corp. [*NYSE symbol*] (CTT)
**NCC**........... National Clearing Corporation [*National Association of Securities Dealers*]
**NCC**........... National Clients Council (EA)
**NCC**........... National Climatic Center [*National Oceanic and Atmospheric Administration*]
**NCC**........... National Coaches Council [*Later, ANCC*] (EA)
**NCC**........... National Coal Council [*Department of Energy*] [*Arlington, VA*] (EGAO)
**NCC**........... National Communications Club (EA)
**NCC**........... National Communications Command [*Army*] (RDA)
**NCC**........... National Company of Crossbowmen [*Defunct*] (EA)
**NCC**........... National Computer Center [*IRS*]
**NCC**........... National Computer Conference
**NCC**........... National Computing Centre [*Manchester, England*]
**NCC**........... National Conference on Citizenship (EA)
**NCC**........... National Congressional Club (EA)
**NCC**........... National Consumer Council [*British*] (ILCA)
**NCC**........... National Consumers Congress [*Later, NCL*]
**NCC**........... National Container Committee [*Later, Uniform Classification Committee*] (EA)
**NCC**........... National Coordinating Committee for the Promotion of History (EA)
**NCC**........... National Coordinating Council on Drug Abuse Education and Information [*Later, NCCDE*] (EA)
**NCC**........... National Coordination Committee [*Responsible for administering the Work Incentive Program*]
**NCC**........... National Core Curriculum [*Australia*]
**NCC**........... National Cotton Council of America (EA)
**NCC**........... National Council Against Conscription [*World War I*] [*Great Britain*]
**NCC**........... National Council of Churches of Christ in the USA (EA)
**NCC**........... National Counselor Certification [*Psychology*]
**NCC**........... National Crime Commission
**NCC**........... National Cryptologic Command [*National Security Agency*]

**NCC**.......... National Cultural Center [*Later, John F. Kennedy Center for the Performing Arts*]
**NCC**.......... National Curriculum Council [*British*] (ECON)
**NCC**.......... Native Council of Canada
**NCC**.......... Nature Conservancy Council [*British*]
**NCC**.......... Navajo Community College [*Tsaile, AZ*]
**NCC**.......... Naval Component Command (CINC)
**NCC**.......... Navigation Computer Control
**NCC**.......... Navigation Control Console
**NCC**.......... Navy Command Center (MCD)
**NCC**.......... Navy Cost Center
**NCC**.......... Network of Concerned Correspondents (EA)
**NCC**.......... Network Control Center [*Telecommunications*]
**NCC**.......... Network Coordination Center [*NASA*]
**NCC**.......... New Chancery Cases (Younge and Collyer) [*1841-43*] [*England*] [*A publication*] (DLA)
**NCC**.......... New Common Carriers
**NCC**.......... New Computer Center [*Social Security Administration*]
**NCC**.......... New Construction and Conversion [*Navy*] (AFIT)
**NCC**.......... New Consultants and Consulting Organizations Directory [*A publication*]
**NCC**.......... Newfoundland Capital Corporation Ltd. [*Toronto Stock Exchange symbol*]
**NCC**.......... Newspaper Comics Council [*Later, NFC*] (EA)
**NCC**.......... Niagara County Community College [*UTLAS symbol*]
**NCC**.......... Nitrogen Charging Console
**NCC**.......... Noise Control Committee
**NCC**.......... Nominal Corrective Combination (MCD)
**NCC**.......... Noncancelable Commitment (SDI)
**NCC**.......... Noncarbohydrate Craver [*Nutrition*]
**NCC**.......... Noncombatant Corps [*British*]
**NCC**.......... NORAD Control Center [*Military*]
**NCC**.......... Nordic Choral Committee (EAIO)
**NCC**.......... Normal-Control Children [*Psychology*]
**NCC**.......... North Calotte Committee [*See also NKK*] [*Nordic Council of Ministers*] [*Rovaniemi, Finland*] (EAIO)
**NCC**.......... North Central College [*Naperville, IL*]
**NCC**.......... Northwest Christian College [*Oregon*]
**NCC**.......... Numerical Control Code
**NCC**.......... Nursing Clerical Coordinator
**NcC**.......... Public Library of Charlotte and Mecklenburg County, Charlotte, NC [*Library symbol*] [*Library of Congress*] (LCLS)
**NCCA**........ Nash Car Club of America (EA)
**NCCA**........ National Catholic Camping Association [*Defunct*] (EA)
**NCCA**........ National Cedar Chest Association [*Defunct*] (EA)
**NCCA**........ National Center for Child Advocacy
**NCCA**........ National Center for Community Action (EA)
**NCCA**........ National Chemical Credit Association (EA)
**NCCA**........ National Clergy Council on Alcoholism and Related Drug Problems (EA)
**NCCA**........ National Coil Coaters Association (EA)
**NCCA**........ National Collegiate Conference Association (EA)
**NCCA**........ National Columbia Challenger Association (EA)
**NCCA**........ National Commission for the Certification of Acupuncture (EA)
**NCCA**........ National Committee on Central America (EA)
**NCCA**........ National Concrete Contractors Association [*Later, ASCC*] (EA)
**NCCA**........ National Cotton Council of America [*Memphis, TN*]
**NCCA**........ National Council for Critical Analysis (EA)
**NCCA**........ National Council for Culture and Art (EA)
**NCCA**........ National Court Clubs Association [*Later, IRSA*] (EA)
**NCCA**........ Negligence and Compensation Cases, Annotated [*A publication*] (DLA)
**NCCA**........ Nordic Committee for Central Africa (EA)
**NCCAA**..... National Christian College Athletic Association (EA)
**NCCAC**..... National Catholic Conference of Airport Chaplains (EA)
**NCCACS**... National Council of Columbia Associations in Civil Service (EA)
**NCCA 3d**... Negligence and Compensation Cases, Annotated, Third Series [*A publication*] (DLA)
**NCCAE**..... National Council of County Association Executives (EA)
**NCCAFV**... National Council on Child Abuse and Family Violence (EA)
**NcCaLM**.... United States Naval Medical Field Research Laboratory, Camp Lejeune, NC [*Library symbol*] [*Library of Congress*] (LCLS)
**NcCaLMC**... United States Marine Corps, Marine Corps Base General Library, Camp Lejeune, NC [*Library symbol*] [*Library of Congress*] (LCLS)
**NcCaLNM**... United States Navy, Naval Regional Medical Center, Library, Camp Lejeune, NC [*Library symbol*] [*Library of Congress*] (LCLS)
**NCCAN**..... National Center on Child Abuse and Neglect [*Department of Health and Human Services*] [*Washington, DC*]
**NCCA NS**... Negligence and Compensation Cases, Annotated, New Series [*A publication*] (DLA)
**NcCar**........ Moore County Library, Carthage, NC [*Library symbol*] [*Library of Congress*] (LCLS)
**NCCAS**...... National Center of Communication Arts and Sciences (EA)
**NCCAS**...... National Council for Clean Air and Streams
**NCCAT**..... National Committee for Clear Air Turbulence (KSC)
**NC Cave Surv**... North Carolina Cave Survey [*A publication*]
**NCCB**........ National Carpenters Craft Board [*Defunct*] (EA)
**NCCB**........ National Citizens Committee for Broadcasting (EA)
**NCCB**........ National Conference of Catholic Bishops (EA)
**NCCB**........ National Consumer Cooperative Bank
**NCCB**........ National Council to Combat Blindness [*Also known as Fight for Sight - FS*] (EA)
**NCCBA**..... National Caucus and Center on Black Aged (EA)
**NCCBI**....... National Coordinating Committee of the Beverage Industry
**NCCBMI**... National Consortium for Computer Based Music Instruction [*University of Delaware*] [*Research clearinghouse*] (EA)
**NCCC**........ National Cambodia Crisis Committee [*Defunct*] (EA)
**NCCC**........ National Cancer Cytology Center [*Later, NCC*] (EA)
**NCCC**........ National Catholic Cemetery Conference (EA)
**NCCC**........ National Conference of Catholic Charities (EA)
**NCCC**........ National Conservative Congressional Committee (EA)
**NCCC**........ National Consumer Credit Consultants (EA)
**NCCC**........ National Council of Churches of Christ in the USA [*Later, NCC*] (EA)
**NCCC**........ National Council of Community Churches [*Later, ICCC*] (EA)
**NCCC**........ National Council of Corvette Clubs (EA)
**NCCC**........ Norris Cotton Cancer Center[*Dartmouth-Hitchcock Medical Center*] [*Research center*] (RCD)
**NCCCC**...... National Coalition for Campus Child Care (EA)
**NCCCCA**... National Collegiate Cross Country Coaches Association [*Later, USCCCA*] (EA)
**NCCCD**..... National Center for Computer Crime Data (EA)
**NCCCD**..... National Center Confraternity of Christian Doctrine (EA)
**NcCCel**...... Celanese Fibers Co., Technical Information Center, Charlotte, NC [*Library symbol*] [*Library of Congress*] (LCLS)
**NCCCLC**... Naval Command Control Communications Laboratory Center
**NcCCP**....... Central Piedmont Community College, Charlotte, NC [*Library symbol*] [*Library of Congress*] (LCLS)
**NCCCP**...... National Center for Community Crime Prevention (EA)
**NCCCR**...... National Citizens Committee for Community Relations [*Defunct*]
**NCCCWA**... National Cotton Compress and Cotton Warehouse Association [*Later, CWAA*] (EA)
**NCCD**........ National Center for Chronic Disease Control [*Public Health Service*]
**NCCD**........ National College for Criminal Defense (EA)
**NCCD**........ National Council for Community Development (EA)
**NCCD**........ National Council on Crime and Delinquency (EA)
**NCCD**........ National Council for Criminal Defense (EA)
**NCCDCI**.... Nordic Contact Committee Concerning Day Care Institutions [*Copenhagen, Denmark*] (EAIO)
**NCCDE**..... National Coordinating Council on Drug Education [*Formerly, NCC*]
**NCCDL**..... National College of Criminal Defense Lawyers and Public Defenders (DLA)
**NCCDPC**... NATO Command, Control, and Information Systems and Automatic Data Processing Committee (NATG)
**NCCD-R & I**... National Council on Crime and Delinquency, Research and Information Division [*Research center*] (RCD)
**NCCDS**...... National Cooperative Crohn's Disease Study
**NCCE**........ National Center for Community Education (EA)
**NCCE**........ National Coalition for Consumer Education (EA)
**NCCE**........ National Commission for Cooperative Education (EA)
**NCCE**........ National Committee for Citizens in Education (EA)
**NCCE**........ Nordic Committee for Commercial Education [*See also NKH*] [*Odense, Denmark*] (EAIO)
**NCCED**..... National Congress for Community Economic Development (EA)
**NCCEM**.... National Coordinating Council on Emergency Management (EA)
**NCCEM**.... National Council of Catholic Employers and Managers (EA)
**NC Cent LJ**... North Carolina Central Law Journal [*A publication*]
**NC Central L J**... North Carolina Central Law Journal [*A publication*]
**NCCEWV**... National Coordinating Committee to End the War in Vietnam [*Defunct*]
**NCCF**......... National Cancer Care Foundation (EA)
**NCCF**......... National Commission on Consumer Finance [*Terminated*]
**NCCF**......... National Council on Community Foundations [*Later, CF*] (EA)
**NCCF**......... Network Communications Control Facility [*IBM program product*]
**NCCFL**...... National Catholic Conference on Family Life (EA)
**NCCG**........ National Council on Compulsive Gambling [*Later, NAPG*] (EA)
**NCCGDP**.. National Council of Chairmen of Graduate Departments of Psychology
**NcCGS**....... Church of Jesus Christ of Latter-Day Saints, Genealogical Society Library, Charlotte North Carolina Branch, Charlotte, NC [*Library symbol*] [*Library of Congress*] (LCLS)
**NcCh**.......... Chapel Hill Public Library, Chapel Hill, NC [*Library symbol*] [*Library of Congress*] (LCLS)
**NCCH**........ National Council of Community Hospitals (EA)
**NCCH**........ National Council to Control Handguns [*Later, HCI*] (EA)
**NCCHB**..... National Committee on Concerns of Hispanics and Blacks (EA)

**NCCHC**..... National Commission on Correctional Health Care (EA)
**NCCHE**..... National Chicano Council for Higher Education (EA)
**NCCHI**...... National Cap and Cloth Hat Institute (EA)
**NCCHR**..... National Commission on Confidentiality of Health Records [*Defunct*] (EA)
**NCCHS**..... National Commission on Community Public Health Services
**NcCI**.......... IBM Corp., Library/15C, Charlotte, NC [*Library symbol*] [*Library of Congress*] (LCLS)
**NCCI**......... National Commission on Coping with Interdependence (EA)
**NCCI**......... National Council on Compensation Insurance [*New York, NY*] (EA)
**NCCI**......... North Central Computer Institute [*Research center*] (RCD)
**NCCI**......... Nutri-Cheese Company [*Oak Park, IL*] [*NASDAQ symbol*] (NQ)
**NCC/IBL**... Nederlandse Centrale Catalogus/Interbibliothecair Leenverkeer System [*Netherlands Central Catalogue/Interlibrary Loan System*] [*Consortium of the Royal Library and University Libraries*] [*Information service or system*] (IID)
**NCCIJ**....... National Catholic Conference for Interracial Justice (EA)
**NCCIP**....... National Center for Clinical Infant Programs (EA)
**NCCIP**....... Nordic Cooperation Committee for International Politics, Including Conflict and Peace Research (EA)
**NCCIS**....... NATO Command, Control, and Information System (NATG)
**NcCJ**.......... Johnson C. Smith University, Charlotte, NC [*Library symbol*] [*Library of Congress*] (LCLS)
**NCCJ**......... National Conference of Christians and Jews (EA)
**NCCJP & A** ... National Clearinghouse for Criminal Justice Planning and Architecture (EA)
**NCCL**......... National Citizen Communication Lobby (EA)
**NCCL**......... National Council of Canadian Labour
**NCCL**......... National Council of Catholic Laity (EA)
**NCCL**......... National Council for Civil Liberties [*British*]
**NCCL**......... National Council of Coal Lessors (EA)
**NcCla**......... Hocutt-Ellington Memorial Library, Clayton, NC [*Library symbol*] [*Library of Congress*] (LCLS)
**NCC-LAW** ... North Carolina Center for Laws Affecting Women, Inc. [*Research center*] (RCD)
**NcClH**........ Haywood Technical Institute, Clyde, NC [*Library symbol*] [*Library of Congress*] (LCLS)
**NcCli**.......... Sampson-Clinton Public Library, Clinton, NC [*Library symbol*] [*Library of Congress*] (LCLS)
**NcCliS**....... Sampson Technical Institute, Clinton, NC [*Library symbol*] [*Library of Congress*] (LCLS)
**NCCLS**...... National Committee for Clinical Laboratory Standards (EA)
**NCCLS**...... National Consumer Center for Legal Services [*Later, NRCCLS*] (EA)
**NcCM**........ Mecklenburg County Medical Society, Charlotte, NC [*Library symbol*] [*Library of Congress*] (LCLS)
**NCCM**....... National Council of Catholic Men (EA)
**NCCMA**.... National Corporate Cash Management Association (EA)
**NCCMCU** ... National Committee to Commemorate the Millenium of Christianity in the Ukraine (EA)
**NCCMGI**.. National Clearinghouse for Corporate Matching Gift Information (EA)
**NCCMHC** ... National Council of Community Mental Health Centers (EA)
**NCCMHS** ... National Consortium for Child Mental Health Services (EA)
**NcCML**...... Medical Library of Mecklenburg County, Inc., Charlotte, NC [*Library symbol*] [*Library of Congress*] (LCLS)
**NCCML**.... National Committee for Careers in the Medical Laboratory [*Defunct*] (EA)
**NCCMP**.... National Coordinating Committee for Multiemployer Plans (EA)
**NCCMT**.... National Committee for Careers in Medical Technology [*Later, NCCML*] (EA)
**NCCN**........ National Council of Catholic Nurses [*Defunct*] (EA)
**NCCNA**..... National Clearinghouse on Child Neglect and Abuse [*HEW*]
**NCCNHR** ... National Citizens Coalition for Nursing Home Reform (EA)
**NcCo**.......... Concord Public Library, Concord, NC [*Library symbol*] [*Library of Congress*] (LCLS)
**NCCO**........ Enseco, Inc. [*Cambridge, MA*] [*NASDAQ symbol*] (NQ)
**NCCO**........ Neodymium, Cerium, Copper, Oxide [*Inorganic chemistry*]
**NcCoB**....... Barber-Scotia College, Concord, NC [*Library symbol*] [*Library of Congress*] (LCLS)
**NcCoCH**.... Cabarrus County Health Department, Concord, NC [*Library symbol*] [*Library of Congress*] (LCLS)
**NcCoi**......... Currituck County Public Library, Coinjock, NC [*Library symbol*] [*Library of Congress*] (LCLS)
**NcCol**......... Polk County Public Library, Columbus, NC [*Library symbol*] [*Library of Congress*] (LCLS)
**NcCola**....... Tyrrell County Public Library, Columbia, NC [*Library symbol*] [*Library of Congress*] (LCLS)
**NcConC**..... Concordia College, Conover, NC [*Library symbol*] [*Library of Congress*] [*Obsolete*] (LCLS)
**NC Conf**..... North Carolina Conference Reports [*A publication*] (DLA)
**NC Conf Rep** ... North Carolina Conference Reports [*A publication*] (DLA)
**NcCorD**...... Duke Power Co., Information Resource Center, Cornelius, NC [*Library symbol*] [*Library of Congress*] (LCLS)
**NCCOS**..... National Committee for Certificates in Office Studies [*British*]
**NCCP**........ National Clearinghouse for Commuter Programs (EA)
**NCCP**........ National Coordinated Cataloging Program [*Library science*]
**NCCP**........ National Council on City Planning
**NCCP**........ NATO Commanders Communications Publication (NATG)
**NCCP**........ Navigation Control Console Panel
**NCCP**........ Northern California Cancer Program [*Research center*] (RCD)
**NCCPA**...... National Cinder Concrete Products Association (EA)
**NCCPA**...... National Commission on Certification of Physician's Assistants (EA)
**NCCPA**...... National Council of College Publications Advisers (EA)
**NCCPAP**... National Conference of CPA [*Certified Public Accountant*] Practitioners [*New York, NY*] (EA)
**NCCPB**...... National Council of Commercial Plant Breeders (EA)
**NCCPC**...... NATO Civil Communications Planning Committee (NATG)
**NCCPL**...... National Community Crime Prevention League (EA)
**NcCpM**...... United States Marine Corps, Air Station, Cherry Point, NC [*Library symbol*] [*Library of Congress*] (LCLS)
**NCC Proc**... National Computer Conference. Proceedings [*A publication*]
**NCCPV**...... National Commission on the Causes and Prevention of Violence (EA)
**NcCQ**......... Queens College, Charlotte, NC [*Library symbol*] [*Library of Congress*] (LCLS)
**nccr---**......... Costa Rica [*MARC geographic area code*] [*Library of Congress*] (LCCP)
**NCCR**........ National Coalition for Cancer Research (EA)
**NCCR**........ National Committee for Cultural Resources
**NCCR**........ National Council for Children's Rights (EA)
**NCCR**........ National Council for Community Relations [*Later, NCMPR*] (EA)
**NCCR**........ New Construction/Conversion Requirements System [*Navy*]
**NCCRE**...... National Consumers Committee for Research and Education [*Later, NCL*] (EA)
**NCC Res Rep Dig** ... Nature Conservancy Council. Research Reports Digest [*A publication*]
**NCCRI**....... National Catholic Coalition for Responsible Investment (EA)
**NcCS**.......... Charlotte-Mecklenburg Schools, Staff Development Center, Charlotte, NC [*Library symbol*] [*Library of Congress*] (LCLS)
**NCCS**......... National Carriers Contract Services [*National Freight Consortium*] [*British*]
**NCCS**......... National Catholic Committee on Scouting (EA)
**NCCS**......... National Catholic Community Service [*Defunct*] (EA)
**NCCS**......... National Catholic Conference for Seafarers (EA)
**NCCS**......... National Center for Charitable Statistics (EA)
**NCCS**......... National Center for Constitutional Studies (EA)
**NCCS**......... National Christ Child Society (EA)
**NCCS**......... National Climbing Classification System
**NCCS**......... National Coalition for Cancer Survivorship (EA)
**NCCS**......... National Command and Control System
**NCCS**......... National Council for Community Services to International Visitors [*Later, NCIV*]
**NC & CS**..... Navigation Command and Control System
**NCCS**......... Navy Camera Control System
**NCCS**......... Navy Command and Control System (NVT)
**NCCS**......... Nordic Church Council for Seamen (EAIO)
**NCCS**......... Nordic Council for Church Studies (EA)
**NCCSA**...... National Council for the Church and Social Action (EA)
**NCCSC**...... National Coordinating Center in Solidarity with Chile [*Later, NCC*] (EA)
**NCCSCE**... National Council on Community Services and Continuing Education (EA)
**NCCSS**...... North Central Conference on Summer Schools (EA)
**NCCTA**..... National Council of Chemical Technician Affiliates
**NCCTS**..... National Catholic Conference for Total Stewardship (EA)
**NCCU**........ National Conference of Canadian Universities
**NCCU**........ Newborn Convalescent Care Unit [*Medicine*]
**NCCU**........ North Carolina Central University [*Durham*]
**NcCU**......... University of North Carolina at Charlotte, Charlotte, NC [*Library symbol*] [*Library of Congress*] (LCLS)
**NCCUSL**... National Conference of Commissioners on Uniform State Laws (EA)
**NcCuW**...... Western Carolina University, Cullowhee, NC [*Library symbol*] [*Library of Congress*] (LCLS)
**NCCV**........ National Center for Church Vocations [*Later, NCVC*] (EA)
**NCCV**........ New Construction and Conversion [*Navy*]
**NCCW**....... National Chamber of Commerce for Women [*New York, NY*] (EA)
**NCCW**....... National Council of Career Women (EA)
**NCCW**....... National Council of Catholic Women (EA)
**NCCWAO** ... National Council of Community World Affairs Organizations (EA)
**NCCWHO** ... National Citizens Committee for the World Health Organization [*Later, AAWH*] (EA)
**NCCY**........ National Committee for Children and Youth [*Later, NCOCY*] (EA)
**NCCY**........ National Council of Catholic Youth [*Defunct*] (EA)
**NCCYSA**... National Conference of Catholics in Youth Serving Agencies [*Defunct*] (EA)
**nccz---**......... Canal Zone [*MARC geographic area code*] [*Library of Congress*] (LCCP)
**NcD**........... Duke University, Durham, NC [*Library symbol*] [*Library of Congress*] (LCLS)
**NCD**.......... National Center for the Diaconate [*Later, NAAND*] (EA)
**NCD**.......... National Commission for Democracy [*Political party*] [*Ghana*]

**NCD**........... National Commission on Diabetes
**NCD**........... National Control Data
**NCD**........... National Council on Drugs (EA)
**NCD**........... Navy Contracting Directives (MCD)
**NCD**........... Negotiable Certificate of Deposit (ADA)
**NCD**........... Negotiated Critical Dates [*Telecommunications*] (TEL)
**NCD**........... Nemine Contradicente [*No One Contradicting*] [*Latin*] [*Legal term*] (DLA)
**NCD**........... Network Cryptographic Device
**NCD**........... Nicotinamide Cytosine Dinucleotide [*Biochemistry*]
**NCD**........... No Can Do [*From pidgin English*]
**NCD**........... No Claim Discount [*Insurance*] (AIA)
**NCD**........... Nordic Committee on Disability (EAIO)
**NCD**........... Nordic Council for the Deaf [*See also DNR*] (EAIO)
**NCD**........... Normal Childhood Disorders [*Medicine*]
**NCD**........... Normalized Cumulative Deviation
**NCD**........... North Canadian Oils Ltd. [*AMEX symbol*] (SPSG)
**NCD**........... North Central Dairy Forwarders Tariff Bureau, Minneapolis MN [*STAC*]
**NCD**........... North Central Division [*Army Engineers*]
**NCD**........... Norton Change Directory [*Data processing*]
**NCD**........... Not Considered Disqualifying
**NCD**........... Notice of Credit Due
**NCD**........... Nova Scotia College of Art and Design Library [*UTLAS symbol*]
**NC³D**......... National Coordinating Center for Curriculum Development
**NCDA**........ National Career Development Association (EA)
**NCDA**........ National Center for Drug Analysis [*St. Louis*] [*FDA*]
**NCDA**........ National Ceramic Dealers Association (EA)
**NCDA**........ National College of District Attorneys (EA)
**NCDA**........ National Community Development Association (EA)
**NCDA**........ National Council on Drug Abuse [*Defunct*] (EA)
**NCDAC**..... National Civil Defense Advisory Council (EA)
**NcDaD**....... Davidson College, Davidson, NC [*Library symbol*] [*Library of Congress*] (LCLS)
**NCDAI**...... National Clearinghouse for Drug Abuse Information [*Public Health Service*] [*Rockville, MD*]
**NcDalG**...... Gaston College, Dallas, NC [*Library symbol*] [*Library of Congress*] (LCLS)
**NcDan**........ Stokes County Public Library, Danbury, NC [*Library symbol*] [*Library of Congress*] (LCLS)
**NCDAPA**.. National Curtain, Drapery, and Allied Products Association [*Later, HFPA*]
**NcD-B**........ Duke University, Fuqua School of Business, Durham, NC [*Library symbol*] [*Library of Congress*] (LCLS)
**NCDB**........ National Center for Drugs and Biologics [*FDA*]
**NCDBC**..... National Center for the Development of Bilingual Curriculum (EA)
**NCDC**........ National Catholic Development Conference (EA)
**NCDC**........ National Center for Disease Control [*Public Health Service*]
**NCDC**........ National Climatic Data Center [*National Oceanic and Atmospheric Administration*] [*Information service or system*] (IID)
**NCDC**........ National Coalition for a Democratic Constitution [*Political group*] [*Republic of Korea*]
**NCDC**........ National Committee for the Day Care of Children [*Later, DCCA*]
**NCDC**........ National Communicable Disease Center (MCD)
**NCDC**........ National Criminal Defense College (EA)
**NCDC**........ Naval Contract Distribution Center
**NCDC**........ New Community Development Corporation [*HUD*]
**NCDC**........ Nitro(carboxyphenyl)diphenylcarbamate [*Biochemistry*]
**NCDC**........ Norchenodeoxycholic Acid [*Biochemistry*]
**NCDCA**..... National Child Day Care Association (EA)
**NCDCF**...... National Civil Defense Computer Facility
**NCDCV**..... Neonatal Calf Diarrhea Coronavirus
**NcD-D**....... Duke University, Divinity School, Durham, NC [*Library symbol*] [*Library of Congress*] (LCLS)
**NCDD**........ No Change in the Due Date (AFM)
**NCDDRE-CCD** ... National Conference of Diocesan Directors of Religious Education - CCD [*Continuing Christian Development*] (EA)
**NcDe**.......... Denton Public Library, Denton, NC [*Library symbol*] [*Library of Congress*] (LCLS)
**NCDE**........ National Coalition for Democracy in Education [*Defunct*] (EA)
**NC Dent J** ... North Carolina Dental Journal [*A publication*]
**NC Dep Conserv Dev Div Miner Resour Bull** ... North Carolina. Department of Conservation and Development. Division of Mineral Resources. Bulletin [*A publication*]
**NC Dep Conserv Dev Econ Pap** ... North Carolina. Department of Conservation and Development. Economic Paper [*A publication*]
**NC Dep Nat Econ Resour Groundwater Sect Rep Invest** ... North Carolina. Department of Natural and Economic Resources. Groundwater Section. Report of Investigation [*A publication*]
**NC Dep Nat Econ Resour Reg Geol Ser** ... North Carolina. Department of Natural and Economic Resources. Regional Geology Series [*A publication*]
**NCDF**........ National Computer Dealer Forum (EA)
**NCDH**....... National Committee Against Discrimination in Housing (EA)
**NCDHM**... National Children's Dental Health Month [*American Dental Association*]
**NC Div Ground Water Ground Water Bull** ... North Carolina. Division of Ground Water. Ground Water Bulletin [*A publication*]
**NC Div Ground Water Ground Water Circ** ... North Carolina. Division of Ground Water. Ground Water Circular [*A publication*]
**NC Div Miner Resour Bull** ... North Carolina. Department of Conservation and Development. Division of Mineral Resources. Bulletin [*A publication*]
**NC Div Miner Resour Inf Circ** ... North Carolina. Division of Mineral Resources. Information Circular [*A publication*]
**NC Div Resour Plann Eval Miner Resour Sect Bull** ... North Carolina. Division of Resource Planning and Evaluation. Mineral Resources Section. Bulletin [*A publication*]
**NC Div Resour Plann Eval Miner Resour Sect Educ Ser** ... North Carolina. Division of Resource Planning and Evaluation. Mineral Resources Section. Educational Series [*A publication*]
**NC Div Resour Plann Eval Miner Resour Sect Reg Geol Ser** ... North Carolina. Division of Resource Planning and Evaluation. Mineral Resources Section. Regional Geology Series [*A publication*]
**NC Div Resour Plann Eval Reg Geol Ser** ... North Carolina. Division of Resource Planning and Evaluation. Regional Geology Series [*A publication*]
**NC Div Water Resour Div Stream Sanit Hydrol Bull** ... North Carolina. Department of Water Resources. Division of Stream Sanitation and Hydrology. Bulletin [*A publication*]
**NcD-L**......... Duke University, School of Law, Durham, NC [*Library symbol*] [*Library of Congress*] (LCLS)
**NCDM**....... Numerically Controlled Drafting Machine (MCD)
**NcD-MC**.... Duke University, Medical Center, Durham, NC [*Library symbol*] [*Library of Congress*] (LCLS)
**NCDO**........ Navy Central Disbursing Office
**NcDo**.......... Surry County-Dobson Library, Dobson, NC [*Library symbol*] [*Library of Congress*] (LCLS)
**NcDoS**....... Surry Community College, Dobson, NC [*Library symbol*] [*Library of Congress*] (LCLS)
**NCDP**........ Namibie Christelike Demokratiese Party [*Namibian Christian Democratic Party*] [*Political party*] (PPW)
**NCDP**........ Navigation Control/Display Panel (MCD)
**NCDPEH**.. National Coalition for Disease Prevention and Environmental Health
**NCDRC**..... National Catholic Disaster Relief Committee (EA)
**NCDS**........ National Center for Dispute Settlement [*American Arbitration Association*] [*Later, CDS*]
**NCDS**........ Naval Combat Data System
**NCDS**........ Navy Combat Direction System (MCD)
**NCDT**........ National Council for Drama Training [*British*]
**NCDT**........ Noble-Collip Drum Trauma [*Physiology*]
**NCDT**........ Non-Chargeable Downtime
**NCDT**........ North Carolina Dance Theater
**NCDT & E** ... Naval Combat Demolition Training and Experimental Base [*Maui, HI*] (KSC)
**NCDT & EBASE** ... Naval Combat Demolition Training and Experimental Base [*Maui, HI*]
**NCDTO**..... National Council of Dance Teacher Organizations [*Later, NDCA*] (EA)
**NcDu**.......... Dunn Public Library, Dunn, NC [*Library symbol*] [*Library of Congress*] (LCLS)
**NCDU**........ Naval Combat Demolition Unit
**NCDU**........ Navigation Control and Display Unit
**NcDubB**..... Bladen Technical College, Dublin, NC [*Library symbol*] [*Library of Congress*] (LCLS)
**NcDur**........ Durham City-County Public Library, Durham, NC [*Library symbol*] [*Library of Congress*] (LCLS)
**NcDurBC**... Blue Cross & Blue Shield of North Carolina, Durham, NC [*Library symbol*] [*Library of Congress*] (LCLS)
**NcDurBD**... Becton, Dickinson & Co., Research Center Library, Research Triangle Park, Durham, NC [*Library symbol*] [*Library of Congress*] (LCLS)
**NcDurC**..... North Carolina Central University, Durham, NC [*Library symbol*] [*Library of Congress*] (LCLS)
**NcDurCL**... North Carolina Central University, School of Library Science, Durham, NC [*Library symbol*] [*Library of Congress*] (LCLS)
**NcDurCR**... Chemstrand Research Center, Inc., Durham, NC [*Library symbol*] [*Library of Congress*] (LCLS)
**NcDurEP**... United States Environmental Protection Agency, Office of Administration, Library Services Branch, Park, Durham, NC [*Library symbol*] [*Library of Congress*] (LCLS)
**NcDurGH**... Durham County General Hospital, Medical Library, Durham, NC [*Library symbol*] [*Library of Congress*] (LCLS)
**NcDurHS**... United States National Environmental Health Sciences Center, Durham, NC [*Library symbol*] [*Library of Congress*] (LCLS)
**NcDurIBM**... International Business Machines Corp., IBM CPD Library, Durham, NC [*Library symbol*] [*Library of Congress*] (LCLS)
**NcDurIF**.... International Fertility Research Program, Durham, NC [*Library symbol*] [*Library of Congress*] (LCLS)

**NcDurL**...... Liggett & Myers, Inc. [*Later, Liggett Group, Inc.*], Durham, NC [*Library symbol*] [*Library of Congress*] (LCLS)
**NcDurM**.... Monsanto Triangle Park Development Center, Durham, NC [*Library symbol*] [*Library of Congress*] (LCLS)
**NcDurNH**... National Humanities Center, Durham, NC [*Library symbol*] [*Library of Congress*] (LCLS)
**NcDurRT**... Research Triangle Institute, Technical Library, Durham, NC [*Library symbol*] [*Library of Congress*] (LCLS)
**NcDurSci**... North Carolina School of Science and Mathematics, Durham, NC [*Library symbol*] [*Library of Congress*] (LCLS)
**NcDurST**... North Carolina Science and Technology Research Center, Durham, NC [*Library symbol*] [*Library of Congress*] (LCLS)
**NcDurT**...... Durham Technical Institute, Durham, NC [*Library symbol*] [*Library of Congress*] (LCLS)
**NcDurUC**.. Union Carbide Agricultural Products Co., Inc., Research Triangle Park, Durham, NC [*Library symbol*] [*Library of Congress*] (LCLS)
**NcDurV**..... United States Veterans Administration Hospital, Durham, NC [*Library symbol*] [*Library of Congress*] (LCLS)
**NcDurW**.... Wellcome Research Laboratories, Durham, NC [*Library symbol*] [*Library of Congress*] (LCLS)
**NcDurW-Gv**... Burroughs Wellcome & Co., Greenville, NC [*Library symbol*] [*Library of Congress*] (LCLS)
**NCDV**........ Nebraska Calf Diarrhea Virus
**NCDVD**..... National Conference of Diocesan Vocation Directors (EA)
**NcD-W**...... Duke University, Woman's College, Durham, NC [*Library symbol*] [*Library of Congress*] (LCLS)
**NcE**............ Bladen County Public Library, Elizabethtown, NC [*Library symbol*] [*Library of Congress*] (LCLS)
**NCe**............ Middle Country Public Library, Centereach, NY [*Library symbol*] [*Library of Congress*] (LCLS)
**NCE**........... Nasa Cotopaxi [*Ecuador*] [*Seismograph station code, US Geological Survey*] (SEIS)
**NCE**........... National College of Education [*Illinois*]
**NCE**........... National Committee on the Emeriti (EA)
**NCE**........... Navy Calibration Equipment List
**NCE**........... Navy Civil Engineer [*A publication*]
**NCE**........... Network Connection Element
**NCE**........... Network Control Elements (MCD)
**NCE**........... Neuritis of the Cauda Equina [*Medicine*]
**NCE**........... New Catholic Edition [*Bible*]
**NCE**........... New Catholic Encyclopedia [*A publication*]
**NCE**........... Newark College of Engineering [*New Jersey*]
**NCE**........... Nice [*France*] [*Airport symbol*] (OAG)
**NCE**........... No Change in Estimates
**NCE**........... Nonconvulsive Epilepsy [*Medicine*]
**NCE**........... Normal Calomel Electrode [*Electrochemistry*]
**NCE**........... Normal Chick Embryo
**NCE**........... North Carolina Music Educator [*A publication*]
**NCE**........... Nuclear Capability Exercise [*Army*] (AABC)
**NCEA**........ N-(Carboxyethyl)alanine [*Biochemistry*]
**NCEA**........ National Catholic Educational Association (EA)
**NCEA**........ National Center for Economic Alternatives (EA)
**NCEA**........ National Christian Education Association (EA)
**NCEA**........ National College Education and Admissions Foundation (EA)
**NCEA**........ National Community Education Association (EA)
**NCEA**........ National Consortium for Education Access (EA)
**NcEB**......... Bladen Technical Institute, Elizabethtown, NC [*Library symbol*] [*Library of Congress*] (LCLS)
**NCEB**........ National Center for Educational Brokering [*Defunct*] (EA)
**NCEB**........ National Council for Environmental Balance (EA)
**NCEB**........ NATO Communications Electronics Board
**NCEBVS**... National Chronic Epstein-Barr Virus Syndrome Association (EA)
**NCEC**........ National Center for Educational Communication [*Office of Education*]
**NCEC**........ National Chemical Emergency Centre [*Atomic Energy Authority*] [*Didcot, Oxon., England*]
**NCEC**........ National Christian Education Council [*Church of England*]
**NCEC**........ National Commission for Electrologist Certification (EA)
**NCEC**........ National Committee for an Effective Congress (EA)
**NCEC**........ National Construction Employers Council (EA)
**NCEC**........ North Coast Export Company [*An association*] [*Defunct*] (EA)
**NCECA**..... National Council on Education for the Ceramic Arts (EA)
**NC Ecc**....... Notes of Cases, English Ecclesiastical and Maritime Courts [*1841-50*] [*A publication*] (DLA)
**NCECD**..... National Commission for Economic Conversion and Disarmament (EA)
**NCECE**...... National Council of Elected County Executives (EA)
**NCECF**...... National Children's Eye Care Foundation (EA)
**NCECG**..... National Coalition to Expand Charitable Giving (EA)
**NCED**....... National Center on Employment of the Deaf (EA)
**NCEDL**...... National Committee for Effective Design Legislation (EA)
**NcEdR-R**... Rockingham County Public Library, Reidsville Branch Library, Reidsville, NC [*Library symbol*] [*Library of Congress*] (LCLS)
**NcEdt**......... Shepard-Pruden Memorial Library, Edenton, NC [*Library symbol*] [*Library of Congress*] (LCLS)
**NCEE**........ National Catholic Educational Exhibitors (EA)
**NCEE**........ National Center on Education and Employment [*New York, NY*] [*Department of Education*] (GRD)
**NCEE**........ National Congress for Educational Excellence (EA)
**NCEE**........ National Council of Engineering Examiners (EA)
**NCEEF**...... National Committee for Electrical Engineering Films
**NCEER**...... National Center for Earthquake Engineering Research [*Buffalo, NY*] (GRD)
**NCEF**......... National Calling and Emergency Frequencies (CET)
**NCEF**......... Non-Circumcision Educational Foundation (EA)
**NCEFF**....... National Committee for Education in Family Finance (EA)
**NCEFR**...... National Council of Erectors, Fabricators, and Riggers (EA)
**NCEFT**...... National Commission on Electronic Fund Transfers
**NCEGA**..... Noise Control Engineering [*A publication*]
**NCEHAI**... National Committee on Ethics of the Hearing Aid Industry [*Defunct*] (EA)
**NCEHELP**... National Conference of Executives of Higher Education Loan Plans [*Later, NCHELP*] (EA)
**NCEHP**..... National Center for the Exploration of Human Potential (EA)
**NCEHS**..... National Center for Environmental Health Strategies (EA)
**NcEl**........... Kemp Memorial Library, Ellerbe, NC [*Library symbol*] [*Library of Congress*] (LCLS)
**NCEL**......... Nationwide Cellular Service, Inc. [*Valley Stream, NY*] [*NASDAQ symbol*] (NQ)
**NCEL**......... Naval Civil Engineering Laboratory
**NCEL**......... Navy Contractor Experience List
**NcElc**......... East Albemarle Regional Library, Elizabeth City, NC [*Library symbol*] [*Library of Congress*] (LCLS)
**NcElcA**...... College of the Albemarle, Elizabeth City, NC [*Library symbol*] [*Library of Congress*] (LCLS)
**NcElcE**....... Elizabeth City State University, Elizabeth City, NC [*Library symbol*] [*Library of Congress*] (LCLS)
**NcElcP**....... Pasquotank-Camden Library, Elizabeth City, NC [*Library symbol*] [*Library of Congress*] (LCLS)
**NcElcR**....... Roanoke Bible College, Mary E. Griffith Memorial Library, Elizabeth City, NC [*Library symbol*] [*Library of Congress*] (LCLS)
**NcElk**......... Elkin Public Library, Elkin, NC [*Library symbol*] [*Library of Congress*] (LCLS)
**NcElon**....... Elon College, Elon College, NC [*Library symbol*] [*Library of Congress*] (LCLS)
**NcElonCH**... Historical Society of the Southern Convention, Congregation of Christian Churches, Elon College, NC [*Library symbol*] [*Library of Congress*] (LCLS)
**NcElonP**.... Primitive Baptist Library, Elon College, NC [*Library symbol*] [*Library of Congress*] (LCLS)
**NCEM**....... National Center for Electron Microscopy [*Berkeley, CA*] [*Lawrence Berkeley Laboratory*] [*Department of Energy*]
**NCEMC**.... National Committee on the Education of Migrant Children [*of the National Child Labor Committee*] (EA)
**NCEMCH**... National Center for Education in Maternal and Child Health (EA)
**NCEMMH**... National Center, Educational Media and Materials for the Handicapped [*Defunct*] (EA)
**NCEMP**..... National Center for Energy Management and Power
**NcEn**.......... Lilly Pike Sullivan Municipal Library, Enfield, NC [*Library symbol*] [*Library of Congress*] (LCLS)
**NCEN**........ National Commission on Egg Nutrition
**NCEN**........ North Central
**N Cen Assn Q**... North Central Association. Quarterly [*A publication*]
**NcEnk**........ American Enka Corp., Enka, NC [*Library symbol*] [*Library of Congress*] (LCLS)
**N Cent**........ Nineteenth Century [*A publication*]
**N Cent Corn Breed Res Comm Minutes Meet**... North Central Corn Breeding Research Committee. Minutes of Meeting [*A publication*]
**N Cent School L Rev**... North Central School Law Review [*A publication*] (DLA)
**NCEO**........ National Center for Employee Ownership (EA)
**NCEO**........ National Center for Exploitation of the Oceans
**NCEOA**..... National Council of Educational Opportunity Associations (EA)
**NCEP**......... National Center for Education in Politics [*Defunct*] (EA)
**NCEP**......... National Cholesterol Education Program Coordinating Committee [*National Institutes of Health*] (EGAO)
**NCEP**......... National Council on Employment Policy (EA)
**NCEP**......... National Council for the Encouragement of Patriotism (EA)
**NcEr**........... Erwin Public Library, Erwin, NC [*Library symbol*] [*Library of Congress*] (LCLS)
**NCER**........ National Center for Earthquake Research [*US Geological Survey*]
**NCER**........ National Conference on Electromagnetic Relays
**NCER**........ National Council on Educational Research [*Department of Education*] [*Washington, DC*] [*Later, NCERI*]
**NCERACCS**... National Coalition to End Racism in America's Child Care System (EA)
**NCERD**..... National Center for Educational Research and Development [*HEW*]
**nces---**........ El Salvador [*MARC geographic area code*] [*Library of Congress*] (LCCP)
**NCES**......... National Center for Education Statistics [*Office of Education*] [*Later, CES*]
**NCES**......... New Careers in Employment Security (OICC)

**NCES**......... North Central Experiment Station [*University of Minnesota*] [*Research center*] (RCD)
**NCES**......... North Country Educational Services [*Library network*]
**NCESA**...... National Class E Scow Association (EA)
**NCESGR**... National Committee for Employer Support of the Guard and Reserve (EA)
**NCET**........ National Capital Real Estate Trust [*San Francisco, CA*] [*NASDAQ symbol*] (NQ)
**NCET**........ National Center for Educational Technology [*Office of Education*]
**NCET**........ National Coastal Ecosystems Team [*Office of Biological Services, United States Fish and Wildlife Service*] (MSC)
**NCET**........ National Council for Educational Technology [*British*]
**NCEW**....... National Conference of Editorial Writers (EA)
**NCEY**........ National Committee on Employment of Youth [*National Child Labor Committee*] (EA)
**NCEZ**........ National Coalition for Enterprise Zones [*San Diego, CA*] (EA)
**NCF**........... Narramore Christian Foundation (EA)
**NCF**........... National Cancer Foundation
**NCF**........... National Chamber Foundation (EA)
**NCF**........... National Civics Federation
**NCF**........... National Commission on a Free and Responsible Media (EA)
**NCF**........... National Communications Forum [*National Engineering Consortium, Inc.*] [*Chicago, IL*] [*Telecommunications*] (TSSD)
**NCF**........... National Conservative Foundation (EA)
**NCF**........... National Craniofacial Foundation [*Later, ICF*] (EA)
**NCF**........... National Cristina Foundation (EA)
**NCF**........... Naval Communications Facility (MUGU)
**NCF**........... Naval Construction Force (NVT)
**NCF**........... Nerve Cell Food
**NCF**........... Net Cash Flow
**NCF**........... Neutrophil Chemotactic Factor [*Hematology*]
**NCF**........... Neutrophil Cytosol Factor [*Cytology*]
**NCF**........... Newton-Cotes Formula [*Mathematics*]
**NCF**........... Nineteenth-Century Fiction [*A publication*]
**NCF**........... No Conscription Fellowship [*England, World War I*]
**NCF**........... Nominal Characteristics File (IEEE)
**NCF**........... Noncold Front [*Meteorology*]
**NCF**........... Nonflammable Cellulosic Foam
**NCF**........... North Carolina Folklore [*A publication*]
**NCF**........... Nuclear Capable Forces (MCD)
**NCF**........... Nucleonics Calibration Facility (RDA)
**NCF**........... Nurses Christian Fellowship (EA)
**NCFA**........ Narcolepsy and Cataplexy Foundation of America (EA)
**NCFA**........ National Cat Fanciers' Association [*Defunct*] (EA)
**NCFA**........ National Collection of Fine Arts [*Later, National Museum of American Art*]
**NCFA**........ National Collegiate Football Association (EA)
**NCFA**........ National Commercial Finance Association (EA)
**NCFA**........ National Committee for Adoption (EA)
**NCFA**........ National Consumer Finance Association (EA)
**NCFA**........ Naval Campus for Achievement (NVT)
**NCFA**........ North Central Field Area
**NCFAE**...... National Council of Forestry Association Executives (EA)
**NcFayC**...... Cumberland County Public Library, Fayetteville, NC [*Library symbol*] [*Library of Congress*] (LCLS)
**NcFayC-F**.. Cumberland County Public Library, North Carolina Foreign Language Center, Fayetteville, NC [*Library symbol*] [*Library of Congress*] (LCLS)
**NcFayCFH**... Cape Fear Valley Hospital, Medical Library, Fayetteville, NC [*Library symbol*] [*Library of Congress*] (LCLS)
**NcFayH**..... Fayetteville Area Health Education Foundation, Inc., Fayetteville, NC [*Library symbol*] [*Library of Congress*] (LCLS)
**NcFayM**.... Methodist College, Fayetteville, NC [*Library symbol*] [*Library of Congress*] (LCLS)
**NcFayR**...... Rutledge College, Fayetteville, NC [*Library symbol*] [*Library of Congress*] (LCLS)
**NcFayS**...... Fayetteville State University, Fayetteville, NC [*Library symbol*] [*Library of Congress*] (LCLS)
**NcFayT**...... Fayetteville Technical Institute, Fayetteville, NC [*Library symbol*] [*Library of Congress*] (LCLS)
**NcFayV**...... United States Veterans Administration Medical Center, Fayetteville, NC [*Library symbol*] [*Library of Congress*] (LCLS)
**NcFb**.......... United States Army, Special Services Library System, Fort Bragg, NC [*Library symbol*] [*Library of Congress*] (LCLS)
**NcFbH**....... United States Army, Womack Army Hospital, Fort Bragg, NC [*Library symbol*] [*Library of Congress*] (LCLS)
**NcFbIM**..... United States Army, Institute for Military Assistance, Marquat Memorial Library, Fort Bragg, NC [*Library symbol*] [*Library of Congress*] (LCLS)
**NcFc**.......... Mooneyham Public Library, Forest City, NC [*Library symbol*] [*Library of Congress*] (LCLS)
**NCFC**......... National Coalition for a Free Cuba (EA)
**NCFC**......... National Commercial Finance Conference [*Later, NCFA*] (EA)
**NCFC**......... National Council of Farmer Cooperatives (EA)
**NCFCA**....... National Congress of Floor Covering Associations (EA)
**NCFD**........ National Corporate Fund for Dance (EA)
**NCFDA**..... National Council on Federal Disaster Assistance
**NCFDAL**... National Committee for Fair Divorce and Alimony Laws (EA)
**NCFE**......... National Center for Financial Education (EA)
**NCFE**......... National Committee for Full Employment [*Washington, DC*] (EA)
**NCFE**......... National Commodity Futures Examination
**NCFEI**....... National Center for Financial and Economic Information Services [*Ministry of Finance and National Economy*] [*Saudi Arabia*] (ECON)
**NCFEPS**.... National Commission for Full Employment Policy Studies (OICC)
**NCFES**...... North Central Forest Experiment Station [*St. Paul, MN*] [*Department of Agriculture*] (GRD)
**NCFFR**...... National Commission on Fraudulent Financial Reporting [*Defunct*] (EA)
**NCFIS**....... National Center for Freedom of Information Studies (EA)
**NCFJE**...... National Committee for the Furtherance of Jewish Education (EA)
**NCFL**......... National Catholic Forensic League (EA)
**NCFLIS**..... National Council on Foreign Language and International Studies (EA)
**NCFLN**...... Northern California Foreign Language Newsletter [*A publication*]
**NCFM**........ National Commission on Food Marketing
**NCFMF**..... National Committee for Fluid Mechanics Films
**NCFMS**..... Naval Comptroller Financial Management Service
**NCFNP**...... National Committee for a Freedom Now Party [*Defunct*] (EA)
**NC Folk**..... North Carolina Folklore [*A publication*]
**NCFP**......... National Conference on Fluid Power (EA)
**NCFPC**...... National Center for Fish Protein Concentrate [*Fish and Wildlife Service*]
**NCFPC**...... National Commission on Fire Prevention and Control
**NCFPI**....... National Clearinghouse for Family Planning Information [*Database*]
**NCFPS**...... National Center for Family Planning Services [*Health Services and Mental Health Administration, HEW*]
**NcFr**........... Macon County Public Library, Franklin, NC [*Library symbol*] [*Library of Congress*] (LCLS)
**NCFR**......... National Council for Family Reconciliation (EA)
**NCFR**......... National Council on Family Relations (EA)
**NCFR**......... National Council on Family Relations. Newsletter [*A publication*]
**NCFRF**...... National Cystic Fibrosis Research Foundation [*Later, Cystic Fibrosis Foundation*] (EA)
**NcFrt**.......... Franklinton Public Library, Franklinton, NC [*Library symbol*] [*Library of Congress*] (LCLS)
**NCFS**......... National College of Foot Surgeons (EA)
**NCFS**......... National Committee on Films for Safety [*Defunct*] (EA)
**NCFS**......... Nineteenth-Century French Studies [*A publication*]
**NCFS**......... Noncontingent Footshock
**NCFSD**...... NORAD Cost Factors and System Data [*Military*] (MCD)
**NCFSK**...... Noncoherent Frequency Shift Keying
**NCFSU**...... Naval Construction Force Support Unit (NVT)
**NCFT**......... National Council for Families and Television (EA)
**NCFTF**....... National Consumer Fraud Task Force (EA)
**NCFTJ**...... National Conference on Federal Trial Judges (EA)
**NcFv**........... Farmville Public Library, Farmville, NC [*Library symbol*] [*Library of Congress*] (LCLS)
**NCFVP**...... National Center for Film and Video Preservation (EA)
**NCFVSI**..... National Council for Fishing Vessel Safety and Insurance (EA)
**NCG**........... Coast Guard Publication [*Later, NAVCG*]
**NcG**............ Greensboro Public Library, Greensboro, NC [*Library symbol*] [*Library of Congress*] (LCLS)
**NCG**........... National Council for the Gifted (EA)
**NCG**........... Network Control Group [*Manned Space Flight Network*]
**NCG**........... Nickel-Coated Graphite [*Materials technology*]
**NCG**........... Noncondensible Gases
**NCG**........... Nova-Cogesco Resources, Inc. [*Toronto Stock Exchange symbol*]
**NCG**........... Nuclear Cratering Group [*Later, EERA*] [*Army*]
**NCG**........... Null Command Generator
**NCG**........... Numerical Control Graphics (MCD)
**NcGa**.......... Gaston-Lincoln Regional Library, Gastonia, NC [*Library symbol*] [*Library of Congress*] (LCLS)
**NCGA**........ National Church Goods Association (EA)
**NCGA**........ National Computer Graphics Association (EA)
**NCGA**........ National Corn Growers Association (EA)
**NCGA**........ National Cotton Ginners' Association (EA)
**NCGA**........ National Council on Governmental Accounting (EA)
**NcGA**......... North Carolina Agricultural and Technical State University, Greensboro, NC [*Library symbol*] [*Library of Congress*] (LCLS)
**NcGaH**....... Gaston Memorial Hospital, Inc., Medical Library, Gastonia, NC [*Library symbol*] [*Library of Congress*] (LCLS)
**NcGav**........ Gates County Library, Gatesville, NC [*Library symbol*] [*Library of Congress*] (LCLS)
**NcGB**......... Bennett College, Greensboro, NC [*Library symbol*] [*Library of Congress*] (LCLS)
**NcGBI**........ Burlington Industries, Inc., Information Services Library, Greensboro, NC [*Library symbol*] [*Library of Congress*] (LCLS)

**NcGBur**...... Burlington Industries, Inc., Information Services Library, Greensboro, NC [*Library symbol*] [*Library of Congress*] (LCLS)
**NcGC**......... Greensboro College, Greensboro, NC [*Library symbol*] [*Library of Congress*] (LCLS)
**NCGC**......... National Catholic Guidance Conference [*Later, ARVIC*] (EA)
**NCGCC**..... National Convention of Gospel Choirs and Choruses (EA)
**NcGCG**...... Ciba-Geigy Corp., Technical Information Service, Greensboro, NC [*Library symbol*] [*Library of Congress*] (LCLS)
**NcGCH**...... Wesley Long Community Hospital, Inc., Greensboro, NC [*Library symbol*] [*Library of Congress*] (LCLS)
**NcGCL**....... Center for Creative Leadership, Greensboro, NC [*Library symbol*] [*Library of Congress*] (LCLS)
**NcGCM**..... Cone Mills Corp., Greensboro, NC [*Library symbol*] [*Library of Congress*] (LCLS)
**NCGE**........ National Council for Geographic Education (EA)
**NCGE/J**.... Journal of Geography. National Council of Geographic Education [*A publication*]
**NC Gen Stat** ... General Statutes of North Carolina [*A publication*] (DLA)
**NCGEP**...... National Council on Graduate Education in Psychology
**NcGf**.......... Granite Falls Public Library, Granite Falls, NC [*Library symbol*] [*Library of Congress*] (LCLS)
**NcGG**......... Guilford College, Greensboro, NC [*Library symbol*] [*Library of Congress*] (LCLS)
**NCGG**........ National Committee for Geodesy and Geophysics (MCD)
**NcGGil**....... Gilbarco Corp. Library, Greensboro, NC [*Library symbol*] [*Library of Congress*] (LCLS)
**NcGGT**...... Guilford Technical Community College, Learning Resource Center, Greensboro, NC [*Library symbol*] [*Library of Congress*] (LCLS)
**NcGH**........ Moses H. Cone Memorial Hospital, Medical Library, Greensboro, NC [*Library symbol*] [*Library of Congress*] (LCLS)
**NCGH**....... Nippon Chugoku Gakkaiho [*Bulletin of the Sinological Society of Japan*] [*A publication*]
**NCGIC**...... National Cartographic and Geographic Information Center [*Geological Survey*] [*Reston, VA*] [*Database*]
**NCGIF**....... National Cherry Growers and Industries Foundation (EA)
**NCGIS**....... National Council of Guilds for Infant Survival (EA)
**NcGL**......... Lorillard Research Center, Greensboro, NC [*Library symbol*] [*Library of Congress*] (LCLS)
**NCGLC**..... National Caucus of Gay and Lesbian Counselors (EA)
**NCGMCTC** ... National Chevy/GMC Truckin' Club [*Defunct*] (EA)
**NcGo**.......... Wayne County Public Library, Goldsboro, NC [*Library symbol*] [*Library of Congress*] (LCLS)
**NcGoCH**.... Cherry Hospital, Learning Resource Center, Goldsboro, NC [*Library symbol*] [*Library of Congress*] (LCLS)
**NcGoO**....... O'Berry Center, Professional Library, Goldsboro, NC [*Library symbol*] [*Library of Congress*] (LCLS)
**NcGoW**...... Wayne Community College, Goldsboro, NC [*Library symbol*] [*Library of Congress*] (LCLS)
**NcGPS**....... Greensboro Public Schools, Greensboro, NC [*Library symbol*] [*Library of Congress*] (LCLS)
**NCGR**........ National Clonal Germplasm Repository [*Corvallis, OR*] [*Agricultural Research Service*] [*Department of Agriculture*] (GRD)
**NCGR**........ National Council on Gene Resources (EA)
**NCGR**........ National Council for GeoCosmic Research (EA)
**NcGrE**........ East Carolina University, Greenville, NC [*Library symbol*] [*Library of Congress*] (LCLS)
**NcGrE-H**... East Carolina University, Health Sciences Library, Greenville, NC [*Library symbol*] [*Library of Congress*] (LCLS)
**NcGrP**........ Pitt Technical Institute, Greenville, NC [*Library symbol*] [*Library of Congress*] (LCLS)
**NcGrS**........ Sheppard Memorial Library, Greenville, NC [*Library symbol*] [*Library of Congress*] (LCLS)
**NCGS**........ Fra Ny-Carlsberg Glyptoteks Sammlingen [*A publication*]
**NCGS**........ National Cooperative Gallstone Study
**NCGS**........ New Century Gilders Society [*A union*] [*British*]
**NCGS B**..... North Carolina Geological Survey. Bulletin [*A publication*]
**NCGSTDS** ... National Coalition of Gay Sexually Transmitted Disease Services [*Defunct*] (EA)
**ncgt---**......... Guatemala [*MARC geographic area code*] [*Library of Congress*] (LCCP)
**NcGU**......... University of North Carolina at Greensboro, Greensboro, NC [*Library symbol*] [*Library of Congress*] (LCLS)
**NcGWE**..... Western Electric Co., Legal Library, Greensboro, NC [*Library symbol*] [*Library of Congress*] (LCLS)
**NCGWR**.... National Center for Ground Water Research [*Stillwater, OK*] [*Environmental Protection Agency*] (GRD)
**NCH**.......... Hamilton & Kirkland Colleges, Clinton, NY [*Library symbol*] [*Library of Congress*] (LCLS)
**NCH**.......... Nachingwea [*Tanzania*] [*Airport symbol*] (OAG)
**NCH**.......... National Center on Educational Media and Materials for the Handicapped, Columbus, OH [*OCLC symbol*] [*Inactive*] (OCLC)
**NCH**.......... National Center for Homeopathy (EA)
**NCH**.......... National Children's Home [*British*]
**NCH**.......... National Clearinghouse [*Public Health Service*]
**NCH**.......... National Coalition for the Homeless (EA)
**NCH**.......... National Cocaine Hotline
**NCH**.......... National Committee on Housing
**NCH**.......... National Council on the Humanities [*Washington, DC*]
**NCH**.......... NCH Corp. [*Formerly, National Chemsearch Corp.*] [*NYSE symbol*] (SPSG)
**NCH**.......... Network Connection Handler
**n/ch**........... Nosso Cheque [*Our Check*] [*Business term*] [*Portuguese*]
**NCH**.......... Notched
**NCha**.......... Chatham Public Library, Chatham, NY [*Library symbol*] [*Library of Congress*] (LCLS)
**NcHa**......... Hamlet Public Library, Hamlet, NC [*Library symbol*] [*Library of Congress*] (LCLS)
**NCHA**........ National Campers and Hikers Association (EA)
**NCHA**........ National Capital Housing Authority
**NCHA**........ National Crossbow Hunters Association (EA)
**NCHA**........ National Cutting Horse Association (EA)
**NcHal**........ Halifax County Library, Halifax, NC [*Library symbol*] [*Library of Congress*] (LCLS)
**NChap**....... Chappaqua Library, Chappaqua, NY [*Library symbol*] [*Library of Congress*] (LCLS)
**NcHaR**....... Richmond Technical Institute, Hamlet, NC [*Library symbol*] [*Library of Congress*] (LCLS)
**NcHav**........ Havelock-Craven County Public Library, Havelock, NC [*Library symbol*] [*Library of Congress*] (LCLS)
**NcHay**........ Moss Memorial Library, Hayesville, NC [*Library symbol*] [*Library of Congress*] (LCLS)
**NCHC**........ National Clogging and Hoedown Council (EA)
**NCHC**........ National Collegiate Honors Council (EA)
**NCHC**........ National Council of Health Centers [*Formerly, NCHCS*] [*Later, AHCA*] (EA)
**NCHCA**..... National Commission for Health Certifying Agencies (EA)
**NCHCS**..... National Council of Health Care Services (EA)
**NCHCT**..... National Center for Health Care Technology [*US Congress agency*]
**NCHDI**...... National Center for Hearing Dog Information [*Later, HDRC*] (EA)
**NcHe**.......... H. Leslie Perry Memorial Library, Henderson, NC [*Library symbol*] [*Library of Congress*] (LCLS)
**NCHE**........ National Center for Health Education (EA)
**NCHE**........ National Center for Health Education. Newsletter [*A publication*]
**NCHE**........ National Committee on Household Employment
**NCheH**...... Saint Joseph Intercommunity Hospital, Cheektowaga, NY [*Library symbol*] [*Library of Congress*] (LCLS)
**NCHELP**... National Council of Higher Education Loan Programs (EA)
**NCHEML**... National Chemical Laboratory (MCD)
**NCHEMS**... National Center for Higher Education Management Systems (EA)
**NCHER**..... National Center for Homecare Education and Research (EA)
**NCHES**..... National Child Health and Education Study [*University of Bristol*] [*British*]
**NcHeV**....... Vance County Technical Institute, Henderson, NC [*Library symbol*] [*Library of Congress*] (LCLS)
**NcHf**.......... Perquimans County Library, Hertford, NC [*Library symbol*] [*Library of Congress*] (LCLS)
**NCHFCI**.... National Committee to Honor the Fourteenth Centennial of Islam (EA)
**NCHGD**.... National Clearinghouse for Human Genetic Diseases [*Later, NCEMCH*] [*Public Health Service*] [*Information service or system*] (IID)
**NCHHA**.... National Council of Homemakers and Home Health Aides
**NCHHHSO** ... National Coalition of Hispanic Health and Human Services Organizations (EA)
**NCHI**......... National Council of the Housing Industry (EA)
**NcHil**......... Confederate Memorial Library, Hillsboro, NC [*Library symbol*] [*Library of Congress*] (LCLS)
**N Chip**....... [*N.*] Chipman's Vermont Reports [*1789-91*] [*A publication*] (DLA)
**N Chipm**.... [*N.*] Chipman's Vermont Reports [*1789-91*] [*A publication*] (DLA)
**N Chip (VT)** ... [*N.*] Chipman's Vermont Reports [*1789-91*] [*A publication*] (DLA)
**NC His As** ... State Literary and Historical Association of North Carolina. Proceedings [*A publication*]
**NC His R**... North Carolina Historical Review [*A publication*]
**NC Hist R**... North Carolina Historical Review [*A publication*]
**NC Hist Rev** ... North Carolina Historical Review [*A publication*]
**NCHLA**..... National Committee for a Human Life Amendment (EA)
**NCHLRR**.. National Commission on Human Life, Reproduction, and Rhythm (EA)
**NCHLS**..... National Council on Health Laboratory Services (EA)
**NCHM**...... National Center for Housing Management (EA)
**NCHMHHSO** ... National Coalition of Hispanic Mental Health and Human Services Organizations [*Later, NCHHHSO*]
**NCHMI**..... National Centers for Health and Medical Information, Inc. [*Research center*] (RCD)
**NCHMT**.... National Capital Historical Museum of Transportation (EA)
**NChn**......... Numismatic Chronicle [*London*] [*A publication*]
**ncho---**........ Honduras [*MARC geographic area code*] [*Library of Congress*] (LCCP)
**NCHO**....... National Chicano Health Organization (EA)

**NcHp** ......... High Point Public Library, High Point, NC [*Library symbol*] [*Library of Congress*] (LCLS)
**NCHP** ........ National Corporation for Housing Partnerships
**NCHP** ........ Nickel-Chromium Honeycomb Panel
**NCHPA** ..... National Center for Health Promotion and Aging (EA)
**NcHpC** ....... High Point College, High Point, NC [*Library symbol*] [*Library of Congress*] (LCLS)
**NCHPD** ..... National Council on Health Planning and Development
**N Ch R** ....... [*H.*] Finch's Chancery Reports [*1673-81*] [*England*] [*A publication*] (DLA)
**NCHR** ........ National Coalition for Haitian Refugees (EA)
**N Ch R** ....... Nelson's English Chancery Reports [*A publication*] (DLA)
**NCHR** ........ North Carolina Historical Review [*A publication*]
**NChr** .......... Numismatic Chronicle [*London*] [*A publication*]
**N Chret Isr** ... Nouvelles Chretiennes d'Israel [*A publication*]
**NChrIsr** ..... Nouvelles Chretiennes d'Israel [*Jerusalem*] [*A publication*]
**NCHRP** ..... National Cooperative Highway Research Program
**NCHRP Prog Rep** ... National Cooperative Highway Research Program. Report [*A publication*]
**NCHRP Rep** ... National Cooperative Highway Research Program. Report [*A publication*]
**NCHRP Synthesis Highw Prac** ... National Cooperative Highway Research Program. Synthesis of Highway Practice [*A publication*]
**NCHRTM** ... National Clearing House of Rehabilitation Training Materials [*Oklahoma State University*] [*Information service or system*] (IID)
**NcHs** .......... Hudson Library, Highlands, NC [*Library symbol*] [*Library of Congress*] (LCLS)
**NCHS** ........ National Center for Health Statistics [*Public Health Service*] [*Hyattsville, MD*] [*Originator and database*]
**NCHS** ........ National Committee on Homemaker Service [*Superseded by NHC*] (EA)
**NCHS (Natl Cent Health Stat) Adv Data** ... NCHS (National Center for Health Statistics) Advance Data [*A publication*]
**NCHSR** ..... National Center for Health Services Research and Health Care Technology Assessment [*Rockville, MD*] [*Public Health Service*] (GRD)
**NCHSRD** .. National Center for Health Services Research and Development [*Later, NCHSR*] [*HEW*]
**NCHSR & D** ... National Center for Health Services Research and Development [*Later, NCHSR*] [*HEW*]
**NcHu** ......... Hudson Public Library, Hudson, NC [*Library symbol*] [*Library of Congress*] (LCLS)
**N Church R** ... New Church Review [*A publication*]
**NcHv** .......... Henderson County Public Library, Hendersonville, NC [*Library symbol*] [*Library of Congress*] (LCLS)
**NcHvH** ...... Blue Ridge Technical Institute, Hendersonville, NC [*Library symbol*] [*Library of Congress*] (LCLS)
**NcHvME** ... Mother Earth News, Hendersonville, NC [*Library symbol*] [*Library of Congress*] (LCLS)
**NCHVRFE** ... National College for Heating, Ventilating, Refrigeration, and Fan Engineering (MCD)
**NCHW** ...... National Council of Hispanic Women (EA)
**NCHWPPTA** ... National Conference of Health, Welfare, and Pension Plans, Trustees and Administrators [*Later, International Foundation of Employee Benefit Plans*] (EA)
**NcHy** ......... Elbert Ivey Memorial Library, Hickory, NC [*Library symbol*] [*Library of Congress*] (LCLS)
**NcHyC** ....... Catawba Valley Technical Institute, Hickory, NC [*Library symbol*] [*Library of Congress*] (LCLS)
**NcHyL** ....... Lenoir Rhyne College, Hickory, NC [*Library symbol*] [*Library of Congress*] (LCLS)
**NcHyS** ....... Siecor Corp., Technical Information Center, Hickory, NC [*Library symbol*] [*Library of Congress*] (LCLS)
**NCi** ............ Central Islip Public Library, Central Islip, NY [*Library symbol*] [*Library of Congress*] (LCLS)
**nCi** ............. Nanocurie
**NCI** ........... Naphthalene Creosote, Iodoform [*Powder for lice*]
**NCI** ........... National Cancer Institute [*National Institutes of Health*] [*Department of Health and Human Services*] [*Database producer*] [*Bethesda, MD*]
**NCI** ........... National Captioning Institute (EA)
**NCI** ........... National Cheese Institute (EA)
**NCI** ........... National Computer Index [*National Computing Centre Ltd.*] [*Great Britain*] [*Information service or system*] (CRD)
**NCI** ........... National Computer Institute (MCD)
**NCI** ........... National Council for Inordinacy (EA)
**NCI** ........... National Critics Institute (EA)
**NCI** ........... Natural Casing Institute [*Later, International Natural Sausage Casing Institute*] (EA)
**NCI** ........... Naval Cost Inspector
**NCI** ........... Navigation Control Indicator (MCD)
**NCI** ........... Necocli [*Colombia*] [*Airport symbol*] (OAG)
**NCI** ........... Negative Chemical Ionization [*Spectrometry*]
**NCI** ........... Network Communications International [*Telecommunications service*] (TSSD)
**NCI** ........... Neutral Countries Intelligence [*of Ministry of Economic Warfare*] [*British*] [*World War II*]
**NCI** ........... New Creation Institute (EA)
**NCI** ........... No Common Interest
**NCI** ........... No-Cost Item (AAG)
**NCI** ........... No Currency Involved
**NCI** ........... Nomenclature Control Index (MCD)
**NCI** ........... Nominal Correction I [*Phasing maneuver*] (MCD)
**NCI** ........... Noncoded Information [*Data processing*] (IBMDP)
**NCI** ........... North Conway Institute (EA)
**NCI** ........... Notice of Change Inception (MCD)
**NCI** ........... Notice of Change Incorporation (MCD)
**NCI** ........... Notiziario Culturale Italiano [*A publication*]
**NCI** ........... Nouvelles Chretiennes d'Israel [*Jerusalem*] [*A publication*]
**NCI** ........... Nuclear Capability Inspection (CINC)
**NCI** ........... Nuclear Contour Index [*Cytology*]
**NCI** ........... Nuclear Control Institute (EA)
**NCI** ........... Nurse Competency Inventory
**NCI** ........... Nursing Citation Index
**NCI** ........... Office of New Concepts and Initiatives [*Air Force*] (TEL)
**NCI** ........... Southwest New Jersey Consortium for Health Information Service, Voorhees, NJ [*OCLC symbol*] (OCLC)
**NCIA** ......... National Cavity Installation Association [*British*]
**NCIA** ......... National Center on Institutions and Alternatives (EA)
**NCIA** ......... National Crop Insurance Association [*Shawnee Mission, KS*] (EA)
**NCIAA** ...... Nuovo Cimento. Sezione A [*A publication*]
**NCIAC** ....... National Construction Industry Arbitration Committee (EA)
**NCIAED** .... National Center for Information and Advice on Educational Disadvantage
**NCIB** ......... National Charities Information Bureau (EA)
**NCIB** ......... National Collection of Industrial Bacteria [*British*]
**NCIBA** ....... Nuovo Cimento. Sezione B [*A publication*]
**NCIC** ......... National Cancer Institute of Canada
**NCIC** ......... National Career Information Center [*Defunct*] (EA)
**NCIC** ......... National Cartographic Information Center [*United States Geological Survey*] [*Reston, VA*]
**NCIC** ......... National Commission on the Indian Canadian
**NCIC** ......... National Congress of Italian Canadians
**NCIC** ......... National Construction Industry Council (EA)
**NCIC** ......... National Crime Information Center [*FBI*] [*Washington, DC*]
**NCIC** ......... National Crop Insurance Council [*Inactive*] (EA)
**NCIC** ......... Network Communications Interface Common (MCD)
**NCIC** ......... Non-Circumcision Information Center (EA)
**NCIC** ......... Northwest Coastal Information Center [*Marine science*] (MSC)
**NCICA** ....... National Counter Intelligence Corps Association (EA)
**NCIC Ops** ... North Carolina Industrial Commission Advance Sheets [*A publication*] (DLA)
**NCICU** ...... National Council of Independent Colleges and Universities [*Later, NAICU*]
**NCID** ......... National Council for Industrial Defense (EA)
**NCIDQ** ...... National Council for Interior Design Qualification (EA)
**NCIES** ....... National Center for the Improvement of Educational Systems [*Office of Education*]
**NCIES** ....... National Committee for International Education through Satellites (EA)
**NCIESD** .... National Conference on International Economic and Social Development [*Later, IDC*]
**NCIH** ......... National Conference on Industrial Hydraulics
**NCIH** ......... National Council for International Health (EA)
**NCIHC** ...... National Council for Interior Horticultural Certification (EA)
**NCII** .......... National Council for Industrial Innovation (EA)
**NCIJC** ....... National Council of Independent Junior Colleges [*Defunct*]
**NCIL** .......... National Council on Independent Living (EA)
**NCIMA** ..... National Cancer Institute. Monographs [*United States*] [*A publication*]
**NCIMA** ..... National Cellulose Insulation Manufacturers Association
**NCIMC** ..... National Council of Industrial Management Clubs [*Later, IMC*] (EA)
**NCI Monogr** ... NCI [*National Cancer Institute*] Monographs [*US*] [*A publication*]
**NCIMS** ...... National Conference on Interstate Milk Shipments
**NCIMS** ...... Negative Chemical Ionization Mass Spectra
**NCIMS** ...... Numerical Control Information Management System (MCD)
**NCIN** ......... National Credit Information Network
**NCIN** ......... North Carolina Information Network [*Library network*]
**NCINAS** .... National Council of Industrial Naval Air Stations (EA)
**NCINASEO** ... National Council of Industrial Naval Air Stations Employee Organizations [*Formerly, NCNASEO*] (EA)
**NCIO** ......... National Congress of Inventors Organizations (EA)
**NCIO** ......... National Council on Indian Opportunity (EA)
**NCIP** .......... National Council for Industrial Peace [*Defunct*] (EA)
**NCIP** .......... North American Collections Inventory Project [*Established 1982*] [*Library science*]
**NCIPA** ....... National Committee for Independent Political Action (EA)
**NCIPLA** .... National Council of Intellectual Property Law Associations (EA)
**NCIR** ......... National Center for Immigrants' Rights [*Later, NILC*] (EA)
**NCIR** ......... National Center for Initiative Review (EA)
**NCIR** ......... National Conference on Industrial Research
**NCirc** ......... Numismatic Circular [*A publication*]
**NCIRF** ....... National Center for Initiative Review Foundation (EA)
**NCIRLS** .... North Central Regional Library System [*Library network*]
**NCIS** .......... National Chemical Information System (DIT)
**NCIS** .......... National Controls, Incorporated [*NASDAQ symbol*] (NQ)

**NCIS** ........ National Credit Information Service [*TRW, Inc.*] [*Long Beach, CA*] [*Credit-information databank*]
**NCIS** ........ National Crop Insurance Services (EA)
**NCIS** ........ Navy Cost Information System
**NCIS** ........ Nuclear Criticality Information System [*Lawrence Livermore National Laboratory*] [*Information service or system*] (IID)
**NCISC** ....... Naval Counterintelligence Support Center
**NCISD** ....... National Coalition on Immune System Disorders (EA)
**NCISE** ....... National Center for Improving Science Education (EA)
**NCiSH** ....... Central Islip State Hospital, Central Islip, NY [*Library symbol*] [*Library of Congress*] (LCLS)
**NCISS** ....... National Council of Investigation and Security Services (EA)
**NCIT** ........ National Committee for Insurance Taxation (EA)
**NCIT** ........ National Council of Independent Truckers [*Defunct*] (EA)
**NCITD** ...... National Council on International Trade Documentation [*In association name: NCITD - The International Trade Facilitation Council*] (EA)
**NCITR** ....... National Center for Intermedia Transport Research [*Los Angeles, CA*] (GRD)
**NCIU** ........ Network Common Interference Unit (MCD)
**NCIV** ........ National Council for International Visitors (EA)
**NCJ** .......... Johnson C. Smith University, James B. Duke Memorial Library, Charlotte, NC [*OCLC symbol*] (OCLC)
**NCJA** ........ National Criminal Justice Association (EA)
**NcJa** ......... Onslow County Public Library, Jacksonville, NC [*Library symbol*] [*Library of Congress*] (LCLS)
**NcJaC** ........ Coastal Carolina Community College, Jacksonville, NC [*Library symbol*] [*Library of Congress*] (LCLS)
**NcJac** ........ Northampton County Memorial Library, Jackson, NC [*Library symbol*] [*Library of Congress*] (LCLS)
**NcJaMC** .... United States Marine Corps, Marine Corps Air Station, Special Services for Station Library, New River Base, Jacksonville, NC [*Library symbol*] [*Library of Congress*] (LCLS)
**NCJAR** ...... National Council for Japanese American Redress [*Defunct*] (EA)
**NCJAVM** ... National Council on Jewish Audio-Visual Materials (EA)
**NCJC** ........ National Conference of Judicial Councils [*Defunct*] (EA)
**NCJCC** ...... National Council of Jewish Correctional Chaplains [*Later, AJCCA*] (EA)
**NCJCJ** ....... National Council of Juvenile Court Judges [*Later, NCJFCJ*] (EA)
**NCJCS** ...... National Conference of Jewish Communal Service [*Later, CJCS*] (EA)
**NCJD** ........ National Coalition for a Just Draft (EA)
**NCJD** ........ National Congress of Jewish Deaf (EA)
**NCJE** ........ National Council for Jewish Education [*Later, CJE*] (EA)
**NCJF** ........ National Center for Jewish Film (EA)
**NCJFCJ** .... National Council of Juvenile and Family Court Judges (EA)
**NcJG** ......... Guilford Technical Institute, Jamestown, NC [*Library symbol*] [*Library of Congress*] (LCLS)
**NCJ Int'l L and Com Reg** ... North Carolina Journal of International Law and Commercial Regulation
**NCJISN** .... National Council of Jewish Invalids Survivors of Nazism [*Later, CHSD*] (EA)
**NCJISS** ..... National Criminal Justice Information and Statistics Service
**NCJJ** ......... National Center for Jobs and Justice (EA)
**NCJJ** ......... National Center for Juvenile Justice (EA)
**NCJ of L** .... North Carolina Journal of Law [*A publication*] (DLA)
**NCJMS** ..... National Center for Job Market Studies [*Commercial firm*] [*Washington, DC*] (EA)
**NcJo** .......... Jonesville-Arlington Public Library, Jonesville, NC [*Library symbol*] [*Library of Congress*] (LCLS)
**NCJO** ........ National Council of Junior Outdoorsmen (EA)
**NCJPS** ....... National Center for Jewish Policy Studies
**NCJR** ........ National Coalition for Jail Reform (EA)
**NCJRS** ...... National Criminal Justice Reference Service [*Department of Justice*] [*Information service or system*]
**NCJSB** ...... National Commission on Jobs and Small Business [*Defunct*] (EA)
**NCJSC** ...... National Criminal Justice Statistics Center
**NCJT** ........ Nordic Committee of Journalism Teachers (EA)
**NCJW** ....... National Council of Jewish Women (EA)
**NCK** .......... Camden County College, Voorhees, NJ [*OCLC symbol*] (OCLC)
**NcK** ........... Kinston-Lenoir County Public Library, Kinston, NC [*Library symbol*] [*Library of Congress*] (LCLS)
**NCK** .......... Nagycenk [*Hungary*] [*Geomagnetic observatory code*]
**NCK** .......... Neck
**NCK** .......... Nickelodeon Industries Corp. [*Vancouver Stock Exchange symbol*]
**NCK** .......... Norman, Craig & Kummel [*Advertising agency*]
**NcKa** ......... Cannon Memorial YMCA Public Library, Kannapolis, NC [*Library symbol*] [*Library of Congress*] (LCLS)
**NcKbMR** ... North Carolina Marine Resources Center, Fort Fisher, Kure Beach, NC [*Library symbol*] [*Library of Congress*] (LCLS)
**NcKC** ........ Kinston-Lenoir County Public Library, Caswell Center Library, Kinston, NC [*Library symbol*] [*Library of Congress*] (LCLS)
**NcKeD** ...... Duplin County, Dorothy Wightman Library, Kenansville, NC [*Library symbol*] [*Library of Congress*] (LCLS)
**NcKeS** ....... James Sprunt Technical Institute, Kenansville, NC [*Library symbol*] [*Library of Congress*] (LCLS)
**NcKg** ......... King Public Library, King, NC [*Library symbol*] [*Library of Congress*] (LCLS)
**NcKiK** ....... Kittrell College, Kittrell, NC [*Library symbol*] [*Library of Congress*] (LCLS)
**NcKL** ........ Lenoir Community College, Kinston, NC [*Library symbol*] [*Library of Congress*] (LCLS)
**NCKL** ........ North Central Kansas Libraries System [*Library network*]
**NcKm** ........ Jacob S. Mauney Memorial Library, Kings Mountain, NC [*Library symbol*] [*Library of Congress*] (LCLS)
**NCKWM** ... National Committee for the Korean War Memorial [*Later, KWVM*] (EA)
**NCL** .......... Camden County Library, Voorhees, NJ [*OCLC symbol*] (OCLC)
**NCL** .......... National Carriers Limited [*British*] (DCTA)
**NCL** .......... National Central Library [*United Kingdom*]
**NCL** .......... National Character Laboratory (EA)
**NCL** .......... National Chemical Laboratory
**NCL** .......... National Civic League (EA)
**NCL** .......... National Coalition for Literacy (EA)
**NCL** .......... National Consumers League (EA)
**NCL** .......... National Council of Labour [*British*] (DCTA)
**NCL** .......... Navy Calibration Laboratory
**NCL** .......... Navy Code Logistic [*Plan*]
**NCL** .......... Network Control Language
**NCL** .......... Neuronal Ceroid Lipofuscinosis [*Medicine*]
**NCL** .......... New Caledonia [*ANSI three-letter standard code*] (CNC)
**NCL** .......... Newcastle [*England*] [*Airport symbol*] (OAG)
**NCL** .......... Nichols [*S. E.*], Inc. [*AMEX symbol*] (SPSG)
**NCL** .......... Node Compatibility List [*Telecommunications*] (TEL)
**NCL** .......... Noise Control Laboratory [*Pennsylvania State University*] [*Research center*] (RCD)
**NCL** .......... Norfolk, VA [*Location identifier*] [*FAA*] (FAAL)
**NCL** .......... North Carolina Law Review [*A publication*]
**NCL** .......... Norwegian Caribbean Lines
**NCL** .......... Nossos Classicos [*A publication*]
**NCL** .......... Notes on Contemporary Literature [*A publication*]
**NCL** .......... Numerically Controlled Lathe
**NcL** ........... Scotland County Memorial Library, Laurinburg, NC [*Library symbol*] [*Library of Congress*] (LCLS)
**NCLA** ........ National C-Lark Association (EA)
**NCLA** ........ National Council of Local Administrators of Vocational Education and Practical Arts (EA)
**NCLAN** ..... National Crop Loss Assessment Network
**NC Law R** .. North Carolina Law Review [*A publication*]
**NC Law Repos** ... North Carolina Law Repository [*A publication*] (DLA)
**NC Law Repository** ... North Carolina Law Repository (Reprint) [*A publication*] (DLA)
**NCLB** ........ North Central Laboratories, Inc. [*NASDAQ symbol*] (NQ)
**NCLC** ........ National Catholic Liturgical Conference (EA)
**NCLC** ........ National Caucus of Labor Committees
**NCLC** ........ National Chamber Litigation Center (EA)
**NCLC** ........ National Child Labor Committee (EA)
**NCLC** ........ National Consumer Law Center (EA)
**NCLC** ........ National Council of Labour Colleges
**NCLC** ........ National Council on Legal Clinics [*Later, CLEPR*]
**NCLC** ........ Nineteenth Century Literary Criticism [*A publication*]
**NCLC** ........ Noncombatant Labour Corps [*British*]
**NCLCH** ..... National Civil Liberties Clearing House [*Defunct*] (EA)
**NCLCI** ...... National Christian Leadership Conference for Israel (EA)
**NCLD** ........ National Center for Law and the Deaf (EA)
**NCLD** ........ National Center for Learning Disabilities (EA)
**NCLD** ........ Williamsport District Library Center [*Library network*]
**NCLE** ........ National Contact Lens Examiners (EA)
**NC League Nurs News** ... NC [*North Carolina*] League for Nursing News [*A publication*]
**NcLeC** ........ Caldwell County Public Library, Lenoir, NC [*Library symbol*] [*Library of Congress*] (LCLS)
**NcLeCT** ..... Caldwell Community College and Technical Institute, Lenoir, NC [*Library symbol*] [*Library of Congress*] (LCLS)
**NCLEHA** .. National Conference of Local Environmental Health Administrators (EA)
**NCLER** ...... National Clearinghouse on Licensure, Enforcement, and Regulation (EA)
**NCLEX** ...... National Council Licensure Examination
**NCLEX-RN** ... National Council Licensure Examination for Registered Nurses
**NCLF** ........ National Coalition to Legalize Freedom (EA)
**NCLG** ........ National Committee for Latin and Greek (EA)
**NCLG** ........ National Conference of Lieutenant Governors (EA)
**NCLH** ........ National Center for Law and the Handicapped [*Defunct*] (EA)
**NCLHA** ..... National Conference of Law Historians of America (EA)
**NCLI** ......... National City Lines, Incorporated [*NASDAQ symbol*] (NQ)
**NCLI** ......... National Committee for Labor Israel [*Later, NCLIIHC*] (EA)
**NC Lib** ...... North Carolina Libraries [*A publication*]
**NCLIIHC** .. National Committee for Labor Israel-Israel Histadrut Campaign (EA)
**NcLil** ......... Harnett County Public Library, Lillington, NC [*Library symbol*] [*Library of Congress*] (LCLS)

**NcLiL**......... Lincoln County Memorial Library, Lincolnton, NC [*Library symbol*] [*Library of Congress*] (LCLS)
**NClinc**........ Clinton Corners Reading Center, Clinton Corners, NY [*Library symbol*] [*Library of Congress*] (LCLS)
**NClio**.......... La Nouvelle Clio [*Brussels*] [*A publication*]
**NCLIS** ....... National Commission on Libraries and Information Science [*Washington, DC*]
**NCLIS** ....... National Council for Languages and International Studies (EA)
**NcLit**.......... Littleton Public Library, Littleton, NC [*Library symbol*] [*Library of Congress*] (LCLS)
**NCLJ**.......... North Carolina Law Journal [*A publication*] (DLA)
**NcLjUM**.... United Methodist Church, Commission on Archives and History, Lake Junaluska, NC [*Library symbol*] [*Library of Congress*] (LCLS)
**NcLk**.......... Rockingham County Library, Leakesville, NC [*Library symbol*] [*Library of Congress*] (LCLS)
**NCLLF**...... National Civil Liberties Legal Foundation [*Inactive*] (EA)
**NcLo**.......... Franklin County Library, Louisburg, NC [*Library symbol*] [*Library of Congress*] (LCLS)
**NcLoC**........ Louisburg College, Louisburg, NC [*Library symbol*] [*Library of Congress*] (LCLS)
**NCL Occ Newsl** ... National Central Library. Occasional Newsletter [*A publication*]
**NCLP**......... National Conference on Law and Poverty
**NCLP**......... Numerically Controlled Line Plotter
**NCLPWA** ... National Council of Local Public Welfare Administrators (EA)
**NCLR** ........ National Center for Legislative Research (EA)
**NCLR** ........ National Coalition for Land Reform (EA)
**NCLR** ........ National Council of La Raza (EA)
**NCLR** ........ National Council for Labor Reform (EA)
**NCLR** ........ North Carolina Law Review [*A publication*]
**NCL Rep**.... North Carolina Law Repository [*A publication*] (DLA)
**NCL Reps**.. North Carolina Law Repository (Reprint) [*A publication*] (DLA)
**NC L Rev**... North Carolina Law Review [*A publication*]
**NCLRSMQ** ... National Campaign for Land Rights and Self-Management in Queensland [*Australia*]
**NCLS**......... National Clearinghouse for Legal Services [*Legal Services Corp.*] [*Information service or system*] (IID)
**NCLS**......... National Committee for Liberation of Slovakia (EA)
**NCLS**......... National Conference of Lawyers and Scientists [*Joint project of the American Association for the Advancement of Science and the American Bar Association*]
**NCLS**......... North Country Library System [*Library network*]
**NcLS**.......... Saint Andrews Presbyterian College, Laurinburg, NC [*Library symbol*] [*Library of Congress*] (LCLS)
**NCL & SW** ... National Conference of Lawyers and Social Workers
**NCLT**......... Night Carrier Landing Trainer [*Navy*]
**NCLTA**...... National Cigar Leaf Tobacco Association (EA)
**NcLu**.......... Robeson County Public Library, Lumberton, NC [*Library symbol*] [*Library of Congress*] (LCLS)
**NcLuH**....... Southeastern General Hospital, Medical Library, Lumberton, NC [*Library symbol*] [*Library of Congress*] (LCLS)
**NcLuR** ....... Robeson Technical Institute, Lumbarton, NC [*Library symbol*] [*Library of Congress*] (LCLS)
**NcLxD**....... Davidson County Public Library, Lexington, NC [*Library symbol*] [*Library of Congress*] (LCLS)
**NcLxDC** .... Davidson County Community College, Lexington, NC [*Library symbol*] [*Library of Congress*] (LCLS)
**NCm**........... Center Moriches Free Public Library, Center Moriches, NY [*Library symbol*] [*Library of Congress*] (LCLS)
**NCM**.......... Court Martial Reports, Navy Cases [*A publication*] (DLA)
**NCM**.......... Mars Hill College, Mars Hill, NC [*OCLC symbol*] (OCLC)
**NCM**.......... National Committee on Mathematics [*Australian Academy of Science*]
**NCM**.......... National Commuter Airlines [*Miami, FL*] [*FAA designator*] (FAAC)
**NCM**.......... National Congress for Men (EA)
**NCM**.......... National Contract Management Journal [*A publication*]
**NCM**.......... National Cursillo Movement (EA)
**NCM**.......... Navy Commendation Medal
**NCM**.......... Navy Correspondence Manual
**NCM**.......... Nederlandsche Creditverzekring Maatschappij [*Export credit agency*] [*Netherlands*]
**NCM**.......... Net Control Master (MCD)
**NCM**.......... Network Control Module
**NCM**.......... Nicaraguan Campaign Medal
**NCM**.......... Nitrocellulose Membrane
**NCM**.......... Noise Canceling Microphone
**NCM**.......... Noncorrosive Metal
**NCM**.......... Noncrew Member
**NCM**.......... Nordic Council on Medicines [*See also NLN*] (EAIO)
**NCM**.......... Nordic Council of Ministers (EAIO)
**NCM**.......... Normal Human Colon Mucosal [*Cells*]
**NCM**.......... North Carolina Motor Carriers Association [*STAC*]
**NCM**.......... Northern Conservatory of Music [*Maine*]
**NCM**.......... Numerical Controlled Machine
**NCM**.......... Nuveen California Municipal Income [*NYSE symbol*] (SPSG)
**NCMA**....... National Campus Ministry Association (EA)
**NCMA**....... National Catalog Managers Association (EA)
**NCMA**....... National Ceramic Manufacturers Association
**NCMA**....... National Concrete Masonry Association (EA)
**NCMA**....... National Contract Management Association (EA)
**NCMA**....... National Council of Millinery Associations (EA)
**NCMA**....... National Council of Moving Associations (EA)
**NCMA**....... Naval Civilian Manager's Association (EA)
**NCMA**....... Newspaper Credit Managers' Association (EA)
**NcMad**....... Madison Public Library, Madison, NC [*Library symbol*] [*Library of Congress*] (LCLS)
**NCMAF** .... National Conference on Ministry to the Armed Forces (EA)
**NcMaM**..... McDowell Technical Institute, Marion, NC [*Library symbol*] [*Library of Congress*] (LCLS)
**NcMaMC**.. McDowell County Public Library, Marion, NC [*Library symbol*] [*Library of Congress*] (LCLS)
**NcMan**....... Dare County Library, Manteo, NC [*Library symbol*] [*Library of Congress*] (LCLS)
**NcManMR** ... North Carolina Marine Resources Center, Roanoke Island Resource Library, Manteo, NC [*Library symbol*] [*Library of Congress*] (LCLS)
**NcMarM** ... Madison County Public Library, Marshall, NC [*Library symbol*] [*Library of Congress*] (LCLS)
**NcMax**....... Gilbert Patterson Memorial Public Library, Maxton, NC [*Library symbol*] [*Library of Congress*] (LCLS)
**NCMB**....... Nordic Council for Marine Biology (EAIO)
**NCMBBJ**.. Novedades Cientificas. Contribuciones Ocasionales del Museo de Historia Natural La Salle [*Caracas*]. Serie Botanica [*A publication*]
**NCMC**....... N-Carboxymethylchitosan [*Biochemistry*]
**NCMC**....... National Capital Management Corp. [*NASDAQ symbol*] (NQ)
**NCMC**....... National Coalition for Marine Conservation (EA)
**NCMC**....... Natural Cell-Mediated Cytotoxicity [*Immunochemistry*]
**NCMC**....... NORAD Cheyenne Mountain Complex [*Military*] (AABC)
**NCMC**....... Nordic Council for Music Conservatories (EA)
**NcMcC** ...... Carteret Technical Institute, Morehead City, NC [*Library symbol*] [*Library of Congress*] (LCLS)
**NcMccH** .... McCain Hospital, Medical Library, McCain, NC [*Library symbol*] [*Library of Congress*] (LCLS)
**NcMccS**..... Sandhills Youth Center, McCain, NC [*Library symbol*] [*Library of Congress*] (LCLS)
**NCMCG**.... National Construction Machinery Credit Group [*Park Ridge, IL*] (EA)
**NCMD**....... National Center for Municipal Development (EA)
**NCMDA**.... National Coin Machine Distributors Association (EA)
**NCMDA**.... National Commission on Marijuana and Drug Abuse [*Presidential advisory committee, terminated 1973*]
**NCMDLRJO** ... National Council of Marriage and Divorce Law Reform and Justice Organizations (EA)
**NCME**....... National Center for Mediation Education (EA)
**NCME**....... National Council on Measurement in Education (EA)
**NCME**....... Network for Continuing Medical Education (EA)
**NCME**....... Northern Counties Motor & Engineering Co. Ltd. [*British*] (DCTA)
**NCME**....... Numerically Controlled Machine Equipment
**NCMEA** .... National Catholic Music Educators Association [*Later, NPM*] (EA)
**NCMEC** .... National Center for Missing and Exploited Children (EA)
**NC Med J** ... North Carolina Medical Journal [*A publication*]
**NCMESD** ... National Coalition for More Effective School Discipline (EA)
**NCMET** .... Nonclosed Shell Many Electron Theory [*Physics*]
**NcMf**......... Murfreesboro Public Library, Murfreesboro, NC [*Library symbol*] [*Library of Congress*] (LCLS)
**NCMF** ....... National Carvers Museum Foundation (EA)
**NCMF** ....... National Church Music Fellowship [*Defunct*]
**NcMfC**....... Chowan College, Murfreesboro, NC [*Library symbol*] [*Library of Congress*] (LCLS)
**NCMFST**.. National Committee for Motor Fleet Supervisor Training (EA)
**NcMG**........ Graham Evangelistic Association, Montreat, NC [*Library symbol*] [*Library of Congress*] (LCLS)
**NCMG**....... Mangaia [*Cook Islands*] [*ICAO location identifier*] (ICLI)
**NCMH** ...... National Committee on Maternal Health (EA)
**NCMH** ...... National Council for Monday Holidays
**NcMhC**...... Mars Hill College, Mars Hill, NC [*Library symbol*] [*Library of Congress*] (LCLS)
**NcMHi** ...... Historical Foundation of the Presbyterian and Reformed Churches, Montreat, NC [*Library symbol*] [*Library of Congress*] (LCLS)
**NCMHI**..... National Clearinghouse for Mental Health Information [*Public Health Service*] [*Rockville, MD*] [*Database*] [*HEW*]
**NCMI**........ National Coin Machine Institute (EA)
**NCMI**........ National Committee Against Mental Illness (EA)
**NCMI**........ National Council of Music Importers [*Later, NCMIE*]
**NCMIE**..... National Council of Music Importers and Exporters (EA)
**NC Miner Resour Sect Reg Geol Ser** ... North Carolina. Mineral Resources Section. Regional Geology Series [*A publication*]
**NcMiP**....... Pfciffcr College, Misenheimer, NC [*Library symbol*] [*Library of Congress*] (LCLS)
**NCMK**....... Mauke [*Cook Islands*] [*ICAO location identifier*] (ICLI)
**NCMLB**..... National Council of Mailing List Brokers [*Later, MLBPA*] (EA)
**NcMM**....... Montreat-Anderson College, Montreat, NC [*Library symbol*] [*Library of Congress*] (LCLS)

**NCmM**....... Museum Manor of Saint George, Center Moriches, NY [*Library symbol*] [*Library of Congress*] (LCLS)
**NCMN**....... Manuae [*Cook Islands*] [*ICAO location identifier*] (ICLI)
**NCMO**....... Navigational Aids/Communications Management Office [*Air Force*] (CET)
**NcMoBH**... Broughton Hospital, Staff Library, Morganton, NC [*Library symbol*] [*Library of Congress*] (LCLS)
**NcMoc**....... Davie County Public Library, Mocksville, NC [*Library symbol*] [*Library of Congress*] (LCLS)
**NcMoM**..... Morganton-Burke Library, Inc., Morganton, NC [*Library symbol*] [*Library of Congress*] (LCLS)
**NcMon**....... Union County Public Library, Monroe, NC [*Library symbol*] [*Library of Congress*] (LCLS)
**NcMoW**..... Western Piedmont Community College, Morganton, NC [*Library symbol*] [*Library of Congress*] (LCLS)
**NcMoWC**.. Western Carolina Center, Staff Library, Morganton, NC [*Library symbol*] [*Library of Congress*] (LCLS)
**NCMP**....... National Commission for Manpower Policy [*Department of Labor*]
**NCMP**....... National Commission on Materials Policy
**NCMPA**.... National Corrugated Metal Pipe Association [*Later, NCSPA*] (EA)
**NCMPR**.... National Council for Marketing and Public Relations (EA)
**NCMR**....... Matiaro [*Cook Islands*] [*ICAO location identifier*] (ICLI)
**NCMR**....... National Committee for Monetary Reform (EA)
**NCMR**....... Nonconforming Material Report
**NCMR**....... North Canterbury Mounted Rifles [*British military*] (DMA)
**NCMRED**... National Council on Marine Resources and Engineering Development [*Later, ICMSE*]
**NCMS**....... National Center for Manufacturing Sciences [*Research center*]
**NCMS**....... National Classification Management Society (EA)
**NCMS**....... National Council of Marine Sciences
**NCMT**....... Numerically Controlled Machine Tool
**NcMta**........ Mount Airy Public Library, Mount Airy, NC [*Library symbol*] [*Library of Congress*] (LCLS)
**NCMTA**.... National Council of Marine Trade Associations
**NcMtC**....... Mount Olive College, Mount Olive, NC [*Library symbol*] [*Library of Congress*] (LCLS)
**NCMTE**.... National Council on Medical Technology Education [*Defunct*]
**NCMTI**...... Noncoherent Moving Target Indicator (MCD)
**NcMu**......... Murphy Public Library, Murphy, NC [*Library symbol*] [*Library of Congress*] (LCLS)
**NcMuN**...... Nantahala Regional Library, Murphy, NC [*Library symbol*] [*Library of Congress*] (LCLS)
**NcMuT**...... Tri-County Technical Institute, Murphy, NC [*Library symbol*] [*Library of Congress*] (LCLS)
**NcMv**......... Mooresville Public Library, Mooresville, NC [*Library symbol*] [*Library of Congress*] (LCLS)
**NCMZAM**... Novedades Cientificas. Serie Zoologia [*A publication*]
**n-cn---**........ Canada [*MARC geographic area code*] [*Library of Congress*] (LCCP)
**NCN**........... National Christian Network [*Cable-television system*]
**NCN**........... National Computer Network Corp. [*Information service or system*] (IID)
**NCN**........... Navy Control Number (MCD)
**NCN**........... Netherlands American Trade [*A publication*]
**NCN**........... Network Control Node
**NCN**........... Nixdorf Communications Network [*Nixdorf*] [*Federal Republic of Germany*]
**NCN**........... Norcen Energy Resources Ltd. [*Toronto Stock Exchange symbol*] [*AMEX symbol*]
**NCNA**........ National Council on Noise Abatement (EA)
**NCNA**........ New China News Agency
**n-cn-ab**....... Alberta [*MARC geographic area code*] [*Library of Congress*] (LCCP)
**NCNASEO**... National Council of Naval Air Stations Employee Organizations [*Later, NCINASEO*] (EA)
**NCNB**........ National Center for Nonprofit Boards (EA)
**n-cn-bc**....... British Columbia [*MARC geographic area code*] [*Library of Congress*] (LCCP)
**NcNbC**....... Craven Technical Institute, New Bern, NC [*Library symbol*] [*Library of Congress*] (LCLS)
**NcNbCP**.... Craven-Pamlico-Carteret Regional Library, New Bern, NC [*Library symbol*] [*Library of Congress*] (LCLS)
**NCNC**........ National Captive Nations Committee (EA)
**NCNC**........ National Council of Nigeria and the Cameroons [*Political party*]
**NCNE**........ National Campaign for Nursery Education [*British*]
**NCNE**........ National Center for Neighborhood Enterprise (EA)
**NCNEVAW**... National Communications Network for the Elimination of Violence Against Women [*Absorbed by NCADV*] (EA)
**NcNew**....... Avery-Morrison Public Library, Newland, NC [*Library symbol*] [*Library of Congress*] (LCLS)
**NCNG**........ North Carolina Natural Gas Corp. [*NASDAQ symbol*] (NQ)
**NCNGD**..... Not Crushed or Not Ground
**NCNGO**.... National Committee of Non-Governmental Organisations [*Australia*]
**n-cnh--**........ Hudson Bay [*MARC geographic area code*] [*Library of Congress*] (LCCP)
**n-cnm--**....... Maritime Provinces [*MARC geographic area code*] [*Library of Congress*] (LCCP)
**n-cn-mb**...... Manitoba [*MARC geographic area code*] [*Library of Congress*] (LCCP)
**n-cn-nf**........ Newfoundland [*MARC geographic area code*] [*Library of Congress*] (LCCP)
**n-cn-nk**....... New Brunswick [*MARC geographic area code*] [*Library of Congress*] (LCCP)
**n-cn-ns**....... Nova Scotia [*MARC geographic area code*] [*Library of Congress*] (LCCP)
**n-cn-nt**........ Northwest Territories [*MARC geographic area code*] [*Library of Congress*] (LCCP)
**N/CNO**...... Navy/Chief of Naval Operations (AAG)
**n-cn-on**....... Ontario [*MARC geographic area code*] [*Library of Congress*] (LCCP)
**NCNP**........ National Child Nutrition Project (EA)
**n-cnp--**........ Prairie Provinces [*MARC geographic area code*] [*Library of Congress*] (LCCP)
**n-cn-pi**........ Prince Edward Island [*Canada*] [*MARC geographic area code*] [*Library of Congress*] (LCCP)
**NCNPSA**... National Conference of Non-Profit Shipping Associations (EA)
**ncnq---**........ Nicaragua [*MARC geographic area code*] [*Library of Congress*] (LCCP)
**n-cn-qu**....... Quebec [*MARC geographic area code*] [*Library of Congress*] (LCCP)
**NCNR**........ Greensboro News and Record [*A publication*]
**NCNR**........ National Center for Nursing Research [*Bethesda, MD*] [*Department of Health and Human Services*] (GRD)
**NCNS**........ Nassau [*Cook Islands*] [*ICAO location identifier*] (ICLI)
**NCNS**........ National Catholic News Service (EA)
**NCNS**........ North Central Name Society (EA)
**n-cn-sn**....... Saskatchewan [*MARC geographic area code*] [*Library of Congress*] (LCCP)
**NcNt**.......... Catawba County Library, Newton, NC [*Library symbol*] [*Library of Congress*] (LCLS)
**NCNTUCW**... National Commission on New Technological Uses of Copyrighted Works [*Terminated, 1978*] [*Library of Congress*]
**NCNW**....... National Congress of Neighborhood Women (EA)
**NCNW**....... National Council of Negro Women (EA)
**NCNW**....... Nearly Certain New Work (MCD)
**NcNw**......... Wilkes County Public Library, North Wilkesboro, NC [*Library symbol*] [*Library of Congress*] (LCLS)
**NcNwA**...... Appalachian Regional Library, North Wilkesboro, NC [*Library symbol*] [*Library of Congress*] (LCLS)
**NCNY**........ Netherland Club of New York (EA)
**NCNY**........ Newswomen's Club of New York (EA)
**n-cn-yk**....... Yukon Territory [*MARC geographic area code*] [*Library of Congress*] (LCCP)
**NCo**........... Commack Public Library, Commack, NY [*Library symbol*] [*Library of Congress*] (LCLS)
**NCO**........... National Council of Obesity (EA)
**NCO**........... Nationalist Chams Organization (EA)
**NCO**........... Net Control (CAAL)
**NCO**........... Network Control Office [*Telecommunications*] (TEL)
**NCO**........... New Consultants [*A publication*]
**NCO**........... Noncombat Operations [*Military*] (CAAL)
**NCO**........... Noncombatant Evacuation Order [*Navy*] (CINC)
**NCO**........... Noncommissioned Officer [*Military*]
**NCO**........... Norsar Array Site 01C00 [*Norway*] [*Seismograph station code, US Geological Survey*] (SEIS)
**NCO**........... North Canadian Oils Ltd. [*Toronto Stock Exchange symbol*]
**NCO**........... North Carolina Department of Transportation, Raleigh, NC [*OCLC symbol*] (OCLC)
**NCO**........... Number-Controlled Oscillator
**NCO**........... Nuveen California Municipal Market Opportunities [*NYSE symbol*] (SPSG)
**NCOA**........ National Campground Owners Association (EA)
**NCOA**........ National Change of Address Service [*US Postal Service*]
**NCOA**........ National Chevelle Owners Association (EA)
**NCOA**........ National Condominium Owners Association [*Defunct*]
**NCOA**........ National Corvette Owners' Association (EA)
**NCOA**........ National Council on the Aging (EA)
**NCOA**........ Non-Commissioned Officers Association of the United States of America (EA)
**NCOA**........ Noncommissioned Officer Academy [*Military*] (AABC)
**NCOBPS**... National Conference of Black Political Scientists (EA)
**NCOBQ**..... Noncommissioned Officer Bachelor Quarters [*Military*] (AFM)
**NCobUA**.... State University of New York, Agricultural and Technical College at Cobleskill, Cobleskill, NY [*Library symbol*] [*Library of Congress*] (LCLS)
**NCOC**........ National Council on Organized Crime (EA)
**NCOC**........ NORAD Combat Operations Center [*Military*] (FAAC)
**NCOCY**..... National Council of Organizations for Children and Youth (EA)
**NCOD**........ National Catholic Office for the Deaf (EA)
**NCODE**..... National Clearinghouse on Development Education [*Information service or system*] (EISS)
**NCODP**..... Noncommissioned Officer Development Program [*Army*] (INF)
**NCO-ER**.... Noncommissioned Officer Evaluation Reporting [*Army*] (INF)
**NCOES**...... Noncommissioned Officer Education System [*Military*] (AABC)

**NcOG**......... Richard H. Thornton Memorial Library, Oxford, NC [*Library symbol*] [*Library of Congress*] (LCLS)
**NCOGD**..... National Council for the Observance of Grandparent's Day (EA)
**NCOHC**..... Northern California Occupational Health Center [*University of California*] [*Research center*] (RCD)
**NCoHS**...... Northumberland County Historical Society. Proceedings [*A publication*]
**NCoHSP**.... Northumberland County Historical Society. Proceedings [*A publication*]
**NCOI**......... National Council for the Omnibus Industry [*British*]
**NCOIC**...... Noncommissioned Officer-in-Charge [*Military*]
**NCOIL**....... National Conference of Insurance Legislators (EA)
**NCOL**........ National Color Laboratories, Inc. [*NASDAQ symbol*] (NQ)
**NCOL**........ National Council on Occupational Licensing [*Formerly, COL*] [*Defunct*] (EA)
**N Col**.......... New Colophon [*A publication*]
**NCOLG**..... National Coordinating Office for Latin and Greek [*Later, NCLG*] (EA)
**NCOLP**..... Noncommissioned Officer Logistics Program [*Army*] (AABC)
**NCOLS**...... Noncommissioned Officers' Leadership School [*Air Force*] (AFM)
**NCOMBL**... Noncombustible (MSA)
**NCOMD**.... National Committee on the Observance of Mothers' Day [*Later, MDC*] (EA)
**NCOMDR**... National Clearinghouse on Marital and Date Rape (EA)
**NCOMM**... Naval Communications Command
**NCOMP**.... National Catholic Office for Motion Pictures [*Later, Office for Film and Broadcasting*]
**NCOMR**.... National Clearinghouse on Marital Rape [*Later, NCOMDR*] (EA)
**NConL**....... Notes on Contemporary Literature [*A publication*]
**NCooHi**..... New York State Historical Association, Cooperstown, NY [*Library symbol*] [*Library of Congress*] (LCLS)
**NCOOM**... Noncommissioned Officers' Open Mess [*Military*] (AFM)
**NCop**.......... Copiague Memorial Public Library, Copiague, NY [*Library symbol*] [*Library of Congress*] (LCLS)
**NCOP**........ National Council on Philanthropy [*Later, IS*] (EA)
**NCOPA**..... National Conference of Police Associations (EA)
**NCOPD**..... National Catholic Office for Persons with Disabilities (EA)
**NCOPDP**.. Noncommissioned Officer Professional Development Program [*Army*] (INF)
**NCOPF**...... National Council for One Parent Families [*British*]
**NCopH**...... Lakeside Hospital, Copiague, NY [*Library symbol*] [*Library of Congress*] (LCLS)
**NCorf**......... Corfu Free Library, Corfu, NY [*Library symbol*] [*Library of Congress*] (LCLS)
**NCorn**........ Cornwall Public Library, Cornwall, NY [*Library symbol*] [*Library of Congress*] (LCLS)
**NCornB**...... Harvard Black Rock Forest, Cornwall, NY [*Library symbol*] [*Library of Congress*] (LCLS)
**NCorni**....... Corning Public Library, Corning, NY [*Library symbol*] [*Library of Congress*] (LCLS)
**NCorniC**.... Corning Glass Works, Corning, NY [*Library symbol*] [*Library of Congress*] (LCLS)
**NCorniCC**... Corning Community College, Corning, NY [*Library symbol*] [*Library of Congress*] (LCLS)
**NCorniFL**... College Center of the Finger Lakes, Corning, NY [*Library symbol*] [*Library of Congress*] (LCLS)
**NCorniM**... Corning Museum of Glass, Corning, NY [*Library symbol*] [*Library of Congress*] (LCLS)
**NCorniS**..... Southern Tier Library System, Corning, NY [*Library symbol*] [*Library of Congress*] (LCLS)
**NCort**......... Cortland Free Library, Cortland, NY [*Library symbol*] [*Library of Congress*] (LCLS)
**NCORT**..... National Catholic Office for Radio and Television [*Later, Office for Film and Broadcasting*]
**NCortHi**..... Cortland County Historical Society, Cortland, NY [*Library symbol*] [*Library of Congress*] (LCLS)
**NCortSC**.... Smith-Corona Laboratory, Cortland, NY [*Library symbol*] [*Library of Congress*] (LCLS)
**NCortU**...... State University of New York, College at Cortland, Cortland, NY [*Library symbol*] [*Library of Congress*] (LCLS)
**NCOS**........ Comite de Liaison des Organisations Non-Gouvernementales de Developpement aupres des Communautes Europeennes [*Liaison Committee of Development Non-Governmental Organizations to the European Communities*] (EAIO)
**NCOS**........ National Centre for Orchestral Studies [*Goldsmiths' College*] [*British*] (CB)
**NCOS**........ National Commission on Space [*Terminated, 1986*] (EGAO)
**NCOS**........ National Council on Stuttering (EA)
**NCOS**........ Non-Concurrent Operating System [*Sperry UNIVAC*]
**NCOSCC**... National Central Office for the Suppression of Counterfeit Currency [*British*]
**NCOSTA**... National Council of Officers of State Teachers Associations (EA)
**NCOTL**..... National Committee of Teacher-Librarians [*Proposed*] [*Australia*]
**NcOtV**........ United States Veterans Administration Hospital, Oteen, NC [*Library symbol*] [*Library of Congress*] (LCLS)
**NCOWFL**... National Center on Women and Family Law (EA)
**NCoxHi**..... Greene County Historical Society, Inc., Coxsakie, NY [*Library symbol*] [*Library of Congress*] (LCLS)
**NcP**........... Given Memorial Library, Pinehurst, NC [*Library symbol*] [*Library of Congress*] (LCLS)
**NCP**........... N-Chlorothiophosphoramide [*Organic chemistry*]
**NCP**........... National Cancer Program [*National Institutes of Health*]
**NCP**........... National Car Parks [*British*]
**NCP**........... National Caries Program [*Public Health Service*] (GRD)
**NCP**........... National Choreography Project
**NCP**........... National Circus Project (EA)
**NCP**........... National Climate Program [*National Oceanic and Atmospheric Administration*] [*Rockville, MD*]
**NCP**........... National Collegiate Players (EA)
**NCP**........... National Commission on Productivity [*Later, National Productivity Council*]
**NCP**........... National Contingency Plan [*Hazardous wastes*] [*Environmental Protection Agency*]
**NCP**........... National Convention Party [*Gambia*] [*Political party*] (PPW)
**NCP**........... National Council on Philanthropy [*Later, IS*]
**NCP**........... Naval Capabilities Plan
**NCP**........... Nepali Congress Party [*Political party*] (PD)
**NCP**........... Net Combat Power
**NCP**........... Net Control Procedure
**NCP**........... Netherlands and Colonial Philately
**NCP**........... Network Control Point [*Telecommunications*]
**NCP**........... Network Control Processor [*Telecommunications*] (TSSD)
**NCP**........... Network Control Program [*IBM Corp.*] [*Telecommunications*] (BUR)
**NCP**........... Network Control Protocol [*Telecommunications*]
**NCP**........... New Call to Peacemaking (EA)
**NCP**........... New Communities Program [*Defunct*] (EA)
**NCP**........... New Community Projects [*A publication*]
**NCP**........... Nickel-Chromium Panel
**NCP**........... Nitrogen Charge Panel [*Later, MRAC*] (AAG)
**NCP**........... No-Copy Paper
**NCP**........... Noctilucent Cloud Particles
**NCP**........... Noncollagen Protein
**NCP**........... Normal Circular Pitch (MSA)
**NCP**........... North Celestial Pole [*Astronomy*]
**NCP**........... Nuclear Contingency Plan (MCD)
**NCP**........... Nursing Care Plan
**NCP**........... Nuveen California Performance Plus Municipal [*NYSE symbol*] (SPSG)
**NCPA**........ National Center for Policy Alternatives [*Later, CPA*] (EA)
**NCPA**........ National Coalition of Patriotic Americans (EA)
**NCPA**........ National Committee for the Prevention of Alcoholism and Drug Dependency [*Later, NCPADD*] (EA)
**NCPA**........ National Composition and Prepress Association (EA)
**NCPA**........ National Conservation Policy Act [*1979*]
**NCPA**........ National Cottonseed Products Association (EA)
**NCPA**........ National Crime Prevention Association [*Defunct*] (EA)
**NCPAC**...... National Conservative Political Action Committee (EA)
**NCPAD**..... National Council on Psychological Aspects of Disability (EA)
**NCPADD**.. National Committee for the Prevention of Alcoholism and Drug Dependency (EA)
**NCPAG**..... National CPA [*Certified Public Accountant*] Group [*Later, BKR International*] (EA)
**NCPAMT**... National Coalition of Psychiatrists Against Motorcoach Therapy (EA)
**NCPAS**...... National Computer Program Abstract Service, Inc. (IID)
**NC/PAT**.... National Council for the Public Assessment of Technology [*Defunct*]
**NcPb**.......... Pinebluff Public Library, Pinebluff, NC [*Library symbol*] [*Library of Congress*] (LCLS)
**NCPC**........ National Capital Planning Commission [*Formerly, NCPPC*]
**NCPC**........ National Capital Planning Committee [*Australia*]
**NCPC**........ National Chrysler Products Club (EA)
**NCPC**........ National Citizens Participation Council (EA)
**NCPC**........ National Coal Policy Conference [*Defunct*] (EA)
**NCPC**........ National Collegiate Poultry Club
**NCPC**........ National Crime Prevention Council (EA)
**NCPC**........ Nose Cone Protective Covering [*Aviation*]
**NCPCA**...... National Center for the Prosecution of Child Abuse (EA)
**NCPCA**...... National Committee for Peace in Central America (EA)
**NCPCA**...... National Committee for Prevention of Child Abuse (EA)
**NCPCC**...... National Clearinghouse for Poison Control Centers (EA)
**NCPCINST**... Naval Civilian Personnel Command Instructions (MCD)
**NCPCO**..... National Climate Program Coordinating Office
**NCPCR**...... National Center for Prevention and Control of Rape [*National Institutes of Health*]
**NCPD**........ Navy Current Procurement Directive
**NCPDM**.... National Council of Physical Distribution Management
**NCPDP**..... National Council for Prescription Drug Programs (EA)
**NCPDS**...... Navy Civilian Personnel Data System
**NCPE**......... National Committee on Pay Equity (EA)
**NCPE**......... Noncardiac Pulmonary Edema [*Medicine*]
**NCPEA**...... National College Physical Education Association [*Later, NCPEAM*] (EA)
**NCPEA**...... National Conference of Professors of Educational Administration [*Later, NAPEHE*] (EA)

**NCPEAM** ... National College Physical Education Association for Men [*Later, NAPEHE*]
**NCPEARL** ... National Coalition for Public Education and Religious Liberty (EA)
**NCPEG** ...... Navy Contractor Performance Evaluation Group
**NCPEP** ...... New Century Policies Educational Programs (EA)
**NCPERL** ... National Coalition for Public Education and Religious Liberty (EA)
**NCPERS** ... National Conference on Public Employee Retirement Systems (EA)
**NcPeS** ........ Pembroke State University, Pembroke, NC [*Library symbol*] [*Library of Congress*] (LCLS)
**NC Pestic Manual** ... North Carolina Pesticide Manual [*A publication*]
**NCPF** ......... National Council on Private Forests (EA)
**NcPfO** ........ Olin Corp., Ecusta-Film Technical Library, Pisgah Forest, NC [*Library symbol*] [*Library of Congress*] (LCLS)
**NCPG** ........ National Catholic Pharmacists Guild of the United States (EA)
**NCPG** ........ National Council on Problem Gambling (EA)
**NCPH** ........ National Council on Public History [*Database producer*] (EA)
**NCPI** .......... National Clay Pipe Institute (EA)
**NCPI** .......... National Committee on Property Insurance [*Boston, MA*] (EA)
**NCPI** .......... National Conference on Parent Involvement (EA)
**NCPI** .......... National Crime Prevention Institute (EA)
**NCPI** .......... Navy Civilian Personnel Instructions
**NCPIE** ....... National Council of Patient Information and Education (EA)
**NCPL** ......... National Center for Preservation Law (EA)
**NCPL** ......... National Collegiate Parachuting League (EA)
**NCPLA** ...... National Council of Patent Law Associations [*Later, NCIPLA*] (EA)
**NCPLD** ...... Noncoupled
**NcPly** ......... Washington County Library, Plymouth, NC [*Library symbol*] [*Library of Congress*] (LCLS)
**NcPlyP** ....... Pettigrew Regional Library, Plymouth, NC [*Library symbol*] [*Library of Congress*] (LCLS)
**NcPm** ......... Charles H. Stone Memorial Library, Pilot Mountain, NC [*Library symbol*] [*Library of Congress*] (LCLS)
**NCPM** ........ National Clay Pot Manufacturers (EA)
**NCPM** ........ National Conference of Personal Managers (EA)
**NCPMA** .... Noise Control Products and Materials Association [*Later, NCA*] (EA)
**ncpn---** ........ Panama [*MARC geographic area code*] [*Library of Congress*] (LCCP)
**NCPNFUNW** ... National Coalition for a Policy of No-First-Use of Nuclear Weapons (EA)
**NCPO** ........ National Chronic Pain Outreach Association (EA)
**NCPO** ........ Nordic Council for Physical Oceanography (EA)
**NcPo** .......... United States Air Force, Pope Air Force Base, Base Library, Pope AFB, NC [*Library symbol*] [*Library of Congress*] (LCLS)
**NcPolA** ...... Anson Technical College, Learning Resources Center, Polk Campus, Polkton, NC [*Library symbol*] [*Library of Congress*] (LCLS)
**NCPP** ......... National Coal Policy Project
**NCPP** ......... National Council on Public Policy (EA)
**NCPP** ......... National Council on Public Polls (EA)
**NCPPC** ...... National Capital Park and Planning Commission [*Later, NCPC*]
**NCPPR** ...... National Center for Public Policy Research (EA)
**NCPQWL** ... National Center for Productivity and Quality of Working Life [*Later, National Productivity Council*]
**NCPR** ........ National Championship Poker Run [*American Motorcyclists Association*]
**NCPR** ........ National Congress of Petroleum Retailers [*Later, SSDA*] (EA)
**NCPRP** ...... National Coastal Pollution Research Program [*Environmental Protection Agency*] (MSC)
**NCPRR** ...... National Congress for Puerto Rican Rights (EA)
**NCPRV** ...... National Congress of Puerto Rican Veterans (EA)
**NCPRV** ...... National Council of Puerto Rican Volunteers (EA)
**NCPS** ......... National Cat Protection Society (EA)
**NCPS** ......... National Circus Preservation Society (EA)
**NCPS** ......... National Coalition to Prevent Shoplifting (EA)
**NCPS** ......... National Commission on Product Safety
**NCPS** ......... National Commission on the Public Service (EA)
**NCPS** ......... Non-Contributory Pension Scheme (DLA)
**NCPS** ......... Nuclear Contingency Planning System (MCD)
**NCPSA** ...... National Child Passenger Safety Association [*Later, NPSA*] (EA)
**NCPSC** ...... National Committee on Paper Stock Conservation
**NCPSF** ...... National Council of Professional Services Firms [*Later, PSC*] (EA)
**NCPSIDS** ... National Center for the Prevention of Sudden Infant Death Syndrome (EA)
**NCPSSM** .. National Committee to Preserve Social Security and Medicare (EA)
**NCPT** ......... National Conference on Power Transmission (EA)
**NCPT** ......... National Congress of Parents and Teachers [*Later, National PTA*] (EA)
**NCPT** ......... Navy Central Planning Team [*NATO*] (NATG)
**NCPTA** ...... National Confederation of Parent Teacher Associations [*British*]
**NCPTCAN** ... National Center for the Prevention and Treatment of Child Abuse and Neglect (EA)
**NCPTF** ...... National Campaign for a Peace Tax Fund (EA)
**NCPTO** ..... National China Painting Teachers Organization [*Later, IPAT*] (EA)
**NCPTWA** ... National Clearinghouse for Periodical Title Word Abbreviations [*ANSI*]
**NCPUA** ..... National Committee on Pesticide Use in Agriculture [*Canada*]
**NCPW** ....... National Country Party of Western Australia [*Political party*]
**NCPWB** ..... National Certified Pipe Welding Bureau (EA)
**NCPY** ........ Penrhyn [*Cook Islands*] [*ICAO location identifier*] (ICLI)
**NCPYA** ...... National Conference of Public Youth Agencies [*Defunct*] (EA)
**NCQ** ......... Marietta, GA [*Location identifier*] [*FAA*] (FAAL)
**NCQA** ........ National Committee for Quality Assurance (EA)
**NCQHC** ..... National Committee for Quality Health Care (EA)
**NCQIE** ...... National Coalition for Quality Integrated Education (EA)
**NCR** .......... Cooperatie [*A publication*]
**NCR** .......... National Capital Region
**NCR** .......... National Cash Register Co. [*Later, NCR Corp.*] [*Computer manufacturer*]
**NCR** .......... National Catholic Reporter [*A publication*]
**NCR** .......... National Civic Review [*A publication*]
**NCR** .......... National Coalition for Research in Neurological and Communicative Disorders (EA)
**NCR** .......... National Council of Resistance for Liberty and Independence [*Iran*] (PD)
**NCR** .......... Naval Construction Regiment (NVT)
**NCR** .......... Navy Code Room
**NCR** .......... NCR Corp. [*Formerly, National Cash Register Co.*] [*NYSE symbol*] (SPSG)
**NCR** .......... Network Change Request [*NASA*] (KSC)
**NCR** .......... Network Control Room [*Television*]
**NCR** .......... Neutrophil Complement Rosettes [*Hematology*]
**NCR** .......... New Cinema Review [*A publication*]
**N Cr** .......... New York Criminal Reports [*A publication*] (DLA)
**NCR** .......... Nickerson, C. R., San Francisco CA [*STAC*]
**NCR** .......... Nicorandil [*Biochemistry*]
**NCR** .......... Nitrile-Chloroprene Rubber
**NCR** .......... No Calibration Required (MCD)
**NCR** .......... No Canadian Rights
**NCR** .......... No Carbon Required (NG)
**NCR** .......... Noncoding Region [*Genetics*]
**NCR** .......... Nonconformance Record [*NASA*] (KSC)
**NCR** .......... Nonconformance Report [*Nuclear energy*] (NRCH)
**NCR** .......... Nonconserved Region [*Genetics*]
**NCR** .......... Northern Central Railway [*British*] (ROG)
**NCR** .......... Notification of Change Report (NRCH)
**NCR** .......... Nucal Resources Ltd. [*Vancouver Stock Exchange symbol*]
**NCR** .......... Nuclear (AAG)
**NCR** .......... Nuclear Cytoplasmic Ratio [*Cytology*]
**NCR** .......... Ontario Library Service - Voyageur [*UTLAS symbol*]
**NcR** .......... Wake County Public Libraries, Raleigh, NC [*Library symbol*] [*Library of Congress*] (LCLS)
**NcRa** ......... Hoke County Public Library, Raeford, NC [*Library symbol*] [*Library of Congress*] (LCLS)
**NCRA** ....... National Cellular Resellers' Association (EA)
**NCRA** ....... National Center on Rural Aging (EA)
**NCRA** ....... National Coalition of Redevelopment Agencies (EA)
**NCRA** ....... National Cooperative Refinery Association [*Commercial firm*] (EA)
**NCRA** ....... National Cooperative Research Act [*1984*]
**NCRA** ....... National Correctional Recreational Association (EA)
**NCRA** ....... National Council of Research Administrators
**NCRAC** ..... National Community Relations Advisory Council [*Later, NJCRAC*] (EA)
**NCR Bus and Econ** ... North Carolina Review of Business and Economics [*A publication*]
**NCRC** ....... National Catholic Resettlement Council (EA)
**NCRC** ....... National Cave Rescue Commission
**NCRC** ....... National Committee for a Representative Congress (EA)
**NCRC** ....... Nickel-Cadmium Rechargeable Cell
**NCRC/AODA** ... National Certification Reciprocity Consortium/Alcoholism and Other Drug Abuse (EA)
**NCRCH** ..... Nordic Committee of the Research Councils for the Humanities (EA)
**NcRCPL** .... Carolina Power & Light Co., Technical Library, Raleigh, NC [*Library symbol*] [*Library of Congress*] (LCLS)
**NCRCRD** .. North Central Regional Center for Rural Development [*Iowa State University*] [*Research center*] (RCD)
**NCRD** ....... National Council to Repeal the Draft [*Defunct*] (EA)
**NCRD** ....... National Council on Resource Development (EA)
**NcRDC** ...... North Carolina Department of Corrections, Central Prison School, Raleigh, NC [*Library symbol*] [*Library of Congress*] (LCLS)
**NCRDC** ..... Northern Colorado Research-Demonstration Center [*Colorado State University*] [*Research center*] (RCD)
**NcRDD** ...... North Carolina Department of Human Resources, Dorothea Dix Hospital, F. T. Fuller Staff Library, Raleigh, NC [*Library symbol*] [*Library of Congress*] (LCLS)
**NCRDS** ...... National Coal Resources Data System [*Geological Survey*] [*Databank*] [*Information service or system*] (IID)

**NCRDTA** .. National Council of Refuse Disposal Trade Associations
**NCRE** ........ National Conference on Research in English (EA)
**NCRE** ........ National Council on Rehabilitation Education (EA)
**NCRE** ........ Naval Construction Research Establishment [*British*] (AAG)
**NCREA** ..... National Council of Religious Education in Australia
**NcReH** ....... Annie Penn Hospital, Medical Library, Reidsville, NC [*Library symbol*] [*Library of Congress*] (LCLS)
**NCREIF** .... National Council of Real Estate Investment Fiduciaries (EA)
**NCREL** ...... North Central Regional Educational Laboratory [*Elmhurst, IL*] [*Department of Education*] (GRD)
**NC Rep** ...... North Carolina Reports [*A publication*] (DLA)
**NC Rep Appendix** ... North Carolina Reports, Appendix [*A publication*] (DLA)
**NC Reports** ... North Carolina Reports [*A publication*] (DLA)
**NcRf** ........... Eden Public Library, Eden, NC [*Library symbol*] [*Library of Congress*] (LCLS)
**NCRFCL** ... National Commission on Reform of Federal Criminal Laws
**NCRFP** ...... National Council for a Responsible Firearms Policy [*Defunct*] (EA)
**NCRFRA** ... National Committee to Repeal the Federal Reserve Act (EA)
**NCRFSCU** ... National Commission on the Role and Future of State Colleges and Universities (EA)
**NCRG** ......... Avarua/Rarotonga International [*Cook Islands*] [*ICAO location identifier*] (ICLI)
**NcRGM** ..... North Carolina Department of Human Resources, The Governor Morehead School, Raleigh, NC [*Library symbol*] [*Library of Congress*] (LCLS)
**NcRGS** ....... Church of Jesus Christ of Latter-Day Saints, Genealogical Society Library, Raleigh Branch, Raleigh, NC [*Library symbol*] [*Library of Congress*] (LCLS)
**NCRH** ........ National Center for Radiological Health [*Public Health Service*]
**NCRH** ........ North Coast Railroad Historical Society (EA)
**NcRH** ......... W. W. Holding Technical Institute, Raleigh, NC [*Library symbol*] [*Library of Congress*] (LCLS)
**NcRHR** ...... North Carolina Department of Human Resources, Public Health Library, Raleigh, NC [*Library symbol*] [*Library of Congress*] (LCLS)
**NCRI** ......... National Coastal Resources Research and Development Institute [*Newport, OR*] [*Department of Commerce*] (GRD)
**NCRI** ......... National Consumer Research Institute (EA)
**NCRIC** ....... National Chemical Response and Information Center [*Established by the Chemical Manufacturers Association to provide information and advice during emergencies*]
**NCRIPTAL** ... National Center for Research to Improve Postsecondary Teaching and Learning [*Ann Arbor, MI*] [*Department of Education*] (GRD)
**NCRIS** ....... National Committee to Restore Internal Security (EA)
**NCRK** ........ Rakahanga [*Cook Islands*] [*ICAO location identifier*] (ICLI)
**NCRL** ........ National Canners Association Research Laboratory
**NCRLC** ...... National Catholic Rural Life Conference (EA)
**NCRLC** ...... National Committee on Regional Library Cooperation
**NCRLS** ...... National Committee of Religious Leaders of Safety (EA)
**NcRM** ........ Meredith College, Raleigh, NC [*Library symbol*] [*Library of Congress*] (LCLS)
**NCRM** ....... National Conference on Radiation Measurements
**NCRM** ....... Nordic Council for Railway Music (EA)
**NcRm** ......... Thomas Hackney Braswell Memorial Library, Rocky Mount, NC [*Library symbol*] [*Library of Congress*] (LCLS)
**NcRMA** ..... North Carolina Museum of Art in Raleigh, Raleigh, NC [*Library symbol*] [*Library of Congress*] (LCLS)
**NcRmE** ...... Edgecombe Technical College, Learning Resources Center, Rocky Mount, NC [*Library symbol*] [*Library of Congress*] (LCLS)
**NcRMG** ..... Measurements Group, Inc., Raleigh, NC [*Library symbol*] [*Library of Congress*] (LCLS)
**NCRMM** ... Nouvelle Critique. Revue du Marxisme Militant [*A publication*]
**NcRmN** ...... Nash Technical Institute, Rocky Mount, NC [*Library symbol*] [*Library of Congress*] (LCLS)
**NcRMNH** ... North Carolina State Museum of Natural History, Raleigh, NC [*Library symbol*] [*Library of Congress*] (LCLS)
**NcRMNH-B** ... North Carolina State Museum of Natural History, H. H. Brimley Memorial Library, Raleigh, NC [*Library symbol*] [*Library of Congress*] (LCLS)
**NCRND** ..... National Committee for Research in Neurological Disorders [*Later, NCR*] (EA)
**NCRNT** ..... National Committee for Rescue from NAZI Terror [*British*]
**NcRo** .......... Rockingham-Richmond County Library, Rockingham, NC [*Library symbol*] [*Library of Congress*] (LCLS)
**NcRob** ........ Bemis Memorial Library, Robbinsville, NC [*Library symbol*] [*Library of Congress*] (LCLS)
**NcRobS** ...... Snowbird Community Library, Robbinsville, NC [*Library symbol*] [*Library of Congress*] (LCLS)
**NCroh** ........ Croton Free Library, Croton-On-Hudson, NY [*Library symbol*] [*Library of Congress*] (LCLS)
**NCrohH** ..... Hudson Institute, Croton-On-Hudson, NY [*Library symbol*] [*Library of Congress*] (LCLS)
**NcRoS** ........ Sandhills Regional Library, Rockingham, NC [*Library symbol*] [*Library of Congress*] (LCLS)
**NcRov** ........ Robersonville Public Library, Robersonville, NC [*Library symbol*] [*Library of Congress*] (LCLS)
**NcRox** ........ Person County Public Library, Roxboro, NC [*Library symbol*] [*Library of Congress*] (LCLS)
**NcRoxP** ..... Person Technical Institute, Roxboro, NC [*Library symbol*] [*Library of Congress*] (LCLS)
**NCRP** ........ National Climatic Research Program
**NCRP** ........ National Committee for Responsible Patriotism (EA)
**NCRP** ........ National Committee for Responsive Philanthropy (EA)
**NCRP** ........ National Council on Radiation Protection and Measurements [*Later, NCRPM*]
**NCRP** ........ National Council for Research and Planning (EA)
**NcRP** ......... Peace College, Raleigh, NC [*Library symbol*] [*Library of Congress*] (LCLS)
**NCRPC** ...... National Capital Regional Planning Council [*Terminated, 1966*]
**NCRPCV** ... National Council of Returned Peace Corps Volunteers (EA)
**NCRPD** ..... National Committee on Recreation for People with Disabilities [*Australia*]
**NCRPE** ...... National Council on Religion and Public Education (EA)
**NCRPM** .... National Council on Radiation Protection and Measurements (EA)
**NCRP Rep** ... National Council on Radiation Protection and Measurements. Reports [*A publication*]
**NCRR** ........ National Center for Resource Recovery [*Defunct*]
**NCRR** ........ National Credit Union Administration Rules and Regulations
**NCRR** ........ Nordic Council of Reindeer Research (EAIO)
**NcRr** .......... Roanoke Rapids Public Library, Roanoke Rapids, NC [*Library symbol*] [*Library of Congress*] (LCLS)
**NCRR Bull** ... NCRR [*National Center for Resource Recovery*] Bulletin [*United States*] [*A publication*]
**NCRRC** ..... National Committee to Reopen the Rosenberg Case (EA)
**NCRRRC** ... North Country Reference and Research Resources Council [*Information service or system*] (IID)
**NCRS** ......... National Clearinghouse on Revenue Sharing [*Defunct*]
**NCRS** ......... National Committee for Rural Schools [*Defunct*] (EA)
**NCRS** ......... National Corvette Restorers Society (EA)
**NcRS** .......... North Carolina State University at Raleigh, Raleigh, NC [*Library symbol*] [*Library of Congress*] (LCLS)
**NCRSA** ...... National Commercial Refrigeration Sales Association (EA)
**NcRSA** ....... Saint Augustine's College, Raleigh, NC [*Library symbol*] [*Library of Congress*] (LCLS)
**NCRSAQ** ... US National Clearinghouse for Drug Abuse Information. Report Series [*A publication*]
**NcRSh** ....... Shaw University, Raleigh, NC [*Library symbol*] [*Library of Congress*] (LCLS)
**NcRSM** ...... Saint Mary's Junior College, Raleigh, NC [*Library symbol*] [*Library of Congress*] (LCLS)
**NcRS-V** ...... North Carolina State University, School of Veterinary Medicine, Raleigh, NC [*Library symbol*] [*Library of Congress*] (LCLS)
**NCRTE** ...... National Center for Research on Teacher Education [*East Lansing, MI*] [*Department of Education*] (GRD)
**NCR/TSI** ... NCR Telecommunication Services, Incorporated (TSSD)
**NcRu** .......... Norris Public Library, Rutherfordton, NC [*Library symbol*] [*Library of Congress*] (LCLS)
**NCRUCE** ... National Conference of Regulatory Utility Commission Engineers (EA)
**NcRuR** ....... Rutherford County Library, Inc., Rutherfordton, NC [*Library symbol*] [*Library of Congress*] (LCLS)
**NCRV** ........ National Committee for Radiation Victims (EA)
**NCRVD** ..... National Conference of Religious Vocation Directors [*Later, NRVC*] (EA)
**NCRVDM** ... National Conference of Religious Vocation Directors of Men [*Later, NCRVD*] (EA)
**NCRVE** ...... National Center for Research in Vocational Education (EA)
**NCRW** ....... National Council for Research on Women (EA)
**NcRWCM** ... Wake County Hospital System, Wake County Medical Center, Raleigh, NC [*Library symbol*] [*Library of Congress*] (LCLS)
**NCRWS** ..... National Campaign for Radioactive Waste Safety (EA)
**NCRY** ........ National Commission on Resources for Youth
**NCS** ........... N-Chlorosuccinimide [*Organic chemistry*]
**NCS** ........... National Cartoonists Society (EA)
**NCS** ........... National Cemetery System
**NCS** ........... National Center for Stuttering (EA)
**NCS** ........... National Chrysanthemum Society (EA)
**NCS** ........... National Commemorative Society [*Defunct*]
**NCS** ........... National Committee on Safety
**NCS** ........... National Communications System [*DoD*]
**NCS** ........... National Computer Systems, Inc.
**NCS** ........... National Conference on Solicitations (EA)
**NCS** ........... National Consensus Standards (MCD)
**NCS** ........... National Convenience Stores, Inc. [*NYSE symbol*] (SPSG)
**NCS** ........... National Corrosion Service [*British*] (IRUK)
**NCS** ........... National Council of Stutterers [*Later, NCOS*] (EA)
**NCS** ........... National Crime Stoppers [*Later, ACF*] (EA)
**NCS** ........... National Crime Survey [*University of Michigan*] [*Database*]
**NCS** ........... National Cryptologic School [*National Security Agency*]
**NCS** ........... Naval Canteen Service [*British military*] (DMA)
**NCS** ........... Naval Communications Station [*or System*]

**NCS** .......... Naval Control of Shipping [*NATO*] (NATG)
**NCS** .......... Navigation Control Simulator
**NCS** .......... Navigational Computer Set (MCD)
**NCS** .......... NCR [*NCR Corp.*] Century Software
**NCS** .......... Nearest Cross Street (ADA)
**NCS** .......... Needlework and Craft Showcase (ITD)
**NCS** .......... Neocarzinostatin [*Zinostatin*] [*Antineoplastic drug*]
**NCS** .......... Net Control Station [*Communications*] [*Amateur radio*]
**NCS** .......... Network Control System
**NCS** .......... Network Coordination Station
**NCS** .......... Newborn Calf Serum [*Immunology*]
**NCS** .......... Newcastle [*South Africa*] [*Airport symbol*] (OAG)
**NCS** .......... Nineteenth Century Series [*A publication*]
**NCS** .......... No Checking Signal [*Telecommunications*] (TEL)
**NCS** .......... Noncallable Security [*Investment term*]
**NCS** .......... Noncritical Sensitive [*DoD*]
**NCS** .......... Noncrystalline Solid [*Physics*]
**NCS** .......... Nonwater Cooling System
**NCS** .......... North Carolina State Library, Raleigh, NC [*OCLC symbol*] (OCLC)
**NCS** .......... Northern Cross Society (EA)
**NCS** .......... Nuclear-Chicago Solubilizer
**NCS** .......... Nuclear Criticality Safety (NRCH)
**NCS** .......... Nucleolar Channel System
**NCS** .......... Nueva Concepcion [*El Salvador*] [*Seismograph station code, US Geological Survey*] [*Closed*] (SEIS)
**NCS** .......... Numerical Category Scaling
**NCS** .......... Numerical Control Society [*Later, NCS/AIMTECH*] (EA)
**NCS** .......... Nutation Control System (MCD)
**NCSA** ........ National Capital Speakers Association (EA)
**NCSA** ........ National Carl Schurz Association (EA)
**NCSA** ........ National Center for Statistics and Analysis [*National Highway Traffic Safety Administration*] [*Washington, DC*] (GRD)
**NCSA** ........ National Center for Supercomputing Applications [*National Science Foundation*] [*University of Illinois*] [*Research center*] (RCD)
**NCSA** ........ National Church Secretaries Association (EA)
**NCSA** ........ National Club Sports Association (EA)
**NCSA** ........ National Coffee Service Association [*Vienna, VA*] (EA)
**NCSA** ........ National Collegiate Ski Association (EA)
**NCSA** ........ National Confectionery Salesmen's Association of America (EA)
**NCSA** ........ National Construction Software Association (EA)
**NCSA** ........ National Contract Sweepers Association [*Later, NCSI*] (EA)
**NCSA** ........ National Council of Seamen's Agencies [*Later, ICOSA*] (EA)
**NCSA** ........ National Crushed Stone Association [*Later, NSA*] (EA)
**NCSA** ........ National Cued Speech Association (EA)
**NCSA** ........ National Customs Service Association [*Later, NTEU*] (EA)
**NCSA** ........ Native Counselling Services of Alberta. Newsletter [*A publication*]
**NCSA** ........ Newsletter. Copyright Society of Australia [*A publication*] (APTA)
**NCSA** ........ Newspaper Collectors Society of America (EA)
**NCSAB** ...... National Council of State Agencies for the Blind (EA)
**NCSABMT** ... National Campaign to Save the ABM [*Antiballistic missile*] Treaty (EA)
**NcSaC** ........ Central Carolina Technical Institute, Sanford, NC [*Library symbol*] [*Library of Congress*] (LCLS)
**NCSAC** ...... National Catholic Social Action Conference [*Defunct*] (EA)
**NCSAC** ...... Nuclear Cross Sections Advisory Committee
**NCSAG** ..... Nuclear Cross Section Advisory Group (NRCH)
**NCS/AIMTECH** ... Numerical Control Society/AIMTECH [*Association for Integrated Manufacturing Technology*] (EA)
**NcSaL** ........ Lee County Library, Sanford, NC [*Library symbol*] [*Library of Congress*] (LCLS)
**NcSal** ......... Rowan Public Library, Salisbury, NC [*Library symbol*] [*Library of Congress*] (LCLS)
**NcSalC** ....... Catawba College, Salisbury, NC [*Library symbol*] [*Library of Congress*] (LCLS)
**NcSalL** ....... Livingstone College, Salisbury, NC [*Library symbol*] [*Library of Congress*] (LCLS)
**NcSalR** ....... Rowan Technical Institute, Salisbury, NC [*Library symbol*] [*Library of Congress*] (LCLS)
**NcSalRH** ... Rowan Memorial Hospital Area, Health Education Center, Salisbury, NC [*Library symbol*] [*Library of Congress*] (LCLS)
**NcSal-S** ...... Rowan Public Library, South Rowan Branch, Landis, NC [*Library symbol*] [*Library of Congress*] (LCLS)
**NcSalVA** .... United States Veterans Administration Center, Medical Library, Salisbury, NC [*Library symbol*] [*Library of Congress*] (LCLS)
**NCSASR** ... National Center for Small-Angle Scattering Research [*Oak Ridge, TN*] [*Department of Energy*] (GRD)
**NCSAW** ..... National Catholic Society for Animal Welfare [*Later, ISAR*] (EA)
**NCSBCS** .... National Conference of States on Building Codes and Standards (EA)
**NCSBEE** ... National Council of State Boards of Engineering Examiners [*Later, NCEE*] (EA)
**NCSBI** ....... National Council for Small Business Innovation
**NcSbJ** ........ North Carolina Justice Academy, Salemburg, NC [*Library symbol*] [*Library of Congress*] (LCLS)
**NCSBMD** ... National Council for Small Business Management Development [*Later, ICSB*] (EA)
**NCSBN** ...... National Council of State Boards of Nursing (EA)
**NcSbP** ....... Southwood College, Salemburg, NC [*Library symbol*] [*Library of Congress*] (LCLS)
**NCSC** ........ National Catholic Stewardship Council (EA)
**NCSC** ........ National Center for State Courts (EA)
**NCSC** ........ National Child Safety Council (EA)
**NCSC** ........ National Communication System Circulars
**NCSC** ........ National Computer Security Council
**NCSC** ........ National Council on Schoolhouse Construction [*Later, CEFP*] (EA)
**NCSC** ........ National Council of Senior Citizens (EA)
**NCSC** ........ Naval Coastal Systems Center [*Panama City, FL*]
**NCSC** ........ Navy Command Support Center (MCD)
**NCSC** ........ North Carolina State College
**Nc-SC** ........ North Carolina State Supreme Court, Raleigh, NC [*Library symbol*] [*Library of Congress*] (LCLS)
**NCSCBHEP** ... National Center for the Study of Collective Bargaining in Higher Education and the Professions (EA)
**NCSCCY** ... National Council of State Committees for Children and Youth (EA)
**NCSCEE** ... National Council of State Consultants in Elementary Education (EA)
**NCSCI** ....... National Center for Standards and Certification Information [*National Institute of Standards and Technology*] [*Gaithersburg, MD*] [*Database*]
**NCSCJ** ...... National Conference of Special Court Judges (EA)
**NCSCJPA** ... National Conference of State Criminal Justice Planning Administrators [*Later, NCJA*] (EA)
**NCSCL** ...... National Committee for Sexual Civil Liberties (EA)
**NCSC Manual** ... National Companies and Securities Commission. Manual [*A publication*] (APTA)
**NcScn** ......... Scotland Neck Memorial Library, Scotland Neck, NC [*Library symbol*] [*Library of Congress*] (LCLS)
**NCSCPAS** ... National Center for the Study of Corporal Punishment and Alternatives in the Schools (EA)
**NCSCR** ...... North Carolina State College Reactor
**NCSCT** ...... National Center for School and College Television
**NCSD** ........ National Child Safety Development [*British*]
**NCSD** ........ National Council on Student Development (EA)
**NCSDHA Dent Hyg** ... NCSDHA [*Northern California State Dental Hygienists Association*] Dental Hygienist [*A publication*]
**NCSE** ......... National Center for Science Education (EA)
**NCSE** ......... National Commission on Safety Education [*Defunct*] (EA)
**NCSE** ......... National Committee on Secondary Education [*of NASSP*]
**NCSE** ......... National Council for Special Education [*British*]
**NCSEA** ...... National Child Support Enforcement Association (EA)
**NCSEA** ...... National Community School Education Association [*Later, NCEA*] (EA)
**NCSEA** ...... National Council of State Education Associations (EA)
**NCSEER** ... National Council for Soviet and East European Research (EA)
**NCSEES** .... Nordic Committee for Soviet and East European Studies (EA)
**NCSEMSTC** ... National Council of State Emergency Medical Services Training Coordinators (EA)
**NC Sess Laws** ... Session Laws of North Carolina [*A publication*] (DLA)
**NCSEX** ...... Naval Control of Shipping Exercises
**NCSF** ......... National Catholic Society of Foresters (EA)
**NCSF** ......... National College Student Foundation [*Defunct*] (EA)
**NCSFA** ...... National Conference of State Fleet Administrators (EA)
**NCSFI** ....... National Coalition to Stop Food Irradiation (EA)
**NCSFP** ...... National Council on Synthetic Fuels Production [*Later, CSF*] (EA)
**NCSFWI** ... National Coalition to Stop Food and Water Irradiation (EA)
**NCSG** ........ National Chimney Sweep Guild (EA)
**NCSGC** ...... National Council of State Garden Clubs (EA)
**NCSGSO** ... National Conference of State General Service Officers [*Later, NASDAGS*] (EA)
**NcSh** .......... Cleveland County Memorial Library, Shelby, NC [*Library symbol*] [*Library of Congress*] (LCLS)
**NCsh** .......... Cold Spring Harbor Public Library, Cold Spring Harbor, NY [*Library symbol*] [*Library of Congress*] (LCLS)
**NCSH** ........ National Clearinghouse for Smoking and Health [*Public Health Service*]
**NCSH** ........ Newton College of the Sacred Heart [*Later, Newton College*] [*Massachusetts*]
**NCshB** ....... Cold Spring Harbor Biological Laboratory, Cold Spring Harbor, NY [*Library symbol*] [*Library of Congress*] (LCLS)
**NcShC** ....... Cleveland County Technical Institute, Shelby, NC [*Library symbol*] [*Library of Congress*] (LCLS)
**NCSHPO** .. National Conference of State Historic Preservation Officers (EA)
**NCSHSA** ... National Council of State Human Service Administrators (EA)
**NCshWM** ... Whaling Museum Society, Inc., Cold Spring Harbor, NY [*Library symbol*] [*Library of Congress*] (LCLS)
**NCSI** .......... National Communication System Instructions
**NCSI** .......... National Contract Sweepers Institute (EA)
**NCSI** .......... National Council of Self-Insurers [*Chicago, IL*] (EA)
**NCSI** .......... National Council for Stream Improvement (EA)

**NCSIT** ....... National Coalition to Support Indian Treaties (EA)
**NCSJ** ......... National College of the State Judiciary (DLA)
**NCSJ** ......... National Conference on Soviet Jewry (EA)
**NcSj** .......... United States Air Force, Seymour Johnson Air Force Base, Base Library, Seymour Johnson AFB, NC [*Library symbol*] [*Library of Congress*] (LCLS)
**NCSL**......... National Center for Service-Learning (EA)
**NCSL**......... National Civil Service League [*Inactive*] (EA)
**NCSL**......... National Conference of Standards Laboratories (EA)
**NCSL**......... National Conference of State Legislatures (EA)
**NCSL**......... Naval Coastal Systems Laboratory [*Later, NCSC*]
**NCSL**......... Naval Code and Signal Laboratory
**NCSLA**....... National Conference of State Liquor Administrators (EA)
**NCSLL** ...... National Conference of State Legislative Leaders [*Later, NCSL*] (EA)
**NCSLO**...... Naval Control of Shipping Liaison Officer
**NCSM** ....... National Communication System Memoranda
**NCSM** ....... National Council of Supervisors of Mathematics (EA)
**NcSmJ** ....... Johnston County Technical Institute, Smithfield, NC [*Library symbol*] [*Library of Congress*] (LCLS)
**NCSMX**...... National Campaign to Stop the MX [*Defunct*] (EA)
**NcSn** ......... Greene County Public Library, Snow Hill, NC [*Library symbol*] [*Library of Congress*] (LCLS)
**NCSN** ........ National Computer Service Network (EA)
**NCSN** ........ National Council for School Nurses [*of AAHPER*]
**NCSNE**...... Naval Control of Shipping in Northern European Command Area [*NATO*] (NATG)
**NCSO** ........ National Council of Salesmen's Organizations [*New York, NY*] (EA)
**NCSO** ........ Naval Control Service Office [*World War II British Routing Service*]
**NCSO** ........ Naval Control of Shipping Officer
**NCSO** ........ Naval Control of Shipping Operations
**NcSopS-L**.. Southport-Brunswick County Library, Leland Branch Library, Leland, NC [*Library symbol*] [*Library of Congress*] (LCLS)
**NcSopS-W** ... Southport-Brunswick County Library, West Brunswick Branch Library, Shallotte, NC [*Library symbol*] [*Library of Congress*] (LCLS)
**NCSORG** .. Naval Control of Shipping Organization
**NCSP**......... National Center for Surrogate Parenting [*Later, IAI*] [*Commercial firm*] (EA)
**NCSP**......... National Conference on State Parks [*Later, NRPA*] (EA)
**NCSP**......... National Crime Stop Program (EA)
**NCSP**......... Nordic Committee on Salaries and Personnel [*Nordic Council of Ministers*] [*Copenhagen, Denmark*] (EAIO)
**NcSp** .......... Southern Pines Public Library, Southern Pines, NC [*Library symbol*] [*Library of Congress*] (LCLS)
**NcSpa** ........ Alleghany County Public Library, Sparta, NC [*Library symbol*] [*Library of Congress*] (LCLS)
**NCSPA**...... National Corrugated Steel Pipe Association (EA)
**NCSPAA** ... National Council of School Press and Advisers Association
**NCSPAE** ... National Council of State Pharmaceutical Association Executives (EA)
**NCSPAS**.... National Conference of State Pharmaceutical Association Secretaries [*Later, NCSPAE*]
**NcSph** ........ Spring Hope Public Library, Spring Hope, NC [*Library symbol*] [*Library of Congress*] (LCLS)
**NcSpi** ......... Spindale Public Library, Spindale, NC [*Library symbol*] [*Library of Congress*] (LCLS)
**NcSpiI**........ Isothermal Community College, Spindale, NC [*Library symbol*] [*Library of Congress*] (LCLS)
**NcSppA** ..... Avery-Mitchell-Yancey Regional Library, Spruce Pine, NC [*Library symbol*] [*Library of Congress*] (LCLS)
**NcSppM** .... Mayland Technical Institute, Spruce Pine, NC [*Library symbol*] [*Library of Congress*] (LCLS)
**NCSPS** ...... National Committee for Support of the Public Schools [*Later, NCCE*] (EA)
**NcSpS**........ Sandhills Community College, Southern Pines, NC [*Library symbol*] [*Library of Congress*] (LCLS)
**NCSPWA**.. National Council of State Public Welfare Administrators [*Later, NCSHSA*] (EA)
**NCSR**......... National Centre for Systems Reliability [*British*] (CB)
**NCSRA**....... National Conference of State Retail Associations (EA)
**NCSRLL**.... North Carolina Studies in Romance Languages and Literatures [*A publication*]
**NCSS**......... National Center for Social Statistics [*HEW*]
**NCSS**......... National Collegiate Sports Services (EA)
**NCSS**......... National Commission on Supplies and Shortages [*Terminated, 1977*]
**NCSS**......... National Conference of Shomrim Societies (EA)
**NCSS**......... National Conference of State Societies (EA)
**NCSS**......... National Conference on Student Services (EA)
**NCSS**......... National Conversational Software Systems, Inc.
**NCSS**......... National Cooperative Soil Survey
**NCSS**......... National Council of Social Service [*British*]
**NCSS**......... National Council for the Social Studies (EA)
**NCSS**......... National Crash Severity Study [*National Highway Traffic Safety Administration*]
**NCSS**......... Nordic Council of Ski Schools (EAIO)
**NCSSA** ...... Naval Command Systems Support Activity
**NCSSAD**... National Council of Secondary School Athletic Directors (EA)
**NCSSB** ...... National Coalition for Seat Belts on School Buses (EA)
**NCSS B** ..... National Council for the Social Studies. Bulletin [*A publication*]
**NCSSC** ...... Naval Command Systems Support Center
**NCSSFL**.... National Council of State Supervisors of Foreign Languages (EA)
**NCSSIA**..... National Council of State Self-Insurers Associations [*Later, NCSI*] (EA)
**NCSSM** ..... National Council of State Supervisors of Music (EA)
**NCSSM** ..... North Carolina School of Science and Mathematics [*Free, residential public high school for gifted students*]
**NCSSMA** .. National Council of Social Security Management Associations (EA)
**NCSS Read** ... National Council for the Social Studies. Readings [*A publication*]
**NCSS Res B** ... National Council for the Social Studies. Research Bulletin [*A publication*]
**NCSSSA**.... National Conference of State Social Security Administrators (EA)
**NCSSW**..... Nordic Committee of Schools of Social Work (EAIO)
**NCSS Yearb** ... National Council for the Social Studies. Yearbook [*A publication*]
**NcSt**........... Iredell Public Library, Statesville, NC [*Library symbol*] [*Library of Congress*] (LCLS)
**NCST**......... National Coalition for Science and Technology [*Defunct*] (EA)
**NCSTAR**... National Committee of Shatnez Testers and Researchers (EA)
**NCSTAS** ... National Council of Scientific and Technical Art Societies [*Later, IG*] (EA)
**NC State Coll Agric Eng Eng Exp Stn Bull** ... North Carolina State College of Agriculture and Engineering. Engineering Experiment Station. Bulletin [*A publication*]
**NC State Coll Dep Eng Res Bull** ... North Carolina State College. Department of Engineering Research. Bulletin [*A publication*]
**NC State Coll Dept Eng Research Bull** ... North Carolina State College. Department of Engineering Research. Bulletin [*A publication*]
**NC State Coll Sch Agric Annu Rep** ... North Carolina State College. School of Agriculture. Annual Report [*A publication*]
**NC State Univ Dep Eng Res Bull** ... North Carolina State University. Department of Engineering. Research Bulletin [*A publication*]
**NC State Univ Eng Sch Bull** ... North Carolina State University. Engineering School Bulletin [*A publication*]
**NC State Univ Miner Res Lab Lab Notes** ... North Carolina State University. Minerals Research Laboratory. Laboratory Notes [*A publication*]
**NC State Univ Miner Res Lab Rep** ... North Carolina State University. Minerals Research Laboratory. Report [*A publication*]
**NC State Univ Sch Agric Life Sci Annu Rep** ... North Carolina State University. School of Agriculture and Life Sciences. Annual Report [*A publication*]
**NC St B Newsl** ... North Carolina State Bar Newsletter [*A publication*]
**NC St BQ**... North Carolina State Bar Quarterly [*A publication*]
**NCSTD**...... National Council of State Travel Directors (EA)
**NC & ST L** ... Nashville, Chattanooga & St. Louis Railway
**NcStMC** .... Mitchell College, Statesville, NC [*Library symbol*] [*Library of Congress*] (LCLS)
**NcStpR** ...... Robeson Technical Institute, St. Pauls, NC [*Library symbol*] [*Library of Congress*] [*Obsolete*] (LCLS)
**NCSTR**...... NATO Communication System Technical Recommendation (NATG)
**NC Str**........ Strange's Notes of Cases, Madras [*1798-1816*] [*A publication*] (DLA)
**NC/STRC** ... North Carolina Science and Technology Research Center [*North Carolina Department of Commerce*] [*Research center*] (RCD)
**NCSTS** ...... National Conference of State Transportation Specialists (EA)
**NCSTSR**.... National Conference of Superintendents of Training Schools and Reformatories [*Later, International Conference of Administrators Residential Centers for Youth - ICA*] (EA)
**NCSU** ........ North Carolina State University [*Raleigh*]
**NcSupB**...... Brunswick Technical College, Supply, NC [*Library symbol*] [*Library of Congress*] (LCLS)
**NCSW** ........ National Conference on Social Welfare (EA)
**NCSW** ........ National Conference of Social Workers
**NcSw**.......... Swannanoa Public Library, Swannanoa, NC [*Library symbol*] [*Library of Congress*] (LCLS)
**NCSWCL**.. National [*Presidential*] Commission on State Workmen's Compensation Laws
**NCSWD** .... National Center for Solid Waste Disposal [*Later, National Center for Resource Recovery*] (EA)
**NCSWD** .... National Council for the Single Woman and Her Dependants (EA)
**NCSWDI**... National Combination Storm Window and Door Institute [*Defunct*] (EA)
**NcSwW**...... Warren Wilson College, Swannanoa, NC [*Library symbol*] [*Library of Congress*] (LCLS)
**NCSX**.......... Shipping Control Exercise [*NATO exercises*] (NATG)
**NcSy** .......... Jackson County Public Library, Sylva, NC [*Library symbol*] [*Library of Congress*] (LCLS)
**NCSY**......... National Conference of Synagogue Youth (EA)

**NcSyS** ........ Southwestern Technical Institute, Sylva, NC [*Library symbol*] [*Library of Congress*] (LCLS)
**NCT** .......... Name Changed To
**NCT** .......... National Centre of Tribology [*Risley Nuclear Laboratories*] [*British*] (CB)
**NCT** .......... National Childbirth Trust [*British*]
**NCT** .......... National Corruption Tribunal [*Australia*]
**N Ct** .......... Native Court [*Ghana*] [*A publication*] (DLA)
**NCT** .......... Neoclassical Radiation Theory
**NCT** .......... Network Control Terminal (MCD)
**NCT** .......... Neural Crest Tumor [*Oncology*]
**NCT** .......... New Curing Technology
**NCT** .......... Night Closing Trunks [*Telecommunications*] (TEL)
**NCT** .......... Nordic Cooperation on Telecommunications (EAIO)
**NCT** .......... North Coast Industries Ltd. [*Vancouver Stock Exchange symbol*]
**NCT** .......... Number Connection Test
**NcTA** ......... Edgecombe County Memorial Library, Tarboro, NC [*Library symbol*] [*Library of Congress*] (LCLS)
**NCTA** ........ National Cable Television Association (EA)
**NCTA** ........ National Capital Transportation Agency [*Functions transferred to Washington Metropolitan Area Transit Authority*]
**NCTA** ........ National Cattle Theft Act
**NCTA** ........ National Ceramic Teachers Association (EA)
**NCTA** ........ National Christmas Tree Association (EA)
**NCTA** ........ National Council for Technological Awards [*British*]
**NCTA** ........ National Council for the Traditional Arts (EA)
**NCTA** ........ Navajo Code Talkers Association (EA)
**NCTA** ........ North Country Trail Association (EA)
**ncta** ........... Nuestra Cuenta [*Our Account*] [*Business term*] [*Spanish*]
**NcTaE** ........ Edgecombe County Technical Institute, Tarboro, NC [*Library symbol*] [*Library of Congress*] (LCLS)
**NCTAM** .... National Committee for Theoretical and Applied Mechanics [*British*]
**NcTa-P** ...... Edgecombe County Memorial Library, Pinetops Branch, Pinetops, NC [*Library symbol*] [*Library of Congress*] (LCLS)
**NcTayA** ..... Alexander County Public Library, Taylorsville, NC [*Library symbol*] [*Library of Congress*] (LCLS)
**NCTC** ........ National Cancer Institute Tissue Culture [*Medium*]
**NCTC** ........ National Catholic Theatre Conference (EA)
**NCTC** ........ National Collection of Type Cultures [*British*]
**NCTC** ........ Naval Communications Training Center
**NCTC** ........ Naval Construction Training Center
**NCTCA** ..... National Collegiate Track Coaches Association (EA)
**NCTCP** ...... National Coalition of Title I/Chapter I Parents (EA)
**NCTD** ........ National College of Teachers of the Deaf [*British*]
**NCTE** ........ National Council of Teachers of English (EA)
**NCTE** ........ National Council for Textile Education (EA)
**NCTE** ........ National Council for Torah Education (EA)
**NCTE** ........ Network Channel Terminating Equipment [*Telecommunications*]
**NCTE** ........ No-Cost Time Extension (MCD)
**NCTE** ........ North Central Turfgrass Exposition [*Illinois Turfgrass Foundation*] (TSPED)
**NCTEPS** .... National Commission on Teacher Education and Professional Standards [*Defunct*] (EA)
**NC Term R** ... North Carolina Term Reports [*A publication*] (DLA)
**NC Term Rep** ... North Carolina Term Reports [*A publication*] (DLA)
**NCTF** ........ National Corporate Theatre Fund (EA)
**NCTFC** ...... North Central Texas Film Cooperative [*Library network*]
**NCTGA** ..... National Christmas Tree Growers Association [*Later, National Christmas Tree Association*] (EA)
**NcTh** .......... Thomasville Public Library, Thomasville, NC [*Library symbol*] [*Library of Congress*] (LCLS)
**NCTI** ......... National Cable Television Institute (EA)
**NCTIP** ....... National Coalition of ESEA [*Elementary and Secondary Education Act*] Title I Parents (EA)
**NCTIP** ....... National Committee on the Treatment of Intractable Pain (EA)
**NCTJ** ......... National Council for the Training of Journalists [*British*]
**NCTM** ....... National Council of Teachers of Mathematics (EA)
**NCTO** ........ Naval Central Torpedo Office
**NCTO** ........ Navy Clothing and Textile Supply Office
**NCTP** ........ National Cryptologic Training Plan (MCD)
**NcTr** .......... Montgomery County Public Library, Troy, NC [*Library symbol*] [*Library of Congress*] (LCLS)
**NCTR** ........ National Center for Telephone Research [*Commercial firm*] [*Louis Harris and Associates*] (EA)
**NCTR** ........ National Center for Therapeutic Riding (EA)
**NCTR** ........ National Center for Toxicological Research [*Department of Health and Human Services*] [*Jefferson, AR*]
**NCTR** ........ National Council on Teacher Retirement (EA)
**NCTR** ........ Naval Commercial Traffic Regulations
**NCTR** ........ Nineteenth-Century Theatre Research [*A publication*]
**NCTR** ........ Noncooperative Target Recognition (MCD)
**NCTR** ........ Nordic Council for Tax Research (EA)
**NCTR** ........ Taylor's North Carolina Term Reports [*A publication*] (DLA)
**NCTRC** ...... National Council for Therapeutic Recreation Certification (EA)
**NCT Rep** .... North Carolina Term Reports [*A publication*] (DLA)
**NCTRF** ...... Navy Clothing and Textile Research Facility [*Natick, MA*]
**NCTRH** ..... National Council for Therapy and Rehabilitation through Horticulture (EA)
**NcTrM** ....... Montgomery Technical Institute, Troy, NC [*Library symbol*] [*Library of Congress*] (LCLS)
**NCTRU** ..... Navy Clothing and Textile Research Unit (MCD)
**NCTS** ......... NADOW [*National Association for Training the Disabled in Office Work*] Computer Training Scheme [*Australia*]
**NCTS** ......... National Council of Technical Schools (EA)
**NCTS** ......... Navy Civilian Technical Specialist (MCD)
**NCTS** ......... Northeast Corridor Transportation System [*Boston to Washington high-speed transportation*]
**NCTSI** ....... National Council of Technical Service Industries [*Later, Contract Services Association of America - CSA*]
**NCTT** ........ National Committee on Tunneling Technology
**NCTT** ........ Nuclear Certification Test Team (MCD)
**NCTTF** ...... Northern Counties Textile Trades' Federation [*British*] (DCTA)
**NCTU** ........ Northern Carpet Trades Union [*British*] (DCTA)
**NCTV** ........ National Coalition on Television Violence (EA)
**NCTV** ........ National College Television [*Cable-television system*]
**NCTW** ....... National Conference of Tuberculosis Workers [*Later, CLAS*] (EA)
**NCTWU** .... National Cigar and Tobacco Workers' Union [*British*]
**NcTy** .......... Lanier Library Association, Inc., Tryon, NC [*Library symbol*] [*Library of Congress*] (LCLS)
**NcTyI** ......... Isothermal Community College, Polk Campus, Tryon, NC [*Library symbol*] [*Library of Congress*] (LCLS)
**NCu** ............ Cuba Library, Cuba, NY [*Library symbol*] [*Library of Congress*] (LCLS)
**NCU** ........... National Commercial Union Ltd. [*Australia*]
**NCU** ........... National Communications Union [*British*]
**NCU** ........... National Conference for Unification [*Republic of Korea*] [*Political party*] (PPW)
**NCU** ........... National Cutlery Union [*British*]
**NCU** ........... National Cyclists' Union [*British*]
**NCU** ........... Navigation Computer Unit
**NCU** ........... Navigation Control and Display Unit (MCD)
**NCU** ........... Network Control Unit [*Data processing*]
**NCU** ........... New Cinch Uranium [*Vancouver Stock Exchange symbol*]
**NCU** ........... Nitrogen Control Unit (AAG)
**NCU** ........... Nonconforming Use (ADA)
**ncu** ............. North Carolina [*MARC country of publication code*] [*Library of Congress*] (LCCP)
**NCU** ........... Nozzle Control Unit [*NASA*]
**NCU** ........... Union College, Lincoln, NE [*OCLC symbol*] (OCLC)
**NcU** ............ University of North Carolina, Chapel Hill, NC [*Library symbol*] [*Library of Congress*] (LCLS)
**NCUA** ......... National Credit Union Administration
**NCUAAE** .. National Council of Urban Administrators of Adult Education (OICC)
**NCUA Q** .... National Credit Union Administration. Quarterly [*A publication*]
**NcU-BPR** .. University of North Carolina, Bureau of Public Records, Collection and Research, Chapel Hill, NC [*Library symbol*] [*Library of Congress*] (LCLS)
**NCUC** ........ North Carolina Utilities Commission Reports [*A publication*] (DLA)
**NCUC** ........ Nuclear Chemistry Users Committee
**NCU(E)** ..... National Communications Union, Engineering Group [*British*]
**NCUEA** ..... National Center for Urban Ethnic Affairs (EA)
**NCUEA** ..... National Council of Urban Education Associations (EA)
**NCUES** ...... National Center for Urban Environmental Studies [*Defunct*] (EA)
**NCUG** ........ Nevada COBOL [*Common Business-Oriented Language*] Users Group (EA)
**NcU-H** ....... University of North Carolina, Division of Health Affairs, Chapel Hill, NC [*Library symbol*] [*Library of Congress*] (LCLS)
**NCUI** ......... National Center for Urban and Industrial Health [*Public Health Service*]
**NcU-IG** ...... University of North Carolina, Institute of Government Library, Chapel Hill, NC [*Library symbol*] [*Library of Congress*] (LCLS)
**NcU-L** ........ University of North Carolina, Law Library, Chapel Hill, NC [*Library symbol*] [*Library of Congress*] (LCLS)
**NcU-LS** ..... University of North Carolina at Chapel Hill, Library School, Chapel Hill, NC [*Library symbol*] [*Library of Congress*] (LCLS)
**NCult** ......... Nuova Cultura [*A publication*]
**NCUMA** .... National Credit Union Management Association (EA)
**NCUMC** .... National Council for the Unmarried Mother and Her Child [*British*] (ILCA)
**NcU-MS** .... University of North Carolina, Institute of Marine Sciences, Morehead City, NC [*Library symbol*] [*Library of Congress*] (LCLS)
**NCUP** ........ No Commission until Paid
**NCUPI** ....... National Coalition for Universities in the Public Interest (EA)
**NCUPM** .... National Council of United Presbyterian Men (EA)
**NcU-Pop** .... University of North Carolina, Carolina Population Center, Technical Information Service, Chapel Hill, NC [*Library symbol*] [*Library of Congress*] (LCLS)

**NCUPRSE** ... National Consortium of Universities Preparing Rural Special Educators (EA)
**NCUR** ........ National Committee for Utilities Radio (MCD)
**NCURA** ........ National Council of University Research Administrators (EA)
**NCUSA** ..... Navy Club of the United States of America (EA)
**NCUSAA**... Navy Club of the United States of America Auxiliary (EA)
**NCUSAR**... National Council on US-Arab Relations (EA)
**NCUSCR**... National Committee on United States-China Relations (EA)
**NCUSCT**... National Council for US-China Trade [*Later, USCBC*] (EA)
**NCUSIF** .... National Credit Union Share Insurance Fund
**NCUSIOGT** ... National Council of the United States, International Organization of Good Templars (EA)
**NCUTLO** .. National Committee on Uniform Traffic Laws and Ordinances (EA)
**NCUUA**..... National Council for Universal and Unconditional Amnesty [*For Vietnam-War resisters*] [*Defunct*] (EA)
**NCV**........... Navigation Computer Unit
**NCV**........... Nerve Conduction Velocity [*Electrophysiology*]
**NCV**........... No Commercial Value [*Business term*]
**NCV**........... No Core Value [*Business term*]
**NCV**........... No Customs Value (DS)
**NCV**........... Non-Cholera Vibrios [*Microbiology*]
**NCV**........... Normalized Critical View
**NCVA**......... National Center for Voluntary Action [*Later, NVC*]
**NcVal**......... Valdese Public Library, Valdese, NC [*Library symbol*] [*Library of Congress*] (LCLS)
**NCVC** ........ National Catholic Vocation Council (EA)
**NCVC** ........ National Congress on Volunteerism and Citizenship [*Bicentennial event, 1976*]
**NCVE** ........ National Council on Vocational Education [*Department of Education*] [*Washington, DC*] (EGAO)
**NCVO**........ National Council for Voluntary Organisations [*British*] (ILCA)
**NCVOTE** .. National Center for Vocational, Occupational, and Technical Education [*Office of Education*]
**NCVP** ........ Natural Circulation Verification Program [*Nuclear energy*] (NRCH)
**NCVP** ........ Noncapsid Viral Protein [*Biochemistry*]
**NCVQ**........ National Council for Vocational Qualifications [*British*]
**NCVR**......... National Conference of Vicars for Religious (EA)
**NCVS**......... National Credential Verification Service (MCD)
**NCW**.......... National Council of Women of the United States (EA)
**NCW**.......... New Catholic World [*A publication*]
**NCW**.......... Newberry College, Newberry, SC [*OCLC symbol*] (OCLC)
**NCW**.......... Nose Cone Warhead [*Aviation*] (NATG)
**NCW**.......... Not Complied With [*Military*]
**NcW**........... Wilmington Public Library, Wilmington, NC [*Library symbol*] [*Library of Congress*] (LCLS)
**NcWa**......... George H. and Laura E. Brown Library, Washington, NC [*Library symbol*] [*Library of Congress*] (LCLS)
**NCWA**........ National Candy Wholesalers Association (EA)
**NCWA**........ NATO Civil Wartime Agency (NATG)
**NcWaB** ...... Beaufort County Technical Institute, Washington, NC [*Library symbol*] [*Library of Congress*] (LCLS)
**NcWaBHM** ... Beaufort, Hyde, Martin Regional Library, Washington, NC [*Library symbol*] [*Library of Congress*] (LCLS)
**NcWad**....... Anson County Library, Wadesboro, NC [*Library symbol*] [*Library of Congress*] (LCLS)
**NcWal**......... Thelma Dingus Bryant Library, Wallace, NC [*Library symbol*] [*Library of Congress*] (LCLS)
**NCWAO**.... National Council of World Affairs Organizations (EA)
**NcWarW** ... Warren County Memorial Library, Warrenton, NC [*Library symbol*] [*Library of Congress*] (LCLS)
**NCWAS**..... National Coal Workers Autopsy Study
**NcWaw** ...... Warsaw Public Library, Warsaw, NC [*Library symbol*] [*Library of Congress*] (LCLS)
**NcWayH**.... Haywood County Public Library, Waynesville, NC [*Library symbol*] [*Library of Congress*] (LCLS)
**NcWayH-C** ... Haywood County Public Library, Canton Branch, Canton, NC [*Library symbol*] [*Library of Congress*] (LCLS)
**NCWBA** .... National Conference of Women's Bar Associations (EA)
**NCWC** ....... National Catholic Welfare Conference [*Later, USCC*] (EA)
**NCWC** ....... National Council of Women of Canada
**NCWC** ....... National Council of Women Chiropractors (EA)
**NcWc** ......... Walnut Cove Public Library, Walnut Cove, NC [*Library symbol*] [*Library of Congress*] (LCLS)
**NcW-C**....... Wilmington Public Library, College Square Branch, Wilmington, NC [*Library symbol*] [*Library of Congress*] (LCLS)
**NcWCF**...... Cape Fear Technical Institute, Wilmington, NC [*Library symbol*] [*Library of Congress*] (LCLS)
**NCWD**....... National Coalition for Women in Defense (EA)
**NcWea** ....... Bess Tilson Sprinkle Memorial Library, Weaverville, NC [*Library symbol*] [*Library of Congress*] (LCLS)
**NcWel** ........ Weldon Memorial Library, Weldon, NC [*Library symbol*] [*Library of Congress*] (LCLS)
**NcWelc** ...... North Davidson Public Library, Welcome, NC [*Library symbol*] [*Library of Congress*] (LCLS)
**NcWelH**..... Halifax County Technical Institute, Weldon, NC [*Library symbol*] [*Library of Congress*] (LCLS)
**NcWeR** ...... Rockingham Community College, Wentworth, NC [*Library symbol*] [*Library of Congress*] (LCLS)
**NCWFC**..... National Council of Women of Free Czechoslovakia (EA)
**NCWFD** .... National Committee for World Food Day [*Later, USNCWFD*] (EA)
**NcWfSB**..... Southeastern Baptist Theological Seminary, Wake Forest, NC [*Library symbol*] [*Library of Congress*] (LCLS)
**NCWGA**.... Natural Colored Wool Growers Association (EA)
**NcWGE** ..... General Electric Co., WMD Technical Library, Wilmington, NC [*Library symbol*] [*Library of Congress*] (LCLS)
**NCWGE**.... National Coalition for Women and Girls in Education (EA)
**NcWhC**...... Columbus County Public Library, Whiteville, NC [*Library symbol*] [*Library of Congress*] (LCLS)
**NcWhS** ...... Southeastern Community College, Whiteville, NC [*Library symbol*] [*Library of Congress*] (LCLS)
**NcWil**......... Wilson County Public Library, Wilson, NC [*Library symbol*] [*Library of Congress*] (LCLS)
**NcWilA**...... Atlantic Christian College, Wilson, NC [*Library symbol*] [*Library of Congress*] (LCLS)
**NcWilC**...... Carolina Discipliana Library, Wilson, NC [*Library symbol*] [*Library of Congress*] (LCLS)
**NcWilE**...... North Carolina Department of Human Resources, Eastern North Carolina School for the Deaf, Wilson, NC [*Library symbol*] [*Library of Congress*] (LCLS)
**NcWill** ....... Martin Memorial Library, Williamston, NC [*Library symbol*] [*Library of Congress*] (LCLS)
**NcWillM** ... Martin Technical Institute, Williamston, NC [*Library symbol*] [*Library of Congress*] (LCLS)
**NcWilW**..... Wilson County Technical Institute, Wilson, NC [*Library symbol*] [*Library of Congress*] (LCLS)
**NcWin**........ Wingate College, Wingate, NC [*Library symbol*] [*Library of Congress*] (LCLS)
**NcWind**...... Lawrence Memorial Library, Windsor, NC [*Library symbol*] [*Library of Congress*] (LCLS)
**NcWintA** ... Albermarle Regional Library, Winton, NC [*Library symbol*] [*Library of Congress*] (LCLS)
**NCWIS**...... New Computerized World Information Service [*Information service or system*] (IID)
**NcWiW**...... Wilkes Community College, Wilkesboro, NC [*Library symbol*] [*Library of Congress*] (LCLS)
**NcWj**.......... Ashe County Public Library, West Jefferson, NC [*Library symbol*] [*Library of Congress*] (LCLS)
**NCWM**...... National Conference on Weights and Measures (EA)
**NCWM**..... National Congress of Women in Music (EA)
**NcWN**........ New Hanover County Public Library, Wilmington, NC [*Library symbol*] [*Library of Congress*] (LCLS)
**NcWN-C**... New Hanover County Public Library, Carolina Beach Branch Library, Carolina Beach, NC [*Library symbol*] [*Library of Congress*] (LCLS)
**NCW News** ... NCW News (National Council of Women of New South Wales) [*A publication*] (APTA)
**NCWPA** .... National Committee for Women in Public Administration (EA)
**NCWPTF**.. National Council for a World Peace Tax Fund (EA)
**NCWQ**....... National Commission on Water Quality [*National Academy of Sciences*]
**NCWR**....... Nordic Council for Wildlife Research (EAIO)
**NCWRU**.... North Central Watershed Research Unit [*Department of Agriculture*] (GRD)
**NcWs** ......... Forsyth County Public Library System, Winston-Salem, NC [*Library symbol*] [*Library of Congress*] (LCLS)
**NCWSA**..... National Collegiate Water Ski Association (EA)
**NcWs-C** ..... Forsyth County Public Library, Clemmons Branch Library, Clemmons, NC [*Library symbol*] [*Library of Congress*] (LCLS)
**NcWs-E** ..... Forsyth County Public Library, East Winston Branch, Winston-Salem, NC [*Library symbol*] [*Library of Congress*] (LCLS)
**NcWsF**....... Forsyth Technical Institute, Winston-Salem, NC [*Library symbol*] [*Library of Congress*] (LCLS)
**NcWs-K**..... Forsyth County Public Library, Kernersville Branch Library, Kernersville, NC [*Library symbol*] [*Library of Congress*] (LCLS)
**NcWsM** ..... Moravian Archives, Winston-Salem, NC [*Library symbol*] [*Library of Congress*] (LCLS)
**NcWsMES** ... Museum of Early Southern Decorative Arts, MESDA Library, Winston-Salem, NC [*Library symbol*] [*Library of Congress*] (LCLS)
**NcWsMM** ... Moravian Music Foundation, Winston-Salem, NC [*Library symbol*] [*Library of Congress*] (LCLS)
**NcWsN** ...... North Carolina School of the Arts, Winston-Salem, NC [*Library symbol*] [*Library of Congress*] (LCLS)
**NcWs-R** ..... Forsyth County Public Library, Reynolda Manor Branch, Winston-Salem, NC [*Library symbol*] [*Library of Congress*] (LCLS)
**NcWsRI**..... Reynolds Industries, Corporate Library, Winston-Salem, NC [*Library symbol*] [*Library of Congress*] (LCLS)
**NcWsR-M** ... Reynolds Tobacco Co., Marketing Development Intelligence Center, Winston-Salem, NC [*Library symbol*] [*Library of Congress*] (LCLS)
**NcWsR-R** .. Reynolds Tobacco Co., Research and Development Technical Information Services, Winston-Salem, NC [*Library symbol*] [*Library of Congress*] (LCLS)

**NcWs-RS**... Forsyth County Public Library, Rural Hall/Stanleyville Branch Library, Rural Hall, NC [*Library symbol*] [*Library of Congress*] (LCLS)
**NcWs-S**..... Forsyth County Public Library, Southside Branch, Winston-Salem, NC [*Library symbol*] [*Library of Congress*] (LCLS)
**NcWsS**....... Salem College, Winston-Salem, NC [*Library symbol*] [*Library of Congress*] (LCLS)
**NcWsU**...... Winston-Salem State University, Winston-Salem, NC [*Library symbol*] [*Library of Congress*] (LCLS)
**NcWsW**..... Wake Forest University, Winston-Salem, NC [*Library symbol*] [*Library of Congress*] (LCLS)
**NcWsW-B**... Wake Forest University, Babcock Graduate School of Management, Winston-Salem, NC [*Library symbol*] [*Library of Congress*] (LCLS)
**NcWsWE**... Western Electric Co., Lexington Road Technical Library, Winston-Salem, NC [*Library symbol*] [*Library of Congress*] (LCLS)
**NcWsWE-R**... Western Electric Co., Reynolda Road Technical Library, Winston-Salem, NC [*Library symbol*] [*Library of Congress*] (LCLS)
**NcWsW-L**... Wake Forest University, Law Library, Winston-Salem, NC [*Library symbol*] [*Library of Congress*] (LCLS)
**NcWsW-M**... Wake Forest University, Bowman Gray School of Medicine, Wake Forest, NC [*Library symbol*] [*Library of Congress*] (LCLS)
**NCWTF**..... Naval Commander Western Task Force
**NCWTM**... National Council on Wholistic Therapeutics and Medicine [*Inactive*] (EA)
**NCWU**....... National Catholic Women's Union (EA)
**NcWU**........ University of North Carolina at Wilmington, Wilmington, NC [*Library symbol*] [*Library of Congress*] (LCLS)
**NCWW**...... National Commission on Working Women (EA)
**NCWX**....... No Change in Weather [*Aviation*] (FAAC)
**NCX**.......... Corpus Christi, TX [*Location identifier*] [*FAA*] (FAAL)
**NCX**.......... NCN Exploration & Development [*Vancouver Stock Exchange symbol*]
**NCX**.......... North Carolina Central University, Durham, NC [*OCLC symbol*] (OCLC)
**NCY**.......... Annecy [*France*] [*Airport symbol*] (OAG)
**NcY**........... Hyconeechee Regional Library, Yanceyville, NC [*Library symbol*] [*Library of Congress*] (LCLS)
**NCY**.......... National Collaboration for Youth (EA)
**N-CY**......... Natural-Colored Yellow [*Diamonds*]
**NCY**.......... New Century Resources [*Vancouver Stock Exchange symbol*]
**NCY**.......... North Central Yiddish (BJA)
**NCY**.......... Yorktown, VA [*Location identifier*] [*FAA*] (FAAL)
**NcYad**........ Yadkin County Public Library, Yadkinville, NC [*Library symbol*] [*Library of Congress*] (LCLS)
**NCYBD**..... Nuclear Canada Yearbook [*A publication*]
**NCYC**........ National Catholic Youth Council
**NCYC**........ National Collection of Yeast Cultures [*AFRC Institute of Food Research*] [*Great Britain*] [*Information service or system*] (IID)
**NCYC**........ National Council of Yacht Clubs (EA)
**N CYC BN**... Northern Cyclist Battalion [*British military*] (DMA)
**NCYC CAT**... National Collection of Yeast Cultures Catalogue [*Norwich Laboratory*] [*Norfolk, England*] [*Information service or system*] [*A publication*] (IID)
**NCYF**........ National Crusaders Youth Federation (EA)
**NCYFS**...... National Children and Youth Fitness Study [*HHS*]
**NcYG**........ Gunn Memorial Public Library, Yanceyville, NC [*Library symbol*] [*Library of Congress*] (LCLS)
**NCYI**........ National Council of Young Israel (EA)
**NCYL**........ National Center for Youth Law (EA)
**NcYo**......... Youngsville Public Library, Youngsville, NC [*Library symbol*] [*Library of Congress*] (LCLS)
**NCYOF**..... National CYO [*Catholic Youth Organizations*] Federation (EA)
**NCYP**........ National Conference of Yeshiva Principals (EA)
**NCYRE**...... National Council for Year-Round Education [*Later, NAYRE*] (EA)
**NCYSP**...... National Committee on Youth Suicide Prevention (EA)
**NCYWA**.... Nordic Child and Youth Welfare Alliance (EA)
**ND**............ Aerospatiale [*Societe Nationale Industrielle Aerospatiale*] [*France*] [*ICAO aircraft manufacturer identifier*] (ICAO)
**ND**............ Diploma in Naturopathy [*British*]
**ND**............ Doctor of Naturopathy
**ND**............ I am not able to deliver message addressed to aircraft [*Telecommunications*] (FAAC)
**ND**............ La Nueva Democracia [*New York*] [*A publication*]
**N-D**........... N-Dimensional (MCD)
**N f D**.......... Nachrichten fuer Dokumentation [*A publication*]
**ND**............ Named (ROG)
**ND**............ Narrowband Distributive Services [*Telecommunications*]
**ND**............ NASA Document (KSC)
**ND**............ National Debt
**ND**............ Natural Death [*Medicine*]
**ND**............ Natural Draught
**ND**............ Naval Dispensary
**ND**............ Naval Distillate Fuel (NVT)
**ND**............ Naval District
**ND**............ Naval Draftsman (ROG)
**ND**............ Navigation Display (MCD)
**ND**............ Navy Department
**ND**............ Nea Demokratia [*New Democracy*] [*Greek*] [*Political party*] (PPE)
**ND**............ Need (FAAC)
**N/D**........... Need Date (MCD)
**ND**............ Negative Declaration (NRCH)
**Nd**............ Neodymium [*Chemical element*]
**ND**............ Neoplastic Disease [*Medicine*]
**ND**............ Nervous Debility [*Medicine*]
**ND**............ Net Debt
**ND**............ Neues Deutschland [*A publication*]
**ND**............ Neurologic Deficit [*Medicine*]
**ND**............ Neurotic Depression [*Psychiatry*]
**ND**............ Neutral Density [*Photography*]
**ND**............ New Deal (DAS)
**ND**............ New Deck [*On ships*]
**ND**............ New Democracy [*Political party*] [*Greece*]
**ND**............ New Directions [*A publication*]
**ND**............ New Directions [*Later, Democratic Alternatives - DA*] (EA)
**ND**............ New Dramatists (EA)
**ND**............ New Drug
**ND**............ New Drugs [*A publication*]
**ND**............ Newcastle Disease [*Virus*] [*Also, NDV*]
**Nd**............ Newfoundland Reports [*A publication*] (DLA)
**ND**............ Newsletters Directory [*Later, NIP*] [*A publication*]
**ND**............ Next Day [*Stock exchange term*] (SPSG)
**ND**............ Next Day's Delivery
**ND**............ Nickajack Dam [*TVA*]
**ND**............ Nippondenso Co. [*Toyota Motor Corp.*]
**ND**............ No Data
**ND**............ No Date [*of publication*]
**ND**............ No Decision [*Sports*]
**N/D**........... No Defects
**ND**............ No Detect
**ND**............ No Discount [*Business term*] (DS)
**ND**............ No Disease [*Medicine*]
**ND**............ No Drawing [*Engineering*]
**ND**............ Node Dissection [*Medicine*]
**N & D**........ Nodular and Diffuse Lymphoma [*Oncology*]
**ND**............ Non Disponible [*Not Available*] [*French*]
**ND**............ Nondelay [*Military*]
**ND**............ Nondelivery [*Shipping*]
**N/D**........... Nondestructive
**ND**............ Nondiabetic [*Medicine*]
**ND**............ Nondirectional Antenna
**ND**............ Nondisabling [*Medicine*]
**ND**............ Nonduty [*Military*]
**ND**............ Nordair Ltd. [*Canada*] [*ICAO designator*] (OAG)
**ND**............ Normal Delivery [*Obstetrics*]
**ND**............ North Dakota [*Postal code*]
**ND**............ North Dakota Music Educator [*A publication*]
**ND**............ North Dakota Reports [*A publication*]
**Nd**............ North Dakota State Library, Bismarck, ND [*Library symbol*] [*Library of Congress*] (LCLS)
**ND**............ North Dakota Supreme Court Reports [*1890-1953*] [*A publication*] (DLA)
**ND**............ Northern District (DLA)
**ND**............ Nose Down [*Aviation*]
**ND**............ Nostra Domina [*Our Lady*] [*Latin*]
**ND**............ Not Dated [*Banking, bibliography*]
**ND**............ Not Detected [*or Detectable*] [*Medicine*]
**ND**............ Not Determined [*Medicine*]
**ND**............ Not Diagnosed [*Medicine*]
**ND**............ Not Done
**ND**............ Nothing Doing [*Amateur radio slang*]
**N-D**........... Notre-Dame [*Our Lady*] [*French*]
**ND**............ Nowe Drogi [*A publication*]
**ND**............ Nuclear Device (AAG)
**Nd**............ Number of Dissimilar Matches
**ND**............ Number of Document [*Online database field identifier*]
**ND**............ Nuovo Didaskaleion [*A publication*]
**ND**............ Nursing Doctorate
**ND**............ Romania [*License plate code assigned to foreign diplomats in the US*]
**ND**............ University of Notre Dame [*Indiana*]
**NDA**.......... Bandanaira [*Indonesia*] [*Airport symbol*] (OAG)
**NDA**.......... National Dance Association (EA)
**NDA**.......... National Defense Act
**NDA**.......... National Defense Area (AABC)
**NDA**.......... National Dental Association (EA)
**NDA**.......... National Denturist Association (EA)
**NDA**.......... National Diploma in Agriculture [*British*]
**NDA**.......... National Dome Association [*Later, NDC*] (EA)
**NDA**.......... National Door Association [*Defunct*]
**NDA**.......... NAUI [*National Association of Underwater Instructors*] Diving Association (EA)
**NDA**.......... Naval Discipline Act [*British military*] (DMA)
**NDA**.......... Neutral Detector Assembly
**NDA**.......... Nevada (ROG)

**NDA**.......... New Desk Accessories [*Utility program*] [*Apple Computers, Inc.*] [*Data processing*]
**NDA**.......... New Drug Application [*FDA*]
**NDA**.......... Ninos de las Americas [*Children of the Americas*] (EAIO)
**NDA**.......... No Data Available [*Data processing*]
**NDA**.......... No Detectable Activity
**NDA**.......... Nonadecanoic Acid [*Organic chemistry*]
**NDA**.......... Nondestructive Assay
**NDA**.......... Nondimensional Analysis
**NDA**.......... Nonresonant Deflection Amplifier
**NDA**.......... Nordair Ltd. [*Toronto Stock Exchange symbol*]
**NDA**.......... Nuclear Device Association (AAG)
**NDA**.......... [*The*] Nuzi Dialect of Akkadian [*A publication*] (BJA)
**NDAA**........ National Dental Assistants Association (EA)
**NDAA**........ National District Attorneys Association (EA)
**NDAB**........ Numerical Data Advisory Board [*National Academy of Sciences*] [*Information service or system*] (IID)
**NDAC**........ National Data Communications, Inc. [*NASDAQ symbol*] (NQ)
**NDAC**........ National Defense Advisory Commission [*World War II*]
**NDAC**........ North Dakota Agricultural College
**NDAC**........ Nuclear Defense Affairs Committee [*NATO*]
**ND Acad Sci Proc** ... North Dakota Academy of Science. Proceedings [*A publication*]
**NDACS**..... Network Diagnostic and Control Systems (ADA)
**NDACSS**... Navy Department Advisory Committee on Structural Steel
**NDADD8**... New Drugs Annual. Cardiovascular Drugs [*A publication*]
**ND Admin Code** ... North Dakota Administrative Code [*A publication*] (DLA)
**NDAFA**..... National Directory of Accounting Firms and Accountants [*A publication*]
**ND Ag Exp** ... North Dakota. Agricultural Experiment Station. Publications [*A publication*]
**ND Agr E**... National Diploma in Agricultural Engineering [*British*]
**ND Agric Exp Stn Bull** ... North Dakota. Agricultural Experiment Station. Bulletin [*A publication*]
**N DAK**....... North Dakota (AAG)
**N Dak**........ North Dakota Reports [*A publication*] (DLA)
**N Dak Acad Sci Proc** ... North Dakota Academy of Science. Proceedings [*A publication*]
**N Dak Agr Coll Exp Sta Bien Rep** ... North Dakota Agricultural College. Experiment Station. Biennial Report [*A publication*]
**N Dak Farm Res Bimon Bull** ... North Dakota Farm Research. Bimonthly Bulletin. North Dakota Agricultural College. Agricultural Experiment Station [*A publication*]
**N Dak Fm Res** ... North Dakota Farm Research [*A publication*]
**N Dak Geol Surv Bull** ... North Dakota. Geological Survey. Bulletin [*A publication*]
**N Dak Geol Surv Circ** ... North Dakota. Geological Survey. Circular [*A publication*]
**N Dak Geol Surv Misc Ser** ... North Dakota. Geological Survey. Miscellaneous Series [*A publication*]
**N Dak Geol Surv Rep Invest** ... North Dakota. Geological Survey. Report of Investigations [*A publication*]
**N Dak G S Bien Rp** ... North Dakota. Geological Survey. Biennial Report [*A publication*]
**N Dak His S** ... North Dakota State Historical Society. Collections [*A publication*]
**N Dak History** ... North Dakota History [*A publication*]
**N Dak Lib Notes** ... North Dakota Library Notes [*A publication*]
**N Dak M**.... North Dakota Magazine [*A publication*]
**N Dak Outdoors** ... North Dakota Outdoors [*A publication*]
**N Dak Research Found Bull Circ** ... North Dakota Research Foundation Bulletin. Circular [*A publication*]
**ND Ala**....... United States District Court for the Northern District of Alabama (DLA)
**NDA & LB** ... Naval District Affairs and Logistics Branch
**N Dame J Ed** ... Notre Dame Journal of Education [*A publication*]
**NDAP**........ Nationalsozialistische Deutsche Arbeiterpartei [*National Socialist German Workers' Party, 1919-45*] [*Political party*] (PPW)
**NDAPTA**... National Drivers Association for the Prevention of Traffic Accidents (EA)
**NDAT**........ Nashriyye(H)-Ye Daneshkade(H)-Ye Adabiyyat va Olum-E Ensani-Ye Tabriz [*A publication*]
**NDAT**........ Nondestructible Aiming Target
**NDB**.......... Naval Disciplinary Barracks
**NDB**.......... Navy Department Bulletin [*A publication*]
**NDB**.......... Net Debit Balance
**NDB**.......... Neue Deutsche Biographie [*A publication*]
**NDB**.......... Nondirectional Beacon (AFM)
**NDB**.......... Nouadhibou [*Mauritania*] [*Airport symbol*] (OAG)
**NDB**.......... Nuclear Depth Bomb (NVT)
**NDB**.......... Numeric Data Base [*INPADOC*] [*Data processing*]
**NDBA**........ National Deaf Bowling Association (EA)
**NDBA**........ New Directions in Biblical Archaeology [*A publication*] (BJA)
**NDBB**........ North Dakota Bar Brief [*A publication*] (DLA)
**NdBC**........ Bismarck Junior College, Bismarck, ND [*Library symbol*] [*Library of Congress*] (LCLS)
**NDBC**........ National Data Buoy Center [*National Oceanic and Atmospheric Administration*] [*Also, an information service or system*] (IID)
**NDBC**........ National Day of Bread Committee [*Defunct*] (EA)
**NDBC**........ National Dry Bean Council (EA)
**NDBC**........ National Duckpin Bowling Congress (EA)
**NDBCA**..... Navy Department Board of Contract Appeals
**NDBDP**..... National Data Buoy Development Project [*Later, NDBO*] [*Coast Guard*] (MSC)
**NdBH**........ Bismarck Hospital, School of Nursing Library, Bismarck, ND [*Library symbol*] [*Library of Congress*] (LCLS)
**NdBHD**..... North Dakota State Health Department, Bismarck, ND [*Library symbol*] [*Library of Congress*] (LCLS)
**NdBHwy**.... North Dakota State Highway Department, Bismarck, ND [*Library symbol*] [*Library of Congress*] (LCLS)
**NDBLO**..... Not to Descend Below [*Aviation*] (FAAC)
**NdBM**........ Mary College, Bismarck, ND [*Library symbol*] [*Library of Congress*] (LCLS)
**NDBMS**.... Network Database Management System
**NDBO**........ NOAA [*National Oceanic and Atmospheric Administration*] Data Buoy Office [*or Operation*] (IID)
**NdBoU**....... North Dakota State University, Bottineau Branch, Bottineau, ND [*Library symbol*] [*Library of Congress*] (LCLS)
**NdBPI**........ North Dakota State Department of Public Instruction, Bismarck, ND [*Library symbol*] [*Library of Congress*] (LCLS)
**NDBPSA**... Non-Denominational Bible Prophecy Study Association (EA)
**NdBPW**..... North Dakota State Public Welfare Board, Bismarck, ND [*Library symbol*] [*Library of Congress*] (LCLS)
**NdBQ**........ Quain and Ramstad Clinic, Bismarck, ND [*Library symbol*] [*Library of Congress*] (LCLS)
**NDBS**........ National Data Buoy System
**NDBS**........ Naval Despatch Boat Service
**NDBSB**...... Nogyo Doboku Shikenjo Hokoku [*A publication*]
**NDBULCUMED** ... Navy Department Bulletins, Cumulative Editions [*A publication*]
**NdBV**......... Bismarck [*Veterans Memorial*] Public Library, Bismarck, ND [*Library symbol*] [*Library of Congress*] (LCLS)
**NDBZ**........ Neue Deutsche Beamtenzeitung [*A publication*]
**Nd B Zt**..... Neudeutsche Bauzeitung [*A publication*]
**NDC**.......... Natick Development Center [*Massachusetts*] [*Army*]
**NDC**.......... National Dairy Council (EA)
**NDC**.......... National Data Communication
**NDC**.......... National Data Corporation [*Fairfield, NJ*] [*Database vendor*]
**NDC**.......... National Defence College [*British*]
**NDC**.......... National Defence Committee [*Ghana*] [*Political party*] (PPW)
**NDC**.......... National Defence Company [*British military*] (DMA)
**NDC**.......... National Defence Contribution [*British*]
**NDC**.......... National Defence Corps [*British*]
**NDC**.......... National Defense Council (KSC)
**NDC**.......... National Democratic Club (EA)
**NDC**.......... National Design Council [*Canada*]
**NDC**.......... National DeSoto Club (EA)
**NDC**.......... National Development Council (EA)
**NDC**.......... National Dome Council (EA)
**NDC**.......... National Drug Code [*FDA*]
**NDC**.......... National Duckling Council (EA)
**NDC**.......... NATO Defense College [*Also, NADC, NADEFCOL*] (NATG)
**NDC**.......... Naval Data Center
**NDC**.......... Naval Dental Clinic
**NDC**.......... Navigation Display and Computer (MCD)
**NDC**.......... Network Diagnostic Control
**NDC**.......... New Democratic Coalition
**NDC**.......... New Die Cast [*Honda Motor Co. Ltd.*]
**NDC**.......... New Dramatists Committee [*Later, ND*] (EA)
**NDC**.......... Nippon Decimal Classification [*Library science*]
**NDC**.......... No Date Club [*Brooklyn girls - no dates for the duration*] [*World War II*]
**NDC**.......... No Direct Charge
**NDC**.......... NORAD Direction Center [*Military*]
**NDC**.......... Normalized Device Coordinates [*Data processing*]
**NDC**.......... Northwest Drama Conference (EA)
**NDC**.......... Notre Dame College [*Missouri, New Hampshire, Ohio*]
**NDC**.......... Notre Dame College, Manchester, NH [*OCLC symbol*] [*Inactive*] (OCLC)
**NDC**.......... Noyes Data Corporation
**NDC**.......... Nuclear Data Committee (NRCH)
**NDC**.......... Nuclear Design Calculations [*Program*]
**NDC**.......... Nuclear Design and Construction [*British*]
**NDCA**........ Naphthalenedicarboxylic Acid [*Organic chemistry*]
**NDCA**........ National Dance Council of America (EA)
**NDCA**........ National Deaf Children's Association [*British*]
**NDCA**........ National Drilling Contractors Association (EA)
**NDCA**........ Nuclear Development Corporation of America
**NDCAB**..... Nippon Dental College. Annual Publications [*A publication*]
**ND Cal**....... United States District Court for the Northern District of California (DLA)
**NdCan**........ Cando Public Library, Cando, ND [*Library symbol*] [*Library of Congress*] (LCLS)
**NDCC**........ National Defense Cadet Corps
**NDCC**........ Navy Department Corrosion Committee

**NDCC**........ Nondirectional Cross-Country (MCD)
**NDCC**........ North Dakota Century Code [*A publication*]
**NDCCC**..... National Defense Communications Control Center (MCD)
**NDCD**........ National Drug Code Directory [*A publication*] [*FDA*]
**NDCDAR**.. National Defense Committee of the Daughters of the American Revolution (EA)
**NDCDDI**... New Directions for Child Development [*A publication*]
**ND Cent Code** ... North Dakota Century Code [*A publication*] (DLA)
**NDCF**........ National Defense Council Foundation (EA)
**NdCo**.......... Cooperstown Public Library, Cooperstown, ND [*Library symbol*] [*Library of Congress*] (LCLS)
**NDCO**........ Noble Drilling Corp. [*NASDAQ symbol*] (NQ)
**NDColl**...... National Defence College [*British*]
**NDCP**........ Navy Decision Coordinating Paper
**NDCP**........ Navy Development Concept Paper (CAAL)
**NDC-PS**.... No Drawing Change Project Slip
**NdCr**.......... Divide County Library, Crosby, ND [*Library symbol*] [*Library of Congress*] (LCLS)
**NDCT**........ Natural Draft Cooling Tower [*Nuclear energy*] (NRCH)
**NDD**.......... Duke University Library, Durham, NC [*OCLC symbol*] (OCLC)
**NDd**.......... Dundee Library, Dundee, NY [*Library symbol*] [*Library of Congress*] (LCLS)
**NDD**.......... National Diploma in Dairying [*British*]
**NDD**.......... National Diploma in Design [*British*]
**NDD**.......... Navigation and Direction Division [*British military*] (DMA)
**NDD**.......... Net Defence Department [*Navy*] [*British*]
**NDD**.......... New Democratic Dimensions (EA)
**NDD**.......... Nitro(dimethyl)dihydrobenzofuran [*Organic chemistry*]
**NDD**.......... Nondeferred Development (MCD)
**NDD**.......... Nuclear Detection Device (MCD)
**NDD**.......... Sumbe [*Angola*] [*Airport symbol*] (OAG)
**NDDC**........ National Defeat Dukakis Campaign (EA)
**NDDC**........ NORAD Division Direction Center [*Military*] (AABC)
**NdDe**.......... Devils Lake Carnegie Library, Devils Lake, ND [*Library symbol*] [*Library of Congress*] (LCLS)
**NdDeH**...... Mercy Hospital, Devils Lake, ND [*Library symbol*] [*Library of Congress*] (LCLS)
**NDDEIC**... National Digestive Diseases Education and Information Clearinghouse [*Public Health Service*] [*Later, NDDIC*] (IID)
**NdDeL**....... Lake Region Junior College, Devils Lake, ND [*Library symbol*] [*Library of Congress*] (LCLS)
**NDDG**........ National Diabetes Data Group [*British*]
**NdDi**.......... Dickinson Public Library, Dickinson, ND [*Library symbol*] [*Library of Congress*] (LCLS)
**NDDIC**...... National Digestive Diseases Information Clearinghouse (EA)
**NdDiS**........ Dickinson State College, Dickinson, ND [*Library symbol*] [*Library of Congress*] (LCLS)
**NdDiStJ**.... Saint Joseph Hospital, Dickinson, ND [*Library symbol*] [*Library of Congress*] (LCLS)
**Ndd Jb**....... Niederdeutsches Jahrbuch [*A publication*]
**NDDO**....... Neglect of Diatomic Differential Overlap [*Quantum mechanics*]
**NDDP**........ NATO Defense Data Program (AABC)
**NDD & RF**... Naval Dry Dock and Repair Facility
**NDE**........... Mandera [*Kenya*] [*Airport symbol*] (OAG)
**NDE**........... N-Demethylencainide [*Organic chemistry*]
**NDE**........... National Defense Education
**NDE**........... National Defense Emergency [*Headquarters*] (MCD)
**NDE**........... National Dinghy Exhibition [*London, England*]
**NDE**........... Navy Department Establishments [*British*]
**NDE**........... Near-Death Experience
**NDE**........... Nevada Desert Experience (EA)
**NDE**........... No Date Established
**NDE**........... No Delay Expected
**NDE**........... Nondestructive Evaluation
**NDE**........... Nondestructive Examination [*Nuclear energy*] (NRCH)
**NDE**........... Nonlinear Differential Equations
**NDEA**........ National Defense Education Act [*1958*]
**NDEA**........ National Defense Emergency Authorization
**NDEA**........ Nitrosodiethylamine [*Organic chemistry*]
**NDEC**........ NDE Environmental Corp. [*NASDAQ symbol*] (NQ)
**NDEI**......... National Defense Education Institute
**NDEITA**.... National Dance-Exercise Instructor's Training Association (EA)
**NDEJ**......... Notre Dame English Journal [*A publication*]
**NDEL**......... Non-Destructive Evaluation Laboratory [*NASA*]
**NDELA**..... Nitrosodiethanolamine [*Organic chemistry*] [*Also, NDEOL*]
**NdEIN**....... State Normal and Industrial School, Ellendale, ND [*Library symbol*] [*Library of Congress*] [*Obsolete*] (LCLS)
**NdEIT**........ Trinity Bible Institute, Ellendale, ND [*Library symbol*] [*Library of Congress*] (LCLS)
**NDemP**...... National Democratic Party [*British*]
**NDEOL**..... Nitrosodiethanolamine [*Organic chemistry*] [*Also, NDELA*]
**NDER**......... National Defense Executive Reserve
**NDERR**..... National Defense Executive Reserve Roster [*of the CSC*]
**NDES**......... Normal Digital Echo Suppressor [*Telecommunications*] (TEL)
**NDETP**...... National Drug Education Training Program [*HEW*]
**NDeUA**...... State University of New York, Agricultural and Technical College at Delhi, Delhi, NY [*Library symbol*] [*Library of Congress*] (LCLS)
**NDEW**....... Nuclear Directed-Energy Weapon
**NDEW**....... Nuclear-Driven Directed-Energy Weapon
**NDex**.......... Dexter Free Library, Dexter, NY [*Library symbol*] [*Library of Congress*] (LCLS)
**NDEX**........ Newspaper Index [*Bell & Howell Co.*] [*Database*]
**NDf**............ Dobbs Ferry Public Library, Dobbs Ferry, NY [*Library symbol*] [*Library of Congress*] (LCLS)
**NdF**............ Fargo Public Library, Fargo, ND [*Library symbol*] [*Library of Congress*] (LCLS)
**NDF**........... Nacelle Drag Efficiency [*Factor*] [*Aerospace*]
**NDF**........... Nandi [*Fiji*] [*Seismograph station code, US Geological Survey*] (SEIS)
**NDF**........... National Democratic Front [*Iran*] [*Political party*] (PD)
**NDF**........... National Democratic Front [*Yemen*] [*Political party*] (PD)
**NDF**........... National Democratic Front [*Pakistan*] [*Political party*] (FEA)
**NDF**........... National Democratic Front [*An association*] (EA)
**NDF**........... National Democratic Front [*Burma*] [*Political party*] (FEA)
**NDF**........... National Democratic Front [*Philippines*] [*Political party*] (FEA)
**NDF**........... National Diploma in Forestry [*British*]
**NDF**........... National Dividend Foundation (EA)
**NDF**........... National Drilling Federation [*Later, IDF*] (EA)
**NDF**........... Naval Dairy Farm
**NDF**........... Naval Defence Force [*British military*] (DMA)
**NDF**........... Nederlands-Duitse Kamer van Koophandel. Mededelingen [*A publication*]
**NDF**........... Neue Deutsche Forschung [*A publication*]
**NDF**........... Neutral Density Filter
**NDF**........... Neutral Detergent Fiber [*Food analysis*]
**NDF**........... New Democratic Forum (EA)
**NDF**........... New Dimensions Foundation (EA)
**NDF**........... No Defect Found
**NDF**........... Nondipole Field [*Electromagnetism*]
**NDFA**........ National Dietary Foods Association [*Later, NNFA*] (EA)
**NdFA**......... North Dakota State University, Fargo, ND [*Library symbol*] [*Library of Congress*] (LCLS)
**ND Farm Res** ... North Dakota Farm Research [*A publication*]
**ND Farm Res ND Agric Exp Stn** ... North Dakota Farm Research. North Dakota Agricultural Experiment Station [*A publication*]
**NdFC**......... Cass County Court House, Fargo, ND [*Library symbol*] [*Library of Congress*] (LCLS)
**NDFC**........ National Days Fan Club (EA)
**NdFD**......... Dakota Clinic, Fargo, ND [*Library symbol*] [*Library of Congress*] (LCLS)
**NDFEA**..... Northwest Dried Fruit Export Association (EA)
**NDFKAH**.. Endemic Diseases Bulletin. Nagasaki University [*A publication*]
**NDFL**........ National Defense Foreign Language [*Fellowship*]
**ND Fla**....... United States District Court for the Northern District of Florida (DLA)
**NdFM**........ Masonic Grand Lodge Library, Fargo, ND [*Library symbol*] [*Library of Congress*] (LCLS)
**NDfM**........ Mercy College, Dobbs Ferry, NY [*Library symbol*] [*Library of Congress*] (LCLS)
**NDFN**........ Nauchnye Doklady Vysshei Shkoly Filologicheskie Nauki [*Moscow*] [*A publication*]
**NdFN**......... Neuropsychiatric Hospital, Fargo, ND [*Library symbol*] [*Library of Congress*] (LCLS)
**NDfS**.......... Stauffer Chemical Co., Eastern Research Center, Dobbs Ferry, NY [*Library symbol*] [*Library of Congress*] (LCLS)
**NdFStJ**...... Saint John's Hospital, Fargo, ND [*Library symbol*] [*Library of Congress*] (LCLS)
**NdFStL**...... Saint Luke's Hospital, Fargo, ND [*Library symbol*] [*Library of Congress*] (LCLS)
**NdFStLN**... Saint Luke's School of Nursing, Fargo, ND [*Library symbol*] [*Library of Congress*] (LCLS)
**NdFVA**...... United States Veterans Administration Hospital, Fargo, ND [*Library symbol*] [*Library of Congress*] (LCLS)
**NDFW**....... New Directions for Women [*A publication*]
**NDFYP**...... Navy Department Five Year Plan
**NdG**........... Grand Forks Public Library, Grand Forks, ND [*Library symbol*] [*Library of Congress*] (LCLS)
**NDG**.......... National Dance Guild [*Later, ADG*]
**NDG**.......... No Date Given (AFM)
**NDGA**........ National Depression Glass Association (EA)
**NDGA**........ National Dog Groomers Association (EA)
**NDGA**........ Nordihydroguaiaretic Acid [*Antioxidant, food additive*]
**ND GA**....... United States District Court for the Northern District of Georgia (DLA)
**NDGAA**..... National Dog Groomers Association of America (EA)
**NDGE**........ NATO Air Defense Ground Environment
**ND Geol Surv Bull** ... North Dakota. Geological Survey. Bulletin [*A publication*]
**ND Geol Surv Circ** ... North Dakota. Geological Survey. Circular [*A publication*]
**ND Geol Surv Educ Ser** ... North Dakota. Geological Survey. Educational Series [*A publication*]
**ND Geol Surv Misc Map** ... North Dakota. Geological Survey. Miscellaneous Map [*A publication*]
**ND Geol Surv Misc Ser** ... North Dakota. Geological Survey. Miscellaneous Series [*A publication*]

**NDGI**......... Nachrichten. Deutsche Gesellschaft fuer Islamkunde [*A publication*]
**NdGIT**....... United States Air Force Institute of Technology, Grand Forks AFB, ND [*Library symbol*] [*Library of Congress*] (LCLS)
**NDGKA**..... Nogyo Doboku Gakkai Ronbunshu [*A publication*]
**NDGL**........ Neodymium-Doped Glass LASER
**NDGO**....... Navy Department General Order
**NdGrC**....... Carnegie Bookmobile Library, Grafton, ND [*Library symbol*] [*Library of Congress*] (LCLS)
**NDGS**........ National Defense General Staff (NATG)
**NDGS**........ National Duncan Glass Society (EA)
**NdGUH**..... Grand Forks United Hospital, Grand Forks, ND [*Library symbol*] [*Library of Congress*] (LCLS)
**NDGW**...... Native Daughters of the Golden West (EA)
**NDGXA**..... Miscellaneous Series. North Dakota Geological Survey [*A publication*]
**NDH**.......... National Diploma in Horticulture [*British*]
**NDH**.......... Natural Disaster Hospitals [*Public Health Service*]
**NDH**.......... Neue Deutsche Hefte [*A publication*]
**NDH**.......... New Departure Hyatt Division [*General Motors Corp.*]
**NDH**.......... Nordic Economic Outlook [*A publication*]
**NDH**.......... North Dakota History [*A publication*]
**NDH**.......... Royal North Devonshire Yeomanry Hussars [*British military*] (DMA)
**NdHa**......... Harvey Public Library, Harvey, ND [*Library symbol*] [*Library of Congress*] (LCLS)
**NDHA**....... National Dental Hygienists' Association (EA)
**NDHA**....... National District Heating Association [*Later, IDHCA*] (EA)
**NDHFP**..... New Developments Human Factors Program [*Navy*]
**NDHi**......... North Dakota History [*A publication*]
**NdHi**.......... State Historical Society of North Dakota, Bismarck, ND [*Library symbol*] [*Library of Congress*] (LCLS)
**ND His Q**.. North Dakota Historical Quarterly [*A publication*]
**ND Hist**..... North Dakota History [*A publication*]
**NDHQ**....... National Defence Headquarters [*Canada*]
**NDHR**....... NDH-Rapport. Norland Distrikshogskole [*A publication*]
**NDHS**........ Nimbus Data Handling System
**NDHX**....... Natural Draft Heat Exchanger [*Nuclear energy*] (NRCH)
**NDI**........... Dickinson State College, Dickinson, ND [*OCLC symbol*] (OCLC)
**NDI**........... Namudi [*Papua New Guinea*] [*Airport symbol*] (OAG)
**NDI**........... National Dance Institute (EA)
**NDI**........... Nephrogenic Diabetes Insipidus [*Endocrinology*]
**NDI**........... Network Development and Implementation Group [*National Research Council of Canada*]
**NDI**........... New Delhi [*Delhi*] [*India*] [*Seismograph station code, US Geological Survey*] (SEIS)
**NDI**........... Nissan Design International
**NDI**........... Non-Combat Development Item
**NDI**........... Nondestructive Inspection (AFM)
**NDI**........... Nondevelopment Item (MCD)
**NDI**........... Nuclear Data, Inc. [*Later, MPB*] [*AMEX symbol*] (SPSG)
**NDI**........... Numerical Designation Index (IEEE)
**NDIC**......... National Datacomputer, Inc. [*NASDAQ symbol*] (NQ)
**NDIC**......... National Diabetes Information Clearinghouse [*Public Health Service*] (IID)
**NDIC**......... NATO Defense Information Complex (NATG)
**NDIC**......... Nuclear Data Information Center [*ORNL*]
**NDIC**......... Nuclear Desalination Information Center
**NDICE**....... Non-Developmental Items Candidate Evaluation
**NDIIA**....... National Democratic Institute for International Affairs (EA)
**ND Ill**......... United States District Court for the Northern District of Illinois (DLA)
**NDim**......... Nuove Dimensioni [*A publication*]
**NDIMC**..... NATO Defense Information Management Committee (NATG)
**ND Ind**....... United States District Court for the Northern District of Indiana (DLA)
**ND Iowa**..... United States District Court for the Northern District of Iowa (DLA)
**NDIR**......... Nondispersive Infrared [*Analyzer*]
**NDIS**......... National Drug Information Service [*Australian Commonwealth Department of Health*] [*Information service or system*] (CRD)
**NDIS**......... Nissan's Direct Ignition System [*Automotive engineering*]
**NDIS**......... North Dakota State Industrial School
**NDIU**......... National Drugs Intelligence Unit [*Metropolitan Police*] [*British*]
**NDIY**......... North Devon Imperial Yeomanry [*British military*] (DMA)
**NdJ**............ Alfred Dickey Free Library, Jamestown, ND [*Library symbol*] [*Library of Congress*] (LCLS)
**NDJ**........... Jamestown College, Jamestown, ND [*OCLC symbol*] (OCLC)
**NDJ**........... N'Djamena [*Chad*] [*Airport symbol*] (OAG)
**Nd Jb**......... Niederdeutsches Jahrbuch [*A publication*]
**Nd Jb**......... Niederdeutsches Jahrbuch fuer Volkskunde [*A publication*]
**NdJC**......... Jamestown College, Jamestown, ND [*Library symbol*] [*Library of Congress*] (LCLS)
**NdJF**......... North Dakota Farmers Union Resource Library, Jamestown, ND [*Library symbol*] [*Library of Congress*] (LCLS)
**NdJN**......... Northern Prairie Wildlife Research Center, Jamestown, ND [*Library symbol*] [*Library of Congress*] (LCLS)
**NdJSH**...... State Hospital, Jamestown, ND [*Library symbol*] [*Library of Congress*] (LCLS)
**NDK**.......... Namorik [*Marshall Islands*] [*Airport symbol*] (OAG)
**NDK**.......... South Weymouth, MA [*Location identifier*] [*FAA*] (FAAL)
**Nd Kbl**....... Korrespondenzblatt. Verein fuer Niederdeutsche Sprachforschung [*A publication*]
**NDKGA**..... Nippon Daicho Komonbyo Gakkai Zasshi [*A publication*]
**NDKGAU**... Journal. Japan Society of Colo-Proctology [*A publication*]
**NDKIA**...... Nagoya Daigaku Kankyo Igaku Kenkyusho Nenpo [*A publication*]
**Nd Ko Bl**.... Korrespondenzblatt. Verein fuer Niederdeutsche Sprachforschung [*A publication*]
**NDKSBX**... Journal. Agricultural Laboratory [*Chiba*] [*A publication*]
**NDL**.......... Duke University, Law Library, Durham, NC [*OCLC symbol*] (OCLC)
**NDL**.......... National Defence Headquarters Library [*UTLAS symbol*]
**NDL**.......... National Democratic League [*Early British political party*]
**NDL**.......... National Demographics & Lifestyles, Inc.
**NDL**.......... National Diet Library [*Japan*] (DIT)
**NDL**.......... Natural Daylight
**NDL**.......... Needle (MSA)
**NDL**.......... Network Definition Language [*Burroughs Corp.*]
**NDL**.......... Neudrucke Deutscher Literaturwerke [*A publication*]
**NDL**.......... Neue Deutsche Literatur [*A publication*]
**NDL**.......... Ni-Cal Developments Ltd. [*Vancouver Stock Exchange symbol*]
**NDL**.......... Norddeutscher Lloyd [*German steamship company*]
**Nd-L**.......... North Dakota State Law Library, Bismarck, ND [*Library symbol*] [*Library of Congress*] (LCLS)
**NDL**.......... Notre Dame Lawyer [*A publication*]
**NDL**.......... Nuclear Data Link System [*Nuclear Regulatory Commission*]
**NDL**.......... Nuclear Defense Laboratory [*Army*]
**NDL**.......... Numerical Drawing List
**ND Laws**..... Laws of North Dakota [*A publication*]
**NDLB**........ National Dock Labour Board [*British*]
**NDLC**........ Network Data Link Control
**NdLibC**...... North Dakota State Library Commission, Bismarck, ND [*Library symbol*] [*Library of Congress*] (LCLS)
**NDLOA**..... National Disabled Law Officers Association (EA)
**NDLP**........ NDL Products, Inc. [*NASDAQ symbol*] (NQ)
**NDLR**........ North Dakota Law Review [*A publication*]
**NDL Rev**.... North Dakota Law Review [*A publication*]
**ND L Review**... North Dakota Law Review [*A publication*]
**NDLT**........ N-Channel Depletion-Load Triode Inverter
**NDM**......... Ferrocarriles Nacionales de Mexico [*AAR code*]
**NDM**......... Mary College, Library, Bismarck, ND [*OCLC symbol*] (OCLC)
**NDM**......... National Dried (Milk) [*Brand name for the British government's dried milk for babies - manufacturer undisclosed*]
**NDM**......... Negative Differential Mobility (IEEE)
**NDM**......... Neutron Dose Monitor
**NDM**......... New Democratic Movement (EA)
**NDM**......... New Dimensions in Medicine
**NdM**.......... Niederdeutsche Mitteilungen [*A publication*]
**NDM**......... NOAA [*National Oceanic and Atmospheric Administration*] Directives Manual (NOAA)
**NDM**......... Nomad Energy & Resources [*Vancouver Stock Exchange symbol*]
**NDM**......... North Durham Militia [*British military*] (DMA)
**NDMA**....... N-Nitrosodimethylamine [*Also, DMN, DMNA*] [*Organic chemistry*]
**NDMA**....... National Dimension Manufacturers Association (EA)
**NDMA**....... National Door Manufacturers Association [*Later, NWWDA*]
**NDMA**....... National Dress Manufacturers Association [*Later, AMA*] (EA)
**NDMA**....... Nonprescription Drug Manufacturers Association (EA)
**NdMan**...... Mandan Public Library, Mandan, ND [*Library symbol*] [*Library of Congress*] (LCLS)
**NdManMH**... North Dakota Memorial Mental Health and Retardation Center, Mandan, ND [*Library symbol*] [*Library of Congress*] (LCLS)
**NdManN**... North Dakota Industrial School, Mandan, ND [*Library symbol*] [*Library of Congress*] (LCLS)
**NdManNG**... United States Northern Great Plains Research Center, Mandan, ND [*Library symbol*] [*Library of Congress*] (LCLS)
**NdMayS**.... Mayville State College, Mayville, ND [*Library symbol*] [*Library of Congress*] (LCLS)
**NDMB**....... National Defense Mediation Board [*World War II*]
**NDMC**....... N-Desmethylclobazam [*Biochemistry*]
**NDMC**....... NATO Defense Manpower Committee (NATG)
**NDMDA**.... National Depressive and Manic Depressive Association (EA)
**NDMG**...... Norddeutsche Missionsgesellschaft [*A publication*]
**NdMin**....... Minot Public Library, Minot, ND [*Library symbol*] [*Library of Congress*] (LCLS)
**NdMinAF**... United States Air Force, Base Library, Minot AFB, ND [*Library symbol*] [*Library of Congress*] (LCLS)
**NdMinIT**... United States Air Force Institute of Technology, Minot AFB, ND [*Library symbol*] [*Library of Congress*] (LCLS)
**NdMinN**.... Northwest Bible College, Minot, ND [*Library symbol*] [*Library of Congress*] (LCLS)
**NdMinS**.... Minot State College, Minot, ND [*Library symbol*] [*Library of Congress*] (LCLS)

**NdMinT-M** ... Trinity Medical Center, August Cameron Medical Library, Minot, ND [*Library symbol*] [*Library of Congress*] (LCLS)
**NdMinT-N** ... Trinity Medical Center, School of Nursing, Minot, ND [*Library symbol*] [*Library of Congress*] (LCLS)
**ND Miss** .... United States District Court for the Northern District of Mississippi (DLA)
**Nd Mitt** ...... Niederdeutsche Mitteilungen [*A publication*]
**NDML** ........ Neutral Data Manipulation Language [*Data processing*]
**NdMo** ........ Mott Public Library, Mott, ND [*Library symbol*] [*Library of Congress*] (LCLS)
**NDMS** ........ National Disaster Medical System
**NDMS** ........ Network Design and Management System
**NDMS** ........ Noise Deficiency Management System
**NDMSP** ..... Navy Department Mobilization Security Plan (NG)
**NDMTB** .... Nondeployment Mobilization Troop Basis (AABC)
**NDN** .......... National Diffusion Network [*Department of Education*] [*Information service or system*] (IID)
**NDN** .......... National Directory of Newsletters and Reporting Services [*A publication*]
**NDN** .......... Nu-Dawn Resources, Inc. [*Vancouver Stock Exchange symbol*]
**nDNA** ........ Deoxyribonucleic Acid, Nuclear [*Biochemistry, genetics*]
**NDNHI** ..... North Dakota Natural Heritage Inventory [*North Dakota State Department of Natural Resources*] [*Bismarck*] [*Information service or system*] (IID)
**NDNT** ........ Not Dressed nor Tanned
**NDNY** ........ United States District Court for the Northern District of New York (DLA)
**NDO** .......... National Debt Office [*British*]
**NDO** .......... Navy Disbursing Office
**NDO** .......... Negotiate Downward Only (MCD)
**NDO** .......... Network Development Office [*Library of Congress*]
**NDOC** ........ Neurological Dysfunctions of Children [*Test*]
**ND Ohio** .... United States District Court for the Northern District of Ohio (DLA)
**ND Okla** .... United States District Court for the Northern District of Oklahoma (DLA)
**NDOP** ........ Navy Designated Overhaul Point (CAAL)
**NDOS** ........ National Defense Operations Section [*FCC*]
**NDp** .......... Deer Park Public Library, Deer Park, NY [*Library symbol*] [*Library of Congress*] (LCLS)
**NDP** .......... National Democracy Party [*Chat Prachathippatai*] [*Thailand*] [*Political party*] (PPW)
**NDP** .......... National Democratic Party [*Pakistan*] [*Political party*] (PD)
**NDP** .......... National Democratic Party [*Egypt*] [*Political party*] (PPW)
**NDP** .......... National Democratic Party [*Solomon Islands*] [*Political party*] (PPW)
**NDP** .......... National Democratic Party [*India*] [*Political party*] (PPW)
**NDP** .......... National Democratic Party [*Namibia*] [*Political party*] (PPW)
**NDP** .......... National Democratic Party [*Grenada*] [*Political party*] (PPW)
**NDP** .......... National Democratic Party [*Iraq*] [*Political party*] (BJA)
**NDP** .......... National Democratic Party [*Parti National Democratique*] [*Morocco*] [*Political party*] (PPW)
**NDP** .......... National Democratic Party [*Rhodesia and Nyasaland*] [*Political party*]
**NDP** .......... National Determination Party (EA)
**NDP** .......... National Development Party [*Montserrat*] [*Political party*] (EY)
**NDP** .......... National Diocesan Press [*Later, Episcopal Communicators*] (EA)
**NDP** .......... National Diploma in Poultry Husbandry [*British*]
**NDP** .......... National Disclosure Policy [*Military*] (MCD)
**NDP** .......... Nationaldemokratische Partei [*National Democratic Party*] [*Austria*] [*Political party*] (PPW)
**NDP** .......... Nationaldemokratische Partei Deutschlands [*German National Democratic Party*] [*German Democratic Republic*] [*Political party*]
**NDP** .......... Nationalist Democracy Party [*Turkey*] [*Political party*] (PPW)
**NDP** .......... Nationwide Demonstration Program
**NDP** .......... Navy Department Personnel
**NDP** .......... Neighborhood Development Program [*Urban renewal*]
**NDP** .......... Neue Deutsche Presse [*A publication*]
**NDP** .......... Neurological Disorders Program [*National Institute of Neurological and Communicative Disorders and Stroke*]
**NDP** .......... Neutron Depth Profiling [*Analytical chemistry*]
**NDP** .......... New Democratic Party [*Facetious translations: "Never Dies Politically," "No Dreams of Prosperity"*] [*Canada*] [*Political party*] (PPW)
**NDP** .......... New Democratic Party [*Shinmin-Dang*] [*Republic of Korea*] [*Political party*] (PPW)
**NDP** .......... New Democratic Party [*St. Vincent*] [*Political party*] (PPW)
**NDP** .......... Night Defensive Positions [*Military*]
**NDP** .......... Normal Diametral Pitch (MSA)
**NDP** .......... Nuclear Desalination Plant
**NDP** .......... Nuclear Disarmament Party [*Australia*]
**NDP** .......... Nucleoside Diphosphate [*Biochemistry*]
**NDP** .......... Numeric Data Processor
**NDP** .......... Pensacola, FL [*Location identifier*] [*FAA*] (FAAL)
**NDPA** ........ National Decorated Packaging Association
**NDPA** ........ National Decorating Products Association (EA)
**NDPA** ........ Nitrosodipropylamine [*Also, DPN, DPNA*] [*Organic chemistry*]
**NDPBC** ...... National Duck Pin Bowling Congress [*Later, NDBC*] (EA)
**NDPC** ........ National Democratic Policy Committee (EA)
**NDPC** ........ National [*Military Information*] Disclosure Policy Committee
**NDPC** ........ National Dropout Prevention Center (EA)
**NDPC** ........ National Drowning Prevention Coalition (EA)
**NDPD** ........ Nationaldemokratische Partei Deutschlands [*German National Democratic Party*] [*German Democratic Republic*]
**NDPhA** ...... N-Nitrosodiphenylamine [*Organic chemistry*]
**NDPIC** ....... Navy Department Program Information Center
**NDPK** ........ Nucleotide Diphosphate Kinase [*An enzyme*]
**NDPN** ........ National Dropout Prevention Network (EA)
**NDPP** ........ (Nitrobenzyl)(Diethylaminophenylazo)-pyridinium Bromide [*Reagent*]
**NDPR** ........ NATO Defense Planning Review (NATG)
**NDPR** ........ Nuclear Duty Position Roster (MCD)
**NDPRP** ...... National Defense Project Rating Plan
**NDPS** ........ National Data Processing Service [*British*] (DCTA)
**NDQ** .......... NASA Delta Quotation (MCD)
**NDQ** .......... North Dakota Quarterly [*A publication*]
**ND Quar J** ... North Dakota University. Quarterly Journal [*A publication*]
**NDR** .......... National Derby Rallies (EA)
**NDR** .......... National Dog Registry (EA)
**NDR** .......... National Driver Register
**NDR** .......... National Drug Co. [*Research code symbol*]
**NDR** .......... Negative Differential Resistance [*Electronics*]
**NDR** .......... Network Data Reduction
**NDR** .......... Neue Deutsche Rundschau [*A publication*]
**NDR** .......... Neutral Detergent Residue [*Food analysis*]
**NDR** .......... New Dimensions Radio (EA)
**NDR** .......... Nondestructive Read [*Data processing*]
**NDR** .......... Norddeutscher Rundfunk [*Radio network*] [*Federal Republic of Germany*]
**NDR** .......... Normal Daily Requirement [*Military*]
**NDR** .......... Normotensive Donor Rat
**NDR** .......... North Dakota Law Review [*A publication*]
**NDR** .......... Nuclear Double Resonance [*Analytical chemistry*]
**NDR** .......... Revue de la Navigation Fluviale Europeenne. Ports et Industries [*A publication*]
**NDRA** ........ Nostalgia Drag Race Association (EA)
**NDRB** ........ New Developments Research Branch [*Navy*] (MCD)
**NDRC** ........ National Defense Research Committee [*of Office of Scientific Research and Development*] [*World War II*]
**NDRCAJ** ... Contributions. Department of Geology and Mineralogy. Niigata University [*A publication*]
**ND REC Mag** ... North Dakota REC [*Rural Electric Cooperatives*] Magazine [*A publication*]
**ND Res Found Bull** ... North Dakota Research Foundation Bulletin [*A publication*]
**ND Res Rep ND Agric Exp Stn** ... North Dakota Research Report. North Dakota Agricultural Experiment Station [*A publication*]
**NDRF** ........ National Debt Repayment Foundation (EA)
**NDRF** ........ National Defense Reserve Fleet [*Maritime Administration, Department of Commerce*]
**NDRG** ........ NATO Defense Research Group (NATG)
**NDRHE4** ... Sado Marine Biological Station. Niigata University. Special Publication [*A publication*]
**Nd Rhein Jb** ... Niederrheinisches Jahrbuch [*A publication*]
**NDRI** ......... National Diabetes Research Interchange [*Research center*] (RCD)
**NDRI** ......... Naval Dental Research Institute
**NDRL** ........ Notre Dame Radiation Laboratory [*University of Notre Dame*] [*Research center*] (RCD)
**NDRM** ....... Neesby Delayed Release Mechanism [*Medicine*]
**NDRO** ....... Nondestructive Readout [*Data processing*]
**NDRS** ........ National Driver Register Service [*Department of Transportation*]
**NDRS** ........ Nuclear Definition and Reporting System (AAG)
**NDRSWG** ... NATO Data Requirements and Standards Working Group (NATG)
**NDRW** ....... Nondestructive Read/Write [*Data processing*]
**NDryT** ....... Tompkins-Cortland Community College, Division of Instructional and Learning Resources, Dryden, NY [*Library symbol*] [*Library of Congress*] (LCLS)
**NDS** .......... Congregation of Notre Dame de Sion [*Roman Catholic women's religious order*]
**NDS** .......... National Decision Systems [*Information service or system*] (IID)
**NDS** .......... National Defense Stockpile [*Collection of materials essential to the defense industry*]
**NDS** .......... Naval Dental School
**NDS** .......... Navigation Development Satellite (MCD)
**NDS** .......... Navigation Display System
**NDS** .......... Navy Data System
**NDS** .......... Navy Directive System (NVT)
**NDS** .......... Navy Director System (NVT)
**NDS** .......... Navy Display System
**NDS** .......... Neurologic Disability Score
**NDS** .......... Nicholas Data [*Vancouver Stock Exchange symbol*]
**NdS** .......... Niederdeutsche Studien [*A publication*]
**NDS** .......... Non-Developmental Software
**NDS** .......... Noncommunications Detection System (MCD)

**NDS** .......... Nonparametric Detection Scheme [*Communication signal*]
**NDS** .......... Nordic Demographic Society (EA)
**NDS** .......... North Dakota State Library Commission, Bismarck, ND [*OCLC symbol*] (OCLC)
**NDS** .......... Nuclear Data Sheets [*National Academy of Sciences*]
**NDS** .......... Nuclear Detection Satellite
**NDS** .......... Nuclear Detonation Detection System
**NDSA** ........ National Directory of State Agencies [*United States*] [*A publication*]
**NDSA** ........ National Disposal Services Association (EA)
**NDSAA** ..... Nuclear Data. Section A [*A publication*]
**NDSB** ........ Narcotic Drugs Supervisory Body [*UN*]
**NDSB** ........ Navy Dependents School Branch
**NDSC** ........ National Down Syndrome Congress (EA)
**NDSE** ........ Nondeliverable Support Equipment
**NDSEG** ...... National Defense Science and Engineering Graduate
**ND Sess Laws** ... Laws of North Dakota [*A publication*] (DLA)
**NDSF** ......... North Dakota School of Forestry
**NDSFB** ...... Nogyo Doboku Shikenjo Giho, F. Sogo [*A publication*]
**Nds GV Bl** ... Niedersaechsisches Gesetz- und Verordnungsblatt [*A publication*]
**NDSK** ........ Nydanske Studier. Almen Kommunikationsteori [*A publication*]
**NDSL** ........ National Direct [*formerly, Defense*] Student Loan
**NDSM** ....... National Defense Service Medal [*Military decoration*]
**NDSN** ....... Nordson Corp. [*NASDAQ symbol*] (NQ)
**NDSOS** ..... Navy Deep Sea Oceanographic System
**Nds Rpfl** ..... Niedersaechsische Rechtspflege [*A publication*]
**NDSS** ......... National Down Syndrome Society (EA)
**ND State Lab Dep Bull** ... North Dakota. State Laboratories Department. Bulletin [*A publication*]
**NDSU** ........ North Dakota State University
**NDT** .......... Ferrocarril Nacional de Tehuantepec [*AAR code*]
**NDT** .......... National Diploma in the Science and Practice of Turfculture and Sports Ground Management [*British*]
**NDT** .......... Net Data Throughout
**NDT** .......... Neuro-Developmental Treatment [*Physical therapy*]
**NDT** .......... Nevada Dance Theatre
**NDT** .......... New Dimensions [*Vancouver Stock Exchange symbol*]
**NDT** .......... Nil-Ductility Temperature [*Metallurgy*]
**NDT** .......... Nil-Ductility Transition [*Metallurgy*] (IEEE)
**NDT** .......... Nondestructive Testing
**NDTA** ........ National Data Corp. [*NASDAQ symbol*] (NQ)
**NDTA** ........ National Defense Transportation Association (EA)
**NDTA** ........ National Dental Technicians Association (EA)
**NDTA** ........ Neurodevelopmental Treatment Association (EA)
**NDTC** ........ National Drug Trade Conference (EA)
**NDTC** ........ Naval Device Training Center
**NDTC** ........ Nondestructive Testing Center (IEEE)
**NDT & E** .... Nondestructive Testing and Evaluation Programs [*Pennsylvania State University*] [*Research center*] (RCD)
**ND Tex** ...... United States District Court for the Northern District of Texas (DLA)
**NDTF** ........ Nondestructive Test Facility (MCD)
**Ndt F** .......... Norddeutsche Familienkunde [*A publication*]
**NDTI** ......... National Disease and Therapeutic Index [*A publication*]
**NDTI** ......... Nondestructive Testing and Inspection
**NDTIB** ....... Nondestructive Testing and Inspection Building
**NDT Int** ..... Non-Destructive Testing International [*A publication*]
**NDTI Rev** .. NDTI [*National Disease and Therapeutic Index*] Review [*United States*] [*A publication*]
**NDTL** ........ Nondestructive Test Laboratory (MCD)
**NDTMA** .... National Drain Tile Manufacturers Association [*Defunct*] (EA)
**NDT News** ... Non-Destructive Testing News [*A publication*]
**NDTP** ........ Nuclear Data Tape Program
**NDTRAN** .. Notre Dame Translator [*Programming language*] [*1977*] [*Data processing*] (CSR)
**NDTSB** ...... Nuclear Data Sheets [*A publication*]
**NDTT** ........ Nil-Ductility Transition Temperature [*Metallurgy*]
**NDU** .......... National Defense University [*DoD*]
**NDU** .......... National Defense University, Washington, DC [*OCLC symbol*] (OCLC)
**NDU** .......... National Democratic Union [*Zimbabwe*] [*Political party*] (PPW)
**NDU** .......... NDU Resources [*Vancouver Stock Exchange symbol*]
**N/D/U** ....... None Done Up [*Bookselling*]
**ndu** ............ North Dakota [*MARC country of publication code*] [*Library of Congress*] (LCCP)
**NDU** .......... Nuclear Data Unit [*International Atomic Energy Agency*] (DIT)
**NDU** .......... Rundu [*Namibia*] [*Airport symbol*] (OAG)
**NdU** ........... University of North Dakota, Grand Forks, ND [*Library symbol*] [*Library of Congress*] (LCLS)
**NDUC** ........ Nimbus Data Utilization Center
**NdU-El** ...... University of North Dakota, Ellendale Branch, Ellendale, ND [*Library symbol*] [*Library of Congress*] [*Obsolete*] (LCLS)
**NDUF** ........ National Democratic United Front [*Later, FNDF*] [*Burma*] [*Political party*] (PD)
**NdU-L** ....... University of North Dakota, Law Library, Grand Forks, ND [*Library symbol*] [*Library of Congress*] (LCLS)
**NdU-M** ...... University of North Dakota, Medical Library, Grand Forks, ND [*Library symbol*] [*Library of Congress*] (LCLS)
**NDunBH** ... Brooks Memorial Hospital Medical Center, Dunkirk, NY [*Library symbol*] [*Library of Congress*] (LCLS)
**NDUP** ........ Nonduplicate
**NDUSTA** .. New Duty Station [*Navy*]
**NDUV** ........ Nondispersive Ultraviolet
**NDV** .......... Nachrichtendienst. Deutscher Verein fuer Oeffentliche und Private Fuersorge [*A publication*]
**NDV** .......... Newcastle Disease Virus [*Also, ND*]
**NDV** .......... Not to Delay Delivery
**NDV** .......... Not to Delay Vessel
**NDV** .......... Notes et Documents Voltaiques [*A publication*]
**NDV** .......... Nuclear Delivery Vehicle
**NDV** .......... Valley City State College, Valley City, ND [*OCLC symbol*] (OCLC)
**NDV** .......... Washington, DC [*Location identifier*] [*FAA*] (FAAL)
**NdVc** .......... Valley City Public Library, Valley City, ND [*Library symbol*] [*Library of Congress*] (LCLS)
**NdVcT** ....... Valley City State College, Valley City, ND [*Library symbol*] [*Library of Congress*] (LCLS)
**NDVI** ......... Normalized Difference Vegetation Index [*Plant biota*]
**NDVS** ........ Naucnye Doklady Vyssej Skoly [*A publication*]
**NDVS-F** .... Naucnye Doklady Vyssej Skoly Filologiceskie Nauki [*A publication*]
**NDVTB** ...... Nederlands Tijdschrift voor Vacuumtechniek [*A publication*]
**NDW** ......... Naval District Washington
**NDW** ......... Niederdeutsches Wort [*A publication*]
**NDW** ......... North Dakota State School of Science, Mildred Johnson Library, Wahpeton, ND [*OCLC symbol*] (OCLC)
**NDWAC** .... National Drinking Water Advisory Council [*Environmental Protection Agency*]
**NdWah** ...... Leach Public Library, Wahpeton, ND [*Library symbol*] [*Library of Congress*] (LCLS)
**NdWahS** .... North Dakota State School of Science, Wahpeton, ND [*Library symbol*] [*Library of Congress*] (LCLS)
**NDWBA** .... National Deaf Women's Bowling Association (EA)
**NdWi** ......... James Memorial Library, Williston, ND [*Library symbol*] [*Library of Congress*] (LCLS)
**NdWiU** ...... University of North Dakota, Williston Branch, Williston, ND [*Library symbol*] [*Library of Congress*] (LCLS)
**NdWiW** ..... West Plains Rural Library, Williston, ND [*Library symbol*] [*Library of Congress*] (LCLS)
**NDWP** ....... National Demonstration Water Project (EA)
**NDWRRI** .. North Dakota Water Resources Research Institute [*Fargo, ND*] [*Department of the Interior*] (GRD)
**NDWU** ...... National Domestic Workers Union (EA)
**NDX** .......... Northern Dynasty Explorations Ltd. [*Toronto Stock Exchange symbol*] [*Vancouver Stock Exchange symbol*]
**NDxhBJ** .... Burr's Lane Junior High School, Dix Hills, NY [*Library symbol*] [*Library of Congress*] (LCLS)
**NDxhHH-E** ... Half Hollow Hills High School East, Dix Hills, NY [*Library symbol*] [*Library of Congress*] (LCLS)
**NDxhHH-W** ... Half Hollow Hills High School West, Dix Hills, NY [*Library symbol*] [*Library of Congress*] (LCLS)
**NDxhHT** ... Half Hollow Hills District Teacher's Center, Dix Hills, NY [*Library symbol*] [*Library of Congress*] (LCLS)
**NDY** .......... Dahlgren, VA [*Location identifier*] [*FAA*] (FAAL)
**NDY** .......... Neodymium-Doped Yttralox [*Ceramic*]
**NDY** .......... Nonresonant Deflection Yoke
**NDY** .......... Sanday [*Scotland*] [*Airport symbol*] (OAG)
**Nd:YAG** ..... Neodymium-Doped: Yttrium Aluminum Garnet [*LASER technology*]
**NDYL** ........ Neodymium-Doped YAG [*Yttrium Aluminum Garnet*] LASER
**NDZ** .......... Milton, FL [*Location identifier*] [*FAA*] (FAAL)
**NDZKA** ..... Noodzaak [*A publication*]
**Nd Z Vk** ..... Niederdeutsche Zeitschrift fuer Volkskunde und Blaetter fuer Niedersaechsische Heimatpflege [*A publication*]
**Ne** .............. Algemeen Rijksarchief te s'Gravenhage (Central State Archives), The Hague, Netherlands [*Library symbol*] [*Library of Congress*] (LCLS)
**NE** ............. Left Nationalists [*Spain*] [*Political party*] (PPW)
**NE** ............. Narcotics Education [*An association*] (EA)
**NE** ............. National Emergency
**NE** ............. National Exchequer [*British*]
**NE** ............. National Executive (ADA)
**NE** ............. National Exhibition [*British*]
**NE** ............. Naval Engineer [*Academic degree*]
**NE** ............. Navy Evaluation
**NE** ............. Near East (BJA)
**NE** ............. Nebraska [*Postal code*]
**NE** ............. Nebraska Music Educator [*A publication*]
**NE** ............. Negative Expectancy [*Psychometrics*]
**Ne** .............. Nehemiah [*Old Testament book*] (BJA)
**NE** ............. Neiva [*Sociedade Construtora Aeronautica Neiva Ltda.*] [*Brazil*] [*ICAO aircraft manufacturer identifier*] (ICAO)
**NE** ............. Neomycin [*Antibacterial compound*]
**NE** ............. Neon [*Chemical element*]
**ne** .............. Nephelite [*CIPW classification*] [*Geology*]
**NE** ............. Nephropathia Epidemica [*Medicine*]
**NE** ............. Nerve Excitability [*Test*]

**NE**.......... Net Earnings
**ne**.......... Netherlands [*MARC country of publication code*] [*Library of Congress*] (LCCP)
**NE**.......... Netherlands
**NE**.......... Neumann-Electroporation [*Gene technology*]
**NE**.......... Neurologic Examination [*Medicine*]
**NE**.......... Neutral Excitation
**Ne**.......... Neva [*A publication*]
**NE**.......... New Edition
**NE**.......... New Editions [*Record label*]
**NE**.......... New Engine [*On ships*]
**NE**.......... New England
**NE**.......... [*The*] New English Bible [*1961*] [*A publication*] (BJA)
**NE**.......... News Editor (ADA)
**NE**.......... Nickel Equivalent [*Coinage*]
**NE**.......... Niger [*ANSI two-letter standard code*] (CNC)
**NE**.......... Night Experimental [*British military*] (DMA)
**NE**.......... Nileair [*Egypt*] [*ICAO designator*] (FAAC)
**NE**.......... No Earthly Chance (DSUE)
**NE**.......... No Effects
**NE**.......... Nodal Exchange (MCD)
**NE**.......... Non-English Speaker [*Airline notation*]
**NE**.......... Nonessential
**NE**.......... Nordelbingen [*A publication*]
**NE**.......... Norepinephrine [*Also known as NA: Noradrenaline*] [*Biochemistry*]
**NE**.......... Normal Excitability [*Medicine*]
**NE**.......... Normally Energized (NRCH)
**NE**.......... North Eastern Reporter [*A publication*] (DLA)
**NE**.......... Northeast
**NE**.......... Northeast Airlines, Inc. [*Obsolete*]
**NE**.......... Not Enlarged [*Medicine*]
**NE**.......... Not Entitled [*British military*] (DMA)
**NE**.......... Not Equal [*Relational operator*]
**NE**.......... Not Evaluated (INF)
**NE**.......... Not Examined [*Medicine*]
**N/E**.......... Not Exceeding
**NE**.......... Not Explosive
**NE**.......... Notice of Exception (MCD)
**NE**.......... Nuclear Engineer
**NE**.......... Nuclear Envelope [*Cytology*]
**NE**.......... Nuclear Explosive
**NE**.......... Nuclear Extract [*Cytology*]
**NE**.......... Nueva Estafeta [*A publication*]
**NE**.......... Numismatica i Epigrafica [*A publication*]
**NEa**.......... Eastchester Public Library, Eastchester, NY [*Library symbol*] [*Library of Congress*] (LCLS)
**NEA**.......... Nashville Entertainment Association (EA)
**NEA**.......... National Economic Association (EA)
**NEA**.......... National Editorial Association [*Later, NNA*] (EA)
**NEA**.......... National Education Association (EA)
**NEA**.......... National Electronic Associations [*Later, NESSDA*]
**NEA**.......... National Employment Association [*Later, NAPC*] (EA)
**NEA**.......... National Endowment for the Arts
**NEA**.......... National Energy Accounts [*Department of Commerce*] [*Information service or system*] (IID)
**NEA**.......... National Erectors Association (EA)
**NEA**.......... Natural Energy Association [*British*]
**NEA**.......... Near-Earth Asteroid [*Astronomy*]
**NEA**.......... Near Eastern Affairs [*Department of State*]
**NEA**.......... Nearctic Resources, Inc. [*Toronto Stock Exchange symbol*]
**NEA**.......... Neath [*Welsh depot code*]
**NEA**.......... Negative Electron Affinity [*Photocathode*]
**NEA**.......... Nelson & Albemarle Railway [*AAR code*]
**NEA**.......... Nenana [*Alaska*] [*Seismograph station code, US Geological Survey*] (SEIS)
**NEA**.......... Network Equivalent Analysis
**NEA**.......... New England Airlines, Inc. [*Westerly, RI*] [*FAA designator*] (FAAC)
**NEA**.......... New Entitlement Authority
**NEA**.......... Newspaper Enterprise Association [*A syndicate*]
**NEA**.......... Noise-Equivalent Angle (MCD)
**NEA**.......... Northeast Airlines, Inc. [*Obsolete*]
**NEA**.......... Northeast Asia (CINC)
**NEA**.......... Northern Examining Association [*British*]
**NEA**.......... Nuclear Energy Agency [*OECD*] [*Paris*] (IEEE)
**NEA**.......... Null Error Amplifier
**NEA**.......... Nutrition Education Association (EA)
**NEA**.......... OECD [*Organization for Economic Cooperation and Development*] Nuclear Energy Agency [*See also AEN*] (EAIO)
**NeAA**.......... Gemeente Archief van Amsterdam, Amsterdam, Netherlands [*Library symbol*] [*Library of Congress*] (LCLS)
**NEAA**.......... National Employment Assistance Act (OICC)
**NEAA**.......... Norwegian Elkhound Association of America (EA)
**NEAATS**... Northeast Asia Association of Theological Schools
**NEABFGP** ... New England Advisory Board for Fish and Game Problems (EA)
**NEabG**.......... Genesee County Landmark Society, East Bethany, NY [*Library symbol*] [*Library of Congress*] (LCLS)
**NEAC**.......... New English Art Club [*British*]
**NEAC**.......... Nippon Electric Automatic Computer (IEEE)
**NEAC**.......... Northeast Air Command
**NEACDS**... Naval Emergency Air Cargo Delivery System (CAAL)
**NEACH**..... New England Automated Clearing House Association
**NEACP**...... National Emergency Airborne Command Post [*Pronounced "kneecap"*] [*Modified Boeing 747 jet to be used as a military control center by the President or Vice President during a nuclear war or other crisis*]
**NEACSS** ... New England Association of Colleges and Secondary Schools [*Later, NEASC*] (EA)
**NEA-DB**.... NEA [*Nuclear Energy Agency*] Data Bank [*OECD*] [*Information service or system*] (IID)
**NEADS**...... Near East and African Development Service
**NEADS**...... Network Engineering Administrative Data System [*AT & T*]
**NEADS**...... Northeast Atlantic Dynamics Studies [*Marine science*] (MSC)
**NEADW**.... Northeast Atlantic Deep Water [*Oceanography*]
**NEAF**.......... Near East Air Force [*British*]
**NEAFC**....... North-East Atlantic Fisheries Commission [*London, England*] (EAIO)
**NEAGC**..... National Early American Glass Club (EA)
**NeaH**.......... Nea Hestia [*A publication*]
**NEAHI**...... Near East Animal Health Institute
**NEA J**.......... National Education Association. Journal [*A publication*]
**NEAM**.......... Nonvolatile Electrically Alterable Memory
**NEAN**.......... National Execution Alert Network (EA)
**NEANMCC** ... Navy Element Alternate National Military Command Center (MCD)
**NEanpHE** ... Harley Avenue Elementary School, East Northport, NY [*Library symbol*] [*Library of Congress*] (LCLS)
**NeAO**.......... Rijksinstituut voor Orlogsdocumentatie, Amsterdam, Netherlands [*Library symbol*] [*Library of Congress*] (LCLS)
**NEAP**.......... National Energy Audit Program [*Canada*]
**Neap**.......... Neapolis [*A publication*]
**NEAPD**..... Northeastern Air Procurement District
**Neapoli** ...... [*Sebastianus*] Neapolitanus [*Flourished, 14th-15th century*] [*Authority cited in pre-1607 legal work*] (DSA)
**NEAR**.......... National Emergency Alarm Repeater [*Civil defense warning system for homes*]
**NEAR**.......... Nationwide/Worldwide Emergency Ambulance Return
**NEAR**.......... Near Earth Asteroid Rendezvous (MCD)
**NEAR**.......... New England Action Research Project
**NEARA**..... New England Antiquities Research Association (EA)
**Near East**... Near East and India [*A publication*]
**NEARELF** ... Near East Land Forces [*British military*] (DMA)
**NEA Res Bul** ... National Education Association. Research Bulletin [*A publication*]
**NEA Res Div Rept** ... National Education Association. Research Division. Reports [*A publication*]
**NEARNAVDIST** ... Nearest Naval District
**NEARP**...... New England Appalachian Research Project [*University of Maine at Orono*] [*Research center*] (RCD)
**NEARS**...... Navy Evaluation of Advanced Reconnaissance Systems
**NEARTIP** ... Near-Term Improvement Program [*For torpedos*] (MCD)
**NEAS**.......... National Engineering Aptitude Search
**NEAS**.......... Near East Archaeological Society (EA)
**NEAS**.......... Newsletter of Engineering Analysis Software [*A publication*] (MCD)
**NEASA**...... Near Eastern, African, and South Asian Affairs [*Department of State*]
**NEASB**...... Near East Archaeological Society. Bulletin [*A publication*]
**NEASC**...... New England Association of Schools and Colleges (EA)
**NEASCUS** ... New England Association of School, College, and University Staffing
**NE Asia J Th** ... Northeast Asia Journal of Theology [*A publication*]
**NEASP**...... Navy Enlisted Advanced School Program
**NEaspHS** .. Eastport High School, Eastport, NY [*Library symbol*] [*Library of Congress*] (LCLS)
**NeAT**.......... Koninklijk Instituut voor de Tropen, Amsterdam, Netherlands [*Library symbol*] [*Library of Congress*] (LCLS)
**NEAT**.......... Navy Electronics Application Trainer
**NEAT**.......... Navy Embarked Advisory Team
**NEAT**.......... NCR [*NCR Corp.*] Electronic Autocoding Technique [*Data processing*]
**NEAT**.......... New Enhanced Technology
**NEATO**..... North East Asian Treaty Organization (NATG)
**NeAU**.......... University of Amsterdam, Amsterdam, Netherlands [*Library symbol*] [*Library of Congress*] (LCLS)
**NEAuC**...... Christ the King Seminary, East Aurora, NY [*Library symbol*] [*Library of Congress*] (LCLS)
**NEAuF**...... Fisher-Price Toys, East Aurora, NY [*Library symbol*] [*Library of Congress*] (LCLS)
**NEAuH**...... Elbert Hubbard Library Museum, East Aurora, NY [*Library symbol*] [*Library of Congress*] (LCLS)
**NEAuS**...... Saint John Vianney Seminary, East Aurora, NY [*Library symbol*] [*Library of Congress*] (LCLS)
**NEawNE** ... North Side Elementary School, East Williston, NY [*Library symbol*] [*Library of Congress*] (LCLS)
**NEB**.......... Bank of New England Corp. [*NYSE symbol*] (SPSG)
**NEB**.......... Department of Aeronautics, State of Nebraska [*Lincoln, NE*] [*FAA designator*] (FAAC)

**NEB**.......... National Energy Board [*Canada*]
**NEB**.......... National Enterprise Board [*Later, BTG*] [*British*]
**NEB**.......... National Environment Board [*Thailand*] (DS)
**NEB**.......... Nebelwerfer [*German six-barrelled mortar*] (DSUE)
**NEB**.......... Nebraska
**Neb**............ Nebraska Reports [*A publication*]
**Neb**............ Nebraska Supreme Court Reports [*A publication*] (DLA)
**Neb**............ [*Helius Antonius*] Nebrissensis [*Deceased, 1522*] [*Authority cited in pre-1607 legal work*] (DSA)
**NEB**.......... Nebula [*Spray*] [*Pharmacy*]
**Neb**............ Nebula Science Fiction [*A publication*]
**NEB**.......... Neuroepithelial Bodies [*Anatomy*]
**NEB**.......... New England Journal of Business and Economics [*A publication*]
**NEB**.......... New England Motor Rate Bureau Inc., Burlington MA [*STAC*]
**NEB**.......... [*The*] New English Bible [*1961*] [*A publication*]
**NEB**.......... Nissim Ezra Benjamin [*Shanghai*] (BJA)
**NEB**.......... Noise-Equivalent Bandwidth
**NEB**.......... Nonenzymatic Maillard Browning [*Food technology*]
**NEB**.......... North Equatorial Belt [*Planet Jupiter*]
**NEB**.......... Nuclear Envelope Breakdown [*Also, NEBD*] [*Cytology*]
**Neb**............ United States District Court for the District of Nebraska (DLA)
**NEBAC**...... National Ethnic Broadcasting Advisory Council [*Australia*]
**Neb Admin R** ... Nebraska Administrative Rules and Regulations [*A publication*] (DLA)
**Neb Admin R & Regs** ... Nebraska Administrative Rules and Regulations [*A publication*]
**Neb Ag Exp** ... Nebraska. Agricultural Experiment Station. Publications [*A publication*]
**Neb Agric Exp Stn Annu Rep** ... Nebraska. Agricultural Experiment Station. Annual Report [*A publication*]
**Neb Agric Exp Stn Circ** ... Nebraska. Agricultural Experiment Station. Circular [*A publication*]
**NEBB**........ National Environmental Balancing Bureau (EA)
**NEBBA**...... Neue Bergbautechnik [*A publication*]
**NEBBA**...... Northeastern Bird-Banding Association [*Later, AFO*] (EA)
**NEBD**........ Nuclear Envelope Breakdown [*Also, NEB*] [*Cytology*]
**NEbE**......... Northeast by East
**Neb Ed J**.... Nebraska Educational Journal [*A publication*]
**NebH**......... Nebraska History [*A publication*]
**NEBHE**..... New England Board of Higher Education [*Information service or system*]
**Neb His**...... Nebraska History [*A publication*]
**Neb His M** ... Nebraska History. Magazine [*A publication*]
**Neb His S**.. Nebraska State Historical Society. Collections [*A publication*]
**Neb Hist**.... Nebraska History [*A publication*]
**NEBI**.......... National Employee Benefits Institute [*Washington, DC*] (EA)
**NEBIC**....... New England Bibliographic Instruction Collection
**NEBIS**....... North of England Biotechnology Information Service [*University of Newcastle-Upon-Tyne Medical School*] [*England*] [*Information service or system*] (IID)
**NEBIT**....... New and Expanding Business and Industry Training (OICC)
**Neb J Econ and Bus** ... Nebraska Journal of Economics and Business [*A publication*]
**NEBK**........ National Enterprise Bank [*Washington, DC*] (NQ)
**Neb Laws**... Laws of Nebraska [*A publication*]
**Neb LB**....... Nebraska Law Bulletin [*A publication*] (DLA)
**Neb Leg N** ... Nebraska Legal News [*A publication*] (DLA)
**Neb Lib Assn Q** ... Nebraska Library Association. Quarterly [*A publication*]
**Neb LR**...... Nebraska Law Review [*A publication*]
**Neb L Rev**.. Nebraska Law Review [*A publication*]
**NEBM**....... No Eating between Meals
**NEBMA**.... Neben-Munitionsanstalt [*Branch ammunition depot*] [*German military - World War II*]
**NEbN**......... Northeast by North
**NEBR**........ Nebraska (AAG)
**Nebr**........... Nebraska Reports [*A publication*] (DLA)
**Nebr**........... [*Helius Antonius*] Nebrissensis [*Deceased, 1522*] [*Authority cited in pre-1607 legal work*] (DSA)
**NEBR**........ New Breed. Association of Metis and Non-Status Indians of Saskatchewan [*A publication*]
**Nebr Ac Sc Pub Pr** ... Nebraska Academy of Sciences. Publications. Proceedings [*A publication*]
**Nebr Agric Exp Stn Annu Rep** ... Nebraska. Agricultural Experiment Station. Annual Report [*A publication*]
**Nebr Agric Exp Stn Bull** ... Nebraska. Agricultural Experiment Station. Bulletin [*A publication*]
**Nebr Agric Exp Stn Res Bull** ... Nebraska. Agricultural Experiment Station. Research Bulletin [*A publication*]
**Nebraska Acad Sci Proc** ... Nebraska Academy of Sciences and Affiliated Societies. Proceedings [*A publication*]
**Nebraska Geol Survey Paper** ... Nebraska Geological Survey. Paper [*A publication*]
**Nebraska L Rev** ... Nebraska Law Review [*A publication*]
**Nebraska Univ State Mus Bull** ... Nebraska. University. State Museum. Bulletin [*A publication*]
**Nebr BA**..... Nebraska State Bar Journal [*A publication*]
**Nebr Bird Rev** ... Nebraska Bird Review [*A publication*]
**Neb RC**...... Nebraska Railway Commission Reports [*A publication*] (DLA)
**Nebr Conserv Bull** ... Nebraska Conservation Bulletin [*A publication*]
**Nebr Energy News** ... Nebraska Energy News [*A publication*]
**NEBRET**... Nematologia Brasileira [*A publication*]
**Neb Rev Stat** ... Revised Statutes of Nebraska [*A publication*] (DLA)
**Nebr Exp Stn Q** ... Nebraska Experiment Station Quarterly [*A publication*]
**Nebr Farm Ranch Econ** ... Nebraska Farm Ranch Economics [*A publication*]
**Nebr Geol Surv Bull** ... Nebraska Geological Survey. Bulletin [*A publication*]
**Nebris**........ [*Helius Antonius*] Nebrissensis [*Deceased, 1522*] [*Authority cited in pre-1607 legal work*] (DSA)
**Nebr LB**..... Nebraska Law Bulletin [*A publication*] (DLA)
**Nebr L Rev** ... Nebraska Law Review [*A publication*]
**Nebr Med J** ... Nebraska Medical Journal [*A publication*]
**Nebr Nurse** ... Nebraska Nurse [*A publication*]
**Nebr State Med J** ... Nebraska State Medical Journal [*A publication*]
**Nebr State Mus Bull** ... Nebraska State Museum. Bulletin [*A publication*]
**Nebr St Bd Agr An Rp** ... Nebraska State Board of Agriculture. Annual Report [*A publication*]
**Nebr St Hist Soc Pr** ... Nebraska State Historical Society. Proceedings and Collections [*A publication*]
**Nebr St Med J** ... Nebraska State Medical Journal [*A publication*]
**Nebr Symp Motiv** ... Nebraska Symposium on Motivation [*A publication*]
**Nebr Univ Agric Exp Stn Annu Rep** ... Nebraska. University. Agricultural Experiment Station. Annual Report [*A publication*]
**Nebr Univ Coll Agric Home Econ Ext Serv Ext Circ** ... Nebraska. University. College of Agriculture and Home Economics. Extension Service. Extension Circular [*A publication*]
**Nebr Univ Eng Exp Stn Bull** ... Nebraska. University. Engineering Experiment Station. Bulletin [*A publication*]
**Nebr Univ Studies** ... Nebraska. University. Studies [*A publication*]
**Nebr Water Surv Pap** ... Nebraska Water Survey Paper [*A publication*]
**Nebr Wheat Variety Estimate Nebr Grain Impr Ass** ... Nebraska Wheat Variety Estimate. Nebraska Grain Improvement Association [*A publication*]
**NEBS**......... New England Business Service, Inc. [*NASDAQ symbol*] (NQ)
**Neb SBJ**..... Nebraska State Bar Journal [*A publication*]
**NEBSS**...... National Examinations Board in Supervisory Studies [*British*]
**Neb St BJ**.. Nebraska State Bar Journal [*A publication*]
**Neb Sup Ct J** ... Nebraska Supreme Court Journal [*A publication*] (DLA)
**NEBTA**...... Nederlands Bosbouw Tijdschrift [*A publication*]
**NEBUL**...... Nebula [*Spray*] [*Pharmacy*]
**NEBULA**... Natural Electronic Business User's Language [*International Computers Ltd.*]
**Neb (Unof)** ... Nebraska Unofficial Reports [*A publication*] (DLA)
**Neb Unoff**.. Nebraska Unofficial Reports [*A publication*] (DLA)
**NEBW**....... Nonvacuum Electron Beam Welding
**Neb WCC**.. Nebraska Workmen's Compensation Court. Bulletin [*A publication*] (DLA)
**NEC**.......... National Economic Council [*Defunct*] (EA)
**NEC**.......... National Economists Club (EA)
**NEC**.......... National Ecumenical Coalition (EA)
**NEC**.......... National Education Center for Paraprofessionals in Mental Health (EA)
**NEC**.......... National Education Corporation [*NYSE symbol*] (SPSG)
**NEC**.......... National Egg Council [*Later, PEIA*] (EA)
**NEC**.......... National Electrical Code
**NEC**.......... National Emblem Club (EA)
**NEC**.......... National Emergency Council [*Abolished, 1939*]
**NEC**.......... National Employers' Committee
**NEC**.......... National Engineering Consortium (EA)
**NEC**.......... National Entertainment Conference [*Later, NECAA*] (EA)
**NEC**.......... National Exchange Club (EA)
**NEC**.......... National Executive Committee [*British*] (DCTA)
**NEC**.......... National Exhibition Centre [*British*]
**NEC**.......... National Extension College [*England*]
**NEC**.......... Naval Examining Center
**NEC**.......... Naval Exercise Coordinator (CINC)
**NEC**.......... Naval Exhibit Center
**NEC**.......... Navy Enlisted Classification (NG)
**NEC**.......... Navy Enlisted Code
**NEC**.......... Nebraska State Railway Commission [*STAC*]
**NEC**.......... Necessary (AABC)
**NEC**.......... Necochea [*Argentina*] [*Airport symbol*] (OAG)
**NEC**.......... Necrotizing Enterocolitis [*Medicine*]
**NEC**.......... Negro Ensemble Company [*A theatre group*]
**NEC**.......... Netherlands Electrotechnical Committee
**NEC**.......... Neuroendocrine Cell [*Cytology*]
**NEC**.......... New England College, Henniker, NH [*OCLC symbol*] (OCLC)
**NEC**.......... New England Commuter, Inc. [*North Andover, MA*] [*FAA designator*] (FAAC)
**NEC**.......... New England Council (EA)
**NEC**.......... Nippon Electric Company [*Japan*]
**NEC**.......... Nippon Electric Company News [*Japan*] [*A publication*]
**NEC**.......... No Eye Contact [*Psychology*]
**NEC**.......... North East Corner [*Freemasonry*]
**NEC**.......... North Equatorial Current [*Oceanography*] (MSC)
**NEC**.......... Northeast Conference on the Teaching of Foreign Languages (EA)
**NEC**.......... Northern Europe Committee [*NATO*] (NATG)
**NEC**.......... Northern European Command [*NATO*] (NATG)
**NEC**.......... Not Elsewhere Classified
**NEC**.......... Notes of English Ecclesiastical Cases [*A publication*] (DLA)
**NEC**.......... Nuclear Energy Center (NRCH)
**NEC**.......... Nucleus of Epidermal Cell

**NECA**........ N-Ethylcarboxamide Adenosine [*Biochemistry*]
**NECA**........ National Electrical Contractors Association (EA)
**NECA**........ National Employment Counselors Association (EA)
**NECA**........ National Episcopal Coalition on Alcohol [*Later, NECAD*] (EA)
**NECA**........ National Exchange Carrier Association (EA)
**NECA**........ National Explorers and Collectors Association (EA)
**NECA**........ Near East College Association (EA)
**NECA**........ Numismatic Error Collectors of America (EA)
**NECAA**..... National Entertainment and Campus Activities Association [*Formerly, NEC*] (EA)
**NECAD**..... National Episcopal Coalition on Alcohol and Drugs (EA)
**NECAP**...... NASA Energy-Cost Analysis Program
**NECAP**...... Navigation Equipment Capability Analysis (KSC)
**NECAP**...... Nutmeg Electric Companies Atomic Project
**NECC**........ National Education Computer Center
**NECC**........ National Education Crisis Committee [*South Africa*]
**NECC**........ New England Congressional Caucus (EA)
**NECC**........ New England Critical Care, Inc. [*NASDAQ symbol*] (NQ)
**NECC**........ North Equatorial Countercurrent [*Oceanography*]
**NECC**........ Northeast Computer Center [*Military*] (AABC)
**NECC**........ Northern Essex Community College [*Haverhill, MA*]
**NECCB**...... National Education Council of the Christian Brothers [*Later, RECCB*] (EA)
**NECCO**..... New England Confectionery Company
**NECCO**..... Northern Essex Community College [*Haverhill, MA*]
**NECCTA**... National Educational Closed-Circuit Television Association [*British*]
**NECDC**..... New England Consumer Development Council
**NECF**......... National Exchange Club Foundation for the Prevention of Child Abuse (EA)
**NECG**........ National Engineering Council for Guidance (EA)
**NECG**........ New Ecologist [*A publication*]
**NECH**........ National Employment Clearing House [*American Chemical Society*]
**NECH**........ National Event Clearinghouse Database [*National Event Clearinghouse, Inc.*] [*Information service or system*] (CRD)
**NECHE**..... Northeastern Colorado Hail Experiment
**NECHI**...... Northeastern Consortium for Health Information [*Library network*]
**NECIES**.... North East Coast Institution of Engineers and Shipbuilders (FAIO)
**NECIP**....... Northeast Corridor Improvement Project [*Department of Transportation*]
**NECIS**....... NEC Information Systems, Inc. [*Boxborough, MA*]
**N Ecl**.......... New Eclectic [*A publication*]
**NECLC**...... National Emergency Civil Liberties Committee (EA)
**NECM**....... New England Conservatory of Music [*Boston, MA*]
**NECMA**.... New England County Metropolitan Areas
**NECNVA**.. New England Committee for Nonviolent Action [*Later, CNVA*] (EA)
**NECO**........ Nuclear Engineering Company, Inc.
**NECOS**...... Communication Net Control Station [*Navy*] (NVT)
**NECOS**...... Northern European Chiefs of Staff [*NATO*] (NATG)
**NECP**......... National Eye Care Project [*Foundation of the American Academy of Ophthalmology*] (EA)
**NECP**......... New England College of Pharmacy
**NECP**......... Nonengineering Change Proposal
**NECPA**...... National Emergency Command Post Afloat
**NECPA**...... National Energy Conservation Policy Act [*1978*]
**NECPL**...... NATO Exploratory Conference on Production Logistics (NATG)
**NECPR**...... New External Cardiopulmonary Resuscitation
**NEC Res Dev**... NEC [*Nippon Electric Company*] Research and Development [*A publication*]
**NEC Res and Dev**... NEC [*Nippon Electric Company*] Research and Development [*A publication*]
**NEC Rev**.... NEC [*Nippon Electric Company*] Review [*A publication*]
**NECS**......... National Electrical Code Standards
**NECS**......... National Elephant Collectors Society (EA)
**NECS**......... Nationwide Educational Computer Service (IEEE)
**NECSS**...... Nuclear Energy Center Site Survey (NRCH)
**NECT**........ National Environmental Controls, Inc. [*NASDAQ symbol*] (NQ)
**NECTA**...... National Electric Comfort Trade Association [*Defunct*] (EA)
**NECTP**...... Northeast Corridor Transportation Project
**NECY**........ Necessary
**NED**........... Naphthylethylenediamine Dihydrochloride [*Organic chemistry*]
**NED**........... National Endowment for Democracy (EA)
**NED**........... Naval Equipment Department [*British military*] (DMA)
**NED**........... Navigation Error Data (MUGU)
**Ned**............ Nedarim (BJA)
**NED**........... New Editor [*Computer program*] [*Air Force*] (MCD)
**NED**........... New England Division [*Army Engineers*]
**NED**........... New English Dictionary [*i.e., the Oxford English Dictionary*]
**NED**........... Newark [*Delaware*] [*Seismograph station code, US Geological Survey*] (SEIS)
**NED**........... No Evidence of Disease
**NED**........... No Expiration Date
**NED**........... Normal Equivalent Deviation
**NED**........... North, East, and Down
**NED**........... Northeastern University, Boston, MA [*OCLC symbol*] (OCLC)
**NED**........... Nuclear Energy Division [*General Electric Co.*]
**NED**........... Nuclear Engineering Directorate [*Army*]
**N E 2d**........ North Eastern Reporter. Second Series [*A publication*]
**NE 2d**......... Northeastern Reporter, Second Series [*A publication*] (DLA)
**NEDA**........ National Economic Development Association
**NEDA**........ National Electronic Distributors Association (EA)
**NEDA**........ National Emergency Defense Airlift
**NEDA**........ National Environmental Development Association (EA)
**NEDA**........ National Equipment Distributors Association (EA)
**NEDA**........ National Exhaust Distributors Association [*Later, NEDA/USA*] (EA)
**Neda**........... Nedarim (BJA)
**NedA**.......... Nederlandsch Archievenblad [*A publication*]
**NEDA/GRND**... National Environmental Development Association/Ground Water Project (EA)
**Ned Akad Wet Afd Natuurkd Verh Eerste Reeks**... Nederlandse Akademie van Wetenschappen, Afdeling Natuurkunde. Verhandelingen. Eerste Reeks [*A publication*]
**Ned Akad Wet Proc Ser B**... Nederlandse Akademie van Wetenschappen [*Koninklijke*]. Proceedings. Series B. Physical Sciences [*A publication*]
**Ned AKG**... Nederlandsch Archief voor Kerkgeschiedenis [*A publication*]
**NEDA/USA**... National Exhaust Distributors Association/Undercar Specialists Association (EA)
**Ned Bosb Tijdschr**... Nederlands Bosbouw Tijdschrift [*A publication*]
**NEDC**........ National Economic Development Council [*Nickname: Neddie*] [*British*]
**NeDC**......... New England Document Conservation Center, Andover, MA [*Library symbol*] [*Library of Congress*] (LCLS)
**NEDCC**..... New England Document Conservation Center [*Information service or system*] (IID)
**Ned Chem Ind**... Nederlandse Chemische Industrie [*A publication*]
**NEDCO**..... Northeast Dairy Cooperative Federation (EA)
**Ned Dendrol Ver Jaarb**... Nederlandse Dendrologische Vereniging. Jaarboek [*A publication*]
**NEDECO**.. Netherlands Engineering Consultants
**Ned Entomol Ver Jaarb**... Nederlandse Entomologische Vereniging. Jaarboek [*A publication*]
**NEDEP**...... Navy Enlisted Dietetic Education Program
**NEDEPA**... Nea Demokratiki Parataxi [*Cyprus*] [*Political party*] (PPE)
**Nederl Akad Wetensch Indag Math**... Koninklijke Nederlandse Akademie van Wetenschappen. Indagationes Mathematicae ex Actis Quibus Titulus [*A publication*]
**Nederl Akad Wetensch Proc Ser A**... Koninklijke Nederlandse Akademie van Wetenschappen. Proceedings. Series A. Mathematical Sciences [*A publication*]
**Nederl Akad Wetensch Proc Ser B**... Koninklijke Nederlandse Akademie van Wetenschappen. Proceedings. Series B. Physical Sciences [*Later, Koninklijke Nederlandse Akademie van Wetenschappen. Proceedings. Series B. Palaeontology, Geology, Physics, and Chemistry*] [*A publication*]
**Nederl Akad Wetensch Verslag Afd Natuurk**... Koninklijke Nederlandse Akademie van Wetenschappen. Verslag van de Gewone Vergadering van de Afdeling Natuurkunde [*A publication*]
**Nederlandsch Hist Inst Rome Med**... Nederlandsch Historisch Instituut te Rome. Mededeelingen [*A publication*]
**Nederlandse Oudheidkundige Bond Bull**... Nederlandse Oudheidkundige Bond. Bulletin [*A publication*]
**Nederlands Kunsthist Jaar**... Nederlands Kunsthistorisch Jaarboek [*A publication*]
**Nederl-Ind Blad Diergeneesk**... Nederlandsch-Indische Bladen voor Diergeneeskunde [*A publication*]
**Nederl Lancet**... Nederlandsch Lancet [*A publication*]
**NeDF**......... New England Data Film, Inc., Milford, CT [*Library symbol*] [*Library of Congress*] (LCLS)
**Ned Gem**.... Nederlandse Gemeente [*A publication*]
**Ned Geol Mijnbouwkd Genoot Verh**... Nederlands Geologisch Mijnbouwkundig Genootschap [*Koninklijk*]. Verhandelingen [*A publication*]
**NedGerefTTs**... Nederduitse Gereformeerde Teologiese Tydskrif [*Kaapstad*] [*A publication*]
**NE Dialog**... Northeast Dialog [*A publication*]
**Ned Ind Eigendom**... Nederland Industriele Eigendom [*A publication*]
**NEDIPA**.... Nea Demokratiki Parataxi [*Cyprus*] [*Political party*] (PPW)
**NEDIS**....... National Environmental Data and Information Service [*Marine science*] (MSC)
**Ned Jbl**...... Nederlands Juristenblad [*A publication*]
**Ned Jpd**..... Nederlandse Jurisprudentie [*A publication*]
**Ned Kruidkd Arch**... Nederlandsch Kruidkundig Archief [*A publication*]
**NedL**.......... Nederlandse Leeuw [*A publication*]
**NEDL**......... New England Deposit Library
**NEDLC**...... National Economic Development and Law Center [*Berkeley, CA*] [*Research center*] (EA)
**Ned Maandschr Geneeskd**... Nederlandsch Maandschrift voor Geneeskunde [*A publication*]
**Ned Melk Zuiveltijdschr**... Nederlands Melk-en Zuiveltijdschrift [*A publication*]
**Ned Mil Geneeskd Tijdschr**... Nederlands Militair Geneeskundig Tijdschrift [*A publication*]
**NEDN**........ Naval Environmental Data Network

**NEDO**........ National Economic Development Office [*British*]
**NEDO Frcst** ... National Economic Development Office. Construction Forecasts [*United Kingdom*] [*A publication*]
**NEDP**........ Neighbourhood Employment Development Program [*Australia*]
**NEDRES**... National Environmental Data Referral Service [*National Oceanic and Atmospheric Administration*] [*Washington, DC*] [*Online database*]
**Nedrl Tijdsch v Intl R** ... Nederlands Tijdschrift voor Internationaal Recht [*Netherlands*] [*A publication*] (DLA)
**Ned Rubberind** ... Nederlandse Rubberindustrie [*A publication*]
**NEDS**........ National Emissions Data System [*Environmental Protection Agency*] [*Information service or system*]
**NEDS**........ Naval Environmental Data System (CAAL)
**NEDS**........ Naval Environmental Display Station (CAAL)
**NEDS**........ New Enlisted Distribution System (NVT)
**NEDS**........ Nonviolent Explosive Destructive System (MCD)
**Ned Scheepsstudiecent TNO Rep** ... Nederlands Scheepsstudiecentrum TNO. Report [*A publication*]
**Ned Staatscourant** ... Nederlandse Staatscourant [*A publication*]
**Ned Stcrt**.... Nederlandse Staatscourant [*A publication*]
**NEDT**........ National Educational Development Test
**NEDT**........ Noise-Equivalent Differential Temperature
**Ned T v Gen** ... Nederlands Tijdschrift voor Geneeskunde [*A publication*]
**NeDTH**...... Technische Hogeschool Delft, Delft, Netherlands [*Library symbol*] [*Library of Congress*] (LCLS)
**NedThT**..... Nederlands Theologisch Tijdschrift [*Wageningen*] [*A publication*]
**Ned Tijdschr** ... Nederlands Tijdschrift voor Internationaal Recht [*A publication*]
**Ned Tijdschr Geneeskd** ... Nederlands Tijdschrift voor Geneeskunde [*A publication*]
**Ned Tijdschr Gerontol** ... Nederlands Tijdschrift voor Gerontologie [*A publication*]
**Ned Tijdschr Hyg Microbiol Serol** ... Nederlandsch Tijdschrift voor Hygiene, Microbiologie, en Serologie [*A publication*]
**Ned Tijdschr Natuurk** ... Nederlands Tijdschrift voor Natuurkunde [*A publication*]
**Ned Tijdschr Natuurk A** ... Nederlands Tijdschrift voor Natuurkunde. Series A [*A publication*]
**Ned Tijdschr Natuurkd** ... Nederlands Tijdschrift voor Natuurkunde [*A publication*]
**Ned Tijdschr Natuurkd A** ... Nederlands Tijdschrift voor Natuurkunde. Series A [*A publication*]
**Ned Tijdschr Psychol** ... Nederlands Tijdschrift voor de Psychologie en Haar Grensgebieden [*A publication*]
**Ned Tijdschr Tandheelkd** ... Nederlands Tijdschrift voor Tandheelkunde [*A publication*]
**Ned Tijdschr Vacuumtech** ... Nederlands Tijdschrift voor Vacuumtechniek [*A publication*]
**Ned Tijdschr Verloskd Gynaecol** ... Nederlandsch Tijdschrift voor Verloskunde en Gynaecologie [*A publication*]
**NEDTRA**... Naval Education and Training Command (MCD)
**Ned Ts Geneesk** ... Nederlandsch Tijdschrift voor Geneeskunde [*A publication*]
**Ned Ts Verlosk** ... Nederlandsch Tijdschrift voor Verloskunde en Gynaecologie [*A publication*]
**NedTT**....... Nederlands Theologisch Tijdschrift [*Wageningen*] [*A publication*]
**NedTTs**...... Nederlands Theologisch Tijdschrift [*Wageningen*] [*A publication*]
**Ned Ver Klin Chem Tijdschr** ... Nederlandse Vereniging voor Klinische Chemie. Tijdschrift [*A publication*]
**NEE**.......... National Electrical Effect
**NEE**.......... National Electrology Educators (EA)
**NEE**.......... New England Economic Review. Federal Reserve Bank of Boston [*A publication*]
**NEE**.......... Noise-Equivalent Energy (MCD)
**NEE**.......... Norethindrone/Ethinyl Estradiol [*Oral contraceptive*]
**NEEB**........ North Eastern Electricity Board [*British*]
**NEEC**........ National Export Expansion Council [*Terminated, 1973*] [*Department of Commerce*]
**NEEC**........ NEECO, Inc. [*Canton, MA*] [*NASDAQ symbol*] (NQ)
**NEEC**........ Nuclear Explosion Effects Center
**NEED**........ National Environmental Education Development [*Program of National Park Service*] [*Defunct*]
**NEED**........ Native Employment and Educational Development [*Canada*]
**NEED**........ Near East Emergency Donations
**Need**.......... Needham's Annual Summary of Tax Cases [*England*] [*A publication*] (DLA)
**NEED**........ Negro Education Emergency Drive
**NEED**........ New Employment Expansion and Development [*Canada*]
**Needlework Bul** ... Needlework Bulletin for Teachers in Secondary Schools [*A publication*] (APTA)
**NEEDS**...... NASA End-to-End Data Systems
**NEEDS**...... Neighborhood Environmental Evaluation and Decision System [*Health Services and Mental Health Administration*]
**NEEDS**...... New England Educational Data Systems
**NEEDS-IR** ... NIKKEI Economic Electronic Databank Service - Information Retrieval [*Japan*] [*Information service or system*] (IID)
**NEEDS-TS** ... NIKKEI Economic Electronic Databank Service - Time Sharing [*Japan*] [*Information service or system*] (IID)
**NeEinP**...... Philips Research Laboratories, Eindhoven, Netherlands [*Library symbol*] [*Library of Congress*] (LCLS)
**NeEinT**...... Technische Hogeschool te Eindhoven, Eindhoven, Netherlands, [*Library symbol*] [*Library of Congress*] (LCLS)
**NEEL**......... National Environmental Education Landmarks [*Department of the Interior*]
**NEELS**...... National Emergency Equipment Locator System [*Environment Canada*] [*Information service or system*] (CRD)
**NEEMIS**.... New England Energy Management Information System
**Ne Engl J Med** ... New England Journal of Medicine [*A publication*]
**NEEP**......... Negative End Expiratory Pressure [*Medicine*]
**NEEP**......... Nuclear Electronics Effects Program
**NE'ER**....... Never (ROG)
**NEERI**....... National Environmental Engineering Research Institute
**NEERS**...... National Earthquake Early Reporting System (NOAA)
**NEES**......... Naval Engineering Experiment Station
**NEES**......... New England Electric System
**NEESA**...... Naval Energy and Environmental Support Activity
**NEESAB** ... National Energy Extension Service Advisory Board [*Department of Energy*] [*Washington, DC*] (EGAO)
**NEETS**...... Naval Electronics Environmental Training System (MCD)
**NEEWSSOP** ... NATO Europe Early Warning System Standard Operating Procedures (NATG)
**NEF**........... National Educators Fellowship [*Later, CEAI*]
**NEF**........... National Energy Foundation (EA)
**NEF**........... National Extra Fine [*Thread*]
**NEF**........... Naval Emergency Fund [*A budget category*]
**NEF**........... Near East Foundation (EA)
**Nef**............ Nef: Cahier Trimestriel [*A publication*]
**NEF**........... Negative-Regulatory Factor [*Genetics*]
**NeF**........... Nephritic Factor [*Clinical medicine*]
**NEF**........... New Education Fellowship [*Later, WEF*]
**NEF**........... Noise-Equivalent Flux
**NEF**........... Noise Exposure Forecast [*Aircraft*]
**NEF**........... Nordiska Ekonomiska Forskningsradet [*Nordic Economic Research Council - NERC*] (EAIO)
**NEF**........... Northeast Folklore [*A publication*]
**NEF**........... Notas y Estudios de Filosofia [*A publication*]
**NEF**........... Nurses Educational Funds (EA)
**NEF**........... Scudder New Europe Fund [*NYSE symbol*] (SPSG)
**NEFA**........ Narcotic Educational Foundation of America (EA)
**NEFA**........ Nonesterified Fatty Acid [*Biochemistry*]
**NEFARS**... Nuclear Effects from Analysis of Residual Signatures
**NEFC**......... Near East Forestry Commission
**NEFC**......... Northeast Fisheries Center [*Department of Commerce*] [*Woods Hole, MA*]
**NEFCO**..... New England Fish Company
**NEFD**........ Noise-Equivalent Flux Density
**NEFDA**..... New England Fisheries Development Association (EA)
**NEFDF**...... New England Fisheries Development Foundation [*Later, NEFDA*] (EA)
**NEFE**......... New England Fish Exchange (EA)
**NEFES**...... Northeastern Forest Experiment Station [*Department of Agriculture*] [*Broomall, PA*] (GRD)
**NEFI**.......... New England Fuel Institute
**NEFMC**..... New England Fisheries Management Council
**NEFNB**...... Neftepererabotka i Neftekhimiya [*A publication*]
**NEFO**........ National Electronics Facilities Organization
**NEFOS**...... New Emerging Forces
**NEFP**......... New England Free Press [*Publisher*]
**NEFPS**...... National Enginemen and Firemen's Protection Society [*A union*] [*British*]
**NEFSA**...... National Education Field Service Association [*Defunct*] (EA)
**Neftegazovaya Geol Geofiz** ... Neftegazovaya Geologiya i Geofizika [*A publication*]
**Neftegazov Geol Geofiz** ... Neftegazovaya Geologiya i Geofizika [*A publication*]
**Neftepererab Neftekhim (Kiev)** ... Neftepererabotka i Neftekhimiya (Kiev) [*A publication*]
**Neftepererab Neftekhim (Moscow)** ... Neftepererabotka i Neftekhimiya (Moscow) [*A publication*]
**Neftepromysl Delo** ... Neftepromyslovoe Delo [*A publication*]
**Neftepromysl Delo (Moscow)** ... Neftepromyslovoe Delo (Moscow) [*A publication*]
**Neftepromysl Delo Ref Nauchno-Tekh Sb** ... Neftepromyslovoye Delo Referativnyy Nauchno-Tekhnicheskiy Sbornik [*A publication*]
**Neft Gazova Promst Sredn Azii** ... Neftyanaya i Gazovaya Promyshlennost Srednei Azii [*A publication*]
**Neft Gazov Prom-St'** ... Neftyanaya i Gazovaya Promyshlennost' [*A publication*]
**Neft Gazov Promst Sredn Azii** ... Neftyanaya i Gazovaya Promyshlcnnost Srednei Azii [*A publication*]
**Neft Khim**.. Neft i Khimiya [*A publication*]
**Neft Khoz**... Neftyanoe Khozyaistvo [*A publication*]
**Neft Slants Khoz** ... Neftyanoe i Slantsevoe Khozyaistvo [*A publication*]
**Neft Vuglishtna Geol** ... Neftena i Vuglishtna Geologiya [*Bulgaria*] [*A publication*]
**NEFZB**...... Neirofiziologila [*A publication*]

**NEG**.......... National Environmental Group [*AMEX symbol*] (SPSG)
**NEG**.......... Nederlandse Gemeente [*A publication*]
**Neg**.......... Nega'im (BJA)
**NEG**.......... Negate a Binary Number [*Data processing*]
**NEG**.......... Negative (AAG)
**NEG**.......... Neglect [*FBI standardized term*]
**NEG**.......... Negligible (AAG)
**NEG**.......... Negotiable (ADA)
**NEG**.......... Negril [*Jamaica*] [*Airport symbol*] (OAG)
**NEG**.......... Negro
**NEGA**........ National Ex-Offender Grant Alliance (EA)
**Negb**.......... Negotiable
**Neg C**......... Negligence Cases [*Commerce Clearing House*] [*A publication*] (DLA)
**Neg Cas**...... Bloomfield's Manumission (or Negro) Cases [*New Jersey*] [*A publication*] (DLA)
**NEGD**........ Negotiated (ROG)
**NEGDEF**... Navy Enlisted Ground Defense Emergency Force
**Neg Ed Rev** ... Negro Educational Review [*A publication*]
**Neg His Bull** ... Negro History Bulletin [*A publication*]
**Neg Inst**..... Negotiable Instrument [*Legal term*] (DLA)
**Negl**.......... Negligence
**Negl Cas**.... Negligence Cases [*Commerce Clearing House*] [*A publication*] (DLA)
**Negl Cas 2d** ... Negligence Cases, Second Series [*Commerce Clearing House*] [*A publication*] (DLA)
**Negl & Comp Cas Ann** ... Negligence and Compensation Cases, Annotated [*A publication*] (DLA)
**Negl & Comp Cas Ann 3d** ... Negligence and Compensation Cases, Annotated, Third Series [*A publication*] (DLA)
**Negl & Comp Cas Ann (NS)** ... Negligence and Compensation Cases, Annotated, New Series [*A publication*] (DLA)
**NEGN**........ Negotiation (ROG)
**NEGOA**..... Northeast Gulf of Alaska [*Marine science*] (MSC)
**NEGPR**...... Negative Print
**NEGRO**..... National Economic Growth and Reconstruction Organization [*Black entrepreneurial organization*]
**NEGRO**..... New England Grass Roots Organization
**Negro Cas**.. Bloomfield's Manumission (or Negro) Cases [*New Jersey*] [*A publication*] (DLA)
**Negro D**..... Negro Digest [*A publication*]
**Negro Ed R** ... Negro Educational Review [*A publication*]
**Negro Educ R** ... Negro Educational Review [*A publication*]
**Negro H B** ... Negro History Bulletin [*A publication*]
**Negro His B** ... Negro History Bulletin [*A publication*]
**Negro Hist B** ... Negro History Bulletin [*A publication*]
**Negro Hist Bul** ... Negro History Bulletin [*A publication*]
**Negro Hist Bull** ... Negro History Bulletin [*A publication*]
**NEGRS**...... Negative Report Submitted [*Army*] (AABC)
**NEGRSBM** ... Negative Report Submitted [*Army*] (AABC)
**negt**........... Negociant [*Merchant, Trader*] [*Business term*] [*French*]
**Negusan**..... [*Antonius*] Negusantius de Fano [*Flourished, 16th century*] [*Authority cited in pre-1607 legal work*] (DSA)
**NEGX**........ Negate a Binary Number with Extend [*Data processing*]
**NEH**.......... East Carolina University, Health Sciences Library, Greenville, NC [*OCLC symbol*] (OCLC)
**NEh**........... East Hampton Free Library, East Hampton, NY [*Library symbol*] [*Library of Congress*] (LCLS)
**NEH**.......... I am connecting you to a station which will accept traffic for the station you request [*Telecommunications*] (FAAC)
**NEH**.......... National Endowment for the Humanities
**Neh**........... Nehemiah [*Old Testament book*]
**NEH**.......... Nuclear Effects Handbook
**NEHA**........ National Environmental Health Association (EA)
**NEHA**........ National Executive Housekeepers Association (EA)
**NeHB**......... Bureau voor de Industriele Eigendom, Bibliotheek Octrooiraad, The Hague, Netherlands [*Library symbol*] [*Library of Congress*] (LCLS)
**NEHC**........ National Extension Homemakers Council (EA)
**NEHEP**..... National Eye Health Education Program [*Information service or system*] (EISS)
**Nehezip Muesz Egy Koezl** ... Nehezipari Mueszaki Egyetem Koezlemenyei [*A publication*]
**Nehezip Musz Egy Miskolc Idegennyelvu Kozl** ... Nehezipari Mueszaki Egyetem, Miskolc, Idegennyelvu Koezlemenyei [*A publication*]
**Nehezip Musz Egy Miskolc Kozl** ... Nehezipari Mueszaki Egyetem, Miskolc, Koezlemenyei [*A publication*]
**Nehezvegyip Kut Intez Kozl** ... Nehezvegyipari Kutato Intezet Kozlemenyei [*A publication*]
**NEHF**........ National Eye and Health Foundation (EA)
**NEHGR**..... New England Historical and Genealogical Register [*A publication*]
**NEHGS**..... New England Historic Genealogical Society (EA)
**NeHKB**...... Koninklijke Bibliotheek [*Royal Library*], The Hague, Netherlands [*Library symbol*] [*Library of Congress*] (LCLS)
**Nehorlavost Polym Mater** ... Nehorlavost Polymernych Materialov [*A publication*]
**NEHRP**..... National Earthquake Hazards Reduction Program [*Federal Emergency Management Agency*] [*Washington, DC*] (EGAO)
**NeHSU**...... Staatsuitgeverij Christoffel Plantijnstaat (State Printing Office), The Hague, Netherlands [*Library symbol*] [*Library of Congress*] (LCLS)
**NEi**........... East Islip Public Library, East Islip, NY [*Library symbol*] [*Library of Congress*] (LCLS)
**NEI**........... Narcotics Education, Incorporated (EA)
**NEI**........... National Enterprises, Incorporated [*NYSE symbol*] (SPSG)
**NEI**........... National Eye Institute [*Formerly, NINDB*] [*Department of Health and Human Services*] [*National Institutes of Health*] [*Bethesda, MD*]
**NEI**........... Neipperg [*Federal Republic of Germany*] [*Seismograph station code, US Geological Survey*] (SEIS)
**NEI**........... Netherlands East Indies
**NEI**........... New Enterprise Institute [*University of Southern Maine*] [*Research center*] (RCD)
**NEI**........... New Equipment Introduction [*Army*] (AABC)
**NEI**........... Noise-Equivalent Input
**NEI**........... Noise-Equivalent Intensity
**NEI**........... Non Est Inventus [*It Has Not Been Found or Discovered*] [*Latin*]
**NEI**........... Nordic Energy Index [*Database*] [*Nordic Atomic Libraries Joint Secretariat*] [*Denmark*] [*Information service or system*] (IID)
**NEI**........... Northern Electric Industries [*British*]
**NEI**........... Northern Engineering Industries [*Commercial firm*] [*British*]
**NEI**........... Not Elsewhere Indicated
**NEI**........... Nouvelles Equipes Internationales [*Later, European Christian Democratic Union*]
**NEI**........... Nuclear Engineering International [*A publication*]
**NEIAL**....... North East Iowa Academic Libraries [*Library network*]
**NEIB**......... National Export Import Bank [*Egypt*] (IMH)
**NEIC**......... National Earthquake Information Center [*US Geological Survey*]
**NEIC**......... National Electronic Information Corporation [*Information service or system*] (IID)
**NEIC**......... National Employers Industrial Council [*Australia*]
**NEIC**......... National Energy Information Center [*Department of Energy*] [*Washington, DC*]
**NEIC**......... New England Information Center [*Information service or system*]
**NEIC**......... News from Iceland [*A publication*]
**NEIC**......... North East Insurance Company [*NASDAQ symbol*] (NQ)
**NEICA**....... National Energy Information Center Affiliate [*University of New Mexico*] (IID)
**NEICE**....... North of England Institute for Christian Education
**NEIDA**...... Network of Educational Innovation for Development in Africa (EAIO)
**NEIED**....... National Educational Institute for Economic Development (EA)
**NEIF**......... Near-Earth Instrumentation Facility [*NASA*] (KSC)
**NEII**.......... National Elevator Industry, Incorporated (EA)
**NEIL**......... Neon Indicating Light
**NEIL**......... Nordic Energy Index, Literature [*Database*] [*Nordic Atomic Libraries Joint Secretariat*] [*Information service or system*] (CRD)
**NEILA8**..... Contributions d'Istanbul a la Science Clinique [*A publication*]
**NEIN**......... News Inuit. News Releases from Inuit Tapirisat of Canada [*A publication*]
**NEINEI**..... NESDIS [*National Environmental Satellite Data and Information Service*] Environmental Inventory [*A publication*]
**NEIPG**....... National Electronic Industries Procurement Group
**NEIR**......... Narrative End Item Report [*NASA*] (KSC)
**NEIR**......... Neither (ROG)
**NEI Rev**.... NEI [*Northern Engineering Industries*] Review [*England*] [*A publication*]
**NEIRLS**..... Northeast Regional Library System [*Library network*]
**Neirokhim Fiziol Sinapticheskikh Protsessov** ... Neirokhimiya i Fiziologiya Sinapticheskikh Protsessov [*A publication*]
**NEIS**......... National Earthquake Information Service [*United States Geological Survey*] (IID)
**NEIS**......... National Emissions Inventory System [*Database*] [*Environment Canada*] [*Information service or system*] (CRD)
**NEIS**......... National Engineering Information System (BUR)
**NEIS**......... National Environmental Information Symposium
**NEIS**......... New Enterprise Incentive Scheme [*Australia*]
**NEISA**....... New England Intercollegiate Sailing Association
**NEISS**....... National Electronic Injury Surveillance System [*Consumer Product Safety Commission*] [*Washington, DC*] [*Databank*]
**NEIT**......... New Equipment Introductory Team [*Army*] (AABC)
**NEIULS**.... Northeast Iowa Union List of Serials
**NEIX**......... Nordic Energy Index [*Database*] [*Nordic Atomic Libraries Joint Secretariat*] [*Information service or system*] (CRD)
**NEJ**.......... Northeast Journal of Business and Economics [*A publication*]
**NEJ**.......... Seattle, WA [*Location identifier*] [*FAA*] (FAAL)
**NEJA**........ National Entertainment Journalists Association (EA)

**NEJ Crim and Civ Con** ... New England Journal on Criminal and Civil Confinement [*A publication*]
**NEJM**........ New England Journal of Medicine [*A publication*]
**NEJMA**..... New England Journal of Medicine [*A publication*]
**NEJMAG** ... New England Journal of Medicine [*A publication*]
**NEJPA**...... Neues Jahrbuch fuer Geologie und Palaeontologie. Abhandlungen [*A publication*]
**NEJS**......... Near Eastern and Judaistic Studies (BJA)
**NEJWMC** ... North Eastern Jewish War Memorial Centre [*Australia*]
**NEK**........... Naval Equerry to the King
**Nek Aktual Vopr Biol Med** ... Nekotorye Aktual'nye Voprosy Biologii i Meditsiny [*A publication*]
**NEKASA**... New England Knitwear and Sportswear Association (EA)
**NEKDA**..... New England Kiln Drying Association (EA)
**Nek Filos Probl Gos Prava** ... Nekotorye Filosofskie Problemy Gosudarstva i Prava [*A publication*]
**NEKL**........ Northeast Kansas Library System [*Library network*]
**NEKOA**..... New England Knitted Outerwear Association [*Later, NEKASA*] (EA)
**Nekot Probl Biokibern Primen Elektron Biol Med** ... Nekotorye Problemy Biokibernetiki Primenenie Elektroniki v Biologii i Meditsine [*Ukrainian SSR*] [*A publication*]
**Nek Vopr Eksp Fiz** ... Nekotorye Voposry Eksperimental'noi Fiziki [*USSR*] [*A publication*]
**Nek Vopr Inzh Fiz** ... Nekotorye Voprosy Inzhenernoi Fiziki [*A publication*]
**Nek Vopr Stroit Skvazhin Oslozhnennykh Usloviyakh Uzb** ... Nekotorye Voprosy Stroitel'stva Skvazhin v Oslozhnennykh Usloviyakh Uzbekistana [*A publication*]
**NEL**........... East Carolina University, Department of Library Science, Greenville, NC [*OCLC symbol*] (OCLC)
**Nel**............ [*H.*] Finch's Chancery Reports [*1673-81*] [*England*] [*A publication*] (DLA)
**NEl**............ Greenburgh Public Library, Elmsford, NY [*Library symbol*] [*Library of Congress*] (LCLS)
**NEL**........... Lakehurst, NJ [*Location identifier*] [*FAA*] (FAAL)
**NEL**........... National Emancipation League [*Nigeria*]
**NEL**........... National Engineering Laboratory [*Superseded IAT*] [*Gaithersburg, MD*] [*National Institute of Standards and Technology*]
**NEL**........... National Epilepsy League [*Later, EFA*] (EA)
**NEL**........... Naval Command Control Communications Laboratory Center
**NEL**........... Naval Electronics Laboratory
**NEL**........... Naval Explosive Laboratory
**NEL**........... Nelson [*Nevada*] [*Seismograph station code, US Geological Survey*] (SEIS)
**NEL**........... Nelson Aviation, Inc. [*Alcoa, TN*] [*FAA designator*] (FAAC)
**Nel**............ Nelson's English Chancery Reports [*A publication*] (DLA)
**NEL**........... New English Library [*Publishers*] [*British*]
**NEL**........... NewTel Enterprises Ltd. [*Toronto Stock Exchange symbol*]
**NEL**........... No Effect Level (ADA)
**NEL**........... Nonspecific Excitability Level [*Animal behavior*]
**NEL**........... Nuclear Energy Laboratory [*Research center*] (RCD)
**NEL**........... Nuclear Engineering Laboratory [*University of Utah*] [*Research center*] (RCD)
**NELA**........ National Electric Light Association
**NELA**........ New England Library Association
**NELA**........ Northeastern Loggers Association (EA)
**NELA Bul** ... National Electric Light Association. Bulletin [*A publication*]
**NELA Newsl** ... NELA [*New England Library Association*] Newsletter [*A publication*]
**NELAT**...... Navy Electronics Laboratory Assembly Tester
**NELB**........ New England Library Board [*Library network*]
**NELC**........ Naval Electronics Laboratory Center [*Later, NOSC*]
**NELCON NZ** ... National Electronics Conference, New Zealand [*IEEE*]
**Nel CR**...... Nelson's English Chancery Reports [*A publication*] (DLA)
**NEld**.......... Sunshine Hall Free Library, Eldred, NY [*Library symbol*] [*Library of Congress*] (LCLS)
**NELEC**...... Nonelectric
**N Elec Telesis** ... Northern Electric Telesis [*A publication*]
**NELED**...... Neuroscience Letters [*A publication*]
**NELEX**...... Naval Electronics Systems Command Headquarters
**NELIA**....... Nuclear Energy Liability Insurance Association [*Later, ANI*] (EA)
**NELIAC**.... Naval Electronics Laboratory International ALGOL Compilers
**NELINET** ... New England Library Information Network
**NELIS**....... Noncommunications Emitter Location and Identification System (MCD)
**NELIS-A**... Noncommunications Emitter Location and Identification System - Airborne
**NELL**......... Nellcor, Inc. [*NASDAQ symbol*] (NQ)
**Nell**.......... Nell's Reports [*1845-55*] [*Ceylon*] [*A publication*] (DLA)
**NELLCO**... New England Law Library Consortium, Inc. [*Harvard Law School*] [*Information service or system*] (IID)
**NElle**......... Ellenville Public Library, Ellenville, NY [*Library symbol*] [*Library of Congress*] (LCLS)
**NELM**....... [*US*] Naval Forces, Eastern Atlantic and Mediterranean
**NElm**......... Steele Memorial Library of Elmira and Chemung County, Elmira, NY [*Library symbol*] [*Library of Congress*] (LCLS)
**NELMA**.... Northeastern Lumber Manufacturers Association (EA)
**NElmC**....... Elmira College, Elmira, NY [*Library symbol*] [*Library of Congress*] (LCLS)
**NElmhC**..... City Hospital at Elmhurst, Elmhurst, NY [*Library symbol*] [*Library of Congress*] (LCLS)
**NElmHi**..... Chemung County Historical Society, Elmira, NY [*Library symbol*] [*Library of Congress*] (LCLS)
**NElmM**...... Mount Saviour Monastery, Elmira, NY [*Library symbol*] [*Library of Congress*] (LCLS)
**NElmo**........ Elmont Public Library, Elmont, NY [*Library symbol*] [*Library of Congress*] (LCLS)
**NElmoCE**.. Covert Elementary School, Elmont, NY [*Library symbol*] [*Library of Congress*] (LCLS)
**NElmoSE**... Stewart Elementary School, Elmont, NY [*Library symbol*] [*Library of Congress*] (LCLS)
**NElmP**....... Elmira Psychiatric Center, Elmira, NY [*Library symbol*] [*Library of Congress*] (LCLS)
**NELOS**...... Navy Electronics Laboratory Operating System
**NELP**......... National Employment Law Project [*New York, NY*] (EA)
**NELP**......... North East London Polytechnic [*School*] [*England*]
**NELPAC**... National Engineering Laboratory's Thermophysical Properties Package [*British*] [*Information service or system*] (IID)
**NELPIA**.... Nuclear Energy Liability Property Insurance Association [*Later, ANI*]
**NELR**........ Nelson Research & Development Co. [*NASDAQ symbol*] (NQ)
**NeLR**......... Rijksuniversiteit Leiden, Leiden, Netherlands [*Library symbol*] [*Library of Congress*] (LCLS)
**NELRC**...... National Epilepsy Library and Resource Center [*Epilepsy Foundation of America*] [*Information service or system*] (IID)
**NEL Reports** ... National Engineering Laboratory. Reports [*A publication*]
**Nels**........... [*H.*] Finch's Chancery Reports [*1673-81*] [*England*] [*A publication*] (DLA)
**NELS**......... National Environmental Laboratories [*Proposed*]
**Nels**........... Nelson's English Chancery Reports [*A publication*] (DLA)
**NELSA**...... Northeast Library Service Area [*Library network*]
**Nels Abr**..... Nelson's Abridgment of the Common Law [*A publication*] (DLA)
**Nels Cler**.... Nelson's Rights of the Clergy [*A publication*] (DLA)
**Nels F**......... Finch's English Chancery Reports, by Nelson [*1673-81*] [*A publication*] (DLA)
**Nels Fol**..... Finch's English Chancery Reports, by Nelson [*1673-81*] [*A publication*] (DLA)
**Nels Fol Rep** ... [*H.*] Finch's Chancery Reports, by Nelson [*21 English Reprint*] [*A publication*] (DLA)
**Nels Lex Man** ... Nelson's Lex Maneriorum [*A publication*] (DLA)
**Nelson (Eng)** ... [*H.*] Finch's Chancery Reports, by Nelson [*21 English Reprint*] [*A publication*] (DLA)
**Nelson (Eng)** ... Nelson's English Chancery Reports [*A publication*] (DLA)
**Nelson Loose-Leaf Med** ... Nelson Loose-Leaf Medicine [*A publication*]
**Nelson's Rep** ... Nelson Tempore Finch [*1673-81*] [*A publication*] (DLA)
**Nels 8vo**..... Nelson's English Chancery Reports [*A publication*] (DLA)
**NeLV**......... Koninklijk Instituut voor Taal-, Land-, en Volkenkunde, Leiden, Netherlands [*Library symbol*] [*Library of Congress*] (LCLS)
**NELWA**.... New England Lumber Women's Association (EA)
**NELY**........ Northeasterly [*Meteorology*] (FAAC)
**NEm**.......... East Meadow Public Library, East Meadow, NY [*Library symbol*] [*Library of Congress*] (LCLS)
**NEM**.......... Metropolitan Technical Community College, Omaha, NE [*OCLC symbol*] (OCLC)
**NEM**.......... N-Ethylmaleimide [*Also, NEMI*] [*Organic chemistry*]
**NEM**.......... N-Ethylmorpholine [*Organic chemistry*]
**NEM**.......... Nahrung Einheit, Milch [*Nourishment Unit, Milk*] [*German*]
**NEM**.......... National Employers Mutual Insurance [*Australia*]
**Nem**........... Neman [*Moscow*] [*A publication*]
**Nem**........... Nemean [*of Pindar*] [*Classical studies*] (OCD)
**NEM**.......... Nemuro [*Japan*] [*Seismograph station code, US Geological Survey*] (SEIS)
**NEM**.......... New England Magazine [*A publication*]
**NeM**.......... New England Micrographics, Inc., Waltham, MA [*Library symbol*] [*Library of Congress*] (LCLS)
**NEM**.......... New Mexico Musician [*A publication*]
**NEM**.......... Newmont Mining Corp. [*NYSE symbol*] (SPSG)
**NEM**.......... Nonelectronic Maintenance
**NEM**.......... Noram Environment [*Vancouver Stock Exchange symbol*]
**NEM**.......... Not Elsewhere Mentioned
**NEMA**....... National Eclectic Medical Association [*Defunct*] (EA)
**NEMA**....... National Educational Management Association (EA)
**NEMA**....... National Electrical Manufacturers Association (EA)
**NEMA**....... National Emergency Management Association (EA)
**NEMA**....... National Emergency Medicine Association (EA)
**NEMA**....... Nematode [*Threadworm*]
**NEMAC**.... National Energy Management Advisory Committee [*British*]
**NEMAC**.... Normal Error Model Analysis Chart
**NEMAG**.... Negative Effective Mass Amplifiers and Generators
**NEMAS**..... New England Marine Advisory Service
**NEMAS**..... Nursing Education Module Authoring System
**Nematol**..... Nematologica [*A publication*]
**NEMATOL** ... Nematology
**Nematol Mediterr** ... Nematologia Mediterranea [*A publication*]

**NEmBGE** .. Bowling Green Elementary School, East Meadow, NY [*Library symbol*] [*Library of Congress*] (LCLS)
**NEmBWE** ... Barnum Woods Elementary School, East Meadow, NY [*Library symbol*] [*Library of Congress*] (LCLS)
**NEMC** ....... New England Medical Center [*Boston, MA*]
**NEMCA** .... NATO Electromagnetic Compatibility Agency (NATG)
**NEMCC** .... Nonessential Motor Control Center (AAG)
**NEMCH**.... New England Medical Center Hospitals
**NEmCJS** ... W. T. Clarke Junior-Senior High School, East Meadow, NY [*Library symbol*] [*Library of Congress*] (LCLS)
**NEM CON** ... Nemine Contradicente [*No One Contradicting*] [*Latin*] [*Legal term*]
**NEMD**....... Nonspecific Esophageal Motor Dysfunction [*Medicine*]
**NEMDA**.... Northeastern Minnesota Development Association
**NEM DISS** ... Nemine Dissentiente [*No One Dissenting*] [*Latin*]
**NEMEA** .... New England Media Evaluators Association
**NEMEDRI** ... North European and Mediterranean Routing Information [*Naval Oceanographic Office*]
**NEMEX** .... National Energy Management Exhibition and Conference (ITD)
**NEMG "T"RL** ... New England MG "T" Register Limited (EA)
**NEmH** ....... Meadowbrook Hospital, East Meadow, NY [*Library symbol*] [*Library of Congress*] (LCLS)
**NEMI** ........ N-Ethylmaleimide [*Also, NEM*] [*Organic chemistry*]
**NEMI** ........ National Elevator Manufacturing Industry [*Later, NEII*] (EA)
**NEMIC**...... New England Materials-Instruction Center
**NEMISYS** ... New Mexico Information System [*Library network*]
**NEmMC** .... Nassau County Medical Center, East Meadow, NY [*Library symbol*] [*Library of Congress*] (LCLS)
**NEmMcE** .. McVey Elementary School, East Meadow, NY [*Library symbol*] [*Library of Congress*] (LCLS)
**NEmME** .... Meadowbrook Elementary School, East Meadow, NY [*Library symbol*] [*Library of Congress*] (LCLS)
**NEmNHi** ... Nassau County Historical Museum, East Meadow, NY [*Library symbol*] [*Library of Congress*] (LCLS)
**NEMO**....... Naval Experimental Manned Observatory
**NEMO**....... Never Ever Mention Outside [*Secret computer toy project of Axlon, Inc.*]
**NEMO**....... Nonempirical Molecular Orbitals [*Atomic physics*]
**NEMO**....... Nuclear Exchange Model
**NEMP**....... National Energy Management Program [*Australia*]
**NEMP**....... Nuclear Electromagnetic Propagation
**NEMP**....... Nuclear Electromagnetic Pulse (AABC)
**NEmPE**...... Parkway Elementary School, East Meadow, NY [*Library symbol*] [*Library of Congress*] (LCLS)
**NEMPS**..... National Environmental Monitoring and Prediction System (MCD)
**NEMQO**.... Non Est Mortale Quod Opto [*It Is No Mortal Thing I Desire*] [*Latin*] [*Motto of Friedrich III, Duke of Schleswig-Holstein-Gottorp (1597-1659)*]
**NEMR**....... National E [*Electronic*]-Mail Registry [*Information service or system*] (TSSD)
**NEMRA** .... National Electrical Manufacturers Representatives Association (EA)
**NEMRB** .... New England Motor Rate Bureau
**NEMRIP**... New England Marine Resources Information Program [*University of Rhode Island*] [*Later, NEMAS*]
**NEMS** ....... National Exchange Market System
**NEMS** ....... Near-Earth Magnetospheric Satellite
**NEMS** ....... Nimbus E Microwave Spectrometer [*Meteorology*]
**NEMSB**..... Newsletter. Environmental Mutagen Society [*A publication*]
**NEMSPA**.. National EMS [*Emergency Medical Service*] Pilots Association (EA)
**NEMVAC** ... Noncombatant Emergency and Evacuation Plan (NVT)
**Nemzetkozi Mezogazd Sz** ... Nemzetkozi Mezogazdasagi Szemle [*A publication*]
**NEN**........... New Eyes for the Needy (EA)
**NEN**........... Northstar Energy Corp. [*Toronto Stock Exchange symbol*]
**NEN**........... Whitehouse, FL [*Location identifier*] [*FAA*] (FAAL)
**NENA**........ New Nation. Manitoba Native Newspaper [*A publication*]
**NENAD3**... Neue Entomologische Nachrichten [*A publication*]
**NENB** ........ Nevada National Bancorporation [*NASDAQ symbol*] (NQ)
**NENBD**..... New England Business [*A publication*]
**NENCL** ..... Nonenclosure
**NENEP** ..... Navy Enlisted Nursing Education Program
**NENG**........ New England
**N Eng**......... New Englander [*A publication*]
**N Eng Hist Geneal Reg** ... New England Historical and Genealogical Register [*A publication*]
**N Eng J Med** ... New England Journal of Medicine [*A publication*]
**N Eng J Prison L** ... New England Journal on Prison Law [*A publication*] (DLA)
**N England J Med** ... New England Journal of Medicine [*A publication*]
**N Engl Bus** ... New England Business [*A publication*]
**N Engl Dairyman** ... New England Dairyman [*A publication*]
**N Engl Econ Rev** ... New England Economic Review [*A publication*]
**N Engl Eng** ... New England Engineer [*A publication*]
**N Engl Fruit Meet Proc Annu Meet Mass Fruit Grow Assoc** ... New England Fruit Meetings. Proceedings. Annual Meeting. Massachusetts Fruit Growers' Association [*A publication*]
**N Engl Galaxy** ... New England Galaxy [*A publication*]
**N Engl J Med** ... New England Journal of Medicine [*A publication*]
**N Engl J Med Med Prog Ser** ... New England Journal of Medicine. Medical Progress Series [*A publication*]
**N Engl L Rev** ... New England Law Review [*A publication*]
**N Eng LR**... New England Law Review [*A publication*]
**N Eng L Rev** ... New England Law Review [*A publication*]
**N Eng Mag** ... New England Magazine [*A publication*]
**N Eng Q**..... New England Quarterly. An Historical Review of the New England Life and Letters [*A publication*]
**N Eng Rep** ... New England Reporter [*A publication*] (DLA)
**N Eng Rev** ... New England Review [*A publication*]
**N Eng Soc Stud Bull** ... New England Social Studies Bulletin [*A publication*]
**NEnI**.......... International Business Machines Corp., Systems Development Library, Endicott, NY [*Library symbol*] [*Library of Congress*] (LCLS)
**NENJA**...... NERC [*National Electronics Research Council*] News Journal [*A publication*]
**NENKA**..... Nenryo Kyokai-Shi [*A publication*]
**N ENMLD** ... Not Enameled [*Freight*]
**NENO** ....... News of Norway [*A publication*]
**NENOA8**... Japanese Journal of Tropical Agriculture [*A publication*]
**NENT**........ National Entertainment Corp. [*Las Vegas, NV*] [*NASDAQ symbol*] (NQ)
**NENV**........ Nautilus Environmedic [*NASDAQ symbol*] (NQ)
**NEO**........... National Electrolysis Organization [*Later, SCME*] (EA)
**NEO**........... National Energy Office [*Executive Office of the President*]
**NEO**........... Near-Earth Orbit
**NEO**........... Neoarsphenamine [*or Neosalvarsan*] [*Medicine*]
**NEO**........... Neocomian [*Paleontology*]
**NEO**........... Neomycin [*Antibiotic compound*]
**NEO**........... Neonatal [*Medicine*]
**Neo**............. Neophilologus [*A publication*]
**NEO**........... Noncombatant Evacuation Order [*Army*] (AABC)
**NEO**........... Northeast Oklahoma R. R. [*AAR code*]
**NEO**........... Northeastern Operations Office [*NASA*]
**NEO**........... Pensacola, FL [*Location identifier*] [*FAA*] (FAAL)
**NEOB**........ Neo-Bionics, Inc. [*NASDAQ symbol*] (NQ)
**NEOB**........ New Executive Office Building [*Washington, DC*]
**NEOC**........ National Earth Observations Center [*National Oceanic and Atmospheric Administration*]
**NEOCOMP** ... New Computational Formulas
**NEOCON** ... National Exposition of Contract Interior Furnishings
**NEOCON** ... Neoconservative
**NEOCON** ... Neomycin, Colistin, Nystatin [*Antineoplastic drug regimen*]
**NEOCS**...... Navy Enlisted Occupational Classification System (NVT)
**NEODF** ..... Naval Explosive Ordnance Disposal Facility
**NEO-DHC** ... Neohesperidin Dihydrochalcone [*Also, NHDC*] [*Sweetening agent*]
**NEOF** ........ No Evidence of Failure (MCD)
**NEOF** ........ Nordic Engineer Officers' Federation (EA)
**NEOG**........ Neogen Corp. [*NASDAQ symbol*] (NQ)
**NEOL**........ Neolens, Inc. [*Miami, FL*] [*NASDAQ symbol*] (NQ)
**NEOL**........ Neologism
**NEOLA4**.... Neoplasma [*Bratislava*] [*A publication*]
**NEOMAL** ... Northeastern Ohio Major Academic Libraries [*The College of Wooster*] [*Wooster, OH*] [*Library network*] [*Later, NEOMARL*]
**NEOMARL** ... Northeast Ohio Major Academic and Research Libraries [*Library network*] [*Information service or system*] (IID)
**NEONA**..... Nenryo Oyobi Nensho [*A publication*]
**Neonatal Netw** ... Neonatal Network [*A publication*]
**Neonat Network** ... Neonatal Network. Journal of Neonatal Nursing [*A publication*]
**NEOP**........ New England Order of Protection [*Later, Woodmen of the World Life Insurance Society*] (EA)
**Neoph** ........ Neophilologus [*A publication*]
**Neophil** ...... Neophilologus [*A publication*]
**Neophilolog** ... Neophilologus [*A publication*]
**NEO-PI** ..... NEO [*Neuroticism, Extraversion, Openness to Experience*] Personality Inventory [*Personality development test*] [*Psychology*]
**Neorg Lyuminofory Prikl Naznacheniya** ... Neorganicheskie Lyuminofory Prikladnogo Naznacheniya [*A publication*]
**Neorg Mater** ... Neorganicheskie Materialy [*USSR*] [*A publication*]
**Neosan Avic** ... Neosan Avicola [*A publication*]
**NEOU**........ Navigators' and Engineering Officers' Union [*British*]
**NEOVA**..... Air-Cushion Vehicle built by Neoteric Engineering Affiliates [*Australia*] [*Usually used in combination with numerals*]
**N/EP**.......... Name on End-Paper [*Antiquarian book trade*]
**NEP** ........... National Education Program (EA)
**NEP** ........... National Emphasis Program [*Occupational Safety and Health Administration*]
**NEP** ........... National Energy Program [*or Plan*] [*Canada*]
**NEP** ........... Natural Effects Processor
**NEP** ........... Near-Earth Phase [*NASA*]
**NEP** ........... Nearest Equivalent Product
**NEP** ........... Negative Equally Probable
**NEP** ........... Negative Expiratory Pressure [*Medicine*]
**NEP** ........... Nemzeti Egyseg Partja [*Party of National Unity*] [*Hungary*] [*Political party*] (PPE)
**nep**............. Nepali [*MARC language code*] [*Library of Congress*] (LCCP)

**NEP** .......... Nepean Public Library [*UTLAS symbol*]
**NEP** .......... Nephrology [*Medical specialty*] (DHSM)
**Nep**............ Nepos [*First century BC*] [*Classical studies*] (OCD)
**NEP** .......... Neptune (ROG)
**N-Ep** .......... Neutralizing Epitope [*Immunogenetics*]
**NEP** .......... New Economic Policy [*Program of USSR, 1921-28; also US wage/price freeze and controls of Nixon Administration, 1971*]
**NEP** .......... New Edition Pending [*Publishing*]
**NEP** .......... New England Plant (NRCH)
**NEP** .......... New Equipment Practice
**NEP** .......... Noise-Equivalent Power
**NEP** .......... Non-English-Proficient
**NEP** .......... Nonelectronic Part
**NEP** .......... Nonelutable Polar Compounds [*Analytical chemistry*]
**NEP** .......... Normal Entry Point (MCD)
**NEP** .......... Nu Pacific Resources Ltd. [*Vancouver Stock Exchange symbol*]
**NEP** .......... Nuclear Electric Propulsion [*System*]
**NEPA** ........ National Enginemen's Protection Association [*A union*] [*British*]
**NEPA** ........ National Euchre Players Association (EA)
**NEPA** ........ Northeast Pacific Area
**NEPA** ........ Nuclear Energy for Propulsion of Aircraft
**NEPAB**...... Neuropaediatrie [*A publication*]
**Nepalese J Agric** ... Nepalese Journal of Agriculture [*A publication*]
**Nepal Gaz** .. Nepal Gazette [*A publication*]
**Nepali Math Sci Rep** ... Nepali Mathematical Sciences Report [*A publication*]
**NEPB**......... National Energy Protection Board
**NEPBC**...... Northeastern Pennsylvania Bibliographic Center [*King's College*] [*Wilkes-Barre, PA*] [*Library network*]
**NEPC**......... New England Power Company
**NEPC**......... Nigerian Export Promotion Council (GEA)
**NEPCC**...... North East Pacific Culture Collection [*of marine organisms*] [*University of British Columbia*]
**NEPCO** ..... New England Provision Company
**NEPCON** .. National Electronic Packaging and Production Conference
**NEPD** ........ Noise-Equivalent Power Density
**NEPDB**...... Navy Environmental Protection Data Base [*Obsolete*]
**NEPE**......... National Emergency Planning Establishment [*Canada*]
**NEPE**......... Nez Perce National Historical Park
**NEPEA**...... Nepegeszseguegy [*A publication*]
**NEPEA**...... New England Project on Education of the Aging [*Defunct*] (EA)
**NEPEC**...... National Earthquake Prediction Evaluation Council [*US Geological Survey*]
**NEPEEQ**... Neuroendocrine Perspectives [*Elsevier Book Series*] [*A publication*]
**Nepeg**......... Nepegeszseguegy [*A publication*]
**NEPEX**...... New England Power Exchange
**NEPHAT** .. Northeastern Pacific Hurricane Analog Tracker
**N Ephem Sem Epigr** ... Neue Ephemeris fuer Semitische Epigraphik [*A publication*]
**NEPHGE** .. Nonequilibrium pH Gradient Gel Electrophoresis
**NEPHIS**.... Nested Phrase Indexing System [*Automated indexing system*] [*University of Western Ontario*]
**Nephrol Nurse** ... Nephrology Nurse [*A publication*]
**Nephro Nurse** ... Nephrology Nurse [*A publication*]
**N Eph Sem Ep** ... Neue Ephemeris fuer Semitische Epigraphik [*A publication*]
**NEPIA**....... Nuclear Energy Property Insurance Association [*Later, ANI*] (EA)
**NEPL**......... National Endowment for the Preservation of Liberty [*Foundation created by Carl Channell to collect funds for Nicaraguan CONTRAs*]
**NEPMA** .... National Engine Parts Manufacturers Association (EA)
**NEPMU** .... Navy Environmental and Preventive Medicine Unit (NVT)
**NEPN** ........ Near-Earth Phase Network [*NASA*] (KSC)
**NEPO** ........ NATO Equipment Policy Objective (NATG)
**NEPOOL** .. New England Power Pool
**NEPP**......... National Energy Policy Plan
**NEPPCO**... Northeastern Poultry Producers Council [*Later, PEIA*] (EA)
**NEPR** ........ NATO Electronic Parts Recommendations (AABC)
**NEPR** ........ Nuclear Explosion Pulse Reaction (AAG)
**NEPRAC**... National Electron Probe Resource for Analysis of Cells [*Harvard University*] [*Research center*] (RCD)
**Nepr Ertes** ... Neprajzi Ertesito [*A publication*]
**NEPRF**...... Naval Environmental Prediction Research Facility
**NEPRILS**.. New Professionals in Information and Library Studies [*Western Australian Institute of Technology*]
**Nepr Koezl** ... Neprajzi Koezlemenyek [*A publication*]
**NEPRS**...... New Equipment Personnel Requirements Summary [*Army*]
**NEPS**......... National Economic Projections Series [*NPA Data Services, Inc.*] [*Information service or system*] (CRD)
**NEPS**......... National Estuarine Pollution Study [*Federal Water Quality Administration*] (MSC)
**NEPSS** ...... Navy Environmental Protection Support Service
**NEPSWL** .. New England Plant, Soil, and Water Laboratory [*Department of Agriculture*] [*Research center*] (RCD)
**NEPT**......... No Evidence of Pulmonary Tuberculosis [*Medicine*]
**NEPTUNE** ... North-Eastern Electronic Peak Tracing Unit and Numerical Evaluator (IEEE)
**NEPU**........ Northern Elements Progression Union [*Political party*] [*Nigeria*]
**NEQ**.......... Nederlands Economisch Persbureau en Adviesbureau [*NEPAB*]. Nieuwsbrief [*A publication*]
**NEQ**.......... New England Quarterly [*A publication*]
**NE Quar** .... New England Quarterly [*A publication*]
**NEr** ........... East Rockaway Public Library, East Rockaway, NY [*Library symbol*] [*Library of Congress*] (LCLS)
**NER** .......... National Educational Radio
**NER** .......... National and English Review [*A publication*]
**NER** .......... National Institute Economic Review [*A publication*]
**NER** .......... Near East Report [*A publication*] (BJA)
**NER** .......... NERCO, Inc. [*NYSE symbol*] (SPSG)
**Ner** ............ Neriglissar (BJA)
**Ner** ............ Nero [*of Suetonius*] [*Classical studies*] (OCD)
**NER** .......... Nervine [*Medicine*] (ROG)
**NER** .......... Network for Economic Rights [*Defunct*] (EA)
**NER** .......... Neutral External Rotation [*Sports medicine*]
**NER** .......... Never-Exceed Redline [*Aerospace*] (AAG)
**NER** .......... New England Reporter [*A publication*] (DLA)
**NER** .......... New England Review [*A publication*]
**NER** .......... New England Review and Bread Loaf Quarterly [*A publication*]
**NER** .......... Niger [*ANSI three-letter standard code*] (CNC)
**NER** .......... Noise-Equivalent Radiance
**NER** .......... Nonconformance Event Record [*NASA*] (KSC)
**NER** .......... Nonionizing Electromagnetic Radiation
**NER** .......... North Eastern Railway [*British*]
**NER** .......... North Eastern Reporter [*Commonly cited NE*] [*A publication*] (DLA)
**NER** .......... Northeastern Regional Library, Cimarron, NM [*OCLC symbol*] (OCLC)
**NERA** ........ National Economic Research Associates
**NERA** ........ National Emergency Relief Administration
**NERA** ........ Naval Enlisted Reserve Association (EA)
**Nera** .......... Nera & Musica [*Record label*] [*Norway*]
**Nera** .......... [*Lucius*] Neratius Priscus [*Flourished, 1st century*] [*Authority cited in pre-1607 legal work*] (DSA)
**NERAC** ..... New England Research Application Center [*University of Connecticut*]
**NERADN**.. Neuroscience Research [*A publication*]
**NERAIC**.... North European Region Air Information Center (NATG)
**NERBC**...... New England River Basin Commission
**NERBS**...... National Electric Rate Book by States [*A publication*]
**NERC**........ National Electronics Research Council
**NERC** ........ National Environment Resource Council [*British*] (NRCH)
**NERC** ........ National Environmental Research Center [*Environmental Protection Agency*] [*Later, CERL*]
**NERC** ........ National Equal Rights Council (EA)
**NERC** ........ Natural Environment Research Council [*Research center*] [*British*] (IRC)
**NERC** ........ New England Regional Commission [*Department of Commerce*] [*Terminated, 1981*]
**NERC** ........ Newton-Evans Research Company, Inc. [*Ellicott City, MD*] [*Information service or system*] (TSSD)
**NERC** ........ Nordic Economic Research Council (EA)
**NERC** ........ North American Electric Reliability Council (EA)
**NERC** ........ Nuclear Energy Research Center [*Also, CEEN, SCK*] [*Belgium*]
**NERC** ........ Regional Conference for the Near East [*UN Food and Agriculture Organization*]
**NErCE**....... Centre Elementary School, East Rockaway, NY [*Library symbol*] [*Library of Congress*] (LCLS)
**NERCIC** .... Northeast Regional Coastal Information Center [*Marine science*] (MSC)
**NERC News J** ... NERC [*National Electronics Research Council*] News Journal [*England*] [*A publication*]
**NERCOE**... New England Resource Center for Occupational Education
**N Ercolani** ... Nuovo Ercolani [*A publication*]
**NERCOM** ... New England Regional Commission [*Department of Commerce*] [*Terminated, 1981*] (EGAO)
**NERCOMM** ... New England Regional Commission [*Department of Commerce*] [*Terminated, 1981*] (NOAA)
**NERComP** ... New England Regional Computing Program, Inc. [*Boston, MA*]
**NERCP**...... Naval European Research Contract Program (NG)
**NERDA** ..... New England Rural Development Association
**NERDAS**... NASA Earth Resources Data Annotation System (MCD)
**NERDC** ..... Northeast Regional Data Center [*University of Florida*] [*Research center*] (RCD)
**NERD & D** ... National Energy Research, Development, and Demonstration Program [*Australia*]
**N E Reg**...... New England Historical and Genealogical Register [*A publication*]
**NEREM** .... Northeast Electronics Research and Engineering Meeting
**NEREM Rec** ... NEREM [*Northeast Electronics Research and Engineering Meeting*] Record [*A publication*]
**NE Rep** ...... New England Reporter [*A publication*] (DLA)
**NE Rep** ...... North Eastern Reporter [*Commonly cited NE*] [*A publication*] (DLA)
**NE Reporter** ... North Eastern Reporter [*Commonly cited NE*] [*A publication*] (DLA)
**NE Repr**..... North Eastern Reporter [*Commonly cited NE*] [*A publication*] (DLA)

**NERF**......... National Eye Research Foundation [*Later, NEHF*] (EA)
**NERHL**..... Northeastern Radiological Health Laboratory [*Massachusetts*]
**NERIC Bull** ... NERIC [*Nuclear Engineering Research in Cambridge*] Bulletin [*A publication*]
**NERIS**....... National Educational Resources Information Service [*British*]
**NERL**........ National Ecological Research Laboratory [*Environmental Protection Agency*]
**NERMLS**.. New England Regional Medical Library Service (EA)
**NERN**........ Northeastern (FAAC)
**NERO**........ National Energy Resources Organization (EA)
**NERO**........ Near-Earth Rescue and Operations [*NASA*]
**NERO**........ Nuclear Effects Rocket Operations
**NERO**........ Sodium [*Na*] Experimental Reactor of Zero Power [*British*] (DEN)
**NEROC**..... Northeast Radio Observatory Corporation
**NERP**........ National Environmental Research Park [*Marine science*] (MSC)
**NERPG**...... Northern European Regional Planning Group [*NATO*] (NATG)
**NERPRC**... New England Regional Primate Research Center [*Harvard University*] [*Research center*] (RCD)
**NERRA**..... New Equipment Resources Requirements Analysis [*Army*] (AABC)
**NErRE**....... Rhame Elementary School, East Rockaway, NY [*Library symbol*] [*Library of Congress*] (LCLS)
**NERSA**...... Northeast Rail Service Act [*1981*] [*Also, NRSA*]
**NERSE**...... Nutrition, Exercise, Relaxation, Sleep, and Enjoyment
**NERSICA** ... National Established Repair, Service, and Improvement Contractors Association [*Later, National Remodelers Association*]
**NERSP**...... Navy Environmental Remote Sensing Program
**NERU**........ Nursing Education Research Unit
**Nerudn Stroit Mater** ... Nerudnye Stroitel'nye Materialy [*A publication*]
**NERV**........ Nervous [*Medicine*]
**NERV**........ Nuclear Emulsion Recovery Vehicle (MUGU)
**NERV**........ Nuclear Energy Research Vehicle
**NERVA**..... Nervenarzt [*A publication*]
**NERVA**..... Nuclear Engine for Rocket Vehicle Application [*NASA*]
**Nerv Child** ... Nervous Child [*A publication*]
**Nervn Sist** ... Nervnaya Sistema [*A publication*]
**Nerv Sist**.... Nervnaia Sistema [*A publication*]
**Nerv Sist Leningr Gos Univ Fiziol Inst** ... Nervnaya Sistema Leningradskij Gosudarstvennyj Universitet Imeni A. A. Zhdanova Fiziologicheskij Institut [*A publication*]
**Nerv Syst Electr Curr** ... Nervous System and Electric Currents [*A publication*]
**NERX**........ NeoRx Corp. [*NASDAQ symbol*] (NQ)
**NES**........... N-Ethylsuccinimide [*Organic chemistry*]
**NES**........... National Eczema Society [*British*]
**NES**........... National Energy Software [*Department of Energy*] [*Information service or system*] (CRD)
**NES**........... National Energy Strategy [*Department of Energy*] (ECON)
**NES**........... National Estimating Society [*Later, SCEA*] (EA)
**NES**........... National Eutrophication Survey [*Environmental Protection Agency*]
**NES**........... Naval Examination Service [*British military*] (DMA)
**NES**........... Naval Experimenting Station
**NES**........... Near Eastern Society (EA)
**NES**........... Near Eastern Studies [*A publication*] (BJA)
**NES**........... Nesmont Industry [*Vancouver Stock Exchange symbol*]
**NES**........... Neurobehavioral Evaluation System
**NES**........... New Earnings Survey [*British*]
**NES**........... New England Electric System [*NYSE symbol*] (SPSG)
**NES**........... News Election Service [*Vote-counting consortium of the major TV networks and two wire services*]
**NES**........... Nintendo Entertainment System [*Video game*]
**NES**........... Noise-Equivalent Signal (IEEE)
**NES**........... Non-English-Speaking (ADA)
**NES**........... Nonerasable Storage [*Data processing*]
**NES**........... Nordic Ergonomic Society (EAIO)
**NES**........... Nordiska Ergonomisallskapet [*Nordic Ergonomic Society*] (EAIO)
**NES**........... Not Elsewhere Specified
**N60ES**........ North of 60. Environmental Studies [*Canada*] [*A publication*]
**NESA**......... John H. Nelson Environmental Study Area [*University of Kansas*] [*Research center*] (RCD)
**NESA**......... National Eagle Scout Association (EA)
**NESA**......... National Electric Sign Association (EA)
**NESA**......... National Emission Standards Act [*1967*]
**NESA**......... National Employment Service Act [*1933*]
**NESA**......... National Energy Specialist Association (EA)
**NESA**......... National Environmental Specialist Association (EA)
**NESA**......... National Environmental Study Areas Program [*National Park Service*] [*Defunct*]
**NESA**......... Near East and South Asia [*Department of State*]
**NE/SA**........ Near East/South Asia Council of Overseas Schools (EA)
**NESA**......... New England School of Art
**NESAC**...... National Environmental Services Administration Committee [*Marine science*] (MSC)
**NESADS**... Notas e Estudos. Secretaria de Estado das Pescas. Serie Recursos e Ambiente Aquatico [*A publication*]
**NESB**......... National Environmental Specimen Bank [*Energy Research and Development Administration*]
**NESB**......... NESB Corp. [*NASDAQ symbol*] (NQ)
**NESB**......... Non-English-Speaking Background (ADA)
**NESB**......... Number of Equally Strong Beams [*Military*] (CAAL)
**NESBA**...... National Earth Shelter Builders Association (EA)
**NESC**......... National Electrical Safety Code
**NESC**......... National Energy Software Center [*Department of Energy*] [*Information service or system*] (IID)
**NESC**......... National Environmental Satellite Center [*Formerly, National Weather Satellite Center*] [*Later, National Environmental Satellite Service*]
**NESC**......... National Executive Service Corps [*New York, NY*] (EA)
**NESC**......... Naval Electronics Systems Command
**NESC**......... Nuclear Engineering and Scientific Congress (MCD)
**NESCA**...... National Environmental Systems Contractors Association [*Later, ACCA*] (EA)
**NESCAC**... New England Small College Athletic Conference
**Ne Sci**........ New Scientist [*A publication*]
**NESCNSC** ... Net Evaluation Subcommittee, National Security Council (AABC)
**NESCO**...... National Energy Supply Corporation [*Proposed*]
**NESCO**...... National Engineering Science Company
**NESCO**...... Naval Environmental Support Office [*Marine science*] (MSC)
**NESCO**...... Nigerian Electricity Supply Corporation African Workers' Union
**NESCTM**.. National Environmental Satellite Center Technical Memoranda (NOAA)
**NESCWS**.. Nonessential Services Chilled Water System [*Nuclear energy*] (NRCH)
**NESDA**...... National Electronic Service Dealers Association [*Later, NESSDA*] (EA)
**NESDA**...... National Equipment Servicing Dealers Association (EA)
**NESDB**...... National Economic and Social Development Board [*Thailand*] (DS)
**NESDEC**... New England School Development Council (EA)
**NESDIS**.... National Environmental Satellite, Data, and Information Service [*Washington, DC*] [*National Oceanic and Atmospheric Administration*] (GRD)
**NESDIS (Natl Environ Satell Data Inf Serv) Environ Inventory** ... NESDIS (National Environmental Satellite Data and Information Service) Environmental Inventory [*A publication*]
**NESE**......... Neue Ephemeris fuer Semitische Epigraphik [*Wiesbaden*] [*A publication*] (BJA)
**NESEA**...... Naval Electronic Systems Engineering Activity
**NESEC**...... Naval Electronics Systems Engineering Center (MCD)
**NESEP**...... Navy Enlisted Scientific Education Program
**NESF**......... Normal Engineered Safety Features [*Nuclear energy*] (NRCH)
**NESHAP**... National Emission Standards for Hazardous Air Pollutants [*Environmental Protection Agency*]
**NESI**......... Nesika [*A publication*]
**NESIP**....... Naval Explosive Safety Improvement Program
**NESL**......... Northeast Shipbuilders Ltd. [*Commercial firm*] [*British*]
**NESLA**...... New England Shoe and Leather Association (EA)
**NEsM**........ Mount Saint Alphonsus Seminary, Esopus, NY [*Library symbol*] [*Library of Congress*] (LCLS)
**NESMRA** ... New England Super-Modified Racing Association
**NESN**........ NATO English-Speaking Nations
**NESN**........ New England Sports Network [*Cable-television system*]
**NESO**........ Naval Electronic Sensor Operator [*Canadian Navy*]
**NESO**........ Naval Engineering Service Office (MCD)
**NESO**........ Navy Environmental Support Office [*Obsolete*]
**NESOSC**... New England Society of Open Salts Collectors (EA)
**NESP**......... National Environmental Studies Project (EA)
**NESP**......... Nurse Education Support Program
**NESP Rep** ... NESP [*National Environmental Studies Project*] Report [*United States*] [*A publication*]
**NESR**......... Natural Environment Support Room (MCD)
**NESR**......... Noise-Equivalent Spectral Radiance [*Physics*]
**NESRA**...... National Employee Services and Recreation Association (EA)
**NESS**......... National Easter Seal Society (EA)
**NESS**......... National Emergency Steel Specification [*World War II*]
**NESS**......... National Environmental Satellite Service [*National Oceanic and Atmospheric Administration*] [*Telecommunications*] (TEL)
**NESS**......... Northeast Satellite Systems [*Avoca, PA*] [*Telecommunications*] (TSSD)
**NESS**......... Nuclear Effects Simulation Study
**NESSDA**... National Electronic Sales and Service Dealers Association (EA)
**NEssDS**..... Dunlap Society, Essex, NY [*Library symbol*] [*Library of Congress*] (LCLS)
**NESSEC**.... Naval Electronics Systems Security Engineering Center (MCD)
**NEST**......... National Emergency Survivable Troop System (AABC)
**NEST**......... Naval Experimental Satellite Terminal (IEEE)
**NEST**......... Nestor, Inc. [*NASDAQ symbol*] (NQ)
**NEST**......... New El Salvador Today (EA)
**NEST**......... New and Emerging Sciences and Technologies
**NEST**......... New Expanding Shelter Technology [*Residential construction*]
**NEST**......... Nonelectric Stimulus Transfer
**NEST**......... Nuclear Effects Support Team
**NEST**......... Nuclear Emergency Search Team [*Department of Energy*]

**NEST**......... Nuclear Explosive Simulation Technique
**NESTA**...... National Earth Science Teachers Association (EA)
**Nest Chr** .... Nestor-Chronik [*A publication*]
**NESTED**... Naval Electronic Systems Test and Evaluation Detachment
**NESTEF**.... Naval Electronic Systems Test and Evaluation Facility
**Nestle Nutr Workshop Ser** ... Nestle Nutrition Workshop Series [*A publication*]
**NESTOR**... Neutron Source Thermal Reactor [*British*] (DEN)
**NESTS** ...... Nonelectric Stimulus Transfer System
**NET** .......... Centre for Agricultural Publications and Documents, Wageningen, Netherlands [*OCLC symbol*] (OCLC)
**NET** .......... Nasoendotracheal Tube [*Medicine*]
**NET** .......... National Educational Television [*Later, EBC*]
**NET** .......... Negative Entropy Trap
**NET** .......... Net Energy Thrust
**NET** .......... Net Equivalent Temperature
**NET** .......... Net Explosive Weight (MSA)
**NET** .......... NETI Technologies, Inc. [*Vancouver Stock Exchange symbol*]
**NET** .......... Netto [*Lowest*]
**NET** .......... Network [*Telecommunications*] (AAG)
**NET** .......... Neuroelectric Therapy [*Substance detoxification*]
**NET** .......... New Equipment Training [*Army*] (AABC)
**NET** .......... New Era Technologies, Inc. [*Washington, DC*] [*Telecommunications*] (TSSD)
**NET** .......... Newton Emission Theory [*Physics*]
**NET** .......... Next European Torus [*Nuclear energy*]
**NET** .......... Nimbus Experiment Team [*NASA*]
**NET** .......... Nitrigin Eireann Teoranta [*Nationalized industry*] [*Ireland*] (EY)
**NET** .......... No Evidence of Tumor [*Medicine*]
**NET** .......... Noise-Equivalent Temperature
**NET** .......... Nonradiative Energy Transfer [*Physics*]
**NET** .......... Norethisterone [*Oral contraceptive ingredient*]
**NET** .......... North European Oil Royalty Trust [*NYSE symbol*] (SPSG)
**NET** .......... Not Earlier Than
**NET** .......... Nuclear Effects Test
**NET** .......... Nuclear Emergency Teams [*DASA*]
**NET** .......... Nuclear Energy Team
**NET** .......... Nuclear Engineer Trainee
**NET** .......... Number of Element Types
**NETA** ........ International Electrical Testing Association (EA)
**NETA** ........ National Employment and Training Association [*Upland, CA*] (EA)
**NETA** ........ National Environmental Training Association (EA)
**NETA** ........ Northeast Test Area [*Military*] (MCD)
**NETAC**...... Nuclear Energy Trade Associations' Conference
**NETAPPS** ... Net Ad-Produced Purchases [*Advertising*]
**NETBIOS** ... Network Basic Input/Output System [*Computer software*]
**NETC** ........ National Emergency Training Center
**NETC** ........ National Emergency Transportation Center
**NETC** ........ Naval Education and Training Center [*or Command*] (NVT)
**NETC** ........ New England Theatre Conference (EA)
**NETC** ........ New England Trail Conference (EA)
**NETC** ........ No Explosion of the Total Contents [*Business term*] (DCTA)
**NETC** ........ Northeast Transportation Coalition
**NETCHE** .. Nebraska Educational Television Council for Higher Education, Inc. [*Library network*]
**NETCO** ..... North Western Employes Transportation Corporation [*Successor to Chicago & North Western Railway*]
**NETCOM** ... Network Control Communications [*Deep Space Instrumentation Facility, NASA*]
**NETDC** ..... New England Trophoblastic Disease Center
**NETDS**...... Near-Earth Tracking and Data System
**NETF**........ Nuclear Energy Test Facility (AFM)
**NETF**........ Nuclear Engineering Test Facility (AAG)
**NETG** ........ Network General Corp. [*NASDAQ symbol*] (CTT)
**NETH**........ National Employ the Handicapped Week
**NETH**........ Netherlands
**NETHA**..... Nederlandsch Tijdschrift voor Hygiene, Microbiologie, en Serologie [*A publication*]
**Neth Ant**.... Netherlands Antilles
**Neth Energy Res Found ECN Rep** ... Netherlands Energy Research Foundation. ECN [*Energieonderzoek Centrum Nederland*] Report [*A publication*]
**Netherl Intl L Rev** ... Netherlands Yearbook of International Law [*The Hague, Netherlands*] [*A publication*] (DLA)
**Neth Fertil Tech Bull** ... Netherlands Fertilizer Technical Bulletin [*A publication*]
**Neth Geol Dienst Toelichting Geol Kaart Ned 1:50,000** ... Netherlands. Geologische Dienst. Toelichting bij de Geologische Kaart van Nederland 1:50,000 [*A publication*]
**Neth Geol Sticht Meded Nieuwe Ser** ... Netherlands. Geologische Stichting. Mededelingen. Nieuwe Serie [*A publication*]
**Neth Inst Sea Res Publ Ser** ... Netherlands. Institute for Sea Research. Publication Series [*A publication*]
**Neth Int'l L Rev** ... Netherlands International Law Review [*A publication*] (DLA)
**Neth J Agric Sci** ... Netherlands Journal of Agricultural Science [*A publication*]
**Neth J Agr Sci** ... Netherlands Journal of Agricultural Science [*A publication*]
**Neth J Med** ... Netherlands Journal of Medicine [*A publication*]
**Neth J Plant Pathol** ... Netherlands Journal of Plant Pathology [*A publication*]
**Neth J Sea** ... Netherlands Journal of Sea Research [*A publication*]
**Neth J Sea Res** ... Netherlands Journal of Sea Research [*A publication*]
**Neth J Surg** ... Netherlands Journal of Surgery [*A publication*]
**Neth J Vet Sci** ... Netherlands Journal of Veterinary Science [*A publication*]
**Neth J Zool** ... Netherlands Journal of Zoology [*A publication*]
**Neth Milk D** ... Netherlands Milk and Dairy Journal [*A publication*]
**Neth Milk Dairy J** ... Netherlands Milk and Dairy Journal [*A publication*]
**Neth Nitrogen Tech Bull** ... Netherlands Nitrogen Technical Bulletin [*A publication*]
**Neth P**........ Netherlands Pharmacopoeia [*A publication*]
**Neth Rijks Geol Dienst Jaarversl** ... Netherlands. Rijks Geologische Dienst. Jaarverslag [*A publication*]
**Neth Rijks Geol Dienst Meded Nieuwe Ser** ... Netherlands. Rijks Geologische Dienst. Mededelingen. Nieuwe Serie [*A publication*]
**Neth Stat**.... Statistical Yearbook of the Netherlands [*A publication*]
**Neth Sticht Bodemkartering Bodemkund Stud** ... Netherlands. Stichting voor Bodemkartering. Bodemkundige Studies [*A publication*]
**NETHW**.... National Employ the Handicapped Week (OICC)
**Neth YB Int'l Law** ... Netherlands Yearbook of International Law [*A publication*] (DLA)
**NETI**.......... NETI Technologies, Inc. [*Ann Arbor, MI*] [*NASDAQ symbol*] (NQ)
**NETI**.......... Network Technologies International, Inc. [*Ann Arbor, MI*] [*Telecommunications*] (TSSD)
**NETJA** ...... Nederlands Tijdschrift voor Geneeskunde [*A publication*]
**NETL**......... National Export Traffic League [*New York, NY*] (EA)
**NETL**......... Nuclear Engineering Teaching Laboratory [*University of Texas at Austin*] [*Research center*] (RCD)
**NETLS** ...... Northeast Texas Library System [*Library network*]
**NETLS/DPL** ... Northeast Texas Library System/Dallas Public Library Film Service [*Library network*]
**NET LTD** .. Nigerian External Telecommunications Limited [*Lagos*] (TSSD)
**NETMA** .... Nobody Ever Tells Me Anything [*Executive complaint*]
**NETMIS** ... Naval Education and Training Management Information System (MCD)
**NETOPS** ... Nuclear Emergency Team Operations (AFM)
**NETP**......... New Equipment Training Program [*Army*] (AABC)
**NETR** ........ NATO Electronic Technical Recommendation (NATG)
**NETR** ........ No Essential Traffic Reported [*Aviation*]
**NETR** ........ Nuclear Engineering Test Reactor [*Air Force*]
**NETRA**...... New England Trail Rider Association (EA)
**NETRB**..... New England Territory Railroad Bureau
**NETRC**...... National Educational Television and Radio Center [*Later, EBC*] (EA)
**NETR-FTC** ... New England Territory Railroads Freight Traffic Committee
**NE TR S NUM** ... Ne Tradas sine Nummo [*Cash on Delivery*] [*Latin*]
**NETS**......... National Electronics Teachers' Service [*Defunct*]
**NETS**......... Nationwide Emergency Telecommunications System [*DoD*]
**NETS**......... Navy Engineering Technical Services (NG)
**NETS**......... Nebraska Electronic Transfer System
**NETS**......... Network for Electronic Transfers System
**NETS**......... Network Techniques
**NETS**......... Network Testing Section [*Social Security Administration*]
**NETS**......... New Examiner Training School [*Federal Home Loan Bank Board*]
**NETSET** ... Network Synthesis and Evaluation Technique [*Data processing*]
**NETSO**...... Northern European Transhipment Organization [*NATO*] (NATG)
**NETSS** ...... National Exhibitions Touring Support Scheme [*Australia*]
**Ne T T**........ Nederlands Theologisch Tijdschrift [*A publication*]
**NETT** ........ Net Tons [*Shipping*]
**NETT** ........ Network Environmental Technology Transfer [*An association*] [*Europe*]
**NETT** ........ New Employment, Transition, and Training [*Department of Labor*] (OICC)
**NETT** ........ New Equipment Training Team [*Army*]
**NETTEL** ... Network Telecommunications, Inc. [*Denver, CO*] [*Telecommunications*] (TSSD)
**NETTSP**.... New Equipment Training Test Support Package (MCD)
**NETV** ........ Nebraska ETV [*Educational Television*] Network [*Lincoln, NE*] [*Telecommunications*] (TSSD)
**NETW** ....... Network Control Corp. [*Danbury, CT*] [*NASDAQ symbol*] (NQ)
**NEU**........... Neuchatel [*Switzerland*] [*Geomagnetic observatory code*]
**NEU**........... Neuchatel [*Switzerland*] [*Seismograph station code, US Geological Survey*] [*Closed*] (SEIS)
**Neu**............ Neuraminic Acid [*Biochemistry*]
**NEUC**........ National Engine Use Council [*Defunct*] (EA)
**NEUDA**..... Neue Deliwa-Zeitschrift [*A publication*]
**Neue Arzneim Spez** ... Neue Arzneimittel und Spezialitaeten [*A publication*]
**Neue Arzneim Spez Geheimm** ... Neue Arzneimittel. Spezialitaeten und Geheimmittel [*A publication*]
**Neue Aspekte Trasylol-Ther** ... Neue Aspekte der Trasylol-Therapie [*A publication*]
**Neue Beitr Gesch Deutsch Altert** ... Neue Beitraege zur Geschichte des Deutschen Altertums [*A publication*]

**Neue Bergbautech** ... Neue Bergbautechnik [*Wissenschaftliche Zeitschrift fuer Bergbau, Geowissenschaften und Aufbereitung*] [*A publication*]
**Neue Deliwa-Z** ... Neue Deliwa-Zeitschrift [*A publication*]
**Neue Denkschr Naturhist Mus Wien** ... Neue Denkschriften des Naturhistorischen Museums in Wien [*A publication*]
**Neue Dtsch Pap Ztg** ... Neue Deutsche Papier-Zeitung [*A publication*]
**Neue Entwicklungspol** ... Neue Entwicklungspolitik [*A publication*]
**Neue Ges**.... Neue Gesellschaft [*A publication*]
**Neue Gesellsch** ... Neue Gesellschaft [*A publication*]
**Neue Jurist Wochenschr** ... Neue Juristische Wochenschrift [*A publication*]
**Neue Med W** ... Neue Medizinische Welt [*A publication*]
**Neue Mitt Landwirtsch** ... Neue Mitteilungen fuer die Landwirtschaft [*A publication*]
**Neue Muench Beitr Gesch Med Medizinhist** ... Neue Muenchner Beitraege zur Geschichte der Medizin und Naturwissenschaften. Medizinhistorische Reihe [*A publication*]
**Neue Muench Beitr Gesch Med Naturwiss Medizinhist Reihe** ... Neue Muenchner Beitraege zur Geschichte der Medizin und Naturwissenschaften. Medizinhistorische Reihe [*A publication*]
**Neue Mz** .... Neue Musikzeitung [*A publication*]
**Neue Oesterr Z Kinderheilkd** ... Neue Oesterreichische Zeitschrift fuer Kinderheilkunde [*A publication*]
**Neue Oest Z Kinderheilk** ... Neue Oesterreichische Zeitschrift fuer Kinderheilkunde [*A publication*]
**Neue Ordnung** ... Neue Ordnung in Kirche, Staat, Gesellschaft, Kultur [*A publication*]
**Neue Phys** ... Neue Physik [*A publication*]
**Neue Pol Lit** ... Neue Politische Literatur [*A publication*]
**Neue Rund** ... Neue Rundschau [*A publication*]
**Neue Rundsch** ... Neue Rundschau [*A publication*]
**Neues Arch Niedersachs** ... Neues Archiv fuer Niedersachsen [*A publication*]
**Neues Jahrb Geologie u Palaeontologie Monatsh** ... Neues Jahrbuch fuer Geologie und Palaeontologie. Monatshefte [*A publication*]
**Neues Jahrb Geol Palaeontol Abh** ... Neues Jahrbuch fuer Geologie und Palaeontologie. Abhandlungen [*A publication*]
**Neues Jahrb Geol Palaeontol Abh B** ... Neues Jahrbuch fuer Geologie und Palaeontologie. Abhandlungen B [*A publication*]
**Neues Jahrb Geol Palaeontol Monatsh** ... Neues Jahrbuch fuer Geologie und Palaeontologie. Monatshefte [*A publication*]
**Neues Jahrb Mineral Abh** ... Neues Jahrbuch fuer Mineralogie. Abhandlungen [*A publication*]
**Neues Jahrb Mineral Geol Palaeontol Abh Abt A** ... Neues Jahrbuch fuer Mineralogie, Geologie, und Palaeontologie. Abhandlungen. Abteilung A. Mineralogie, Petrographie [*A publication*]
**Neues Jahrb Mineral Geol Palaeontol Abh Abt B** ... Neues Jahrbuch fuer Mineralogie, Geologie, und Palaeontologie. Abhandlungen. Abteilung B. Geologie, Palaeontologie [*A publication*]
**Neues Jahrb Mineral Geol Palaeontol Monatsh Abt 1** ... Neues Jahrbuch fuer Mineralogie, Geologie, und Palaeontologie. Monatshefte. Abteilung 1. Mineralogie, Gesteinskunde [*A publication*]
**Neues Jahrb Mineral Geol Palaeontol Monatsh Abt 2** ... Neues Jahrbuch fuer Mineralogie, Geologie, und Palaeontologie. Monatshefte. Abteilung 2. Geologie, Palaeontologie [*A publication*]
**Neues Jahrb Mineral Geol Palaeontol Ref** ... Neues Jahrbuch fuer Mineralogie, Geologie, und Palaeontologie. Referate [*A publication*]
**Neues Jahrb Mineral Monatsh** ... Neues Jahrbuch fuer Mineralogie. Monatshefte [*A publication*]
**Neues Jahrb Mineralogie Abh** ... Neues Jahrbuch fuer Mineralogie. Abhandlungen [*A publication*]
**Neues Jahrb Mineralogie Monatsh** ... Neues Jahrbuch fuer Mineralogie. Monatshefte [*A publication*]
**Neues Jahrbuch Geologie u Palaeontologie Abh Monatsh** ... Neues Jahrbuch fuer Geologie und Palaeontologie. Abhandlungen. Monatshefte [*A publication*]
**Neues Jahrbuch Geol Palaeontol Abhandl** ... Neues Jahrbuch fuer Geologie und Palaeontologie. Abhandlungen [*A publication*]
**Neues Jahrbuch Geol Palaeontol Monatsh** ... Neues Jahrbuch fuer Geologie und Palaeontologie. Monatshefte [*A publication*]
**Neues Jahrbuch Mineralogie Abh Monatsh** ... Neues Jahrbuch fuer Mineralogie. Abhandlungen. Monatshefte [*A publication*]
**Neues Jb Miner Geol Palaeont Mh** ... Neues Jahrbuch fuer Mineralogie, Geologie, und Palaeontologie. Monatshefte [*A publication*]
**Neues J Pharm** ... Neues Journal der Pharmacie [*A publication*]
**Neues J Phys** ... Neues Journal der Physik [*A publication*]
**Neues Optiker Jl** ... Neues Optiker Journal [*A publication*]
**Neuesten Entdeckungen Chem** ... Neuesten Entdeckungen in der Chemie [*A publication*]
**Neuestes Chem Arch** ... Neuestes Chemisches Archiv [*A publication*]
**Neue Tech** ... Neue Technik [*A publication*]
**Neue Tech A** ... Neue Technik. Abteilung A. Automatik und Industrielle Elektronik [*Switzerland*] [*A publication*]
**Neue Tech B** ... Neue Technik. Abteilung B. Kerntechnik [*Switzerland*] [*A publication*]
**Neue Tech Buero** ... Neue Technik im Buero [*A publication*]
**Neue Verpack** ... Neue Verpackung [*West Germany*] [*A publication*]
**Neue Wirtsch** ... Neue Wirtschaft [*A publication*]
**Neue ZFM** ... Neue Zeitschrift fuer Musik [*A publication*]
**Neue Z Mission** ... Neue Zeitschrift fuer Missionswissenschaft/Nouvelle Revue de Science Missionaire [*A publication*]
**Neue Z Miss Wiss** ... Neue Zeitschrift fuer Missionswissenschaft [*A publication*]
**Neue Z Ruebenzucker Ind** ... Neue Zeitschrift fuer Ruebenzucker-Industrie [*A publication*]
**Neue Z Sys Th** ... Neue Zeitschrift fuer Systematische Theologie und Religionsphilosophie [*A publication*]
**Neue Zuer Ztg** ... Neue Zuericher Zeitung [*Switzerland*] [*A publication*]
**Neue Z Verwaltungsr** ... Neue Zeitschrift fuer Verwaltungsrecht [*A publication*]
**NEUFCH**.. Neufchatel [*Imprint*] (ROG)
**NEUG**........ National Epson Users Group (EA)
**NEUIDS**.... Neurochemistry International [*A publication*]
**Neujahrsblatt Naturforsch Ges Zur** ... Neujahrsblatt. Naturforschende Gesellschaft in Zuerich [*A publication*]
**Neujahrsbl Naturforsch Ges Zuer** ... Neujahrsblatt. Naturforschenden Gesellschaft in Zuerich [*A publication*]
**Neujahrsbl Naturforsch Ges Zuerich** ... Neujahrsblatt Herausgegeben von der Naturforschenden Gesellschaft in Zuerich [*A publication*]
**Neujahrsbl Sachs** ... Neujahrsblaetter Herausgegeben von der Historischen Kommission fuer die Provinz Sachsen [*A publication*]
**NEUM**....... Non-European Unity Movement [*South Africa*] (PD)
**Neumol Cir Torax** ... Neumologia y Cirugia de Torax [*A publication*]
**NEUND9**... Neurology and Neurobiology [*New York*] [*A publication*]
**NE Univ Bul** ... New England University. Bulletin [*A publication*] (APTA)
**NE Univ External Stud Gaz** ... University of New England. External Studies Gazette [*A publication*] (APTA)
**NE Univ Union Rec** ... University of New England. Union Record [*A publication*] (APTA)
**NeuP**.......... Neuphilologische Monatsschrift [*A publication*]
**Neuphil Mit** ... Neuphilologische Mitteilungen [*A publication*]
**Neuphilol M** ... Neuphilologische Mitteilungen [*A publication*]
**Neuphilol Mitt** ... Neuphilologische Mitteilungen [*A publication*]
**NeUR**......... Rijksuniversiteit te Utrecht, Utrecht, Netherlands [*Library symbol*] [*Library of Congress*] (LCLS)
**NEURA**..... Neurology [*A publication*]
**NEUREM** ... Neurourology and Urodynamics [*A publication*]
**NEURO**..... Neurology [*or Neurological*]
**Neurobehav Toxicol** ... Neurobehavioral Toxicology [*A publication*]
**Neurobehav Toxicol Teratol** ... Neurobehavioral Toxicology and Teratology [*A publication*]
**Neurobiol Aging** ... Neurobiology of Aging [*A publication*]
**Neurobiol Biochem Morphol** ... Neurobiology, Biochemistry, and Morphology [*A publication*]
**Neurochem Int** ... Neurochemistry International [*A publication*]
**Neurochem Pathol** ... Neurochemical Pathology [*A publication*]
**Neurochem Res** ... Neurochemical Research [*A publication*]
**Neuro Chir** ... Neuro-Chirurgie [*A publication*]
**Neurochira** ... Neurochirurgia [*A publication*]
**Neuro-Chire** ... Neuro-Chirurgie [*A publication*]
**Neuroc Path** ... Neurochemical Pathology [*A publication*]
**Neuroendocr** ... Neuroendocrinology [*A publication*]
**Neuroendocrinol Lett** ... Neuroendocrinology Letters [*A publication*]
**Neuroendocr Perspect** ... Neuroendocrine Perspectives [*A publication*]
**NEUROL** .. Neurology
**Neurol Centralbl** ... Neurologisches Centralblatt [*A publication*]
**Neurol Clin** ... Neurologic Clinics [*A publication*]
**Neurol India** ... Neurology India [*A publication*]
**Neurol Med-Chir** ... Neurologia Medico-Chirurgica [*A publication*]
**Neurol Neurobiol (NY)** ... Neurology and Neurobiology (New York) [*A publication*]
**Neurol Neurochir Pol** ... Neurologia i Neurochirurgia Polska [*A publication*]
**Neurol Neurochir Psychiatr Pol** ... Neurologia, Neurochirurgia, i Psychiatria Polska [*Poland*] [*A publication*]
**Neurol Neurocir Psiquiatr** ... Neurologia, Neurocirurgia, Psiquiatria [*A publication*]
**Neurol Psihiatr Neurochir (Buchar)** ... Neurologia Psihiatria Neurochirurgia (Bucharest) [*A publication*]
**Neurol Psychiatr (Bucur)** ... Neurologie et Psychiatrie (Bucuresti) [*A publication*]
**Neurol Res** ... Neurological Research [*A publication*]
**Neurol Ser One Neural Mech Mov** ... Neurology. Series One. Neural Mechanisms of Movement [*A publication*]
**Neurol Surg** ... Neurological Surgery [*A publication*]
**Neuropadiat** ... Neuropaediatrie [*A publication*]
**Neurop Ap N** ... Neuropathology and Applied Neurobiology [*A publication*]
**Neuropathol Appl Neurobiol** ... Neuropathology and Applied Neurobiology [*A publication*]
**Neuropatol Pol** ... Neuropatologia Polska [*A publication*]
**Neuropharm** ... Neuropharmacology [*A publication*]
**Neurophysiology (Engl Transl Neirofiziologiya)** ... Neurophysiology (English Translation of Neirofiziologiya) [*A publication*]
**Neuropsichiatr Infant** ... Neuropsichiatria Infantile [*A publication*]
**Neuropsychiatr Enfance Adolesc** ... Neuropsychiatrie de l'Enfance et de l'Adolescence [*A publication*]
**Neuropsycho** ... Neuropsychologia [*A publication*]
**Neuroptera Int** ... Neuroptera International [*A publication*]
**Neuroradiol** ... Neuroradiology [*A publication*]
**Neurosci Behav Physiol** ... Neuroscience and Behavioral Physiology [*A publication*]

**Neurosci Biobehav Rev** ... Neuroscience and Biobehavioral Reviews [*A publication*]
**Neurosci L** ... Neuroscience Letters [*A publication*]
**Neurosci Lett** ... Neuroscience Letters [*A publication*]
**Neurosci Lett Suppl** ... Neuroscience Letters. Supplement [*A publication*]
**Neurosci Res** ... Neurosciences Research [*A publication*]
**Neurosci Res Program Bull** ... Neurosciences Research. Program Bulletin [*A publication*]
**Neurosci Res (Shannon Irel)** ... Neuroscience Research (Shannon, Ireland) [*A publication*]
**Neurosci Res Suppl** ... Neuroscience Research. Supplement [*A publication*]
**Neurosci Res Symp Summ** ... Neurosciences Research. Symposium Summaries [*A publication*]
**Neurosci Ser** ... Neuroscience Series [*A publication*]
**Neurosci Symp** ... Neuroscience Symposia [*A publication*]
**Neurosci Transl** ... Neuroscience Translations [*A publication*]
**Neurospora Newsl** ... Neurospora Newsletter [*A publication*]
**Neurosurg Rev** ... Neurosurgical Review [*A publication*]
**Neurourol Urodyn** ... Neurourology and Urodynamics [*A publication*]
**NeuS** .......... Neuere Sprachen [*A publication*]
**NEUS** ........ New Extensions for Utilizing Scientists, Inc.
**NEUS** ........ Northeastern United States
**NEUS** ........ Nuclear-Electric Unmanned Spacecraft
**Neu Spr** ...... Neuere Sprachen [*A publication*]
**NEUSSN** ... Northeastern United States Seismic Network (NRCH)
**NEUT** ........ Neuter
**NEUT** ........ Neutral (AAG)
**neut** ............ Neutrophil [*Hematology*]
**neut equiv** ... Neutralization Equivalent [*Chemistry*]
**NEV** ........... Net Economic Value
**NEV** ........... Neutral-to-Earth Voltage [*Electrical power transmission*]
**NEV** ........... Nevada (AAG)
**NEV** ........... Nevada Airlines, Inc. [*Las Vegas, NV*] (FAAC)
**Nev** ............ Nevada Reports [*A publication*]
**Nev** ............ Nevada Supreme Court Reports [*A publication*] (DLA)
**NEV** ........... Nevis [*Leeward Islands*] [*Airport symbol*] (OAG)
**NEV** ........... Nuevo Energy Co. [*NYSE symbol*] (SPSG)
**NEVA** ........ Nevada Resources [*NASDAQ symbol*] (NQ)
**NEVA** ........ North Eastern Vecturists Association
**Nevada Bur Mines Map** ... Nevada. Bureau of Mines. Map [*A publication*]
**Nevada Rep** ... Nevada Reports [*A publication*] (DLA)
**Nevada Repts** ... Nevada Reports [*A publication*] (DLA)
**Nevada Univ Center Water Resources Research Proj Rept** ... Nevada University. Desert Research Institute. Center for Water Resources Research. Project Report [*A publication*]
**Nevada Univ Desert Research Inst Tech Rept** ... Nevada. University. Desert Research Institute. Technical Report [*A publication*]
**Nev Admin Code** ... Nevada Administrative Code [*A publication*] (DLA)
**Nev Ag Exp** ... Nevada. Agricultural Experiment Station. Publications [*A publication*]
**Nev Agric Exp Stn B** ... Nevada. Agricultural Experiment Station. B [*A publication*]
**Nev Agric Exp Stn Circ** ... Nevada. Agricultural Experiment Station. Circular [*A publication*]
**Nev Agric Exp Stn R** ... Nevada. Agricultural Experiment Station. R [*A publication*]
**Nev Agric Exp Stn Ser B** ... Nevada. Agricultural Experiment Station. Series B [*A publication*]
**Nev Agric Exp Stn T** ... Nevada. Agricultural Experiment Station. T [*A publication*]
**Nev Agric Exp Stn Tech Bull** ... Nevada. Agricultural Experiment Station. Technical Bulletin [*A publication*]
**NEVATV** ... Nebraska VA Television Network [*Telecommunications service*] (TSSD)
**Nev Bur Mines Bull** ... Nevada. Bureau of Mines. Bulletin [*A publication*]
**Nev Bur Mines Geol Bull** ... Nevada. Bureau of Mines and Geology. Bulletin [*A publication*]
**Nev Bur Mines Geol Rep** ... Nevada. Bureau of Mines and Geology. Report [*A publication*]
**Nev Bur Mines Rep** ... Nevada. Bureau of Mines. Report [*A publication*]
**Nev Dep Conserv Nat Resour Water Resour Bull** ... Nevada. Department of Conservation and Natural Resources. Water Resources Bulletin [*A publication*]
**Nev Dep Conserv Nat Resour Water Resour Inf Ser** ... Nevada. Department of Conservation and Natural Resources. Water Resources Information Series [*A publication*]
**Nev Dep Conserv Nat Resour Water Resour Reconnaissance Ser** ... Nevada. Department of Conservation and Natural Resources. Water Resources Reconnaissance Series [*A publication*]
**Nev Div Water Resour Water Resour Bull** ... Nevada. Division of Water Resources. Water Resources Bulletin [*A publication*]
**Nev Div Water Resour Water Resour Reconnaissance Ser** ... Nevada. Division of Water Resources. Water Resources Reconnaissance Series [*A publication*]
**NEVE** ........ Nonempirical Valence-Electron [*Physics*]
**Nevelestud Kozlem** ... Nevelestudomanyi Koezlemenyek [*A publication*]
**Nev Highways and Parks** ... Nevada Highways and Parks [*A publication*]
**NEVLESS** ... Nevertheless (ROG)
**Nev & M** .... Nevile and Manning's English King's Bench Reports [*A publication*] (ILCA)
**Nev & Mac** ... Neville and Macnamara's Railway Cases [*1855-1950*] [*A publication*] (DLA)
**Nev & MacN** ... Neville and Macnamara's Railway and Canal Cases [*1855-1950*] [*A publication*] (DLA)
**Nev & Man** ... Nevile and Manning's English King's Bench Reports [*A publication*] (DLA)
**Nev & Man Mag Cas** ... Nevile and Manning's English Magistrates' Cases [*A publication*] (DLA)
**Nev & Mcn** ... Neville and Macnamara's Railway Cases [*England*] [*A publication*] (DLA)
**Nev & M (Eng)** ... Nevile and Manning's English King's Bench Reports [*A publication*] (DLA)
**Nev & MKB** ... Nevile and Manning's English King's Bench Reports [*A publication*] (DLA)
**Nev & MMC** ... Nevile and Manning's English Magistrates' Cases [*A publication*] (DLA)
**Nev Nurses Assoc Q Newslett** ... Nevada Nurses' Association. Quarterly Newsletter [*A publication*]
**Nev Off State Eng Water Resour Bull** ... Nevada. Office of the State Engineer. Water Resources Bulletin [*A publication*]
**Nev & P**...... Nevile and Perry's English King's Bench Reports [*1836-38*] [*A publication*] (DLA)
**Nev & P**...... Nevile and Perry's English Magistrates' Cases [*1836-37*] [*A publication*] (DLA)
**Nev & PKB** ... Nevile and Perry's English King's Bench Reports [*1836-38*] [*A publication*] (DLA)
**Nev & P Mag Cas** ... Nevile and Perry's English Magistrates' Cases [*1836-37*] [*A publication*] (DLA)
**Nev & PMC** ... Nevile and Perry's English Magistrates' Cases [*1836-37*] [*A publication*] (DLA)
**Nev PSC Op** ... Nevada Public Service Commission Opinions [*A publication*] (DLA)
**Nev R Bus and Econ** ... Nevada Review of Business and Economics [*A publication*]
**Nev Rev Stat** ... Nevada Revised Statutes [*A publication*] (DLA)
**Nev Rev Stat Ann (Michie)** ... Nevada Revised Statutes, Annotated (Michie) [*A publication*]
**Nev RNformation** ... Nevada RNformation [*A publication*]
**Nevrol Psikhiat Nevrokhir** ... Nevrologiya, Psikhiatriya, i Nevrokhirurgiya [*Neurology, Psychiatry, and Neurosurgery*] [*A publication*]
**Nevrol Psikhiatr** ... Nevrologiya i Psikhiatriya [*A publication*]
**Nevrol Psikhiatr Nevrokhir** ... Nevrologiya, Psikhiatriya, i Nevrokhirurgiya [*A publication*]
**Nevropatol Psikhiat** ... Nevropatologiya i Psikhiatriya [*A publication*]
**Nev SBJ** ..... Nevada State Bar Journal [*A publication*] (DLA)
**Nev Stat** ..... Statutes of Nevada [*A publication*]
**Nev State Engineer's Office Water Res Bull** ... Nevada. State Engineer's Office. Water Resources Bulletin [*A publication*]
**Nev State Eng Water Resour Bull** ... Nevada. State Engineer. Water Resources Bulletin [*A publication*]
**Nev State Mus Anthropol Pap** ... Nevada State Museum. Anthropological Papers [*A publication*]
**Nev Stats**.... Statutes of Nevada [*A publication*] (DLA)
**Nev St Bar J** ... Nevada State Bar Journal [*A publication*] (DLA)
**Nev Univ Dp G M B** ... Nevada University. Department of Geology and Mining. Bulletin [*A publication*]
**Nev Univ Max C Fleischmann Coll Agric B** ... Nevada University. Max C. Fleischmann College of Agriculture. Series B [*A publication*]
**Nev Univ Max C Fleischmann Coll Agric R** ... Nevada University. Max C. Fleischmann College of Agriculture. Series R [*A publication*]
**Nev Wildl**... Nevada Wildlife [*A publication*]
**NEW** .......... National Electronics Week
**NEW** .......... National Energy Watch [*Edison Electric Institute*]
**NEW** .......... Native Egg White
**NEW** .......... Navy Early Warning
**NEW** .......... Net Economic Welfare [*Economic indicator*]
**NEW** .......... Net Explosive Weight (AFM)
**New** ............ New Age [*A publication*]
**NEW** .......... New College of California, San Francisco, CA [*OCLC symbol*] (OCLC)
**NEW** .......... New England Business [*A publication*]
**NEW** .......... New Orleans, LA [*Location identifier*] [*FAA*] (FAAL)
**new** ............ Newari [*MARC language code*] [*Library of Congress*] (LCCP)
**NEW** .......... Newcor, Inc. [*AMEX symbol*] (SPSG)
**New** ............ Newell's Illinois Appeal Reports [*A publication*] (DLA)
**NEW** .......... Newport [*Washington*] [*Seismograph station code, US Geological Survey*] (SEIS)
**NEW** .......... Newport [*Quebec*] [*Geomagnetic observatory code*]
**NEW** .......... Newtec Industries Ltd. [*Vancouver Stock Exchange symbol*]
**NEW** .......... Newton
**NEW** .......... Nuclear Energy Women (EA)
**NEW** .......... Onderneming [*A publication*]
**NEw** ............ Thomas E. Ryan Public Library, East Williston, NY [*Library symbol*] [*Library of Congress*] (LCLS)
**NEWA** ....... National Electrical Wholesalers Association
**NewA** ......... New African [*A publication*]
**NEWA** ....... Nuclear Energy Writers Association [*Defunct*]
**NEWAC** .... NATO Electronic Warfare Advisory Committee (NATG)
**New A C P** ... New American and Canadian Poetry [*A publication*]

**NewAD**...... Newspaper Archive Developments Ltd., New Haven, CT [*Library symbol*] [*Library of Congress*] (LCLS)
**New Africa** ... New African [*A publication*]
**New Am**..... New America [*A publication*]
**New Am Cyc** ... New American Cyclopaedia [*A publication*] (ROG)
**New Am Mercury** ... New American Mercury [*A publication*]
**New Ann Reg** ... New Annual Register [*London*] [*A publication*] (DLA)
**New Argent** ... Newsletter Argentina [*A publication*]
**Newark Eng Notes** ... Newark Engineering Notes [*A publication*]
**Newark L Rev** ... University of Newark. Law Review [*A publication*] (DLA)
**New A'sian Post** ... New Australasian Post [*A publication*] (APTA)
**N E Water Works Assn J** ... New England Water Works Association. Journal [*A publication*]
**Newb**.......... Newberry's United States District Court, Admiralty Reports [*A publication*] (DLA)
**NEWB**....... Newbury [*Municipal borough in England*]
**Newb Adm** ... Newberry's United States District Court, Admiralty Reports [*A publication*] (DLA)
**New Benl**.... New Benloe's Reports, English King's Bench [*1531-1628*] [*A publication*] (DLA)
**New B Eq Ca** ... New Brunswick Equity Cases [*A publication*] (DLA)
**New B Eq Rep** ... New Brunswick Equity Reports [*A publication*] (DLA)
**Newberry** ... Newberry's United States District Court, Admiralty Reports [*A publication*] (DLA)
**Newberry Adm (F)** ... Newberry's United States District Court, Admiralty Reports [*A publication*] (DLA)
**Newberry Lib Bul** ... Newberry Library. Bulletin [*A publication*]
**Newberry's Ad Rep** ... Newberry's United States District Court, Admiralty Reports [*A publication*] (DLA)
**New Biol**.... New Biology [*A publication*]
**New Blckfrs** ... New Blackfriars [*A publication*]
**New Bldg Projects** ... New Building Projects [*A publication*]
**Newbon**...... Newbon's Private Bills Reports [*1895-99*] [*England*] [*A publication*] (DLA)
**New Bot**.... New Botanist [*A publication*]
**New Br**....... New Brunswick Reports [*A publication*] (DLA)
**New Br Eq (Can)** ... New Brunswick Equity Reports [*Canada*] [*A publication*] (DLA)
**New Br Eq Cas (Can)** ... New Brunswick Equity Cases [*Canada*] [*A publication*] (DLA)
**New Br R** ... New Brunswick Reports [*A publication*] (DLA)
**New Brunswick Dept Lands and Mines Ann Rept** ... New Brunswick. Department of Lands and Mines. Annual Report [*A publication*]
**Newbyth**..... Newbyth's Manuscript Decisions, Scotch Session Cases [*A publication*] (DLA)
**New C**........ New Collage [*A publication*]
**NEWC**....... Newcastle [*Name of two cities in England*]
**New Caledonia Bull Geol** ... New Caledonia. Bulletin Geologique [*A publication*]
**New Can F** ... New Canadian Film [*A publication*]
**New Cas**..... New Cases (Bingham's New Cases) [*A publication*] (DLA)
**New Cas Eq** ... New Cases in Equity [*8, 9 Modern Reports*] [*1721-55*] [*A publication*] (DLA)
**Newcastle Chamber of Commerce J** ... Newcastle Chamber of Commerce Journal [*A publication*] (APTA)
**Newcastle Ch Comm J** ... Newcastle Chamber of Commerce Journal [*A publication*] (APTA)
**Newcastle Inst Ed J** ... Institutes of Education of the Universities of Newcastle Upon Tyne and Durham. Journal [*A publication*]
**Newcastle Teach Coll Bul** ... Newcastle Teachers College. Bulletin [*A publication*] (APTA)
**Newcastle Teach Coll Bull** ... Newcastle Teachers College. Bulletin [*A publication*] (APTA)
**Newcastle Univ Gaz** ... Gazette. University of Newcastle [*A publication*] (APTA)
**Newcastle Univ Phys Dep Res Pub** ... University of Newcastle. Department of Physics. Research Publication [*A publication*] (APTA)
**NEWCC**.... Northeastern Weed Control Conference [*Later, NEWSS*] (EA)
**New Cent Res Inst Electr Power Ind** ... News. Central Research Institute of Electrical Power Industry [*Japan*] [*A publication*]
**New China** ... New China Magazine [*A publication*]
**New Church R** ... New Church Review [*A publication*]
**New Civ Eng** ... New Civil Engineer [*United Kingdom*] [*A publication*]
**New Civ Engnr** ... New Civil Engineer [*A publication*]
**New Civ Engr** ... New Civil Engineer [*A publication*]
**New Civil Engr** ... New Civil Engineer [*A publication*]
**NEWC L**.... Newcastle-Under-Lyme [*City in England*] (ROG)
**NEWCN**.... New Construction [*Navy*]
**Newcomen Soc Trans** ... Newcomen Society. Transactions [*A publication*]
**New Commun** ... New Community [*A publication*]
**New Cov**..... New Covenant [*A publication*]
**NEWD**....... Newsday [*A publication*]
**New Dent** ... New Dentist [*A publication*]
**New Dir Child Dev** ... New Directions for Child Development [*A publication*]
**New Dir Com** ... New Directions for Community Colleges [*A publication*]
**New Direct** ... New Directions [*A publication*]
**New Direct Com Coll** ... New Directions for Community Colleges [*A publication*]
**New Direct Higher Educ** ... New Directions for Higher Education [*A publication*]
**New Direct Inst Res** ... New Directions for Institutional Research [*A publication*]
**New Dir Hig** ... New Directions for Higher Education [*A publication*]
**New Dir Ment Health Serv** ... New Directions for Mental Health Services [*A publication*]
**New Dom** ... New Dominion Monthly [*A publication*]
**New Drugs Annu Cardiovasc Drugs** ... New Drugs Annual. Cardiovascular Drugs [*A publication*]
**NEWE**....... Newport Electronics, Inc. [*NASDAQ symbol*] (NQ)
**New Ecol**.... New Ecologist [*United Kingdom*] [*A publication*]
**New Edinburgh Rev** ... New Edinburgh Review [*A publication*]
**New Educ**... New Education [*A publication*] (APTA)
**Newel**......... Newelectronics [*A publication*]
**New Electron** ... New Electronics [*A publication*]
**Newell**........ Newell's Appeals Reports [*48-90 Illinois*] [*A publication*] (DLA)
**Newell Defam** ... Newell on Defamation, Slander, and Libel [*A publication*] (DLA)
**Newell Eject** ... Newell's Treatise on the Action of Ejectment [*A publication*] (DLA)
**Newell Mal Pros** ... Newell's Treatise on Malicious Prosecution [*A publication*] (DLA)
**Newell Sland & L** ... Newell on Slander and Libel [*A publication*] (DLA)
**New Eng**..... New Engineer [*United States*] [*A publication*]
**New Eng**..... New England Reporter [*A publication*] (DLA)
**New Eng**..... New Englander [*A publication*]
**New Eng Bs** ... New England Business [*A publication*]
**New Eng Hist** ... New England Historical and Genealogical Register [*A publication*]
**New Eng Hist Geneal Reg** ... New England Historical and Genealogical Register [*A publication*]
**New Eng J Crim & Civil Confinement** ... New England Journal on Criminal and Civil Confinement [*A publication*]
**New Eng J Prison** ... New England Journal of Prison Law [*A publication*]
**New Eng J Prison L** ... New England Journal of Prison Law [*A publication*]
**New England Bus** ... New England Business [*A publication*]
**New England Econ Indicators** ... New England Economic Indicators [*A publication*]
**New England Econ R** ... New England Economic Review [*A publication*]
**New England J Bus and Econ** ... New England Journal of Business and Economics [*A publication*]
**New England J Human Services** ... New England Journal of Human Services [*A publication*]
**New England Jl Photogr Hist** ... New England Journal of Photographic History [*A publication*]
**New England J Prison L** ... New England Journal of Prison Law [*A publication*]
**New England L Rev** ... New England Law Review [*A publication*]
**New England Water Works Assoc Jour** ... New England Water Works Association. Journal [*A publication*]
**New Engl J Hum Serv** ... New England Journal of Human Services [*A publication*]
**New Engl J Med** ... New England Journal of Medicine [*A publication*]
**New Eng L Rev** ... New England Law Review [*A publication*]
**New Engl Univ Bull** ... New England University. Bulletin [*A publication*]
**New Engl Univ Explor Soc Rep** ... University of New England. Exploration Society. Report [*A publication*] (APTA)
**New Eng M ns** ... New England Magazine (New Series) [*A publication*]
**New Eng Mag** ... New England Magazine [*A publication*]
**New Eng Q** ... New England Quarterly [*A publication*]
**New Eng R** ... New England Reporter [*A publication*] (DLA)
**New Eng Rep** ... New England Reporter [*A publication*] (DLA)
**New Entomol** ... New Entomologist [*A publication*]
**New Ent (Ueda)** ... New Entomologist (Ueda) [*A publication*]
**New Equip News** ... New Equipment News [*South Africa*] [*A publication*]
**New Era**..... New Era in Home and School [*A publication*]
**New Era Nurs Image Int** ... New Era Nursing Image International [*A publication*]
**Newer Methods Nutr Biochem** ... Newer Methods of Nutritional Biochemistry [*A publication*]
**Newer Methods Nutr Biochem Appl Interpret** ... Newer Methods of Nutritional Biochemistry with Applications and Interpretations [*A publication*]
**Newer Met Ind** ... Newer Metal Industry [*Japan*] [*A publication*]
**NEWF**....... Newfoundland [*with Labrador, a Canadian province*]
**NEWFLD** ... Newfoundland [*with Labrador, a Canadian province*]
**Newfld LR** ... Newfoundland Law Reports [*A publication*] (DLA)
**Newf LR**..... Newfoundland Law Reports [*A publication*] (DLA)
**NEWFO**.... Newfoundland [*with Labrador, a Canadian province*]
**New Food Ind** ... New Food Industry [*Japan*] [*A publication*]
**Newfoundland Dep Mines Energy Miner Dev Div Rep Act** ... Newfoundland. Department of Mines and Energy. Mineral Development Division. Report of Activities [*A publication*]
**Newfoundland Geol Survey Inf Circ Rept** ... Newfoundland. Geological Survey. Information Circular. Report [*A publication*]
**Newfoundland Geol Surv Inf Circ** ... Newfoundland. Geological Survey. Information Circular [*A publication*]
**Newfoundland Geol Surv Rep** ... Newfoundland. Geological Survey. Report [*A publication*]
**Newfoundland J Geol Educ** ... Newfoundland Journal of Geological Education [*A publication*]

**Newfoundland and Labrador Mineral Resources Div Bull** ... Newfoundland and Labrador. Department of Mines, Agriculture, and Resources. Mineral Resources Division. Bulletin [*A publication*]
**Newfoundland Labrador Miner Dev Div Rep** ... Newfoundland and Labrador. Mineral Development Division. Report [*A publication*]
**Newfoundland Labrador Miner Resour Div Inf Circ** ... Newfoundland and Labrador. Mineral Resources Division. Information Circular [*A publication*]
**Newfoundland Labrador Miner Resour Div Miner Resour Rep** ... Newfoundland and Labrador. Mineral Resources Division. Mineral Resources Report [*A publication*]
**Newfoundl LR** ... Newfoundland Law Reports [*A publication*] (DLA)
**Newfoundl R** ... Newfoundland Reports [*A publication*] (DLA)
**Newfoundl Sel Cas** ... Newfoundland Select Cases [*A publication*] (DLA)
**NEWFS** ..... New England Wild Flower Society (EA)
**Newf S Ct** ... Newfoundland Supreme Court Decisions [*A publication*] (DLA)
**Newf Sel Cas** ... Newfoundland Select Cases [*A publication*] (DLA)
**New Ger Cr** ... New German Critique [*A publication*]
**New Germ** ... New German Critique [*A publication*]
**New Germ Crit** ... New German Critique [*A publication*]
**New Ger Stud** ... New German Studies [*A publication*]
**New Grove** ... New Grove Dictionary of Music and Musicians [*A publication*]
**New Grove Jazz** ... New Grove Dictionary of Jazz [*A publication*]
**New Grove Mus Inst** ... New Grove Dictionary of Musical Instruments [*A publication*]
**New Guinea Agric Gaz** ... New Guinea Agricultural Gazette [*A publication*]
**New Guinea Austral Pacific SE Asia** ... New Guinea and Australia, the Pacific, and South East Asia [*A publication*]
**New Guinea Res B** ... New Guinea Research Bulletin [*A publication*]
**New Hamp** ... New Hampshire Reports [*A publication*] (DLA)
**New Hamp BJ** ... New Hampshire Bar Journal [*A publication*]
**New Hamp R** ... New Hampshire Reports [*A publication*] (DLA)
**New Hamp Rep** ... New Hampshire Reports [*A publication*] (DLA)
**New Hampshire Rep** ... New Hampshire Reports [*A publication*] (DLA)
**New Harb** .. New Harbinger [*A publication*]
**New Haven Sym** ... New Haven Symphony Orchestra. Program Notes [*A publication*]
**New Hebrides Geol Surv Annu Rep** ... New Hebrides. Geological Survey. Annual Report [*A publication*]
**New Hebrides Geol Surv Rep** ... New Hebrides. Geological Survey. Report [*A publication*]
**New Hor Educ** ... New Horizons in Education [*A publication*] (APTA)
**New Horiz Educ** ... New Horizons in Education [*A publication*] (APTA)
**New Horizons in Educ** ... New Horizons in Education [*A publication*] (APTA)
**New Hungarian Q** ... New Hungarian Quarterly [*A publication*]
**New Hungar Quart** ... New Hungarian Quarterly [*A publication*]
**New Hung Q** ... New Hungarian Quarterly [*A publication*]
**NEWIL** ...... Northeast Wisconsin Intertype Libraries [*Library network*]
**New Inf Syst Serv** ... New Information Systems and Services [*United States*] [*A publication*]
**New Int** ...... New Internationalist [*England*] [*A publication*]
**New Int Clin** ... New International Clinics [*A publication*]
**New Inter** ... New Internationalist [*A publication*] (APTA)
**New Intl** ..... New International Review [*A publication*]
**New Int Realities** ... New International Realities [*United States*] [*A publication*]
**New Ir Jur** ... New Irish Jurist and Local Government Review [*1900-05*] [*A publication*] (DLA)
**NEWISA** ... New England Women's Intercollegiate Sailing Association
**New Istanbul Contrib Clin Sci** ... New Istanbul Contribution to Clinical Science [*A publication*]
**New Jers Beekprs Ass News** ... New Jersey Beekeepers Association. News [*A publication*]
**New Jersey** ... New Jersey Law Reports [*A publication*] (DLA)
**New Jersey Div Water Policy and Supply Spec Rept** ... State of New Jersey. Department of Conservation and Economic Development. Division of Water Policy and Supply. Special Report [*A publication*]
**New Jersey Div Water Policy and Supply Water Resources Circ** ... State of New Jersey. Department of Conservation and Economic Development. Division of Water Policy and Supply. Water Resources Circular [*A publication*]
**New Jersey Eq** ... New Jersey Equity Reports [*A publication*] (DLA)
**New Jersey Equity** ... New Jersey Equity Reports [*A publication*] (DLA)
**New Jersey Leg Rec** ... New Jersey Legal Record [*A publication*] (DLA)
**New Jersey LJ** ... New Jersey Law Journal [*A publication*]
**New Jersey L Rev** ... New Jersey Law Review [*A publication*] (DLA)
**New Jersey SBA Qu** ... New Jersey State Bar Association. Quarterly [*A publication*] (DLA)
**New Jers St Hort Soc News** ... New Jersey State Horticultural Society. News [*A publication*]
**New Journ** ... New Journalist [*A publication*]
**New J Stat & Oper Res** ... New Journal of Statistics and Operational Research [*A publication*]
**NewL** .......... New Leader [*A publication*]
**New L** ......... New Letters [*A publication*]
**New Law J** ... New Law Journal [*A publication*]
**NEWLC** ..... NATO Electronic Warfare Liaison Committee
**Newl Ch PR** ... Newland's Chancery Practice [*A publication*] (DLA)
**Newl Ch Prac** ... Newland's Chancery Practice [*A publication*] (DLA)
**Newl Cont** .. Newland on Contracts [*1806*] [*A publication*] (DLA)
**New Left** .... New Left Review [*A publication*]
**New Left R** ... New Left Review [*A publication*]
**New Lib** ...... New Liberal Review [*A publication*]
**New Libr Wld** ... New Library World [*A publication*]
**New Lib W** ... New Library World [*A publication*]
**New Lib World** ... New Library World [*A publication*]
**New Lit His** ... New Literary History [*A publication*]
**New Lit Hist** ... New Literary History [*A publication*]
**New Lit Ideol** ... New Literature and Ideology [*A publication*]
**New L J** ...... New Law Journal [*A publication*]
**NEWLON** ... New London, Connecticut [*Navy*]
**NEWM** ...... New England and World Missions (EA)
**NEW M** ..... New Mexico (ROG)
**New Mag Cas** ... New Magistrates' Cases (Bittleston, Wise, and Parnell) [*1844-51*] [*A publication*] (DLA)
**New Math Library** ... New Mathematical Library [*A publication*]
**Newm Conv** ... Newman on Conveyancing [*A publication*] (DLA)
**New Med J** ... New Medical Journal [*A publication*]
**New Met Tech** ... New Metals and Technics [*Japan*] [*A publication*]
**New Mex BA** ... New Mexico State Bar Association, Minutes [*A publication*] (DLA)
**New Mex Geol** ... New Mexico Geology [*A publication*]
**New Mex Hist Rev** ... New Mexico Historical Review [*A publication*]
**New Mexico Bur Mines and Mineral Resources Bull** ... New Mexico. Bureau of Mines and Mineral Resources. Bulletin. New Mexico Institute of Mining and Technology [*A publication*]
**New Mexico Bur Mines and Mineral Resources Circ** ... New Mexico. Bureau of Mines and Mineral Resources. Circular. New Mexico Institute of Mining and Technology [*A publication*]
**New Mexico Bur Mines and Mineral Resources Geol Map** ... New Mexico. Bureau of Mines and Mineral Resources. Geologic Map. New Mexico Institute of Mining and Technology [*A publication*]
**New Mexico Bur Mines and Mineral Resources Mem** ... New Mexico Bureau of Mines and Mineral Resources. Memoir. New Mexico Institute of Mining and Technology [*A publication*]
**New Mexico Geol Soc Spec Pub** ... New Mexico Geological Society. Special Publication [*A publication*]
**New Mexico Libr Bull** ... New Mexico Library Bulletin [*A publication*]
**New Mexico L Rev** ... New Mexico Law Review [*A publication*]
**New Mexico State Engineer Tech Rept** ... New Mexico State Engineer. Technical Report [*A publication*]
**New Mexico Univ Pubs Meteoritics** ... New Mexico University. Publications in Meteoritics [*A publication*]
**New Mex L Rev** ... New Mexico Law Review [*A publication*]
**New Mex SBA** ... New Mexico State Bar Association, Report of Proceedings [*A publication*] (DLA)
**NEW MOONS** ... NASA Evaluation with Models of Optimized Nuclear Spacecraft
**New Nat Brev** ... New Natura Brevium [*A publication*] (DLA)
**New NB** ..... New Natura Brevium [*A publication*] (DSA)
**New Nippon Electr Tech Rev** ... New Nippon Electric Technical Review [*A publication*]
**New O R** ..... New Orleans Review [*A publication*]
**New Orleans Ac Sc Papers** ... New Orleans Academy of Sciences. Papers [*A publication*]
**New Orleans Med Surg J** ... New Orleans Medical and Surgical Journal [*A publication*]
**New Orleans Port Rec** ... New Orleans Port Record [*A publication*]
**New Orl Rev** ... New Orleans Review [*A publication*]
**NEWOT** .... Naval Electronic Warfare Operator Trainer (MCD)
**NEWP** ....... Newport [*England*]
**NEWP** ....... Newport Corp. [*NASDAQ symbol*] (NQ)
**New Per Ind** ... New Periodicals Index [*A publication*]
**NEWPEX** ... Northeast Wood Products Expo [*In company name, NEWPEX, Inc.*] (TSPED)
**New Phys** ... New Physics [*A publication*]
**New Phys (Korean Phys Soc)** ... New Physics (Korean Physical Society) [*A publication*]
**New Phys Suppl** ... New Physics. Supplement [*A publication*]
**New Phytol** ... New Phytologist [*A publication*]
**NEWPIL** ... NADGE [*NATO Air Defense Ground Environment*] Early Warning Program Information Leaflet (NATG)
**New Polit** ... New Political Science [*A publication*]
**New Polit** ... New Politics [*A publication*]
**New Pol Sci** ... New Political Science [*A publication*]
**Newport N H Soc Pr** ... Newport Natural History Society. Proceedings [*A publication*]
**NEWPOSITREP** ... New [*Corrected*] Position Report (NVT)
**New Pract Case** ... New Practice Cases [*1844-48*] [*A publication*] (DLA)
**New Pr Cases** ... New Practice Cases [*1844-48*] [*A publication*] (DLA)
**New Princ** .. New Princeton Review [*A publication*]
**New Publ Bur Mines** ... New Publications. Bureau of Mines [*Washington, DC*] [*A publication*]
**New Q** ........ New Quarterly Review [*A publication*]
**NEWQ** ....... Newquay [*Urban district in England*]
**NEWR** ....... New England Realty Associates Ltd. [*NASDAQ symbol*] (NQ)
**New R** ........ [*The*] New Republic [*A publication*]
**New R** ........ New Review [*A publication*]

**NEWRADS** ... Nuclear Explosion Warning and Radiological Data System
**New Real**.... New Realities [*A publication*]
**New Rena**... New Renaissance [*A publication*]
**New Rep**..... Bosanquet and Puller's New Reports, English Common Pleas [*1804-07*] [*A publication*] (DLA)
**New Rep**..... New Reports [*1862-65*] [*England*] [*A publication*] (DLA)
**New Rep**..... [*The*] New Republic [*A publication*]
**New Repub** ... [*The*] New Republic [*A publication*]
**New Res Plant Anat** ... New Research in Plant Anatomy [*A publication*]
**New Rev**..... New Review [*A publication*]
**NEWRIT**... Northeast Water Resources Information Terminal (IID)
**New Riv R** ... New River Review [*A publication*]
**NEWS** ....... Naval Electronic Warfare Simulator
**NEWS** ....... Neighborhood Environmental Workshops (EA)
**NEWS** ....... Network Extensible Window System [*Data processing*]
**NEWS** ....... New England Weekly Survey [*A publication*] (APTA)
**NEWS** ....... New England Wild Flower Society (EA)
**NEWS** ....... New European Wide Warranty System [*General Motors Corp.*]
**NEWS** ....... New Product Early Warning System
**New S**......... New Scholar [*A publication*]
**NewS**.......... New Statesman [*A publication*]
**News** .......... News from Nowhere [*A publication*]
**News Bull Indian Dent Assoc** ... News Bulletin. Indian Dental Association [*A publication*]
**News Bull Soc Vertebr Paleontol** ... News Bulletin. Society of Vertebrate Paleontology [*A publication*]
**Newscast Reg 4 Amer Iris Soc** ... Newscast Region 4. American Iris Society [*A publication*]
**New Sch Ex** ... New Schools Exchange. Newsletter [*A publication*]
**New Schl**.... New Schools Exchange. Newsletter [*A publication*]
**New Schol** ... New Scholasticism [*A publication*]
**New Scholas** ... New Scholasticism [*A publication*]
**New Sci**...... New Scientist [*A publication*]
**New Scient** ... New Scientist [*A publication*]
**New Sci (London)**... New Scientist (London) [*A publication*]
**News CIMMYT** ... News. Centro Internacional de Mejoramiento de Maiz y Trigo [*A publication*]
**New Sci Sci J** ... New Scientist and Science Journal [*A publication*]
**News Comment** ... News and Comments [*American Academy of Pediatrics*] [*A publication*]
**News Ed Am Chem Soc** ... News Edition. American Chemical Society [*A publication*]
**News Eng**... News in Engineering [*A publication*]
**New Series** ... Martin's Louisiana Reports, New Series [*A publication*] (DLA)
**New Sess Cas** ... New Session Cases (Carrow, Hamerton, and Allen) [*1844-51*] [*A publication*] (DLA)
**News Farmer Coop** ... News for Farmer Cooperatives [*A publication*]
**News Farmer Coops** ... News for Farmer Cooperatives [*A publication*]
**Newsfront**.. Newsfront International [*A publication*]
**News Geotherm Energy Convers Technol** ... News of Geothermal Energy Conversion Technology [*United States*] [*A publication*]
**New Silver Technol** ... New Silver Technology [*A publication*]
**News Jrl**..... News Journal [*A publication*]
**NEWSL**..... Newsletter
**Newsl Am Acad Health Adm** ... Newsletter. American Academy of Health Administration [*A publication*]
**Newsl Am Acad Implant Dent** ... Newsletter. American Academy of Implant Dentistry [*A publication*]
**Newsl Am Assoc Equine Pract** ... Newsletter. American Association of Equine Practitioners [*A publication*]
**Newsl Appl Nucl Methods Biol Agric** ... Newsletter on the Application of Nuclear Methods in Biology and Agriculture [*Netherlands*] [*A publication*]
**Newsl Aust Coll Ed Qd** ... Australian College of Education. Queensland Chapter. Newsletter [*A publication*]
**Newsl Aust Conserv Fdn** ... Australian Conservation Foundation. Newsletter [*A publication*] (APTA)
**Newsl Aust Conserv Found** ... Australian Conservation Foundation. Newsletter [*A publication*] (APTA)
**Newsl Aust Inst Aborig St** ... Newsletter. Australian Institute of Aboriginal Studies [*A publication*]
**Newsl Aust Natn Ass Ment Hlth** ... Australian National Association for Mental Health. Newsletter [*A publication*]
**Newsl Aust NZ Soc Nucl Med** ... Newsletter. Australian and New Zealand Society of Nuclear Medicine [*A publication*]
**Newsl Biomed Saf Stand** ... Newsletter of Biomedical Safety and Standards [*A publication*]
**Newsl Br Univ Film Video Counc** ... Newsletter. British Universities Film and Video Council [*A publication*]
**Newsl Comm Eur Communit** ... Newsletter. Commission of the European Communities [*A publication*]
**Newsl Commonw Sci Counc Earth Sci Programme** ... Newsletter. Commonwealth Science Council. Earth Sciences Programme [*A publication*]
**Newsl Commw Geol Liaison Off** ... Newsletter. Commonwealth Geological Liaison Office [*A publication*]
**Newsl Coop Invest Mediterr** ... Newsletter of the Cooperative Investigations in the Mediterranean [*A publication*]
**Newsl Counc Eur Doc Ctre Educ Eur** ... Newsletter. Council of Europe. Documentation Centre for Education in Europe [*A publication*]
**Newsl Environ Mutagen Soc** ... Newsletter. Environmental Mutagen Society [*A publication*]
**News Lepid Soc** ... News. Lepidopterists' Society [*A publication*]
**Newslet**...... Newsletter. American Symphony Orchestra League, Inc. [*A publication*]
**News Lett Assoc Off Seed Anal** ... News Letter. Association of Official Seed Analysts [*A publication*]
**Newslett Ass Offic Seed Anal** ... Newsletter. Association of Official Seed Analysis [*A publication*]
**Newsletter Comp Stud Communism** ... Newsletter on Comparative Studies of Communism [*A publication*]
**Newsletter R Aust Hist Soc** ... Royal Australian Historical Society. Newsletter [*A publication*] (APTA)
**Newsletter WSEO** ... Newsletter. Washington State Energy Office [*A publication*]
**News Lett Florence Nightingale Int Nurs Assoc** ... News Letter. Florence Nightingale International Nurses Association [*A publication*]
**News Lett India Popul Proj UP** ... News Letter. India Population Project UP [*A publication*]
**News Lett Int Coll Dent** ... News Letter. International College of Dentists [*A publication*]
**Newslett Int Rice Comm** ... Newsletter. International Rice Commission [*A publication*]
**News Lett Popul Cent (Bangalore)** ... News Letter. Population Centre (Bangalore) [*A publication*]
**Newslett Stratigr** ... Newsletter on Stratigraphy [*A publication*]
**Newslett Tree Impr Introd** ... Newsletter of Tree Improvement and Introduction [*A publication*]
**Newsl Fusion Energy Found** ... Newsletter. Fusion Energy Foundation [*A publication*]
**Newsl Geol Soc (London)** ... Newsletter. Geological Society (London) [*A publication*]
**Newsl Geol Soc NZ** ... Newsletter. Geological Society of New Zealand [*A publication*]
**Newsl Geol Soc Zambia** ... Newsletter. Geological Society of Zambia [*A publication*]
**Newsl Geosci Inf Soc** ... Newsletter. Geoscience Information Society [*A publication*]
**Newsl Gov West Aus** ... Newsletter. Government of Western Australia. Mining [*A publication*]
**Newsl-IGCP Proj 167** ... Newsletter. International Geological Correlation Programme. Project 167 [*A publication*]
**Newsl Indones Min Assoc** ... Newsletter. Indonesian Mining Association [*A publication*]
**Newsl Inst Foresters Aust** ... Institute of Foresters of Australia. Newsletter [*A publication*] (APTA)
**Newsl Int Coll Dent India Sect** ... Newsletter. International College of Dentists. India Section [*A publication*]
**Newsl Intellectual Freedom** ... Newsletter on Intellectual Freedom [*A publication*]
**Newsl Int Geol Correl Programme Proj 156 Phosphorites** ... Newsletter. International Geological Correlation Programme. Project 156. Phosphorites [*A publication*]
**Newsl Int Rice Comm** ... Newsletter. International Rice Commission [*A publication*]
**Newsl Int Soc Bass** ... Newsletter. International Society of Bassists [*A publication*]
**Newsl Int Soc Radiogr Radiol Tech** ... Newsletter. International Society of Radiographers and Radiological Technicians [*A publication*]
**Newsl Int Union Biol Sci** ... Newsletter. International Union of Biological Sciences [*A publication*]
**Newsl Isot Generator Inf Cent** ... Newsletter. Isotopic Generator Information Centre [*France*] [*A publication*]
**Newsl Lab Hist Assoc** ... Newsletter. Labour History Association [*A publication*]
**Newsl Lang Teach Assoc** ... Newsletter. Language Teachers Association [*A publication*]
**Newsl League Int Fd Educ** ... Newsletter. League for International Food Education [*A publication*]
**Newsl Leg Act** ... Newsletter on Legislative Activities [*Council of Europe*] [*A publication*] (DLA)
**Newsl Mar Technol Soc** ... Newsletter. Marine Technology Society [*A publication*]
**Newsl NEA Comput Program Libr** ... Newsletter. NEA [*National Education Association*] Computer Program Library [*United States*] [*A publication*]
**Newsl NEA Data Bank** ... Newsletter. NEA [*Nuclear Energy Agency*] Data Bank [*A publication*]
**Newsl New Zealand Archaeol Assoc** ... Newsletter. New Zealand Archaeological Association [*A publication*]
**Newsl NZ Archaeol Assoc** ... Newsletter. New Zealand Archaeological Association [*A publication*]
**Newsl NZ Map Circle** ... Newsletter. New Zealand Mapkeepers Circle [*A publication*]
**Newsl Peak Dist Mines Hist Soc** ... News-Letter. Peak District Mines Historical Society [*A publication*]
**Newsl R & D Uranium Explor Tech** ... Newsletter. R and D in Uranium Exploration Techniques [*A publication*]

**Newsl Somerset Mines Res Group** ... Newsletter. Somerset Mines Research Group [*A publication*]
**Newsl Springfield Dent Soc** ... Newsletter. Springfield Dental Society [*A publication*]
**Newsl Statist Soc Aust** ... Statistical Society of Australia. Newsletter [*A publication*]
**Newsl Stat Soc Aust** ... Statistical Society of Australia. Newsletter [*A publication*] (APTA)
**Newsl Stratigr** ... Newsletters on Stratigraphy [*A publication*]
**Newsl Wildl Dis Assoc** ... Newsletter. Wildlife Disease Association [*A publication*]
**Newsl Wis League Nurs** ... Newsletter. Wisconsin League for Nursing [*A publication*]
**News Media and L** ... News Media and the Law [*A publication*]
**News Notes Calif Libr** ... News Notes of California Libraries [*A publication*]
**News Notes Calif Libs** ... News Notes of California Libraries [*A publication*]
**News Obser** ... News and Observer [*A publication*]
**New Soc** ..... New Society [*A publication*]
**New Soc (London)** ... New Society (London) [*A publication*]
**New South Wales Mag** ... New South Wales Magazine [*A publication*] (APTA)
**New South Wales Soil Conserv Serv J** ... New South Wales. Soil Conservation Service. Journal [*A publication*] (APTA)
**New South Wales Univ Sch Civ Eng UNICIV Rep** ... University of New South Wales. School of Civil Engineering. UNICIV Report [*A publication*] (APTA)
**New So WL** ... New South Wales Law Reports [*A publication*]
**New So W St** ... New South Wales State Reports [*A publication*]
**New So WWN** ... New South Wales Weekly Notes [*A publication*]
**News Pestic Rev Nat Agr Chem Ass** ... News and Pesticide Review. National Agricultural Chemicals Association [*A publication*]
**NEWSS** ..... Northeastern Weed Science Society [*Formerly, NEWCC*] (EA)
**NewSt** ........ New Statesman [*A publication*]
**New Statesm** ... New Statesman [*A publication*]
**News Views Ohio League Nurs** ... News and Views. Ohio League for Nursing [*A publication*]
**News W** ...... News Weekly [*A publication*] (APTA)
**Newswk** ...... Newsweek [*A publication*]
**News Xinhua News Agency** ... News from Xinhua News Agency [*China*] [*A publication*]
**NEW T** ...... Newcastle-Upon-Tyne [*City in England*] (ROG)
**NEWT** ....... Newton [*England*]
**New Tech Biophys Cell Biol** ... New Techniques in Biophysics and Cell Biology [*A publication*]
**New Tech Books** ... New Technical Books [*A publication*]
**New Term Rep** ... Dowling and Ryland's English King's Bench Reports [*A publication*] (DLA)
**New Term Rep** ... New Term Reports [*A publication*] (DLA)
**New Test Abstr** ... New Testament Abstracts [*A publication*]
**New Test St** ... New Testament Studies [*A publication*]
**New Test Stud** ... New Testament Studies [*A publication*]
**New Times** ... New Womens Times [*A publication*]
**New Towns Bull** ... New Towns Bulletin [*A publication*]
**New Trends Chem Teach** ... New Trends in Chemistry Teaching [*A publication*]
**NEWTS** ..... Naval Electronic Warfare Training System
**New University** ... New University and New Education [*A publication*]
**New Univ Q** ... New Universities. Quarterly [*A publication*]
**New Univ Quart** ... New Universities. Quarterly [*A publication*]
**NEWW** ...... New World Computer [*NASDAQ symbol*] (NQ)
**New World A** ... New World Archaeological Record [*A publication*]
**New World R** ... New World Review [*A publication*]
**New W R** .... New World Review [*A publication*]
**New York** ... New York Magazine [*A publication*]
**New York Acad Sci Trans** ... New York Academy of Sciences. Transactions [*A publication*]
**New York Att'y Gen Annual Rep** ... New York Attorney General Reports [*A publication*] (DLA)
**New York City BA Bul** ... Bulletin. Association of the Bar of the City of New York [*A publication*] (DLA)
**New York City Board Education Curriculum Bull** ... New York City Board of Education. Curriculum Bulletins [*A publication*]
**New York J Med** ... New York State Journal of Medicine [*A publication*]
**New York Law School Law R** ... New York Law School. Law Review [*A publication*]
**New York R** ... New York Court of Appeals Reports [*A publication*] (DLA)
**New York Rep** ... New York Court of Appeals Reports [*A publication*] (DLA)
**New York State Mus and Sci Service Map and Chart Ser** ... New York State Museum and Science Service. Map and Chart Series [*A publication*]
**New York State Mus and Sci Service Mem** ... New York State Museum and Science Service. Memoir [*A publication*]
**New York Supp** ... New York Supplement [*A publication*] (DLA)
**New York Univ J Internat Law and Politics** ... New York University. Journal of International Law and Politics [*A publication*]
**New York Univ Law R** ... New York University. Law Review [*A publication*]
**New York Water Resources Comm Bull** ... New York Conservation Department. Water Resources Commission. Bulletin [*A publication*]
**New York Water Resources Comm Rept Inv** ... New York Conservation Department. Water Resources Commission. Report of Investigation [*A publication*]
**New Y Q** .... New York Quarterly [*A publication*]
**New Y R B** ... New York Review of Books [*A publication*]
**New Yugo L** ... New Yugoslav Law [*A publication*] (DLA)
**NEWZAD** ... New Zealand Army Detachment (CINC)
**New Zealand Archt** ... New Zealand Architect [*A publication*]
**New Zealand Econ Pap** ... New Zealand Economic Papers [*A publication*]
**New Zealand Jour Geology and Geophysics** ... New Zealand Journal of Geology and Geophysics [*A publication*]
**New Zealand J Publ Adm** ... New Zealand Journal of Public Administration [*A publication*]
**New Zealand J Sci Tech** ... New Zealand Journal of Science and Technology [*A publication*]
**New Zealand Math Mag** ... New Zealand Mathematics Magazine [*A publication*]
**New Zealand MJ** ... New Zealand Medical Journal [*A publication*]
**New Zealand Oper Res** ... New Zealand Operational Research [*A publication*]
**New Zealand Soc Wker** ... New Zealand Social Worker [*A publication*]
**New Zeal Dep Sci Ind Res Bull** ... New Zealand. Department of Scientific and Industrial Research. Bulletin [*A publication*]
**New Zeal Geol Surv Bull** ... New Zealand. Geological Survey. Bulletin [*A publication*]
**New Zeal J Geol Geophys** ... New Zealand Journal of Geology and Geophysics [*A publication*]
**New Zeal Jur R** ... New Zealand Jurist Reports [*A publication*] (DLA)
**New Zeal L** ... New Zealand Law Reports [*A publication*] (DLA)
**New Zeal LJ** ... New Zealand Law Journal [*A publication*]
**New Zeal LR** ... New Zealand Law Reports [*A publication*] (DLA)
**New Zeal Med J** ... New Zealand Medical Journal [*A publication*]
**NEX** .......... National Exchange, Inc. [*McLean, VA*] [*Telecommunications*] (TSSD)
**NEX** .......... Nonepoxide Xanthophyll [*Organic chemistry*]
**NEX** .......... Nose to Ear to Xiphoid [*Medicine*]
**N EX** ......... Not Exceeding [*Freight*]
**NEXAFS** .... Near-Edge X-Ray Absorption Fine Structure [*For study of surfaces*]
**NEXAIR** .... Next Generation Upper Air System [*National Weather Service*]
**NEXCO** ..... National Association of Export Companies [*New York, NY*] (EA)
**NEXIS** ....... [*A*] newspaper database [*Mead Data Control*]
**NEXRAD** .. Next Generation Weather RADAR [*National Weather Service*]
**NEXT** ........ Hooker Enterprises, Inc. [*Naples, FL*] [*NASDAQ symbol*] (NQ)
**NEXT** ........ Nationwide Evaluation of X-Ray Trends
**NEXT** ........ NATO Experimental Tactics (NATG)
**NEXT** ........ Near-End Crosstalk [*Bell System*]
**NEXT** ........ New/Experimental Techniques (MCD)
**Next Year** ... Next Year Country [*A publication*]
**NEXUS** ...... Nature and Earth United with Science [*Brand of hair products*]
**NEY** .......... Neomycin Egg Yolk [*Agar*] [*Microbiology*]
**NEY** .......... Neyland [*British depot code*]
**NEY** .......... Northeastern Yiddish [*Language, etc.*] (BJA)
**NEYO** ........ New York City National Park Service Group
**Nezelezne Kovy Technickoekon Zpravodaj** ... Nezelezne Kovy. Technickoekonomicky Zpravodaj [*Czechoslovakia*] [*A publication*]
**NEZP** ......... Nezperce Railroad Co. [*AAR code*]
**NEZSA** ...... Bulletin. New Zealand Department of Scientific and Industrial Research [*A publication*]
**NEZTA** ...... New Zealand Veterinary Journal [*A publication*]
**NF** ............. Eaton Laboratories, Inc. [*Research code symbol*]
**NF** ............. Fujisawa Pharmaceutical Co. [*Japan*] [*Research code symbol*]
**NF** ............. Nafcillin [*An antibiotic*]
**nF** .............. Nanofarad
**NF** ............. Narodni Fronta [*National Front*] [*Czechoslovakia*] [*Political party*] (PPE)
**NF** ............. National Airways Corp. [*South Africa*] [*ICAO designator*] (FAAC)
**NF** ............. National Fine [*Thread*]
**NF** ............. National Formulary [*A publication listing standard drugs*]
**NF** ............. National Foundation
**NF** ............. National Front [*British*]
**NF** ............. Natural Flood (MCD)
**NF** ............. Natural Food (MCD)
**NF** ............. Near Face [*Technical drawings*]
**NF** ............. Nebramycin Factor [*An antibacterial compound*]
**NF** ............. Neerlandia Franciskana [*A publication*]
**NF** ............. Negro Female
**NF** ............. Neighborhood Final Fade
**NF** ............. Nephritic Factor [*Clinical medicine*]
**NF** ............. Nested or Flat [*Freight*]
**NF** ............. Neue Folge [*New Series*] [*Bibliography*] [*German*]
**NF** ............. Neue Forschungen [*A publication*]
**NF** ............. Neues Forum [*A publication*]
**NF** ............. Neurofibromatosis [*Medicine*]
**NF** ............. Neurofibromatosis, Inc. [*An association*] (EA)
**NF** ............. Neurofilament [*Neurophysiology*]
**NF** ............. Neutral Fraction
**NF** ............. Neutron Flux [*Nuclear energy*] (NRCH)

NF ............. New French [*Language, etc.*] (ROG)
NF ............. New York Folklore. Quarterly [*A publication*]
NF ............. Newfoundland [*with Labrador, a Canadian province*] [*Postal code*]
NF ............. Newfoundland Reports [*A publication*] (DLA)
NF ............. Newspaper Fund (EA)
NF ............. Nichibei Fujinkai [*An association*] (EA)
NF ............. Niederfrequenz [*Audio Frequency*] [*German military - World War II*]
NF ............. Nieman Foundation (EA)
NF ............. Nigerian Field [*A publication*]
NF ............. Night Fighter Aircraft
NF ............. Nitrofluoranthene [*Organic chemistry*]
NF ............. No Fly [*Shrewd tradesman*] [*Slang*] [*British*] (DSUE)
NF ............. No Fool
NF ............. No Form (AAG)
NF ............. No Funds [*Banking*]
NF ............. Nobel Foundation (EA)
NF ............. Noise Factor
NF ............. Noise Figure
NF ............. Noise Frequency (MSA)
NF ............. Noise Fuse (MCD)
NF ............. None Found [*Medicine*]
NF ............. Nonferrous
NF ............. Nonfiler [*IRS*]
NF ............. Nonfiltered
NF ............. Nonfundable
NF ............. Nonwhite Female
NF ............. Noranda Forest, Inc. [*Toronto Stock Exchange symbol*] [*Vancouver Stock Exchange symbol*]
NF ............. Nordiska Fabriksarbetarefederationen [*Nordic Federation of Factory Workers Unions - NFFWU*] (EAIO)
NF ............. Nordmanns-Forbunder [*Norsemen's Federation*] (EA)
NF ............. Norfolk [*Virginia*] [*Navy Yard*]
NF ............. Norfolk Island [*ANSI two-letter standard code*] (CNC)
NF ............. Normal Flow [*Medicine*]
NF ............. Normal Formula
NF ............. Norman French [*Language, etc.*]
NF ............. Norsemen's Federation (EA)
NF ............. Norsk Front [*Norwegian Front*] (PD)
NF ............. North Following [*Astronomy*]
NF ............. Northeast Folklore [*A publication*]
NF ............. Northern French [*Language, etc.*] (ROG)
NF ............. Northland Free Press [*Slave Lake, Alberta*] [*A publication*]
NF ............. Northumberland Fusiliers [*British military*] (DMA)
NF ............. Nose Fairing [*Missiles*]
NF ............. Nose Fuse [*Aviation*]
NF ............. Not Fertilized
NF ............. Not Fordable [*Maps and charts*]
NF ............. Not Found [*Telephone listing*] [*Telecommunications*] (TEL)
NF ............. Nouveau Franc [*New Franc*] [*Monetary unit*] [*Introduced in 1960*] [*France*]
NF ............. Nuclear Factor [*Cytology*]
NF ............. Nuclear Red Fast [*A dye*]
NF ............. Nutrition Foundation [*Later, ILSI-NF*]
NF ............. Royal Northumberland Fusiliers [*Military unit*] [*British*]
N3F ............ National Fantasy Fan Federation (EA)
NFA ........... Cast Metals Association (EA)
NFA ........... Nachrichten fuer Aussenhandel [*A publication*]
NFA ........... Naga Federal Army [*India*]
NFA ........... Natal Field Artillery [*British military*] (DMA)
NFA ........... National Faculty Association of Community and Junior Colleges [*Later, NEA Higher Education Council*]
NFA ........... National Families in Action (EA)
NFA ........... National Film Archive [*British Film Institute*]
NFA ........... National Film, Television, and Sound Archives [*Ottawa*] [*UTLAS symbol*]
NFA ........... National Fire Academy
NFA ........... National Firearms Act
NFA ........... National Firearms Association [*Canada*]
NFA ........... National Fitness Association [*Later, NHCA*] (EA)
NFA ........... National Florist Association (EA)
NFA ........... National Flute Association (EA)
NFA ........... National Food Administration
NFA ........... National Food Authority [*Philippines*] (DS)
NFA ........... National Foremen's Association [*A union*] [*British*]
NFA ........... National Forensic Association (EA)
NFA ........... National Foundation for Asthma (EA)
NFA ........... National Foundry Association (EA)
NFA ........... National Freedom Academy (EA)
NFA ........... National Front of Ahvaz [*Iran*]
NFA ........... National Frumps of America (EA)
NFA ........... National Futures Association (EA)
NFA ........... Native Fish Australia
NFA ........... Natural Food Associates (EA)
NFA ........... Naval Fuel Annex
NFA ........... New Farmers of America [*Later, FFA*] (EA)
NFA ........... New Fighter Aircraft (MCD)
NFA ........... New South Wales Farmers' Association [*Australia*]
NFA ........... Night Fighter Association
NFA ........... Nitrogen Filling Assembly
NFA ........... Nixon Family Association (EA)
NFA ........... No Fire Area [*Military*] (INF)
NFA ........... No Fixed Abode
NFA ........... No Further Action
NFA ........... Non-Financial Agreement (OICC)
NFA ........... Nondeterministic Finite Automaton
NFA ........... Nonhydroxylated Fatty Acid [*Organic chemistry*]
NFA ........... Northwest Festivals Association (EA)
NFA ........... Northwest Fisheries Association (EA)
NFA ........... Northwest Forestry Association (EA)
NFA ........... Not for Attribution [*Military*]
NFA ........... Nuclear Free America (EA)
NFAA ........ National Federation of Advertising Agencies [*Later, IFAA*] (EA)
NFAA ........ National Field Archery Association (EA)
NFAA ........ National Forum for the Advancement of Aquatics (EA)
NFAA ........ National Foundation for Advancement in the Arts (EA)
NFAA ........ Nordic Forwarding Agents Association (EA)
NFAA ........ Northern Federation of Advertisers Associations [*Stockholm, Sweden*] (EAIO)
NFAA ........ Nuclear Fuel Assurance Act
NFAAUM ... National Federation of Asian American United Methodists (EA)
NFAC ........ Arnolds Cove Public Library, Newfoundland [*Library symbol*] [*National Library of Canada*] (NLC)
NFAC ........ National Food and Agricultural Council [*Philippines*] (DS)
NFAC ........ National Foreign Assessment Center [*CIA*]
NFAC ........ National Foundation for Asthmatic Children at Tucson [*Later, NFA*] (EA)
NFAC ........ National Franchise Association Coalition (EA)
NFAC ........ National Full-Scale Aerodynamics Complex [*Ames Research Center, CA*] [*NASA*]
NFAC ........ Naval Facilities Engineering Command Headquarters
NFAC ........ NFA Corporation [*NASDAQ symbol*] (NQ)
NFACJC .... National Faculty Association of Community and Junior Colleges [*Later, NEA Higher Education Council*]
NFAF ......... Naval Fleet Auxiliary Force
NFAH ........ National Federation of American Hungarians (EA)
NFAH ........ National Foundation on the Arts and Humanities
NFAHA ..... National Foundation on the Arts and Humanities Act [*1965*]
NFaiB ........ Board of Cooperative Educational Services - Monroe I, Fairport, NY [*Library symbol*] [*Library of Congress*] (LCLS)
NFAIO ...... National Federation of Asian Indian Organizations in America [*Later, NFIAA*] (EA)
NFAIS ....... National Federation of Abstracting and Information Services (EA)
NFAIS Newsl ... NFAIS [*National Federation of Abstracting and Indexing Services*] Newsletter [*United States*] [*A publication*]
NFAM ....... Network File Access Method
NFANA ...... Norwegian Fjord Association of North America (EA)
NFAOD ..... Numerical Functional Analysis and Optimization [*A publication*]
NFAP ......... Nerve Fiber Action Potentials [*Neurophysiology*]
NFAP ......... Network File Access Protocol
NFAP ......... Nuclear Free Australia Party [*Political party*] (ADA)
NFar .......... Farmingdale Public Library, Farmingdale, NY [*Library symbol*] [*Library of Congress*] (LCLS)
NFarB ........ BioResearch, Inc., Farmingdale, NY [*Library symbol*] [*Library of Congress*] (LCLS)
NFarEE ..... East Memorial Elementary School, Farmingdale, NY [*Library symbol*] [*Library of Congress*] (LCLS)
NFarF ........ Fairchild-Hiller Corp. [*Later, Fairchild Industries, Inc.*], Republic Aviation Division, Farmingdale, NY [*Library symbol*] [*Library of Congress*] (LCLS)
NFARS ...... NORAD Forward Automated Reporting System (MCD)
NFarUA ..... State University of New York, Agricultural and Technical College at Farmingdale, Farmingdale, NY [*Library symbol*] [*Library of Congress*] (LCLS)
NFASG ...... National Fashion Accessories Salesmen's Guild (EA)
NFAT ........ Nuclear Factor of Activated T-Cells [*Genetics*]
NFay .......... Fayetteville Free Library, Fayetteville, NY [*Library symbol*] [*Library of Congress*] (LCLS)
NFB ........... Booth Memorial Hospital, Flushing, NY [*Library symbol*] [*Library of Congress*] (LCLS)
NFB ........... Mount Clemens, MI [*Location identifier*] [*FAA*] (FAAL)
NFB ........... National Federation of the Blind (EA)
NFB ........... National Film Board [*of Canada*]
NFB ........... National Film Board of Canada [*UTLAS symbol*]
NFB ........... Naval Frontier Base
NFB ........... Negative Feedback (DEN)
NFB ........... New Fibers International [*Vancouver Stock Exchange symbol*]
NFB ........... Niagara Frontier Tariff Bureau, Inc., Buffalo NY [*STAC*]
NFB ........... Nonfermenting Bacteria
NFB ........... North Fork Bancorp [*NYSE symbol*] (SPSG)
NFBA ........ National Family Business Association [*Tarzana, CA*] (EA)
NFBA ........ National Farm Borrowers Association (EA)
NFBA ........ National Food Brokers Association (EA)
NFBA ........ National Frame Builders Association (EA)
NFBC ........ National Family Business Council [*Northbrook, IL*] (EA)
NFBC ........ National Film Board of Canada

**NFBC**......... Newfoundland Base Command [*Army*] [*World War II*]
**NFBF**......... Bishops Falls Public Library, Newfoundland [*Library symbol*] [*National Library of Canada*] (NLC)
**NFBF**......... National Farm Bureau Federation
**NFBI**.......... Bell Island Public Library, Newfoundland [*Library symbol*] [*National Library of Canada*] (NLC)
**NFBI**.......... Netherlands Flower-Bulb Institute [*Defunct*] (EA)
**NFBI**.......... Nonresidential Fixed Business Investment (MCD)
**NFBN**......... National Food Bank Network (EA)
**NFBO**......... Bonavista Public Library, Newfoundland [*Library symbol*] [*National Library of Canada*] (NLC)
**NFBOT**...... Botwood Public Library, Newfoundland [*Library symbol*] [*National Library of Canada*] (NLC)
**NFBPA**...... National Forum for Black Public Administrators (EA)
**NFBPT**...... National Federation for Biblio/Poetry Therapy (EA)
**NFBPWC**.. National Federation of Business and Professional Women's Clubs (EA)
**NFBQ**......... Rural District Memorial Library, Badgers Quay, Newfoundland [*Library symbol*] [*National Library of Canada*] (NLC)
**NFBR**......... Bay Roberts Public Library, Newfoundland [*Library symbol*] [*National Library of Canada*] (NLC)
**NFBRI**....... Brigus Public Library, Newfoundland [*Library symbol*] [*National Library of Canada*] (NLC)
**NFBS**......... National Freehold Building Society [*British*]
**NFBTE**...... National Federation of Building Trades Employers [*British*] (DCTA)
**NFBTO**...... National Federation of Building Trades Operatives [*British*]
**NFBU**......... Buchans Public Library, Newfoundland [*Library symbol*] [*National Library of Canada*] (NLC)
**NFBU**......... National Federation of Bus Users [*British*]
**NFBU**......... National Fire Brigades Union (ROG)
**NFBUR**...... Burgeo Public Library, Newfoundland [*Library symbol*] [*National Library of Canada*] (NLC)
**NFBURI**.... Burin Public Library, Newfoundland [*Library symbol*] [*National Library of Canada*] (NLC)
**NFBV**......... Baie Verte Public Library, Newfoundland [*Library symbol*] [*National Library of Canada*] (NLC)
**NFBWA**..... National Federation of Buddhist Women's Associations [*Later, BCAFBWA*] (EA)
**NFBWW**... Nordic Federation of Building and Wood Workers (EA)
**NFC**........... Carbonear Public Library, Newfoundland [*Library symbol*] [*National Library of Canada*] (NLC)
**NFC**........... Name Formula Card
**NFC**........... National Farm Coalition (EA)
**NFC**........... National Federated Craft (EA)
**NFC**........... National Fenestration Council [*Later, PGMC*] (EA)
**NFC**........... National Fertiliser Corporation [*Thailand*]
**NFC**........... National Film Carriers (EA)
**NFC**........... National Fire Code
**NFC**........... National Firebird Club (EA)
**NFC**........... National Food Conference Association (EA)
**NFC**........... National Football Conference [*of NFL*]
**NFC**........... National Forensic Center (EA)
**NFC**........... National Fraternal Congress [*Later, NFCA*]
**NFC**........... National Freight Corp. [*British*]
**NFC**........... National Fructose Center (EA)
**NFC**........... National Fund Chairman [*or Co-chairman*] [*Red Cross*]
**NFC**........... Navy Federal Credit Union
**NFC**........... Navy Finance Center
**NFC**........... Negative Factor Counting
**NFC**........... Negative Feedback Circuit
**nfc**............. Newfoundland [*MARC country of publication code*] [*Library of Congress*] (LCCP)
**NFC**........... News for Farmer Cooperatives [*A publication*]
**NFC**........... Newsline Fan Club (EA)
**NFC**........... Newspaper Features Council (EA)
**NFC**........... NFC PLC ADS [*AMEX symbol*] (SPSG)
**NFC**........... Nighttime Fatal Crash
**NFC**........... No Further Clearance Required (KSC)
**NFC**........... No Further Consequences (NRCH)
**NFC**........... Nordisk Forening for Cellforskning [*Nordic Society for Cell Biology - NSCB*] (EAIO)
**NFC**........... Nose Fairing Container [*Missiles*]
**NFC**........... Not Favorably Considered
**NFCA**......... Carmanville Public Library, Newfoundland [*Library symbol*] [*National Library of Canada*] (NLC)
**NFCA**......... National Fraternal Congress of America [*Naperville, IL*] (EA)
**NFCA**......... National Fuel Credit Association [*Defunct*]
**NFCA**......... Nonfuel Core Array [*Nuclear energy*] (NRCH)
**NFCA**......... Northern Fishing Companies' Association [*Australia*]
**NFCAA**...... National Fencing Coaches Association of America (EA)
**NFCADA**... National Family Council Against Drug Abuse [*Formerly, NFCDA*] (EA)
**NFCARW**... National Federation of Cuban-American Republican Women (EA)
**NFCAT**...... Joseph E. Clouter Memorial Library, Catalina, Newfoundland [*Library symbol*] [*National Library of Canada*] (NLC)
**NFCB**......... Corner Brook City Public Library, Newfoundland [*Library symbol*] [*National Library of Canada*] (NLC)
**NFCB**......... National Federation of Community Broadcasters (EA)
**NFCBF**...... Newfoundland Department of Forest Resources and Lands, Corner Brook, New Foundland [*Library symbol*] [*National Library of Canada*] (NLC)
**NFCBFT**.... Fisher Institute of Applied Arts and Technology, Corner Brook, Newfoundland [*Library symbol*] [*National Library of Canada*] (NLC)
**NFCBM**..... Sir Wilfred Grenfell College, Memorial University, Corner Brook, Newfoundland [*Library symbol*] [*National Library of Canada*] (NLC)
**NFCBR**...... Regional Library, Corner Brook, Newfoundland [*Library symbol*] [*National Library of Canada*] (NLC)
**NFCBRO**.. National Federation of Citizen Band Radio Operators (EA)
**NFCBW**..... Western Memorial Hospital, Corner Brook, Newfoundland [*Library symbol*] [*National Library of Canada*] (NLC)
**NFCC**......... National Farm-City Council (EA)
**NFCC**......... National Foundation for Consumer Credit [*Silver Spring, MD*] (EA)
**NFCC**......... National Free Clinic Council [*Superseded by NCAHCP*]
**NFCCE**...... National Fellowship of Child Care Executives (EA)
**NFCCS**...... National Federation of Catholic College Students [*Defunct*] (EA)
**NFCDA**..... National Family Council on Drug Addiction [*Later, NFCADA*] (EA)
**NFCDCU**.. National Federation of Community Development Credit Unions [*New York, NY*] (EA)
**NFCE**......... Centreville Public Library, Newfoundland [*Library symbol*] [*National Library of Canada*] (NLC)
**NFCEO**..... National Foundation for Conservation and Environmental Officers (EA)
**NFCF**......... Churchill Falls Public Library, Newfoundland [*Library symbol*] [*National Library of Canada*] (NLC)
**NFCG**......... National Federation of Consumer Groups [*British*] (ILCA)
**NFCGC**...... National Federation of Coffee Growers of Colombia [*See also FNCC*] (EA)
**NFCGH**..... Carbonear General Hospital, Newfoundland [*Library symbol*] [*National Library of Canada*] (NLC)
**NFCH**......... Cow Head Public Library, Newfoundland [*Library symbol*] [*National Library of Canada*] (NLC)
**NFCI**.......... Change Islands Public Library, Newfoundland [*Library symbol*] [*National Library of Canada*] (NLC)
**NFCJ**.......... National Forum on Criminal Justice [*Formerly, NICD*] [*Inactive*] (EA)
**NFCL**......... Clarenville Public Library, Newfoundland [*Library symbol*] [*National Library of Canada*] (NLC)
**NFC-L**....... National Fisheries Center - Leetown [*Department of the Interior*] (GRD)
**NFCM**....... National Front Constitutional Movement [*British*]
**NFCO**........ Cormack Public Library, Newfoundland [*Library symbol*] [*National Library of Canada*] (NLC)
**NFCP**......... Channel/Port Aux Basques Public Library, Newfoundland [*Library symbol*] [*National Library of Canada*] (NLC)
**NFCPG**...... National Federation of Catholic Physicians' Guilds (EA)
**NFCPO**...... National Forum of Catholic Parent Organizations [*Defunct*] (EA)
**NFCR**......... 1963 Falcon Convertible Registry (EA)
**NFCR**......... National Foundation for Cancer Research (EA)
**NFCRC**...... National Fisheries Contaminant Research Center (EA)
**NFCS**......... National Federation of Catholic Seminarians [*Defunct*] (EA)
**NFCS**......... Night Fire [*Rifle*] Control Sight
**NFCS**......... Nuclear Forces Communications Satellite
**NFCSG**...... Cape St. George Public Library, Newfoundland [*Library symbol*] [*National Library of Canada*] (NLC)
**NFCT**......... Nonfederal Control Tower [*For chart use only*]
**NFCTA**...... National Federation of Continuative Teachers' Associations [*British*]
**NFCTA**...... National Fibre Can and Tube Association [*Later, CCTI*] (EA)
**NFCU**......... Navy Federal Credit Union
**NFCUS**...... National Federation of Canadian University Students
**NFCW**........ Cartwright Public Library, Newfoundland [*Library symbol*] [*National Library of Canada*] (BIB)
**NFCYM**..... National Federation for Catholic Youth Ministry (EA)
**NFD**........... Dover Public Library, Newfoundland [*Library symbol*] [*National Library of Canada*] (BIB)
**NFD**........... National Faculty Directory [*A publication*]
**NFD**........... National Fax Directory [*A publication*]
**NFD**........... National Federation for Decency (EA)
**NFD**........... Naval Fuel Depot
**NFD**........... Neurofibrillary Degeneration [*Medicine*]
**NFD**........... Neutron Flux Density [*Nuclear energy*]
**NFD**........... Newfoundland [*with Labrador, a Canadian province*]
**NFD**........... Newfoundland Tracking Station
**NFD**........... No Fixed Date
**NFD**........... No Foreign Dissemination [*Intelligence classification*] (MCD)
**NFD**........... Norfolk, Franklin & Danville Railway Co. [*AAR code*]
**NFD**........... Northern Frontier District [*Kenya*]
**NFDA**......... National Fastener Distributors Association (EA)
**NFDA**......... National Food Distributors Association (EA)
**NFDA**......... National Funeral Directors Association (EA)
**NFDC**......... Dark Cove Public Library, Newfoundland [*Library symbol*] [*National Library of Canada*] (NLC)
**NFDC**......... National Father's Day Committee (EA)

**NFDC** ........ National Fertilizer Development Center [*Tennessee Valley Authority*] [*Muscle Shoals, AL*]
**NFDC** ........ National Flight Data Center [*FAA*]
**NFDCAMD** ... National Food, Drug, and Cosmetic Association of Manufacturers and Distributors [*Defunct*] (EA)
**NFDD** ........ National Flight Data Digest (FAAC)
**NFDF** ........ National Flag Day Foundation (EA)
**NFDH** ........ Daniels Harbour Public Library, Newfoundland [*Library symbol*] [*National Library of Canada*] (NLC)
**NFDH** ........ National Foundation of Dentistry for the Handicapped (EA)
**NFDL** ........ Deer Lake Public Library, Newfoundland [*Library symbol*] [*National Library of Canada*] (NLC)
**NFDM** ........ Nonfat Dry Milk
**NFDMA** .... National Funeral Directors and Morticians Association (EA)
**NFDRS** ..... National Fire Danger Rating System [*US Forest Service*]
**NFDW** ....... National Federation of Democratic Women (EA)
**NFE** .......... Fentress, VA [*Location identifier*] [*FAA*] (FAAL)
**NFE** .......... National Faculty Exchange (EA)
**NFE** .......... Naval Facilities Engineering Command, Alexandria, VA [*OCLC symbol*] (OCLC)
**NFE** .......... Network Front End
**NFE** .......... Nitrogen-Free Extract [*Analytical chemistry*]
**NFE** .......... Nonformal Education
**NFE** .......... Nose Fairing Exit [*Missiles*]
**NFE** .......... Not Fully Equipped [*of aircraft*] [*Air Force*]
**NFEA** ........ National Federation of Export Associations [*New York, NY*] (EA)
**NFEA** ........ Newspaper Farm Editors of America (EA)
**NFEA** ........ Non-Fleet Experienced Aviator (NVT)
**NFEAC** ...... National Foundation for Education in American Citizenship (EA)
**NFEC** ........ National Food and Energy Council (EA)
**NFEC** ........ National Foundation for Environmental Control (EA)
**NFEC** ........ Naval Facilities Engineering Command [*Formerly, Bureau of Yards and Docks*] (IEEE)
**NFEC** ........ Newspaper Food Editors Conference (EA)
**NFECC** ...... National Fusion Energy Computer Center [*Lawrence Livermore National Laboratory*] (MCD)
**NFED** ........ National Foundation for Ectodermal Dysplasias (EA)
**NFEFD** ...... Newsletter. Fusion Energy Foundation [*A publication*]
**NFER** ........ National Foundation for Educational Research in England and Wales (IID)
**NFER** ........ National Foundation for Eye Research (EA)
**NFERF** ...... National Fisheries Education and Research Foundation (EA)
**NFETA** ...... National Foundry and Engineering Training Association [*British*]
**NFEW** ........ National Forum for Executive Women [*Washington, DC*] (EA)
**NFEWA** ..... Newspaper Food Editors and Writers Association (EA)
**NFEXF** ...... New Frontier Petroleum Corp. [*NASDAQ symbol*] (NQ)
**NFF** ........... Fogo Public Library, Newfoundland [*Library symbol*] [*National Library of Canada*] (NLC)
**NFF** ........... Jacksonville, FL [*Location identifier*] [*FAA*] (FAAL)
**NFF** ........... Natal Field Force [*British military*] (DMA)
**NFF** ........... National Fatherland Front [*Political party*] [*Afghanistan*] (FEA)
**NFF** ........... National Federation of Fishermen [*Inactive*] (EA)
**NFF** ........... National Fitness Foundation (EA)
**NFF** ........... National Flag Foundation (EA)
**NFF** ........... National Football Foundation and Hall of Fame (EA)
**NFF** ........... National Forum Foundation (EA)
**NFF** ........... NATO [*North Atlantic Treaty Organization*] Review [*A publication*]
**NF & F** ....... Natural Food and Farming [*A publication*]
**NFF** ........... Naval Fuel Facility
**NFF** ........... Nemzeti Fueggetlensegi Front [*National Independence Front*] [*Hungary*] [*Political party*] (PPE)
**NFF** ........... New Forests Fund (EA)
**NFF** ........... No Fault Found (MCD)
**Nff** ............ Nordisk Forening for Folkendansforskning [*Nordic Association for Folk Dance Research*] (EAIO)
**NFF** ........... Nuclear Freeze Foundation (EA)
**NFF** ........... Numbered Fleet Flagship [*Navy*]
**NFFA** ......... Ba [*Fiji*] [*ICAO location identifier*] (ICLI)
**NFFA** ......... National Flying Farmers Association [*Later, International Flying Farmers*]
**NFFA** ......... National Folk Festival Association [*Later, National Council for the Traditional Arts*]
**NFFA** ......... National Frozen Food Association (EA)
**NFFAO** ...... National FFA [*Future Farmers of America*] Organization (EA)
**NFFC** ......... Nancy Fisher Fan Club (EA)
**NFFC** ......... National Family Farm Coalition (EA)
**NFFC** ......... National Film Finance Corporation [*British*]
**NFFDA** ...... National Frozen Food Distributors Association [*Later, NFFA*]
**NFFDF** ...... National Fraternal Flag Day Foundation (EA)
**NFFE** ......... National Federation of Federal Employees (EA)
**NFFF** ......... Nandi [*Fiji*] [*ICAO location identifier*] (ICLI)
**NFFF** ......... National Fantasy Fan Federation
**NFFGB** ...... National Federation of Flemish Giant Breeders [*Later, NFFGRB*]
**NFFGRB** ... National Federation of Flemish Giant Rabbit Breeders (EA)
**NFFH** ........ Fox Harbour Public Library, Newfoundland [*Library symbol*] [*National Library of Canada*] (NLC)
**NFFI** .......... Not Fit for Issue [*Navy*]
**NFFL** ......... Northern Forest Fire Laboratory [*Later, Intermountain Fire Sciences Laboratory*] [*Research center*] (RCD)
**NFFN** ........ Nandi/International [*Fiji*] [*ICAO location identifier*] (ICLI)
**NFFO** ........ Fortune Public Library, Newfoundland [*Library symbol*] [*National Library of Canada*] (NLC)
**NFFO** ........ Malolo Lailai [*Fiji*] [*ICAO location identifier*] (ICLI)
**NFFO** ........ National Federation of Fishermen's Organisations (EAIO)
**NFFR** ........ Freshwater Public Library, Newfoundland [*Library symbol*] [*National Library of Canada*] (NLC)
**NFFR** ........ National Foundation for Facial Reconstruction (EA)
**NFFR** ........ Rabi [*Fiji*] [*ICAO location identifier*] (ICLI)
**NFFS** ......... National Foundation of Funeral Service (EA)
**NFFS** ......... Non-Ferrous Founders Society (EA)
**NFFWU** ..... Nordic Federation of Factory Workers Unions (EA)
**NFG** .......... Gander Public Library, Newfoundland [*Library symbol*] [*National Library of Canada*] (NLC)
**NFG** .......... Nagaland Federal Government [*India*]
**NFG** .......... National Fuel Gas Co. [*NYSE symbol*] (SPSG)
**NFG** .......... Northwest Fruit Growers (EA)
**NFG** .......... Oceanside, CA [*Location identifier*] [*FAA*] (FAAL)
**NFGA** ........ Garnish Public Library, Newfoundland [*Library symbol*] [*National Library of Canada*] (NLC)
**NFGAU** ..... Gaultois Public Library, Newfoundland [*Library symbol*] [*National Library of Canada*] (BIB)
**NFGB** ........ Grand Bank Public Library, Newfoundland [*Library symbol*] [*National Library of Canada*] (NLC)
**NFGBM** .... Medical Library, Melville Hospital, Goose-Bay, Newfoundland [*Library symbol*] [*National Library of Canada*] (BIB)
**NFGBM** .... National Fellowship of Grace Brethren Ministers (EA)
**NFGC** ........ National Federation of Grain Cooperatives [*Later, NCFC*] (EA)
**NFGCA** ..... National Federation of Grandmother Clubs of America (EA)
**NFGF** ........ Regional Library, Grand Falls, Newfoundland [*Library symbol*] [*National Library of Canada*] (NLC)
**NFGFC** ...... Central Region Libraries, Grand Falls, Newfoundland [*Library symbol*] [*National Library of Canada*] (NLC)
**NFGFH** ..... Central Newfoundland Hospital, Grand Falls, Newfoundland [*Library symbol*] [*National Library of Canada*] (NLC)
**NFGFHA** .. Harmsworth Public Library, Grand Falls, Newfoundland [*Library symbol*] [*National Library of Canada*] (NLC)
**NFGJPH** ... James Paton Memorial Hospital, Gander, Newfoundland [*Library symbol*] [*National Library of Canada*] (NLC)
**NFGL** ........ Glenwood Public Library, Newfoundland [*Library symbol*] [*National Library of Canada*] (NLC)
**NFGLO** ..... Glovertown Public Library, Newfoundland [*Library symbol*] [*National Library of Canada*] (NLC)
**NFGMIC** ... National Federation of Grange Mutual Insurance Companies [*Glastonbury, CT*] (EA)
**NFGND** ..... National Foundation for Genetics and Neuromuscular Disease [*Later, NGF*]
**NFGNE** ..... National Fund for Graduate Nursing Education [*Defunct*]
**NFGO** ........ Goulds Public Library, Newfoundland [*Library symbol*] [*National Library of Canada*] (BIB)
**NFGOCM** ... National Forum of Greek Orthodox Church Musicians (EA)
**NFGOPC** ... National Federation of the Grand Order of Pachyderm Clubs (EA)
**NFGR** ........ Greenspond Public Library, Newfoundland [*Library symbol*] [*National Library of Canada*] (NLC)
**NFGS** ......... National Federation of Gramophone Societies (EAIO)
**NFH** .......... Holyrood Public Library, Newfoundland [*Library symbol*] [*National Library of Canada*] (BIB)
**NFH** .......... National Fish Hatchery
**NFH** .......... Native Field Hospital [*British military*] (DMA)
**NFHA** ........ National Fox Hunters Association (EA)
**NFHANA** ... Norwegian Fjord Horse Association of North America [*Later, NFANA*] (EA)
**NFHAS** ..... National Faculty of Humanities, Arts, and Sciences (EA)
**NFHB** ........ Harbour Breton Public Library, Newfoundland [*Library symbol*] [*National Library of Canada*] (NLC)
**NFHBA** ..... Hare Bay Public Library, Newfoundland [*Library symbol*] [*National Library of Canada*] (NLC)
**NFHC** ........ National Federation of Hispanics in Communication (EA)
**NFHC** ........ National Federation of Housing Counselors (EA)
**NFHC** ........ National Foot Health Council [*Defunct*] (EA)
**NFHC** ........ National Foundation for History of Chemistry (EA)
**NFHCF** ...... National Flotation Health Care Foundation (EA)
**NFHD** ........ National Foundation for the Handicapped and Disabled [*Defunct*] (EA)
**NFHE** ........ Hermitage Public Library, Newfoundland [*Library symbol*] [*National Library of Canada*] (NLC)
**NFHE** ........ Non-Irradiated Fuel Handling Equipment [*Nuclear energy*] (NRCH)
**NFHEA** ..... National Farm Home Editors Association [*Defunct*] (EA)
**NFHG** ........ Harbour Grace Public Library, Newfoundland [*Library symbol*] [*National Library of Canada*] (NLC)
**NFHH** ........ Harrys Harbour Public Library, Newfoundland [*Library symbol*] [*National Library of Canada*] (NLC)

**NFhM**........ Medical Society of the County of Queens, Forest Hills, NY [*Library symbol*] [*Library of Congress*] (LCLS)
**NFHO**........ Caaf Ho Nandi [*Fiji*] [*ICAO location identifier*] (ICLI)
**NFHO**........ National Federation of Housestaff Organizations (EA)
**NFHPER**... National Foundation for Health, Physical Education, and Recreation [*Defunct*]
**NFHRL**..... National Fish Health Research Laboratory [*Department of the Interior*] [*Kearneysville, WV*] (GRD)
**NFHTP**...... National Federation of Hebrew Teachers and Principals [*Defunct*] (EA)
**NFHV**........ Happy Valley Public Library, Newfoundland [*Library symbol*] [*National Library of Canada*] (NLC)
**NFI**............ Narrow Fabrics Institute (EA)
**NFI**............ National Fisheries Institute (EA)
**NFI**............ Natural Food Institute (EA)
**NFI**............ Naturfreunde-Internationale [*International Friends of Nature - IFN*] (EAIO)
**NFI**............ New Signet Resources [*Vancouver Stock Exchange symbol*]
**NFI**............ News Features of India [*Press agency*]
**NFI**............ NFIB [*National Federation of Independent Business*] Quarterly Economic Report [*A publication*]
**NFI**............ No Further Service (Inspections)
**NFI**............ Noise Figure Indicator
**NFI**............ Not Further Identified (MCD)
**NFIA**.......... National Feed Ingredients Association (EA)
**NFIA**.......... National Flood Insurers Association [*Defunct*] (EA)
**NFIA**.......... Nonappropriated Fund Instrumentalities Act
**NFIAA**....... National Federation of Indian American Associations (EA)
**NFIB**.......... National Federation of Independent Business [*San Mateo, CA*] (EA)
**NFIB**.......... National Foreign Intelligence Board [*Formerly, USIB*] [*Military*]
**NFIC**.......... National Foundation for Ileitis and Colitis (EA)
**NFICA**........ National Federation Interscholastic Coaches Association (EA)
**NFICSC**..... National Foundation for Ileitis and Colitis Sports Council (EA)
**NFID**.......... National Foundation for Infectious Diseases (EA)
**NFIE**.......... National Foundation for the Improvement of Education (EA)
**NFIL**.......... Nuclear Factor Interleukin [*Genetics*]
**NFIMA**....... National Federation Interscholastic Music Association (EA)
**NFIOA**...... National Federation Interscholastic Officials Association (EA)
**NFIP**.......... National Flood Insurance Program [*Federal Emergency Management Agency*]
**NFIP**.......... National Foreign Intelligence Program [*DoD*]
**NFIP**.......... National Foundation for Infantile Paralysis [*Later, MDBDF*]
**NFIR**.......... National Federation of Indian Railwaymen
**NFIRF**....... Nature Farming International Research Foundation (EAIO)
**NFIS**.......... Naval Fighting Instruction School
**NFisi**.......... Fishers Island Library Association, Fishers Island, NY [*Library symbol*] [*Library of Congress*] (LCLS)
**NFisk**......... Blodgett Memorial Library, Fishkill, NY [*Library symbol*] [*Library of Congress*] (LCLS)
**NFISYD**.... National Federation of Independent Scrap Yard Dealers (EA)
**NFIU**......... National Federation of Independent Unions (EA)
**NFJ**............ Milton, FL [*Location identifier*] [*FAA*] (FAAL)
**Nf J**............ Nordfriesisches Jahrbuch [*A publication*]
**NFJC**.......... National Foundation for Jewish Culture (EA)
**NFJGD**....... National Foundation for Jewish Genetic Diseases (EA)
**NFJGG**...... Neue Folge des Jahrbuchs der Goethe Gesellschaft [*A publication*]
**NFJM**........ National Foundation for Junior Museums [*Later, NSYF*]
**NFJMC**..... National Federation of Jewish Men's Clubs (EA)
**NFJU**......... Nordic Federation of Journalists' Unions (EAIO)
**NFK**........... Norfolk Island [*ANSI three-letter standard code*] (CNC)
**NFKK**........ Nordisk Forening for Klinisk Kemi [*Scandinavian Society for Clinical Chemistry - SSCC*] [*Helsinki, Finland*] (EAIO)
**NFKP**......... Kings Point Public Library, Newfoundland [*Library symbol*] [*National Library of Canada*] (NLC)
**NFL**........... Fallon, NV [*Location identifier*] [*FAA*] (FAAL)
**NFL**........... Labrador City Public Library, Newfoundland [*Library symbol*] [*National Library of Canada*] (NLC)
**NFL**........... National Federation of Laymen (EA)
**NFL**........... National Football League (EA)
**NFL**........... National Forensic League (EA)
**NFL**........... National Fund Leadership [*Group*] [*Red Cross*]
**NFL**........... Naval Standard Flange (MSA)
**NFL**........... New Found Land [*A publication*]
**NFL**........... Newfoundland Light & Power Co. Ltd. [*Toronto Stock Exchange symbol*]
**NFL**........... Newfoundland and Prince Edward Island Reports [*Maritime Law Book Company Ltd.*] [*Canada*] [*Information service or system*] (CRD)
**NFL**........... Newlands Field Laboratory [*University of Nevada - Reno*] [*Research center*] (RCD)
**NFL**........... No Fire Line [*Military*]
**NFL**........... No Phone Listed [*Cablegram marking*] [*British*]
**NFL**........... Normal Female Liver [*Hepatology*]
**NFL**........... Northaire Freight Lines Ltd. [*Davisburg, MI*] [*FAA designator*] (FAAC)
**NFL**........... Nurses for Laughter
**NFLA**......... L'Anse Au Loup Public Library, Newfoundland [*Library symbol*] [*National Library of Canada*] (NLC)
**NFLA**......... National Football League Alumni (EA)
**NFLA**......... National Front for the Liberation of Angola (EA)
**NFLCC**...... National Fishing Lure Collectors Club (EA)
**NFLCP**...... National Federation of Local Cable Programmers (EA)
**NFLD**........ Newfoundland [*with Labrador, a Canadian province*]
**Nfld**........... Newfoundland Supreme Court Decisions [*Canada*] [*A publication*] (DLA)
**Nfld LR**...... Newfoundland Law Reports [*A publication*] (DLA)
**Nfld & PEIR**... Newfoundland and Prince Edward Island Reports [*A publication*]
**Nfld Q**........ Newfoundland Quarterly [*A publication*]
**Nfld R**........ Newfoundland Reports [*A publication*] (DLA)
**Nfld Rev Stat**... Newfoundland Revised Statutes [*Canada*] [*A publication*] (DLA)
**Nfld Sel Cas**... Newfoundland Select Cases [*A publication*] (DLA)
**Nfld Stat**.... Newfoundland Statutes [*Canada*] [*A publication*] (DLA)
**NFLE**......... Lewisporte Public Library, Newfoundland [*Library symbol*] [*National Library of Canada*] (NLC)
**NFLF**......... National Family Life Foundation (EA)
**NFLF**......... Nylon Full-Line Filter
**NFLHB**...... Blow Me Down School/Public Library, Lark Harbour, Newfoundland [*Library symbol*] [*National Library of Canada*] (NLC)
**NFLI**.......... Northern Fraternal Life Insurance (EA)
**NFLIO**....... Training Department, Iron Ore Co. of Canada, Labrador City, Newfoundland [*Library symbol*] [*National Library of Canada*] (NLC)
**NFLO**........ Lourdes Public Library, Newfoundland [*Library symbol*] [*National Library of Canada*] (NLC)
**NFlp**.......... Floral Park Public Library, Floral Park, NY [*Library symbol*] [*Library of Congress*] (LCLS)
**NFLPA**...... National Football League Players Association (EA)
**NFLPA**...... National Free Lance Photographers Association (EA)
**NFLPN**...... National Federation of Licensed Practical Nurses (EA)
**NFLS**......... La Scie Public Library, Newfoundland [*Library symbol*] [*National Library of Canada*] (NLC)
**NFLS**......... Nicolet Federated Library System [*Library network*]
**NFLSV**...... National Front for the Liberation of South Vietnam
**NFLTHC**... National Foundation for Long Term Health Care (EA)
**NFLU**........ Lumsden Public Library, Newfoundland [*Library symbol*] [*National Library of Canada*] (NLC)
**NFM**.......... Conception Bay South Public Library, Manuels, Newfoundland [*Library symbol*] [*National Library of Canada*] (NLC)
**NFM**.......... Midland Lutheran College, Fremont, NE [*OCLC symbol*] (OCLC)
**NFM**.......... Narrowband Frequency Modulation [*Radio*]
**NFM**.......... Next Full Moon [*Freemasonry*] (ROG)
**NFM**.......... Noise Figure Meter
**NFM**.......... Nonferrous Metal
**NFM**.......... North-Finding Module (RDA)
**NFM**.......... Northern Fowl Mite [*Immunology*]
**NFMA**....... Marystown Public Library, Newfoundland [*Library symbol*] [*National Library of Canada*] (NLC)
**NFMA**....... National Footwear Manufacturers Association [*Later, FIA*]
**NFMA**....... Northwest Farm Managers Association (EA)
**NFMA**....... November, February, May, and August [*Denotes quarterly payments of interest or dividends in these months*] [*Business term*]
**NFMAA**.... National Federation Music Adjudicator Association (EA)
**NFMC**....... National Federation of Music Clubs (EA)
**NFMC**....... National Film Music Council [*Defunct*]
**NFMD**....... National Foundation for Muscular Dystrophy
**NFME**....... National Fund for Medical Education (EA)
**NFME**....... Nordic Federation for Medical Education (EAIO)
**NF Med Dt**... Naturforschung und Medizin in Deutschland [*A publication*]
**NFMHJ**..... John B. Wheeler Memorial Library, Musgrave Harbour, Newfoundland [*Library symbol*] [*National Library of Canada*] (NLC)
**NFMHO**.... National Foundation Manufactured Home Owners (EA)
**NFMLTA**.. National Federation of Modern Language Teachers Associations (EA)
**NFMM**...... National Fellowship of Methodist Musicians (EA)
**NFMN**...... National Fallout Monitoring Network
**NFMOA**.... National Fish Meal and Oil Association (EA)
**NFMP**....... Mount Pearl Public Library, Newfoundland [*Library symbol*] [*National Library of Canada*] (NLC)
**NFMP**....... Nonferrous Metal Powder
**NFMPC**..... Non-Ferrous Metals Producers Committee (EA)
**NFMR**....... National Foundation for Metabolic Research [*Defunct*] (EA)
**NFMR**....... Nordisk Forening for Medisinsk Radiologi [*Scandinavian Radiological Society - SRS*] (EAIO)
**NFMS**....... National Federation of Music Societies [*British*]
**NFMS**....... Navy Fleet Material Support (MCD)
**NFMS**....... Nitrogen Flow Measuring System
**NFMS**....... Noise Figure Meter System
**NFMSAEG**... Naval Fleet Missile System Analysis and Evaluation Group
**NFMSAEGA**... Naval Fleet Missile System Analysis and Evaluation Group Annex (MCD)
**NFN**.......... Newly Founded Nest [*Ornithology*]
**NFN**.......... No Form Necessary

**NFN** ........ No Further Need (MUGU)
**NFN** ........ Nouvelle Front NAZI [*New NAZI Front*] [*French*] (PD)
**NFNA** ........ National Flight Nurses Association (EA)
**NFNA** ........ Nausori/International [*Fiji*] [*ICAO location identifier*] (ICLI)
**NFNA** ........ Norris Arm Public Library, Newfoundland [*Library symbol*] [*National Library of Canada*] (NLC)
**NFNB** ........ Bureta [*Fiji*] [*ICAO location identifier*] (ICLI)
**NFND** ........ Deumba [*Fiji*] [*ICAO location identifier*] (ICLI)
**NFND** ........ National Foundation for Neuromuscular Diseases [*Later, NGF*] (EA)
**NFNG** ........ Ngau [*Fiji*] [*ICAO location identifier*] (ICLI)
**NFNH** ........ Lauthala Islands [*Fiji*] [*ICAO location identifier*] (ICLI)
**NFNID** ........ National Foundation for Non-Invasive Diagnostics (EA)
**NFNK** ........ Lakemba [*Fiji*] [*ICAO location identifier*] (ICLI)
**NFNL** ........ Lambasa [*Fiji*] [*ICAO location identifier*] (ICLI)
**NFNLA** ........ NFAIS [*National Federation of Abstracting and Indexing Services*] Newsletter [*A publication*]
**NFNLI** ........ Labrador Inuit Association, Nain, Newfoundland [*Library symbol*] [*National Library of Canada*] (NLC)
**NFNLI** ........ Labrador Unit Association, Nain, Newfoundland [*Library symbol*] [*National Library of Canada*] (NLC)
**NFNM** ........ Matei [*Fiji*] [*ICAO location identifier*] (ICLI)
**NFNN** ........ Vanuabalavu [*Fiji*] [*ICAO location identifier*] (ICLI)
**NFNO** ........ Koro [*Fiji*] [*ICAO location identifier*] (ICLI)
**NFNP** ........ Norris Point Public Library, Newfoundland [*Library symbol*] [*National Library of Canada*] (NLC)
**NFNR** ........ Rotuma [*Fiji*] [*ICAO location identifier*] (ICLI)
**NFNS** ........ Savusavu [*Fiji*] [*ICAO location identifier*] (ICLI)
**N FNSHD** ... Not Finished [*Freight*]
**NFNTU** ........ National Federation of Furniture Trade Union [*British*]
**NFNU** ........ Bua [*Fiji*] [*ICAO location identifier*] (ICLI)
**NFNU** ........ National Federation of Nurses' Unions [*See also FNSII*]
**NFNV** ........ Vatukoula [*Fiji*] [*ICAO location identifier*] (ICLI)
**NFNW** ........ Wakaya [*Fiji*] [*ICAO location identifier*] (ICLI)
**NFNWF** ........ Navy Fleet Numerical Weather Facility [*Marine science*] (MSC)
**NFO** ........ National Family Opinion
**NFO** ........ National Farmers Organization (EA)
**NFO** ........ Naval Flight Officer
**NFO** ........ Navy Finance Office
**NFO** ........ News from the Ukraine [*A publication*]
**NFO** ........ Norvell Family Organization (EA)
**NFO** ........ Not Fully Open (MCD)
**NFOBA** ........ National Fats and Oils Brokers Association [*Defunct*] (EA)
**NFOF** ........ Fiji [*Fiji*] [*ICAO location identifier*] (ICLI)
**NFOIO** ........ Naval Field Operational Intelligence Office (NVT)
**NFOO** ........ Naval Forward Observing Officer [*British military*] (DMA)
**NFOP** ........ Old Perlican Public Library, Newfoundland [*Library symbol*] [*National Library of Canada*] (NLC)
**NFoPA** ........ National Forest Products Association [*Washington, DC*]
**NFOSG** ........ Naval Field Operations Support Group
**NFOV** ........ Narrow Field of View
**NFP** ........ Marietta, GA [*Location identifier*] [*FAA*] (FAAL)
**NFP** ........ N-Formylmethionylphenylalanine [*Biochemistry*]
**NFP** ........ Nandrolone Furylpropionate [*Pharmacology*]
**NFP** ........ National Federation of Parents for Drug-Free Youth (EA)
**NFP** ........ National Federation Party [*Fiji*] [*Political party*] (PPW)
**NFP** ........ National Fire Academy Library, Emmitsburg, MD [*OCLC symbol*] (OCLC)
**NFP** ........ National Focal Points (DCTA)
**NFP** ........ Nationalist Front for Progress [*Political party*] [*Solomon Islands*] (FEA)
**NFP** ........ Natural Family Planning
**NFP** ........ Neighborhood Facilities Program (OICC)
**NFP** ........ Neue Freie Presse [*A publication*]
**NFP** ........ Neurofilament Protein [*Neurophysiology*]
**NFP** ........ New Federalist Party (EA)
**NFP** ........ New Forests Project (EA)
**NFP** ........ Nonflare Proton
**NFP** ........ Norfolk Petroleum Ltd. [*Vancouver Stock Exchange symbol*]
**NFP** ........ Normal Failure Period
**NFP** ........ Northern Frontier Province [*Kenya*]
**NFP** ........ Not for Profit (ADA)
**NFP** ........ Not for Publication (ADA)
**NFP** ........ Placentia Public Library, Newfoundland [*Library symbol*] [*National Library of Canada*] (NLC)
**NFPA** ........ National Federation of Paralegal Associations (EA)
**NFPA** ........ National Fire Protection Association (EA)
**NFPA** ........ National Flaxseed Processors Association (EA)
**NFPA** ........ National Flexible Packaging Association [*Later, FPA*] (EA)
**NFPA** ........ National Flight Paramedics Association (EA)
**NFPA** ........ National Fluid Power Association (EA)
**NFPA** ........ National Food Processors Association (EA)
**NFPA** ........ National Forest Products Association (EA)
**NFPA** ........ National Foster Parent Association (EA)
**NFPA** ........ Natural Family Planning Association of Connecticut (EA)
**NFPA** ........ Pasadena Public Library, Newfoundland [*Library symbol*] [*National Library of Canada*] (NLC)
**NFPB** ........ National Friends of Public Broadcasting (EA)
**NFPC** ........ National Federation of Priests' Councils (EA)
**NFPC** ........ Pouch Cove Public Library, Newfoundland [*Library symbol*] [*National Library of Canada*] (NLC)
**NFPCA** ........ National Fire Prevention and Control Administration [*Later, United States Fire Administration*] [*Department of Commerce*]
**NFPDB** ........ NATO Force Planning Data Base (NATG)
**NFPE** ........ NATO Force Planning Exercise (NATG)
**NFPE** ........ Non-Financial Public Enterprise [*British*]
**NFPEC** ........ Curran Memorial Library, Port Au Port East, Newfoundland [*Library symbol*] [*National Library of Canada*] (NLC)
**NFPEDA** ... National Farm and Power Equipment Dealers Association [*Later, NAEDA*] (EA)
**NF/PFOG** ... National Federation of Parents and Friends of Gays (EA)
**NFPI** ........ National Frozen Pizza Institute (EA)
**NFP Jb** ........ Jahrbuch der Neuen Freien Presse [*A publication*]
**NFPL** ........ Point Leamington Public Library, Newfoundland [*Library symbol*] [*National Library of Canada*] (NLC)
**NFPLA** ........ National Foundation for Professional Legal Assistants (EA)
**NFPM** ........ Nuclear Flight Propulsion Module (KSC)
**NFPMA** ........ National Feeder Pig Marketing Association (EA)
**NFPMA** ........ National Foundation for Peroneal Muscular Atrophy (EA)
**NFPMC** ........ National Farm Products Marketing Council [*Canada*]
**NFPO** ........ National Federation of Professional Organizations (EA)
**NFPOC** ........ National Federation of Post Office Clerks [*Later, APWU*]
**NFPOD** ........ National Foundation for the Prevention of Oral Disease (EA)
**NFPRHA** ... National Family Planning and Reproductive Health Association (EA)
**NFPS** ........ Naval Flight Preparatory School
**NFPS** ........ Naval Future Policy Staff [*British*]
**NFPS** ........ Navy Field Purchase Systems (NG)
**NFPS** ........ Nuclear Flight Propulsion System (AAG)
**NFPS** ........ Port Saunders Public Library, Newfoundland [*Library symbol*] [*National Library of Canada*] (NLC)
**NFPTC** ........ National Federation of Postal and Telegraph Clerks [*A union*] [*British*]
**NFPW** ........ National Federation of Press Women (EA)
**NFPW** ........ Port Au Port West School/Public Library, Newfoundland [*Library symbol*] [*National Library of Canada*] (NLC)
**NFQ** ........ Night Frequency [*Aviation*] (FAAC)
**NFQC** ........ Queens College, Flushing, NY [*Library symbol*] [*Library of Congress*] (LCLS)
**NFR** ........ National Field Research [*British*]
**NFR** ........ National Film Board Reference Library [*UTLAS symbol*]
**NFR** ........ Negative Flux Rate (IEEE)
**NFR** ........ Nephron Filtration Rate [*Physiology*]
**NFR** ........ New Frontier Petroleum Corp. [*Vancouver Stock Exchange symbol*]
**NFR** ........ No Further Requirement
**NFR** ........ Nordisk Forening for Rehabilitering [*Nordic Association for Rehabilitation*] (EAIO)
**N FR** ........ Northern French [*Language, etc.*] (ROG)
**NFR** ........ Nuclear Fission Reactor
**NFR** ........ Nursing Field Representative [*Red Cross*]
**NFRA** ........ National Forest Recreation Association (EA)
**NFRA** ........ National Furniture Removers' Association [*Australia*]
**NFRA** ........ Robert's Arm Public Library, Newfoundland [*Library symbol*] [*National Library of Canada*] (BIB)
**NFRC** ........ National Finals Rodeo Committee (EA)
**NFRC** ........ National Forest Reservation Commission [*Terminated, 1976; functions transferred to Department of Agriculture*]
**NFRC** ........ Northeast Financial Resources Corporation [*Reno, NV*] [*NASDAQ symbol*] (NQ)
**NFRCC** ........ Nordic Forest Research Cooperation Committee (EAIO)
**NFred** ........ Darwin R. Barker Library Association, Fredonia, NY [*Library symbol*] [*Library of Congress*] (LCLS)
**NFredU** ........ State University of New York, College at Fredonia, Fredonia, NY [*Library symbol*] [*Library of Congress*] (LCLS)
**NFree** ........ Freeport Memorial Library, Freeport, NY [*Library symbol*] [*Library of Congress*] (LCLS)
**NFreeAE** ... Archer Elementary School, Freeport, NY [*Library symbol*] [*Library of Congress*] (LCLS)
**NFreeCE** ........ Columbus Elementary School, Freeport, NY [*Library symbol*] [*Library of Congress*] (LCLS)
**NFreeDH** ... Doctors Hospital, Freeport, NY [*Library symbol*] [*Library of Congress*] (LCLS)
**NFreeDJ** ........ Dodd Junior High School, Freeport, NY [*Library symbol*] [*Library of Congress*] (LCLS)
**NFreeH** ........ Freeport Hospital, Freeport, NY [*Library symbol*] [*Library of Congress*] (LCLS)
**NFreeHS** ... Freeport High School, Freeport, NY [*Library symbol*] [*Library of Congress*] (LCLS)
**NFRH** ........ Rocky Harbour Public School, Newfoundland [*Library symbol*] [*National Library of Canada*] (NLC)
**NFRM** ........ National Foundation for Research in Medicine (EA)
**NFRMC** ........ National Foundation for Rural Medical Care (EA)
**NFRN** ........ National Federation of Retail Newsagents [*British*]
**NFRP** ........ Marie S. Penney Memorial Library, Ramea, Newfoundland [*Library symbol*] [*National Library of Canada*] (NLC)
**NFRRC** ........ Nuclear Fuel Recovery and Receiving Center (NRCH)
**NFRS** ........ National Fancy Rat Society [*British*]
**NFRW** ........ National Federation of Republican Women (EA)

**NFS**........... Fayetteville State University, Fayetteville, NC [*OCLC symbol*] (OCLC)
**NFs**........... Franklin Square Public Library, Franklin Square, NY [*Library symbol*] [*Library of Congress*] (LCLS)
**NFS**........... National Federation of Settlements [*Later, UNCA*]
**NFS**........... National Fertility Study
**NFS**........... National Field Service Corp. [*Suffern, NY*] [*Telecommunications*] (TSSD)
**NFS**........... National Film Society (EA)
**NFS**........... National Fire Service [*British*]
**NFS**........... National Flying Service [*British*]
**NFS**........... National Food Situation [*Series*] [*A publication*]
**NFS**........... National Food Survey [*British*]
**NFS**........... National Fuchsia Society (EA)
**NFS**........... Naval Flying Station [*British*]
**NFS**........... Navy Facilities System
**NFS**........... Navy Field Service
**NFS**........... Network File System [*Sun Microsystems, Inc.*]
**NFS**........... Neutron Flux Spectra [*Nuclear energy*]
**NFS**........... Nitrofuraldehyde Semicarbazone [*Germicide*]
**NFS**........... Nitrogen Flow System
**NFS**........... Noise Frequency Spectrum
**NFS**........... Nonfriendly Submarines (MCD)
**NFS**........... Nordens Fackliga Samorganisation [*Council of Nordic Trade Unions*] (EAIO)
**NFS**........... Nordiska Forbundet for Statskunskap [*Nordic Political Science Association - NPSA*] (EAIO)
**NFS**........... Not on Flying Status
**NFS**........... Not for Sale
**NFS**........... Nottingham French Studies [*A publication*]
**NFS**........... Nozzle Flow Sensor (MCD)
**NFS**........... Nuclear Fuel Services Plant (NRCH)
**NFSA**......... National Federation of Sea Anglers [*British*]
**NFSA**......... National Fertilizer Solutions Association (EA)
**NFSA**......... National Film and Sound Archive [*Australia*]
**NFSA**......... National Fire Sprinkler Association (EA)
**NFSA**......... National Food Service Association (EA)
**NFSA**......... Navy Field Safety Association (EA)
**NFSA**......... New Fuel Storage Area (NRCH)
**NFSA**......... News from Saudi Arabia [*A publication*] (BJA)
**NFSA**......... Provincial Archives of Newfoundland and Labrador, St. John's, Newfoundland [*Library symbol*] [*National Library of Canada*] (NLC)
**NFSAG**...... Research Station, Agriculture Canada [*Station de Recherches, Agriculture Canada*] St. John's, Newfoundland [*Library symbol*] [*National Library of Canada*] (NLC)
**NFSAIC**.... Charles Curtis Memorial Hospital, International Grenfell Association, St. Anthony, Newfoundland [*Library symbol*] [*National Library of Canada*] (NLC)
**NFSAIS**..... National Federation of Science Abstracting and Indexing Services [*Later, NFAIS*] (EA)
**NFSAL**...... St. Alban's Public Library, Newfoundland [*Library symbol*] [*National Library of Canada*] (NLC)
**NFSAN**...... St. Anthony Public Library, Newfoundland [*Library symbol*] [*National Library of Canada*] (NLC)
**NFSANS**... Naskapi School/Public Library, Sops Arm, Newfoundland [*Library symbol*] [*National Library of Canada*] (NLC)
**NFSB**......... Spaniards Bay Public Library, Newfoundland [*Library symbol*] [*National Library of Canada*] (NLC)
**NFSBC**...... Boys' Club, St. John's, Newfoundland [*Library symbol*] [*National Library of Canada*] (NLC)
**NFSBCS**.... Cape Shore Public Library, St. Brides, Newfoundland [*Library symbol*] [*National Library of Canada*] (NLC)
**NFSBS**....... Bay St. George Community College, Stephenville, Newfoundland [*Library symbol*] [*National Library of Canada*] (NLC)
**NFSC**......... National Federation of Stamp Clubs (EA)
**NFSC**......... Seal Cove Public Library, Newfoundland [*Library symbol*] [*National Library of Canada*] (NLC)
**NFSCA**...... Children's and Adults' Library, St. John's, Newfoundland [*Library symbol*] [*National Library of Canada*] (NLC)
**NFSCAEE**... Environment Division, Newfoundland Department of Consumer Affairs and Environment, St. John's, Newfoundland [*Library symbol*] [*National Library of Canada*] (NLC)
**NFSCF**...... Newfoundland and Labrador Institute of Fisheries and Marine Technology (Marine Institute), St. John's, New Foundland [*Library symbol*] [*National Library of Canada*] (NLC)
**NFSCJ**....... Dr. Charles A. Janeway Child Health Centre, St. John's, Newfoundland [*Library symbol*] [*National Library of Canada*] (NLC)
**NFSCR**...... Children's Rehabilitation Centre, St. John's, Newfoundland [*Library symbol*] [*National Library of Canada*] (NLC)
**NFSCSW**... National Federation of Societies for Clinical Social Work (EA)
**NFSCT**...... Cabot Institute of Applied Arts and Technology, St. John's, Newfoundland [*Library symbol*] [*National Library of Canada*] (NLC)
**NFSCTM**.. Topsail Campus Resource Centre, Cabot Institute of Applied Arts and Technology, St. John's, Newfoundland [*Library symbol*] [*National Library of Canada*] (NLC)
**NFSD**......... National Federation of Spiritual Directors (EA)
**NFSD**......... National Fraternal Society of the Deaf [*Mount Prospect, IL*] (EA)
**NFSD**......... Nonfused (MSA)
**NFSE**......... National Federation of Sales Executives [*Later, Sales and Marketing Executives International*]
**NFSE**......... National Federation of Self Employed [*British*]
**NFSEC**...... Newfoundland Forest Research Centre, Environment Canada [*Centre de Recherches Forestieres de Terre-Neuve, Environnement Canada*] St. John's, Newfoundland [*Library symbol*] [*National Library of Canada*] (NLC)
**NFSEEP**.... National Foundation for the Study of Equal Employment [*Washington, DC*] (EA)
**NFSF**......... National Freedom Shrine Foundation (EA)
**NFSF**......... NFS Financial Corp. [*Nashua, NH*] [*NASDAQ symbol*] (NQ)
**NFSF**......... North-West Atlantic Fisheries Centre, Fisheries and Oceans Canada [*Centre de Pecheries de l'Atlantique du Nord-Ouest, Peches et Oceans Canada*] St. John's, Newfoundland [*Library symbol*] [*National Library of Canada*] (NLC)
**NFSFJG**.... St. Judes Central High School Public Library/Bay St. George South Public Library Library, St. Fintans, Newfoundland [*Library symbol*] [*National Library of Canada*] (NLC)
**NFSFS**....... Newfoundland Forest Service, St. John's, Newfoundland [*Library symbol*] [*National Library of Canada*] (NLC)
**NFSG**......... National Federation of Students of German (EA)
**NFSG**......... Newfoundland Public Library Services, St. John's, Newfoundland [*Library symbol*] [*National Library of Canada*] (NLC)
**NFSG**......... Provinical Reference and Resource Library, Newfoundland Public Library Services, St. John's, New Foundland [*Library symbol*] [*National Library of Canada*] (NLC)
**NFSGE**...... St. Georges Public Library, Newfoundland [*Library symbol*] [*National Library of Canada*] (NLC)
**NFSGGH**.. C. A Pippy Jr. Medical Library, Grace General Hospital, St. John's, Newfoundland [*Library symbol*] [*National Library of Canada*] (NLC)
**NFSGGHN**... School of Nursing, Grace General Hospital, St. John's, Newfoundland [*Library symbol*] [*National Library of Canada*] (NLC)
**NFSGH**..... General Hospital Corp., St. John's, Newfoundland [*Library symbol*] [*National Library of Canada*] (NLC)
**NFSGHN**.. Nursing Education, General Hospital Corp., St. John's, Newfoundland [*Library symbol*] [*National Library of Canada*] (NLC)
**NFSGO**..... Gosling Library, St. John's, Newfoundland [*Library symbol*] [*National Library of Canada*] (NLC)
**NFSGWS**.. Newsletter. Folklore Society of Greater Washington. Supplement [*A publication*]
**NFSH**........ National Federation of Spiritual Healers (EA)
**NFSH**........ Southern Harbour Public Library, Newfoundland [*Library symbol*] [*National Library of Canada*] (NLC)
**NFSHC**...... National Federation of State Humanities Councils (EA)
**NFSHE**...... Health Education Division, Newfoundland Department of Health, St. John's, Newfoundland [*Library symbol*] [*National Library of Canada*] (NLC)
**NFSHPH**.. Public Health Nursing Division, Newfoundland Department of Health, St. John's, Newfoundland [*Library symbol*] [*National Library of Canada*] (NLC)
**NFSHSA**... National Federation of State High School Associations (EA)
**NFSHSAA**... National Federation of State High School Athletic Associations [*Later, NFSHSA*] (EA)
**NFSI**.......... National FSI, Inc. [*Dallas, TX*] [*NASDAQ symbol*] (NQ)
**NFSICA**.... Institute of Chartered Accountants of Newfoundland, St. John's, Newfoundland [*Library symbol*] [*National Library of Canada*] (NLC)
**NFsJE**....... John Street Elementary School, Franklin Square, NY [*Library symbol*] [*Library of Congress*] (LCLS)
**NFSJL**....... Law Library, Newfoundland Department of Justice, St. John's, Newfoundland [*Library symbol*] [*National Library of Canada*] (NLC)
**NFSK**......... Kindale Public Library, Stephenville, Newfoundland [*Library symbol*] [*National Library of Canada*] (NLC)
**NFSK**......... Narrowband Frequency Shift Keying (MCD)
**NFSL**......... Legislative Library, St. John's, Newfoundland [*Library symbol*] [*National Library of Canada*] (NLC)
**NFSL**......... Newman Savings Bank [*NASDAQ symbol*] (NQ)
**NFSL**......... Nucleus Fleet Sealift
**NFSLA**...... St. Lawrence Public Library, Newfoundland [*Library symbol*] [*National Library of Canada*] (NLC)
**NFSLG**...... St. Lunaire-Griquet Public Library, St. Lunaire, Newfoundland [*Library symbol*] [*National Library of Canada*] (NLC)
**NFSLP**....... Central Records Library, Newfoundland Light and Power Co. Ltd., St. John's, Newfoundland [*Library symbol*] [*National Library of Canada*] (NLC)
**NFSLS**....... Law Society of Newfoundland, St. John's, Newfoundland [*Library symbol*] [*National Library of Canada*] (NLC)
**NFSM**........ Memorial University, St. John's, Newfoundland [*Library symbol*] [*National Library of Canada*] (NLC)
**NFSM**........ National Fraternity of Student Musicians (EA)

**NFSM** ........ Queen Elizabeth II Library, Memorial University of Newfoundland, St. John's, Newfoundland [*Library symbol*] [*National Library of Canada*] (NLC)
**NFSMA** ..... National Fruit and Syrup Manufacturers Association (EA)
**NFSMA** ..... Provincial Planning Office, Newfoundland Department of Municipal Affairs, St. John's, Newfoundland [*Library symbol*] [*National Library of Canada*] (NLC)
**NFSME** ..... Newfoundland Department of Mines and Energy, St. John's, Newfoundland [*Library symbol*] [*National Library of Canada*] (NLC)
**NFSMEC** .. Curriculum Materials Centre, Education Library, Memorial University, St. John's, Newfoundland [*Library symbol*] [*National Library of Canada*] (NLC)
**NFSMED** .. Education Library, Memorial University, St. John's, Newfoundland [*Library symbol*] [*National Library of Canada*] (NLC)
**NFSMEM** ... Publications and Information Section, Mineral Development Division Library, Newfoundland Department of Mines and Energy, St. John's, Newfoundland [*Library symbol*] [*National Library of Canada*] (NLC)
**NFSMG** ..... Department of Geography, Memorial University, St. John's, Newfoundland [*Library symbol*] [*National Library of Canada*] (NLC)
**NFSMLS** ... Library Studies Program, Memorial University of Newfoundland, St. John's, Newfoundland [*Library symbol*] [*National Library of Canada*] (BIB)
**NFSMM** .... Health Sciences Library, Memorial University, St. John's, Newfoundland [*Library symbol*] [*National Library of Canada*] (NLC)
**NFSMMH** ... Maritime History Archive, Memorial University, St. John's, Newfoundland [*Library symbol*] [*National Library of Canada*] (BIB)
**NFSMO** .... Ocean Engineering Centre, Memorial University, St. John's, Newfoundland [*Library symbol*] [*National Library of Canada*] (NLC)
**NFSN** ........ NATO French-Speaking Nations
**NFS & NC** ... National Federation of Settlements and Neighborhood Centers [*Later, UNCA*] (EA)
**NFSNI** ....... National Research Council IRAP [*Industrial Research Assistance Program*], St. John's, Newfoundland [*Library symbol*] [*National Library of Canada*] (NLC)
**NFSNL** ...... Newfoundland and Labrador Hydro, St. John's, Newfoundland [*Library symbol*] [*National Library of Canada*] (NLC)
**NFSNLD** ... Newfoundland and Labrador Development Corp., St. John's, Newfoundland [*Library symbol*] [*National Library of Canada*] (NLC)
**NFSNM** ..... Marine Dynamics Branch, Canada Institute for Scientific and Technical Information, National Research Council [*Direction de la Dynamique Marine Institut Canadien de l'Information Scientifique et Technique, Conseil National de Recherches*], St. John's, Newfoundland [*Library symbol*] [*National Library of Canada*] (NLC)
**NFSNO** ..... National Federation for Specialty Nursing Organizations (EA)
**NFSO** ........ Navy Fuel Supply Office
**NFSP** ......... Nonflight Switch Panel (NASA)
**NFSP** ......... Springdale Public Library, Newfoundland [*Library symbol*] [*National Library of Canada*] (NLC)
**NFSPR** ...... Provincial Reference Library, St. John's, Newfoundland [*Library symbol*] [*National Library of Canada*] (NLC)
**NFSPS** ....... National Federation of State Poetry Societies (EA)
**NFSQ** ........ Queen's College, St. John's, Newfoundland [*Library symbol*] [*National Library of Canada*] (NLC)
**NFSRD** ...... Newfoundland Department of Rural Development, St. John's, Newfoundland [*Library symbol*] [*National Library of Canada*] (NLC)
**NFSREX** ... Canada Department of Regional Industrial Expansion [*Ministere de l'Expansion Industrielle Regionale*] St. John's, Newfoundland [*Library symbol*] [*National Library of Canada*] (NLC)
**NFSS** ......... National Fallout Shelter Survey [*Civil Defense*]
**NFSS** ......... National Federation of Sailing Schools [*British*]
**NFSS** ......... National Finch and Softbill Society (EA)
**NFSS** ......... Nucleus Fleet Scientific Support
**NFSSC** ....... St. Clare's Mercy Hospital, St. John's, Newfoundland [*Library symbol*] [*National Library of Canada*] (NLC)
**NFSSCN** ... School of Nursing, St. Clare's Mercy Hospital, St. John's, Newfoundland [*Library symbol*] [*National Library of Canada*] (NLC)
**NFSSW** ..... Newfoundland Status of Women Council, St. John's, Newfoundland [*Library symbol*] [*National Library of Canada*] (NLC)
**NFST** ......... Newfoundland Department of Tourism, St. John's, Newfoundland [*Library symbol*] [*National Library of Canada*] (NLC)
**NFSTA** ...... Newfoundland Teachers' Association, St. John's, Newfoundland [*Library symbol*] [*National Library of Canada*] (NLC)
**NFSTC** ...... Stephenville Crossing Public Library, Newfoundland [*Library symbol*] [*National Library of Canada*] (NLC)
**NFSTCG** ... Canadian Coast Guard [*Garde Cotiere Canadienne*] St. John's, Newfoundland [*Library symbol*] [*Obsolete*] [*National Library of Canada*] (NLC)
**NFSTPG** ... National Foundation for the Study and Treatment of Pathological Gambling [*Defunct*] (EA)
**NFSTR** ...... Medical Library, Sir Thomas Roddick Hospital, Stephenville, Newfoundland [*Library symbol*] [*National Library of Canada*] (NLC)
**NFSU** ......... Nonflying Support Unit
**NFSU** ......... Summerford Public Library, Newfoundland [*Library symbol*] [*National Library of Canada*] (NLC)
**NFSU** ......... Suva/Nausori [*Fiji*] [*ICAO location identifier*] (ICLI)
**NFSVP** ...... National Forest Service Volunteers Program (EA)
**NFSWH** .... Health Services, Waterford Hospital, St. John's, Newfoundland [*Library symbol*] [*National Library of Canada*] (NLC)
**NFT** ........... N-Formimidoylthienamycin [*Biochemistry*]
**NFT** ........... National Film and Television Sound Archives [*National Film Board of Canada*] [*UTLAS symbol*]
**NFT** ........... National Film Theatre [*British*]
**NFT** ........... Navy Flight Test (MCD)
**NFT** ........... Networks File Transfer
**NFT** ........... Neurofibrillary Tangle [*Brain anatomy*]
**NFT** ........... New Frontiers in Theology [*A publication*] (BJA)
**NFT** ........... Newfoundland Telephone Co. Ltd. [*Toronto Stock Exchange symbol*]
**NFT** ........... No Filing Time [*Aviation*]
**NFT** ........... Normal Fuel-Oil Tank (MSA)
**NFT** ........... Nutrient Film Technique
**NFTA** ........ National Feminist Therapist Association (EA)
**NFTA** ........ National Freight Transportation Association [*Rocky River, OH*] (EA)
**NFTA** ........ Netherlands Foreign Trade Agency
**NFTA** ........ New Feminist Talent Associates (EA)
**NFTA** ........ Night-Fire [*Rifle*] Training Aid [*Army*] (INF)
**NFTA** ........ Nitrogen Fixing Tree Association [*University of Hawaii*] [*Research center*] (RCD)
**NFTB** ......... National Federation of Temple Brotherhoods (EA)
**NFTB** ......... Naval Fleet Training Base
**NFTB** ......... Niagara Frontier Tariff Bureau
**NFTB** ......... Nuclear Flight Test Base
**NFTBEA** ... Netherlands Fertilizer Technical Bulletin [*A publication*]
**NFTC** ......... National Foreign Trade Council [*New York, NY*] (EA)
**NFTC** ......... National Furniture Traffic Conference (EA)
**NFTD** ........ Normal, Full Term Delivery [*Obstetrics*]
**NFTE** ......... Eua [*Tonga*] [*ICAO location identifier*] (ICLI)
**NFTF** ......... Tongatapu/Fua'Amotu International [*Tonga*] [*ICAO location identifier*] (ICLI)
**NFTL** ......... Ha'Apai Lifuka [*Tonga*] [*ICAO location identifier*] (ICLI)
**NFTN** ........ Nuku'Alofa [*Tonga*] [*ICAO location identifier*] (ICLI)
**NFTO** ........ Niuafo'Ou [*Tonga*] [*ICAO location identifier*] (ICLI)
**NFTO** ........ Torbay Public Library, Newfoundland [*Library symbol*] [*National Library of Canada*] (NLC)
**NFTP** ......... Niuatoputapu [*Tonga*] [*ICAO location identifier*] (ICLI)
**NFTR** ......... Trepassey Public Library, Newfoundland [*Library symbol*] [*National Library of Canada*] (NLC)
**NFTS** ......... National Federation of Temple Sisterhoods (EA)
**NFTS** ......... National Film and Television School [*British*]
**NFTS** ......... Naval Flight Training School
**NFTSA** ...... National Film, Television, and Sound Archives [*Canada*]
**NFtT** .......... Fort Ticonderoga Association Museum and Library, Fort Ticonderoga, NY [*Library symbol*] [*Library of Congress*] (LCLS)
**NFTV** ......... Vava'u [*Tonga*] [*ICAO location identifier*] (ICLI)
**NFTW** ....... National Federation of Telephone Workers [*Later, CWA*]
**NFTW** ....... National Federation of Tobacco Workers [*A union*] [*British*]
**NFTW** ....... Twillingate Public Library, Newfoundland [*Library symbol*] [*National Library of Canada*] (NLC)
**NFTY** ......... North American Federation of Temple Youth (EA)
**NFTZ** ......... Non Free Trade Zone (DS)
**NFU** ........... National Farmers' Union [*British*]
**NFU** ........... Niho Fukushi University [*UTLAS symbol*]
**NFU** ........... Not for Us [*Communications*]
**NFU** ........... Unitas. Economic Quarterly Review [*A publication*]
**NFUCWC** ... National Foundation for Unemployment Compensation and Workers Compensation (EA)
**NFUF** ........ Codroy Valley Public Library, Upper Ferry, Newfoundland [*Library symbol*] [*National Library of Canada*] (NLC)
**NFUI** ......... Upper Island Cove Public Library, Newfoundland [*Library symbol*] [*National Library of Canada*] (NLC)
**NFULDA** ... Fondation Universitaire Luxembourgeoise. Serie Notes de Recherche [*A publication*]
**NFV** ........... National Field Volunteer [*Red Cross*]
**NFV** ........... New Zealand Foreign Affairs Review [*A publication*]
**NFV** ........... No Further Visits [*Medicine*]
**NFV** ........... Nordischer Friseurverband [*Nordic Association of Hairdressers*] (EAIO)
**NFV** ........... Point Barrow, AK [*Location identifier*] [*FAA*] (FAAL)
**NFV** ........... Victoria Public Library, Newfoundland [*Library symbol*] [*National Library of Canada*] (NLC)
**NFVA** ........ Net Free Vent Area [*Roofing*]
**NFVC** ........ National Frozen Vegetable Council [*Later, FVC*] (EA)

**NFVLS** ...... National Federation of Voluntary Literacy Schemes [*British*]
**NFVOA** ..... Northern Fishing Vessel Owners Association [*Defunct*] (EA)
**NFW** .......... Lakehurst, NJ [*Location identifier*] [*FAA*] (FAAL)
**NFW** .......... Non-Fuel-Wasting (MCD)
**NFWA** ....... National Farm Workers of America
**NFWA** ....... National Furniture Warehousemen's Association [*Later, NMSA*] (EA)
**NFWA** ....... Wabush Public Library, Newfoundland [*Library symbol*] [*National Library of Canada*] (NLC)
**NFWD** ....... New Field Wildcat Drilling [*Petroleum technology*]
**NFWE** ....... Edgar L. M. Roberts Memorial Library, Woodypoint, Newfoundland [*Library symbol*] [*National Library of Canada*] (NLC)
**NFWE** ....... National Federation of Woman's Exchanges (EA)
**NFWH** ....... National Foundation for Wholistic Medicine [*Inactive*] (EA)
**NFWH** ....... Whitbourne Public Library, Newfoundland [*Library symbol*] [*National Library of Canada*] (NLC)
**NFWI** ........ National Federation of Women's Institutes [*British*]
**NFWI** ........ Windsor Memorial Public Library, Newfoundland [*Library symbol*] [*National Library of Canada*] (NLC)
**NFWIN** ..... Winterton Public Library, Newfoundland [*Library symbol*] [*National Library of Canada*] (NLC)
**NFWM** ...... National Farm Worker Ministry (EA)
**NFWT** ....... National Foundation of Wheelchair Tennis (EA)
**NFWV** ....... Wesleyville Public Library, Newfoundland [*Library symbol*] [*National Library of Canada*] (NLC)
**NFWW** ...... National Federation of Women Workers [*British*]
**NFXD** ........ National Fax Directory [*A publication*]
**NFXF** ........ National Fragile X Foundation (EA)
**NFY** .......... Notify [*Telecommunications*] (TEL)
**NFYD** ........ Notified [*Telecommunications*] (TEL)
**NFYFC** ..... National Federation of Young Farmers' Clubs (EAIO)
**NFZ** .......... National Front of Zimbabwe (PPW)
**NFZ** .......... (Nitro)furfuralsemicarbazone [*Organic chemistry*]
**NFZ** .......... No Fire Zone [*Military*]
**NFZ** .......... Nuclear Free Zone (AFM)
**NFZR** ........ Nuclear Free Zone Registry (EA)
**NG** ............ Gill Aviation Ltd. [*ICAO designator*] (FAAC)
**ng** ............. Nanogram
**NG** ............ Narrow Gauge
**NG** ............ Nasogastric [*Medicine*]
**NG** ............ National Gallery [*London*]
**NG** ............ National Gathering [*Jordan*] [*A publication*] (BJA)
**NG** ............ National Grange (EA)
**NG** ............ National Grid [*British Ordnance Survey maps*]
**NG** ............ National Guard [*or Guardsman*]
**NG** ............ Natural, Grazed [*Agriculture*]
**N & G** ........ Navigation and Guidance [*G & N is preferred*] [*NASA*] (KSC)
**NG** ............ Navy General [*MCD files*]
**NG** ............ NAZI Government (BJA)
**NG** ............ Nephridial Gland
**NG** ............ Neue Germanistik [*A publication*]
**NG** ............ Neue Gesellschaft [*A publication*]
**NG** ............ New Genus
**NG** ............ New Gnostics Special Interest Group (EA)
**NG** ............ New Granada
**NG** ............ New Group
**NG** ............ New Growth [*Medicine*]
**NG** ............ New Guard [*A publication*]
**NG** ............ New Guinea
**NG** ............ Newly Generated
**NG** ............ Nieuwe Gids [*A publication*]
**ng** ............. Niger [*MARC country of publication code*] [*Library of Congress*] (LCCP)
**NG** ............ Nigeria [*ANSI two-letter standard code*] (CNC)
**NG** ............ Nitrogen Gauge (MCD)
**NG** ............ Nitroglycerin [*Also, GTN, NTG*] [*Explosive, vasodilator*]
**NG** ............ Nitroguanidine [*Organic chemistry*]
**NG** ............ No Go [*i.e., an unacceptable arrangement*]
**NG** ............ No Good [*Similar to IC - Inspected and Condemned*]
**NG** ............ No Gum [*Philately*]
**NG** ............ Noble Gases [*Nuclear energy*] (NRCH)
**NG** ............ Noble Grand
**NG** ............ Noble Guard [*Freemasonry*] (ROG)
**NG** ............ Nongraduate
**NG** ............ Normal Graduate
**NG** ............ Normotensive Group [*Cardiology*]
**NG** ............ Norwegian
**NG** ............ Norwegium [*Chemistry*] (ROG)
**NG** ............ Nose Gear [*Aviation*] (MCD)
**NG** ............ Not Given (ADA)
**NG** ............ Not Good
**NG** ............ Not Guilty
**NG** ............ Nota Genitiva
**NG** ............ Royal North Gloucestershire Militia [*British military*] (DMA)
**NGA** .......... Associated Natural Gas Corp. [*NYSE symbol*] (SPSG)
**NGA** .......... National Gallery of Art [*Washington, DC*]
**NGA** .......... National Gallery of Art, Washington, DC [*OCLC symbol*] (OCLC)
**NGA** .......... National Gallery of Canada Library [*UTLAS symbol*]
**NGA** .......... National Gardening Association (EA)
**NG & A** ...... National Gift and Art Association (EA)
**NGA** .......... National Glass Association (EA)
**NGA** .......... National Gliding Association [*Later, SSA*]
**NGA** .......... National Governors' Association (EA)
**NGA** .......... National Grant Agency
**NGA** .......... National Graphical Association [*British printers' union*]
**NGA** .......... National Greyhound Association (EA)
**NGA** .......... National Grocers Association (EA)
**NGA** .......... NATO Guidelines Area (NATG)
**NGA** .......... Needlework Guild of America [*Later, NGAI*] (EA)
**NGA** .......... Nigeria [*ANSI three-letter standard code*] (CNC)
**NGA** .......... Nutrient Gelative Agar [*Microbiology*]
**NGA** .......... Nutrient Glucose Agar [*Microbiology*]
**NGA** .......... Young [*Australia*] [*Airport symbol*] (OAG)
**NGAA** ........ National Girls Athletic Association [*Defunct*]
**NGAA** ........ Natural Gasoline Association of America [*Later, GPA*]
**NGAB** ........ Abaiang [*Kiribati*] [*ICAO location identifier*] (ICLI)
**NGaC** ......... Capuchin Theological Seminary, Garrison, NY [*Library symbol*] [*Library of Congress*] (LCLS)
**NGAD** ........ Nobody Gives a Damn
**NGADA** ..... National Graphic Arts Dealers Association (EA)
**NGAI** ......... NGA [*Needlework Guild of America*], Inc. (EA)
**NGAL** ........ Chestatee Regional Library [*Library network*]
**NGAM** ....... Noble Gas Activity Monitor (IEEE)
**NGAO** ....... New Governmental Advisory Organizations [*A publication*]
**NGARP** ..... National Guard and Army Reserve Policy
**N Gas M 1990** ... Natural Gas Market through 1990 [*A publication*]
**NGAUS** ..... National Guard Association of the United States (EA)
**NGAYA** ..... National Gay Alliance for Young Adults (EA)
**NGAZ** ........ NATO Gazetteer (MCD)
**NGB** .......... National Garden Bureau (EA)
**NGB** .......... National Governing Body [*United States Olympic Committee*]
**NGB** .......... National Guard Bureau [*Army*]
**ngb** ............ Natural Gum Blend [*Philately*]
**NGB** .......... Neues Goettinger Bibelwerk [*A publication*] (BJA)
**NGB** .......... Nippon Gijutsu Boeki Co. Ltd. [*Japan*] [*Information service or system*] (IID)
**NGBR** ........ Beru [*Kiribati*] [*ICAO location identifier*] (ICLI)
**NGBRI** ...... Not Guilty by Reason of Insanity
**NGc** ........... Garden City Public Library, Garden City, NY [*Library symbol*] [*Library of Congress*] (LCLS)
**NGC** .......... Gloucester County College, Voorhees, NJ [*OCLC symbol*] (OCLC)
**NGC** .......... National Gallery of Canada
**NGC** .......... National Gasohol Commission [*Defunct*] (EA)
**NGC** .......... National Giro Centre [*British*] (DCTA)
**NGC** .......... National Glass Clubs (EA)
**NGC** .......... National Gloster Club (EA)
**NGC** .......... National Governors Conference [*Later, NGA*]
**NGC** .......... National Guild of Churchmen (EA)
**NGC** .......... National Guinea Club
**ngc** ............ Natural Gum Crease [*Philately*]
**NGC** .......... Near Galactic Catalog
**NGC** .......... New General Catalogue [*Astronomy*]
**NGC** .......... New Generation Computing [*A publication*]
**NGC** .......... New German Critique [*A publication*]
**NGC** .......... Newmont Gold Company [*NYSE symbol*] (SPSG)
**NGC** .......... Noise Generator Card
**NGC** .......... Nordic Geodetic Commission (EA)
**NGC** .......... North Georgia College [*Dahlonaga*]
**NGC** .......... Nozzle Gap Control [*Aerospace*] (AAG)
**NGC** .......... Nucleus Reticularis Gigantocellularis [*Brain anatomy*]
**NGcA** ......... Adelphi University, Garden City, NY [*Library symbol*] [*Library of Congress*] (LCLS)
**Ng-CAM** .... Neuralglial Cell Adhesion Model [*Biochemistry*]
**NGCC** ........ National Guard Computer Center
**NGCC** ........ North German Coal Control [*Post-World War II*]
**NGcCC** ...... Nassau Community College, Garden City, NY [*Library symbol*] [*Library of Congress*] (LCLS)
**NGCDO** ..... North German Coal Distribution Organization [*Post-World War II*]
**NGcE** ......... Endo Laboratories, Inc., Garden City, NY [*Library symbol*] [*Library of Congress*] (LCLS)
**NGcG** ......... George Mercer, Jr., School of Theology, Garden City, NY [*Library symbol*] [*Library of Congress*] (LCLS)
**NGCIC** ...... Natural Gas Consumers Information Center (EA)
**NGCM** ....... Navy Good Conduct Medal
**NGcMH** .... Mineola High School, Garden City Park, NY [*Library symbol*] [*Library of Congress*] (LCLS)
**NGCMS** .... National Guild of Community Music Schools [*Later, NGCSA*] (EA)
**NGcN** ......... Nassau Academy of Medicine, Garden City, NY [*Library symbol*] [*Library of Congress*] (LCLS)
**NGcNe** ....... Newsday, Garden City, NY [*Library symbol*] [*Library of Congress*] (LCLS)
**NGcNLS** .... Nassau Library System, Garden City, NY [*Library symbol*] [*Library of Congress*] (LCLS)
**NGCP** ........ National Guild of Catholic Psychiatrists (EA)
**NGcR** ......... Nassau County Research Library, Garden City, NY [*Library symbol*] [*Library of Congress*] (LCLS)
**NGCSA** ..... National Guild of Community Schools of the Arts (EA)

**NGcSS**....... Scully, Scott, Murphy, and Presser, Garden City, NY [*Library symbol*] [*Library of Congress*] (LCLS)
**NGD**.......... National Grassland Demonstration [*British*]
**NGD**.......... National Guild of Decoupeurs (EA)
**NGD**.......... New Golden Sceptre Minerals Ltd. [*Toronto Stock Exchange symbol*] [*Vancouver Stock Exchange symbol*]
**Ngd**............ Nitrosoguanidine [*Biochemistry*]
**NGDA**........ National Glass Dealers Association [*Later, NGA*] (EA)
**NGDB**........ National Geochemical Data Bank [*Natural Environment Research Council*] [*Information service or system*] (IID)
**NGDBFC**... Nitty Gritty Dirt Band Fan Club (EA)
**NGDC**........ National Geophysical Data Center [*Later, NGSDC*] [*National Oceanic and Atmospheric Administration*] [*Boulder, CO*] (MCD)
**NGD & MTC**... National Guide Dog and Mobility Training Centre [*Australia*]
**NGDS**........ Naval Graduate Dental School
**NGE**........... Navigation Guidance Equipment (MCD)
**NGE**........... New York State Electric & Gas Corp. [*NYSE symbol*] (SPSG)
**NGE**........... N'Gaoundere [*Cameroon*] [*Airport symbol*] (OAG)
**NGEC**........ National Gypsy Education Council [*British*]
**NGEN**........ New Generation Foods, Inc. [*NASDAQ symbol*] (NQ)
**NGEN**........ Noise Generator (MSA)
**NGenoA**..... Livingston County Archives, Geneseo, NY [*Library symbol*] [*Library of Congress*] (LCLS)
**NGenoLS**... Livingston-Steuben-Wyoming Educational Communication Center (BOCES), Geneseo, NY [*Library symbol*] [*Library of Congress*] (LCLS)
**NGenoU**..... State University of New York, College at Geneseo, Geneseo, NY [*Library symbol*] [*Library of Congress*] (LCLS)
**NGEPSSC**... Navy Graduate Education Program Select Study Committee [*Terminated, 1975*] (EGAO)
**N Ges**......... Neue Gesellschaft [*A publication*]
**NGET**........ Norsk Geografisk Tidsskrift [*A publication*]
**NGF**........... Kaneohe, HI [*Location identifier*] [*FAA*] (FAAL)
**NGF**........... National Gaucher Foundation (EA)
**NGF**........... National Genetics Foundation (EA)
**NGF**........... National Golf Foundation (EA)
**NGF**........... Natural Guard Fund (EA)
**NGF**........... Naval Gun Factory [*Later, NWF*]
**NGF**........... Naval Gunfire
**NGF**........... Nerve Growth Factor [*A protein*] [*Biochemistry*]
**NGF**........... Nevada Goldfields Corp. [*Toronto Stock Exchange symbol*]
**NGF**........... New Games Foundation (EA)
**NGF**........... New Guinea Force [*Army*] [*World War II*]
**NGF**........... Nomina Geographica Flandrica [*A publication*]
**NGF**........... Northern Group of Forces [*USSR*] (NATG)
**NGFA**........ National Grain and Feed Association (EA)
**NGFC**........ Nevada Goldfields Corp. [*NASDAQ symbol*] (NQ)
**NGFEX**...... Naval Gunfire Exercise (NVT)
**NGFF**........ Funafuti [*Tuvalu*] [*ICAO location identifier*] (ICLI)
**NGFLO**..... Naval Gunfire Liaison Officer
**NGFLT**..... Naval Gunfire Liaison Team
**NGFO**........ Nanumea [*Tuvalu*] [*ICAO location identifier*] (ICLI)
**NGFO**........ Naval Gunfire Officer
**NGFR**........ Nerve Growth Factor Receptor [*Neurobiology*]
**NGFS**........ Naval Gunfire Support (NVT)
**NGFT**........ National Guard on Field Training Exercises
**NGFT**........ Naval Gunfire Liaison Team (MUGU)
**NGFTB**...... Nordic Group for Forest Tree Breeding (EAIO)
**NGFU**........ Funafuti/International [*Tuvalu*] [*ICAO location identifier*] (ICLI)
**NGG**.......... Nachrichten. Gesellschaft der Wissenschaften zu Goettingen [*A publication*]
**NGG**.......... Negative Grid Generator
**NGGA**........ National Greentown Glass Association (EA)
**NGGW**....... Nachrichten. Gesellschaft der Wissenschaften zu Goettingen [*A publication*]
**NGH**.......... Hobart and William Smith Colleges, Geneva, NY [*Library symbol*] [*Library of Congress*] (LCLS)
**NGH**.......... Nachrichten der Giessener Hochschulgesellschaft [*A publication*]
**NGH**.......... NASA Grant Handbook
**NGH**.......... National Guard [*Hawaii*] [*Seismograph station code, US Geological Survey*] (SEIS)
**NGH**.......... National Guild of Hypnotists (EA)
**NGHA**........ 91st General Hospital Association (EA)
**NGHEF**..... National Gay Health Education Foundation (EA)
**NGI**........... N-W Group, Inc. [*Toronto Stock Exchange symbol*]
**NGI**........... National Garden Institute
**NGI**........... Nederlandse Genootschap voor Informatica [*Netherlands Society for Informatics*] [*Information service or system*] (IID)
**NGI**........... Ngau [*Fiji*] [*Airport symbol*] (OAG)
**NGI**........... Not Guilty by Reason of Insanity
**NGIC**......... National Geodetic Information Center [*National Oceanic and Atmospheric Administration*] (IID)
**NGiG**......... Gibco/Invenex, Grand Island, NY [*Library symbol*] [*Library of Congress*] (LCLS)
**NGiHC**...... Hooker Chemicals & Plastics Corp., Corporate Technical and Services Center Research Library, Grand Island, NY [*Library symbol*] [*Library of Congress*] (LCLS)
**NGIPSCA**... National GI Pipe Smokers Club of America (EA)
**NgIU**.......... University of Ibadan, Ibadan, Nigeria [*Library symbol*] [*Library of Congress*] (LCLS)
**NGJ**........... Beaufort, SC [*Location identifier*] [*FAA*] (FAAL)
**NGJ**........... Nigerian Geographical Journal [*A publication*]
**NGJA**........ National Gymnastics Judges Association (EA)
**NGJC**........ North Greenville Junior College [*South Carolina*]
**NGK**........... New Greek [*Language, etc.*]
**NGK**........... Niemegk [*German Democratic Republic*] [*Geomagnetic observatory code*]
**NGKBA**..... Nogyo Gijutsu Kenkyusho Hokoku. B. Dojo Hiryo [*A publication*]
**NGKCA**..... Nogyo Gijutsu Kenkyusho Hokoku. C. Byori Konchu [*A publication*]
**NGKDA**..... Nogyo Gijutsu Kenkyusho Hokoku. D. Seiri, Iden, Sakumotsu Ippan [*A publication*]
**NGKJB**...... Nippon Genshiryokusen Kaihatsu Jigyodan Nenpo [*A publication*]
**NGKNA**..... Nippon Genshiryoku Kenkyusho Nenpo [*A publication*]
**NGKYA3**... Folia Ophthalmologica Japonica [*A publication*]
**n-gl---**......... Greenland [*MARC geographic area code*] [*Library of Congress*] (LCCP)
**NGl**............ Harborfields Public Library, Greenlawn, NY [*Library symbol*] [*Library of Congress*] (LCLS)
**NGL**........... Natural Gas Liquids
**NGL**........... Natural Ground Level
**NGL**........... Neodymium Glass LASER
**NGL**........... Neon Glow Lamp
**NGL**........... No Gimbal Lock
**NGL**........... No Greater Love (EA)
**NGL**........... Normalair-Garrett Ltd. [*British*] (IRUK)
**NGL**........... North Gasline [*Alaska*] [*Seismograph station code, US Geological Survey*] (SEIS)
**NGlc**........... Glen Cove Public Library, Glen Cove, NY [*Library symbol*] [*Library of Congress*] (LCLS)
**NGlcC**........ Community Hospital at Glen Cove, Glen Cove, NY [*Library symbol*] [*Library of Congress*] (LCLS)
**NGlcM**....... Garvie's Point Museum, Glen Cove, NY [*Library symbol*] [*Library of Congress*] (LCLS)
**NGlcMS**.... Glen Cove Middle School, Glen Cove, NY [*Library symbol*] [*Library of Congress*] (LCLS)
**NGlcP**........ Pall Corp., Glen Cove, NY [*Library symbol*] [*Library of Congress*] (LCLS)
**NGlcW**....... Webb Institute of Naval Architecture, Glen Cove, NY [*Library symbol*] [*Library of Congress*] (LCLS)
**NGlf**........... Crandall Library, Glens Falls, NY [*Library symbol*] [*Library of Congress*] (LCLS)
**NGlfAC**..... Adirondack Community College, Glens Falls, NY [*Library symbol*] [*Library of Congress*] (LCLS)
**NGlH**......... Hazeltine Corp., Greenlawn, NY [*Library symbol*] [*Library of Congress*] (LCLS)
**NGlhC**....... New York Chiropractic College, Glen Head, NY [*Library symbol*] [*Library of Congress*] (LCLS)
**NGlhES**..... Glen Head Elementary School, Glen Head, NY [*Library symbol*] [*Library of Congress*] (LCLS)
**NGlhNJ**..... North Shore Junior High School, Glen Head, NY [*Library symbol*] [*Library of Congress*] (LCLS)
**NGLIOGT**... National Grand Lodge, International Order of Good Templars [*Later, NCUSIOGT*] (EA)
**NGLO**........ Naval Gunfire Liaison Officer
**NGLR**........ Neodymium Glass LASER Rod
**NGLTF**....... National Gay and Lesbian Task Force (EA)
**NGlwES**..... Glenwood Landing Elementary School, Glenwood Landing, NY [*Library symbol*] [*Library of Congress*] (LCLS)
**N GLZD**.... Not Glazed [*Freight*]
**NGM**......... National Geographic Magazine [*A publication*]
**NGM**......... Neutron-Gamma Monte Carlo [*Data processing*]
**NGM**......... New Ridge Resources [*Vancouver Stock Exchange symbol*]
**NGM**......... Nitrogen Generation Module (NASA)
**NGM**......... Noise Generation Mechanism
**NGMA**....... Maiana [*Kiribati*] [*ICAO location identifier*] (ICLI)
**NGMA**....... National Gadget Manufacturers Association
**NGMA**....... National Gas Measurement Association (EA)
**NGMA**....... National Gospel Music Association (EA)
**NGMA**....... National Greenhouse Manufacturers Association (EA)
**NGMK**....... Marakei [*Kiribati*] [*ICAO location identifier*] (ICLI)
**ng/ml**......... Nanograms per Milliliter
**NGMN**....... Makin [*Kiribati*] [*ICAO location identifier*] (ICLI)
**NGMSA**..... Nauchnye Trudy Nauchno-Issledovatel'skii Gornometallurgicheskii Institut [*Yerevan*] [*A publication*]
**NGN**.......... Nagano [*Japan*] [*Seismograph station code, US Geological Survey*] (SEIS)
**NGN**.......... Nargana [*Panama*] [*Airport symbol*] (OAG)
**NGN**.......... National Geographic Names Data Base [*Geological Survey*] [*Database*]
**NGN**.......... News Group Newspapers [*British*]
**NGN**.......... Nomina Geographica Neerlandica [*A publication*]
**NGN**.......... NRG Resources Ltd. [*Vancouver Stock Exchange symbol*]

**NGNA** ....... Neutrogena Corp. [*NASDAQ symbol*] (NQ)
**NGNF** ........ National Guard Not in Federal Service
**NG/NS** ...... Next Generation/Notional System [*Army*]
**NGNU** ....... Nikunau [*Kiribati*] [*ICAO location identifier*] (ICLI)
**NGNVO** .... Nachrichten. Gesellschaft fuer Natur- und Voelkerkunde Ostasiens [*A publication*]
**NGO** .......... Nago [*Ryukyu Islands*] [*Seismograph station code, US Geological Survey*] (SEIS)
**NGO** .......... Nagoya [*Japan*] [*Airport symbol*] (OAG)
**NGO** .......... National Gas Outlet [*Thread*]
**NGO** .......... Naval Gunfire Officer
**NGO** .......... Navy Guidance Official [*British*]
**NGO** .......... Nongovernmental Observer
**NGO** .......... Nongovernmental Organization [*Generic term*]
**NGOC** ........ North German Oil Control [*Post-World War II*]
**NGOCD** ..... Non-Governmental Organization Committee on Disarmament (EA)
**NGOCS** ..... National Guard Officer Candidate School
**NGoH** ........ Hillside Hospital, Glen Oaks, NY [*Library symbol*] [*Library of Congress*] (LCLS)
**NGON** ....... Onotoa [*Kiribati*] [*ICAO location identifier*] (ICLI)
**NGos** .......... Goshen Library and Historical Society, Goshen, NY [*Library symbol*] [*Library of Congress*] (LCLS)
**NGosA** ....... Arden Hill Hospital Medical Library, Goshen, NY [*Library symbol*] [*Library of Congress*] (LCLS)
**NGou** .......... Reading Room Association Library, Gouveneur, NY [*Library symbol*] [*Library of Congress*] (LCLS)
**NGowH** ...... Tri-County Memorial Hospital, Gowanda, NY [*Library symbol*] [*Library of Congress*] (LCLS)
**NGP** ........... Corpus Christi, TX [*Location identifier*] [*FAA*] (FAAL)
**NGP** ........... Greensboro Public Library, Greensboro, NC [*OCLC symbol*] (OCLC)
**NGP** ........... Nano Glass Pellet
**NGP** ........... Network Graphics Protocol
**NGP** ........... Neue Grosse Partei [*New Great Party*] [*Federal Republic of Germany*] [*Political party*] (PPW)
**NGP** ........... New Gatineau Pulp [*Pulp and paper technology*]
**Ngp** ............ Nominal Group [*Linguistics*]
**NGP** ........... North Galactic Pole
**NGP** ........... Northern Galactic Pole
**NGPA** ........ National Guard Personnel, Army
**NGPA** ........ Natural Gas Policy Act [*1978*]
**NGPA** ........ Natural Gas Processors Association [*Later, GPA*] (EA)
**NGPEC** ...... National Guard Professional Education Center [*North Little Rock, AR*]
**NGPI** ......... New Guinea Periodicals Index [*A publication*]
**NGPP** ......... National Guild of Professional Paperhangers (EA)
**NGPRS** ...... Northern Great Plains Research Center [*Department of Agriculture*] [*Research center*] (RCD)
**NGPSA** ...... Natural Gas Pipeline Safety Act [*1968*]
**NGPSA** ...... Natural Gas Processors Suppliers Association [*Later, GPSA*] (EA)
**NGPSA** ...... Neftyanaya i Gazovaya Promyshlennost' [*A publication*]
**NGPT** ........ National Guild of Piano Teachers (EA)
**NGQ** .......... Nongovernment Quarters (AFM)
**NGQ** .......... Numismatic Gazette Quarterly [*A publication*]
**NGR** ........... Narrow Gauge Railways Ltd. [*Wales*]
**NGR** ........... Narrow Gauze Roll [*Medicine*]
**NGR** ........... National Guard Register
**NGR** ........... National Guard Regulations
**N GR** .......... New Greek [*Language, etc.*] (ROG)
**N-GR** ......... New York State Library, General Reference Library, Albany, NY [*Library symbol*] [*Library of Congress*] (LCLS)
**NGR** ........... Nigerum [*Papua New Guinea*] [*Airport symbol*] (OAG)
**NGR** ........... Non-Grain-Raising [*Coating technology*]
**NGR** ........... Norgold Resources [*Vancouver Stock Exchange symbol*]
**NGRA** ........ National Gay Rights Advocates (EA)
**NGRC** ........ National Government of the Republic of China
**NGREEG** .. National Geographic Research [*A publication*]
**NG Research Bul** ... New Guinea Research Bulletin [*A publication*] (APTA)
**NGRF** ........ National Ghost Ranch Foundation (EA)
**NGRI** ......... Not Guilty by Reason of Insanity
**NGrl** ........... Greenwood Lake Public Library, Greenwood, NY [*Library symbol*] [*Library of Congress*] (LCLS)
**NGrlHS** ..... Harborfields High School, Greenlawn, NY [*Library symbol*] [*Library of Congress*] (LCLS)
**NGrn** .......... Great Neck Library, Great Neck, NY [*Library symbol*] [*Library of Congress*] (LCLS)
**NGrnBE** ..... Baker Elementary School, Great Neck, NY [*Library symbol*] [*Library of Congress*] (LCLS)
**NGrnKE** .... Kennedy Elementary School, Great Neck, NY [*Library symbol*] [*Library of Congress*] (LCLS)
**NGrnKJE** .. Kensington-Johnson Elementary School, Great Neck, NY [*Library symbol*] [*Library of Congress*] (LCLS)
**NGrnLE** ..... Lakeville Elementary School, Great Neck, NY [*Library symbol*] [*Library of Congress*] (LCLS)
**NGrnMS** ... Great Neck South Middle School, Great Neck, NY [*Library symbol*] [*Library of Congress*] (LCLS)
**NGrnNA** .... Network Analysis Corp., Great Neck, NY [*Library symbol*] [*Library of Congress*] (LCLS)
**NGrnPE** ..... Parkville Elementary School, Great Neck, NY [*Library symbol*] [*Library of Congress*] (LCLS)
**NGrnS** ....... Sperry Rand Corp., Sperry Gyroscope Division, Great Neck, NY [*Library symbol*] [*Library of Congress*] (LCLS)
**NGrnSH** .... Great Neck South Senior High School, Great Neck, NY [*Library symbol*] [*Library of Congress*] (LCLS)
**NGrnSRE** .. Saddle Rock Elementary School, Great Neck, NY [*Library symbol*] [*Library of Congress*] (LCLS)
**NGroT** ....... Tompkins-Cortland Community College, Groton, NY [*Library symbol*] [*Library of Congress*] [*Obsolete*] (LCLS)
**NGrpAg** ..... United States Department of Agriculture, Plum Island Animal Disease Laboratory Library, Greenport, NY [*Library symbol*] [*Library of Congress*] (LCLS)
**NGRPD** ..... GREMP [*Geothermal Reservoir Engineering Management Program*] News [*A publication*]
**NGrpEH** .... Eastern Long Island Hospital, Greenport, NY [*Library symbol*] [*Library of Congress*] (LCLS)
**NGRS** ........ Narrow Gauge Railway Society [*British*]
**NGRS** ........ National Geodetic Reference System [*National Oceanic and Atmospheric Administration*]
**NGRS** ........ National Goals Research Staff
**NGS** ........... Alpha Airlines, Inc. [*Jamaica, NY*] [*FAA designator*] (FAAC)
**NGS** ........... Nagasaki [*Japan*] [*Seismograph station code, US Geological Survey*] (SEIS)
**NGS** ........... Nagasaki [*Japan*] [*Airport symbol*] (OAG)
**NGS** ........... National Gardens Scheme Charitable Trust (EAIO)
**NGS** ........... National Gas Straight [*Thread*]
**NGS** ........... National Genealogical Society (EA)
**NGS** ........... National Geodetic Survey [*National Oceanic and Atmospheric Administration*]
**NGS** ........... National Geographic Service
**NGS** ........... National Geographic Society (EA)
**NGS** ........... National Geriatrics Society (EA)
**NGS** ........... National Gladiolus Society (EA)
**NGS** ........... National Goldfish Society
**NGS** ........... National Graniteware Society (EA)
**NGS** ........... Natural Ground Surface
**NGS** ........... Naval Gunfire Support
**N & GS** ...... Navigation and Guidance Subsystem [*NASA*] (KSC)
**NGS** ........... Neue Geisteswissenschaftliche Studien [*A publication*]
**NGS** ........... Neutral Gear Switch [*Automotive engineering*]
**NGS** ........... Neutral Grain Spirits
**NGS** ........... New German Studies [*A publication*]
**NGS** ........... Niagara Share Corp. [*NYSE symbol*] (SPSG)
**NGS** ........... Nieuw-Guinea Studien [*A publication*]
**NGS** ........... No Gallstones [*Medicine*]
**NGS** ........... Non-Immune [*or Normal*] Goat Serum
**NGS** ........... Nucleonic Gauging System
**NGSA** ........ National Golf Salesmen Association [*Defunct*] (EA)
**NGSA** ........ Natural Gas Supply Association (EA)
**NGSA** ........ Nerve Growth Stimulating Activity [*Biochemistry*]
**NGSC** ........ National Gay Student Center [*Defunct*] (EA)
**NGSC** ........ National Gender Selection Center (EA)
**NGSCO** ..... National Geodetic Survey Operations Center [*National Oceanic and Atmospheric Administration*]
**NGSDC** ..... National Geophysical and Solar-Terrestrial Data Center [*National Oceanic and Atmospheric Administration*] (IID)
**NGSEF** ...... National Geographic Society Education Foundation (EA)
**NGSF** ........ Noble Gas Storage Facility (NRCH)
**NGSFO** ..... Naval Gunfire Support Forward Observer [*British*]
**NGSIC** ....... National Geodetic Survey Information Center [*National Oceanic and Atmospheric Administration*] (IID)
**NGSM** ....... National Gold Star Mothers (EA)
**NGSMA** .... Natural Gasoline Supply Men's Association [*Later, GPSA*]
**NGS/NGM** ... National Geographic Magazine. National Geographic Society [*A publication*]
**NGSP** ......... National Geodetic Satellite Program [*NASA*]
**NGSP** ......... National Guilds of St. Paul (EA)
**NGSP** ......... Nonglycosylated Serum Protein
**NGSQ** ........ National Genealogical Society. Quarterly [*A publication*]
**NGSTDC** ... National Geophysical and Solar-Terrestrial Data Center [*National Oceanic and Atmospheric Administration*]
**NGT** ........... Berclair, TX [*Location identifier*] [*FAA*] (FAAL)
**NGT** ........... Nagatsuro [*Irozaki*] [*Japan*] [*Seismograph station code, US Geological Survey*] (SEIS)
**NGT** ........... NASA Ground Terminal (MCD)
**NGT** ........... National Gas Taper [*Thread*]
**NGT** ........... National Guard Technician (MCD)
**NGT** ........... Next Generation Trainer [*Air Force*]
**NGT** ........... Night
**NGT** ........... Noise Generator Tube
**NGT** ........... Nominal Grouping Technique
**NGT** ........... Nonsymmetric Gravitational Theory
**NGT** ........... Northern General Transport Co. [*British*] (DCTA)
**NGTA** ........ Next Generation Trainer Aircraft (MCD)
**NGTA** ........ Nonguaranteed Trade Arrears (IMH)
**NGTA** ........ Tarawa/Bonriki International [*Kiribati*] [*ICAO location identifier*] (ICLI)
**NGTB** ........ Abemama [*Kiribati*] [*ICAO location identifier*] (ICLI)
**NGTC** ........ National Grain Trade Council (EA)

**NGTE** ........ National Gas Turbine Establishment [*British*]
**NGTE** ........ Tabiteuea (North) [*Kiribati*] [*ICAO location identifier*] (ICLI)
**NGTF** ........ National Gay Task Force [*Later, NGLTF*] (EA)
**NGTG** ........ NCAR [*National Center for Atmospheric Research*] GARP [*Global Atmospheric Research Program*] Task Group
**NGTM** ........ Tamana [*Kiribati*] [*ICAO location identifier*] (ICLI)
**NGTO** ........ Nonouti [*Kiribati*] [*ICAO location identifier*] (ICLI)
**NGTR** ........ Arorae [*Kiribati*] [*ICAO location identifier*] (ICLI)
**NGTS** ........ Tabiteuea (South) [*Kiribati*] [*ICAO location identifier*] (ICLI)
**NGTT** ........ Tarawa/Betio [*Kiribati*] [*ICAO location identifier*] (ICLI)
**NGTU** ........ Butaritari [*Kiribati*] [*ICAO location identifier*] (ICLI)
**nGU** .......... Nano-Goldblatt Units [*Clinical chemistry*]
**NGU** .......... Nongonococcal Urethritis [*Medicine*]
**NGU** .......... Norfolk, VA [*Location identifier*] [*FAA*] (FAAL)
**NGU** .......... University of North Carolina, Greensboro, Greensboro, NC [*OCLC symbol*] (OCLC)
**N Guin** ....... New Guinea
**NGUK** ........ Aranuka [*Kiribati*] [*ICAO location identifier*] (ICLI)
**NGuNA** ..... New York State Nurses Association, Guilderland, NY [*Library symbol*] [*Library of Congress*] (LCLS)
**NGUS** ........ National Guard of the United States
**NGV** .......... Natural Gas Vehicle
**NGV** .......... New Goldcore Ventures [*Vancouver Stock Exchange symbol*]
**NGV** .......... Nozzle Guide Vanes [*Aviation*] (AIA)
**NGV Bl** ...... Niedersaechsisches Gesetz- und Verordnungsblatt [*A publication*]
**NGVC** ........ National Guard Volunteer Corps [*British military*] (DMA)
**NGvP** ........ Long Island University, C. W. Post Center, Greenvale, NY [*Library symbol*] [*Library of Congress*] (LCLS)
**NGVR** ........ New Guinea Volunteer Reserve
**NGW** ......... Corpus Christi, TX [*Location identifier*] [*FAA*] (FAAL)
**NGW** ......... Gardner-Webb College, Boiling Springs, NC [*OCLC symbol*] (OCLC)
**NGW** ......... National Gallery of Art, Washington, DC
**NGW** ......... No Gift Wrap [*Mail-order catalogs*]
**NGWG** ....... Nachrichten. Gesellschaft der Wissenschaften zu Goettingen. Philologisch-Historische Klasse [*A publication*]
**NGW (Goett)** ... Nachrichten. Gesellschaft der Wissenschaften (Goettingen) [*A publication*]
**NGWGott** .. Nachrichten. Gesellschaft der Wissenschaften zu Goettingen [*A publication*]
**NGWIC** ..... National Ground Water Information Center [*National Water Well Association*] [*Information service or system*] (IID)
**NGWO** ...... Non-Government Welfare Organisation [*Australia*]
**NGX** .......... Northgate Exploration Ltd. [*NYSE symbol*] [*Toronto Stock Exchange symbol*] (SPSG)
**NGYN** ........ National Gay Youth Network (EA)
**NGZ** .......... Alameda, CA [*Location identifier*] [*FAA*] (FAAL)
**NH** ............ All Nippon Airways Co. Ltd. [*Japan*] [*ICAO designator*] (FAAC)
**NH** ............ Editions Nouveaux Horizons [*US government imprint*]
**NH** ............ Hamilton Public Library, Hamilton, NY [*Library symbol*] [*Library of Congress*] (LCLS)
**nH** ............ Nanohenry (IEEE)
**NH** ............ National Hunt [*British*]
**NH** ............ Natural History [*A publication*]
**NH** ............ Naval Home [*Philadelphia, PA*]
**NH** ............ Naval Hospital
**NH** ............ Nebraska History [*A publication*]
**NH** ............ Neo-Hebrew (BJA)
**NH** ............ Neonatal Hypothyroidism [*Cretinism*] [*Medicine*]
**NH** ............ Never Hinged [*Philately*]
**NH** ............ New Hampshire [*Postal code*]
**NH** ............ New Hampshire Quarter Notes [*A publication*]
**NH** ............ New Hampshire Reports [*A publication*]
**Nh** ............ New Hampshire State Library, Concord, NH [*Library symbol*] [*Library of Congress*] (LCLS)
**NH** ............ New Hampshire Supreme Court Reports [*A publication*] (DLA)
**NH** ............ New Haven [*Connecticut*]
**NH** ............ New High [*Investment term*]
**NH** ............ New York, New Haven & Hartford R. R. [*AAR code*]
**N/H** .......... Next Higher Assembly [*Engineering*]
**NH** ............ Nominal Height (MCD)
**NH** ............ Nonhandicapped
**NH** ............ Nonhygroscopic
**NH** ............ Norfolk Howard [*Refers to a bed-bug*] [*Slang*] (DSUE)
**NH** ............ Northern Canada Mines Ltd. [*Toronto Stock Exchange symbol*]
**NH** ............ Northern Hemisphere
**NH** ............ Northern History [*A publication*]
**Nh** ............ Northern Hogsucker [*Ichthyology*]
**NH** ............ Northumberland Hussars [*British military*] (DMA)
**NH** ............ Not Held
**N & H** ........ Nott and Hopkins' Reports [*United States Court of Claims*] [*A publication*] (DLA)
**N & H** ........ Nott and Huntington's Reports [*1-7 United States Court of Claims*] [*A publication*] (DLA)
**NH** ............ Nursing Home
**NHA** .......... American Foundation for Management Research, Hamilton, NY [*Library symbol*] [*Library of Congress*] (LCLS)
**NHA** .......... Nahanni Mines Ltd. [*Toronto Stock Exchange symbol*]
**NHA** .......... National Fashion Accessories Association (EA)
**NHA** .......... National Handbag Association (EA)
**NHA** .......... National Hay Association (EA)
**NHA** .......... National Health Agencies (EA)
**NHA** .......... National Health Association
**NHA** .......... National Hearing Association (EA)
**NHA** .......... National Heritage Act [*Protects national treasures from sale out of the country*] [*British*]
**NHA** .......... National Hide Association [*Later, USHSLA*] (EA)
**NHA** .......... National Hobo Association (EA)
**NHA** .......... National Hockey Association [*to 1917*]
**NHA** .......... National Holiness Association [*Later, CHA*] (EA)
**NHA** .......... National Homeowners Association (EA)
**NHA** .......... National Homeschool Association (EA)
**NHA** .......... National Housing Act [*1934, 1954*]
**NHA** .......... National Housing Administration
**NHA** .......... National Housing Agency [*Superseded by HHFA, 1947; then by HUD, 1965*]
**NHA** .......... National Humanities Alliance (EA)
**NHA** .......... National Hunters Association (EA)
**NHA** .......... National Hydropower Association (EA)
**NHA** .......... National Hypertension Association (EA)
**NHA** .......... National Hypoglycemia Association (EA)
**NHA** .......... Nationwide Hotel Association
**NHA** .......... New Homemakers of America [*Later, FHA*] (EA)
**NHA** .......... New Humanity Alliance (EA)
**NHA** .......... Next Higher Assembly [*Engineering*]
**NHA** .......... Next Higher Authority (MUGU)
**NHA** .......... Nhatrang [*Vietnam*] [*Seismograph station code, US Geological Survey*] [*Closed*] (SEIS)
**NHA** .......... Nonhydrogen Atom [*Chemistry*]
**NHA** .......... Northwest Hardwood Association [*Later, WHA*] (EA)
**NHAC** ........ National Health Awareness Center [*Later, NHSAC*] (EA)
**NHACE** ..... National Hispanic Association of Construction Enterprises (EA)
**NHACFC** .. National Health Agencies for the Combined Federal Campaign [*Formerly, FSCNHA*] [*Later, NVHA*] (EA)
**NH Act** ...... National Housing Act [*1934, 1954*] (DLA)
**NH Admin Code** ... New Hampshire Code of Administrative Rules [*A publication*] (DLA)
**NHAES** ..... New Hampshire Agricultural Experiment Station [*University of New Hampshire*] [*Research center*] (RCD)
**NH Ag Exp** ... New Hampshire Agricultural Experiment Station. Publications [*A publication*]
**NHAIAC** ... National Highway Accident and Injury Analysis Center
**NHAM** ...... National Hose Assemblies Manufacturers Association [*Defunct*]
**NHAM** ...... North-Holland Series in Applied Mathematics and Mechanics [*Elsevier Book Series*] [*A publication*]
**NHamB** ..... Hampton Bays Public Library, Hampton Bays, NY [*Library symbol*] [*Library of Congress*] [*Obsolete*] (LCLS)
**NHamH** ..... Hilbert College, Hamburg, NY [*Library symbol*] [*Library of Congress*] (LCLS)
**N Hamp** ..... New Hampshire Reports [*A publication*] (DLA)
**NHampB** ... Hampton Bays Public Library, Hampton Bays, NY [*Library symbol*] [*Library of Congress*] (LCLS)
**N Hamp Rep** ... New Hampshire Reports [*A publication*] (DLA)
**N Hampshire Rep** ... New Hampshire Reports [*A publication*] (DLA)
**NHANES** .. National Health and Nutritional Examination Survey
**NHapSA** .... Suffolk Academy of Medicine, Hauppauge, NY [*Library symbol*] [*Library of Congress*] (LCLS)
**Nh-Ar** ......... New Hampshire Department of Administration and Control, Division of Archives and Records Management, Concord, NH [*Library symbol*] [*Library of Congress*] (LCLS)
**NHAR** ....... Next Higher Assembly Removal Frequency [*Engineering*] (MCD)
**NHarC** ....... Harriman College, Harriman, NY [*Library symbol*] [*Library of Congress*] (LCLS)
**NHARC** ..... Nursing Home Advisory and Research Council (EA)
**NHarn** ........ Harrison Public Library, Harrison, NY [*Library symbol*] [*Library of Congress*] (LCLS)
**NHas** ......... Hastings-On-Hudson Public Library, Hastings-On-Hudson, NY [*Library symbol*] [*Library of Congress*] (LCLS)
**NHAS** ........ National Healthcare Antifraud Association [*Address unknown*] (EA)
**NHAS** ........ National Hearing Aid Society (EA)
**NHASA** ..... National Handbag and Accessories Salesmen's Association (EA)
**NHasI** ........ Institute of Society, Ethics, and Life Sciences, The Hastings Center, Hastings-On-Hudson, NY [*Library symbol*] [*Library of Congress*] (LCLS)
**NHAT** ........ Neutron Hardness Assurance Test
**NHauS** ....... Suffolk County Department of Health Service, Hauppauge, NY [*Library symbol*] [*Library of Congress*] (LCLS)
**NHAW** ...... Northamerican Heating and Airconditioning Wholesalers Association (EA)
**NHB** .......... NASA Handbook (KSC)
**NHB** .......... National Harbours Board [*Canada*]
**NHB** .......... National Naval Medical Center [*Maryland*] [*Seismograph station code, US Geological Survey*] [*Closed*] (SEIS)
**NHB** .......... Nederlandsche Historiebladen [*A publication*]

**NHB** .......... Negro History Bulletin [*A publication*]
**NHB** .......... New Hibernian [*Vancouver Stock Exchange symbol*]
**NHB** .......... Nitro(hydroxy)benzoic Acid [*Organic chemistry*]
**NHBC**........ National House Building Council [*British*]
**NHBE**........ Normal Human Bronchial Epithelial [*Cells*]
**NHB J** ....... New Hampshire Bar Journal [*A publication*]
**NHBl** ......... Nassauische Heimatblaetter [*A publication*]
**NHBPCC**... National High Blood Pressure Coordinating Committee
**NHBPEP**... National High Blood Pressure Education Program
**NHBRC**..... National House-Builders Registration Council [*British*] (ILCA)
**NH Bsns** .... Seacoast New Hampshire. Business Digest [*A publication*]
**NH Bsns Rv** ... New Hampshire Business Review [*A publication*]
**NHBW**....... National Hook-Up of Black Women (EA)
**NHC** .......... Colgate University, Hamilton, NY [*Library symbol*] [*Library of Congress*] (LCLS)
**NHC** .......... N-Hexylcarborane [*Rocket fuel*] (RDA)
**NHC** .......... National Havurah Committee (EA)
**NHC** .......... National Health Council (EA)
**NHC** .......... National Healthcorp LP [*AMEX symbol*] (SPSG)
**NHC** .......... National Homecaring Council [*Later, FHH*] (EA)
**NHC** .......... National Horse Carriers Association, Inc., Frankfort KY [*STAC*]
**NHC** .......... National Housing Center (EA)
**NHC** .......... National Housing Conference (EA)
**NHC** .......... National Housing Council [*of the HHFA*] [*Abolished, 1965*]
**NHC** .......... National Humanities Center (EA)
**NHC** .......... National Hunt Cup [*British*] (ROG)
**NHC** .......... National Hurricane Center [*National Weather Service*]
**NHC** .......... Native High Court Reports [*South Africa*] [*A publication*] (DLA)
**NHC** .......... Natural Hydrocarbon [*Organic chemistry*]
**NHC** .......... Navy Department Library, Naval Historical Center, Washington, DC [*OCLC symbol*] (OCLC)
**NHC** .......... Neighborhood Health Center [*Generic term*] (DHSM)
**NHC** .......... Neohemocyte [*An artificial red blood cell*]
**NHC** .......... New Haven [*Yale*] [*Connecticut*] [*Seismograph station code, US Geological Survey*] [*Closed*] (SEIS)
**NHC** .......... Nicaraguan Humanitarian Coalition (EA)
**NHC** .......... Northwest Horticultural Council (EA)
**NH & C**...... Railway and Canal Cases [*1835-55*] [*England*] [*A publication*] (DLA)
**N4-HC** ....... National 4-H Council (EA)
**NHCA**........ National Hairdressers and Cosmetologists Association (EA)
**NHCA**........ National Health Club Association (EA)
**NHCA**........ National Hearing Conservation Association (EA)
**NHCA**........ National Hispanic Congress on Alcoholism (EA)
**NHCA**........ National Hispanic Council on Aging (EA)
**NHCC**........ NASA Headquarters Computer Center
**N-HCC** ...... Nash-Healey Car Club (EA)
**NHCC**........ National Havurah Coordinating Committee (EA)
**NHCC**........ National Health Care Campaign (EA)
**NHCC**........ National Health Corporation [*NASDAQ symbol*] (NQ)
**NHCC**........ National Hebrew Culture Council (EA)
**NHCES** ..... National Health Care Expenditures Study (DHSM)
**NHCFD**..... National Health Care Foundation for the Deaf [*Later, Deaf-REACH*] (EA)
**NHCG** ....... North-Holland Series in Crystal Growth [*Elsevier Book Series*] [*A publication*]
**NHCI**......... National Healthcare, Incorporated [*Dothan, AL*] [*NASDAQ symbol*] (NQ)
**NhCla** ........ Fiske Free Library, Claremont, NH [*Library symbol*] [*Library of Congress*] (LCLS)
**NH Code Admin R** ... New Hampshire Code of Administrative Rules [*A publication*]
**NHCP**........ National HUMINT Collection Plan (MCD)
**NHCP**........ Nonhistone Chromosomal Protein [*Genetics*]
**NHCS**........ National Health Care Systems, Inc. [*NASDAQ symbol*] (NQ)
**NHCS**........ National Home Center Show (ITD)
**NHCSA** ..... National Historic Communal Societies Association [*Later, CSA*] (EA)
**NhCSp**....... Saint Paul's School, Concord, NH [*Library symbol*] [*Library of Congress*] (LCLS)
**NhCT**......... New Hampshire Technical Institute, Concord, NH [*Library symbol*] [*Library of Congress*] (LCLS)
**NHCU** ....... Nursing Home Care Unit [*Veterans Administration*]
**NHCUC**..... New Hampshire College and University Council, Library Policy Committee [*Library network*]
**NhD** ........... Dartmouth College, Hanover, NH [*Library symbol*] [*Library of Congress*] (LCLS)
**NHD** .......... National History Day (EA)
**NHD** .......... New Harding Group, Inc. [*Toronto Stock Exchange symbol*]
**NHD** .......... New Housing District [*Australia*]
**NHD** .......... Not Heard [*Communications*]
**NHDA** ....... National Huntington's Disease Association [*Later, HDSA*] (EA)
**NHDAA** .... National Home Demonstration Agents' Association [*Later, NAEHE*] (EA)
**NhD-BE**..... Dartmouth College, Business Administration and Engineering Library, Hanover, NH [*Library symbol*] [*Library of Congress*] (LCLS)
**NHDC** ....... National Home Demonstration Council [*Later, NEHC*] (EA)
**NHDC** ....... NATO HAWK Documentation Center [*Missiles*] (NATG)
**NHDC** ....... Naval Historical Display Center
**NHDC** ....... Neohesperidin Dihydrochalcone [*Also, NEO-DHC*] [*Sweetening agent*]
**NhD-D**....... Dartmouth College, Dana Biomedical Library, Hanover, NH [*Library symbol*] [*Library of Congress*] (LCLS)
**NH Dep Resour Econ Dev Bull** ... New Hampshire Department of Resources and Economic Development. Bulletin [*A publication*]
**NHDI**......... NHD Stores, Incorporated [*NASDAQ symbol*] (NQ)
**NHDI**......... Notch Die [*Tool*] (AAG)
**NHDIDW** ... Nutrition in Health and Disease [*A publication*]
**NH Div Econ Dev Miner Resour Surv** ... New Hampshire Division of Economic Development. Mineral Resources Survey [*A publication*]
**NhD-K** ....... Dartmouth College, Kresge Physical Sciences Library, Hanover, NH [*Library symbol*] [*Library of Congress*] (LCLS)
**NHDNA** .... Nucleohistone Deoxyribonucleic Acid
**NhDo** ......... Dover Public Library, Dover, NH [*Library symbol*] [*Library of Congress*] (LCLS)
**NHDS**........ National Hospital Discharge Survey
**NHDS**........ Nonhazardous Dry Solid [*Shipping classification*]
**NHDSC** ..... National Hot Dog and Sausage Council (EA)
**NHE** .......... National Housing Endowment (EA)
**NHE** .......... Nederlandse Energiehuishouding. Witkomsten van Maandtellingen en Kwartaaltellingen [*A publication*]
**NHE** .......... Nitrogen Heat Exchange
**NHE** .......... Normal Hydrogen Electrode
**NHE** .......... North Hennepin Community College Library, Brooklyn Park, MN [*OCLC symbol*] (OCLC)
**NHEA**........ National Higher Education Association (EA)
**N HEB** ....... New Hebrew [*Language, etc.*] (ROG)
**N HEB** ....... New Hebrides (ROG)
**NHEDLP** .. National Housing and Economic Development Law Project
**NHEF**......... National Health Education Foundation
**NHEIAY** ... Japanese Journal of Smooth Muscle Research [*A publication*]
**NHEK**........ Normal Human Epidermal Keratinocyte
**NHeLP** ...... National Health Law Program (EA)
**NHem** ........ Hempstead Public Library, Hempstead, NY [*Library symbol*] [*Library of Congress*] (LCLS)
**NHEM** ...... Normal Human Epidermal Melanocyte [*Cytology*]
**NHemB**...... Burns & Roe, Inc., Branch Library, Hempstead, NY [*Library symbol*] [*Library of Congress*] (LCLS)
**NHemGH** .. Hempstead General Hospital, Medical Center, Hempstead, NY [*Library symbol*] [*Library of Congress*] (LCLS)
**NHemH** ..... Hofstra University, Hempstead, NY [*Library symbol*] [*Library of Congress*] (LCLS)
**NHEML**.... National Hurricane and Experimental Meteorology Laboratory [*Marine science*] (MSC)
**NHemNH** ... Nassau County Department of Health, Hempstead, NY [*Library symbol*] [*Library of Congress*] (LCLS)
**NHemNHR** ... Nassau County Department of Health, Division of Laboratories and Research, Hempstead, NY [*Library symbol*] [*Library of Congress*] (LCLS)
**NHen** ......... Henderson Free Library, Henderson, NY [*Library symbol*] [*Library of Congress*] (LCLS)
**NHEN** ....... National Holistic Education Network (EA)
**NHENMA** ... National Hand Embroidery and Novelty Manufacturers Association (EA)
**NHEP** ........ Nicaragua-Honduras Education Project (EA)
**NHER**........ National Heritage Industries, Inc. [*NASDAQ symbol*] (NQ)
**NHerkCHi** ... Herkimer County Historical Society, Herkimer, NY [*Library symbol*] [*Library of Congress*] (LCLS)
**NHES** ........ National Health Enhancement Systems, Inc. [*Phoenix, AZ*] [*NASDAQ symbol*] (NQ)
**NHESA** ..... National Higher Education Staff Association [*Defunct*] (EA)
**NHESP**...... Natural Heritage and Endangered Species Program [*Massachusetts State Division of Fisheries and Wildlife*] [*Also, an information service or system*] (IID)
**NHew**......... Hewlett-Woodmere Public Library, Hewlett, NY [*Library symbol*] [*Library of Congress*] (LCLS)
**NHewE** ....... Hewlett Elementary School, Hewlett, NY [*Library symbol*] [*Library of Congress*] (LCLS)
**NHewFE**.... Franklin Elementary School, Hewlett, NY [*Library symbol*] [*Library of Congress*] (LCLS)
**NHewOE**... Ogden Elementary School, Hewlett, NY [*Library symbol*] [*Library of Congress*] (LCLS)
**NhExP** ....... Phillips Exeter Academy, Exeter, NH [*Library symbol*] [*Library of Congress*] (LCLS)
**NHF**........... National Handicapped Foundation (EA)
**NHF**........... National Headache Foundation (EA)
**NHF**........... National Health Federation (EA)
**NHF**........... National Hemophilia Foundation (EA)
**NHF**........... National Humanities Faculty [*Later, NFHAS*] (EA)
**NHF**........... National Hunting and Fishing [*In "NHF" Day*] [*National Rifle Association*]
**NHF**........... National Hydrocephalus Foundation (EA)
**NHF**........... Nausori Highlands [*Fiji*] [*Seismograph station code, US Geological Survey*] (SEIS)
**NHF**........... Naval Historical Foundation (EA)
**NHF**........... New Halfa [*Sudan*] [*Airport symbol*] (OAG)

**NHF**.......... Nordisk Herpetologisk Forening [*Scandinavian Herpetological Society - SHS*] (EAIO)
**NHF**.......... Nordisk Hydrologisk Forening [*Nordic Association for Hydrology - NAH*] (EAIO)
**NHF**.......... Nordiska Handikappforbundet [*Nordic Association for the Handicapped - NAH*] (EAIO)
**NHFA**........ National Home Furnishings Association (EA)
**NHFF**........ National Historical Fire Foundation (EA)
**NHFL**........ National Home Fashions League (EA)
**NHFP**........ New Hebrides Federal Party [*Political party*] (PPW)
**NhFr**.......... Franklin Public Library, Franklin, NH [*Library symbol*] [*Library of Congress*] (LCLS)
**NHFRA**..... National Hay Fever Relief Association [*Defunct*] (EA)
**NHG**.......... New High German [*Language, etc.*]
**NHG**.......... Newhawk Gold Mines Ltd. [*Toronto Stock Exchange symbol*] [*Vancouver Stock Exchange symbol*]
**NHG**.......... Normal Human Globulin [*or anticancer substance derived from NHG*] [*Biochemistry*]
**NHG**.......... Northern Hemisphere Glaciation
**NHGZA**..... Nippon Igaku Hoshasen Gakkai Zasshi [*A publication*]
**NHH**.......... Neither Help nor Hinder
**NhHaCR**.... United States Army, Cold Regions Research and Engineering Laboratory, Hanover, NH [*Library symbol*] [*Library of Congress*] (LCLS)
**NhHen**....... Tucker Free Library, Henniker, NH [*Library symbol*] [*Library of Congress*] (LCLS)
**NhHenN**.... New England College, Henniker, NH [*Library symbol*] [*Library of Congress*] (LCLS)
**NhHi**.......... New Hampshire Historical Society, Concord, NH [*Library symbol*] [*Library of Congress*] (LCLS)
**NH His S**... New Hampshire Historical Society. Proceedings [*A publication*]
**NhHopA**.... New Hampshire Antiquarian Society, Hopkinton, NH [*Library symbol*] [*Library of Congress*] (LCLS)
**NHHRA**.... National Hereford Hog Record Association (EA)
**NH-HY**...... Harvard University, Harvard-Yenching Institute [*Chinese-Japanese Library*], Cambridge, MA [*Library symbol*] [*Library of Congress*] (LCLS)
**NHI**........... Jacksonville, FL [*Location identifier*] [*FAA*] (FAAL)
**NHI**........... Naphtali Herz Imber (BJA)
**NHI**........... Nathan Hale Institute (EA)
**NHI**........... National Health Insurance [*British*]
**NHI**........... National Heart Institute [*Later, NHLI, NHLBI*] [*National Institutes of Health*]
**NHI**........... National Highway Institute
**NHI**........... National Hobby Institute [*Defunct*]
**NHI**........... National Humanities Institute (EA)
**NHI**........... Nelson Holdings International Ltd. [*Toronto Stock Exchange symbol*] [*Vancouver Stock Exchange symbol*]
**NHi**........... New York Historical Society, New York, NY [*Library symbol*] [*Library of Congress*] (LCLS)
**NHIC**......... NASA Hazards Identification Committee (KSC)
**NHIC**......... National Health Information Clearinghouse [*Public Health Service*] [*Later, ODPHP Health Information Center*] (IID)
**NHIC**......... National Home Improvement Council [*Later, NARI*] (EA)
**NHIC**......... Nichols-Homeshield, Incorporated [*Dallas, TX*] [*NASDAQ symbol*] (NQ)
**NHick**........ Hicksville Free Public Library, Hicksville, NY [*Library symbol*] [*Library of Congress*] (LCLS)
**NHickAd**... Hicksville Administration, Hicksville, NY [*Library symbol*] [*Library of Congress*] (LCLS)
**NHickBE**... Burns Elementary School, Hicksville, NY [*Library symbol*] [*Library of Congress*] (LCLS)
**NHickCE**... Old Country Elementary School, Hicksville, NY [*Library symbol*] [*Library of Congress*] (LCLS)
**NHickDLE**... Dutch Lane Elementary School, Hicksville, NY [*Library symbol*] [*Library of Congress*] (LCLS)
**NHickEE**... East Elementary School, Hicksville, NY [*Library symbol*] [*Library of Congress*] (LCLS)
**NHickFE**... Fork Elementary School, Hicksville, NY [*Library symbol*] [*Library of Congress*] (LCLS)
**NHickLE**... Lee Elementary School, Hicksville, NY [*Library symbol*] [*Library of Congress*] (LCLS)
**NHickSH**.. Hicksville Senior High School, Hicksville, NY [*Library symbol*] [*Library of Congress*] (LCLS)
**NHickWE**... Willet Elementary School, Hicksville, NY [*Library symbol*] [*Library of Congress*] (LCLS)
**NHIF**......... National Head Injury Foundation (EA)
**NHig**.......... Highland Free Library, Highland, NY [*Library symbol*] [*Library of Congress*] (LCLS)
**NHigfL**...... Ladycliff College, Highland Falls, NY [*Library symbol*] [*Library of Congress*] (LCLS)
**NHigm**....... Rushmore Memorial Library, Highland Mills, NY [*Library symbol*] [*Library of Congress*] (LCLS)
**NHIP**......... Nursing Home Improvement Program [*National Institute of Mental Health*]
**NHIR**......... Natural History Information Retrieval System [*Smithsonian Institution*]
**NHIR**......... New Hope & Ivyland Railroad Co. [*AAR code*]
**NHIS**......... Nursing Home Information Service (EA)
**NHIY**........ Northumberland Hussars Imperial Yeomanry [*British military*] (DMA)
**NHJ**........... Nathaniel Hawthorne Journal [*A publication*]
**NHJ**........... Neue Heidelberger Jahrbuecher [*A publication*]
**NHJ**........... New Hampshire Bar Journal [*A publication*]
**NHJB**........ Neue Heidelberger Jahrbuecher [*A publication*]
**NHjI**.......... International Business Machines Corp., Components Division Library, Hopewell Junction, NY [*Library symbol*] [*Library of Congress*] (LCLS)
**NHK**.......... Frank Aviation, Inc. [*Dallas, TX*] [*FAA designator*] (FAAC)
**NHK**.......... Patuxent River, MD [*Location identifier*] [*FAA*] (FAAL)
**NhKe**.......... Keene Public Library, Keene, NH [*Library symbol*] [*Library of Congress*] (LCLS)
**NhKeHi**..... Historical Society of Cheshire County, Keene, NH [*Library symbol*] [*Library of Congress*] (LCLS)
**NhKeK**....... Keene State College, Keene, NH [*Library symbol*] [*Library of Congress*] (LCLS)
**NHK Lab Note**... NHK [*Nippon Hoso Kyokai*] Laboratories Note [*A publication*]
**NHKNA**.... Nippon Hoshasen Kobunshi Kenkyu Kyokai Nempo [*A publication*]
**NHK Tech J**... NHK [*Nippon Hoso Kyokai*] Technical Journal [*A publication*]
**NHK Tech Monogr**... NHK [*Nippon Hoso Kyokai*] Technical Monograph [*A publication*]
**NHKYA**..... National Hand Knitting Yarn Association [*Later, NHKYC*] (EA)
**NHKYC**..... National Hand Knitting Yarn Committee [*Defunct*] (EA)
**NHL**.......... National Historic Landmark
**NHL**.......... National Hockey League (EA)
**NHL**.......... Negro Heritage Library
**NHL**.......... Newhall Land & Farming Co. [*NYSE symbol*] (SPSG)
**NHL**.......... Nodular Histiocytic Lymphoma [*Oncology*]
**NHL**.......... Non-Hodgkin's Lymphoma [*Oncology*]
**NHL**.......... Nordic Federation of Heart and Lung Associations (EA)
**NHL**.......... Normal Human Lymphocyte
**NHL**.......... Northcal Resources [*Vancouver Stock Exchange symbol*]
**NHL**.......... Notes from Hume's Lectures [*A publication*] (DLA)
**NHLA**........ National Hardwood Lumber Association (EA)
**NHLA**........ National Health Lawyers Association (EA)
**NHLA**........ National Housewives' League of America (EA)
**NH Laws**.... Laws of the State of New Hampshire [*A publication*]
**NHLBAC**.. National Heart, Lung, and Blood Advisory Council [*National Institutes of Health*]
**NHLBCA**.. National Hockey League Booster Clubs Association (EA)
**NHLBI**...... National Heart, Lung, and Blood Institute [*National Institutes of Health*] [*Bethesda, MD*]
**NHLC**........ National Hispanic Leadership Conference (EA)
**NHLC**........ National Home Loans Corporation [*British*]
**NhLe**.......... Lebanon Public Library, Lebanon, NH [*Library symbol*] [*Library of Congress*] (LCLS)
**NhLeHi**...... Lebanon Historical Society, Lebanon, NH [*Library symbol*] [*Library of Congress*] (LCLS)
**NHLI**......... National Health Laboratories, Incorporated [*NASDAQ symbol*] (NQ)
**NHLI**......... National Heart and Lung Institute [*Later, NHLBI*] [*National Institutes of Health*]
**NHLP**........ National Housing Law Project (EA)
**NHLPA**..... National Hockey League Player's Association (EA)
**NHL Rep**... New Hampshire Law Reporter [*A publication*] (DLA)
**NHLS**........ North-Holland Linguistic Series [*Elsevier Book Series*] [*A publication*]
**NhM**.......... Manchester City Library, Manchester, NH [*Library symbol*] [*Library of Congress*] (LCLS)
**NHM**......... Natural History Museum [*British*]
**NHM**......... Niihama [*Japan*] [*Seismograph station code, US Geological Survey*] [*Closed*] (SEIS)
**NHM**......... No Hot Metal [*Photocomposition*]
**NHM**......... Nonhostile Missing [*Military*] (CINC)
**NHM**......... Normal Human Milk
**NHM**......... Nozzle Hinge Moment
**NHM**......... Nuclear Hyperfine Magnetic [*Rare-earth alloy*]
**NHM**......... University of New Hampshire, Durham, NH [*OCLC symbol*] (OCLC)
**NHMA**...... National Handle Manufacturers Association [*Defunct*] (EA)
**NHMA**...... National Housewares Manufacturers Association (EA)
**NHMC**...... National Hispanic Media Conference (EA)
**NHMC**...... Normal Human Mammary Cell
**NHMDAP**... National Health and Medical Research Council [*Canberra*]. Medical Research [*A publication*]
**NHMILCOM**... NATO HAWK Military Committee [*Missiles*] (AABC)
**NHML**....... North-Holland Mathematical Library [*Elsevier Book Series*] [*A publication*]
**NhMND**.... Notre Dame College, Manchester, NH [*Library symbol*] [*Library of Congress*] (LCLS)
**NHMO**...... National HMO Corp. [*NASDAQ symbol*] (NQ)
**NHMO**...... NATO HAWK Management Office [*Missiles*] (NATG)
**NHMRC**.... National Hotel & Motel Reservations Corporation
**NHMS**....... North-Holland Mathematics Studies [*Elsevier Book Series*] [*A publication*]

**NhMSA** ..... Saint Anselm's College, Manchester, NH [*Library symbol*] [*Library of Congress*] (LCLS)
**NHMT** ...... North-Holland Medieval Translations [*Elsevier Book Series*] [*A publication*]
**NhMV** ....... United States Veterans Administration Hospital, Manchester, NH [*Library symbol*] [*Library of Congress*] (LCLS)
**NHN** .......... Northern Horizon [*Vancouver Stock Exchange symbol*]
**NhNa** ......... Nashua Public Library, Nashua, NH [*Library symbol*] [*Library of Congress*] (LCLS)
**NhNaR** ...... Rivier College, Nashua, NH [*Library symbol*] [*Library of Congress*] (LCLS)
**NhNaS** ....... Sanders Associates, Inc., Technical Library, Nashua, NH [*Library symbol*] [*Library of Congress*] (LCLS)
**NhNelC** ..... Colby Junior College for Women [*Later, CSC*], New London, NH [*Library symbol*] [*Library of Congress*] (LCLS)
**NHNP** ....... New Hebrides National Party [*Political party*] (FEA)
**NHNR** ....... National Highway Needs Report [*Department of Transportation*]
**NHO** .......... National Hospice Organization (EA)
**NHO** .......... Navy Hydrographic Office [*Later, NOO*]
**NHOA** ........ National Hemi Owners Association (EA)
**NHochland** ... Neues Hochland [*A publication*]
**NHOKA** .... NHK (Nippon Hoso Kyokai) Technical Monograph [*A publication*]
**NHolb** ........ Sachem Public Library, Holbrook, NY [*Library symbol*] [*Library of Congress*] (LCLS)
**NHolbHS** .. Sachem High School North, Holbrook, NY [*Library symbol*] [*Library of Congress*] (LCLS)
**NHolbSJ** ... Seneca Junior High School, Holbrook, NY [*Library symbol*] [*Library of Congress*] (LCLS)
**NHoll** ......... Community Free Library, Holley, NY [*Library symbol*] [*Library of Congress*] (LCLS)
**N & Hop**..... Nott and Hopkins' Reports [*United States Court of Claims*] [*A publication*] (DLA)
**NHorW** ...... Westinghouse Electric Corp., Engineering Library, Horseheads, NY [*Library symbol*] [*Library of Congress*] (LCLS)
**NHOS** ........ Naval Hospital
**NHP** ........... National Hamiltonian Party (EA)
**NHP** ........... National Housing Partnership [*HUD*]
**NHP** ........... National Humanitarian Party [*Australia*] [*Political party*]
**NHP** ........... Nationwide Health Properties, Inc. [*NYSE symbol*] (SPSG)
**NHP** ........... Neighborhood Health Program [*Generic term*]
**NHP** ........... Network Host Protocol
**NHP** ........... New Haven Free Public Library, New Haven, CT [*OCLC symbol*] (OCLC)
**NHP** ........... New Health Practitioners [*Nurse practitioners and physician assistants*]
**NHP** ........... Nitrogen High Pressure
**NHP** ........... Nominal Horsepower
**NHP** ........... Noninverted Hand Position [*Neuropsychology*]
**NHP** ........... Normal Hearing Peer [*of the hearing-impaired*]
**NHP** ........... Normal Human-Pooled Plasma
**NHP** ........... Nuclear Heart Pacer
**NHPA** ........ National Hispanic Psychological Association (EA)
**NHPA** ........ National Horseshoe Pitchers Association of America (EA)
**NHPAA** ..... National Horseshoe Pitchers Association of America (EA)
**NHPC** ........ National Historical Publications Commission [*Later, NHPRC*]
**NHPDA** ..... National Honey Packers and Dealers Association (EA)
**NHPF** ........ National Health Policy Forum (EA)
**NhPHi** ....... Peterborough Historical Society, Peterborough, NH [*Library symbol*] [*Library of Congress*] (LCLS)
**NHPIC** ...... National Health Planning Information Center [*Public Health Service*] [*Database*] (IID)
**NHpJR** ...... James Roosevelt Library, Hyde Park, NY [*Library symbol*] [*Library of Congress*] [*Obsolete*] (LCLS)
**NHPLO** ..... NATO HAWK Production and Logistics Organization [*Missiles*] [*Rueil-Malmaison, France*] (NATG)
**NhPlS** ........ Plymouth State College of the University of New Hampshire, Plymouth, NH [*Library symbol*] [*Library of Congress*] (LCLS)
**NHPMA** .... Northern Hardwood and Pine Manufacturers Association (EA)
**NHPO** ....... NATO HAWK Production Organization [*Missiles*]
**NhPoA** ....... Portsmouth Athenaeum, Portsmouth, NH [*Library symbol*] [*Library of Congress*] (LCLS)
**NhPoS** ....... Strawbery Banke, Portsmouth, NH [*Library symbol*] [*Library of Congress*] (LCLS)
**NHPP** ........ National Health Professions Placement Network
**NHPP** ........ National Hormone and Pituitary Program (EA)
**NHpR** ........ Franklin D. Roosevelt Library, Hyde Park, NY [*Library symbol*] [*Library of Congress*] [*Obsolete*] (LCLS)
**NHPRC** ..... National Historical Publications and Records Commission [*Formerly, NHPC*] [*Washington, DC*]
**NH Progr Rep** ... New Hampshire Progress Report [*A publication*]
**NHPSCR**... New Hampshire Public Service Commission Reports [*A publication*] (DLA)
**NHQ** .......... NASA Headquarters
**NHQ** .......... National Headquarters
**NHQ** .......... New Hungarian Quarterly [*A publication*]
**NHQ** .......... Nuclear Hyperfine Quadrupolar [*Rare-earth alloy*]
**NHQC** ........ National Hispanic Quincentennial Commission (EA)
**NHR** .......... National Heritage, Inc. [*NYSE symbol*] (SPSG)
**NHR** .......... National Housewives Register [*British*]
**NHR** .......... National Hunt Rules [*British*]
**NHR** .......... Net Histocompatibility Ratio
**NHR** .......... New Hampshire Reports [*A publication*] (DLA)
**NHR** .......... North Hart Resources [*Vancouver Stock Exchange symbol*]
**NHR** .......... Nova/Husky Research Corp. [*UTLAS symbol*]
**NHRA** ....... National Hot Rod Association (EA)
**NHRA** ....... National Housing and Rehabilitation Association (EA)
**NHRA** ....... Next Higher Repairable Assembly (MCD)
**NHRAC**..... National Health Resources Advisory Committee [*Terminated, 1978*] [*General Services Administration*] (EGAO)
**NHRAIC** ... Natural Hazards Research and Applications Information Center [*University of Colorado - Boulder*] [*Research center*] (RCD)
**NHRC**........ National Human Rights Committee (EA)
**NHRC**........ Naval Health Research Center (GRD)
**NHRCPPUS** ... National Human Rights Campaign for Political Prisoners in the US (EA)
**NHRD** ....... National Hardgoods Distributors, Inc. [*NASDAQ symbol*] (NQ)
**NHRD** ....... National Health Planning and Resource Development Act [*1974*] (DHSM)
**NHRDP**..... National Health Research and Development Program [*Canada*]
**NHRE**........ National Hail Research Experiment
**NH Rep**...... New Hampshire Reports [*A publication*] (DLA)
**NH Rev Stat Ann** ... New Hampshire Revised Statutes, Annotated [*A publication*] (DLA)
**NHRI**......... National Hydrology Research Institute [*Canada*]
**NHRI Paper** ... National Hydrology Research Institute. Paper [*A publication*]
**NHRL**........ National Hurricane Research Laboratory [*Later, AOML*]
**NHRL**........ Northern Hemisphere Reference Line [*Geology*]
**NHRP**........ National Heart Research Project (EA)
**NHRP**........ National Hurricane Research Project
**NHRR**........ New Haven Railroad
**NHRS**........ New Hampshire Revised Statutes [*A publication*] (DLA)
**NHRSS**...... Newcastle and Hunter River Steam Ship Co. [*Australia*]
**N & HRSS Co** ... Newcastle and Hunter River Steam Ship Co. [*Australia*]
**NH Rulemaking Reg** ... New Hampshire Rulemaking Register [*A publication*]
**N H Rv**....... Natural History Review [*A publication*]
**NHS**........... Das Nordhebraeische Sagenbuch [*A publication*] (BJA)
**NhS**............ Kelley Memorial Library, Salem, NH [*Library symbol*] [*Library of Congress*] (LCLS)
**NHS**........... N-Hydroxysuccinimide [*Organic chemistry*]
**NHS**........... Nag Hammadi Studies [*A publication*] (BJA)
**NHS**........... Nathaniel Hawthorne Society (EA)
**NHS**........... National Handcraft Society [*Commercial firm*] (EA)
**NHS**........... National Handicapped Sports (EA)
**NHS**........... National Health Service [*British*]
**NHS**........... National Health Survey
**NHS**........... National Historical Society [*Commercial firm*] (EA)
**NHS**........... National Honor Society (EA)
**NHS**........... National Huguenot Society (EA)
**NHS**........... Natural Human Serum
**NHS**........... Naval Honor Schools (AFIT)
**NH & S**...... Needham, Harper & Steers [*Advertising agency*]
**NHS**........... Neighborhood Housing Services [*Generic term*]
**NHS**........... New Hampshire State Library, Concord, NH [*OCLC symbol*] (OCLC)
**NHS**........... Nikon Historical Society (EA)
**NHS**........... Normal Horse Serum
**NHS**........... Normal Human Serum
**NHS**........... North Hampton [*South Carolina*] [*Seismograph station code, US Geological Survey*] [*Closed*] (SEIS)
**NH & S**...... Nuclear Hardening and Survivability
**NHSA**........ National Head Start Association (EA)
**NHSA**........ National Heart Savers Association (EA)
**NHSA**........ National Highway Safety Administration [*Formerly, NHSB; later, NHTSA*] [*Department of Transportation*]
**NHSA**........ National Home Service Association [*Defunct*] (EA)
**NHSA**........ National Horse Show Association of America (EA)
**NHSA**........ Negro Historical Society of America
**NHSA**........ Neighborhood Housing Services of America (EA)
**NHSAA**...... National Horse Show Association of America (EA)
**NHSAC**..... National Health and Safety Awareness Center (EA)
**NHSAC**..... National Highway Safety Advisory Committee
**NHSACA** .. National High School Athletic Coaches Association (EA)
**NHSAS** ..... National Health Service Audit Staff [*Department of Health and Social Security*] [*British*]
**NHSB**........ National High School Band Institute (EA)
**NHSB**........ National Highway Safety Bureau [*Later, NHSA, NHTSA*] [*Department of Transportation*]
**NHSB**........ New Hampshire Savings Bank Corp. [*NASDAQ symbol*] (NQ)
**NHSBVA** .. National High School Boys Volleyball Association (EA)
**NHSC**........ National Health Service Corps [*Department of Health and Human Services*]
**NHSC**........ National Home Study Council (EA)
**NHSC**........ North-Holland Systems and Control Series [*Elsevier Book Series*] [*A publication*]
**NHSCP** ..... National Household Survey Capability Program [*United Nations*]

**NHSCVO** .. National Health Screening Council for Volunteer Organizations (EA)
**NHSD** ........ National Health Survey Division [*of OSG*]
**NHSD** ........ NATO HAWK Support Department [*Missiles*] (NATG)
**NHSF** ........ National Hispanic Scholarship Fund (EA)
**NHSF** ........ National Horse Show Foundation (EA)
**NHsH** ........ Half Hollow Hills Community Public Library, Huntington Station, NY [*Library symbol*] [*Library of Congress*] (LCLS)
**N H Soc NB B** ... Natural History Society of New Brunswick. Bulletin [*A publication*]
**NHSP** ........ N-Hydroxysuccinimidyl Palmitate [*Organic chemistry*]
**NHSQ** ........ Nevada Historical Society Quarterly [*A publication*]
**NHSR** ........ National Hospital Service Reserve [*British*]
**NHSRA** ..... National Handicapped Sports and Recreation Association [*Later, NHS*] (EA)
**NHSRA** ..... National High School Rodeo Association (EA)
**NHSS** ........ National Herb Study Society (EA)
**NHSS** ........ North-Holland Studies in Silver [*Elsevier Book Series*] [*A publication*]
**NHsS** ......... South Huntington Public Library, Huntington Station, NY [*Library symbol*] [*Library of Congress*] (LCLS)
**NHSSD** ..... North-Holland Series in Systems and Software Development [*Elsevier Book Series*] [*A publication*]
**NH State Plan Devel Comm Mineral Res Survey** ... New Hampshire State Planning and Development Commission. Mineral Resources Survey [*A publication*]
**NH State Plann Dev Comm Miner Resour Surv** ... New Hampshire State Planning and Development Commission. Mineral Resources Survey [*A publication*]
**NHsW** ....... Walt Whitman Birthplace Association, Huntington Station, NY [*Library symbol*] [*Library of Congress*] (LCLS)
**NHT** .......... Corpus Christi, TX [*Location identifier*] [*FAA*] (FAAL)
**NHT** .......... International Herald Tribune [*A publication*]
**NHT** .......... Nationwide Housing Trust [*British*]
**NHT** .......... Nernst Heat Theorem [*Physics*]
**NHT** .......... Nursing Home Type (ADA)
**NHTB** ........ New Hampshire Thrift Bancshares, Inc. [*NASDAQ symbol*] (NQ)
**NHTD** ....... NASA Headquarters Telephone Directory
**NHTPC** ..... National Housing and Town Planning Council [*British*]
**NHTSA** ..... National Highway Traffic Safety Administration [*Formerly, NHSB, NHSA*] [*Department of Transportation*]
**NHTU** ....... Naval Hovercraft Trials Unit
**NHu** .......... Huntington Public Library, Huntington, NY [*Library symbol*] [*Library of Congress*] (LCLS)
**nhu** ............ New Hampshire [*MARC country of publication code*] [*Library of Congress*] (LCCP)
**NhU** .......... University of New Hampshire, Durham, NH [*Library symbol*] [*Library of Congress*] (LCLS)
**NHUBW** ... National Hook-Up of Black Women (EA)
**NHUC** ....... National Highway Users Conference [*Later, HUF*]
**NHuCE** ...... Cuba Hill Elementary School, Huntington, NY [*Library symbol*] [*Library of Congress*] (LCLS)
**NHudC** ...... Columbia-Greene Community College, Hudson, NY [*Library symbol*] [*Library of Congress*] (LCLS)
**NHudDAR** ... Daughters of the American Revolution, Hendrick Hudson Chapter, Hudson, NY [*Library symbol*] [*Library of Congress*] (LCLS)
**NHudHi** ..... Columbia County, New York Official Historian, Hudson, NY [*Library symbol*] [*Library of Congress*] (LCLS)
**NHuEJ** ...... Elwood Junior High School, Huntington, NY [*Library symbol*] [*Library of Congress*] (LCLS)
**NHuFJ** ...... Finley Junior High School, Huntington, NY [*Library symbol*] [*Library of Congress*] (LCLS)
**NHuH** ........ Huntington Hospital, Huntington, NY [*Library symbol*] [*Library of Congress*] (LCLS)
**NHuHi** ...... Huntington Historical Society, Huntington, NY [*Library symbol*] [*Library of Congress*] (LCLS)
**NHuHS** ..... Huntington High School, Huntington, NY [*Library symbol*] [*Library of Congress*] (LCLS)
**NHuI** ......... Immaculate Conception Seminary, Huntington, NY [*Library symbol*] [*Library of Congress*] (LCLS)
**N & Hunt** ... Nott and Huntington's Reports [*1-7 United States Court of Claims*] [*A publication*] (DLA)
**NHusk** ....... KLD Associates, Inc., Huntington Station, NY [*Library symbol*] [*Library of Congress*] (LCLS)
**NHusMJ** ... Memorial Junior High School, Huntington Station, NY [*Library symbol*] [*Library of Congress*] (LCLS)
**NHusWH** .. Walt Whitman High School, Huntington Station, NY [*Library symbol*] [*Library of Congress*] (LCLS)
**NHuTJ** ...... R. K. Toaz Junior High School, Huntington, NY [*Library symbol*] [*Library of Congress*] (LCLS)
**NHV** .......... Nea Helliniki Vivliothiki [*A publication*]
**NHV** .......... Nuku Hiva [*French Polynesia*] [*Airport symbol*] (OAG)
**NHVKSG** .. Neujahrsblatt. Historischer Verein des Kantons St. Gallen [*A publication*]
**NHvL** ......... Long Island Lighting Co., Hicksville, NY [*Library symbol*] [*Library of Congress*] (LCLS)
**NHW** ......... National Health and Welfare Mutual Life Insurance Association [*Formerly, NHWRA*] (EA)
**NHW** ......... Neighbourhood Watch [*Australia*]
**NHW** ......... Neuhebraeisches Woerterbuch [*A publication*] (BJA)
**NHW** ......... New Hospital for Women [*1904*] [*British*] (ROG)
**NHW** ......... Night Hawk Resources Ltd. [*Vancouver Stock Exchange symbol*]
**NhWalHi** ... Walpole Historical Society, Walpole, NH [*Library symbol*] [*Library of Congress*] (LCLS)
**NHWRA** .... National Health and Welfare Retirement Association [*Later, NHW*] (EA)
**NHWS** ....... National Hurricane Warning Service [*National Weather Service*]
**NHWU** ...... Non-Heatset Web Unit (EA)
**NHX** ......... Albany, GA [*Location identifier*] [*FAA*] (FAAL)
**NHY** .......... Norsk Hydro AS [*NYSE symbol*] (SPSG)
**NHY** .......... Northumberland Hussars Yeomanry [*British military*] (DMA)
**NHyF** ......... General Services Administration, National Archives and Record Service, Franklin D. Roosevelt Library, Hyde Park, NY [*Library symbol*] [*Library of Congress*] (LCLS)
**NHZ** .......... Brunswick, ME [*Location identifier*] [*FAA*] (FAAL)
**NI** .............. Aeronica [*Nicaragua*] [*ICAO designator*] (FAAC)
**NI** .............. Das Neue Israel [*A publication*] (BJA)
**NI** .............. NAMBA [*North American Model Boating Association*] International (EA)
**NI** .............. Nation Institute (EA)
**NI** .............. Nation of Ishmael [*An association*] (EA)
**NI** .............. National Income
**NI** .............. National Insurance [*British*]
**NI** .............. National Intervenors [*Defunct*] (EA)
**NI** .............. Native Infantry [*Indian Armed Forces regiment*]
**NI** .............. Naucno-Issledovatel'skij [*A publication*]
**NI** .............. Nautical Institute [*London, England*] (EAIO)
**NI** .............. Naval Instructor [*British*]
**NI** .............. Naval Intelligence
**NI** .............. Need International [*An association*] (EA)
**NI** .............. Negotiable Instrument
**NI** .............. Net Income
**NI** .............. Net Interest
**NI** .............. Netherlands Indies [*Later, Republic of Indonesia*]
**NI** .............. Network International (EA)
**NI** .............. Neurointermediate Lobe [*Of the pituitary*]
**NI** .............. Neurological Impairment
**NI** .............. Neurological Institute
**NI** .............. Neurologically Intact [*Medicine*]
**NI** .............. New Impression [*Publishing*]
**NI** .............. New Internationalist [*A publication*]
**NI** .............. New Ireland
**NI** .............. New Issue [*Publishing*]
**NI** .............. News International [*An association*] (EA)
**NI** .............. Niagara Institute (EA)
**NI** .............. Nicaragua [*ANSI two-letter standard code*] (CNC)
**Ni** .............. Nickel [*Chemical element*]
**Ni** .............. Nicolaus Furiosus [*Flourished, 12th century*] [*Authority cited in pre-1607 legal work*] (DSA)
**Ni** .............. Nicolaus de Tudeschis [*Deceased, 1445*] [*Authority cited in pre-1607 legal work*] (DSA)
**NI** .............. Night (AABC)
**NI** .............. NIPSCO Industries [*NYSE symbol*] (SPSG)
**NI** .............. Nitrogen
**NI** .............. No Imprint (ADA)
**NI** .............. No Information
**NI** .............. No Interaction [*Medicine*]
**NI** .............. No Issue
**NI** .............. Noise Index
**N/I** ............ Noise to Interference Ratio [*Telecommunications*] (TEL)
**NI** .............. Noninductive (DEN)
**NI** .............. Nonintervention
**NI** .............. Noninvasive Index [*Medicine*]
**NI** .............. Norfolk Island [*Australia*] (ADA)
**NI** .............. Normal Impurity [*Metals*]
**NI** .............. Normal Inferior
**NI** .............. Northern Indiana Railway
**NI** .............. Northern Ireland
**NI** .............. Northern Ireland Law Reports [*A publication*] (DLA)
**NI** .............. Not Identified
**NI** .............. Not Illustrated [*Publishing*]
**NI** .............. Not In
**NI** .............. Not Informed
**NI** .............. Not Inoculated
**NI** .............. Not Interested
**NI** .............. Not Isolated
**NI** .............. Not Issued (AAG)
**NI** .............. Notice of Information [*Data processing*]
**NI** .............. Nuclear Instrumentation (NRCH)
**NI** .............. Nuclear Island (NRCH)
**NI** .............. Numerical Index (BUR)
**NI** .............. Numismatics International (EA)
**NI** .............. Nuova Italia [*A publication*]
**NI** .............. Tompkins County Public Library, Ithaca, NY [*Library symbol*] [*Library of Congress*] (LCLS)
**NIA** ........... National Ice Association [*Later, PIA*] (EA)
**NIA** ........... National Iceboat Authority

**NIA** ........... National Impala Association (EA)
**NIA** ........... National Income Accounts
**NIA** ........... National Inholders Association [*Database producer*] (EA)
**NIA** ........... National Institute on Aging [*National Institutes of Health*] [*Bethesda, MD*]
**NIA** ........... National Insulator Association (EA)
**NIA** ........... National Insurance Association [*Chicago, IL*] (EA)
**NIA** ........... National Intelligence Authority [*1946-1947*]
**NIA** ........... National International Academy
**NIA** ........... National Involvement Association (EA)
**NIA** ........... National Irrigation Administration [*Philippines*] (DS)
**NIA** ........... Navy Industrial Association [*Later, NSIA*]
**NIA** ........... Neighborhoods-in-Action [*An association*] (EA)
**NIA** ........... Nephelometric Immunoassay
**NIA** ........... Newspaper Institute of America (EA)
**NIA** ........... Nickel-Iron Alloy
**NIA** ........... No Information Available
**NIA** ........... No Input Acknowledge [*Data processing*]
**NIA** ........... Nordic Institute in Aland [*See also NIPA*] [*Mariehamn, Aland, Finland*] (EAIO)
**NIA** ........... Norfolk Island [*Australia*] [*Seismograph station code, US Geological Survey*] [*Closed*] (SEIS)
**NIA** ........... Nutrition Institute of America [*Inactive*] (EA)
**NIAA** ......... National Indian Athletic Association (EA)
**NIAA** ......... National Industrial Advertisers Association [*Later, B/PAA*]
**NIAA** ......... National Institute of Animal Agriculture [*Defunct*] (EA)
**NIAAA** ...... National Institute on Alcohol Abuse and Alcoholism [*Rockville, MD*] [*Public Health Service*] [*Department of Health and Human Services*]
**NIAAA** ...... National Interscholastic Athletic Administrators Association (EA)
**NIAB** ......... National Institute of Agricultural Botany [*Research center*] [*British*] (IRC)
**NIABS** ....... National Institute for Applied Behavioral Science
**NIAC** ......... NASA Industrial Application Center [*University of Southern California*] [*Los Angeles*] [*Information service or system*] (IID)
**NIAC** ......... NASA Industrial Applications Center [*University of Pittsburgh*] [*Pittsburgh, PA*]
**NIAC** ......... National Industry Advisory Committee [*FCC*] [*Terminated, 1986*]
**NIAC** ......... National Information and Analysis Center
**NIAC** ......... National Insulation and Abatement Contractors Association (EA)
**NIAC** ......... National Insurance Advisory Committee [*British*] (DCTA)
**NIAC** ......... Northern Ireland Automation Centre [*Queen's University of Belfast*] (CB)
**NIAC** ......... Nuclear Insurance Association of Canada
**NIAC** ......... Nutritional Information and Analysis Center [*Illinois Institute of Technology and Institute of Food Technologists*] (IID)
**NIACA** ...... National Indirect Air Carrier Association (EA)
**NIACE** ....... National Institute of Adult Continuing Education [*British*]
**NIACE** ....... National Institute for the Advancement of Career Education (EA)
**NIAD** ......... National Institute on Adult Daycare (EA)
**NIADA** ...... National Independent Automobile Dealers Association (EA)
**NIADA** ...... National Institute of American Doll Artists (EA)
**NIADDK** ... National Institute of Arthritis, Diabetes, and Digestive and Kidney Diseases [*National Institutes of Health*] (EA)
**NIAE** ......... National Institute of Agricultural Engineering [*Research center*] [*British*] (IRC)
**NIAE** ......... National Institute for Architectural Education (EA)
**NIAF** ......... National Italian American Foundation (EA)
**NIAG** ......... NATO Industrial Advisory Group (MCD)
**NIAG** ......... Niagara (ROG)
**NIAHAI** .... National Institute of Animal Health. Quarterly [*Yatabe*] [*A publication*]
**NIAID** ....... National Institute of Allergy and Infectious Diseases [*of National Institutes of Health*] [*Department of Health and Human Services*] [*Bethesda, MD*]
**NIAJ** .......... Niagara Junction Railway Co. [*Absorbed into Consolidated Rail Corp.*] [*AAR code*]
**NIAL** ......... National Institute of Arts and Letters [*Later, AAIAL*] (EA)
**NIALSA** .... Northwest Indiana Area Library Services Authority [*Library network*]
**NIAM** ........ National Imaging, Inc. [*NASDAQ symbol*] (NQ)
**NIAM** ........ National Institute of Advertising Management
**NIAMD** ..... National Institute of Arthritis and Metabolic Diseases [*Later, NIAMDD, NIADDK*] [*National Institutes of Health*]
**NIAMDD** .. National Institute of Arthritis, Metabolism, and Digestive Diseases [*Formerly, NIAMD*] [*Later, NIADDK*] [*National Institutes of Health*]
**NIAMS** ...... National Institute of Arthritis and Musculoskeletal and Skin Diseases [*Bethesda, MD*] [*Department of Health and Human Services*] (GRD)
**NIAP** ......... National Income and Products [*Economics*]
**NIAP** ......... Noninverting Amplifier Pair
**NIAR** ......... National Institute of Atmospheric Research
**NIAR** ......... Neutron-Induced Autoradiography
**NIAS** .......... National Institute for Advanced Studies (EA)
**NIAS** .......... National Institute of Aeronautical Sciences
**NIAS** .......... Nordisk Institut for Asienstudier [*Nordic Institute of Asian Studies*] (EAIO)
**NIASA** ....... National Insurance Actuarial and Statistical Association [*Later, ISO*]
**NIASE** ....... National Institute for Automotive Service Excellence
**NIAWR** ..... National Institute on Aging, Work, and Retirement [*Washington, DC*] (EA)
**NIB** ............ National Identification Bureau [*British*]
**NIB** ............ National Industries for the Blind (EA)
**NIB** ............ National Information Bureau [*Information service or system*] (EA)
**NIB** ............ National Institute for the Blind (EA)
**NIB** ............ Navigation Information Bulletin
**NIB** ............ Negative Impedance Booster [*Electronics*]
**NIB** ............ Negative Ion Beam
**NIB** ............ Negative Ion Blemish
**NIB** ............ Network Interface Board
**NIB** ............ Nigeria International Bank Ltd.
**NIB** ............ Node Initialization Block [*Data processing*] (IBMDP)
**NIB** ............ Noninterference Basis
**NIBA** ......... National Industrial Belting Association (EA)
**NIBA** ......... National Insurance Brokers Association [*Australia*]
**NIBA** ......... National Insurance Buyers Association
**NIBC** ......... National Industrial Bancorp, Inc. [*Hartford, CT*] [*NASDAQ symbol*] (NQ)
**NIBC** ......... Northern Ireland Base Command [*World War II*]
**NIBCA** ....... National Intercollegiate Boxing Coaches Association (EA)
**NIBESA** .... National Independent Bank Equipment and Systems Association [*Park Ridge, IL*] (EA)
**NIBID** ........ National Investment Bank for Industrial Development [*Greece*]
**NIBJL** ....... National Information Bureau for Jewish Life (EA)
**NIBL** ......... National Industrial Basketball League (EA)
**NIBM** ........ National Institute for Burn Medicine (EA)
**NIBMAR** ... No Independence before Majority African Rule [*British policy in regard to Rhodesia*]
**NIBN** ......... National Indian Brotherhood. Newsletter [*A publication*]
**NIBOR** ...... New York Interbank Official Rate
**NIBRA** ....... National Independent Bicycle Rep Association (EA)
**NIBS** ......... National Institute of Building Sciences (EA)
**NIBS** ......... Neural, Informational, and Behavioral Science
**NIBS Bull Biol Res** ... Nippon Institute for Biological Science. Bulletin. Biological Research [*A publication*]
**NIBSC** ....... National Institute for Biological Standards and Control [*British*]
**NIBTN** ...... Nitroisobutametriol Trinitrate [*An explosive*]
**NIC** ............ Cornell University, Ithaca, NY [*Library symbol*] [*Library of Congress*] (LCLS)
**NIC** ............ National Impeachment Coalition (EA)
**NIC** ............ National Incomes Commission [*Nickname: Nicky*] [*British*]
**NIC** ............ National Indications Center [*Disbanded*] [*DoD*]
**NIC** ............ National Industrial Council (EA)
**NIC** ............ National Institute of Corrections [*Department of Justice*]
**NIC** ............ National Institute of Creativity [*Defunct*] (EA)
**NIC** ............ National Institute of Credit [*New York, NY*] (EA)
**NIC** ............ National Insurance Certificate [*British*]
**NIC** ............ National Insurance Contributions [*British*]
**NIC** ............ National Interagency Council on Smoking and Health [*New York, NY*]
**NIC** ............ National Interfraternity Conference (EA)
**NIC** ............ National Interrogation Center [*Military*]
**NIC** ............ National Interstate Council of State Boards of Cosmetology (EA)
**NIC** ............ National Inventors Council [*Terminated, 1974*] [*National Institute of Standards and Technology*]
**NIC** ............ Naval Intelligence Code [*World War II*] [*British*]
**NIC** ............ Naval Intelligence Command
**NIC** ............ Navigation Information Center
**NIC** ............ Navy Information Center
**NIC** ............ Nearly Instantaneous Compounding (MCD)
**NIC** ............ Negative Immittance Converter [*Electronics*]
**NIC** ............ Negative Impedance Converter [*Electronics*]
**NIC** ............ Negative Ion Chamber
**NIC** ............ Neighborhood Info Centers Project (EA)
**NIC** ............ Net Interest Cost [*Investment term*]
**NIC** ............ Netherlands Information Combine [*Information service or system*] [*Delft*] (IID)
**NIC** ............ Network Information Center [*Advanced Research Projects Agency*] [*DoD*]
**NIC** ............ Network Interface Card [*Data processing*]
**NIC** ............ Network Interface Control
**NIC** ............ New Initial Commissions [*Business term*]
**NIC** ............ New International Commentary on the New Testament [*A publication*] (BJA)
**NIC** ............ Newly Industrialized [*or Industrializing*] Country
**NIC** ............ Newspaper Indexing Center [*Flint, MI*]
**NIC** ............ Newsprint Information Committee (EA)
**Nic** ............. Nicander [*Second century BC*] [*Classical studies*] (OCD)
**NIC** ............ Nicaragua [*ANSI three-letter standard code*] (CNC)
**NIC** ............ Nicaraguan Information Center (EA)
**NIC** ............ Nickling Resources, Inc. [*Vancouver Stock Exchange symbol*]
**Nic** ............. Nicolaus de Tudeschis [*Deceased, 1445*] [*Authority cited in pre-1607 legal work*] (DSA)

**NIC**........... Nicolet Instrument Corporation [*NYSE symbol*] (SPSG)
**nic**.............. Niger-Congo [*MARC language code*] [*Library of Congress*] (LCCP)
**NIC**........... Nineteen-Hundred Indexing and Cataloging (DIT)
**NI & C**........ Nippon Information and Communication [*Joint venture of IBM Corp. Japan and Nippon Telegraph and Telephone*]
**NIC**........... Non-Intel [*Corp.*]-Compatible Chips [*Data processing*]
**NIC**........... Non-Intervention in Chile [*An association*] (EA)
**NIC**........... Nordic Immigration Committee [*Norrkoping, Sweden*] (EAIO)
**NIC**........... Northern Illinois Commuter [*Plainfield, IL*] [*FAA designator*] (FAAC)
**NIC**........... Not in Contact [*Electronics*] (DEN)
**NIC**........... Not in Contract [*Technical drawings*]
**NIC**........... Nuclear Industry Consortium [*Also known as GPIN*] [*Belgium*]
**NIC**........... Nudist Information Center (EA)
**NICA**......... National Indian Counselors Association (EA)
**NICA**......... National Insulation Contractors Association [*Later, NIAC*] (EA)
**NICA**......... National Interfaith Coalition on Aging (EA)
**NICA**......... Netherlands Indies Civil Affairs Organization [*World War II*]
**NICAD**...... Nickel Cadmium (NG)
**Nic Adult Bast** ... Nicolas' Adulterine Bastardy [*1836*] [*A publication*] (DLA)
**NICAN**...... National Information Communication Awareness Network [*Australia*]
**NICAP**....... National Investigations Committee on Aerial Phenomena [*Defunct*] (EA)
**NICAR**....... Nicaragua
**Nicaragua Servicio Geol Nac Bol** ... Nicaragua Servicio Geologico Nacional. Boletin [*A publication*]
**NICARD**.... Navy/Industry Cooperative Research and Development Program (MCD)
**Nicar Inst Invest Sism Bol** ... Nicaragua Instituto de Investigaciones Sismicas. Boletin [*A publication*]
**Nicar Med** ... Nicaragua Medica [*A publication*]
**NICATELSAT** ... Nicaraguan Telecommunication by Satellite [*Commercial firm*]
**NICB**......... National Industrial Conference Board [*Later, TCB*] (EA)
**Nic Bel**....... Nicolaus Bellonus [*Flourished, 1542-47*] [*Authority cited in pre-1607 legal work*] (DSA)
**Nic Boe**...... Nicolaus Boerius [*Authority cited in pre-1607 legal work*] (DSA)
**NICC**......... National Industrial Conservation Conference
**NICC**......... National Inventory Control Center (MCD)
**NICC**......... Nevis Island Cultural Center of the US (EA)
**NICCYH** ... National Information Center for Children and Youth with Handicaps (EA)
**NICD**......... National Information Center on Deafness (EA)
**NICD**......... National Institute on Crime and Delinquency [*Later, NFCJ*] (EA)
**NICD**......... Nickel Cadmium (MCD)
**NICDA**...... National Imported Car Dealers Association (EA)
**NICE**......... National Information Conference and Exposition [*Associated Information Managers*]
**NICE**......... National Institute of Careers, Inc. [*Miramar, FL*] [*NASDAQ symbol*] (NQ)
**NICE**......... National Institute of Ceramic Engineers (EA)
**NICE**......... National Institute for Computers in Engineering (EA)
**Nice**........... [*Antonius*] Nicenus [*Authority cited in pre-1607 legal work*] (DSA)
**NICE**......... Normal Input-Output Control Executive [*Data processing*]
**NICE**......... Northern Indiana Consortium for Education [*Library network*]
**NICEC**....... National Institute for Careers Education and Counselling [*Research center*] [*British*] (IRC)
**NICEDD** ... National Institute for Continuing Education in Developmental Disabilities (EA)
**Nice Hist**.... Nice Historique [*A publication*]
**NICEIC**..... National Inspection Council for Electrical Installation Contracting [*British*]
**NICEL**....... National Institute for Citizen Education in the Law (EA)
**Nic Elec**....... Nicolson's Elections in Scotland [*A publication*] (DLA)
**NICEM**...... National Information Center for Educational Media [*Later, A V Online*] (EA)
**Nice Med** ... Nice Medical [*A publication*]
**NICET**....... National Institute for Certification in Engineering Technologies (EA)
**Nic & Fl Reg** ... Nicoll and Flaxman on Registration [*A publication*] (DLA)
**NICG**......... National Interagency Coordination Group [*National Atmospheric Electricity Hazards Program*] (MCD)
**NICH**......... National Information Center for the Handicapped (EA)
**NICH**......... Non-Intervention in Chile [*An association*] (EA)
**Nic Ha C**.... Nicholl, Hare, and Carrow's Railway and Canal Cases [*1835-55*] [*A publication*] (DLA)
**Nich Adult Bast** ... Nicholas on Adulterine Bastardy [*A publication*] (DLA)
**NICHAS**.... Journal. Nihon University Medical Association [*A publication*]
**Nic H & C**.. Nicholl, Hare, and Carrow's Railway and Canal Cases [*1835-55*] [*A publication*] (ILCA)
**NICHD**...... National Institute of Child Health and Human Development [*National Institutes of Health*] [*Bethesda, MD*] (GRD)
**Nich H & C** ... Nicholl, Hare, and Carrow's Railway and Canal Cases [*1835-55*] [*A publication*] (DLA)
**NICHHD**... National Institute of Child Health and Human Development [*National Institutes of Health*]
**Nich Ig Zass** ... Nichidai Igaku Zasshi [*A publication*]
**Nicholl H & C** ... Nicholl, Hare, and Carrow [*1835-55*] [*A publication*] (DLA)
**Nicholls State Univ Prof Pap Ser Biol** ... Nicholls State University. Professional Papers Series. Biology [*A publication*]
**Nichols-Cahill** ... Nichols-Cahill's Annotated New York Civil Practice Acts [*A publication*] (DLA)
**Nicholson**... Nicholson's Manuscript Decisions, Scotch Session Cases [*A publication*] (DLA)
**NICHROME** ... Nickel Chromium [*Alloy*] [*Trade name*]
**NICI**.......... National Insulation Certification Institute (EA)
**NICI**.......... Negative Ion Chemical Ionization [*Spectrometry*]
**NICIMS**.... Negative Ion Chemical Ionization Mass Spectroscopy
**NICIS**........ Nikon Intracellular Calcium Ion System
**NICJ**.......... National Institute for Consumer Justice
**NICK**......... Name Information Correlation Key
**nick**............ Nickname
**NICKA3**.... Japanese Journal of Zootechnical Science [*A publication*]
**Nickel Ber** ... Nickel Berichte [*A publication*]
**Nickel Bull** ... Nickel Bulletin [*A publication*]
**Nickel Steel Top** ... Nickel Steel Topics [*A publication*]
**Nickel Top** ... Nickel Topics [*A publication*]
**NICL**.......... Nickel Resoures Development Corp. [*NASDAQ symbol*] (NQ)
**NICLC**....... National Institute on Community-Based Long-Term Care (EA)
**NICLOG** ... National Information Center for Local Government Records [*Canada*]
**NICM**........ National Institute for Campus Ministries (EA)
**NICMA**..... National Ice Cream Mix Association (EA)
**NICMA**..... National Industrial Cafeteria Managers Association [*Later, SFM*] (EA)
**NICN**......... Navy Item Control Number (MCD)
**NICNT**...... New International Commentary on the New Testament [*A publication*] (BJA)
**NICO**......... National Insurance Consumer Organization (EA)
**NICO**......... Navy Inventory Control Office
**Nico**........... Nicolaus de Tudeschis [*Deceased, 1445*] [*Authority cited in pre-1607 legal work*] (DSA)
**NICOA**...... National Independent Coal Operators Association (EA)
**NICOA**...... National Indian Council on Aging (EA)
**Nico Alex**... Nicolaus de Alexandria [*Authority cited in pre-1607 legal work*] (DSA)
**NICOL**...... New Integrated Computer Language
**NICOL**...... Nineteen-Hundred Commercial Language
**Nicolas**....... Proceedings and Ordinances of the Privy Council, Edited by Sir Harry Nicolas [*A publication*] (DLA)
**NICOP**...... Navy Industry Cooperation Plan
**NICOP**...... Nickel Copper
**NICORD**... Navy/Industry Cooperative Research and Development Program
**NICOS**....... Newfoundland Institute for Cold Ocean Science [*Memorial University of Newfoundland*] [*Canada*] [*Research center*] (RCD)
**NICOV**...... National Information Center on Volunteerism [*Later, NVC*] (EA)
**NICP**.......... National Inventory Control Point [*Military*]
**NICP**.......... NOAA [*National Oceanic and Atmospheric Administration*] Interoceanic Canal Project (NOAA)
**NICP**.......... Nuclear Incident Control Plan
**Nic R**.......... Nicolaus Rufulus [*Flourished, 13th century*] [*Authority cited in pre-1607 legal work*] (DSA)
**NICRA**....... National Ice Cream Retailers Association [*Later, NICYRA*] (EA)
**NICRA**....... Northern Ireland Civil Rights Association
**NICRAD**.... Navy/Industry Cooperative Research and Development
**NICRISP**... Navy Integrated Comprehensible Repairable Item Scheduling Program
**NICRO**...... National Institute for Crime Prevention and Rehabilitation of Offenders
**NICS**.......... National Institute for Chemical Studies (EA)
**NICS**.......... National Insurance Contributions System [*Department of Health and Social Security*] [*British*]
**NICS**.......... NATO Integrated Communications System (NATG)
**NICS**.......... Network Integrity Control System
**NICS**.......... Nissan's Induction Control System [*Automotive engineering*]
**NICSE**....... National Institute for Child Support Enforcement [*Commercial firm*] (EA)
**NICSEM**... National Information Center for Special Education Materials [*University of Southern California*] [*Los Angeles, CA*]
**NICSH**...... National Interagency Council on Smoking and Health [*Inactive*] (EA)
**Nic Sic Do** ... Nicolaus (Siculus Doctor) de Tudeschis [*Deceased, 1445*] [*Authority cited in pre-1607 legal work*] (DSA)
**NICSMA**... NATO Integrated Communications System Management Agency (NATG)
**NICSO**....... NATO Integrated Communications System Organization [*Brussels, Belgium*] (NATG)
**NIC-TRANS** ... Naval Intelligence Command - Translation Division
**NICU**......... Neonatal [*or Newborn*] Intensive Care Unit
**NICU**......... Neurological Intensive Care Unit [*Medicine*]

**NICUFO** ... National Investigations Committee on Unidentified Flying Objects (EA)
**NICWM** .... National Information Center on Women and the Military [*Later, WMP*] (EA)
**NICYRA** .... National Ice Cream and Yogurt Retailers Association (EA)
**NID** ............ Inyokern, CA [*Location identifier*] [*FAA*] (FAAL)
**NID** ............ National Institute of Drycleaning [*Later, IFI*] (EA)
**NID** ............ National Institute of Dyslexia (EA)
**NID** ............ National Intelligence Daily [*Central Intelligence Agency*] [*A publication*]
**NID** ............ [*US*] Naval Intelligence Division [*Usually, ONI*]
**NID** ............ Naval Intelligence Division [*British*]
**NID** ............ Network In-Dial [*Automatic Voice Network*] (CET)
**NID** ............ Network Interface Device [*Telecommunications*]
**NID** ............ New International Dictionary [*Webster's*] [*A publication*]
**Nid** ............ Niddah (BJA)
**NID** ............ Non-Internal Development [*DoD*]
**NID** ............ Nonequilibrium Ionospheric Disturbance [*Geophysics*]
**NID** ............ Nonillusion Direction [*Ophthalmology*]
**NID** ............ Northern Ireland District
**NID** ............ Nuclear Instruments and Detectors [*IEEE*] (MCD)
**NIDA** ......... 99th Infantry Division Association (EA)
**NIDA** ......... National Independent Dairy-Food Association (EA)
**NIDA** ......... National Industrial Distributors Association [*Philadelphia, PA*] (EA)
**NIDA** ......... National Institute on Drug Abuse [*Department of Health and Human Services*] [*Rockville, MD*]
**NIDA** ......... National Insurance Development Act of 1975
**NIDA** ......... Northeastern Industrial Developers Association
**NIDA** ......... Numerically Integrated Differential Analyzer [*Data processing*]
**NIDA Res Monogr** ... National Institute on Drug Abuse. Research Monograph [*A publication*]
**NIDC** ......... National Insurance Development Corp. [*Government-sponsored organization*]
**NIDC** ......... National Investment and Development Corporation [*Philippines*] (DS)
**NIDC** ......... Newly Industrialized Developing Country
**NIDCC** ...... National Internal Defense Coordination Center [*Army*] (AABC)
**NIDDK** ...... National Institute of Diabetes and Digestive and Kidney Diseases [*Public Health Service*] [*Also, an information service or system*] (IID)
**NIDDM** ..... Non-Insulin-Dependent Diabetes Mellitus [*Medicine*]
**NIDI** .......... Nederlands Interuniversitair Demografisch Institut
**NiDI** .......... Nickel Development Institute (EAIO)
**NIDL** .......... Network Interface Definition Language [*Data processing*]
**NIDLR** ........ Office of the Director of Law Reform, Northern Ireland (DLA)
**NIDM** ........ National Institute for Disaster Mobilization (EA)
**NIDN** ......... Navy Intelligence Data Network (MCD)
**NIDOC** ...... National Information and Documentation Center
**NIDOCD** ... National Institute on Deafness and Other Communication Disorders [*NIH*]
**NIDR** ......... National Institute of Dental Research [*Public Health Service*] [*Bethesda, MD*]
**NIDR** ......... National Institute for Dispute Resolution (EA)
**NIDRR** ...... National Institute on Disability and Rehabilitation Research [*Washington, DC*] [*Department of Education*] (GRD)
**NIDS** ......... National Institute of Diaper Services [*Defunct*] (EA)
**NIDS** ......... National Inventory of Documentary Sources [*British*]
**NIDS** ......... National Investor Data Service (EA)
**NIDS** ......... Navigation Instrument Development Unit
**NIDS** ......... Network Interface Data System (MCD)
**NIDZA** ...... Nippon Ika Daigaku Zasshi [*A publication*]
**NIDZAJ** .... Journal. Nippon Medical School [*A publication*]
**NIE** ............ NASA Interface Equipment (MCD)
**NIE** ............ National Institute of Education [*Department of Education*] [*Washington, DC*]
**NIE** ............ National Institute of Education, Washington, DC [*OCLC symbol*] (OCLC)
**NIE** ............ National Intelligence Estimate
**NIE** ............ Negative Ion Erosion
**NIE** ............ Neutron Ionization Effect
**NIE** ............ Niedzica [*Poland*] [*Seismograph station code, US Geological Survey*] (SEIS)
**NIE** ............ Not Included Elsewhere
**NIEA** ......... National Indian Education Association (EA)
**NIEAC** ....... National Indian Education Advisory Committee [*Terminated, 1974*] [*Department of the Interior*] (EGAO)
**NIECC** ....... National Industrial Energy Conservation Council (MCD)
**Niederdeu Mit** ... Niederdeutsche Mitteilungen [*A publication*]
**Niederdt Jb** ... Jahrbuch des Vereins fuer Niederdeutsche Sprachforschung [*A publication*]
**Niederdt Kbl** ... Korrespondenzblatt des Vereins fuer Niederdeutsche Sprachforschung [*A publication*]
**Niederoest Imker** ... Niederoesterreichesche Imker [*A publication*]
**Niederrhein Ges Bonn Szb** ... Niederrheinische Gesellschaft fuer Natur und Heilkunde zu Bonn. Sitzungsberichte [*A publication*]
**Niederrhein Jahrb** ... Niederrheinisches Jahrbuch [*A publication*]
**Niedersaechs Ministerialbl** ... Niedersaechsisches Ministerialblatt [*A publication*]
**Nied Jb LG** ... Niedersaechsisches Jahrbuch fuer Landesgeschichte [*A publication*]
**NIEHS** ....... National Institute of Environmental Health Sciences [*National Institutes of Health*] [*Research Triangle Park, NC*]
**NIEI** ........... National Institute of Electromedical Information (EA)
**NIEIR** ........ National Institute of Economic and Industry Research [*Australia*]
**NIELA** ....... Nielsen [*A. C.*] Cl A [*NASDAQ symbol*] (NQ)
**Nielson Rs** ... Nielson Researcher [*A publication*]
**NIEM** ........ National Industrial Engineering Mission (AABC)
**NIEMS** ...... National Industrial Energy Management Scheme [*Australia*]
**Niem Z** ....... Niemeyers Zeitschrift fuer Internationales Recht [*A publication*]
**Nien San Ann Univ Cantho** ... Nien San. Annals. University of Cantho [*A publication*]
**Nient Cul** ... Nient Culpable [*Not Guilty*] [*Latin*] [*Legal term*] (DLA)
**NIEO** ......... New International Economic Order
**NIER** ......... National Industrial Equipment Reserve [*of DMS*]
**NIERC** ....... Northern Ireland Economic Research Centre
**Nieren- Hochdruckkr** ... Nieren- und Hochdruckkrankheiten [*A publication*]
**NIES** .......... National Intelligence Estimates [*Summaries of foreign policy information and advice prepared for the president*] [*Known informally as "knees"*]
**NIESR** ....... National Institute of Economic and Social Research [*British*]
**NIETB** ....... National Imagery Exploitation Target Base (MCD)
**NIETU** ...... National Independent Enginemen's Trade Union [*British*]
**NietzscheS** ... Nietzsche Studien [*A publication*]
**NIEU** ......... Negro Industrial and Economic Union
**Nieuw Arch Wisk** ... Nieuw Archief voor Wiskunde [*A publication*]
**Nieuwe Verh Bataafsch Genoot Proefonderv Wijsbegeerte** ... Nieuwe Verhandelingen van het Bataafsch Genootschap der Proefondervindelijke Wijsbegeerte [*A publication*]
**Nieuw Tijdschr Wisk** ... Nieuw Tijdschrift voor Wiskunde [*A publication*]
**NIEX** ......... Niagara Exchange Corp. [*Buffalo, NY*] [*NASDAQ symbol*] (NQ)
**NIF** ............ National Ichthyosis Foundation (EA)
**NIF** ............ National Income Forecasting (ADA)
**NIF** ............ National Institute for the Family (EA)
**NIF** ............ National Interfraternity Foundation (EA)
**NIF** ............ National Inventors Foundation (EA)
**NIF** ............ National Iranian Front
**NIF** ............ National Islamic Front [*Sudan*]
**NIF** ............ National Issues Forums (EA)
**NIF** ............ Navy Industrial Fund
**NIF** ............ Negative Inspiratory Force [*Medicine*]
**NIF** ............ Network Information Files [*Burroughs Corp.*]
**NIF** ............ Neutrophil Migration Inhibition Factor
**NIF** ............ New Israel Fund (EA)
**NIF** ............ Newsletter on Intellectual Freedom [*A publication*]
**NIF** ............ Nickel-Iron Film
**NIF** ............ Nifedipine [*Pharmacology*]
**NIF** ............ Nippon Facts [*A publication*]
**NIF** ............ Noise Improvement Factor (IEEE)
**NIF** ............ Nomura International Finance [*Japan*]
**NIF** ............ Nordiska Institutet for Folkdiktning [*Nordic Institute of Folklore*] (EAIO)
**NIF** ............ Not in File
**NIF** ............ Not Industrially Funded [*Military*]
**NIF** ............ Note-Issuance Facility [*Banking*]
**NIF** ............ Nuclear Information File (AFM)
**NIFA** .......... National Intercollegiate Flying Association (EA)
**NIFAA** ........ Nuovo Cimento. Societa Italiana di Fisica. Sezione A [*A publication*]
**NIFAC** ....... Night Forward Air Controller [*Aircraft*]
**NIFADCS** ... National Institute of Furnace and Air Duct Cleaning Specialists (EA)
**NIFB** .......... National Institute of Farm Brokers [*Later, NIFLB*] (EA)
**NIFBA** ........ Nuovo Cimento. Societa Italiana di Fisica. Sezione B [*A publication*]
**NIFCA** ........ Nuovo Cimento. Societa Italiana di Fisica. Sezione C [*A publication*]
**NIFDA** ....... National Institutional Food Distributor Associates (EA)
**NIFE** .......... Nomenclature-in-Federal Employment
**NIFER** ........ National Institute for Full Employment Research [*Department of Labor*] (OICC)
**NIFES** ....... National Industrial Fuel Efficiency Service [*British*]
**NIFF** .......... Nordiska Ickekommersielles Fonogramproducenters Forening [*Nordic Association of Non-Commercial Phonogram Producers - NANPP*] (EAIO)
**NIFFTE** ..... Noncooperative Identification Friend or Foe Technology Evaluation (RDA)
**NIFI** ........... National Institute for the Foodservice Industry (EA)
**NIFL** .......... Finger Lakes Library System, Ithaca, NY [*Library symbol*] [*Library of Congress*] (LCLS)
**NIFLB** ....... National Institute of Farm and Land Brokers [*Later, FLI*] (EA)
**NIFO** ......... Next In, First Out [*Queuing technique*]
**NIFS** .......... National Institute for Farm Safety (EA)
**NIFTE** ....... Neon Indicator Functional Test Equipment
**NIFTI** ........ Near-Isotropic Flux Turbulence Instrument [*Oceanography*]
**NIFTS** ........ Naval Integrated Flight Training System (MCD)
**NI/FWM** ... New, Incorporated/Fourth World Movement (EA)

**NIG**........... Nationwide Investigations Group [*British*]
**NIG**........... Naval Inspector General
**NIG**........... Negative Ion Generator (ADA)
**NIG**........... Niger [*Black*] [*Pharmacy*]
**NIG**........... Nigeria
**NIG**........... Nikunau [*Kiribati*] [*Airport symbol*] (OAG)
**NIG**........... Nude Ionization Gauge
**NIGA**......... Neutron-Induced Gamma Activity (AABC)
**NIGA**......... Nuclear-Induced Ground Radioactivity (NATG)
**NIGAB**...... Annual Report. National Institute of Genetics [*English Edition*] [*Japan*] [*A publication*]
**Nig Ann Int'l L**... Nigerian Annual of International Law [*A publication*] (DLA)
**Nig Bar J**... Nigerian Bar Journal [*A publication*] (DLA)
**Nig BJ**........ Nigerian Bar Journal [*A publication*] (DLA)
**NIGCS**....... National Imperial Glass Collectors Society (EA)
**NIGDA**...... National Industrial Glove Distributors Association (EA)
**Niger Annu Rep Fed Dep Agric Res**... Nigeria. Annual Report. Federal Department of Agricultural Research [*A publication*]
**Niger Annu Rep Geol Surv Dep**... Nigeria. Annual Report. Geological Survey Department [*A publication*]
**Niger Dent J**... Nigerian Dental Journal [*A publication*]
**Niger Dep For Res Programme Work**... Nigeria. Department of Forest Research. Programme of Work [*A publication*]
**Niger Dep For Res Tech Note**... Nigeria. Department of Forest Research. Technical Note [*A publication*]
**Niger Entomol Mag**... Nigerian Entomologists' Magazine [*A publication*]
**Niger Fed Annu Rep Geol Surv**... Nigeria Federation. Annual Report. Geological Survey [*A publication*]
**Niger Fed Dep Agric Res Memor**... Nigeria Federal Department of Agricultural Research. Memorandum [*A publication*]
**Niger Field**... Nigerian Field [*A publication*]
**Niger Fld**.... Nigerian Field [*A publication*]
**Niger For Inform Bull**... Nigerian Forestry Information. Bulletin [*A publication*]
**Niger Geol Surv Div Annu Rep**... Nigeria Geological Survey Division. Annual Report [*A publication*]
**Nigeria Annu Rep Fed Dep Agric Res**... Nigeria. Annual Report. Federal Department of Agricultural Research [*A publication*]
**Nigeria Bar J**... Nigerian Bar Journal. Annual Journal of the Nigeria Bar Association [*Lagos, Nigeria*] [*A publication*] (DLA)
**Nigeria Cocoa Res Inst Annu Rep**... Nigeria Cocoa Research Institute. Annual Report [*A publication*]
**Nigeria Dep For Res Programme Work**... Nigeria. Department of Forest Research. Programme of Work [*A publication*]
**Nigeria Dep For Res Tech Note**... Nigeria. Department of Forest Research. Technical Note [*A publication*]
**Nigeria Fed Dep Agric Res Memo**... Nigeria Federal Department of Agricultural Research. Memorandum [*A publication*]
**Nigeria Fed Dep Fish Annu Rep**... Nigeria Federal Department of Fisheries. Annual Report [*A publication*]
**Nigeria Fed Dep Fish Fed Fish Occas Pap**... Nigeria Federal Department of Fisheries. Federal Fisheries. Occasional Paper [*A publication*]
**Nigeria Fed Dep For Res Annu Rep**... Nigeria Federal Department of Forest Research. Annual Report [*A publication*]
**Nigeria Fed Dep For Res Res Pap (For Ser)**... Nigeria Federal Department of Forest Research. Research Paper (Forest Series) [*A publication*]
**Nigeria Fed Dep For Res Res Pap (Savanna Ser)**... Nigeria Federal Department of Forest Research. Research Paper (Savanna Series) [*A publication*]
**Nigeria For Inf Bull**... Nigeria Forestry Information Bulletin [*A publication*]
**Nigeria Geogr J**... Nigerian Geographical Journal [*A publication*]
**Nigeria LR**... Nigeria Law Reports [*A publication*] (DLA)
**Nigerian Agric J**... Nigerian Agricultural Journal [*A publication*]
**Nigerian Agr J**... Nigerian Agricultural Journal [*A publication*]
**Nigerian Ann Int'l L**... Nigerian Annual of International Law [*A publication*] (DLA)
**Nigerian Entomol Mag**... Nigerian Entomologists' Magazine [*A publication*]
**Nigerian Inst Oil Palm Res Annu Rep**... Nigerian Institute for Oil Palm Research. Annual Report [*A publication*]
**Nigerian J Econ and Social Studies**... Nigerian Journal of Economic and Social Studies [*A publication*]
**Nigerian J Entomol**... Nigerian Journal of Entomology [*A publication*]
**Nigerian J For**... Nigerian Journal of Forestry [*A publication*]
**Nigerian J Internat Studies**... Nigerian Journal of International Studies [*A publication*]
**Nigerian J Paediatr**... Nigerian Journal of Paediatrics [*A publication*]
**Nigerian J Sci**... Nigerian Journal of Science [*A publication*]
**Nigerian Lib**... Nigerian Libraries [*A publication*]
**Nigerian Libr**... Nigerian Libraries [*A publication*]
**Nigerian LJ**... Nigerian Law Journal [*A publication*] (DLA)
**Nigerian Med J**... Nigerian Medical Journal [*A publication*]
**Nigerian Stored Prod Res Inst Annu Rep**... Nigerian Stored Products Research Institute. Annual Report [*A publication*]
**Nigeria Savanna For Res Stn Samaru Zaria Annu Rep**... Nigeria Savanna Forestry Research Station. Samaru Zaria Annual Report [*A publication*]
**Nigeria Savanna For Res Stn Ser Res Pap**... Nigeria Savanna Forestry Research Station. Series Research Paper [*A publication*]
**Niger Inst Oil Palm Res Annu Rep**... Nigerian Institute for Oil Palm Research. Annual Report [*A publication*]
**Niger J Anim Prod**... Nigerian Journal of Animal Production [*A publication*]
**Niger J Entomol**... Nigerian Journal of Entomology [*A publication*]
**Niger J For**... Nigerian Journal of Forestry [*A publication*]
**Niger J Sci**... Nigerian Journal of Science [*A publication*]
**Niger Mag**... Nigeria Magazine [*A publication*]
**Niger Med J**... Nigerian Medical Journal [*A publication*]
**Niger Nurse**... Nigerian Nurse [*A publication*]
**Niger Pl Dev**... Plan Quinquennal de Developpement Economique et Social, 1979-1983 (Niger) [*A publication*]
**NIGHAE**... Archiv fuer Japanische Chirurgie [*A publication*]
**NIGHTCAP**... Night Combat Air Patrol [*Military*] (NVT)
**Nig J Contemp L**... Nigerian Journal of Contemporary Law [*A publication*]
**NIGLA**...... Nauchno-Tekhnicheskaya Informatsiya. Tsentral'nyi Institut Nauchno-Tekhnicheskoi Informatsii Bumazhnoi i Drevoobrabatyvayushchei Promyshlennosti, Tsellyulozno-Baumazhnaya, Gidroliznaya i Lesokhimicheskaya Promyshlennost [*A publication*]
**Nig Lawy Q**... Nigeria Lawyer's Quarterly [*A publication*] (DLA)
**Nig LJ**........ Nigerian Law Journal [*A publication*] (DLA)
**Nig LQ**....... Nigeria Lawyer's Quarterly [*A publication*] (ILCA)
**Nig LQR**.... Nigerian Law Quarterly Review [*A publication*] (DLA)
**Nig LR**....... Nigeria Law Reports [*A publication*] (DLA)
**NigM**......... Nigeria Magazine [*A publication*]
**NIGMS**...... National Institute of General Medical Sciences [*National Institutes of Health*] [*Bethesda, MD*]
**NIGP**......... National Institute of Governmental Purchasing (EA)
**Nigr**........... Nigrinus [*of Lucian*] [*Classical studies*] (OCD)
**NIH**........... Hoffmann-La Roche, Inc. [*Research code symbol*]
**NIH**........... National Institute on the Holocaust [*Later, AFIP*] (EA)
**NIH**........... National Institute for the Humanities [*Yale University*] [*National Endowment for the Humanities*]
**NIH**........... National Institutes of Health [*Public Health Service*] [*Bethesda, MD*]
**NIH**........... National Institutes of Health. Publications [*A publication*]
**NIH**........... New Inn Hall [*British*] (ROG)
**NIH**........... Nonimmune Hydrops [*Medicine*]
**NIH**........... North Irish Horse [*Military unit*] [*British*]
**NIH**........... Not Invented Here Syndrome [*Business Management*]
**NIHAE Bull**... NIHAE [*National Institute of Health Administration and Education*] Bulletin [*A publication*]
**NIHB**......... National Indian Health Board (EA)
**NIHC**......... Northern Ireland House of Commons
**NIH Consensus Dev Conf Summ**... NIH [*National Institutes of Health*] Consensus Development. Conference Summary [*A publication*]
**NIHF**......... Nonimmune Hydrops Fetalis [*Medicine*]
**NIHHD**..... National Institute of Health and Human Development
**NIHi**.......... DeWitt Historical Society of Tompkins County, Ithaca, NY [*Library symbol*] [*Library of Congress*] (LCLS)
**NIHJ**......... National Institutes of Health, Japan
**NIHL**......... Noise-Induced Hearing Loss
**NIHOD**..... Nieren- und Hochdruckkrankheiten [*A publication*]
**Nihon Chikusan Gakkai Ho Jap J Zootech**... Nihon Chikusan Gakkai Ho/Japanese Journal of Zootechnical Science [*A publication*]
**Nihon Juishikai Zasshi J Jap Vet Med Assoc**... Nihon Juishikai Zasshi/Journal. Japan Veterinary Medical Association [*A publication*]
**Nihon Oyo Dobutsu Konchu Gakkai Shi Jap J Appl Entomol Zool**... Nihon Oyo Dobutsu Konchu Gakkai Shi/Japanese Journal of Applied Entomology and Zoology [*A publication*]
**Nihon Ringakkai Shi J Jap For Soc**... Nihon Ringakukai Shi. Journal. Japanese Forestry Society [*A publication*]
**Nihon Sanshigaku Zasshi J Seric Sci Jap**... Nihon Sanshigaku Zasshi. Journal of Sericultural Science of Japan [*A publication*]
**Nihon Seirigaku Zasshi Jap**... Nihon Seirigaku Zasshi/Journal. Physiological Society of Japan [*A publication*]
**Nihon Senchu Kenkyukai Shi Jap J Nematol**... Nihon Senchu Kenkyukai Shi/Japanese Journal of Nematology [*A publication*]
**Nihon Shokubutsu Byori Gakkaiho Ann Phytopathol Soc Jap**... Nihon Shokubutsu Byori Gakkaiho/Annals. Phytopathological Society of Japan [*A publication*]
**Nihon Univ Dent J**... Nihon University. Dental Journal [*Japan*] [*A publication*]
**Nihon Univ J Med**... Nihon University. Journal of Medicine [*A publication*]
**Nihon Univ J Radiat Med Biol**... Nihon University. Journal of Radiation Medicine and Biology [*Japan*] [*A publication*]
**Nihon Univ Med J**... Nihon University. Medical Journal [*Japan*] [*A publication*]
**Nihon Univ Mishima Coll Humanit Sci Annu Rep Res**... Nihon University. Mishima College of Humanities and Sciences. Annual Report of the Researches [*A publication*]
**Nihon Univ Mishima Coll Humanit Sci Annu Rep Res Nat Sci**... Nihon University. Mishima College of Humanities and Sciences. Annual Report of the Researches. Natural Sciences [*A publication*]
**NIHR**......... National Institute of Handicapped Research [*Department of Health and Human Services*] [*Washington, DC*] [*Later, NIDRR*]

**NIHS** ........ National Institute of Hypertension Studies - Institute of Hypertension School of Research (EA)
**NIHS** ........ NAVEUR Intelligence Highlights Summary (MCD)
**NIHTA** ...... Northern Ireland Head Teachers' Association
**NIHYSOB** ... Now I Have You, Son of a Bitch [*Term coined by Kenneth Blanchard, author of "The One-Minute Manager"*]
**NII** ............ National Intergroup, Incorporated [*NYSE symbol*] (SPSG)
**NII** ............ NATO Item Identification (NATG)
**NII** ............ Niigata [*Japan*] [*Seismograph station code, US Geological Survey*] (SEIS)
**NII** ............ Nuclear Installations Inspectorate [*British*]
**NIIA** .......... Nonisotropic Immunoassay
**NIIC** .......... Ithaca College, Ithaca, NY [*Library symbol*] [*Library of Congress*] (LCLS)
**NIIC** .......... National Injury Information Clearinghouse [*Consumer Product Safety Commission*]
**NIIC** .......... NORAD Intelligence Indications Center (MCD)
**NIICP** ........ No Increase in Contract Price
**NIICU** ....... National Institute of Independent Colleges and Universities (EA)
**NIIG** .......... NATO Item Identification Guide (NATG)
**Niigata Agric For Res** ... Niigata Agriculture and Forestry Research [*A publication*]
**Niigata Agric Sci** ... Niigata Agricultural Science [*A publication*]
**Niigata Agr Sci** ... Niigata Agricultural Science [*A publication*]
**Niigata Med J** ... Niigata Medical Journal [*Japan*] [*A publication*]
**Niigata Univ Sci Rep Ser E** ... Niigata University. Science Reports. Series E (Geology and Mineralogy) [*A publication*]
**NIIN** .......... National Item Identification Number (MCD)
**NIIP** .......... National Institute of Industrial Psychology [*British*]
**NIIP** .......... Net International Investment Position
**NIIRS** ........ National Imagery Interpretation Rating Scale (MCD)
**NIIS** .......... National Institute of Infant Services [*Later, NADS*]
**NIIS** .......... New Image Industries, Inc. [*NASDAQ symbol*] (NQ)
**NIIS** .......... Niagara Institute for International Studies [*Canada*]
**NIJ** ............ National Institute of Justice [*Washington, DC*] [*Department of Justice*]
**NIJ** ............ New Irish Jurist [*A publication*] (DLA)
**NIJD** .......... National Institute of Judicial Dynamics (EA)
**NIJH** .......... National Institute for Jewish Hospice (EA)
**Nijhoff Internat Philos Ser** ... Nijhoff International Philosophy Series [*A publication*]
**NIJJDP** ..... National Institute for Juvenile Justice and Delinquency Prevention
**NIJKA** ....... Nippon Jozo Kyokai Zasshi [*A publication*]
**NIJR** .......... New Irish Jurist [*A publication*] (DLA)
**NIK** ............ Boston, MA [*Location identifier*] [*FAA*] (FAAL)
**NIK** ............ Nickel [*Watchmaking*] (ROG)
**NIK** ............ Nickel Rim Mines Ltd. [*Toronto Stock Exchange symbol*]
**NIK** ............ Nikolski [*Alaska*] [*Seismograph station code, US Geological Survey*] [*Closed*] (SEIS)
**nik** ............. Northern Ireland [*MARC country of publication code*] [*Library of Congress*] (LCCP)
**NIK** ............ Novye Inostrannyye Knigi [*New Foreign Books*] [*A publication*]
**NIK** ............ Nyelv-Es Irodalomtudomanyi Koezlemenyek [*A publication*]
**NIKGA** ...... Nippon Kinzoku Gakkaishi [*A publication*]
**NIKHD** ...... Niigata-Ken Kogai Kenkyusho Kenkyu Hokoku
**NIKKA** ...... Nippon Kogyo Kaishi [*A publication*]
**NIKKEI** ..... Nihon Keizai Shimbun, Inc. [*Tokyo, Japan*] (IID)
**Nikko Mater** ... Nikko Materials [*A publication*]
**NIL** ............ I have nothing to send to you [*Telecommunications*] (FAAC)
**NIL** ............ Nederland Israel [*A publication*]
**NIL** ............ Negotiable Instruments Law (DLA)
**NIL** ............ Neurointermediate Lobe [*Neuroanatomy*]
**NIL** ............ Nilore [*Pakistan*] [*Seismograph station code, US Geological Survey*] (SEIS)
**NIL** ............ Nitrogen Inerting Line (IEEE)
**NIL** ............ No Limit (NASA)
**NIL** ............ Not in Labor [*Medicine*]
**NILA** .......... National Industrial Leather Association [*Later, NIBA*] (EA)
**NILab** ........ Northern Ireland Labour Party [*Political party*]
**NILB** .......... National Indian Lutheran Board (EA)
**NILC** .......... National Immigration Law Center (EA)
**NILE** .......... National Institute of Labor Education [*Defunct*] (EA)
**NILE** .......... Naval Inflatable Life-Saving Equipment [*British military*] (DMA)
**NILE & CJ** ... National Institute of Law Enforcement and Criminal Justice [*Law Enforcement Assistance Administration*]
**NILECJ** ..... National Institute of Law Enforcement and Criminal Justice [*Law Enforcement Assistance Administration*]
**Niles Reg** ... Niles' Weekly Register [*A publication*] (DLA)
**NILFP** ....... National Institute of Locker and Freezer Provisioners [*Later, AAMP*] (EA)
**NILGOSC** ... Northern Ireland Local Government Officers Superannuation Committee
**NIlH** .......... Herkimer County Community College, Ilion, NY [*Library symbol*] [*Library of Congress*] (LCLS)
**NILI** .......... Netsah Israel Lo Yeshakker (BJA)
**NILI** .......... Newark Island Layered Intrusion [*Canada*] [*Geology*]
**NI Libr** ....... Northern Ireland Libraries [*A publication*]
**NILKY** ....... No Income, Lots of Kids [*Lifestyle classification*]
**N Ill LR** ...... Northern Illinois University. Law Review [*A publication*]
**N Ill UL Rev** ... Northern Illinois University. Law Review [*A publication*]
**NILN** .......... Nylon Insert Lock Nut
**NILO** .......... Naval Intelligence Liaison Officer (NVT)
**NILP** .......... Northern Ireland Labour Party [*Political party*] (PPW)
**NILPT** ........ National Institute for Low Power Television (EA)
**NILQ** .......... Northern Ireland Legal Quarterly [*A publication*]
**NILR** .......... Netherlands International Law Review [*A publication*]
**NILR** .......... Northern Ireland Law Reports [*A publication*] (DLA)
**NILRC** ....... Northern Illinois Learning Resources Cooperative [*Library network*]
**Nil Reg** ....... Niles' Weekly Register [*A publication*] (DLA)
**NIL Rev** ..... Netherlands International Law Review [*A publication*]
**NILS** .......... Naval Intelligence Locating Summary (MCD)
**NILS** .......... Northern Illinois Library System [*Library network*]
**NILS** .......... Nuclear Instrument Landing System
**NILT** .......... National Institute for Lay Training (EA)
**NIM** ........... Naval Inspector of Machinery
**NIM** ........... Net Interest Margin [*Banking*]
**NIM** ........... Network Injection Molding
**NIM** ........... Network Interface Machine [*Datapac*]
**NIM** ........... Network Interface Module [*Telecommunications*] (TSSD)
**NIM** ........... Network Interface Monitor
**NIM** ........... Niamey [*Niger*] [*Airport symbol*] (OAG)
**NIM** ........... Night Intruder Mission [*Air Force*]
**NIM** ........... No Immediate Miracles [*Acronym and facetious translation derived from turning President Gerald Ford's anti-inflation WIN buttons upside down*] [*See WIN entry*]
**NIM** ........... Noninterrupt Mode
**NIM** ........... NORAD Intelligence Memorandum (MCD)
**NIM** ........... Normal Integration Mode
**NIM** ........... North Irish Militia [*Military unit*] [*British*]
**NIM** ........... Nothing in Mind [*Acronym and facetious translation derived from turning President Gerald Ford's anti-inflation WIN buttons upside down*] [*See WIN entry*]
**NIM** ........... Nuclear Instrumentation Module
**NIM** ........... Nylon Insulation Material
**NIM** ........... University of North Carolina at Asheville, Asheville, NC [*OCLC symbol*] (OCLC)
**NIMA** ........ National Insulation Manufacturers Association [*Later, Thermal Insulation Manufacturers Association*] (EA)
**NIMA** ........ Noninherited Maternal Antigen [*Genetics*] [*Immunology*]
**NIMAB** ..... National Indian Manpower Advisory Board
**NIMAC** ..... National Interscholastic Music Activities Commission [*Defunct*] (EA)
**NIMBIN** .... Nuclear Instrumentation Modular Bin
**NIMBY** ..... Not in My Back Yard [*i.e., garbage incinerators, prisons, roads, etc.*]
**NIMC** ........ National Institute of Management Counsellors (EA)
**NIMC** ........ National Institute of Municipal Clerks [*Later, IIMC*]
**NIMC** ........ Nodding Image Motion Compensation [*Instrumentation*]
**NIMCGA** .. Northern Indiana Muck Crop Growers Association [*Defunct*] (EA)
**NIMCP** ..... NATO Information Management Control Point (NATG)
**NIME** ........ National Institute for Multicultural Education (EA)
**NIMEY** ..... Not in My Election Year [*Slang*]
**NIMFR** ..... National Institutes of Marriage and Family Relations (EA)
**NIMH** ........ National Institute of Medical Herbalists [*British*]
**NIMH** ........ National Institute of Mental Health [*Rockville, MD*] [*Department of Health and Human Services*]
**NIMH** ........ National Institute of Mental Health. Publications [*A publication*]
**NIMIS** ....... National Instructional Materials Information System
**NIMIT** ....... Nimbus Integration and Test [*NASA*] (KSC)
**NIMJ** ......... Near Infrared Miniaturized Jammer
**NIMLO** ..... National Institute of Municipal Law Officers (EA)
**NIMLO Mun L Rev** ... National Institute of Municipal Law Officers. Municipal Law Review [*A publication*] (DLA)
**NIMMA** .... Northern Ireland Mixed Marriage Association
**NIMMP** .... National Institute of Marine Medicine and Pharmacology [*Proposed*] [*National Institutes of Health*]
**NIMMS** .... Nineteen-Hundred Integrated Modular Management System
**NIMP** ........ National Intern Matching Program [*Later, NRMP*] (EA)
**NIMPA** ..... National Independent Meat Packers Association [*Later, NMA*] (EA)
**NIMPH** ..... Network Interface Message Processing Host [*NERComP*]
**NIMPHE** .. Nuclear Isotope Monopropellant Hydrazine Engine
**NIMR** ........ National Institute for Medical Research
**NIMR** ........ Navy Industrial Management Reviews (NG)
**NIMRD** ..... Nuclear Instruments and Methods in Physics Research [*A publication*]
**NIM Res Dig** ... NIM [*National Institute for Metallurgy*] Research Digest [*United States*] [*A publication*]
**NIMROD** ... Northern Illinois Meteorological Research on Downbursts [*National Center for Atmospheric Research*]
**NIMRS** ...... Navy Integrated Message Reporting System (MCD)
**NIMS** ........ Fairhaven International Ltd. [*NASDAQ symbol*] (NQ)
**NIMS** ........ National Information Management System
**NIMS** ........ National Ingredient Marketing Specialists (EA)

**NIMS** ........ Nationwide Improved Mail Service [*Postal Service*]
**NIMSC** ...... Nonconsumable Item Materiel Support Code [*Military*] (AFIT)
**NIMSCO** ... NODC [*National Oceanographic Data Center*] Index to Instrument Measures Subsurface e Current Observations [*Marine science*] (MSC)
**NIMSLO** ... Camera producing three-dimensional photographs [*Product is named after Jerry Nims, chairman of the photography company that produces it, and Allen Lo, its inventor*]
**NIMSR** ...... Nonconsumable Item Materiel Support Request [*Military*] (AFIT)
**NIMT** ........ National Institute for Music Theater (EA)
**NIMTECH** ... New and Improved Technology [*British*]
**NIMU** ........ Non-Invasive Monitoring Systems, Inc. [*NASDAQ symbol*] (NQ)
**NIN** ............ National Information Network [*ASTIA*]
**NIN** ............ National Inservice Network
**NIN** ............ Neighbors in Need [*An association*]
**NIN** ............ New Products International [*A publication*]
**NIN** ............ Ninilchik [*Alaska*] [*Seismograph station code, US Geological Survey*] [*Closed*] (SEIS)
**NIN** ............ Ninilchik, AK [*Location identifier*] [*FAA*] (FAAL)
**NIN** ............ Norsat International, Inc. [*Vancouver Stock Exchange symbol*]
**NINA** ......... No Irish Need Apply [*Classified advertising*]
**NINCDS** .... National Institute of Neurological and Communicative Disorders and Stroke [*Formerly, NINDS*] [*Public Health Service*] [*Bethesda, MD*]
**NINDB** ...... National Institute of Neurological Diseases and Blindness [*Later, NEI, NINDS*] [*National Institutes of Health*]
**NINDS** ...... National Institute of Neurological Diseases and Stroke [*Formerly, NINDB*] [*Later, NINCDS*] [*National Institutes of Health*]
**NIndTP** ...... National Independent Teenage Party [*British*]
**NINE** .......... National Infertility Network Exchange [*An association*] (EA)
**Nine Cen Mus** ... Nineteenth Century Music [*A publication*]
**Nine Ct** ....... Nineteenth Century [*A publication*]
**Nine-Ct Fic** ... Nineteenth-Century Fiction [*A publication*]
**Nine-Ct Fr** ... Nineteenth-Century French Studies [*A publication*]
**Nine Ct Mus** ... Nineteenth Century Music [*A publication*]
**Nine Ct The** ... Nineteenth-Century Theatre Research [*A publication*]
**NINF Informasjon Nor Inst Naeringsmidforsk** ... NINF Informasjon. Norsk Institutt for Naeringsmiddelforskning [*A publication*]
**NINFRA** .... National Independent Nursery Furniture Retailers Association (EA)
**NINIA** ....... Nephelometric Inhibition Immunoassay [*Analytical chemistry*]
**Nink** ........... No Income, No Kids [*Lifestyle classification*]
**NINND2** .... Neuroptera International [*A publication*]
**NINOW** ..... Non-Interest-Bearing Negotiable Order of Withdrawal [*Banking*]
**NINS** ......... Northern Ireland News Service [*Information service or system*] (EISS)
**NINST** ....... Nose Instantaneous [*Aerospace*]
**N Instr Meth** ... Nuclear Instruments and Methods [*Later, Nuclear Instruments and Methods in Physics Research*] [*A publication*]
**NINTD** ...... New Internationalist [*A publication*]
**Ninth District Q** ... Ninth District Quarterly [*A publication*]
**NIO** ............ National Institute of Oceanography [*British*] (IID)
**NIO** ............ National Intelligence Officer (MCD)
**NIO** ............ Naval Inspector of Ordnance
**NIO** ............ Navigational Information Office
**NIO** ............ Navy Institute of Oceanography
**NIO** ............ Niobium [*See Cb*] [*Chemical element*] (ROG)
**NIO** ............ Nioki [*Zaire*] [*Airport symbol*] (OAG)
**NIO** ............ Northern Ireland Office
**NIOBE** ...... Numerical Integration of the Boltzmann Transport Equation
**NIOD** ......... Network In-Out Dial [*Automatic Voice Network*] (CET)
**NIOG** ......... Nationalized Industries Overseas Group [*British*] (DCTA)
**NIOGA** ...... Nippon Onkyo Gakkaishi [*A publication*]
**NIOHS** ...... National Institute of Occupational Health and Safety [*Australia*]
**NIOK** ......... National Institute for Overseas Koreans (EA)
**NIOP** ......... National Institute of Oilseed Products (EA)
**NIOS** ......... Northern Ireland Orchid Society (EAIO)
**NIOSH** ...... National Institute for Occupational Safety and Health [*Public Health Service*] [*Cincinnati, OH*] [*Database producer*]
**NIOSH** ...... National Institute of Occupational Safety and Health. Publications [*A publication*]
**NIOSH/OSHA Current Intell Bull** ... NIOSH/OSHA Current Intelligence Bulletin [*A publication*]
**NIOSH Surv** ... NIOSH [*National Institute for Occupational Safety and Health*] Survey [*A publication*]
**NIOSH Tech Inf** ... NIOSH [*National Institute for Occupational Safety and Health*] Technical Information [*A publication*]
**NIOSHTIC** ... National Institute for Occupational Safety and Health Technical Information Center [*Database*] [*NIOSH*] [*Information service or system*] (CRD)
**NIOTC** ...... Naval Inshore Operations Training Center (NVT)
**NIp** ............ Island Park Public Library, Island Park, NY [*Library symbol*] [*Library of Congress*] (LCLS)
**NIP** ............ Jacksonville, FL [*Location identifier*] [*FAA*] (FAAL)
**NIP** ............ NADGE [*NATO Air Defense Ground Environment*] Improvement Plan (NATG)
**NIP** ............ Namibia Independence Party [*Political party*] (PPW)
**NIP** ............ National Identification Program for the Advancement of Women in Higher Education Administration (EA)
**NIP** ............ National Independence Party [*Namibia*] [*Political party*] (PPW)
**NIP** ............ National Information Policy [*Australia*]
**NIP** ............ National Institute of Polarology [*British*] (IRUK)
**NIP** ............ National Intelligence Priorities (MCD)
**NIP** ............ National Inventory Programme [*National Museums of Canada*] [*Later, CHIN*]
**NIP** ............ Naval Institute Press [*Publisher*]
**NIP** ............ Naval Intelligence Professionals (EA)
**NIP** ............ Navy Interceptor Program
**NIP** ............ Neighbourhood Improvement Program [*Canada*]
**NIP** ............ Network Input Processor [*Data processing*] (MCD)
**NIP** ............ Network Interface Processor (MCD)
**NIP** ............ New Ideas in Psychology [*A publication*]
**NIP** ............ New Impact Resources, Inc. [*Vancouver Stock Exchange symbol*]
**NIP** ............ New Incentive Package (ADA)
**NIP** ............ Newhall Investment Properties [*NYSE symbol*] (SPSG)
**NIP** ............ Newsletters in Print [*Formerly, ND*] [*A publication*]
**NIP** ............ Nipple (AAG)
**NIP** ............ Nipponese
**NIP** ............ Nonimpact Printer
**NIP** ............ Normal Impact Point
**NIP** ............ Normal Investment Practice
**NIP** ............ Notice of Intelligence Potential [*Military*] (AFM)
**NIP** ............ Notice of Intent to Purchase [*DoD*]
**NIP** ............ Nucleus Initialization Program [*Data processing*]
**NIP** ............ Numeric Indicator Performance
**NIP** ............ Numero d'Identification Personnel [*Personal Identification Number - PIN*]
**NIPA** ......... National Income and Product Accounts [*The WEFA Group*] [*Information service*] [*Information service or system*] (CRD)
**NIPA** ......... National Institute of Pension Administrators [*Santa Ana, CA*] (EA)
**NIPA** ......... National Institute of Public Affairs
**NIPA** ......... Noninherited Paternal Antigen [*Genetics*] [*Immunology*]
**NIPA** ......... Noninterference Performance Assessment
**NIPA** ......... Nordens Institut pa Aland [*Nordic Institute in Aland - NIA*] [*Mariehamn, Aland, Finland*] (EAIO)
**NIPA** ......... Northern Ireland Police Authority
**NIPA** ......... Notice of Initiation of Procurement Action (NRCH)
**NIPAA** ....... Nippon Shokakibyo Gakkai Zasshi [*A publication*]
**NIPAGRAM** ... National Income and Product Account Data by Mailgram [*NTIS*]
**NIPALS** ..... Noniterative Partial Least Squares [*Algorithm*]
**NIPC** .......... N-Isopropylcarbazole [*Organic chemistry*]
**NIPCC** ....... National Industrial Pollution Control Council [*Terminated, 1973*] [*Department of Commerce*]
**NIPD** ......... Not in the Public Domain
**NIPDA** ...... Nihon Daigaku Nojuigakubu Gakujutsu Kenkyu Hokoku [*A publication*]
**NIPDWR** ... National Interim Primary Drinking Water Regulations [*Environmental Protection Agency*]
**NIPDWS** ... National Interim Primary Drinking Water Standards [*Environmental Protection Agency*]
**NIPEA** ....... Nippon Genshiryoku Kenkyusho Kenkyu Hokoku [*A publication*]
**NIPER** ....... National Institute for Petroleum and Energy Research [*Formerly, BETC*] [*Department of Energy*] [*Bartlesville, OK*]
**NIPF** .......... Northern Ireland Peace Forum
**NIPFDA** .... National Independent Poultry and Food Distributors Association (EA)
**NIPGM** ..... National Institute on Park and Grounds Management (EA)
**NIPH** ......... National Institute of Public Health
**NIPHA** ....... Nippon Hoshasen Gijutsu Gakkai Zasshi [*A publication*]
**NIPH Ann** ... NIPH [*National Institute of Public Health*] Annals [*A publication*]
**NIPHLE** .... National Institute of Packaging, Handling, and Logistic Engineers (EA)
**NIPH (Natl Inst Public Health) Ann (Oslo)** ... NIPH (National Institute of Public Health) Annals (Oslo) [*A publication*]
**NIPILS** ...... New Irish Professionals in London [*Lifestyle classification*]
**NIPIMS** .... NAVMAT Instructional Procurement Inventory Monitoring System (MCD)
**NIPIR** ........ Nuclear Immediate Photo Interpretation Report (MCD)
**Nip Kag Kai** ... Nippon Kagaku Kaishi [*A publication*]
**NIPM** ........ National Institute of Public Management (EA)
**NIPN** ......... NEC Corp. [*NASDAQ symbol*] (NQ)
**NIP/NLG** .. National Immigration Project of the National Lawyers Guild (EA)
**NIPO** ......... Negative Input, Positive Output
**NIPOLOS** ... Nonimpact Off-Line Operating System [*Data processing*]
**NIPP** .......... National Institute for Public Policy (EA)
**NIPP** .......... National Intelligence Projection for Planning (AFM)

**NIPP**.......... Net Income per Partner [*Business term*]
**NIPP**.......... Nonimpact Printing Process (MCD)
**NIPPE**....... National Income per Person Employed
**Nippon Acta Radiol** ... Nippon Acta Radiologica [*Japan*] [*A publication*]
**Nippon Dent Coll Annu Publ** ... Nippon Dental College. Annual Publications [*A publication*]
**Nippon Dojo Hiryogaku Zasshi J Sci Soil Manure** ... Nippon Dojo Hiryogaku Zasshi/Journal of the Science of Soil and Manure [*Japan*] [*A publication*]
**Nippon Kagaku Kaishi J Chem Soc Jap Chem** ... Nippon Kagaku Kaishi/Journal. Chemical Society of Japan. Chemistry and Industrial Chemistry [*A publication*]
**Nippon Kokan Tech Bull** ... Nippon Kokan Technical Bulletin [*A publication*]
**Nippon Kokan Tech Rep** ... Nippon Kokan Technical Reports [*A publication*]
**Nippon Kokan Tech Rep Overseas** ... Nippon Kokan Technical Reports Overseas [*A publication*]
**Nippon Nogei Kagakukai Shi J Agric Chem Soc Jap** ... Nippon Nogei Kagakukai-Shi/Journal. Agricultural Chemical Society of Japan [*A publication*]
**Nippon Noyaku Gakkaishi/J Pestic Sci** ... Nippon Noyaku Gakkaishi/Journal of Pesticide Science [*A publication*]
**Nippon-Orient** ... Nippon-Orient-Gakkai-Geppo [*A publication*]
**Nippon Sochi Gakkai Shi J Jap Soc Grassl Sci** ... Nippon Sochi Gakkai Shi/Journal. Japanese Society of Grassland Science [*A publication*]
**Nippon Stainless Tech Rep** ... Nippon Stainless Technical Report [*A publication*]
**Nippon Steel Tech Rep** ... Nippon Steel Technical Report [*A publication*]
**Nippon Steel Tech Rep (Jpn Ed)** ... Nippon Steel Technical Report (Japanese Edition) [*A publication*]
**Nippon Steel Tech Rep (Overseas)** ... Nippon Steel Technical Report (Overseas) [*A publication*]
**NIPR**.......... National Industrial Plant Reserve
**NIPR**.......... Naval Intelligence Publication Register (NVT)
**NI PRI**....... Nisi Prius [*Unless Before*] [*Legal term*] [*Latin*]
**NIPRM**...... National Institute of Polar Research. Memoirs. Special Issue [*A publication*]
**NIPRMAA** ... National Institute of Polar Research. Memoirs. Series A. Aeronomy [*A publication*]
**NIPRMBMT** ... National Institute of Polar Research. Memoirs. Series B. Meteorology [*A publication*]
**NIPRMCES** ... National Institute of Polar Research. Memoirs. Series C. Earth Sciences [*A publication*]
**NIPRMEB** ... National Institute of Polar Research. Memoirs. Series E. Biology and Medical Science [*A publication*]
**NIPRMFL** ... National Institute of Polar Research. Memoirs. Series F. Logistics [*A publication*]
**NIPRMS** ... National Institute of Polar Research. Memoirs. Special Issue [*A publication*]
**NIPRORUDA Sb Nauchni Tr Ser Obogat** ... NIPRORUDA [*Nauchnoizsledovatelski i Proektantski Institut za Rudodobiv i Obogatyavane*] Sbornik Nauchni Trudove. Seriya. Obogatyavanne [*A publication*]
**NIPRSMS** ... National Institute of Polar Research. Special Map Series [*A publication*]
**NIPS**.......... National Information Processing System [*Military*]
**NIPS**.......... National Institute for Public Services
**NIPS**.......... National Inventory of Pollution Sources [*Database*] [*Environment Canada*] [*Information service or system*] (CRD)
**NIPS**.......... Nationwide Integrated Postal Service [*Postal Service*]
**NIPS**.......... Naval Intelligence Processing System
**NIPS**.......... Navy Information Policy Summaries (NG)
**NIPS**.......... New Inventory Pricing Systems (MCD)
**NIPS**.......... Nippon Information Processing System [*Nippon Shuppan Hanbai, Inc.*] [*Database*]
**NIPSA**....... Northern Ireland Public Service Alliance (EAIO)
**NIPSSA**..... Naval Intelligence Processing System Support Activity
**NIP & TB**.. Northern Ireland Postal and Telecommunications Board
**NIPTS**....... Noise-Induced Permanent Threshold Shift [*Hearing*]
**NIQ**........... National Institute Economic Review [*London*] [*A publication*]
**NIR**............ Beeville, TX [*Location identifier*] [*FAA*] (FAAL)
**NIr**............ Irvington Public Library, Irvington, NY [*Library symbol*] [*Library of Congress*] (LCLS)
**NIR**............ National Inventory Record [*DoD*]
**NIR**............ Near Infrared Region
**NIR**............ Nerve Impulse Recorder
**NIR**............ Netherlands International Law Review [*A publication*]
**NIR**............ New Ireland Review [*A publication*] (ROG)
**NIR**............ Next Inferior Rank
**NIR**............ No Individual Requirement (MSA)
**NIR**............ Non-Insulin-Requiring [*Medicine*]
**NIR**............ Noninductive Resistor
**N Ir**........... Northern Ireland Law Reports [*A publication*] (DLA)
**NIR**............ Northern Ireland Railways Co. Ltd.
**NIR**............ Nose Impact Rocket (NATG)
**NIRA**......... National Industrial Recovery Act [*1933*]
**NIRA**......... National Industrial Recreation Association [*Later, NESRA*] (EA)
**NIRA**......... National Industrial Reserve Act of 1948
**NIRA**......... National Intercollegiate Rodeo Association (EA)
**NIRA**......... Near Infrared Reflectance Analysis
**NIRA**......... Niravoice, Inc. [*NASDAQ symbol*] (NQ)
**NIRAP**....... Naval Industrial Reserve Aircraft Plant (MUGU)
**NIRAS**....... National Institute of Research and Advanced Studies [*Proposed*]
**NIRB**......... National Industrial Recovery Board [*Terminated, 1935*]
**NIRB**......... Nuclear Insurance Rating Bureau
**NIRC**......... National Industrial Relations Court [*British*]
**NIRC**......... National Information Retrieval Colloquium [*Later, Benjamin Franklin Colloquium on Information Science*]
**NIRC**......... National Institute of Rug Cleaning [*Superseded by AIDS International*] (EA)
**NIRC**......... Negative Ion Recombination Chamber
**NIRCF**....... National Immigration, Refugee and Citizenship Forum (EA)
**NIRD**......... National Institute for Research in Dairying [*British*]
**NIRDR**...... Nonintegrated RADAR (MCD)
**NIRE**......... National Institute for Rehabilitation Engineering (EA)
**N IRE**........ Northern Ireland
**NIREB**....... National Institute of Real Estate Brokers [*Later, Realtors National Marketing Institute*] (EA)
**NIRED**...... New International Realities [*A publication*]
**N Ireland Rec Agr Res** ... Northern Ireland Record of Agricultural Research [*A publication*]
**N Ire LQ**.... Northern Ireland Legal Quarterly [*A publication*]
**NIREX**....... Nuclear Industry Radioactive Waste Executive [*British*] (ECON)
**NIRI**.......... National Information Research Institute
**NIRI**.......... National Investor Relations Institute [*Washington, DC*] (EA)
**N Ir Legal Q** ... Northern Ireland Legal Quarterly [*A publication*]
**N Ir LQ**...... Northern Ireland Legal Quarterly [*A publication*]
**N Ir LR**...... Northern Ireland Law Reports [*A publication*] (DLA)
**NIRM**........ Network for Information Retrieval in Mammology
**NIRMA**..... Nuclear Information and Records Management Association (EA)
**NIRMP**...... National Intern and Resident Matching Program [*Later, NRMP*] (EA)
**NIRNS**....... National Institute for Research in Nuclear Science [*British*]
**NIRO**......... Nike-Iroquois [*Rockets*]
**NIROC**...... National Institute of Red Orange Canaries and All Other Cage Birds (EA)
**NIROP**...... Naval Industrial Reserve Ordnance Plant (MCD)
**NIRPL**....... Navy Industrial Readiness Planning List (NG)
**N Ir Pub Gen Acts** ... Northern Ireland Public General Acts [*A publication*] (DLA)
**N Ir Rev Stat** ... Northern Ireland Revised Statutes [*A publication*]
**NIRS**.......... Near Infrared Reflectance Spectroscopy [*Britton Chance*]
**NIRS**.......... Nuclear Information and Resource Service (EA)
**NIRSA**....... National Intramural-Recreational Sports Association (EA)
**NIRSA**....... NIRSA. Journal of the National Intramural-Recreational Sports Association [*A publication*]
**N Ir Stat**..... Northern Ireland Statutes [*A publication*] (DLA)
**NIRT**......... National Income Realty Trust [*NASDAQ symbol*] (NQ)
**NI & RT**..... Numerical Index and Requirement Table (MCD)
**NIRTS**....... New Integrated Range Timing System
**NIRTV**....... National Iranian Radio and Television
**NIrvH**........ Lake Shore Hospital, Irving, NY [*Library symbol*] [*Library of Congress*] (LCLS)
**NIs**............ Islip Public Library, Islip, NY [*Library symbol*] [*Library of Congress*] (LCLS)
**NIS**............ N-Iodosuccinimide [*Organic chemistry*]
**NIS**............ National Income Statistics [*British*]
**NIS**............ National Information Systems [*Later, GIP*] [*UNESCO*] (BUR)
**NIS**............ National Information Systems, Inc. [*Information service or system*] (IID)
**NIS**............ National Institute of Science (EA)
**NIS**............ National Insurance Surcharge [*A separately accounted tax on employment*] [*British*]
**NIS**............ National Intelligence Survey
**NIS**............ National Interdepartmental Seminar [*Military*]
**NIS**............ NATO Identification System
**NIS**............ Naval Intelligence School
**NIS**............ Naval Investigative Service
**NIS**............ Navy Inspection Service
**NIS**............ Negative Ion Source
**NIS**............ Neighborhood Information Service
**NIS**............ Network Information System [*AT & T*]
**NIS**............ Network Interface System
**NIS**............ Neutron Inelastic Scattering
**NIS**............ Neutron Instrumentation System (IEEE)
**NIS**............ News and Information Service [*National Broadcasting Co.*]
**NIS**............ Nickel-Iron System
**NIS**............ Night Illumination System
**NIS**............ No Intermediate Storage [*Industrial engineering*]
**NIS**............ Noise Information System [*Environmental Protection Agency*] (IID)
**NIS**............ Nonconsumable Item Subgroup [*Military*] (AFIT)
**NIS**............ Not in Stock
**NIS**............ Not in System (FAAC)
**NIS**............ Nuclear Instrumentation System (NRCH)
**NISA**.......... National Inconvenienced Sportsmen's Association [*Later, NHSRA*] (EA)

**NISA**.......... National Industrial Sand Association (EA)
**NISA**.......... National Industrial Service Association [*Later, EASA*]
**NISA**.......... National Industrial Stores Association (EA)
**NISA**.......... National Institute of Supply Associations
**NISA**.......... Numerically Integrated Elements for System Analysis (MCD)
**NISAA**........ Nippon Sakumotsu Gakkai Kiji [*A publication*]
**NISARC**.... National Information Storage and Retrieval Center
**NISBCO**.... National Interreligious Service Board for Conscientious Objectors (EA)
**Nisbet**......... Nisbet of Dirleton's Scotch Session Cases [*1665-77*] [*A publication*] (DLA)
**NISBS** ....... National Institute of Social and Behavioral Science (EA)
**NISC**.......... National Independent Study Center [*Civil Service Commission*]
**NISC**.......... National Industrial Security Corporation [*St. Louis, MO*] [*NASDAQ symbol*] (NQ)
**NISC**.......... National Industrial Space Committee
**NISC**.......... National Information Services Corporation (EISS)
**NISC**.......... National Institute of Senior Centers (EA)
**NISC**.......... National Intelligence Study Center (EA)
**NISC**.......... National Inter Seminary Council
**NISC**.......... National Intramural Sports Council
**NISC**.......... Naval Intelligence Support Center
**NISCA**....... National Interscholastic Swimming Coaches Association of America (EA)
**NISCO**....... Nuclear Installation Services Company (NRCH)
**NISCR**....... South Central Research Library Council, Ithaca, NY [*Library symbol*] [*Library of Congress*] (LCLS)
**NISC-TRANS** ... Naval Intelligence Support Center Translation Division
**NISCUE**.... National Institute for State Credit Union Examination [*McLean, VA*] (EA)
**NISD** ......... National Institute of Steel Detailing (EA)
**NISE**.......... Neighborhood Information Sharing Exchange [*Defunct*] (EA)
**NISE**.......... Normalized Integral Squared Error
**NISEA**....... Nippon Seirigaku Zasshi [*A publication*]
**NISEC** ....... National Institute for the Study of Educational Change
**NISEE** ....... National Information Service for Earthquake Engineering (EA)
**NISFAY** .... Acta Obstetrica et Gynaecologica Japonica [*Japanese Edition*] [*A publication*]
**NISG** ......... National Institute of Student Governments [*Defunct*] (EA)
**NISG** ......... Navy Installation Survey Group
**NISGA**....... Nisshin Seiko Giho [*A publication*]
**NISGAZ**.... National Intelligence Survey Gazetteer
**NISGUA**.... Network in Solidarity with the People of Guatemala (EA)
**NISH** ......... National Industries for the Severely Handicapped (EA)
**NISH** ......... National Information Sources on the Handicapped [*Clearinghouse on the Handicapped*] [*Database*]
**NISH** ......... National Institute of Senior Housing (EA)
**NISHB**....... Nichidai Shigaku [*A publication*]
**Nishinihon J Dermatol** ... Nishinihon Journal of Dermatology [*A publication*]
**Nishinihon J Urol** ... Nishinihon Journal of Urology [*A publication*]
**NISHQ**...... Naval Investigative Service Headquarters
**NI-SIL**....... Nickel-Silver (KSC)
**Nisi Prius & Gen T Rep** ... Nisi Prius and General Term Reports [*Ohio*] [*A publication*] (DLA)
**Nisi Prius Rep** ... Ohio Nisi Prius Reports [*A publication*] (DLA)
**NISLAPP**.. National Institute for Science, Law, and Public Policy (EA)
**NISMF**...... Naval Inactive Ship Maintenance Facility
**NISO** ......... National Information Standards Organization - Z39 (EA)
**NISO** ......... Naval Investigative Service Office (NVT)
**NISOA** ...... National Intercollegiate Soccer Officials Association (EA)
**NISOD** ...... National Institute for Staff and Organizational Development (OICC)
**NISP**.......... National Information System for Psychology
**NISP**.......... Navy Integrated Space Program (NG)
**NISR**.......... National Intelligence Situation Report (MCD)
**NISR**.......... Navy Initial Support Requirement (AFIT)
**NISRA**....... National Intercollegiate Squash Racquets Association (EA)
**NISRA**....... Naval Investigative Service Resident Agent (NVT)
**NISS** .......... National Institute of Social Sciences (EA)
**NISS** .......... New Information Systems and Services [*A publication*]
**Nissan Diesel Rev** ... Nissan Diesel Review [*Japan*] [*A publication*]
**Nisseki Tech Rev** ... Nisseki Technical Review [*Japan*] [*A publication*]
**Nisshin Steel Tech Rep** ... Nisshin Steel Technical Report [*A publication*]
**NISSM**...... Navy Interim Surface Ship Model (CAAL)
**NISSPO** .... NATO Identification System Special Project Office
**NIST**.......... National Institute of Science and Technology [*Manila, Philippines*]
**NIST**.......... National Institute of Standards and Technology [*Formerly, NBS*] [*Department of Commerce*] [*Gaithersburg, MD*]
**NISTARS** ... Naval Integrated Storage Tracking and Retrieval System
**NISTF** ....... National Information Systems Task Force [*Society of American Archivists*] [*Information service or system*] (IID)
**NISW**......... National Institute of Social Work [*British*]
**NISWA**...... National Indian Social Workers Association (EA)
**NIT** ............ Midwest Aviation Corp. [*Davenport, IA*] [*FAA designator*] (FAAC)
**NIT** ............ National Institute of Technology
**NIT** ............ National Instructional Television [*Superseded by AIT*] (EA)
**NIT** ............ National Intelligence Test [*Psychology*]
**NIT** ............ National Invitation Tournament [*Basketball*]
**NIT** ............ Negative Income Tax
**NIT** ............ New Information Technology
**NIT** ............ Nitrum [*Chemistry*] (ROG)
**NIT** ............ None in Town [*Bookselling*]
**NIT** ............ Normal Incidence Technique [*Structural testing*]
**NIT** ............ Nuclear Irradiation Test
**NIt**............. Nuova Italia [*A publication*]
**NIT** ............ Nurses in Transition (EA)
**NITA** ......... Journal. National Intravenous Therapy Association [*A publication*]
**NITA** ......... National Indoor Tennis Association [*Formerly, ITA*] [*Later, NTA*] (EA)
**NITA** ......... National Industrial Television Association [*Later, ITVA*] (EA)
**NITA** ......... National Institute for Trial Advocacy (EA)
**NITA** ......... National Intravenous Therapy Association [*Later, INS*] (EA)
**NITAJ** ....... Journal. National Intravenous Therapy Association [*A publication*]
**NITB**.......... Northern Ireland Tourist Board
**NITC** ......... National Information Technology Council [*Australia*]
**NITC** ......... National Intelligence Tasking Center [*CIA*]
**NITE**.......... Navy Integrated Terminal Evaluation
**NITE**.......... Night Imaging Thermal Equipment [*Army*] (INF)
**NITEDEVRON** ... Night Development Squadron
**NITEOP**.... Night Imaging Through Electro-Optic Package [*Military*] [*British*]
**NITEWOG** ... Naval Integrated Test and Evaluation Working Group (MCD)
**NITFSJ** ..... National Interreligious Task Force on Soviet Jewry (EA)
**NITINOL** ... Nickel Titanium Naval Ordnance Laboratory [*An alloy named by William Buehler of the NOL*] (KSC)
**NITL**.......... National Industrial Traffic League (EA)
**NITL**.......... National Industrial Transportation League (EA)
**NITM** ........ National Income Tax Magazine [*A publication*] (DLA)
**NITMDA** .. National Indoor Track Meet Directors Association (EA)
**NITP**.......... National Industrial Training Program [*Canada*]
**NITP**.......... National Institutional Training Program [*Canada*]
**NITP**.......... Nibbling Template
**NITPA**....... National Institutional Teacher Placement Association [*Later, ASCUS*]
**NITPICKERS** ... National Institute of Technical Processors, Information Consultants, Keyword Experts, and Retrieval Specialists [*Fictitious organization*]
**NITRAS** .... Navy Integrated Training Resources and Administration System (NVT)
**NITRC**....... National Indian Training and Research Center (EA)
**NITRO** ...... Nitrogen [*Chemical symbol is N*]
**nitro**............ Nitroglycerin [*Pharmacy*]
**NITROS**.... Nitrostarch (AAG)
**NITSTL**..... Nitride Steel
**NITTA**....... Nauchno-Issledovatel'skie Trudy Tsentral'nogo Nauchno-Issledovatel'skogo Instituta Kozhevenno-Obuvnoi Promyshlennosti [*A publication*]
**NITUC** ...... National Independent Truckers Unity Council (EA)
**NIU**............ NATO Interface Unit (MCD)
**NIU**............ Naval Intelligence Unit
**NIU**............ Navigation Interface Unit [*Navy*] (CAAL)
**NIU**............ Network Interface Unit [*Data processing*]
**NIU**............ Niue [*ANSI three-letter standard code*] (CNC)
**NIU**............ Niumate [*Tonga*] [*Seismograph station code, US Geological Survey*] [*Closed*] (SEIS)
**NIU**............ Northern Illinois University [*Dekalb, IL*]
**NIU**............ University of Northern Iowa, Cedar Falls, IA [*OCLC symbol*] (OCLC)
**NIUC** ......... National Independent Union Council [*Later, NFIU*]
**NIUE** ......... Alofi/Niue International [*Niue Island*] [*ICAO location identifier*] (ICLI)
**NIUF** ......... National Inshore Union of Fishermen [*British*]
**NIUW**........ National Institute for Urban Wildlife (EA)
**NIV** ............ National Institute of Victimology (EA)
**NIV** ............ Negative Ion Vacancy
**NIV** ............ New International Version [*of the Bible*] [*A publication*]
**NIV** ............ Newbury International Ventures, Inc. [*Vancouver Stock Exchange symbol*]
**NIV** ............ Nivalenol [*A mycotoxin*]
**NIV** ............ Nodule-Inducing Virus
**NIVA** ......... National Independent Vendors Association [*Defunct*] (EA)
**NIVC** ......... National Interactive Video Centre [*British*]
**NIVEA**....... Night Vision Equipment for Armor
**NIW** ........... National Industrial Workers Union
**NIW** ........... Naval Inshore Warfare Project
**NIW** ........... Nieuw Israelitisch Weekblad [*A publication*]
**NIW** ........... Nonlethal Incapacitating Weapon
**NIWC** ........ National Institute for Women of Color (EA)
**NIWC** ........ Naval Inshore Warfare Command (NVT)
**NIWFA**...... National Intercollegiate Women's Fencing Association (EA)
**NIWG**........ National Institute for the Word of God (EA)
**NIWKC** ..... National Institute of Wood Kitchen Cabinets [*Later, KCMA*]
**NIWL** ........ National Institute for Work and Learning (EA)
**NIWS**......... National Institute on Workshop Standards [*Defunct*] (EA)
**NIWS**......... National Integrated Wage Structure (ADA)
**NIWS**......... News Information Weekly Service
**NIWTU** ..... Naval Inshore Warfare Task Unit (MCD)
**NIWU**........ National Industrial Workers Union (EA)

**NIX**........... Nioro [*Mali*] [*Airport symbol*] (OAG)
**NIX**........... Nix-o-Tine Pharmacy [*Vancouver Stock Exchange symbol*]
**Nix**........... Nixa [*Record label*] [*Great Britain, etc.; including Vanguard label re-issues*]
**NIX**........... Pacific Beach, WA [*Location identifier*] [*FAA*] (FAAL)
**Nix Dig**...... Nixon's Digest of Laws [*New Jersey*] [*A publication*] (DLA)
**Nix F**.......... Nixon's Forms [*A publication*] (DLA)
**NIXX**......... Nix-O-Tine Pharmaceuticals Ltd. [*NASDAQ symbol*] (NQ)
**NIY**........... Norfolk, VA [*Location identifier*] [*FAA*] (FAAL)
**NIY**........... Northamptonshire Imperial Yeomanry [*British military*] (DMA)
**NIY**........... Northumberland Imperial Yeomanry [*British military*] (DMA)
**NIYB**......... New International Year Book [*A publication*]
**NIYC**......... National Indian Youth Council (EA)
**NIZ**........... Nizhne-Angarsk [*USSR*] [*Seismograph station code, US Geological Survey*] (SEIS)
**NIZC**......... National Industrial Zoning Committee (EA)
**Nizkotemp Vak Materialoved**... Nizkotemperaturnoe i Vakuumnoe Materialovedenie [*Ukrainian SSR*] [*A publication*]
**NIZO Nieuws**... Nederlands Instituut voor Zuiverlonderzoek Nieuws [*A publication*]
**NJ**............. Namakwaland Lugdiens Bpk [*South Africa*] [*ICAO designator*] (ICDA)
**nJ**.............. Nanojoule
**NJ**............. Napierville Junction Railway Co. [*AAR code*]
**NJ**............. Nas Jezik [*A publication*]
**NJ**............. Nasojejunal [*Medicine*]
**NJ**............. Nederlandse Jurisprudentie (Uitspraken in Burgerlijke, Straf-, en Onteigeningszaken) [*Netherlands*] [*A publication*] (DLA)
**NJ**............. Neue Justiz [*German Democratic Republic*] [*A publication*]
**NJ**............. Neue Justiz. Zeitschrift fuer Recht und Rechtswissenschaft [*Berlin, German Democratic Republic*] [*A publication*] (DLA)
**NJ**............. New Japan Aircraft Maintenance Co. Ltd. [*Japan*] [*ICAO aircraft manufacturer identifier*] (ICAO)
**NJ**............. New Jason [*Charter-party clause*] [*Business term*] (DS)
**NJ**............. New Jersey [*Postal code*]
**NJ**............. New Jersey Reports [*A publication*]
**Nj**.............. New Jersey State Library, Trenton, NJ [*Library symbol*] [*Library of Congress*] (LCLS)
**NJ**............. New Jersey Supreme Court Reports [*A publication*] (DLA)
**NJ**............. New Journalism [*Refers to specific style, as that of writer Tom Wolfe*]
**NJ**............. New Judaea [*London*] [*A publication*]
**NJ**............. Niederdeutsches Jahrbuch [*A publication*]
**NJ**............. Northern Journal [*Atlin, British Columbia*] [*A publication*]
**NJ**............. Not Appropriated
**NJ**............. Notice of Judgment (Official) [*Legal term*] (DLA)
**NJ**............. Nylon Jacket
**NJA**........... National Jail Association [*Later, AJA*] (EA)
**NJA**........... National Jogging Association [*Later, ARFA*] (EA)
**NJA**........... National Jousting Association (EA)
**NJA**........... National Judges Association (EA)
**NJ (A)**........ Nederlandse Jurisprudentie (Administratiefrechtelijke Beslissingen) [*Netherlands*] [*A publication*] (DLA)
**NJA**........... Neue Jahrbuecher fuer das Klassische Altertum [*A publication*]
**NJA**........... New Jewish Agenda (EA)
**NJA**........... Nozzle Jetevator Assembly
**NJA**........... Nytt Juridiskt Arkiv [*Sweden*] [*A publication*] (DLA)
**NJAA**......... National Junior Angus Association (EA)
**NJAB**......... Neue Jahrbuecher fuer Antike und Deutsche Bildung [*A publication*]
**NjAc**.......... Atlantic City Free Public Library, Atlantic City, NJ [*Library symbol*] [*Library of Congress*] (LCLS)
**NJAC**......... National Joint Advisory Council [*on labor-management relations*] [*British*]
**NJAC**......... New Jersey Administrative Code [*A publication*]
**NjAcCoC**... Atlantic County Clerk, Atlantic City, NJ [*Library symbol*] [*Library of Congress*] (LCLS)
**NjAcFA**..... United States Federal Aviation Administration, National Aviation Facilities Experimental Center, Atlantic City, NJ [*Library symbol*] [*Library of Congress*] (LCLS)
**NjAcJ**......... Jewish Record, Atlantic City, NJ [*Library symbol*] [*Library of Congress*] (LCLS)
**NjAcP**........ Press Publishing Co., Atlantic City, NJ [*Library symbol*] [*Library of Congress*] (LCLS)
**NjAcPI**....... Popolo Italiano, Atlantic City, NJ [*Library symbol*] [*Library of Congress*] (LCLS)
**NjAcR**........ Atlantic City Reporter, Atlantic City, NJ [*Library symbol*] [*Library of Congress*] (LCLS)
**NJADB**...... Neue Jahrbuecher fuer Antike und Deutsche Bildung [*A publication*]
**NJ Admin**.. New Jersey Administrative Reports [*A publication*]
**NJ Admin Code**... New Jersey Administrative Code [*A publication*] (DLA)
**NJAF**......... Northern Journal of Applied Forestry [*A publication*]
**NJAG**........ National Jewish Artisans Guild (EA)
**NJ Ag**......... New Jersey Agriculture [*A publication*]
**NJ Ag Dept**... New Jersey. Department of Agriculture. Publications [*A publication*]
**NJ Ag Exp**... New Jersey. Agricultural Experiment Station. Publications [*A publication*]
**NJ Agr**....... New Jersey Agriculture [*A publication*]
**NJ Agr Expt Sta Bull**... New Jersey. Agricultural Experiment Station. Bulletin [*A publication*]
**NJ Agric**.... New Jersey Agriculture [*A publication*]
**NJ Agric Exp Stn Bull**... New Jersey. Agricultural Experiment Station. Bulletin [*A publication*]
**NJ Agric Exp Stn Circ**... New Jersey. Agricultural Experiment Station. Circular [*A publication*]
**NJAIC**....... New Jersey Asparagus Industry Council (EA)
**NjAl**.......... Allentown Public Library, Allentown, NJ [*Library symbol*] [*Library of Congress*] (LCLS)
**NjAlA**........ Allentown Printing Service, Allentown, NJ [*Library symbol*] [*Library of Congress*] (LCLS)
**NjAlB**........ Allentown Borough Hall, Allentown, NJ [*Library symbol*] [*Library of Congress*] (LCLS)
**NjAlHi**....... Allentown Historical Society, Allentown, NJ [*Library symbol*] [*Library of Congress*] (LCLS)
**NJam**......... James Prendergast Free Library, Jamestown, NY [*Library symbol*] [*Library of Congress*] (LCLS)
**NJamC**...... Chautauqua-Cattaraugus Library System, Jamestown, NY [*Library symbol*] [*Library of Congress*] (LCLS)
**NJamCC**.... Jamestown Community College, Jamestown, NY [*Library symbol*] [*Library of Congress*] (LCLS)
**NJamH**...... Jamestown General Hospital, Jamestown, NY [*Library symbol*] [*Library of Congress*] (LCLS)
**NJamW**..... Woman's Christian Association Hospital, Jamestown, NY [*Library symbol*] [*Library of Congress*] (LCLS)
**NJAR**........ New Jersey Administrative Reports [*A publication*]
**NjAs**.......... Asbury Park Free Public Library, Asbury Park, NJ [*Library symbol*] [*Library of Congress*] (LCLS)
**NjAsP**........ Asbury Park Press, Asbury Park, NJ [*Library symbol*] [*Library of Congress*] (LCLS)
**NjAsS**........ Spotlight Magazine, Asbury Park, NJ [*Library symbol*] [*Library of Congress*] (LCLS)
**NjAt**........... Atlantic Highlands Public Library Association, Atlantic Highlands, NJ [*Library symbol*] [*Library of Congress*] (LCLS)
**NjAuV**........ Weekly Visitor, Audubon, NJ [*Library symbol*] [*Library of Congress*] (LCLS)
**NjAveT**...... Tabloid Lithographers, Inc., Avenel, NJ [*Library symbol*] [*Library of Congress*] (LCLS)
**NjAvH**....... Herald, Avalon, NJ [*Library symbol*] [*Library of Congress*] (LCLS)
**NJB**........... Appalachian State University, Boone, NC [*OCLC symbol*] (OCLC)
**NjB**............ Bridgeton Free Public Library, Bridgeton, NJ [*Library symbol*] [*Library of Congress*] (LCLS)
**NJB**........... Nederlands Juristenblad [*A publication*]
**N Jb**.......... Neue Jahrbuecher fuer das Klassische Altertum [*A publication*]
**N Jb**.......... Neue Jahrbuecher fuer Philologie und Paedagogik [*A publication*]
**NJb**........... Neue Jahrbuecher fuer Wissenschaft und Jugendbildung [*A publication*]
**NJb**........... Niederdeutsches Jahrbuch [*A publication*]
**NjBa**.......... Bayonne Free Public Library, Bayonne, NJ [*Library symbol*] [*Library of Congress*] (LCLS)
**N Jb A**........ Neue Jahrbuecher fuer das Klassische Altertum [*A publication*]
**NjBaF**........ Facts of Bayonne Publishing Co., Bayonne, NJ [*Library symbol*] [*Library of Congress*] (LCLS)
**NjBaFAR**... Federal Archives and Records Center, General Services Administration, Bayonne, NJ [*Library symbol*] [*Library of Congress*] (LCLS)
**NjBaNSRF**... United States Naval Supply Research and Development Facility, Bayonne, NJ [*Library symbol*] [*Library of Congress*] (LCLS)
**NjBAP**....... Cumberland County Advertiser-Press, Inc., Bridgeton, NJ [*Library symbol*] [*Library of Congress*] (LCLS)
**NjBarHi**..... Barrington Historical Society, Barrington, NJ [*Library symbol*] [*Library of Congress*] (LCLS)
**NjBas**......... Bernards Township Library, Inc., Basking Ridge, NJ [*Library symbol*] [*Library of Congress*] (LCLS)
**NjBb**.......... Bound Brook Memorial Library, Bound Brook, NJ [*Library symbol*] [*Library of Congress*] (LCLS)
**NjBbA**........ American Cyanamid Co., Organic Chemicals Division, Bound Brook, NJ [*Library symbol*] [*Library of Congress*] (LCLS)
**NjBbC**........ Bound Brook Chronicle, Bound Brook, NJ [*Library symbol*] [*Library of Congress*] (LCLS)
**N Jb Beil Bd**... Neues Jahrbuch fuer Mineralogie, Geologie, und Palaeontologie. Beilage Band [*A publication*]
**NJBBF**....... National Judo Black Belt Federation of the USA (EA)
**NjBbU**........ Union Carbide Plastics Co., Bound Brook, NJ [*Library symbol*] [*Library of Congress*] (LCLS)
**NjBCoC**..... Cumberland County Clerk, Bridgeton, NJ [*Library symbol*] [*Library of Congress*] (LCLS)
**NjBe**.......... Belleville Free Public Library, Belleville, NJ [*Library symbol*] [*Library of Congress*] (LCLS)
**NjBeA**........ Ad-Print, Belleville, NJ [*Library symbol*] [*Library of Congress*] (LCLS)

**NjBeacO**.... Daily Observer, Beachwood, NJ [*Library symbol*] [*Library of Congress*] (LCLS)
**NJBEA Newsletter** ... New Jersey Business Education Association. Newsletter [*A publication*]
**NjBel**.......... Belmar Public Library, Belmar, NJ [*Library symbol*] [*Library of Congress*] (LCLS)
**NjBelvCoC** ... Warren County Clerk, Belvidere, NJ [*Library symbol*] [*Library of Congress*] (LCLS)
**NjBelvW**.... Warren County Library, Belvidere, NJ [*Library symbol*] [*Library of Congress*] (LCLS)
**NjBer** ......... Bergenfield Free Public Library, Bergenfield, NJ [*Library symbol*] [*Library of Congress*] (LCLS)
**NjBerl** ........ Marie Fleche Memorial Library, Berlin, NJ [*Library symbol*] [*Library of Congress*] (LCLS)
**NjBern** ....... Bernardsville Library Association, Bernardsville, NJ [*Library symbol*] [*Library of Congress*] (LCLS)
**NjBernN** .... Bernardsville News, Bernardsville, NJ [*Library symbol*] [*Library of Congress*] (LCLS)
**NjBeT** ........ Belleville Telegram, Belleville, NJ [*Library symbol*] [*Library of Congress*] (LCLS)
**NjBh** .......... Berkley Heights Public Library, Berkley Heights, NJ [*Library symbol*] [*Library of Congress*] (LCLS)
**N Jb KA**..... Neue Jahrbuecher fuer das Klassische Altertum [*A publication*]
**NjBl** ........... Bloomfield Public Library, Bloomfield, NJ [*Library symbol*] [*Library of Congress*] (LCLS)
**NjBla**.......... Gloucester Township [*Blackwood*] Library, Blackwood, NJ [*Library symbol*] [*Library of Congress*] (LCLS)
**NjBlaC**....... Camden County College, Blackwood, NJ [*Library symbol*] [*Library of Congress*] (LCLS)
**NjBlaCG**.... Camden-Gloucester Newspapers, Blackwood, NJ [*Library symbol*] [*Library of Congress*] (LCLS)
**NjBlaiP**...... Blairstown Press, Blairstown, NJ [*Library symbol*] [*Library of Congress*] (LCLS)
**NjBlC**......... Bloomfield College, Bloomfield, NJ [*Library symbol*] [*Library of Congress*] (LCLS)
**NjBlHi**....... Historical Society of Bloomfield, Bloomfield, NJ [*Library symbol*] [*Library of Congress*] (LCLS)
**NjBlI**.......... Independent Press, Bloomfield, NJ [*Library symbol*] [*Library of Congress*] (LCLS)
**NjBlM**........ Academy of Medicine of New Jersey, Bloomfield, NJ [*Library symbol*] [*Library of Congress*] (LCLS)
**NjBlS**......... Shering Corp., Bloomfield, NJ [*Library symbol*] [*Library of Congress*] (LCLS)
**NjBlW**........ Westinghouse Electric Corp., Lamp Division, Bloomfield, NJ [*Library symbol*] [*Library of Congress*] (LCLS)
**NjBN**.......... Bridgeton Evening News, Bridgeton, NJ [*Library symbol*] [*Library of Congress*] (LCLS)
**NjBo**........... Bogota Public Library, Bogota, NJ [*Library symbol*] [*Library of Congress*] (LCLS)
**NJBO** ........ Nordic Journal of Botany [*A publication*]
**NjBoo**......... Holmes Library, Boonton, NJ [*Library symbol*] [*Library of Congress*] (LCLS)
**NjBooT** ...... Times-Bulletin, Boonton, NJ [*Library symbol*] [*Library of Congress*] (LCLS)
**NjBorHi**..... Bordentown Historical Society, Bordentown, NJ [*Library symbol*] [*Library of Congress*] (LCLS)
**NjBorL**....... Lorraine Publishing, Inc., Bordentown, NJ [*Library symbol*] [*Library of Congress*] (LCLS)
**NjBriCN**.... Plainfield Courier-News, Bridgewater, NJ [*Library symbol*] [*Library of Congress*] (LCLS)
**NjBrigT** ..... Brigantine Times, Brigantine, NJ [*Library symbol*] [*Library of Congress*] (LCLS)
**NjBro** ......... Mendham Township Library, Brookside, NJ [*Library symbol*] [*Library of Congress*] (LCLS)
**NjBrS**......... Seacoast Newspapers, Brick Town, NJ [*Library symbol*] [*Library of Congress*] (LCLS)
**NjBu**........... Library Co. of Burlington, Burlington, NJ [*Library symbol*] [*Library of Congress*] (LCLS)
**NjBuHi** ...... Burlington County Historical Society, Burlington, NJ [*Library symbol*] [*Library of Congress*] (LCLS)
**NJ Bur Geol Topogr Bull** ... New Jersey. Bureau of Geology and Topography. Bulletin [*A publication*]
**NJ Bus**....... New Jersey Business [*A publication*]
**NjButA**....... Argus Printing & Publishing Co., Butler, NJ [*Library symbol*] [*Library of Congress*] (LCLS)
**N Jb WJ** .... Neue Jahrbuecher fuer Wissenschaft und Jugendbildung [*A publication*]
**NjbWJB** .... Neue Jahrbuecher fuer Wissenschaft und Jugendbildung [*A publication*]
**NjC**............. Chatham Public Library, Chatham, NJ [*Library symbol*] [*Library of Congress*] (LCLS)
**NJC** ........... Natchez Junior College [*Mississippi*]
**NJC** ........... National Jewish Coalition (EA)
**NJC** ........... National Judicial College (EA)
**NJC** ........... Navarro Junior College [*Texas*]
**NJC** ........... Navy Job Classification Manual
**NJC** ........... New Jersey Central Railroad
**NJC** ........... Newcastle Jockey Club [*Australia*]
**NJC** ........... Newton Junior College [*Massachusetts*]
**NJC** ........... Norfolk Junior College [*Nebraska*]
**NjCa**........... Camden Free Public Library, Camden, NJ [*Library symbol*] [*Library of Congress*] (LCLS)
**NJCAA**...... National Job Corps Alumni Association [*Washington, DC*] (EA)
**NJCAA**...... National Junior College Athletic Association (EA)
**NjCaC**........ Cooper Medical Center, Camden, NJ [*Library symbol*] [*Library of Congress*] (LCLS)
**NjCaHi**...... Camden County Historical Society, Camden, NJ [*Library symbol*] [*Library of Congress*] (LCLS)
**NjCal** ......... Caldwell Free Public Library, Caldwell, NJ [*Library symbol*] [*Library of Congress*] (LCLS)
**NjCalC**....... Caldwell College, Caldwell, NJ [*Library symbol*] [*Library of Congress*] (LCLS)
**NjCalP**....... Caldwell Progress, Caldwell, NJ [*Library symbol*] [*Library of Congress*] (LCLS)
**NjCaN**........ Camden News, Camden, NJ [*Library symbol*] [*Library of Congress*] (LCLS)
**NjCapS**...... Star and Wave, Cape May, NJ [*Library symbol*] [*Library of Congress*] (LCLS)
**NJCAPT & C** ... National Joint Council for Administrative, Professional, Technical, and Clerical Staff [*British*]
**NjCaRD**..... Radio Corp. of America, Communications Systems Division, Camden, NJ [*Library symbol*] [*Library of Congress*] (LCLS)
**NjCarpD**.... E. I. Du Pont de Nemours & Co., Carney's Point Development Laboratory, Carney's Point, NJ [*Library symbol*] [*Library of Congress*] (LCLS)
**NjCaSH**..... Catholic Star Herald, Camden, NJ [*Library symbol*] [*Library of Congress*] (LCLS)
**NjCaUR**..... Union Reporter, Camden, NJ [*Library symbol*] [*Library of Congress*] (LCLS)
**NJCBI** ....... National Joint Council for the Building Industry [*British*] (DCTA)
**NjCC**.......... Chatham Courier, Chatham, NJ [*Library symbol*] [*Library of Congress*] (LCLS)
**NJCC**......... National Joint Computer Committee [*of ACM, AIEE, IRE*] [*Superseded by AFIPS*]
**NJCC**......... Northeastern Junior College of Colorado [*Sterling*]
**NJCCA**...... National Japanese Canadian Citizens' Association
**NJCCOE**... Nordic Joint Committee of Commercial and Office Executives (EA)
**NJCDE**...... Nordic Joint Committee for Domestic Education (EA)
**NjCE**.......... Chatham Township Echoes, Chatham, NJ [*Library symbol*] [*Library of Congress*] (LCLS)
**NJCEC**....... NATO Joint Communications-Electronics Committee (NATG)
**NJCF**......... National Juvenile Court Foundation (EA)
**NjCg**.......... Cedar Grove Public Library, Cedar Grove, NJ [*Library symbol*] [*Library of Congress*] (LCLS)
**NjCh** .......... Cherry Hill Free Public Library, Cherry Hill, NJ [*Library symbol*] [*Library of Congress*] (LCLS)
**NJ Ch** ........ New Jersey Equity Reports [*A publication*] (DLA)
**NJCHC** ..... National Joint Council for Handicapped Children [*British*]
**NjChCP** ..... Courier Post, Cherry Hill, NJ [*Library symbol*] [*Library of Congress*] (LCLS)
**NJCHD** ..... Nouveau Journal de Chimie [*A publication*]
**NjChe**......... Chester Free Public Library, Chester, NJ [*Library symbol*] [*Library of Congress*] (LCLS)
**NjChJ** ........ Jewish Federation of Camden County, Cherry Hill, NJ [*Library symbol*] [*Library of Congress*] (LCLS)
**NjChM** ...... Cherry Hill Medical Center, Cherry Hill, NJ [*Library symbol*] [*Library of Congress*] (LCLS)
**NjChSG**..... Shoppers Guide, Cherry Hill, NJ [*Library symbol*] [*Library of Congress*] (LCLS)
**NjChSN**..... Suburban Newspaper Group, Cherry Hill, NJ [*Library symbol*] [*Library of Congress*] (LCLS)
**NjCiL**......... Cinnaminson Little Paper, Cinnaminson, NJ [*Library symbol*] [*Library of Congress*] (LCLS)
**NjCl** ........... Clark Free Public Library, Clark, NJ [*Library symbol*] [*Library of Congress*] (LCLS)
**NJCL**......... Network Job Control Language
**NJCLAFB** ... National Joint Council for Local Authority Fire Brigades [*British*]
**NJCLD**...... National Joint Committee for Learning Disabilities
**NJCLE** ...... Institute for Continuing Legal Education, New Jersey (DLA)
**NjClif**......... Clifton Public Library, Clifton, NJ [*Library symbol*] [*Library of Congress*] (LCLS)
**NjClifB** ...... New Jersey Business Review, Clifton, NJ [*Library symbol*] [*Library of Congress*] (LCLS)
**NjClifI** ....... Clifton Independent Prospector, Clifton, NJ [*Library symbol*] [*Library of Congress*] (LCLS)
**NjClifL**....... Clifton Leader, Clifton, NJ [*Library symbol*] [*Library of Congress*] (LCLS)
**NjClifP**....... Clifton Publishing Co., Clifton, NJ [*Library symbol*] [*Library of Congress*] (LCLS)
**NjClifPE**.... Post Eagle Publishing Co., Clifton, NJ [*Library symbol*] [*Library of Congress*] (LCLS)
**NjClifW** ..... Woodward-Clyde Consultants, Clifton, NJ [*Library symbol*] [*Library of Congress*] (LCLS)
**NjClinH**..... Hunterdon Review, Clinton, NJ [*Library symbol*] [*Library of Congress*] (LCLS)

**NjClp** ......... Cliffside Park Public Library, Cliffside Park, NJ [*Library symbol*] [*Library of Congress*] (LCLS)
**NjClpP** ....... Palisades Printing Corp., Cliffside Park, NJ [*Library symbol*] [*Library of Congress*] (LCLS)
**NjCmCo** ..... Cape May County Library, Cape May Court House, NJ [*Library symbol*] [*Library of Congress*] (LCLS)
**NjCmCoC** .. Cape May County Clerk, Cape May Court House, NJ [*Library symbol*] [*Library of Congress*] (LCLS)
**NjCmG** ....... Cape May County Gazette, Cape May Court House, NJ [*Library symbol*] [*Library of Congress*] (LCLS)
**NjCo** .......... Collingswood Free Public Library, Collingswood, NJ [*Library symbol*] [*Library of Congress*] (LCLS)
**NjCoB** ......... Christian Beacon, Collingswood, NJ [*Library symbol*] [*Library of Congress*] (LCLS)
**NjCoC** ........ Collingswood Publishing Co., Collingswood, NJ [*Library symbol*] [*Library of Congress*] (LCLS)
**NjColS** ....... South Jersey Ad-Visor, Cologne, NJ [*Library symbol*] [*Library of Congress*] (LCLS)
**NjConC** ...... College of Saint Elizabeth, Convent Station, NJ [*Library symbol*] [*Library of Congress*] (LCLS)
**NjCoT** ........ Camden County Times, Collingswood, NJ [*Library symbol*] [*Library of Congress*] (LCLS)
**NjCr** .......... Cranford Public Library, Cranford, NJ [*Library symbol*] [*Library of Congress*] (LCLS)
**NJCRAC** ... National Jewish Community Relations Advisory Council (EA)
**NjCrbP** ...... Cranbury Press, Cranbury, NJ [*Library symbol*] [*Library of Congress*] (LCLS)
**NjCrC** ........ Cranford Citizen & Chronicle, Cranford, NJ [*Library symbol*] [*Library of Congress*] (LCLS)
**NjCrHi** ....... Cranford Historical Society, Cranford, NJ [*Library symbol*] [*Library of Congress*] (LCLS)
**NjCrU** ........ Union College, Cranford, NJ [*Library symbol*] [*Library of Congress*] (LCLS)
**NJCS** ......... National Jewish Committee on Scouting (EA)
**NJCSA** ...... National Juvenile Court Services Association (EA)
**NJCSE** ...... National Jewish Civil Service Employees (EA)
**NjD** ........... Dover Public Library, Dover, NJ [*Library symbol*] [*Library of Congress*] (LCLS)
**NjDA** ......... Daily Advance, Dover, NJ [*Library symbol*] [*Library of Congress*] (LCLS)
**NJDA** ......... National Juvenile Detention Association (EA)
**NjDe** .......... Denville Free Public Library, Denville, NJ [*Library symbol*] [*Library of Congress*] (LCLS)
**NjDeC** ........ Citizen of Morris County, Denville, NJ [*Library symbol*] [*Library of Congress*] (LCLS)
**NJ Dep Conserv Econ Develop Geol Rep Ser** ... New Jersey. Department of Conservation and Economic Development. Geologic Report Series [*A publication*]
**NJ Dep Environ Prot Div Nat Resour Bur Geol Topogr Bull** ... New Jersey. Department of Environmental Protection. Division of Natural Resources. Bureau of Geology and Topography. Bulletin [*A publication*]
**NJDFC** ...... New Jersey Devils Fan Club (EA)
**NJ Div Water Policy Supply Spec Rep** ... New Jersey. Division of Water Policy and Supply. Special Report [*A publication*]
**NJ Div Water Policy Supply Water Resour Cir** ... New Jersey. Division of Water Policy and Supply. Water Resources Circular [*A publication*]
**NjDPA** ....... United States Army, Armament Research and Development Command, Science and Technical Library, Dover Site, Dover, NJ [*Library symbol*] [*Library of Congress*] (LCLS)
**NJ Dp Conservation An Rp** ... New Jersey. Department of Conservation and Development. Annual Report [*A publication*]
**NJDW** ....... Neue Jahrbuecher fuer Deutsche Wissenschaft [*A publication*]
**NJe** ............ Nas Jezik [*A publication*]
**NJE** ........... Nebraska Journal of Economics and Business [*A publication*]
**NJE** ........... Network Job Entry
**NJE** ........... New Jersey Equity Reports [*A publication*] (DLA)
**Nj-E** .......... New Jersey State Library, Department of Education, Trenton, NJ [*Library symbol*] [*Library of Congress*] (LCLS)
**NJE** ........... Nigerian Journal of Economic and Social Studies [*A publication*]
**NJE** ........... Office of Cancer and Toxic Substances Research, Trenton, NJ [*OCLC symbol*] (OCLC)
**NjEa** .......... Eatontown Public Library, Eatontown, NJ [*Library symbol*] [*Library of Congress*] (LCLS)
**NjEb** .......... East Brunswick Public Library, East Brunswick, NJ [*Library symbol*] [*Library of Congress*] (LCLS)
**NjEbGS** ..... Church of Jesus Christ of Latter-Day Saints, Genealogical Society Library, East Brunswick Stake Branch, East Brunswick, NJ [*Library symbol*] [*Library of Congress*] (LCLS)
**NjEbS** ........ Sentinel Publishing Co., East Brunswick, NJ [*Library symbol*] [*Library of Congress*] (LCLS)
**NjEdE** ........ Engelhard Minerals & Chemicals Corp. [*Later, Engelhard Corp.*], Research Library, Edison, NJ [*Library symbol*] [*Library of Congress*] (LCLS)
**NjEdM** ....... Middlesex County College, Edison, NJ [*Library symbol*] [*Library of Congress*] (LCLS)
**NjEgN** ........ Egg Harbor News, Egg Harbor City, NJ [*Library symbol*] [*Library of Congress*] (LCLS)
**NjEh** .......... East Hanover Public Library, East Hanover, NJ [*Library symbol*] [*Library of Congress*] (LCLS)
**NjEli** .......... Elizabeth Free Public Library, Elizabeth, NJ [*Library symbol*] [*Library of Congress*] (LCLS)
**NjEliCoC** ... Union County Clerk, Elizabeth, NJ [*Library symbol*] [*Library of Congress*] (LCLS)
**NjEliJ** ........ Daily Journal, Elizabeth, NJ [*Library symbol*] [*Library of Congress*] (LCLS)
**NjElT** ......... Elmer Times, Elmer, NJ [*Library symbol*] [*Library of Congress*] (LCLS)
**NjEn** .......... Englewood Library, Englewood, NJ [*Library symbol*] [*Library of Congress*] (LCLS)
**NjEncL** ...... Thomas J. Lipton, Inc., Englewood Cliffs, NJ [*Library symbol*] [*Library of Congress*] (LCLS)
**NjEncStP** ... Saint Peter's College, Englewood Cliffs, NJ [*Library symbol*] [*Library of Congress*] (LCLS)
**NJE/NJI** ... Network Job Entry, Including Network Job Interface
**NjEnP** ........ Englewood Press, Englewood, NJ [*Library symbol*] [*Library of Congress*] (LCLS)
**NjEnPa** ...... Palisades Newspapers, Englewood, NJ [*Library symbol*] [*Library of Congress*] (LCLS)
**NjEnS** ........ North Jersey Suburbanite, Englewood, NJ [*Library symbol*] [*Library of Congress*] (LCLS)
**NjEo** .......... East Orange Free Public Library, East Orange, NJ [*Library symbol*] [*Library of Congress*] (LCLS)
**NjEoA** ........ Advocate, East Orange, NJ [*Library symbol*] [*Library of Congress*] (LCLS)
**NjEoS** ........ Sokol USA, East Orange, NJ [*Library symbol*] [*Library of Congress*] (LCLS)
**NjEoU** ........ Upsala College, East Orange, NJ [*Library symbol*] [*Library of Congress*] (LCLS)
**NjEoV** ........ United States Veterans Administration Hospital, East Orange, NJ [*Library symbol*] [*Library of Congress*] (LCLS)
**NJ Eq** ......... New Jersey Equity Reports [*A publication*] (DLA)
**NJ Eq R** ..... New Jersey Equity Reports [*A publication*] (DLA)
**NJ Equity** .. New Jersey Equity Reports [*A publication*] (DLA)
**NJer** .......... Jericho Public Library, Jericho, NY [*Library symbol*] [*Library of Congress*] (LCLS)
**NJerC** ........ Long Island Association of Commerce and Industry, Jericho, NY [*Library symbol*] [*Library of Congress*] (LCLS)
**NJerHS** ..... Jericho Senior High School, Jericho, NY [*Library symbol*] [*Library of Congress*] (LCLS)
**NJerJE** ...... George Jackson Elementary School, Jericho, NY [*Library symbol*] [*Library of Congress*] (LCLS)
**NJerS** ........ Staff Supermarket Associates, Inc., Jericho, NY [*Library symbol*] [*Library of Congress*] (LCLS)
**N Jersey R** ... New Jersey Law Reports [*A publication*] (DLA)
**NJESS** ....... Nigerian Journal of Economic and Social Studies [*A publication*]
**NjEwB** ....... Bergen Citizen, Edgewater, NJ [*Library symbol*] [*Library of Congress*] (LCLS)
**NjEwJJ** ...... Johnson & Johnson Dental Product Co., East Windsor, NJ [*Library symbol*] [*Library of Congress*] (LCLS)
**NJF** ........... Cherry Point, NC [*Location identifier*] [*FAA*] (FAAL)
**NjF** ............ Fair Lawn Free Public Library, Fair Lawn, NJ [*Library symbol*] [*Library of Congress*] (LCLS)
**NJF** ........... Nordiska Journalistforbundet [*Nordic Association of Journalists Unions - NAJU*] (EAIO)
**NJF** ........... Nordiske Jordbrugsforskeres Forening [*Nordic Agricultural Research Workers Association - NARWA*] (EAIO)
**NJF** ........... Scandinavian Agricultural Research Workers' Association
**NJFA** ......... National Justice Foundation of America (EA)
**NJFAA** ...... Federal Aviation Administration, Eastern Region Library, Jamaica, NY [*Library symbol*] [*Library of Congress*] (LCLS)
**NJFC** ......... Norma Jean Fan Club (EA)
**NJFD** ......... Notices of Judgment, United States Food and Drug Administration [*A publication*] (DLA)
**NjFdA** ........ United States Army, Special Services Post Library, Fort Dix, NJ [*Library symbol*] [*Library of Congress*] (LCLS)
**NjFf** ........... Fairfield Free Public Library, Fairfield, NJ [*Library symbol*] [*Library of Congress*] (LCLS)
**NjFhUGA** ... United States Golf Association, Far Hills, NJ [*Library symbol*] [*Library of Congress*] (LCLS)
**NjFlCoC** .... Hunterdon County Clerk, Flemington, NJ [*Library symbol*] [*Library of Congress*] (LCLS)
**NjFlD** ......... Hunterdon County Democrat, Flemington, NJ [*Library symbol*] [*Library of Congress*] (LCLS)
**NjFlH** ........ Hunterdon County Library, Flemington, NJ [*Library symbol*] [*Library of Congress*] (LCLS)
**NjFlHi** ....... Hunterdon County Historical Society, Flemington, NJ [*Library symbol*] [*Library of Congress*] (LCLS)
**NjFlM** ........ Hunterdon Medical Center, Flemington, NJ [*Library symbol*] [*Library of Congress*] (LCLS)
**NjFmE-TD** ... United States Army, Electronics Command, Technical Documents Branch, Fort Monmouth, NJ [*Library symbol*] [*Library of Congress*] (LCLS)
**NjFmS** ....... United States Army, Signal School, Fort Monmouth, NJ [*Library symbol*] [*Library of Congress*] (LCLS)
**NjFNB** ....... Shopper-News Beacon, Fair Lawn, NJ [*Library symbol*] [*Library of Congress*] (LCLS)

**NjFp**.......... Florham Park Public Library, Florham Park, NJ [*Library symbol*] [*Library of Congress*] (LCLS)
**NjFpEx**...... Exxon Research & Engineering Co., Engineering Information Center, Florham Park, NJ [*Library symbol*] [*Library of Congress*] (LCLS)
**NjFpN**........ Florham Park Community News, Florham Park, NJ [*Library symbol*] [*Library of Congress*] (LCLS)
**NjFr**........... Freehold Public Library, Freehold, NJ [*Library symbol*] [*Library of Congress*] (LCLS)
**NJFR**......... National Joint Fiction Reserve
**NjFraS**....... Suburban News, Franklin Lakes, NJ [*Library symbol*] [*Library of Congress*] (LCLS)
**NjFrCoC**.... Clerk of Monmouth County, Freehold, NJ [*Library symbol*] [*Library of Congress*] (LCLS)
**NjFrHi**....... Monmouth County Historical Association, Freehold, NJ [*Library symbol*] [*Library of Congress*] (LCLS)
**NjFrM**....... Monmouth County Library, Freehold, NJ [*Library symbol*] [*Library of Congress*] (LCLS)
**NjFrS**......... Schreiber Publishing Co., Freehold, NJ [*Library symbol*] [*Library of Congress*] (LCLS)
**NjFrtD**....... Delaware Valley News, Frenchtown, NJ [*Library symbol*] [*Library of Congress*] (LCLS)
**NjFrvA**....... Advertiser, Franklinville, NJ [*Library symbol*] [*Library of Congress*] (LCLS)
**NjFvW**....... West New Yorker, Inc., Fairview, NJ [*Library symbol*] [*Library of Congress*] (LCLS)
**NJG**........... Glassboro State College, Glassboro, NJ [*OCLC symbol*] (OCLC)
**NJG**........... Nice Jewish Girl [*Slang*]
**NjGaB**........ Bergen Gazette, Inc., Garfield, NJ [*Library symbol*] [*Library of Congress*] (LCLS)
**NjGaG**....... Garfield Guardian, Garfield, NJ [*Library symbol*] [*Library of Congress*] (LCLS)
**NjGb**.......... Glassboro Public Library, Glassboro, NJ [*Library symbol*] [*Library of Congress*] (LCLS)
**NjGbS**........ Glassboro State College, Glassboro, NJ [*Library symbol*] [*Library of Congress*] (LCLS)
**NJ Geol Topogr Bull**... New Jersey. Bureau of Geology and Topography. Bulletin [*A publication*]
**NJGFE**...... Nordic Joint Group for Forest Entomology (EA)
**NjGiD**........ E. I. Du Pont de Nemours & Co., Eastern Laboratory Library, Gibbstown, NJ [*Library symbol*] [*Library of Congress*] (LCLS)
**NJGKA**...... Nippon Jinzo Gakkaishi [*A publication*]
**NjGl**........... Gloucester City Library, Gloucester City, NJ [*Library symbol*] [*Library of Congress*] (LCLS)
**NjGlN**........ Gloucester City News, Gloucester City, NJ [*Library symbol*] [*Library of Congress*] (LCLS)
**NjGlri**......... Glen Ridge Free Public Library, Glen Ridge, NJ [*Library symbol*] [*Library of Congress*] (LCLS)
**NjGlriA**...... Associated Technical Services, Inc., Glen Ridge, NJ [*Library symbol*] [*Library of Congress*] (LCLS)
**NjGrbR**...... Raritan Valley Hospital, Greenbrook, NJ [*Library symbol*] [*Library of Congress*] (LCLS)
**NjGrHi**...... Cumberland County Historical Society, Greenwich, NJ [*Library symbol*] [*Library of Congress*] (LCLS)
**NJ G S**....... New Jersey. Geological Survey [*A publication*]
**NJGSC**...... National Jewish Girl Scout Committee (EA)
**NjH**............ Haddonfield Public Library, Haddonfield, NJ [*Library symbol*] [*Library of Congress*] (LCLS)
**NJH**........... New Jersey History [*A publication*]
**NJHA**........ National Junior Horticultural Association (EA)
**NjHaC**....... Centenary College for Women, Hackettstown, NJ [*Library symbol*] [*Library of Congress*] (LCLS)
**NjHack**...... Johnson Free Public Library, Hackensack, NJ [*Library symbol*] [*Library of Congress*] (LCLS)
**NjHackR**... Bergen Record, Hackensack, NJ [*Library symbol*] [*Library of Congress*] (LCLS)
**NjHam**....... Hammonton Public Library, Hammonton, NJ [*Library symbol*] [*Library of Congress*] (LCLS)
**NjHamN**.... News Publishing Co., Hammonton, NJ [*Library symbol*] [*Library of Congress*] (LCLS)
**NjHanS**...... Sandoz, Inc., Hanover, NJ [*Library symbol*] [*Library of Congress*] (LCLS)
**NjHarN**..... Diamond Shamrock Corp., Harrison, NJ [*Library symbol*] [*Library of Congress*] (LCLS)
**NjHarR**...... Radio Corp. of America, Electronics Division, Harrison, NJ [*Library symbol*] [*Library of Congress*] (LCLS)
**NjHas**........ Hasbrouck Heights Free Public Library, Hasbrouck Heights, NJ [*Library symbol*] [*Library of Congress*] (LCLS)
**NjHaS**........ Star Gazette, Hackettstown, NJ [*Library symbol*] [*Library of Congress*] (LCLS)
**NjHasO**..... Observer, Hasbrouck Heights, NJ [*Library symbol*] [*Library of Congress*] (LCLS)
**NjHawD**.... Dodds Publishing Co., Hawthorne, NJ [*Library symbol*] [*Library of Congress*] (LCLS)
**NjHawP**..... Hawthorne Press, Inc., Hawthorne, NJ [*Library symbol*] [*Library of Congress*] (LCLS)
**NjHb**......... Hillsborough Public Library, Hillsborough, NJ [*Library symbol*] [*Library of Congress*] (LCLS)
**NJHC**........ National Jewish Hospitality Committee (EA)
**NjHh**.......... Haddon Heights Public Library, Haddon Heights, NJ [*Library symbol*] [*Library of Congress*] (LCLS)
**NJHHCC**.. National Joint Heavy and Highway Construction Committee (EA)
**NjHHi**........ Historical Society of Haddonfield, Haddonfield, NJ [*Library symbol*] [*Library of Congress*] (LCLS)
**NjHi**........... New Jersey Historical Society, Newark, NJ [*Library symbol*] [*Library of Congress*] (LCLS)
**NjHibP**...... High Bridge Painting Co., High Bridge, NJ [*Library symbol*] [*Library of Congress*] (LCLS)
**NjHig**......... Hightstown Memorial Library, Hightstown, NJ [*Library symbol*] [*Library of Congress*] (LCLS)
**NjHigG**...... Hightstown Gazette, Hightstown, NJ [*Library symbol*] [*Library of Congress*] (LCLS)
**NjHigN**...... NL Industries, Inc., Hightstown, NJ [*Library symbol*] [*Library of Congress*] (LCLS)
**NjHigP**...... Peddie School, Hightstown, NJ [*Library symbol*] [*Library of Congress*] (LCLS)
**NjHil**.......... Hillside Free Public Library, Hillside, NJ [*Library symbol*] [*Library of Congress*] (LCLS)
**NjHilT**....... Hillside Times, Hillside, NJ [*Library symbol*] [*Library of Congress*] (LCLS)
**NJ His S**.... New Jersey Historical Society. Proceedings [*A publication*]
**NJ His S Col**... New Jersey Historical Society. Collections [*A publication*]
**NJ Hist**...... New Jersey History [*A publication*]
**NJHistS**.... New Jersey Historical Society. Proceedings [*A publication*]
**NJH/NAC**... National Jewish Hospital/National Asthma Center [*Later, National Jewish Center for Immunology and Respiratory Medicine*] (EA)
**NjHo**.......... Hoboken Free Public Library, Hoboken, NJ [*Library symbol*] [*Library of Congress*] (LCLS)
**NjHoGF**..... General Foods Corp., Hoboken, NJ [*Library symbol*] [*Library of Congress*] (LCLS)
**NjHolB**...... Bell Telephone Laboratories, Inc., Technical Information Library, Holmdel, NJ [*Library symbol*] [*Library of Congress*] (LCLS)
**NjHop**........ Hopewell Public Library, Hopewell, NJ [*Library symbol*] [*Library of Congress*] (LCLS)
**NjHopM**.... Hopewell Museum, Hopewell, NJ [*Library symbol*] [*Library of Congress*] (LCLS)
**NjHopN**..... Hopewell Valley News, Hopewell, NJ [*Library symbol*] [*Library of Congress*] (LCLS)
**NjHoS**........ Stevens Institute of Technology, Hoboken, NJ [*Library symbol*] [*Library of Congress*] (LCLS)
**NjHowB**..... Booster Press, Howell, NJ [*Library symbol*] [*Library of Congress*] (LCLS)
**NJHS**......... National Junior Honor Society (EA)
**NJHS**......... New Jersey Historical Society. Proceedings [*A publication*]
**NJHSP**....... New Jersey Historical Society. Proceedings [*A publication*]
**NjI**.............. Free Public Library of Irvington, Irvington, NJ [*Library symbol*] [*Library of Congress*] (LCLS)
**NJI**............. Network Job Interface
**NJI**............. New Jersey Institute of Technology, Newark, NJ [*OCLC symbol*] (OCLC)
**NJIC**.......... National Joint Industrial Council [*Pharmacology*] [*British*]
**NJIFR**........ Notices of Judgment, Federal Insecticide, Fungicide, and Rodenticide Act [*A publication*] (DLA)
**NJIGA**........ Nippon Jibi-Inko-Ka Gakkai Kaiho Kaiho [*A publication*]
**NJII**........... New Jersey, Indiana & Illinois Railroad Co. [*AAR code*]
**NJIS**.......... National Jewish Information Service (for the Propagation of Judaism) (EA)
**NJIT**.......... New Jersey Institute of Technology [*Newark*]
**NjJ**............. Jersey City Free Public Library, Jersey City, NJ [*Library symbol*] [*Library of Congress*] (LCLS)
**NJJ**............ Jersey City State College, Jersey City, NJ [*OCLC symbol*] (OCLC)
**NJJ**............ Niijima [*Japan*] [*Seismograph station code, US Geological Survey*] [*Closed*] (SEIS)
**NjJa**........... Library at Jamesburg, Jamesburg, NJ [*Library symbol*] [*Library of Congress*] (LCLS)
**NjJacN**....... Jackson News, Jackson, NJ [*Library symbol*] [*Library of Congress*] (LCLS)
**NjJacP**....... Jackson Township Publishing Co., Jackson, NJ [*Library symbol*] [*Library of Congress*] (LCLS)
**NjJJ**........... Jewish Standard, Jersey City, NJ [*Library symbol*] [*Library of Congress*] (LCLS)
**NjJJJ**......... Jersey Journal, Jersey City, NJ [*Library symbol*] [*Library of Congress*] (LCLS)
**NJ J Pharm**... New Jersey. Journal of Pharmacy [*A publication*]
**NjJS**........... Jersey City State College, Jersey City, NJ [*Library symbol*] [*Library of Congress*] (LCLS)
**NjJStP**....... Saint Peter's College, Jersey City, NJ [*Library symbol*] [*Library of Congress*] (LCLS)
**NjJUB**....... Urner-Barry Publications, Jersey City, NJ [*Library symbol*] [*Library of Congress*] (LCLS)
**NJK**........... El Centro, CA [*Location identifier*] [*FAA*] (FAAL)
**NJK**........... Kean College of New Jersey, Union, NJ [*OCLC symbol*] (OCLC)
**NjK**............ Kearny Public Library, Kearny, NJ [*Library symbol*] [*Library of Congress*] (LCLS)
**NJK**........... Nastava Jezika i Knjizevnosti u Srednoj Skoli [*A publication*]

**NJKA**......... Neue Jahrbuecher fuer das Klassische Altertum [*A publication*]
**NJKAGDL**... Neue Jahrbuecher fuer das Klassische Altertum, Geschichte, und Deutsche Literatur [*A publication*]
**NjKey**......... Keyport Free Public Library, Keyport, NJ [*Library symbol*] [*Library of Congress*] (LCLS)
**NjKO**......... Kearny Observer, Kearny, NJ [*Library symbol*] [*Library of Congress*] (LCLS)
**NjKWT**...... Western Electric Co., Kearny, NJ [*Library symbol*] [*Library of Congress*] (LCLS)
**NjL**............ Lodi Memorial Library, Lodi, NJ [*Library symbol*] [*Library of Congress*] (LCLS)
**NJL**............ New Jersey Law Reports [*A publication*] (DLA)
**NJL**............ New Jersey State Library, Trenton, NJ [*OCLC symbol*] (OCLC)
**NJL**............ Nordic Journal of Linguistics [*A publication*]
**NjLaHi**...... Lake Hopatcong Historical Society, Lake Hopatcong, NJ [*Library symbol*] [*Library of Congress*] (LCLS)
**NjLak**......... Lakewood Public Library, Lakewood, NJ [*Library symbol*] [*Library of Congress*] (LCLS)
**NjLakC**...... Ocean County Citizen, Lakewood, NJ [*Library symbol*] [*Library of Congress*] (LCLS)
**NjLakG**...... Georgian Court College, Lakewood, NJ [*Library symbol*] [*Library of Congress*] (LCLS)
**NjLakhM**.. Manchester Publishing Co., Lakehurst, NJ [*Library symbol*] [*Library of Congress*] (LCLS)
**NjLakT**...... Ocean County Daily Times, Lakewood, NJ [*Library symbol*] [*Library of Congress*] (LCLS)
**NjLamB**..... Lambertville Beacon, Lambertville, NJ [*Library symbol*] [*Library of Congress*] (LCLS)
**NJ Law**...... New Jersey Law Reports [*A publication*] (DLA)
**NJ Law**...... New Jersey Lawyer [*A publication*]
**NJ Law J**... New Jersey Law Journal [*A publication*]
**NJ Law N**.. New Jersey Law News [*A publication*] (DLA)
**NjLawR**..... Rider College, Lawrenceville, NJ [*Library symbol*] [*Library of Congress*] (LCLS)
**NJ Law Rep**... New Jersey Law Reports [*A publication*] (DLA)
**NJ Laws**..... Laws of New Jersey [*A publication*]
**NJ Lawy**..... New Jersey Lawyer [*A publication*]
**NJLC**......... National Juvenile Law Center [*Later, NCYL*] (EA)
**NjLe**.......... Leonia Public Library, Leonia, NJ [*Library symbol*] [*Library of Congress*] (LCLS)
**NJ League Nurs News**... New Jersey League for Nursing. News [*A publication*]
**NjLedW**..... West Morris Star Journal, Ledgewood, NJ [*Library symbol*] [*Library of Congress*] (LCLS)
**NJ Leg Rec**... New Jersey Legal Record [*A publication*] (DLA)
**NjLF**.......... Felician College, Lodi, NJ [*Library symbol*] [*Library of Congress*] (LCLS)
**NjLf**........... Little Falls Free Public Library, Little Falls, NJ [*Library symbol*] [*Library of Congress*] (LCLS)
**NJLFC**....... New Jersey Film Circuit [*Library network*]
**NjLh**.......... Lake Hiawatha Public Library, Lake Hiawatha, NJ [*Library symbol*] [*Library of Congress*] (LCLS)
**NjLhP**........ Pennysaver Publishing Co., Lake Hiawatha, NJ [*Library symbol*] [*Library of Congress*] (LCLS)
**NjLi**........... Free Public Library of Livingston, Livingston, NJ [*Library symbol*] [*Library of Congress*] (LCLS)
**NJ Lib**........ New Jersey Libraries [*A publication*]
**NJ Libr**...... New Jersey Libraries [*A publication*]
**NjLin**.......... Linden Free Public Library, Linden, NJ [*Library symbol*] [*Library of Congress*] (LCLS)
**NjLincB**..... Brookdale Community College, Lincroft, NJ [*Library symbol*] [*Library of Congress*] (LCLS)
**NjLinEx**..... Exxon Research & Engineering Co., Company and Literature Information Center Library, Linden, NJ [*Library symbol*] [*Library of Congress*] (LCLS)
**NjLinEx-M**... Exxon Research & Engineering Co., Medical Research Library, Linden, NJ [*Library symbol*] [*Library of Congress*] (LCLS)
**NjLivStB**.... Saint Barnabas Medical Center, Staff Library, Livingston, NJ [*Library symbol*] [*Library of Congress*] (LCLS)
**NjLiW**........ West Essex Tribune, Livingston, NJ [*Library symbol*] [*Library of Congress*] (LCLS)
**NJLJ**.......... New Jersey Law Journal [*A publication*]
**NjLob**......... Long Branch Public Library, Long Branch, NJ [*Library symbol*] [*Library of Congress*] (LCLS)
**NjLp**........... Lincoln Park Public Library, Lincoln Park, NJ [*Library symbol*] [*Library of Congress*] (LCLS)
**NjLP**.......... Paci Press, Lodi, NJ [*Library symbol*] [*Library of Congress*] (LCLS)
**NjLpBHi**.... Beavertown Historical Society, Lincoln Park, NJ [*Library symbol*] [*Library of Congress*] (LCLS)
**NjLpH**....... Lincoln Herald, Lincoln Park, NJ [*Library symbol*] [*Library of Congress*] (LCLS)
**NJL Rep**.... New Jersey Law Reports [*A publication*] (DLA)
**NJL Rev**.... New Jersey Law Review [*A publication*] (DLA)
**NjLwR**....... Record Breeze, Lindenwold, NJ [*Library symbol*] [*Library of Congress*] (LCLS)
**NjLy**........... Lyndhurst Public Library, Lyndhurst, NJ [*Library symbol*] [*Library of Congress*] (LCLS)
**NjLyL**........ Leader Publications, Lyndhurst, NJ [*Library symbol*] [*Library of Congress*] (LCLS)
**NjLyoV**...... United States Veterans Administration Hospital, Lyons, NJ [*Library symbol*] [*Library of Congress*] (LCLS)
**NjM**........... Free Public Library of the Borough of Madison, Madison, NJ [*Library symbol*] [*Library of Congress*] (LCLS)
**NJM**.......... Montclair State College, Upper Montclair, NJ [*OCLC symbol*] (OCLC)
**NJM**.......... National Jewish Monthly [*A publication*]
**NJM**.......... Neue Juedische Monatshefte [*A publication*]
**NJM**.......... New Jersey Miscellaneous Reports [*A publication*] (DLA)
**NJM**.......... New JEWEL Movement [*Grenada*]
**NJM**.......... Nouvelles Juives Mondiales [*Paris*] [*A publication*]
**NJM**.......... Swansboro, NC [*Location identifier*] [*FAA*] (FAAL)
**NJMA**........ National Jail Managers Association [*Later, AJA*] (EA)
**NjMah**....... Free Public Library of the Township of Mahwah, Mahwah, NJ [*Library symbol*] [*Library of Congress*] (LCLS)
**NjMahR**.... Ramapo College of New Jersey, Mahwah, NJ [*Library symbol*] [*Library of Congress*] (LCLS)
**NjMal**........ Franklin Township Public Library, Malaga, NJ [*Library symbol*] [*Library of Congress*] (LCLS)
**NjMan**....... Manasquan Public Library, Manasquan, NJ [*Library symbol*] [*Library of Congress*] (LCLS)
**NjManhT**.. Times Beacon Co., Manahawkin, NJ [*Library symbol*] [*Library of Congress*] (LCLS)
**NjManS**..... Coast Star, Manasquan, NJ [*Library symbol*] [*Library of Congress*] (LCLS)
**NjMap**....... Maplewood Memorial Library, Maplewood, NJ [*Library symbol*] [*Library of Congress*] (LCLS)
**NjMapW**... Worrall Publishing Co., Maplewood, NJ [*Library symbol*] [*Library of Congress*] (LCLS)
**NjMat**........ Matawan Joint Free Public Library, Matawan, NJ [*Library symbol*] [*Library of Congress*] (LCLS)
**NjMatB**..... Bayshore Independent, Matawan, NJ [*Library symbol*] [*Library of Congress*] (LCLS)
**NjMatHi**.... Madison Township Historical Society, Matawan, NJ [*Library symbol*] [*Library of Congress*] (LCLS)
**NjMayO**.... Our Town, Maywood, NJ [*Library symbol*] [*Library of Congress*] (LCLS)
**NJMC**........ National Jewish Music Council [*Later, Jewish Welfare Board Jewish Music Council*] (EA)
**NjMcUSAF**... United States Air Force, Base Library, McGuire Air Force Base, NJ [*Library symbol*] [*Library of Congress*] (LCLS)
**NjMD**........ Drew University, Madison, NJ [*Library symbol*] [*Library of Congress*] (LCLS)
**NJMDC**..... NORAD Joint Manual Direction Center [*Military*]
**NjMD-T**.... Drew University, Theological School, Madison, NJ [*Library symbol*] [*Library of Congress*] (LCLS)
**NjMe**.......... Free Public Library, Metuchen, NJ [*Library symbol*] [*Library of Congress*] (LCLS)
**NjME**......... Madison Eagle, Madison, NJ [*Library symbol*] [*Library of Congress*] (LCLS)
**NJ Med**...... New Jersey Medicine [*A publication*]
**NjMedR**..... Central Record, Medford, NJ [*Library symbol*] [*Library of Congress*] (LCLS)
**NjMen**....... Mendham Public Library, Mendham, NJ [*Library symbol*] [*Library of Congress*] (LCLS)
**NjMenO**.... Observer-Tribune, Mendham, NJ [*Library symbol*] [*Library of Congress*] (LCLS)
**NjMF**......... Fairleigh Dickinson University, Madison, NJ [*Library symbol*] [*Library of Congress*] (LCLS)
**NjMhB**...... Burlington County Area Reference Library, Mount Holly, NJ [*Library symbol*] [*Library of Congress*] (LCLS)
**NjMhCoC**... Burlington County Clerk, Mount Holly, NJ [*Library symbol*] [*Library of Congress*] (LCLS)
**NjMhH**...... Burlington County Herald, Mount Holly, NJ [*Library symbol*] [*Library of Congress*] (LCLS)
**NjMHi**....... Madison Historical Society, Madison, NJ [*Library symbol*] [*Library of Congress*] (LCLS)
**NjMhL**....... Burlington County Lyceum [*Mount Holly Public Library*], Mount Holly, NJ [*Library symbol*] [*Library of Congress*] (LCLS)
**NjMhPM**... Burlington County Prison Museum, Mount Holly, NJ [*Library symbol*] [*Library of Congress*] (LCLS)
**NJMI**......... Mary Immaculate Hospital, School of Nursing, Jamaica, NY [*Library symbol*] [*Library of Congress*] (LCLS)
**NjMi**.......... Middletown Township Free Public Library, Middletown, NJ [*Library symbol*] [*Library of Congress*] (LCLS)
**NJMI**......... New Junior Maudsley Inventory [*Psychology*]
**NjMiA**....... Advisor, Middletown, NJ [*Library symbol*] [*Library of Congress*] (LCLS)
**NJMIA**...... Neues Jahrbuch fuer Mineralogie. Abhandlungen [*A publication*]
**NjMiC**....... Courier, Middletown, NJ [*Library symbol*] [*Library of Congress*] (LCLS)
**NjMid**........ Middlesex Public Library, Middlesex, NJ [*Library symbol*] [*Library of Congress*] (LCLS)
**NjMil**......... Millburn Free Public Library, Millburn, NJ [*Library symbol*] [*Library of Congress*] (LCLS)
**NjMilt**........ Milltown Public Library, Milltown, NJ [*Library symbol*] [*Library of Congress*] (LCLS)
**NjMilv**....... Millville Public Library, Millville, NJ [*Library symbol*] [*Library of Congress*] (LCLS)

**NjMilvHi**... Wheaton Historical Association, Millville, NJ [*Library symbol*] [*Library of Congress*] (LCLS)
**NjMilvM**... Millville Daily, Millville, NJ [*Library symbol*] [*Library of Congress*] (LCLS)
**NJ Mis**....... New Jersey Miscellaneous Reports [*A publication*] (DLA)
**NJ Misc**..... New Jersey Miscellaneous Reports [*A publication*] (DLA)
**NJ Mis R**... New Jersey Miscellaneous Reports [*A publication*] (DLA)
**NjMj**.......... South Brunswick Free Public Library, Monmouth Junction, NJ [*Library symbol*] [*Library of Congress*] (LCLS)
**NjMlA**....... Atlantic County Library, Mays Landing, NJ [*Library symbol*] [*Library of Congress*] (LCLS)
**NjMlAC**..... Atlantic Community College, Mays Landing, NJ [*Library symbol*] [*Library of Congress*] (LCLS)
**NjMlCoC**... Atlantic County Clerk, Mays Landing, NJ [*Library symbol*] [*Library of Congress*] (LCLS)
**NjMlR**....... Atlantic County Record, Mays Landing, NJ [*Library symbol*] [*Library of Congress*] (LCLS)
**NjMo**......... Joint Free Public Library of Morristown and Morris Township, Morristown, NJ [*Library symbol*] [*Library of Congress*] (LCLS)
**NjMoAT**.... American Telephone & Telegraph Co., Morristown Corporate Marketing Library, Morristown, NJ [*Library symbol*] [*Library of Congress*] (LCLS)
**NjMoCoC**.. Morris County Clerk, Morristown, NJ [*Library symbol*] [*Library of Congress*] (LCLS)
**NjMoH**...... Morristown Memorial Hospital, Morristown, NJ [*Library symbol*] [*Library of Congress*] (LCLS)
**NjMoHP**.... Morristown National Historical Park, Morristown, NJ [*Library symbol*] [*Library of Congress*] (LCLS)
**NjMon**....... Montclair Free Public Library, Montclair, NJ [*Library symbol*] [*Library of Congress*] (LCLS)
**NjMonM**... Montclair Times, Montclair, NJ [*Library symbol*] [*Library of Congress*] (LCLS)
**NjMor**........ Moorestown Free Library, Moorestown, NJ [*Library symbol*] [*Library of Congress*] (LCLS)
**NjMorR**..... Radio Corp. of America, Missile and Surface Radar Division, Moorestown, NJ [*Library symbol*] [*Library of Congress*] (LCLS)
**NjMou**....... Mountain Lakes Public Library, Mountain Lakes, NJ [*Library symbol*] [*Library of Congress*] (LCLS)
**NjMouHi**... Mountain Lakes Historical Society, Mountain Lakes, NJ [*Library symbol*] [*Library of Congress*] (LCLS)
**NjMov**........ Montvale Free Public Library, Montvale, NJ [*Library symbol*] [*Library of Congress*] (LCLS)
**NjMovL**..... Lehn & Fink Products Co., Montvale, NJ [*Library symbol*] [*Library of Congress*] (LCLS)
**NjMp**......... Morris Plains Public Library, Morris Plains, NJ [*Library symbol*] [*Library of Congress*] (LCLS)
**NJMP**........ New Jewish Media Project [*Absorbed by JMS*] (EA)
**NjMpN**...... Morris News-Bee, Morris Plains, NJ [*Library symbol*] [*Library of Congress*] (LCLS)
**NjMpW**..... Warner-Lambert Research Institute, Morris Plains, NJ [*Library symbol*] [*Library of Congress*] (LCLS)
**NJMR**....... Nordisk Verbane Musik Rad [*Nordic Council for Railway Music - NCRM*] (EAIO)
**NjMs**.......... Maple Shade Public Library, Maple Shade, NJ [*Library symbol*] [*Library of Congress*] (LCLS)
**NJMS**........ New Jersey Medical School [*Newark*]
**NjMsP**....... Maple Shade Progress Press, Maple Shade, NJ [*Library symbol*] [*Library of Congress*] (LCLS)
**NjMuA**...... Air Reduction Co., Inc., Central Research Department Library, Murray Hill, NJ [*Library symbol*] [*Library of Congress*] (LCLS)
**NjMuB**....... Bell Telephone Laboratories, Inc., Murray Hill, NJ [*Library symbol*] [*Library of Congress*] (LCLS)
**NjMuhHi**... Harrison Township Historical Society, Mullica Hill, NJ [*Library symbol*] [*Library of Congress*] (LCLS)
**NJN**........... College of Medicine and Dentistry of New Jersey, Newark, NJ [*OCLC symbol*] (OCLC)
**NJN**........... Neue Juedische Nachrichten [*A publication*]
**NJN**........... New Jersey Network [*Trenton*] [*Telecommunications service*] (TSSD)
**NjN**............ Newark Public Library, Newark, NJ [*Library symbol*] [*Library of Congress*] (LCLS)
**NjNA**......... United States Attorney's Office, Law Library, Newark, NJ [*Library symbol*] [*Library of Congress*] (LCLS)
**NjNAA**...... New Jersey Afro-American, Newark, NJ [*Library symbol*] [*Library of Congress*] (LCLS)
**NjNb**.......... New Brunswick Free Public Library, New Brunswick, NJ [*Library symbol*] [*Library of Congress*] (LCLS)
**NJNB**........ New Jersey National Corp. [*NASDAQ symbol*] (NQ)
**NjNbH**....... Home News, New Brunswick, NJ [*Library symbol*] [*Library of Congress*] (LCLS)
**NjNbJJ**...... Johnson & Johnson, Research Center, New Brunswick, NJ [*Library symbol*] [*Library of Congress*] (LCLS)
**NjNbM**...... Middlesex General Hospital, New Brunswick, NJ [*Library symbol*] [*Library of Congress*] (LCLS)
**NjNbS**........ New Brunswick Theological Seminary, New Brunswick, NJ [*Library symbol*] [*Library of Congress*] (LCLS)
**NjNbSI**...... Squibb-Beechnut, Inc., New Brunswick, NJ [*Library symbol*] [*Library of Congress*] (LCLS)
**NjNbSp**...... New Brunswick Spokesman, New Brunswick, NJ [*Library symbol*] [*Library of Congress*] (LCLS)
**NjNbStP**.... Saint Peter's Medical Center, New Brunswick, NJ [*Library symbol*] [*Library of Congress*] (LCLS)
**NjNC**......... New Jersey Institute of Technology, Newark, NJ [*Library symbol*] [*Library of Congress*] (LCLS)
**NjNCM**..... New Jersey College of Medicine and Dentistry, Newark, NJ [*Library symbol*] [*Library of Congress*] (LCLS)
**NjNE**.......... Essex County College, Newark, NJ [*Library symbol*] [*Library of Congress*] (LCLS)
**NjNeP**........ New Egypt Press, New Egypt, NJ [*Library symbol*] [*Library of Congress*] (LCLS)
**NjNet**......... Dennis Memorial Library, Newton, NJ [*Library symbol*] [*Library of Congress*] (LCLS)
**NjNetcN**.... News Leader, Netcong, NJ [*Library symbol*] [*Library of Congress*] (LCLS)
**NjNetCoC**... Sussex County Clerk, Newton, NJ [*Library symbol*] [*Library of Congress*] (LCLS)
**NjNetDB**.... Don Bosco College, Newton, NJ [*Library symbol*] [*Library of Congress*] (LCLS)
**NjNetH**...... New Jersey Herald, Newton, NJ [*Library symbol*] [*Library of Congress*] (LCLS)
**NjNetS**....... Sussex County Library, Newton, NJ [*Library symbol*] [*Library of Congress*] (LCLS)
**NjNetSHi**.. Sussex County Historical Society, Newton, NJ [*Library symbol*] [*Library of Congress*] (LCLS)
**NjNhBHi**... Bergen County Historical Society, North Hackensack, NJ [*Library symbol*] [*Library of Congress*] (LCLS)
**NjNI**........... Ironbound Crier, Newark, NJ [*Library symbol*] [*Library of Congress*] (LCLS)
**NjNIM**....... International Musician, Newark, NJ [*Library symbol*] [*Library of Congress*] (LCLS)
**NjNIT**........ Italian Tribune, Newark, NJ [*Library symbol*] [*Library of Congress*] (LCLS)
**NjNJL**....... Jewish Ledger, Newark, NJ [*Library symbol*] [*Library of Congress*] (LCLS)
**NjNJN**....... Jewish News, Newark, NJ [*Library symbol*] [*Library of Congress*] (LCLS)
**NjNL**.......... Luso-Americano, Newark, NJ [*Library symbol*] [*Library of Congress*] (LCLS)
**NjNLH**...... New Jersey Labor Herald, Newark, NJ [*Library symbol*] [*Library of Congress*] (LCLS)
**NjNN**......... Nite-Lite, Newark, NJ [*Library symbol*] [*Library of Congress*] (LCLS)
**NjNoA**....... Atlantic County Advertiser, Northfield, NJ [*Library symbol*] [*Library of Congress*] (LCLS)
**NjNoa**........ North Arlington Free Public Library, North Arlington, NJ [*Library symbol*] [*Library of Congress*] (LCLS)
**NjNor**......... Norwood Public Library, Norwood, NJ [*Library symbol*] [*Library of Congress*] (LCLS)
**NjNp**.......... New Providence Memorial Library, New Providence, NJ [*Library symbol*] [*Library of Congress*] (LCLS)
**NjNpD**....... Dispatch, New Providence, NJ [*Library symbol*] [*Library of Congress*] (LCLS)
**NjNpHi**...... New Providence Historical Society, New Providence, NJ [*Library symbol*] [*Library of Congress*] (LCLS)
**NjNpI**......... Independent Press, New Providence, NJ [*Library symbol*] [*Library of Congress*] (LCLS)
**NjNT**.......... Tribuna di North Jersey, Newark, NJ [*Library symbol*] [*Library of Congress*] (LCLS)
**NjNu**.......... Nutley Free Public Library, Nutley, NJ [*Library symbol*] [*Library of Congress*] (LCLS)
**NjNuH**....... Hoffmann-La Roche, Inc., Scientific Library, Nutley, NJ [*Library symbol*] [*Library of Congress*] (LCLS)
**NjNuHi**...... Nutley Historical Society, Nutley, NJ [*Library symbol*] [*Library of Congress*] (LCLS)
**NJ Nurse**... New Jersey Nurse [*A publication*]
**NjNuS**........ Sun-Bank Newspapers, Nutley, NJ [*Library symbol*] [*Library of Congress*] (LCLS)
**NJNY**........ New Jersey & New York R. R. [*AAR code*]
**NjO**............ Free Public Library of the City of Orange, Orange, NJ [*Library symbol*] [*Library of Congress*] (LCLS)
**NjOak**........ Oakland Public Library, Oakland, NJ [*Library symbol*] [*Library of Congress*] (LCLS)
**NjOaS**........ Shore Publishers, Inc., Oakhurst, NJ [*Library symbol*] [*Library of Congress*] (LCLS)
**NjOcM**...... Ocean City Historical Museum, Ocean City, NJ [*Library symbol*] [*Library of Congress*] (LCLS)
**NjOcS**........ Sentinel Ledger, Ocean City, NJ [*Library symbol*] [*Library of Congress*] (LCLS)
**NJOG**........ Northern Offshore. Norwegian Journal of Oil and Gas [*A publication*]
**NjOgT**........ Ocean Grove Times, Ocean Grove, NJ [*Library symbol*] [*Library of Congress*] (LCLS)
**NjOrd**......... Oradell Public Library, Oradell, NJ [*Library symbol*] [*Library of Congress*] (LCLS)
**NjOrdB**...... Burns & Roe, Inc., Oradell, NJ [*Library symbol*] [*Library of Congress*] (LCLS)
**NJosnU**..... United Health Services, Wilson Hospital, Johnson City, NY [*Library symbol*] [*Library of Congress*] (LCLS)

**NJostF** ....... Fulton-Montgomery Community College, Johnstown, NY [*Library symbol*] [*Library of Congress*] (LCLS)
**NjOtR** ........ Fleming H. Revell Co., Old Tappan, NJ [*Library symbol*] [*Library of Congress*] (LCLS)
**N Jour Med Chir Pharm (Paris)** ... Nouveau Journal de Medecine, Chirurgie, et Pharmacie (Paris) [*A publication*]
**N Jour Pharm (Leipzig)** ... Neues Journal der Pharmacie fuer Aerzte Apotheker und Chemiker (Leipzig) [*A publication*]
**NjOW** ........ Worrall Publications, Inc., Orange, NJ [*Library symbol*] [*Library of Congress*] (LCLS)
**NJP** ........... National Jury Project (EA)
**NJP** ........... Nederlandse Jurisprudentie. Uitspraken in Burgerlijke en Strafzaken [*A publication*]
**NJP** ........... Network Job Processing
**NJP** ........... Neue Jahrbuecher fuer Paedogogik [*A publication*]
**NJP** ........... Neue Jahrbuecher fuer Philologie und Paedagogik [*A publication*]
**NJP** ........... Nonjudicial Punishment [*Military*]
**NjP** ............ Princeton University, Princeton, NJ [*Library symbol*] [*Library of Congress*] (LCLS)
**NJP** ........... Warminster, PA [*Location identifier*] [*FAA*] (FAAL)
**NJP** ........... William Patterson College of New Jersey, Wayne, NJ [*OCLC symbol*] (OCLC)
**NjPA** .......... American Cyanamid Co., Agricultural Division, Princeton, NJ [*Library symbol*] [*Library of Congress*] (LCLS)
**NJPA** ......... National Juice Products Association (EA)
**NjPalN** ....... Bergen News, Palisades Park, NJ [*Library symbol*] [*Library of Congress*] (LCLS)
**NjPar** ......... Paramus Public Library, Paramus, NJ [*Library symbol*] [*Library of Congress*] (LCLS)
**NjParB** ....... Bergen Community College, Paramus, NJ [*Library symbol*] [*Library of Congress*] (LCLS)
**NjParkHi** ... Pascack Historical Society and Museum, Park Ridge, NJ [*Library symbol*] [*Library of Congress*] (LCLS)
**NjParkP** ..... Pascack Publications Corp., Park Ridge, NJ [*Library symbol*] [*Library of Congress*] (LCLS)
**NjParR** ....... Ridgewood Newspapers, Paramus, NJ [*Library symbol*] [*Library of Congress*] (LCLS)
**NjParT** ....... Town News, Paramus, NJ [*Library symbol*] [*Library of Congress*] (LCLS)
**NjPas** ......... Passaic Public Library, Passaic, NJ [*Library symbol*] [*Library of Congress*] (LCLS)
**NjPasC** ...... Passaic Citizen, Passaic, NJ [*Library symbol*] [*Library of Congress*] (LCLS)
**NjPasCS** .... Catholic Sokol Printing Co., Passaic, NJ [*Library symbol*] [*Library of Congress*] (LCLS)
**NjPasE** ....... Eastern Catholic Life, Passaic, NJ [*Library symbol*] [*Library of Congress*] (LCLS)
**NjPasH** ...... Herald News, Passaic, NJ [*Library symbol*] [*Library of Congress*] (LCLS)
**NjPat** .......... Paterson Free Public Library, Paterson, NJ [*Library symbol*] [*Library of Congress*] (LCLS)
**NjPatCoC** .. Passaic County Clerk, Paterson, NJ [*Library symbol*] [*Library of Congress*] (LCLS)
**NjPatNe** ..... News, Paterson, NJ [*Library symbol*] [*Library of Congress*] (LCLS)
**NjPatPHi** ... Passaic County Historical Society, Paterson, NJ [*Library symbol*] [*Library of Congress*] (LCLS)
**NjPatSA** .... Saint Anthony's Guild, Franciscan Monastery, Paterson, NJ [*Library symbol*] [*Library of Congress*] (LCLS)
**NjPatV** ...... Voce Italiana, Paterson, NJ [*Library symbol*] [*Library of Congress*] (LCLS)
**NjPauR** ...... Record, Paulsboro, NJ [*Library symbol*] [*Library of Congress*] (LCLS)
**NjPauS** ...... Mobil Research & Development Corp., Paulsboro, NJ [*Library symbol*] [*Library of Congress*] (LCLS)
**NjPD** .......... Daily Princetonian, Princeton, NJ [*Library symbol*] [*Library of Congress*] (LCLS)
**NJPDDATC** ... National Joint Painting, Decorating, and Drywall Apprenticeship and Training Committee (EA)
**NjPE** .......... Educational Testing Service, Princeton, NJ [*Library symbol*] [*Library of Congress*] (LCLS)
**NjPeB** ........ Burlington County College, Pemberton, NJ [*Library symbol*] [*Library of Congress*] (LCLS)
**NjPegR** ...... Penns Grove Record, Penns Grove, NJ [*Library symbol*] [*Library of Congress*] (LCLS)
**NjPenP** ...... Pennsauken Resume, Pennsauken, NJ [*Library symbol*] [*Library of Congress*] (LCLS)
**NjPeqB** ...... Beacon, Pequannock, NJ [*Library symbol*] [*Library of Congress*] (LCLS)
**NjPera** ........ Perth Amboy Free Public Library, Perth Amboy, NJ [*Library symbol*] [*Library of Congress*] (LCLS)
**NjPeraSo** ... Universum Sokol Publishers, Perth Amboy, NJ [*Library symbol*] [*Library of Congress*] (LCLS)
**NjPeraSt** .... Saint John's Church, Perth Amboy, NJ [*Library symbol*] [*Library of Congress*] (LCLS)
**NjPERS** ..... E. R. Squibb & Sons, Princeton, NJ [*Library symbol*] [*Library of Congress*] (LCLS)
**NjPeT** ........ Times Advertising Printing Co., Pemberton, NJ [*Library symbol*] [*Library of Congress*] (LCLS)
**NjPF** .......... FMC Corp., Princeton, NJ [*Library symbol*] [*Library of Congress*] (LCLS)
**NjP-G** ........ Princeton University, Gest Library, Princeton, NJ [*Library symbol*] [*Library of Congress*] (LCLS)
**NjPh** ........... Phillipsburg Free Public Library, Phillipsburg, NJ [*Library symbol*] [*Library of Congress*] (LCLS)
**NJPHA** ...... National Junior Polled Hereford Association (EA)
**NJPHC** ...... National Junior Polled Hereford Council [*Later, NJPHA*] (EA)
**NjPHi** ........ Historical Society of Princeton, Princeton, NJ [*Library symbol*] [*Library of Congress*] (LCLS)
**NjPhP** ........ Free Press, Phillipsburg, NJ [*Library symbol*] [*Library of Congress*] (LCLS)
**NJ Ph P** ..... Neue Jahrbuecher fuer Philologie und Paedagogik [*A publication*]
**NjPI** .......... Institute for Advanced Study, Princeton, NJ [*Library symbol*] [*Library of Congress*] (LCLS)
**NjPi** ........... McCowan Memorial Library, Pitman, NJ [*Library symbol*] [*Library of Congress*] (LCLS)
**NjPJ** .......... Robert Wood Johnson Foundation Library, Princeton, NJ [*Library symbol*] [*Library of Congress*] (LCLS)
**NjPl** ........... Emanuel Einstein Free Public Library, Pompton Lakes, NJ [*Library symbol*] [*Library of Congress*] (LCLS)
**NjPla** .......... Plainfield Public Library, Plainfield, NJ [*Library symbol*] [*Library of Congress*] (LCLS)
**NjPlaM** ...... Muhlenberg Hospital, Plainfield, NJ [*Library symbol*] [*Library of Congress*] (LCLS)
**NjPlaSDB** ... Seventh Day Baptist Historical Society, Plainfield, NJ [*Library symbol*] [*Library of Congress*] (LCLS)
**NjPlaT** ....... Plainfield Times, Plainfield, NJ [*Library symbol*] [*Library of Congress*] (LCLS)
**NjPlaV** ....... Voice, Plainfield, NJ [*Library symbol*] [*Library of Congress*] (LCLS)
**NjPleM** ...... Mainland Journal, Pleasantville, NJ [*Library symbol*] [*Library of Congress*] (LCLS)
**NjPM** ......... Mobil Research & Development Corp., Central Research Division Library, Princeton, NJ [*Library symbol*] [*Library of Congress*] (LCLS)
**NJPMB** ...... Navy Jet-Propelled-Missile Board
**NjPMC** ...... Medical Center at Princeton, Princeton, NJ [*Library symbol*] [*Library of Congress*] (LCLS)
**NJPMP** ..... Navy Jet-Propelled-Missile Board (MCD)
**NjPoiO** ...... Ocean County Leader, Point Pleasant Beach, NJ [*Library symbol*] [*Library of Congress*] (LCLS)
**NjPoR** ........ Richard Stockton State College, Pomona, NJ [*Library symbol*] [*Library of Congress*] (LCLS)
**NjPP** .......... Princeton Packet, Inc., Princeton, NJ [*Library symbol*] [*Library of Congress*] (LCLS)
**NjPpE** ........ Eastern Historical Commission, Prospect Park, NJ [*Library symbol*] [*Library of Congress*] (LCLS)
**NjP-Pop** ..... Princeton University, Office of Population Research, Princeton, NJ [*Library symbol*] [*Library of Congress*] (LCLS)
**NjPPP** ........ Princeton Public Library, Princeton, NJ [*Library symbol*] [*Library of Congress*] (LCLS)
**NjPRCA** .... Radio Corporation of America, Laboratories Division, Princeton, NJ [*Library symbol*] [*Library of Congress*] (LCLS)
**NjPS** .......... Princeton Shopping News, Princeton, NJ [*Library symbol*] [*Library of Congress*] (LCLS)
**NjPStJ** ....... Saint Joseph's College, Princeton, NJ [*Library symbol*] [*Library of Congress*] (LCLS)
**NjPT** .......... Princeton Theological Seminary, Princeton, NJ [*Library symbol*] [*Library of Congress*] (LCLS)
**NjPTe** ........ Textile Research Institute, Princeton, NJ [*Library symbol*] [*Library of Congress*] (LCLS)
**NjPTT** ....... Town Topics, Inc., Princeton, NJ [*Library symbol*] [*Library of Congress*] (LCLS)
**NjPW** ......... Western Electric Co., Inc., Engineering Research Center, Princeton, NJ [*Library symbol*] [*Library of Congress*] (LCLS)
**NjPwAT** ..... American Telephone & Telegraph Co. Resource Center, Piscataway, NJ [*Library symbol*] [*Library of Congress*] (LCLS)
**NjPwC** ....... Colgate-Palmolive Co., Technical Information Center, Piscataway, NJ [*Library symbol*] [*Library of Congress*] (LCLS)
**NjPwIE** ...... Institute of Electrical and Electronics Engineers, Piscataway, NJ [*Library symbol*] [*Library of Congress*] (LCLS)
**NJQ** .......... Queens Borough Public Library, Jamaica, NY [*Library symbol*] [*Library of Congress*] (LCLS)
**NJQH** ........ Queens Hospital Center, Jamaica, NY [*Library symbol*] [*Library of Congress*] (LCLS)
**NJR** ........... New Jersey Register [*A publication*] (DLA)
**NJR** ........... New Jersey Resources Corp. [*NYSE symbol*] (SPSG)
**NJR** ........... New JEWEL Regime [*Grenada*] (INF)
**NJR** ........... Nonjob Routed [*Military*] (AFIT)
**NJR** ........... Rutgers-[*The*] State University, New Brunswick, NJ [*OCLC symbol*] (OCLC)
**NjR** ............ Rutgers-[*The*] State University, New Brunswick, NJ [*Library symbol*] [*Library of Congress*] (LCLS)
**NJRA** ......... National Juvenile Restitution Association [*Later, ARA*] (EA)
**NJRA** ......... NJR Association [*Beirut, Lebanon*] (EAIO)

**NjRah** ........ Rahway Public Library, Rahway, NJ [*Library symbol*] [*Library of Congress*] (LCLS)
**NjRahB** ...... Bauer Publishing & Printing Ltd., Rahway, NJ [*Library symbol*] [*Library of Congress*] (LCLS)
**NjRahM** .... Merck, Sharp & Dohme [*Later, Merck & Co., Inc.*] Research Laboratory, Research Library, Rahway, NJ [*Library symbol*] [*Library of Congress*] (LCLS)
**NjRam** ........ Ramsey Free Public Library, Ramsey, NJ [*Library symbol*] [*Library of Congress*] (LCLS)
**NjRamH** .... Home and Store News, Ramsey, NJ [*Library symbol*] [*Library of Congress*] (LCLS)
**NjRamI** ...... Immaculate Conception Theological Seminary, Ramsey, NJ [*Library symbol*] [*Library of Congress*] (LCLS)
**NjRarO** ...... Ortho Pharmaceutical Corp., Raritan, NJ [*Library symbol*] [*Library of Congress*] (LCLS)
**NjRarOD** ... Ortho Diagnostics, Raritan, NJ [*Library symbol*] [*Library of Congress*] (LCLS)
**NjRb** .......... Red Bank Public Library, Red Bank, NJ [*Library symbol*] [*Library of Congress*] (LCLS)
**NjRbR** ........ Daily Register, Red Bank, NJ [*Library symbol*] [*Library of Congress*] (LCLS)
**NJRC** ......... National Jewish Resource Center (EA)
**NJRC** ......... New Jersey Board of Railroad Commissioners Annual Reports [*A publication*] (DLA)
**NjRdR** ........ Riverdale Publishing Co., Riverdale, NJ [*Library symbol*] [*Library of Congress*] (LCLS)
**NJ Reg** ....... New Jersey Register [*A publication*]
**NJ Rep** ....... New Jersey Law Reports [*A publication*] (DLA)
**NJ Re Tit N** ... New Jersey Realty Title News [*A publication*] (DLA)
**NJ Rev Stat** ... New Jersey Revised Statutes [*A publication*] (DLA)
**NjRf** ........... Ridgefield Public Library, Ridgefield, NJ [*Library symbol*] [*Library of Congress*] (LCLS)
**NjRh** .......... Rocky Hill Public Library, Rocky Hill, NJ [*Library symbol*] [*Library of Congress*] (LCLS)
**NjRiv** .......... Riverside Public Library, Riverside, NJ [*Library symbol*] [*Library of Congress*] (LCLS)
**NjRive** ........ River Edge Free Public Library, River Edge, NJ [*Library symbol*] [*Library of Congress*] (LCLS)
**NjR-L** .......... Rutgers-[*The*] State University, Rutgers-Camden School of Law, Camden, NJ [*Library symbol*] [*Library of Congress*] (LCLS)
**NjRo** ........... Roseland Public Library, Roseland, NJ [*Library symbol*] [*Library of Congress*] (LCLS)
**NjRocM** ..... Morris County News, Rockaway, NJ [*Library symbol*] [*Library of Congress*] (LCLS)
**NjRos** ......... Roselle Free Public Library, Roselle, NJ [*Library symbol*] [*Library of Congress*] (LCLS)
**NJROTC** ... Naval Junior Reserve Officer Training Corps
**NjRp** .......... Ridgefield Park Free Public Library, Ridgefield Park, NJ [*Library symbol*] [*Library of Congress*] (LCLS)
**NjRpS** ........ Sun Bulletin, Ridgefield Park, NJ [*Library symbol*] [*Library of Congress*] (LCLS)
**NjR-S** .......... Rutgers-[*The*] State University, College of South Jersey, Camden, NJ [*Library symbol*] [*Library of Congress*] (LCLS)
**NjRu** ........... Rutherford Free Public Library, Rutherford, NJ [*Library symbol*] [*Library of Congress*] (LCLS)
**NjRuB** ........ Becton, Dickinson & Co., Rutherford, NJ [*Library symbol*] [*Library of Congress*] (LCLS)
**NjRuF** ......... Fairleigh Dickinson University, Rutherford, NJ [*Library symbol*] [*Library of Congress*] (LCLS)
**NjRw** .......... Ridgewood Library, Ridgewood, NJ [*Library symbol*] [*Library of Congress*] (LCLS)
**NjRwN** ........ Ridgewood News, Ridgewood, NJ [*Library symbol*] [*Library of Congress*] (LCLS)
**NjRwPHi** ... Paramus Historical and Preservation Society, Ridgewood, NJ [*Library symbol*] [*Library of Congress*] (LCLS)
**NJS** ............ New Jersey Superior Court Reports [*A publication*] (DLA)
**NJS** ............ Noise Jammer Simulator [*Telecommunications*] (TEL)
**NJS** ............ Norwegian Bankers Association. Financial Review [*A publication*]
**NJS** ............ Stockton State College, Pomona, NJ [*OCLC symbol*] (OCLC)
**NjS** ............. Summit Free Public Library, Summit, NJ [*Library symbol*] [*Library of Congress*] (LCLS)
**NJSA** ......... New Jersey Statutes Annotated [*A publication*]
**NjSabN** ...... News Dispatch, Saddle Brook, NJ [*Library symbol*] [*Library of Congress*] (LCLS)
**NjSalCoC** ... Salem County Clerk, Salem, NJ [*Library symbol*] [*Library of Congress*] (LCLS)
**NjSalHi** ..... Salem County Historical Society, Salem, NJ [*Library symbol*] [*Library of Congress*] (LCLS)
**NjSalS** ....... Sunbeam Publishing Co., Salem, NJ [*Library symbol*] [*Library of Congress*] (LCLS)
**NJSB** ......... New Jersey Savings Bank [*NASDAQ symbol*] (NQ)
**NJSBAQ** ... New Jersey State Bar Association. Quarterly [*A publication*] (DLA)
**NjSbB** ........ Beachcomber, Ship Bottom, NJ [*Library symbol*] [*Library of Congress*] (LCLS)
**NjSbbU** ...... Saint Sophia Ukrainian Orthodox Seminary, South Bound Brook, NJ [*Library symbol*] [*Library of Congress*] (LCLS)
**NJSBJ** ....... New Jersey State Bar Journal [*A publication*] (DLA)
**NJSBTA Ops** ... New Jersey State Board of Tax Appeals, Opinions [*A publication*] (DLA)
**NjSC** .......... Ciba Pharmaceutical Co., Research Library, Summit, NJ [*Library symbol*] [*Library of Congress*] (LCLS)
**NjSCC** ....... Summit City Clerk, Summit, NJ [*Library symbol*] [*Library of Congress*] (LCLS)
**NJ Sch Libn** ... New Jersey School Librarian [*A publication*]
**NjScp** ......... Scotch Plains Public Library, Scotch Plains, NJ [*Library symbol*] [*Library of Congress*] (LCLS)
**NjScpT** ....... Times, Scotch Plains, NJ [*Library symbol*] [*Library of Congress*] (LCLS)
**NJSD** ......... National Joint Service Delegations (NATG)
**NJSDC** ...... New Jersey State Data Center [*New Jersey State Department of Labor*] [*Trenton*] [*Information service or system*] (IID)
**NjSe** .......... Secaucus Free Public Library, Secaucus, NJ [*Library symbol*] [*Library of Congress*] (LCLS)
**NjSeH** ........ Secaucus Home News, Secaucus, NJ [*Library symbol*] [*Library of Congress*] (LCLS)
**NJ Sess Law Serv** ... New Jersey Session Law Service [*A publication*] (DLA)
**NJ Sess Law Serv (West)** ... New Jersey Session Law Service (West) [*A publication*]
**NjSewG** ...... Gloucester County College, Sewell, NJ [*Library symbol*] [*Library of Congress*] (LCLS)
**NjSewHi** .... Washington Township Historical Society, Sewell, NJ [*Library symbol*] [*Library of Congress*] (LCLS)
**NJSGA** ...... National Junior Santa Gertrudis Association (EA)
**NjSGS** ........ Church of Jesus Christ of Latter-Day Saints, Genealogical Society Library, Caldwell Branch, Summit, NJ [*Library symbol*] [*Library of Congress*] (LCLS)
**NjSH** .......... Summit Herald, Summit, NJ [*Library symbol*] [*Library of Congress*] (LCLS)
**NjShO** ........ Ocean County Review, Seaside Heights, NJ [*Library symbol*] [*Library of Congress*] (LCLS)
**NJSHS** ...... National Junior Science and Humanities Symposium
**NjSicTR** ..... Cape May County Times and Seven Mile Beach Reporter, Sea Isle City, NJ [*Library symbol*] [*Library of Congress*] (LCLS)
**NJSN** ......... National Job Sharing Network (EA)
**NJSNA News** ... NJSNA [*New Jersey State Nurses Association*] Newsletter [*Later, New Jersey Nurse*] [*A publication*]
**NJSNA Newsl** ... NJSNA [*New Jersey State Nurses Association*] Newsletter [*Later, New Jersey Nurse*] [*A publication*]
**NJSO** ......... National Jazz Service Organization (EA)
**NjSo** .......... Somerville Free Public Library, Somerville, NJ [*Library symbol*] [*Library of Congress*] (LCLS)
**NjSoa** ......... South Amboy Public Library, South Amboy, NJ [*Library symbol*] [*Library of Congress*] (LCLS)
**NjSoaP** ....... South Amboy Publishing Co., South Amboy, NJ [*Library symbol*] [*Library of Congress*] (LCLS)
**NjSobC** ...... Central Post, South Brunswick, NJ [*Library symbol*] [*Library of Congress*] (LCLS)
**NjSoCo** ...... Somerset County Library, Somerville, NJ [*Library symbol*] [*Library of Congress*] (LCLS)
**NjSoCoC** .... Somerset County Clerk, Somerville, NJ [*Library symbol*] [*Library of Congress*] (LCLS)
**NjSoE** ........ Ethicon, Inc., Somerville, NJ [*Library symbol*] [*Library of Congress*] (LCLS)
**NjSoH** ........ Somerset Hospital, Somerville, NJ [*Library symbol*] [*Library of Congress*] (LCLS)
**NjSoHR** ..... Hoechst-Roussel Pharmaceuticals, Inc., Somerville, NJ [*Library symbol*] [*Library of Congress*] (LCLS)
**NjSoM** ....... Somerset Messenger-Gazette, Somerville, NJ [*Library symbol*] [*Library of Congress*] (LCLS)
**NjSomHi** .... Atlantic County Historical Society, Somers Point, NJ [*Library symbol*] [*Library of Congress*] (LCLS)
**NjSoo** ........ South Orange Public Library, South Orange, NJ [*Library symbol*] [*Library of Congress*] (LCLS)
**NjSooS** ....... Seton Hall University, South Orange, NJ [*Library symbol*] [*Library of Congress*] (LCLS)
**NjSooS-L** ... Seton Hall University, Law Library, Newark, NJ [*Library symbol*] [*Library of Congress*] (LCLS)
**NjSop** ........ South Plainfield Free Public Library, South Plainfield, NJ [*Library symbol*] [*Library of Congress*] (LCLS)
**NjSopA** ...... American Smelting & Refining Co., Research Department Library, South Plainfield, NJ [*Library symbol*] [*Library of Congress*] (LCLS)
**NjSopP** ...... PAMCAM, Inc., South Plainfield, NJ [*Library symbol*] [*Library of Congress*] (LCLS)
**NjSoS** ........ Somerset County College, Somerville, NJ [*Library symbol*] [*Library of Congress*] (LCLS)
**NjSosS** ....... Somerset Spectator, Somerset, NJ [*Library symbol*] [*Library of Congress*] (LCLS)
**NjSoVA** ..... United States Veterans Administration Supply Depot, Somerville, NJ [*Library symbol*] [*Library of Congress*] (LCLS)
**NjSp** .......... Springfield Free Public Library, Springfield, NJ [*Library symbol*] [*Library of Congress*] (LCLS)
**NjSpl** ......... Spring Lake Public Library, Spring Lake, NJ [*Library symbol*] [*Library of Congress*] (LCLS)
**NjSpW** ....... Western Electric Co., Springfield, NJ [*Library symbol*] [*Library of Congress*] (LCLS)

**NJSRB** ...... Netherlands Journal of Sea Research [*A publication*]
**NJST** ......... New Jersey Steel Corp. [*NASDAQ symbol*] (NQ)
**NjSt** ........... Passaic Township Public Library, Stirling, NJ [*Library symbol*] [*Library of Congress*] (LCLS)
**NJ Stat Ann (West)** ... New Jersey Statutes, Annotated (West) [*A publication*] (DLA)
**NJ St BJ** .... New Jersey State Bar Journal [*A publication*] (DLA)
**NjStR** ......... Recorder Publishing Co., Stirling, NJ [*Library symbol*] [*Library of Congress*] (LCLS)
**NjStrK** ....... John F. Kennedy Memorial Hospital, Stratford, NJ [*Library symbol*] [*Library of Congress*] (LCLS)
**NjSu** ........... Roxbury Public Library, Succasunna, NJ [*Library symbol*] [*Library of Congress*] (LCLS)
**NJ Success** ... New Jersey Success [*A publication*]
**NJSUD** ...... Netherlands Journal of Surgery [*A publication*]
**NJ Sup** ....... New Jersey Superior Court Reports [*A publication*] (DLA)
**NJ Super** .... New Jersey Superior Court Reports [*A publication*] (DLA)
**NjSw** .......... Swedesboro Free Public Library, Swedesboro, NJ [*Library symbol*] [*Library of Congress*] (LCLS)
**NjSwN** ....... Swedesboro News, Swedesboro, NJ [*Library symbol*] [*Library of Congress*] (LCLS)
**NJT** ........... National Jewish Television [*Cable-television system*]
**NjT** ............ Trenton Free Public Library, Trenton, NJ [*Library symbol*] [*Library of Congress*] (LCLS)
**NJT** ............ Trenton State College, Trenton, NJ [*OCLC symbol*] (OCLC)
**NJ Tax** ....... New Jersey Tax Court Reports [*A publication*]
**NjTCP** ....... Commercial Printing Co., Trenton, NJ [*Library symbol*] [*Library of Congress*] (LCLS)
**NjTea** ......... Teaneck Public Library, Teaneck, NJ [*Library symbol*] [*Library of Congress*] (LCLS)
**NjTeaF** ....... Fairleigh Dickinson University, Teaneck, NJ [*Library symbol*] [*Library of Congress*] (LCLS)
**NjTeaL** ...... Luther College, Teaneck, NJ [*Library symbol*] [*Library of Congress*] (LCLS)
**NjTen** ......... Tenafly Public Library, Tenafly, NJ [*Library symbol*] [*Library of Congress*] (LCLS)
**NJTL** ......... National Junior Tennis League (EA)
**NjTM** ......... Monitor, Trenton, NJ [*Library symbol*] [*Library of Congress*] (LCLS)
**NjTMC** ...... Mercer County Community College, Trenton, NJ [*Library symbol*] [*Library of Congress*] (LCLS)
**NjTPP** ........ Planned Parenthood of Mercer Area, Trenton, NJ [*Library symbol*] [*Library of Congress*] (LCLS)
**NjTR** .......... Rider College, Trenton, NJ [*Library symbol*] [*Library of Congress*] (LCLS)
**NjTrCo** ....... Ocean County Public Library, Toms River, NJ [*Library symbol*] [*Library of Congress*] (LCLS)
**NjTrCoC** .... Ocean County Clerk, Toms River, NJ [*Library symbol*] [*Library of Congress*] (LCLS)
**NjTrO** ........ Ocean County College, Toms River, NJ [*Library symbol*] [*Library of Congress*] (LCLS)
**NjTrR** ........ Reporter, Toms River, NJ [*Library symbol*] [*Library of Congress*] (LCLS)
**NjTS** .......... Trenton State College, Trenton, NJ [*Library symbol*] [*Library of Congress*] (LCLS)
**NjTSch** ...... Schweats, Inc., Trenton, NJ [*Library symbol*] [*Library of Congress*] (LCLS)
**NjTStF** ....... Saint Francis Medical Center, Health Science Library, Trenton, NJ [*Library symbol*] [*Library of Congress*] (LCLS)
**NjTTr** ........ Trentonian, Trenton, NJ [*Library symbol*] [*Library of Congress*] (LCLS)
**NjTTT** ....... Trenton Times Newspapers, Trenton, NJ [*Library symbol*] [*Library of Congress*] (LCLS)
**nju** .............. New Jersey [*MARC country of publication code*] [*Library of Congress*] (LCCP)
**NJU** ........... Nordic Judo Union (EAIO)
**NJU** ........... Northern Jiaotong Univeristy [*People's Republic of China*]
**NjU** ............ Union Township Public Library, Union, NJ [*Library symbol*] [*Library of Congress*] (LCLS)
**NjUbI** ......... International Flavors & Fragrances, Inc., Union Beach, NJ [*Library symbol*] [*Library of Congress*] (LCLS)
**NjUc** ........... Union City Free Public Library, Union City, NJ [*Library symbol*] [*Library of Congress*] (LCLS)
**NjUcD** ........ Dispatch, Union City, NJ [*Library symbol*] [*Library of Congress*] (LCLS)
**NjUcS** ........ Shield, Union City, NJ [*Library symbol*] [*Library of Congress*] (LCLS)
**NjUcSM** .... Saint Michael's Passionist Monastery, Union City, NJ [*Library symbol*] [*Library of Congress*] (LCLS)
**NJUGA** ..... Nippon Junkanki Gakushi [*A publication*]
**NjUJ** .......... Jewish Community News, Union, NJ [*Library symbol*] [*Library of Congress*] (LCLS)
**NjUN** ......... Kean College of New Jersey, Union, NJ [*Library symbol*] [*Library of Congress*] (LCLS)
**NjUpM** ...... Montclair State College, Upper Montclair, NJ [*Library symbol*] [*Library of Congress*] (LCLS)
**NjUpM-C** .. China Institute of New Jersey, Montclair State College, Upper Montclair, NJ [*Library symbol*] [*Library of Congress*] (LCLS)
**NjUS** .......... Suburban Publishing Co., Union, NJ [*Library symbol*] [*Library of Congress*] (LCLS)
**NjUsrHi** ..... Upper Saddle River Historical Committee, Upper Saddle River, NJ [*Library symbol*] [*Library of Congress*] (LCLS)
**NJUZA9** .... Japanese Journal of Veterinary Science [*A publication*]
**NJV** ........... Nederlandse Juristenvereniging [*Netherlands Lawyers Association*] (ILCA)
**NjV** ............ Vineland Free Public Library, Vineland, NJ [*Library symbol*] [*Library of Congress*] (LCLS)
**NjVC** .......... Cumberland County College, Vineland, NJ [*Library symbol*] [*Library of Congress*] (LCLS)
**NJVGA** ...... National Junior Vegetable Growers Association [*Later, NJHA*] (EA)
**NjVHi** ........ Vineland Historical and Antiquarian Society, Vineland, NJ [*Library symbol*] [*Library of Congress*] (LCLS)
**NjVT** .......... Times Journal, Vineland, NJ [*Library symbol*] [*Library of Congress*] (LCLS)
**NJW** .......... Neue Jahrbuecher fuer Wissenschaft und Jugendbildung [*A publication*]
**NJW** .......... Neue Juristische Wochenschrift [*A publication*]
**NJW** .......... Norris Junction [*Wyoming*] [*Seismograph station code, US Geological Survey*] (SEIS)
**NjW** ........... Wayne Public Library, Wayne, NJ [*Library symbol*] [*Library of Congress*] (LCLS)
**NjWa** ......... Warren Township Public Library, Warren, NJ [*Library symbol*] [*Library of Congress*] (LCLS)
**NjWas** ........ Washington Free Public Library, Washington, NJ [*Library symbol*] [*Library of Congress*] (LCLS)
**NjWasW** .... Washington Star, Washington, NJ [*Library symbol*] [*Library of Congress*] (LCLS)
**NJ Water Resour Spec Rep** ... New Jersey. Division of Water Resources. Special Report [*A publication*]
**NJWB** ........ National Jewish Welfare Board [*Later, JWB*]
**NjWdHi** ..... Gloucester County Historical Society, Woodbury, NJ [*Library symbol*] [*Library of Congress*] (LCLS)
**NjWdT** ....... Woodbury Daily Times, Woodbury, NJ [*Library symbol*] [*Library of Congress*] (LCLS)
**NjWef** ........ Westfield Memorial Library, Westfield, NJ [*Library symbol*] [*Library of Congress*] (LCLS)
**NjWefW** .... Wyckoff Printing Co., Westfield, NJ [*Library symbol*] [*Library of Congress*] (LCLS)
**NjWem** ....... Haddon Township Free Library, Westmont, NJ [*Library symbol*] [*Library of Congress*] (LCLS)
**NjWemT** .... Camden County Times, Westmont, NJ [*Library symbol*] [*Library of Congress*] (LCLS)
**NjWesny** .... West New York Public Library, West New York, NJ [*Library symbol*] [*Library of Congress*] (LCLS)
**NjWew** ....... Westwood Free Public Library, Westwood, NJ [*Library symbol*] [*Library of Congress*] (LCLS)
**NjWewP** .... Pascack Valley Community Life, Westwood, NJ [*Library symbol*] [*Library of Congress*] (LCLS)
**NjWewW** ... Westwood Publications, Westwood, NJ [*Library symbol*] [*Library of Congress*] (LCLS)
**NjWF** ......... Fairleigh Dickinson University, Wayne, NJ [*Library symbol*] [*Library of Congress*] (LCLS)
**NjWhi** ........ Whippanong Public Library, Whippany, NJ [*Library symbol*] [*Library of Congress*] (LCLS)
**NjWhiB** ..... Bell Telephone Laboratories, Inc., Technical Information Library, Whippany, NJ [*Library symbol*] [*Library of Congress*] (LCLS)
**NjWhiM** .... Morris County Free Library, Whippany, NJ [*Library symbol*] [*Library of Congress*] (LCLS)
**NjWhiR** ..... Regional Weekly News, Whippany, NJ [*Library symbol*] [*Library of Congress*] (LCLS)
**NjWhsH** .... Hunterdon Review, Whitehouse Station, NJ [*Library symbol*] [*Library of Congress*] (LCLS)
**NjWi** .......... Willingboro Public Library, Willingboro, NJ [*Library symbol*] [*Library of Congress*] (LCLS)
**NjWilH** ...... Williamstown High School, Williamstown, NJ [*Library symbol*] [*Library of Congress*] (LCLS)
**NjWiT** ........ Burlington County Times, Willingboro, NJ [*Library symbol*] [*Library of Congress*] (LCLS)
**NJWJ** ........ Neue Jahrbuecher fuer Wissenschaft und Jugendbildung [*A publication*]
**NjWlM** ...... Monmouth College, West Long Beach, NJ [*Library symbol*] [*Library of Congress*] (LCLS)
**NjWMN** .... Matzner Suburban Newspapers, Wayne, NJ [*Library symbol*] [*Library of Congress*] (LCLS)
**NjWo** ......... West Orange Free Public Library, West Orange, NJ [*Library symbol*] [*Library of Congress*] (LCLS)
**NjWoE** ....... Edison National Historic Site, West Orange, NJ [*Library symbol*] [*Library of Congress*] (LCLS)
**NjWolA** ..... Alphonsus College, Woodcliff Lake, NJ [*Library symbol*] [*Library of Congress*] (LCLS)
**NjWoo** ........ Free Public Library of Woodbridge, Woodbridge, NJ [*Library symbol*] [*Library of Congress*] (LCLS)
**NjWooN** .... News-Tribune, Woodbridge, NJ [*Library symbol*] [*Library of Congress*] (LCLS)
**NjWor** ........ Wood Ridge Memorial Library, Wood Ridge, NJ [*Library symbol*] [*Library of Congress*] (LCLS)
**NjWP** ......... William Paterson College of New Jersey, Wayne, NJ [*Library symbol*] [*Library of Congress*] (LCLS)
**NJWPC** ..... National Jobs with Peace Campaign (EA)

**NjWwHi** .... Wildwood Historical Commission, Wildwood, NJ [*Library symbol*] [*Library of Congress*] (LCLS)
**NjWwL** ...... Wildwood Leader, Wildwood, NJ [*Library symbol*] [*Library of Congress*] (LCLS)
**NjWwP** ...... National Association of Precancel Collectors, Wildwood, NJ [*Library symbol*] [*Library of Congress*] (LCLS)
**NjWy** ......... Wyckoff Free Public Library, Wyckoff, NJ [*Library symbol*] [*Library of Congress*] (LCLS)
**NjWyN** ...... Wyckoff News, Wyckoff, NJ [*Library symbol*] [*Library of Congress*] (LCLS)
**NJY** ........... Newjay Resources Ltd. [*Vancouver Stock Exchange symbol*]
**NJY** ........... York College of the City University of New York, Jamaica, NY [*Library symbol*] [*Library of Congress*] (LCLS)
**NjZaA** ........ Alma White College, Zarephath, NJ [*Library symbol*] [*Library of Congress*] (LCLS)
**Nk** .............. Naik [*British military*] (DMA)
**NK** .............. Narodna Kultura [*Sofia*] [*A publication*]
**NK** .............. Nasza Ksiegarnia [*A publication*]
**NK** .............. National Air Express Sudan [*ICAO designator*] (FAAC)
**NK** .............. Natural Killer [*Cell*] [*Immunochemistry*]
**NK** .............. Neck (AAG)
**NK** .............. Neon Komma [*New Party*] [*Greek*] [*Political party*] (PPE)
**NK** .............. New Kingdom [*Egyptology*] (ROG)
**NK** .............. New Korea [*A publication*]
**NK** .............. Next of Kin
**NK** .............. Nippon Kaiji Kyokai [*Japanese ship classification society*] (DS)
**NK** .............. Nomenklature Kommission [*Commission on Nomenclature*] [*Anatomy*] [*German*]
**NK** .............. Nordiska Kemistradet [*Chemical Societies of the Nordic Countries*] (EAIO)
**NK** .............. North Korean
**NK** .............. Not Known
**NK** .............. Nowe Kultura [*A publication*]
**NK** .............. Numizmatikai Koezloeny [*A publication*]
**NK** .............. Nyelvtudomanyi Koezlemenyek [*A publication*]
**NKa** ............ Katonah Village Library, Katonah, NY [*Library symbol*] [*Library of Congress*] (LCLS)
**NKA** ........... National Kindergarten Association [*Defunct*] (EA)
**NKA** ........... Neurokinin A [*Biochemistry*]
**NKA** ........... Nikiskha [*Alaska*] [*Seismograph station code, US Geological Survey*] (SEIS)
**NKA** ........... Norcanair [*Prince Albert, SK*] [*FAA designator*] (FAAC)
**NKA** ........... Nordisk Kontaktorgan for Atomenergisporgsmal [*Nordic Liaison Committee for Atomic Energy*] (EAIO)
**NKA** ........... North Korean Army (CINC)
**NKA** ........... Now Known As (DLA)
**NKABEA** ... National Korean American Bilingual Educators Association (EA)
**NKAF** ........ Natural Killer-Cell Activating Factor [*Immunology*]
**NKAF** ........ North Korean Air Force (CINC)
**NKAKB** ..... Nippon Kagaku Kaishi [*A publication*]
**NKB** ........... Neurokinin B [*Biochemistry*]
**NKB** ........... Nordiska Kommitten for Byggbestammelser [*Nordic Committee on Building Regulations - NCBR*] [*Espoo, Finland*] (EAIO)
**NKB** ........... Nordiske Kristne Buddhistmission [*Christian Mission to Buddhists - CMB*] [*Arhus, Denmark*] (EAIO)
**NKBA** ........ National Kitchen and Bath Association (EA)
**NKBK** ........ Connecticut Bancorp, Inc. [*Norwalk, CT*] [*NASDAQ symbol*] (NQ)
**NK Bl** ......... Neuburger Kollektaneenblatt [*A publication*]
**NKC** ........... National Kidney Centre [*British*] (CB)
**nkc** ............. New Brunswick [*MARC country of publication code*] [*Library of Congress*] (LCCP)
**NKC** ........... Nouakchott [*Mauritania*] [*Airport symbol*] (OAG)
**NKCA** ........ National Kitchen Cabinet Association [*Later, KCMA*] (EA)
**NKCA** ........ National Knife Collectors Association (EA)
**NKCF** ........ Natural Killer (Cell) Cytotoxic Factor [*Immunochemistry*]
**NKCHD** ..... Nippon Kikai Gakkai Ronbunshu. C Hen [*A publication*]
**NKCP** ........ North Kalimantan Communist Party [*Malaysia*] [*Political party*] (PD)
**NKDF** ........ National Kidney Disease Foundation [*Later, NKF*] (EA)
**NKDS** ........ Navy Key Distribution System (CAAL)
**NKE** ........... Nake [*Ryukyu Islands*] [*Seismograph station code, US Geological Survey*] [*Closed*] (SEIS)
**NKE** ........... Nike, Inc. Class B [*NYSE symbol*] (SPSG)
**NKE** ........... Nortek Capital Corp. [*Formerly, Nortek Energy Corp.*] [*Vancouver Stock Exchange symbol*]
**NKendOHi** ... Orleans County Historical Society, Kendall, NY [*Library symbol*] [*Library of Congress*] (LCLS)
**NKEP** ........ Narodnyj Komissariat Elektrostancij i Elektropromyslennosti [*A publication*]
**NKEWA** .... New Kuban Education and Welfare Association (EA)
**NKEZA** ..... Nippon Koshu Eisei Zasshi [*A publication*]
**NKEZA4** ... Japanese Journal of Public Health [*A publication*]
**NKF** ........... National Kidney Foundation (EA)
**NKF** ........... Nordisk Konstforbund [*Nordic Art Association*] (EAIO)
**NKFO** ........ Nordisk Kollegium for Fysisk Oceanografi [*Nordic Council for Physical Oceanography - NCPO*] (EAIO)
**NKFTA** ...... National Kosher Food Trade Association (EA)
**NKG** ........... Nanjing [*China*] [*Airport symbol*] (OAG)
**NkG** ........... Newton K. Gregg, Novato, CA [*Library symbol*] [*Library of Congress*] (LCLS)
**NKGAD** ..... Nippon Kikai Gakkai Ronbunshu. A Hen [*A publication*]
**NKGBD** ..... Nippon Kikai Gakkai Ronbunshu. B Hen [*A publication*]
**NKGB-NKVD** ... Narodnyi Komissariat Gosudarstvennoe Bezopasnosti-Narodnyi Komissariat Vnutrennikh Del [*Later, KGB*]
**NKGRB** ..... Nippon Kenchiku Gakkai Ronbun Hokoku-shu [*A publication*]
**NKGWG** .... Nachrichten der Koeniglichen Gesellschaft der Wissenschaften zu Goettingen [*A publication*]
**NKGZAE** .. Acta Haematologica Japonica [*A publication*]
**NKH** .......... Kaneohe Bay, HI [*Location identifier*] [*FAA*] (FAAL)
**NKH** .......... Nordisk Komite for Handelsundervisning [*Nordic Committee for Commercial Education - NCCE*] [*Odense, Denmark*] (EAIO)
**NKHA** ....... National Kerosene Heater Association (EA)
**NKHA** ....... Nonketotic Hyperosmolar Acidosis [*Medicine*]
**NKHHC** .... Nonketotic Hyperosmolar Hyperglycemis Coma [*Also, HHNK*] [*Medicine*]
**NKHJ** ........ Nederlandsch Kunsthistorisch Jaarboek [*A publication*]
**NKHOAK** ... Bulletin. Agricultural Chemicals Inspection Station [*Tokyo*] [*A publication*]
**NKI** ........... Nikolski [*Alaska*] [*Seismograph station code, US Geological Survey*] (SEIS)
**NKiB** .......... Benedictine Hospital, Medical Library, Kingston, NY [*Library symbol*] [*Library of Congress*] (LCLS)
**NKiC** .......... Children's Home of Kingston, Kingston, NY [*Library symbol*] [*Library of Congress*] (LCLS)
**NKiHL** ....... Kingston Hospital Libraries, Kingston, NY [*Library symbol*] [*Library of Congress*] (LCLS)
**NKiI** ........... International Business Machines Corp., Kingston, NY [*Library symbol*] [*Library of Congress*] (LCLS)
**NKIN** ......... Nankin Express, Inc. [*NASDAQ symbol*] (NQ)
**NKipM** ...... United States Merchant Marine Academy, Kings Point, NY [*Library symbol*] [*Library of Congress*] (LCLS)
**NKJV** ......... New King James Version of the Bible [*A publication*]
**NKK** .......... Nordiska Kor Kommitten [*Arhus, Denmark*] (EAIO)
**NKK** .......... Nordkalottkommitten [*North Calotte Committee - NCC*] [*Rovaniemi, Finland*] (EAIO)
**NKK** .......... Novo-Kazalinsk [*USSR*] [*Geomagnetic observatory code*]
**NKKGAB** .. Japanese Poultry Science [*A publication*]
**NKKOB** ..... Nara Kogyo Koto Senmon Gakko Kenkyu Kiyo [*A publication*]
**NKL** .......... Nemeth-Kellner Leukemia
**NKL** .......... New Keel [*On ships*]
**NKL** .......... New Kelore Mines Ltd. [*Toronto Stock Exchange symbol*]
**NKL** .......... Nickel
**NKL C** ....... Nickel Copper [*Freight*]
**NKM** ......... Nakhla [*Morocco*] [*Seismograph station code, US Geological Survey*] (SEIS)
**NKM** ......... University of North Carolina at Charlotte, Charlotte, NC [*OCLC symbol*] (OCLC)
**NKMA** ....... National Knitwear Manufacturers Association (EA)
**NKMB** ....... Nordisk Kollegium for Marinbiologi [*Nordic Council for Marine Biology - NCMB*] (EAIO)
**NKN** .......... North Korean Navy (CINC)
**NKO** .......... Narodnyi Komissariat Oborony [*People's Commissariat of Defense*] [*Existed until 1946*] [*USSR*]
**NKO** .......... Need to Know Only [*Espionage*]
**NKOA** ........ National Knitted Outerwear Association [*Later, NKSA*] (EA)
**N Ko Bl H Sch** ... Neues Korrespondenzblatt fuer die Hoeheren Schulen in Wuerttemberg [*A publication*]
**NKOGA** ..... Nippon Kokoka Gakkai Zasshi [*A publication*]
**NKOKD** ..... Nichidai Koko Kagaku [*A publication*]
**NKP** .......... Nakorn Phanom [*Air base northeast of Bangkok*]
**NKP** .......... Nasionale Konserwatiewe Party [*National Conservative Party*] [*South Africa*] [*Political party*] (PPW)
**NKP** .......... New Kensington [*Pennsylvania*] [*Seismograph station code, US Geological Survey*] [*Closed*] (SEIS)
**NKP** .......... Norges Kommunistiske Parti [*Norwegian Communist Party*] [*Political party*] (PPE)
**NKPA** ........ National Kraut Packers Association (EA)
**NKPA** ........ North Korean People's Army
**NKpaH** ...... Kings Park State Hospital, Kings Park, NY [*Library symbol*] [*Library of Congress*] (LCLS)
**NKpK** ........ Keuka College, Keuka Park, NY [*Library symbol*] [*Library of Congress*] (LCLS)
**NKR** .......... Nakanohara [*Japan*] [*Seismograph station code, US Geological Survey*] (SEIS)
**NKR** .......... New Kenrell Resources [*Vancouver Stock Exchange symbol*]
**NKR** .......... Nordisk Konservatorierad [*Nordic Council for Music Conservatories - NCMC*] (EAIO)
**N Kr** .......... Norveg Korona [*Norwegian Krone*] [*Monetary unit*] [*Hungary*]
**N KR** ......... Norwegian Krone [*Monetary unit*]
**NKRA** ........ Neue Keilschriftliche Rechtsurkunden aus der el-Amarna-Zeit [*Koschaker*] [*A publication*]
**NKRC** ........ No Known Relatives or Concerned
**NKS** .......... Nederlandsche Katholieke Stemmen [*A publication*]
**NKS** .......... Network of Kindred Spirits (EA)
**NKS** .......... Nordisk Kirkelig Studierad [*Nordic Council for Adult Studies in Chruch - NCASC*] (EAIO)
**NKs** ........... Nowe Ksiazki [*A publication*]

**NKSA**........ National Knitwear and Sportswear Association (EA)
**NKSA**........ Newsletter. Kafka Society of America [*A publication*]
**NKSHB**..... Naikai-Ku Suisan Kenkyusho Kenkyu Hokoku [*A publication*]
**NKSKA**..... Nippon Kagaku Seni Kenkyusho Koenshu [*A publication*]
**NKT**........... Cherry Point, NC [*Location identifier*] [*FAA*] (FAAL)
**NKT**........... Nankipoo [*Tennessee*] [*Seismograph station code, US Geological Survey*] (SEIS)
**NKT**........... None Kept in Town
**NKT**........... Norske Klassiker-Tekster [*A publication*]
**NKT**........... Nursery and Kindergarten Teachers [*A publication*]
**NKTAD**..... Journal. Gyeongsang National University. Natural Sciences [*A publication*]
**NKTRA**..... Nippon Kokan Technical Reports Overseas [*A publication*]
**Nku**............ Naamkunde [*A publication*]
**NKU**........... Nakusp Resources Ltd. [*Vancouver Stock Exchange symbol*]
**NKU**........... Nkaus [*Lesotho*] [*Airport symbol*] (OAG)
**NKUDIC**... National Kidney and Urologic Diseases Information Clearinghouse (EA)
**NKUSA**..... Neturei Karta of USA (EA)
**NKVD**........ Narodnyi Komissariat Vnutrennikh Del [*People's Commissariat of Internal Affairs (1917-1946)*] [*Also known as NARKOMVNUDEL*] [*Soviet secret police organization*]
**NKX**........... San Diego, CA [*Location identifier*] [*FAA*] (FAAL)
**NKYLR**...... Northern Kentucky Law Review [*A publication*]
**N KY L Rev**... Northern Kentucky Law Review [*A publication*]
**NKYRA**..... Nippon Kyobu Rinsho [*A publication*]
**NKyrKTs**... Ny Kyrklig Tidsskrift [*Uppsala*] [*A publication*]
**N Ky St LF**... Northern Kentucky State Law Forum [*A publication*] (DLA)
**NKYZA2**... Japanese Journal of Thoracic Diseases [*A publication*]
**NKZ**........... Neue Kirchliche Zeitschrift [*A publication*]
**NKZ**........... Nuclear Killing Zone [*Military*] [*British*]
**NKZAA**..... Nippon Kyobu Geka Gakkai Zasshi [*A publication*]
**NKZKA**..... Nippon Kinzoku Gakkai Kaiho [*A publication*]
**NL**............. Air Liberia [*ICAO designator*] (FAAC)
**NL**............. Canadian Communications Network Letter [*Telecommunications service*] [*A publication*] (TSSD)
**nl-----**.......... Great Lakes [*MARC geographic area code*] [*Library of Congress*] (LCCP)
**NL**............. Lima Public Library, Lima, NY [*Library symbol*] [*Library of Congress*] (LCLS)
**NL**............. Nailable [*Technical drawings*]
**NL**............. Natick Laboratories [*Army*] (MCD)
**NL**............. National League of Professional Baseball Clubs (EA)
**NL**............. National Liberal [*British politics*]
**NL**............. National Library [*Canada*]
**NL**............. Natur und Landschaft [*A publication*]
**NL**............. Natural Language [*Computer software*]
**NL**............. Naturalist's Library [*A publication*]
**NL**............. Naval Lighter
**NL**............. Navigating Lieutenant [*Navy*] [*British*] (ROG)
**N/L**........... Navigation/Localizer (IEEE)
**NL**............. Navy League of the United States
**NL**............. Navy List [*British military*] (DMA)
**NL**............. Nebenlager [*Branch Camp*] [*German military - World War II*]
**NL**............. Nelson's Lutwyche, English Common Pleas Reports [*A publication*] (DLA)
**NL**............. Neon Lamp (KSC)
**NL**............. Net Loss
**NL**............. Netherlands [*ANSI two-letter standard code*] (CNC)
**NL**............. Neuland [*A publication*]
**NL**............. Neurilemmona [*Oncology*]
**nl**.............. New Caledonia [*MARC country of publication code*] [*Library of Congress*] (LCCP)
**NL**............. New Latin [*Language, etc.*]
**NL**............. New Law Journal [*A publication*]
**NL**............. New Leader [*A publication*]
**NL**............. New Line [*Data processing*]
**NL**............. New London, Connecticut [*Navy*]
**N-L**........... New York State Library, Law Library, Albany, NY [*Library symbol*] [*Library of Congress*] (LCLS)
**NL**............. Night Letter
**NL**............. NL Industries, Inc. [*Formerly, National Lead Co.*] [*NYSE symbol*] (SPSG)
**NL**............. No Layers [*Aviation*] (FAAC)
**NL**............. No Liability (ADA)
**NL**............. No License [*Traffic offense charge*]
**NL**............. No Limit (NASA)
**NL**............. No Liner (DS)
**NL**............. No Load
**NL**............. Non-Labeled [*Tape*] [*Data processing*]
**NL**............. Non Licet [*It Is Not Permitted*] [*Latin*]
**NL**............. Non Liquet [*It Is Not Clear*] [*Latin*]
**NL**............. Non Longe [*Not Far*] [*Latin*]
**NL**............. Nonlinear
**NL**............. Nonlocking
**n/l**............. Normal Limits
**NL**............. Normal Lungs
**NL**............. North Latitude
**NL**............. Norwiny Literackie [*A publication*]
**NL**............. Nose Left [*Aviation*] (MCD)
**NL**............. Not Listed (AFM)
**NL**............. Not Located
**NL**............. Nouvelles Litteraires [*A publication*]
**NL**............. Numismatic Literature [*A publication*]
**NL**............. Nurses for Laughter (EA)
**NLA**........... National Landscape Association (EA)
**NLA**........... National Leather Association (EA)
**NLA**........... National Leukemia Association (EA)
**NLA**........... National Liberation Army [*Bolivia*]
**NLA**........... National Librarians Association (EA)
**NLA**........... National Libraries Authority
**NLA**........... National Library Act
**NLA**........... National Library of Australia
**NLA**........... National Library of Canada, Cataloguing Branch [*UTLAS symbol*]
**NLA**........... National Lime Association (EA)
**NLA**........... National Limousine Association (EA)
**NLA**........... National Locksmiths Association (EA)
**NLA**........... NATO Lot Acceptance (MCD)
**NLA**........... Ndola [*Zambia*] [*Airport symbol*] (OAG)
**NLA**........... Neuroleptic Anesthesia
**NLA**........... New Libertarian Alliance (EA)
**NLA**........... Next Lower Assembly (MCD)
**NLA**........... Nine Lives Associates (EA)
**NLA**........... Nonlinear Amplifier
**NLA**........... Nonuniform Linear Array
**NLA**........... Norsk Litteraer Aarbok [*A publication*]
**NLA**........... Northwestern Lumbermen's Association (EA)
**NLAA**......... National Legal Aid Association
**NLAAM**.... N-Desmethyl-levo-alpha-Acetylmethadol [*Opiate*]
**NLABS**...... Natick Laboratories [*Army*] (AABC)
**NLAC**........ National Listen America Club (EA)
**NLacOH**.... Our Lady of Victory Hospital, Lackawanna, NY [*Library symbol*] [*Library of Congress*] (LCLS)
**NLADA**..... National Legal Aid and Defender Association (EA)
**NLADA Brief**... National Legal Aid and Defender Association Briefcase [*A publication*] (DLA)
**NLakrHS**... Sachem High School South, Lake Ronkonkoma, NY [*Library symbol*] [*Library of Congress*] (LCLS)
**NLAPW**..... National League of American Pen Women (EA)
**NLar**.......... Larchmont Public Library, Larchmont, NY [*Library symbol*] [*Library of Congress*] (LCLS)
**NLAS**......... National Lum and Abner Society (EA)
**NLAS**......... Nouvelles Litteraires, Artistiques, et Scientifiques [*A publication*]
**NLauR**....... New Laurel Review [*A publication*]
**NLaw**......... Peninsula Public Library, Lawrence, NY [*Library symbol*] [*Library of Congress*] (LCLS)
**NLawCE**.... Central Elementary School, Lawrence, NY [*Library symbol*] [*Library of Congress*] (LCLS)
**NLawChE**... Cedarhurst Elementary School, Lawrence, NY [*Library symbol*] [*Library of Congress*] (LCLS)
**NLawDE**.... Donahue Elementary School, Lawrence, NY [*Library symbol*] [*Library of Congress*] (LCLS)
**NLawJH**.... Lawrence Junior High School, Lawrence, NY [*Library symbol*] [*Library of Congress*] (LCLS)
**NLawPE**.... Peninsula Elementary School, Lawrence, NY [*Library symbol*] [*Library of Congress*] (LCLS)
**NLawWE**... Wansee Elementary School, Lawrence, NY [*Library symbol*] [*Library of Congress*] (LCLS)
**NLB**........... National Library for the Blind
**NLB**........... National Library of Canada, Locations Division [*UTLAS symbol*]
**NLB**........... National Lighting Bureau (EA)
**NLB**........... Newberry Library. Bulletin [*A publication*]
**NLB**........... No Lunch Break
**NLB**........... Northeast Louisiana Business Review [*A publication*]
**NLB**........... Nuclear Light Bulb
**NLB**........... Numismatisches Literatur-Blatt [*A publication*]
**NLBA**......... National Lead Burning Association (EA)
**NLBA**......... National Licensed Beverage Association (EA)
**NLBC**......... National Livestock Brand Conference [*Later, International Livestock Brand Conference*]
**NLBD**......... National League of the Blind and Disabled [*A union*] [*British*] (DCTA)
**NLBK**......... National Loan Bank [*NASDAQ symbol*] (NQ)
**NLBMDA**... National Lumber and Building Material Dealers Association (EA)
**NLBRA**...... National Little Britches Rodeo Association (EA)
**NLBW**........ NorthLand Bank of Wisconsin, SSB [*NASDAQ symbol*] (NQ)
**NLC**........... Lemoore, CA [*Location identifier*] [*FAA*] (FAAL)
**NLC**........... NADGE [*NATO Air Defense Ground Environment*] Logistics Committee (NATG)
**NLC**........... Nalco Chemical Co. [*NYSE symbol*] (SPSG)
**NLC**........... National Laboratory Center [*Bureau of Alcohol, Tobacco, and Firearms*] [*Rockville, MD*] (GRD)
**NLC**........... National Lawyers Club (EA)
**NLC**........... National Leadership Committee [*Military*]
**NLC**........... National Leadership Council (EA)
**NLC**........... National League of Cities (EA)
**NLC**........... National Legislative Conference [*Later, NCSL*] (EA)

**NLC** .......... National Legislative Council [*Later, NCSL*]
**NLC** .......... National Liberal Club [*British*]
**NLC** .......... National Liberation Committee [*South Africa*]
**NLC** .......... National Liberty Committee (EA)
**NLC** .......... National Library of Canada
**NLC** .......... National Library of Canada, Ottawa, ON, Canada [*OCLC symbol*] (OCLC)
**NLC** .......... National Library of China
**NLC** .......... National Lifeguard Championships (EA)
**NLC** .......... National Location Code [*Civil Defense*]
**NLC** .......... National Logistical Command (MCD)
**NLC** .......... National Lutheran Council [*Later, LC/USA*] (EA)
**NLC** .......... Nederlandsche Landbouwcooperatie [*A publication*]
**NLC** .......... Negro Labor Committee [*Defunct*] (EA)
**NLC** .......... New Liberal Club [*Shin Jiyu Club*] [*Japan*] (PPW)
**NLC** .......... New Line Character [*Keyboard*] [*Data processing*] (MDG)
**NLC** .......... New Location Code [*Military*]
**NLC** .......... New London Commentary [*A publication*]
**NLC** .......... New Orleans & Lower Coast Railroad Co. [*AAR code*]
**NLC** .......... News and Letters Committee (EA)
**NLC** .......... Noctilucent Clouds
**NLC** .......... Noise-Level Cable
**NLC** .......... Nordic Literature Committee [*Copenhagen, Denmark*] (EAIO)
**NLC** .......... Northern Libraries Colloquy (EA)
**NLC** .......... Northland Library System [*Library network*]
**NLCA** .......... Norlaudanosolinecarboxylic Acid [*Biochemistry*]
**NLCA** .......... Norlithocholic Acid [*Biochemistry*]
**NLCAA** ..... National Little College Athletic Association [*Later, NSCAA*] (EA)
**NLCAB** ...... National Library of Canada Advisory Board
**NLCACBC** ... National League of Cuban American Community-Based Centers (EA)
**NLCC** ........ National Library Clearing Centre [*Australia*]
**NLCD** ........ National Liberation Council Decree [*1966-69*] [*Ghana*] [*A publication*] (DLA)
**NLCH** ........ National Legislative Council for the Handicapped (EA)
**NLCHAIBS** ... Newberry Library. Center for the History of the American Indian. Bibliographical Series [*A publication*]
**NLCM** ....... National Lutheran Campus Ministry (EA)
**NLCMDD** ... National Legal Center for the Medically Dependent and Disabled (EA)
**NLCOA** ..... National Leadership Coalition on AIDS [*Acquired Immune Deficiency Syndrome*] (EA)
**NLCP** ........ Navy Logistics Capabilities Plan
**NLCPI** ....... National Legal Center for the Public Interest (EA)
**NLCS** ......... National Computer Systems, Inc. [*NASDAQ symbol*] (NQ)
**NLCS** ......... National League Championship Series [*Baseball*]
**NLCS** ......... National Lutheran Commission on Scouting [*Defunct*] (EA)
**NLCS** ......... Nordic Leather Chemists Society [*Formerly, IVLIC Scandinavian Section*] (EA)
**NLCSDHRES** ... National Labor Committee in Support of Democracy and Human Rights in El Salvador (EA)
**NLCSJ** ....... National Lawyers Committee for Soviet Jewry (EA)
**NLCWC** ..... National Lincoln-Civil War Council (EA)
**NLD** .......... NASA Launch Director
**NLD** .......... National League for Democracy [*Burma*] [*Political party*]
**NLD** .......... National Legion of Decency [*Later, National Catholic Office for Motion Pictures*] (EA)
**NLD** .......... Naval Electrical Department [*British military*] (DMA)
**NLD** .......... Naval Lighter [*Pontoon*] Dock
**NLD** .......... Necrobiosis Lipoidica Diabeticorum [*Medicine*]
**NLD** .......... Netherlands [*ANSI three-letter standard code*] (CNC)
**NLD** .......... No Load (MSA)
**NLD** .......... Northland Bank [*Toronto Stock Exchange symbol*] [*Vancouver Stock Exchange symbol*]
**NLD** .......... Not in Line of Duty [*as of an injury*] [*Military*]
**NLD** .......... Nuevo Laredo [*Mexico*] [*Airport symbol*] (OAG)
**NLDA** ........ National Livestock Dealers Association [*Later, Livestock Marketing Association*] (EA)
**NLDA** ........ National Luggage Dealers Association (EA)
**NLDB** ........ Natural Language Data Base
**NLDC** ........ National Legal Data Center [*Defunct*] (EA)
**NLDF** ........ Naval Local Defense Forces
**NLDV** ........ National League of Disabled Voters (EA)
**NLE** .......... National Livestock Exchange (EA)
**NLE** .......... Nonlinear Element
**Nle** ............ Norleucine [*A nonessential amino acid*] [*Biochemistry*]
**NLE** .......... Nuclear Engineering International [*A publication*]
**NLEA** ........ National Lumber Exporters Association [*Later, AHEC*] (EA)
**NLEACH** .. Northleach [*England*]
**NLEC** ......... National Law Enforcement Council (EA)
**NLEC** ......... National Lutheran Educational Conference [*Later, LECNA*] (EA)
**NLEF** ......... National Legislative Education Foundation (EA)
**NLEF** ......... National Lupus Erythematosus Foundation (EA)
**NLEMA** .... National Lutheran Editors and Managers Association [*Defunct*] (EA)
**NLEOMF** ... National Law Enforcement Officers Memorial Fund (EA)
**NLer** .......... Woodward Memorial Library, LeRoy, NY [*Library symbol*] [*Library of Congress*] (LCLS)
**NLerHi** ...... LeRoy Historical Society, LeRoy, NY [*Library symbol*] [*Library of Congress*] (LCLS)
**NLETDU** ... Neuroendocrinology Letters [*A publication*]
**NLETS** ...... National Law Enforcement Telecommunications System
**NLev** .......... Levittown Public Library, Levittown, NY [*Library symbol*] [*Library of Congress*] (LCLS)
**NLevI** ......... Island Trees Public Library, Levittown, NY [*Library symbol*] [*Library of Congress*] (LCLS)
**NLevIH** ..... Island Trees High School, Levittown, NY [*Library symbol*] [*Library of Congress*] (LCLS)
**NLevIJ** ....... Island Trees Memorial Junior High School, Levittown, NY [*Library symbol*] [*Library of Congress*] (LCLS)
**NLew** ......... Lewiston Public Library, Lewiston, NY [*Library symbol*] [*Library of Congress*] (LCLS)
**NLewStM** ... Mount Saint Mary's Hospital, Lewiston, NY [*Library symbol*] [*Library of Congress*] (LCLS)
**NLf** ............ Little Falls Public Library, Little Falls, NY [*Library symbol*] [*Library of Congress*] (LCLS)
**NLF** .......... National Fuelcorp Ltd. [*Vancouver Stock Exchange symbol*]
**NLF** .......... National League of Families of Prisoners and Missing in Southeast Asia
**NLF** .......... National Legal Foundation (EA)
**NLF** .......... National Liberal Federation [*British*]
**NLF** .......... National Liberation Front [*Burma*] [*Political party*] (PD)
**NLF** .......... National Liberation Front [*Vietnam*] [*Political party*]
**NLF** .......... National Liberation Front [*South Africa*] [*Political party*] (PD)
**NLF** .......... National Liberation Front [*Aden*] [*Political party*]
**NLF** .......... Navigation Light Flasher
**NLF** .......... Nearest Landing Field
**NLF** .......... Neutral Lipid Fraction [*Biochemistry*]
**NLF** .......... New Leadership Fund (EA)
**NLF** .......... No-Load Funds
**NLF** .......... North Luzon Force [*Army*] [*World War II*]
**NLFA** ........ National Lamb Feeders Association (EA)
**NLFA** ........ National Livestock Feeders Association [*Later, NCA*] (EA)
**NLFED** ...... Naval Landing Force Equipment Depot
**NLFM** ....... Noise-Level Frequency Monitor
**NLFMA** ..... National Law Firm Marketing Association (EA)
**NLFPA** ...... National Liberation Front Party Apparatus [*Algeria*]
**NLFSV** ...... National Liberation Front of South Vietnam [*Political party*]
**NLFT** ........ No-Load Frame Time
**NLG** .......... National Gas & Oil Corp. [*AMEX symbol*] (SPSG)
**NLG** .......... National Lawyers Guild (EA)
**NLG** .......... Nelson Lagoon [*Alaska*] [*Airport symbol*] (OAG)
**NLG** .......... North Louisiana & Gulf Railroad Co. [*AAR code*]
**NLG** .......... Nose Landing Gear [*Aviation*]
**NLG** .......... Null Line Gap
**NLG** .......... Numismatic Literary Guild (EA)
**NLGA** ........ National Lumber Grading Agency [*Canada*]
**NLGAWVA** ... National Legion of Greek-American War Veterans in America (EA)
**NLGC** ........ Noise-Level Gain Control (MCD)
**NLGDA** ..... National Lawn and Garden Distributors Association (EA)
**NLGHF** ..... National Lesbian and Gay Health Foundation (EA)
**NLGI** ......... National Lubricating Grease Institute (EA)
**NLGI Spokesman** ... NLGI [*National Lubricating Grease Institute*] Spokesman [*A publication*]
**NLGPDC** ... National Lawyer's Guild Peace and Disarmament Committee [*Later, NLGPDS*] (EA)
**NLGPDS** ... National Lawyer's Guild Peace and Disarmament Subcommittee (EA)
**NLGQ** ........ National Lawyers Guild Quarterly [*A publication*] (DLA)
**NLH** .......... New Lao Hak [*Lao Patriotic Front*] [*Vietnam*] [*Political party*] (CINC)
**NLH** .......... New Life Hamlet [*See also NLHS, NLHZ*] [*Military*] [*Vietnam*]
**NLH** .......... New Literary History [*A publication*]
**NLHA** ........ National Leased Housing Association [*Washington, DC*] (EA)
**NLHRSA** ... National Left-Handers Racquet Sports Association (EA)
**NLHS** ........ New Lao Hak Sat [*New Life Hamlet*] [*See also NLH*] [*Military*] [*Vietnam*] (CINC)
**NLHZ** ........ New Lao Hak Zat [*New Life Hamlet*] [*See also NLH, NLHS*] [*Military*] [*Vietnam*] (CINC)
**NLI** ............ National Landscape Institute
**NLI** ............ National Leadership Institute (EA)
**NLI** ............ National Limestone Institute [*Later, NSA*] (EA)
**NLI** ............ Neodymium LASER Illuminator
**NLI** ............ Newmark & Lewis, Incorporated [*AMEX symbol*] (SPSG)
**NLI** ............ Noise Limit Indicator
**NLI** ............ Nonlinear Interpolating (IEEE)
**NLI** ............ Northern Lights College Library [*UTLAS symbol*]
**NLib** .......... Liberty Public Library, Liberty, NY [*Library symbol*] [*Library of Congress*] (LCLS)
**NLicL** ......... LaGuardia Community College of the City University of New York, Long Island City, NY [*Library symbol*] [*Library of Congress*] (LCLS)
**NLicP** ......... PepsiCo, Inc., Research Library, Long Island, NY [*Library symbol*] [*Library of Congress*] (LCLS)
**NLIF** .......... Nonlinear Interference Filter [*Electronics*]
**NLIHC** ...... National Low Income Housing Coalition (EA)

**NLin**.......... Lindenhurst Memorial Library, Lindenhurst, NY [*Library symbol*] [*Library of Congress*] (LCLS)
**NLin**.......... Nonlinear
**NLing**......... Notes on Linguistics [*A publication*]
**NLIS**.......... National Lesbian Information Service
**NLIS**.......... Navy Logistics Information System
**NLISA**....... National League of Insured Savings Associations [*Later, NSLL*] (EA)
**NListy**........ Numismaticke Listy [*A publication*]
**NLit**.......... Neue Literatur [*A publication*]
**NLiW**......... Nowiny Literackie i Wydawnicze [*A publication*]
**NLJ**........... Nagpur Law Journal [*India*] [*A publication*] (DLA)
**NLJ**........... New Law Journal [*A publication*] (ILCA)
**NLJMA**..... Netherlands Journal of Medicine [*A publication*]
**NLK**........... Neuroleukin [*Biochemistry*]
**NLK**........... Norfolk Island [*Airport symbol*] (OAG)
**NLKF**......... Nonlinear Kalman Filter
**NLL**........... National Lacrosse League [*Disbanded*]
**NLL**........... National Lending Library for Science and Technology [*Later, BLLD*] [*British Library*]
**NLL**........... National Liberal League [*Later, NLSCS*] (EA)
**NLL**........... Negative Logic Level
**NLL**........... New England School of Law Library, Boston, MA [*OCLC symbol*] (OCLC)
**NLL**........... New Library of Law [*Harrisburg, PA*] [*A publication*] (DLA)
**NLL**........... New Library of Law and Equity [*England*] [*A publication*] (DLA)
**NLL**........... New Life League (EA)
**NLL**........... Northern Limit Line [*Korea*]
**NLL**........... Nullagine [*Australia*] [*Airport symbol*] (OAG)
**NLLC**......... National Labor Law Center (EA)
**NLL Rev**.... NLL Review [*A publication*]
**NLLSQ**...... Nonlinear Least Squares [*Computer program*]
**NLLST**...... National Lending Library for Science and Technology [*Later, BLL*] [*British*]
**NLL Transl Bull** ... National Lending Library. Translations Bulletin [*A publication*]
**NLM**.......... National Language Mediator
**NLM**.......... National Library of Medicine [*Public Health Service*] [*Bethesda, MD*] [*Database producer*]
**NLM**.......... National Library of Medicine, Bethesda, MD [*OCLC symbol*] (OCLC)
**NLM**.......... Naval Ordnance Lab [*Maryland*] [*Seismograph station code, US Geological Survey*] [*Closed*] (SEIS)
**NLM**.......... Nederlands Luchtvaart Maatschappij [*Airline*] [*Netherlands*]
**NLM**.......... Neues Lausitzisches Magazin [*A publication*]
**NLM**.......... New Library of Music [*A publication*]
**NLM**.......... Noise-Level Monitor [*SONAR*]
**NLM**.......... Nonlinear Mapping (MCD)
**NLM**.......... Nuclear Level Mixing [*Physics*]
**NLMA**....... National Lumber Manufacturers Association [*Later, NFPA*] (EA)
**NLMA**....... Northeastern Lumber Manufacturers Association
**NLMC**....... National League of Masonic Clubs (EA)
**NLMC**....... National Library of Medicine. Current Catalog [*A publication*]
**NLMC**....... Nordic Labour Market Committee (EAIO)
**NLMC**....... North Lily Mining Company [*Moss Beach, CA*] [*NASDAQ symbol*] (NQ)
**NLMF**....... National Labor-Management Foundation (EA)
**NLMF**....... Nucleus of Longitudinal Muscle Fiber
**NLMFA**..... No-Load Mutual Fund Association (EA)
**NLM News** ... National Library of Medicine. News [*A publication*]
**NLMS**........ Navy Logistics Management School
**NLMS**........ Numerical Largeness of More Significant [*Statistics*]
**NLM Tech Bull** ... National Library of Medicine. Technical Bulletin [*A publication*]
**NLMWT**... National Liberation Movement of Western Togoland
**NLN**........... National League for Nursing (EA)
**NLN**........... National Library Network
**NLN**........... Neo-Latin News [*Queens College*] [*A publication*]
**NLN**........... Nepean Libraries Network [*Australia*]
**NLN**........... New Line Cinema [*AMEX symbol*] (SPSG)
**NLN**........... New Lintex Minerals [*Vancouver Stock Exchange symbol*]
**NLN**........... No Longer Needed (AABC)
**NLN**........... Nordiska Lakemedelsnamnden [*Nordic Council on Medicines - NCM*] (EAIO)
**NLN**........... Northwest Missouri Library Network [*Library network*]
**NLNA**........ National Landscape Nurserymen's Association [*Later, NLA*] (EA)
**NLN News** ... NLN (National League for Nursing) News [*A publication*]
**NLN Publ**.. National League for Nursing. Publications [*A publication*]
**NLNR**........ Nonlinear (MSA)
**NLNS**........ New Lightweight Night Sight (INF)
**NLO**........... Nasolacrimal Occlusion [*Medicine*]
**NLO**........... Naval Liaison Officer
**NLO**........... No-Limit Order
**NLO**........... Nonlinear Optics (IEEE)
**NLob**.......... Long Beach Public Library, Long Beach, NY [*Library symbol*] [*Library of Congress*] (LCLS)
**NLobES**..... East School, Long Beach, NY [*Library symbol*] [*Library of Congress*] (LCLS)
**NLobH**....... Long Beach Memorial Hospital, Long Beach, NY [*Library symbol*] [*Library of Congress*] (LCLS)
**NLobJH**.... Long Beach Junior High School, Long Beach, NY [*Library symbol*] [*Library of Congress*] (LCLS)
**NLobLE**..... Lido Elementary School, Long Beach, NY [*Library symbol*] [*Library of Congress*] (LCLS)
**NLobLS**..... Lindell Boulevard School, Long Beach, NY [*Library symbol*] [*Library of Congress*] (LCLS)
**NLobMS**.... Magnolia School, Long Beach, NY [*Library symbol*] [*Library of Congress*] (LCLS)
**NLobSH**.... Long Beach Senior High School, Long Beach, NY [*Library symbol*] [*Library of Congress*] (LCLS)
**NLobWE**... West Elementary School, Long Beach, NY [*Library symbol*] [*Library of Congress*] (LCLS)
**NLock**........ Lockport Public Library, Lockport, NY [*Library symbol*] [*Library of Congress*] (LCLS)
**NLockH**..... Lockport Memorial Hospital, Doctor's Library, Lockport, NY [*Library symbol*] [*Library of Congress*] (LCLS)
**NLockMt**... Mount View Health Facility, Lockport, NY [*Library symbol*] [*Library of Congress*] (LCLS)
**NLockNHi**... Niagara County Historical Society, Lockport, NY [*Library symbol*] [*Library of Congress*] (LCLS)
**NLOGM**.... Navy Liaison Office for Guided Missiles (MCD)
**NLOMA**.... National Lutheran Outdoors Ministry Association (EA)
**NLON**........ New London, Inc. [*NASDAQ symbol*] (NQ)
**NLONTEVDET** ... New London Test and Evaluation Detachment [*Navy*]
**NLOP**........ Nonlinear Optical Polymer
**NLOrLanyard** ... Netherlands Orange Lanyard [*Military decoration*] (AABC)
**NLOS**........ Natural Language Operating System
**NLOS**........ Nonline of Sight
**NLOS-AT/AD** ... Nonline-of-Sight Antitank/Air Defense Vehicle [*Army*]
**NLouvGS**... Church of Jesus Christ of Latter-Day Saints, Genealogical Society Library, Albany New York Stake Branch, Loudonville, NY [*Library symbol*] [*Library of Congress*] (LCLS)
**NLouvS**....... Siena College, Loudonville, NY [*Library symbol*] [*Library of Congress*] (LCLS)
**NLowLH**.... Lewis County General Hospital, Medical Library, Lowville, NY [*Library symbol*] [*Library of Congress*] (LCLS)
**NLp**............ Lake Placid Public Library, Lake Placid, NY [*Library symbol*] [*Library of Congress*] (LCLS)
**NLP**........... Narodnoliberalna Partiia [*National Liberal Party*] [*Bulgaria*] [*Political party*] (PPE)
**NLP**........... National Land for People [*An association*] (EA)
**NLP**........... National Language Policy [*Australia*]
**NLP**........... National League of Postmasters of the United States
**NLP**........... National Liberation Party [*Gambia*] [*Political party*] (PPW)
**NLP**........... National Productivity Review [*A publication*]
**NLP**........... National Realty LP [*AMEX symbol*] (SPSG)
**NLP**........... Natural Language Processing [*Data processing*]
**NLP**........... Neglected Language Program
**NLP**........... Neighborhood Loan Program
**NLP**........... Nelspruit [*South Africa*] [*Airport symbol*] (OAG)
**NLP**........... Net Level Premium [*Insurance*]
**NLP**........... Neurolinguistic Programming
**NLP**........... No Light Perception [*Ophthalmology*]
**NLP**........... Nonlinear Programming [*Algorithm*]
**NLPC**......... n-Laurylpyridinium Chloride [*Detergent*]
**NLPGA**...... National LP-Gas Association (EA)
**NLPGA Times** ... National LP-Gas Association Times [*United States*] [*A publication*]
**NLPI**.......... National Lampoon, Incorporated [*NASDAQ symbol*] (NQ)
**NLPLG**...... National Language Policy Liaison Group [*Australia*]
**NLPM**........ National League of Postmasters of the United States (EA)
**NLPNEF**... National Licensed Practical Nurses Educational Foundation (EA)
**NLPR**......... National Laboratory of Psychical Research [*British*]
**NLPS**......... Natural Language Processing Segment [*Data processing*]
**NLpSA**....... Lake Placid School of Art, Fine Arts Library, Lake Placid, NY [*Library symbol*] [*Library of Congress*] (LCLS)
**NLpT**......... Tissue Culture Association, Lake Placid, NY [*Library symbol*] [*Library of Congress*] (LCLS)
**NLPTL**....... National Lutheran Parent-Teacher League (EA)
**NLQ**........... Natural Language Query [*Software*] [*Battelle Software Products Center*]
**NLQ**........... Near Letter Quality [*Computer printer*]
**NLQ**........... Nigeria Lawyer's Quarterly [*A publication*] (DLA)
**NLQR**......... Nigeria Law Quarterly Review [*A publication*] (DLA)
**NLR**........... Dine Bizaad Nanil' Iih/Navajo Language Review [*A publication*]
**NLR**........... Nagpur Law Reports [*India*] [*A publication*] (DLA)
**NLR**........... Natal Law Reports [*India*] [*A publication*] (DLA)
**NLR**........... National Liquid Reserves Money Market Fund
**NLR**........... National Review (London) [*A publication*]
**NLR**........... NATO Liaison Representative (MCD)
**NLR**........... Neodymium LASER Range-Finder
**NLR**........... New Law Reports [*Ceylon*] [*A publication*] (DLA)
**N-LR**.......... New York State Library, Legislative Reference Library, Albany, NY [*Library symbol*] [*Library of Congress*] (LCLS)
**NLR**........... Newfoundland Law Reports [*A publication*] (DLA)
**NLR**........... Nigeria Law Reports [*A publication*] (DLA)

**NLR** .......... Noise Load Ratio
**NLR** .......... Nolan Resources Ltd. [*Vancouver Stock Exchange symbol*]
**NLR** .......... Nonlinear Regression [*Mathematics*]
**NLR** .......... Nonlinear Resistive
**NLR** .......... North London Railway [*British*]
**NLR** .......... Nyasaland Law Reports [*A publication*] (DLA)
**NLR** .......... South African Law Reports, Natal Province Division [*1910-46*] [*A publication*] (DLA)
**NLRA** ........ National Labor Relations Act [*1935*]
**NLRA** ........ National Lakes and Rivers Association [*Defunct*] (EA)
**NLRB** ........ National Labor Relations Board [*Department of Labor*] [*Washington, DC*]
**NLRB** ........ National Labor Relations Board Decisions and Orders [*A publication*] (DLA)
**NLRB Ann Rep** ... National Labor Relations Board Annual Report [*A publication*] (DLA)
**NLRB Dec** ... National Labor Relations Board Decisions [*A publication*] (DLA)
**NLRB Dec CCH** ... NLRB [*National Labor Relations Board*] Decisions. Commerce Clearing House [*A publication*]
**NLRBP** ...... National Labor Relations Board Professional Association
**NLRBPA** ... National Labor Relations Board Professional Association (EA)
**NLRBU** ..... National Labor Relations Board Union (EA)
**NLRCA** ...... National Lilac Rabbit Club of America (EA)
**NLRCCAP** ... National Legal Resource Center for Child Advocacy and Protection [*Later, ABACCL*] (EA)
**Nl Res Men Health & Behav Sc** ... Newsletter for Research in Mental Health and Behavioral Sciences [*A publication*]
**N L Rev** ...... New Literature Review [*A publication*]
**NL Rev** ....... Northeastern Law Review [*A publication*] (DLA)
**NLRG** ........ Navy Long-Range Guidance
**NLR (OS)** .. Natal Law Reports, Old Series [*1867-72*] [*South Africa*] [*A publication*] (DLA)
**NLRSS** ...... Navy Long-Range Strategic Study
**NLRU** ........ Nordens Liberale og Radikale Ungdom [*Nordic Liberal and Radical Youth*] (EAIO)
**NLS** .......... Nassau Library System [*Library network*]
**NLS** .......... National Language Support [*Data processing*] (PCM)
**NLS** .......... National Lending Service [*Australia*]
**NLS** .......... National Library Service for the Blind and Physically Handicapped [*Also, NLS/BPH*] [*Library of Congress*]
**NLS** .......... National Longitudinal Survey [*Statistics*]
**NLS** .......... National Longitudinal Surveys of Labor Market Experience [*Ohio State University*] [*Columbus*] [*Information service or system*] (IID)
**NLS** .......... Natural Law Society (EA)
**NLS** .......... Natuur en Milieu [*A publication*]
**NLS** .......... Navigating Light System
**NLS** .......... Negative Lens Systems
**NLS** .......... Neodymium LASER System
**NLS** .......... Network Library System
**NLS** .......... No-Load Speed
**NLS** .......... No-Load Start
**NLS** .......... Non-Linear Least Squares [*Statistics*]
**NLS** .......... Nonlinear Smoothing
**NLS** .......... Nonlinear Systems
**NLS** .......... Nordic Language Secretariat [*See also SLN*] [*Oslo, Norway*] (EAIO)
**NLS** .......... Nordiske Laererorganisationers Samrad [*Council of Nordic Teachers' Association*] (EAIO)
**NLS** .......... North Carolina Central University, School of Library Science, Durham, NC [*OCLC symbol*] (OCLC)
**NLS** .......... Nuclear Location Sequence [*Cytology*]
**NLS** .......... On-Line System [*Stanford Research Institute*] [*Data processing*]
**NLSA** ......... National Liquor Stores Association (EA)
**NLSA** ......... National Lithuanian Society of America (EA)
**NLSA** ......... National Locksmith Suppliers Association (EA)
**NLSBA** ...... National Lincoln Sheep Breeders' Association (EA)
**NLS/BPH** ... National Library Service for the Blind and Physically Handicapped [*Also, NLS*] [*Library of Congress*] [*Data processing*] (IID)
**NLSC** ......... Navy Lockheed Service Center
**NLSC** ......... Northeastern Louisiana State College
**NLSCS** ...... National League for Separation of Church and State (EA)
**NLsH** ......... Frederic R. Harris, Inc., Lake Success, NY [*Library symbol*] [*Library of Congress*] (LCLS)
**NLSI** .......... National Library of Science and Invention [*British*] (DIT)
**NLSI** .......... Nationwide Legal Services, Incorporated [*Hartsdale, NY*] [*NASDAQ symbol*] (NQ)
**NLSL** ......... North Land Savings & Loan Association [*Ashland, WI*] [*NASDAQ symbol*] (NQ)
**NLsM** ........ Medical Society of the State of New York, Lake Success, NY [*Library symbol*] [*Library of Congress*] (LCLS)
**NLSMA** ..... National Longitudinal Study of Mathematical Abilities
**NLSMB** ..... National Live Stock and Meat Board (EA)
**NLSP** ......... Neighborhood Legal Services Program
**NLSPA** ....... National Live Stock Producers Association (EA)
**NLSPN** ...... National List of Scientific Plant Names [*Department of Agriculture*] (IID)
**NLSS** ......... Navy Logistics Systems School
**NLSS** ......... New London Submarine School [*Navy*] (MCD)
**NLST** ......... Nonlisted Name [*Telecommunications*] (TEL)
**NLT** .......... Net Long Ton
**NLT** .......... New London Training Unit [*Navy*]
**NLT** .......... Night Letter [*Telegraphic communications*]
**NLT** .......... Normal Lube-Oil Tank (MSA)
**NLT** .......... Normal Lymphocyte Transfer [*Immunochemistry*]
**NLT** .......... Not Later Than
**NLT** .......... Not Less Than
**NLTA** ........ National League of Teachers' Associations [*Defunct*] (EA)
**NLTC** ......... National Livestock Tax Committee [*Later, NCA*] (EA)
**NLTE** ......... Nonlocal Thermodynamic Equilibrium
**NLTF** ......... National Leather Trades Federation [*A union*] [*British*]
**NLTNIF** .... National Low-Temperature Neutron Irradiation Facility [*Oak Ridge, TN*] [*Department of Energy*] (GRD)
**NLTRA** ...... National Land Title Reclamation Association (EA)
**NLTS** ......... Near Launch Tracking System
**NLTSD** ...... National Times [*A publication*]
**NLUF** ......... National LASER Users Facility [*Rochester, NY*] [*Department of Energy*] (GRD)
**NLUS** ........ Navy League of the United States (EA)
**NLUTS** ...... National Labourers' Union Trade Society [*British*]
**NLv** ........... Locust Valley Public Library, Locust Valley, NY [*Library symbol*] [*Library of Congress*] (LCLS)
**NLV** .......... Narcissus Latent Virus
**NLvBI** ........ Bayville Intermediate School, Locust Valley, NY [*Library symbol*] [*Library of Congress*] (LCLS)
**NLvHS** ...... Locust Valley High School, Locust Valley, NY [*Library symbol*] [*Library of Congress*] (LCLS)
**NLvI** .......... Locust Valley Intermediate School, Locust Valley, NY [*Library symbol*] [*Library of Congress*] (LCLS)
**NLVP** ......... NASA Launch Vehicle Planning Project (MCD)
**NLVR** ........ Nonlinear Vacuum Regulator Valve [*Automotive engineering*]
**NLW** ......... National Lawyers Wives (EA)
**NLW** ......... National Library Week
**NLW** ......... Neue Literarische Welt [*A publication*]
**NLW** ......... Nominal Line Width
**NLW** ......... Nowiny Literackie i Wydawnicze [*A publication*]
**NLWF** ........ Futuna/Pointe Vele [*Wallis and Futuna Islands*] [*ICAO location identifier*] (ICLI)
**NLWJ** ........ National Library of Wales. Journal [*A publication*]
**NLW Journ** ... National Library of Wales. Journal [*A publication*]
**NLWW** ...... Wallis/Hifo [*Wallis and Futuna Islands*] [*ICAO location identifier*] (ICLI)
**NLX** .......... NLX Resources, Inc. [*Toronto Stock Exchange symbol*]
**NLY** .......... Northerly
**NLynd** ........ Yates Community Library, Lyndonville, NY [*Library symbol*] [*Library of Congress*] (LCLS)
**NLyndHi** ... Lyndonville Historical Society, Lyndonville, NY [*Library symbol*] [*Library of Congress*] (LCLS)
**NLynWPE** ... Waverly Park Elementary School, Lynbrook, NY [*Library symbol*] [*Library of Congress*] (LCLS)
**NLZ** .......... Numismatische Literatur-Zeitung [*A publication*]
**nm-----** ....... Gulf of Mexico [*MARC geographic area code*] [*Library of Congress*] (LCCP)
**NM** ........... Mount Cook Airlines [*New Zealand*] [*ICAO designator*] (FAAC)
**NM** ........... Nachmittag [*Afternoon*] [*German*]
**nm** ............ Nanometer
**nM** ............ Nanomole
**NM** ........... Narrow Market [*Investment term*]
**NM** ........... National Magazine Co. Ltd. [*Publisher*] [*British*]
**NM** ........... National Match
**NM** ........... National Media Corp. [*NYSE symbol*] (SPSG)
**NM** ........... National Motor Volunteers [*British military*] (DMA)
**NM** ........... National Music Council. Bulletin [*A publication*]
**NM** ........... Nationalist Movement (EA)
**NM** ........... Nations Ministries (EA)
**NM** ........... Natriuretic Material [*Physiology*]
**NM** ........... Naturally Occurring Mutants
**NM** ........... Naturwissenschaft und Medizin [*A publication*]
**NM** ........... Nautical Mile [*6,080 feet*]
**NM** ........... Naval Magazine [*A publication*]
**NM** ........... Naval Mission (AFIT)
**NM** ........... Navigation Multiplexer [*Navy*] (CAAL)
**NM** ........... Navy Mines (MCD)
**NM** ........... Near Match (MCD)
**nm** ............ Near-Metacentric [*Botany*]
**NM** ........... Near Mint [*Condition*] [*Numismatics, deltiology, etc.*]
**NM** ........... Negro Male
**NM** ........... Neiman-Marcus
**NM** ........... Net Imports [*Economics*]
**NM** ........... Netherlands Museum [*Later, HHT*] (EA)
**NM** ........... Network Manager (MCD)
**NM** ........... Neuphilologische Mitteilungen [*A publication*]
**NM** ........... Neuromuscular
**NM** ........... Neusprachliche Mitteilungen aus Wissenschaft und Praxis [*A publication*]
**N & M** ........ Nevile and Manning's English King's Bench Reports [*A publication*] (DLA)
**NM** ........... New Measurement
**NM** ........... New Mexico [*Postal code*]

**NM** .......... New Mexico Reports [*A publication*]
**Nm** .......... New Mexico State Library, Santa Fe, NM [*Library symbol*] [*Library of Congress*] (LCLS)
**NM** .......... New Mexico Supreme Court Reports [*A publication*] (DLA)
**NM** .......... New Mexico Territorial Court (DLA)
**NM** .......... New Moon [*Moon phase*]
**N-M** .......... New York State Library, Medical Library, Albany, NY [*Library symbol*] [*Library of Congress*] (LCLS)
**NM** .......... Newly Molded
**N/m** .......... Newton per Meter
**Nm** .......... Nicotiana mesophilia [*Tobacco*]
**NM** .......... Nictitating Membrane [*Animal anatomy*]
**NM** .......... Niederdeutsche Mitteilungen [*A publication*]
**NM** .......... Night Message
**NM** .......... Nitrogen Mustard [*Also, HN, M, MBA*] [*Antineoplastic drug, war-gas base*]
**NM** .......... No Mark
**NM** .......... No Message
**NM** .......... Nocte et Mane [*Night and Morning*] [*Pharmacy*]
**N et M** .......... Nocte et Mane [*Night and Morning*] [*Pharmacy*]
**NM** .......... Nodular Melanoma [*Oncology*]
**NM** .......... Noise Meter (MSA)
**NM** .......... Nomen Masculinam [*Masculine Noun*] [*Latin*] (ROG)
**NM** .......... Nonmetallic
**NM** .......... Nonmotile [*Microbiology*]
**NM** .......... Nonwhite Male
**NM** .......... Nordiska Metallarbetaresekretariatet [*Nordic Metalworkers Secretariat - NMS*] (EAIO)
**NM** .......... NorthEastern Mortgage Co., Inc. [*AMEX symbol*] (SPSG)
**NM** .......... Northern Miner [*A publication*]
**NM** .......... Northern Miscellany [*A publication*]
**N/M** .......... Not Marked [*Business term*]
**NM** .......... Not Married
**NM** .......... Not Measurable [*or Measured*]
**n/m** .......... Not Mentioned [*Medicine*]
**NM** .......... Notice to Mariners
**NM** .......... Noun Modifier [*Linguistics*]
**N & M** .......... November and May [*Denotes semiannual payments of interest or dividends in these months*] [*Business term*]
**NM** .......... Nuclear Magnetic
**NM** .......... Nuclear Magnetron (MSA)
**NM** .......... Nuclear Medicine
**Nm** .......... Numbers [*Old Testament book*]
**NM** .......... Numismatiska Meddelanden [*A publication*]
**NM** .......... Nutmeg (ADA)
**NM** .......... Nux Moschata [*Nutmeg*] [*Pharmacology*] (ROG)
**NmA** .......... Albuquerque Public Library, Albuquerque, NM [*Library symbol*] [*Library of Congress*] (LCLS)
**NMA** .......... Miami, FL [*Location identifier*] [*FAA*] (FAAL)
**NMA** .......... N-Methylaspartate [*Organic chemistry*]
**NMA** .......... N-Methylaspartic Acid [*An amino acid*]
**NMA** .......... N-Methylolacrylamide [*Organic chemistry*]
**NMA** .......... Naphthalenemethylamine [*Reagent*] [*Organic chemistry*]
**NMA** .......... Nashville Music Association [*Later, NEA*] (EA)
**NMA** .......... National Management Association [*Dayton, OH*] (EA)
**NMA** .......... National Management Award [*GAMC*]
**NMA** .......... National Marina Association (EA)
**NMA** .......... National Meat Association [*Formerly, NIMPA*] (EA)
**NMA** .......... National Medical Association (EA)
**NMA** .......... National Microfilm Association [*Later, National Micrographics Association, now AIIM*] [*Trade association*]
**NMA** .......... National Micrographics Association [*Later, AIIM*] [*Trade association*] (EA)
**NMA** .......... National Midwives Association (EA)
**NMA** .......... National Military Authority (NATG)
**NMA** .......... National Mime Association [*Later, NMTA*] (EA)
**NMA** .......... National Motorists Association (EA)
**NMA** .......... National Museum of Antiquities in Scotland
**NMA** .......... National Mustang Association (EA)
**NMA** .......... NATO Military Authorities (NATG)
**NMA** .......... Natural Marketing Association [*Woodland Hills, CA*] (EA)
**NMA** .......... Navy Mutual Aid Association (EA)
**NMA** .......... Negligee Manufacturers Association [*Later, IAMA*]
**NMA** .......... Netherlands Military Administration [*World War II*]
**NMA** .......... Neurogenic Muscular Atrophy [*Medicine*]
**NMA** .......... New Music Articles [*A publication*]
**NMA** .......... Nicaragua Medical Aid (EA)
**NMA** .......... Noma Industries Ltd. [*Toronto Stock Exchange symbol*]
**NMA** .......... Non-Marine Association [*Lloyd's Underwriters*] (AIA)
**NMA** .......... Nonmass Analyzed [*Photovoltaic energy systems*]
**NMA** .......... Nonmedical Attendant (AABC)
**NMA** .......... Nonprofit Management Association (EA)
**NMA** .......... Nonresonant Magnetic Amplifier
**NMA** .......... Normal Method of Acquisition (MCD)
**NMA** .......... Northwest Mining Association (EA)
**NMA** .......... Nuveen Municipal Advantage Fund [*NYSE symbol*] (SPSG)
**NMA** .......... University of Albuquerque, Albuquerque, NM [*OCLC symbol*] (OCLC)
**NMa** .......... Wead Library, Malone, NY [*Library symbol*] [*Library of Congress*] (LCLS)
**NMAA** .......... National Machine Accountants Association [*Later, DPMA*]
**NMAA** .......... National Metal Awning Association [*Defunct*] (EA)
**NMAA** .......... National Mobilization Against AIDS [*Acquired Immune Deficiency Syndrome*] (EA)
**NMAA** .......... National Museum of African Art [*Smithsonian Institution*]
**NMAA** .......... Navy Mutual Aid Association
**NmAACF** .. ACF Industries, Inc., Albuquerque, NM [*Library symbol*] [*Library of Congress*] (LCLS)
**NmAAF** ..... United States Air Force, Weapons Laboratory, Kirtland Air Force Base, Albuquerque, NM [*Library symbol*] [*Library of Congress*] (LCLS)
**NmAAM** .... United States Army, Medical Library, Sandia Base, Albuquerque, NM [*Library symbol*] [*Library of Congress*] (LCLS)
**NMAA Newsletter** ... Nursing Mothers' Association of Australia. Newsletter [*A publication*] (APTA)
**NMAB** ....... N-Monochloro(amino)butyric Acid [*Organic chemistry*]
**NMAB** ....... National Market Advisory Board [*SEC*]
**NMAB** ....... National Materials Advisory Board (EA)
**N-MAb** ...... Neutralizing Monoclonal Antibody [*Immunology*]
**NMAC** ....... National Medical Audiovisual Center [*of the National Library of Medicine*] [*Absorbed by LHNCBC*] (EA)
**NMAC** ....... National Minority AIDS [*Acquired Immune Deficiency Syndrome*] Council (EA)
**NMAC** ....... Naval Missile and Astronautics Center
**NMAC** ....... Near Midair Collision
**NMAC** ....... Nissan Motor Acceptance Corp.
**NM Acad Sci Bull** ... New Mexico Academy of Science. Bulletin [*A publication*]
**N & Macn** .. Neville and Macnamara's Railway and Canal Cases [*1855-1950*] [*A publication*] (DLA)
**NmADAS** .. United States Defense Atomic Support Agency, Sandia Base, Albuquerque, NM [*Library symbol*] [*Library of Congress*] (LCLS)
**NmA-EP** .... Albuquerque Public Library, Ernie Pyle Memorial Branch, Albuquerque, NM [*Library symbol*] [*Library of Congress*] (LCLS)
**NMAF** ....... National Medical Association Foundation [*Defunct*] (EA)
**NMAG** ....... Naval Magazine [*A publication*]
**NMAG** ....... Nonmagnetic (MSA)
**N Mag Ca** .. New Magistrates' Cases [*England*] [*A publication*] (DLA)
**NmAGen** .... New Mexico Genealogical Society, Inc., Albuquerque, NM [*Library symbol*] [*Library of Congress*] (LCLS)
**NM Ag Exp** ... New Mexico. Agricultural Experiment Station. Publications [*A publication*]
**N Mag Hanau** ... Neues Magazin fuer Hanauische Geschichte [*A publication*]
**NM Agric Exp Stn Bull** ... New Mexico. Agricultural Experiment Station. Bulletin [*A publication*]
**NM Agric Exp Stn Res Rep** ... New Mexico. Agricultural Experiment Station. Research Report [*A publication*]
**NmAGS** ..... Church of Jesus Christ of Latter-Day Saints, Genealogical Society Library, Albuquerque Branch, Albuquerque, NM [*Library symbol*] [*Library of Congress*] (LCLS)
**NMah** ........ Mahopac Library Association, Mahopac, NY [*Library symbol*] [*Library of Congress*] (LCLS)
**NMAHSTC** ... National Museum of American History, Science, Technology, and Culture [*Smithsonian Institution*]
**NMA Journal** ... National Microfilm Association. Journal [*A publication*]
**NmAl** ........ Alamogordo Public Library, Alamogordo, NM [*Library symbol*] [*Library of Congress*] (LCLS)
**NmAL** ........ Lovelace Foundation for Medical Education and Research, Albuquerque, NM [*Library symbol*] [*Library of Congress*] (LCLS)
**NMAL** ....... Notes on Modern American Literature [*A publication*]
**NmA-LG** .... Albuquerque Public Library, Los Griegos Branch, Albuquerque, NM [*Library symbol*] [*Library of Congress*] (LCLS)
**NMalv** ........ Malverne Public Library, Malverne, NY [*Library symbol*] [*Library of Congress*] (LCLS)
**NMalvDE** ... Davison Elementary School, Malverne, NY [*Library symbol*] [*Library of Congress*] (LCLS)
**NMalvLE** .. Lindner Elementary School, Malverne, NY [*Library symbol*] [*Library of Congress*] (LCLS)
**NMam** ....... Mamaroneck Free Library, Mamaroneck, NY [*Library symbol*] [*Library of Congress*] (LCLS)
**NmAM** ...... Montessori School, Albuquerque, NM [*Library symbol*] [*Library of Congress*] (LCLS)
**NMANDX** ... Nuclear Medicine Annual [*A publication*]
**NManh** ...... Manhasset Public Library, Manhasset, NY [*Library symbol*] [*Library of Congress*] (LCLS)
**NManhH** ... North Shore Hospital, Manhasset, NY [*Library symbol*] [*Library of Congress*] (LCLS)
**NManhJSH** ... Manhasset Junior-Senior High School, Manhasset, NY [*Library symbol*] [*Library of Congress*] (LCLS)
**NManhM** .. Manhasset Medical Center Hospital, Manhasset, NY [*Library symbol*] [*Library of Congress*] (LCLS)
**NMAP** ....... Navy Military Assistance Programs
**NmA-PP** .... Albuquerque Public Library, Prospect Park Branch, Albuquerque, NM [*Library symbol*] [*Library of Congress*] (LCLS)
**NM App** ..... New Mexico Court of Appeals (DLA)
**NmAr** ........ Artesia Public Library, Artesia, NM [*Library symbol*] [*Library of Congress*] (LCLS)

**NMar**......... Marcellus Free Library, Marcellus, NY [*Library symbol*] [*Library of Congress*] (LCLS)
**Nm-Ar**......... New Mexico State Records Center and Archives, Santa Fe, NM [*Library symbol*] [*Library of Congress*] (LCLS)
**NMARC**.... Navy and Marine Corps Acquisition Review Committee [*Terminated, 1975*] (MCD)
**NMarcP**..... Marcy Psychiatric Center, Marcy, NY [*Library symbol*] [*Library of Congress*] (LCLS)
**NMas**......... Henry H. Warren Memorial Library, Massena, NY [*Library symbol*] [*Library of Congress*] (LCLS)
**NMAS**....... National Marine Advisory Service [*National Oceanic and Atmospheric Administration*] (MSC)
**NmAS**........ Sandia Corp., Albuquerque, NM [*Library symbol*] [*Library of Congress*] (LCLS)
**NMass**....... Massapequa Public Library, Massapequa, NY [*Library symbol*] [*Library of Congress*] (LCLS)
**NMassBE**... Birch Elementary School, Massapequa, NY [*Library symbol*] [*Library of Congress*] (LCLS)
**NMassBH**... Berner High School, Massapequa, NY [*Library symbol*] [*Library of Congress*] (LCLS)
**NMassELE**... East Lake Elementary School, Massapequa, NY [*Library symbol*] [*Library of Congress*] (LCLS)
**NMassFE**.. Fairfield Elementary School, Massapequa, NY [*Library symbol*] [*Library of Congress*] (LCLS)
**NMassHE**... Hawthorn Elementary School, Massapequa, NY [*Library symbol*] [*Library of Congress*] (LCLS)
**NMassLE**.. Lockhart Elementary School, Massapequa, NY [*Library symbol*] [*Library of Congress*] (LCLS)
**NMassUE**... Unqua Elementary School, Massapequa, NY [*Library symbol*] [*Library of Congress*] (LCLS)
**NMat**......... Mattituck Free Library, Mattituck, NY [*Library symbol*] [*Library of Congress*] (LCLS)
**NMAT**....... Night-Time Marine Air Temperature
**NMATP**.... Navy Military Assistance Training Program (NG)
**NmAU**....... University of Albuquerque, Albuquerque, NM [*Library symbol*] [*Library of Congress*] (LCLS)
**NmAVA**..... United States Veterans Administration Hospital, Albuquerque, NM [*Library symbol*] [*Library of Congress*] (LCLS)
**NMb**.......... Mastics-Moriches-Shirley Community Library, Mastic Beach, NY [*Library symbol*] [*Library of Congress*] (LCLS)
**NMB**.......... National Marine Board [*British*] [*World War II*]
**NMB**.......... National Maritime Board
**NMB**.......... National Mediation Board [*Department of Labor*]
**NMB**.......... National Metric Board
**NMB**.......... National Motel Brokers (EA)
**NMB**.......... National Mutual Benefit [*Madison, WI*] (EA)
**NMB**.......... Naval Meteorological Branch [*British*]
**NMB**.......... Naval Minecraft Base
**NMB**.......... Naval Model Basin
**NMB**.......... Neuromuscular Blockade [*Medicine*]
**NMB**.......... New Methylene Blue [*Organic chemistry*]
**NMB**.......... No Military Branch
**NMB**.......... Noise, Measurement Buoy
**NMB**.......... Not Member of a Branch
**NMBA**........ National Marine Bankers Association [*Chicago, IL*] (EA)
**NMBC**....... [*The*] Merchants Bancorp, Inc. [*Norwalk, CT*] [*NASDAQ symbol*] (NQ)
**NMBC**....... National Minority Business Campaign [*Later, NMBD*] (EA)
**NMBC**....... National Minority Business Council [*New York, NY*] (EA)
**NMbCH**.... Bayview Community Hospital, Mastic Beach, NY [*Library symbol*] [*Library of Congress*] (LCLS)
**NMBD**....... National Minority Business Directories [*Minneapolis, MN*] (EA)
**NmBeN**...... Northwestern Regional Library, Belen, NM [*Library symbol*] [*Library of Congress*] (LCLS)
**NMBF**....... National Manufacturers of Beverage Flavors [*Defunct*] (EA)
**NMBHF**.... Naismith Memorial Basketball Hall of Fame (EA)
**NMBJD**..... New Mexico Business Journal [*A publication*]
**NMBMMR**... New Mexico Bureau of Mines and Mineral Resources [*New Mexico Institute of Mining and Technology*] [*Research center*] (RCD)
**NMBQAA**... Naturalia Monspeliensia. Serie Botanique [*A publication*]
**NMBR**....... NATO Military Basic Requirement (MCD)
**NMBR**....... Number (FAAC)
**NMbrB**...... Bennett College, Millbrook, NY [*Library symbol*] [*Library of Congress*] (LCLS)
**NMBS**....... Nationale Maatschappij der Belgische Spoorwegen [*Railway*] [*Belgium*] (EY)
**NMBT**....... New Main Battle Tank [*Military*] (RDA)
**NMBT**....... New Milford Bank & Trust Co. [*NASDAQ symbol*] (CTT)
**NM Bur Mines Miner Resour Bull**... New Mexico. Bureau of Mines and Mineral Resources. Bulletin [*A publication*]
**NM Bur Mines Miner Resour Cir**... New Mexico. Bureau of Mines and Mineral Resources. Circular [*A publication*]
**NM Bur Mines Miner Resour Circ**... New Mexico. Bureau of Mines and Mineral Resources. Circular [*A publication*]
**NM Bur Mines Miner Resour Hydrol Rep**... New Mexico. Bureau of Mines and Mineral Resources. Hydrologic Report [*A publication*]
**NM Bur Mines Miner Resour Mem**... New Mexico. Bureau of Mines and Mineral Resources. Memoir [*A publication*]
**NM Bur Mines Miner Resour Miner Resour Rep**... New Mexico. Bureau of Mines and Mineral Resources. Mineral Resources Report [*A publication*]
**NM Bur Mines Miner Resour Prog Rep**... New Mexico. Bureau of Mines and Mineral Resources. Progress Report [*A publication*]
**NM Bur Mines Miner Resour Target Explor Rep**... New Mexico. Bureau of Mines and Mineral Resources. Target Exploration Report [*A publication*]
**NM Bur Mines Miner Rsour Ground Water Rep**... New Mexico. Bureau of Mines and Mineral Resources. Ground Water Report [*A publication*]
**NM Bus J**.. New Mexico Business Journal [*A publication*]
**NmC**.......... Carlsbad Public Library, Carlsbad, NM [*Library symbol*] [*Library of Congress*] (LCLS)
**NMC**.......... Marine Corps Publications [*Later, NAVMC*]
**NMC**.......... Meredith College, Raleigh, NC [*OCLC symbol*] (OCLC)
**NMC**.......... Natal Medical Corps [*British military*] (DMA)
**NMC**.......... National Magazine Company
**NMC**.......... National Mail Centers, Inc. [*Telecommunications service*] (TSSD)
**NMC**.......... National Manpower Council
**NMC**.......... National Maritime Council (EA)
**NMC**.......... National Mastitis Council (EA)
**NMC**.......... National Medical Care
**NMC**.......... National Message Center [*Overland Park, KS*] (TSSD)
**NMC**.......... National Meteorological Center [*National Oceanic and Atmospheric Administration*] [*Information service or system*] (IID)
**NMC**.......... National Migrant Clearinghouse (OICC)
**NMC**.......... National Military Council [*Surinam*] (PD)
**NMC**.......... National Motorsports Committee (EA)
**NMC**.......... National Museum of Canada
**NMC**.......... National Music Camp [*Interlochen, MI*]
**NMC**.......... National Music Council (EA)
**NMC**.......... NATO Manual on Codification (NATG)
**NMC**.......... NAVA [*National Audio-Visual Association*] Materials Council (EA)
**NMC**.......... Naval Material Command [*Formerly, NMSE*]
**NMC**.......... Naval Medical Center [*Bethesda, MD*]
**NMC**.......... Naval Memorandum Correction (NVT)
**NMC**.......... Naval Missile Center [*Point Mugu, CA*]
**NMC**.......... Naval Mission Center (KSC)
**NMC**.......... Navigation Map Computer
**NMC**.......... Navy Mail Clerk
**N & MC**..... Navy and Marine Corps [*Medal*]
**NMC**.......... Navy Memorandum Correction
**NMC**.......... Nebraska Motor Carriers Association, Petroleum Carriers' Conference, Inc., Omaha NE [*STAC*]
**NMC**.......... Net Matchable Cost
**NMC**.......... Network Management Center [*Data processing*]
**NMC**.......... Network Management Console [*Industrial Networking, Inc.*]
**NMC**.......... Network Measurement Center
**NMC**.......... Nine Mile Canyon [*California*] [*Seismograph station code, US Geological Survey*] (SEIS)
**NMC**.......... No More Credit [*Business term*] (ADA)
**NMC**.......... Non-Metropolitan Counties [*British*]
**NMC**.......... Northern Montana College [*Havre*]
**NMC**.......... Northwestern Michigan College [*Traverse City*]
**NMC**.......... Not Mission Capable (MCD)
**N & Mc**...... Nott and McCord's South Carolina Reports [*A publication*] (DLA)
**NMC**.......... Nuclear Medicine Communications [*A publication*]
**NMC**.......... Nuclear Metal Conference
**NMC**.......... Numac Oil & Gas Ltd. [*AMEX symbol*] [*Toronto Stock Exchange symbol*] (SPSG)
**NMC**.......... Nursery Marketing Council (EA)
**NMC**.......... Public Archives of Canada, National Map Collection [*UTLAS symbol*]
**NMC**.......... San Francisco, CA [*Location identifier*] [*FAA*] (FAAL)
**NMCA**....... National Meat Canners Association (EA)
**NMCA**....... National Military Command Authority (NVT)
**NMCA**....... National Motorcycle Commuter Association [*Defunct*] (EA)
**NMCA**....... National Musclecar Association (EA)
**NMCA**....... Navy Mothers' Clubs of America (EA)
**N-McAb**..... Neutralizing Monoclonal Antibody [*Immunology*]
**NMCB**....... National Munitions Control Board [*World War II*]
**NMCB**....... National Museum of Canada Bulletin [*A publication*]
**NMCB**....... Navy Mobile Construction Battalion (CINC)
**NMC Bul**... National Music Council. Bulletin [*A publication*]
**NMCC**....... National Manpower Coordinating Committee [*Department of Labor*]
**NMCC**....... National Military Command Center [*DoD*]
**NMCC**....... Navy-Marine Corps Council (EA)
**NMCC**....... Network Management Control Center [*Telecommunications*]
**NMCC**....... Northeast-Midwest Congressional Coalition (EA)
**N & McC**... Nott and McCord's South Carolina Reports [*A publication*] (DLA)
**NMCCDDA**... National Model Cities Community Development Directors Association [*Later, NCDA*] (EA)
**NMCCFCS**... National Museum of Man. Mercury Series. Canadian Centre for Folk Culture Studies. Papers [*A publication*]

**NMCCIS**..... NATO Military Command and Control and Information System (NATG)
**NMCDA**.... National Model Cities Directors Association [*Later, NCDA*] (EA)
**NMCEC**..... Navy-Marine Corps Exhibit Center
**NMCGB**.... National Music Council of Great Britain (EAIO)
**NMCGRF**... Navy-Marine Corps-Coast Guard Residence Foundation
**NMCHC**.... National Maternal and Child Health Clearinghouse (EA)
**NmCiN**...... Northeastern Regional Library, Cimarron, NM [*Library symbol*] [*Library of Congress*] (LCLS)
**NMCJS**..... Naval Member, Canadian Joint Staff
**NmCl**......... Clovis-Carver Public Library, Clovis, NM [*Library symbol*] [*Library of Congress*] (LCLS)
**NMCL**........ Navy Missile Center Laboratory (KSC)
**NmCla**........ Albert W. Thompson Memorial Library, Clayton, NM [*Library symbol*] [*Library of Congress*] (LCLS)
**NMCLA**.... Bethesda Military Librarians Group [*Library network*]
**NmClA**........ United States Air Force, Cannon Air Force Base, Clovis, NM [*Library symbol*] [*Library of Congress*] (LCLS)
**NMCLK**.... Navy Mail Clerk
**NMCM**...... Navy and Marine Corps Medal [*Military decoration*]
**N & MCM**... Navy and Marine Corps Medal [*Military decoration*]
**NMCM**...... Not Mission Capable, Maintenance (NVT)
**NMCMASC**... National Museums of Canada. Mercury Series. Archaeological Survey of Canada. Papers [*A publication*]
**NMCMCES**... National Museums of Canada. National Museum of Man. Mercury Series. Canadian Ethnology Service. Papers [*A publication*]
**NMCMED**... National Museums of Canada. Mercury Series. Ethnology Division. Papers [*A publication*]
**NMCMSDP**... National Museums of Canada. Mercury Series. Directorate Paper [*A publication*]
**N & McN**... Neville and Macnamara's Railway and Canal Cases [*1855-1950*] [*A publication*] (DLA)
**NMCO**....... Navy Material Cataloging Office
**NMCOM**... Naval Material Command [*Formerly, NMSE*] (MCD)
**NmCP**........ United States Potash Co., Carlsbad, NM [*Library symbol*] [*Library of Congress*] (LCLS)
**NMCPA**.... National Museums of Canada. Publications in Archaeology [*A publication*]
**NMCPB**..... National Museums of Canada. Publications in Botany [*A publication*]
**NMCPBO**... National Museums of Canada. Publications in Biological Oceanography [*A publication*]
**NMCPE**..... National Museums of Canada. Publications in Ethnology [*A publication*]
**NMCPFC**.. National Museums of Canada. Publications in Folk Culture [*A publication*]
**NMCPNS**... National Museums of Canada. Publications in Natural Sciences [*A publication*]
**NMCPZ**..... National Museums of Canada. Publications in Zoology [*A publication*]
**NMCRB**.... Navy Military Construction Review Board
**NMCRC**.... Navy-Marine Corps Reserve Center (NVT)
**NMCRTC**... Navy and Marine Corps Reserve Training Center
**NMCS**....... National Medic-Card [*Commercial firm*] (EA)
**NMCS**....... National Military Command System
**NMCS**....... Navy Mine Countermeasures Station (MUGU)
**NMCS**....... Not Mission Capable, Supply (MCD)
**NMCS**....... Nuclear Materials Control System (IEEE)
**NMCSA**.... Navy Material Command Support Activity
**NMCSS**..... National Military Command System Standards (AFM)
**NMCSSC**.. National Military Command System Support Center (AABC)
**NMCUES**... National Medical Care Utilization and Expenditure Survey [*Department of Health and Human Services*] [*A publication*] (DHSM)
**NmD**.......... Deming Public Library, Deming, NM [*Library symbol*] [*Library of Congress*] (LCLS)
**NMD**......... Nahost und Mittelostverein eV. Rundschreiben [*A publication*]
**NMD**......... NASA Management Delegations (MCD)
**NMD**......... Naval Mine Depot
**NMD**......... Navy Marine Diesel Fuel
**NMD**......... Nonmonetary Determination [*Unemployment insurance*] (OICC)
**NMD**......... Nu-Media Industry International [*Vancouver Stock Exchange symbol*]
**NMDA**....... N-Methyl-D-Aspartic Acid [*An amino acid*]
**NMDA**....... National Marine Distributors Association (EA)
**NMDA**....... National Medical and Dental Association (EA)
**NMDA**....... National Metal Decorators Association (EA)
**NMDA**....... National Midas Dealers Association (EA)
**NMDA**....... National Motor Drivers' Association [*A union*] [*British*]
**NMDA**....... National Motorcycle Dealers Association [*Later, NMRA*] (EA)
**NMDA**....... Nonresonant Magnetic Deflection Amplifier
**NMDCEF**... National Medico-Dental Conference for the Evaluation of Fluoridation [*Later, Medical-Dental Committee on Evaluation of Fluoridation*] (EA)
**NM Dent J**... New Mexico Dental Journal [*A publication*]
**NM Dep Game Fish Bull**... New Mexico. Department of Game and Fish. Bulletin [*A publication*]
**NMDG**...... N-Methyl-D-Glucamine [*Biochemistry*]
**NMDJA**..... Netherlands Milk and Dairy Journal [*A publication*]
**NMDL**....... Naval Mine Defense Laboratory [*Naval Facilities Engineering Command*] [*Panama City, FL*]
**NMDL**....... Navy Management Data List (NG)
**NMDL**....... Navy Material Data List
**NMDP**....... National Marrow Donor Program [*National Institutes of Health*] (IID)
**NMDR**....... Nuclear Magnetic Double Resonance
**NMDRP**.... National Military Discharge Review Project (EA)
**NMDS**....... Naval Mine Disposal School
**NMDS**....... New Music Distribution Service (EA)
**NMDS**....... Nonmetric Multidimensional Scaling [*Statistics*]
**NMDTA**.... Novosti Meditsinskoi Tekhniki [*A publication*]
**NMDU**...... Newspaper and Mail Deliverers Union of New York and Vicinity (EA)
**NMDX**....... National Medplex Corp. [*NASDAQ symbol*] (NQ)
**NMDY**....... Nonresonant Magnetic Deflection Yoke
**NMDY**....... Normandy Oil & Gas Co. [*Fort Worth, TX*] [*NASDAQ symbol*] (NQ)
**NMDZ**....... NATO Maritime Defense Zone (NATG)
**NmE**........... Espanola Public Library, Espanola, NM [*Library symbol*] [*Library of Congress*] (LCLS)
**NME**.......... National Marriage Encounter (EA)
**NME**.......... National Medical Enterprises, Inc. [*NYSE symbol*] (SPSG)
**NME**.......... National Military Establishment [*Designated Department of Defense, 1949*]
**NME**.......... Necrolytic Migratory Erythema [*Dermatology*]
**NME**.......... New Middle East [*London*] [*A publication*]
**NME**.......... New Musical Express [*A publication*]
**NME**.......... Nightmute [*Alaska*] [*Airport symbol*] (OAG)
**NME**.......... Noise-Measuring Equipment
**NME**.......... Nonsupervisory Manufacturing Engineer
**NMEA**....... National Marine Educators Association (EA)
**NMEA**....... National Marine Electronics Association (EA)
**NMEBA**.... National Marine Engineers' Beneficial Association (EA)
**NMEC**....... National Metric Education Center [*Western Michigan University*]
**NMED**....... Inmed Corp. [*Norcross, GA*] [*NASDAQ symbol*] (NQ)
**NMed**......... Lee-Whedon Memorial Library, Medina, NY [*Library symbol*] [*Library of Congress*] (LCLS)
**NMedH**..... Medina Memorial Hospital, Medina, NY [*Library symbol*] [*Library of Congress*] (LCLS)
**NMEF**....... Naval Mine Engineering Facility
**NMEG**....... Nisei Mass Evacuation Group
**NMEIA**..... National Machine Embroidery Instructors Association (EA)
**NMEIA**..... Nauchnye Trudy Moskovskogo Inzhenerno-Ekonomicheskogo Instituta [*A publication*]
**NMEIAA**... National Machine Embroidery Instructors Association of America (EA)
**NMEL**....... Navy Marine Engineering Laboratory [*Later, David W. Taylor Naval Ship Research and Development Center*] (KSC)
**NMelA**....... Airborne Institute Laboratories, Melville, NY [*Library symbol*] [*Library of Congress*] (LCLS)
**NMelH**...... Holzmacher, McLendon & Murrell, Inc., Melville, NY [*Library symbol*] [*Library of Congress*] (LCLS)
**NMelL**....... Litcom Library, Melville, NY [*Library symbol*] [*Library of Congress*] (LCLS)
**NMelS**....... Suffolk State School, Melville, NY [*Library symbol*] [*Library of Congress*] (LCLS)
**NMelSC**.... Sagamore Children's Center, Melville, NY [*Library symbol*] [*Library of Congress*] (LCLS)
**NmEN**........ Northern Regional Library, Espanola, NM [*Library symbol*] [*Library of Congress*] (LCLS)
**NMERI**..... New Mexico Engineering Research Institute [*University of New Mexico*] [*Research center*] (RCD)
**NMerk**....... Merrick Public Library, Merrick, NY [*Library symbol*] [*Library of Congress*] (LCLS)
**NMerkF**..... Five Towns College, Merrick, NY [*Library symbol*] [*Library of Congress*] (LCLS)
**NMES**....... Naval Marine Engineering Station
**NMessenger**... Numismatic Messenger [*A publication*]
**NMEX**....... New Mexico
**N Mex Bs Jl**... New Mexico Business Journal [*A publication*]
**N Mex Bur Mines Mineral Resources Bull**... New Mexico State Bureau of Mines and Mineral Resources. Bulletin [*A publication*]
**N Mex Bur Mines Mineral Resources Mem**... New Mexico State Bureau of Mines and Mineral Resources. Memoir [*A publication*]
**N Mex Bus**... New Mexico Business [*A publication*]
**N Mex Ext N**... New Mexico Extension News [*A publication*]
**N Mex Ext News N Mex State Univ Agr Ext Serv**... New Mexico Extension News. New Mexico State University. Agricultural Extension Service [*A publication*]
**N Mex Geol**... New Mexico Geology [*A publication*]
**N Mex Lib**... New Mexico Libraries [*A publication*]
**N Mex L Rev**... New Mexico Law Review [*A publication*]
**N Mex Miner**... New Mexico Miner [*A publication*]
**N Mex State Engineer Office Tech Rept**... New Mexico State Engineer Office. Technical Report [*A publication*]
**NM Ext News**... New Mexico Extension News [*A publication*]
**N Mex Univ B G S**... New Mexico University. Bulletin. Geological Series [*A publication*]

**N Mex Univ Pubs Geology Pubs Meteoritics** ... New Mexico University. Publications in Geology. Publications in Meteoritics [*A publication*]
**NMF** .......... Boston, MA [*Location identifier*] [*FAA*] (FAAL)
**NmF** .......... Farmington Public Library, Farmington, NM [*Library symbol*] [*Library of Congress*] (LCLS)
**NMF** .......... N-Methylformamide [*Antineoplastic compound*]
**NMF** .......... National Marfan Foundation (EA)
**NMF** .......... National Medical Fellowships (EA)
**NMF** .......... National Migraine Foundation [*Later, National Headache Foundation - NHF*] (EA)
**NMF** .......... National Motor Freight Traffic Association Inc., Agent, Washington DC [*STAC*]
**NMF** .......... National Myoclonus Foundation (EA)
**NMF** .......... Naval Missile Facility [*Also, NAVMISFAC*]
**NMF** .......... Navy Management Fund
**NMF** .......... Neuromuscular Foundation of Western Australia
**NMF** .......... New Master File
**NMF** .......... Nonmaster File [*Data processing*]
**NMF** .......... Nonmember Firm [*of NYSE*]
**NMF** .......... Nonmigrating Fraction [*of spermatozoa*] [*Medicine*]
**NMF** .......... Nonprofit Mailers Federation (EA)
**NMF** .......... Nonuniform Magnetic Field
**NMF** .......... Nordiska Maskinbefalsfederationen [*Nordic Engineer Officers' Federation - NEOF*] (EAIO)
**NMFA** ....... National Military Family Association (EA)
**NMFC** ....... National Motor Freight Classification
**NMFCR** ..... National Motor Freight Classification Rules
**NMFEC** ..... National Medical Foundation for Eye Care [*Later, AAO*] (EA)
**NMFECC** ... National Magnetic Fusion Energy Computer Center [*Department of Energy*] (MCD)
**NmFGS** ...... Church of Jesus Christ of Latter-Day Saints, Genealogical Society Library, Farmington Branch, Farmington, NM [*Library symbol*] [*Library of Congress*] (LCLS)
**NMFHAWAREA** ... Naval Missile Facility, Hawaiian Area (MUGU)
**NMFHG** .... National Master Farm Homemakers Guild (EA)
**NMFMA** ... National Mutual Fund Managers Association [*Defunct*] (EA)
**NMFPA** ..... Naval Missile Facility, Point Arguello
**NMFR** ....... NAPALM [*National ADP Program for AMC Logistics Management*] Master File Record
**NMFR** ....... New Mexico Folklore Record [*A publication*]
**NMFRL** ..... Naval Medical Field Research Laboratory [*Camp Lejeune, NC*]
**NmFs** ......... Fort Sumner Public Library, Fort Sumner, NM [*Library symbol*] [*Library of Congress*] (LCLS)
**NMFS** ........ National Marine Fisheries Service [*Formerly, Bureau of Commercial Fisheries*] [*National Oceanic and Atmospheric Administration*] [*Washington, DC*]
**NMFS** ........ National Mortality Followback Survey [*National Center for Health Statistics*]
**NMFS** ........ Night Missile Flash Simulator (MCD)
**NMFT** ....... New Material Flight Tests
**NMFTA** ..... National Motor Freight Traffic Association [*Alexandria, VA*] (EA)
**NMFWA** ... National Military Fish and Wildlife Association (EA)
**NmG** .......... Gallup Public Library, Gallup, NM [*Library symbol*] [*Library of Congress*] (LCLS)
**NMG** .......... Navy Military Government
**NMG** .......... Neiman-Marcus Group [*NYSE symbol*] (SPSG)
**NMG** .......... New Management [*A publication*]
**NM (G)** ...... New Mexico Reports (Gildersleeve) [*1852-89*] [*A publication*] (DLA)
**NMG** .......... New Orleans, LA [*Location identifier*] [*FAA*] (FAAL)
**NMG** .......... Numerical Master Geometry [*System*]
**NMG** .......... San Miguel [*Panama*] [*Airport symbol*] (OAG)
**NMGA** ....... National Military Guidance Association (EA)
**NMGC** ....... National Marriage Guidance Council [*British*] (ILCA)
**NM Geol** .... New Mexico Geology [*A publication*]
**NM Geol Soc Annu Field Conf Guideb** ... New Mexico Geological Society. Annual Field Conference Guidebook [*A publication*]
**NM Geol Soc Field Conf Guideb** ... New Mexico Geological Society. Field Conference Guidebook [*A publication*]
**NM Geol Soc Guideb Annu Field Conf** ... New Mexico Geological Society. Guidebook of Annual Field Conference [*A publication*]
**NM Geol Soc Spec Publ** ... New Mexico Geological Society. Special Publication [*A publication*]
**NMGGA** .... Field Conference Guidebook. New Mexico Geological Society [*A publication*]
**NmGr** ......... Mother Whiteside Memorial Library, Grants, NM [*Library symbol*] [*Library of Congress*] (LCLS)
**NMGRA** .... National Museum and Gallery Registration Association (EA)
**NMGTA** .... Nederlands Militair Geneeskundig Tijdschrift [*A publication*]
**NMH** .......... N-Methylhydroxylamine [*Organic chemistry*]
**NMH** .......... Nautical Miles per Hour
**NMH** .......... New Mexico Highlands [*New Mexico*] [*Seismograph station code, US Geological Survey*] (SEIS)
**NMH** .......... New Mexico Highlands University, Las Vegas, NM [*OCLC symbol*] (OCLC)
**NMH** .......... Newcastle Morning Herald [*A publication*] (APTA)
**NmHa** ........ Hatch Public Library, Hatch, NM [*Library symbol*] [*Library of Congress*] (LCLS)
**NMHA** ...... National Mental Health Association (EA)
**NMHA** ...... National Minority Health Association (EA)
**NMHA** ...... National Mobile Home Association (EA)
**NmHARL** ... Aeromedical Library, 6571st Aeromedical Research Laboratory, Holloman AFB, NM [*Library symbol*] [*Library of Congress*] (LCLS)
**NMHB** ...... National Materials Handling Bureau [*Australia*]
**NMHC** ...... National Materials Handling Centre [*Cranfield Institute of Technology*] [*British*] (CB)
**NMHC** ...... National Multi Housing Council (EA)
**NMHC** ...... Nonmethane Hydrocarbons [*Organic chemistry*]
**NMHCA** .... National Mental Health Consumers' Association (EA)
**NMHCSHC** ... National Mental Health Consumer Self-Help Clearinghouse (EA)
**NMHF** ....... National Manufactured Housing Federation (EA)
**NMHFA** .... National Manufactured Housing Finance Association [*Washington, DC*] (EA)
**NmHi** ......... Historical Society of New Mexico, Santa Fe, NM [*Library symbol*] [*Library of Congress*] (LCLS)
**NM His R** ... New Mexico Historical Review [*A publication*]
**NmHo** ........ Hobbs Public Library, Hobbs, NM [*Library symbol*] [*Library of Congress*] (LCLS)
**NmHoC** ..... New Mexico Junior College, Hobbs, NM [*Library symbol*] [*Library of Congress*] (LCLS)
**NmHORA** ... United States Air Force, Office of Research Analyses, Technical Library, Holloman AFB, Albuquerque, NM [*Library symbol*] [*Library of Congress*] (LCLS)
**NmHoSW** ... College of the Southwest, Hobbs, NM [*Library symbol*] [*Library of Congress*] (LCLS)
**NMHQ** ...... New Mexico Historical Quarterly [*A publication*]
**NM/HR** ..... Nautical Mile/Hour (MCD)
**NMHR** ...... New Mexico Historical Review [*A publication*]
**NMHS** ....... National Maritime Historical Society (EA)
**NMHT** ...... National Museum of History and Technology [*Later, National Museum of American History*] (GRD)
**NMHU** ...... New Mexico Highlands University [*Las Vegas, NM*]
**NMHUJ** .... New Mexico Highlands University. Journal [*A publication*]
**NMI** ........... Minot State College, Minot, ND [*OCLC symbol*] (OCLC)
**NMI** ........... NASA Management Instruction (KSC)
**NMI** ........... National Macaroni Institute (EA)
**NMI** ........... National Manpower Institute [*Later, NIWL*] (EA)
**NMI** ........... National Maritime Institute [*British*]
**NMI** ........... Nautical Mile
**NMi** ........... Neuphilologische Mitteilungen [*A publication*]
**NMI** ........... New Material Introductory [*Team*] [*Military*]
**NMI** ........... No Middle Initial
**NMI** ........... Nonmajor Item (MCD)
**NMI** ........... Nonmasking Interrupt
**NMI** ........... Northeast-Midwest Institute (EA)
**NMI** ........... Northwest Microfilm, Incorporated [*Information service or system*] (IID)
**NMI** ........... Nuclear Metals, Incorporated
**NMI** ........... Nuveen Municipal Income Fund [*NYSE symbol*] (SPSG)
**NMi** ........... Thrall Library, Middletown, NY [*Library symbol*] [*Library of Congress*] (LCLS)
**NMIA** ........ National Military Intelligence Association (EA)
**NMIA** ........ Norske Meteorologiske Institutt. Meteorologiske Annaler [*A publication*]
**NMIAPO** .. New Montreal International Airport Project [*Canada*]
**NMIB** ........ New Material Introductory Briefing [*Military*] (MCD)
**NMIBT** ...... New Material Introductory Briefing Team [*Military*] (MCD)
**NMIC** ........ National Meat Industry Council (EA)
**NMIC** ........ National Micronetics, Inc. [*NASDAQ symbol*] (NQ)
**NMIC** ........ National Military Information Center
**NMIC** ........ National Missile Industry Conference (AAG)
**NMIC** ........ Not Made in Canada [*Business term*]
**NMIDA** ..... N-Methyliminodiacetic Acid [*Organic chemistry*]
**NMidp** ....... Middleport Free Library, Middleport, NY [*Library symbol*] [*Library of Congress*] (LCLS)
**NMidpF** ..... FMC Corp., Niagara Chemical Division, R and D Library, Middleport, NY [*Library symbol*] [*Library of Congress*] (LCLS)
**NMil** .......... Millerton Free Library, Millerton, NY [*Library symbol*] [*Library of Congress*] (LCLS)
**NMIL** ........ New Materiel Introductory Letter [*Army*] (AABC)
**NMilt** ......... Sarah Hull Hallock Free Library, Milton, NY [*Library symbol*] [*Library of Congress*] (LCLS)
**NMIMA** .... Norske Meteorologiske Institutt. Meteorologiske Annaler [*A publication*]
**NMIMAX** ... Nuclear Medicine [*A publication*]
**NMIMT** .... New Mexico Institute of Mining and Technology [*Socorro*]
**NMin** ......... Mineola Memorial Library, Mineola, NY [*Library symbol*] [*Library of Congress*] (LCLS)
**NMinH** ...... Nassau Hospital, Mineola, NY [*Library symbol*] [*Library of Congress*] (LCLS)
**NMinHe** .... Hampton Elementary School, Mineola, NY [*Library symbol*] [*Library of Congress*] (LCLS)
**NMinJE** .... Jackson Avenue Elementary School, Mineola, NY [*Library symbol*] [*Library of Congress*] (LCLS)
**NMinME** ... Meadow Elementary School, Mineola, NY [*Library symbol*] [*Library of Congress*] (LCLS)

**NMinMJ** ... Mineola Junior High School, Mineola, NY [*Library symbol*] [*Library of Congress*] (LCLS)
**NMinNCL** ... Nassau County Law Library, Mineola, NY [*Library symbol*] [*Library of Congress*] (LCLS)
**NMiOC** ..... Orange County Community College, Middletown, NY [*Library symbol*] [*Library of Congress*] (LCLS)
**NMiR**......... Ramapo Catskill Library System, Middletown, NY [*Library symbol*] [*Library of Congress*] (LCLS)
**NMIRA** ..... Nursing Mirror [*A publication*]
**NMIRO**..... Naval Material Industrial Resources Office
**NMIS** ........ National Military Indications System (MCD)
**NMIS** ........ Naval Manpower Information System
**NMis**......... Nova Misao [*A publication*]
**NMIS** ........ Nuclear Materials Information System
**NMIS** ........ Nuclear Materials Inventory System (NRCH)
**NMIT** ........ New Materiel Introductory Team [*Army*] (AABC)
**N Mitt**........ Neuphilologische Mitteilungen [*A publication*]
**NMIU**........ Nordic Meat Industry Union (EA)
**NmJ** ........... Jal Public Library, Jal, NM [*Library symbol*] [*Library of Congress*] (LCLS)
**NMJ** ........... Neuromuscular Junction [*Anatomy*]
**NM (J)**....... New Mexico Reports (Johnson) [*A publication*] (DLA)
**NMJC**........ National Men's Judo Championships [*London, England*]
**NMJC**........ Northeastern Mississippi Junior College [*Senatobia*]
**NMJC**........ Northwest Mississippi Junior College
**NMJL**........ National Mah Jongg League (EA)
**NMK**.......... Cape May, NJ [*Location identifier*] [*FAA*] (FAAL)
**NMK**.......... Niagara Mohawk Power Corp. [*NYSE symbol*] (SPSG)
**NMKL**....... Nordisk Metodikkommitte for Livsmedel [*Nordic Committee on Food Analysis*] (EAIO)
**NML**.......... Narragansett Marine Laboratory [*University of Rhode Island*]
**NML**.......... National Magnet Laboratory
**NML**.......... National Measurement Laboratory [*National Institute of Standards and Technology*] [*Gaithersburg, MD*] (GRD)
**NML**.......... National Municipal League (EA)
**NML**.......... National Music League (EA)
**NML**.......... Native Machine Language [*Data processing*]
**NML**.......... Nautical Mile
**NML**.......... Navy Management List (AFIT)
**NML**.......... New Mathematical Library [*School Mathematics Study Group*]
**NML**.......... New Mexico Law Review [*A publication*]
**Nm-L** ......... New Mexico Supreme Court Law Library, Santa Fe, NM [*Library symbol*] [*Library of Congress*] (LCLS)
**NML**.......... No Man's Land [*Medical slang, cardiology*]
**NML**.......... Normal
**NML**.......... University of New Mexico, School of Law, Albuquerque, NM [*OCLC symbol*] (OCLC)
**NmLa**......... Mesa Public Library, Los Alamos, NM [*Library symbol*] [*Library of Congress*] (LCLS)
**NmLaS** ...... Los Alamos Scientific Laboratory, Los Alamos, NM [*Library symbol*] [*Library of Congress*] (LCLS)
**NmLaS-M** ... Los Alamos Scientific Laboratory, Medical Library, Los Alamos, NM [*Library symbol*] [*Library of Congress*] (LCLS)
**NmLaU**...... University of New Mexico, Los Alamos, NM [*Library symbol*] [*Library of Congress*] (LCLS)
**NM Laws**... Laws of New Mexico [*A publication*]
**NmLc**......... Thomas Branigan Memorial Library, Las Cruces, NM [*Library symbol*] [*Library of Congress*] (LCLS)
**NmLcU** ...... New Mexico State University, Las Cruces, NM [*Library symbol*] [*Library of Congress*] (LCLS)
**NM Lib Newsl** ... New Mexico Libraries. Newsletter [*A publication*]
**NmLor** ....... Lordsburg-Hidalgo Public Library, Lordsburg, NM [*Library symbol*] [*Library of Congress*] (LCLS)
**NmLov** ....... Lovington Public Library, Lovington, NM [*Library symbol*] [*Library of Congress*] (LCLS)
**NmLovS**..... Southeastern Regional Library Center, Lovington, NM [*Library symbol*] [*Library of Congress*] (LCLS)
**NMLR** ....... New Mexico Law Review [*A publication*]
**NMLR** ....... Nigerian Monthly Law Reports [*1964-65*] [*A publication*] (DLA)
**NMLRA** .... National Muzzle Loading Rifle Association (EA)
**NML Rev**... New Mexico Law Review [*A publication*]
**NMLS**........ National Microwave Landing System (MCD)
**NMLT** ....... New Material Laboratory Tests
**NML Tech J** ... NML [*National Metallurgical Laboratory*] Technical Journal [*A publication*]
**NmLv** ......... Las Vegas Carnegie Library, Las Vegas, NM [*Library symbol*] [*Library of Congress*] (LCLS)
**NmLvH**...... New Mexico Highlands University, Las Vegas, NM [*Library symbol*] [*Library of Congress*] (LCLS)
**NmLvSH** ... New Mexico State Hospital, Las Vegas, NM [*Library symbol*] [*Library of Congress*] (LCLS)
**NMM** ........ Meridian, MS [*Location identifier*] [*FAA*] (FAAL)
**NMM** ........ N-Methylmorpholine [*Organic chemistry*]
**NMM** ........ NASA Management Manual
**NMM** ........ National Maritime Museum [*Great Britain*]
**NMM** ........ Neutron Magnetic Moment
**NMM** ........ New Madrid [*Missouri*] [*Seismograph station code, US Geological Survey*] [*Closed*] (SEIS)
**NMM** ........ New Mexico Military Institute, Roswell, NM [*OCLC symbol*] (OCLC)
**NMM** ........ Norsemont Mining [*Vancouver Stock Exchange symbol*]
**NMM** ........ Nuclear Materials Management
**NMM** ........ Nuclear Methods Monographs [*Elsevier Book Series*] [*A publication*]
**NMMA**...... National Macaroni Manufacturers Association [*Later, NPA*] (EA)
**NMMA**...... National Maintenance Management Association (EA)
**NMMA**...... National Marine Manufacturers Association (EA)
**N & M Mag** ... Nevile and Manning's English Magistrates' Cases [*A publication*] (DLA)
**NMMC**...... National Adult Education Clearinghouse (NAEC)/National Multimedia Center for Adult Education [*Information service or system*] [*Defunct*] (IID)
**NMMC**...... National Marina Manufacturers Consortium (EA)
**N & MMC** ... Nevile and Manning's English Magistrates' Cases [*A publication*] (DLA)
**NmMeB**..... Bent-Mescalero School Library, Mescalero, NM [*Library symbol*] [*Library of Congress*] (LCLS)
**NMMFO**... Navy Maintenance Management Field Office
**NMMHOF** ... National Mobile/Manufactured Home Owners Foundation [*Later, NFMHO*] (EA)
**NMMI**...... New Mexico Military Institute [*Roswell*] (MCD)
**NMML**...... National Marine Mammal Laboratory [*National Marine Fisheries Service*]
**NMMLC** ... New Moon Matchbox and Label Club (EA)
**NMMM** .... Navy Maintenance and Material Management System [*Also known as MMM, NMMMS, 3M*]
**NMMMA** ... Memoir. New Mexico Bureau of Mines and Mineral Resources [*A publication*]
**NMMMS**.. Navy Maintenance and Material Management System [*Also known as MMM, NMMM, 3M*]
**NmMS**....... Montezuma Seminary, Montezuma, NM [*Library symbol*] [*Library of Congress*] (LCLS)
**NMMSN**... National Marine Mammal Stranding Network (EA)
**NMMSS**.... Nuclear Materials Management and Safeguards System (NRCH)
**NMMW**..... Near Millimeter Wave System [*Telecommunications*] (TEL)
**NMN** ......... Nicotinamide-Mononucleotide [*Biochemistry*]
**NMN** ......... No Middle Name
**NMN** ......... Normetanephrine [*Also, Methylnorepinephrine*] [*Biochemistry*]
**NMN** ......... NRD Mining Ltd. [*Vancouver Stock Exchange symbol*]
**NMNA** ...... National Male Nurse Association [*Later, AAMN*] (EA)
**NMNase**.... Nicotinamidenucleotide Phosphoribohydrolase [*An enzyme*]
**NMND** ..... Naval Magazine and Net Depot
**NMNFO**.... Navy Maintenance Field Office (NVT)
**NMNH** ...... National Museum of Natural History [*Smithsonian Institution*]
**NMNRU** ... Naval Medical Neuropsychiatric Research Unit
**NMNS**...... National Museum of Natural Sciences [*National Museums of Canada*] [*Research center*] (RCD)
**NM Nurse** ... New Mexico Nurse [*A publication*]
**NMO** ......... Long Beach, CA [*Location identifier*] [*FAA*] (FAAL)
**NMO** ......... National Mobility Office [*British*]
**NMO** ......... Navy Management Office
**NMo**........... Neuphilologische Monatsschrift [*A publication*]
**NMO** ......... Noble Mines & Oils Ltd. [*Toronto Stock Exchange symbol*]
**NMO** ......... Normal Manual Operation (KSC)
**NMO** ......... Normal Mode Operation
**NMO** ......... Norman [*Oklahoma*] [*Seismograph station code, US Geological Survey*] [*Closed*] (SEIS)
**NMO** ......... Nuveen Municipal Market Opportunities [*NYSE symbol*] (SPSG)
**NMOA** ...... National Mail Order Association [*Los Angeles, CA*] (EA)
**NMOC**....... Non-Methane Organic Compound [*Environmental chemistry*]
**NMOCOD** ... [*The*] Nonmateriel Objectives Coordinating Document [*Army*] (RDA)
**N Mon**........ Neuphilologische Monatsschrift [*A publication*]
**NMoN** ....... New York Ocean Science Laboratory, Montauk, NY [*Library symbol*] [*Library of Congress*] (LCLS)
**NMONA** .... National Mail Order Nurserymen's Association [*Later, MAN*] (EA)
**NMontr**...... Hendrick Hudson Free Library, Montrose, NY [*Library symbol*] [*Library of Congress*] (LCLS)
**NMontrVA** ... United States Veterans Administration Hospital, Montrose, NY [*Library symbol*] [*Library of Congress*] (LCLS)
**NMOP**....... National Mission Operating Procedures (AAG)
**NMOR**....... Nitrosomorpholine [*Also, NNM*] [*Organic chemistry*]
**NMOS**....... Negative Channel Metal-Oxide Semiconductor
**NMOS**....... Nonvolatile Metal-Oxide Semiconductor (MCD)
**NMOSAW** ... Naval and Military Order of the Spanish-American War (EA)
**NMP**.......... N-Methylphenazium [*Organic chemistry*]
**NMP**.......... N-Methylpyrrolidone [*Organic chemistry*]
**NMP**.......... National Maintenance Point [*Military*] (AABC)
**NMP**.......... National Meter Programming (NRCH)
**NMP**.......... Naval Management Program
**NMP**.......... Naval Medical Publication
**NMP**.......... Naval Message Processing (MCD)
**NMP**.......... Navigational Microfilm Projector
**NMP**.......... Navy Manning Plan (NVT)

**NMP** ........ Nederlands Middenstands Partij [*Netherlands Middle Class Party*] [*Political party*] (PPE)
**NMP** ........ Net Material Product [*Economics*]
**NM/P** ........ New Material/Process (MCD)
**NMP** ........ Not Machine Pressed
**NMP** ........ Nucleoside Monophosphate [*Biochemistry*]
**NmP** ........ Portales Public Library, Portales, NM [*Library symbol*] [*Library of Congress*] (LCLS)
**NMPA** ........ National Meat Processors Association [*Australia*]
**NMPA** ........ National Motorsports Press Association (EA)
**NMPA** ........ National Music Publishers' Association (EA)
**NMPA** ........ NATO Maritime Patrol Aircraft (NATG)
**NMPA** ........ New Mexico Philatelic Association (EA)
**NMPA** ........ Nitrosomethylpropylamine [*Organic chemistry*]
**NMPASC** ... NATO Maritime Patrol Aircraft Steering Committee (NATG)
**NMPATA** ... National Music Printers and Allied Trades Association (EA)
**NMPB** ........ National Millinery Planning Board [*Defunct*] (EA)
**NMPC** ........ National Maintenance Publications Center [*Army*] (AABC)
**NMPC** ........ National Minority Purchasing Council [*Later, NMSDC*] (EA)
**NMPC** ........ National Moratorium on Prison Construction [*Defunct*] (EA)
**NMPD** ........ Nitromethylpropanediol [*Organic chemistry*]
**NMPDN** .... National Materials Property Data Network (EA)
**NmPE** ........ Eastern New Mexico University, Portales, NM [*Library symbol*] [*Library of Congress*] (LCLS)
**NMPF** ........ National Milk Producers Federation (EA)
**NMPF** ........ Normal Magnitude Probability Function
**NMPG** ........ New Mexico Proving Ground [*Army*]
**NMPL** ........ New Material Planning Letter (MCD)
**NMPNC** .... Naval Medical Program for Nuclear Casualties
**NMPNS** .... Nine Mile Point Nuclear Station (NRCH)
**NMPO** ........ Navy Motion Picture Office
**NMPO** ........ Nordic Master Painters' Organization (EA)
**NMPP** ........ Nautical Miles per Pound (MCD)
**NMPP** ........ Nouvelles Messageries de la Presse Parisienne [*Paris press distribution agency*]
**NMPS** ........ Nautical Miles per Second
**NMPS** ........ Navy Motion Picture Service
**NMPTP** ..... N-Methyl(phenyl)tetrahydropyridine [*Biochemistry*]
**NMPX** ........ Navy Motion Picture Exchange
**NMQ** ........ New Mexico Quarterly [*A publication*]
**NMQR** ........ New Mexico Quarterly. Review [*A publication*]
**NMQR** ........ New Music Quarterly Review [*Record label*]
**NMQUE** .... Nocte Maneque [*Night and Morning*] [*Pharmacy*]
**NMR** ........ Centre for Nuclear Magnetic Resonance [*University of Warwick*] [*British*] (CB)
**NMR** ........ N. M. De Rothschild & Co. [*Merchant bank*] [*British*]
**NMR** ........ Natal Mounted Rifles [*British military*] (DMA)
**NMR** ........ National Military Representatives with SHAPE [*NATO*]
**NMR** ........ National Missile Range (KSC)
**NMR** ........ National Museum of Racing (EA)
**NMR** ........ Natural Magnetic Remanence [*Geophysics*]
**NMR** ........ Nautical Mile Radius Of (FAAC)
**NMR** ........ Naval Medical Research Institute, Washington, DC [*OCLC symbol*] (OCLC)
**NMR** ........ Naval Missile Range
**NMR** ........ Navy Management Review [*A publication*]
**NMR** ........ Neomar Resources Ltd. [*Toronto Stock Exchange symbol*]
**NMR** ........ New Magazine Review [*A publication*]
**NMR** ........ New Material Release (MCD)
**NMR** ........ New Mexico Review [*A publication*]
**NMR** ........ Nictitating Membrane Response [*Neurophysiology*]
**NMR** ........ No Maintenance Requirement (NVT)
**NMR** ........ No Master Record [*Military*] (AFIT)
**NMR** ........ Nonconforming Material Report (MCD)
**NMR** ........ Normal Mode Rejection
**NMR** ........ NOTAM Monitor Review (FAAC)
**NMR** ........ Nuclear Magnetic Relaxation
**NMR** ........ Nuclear Magnetic Resonance [*Also, NUMAR*] [*Atomic physics*]
**NmR** ........ Roswell Carnegie Library, Roswell, NM [*Library symbol*] [*Library of Congress*] (LCLS)
**NMR** ........ San Juan, PR [*Location identifier*] [*FAA*] (FAAL)
**NmRa** ........ Arthur Johnson Memorial Library, Raton, NM [*Library symbol*] [*Library of Congress*] (LCLS)
**NMRA** ........ National Marine Representatives Association (EA)
**NMRA** ........ National Mine Rescue Association
**NMRA** ........ National Mobile Radio Association (EA)
**NMRA** ........ National Model Railroad Association (EA)
**NMRA** ........ National Motorcycle Racing Association (EA)
**NMRA** ........ National Motorcycle Retailers Association (EA)
**NMRAS** .... Nuclear Material Report and Analysis System [*Energy Research and Development Administration*]
**NMRB** ........ National Mutual Royal Bank [*Australia*] (ADA)
**NMRC** ........ National Maritime Research Center [*Maritime Administration*] [*Also, an information service or system*] (IID)
**NMRC** ........ Navy Material Redistribution Center
**NMRC** ........ NMR Centers, Inc. [*Newport Beach, CA*] [*NASDAQ symbol*] (NQ)
**NMR & DA** ... Navy Material Redistribution and Disposition Administration
**NMRDC** .... Naval Medical Research and Development Command (MCD)
**NMR & DO** ... Navy Material Redistribution and Disposal Office [*or Officer*]
**NmRE** ........ Eastern New Mexico University, Roswell Campus, Roswell, NM [*Library symbol*] [*Library of Congress*] (LCLS)
**NMRG** ........ Navy Mid-Range Guidance
**NMRI** ........ National Mass Retailing Institute [*New York, NY*] (EA)
**NMRI** ........ Naval Medical Research Institute
**NMRI** ........ Nuclear Magnetic Resonance Imaging
**NMRL** ........ Naval Medical Research Laboratory
**NMRLIT** ... Nuclear Magnetic Resonance Literature System [*Chemical Information Systems, Inc.*] [*Information service or system*]
**NmRM** ........ New Mexico Military Institute, Roswell, NM [*Library symbol*] [*Library of Congress*] (LCLS)
**NMRN** ........ National Meteorological Rocket Network
**NMRNB** .... Nuclear Magnetic Resonance [*A publication*]
**NMRNBE** ... Specialist Periodical Reports. Nuclear Magnetic Resonance [*A publication*]
**NMRO** ........ Navy Mid-Range Objectives
**NMRP** ........ National Migrant Resource Program (EA)
**NMRP** ........ Nuclear Magnetic Resonance Program
**NMRR** ........ NMR of America, Inc. [*NASDAQ symbol*] (NQ)
**NMRS** ........ National Mobile Radio System [*Later, Telocator Network of America*] (EA)
**NMRS** ........ Navy Manpower Requirements System (NVT)
**NMRS** ........ Numerous (FAAC)
**NMRT** ........ New Members Round Table [*American Library Association*]
**NMRT** ........ Nimbus Meteorological Radiation Tape [*NASA*]
**NMRTC** .... Navy and Marine Corps Reserve Training Center
**NMRU** ........ Naval Medical Research Unit
**NmRu** ........ Ruidoso Public Library, Ruidoso, NM [*Library symbol*] [*Library of Congress*] (LCLS)
**NMRX** ........ Numerax, Inc. [*NASDAQ symbol*] (NQ)
**NMS** ........ Ancient Egyptian Arabic Order Nobles of the Mystic Shrine (EA)
**NM & S** ..... Bureau of Medicine and Surgery Publications [*Navy*]
**NMS** ........ Namsang [*Burma*] [*Airport symbol*] (OAG)
**NMS** ........ National Management Systems [*Information service or system*] (IID)
**NMS** ........ National Market System
**NMS** ........ National Master Specification [*Construction Specifications Canada*] [*Information service or system*] (IID)
**NMS** ........ National Measurement System [*National Institute of Standards and Technology*]
**NMS** ........ National Medicine Society [*British*]
**NMS** ........ National Mine Service Co. [*NYSE symbol*] (SPSG)
**NMS** ........ National Mobility Scheme [*British*]
**NMS** ........ Naval Medical School (MCD)
**NMS** ........ Naval Meteorological Service
**NMS** ........ Navy Mid-Range Study
**NMS** ........ Network Management Services [*Ohio Bell Communications, Inc.*] [*Cleveland, OH*] [*Telecommunications*] (TSSD)
**NMS** ........ Network Management Signal [*Telecommunications*] (TEL)
**NMS** ........ Network Measurement System [*Computer network*]
**NMS** ........ Neuroleptic Malignant Syndrome
**NMS** ........ Neutral Mass Spectrometer [*Instrumentation*]
**NMS** ........ Neutron Monitoring System [*Nuclear energy*] (NRCH)
**NMS** ........ New Mexico State Library, Santa Fe, NM [*OCLC symbol*] (OCLC)
**NMS** ........ New Mexico Statutes [*A publication*] (DLA)
**NMS** ........ New Music Seminar
**NMS** ........ Nitrogen Measuring System
**NMS** ........ Noise Measuring Set [*Telecommunications*] (TEL)
**NMS** ........ Nonmajor System (MCD)
**NMS** ........ Nordic Metalworkers Secretariat (EA)
**NMS** ........ Normal Market Size Transaction
**NMS** ........ Normal Mouse Serum
**NMS** ........ Nottingham Medieval Studies [*A publication*]
**NMS** ........ Nuclear Materials Safeguards
**NmS** ........ Santa Fe City and County Public Library, Santa Fe, NM [*Library symbol*] [*Library of Congress*] (LCLS)
**NMSA** ........ National Metal Spinners Association (EA)
**NMSA** ........ National Middle School Association (EA)
**NMSA** ........ National Moving and Storage Association (EA)
**NMSA** ........ Nonstandard Metropolitan Statistical Area
**NMSB** ........ Navy Manpower Survey Board
**NMSB** ........ NewMil Bancorp, Inc. [*New Milford, CT*] [*NASDAQ symbol*] (NQ)
**NmSC** ........ College of Santa Fe, Santa Fe, NM [*Library symbol*] [*Library of Congress*] (LCLS)
**NMSC** ........ National Main Street Center (EA)
**NMSC** ........ National Maple Syrup Council [*Later, NAMSC*]
**NMSC** ........ National Merit Scholarship Corporation (EA)
**NMSC** ........ Nerve and Muscle Stimulating Current
**NMSC** ........ Non-Military Supplies Committee [*Combined Production and Resources Board*] [*British*] [*World War II*]
**NMSC** ........ Northeast-Midwest Senate Coalition (EA)
**NMSC** ........ Northwest Missouri State College [*Later, Northwest Missouri State University*]
**NmSc** ........ Silver City Public Library, Silver City, NM [*Library symbol*] [*Library of Congress*] (LCLS)
**NMSCS** ..... Northwest Missouri State College Studies [*A publication*]

**NmScSW** ... Southwestern Regional Library, Silver City, NM [*Library symbol*] [*Library of Congress*] (LCLS)
**NmScW** ..... Western New Mexico University, Silver City, NM [*Library symbol*] [*Library of Congress*] (LCLS)
**NMSD** ....... National Match Support Detachment [*Ammunition supplier*]
**NMSD** ....... Naval Medical Supply Depot
**NMSD** ....... Next Most Significant Digit [*Data processing*]
**NMSDC** .... National Minority Supplier Development Council (EA)
**NMSE** ....... Naval Material Support Establishment [*After 1966, NAVMAT, NMCOM, NMC*]
**NMSHC** .... Bureau of Medicine and Surgery Hospital Corps Publication [*Later, NAVMED*] [*Navy*]
**NMSI** ....... National Mini-Storage Institute (EA)
**NmSM** ....... Museum of New Mexico, Santa Fe, NM [*Library symbol*] [*Library of Congress*] (LCLS)
**NMSM** ....... New Mexico School of Mines (AAG)
**NmSM-A** ... Museum of New Mexico, Laboratory of Anthropology, Santa Fe, NM [*Library symbol*] [*Library of Congress*] (LCLS)
**NMSO** ....... NATO Maintenance and Support Operation (AFM)
**NMSO** ....... Naval Manpower Survey Office (NVT)
**NMSO** ....... Nuclear Missile Safety Office [*or Officer*] (AFM)
**NmSo** ......... Socorro Public Library, Socorro, NM [*Library symbol*] [*Library of Congress*] (LCLS)
**NmSoI** ....... New Mexico Institute of Mining and Technology, Socorro, NM [*Library symbol*] [*Library of Congress*] (LCLS)
**NM Sol Energy Assoc Southwest Bull** ... New Mexico Solar Energy Association. Southwest Bulletin [*A publication*]
**NMSP** ........ N-Methylspiperone [*Biochemistry*]
**NmSP** ........ New Mexico State Penitentiary Library, Santa Fe, NM [*Library symbol*] [*Library of Congress*] (LCLS)
**NMSP** ........ New Mon State Party [*Burma*] [*Political party*]
**NmSp** ......... Springer Public Library, Springer, NM [*Library symbol*] [*Library of Congress*] (LCLS)
**NMSQT** .... National Merit Scholarship Qualifying Test
**NmSr** ......... Moise Memorial Library, Santa Rosa, NM [*Library symbol*] [*Library of Congress*] (LCLS)
**NMSRA** .... National Master Shoe Rebuilders Association (EA)
**NMSRC** ..... National Middle School Resource Center (EA)
**NMSS** ........ National Multiple Sclerosis Society (EA)
**NMSS** ........ National Multipurpose Space Station
**NMSS** ........ Office of Nuclear Materials Safety and Safeguards [*Nuclear Regulatory Commission*]
**NMSSA** ..... NATO Maintenance Supply Service Agency [*Later, NAMSO*]
**NMSSS** ..... NATO Maintenance Supply Service System
**NMSST** ..... Naval Manpower Shore Survey Team (NVT)
**NmSStJ** ..... Saint John's College in Santa Fe, Santa Fe, NM [*Library symbol*] [*Library of Congress*] (LCLS)
**NMST** ....... New Materials System Test [*Obsolete*] [*Nuclear energy*]
**NM Stat Ann** ... New Mexico Statutes, Annotated [*A publication*] (DLA)
**NM State Bur Mines Miner Resour Annu Rep** ... New Mexico State Bureau of Mines and Mineral Resources. Annual Report [*A publication*]
**NM State Bur Mines Miner Resour Bull** ... New Mexico State Bureau of Mines and Mineral Resources. Bulletin [*A publication*]
**NM State Bur Mines Miner Resour Circ** ... New Mexico State Bureau of Mines and Mineral Resources. Circular [*A publication*]
**NM State Bur Mines Miner Resour Geol Map** ... New Mexico State Bureau of Mines and Mineral Resources. Geologic Map [*A publication*]
**NM State Bur Mines Miner Resour Mem** ... New Mexico State Bureau of Mines and Mineral Resources. Memoir [*A publication*]
**NM State Eng Basic Data Rep** ... New Mexico State Engineer. Basic Data Report [*A publication*]
**NMSU** ....... Naval Motion Study Unit [*British*]
**NMSU** ....... New Mexico State University
**NmSuAF** .... United States Air Force, Sacramento Peak Observatory, Sunspot, NM [*Library symbol*] [*Library of Congress*] (LCLS)
**NMSVA** .... Navy Mail Service Veterans Association (EA)
**NMT** .......... Barrow, AK [*Location identifier*] [*FAA*] (FAAL)
**NMT** .......... N-Monomethyltryptamine [*Organic chemistry*]
**NMT** .......... N-Myristoyl Acyltransferase [*An enzyme*]
**NMT** .......... National Museum of Transport [*Later, TMA*] (EA)
**NMT** .......... Neuromuscular Tension [*Medicine*]
**NMT** .......... New Mexico Institute of Mining and Technology, Socorro, NM [*OCLC symbol*] (OCLC)
**NMT** .......... No More Trouble [*Coates' brand of cotton thread*] (ROG)
**NMT** .......... Noble-Metal-Coated Titanium [*Anode*]
**NMT** .......... Nonmetalic [*Technical drawings*]
**NMT** .......... Nordic Mobile Telephone [*Radio-telephone system for car users*] [*Denmark, Finland, Norway, Sweden*]
**NMT** .......... Northwest Marine Trade Association (EA)
**NMT** .......... Not More Than
**NMT** .......... Notification of Master Tool (NASA)
**NMT** .......... Nuclear Medicine Technology
**NMT** .......... Number of Module Types
**NMTA** ....... National Manpower Training Association [*Later, NETA*] (EA)
**NMTA** ....... National Metal Trades Association [*Later, AAIM*] (EA)
**NMTA** ....... National Movement Theatre Association (EA)
**NMTBA** .... National Machine Tool Builders' Association [*Later, AMT*] (EA)
**NMTBD** .... No More to Be Done [*Medicine*]
**NMTC** ....... Naval Mine Testing Center (MCD)
**NMTC** ....... Naval Missile Testing Center
**NMTC** ....... North Metropolitan Tramways Company [*British*] (ROG)
**NMTC** ....... Nucleon-Meson Transport Code
**NMTCB** ..... Nuclear Medicine Technology Certification Board (EA)
**NMTD** ....... Nuclear Materials Transfer Document
**NMTF** ....... Naval Mine Test Facility
**NMTGS** ..... National Mortgage Fund [*NASDAQ symbol*] (NQ)
**NMTHC** .... Nonmethane Total Hydrocarbons [*Organic chemistry*]
**NmTHF** ..... Harwood Foundation, Taos, NM [*Library symbol*] [*Library of Congress*] (LCLS)
**NMTI** ....... Neuromedical Technologies, Inc. [*NASDAQ symbol*] (NQ)
**NMtK** ........ Mount Kisco Public Library, Mount Kisco, NY [*Library symbol*] [*Library of Congress*] (LCLS)
**NmTKC** ..... Kit Carson Memorial Foundation, Inc., Taos, NM [*Library symbol*] [*Library of Congress*] (LCLS)
**NMTO** ....... Navy Material Transportation Office
**NMTR** ....... Nuclear Materials Transfer Report
**NmTr** ......... Truth Or Consequences Public Library, Truth Or Consequences, NM [*Library symbol*] [*Library of Congress*] (LCLS)
**NMTS** ....... National Milk Testing Service
**NMTS** ....... Navy Military Technical Specialist (MCD)
**NMTS** ....... Noise Measurement Test Set
**NMTSD7** .. Nouvelle Revue de Medecine de Toulouse. Supplement [*A publication*]
**NmTu** ......... Tucumcari Public Library, Tucumcari, NM [*Library symbol*] [*Library of Congress*] (LCLS)
**NmTuE** ...... Eastern Plains Regional Library, Tucumcari, NM [*Library symbol*] [*Library of Congress*] (LCLS)
**NMtv** ......... Mount Vernon Public Library, Mount Vernon, NY [*Library symbol*] [*Library of Congress*] (LCLS)
**NMTX** ....... Novametrix Medical Systems, Inc. [*NASDAQ symbol*] (NQ)
**NMU** ......... Brunswick, ME [*Location identifier*] [*FAA*] (FAAL)
**NMU** ......... National Maritime Union of America (EA)
**NMU** ......... National Museums of Canada Library [*UTLAS symbol*]
**NMU** ......... Network Monitor Unit [*Telecommunications*] (TSSD)
**NMU** ......... Neuromuscular Unit [*Medicine*]
**nmu** ........... New Mexico [*MARC country of publication code*] [*Library of Congress*] (LCCP)
**NMU** ......... Nitrosomethylurea [*Also, MNU*] [*Organic chemistry*]
**NMU** ......... Nordic Musicians' Union (EA)
**NMU** ......... Northern Michigan University [*Marquette*]
**NmU** .......... University of New Mexico, Albuquerque, NM [*Library symbol*] [*Library of Congress*] (LCLS)
**NMUC** ....... National Medical Utilization Committee [*HEW*]
**NmU-L** ....... University of New Mexico, Law Library, Albuquerque, NM [*Library symbol*] [*Library of Congress*] (LCLS)
**NmU-M** ..... University of New Mexico, Library of the Medical Sciences, School of Medicine and Bernalillo County Medical Society, Albuquerque, NM [*Library symbol*] [*Library of Congress*] (LCLS)
**N Munster Antiq J** ... North Munster Antiquarian Journal [*A publication*]
**NMuP** ........ Muttontown Preserve, Muttontown, NY [*Library symbol*] [*Library of Congress*] (LCLS)
**N Music R** ... New Music Review [*A publication*]
**NMV** .......... Nitrogen Manual Valve (MCD)
**NMVCA** ..... National Military Vehicle Collectors Association [*Defunct*]
**NMVOC** .... Nonmethane Volatile Organic Carbon [*Environmental chemistry*]
**NMVP** ....... Navy Manpower Validation Program (NG)
**NMVSA** .... Navy Manpower Validation Support Activity
**NMVSAC** ... National Motor Vehicle Safety Advisory Council (EA)
**NMVTA** .... National Motor Vehicle Theft Act
**NMvUA** ..... State University of New York, Agricultural and Technical College at Morrisville, Morrisville, NY [*Library symbol*] [*Library of Congress*] (LCLS)
**NMW** ........ Astoria, OR [*Location identifier*] [*FAA*] (FAAL)
**NMW** ........ Normal Molecular Weight
**NMW** ........ Notes on Mississippi Writers [*A publication*]
**NMW** ........ Western Carolina University, Cullowhee, NC [*OCLC symbol*] (OCLC)
**NMWA** ...... National Military Wives Association [*Later, NMFA*] (EA)
**NMWA** ...... National Mineral Wool Association [*Later, MIMA*]
**NMWC** ...... National Migrant Workers Council [*Farmington Hills, MI*] (EA)
**NMWC** ...... Nelson, Marlborough, and West Coast Regiment [*British military*] (DMA)
**NMWC** ...... New Mexico Western College
**NMWIA** .... National Mineral Wool Insulation Association [*Formerly, NMWA*] [*Later, MIMA*] (EA)
**NM Wildl** .. New Mexico Wildlife [*A publication*]
**NMWL** ...... Normal Molecular Weight, Low in Extractables
**NmWM** ..... White Sands Missile Range Library, White Sands Missile Range, NM [*Library symbol*] [*Library of Congress*] (LCLS)
**NMWP** ...... National Migrant Worker Program [*Department of Labor*]
**NMWQL** ... National Marine Water Quality Laboratory [*Environmental Protection Agency*] (MSC)
**NMWS** ...... Naval Mine Warfare School

**NMWTC** ... Naval Mine Warfare Training Center
**NMWTS** ... Naval Mine Warfare Test Station
**NMWTS** ... Naval Mine Warfare Training School
**n-mx---** ... Mexico [*MARC geographic area code*] [*Library of Congress*] (LCCP)
**NMxB** ... Board of Cooperative Educational Services, Regional Resource Center, Mexico, NY [*Library symbol*] [*Library of Congress*] (LCLS)
**NMY** ... Mayville State College, Mayville, ND [*OCLC symbol*] (OCLC)
**NMY** ... Nonresonant Magnetic Yoke
**NMyM** ... Maryknoll Fathers Seminary, Maryknoll, NY [*Library symbol*] [*Library of Congress*] (LCLS)
**NMZ** ... Norman Resources Ltd. [*Vancouver Stock Exchange symbol*]
**NMZ** ... Willow Grove, PA [*Location identifier*] [*FAA*] (FAAL)
**NMZA** ... Metro Mobile Centers, Inc. [*AMEX symbol*] (CTT)
**NN** ... Anonimo [*Anonymous, Joint-Stock*] [*Portuguese*]
**nn** ... Footnotes (DLA)
**NN** ... Names
**NN** ... NASA Notice
**NN** ... National Neighbors (EA)
**NN** ... Natural, Nongrazed [*Agriculture*]
**NN** ... Nearest Neighbor [*Mathematics*] [*Computer search term*]
**NN** ... Necessary Nuisance [*i.e., a husband*] [*Slang*]
**NN** ... Nerves
**NN** ... Neurotics Nomine [*British*]
**NN** ... Neutral and Nonaligned [*Nations*]
**NN** ... Nevada Northern Railway Co. [*AAR code*]
**nn** ... New Hebrides [*MARC country of publication code*] [*Library of Congress*] (LCCP)
**NN** ... New Nationals [*Political party*] [*Australia*]
**NN** ... New Nigerian [*A publication*]
**NN** ... New York Public Library, New York, NY [*Library symbol*] [*Library of Congress*] (LCLS)
**NN** ... News of the North [*A publication*]
**NN** ... Newspaper News [*A publication*]
**NN** ... Nicaragua Network (EA)
**NN** ... Nigerian Navy
**NN** ... No Name
**NN** ... Non-Nuclear Lance (MCD)
**NN** ... Noon
**NN** ... Normalnull [*Mean Sea Level*] [*German*]
**N/N** ... Not to Be Noted [*Business term*]
**NN** ... Not Nested [*Freight*]
**NN** ... Not Normal
**N/N** ... Not North Of
**NN** ... Notes
**NN** ... Notes [*Finance*]
**NN** ... Nouns
**NN** ... Nouvelle Normes [*New Standards*] [*French government hotel rating system*]
**NN** ... Nuclear Network (EA)
**NN** ... Nucleon-Nucleon
**NN** ... Nucleosides and Nucleotides [*A publication*]
**NN** ... Numismatic News Weekly [*A publication*]
**NN** ... Nurturing Network [*An association*] (EA)
**N2N** ... Project Neighbor to Neighbor (EA)
**NNA** ... American Geographical Society, New York, NY [*Library symbol*] [*Library of Congress*] (LCLS)
**NNA** ... N-Nitrosamine [*Organic chemistry*]
**NNA** ... Nana [*Peru*] [*Seismograph station code, US Geological Survey*] (SEIS)
**NNA** ... National Neckwear Association (EA)
**NNA** ... National Needlework Association (EA)
**NNA** ... National Newman Apostolate
**NNA** ... National News Agency [*Lebanon*]
**NNA** ... National Newspaper Association (EA)
**NNA** ... National Notary Association (EA)
**NNA** ... National Notion Association [*Later, AHSA*] (EA)
**NNA** ... National Numismatic Association (EA)
**NNA** ... Neutral/Nonaligned [*Countries*]
**NNA** ... New Nadina Explorations [*Vancouver Stock Exchange symbol*]
**NNA** ... New Network Architecture
**NNA** ... Nonhistone Nucleoprotein Antibodies [*Immunochemistry*]
**NNA** ... Nordisk Numismatisk Arsskrift [*A publication*]
**NNAA** ... Augusta Warshaw Advertising Library, New York, NY [*Library symbol*] [*Library of Congress*] (LCLS)
**NNAA** ... National Newman Alumni Association [*Defunct*] (EA)
**NNAAl** ... American Alpine Club, New York, NY [*Library symbol*] [*Library of Congress*] (LCLS)
**NNAAr** ... American Arbitration Association, New York, NY [*Library symbol*] [*Library of Congress*] (LCLS)
**NNAB** ... American Bible Society, New York, NY [*Library symbol*] [*Library of Congress*] (LCLS)
**NNABA** ... American Bankers Association, New York, NY [*Library symbol*] [*Library of Congress*] (LCLS)
**NNAC** ... National Native American Cooperative (EA)
**NNAC** ... National Noise Abatement Council [*Defunct*]
**NNACC** ... National Native American Chamber of Commerce (EA)
**NNACS** ... American Cancer Society, New York, NY [*Library symbol*] [*Library of Congress*] (LCLS)
**NNAD** ... Anti-Defamation League of B'nai B'rith, New York, NY [*Library symbol*] [*Library of Congress*] (LCLS)
**NNADAP** .. National Native Alcohol and Drug Abuse Program [*Canada*]
**NNAdv** ... American Association of Advertising Agencies, New York, NY [*Library symbol*] [*Library of Congress*] (LCLS)
**NNAF** ... American Foundation for the Blind, New York, NY [*Library symbol*] [*Library of Congress*] (LCLS)
**NNAFS** ... National Newman Association of Faculty and Staff [*Defunct*] (EA)
**NNAG** ... American Gas Association, New York, NY [*Library symbol*] [*Library of Congress*] (LCLS)
**NNAG** ... NATO Naval Advisory Group (NATG)
**NNAG** ... NATO Naval Armaments Group (NATG)
**NNAI** ... American Irish Historical Society, New York, NY [*Library symbol*] [*Library of Congress*] (LCLS)
**NNAIA** ... American Institute of Certified Public Accountants, New York, NY [*Library symbol*] [*Library of Congress*] (LCLS)
**NNAIP** ... American Institute of Physics, New York, NY [*Library symbol*] [*Library of Congress*] (LCLS)
**NNAJ** ... American Jewish Committee, New York, NY [*Library symbol*] [*Library of Congress*] (LCLS)
**NNAJN** ... American Journal of Nursing Co., New York, NY [*Library symbol*] [*Library of Congress*] (LCLS)
**NNAKC** ... American Kennel Club, New York, NY [*Library symbol*] [*Library of Congress*] (LCLS)
**NNAL** ... American Academy of Arts and Letters, New York, NY [*Library symbol*] [*Library of Congress*] (LCLS)
**NNAMA** ... American Management Associations, New York, NY [*Library symbol*] [*Library of Congress*] (LCLS)
**NNAMM** .. American Merchant Marine Library Association, New York, NY [*Library symbol*] [*Library of Congress*] (LCLS)
**NNAN** ... American Numismatic Society, New York, NY [*Library symbol*] [*Library of Congress*] (LCLS)
**NNAn** ... Anthology Film Archives, New York, NY [*Library symbol*] [*Library of Congress*] (LCLS)
**NNan** ... Nanuet Public Library, Nanuet, NY [*Library symbol*] [*Library of Congress*] (LCLS)
**NNAP** ... New Native People [*A publication*]
**NNAPS** ... Night Navigation and Pilotage System
**NNAPW** ... National Network of Asian and Pacific Women (EA)
**NNASA** ... American National Standards Institute, New York, NY [*Library symbol*] [*Library of Congress*] (LCLS)
**NNASF** ... American-Scandinavian Foundation, New York, NY [*Library symbol*] [*Library of Congress*] (LCLS)
**NNASovM** ... American-Soviet Medical Society, New York, NY [*Library symbol*] [*Library of Congress*] [*Obsolete*] (LCLS)
**NNASP** ... American Society for Psychical Research, New York, NY [*Library symbol*] [*Library of Congress*] (LCLS)
**NNAT** ... American Telephone & Telegraph Co., Corporate Research Library, New York, NY [*Library symbol*] [*Library of Congress*] (LCLS)
**NNAuS** ... National Audubon Society, New York, NY [*Library symbol*] [*Library of Congress*] (LCLS)
**N/NAVEXOS** ... Navy/Executive Offices (AAG)
**NNAVS** ... Association for Voluntary Sterilization, Inc., International Project, New York, NY [*Library symbol*] [*Library of Congress*] (LCLS)
**NNAy** ... American Home Products Corp., Ayerst Medical Library, New York, NY [*Library symbol*] [*Library of Congress*] (LCLS)
**NNB** ... Association of the Bar of the City of New York, New York, NY [*Library symbol*] [*Library of Congress*] (LCLS)
**NNB** ... National Needlecraft Bureau (EA)
**NNB** ... National News Bureau [*Commercial firm*] (EA)
**NNB** ... New Natura Brevium [*A publication*] (DSA)
**NN-B** ... New York Public Library, Albert A. and Henry W. Berg Collection, New York, NY [*Library symbol*] [*Library of Congress*] (LCLS)
**NNb** ... North Babylon Public Library, North Babylon, NY [*Library symbol*] [*Library of Congress*] (LCLS)
**NNB** ... Northumberland and Newcastle Board of Education [*UTLAS symbol*]
**NNb** ... Numismatisches Nachrichtenblatt. Organ des Verbandes der Deutschen Muenzvereine [*A publication*]
**NNBa** ... Barnard College, Columbia University, New York, NY [*Library symbol*] [*Library of Congress*] (LCLS)
**NNBA** ... National Nurses in Business Association (EA)
**NNBB** ... Native News and BIA [*Bureau of Indian Affairs*] Bulletin [*A publication*]
**NNBBC** ... Bernard M. Baruch College of the City University of New York, New York, NY [*Library symbol*] [*Library of Congress*] (LCLS)
**NNBC** ... Bronx Community College, New York, NY [*Library symbol*] [*Library of Congress*] (LCLS)
**NNBC** ... National Network of Bilingual Centers (EA)
**NNbe** ... North Bellmore Public Library, North Bellmore, NY [*Library symbol*] [*Library of Congress*] (LCLS)
**NNbeDE** ... Dinkelmeyer Elementary School, North Bellmore, NY [*Library symbol*] [*Library of Congress*] (LCLS)
**NNbeGE** ... Gunther Elementary School, North Bellmore, NY [*Library symbol*] [*Library of Congress*] (LCLS)

**NNbePE**..... Park Elementary School, North Bellmore, NY [*Library symbol*] [*Library of Congress*] (LCLS)
**NNBeS**....... Bentley School, New York, NY [*Library symbol*] [*Library of Congress*] (LCLS)
**NNbeSME**... Saw Mill Elementary School, North Bellmore, NY [*Library symbol*] [*Library of Congress*] (LCLS)
**NNBG**........ New York Botanical Garden, Bronx, NY [*Library symbol*] [*Library of Congress*] (LCLS)
**NNBI**......... Beth Israel Medical Center, New York, NY [*Library symbol*] [*Library of Congress*] (LCLS)
**NNBIS**....... National Narcotics Border Interdiction System
**NNBL**........ National Negro Business League [*Later, National Business League*]
**NNBLI**....... British Information Services, New York, NY [*Library symbol*] [*Library of Congress*] (LCLS)
**NNBMC**.... Borough of Manhattan Community College, New York, NY [*Library symbol*] [*Library of Congress*] (LCLS)
**NN-Br**........ New York Public Library, Branch Library System, New York, NY [*Library symbol*] [*Library of Congress*] (LCLS)
**NNBS**........ Biblical Seminary in New York, New York, NY [*Library symbol*] [*Library of Congress*] (LCLS)
**NNBSC**...... Bank Street College of Education, New York, NY [*Library symbol*] [*Library of Congress*] (LCLS)
**NNBYA**..... Nature: New Biology [*A publication*]
**NNC**........... Columbia University, New York, NY [*Library symbol*] [*Library of Congress*] (LCLS)
**NNC**........... Naga National Council [*India*] (PD)
**NNC**........... Natal Native Contingent [*British military*] (DMA)
**NNC**........... National Namibia Concerns (EA)
**NNC**........... National Neighborhood Coalition (EA)
**NNC**........... National News Council (EA)
**NNC**........... National Nomad Club [*Defunct*] (EA)
**NNC**........... National Nuclear Corporation [*British*]
**NNC**........... National Nudist Council (EA)
**NNC**........... National Nutrition Consortium (EA)
**NNC**........... Navy Nurse Corps
**NNC**........... Neutral Nations Committee [*CINCPAC*] (CINC)
**NN/C**......... Night Noise Group C [*Aircraft*]
**NNC**........... Nolan, Norton & Co., Inc., Lexington, MA [*OCLC symbol*] (OCLC)
**NNC**........... Northern Navigation Company Ltd. [*AAR code*]
**NNC**........... Northwest Nazarene College [*Nampa, ID*]
**NNC**........... Nudist National Committee (EA)
**NNC-A**...... Columbia University, Avery Library of Architecture, New York, NY [*Library symbol*] [*Library of Congress*] (LCLS)
**NNCA**........ National Newman Chaplains Association [*Later, CCMA*] (EA)
**NNCAA**..... National Negro County Agents Association (EA)
**NNCar**....... Carnegie Corp. of New York, New York, NY [*Library symbol*] [*Library of Congress*] (LCLS)
**NNC-B**....... Columbia University, Biological Sciences Library, New York, NY [*Library symbol*] [*Library of Congress*] (LCLS)
**NNCBS**...... Columbia Broadcasting System, Inc., New York, NY [*Library symbol*] [*Library of Congress*] (LCLS)
**NNCC**........ Chemists' Club, New York, NY [*Library symbol*] [*Library of Congress*] (LCLS)
**NNCC**........ National Network Control Centre [*Communications*] [*British*]
**NNCCVTE**... National Network for Curriculum Coordination in Vocational and Technical Education (OICC)
**NNCE**........ Carnegie Endowment for International Peace, New York, NY [*Library symbol*] [*Library of Congress*] (LCLS)
**NNC-EA**.... Columbia University, East Asiatic Library, New York, NY [*Library symbol*] [*Library of Congress*] (LCLS)
**NNCEF**...... Child Education Foundation, New York, NY [*Library symbol*] [*Library of Congress*] [*Obsolete*] (LCLS)
**NNCenC**.... Century Association, New York, NY [*Library symbol*] [*Library of Congress*] (LCLS)
**NNCEP**..... Centro de Estudios Puertorriquenos, New York, NY [*Library symbol*] [*Library of Congress*] (LCLS)
**NNCF**........ Commonwealth Fund, New York, NY [*Library symbol*] [*Library of Congress*] (LCLS)
**NNCF**........ National Newman Club Federation [*Defunct*] (EA)
**NNCFo**...... Council on Foundations, New York, NY [*Library symbol*] [*Library of Congress*] (LCLS)
**NNCFR**..... Council on Foreign Relations, New York, NY [*Library symbol*] [*Library of Congress*] (LCLS)
**NNC-G**...... Columbia University, Lamont-Doherty Geological Observatory, Palisades, NY [*Library symbol*] [*Library of Congress*] (LCLS)
**NNCI**......... College of Insurance, New York, NY [*Library symbol*] [*Library of Congress*] (LCLS)
**NNCit**........ Cities Service Co., Corporate Library, New York, NY [*Library symbol*] [*Library of Congress*] (LCLS)
**NNC-L**....... Columbia University, Law Library, New York, NY [*Library symbol*] [*Library of Congress*] (LCLS)
**NNC-M**..... Columbia University, Medical Library, New York, NY [*Library symbol*] [*Library of Congress*] (LCLS)
**NNCN**....... Northern Nigeria Case Notes [*A publication*] (DLA)
**NNCo**......... Collectors Club, New York, NY [*Library symbol*] [*Library of Congress*] (LCLS)
**NNcoM**...... Moore-Cottrell Subscription Agencies, Inc., North Cohocton, NY [*Library symbol*] [*Library of Congress*] (LCLS)
**NNConE**.... Consolidated Edison Co., Inc., New York, NY [*Library symbol*] [*Library of Congress*] (LCLS)
**NNCoo**....... Cooper Union for the Advancement of Science and Art, New York, NY [*Library symbol*] [*Library of Congress*] (LCLS)
**NNCorM**... Cornell University, Medical College, New York, NY [*Library symbol*] [*Library of Congress*] (LCLS)
**NNCorM-D**... Cornell University, Medical College, Oskar Diethelm Historical Library, New York, NY [*Library symbol*] [*Library of Congress*] (LCLS)
**NNC-P**....... Columbia University, College of Pharmacy, New York, NY [*Library symbol*] [*Library of Congress*] (LCLS)
**NNCP**........ Pfizer, Inc., New York, NY [*Library symbol*] [*Library of Congress*] (LCLS)
**NNCPL**...... College of Police Science, New York, NY [*Library symbol*] [*Library of Congress*] (LCLS)
**NNCPM**.... New York College of Podiatric Medicine, New York, NY [*Library symbol*] [*Library of Congress*] (LCLS)
**NNC-Pop**... Columbia University, International Institute for the Study of Human Reproduction, Center for Population and Family Health, New York, NY [*Library symbol*] [*Library of Congress*] (LCLS)
**NNC-Ps**..... Columbia University, Psychology Library, New York, NY [*Library symbol*] [*Library of Congress*] (LCLS)
**NNcR**........ Roberts Wesleyan College, North Chili, NY [*Library symbol*] [*Library of Congress*] (LCLS)
**NNCre**....... Creedmore Psychiatric Center, Queens Village, New York, NY [*Library symbol*] [*Library of Congress*] (LCLS)
**NNCS**........ Child Study Association of America, New York, NY [*Library symbol*] [*Library of Congress*] (LCLS)
**NNCSC**..... National Neutron Cross Section Center [*AEC*] (MCD)
**NNC-T**....... Columbia University, Teachers College, New York, NY [*Library symbol*] [*Library of Congress*] (LCLS)
**NNC-Typ**... Columbia University, American Typefounders' Library, New York, NY [*Library symbol*] [*Library of Congress*] (LCLS)
**NNCU-G**... City University of New York, Graduate Center, New York, NY [*Library symbol*] [*Library of Congress*] (LCLS)
**NNCU-L**.... City University of New York, Law School, Flushing, NY [*Library symbol*] [*Library of Congress*] (LCLS)
**NNCU-T**.... City University of New York, Division of Teacher Education, New York, NY [*Library symbol*] [*Library of Congress*] (LCLS)
**NNCX**........ Newbridge Networks Corp. [*NASDAQ symbol*] (NQ)
**NND**.......... Dover Publications, New York, NY [*Library symbol*] [*Library of Congress*] (LCLS)
**NND**.......... National Network Dialing [*Telecommunications*] (TEL)
**NND**.......... National Number Dialing [*Telecommunications*] (DCTA)
**NND**.......... Naval Net Depot
**NND**.......... Neo-Natal Death [*Medicine*]
**NND**.......... New and Nonofficial Drugs [*AMA*]
**NNDC**........ National Naval Dental Center
**NNDC**........ National New Democratic Coalition (EA)
**NNDC**........ National Nuclear Data Center [*Department of Energy*] [*Database producer*] (IID)
**NNDE**........ Nearest-Neighbor Distance Error [*Algorithm*]
**NNDP**........ Naga National Democratic Party [*India*] [*Political party*] (PPW)
**NNDPA**...... N-Nitrosodiphenylamine [*Organic chemistry*]
**NNDPW**.... Davis, Polk & Wardwell, Law Library, New York, NY [*Library symbol*] [*Library of Congress*] (LCLS)
**NNDR**........ National Non-Domestic Rate [*British*]
**NNDTC**..... National Nondestructive Testing Centre [*Atomic Energy Authority*] [*Information service or system*] (IID)
**NNE**.......... Engineering Societies Library, New York, NY [*Library symbol*] [*Library of Congress*] (LCLS)
**NNE**.......... Nonneuron-Specific Enolase [*An enzyme*]
**NNE**.......... Nonstandard Negro English
**NNE**.......... North-Northeast
**NNEA**........ National Negro Evangelical Association [*Later, NBEA*]
**NNEB**........ National Nursery Examination Board
**NNebg**........ Newburgh Free Library, Newburgh, NY [*Library symbol*] [*Library of Congress*] (LCLS)
**NNebgE**..... Epiphany Apostolic College, Newburgh, NY [*Library symbol*] [*Library of Congress*] (LCLS)
**NNebgL**..... Ninth Judicial District Law Library, Newburgh, NY [*Library symbol*] [*Library of Congress*] (LCLS)
**NNEC**........ Explorers Club, New York, NY [*Library symbol*] [*Library of Congress*] (LCLS)
**NNec**.......... New City Free Library, New City, NY [*Library symbol*] [*Library of Congress*] (LCLS)
**NNECA**..... National Network of Episcopal Clergy Associations (EA)
**NNECH**..... National Nutrition Education Clearing House [*Society for Nutrition Education*] (IID)
**NNEF**........ Educational Film Library Association, New York, NY [*Library symbol*] [*Library of Congress*] (LCLS)
**NNef**.......... Newfane Public Library, Newfane, NY [*Library symbol*] [*Library of Congress*] (LCLS)
**NNefH**....... Inter-Community Memorial Hospital, Newfane, NY [*Library symbol*] [*Library of Congress*] (LCLS)
**NNegbM**.... Mount St. Mary College, Newburgh, NY [*Library symbol*] [*Library of Congress*] (LCLS)

**NNegbWM** ... Washington's Headquarters Museum, Newburgh, NY [*Library symbol*] [*Library of Congress*] (LCLS)
**NNehpHH** ... Herricks High School, New Hyde Park, NY [*Library symbol*] [*Library of Congress*] (LCLS)
**NNEL** ........ Equitable Life Assurance Society of the United States, Medical Library, New York, NY [*Library symbol*] [*Library of Congress*] (LCLS)
**NNEL-M** ... Equitable Life Assurance Society of the United States, Medical Library, New York, NY [*Library symbol*] [*Library of Congress*] (LCLS)
**NNepa** ........ Elting Memorial Library, New Paltz, NY [*Library symbol*] [*Library of Congress*] (LCLS)
**NNepaSU** .. State University of New York, College at New Paltz, New Paltz, NY [*Library symbol*] [*Library of Congress*] (LCLS)
**NNer** .......... New Rochelle Public Library, New Rochelle, NY [*Library symbol*] [*Library of Congress*] (LCLS)
**NNerAIS** ... United States Army, Information School, Fort Slocum, New Rochelle, NY [*Library symbol*] [*Library of Congress*] (LCLS)
**NNerC** ....... College of New Rochelle, New Rochelle, NY [*Library symbol*] [*Library of Congress*] (LCLS)
**NNerI** ........ Iona College, New Rochelle, NY [*Library symbol*] [*Library of Congress*] (LCLS)
**NNERN** ..... North-Northeastern [*Meteorology*] (FAAC)
**NNES** ........ National Nuclear Energy Series [*of AEC-sponsored books*]
**NNET** ........ [*The*] Nostalgia Network, Inc. [*NASDAQ symbol*] (NQ)
**NNEU** ........ Naval Nuclear Evaluation Unit
**NNEW** ....... Ernst & Whinney, Audit Management Services, New York, NY [*Library symbol*] [*Library of Congress*] (LCLS)
**NNEW** ....... New York Newsday [*A publication*]
**NNEWD** .... North-Northeastward [*Meteorology*] (FAAC)
**NNF** ........... Fordham University, New York, NY [*Library symbol*] [*Library of Congress*] (LCLS)
**NNF** ........... Namibia National Front [*Political party*] (PPW)
**NNF** ........... National Nephrosis Foundation [*Later, NKF*]
**NNF** ........... National Newman Foundation [*Defunct*] (EA)
**NNF** ........... National Newspaper Foundation (EA)
**NNF** ........... National Nothing Foundation [*Defunct*] (EA)
**NNF** ........... Nordisk Neurokirurgisk Forening [*Scandinavian Neurosurgical Society - SNS*] (EAIO)
**NNF** ........... Nordisk Neurologisk Forening [*Scandinavian Neurological Association - SNA*] (EAIO)
**NNF** ........... Northern Nurses Federation [*Norway*]
**NNFA** ......... National Nutritional Foods Association (EA)
**NNFB** ......... Ford, Bacon & Davis, Inc., New York, NY [*Library symbol*] [*Library of Congress*] (LCLS)
**NNFBC** ...... First Boston Corporation, New York, NY [*Library symbol*] [*Library of Congress*] (LCLS)
**NNFC** ......... Finch College, New York, NY [*Library symbol*] [*Library of Congress*] (LCLS)
**NNFE** ......... Free Europe Committee, New York, NY [*Library symbol*] [*Library of Congress*] (LCLS)
**NNFF** ......... Ford Foundation, New York, NY [*Library symbol*] [*Library of Congress*] (LCLS)
**NNFF** ......... National Neurofibromatosis Foundation (EA)
**NNFF** ......... Not Nested or Folded Flat [*Freight*]
**NNFF-FL** .. Ford Foundation, Ford Foundation Library, New York, NY [*Library symbol*] [*Library of Congress*] (LCLS)
**NNFI** ......... French Institute/Alliance Francaise, New York, NY [*Library symbol*] [*Library of Congress*] (LCLS)
**NNFIT** ....... Fashion Institute of Technology, New York, NY [*Library symbol*] [*Library of Congress*] (LCLS)
**NNF-L** ....... Fordham University, Law Library, New York, NY [*Library symbol*] [*Library of Congress*] (LCLS)
**NNFL** ......... Religious Society of Friends [*Quakers*], New York, NY [*Library symbol*] [*Library of Congress*] (LCLS)
**NNF-LC** .... Fordham University, Library at Lincoln Center, New York, NY [*Library symbol*] [*Library of Congress*] (LCLS)
**NNFM** ....... Grand Lodge of New York, F & AM Library and Museum, New York, NY [*Library symbol*] [*Library of Congress*] (LCLS)
**NNF Nytt** .. NNF. Nytt Meddelelser fra Norsk Numismatisk Forening [*A publication*]
**NNFoC** ...... Foundation Center Library, New York, NY [*Library symbol*] [*Library of Congress*] (LCLS)
**NNFoM** ..... Forbes Magazine, Inc., New York, NY [*Library symbol*] [*Library of Congress*] (LCLS)
**NNFP** ......... Nuclear Nitrogen Fixation Plant
**NNFr** ......... Frick Art Reference Library, New York, NY [*Library symbol*] [*Library of Congress*] (LCLS)
**NNF-RS** .... Fordham University, Institute of Contemporary Russian Studies, New York, NY [*Library symbol*] [*Library of Congress*] (LCLS)
**NNFS** ......... Nordic Narrow/16mm Film Society (EA)
**NNFT** ......... National Federation of Textiles, New York, NY [*Library symbol*] [*Library of Congress*] (LCLS)
**NNFU** ......... Nuclear Nonfirst Use
**NNG** .......... General Theological Seminary of the Protestant Episcopal Church, New York, NY [*Library symbol*] [*Library of Congress*] (LCLS)
**NNG** .......... Nanning [*China*] [*Airport symbol*] (OAG)
**NNG** .......... National Network of Grantmakers (EA)
**NNGA** ........ Northern Nut Growers Association (EA)
**NNGBSW** ... National Network of Graduate Business School Women [*Knoxville, TN*] (EA)
**NNGNA** .... Novosti Neftyanoi i Gazovoi Tekhniki, Neftepererabotka, i Neftekhimiya [*A publication*]
**NNGoe** ....... Goethe House, German Cultural Institute, New York, NY [*Library symbol*] [*Library of Congress*] (LCLS)
**NNGr** ......... Grolier Club, New York, NY [*Library symbol*] [*Library of Congress*] (LCLS)
**NNGS** ........ Church of Jesus Christ of Latter-Day Saints, Genealogical Society Library, New York Branch, New York, NY [*Library symbol*] [*Library of Congress*] (LCLS)
**NNGu** ........ Solomon R. Guggenheim Museum, New York, NY [*Library symbol*] [*Library of Congress*] (LCLS)
**NNGZAZ** .. Folia Endocrinologica Japonica [*A publication*]
**NNGZB** ..... Neujahrsblatt. Naturforschende Gesellschaft in Zuerich [*A publication*]
**NNGZB2** ... Neujahrsblatt. Naturforschende Gesellschaft in Zuerich [*A publication*]
**NNH** .......... Hispanic Society of America, New York, NY [*Library symbol*] [*Library of Congress*] (LCLS)
**NNH** .......... Natal Native Horse [*British military*] (DMA)
**NNH** .......... National Humanities Center, Research Triangle Park, NC [*OCLC symbol*] (OCLC)
**NNH** .......... Neuva Narrativa Hispanoamericana [*A publication*]
**NNH** .......... NHI Nelson Holdings International Ltd. [*AMEX symbol*] (SPSG)
**NNH** .......... Nordiska Namnden for Handikappfragor [*Nordic Committee on Disability - NCD*] (EAIO)
**NNHA** ........ National Novice Hockey Association [*Later, HNA*] (EA)
**NNHC** ....... Hostos Community College, New York, NY [*Library symbol*] [*Library of Congress*] (LCLS)
**NNHC** ....... Natal Native High Court Reports [*1899-1915*] [*South Africa*] [*A publication*] (DLA)
**NNHCF-C** ... Holy Cross Friary, Juniper Carol Library, New York, NY [*Library symbol*] [*Library of Congress*] (LCLS)
**NNHE** ....... New York City Board of Higher Education, New York, NY [*Library symbol*] [*Library of Congress*] (LCLS)
**NNHeb** ...... Hebrew Union College - Jewish Institute of Religion, New York, NY [*Library symbol*] [*Library of Congress*] (LCLS)
**NNHH** ....... Harlem Hospital Center, Medical Library, New York, NY [*Library symbol*] [*Library of Congress*] (LCLS)
**NNHL** ....... National Novice Hockey League [*Later, NNHA*] (EA)
**NNHol** ...... Holland Society of New York, New York, NY [*Library symbol*] [*Library of Congress*] (LCLS)
**NNHor** ...... Horticultural Society of New York, Inc., New York, NY [*Library symbol*] [*Library of Congress*] (LCLS)
**NNhp** ......... New Hyde Park Public Library, New Hyde Park, NY [*Library symbol*] [*Library of Congress*] (LCLS)
**NNhpH** ...... Hillside Public Library, New Hyde Park, NY [*Library symbol*] [*Library of Congress*] (LCLS)
**NNhpJ** ....... Long Island Jewish Hospital, New Hyde Park, NY [*Library symbol*] [*Library of Congress*] (LCLS)
**NNHR** ....... New York City Human Resources Administration, New York, NY [*Library symbol*] [*Library of Congress*] (LCLS)
**NNHS** ........ Hospital for Special Surgery, New York, NY [*Library symbol*] [*Library of Congress*] (LCLS)
**NNhS** ......... Special Metals Corp., New Hartford, NY [*Library symbol*] [*Library of Congress*] (LCLS)
**NNHuC** ..... Hunter College of the City University of New York, New York, NY [*Library symbol*] [*Library of Congress*] (LCLS)
**NNI** ............ National Newspaper Index [*Information Access Co.*] [*Bibliographic database*] [*Information service or system*] (IID)
**NNI** ............ Net National Income [*Economics*]
**NNI** ............ Net-Net Income [*Business term*]
**NNI** ............ Network Node Interface [*Data processing*]
**NNI** ............ Noise and Number Index
**NNI** ............ Nonnuclear Instrumentation (NRCH)
**NNI** ............ Nucleon-Nucleon Interaction
**NNI** ............ Office of Naval Intelligence Publications
**NNIA** ......... American Institute of Aeronautics and Astronautics, New York, NY [*Library symbol*] [*Library of Congress*] (LCLS)
**NNia** .......... Niagara Falls Public Library, Niagara Falls, NY [*Library symbol*] [*Library of Congress*] (LCLS)
**NNiaA** ....... Airco Speer Research & Development Laboratories, Niagara Falls, NY [*Library symbol*] [*Library of Congress*] (LCLS)
**NNiaB** ........ Bell Aerospace Textron, Technical Library, Niagara Falls, NY [*Library symbol*] [*Library of Congress*] (LCLS)
**NNiaC** ........ Niagara County Community College, Niagara Falls, NY [*Library symbol*] [*Library of Congress*] (LCLS)
**NNiaCa** ...... Carborundum Co., Niagara Falls, NY [*Library symbol*] [*Library of Congress*] (LCLS)
**NNiaD** ....... E. I. Du Pont de Nemours & Co., Electrochemical Department, Niagara Falls, NY [*Library symbol*] [*Library of Congress*] (LCLS)
**NNiaEM** .... Elkem Metals Co., Niagara Falls, NY [*Library symbol*] [*Library of Congress*] (LCLS)
**NNiaH** ....... Hooker Chemical Corp. [*Later, Hooker Chemicals & Plastics Corp.*], Niagara Falls, NY [*Library symbol*] [*Library of Congress*] (LCLS)

**NNiaHC** .... Hooker Chemicals & Plastics Corp., Business Library, Niagara Falls, NY [*Library symbol*] [*Library of Congress*] (LCLS)
**NNiaM** ...... Moore Business Forms, Niagara Falls, NY [*Library symbol*] [*Library of Congress*] (LCLS)
**NNiaMed** .. Niagara Falls Memorial Medical Center, Medical Library, Niagara Falls, NY [*Library symbol*] [*Library of Congress*] (LCLS)
**NNiaN** ....... National Lead Co., Research Library, Niagara Falls, NY [*Library symbol*] [*Library of Congress*] (LCLS)
**NNiaNC** .... NIACET Corporation, Niagara Falls, NY [*Library symbol*] [*Library of Congress*] (LCLS)
**NNiaNL**..... Nioga Library System, Niagara Falls, NY [*Library symbol*] [*Library of Congress*] (LCLS)
**NNiaTC** ..... TAM Ceramics, Inc., Niagara Falls, NY [*Library symbol*] [*Library of Congress*] (LCLS)
**NNiaTV**..... Trott Vocational High School, Niagara Falls, NY [*Library symbol*] [*Library of Congress*] (LCLS)
**NNiaU** ....... Niagara University, Niagara University, NY [*Library symbol*] [*Library of Congress*] (LCLS)
**NNiaUC** .... Union Carbide Corp., Niagara Falls, NY [*Library symbol*] [*Library of Congress*] (LCLS)
**NNICC** ...... National Narcotics Intelligence Consumers Committee [*Drug Enforcement Administration*] [*Washington, DC*] (EGAO)
**NNIIE**........ Institute of International Education, New York, NY [*Library symbol*] [*Library of Congress*] (LCLS)
**NNIMD**..... Institute for Muscle Disease, New York, NY [*Library symbol*] [*Library of Congress*] [*Obsolete*] (LCLS)
**NNIND**...... International Nickel Co., Technical Library, New York, NY [*Library symbol*] [*Library of Congress*] (LCLS)
**NNInS** ....... Insurance Society of New York, New York, NY [*Library symbol*] [*Library of Congress*] (LCLS)
**NNIP** ......... Institute of Public Administration, New York, NY [*Library symbol*] [*Library of Congress*] (LCLS)
**NNIPF**....... International Planned Parenthood Federation, Documentation and Publications Center, New York, NY [*Library symbol*] [*Library of Congress*] (LCLS)
**NNIR** ......... Industrial Relations Counselors, New York, NY [*Library symbol*] [*Library of Congress*] (LCLS)
**NNIRR** ...... National Network for Immigrant and Refugee Rights (EA)
**NNIS** ......... Library for Intercultural Studies, Inc., New York, NY [*Library symbol*] [*Library of Congress*] (LCLS)
**NNIS** ......... Nonnuclear Instrumentation System (NRCH)
**NNJ** ........... Jewish Theological Seminary of America, New York, NY [*Library symbol*] [*Library of Congress*] (LCLS)
**NNJ** ........... Nakano [*Japan*] [*Seismograph station code, US Geological Survey*] (SEIS)
**NNJef** ........ Jefferson School of Social Science, New York, NY [*Library symbol*] [*Library of Congress*] [*Obsolete*] (LCLS)
**NNJH**........ Joint Health Library, New York, NY [*Library symbol*] [*Library of Congress*] [*Obsolete*] (LCLS)
**NNJHK**..... Jenny Hunter's Kindergarten and Primary Training School, New York, NY [*Library symbol*] [*Library of Congress*] [*Obsolete*] (LCLS)
**NNJJ** ......... John Jay College of Criminal Justice, New York, NY [*Library symbol*] [*Library of Congress*] (LCLS)
**NNJu** ......... Juilliard School of Music, New York, NY [*Library symbol*] [*Library of Congress*] (LCLS)
**NNK** .......... Naknek [*Alaska*] [*Airport symbol*] (OAG)
**NNK** .......... Nic-Nik Resources [*Vancouver Stock Exchange symbol*]
**NNK** .......... Nonnuclear Kill
**NNKKAA**.. Journal. Agricultural Chemical Society of Japan [*A publication*]
**NNKKB**..... Nainen Kikan [*A publication*]
**NNL**........... Beeville, TX [*Location identifier*] [*FAA*] (FAAL)
**NNL**........... Herbert H. Lehman College of the City University of New York, New York, NY [*Library symbol*] [*Library of Congress*] (LCLS)
**NN-L** ......... New York Public Library, Research Library for the Performing Arts at Lincoln Center, New York, NY [*Library symbol*] [*Library of Congress*] (LCLS)
**NNL**........... Nigeria Newsletter [*A publication*]
**NNL**........... Ninilchik [*Alaska*] [*Seismograph station code, US Geological Survey*] (SEIS)
**NNL**........... Nondalton [*Alaska*] [*Airport symbol*] (OAG)
**NNLBI**....... Leo Baeck Institute, New York, NY [*Library symbol*] [*Library of Congress*] (LCLS)
**NNLC**........ Lutheran Council in the USA, New York, NY [*Library symbol*] [*Library of Congress*] (LCLS)
**NNLC**........ Ngwane National Liberatory Congress [*Swaziland*]
**NNLDA**..... National Network of Learning Disabled Adults (EA)
**NNLehman** ... Lehman Corp., New York, NY [*Library symbol*] [*Library of Congress*] (LCLS)
**NNLH** ....... Lenox Hill Hospital, Medical Library, New York, NY [*Library symbol*] [*Library of Congress*] (LCLS)
**NNLI** ......... New York Law Institute, New York, NY [*Library symbol*] [*Library of Congress*] (LCLS)
**NNLN**........ Northern Nigeria Legal Notes [*A publication*] (DLA)
**NNLR**........ Northern Nigeria Law Reports [*A publication*] (DLA)
**NNLS** ........ New York Law School Library, New York, NY [*Library symbol*] [*Library of Congress*] (LCLS)
**NNM** ......... American Museum of Natural History, New York, NY [*Library symbol*] [*Library of Congress*] (LCLS)
**NNM** ......... Davidson College, Davidson, NC [*OCLC symbol*] (OCLC)
**NNM** ......... N-Nitrosomorpholine [*Also, NMOR*] [*Organic chemistry*]
**NNM** ......... Neueste Nachrichten aus dem Morgenlande [*A publication*]
**NN-M** ........ New York Public Library, Municipal Reference Library, New York, NY [*Library symbol*] [*Library of Congress*] (LCLS)
**NNM** ......... Next (or Nearest) New Moon [*Freemasonry*] (ROG)
**NNM** ......... No Neutral Mode
**NNm** .......... North Merrick Public Library, North Merrick, NY [*Library symbol*] [*Library of Congress*] (LCLS)
**NNM** ......... Numismatic Notes and Monographs [*A publication*]
**NNM** ......... Nuveen New York Municipal Income [*AMEX symbol*] (SPSG)
**NNMa** ....... Marymount Manhattan College, New York, NY [*Library symbol*] [*Library of Congress*] (LCLS)
**NNMAI**..... Museum of the American Indian, New York, NY [*Library symbol*] [*Library of Congress*] (LCLS)
**NNMan** ..... Manhattan College, New York, NY [*Library symbol*] [*Library of Congress*] (LCLS)
**NNMB**....... Methodist Board of Missions, New York, NY [*Library symbol*] [*Library of Congress*] (LCLS)
**NNMC**....... Mannes College of Music, New York, NY [*Library symbol*] [*Library of Congress*] (LCLS)
**NNMC**....... National Naval Medical Center [*Bethesda, MD*]
**NNMcGraw** ... McGraw-Hill, Inc., New York, NY [*Library symbol*] [*Library of Congress*] (LCLS)
**NNME**....... Mid-European Studies Center, New York, NY [*Library symbol*] [*Library of Congress*] (LCLS)
**NNMec**...... General Society of Mechanics and Tradesmen, New York, NY [*Library symbol*] [*Library of Congress*] (LCLS)
**NNMel** ...... Andrew W. Mellon Foundation, New York, NY [*Library symbol*] [*Library of Congress*] (LCLS)
**NN-Mel** ..... New York Public Library, Mellon Microfilm Collection, New York, NY [*Library symbol*] [*Library of Congress*] (LCLS)
**NNMer**...... Mercantile Library Association, New York, NY [*Library symbol*] [*Library of Congress*] (LCLS)
**NNMF**....... Markle Foundation, New York, NY [*Library symbol*] [*Library of Congress*] (LCLS)
**NNMH**...... Montefiore Hospital, New York, NY [*Library symbol*] [*Library of Congress*] (LCLS)
**NNMi**........ Millenium Film Workshop, New York, NY [*Library symbol*] [*Library of Congress*] (LCLS)
**NNML**....... Metropolitan Life Insurance Co., New York, NY [*Library symbol*] [*Library of Congress*] (LCLS)
**NNMLC**.... Medical Library Center of New York, New York, NY [*Library symbol*] [*Library of Congress*] (LCLS)
**NNMM** ..... Metropolitan Museum of Art, New York, NY [*Library symbol*] [*Library of Congress*] (LCLS)
**NNMMA** .. Museum of Modern Art, New York, NY [*Library symbol*] [*Library of Congress*] (LCLS)
**NNMMA-F** ... Museum of Modern Art, Film Study Center, New York, NY [*Library symbol*] [*Library of Congress*] (LCLS)
**NNMM-CI** ... Metropolitan Museum of Art, Costume Institute, New York, NY [*Library symbol*] [*Library of Congress*] (LCLS)
**NNMoMA** ... Museum of Modern Art, New York, NY [*Library symbol*] [*Library of Congress*] (LCLS)
**NNMP**....... Motion Picture Association of America, Inc., Research Department Library, New York, NY [*Library symbol*] [*Library of Congress*] (LCLS)
**NNMPA**.... Museum of Primitive Art, New York, NY [*Library symbol*] [*Library of Congress*] (LCLS)
**NN-MPH** .. New York Public Library, Public Health Division, New York, NY [*Library symbol*] [*Library of Congress*] (LCLS)
**NNMR**....... Missionary Research Library, New York, NY [*Library symbol*] [*Library of Congress*] (LCLS)
**NNMRR**.... New York Metropolitan Reference and Research Library Agency, Inc., New York, NY [*Library symbol*] [*Library of Congress*] (LCLS)
**NNMS**....... Manhattan State Hospital, New York, NY [*Library symbol*] [*Library of Congress*] (LCLS)
**NNMSB** .... Nonnuclear Munitions Safety Board [*Military*]
**NNMSCP** ... Nonnuclear Munitions Safety Control Program [*Military*]
**NNMSG**.... Nonnuclear Munitions Safety Group [*Air Force*] (AFM)
**NNMSGP** ... Nonnuclear Munitions Safety Group [*Air Force*]
**NNMSK**.... Memorial Sloan-Kettering Cancer Center, New York, NY [*Library symbol*] [*Library of Congress*] (LCLS)
**NNMSM**... Manhattan School of Music, New York, NY [*Library symbol*] [*Library of Congress*] (LCLS)
**NNMtS**...... Mount Sinai Hospital, New York, NY [*Library symbol*] [*Library of Congress*] (LCLS)
**NNMtSM** ... Mount Sinai School of Medicine of the City University of New York, New York, NY [*Library symbol*] [*Library of Congress*] (LCLS)
**NNMtSV**... College of Mount Saint Vincent, New York, NY [*Library symbol*] [*Library of Congress*] (LCLS)
**NNMus**...... Museum of the City of New York, New York, NY [*Library symbol*] [*Library of Congress*] (LCLS)
**NNN** .......... N-Nitrosonornicotine [*Organic chemistry*]
**NNN** .......... National Navy Notice
**NNN** .......... National Nostalgic Nova (EA)
**NNN** .......... Nitrosonornicotine [*Organic chemistry*]
**NNN** .......... No National Name
**NNN** .......... No No Nanette [*Broadway musical*]

**NNN** .......... Noramco Mining Corp. [*Toronto Stock Exchange symbol*] [*Vancouver Stock Exchange symbol*]
**NNNA** ....... No Name, No Address
**NNNAM** ... New York Academy of Medicine, New York, NY [*Library symbol*] [*Library of Congress*] (LCLS)
**NNNASA** .. National Aeronautical and Space Administration, Institute for Space Studies, New York, NY [*Library symbol*] [*Library of Congress*] (LCLS)
**NNNBC** ..... National Broadcasting Co., Inc., General Library, New York, NY [*Library symbol*] [*Library of Congress*] (LCLS)
**NNNBC-I** ... National Broadcasting Co., Inc., Information Unit, Research Department, New York, NY [*Library symbol*] [*Library of Congress*] (LCLS)
**NNNC** ....... New York Chamber of Commerce, New York, NY [*Library symbol*] [*Library of Congress*] (LCLS)
**NNNCL** ..... New York County Lawyers Association, New York, NY [*Library symbol*] [*Library of Congress*] (LCLS)
**NNNDO** .... Neglect of Non-Neighbor Differential Overlap [*Physics*]
**NNNE** ........ Nigiqpaq Northwind News [*Barrow, Alaska*] [*A publication*]
**NNNeI** ....... Netherlands Information Service, New York, NY [*Library symbol*] [*Library of Congress*] (LCLS)
**NNNGB** ..... New York Genealogical and Biographical Society, New York, NY [*Library symbol*] [*Library of Congress*] (LCLS)
**NNNH** ....... National Health Agencies Library, New York, NY [*Library symbol*] [*Library of Congress*] [*Obsolete*] (LCLS)
**NNNHi** ...... Naval History Society, New York, NY [*Library symbol*] [*Library of Congress*] [*Obsolete*] (LCLS)
**NNNM** ...... New York Medical College, Flower and Fifth Avenue Hospitals, New York, NY [*Library symbol*] [*Library of Congress*] (LCLS)
**NNNN** ....... End of Message [*Aviation code*] (FAAC)
**NNNPsan** ... New York Psychoanalytic Institute, New York, NY [*Library symbol*] [*Library of Congress*] (LCLS)
**NNNPSC** ... National No-Nukes Prison Support Collective (EA)
**NNNPsI** .... New York State Department of Mental Hygiene, Psychiatric Institute, New York, NY [*Library symbol*] [*Library of Congress*] (LCLS)
**NNNS** ........ New School for Social Research, New York, NY [*Library symbol*] [*Library of Congress*] (LCLS)
**NNNSB** ..... National Society for the Prevention of Blindness, New York, NY [*Library symbol*] [*Library of Congress*] (LCLS)
**NNNT** ........ New York Theological Seminary, New York, NY [*Library symbol*] [*Library of Congress*] (LCLS)
**NNNTSH** ... Naukove Tovarystvo Imeni Shevchenka (Shevchenko Scientific Society, Inc.), New York, NY [*Library symbol*] [*Library of Congress*] (LCLS)
**NNNWA** ... N. W. Ayer & Son, New York, NY [*Library symbol*] [*Library of Congress*] (LCLS)
**NNO** .......... Naga Nationalist Organization [*India*]
**NNO** .......... Nord-Nord-Ouest [*North-Northwest*] [*French*]
**NNO** .......... Northern Orion Explorations [*Vancouver Stock Exchange symbol*]
**NNO** .......... Nuveen New York Municipal Market Opportunities [*NYSE symbol*] (SPSG)
**NNOA** ....... National Naval Officers Association (EA)
**NNOC** ....... National Network Operations Center [*Telecommunications*] [*Ottawa, ON*] (TSSD)
**NNOPE** ..... Naturists and Nudists Opposing Pornographic Exploitation (EA)
**NNopo** ....... Northport Public Library, Northport, NY [*Library symbol*] [*Library of Congress*] (LCLS)
**NNopo-E** ... Northport Public Library, East Northport Branch, East Northport, NY [*Library symbol*] [*Library of Congress*] (LCLS)
**NNopoVA** ... United States Veterans Administration Hospital, Northport, NY [*Library symbol*] [*Library of Congress*] (LCLS)
**NNorP** ....... Norwich Pharmacal Co., Norwich, NY [*Library symbol*] [*Library of Congress*] (LCLS)
**NNOt** ......... New York Orthopaedic Hospital, New York, NY [*Library symbol*] [*Library of Congress*] (LCLS)
**NNot** .......... North Tonawanda Public Library, North Tonawanda, NY [*Library symbol*] [*Library of Congress*] (LCLS)
**NNotD** ....... DeGraff Memorial Hospital, North Tonawanda, NY [*Library symbol*] [*Library of Congress*] (LCLS)
**NNotHC** .... Hooker Chemicals & Plastics Corp., Durez Division Library, North Tonawanda, NY [*Library symbol*] [*Library of Congress*] (LCLS)
**NNotL** ........ Lawless Container Corp., North Tonawanda, NY [*Library symbol*] [*Library of Congress*] (LCLS)
**NNP** ........... Needle-Nosed Probe
**NNP** ........... Negative Node Point
**NNP** ........... Nerve Net Pulse [*Neurobiology*]
**NNP** ........... Net National Product [*Economics*]
**NNP** ........... Nuveen New York Performance Plus Municipal [*NYSE symbol*] (SPSG)
**NNPA** ........ National Negro Press Association [*Defunct*] (EA)
**NNPA** ........ National Newspaper Promotion Association [*Later, INPA*] (EA)
**NNPA** ........ National Newspaper Publishers Association (EA)
**NNPA** ........ Nuclear Nonproliferation Act [*1975*]
**NNPA** ........ Port Authority of New York and New Jersey, New York, NY [*Library symbol*] [*Library of Congress*] (LCLS)
**NNParS** ..... Parsons School of Design, New York, NY [*Library symbol*] [*Library of Congress*] (LCLS)
**NNPaul** ...... Paul, Weiss, Rifkind, Wharton & Garrison, Law Library, New York, NY [*Library symbol*] [*Library of Congress*] (LCLS)
**NNPaW** ..... Payne Whitney Clinic, New York, NY [*Library symbol*] [*Library of Congress*] (LCLS)
**NNPC** ........ Pace College, New York, NY [*Library symbol*] [*Library of Congress*] (LCLS)
**NNPC-L** .... Pace University, Law Library, White Plains, NY [*Library symbol*] [*Library of Congress*] (LCLS)
**NNPE-NC** ... National Council of the Protestant Episcopal Church, New York, NY [*Library symbol*] [*Library of Congress*] (LCLS)
**NNPennie** .. Pennie, Edmonds, Morton, Taylor & Adams, New York, NY [*Library symbol*] [*Library of Congress*] (LCLS)
**NNPf** ......... Carl H. Pforzheimer Library, New York, NY [*Library symbol*] [*Library of Congress*] (LCLS)
**NNPH-O** ... Institute of Ophthalmology, Presbyterian Hospital, New York, NY [*Library symbol*] [*Library of Congress*] (LCLS)
**NNPHR** ..... New York City Public Health Research Laboratory, New York, NY [*Library symbol*] [*Library of Congress*] (LCLS)
**NNPHW** .... National New Professional Health Workers [*Later, NPSAPHA*] (EA)
**NNPlan** ...... Planning Assistance, Inc., New York, NY [*Library symbol*] [*Library of Congress*] (LCLS)
**NNPM** ....... Pierpont Morgan Library, New York, NY [*Library symbol*] [*Library of Congress*] (LCLS)
**NNPopC** .... Population Council, New York, NY [*Library symbol*] [*Library of Congress*] (LCLS)
**NNPPA** ..... Neurologia, Neurochirurgia, i Psychiatria Polska [*A publication*]
**NNPPFA** ... Planned Parenthood Federation of America, Inc., Katharine Dexter McCormick Library, New York, NY [*Library symbol*] [*Library of Congress*] (LCLS)
**NNPPNYC** ... Planned Parenthood of New York City, Inc., Abraham Stone Memorial Library, Margaret Sanger Center, New York, NY [*Library symbol*] [*Library of Congress*] (LCLS)
**NNPRM** .... United Presbyterian Mission Library of the United Presbyterian Church in the USA, New York, NY [*Library symbol*] [*Library of Congress*] (LCLS)
**NNPS** ........ Norco Nuclear Power Station (NRCH)
**NNPU** ........ Naval Nuclear Power Unit [*Obsolete*]
**NNR** ........... City College of City University of New York, New York, NY [*Library symbol*] [*Library of Congress*] (LCLS)
**NNR** ........... National Number Routed [*Telecommunications*] (TEL)
**NNR** ........... Nearest-Neighbor Rule [*Mathematics*]
**NNR** ........... Nevada North Resources [*Vancouver Stock Exchange symbol*]
**NNR** ........... New and Nonofficial Remedies [*A publication*]
**NNR** ........... Nordiska Nykterhetsradet [*Nordic Temperance Council - NTC*] (EAIO)
**NNRA** ........ National Negro Republican Assembly [*Defunct*]
**NNRB** ........ Recording for the Blind, Inc., New York, NY [*Library symbol*] [*Library of Congress*] (LCLS)
**NNRDC** ..... National Nuclear Rocket Development Center [*Also known as NRDS*]
**NNRDF** ..... National Nuclear Rocket Development Facility (AAG)
**NNRecA** .... National Recreation Association [*Later, NRPA*], New York, NY [*Library symbol*] [*Library of Congress*] (LCLS)
**NNreP** ....... Regional Plan Association, Inc., Library, New York, NY [*Library symbol*] [*Library of Congress*] (LCLS)
**NNRF** ........ National Neurological Research Foundation (EA)
**NNRF** ........ Non-Negotiable Report of Findings [*Societe Generale de Surveillance SA*] (DS)
**NNRF** ........ Nouvelle Nouvelle Revue Francaise [*A publication*]
**NNRH** ........ Roosevelt Hospital, Medical Library, New York, NY [*Library symbol*] [*Library of Congress*] (LCLS)
**NNRIS** ....... Nebraska Natural Resources Information System [*Nebraska State Natural Resources Commission*] [*Lincoln*] [*Information service or system*] (IID)
**NNRo** ......... Theodore Roosevelt Association, New York, NY [*Library symbol*] [*Library of Congress*] (LCLS)
**NNRocF** ..... Rockefeller Foundation, New York, NY [*Library symbol*] [*Library of Congress*] (LCLS)
**NNRocFA** ... Rockefeller Family & Associates, Inc., Office Library, New York, NY [*Library symbol*] [*Library of Congress*] (LCLS)
**NNRoI** ....... Rochdale Institute, New York, NY [*Library symbol*] [*Library of Congress*] (LCLS)
**NNRom** ...... Romanian Library, New York, NY [*Library symbol*] [*Library of Congress*] (LCLS)
**NNRRB** ..... R. R. Bowker Co., New York, NY [*Library symbol*] [*Library of Congress*] (LCLS)
**NNRT** ........ Racquet and Tennis Club, New York, NY [*Library symbol*] [*Library of Congress*] (LCLS)
**NNRU** ....... Rockefeller University, New York, NY [*Library symbol*] [*Library of Congress*] (LCLS)
**NNRU-P** .... Rockefeller University, Population Council, Bio-Medical Library, New York, NY [*Library symbol*] [*Library of Congress*] (LCLS)
**NNRYS** ..... National Network of Runaway and Youth Services (EA)

**NNS**.......... National Narrowcast Service [*Public Broadcasting Service*] [*Arlington, VA*] [*Telecommunications service*] (TSSD)
**NNS**.......... National Natality Survey
**NNS**.......... National Newspaper Syndicate
**NNS**.......... Navy Navigation Satellite
**NNS**.......... Neural Network Simulator
**NNS**.......... New York Society Library, New York, NY [*Library symbol*] [*Library of Congress*] (LCLS)
**NNS**.......... Nonnuclear Safety (NRCH)
**NNS**.......... Nonnutritive Sweetener
**NNs**.......... North Salem Free Library, North Salem, NY [*Library symbol*] [*Library of Congress*] (LCLS)
**NNS**.......... Nucleon-Nucleon Scattering
**NNSA**........ National Nurses Society on Addictions (EA)
**NNSaB**...... Salomon Brothers, New York, NY [*Library symbol*] [*Library of Congress*] (LCLS)
**NNSAE**..... Society of Automotive Engineers, New York, NY [*Library symbol*] [*Library of Congress*] (LCLS)
**NNSAR**..... Sons of the American Revolution, Empire State Society Library, New York, NY [*Library symbol*] [*Library of Congress*] (LCLS)
**NNSAS**...... Skadden, Arps, Slate, Meagher & Flom, New York, NY [*Library symbol*] [*Library of Congress*] (LCLS)
**NNSB**........ Simmons-Boardman Publishing Corp., New York, NY [*Library symbol*] [*Library of Congress*] [*Obsolete*] (LCLS)
**NNSC**........ Neutral Nations Supervisory Commission
**NN-Sc**........ New York Public Library, Schomburg Collection, New York, NY [*Library symbol*] [*Library of Congress*] (LCLS)
**NNSeag**..... Joseph E. Seagram & Sons, Inc., New York, NY [*Library symbol*] [*Library of Congress*] (LCLS)
**NNSG**........ NASCOM [*NASA Communications Network*] Network Scheduling Group
**NNSIHi**..... Staten Island Historical Society, New York, NY [*Library symbol*] [*Library of Congress*] (LCLS)
**NNSII**........ Staten Island Institute of Arts and Sciences, New York, NY [*Library symbol*] [*Library of Congress*] (LCLS)
**NNSJD**...... Cathedral of Saint John the Divine, New York, NY [*Library symbol*] [*Library of Congress*] (LCLS)
**NNSL**........ Newport News Savings Bank [*NASDAQ symbol*] (NQ)
**NNSN**........ No National Stock Number (AABC)
**NNSNP**..... National Network in Solidarity with the Nicaraguan People (EA)
**NNSPG**..... National Network in Solidarity with the People of Guatemala (EA)
**NNSPo**...... Standard & Poor's Corp., New York, NY [*Library symbol*] [*Library of Congress*] (LCLS)
**NNSR**........ Sons of the Revolution in the State of New York, New York, NY [*Library symbol*] [*Library of Congress*] (LCLS)
**NNSS**......... Navy Navigational Satellite System
**NNStJ**....... St. John's University, Jamaica, NY [*Library symbol*] [*Library of Congress*] (LCLS)
**NNStL**....... Saint Luke's Hospital, Richard Walker Bolling Memorial Medical Library, New York, NY [*Library symbol*] [*Library of Congress*] (LCLS)
**NNStOD**... Standard Oil Co. (New Jersey), New York, NY [*Library symbol*] [*Library of Congress*] (LCLS)
**NNSTWG**... Nonnuclear Survivability Technology Working Group (AFIT)
**NNSU-MC**... State University of New York, Maritime College, Fort Schuyler, Bronx, NY [*Library symbol*] [*Library of Congress*] (LCLS)
**NNSU-Op**... State University of New York, College of Optometry, New York, NY [*Library symbol*] [*Library of Congress*] (LCLS)
**NNSW**........ Nonnuclear Strategic Warfare
**NNSWM**... National Network for Social Work Managers (EA)
**NNSY**........ Norfolk Naval Shipyard [*Portsmouth, VA*]
**NNT**.......... Nan [*Thailand*] [*Airport symbol*] (OAG)
**NNT**.......... Nanotec Canada, Inc. [*Vancouver Stock Exchange symbol*]
**NNT**.......... New York Times, New York, NY [*Library symbol*] [*Library of Congress*] (LCLS)
**NNT**.......... Notice Number Tracking (MCD)
**NNTAICH**... Technical Assistance Information Clearing House, New York, NY [*Library symbol*] [*Library of Congress*] (LCLS)
**NNTax**....... Tax Foundation, Inc., New York, NY [*Library symbol*] [*Library of Congress*] (LCLS)
**NNTC**........ National Nondestructive Testing Centre [*Atomic Energy Authority*] [*Information service or system*] (IID)
**NNTC**........ Norwich and Norfolk Terrier Club (EA)
**NNTC**........ Teachers College, New York, NY [*Library symbol*] [*Library of Congress*] (LCLS)
**NNTF**........ Traphagen School of Fashion, New York, NY [*Library symbol*] [*Library of Congress*] (LCLS)
**NNTM**....... Tobacco Merchants Association of the United States, New York, NY [*Library symbol*] [*Library of Congress*] (LCLS)
**NNTN**........ Not Necessarily the News [*Cable television comedy program*]
**NNTP**........ National Nuclear Test Plan [*Later, NNTRP*]
**NNTRP**..... National Nuclear Test Readiness Program [*Formerly, NNTP*]
**NNTT**........ National New Technology Telescope [*Proposed*] [*National Science Foundation*]
**NNU**.......... New York University, New York, NY [*Library symbol*] [*Library of Congress*] (LCLS)
**NNU**.......... Nordic Numismatic Union (EAIO)
**NNU-B**...... New York University, Graduate School of Business Administration, New York, NY [*Library symbol*] [*Library of Congress*] (LCLS)
**NNU-C**...... New York University, School of Commerce, New York, NY [*Library symbol*] [*Library of Congress*] (LCLS)
**NNU-D**...... New York University, College of Dentistry, New York, NY [*Library symbol*] [*Library of Congress*] (LCLS)
**NNU-ES**.... New York University, Engineering and Science Library, New York, NY [*Library symbol*] [*Library of Congress*] (LCLS)
**NNU-F**...... New York University, Fales Collection, New York, NY [*Library symbol*] [*Library of Congress*] (LCLS)
**NNU-FA**.... New York University, Institute of Fine Arts, New York, NY [*Library symbol*] [*Library of Congress*] (LCLS)
**NNU-G**...... New York University, Wall Street Library, New York, NY [*Library symbol*] [*Library of Congress*] (LCLS)
**NNU-H**...... New York University, University Heights Library, Bronn, NY [*Library symbol*] [*Library of Congress*] (LCLS)
**NNUH**....... United Hospital Fund of New York, New York, NY [*Library symbol*] [*Library of Congress*] (LCLS)
**NNU-IEM**... New York University, Institute of Environmental Medicine, Tuxedo Park, NY [*Library symbol*] [*Library of Congress*] (LCLS)
**NNU-L**...... New York University, School of Law, New York, NY [*Library symbol*] [*Library of Congress*] (LCLS)
**NNU-M**..... New York University, Medical Center, New York, NY [*Library symbol*] [*Library of Congress*] (LCLS)
**NNUM**...... Nordisk Numismatisk Unions Medlemsblad [*A publication*]
**NNUN**....... United Nations Library, New York, NY [*Library symbol*] [*Library of Congress*] (LCLS)
**NNUnC**..... University Club, New York, NY [*Library symbol*] [*Library of Congress*] (LCLS)
**NNUN-CF**... United Nations Childrens Fund, New York, NY [*Library symbol*] [*Library of Congress*] (LCLS)
**NNUni**....... Unipub, Inc., New York, NY [*Library symbol*] [*Library of Congress*] (LCLS)
**NNUnionC**... Union Club, New York, NY [*Library symbol*] [*Library of Congress*] (LCLS)
**NNUnionL**... Union League Club, New York, NY [*Library symbol*] [*Library of Congress*] (LCLS)
**NNUN-PA**... United Nations Fund for Population Activities, New York, NY [*Library symbol*] [*Library of Congress*] (LCLS)
**NNUN-W**... United Nations, Woodrow Wilson Memorial Library, New York, NY [*Library symbol*] [*Library of Congress*] (LCLS)
**NNU-T**...... New York University, Tamiment Library, New York, NY [*Library symbol*] [*Library of Congress*] (LCLS)
**NNUT**........ Union Theological Seminary, New York, NY [*Library symbol*] [*Library of Congress*] (LCLS)
**NNUT-Mc**... Union Theological Seminary, McAlpin Collection, New York, NY [*Library symbol*] [*Library of Congress*] (LCLS)
**NNUVAN**... Ukrainian Academy of Arts and Sciences in the United States, New York, NY [*Library symbol*] [*Library of Congress*] (LCLS)
**NNUVE**..... Nonnegative Unbiased Variance Estimator [*Statistics*]
**NNU-W**..... New York University, Washington Square Library, New York, NY [*Library symbol*] [*Library of Congress*] (LCLS)
**NNU-We**... New York University, Joe Weinstein Residence Halls Library, New York, NY [*Library symbol*] [*Library of Congress*] (LCLS)
**NNV**.......... National Naval Volunteers
**NNVAB**..... United States Veterans Administration Hospital, Bronx, NY [*Library symbol*] [*Library of Congress*] (LCLS)
**NNVAM**.... United States Veterans Administration Hospital (Manhattan), New York, NY [*Library symbol*] [*Library of Congress*] (LCLS)
**NNVPA**..... Nauchni Trudove. Nauchnoizsledovatelski Institut po Vinarska i Pivovarna Promishlenost [*A publication*]
**NNW**......... North-Northwest
**NNWB**....... Navy Nuclear Weapons Bulletin [*A publication*]
**NNWB**....... Net National Well Being
**NNWC**....... Nonnuclear Weapons Country
**NNWF**....... National Network of Women's Funds (EA)
**NNWFG**.... Wilkie, Farr & Gallagher, New York, NY [*Library symbol*] [*Library of Congress*] (LCLS)
**NNWG**...... Wenner-Gren Foundation for Anthropological Research, New York, NY [*Library symbol*] [*Library of Congress*] (LCLS)
**NNWH**...... Nonnormal Working Hours
**NNWH**...... Walter Hampden Memorial Library, New York, NY [*Library symbol*] [*Library of Congress*] (LCLS)
**NNWhit**..... Whitney Museum of American Art, New York, NY [*Library symbol*] [*Library of Congress*] (LCLS)
**NNWM**..... William Douglas McAdams, Inc., Medical Library, New York, NY [*Library symbol*] [*Library of Congress*] (LCLS)
**NNWML**.... Wagner College, Staten Island, NY [*Library symbol*] [*Library of Congress*] (LCLS)
**NNWRN**... North-Northwestern [*Meteorology*] (FAAC)
**NNWS**....... National Network of Women in Sales (EA)
**NNWS**....... Nonnuclear Weapons State
**NNWSDT**... Nestle Nutrition Workshop Series [*A publication*]
**NNWSI**..... Nevada Nuclear Waste Storage Investigations
**NNWWD**... North-Northwestward [*Meteorology*] (FAAC)
**NNY**.......... Nanyang [*China*] [*Airport symbol*] (OAG)

**NNY**.......... Nuveen New York Municipal Fund [*NYSE symbol*] (SPSG)
**NNy**.......... Nyack Library, Nyack, NY [*Library symbol*] [*Library of Congress*] (LCLS)
**NNYAB**..... National Network of Youth Advisory Boards (EA)
**NNYC**........ Yale Club, New York, NY [*Library symbol*] [*Library of Congress*] (LCLS)
**NNYD**........ Norfolk Navy Yard [*Virginia*] [*Later, Norfolk Naval Shipyard*]
**NNYI**......... YIVO Institute for Jewish Research, New York, NY [*Library symbol*] [*Library of Congress*] (LCLS)
**NNyM**....... Nyack Missionary College, Nyack, NY [*Library symbol*] [*Library of Congress*] (LCLS)
**NNYMCA-GC**... Young Men's Christian Association, Grand Central Branch Library, New York, NY [*Library symbol*] [*Library of Congress*] (LCLS)
**NNYMCA-NC**... Young Men's Christian Association, National Council Historical Library, New York, NY [*Library symbol*] [*Library of Congress*] (LCLS)
**NNYU**....... Yeshiva University, New York, NY [*Library symbol*] [*Library of Congress*] (LCLS)
**NNYU-HJ**... Yeshiva University, Mendel Gottesman Library of Hebraica Judaica, New York, NY [*Library symbol*] [*Library of Congress*] (LCLS)
**NNYU-M**.. Yeshiva University, Albert Einstein College of Medicine, Bronx, NY [*Library symbol*] [*Library of Congress*] (LCLS)
**NNYU-S**.... Yeshiva University, Stern College, New York, NY [*Library symbol*] [*Library of Congress*] (LCLS)
**NNZ**.......... New York Zoological Society, New York, NY [*Library symbol*] [*Library of Congress*] (LCLS)
**NNZ**.......... Point Sur, CA [*Location identifier*] [*FAA*] (FAAL)
**NNZi**........ Zionist Archives and Library, New York, NY [*Library symbol*] [*Library of Congress*] (LCLS)
**NO**............ Flugfelag Nordurlands [*Iceland*] [*ICAO designator*] (FAAC)
**NO**............ Lifts Not Operating [*Skiing*]
**N/O**........... [*In the*] Name Of [*Business term*]
**NO**............ Narcotics Officer
**NO**............ Narodnoe Obrazovanie [*Moscow*] [*A publication*]
**NO**............ National Observer [*A publication*]
**NO**............ National Office
**NO**............ National Outlook: an Australian Christian Monthly [*A publication*] (APTA)
**NO**............ Native Officer [*British military*] (DMA)
**NO**............ Natural Orbital [*Physical chemistry*]
**NO**............ Natural Order [*Botany*]
**NO**............ Naval Observatory [*Navy*]
**NO**............ Naval Officer
**NO**............ Navigation Officer
**NO**............ Negative [*British naval signaling*]
**NO**............ Neurooncology [*Elsevier Book Series*] [*A publication*]
**NO**............ New Options (EA)
**NO**............ New Order (EA)
**NO**............ New Orient [*Prague*] [*A publication*]
**NO**............ New Orleans [*Louisiana*]
**NO**............ New Outlook [*Tel Aviv*] [*A publication*]
**NO**............ Nitrogen Oxide [*Emission control*] [*Automotive engineering*]
**N/O**........... No Orders [*Business term*]
**NO**............ No Palpable Nodes [*Oncology*]
**No**............ Nobelium [*Chemical element*]
**n/o**............ None Obtained [*Medicine*]
**NO**............ Nonofficial
**NO**............ Nonoriginal
**NO**............ Nord-Ouest [*Northwest*] [*French*]
**NO**............ Normally Open [*Switch*]
**NO**............ North
**NO**............ North Central Airlines, Inc.
**NO**............ Northern Times [*A publication*]
**NO**............ Norway [*ANSI two-letter standard code*] (CNC)
**no**............ Norway [*MARC country of publication code*] [*Library of Congress*] (LCCP)
**NO**............ Nose [*Horse racing*]
**NO**............ Not Operational (FAAC)
**NO**............ Not Or [*Logical operator*] [*Data processing*]
**N/O**........... Not Otherwise
**NO**............ Not Our Publication
**N/O**........... Not Out [*Bookselling*]
**NO**............ Notes [*Online database field identifier*]
**No**............ Notes [*A publication*]
**n/o**............ Notre Ordre [*Our Order*] [*Business term*] [*French*]
**N O**........... Nouvel Observateur [*A publication*]
**NO**............ Nova Obzorija [*A publication*]
**NO**............ November (ADA)
**N O**........... Novy Orient. Casopis Orientalniho Ustava v Praze [*A publication*]
**NO**............ Nuestra Orden [*Our Order*] [*Spanish*] [*Business term*]
**NO**............ Number (EY)
**NO**............ Numero [*In Number*] [*Pharmacy*] (ROG)
**NO**............ Nursing Officer [*British*]
**NO**............ Oneida Library, Oneida, NY [*Library symbol*] [*Library of Congress*] (LCLS)
**NOA**.......... National Oceanographic Association
**NOA**.......... National Officers Association (EA)
**NOA**.......... National Onion Association (EA)
**NOA**.......... National Opera Association (EA)
**NOA**.......... National Optical Association [*Later, NAOO*]
**NOA**.......... National Optometric Association (EA)
**NOA**.......... National Orchestral Association (EA)
**NOA**.......... National Outboard Association (EA)
**NOA**.......... National Outdoorsmen's Association (EA)
**NOA**.......... NATO Oil Authority (NATG)
**NOA**.......... Nature of Action [*Military*] (AFM)
**NOA**.......... New London, CT [*Location identifier*] [*FAA*] (FAAL)
**NOA**.......... New Obligational Authority
**NOA**.......... Northwest Orient Airlines, Inc.
**NOA**.......... Not Operationally Assigned
**N-O-A**........ Not-Or-And [*Data processing*]
**NOA**.......... Not Otherwise Authorized
**NOA**.......... Nueva Organizacion Antiterrorista [*New Anti-Terrorist Organization*] [*Guatemala*] (PD)
**NOA**.......... University of North Carolina, Chapel Hill Library School, Chapel Hill, NC [*OCLC symbol*] (OCLC)
**NOAA**........ Nonoperating Aircraft Authorization
**NOAADN**... National Organization for Advancement of Associate Degree Nursing (EA)
**NOAA-JTRE**... National Oceanic and Atmospheric Administration Joint Tsunami Research Effort
**NOAA-PMEL**... National Oceanic and Atmospheric Administration Pacific Marine Environmental Laboratory
**NOAA Tech Rep NMFS Circ**... NOAA [*National Oceanic and Atmospheric Administration*] Technical Report. NMFS [*National Marine Fisheries Service*] Circular [*A publication*]
**NOAA Tech Rep NMFS SSRF**... NOAA [*National Oceanic and Atmospheric Administration*] Technical Report. NMFS [*National Marine Fisheries Service*] SSRF [*Special Scientific Report Fisheries*] [*A publication*]
**NOAB**........ National Outdoor Advertising Bureau [*Defunct*] (EA)
**NOAB**........ North American Bancorporation, Inc. [*NASDAQ symbol*] (CTT)
**NOAC**........ No Action Necessary (FAAC)
**NOAC**........ Nordic Committee for Accelerator Based Research (EAIO)
**NOAC**........ Nuclear Operations Analysis Center [*Department of Energy*] [*Information service or system*] (IID)
**NOACT**..... Naval Overseas Air Cargo Terminal
**NOACT**..... No Action (MUGU)
**NOACTLANT**... Naval Ordnance Activities, Atlantic
**NOACTPAC**... Naval Ordnance Activities, Pacific
**NOaD**........ Dowling College, Oakdale, NY [*Library symbol*] [*Library of Congress*] (LCLS)
**NOAD**....... Northern Adventures [*A publication*]
**NOADN**.... National Oceanic and Atmospheric Data Network
**NOAF**........ Northern Affairs. Ontario Ministry of Northern Affairs [*A publication*]
**NOaf**.......... Oakfield Public Library (Haxton Memorial), Oakfield, NY [*Library symbol*] [*Library of Congress*] (LCLS)
**NOAFIRM**... Affirmative Replies Neither Required nor Desired (MUGU)
**NOAG**....... Naval Objectives Analysis Group
**NOAH**....... National Ocean Agency Headquarters
**NOAH**....... National Organization for Albinism and Hypopigmentation (EA)
**NOAH**....... Noarko Resources, Inc. [*NASDAQ symbol*] (NQ)
**NOAH**....... Norwegian Adapted HAWK [*Hughes Aircraft Co.*]
**Noah's Ark Toy Libr Handicapped Child Newsletter**... Noah's Ark Toy Library for Handicapped Children. Newsletter [*A publication*] (APTA)
**NOaJH**....... Oakdale-Bohemia Junior High School, Oakdale, NY [*Library symbol*] [*Library of Congress*] (LCLS)
**NOALA**..... Noise-Operated Automatic Level Adjustment
**NOALA**..... Nova Acta Leopoldina [*A publication*]
**NOAM**...... Noan Mizrachi [*American Zionist organization*]
**No Am**....... North American Review [*A publication*]
**NOAM**...... Nuclear Ordnance Air Force Materiel [*Military*] (AFIT)
**No Am R**.... North American Review [*A publication*]
**No Am Rev**... North American Review [*A publication*]
**NOAMTRAC**... North America Trail Complex (EA)
**NOAO**....... National Optical Astronomy Observatories [*Tucson, AZ*] [*National Science Foundation*]
**NOAO**....... Navy Officers, Accounts Office (MUGU)
**NOAP**........ National Ocean Access Project (EA)
**NOAP**........ Naval Overseas Air Cargo Terminal, Pearl (MUGU)
**NOAP**........ Navy Oil Analysis Program (NG)
**NOAPP**..... National Organization of Adolescent Pregnancy and Parenting (EA)
**NOAR**........ National Organization for an American Revolution (EA)
**NOAR**........ Norwegian Archaeological Review [*A publication*]
**NOARDP**.. Novitates Arthropodae [*A publication*]
**NOART**..... New Orleans Army Terminal
**NOAX**........ NEOAX, Inc. [*Lawrenceville, NJ*] [*NASDAQ symbol*] (NQ)
**NoB**........... Namm och Bygd [*A publication*]
**NOB**........... National Oil Board (NATG)
**NOB**........... Naval Operating Base
**NOB**........... Naval Order of Battle
**NOB**........... Naval Ordnance Bulletin [*A publication*]
**NOB**........... New Orient Bimonthly [*A publication*]

**NOB**.......... Nobeoka [*Japan*] [*Seismograph station code, US Geological Survey*] (SEIS)
**NOB**.......... Nobile [*Nobly*] [*Music*] (ROG)
**NOB**.......... Nobis [*With Us*] [*Latin*] (ROG)
**NOB**.......... Nonobese [*A diabetic mouse strain*]
**NOB**.......... Norges Bank. Economic Bulletin [*A publication*]
**NOB**.......... North Bay Cooperative Library System, Santa Rosa, CA [*OCLC symbol*] (OCLC)
**NOB**.......... Norwest Corp. [*NYSE symbol*] (SPSG)
**NOB**.......... Not on Bonus
**NOB**.......... Nuclear Order of Battle (AFM)
**NOB**.......... Number of Bursts
**NOB**.......... San Francisco, CA [*Location identifier*] [*FAA*] (FAAL)
**NOBC**........ National Office for Black Catholics (EA)
**NOBC**........ National Order of Battlefield Commissions (EA)
**NOBC**........ National Organization of Bar Counsel (EA)
**NOBC**........ Naval Officer Billet Classifications [*or Code*]
**NOBCA**..... National Organization of Black College Alumni (EA)
**NOBCCE**... National Organization of Black Chemists and Chemical Engineers [*Later, NOPABCCE*] (EA)
**NOBCChE** ... National Organization for Professional Advancement of Black Chemists and Chemical Engineers
**NOBCO**..... National Organization of Black County Officials (EA)
**NOBDUCHAR** ... Naval Operating Base, Dutch Harbor, Aleutians
**NOBE**........ Nordstrom, Inc. [*NASDAQ symbol*] (NQ)
**NoBeFi**....... Fiskeridirektoratet [*Directorate of Fisheries*], Bergen-Nordens, Norway [*Library symbol*] [*Library of Congress*] (LCLS)
**NOBELS**... New Office and Business Education Learning System
**Nobel Symp** ... Nobel Symposium [*A publication*]
**NoBeU**....... Universitetet i Bergen [*University of Bergen*], Bergen, Norway [*Library symbol*] [*Library of Congress*] (LCLS)
**NOBFRAN** ... Naval Operating Base, San Francisco, California
**NOBH**........ Nobility Homes, Inc. [*NASDAQ symbol*] (NQ)
**NOBIN**...... Stichting Nederlands Orgaan voor de Bevordering van de Informatieverzorging [*Netherlands Organization for Information Policy*] [*Information service or system*] [*Defunct*] (IID)
**NOBKSS**... Norges Bank. Skrifter Series [*A publication*]
**NOBL**........ Nobel Insurance Ltd. [*NASDAQ symbol*] (NQ)
**NOBLE**..... National Organization of Black Law Enforcement Executives (EA)
**Noble**.......... Noble's Current Court Decisions [*New York*] [*A publication*] (DLA)
**NOBNEWT** ... Naval Operating Base, Newport, Rhode Island
**No Brit**....... North British Review [*A publication*]
**NOBS**........ Naval Observatory [*Navy*]
**N Obs**......... Nihil Obstat [*Official Approval*] [*Latin*]
**NOBS**........ Nonanoyloxybenzene Sulfonate [*Laundry bleach activator*]
**NOBSOLO** ... Naval Operating Base, Coco Solo, Canal Zone
**NOBSY**..... Naval Observatory [*Navy*]
**NOBT**........ New Orleans Board of Trade (EA)
**NOBTRIN** ... Naval Operating Base, Trinidad
**NOBTS**...... Naval Order of Battle Textual Summary (MCD)
**NOC**.......... National Oceanographic Center [*Marine science*] (MSC)
**NOC**.......... National Offshore Council (EA)
**NOC**.......... National Online Circuit (EA)
**NOC**.......... National Opportunity Camps for the Pre-Teen Child (EA)
**NOC**.......... Naval Officer Commanding [*Australia*]
**NOC**.......... Naval Operations Center (NVT)
**NOC**.......... Navy Officer's Classification
**NOC**.......... Network Operation Center [*Bell System*]
**NOC**.......... Network Operations Control [*NASA*] (KSC)
**NOC**.......... New Orleans Consortium [*Library network*]
**noc**............ Noctis [*Night*] [*Medicine*]
**NOC**.......... Nominal Operating Cell [*Photovoltaic energy systems*]
**NOC**.......... Non-Ionic Organic Contaminant [*Environmental chemistry*]
**NOC**.......... Norris Communications Corp. [*Vancouver Stock Exchange symbol*]
**NOC**.......... Northrop Corporation [*NYSE symbol*] (SPSG)
**NOC**.......... Northwest Ohio Consortium [*Library network*]
**NOC**.......... Norwegian Government Office of Culture [*Record label*]
**NOC**.......... Not Otherwise Classified
**NOC**.......... Notation of Content [*Aerospace*]
**NOC**.......... Notice of Change (MCD)
**NOC**.......... Notice of Contents [*Indexing*]
**NoC**........... Nouveaux Cahiers [*A publication*]
**NOC**.......... Nuclear Operations Center (MCD)
**NOC**.......... Nuclear Ordnance Commission [*Military*] (AFIT)
**NOC**.......... Numerical Optimisation Centre [*British*]
**NOC**.......... Nuttall Ornithological Club (EA)
**NOc**........... Oceanside Free Library, Oceanside, NY [*Library symbol*] [*Library of Congress*] (LCLS)
**NOC**.......... University of North Carolina, Chapel Hill, Chapel Hill, NC [*OCLC symbol*] (OCLC)
**NOCA**........ North Cascades National Park
**No Ca Ecc & Mar** ... Notes of Cases, English Ecclesiastical and Maritime Courts [*1841-50*] [*A publication*] (DLA)
**No Ca Fo**.... North Carolina Folklore [*A publication*]
**No Cages**.... No More Cages [*A publication*]
**No Car Hist Rev** ... North Carolina Historical Review [*A publication*]
**No Car Law Rev** ... North Carolina Law Review [*A publication*]
**NOcaS**....... Shaker Museum Foundation, Inc., Old Catham, NY [*Library symbol*] [*Library of Congress*] (LCLS)
**No Cas LJ** ... Notes of Cases, Law Journal [*A publication*] (DLA)
**No of Cas Madras** ... Notes of Cases at Madras (Strange) [*A publication*] (DLA)
**NOCB**........ New Orleans City Ballet
**NOCC**........ NATO Oil Crisis Contingent (NATG)
**NOCC**........ Navigation Operational Checkout Computer
**NOCC**........ Navigation Operator's Control Console
**NOCC**........ Network Operations Control Center [*Manned Space Flight Network, NASA*]
**NOCCC**...... No Control Circuit Contacts (MSA)
**NOCD**........ Not Our Class, Dear [*Slang*]
**NOCE**........ New Orleans Commodity Exchange (EA)
**NOCERCC** ... National Organization for Continuing Education of Roman Catholic Clergy (EA)
**NOCF**........ National Office Computer Facility [*IRS*]
**NOcH**........ South Nassau Communities Hospital, Oceanside, NY [*Library symbol*] [*Library of Congress*] (LCLS)
**NOCHA**.... National Off-Campus Housing Association [*Defunct*] (EA)
**NOCIG**...... Night Only Calligraphic Image Generator
**NOC II**....... Nuclear Operations Concept II [*Military*]
**NO-CIRC**.. National Organization of Circumcision Information Resource Centers (EA)
**NOCM**....... National Organization for Changing Men (EA)
**NOCM**....... Nuclear Ordnance Commodity Manager (AFM)
**NOCO**....... Noise Correlation
**NOCO**....... Nuclear Ordnance Catalog Office [*DoD*]
**NOCOA**..... Noise Control [*A publication*]
**NOCONIT** ... No Continuing Interest (NG)
**NOCONTRACT** ... Not Releasable to Contractors (MCD)
**NOCOPS**.. NORAD Combat Operations System (MCD)
**NOCOR**..... Neglect of Core Orbitals [*Physical chemistry*]
**No Cordilleran** ... Northern Cordilleran [*A publication*]
**NOCOST**.. [*Authorization Issued with Understanding of*] No Entitlement to Reimbursement for Mileage or Expenses [*Military*]
**NOCP**........ Network Operator Control Program
**NOCSAE**... National Operating Committee on Standards for Athletic Equipment (EA)
**NOCT**........ Navy Overseas Cargo Terminals
**NOCT**........ Nocte [*At Night*] [*Pharmacy*] (ROG)
**NOCT**........ Nominal [*or Normal*] Operating Cell Temperature [*Photovoltaic energy systems*]
**NOCT MANEQ** ... Nocte Maneque [*Night and Morning*] [*Pharmacy*]
**NOD**.......... National Organization on Disability (EA)
**NOD**.......... Naval Ordnance Department [*British*]
**NOD**.......... Naval Ordnance Depot
**NOD**.......... Navy Operational Deception (MCD)
**NOD**.......... Network Operations Directive [*NASA*] (KSC)
**NOD**.......... Network Out-Dial [*Automatic Voice Network*] (CET)
**NOD**.......... New Offshore Dischargement (NATG)
**NOD**.......... News of the Day [*A publication*]
**NOD**.......... Night Observation Device
**NOD**.......... Noise Output Device
**NOD**.......... Nonobese Diabetic [*Mouse strain*]
**NOD**.......... Norris Dam [*TVA*]
**NODA**....... National Operatic and Dramatic Association (EAIO)
**NODA**....... National Orientation Directors Association (EA)
**NODA**....... National Outdoor Drama Association (EA)
**NODA**....... Normal-Octyl & -Deyl Adipate [*Organic chemistry*]
**NODAC**..... Naval Ordnance Data Automation Center
**No Dak Hist** ... North Dakota History [*A publication*]
**No Dak Hist Quar** ... North Dakota Historical Quarterly [*A publication*]
**No Dak Quar** ... North Dakota Quarterly [*A publication*]
**NODAL**..... Network-Oriented Data Acquisition Language
**NODAN**.... Noise-Operated Device for Antinoise [*Telecommunications*] (TEL)
**NODAP**..... Nonlinear Distortion Analysis Program [*Bell System*]
**NODC**........ National Oceanographic Data Center [*Washington, DC*] [*National Oceanic and Atmospheric Administration*] [*Databank originator*]
**NODC**........ Naval Oceanographic Distribution Center
**NODC**........ Naval Operating Development Center
**NODCAB**.. National Oceanographic Data Center Advisory Board [*National Oceanic and Atmospheric Administration*] (NOAA)
**NODCC**...... Noble Order, Descendants of the Conqueror and His Companions (EA)
**NODDS**..... Naval Oceanographic Data Distribution System
**NODE**........ Northern Development, Incorporating Arctic Digest [*A publication*]
**NODECA**.. Norwegian Defense Communications Agency (NATG)
**NODEL**..... Not to Delay
**NODESTA** ... Will Not Depart This Station [*Army*] (AABC)
**NODEX**..... New Offshore Dischargement Exercise (NATG)
**NODI**........ Notice of Delayed [*or Delinquent*] Item
**NODIS**...... No Distribution [*Military security classification*] (AFM)
**NODIS**...... Northern Ohio Data and Information Service [*Cleveland State University*] [*Information service or system*] (IID)
**NODL**........ National Office for Decent Literature [*Defunct*]
**NODL**........ Not on Drawing List (MCD)
**No D Law**... Notre Dame Law Review [*A publication*]

**NODLR**..... Night Observation Device, Long-Range [*Army*] (RDA)
**NODM**...... Ferrocarril Nor-Oeste de Mexico [*Mexico North Western Railroad*] [*AAR code*]
**NODMR**.... Night Observation Device, Medium-Range [*Army*]
**NODRA**..... National One Design Racing Association (EA)
**NODS**........ Navy Overseas Dependents School
**NOE**........... Nap of the Earth [*Night helicopter flight*] [*Army*]
**NOE**........... No Ophthalmologic Examination [*Medicine*]
**NOE**........... No Other Entry (ADA)
**NOE**........... NORAD Operational Evaluation (MCD)
**NOE**........... Norden-Norddeich [*Germany*] [*Airport symbol*]
**NOE**........... Not Otherwise Enumerated
**NOE**........... Notice of Exception
**NOE**........... Notice of Execution
**NOE**........... Nuclear Overhauser Effect
**No East As J Theo** ... Northeast Asia Journal of Theology [*A publication*]
**No East Rep** ... Northeastern Reporter [*Commonly cited NE*] [*A publication*] (DLA)
**NOEB**........ NATO Oil Executive Board (NATG)
**NOEB-E**.... NATO Oil Executive Board - East
**NOEB-W**... NATO Oil Executive Board - West
**NOEC**........ No Effects Concentration [*British environmental standard*]
**NOEC**........ No Observed Effect Concentration [*Toxicology*]
**NOECOMM** ... Nap-of-the-Earth Communications [*Night helicopter flight*]
**NOED**........ New Oxford English Dictionary [*Proposed*]
**NOEDS**..... Nuclear Overhauser Enhancement Difference Spectrometry
**NoEF**......... Northeast Folklore [*A publication*]
**NOEHI**...... No One Else Has It [*Lexicography*]
**NOEL**........ National Organization of Episcopalians for Life (EA)
**NOEL**........ National Ornament and Electric Lights Christmas Association (EA)
**NOEL**........ No Observed Effect Level [*Toxicology*]
**NOELS**...... New Office Education Learning System
**NOEN**....... Northern Engineer [*A publication*]
**NOEP**........ Neue Oekonomische Politik [*New Economic Policy*] [*Germany*]
**Noerdlinger Bienenztg** ... Noerdlinger Bienenzeitung [*A publication*]
**NOES**........ National Operational Environmental Satellite Service (MCD)
**NOESS**...... National Operational Environmental Satellite System
**NOESY**..... Nuclear Overhauser Effect Spectroscopy
**NOEU**........ Naval Ordnance Experimental Unit
**Noevenyved Kutato Intez Evkoen (Budapest)** ... Noevenyvedelmi Kutato Intezet Evkoenyve (Budapest) [*A publication*]
**Noevenyved Tud Tanacskozas Koezlem** ... Noevenyved Tudomanyos Tanacskozas Koezlemenyei [*A publication*]
**NOF**........... National Optical Font [*Typography*]
**NOF**........... National Osteopathic Foundation (EA)
**NOF**........... National Osteoporosis Foundation (EA)
**NOF**........... Naval Operating Facility
**NOF**........... Naval Ordnance Facility
**NOF**........... NCR [*NCR Corp.*] Optical Font (MCD)
**NOF**........... Network Operations and Facilities
**NOF**........... Network Operations Forum [*Exchange Carriers Standards Association*] [*Telecommunications*]
**NOF**........... Neurite Outgrowth Factor [*Biochemistry*]
**NOF**........... Nickel Offsets Ltd. [*Toronto Stock Exchange symbol*]
**NOF**........... NOTAM Office
**NOF**........... St. Petersburg, FL [*Location identifier*] [*FAA*] (FAAL)
**NOFA**........ National Office Furniture Association [*Later, NOPA*] (EA)
**NOFA**........ Natural Organic Farmers Association (EA)
**NOFI**......... National Oil Fuel Institute [*Later, NOJC*] (EA)
**NOFIN**...... No Further Information
**NOFMA**.... National Oak Flooring Manufacturers Association (EA)
**NOFOA**..... Naval Office for Occupied Areas [*World War II*]
**NOFODIS** ... No Foreign Dissemination [*Intelligence classification*]
**NOFORN** ... Not Releasable to Foreign Nationals [*Military security classification*]
**NOFRC**..... Northern Forest Research Centre [*Canadian Forestry Service of Agriculture Canada*] [*Research center*] (RCD)
**NOFS**........ National Option and Futures Society (EA)
**NOFT**........ Naval Overseas Freight Terminal
**NOFT**........ Notification of Foreign Travel (AFM)
**NOG**.......... Northern Offshore. Norwegian Journal of Oil and Gas [*A publication*]
**NOG**.......... NSAPAC Operations Group
**NOG**.......... Nuclear Ordnance Group [*Air Force*] (MCD)
**NOG**.......... Numbering
**NOg**........... Ogdensburg Public Library, Ogdensburg, NY [*Library symbol*] [*Library of Congress*] (LCLS)
**NOGA**....... National Osteopathic Guild Association (EA)
**NOGAD**.... Noise-Operated Gain-Adjusting Device
**Nogaku Iho Agric Bull Saga Univ Nogaku-Bu** ... Nogaku Iho. Agricultural Bulletin of Saga University. Saga Daigaku. Nogaku-Bu [*A publication*]
**Nogaku Shusho J Agric Sci (Setagoya)** ... Nogaku Shuho. Journal of Agricultural Science (Setagoya) [*A publication*]
**NOGAPS**... Navy Operational Global Atmospheric Prediction System
**NOGC**....... Nicklos Oil & Gas [*NASDAQ symbol*] (NQ)
**NOGDA**.... Nogyo Doboku Gakkai-Shi [*A publication*]
**NOGGA**.... National Ornamental Goldfish Growers Association (EA)
**NOgH**........ A. Barton Hepburn Hospital, Ogdensburg, NY [*Library symbol*] [*Library of Congress*] (LCLS)
**NOGKAV** ... Agricultural Research [*Kurashiki*] [*A publication*]
**NOGL**........ Naval Ordnance Gauge Laboratory
**NOGL**........ Nizam's Own Golgonda Lancers [*British military*] (DMA)
**NOGLSTP** ... National Organization of Gay and Lesbian Scientists and Technical Professionals (EA)
**NOgM**....... Mater Dei College, Ogdensburg, NY [*Library symbol*] [*Library of Congress*] (LCLS)
**NOGS**........ Night Observation Gunship (MCD)
**NOgSH**...... Saint Lawrence State Hospital, Ogdensburg, NY [*Library symbol*] [*Library of Congress*] (LCLS)
**NOGS Log** ... New Orleans Geographical Society. Log [*A publication*]
**NOGT**........ Norsk Geologisk Tidsskrift [*A publication*]
**NOGU**........ Norges Geologiske Undersoekelse [*A publication*]
**NOGUA**.... Noguchi Kenkyusho Jiho [*A publication*]
**NOgW**....... Wadhams Hall Seminary College, Ogdensburg, NY [*Library symbol*] [*Library of Congress*] (LCLS)
**Nogyo Doboku Shikenjo Hokoku Bull Natl Res Inst Agric Eng** ... Nogyo Doboku Shikenjo Hokoku/Bulletin. National Research Institute of Agricultural Engineering [*A publication*]
**Nogyo Gijutsu J Agric** ... Nogyo Gijutsu/Journal of Agricultural Science [*A publication*]
**Nogyo Kikai Gakkai Shi J Soc Agric Mach** ... Nogyo Kikai Gakkai Shi/ Journal. Society of Agricultural Machinery [*Japan*] [*A publication*]
**Nogyo Oyobi Engei/Agric Hortic** ... Nogyo Oyobi Engei/Agriculture and Horticulture [*A publication*]
**NOH**.......... Chicago, IL [*Location identifier*] [*FAA*] (FAAL)
**NOH**.......... Night Observation Helicopter (MCD)
**NOH**.......... University of North Carolina, Health Science Library, Chapel Hill, NC [*OCLC symbol*] (OCLC)
**NOHA**....... Nutrition for Optimal Health Association (EA)
**NOHIMS**.. Navy Occupational Health Information Management System
**N Ohio Bus** ... Northern Ohio Business Journal [*A publication*]
**NOHL**....... North Hills Electronics, Inc. [*NASDAQ symbol*] (NQ)
**NoHo**......... North of Houston Street [*Artists' colony in New York City*] [*See also SoHo, SoSo, TriBeCa*]
**NOHO**....... Northern Housing [*A publication*]
**NOHOL**.... Not Holding [*a given course or altitude*] [*Aviation*]
**NOHP**....... Not Otherwise Herein Provided
**NOHS**....... National Organization of Human Services (EA)
**NOHSC**..... National Occupational Health and Safety Commission [*Australia*]
**NOHSE**..... National Organization of Human Service Education (EA)
**NOHSN**.... National Organization of Hospital Schools of Nursing [*Defunct*] (EA)
**NOHY**....... Nordic Hydrology [*A publication*]
**NOI**........... Detroit, MI [*Location identifier*] [*FAA*] (FAAL)
**NOI**........... National Opera Institute (EA)
**NOI**........... NAVWEPS ORDALT Instruction (MCD)
**NOI**........... Net Operating Income
**NOI**........... Netherlands Offset Industry
**NOI**........... Nonoperational Intelligence
**NOI**........... Not Otherwise Identified (NG)
**NOI**........... Not Otherwise Indexed
**NOI**........... Notice of Inquiry (IEEE)
**NOI**........... Notice of Intent (MCD)
**NOIA**........ National Ocean Industries Association (EA)
**NOIAW**..... National Organization of Italian-American Women (EA)
**NOIBN**...... Not Otherwise Identified [*or Indicated*] by Name [*Military*] (AABC)
**NOIBN**...... Not Otherwise Indexed by Name [*Tariffs*]
**NOIC**......... National Oceanographic Instrumentation Center [*National Oceanic and Atmospheric Administration*]
**NOIC**......... National Osteopathic Interfraternity Council (EA)
**NOIC**......... Naval Officer-in-Charge
**NOICC**...... National Occupational Information Coordinating Committee [*Washington, DC*]
**NOIFN**...... No Information Available (FAAC)
**NOIL**......... Norris Oil Co. [*NASDAQ symbol*] (NQ)
**NOIO**......... Naval Ordnance Inspecting Officer
**NOIRB**...... Non-Ionizing Radiation [*A publication*]
**No Ire L Q** ... Northern Ireland Legal Quarterly [*A publication*]
**NOIS**......... National Occupational Information Service
**NOISE**....... National Organization for Improving School Environments (EA)
**NOISE**....... National Organization to Insure a Sound-Controlled Environment (EA)
**NOISE**....... National Organization to Insure Survival Economics (EA)
**NOISE**....... Noise Information Service
**Noise Control Eng** ... Noise Control Engineering [*A publication*]
**Noise Control Eng J** ... Noise Control Engineering Journal [*A publication*]
**Noise Control Engrg** ... Noise Control Engineering [*A publication*]
**Noise Control Vib** ... Noise Control, Vibration Isolation [*Later, Noise and Vibration Control Worldwide*] [*A publication*]
**Noise Control Vib Isol** ... Noise Control, Vibration Isolation [*Later, Noise and Vibration Control Worldwide*] [*A publication*]
**Noise Control and Vib Reduct** ... Noise Control and Vibration Reduction [*Later, Noise and Vibration Control Worldwide*] [*A publication*]

**Noise Control Vibr Reduct** ... Noise Control and Vibration Reduction [*Later, Noise and Vibration Control Worldwide*] [*A publication*]
**Noise Reg Rep** ... Noise Regulation Reporter [*Bureau of National Affairs*] [*A publication*] (DLA)
**Noise Reg Rep BNA** ... Noise Regulation Reporter. Bureau of National Affairs [*A publication*]
**Noise Vib Bull** ... Noise and Vibration Bulletin [*A publication*]
**Noise Vib Control** ... Noise and Vibration Control [*A publication*]
**Noise & Vib Control Worldwide** ... Noise and Vibration Control Worldwide [*A publication*]
**Noise Vibr Contr Worldwide** ... Noise and Vibration Control Worldwide [*A publication*]
**NOITU** ...... National Organization of Industrial Trade Unions (EA)
**NOIWON** ... National Operations and Intelligence Watch Officers Network (MCD)
**NOIZ** ......... Micronetics, Inc. [*NASDAQ symbol*] (NQ)
**NOJ** ........... Kodiak, AK [*Location identifier*] [*FAA*] (FAAL)
**NOJB** ........ Norwegian Journal of Botany [*A publication*]
**NOJC** ........ National Oil Jobbers Council [*Later, PMAA*] (EA)
**NOJC** ........ New Orleans Jazz Club (EA)
**NOJC** ........ Northern Oklahoma Junior College
**NOJO** ........ Northern Journal [*Canada*] [*A publication*]
**NOJOA** ..... Nordisk Jordbrugsforskning [*A publication*]
**NOJSM** ..... National Office of Jesuit Social Ministries (EA)
**NOJZ** ........ Norwegian Journal of Zoology [*A publication*]
**NOK** .......... Next of Kin
**NOK** .......... Noril'sk [*USSR*] [*Geomagnetic observatory code*]
**NOKD** ........ Not Our Kind, Dear [*Slang*]
**NOKIAB** ... Journal of Agricultural Meteorology [*A publication*]
**NOKL** ........ Northwestern Oklahoma Railroad Co. [*AAR code*]
**Nok Mort** ... Nokes' Mortgages and Receiverships [*3rd ed.*] [*1951*] [*A publication*] (DLA)
**NOKW** ....... NAZI Oberkommando der Wehrmacht [*NAZI Armed Forces High Command*] [*World War II*] [*German*] (BJA)
**NOL** .......... National Old Lacers [*Later, IOL*] (EA)
**NOL** .......... National Ordnance Laboratory
**NOL** .......... Naval Ordnance Laboratory [*Later, NSWC*]
**NOL** .......... Net Operating Loss
**NOL** .......... New Orleans - Loyola [*Louisiana*] [*Seismograph station code, US Geological Survey*] (SEIS)
**NOL** .......... Noel Industries, Inc. [*AMEX symbol*] (SPSG)
**Nol** ............ Nolan's English Magistrates' Cases [*A publication*] (DLA)
**Nol** ............ Nolan's English Settlement Cases [*A publication*] (DLA)
**NOL** .......... Normal Operational Loss [*Nuclear energy*]
**NOL** .......... Normal Overload
**NOL** .......... Northland Oils Ltd. [*Toronto Stock Exchange symbol*]
**NOl** ........... Olean Public Library, Olean, NY [*Library symbol*] [*Library of Congress*] (LCLS)
**NOLA** ........ National Association for Outlaw and Lawman History (EA)
**NOLA** ........ Northeastern Ohio Library Association [*Library network*]
**NOLAC** ..... National Organization of Liaison for Allocation of Circuit (NATG)
**Nolan** ........ Nolan on the Poor Laws [*A publication*] (DLA)
**Nolan** ........ Nolan's English Magistrates' Cases [*A publication*] (DLA)
**NOLB** ........ Novaferon Laboratories, Inc. [*NASDAQ symbol*] (NQ)
**NOLC** ........ National Obscenity Law Center (IID)
**NOLC** ........ National One-Liners Club (EA)
**NOLC** ........ Naval Ordnance Laboratory Corona
**NOlD** ........ Dresser Industries, Inc., Dresser Clark Division, Olean, NY [*Library symbol*] [*Library of Congress*] (LCLS)
**NOLD** ........ Noland Co. [*NASDAQ symbol*] (NQ)
**NOLD** ........ Northland [*A publication*]
**NOLDC** ..... Non-Oil Less-Developed Country
**NOLEO** ..... Notice to Law Enforcement Officials
**NOlH** ........ Olean General Hospital, Olean, NY [*Library symbol*] [*Library of Congress*] (LCLS)
**NOLI** ......... Northern Lights. Diocese of Yukon [*A publication*]
**Nol Mag** ..... Nolan's English Magistrates' Cases [*A publication*] (DLA)
**NOL-MDI** ... Naval Ordnance Laboratory Miss Distance Indicator
**NOLO** ........ No Live Operator (NG)
**NOLOC** ..... No Location (AABC)
**NOLPE** ..... National Organization on Legal Problems of Education (EA)
**NOLPE Sch LJ** ... NOLPE [*National Organization on Legal Problems of Education*] School Law Journal [*A publication*] (DLA)
**NOLPE School LJ** ... NOLPE [*National Organization on Legal Problems of Education*] School Law Journal [*A publication*] (DLA)
**NOLPE School L Rep** ... NOLPE [*National Organization on Legal Problems of Education*] School Law Reporter [*A publication*] (DLA)
**Nol PL** ....... Nolan on the Poor Laws [*A publication*] (DLA)
**NOL PROS** ... Nolle Prosequi [*Unwilling to Prosecute*] [*Legal term*] [*Latin*]
**NOLS** ........ National Oceanographic Laboratory System
**NOLS** ........ National Organization for Legal Services (EA)
**NOLS** ........ National Outdoor Leadership School
**NOlSFH** .... Saint Francis Hospital, Olean, NY [*Library symbol*] [*Library of Congress*] (LCLS)
**NOLTF** ...... Naval Ordnance Laboratory Test Facility
**NOL/WO** ... Naval Ordnance Laboratory, White Oak [*Maryland*]
**NOM** ......... National Online Meeting [*Conference*] (IT)
**NOM** ......... National Organization for Men (EA)
**NOM** ......... Network Operations Manager [*Manned Space Flight Network, NASA*]
**NOM** ......... Network Output Multiplexer [*Telecommunications*] (MCD)
**NOM** ......... Newspapers on Microfilm
**NOM** ......... Nomad River [*Papua New Guinea*] [*Airport symbol*] (OAG)
**NOM** ......... Nome [*Alaska*] [*Seismograph station code, US Geological Survey*] [*Closed*] (SEIS)
**NOM** ......... Nomenclature (AAG)
**NOM** ......... Nominal (AAG)
**NOM** ......... Nominate (AFM)
**NOM** ......... Nominative
**Nom** ........... Nomisma. Untersuchungen auf dem Gebiete der Antiken Munskunde [*A publication*]
**NOM** ......... Norbeau Mines, Inc. [*Toronto Stock Exchange symbol*]
**NoM** .......... Novyj Mir [*A publication*]
**NOM** ......... Number of Open Microphones
**NOM** ......... Opa Locka, FL [*Location identifier*] [*FAA*] (FAAL)
**NOMA** ...... National Office Management Association [*Later, AMS*]
**NOMA** ...... National Oil Marketers Association [*Defunct*] (EA)
**NOMA** ...... National Organization of Minority Architects (EA)
**NOMAD** ... [*A*] programming language (CSR)
**NOMAD** ... Navy Oceanographic Meteorological Automatic Device
**NOMb** ....... Nitric Oxide Myoglobin [*Food technology*]
**NOMBOS** ... Nonmine Bottom Objects [*Navy*] (NVT)
**NOMC** ....... National Organization for Migrant Children [*Later, NCEMC*] (EA)
**nom cons** .... Nomen Conservandum [*Retained Name*] [*Biology, taxonomy*]
**NOMDA** ... National Office Machine Dealers Association (EA)
**nom dub** ...... Nomen Dubium [*Doubtful Name*] [*Biology, taxonomy*]
**NOMEN** .... Nomenclature (AFM)
**Nomencl Chim** ... Nomenclatura Chimica [*A publication*]
**NOMES** .... New England Offshore Mining Experiment Study (NOAA)
**NOMI** ........ Nonocclusive Mesenteric Ischemia [*Medicine*]
**No Miner** ... Northern Miner [*A publication*]
**NOMIS** ..... National Online Manpower Information System [*Manpower Services Commission*] [*Information service or system*] (IID)
**NOMIS** ..... Naval Ordnance Management Information System
**Nom Khron** ... Nomismatika Khronika [*A publication*]
**NOML** ....... Nominal (ROG)
**NOMMA** .. National Ornamental and Miscellaneous Metals Association (EA)
**NOMN** ...... Nomination
**nom nov** ...... Nomen Novum [*New Name*] [*Biology, taxonomy*]
**nom nud** ..... Nomen Nudum [*Invalid Name*] [*Biology, taxonomy*] [*Latin*]
**Nomograficheskii Sb** ... Nomograficheskii Sbornik [*A publication*]
**Nomos** ........ Nomos. Yearbook of the American Society of Political and Legal Philosophy [*A publication*]
**NOMOTC** ... National Organization of Mothers of Twins Clubs (EA)
**nom rej** ....... Nomen Rejiciendum [*Rejected Name*] [*Biology, taxonomy*]
**NOMRP** .... Normal Return Point (MCD)
**NOMS** ....... Nuclear Operations Monitoring System (MCD)
**NOMSA** .... National Office Machine Service Association [*Paramount, CA*] (EA)
**NOMSS** ..... National Operational Meteorological Satellite System
**NOMTF** .... Naval Ordnance Missile Test Facility
**NOMTS** .... Naval Ordnanace Missile Test Station [*White Sands Missile Range, NM*] (GRD)
**NOMUS** .... Nordisk Musikkomite [*Nordic Music Committee*] (EAIO)
**NOMW** ..... National Organization of Mall Walkers (EA)
**NON** .......... National Organization for Non-Parents [*Later, NAOP*]
**NON** .......... Nonouti [*Kiribati*] [*Airport symbol*] (OAG)
**NON** .......... Normine Resources Ltd. [*Vancouver Stock Exchange symbol*]
**NON** .......... North Norway (NATG)
**No N** ........... Novae Narrationes [*New Counts*] [*1516*] [*A publication*] (DLA)
**NONA** ....... Notice of Nonavailability
**Nonacq** ....... Nonacquiescence by Commissioner in a Tax Court or Board of Tax Appeals Decision [*United States*] [*Legal term*] (DLA)
**NONADD** ... Nonadditivity [*Statistics*]
**NON AL OCC** ... Non Alibi Occurrit [*It Occurs in No Other Place*] [*Latin*] (ROG)
**NON-BUS** ... Nonbusiness [*IRS*]
**NONCIT** ... Noncitizen (AABC)
**NONCNST** ... Nonconsent
**NONCOHO** ... Noncoherent Oscillator (MCD)
**NON COM** ... Non Compos Mentis [*Not in Sound Mind*] [*Latin*] (ROG)
**NONCOM** ... Noncommissioned Officer [*Military*]
**NONCOMECM** ... Noncommunications Electronics Countermeasures [*Military*] (AABC)
**NONCOMJAM** ... Noncommunications Jamming [*Military*] (AABC)
**NONCON** ... Nonconformist
**NON CUL** ... Non Culpabilis [*Not Guilty*] [*Latin*] (ROG)
**NON-CUM** ... Non-Cumulative [*Business term*]
**Non-Destr T** ... Non-Destructive Testing [*A publication*]
**Non-Destr Test** ... Non-Destructive Testing [*A publication*]
**Non-Destr Test (Aust)** ... Non-Destructive Testing (Australia) [*A publication*]
**Nondestr Test (Chicago)** ... Non-Destructive Testing (Chicago) [*A publication*]
**Non-Destr Test (Guilford Eng)** ... Non-Destructive Testing (Guilford, England) [*A publication*]
**Non-Destr Test Int** ... Non-Destructive Testing International [*A publication*]
**Non-Dest Test** ... Non-Destructive Testing [*A publication*]

**NONE** ....... New Orleans & Northeastern R. R. [*AAR code*]
**NONEG**..... Negative Replies Neither Required nor Desired
**NOneoC**..... Hartwick College, Oneonta, NY [*Library symbol*] [*Library of Congress*] (LCLS)
**NOneoU** .... State University of New York, College at Oneonta, Oneonta, NY [*Library symbol*] [*Library of Congress*] (LCLS)
**Non-Ferrous Met (China)** ... Non-Ferrous Metals (China) [*A publication*]
**NONFLMB** ... Nonflammable
**NonFMerch** ... Non-Foods Merchandising [*A publication*]
**NON-FRAG** ... Non-Fragmentation [*Bomb*]
**Nonfuel M** ... Future of Nonfuel Minerals in the United States and World. Input-Output Projections, 1980-2030 [*A publication*]
**N/ONI**....... Navy/Office of Naval Intelligence (AAG)
**Non-Ioniz Radiat** ... Non-Ionizing Radiation [*A publication*]
**Nonlinear Anal** ... Nonlinear Analysis [*A publication*]
**Nonlinear Anal Theory Methods and Appl** ... Nonlinear Analysis Theory. Methods and Applications [*A publication*]
**Nonlinear Vibr Probl** ... Nonlinear Vibration Problems [*A publication*]
**Nonmet Miner Process** ... Nonmetallic Minerals Processing [*A publication*]
**NON-MSA** ... Non-Standard Metropolitan Statistical Area (OICC)
**Nonmunjip Inha Tech Jr Coll** ... Nonmunjip. Inha Technical Junior College [*A publication*]
**NON-NSN** ... Not Assigned a National Stock Number
**NON OBS** ... Non Obstante [*Notwithstanding*] [*Latin*]
**NON OBST** ... Non Obstante [*Notwithstanding*] [*Latin*] (ROG)
**NONP**........ Nonpackaged
**NONP**........ Nonpareil (ADA)
**NONPAYT** ... Nonpayment (ROG)
**Nonpet Veh Fuels Symp** ... Nonpetroleum Vehicle Fuels Symposium [*A publication*]
**NONPROF** ... Nonprofessional
**NON PROS** ... Non Prosequitur [*Does Not Prosecute*] [*Latin*]
**N/ONR**...... Navy/Office of Naval Research (AAG)
**NON REP** ... Non Repetatur [*Do Not Repeat*] [*Pharmacy*]
**Non Repetat** ... Non Repetatur [*Do Not Repeat*] [*Pharmacy*]
**NONSAP** .. Nonlinear Structural Analysis Program [*Data processing*]
**NON SEQ** ... Non Sequitur [*It Does Not Follow*] [*Latin*]
**NON-SLIP** ... Non-Speech Language Initiation Program
**NONSTD** .. Nonstandard
**NONStY**.... Non-Standard Yiddish (BJA)
**NONSUB** .. Nonsubmarine [*Navy*] (NVT)
**NONSYN** ... Nonsynchronous
**NONT** ....... Northern Ontario Business [*A publication*]
**N Ontario B** ... Northern Ontario Business [*A publication*]
**NONTSDSL** ... Not Included in Technical Service Demand Stockage Lists [*Army*] (AABC)
**NONUM**... Notional Number (NVT)
**NON-VON** ... Non-Von Neumann [*Experimental computer, not based on the principles of Von Neumann computer design, under construction at Columbia University*]
**NON-VTG** ... Non-Voting [*Business term*]
**Nonwn Fabr** ... International Directory of the Nonwoven Fabrics Industry [*A publication*]
**Nonwoven Pat Dig** ... Nonwoven Patents Digest [*A publication*]
**Nonwovn In** ... Nonwovens Industry [*A publication*]
**NOO**.......... Naoro [*Papua New Guinea*] [*Airport symbol*] (OAG)
**NOO**.......... Naval Oceanographic Office [*Also known as NAVOCEANO; formerly, HO, NHO, USNHO*]
**NOO**.......... Naval Oceanographic Office, Washington, DC [*OCLC symbol*] [*Inactive*] (OCLC)
**NOO**.......... Nevada Operations Office [*Department of Energy*]
**NOO**.......... Notice of Obligation [*Military*] (AFM)
**NOOD**....... Nitric Oxide Optical Detector
**NOODDJ** ... Notulae Odonatologicae [*A publication*]
**NOOIAC**... National Offshore Operations Industry Advisory Committee [*Coast Guard*]
**NO-OP**...... Flight Not Operating [*Travel industry*]
**NOOP**........ No Operation [*Data processing*]
**NOOS**........ Nuclear Orbit-to-Orbit Shuttle [*NASA*]
**NOO-SP**.... Naval Oceanographic Office Special Publication
**NOOU**....... Not One of Us [*Slang*]
**NoOU** ........ Universitetet i Oslo [*University of Oslo*], Oslo, Norway [*Library symbol*] [*Library of Congress*] (LCLS)
**NoOU-M**... Universitetet i Oslo, Matematisk-Naturvitenskapelige Fakultet [*University of Oslo, Department of Mathematics and Natural Sciences*], Oslo, Norway [*Library symbol*] [*Library of Congress*] (LCLS)
**NOP**.......... Brooklyn, NY [*Location identifier*] [*FAA*] (FAAL)
**NOP**.......... National Onderzoek Persmedia [*Database*] [*Stichting Nationaal Onderzoek Persmedia*] [*Netherlands*] [*Information service or system*] (CRD)
**NOP**.......... National Opinion Poll
**NOP**.......... Naval Oceanographic Publication
**NOP**.......... Naval Officer Procurement
**NOP**.......... Naval Ordnance Plant
**NOP**.......... Navigation Operating Procedure
**NOP**.......... Navy Objectives Plan
**NOP**.......... Network Operations Procedure [*Manned Space Flight Network, NASA*]
**NOP**.......... New Orleans Poetry Journal [*A publication*]
**NOP**.......... No Operation [*Data processing*]
**NOP**.......... Noncoherent Optical Processor
**NOP**.......... Nonoperating (KSC)
**NOP**.......... Normal Operating Procedure (NRCH)
**NOP**.......... North Oscura Peak [*White Sands Missile Range*] [*Army*]
**NOP**.......... Not Otherwise Provided
**NOP**.......... Not Our Publication
**NOP**.......... Notice of Procurement [*Navy*] (NG)
**NOP**.......... Nuclear Operations Plan (MCD)
**NOP**.......... Nuclear Ordnance Platoon [*Marine Corps*] (NVT)
**NOP**.......... Null Operation [*Data processing*]
**NOP**.......... Number of Openings [*Technical drawings*]
**NOP**.......... Number of Passes (MSA)
**NOPA**........ National Office Products Association (EA)
**NOPA**........ National Oilseed Processors Association (EA)
**NOPA**........ Network Operations Performance Analysis [*Manned Space Flight Network, NASA*]
**NOPA**........ Norsk Polarinstitutt. Aarbok [*A publication*]
**NOPABCCE** ... National Organization for Professional Advancement of Black Chemists and Chemical Engineers (EA)
**NOPB**........ New Orleans Public Belt Railroad [*AAR code*]
**NOPCL**...... Naval Officer Personnel Circular Letter
**NOPCO**..... National Oil Products Company [*Later, NOPCO Chemical Co.*]
**NOPD**........ New Orleans Police Department [*Initialism also used as title of TV series*]
**NOPE**........ National Organization of Poll-Ettes (EA)
**NOPE**........ Naturists and Nudists Opposing Pornographic Exploitation (EA)
**NOPE**........ New Orleans Port of Embarkation
**NOPE**........ No Promotion [*Refers to lack of publicity in the record business*]
**NOPE**........ Northern Perspectives. Canadian Arctic Resources Committee [*A publication*]
**NOPEC** ..... Non-OPEC [*Oil producing countries which are not members of OPEC*]
**NoPEF**....... Nordiska Projektexportfonden [*Nordic Project Fund*] [*Helsinki, Finland*] (EAIO)
**NOPEOL** .. National Organization to Promote English as the Official Language (EA)
**NOPF**........ Naval Ordnance Plant, Forest Park [*Illinois*]
**NOPH** ....... Norsk Polarinstitutt. Polarhandbok [*A publication*]
**NOPHYSRET** ... Not Required to Take New Physical Provided No Material Change since Recent Retirement Physical [*Military*]
**NOPI**......... Naval Ordnance Plant Institute (MCD)
**NOPL**......... Naval Ordnance Plant, Louisville [*Kentucky*]
**NOPM**........ Norsk Polarinstitutt. Meddelelser [*A publication*]
**NOP-N**...... Nordiska Publiceringsnamnden for Naturvetenskap [*Nordic Publishing Board in Science*] (EAIO)
**NOPN**........ Normally Open [*Switch*]
**NOPOL**..... No Pollution
**NOPPA**..... National Ocean Pollution Planning Act of 1978
**NOPPA**..... Nitroso(oxopropyl)propylamine [*Organic chemistry*]
**NOPR**........ Notice of Proposed Rule Making [*Federal Energy Regulatory Commission*]
**NOPRI**...... National Orthotic and Prosthetic Research Institute (EA)
**NOPROCAN** ... If Not Already Processed, Orders Cancelled [*Military*]
**NOPS**........ National Ocean Policy Study [*US Senate*]
**NOPS**........ Nike Operator Proficiency Scale [*Army*]
**NOPS**........ Noncoherent Optical Processing System
**NOPS**........ Norsk Polarinstitutt. Skrifter [*A publication*]
**NOPSA**..... Nordisk Psykologi [*A publication*]
**NOPT**........ No Procedure Turn Required [*Aviation*]
**NoPVDM**.. N'Oubliez Pas Vos Decorations Maconniques [*Do Not Forget Your Masonic Regalia*] [*French*] [*Freemasonry*]
**NO-PYR**.... N-Nitrosopyrrolidine [*Also, NYPR*] [*Biochemistry, organic chemistry*]
**NOQ**.......... Northwest Ohio Quarterly [*A publication*]
**NOQUIS**... Nucleonic Oil Quantity Indication System [*Air Force*]
**NOR**.......... National Organization for Rehabilitation [*Ireland*]
**NOR**.......... New Orleans Review [*A publication*]
**NOR**.......... Nitrogen Oxide Reduction [*Research in automotive air pollution*]
**nor**............ Nitrogen ohne Radikal [*Chemical prefix*]
**NOR**.......... Non-Ordinary Resident [*British*]
**NOR**.......... Nonoperational Ready (NVT)
**NOR**.......... Noranda, Inc. [*Toronto Stock Exchange symbol*] [*Vancouver Stock Exchange symbol*]
**NOR**.......... Norbornadiene [*Also, NBD*] [*Organic chemistry*]
**NOR**.......... Nord [*Greenland*] [*Seismograph station code, US Geological Survey*] [*Closed*] (SEIS)
**NOR**.......... Nordfjordur [*Iceland*] [*Airport symbol*] (OAG)
**NOR**.......... Nordisk Organ for Reinforskning [*Nordic Council of Reindeer Research*] (EAIO)
**Nor**............ Norma [*Constellation*]
**NOR**.......... Normal (KSC)
**NOR**.......... Normalisatie [*A publication*]
**NOR**.......... Norman
**NOR**.......... Normandale Community College, Bloomington, MN [*OCLC symbol*] (OCLC)
**Nor**............ Norseman [*London*] [*A publication*]
**NOR**.......... Norstar Bancorp., Inc. [*NYSE symbol*] (SPSG)
**NOR**.......... North

**NOR** .......... North Central Airlines, Inc.
**NoR**........... Northern Review [*A publication*]
**NOR** .......... Norway [*ANSI three-letter standard code*] (CNC)
**nor** .............. Norwegian [*MARC language code*] [*Library of Congress*] (LCCP)
**NOR** .......... Norwich [*City in England*] (ROG)
**NOR** .......... Not Operationally Ready [*Military*] (AFM)
**NOR** .......... Not Or [*Logical operator*] [*Data processing*]
**NOR** .......... Notice of Readiness [*Shipping*]
**NOR** .......... Notice of Revision
**NOR** .......... Nucleolar Organizer Region [*in chromosomes*]
**NOR** .......... Number of Rounds [*Military*] (CINC)
**NOR** .......... San Diego, CA [*Location identifier*] [*FAA*] (FAAL)
**NORA**........ National Online Regulatory Access [*Data Development, Inc.*] [*Information service or system*] (CRD)
**NORA**........ Northern Raven [*A publication*]
**NORA**........ Norwegian Zero Power Reactor Assembly
**NORAC**..... No Radio Contact [*Aviation*]
**NORAD**..... North American Air Defense [*Integrated United States-Canada command*]
**NORAD**..... Norwegian Agency for International Development
**NORADCOC** ... North American Air Defense Combat Operations Center [*Military*] (AFM)
**NORADCRU** ... North American Air Defense Orientation Cruise (NVT)
**NORADEX** ... North American Air Defense Exercise (NVT)
**NorAE** ........ Norwegian Antarctic Expedition [*1956-*]
**NORAID**... Irish Northern Aid Committee (EA)
**NORAP**..... Northwestern Alumni Players
**Nor Apotekerforen Tidsskr** ... Norges Apotekerforenings Tidsskrift [*A publication*]
**Nor Arch Rev** ... Norwegian Archaeological Review [*A publication*]
**NORASDEFLANT** ... North American Antisubmarine Defense Force, Atlantic (NATG)
**NORATS**... Navy Operational Radio and Telephone Switchboard (NVT)
**NOrb**.......... Orangeburg Public Library, Orangeburg, NY [*Library symbol*] [*Library of Congress*] (LCLS)
**NORBA** ..... National Off-Road Bicycle Association [*Later, USCF*] (EA)
**NOrbR**....... Rockland State Hospital, Medical Library, Orangeburg, NY [*Library symbol*] [*Library of Congress*] (LCLS)
**NORBS** ..... Northern Base Section [*Corsica*]
**NORC**........ National Oceanographic Records Center
**NORC**........ National Opinion Research Center [*University of Chicago*]
**NORC**........ Naturally Occurring Retirement Community
**NORC**........ Naval Ordnance Research Calculator [*or Computer*] [*Naval Ordnance Proving Ground*]
**Norc** ........... Norcross' Reports [*23-24 Nevada*] [*A publication*] (DLA)
**NORC**........ Nuclear Ordnance Record Card (NVT)
**NOrc**.......... Orchard Park Public Library, Orchard Park, NY [*Library symbol*] [*Library of Congress*] (LCLS)
**NORCALSEC** ... Northern California Section, Western Sea Frontier
**NOrcE** ....... Erie Community College-South, Orchard Park, NY [*Library symbol*] [*Library of Congress*] (LCLS)
**NORCO**..... National Oil Recovery Corporation
**NORCUS** .. Northwest College and University Association for Science [*Richland, WA*] [*Department of Energy*] (GRD)
**NORD** ....... Bureau of Ordnance Publication [*Later, NAVORD*] [*Navy*]
**NORD** ....... National Organization for Rare Disorders (EA)
**NORD** ....... Naval Ordnance
**Nord**........... Nordia [*A publication*]
**NORD** ....... Norsk Data [*Manufacturer and computer series*] [*Norway*]
**NORDA**..... Naval Ocean Research and Development Activity [*Bay St. Louis, MS*]
**Nord Adm Tss** ... Nordisk Administrativt Tidsskrift [*A publication*]
**Nord Betong** ... Nordisk Betong [*A publication*]
**Nord Bitidskr** ... Nordisk Bitidskrift [*A publication*]
**Nord Bl Chem** ... Nordische Blaetter fuer die Chemie [*A publication*]
**Nord Datanytt Data** ... Nordisk Datanytt Med Data [*A publication*]
**Nordd J Mv G** ... Norddeutsches Jahrbuch fuer Muenzkunde und Verwandte Gebiete [*A publication*]
**Norddtsch Farben Ztg** ... Norddeutsche Farben Zeitung [*A publication*]
**NORDEK** .. Norway, Denmark, Finland, Sweden [*Nordic Economic Community*] [*Trade bloc*]
**NORDEL** .. Organization for Nordic Electrical Cooperation (EA)
**Nordeuropaeisk Mejeri-Tidsskr** ... Nordeuropaeisk Mejeri-Tidsskrift [*A publication*]
**Nord Fotohist Jl** ... Nordisk Fotohistorisk Journal [*A publication*]
**Nord Hydrol** ... Nordic Hydrology [*A publication*]
**Nord Hyg Tidskr** ... Nordisk Hygienisk Tidskrift [*A publication*]
**Nord Hyg Tidskr Suppl** ... Nordisk Hygienisk Tidskrift. Supplementum [*A publication*]
**NORDIATRANS** ... Association for Nordic Transplant and Dialysis Personnel (EAIO)
**Nordic Hydrol** ... Nordic Hydrology [*A publication*]
**NORDICOM** ... Nordic Documentation Center for Mass Communication Research [*Finland*] [*Database originator*] [*Information service or system*] (IID)
**NORDINFO** ... Nordiska Samarbetsorganet for Vetenskaplig Information [*Nordic Council for Scientific Information and Research Libraries*] [*Espoo, Finland*] (EAIO)
**Nordisk Mat Tidskr** ... Nordisk Matematisk Tidskrift [*A publication*]
**Nordisk Tid** ... Nordisk Tidskrift foer Bok- och Biblioteksvaesen [*A publication*]
**Nordisk Tids Bok & Bibl** ... Nordisk Tidskrift foer Bok- och Biblioteksvaesen [*A publication*]
**NORDITA** ... Nordic Institute for Theoretic Atomic Physics (EY)
**NORDITA** ... Nordisk Institut for Teoretisk Atomfysik [*Nordic Institute for Theoretical Atomic Physics*] (EAIO)
**Nord J Bot** ... Nordic Journal of Botany [*A publication*]
**Nord Jordbrforsk** ... Nordisk Jordbrugsforskning [*A publication*]
**Nord Jordbrugsforsk** ... Nordisk Jordbrugsforskning [*A publication*]
**Nord Jordbrugsforsk Suppl** ... Nordisk Jordbrugsforskning. Supplement [*A publication*]
**Nord Med** .. Nordisk Medicin [*A publication*]
**Nord Med Ark** ... Nordiskt Medicinskt Arkiv [*A publication*]
**Nord Med Ark Afd 2 Med** ... Nordiskt Medicinskt Arkiv Afdeling 2. Inre Medicine Arkiv foer Inre Medicin [*A publication*]
**Nord Medicinhist Arsb** ... Nordisk Medicinhistorisk Aarsbok [*A publication*]
**Nord Med Tidskr** ... Nordisk Medicinsk Tidskrift [*A publication*]
**Nord Mejeri Tidsskr** ... Nordisk Mejeri Tidsskrift [*A publication*]
**Nord Mus** .. Nordisk Musikkultur [*A publication*]
**NORDO** .... No Radio
**Nord P**........ Nordic Pharmacopoeia [*A publication*]
**NORDPLAN** ... Nordic Institute for Studies in Urban and Regional Planning [*Stockholm, Sweden*] (EAIO)
**Nord Psykiatr Tidsskr** ... Nordisk Psykiatrisk Tidsskrift [*A publication*]
**Nord Psykol** ... Nordisk Psykologi [*A publication*]
**NordREFO** ... Nordiskt Institut foer Regionalpolitisk Forskning [*Nordic Institute of Regional Policy Research*] [*Research center*] [*Finland*] (IRC)
**NORDSAM** ... Nordiska Samarbetskommitten for Internationell Politik [*Nordic Cooperation Committee for International Politics, Including Conflict and Peace Research*] (EAIO)
**NORDSAT** ... Scandinavian Countries Broadcast Satellite (MCD)
**Nordser**...... Nordisk Samkatalog foer Seriella Medicinska Publikationer [*Karolinska Institutets Bibliotek och Informationscentral*] [*Sweden*] [*Information service or system*] (CRD)
**NORDTEL** ... Nordiskt Samarbete Inom Telekommunikation [*Nordic Cooperation on Telecommunications*] (EAIO)
**Nord Tid** .... Nordisk Tidskrift foer Bok- och Biblioteksvaesen [*A publication*]
**Nord Tidskr** ... Nordisk Tidskrift foer Bok- och Biblioteksvaesen [*A publication*]
**Nord Tidskr Dov** ... Nordisk Tidskrift foer Dovundervisningen [*A publication*]
**Nord Tidskr Fotogr** ... Nordisk Tidskrift foer Fotografi [*A publication*]
**Nord Tidskrift** ... Nordisk Tidsskrift foer Filologi [*A publication*]
**Nord Tidskr Medicotek** ... Nordisk Tidskrift foer Medicoteknik [*A publication*]
**Nord Tidskr f Vetensk** ... Nordisk Tidskrift foer Vetenskap, Konst, och Industri [*A publication*]
**Nord Tidsskr Kriminalvidensk** ... Nordisk Tidsskrift foer Kriminalvidenskab [*A publication*]
**Nord Tidsskr Logop Foniat** ... Nordisk Tidsskrift foer Logopedi og Foniatri [*A publication*]
**Nord Utredningsser** ... Nordisk Utredningsserie [*A publication*]
**Nord Veterinaermed** ... Nordisk Veterinaermedicin [*A publication*]
**Nord Veterinaermed Suppl** ... Nordisk Veterinaermedicin. Supplementum [*A publication*]
**Nord Vetmed** ... Nordisk Veterinaermedicin [*A publication*]
**Nordwestdt Imkerztg** ... Nordwestdeutsche Imkerzeitung [*A publication*]
**Nord World** ... Nordic World [*A publication*]
**NORE**........ Northeast
**NOREASTNAVFACENGCOM** ... Northeast Division Naval Facilities Engineering Command
**NOREC** ..... No Record
**NOREC** ..... Northern Environmental Council [*Defunct*] (EA)
**NORECHAN** ... Northeast Subarea Channel (NATG)
**NORED**..... Norsk Olje Revy [*A publication*]
**NOREF** ..... No Reference
**Norelco Rep** ... Norelco Reporter [*A publication*]
**Nor Entomol Tidsskr** ... Norsk Entomologisk Tidsskrift [*A publication*]
**NOREP** ..... No Reply Received
**NOREP** ..... No Report Prepared [*or Received*] (FAAC)
**NORESS**... Norwegian Regional Seismic Array
**NOREX**..... Nuclear Operational Readiness Exercise (NVT)
**NORF**........ Norfolk [*County in England*]
**Nor Fag Foto** ... Norsk Fag Foto [*A publication*]
**Nor Farm Tidsskr** ... Norsk Farmaceutisk Tidsskrift [*A publication*]
**NORFISH** ... North Pacific Fisheries Project (NOAA)
**Nor Fisk**..... Norges Fiskerier [*A publication*]
**Nor Fiskeritid** ... Norsk Fiskeritidende [*A publication*]
**NORFLK**... Norfolk [*County in England*]
**Norfolk A**... Norfolk Archaeology [*A publication*]
**Norfolk Arch** ... Norfolk Archacology [*A publication*]
**Norfolk Archaeol** ... Norfolk Archaeology [*A publication*]
**Nor Fotogr Tidsskr** ... Norsk Fotografisk Tidsskrift [*A publication*]
**Nor Fr** ........ Norman French [*Language, etc.*] (DLA)
**NORGD**..... National Organization for the Rights of Guide Dogs (EA)
**Nor Geol Tidsskr** ... Norsk Geologisk Tidsskrift [*A publication*]
**Nor Geol Unders** ... Norges Geologiske Undersoekelse [*A publication*]

**Nor Geol Unders Bull** ... Norges Geologiske Undersoekelse. Bulletin [*A publication*]
**Nor Geol Unders Skr** ... Norges Geologiske Undersoekelse. Skrifter [*A publication*]
**Norges Bank Econ Bul** ... Norges Bank. Economic Bulletin [*A publication*]
**Norg Geol Unders (Publ)** ... Norges Geologiske Undersoekelse (Publikasjoner) [*A publication*]
**Norg Geotek Inst Publ** ... Norges Geotekniske Institut. Publikasjon [*Oslo*] [*A publication*]
**NORGLAC** ... Northern Great Lakes Area Council
**NORGRAPH** ... Northeast Graphics Conference and Printing Show [*Printing Industry Association of Connecticut and Western Massachusetts*] (TSPED)
**Nor Hvalfanst Tid** ... Norsk-Hvalfangst-Tidende [*A publication*]
**NORI**......... National Office for the Rights of the Indigent [*Later, LDF*]
**NORIANE** ... Normes et Reglements Informations Automatisees Accessibles en Ligne [*Automated Standards and Regulations Information Online*] [*Database*] [*French Association for Standardization*] [*Information service or system*] (IID)
**NORIMB** .. Norimberge [*Nuremberg*] [*Imprint*] (ROG)
**Nor Inst Tang- Tareforsk Rep** ... Norsk Institutt for Tang- og Tareforskning. Report [*A publication*]
**NORIP** ...... NORAD Intelligence Plan [*Military*] (AABC)
**NORIS**....... North Island (MUGU)
**NORJ** ........ Northward Journal [*A publication*]
**NORK**........ [*The*] New Orleans Rhythm Kings [*Jazz band*]
**NORK**........ Norsk Data AS [*NASDAQ symbol*] (NQ)
**NORL**........ Nordic Limited, Inc. [*NASDAQ symbol*] (NQ)
**NORL**........ Northian Newsletter [*A publication*]
**Nor Landbrukshogsk Foringsforsok Beret** ... Norges Landbrukshogskole Foringsforsokene Beretning [*A publication*]
**NORLANT** ... North Atlantic Area (MUGU)
**NORLANTEX** ... North Atlantic - Training Exercise (MCD)
**N Orlean Bs** ... New Orleans Business [*A publication*]
**N Orleans CB** ... New Orleans City Business [*A publication*]
**NORLEU** .. Norleucine [*A nonessential amino acid*] [*Biochemistry*]
**N Orl Med and S J** ... New Orleans Medical and Surgical Journal [*A publication*]
**Nor Lovtid** ... Norsk Lovtidend [*A publication*]
**Nor Lovtid Avd I** ... Norsk Lovtidend Avdeling I [*Norway*] [*A publication*]
**NORM**....... National Office Resources Management [*IRS*]
**NORM**....... National Organization for Raw Materials (EA)
**Norm**......... Norma [*Constellation*]
**NORM**....... Normal [*or Normalize*] (AAG)
**NORM**....... Norman [*or Normandy*]
**NORM**....... Normative Operating Reporting Method
**NORM**....... Normetal [*AAR code*]
**NORM**....... Not Operational Ready Materiel [*Military*] (AFIT)
**NORM**....... Not Operationally Ready Maintenance [*Military*] (NG)
**NORM**....... Nuclear Operational Readiness Maneuver (NVT)
**NORM**....... Nuclear Ordnance Readiness Manpower
**Nor Mag Laegevidensk** ... Norsk Magasin foer Laegevidenskapen [*A publication*]
**Normalfrequenzen** ... Normalfrequenzen und Normalzeit der Frequenz-Technischen Zentralstelle der Berliner Post [*A publication*]
**NORMATERM** ... Normalisation, Automatisation de la Terminologie [*Standardization and Automation of Terminology*] [*Databank*] [*France*] [*Information service or system*] (IID)
**Nor Met Arb** ... Norsk Meteorologisk Arbok [*A publication*]
**NORM(F)** ... Not Operationally Ready Maintenance - Flyable [*Military*] (MCD)
**NORM(G)** ... Not Operationally Ready Maintenance - Grounded [*Military*] (MCD)
**Norm Instr and Prim Plans** ... Normal Instructor and Primary Plans [*A publication*]
**NORML**.... National Organization for the Reform of Marijuana Laws (EA)
**Norm Pathol Anat (Stuttg)** ... Normale und Pathologische Anatomie (Stuttgart) [*A publication*]
**NORMSHOR** ... Normal Tour of Shore Duty
**Nor Myrselsk Medd** ... Norske Myrselskap. Meddelelser [*A publication*]
**Nor Nat**...... Norsk Natur [*A publication*]
**NORO** ........ Not Operationally Ready Other [*Military*] (AFM)
**NOROD** .... Noroil [*A publication*]
**NOROEC**.. NORAD Operational Employment Concept [*Military*] (AABC)
**Nor Olje Revy** ... Norsk Olje Revy [*A publication*]
**Noro-Psikiyatri Ars** ... Noro-Psikiyatri Arsivi [*A publication*]
**NORP**........ New Oil Reference Price
**NORP**........ NORPAC Explorations Services [*NASDAQ symbol*] (NQ)
**NORP**........ Norpic [*A publication*]
**NORPAC** .. Naval Overhaul and Repair Pacific (MUGU)
**NORPAC** .. North Pacific [*Military*]
**NORPAC** .. Northern Pacific Railway Co.
**Nor Pat** ...... Norman. Letters Patent [*1853*] [*A publication*] (DLA)
**NORPAX** .. North Pacific Experiment [*National Science Foundation*]
**Nor Pelsdyrbl** ... Norsk Pelsdyrblad [*A publication*]
**NORPI** ...... No Pilot Balloon Observation Will Be Filed Next Collection Unless Weather Changes Significantly [*National Weather Service*] (FAAC)
**NOrpOHi** .. Oyster Pond Historical Society, Orient Point, NY [*Library symbol*] [*Library of Congress*] (LCLS)
**Nor Polarinst Aarbok** ... Norsk Polarinstitutt. Aarbok [*A publication*]
**Nor Polarinst Medd** ... Norsk Polarinstitutt. Meddelelser [*A publication*]
**Nor Polarinst Polarhandb** ... Norsk Polarinstitutt. Polarhandbok [*A publication*]
**Nor Polarinst Skr** ... Norsk Polarinstitutt. Skrifter [*A publication*]
**Nor Prin**..... Northern Principal [*A publication*]
**Nor Pro Pr** ... North's Probate Practice [*Illinois*] [*A publication*] (DLA)
**NORQR**..... NORAD Qualitative Requirement [*Military*] (AABC)
**NORR**........ No Reply Received (FAAC)
**Norr** ........... Norris' Reports [*82-96 Pennsylvania*] [*A publication*] (DLA)
**NORRA**..... National Off-Road Racing Association
**NORRD**..... No Reply Received (NOAA)
**Norris**......... Norris' Reports [*82-96 Pennsylvania*] [*A publication*] (DLA)
**Norris & L Perpetuities** ... Norris and Leach on Rule Against Perpetuities [*A publication*] (DLA)
**Norris Seamen** ... Norris' Law of Seamen [*A publication*] (DLA)
**Norrlands Skogsvforb Tidskr (Stockh)** ... Norrlands Skogsvardsforbunds Tidskrift (Stockholm) [*A publication*]
**Norr Peake** ... Norris' Edition of Peake's Law of Evidence [*A publication*] (DLA)
**NORRS** ..... Naval Operational Readiness Reporting Systems
**NORS**........ National Organization for River Sports (EA)
**NORS**........ New Old Replacement Stock [*Automotive parts*]
**NORS**........ Norseman [*A publication*]
**NORS**........ Not Operationally Ready Supply [*Military*]
**NORS**........ Not Operationally Ready System [*Military*]
**NORSAIR** ... Not Operationally Ready Supply Aviation Items Report [*Military*]
**NORSAM** ... Nordiskt Samrad for en Aktiv Alderdom [*Nordic Association for Active Aging*] [*Helsinki, Finland*] (EAIO)
**NORSAR**... Norwegian Seismic Array [*Royal Norwegian Council for Scientific and Industrial Research*] [*Kjeller, Norway*]
**NORSAT**... Norwegian Satellite System
**NORSE** ..... Norsul Oil & Mining [*NASDAQ symbol*] (NQ)
**NORSEACENT** ... North Sea Subarea (NATG)
**NORSEC**... Northern Security Exhibition [*British*] (ITD)
**NORSEX**... Norwegian Remote Sensing Experiment [*in marginal ice zone*]
**NORSF**...... Not Operationally Ready Supply Flyable [*Military*] (MCD)
**NORSG** ..... Not Operationally Ready Supply Grounded [*Military*] (NG)
**Norsk Data** ... Norsk Datatidende [*A publication*]
**Norsk Entomol Tidsskr** ... Norsk Entomologisk Tidsskrift [*A publication*]
**Norsk Ent Tidsskr** ... Norsk Entomologisk Tidsskrift [*A publication*]
**Norske Vid-Akad Oslo Mat-Natur Kl Skr** ... Norske Videnskaps-Akademi i Oslo. Matematisk-Naturvidenskapelig Klasse. Skrifter [*A publication*]
**Norske Vid Selsk Forh (Trondheim)** ... Kongelige Norske Videnskabers Selskab. Foerhandlinger (Trondheim) [*A publication*]
**Norske Vid Selsk Skr (Trondheim)** ... Kongelige Norske Videnskabers Selskab. Skrifter (Trondheim) [*A publication*]
**Norsk Farm T** ... Norsk Farmaceutisk Tidsskrift [*A publication*]
**Norsk Geogr Tidsskr** ... Norsk Geografisk Tidsskrift [*A publication*]
**Norsk Geogr Ts** ... Norsk Geografisk Tidsskrift [*A publication*]
**Norsk Geog Tid** ... Norsk Geografisk Tidsskrift [*A publication*]
**Norsk Geol** ... Norsk Geologisk Tidsskrift [*A publication*]
**Norsk Geol Tids** ... Norsk Geologisk Tidsskrift [*A publication*]
**Norsk Geol Tidsskr** ... Norsk Geologisk Tidsskrift [*A publication*]
**Norsk Hagetid** ... Norsk Hagetidend [*A publication*]
**Norskind**.... Norsk Skogindustri [*A publication*]
**Norsk Mag Laegevidensk** ... Norsk Magazin foer Laegevidenskaben [*A publication*]
**Norsk Mus** ... Norsk Musikerblad [*A publication*]
**Nor Skogbruk** ... Norsk Skogbruk [*A publication*]
**Nor Skogind** ... Norsk Skogindustri [*A publication*]
**Norsk Polarinst Aarbok** ... Norsk Polarinstitutt. Aarbok [*A publication*]
**Norsk Skog** ... Norsk Skogindustri [*A publication*]
**Norsk Skogbr** ... Norsk Skogbruk [*A publication*]
**Norsk Tekstiltid** ... Norsk Tekstiltidende [*A publication*]
**Norsk Vet Tid** ... Norsk Veterinaer-Tidsskrift [*A publication*]
**Norsk Vet-Tidsskr** ... Norsk Veterinaer-Tidsskrift [*A publication*]
**NORSN**..... Not Operationally Ready Supply Nongrounded [*Military*] (NG)
**NORSNET** ... National Oceanographic Reference Station Network (NOAA)
**NORSOLS** ... Northern Solomons Area
**NORST** ..... No Restrictions (FAAC)
**NORT**........ North [*A publication*]
**NORT**........ Nuclear Ordnance Readiness Test (NVT)
**Nor Tannlaegeforen Tid** ... Norske Tannlaegeforenings Tidende [*A publication*]
**NORTEB**... Norwegian Telecommunications Users Group (TSSD)
**Nor Tek Naturvitensk Forskningsrad Metall Kom Medd** ... Norges Teknisk Naturvitenskapelige Forskningsrad. Metallurgisk Komite. Meddelelse [*A publication*]
**Nor Tek Vitenskapsakad Medd** ... Norges Tekniske Vitenskapsakademi. Meddelelse [*A publication*]
**North**.......... Northampton County Reporter [*Pennsylvania*] [*A publication*] (DLA)
**NORTH**..... Northern Operations of Rail Transportation and Highways [*Alaska*]
**North**.......... Reports Tempore Northington [*Eden. English Chancery Reports*] [*1757-67*] [*A publication*] (DLA)
**NORTHAG** ... North [*European*] Army Group [*NATO*]

**Northam**..... Northampton Law Reporter [*Pennsylvania*] [*A publication*] (DLA)
**North Amer Fauna** ... North American Fauna [*A publication*]
**North Am Flora** ... North American Flora [*A publication*]
**North Am Flora Ser II** ... North American Flora. Series II [*A publication*]
**North Am Gladiolus Counc Bull** ... North American Gladiolus Council. Bulletin [*A publication*]
**Northam Law Rep** ... Northampton County Law Reporter [*Pennsylvania*] [*A publication*] (DLA)
**Northam L Rep** ... Northampton Law Reporter [*Pennsylvania*] [*A publication*] (DLA)
**Northamp A** ... Northampton Archaeology [*A publication*]
**Northamp Co Repr** ... Northampton County Reporter [*Pennsylvania*] [*A publication*] (DLA)
**North Am Pomona** ... North American Pomona [*A publication*]
**North Am Pract** ... North American Practitioner [*A publication*]
**Northampton Co Rep** ... Northampton County Reporter [*Pennsylvania*] [*A publication*] (DLA)
**Northamptonshire Archaeol** ... Northamptonshire Archaeology [*A publication*]
**North Am R** ... North American Review [*A publication*]
**North Am Vet** ... North American Veterinarian [*A publication*]
**NORTHANTS** ... Northamptonshire [*County in England*]
**North Car J Int'l L & Comm** ... North Carolina Journal of International Law and Commercial Regulation [*A publication*] (DLA)
**North Car Med J** ... North Carolina Medical Journal [*A publication*]
**North Carolina Cent LJ** ... North Carolina Central Law Journal [*A publication*]
**North Carolina College LJ** ... North Carolina College Law Journal [*A publication*] (DLA)
**North Carolina Div Ground Water Ground Water Bull** ... North Carolina. Department of Water and Air Resources. Division of Ground Water. Ground Water Bulletin [*A publication*]
**North Carolina Div Mineral Resources Geol Map Ser** ... North Carolina. Department of Conservation and Development. Division of Mineral Resources. Geologic Map Series [*A publication*]
**North Carolina Div Mineral Resources Inf Circ** ... North Carolina. Department of Conservation and Development. Division of Mineral Resources. Information Circular [*A publication*]
**North Carolina Div Mineral Resources Spec Pub** ... North Carolina. Department of Conservation and Development. Division of Mineral Resources. Special Publication [*A publication*]
**North Carolina Lib** ... North Carolina Libraries [*A publication*]
**North Cavern Mine Res Soc Occas Publ** ... Northern Cavern and Mine Research Society. Occasional Publication [*A publication*]
**North Cent Assn Q** ... North Central Association. Quarterly [*A publication*]
**North Cent Reg Ext Publ** ... North Central Regional Extension Publication [*A publication*]
**North Co**.... North Country Anvil [*A publication*]
**North Co**.... Northampton County Reporter [*Pennsylvania*] [*A publication*] (DLA)
**North Co Rep** ... Northampton County Reporter [*Pennsylvania*] [*A publication*] (DLA)
**North Co R (PA)** ... Northampton County Reporter [*Pennsylvania*] [*A publication*] (DLA)
**North Country Lib** ... North Country Libraries [*A publication*]
**NORTHD** .... Northumberland [*County in England*] (ROG)
**North Dakota Acad Sci Proc** ... North Dakota Academy of Science. Proceedings [*A publication*]
**North Dakota Geol Survey Bull** ... North Dakota. Geological Survey. Bulletin [*A publication*]
**North Dakota Geol Survey Misc Map** ... North Dakota. Geological Survey. Miscellaneous Map [*A publication*]
**North Dakota Geol Survey Misc Ser** ... North Dakota. Geological Survey. Miscellaneous Series [*A publication*]
**North Dakota Geol Survey Rept Inv** ... North Dakota. Geological Survey. Report of Investigations [*A publication*]
**North Dakota L Rev** ... North Dakota Law Review [*A publication*]
**North East Coast Inst Eng Shipbuild Trans** ... North East Coast Institution of Engineers and Shipbuilders. Transactions [*A publication*]
**Northeast Electron Res Eng Meet Rec** ... Northeast Electronics Research and Engineering Meeting Record [*A publication*]
**Northeast Environ Sci** ... Northeastern Environmental Science [*A publication*]
**Northeastern Ind World** ... Northeastern Industrial World [*A publication*]
**Northeast Geol** ... Northeastern Geology [*A publication*]
**Northeast Gulf Sci** ... Northeast Gulf Science [*A publication*]
**Northeast Wood Util Counc Inc Bull** ... Northeastern Wood Utilization Council, Incorporated. Bulletin [*A publication*]
**North Eng (Fairbanks)** ... Northern Engineer (Fairbanks) [*A publication*]
**Northern Archt** ... Northern Architect [*A publication*]
**Northern Cal R Bus and Econ** ... Northern California Review of Business and Economics [*A publication*]
**Northern Hist** ... Northern History. A Review of the History of the North of England [*A publication*]
**Northern Ireland Lib** ... Northern Ireland Libraries [*A publication*]
**Northern KY Law R** ... Northern Kentucky Law Review [*A publication*]
**Northern L** ... Northern Lights [*A publication*]
**Northern Logger** ... Northern Logger and Timber Processor [*A publication*]
**Northern Scot** ... Northern Scotland [*A publication*]
**Northern Stud** ... Northern Studies [*England*] [*A publication*]
**North Fur Trade** ... Northern Fur Trade [*A publication*]
**North & G** ... North and Guthrie's Appeals Reports [*68-80 Missouri*] [*A publication*] (DLA)
**North Hist** ... Northern History [*A publication*]
**North-Holland Math Library** ... North-Holland Mathematical Library [*A publication*]
**North-Holland Math Stud** ... North-Holland Mathematics Studies [*Elsevier Book Series*] [*A publication*]
**North-Holland Math Studies** ... North-Holland Mathematics Studies [*A publication*]
**North-Holland Ser in Appl Math and Mech** ... North-Holland Series in Applied Mathematics and Mechanics [*A publication*]
**North-Holland Ser Appl Math Mech** ... North-Holland Series in Applied Mathematics and Mechanics [*Elsevier Book Series*] [*A publication*]
**North Holland Ser Gen Systems Res** ... North-Holland Series in General Systems Research [*A publication*]
**North Holland Ser System Sci Engrg** ... North-Holland Series in Systems Science and Engineering [*A publication*]
**North Holland Syst Control Ser** ... North-Holland Systems and Control Series [*Elsevier Book Series*] [*A publication*]
**North Ireland LQ** ... Northern Ireland Legal Quarterly [*A publication*]
**North Irel Mem Geol Surv** ... Northern Ireland. Memoirs. Geological Survey [*A publication*]
**North Irel Minist Agric Annu Rep Res Tech Work** ... North Ireland Ministry of Agriculture. Annual Report on Research and Technical Work [*A publication*]
**North Irel Minist Agric Rec Agric Res** ... North Ireland Ministry of Agriculture. Record of Agricultural Research [*A publication*]
**North Irel Minist Agric Rec Agricultural Res** ... Northern Ireland. Ministry of Agriculture. Record of Agricultural Research [*A publication*]
**North Ken'y SL Rev** ... Northern Kentucky State Law Review [*A publication*] (DLA)
**North KY LR** ... Northern Kentucky Law Review [*A publication*]
**North Log Timber Process** ... Northern Logger and Timber Processer [*A publication*]
**North Miner** ... Northern Miner [*A publication*]
**NORTH'N** ... Northampton [*City in England*] (ROG)
**North Nigeria Reg Res Stn Tech Rep** ... Northern Nigeria. Regional Research Station. Technical Report [*A publication*]
**North Nut Grow Assoc Annu Rep** ... Northern Nut Growers Association. Annual Report [*A publication*]
**North Offshore** ... Northern Offshore [*A publication*]
**North Pac Fur Seal Comm Proc Annu Meet** ... North Pacific Fur Seal Commission. Proceedings of the Annual Meeting [*A publication*]
**North Pr**..... North's Probate Practice [*Illinois*] [*A publication*] (DLA)
**North Queensl Conf Australas Inst Min Metall** ... North Queensland Conference. Australasian Institute of Mining and Metallurgy [*A publication*] (APTA)
**North Queensl Nat** ... North Queensland Naturalist [*A publication*]
**North R**...... Northern Review [*A publication*]
**North Rhod Geol Surv Bull** ... Northern Rhodesia. Geological Survey. Bulletin [*A publication*]
**North Rhod Geol Surv Rep** ... Northern Rhodesia. Geological Survey. Report [*A publication*]
**Northrop ULJ** ... Northrop University. Law Journal of Aerospace, Energy, and the Environment [*A publication*] (DLA)
**Northrop ULJ Aero Energy and Envt** ... Northrop University. Law Journal of Aerospace, Energy, and the Environment [*A publication*]
**North Scot** ... Northern Scotland [*A publication*]
**North Scotl Coll Agric Bull** ... North of Scotland College of Agriculture. Bulletin [*A publication*]
**North Sea Oil Inf Sheet** ... North Sea Oil Information Sheet [*A publication*]
**North Staffordshire J Field Stud** ... North Staffordshire Journal of Field Studies [*A publication*]
**North St L** ... North. Study of the Laws [*1824*] [*A publication*] (DLA)
**North Stud** ... Northern Studies [*A publication*]
**North UL Rev** ... Northwestern University. Law Review [*A publication*]
**NORTHUM** ... Northumberland [*County in England*]
**Northum** .... Northumberland County Legal News [*Pennsylvania*] [*A publication*] (DLA)
**NORTHUMB** ... Northumberland [*County in England*] (ROG)
**Northumb Co** ... Northumberland County Legal News [*Pennsylvania*] [*A publication*] (DLA)
**Northumberland Co Leg Jour** ... Northumberland Legal Journal [*Pennsylvania*] [*A publication*] (DLA)
**Northumberland LJ** ... Northumberland Legal Journal [*Pennsylvania*] [*A publication*] (DLA)
**Northumb Legal J** ... Northumberland Legal Journal [*Pennsylvania*] [*A publication*] (DLA)
**Northumb LJ** ... Northumberland Legal Journal News [*Pennsylvania*] [*A publication*] (DLA)
**Northumb LN** ... Northumberland Legal Journal [*Pennsylvania*] [*A publication*] (DLA)
**Northum Co Leg N** ... Northumberland County Legal News [*Pennsylvania*] [*A publication*] (ILCA)
**Northum Leg J** ... Northumberland Legal Journal [*Pennsylvania*] [*A publication*] (DLA)

**Northum Leg J (PA)** ... Northumberland Legal Journal [*Pennsylvania*] [*A publication*] (DLA)
**Northum Leg N (PA)** ... Northumberland County Legal News [*Pennsylvania*] [*A publication*] (DLA)
**Northwest Anthropol Res Notes** ... Northwest Anthropological Research Notes [*A publication*]
**Northwest Atl Fish Organ Annu Rep** ... Northwest Atlantic Fisheries Organization. Annual Report [*A publication*]
**Northwest Atl Fish Organ Sci Counc Stud** ... Northwest Atlantic Fisheries Organization. Scientific Council. Studies [*A publication*]
**Northwest Atl Fish Organ Stat Bull** ... Northwest Atlantic Fisheries Organization. Statistical Bulletin [*A publication*]
**Northwest Dent** ... Northwest Dentistry [*A publication*]
**Northwest Environ J** ... Northwest Environmental Journal [*A publication*]
**Northwestern J Internat Law and Bus** ... Northwestern Journal of International Law and Business [*A publication*]
**Northwestern UL Rev** ... Northwestern University. Law Review [*A publication*]
**Northwestern Univ Dept Geography Studies Geography** ... Northwestern University. Department of Geography. Studies in Geography [*A publication*]
**Northwestern Univ Law R** ... Northwestern University. Law Review [*A publication*]
**Northwestern Univ L Rev** ... Northwestern University. Law Review [*A publication*]
**Northwest Geol** ... Northwest Geology [*A publication*]
**Northwest J Int'l L & Bus** ... Northwestern Journal of International Law and Business [*A publication*]
**Northwest Lancet** ... Northwestern Lancet [*A publication*]
**Northwest Livestock Dir** ... Northwest Livestock Directory [*A publication*]
**Northwest Lumberman** ... Northwestern Lumberman [*A publication*]
**Northwest Med** ... Northwest Medicine [*A publication*]
**Northwest Miller** ... Northwestern Miller [*A publication*]
**North West Newsl** ... North Western Newsletter [*A publication*]
**Northwest Ohio Q** ... Northwest Ohio Quarterly [*A publication*]
**Northwest Sci** ... Northwest Science [*A publication*]
**Northwest Univ Dent Res Grad Study Bull** ... Northwestern University. Dental Research and Graduate Study Bulletin [*A publication*]
**North WLJ** ... Northwestern Law Journal [*A publication*] (DLA)
**Northw L Rev** ... Northwestern University. Law Review [*A publication*]
**Northw Med** ... Northwest Medicine [*A publication*]
**Northw Ohio Quar** ... Northwest Ohio Quarterly [*A publication*]
**Northw Rep** ... Northwestern Reporter [*Commonly cited NW*] [*A publication*] (DLA)
**Northw U La** ... Northwestern University. Law Review [*A publication*]
**Northw Univ Law Rev** ... Northwestern University. Law Review [*A publication*]
**NORTLANT** ... North Atlantic
**Nort LC**...... Norton's Leading Cases on Inheritance [*India*] [*A publication*] (DLA)
**Norton**........ Norton's Cases on Hindu Law of Inheritance [*1870-71*] [*India*] [*A publication*] (DLA)
**Norton**........ Norton's Literary Letter [*A publication*]
**NORTR**..... Nortronics Corp.
**Nor Tr Bul** ... Norwegian Trade Bulletin [*A publication*]
**Nor TT**....... Norsk Teologisk Tidsskrift [*A publication*]
**NorTTs**...... Norsk Teologisk Tidsskrift [*Oslo*] [*A publication*]
**NORV**........ Norveg. Journal of Norwegian Ethnology [*A publication*]
**NORVA**..... Norfolk, Virginia [*Navy*]
**NORVAGRP** ... Norfolk, Virginia Group [*Navy*]
**NORVAL**.. Norvaline [*Biochemistry*]
**Nor Vel**...... Norges Vel [*A publication*]
**Nor Veritas Publ** ... Norske Veritas. Publication [*A publication*]
**Nor Veterinaertidsskr** ... Norsk Veterinaertidsskrift [*A publication*]
**Nor Vet-Tidsskr** ... Norsk Veterinaer-Tidsskrift [*A publication*]
**NORVIC** ... Norvicensis [*Norwich*] [*Imprint*] (ROG)
**Nor Vidensk-Akad Oslo Arbok** ... Norske Videnskaps-Akademi i Oslo. Aarbok [*A publication*]
**Nor Vidensk-Akad Oslo Mat Natur Kl N Ser** ... Norske Videnskaps-Akademi i Oslo. Matematisk-Naturvidenskapelig Klasse. Skrifter. Ny Serie [*A publication*]
**Nor Vidensk-Akad Skr** ... Norske Videnskaps-Akademi. Skrifter [*A publication*]
**Nor Vidensk Selsk Mus Misc** ... Norske Videnskabers Selskab. Museet. Miscellanea [*A publication*]
**NORVIPS** ... Northrup Voice Interruption Priority System (MUGU)
**Norv Pharm Acta** ... Norvegica Pharmaceutica Acta [*A publication*]
**Nor VVS**.... Norsk VVS [*Norsk Forening foer Varme-, Ventilasjon-, og Sanitaerteknikk*] [*Norway*] [*A publication*]
**NORW**....... Norway [*or Norwegian*]
**NORW**....... Norwich [*City in England*] (ROG)
**NORWAID** ... Norwegian Aid Society for Refugees and International Development
**Norw AR**.... Norwegian Archaeological Review [*A publication*]
**Norw Archaeol Rev** ... Norwegian Archaeological Review [*A publication*]
**Norway Bud** ... National Budget of Norway [*A publication*]
**Norway Geol Undersoekelse Bull** ... Norway. Geologiske Undersoekelse. Bulletin [*A publication*]
**Norwegian** ... Norwegian American Commerce [*A publication*]
**Norwegian-Am Stud and Rec** ... Norwegian-American Studies and Records [*A publication*]
**Norwegian Commer Banks Fin R** ... Norwegian Commercial Banks. Financial Review [*A publication*]
**NORWELD** ... Northwest Library District [*Library network*]
**NORWESSEAFRON** ... Northwestern Sea Frontier
**NORWESSEC** ... Northwestern Sector, Western Sea Frontier
**Nor'-West F** ... Nor'-West Farmer [*A publication*]
**NORWESTLANT** ... Northwest Atlantic [*Military*]
**NORWESTNAVFACENGCOM** ... Northwest Division Naval Facilities Engineering Command
**Norw Geotech Inst Publ** ... Norwegian Geotechnical Institute. Publication [*A publication*]
**NORWICH** ... Knickers Off Ready When I Come Home [*Correspondence*] (DSUE)
**Norw J Bot** ... Norwegian Journal of Botany [*A publication*]
**Norw J Entomol** ... Norwegian Journal of Entomology [*A publication*]
**Norw J Zool** ... Norwegian Journal of Zoology [*A publication*]
**Norw Marit Res** ... Norwegian Maritime Research [*A publication*]
**Norw Oil Rev** ... Norwegian Oil Review [*A publication*]
**Norw Petrol Dir Pap** ... Norwegian Petroleum Directorate. Paper [*A publication*]
**Norw Shipp News** ... Norwegian Shipping News [*A publication*]
**(Norw) Stat** ... Statistisk Manedskefte (Norway) [*A publication*]
**Norwy Econ** ... Economic Policy and Developments in Norway [*A publication*]
**Norw Yrbk** ... Statistical Yearbook of Norway [*A publication*]
**NOS**.......... National Ocean Service [*Formerly, Coast and Geodetic Survey*] [*Washington, DC*] [*National Oceanic and Atmospheric Administration*]
**NOS**.......... National Ocean Survey (NOAA)
**NOS**.......... National Office Staff [*American Occupational Therapy Association*]
**NOS**.......... National Operational Satellite
**NOS**.......... National Oratorio Society (EA)
**NOS**.......... National Osteoporosis Society [*British*]
**NOS**.......... NATO Office of Security (NATG)
**NOS**.......... Naval Ordnance Station
**NOS**.......... Nederlandse Omroep Stichtung [*Radio and television network*] [*Netherlands*]
**NOS**.......... Network Operating System
**NOS**.......... New Old Stock [*Automotive parts*]
**NOS**.......... News on Sunday [*A publication*]
**NOS**.......... Night Observation Sight [*Air Force*]
**NOS**.......... Night Observation System [*Navy*] (CAAL)
**NOS**.......... Night Operation System [*Aviation*]
**NOS**.......... Nimbus Operational System
**NOS**.......... Non-Ocular Source [*Physiology*]
**NOS**.......... Nonoriented Satellite
**NOS**.......... Nopaline Synthase [*An enzyme*]
**NOS**.......... Nordiska Odontologiska Studenter [*Council of Nordic Dental Students*] (EAIO)
**NOS**.......... Northern State College Library, Aberdeen, SD [*OCLC symbol*] (OCLC)
**NOS**.......... Northstar Resources Ltd. [*Toronto Stock Exchange symbol*]
**NOS**.......... Nossi-Be [*Madagascar*] [*Airport symbol*] (OAG)
**NOS**.......... Not Otherwise Specified (AFM)
**NOS**.......... Not Otherwise Stated
**NOS**.......... Not on Shelf (ADA)
**NOS**.......... Nouvel Ordre Social [*New Social Order*] [*Switzerland*] (PD)
**NOS**.......... Numbers (AAG)
**NOs**........... Oswego City Library, Oswego, NY [*Library symbol*] [*Library of Congress*] (LCLS)
**NOSA**........ National Outerwear and Sportswear Association (EA)
**NOSALF** ... Nordiska Samfundet for Latinamerika Forskning [*Nordic Association for Research on Latin America*] [*Stockholm, Sweden*] (EAIO)
**NOSBE**...... Network Operating System/Batch Environment
**NOSC**........ Naval Ocean Systems Center [*Formerly, NELC*]
**NOSC**........ Naval Ordnance Systems Command [*Later, Naval Sea Systems Command*]
**NOSC**........ Nonoscillating
**NOSCP**...... National Ocean Sediment Coring Program (NOAA)
**NOSE**........ National Odd Shoe Exchange (EA)
**NOSE**........ Neighbors Opposing Smelly Emissions [*Student legal action organization*]
**NOSEC**...... Information which does not affect national security
**NOSGLANT** ... Naval Operations Support Group, Atlantic
**NOSGPAC** ... Naval Operations Support Group, Pacific
**NOS-H**...... Nordiska Samarbetsnamnden for Humanistisk Forskning [*Nordic Committee of the Research Councils for the Humanities - NCRCH*] (EA)
**NOsHi**....... Oswego County Historical Society, Oswego, NY [*Library symbol*] [*Library of Congress*] (LCLS)
**NOsI**.......... International Business Machines Corp., Oswego, NY [*Library symbol*] [*Library of Congress*] (LCLS)
**NOSI**......... Now Simultaneous (FAAC)
**NOSIC**....... Naval Ocean Surveillance Information Center
**NOSIC**....... Naval Operations Support Information Center [*Navy*]
**NOSIE**....... Nurses Observation Scale for Inpatient Evaluation [*Psychiatry*]
**NOSIG**...... No Significant Change [*Used to qualify weather phenomena*]

**NOSIH** ...... Naval Ordnance Station, Indian Head (MCD)
**NOSK** ........ Norsk Skogindustri [*A publication*]
**NOSKA** ....... Norsk Skogindustri [*A publication*]
**NOSL** ........ Naval Ordnance Station, Louisville [*Kentucky*]
**NOSL** ........ Night-Day Optical Survey of Lightning [*NASA*]
**NOSLA** ..... National Oil Scouts and Landmen's Association [*Later, IOSA*]
**NOS-LSCR** ... National Ocean Survey Lake Survey Center [*National Oceanic and Atmospheric Administration*]
**NOSM** ....... Navy Occupation Service Medal
**NOSMO** .... Norden Optics Setting, Mechanized Operation [*Air Force bombsight*]
**NOS-N** ...... Samarbetsnamnden for de Nordiska Naturvetenskapliga Forskningraden [*Joint Committee of the Nordic Natural Science Research Councils - JCNNSRC*] (EA)
**NOSO** ........ Naval Ordnance Supply Office (MUGU)
**Nos Oiseaux Bull Romande Etude Prot Oiseaux** ... Nos Oiseaux. Bulletin de la Societe Romande pour l'Etude et la Protection des Oiseaux [*A publication*]
**Nosokom Chron** ... Nosokomeiaka Chronika [*A publication*]
**Nosokomeiaka Chron** ... Nosokomeiaka Chronika [*A publication*]
**NOSP** ........ National Ophthalmic Speakers Programme [*Canada*]
**NOSP** ........ Naval Ordnance Special Projects
**NOSP** ........ Network Operation Support Program [*Data processing*]
**NOSP** ........ Network Operations Support Plan [*NASA*] (KSC)
**NOSR** ........ National Office for Social Responsibility (EA)
**NOSS** ........ National Ocean Survey System [*Cooperative program of governmental agencies*]
**NOSS** ........ National Oceanic Satellite System (MCD)
**NOSS** ........ National Orbiting Space Station
**NOSS** ........ Nimbus Operational Satellite System [*GSFC/USWB*]
**NOS-S** ....... Nordiska Samarbetsnamnden for Samhallsforskning [*Joint Committee of Nordic Social Science Research Councils*] (EAIO)
**NOss** .......... Ossining Public Library, Ossining, NY [*Library symbol*] [*Library of Congress*] (LCLS)
**NOSSA** ...... New Orleans Steamship Association (EA)
**NOSSCR** ... National Organization of Social Security Claimants' Representatives (EA)
**NOSSO** ..... Naval Ordnance Systems Support Office (MCD)
**NOSSOLANT** ... Naval Ordnance Systems Support Office, Atlantic
**NOSSOPAC** ... Naval Ordnance Systems Support Office, Pacific
**NOST** ........ Knights of the Square Table (EA)
**NOST** ........ Nuclear Operational Systems Test
**NOSTA** ..... National Ocean Science and Technology Agency
**NOSTA** ..... Naval Ophthalmic Support and Training Activity
**NOSTA** ..... Norges Offisielle Statistikk [*A publication*]
**NOSTS** ...... National Ocean Survey Tide Station [*Marine science*] (MSC)
**NOsU** ........ State University of New York, College at Oswego, Oswego, NY [*Library symbol*] [*Library of Congress*] (LCLS)
**NOSUM** .... Notice to Airmen Summary (FAAC)
**NOSYAV** .. Museum National d'Histoire Naturelle. Notulae Systematicae [*A publication*]
**NOT** .......... New Orleans Terminal [*AAR code*]
**NOT** .......... Noront Resources Ltd. [*Vancouver Stock Exchange symbol*]
**NOT** .......... Notation (ROG)
**NOT** .......... Noted
**NOT** .......... Notes on Translation [*A publication*]
**NOT** .......... Notice (ROG)
**NOT** .......... Nucleus of the Optic Tract [*Eye anatomy*]
**NOTA** ........ National Organ Transplant Act [*1984*]
**NOTA** ........ None of the Above [*Politics*]
**NOTACGENSEA** ... Nontactical Generator, Southeast Asia
**NOTACK** .. No Attack Area [*Military*] (NVT)
**NOTAD** ..... Notice to Airmen Address
**NOTAEI** .... National Old Timers' Association of the Energy Industry (EA)
**Not Af** ........ Notes Africaines [*A publication*]
**Not Agric Fund Serv Agric** ... Noticias Agricolas. Fundacion Servicio para el Agricultor [*A publication*]
**Not Agric Serv Shell Agric** ... Noticias Agricolas. Servicio Shell para el Agricultor [*A publication*]
**Nota Inf Inst Nac Invest Forest (Mex)** ... Nota Informativa. Instituto Nacional de Investigaciones Forestales (Mexico) [*A publication*]
**Nota Invest Cent Invest Pesq (Bauta Cuba)** ... Nota sobre Investigaciones. Centro de Investigaciones Pesqueras (Bauta, Cuba) [*A publication*]
**NOTAL** ..... Not at All
**NOTAL** ..... Not to, nor Needed by, All
**Not Allumiere** ... Notiziario. Museo Civico ed Associazione Archeologica di Allumiere [*A publication*]
**NOTAM** .... Notice to Airmen
**Not Am Math** ... Notices. American Mathematical Society [*A publication*]
**Not Ammin Sanit** ... Notiziario dell'Amministrazione Sanitaria [*A publication*]
**NOTAMS** ... Notice to Airmen [*A publication*] (APTA)
**NOTAP** ..... Navy Occupational Task Analysis Program (NVT)
**NOTAR** ..... No-Tail Rotor [*Helicopters*]
**NOTARC** .. National Old Timers Auto Racing Club (EA)
**NOTAS** ..... Notice to Airmen Summary
**Notas Agron** ... Notas Agronomicas [*A publication*]
**Notas Algebra Anal** ... Notas de Algebra y Analisis [*Bahia Blanca*] [*A publication*]
**Notas Cent Biol Aquat Trop (Lisb)** ... Notas. Centro de Biologia Aquatica Tropical (Lisbon) [*A publication*]
**Notas Cient Ser M Mat** ... Notas Cientificas. Serie M. Matematica [*Lima*] [*A publication*]
**Notas Ci Ser M Mat** ... Notas Cientificas. Serie M. Matematica [*A publication*]
**Notas Comun Inst Geol Min Esp** ... Notas y Comunicaciones. Instituto Geologico y Minero de Espana [*A publication*]
**Notas Divulg Inst Munic Bot (Buenos Aires)** ... Notas de Divulgacion del Instituto Municipal de Botanica (Buenos Aires) [*A publication*]
**Notas Estud Inst Biol Marit (Lisb)** ... Notas e Estudos. Instituto de Biologia Maritima (Lisbon) [*A publication*]
**Notas Estud Secr Estado Pescas Ser Recur Ambiente Aquat** ... Notas e Estudos. Secretaria de Estado das Pescas. Serie Recursos e Ambiente Aquatico [*A publication*]
**Notas Fis** .... Notas de Fisica [*A publication*]
**Notas Fis Cent Bras Pesqui Fis** ... Notas de Fisica. Centro Brasileiro de Pesquisas Fisicas [*A publication*]
**Notas Geom Topol** ... Notas de Geometria y Topologia [*Bahia Blanca*] [*A publication*]
**Nota Silvic Adm Nac Bosques (Argent)** ... Notas Silvicolas. Administracion Nacional de Bosques (Buenos Aires, Argentina) [*A publication*]
**Notas Inst Mat Estatist Univ Sao Paulo Ser Mat** ... Notas. Instituto de Matematica e Estatistica da Universidade de Sao Paulo. Serie Matematica [*A publication*]
**Notas Mat** ... Notas de Matematica [*Amsterdam*] [*A publication*]
**Notas Mat Discreta** ... Notas de Matematica Discreta [*A publication*]
**Notas Mimeogr Cent Biol Aquat Trop (Lisb)** ... Notas Mimeografadas. Centro de Biologia Aquatica Tropical (Lisbon) [*A publication*]
**Notas Mus La Plata Antropol** ... Notas. Museo de La Plata. Antropologia [*A publication*]
**Notas Mus La Plata Bot** ... Notas. Museo de La Plata. Botanica [*A publication*]
**Notas Mus La Plata Paleontol** ... Notas. Museo de La Plata. Paleontologia [*A publication*]
**Notas Mus La Plata Zool** ... Notas. Museo de La Plata. Zoologia [*A publication*]
**Notas Pobl** ... Notas de Poblacion [*A publication*]
**Notas Prelim Estud Serv Geol Mineral Braz** ... Notas Preliminares e Estudos. Servico Geologico e Mineralogico do Brazil [*A publication*]
**Notas Quir Sanat Deschamps** ... Notas Quirurgicas. Sanatorio Deschamps [*A publication*]
**Notas Tec Inst Pesqui Mar (Rio De J)** ... Notas Tecnicas. Instituto de Pesquisas da Marinha (Rio De Janeiro) [*A publication*]
**Notas Tec Inst Pesqui Mar (Rio De Janeiro)** ... Notas Tecnicas. Instituto de Pesquisas da Marinha (Rio De Janeiro) [*A publication*]
**Nota Tec For Esc Ingen For Univ Chile** ... Notas Tecnico Forestales. Escuela de Ingenieria Forestal. Universidad de Chile [*A publication*]
**Nota Tec Inst For (Chile)** ... Nota Tecnica. Instituto Forestal (Santiago De Chile) [*A publication*]
**Nota Tec Inst Nac Invest For (Mex)** ... Nota Tecnica. Instituto Nacional de Investigaciones Forestales (Mexico) [*A publication*]
**Nota Tecnol For Adm Nac Bosques (Argent)** ... Notas Tecnological Forestales. Administracion Nacional de Bosques (Buenos Aires, Argentina) [*A publication*]
**Notatki Ornitol** ... Notatki Ornitologiczne [*A publication*]
**NOTB** ........ National Ophthalmic Treatment Board [*British*]
**NOTBA** ..... National Ophthalmic Treatment Board Association [*British*]
**Not Biol** ...... Notationes Biologicae [*A publication*]
**NOTC** ........ Naval Ordnance Test Center (KSC)
**NOTC** ........ NOAA [*National Oceanic and Atmospheric Administration*] Operational Telecommunications Coordinator (NOAA)
**Not Cas** ...... Notes of Cases, English Ecclesiastical and Maritime Courts [*1841-50*] [*A publication*] (DLA)
**Not Cas** ...... Notes of Cases at Madras (Strange) [*A publication*] (DLA)
**Not Cas Ecc & M** ... Notes of Cases, English Ecclesiastical and Maritime Courts [*1841-50*] [*A publication*] (DLA)
**Not Cas Madras** ... Notes of Cases at Madras (Strange) [*A publication*] (DLA)
**Notc on Fac** ... Notcutt on Factories and Workshops [*2nd ed.*] [*1879*] [*A publication*] (DLA)
**NOT i Ch** ... Naucnaja Organizacija Truda i Chozjajstvo [*A publication*]
**Not Chim Ind** ... Notiziario Chimico-Industriale [*A publication*]
**Not Chiostro Mon Magg** ... Notizie dal Chiostro del Monastero Maggiore [*A publication*]
**NOTCOMM** ... Not Commissioned [*Military*]
**Not Com Naz Energ Nucl** ... Notiziario. Comitato Nazionale per l'Energia Nucleare [*A publication*]
**Not Dec** ...... Notes of Decisions [*Martin's North Carolina Reports*] [*A publication*] (DLA)
**Not Dig** ...... Boddam and Greenwood's Notanda Digest [*A publication*] (DLA)
**Not Dign** .... Notitia Dignitatum [*Classical studies*] (OCD)
**note** ............ Footnote in Cross-Reference (DLA)
**NOTEA** ..... Novosti Tekhniki [*A publication*]
**Note Apunti Sper Ent Agr** ... Note ed Apunti Sperimentale di Entomologia Agraria [*A publication*]
**Noteb Empirical Petrol** ... Notebook of Empirical Petrology [*A publication*]
**Note Econ** .. Note Economiche [*A publication*]

**NOTEF**...... National Organ Transplant Education Foundation (EA)
**Note Fruttic** ... Note de Frutticultura [*A publication*]
**Note Inf Tech Lab Cent Ponts Chaussees** ... Note d'Information Technique. Laboratoire Central des Ponts et Chaussees [*A publication*]
**Note Lab Biol Mar Pesca-Fano** ... Note. Laboratorio di Biologia Marina e Pesca-Fano [*A publication*]
**Note Mat** ... Note di Matematica [*A publication*]
**NOTEMPS** ... Nontemporary Storage System (MCD)
**Not Enol Aliment** ... Notiziario Enologico ed Alimentare [*A publication*]
**Not Entomol** ... Notulae Entomologicae [*A publication*]
**Note Recens & Not** ... Note Recensioni e Notizie [*A publication*]
**Note Rech Dep Exploit Util Bois Univ Laval** ... Note de Recherches. Departement d'Exploitation et Utilisation des Bois. Universite Laval [*A publication*]
**Note Rech Miner Explor Res Inst McGill Univ** ... Note de Recherche. Mineral Exploration Research Institute. McGill University [*A publication*]
**Note Rec Roy Soc London** ... Notes and Records. Royal Society of London [*A publication*]
**Note Riv Psichiat** ... Note e Riviste di Psichiatria [*A publication*]
**Note Riv Psichiatr** ... Note e Riviste di Psichiatria [*A publication*]
**NOTES**...... National Organization of Telecommunications Engineers and Scientists [*Washington, DC*] [*Telecommunications*] (TSSD)
**No Tes**........ Novum Testamentum [*A publication*]
**Notes Afr** ... Notes Africaines [*A publication*]
**Notes Agric Res Cent Herb (Egypt)** ... Notes. Agricultural Research Centre Herbarium (Egypt) [*A publication*]
**Notes Appl Sci NPL** ... Notes on Applied Science. National Physical Laboratory [*A publication*]
**Notes Appl Sci UK Natl Phys Lab** ... Notes on Applied Science. United Kingdom National Physical Laboratory [*A publication*]
**Notes Bot Sch Trinity Coll (Dublin)** ... Notes. Botanical School of Trinity College (Dublin) [*A publication*]
**Notes of Ca** ... Notes of Cases [*England*] [*A publication*] (DLA)
**Notes of Cas** ... Notes of Cases, English Ecclesiastical and Maritime Courts [*1841-50*] [*A publication*] (DLA)
**Notes of Cases** ... Notes of Cases, English Ecclesiastical and Maritime Courts [*1841-50*] [*A publication*] (DLA)
**Notes Docum UN Unit Apartheid** ... Notes and Documents. United Nations Unit on Apartheid [*A publication*]
**Notes Ent Chin** ... Notes d'Entomologie Chinoise [*A publication*]
**Notes Etud Doc** ... Notes et Etudes Documentaires [*A publication*]
**Notes et Etud Docum** ... Notes et Etudes Documentaires [*A publication*]
**Notes et Etud Docum Ser Problemes Am Latine** ... Notes et Etudes Documentaires. Serie Problemes d'Amerique Latine [*A publication*]
**Notes Higher Ed** ... Notes on Higher Education [*A publication*]
**Notes on Higher Educ** ... Notes on Higher Education [*A publication*] (APTA)
**Notes Inf CEA** ... Notes d'Information CEA [*Comissariat a l'Energie Atomique*] [*A publication*]
**Notes Inform Statist Banque Centr Afr Ouest** ... Notes d'Information et Statistiques. Banque Centrale des Etats de l'Afrique de l'Ouest [*A publication*]
**Notes Maroc** ... Notes Marocaines [*A publication*]
**Notes et Mem Moyen-Orient** ... Notes et Memoires sur le Moyen-Orient [*A publication*]
**Notes Mem Moyen-Orient** ... Notes et Memoires sur le Moyen-Orient [*A publication*]
**Notes Mem Serv Geol Maroc** ... Notes et Memoires. Service Geologique du Maroc [*A publication*]
**Notes Mem Serv Geol (Rabat)** ... Notes et Memoires du Service Geologique (Rabat) [*A publication*]
**Notes Mem UAR Hydrobiol Dep** ... Notes and Memoirs. United Arab Republic. Hydrobiological Department [*A publication*]
**Notes Pure Math** ... Notes on Pure Mathematics [*A publication*] (APTA)
**Notes on Pure Math** ... Notes on Pure Mathematics [*A publication*]
**Notes & Quer** ... Notes and Queries [*A publication*]
**Notes Quer** ... Notes and Queries [*A publication*]
**Notes Queries Soc West Highl Isl Hist Res** ... Notes and Queries. Society of West Highland and Island Historical Research [*A publication*]
**Notes R Bot Gard (Edinb)** ... Notes. Royal Botanic Garden (Edinburgh) [*A publication*]
**Notes R Bot Gdn (Edinb)** ... Notes. Royal Botanic Garden (Edinburgh) [*A publication*]
**Notes Read** ... Notes and Queries for Readers and Writers, Collectors, and Librarians [*A publication*]
**Notes and Records Roy Soc London** ... Notes and Records. Royal Society of London [*A publication*]
**Notes Rec R** ... Notes and Records. Royal Society of London [*A publication*]
**Notes Rec Roy London** ... Notes and Records. Royal Society of London [*A publication*]
**Notes Rec R Soc Lond** ... Notes and Records. Royal Society of London [*A publication*]
**Notes on Sc Build** ... Notes on the Science of Building [*Australia Commonwealth Experimental Building Station*] [*A publication*] (APTA)
**Notes Sci Bldg** ... Notes on the Science of Building [*Australia Commonwealth Experimental Building Station*] [*A publication*] (APTA)
**Notes Sci Build** ... Notes on the Science of Building [*Australia Commonwealth Experimental Building Station*] [*A publication*] (APTA)
**Notes on the Science of Bldg** ... Notes on the Science of Building [*Australia Commonwealth Experimental Building Station*] [*A publication*]
**Notes Serv Geol Maroc** ... Notes du Service Geologique du Maroc [*A publication*]
**Notes Soil Tech** ... Notes on Soil Technique [*Australia Commonwealth Scientific and Industrial Research Organisation. Division of Soils*] [*A publication*] (APTA)
**No Test**...... Novum Testamentum (DSA)
**Notes Tech Hydrol** ... Notes Techniques en Hydrologie [*A publication*]
**Notes on Univ Ed** ... Notes on University Education [*A publication*] (APTA)
**Notes on US** ... Notes on United States Reports [*A publication*] (DLA)
**Notes Water Pollut (Stevenage)** ... Notes on Water Pollution (Stevenage) [*A publication*]
**Notes Water Res** ... Notes on Water Research [*A publication*]
**Note Tech Centre Tech For Trop** ... Note Technique. Centre Technique Forestier Tropicale [*A publication*]
**Note Tech Cent Tech For Trop (Nogent Sur Marne Fr)** ... Note Technique. Centre Technique Forestier Tropical (Nogent-Sur-Marne, France) [*A publication*]
**Note Tech Dep Exploit Util Bois Univ Laval** ... Note Technique. Departement d'Exploitation et Utilisation des Bois. Universite Laval [*A publication*]
**Note Tech Inst Rebois Tunis** ... Note Technique. Institut de Reboisement de Tunis [*A publication*]
**NO-TFA**.... National Old-Time Fiddlers' Association (EA)
**Not Farm** ... Noticias Farmaceuticas [*A publication*]
**Not Farm (Coimbra)** ... Noticias Farmaceuticas (Coimbra) [*A publication*]
**Not Galapagos** ... Noticias de Galapagos [*A publication*]
**Notic Agr Serv Shell Agr** ... Noticias Agricolas. Servicio Shell para el Agricultor [*A publication*]
**Notic Arqueol Hispan Prehist** ... Noticiario Arqueologico Hispanico Prehistoria [*A publication*]
**Notices Amer Math Soc** ... Notices. American Mathematical Society [*A publication*]
**Notic Geomorfol** ... Noticia Geomorfologica [*A publication*]
**Noticiario Inst Forestal** ... Noticiario Instituto Forestal [*A publication*]
**Noticias**...... Brasil. Instituto Brasileiro de Bibliographia e Documentacao. Noticias [*A publication*]
**NOTIF**....... Notification
**NOTIN**...... Notification (ROG)
**NOTIP**....... Night Observation Television in a Pod
**NOTIS**....... Network Operations Trouble Information System [*Telecommunications*] (TEL)
**NOTIS**....... Northwestern Online Total Integrated System [*Northwestern University Library*] [*Library automation project*] [*Information service or system*] (IID)
**Not Ist Autom Univ Roma** ... Notiziario. Istituto di Automatica. Universita di Roma [*A publication*]
**Not Ist Vaccinogeno Antituberc** ... Notiziario. Istituto Vaccinogeno Antitubercolare [*A publication*]
**Notizbl Hess Landesamtes Bodenforsch Wiesb** ... Notizblatt. Hessisches Landesamt fuer Bodenforschung zu Wiesbaden [*A publication*]
**Notiz Cam Cam Commer Ind Agr Cuneo** ... Notiziario Camerale. Camera di Commercio. Industria e Agricoltura di Cuneo [*A publication*]
**Notiz Farm** ... Notiziario Farmaceutico [*A publication*]
**Notiz IRI**.... Notizie IRI [*Istituto per la Ricostruzione Industriale*] [*A publication*]
**Notiz Malatt Piante** ... Notiziario sulle Malattie delle Piante [*A publication*]
**Notiz Mal Piante** ... Notiziario sulle Malattie delle Piante [*A publication*]
**Not J**.......... Notaries Journal [*A publication*] (DLA)
**N-O-T-L**.... Niagara-On-The-Lake [*Ontario*]
**NOTL**........ Northline Association of Canadian Universities for Northern Studies [*A publication*]
**NOTL**........ Notarial (ROG)
**NOTM**....... New Orleans, Texas & Mexico [*AAR code*]
**No TM**....... Norsk Tidsskrift vor Misjon [*A publication*]
**Not Mal Piante** ... Notiziario sulle Malattie delle Piante [*A publication*]
**Not Man A** ... Not Man Apart [*A publication*]
**Not Mar**..... Notes Marocaines [*A publication*]
**NOTMAR** ... Notice to Mariner (NVT)
**Not Mens Mus Nac Hist Nat** ... Noticiario Mensual. Museo Nacional de Historia Natural [*A publication*]
**Not Mineral Sicil Calabrese** ... Notizie di Mineralogia Siciliana e Calabrese [*A publication*]
**NoTN**......... Norges Tekniske Vitenskapsakademi [*Norwegian Academy for Technical Sciences*], Trondheim, Norway [*Library symbol*] [*Library of Congress*] (LCLS)
**NOTN** ....... Nortext News [*A publication*]
**Not Nat Acad Nat Sci Philadelphia** ... Notulae Naturae. Academy of Natural Sciences of Philadelphia [*A publication*]
**Not Nat (Phila)** ... Notulae Naturae (Philadelphia) [*A publication*]
**NOTNO**.... Notional Number (NVT)
**NOTO** ....... Non-Official Trade Organisation [*British*]
**NOTO** ....... Numbering Tool (AAG)
**NOTOA6**... Brain and Nerve [*Tokyo*] [*A publication*]
**Not Odonatol** ... Notulae Odonatologicae [*A publication*]

**NOTOF** ..... Notice to Airmen Office
**Not Op** ....... Wilmot's Notes of Opinions and Judgments [*A publication*] (DLA)
**NOTOX** ...... Not to Exceed (NOAA)
**NOTP** ......... New Orleans Times-Picayune [*A publication*]
**Not Quir Sanat Desch** ... Notas Quirurgicas del Sanatorio Deschamps [*A publication*]
**NOTR** ........ National Order of Trench Rats (EA)
**Notr Dame E** ... Notre Dame English Journal [*A publication*]
**Notre Dame Eng J** ... Notre Dame English Journal [*A publication*]
**Notre Dame Est Plan Inst** ... Notre Dame Estate Planning Institute. Proceedings [*A publication*] (DLA)
**Notre Dame Est Plan Inst Proc** ... Notre Dame Estate Planning Institute. Proceedings [*A publication*]
**Notre Dame Inst on Char Giving Found and Tr** ... Notre Dame Institute on Charitable Giving. Foundations and Trusts [*A publication*]
**Notre Dame J Formal Logic** ... Notre Dame Journal of Formal Logic [*A publication*]
**Notre Dame J Form Log** ... Notre Dame Journal of Formal Logic [*A publication*]
**Notre Dame J Leg** ... Notre Dame Journal of Legislation [*A publication*] (DLA)
**Notre Dame L** ... Notre Dame Lawyer [*A publication*]
**Notre Dame Law** ... Notre Dame Lawyer [*A publication*]
**Notre Dame Law R** ... Notre Dame Law Review [*A publication*]
**Notre Dame L Rev** ... Notre Dame Law Review [*A publication*]
**Notre Dame Sci Q** ... Notre Dame Science Quarterly [*United States*] [*A publication*]
**Not Ric Sci** ... Notiziario de "La Ricerca Scientifica" [*A publication*]
**NOTRTR** .. National Organization of Test, Research, and Training Reactors [*Later, TRTR*] (EA)
**NOTS** ........ Naval Ordnance Test Station
**NOTS** ........ Naval Overseas Transport Service
**NOTS** ........ NOAA [*National Oceanic and Atmospheric Administration*] Operational Telecommunications System (NOAA)
**NOT SAFE** ... National Organization Taunting Safety and Fairness Everywhere (EA)
**Not Soc Ital Fitosoc** ... Notiziario. Societa Italiana di Fitosociologia [*A publication*]
**Not Syst** ..... Notulae Systematicae [*A publication*]
**No TT** ........ Norsk Teologisk Tidsskrift [*A publication*]
**Nott Fr St** ... Nottingham French Studies [*A publication*]
**Nott & Hop** ... Nott and Hopkins' Reports [*United States Court of Claims*] [*A publication*] (DLA)
**Nott & Hunt** ... Nott and Huntington's Reports [*1-7 United States Court of Claims*] [*A publication*] (DLA)
**Nottingham Medieval Stud** ... Nottingham Medieval Studies [*A publication*]
**Nottingham Univ Min Dep Mag** ... Nottingham University. Mining Department Magazine [*England*] [*A publication*]
**NOTTM** .... Nottingham [*County in England*]
**Nott & McC** ... Nott and McCord's South Carolina Reports [*A publication*] (DLA)
**Nott & M'C (SC)** ... Nott and M'Cord's South Carolina Reports [*A publication*] (DLA)
**Nott Mech L** ... Nott on the Mechanics' Lien Law [*A publication*] (DLA)
**NOTTS** ...... Nottinghamshire [*County in England*]
**NOTU** ........ Naval Operational Training Unit
**NOTU** ........ Naval Ordnance Test Unit
**NoTU** ......... Universitetet i Trondheim [*University of Trondheim*], Trondheim, Norway [*Library symbol*] [*Library of Congress*] (LCLS)
**Notulae Entomol** ... Notulae Entomologicae [*A publication*]
**Notul Ent** ... Notulae Entomologicae [*A publication*]
**NOTUN** .... Notice of Unreliability
**NoTU-T** ..... Universitetet i Trondheim, Norges Tekniske Hogskole [*University of Trondheim, Norwegian Institute of Technology*], Trondheim-NTH, Norway [*Library symbol*] [*Library of Congress*] (LCLS)
**NoTU-V** ..... Universitetet i Trondheim, Kongelige Norske Videnskabers Selskabs [*University of Trondheim, Royal Norwegian Society of Sciences and Letters*], Trondheim, Norway [*Library symbol*] [*Library of Congress*] (LCLS)
**Not W** ........ Notarieel Weekblad [*A publication*]
**NOTWG** .... Notwithstanding
**NOTWSTG** ... Notwithstanding
**NOTWT** .... Do Not Transmit by Radio (NATG)
**NOTY** ........ Notary (ROG)
**NOU** .......... Naval Ordnance Unit
**NOU** .......... Noumea [*New Caledonia*] [*Airport symbol*] (OAG)
**NOU** .......... Noumea [*New Caledonia*] [*Seismograph station code, US Geological Survey*] (SEIS)
**NOU** .......... Sitka, AK [*Location identifier*] [*FAA*] (FAAL)
**NOUS** ........ Naval Order of the United States (EA)
**NOUTD** ..... Nordisk Utredningsserie [*A publication*]
**Nouv Arch** ... Nouvelles Archives des Missions Scientifiques [*A publication*]
**Nouv Arch Hosp** ... Nouvelles Archives Hospitalieres [*A publication*]
**Nouv Autom** ... Nouvel Automatisme [*A publication*]
**Nouv Avic** .. Nouvelles de l'Aviculture [*A publication*]
**Nouv Cah** ... Nouveaux Cahiers [*A publication*]
**Nouv Caledoniennes** ... Nouvelles Caledoniennes [*A publication*]
**Nouv Chine** ... Nouvelle Chine [*A publication*]
**Nouv Clio** ... La Nouvelle Clio [*A publication*]
**Nouv Crit** ... Nouvelle Critique [*A publication*]
**Nouv Critique** ... Nouvelle Critique [*A publication*]
**Nouveau Cours de Math** ... Nouveau Cours de Mathematiques [*A publication*]
**Nouvel Autom** ... Nouvel Automatisme [*A publication*]
**Nouv Etud Hongroises** ... Nouvelles Etudes Hongroises [*A publication*]
**Nouv Hongrie** ... Nouvelles de Hongrie [*A publication*]
**Nouv J Chim** ... Nouveau Journal de Chimie [*A publication*]
**NouvLitt** ..... Nouvelles Litteraires [*Paris*] [*A publication*]
**Nouv Med** .. Nouveautes Medicales [*A publication*]
**Nouv Polit Agric Commune** ... Nouvelles de la Politique Agricole Commune [*A publication*]
**Nouv Presse** ... Nouvelle Presse Medicale [*A publication*]
**Nouv Presse Med** ... Nouvelle Presse Medicale [*A publication*]
**Nouv R Deux Mondes** ... Nouvelle Revue des Deux Mondes [*A publication*]
**Nouv Rev** .... Nouvelle Revue de Droit Francais [*Paris*] [*A publication*] (DLA)
**Nouv Rev Entomol** ... Nouvelle Revue d'Entomologie [*A publication*]
**Nouv Rev Fr** ... Nouvelle Revue Francaise [*A publication*]
**Nouv Rev Fr Hematol** ... Nouvelle Revue Francaise d'Hematologie. Blood Cells [*A publication*]
**Nouv Rev Fr Hematol Blood Cells** ... Nouvelle Revue Francaise d'Hematologie. Blood Cells [*A publication*]
**Nouv Rev Med Toulouse Suppl** ... Nouvelle Revue de Medecine de Toulouse. Supplement [*A publication*]
**Nouv Rev Opt** ... Nouvelle Revue d'Optique [*A publication*]
**Nouv Rev Opt Appl** ... Nouvelle Revue d'Optique Appliquee [*A publication*]
**Nouv Rev Son** ... Nouvelle Revue du Son [*A publication*]
**Nouv Rev Theo** ... Nouvelle Revue Theologique [*A publication*]
**Nouv R F Hem** ... Nouvelle Revue Francaise d'Hematologie. Blood Cells [*A publication*]
**Nouv R Francaise** ... Nouvelle Revue Francaise [*A publication*]
**Nouv R Int** ... Nouvelle Revue Internationale [*A publication*]
**Nouv R Opt** ... Nouvelle Revue d'Optique [*A publication*]
**Nouv R Social** ... Nouvelle Revue Socialiste [*A publication*]
**Nouv Rythmes Monde** ... Nouveaux Rythmes du Monde [*A publication*]
**NOV** .......... Huambo [*Angola*] [*Airport symbol*] (OAG)
**NOV** .......... Nodamura Virus
**NOV** .......... Non Obstante Veredicto [*Judgment Notwithstanding*] [*Latin*] [*Legal term*] (DLA)
**NOV** .......... Notice of Violation [*Nuclear energy*] (NRCH)
**NOV** .......... Novamin, Inc. [*Toronto Stock Exchange symbol*]
**NOV** .......... Novara [*Sicily*] [*Seismograph station code, US Geological Survey*] (SEIS)
**NOV** .......... Novation [*Legal term*] (DLA)
**NOV** .......... Novel (ROG)
**Nov** ............ Novellae [*Classical studies*] (OCD)
**Nov** ............ Novels [*Roman law*] [*A publication*]
**NOV** .......... November (AAG)
**Nov** ............ Noverim [*A publication*]
**NOV** .......... Novitiate (ROG)
**NOVA** ........ National Organization for Victim Assistance (EA)
**NOVA** ........ National Outdoor Volleyball Association (EA)
**NOVA** ........ National Overhead Evaluation Assessment [*Term for the restructuring process begun at E. F. Hutton after the October 1987 stock market collapse*]
**NOVA** ........ Network Organization via Advanced Architecture [*Marubeni Corp.*]
**NOVA** ........ Nova Natural Resources Corp. [*NASDAQ symbol*] (NQ)
**NOVA** ........ Nurses Organization of Veterans Affairs (EA)
**NOVA** ........ Nutritional Oncology Vascular Access
**Nova Acta Leopold** ... Nova Acta Leopoldina [*A publication*]
**Nova Acta Leopold Suppl** ... Nova Acta Leopoldina. Supplementum [*A publication*]
**Nova Acta Regiae Soc Sci Ups** ... Nova Acta Regiae Societatis Scientiarum Upsaliensis [*A publication*]
**Nova Acta Regiae Soc Sci Ups C** ... Nova Acta Regiae Societatis Scientiarum Upsaliensis. Seria C [*A publication*]
**Nova Acta R Soc Sc Upsaliensis** ... Nova Acta Regiae Societatis Scientiarum Upsaliensis [*A publication*]
**Nova Guinea Geol** ... Nova Guinea. Geology [*A publication*]
**Nova Hedwigia Z Kryptogamenkd** ... Nova Hedwigia Zeitschrift fuer Kryptogamenkunde [*A publication*]
**Nova LJ** ..... Nova Law Journal [*A publication*]
**Nova Proizv** ... Nova Proizvodnja [*A publication*]
**Nova Proizvod** ... Nova Proizvodnya [*A publication*]
**Nova Scotia Dept Mines Ann Rept Mem** ... Nova Scotia. Department of Mines. Annual Report. Memoir [*A publication*]
**Nova Scotia Hist Rev** ... Nova Scotia Historical Review [*A publication*]
**Nova Scotia Med Bull** ... Nova Scotia Medical Bulletin [*A publication*]
**Nova Scotian Inst Sci Proc** ... Nova Scotian Institute of Science. Proceedings [*A publication*]
**NOVC** ........ Northview Corporation [*San Diego, CA*] [*NASDAQ symbol*] (NQ)
**Nov Com Fragm** ... Novae Comoediae Fragmenta in Papyris Reperta Exceptis Menandreis [*A publication*] (OCD)
**Nov Comm Acad Sci Imp Petrop** ... Novi Commentarii Academiae Scientiarum Imperalis Petropolitanae [*A publication*]
**NOVDA** ..... Norsk Veterinaer-Tidsskrift [*A publication*]
**Nov Dannye Geol Polezn Iskop Zapadn Sib** ... Novye Dannye po Geologii i Poleznym Iskopaemym Zapadnoi Sibiri [*A publication*]

**NOVE**........ NOMOS Verlagskatalog [*NOMOS Datapool*] [*Information service or system*] (IID)
**No Ve**......... Nova et Vetera [*A publication*]
**NOVEA**..... Novenytermeles [*A publication*]
**Noved Cient Ser Zool** ... Novedades Cientificas. Serie Zoologia [*A publication*]
**Noveishaya Tektonika Noveishie Otlozh Chel** ... Noveishaya Tektonika. Noveishie Otlozheniya i Chelovek [*A publication*]
**NOVEL**..... Narrative Output Vocabulary Editing Language [*Psychiatric test*]
**Novenynemes Novenytermesz Kutato Intez Koezl Sopronhorpacs** ... Novenynemesitesi es Novenytermesztesi Kutato Intezet. Sopronhorpacs Koezlemenyei [*A publication*]
**Novenytermeles Crop Prod** ... Novenytermeles/Crop Production [*A publication*]
**Novenyved Idoszeru Kerdesei** ... Novenyvedelem Idoszeru Kerdesei [*A publication*]
**No et Vet Test** ... Novi et Veteris Testamenti (DSA)
**Nove Virobnitstvi Budiv Mater** ... Nove u Virobnitstvi Budivel'nikh Materialiv [*A publication*]
**Nov Fiz Metody Obrab Pishch Prod** ... Novye Fizicheskie Metody Obrabotki Pishchevykh Produktov [*A publication*]
**Novgorod Golovn Gos Pedagog Inst Uch Zap** ... Novgorodskii Golovnoi Gosudarstvennyi Pedagogicheskii Institut. Uchenye Zapiski [*A publication*]
**Novgorod Golovn Gos Ped Inst Ucen Zap** ... Novgorodskii Golovnoi Gosudarstvennyi Pedagogicheskii Institut. Ucenye Zapiski [*A publication*]
**NOVICE**.... Night Operational Vision and the Individual Combat Engineer (MCD)
**NoVidSF**.... Det Kongelige Norske Videnskabers Selskabs Forhandlinger [*A publication*]
**Novinky Poligr Prum** ... Novinky v Poligrafichem Prumyslu [*A publication*]
**Novi Probl Pediatr** ... Novi Problemi v Pediatriyata [*A publication*]
**Nov Issled Khim Metall Obogashch** ... Novye Issledovaniya v Khimii, Metallurgii, i Ogobashchenii [*A publication*]
**Nov Issled Metall Khim Obogashch** ... Novye Issledovaniya v Metallurgii, Khimii, i Obogashchenii [*A publication*]
**Nov Issled Pedagog Naukakh** ... Novye Issledovaniya v Pedagogicheskikh Naukakh [*A publication*]
**Nov Issled Psikhol Vozrastn Fiziol** ... Novye Issledovaniya v Psikhologii i Vozrastnoi Fiziologii [*A publication*]
**Novit Arthropodae** ... Novitates Arthropodae [*A publication*]
**Novi Zb Mat Prob** ... Novi Zbornik Matematickih Problema [*A publication*]
**Nov Khir Arkh** ... Novyi Khirurgicheskii Arkhiv [*A publication*]
**NOVL**........ Novell, Inc. [*NASDAQ symbol*] (NQ)
**Nov Lek Rast Sib Ikh Lech Prep Primen** ... Novye Lekarstvennye Rasteniya Sibiri Ikh Lechebnye Preparaty i Primenenie [*A publication*]
**Nov Lek Sredstva** ... Novye Lekarstvennye Sredstva [*A publication*]
**NOVM**...... No Obvious Value Mail [*Postal service*]
**NovM**......... Novyj Mir [*A publication*]
**Nov Maloizvestnye Vidy Fauny Sib** ... Novye i Maloizvestnye Vidy Fauny Sibiri [*A publication*]
**Nov Mashinostr** ... Novoe v Mashinostroenii [*A publication*]
**Nov Med**.... Novosti Meditsiny [*A publication*]
**Nov Med Priborostr** ... Novosti Meditsinskogo Priborostroeniya [*USSR*] [*A publication*]
**Nov Med Tek** ... Novosti Meditsinskoi Tekhniki [*A publication*]
**Nov Med Tekh** ... Novosti Meditsinskoi Tekhniki [*A publication*]
**NOVN**....... Noven Pharmaceuticals, Inc. [*NASDAQ symbol*] (NQ)
**Nov Neftepererab** ... Novosti Neftepererabotki [*A publication*]
**Nov Neft Gazov Tekh Gazov Delo** ... Novosti Neftyanoi i Gazovoi Tekhniki Gazovoe Delo [*A publication*]
**Nov Neft Gazov Tekh Geol** ... Novosti Neftyanoi i Gazovoi Tekhniki. Geologiya [*A publication*]
**Nov Neft Gazov Tekh Neftepererab Neftekhim** ... Novosti Neftyanoi i Gazovoi Tekhniki, Neftepererabotka, i Neftekhimiya [*USSR*] [*A publication*]
**Nov Neft Gazov Tekh Neftepromysl Delo** ... Novosti Neftyanoi i Gazovoi Tekhniki Neftepromyslovoe Delo [*A publication*]
**Nov Neft Gazov Tekh Transp Khranenie Nefti Nefteprod** ... Novosti Neftyanoi i Gazovoi Tekhniki Transport i Khranenie Nefti i Nefteproduktov [*A publication*]
**Nov Neft Gaz Tekh Neft Oborudovanie Sredstva Avtom** ... Novosti Neftyanoi i Gazovoi Tekhniki Neftyanoe Oborudovanie i Sredstva Avtomatizatsii [*A publication*]
**Nov Neft Tekh** ... Novosti Neftyanoi Tekhniki [*A publication*]
**Nov Neft Tekh Geol** ... Novosti Neftyanoi Tekhniki. Geologiya [*A publication*]
**Nov Neft Tekh Neftepererab** ... Novosti Neftyanoi Tekhniki Neftepererabotka [*A publication*]
**Nov Neft Tekh Neftepromysl Delo** ... Novosti Neftyanoi Tekhniki Neftepromyslovoe Delo [*A publication*]
**Nov Neft Tekh Stroit Montazh** ... Novosti Neftyanoi Tekhniki Stroitel'stvo i Montazh [*A publication*]
**Nov Novejs Ist** ... Novaja i Novejsaga Istorija [*A publication*]
**NOVO**....... Novo Corp. [*NASDAQ symbol*] (NQ)
**Novosibirsk Gos Ped Inst Naucn Trudy** ... Novosibirskii Gosudarstvennyi Pedagogiceskii Institut Naucnye Trudy [*A publication*]
**Novos Taxa Ent** ... Novos Taxa Entomologicos [*A publication*]
**Novos Taxa Entomol** ... Novos Taxa Entomologicos [*A publication*]
**Nov Pishch Promsti** ... Novosti Pishchevoi Promyshlennosti [*A publication*]
**Nov Proizvod Khim Istochnikov Toka** ... Novoe v Proizvodstve Khimicheskikh Istochnikov Toka [*USSR*] [*A publication*]
**NOVR**........ Novar Electronics Corp. [*NASDAQ symbol*] (NQ)
**Nov Razrab Elem Radiotekh Ustroistv** ... Novye Razrabotki Elementov Radiotekhnicheskikh Ustroistv [*A publication*]
**Nov Rec**...... Novisima Recopilacion de las Leyes de Espana [*Latest Compilation of Spanish Law*] [*A publication*] (DLA)
**Nov Recop** ... Novisima Recopilacion [*Latest Compilation*] [*Spanish law*] [*A publication*] (DLA)
**NOVS**........ National Office of Vital Statistics [*Public Health Service*] [*Obsolete*]
**Nov Sc Dec** ... Nova Scotia Decisions [*A publication*] (DLA)
**Nov Sc LR** ... Nova Scotia Law Reports [*A publication*] (DLA)
**Nov Sorbenty Khromatogr** ... Novye Sorbenty diya Khromatografii [*A publication*]
**Nov Tekh** ... Novosti Tekhniki [*USSR*] [*A publication*]
**Nov Tekh Astron** ... Novaya Tekhnika v Astronomii [*A publication*]
**Nov Tekh Buren** ... Novosti Tekhniki Bureniya [*A publication*]
**Nov Tekh Neftedobychi** ... Novosti Tekhniki Neftedobychi [*A publication*]
**Nov Termoyad Issled SSSR Inf Byull** ... Novosti Termoyadernykh Issledovanii v SSSR Informatsionnyi Byulleten [*USSR*] [*A publication*]
**NovTest**..... Novum Testamentum [*A publication*]
**Novum Gebrauchs** ... Novum Gebrauchsgraphik [*A publication*]
**Novum Test** ... Novum Testamentum [*A publication*]
**NOVUS**..... Novus Property SBI [*NASDAQ symbol*] (NQ)
**NOVX**........ Nova Pharmaceutical Corp. [*NASDAQ symbol*] (NQ)
**NovZ**.......... Novyj Zurnal [*A publication*]
**Nov Zhizni Nauke Tekh Khim** ... Novoe v Zhizni, Nauke, Tekhnike. Khimiya [*A publication*]
**Nov Zhizni Nauke Tekh Ser Biol** ... Novoe v Zhizni, Nauke, Tekhnike. Seriya Biologiia [*A publication*]
**Nov Zhizni Nauke Tekh Ser Fiz** ... Novoe v Zhizni, Nauke, Tekhnike. Seriya Fizika [*USSR*] [*A publication*]
**Nov Zhizni Nauke Tekh Ser IX Fiz Mat Astron** ... Novoe v Zhizni, Nauke, Tekhnike. Seriya IX. Fizika, Matematika, Astronomiya [*USSR*] [*A publication*]
**Nov Zhizni Nauke Tekh Ser Khim** ... Novoe v Zhizni, Nauke, Tekhnike. Seriya Khimiya [*A publication*]
**Nov Zhizni Nauke Tekh Ser Kosmonavt Astron** ... Novoe v Zhizni, Nauke, Tekhnike. Seriya Kosmonavtika Astronomiya [*USSR*] [*A publication*]
**Nov Zhizni Nauke Tekh Ser Tekh** ... Novoe v Zhizni, Nauke, Tekhnike. Seriya Tekhnika [*USSR*] [*A publication*]
**NOW**......... National Organization for Women (EA)
**NOW**......... National Organizations of the World [*A publication*]
**NOW**......... National Overhaul Warranty [*Automotive engineering*]
**NOW**......... Negotiable Order of Withdrawal [*Banking*]
**NOW**......... Neighbors of Woodcraft [*Portland, OR*] (EA)
**NOW**......... Network Order Wire [*Military*] (CAAL)
**NOW**......... Northway Explorations Ltd. [*Toronto Stock Exchange symbol*]
**NOW**......... Port Angeles, WA [*Location identifier*] [*FAA*] (FAAL)
**NOWAI**..... Neshei Ubenos Agudath Israel [*Antwerp*] (BJA)
**Nowa Tech Inz Sanit** ... Nowa Technika w Inzynierii Sanitarnej [*A publication*]
**NOWC**....... Northwest Pennsylvania Corporation [*NASDAQ symbol*] (NQ)
**Nowe Roln** ... Nowe Rolnictwo [*A publication*]
**Nowest R**.... Northwest Review [*A publication*]
**No West Rep** ... Northwestern Reporter [*Commonly cited NW*] [*A publication*] (DLA)
**NOweWJ**... Wheatley Junior-Senior High School, Old Westbury, NY [*Library symbol*] [*Library of Congress*] (LCLS)
**NOWIS**..... National Older Workers Information System [*American Association of Retired Persons*] [*Information service or system*] [*Defunct*] (IID)
**NOWL**....... National Order of Women Legislators (EA)
**NOW LDEF** ... NOW [*National Organization for Women*] Legal Defense and Education Fund (EA)
**Now Lek**..... Nowiny Lekarskie [*A publication*]
**NOwNC**..... New York College of Osteopathic Medicine, Old Westbury, NY [*Library symbol*] [*Library of Congress*] (LCLS)
**NOwNI**....... New York Institute of Technology, Old Westbury, NY [*Library symbol*] [*Library of Congress*] (LCLS)
**NOwNI-C** ... New York Institute of Technology, Commack Center Library, Commack, NY [*Library symbol*] [*Library of Congress*] (LCLS)
**NOwNI-N** ... New York Institute of Technology, New York, NY [*Library symbol*] [*Library of Congress*] (LCLS)
**NOWPA**.... National Osteopathic Women Physician's Association (EA)
**NOWP-OM** ... National Older Workers Programs - Operation Mainstream [*Department of Labor*]
**NOWR**....... Northwater. Institute of Water Resources. University of Alaska [*A publication*]
**NOWR**....... Nuclear Ordnance War Reserve [*Military*] (AFIT)
**NOWRAD** ... Nowra RADAR [*Radio Detection and Ranging*] [*Australia*]
**NOWSA**.... National One-Write Systems Association (EA)
**NOWT**....... North-West Telecommunications, Inc. [*NASDAQ symbol*] (NQ)

**NOWT**....... Northern Women Talk [*Canada*] [*A publication*]
**NOwU**....... State University of New York, College at Old Westbury, Oyster Bay, NY [*Library symbol*] [*Library of Congress*] (LCLS)
**NOWUS**.... Normal Operation with Unscram [*Nuclear energy*] (NRCH)
**NOWWN**.. National Organization of World War Nurses (EA)
**NOX**......... Nitrous Oxide [*or NOx*] [*Laughing gas*]
**NOx**.......... Oxford Memorial Library, Oxford, NY [*Library symbol*] [*Library of Congress*] (LCLS)
**NOXA**........ Naphthoxyacetic Acid [*Organic chemistry*]
**NOXL**........ Noxell Corp. [*NASDAQ symbol*] (NQ)
**NOXO**....... Noxso Corp. [*NASDAQ symbol*] (NQ)
**NOXZEMA**... Knocks Eczema [*Acronym, brand name for skin cream, said to be taken from this phrase*]
**NOY**.......... Not Out Yet
**Noy**............ Noy's English King's Bench Reports [*1559-1649*] [*A publication*] (DLA)
**NOy**.......... Oyster Bay-East Norwich Public Library, Oyster Bay, NY [*Library symbol*] [*Library of Congress*] (LCLS)
**Noy Ch U**... Noyes on Charitable Uses [*A publication*] (DLA)
**Noye**.......... Grounds and Maxims of English Law, by William Noye [*A publication*] (DLA)
**Noy (Eng)**.. Noy's English King's Bench Reports [*1559-1649*] [*A publication*] (DLA)
**Noyes**........ Catalog of New Publications. Noyes Data Corp. [*A publication*]
**Noye's Max**... Maxims of the Laws of England, by William Noye [*A publication*] (DLA)
**NOyHS**...... Oyster Bay High School, Oyster Bay, NY [*Library symbol*] [*Library of Congress*] (LCLS)
**Noy Max**.... Noy's Maxims [*A publication*] (DLA)
**NOZ**.......... Elizabeth City, NC [*Location identifier*] [*FAA*] (FAAL)
**NOZ**.......... New Process Co. [*AMEX symbol*] [*Later, BL*] (SPSG)
**NOZ**.......... Normal Operating Zone (FAAC)
**NoZ**........... Novy Zivot [*A publication*]
**NOZ**.......... Nozzle (AAG)
**NOZE**........ US National Ozone Expedition [*1986*] [*McMurdo Station, Antarctica*]
**NP**............. Adriance Memorial Library, Poughkeepsie, NY [*Library symbol*] [*Library of Congress*] (LCLS)
**np----**......... Great Plains [*MARC geographic area code*] [*Library of Congress*] (LCCP)
**NP**............. Heavylift Cargo Airlines [*Great Britain*] [*ICAO designator*] (FAAC)
**NP**............. Nacionalista Party [*Philippines*]
**NP**............. Nameplate
**NP**............. NAPALM [*Naphthenic and Palmitic Acids*] (NATG)
**NP**............. Nasionale Party van Suid-Afrika [*National Party of South Africa*] [*Political party*] (PPW)
**NP**............. Nasionale Party van Suidwesafrika [*National Party of South West Africa*] [*Namibia*] [*Political party*] (PPW)
**NP**............. Nasopharyngeal [*or Nasopharynx*] [*Medicine*]
**NP**............. Nasza Przeszlosc [*A publication*]
**NP**............. Nation Party [*Millet Partisi*] [*Turkey*] [*Political party*] (PPW)
**NP**............. National Parks [*A publication*]
**NP**............. National Party [*Papua New Guinea*] [*Political party*] (PPW)
**NP**............. National Pipe [*Thread*]
**NP**............. National Police (CINC)
**NP**............. National Porkettes (EA)
**NP**............. National Publishing Co. [*Philadelphia*]
**NP**............. Nationalist Parnellite [*British*] (ROG)
**NP**............. Nationalist Party [*Malta*] [*Political party*] (PPE)
**NP**............. Nationalist Party [*Partido Nacionalista*] [*Philippines*] [*Political party*] (PPW)
**NP**............. Native Press [*A publication*]
**NP**............. Nauka Polska [*A publication*]
**NP**............. Naval Party [*British military*] (DMA)
**NP**............. Naval Patrol [*British military*] (DMA)
**NP**............. Naval Pattern [*British military*] (DMA)
**NP**............. Naval Pension [*British*] (ROG)
**NP**............. Naval Police [*British*] (ROG)
**NP**............. Naval Prison
**NP**............. Naval Publication (IEEE)
**NP**............. Nea Poreia [*A publication*]
**NP**............. Neap Tide
**NP**............. Near Point
**np**............. Nedsat Pris [*Reduced Price*] [*Danish, Norwegian*]
**NP**............. Needle Position [*on dial*]
**NP**............. Negative Prescreening [*Marketing*]
**NP**............. Negative Pressure (NRCH)
**NP**............. Neo-Punic (BJA)
**Np**............. Neophilologus [*A publication*]
**np**............. Nepal [*MARC country of publication code*] [*Library of Congress*] (LCCP)
**NP**............. Nepal [*ANSI two-letter standard code*] (CNC)
**Np**............. Neper [*A unit on a natural logarithmic scale*]
**Np**............. Neptunium [*Chemical element*]
**NP**............. Net Position [*Business term*]
**NP**............. Net Proceeds
**NP**............. Net Profit
**NP**............. Network Planning [*Data processing*]
**NP**............. Network Program (NASA)
**NP**............. Network Project [*An association*] (EA)
**NP**............. Neupunische Inschriften [*A publication*]
**NP**............. Neuritic Plaque [*Pathology*]
**N/P**........... Neuro-Psychiatry [*Medical Officer designation*] [*British*]
**NP**............. Neuroendocrine Perspectives [*Elsevier Book Series*] [*A publication*]
**NP**............. Neuropathology [*Medicine*]
**NP**............. Neurophysin [*Biochemistry*]
**NP**............. Neurophysiological
**NP**............. Neuropsychiatric
**N & P**......... Nevile and Perry's English King's Bench Reports [*1836-38*] [*A publication*] (DLA)
**NP**............. New Paragraph
**NP**............. New Party (EA)
**NP**............. New Patient
**NP**............. New Pattern [*British military*] (DMA)
**np**............. New Pence [*Monetary unit in Great Britain since 1971*]
**NP**............. New Permutations
**NP**............. New Philosophy [*A publication*]
**NP**............. New Point [*Used in correcting manuscripts, etc.*]
**NP**............. New Providence
**NP**............. Newport [*Rhode Island*]
**N/P**........... Newspaper
**NP**............. Nickel Plated [*Guns*]
**NP**............. Nippon Investment Corp. [*Vancouver Stock Exchange symbol*]
**NP**............. Nisi Prius [*Unless Before*] [*Legal term*] [*Latin*]
**NP**............. Nitrophenide [*Pharmacology*]
**NP**............. Nitrophenoacetylamino Caproate
**NP**............. Nitroprusside [*A vasodilator*]
**NP**............. Nitropyrene [*Organic chemistry*]
**NP**............. Nitrosopiperidine [*Organic chemistry*]
**NP**............. No Paging
**NP**............. No Parity
**NP**............. No Place [*of publication*] [*Bibliography*]
**NP**............. No Predators [*Ecology*]
**NP**............. No Print [*Telecommunications*] (TEL)
**NP**............. No Prospect [*In sports*]
**NP**............. No Protest [*Banking*]
**NP**............. Nobel Prize
**NP**............. Nomen Proprium [*Proper Name*] [*Pharmacy*]
**NP**............. Nondeterministic Polynomial [*Mathematics*]
**NP**............. Nonpapillate [*Type of seed*] [*Botany*]
**NP**............. Nonparticipating [*Insurance or finance*]
**N/P**........... Nonpayment (ROG)
**NP**............. Nonperson
**NP**............. Nonpolarized [*Data processing*]
**NP**............. Nonpractising Member [*Chiropody*] [*British*]
**NP**............. Nonprocurable
**NP**............. Nonpropelled (AAG)
**NP**............. Nonylphenol [*Organic chemistry*]
**NP**............. Normal Phase [*Chromatography*]
**NP**............. Normal Pitch (ADA)
**NP**............. Normal Pregnancy [*Medicine*]
**NP**............. Normal Pressure
**NP**............. North Pole [*Also, PN*]
**NP**............. Northern Pine [*Utility pole*] [*Telecommunications*] (TEL)
**NP**............. Not Perceptible [*Medicine*]
**NP**............. Not Performed
**NP**............. Not Planned
**NP**............. Not Practiced [*Medicine*]
**NP**............. Not Preferred
**NP**............. Not Printed (ILCA)
**N/P**........... Not Provided (KSC)
**NP**............. Notary Public
**N/P**........... Notes Payable
**NP**............. Noun Phrase [*Linguistics*]
**NP**............. Nova Placita [*A publication*] (DLA)
**NP**............. Nucleoplasmic [*Index*] [*Cytology*]
**NP**............. Nucleoprotein [*Biochemistry*]
**NP**............. Nucleoside Phosphorylase [*An enzyme*]
**NP**............. Nurse Practitioner
**NP**............. Nursing Procedure
**np**............. Ny Pris [*List Price*] [*Danish, Norwegian*]
**NP**............. Ohio Nisi Prius Reports [*A publication*] (DLA)
**NP0**........... Negative-Positive-Zero
**NPA**.......... Committee for a National Peace Academy [*Later, N-PAC*] (EA)
**NPA**.......... N-Propylamine [*Organic chemistry*]
**NPA**.......... Naphthylphthalamic Acid [*Organic chemistry*]
**NPA**.......... National Paddleball Association (EA)
**NPA**.......... National Panel of Arbitrators
**NPA**.......... National Paperboard Association [*Later, API*]
**NPA**.......... National Paralegal Association (EA)
**NPA**.......... National Parking Association (EA)
**NPA**.......... National Parks and Access to the Countryside Act [*Town planning*] [*British*]
**NPA**.......... National Parks Association [*Later, NPCA*] (EA)
**NPA**.......... National Particleboard Association (EA)
**NPA**.......... National Pasta Association (EA)
**NPA**.......... National Patrolmen's Association
**NPA**.......... National Pawnbrokers Association (EA)
**NPA**.......... National Payphone Association (EA)

**NPA** National Peace Academy
**NPA** National Pediculosis Association (EA)
**NPA** National People's Action (EA)
**NPA** National Perinatal Association (EA)
**NPA** National Peripheral Association (EA)
**NPA** National Personnel Associates
**NPA** National Pet Association [*Defunct*] (EA)
**NPA** National Petroleum Association [*Later, NPRA*]
**NPA** National Pharmaceutical Association [*Washington, DC*]
**NPA** National Phlebotomy Association (EA)
**NPA** National Pigeon Association (EA)
**NPA** National Pilots Association [*Defunct*] (EA)
**NPA** National Pituitary Agency [*Later, NHPP*]
**NPA** National Planning Association (EA)
**NPA** National Plastercraft Association (EA)
**NPA** National Podiatry Association [*Later, NPMA*] (EA)
**NPA** National Poker Association (EA)
**NPA** National Ports Authority [*British*]
**NPA** National Postmasters Auxiliary (EA)
**NPA** National Preservers Association [*Later, International Jelly and Preserve Association*] (EA)
**NPA** National Priority Area [*Military*]
**NPA** National Proctologic Association (EA)
**NPA** National Production Authority [*Functions merged into BDSA, 1953*]
**NPA** National Prohibition Act
**NPA** National Psychological Association (EA)
**NPA** National Public Accountant [*A publication*]
**NPA** Naval Procurement Account
**NPA** Navy Postal Affairs Section Publication
**NPA** Navy Purchasing Activity (AFIT)
**NPA** Near Point Accommodation [*Ophthalmology*]
**NPA** Network Program Analysis by ADI [*Area of Dominant Influence*] [*Arbitron Ratings Co.*] [*Information service or system*] (CRD)
**NPA** Neutrons per Absorption (DEN)
**NPA** New People's Army [*Philippines*] (PD)
**NPA** New Populist Action [*Defunct*] (EA)
**NPA** New Product Announcements [*Predicasts, Inc.*] [*Cleveland, OH*] [*Information service or system*] (IID)
**NPA** Newspaper Publishers' Association [*British*] (DCTA)
**NPA** Nine Pin Association [*Schauenburg, Federal Republic of Germany*] (EAIO)
**NPA** No Price Available [*Business term*] (ADA)
**NPA** Nonbuffered Pyrophosphatase Activity
**NPA** Normal Pressure Angle
**NPA** North Pacific Airlines [*Anchorage, AK*] [*FAA designator*] (FAAC)
**NPA** Northern Pipeline Agency [*Ottawa, ON*]
**NPA** Nuclear Plant Analyzer (NRCH)
**NPA** Numbering Plan Area [*Bell System*] [*Telecommunications*]
**NPA** Numerical Production Analysis (IEEE)
**NPA** Pensacola, FL [*Location identifier*] [*FAA*] (FAAL)
**NPA** PTS [*Predicasts, Inc.*] New Product Announcements/Plus [*Information service or system*] (EISS)
**NPAA** National Park Academy of the Arts (EA)
**NPAA** National Photographic Art Archive [*Victoria and Albert Museum*] [*British*]
**NPAA** National Postal Arts Association (EA)
**NPAAC** National Pathology Accreditation Advisory Council [*Australia*]
**NPAB** Navy Price Adjustment Board
**N-PAC** National Peace Academy Campaign [*Formerly, NPA*] (EA)
**NPAC** National Peace Action Coalition
**NPAC** National Political Action Committee (EA)
**NPAC** National Program for Acquisitions and Cataloging [*Library of Congress*]
**NPAC** Navy Procurement Assignment Committee
**NPAC** Northeast Parallel Architectures Center [*Syracuse University*] [*Research center*] (RCD)
**NPAC** Northern Pipeline Agency Canada [*See also APNC*]
**NPAC** Northern Pipeline Agency News Releases and Communiques [*A publication*]
**NPACI** National Production Advisory Council on Industry [*British*]
**NPACOE** National Panhellenic Association of Central Office Executives (EA)
**NPACSE** National Political Action Committee for Scientists and Engineers
**NPACT** National Public Affairs Center for Television [*Defunct*]
**NPAED** National Progress Association for Economic Development (EA)
**NPAF** National Peace Academy Foundation (EA)
**NPA(G)R** National Parks and Access to the Countryside (Grants) Regulations [*Town planning*] [*British*]
**NPAI** Nevada Public Affairs Institute [*University of Nevada - Reno*] [*Research center*] (RCD)
**NPals** Palisades Free Library, Palisades, NY [*Library symbol*] [*Library of Congress*] (LCLS)
**NPAM** Nonpermanent Active Militia
**NPANX** Naval Potomac Annex
**NPAP** National Psychological Association for Psychoanalysis (EA)
**NPAR** National Paragon Corp. [*NASDAQ symbol*] (NQ)
**NP/ARCA** National Pacific/Asian Resource Center on Aging (EA)
**NPAS** Normalized Photoacoustic Signal [*Instrumentation*]
**NPASO** National Postsecondary Agriculture Student Organization (EA)
**NPat** Patchogue Library, Patchogue, NY [*Library symbol*] [*Library of Congress*] (LCLS)
**NPatB** Brookhaven Town Hall, Historical Collection, Patchogue, NY [*Library symbol*] [*Library of Congress*] (LCLS)
**NPatBH** Brookhaven Memorial Hospital, Patchogue, NY [*Library symbol*] [*Library of Congress*] (LCLS)
**NPatSJ** Saint Joseph's College, Patchogue, NY [*Library symbol*] [*Library of Congress*] (LCLS)
**NPB** NADGE [*NATO Air Defense Ground Environment*] Policy Board (NATG)
**NPB** National Parole Board [*Canada*]
**NPB** National Plant Board (EA)
**NPB** National Prayer Breakfast (EA)
**NPB** National Productivity Board [*Australia*]
**NPB** Newspaper Bag (ROG)
**NPB** Nodal Premature Beat [*Cardiology*]
**NPB** Nonplasminogen Binding [*Hematology*]
**NPB** Nonprimate Biosatellite
**NPB** Norfolk & Portsmouth Belt Line Railroad Co. [*AAR code*]
**NPBA** National Palomino Breeders Association [*Inactive*]
**NPBA** National Paper Box Association [*Formerly, NPBMA; later NP & PA*] (EA)
**NPBA** National Perinatal Bereavement Association [*Defunct*] (EA)
**NPBA** National Pocket Billiards Association (EA)
**NPBA** National Police Bloodhound Association (EA)
**NPBA** National Poro Beautician Association [*Defunct*] (EA)
**NPBA** Natural Product Broker Association [*St. Augustine, FL*] (EA)
**NPBC** National Penn Bancshares, Inc. [*NASDAQ symbol*] (NQ)
**NPBC** National Progressive Broadcast Coalition (EA)
**NPBE** National Political Button Exchange [*An association*] [*Defunct*] (EA)
**NPBE** Nitrophenyl Butyl Ether [*Organic chemistry*]
**NPBE** Nonlinear Poisson-Boltzmann Equation [*Physical chemistry*]
**NPBEA** National Poultry, Butter, and Egg Association [*Defunct*] (EA)
**NPBI** National Pretzel Bakers Institute [*Defunct*] (EA)
**NPBMA** National Paper Box Manufacturers Association (EA)
**NPBOA** National Party Boat Owners Alliance (EA)
**NPBRO** Naval Plant Branch Representative Office
**NPBSA** National Paper Box Supplies Association [*Defunct*] (EA)
**NPC** NASA Procurement Circular
**NPC** NASA Publication Control (KSC)
**NPC** Nasopharyngeal Carcinoma [*Medicine*]
**NPC** National Panhellenic Conference (EA)
**NPC** National Patent Council (EA)
**NPC** National Peace Council [*British*]
**NPC** National Peach Council (EA)
**NPC** National Peanut Council (EA)
**NPC** National People's Congress [*People's Republic of China*] [*Political party*] (PPW)
**NPC** National People's Congress [*Nigeria*] [*Political party*]
**NPC** National Periodicals Center
**NPC** National Personnel Consultants [*Later, NAPC*] (EA)
**NPC** National Petroleum Council [*Department of Energy*] (EA)
**NPC** National Pharmaceutical Council (EA)
**NPC** National Philatelic Collections [*Smithsonian Institution*]
**NPC** National Playwrights Conference (EA)
**NPC** National Plumbing Code
**NPC** National Poetry Circle [*Cambridge*] [*British*]
**NPC** National Ports Council [*British*]
**NPC** National Potato Council (EA)
**NPC** National Power Corporation [*Philippines*] (DS)
**NPC** National Press Club (EA)
**NPC** National Prime Contractor (NATG)
**NPC** National Processing Centre [*Marine science*] (MSC)
**NPC** National Productivity Council [*Inactive*]
**NPC** National Publicity Council for Health and Welfare Services [*Later, NPRC*]
**NPC** Native Preacher Company [*An association*] (EA)
**NPC** NATO Parliamentarians' Conference
**NPC** NATO Pipeline Committee
**NPC** NATO Programming Center (NATG)
**NPC** Naval Personnel Committee [*British military*] (DMA)
**NPC** Naval Photographic Center
**NPC** Navy Policy Council
**NPC** Navy Procurement Circular
**NPC** Near Point of Convergence [*Ophthalmology*]
**NPC** Needle Punch Card
**NPC** Neplanocin A [*Biochemistry*]
**NPC** Neuropsychiatry Clerical Procedure [*Navy*]
**NPC** Neuropsychiatry Clerical Technician [*Navy*]
**NPC** New Practice Cases [*Legal*] [*British*]
**NPC** New Practice Cases. Bail Court [*1844-48*] [*A publication*] (DLA)
**NPC** News and Periodicals Corporation [*Burma*] (DS)
**NPC** Ninety Pound Charge
**NPC** Nisi Prius Cases [*England*] [*A publication*] (DLA)
**NPC** Nitrogen Purge Control (NASA)
**NPC** No Previous Carrier [*Insurance*]

**NPC**.......... Nominal Protection Coefficient [*Business term*]
**NPC**.......... Nonprinting Character [*Data processing*]
**NPC**.......... Normal Phase Chromatography
**NPC**.......... North Pacific Coast Freight Bureau, Seattle WA [*STAC*]
**NPC**.......... North Pacific Industry [*Vancouver Stock Exchange symbol*]
**NPC**.......... North Polar Cap [*A filamentary mark on Mars*]
**NPC**.......... Northern Peoples Congress [*Nigerian*]
**NPC**.......... Nuclear Power Company (NRCH)
**NPC**.......... Public Library of Charlotte and Mecklenburg County, Charlotte, NC [*OCLC symbol*] (OCLC)
**NPCA**........ National Paint and Coatings Association (EA)
**NPCA**........ National Parks and Conservation Association (EA)
**NPCA**........ National Pest Control Association (EA)
**NPCA**........ National Plastercraft Association (EA)
**NPCA**........ National Precast Concrete Association (EA)
**NPCA**........ National Progressive Consumers Alliance (EA)
**NPCBW**..... National Political Congress of Black Women (EA)
**NPCC**........ National Pop Can Collectors (EA)
**NPCC**........ North Peralta Community College [*California*]
**NPCC**........ Northeast Power Coordinating Council [*Regional power council*]
**NPC/COES**... National Panhellenic Conference of Central Office Executives (EA)
**NPCD**........ National Association of Parish Coordinators/Directors of Religious Education (EA)
**NPCF**......... National Pollution Control Foundation
**NPCFB**...... North Pacific Coast Freight Bureau
**NPCI**.......... National Potato Chip Institute [*Later, SFA*]
**N-PCL**....... Not-for-Profit Corporation Law [*New York, NY*] [*A publication*]
**NP-CLT**..... Neuropsychiatry Clerical Procedure Technician [*Navy*]
**NPCM**....... National Parks and Conservation Magazine [*Later, National Parks Magazine*] [*A publication*]
**NPCN**........ National Poison Center Network (EA)
**NPCNU**..... Neopentyl(chloroethyl)nitrosourea [*Biochemistry*]
**NPCO**........ [*The*] New Paraho Corporation [*NASDAQ symbol*] (NQ)
**N-P, Complete**... Nondeterministic Polynomial Complete Problem [*Mathematics*]
**NPCP**......... Nairobi Peoples' Convention Party
**NPCP**......... National Prostatic Cancer Project
**NPCR**........ No Periodic Calibration Required (MCD)
**NPCR**........ No Programmed Calibration Required (MCD)
**NP-CT**....... Naval Personnel Conversion Tables
**NPCW**....... National Pork Council Women (EA)
**NPD**.......... N-Player Prisoneris Dilemma
**NPD**.......... NASA Policy Directive
**NPD**.......... National Paint Distributors (EA)
**NPD**.......... National Patent Development Corp. [*AMEX symbol*] (SPSG)
**NPD**.......... National Policy Debate [*Nuclear energy*] (NRCH)
**NPD**.......... National Power Demonstration (IEEE)
**NPD**.......... National Program for Dermatology
**NPD**.......... Nationaldemokratische Partei Deutschlands [*National Democratic Party of Germany*] [*Federal Republic of Germany*] [*Political party*] (PPE)
**NPD**.......... Navy Procurement Directives
**NPD**.......... Nees Politikes Dynameis [*New Political Forces*] [*Greek*] [*Political party*] (PPE)
**NPD**.......... Network Protection Device [*Telecommunications*] (TEL)
**NPD**.......... New Products and Processes Highlights [*A publication*]
**NPD**.......... New Providence Development Co. Ltd. [*Toronto Stock Exchange symbol*]
**NPD**.......... Niemann-Pick Disease [*Medicine*]
**NPD**.......... Night Perimeter Defense
**NPD**.......... Nitrogen-Phosphorus Detector [*Analytical instrumentation*]
**NPD**.......... Nitrogen, Phosphorus Gas Chromatographic Detector [*Spectroscopy*]
**NPD**.......... No Payroll Division
**NP or D**..... No Place or Date
**NPD**.......... Nominal Percent Defective
**NPD**.......... North Pacific Division [*Army*] [*World War II*]
**NPD**.......... North Pacific Drift [*Oceanography*]
**NPD**.......... North Polar Distance
**NPD**.......... Nouveau Parti Democratique [*New Democratic Party*] [*Canada*] [*Political party*] (EAIO)
**NPD**.......... Nuclear Power Demonstration [*of a reactor*]
**NPD**.......... South African Law Reports, Natal Province Division [*A publication*] (DLA)
**NPDA**........ National Plywood Distributors Association (EA)
**NPDA**........ National Pyrotechnic Distributors Association [*Absorbed by APA*] (EA)
**NPDA**........ Network Problem Determination Application [*Data processing*]
**NPDAA**..... National Pharmaceutical Direct Advertising Association [*Defunct*] (EA)
**NPDB**........ National Practitioner Data Bank [*Information service or system*] (EISS)
**NPDB**........ Nuclear Plant Databank (NRCH)
**NPDBA**..... National Pet Dealers and Breeders Association (EA)
**NPDC**........ Dutchess Community College, Poughkeepsie, NY [*Library symbol*] [*Library of Congress*] (LCLS)
**NPDC**........ National Patent Development Corporation
**NPDC**........ National Peace Day Celebration (EA)
**NPDC**........ National Planning Data Corporation [*Information service or system*] (IID)
**NPDC**........ National Poetry Day Committee (EA)
**NPDCM**.... Dutchess County Mental Health Center, Poughkeepsie, NY [*Library symbol*] [*Library of Congress*] (LCLS)
**NPDDE**..... Nitrophenyl Dodecyl Ether [*Organic chemistry*]
**NPDE**........ Nonlinear Partial Differential Equation
**NPDES**...... National Pollutant Discharge Elimination System [*Environmental Protection Agency*]
**NPDF**........ Normal Probability Distribution Function
**NPDI**......... Nonperformance of Duty because Imprisoned [*Navy*]
**NPDL**........ Nodular Poorly Differentiated Lymphocyte
**NPDNA**..... Nucleoprotamine Deoxyribonucleic Acid
**NPDO**........ Nacelle Product Development Organization (MCD)
**NPDP**........ National Procurement Development Program [*Australia*]
**NPDR**........ NCO Professional Development Ribbon [*Military decoration*]
**NPDS**........ Nuclear Particle Detection System (KSC)
**NPDW**....... North Pacific Deep Water [*Oceanography*]
**NPDWG**.... Networking Project for Disabled Women and Girls (EA)
**NPDWR**.... National Primary Drinking Water Regulations [*Environmental Protection Agency*]
**NPE**........... Elizabeth City State University, Elizabeth City, NC [*OCLC symbol*] (OCLC)
**NPE**........... Napier [*New Zealand*] [*Airport symbol*] (OAG)
**NPE**........... Nasal Physical Examination
**NPE**........... National Plastic Exposition
**NPE**........... Naval Pilot Evaluation (MUGU)
**NPE**........... Navy Preliminary Evaluation
**NPE**........... New Preliminary Evaluation (MCD)
**NPE**........... Nonpolluting Engine [*Rocketdyne/Commonwealth Edison Co.*]
**NPE**........... Nonpotential Energy [*of molecules*]
**NPE**........... Nonylphenol Ethoxylate [*Organic chemistry*]
**NPE**........... Nuclear Photographic Emulsion
**NPEA**........ National Patio Enclosure Association (EA)
**NPEA**........ National Printing Equipment Association [*Later, NPES*] (EA)
**NPEB**......... Nonparametric Empirical Bayes [*Statistics*]
**NPEC**......... National Panhellenic Editors Conference (EA)
**NPEC**......... Nuclear Power Engineering Committee [*Nuclear Regulatory Commission*] (NRCH)
**NPED**........ Nuclear-Powered Energy Depot
**NPee**.......... Field Library, Inc., Peekskill, NY [*Library symbol*] [*Library of Congress*] (LCLS)
**NPEE**......... NP Energy Corp. [*NASDAQ symbol*] (NQ)
**NPEF**......... New Product Evaluation Form
**N & PEIR**.. Newfoundland and Prince Edward Island Reports [*A publication*]
**NPel**........... Pelham Public Library, Pelham, NY [*Library symbol*] [*Library of Congress*] (LCLS)
**NPELRA**... National Public Employer Labor Relations Association (EA)
**NPEO**........ Nonylphenol Polyethoxylate [*Organic chemistry*]
**NPER**........ National Public Employment Reporter Database [*Information service or system*] (IID)
**NPerbA**...... J. N. Adam Developmental Center, Perrysburg, NY [*Library symbol*] [*Library of Congress*] (LCLS)
**NPES**......... National Printing Equipment Show
**NPES**......... National Printing Equipment and Supply Association (EA)
**NPESO**...... NAVSHIPS [*Naval Ship Systems Command*] Plant Equipment Support Office
**NPET**......... Newport Petroleums [*NASDAQ symbol*] (NQ)
**NPET**......... Nonpetroleum
**NPF**........... Names Project Foundation (EA)
**NPF**........... National Paraplegia Foundation (EA)
**NPF**........... National Park Foundation (EA)
**NPF**........... National Parkinson Foundation (EA)
**NPF**........... National Pharmaceutical Foundation (EA)
**NPF**........... National Piano Foundation (EA)
**NPF**........... National Pig Fair [*British*] (ITD)
**NPF**........... National Poetry Foundation (EA)
**NPF**........... National Press Foundation (EA)
**NPF**........... National Progressive Front [*Syria*] [*Political party*] (PPW)
**NPF**........... National Progressive Front [*Iraq*] [*Political party*] (PPW)
**NPF**........... National Psoriasis Foundation (EA)
**NPF**........... Naval Parachute Facility (MCD)
**NPF**........... Naval Powder Factory
**NPF**........... Naval Procurement Fund [*Budget appropriation title*]
**NPF**........... Net Propulsion Force (MCD)
**NPF**........... Network Pulse Forming
**NPF**........... Neutrons per Fission (DEN)
**NPF**........... Newtonian Potential Function [*Mathematics*]
**NPF**........... Nicaragua Peace Fleet (EA)
**NPF**........... Nonpublic Funds [*Canadian Forces*]
**NPF**........... Nordisk Plastikkirurgisk Forening [*Scandinavian Association of Plastic Surgeons - SAPS*] (EAIO)
**NPF**........... North Pyrenean Fault [*Geology*]
**NPF**........... Not Provided For
**NPF**........... Nuclear Power Facility (NRCH)
**NPFA**......... National Peanut Festival Association (EA)
**NPFA**......... National Playing Fields Association [*British*]
**NPFC**......... National Pro-Family Coalition (EA)
**NPFC**......... Naval Publications and Forms Center
**NPFC**......... North Pacific Fisheries Commission (NOAA)

**NPFC** North Pacific Fur Seal Commission [*Inactive*]

**NPFF** National Police Field Force [*Military*]

**NPFF** Normal Probability Frequency Function

**NPFFA** National Prepared Frozen Food Association (EA)

**NPFFG** National Plant, Flower, and Fruit Guild (EA)

**NPFFPA** National Prepared Frozen Food Processors Association [*Later, NPFFA*] (EA)

**NPfG** Nordpfalzer Geschichtsverein [*A publication*]

**NPFI** National Plant Food Institute [*Later, TFI*] (EA)

**NPFID** Nitrogen-Phosphorus-Flame Ionization Detector [*Instrumentation*]

**NPFO** Nuclear Power Field Office (IEEE)

**NPF & PP** Naval Prison Farms and Prison Personnel [*Budget appropriation title*]

**NPFRC** North Pacific Fisheries Research Center [*National Oceanic and Atmospheric Administration*]

**NPFS** Naval Preflight School

**NPFS** No Prior or Current Federal Service (AABC)

**NPFSC** North Pacific Fur Seal Commission [*Inactive*]

**NPFT** Neurotic Personality Factor Test [*Psychology*]

**NPFTA** National Personal Fitness Trainers Association (EA)

**NPFZ** North Pyrenean Fault Zone [*Geology*]

**NPG** National Peace Garden (EA)

**NPG** National Portrait Gallery [*Smithsonian Institution*]

**NPG** NATO Planning Group (NATG)

**NPG** Naval Proving Ground [*Dahlgren, VA*]

**NPG** Negative Population Growth (EA)

**NPG** Neopentylglycol [*Organic chemistry*]

**NPG** New Performance Gallery [*San Francisco*]

**NPG** Not Paged [*Publishing*]

**NPG** Nuclear Planning Group [*NATO*]

**NPG** [*The*] Nuclear Power Group [*British*] (NRCH)

**NPG** Ontario Library Service Nipigon/Thunder Bay Public Library [*UTLAS symbol*]

**NPGA** National Pygmy Goat Association (EA)

**NPGB** (Nitrophenyl)guanidinobenzoate [*Organic chemistry*]

**NPGC** National Pell Grant Coalition (EA)

**NPG-GMA** N-Phenylglycine Glycidyl Methacrylate [*Organic chemistry*]

**NPGLINAC** Naval Postgraduate School Linear Accelerator

**NPGPA** Non-Powder Gun Products Association (EA)

**NPGS** National Plant Germplasm System [*Department of Agriculture*]

**NPGS** Naval Postgraduate School

**NPGS** Nuclear Power Generating Station (NRCH)

**NPGTC** National Prairie Grouse Technical Council (EA)

**NP & GT Rep** Nisi Prius and General Term Reports [*Ohio*] [*A publication*] (DLA)

**NPH** Association of Nordic Paper Historians [*See also FNPH*] [*Stockholm, Sweden*] (EAIO)

**NPH** Nalcap Holdings, Inc. [*Vancouver Stock Exchange symbol*]

**NPH** Natural Period in Heave

**NPh** Neophilologus [*A publication*]

**NPH** Nephi [*Utah*] [*Airport symbol*] (OAG)

**NPH** Neurophysin [*Biochemistry*]

**NPH** Neutral Protamine Hagedorn [*Insulin suspension*]

**NPH** No Profit Here [*Business term*]

**NPH** Normal Paraffin Hydrocarbon

**NPH** Normal Pressure Hydrocephalus [*Medicine*]

**NPH** North American Philips Corp. [*NYSE symbol*] (SPSG)

**NPH** North Pit [*Hawaii*] [*Seismograph station code, US Geological Survey*] (SEIS)

**NPh** Northern Phoenician (BJA)

**NPHA** National Peer Helpers Association (EA)

**NPhA** National Pharmaceutical Association (EA)

**NPHA** National Plott Hound Association (EA)

**NPHB** Nonphotochemical Hole Burning [*Spectrometry*]

**NPhD** Doctor of Natural Philosophy

**NPHE** Nitrophenyl Hexyl Ether [*Organic chemistry*]

**NPHI** Nalcap Holdings, Inc. [*NASDAQ symbol*] (NQ)

**NphM** Neuphilologische Mitteilungen [*A publication*]

**Nph Mitt** Neuphilologische Mitteilungen [*A publication*]

**NPHOE** Nitrophenyl Hydroxyoctyl Ether [*Organic chemistry*]

**NPHPRS** National Public Health Program Reporting System [*Department of Health and Human Services*]

**NPhR** Neue Philologische Rundschau [*A publication*] (BJA)

**NPHR** Notice Papers - House of Representatives [*A publication*] (APTA)

**NPHWA** National Presbyterian Health and Welfare Association [*Later, PHEWA*]

**NPHYBI** Neurophysiology [*English translation of Neirofiziologiya*] [*A publication*]

**NphZ** Neuphilologische Zeitschrift [*A publication*]

**NPI** International Business Machines Corp., Systems Development Division, Poughkeepsie, NY [*Library symbol*] [*Library of Congress*] (LCLS)

**NPI** National Paralegal Institute (EA)

**NPI** National Parkinson Institute

**NPI** National Pastoral Institute, Melbourne [*Australia*]

**NPI** National Provident Institution [*Wales*]

**NPI** National Purchasing Institute (EA)

**NPI** Net Premium Income [*Insurance*] (AIA)

**NPI** NeuroPsychiatric Institute [*UCLA*]

**NPI** New Periodicals Index [*A publication*]

**NPI** Newsletter. Portuguese Industrial Association [*A publication*]

**NPI** No Present Illness

**NPI** No Previous Information [*to tip off a US Customs Service seizure*]

**NPI** Nonprecision Instrument (FAAC)

**NPI** Nonprocedural Interface [*Data processing*]

**NPI** Normick Perron, Inc. [*Toronto Stock Exchange symbol*]

**NPI** North Pocatello Valley [*Idaho*] [*Seismograph station code, US Geological Survey*] (SEIS)

**NPI** Nuveen Premium Income Municipal Fund, Inc. [*NYSE symbol*] (SPSG)

**NPIA** Nanny Pop-Ins Association [*Defunct*] (EA)

**NPIA** National Photography Instructors Association (EA)

**NPIAW** National Photographic Index of Australian Wildlife

**NPIC** National Pesticide Information Clearinghouse [*Later, NPTN*] (EA)

**NPIC** National Pharmacy Insurance Council [*Defunct*] (EA)

**NPIC** National Photographic Interpretation Center [*CIA*]

**NPIC** Naval Photographic Interpretation Center

**NPie** Piermont Public Library, Piermont, NY [*Library symbol*] [*Library of Congress*] (LCLS)

**NPIF** National Peace Institute Foundation (EA)

**NPIN** Negative-Positive-Intrinsic-Negative [*Electron device*] (MSA)

**NPIP** National Poultry Improvement Plan (EA)

**NPiPNA** N-Paraffins, iso-Paraffins, Naphthenes and Aromatics [*Gasoline analysis*]

**NPIR** No Periodic Inspection Required [*Military*] (AFIT)

**NPIRG** National Public Interest Research Group (EA)

**NPIRI** National Printing Ink Research Institute (EA)

**NPIRS** National Pesticide Information Retrieval System [*Purdue University*] [*West Lafayette, IN*] [*Database*]

**NPIS** National Physics Information System [*American Institute of Physics*] [*New York, NY*] (DIT)

**NP/IS** National Premium Incentive Show (ITD)

**NPIS** New Product Information Service [*Department of Commerce*]

**NPIS** Nuclear Plant Island Structure (NRCH)

**NPITC** National Plastics Industry Training Committee [*Australia*]

**NPITI** National Project for the Improvement of Televised Instruction [*National Association of Educational Broadcasters*]

**NPJ** Corpus Christi, TX [*Location identifier*] [*FAA*] (FAAL)

**NPj** Port Jefferson Free Library, Port Jefferson, NY [*Library symbol*] [*Library of Congress*] (LCLS)

**NPjES** Port Jefferson Elementary School, Port Jefferson, NY [*Library symbol*] [*Library of Congress*] (LCLS)

**NPjMH** John T. Mather Memorial Hospital, Port Jefferson, NY [*Library symbol*] [*Library of Congress*] (LCLS)

**NPJO** Northern Projects Journal. British Columbia Hydro [*A publication*]

**NPJPA** National Prune Juice Packers Association (EA)

**NPjs** Port Jefferson Station-Terryville Public Library, Port Jefferson Station, NY [*Library symbol*] [*Library of Congress*] (LCLS)

**NPjSCH** Saint Charles Hospital, Port Jefferson, NY [*Library symbol*] [*Library of Congress*] (LCLS)

**NPJT** Nonparoxysmal Atrioventricular Junction Tachycardia [*Cardiology*]

**NPjVH** Earl L. Vandermeulen High School, Port Jefferson, NY [*Library symbol*] [*Library of Congress*] (LCLS)

**NPK** National Presto Industries, Inc. [*NYSE symbol*] (SPSG)

**NPK** Nationale Partij Kombinatie [*National Party Alliance*] [*Surinam*] [*Political party*] (PPW)

**NPK** Nitrogen, Phosphorus, Potassium [*Fertilizer components*]

**NPK** Noble Peak Resources Ltd. [*Vancouver Stock Exchange symbol*]

**NPK** Nodal Point Keying

**NPKZA** Nippon Kagaku Zasshi [*A publication*]

**NPL** Free Public Library of Newark, Newark, NJ [*OCLC symbol*] (OCLC)

**NPL** Nameplate (MSA)

**NPL** Naples [*Italy*] [*Seismograph station code, US Geological Survey*] [*Closed*] (SEIS)

**NPL** National Physical Laboratory [*Research center*] [*British*] (IRC)

**NPL** National Physics Laboratory (KSC)

**NPL** National Policy on Languages [*Australia*]

**NPL** National Priorities List [*Hazardous wastes*] [*Environmental Protection Agency*]

**NPL** National Properties Ltd. [*Australia*]

**NPL** National Puzzlers' League (EA)

**NPL** Neon Pilot Light

**NPL** Neoproteolipid [*Hematology*]

**NPL** Nepal [*ANSI three-letter standard code*] (CNC)

**NPL** Nepheline Resources Ltd. [*Vancouver Stock Exchange symbol*]

**NPL** New Plymouth [*New Zealand*] [*Airport symbol*] (OAG)

**NPL** New Product Line

**NPL** New Programming Language [*1974*] [*Later, PL/1*] [*Data processing*]

**NPL** Newfoundland Public Library Services [*UTLAS symbol*]

**NPL** Noise Pollution Level

**NPL** Nonpartisan League [*Political party in North Dakota opposed by the IVA*]

**NPL**.......... Nonpersonal Liability
**NPL**.......... Nonstandard Parts List (MCD)
**NPL**.......... Normal Power Level (KSC)
**NPL**.......... Northwest Pipeline Corp. [*NYSE symbol*] (SPSG)
**NPL**.......... Novgorodskaja Pervaja Letopis' Starsego i Mladsego Izvodov [*A publication*]
**NPL**.......... Numerical Parts List (MCD)
**NPL**.......... Numerical Preference List [*Military*] (AFIT)
**NPl**.......... Plainview-Old Bethpage Public Library, Plainview, NY [*Library symbol*] [*Library of Congress*] (LCLS)
**NPla**.......... Plattsburgh Public Library, Plattsburgh, NY [*Library symbol*] [*Library of Congress*] (LCLS)
**NPlaB**........ Bellarmine College, Plattsburgh, NY [*Library symbol*] [*Library of Congress*] (LCLS)
**NPlaC**........ Champlain College, Plattsburgh, NY [*Library symbol*] [*Library of Congress*] [*Obsolete*] (LCLS)
**NPlaCC**..... Clinton Community College, Plattsburgh, NY [*Library symbol*] [*Library of Congress*] (LCLS)
**NPlaCEF**... Clinton-Essex-Franklin Library System, Plattsburgh, NY [*Library symbol*] [*Library of Congress*] (LCLS)
**NPlaCN**..... Champlain Valley School of Nursing, Plattsburgh, NY [*Library symbol*] [*Library of Congress*] (LCLS)
**NPlaP**........ Champlain Valley Physicians Hospital, Plattsburgh, NY [*Library symbol*] [*Library of Congress*] (LCLS)
**NPlaU**........ State University of New York, College at Plattsburgh, Plattsburgh, NY [*Library symbol*] [*Library of Congress*] (LCLS)
**NPlBE**....... Old Bethpage Elementary School, Plainview, NY [*Library symbol*] [*Library of Congress*] (LCLS)
**NPLC**......... National Pedigree Livestock Council (EA)
**NPLC**......... National Product Liability Council (EA)
**NPLC**......... Normal Phase Liquid Chromatography
**NPlCH**....... Central General Hospital, Plainview, NY [*Library symbol*] [*Library of Congress*] (LCLS)
**NPLD**........ National Pro-Life Democrats (EA)
**NPle**.......... Mount Pleasant Public Library, Pleasantville, NY [*Library symbol*] [*Library of Congress*] (LCLS)
**NPLEI**....... National Police Law Enforcement Institute (EA)
**NPleP**........ Pace University Westchester, Pleasantville, NY [*Library symbol*] [*Library of Congress*] (LCLS)
**NPLF**......... National Preservation Loan Fund [*National Trust for Historic Preservation*]
**NPLG**........ Navy Program Language Group
**NPLG**........ Night Plane Guard Station (NVT)
**NPLG**........ Night Plane Landing Guard (NVT)
**NPlGS**....... Church of Jesus Christ of Latter-Day Saints, Genealogical Society Library, Plainview Branch, Plainview, NY [*Library symbol*] [*Library of Congress*] (LCLS)
**NPlJE**........ Jamaica Elementary School, Plainview, NY [*Library symbol*] [*Library of Congress*] (LCLS)
**NPlKH**....... John F. Kennedy High School, Plainview, NY [*Library symbol*] [*Library of Congress*] (LCLS)
**NPlMC**...... Nassau County Medical Center, Plainview Division, Plainview, NY [*Library symbol*] [*Library of Congress*] (LCLS)
**NPLO**........ NATO Production and Logistics Organization (NATG)
**NPlockie**.... Notatki Plockie [*A publication*]
**NP-L PAC**... National Pro-Life Political Action Committee (EA)
**NPlPE**........ Pasadena Elementary School, Plainview, NY [*Library symbol*] [*Library of Congress*] (LCLS)
**NPlPwE**..... Parkway Elementary School, Plainview, NY [*Library symbol*] [*Library of Congress*] (LCLS)
**NPLR**......... Nyasaland Protectorate Law Reports [*A publication*] (ILCA)
**NPlSH**....... Plainview-Old Bethpage Senior High School, Plainview, NY [*Library symbol*] [*Library of Congress*] (LCLS)
**N/PLT**....... Name Plate [*Automotive engineering*]
**NPLTC**...... National Public Law Training Center (EA)
**N PLUR**..... Neuter Plural [*Grammar*] (OCD)
**NPM**.......... Marist College, Poughkeepsie, NY [*Library symbol*] [*Library of Congress*] (LCLS)
**NPM**.......... Narrowband Phase Modulation (DEN)
**NPM**.......... National Association of Pastoral Musicians (EA)
**NPM**.......... Natural Particulate Matter [*Oceanography*]
**NPM**.......... Naval Provost Martial [*British*]
**NPM**.......... Navy Programming Manual
**NPM**.......... Neonatal-Perinatal Medicine [*Medical specialty*] (DHSM)
**Np/m**.......... Neper per Meter
**NPM**.......... Neuphilologische Mitteilungen [*A publication*]
**NPM**.......... Neuphilologische Monatsschrift [*A publication*]
**NPM**.......... New Privateer Mines [*Vancouver Stock Exchange symbol*]
**NPM**.......... Non-Print Media [*Advertising*]
**NPM**.......... North Pahute Mesa [*Nevada*] [*Seismograph station code, US Geological Survey*] (SEIS)
**NPMA**....... National Piano Manufacturers Association of America [*Later, PMAI*] (EA)
**NPMA**....... National Podiatric Medical Association (EA)
**NPMA**....... National Property Management Association (EA)
**NPMA**....... Newspaper Purchasing Management Association (EA)
**N & P Mag**... Nevile and Perry's English Magistrates' Cases [*1836-37*] [*A publication*] (DLA)
**NPMC**....... National Pecan Marketing Council (EA)
**N & PMC**... Nevile and Perry's English Magistrates' Cases [*1836-37*] [*A publication*] (DLA)
**NPMG**....... NATO Patriot Management Group (MCD)
**NPMH**....... Mid-Hudson Libraries, Poughkeepsie, NY [*Library symbol*] [*Library of Congress*] (LCLS)
**NPMHU**.... National Postal Mail Handlers Union (EA)
**NPMI**........ Nordic Pool for Marine Insurance [*Helsinki, Finland*] (EA)
**NPMP**....... National Pesticide Monitoring Program [*Later, National Contaminant Biomonitoring Program*] [*US Fish and Wildlife Service*]
**NPMR**....... National Premium Manufacturers Representatives [*Later, IMRA*] (EA)
**NPMTC**..... Navy Pacific Missile Test Center (MCD)
**NPMTT**..... Nuclear Propulsion Mobile Training Team [*Military*] (CAAL)
**NPN**.......... NASA Part Number (MCD)
**NPN**.......... National Party of Nigeria [*Political party*] (PPW)
**NPN**.......... National Performance Network (EA)
**NPN**.......... National Petroleum News [*A publication*]
**NPN**.......... National Prevention Network (EA)
**N-P-N**........ Negative-Positive-Negative [*Transistor*] (CET)
**NPN**.......... New Product Network [*Television*]
**NPN**.......... New Pseudonyms and Nicknames [*A publication*]
**NPN**.......... Nonprotein Nitrogen [*Analytical chemistry*]
**NPNA**........ No Protest Nonacceptance [*Banking*]
**NP News**.... National Petroleum News [*A publication*]
**NPNMA**..... Nevrologiya, Psikhiatriya, i Nevrokhirurgiya [*A publication*]
**NPNP**........ Negative-Positive-Negative-Positive [*Transistor*]
**NP NS**........ Ohio Nisi Prius Reports, New Series [*A publication*] (DLA)
**NPO**.......... Naphthylphenyloxazole [*Biochemical analysis*]
**NPO**.......... National [*or New*] Post Office Building
**NPO**.......... National Project Office
**NPO**.......... Naval Port Officer
**NPO**.......... Navy Post Office
**NPO**.......... Navy Program Objectives (NG)
**NPO**.......... Navy Purchasing Office
**NPO**.......... Neighborhood Patrol Office [*or Officer*]
**NPO**.......... New Personnel Orientation (MCD)
**NPO**.......... New Philharmonic Orchestra [*British*]
**NPO**.......... Nil per Os [*Nothing by Mouth*] [*Medicine*]
**NPO**.......... No Part on Order (MCD)
**NPO**.......... Norpet Resources Ltd. [*Toronto Stock Exchange symbol*]
**NPO**.......... Not Pickled Ordinary [*Metal industry*]
**NPO**.......... Nuclear Plant Operator (NRCH)
**NPO**.......... Nuclear Propulsion Office
**NPO**.......... Strategic Systems Project Office, Washington, DC [*OCLC symbol*] (OCLC)
**NPOAA**..... National Police Officers Association of America (EA)
**NPOC**........ Nonpurgeable Organic Carbon
**NPOE**........ Nitrophenyl Octyl Ether [*Organic chemistry*]
**NPOEV**...... Nuclear-Powered Ocean Engineering Vehicle [*Minisub*]
**NP Ohio**.... Ohio Nisi Prius Reports [*A publication*] (DLA)
**NPOLA**..... Navy Purchasing Office, Los Angeles
**NPOMHWMGL**... National Post Office Mail Handlers, Watchmen, Messengers, and Group Leaders [*Later, NPMHU*] (EA)
**NPOPR**..... Not Paid on Prior Rolls
**NPoq**......... Beekman Community Library Reading Center, Poughquag, NY [*Library symbol*] [*Library of Congress*] (LCLS)
**NP & OSR**... Naval Petroleum and Oil Shale Reserve
**NPOST**....... Nonperturbative Open-Shell Theory [*Physics*]
**NPot**.......... Potsdam Public Library, Potsdam, NY [*Library symbol*] [*Library of Congress*] (LCLS)
**NPotC**........ Clarkson College of Technology, Potsdam, NY [*Library symbol*] [*Library of Congress*] (LCLS)
**NPotU**........ State University of New York, College at Potsdam, Potsdam, NY [*Library symbol*] [*Library of Congress*] (LCLS)
**NPP**.......... N-Pentylpalmitamide [*Organic chemistry*]
**NPP**.......... National Peach Partners (EA)
**NPP**.......... National People's Party [*Political party*] [*Pakistan*] (FEA)
**NPP**.......... National Periodicals Publications, Inc.
**NPP**.......... National Policy Paper [*Army*] (AABC)
**NPP**.......... National Prison Project (EA)
**NPP**.......... National Progressive Party [*Iraq*] [*Political party*] (BJA)
**NPP**.......... National Prohibition Party (EA)
**NPP**.......... National Promotion Plan (FAAC)
**NPP**.......... Naval Propellant Plant
**NPP**.......... Negative Picture Phase
**NPP**.......... Nemzeti Paraszt Part [*National Peasant Party*] [*Hungary*] [*Political party*] (PPE)
**NPP**.......... Neodymium Pentaphosphate [*Inorganic chemistry*]
**NPP**.......... Net Primary Productivity
**NPP**.......... Network Protocol Processor
**NPP**.......... New People's Party [*Political party*] [*Democratic People's Republic of Korea*] (FEA)
**NPP**.......... New Progressive Party [*Puerto Rico*] [*Political party*]
**NPP**.......... Nigerian People's Party [*Political party*] (PPW)
**NPP**.......... Nitrophenyl Phosphate [*Biochemical analysis*]
**NPP**.......... No Passed Proof
**NPP**.......... Non-Penetrating Periscope [*DARPA*]
**NPP**.......... Normal Pool Plasma [*Clinical chemistry*]
**NPP**.......... North American Power [*Vancouver Stock Exchange symbol*]
**NPP**.......... Nuclear Power Plant (IEEE)

**NPP** .......... Nuveen Performance Plus Municipal [*NYSE symbol*] (SPSG)
**NP & PA** .... National Paperbox and Packaging Association (EA)
**NPPA** ........ National Pickle Packers Association [*Later, PPI*]
**NPPA** ........ National Press Photographers Association (EA)
**NPPA** ........ National Probation and Parole Association [*Later, NCCD*]
**NPPA** ........ National and Provincial Parks Association. Newsletter [*A publication*]
**NPPAC** ...... National and Provincial Parks Association of Canada
**NPPB** ........ National Poisons and Pesticides Board [*Sweden*]
**NPPB** ........ National Potato Promotion Board (EA)
**NPPC** ........ National Pork Producers Council (EA)
**NPPC** ........ National Power Policy Committee [*World War II*]
**NPPC** ........ Navy Programming Planning Council
**NPPC** ........ Nuclear Power Plant Company Ltd.
**NPPC** ........ Numeric Parts Preference Code [*Military*] (AFIT)
**NPPD** ........ (Nitrophenyl)pentadienal [*Organic chemistry*] [*Tracer chemical*]
**NPPE** ........ Nitrophenyl Pentyl Ether [*Organic chemistry*]
**NPPE** ........ Nuclear Power Propulsion Evaluation (NG)
**NPPF** ........ National Poultry Producers Federation [*Defunct*] (EA)
**NPPI** ......... Navy Program Progress Item (CAAL)
**NPPL** ........ Neuropsychopharmacology Laboratory [*Wayne State University*] [*Research center*]
**NPPM** ....... Northern Parks and Playgrounds Movement [*Australia*]
**NPPN** ........ Nitroxyperoxypropyl Nitrate [*Environmental chemistry*]
**NPPN** ........ NUDO [*Namibia United Democratic Organization*] Progressive Party of Namibia [*Political party*] (PPW)
**NPPO** ........ Navy Program Planning Office
**NPPO** ........ Navy Publications and Printing Office
**NPPR** ........ Navy Program Progress Report
**NPPR** ........ Nonproductive Procurement Directive
**NPPRE** ...... Nitrophenyl Propyl Ether [*Organic chemistry*]
**NPPS** ........ Navy Planning and Programming System
**NPPS** ........ Navy Publications and Printing Service
**NPPSBO** ... Navy Publications and Printing Service Branch Office
**NPPSMO** ... Navy Publications and Printing Service Management Office
**NPPSO** ...... Navy Publications and Printing Service Office
**NPPTA** ...... National Public Parks Tennis Association (EA)
**NPPW** ....... National Poison Prevention Week
**NPR** .......... Napier [*New Zealand*] [*Seismograph station code, US Geological Survey*] [*Closed*] (SEIS)
**NPR** .......... Narodowa Partia Robotnicza [*National Workers Party*] [*Poland*] [*Political party*] (PPE)
**NPR** .......... National Parks and Access to the Countryside Regulations [*Town planning*] [*British*]
**NPR** .......... National Productivity Review [*A publication*]
**NPR** .......... National Public Radio [*Washington, DC*] [*Telecommunications*] (TSSD)
**NPR** .......... Naval Petroleum Reserves
**NPR** .......... Naval Plant Representative
**NPR** .......... Navy Procurement Regulation
**NPR** .......... Negro Puerto Rican
**NPR** .......... Neoricans in Puerto Rico (EA)
**NPR** .......... Neptune Resources Corp. [*Toronto Stock Exchange symbol*]
**NPR** .......... Net Pool Return
**NPR** .......... Net Protein Ratio [*Nutrition*]
**NPR** .......... New Plan Realty Trust SBI [*NYSE symbol*] (SPSG)
**NPR** .......... New Production Reactor [*Department of Energy*]
**NPR** .......... Night Press Rates [*of newspapers*]
**NPR** .......... Nisi Prius Reports [*A publication*] (DLA)
**NPR** .......... Noise Power Ratio
**NPR** .......... Noise Prediction and Reduction
**NPR** .......... Nonproduction Release (MCD)
**NPR** .......... North Polar Region
**NPR** .......... Nozzle Pressure Ratio [*Aviation*]
**NPR** .......... Nuclear Paramagnetic Resonance (MCD)
**NPR** .......... Nuclear Power Reactor
**NPR** .......... Nuclear Pulse Rocket [*NASA*]
**NPr** ........... Pearl River Public Library, Pearl River, NY [*Library symbol*] [*Library of Congress*] (LCLS)
**NPrA** ......... American Cyanamid Co., Lederle Laboratories, Pearl River, NY [*Library symbol*] [*Library of Congress*] (LCLS)
**NPRA** ........ National Personal Robot Association [*Later, NSRA*] (EA)
**NPRA** ........ National Petroleum Refiners Association (EA)
**NPRA** ........ Naval Personnel Research Activity
**NPRA** ........ Newspaper Personnel Relations Association (EA)
**NPRC** ........ National Personnel Records Center [*National Archives and Records Service*]
**NPRC** ........ National Polystyrene Recycling Co.
**NPRC** ........ National Project on Resource Coordination for Justice Statistics and Information [*Canada*]
**NPRC** ........ National Public Relations Council of Health and Welfare Services [*Formerly, NPC*]
**NPRC** ........ National Puerto Rican Coalition (EA)
**NPRC** ........ Newspaper Production and Research Center
**NPRC** ........ Nuclear Power Range Channel (IEEE)
**NPRC (CPR)** ... National Personnel Records Center (Civilian Personnel Records) [*National Archives and Records Service*] (AFM)
**NPRCG** ..... Nuclear Public Relations Contact Group
**NPRC (MPR)** ... National Personnel Records Center (Military Personnel Records) [*National Archives and Records Service*] (AFM)
**NPRD** ........ NASA Procurement Regulation Directive
**NPRD** ........ Nonelectronic Parts Reliability Data (MCD)
**NPRD** ........ Nuclear Plant Reliability Data
**NPRDA** ..... National Precure Retread Dealers Association (EA)
**NPRDC** ..... Navy Personnel Research and Development Center (GRD)
**NPRDL** ..... Naval Personnel Research and Development Laboratory
**NPRDS** ..... Nuclear Plant Reliability Data System (NRCH)
**NPRF** ........ National Puerto Rican Forum (EA)
**NPRF** ........ Northrop Pulse Radiation Facility
**NPRI** ......... National Psychiatric Reform Institute
**N Princ** ...... New Princeton Review [*A publication*]
**NPRL** ........ Navy Prosthetics Research Laboratory
**NPRL** ........ No Parallel Traffic [*Aviation*] (FAAC)
**NPRL** ........ Nonprocedural Referencing Language
**NPRM** ....... Notice of Proposed Rule Making [*Federal agencies*]
**NPRN** ....... Neoprene [*Synthetic rubber*]
**NPRO** ....... N-Nitrosoproline [*Organic chemistry*]
**NPRO** ....... Naval Petroleum Reserves Office
**NPRO** ....... Navy Plant Representative Office
**NPRR** ........ National Public Relations Roundtable [*Defunct*]
**NPRR** ........ Net Pool Return Rule
**NPRRDF** ... Natural Product Reports [*A publication*]
**NPRS** ........ NASA Procurement Regulation Supplement
**NPRS** ........ Nonpersistent (FAAC)
**NPRV** ........ Nitrogen Pressure Relief Valve (MCD)
**NPRWC** .... National Puerto Rican Women's Caucus (EA)
**NPS** .......... Honolulu, HI [*Location identifier*] [*FAA*] (FAAL)
**NPS** .......... NASA Planning Studies (KSC)
**NPS** .......... National Park Service [*Department of the Interior*]
**NPS** .......... National Parole Service [*Canada*]
**NPS** .......... National Periodicals System
**NPS** .......... National Philatelic Society [*Defunct*] (EA)
**NPS** .......... National Phone Services, Inc.
**NPS** .......... National Poetry Series
**NPS** .......... National Prisoner Statistics [*An association*]
**NPS** .......... Nationale Partij Suriname [*Surinam National Party*] [*Political party*] (PPW)
**NPS** .......... Nature: Physical Science [*A publication*]
**NPS** .......... Naval Postgraduate School
**NPS** .......... Navy Personnel Survey
**NPS** .......... Navy Primary Standards (MSA)
**NPS** .......... Neapolis [*Greece*] [*Seismograph station code, US Geological Survey*] (SEIS)
**NPS** .......... Negative Potential Shifts [*Neurophysiology*]
**NPS** .......... Network Processing Supervisor [*Honeywell, Inc.*]
**NPS** .......... New Palaeographical Society [*A publication*]
**NPS** .......... Night Photographic System
**NPS** .......... Nitrophenyl Sulfenyl [*Organic chemistry*]
**Nps** ........... Nitrophenylthio(nitrophenylsulfonyl) [*Biochemistry*]
**NPS** .......... No Prior Service [*Military*]
**NPS** .......... Nonperishable Subsistence
**NPS** .......... Nonpoint Pollution Source [*Agricultural engineering*]
**NPS** .......... Normal Pipe Size
**NPS** .......... Normalized Plateau Slope
**NPS** .......... North Polar Sequence
**NPS** .......... Northwestern Public Service Co. [*NYSE symbol*] (SPSG)
**NPS** .......... Notice Papers - Senate [*A publication*] (APTA)
**NPS** .......... Nuclear and Plasma Sciences (MCD)
**NPS** .......... Nuclear Power Source
**NPS** .......... Nuclear Power System
**NPS** .......... Nuclear-Powered Ship (NVT)
**NPS** .......... Numerical Plotting System (NRCH)
**NPSA** ........ National Passenger Safety Association (EA)
**NPSA** ........ National Pecan Shellers Association (EA)
**NPSA** ........ National Pegboard Systems Association (EA)
**NPSA** ........ National Psychic Science Association (EA)
**NPSA** ........ New Program Status Area (IEEE)
**NPSA** ........ Nordic Political Science Association (EAIO)
**NPSA** ........ Novitiate of Saint Andrew-On-Hudson, Poughkeepsie, NY [*Library symbol*] [*Library of Congress*] (LCLS)
**NPSAPHA** ... New Professionals Section of the American Public Health Association (EA)
**NPSB** ........ National Prisoner Statistics Bulletin [*Department of Justice*]
**NPSB** ........ News Print Service Bureau
**NPSC** ........ Naval Personnel Separation Center
**NPSC** ........ Nursing Policy Studies Centre [*University of Warwick*] [*British*] (CB)
**NPS-CL** ..... Nitrophenyl Sulfenyl Chloride
**NPS/CPSU/UW** ... National Park Service Cooperative Park Studies Unit, University of Washington [*Research center*] (RCD)
**NPSD** ........ Naval Photographic Services Depot
**NPSD** ........ Noise Power Spectre Density
**NPSE** ........ National Premium Sales Executives (EA)
**NPSF** ........ National Straight Pipe Threads for Dry Seal Pressure Tight Joints
**NPSG** ........ NPS Technologies Group, Inc. [*Secaucus, NJ*] [*NASDAQ symbol*] (NQ)
**NPSH** ........ National Straight Pipe Threads for Hose Couplings and Nipples
**NPSH** ........ Net Positive Suction Head [*Pumps*]
**NPSH** ........ Nonprotein Sulfhydryl [*Biochemistry*]

**NPSHR** ..... Net Positive Suction Head Required [*Chemical or food processing*]
**NPSI** .......... Networked Picture Systems, Inc. [*NASDAQ symbol*] (NQ)
**NPSI** .......... Nursing Performance Simulation Instrument
**NPSL** .......... National Professional Soccer League [*Later, NASL*]
**NPSL** .......... National Straight Pipe Threads for Locknuts and Locknut Pipe Threads
**NPSO** ......... Nonpaired Spatial Orbitals [*Atomic physics*]
**NPSP** ......... Net Positive Static Pressure (NASA)
**NPSP** ......... Net Positive Suction Pressure [*Cryogenics*]
**NPsP** .......... Paul Smiths College, Paul Smiths, NY [*Library symbol*] [*Library of Congress*] (LCLS)
**NPSPA** ...... National Pecan Shellers and Processors Association (EA)
**NPSR** ......... No Primary Staff Responsibility [*Army*] (AABC)
**NPSRA** ...... National Professional Squash Racquets Association (EA)
**NPSRC** ...... National Professional Standards Review Council [*HEW*] [*Terminated, 1982*] (EGAO)
**NPSRI** ........ National Public Services Research Institute
**NPSS** ......... IEEE Nuclear and Plasma Sciences Society (EA)
**NPSS** ......... National Police and Security Service [*Republic of Vietnam*] (CINC)
**NPSS** ......... Noms Propres Sud-Semitiques [*A publication*] (BJA)
**NPSS** ......... Non-Public School Section [*American Association of School Librarians*]
**NPSS** ......... Nuclear and Plasma Science Symposium (MCD)
**N Ps St** ....... Neue Psychologische Studien [*A publication*]
**NPST** ......... Native Pituitary-Derived Somatotropin [*Endocrinology*]
**NPST** ......... Native Porcine Somatotropin [*Endocrinology*]
**NPSU** ......... National Perinatal Statistics Unit [*Australia*]
**NPSWL** ..... New Program Status Word Location
**NPSWU** .... Newpark Resources Uts [*NASDAQ symbol*] (NQ)
**NPT** ........... Executive Aviation Services [*Long Beach, CA*] [*FAA designator*] (FAAC)
**NPT** ........... Nasal Provocation Test [*Immunology*]
**NPT** ........... National Petroleum Corp. Ltd. [*Toronto Stock Exchange symbol*]
**NPT** ........... National Taper Pipe [*Thread*]
**NPT** ........... Navy Pointer Tracker (MCD)
**NPT** ........... NECO Enterprises [*AMEX symbol*] (SPSG)
**NPT** ........... Neomycin Phosphotransferase [*An enzyme*]
**NPT** ........... Neoprecipitin Test [*Oncology*]
**NPT** ........... Network Planning Technique [*Data processing*] (IEEE)
**NPT** ........... Neuropsychiatry
**NPT** ........... Neuropsychiatry Technician [*Navy*]
**NPT** ........... New Periodical Titles [*of British Union Catalogue of Periodicals*]
**NPT** ........... Newport [*Rhode Island*] [*Airport symbol*] (OAG)
**NPT** ........... Newport Ebbw Junction [*British depot code*]
**NPT** ........... Nocturnal Penile Tumescence [*Psychiatry*]
**NPT** ........... Nonproliferation Treaty [*to halt the spread of nuclear weapons*]
**NPT** ........... Nonpyramidal Tract
**NPT** ........... Normal Pressure and Temperature
**NPT** ........... Portland Terminal R. R. Co. [*Formerly, Northern Pacific Terminal R. R.*] [*AAR code*]
**NPTA** ........ National Paper Trade Association (EA)
**NPTA** ........ National Passenger Traffic Association [*Later, NBTA*] (EA)
**NPTA** ........ National Perishable Transportation Association (EA)
**NPTA** ........ National Piano Travelers Association (EA)
**NPTA** ........ National Postal Transport Association [*Later, APWU*]
**NPTA** ........ New Periodical Title Abbreviations [*A publication*]
**NPTC** ........ National Postal and Travelers Censorship [*Army*] (AABC)
**NPtc** .......... Port Chester Public Library, Port Chester, NY [*Library symbol*] [*Library of Congress*] (LCLS)
**NPTCO** ..... National Postal and Travelers Censorship Organization [*Army*] (AABC)
**NPtcU** ........ United Hospital, Port Chester, NY [*Library symbol*] [*Library of Congress*] (LCLS)
**NPTD** ........ Nitrogen Phosphorus Thermionic Detector [*Instrumentation*]
**NPte** .......... Port Ewen Free Library, Port Ewen, NY [*Library symbol*] [*Library of Congress*] (LCLS)
**NPTF** ......... National Taper Pipe Threads for Dry Seal Pressure Tight Joints
**NPTF** ......... Nuclear Power Task Force
**NPTF** ......... Nuclear Proof Test Facility [*Proposed, but never built*] (NRCH)
**NPTFB** ...... National Park Trust Fund Board [*Later, NPF*]
**NPTG** ........ Nuclear Power Task Group [*Navy*] (MCD)
**NPtjer** ........ Port Jervis Free Public Library, Port Jervis, NY [*Library symbol*] [*Library of Congress*] (LCLS)
**NPTL** ......... National Police Testing Laboratories (EA)
**NPTN** ........ National Pesticide Telecommunication Network (EA)
**NPTR** ........ National Parachute Test Range (MCD)
**NPTR** ........ National Taper Pipe Threads for Railing Fixtures
**NPTRL** ...... Naval Personnel and Training Research Laboratory [*Formerly, Personnel Research Activity*]
**NPtw** .......... Port Washington Public Library, Port Washington, NY [*Library symbol*] [*Library of Congress*] (LCLS)
**NptwDE** ..... Daly Elementary School, Port Washington, NY [*Library symbol*] [*Library of Congress*] (LCLS)
**NPtwGE** .... Guggenheim Elementary School, Port Washington, NY [*Library symbol*] [*Library of Congress*] (LCLS)
**NptwME** .... Manorhaven Elementary School, Port Washington, NY [*Library symbol*] [*Library of Congress*] (LCLS)
**NPtwMSE** ... Main Street Elementary School, Port Washington, NY [*Library symbol*] [*Library of Congress*] (LCLS)
**NPtwSSE** ... South Salem Elementary School, Port Washington, NY [*Library symbol*] [*Library of Congress*] (LCLS)
**NPTWZI** ... North Pacific Trade Winds Zone Investigation (NOAA)
**NPU** ........... National Postal Union [*Later, APWU*]
**NPU** ........... Natural Product Update [*A publication*]
**NPU** ........... Naval Parachute Unit
**NPU** ........... Navigation Processor Unit (MCD)
**NPU** ........... Ne Plus Ultra [*No Further; i.e., the pinnacle of attainment*] [*French*]
**NPU** ........... Net Protein Utilization [*Nutrition*]
**NPU** ........... Network Processing Unit
**NPU** ........... Neue Verpackung. Zeitschrift fuer die Gesamte Verpackungswirtschaft des Inlandes und Auslandes [*A publication*]
**NPU** ........... Nitrogen Pressure Unit (MCD)
**NPU** ........... Nitrogen Purge Unit (MCD)
**NPU** ........... Nordic Postal Union (EA)
**NPU** ........... Not Passed Urine [*Medicine*]
**NPUP** ........ National Progressive Unionist Party [*Egypt*] [*Political party*] (PPW)
**NPur** .......... Purchase Free Library, Purchase, NY [*Library symbol*] [*Library of Congress*] (LCLS)
**NPurMC** .... Manhattanville College, Purchase, NY [*Library symbol*] [*Library of Congress*] (LCLS)
**NPurU** ....... State University of New York, College at Purchase, Purchase, NY [*Library symbol*] [*Library of Congress*] (LCLS)
**NPurW** ...... Westchester Academy of Medicine, Purchase, NY [*Library symbol*] [*Library of Congress*] (LCLS)
**NPV** ........... National Present Volume Method [*Management*]
**NPV** ........... Naturpolitische Volkspartei [*People's Party for Nature Policy*] [*Federal Republic of Germany*] [*Political party*] (PPW)
**NPV** ........... Negative Predictive Value [*Experimentation*]
**NPV** ........... Net Present Value [*Accounting*]
**NPV** ........... New Plymouth Ventures, Inc. [*Vancouver Stock Exchange symbol*]
**NPV** ........... Nitrogen Pressure Valve (KSC)
**NPV** ........... No Par Value [*Stock exchange term*]
**NPV** ........... Nonpropulsive Vent (KSC)
**NPV** ........... Nuclear Polyhedrosis Virus
**NPV** ........... Vassar College, Poughkeepsie, NY [*Library symbol*] [*Library of Congress*] (LCLS)
**NPVCE** ...... Net Present Value for Current Expendable Launch Vehicles [*NASA*] (KSC)
**NPVLA** ...... National Paint, Varnish, and Lacquer Association [*Later, NPCA*] (EA)
**NPVNE** ..... Net Present Value for New Expendable Launch Vehicles [*NASA*] (KSC)
**NPVS** ......... No-Par-Value Stock [*Stock exchange term*]
**NPVSH** ..... Net Present Value for Space Shuttle [*NASA*] (KSC)
**NPW** .......... International Union of Allied Novelty and Production Workers
**NPW** .......... National Party of Western Australia [*Political party*]
**NPW** .......... Network for Professional Women [*Hartford, CT*] (EA)
**NPWA** ....... National Pure Water Association [*British*]
**NPWC** ....... Navy Public Works Center
**NPWD** ....... Navy Public Works Department
**NPWOA** .... National Piggly Wiggly Operators Association (EA)
**NPWR** ....... Nationwide Power Corp. [*NASDAQ symbol*] (NQ)
**NPWRC** .... Northern Prairie Wildlife Research Center [*Jamestown, ND*] [*Department of the Interior*] (GRD)
**NPWS** ........ NATO Planning Workshop (NATG)
**NPX** .......... New Pioneer Exploration [*Vancouver Stock Exchange symbol*]
**NPY** .......... Neuropeptide Y [*Biochemistry*]
**NPy** ........... Penn Yan Public Library, Penn Yan, NY [*Library symbol*] [*Library of Congress*] (LCLS)
**NPYR** ........ Nitrosopyrrolidine [*Also, NYPYR*] [*Organic chemistry*]
**NPYRR** ...... N-Nitrosopyrrolidine [*Organic chemistry*]
**NPZ** ........... New Plymouth [*New Zealand*] [*Seismograph station code, US Geological Survey*] [*Closed*] (SEIS)
**NPZ** ........... North Pyrenean Zone [*Geology*]
**NQ** ............. Net Quick Assets
**NQ** ............. Neural Quantum [*Theory*] [*Sensory discrimination*]
**nq** .............. Nicaragua [*MARC country of publication code*] [*Library of Congress*] (LCCP)
**NQ** ............. Northwest Territorial Airlines [*Canada*] [*ICAO designator*] (FAAC)
**N & Q** ......... Notes and Queries [*A publication*]
**NQ** ............. Notes and Queries [*A publication*]
**NQ** ............. Quoque Library, Quoque, NY [*Library symbol*] [*Library of Congress*] (LCLS)
**NQA** .......... Memphis, TN [*Location identifier*] [*FAA*] (FAAL)
**NQA** .......... National Quality Award [*LIMRA, NALU*]
**NQA** .......... National Quilting Association (EA)
**NQA** .......... Net Quick Assets
**NQA** .......... North Carolina Agricultural and Technical State University, Greensboro, NC [*OCLC symbol*] (OCLC)
**NQAA** ........ Nuclear Quality Assurance Agency
**NQB** .......... National Quotation Bureau [*Stock market*]

**NQB**.......... No Qualified Bidders (FAAC)
**NQC**.......... NASA Quality Control (KSC)
**NQC**.......... National Quotations Committee [*of the National Association of Securities Dealers*]
**NQC**.......... Northern Queensland Co. [*Australia*]
**NQC**.......... Nuveen California Investment Quality Municipal Fund [*NYSE symbol*] (SPSG)
**NQCC**........ North Queensland Conservation Council [*Australia*]
**NQD**.......... Nonquaded [*Telecommunications*] (TEL)
**NQD**.......... Notice of Quality Discrepancy
**N QD Nat**.. North Queensland Naturalist [*A publication*] (APTA)
**NQHR**....... National Quarter Horse Registry (EA)
**NQI**.......... Kingsville, TX [*Location identifier*] [*FAA*] (FAAL)
**NQI**.......... Nuveen Insurance Quality Municipal [*NYSE symbol*] (SPSG)
**NQIC**......... National Quality Information Centre [*Institute of Quality Assurance*] [*Information service or system*] (IID)
**NQKA**........ Northwest Quoin Key Association (EA)
**NQL**.......... National Quick Lube [*Vancouver Stock Exchange symbol*]
**NQL**.......... North Queensland Libraries: A Directory [*Australia*] [*A publication*]
**NQL**.......... Nouveau Quartier Latin [*Paris bookstore*]
**NQL**.......... Nuclear Quadrupole Interaction [*Physics*]
**N Qld Nat**.. North Queensland Naturalist [*A publication*] (APTA)
**NQLL**......... National Quick Lube Ltd. [*NASDAQ symbol*] (NQ)
**NQM**.......... Midway/Henderson Naval Station, HI [*Location identifier*] [*FAA*] (FAAL)
**NQM**.......... Nuovi Quaderni del Meridione [*A publication*]
**NQM**.......... Nuveen Investment Quality Municipal [*NYSE symbol*] (SPSG)
**NQN**.......... Neuquen [*Argentina*] [*Airport symbol*] (OAG)
**NQN**.......... Nuveen New York Investment Quality Municipal Fund [*NYSE symbol*] (SPSG)
**NQNS**........ Notes and Queries. New Series [*A publication*]
**NQO**.......... Nitroquinoline Oxide [*Organic chemistry*]
**NQPA**........ National Quarter Pony Association (EA)
**NQPC**........ National Quartz Producers Council (EA)
**NQR**.......... New Quebec Raglan Mines Ltd. [*Toronto Stock Exchange symbol*]
**NQR**.......... North Queensland Resources [*Australia*]
**NQR**.......... Nuclear Quadrupole Resonance [*Frequencies*]
**NQRC**........ National Quadraphonic Radio Committee
**NQ Register** ... North Queensland Register [*A publication*] (APTA)
**NQRL**......... Nor-Quest Resources Limited [*NASDAQ symbol*] (NQ)
**NQRR**........ Nuclear Quadrupole Resonance Response
**NQT**.......... Nonlanguage Qualification Test
**NQT**.......... Nor-Quest Resources Ltd. [*Vancouver Stock Exchange symbol*]
**NQU**.......... Not Quite Us [*Lower in social status*] [*Slang*] [*British*]
**NQU**.......... Nuqui [*Colombia*] [*Airport symbol*] (OAG)
**N QUEENSD** ... North Queensland [*Australia*] (ROG)
**N Queensl Nat** ... North Queensland Naturalist [*A publication*]
**NQX**.......... Key West, FL [*Location identifier*] [*FAA*] (FAAL)
**NQX**.......... North Queensland Express [*Australia*]
**NQY**.......... Newquay [*England*] [*Airport symbol*] (OAG)
**NR**............. Bosanquet and Puller's New Reports, English Common Pleas [*1804-07*] [*A publication*] (DLA)
**NR**............. CSE Aviation Ltd. [*Great Britain*] [*ICAO designator*] (FAAC)
**NR**............. [*The*] Item Requested Is Current but Is No Longer Maintained [*Advice of supply action code*] [*Army*]
**NR**............. Nachrichtenregiment [*Signal Regiment*] [*German military - World War II*]
**NR**............. Narrow Resonance [*Nuclear energy*] (NRCH)
**NR**............. Nase Rec [*Prague*] [*A publication*]
**NR**............. Nassau Review [*A publication*]
**NR**............. Natal Reports [*South Africa*] [*A publication*] (DLA)
**NR**............. Nation Review [*A publication*] (APTA)
**NR**............. National Recovery Act
**NR**............. National Recovery Administration [*Voided by Supreme Court, 1935*]
**NR**............. National Report (OICC)
**NR**............. National Reporter [*Maritime Law Book Company Ltd.*] [*Canada*] [*Information service or system*] (CRD)
**NR**............. National Reserve [*British military*] (DMA)
**NR**............. National Review [*A publication*]
**NR**............. NATO Restricted (NATG)
**NR**............. Natural Resources
**NR**............. Natural Rubber
**NR**............. Naturwissenschaftliche Rundschau [*A publication*]
**NR**............. Naucnyj Rabotnik [*A publication*]
**NR**............. Nauka i Religija [*A publication*]
**NR**............. Nauru [*ANSI two-letter standard code*] (CNC)
**NR**............. Naval Rating
**NR**............. Naval Reserve
**NR**............. Navigational RADAR
**NR**............. Navy Regulations
**NR**............. Near (EY)
**NR**............. Negative Resistance [*Electronics*]
**NR**............. Net Register [*Shipping*]
**NR**............. Neue Rundschau [*A publication*]
**NR**............. Neues Reich in Aegypten [*A publication*]
**NR**............. Neural Retina [*Ophthalmology*]
**NR**............. Neutral Red [*An indicator*]
**NR**............. New Records [*A publication*]
**NR**............. New Reports [*1862-65*] [*England*] [*A publication*] (DLA)
**NR**............. [*The*] New Republic [*A publication*]
**NR**............. Newhall Resources [*NYSE symbol*] (SPSG)
**NR**............. News Release [*A publication*]
**NR**............. Next Renewal
**NR**............. Nicaraguan Resistance [*An association*] (EA)
**NR**............. Nicolaus Rufulus [*Flourished, 13th century*] [*Authority cited in pre-1607 legal work*] (DSA)
**nr**............... Nigeria [*MARC country of publication code*] [*Library of Congress*] (LCCP)
**NR**............. Nigeria Regiment [*British military*] (DMA)
**NR**............. Nitrate Reductase [*An enzyme*]
**NR**............. Nitrile Rubber [*Organic chemistry*]
**N/R**........... No Record (AAG)
**NR**............. No Refill [*Pharmacy*]
**NR**............. No Release (AAG)
**NR**............. No Remittance
**NR**............. No Report [*Medicine*]
**NR**............. No Requirement
**NR**............. No Residency Requirement [*Voter registration*]
**NR**............. No Response [*Medicine*]
**NR**............. No Risk [*Business term*]
**NR**............. Noise Rating (NASA)
**NR**............. Noise Ratio
**NR**............. Noise Ration
**NR**............. Noise-Reduction [*Audio technology*]
**NR**............. Non-Rebreathing
**NR**............. Non Repetatur [*Do Not Repeat*] [*Pharmacy*]
**NR**............. Nonconformance Report [*Nuclear energy*] (NRCH)
**NR**............. Nonrated
**NR**............. Nonreactive [*Relay*]
**NR**............. Nonrecoverable (IEEE)
**NR**............. Nonrefundable [*Airline fare code*]
**NR**............. Nonregistered (AABC)
**NR**............. Nonresident [*British*]
**NR**............. Nonresponder [*Strain of mice*]
**NR**............. Nonreturnable [*Beverage bottles*]
**NR**............. Nonspecific Gene Resistance [*Genetics*]
**NR**............. Norfolk Rangers [*British military*] (DMA)
**NR**............. Norgold Russet Potato
**NR**............. Normal Range
**NR**............. Normal Responder
**NR**............. North American Rockwell Corp. [*Later, ROK*] [*NYSE symbol*] (SPSG)
**NR**............. North Riding [*England*] (ROG)
**NR**............. North River [*New York, New Jersey*]
**NR**............. Northern News Report
**NR**............. Northern Range [*Navigation*]
**NR**............. Northern Rhodesia [*Later, Zambia*]
**NR**............. Northwest Review [*A publication*]
**NR**............. Nose Right [*Aviation*] (MCD)
**NR**............. Not Rated
**NR**............. Not Readable
**NR**............. Not Recorded
**N/R**........... Not Remarkable [*Medicine*]
**NR**............. Not Reported
**NR**............. Not Required
**N/R**........... Not Responsible For
**N/R**........... Notes Receivable
**NR**............. Notice of Rating Required [*Civil Service*]
**N/R**........... Notice of Readiness [*Shipping*]
**NR**............. Nova Revija [*A publication*]
**NR**............. Nuchal Rigidity [*Medicine*]
**NR**............. Nuclear Radiology [*Medical specialty*] (DHSM)
**NR**............. Nuclear Reactor
**NR**............. Nuclear Research Submarine (MCD)
**NR**............. Nuestra Remesa [*Our Remittance*] [*Spanish*] [*Business term*]
**NR**............. Nufort Resources, Inc. [*Toronto Stock Exchange symbol*]
**NR**............. Number (AAG)
**NR**............. Number of Runs
**NR**............. Numismatic Review [*A publication*]
**NR**............. Nurse
**NR**............. Nursing Representative [*Red Cross*]
**NR**............. Nutritive Ratio
**NR**............. Nystagmus Recorder
**NR**............. Rochester Public Library, Rochester, NY [*Library symbol*] [*Library of Congress*] (LCLS)
**nr----**......... Rocky Mountain Region [*MARC geographic area code*] [*Library of Congress*] (LCCP)
**NR**............. Submersible Research Vehicle (Nuclear Propulsion) [*Navy ship symbol*]
**NRA**........... Coupeville, WA [*Location identifier*] [*FAA*] (FAAL)
**NRA**........... Narrandera [*Australia*] [*Airport symbol*] (OAG)
**NRA**........... National Reclamation Association [*Later, National Water Resources Association*] (EA)
**NRA**........... National Recovery Act
**NRA**........... National Recovery Administration [*Voided by Supreme Court, 1935*]
**NRA**........... National Recreation Association [*Later, NRPA*] (EA)
**NRA**........... National Reform Association (EA)

**NRA** .......... National Register of Archives [*Historical Manuscripts Commission*] [*British*]
**NRA** .......... National Rehabilitation Association (EA)
**NRA** .......... National Remodelers Association [*Later, NARI*]
**NRA** .......... National Renderers Association (EA)
**NRA** .......... National Resistance Army [*Uganda*] (PD)
**NRA** .......... National Restaurant Association (EA)
**NRA** .......... National Rifle Association of America (EA)
**NRA** .......... National Rivers Authority [*British*]
**NRA** .......... National Roommate Association [*Later, ASRS*] (EA)
**NRA** .......... NATO Refugees Agency (NATG)
**NRA** .......... Naval Radio Activity
**NRA** .......... Naval Reserve Association (EA)
**NRA** .......... Net Rentable Area (ADA)
**NRA** .......... Network Resolution Area
**NRA** .......... New Era Development Ltd. [*Vancouver Stock Exchange symbol*]
**NRA** .......... New Regional Airliner
**NRA** .......... No Repair Action [*Military*]
**NRA** .......... Nonregistered Accountable [*Military*]
**NRA** .......... Nonresident Alien
**NRA** .......... North River [*Alaska*] [*Seismograph station code, US Geological Survey*] (SEIS)
**NRA** .......... Northrop Radio Service, Inc. [*Palos Verdes, CA*] [*FAA designator*] (FAAC)
**NRA** .......... Nothing Recorded Against [*Security investigation result*] [*British*]
**NRA** .......... Nouvelle Revue Apologetique [*A publication*]
**NRA** .......... Nuclear Radiation Absorber
**NRA** .......... Nuclear Reaction Analysis
**NRA** .......... Nuclear Regulatory Agency
**NRA** .......... Nucleus Raphe Alatus [*Neurology*]
**NRA** .......... St. Augustine's College, Raleigh, NC [*OCLC symbol*] (OCLC)
**NRAA** ........ National Railway Appliances Association [*Later, REMSA*] (EA)
**NRAA** ........ National Renal Administrators Association (EA)
**NRAA** ........ National Rifle Association of America
**NRAA** ........ National Rifle Association of Australia
**NRAB** ........ American Baptist Historical Society, Rochester, NY [*Library symbol*] [*Library of Congress*] (LCLS)
**NRAB** ........ National Railroad Adjustment Board
**NRAB** ........ National Railroad Adjustment Board Awards [*A publication*] (DLA)
**NRAB** ........ Naval Reserve Aviation Base
**NRAB (2d D)** ... United States National Railroad Adjustment Board Awards, Second Division [*A publication*] (DLA)
**NRAB (3d D)** ... United States National Railroad Adjustment Board Awards, Third Division [*A publication*] (DLA)
**NRAB (1st D)** ... United States National Railroad Adjustment Board Awards, First Division [*A publication*] (DLA)
**NRAB (4th D)** ... United States National Railroad Adjustment Board Awards, Fourth Division [*A publication*] (DLA)
**NRAC** ........ National Resources Analysis Center
**NRAC** ........ Naval Research Advisory Committee
**NRACCO** .. Navy Regional Air Cargo Central [*or Control*] Office
**NRAD** ........ National Racquetball Association of the Deaf (EA)
**NRAD** ........ No Risk After Discharge [*Shipping*]
**NRADUSA** ... National Racquetball Association of the Deaf of the USA [*Later, NRAD*] (EA)
**NRAF** ........ Naval Reserve Auxiliary Field
**NRAG** ........ Naval Research Advisory Group (KSC)
**NRAI** ......... National Residential Appraisers Institute (EA)
**NRAL** ........ New York State Appellate Division, Law Library, Rochester, NY [*Library symbol*] [*Library of Congress*] (LCLS)
**NRam** ......... New Rambler [*A publication*]
**NRAM** ....... Non-Volatile Random Access Memory [*Data processing*]
**NRAMEG** ... National Restaurant Association Marketing Executives Group [*Defunct*] (EA)
**NRAMRG** ... National Restaurant Association Market Research Group [*Defunct*] (EA)
**NRans** ........ Ransomville Free Library, Ransomville, NY [*Library symbol*] [*Library of Congress*] (LCLS)
**NRAO** ........ National Radio Astronomy Observatory [*Charlottesville, VA*] [*National Science Foundation*] (GRD)
**NRAO** ........ Navy Regional Accounts Office
**NRAP** ........ Naturally Radioactive Product (NRCH)
**NRA Report** ... NRA [*National Restaurant Association*] Washington Report [*A publication*]
**NRAS** ........ National Radio Astronomy Observatory [*Charlottesville, VA*] [*National Science Foundation*] (GRD)
**NRAS** ........ Navy Readiness Analysis System
**NRAS** ........ Nuclear Release Authentication System [*Seventh Army*] (AABC)
**NRASF** ...... National Registry of Ambulatory Surgical Facilities (EA)
**NRAT** ........ Nonrationed (AABC)
**NRB** .......... Mayport, FL [*Location identifier*] [*FAA*] (FAAL)
**NRB** .......... National Religious Broadcasters (EA)
**NRB** .......... National Research Bureau [*Commercial firm*] (EA)
**NRB** .......... Natural Rubber Bureau [*Later, MRB*] (EA)
**NRB** .......... Naval Reactor Branch (MUGU)
**NRB** .......... Naval Repair Base
**NRB** .......... Navy Recruiting Bureau
**NRB** .......... Navy Reservation Bureau
**NRB** .......... New Redundancy Benefit [*To reduce unemployment*] [*British*]
**NRB** .......... Nonconformance Review Board [*Nuclear Regulatory Commission*] (NRCH)
**NRB** .......... Nouvelle Revue de Bretagne [*A publication*]
**NRB** .......... Nuclear Reactors Branch [*AEC*]
**NRBA** ........ National Radio Broadcasters Association [*Absorbed by NAB*] (EA)
**NRBC** ........ National Rare Blood Club [*Later, NRBC/NYBC*] (EA)
**NRBC** ........ Nucleated Red Blood Cell
**NRBC/NYBC** ... National Rare Blood Club/New York Blood Center (EA)
**NRBE** ........ Native Races of the British Empire [*A publication*]
**NRBF** ......... Number of Rounds between Failures [*Quality control*] (MCD)
**NRBL** ........ Bausch & Lomb, Inc., Rochester, NY [*Library symbol*] [*Library of Congress*] (LCLS)
**NRBL-S** ..... Bausch & Lomb, Inc., SOFLENS Division, Technical Information Center, Rochester, NY [*Library symbol*] [*Library of Congress*] (LCLS)
**NRBP** ........ New Reports of Bosanquet and Puller [*A publication*] (DLA)
**NRBQ** ........ New Rhythm and Blues Quartet [*Rock music group*]
**NRC** .......... Crows Landing, CA [*Location identifier*] [*FAA*] (FAAL)
**NRC** .......... National Racquetball Club (EA)
**NRC** .......... National Radio Club (EA)
**NRC** .......... National Railroad Construction and Maintenance Association, Inc. (EA)
**NRC** .......... National Ramah Commission (EA)
**NRC** .......... National Reading Conference (EA)
**NRC** .......... National Realty Club [*New York, NY*] (EA)
**NRC** .......... National Realty Committee [*Washington, DC*] (EA)
**NRC** .......... National Records Center
**NRC** .......... National Recycling Coalition (EA)
**NRC** .......... National Redemption Council [*Ghana*]
**NRC** .......... National Referee Council [*Australia*]
**NRC** .......... National Referral Center [*Defunct*] (EA)
**NRC** .......... National Remodelers Council [*Later, NAHB/RC*] (EA)
**NRC** .......... National Reprographic Centre for Documentation [*British*]
**NRC** .......... National Republican Club (EA)
**NRC** .......... National Republican Convention [*Nigeria*] [*Political party*]
**NRC** .......... National Research Center (NATG)
**NRC** .......... National Research Corporation
**NRC** .......... National Research Council [*Washington, DC*] [*National Academy of Sciences*]
**NRC** .......... National Research Council, Canada [*Research center*] (IRC)
**NRC** .......... National Resistance Committee (EA)
**NRC** .......... National Resource Center for Paraprofessionals in Special Education and Related Human Services (EA)
**NRC** .......... National Resources Committee [*Functions transferred to National Resources Planning Board*]
**NRC** .......... National Response Center [*Environmental Protection Agency*]
**NRC** .......... National Retreat Centre [*British*] (CB)
**NRC** .......... National Riding Committee [*Later, ANRC*] (EA)
**NRC** .......... National Rocket Club [*Later, NSC*]
**NRC** .......... National Rural Center (EA)
**NRC** .......... Natural Resources Center [*University of Alabama*] [*Research center*] (RCD)
**NRC** .......... Natural Resources Council of America (EA)
**NRC** .......... Natural Rights Center (EA)
**NRC** .......... Naval Records Club [*Later, INRO*]
**NRC** .......... Naval Research Company - Reserves
**NRC** .......... Naval Retraining Command
**NRC** .......... Navy Reconnaissance Center (MCD)
**NRC** .......... Navy Reserve Centers (NVT)
**NRC** .......... Negative Resistance Characteristic [*Electrophysiology*]
**NRC** .......... Net Replacement Cost [*Accounting*]
**NRC** .......... Netherlands Red Cross
**NRC** .......... Network Reliability Coordinator
**NRC** .......... Neutron Radiation Capture
**NRC** .......... New Research Centers [*A publication*]
**NRC** .......... New Right Coalition (EA)
**NRC** .......... Newspaper Research Council (EA)
**NRC** .......... Nieuwe Rotterdamsche Courant [*A publication*]
**NRC** .......... Noise Reduction Coefficient [*of insulation*]
**NRC** .......... Nonrecurring Costs [*Accounting*] (KSC)
**NRC** .......... Norco Resources [*Vancouver Stock Exchange symbol*]
**NRC** .......... Normal Retinal Correspondence
**NRC** .......... North Carolina State University, Raleigh, NC [*OCLC symbol*] (OCLC)
**NRC** .......... Not Recommended for Children (ADA)
**NRC** .......... Not Routine Care [*Medicine*]
**NRC** .......... Nouvelle Revue Canadienne [*A publication*]
**NRC** .......... Nouvelle Revue Critique [*A publication*]
**NRC** .......... Nuclear Radiation Center [*Washington State University*] [*Research center*] (RCD)
**NRC** .......... Nuclear Recycling Consultants (EA)
**NRC** .......... Nuclear Regulatory Commission [*Washington, DC*]
**NRC** .......... Nuclear Research Council
**NRC** .......... Nutrition-Related Complications [*Medicine*]
**NRCA** ........ National Reamer Collectors Association (EA)
**NRCA** ........ National Rebel Class Association (EA)
**NRCA** ........ National Recovery and Collection Association (EA)

**NRCA**........ National Redbone Coonhound Association (EA)
**NRCA**........ National Rehabilitation Counseling Association (EA)
**NRCA**........ National Resources Council of America
**NRCA**........ National Retail Credit Association [*Later, ICA*]
**NRCA**........ National Roofing Contractors Association (EA)
**NRC-ACAC** ... National Research Council Army Countermine Advisory Committee
**NRCAGTM** ... National Research Council of Canada. Associate Committee on Geotechnical Research. Technical Memorandum [*A publication*]
**NRCBRN** .. National Research Council. Building Research Note [*A publication*]
**NRCBRRP** ... National Research Council of Canada. Division of Building Research. Research Paper [*A publication*]
**NRCBRTP** ... National Research Council of Canada. Division of Building Research. Technical Paper [*A publication*]
**NRCC**........ National Registry in Clinical Chemistry (EA)
**NRCC**........ National Republican Coalition for Choice (EA)
**NRCC**........ National Republican Congressional Committee (EA)
**NRCC**........ National Research Council of Canada
**NRCC**........ National Resource for Computation in Chemistry [*Lawrence Berkeley Laboratory*] [*Terminated, 1981*]
**NRCC**........ NORAD Region Combat Center [*Military*]
**NRCC Bull** ... NRCC [*National Research Council of Canada*] Bulletin [*A publication*]
**NRCCLS** ... National Resource Center for Consumers of Legal Services (EA)
**NRCCS**...... National Research Council Committee on Salmonella (EA)
**NRCCTT**... National Research Council of Canada. Technical Translation [*A publication*]
**NRCD**........ National Redemption Council Decree [*Ghana*] [*A publication*] (DLA)
**NRCd**......... National Reprographic Centre for Documentation [*Hatfield Polytechnic Institute*] [*Hertfordshire, England*] [*Evaluation and information group*] [*Information service or system*]
**NRCDA**..... North Region Cooperative Development Agency [*British*]
**NRCDBP**... National Research Council of Canada. Division of Building Research. DBR Paper [*A publication*]
**NRCD Bull** ... National Reprographic Centre for Documentation. Bulletin [*A publication*]
**NRC/DME** ... National Research Council of Canada, Division of Mechanical Engineering [*Research center*] (RCD)
**NRCE**........ National Research Council of Canada. Associate Committee on Ecological Reserves. Newsletter [*A publication*]
**NRCEBF**... National Research Council of Canada. Associate Committee on Scientific Criteria for Environmental Quality. Publication [*A publication*]
**NRCG**........ Numismatic Review and Coin Galleries [*Fixed Price List*] [*A publication*]
**NRCI**......... National Rainbow Coalition, Incorporated (EA)
**NRCI**......... National Red Cherry Institute (EA)
**NRCI**......... Nuclear Regulatory Commission Issuances [*A publication*] (DLA)
**NRCL**........ National Research Council Library (DIT)
**NRCLAZ**... NRCL. National Research Council Laboratories [*Ottawa*] [*A publication*]
**NRCL Natl Res Counc Lab (Ottawa)** ... NRCL. National Research Council Laboratories (Ottawa) [*A publication*]
**NRCLS**...... National Resource Center for Consumers of Legal Services (DLA)
**NRC-MAC** ... National Research Council - Mine Advisory Committee
**NRC/MAI** ... National Railroad Construction and Maintenance Association, Incorporated (EA)
**NRCMC**.... National Resource Center for Minority Contractors (EA)
**NRCMCA** ... National Radiator Core Manufacturing Credit Association [*Later, NRMCA*] (EA)
**NRCMET** ... National Research Council of Canada. Division of Mechanical Engineering. Transportation Newsletter [*A publication*]
**NRCN**........ NRC [*Northern Regions Centre*] Newsletter [*Hokkaido, Japan*] [*A publication*]
**NRC-NAS** ... National Research Council - National Academy of Sciences (AAG)
**NRC (Natl Res Counc Can) Bull** ... NRC (National Research Council of Canada) Bulletin [*A publication*]
**NRC (Natl Res Counc Can) Tech Transl** ... NRC (National Research Council of Canada) Technical Translation [*A publication*]
**NRCO**........ New Russian Chamber Orchestra (BJA)
**NRCP**........ Nonreinforced Concrete Pipe [*Technical drawings*]
**NRCP**........ Norcap Financial Corp. [*Scottsdale, AZ*] [*NASDAQ symbol*] (NQ)
**NRCPS**...... National Research Council on Peace Strategy (EA)
**NRCR**........ Colgate-Rochester Divinity School, Rochester, NY [*Library symbol*] [*Library of Congress*] (LCLS)
**NRC Res News** ... National Research Council. Research News [*A publication*]
**NRC Rev**.... NRC [*National Research Council of Canada*] Review [*A publication*]
**NRCS**........ Normalized RADAR Cross Section
**NRCSA**...... National Registration Center for Study Abroad (EA)
**NRCST**...... National Referral Center for Science and Technology (MCD)
**NRC-TOX** ... National Research Council - Committee on Toxicology
**NRCV**........ Consolidated Vacuum Corp., Rochester, NY [*Library symbol*] [*Library of Congress*] (LCLS)
**NRCWA**.... National Resource Center on Women and AIDS [*Acquired Immune Deficiency Syndrome*] (EA)
**NRCX**........ New Retail Concepts, Inc. [*NASDAQ symbol*] (NQ)
**NR(Cyprus)** ... Numismatic Report (Cyprus) [*A publication*]
**NRD**........... National Bank of Pakistan. Monthly Economic Letter [*A publication*]
**NRD**........... National Range Division [*Air Force*]
**NRD**........... National Range Documentation (MUGU)
**NRD**........... National Registered Designer [*British*]
**NRD**........... Natural Resources Division [*An association*] (EAIO)
**NRD**........... Naval Recruiting Department [*British military*] (DMA)
**NRD**........... Naval Research and Development (KSC)
**NRD**........... Negative Resistance Diode
**N Rd**........... Neue Rundschau [*A publication*]
**NRD**........... No Record of Destination [*Aviation*]
**NRD**........... Nonreplenishable Demand
**NRD**........... Nord Resources Corp. [*NYSE symbol*] (SPSG)
**NRD**........... Norderney [*Federal Republic of Germany*] [*Airport symbol*] (OAG)
**NRD**........... Nordlingen [*Federal Republic of Germany*] [*Seismograph station code, US Geological Survey*] [*Closed*] (SEIS)
**NR/D**......... Not Required, but Desired
**NRD**........... Nuclear Radiation Detector
**NRD**........... Nucleus Raphe Dorsalis [*Neuroanatomy*]
**NRD**........... Office of Naval Research and Development
**NRDC**........ Natick Research and Development Center [*Army*] (INF)
**NRDC**........ National Research & Development Corp. [*Later, BTG*] [*British*]
**NRDC**........ National Retail Distribution Certificate [*British*]
**NRDC**........ National Running Data Center, Inc. (EA)
**NRDC**........ Natural Resources Defense Council (EA)
**NRDC**........ Navy Relief Society, Washington, DC, Auxiliary
**NRDC**........ Navy Research and Development Committee
**NRDCA**..... National Roof Deck Contractors Association (EA)
**NRDEC**..... Natick Research Development and Engineering Center [*Army*] (INF)
**NRDF**........ Nonrecursive Digital Filter [*Navy*]
**NRDFS**...... Naval Radio Direction Finder Service
**NRDI**......... National Rural Development Institute (EA)
**NRDIP**....... Nouvelle Revue de Droit International Prive [*A publication*]
**NRDL**........ Naval Radiological Defense Laboratory
**NRDLS**...... National Rural Development Leaders School (OICC)
**NRDM**....... NRD Mining Ltd. [*NASDAQ symbol*] (NQ)
**NRDO**....... Navy Radio (NOAA)
**NRDR**........ Consolidated NRD Resources Ltd. [*NASDAQ symbol*] (NQ)
**NRDS**........ Nuclear Rocket Detection System [*NASA*]
**NRDS**........ Nuclear Rocket Development Station
**NRDU-V** ... Navy Research and Development Unit - Vietnam (MCD)
**NRE**........... Eastman Kodak Co., Rochester, NY [*Library symbol*] [*Library of Congress*] (LCLS)
**NRE**........... Eco 3. Energies, Environnement, Matieres Premieres [*A publication*]
**NRE**........... National Real Estate Investor [*A publication*]
**NRE**........... National Resource Explorations Ltd. [*Toronto Stock Exchange symbol*] [*Vancouver Stock Exchange symbol*]
**NRE**........... Naval Research Establishment
**NRE**........... Negative Regulatory Element [*Genetics*]
**NRE**........... Negative Resistance Effect
**NRE**........... New York Revised Laws [*A publication*] (DLA)
**NRE**........... Nonrecurring Engineering Expense
**NRE**........... Nonrotating Earth (NATG)
**NRE**........... Northern Reporter. Capital Communications Ltd. [*A publication*]
**NRE**........... Not Receiving Additional Irrigation [*Agriculture*]
**NRE**........... Nuclear Radiation Effect
**NRE**........... Nuclear Rocket Engine (AAG)
**NRE**........... Point Mugu, CA [*Location identifier*] [*FAA*] (FAAL)
**NRE-A**........ Eastman Kodak Co., Apparatus Division, Rochester, NY [*Library symbol*] [*Library of Congress*] (LCLS)
**NREA**........ National Rural Education Association (EA)
**NRE-B**....... Kodak (Near East) Ltd., Beirut, Lebanon [*Library symbol*] [*Library of Congress*] (LCLS)
**NREC**........ NAC Re Corp. [*NASDAQ symbol*] (NQ)
**NREC**........ National Resources Evaluation Center [*of OEP*] [*Nuclear effects*]
**NRECA**..... National Rural Electric Cooperative Association (EA)
**NREd**......... Eastman Dental Center, Basil G. Bibby Library, Rochester, NY [*Library symbol*] [*Library of Congress*] (LCLS)
**NRed**.......... Red Hook Public Library, Red Hook, NY [*Library symbol*] [*Library of Congress*] (LCLS)
**NRE-E**....... Eastman Kodak Co., Engineering Division, Rochester, NY [*Library symbol*] [*Library of Congress*] (LCLS)
**NREEC**...... Natural Resources and Environmental Education Center [*Oklahoma State University*] [*Research center*] (RCD)
**NREF**......... North Russia Expeditionary Force [*World War I*] [*Canada*]
**NREFA**...... National Real Estate Fliers Association [*Later, Real Estate Aviation Chapter*] (EA)

**NREL** ........ CSIRO [*Commonwealth Scientific and Industrial Research Organisation*] News Releases [*Australia*] [*Information service or system*] (CRD)
**NRE-L** ........ Kodak Ltd., Recordak Division, London, United Kingdom [*Library symbol*] [*Library of Congress*] (LCLS)
**NREL** ........ Nouvelle Releve [*A publication*]
**NRE-M** ...... Eastman Kodak Co., Health and Safety Laboratory, Rochester, NY [*Library symbol*] [*Library of Congress*] (LCLS)
**NREM** ....... Nonrapid Eye Movement [*Type of sleep*]
**NREMT** .... National Registry of Emergency Medical Technicians (EA)
**NREN** ........ National Education and Research Network [*Proposed*] [*Federal government*]
**NRena** ........ New Renaissance [*A publication*]
**NRenSA** ..... Saint Anthony-On-Hudson Theological Seminary, Rensselaer, NY [*Library symbol*] [*Library of Congress*] (LCLS)
**NRenSW** .... Sterling-Winthrop Research Institute, Rensselaer, NY [*Library symbol*] [*Library of Congress*] (LCLS)
**NRE-P** ....... Eastman Kodak Co., Photographic Technology Library, Rochester, NY [*Library symbol*] [*Library of Congress*] (LCLS)
**NREP** ........ Name Removed from End-Paper [*Antiquarian book trade*]
**NREP** ........ National Reliability Evaluation Program [*Nuclear Regulatory Commission*]
**NREP** ........ Neutron Resonance Escape Probability [*Nuclear energy*] (NRCH)
**NRep** .......... [*The*] New Republic [*A publication*]
**NRE-R** ....... Eastman Kodak Co., Research Laboratories, Rochester, NY [*Library symbol*] [*Library of Congress*] (LCLS)
**NRERC** ...... National Rural Education Research Consortium [*Inactive*] (EA)
**NRES** ......... Natural Resources, Energy, and Environment [*Office of Management and Budget*]
**NRES** ......... Naval Receiving Station
**NRES** ......... Nichols Research Corp. [*NASDAQ symbol*] (NQ)
**NRETN** ...... Nonreturn
**N Rev Th** .... Nouvelle Revue Theologique [*A publication*]
**NRF** ........... National Republican Foundation (EA)
**NRF** ........... National Research Fellowships [*Australia*]
**NRF** ........... National Research Foundation [*Research center*] (RCD)
**NRF** ........... National Retail Federation (EA)
**NRF** ........... National Roofing Foundation (EA)
**NRF** ........... National Rowing Foundation (EA)
**NRF** ........... National Rural Fellows (EA)
**NRF** ........... Naval Reactor Facility
**NRF** ........... Naval Repair Facility
**NRF** ........... Naval Reserve Fleet [*or Force*]
**NRF** ........... Neurite Retraction Factor [*Biochemistry*]
**NRF** ........... Newport Restoration Foundation (EA)
**NRF** ........... Nitrogen Rejection Facility [*Process engineering*]
**NRF** ........... No Redeeming Features
**NRF** ........... No Reflight
**NRF** ........... No Reinforcement [*Psychology*]
**NRF** ........... Nouvelle Revue Francaise [*French periodical; initials also used on books published by Gallimard*]
**NRF** ........... R. T. French Co., Rochester, NY [*Library symbol*] [*Library of Congress*] (LCLS)
**NRFA** ......... National Retail Florists Association [*Defunct*]
**NRFA** ......... National Retail Furniture Association [*Later, NHFA*] (EA)
**NRFB** ......... Never Removed from Box [*Doll collecting*]
**NRFBS** ...... National Research Foundation for Business Statistics (EA)
**NRFC** ......... National Railroad Freight Committee (EA)
**NRFC** ......... Navy Regional Finance Center
**NRFD** ......... Not Ready for Data
**NRFEA** ...... National Retail Farm Equipment Association [*Later, NFPEDA*]
**NRFF** ......... National Research Foundation for Fertility [*Inactive*] (EA)
**NRFH** ......... Nueva Revista de Filologia Hispanica [*A publication*]
**NRFHE8** ... Report. Sado Marine Biological Station. Niigata University [*A publication*]
**NRFI** .......... Nonrecurring Finished Intelligence (MCD)
**NRFI** .......... Not Ready for Issue
**NRFO** ......... Navy Regional Finance Office
**NRFOD** ..... Natural Resources Forum [*A publication*]
**NRFSA** ...... Navy Radio Frequency Spectrum Activity
**NRFSEA** ... National Reciprocal and Family Support Enforcement Association [*Later, NCSEA*] (EA)
**NRG** ........... Nautical Research Guild (EA)
**NRG** ........... Naval Research Group
**NRG** ........... Northern Rhodesia Gazette [*A publication*] (DLA)
**NRGA** ......... National Rice Growers Association (EA)
**NRGas** ....... Rochester Gas & Electric Corp., Technical Information Center, Rochester, NY [*Library symbol*] [*Library of Congress*] (LCLS)
**NRGC** ........ Nucleus Reticularis Gigantocellularis [*Neuroanatomy*]
**NRGD** ........ Nutri Bevco, Inc. [*Middletown, NY*] [*NASDAQ symbol*] (NQ)
**NRGD-SC** ... Stromberg-Carlson Corp., Rochester, NY [*Library symbol*] [*Library of Congress*] (LCLS)
**NRGE** ......... George Eastman House, Rochester, NY [*Library symbol*] [*Library of Congress*] (LCLS)
**NRGID** ...... Energia [*A publication*]
**NRGN** ........ Neurogen Corp. [*NASDAQ symbol*] (NQ)
**NRGR** ........ General Railway Signal Co., Rochester, NY [*Library symbol*] [*Library of Congress*] (LCLS)
**NRGS** ........ Church of Jesus Christ of Latter-Day Saints, Genealogical Society Library, Rochester Branch, Rochester, NY [*Library symbol*] [*Library of Congress*] (LCLS)
**NRGSD** ..... Energiespectrum [*A publication*]
**NRGXD** ..... Energoexport [*A publication*]
**NRH** .......... Natural Rate Hypothesis [*Economics*]
**NRH** .......... Nodular Regenerative Hyperplasia [*of liver*] [*Medicine*]
**NRH** .......... Nonready Hours
**NRH** .......... Nouvelle Revue de Hongrie [*A publication*]
**NRH** .......... Tweewieler [*A publication*]
**NRHA** ....... National Radio Heritage Association (EA)
**NRHA** ....... National Reining Horse Association (EA)
**NRHA** ....... National Retail Hardware Association (EA)
**NRHA** ....... National Rural Health Association (EA)
**NRhbA** ....... Astor Home for Children, Rhinebeck, NY [*Library symbol*] [*Library of Congress*] (LCLS)
**NRHC** ........ National Rental Housing Council [*Later, NMHC*] (EA)
**NRHC** ........ National Rivers and Harbors Congress [*Later, WRC*]
**NR & HC** ... National Rivers and Harbors Congress [*Later, WRC*]
**NRHC** ........ National Rural Housing Coalition (EA)
**NRHCA** ..... National Rural Health Care Association [*Formerly, NRPCA*] (EA)
**NRHD** ....... Nouvelle Revue Historique de Droit Francais et Etranger [*A publication*]
**NRHDFE** .. Nouvelle Revue Historique de Droit Francais et Etranger [*A publication*]
**NRhDH** ..... Long Island Doctors' Hospital, Roslyn Heights, NY [*Library symbol*] [*Library of Congress*] (LCLS)
**NRHE** ........ Nonregenerative Heat Exchanger [*Nuclear energy*] (NRCH)
**NRHGC** ..... National Republican Heritage Groups (Nationalities) Council (EA)
**NRHi** ......... Rochester Historical Society, Rochester, NY [*Library symbol*] [*Library of Congress*] (LCLS)
**NRHS** ........ National Railway Historical Society (EA)
**NRHX** ........ Nonregenerative Heat Exchanger [*Nuclear energy*] (NRCH)
**NRI** ............ National Radio Institute
**NRI** ............ National Resource Inventory [*US database on erosion*]
**NRI** ............ Net Radio Interface [*Telecommunications*] (TEL)
**NRI** ............ Neuromuscular Research Institute [*Australia*]
**NRI** ............ Neutral Regular Insulin
**NRI** ............ New Records, Incorporated [*Record label*]
**NRI** ............ New Ring Index [*of chemical compounds*] [*A publication*]
**NRI** ............ Nomura Research Institute [*Database producer*] [*Tokyo, Japan*]
**NRI** ............ Nonrecurring Installation Charge [*Telecommunications*] (TEL)
**NRI** ............ Nonrecurring Investment (NASA)
**NRI** ............ Nonresident Instruction (MCD)
**NRI** ............ Noril'sk [*USSR*] [*Seismograph station code, US Geological Survey*] (SEIS)
**NRI** ............ Novagold Resources, Inc. [*Toronto Stock Exchange symbol*]
**NRIA** ......... National Railroad Intermodal Association [*Palos Park, IL*] (EA)
**NRIAD** ...... National Register of Industrial Art Designers [*British*] (DAS)
**NRIC** ......... National Rehabilitation Information Center [*Catholic University of America*] [*Bibliographic Database*] [*Washington, DC*]
**NRIC** ......... Nuclear Research Information Center [*American Nuclear Center*] [*Information service or system*] (IID)
**N Riding Sch Libr Guild Bull** ... North Riding School Library. Guild Bulletin [*A publication*]
**NRIIA** ........ National Republican Institute for International Affairs (EA)
**NRIM** ........ Narrow Resonance Infinite Mass [*Nuclear energy*] (NRCH)
**NRIMS** ...... National Research Institute for Mathematical Sciences [*South Africa*]
**NRINA** ...... Nippon Rinsho [*A publication*]
**NRIP** .......... Number of Rejected Initial Pickups
**NRIPMVLIC** ... Nonresident Interprovince Motor Vehicle Liability Insurance Card [*For travel in Canada*]
**NRIS** .......... Natural Resource Information System [*Department of the Interior*]
**NRIS** .......... New Mexico Natural Resources Information System [*New Mexico State Department of Natural Resources*] [*Santa Fe*] (IID)
**N Ri St** ....... Nuova Rivista Storica [*A publication*]
**N Riv Dir Comm** ... Nuova Rivista di Diritto Commerciale, Diritto dell'Economia, Diritto Sociale [*A publication*]
**N Riv St** ..... Nuova Rivista Storica [*A publication*]
**NRJ** ............ Natural Resources Journal [*A publication*]
**NRK** ........... Normal Rat Kidney
**NRK** ........... Normotensive Rat Kidney
**NRK** ........... Norrkoping [*Sweden*] [*Airport symbol*] (OAG)
**NRK** ........... Norsk Rikskringkasting [*Norwegian Broadcasting Corporation*]
**NRK** ........... Nurek [*USSR*] [*Seismograph station code, US Geological Survey*] [*Closed*] (SEIS)
**NRKF** ........ Normal Rat Kidney Fibroblast [*Cytology*]
**NRkpJH** .... Rocky Point Junior-Senior High School, Rocky Point, NY [*Library symbol*] [*Library of Congress*] (LCLS)

**NRL**.......... Naneco Resources Limited [*Vancouver Stock Exchange symbol*]
**NRL**.......... National Registry for Librarians (EA)
**NRL**.......... National Research Laboratory
**NRL**.......... National Research Library [*Canada*] (DIT)
**NRL**.......... National Resources Library
**NRL**.......... Naval Research Laboratory [*Washington, DC*] [*Seismograph station code, US Geological Survey*] [*Closed*] (SEIS)
**NRL**.......... Naval Research Laboratory [*Washington, DC*] [*Office of Naval Research*] (GRD)
**NRL**.......... Naval Research Laboratory, Washington, DC [*OCLC symbol*] (OCLC)
**NRL**.......... Network Restructuring Language
**NRL**.......... New York Revised Laws [*A publication*] (DLA)
**NRL**.......... Night Ration Locker (MSA)
**NRL**.......... Normal Rated Load
**NRL**.......... Normal Response Level
**NRL**.......... North Ronaldsay [*Scotland*] [*Airport symbol*] (OAG)
**NRL**.......... Nouvelles de la Republique des Lettres [*A publication*]
**NRL**.......... Nuclear Reactor Laboratory [*Massachusetts Institute of Technology*] [*Research center*] (RCD)
**NRLA**........ Network Repair Level Analysis
**NRLA**........ Northeastern Retail Lumbermen's Association (EA)
**NRLC**........ National Railway Labor Conference (EA)
**NRLC**........ National Right to Life Committee (EA)
**NRLCA**...... National Rural Letter Carriers' Association (EA)
**NRLDA**..... National Retail Lumber Dealers Association [*Later, NLBMDA*]
**NRLETF**... National Right to Life Educational Trust Fund (EA)
**NRLF**........ Lincoln First Bank of Rochester, Rochester, NY [*Library symbol*] [*Library of Congress*] (LCLS)
**NRLN**........ Northern Regional Legal Notice [*1954-61*] [*Nigeria*] [*A publication*] (DLA)
**NRLP**........ National Railway Labor Panel [*World War II*]
**NRLQ**........ Naval Research Logistics. Quarterly [*A publication*]
**NRLR**........ Northern Rhodesia Law Reports [*A publication*] (DLA)
**NRLSI**....... National Reference Library of Science and Invention [*of the British Museum*]
**NRL/SVIC**... Naval Research Laboratory Shock and Vibration Information Center [*ONR*]
**NRM**.......... Nara [*Mali*] [*Airport symbol*] (OAG)
**NRM**.......... National Resistance Movement [*Uganda*] (PD)
**NRM**.......... National Revolutionary Movement [*France*]
**NRM**.......... Natural Remanent Magnetism [*or Magnetization*]
**NRM**.......... Natural Resource Management
**NRM**.......... Naval Reserve Medal
**NRM**.......... Nonrecurring Maintenance [*NASA*] (KSC)
**NRM**.......... Norm-Referenced Measurement [*Education*]
**NRM**.......... Normal Response Mode
**NRM**.......... Normalize (DEN)
**NRM**.......... North Rainier Mesa [*Nevada*] [*Seismograph station code, US Geological Survey*] (SEIS)
**NRM**.......... Northair Mines Ltd. [*Toronto Stock Exchange symbol*] [*Vancouver Stock Exchange symbol*]
**NRM**.......... Northern Rocky Mountains
**NRM**.......... NRM Energy Co. Ltd. [*AMEX symbol*] (SPSG)
**NRM**.......... Nuova Rivista Musicale Italiana [*A publication*]
**NRM**.......... Rochester Museum and Science Center, Rochester, NY [*Library symbol*] [*Library of Congress*] (LCLS)
**NRMA**....... National Reloading Manufacturers Association (EA)
**NRMA**....... National Retail Merchants Association [*New York, NY*] (EA)
**NRMA**....... Northern Rivers Mathematical Association [*Australia*]
**NRMA**....... Nuclear Records Management Association (EA)
**NRMADI**.. Non Recedet Malum a Domo Ingrati [*Evil Shall Not Depart from the House of the Ungrateful*] [*Latin*] [*(After Prov., XVII. 13) Motto of Julius, Duke of Braunschweig-Wolfenbuttel (1529-89)*]
**NRMC**....... Monroe Community College, Rochester, NY [*Library symbol*] [*Library of Congress*] (LCLS)
**NRMC**....... National Records Management Council (EA)
**NRMC**....... Naval Records Management Center
**NRMC**....... Naval Regional Medical Center (NVT)
**NRMC**....... Naval Reserve Manpower Center
**NRMCA**.... National Radiator Manufacturing Credit Association (EA)
**NRMCA**.... National Ready Mixed Concrete Association (EA)
**NRMCEN**... Naval Records Management Center
**NRME**....... Notched, Returned, and Mitred Ends [*Construction*]
**NRMEC**.... North American Rockwell Microelectronics Company [*Obsolete*]
**NRMF**....... New Road Map Foundation (EA)
**NRMI**....... Nuova Rivista Musicale Italiana [*A publication*]
**NRML**....... Monroe County Library System, Rochester, NY [*Library symbol*] [*Library of Congress*] (LCLS)
**NRMM**...... National Register of Microform Masters [*Library of Congress*]
**NRMM**...... NATO Reference Mobility Model
**NRMP**...... National Resident Matching Program (EA)
**NRMS**....... National Registry of Medical Secretaries (EA)
**NRMS**....... Natural Resource Management System [*Army Corps of Engineers*] [*Database*]
**NRMS**....... Naval Reserve Midshipmen's School
**NRMS**....... Neutralization-Reionization Mass Spectrometry
**NRMS**....... Norman Rockwell Memorial Society (EA)
**NRMS**....... Nottingham Renaissance and Modern Studies [*A publication*]
**NRMT**....... Northern Rocky Mountain Trench [*Geology*]
**NRMTC**.... Nordoff-Robbins Music Therapy Centre Ltd. [*British*] (CB)
**NRMTDA**... Nouvelle Revue de Medecine de Toulouse [*A publication*]
**NRMU**....... Northern Rhodesia European Mineworkers' Union
**NRMW**...... Margaret Woodbury Strong Museum, Rochester, NY [*Library symbol*] [*Library of Congress*] (LCLS)
**NRN**.......... Naryn [*USSR*] [*Seismograph station code, US Geological Survey*] (SEIS)
**NRN**.......... National Resource Network [*Commercial firm*] (EA)
**NRN**.......... Natural Radioactive Nuclides
**NRN**.......... Northern
**nRNA**........ Ribonucleic Acid, Nuclear [*Biochemistry, genetics*]
**NRNC**........ Nazareth College of Rochester, Rochester, NY [*Library symbol*] [*Library of Congress*] (LCLS)
**NRNFC**..... National Rick Nelson Fan Club (EA)
**NRNLR**..... Northern Region of Nigeria Law Reports [*A publication*] (DLA)
**NRNR**........ National Rotorcraft Noise Reduction [*Program to reduce noise of helicopters*]
**NRO**.......... National Range Operations (RDA)
**NRO**.......... National Reconnaissance Office [*Air Force/CIA*]
**NRO**.......... Naval Research Objectives
**NRO**.......... Navy Retail Office (AFIT)
**NRO**.......... Negative Resistance Oscillator [*Electronics*]
**NRO**.......... Nobeyama Radio Observatory
**NRO**.......... Nonresident-Owned Funds [*Investment term*]
**NROC**........ National Royalty Corporation [*NASDAQ symbol*] (NQ)
**NRock**........ Rockville Centre Public Library, Rockville Centre, NY [*Library symbol*] [*Library of Congress*] (LCLS)
**NRockH**...... Mercy Hospital, Rockville Centre, NY [*Library symbol*] [*Library of Congress*] (LCLS)
**NRockHE**... Hewett Elementary School, Rockville Centre, NY [*Library symbol*] [*Library of Congress*] (LCLS)
**NRockL**...... Lakeview Public Library, Rockville Centre, NY [*Library symbol*] [*Library of Congress*] (LCLS)
**NRockM**.... Molloy College, Rockville Centre, NY [*Library symbol*] [*Library of Congress*] (LCLS)
**NRockWE**... Wilson Elementary School, Rockville Centre, NY [*Library symbol*] [*Library of Congress*] (LCLS)
**NROE**........ Naval Reactor Organic Experiment
**NRom**........ Jervis Library Association, Rome, NY [*Library symbol*] [*Library of Congress*] (LCLS)
**NROM**....... Noble Roman's, Inc. [*NASDAQ symbol*] (NQ)
**NRomA**...... Rome Air Development Center, Rome, NY [*Library symbol*] [*Library of Congress*] (LCLS)
**NRomAF**... United States Air Force, Base Library, Griffiss Air Force Base, Rome, NY [*Library symbol*] [*Library of Congress*] (LCLS)
**NRomAF-R**... United States Air Force, Rome Air Development Center, Griffiss, NY [*Library symbol*] [*Library of Congress*] (LCLS)
**NROO**....... Naval Reactors Operations Office
**NRoos**........ Roosevelt Community Library, Roosevelt, NY [*Library symbol*] [*Library of Congress*] (LCLS)
**NROPS**..... New Riders of the Purple Sage [*Rock music group*]
**NROS**........ Naval Reserve Officer School
**NRosl**......... Bryant Library, Roslyn, NY [*Library symbol*] [*Library of Congress*] (LCLS)
**NRoslH**...... Saint Francis Hospital, Roslyn, NY [*Library symbol*] [*Library of Congress*] (LCLS)
**NRoslHS**... Roslyn High School, Roslyn, NY [*Library symbol*] [*Library of Congress*] (LCLS)
**NRoslhWI**... Willets Road Intermediate School, Roslyn Heights, NY [*Library symbol*] [*Library of Congress*] (LCLS)
**NRoslJH**... Roslyn Junior High School, Roslyn, NY [*Library symbol*] [*Library of Congress*] (LCLS)
**NROSS**...... Navy Remote Ocean Sensing System [*Proposed*]
**NROTC**..... Naval Reserve Officers' Training Corps
**NRP**.......... National Religious Party [*Hamiflaga Hadatit Leumit*] [*Israel*] [*Political party*] (PPW)
**NRP**.......... National Resistance Party [*Political party*] (BJA)
**NRP**.......... National Review Panel [*Work Incentive Program*] [*Department of Labor*]
**N/RP**......... Neoclassical/Rational Planning
**NRP**.......... Neurosciences Research Program [*Massachusetts Institute of Technology*]
**NRP**.......... Nevis Reformation Party [*Political party*]
**NRP**.......... New Republic Party [*South Africa*] [*Political party*] (PPW)
**NRP**.......... New Rhodesia Party [*Political party*]
**NRP**.......... Nonregistered Publication
**NRP**.......... Nonreportable Property [*Military*]
**NRP**.......... Nonstationary Random Process
**NRP**.......... Normal Rated Power
**NRP**.......... Notice of Research Project
**NRP**.......... Nouvelle Revue Pedagogique [*A publication*]
**NRP**.......... Nuclear Reform Project (EA)
**NRP**.......... Nueva Revista del Pacifico [*A publication*]
**NRP**.......... Nuwe Republiekparty [*New Republic Party*] [*Political party*] [*Afrikaans*]
**NRP**.......... People's Republican Party [*Turkey*] [*Political party*]

**NRP** .......... Pfaudler Technical Library, Rochester, NY [*Library symbol*] [*Library of Congress*] (LCLS)
**NRpA** .......... Ayerst Science Laboratory, Rouses Point, NY [*Library symbol*] [*Library of Congress*] (LCLS)
**NRPA** .......... National Recreation and Park Association (EA)
**NRPAC** .......... Naval Reserve Public Affairs Company
**NRPAIN** .......... National Register of Prominent Americans and International Notables (EA)
**NRPB** .......... National Radiological Protection Board [*British*]
**NRPB** .......... National Research Planning Board
**NRPB** .......... National Resources Planning Board [*Abolished, 1943*]
**NRPB** .......... Nickerson RPB Ltd. [*British*] (IRUK)
**NRPBA** .......... Neurosciences Research. Program Bulletin [*A publication*]
**NRPC** .......... National Railroad Passenger Corporation [*Government rail transportation*]
**NRPC** .......... National Register Publishing Company [*Information service or system*] (IID)
**NRPCA** .......... National Rural Primary Care Association [*Later, NRHCA*] (EA)
**NRPF** .......... National Railroad Pension Forum [*Defunct*] (EA)
**NRPF** .......... National Retinitis Pigmentosa Foundation [*Later, RPFFB*] (EA)
**NRPH** .......... Park Ridge Hospital, Medical Library, Rochester, NY [*Library symbol*] [*Library of Congress*] (LCLS)
**NRPIO** .......... Naval Registered Publications Issuing Office
**NRPJ** .......... Nezavisna Radnicka Partija Jugoslavije [*Independent Labor Party of Yugoslavia*] [*Political party*]
**NRPlanP** .......... Planned Parenthood of Rochester and Monroe County, Rochester, NY [*Library symbol*] [*Library of Congress*] (LCLS)
**NRPM** .......... Nonregistered Publications Memoranda
**NRPO** .......... Naval Regional Procurement Office
**NRPP** .......... Pennwalt Corp., Pharmaceutical Division Research Library, Rochester, NY [*Library symbol*] [*Library of Congress*] (LCLS)
**NRPS** .......... New Riders of the Purple Sage [*Rock music group*]
**NRPSA** .......... National Retail Pet Supply Association [*Defunct*] (EA)
**NRPSGA** .......... National Retail Pet Store and Groomers Association (EA)
**NRR** .......... National Records Return [*Australia*]
**NRR** .......... Naval Research Reactor
**NRR** .......... Naval Research Requirement
**NRR** .......... Naval Reserve Requirement (MCD)
**NRR** .......... Net Reproductive Rate
**NRR** .......... Net Retail Requirements
**NRR** .......... No Resume Required
**NRR** .......... North Reno [*Nevada*] [*Seismograph station code, US Geological Survey*] (SEIS)
**NRR** .......... Northern Rhodesia Regiment
**NRR** .......... Nuclear Rocket Reactor
**NRR** .......... Office of Nuclear Reactor Regulation [*Nuclear Regulatory Commission*]
**NRR** .......... Roosevelt Roads, PR [*Location identifier*] [*FAA*] (FAAL)
**NRRA** .......... National Resource Recovery Association (EA)
**NRRA** .......... National Risk Retention Association (EA)
**NRRAS** .......... Navy Readiness Reporting and Analysis System (MCD)
**NRRBA** .......... Bulletin. Radio and Electrical Engineering Division. National Research Council of Canada [*A publication*]
**NRRC** .......... National Rex Rabbit Club (EA)
**NRRC** .......... Naval Research Reserve Company
**NRRC** .......... Northern Regional Research Center [*Formerly, NRRL*] [*Peoria, IL*] [*Department of Agriculture*]
**NRR & C** .......... Russell and Chesley's Nova Scotia Reports [*A publication*] (DLA)
**NRRD** .......... Norstan, Inc. [*NASDAQ symbol*] (NQ)
**NRRE** .......... Netherlands RADAR Research Establishment
**NRRFSS** .......... National Research and Resource Facility for Submicron Structures [*Cornell University*] [*Research center*] (RCD)
**NRRI** .......... National Regulatory Research Institute [*Ohio State University*] [*Research center*] (RCD)
**NRRI** .......... Natural Resources Research Institute [*Research center*] (RCD)
**NRRI** .......... Rochester Institute of Technology, Rochester, NY [*Library symbol*] [*Library of Congress*] (LCLS)
**NRRI-C** .......... Rochester Institute of Technology, Melbert B. Cary, Jr. Graphic Arts Collection, Rochester, NY [*Library symbol*] [*Library of Congress*] (LCLS)
**NRRL** .......... Northern Regional Research Laboratory [*Later, NRRC*] [*Department of Agriculture*]
**NRRO** .......... Nuclear Radiation-Resistant Oils (NRCH)
**NRRP** .......... National Reservoir Research Program [*Department of the Interior*] (GRD)
**NRRP** .......... Sybron Corp., Rochester, NY [*Library symbol*] [*Library of Congress*] (LCLS)
**NRRR** .......... Rochester Reference Research and Resources Council, Rochester, NY [*Library symbol*] [*Library of Congress*] (LCLS)
**NRRS** .......... Naval Radio Research Station
**NRRS** .......... No Remaining Radiation Service [*Unit*] [*Military*]
**NRRTUC** .......... Northern Rhodesian Reformed Trades Union Congress
**NRS** .......... Imperial Beach, CA [*Location identifier*] [*FAA*] (FAAL)
**NRS** .......... National Readership Survey [*British*]
**NRS** .......... National Real Estate Service [*Canada*]
**NRS** .......... National Reemployment Service
**NRS** .......... National Referral System [*British*] (DCTA)
**NRS** .......... National Reporter System [*Database*] [*Maritime Law Book Co. Ltd.*] [*Information service or system*] (CRD)
**NRS** .......... National Runaway Switchboard (EA)
**NRS** .......... Nationwide Refrigeration Supplies [*British*]
**NRS** .......... Naucnye Raboty is Oobscenija Akademii Nauk Uzbekskoj SSR, Otdelenie Obscestvennych Nauk [*A publication*]
**NRS** .......... Naval Radio Station
**NRS** .......... Naval Receiving Station
**NRS** .......... Naval Recruiting Service [*British military*] (DMA)
**NRS** .......... Naval Recruiting Station
**NRS** .......... Naval Research Section [*Library of Congress*] (MCD)
**NRS** .......... Navy Relief Society (EA)
**NRs** .......... Neue Rundschau [*A publication*]
**NRS** .......... Nevada Revised Statutes [*A publication*]
**NRS** .......... New Rural Society [*HUD project*]
**NRS** .......... Newborn Rights Society (EA)
**NRS** .......... Night Reconnaissance System
**NRS** .......... Nitrogen Recharge Station
**NRS** .......... Nonconformance Reporting System (NASA)
**NRS** .......... Normal Rabbit Serum [*Culture medium*]
**NRS** .......... Normal Rat Serum [*Hematology*]
**NRS** .......... North-Holland Research Series in Early Detection and Prevention of Behaviour Disorders [*Elsevier Book Series*] [*A publication*]
**NRS** .......... Nuclear Radiation Shield
**NRS** .......... Nuclear Rocket Shuttle (KSC)
**NRS** .......... Numerical Rating System [*Insurance*]
**NRS** .......... Nuova Rivista Storica [*A publication*]
**NRSA** .......... National Rental Service Association (EA)
**NRSA** .......... National Research Service Awards [*Department of Health and Human Services*]
**NRSA** .......... Natural Rubber Shippers Association (EA)
**NRSA** .......... Northeast Rail Service Act [*1981*] [*Also, NERSA*]
**NRSB** .......... Saint Bernard's Seminary and College, Rochester, NY [*Library symbol*] [*Library of Congress*] (LCLS)
**NRSC** .......... National Radio Systems Committee
**NRSC** .......... National Remote Sensing Centre [*Royal Aircraft Establishment Space Department*] [*British*] (CB)
**NRSC** .......... National Republican Senatorial Committee (EA)
**NRSC** .......... Nordic Road Safety Council [*See also NTR*] [*Helsinki, Finland*] (EAIO)
**NRSCC** .......... National Registry System for Chemical Compounds (DIT)
**NRSCO** .......... Navy Recruiting Station Commanding Officer
**NRSDA** .......... Science Dimension [*A publication*]
**NRSe** .......... Sear-Brown Associates, PC, Rochester, NY [*Library symbol*] [*Library of Congress*] (LCLS)
**NRSF** .......... National Rehabilitation and Service Foundation (EA)
**NRSF** .......... National Reye's Syndrome Foundation (EA)
**NRSFPS** .......... National Reporting System for Family Planning Services [*National Institutes of Health*]
**NRSG** .......... Nursing
**NRSHB2** .......... Annual Report. Hokkaido Branch. Government Forest Experiment Station [*A publication*]
**NRSJ** .......... Saint John Fisher College, Rochester, NY [*Library symbol*] [*Library of Congress*] (LCLS)
**NRSM** .......... Nouvelle Revue de Science Missionaire [*A publication*]
**NRSO** .......... Navy Resale Systems Office
**nrsry** .......... Nursery
**NRSSC** .......... National Rural and Small Schools Consortium (EA)
**NRSSG** .......... Nuclear Reactor Systems Safety Group [*Air Force*]
**NRSSGP** .......... Nuclear Reactor Systems Safety Group [*Air Force*]
**NRSV** .......... Necrotic Ringspot Virus [*of prunes*]
**NRSW** .......... Nuclear River Service Water (IEEE)
**NRSY** .......... Nordiska Forbundet for Studie- och Yrkesvagledning [*Nordic Association for Study and Vocational Guidance - NASVG*] (EAIO)
**NRSZD** .......... Nippon Rinsho Saibo Gakkai Zasshi [*A publication*]
**NRT** .......... Burroughs Wellcome & Co., Research Triangle Park, NC [*OCLC symbol*] (OCLC)
**nrt** .......... Narrator [*MARC relator code*] [*Library of Congress*] (LCCP)
**NRT** .......... National Repertory Theatre Foundation [*Defunct*] (EA)
**NRT** .......... National Response Team for Oil and Hazardous Materials Spills [*Environmental Protection Agency*] [*Washington, DC*] (EGAO)
**NRT** .......... Navy Reserve Training
**NRT** .......... Near-Real Time
**NRT** .......... Neighbours of the Roundtable (EA)
**NRT** .......... Net Register Tons [*Shipping*]
**NRT** .......... Nettoregistertonne [*Net Register Tonnage*] [*German*]
**NRT** .......... Network Readiness Test (KSC)
**NRT** .......... Nonradiating Target
**NRT** .......... Nonreal Time
**NRT** .......... Norm-Referenced Testing [*Education*]
**NRT** .......... Normal Rated Thrust (AAG)
**NRT** .......... Northern Airlines, Inc. [*St. Paul, MN*] [*FAA designator*] (FAAC)
**NRT** .......... Northfield [*Vermont*] [*Seismograph station code, US Geological Survey*] [*Closed*] (SEIS)
**NRT** .......... Norton Co. [*NYSE symbol*] (SPSG)

**NRT** .......... Notion Round Table (EA)
**NRT** .......... Nouvelle Revue Theologique [*A publication*]
**NRT** .......... Nucleus Reticularis Thalami [*Neuroanatomy*]
**NRT** .......... Taylor Instrument Cos., Rochester, NY [*Library symbol*] [*Library of Congress*] (LCLS)
**NRT** .......... Tokyo-Narita [*Japan*] [*Airport symbol*] (OAG)
**NRTA** ........ National Retired Teachers Association, Division of AARP (EA)
**NRTB** ........ Naval Reserve Training Branch
**NRTC** ........ National Retail Trade Centre (EAIO)
**NRTC** ........ Naval Reserve Training Center
**NRTC** ........ Nonreal-Time Conversion Subsystem [*Space Flight Operations Facility, NASA*]
**NRT & CMA** ... National Retail Tea and Coffee Merchants Association
**NRTCOMD** ... Naval Reserve Training Command
**NRTEC**...... National Rural Teacher Education Consortium [*National Rural Development Institute*] [*Later, NRSSC*] (EA)
**N R Technol** ... Natural Rubber Technology [*A publication*]
**NRTh**......... Nouvelle Revue Theologique [*A publication*]
**NRTHUM** ... Northumberland [*County in England*] (ROG)
**NRTI** ......... National Rehabilitation Training Institute [*Defunct*] (EA)
**NRTI** ......... Nooney Realty Trust, Incorporated [*St. Louis, MO*] [*NASDAQ symbol*] (NQ)
**NRTIPT** .... Naval Reserve Training in Port (NVT)
**NRTL** ........ Non-Random Two-Liquid [*Equation of state*]
**NRTN**........ Norton Enterprises, Inc. [*NASDAQ symbol*] (NQ)
**NRTO**........ National Remotivation Therapy Organization (EA)
**NRTOI** ...... National Range Technical Operating Instructions [*NASA*] (KSC)
**NRTP** ........ Nouvelle Revue des Traditions Populaires [*A publication*]
**NRTP** ........ Nucleus Reticularis Tegmenti Pontis [*Neuroanatomy*]
**NRTR** ........ Near-Real-Time Reconnaissance (MCD)
**NRTS**......... National Reactor Test Station [*INEL*] (NRCH)
**NRTS**......... Not Repairable This Ship [*Navy*] (AFIT)
**NRTS**......... Not Reparable This Station
**NRTSC**...... Naval Reconnaissance and Technical Support Center
**NRTWLDEF** ... National Right to Work Legal Defense and Education Foundation [*Also, NRWLDF*] (EA)
**NRU**........... National Reactor Universal
**NRU**........... National Research Universal [*Nuclear reactor*] [*Canada*]
**NRU**........... Natural Resource Unit [*Environmental unit*]
**NRU**........... Nauru [*ANSI three-letter standard code*] (CNC)
**NRu**........... Neue Rundschau [*A publication*]
**NRU**........... Neuropsychiatric Research Unit [*Navy*]
**N Ru**.......... Nicolaus Rufulus [*Flourished, 13th century*] [*Authority cited in pre-1607 legal work*] (DSA)
**NRU**........... Nitrogen Rejection Unit [*Process engineering*]
**NRU**........... Not Recently Used [*Replacement algorithm*] [*Data processing*] (BYTE)
**NRU**........... University of Rochester, Rochester, NY [*Library symbol*] [*Library of Congress*] (LCLS)
**NRU-A** ...... University of Rochester, Memorial Art Gallery, Rochester, NY [*Library symbol*] [*Library of Congress*] (LCLS)
**NRUCFC**... National Rural Utilities Cooperative Finance Corporation (EA)
**NRU-M** ..... University of Rochester, School of Medicine and Dentistry, Rochester, NY [*Library symbol*] [*Library of Congress*] (LCLS)
**NRU-Mus** ... University of Rochester, Eastman School of Music, Rochester, NY [*Library symbol*] [*Library of Congress*] (LCLS)
**N Rund**....... Neue Rundschau [*A publication*]
**NRUSDD**.. US National Park Service. Natural Resources Report [*A publication*]
**NRUTUC**.. Northern Rhodesia United Trades Union Congress
**NRU-W** ..... University of Rochester, Women's College, Rochester, NY [*Library symbol*] [*Library of Congress*] (LCLS)
**NRV**........... Navarre Resources [*Vancouver Stock Exchange symbol*]
**NRV**........... Net Realizable Value
**NRV**........... Neubabylonische Rechts- und Verwaltungsurkunden [*A publication*] (BJA)
**NRV**........... Nonrevenue [*Passengers or cargo*] [*Transportation*]
**NRV**........... North Carolina State University, School of Veterinary Medicine, Raleigh, NC [*OCLC symbol*] (OCLC)
**NRV**........... Northamptonshire Rifle Volunteer Corps [*British military*] (DMA)
**NRVA**........ Net Realizable Value Accounting (ADA)
**NRVC**........ National Religious Vocation Conference (EA)
**NRvCH**....... Central Suffolk Hospital, Riverhead, NY [*Library symbol*] [*Library of Congress*] (LCLS)
**NRVN**........ Northern Raven. New Series [*A publication*]
**NRVOC**..... National RV [*Recreational Vehicle*] Owners Club (EA)
**NRvS** ......... Suffolk County Historical Society, Riverhead, NY [*Library symbol*] [*Library of Congress*] (LCLS)
**NRVSBL** ... Nonreversible
**NRvSL**....... Supreme Court Law Library, Tenth Judical District, Riverhead, NY [*Library symbol*] [*Library of Congress*] (LCLS)
**NRVU**........ Nuova Rivista di Varia Umanita [*A publication*]
**NRW**.......... Narrow (FAAC)
**NRW**.......... New Right Watch [*An association*] (EA)
**NRW**.......... Nonradioactive Waste [*Nuclear energy*] (NRCH)
**NRW**.......... Nuclear RADWASTE (IEEE)
**NR/WA**..... National Rep/Wholesaler Association (EA)
**NRWA**...... National Rural Water Association (EA)
**NRWC**....... National Right to Work Committee (EA)
**NRWG**....... Neutron Radiography Working Group [*EURATOM*]
**NRW-KA**... National Registry of Willys-Knight Automobiles [*Later, W-O-KR*]
**NRWLDEF** ... National Right to Work Legal Defense and Education Foundation [*Later, NRWLDF*] (EA)
**NRWLDF** ... National Right to Work Legal Defense Foundation (EA)
**NRWV**....... Nonradioactive Waste Vent [*Nuclear energy*] (NRCH)
**NRX**........... National Research Experiment [*Canadian reactor*]
**NRX**........... NERVA [*Nuclear Engine for Rocket Vehicle Application*] Reactor Experiment
**NRX**........... Nuclear Engine Reactor Experiment (NRCH)
**NRX**........... Nuclear Reactor, Experimental
**NRX**........... Xerox Corp., Rochester, NY [*Library symbol*] [*Library of Congress*] (LCLS)
**NRX(C)**...... Nonreturn-to-Zero (Change) Recording
**NRy**............ Rye Free Reading Room, Rye, NY [*Library symbol*] [*Library of Congress*] (LCLS)
**NRyHi** ....... Rye Historical Society, Rye, NY [*Library symbol*] [*Library of Congress*] (LCLS)
**NRyS** ......... Sloan-Kettering Institute for Cancer Research, Rye, NY [*Library symbol*] [*Library of Congress*] (LCLS)
**NRZ**........... Neue Ruhr Zeitung [*A publication*]
**NRZ**........... Nonreturn to Zero [*Data transmission*]
**NRZ**........... Null Reception Zone
**NRZ1**......... Nonreturn to Zero Change on One (BUR)
**NRZC** ........ Nonreturn to Zero Change
**NRZI** ......... Nonreturn to Zero Inverted [*Recording method*]
**NRZL** ........ Nonreturn to Zero Level
**NRZM**....... Nonreturn to Zero Mark
**NRZ-S** ....... Non-Return to Zero-Space (MCD)
**NS**.............. Although a Current Publication Presently in Use, the Item Requested Is Not Stocked [*Supply action error code*] [*Army*]
**NS**.............. Graduate of the Royal Naval Staff College, Greenwich [*British*]
**ns**............... Nanosecond [*100 billionth of a second*] [*Also, nsec*]
**NS**.............. Naram-Sin (BJA)
**NS**.............. Narodnye Sotsialisty [*Popular Socialists*] [*Russian*] [*Political party*] (PPE)
**N-S**............ Nassi-Schneiderman [*Data processing*]
**NS**.............. National Savings [*British*]
**NS**.............. National Scientific [*Vancouver Stock Exchange symbol*]
**NS**.............. National Service [*in the armed forces*] [*British*]
**NS**.............. National Society
**NS**.............. National Sojourners (EA)
**NS**.............. National Special [*Thread*]
**NS**.............. National Standard (IEEE)
**NS**.............. Natjonal Samling [*National Union*] [*Norway*] (PD)
**NS**.............. NATO Secret (NATG)
**NS**.............. NATO Surveillance (NATG)
**NS**.............. Natural Sciences
**NS**.............. [*The*] Naturist Society (EA)
**NS**.............. Naval School (MCD)
**NS**.............. Naval Shipyard
**NS**.............. Naval Station
**NS**.............. Naval Stores [*British*]
**NS**.............. NAVSHIPS [*Naval Ship Systems Command*] Publication
**NS**.............. Near Side [*Technical drawings*]
**NS**.............. Near Space
**NS**.............. Nederlandsche Spectator [*A publication*]
**NS**.............. Nederlandse Spoorwegen [*Netherlands Railways*]
**NS**.............. Neo Sumerian (BJA)
**NS**.............. Nephrosclerosis [*Medicine*]
**NS**.............. Nephrotic Syndrome [*Medicine*]
**NS**.............. Nerine Society [*Defunct*] (EA)
**NS**.............. Nervous System
**NS**.............. Net Surplus
**NS**.............. Neue Sachlichkeit [*New Objectivity*] [*Pre-World War II group of German artists*]
**NS**.............. Neuere Sprachen [*A publication*]
**NS**.............. Neukirchener Studienbuecher [*A publication*]
**NS**.............. Neuro-Syphilis [*Medicine*]
**NS**.............. Neuroelectric Society (EA)
**NS**.............. Neurosecretory
**NS**.............. Neurosurgery [*Medicine*]
**NS**.............. Neurotic Score [*Psychology*]
**NS**.............. New Scholasticism [*A publication*]
**NS**.............. New School
**NS**.............. New Scientist [*A publication*]
**NS**.............. New Series [*Bibliography*]
**NS**.............. New Side
**NS**.............. New South Wales [*Australia*] (ADA)
**NS**.............. New Statesman [*A publication*]
**NS**.............. New Style
**NS**.............. New System [*Data processing*]
**NS**.............. Newspaper Society [*British*]
**NS**.............. Next System [*Data processing*]
**N & S** ......... Nicholls and Stops' Reports [*1897-1904*] [*Tasmania*] [*A publication*] [*A publication*] (DLA)

**NS** ............. Nickel Silver [*Used in minting coins*]
**NS** ............. Nickel Steel
**NS** ............. Nietzsche Society (EA)
**NS** ............. Nimbostratus [*Cloud*] [*Meteorology*]
**NS** ............. Nitrogen Supply
**NS** ............. Nitrogen System
**NS** ............. No Sparring (DS)
**NS** ............. No Specimen [*Medicine*]
**N/S** ............. No Stamp [*Deltiology*]
**NS** ............. No Stimulation [*Neurophysiology*]
**NS** ............. No Surgery Performed
**NS** ............. Nobelstiftelsen [*Nobel Foundation - NF*] (EAIO)
**NS** ............. Noble Savage [*A publication*]
**NS** ............. Nockian Society (EA)
**NS** ............. Nonscheduled
**NS** ............. Nonschizophrenic [*Psychology*]
**NS** ............. Nonserviceable (MSA)
**NS** ............. Nonsmutted [*Plant pathology*]
**NS** ............. Nonspecified
**NS** ............. Nonstandard (AABC)
**NS** ............. Nonstatus Candidates May Apply [*Civil Service*]
**NS** ............. Nonstimulation
**NS** ............. Nonstop [*Aviation*]
**NS** ............. Nordisk Speditorforbund [*Nordic Forwarding Agents Association - NFAA*] (EAIO)
**NS** ............. Nordisk Svommeforbund [*Nordic Swimming Federations Association - NSFA*] (EAIO)
**NS** ............. Norfolk Southern Railway Co. [*AAR code*]
**NS** ............. Normal Saline
**NS** ............. Normal Segment
**NS** ............. Normal Serum
**NS** ............. Normally Shut (NRCH)
**NS** ............. Norsk Skogindustri [*A publication*]
**NS** ............. North Sea - Nonrigid Airship [*Royal Naval Air Service*] [*British*]
**NS** ............. North Somerset Imperial Yeomanry [*British military*] (DMA)
**NS** ............. North-South
**NS** ............. Nose [*Horse racing*]
**n/s** ............. Nosso Saque [*Our Draft*] [*Business term*] [*Portuguese*]
**NS** ............. Nostro Signore [*Our Lord*]
**NS** ............. Not Seen
**NS** ............. Not Significant
**NS** ............. Not Specified
**NS** ............. Not Sprinklered [*Insurance*]
**NS** ............. Not Stated
**NS** ............. Not Stocked
**NS** ............. Not Stung
**NS** ............. Not Sufficient
**NS** ............. Not Suppressed
**NS** ............. Not Switchable (MCD)
**NS** ............. Notre Seigneur [*Our Lord*] [*French*]
**NS** ............. Noun Substantive [*Grammar*] (ROG)
**NS** ............. Nourishing Stout [*Brewing*] (ROG)
**NS** ............. Nova Scotia [*Canadian province*] [*Postal code*]
**NS** ............. Nova Scotia Reports [*Information service or system*] [*A publication*]
**NS** ............. Novi Svet [*A publication*]
**NS** ............. Noxious Stimuli
**NS** ............. NS. NorthSouth NordSud NorteSur NorteSul. Canadian Association of Latin American Studies. University of Ottawa [*A publication*]
**NS** ............. Nuclear Safety [*A publication*]
**NS** ............. Nuclear Science
**NS** ............. Nuclear Ship
**NS** ............. Nuclear Shuttle (NASA)
**NS** ............. Nuclear Submarine
**NS** ............. Nuclear Systems
**NS** ............. Numen Supplements [*A publication*]
**NS** ............. Numismatic Society
**NS** ............. Numismatic Studies [*A publication*]
**NS** ............. Numismatica et Sphragistica [*A publication*]
**NS** ............. Nurnberger Flugdienst GmbH & Co. KG, Nurnberg [*West Germany*] [*ICAO designator*] (FAAC)
**NS** ............. Nursing Services
**NS** ............. Nursing Sister [*Navy*] [*British*]
**NS** ............. Nylon Suture [*Medicine*]
**NS** ............. Nzingha Society (EA)
**ns** ............. Sodium Metasilicate [*CIPW classification*] [*Geology*]
**Ns** ............. Surface Refractivity (CET)
**NSa** ........... Bancroft Public Library, Salem, NY [*Library symbol*] [*Library of Congress*] (LCLS)
**NSA** ........... Napoleonic Society of America (EA)
**NSA** ........... National Scrabble Association (EA)
**NSA** ........... National Secretaries Association (International) [*Later, PSI*] (EA)
**NSA** ........... National Security Act (AAG)
**NSA** ........... National Security Agency [*Acronym is facetiously translated as No Such Agency or Never Say Anything because of staffers' reluctance to give interviews*] [*DoD*]
**NSA** ........... National Security Agency, Fort George G. Meade, MD [*OCLC symbol*] (OCLC)
**NSA** ........... National Security Archive
**NSA** ........... National Service Acts [*British*]
**NSA** ........... National Shellfisheries Association (EA)
**NSA** ........... National Sheriffs' Association (EA)
**NSA** ........... National Shipping Authority [*Department of Commerce*]
**NSA** ........... National Showmen's Association (EA)
**NSA** ........... National Shuffleboard Association (EA)
**NSA** ........... National Silo Association [*Later, ISA*] (EA)
**NSA** ........... National Skating Association of Great Britain
**NSA** ........... National Ski Association of America [*Later, United States Ski Association*]
**NSA** ........... National Slag Association (EA)
**NSA** ........... National Slate Association (EA)
**NSA** ........... National Snurfing Association (EA)
**NSA** ........... National Society of Andersonville (EA)
**NSA** ........... National Society of Auctioneers [*Later, National Auctioneers Association*]
**NSA** ........... National Sound Archive [*British Library*]
**NSA** ........... National Speakers Association (EA)
**NSA** ........... National Spiritual Alliance of the USA (EA)
**NSA** ........... National Sports Association (EA)
**NSA** ........... National Sprouting Association (EA)
**NSA** ........... National Standards Association, Inc. [*Bethesda, MD*]
**NSA** ........... National Stereoscopic Association (EA)
**NSA** ........... National Stone Association (EA)
**NSA** ........... National Stroke Association (EA)
**NSA** ........... National Student Association [*Later, USSA*]
**NSA** ........... National Sunflower Association (EA)
**NSA** ........... Nausea (KSC)
**NSA** ........... Naval Stock Account
**NSA** ........... Naval Supply Account
**NSA** ........... Naval Support Activity [*Vietnam*]
**NSA** ........... Navy Scientific Adviser [*Australia*]
**NSA** ........... Navy Supply Annex (AFIT)
**NSA** ........... Neighborhood Strategy Area [*Program*] [*HUD*]
**NSA** ........... Nepal Studies Association (EA)
**NSA** ........... Neurosurgical Society of America (EA)
**NSA** ........... New Sabina Resources Ltd. [*Vancouver Stock Exchange symbol*]
**NSA** ........... New Shipborne Aircraft [*Canada*]
**NSA** ........... Nichiren Shoshu Soka Gakkai of America (EA)
**NSA** ........... Nitrosylsulfuric Acid [*Inorganic chemistry*]
**NSA** ........... No Salt Added
**NSA** ........... No Significant Abnormalities [*Medicine*]
**NSA** ........... Noise Suppressor Assembly
**NSA** ........... Nonylsuccinic Acid [*Organic chemistry*]
**NSA** ........... Noosa [*Australia*] [*Airport symbol*] (OAG)
**NSA** ........... Normal Serum Albumin [*Clinical chemistry*]
**NSA** ........... North Sea Assets [*Investment firm*] [*British*]
**NSA** ........... North-South Acceleration
**NSA** ........... Northeastern Saengerbund of America (EA)
**NSA** ........... Norwegian Seamen's Association (EA)
**NSA** ........... Notizie degli Scavi di Antichita [*A publication*]
**NSA** ........... Nuclear Science Abstracts [*Later, INIS Atomindex*] [*Information service or system*] [*A publication*]
**NSA** ........... Nuclear Suppliers Association (EA)
**NSA** ........... Nuclear Systems Analysis
**NSA** ........... Numen Supplements. Altera Series [*A publication*]
**NSAA** ........ National Sales Achievement Award [*NALU*]
**NSAA** ........ National Ski Areas Association (EA)
**NSAA** ........ National Space and Aeronautics Agency (MCD)
**NSAA** ........ National Supply Association of America [*Later, NSDA*] (EA)
**NSAA** ........ Neue Studien zur Anglistik und Amerikanistik [*A publication*]
**NSAA** ........ Norwegian Singers Association of America (EA)
**NSAAB** ...... National Security Agency Advisory Board [*Fort George G. Meade, MD*] (EGAO)
**NSAAB** ...... Nuclear Science and Applications. Series A. Biological Science [*Pakistan*] [*A publication*]
**NSAAC** ...... Atlantic Co-Operator, Antigonish, Nova Scotia [*Library symbol*] [*National Library of Canada*] (NLC)
**NSABP** ...... National Surgical Adjuvant Breast Project
**NSAC** ........ National Society of Accountants for Cooperatives (EA)
**NSAC** ........ National Society for Autistic Children [*British*]
**NSAC** ........ National Spiritualist Association of Churches (EA)
**NSAC** ........ National Sport Aviation Council [*Inactive*] (EA)
**NSAC** ........ National Student Action Center (EA)
**NSAC** ........ National Student Aid Coalition (EA)
**NSAC** ........ Notices et Memoires. Societe Archeologique de Constantine [*A publication*]
**NSAC** ........ Nova Scotia Agricultural College
**NSAC** ........ NSAC, the National Society for Children and Adults with Autism (EA)
**NSAC** ........ Nuclear Safety Analysis Center [*Electric Power Research Institute*] (NRCH)
**NSACG** ...... Nuclear Strike Alternate Control Group (NATG)
**NSACSS** .... National Security Agency/Central Security Service (AABC)
**NSAD** ........ National Society of Art Directors (EA)
**NSAD** ........ Nuclear Safety Analysis Document (KSC)
**NSADN** ..... Daily News, Amherst, Nova Scotia [*Library symbol*] [*National Library of Canada*] (NLC)

**NSADP**...... Niger State Agricultural Development Project [*Nigeria*] (ECON)
**NSAE**......... National Society of Architectural Engineers (EA)
**NSAE**......... National Society for Art Education [*British*]
**NSAF**......... Naval Supply Account Fund
**NSAFC**...... National Service Armed Forces Act [*British*]
**NSAGT**...... New South African Group Test [*Intelligence test*]
**NSAH**........ Heritage Association of Antigonish, Nova Scotia [*Library symbol*] [*National Library of Canada*] (NLC)
**NSAHW**.... Nordic Secretariat for Agricultural and Horticultural Workers (EAIO)
**NSAI**.......... Nashville Songwriters Association, International (EA)
**NSAI**.......... Need Satisfaction of Activity Interview
**NSAI**.......... Nonsteroidal Anti-Inflammatory [*Pharmacochemistry*]
**NSAIA**....... Nonsteroidal Anti-Inflammatory Agent
**NSAID**....... Nonsteroidal Anti-Inflammatory Drug
**NSAIN**...... Indian and Northern Affairs Canada [*Affaires Indiennes et du Nord Canada*], Amherst, Nova Scotia [*Library symbol*] [*National Library of Canada*] (BIB)
**NSAL**......... National Society of Arts and Letters (EA)
**NSAL**......... Nsukka Studies in African Literature [*A publication*]
**NSalDH**..... Salamanca District Hospital, Salamanca, NY [*Library symbol*] [*Library of Congress*] (LCLS)
**NSALO**..... National Security Agency Liaison Officer
**NSAM**....... National Security Agency Memorandum
**NSAM**....... Naval School of Aviation Medicine
**NSAMC**.... Cumberland Regional Library, Amherst, Nova Scotia [*Library symbol*] [*National Library of Canada*] (NLC)
**NS Am Law Register**... American Law Register (Reprint) [*Ohio*] [*A publication*] (DLA)
**NSammlung**... Neue Sammlung [*A publication*]
**NSAMRMS**... Maritime Resource Management Service [*Service d'Amenagement des Ressources des Maritimes*] Amherst, Nova Scotia [*Library symbol*] [*National Library of Canada*] (NLC)
**NSAN**........ Nissan Motor Co. Ltd. [*NASDAQ symbol*] (NQ)
**NSan**.......... Sanborn-Pekin Free Library, Sanborn, NY [*Library symbol*] [*Library of Congress*] (LCLS)
**NSanF**........ National Sanitation Foundation
**NSANL**...... Non-Sectarian Anti-NAZI League (EA)
**NSanO**....... Orleans-Niagara Board of Cooperative Educational Services, Associates Special Educational Instruction Materials Center, Sanborn, NY [*Library symbol*] [*Library of Congress*] (LCLS)
**NSanO-C**... Orleans-Niagara Board of Cooperative Educational Services, Educational Communications Center, Sanborn, NY [*Library symbol*] [*Library of Congress*] (LCLS)
**NSAP**......... Apia [*Western Samoa*] [*ICAO location identifier*] (ICLI)
**NSAP**......... National Socialist Action Party [*British*]
**NSAP**......... National Society for Animal Protection (EA)
**NSAP**......... Navy Science Assistance Program (CAAL)
**NSAPA**...... Nuclear Science and Applications [*A publication*]
**NSAPAC**... National Security Agency Pacific (CINC)
**NSAPEA**... Nordic Society Against Painful Experiments on Animals (EA)
**NSAR**........ Annapolis Valley Regional Library, Annapolis Royal, NS [*Library symbol*] [*National Library of Canada*] (NLC)
**NSAR**........ Nationalmusei Skriftserie. Analecta Reginensia [*A publication*]
**NSARC**..... Navy Systems Acquisition Review Council
**N-S Arch Ph**... Naunyn-Schmiedeberg's Archives of Pharmacology [*A publication*]
**NSARF**...... Fort Anne Museum, Annapolis Royal, Nova Scotia [*Library symbol*] [*National Library of Canada*] (NLC)
**NSAS**......... Near Infrared Spectral Analysis Software
**NSAS**......... Nonscheduled Air Services (AAG)
**NSAS**......... Nuclear Sealed Authentication System (AABC)
**NSAS**......... St. Francis Xavier University, Antigonish, Nova Scotia [*Library symbol*] [*National Library of Canada*] (NLC)
**NSASAB**... National Security Agency Scientific Advisory Board [*Ft. George G. Meade, MD*] (EGAO)
**NSASC**...... Chemistry Department, St. Francis Xavier University, Antigonish, Nova Scotia [*Library symbol*] [*National Library of Canada*] (NLC)
**NSAT**......... NATO Small Arms Test (MCD)
**NSAU**........ Asau [*Western Samoa*] [*ICAO location identifier*] (ICLI)
**NSau**.......... Saugerties Public Library, Saugerties, NY [*Library symbol*] [*Library of Congress*] (LCLS)
**NSauF**........ Ferroxcube Corp., Suagerties, NY [*Library symbol*] [*Library of Congress*] (LCLS)
**NSA-US**.... National Spiritual Assembly of the Baha'is of the US (EA)
**NSAW**....... National Society of Asphalt Workers [*A union*] [*British*]
**NSay**.......... Sayville Library, Sayville, NY [*Library symbol*] [*Library of Congress*] (LCLS)
**NSB**........... Bimini-North [*Bahamas*] [*Airport symbol*] (OAG)
**NSB**........... Nationaal-Socialistische Beweging [*National Socialist Movement*] [*Netherlands*] [*Political party*] (PPE)
**NSB**........... National Science Board [*National Science Foundation*]
**NSB**........... National Small Business Association [*Later, NSBU*]
**NSB**........... National Socialist Board [*Dutch National Socialist Party of 1931; later, Dutch NAZI Party*] [*Political party*]
**NSB**........... National Socialist Bulletin [*A publication*] (APTA)
**NSB**........... NATO Security Board (NATG)
**NSB**........... Naval Standardization Board
**NSB**........... Naval Submarine Base
**NSB**........... Near Surface Burst (MCD)
**NSB**........... Network of Small Businesses [*Lyndhurst, OH*] (EA)
**NSB**........... Neuerwerbungen Stadtbuecherei Nuernberg [*A publication*]
**NSB**........... Newsprint Service Bureau [*Later, API*] (EA)
**NSB**........... Nonspecific Binder
**NSB**........... Nordisk Sammanslutning for Barnavard [*Nordic Child and Youth Welfare Alliance - NCYWA*] (EA)
**NSB**........... Norges Statsbaner [*Norwegian State Railways*]
**NSB**........... Northeast Federal [*NYSE symbol*] (SPSG)
**NSB**........... Northern Soviet Boundary
**NSB**........... Not Separately Billed
**NSB**........... Notes on the Science of Building [*Australia Commonwealth Experimental Building Station*] [*A publication*] (APTA)
**NSB**........... Nuclear Safety Bureau [*Australia*]
**NSBA**......... National Saanen Breeders Association (EA)
**NSBA**......... National Safe Boating Association (EA)
**NSBA**......... [*The*] National Savings Bank of Albany [*Albany, NY*] [*NASDAQ symbol*] (NQ)
**NSBA**......... National School Boards Association (EA)
**NSBA**......... National Semi-Professional Baseball Association (EA)
**NSBA**......... National Shrimp Breeders Association (EA)
**NSBA**......... National Small Business Association [*Later, NSBU*]
**NSBA**......... National Small Business Awards [*Australia*]
**NSBA**......... National Snaffle Bit Association (EA)
**NSBA**......... National Sugar Brokers Association (EA)
**NSBB**......... National Society for Business Budgeting [*Later, PEI*]
**NSBBA**....... National Small Business Benefits Association (EA)
**NSBC**......... National Safe Boating Council (EA)
**NSBC**......... National Shoeboard Conference (EA)
**NSBC**......... National Student Book Club
**NSBCSH**... Cape Sable Historical Society, Barrington, Nova Scotia [*Library symbol*] [*National Library of Canada*] (NLC)
**NSBD**........ Narrow Spectral Band Detection
**NSBD**........ National Society of Bank Directors [*Formerly, NABD*] [*Later, ASBD*] (EA)
**NSBDM**.... DesBrisay Museum and National Exhibit Centre, Bridgewater, Nova Scotia [*Library symbol*] [*National Library of Canada*] (NLC)
**NSBE**......... National Society of Black Engineers (EA)
**NSBEO**...... National Sonic Boom Evaluation Office [*Air Force*] (MCD)
**NSBET**...... National Society of Biomedical Equipment Technicians (EA)
**NSBF**......... National Scientific Balloon Facility [*Palestine, TX*] [*NASA*]
**NSBGA**...... Nippon Shokubutsu Byori Gakkaiho [*A publication*]
**NSBGAM**... Annals. Phytopathological Society of Japan [*A publication*]
**NSBGCA**... National Small Business Government Contractors Association [*Inactive*] (EA)
**NSBGW**.... National Society of Brushmakers and General Workers [*A union*] [*British*] (DCTA)
**NSbIA**........ Institute of Advanced Studies of World Religions, Stony Brook, NY [*Library symbol*] [*Library of Congress*] (LCLS)
**NSBISS**..... NATO Security Bureau Industrial Security Section (NATG)
**NSBJH**...... James House, Bridgetown, Nova Scotia [*Library symbol*] [*National Library of Canada*] (NLC)
**NSBK**......... North Side Savings Bank [*NASDAQ symbol*] (NQ)
**NSBL**......... Lighthouse Publishing Ltd., Bridgewater, Nova Scotia [*Library symbol*] [*National Library of Canada*] (NLC)
**NSBLE**...... Leader, Berwick, Nova Scotia [*Library symbol*] [*National Library of Canada*] (NLC)
**NSBM**....... Monitor, Bridgetown, Nova Scotia [*Library symbol*] [*National Library of Canada*] (NLC)
**NSBMA**..... National Small Business Men's Association [*Later, NSBU*]
**NSBNL**..... Naval Submarine Base - New London (MCD)
**NSBPA**..... National Shrimp Breeders and Processors Association (EA)
**NSBPH**..... National Library Service for the Blind and Physically Handicapped [*Library of Congress*] [*Washington, DC*] [*Library network*]
**NSBR**......... Register, Berwick, Nova Scotia [*Library symbol*] [*National Library of Canada*] (NLC)
**NSBRH**..... Bear River Historical Society, Nova Scotia [*Library symbol*] [*National Library of Canada*] (NLC)
**NSBRO**..... National Service Board for Religious Objectors [*Later, NISBCO*] (EA)
**NSBS**......... South Shore Regional Library, Bridgewater, Nova Scotia [*Library symbol*] [*National Library of Canada*] (NLC)
**NSbSM**..... Suffolk Museum at Stony Brook, Stony Brook, NY [*Library symbol*] [*Library of Congress*] (LCLS)
**NSBSSA**.... National Strict Baptist Sunday School Association [*British*]
**NSBSSN**.... South Shore News, Bridgewater, Nova Scotia [*Library symbol*] [*National Library of Canada*] (NLC)
**NSbSU**....... State University of New York at Stony Brook, Stony Brook, NY [*Library symbol*] [*Library of Congress*] (LCLS)
**NSbSU-H**... State University of New York at Stony Brook, Health Sciences Library, Stony Brook, NY [*Library symbol*] [*Library of Congress*] (LCLS)
**NSBT**......... National Swiss Battle Tank (MCD)
**NSBT**......... Not Series by Title (MCD)
**NSBU**........ National Small Business United [*Washington, DC*] (EA)
**NSBVCA**... Victoria County Archives and Museum, Baddeck, Nova Scotia [*Library symbol*] [*National Library of Canada*] (NLC)

**NSBWC**..... National Safe Boating Week Committee [*Later, NSBC*]
**NSBWK**..... Western King's Memorial Hospital, Berwick, Nova Scotia [*Library symbol*] [*National Library of Canada*] (NLC)
**NSC**.......... Arthur D. Little, Inc. [*Research code symbol*]
**NSC**.......... Bristol-Myers Co. [*Research code symbol*]
**NSC**.......... Hoffmann-La Roche, Inc. [*Research code symbol*]
**NSC**.......... Names in South Carolina [*A publication*]
**NSC**.......... NASCAR [*National Association for Stock Car Auto Racing*] Street Classics [*Later, WW*] (EA)
**NSC**.......... National Cancer Institute [*Research code symbol*]
**NSC**.......... National Safety Corporation
**NSC**.......... National Safety Council (EA)
**NSC**.......... National Safflower Council [*Inactive*] (EA)
**NSC**.......... National Savings Certificates [*British*] (DAS)
**NSC**.......... National Savings Committee [*British*]
**NSC**.......... National Security Council
**NSC**.......... National Semiconductor Corporation
**NSC**.......... National Shrimp Congress (EA)
**NSC**.......... National Slavic Convention (EA)
**NSC**.......... National Society of Chauffeurs [*A union*] [*British*]
**NSC**.......... National Society of Computer/Genealogists (EA)
**NSC**.......... National Society of Cwens (EA)
**NSC**.......... National Space Club (EA)
**NSC**.......... National Space Council
**NSC**.......... National Spiritualist Church [*British*]
**NSC**.......... National Sports Centre [*Australia*]
**NSC**.......... National Staff Committee [*Nurses and midwives*] [*British*]
**NSC**.......... National Steel Corporation [*Philippines*] (DS)
**NSC**.......... National Stinson Club (EA)
**NSC**.......... National Supply Class [*Military*] (AFIT)
**NSC**.......... National Synthetics Collection [*Smithsonian Institution*]
**NSC**.......... NATO [*North Atlantic Treaty Organization*] Science Committee (EAIO)
**NSC**.......... NATO Steering Committee (NATG)
**NSC**.......... NATO Supply Center (NATG)
**NSC**.......... NATO Supply Classification
**NSC**.......... Naval Coastal Systems Center [*Florida*]
**NSC**.......... Naval Safety Center (MCD)
**NSC**.......... Naval School Command
**NSC**.......... Naval Sea Cadets
**NSC**.......... Naval Supply Center
**NSC**.......... Navigation and Sensor Computer
**NSC**.......... Navigation Star Catalogue
**NSC**.......... Navy Service Center
**NSC**.......... Nederlandse Staatscourant. Officiele Uitgaven van het Koninkrijk der Nederlanden [*A publication*]
**NSC**.......... Netherlands Shippers Council (DS)
**NSC**.......... Network Service Center [*Telecommunications*]
**NSC**.......... Network Switching Center [*Telecommunications*] (TEL)
**NSC**.......... Network Systems Corporation [*Brooklyn Park, MN*] [*Telecommunications*] (TSSD)
**NSC**.......... Neurosecretory Cells
**NSC**.......... New Session Cases [*Scotland*] [*A publication*] (DLA)
**NSC**.......... Newscope Resources Ltd. [*Toronto Stock Exchange symbol*]
**NSC**.......... Newtex SS [*Steamship company*] [*AAR code*]
**NSC**.......... Nicaragua Solidarity Campaign (EAIO)
**NSC**.......... Nippon Steel Corporation [*Japan*]
**NSC**.......... No Significant Change [*Medicine*]
**NSC**.......... Nodal Switching Center
**NSC**.......... Noise Suppression Circuit (DEN)
**NSC**.......... Nomenclature Sequence Code [*Navy*] (AFIT)
**NSC**.......... Non-Service-Connected
**NSC**.......... Norfolk Southern Ry. [*NYSE symbol*] (SPSG)
**NSC**.......... North Stonington [*Connecticut*] [*Seismograph station code, US Geological Survey*] (SEIS)
**NSC**.......... Northeastern State College [*Oklahoma*]
**NSC**.......... Norwegian Shippers Council (DS)
**NSC**.......... Nothing So Called [*Bookselling*]
**NSc**.......... Notizie degli Scavi di Antichita [*A publication*]
**nsc**.......... Nova Scotia [*MARC country of publication code*] [*Library of Congress*] (LCCP)
**NSC**.......... Nuclear Science Center [*Louisiana State University*] [*Research center*] (RCD)
**NSC**.......... Numerical Sequence Code
**NSC**.......... Nursing Sentence Completions [*Nursing school test*]
**NSC**.......... Salem College, Winston-Salem, NC [*OCLC symbol*] (OCLC)
**NSCA**........ NASCOM [*NASA Communications Network*] Assembly
**NSCA**........ National Satellite Cable Association (EA)
**NSCA**........ National Scrip Collectors Association (EA)
**NSCA**........ National Senior Citizens Association [*Commercial firm*] (EA)
**NSCA**........ National Shrimp Canners Association
**NSCA**........ National Ski Credit Association (EA)
**NSCA**........ National Soccer Coaches Association of America (EA)
**NSCA**........ National Society for Clean Air [*British*] (DCTA)
**NSCA**........ National Sound and Communications Association (EA)
**NSCA**........ National Strength and Conditioning Association (EA)
**NSCA**........ Northwest Salmon Canners Association (EA)
**NSCA**........ Nova Scotia College of Art
**NSCA**........ Nutrient Starch Cycloheximide Agar [*Microbiology*]
**NSca**........ Scarsdale Public Library, Scarsdale, NY [*Library symbol*] [*Library of Congress*] (LCLS)
**NSCAA**...... National Small College Athletic Association (EA)
**NSCAA**...... [*The*] National Society for Children and Adults with Autism [*Formerly, NSAC*] (EA)
**NSCAA**...... National Society for Clean Air. Annual Conference. Proceedings [*England*] [*A publication*]
**NSCAA**...... Nutrient Starch Cycloheximide Antibiotic Agar [*Microbiology*]
**NSCAE**...... National Standards Council of American Embroiderers [*Later, CAE*] (EA)
**NSCAEU**... National Service Conference of the American Ethical Union (EA)
**NSCAH**..... National Student Campaign Against Hunger [*Later, NSCAHH*] (EA)
**NSCAHH**... National Student Campaign Against Hunger and Homelessness (EA)
**NSCA J**..... National Strength and Conditioning Association. Journal [*A publication*]
**NSCAMP**... National Stock Control and Maintenance Point [*Army*] (AFIT)
**NSCA (Natl Soc Clean Air) Year Book**... NSCA (National Society for Clean Air) Year Book [*A publication*]
**NSCAR**...... National Society of the Children of the American Revolution (EA)
**NSCAS**...... Archelaus Smith Museum, Centreville (Shelburne Co.), Nova Scotia [*Library symbol*] [*National Library of Canada*] (NLC)
**NSCAT**...... NASA [*or NROSS*] Scatterometer [*Instrumentation*]
**N Scav Ant**... Notizie degli Scavi di Antichita [*A publication*]
**NSCB**......... NBSC Corp. [*NASDAQ symbol*] (NQ)
**NSCB**......... Nordic Society for Cell Biology (EA)
**NSCBDF**... NSCA [*National Society for Clean Air*] Year Book [*A publication*]
**NSCC**......... National Securities Clearing Corporation
**NSCC**......... National Service Coordinating Committee [*Ministry of Labour and National Service*] [*British*] [*World War II*]
**NSCC**......... National Siamese Cat Club (EA)
**NSCC**......... National Social Conditioning Camps [*Later, NOC*] (EA)
**NSCC**......... Naval Sea Cadet Corps (NVT)
**NSCC**......... North Shore Community College [*Beverly, MA*]
**NSCC**......... Nuclear Services Closed Cooling (IEEE)
**NSCCA**...... National Society for Crippled Children and Adults [*Later, NESS*] (EA)
**NSCCA**...... National Sports Car Club of America
**NSCCF**...... Canadian Forces Base, Cornwallis, Nova Scotia [*Library symbol*] [*National Library of Canada*] (NLC)
**NSCCFE**.... Ensign, Canadian Forces Base, Cornwallis, Nova Scotia [*Library symbol*] [*National Library of Canada*] (NLC)
**NSCCM**..... Cumberland County Museum, Amherst, Nova Scotia [*Library symbol*] [*National Library of Canada*] (NLC)
**NSCDA**..... National Society of Colonial Dames of America (EA)
**N Sc Dec**.... Nova Scotia Decisions [*A publication*] (DLA)
**NSCDP**...... Non-Sexist Child Development Project (EA)
**NSCDRF**... National Sickle Cell Disease Research Foundation [*Defunct*] (EA)
**NSCEC**...... National School Curriculum Center for Educational Computing (EA)
**NSCEE**...... National Schools Committee for Economic Education (EA)
**NSCEO**...... National Society of Chief Executive Officers [*Lincolnwood, IL*] (EA)
**NSCF**......... National Skin Cancer Foundation [*Later, SCF*] (EA)
**NSCF**......... National Student Christian Federation [*Later, UCM*] (EA)
**NSCF**......... Naval Small Craft Facilities
**NSCFA**...... National Support Center for Families of the Aging [*Defunct*] (EA)
**NSCH**........ Canso Historical Society, Nova Scotia [*Library symbol*] [*National Library of Canada*] (NLC)
**NSch**.......... New Scholasticism [*A publication*]
**NSch**.......... Schenectady County Public Library, Schenectady, NY [*Library symbol*] [*Library of Congress*] (LCLS)
**NSchC**....... Schenectady County Community College, Schenectady, NY [*Library symbol*] [*Library of Congress*] (LCLS)
**NSchE**........ Ellis Hospital, Schenectady, NY [*Library symbol*] [*Library of Congress*] (LCLS)
**NSchGEKA**... General Electric Co., Knolls Atomic Laboratory, Technical Library, Schenectady, NY [*Library symbol*] [*Library of Congress*] (LCLS)
**NSchGEM**... General Electric Co., Main Library, Schenectady, NY [*Library symbol*] [*Library of Congress*] (LCLS)
**NSchGER**... General Electric Co., Research Laboratory, Schenectady, NY [*Library symbol*] [*Library of Congress*] (LCLS)
**NSchGERB**... General Electric Co., R and D Center, Branch Library, Schenectady, NY [*Library symbol*] [*Library of Congress*] (LCLS)
**NScHLC**.... Capital District Library Council, Schenectady, NY [*Library symbol*] [*Library of Congress*] (LCLS)
**NSchM**...... Mohawk Valley Library Association, Schenectady, NY [*Library symbol*] [*Library of Congress*] (LCLS)
**NSchoCHi**... Schoharie County Historical Society, Schoharie, NY [*Library symbol*] [*Library of Congress*] (LCLS)
**NSchSC**..... Schenectady Chemicals, Inc., Schenectady, NY [*Library symbol*] [*Library of Congress*] (LCLS)
**NSchStC**.... Saint Clare's Hospital, Physicians' Library, Schenectady, NY [*Library symbol*] [*Library of Congress*] (LCLS)

**NSchU**....... Union College, Schenectady, NY [*Library symbol*] [*Library of Congress*] (LCLS)
**NSchwRundschau** ... Neue Schweizer Rundschau [*A publication*]
**NSCI**.......... NASCOM System Control Interface [*NASA*] (MCD)
**NSCI**.......... National Superannuation Committee of Inquiry [*Australia*]
**NSCIA**....... National Spinal Cord Injury Association (EA)
**NSCIC**....... National Security Council Intelligence Committee [*Inactive*]
**NSCIC**....... National Soybean Crop Improvement Council
**NSCID**....... National Security Council Intelligence Directive [*Pronounced "nee-sid"*] (AFM)
**N Scientist** ... New Scientist [*A publication*]
**NSCIF**....... National Spinal Cord Injury Foundation [*Formerly, NPF*] [*Later, NSCIA*] (EA)
**NSCIG**....... National Security Council Interdepartmental Group (MCD)
**N Sci R**....... New Science Review [*A publication*]
**NSCISC**..... National Spinal Cord Injury Statistical Center Database [*University of Alabama in Birmingham*] [*Information service or system*] (CRD)
**NSCL**......... National Superconducting Cyclotron Laboratory [*National Science Foundation*] [*Michigan State University*] [*Research center*] (RCD)
**NSCLC**...... National Senior Citizens Law Center (EA)
**NSCLC**...... Non-Small-Cell Lung Cancer [*Oncology*]
**NSCLS**...... North State Cooperative Library System [*Library network*]
**NSCM**....... National Society of Cycle Makers [*A union*] [*British*]
**NSCM**....... NATO Supply Code for Manufacturing (MCD)
**NSC & MP** ... National Stock Control and Maintenance Point [*Army*] (AABC)
**NSCN**........ National Socialist Council of Nagaland [*India*] (PD)
**NSC (Natl Sci Counc) Symp Ser (Taipei)** ... NSC (National Science Council) Symposium Series (Taipei) [*A publication*]
**NSCNQH** ... North Queens Heritage Society, Caledonia, Nova Scotia [*Library symbol*] [*National Library of Canada*] (NLC)
**NSCO**........ National Scientific Committee on Oceanography
**NSCO**........ Network Systems Corporation [*NASDAQ symbol*] (NQ)
**NSCP**......... National Soil Conservation Program [*Australia*]
**NSCP**......... Naval Stores Conservation Program
**NSCP**......... Navy Staffing Criteria Program
**NSCPA**...... National Society of Certified Public Accountants (EA)
**NSCPC**...... National Student Consumer Protection Council (EA)
**NSCPT**...... National Society for Cardiovascular and Pulmonary Technology (EA)
**NSCR**......... National Society for Cancer Relief [*British*]
**NSCR**......... National Sport Custom Registry (EA)
**NSCR**......... Nuclear Science Center Reactor
**NSCRA**...... NASA [*National Aeronautics and Space Administration*] Contractor Report. CR [*A publication*]
**NSCRC**...... National Stock Car Racing Commission
**NSCRDFO** ... National Study Commission on Records and Documents of Federal Officials
**NSC Rev 1977-8** ... NSC [*National Science Council*] Review 1977-8 [*Taiwan*] [*A publication*]
**NSCS**......... National Sisters Communications Service [*Later, CCM*] (EA)
**NSCS**......... National Small Craft School [*Red Cross*]
**NSCS**......... Navy Supply Corps School
**NSCS**......... North Star Computer Society (EA)
**NSCS**......... Universite Sainte-Anne, Church Point, Nova Scotia [*Library symbol*] [*National Library of Canada*] (NLC)
**NSCSA**...... Centre Acadien, Universite Sainte-Anne, Church Point, Nova Scotia [*Library symbol*] [*National Library of Canada*] (BIB)
**NSCSC**...... National School Calendar Study Committee
**NSCSCC**.... National Standard for Common System Component Characteristics (MCD)
**NSC Special Publication** ... National Science Council. Special Publication [*A publication*]
**NSCSWD**.. No Small Craft or Storm Warnings are Being Displayed [*Weather*]
**NSCT**......... National Students Center for Thailand
**NSCT**......... Niagara, St. Catharines & Toronto [*AAR code*]
**NSCTE**...... National Society of College Teachers of Education [*Later, SPE*] (EA)
**NSCU**........ National Software Coordination Unit [*Australia*]
**NSCVPT** ... National Society for Cardiovascular and Pulmonary Technology (EA)
**NSCVR**..... National Student Campaign for Voter Registration (EA)
**NSCW**....... National Society of Cycle Workers [*A union*] [*British*]
**NS(Czech)** ... Numismaticky Sbornik (Czechoslovakia) [*A publication*]
**NSD**........... Dartmouth Regional Library, Dartmouth, Nova Scotia [*Library symbol*] [*National Library of Canada*] (NLC)
**NSD**........... Ferrosan [*Denmark*] [*Research code symbol*]
**NSD**........... Geldert and Oxley's Nova Scotia Decisions [*7-9 Nova Scotia Reports*] [*1866-75*] [*Canada*] [*A publication*] (DLA)
**NSD**........... National Silage Demonstration [*British*]
**NSD**........... National-Standard Co. [*NYSE symbol*] (SPSG)
**NSD**........... Naval Stores Department [*British military*] (DMA)
**NSD**........... Naval Supply Depot
**NSD**........... Navy Support Date (NG)
**NSD**........... Network Status Display
**NSD**........... New Spirit Research [*Vancouver Stock Exchange symbol*]
**NSD**........... Next Most Significant Digit [*Data processing*]
**NSD**........... No Significant Defects [*or Deficiency*] [*Medicine*]
**NSD**........... No Significant Deviation [*Medicine*]
**NSD**........... No Significant Difference [*Medicine*]
**NSD**........... No Significant Disease [*Medicine*]
**NSD**........... Noise Suppression Device
**NSD**........... Nominal Standard Dose [*Medicine*]
**NSD**........... Non-Self-Destroying
**NSD**........... Normal, Spontaneous Delivery [*Obstetrics*]
**NSD**........... Normal Standard Dose [*Oncology radiation*]
**NSD**........... Norsk Samfunnsvitenskapelig Datatjeneste [*Norwegian Social Science Data Services*] [*Information service or system*] (IID)
**NSD**........... United States Library of Congress, Washington, DC [*OCLC symbol*] (OCLC)
**NSDA**........ National Soft Drink Association (EA)
**NSDA**........ National Sprayer and Duster Association (EA)
**NSDA**........ National Supply Distributors Association [*Dayton, OH*] (EA)
**NSDA**........ National Surplus Dealers Association (EA)
**NSDA**........ Naval Supply Depot Annex
**NSDAB**...... Non-Self-Deployable Aircraft and Boats (MCD)
**NSDAP**...... Nationalsozialistische Deutsche Arbeiterpartei [*National Socialist German Workers' Party, 1919-45*] [*Political party*]
**NSDAP-AO** ... NSDAP Auslands- und Aufbauorganisation (EA)
**NSDAR**..... National Society, Daughters of the American Revolution (EA)
**NSDB**........ Bedford Institute of Oceanography [*Institut Oceanographique de Bedford*] Dartmouth, Nova Scotia [*Library symbol*] [*National Library of Canada*] (NLC)
**NSDB**........ National Science Development Board
**NSDBE**...... National Society, Daughters of the British Empire (EA)
**NSDBR**...... National Society, Daughters of the Barons of Runnemede (EA)
**NSDC**........ Courier, Digby, Nova Scotia [*Library symbol*] [*National Library of Canada*] (NLC)
**NSDC**........ National School Development Council (EA)
**NSDC**........ National Square Dance Convention (EA)
**NSDC**........ National Staff Development Council (EA)
**NSDC**........ Nonsuppurative Destructive Cholangitis [*Medicine*]
**NSDC**........ NORAD Sector Direction Center [*Military*]
**NSDC**........ Northern Shipowners' Defence Club [*See also NORDISK*] (EAIO)
**NSDCM**.... NORAD Sector Direction Center Manual [*Military*]
**N & SDCP** ... Neurological and Sensory Disease Control Program
**NSDD**........ National Security Decision Directive
**NSDDS**...... Dartmouth District School Board, Nova Scotia [*Library symbol*] [*National Library of Canada*] (NLC)
**NSDE**........ Environment Canada [*Environnement Canada*] Dartmouth, Nova Scotia [*Library symbol*] [*National Library of Canada*] (NLC)
**NSDEA**...... National Soda Dispensing Equipment Association (EA)
**NS Dec**....... Nova Scotia Decisions [*A publication*] (DLA)
**NS Dep Lands For Annu Rep** ... Nova Scotia. Department of Lands and Forests. Annual Report [*A publication*]
**NS Dep Mines Annu Rep Mines** ... Nova Scotia. Department of Mines. Annual Report on Mines [*A publication*]
**NS Dep Mines Mem** ... Nova Scotia. Department of Mines. Memoir [*A publication*]
**NSDEQ**..... National Society, Descendants of Early Quakers (EA)
**NSDF**......... National Student Drama Festival [*British*]
**NSDF**......... Navy Standard Distillate Fuel (NVT)
**NSDG**........ Digby General Hospital, Nova Scotia [*Library symbol*] [*National Library of Canada*] (NLC)
**NSDGH**..... Dartmouth General Hospital, Nova Scotia [*Library symbol*] [*National Library of Canada*] (NLC)
**NSDH**........ Hermes Electronics Ltd., Dartmouth, Novia Scotia [*Library symbol*] [*National Library of Canada*] (NLC)
**NSDI**......... National Sales Development Institute
**NSDJA**...... National Sash and Door Jobbers Association (EA)
**NSDL**........ National Soil Dynamics Laboratory [*Auburn, AL*] [*Department of Agriculture*] (GRD)
**NSDL**........ Navy Standard Distribution List (MCD)
**NSDLANT/PAC** ... Naval Supply Depots, Atlantic/Pacific
**NSDLMM** ... National Society of Descendants of Lords of the Maryland Manors (EA)
**NSDM**....... Mirror, Digby, Nova Scotia [*Library symbol*] [*National Library of Canada*] (NLC)
**NSDM**....... National Security Decision Memorandum [*Air Force*]
**NSDM**....... New School for Democratic Management [*Inactive*] (EA)
**NSDMM** ... MacLaren Plansearch Ltd., Dartmouth, Nova Scotia [*Library symbol*] [*National Library of Canada*] (NLC)
**NSDNHM** ... North Highlands Museum, Dingwall, Nova Scotia [*Library symbol*] [*National Library of Canada*] (NLC)
**NSDNSH** .. Nova Scotia Hospital, Dartmouth, Nova Scotia [*Library symbol*] [*National Library of Canada*] (NLC)
**NSDO**....... National Seed and Development Organisation [*British*]
**NSDP**....... National Serials Data Program [*Library of Congress*] (EA)
**NSDP**....... National Society of Denture Prosthetists [*Later, ADP*]
**NSDP**....... Norfolk Sample Drug Program
**NS Dp Mines Rp** ... Nova Scotia. Department of Mines. Report [*A publication*]
**NSDR**....... National Ships Destination Room (NATG)
**NSDR**....... National Silver Dollar Roundtable (EA)

**NSDRV** ..... Dartmouth Regional Vocational School, Dartmouth, Nova Scotia [*Library symbol*] [*National Library of Canada*] (NLC)
**NSDS** ......... Navy School, Diving and Salvage (NVT)
**NSDS** ......... Neutron Spectrometer Digital System
**NSDSA** ...... Naval Sea Data Support Activity (NVT)
**NSDTA** ...... National Staff Development and Training Association (EA)
**NSDUP** ..... National Society, Daughters of Utah Pioneers (EA)
**NSDV** ......... Netted Secure Digital Voice (MCD)
**NSDYA** ..... Nagoya Shiritsu Daigaku Yakugakubu Kenkyu Nempo [*A publication*]
**NSDYAI** .... Annual Report. Faculty of Pharmaceutical Sciences. Nagoya City University [*A publication*]
**NSE** ........... Milton, FL [*Location identifier*] [*FAA*] (FAAL)
**NSE** ........... National Sales Executives
**NSE** ........... National Society for Epilepsy [*British*]
**NSE** ........... National Stock Exchange [*Dissolved, 1975*]
**NSE** ........... National Student Exchange (EA)
**NSE** ........... National Support Elements [*British military*] (DMA)
**NSE** ........... Natural Space Environment
**NSE** ........... Naval Shore Establishment
**NSE** ........... Navier-Stokes Equation
**NSE** ........... Navigation Support Equipment
**NSE** ........... Network SouthEast [*British Rail*] (ECON)
**NSE** ........... Neuron-Specific Enolase [*Formerly, NSP*] [*An enzyme*]
**NSE** ........... Neuropsychological Status Examination [*Psychology*]
**NS & E** ....... New Systems and Enhancements (MCD)
**NSE** ........... Nigerian Stock Exchange
**NSE** ........... Nitroguanidine Support Element (MCD)
**NSE** ........... Nonsecurity Exemption [*Military*]
**NSE** ........... Nonspecific Esterase [*An enzyme*]
**NSE** ........... Northwest Sports Enterprises Ltd. [*Vancouver Stock Exchange symbol*]
**NSE** ........... Norwegian Studies in English [*A publication*]
**NSE** ........... Nuclear Science and Engineering [*A publication*]
**NSE** ........... Nuclear Statistical Equilibrium [*Physics*]
**NSE** ........... Nuclear Support Equipment
**NSE** ........... Nuclear Systems Engineering
**NSEA** ......... National Standards Educators Association (EA)
**NSea** .......... Seaford Public Library, Seaford, NY [*Library symbol*] [*Library of Congress*] (LCLS)
**NSEAD** ...... National Society for Education in Art and Design (EAIO)
**NSeaMH** ... Massapequa General Hospital, Seaford, NY [*Library symbol*] [*Library of Congress*] (LCLS)
**NSeaP** ........ Plainedge Public Library, Seaford, NY [*Library symbol*] [*Library of Congress*] (LCLS)
**NSeaTM** .... Tackapausha Museum, Seaford, NY [*Library symbol*] [*Library of Congress*] (LCLS)
**nsec** ........... Nanosecond [*100 billionth of a second*] [*Also, ns*]
**NSEC** ......... National Service Entertainments Council [*British*]
**NSEC** ......... Naval Ship Engineering Center (MCD)
**NSECINST** ... Naval Ship Engineering Center Instruction
**NSEEC** ...... Naval Shore Electronics Engineering Center [*Terminated, 1966*] (MCD)
**NSEF** ......... National SANE Education Fund (EA)
**NSEF** ......... National Student Educational Fund (EA)
**NSEF** ......... Navy Security Engineering Facility
**NSEF** ......... New Society Educational Foundation (EA)
**NSEGA** ...... Nippon Seikosho Giho [*A publication*]
**NSEGB4** .... Science Reports. Niigata University. Series E. Geology and Mineralogy [*A publication*]
**NSEI** .......... Norsk Selskap for Elektronisk Informasjonselskap [*Norwegian Computer Society*] (CSR)
**NSel** .......... Middle Country Public Library, Selden Branch, Selden, NY [*Library symbol*] [*Library of Congress*] (LCLS)
**NSelC** ........ Suffolk County Community College, Selden, NY [*Library symbol*] [*Library of Congress*] (LCLS)
**NSelC-E** .... Suffolk County Community College, Eastern Campus, Riverhead, NY [*Library symbol*] [*Library of Congress*] (LCLS)
**NSelC-W** ... Suffolk County Community College, Western Campus, Brentwood, NY [*Library symbol*] [*Library of Congress*] (LCLS)
**NSELH** ...... East Lake Ainslie Historical Society, Nova Scotia [*Library symbol*] [*National Library of Canada*] (BIB)
**NSEMA** ..... National Spray Equipment Manufacturers Association (EA)
**NSEN** ........ Northern Science Education News Service. Scavengers College, Alaska [*A publication*]
**NSEP** ......... National Security and Emergency Preparedness
**NSEQ** ........ Nankai Social and Economic Quarterly [*A publication*]
**NSERC** ...... Natural Sciences and Engineering Research Council of Canada [*Research center*] (IRC)
**NSERI** ....... National Solar Energy Research Institute [*Energy Research and Development Administration*]
**NSES** ......... National Security Electronic Surveillance
**NSetSP** ...... Society for the Preservation of Long Island Antiquities, Setauket, NY [*Library symbol*] [*Library of Congress*] (LCLS)
**NSewEH** .... Elmont Memorial High School, Sewanhaka, NY [*Library symbol*] [*Library of Congress*] (LCLS)
**NSewSJ** ..... Stanforth Junior High School, Sewanhaka, NY [*Library symbol*] [*Library of Congress*] (LCLS)
**NSF** ........... Camp Springs, MD [*Location identifier*] [*FAA*] (FAAL)
**NSF** ........... National Salvation Front [*Romania*] [*Political party*]
**NSF** ........... National Sanitation Foundation (EA)
**NSF** ........... National Schizophrenia Fellowship [*British*]
**NSF** ........... National Science Foundation (EA)
**NSF** ........... National Science Foundation, Washington, DC [*OCLC symbol*] (OCLC)
**NSF** ........... National Scoliosis Foundation (EA)
**NSF** ........... National Sex Forum [*Later, ET*] (EA)
**NSF** ........... National Sharecroppers Fund (EA)
**NSF** ........... National Soaring Foundation (EA)
**NSF** ........... National Stockbrokers Forum [*Later, CFC*] (EA)
**NSF** ........... National Strike Force [*Marine science*] (MSC)
**NSF** ........... Naval Stock Fund
**NSF** ........... Naval Supersonic Facility
**NSF** ........... Naval Supply Force
**NSF** ........... Naval Support Force (MCD)
**NSF** ........... Navy Special Fuel
**NSF** ........... Negotiated Search Facility [*Information retrieval*]
**NSF** ........... Net Square Feet (MCD)
**NSF** ........... Neutron Scattering Facility [*Oak Ridge, TN*] [*Oak Ridge National Laboratory*] [*Department of Energy*] (GRD)
**NSF** ........... Nitrogen Supply Flask
**NSF** ........... Nodular Subepidermal Fibrosis [*Dermatology*]
**NSF** ........... Nonsterile Field Soil [*Agronomy*]
**NSF** ........... Nonstock Fund
**NSF** ........... Nordiska Skattevetenskapliga Forskningradet [*Nordic Council for Tax Research - NCTR*] (EAIO)
**NSF** ........... Norges Standardiseringsforbund [*Norwegian Standards Association*] [*Information service or system*] (IID)
**NSF** ........... Not Sufficient Funds [*Banking*]
**NSF** ........... Nuclear Safety Facility
**NSF** ........... Nuclear Structure Facility [*British*]
**NSFA** ......... Faleolo/International [*Western Samoa*] [*ICAO location identifier*] (ICLI)
**NSFA** ......... National Science Foundation Act [*1950*]
**NSFA** ......... Nordic Swimming Federations Association (EA)
**NSFAC** ...... National Student Financial Aid Council [*Later, NASFAA*] (EA)
**NSFB** ......... New School of Family Birthing (EA)
**NSFC** ......... Nancy Sinatra Fan Club (EA)
**NSFC** ......... Nat Stuckey Fan Club [*Inactive*] (EA)
**NSFC** ......... National Society of Film Critics
**NSFCCDLR** ... National Society of Fathers for Child Custody and Divorce Law Reform [*Later, FER*] (EA)
**NSFD** ......... Notice of Structural or Functional Deficiency
**NSFFC** ...... National Save the Family Farm Coalition (EA)
**NSFG** ......... National Survey of Family Growth
**NSFH** ......... North-South Fine, Hundreds
**NSFI** .......... Fagali'I [*Western Samoa*] [*ICAO location identifier*] (ICLI)
**NSF-I** ......... National Science Fair - International
**NSF/IDOE** ... National Science Foundation Office for the International Decade of Ocean Exploration
**NSF Inform** ... NSF [*Namnden foer Skoglig Flygbildteknik*] Information [*A publication*]
**NSfK** .......... Nordiska Samarbetsradet for Kriminologi [*Scandinavian Research Council for Criminology - SRCC*] [*Helsinki, Finland*] (EAIO)
**NSFL** ......... National Sanitation Foundation Laboratory
**NSFNB** ...... NSFI [*Norges Skipaforsknings Institutt*] Nytt [*A publication*]
**NSFNET** ... National Science Foundation Network
**NSFO** ........ National-Sozialistischer Fuersorge Offizier [*NAZI Guidance Officer*] [*German*]
**NSFO** ........ Navy Special [*or Standard*] Fuel Oil
**NSFP** ......... Non-Sodium Fire Protection [*Nuclear energy*] (NRCH)
**NSFPA** ...... National Suppliers to Food Processors Association (EA)
**NSFR** ......... National Society of Fund Raisers [*Later, NSFRE*] (EA)
**NSFR** ......... Nitroxide Stable Free Radical [*For tissue NMR*]
**NSFRC** ...... National Silver Fox Rabbit Club (EA)
**NSFRE** ...... National Society of Fund Raising Executives (EA)
**NSFS** ......... National Society for Shut-Ins (EA)
**NSFS** ......... Nordiska Sallskapet for Stralskydd [*Nordic Society for Radiation Protection - NSRP*] [*Helsinki, Finland*] (EAIO)
**NSfSC** ........ Sullivan County Community College, South Fallsburg, NY [*Library symbol*] [*Library of Congress*] (LCLS)
**NSF SRS** ... National Science Foundation. Science Resources Studies Highlights [*A publication*]
**NSF/STAH** ... National Science Foundation Program for Science and Technology Aid to the Handicapped
**NSF Svy SE** ... Postcensal Survey of Scientists and Engineers. National Science Foundation. Report No. 84-330 [*United States*] [*A publication*]
**NSFT** ......... North-South Fine, Tens
**NSFTD** ...... Normal, Spontaneous, Full Term Delivery [*Obstetrics*]
**NSFTL** ...... National Sanitation Foundation Testing Laboratory, Inc. (MSA)
**NSFU** ......... Needle Stampers' and Filers' Union [*British*]
**NSFU** ......... North-South Fine, Units

**NSF Univ**... Federal Support to Universities, Colleges, and Nonprofit Institutions. Fiscal Year 1982. National Science Foundation. Report No. 84-315 [*United States*] [*A publication*]
**NSFZD**...... Nippon Sanka Fujinka Gakkai Chugoku Shikoku Godo Chihobukai Zasshi [*A publication*]
**NSG**.......... National Society for Graphology (EA)
**NSG**.......... National Supply Group [*Military*] (AFIT)
**NSG**.......... Naval Security Group
**NSG**.......... Neurosecretory Granules
**NSG**.......... Newspaper Systems Group (EA)
**NSG**.......... North Seeking Gyro
**NSG**.......... Not So Good
**NSG**.......... Nursing
**NSGA**........ National Sand and Gravel Association [*Later, NAA*] (EA)
**NSGA**........ National Sporting Goods Association (EA)
**NSGA**........ Naval Security Group Activity
**NSGC**........ National Self Government Committee (EA)
**NSGC**........ National Society of Genetic Counselors (EA)
**NSGC**........ National Swine Growers Council [*Later, NPPC*] (EA)
**NSGCC**...... Coastal Courier, Glace Bay, Nova Scotia [*Library symbol*] [*National Library of Canada*] (NLC)
**NSGCFA**... Aurora, Canadian Forces Base, Greenwood, Nova Scotia [*Library symbol*] [*National Library of Canada*] (NLC)
**NSGCH**..... Naval Security Group Command Headquarters
**NSGCTT**... Nonseminomatous Germ Cell Tumors of the Testes
**NSGD**........ National Sea Grant Depository [*National Oceanic and Atmospheric Administration*] [*Information service or system*] (IID)
**NSGIB**....... NAVSHIPS [*Naval Ship Systems Command*] General Information Book
**NSGKA**..... Nippon Shashin Gakkai Kaishi [*A publication*]
**NSGLS**...... Nordisk Sekretariat for Gartneri- Land-, og Skovarbejderforbund [*Nordic Secretariat for Agricultural and Horticultural Workers - NSAHW*] (EAIO)
**NSGN**........ Noise Generator (CET)
**NSGOC**..... Old Court House Museum, Guysborough, Nova Scotia [*Library symbol*] [*National Library of Canada*] (NLC)
**NSGSR**...... North-Holland Series in General Systems Research [*Elsevier Book Series*] [*A publication*]
**NSGT**........ Non-Self-Governing Territories [*United Nations*]
**NSGTMEM**... National Society of General Tool Makers, Engineers, and Machinists [*A union*] [*British*]
**NSGW**....... National Society of Glass Workers [*A union*] [*British*]
**NSGW**....... Native Sons of the Golden West (EA)
**NSGZD**..... Nippon Shokaki Geka Gakkai Zasshi [*A publication*]
**NSH**.......... Halifax City Regional Library, Nova Scotia [*Library symbol*] [*National Library of Canada*] (NLC)
**NSh**........... John Jermain Memorial Public Library, Sag Harbor, NY [*Library symbol*] [*Library of Congress*] (LCLS)
**NSH**.......... Nashua Corp. [*NYSE symbol*] (SPSG)
**NSH**.......... National Society for Histotechnology (EA)
**NSH**.......... National Society of Hypnotherapists (EA)
**NSH**.......... Naval School of Health Sciences, Bethesda, MD [*OCLC symbol*] (OCLC)
**NSH**.......... Nordisk Samarbeidskomite for Husstellundervisning [*Nordic Joint Committee for Domestic Education - NJCDE*] (EAIO)
**NSH**.......... Northern-Southern Hybrid [*Hemoglobin phenotype of Rana pipiens*]
**NSH**.......... Norwegian Shipping News [*Oslo*] [*A publication*]
**NSH**.......... Not So Hot [*Slang*]
**NSHA**........ National Steeplechase and Hunt Association (EA)
**NSHA**........ National Stock Horse Association (EA)
**NSHAC-FP**... National Self-Help Action Center - Food Program (EA)
**NSHAG**..... Art Gallery of Nova Scotia, Halifax, Nova Scotia [*Library symbol*] [*National Library of Canada*] (NLC)
**NSHANSS**... Synod Office, Diocese of Nova Scotia, Anglican Church of Canada, Halifax, Nova Scotia [*Library symbol*] [*National Library of Canada*] (NLC)
**NSHAR**..... Algas Resources Ltd., Halifax, Nova Scotia [*Library symbol*] [*National Library of Canada*] (NLC)
**NSHAVI**.... [*The*] Atlantic Provinces Resource Centre for the Visually-Impaired, Halifax, Nova Scotia [*Library symbol*] [*National Library of Canada*] (NLC)
**NSHBS**...... Nova Scotia Barristers Society, Halifax, Nova Scotia [*Library symbol*] [*National Library of Canada*] (NLC)
**NSHC**........ Cambridge Military Library, Halifax, Nova Scotia [*Library symbol*] [*National Library of Canada*] (NLC)
**NSHC**........ National Self-Help Clearinghouse (EA)
**NSHC**........ National Silver-Haired Congress (EA)
**NSHC**........ North Sea Hydrographic Commission [*of the International Hydrographic Organization*] [*Belgium*]
**NSHCA**..... Nova Scotia College of Art and Design, Halifax, Nova Scotia [*Library symbol*] [*National Library of Canada*] (NLC)
**NSHCB**..... Music and Record Library, Canadian Broadcasting Corp. [*Musicotheque et Discotheque, Societe Radio-Canada*] Halifax, Nova Scotia [*Library symbol*] [*National Library of Canada*] (NLC)
**NSHCBC**... Canadian British Consultants Ltd., Halifax, Nova Scotia [*Library symbol*] [*National Library of Canada*] (NLC)
**NSHCBF**... Film Library, CBHT-TV, Halifax, Nova Scotia [*Library symbol*] [*National Library of Canada*] (NLC)
**NSHCD**..... Law Library, Cox, Downie & Co., Halifax, Nova Scotia [*Library symbol*] [*National Library of Canada*] (NLC)
**NSHCDD**.. Nova Scotia Commission on Drug Dependency, Halifax, Nova Scotia [*Library symbol*] [*National Library of Canada*] (NLC)
**NSHCFM**... Maritime Command Museum, Canadian Forces Base, Halifax, Nova Scotia [*Library symbol*] [*National Library of Canada*] (BIB)
**NSHCH**..... Camp Hill Hospital, Halifax, Nova Scotia [*Library symbol*] [*National Library of Canada*] (NLC)
**NSHCIC**.... National Solar Heating and Cooling Information Center [*Later, CAREIRS*]
**NSHCIC**.... Nova Scotia Communications and Information Centre, Halifax, Nova Scotia [*Library symbol*] [*National Library of Canada*] (NLC)
**NSHD**........ Dalhousie University, Halifax, Nova Scotia [*Library symbol*] [*National Library of Canada*] (NLC)
**NSHDA**..... Archives, Dalhousie University, Halifax, Nova Scotia [*Library symbol*] [*National Library of Canada*] (BIB)
**NSHDAG**... Nova Scotia Department of the Attorney-General, Halifax, Nova Scotia [*Library symbol*] [*National Library of Canada*] (NLC)
**NSHDCA**.. Nova Scotia Department of Consumer Affairs, Halifax, Nova Scotia [*Library symbol*] [*National Library of Canada*] (NLC)
**NSHDD**..... Nova Scotia Department of Industry, Trade, and Technology, Halifax, Nova Scotia [*Library symbol*] [*National Library of Canada*] (NLC)
**NSHDE**..... Nova Scotia Department of the Environment, Halifax, Nova Scotia [*Library symbol*] [*National Library of Canada*] (NLC)
**NSHDEA**.. Resource Centre, Ecology Action Centre, Dalhousie University, Halifax, Nova Scotia [*Library symbol*] [*National Library of Canada*] (NLC)
**NSHDF**..... Nova Scotia Department of Fisheries, Halifax, Nova Scotia [*Library symbol*] [*National Library of Canada*] (NLC)
**NSHDH**.... Nova Scotia Department of Transportation, Halifax, Nova Scotia [*Library symbol*] [*National Library of Canada*] (NLC)
**NSHDIP**.... Institute of Public Affairs, Dalhousie University, Halifax, Nova Scotia, [*Library symbol*] [*National Library of Canada*] (NLC)
**NSHDIR**... School of Resources and Environmental Studies, Dalhousie University, Halifax, Nova Scotia [*Library symbol*] [*National Library of Canada*] (NLC)
**NSHDL**..... Law School, Dalhousie University, Halifax, Nova Scotia [*Library symbol*] [*National Library of Canada*] (NLC)
**NSHDLS**... School of Library Service, Dalhousie University, Halifax, Nova Scotia [*Library symbol*] [*National Library of Canada*] (NLC)
**NSHDM**.... W. K. Kellogg Health Sciences Library, Dalhousie University, Halifax, Nova Scotia [*Library symbol*] [*National Library of Canada*] (NLC)
**NSHDMA**... Map Library, Dalhousie University, Halifax, Nova Scotia [*Library symbol*] [*National Library of Canada*] (NLC)
**NSHDOL**.. Nova Scotia Department of Labour and Manpower, Halifax, Nova Scotia [*Library symbol*] [*National Library of Canada*] (NLC)
**NSHDOM**... Nova Scotia Department of Mines, Halifax, Nova Scotia [*Library symbol*] [*National Library of Canada*] (NLC)
**NSHDOS**.. Dalhousie Ocean Studies Programme, Dalhousie University, Halifax, Nova Scotia [*Library symbol*] [*National Library of Canada*] (NLC)
**NSHDR**..... Cultural Affairs Library, Nova Scotia Department of Tourism and Culture, Halifax, Nova Scotia [*Library symbol*] [*National Library of Canada*] (NLC)
**NSHDS**..... MacDonald Science Library, Dalhousie University, Halifax, Nova Scotia [*Library symbol*] [*National Library of Canada*] (NLC)
**NSHE**........ [*The*] New Schaff-Herzog Encyclopaedia of Religious Knowledge [*A publication*] (BJA)
**NSHEB**..... North of Scotland Hydro-Electric Board (ECON)
**NShei**......... Shelter Island Public Library Society, Shelter Island, NY [*Library symbol*] [*Library of Congress*] (LCLS)
**NSherb**....... Sherburne Public Library, Sherburne, NY [*Library symbol*] [*Library of Congress*] (LCLS)
**NSHF**........ Fisheries and Oceans Canada [*Peches et Oceans Canada*] Halifax, Nova Scotia [*Library symbol*] [*National Library of Canada*] (NLC)
**NSHF**........ Scotia-Fundy Regional Library, Fisheries and Oceans Canada [*Bibliotheque de la Region Scotia-Fundy, Peches et Oceans Canada*], Halifax, Nova Scotia [*Library symbol*] [*National Library of Canada*] (NLC)
**NSHFIF**.... Federal-Provincial Taxation and Fiscal Relations Library, Nova Scotia Department of Finance, Halifax, Nova Scotia [*Library symbol*] [*National Library of Canada*] (NLC)
**NSHH**....... Nova Scotia Department of Health, Halifax, Nova Scotia [*Library symbol*] [*National Library of Canada*] (NLC)

**NSHHC**..... Halifax County Regional Library, Lower Sackville, Nova Scotia [*Library symbol*] [*National Library of Canada*] (NLC)
**NSHHE**..... Halifax Herald Ltd., Nova Scotia [*Library symbol*] [*National Library of Canada*] (NLC)
**NSHHI**...... Health Services Library, Halifax Infirmary, Nova Scotia [*Library symbol*] [*National Library of Canada*] (NLC)
**NSHHR**..... Nova Scotia Human Rights Commission, Halifax, Nova Scotia [*Library symbol*] [*National Library of Canada*] (NLC)
**NSHHS**..... Hantsport and Area Historical Society, Nova Scotia [*Library symbol*] [*National Library of Canada*] (NLC)
**NSHIA**...... Nankyoku Shiryo [*Antarctic Record*] [*Japan*] [*A publication*]
**NSHIAP**.... Atlantic Regional Library, Parks Canada [*Bibliotheque Regionale de l'Atlantique, Parcs Canada*] Halifax, Nova Scotia [*Library symbol*] [*National Library of Canada*] (NLC)
**NSHIC**...... International Centre for Ocean Development, Halifax, Nova Scotia [*Library symbol*] [*National Library of Canada*] (BIB)
**NS His S**.... Nova Scotia Historical Society. Collections [*A publication*]
**NS Hist**...... Nova Scotia History [*A publication*]
**NSHJ**......... Canada Department of Justice [*Ministere de la Justice*] Halifax, Nova Scotia [*Library symbol*] [*National Library of Canada*] (NLC)
**NSHK**........ University of King's College, Halifax, Nova Scotia [*Library symbol*] [*National Library of Canada*] (NLC)
**NSHKA**..... Nippon Shika Ishikai Zasshi [*A publication*]
**NSHKH**..... Izaak Walton Killam Hospital for Children, Halifax, Nova Scotia [*Library symbol*] [*National Library of Canada*] (NLC)
**NSHKJ**...... School of Journalism, University of King's College, Halifax, Nova Scotia [*Library symbol*] [*National Library of Canada*] (NLC)
**NSHKMGM**... Kitz, Matheson, Green & MacIsaac Law Firm, Halifax, Nova Scotia [*Library symbol*] [*National Library of Canada*] (NLC)
**NSHL**........ Legislative Library, Halifax, Nova Scotia [*Library symbol*] [*National Library of Canada*] (NLC)
**NSHL**........ Northern Star Holdings Ltd. [*Australia*]
**NSHLA**..... Nova Scotia Legal Aid, Halifax, Nova Scotia [*Library symbol*] [*National Library of Canada*] (BIB)
**NSHLP**...... Liberal Party of Nova Scotia, Halifax [*Library symbol*] [*National Library of Canada*] (BIB)
**NSHM**....... Atlantic Regional Laboratory, National Research Council [*Laboratoire Regional de l'Atlantique, Conseil National de Recherches du Canada*] Halifax, Nova Scotia [*Library symbol*] [*National Library of Canada*] (NLC)
**NSHMA**.... Nova Scotia Department of Municipal Affairs, Halifax, Nova Scotia [*Library symbol*] [*National Library of Canada*] (NLC)
**NSHMBA**... National Society of Hispanic MBAs (EA)
**NSHMC**.... Maritime Conservatory of Music, Halifax, Nova Scotia [*Library symbol*] [*National Library of Canada*] (NLC)
**NSHMCA**... Archives, Maritime Conference, United Church of Canada Halifax, Nova Scotia [*Library symbol*] [*National Conference of Commissioners on Uniform State Laws*] (BIB)
**NSHMCR**... Law Library, McInnes, Cooper & Robertson, Halifax, Nova Scotia [*Library symbol*] [*National Library of Canada*] (NLC)
**NSHML**.... Martec Ltd., Halifax, Nova Scotia [*Library symbol*] [*National Library of Canada*] (NLC)
**NSHMM**... Maritime Museum of the Atlantic, Halifax, Nova Scotia [*Library symbol*] [*National Library of Canada*] (NLC)
**NSHMO**.... Mobil Oil Canada Ltd., Halifax, Nova Scotia [*Library symbol*] [*National Library of Canada*] (NLC)
**NSHMS**.... Nova Scotia Museum, Halifax, Nova Scotia [*Library symbol*] [*National Library of Canada*] (NLC)
**NSHMT**.... Regional Library, Canadian Coast Guard [*Bibliotheque Regionale, Garde Cotiere Canadienne*] Dartmouth, Nova Scotia [*Library symbol*] [*National Library of Canada*] (NLC)
**NSHMTT**... Information Resource Centre, Maritime Tel & Tel, Halifax, Nova Scotia [*Library symbol*] [*National Library of Canada*] (NLC)
**NSHN**........ Defence Research Establishment Atlantic, Canada Department of National Defence [*Centre de Recherches pour la Defense Atlantique, Ministere de la Defense Nationale*] Dartmouth, Nova Scotia [*Library symbol*] [*National Library of Canada*] (NLC)
**NSHND**..... Reference and Recreational Library (Stadacona), Canada Department of National Defence [*Bibliotheque de Consultation et de Lecture (Stadacona), Ministere de la Defense Nationale*] Halifax, Nova Scotia [*Library symbol*] [*National Library of Canada*] (NLC)
**NSHNF**..... National Film Board [*Office National du Film*], Halifax, Nova Scotia [*Library symbol*] [*National Library of Canada*] (NLC)
**NSHNI**...... Nova Scotia Nautical Institute, Halifax, Nova Scotia [*Library symbol*] [*National Library of Canada*] (NLC)
**NSHNP**..... Nova Scotia Newspaper Project, Halifax [*Library symbol*] [*National Library of Canada*] (BIB)
**NSHNS**..... Ships Recreational Library, Canadian Forces Base Halifax [*Bibliotheque Recreative, Base des Forces Canadiennes Halifax*], Nova Scotia [*Library symbol*] [*National Library of Canada*] (BIB)
**NSHOQ**.... National Shoes, Inc. [*NASDAQ symbol*] (NQ)
**NShor**........ Shoreham-Wading River Public Library, Shoreham, NY [*Library symbol*] [*Library of Congress*] (LCLS)
**NShorHS**... Shoreham-Wading River High School, Shoreham, NY [*Library symbol*] [*Library of Congress*] (LCLS)
**NSHP**........ Nova Scotia Public Archives, Halifax, Nova Scotia [*Library symbol*] [*National Library of Canada*] (NLC)
**NSHPC**..... Corporate Research and Information Centre, Nova Scotia Power Corp., Halifax, Nova Scotia [*Library symbol*] [*National Library of Canada*] (NLC)
**NSHPH**..... Atlantic School of Theology, Halifax, Nova Scotia [*Library symbol*] [*National Library of Canada*] (NLC)
**NSHPI**....... Planning Information Office, City of Halifax, Nova Scotia [*Library symbol*] [*National Library of Canada*] (NLC)
**NSHPL**...... Nova Scotia Union Catalogue, Nova Scotia Provincial Library, Halifax, Nova Scotia [*Library symbol*] [*National Library of Canada*] (NLC)
**NSHPLX**... Reference Services, Nova Scotia Provinical Library, Halifax, Nova Scotia [*Library symbol*] [*National Library of Canada*] (NLC)
**NSHPW**.... Atlantic Regional Library, Public Works Canada [*Bibliotheque Regionale de l'Atlantique, Travaux Publics Canada*] Halifax, Nova Scotia [*Library symbol*] [*National Library of Canada*] (NLC)
**NSHQ**........ Naval Service Headquarters [*Canada*]
**NSHQ**........ Naval Staff Headquarters [*British military*] (DMA)
**NShr**.......... John C. Hart Memorial Library, Shrub Oak, NY [*Library symbol*] [*Library of Congress*] (LCLS)
**NSHR**........ National Show Horse Registry (EA)
**NSHR**........ Nova Scotia Research Foundation, Dartmouth, Nova Scotia [*Library symbol*] [*National Library of Canada*] (NLC)
**NSHRC**..... National Self-Help Resource Center (EA)
**NSHRC**..... National Shared Housing Resource Center (EA)
**NSHRC**..... Nova Scotia Rehabilitation Centre, Halifax, Nova Scotia [*Library symbol*] [*National Library of Canada*] (NLC)
**NSHRCA**.. Roman Catholic Archdiocesan Archives, Halifax, Nova Scotia [*Library symbol*] [*National Library of Canada*] (BIB)
**NSHRL**..... Nova Scotia Regional Libraries, Halifax, Nova Scotia [*Library symbol*] [*National Library of Canada*] (NLC)
**NSHRP**..... Photogrammetry Division, Nova Scotia Research Foundation, Halifax, Nova Scotia [*Library symbol*] [*Obsolete*] [*National Library of Canada*] (NLC)
**NSHS**........ National Slavic Honor Society (EA)
**NSHS**........ St. Mary's University, Halifax, Nova Scotia [*Library symbol*] [*National Library of Canada*] (NLC)
**NSHSG**..... Sable Gas Systems Ltd., Halifax, Nova Scotia [*Library symbol*] [*National Library of Canada*] (NLC)
**NSHSMC**... Stewart, MacKeen & Covert Law Firm, Halifax, Nova Scotia [*Library symbol*] [*National Library of Canada*] (NLC)
**NSHSP**...... Social Development Division Library, Social Planning Department, City of Halifax, Nova Scotia [*Library symbol*] [*National Library of Canada*] (NLC)
**NSHSPT**... Ferguson Library for Print Handicapped Students, Patrick Power Library, St. Mary's University, Halifax, Nova Scotia [*Library symbol*] [*National Library of Canada*] (NLC)
**NSHSS**...... Nova Scotia Department of Community Services, Halifax, Nova Scotia [*Library symbol*] [*National Library of Canada*] (NLC)
**NSHSW**.... Maritime School of Social Work, Halifax, Nova Scotia [*Library symbol*] [*National Library of Canada*] (NLC)
**NSHT**........ Norsk Slektshistorisk Tidsskrift [*A publication*]
**NSHT**........ Technical University of Nova Scotia, Halifax, Nova Scotia [*Library symbol*] [*National Library of Canada*] (NLC)
**NSHTI**....... Nova Scotia Institute of Technology, Halifax, Nova Scotia [*Library symbol*] [*National Library of Canada*] (NLC)
**NSHTU**..... Nova Scotia Teachers Union, Halifax, Nova Scotia [*Library symbol*] [*National Library of Canada*] (NLC)
**NSHV**........ Mount Saint Vincent University, Halifax, Nova Scotia [*Library symbol*] [*National Library of Canada*] (NLC)
**NSHVA**..... Art Gallery, Mount Saint Vincent University, Halifax, Nova Scotia [*Library symbol*] [*National Library of Canada*] (NLC)
**NSHVGH**... Health Sciences Library, Victoria General Hospital, Halifax, Nova Scotia [*Library symbol*] [*National Library of Canada*] (NLC)
**NSHVH**..... Halifax Regional Vocational School, Nova Scotia [*Library symbol*] [*National Library of Canada*] (NLC)
**NSHVTT**... Nova Scotia Department of Advanced Education and Job Training, Halifax, Nova Scotia [*Library symbol*] [*National Library of Canada*] (NLC)
**NSHW**....... Atlantic Region, Atmospheric Environment Service, Environment Canada [*Bureau Regional de l'Atlantique, Service de l'Environnement Atmospherique, Environnement Canada*] Halifax, Nova Scotia [*Library symbol*] [*National Library of Canada*] (NLC)
**NSHW**....... National Showmanship Services [*NASDAQ symbol*] (NQ)
**NSI**............ Handbook of North-Semitic Inscriptions [*A publication*] (BJA)

**NSI** ........... NASA Standard Initiator (NASA)
**NSI** ........... National Security Index of the American Security Council [*A publication*] (DLA)
**NSI** ........... National Security Information (NRCH)
**NSI** ........... National Service Industries, Inc. [*NYSE symbol*] (SPSG)
**NSI** ........... National Service [*Life*] Insurance
**NSI** ........... National Shoe Institute (EA)
**NSI** ........... National Space Institute [*Later, NSS*] (EA)
**NSi** ........... Nea Sion [*A publication*]
**NSI** ........... Negative Self-Image [*Psychology*]
**NSI** ........... Network Strategies, Incorporated [*Fairfax, VA*] [*Telecommunications*] (TSSD)
**NSI** ........... Next Sequential Instruction
**NSI** ........... Nielsen Station Index [*Nielsen Media Research*] [*Information service or system*]
**NSI** ........... Nitrogen Solubility Index [*Analytical chemistry*]
**NSI** ........... Noise Source Instrumentation
**NSI** ........... Nonsatellite Identification
**NSI** ........... Nonspecific Sexually Transmitted Infection [*Medicine*]
**NSI** ........... Nonstandard Item
**NSI** ........... Nonstocked Item
**NSI** ........... Norsk Senter for Informatikk [*Norwegian Center for Informatics*] [*Information service or system*] (IID)
**NSI** ........... Nuclear Safety Inspection (NVT)
**NSI** ........... Nuclear Safety Institute
**NSI** ........... Nuclear Services International
**NSI** ........... Nuclear Surety Inspection
**NSI** ........... San Nicolas Island, CA [*Location identifier*] [*FAA*] (FAAL)
**NSI-1** ......... NASA [*National Aeronautics and Space Administration*] Standard Initiator - Type 1 [*Formerly, SMSI*] (NASA)
**NSIA** .......... National Security Industrial Association (EA)
**NSIA** .......... National Security and International Affairs [*Office of Management and Budget*]
**NSIAC** ......... National Student Involvement Assistance Center [*Boston University*] [*Defunct*]
**NSIC** .......... National Security Insurance Company [*NASDAQ symbol*] (NQ)
**NSIC** .......... National Spinal Injuries Centre [*Stoke Mandeville Hospital*] [*British*] (CB)
**NSIC** .......... National Strategy Information Center (EA)
**NSIC** .......... Naval Security and Investigative Command
**NSIC** .......... Next Senior in Command [*Navy*]
**NSIC** .......... Noster Salvator Iesus Christus [*Our Savior, Jesus Christ*] [*Latin*]
**NSIC** .......... Nuclear Safety Information Center
**NSIC** .......... Nuclear Strike Information Center
**NSiC** .......... Staten Island Community College, Staten Island, NY [*Library symbol*] [*Library of Congress*] [*Obsolete*] (LCLS)
**NSiCS** ......... College of Staten Island, St. George Campus, Staten Island, NY [*Library symbol*] [*Library of Congress*] (LCLS)
**NSID** .......... National Society of Interior Designers [*Later, ASID*]
**NSIDH** ......... National System of Interstate and Defense Highways (AFIT)
**NSidS** ......... Bendix Corp., Electrical Components Division, Engineering Library, Sidney, NY [*Library symbol*] [*Library of Congress*] (LCLS)
**NSIDS** ......... National Shut-In Day Society (EA)
**NSIDSC** ........ National Sudden Infant Death Syndrome Clearinghouse (EA)
**NSIDSF** ........ National Sudden Infant Death Syndrome Foundation (EA)
**NSIEE** ......... National Society for Internships and Experiential Education (EA)
**NSIF** .......... National Swine Improvement Federation (EA)
**NSIF** .......... Near Space Instrumentation Facility [*NASA*] (KSC)
**NSiIR** ......... New York State Department of Mental Hygiene, Institute for Basic Research in Mental Retardation, Staten Island, NY [*Library symbol*] [*Library of Congress*] (LCLS)
**NSIL** .......... National Seafood Inspection Laboratory [*Pascagoula, MS*] [*Department of Commerce*] (GRD)
**NSILA** ......... Nonsuppressible Insulin-Like Activity [*Cytochemistry*]
**NSiIStC** ....... Saint Columban's Seminary, Silver Creek, NY [*Library symbol*] [*Library of Congress*] [*Obsolete*] (LCLS)
**NSiND** ......... Notre Dame College of Staten Island, Staten Island, NY [*Library symbol*] [*Library of Congress*] (LCLS)
**NS Inst N Sc Pr Tr** ... Nova Scotia Institute of Natural Science. Proceedings and Transactions [*A publication*]
**NSIPA** ......... National Society of Insurance Premium Auditors (EA)
**NSiRC** ......... Richmond College, Staten Island, NY [*Library symbol*] [*Library of Congress*] [*Obsolete*] (LCLS)
**NSIS** .......... National Shut-In Society (EA)
**NSiSV** ......... Saint Vincent's Medical Center of Richmond, Staten Island, NY [*Library symbol*] [*Library of Congress*] (LCLS)
**NSIT** .......... Not Safe in Taxis
**NSITF** ......... National Ship Installations Test Facility
**NSIY** .......... North Somerset Imperial Yeomanry [*British military*] (DMA)
**NSJ** ........... Nuestro Senor Jesucristo [*Our Lord, Jesus Christ*] [*Spanish*]
**NSJB** .......... Niedersaechsisches Jahrbuch [*A publication*]
**NSJBH** ......... Niedersaechsisches Jahrbuch. Hildesheim [*A publication*]
**NSJC** .......... National Society of Journeymen Curriers [*A union*] [*British*]
**NSJC** .......... Noster Salvator Jesus Christus [*Our Savior, Jesus Christ*] [*Latin*]
**NSJC** .......... Notre Seigneur Jesus Christ [*Our Lord, Jesus Christ*] [*French*]
**NSJFS** ......... North Staffordshire Journal of Field Studies [*A publication*]
**NSJLG** ......... Niedersaechsisches Jahrbuch fuer Landesgeschichte [*A publication*]
**NSK** ........... Nippon Seiko Kabushiki Kaisha [*Japan*]
**NSKC** .......... National Safe Kids Campaign (EA)
**NSKER** ......... Efamol Research Institute, Kentville, Nova Scotia [*Library symbol*] [*National Library of Canada*] (NLC)
**NSKIA** ......... Nippon Soshikigaku Kiroku [*A publication*]
**NSKIP** ......... Nordiska Samarbetskommitten for Internationell Politik [*Nordic Cooperation Committee for International Politics, Including Conflict and Peace Research*] (EAIO)
**NSKKR** ......... Kings Regional Vocational School, Kentville, Nova Scotia [*Library symbol*] [*National Library of Canada*] (NLC)
**NSKL** .......... Wildlife Division, Nova Scotia Department of Lands and Forests, Kentville, Nova Scotia [*Library symbol*] [*National Library of Canada*] (NLC)
**NSKOK** ......... Old Kings Courthouse Heritage Museum, Kentville, Nova Scotia [*Library symbol*] [*National Library of Canada*] (NLC)
**NSKR** .......... Research Station, Agriculture Canada [*Station de Recherches, Agriculture Canada*] Kentville, Nova Scotia [*Library symbol*] [*National Library of Canada*] (NLC)
**NSKSA** ......... Nippon Setchaku Kyokaishi [*A publication*]
**NSKVH** ......... Valley Health Services Association, Kentville, Nova Scotia [*Library symbol*] [*National Library of Canada*] (NLC)
**NSKY** .......... New Sky Communications, Inc. [*Rochester, NY*] [*NASDAQ symbol*] (NQ)
**NSL** ........... Det Norske Sprak-og Litteraturselskap [*A publication*]
**NSL** ........... Nasion-Sella Line [*Brain anatomy*]
**NSL** ........... National Science Laboratories (KSC)
**NSL** ........... National Science Library [*Later, Canada Institute for Scientific and Technical Information*] (DIT)
**NSL** ........... National Service League [*British military*] (DMA)
**NSL** ........... National Soccer League (EA)
**NSL** ........... National Standards Laboratory [*Formerly, IBS, IMR*] [*National Institute of Standards and Technology*]
**NSL** ........... National Story League (EA)
**NSL** ........... Naval Submarine League (EA)
**NSL** ........... Naval Supersonic Laboratory
**NSL** ........... Navigating Sub-Lieutenant [*Navy*] [*British*] (ROG)
**NSL** ........... Navy Standards Laboratory
**NSL** ........... Navy Stock List
**NSL** ........... Net Switching Loss [*Telecommunications*] (TEL)
**NSL** ........... New Special Libraries [*A publication*]
**NSL** ........... Nonstandard Label [*Data processing*]
**NSL** ........... Nonstockage List
**NSL** ........... North Air Airlines [*Anchorage, AK*] [*FAA designator*] (FAAC)
**NSL** ........... Northrup Space Laboratories (KSC)
**NSL** ........... Norwood & St. Lawrence Railroad Co. [*AAR code*]
**NSL** ........... Not Stock Listed
**NSL** ........... Nuclear Safety Line
**NSl** ........... Saranac Lake Free Library, Saranac Lake, NY [*Library symbol*] [*Library of Congress*] (LCLS)
**NSLA** .......... Louisbourg Archives, Nova Scotia [*Library symbol*] [*National Library of Canada*] (NLC)
**NSLA** .......... National Society of Literature and the Arts (EA)
**NSLA** .......... National Staff Leasing Association (EA)
**NSLAL** ......... Nova Scotia Land Survey Institute, Lawrencetown, Nova Scotia [*Library symbol*] [*National Library of Canada*] (NLC)
**NSLC** .......... Nuclear Safety and Licensing Commission
**NSLF** .......... Fortress of Louisbourg, Canada National Historic Park [*Forteresse de Louisbourg, Parc Historique National*] Nova Scotia [*Library symbol*] [*National Library of Canada*] (NLC)
**NSLF** .......... Nonself
**NSLFA** ......... Nervnaia Sistema Leningradskii Gosudarstvennii Universitet Imeni A. A. Zhdanova Fiziologicheskii Institut [*A publication*]
**NSLFM** ......... Fisheries Museum of the Atlantic, Lunenburg, Nova Scotia [*Library symbol*] [*National Library of Canada*] (NLC)
**NSLFP** ......... Fort Point Museum, La Have, Nova Scotia [*Library symbol*] [*National Library of Canada*] (NLC)
**NSlH** .......... General Hospital of Saranac Lake, Saranac Lake, NY [*Library symbol*] [*Library of Congress*] (LCLS)
**NSLHS** ......... Lunenburg Heritage Society, Nova Scotia [*Library symbol*] [*National Library of Canada*] (NLC)
**NSLI** .......... National Service Life Insurance
**NSLI** .......... National Street Law Institute (EA)
**NSLIN** ......... Nonstandard Line Item Number [*Army*] (AABC)
**NS Lit Sc Soc Tr** ... Nova Scotia Literary and Scientific Society. Transactions [*A publication*]
**NSLL** .......... National Save-a-Life League (EA)
**NSLL** .......... National Savings and Loan League [*Formerly, NLISA*] (EA)
**NSLLS** ......... Lockeport Little School Museum, Nova Scotia [*Library symbol*] [*National Library of Canada*] (NLC)
**NSlNC** ......... North Country Community College, Saranac Lake, NY [*Library symbol*] [*Library of Congress*] (LCLS)
**NSL News** ... Nova Scotia Law News [*A publication*]
**NSLP** .......... National School Lunch Program [*Department of Agriculture*]
**NSLPE** ......... Progress-Enterprise, Lunenburg, Nova Scotia [*Library symbol*] [*National Library of Canada*] (NLC)

**NSLQCM** ... Queens County Museum, Liverpool, Nova Scotia [*Library symbol*] [*National Library of Canada*] (NLC)
**NSLR** ......... Nova Scotia Law Reports [*A publication*] (DLA)
**NSLRS** ...... National School Labor Relations Service [*Later, LMRS*] (EA)
**NSLS** ......... National Synchrotron Light Source [*Brookhaven National Laboratory*]
**NSLS** ......... North Suburban Library System [*Library network*]
**NSLSA** ...... National Surf Life Saving Association of America [*Later, USLA*] (EA)
**NSLSRA**.... National Society of Live Stock Record Associations (EA)
**NSIT** .......... Trudeau Institute, Saranac Lake, NY [*Library symbol*] [*Library of Congress*] (LCLS)
**N/S-LTI-G/T** ... National/State Leadership Training Institute on Gifted and Talented (EA)
**NSIW** ......... Will Rogers Memorial Fund, Saranac Lake, NY [*Library symbol*] [*Library of Congress*] (LCLS)
**NSM** .......... National Security Management [*Military*]
**NSM** .......... National Security Medal [*Military decoration*]
**NSM** .......... National Selected Morticians (EA)
**NSM** .......... National Semiconductor Corp. [*NYSE symbol*] (SPSG)
**NSM** .......... National Serviceman [*British military*] (DMA)
**NSM** .......... National Socialist Movement (EA)
**NSM** .......... Nationalsozialistische Monatshefte [*A publication*]
**NSM** .......... Naval School of Music
**NSM** .......... Network Security Module
**NSM** .......... Network Status Monitor [*NASA*] (KSC)
**NSM** .......... Neurosecretory Motoneurons
**NSM** .......... Neusprachliche Mitteilungen aus Wissenschaft und Praxis [*A publication*]
**NSM** .......... New Schools Movement [*Defunct*] (EA)
**NSM** .......... New Smoking Material [*A wood cellulose-based tobacco substitute*]
**NSM** .......... Nice Safe Man [*Slang*]
**NSM** .......... Nitsanim [*Israel*] [*Later, AMT*] [*Geomagnetic observatory code*]
**NSM** .......... Noise Source Meter
**NSM** .......... Norseman [*Australia*] [*Airport symbol*] (OAG)
**NSM** .......... North-South Map [*Via orbiter*]
**NSM** .......... Northern Student Movement [*Defunct*] (EA)
**NSM** .......... Numismatic Scrapbook Magazine [*A publication*]
**NSm** ........... Smithtown Public Library, Smithtown, NY [*Library symbol*] [*Library of Congress*] (LCLS)
**NSMA** ....... Maota [*Western Samoa*] [*ICAO location identifier*] (ICLI)
**NSMA** ....... National Scale Men's Association (EA)
**NSMA** ....... National Seasoning Manufacturers Association (EA)
**NSMA** ....... National Second Mortgage Association [*Center Square, PA*] (EA)
**NSMA** ....... National Shoe Manufacturers Association [*Later, FIA*] (EA)
**NSMA** ....... National Soup Mix Association [*Defunct*] (EA)
**NSMAPMAWOL** ... Not So Much a Programme, More a Way of Life [*British television program*]
**NSMATCC** ... NATO Small Arms Test Control Commission (MCD)
**NSMB** ....... Netherlands Ship Model Basin
**NSMC** ....... National Student Marketing Corporation
**NSMC** ....... Naval Submarine Medical Center
**NSMCA** .... National Spirit, Metropolitan Club of America (EA)
**NSMCM** ... Naval Supplement, Manual for Courts-Martial [*United States*] [*A publication*] (DLA)
**NSME** ....... Eastern Counties Regional Library, Mulgrave, Nova Scotia [*Library symbol*] [*National Library of Canada*] (NLC)
**NSME** ....... Nonstandard Measuring Equipment [*Aviation*] (FAAC)
**NS Med Bull** ... Nova Scotia Medical Bulletin [*A publication*]
**NSMEX**..... Examiner, Middleton, Nova Scotia [*Library symbol*] [*National Library of Canada*] (NLC)
**NSMFA**..... North Sea Mine Force Association (EA)
**NSMG**....... Naval School of Military Government
**NSMG & A** ... Naval School of Military Government and Administration
**NSmGH**..... Smithtown General Hospital, Smithtown, NY [*Library symbol*] [*Library of Congress*] (LCLS)
**NSMH**....... Nuclear Systems Material Handbook (NRCH)
**NSML**....... Low-Sodium Meal [*Airline notation*] (ADA)
**NSMM**...... Macdonald Museum, Middleton, Nova Scotia [*Library symbol*] [*National Library of Canada*] (NLC)
**NSMM**...... National Society of Metal Mechanics [*A union*] [*British*] (DCTA)
**NSMO**....... NASTRAN [*NASA Structural Analysis*] Systems Management Office
**NSMOD2** ... US Department of Health and Human Services. National Institute of Mental Health. Science Monographs [*A publication*]
**NSMP**........ National Society of Mural Painters (EA)
**NSMP**........ Navy Support and Mobilization Plan (NVT)
**NSMPA**..... National Screw Machine Products Association (EA)
**NSMPA**..... Nauchnye Trudy Samarkandskii Meditsinskii Institut Imeni Akademika I. P. Pavlova [*A publication*]
**NSMR** ....... National Society for Medical Research (EA)
**NSMR** ....... Non-Store Marketing Report [*A publication*]
**NSMRL**...... Naval Submarine Medical Research Laboratory
**NSMRSE** .. National Study of Mathematics Requirements for Scientists and Engineers
**NSMS**........ National Safety Management Society (EA)
**NSMS**........ National Sheet Music Society (EA)
**NSMS**........ Soldiers Memorial Hospital, Middleton, Nova Scotia [*Library symbol*] [*National Library of Canada*] (NLC)
**NSMSES**... Naval Ship Missile System Engineering Station
**NSMSESDETLANT** ... Naval Ship Missile System Engineering Station Detachment, Atlantic (MUGU)
**NSmSJH** ... Saint John's Smithtown Hospital, Smithtown, NY [*Library symbol*] [*Library of Congress*] (LCLS)
**NSMT** ....... National Society of Medical Technologists
**NSMV** ....... Valley Mirror, Middleton, Nova Scotia [*Library symbol*] [*National Library of Canada*] (NLC)
**NSMW** ...... Naval Schools Mine Warfare
**NSN** ........... Akten Betreffende Naamloze Vennootschappen [*A publication*]
**NSN** ........... Military Sealift Command, Washington, DC [*OCLC symbol*] (OCLC)
**NSN** ........... National Stock Number (MCD)
**NSN** ........... NATO Stock Number (NATG)
**NSN** ........... Nelson [*New Zealand*] [*Airport symbol*] (OAG)
**NS & N** ...... New Statesman and Nation [*A publication*]
**NSN** ........... New Statesman and Nation [*A publication*]
**NSN** ........... Nicotine-Stimulated Neurophysin [*Biochemistry*]
**NSN** ........... No Stock Number
**NSN** ........... North Star Network (EA)
**Nsn**............. Number of Similar Negative Matches
**NSN** ........... Nurses Support Network [*Later, NIT*] (EA)
**NSNA** ........ National Socialist Nederlandse Arbeiders Partij [*Netherlands group favoring integration of the Netherlands into the German reich*] [*World War II*]
**NSNA** ........ National Student Nurses' Association (EA)
**NSNA** ........ Newcomen Society in North America (EA)
**NSNC** ........ Nova Scotia Normal College
**NSNE** ........ Nappan Experimental Farm, Nova Scotia [*Library symbol*] [*National Library of Canada*] (NLC)
**NSNEW** .... National Society of New England Women (EA)
**NSNF** ........ Nonstrategic Nuclear Forces (MCD)
**NSnfG**........ GTE Sylvania, Inc., Electronic Components Group, Seneca Falls, NY [*Library symbol*] [*Library of Congress*] (LCLS)
**NSNGA** ..... Aberdeen Hospital, New Glasgow, Nova Scotia [*Library symbol*] [*National Library of Canada*] (NLC)
**NSNGE** ..... Evening News, New Glasgow, Nova Scotia [*Library symbol*] [*National Library of Canada*] (NLC)
**NSNGH**..... New Glasgow Senior High School, Nova Scotia [*Library symbol*] [*National Library of Canada*] (BIB)
**NSNGP** ..... Pictou-Antigonish Regional Library, New Glasgow, Nova Scotia [*Library symbol*] [*National Library of Canada*] (NLC)
**NSNHC**..... Cabot Archives, Neil's Harbour, Nova Scotia [*Library symbol*] [*National Library of Canada*] (NLC)
**NSNLC**...... North Shore New Life Centre [*Australia*]
**NSNMDR** ... National Stock Number Master Data Records (MCD)
**NSNMK**.... Kentville Publishing, New Minas, Nova Scotia [*Library symbol*] [*National Library of Canada*] (NLC)
**NSNN**........ Northern Science Network Newsletter. UNESCO-MAB Northern Science Network Secretariat [*Edmonton*] [*A publication*]
**NSNRP**...... Nonstock Numbered Repair Parts
**NSO** ........... NASA Support Operation (KSC)
**NSO** ........... National School Orchestra Association. Bulletin [*A publication*]
**NSO** ........... National Service Officer [*Ministry of Labour and National Service*] [*British*] [*World War II*]
**NSO**........... National Solar Observatory [*Tucson, AZ*] [*National Science Foundation*] (GRD)
**NSO** ........... National Standardization Office [*US Army Materiel Command*]
**NSO** ........... National Symphony Orchestra
**NSO** ........... Naval Staff Officer
**NSO** ........... Naval Store Officer [*British*]
**NSO** ........... Neighborhood Service Organization
**NSO** ........... Network Support Office [*NASA*]
**NSO** ........... New American Shoe Co., Inc. [*NYSE symbol*] (SPSG)
**NSO** ........... Next Standing Order
**NSO** ........... No Spares Ordered (AAG)
**NSO** ........... Noise Suppression Oscillator (MCD)
**NSO** ........... Nonferrous Smelter Order [*Environmental Protection Agency*]
**NSO** ........... North State Cooperative Library System, Willows, CA [*OCLC symbol*] (OCLC)
**nso**............. Northern Sotho [*MARC language code*] [*Library of Congress*] (LCCP)
**NSO** ........... Nuclear Safety Office [*or Officer*] [*Air Force*] (AFM)
**NSO** ........... Numeric Stockage Objective [*Items*] [*DoD*]
**NSO** ........... Scone [*Australia*] [*Airport symbol*] (OAG)
**NSo** ........... Somers Library, Somers, NY [*Library symbol*] [*Library of Congress*] (LCLS)
**NSOA** ........ National School Orchestra Association (EA)
**NSOA** ........ National School Orchestra Association. Bulletin [*A publication*]
**NSOA** ........ National Symphony Orchestra Association (EA)
**NSOA** ........ Nuclear Safety Operational Analysis (NRCH)
**NSoa** .......... Rogers Memorial Library, Southampton, NY [*Library symbol*] [*Library of Congress*] (LCLS)
**NSoaH** ....... Southampton Hospital, Southampton, NY [*Library symbol*] [*Library of Congress*] (LCLS)

**NSoaS**........ Long Island University, Southampton College, Southampton, NY [*Library symbol*] [*Library of Congress*] (LCLS)
**NSOB**........ New Senate Office Building
**NSOC**........ National SIGINT Operations Center (MCD)
**NSOC**........ Navy Satellite Operations Center (NVT)
**NSOC**........ Norbornene Spiroorthocarbonate [*Organic chemistry*]
**NSOD**........ Naval School of Ordnance Disposal
**NSOEA**..... National Stationery and Office Equipment Association [*Later, NOPA*] (EA)
**NSOF**........ Navy Special Operations Force (AABC)
**NSOGA**..... National Seniors' Open Golf Association (EA)
**NSoHi**........ Somers Historical Society, Somers, NY [*Library symbol*] [*Library of Congress*] (LCLS)
**NSOJ**........ Journal, Oxford, Nova Scotia [*Library symbol*] [*National Library of Canada*] (NLC)
**NSOM**....... Near Field Scanning Optical Microscopy
**NSoo**.......... Southold Free Library, Southold, NY [*Library symbol*] [*Library of Congress*] (LCLS)
**NSOP**........ National Second Opinion Program (EA)
**NSOPCD**... National Society of Old Plymouth Colony Descendants (EA)
**NSOR**........ No Shop Order Required
**NSos**.......... South Salem Library, South Salem, NY [*Library symbol*] [*Library of Congress*] (LCLS)
**NSOSG**...... North Sea Oceanographical Study Group [*British*]
**N Sov**......... Nas Sovremennik [*A publication*]
**NSP**........... NASA Support Plan (KSC)
**NSP**........... National Salvation Party [*Milli Selamet Partisi*] [*Turkey*] [*Political party*] (PPW)
**NSP**........... National Sea Products Ltd. [*Toronto Stock Exchange symbol*]
**NSP**........... National Seoposengwe Party [*Bophuthatswana*] [*Political party*] (PPW)
**NSP**........... National Ski Patrol System (EA)
**NSP**........... National Socialist Party [*New Zealand*] [*Political party*] (PD)
**NSP**........... National Society of Painters [*A union*] [*British*]
**NSP**........... National Society of Professors [*Later, NEA Higher Education Council*] (EA)
**NSP**........... National Space Program (AAG)
**NSP**........... National Stolen Property
**NSP**........... National Stuttering Project (EA)
**NSP**........... Navy Space Project
**NSP**........... Navy Standard Part
**NSP**........... Navy Support Plan
**NSP**........... Net Social Profitability
**NSP**........... Network Services Protocol [*Digital Equipment Corp.*] [*Telecommunications*] (TEL)
**NSP**........... Network Signal Processor (NASA)
**NSP**........... Network Support Plan [*NASA*] (KSC)
**NSp**........... Neuere Sprachen [*A publication*]
**NSP**........... Neuron-Specific Protein [*Later, NSE*] [*Biochemistry*]
**NSP**........... New Species
**NSP**........... Nominal Stagnation Point
**NSP**........... Non-Self-Propelled
**NSP**........... Nonspecific Prostatitis [*Medicine*] (ADA)
**NSP**........... Nonstandard Holding Pattern [*Aviation*] (FAAC)
**NSP**........... Nonstandard Part
**NSP**........... Nonstorage Protein [*Food technology*]
**NSP**........... Nordiska Sjoforsakringspoolen [*Nordic Pool for Marine Insurance - NPMI*] (EA)
**NSP**........... Normal Serum Pool
**NSP**........... Normal Superphosphate [*Fertilizer*]
**NSP**........... Northern States Power Co. [*NYSE symbol*] (SPSG)
**NSP**........... Nose Shipping Plug
**NSP**........... Not Separately Priced (NG)
**NSP**........... Nuclear Strike Plan [*Army*] (AABC)
**Nsp**........... Number of Similar Positive Matches
**NSP**........... Numeric Space Character [*Data processing*]
**NSP**........... St. Andrews Presbyterian College, Laurinburg, NC [*OCLC symbol*] (OCLC)
**NSPA**......... Advocate, Pictou, Nova Scotia [*Library symbol*] [*National Library of Canada*] (NLC)
**NSPA**......... National Scholastic Press Association (EA)
**NSPA**......... National Shrimp Processors Association (EA)
**NSPA**......... National Socialist Party of America (EA)
**NSPA**......... National Society of Public Accountants [*Alexandria, VA*] (EA)
**NSPA**......... National Soybean Processors Association [*Later, NOPA*] (EA)
**NSPA**......... National Split Pea Association [*Defunct*]
**NSPA**......... National Standard Parts Association [*Later, ASIA*]
**NSPA**......... National State Printing Association (EA)
**NSPA**......... Pictou Advocate, Nova Scotia [*Library symbol*] [*National Library of Canada*] (NLC)
**NSPAC**...... National Security Political Action Committee (EA)
**NSPAR**...... Nonstandard Part Approval Request
**NSpaT**....... Saint Thomas Aquinas College, Sparkill, NY [*Library symbol*] [*Library of Congress*] (LCLS)
**NSPB**......... National Society to Prevent Blindness (EA)
**NSPBB**...... Burning Bush Museum, Pictou, Nova Scotia [*Library symbol*] [*National Library of Canada*] (BIB)
**NSPC**......... National Security Planning Commission
**NSPC**......... National Society of Painters In Casein (EA)
**NSPC**......... National Sound-Program Center [*Telecommunications*] (TEL)
**NSPC**......... National Standard Plumbing Code Committee (EA)
**NSPC**......... National Straight Pipe Threads in Pipe Couplings
**NSPCA**...... National Society of Painters in Casein and Acrylic (EA)
**NSPCA**...... National Society for the Prevention of Cruelty to Animals
**NSPCB**...... National Society for the Preservation of Covered Bridges (EA)
**NSPCC**...... National Society for the Prevention of Cruelty to Children
**NSPCC**...... Naval Ships Parts Control Center (MCD)
**NSPCM**..... National Society for Prevention of Cruelty to Mushrooms (EA)
**NSPD**........ Naval Shore Patrol Detachment
**NSPE**........ National Society of Professional Engineers (EA)
**NSpeB**........ Board of Cooperative Educational Services (BOCES), Spencerport, NY [*Library symbol*] [*Library of Congress*] (LCLS)
**NSPF**......... National Swimming Pool Foundation (EA)
**NSPF**......... Not Specifically Provided For
**NSPFEA**.... National Spray Painting and Finishing Equipment Association [*Later, NSEMA*] (EA)
**NSPG**......... National Security Planning Group
**NSPHM**.... Port Hastings Museum and Archives, Nova Scotia [*Library symbol*] [*National Library of Canada*] (NLC)
**NSPI**.......... National Society for Performance and Instruction (EA)
**NSPI**.......... National Spa and Pool Institute (EA)
**NSPI**.......... Nonstorage Protein Isolate [*Food technology*]
**NSPIE**........ National Society for the Promotion of Industrial Education [*Later, AVA*]
**NSPLO**...... NATO Sidewinder Production and Logistics Organization [*Missiles*] (NATG)
**NSPMH**.... McCulloch House, Pictou, Nova Scotia [*Library symbol*] [*National Library of Canada*] (NLC)
**NSPNC**...... North Cumberland Historical Society, Pugwash, Nova Scotia [*Library symbol*] [*National Library of Canada*] (NLC)
**NSPO**........ NATO Sea Sparrow Project Office (MCD)
**NSPO**........ NATO Sidewinder Production Organization [*Missiles*] (NATG)
**NSPO**........ NATO Sidewinder Program Office [*Missiles*] (NATG)
**NSPO**........ Naval Ship Production Overseer [*British*]
**NSPO**........ Naval Space Projects Office
**NSPO**........ Navy Special Projects Office
**NSPO**........ Nuclear Systems Project Office [*Air Research and Development Command*] [*Air Force*] (AAG)
**NS-POG**.... NAVSHIPS [*Naval Ship Systems Command*] Propulsion Operating Guides
**NSPP**......... National Serials Pilot Project
**NSPP**......... Nuclear Safety Pilot Plant [*ORNL*]
**NSPR**......... National Society for Park Resources (EA)
**NSPR**......... National Society of Patient Representatives of the American Hospital Association (EA)
**NSPR**......... National Society of Pershing Rifles (EA)
**NSPR**......... Record, Parrsboro, Nova Scotia [*Library symbol*] [*National Library of Canada*] (NLC)
**NSPRA**...... National School Public Relations Association (EA)
**NSPRDS**... New Systems Personnel Requirements Data System [*Navy*]
**NSPRM**..... National Society of Professional Resident Managers (EA)
**NS Prov Dep Mines Annu Rep**... Nova Scotia Province. Department of Mines. Annual Report [*A publication*]
**NSPRV**...... Pictou Regional Vocational School, Nova Scotia [*Library symbol*] [*National Library of Canada*] (NLC)
**NSprvCH**... Bertrand Chaffee Hospital, Springville, NY [*Library symbol*] [*Library of Congress*] (LCLS)
**NSPS**......... National Ski Patrol System (EA)
**NSPS**......... National Society of Professional Sanitarians (EA)
**NSPS**......... National Society of Professional Surveyors (EA)
**NSPS**......... National Stockpile Purchase Specification [*for metals*]
**NSPS**......... New Source Performance Standards [*Environmental Protection Agency*]
**NSPS**......... Nonsynchronous Pulse Suppression (MCD)
**NSPS**......... Nuclear Safety Protection System (NRCH)
**NSPS**......... Nuclear Strike Planning System (MCD)
**NSPSH**...... Parrsboro Shore Historical Society, Parrsboro, Nova Scotia [*Library symbol*] [*National Library of Canada*] (BIB)
**NSPSS**....... Scotia Sun, Port Hawkesbury, Nova Scotia [*Library symbol*] [*National Library of Canada*] (NLC)
**NSPST**...... National Society of Pharmaceutical Sales Trainers (EA)
**NSPWA**..... National Society Patriotic Women of America
**NSQ**........... Neuroticism Scale Questionnaire [*Psychology*]
**NSQ**........... Not Sufficient Quantity [*Clinical chemistry*]
**NSQ**........... Nurse Satisfaction Questionnaire
**NSR**........... Mount Vernon, WA [*Location identifier*] [*FAA*] (FAAL)
**NSR**........... National Scientific Register
**NSR**........... National Sculpture Review [*A publication*]
**NSR**........... National Shipping Report [*NATO*]
**NSR**........... National Shipping Representative (NATG)
**NSR**........... National Shorthand Reporter [*A publication*]
**NSR**........... National Singles Registry (EA)
**NSR**........... National Slow Rate (NASA)
**NSR**........... Net Survival Rate
**NSR**........... Neue Schweizer Rundschau [*A publication*]
**NSR**........... Neutron Source Reactor
**NSR**........... Night Sky Radiation
**NSR**........... Nitrile Silicone Rubber [*Organic chemistry*]
**NSR**........... No Staff Responsibility [*Army*] (AABC)
**NSR**........... Nominal Slow Rate [*NASA*] (KSC)

**NSR** .......... Nordic Shooting Region (EAIO)
**NSR** .......... Nordisk Skuespillerrad [*Nordic Actors' Council - NAC*] (EAIO)
**NSR** .......... Nordiska Skidskolans Rad [*Nordic Council of Ski Schools - NCSS*] (EAIO)
**NSR** .......... Nordiska Skogsarbetsstudiernas Rad [*Nordic Research Council on Forest Operations*] [*Spanga, Sweden*] (EAIO)
**NSR** .......... Normal Sinus Rhythm [*Physiology*]
**NSR** .......... Normal Slow Rate Maneuver (NASA)
**NSR** .......... North Sea Observer [*A publication*]
**NSR** .......... North Staffordshire Railway [*British*] (ROG)
**NSR** .......... Northern Sea Route (NATG)
**NSR** .......... Nova Scotia Provincial Library [*UTLAS symbol*]
**NSR** .......... Nova Scotia Regiment [*Canada*] (DMA)
**NSR** .......... Nova Scotia Reports [*Information service or system*] [*A publication*]
**NSR** .......... NSR Resources, Inc. [*Toronto Stock Exchange symbol*]
**NSR** .......... Nuclear Spin Relaxation [*Physics*]
**NSR** .......... Nuclear Structure References [*Brookhaven National Laboratory*] [*Information service or system*]
**NSR** .......... Nutrient Supply Rate [*Oceanography*]
**NSRA** ........ National Service Robot Association (EA)
**NSRA** ........ National Shoe Retailers Association (EA)
**NSRA** ........ National Shorthand Reporters Association (EA)
**NSRA** ........ National Ski Retailers Association (EA)
**NSRA** ........ National Smallbore Rifle Association [*British*]
**NSRA** ........ National Society for Research into Allergy [*British*]
**NSRA** ........ National Street Rod Association (EA)
**NSRA** ........ National Swim and Recreation Association (EA)
**NSRA** ........ Nuclear Safety Research Association [*See also GAKK*] [*Japan*] (NRCH)
**NSRB** ......... National Security Resources Board [*Functions transferred to ODM, 1953*]
**NSRB** ......... Nuclear Safety Review Board (NRCH)
**NSRC** ......... National Silver Rabbit Club (EA)
**NSRC** ......... National Stereophonic Radio Committee
**NSRC** ......... NeoSynthesis Research Centre (EAIO)
**NSRC** ......... North Stratford Railroad Corporation [*AAR code*]
**NSR Coch** ... Cochran's Nova Scotia Reports [*1859*] [*A publication*] (DLA)
**NSR Coh** .... Cohen's Nova Scotia Reports [*A publication*] (DLA)
**NSRD** ........ National Security Resources Development
**NSR 2d** ...... Nova Scotia Reports. Second Series [*A publication*]
**NSRDA** ..... National Standard Reference Data Series. United States National Bureau of Standards [*A publication*]
**NSRDC** ...... National Standards Reference Data Center
**NSRDC** ...... Naval Ship Research and Development Center [*Also, DTNSRDC*]
**NSRDC(AD)** ... Naval Ship Research and Development Center (Annapolis Division)
**NSRDF** ...... Naval Supply Research and Development Facility
**NSRDL** ...... Naval Ship Research and Development Laboratory (MCD)
**NSRDL/A** ... Naval Ship Research and Development Laboratory, Annapolis [*Maryland*]
**NSRDL/PC** ... Naval Ship Research and Development Laboratory, Panama City [*Florida*] [*Later, NCSC*]
**NSRDS** ...... National Standard Reference Data System [*National Institute of Standards and Technology*] [*Gaithersburg, MD*]
**NSRDS Ref Data Rep** ... NSRDS [*National Standards Reference Data System*] Reference Data Report [*United States*] [*A publication*]
**NSREA** ...... Neurosciences Research [*A publication*]
**NSREF** ...... National Society for Real Estate Finance [*Washington, DC*] (EA)
**NS Rep** ....... Nova Scotia Reports [*Information service or system*] [*A publication*]
**NS Rev Stat** ... Nova Scotia Revised Statutes [*Canada*] [*A publication*] (DLA)
**NSRF** ......... National Stroke Recovery Foundation (EA)
**NSRF** ......... Naval Ship Repair Facility (MCD)
**NSRF** ......... Naval Strategic Reserve Fleet
**NSRG & O** ... Nova Scotia Reports, by Geldert and Oxley [*A publication*] (DLA)
**NSRG & R** ... Nova Scotia Reports, by Geldert and Russell [*A publication*] (DLA)
**NSRJ** ......... Nova Scotia Reports (James) [*A publication*] (DLA)
**NSR (James)** ... Nova Scotia Reports (James) [*Canada*] [*A publication*] (DLA)
**NSRL** ......... National SIGINT Requirements List (MCD)
**NSRL** ......... Nuclear Structure Research Laboratory (NRCH)
**NSRMCA** ... National Star Route Mail Contractors Association (EA)
**NSRMP** ..... Net Survival Rate for Monocyclic Process
**NSRN** ......... National School Resource Network (EA)
**NSR Old** .... Oldright's Nova Scotia Reports [*A publication*] (DLA)
**NSRP** ......... National Search and Rescue Plan
**NSRP** ......... National States Rights Party (EA)
**NSRP** ......... Neutral Seat Reference Point (MCD)
**NSRP** ......... Nontechnical Support Real Property
**NSRP** ......... Nordic Society for Radiation Protection [*See also NSFS*] [*Helsinki, Finland*] (EAIO)
**NSRPDU** ... Netherlands Institute for Sea Research. Publication Series [*A publication*]
**NSRQCE** ... National Symposium on Reliability and Quality Control in Electronics (MCD)
**NSRR** ......... Nuclear Safety Research Reactors (NRCH)
**NSRR & C** ... Russell and Chesley's Nova Scotia Reports [*10-12 Nova Scotia Reports*] [*1875-79*] [*A publication*] (DLA)
**NSRR & G** ... Russell and Geldert's Nova Scotia Reports [*A publication*] (DLA)
**NSRS** ......... National Scholarship Research Service [*Information service or system*] (IID)
**NSRS** ......... National Shoreline Refuse Survey [*British*]
**NSRS** ......... National Supply Radio Station (MCD)
**NSRS** ......... Naval Supply Radio Station
**NSRT** ......... Near-Surface Radiation Thermometer
**NSRT** ......... Near Surface Reference Temperature [*Oceanography*]
**NSRT** ......... North South Roundtable (EAIO)
**NSR Thom** ... Thomson's Nova Scotia Reports [*A publication*] (DLA)
**NSRU** ......... North Star Universal, Inc. [*NASDAQ symbol*] (NQ)
**NSrU** ......... Ulster County Community College, Stone Ridge, NY [*Library symbol*] [*Library of Congress*] (LCLS)
**NSRW** ....... Nuclear Service Raw Water (IEEE)
**NSR Wall** .. Wallace's Nova Scotia Reports [*6 Nova Scotia Reports*] [*1884-1907*] [*A publication*] (DLA)
**NSS** ........... National Sculpture Society (EA)
**NSS** ........... National Seismic Stations
**NSS** ........... National Serigraph Society [*Defunct*]
**NSS** ........... National Service Secretariat (EA)
**NSS** ........... National Slovak Society of the USA
**NSS** ........... National Snapdragon Society (EA)
**NSS** ........... National Space Society (EA)
**NSS** ........... National Speleological Society (EA)
**NSS** ........... National Staff Side [*British*]
**NSS** ........... National Stockpile Site
**NSS** ........... National Study Service [*Defunct*] (EA)
**NSS** ........... National Supply System (MCD)
**NS/S** ......... Native Seeds/SEARCH [*Southwestern Endangered Arid-Land Resource Clearing House*] (EA)
**NSS** ........... Naval Sea Systems Command, Washington, DC [*OCLC symbol*] (OCLC)
**NSS** ........... Naval Security Station (NVT)
**NSS** ........... Naval Strategic Study
**NSS** ........... Navigation Subsystem Switchboard
**NSS** ........... Navy Secondary Standards (MSA)
**NSS** ........... Navy Strategic Study
**NSS** ........... Navy Supply System
**NSS** ........... Network Supervisor System
**NSS** ........... Network Support System [*Data processing*]
**NSS** ........... Network Synchronization Subsystem [*Telecommunications*] (TEL)
**NSS** ........... Neurological Soft Signs [*Occupational therapy*]
**NSS** ........... Neuropathy Symptom Score
**NSS** ........... Neutron Spectrometer System
**NSS** ........... [*The*] Newburgh & South Shore Railway Co. [*AAR code*]
**NSS** ........... Nitrogen Supply System [*or Subsystem*] (AAG)
**NSS** ........... Nodding Subdish System
**NSS** ........... Noise Suppressor System (MCD)
**NSS** ........... Non-Salt Sensitive
**NSS** ........... Non-Sea Salt
**NSS** ........... Non-Self-Sustaining [*Container ship*] (MCD)
**NSS** ........... Nonstandard Facilities Setup [*Data processing*]
**NSS** ........... Nordiska Kommitten for Samordning av Elektriska Sakerhetsfragor [*Nordic Committee for Coordination of Electrical Safety Matters*] (EAIO)
**NSS** ........... Nordiska Statistiska Sekretariatet [*Nordic Statistical Secretariat*] (EAIO)
**NSS** ........... Normal Saline Solution
**NSS** ........... Northwest Steam Society (EA)
**NSS** ........... Nortronics System Support
**NSS** ........... NS Group [*NYSE symbol*] (SPSG)
**NSS** ........... Nuclear Steam System (NRCH)
**NSS** ........... Nysvenska Studier [*A publication*]
**NSS** ........... Statuten der Verenigingen [*A publication*]
**NSSA** ......... National Sanitary Supply Association [*Later, ISSA*] (EA)
**NSSA** ......... National Scholastic Surfing Association (EA)
**NSSA** ......... National Science Supervisors Association (EA)
**NSSA** ......... National Senior Sports Association (EA)
**NSSA** ......... National Skeet Shooting Association (EA)
**NSSA** ......... National Sportscasters and Sportswriters Association (EA)
**NSSA** ......... National Suffolk Sheep Association (EA)
**NSSA** ......... National Sunday School Association [*Defunct*] (EA)
**NSSA** ......... Navy Space Systems Activity [*Los Angeles, CA*] (MCD)
**NSSA** ......... Nematological Society of Southern Africa (EAIO)
**NSSA** ......... New York Skirt and Sportswear Association (EA)
**N-SSA** ....... North-South Skirmish Association (EA)
**NSSAB** ...... National Selective Service Appeal Board [*of SSS*] [*Inactive since 1975*]
**NSSAC** ...... National Society, Sons of the American Colonists [*Defunct*] (EA)
**NSSB** ......... National Society of Scabbard and Blade (EA)
**NSSB** ......... Norwich Financial Corp. [*NASDAQ symbol*] (NQ)
**NSS Bull** .... NSS [*National Speleological Society*] Bulletin [*A publication*]
**NSS Bulletin** ... National Speleological Society. Bulletin [*A publication*]

**NSSC**......... Cape Breton Regional Library, Sydney, Nova Scotia [*Library symbol*] [*National Library of Canada*] (NLC)
**NSSC**......... Napco Security Systems, Inc. [*NASDAQ symbol*] (NQ)
**NSSC**......... NASA Safety Standards Committee
**NSSC**......... National Society for the Study of Communication [*Later, ICA*] (EA)
**NSSC**......... National Soil Survey Committee [*Canada*]
**NSSC**......... Naval Sea [*formerly, Ship*] Systems Command
**NSSC**......... Neutral Sulfite Semichemical [*Pulp*]
**NSSCB**...... Cape Breton Post, Sydney, Nova Scotia [*Library symbol*] [*National Library of Canada*] (NLC)
**NSSCBD**... Cape Breton Development Corp., Sydney, Nova Scotia [*Library symbol*] [*National Library of Canada*] (NLC)
**NSSCBH**... Cape Breton Hospital, Sydney, Nova Scotia [*Library symbol*] [*National Library of Canada*] (NLC)
**NSSCC**...... National Space Surveillance Control Center
**NSSCG**...... Canadian Coast Guard College [*College de la Garde Cotiere Canadienne*] Sydney, Nova Scotia [*Library symbol*] [*National Library of Canada*] (NLC)
**NS Sch Bd Assn N**... Nova Scotia School Boards Association. Newsletter [*A publication*]
**NSSCM**..... Shelburne County Museum, Nova Scotia [*Library symbol*] [*National Library of Canada*] (NLC)
**NSSCO**...... Coast Guard, Shelburne, Nova Scotia [*Library symbol*] [*National Library of Canada*] (NLC)
**NSSDC**...... National Space Science Data Center [*NASA*] [*Greenbelt, MD*] (MCD)
**NSSDP**...... National Society of Sons and Daughters of the Pilgrims (EA)
**NSsE**.......... Empire State College, Saratoga Springs, NY [*Library symbol*] [*Library of Congress*] (LCLS)
**NSSE**......... National Society for the Study of Education (EA)
**NSSE**......... National Study of School Evaluation (EA)
**NSSEA**...... National School Supply and Equipment Association (EA)
**NSSET**...... National Symposium on Space Electronics and Telemetry [*IEEE*] (MCD)
**NSSF**......... National Shooting Sports Foundation (EA)
**NSSF**......... National Social Science Foundation [*Proposed in 1966*]
**N/SSF**........ Novice, Society of St. Francis
**NSSFA**...... National Single Service Food Association (EA)
**NSSFC**....... National Severe Storms Forecast Center [*National Oceanic and Atmospheric Administration*]
**NSSFC**....... National Society of Student Film Critics (EA)
**NSSFFA**.... National Soft Serve and Fast Food Association (EA)
**NSSFNS**.... National Scholarship Service and Fund for Negro Students (EA)
**NSSG**......... National Ski Study Group [*Defunct*]
**NSSHA**..... National Spotted Saddle Horse Association (EA)
**NSSHA**..... National Student Speech and Hearing Association [*Later, NSSLHA*] (EA)
**NSSHCF**... Canadian Forces Base Barrington, Stone Horse, Nova Scotia [*Library symbol*] [*National Library of Canada*] (NLC)
**NSSHDC**... National Spanish Speaking Housing Development Corporation
**NSSI**.......... Nuclear Support Services, Incorporated [*NASDAQ symbol*] (NQ)
**NS-SIB**...... NAVSHIPS [*Naval Ship Systems Command*] Ship Information Booklets
**NSSIC**....... National Student Strike Information Center [*Brandeis University*]
**NSSJ**......... New Scientist and Science Journal [*A publication*]
**NSSJB**....... New Scientist and Science Journal [*A publication*]
**NSSJD**...... Community of the Nursing Sisters of St. John the Divine [*Anglican religious community*]
**NSSK**......... National Society of Student Keyboardists (EA)
**NSSL**......... National Seed Storage Laboratory [*Department of Agriculture*] [*Fort Collins, CO*] (GRD)
**NSSL**......... National Service Star Legion (EA)
**NSSL**......... National Severe Storms Laboratory [*National Oceanic and Atmospheric Administration*] [*Research center*]
**NSSL**......... National Society of State Legislators [*Later, NCSL*]
**NSSLC**....... National Social Science and Law Center (EA)
**NSSLHA**... National Student Speech Language Hearing Association (EA)
**NSSLP**....... National Social Science and Law Project (EA)
**NSSM**........ National Security Study Memorandum [*Obsolete*]
**NSSM**........ Navy Spread Spectrum MODEM (MCD)
**NSSMM**.... Memorial High School, Sydney Mines, Nova Scotia [*Library symbol*] [*National Library of Canada*] (NLC)
**NSSMS**..... NATO Sea Sparrow Missile System
**NSSN**......... National Standard Shipping Note (DS)
**NSSNAQ**... NSS [*National Speleological Society*] News [*A publication*]
**NSS (Natl Speleol Soc) News**... NSS (National Speleological Society) News [*A publication*]
**NSSNF**...... Naval Strategic Systems Navigation Facility
**NSSO**........ National Society of Student Organists [*Later, NSSK*] (EA)
**NSSO**........ National Solar Space Observatory [*NASA*]
**NSSO**........ Navy Ships' Store Office [*PX*]
**NS & SO**.... Nervous System and Sense Organs
**NSSP**......... National Severe Storms Project [*National Oceanic and Atmospheric Administration*]
**NSSP**......... National Syrian Socialist Party [*Political party*] [*Lebanon*]
**NSSP**......... Nava Sama Samaja Party [*New Equal Society Party*] [*Sri Lanka*] [*Political party*] (PPW)
**NSSP**......... Nonreporting Secondary Stock Point (AFIT)
**NSSPA**...... NASA [*National Aeronautics and Space Administration*] Special Publications [*A publication*]
**NSSR**......... National Spotted Swine Record (EA)
**NSSR**......... New School for Social Research [*New York, NY*]
**NSSR**......... Record, Springhill, Nova Scotia [*Library symbol*] [*National Library of Canada*] (NLC)
**NSSRI**....... Nervous System Sports-Related Injury [*Medicine*]
**NSSRM**..... Soluth Rawdon Museum, Nova Scotia [*Library symbol*] [*National Library of Canada*] (NLC)
**NSSS**......... National Social Science Survey [*Australia*]
**NSSS**......... National Space Surveillance System
**NSSS**......... Nuclear Steam Supply System [*Vendor*] (NRCH)
**NSsS**.......... Skidmore College, Saratoga Springs, NY [*Library symbol*] [*Library of Congress*] (LCLS)
**NSsSA**....... Southern Adirondack Library System, Saratoga Springs, NY [*Library symbol*] [*Library of Congress*] (LCLS)
**NSSSE**....... National Study of Secondary School Evaluation [*Later, NSSE*] (EA)
**NSSSRH**... St. Rita's Hospital, Sydney, Nova Scotia [*Library symbol*] [*National Library of Canada*] (NLC)
**NSSSS**....... Nuclear Steam Supply Shutoff System (NRCH)
**NSST**......... Northwestern Syntax Screening Test [*Education*]
**NSSTA**...... National Structured Settlements Trade Association (EA)
**NS Stat**...... Nova Scotia Statutes [*Canada*] [*A publication*] (DLA)
**NSSTC**...... National Small Shipments Traffic Conference (EA)
**NSSTE**...... National Society of Sales Training Executives [*Orlando, FL*] (EA)
**NSSU**......... National Steam Service Union [*British*]
**NSSU**......... National Sunday School Union [*British*]
**NSSUP**...... National Society of the Sons of Utah Pioneers (EA)
**NSSVD**...... Naucni Sastanak Slavista u Vulove Dane [*A publication*]
**NSSX**......... National Sanitary Supply Co. [*Cincinnati, OH*] [*NASDAQ symbol*] (NQ)
**NSSX**......... University College of Cape Breton, Sydney, Nova Scotia [*Library symbol*] [*National Library of Canada*] (NLC)
**NSSXA**...... Archives and General Library, College of Cape Breton, Sydney, Nova Scotia [*Library symbol*] [*National Library of Canada*] (NLC)
**NSSYA**...... National Small Sailing Yacht Association (EA)
**NST**........... National Symposium on Telemetering (MCD)
**NS & T**....... Naval Science and Tactics
**NST**........... Navy Shipboard Terminal
**NST**........... Nesting Module (MCD)
**NST**........... Network Support Team [*NASA*] (KSC)
**NST**........... New Scientist [*A publication*]
**NST**........... New Serial Titles [*A publication of Library of Congress*]
**NST**........... New Serial Titles, Library of Congress, Washington, DC [*OCLC symbol*] (OCLC)
**N St**........... New Statesman [*A publication*]
**NST**........... New York Air [*Farmingdale, NY*] [*FAA designator*] (FAAC)
**NST**........... Newfoundland Standard Time [*Aviation*] (AIA)
**NST**........... Noise Source Tube
**NST**........... Nonshivering Thermogenesis [*Physiology*]
**NST**........... Nonslip Tread [*Technical drawings*]
**NST**........... Nonstress Test [*Gynecology*]
**NSt**............ Nordische Studien [*A publication*]
**NST**........... North Solomon Trench [*Geoscience*]
**NST**........... Not Sooner Than
**NST**........... Nouvelle Serie Theologique [*A publication*]
**NSTA**......... National Safe Transit Association (EA)
**NSTA**......... National School Transportation Association (EA)
**NSTA**......... National Science Teachers Association (EA)
**NSTA**......... National Science and Technology Authority [*Information service or system*] (IID)
**NSTA**......... National Security Traders Association [*Later, STA*] (EA)
**NSTA**......... National Shoe Traveler's Association (EA)
**NSTA**......... National Spasmodic Torticollis Association (EA)
**NSTA**......... National Squash Tennis Association (EA)
**NSTA**......... Nova Scotia Agricultural College, Truro, Nova Scotia [*Library symbol*] [*National Library of Canada*] (NLC)
**NS-TAB**..... NAVSHIPS [*Naval Ship Systems Command*] Training Aid Bulletins
**NSTAF**...... National Solar Technical Audience File [*Solar Energy Research Institute*] [*Database*]
**N Staffordshire J Fld Stud**... North Staffordshire Journal of Field Studies [*A publication*]
**NSTAP**...... National Strategic Targeting and Attack Policy (CINC)
**NSTARS**... Navy Standard Tracking and Retrieval System (MCD)
**NStat**......... New Statesman [*A publication*]
**NSTB**......... Biblio-Tech Ltd., Three Fathom Harbor, Nova Scotia [*Library symbol*] [*National Library of Canada*] (NLC)
**NStBU**....... St. Bonaventure University, St. Bonaventure, NY [*Library symbol*] [*Library of Congress*] (LCLS)
**NSTC**......... Colchester - East Hants Regional Library, Truro, Nova Scotia [*Library symbol*] [*National Library of Canada*] (NLC)
**NSTC**......... National Science and Technology Centre [*Australia*]
**NSTC**......... National Security Training Commission [*Expired, 1957*]
**NSTC**......... National Shade Tree Conference [*Later, ISA*]
**NSTC**......... National Spiritualist Teachers Club (EA)

**NSTC** ......... Nineteenth Century Short Title Catalogue [*Avero Publications Ltd.*] [*Information service or system*] [*Great Britain*] (CRD)
**NSTC** ......... Nonsmokers' Travel Club [*Defunct*] (EA)
**NSTC** ......... Nova Scotia Teachers College [*Canada*]
**NSTC** ......... Nova Scotia Technical College
**NSTCH** ..... Colchester Historical Society, Truro, Nova Scotia [*Library symbol*] [*National Library of Canada*] (BIB)
**NST-D** ....... Navy Standard Transmission [*Dension hydraulics*] (CAAL)
**NSTD** ......... Nested [*Packaging*]
**NSTDB** ...... National Strategic Target Data Base (CINC)
**NSTDH** ..... National STD [*Sexually Transmitted Disease*] Hotline (EA)
**NSTDN** ..... Daily News, Truro, Nova Scotia [*Library symbol*] [*National Library of Canada*] (NLC)
**NSTDP** ...... National Society of Tole and Decorative Painters (EA)
**NSTE** ......... National Society of Telephone Employees [*A union*] [*British*]
**NSTEA** ...... Nuclear Structural Engineering [*A publication*]
**NS Tech Coll Dep Civ Eng Essays Timber Struct** ... Nova Scotia Technical College (Halifax). Department of Civil Engineering. Essays on Timber Structures [*A publication*]
**NStem** ........ Nieuwe Stem [*A publication*]
**NSTF** ......... Fraser Culture Centre, Tatamagouche, Nova Scotia [*Library symbol*] [*National Library of Canada*] (NLC)
**NSTF** ......... National Scholarship Trust Fund [*An affiliate of the Graphic Arts Technical Foundation*]
**NSTF** ......... Nuclear Science and Technology Facility [*State University of New York at Buffalo*] [*Research center*] (RCD)
**NSTG** ........ Nuclear Strike Target Graphic (MCD)
**NSTGThK** ... Neue Studien zur Geschichte der Theologie und der Kirche [*A publication*]
**NSTIC** ....... Naval Scientific and Technical Information Centre [*Later, DRIC*] [*British*] (MCD)
**NSTIC** ....... Navy Scientific and Technical Intelligence Center (IEEE)
**NSTIM** ...... Islands Museum and Tourist Bureau, Tiverton, Nova Scotia [*Library symbol*] [*National Library of Canada*] (NLC)
**NSTK** ......... Nastech Pharmaceutical Co., Inc. [*Hauppauge, NY*] [*NASDAQ symbol*] (NQ)
**NSTL** ......... National Space Technology Laboratories [*Formerly, MTF*] [*NASA*] [*Mississippi*]
**NSTL** ......... National Strategic Target Line [*or List*] (AFM)
**NSTL** ......... Nuclear Services and Training Laboratory [*Ohio State University*] [*Research center*] (RCD)
**NSTM** ....... Naval School Transportation Management
**NSTM** ....... Navy Ship Technical Manual (CAAL)
**NSTM** ....... Navy Standard Test Model (CAAL)
**NSTM** ....... Nordiska Skeppstekniska Mote [*Joint Committee of Nordic Marine Technology - JCNMT*] (EAIO)
**NS-TMI** ..... NAVSHIPS [*Naval Ship Systems Command*] Technical Manual Index
**NStN** .......... New Statesman and Nation [*A publication*]
**NSTN** ........ Nonstandard Telephone Number [*Telecommunications*] (TEL)
**NSTO** ........ Non Statutory Training Organisation [*British*]
**NSTOA** ..... National Ski Touring Operators' Association (EA)
**NSTP** ......... Nonstop [*Aviation*] (FAAC)
**NSTP** ......... Nuffield Service Teaching Project
**NSTPS** ...... Law Library, Patterson, Smith, Mathews & Grant, Truro, Nova Scotia [*Library symbol*] [*National Library of Canada*] (NLC)
**NSTR** ......... Naval Sea Systems Command Technical Representative
**NSTR** ......... Northstar Minerals [*NASDAQ symbol*] (NQ)
**NSTR** ......... Record, Truro, Nova Scotia [*Library symbol*] [*National Library of Canada*] (NLC)
**NSTS** ......... National Sea Training Schools [*British*]
**NSTS** ......... National Securities Trading System
**NSTS** ......... National Space Transportation System
**NSTS** ......... Navy Stockpile to Target Sequence
**NSTS** ......... Northwestern States Portland Cement Co. [*NASDAQ symbol*] (NQ)
**NSTT** ......... National Sea Training Trusts [*British*] (DS)
**NSTT** ......... Nova Scotia Teachers' College, Truro, Nova Scotia [*Library symbol*] [*National Library of Canada*] (NLC)
**NSTU** ........ Pago Pago/International, Tutuila Island [*American Samoa*] [*ICAO location identifier*] (ICLI)
**NStv** ........... Narodno Stvaralastvo. Folklor [*A publication*]
**NST-V** ....... Navy Standard Transmission [*Vickers hydraulics*] (CAAL)
**NSU** ........... Naval Scout Unit
**NSU** ........... Neckarsulm [*Location in Wuerttemberg, Germany, of NSU Werke, automobile manufacturer; initialism used as name of its cars*]
**NSU** ........... Nitrogen Supply Unit (AAG)
**NSU** ........... Nonspecific Urethritis [*Medicine*]
**NSU** ........... North Stansbury [*Utah*] [*Seismograph station code, US Geological Survey*] (SEIS)
**NSU** ........... Nuova Sinistra Unita [*New United Left*] [*Italy*] [*Political party*] (PPE)
**NSU** ........... Uitspraken van de Raad voor de Luchtvaart en Scheepvaart [*A publication*]
**NSUA** ........ Nigerian Students Union in the Americas (EA)
**NSuf** ........... Suffern Free Library, Suffern, NY [*Library symbol*] [*Library of Congress*] (LCLS)
**NSufA** ........ Avon Products, Inc., Suffern, NY [*Library symbol*] [*Library of Congress*] (LCLS)
**NSufR** ........ Rockland Community College, Suffern, NY [*Library symbol*] [*Library of Congress*] (LCLS)
**Nsukka Stud** ... Nsukka Studies in African Literature [*A publication*]
**N/Sun Sent** ... News/Sun - Sentinel [*A publication*]
**NSUP** ........ Naval Supply Systems Command Headquarters
**NSUPSC** ... Naval Supply Systems Command [*Formerly, Bureau of Supplies and Accounts*] (MCD)
**NSUR** ........ Compu-Plan, Inc. [*NASDAQ symbol*] (NQ)
**NSURG** ..... Neurosurgery [*Medicine*]
**NSUS** ......... Newcomen Society of the United States (EA)
**NS (USSR)** ... Numizmaticheskii Sbornik Materialy k Katalogu Numizmaticheskogo Sobraniia Gosudarstvennyi Istoricheskii Muzei (USSR) [*A publication*]
**NSV** ........... Akten Betreffende Cooperatieve Verenigingen [*A publication*]
**NSv** ............ Finkelstein Memorial Library, Spring Valley, NY [*Library symbol*] [*Library of Congress*] (LCLS)
**NSV** ........... National Socialist Vanguard (EA)
**NSV** ........... Negative Supply Voltage
**NSV** ........... Net Sales Value (BUR)
**NSV** ........... Netted Secure Voice [*Military*] (CAAL)
**NSV** ........... Neurosecretory Vesicle [*Neuroanatomy*]
**NSV** ........... Nonautomatic Self-Verification [*Data processing*] (MDG)
**NSV** ........... Nonspecific Vaginitis [*Medicine*]
**NSV** ........... Nonspinning Vehicle
**NSV** ........... Nova Scotia Savings & Loans Co. [*Toronto Stock Exchange symbol*]
**NSV** ........... Nuclear Service Vessel
**NSVA** ........ Navy Seabee Veterans of America (EA)
**NSVC** ......... National Sisters Vocation Conference [*Later, NRVC*] (EA)
**NSVEA** ...... Natural-Source Vitamin E Association (EA)
**NSVP** ......... National School Volunteer Program (EA)
**NSVP** ......... National Student Volunteer Program [*Later, NCSL*] (EA)
**NsvS** ........... Nysvenska Studier [*A publication*]
**NSW** .......... National Software Works
**NSW** .......... Naval Special Warfare (NVT)
**NSW** .......... New South Wales [*Australia*]
**NSW** .......... New South Wales Reports, Old and New Series [*Australia*] [*A publication*] (DLA)
**NSW** .......... Northwestern Steel & Wire Co. [*NYSE symbol*] (SPSG)
**NSWA** ....... Acadia University, Wolfville, Nova Scotia [*Library symbol*] [*National Library of Canada*] (NLC)
**NSWA** ....... National Social Welfare Assembly [*Later, National Assembly of National Voluntary Health and Social Welfare Organizations*] (EA)
**NSWA** ....... National Soft Wheat Association [*Later, MNF*] (EA)
**NSWA** ....... National Stripper Well Association (EA)
**NSWA** ....... North Shore Writers Alliance (EA)
**NSWAAT** ... New South Wales Association of Agricultural Teachers [*Australia*]
**NSWABA** ... New South Wales Amateur Boxing Association [*Australia*]
**NSW Ad** .... Law Reports (New South Wales). Vice-Admiralty [*A publication*] (APTA)
**NSW Adm** ... Law Reports (New South Wales). Vice-Admiralty [*A publication*] (APTA)
**NSW Adm** ... New South Wales Reports, Admiralty [*A publication*] (DLA)
**NSWAG** .... Department of Geography, Acadia University, Wolfville, Nova Scotia [*Library symbol*] [*Obsolete*] [*National Library of Canada*] (NLC)
**NSWALC** .. New South Wales Aboriginal Land Council [*Australia*]
**NS Wales L** ... New South Wales Law [*A publication*] (DLA)
**NS Wales LR Eq** ... New South Wales Law Reports, Equity [*A publication*] (DLA)
**NSWAMES** ... New South Wales Adult Migrant Education Service [*Australia*]
**NSWAMH** ... New South Wales Association for Mental Health [*Australia*]
**NSWAR** .... New South Wales Arbitration Reports [*A publication*] (DLA)
**NSW Art Gallery Q** ... New South Wales Art Gallery Quarterly [*A publication*] (APTA)
**NSWB** ....... New South Wales Bankruptcy Cases [*A publication*] (APTA)
**NSWB** ....... New South Wales Bushmen [*British military*] (DMA)
**NSWBC** ..... Black Cultural Centre for Nova Scotia, Westphal [*Library symbol*] [*National Library of Canada*] (BIB)
**NSW Bkptcy Cas** ... New South Wales Bankruptcy Cases [*A publication*] (APTA)
**NSW Bktcy Cas** ... New South Wales Reports, Bankruptcy Cases [*A publication*] (DLA)
**NSWC** ....... National South West Coalition [*Australia*]
**NSWC** ....... Naval Surface Warfare Center [*Silver Spring, MD*] (GRD)
**NSW CAC Report** ... New South Wales Corporate Affairs Commission. Report [*Australia*] [*A publication*]
**NSWCAF** .. Naval Surface Weapons Center Acoustic Facility (GRD)
**NSW Carpenters J** ... New South Wales Carpenters' Journal [*A publication*] (APTA)
**NSWC/DL** ... Naval Surface Weapons Center, Dahlgren Laboratory
**NSWC Eq** ... New South Wales Law Reports, Equity [*A publication*] (DLA)
**NSWCMHJ** ... New South Wales Council for the Mentally Handicapped. Journal [*A publication*] (APTA)
**NSWCN** .... New South Wales College of Nursing [*Australia*]

**NSW Contract Reporter** ... New South Wales Contract Reporter and Prices Current List [*A publication*] (APTA)
**NSW Conv R** ... New South Wales Conveyancing Reports [*A publication*] (APTA)
**NSW Country Trader** ... New South Wales Country Trader and Storekeeper [*A publication*] (APTA)
**NSW CRD** ... New South Wales Court of Review Decisions [*A publication*] (APTA)
**NSWCRL**.. New South Wales Law Reports, Supreme Court [*A publication*] (DLA)
**NSW Ct of App** ... New South Wales Court of Appeal [*Australia*]
**NSWC/WOL** ... Naval Surface Weapons Center, White Oak Laboratory
**NSWDAHAC** ... National Society Women Descendants of the Ancient and Honorable Artillery Company (EA)
**NSW Dep Agric Annu Rep** ... New South Wales. Department of Agriculture. Annual Report [*A publication*]
**NSW Dep Agric Biol Chem Res Inst Annu Plant Dis Surv** ... New South Wales. Department of Agriculture. Biological and Chemical Research Institute. Annual Plant Disease Survey [*A publication*]
**NSW Dep Agric Bull S** ... New South Wales. Department of Agriculture. Bulletin S [*A publication*]
**NSW Dep Agric Chem Branch** ... New South Wales. Department of Agriculture. Chemistry Branch. Bulletin S [*A publication*] (APTA)
**NSW Dep Agric Div Sci Serv Entomol Branch Annu Rep** ... New South Wales. Department of Agriculture. Division of Science Services. Entomology Branch. Annual Report [*A publication*]
**NSW Dep Agric Div Sci Serv Entomol Branch Insect Pest Leafl** ... New South Wales. Department of Agriculture. Division of Science Services. Entomology Branch. Insect Pest Leaflet [*A publication*]
**NSW Dep Agric Plant Dis Surv** ... New South Wales. Department of Agriculture. Plant Disease Survey [*A publication*]
**NSW Dep Agric Rep** ... New South Wales. Department of Agriculture. Report [*A publication*] (APTA)
**NSW Dep Agric Sci Bull** ... New South Wales. Department of Agriculture. Science Bulletin [*A publication*]
**NSW Dep Agric Tech Bull** ... New South Wales. Department of Agriculture. Technical Bulletin [*A publication*] (APTA)
**NSW Dep Mines Chem Lab Rep** ... New South Wales. Department of Mines. Chemical Laboratory Report [*A publication*]
**NSW Dep Mines Coalfields Branch Tech Rep** ... New South Wales. Department of Mines. Coalfields Branch. Technical Report [*A publication*] (APTA)
**NSW Dep Mines Geol Surv Bull** ... New South Wales. Department of Mines. Geological Survey. Bulletin [*A publication*] (APTA)
**NSW Dep Mines Geol Surv Miner Ind NSW** ... New South Wales. Department of Mines. Geological Survey. Mineral Industry of New South Wales [*A publication*] (APTA)
**NSW Dep Mines Geol Surv Rep** ... New South Wales. Department of Mines. Geological Survey. Report [*A publication*] (APTA)
**NSW Dep Mines Mem Geol Surv NSW Geol** ... New South Wales. Department of Mines. Memoirs of the Geological Survey of New South Wales. Geology [*A publication*] (APTA)
**NSW Dep Mines Mem Geol Surv NSW Palaeontol** ... New South Wales. Department of Mines. Memoirs of the Geological Survey of New South Wales. Palaeontology [*A publication*] (APTA)
**NSW Dep Mines Tech Rep** ... New South Wales. Department of Mines. Technical Report [*A publication*] (APTA)
**NSW Dep Mines Tech Rep CF** ... New South Wales. Department of Mines. Coalfields Branch. Technical Report CF [*A publication*] (APTA)
**NSW Dept Mines Chem Lab Rep** ... New South Wales. Department of Mines. Chemical Laboratory. Report [*A publication*] (APTA)
**NSW Ed Gaz** ... Education Gazette (New South Wales) [*A publication*] (APTA)
**NSWEK**..... Eastern King's Memorial Hospital, Wolfville, Nova Scotia [*Library symbol*] [*National Library of Canada*] (NLC)
**NSW Eq**..... Law Reports (New South Wales). Equity [*A publication*] (APTA)
**NSW Eq Rep** ... New South Wales Law Reports, Equity [*A publication*] (DLA)
**NSWFCA**.. New South Wales Foster Care Association [*Australia*]
**NSW Fed INS Clubs Gen Newsletter** ... New South Wales. Federation of Infants and Nursery School Clubs. General Newsletter [*A publication*] (APTA)
**NSW Fed INSC News** ... New South Wales Federation of Infants and Nursery School Clubs. News [*A publication*] (APTA)
**NSW For Comm Dir For Mgmt Res Note** ... New South Wales. Forestry Commission. Division of Forest Management. Research Note [*A publication*] (APTA)
**NSW For Comm Div Wood Technol Bull** ... New South Wales. Forestry Commission. Division of Wood Technology. Bulletin [*A publication*] (APTA)
**NSW For Comm Div Wood Technol Leafl** ... New South Wales. Forestry Commission. Division of Wood Technology. Leaflet [*A publication*] (APTA)
**NSW For Comm Div Wood Technol Pamph** ... New South Wales. Forestry Commission. Division of Wood Technology. Pamphlet [*A publication*] (APTA)
**NSW For Comm Div Wood Technol Proj Rep** ... New South Wales. Forestry Commission. Division of Wood Technology. Project Reports [*A publication*]
**NSW For Comm Div Wood Technol Tech** ... New South Wales. Forestry Commission. Division of Wood Technology. Technical Notes [*A publication*] (APTA)
**NSW For Comm Div Wood Technol Tech Notes** ... New South Wales. Forestry Commission. Division of Wood Technology. Technical Notes [*A publication*]
**NSW For Comm Res Note** ... New South Wales. Forestry Commission. Research Notes [*A publication*] (APTA)
**NSW For Rec** ... New South Wales Forestry Recorder [*A publication*] (APTA)
**NSW Freemason** ... New South Wales Freemason [*A publication*] (APTA)
**NSWG**....... Naval Special Warfare Group (NVT)
**NSWG**....... Nuclear Safety Working Group (CINC)
**NSW Geol Surv Bull** ... New South Wales. Geological Survey. Bulletin [*A publication*] (APTA)
**NSW Geol Surv 1:250 000 Geol Ser** ... New South Wales. Geological Survey. 1:250,000 Geological Series [*A publication*] (APTA)
**NSW Geol Surv Mem Geol** ... New South Wales. Geological Survey. Memoirs. Geology [*A publication*] (APTA)
**NSW Geol Surv Mem Palaeontol** ... New South Wales. Geological Survey. Memoirs. Palaeontology [*A publication*]
**NSW Geol Surv 4-Mile Geol Ser** ... New South Wales. Geological Survey. 4-Mile Geological Series [*A publication*] (APTA)
**NSW Geol Surv Mineral Industry of NSW** ... New South Wales. Geological Survey. Mineral Industry of New South Wales [*A publication*] (APTA)
**NSW Geol Surv Miner Resour** ... New South Wales. Geological Survey. Mineral Resources [*A publication*] (APTA)
**NSW Geol Surv Min Res** ... New South Wales. Geological Survey. Mineral Resources [*A publication*] (APTA)
**NSW Geol Surv Q Notes** ... New South Wales. Geological Survey. Quarterly Notes [*A publication*]
**NSW Geol Surv Rec** ... New South Wales. Geological Survey. Records [*A publication*] (APTA)
**NSW Geol Surv Rep** ... New South Wales. Geological Survey. Report [*A publication*] (APTA)
**NSWGG**.... New South Wales Government Gazette [*A publication*] (APTA)
**NSWH**....... Wolfville Historical Museum, Nova Scotia [*Library symbol*] [*National Library of Canada*] (NLC)
**NSW Herb Contr** ... New South Wales. National Herbarium. Contributions [*A publication*] (APTA)
**NSW Herb Contr Flora Ser** ... New South Wales. National Herbarium. Contributions. Flora Series [*A publication*] (APTA)
**NSWHJ**..... Hants Journal, Windsor, Nova Scotia [*Library symbol*] [*National Library of Canada*] (NLC)
**NSWI**......... National Safe Workplace Institute (EA)
**NSWIC**...... New South Wales Industrial Commission [*Australia*]
**NSWIC**...... New South Wales Investment Corp. [*Australia*]
**NSWIC Ct S** ... New South Wales Industrial Commission in Court Session [*Australia*]
**NSWIER Bul** ... New South Wales Institute for Educational Research. Bulletin [*A publication*] (APTA)
**NSWIG**...... New South Wales Industrial Gazette [*Australia*] [*A publication*]
**NSW Inc Acts** ... New South Wales Incorporated Acts [*A publication*] (DLA)
**NSW Ind Arbtn** ... New South Wales Industrial Arbitration Cases [*A publication*] (DLA)
**NSW Ind Arbtn Cas** ... New South Wales Industrial Arbitration Cases [*A publication*] (DLA)
**NSW Ind Gaz** ... New South Wales Industrial Gazette [*A publication*] (APTA)
**NSW Indus Arb R** ... New South Wales Industrial Arbitration Reports [*A publication*] (DLA)
**NSW Inst Ed Res Bul** ... New South Wales Institute for Educational Research. Bulletin [*A publication*] (APTA)
**NSWJB**..... New South Wales Judgements Bulletin [*Australia*] [*A publication*]
**NSWJT**..... Materials Laboratory Library, Nova Scotia Department of Transportation, Windsor Junction, Nova Scotia [*Library symbol*] [*National Library of Canada*] (NLC)
**NSWKE**..... King's-Edgehill School, Windsor, Nova Scotia [*Library symbol*] [*National Library of Canada*] (NLC)
**NSW Land App** ... New South Wales Land Appeal Court Cases [*A publication*] (DLA)
**NSW Land App Cas** ... Land Appeal Court Cases (New South Wales) [*A publication*] (APTA)
**NSW Land App Cts** ... New South Wales Land Appeal Courts (DLA)
**NSW Law Repts** ... New South Wales Law Reports [*A publication*]
**NSW Lib Bul** ... New South Wales Library Bulletin [*A publication*] (APTA)
**NSW Local Gov't R** ... New South Wales Local Government Reports [*A publication*] (DLA)
**NSWLR**..... New South Wales Law Reports [*A publication*] (APTA)
**NSWLR**..... New South Wales Letters of Registration [*A publication*] (APTA)
**NSWLRC**.. New South Wales Law Reform Commission [*Australia*] (ILCA)
**NSWLVR**.. New South Wales Land and Valuation Court Reports [*A publication*] (APTA)
**NSWMA** ... National Soft Wheat Millers Association [*Later, MNF*] (EA)

**NSWMA**... National Solid Wastes Management Association (EA)
**NSWOP**.... New South Wales Official Publications [*A publication*] (APTA)
**NSWP**........ Non-Soviet Warsaw Pact (NATG)
**NSW Parl Deb**... New South Wales Parliamentary Debates [*A publication*] (APTA)
**NSW Parl Parl Deb**... New South Wales. Parliament. Parliamentary Debates [*A publication*] (APTA)
**NSWPD**..... New South Wales Parliamentary Debates [*A publication*] (APTA)
**NSW Philatelic Ann**... New South Wales Philatelic Annual [*A publication*] (APTA)
**NSW Police News**... New South Wales Police News [*A publication*] (APTA)
**NSW Potato**... New South Wales Potato [*A publication*] (APTA)
**NSWPP**..... National Socialist White People's Party [*Formerly, American NAZI Party*] (EA)
**NSW Presbyterian**... New South Wales Presbyterian [*A publication*] (APTA)
**NSW Priv Com Papers**... New South Wales Privacy Committee. Papers [*Australia*] [*A publication*]
**NSWPTCA**... New South Wales Professional Tennis Coaches Association [*Australia*]
**NSW Pub Acts**... New South Wales Public Acts [*A publication*] (DLA)
**NSW Pub Stat**... New South Wales Public Statutes [*A publication*] (DLA)
**NSWR**....... Industrial Arbitration Reports (New South Wales). New South Wales Reports [*A publication*] (APTA)
**NSW Regs B & Ords**... New South Wales Regulations, By-Laws, and Ordinances [*Australia*] [*A publication*] (DLA)
**NSWS**........ Nuclear Service Water System (NRCH)
**NSWSCR**.. New South Wales Supreme Court Reports [*A publication*] (DLA)
**(NSW) SCR (L)**... Supreme Court Reports (Law) (New South Wales) [*A publication*] (APTA)
**NSW S Ct Cas**... New South Wales Supreme Court Cases [*A publication*] (DLA)
**NSW S Ct R**... New South Wales Supreme Court Reports [*A publication*] (DLA)
**NSWSES**... Naval Ship Weapon Systems Engineering Station [*Port Hueneme, CA*]
**NSWSR**..... New South Wales State Reports [*A publication*] (APTA)
**NSW State Fish Cruise Rep**... New South Wales. State Fisheries Cruise Report [*A publication*]
**NSW Statist Summ**... New South Wales Statistical Summary [*A publication*] (APTA)
**NSW Stat Reg**... New South Wales Statistical Register [*A publication*] (APTA)
**NSW St R**... New South Wales State Reports [*A publication*] (APTA)
**NSWTA**..... National Senior Women's Tennis Association (EA)
**NSWTA**..... New South Wales Typographical Association [*Australia*]
**NSWTG**.... Naval Special Warfare Task Group (CAAL)
**NSWTIA**... New South Wales Taxi Industry Association [*Australia*]
**NSW Timber Worker**... New South Wales Timber Worker [*A publication*] (APTA)
**NSWTPA**.. New South Wales Tennis Professionals Association [*Australia*]
**NSW Univ Engineering Yrbk**... University of New South Wales. Faculty of Engineering. Yearbook [*A publication*] (APTA)
**NSW Univ Inst Highw Traff Res Res Note**... University of New South Wales. Institute of Highway and Traffic Research. Research Note [*A publication*] (APTA)
**NSW Univ Sch Civ Eng UNICIV Rep Ser R**... New South Wales University. School of Civil Engineering. UNICIV Report. Series R [*A publication*]
**NSW Univ UNICIV Rep**... University of New South Wales. School of Civil Engineering. UNICIV Report [*A publication*] (APTA)
**NSW Univ Wat Res Lab Rep**... University of New South Wales. Water Research Laboratory. Report [*A publication*] (APTA)
**NSW Vet Proc**... Proceedings. Australian Veterinary Association. New South Wales Division [*A publication*] (APTA)
**NSWWA**... North Shore Women Writers Alliance [*Later, NSWA*] (EA)
**NSWWASA**... New South Wales Women's Amateur Swimming Association [*Australia*]
**NSW Wat Conserv Irrig Comm Surv Thirty NSW River Valleys Rep**... New South Wales. Water Conservation and Irrigation Commission. Survey of Thirty New South Wales River Valleys. Report [*A publication*] (APTA)
**NSW Weath Rep**... New South Wales Weather Report [*A publication*] (APTA)
**NSWWH**... West Hants Historical Society Museum, Windsor, Nova Scotia [*Library symbol*] [*National Library of Canada*] (NLC)
**NSWWN**... New South Wales Weekly Notes [*A publication*] (APTA)
**NSW Worker's Comp R**... New South Wales Worker's Compensation Reports [*A publication*] (DLA)
**NSY**........... Naval Shipyard
**NSY**........... New Scotland Yard
**NSY**........... North Salopian Yeomanry [*British military*] (DMA)
**NSY**........... North Somerset Yeomanry [*British military*] (DMA)
**NSy**........... Onondaga County Public Library, Syracuse, NY [*Library symbol*] [*Library of Congress*] (LCLS)
**NSY**........... Western Counties Regional Library, Yarmouth, Nova Scotia [*Library symbol*] [*National Library of Canada*] (NLC)
**NSyA**........ Allied Corp., Solvay Process Division, Syracuse, NY [*Library symbol*] [*Library of Congress*] (LCLS)
**NSYA**........ National School Yearbook Association [*Later, NSY/NA*]
**NSyAF**....... United States Air Force, Hancock Air Base Library, Syracuse, NY [*Library symbol*] [*Library of Congress*] (LCLS)
**NSyAg**....... Agway, Inc., Syracuse, NY [*Library symbol*] [*Library of Congress*] (LCLS)
**NSyBL**....... Bristol Laboratories, Syracuse, NY [*Library symbol*] [*Library of Congress*] (LCLS)
**NSyC**......... Carrier Corp., Syracuse, NY [*Library symbol*] [*Library of Congress*] (LCLS)
**NSYC**......... Courrier de la Nouvelle-Ecosse, Yarmouth, Nova Scotia [*Library symbol*] [*National Library of Canada*] (NLC)
**NSyCA**....... United States Court of Appeals, Syracuse, NY [*Library symbol*] [*Library of Congress*] (LCLS)
**NSYCDA**... Archives, Diocese of Yarmouth, Catholic Church, Nova Scotia [*Library symbol*] [*National Library of Canada*] (NLC)
**NSyCH**...... Crouse-Irving Hospital, Syracuse, NY [*Library symbol*] [*Library of Congress*] (LCLS)
**NSYD**........ Naval Shipyard
**NSYDCN**.. Diocese of Central New York, Syracuse, NY [*Library symbol*] [*Library of Congress*] (LCLS)
**NSyEd**....... Educational Opportunity Center, Syracuse, NY [*Library symbol*] [*Library of Congress*] (LCLS)
**NSYF**......... Natural Science for Youth Foundation (EA)
**NSYFG**...... Fundy Group Publications, Yarmouth, Nova Scotia [*Library symbol*] [*National Library of Canada*] (NLC)
**NSyGE**...... General Electric Co., Syracuse, NY [*Library symbol*] [*Library of Congress*] (LCLS)
**NSyGH**...... Community-General Hospital, Syracuse, NY [*Library symbol*] [*Library of Congress*] (LCLS)
**NSYHM**.... Research Library, Yarmouth County Historical Society, Yarmouth, Nova Scotia [*Library symbol*] [*National Library of Canada*] (NLC)
**NSyL**.......... LeMoyne College, Syracuse, NY [*Library symbol*] [*Library of Congress*] (LCLS)
**NSyLG**....... Loretto Geriatric Center, Educational Resource Center, Syracuse, NY [*Library symbol*] [*Library of Congress*] (LCLS)
**NSyMR**..... Maria Regina College, Syracuse, NY [*Library symbol*] [*Library of Congress*] (LCLS)
**NSyN**......... City Normal School, Syracuse, NY [*Library symbol*] [*Library of Congress*] [*Obsolete*] (LCLS)
**NSY/NA**.... National School Yearbook/Newspaper Association [*Defunct*] (EA)
**NSyo**.......... Syosset Public Library, Syosset, NY [*Library symbol*] [*Library of Congress*] (LCLS)
**NSyoBaE**... Baylis Elementary School, Syosset, NY [*Library symbol*] [*Library of Congress*] (LCLS)
**NSyoBE**..... Berry Hill Elementary School, Syosset, NY [*Library symbol*] [*Library of Congress*] (LCLS)
**NSyOC**...... Onondaga Community College, Syracuse, NY [*Library symbol*] [*Library of Congress*] (LCLS)
**NSyoF**........ Fairchild Space and Defense System, Syosset, NY [*Library symbol*] [*Library of Congress*] (LCLS)
**NSyoG**....... United States Geological Survey, Water Resources Division, Syosset, NY [*Library symbol*] [*Library of Congress*] (LCLS)
**NSyoH**....... Syosset Hospital, Syosset, NY [*Library symbol*] [*Library of Congress*] (LCLS)
**NSyOHi**..... Onondaga Historical Association, Syracuse, NY [*Library symbol*] [*Library of Congress*] (LCLS)
**NSyOL**...... Onondaga Library System, Syracuse, NY [*Library symbol*] [*Library of Congress*] (LCLS)
**NSyoP**........ PRD Electronics, Inc., Information Center Library, Syosset, NY [*Library symbol*] [*Library of Congress*] (LCLS)
**NSyoRE**..... Robbins Elementary School, Syosset, NY [*Library symbol*] [*Library of Congress*] (LCLS)
**NSyoSGE**.. South Grove Elementary School, Syosset, NY [*Library symbol*] [*Library of Congress*] (LCLS)
**NSyoSRE**.. Split Rock Elementary School, Syosset, NY [*Library symbol*] [*Library of Congress*] (LCLS)
**NSyoVE**..... Village Elementary School, Syosset, NY [*Library symbol*] [*Library of Congress*] (LCLS)
**NSyoWE**.... Willits Elementary School, Syosset, NY [*Library symbol*] [*Library of Congress*] (LCLS)
**NSyoWhE**... Whitman Elementary School, Syosset, NY [*Library symbol*] [*Library of Congress*] (LCLS)
**NSYR**......... Medical Library, Yarmouth Regional Hospital, Nova Scotia [*Library symbol*] [*National Library of Canada*] (BIB)
**NSyR**......... Syracuse Research Corp., Syracuse, NY [*Library symbol*] [*Library of Congress*] (LCLS)
**NSySC**....... New York State Supreme Court Law Library, Syracuse, NY [*Library symbol*] [*Library of Congress*] (LCLS)
**NSYSD6**.... NSC [*National Science Council*] Symposium Series [*Taipei*] [*A publication*]
**NSySJ**........ Saint Joseph's Hospital, School of Nursing and Medical Library, Syracuse, NY [*Library symbol*] [*Library of Congress*] (LCLS)
**NSYSP**...... National Summer Youth Sports Program
**NSySU-F**... State University of New York, College of Environmental Sciences and Forestry at Syracuse University, Syracuse, NY [*Library symbol*] [*Library of Congress*] (LCLS)

**NSySU-M** ... State University of New York, Upstate Medical Center, Syracuse, NY [*Library symbol*] [*Library of Congress*] (LCLS)
**NSyT** ......... Technology Club of Syracuse, Syracuse, NY [*Library symbol*] [*Library of Congress*] (LCLS)
**NSyU** ......... Syracuse University, Syracuse, NY [*Library symbol*] [*Library of Congress*] (LCLS)
**NSyU-CE** .. Syracuse University, Library of Continuing Education at Syracuse, Syracuse, NY [*Library symbol*] [*Library of Congress*] (LCLS)
**NSyU-G**..... Syracuse University, Educational Resources Center of the All-University Gerontology Center, Syracuse, NY [*Library symbol*] [*Library of Congress*] (LCLS)
**NSyVA** ...... United States Veterans Administration Hospital, Syracuse, NY [*Library symbol*] [*Library of Congress*] (LCLS)
**NSZ** ........... Nederlands-Spaanse Kamer van Koophandel. Spaanse Aanvragen voor Handelskontakten met Nederland [*A publication*]
**NSZKA**...... Nauchnye Trudy Severo-Zapadnyi Nauchno-Issledovatel'skii Institut Sel'skogo Khozyaistva [*A publication*]
**NSZP**......... Nemzeti Szabadelvu Part [*National Liberal Party*] [*Hungary*] [*Political party*] (PPE)
**NT**............. Iraq-Saudi Arabia Neutral Zone [*ANSI two-letter standard code*] (CNC)
**N-T** ........... Nal-Tel [*Race of maize*]
**nT**.............. Nanotesla
**NT**.............. Narrower Term [*Indexing*]
**NT**.............. Naso-Tracheal [*Medicine*]
**NT**.............. National Taranesc [*National Peasant Party*] [*Romania*] [*Political party*] (PPE)
**NT**.............. National Team
**NT**.............. National Theatre [*Great Britain*]
**NT**.............. National Times [*A publication*] (APTA)
**NT**.............. National Trust for Historic Preservation
**NT**.............. Naturalization Test
**NT**.............. Naval Training
**N & T** ......... Navigation and Timing
**NT**.............. Navy Type (MSA)
**NT**.............. Neap Tide
**NT**.............. Near Term
**NT**.............. Neat [*Plain*] [*Bookbinding*] (ROG)
**NT**.............. Neotetrazolium
**NT**.............. Nested-Task [*Data processing*] (BYTE)
**NT**.............. Net Tax [*IRS*]
**N/t** ............ Net Terms [*Business term*] (DS)
**NT**.............. Net Tons [*Shipping*]
**NT**.............. Netilmicin-Ticarcillin [*Antibiotic combination*]
**NT**.............. Nett [*Net*] [*British*] (ROG)
**NT**.............. Network Terminal (MCD)
**NT**.............. Network Termination [*Telecommunications*]
**NT**.............. Neural Tube [*Anatomy*]
**NT**.............. Neurotensin [*Biochemistry*]
**NT**.............. Neurotrophin [*Neurobiology*]
**NT**.............. Neutralization Test [*Chemistry*]
**NT**.............. Neutron Transmitter [*Nuclear energy*] (NRCH)
**NT**.............. Nevada Territory [*Prior to statehood*]
**NT**.............. New Taiwan
**N/T** ........... New Terms [*Business term*]
**NT**.............. New Territories [*Hong Kong*]
**N T** ............ New Testament [*A publication*]
**NT**.............. New Testament [*of the Bible*]
**NT**.............. New Times [*A publication*]
**NT**.............. New Towns [*British*]
**NT**.............. New Translation
**nt** ............... Newton (NASA)
**Nt** ............... Nicotiana tabacum [*Tobacco*]
**NT**.............. Nieuwe Taalgids [*A publication*]
**NT**.............. Night (ROG)
**NT**.............. Night Trunk [*Business term*] (DCTA)
**nt** ............... Nit [*Unit of luminance*]
**N/T** ........... No Terms [*Shipping*]
**NT**.............. No Test
**NT**.............. No Tillage [*Agriculture*]
**NT**.............. No Trace [*Counterintelligence*]
**NT**.............. No Transmission [*Telecommunications*]
**NT**.............. No Trump [*in game of bridge*]
**NT**.............. Non-T Cell [*Cytology*]
**N/T** ........... None in Town [*Bookselling*]
**N/T** ........... Nonmeasured Time
**NT**.............. Nontight (AAG)
**NT**.............. Nontryptophan [*Protein-bound fluorescence*]
**NT**.............. Nordisk Tidskrift [*A publication*]
**NT**.............. Nordisk Tidskrift foer Vetenskap, Konst, och Industri [*A publication*]
**NT**.............. Nordisk Traebeskyttelsesrad [*Nordic Wood Preservation Council - NWPC*] (EAIO)
**NT**.............. Nordiska Transportarbetarefederationen [*Nordic Transportworkers' Federation - NTF*] (EAIO)
**NT**.............. Normal Temperature (ADA)
**NT**.............. Normal Tour
**NT**.............. Northern Air Taxis Ltd. [*Great Britain*] [*ICAO designator*] (FAAC)
**NT**.............. Northern Telecom Ltd. [*NYSE symbol*] (SPSG)
**NT**.............. Northern Territory [*Australia*]
**NT**.............. Northern Times [*Whitehorse, Canada*] [*A publication*]
**NT**.............. Northwest Territories [*Canada*] [*Postal code*]
**NT**.............. Nortriptyline [*Antidepressant drug*]
**N & T** ......... Nose and Throat [*Medicine*]
**NT**.............. Not Tested
**NT**.............. Not Titled [*Accounting*]
**NT**.............. Not Typical
**NT**.............. Note [*Online database field identifier*]
**NT**.............. Novum Testamentum [*New Testament*] [*of the Bible*]
**NT**.............. Novum Testamentum [*A publication*]
**NT**.............. Nuclear Theory [*Elsevier Book Series*] [*A publication*]
**NT**.............. Nuclear Transfer
**NT**.............. Numbering Transmitter
**NT**.............. Nurse Technician
**NT**.............. Thermal Necrosis [*Roentgenology*]
**NT**.............. Troy Public Library, Troy, NY [*Library symbol*] [*Library of Congress*] (LCLS)
**NTA**........... Fujisawa Pharmaceutical Co. [*Japan*] [*Research code symbol*]
**NTA**........... Naphthoyltrifluoroacetone [*Organic chemistry*]
**NTA**........... Narcotics Treatment Administration [*Washington, DC*]
**NTA**........... National Tabletop Association (EA)
**NTA**........... National Tattoo Association (EA)
**NTA**........... National Tax Association [*Later, NTA-TIA*] (EA)
**NTA**........... National Taxidermists Association (EA)
**NTA**........... National Taxpayers Alliance (EA)
**NTA**........... National Technical Association (EA)
**NTA**........... National Telecommunications Agency
**NTA**........... National Tennis Academy [*Commercial firm*] (EA)
**NTA**........... National Tennis Association [*Later, IRJA*] (EA)
**NTA**........... National Threshers Association (EA)
**NTA**........... National Times (Australia) [*A publication*]
**NTA**........... National Tour Association (EA)
**NTA**........... National Translator Association (EA)
**NTA**........... National Trappers Association (EA)
**NTA**........... National Triton Association (EA)
**NTA**........... National Trolleybus Association [*British*]
**NTA**........... National Tuberculosis Association [*Later, American Lung Association*] (EA)
**NTA**........... Naval Technical Assistants
**NTA**........... Navy Technical Assessment (MCD)
**NTA**........... Navy Technician Authorization (NG)
**NTA**........... Near-Terminal Area [*Airports*]
**NTA**........... Neher Tetrode Amplifier
**NTA**........... Net Tangible Assets [*Business term*] (ADA)
**NTA**........... Net Technical Assessment (MCD)
**NtA** ............ Neutestamentliche Abhandlungen [*Muenster*] [*A publication*]
**NTA**........... Nevada Test Site Array [*Nevada*] [*Seismograph station code, US Geological Survey*] (SEIS)
**NTA**........... New Testament Abstracts [*A publication*]
**NTA**........... New Towns Act [*Town planning*] [*British*]
**NTA**........... Nitrilotriacetic Acid [*Organic chemistry*]
**NTA**........... Northern Territory, Australia
**NTA**........... Northern Textile Association (EA)
**NTA**........... Northwest Territory Alliance (EA)
**NTA**........... Norwegian Telecommunications Administration [*Oslo*]
**NTA**........... Nuclear Test Aircraft
**NTA**........... Nurse Training Act
**NTa**............ Warner Library, Tarrytown, NY [*Library symbol*] [*Library of Congress*] (LCLS)
**NTAA**........ National Travelers Aid Association (EA)
**NTAA**........ Tahiti/FAAA [*French Polynesia*] [*ICAO location identifier*] (ICLI)
**NTAB** ........ Nuclear Technical Advisory Board [*American National Standards Institute*]
**NTAbstr** .... New Testament Abstracts [*Weston, MA*] [*A publication*]
**NTA Bul** .... Newfoundland Teachers' Association. Bulletin [*A publication*]
**NTAC** ........ National Technical Assistance Center on Family Violence [*Defunct*] (EA)
**NTAG**........ Network Technical Architecture Group [*Library of Congress*]
**NTaGF** ...... General Foods Technical Center Library, Tarrytown, NY [*Library symbol*] [*Library of Congress*] (LCLS)
**NTaHi** ....... Historical Society of the Tarrytowns, Tarrytown, NY [*Library symbol*] [*Library of Congress*] (LCLS)
**NTAI** ......... Nam Tai Electronics, Inc. [*NASDAQ symbol*] (NQ)
**NTaI** ......... Washington Irving Home, Sleepy Hollow Restorations, Tarrytown, NY [*Library symbol*] [*Library of Congress*] [*Obsolete*] (LCLS)
**NTAJ**......... Newfoundland Teachers' Association. Journal [*A publication*]
**NTaM**........ Marymount College, Tarrytown, NY [*Library symbol*] [*Library of Congress*] (LCLS)
**NTAM**....... New Testament Archaeology Monographs [*A publication*] (BJA)
**NTAN**........ Nitrilotriacetonitrile [*Organic chemistry*]
**NTAP** ........ National Targeting and Attack Policy (CINC)
**NTap**.......... Tappan Free Library, Tappan, NY [*Library symbol*] [*Library of Congress*] (LCLS)

**NTA Proceedings** ... National Tax Association. Proceedings [*A publication*] (DLA)
**NTAR** ........ NetAir International Corp. [*Denver, CO*] [*NASDAQ symbol*] (NQ)
**NTAR** ........ Nonviolent Techniques Against Rape [*An association*] (EA)
**NTAR** ........ Rurutu [*French Polynesia*] [*ICAO location identifier*] (ICLI)
**NTAS** ......... Norwegian Tracking Adjunct System
**NTaS** ......... Sleepy Hollow Restorations, Tarrytown, NY [*Library symbol*] [*Library of Congress*] (LCLS)
**NTAT** ........ Tubuai/Mataura [*French Polynesia*] [*ICAO location identifier*] (ICLI)
**NTATC** ...... National Transportation Apprenticeship and Training Conference [*Bureau of Apprenticeship and Training*] [*Department of Labor*]
**NTA-TIA** ... National Tax Association - Tax Institute of America (EA)
**NTaUC** ...... Union Carbide Corp., Tarrytown Technical Center, Tarrytown, NY [*Library symbol*] [*Library of Congress*] (LCLS)
**NTAVL** ...... Not Available (NOAA)
**NTAW** ....... Northern Territory Aerial Work [*Australia*]
**NTAZA** ..... Nippon Taishitsugaku Zasshi [*A publication*]
**NTB** ........... National Target Base (MCD)
**NTB** ........... National Test Bed [*Military*] (SDI)
**NTB** ........... New Technical Books [*A publication*]
**NTB** ........... No Talent Bum [*Slang*]
**NTB** ........... Nontariff Barrier [*Kennedy Round*]
**NTB** ........... Nontumor-Bearing
**NTB** ........... Norsk Telegrambyra [*Norwegian News Agency*]
**NTB** ........... Northumbria Tourist Board [*British*] (DCTA)
**NTB** ........... Nuclear Test Ban
**NTBA** ........ National Tour Brokers Association (EA)
**NTBB** ........ National Temporal Bone Banks Program of the DRF [*Deafness Research Foundation*] (EA)
**NTBB** ........ Nordisk Tidskrift foer Bok- och Biblioteksvaesen [*A publication*]
**NTBBV** ...... Nordisk Tidskrift foer Bok- och Biblioteksvaesen [*A publication*]
**NTBEDQ** .. Scandinavian Journal of Behaviour Therapy [*A publication*]
**NTBPSC** .... Nepal, Tibet, and Bhutan Philatelic Study Circle (EA)
**NTBR** ........ Not to Be Resuscitated
**NTC** ........... Economisch Dagblad. Dagblad voor het Management [*A publication*]
**NTC** ........... National Tasking Center (MCD)
**NTC** ........... National Teachers Corps
**NTC** ........... National Team Championship [*Swimming*] [*British*] (ROG)
**NTC** ........... National Teen Challenge (EA)
**NTC** ........... National Telecommunications Commission [*Philippines*] (DS)
**NTC** ........... National Telecommunications Conference [*IEEE*]
**NTC** ........... National Telemedia Council (EA)
**NTC** ........... National Television Center [*Telecommunications*] (TEL)
**NTC** ........... National Territorial Command (MCD)
**NTC** ........... National Test Center (NATG)
**NTC** ........... National Thanksgiving Commission (EA)
**NTC** ........... National Theatre Conference (EA)
**NTC** ........... National Thrift Committee [*Defunct*] (EA)
**NTC** ........... National Timesharing Council (EA)
**NTC** ........... National Traditionalist Caucus (EA)
**NTC** ........... National Trails Council (EA)
**NTC** ........... National Training Center [*Red Cross*] [*Charlottesville, VA*]
**NTC** ........... National Translations Center [*John Crerar Library*] [*Information service or system*]
**NTC** ........... National Transportation Center [*Large city situated at a key junction of rail, air, and highway transportation*] [*Postal Service*]
**NTC** ........... National Travel Club [*Commercial firm*] (EA)
**NTC** ........... National Troopers Coalition (EA)
**NTC** ........... Naturally Occurring Top Component [*Virology*]
**NTC** ........... Nautical Training Corps [*British military*] (DMA)
**NTC** ........... Naval Training Center
**NTC** ........... Naval Training Command
**NTC** ........... Negative Temperature Coefficient
**NTC** ........... Neotetrazolium Chloride [*A dye*]
**NTC** ........... Nordic Temperance Council (EA)
**NTC** ........... Nordic Theater Committee [*Later, NTDC*] (EAIO)
**NTC** ........... Normal Tour of Duty Completed
**ntc** ............. Northwest Territories [*MARC country of publication code*] [*Library of Congress*] (LCCP)
**NTC** ........... Norwich Terrier Club [*Later, NNTC*] (EA)
**NTC** ........... Notice
**NTC** ........... Nu-Trans Cooperative (EA)
**NTC** ........... Nucleon Transport Code
**NTCA** ........ N-Nitrosothioazolidine Carboxylic Acid [*Organic chemistry*]
**NTCA** ........ National Telephone Cooperative Association (EA)
**NTCA** ........ National Tile Contractors Association (EA)
**NTCA** ........ National Town Class Association (EA)
**NTCA** ........ National Tribal Chairman's Association (EA)
**NTCA** ........ Northern Territory Cattlemen's Association [*Australia*]
**NTCAVAL** ... Notice of Availability
**NTCB** ........ (Nitro)thiocyanatobenzoic Acid [*Organic chemistry*]
**NTCC** ........ Naval Tactical Communications Center (MCD)
**NTCC** ........ Neutron Transport Computer Code
**NTCC** ........ Nimbus Technical Control Center
**NTCD** ........ Nitro(thiocyano)benzoic Acid [*Organic chemistry*]
**NTCHBA** .. National Trust Closely Held Business Association (EA)
**NTCI** ......... National Training Center - Phase I (MCD)
**NTCLP** ...... Northern Territory Country Liberal Party [*Australia*] [*Political party*] (ADA)
**NTCMA** .... National Traditional Country Music Association [*Later, NTMA*] (EA)
**NTCNB** ..... Nature Canada [*A publication*]
**NTCOGSO** ... Northern Territory Council of Government School Organisations [*Australia*]
**NTCP** ......... Near-Term Construction Permit [*Nuclear energy*] (NRCH)
**NTCS** ......... National Teaching Company Scheme [*Australia*]
**NTCS** ......... Newsletter for Targumic and Cognate Studies [*Toronto*] [*A publication*]
**NTCS** ......... Nonverbal Test of Cognitive Skills [*Intelligence test*]
**NTCSD** ...... Naval Training Center, San Diego
**NTCSOC** ... Naval Telecommunications Command Satellite Operations Center (MCD)
**NTD** ........... Das Neue Testament Deutsch. Neues Goettinger Bibelwerk [*A publication*] (BJA)
**NTD** ........... N-Tone International Ltd. [*Vancouver Stock Exchange symbol*]
**NTD** ........... NASA Test Director (MCD)
**NTD** ........... National Tap Dance Company of Canada
**NTD** ........... National Theatre of the Deaf (EA)
**NTD** ........... Naval Training Department [*British military*] (DMA)
**NTD** ........... Netherlands Trade and News Bulletin [*A publication*]
**NTD** ........... Neural Tube (Closure) Defect [*Medicine*]
**NTD** ........... Neutron Transmutation Doped [*Silicon for semiconductor use*]
**NTD** ........... New Tyee Resources [*Vancouver Stock Exchange symbol*]
**NTD** ........... Nontight Door
**NTD** ........... Nuclear Test Directorate [*Air Force*]
**NTD** ........... Port Hueneme, CA [*Location identifier*] [*FAA*] (FAAL)
**NTDA** ........ Navy Tactical Doctrine Activity (NVT)
**NTDC** ........ Naval Training Devices Center [*Port Washington, LI*]
**NTDC** ........ Nordic Theatre and Dance Committee (EAIO)
**NTDDPA** .. Navy Tactical Doctrine Development and Production Activity
**NTDI** ......... NATO Target Data Inventory (MCD)
**NTDO** ........ Navy Technical Data Office [*of the Office of Naval Material*]
**NTDPMA** ... National Tool, Die, and Precision Machining Association [*Later, NTMA*] (EA)
**NTDRA** ..... National Tire Dealers and Retreaders Association (EA)
**NTDS** ........ Navy Tactical Data System
**NTDSC** ...... Nondestructive Testing Data Support Center [*DoD*] (MCD)
**NTE** ........... Nantes [*France*] [*Airport symbol*] (OAG)
**NTE** ........... Narodna Tvorcist' ta Etnografija [*A publication*]
**NTE** ........... National Teacher Examination
**NTE** ........... National Treasury Employees Union
**NTE** ........... Navy Technical Evaluation (NG)
**NTE** ........... Navy Teletypewriter Exchange [*Later, NTX*]
**NTE** ........... Neutron Transient Effect
**NTE** ........... Northern Eagle Mines [*Vancouver Stock Exchange symbol*]
**NTE** ........... Not to Exceed [*Aviation*]
**NTEA** ........ National Tax Equality Association (EA)
**NTEA** ........ National Telecommunications Electronics Administration
**NTEA** ........ National Time Equipment Association (EA)
**NTEA** ........ National Truck Equipment Association (EA)
**NTEC** ........ National Telecommunications Education Committee [*North American Telecommunications Association*] [*Washington, DC*] [*Telecommunications service*] (TSSD)
**NTEC** ........ Naval Training Equipment Center
**NTECPE** ... Naval Training Equipment Center, Project Engineer
**NTED** ........ Northern Territory Education Department [*Australia*]
**NTEF** ......... National Tennis Educational Foundation [*Later, NTFHF*] (EA)
**NTE/IOTE** ... Navy Technical Evaluation/Initial Operational Test and Evaluation (MCD)
**NTELA** ...... Nachrichtentechnik-Elektronik [*A publication*]
**NTemp** ....... Nostro Tempo [*A publication*]
**NTER** ........ Normalized Transmission Energy Requirement
**N Terr** ........ Northern Territory
**N Terr Austl Ord** ... Northern Territorial Ordinances [*Australia*] [*A publication*] (DLA)
**NTEU** ........ National Treasury Employees Union (EA)
**NTeZ** ......... North Temperate Zone [*Planet Jupiter*]
**NTF** ........... National Tactical Force (NATG)
**NTF** ........... National Tennis Foundation [*Formerly, NTEF*] [*Later, NTFHF*] (EA)
**NTF** ........... National Test Facility [*Military*] (SDI)
**NTF** ........... National Theater File [*Theater Sources, Inc.*] [*Information service or system*] [*Defunct*] (IID)
**NTF** ........... National Transonic Facility [*NASA*]
**NTF** ........... National Turkey Federation (EA)
**NTF** ........... Naval Task Force
**NTF** ........... Navy Technological Forecast
**NTF** ........... Neutestamentliche Forschungen [*A publication*]
**NTF** ........... Nigerian Trust Fund [*African Development Bank*]
**NTF** ........... No Trouble Found
**NTF** ........... Nordic Transportworkers' Federation [*See also NT*] (EAIO)
**NTF** ........... Nordisk Thoraxkirurgisk Forening [*Scandinavian Association for Thoracic and Cardiovascular Surgery - SATCS*] (EAIO)

**NTF** .......... NOTAM to Follow (FAAC)
**NTF** .......... Nuclear Technology/Fusion [*A publication*]
**NTF** .......... Nuclear Test Facility
**NTFA** ........ National Teaching-Family Association (EA)
**NTFA** ........ National Track and Field Association [*Superseded by ANG*] (EA)
**NTFAO** ..... National Task Force on Autocratic Options (EA)
**NTFC**......... National Television Film Council (EA)
**NTFDA** ..... Natturufraedingurinn [*A publication*]
**NTFDC**...... Non Theatrical Film Distributors Council (EA)
**NTFEEG** ... National Task Force on Education for Economic Growth (EA)
**NTFHF**...... National Tennis Foundation and Hall of Fame [*Later, ITHOF*] (EA)
**NTFL**......... National Touch Football Leagues (EA)
**NTFL**......... Northern Territory Football League [*Australia*]
**NTFLDX** ... Fonds de Recherches Forestieres. Universite Laval. Note Technique [*A publication*]
**NTFND** ..... No Trouble Found (FAAC)
**NTFP**......... National Task Force on Prostitution (EA)
**NTFTA**...... National Toy Fox Terrier Association (EA)
**NTFUD** ..... Nuclear Technology/Fusion [*A publication*]
**NTFY**......... Notify (AFM)
**NTG**.......... N-Tolylglycine [*Organic chemistry*]
**NTG**.......... Nederlandsch Tijdschrift voor Geneeskunde [*A publication*]
**NTg**........... Nieuwe Taalgids. Tijdschrift voor Neerlandici [*A publication*]
**NTG**.......... Nitroglycerin [*Also, GTN, NG*] [*Explosive, vasodilator*]
**NTG**.......... Nitrosoguanidine [*Organic chemistry*]
**NTG**.......... Non-Technical Generator [*Army*]
**NTG**.......... Nontactical Generator (RDA)
**NTG**.......... Nontoxic Goiter [*Medicine*]
**NTGA**........ Anaa [*French Polynesia*] [*ICAO location identifier*] (ICLI)
**NTGB**........ Fangatau [*French Polynesia*] [*ICAO location identifier*] (ICLI)
**NTGC**........ Tikehau [*French Polynesia*] [*ICAO location identifier*] (ICLI)
**NTGD**........ Apataki [*French Polynesia*] [*ICAO location identifier*] (ICLI)
**NTGE**........ Reao [*French Polynesia*] [*ICAO location identifier*] (ICLI)
**NTGF**........ Fakarava [*French Polynesia*] [*ICAO location identifier*] (ICLI)
**NTGH**........ Hikueru [*French Polynesia*] [*ICAO location identifier*] (ICLI)
**NTGI**......... Manihi [*French Polynesia*] [*ICAO location identifier*] (ICLI)
**NTGJ**......... Totegegie [*French Polynesia*] [*ICAO location identifier*] (ICLI)
**NTGK**........ Kaukura [*French Polynesia*] [*ICAO location identifier*] (ICLI)
**NTGL**........ Fakahina [*French Polynesia*] [*ICAO location identifier*] (ICLI)
**NTGLA** ..... Nauchnye Trudy Tashkentskii Gosudarstvennyi Universitet Imeni V. I. Lenina [*A publication*]
**NTGM**....... Makemo [*French Polynesia*] [*ICAO location identifier*] (ICLI)
**NTGN**........ Napuka [*French Polynesia*] [*ICAO location identifier*] (ICLI)
**NTGNA**...... Nauchnye Trudy Gosudarstvennyi Nauchno-Issledovatel'skii i Proektnyi Institut Redkometallicheskoi Promyshlennosti [*A publication*]
**NTGO**........ Nitroglycerine Ointment [*Pharmacy*]
**NTGO**........ Tatakoto [*French Polynesia*] [*ICAO location identifier*] (ICLI)
**NTGP**........ Puka Puka [*French Polynesia*] [*ICAO location identifier*] (ICLI)
**NTGQ**........ Pukarua [*French Polynesia*] [*ICAO location identifier*] (ICLI)
**NTGR**........ Aratica [*French Polynesia*] [*ICAO location identifier*] (ICLI)
**NTGR**........ New Testament Greek (BJA)
**NTGS**........ Northwest Territory Genealogical Society (EA)
**NTGT**........ Takapoto [*French Polynesia*] [*ICAO location identifier*] (ICLI)
**NTGTB**...... Northern Territory Government Tourist Bureau [*Australia*]
**NTGU**........ Arutua [*French Polynesia*] [*ICAO location identifier*] (ICLI)
**NTGV**........ Mataiva [*French Polynesia*] [*ICAO location identifier*] (ICLI)
**NTGW**....... Nukutavake [*French Polynesia*] [*ICAO location identifier*] (ICLI)
**NTGY**........ Tureia [*French Polynesia*] [*ICAO location identifier*] (ICLI)
**NTH** .......... Hudson Valley Community College, Troy, NY [*Library symbol*] [*Library of Congress*] (LCLS)
**NTH** .......... New Testament Handbooks [*A publication*]
**NTH** .......... Northern Platinum [*Vancouver Stock Exchange symbol*]
**NTHA**........ National Temple Hill Association (EA)
**NTHAA7**... Brain and Development [*A publication*]
**Nth Apiar**... Northern Apiarist [*A publication*]
**NTHCS** ..... National Toothpick Holder Collector's Society (EA)
**NTHEST**... Northeast
**NTHESTN** ... Northeastern
**Nth Forest Ranger Coll A** ... Northern Forest Ranger College Annual [*A publication*]
**Nth Gdnr** ... Northern Gardener [*A publication*]
**NTHL**........ National Treasure Hunters League (EA)
**Nth Logger** ... Northern Logger [*A publication*]
**NThM**........ New Theatre Magazine [*A publication*]
**NTHMF**..... Northair Mines Ltd. [*NASDAQ symbol*] (NQ)
**Nth Miner** ... Northern Miner [*A publication*]
**NTHN**........ Northern
**NTHP**........ National Trust for Historic Preservation (EA)
**NThS**......... Nieuwe Theologische Studien [*A publication*]
**NThSt**........ Nieuwe Theologische Studien [*A publication*]
**NThT**......... Nieuwe Theologisch Tijdschrift [*A publication*]
**NThTs**....... Nederlands Theologisch Tijdschrift [*A publication*]
**NTHWST** ... Northwest
**NTHWSTN** ... Northwestern
**NTHZ**........ N-Nitrosothiazolidine [*Organic chemistry*]
**NTI**........... Bintuni [*Indonesia*] [*Airport symbol*] (OAG)
**NTI**........... Futuribles [*A publication*]
**NTI**........... Nadic-Terminated Imide [*Polymer technology*]
**NTI**........... National Tactical Interface (MCD)
**NTI**........... National Theatre Institute (EA)
**NTI**........... National Trade Index
**NTI**........... Naval Travel Instructions
**NTI**........... Nesbitt Thomson, Inc. [*Toronto Stock Exchange symbol*] [*Vancouver Stock Exchange symbol*]
**NTI**........... Neuropsychiatric Interest Checklist
**NTI**........... Nielsen Television Index [*Nielsen Media Research*] [*Information service or system*]
**NTI**........... No Travel Involved [*Military*]
**NTI**........... Noise Transmission Impairment [*Telecommunications*]
**NTI**........... Nonthyroidal Illness [*Medicine*]
**NTI**........... Nordman [*Idaho*] [*Seismograph station code, US Geological Survey*] [*Closed*] (SEIS)
**NTIA**......... National Telecommunications and Information Administration [*Department of Commerce*] [*Washington, DC*]
**NTIAA**...... Nauchnye Trudy Instituta Avtomatiki [*A publication*]
**NTIAC**....... Nondestructive Testing Information Analysis Center [*San Antonio, TX*] [*DoD*] (MCD)
**NTIC**......... Immaculate Conception Seminary, College of Philosophy, Troy, NY [*Library symbol*] [*Library of Congress*] (LCLS)
**NTIC**......... National Training and Information Center (EA)
**NTIC**......... Nondestructive Testing Information Center [*Battelle Memorial Institute*] [*Databank*] [*Information service or system*] (IID)
**NTICED**.... National Training Institute for Community Economic Development (EA)
**NTID**......... National Technical Institute for the Deaf [*Rochester Institute of Technology*] [*Research center*]
**NTIF**.......... National Taxpayers' Investigative Fund (EA)
**NTIH**......... Normal Terminate Interrupt Handler (MCD)
**NTIOC**....... No Travel Involved for Officer Concerned [*Military*]
**NTIP**.......... National Turkey Improvement Plan
**NTIPI**........ Nauchnye Trudy Industrial'no-Pedagogicheskogo Instituta [*A publication*]
**NTIPP**....... Navy Technical Information Presentation Program (MCD)
**NTIR**......... Nederlands Tijdschrift voor Internationaal Recht [*Netherlands*] [*A publication*] (ILCA)
**NTIR**......... Nontechnical Intelligence Report
**NTIRA**....... National Trucking Industrial Relations Association (EA)
**NTIS**.......... National Technical Information Service [*Department of Commerce*] [*Springfield, VA*] [*Database producer and database*]
**NTIS**.......... NEC [*Nippon Electric Company*]-Toshiba Information Systems, Inc. [*Japan*]
**NTIS Announc** ... NTIS [*National Technical Information Service*] Trade Announcements [*A publication*]
**NTIS Mater Sci** ... NTIS [*National Technical Information Service*] Materials Science [*A publication*]
**NTJ**........... National Tax Journal [*A publication*]
**NTJ**........... Nigeria Trade Journal [*A publication*]
**NTJ**........... Northern Territory Judgements [*A publication*] (APTA)
**NTK**........... Nauchnye Trudy Krasnodarskogo Pedagogicheskogo Instituta [*A publication*]
**NTK**........... Need to Know (MCD)
**NTK**........... New York Air [*Farmingdale, NY*] [*FAA designator*] (FAAC)
**NTK**........... Nordisk Teaterkomite [*Nordic Theater Committee - NTC*] (EAIO)
**NTK**........... Nortek, Inc. [*NYSE symbol*] (SPSG)
**NTK**........... Nunatak [*Alaska*] [*Seismograph station code, US Geological Survey*] (SEIS)
**NTK**........... Tustin, CA [*Location identifier*] [*FAA*] (FAAL)
**NTKAA**..... Neue Technik. Abteilung A. Automatik und Industrielle Elektronik [*A publication*]
**NTKBA**..... Neue Technik. Abteilung B. Kerntechnik [*A publication*]
**NTKPB**..... Nauchnye Trudy Kurskii Politekhnicheskii Institut [*A publication*]
**NTKR**........ Takaroa [*French Polynesia*] [*ICAO location identifier*] (ICLI)
**NTL**........... Jacksonville, NC [*Location identifier*] [*FAA*] (FAAL)
**NTL**........... National Temperance League [*Later, ACAP*] (EA)
**NTL**........... National Tennis League
**NTL**........... National Textiles Ltd. [*Australia*]
**NTL**........... National Training Laboratories [*Later, NTLI*] (EA)
**NTL**........... Neon Test Light
**NTL**........... Newcastle [*Australia*] [*Airport symbol*] (OAG)
**NTL**........... Night Telegraph Letter
**NTL**........... No Time Lost [*Military*]
**NTL**........... Northern Telecom Limited [*Toronto Stock Exchange symbol*] [*Vancouver Stock Exchange symbol*]
**NTL**........... NovAtel Communications Limited [*UTLAS symbol*]
**NTL**........... Nuclear Technology Laboratory [*Stanford University*] (MCD)
**NTL**........... Nuclear Thermionics Laboratory
**NTL**........... Nuclear Transport Ltd. [*British*] (IRUK)
**NTLA**........ Nebraska Test of Learning Aptitude [*Education*]
**NTLB**........ National Lumber & Supply, Inc. [*NASDAQ symbol*] (NQ)
**NTLC**........ National Tax-Limitation Committee (EA)
**NTLC**........ National Trades and Labour Congress [*Canada*]
**NTLDO**..... Navy Terminal Leave Disbursing Office
**NTLEN**..... Nutlet Length [*Botany*]

**NTLF**......... National Taxpayers Legal Fund (EA)
**NTLF**......... Northern Troops and Landing Force
**NTLI**......... Neurotensin-Like Immunoreactivity
**NTLI**......... NTL Institute (EA)
**NTLLDT**... Intelligence [*A publication*]
**NTLS**......... National Truck Leasing System (EA)
**NTLS**......... Nautilus Funds [*NASDAQ symbol*] (NQ)
**NTLS**......... Northern Territory Library Service [*Australia*]
**NTLTL**...... Newsletter. Teaching Language through Literature [*A publication*]
**NTM**.......... Narrowband Trunk Module [*Telecommunications*]
**NTM**.......... National Technical Means [*For monitoring compliance with the provisions of an agreement*]
**NTM**.......... NAVAIR Test Manual (MCD)
**NTM**.......... Nazarene Theological Seminary, Kansas City, MO [*OCLC symbol*] (OCLC)
**NTM**.......... Net Ton Mile [*Shipping*]
**NTM**.......... New Theatre Magazine [*A publication*]
**NTM**.......... New Tribes Mission (EA)
**NTM**.......... Night Message (MSA)
**NTM**.......... Nontariff Measures
**NtM**.......... Norton Micro Images, Inc., Trenton, NJ [*Library symbol*] [*Library of Congress*] (LCLS)
**NTM**.......... NTM. Schriftenreihe fuer Geschichte der Naturwissenschaften, Technik, und Medizin [*A publication*]
**NTM**.......... Nuestro Tiempo (Madrid) [*A publication*]
**NTMA**....... National Tank Manufacturers Association [*Defunct*] (EA)
**NTMA**....... National Terrazzo and Mosaic Association (EA)
**NTMA**....... National Tooling and Machining Association (EA)
**NTMA**....... National Traditional Music Association (EA)
**NTMD**....... Nuku Hiva [*French Polynesia*] [*ICAO location identifier*] (ICLI)
**NTME**....... Naval Technical Mission in Europe
**NTMI**........ Net Ton of Molten Iron
**NTMICP**... National Topographic Map Inventory Control Point
**NTMJ**........ Naval Technical Mission to Japan
**NTML**....... National Tillage Machinery Laboratory [*Department of Agriculture*] [*Research center*] (GRD)
**NTMLB**..... Nauchni Trudove. Vissh Lesotekhnicheski Institut (Sofia). Seriya Mekhanichna Tekhnologiya na Durvesinata (Bulgaria) [*A publication*]
**NTMN**....... Hiva-Oa/Atuana [*French Polynesia*] [*ICAO location identifier*] (ICLI)
**NTMN**....... National Thrift and Mortgage News [*A publication*]
**NTMP**....... Nike Target Measurements Program
**NTMP**....... Ua Pou [*French Polynesia*] [*ICAO location identifier*] (ICLI)
**NTMSB**..... NTM. Schriftenreihe fuer Geschichte der Naturwissenschaften, Technik, und Medizin [*A publication*]
**NTM Schr Geschichte Natur Tech Medizin** ... NTM. Schriftenreihe fuer Geschichte der Naturwissenschaften, Technik, und Medizin [*A publication*]
**NTM Schr Geschichte Naturwiss Tech Medizin** ... NTM. Schriftenreihe fuer Geschichte der Naturwissenschaften, Technik, und Medizin [*A publication*]
**NTM Schriftenr Gesch Naturwiss Tech Med** ... NTM. Schriftenreihe fuer Geschichte der Naturwissenschaften, Technik, und Medizin [*A publication*]
**NTMTA**.... Nauchnye Trudy Moskovskogo Tekhnologicheskogo Instituta Legkoi Promyshlennosti [*A publication*]
**NTMU**....... Ua Huka [*French Polynesia*] [*ICAO location identifier*] (ICLI)
**NTMUZ**.... Neues Testament fuer Menschen Unserer Zeit [*A publication*]
**NTN**.......... National Telecommunications Network [*Rockville, MD*] (TSSD)
**NTN**.......... National Towing News [*A publication*] (EAAP)
**NTN**.......... Nederland Taiwan Nieuws [*A publication*]
**NTN**.......... Nephrotoxic Nephritis [*Medicine*]
**NTN**.......... Network Terminal Number [*Telecommunications*]
**NTN**.......... Neutral Twisted Nematic [*Data processing*] (PCM)
**NTN**.......... Neutron [*A nuclear particle*] (MSA)
**NTN**.......... New Trade Names [*Later, NBTC*] [*A publication*]
**NTN**.......... Newton College, Newton, MA [*OCLC symbol*] [*Inactive*] (OCLC)
**NTN**.......... Normanton [*Australia*] [*Airport symbol*] (OAG)
**NTN**.......... Norton Co., Coated Abrasive Division, R and D Department, Troy, NY [*Library symbol*] [*Library of Congress*] (LCLS)
**NTN**.......... NTIS [*National Technical Information Service*] Energy Tech Notes [*United States*] [*A publication*]
**NT Neue Tech** ... NT. Neue Technik [*Switzerland*] [*A publication*]
**NTNF**........ Norges Teknisk-Naturvitenskapelige Forskningsraad [*Online database*]
**NTNI**......... National Transaction Network, Inc. [*NASDAQ symbol*] (NQ)
**NTNKA**..... Nederlands Tijdschrift voor Natuurkunde [*A publication*]
**NTNSDQ**.. Intensivbehandlung [*A publication*]
**NTNYT**..... Not the New York Times [*A publication*]
**NTO**.......... Name To (AAG)
**NTO**.......... National Tenants Organization [*Defunct*] (EA)
**NTO**.......... National Turnover [*Economics*]
**NTO**.......... Natural Transition Orbitals [*Atomic physics*]
**NTO**.......... Naval Technology Office [*Arlington, VA*] (GRD)
**NTO**.......... Naval Transport Officer
**NTO**.......... Network Terminal Option [*Data processing*]
**NTO**.......... New Technology Opportunities [*Program*] [*US government*]
**NTO**.......... Nitrogen Tetroxide [*Inorganic chemistry*]
**NTO**.......... No Try On [*Purchaser did not have a fitting*] [*Merchandising slang*]
**NTO**.......... Nontraditional Occupations
**NTO**.......... Not Taken Out [*Insurance*]
**NTO**.......... Santo Antao [*Cape Verde Islands*] [*Airport symbol*] (OAG)
**NTOC**........ Northern Territory Open College [*Australia*]
**NTOFMS**... Neutral Time-of-Flight Mass Spectroscopy [*Aviation*]
**NTOL**........ Near-Term Operating License [*Nuclear energy*] (NRCH)
**NTOL**........ Normal Takeoff and Landing [*Aviation*] (MCD)
**NTOMC**.... National Tung Oil Marketing Cooperative [*Defunct*] (EA)
**NTonHi**..... Historical Society of the Tonawandas, Tonawanda, NY [*Library symbol*] [*Library of Congress*] (LCLS)
**NTonL**....... Union Carbide Corp., Linde Division, Tonawanda, NY [*Library symbol*] [*Library of Congress*] (LCLS)
**NTonS**....... Sheridan Park Hospital, Inc., Tonawanda, NY [*Library symbol*] [*Library of Congress*] (LCLS)
**NTOP**........ New Technology Opportunities Program [*US government*]
**NTORS**..... Naval Torpedo Station
**NTOTC**..... National Training and Operational Technology Center [*Environmental Protection Agency*] (IID)
**NTOTD**..... Neurobehavioral Toxicology and Teratology [*A publication*]
**NTP**.......... Nathian [*Pakistan*] [*Seismograph station code, US Geological Survey*] (SEIS)
**NTP**.......... National Toxicology Program [*Department of Health and Human Services*] [*Research Triangle Park, NC*]
**NTP**.......... National Transportation Policy
**NTP**.......... National Tree Program [*Australia*]
**NTP**.......... Naval Tactical Publication (NVT)
**NTP**.......... Naval Telecommunications Procedures (NVT)
**NTP**.......... Naval Telecommunications Publication (NVT)
**NTP**.......... Navy Technological Projections
**NTP**.......... Navy Training Plan (NVT)
**NTP**.......... Network Terminal Protocol
**NTP**.......... Network Terminating Point [*Telecommunications*] (TEL)
**NTP**.......... Network Termination Processor
**NTP**.......... Network Test Panel [*NASA*] (KSC)
**NTP**.......... Network Time Protocol
**NTP**.......... Nitroprusside [*A vasodilator*]
**NTP**.......... No Title Page [*Bibliography*]
**NTP**.......... Nonzero Temperature Plasma
**NTP**.......... Normal Temperature and Pressure [*Medicine*]
**NTP**.......... Notice to Proceed (KSC)
**NTP**.......... Nuclear Test Plant
**NTP**.......... Nuclear Transportation Project (EA)
**NTP**.......... Nucleoside Triphosphate [*Biochemistry*]
**NTP**.......... Number of Theoretical Plates
**NTP**.......... Numerical Tape Punch
**NTPA**........ National Tractor Pullers Association (EA)
**NTPA**........ National Trotting Pony Association [*Later, ITPA*]
**NTPA**........ Naval Technical Proficiency Assist (NVT)
**NTPA**........ Northern Territory Port Authority [*Australia*]
**NTPC**........ National Technical Processing Center
**NTPC**........ National Temperance and Prohibition Council (EA)
**NTPC**........ Natpac, Inc. [*NASDAQ symbol*] (NQ)
**NTPC**........ Naval Training Publications Center
**NTPC**........ Navy Training Plan Conference
**NTPD**........ Normal Temperature, Pressure Differential (MCD)
**NTPF**........ National Tile Promotion Federation (EA)
**NTPF**........ Near-Term Prepositioning Forces [*Navy*]
**NTPF**........ Number of Terminals per Failure [*Data processing*]
**NTPG**........ National Textile Processors Guild (EA)
**NTPGB**...... Nederlands Tijdschrift voor de Psychologie en Haar Grensgebieden [*A publication*]
**NTPH**........ Nucleosidetriphosphate Pyrophosphatase [*An enzyme*]
**NTPI**......... Navy Technical Proficiency Inspection (NG)
**NTPL**........ Navy Technical Proficiency List
**NTPL**........ Nut Plate (AAG)
**NTPO**........ Nitrilotrimethylenephosphonic Acid [*Organic chemistry*]
**NTPP**........ Normal through Patch Panel (MCD)
**NTPPA**...... Nauchnye Trudy Permskii Politekhnicheskii Institut [*A publication*]
**NTPR**........ Nuclear Targeting Policy Review (MCD)
**NTPR**........ [*Atomospheric*] Nuclear Test Personnel Review (MCD)
**NTPS**........ Naval Test Pilot School
**NTPS**........ Near-Term Prepositioned Ships
**NTPS**........ Northern Territory Public Service [*Australia*]
**NTPSA**...... Northern Territory Public Service Association [*Australia*]
**NTPUB**...... Nauchni Trudove. Plovdivski Universitet. Matematika, Fizika, Khimiya, Biologiya [*A publication*]
**NTQ**.......... Nebennieren, Thymus, Quotient [*Test*] [*Medicine*]
**NTQ**.......... New Theatre Quarterly [*A publication*]
**NTR**.......... Nachrichten Transportrationalisierung [*A publication*]
**NTR**.......... National Tape Repository (EA)
**NTR**.......... National Transcontinental Railway [*Canada*]
**NTR**.......... Navigational Time Reference (AAG)
**NTR**.......... Navy Technical Representative (MCD)
**NTR**.......... Nernst-Thomson Rule [*Physics*]
**NTR**.......... Neutron Test Reactors (KSC)
**NTR**.......... New Technology Report

**NTR**.......... Next Task Register
**NTR**.......... No Texts Required [*Education*]
**NTR**.......... No Traffic Reported [*Aviation*]
**NTR**.......... Noise Temperature Ratio (AAG)
**NTR**.......... Nordisk Tolladministrativt Rad [*Nordic Customs Administrative Council - NCAC*] (EAIO)
**NTR**.......... Nordiska Trafiksakerhetsradet [*Nordic Road Safety Council - NRSC*] [*Helsinki, Finland*] (EAIO)
**NTR**.......... Northern Territory Railway [*Australia*]
**NTR**.......... Northern Territory Reports [*A publication*] (APTA)
**NTR**.......... Nothing to Report
**NTR**.......... Nuclear Test Reactor [*Also known as GETR*]
**NTR**.......... Nutrition
**NTR**.......... Rensselaer Polytechnic Institute, Troy, NY [*Library symbol*] [*Library of Congress*] (LCLS)
**NTRA**........ National Television Rental Association [*British*]
**NTRA**........ National Trailer Rental Association (EA)
**NTRA**........ National Tumor Registrars Association (EA)
**N Trans S Dec**... National Transportation Safety Board Decisions [*A publication*] (DLA)
**NTRC**........ National Tourism Review Commission
**NTRC**........ Natural Toxins Research Center [*Public Health Service*] (GRD)
**NTRDA**..... National Tuberculosis and Respiratory Diseases Association [*Later, American Lung Association*]
**NT Rep**...... New Term Reports, English Queen's Bench [*A publication*] (DLA)
**NT Repts**... New Term Reports, English Queen's Bench [*A publication*] (DLA)
**NTRG**........ New Testament Reading Guide [*Collegeville, MN*] [*A publication*] (BJA)
**NTRK**........ Neoterik Health Technologies, Inc. [*NASDAQ symbol*] (NQ)
**NTRK**........ Noeterik Health Technologies, Inc. [*NASDAQ symbol*] (NQ)
**NTRMA**.... National Tile Roofing Manufacturing Association (EA)
**NTRS**........ National Therapeutic Recreation Society (EA)
**NTRS**........ Nationwide Trailer Rental System
**NTRS**........ Northern Trust Corp. [*NASDAQ symbol*] (NQ)
**NTRS**........ Russell Sage College, Troy, NY [*Library symbol*] [*Library of Congress*] (LCLS)
**NTrZ**.......... North Tropical Zone [*Planet Jupiter*]
**NTS**.......... Namens Trau- und Sterberegister der Judenschaft [*A publication*] (BJA)
**NTS**.......... Narodno Trudovoi Soyuz [*People's Labor Union*] [*Frankfurt, Federal Republic of Germany*] (PD)
**NTS**.......... NASA Test Support
**NTS**.......... National Technical Systems [*Commercial firm*]
**NTS**.......... National Thespian Society [*Later, ITS*] (EA)
**NTS**.......... National Traffic System [*Amateur radio*]
**NTS**.......... National Transportation Statistics [*or Survey*] [*Department of Transportation*]
**NTS**.......... National Travel Survey [*Census Bureau*]
**NTS**.......... National Tulip Society [*Defunct*] (EA)
**NTS**.......... Naukovo Tovarystvo Imeni Sevcenka [*A publication*]
**NTS**.......... Naval Target Subdivision [*G-2, SHAEF*]
**NTS**.......... Naval Telecommunications System (NVT)
**NTS**.......... Naval Torpedo Station
**NTS**.......... Naval Training School
**NTS**.......... Naval Training Station
**NTS**.......... Naval Transportation Service [*Later, MSC*]
**NTS**.......... Navigational Technology Satellite (MCD)
**NTS**.......... Navigator Training Squadron [*Air Force*]
**NTS**.......... Navy Technology Satellite
**NTS**.......... Near Term Schedule (MCD)
**NTS**.......... Negative Torque Signal (MSA)
**NTS**.......... Nevada Test Site [*Department of Energy*]
**NTS**.......... New Testament Studies [*A publication*]
**NTS**.......... New Tube Shelter [*British*]
**NTS**.......... Nieuwe Theologische Studien [*A publication*]
**NTS**.......... Nitroglycerin Transdermal System [*Pharmacy*]
**NTS**.......... Non-Traffic Sensitive [*Costs*] [*Telecommunications*]
**NTS**.......... Nontariff Size
**NTS**.......... Nontemporary Storage [*Personal property*]
**NTS**.......... Nontranscribed Spacer [*Genetics*]
**NTS**.......... Nordiske Teleansattes Samarbeidsorgan [*Nordic Telecommunications Association*] (EAIO)
**NTS**.......... Norsk Tidsskrift foer Sprogvidenskap [*A publication*]
**NTS**.......... Not to Scale [*Drafting*]
**NTS**.......... Notes [*Finance*]
**NTS**.......... Novum Testamentum. Supplements [*Leiden*] [*A publication*]
**NTS**.......... Nuclear Test Stage (AAG)
**NTS**.......... Nucleus Tractus Solitarii [*Brain anatomy*]
**NTS**.......... Number of Theoretical Stages [*Chemical engineering*]
**NTS**.......... Nutrition Today Society (EA)
**NTS**.......... Samaritan Hospital, Troy, NY [*Library symbol*] [*Library of Congress*] (LCLS)
**NTSA**........ National T-Shirt Association (EA)
**NTSA**........ National Tay-Sachs Association [*Later, NTSAD*] (EA)
**NTSA**........ National Technical Services Association (EA)
**NTSA**........ National Traffic Safety Agency [*Federal Highway Administration*]
**NTSA**........ National Training Systems Association (EA)
**NTSA**........ National Transportation Safety Association (EA)
**NTSA**........ National Tuberous Sclerosis Association (EA)
**NTSA**........ Naval Telecommunications System Architect (MCD)
**NTSA**........ Northern Territory Supervising Authority [*Australia*]
**NTSA**........ Norway Technical Science Academy
**NTSAD**...... National Tay-Sachs and Allied Diseases Association (EA)
**NTSB**........ National Traffic Safety Bureau
**NTSB**........ National Transportation Safety Board [*Independent government agency*] [*Washington, DC*]
**NTSC**........ National Tax Strike Coalition (EA)
**NTSC**........ National Technical Systems, Inc. [*NASDAQ symbol*] (NQ)
**NTSC**........ National Television Standard Code [*Video equipment*] (RDA)
**NTSC**........ National Television System Committee [*Formed in 1936*]
**NTSC**........ Nonextrusion Texturized Soy Concentrate
**NTSC**........ North Texas State College [*Later, North Texas State University*]
**NTSCH**...... Naval Training School
**NTSDS**...... Near-Term Swimmer Defense System
**NTSE**........ Naval Telecommunications System Engineer (MCD)
**NTSE**........ Nontactical Support Equipment (MCD)
**NTSEA**...... National Trade Show Exhibitors Association [*Later, IEA*] (EA)
**NTSF**........ Nonextrusion Texturized Soy Flour
**NTSI**.......... Nonextrusion Texturized Soy Isolate
**NTSIAI**..... Naturalista Siciliano [*A publication*]
**NTSK**........ Nordiska Tele-Satelit Kommitton [*Norway*]
**NTSM**....... Saint Mary's Hospital, Troy, NY [*Library symbol*] [*Library of Congress*] (LCLS)
**NTSO**........ NASA Test Support Office (KSC)
**NT Spr**....... Norsk Tidsskrift foer Sprogvidenskap [*A publication*]
**NTsPsych**.. Nederlandsch Tijdschrift voor de Psychologie en Haar Grensgebieden [*A publication*]
**NTSR**........ National Tunis Sheep Registry (EA)
**NTSRP**...... Nontechnical Services Real Property
**NTSRVA**... Nevada Test Site Radiation Victim Association (EA)
**NTSt**.......... New Testament Studies [*A publication*]
**NTSTN**...... Naval Telecommunications System Test Node (CAAL)
**NTStud**...... New Testament Studies [*A publication*]
**NTSuppl**.... Novum Testamentum. Supplements [*Leiden*] [*A publication*]
**NT Suppls**... Novum Testamentum. Supplements [*Leiden*] [*A publication*]
**NTSV**........ Nordisk Tidskrift foer Sprogvidenskap [*A publication*]
**NTsV**......... Nordisk Tidskrift foer Vetenskap, Konst, och Industri [*A publication*]
**NTT**.......... Nederlands Theologisch Tijdschrift [*A publication*]
**NTT**.......... New Technology Telescopes [*Under development*]
**NTT**.......... Nieuw Theologisch Tijdschrift [*A publication*]
**NTT**.......... Nippon Telegraph & Telephone Corp. [*Telecommunications and videotex company*] [*Japan*]
**NTT**.......... Norsk Teologisk Tidsskrift [*A publication*]
**NTT**.......... Nuiatoputapu [*Tonga*] [*Airport symbol*] (OAG)
**NTTA**........ National Tobacco Tax Association (EA)
**NTTB**........ Bora Bora/Motu-Mute [*French Polynesia*] [*ICAO location identifier*] (ICLI)
**NTTBR**...... Nineteen Thirty-Two Buick Registry (EA)
**NTTC**........ National Tank Truck Carriers [*Alexandria, VA*] (EA)
**NTTC**........ Naval Technical Training Center
**NTTC**........ NAVFAC [*Naval Facilities Engineering Command*] Technical Training Center
**NTTCIW**... National Technical Task Committee on Industrial Wastes
**NTTE**........ Tetiaroa [*French Polynesia*] [*ICAO location identifier*] (ICLI)
**NTTF**........ Network Test and Training Facility [*Goddard Space Flight Center*]
**NTTG**........ Rangiroa [*French Polynesia*] [*ICAO location identifier*] (ICLI)
**NTTH**........ Huahine/Fare [*French Polynesia*] [*ICAO location identifier*] (ICLI)
**NTTid**........ Norsk Teologisk Tidsskrift [*A publication*]
**NTTij**......... Nederlands Theologisch Tijdschrift [*A publication*]
**NTTM**....... Moorea/Temae [*French Polynesia*] [*ICAO location identifier*] (ICLI)
**NTTO**........ Hao [*French Polynesia*] [*ICAO location identifier*] (ICLI)
**NTTO**........ Nordisk Tidsskrift foer Teknisk Okonomi [*A publication*]
**NTTP**........ Maupiti [*French Polynesia*] [*ICAO location identifier*] (ICLI)
**NTTR**........ Naval Torpedo Testing Range
**NTTR**........ Nontactical Telecommunications Requirement [*Army*] (AABC)
**NTTR**........ Raiatea/Uturoa [*French Polynesia*] [*ICAO location identifier*] (ICLI)
**NTT Rev**.... NTT [*Nippon Telegraph and Telephone Corporation*] Review [*A publication*]
**NT Ts**......... Nederlands Theologisch Tidsskrift [*A publication*]
**NTTS**........ New Testament Texts and Studies [*A publication*]
**NTTS**........ New Testament Tools and Studies [*A publication*]
**NTTS**........ Nordisk Tidsskrift foer Tale og Stemme [*A publication*]
**NTTSt**....... New Testament Texts and Studies [*A publication*]
**NTTSt**....... New Testament Tools and Studies [*Leiden*] [*A publication*]
**NTTT**........ Tahiti [*French Polynesia*] [*ICAO location identifier*] (ICLI)
**NTTTTI**.... National Truck Tank and Trailer Tank Institute [*Later, Tank Conference of the Truck Trailer Manufacturers Association*]
**NTTX**........ Mururoa [*French Polynesia*] [*ICAO location identifier*] (ICLI)
**NTU**.......... National Taxpayers Union (EA)
**NTU**.......... National Technological University [*Fort Collins, CO*]
**NTU**.......... National Tenants Union (EA)

**NTU**.......... Naval Training Unit
**NTU**.......... Navy Toxicology Unit
**NTU**.......... Nephelometric Turbidity Unit [*Analytical chemistry*]
**NTU**.......... Network Terminating Unit
**NTU**.......... New Threat Upgrade [*Military*] (CAAL)
**NTU**.......... Nonimmune Transfer Utensil [*i.e., spoon*] [*Slang*]
**NTU**.......... Nordisk Trafikskoleunion [*Nordic Union of Motor Schools Associations - NUMSA*] (EAIO)
**NTU**.......... Nordiska Texter och Undersokningar [*A publication*]
**NTU**.......... Normal Trading Unit
**NTU**.......... Northern Territory University [*Australia*]
**NTU**.......... Not Taken Up
**NTU**.......... Nuclear Training Unit (MCD)
**NTU**.......... Number of Transfer Units
**NTU**.......... Oceana, VA [*Location identifier*] [*FAA*] (FAAL)
**NTUC**........ National Trade Union Congress [*Singapore*]
**NTUC**........ National Trade Union of Coopers [*British*]
**NTUC**........ National Trade Union Council [*Hungary*]
**NTUC**........ National Trade Union Council for Human Rights (EA)
**NTUC**........ Newcastle Technical and University College [*Australia*]
**NTUC**........ Nigerian Trade Union Congress
**NTUC**........ Nyasaland Trade Union Congress
**NTuc**.......... Tuckahoe Public Library, Tuckahoe, NY [*Library symbol*] [*Library of Congress*] (LCLS)
**NTucW**...... Westchester County Historical Society, Tuckahoe, NY [*Library symbol*] [*Library of Congress*] (LCLS)
**NTULA3**... Naturalia [*Lisbon*] [*A publication*]
**NTULC**...... Negro Trade Union Leadership Council
**NTU Phytopathol Entomol** ... NTU [*National Taiwan University*] Phytopathologist and Entomologist [*A publication*]
**NTuPSC**.... Sunmount Development Center, Staff Library, Tupper Lake, NY [*Library symbol*] [*Library of Congress*] (LCLS)
**NTURB**..... Natura (Plovdiv, Bulgaria) [*A publication*]
**NTUV**........ Vahitahi [*French Polynesia*] [*ICAO location identifier*] (ICLI)
**NTUWM**... National Trade Union of Woodcutting Machinists [*British*]
**NTUWWM** ... National Trade Union of Wood Working Machinists [*British*]
**NTuxp**........ Tuxedo Park Library, Tuxedo Park, NY [*Library symbol*] [*Library of Congress*] (LCLS)
**NTuxpI**...... International Paper Co., Corporate Research and Development Division, Technical Information Center, Tuxedo Park, NY [*Library symbol*] [*Library of Congress*] (LCLS)
**NTV**.......... Nippon Television Network Corp. [*Japan*]
**NTV**.......... NTV Oil Services Industries, Inc. [*Vancouver Stock Exchange symbol*]
**NTVGA**..... Nederlandsch Tijdschrift voor Verloskunde en Gynaecologie [*A publication*]
**NTVK**........ Nederlandsch Tijdschrift voor Volkskunde [*A publication*]
**NTVLRO**... National Television Licensing and Records Office [*British*]
**NTVMA**.... Nauchni Trudove na Visshiya Meditsinski Institut [*A publication*]
**NTVS**......... Navy Television System
**NTVT**........ Non-Toxic Vinyl Tubing
**NTW**.......... Nose, Tail, Waist [*Aviation*]
**NTW**.......... Nymphenburger Texte zur Wissenschaft [*A publication*]
**NTWA**....... National Turf Writers Association (EA)
**NTWD**....... Netword, Inc. [*NASDAQ symbol*] (NQ)
**NTWH**....... National Theatre Workshop of the Handicapped (EA)
**NTWK**....... Network (MSA)
**NTWK**....... Network Security Corp. [*NASDAQ symbol*] (NQ)
**NTWS**....... New Threat Warning System [*Military*]
**NTWS**....... Nontrack while Scan
**NT WT**..... Net Weight
**NTX**.......... Naval Teletypewriter Exchange [*Formerly, NTE*]
**NTX**.......... Neonatal Thymectomy [*Medicine*]
**NTX**.......... Networking and Expansion [*Data processing*] (PCM)
**NTX**.......... Northern Air Service, Inc. [*Grand Rapids, MI*] [*FAA designator*] (FAAC)
**NTY**.......... Sun City [*South Africa*] [*Airport symbol*] (OAG)
**NTZ**.......... Iraq-Saudi Arabia Neutral Zone [*ANSI three-letter standard code*] (CNC)
**NTZ**.......... Nachrichtentechnische Zeitschrift [*A publication*]
**NTZ**.......... No Transgression Zone (FAAC)
**NTZ**.......... North Temperate Zone
**NTZ**.......... Northern Transgressive Zone [*Geology*]
**NTZ-Commun J** ... NTZ-Communications Journal [*A publication*]
**NTZG**........ Neutestamentliche Zeitgeschichte [*A publication*]
**NTZ Nachr Z NTZ-Commun J** ... NTZ. Nachrichtentechnische Zeitschrift/ NTZ-Communications Journal [*A publication*]
**NTZ Rep**.... NTZ. Nachrichtentechnische Zeitschrift. Report [*A publication*]
**NU**............ Lipnur [*Indonesia*] [*ICAO aircraft manufacturer identifier*] (ICAO)
**NU**............ Name Unknown
**nU**............ Nanounit [*One billionth of a standard unit*]
**NU**............ National Union (EA)
**NU**............ National Unity Party [*British*] [*Political party*]
**NU**............ NATO Unclassified (NATG)
**nu**............ Nauru [*MARC country of publication code*] [*Library of Congress*] (LCCP)
**NU**............ Nebraska University (MCD)
**NU**............ Nebraska Unofficial Reports [*A publication*] (DLA)
**NU**............ New Uses [*Research test*] [*Psychology*]
**NU**............ Niue [*ANSI two-letter standard code*] (CNC)
**NU**............ Northeast Utilities [*NYSE symbol*] (SPSG)
**NU**............ Northern Union [*Rugby*] [*British*] (DAS)
**NU**............ Northrop Unit [*Of hydrolytic enzyme activity*]
**NU**............ Nose Up [*Aviation*]
**NU**............ Nu-Gro Corp. [*Toronto Stock Exchange symbol*]
**Nu**............ Nucleolus [*Cytology*]
**NU**............ Nullified Unpostable [*Data processing*]
**NU**............ Number Unobtainable [*Telecommunications*]
**Nu**............ Numbers [*Old Testament book*] (BJA)
**NU**............ Nunatsiaq News [*A publication*]
**Nu**............ Nusselt Number [*IUPAC*]
**NU**............ Southwest Air Lines Ltd. [*ICAO designator*] (FAAC)
**NUA**.......... Nations Unies des Animaux [*United Animal Nations - UAN*] (EA)
**NUA**.......... Network User Address
**NUA**.......... Network Users Association [*Inactive*] (EA)
**NUA**.......... Nuclear Agency [*Army*]
**NuA**........... Nuova Antologia [*A publication*]
**NUAAW**.... National Union of Agricultural and Allied Workers [*British*]
**NUABA**..... National United Affiliated Beverage Association (EA)
**NUAD**....... Nucleus Average Optical Density [*Microscopy*]
**NUADC**.... National Underwater Accident Data Center
**NUAH**....... Nutrition and Health. A Journal of Preventive Medicine [*A publication*]
**NUAPA**..... Nuclear Applications [*A publication*]
**NUAT**........ Nordisk Union for Alkoholfri Trafikk [*Scandinavian Union for Non-Alcoholic Traffic - SUNAT*] (EA)
**NUATA**..... Nuclear Applications and Technology [*A publication*]
**NUATFAC** ... Nordiska Unionen for Arbetsledare, Tekniska Funktionarer och andra Chefer [*Nordic Confederation of Supervisors, Technicians and Other Managers*] (EAIO)
**NUB**.......... National Union of Busmen [*British*]
**NUB**.......... Northumberland Mines Ltd. [*Toronto Stock Exchange symbol*]
**Nub**........... Nubes [*Clouds*] [*of Aristophanes*] [*Classical studies*] (OCD)
**nub**........... Nubian [*MARC language code*] [*Library of Congress*] (LCCP)
**NUB**.......... Nuernberger Urkundenbuch [*A publication*]
**NUBA**........ National UHF [*Ultrahigh Frequency*] Broadcasters Association (EA)
**NUBE**........ National Union of Bank Employees [*Later, Banking, Insurance, and Finance Union*] (DCTA)
**NUBEDX**.. Nutrition and Behavior [*A publication*]
**NUBF**........ National Union of British Fishermen
**NUBIC**...... Nuclear Bunkered Instrumentation Center (MCD)
**NUBICWOPS** ... Nuclear, Biological, and Chemical Warfare Operations [*Military*]
**NUBOMCWKT** ... National Union of Blastfurnacemen, Ore Miners, Coke Workers, and Kindred Trades [*British*] (DCTA)
**NUBS**........ National Unemployment Benefit System [*Department of Health and Social Security*] [*British*]
**NUBSO**..... National Union of Boot and Shoe Operatives [*British*]
**NUBTC**..... National Union of Boot Top Cutters [*British*]
**NUC**.......... National Unification Council [*Political party*] [*Philippines*] (FEA)
**NUC**.......... National Union of Carriers [*British*]
**NUC**.......... National Union Catalogue [*A publication*] (APTA)
**NUC**.......... National University Consortium for Telecommunications in Teaching (EA)
**NUC**.......... National Urban Coalition (EA)
**NUC**.......... Naval Undersea Center [*Later, NOSC*] (MCD)
**NUC**.......... Navy Unit Commendation [*Military decoration*]
**NUC**.......... New University Conference
**NUC**.......... Nuclear (AFM)
**NUC**.......... Nucleated
**Nuc**........... [*A*] Nucleoside [*Also, N*]
**NUC**.......... Nucorr Petroleums Ltd. [*Toronto Stock Exchange symbol*]
**NUC**.......... San Clemente Island, CA [*Location identifier*] [*FAA*] (FAAL)
**NUCA**........ National Utility Contractors' Association (EA)
**NUCAA**..... National United Church Association of America (EA)
**NUCAD**..... Nutrition and Cancer [*A publication*]
**NUCAL**..... National Union Catalog Author List
**NUCAP**..... Nuclear Cannon Projectile [*Army*]
**NUCAP**..... Nuclear Capability [*Military*]
**NUCAP**..... Nuclear Capability Report (CINC)
**NUCAS**..... Nuclear Authentication System
**NUCAV**..... National Union Catalogue of Audio-Visual Materials [*A publication*] (APTA)
**NUCAW**.... National Union of Clerks and Administrative Workers [*British*]
**NUCBO**..... National Uniform Certification of Building Operators (EA)
**Nuc Compact Compact News Nucl Med** ... Nuc Compact. Compact News in Nuclear Medicine [*West Germany*] [*A publication*]
**NUCD**........ National Union Catalogue of Library Materials for People with Disabilities [*Australia*]
**NUCDEF**... Nuclear Defense (AABC)
**NUCDETS** ... Nuclear Detonation Detection and Reporting System (AABC)
**Nuc E**........ Nuclear Engineer
**NUCEA**..... National University Continuing Education Association (EA)
**Nuc Energy** ... Nuclear Energy [*A publication*]
**Nuc En Pros** ... Nuclear Energy Prospects to 2000 [*A publication*]
**NUCEX**..... Nuclear Exercise [*Also, NUKEX*] (NVT)
**NUCFO**..... Nuclear Force Posture

**NUC:H**...... National Union Catalogue of Library Materials for the Handicapped [*A publication*] (APTA)
**NUCH**....... Nucha [*Nape of the Neck*] [*Latin*] (ROG)
**NUCIA**...... National Union of Cooperative Insurance Agents [*British*]
**NUCINT**... Nuclear Intelligence (MCD)
**NUCISE**.... National Union of Cooperative Insurance Society Employees [*British*]
**NUCL**........ Nuclear
**Nucl**............ Nucleus [*A publication*]
**NUCL**........ Nucleus
**Nucl Acid R**... Nucleic Acids Research [*A publication*]
**Nucl Act**..... Nuclear Active [*A publication*]
**Nucl Active**... Nuclear Active [*A publication*]
**Nucl Appl**... Nuclear Applications [*A publication*]
**Nucl Appl and Technol**... Nuclear Applications and Technology [*A publication*]
**Nucl Appl Technol**... Nuclear Applications and Technology [*A publication*]
**Nuc L Bull**... Nuclear Law Bulletin [*A publication*] (ILCA)
**Nucl Can/Can Nucl**... Nuclear Canada/Canada Nucleaire [*A publication*]
**Nucl Can Yearb**... Nuclear Canada Yearbook [*A publication*]
**Nucl Chem Waste Manage**... Nuclear and Chemical Waste Management [*A publication*]
**Nucl-Chicago Tech Bull**... Nuclear-Chicago Technical Bulletin [*A publication*]
**Nucl Data A**... Nuclear Data. Section A [*A publication*]
**Nucl Data Sect A**... Nuclear Data. Section A [*A publication*]
**Nucl Data Sect B**... Nuclear Data. Section B [*A publication*]
**Nucl Data Sheets**... Nuclear Data Sheets [*A publication*]
**Nucl Data Tables**... Nuclear Data Tables [*A publication*]
**Nucl Data Tables US AEC**... Nuclear Data Tables. United States Atomic Energy Commission [*A publication*]
**NUCLE**..... Nuclear
**Nuclear Eng**... Nuclear Engineering International [*A publication*]
**Nuclear Engng Design**... Nuclear Engineering and Design [*A publication*]
**Nuclear Law Bul**... Nuclear Law Bulletin [*A publication*]
**Nuclear Phys A**... Nuclear Physics. A [*A publication*]
**Nuclear Phys B**... Nuclear Physics. B [*A publication*]
**Nuclear Reg Rep (CCH)**... Nuclear Regulation Reports (Commerce Clearing House) [*A publication*] (DLA)
**Nuclear Sci Abstr**... Nuclear Science Abstracts [*Later, INIS Atomindex*] [*Information service or system*] [*A publication*]
**Nuclear Science Abstr**... Nuclear Science Abstracts [*Later, INIS Atomindex*] [*Information service or system*] [*A publication*]
**Nuclear Sci Engng**... Nuclear Science and Engineering [*A publication*]
**Nucleic Acids Res**... Nucleic Acids Research [*A publication*]
**Nucleic Acids Symp Ser**... Nucleic Acids Symposium Series [*A publication*]
**Nucl Electron Detect Technol**... Nuclear Electronics and Detection Technology [*A publication*]
**Nucl Energy**... Nuclear Energy [*A publication*]
**Nucl Energy Br Nucl Energy Soc**... Nuclear Energy. British Nuclear Energy Society [*A publication*]
**Nucl Energy Dig**... Nuclear Energy Digest [*A publication*]
**Nucl Eng**.... Nuclear Engineer. Institution of Nuclear Engineers [*A publication*]
**Nucl Eng Abstr**... Nuclear Engineering Abstracts [*A publication*]
**Nucl Eng Bull**... Nuclear Engineering Bulletin [*A publication*]
**Nucl Eng Des**... Nuclear Engineering and Design [*A publication*]
**Nucl Eng and Des**... Nuclear Engineering and Design [*A publication*]
**Nucl Eng Des Fusion**... Nuclear Engineering and Design/Fusion [*A publication*]
**Nucl Eng In**... Nuclear Engineering International [*A publication*]
**Nucl Eng Inst Nucl Eng**... Nuclear Engineer. Institution of Nuclear Engineers [*England*] [*A publication*]
**Nucl Eng Int**... Nuclear Engineering International [*A publication*]
**Nucl Engng & Des**... Nuclear Engineering and Design [*A publication*]
**Nucl Engng Int**... Nuclear Engineering International [*A publication*]
**Nucl Engr**... Nuclear Engineer [*A publication*]
**Nucl Eng (Tokyo)**... Nuclear Engineering (Tokyo) [*A publication*]
**NUCLEX**... Nuclear Industries Exhibition
**NUCLEX**... Nuclear Loadout Exercise [*Military*] (NVT)
**Nucl F Supplm**... Nuclear Fusion. Supplement [*A publication*]
**Nucl Fuel Cycle Revis Ed**... Nuclear Fuel Cycle. Revised Edition [*A publication*]
**Nucl Fusion**... Nuclear Fusion [*A publication*]
**Nucl Fusion Res Rep**... Nuclear Fusion Research Report [*Japan*] [*A publication*]
**Nucl Fusion Spec Publ**... Nuclear Fusion. Special Publication [*A publication*]
**Nucl Fusion Suppl**... Nuclear Fusion. Supplement [*A publication*]
**Nucl Geneeskd Bull**... Nucleair Geneeskundig Bulletin [*A publication*]
**Nucl Hematol**... Nuclear Hematology [*A publication*]
**Nucl Ind**..... Nuclear Industry [*A publication*]
**Nucl India**... Nuclear India [*A publication*]
**Nucl Inf**...... Nuclear Information [*A publication*]
**Nucl Instr**... Nuclear Instruments and Methods [*Later, Nuclear Instruments and Methods in Physics Research*] [*A publication*]
**Nucl Instrum**... Nuclear Instruments [*A publication*]
**Nucl Instrum and Methods**... Nuclear Instruments and Methods [*Later, Nuclear Instruments and Methods in Physics Research*] [*A publication*]
**Nucl Instrum Methods**... Nuclear Instruments and Methods [*Later, Nuclear Instruments and Methods in Physics Research*] [*A publication*]
**Nucl Instrum Methods Phys Res**... Nuclear Instruments and Methods in Physics Research [*Netherlands*] [*A publication*]
**Nucl Instrum Methods Phys Res Sect A**... Nuclear Instruments and Methods in Physics Research. Section A. Accelerators, Spectrometers, Detectors, and Associated Equipment [*A publication*]
**Nucl Instrum Methods Phys Res Sect B**... Nuclear Instruments and Methods in Physics Research. Section B. Beam Interactions with Materials and Atoms [*A publication*]
**Nucl Issues**... Nuclear Issues [*A publication*]
**Nucl Law Bull**... Nuclear Law Bulletin [*A publication*]
**Nucl Law Bull Suppl**... Nuclear Law Bulletin. Supplement [*A publication*]
**Nucl Magn Reson**... Nuclear Magnetic Resonance [*A publication*]
**Nucl Mater Manage**... Nuclear Materials Management. Journal of the Institute of Nuclear Materials Management [*A publication*]
**Nucl Med**... Nuclear Medicine [*A publication*]
**Nucl-Med**... Nuclear-Medizin [*A publication*]
**Nucl Med Annu**... Nuclear Medicine Annual [*A publication*]
**Nucl Med Commun**... Nuclear Medicine Communications [*A publication*]
**Nucl Med (Stuttgart)**... Nuclear Medicine (Stuttgart) [*A publication*]
**Nucl-Med (Stuttgart)**... Nuclear-Medizin (Stuttgart) [*A publication*]
**Nucl Med Suppl**... Nuclear-Medizin. Supplementum [*A publication*]
**Nucl-Med Suppl (Stuttgart)**... Nuclear-Medizin. Supplementum (Stuttgart) [*A publication*]
**Nucl Metall**... Nuclear Metallurgy [*A publication*]
**Nucl N**........ Nuclear News [*A publication*]
**Nucl News**... Nuclear News [*A publication*]
**Nucl News (Colombo Sri Lanka)**... Nuclear News (Colombo, Sri Lanka) [*A publication*]
**Nucl News (Hinsdale Ill)**... Nuclear News (Hinsdale, Illinois) [*A publication*]
**Nucl News (La Grange Park Ill)**... Nuclear News (La Grange Park, Illinois) [*A publication*]
**Nucl Newsl Switz**... Nuclear Newsletter from Switzerland [*A publication*]
**Nucl Part Phys Annu**... Nuclear and Particle Physics. Annual [*A publication*]
**Nucl Phys**.. Nuclear Physics [*A publication*]
**Nucl Phys A**... Nuclear Physics. A [*A publication*]
**Nucl Phys B**... Nuclear Physics. B [*A publication*]
**Nucl Phys B Field Theory and Stat Syst**... Nuclear Physics. B. Field Theory and Statistical Systems [*A publication*]
**Nucl Phys B Part Phys**... Nuclear Physics. B. Particle Physics [*A publication*]
**Nucl Pow**.... Nuclear Power [*A publication*]
**Nucl Power**... Nuclear Power [*A publication*]
**Nucl Power Eng**... Nuclear Power Engineering [*A publication*]
**Nucl React Built Being Built Planned**... Nuclear Reactors Built, Being Built, or Planned [*A publication*]
**Nucl Res**..... Nuclear Research [*A publication*]
**Nucl Res Cent "Democritus" (Rep)**... Nuclear Research Center "Democritus" (Report) [*A publication*]
**Nucl Saf**..... Nuclear Safety [*A publication*]
**Nucl Safety**... Nuclear Safety [*A publication*]
**Nucl Sci Abstr**... Nuclear Science Abstracts [*Later, INIS Atomindex*] [*Information service or system*] [*A publication*]
**Nucl Sci Abstr Jpn**... Nuclear Science Abstracts of Japan [*A publication*]
**Nucl Sci Appl**... Nuclear Science and Applications [*Pakistan*] [*A publication*]
**Nucl Sci Appl Sect A**... Nuclear Science Applications. Section A [*A publication*]
**Nucl Sci Appl Sect B**... Nuclear Science Applications. Section B [*A publication*]
**Nucl Sci Appl Ser A**... Nuclear Science and Applications. Series A [*A publication*]
**Nucl Sci Appl Ser B**... Nuclear Science and Applications. Series B [*A publication*]
**Nucl Sci En**... Nuclear Science and Engineering [*A publication*]
**Nucl Sci Eng**... Nuclear Science and Engineering [*A publication*]
**Nucl Sci and Eng**... Nuclear Science and Engineering [*A publication*]
**Nucl Sci Inf Jpn**... Nuclear Science Information of Japan [*A publication*]
**Nucl Sci J**.. Nuclear Science Journal [*A publication*]
**Nucl Sci J (Bandar Baru Bangi Malays)**... Nuclear Science Journal (Bandar Baru Bangi, Malaysia) [*A publication*]
**Nucl Sci J (Taiwan)**... Nuclear Science Journal (Taiwan) [*A publication*]
**Nucl Sci (Taiwan)**... Nuclear Science (Taiwan) [*A publication*]
**Nucl Sci Technol**... Nuclear Science and Technology [*A publication*]
**Nucl Ships**... Nuclear Ships [*Japan*] [*A publication*]
**Nucl Struct Eng**... Nuclear Structural Engineering [*Netherlands*] [*A publication*]
**Nucl Study**... Nuclear Study [*Japan*] [*A publication*]
**Nucl Tech**... Nuclear Technology [*A publication*]
**Nucl Technol**... Nuclear Technology [*A publication*]
**Nucl Technol/Fusion**... Nuclear Technology/Fusion [*A publication*]
**Nucl Technol Suppl**... Nuclear Technology. Supplement [*A publication*]
**Nucl Track Detect**... Nuclear Track Detection [*A publication*]
**Nucl Tracks**... Nuclear Tracks [*A publication*]
**Nucl Tracks Methods Instrum and Appl**... Nuclear Tracks. Methods, Instruments, and Applications [*A publication*]
**Nucl Tracks and Radiat Meas**... Nuclear Tracks and Radiation Measurements [*A publication*]
**NUCM**....... Nuclear Metals, Inc. [*NASDAQ symbol*] (NQ)

**NUCMC**.... National Union Catalog of Manuscript Collections [*Library of Congress*]
**NUCMUN** ... Nuclear Munitions (RDA)
**NUC:N** ...... National Union Catalogue: Nonbook Materials [*Australia*]
**NUCO** ....... National Union of Certified Officers [*British*]
**NUCO** ....... Nucorp, Inc. [*NASDAQ symbol*] (NQ)
**NUCO** ....... Numerical Code (NATG)
**NUCOF**..... National Union Catalogue of Films [*Australia*]
**NUCOIN$** ... Nutrition Consumer Information System [*Under development by Michigan Agricultural Experiment Station and the Michigan Cooperative Extension Service*]
**NUCOM** ... National Union Catalogue of Monographs [*A publication*] (APTA)
**NUCOM** ... Nuclear Effects on Joint Force Communications (MCD)
**NUCOM** ... Numerical Contouring Mechanism
**NUCOMUSIC** ... National Union Catalogue of Music [*A publication*] (APTA)
**NUCOS**..... National Union Catalogue of Serials [*A publication*] (APTA)
**NUCP**........ National Union of Czechoslovak Protestants in America and Canada [*Defunct*] (EA)
**NUCP**........ New Century Entertainment Corp. [*Formerly, New Century Production*] [*NASDAQ symbol*] (NQ)
**NUCPWR** ... Nuclear Powered (NVT)
**NucReaOpBasBad** ... Nuclear Reactor Operator, Basic Badge [*Military decoration*] (AABC)
**NucReaOpFCBad** ... Nuclear Reactor Operator, First-Class Badge [*Military decoration*] (AABC)
**NucReaOpSCBad** ... Nuclear Reactor Operator, Second-Class Badge [*Military decoration*] (AABC)
**NucReaOpSftSupvBad** ... Nuclear Reactor Operator, Shift Supervisor Badge [*Military decoration*] (AABC)
**NUCREP**... Nuclear Damage Report (AABC)
**NUCS**........ National Union of Christian Schools [*Later, CSI*] (EA)
**NUCSA**..... Nucleus [*Paris*] [*A publication*]
**NUCSAM** ... Nuclear Surface-to-Air Missile (NVT)
**NucSciAb**... Nuclear Science Abstracts [*Later, INIS Atomindex*] [*Information service or system*] [*A publication*]
**NUCSE**...... National Union of Czechoslovak Students in Exile (EA)
**NUCSEQ**... Nucleotide Sequencing Search System [*NIH/EPA Chemical Information System*] [*Database*]
**NUCSTAT** ... Nuclear Operational Status Report (NATG)
**NUCUA**..... Nuovo Cimento. Supplemento [*A publication*]
**NUCUAA** ... National United Church Ushers Association of America (EA)
**NUCURES** ... Northeastern University Center for Urban and Regional Economic Studies [*Research center*] (RCD)
**NUCWA**.... Nuclear Weapons Accounting (MCD)
**NUCWAR** ... Nuclear War
**NUCWPN** ... Nuclear Weapon (AABC)
**NUCWPNSTRACEN** ... Nuclear Weapons Training Center
**NUCY**........ NewCentury Bank Corp. [*Bay City, MI*] [*NASDAQ symbol*] (NQ)
**NUD** .......... Adak, AK [*Location identifier*] [*FAA*] (FAAL)
**NUD** .......... National Union of the Deaf [*British*]
**NUD** .......... Naval Unit Disseminator (RDA)
**NUD** .......... Nebraska University Disease or N. Underdahl Disease [*A disease of swine named both for the place where it was originally identified and for the person who isolated the causative agent*]
**NUDAGMW** ... National Union of Domestic Appliance and General Metal-Workers [*British*] (DCTA)
**NUDAP**..... Nuclear Detonating Data Points (MCD)
**NUDAW**.... National Union of Shop Distributive and Allied Workers [*British*]
**NUDBTW** ... National Union of Dyers, Bleachers, and Textile Workers [*British*] (DCTA)
**NUDET**..... Nuclear Detection (MCD)
**NUDET**..... Nuclear Detonation (FAAC)
**NUDET**..... Nuclear Detonation Evaluation Technique (MCD)
**NUDETS**... Nuclear Detection and Reporting System
**NUDETS**... Nuclear Detonation Detection and Reporting System
**NUDIA**...... Nutritio et Dieta [*A publication*]
**NUDO** ....... National United Democratic Organization [*Namibia*] [*Political party*] (PPW)
**NUDORE** ... Nuclear Doctrine Organization and Equipment (MCD)
**NUDWSS** ... National Union of Docks, Wharves, and Shipping Staffs [*British*]
**NUDY**........ ND Resources, Inc. [*NASDAQ symbol*] (NQ)
**NUE**........... Nitrogen Utilization Efficiency [*Ecology*]
**NUE**........... Niue [*Niue Island*] [*Seismograph station code, US Geological Survey*] (SEIS)
**NUE**........... Nucor Corp. [*NYSE symbol*] (SPSG)
**NUE**........... Nuremberg [*West Germany*] [*Airport symbol*] (OAG)
**NUEA**........ National University Extension Association [*Later, NUCEA*] (EA)
**NUENA**..... Nuclear Engineering [*A publication*]
**NUERA**..... Nuclear Extended Range Aircraft [*Proposed*] [*Air Force*]
**NUESNA** .. National Union of Eritrean Students - North America (EA)
**Nuestra Ind Rev Tecnol** ... Nuestra Industria. Revista Tecnologica [*A publication*]
**Nuestra Tierra** ... Nuestra Tierra. Paz y Progreso [*A publication*]
**NUET**........ National Union of Elementary Teachers [*British*]
**Nueva Enferm** ... Nueva Enfermeria [*A publication*]
**Nueva Estaf** ... Nueva Estafeta [*A publication*]
**Nueva Pol**... Nueva Politica [*A publication*]
**NUEW**....... National Union of Eritrean Women - North America (EA)
**NUF**........... National Ulcer Foundation (EA)
**NUF**........... National Unifying Force [*Zimbabwe*] [*Political party*] (PPW)
**NUF**........... National Union of Firemen [*British*] (DAS)
**NUF**........... National Unity Front [*Poland*] [*Political party*] (PPW)
**NUF**........... National Urban Fellows (EA)
**NUF**........... Natural Uranium Fuel
**NUF**........... Nordisk Urologisk Forening [*Scandinavian Association of Urology - SAU*] (EAIO)
**NUFAM**.... Nuclear Fire Planning and Assessment Model (MCD)
**NUFD**........ Naval Unit, Fort Detrick [*Maryland*]
**NUFDC**..... Northgate Universal Floppy Drive Controller [*Data processing*]
**NUFI** ......... National Unfinished Furniture Institute (EA)
**NUFLAT**... National Union of Footwear, Leather, and Allied Trades [*British*] (DCTA)
**NUFLV**...... National United Front for the Liberation of Vietnam (EA)
**NUFON**..... Northern UFO Network [*British*]
**NUFP** ........ Not Used for Production (AAG)
**NUFRONLIV** ... National United Front for the Liberation of Vietnam (EA)
**NUFTIC**.... Nuclear Fuels Technology Information Center (DIT)
**NUFTO**..... National Union of Furniture Trade Operatives [*British*]
**NUG** .......... Federation of NCR [*NCR Corp.*] User Groups (EA)
**NUG** .......... National Union of Glovers [*British*]
**NUG** .......... Necrotizing Ulcerative Gingivitis [*Dentistry*]
**Nu G Bot Ital** ... Nuovo Giornale Botanico Italiano [*A publication*]
**NUGMW** .. National Union of General and Municipal Workers [*British*]
**NUGO** ....... Nugget Oil Corp. [*NASDAQ symbol*] (NQ)
**NUGS**........ Nonutility Generating Source
**NUGSAT** .. National Union of Gold, Silver, and Allied Trades [*British*] (DCTA)
**NUGT**........ Nugget Exploration, Inc. [*NASDAQ symbol*] (NQ)
**NUH** .......... National Underwriter (Life and Health Insurance Edition) [*A publication*]
**NUH** .......... National Union for the Homeless (EA)
**NUH** .......... Nu Horizons Electronics Corp. [*AMEX symbol*] (SPSG)
**NUHADI**... Nuclear Helicopter Air Density Indicating [*System*] [*Army*]
**NUHEA**..... Nuclear Hematology [*A publication*]
**NUHELI** ... Nuclear Helicopter Lift Indicator (KSC)
**NUHKW** ... National Union of Hosiery and Knitwear Workers [*British*] (DCTA)
**NUHW** ...... Nordic Union for Health and Work (EAIO)
**NUI**............ National University of Ireland
**NUI**............ Network User Identifier [*Password*]
**NUI**............ Networks Unlimited, Incorporated [*Brooklyn, NY*] (EA)
**NUI**............ Notebook User Interface [*Penpoint*] [*Data processing*]
**NUI**............ NUI Corp. [*NYSE symbol*] (SPSG)
**NUI**............ Nuiqsut [*Alaska*] [*Airport symbol*] (OAG)
**NUI**............ Patuxent River, MD [*Location identifier*] [*FAA*] (FAAL)
**NUIA**......... National United Italian Associations (EA)
**NUIC** ......... National Urban Indian Council (EA)
**NUIR**......... National Union for Independence and Revolution [*Political party*] [*Chad*]
**NUIS** ......... Navy Unit Identification System (NVT)
**Nuisances et Environ** ... Nuisances et Environnement [*A publication*]
**Nuisances Environ** ... Nuisances et Environnement [*A publication*]
**NUIW**........ National Union of Insurance Workers [*British*] (DCTA)
**NUJ** .......... National Union of Journalists [*British*]
**NUK**........... Nukutavake [*French Polynesia*] [*Airport symbol*] (OAG)
**NUKE**........ Nuclear
**NUKEX**..... Nuclear Exercise [*Also, NUCEX*] (NVT)
**NUKKA**..... Nukleonika [*A publication*]
**Nukl**........... Nukleonika [*A publication*]
**Nukl Energ** ... Nuklearna Energija [*A publication*]
**Nukleonika Suppl** ... Nukleonika. Supplement [*Poland*] [*A publication*]
**NUKOA**..... Nauchno-Issledovatel'skii Trudy Ukrainskii Nauchno-Issledovatel'skii Institut Kozhevenno-Obuvnoi Promyshlennosti [*A publication*]
**NUL**........... National Union for Liberation [*Philippines*] [*Political party*] (PPW)
**NUL**........... National and University Library [*Jerusalem*] (BJA)
**NUL**........... National Urban League (EA)
**NUL**........... New Universal Library [*A publication*]
**NUL**........... New Upper Lateral [*Botany*]
**NUL**........... Nihon University [*UTLAS symbol*]
**NUL**........... Non-GSE [*Ground Support Equipment*] Utilization List [*NASA*] (NASA)
**NUL**........... Northwestern University. Law Review [*A publication*]
**NUL**........... Nu-Lady Gold Mines [*Vancouver Stock Exchange symbol*]
**NUL**........... Nulato [*Alaska*] [*Airport symbol*] (OAG)
**NUL**........... Nulato, AK [*Location identifier*] [*FAA*] (FAAL)
**NUL**........... Null Character [*Keyboard*] [*Data processing*]
**NULAB** ..... Nuclear Active [*A publication*]
**NULAC** ..... Nuclear Liquid Air Cycle Engine
**NULACE**... Nuclear Liquid Air Cycle Engine
**NULBA** ..... National United Licensees Beverage Association [*Later, NUABA*] (EA)
**NULCAIS** ... Northwestern University Library Computer-Assisted Information Service (OLDSS)

**NULCW** .... National Union of Lift and Crane Workers [*British*]
**NULEOA** .. National United Law Enforcement Officers Association (EA)
**NULF** ........ National United Liberation Front [*Political party*] [*Burma*] (FEA)
**NULH** ....... National Underwriter (Life and Health Insurance Edition) [*A publication*]
**NULMW** ... National Union of Lock and Metal Workers [*British*] (DCTA)
**NULO** ........ NASA Unmanned Launch Operations (MCD)
**NULOR** ..... Neuron Location and Ranging
**NULR** ........ Northwestern University. Law Review [*A publication*]
**NULS** ........ National Underwater Laboratory System [*Marine science*] (MSC)
**NULU** ........ New Library Utility
**NUM** ......... Error in Use of Numbers [*Used in correcting manuscripts, etc.*]
**NUm** .......... Narodna Umjetnost [*A publication*]
**NUM** ......... National Union of Mineworkers [*South Africa*]
**Num** ........... Numa [*of Plutarch*] [*Classical studies*] (OCD)
**NUM** ......... Numadu [*Japan*] [*Seismograph station code, US Geological Survey*] [*Closed*] (SEIS)
**NUM** ......... Number [*or Numerator, or Numeric*]
**Num** ........... Numbers [*Old Testament book*]
**NUM** ......... Numeral [*or Numerical*]
**Num** ........... Numismatist [*A publication*]
**NUMA** ...... National Underwater and Marine Agency (MCD)
**NUMA** ...... Nonuniform - Memory - Access [*Data processing*]
**Num Ant Cl** ... Numismatica e Antichita Classiche. Quaderni Ticinesi [*A publication*]
**Num Ant Clas** ... Quaderni Ticinesi. Numismatica e Antichita Classiche [*A publication*]
**NUMAR** .... Nuclear Magnetic Resonance [*Also, NMR*]
**NUMARC** ... Nuclear Management and Resources Council (EA)
**NUMARCOM** ... Nuclear Power for Marine Purposes Committee (MCD)
**NUMAS** .... Numerical Multifactor Assessment System (ADA)
**NUMAST** ... National Union of Marine Aviation and Shipping Transport [*British*]
**NUMB** ....... Numbered
**Numb** ......... Numbers [*Old Testament book*]
**Num Beitr** .. Numismatische Beitraege [*A publication*]
**Num Change** ... Numismatique et Change [*A publication*]
**Num Chron** ... Numismatic Chronicle [*A publication*]
**Num Chron** ... Numismatic Chronicle and Journal [*London*] [*A publication*]
**NumCirc** .... Numismatic Circular [*A publication*]
**NUMDA** ... Nihon University. Journal of Medicine [*A publication*]
**Num Digest** ... Numismatic Digest [*A publication*]
**NUME** ....... Numerica Financial Corp. [*Manchester, NH*] [*NASDAQ symbol*] (NQ)
**NUMEC** .... Nuclear Materials & Equipment Corporation
**Num Epigr** ... Numizmatika i Epigrafika [*A publication*]
**NUMERALS** ... Numerical Analysis System (BUR)
**Numer Control Soc Proc Annu Meet Tech Conf** ... Numerical Control Society Proceedings. Annual Meeting and Technical Conference [*A publication*]
**Numer Eng** ... Numerical Engineering [*A publication*]
**Numer Funct Anal Optim** ... Numerical Functional Analysis and Optimization [*A publication*]
**Numer Funct Anal Optimiz** ... Numerical Functional Analysis and Optimization [*A publication*]
**Numer Heat Transfer** ... Numerical Heat Transfer [*A publication*]
**Numer Math** ... Numerische Mathematik [*A publication*]
**Numer Math Ingenieure Physiker** ... Numerische Mathematik fuer Ingenieure und Physiker [*A publication*]
**Numer Math Ingenieure Physiker (Berl)** ... Numerische Mathematik fuer Ingenieure und Physiker (Berlin) [*A publication*]
**Numer Math J Chinese Univ** ... Numerical Mathematics. A Journal of Chinese Universities [*Nanjing*] [*A publication*]
**Num Hisp** .. Numario Hispanico [*A publication*]
**Numid** ........ Numidian
**NUMIS** ..... Navy Uniform Management Information System
**NUMIS** ..... Numismatics
**Numis** ......... Numismatist [*A publication*]
**Numis Chron 7 Ser** ... Numismatic Chronicle. Series 7 [*A publication*]
**Numis Chron 7 Ser (Engl)** ... Numismatic Chronicle. Series 7 (England) [*A publication*]
**Numis Circ** ... Numismatic Circular [*England*] [*A publication*]
**NUMISM** ... Numismatics
**Numisma (Austral)** ... Numisma: An Occasional Numismatic Magazine (Australia) [*A publication*]
**Numisma Rev Soc IA** ... Numisma. Revista de la Sociedad Ibero-Americana de Estudios Numismaticos [*A publication*]
**Num Israel** ... Numismatics in Israel [*A publication*]
**Num J** ........ Numismatic Journal [*A publication*]
**Num Koezl** ... Numizmatikai Koezloeny [*A publication*]
**NUMM** ..... National Union of Masters and Mates [*British*]
**Num Math** ... Numerische Mathematik [*A publication*]
**NUMMB** ... Nuclear Materials Management [*A publication*]
**NUMMI** .... New United Motor Manufacturing, Incorporated [*Joint venture of Toyota Motor Corp. and General Motors Corp.*]
**Num Moravica** ... Numismatica Moravica [*A publication*]
**Num Nachr Bl** ... Numismatisches Nachrichtenblatt [*A publication*]
**NUMORD** ... Australian Capital Territory Ordinances: Numbered [*Database*]
**NumR** ......... Numbers Rabbah
**NUMR** ........ Numerex Corp. [*NASDAQ symbol*] (NQ)
**NUMREG** ... Australian Capital Territory Regulations: Numbered [*Database*]
**NUMRUL** ... Commonwealth Statutory Rules: Numbered [*Database*] [*Australia*]
**NUMS** ....... Nu-Med, Inc. [*NASDAQ symbol*] (NQ)
**NUMS** ....... Nuclear Materials Security (NRCH)
**NUMS** ....... Numerous (ROG)
**NUMSA** .... Nordic Union of Motor Schools Associations (EAIO)
**Num Sbor** ... Numismaticky Sbornik [*A publication*]
**Num Sfrag** ... Numizmatika i Sfragistika [*A publication*]
**Num Stockholm** ... Numismatica Stockholmiensia. Annual Reports and Acquisitions of the Royal Coin Cabinet. National Museum of Monetary History [*A publication*]
**NUMW** ..... National Unemployed Workers' Movement [*British*]
**Num Z** ........ Numismatische Zeitschrift [*A publication*]
**NUN** .......... Pensacola, FL [*Location identifier*] [*FAA*] (FAAL)
**NUn** ........... Uniondale Public Library, Uniondale, NY [*Library symbol*] [*Library of Congress*] (LCLS)
**NUNA** ....... Not Used on Next Assembly (AAG)
**NUnCE** ...... California Elementary School, Uniondale, NY [*Library symbol*] [*Library of Congress*] (LCLS)
**NUNGAS** .. Acta Agriculturae Sinica [*A publication*]
**NUnH** ........ Uniondale High School, Uniondale, NY [*Library symbol*] [*Library of Congress*] (LCLS)
**NUnLJ** ....... Lawrence Junior High School, Uniondale, NY [*Library symbol*] [*Library of Congress*] (LCLS)
**NUnSE** ...... Smith Elementary School, Uniondale, NY [*Library symbol*] [*Library of Congress*] (LCLS)
**NUnTHJ** ... Turtle Hook Junior High School, Uniondale, NY [*Library symbol*] [*Library of Congress*] (LCLS)
**Nunt Radiol** ... Nuntius Radiologicus [*A publication*]
**NUNW** ...... Nutrition Newsletter [*Canada*] [*A publication*]
**NUnWE** ..... Walnut Elementary School, Uniondale, NY [*Library symbol*] [*Library of Congress*] (LCLS)
**NUO** .......... Nugold Enterprises Corp. [*Vancouver Stock Exchange symbol*]
**Nuo Ant** ..... Nuova Antologia [*A publication*]
**Nuo G Bot Ital** ... Nuovo Giornale Botanico Italiano [*A publication*]
**Nuo Ital** ...... Nuova Italia [*A publication*]
**NUOL** ........ Naval Underwater Ordnance Laboratory (NOAA)
**NUOL** ........ Nursing Outlook [*A publication*]
**NUOM** ...... Northern Union of Operative Masons [*British*]
**NUON** ...... Nunavut Onipkaat. Kitikmeot Inuit Association [*A publication*]
**Nuo Riv Stor** ... Nuova Rivista Storica [*A publication*]
**NUOS** ........ Naval Underwater Ordnance Station
**Nuova Agr Lucana** ... Nuova Agricoltura Lucana [*A publication*]
**Nuova Antol** ... Nuova Antologia [*A publication*]
**Nuova Chim** ... Nuova Chimica [*A publication*]
**Nuova Econ** ... Nuova Economia [*A publication*]
**Nuova Riv Olii Veg Saponi** ... Nuova Rivista Olii Vegetali e Saponi [*A publication*]
**Nuova Riv Stor** ... Nuova Rivista Storica [*A publication*]
**Nuova RM Italiana** ... Nuova Rivista Musicale Italiana [*A publication*]
**Nuova Vet** .. Nuova Veterinaria [*A publication*]
**Nuov Bull** ... Nuovo Bulletino di Archeologia Cristiana [*A publication*]
**Nuov Cim A** ... Nuovo Cimento. A [*A publication*]
**Nuov Cim B** ... Nuovo Cimento. B [*A publication*]
**Nuovi Allevam** ... Nuovi Allevamenti [*A publication*]
**Nuovi Ann Agric** ... Nuovi Annali dell'Agricoltura [*A publication*]
**Nuovi Annali Ig Microbiol** ... Nuovi Annali d'Igiene e Microbiologia [*A publication*]
**Nuovi Ann Ig Microbiol** ... Nuovi Annali d'Igiene e Microbiologia [*A publication*]
**Nuovi Ann Ist Chim-Agr Sper Gorizia Ser 2** ... Nuovi Annali. Istituto Chimico-Agrario Sperimentale di Gorizia. Serie 2 [*A publication*]
**Nuovi Studi Sta Chim-Agr Sper Udine** ... Nuovi Studi. Stazione Chimico-Agraria Sperimentale di Udine [*A publication*]
**Nuovo Arch Ital ORL** ... Nuovo Archivio Italiano di Otologia, Rinologia, e Laringologia [*A publication*]
**Nuovo Arch Ital Otol Rinol Laringol** ... Nuovo Archivio Italiano di Otologia, Rinologia, e Laringologia [*A publication*]
**Nuovo Cim** ... Nuovo Cimento [*A publication*]
**Nuovo Cim A** ... Nuovo Cimento. A [*A publication*]
**Nuovo Cim B** ... Nuovo Cimento. B [*A publication*]
**Nuovo Cim C** ... Nuovo Cimento. C [*A publication*]
**Nuovo Cimento C 1** ... Nuovo Cimento. C. Serie 1 [*A publication*]
**Nuovo Cimento Lett** ... Nuovo Cimento. Lettere [*Italy*] [*A publication*]
**Nuovo Cimento Soc Ital Fis A** ... Nuovo Cimento. Societa Italiana di Fisica. Sezione A [*A publication*]
**Nuovo Cimento Soc Ital Fis B** ... Nuovo Cimento. Societa Italiana di Fisica. Sezione B [*A publication*]
**Nuovo Cimento Suppl** ... Nuovo Cimento. Supplemento [*Italy*] [*A publication*]
**Nuovo G Bot Ital** ... Nuovo Giornale Botanico Italiano [*A publication*]
**Nuovo G Bot Ital (Nuovo Ser)** ... Nuovo Giornale Botanico Italiano (Nuovo Serie) [*A publication*]
**Nuov Riv M** ... Nuova Rivista Musicale Italiana [*A publication*]
**Nuov Riv St** ... Nuova Rivista Storica [*A publication*]
**NUP** ........... National Umma Party [*Political party*] [*Sudan*]

**NUP**.......... National Underwriter (Property and Casualty Insurance Edition) [*A publication*]
**NUP**.......... National Union of Protestants
**NUP**.......... National Unity Party [*Political party*] (EA)
**NUP**.......... Nationalist Unionist Party [*Sudanese*]
**NUP**.......... New Union Party [*Later, IUP*] (EA)
**NUP**.......... Nunapitchuk [*Alaska*] [*Airport symbol*] (OAG)
**NUPAD**..... Nuclear-Powered Active Detection System
**NUpB**......... United States Brookhaven National Laboratory, Upton, NY [*Library symbol*] [*Library of Congress*] (LCLS)
**NUPBB**...... Nuclear Physics. B [*A publication*]
**NUpB-MH** ... United States Brookhaven National Laboratory, Medical Research Center Hospital, Upton, NY [*Library symbol*] [*Library of Congress*] (LCLS)
**NUPBP**...... National Union of Printing, Bookbinding, and Paperworkers [*British*]
**NUPC**........ National Underwriter (Property and Casualty Insurance Edition) [*A publication*]
**NUPC**........ Nupec Resources [*NASDAQ symbol*] (NQ)
**NUPDTU**.. National Union of Painters and Decorators Trade Union [*British*]
**NUPE**........ National Union of Public Employees [*British*]
**NUPEC**..... Nuclear Power Engineering Test Center (NRCH)
**NUPGE**..... National Union of Provincial Government Employees [*Canada*]
**NUPLEX**... Nuclear Complex
**NUPOC**..... Nuclear Propulsion Officer Candidate [*Navy*]
**NUPS**........ Nordic Union of Private Schools (EA)
**NUPSA**..... Neuropsychologia [*A publication*]
**NUQ**.......... Mountain View, CA [*Location identifier*] [*FAA*] (FAAL)
**NUR**.......... Natchez, Urania & Ruston Railway Co. [*AAR code*]
**NUR**.......... National Union of Railwaymen [*British*]
**NUR**.......... Net Unduplicated Research
**Nur**........... Nitrosourea [*Biochemistry*]
**NUR**.......... Nonuniformity Ratio
**NUR**.......... Nurmijarvi [*Finland*] [*Geomagnetic observatory code*]
**NUR**.......... Nurmijarvi [*Finland*] [*Seismograph station code, US Geological Survey*] (SEIS)
**NUR**.......... Nurse (AABC)
**NUR**.......... Nuspar Resources [*Vancouver Stock Exchange symbol*]
**NURB**........ National Uniform Business Rate [*British*]
**NURBS**...... Nonuniform Relational B-Spline [*Micro Cadam 3-D*] [*Data processing*]
**NURC**........ National Undersea Research Center [*Virgin Islands*]
**NURC**........ National Union of Railway Clerks [*British*]
**NURDC**..... Naval Undersea Research and Development Center
**NURE**........ National Uranium Resource Evaluation [*Program*] [*Energy Research and Development Administration*]
**NURE**........ Nunasi Report [*A publication*]
**NURED**..... Nuclear Requirements Determination [*Military*]
**NUREG**..... Nuclear Regulatory Commission
**NUREM**.... Nuclear Requirements Methodology [*Military*]
**NUREP** ..... New York University Resonance Escape Probability [*Code*] [*Nuclear energy*] (NRCH)
**NUREQ**..... Nuclear Requirements [*Military*]
**NUREX**..... Nuclear Requirements Extrapolation [*Model*] (MCD)
**NU/RF** ...... National Urban/Rural Fellows (EA)
**NURO** ....... Neurotech Corp. [*Farmingdale, NY*] [*NASDAQ symbol*] (NQ)
**NURP**........ National Undersea Research Program [*Department of Commerce*] (GRD)
**NURP**........ Nationwide Urban Runoff Program [*Water pollution*]
**NURS**........ Nursery
**NURS**........ Nursing
**Nurs '78**..... Nursing '78 [*A publication*]
**Nurs '82**..... Nursing '82 [*A publication*]
**Nurs '80/'81** ... Nursing '80/'81 [*A publication*]
**Nurs 83/84** ... Nursing '83/'84 [*A publication*]
**Nurs 85/86** ... Nursing '85/'86 [*A publication*]
**Nurs Abstr** ... Nursing Abstracts [*A publication*]
**Nurs Admin Q** ... Nursing Administration. Quarterly [*A publication*]
**Nurs Adm Q** ... Nursing Administration. Quarterly [*A publication*]
**Nurs Care**.. Nursing Care [*A publication*]
**Nurs Careers** ... Nursing Careers [*A publication*]
**Nurs Clin N Am** ... Nursing Clinics of North America [*A publication*]
**Nurs Clin North Am** ... Nursing Clinics of North America [*A publication*]
**Nurs Digest** ... Nursing Digest [*A publication*]
**Nurs Dimens** ... Nursing Dimensions [*A publication*]
**Nurs Econ**.. Nursing Economics [*A publication*]
**NURSEDETS** ... Nurse Detachments [*Army*]
**Nurs Educ Monogr** ... Nursing Education Monographs [*A publication*]
**Nurse Educ** ... Nurse Educator [*A publication*]
**Nurse Educ Oppor Innov** ... Nurse Educators Opportunities and Innovations [*A publication*]
**Nurse Educ Today** ... Nurse Education Today [*A publication*]
**Nurse Inquir** ... Nurse Inquirer [*A publication*]
**Nurse Isr**.... Nurse in Israel [*A publication*]
**Nurse Pract** ... Nurse Practitioner [*A publication*]
**Nurse Practit** ... Nurse Practitioner [*A publication*]
**Nursery Bus** ... Nursery Business [*A publication*]
**Nurserym Gdn Cent** ... Nurseryman and Garden Center [*A publication*]
**Nurs Focus** ... Nursing Focus [*A publication*]
**Nurs Forum** ... Nursing Forum [*A publication*]
**Nurs Forum (Auckl)** ... Nursing Forum (Auckland) [*A publication*]
**Nurs Health Care** ... Nursing and Health Care [*A publication*]
**Nurs Hlth Care** ... Nursing and Health Care [*A publication*]
**Nurs Homes** ... Nursing Homes [*A publication*]
**Nursing (Lond)** ... Nursing (London) [*A publication*]
**Nurs J**........ Nursing Journal [*A publication*]
**Nurs J India** ... Nursing Journal of India [*A publication*]
**Nurs J Singapore** ... Nursing Journal of Singapore [*A publication*]
**Nurs J (S Toms)** ... Nursing Journal (Santo Tomas, Manila) [*A publication*]
**Nurs Law Ethics** ... Nursing Law and Ethics [*A publication*]
**Nurs Leader** ... Nurse Leadership [*A publication*]
**Nurs Leadersh** ... Nursing Leadership [*A publication*]
**Nurs Leadership** ... Nursing Leadership [*A publication*]
**Nurs Life**.... Nursing Life [*A publication*]
**Nurs M**...... Nursing Management [*A publication*]
**Nurs Manage** ... Nursing Management [*A publication*]
**Nurs Mirror** ... Nursing Mirror and Midwives Journal [*Later, Nursing Mirror*] [*A publication*]
**Nurs (Montreal)** ... Nursing (Montreal) [*A publication*]
**Nurs News (Concord)** ... Nursing News (Concord) [*A publication*]
**Nurs News (Conn)** ... Nursing News (Connecticut) [*A publication*]
**Nurs News (Hartford)** ... Nursing News (Hartford) [*A publication*]
**Nurs News (Meriden)** ... Nursing News (Meriden) [*A publication*]
**Nurs News (New Hamp)** ... Nursing News (New Hampshire) [*A publication*]
**Nurs News (So Africa)** ... Nursing News (South Africa) [*A publication*]
**Nurs Outlook** ... Nursing Outlook [*A publication*]
**Nurs Pap**.... Nursing Papers [*A publication*]
**Nurs Papers** ... Nursing Papers [*A publication*]
**Nurs Pract** ... Nursing Practice [*A publication*]
**Nurs Pulse New Engl** ... Nursing Pulse of New England [*A publication*]
**Nurs (Que)** ... Nursing (Quebec) [*A publication*]
**Nurs Res**.... Nursing Research [*A publication*]
**Nurs Res Conf** ... Nursing Research Conference [*A publication*]
**Nurs Res Rep** ... Nursing Research Report [*A publication*]
**Nurs Sci**..... Nursing Science [*A publication*]
**Nurs Stand** ... Nursing Standard [*A publication*]
**Nurs Success Today** ... Nursing Success Today [*A publication*]
**Nurs Times** ... Nursing Times [*A publication*]
**Nurs Update** ... Nursing Update [*A publication*]
**NURSW**.... Nursing System-Wide
**NURVA**..... Nursing Research [*A publication*]
**NURX**........ Nuclear Pharmacy, Inc. [*NASDAQ symbol*] (NQ)
**NUS**.......... National Union of Scalemakers [*British*] (DCTA)
**NUS**.......... National Union of Seamen [*British*]
**NUS**.......... National Union of Students [*British*]
**NUS**.......... National Utility Services [*British*]
**NUS**.......... New Upper Stage [*NASA*] (KSC)
**NUS**.......... Norsup [*Vanuatu*] [*Airport symbol*] (OAG)
**NUS**.......... Nu-Start Resource Corp. [*Vancouver Stock Exchange symbol*]
**NUS**.......... Nuclear Utility Services
**n-us---**........ United States [*MARC geographic area code*] [*Library of Congress*] (LCCP)
**n-usa--**........ Appalachian Area [*MARC geographic area code*] [*Library of Congress*] (LCCP)
**NUSA**........ National Union of Shop Assistants [*British*] (DAS)
**NUSA**........ Neighborhoods USA (EA)
**NUSA**........ Ninth United States Army
**NUSAC**..... Nuclear Sciences Advisory Committee [*Department of Energy/National Science Foundation*]
**n-us-ak**....... Alaska [*MARC geographic area code*] [*Library of Congress*] (LCCP)
**n-us-al**........ Alabama [*MARC geographic area code*] [*Library of Congress*] (LCCP)
**n-us-ar**........ Arkansas [*MARC geographic area code*] [*Library of Congress*] (LCCP)
**NUSAS**...... National Union of South African Students
**NUSAT**..... Northern Utah Satellite
**n-us-az**....... Arizona [*MARC geographic area code*] [*Library of Congress*] (LCCP)
**NUSBA**..... Nuclear Science and Applications. Series B. Physical Sciences [*A publication*]
**NUSC**........ Naval Underwater Systems Center
**n-usc--**........ North Central States [*MARC geographic area code*] [*Library of Congress*] (LCCP)
**n-us-ca**........ California [*MARC geographic area code*] [*Library of Congress*] (LCCP)
**NUSC/NL** ... Naval Underwater Systems Center, New London [*Connecticut*]
**NUSC/NPT** ... Naval Underwater Systems Center, Newport [*Rhode Island*]
**n-us-co**........ Colorado [*MARC geographic area code*] [*Library of Congress*] (LCCP)
**n-us-ct**........ Connecticut [*MARC geographic area code*] [*Library of Congress*] (LCCP)
**NUSD**........ Nucleus Sum Optical Density [*Microscopy*]
**n-us-dc**....... District of Columbia [*MARC geographic area code*] [*Library of Congress*] (LCCP)
**n-us-de**....... Delaware [*MARC geographic area code*] [*Library of Congress*] (LCCP)
**n-use--**........ Northeast (United States) [*MARC geographic area code*] [*Library of Congress*] (LCCP)
**NUSEC**...... Naval Underwater Systems Engineering Center (MUGU)

**NUSFDB**... NUS [*National University of Singapore*] Financial Database [*Information service or system*] (IID)
**n-us-fl**......... Florida [*MARC geographic area code*] [*Library of Congress*] (LCCP)
**n-us-ga**....... Georgia [*MARC geographic area code*] [*Library of Congress*] (LCCP)
**NUSGGMW**... National Union of Stove Grate and General Metal Workers [*British*]
**NUSGW**.... National Union of Stove and Grate Workers [*British*]
**NUSH**........ Northwestern University. Studies in the Humanities [*A publication*]
**NUSH**........ Nucleus Shape [*Microscopy*]
**n-us-hi**........ Hawaii [*MARC geographic area code*] [*Library of Congress*] (LCCP)
**n-us-ia**........ Iowa [*MARC geographic area code*] [*Library of Congress*] (LCCP)
**n-us-id**........ Idaho [*MARC geographic area code*] [*Library of Congress*] (LCCP)
**n-us-il**......... Illinois [*MARC geographic area code*] [*Library of Congress*] (LCCP)
**n-us-in**........ Indiana [*MARC geographic area code*] [*Library of Congress*] (LCCP)
**n-us-ks**....... Kansas [*MARC geographic area code*] [*Library of Congress*] (LCCP)
**n-us-ky**....... Kentucky [*MARC geographic area code*] [*Library of Congress*] (LCCP)
**n-usl--**......... Middle Atlantic States [*MARC geographic area code*] [*Library of Congress*] (LCCP)
**NUSL**........ Naval Underwater Sound Laboratory [*Later, NUSC*]
**n-us-la**........ Louisiana [*MARC geographic area code*] [*Library of Congress*] (LCCP)
**n-usm--**....... Mississippi River and Basin [*MARC geographic area code*] [*Library of Congress*] (LCCP)
**n-us-ma**...... Massachusetts [*MARC geographic area code*] [*Library of Congress*] (LCCP)
**n-us-md**...... Maryland [*MARC geographic area code*] [*Library of Congress*] (LCCP)
**n-us-me**...... Maine [*MARC geographic area code*] [*Library of Congress*] (LCCP)
**n-us-mi**....... Michigan [*MARC geographic area code*] [*Library of Congress*] (LCCP)
**n-us-mn**...... Minnesota [*MARC geographic area code*] [*Library of Congress*] (LCCP)
**n-us-mo**...... Missouri [*MARC geographic area code*] [*Library of Congress*] (LCCP)
**n-us-ms**...... Mississippi [*MARC geographic area code*] [*Library of Congress*] (LCCP)
**n-us-mt**....... Montana [*MARC geographic area code*] [*Library of Congress*] (LCCP)
**NUSMWCHDE**... National Union of Sheet Metal Workers, Coppersmiths, Heating and Domestic Engineers [*British*] (DCTA)
**n-usn--**........ New England [*MARC geographic area code*] [*Library of Congress*] (LCCP)
**n-us-nb**....... Nebraska [*MARC geographic area code*] [*Library of Congress*] (LCCP)
**n-us-nc**....... North Carolina [*MARC geographic area code*] [*Library of Congress*] (LCCP)
**n-us-nd**....... North Dakota [*MARC geographic area code*] [*Library of Congress*] (LCCP)
**n-us-nh**....... New Hampshire [*MARC geographic area code*] [*Library of Congress*] (LCCP)
**n-us-nj**........ New Jersey [*MARC geographic area code*] [*Library of Congress*] (LCCP)
**n-us-nm**...... New Mexico [*MARC geographic area code*] [*Library of Congress*] (LCCP)
**n-us-nv**....... Nevada [*MARC geographic area code*] [*Library of Congress*] (LCCP)
**n-us-ny**....... New York [*MARC geographic area code*] [*Library of Congress*] (LCCP)
**n-uso--**........ Ohio River and Basin [*MARC geographic area code*] [*Library of Congress*] (LCCP)
**n-us-oh**....... Ohio [*MARC geographic area code*] [*Library of Congress*] (LCCP)
**n-us-ok**....... Oklahoma [*MARC geographic area code*] [*Library of Congress*] (LCCP)
**n-us-or**........ Oregon [*MARC geographic area code*] [*Library of Congress*] (LCCP)
**NUSOS**..... Nuclear Underwater Sound Source (NG)
**n-usp--**........ Pacific and Mountain States [*MARC geographic area code*] [*Library of Congress*] (LCCP)
**n-us-pa**....... Pennsylvania [*MARC geographic area code*] [*Library of Congress*] (LCCP)
**n-us-ri**......... Rhode Island [*MARC geographic area code*] [*Library of Congress*] (LCCP)
**NUSRL**...... Navy Underwater Sound Reference Laboratory
**n-uss--**........ Missouri River and Basin [*MARC geographic area code*] [*Library of Congress*] (LCCP)
**n-us-sc**........ South Carolina [*MARC geographic area code*] [*Library of Congress*] (LCCP)
**n-us-sd**....... South Dakota [*MARC geographic area code*] [*Library of Congress*] (LCCP)
**NUSSE**...... Nonuniform Simple Surface Evaporated Model (MCD)
**n-ust--**......... Southwest (United States) [*MARC geographic area code*] [*Library of Congress*] (LCCP)
**n-us-tn**........ Tennessee [*MARC geographic area code*] [*Library of Congress*] (LCCP)
**n-us-tx**........ Texas [*MARC geographic area code*] [*Library of Congress*] (LCCP)
**n-usu--**........ Southern States [*MARC geographic area code*] [*Library of Congress*] (LCCP)
**NUSUM**.... Nuclear Detonation Summary (NVT)
**NUSUM**.... Numerical Summary Report [*Military*] (AFM)
**NuSup**........ Numen Supplements [*Leiden*] [*A publication*]
**n-us-ut**........ Utah [*MARC geographic area code*] [*Library of Congress*] (LCCP)
**n-us-va**....... Virginia [*MARC geographic area code*] [*Library of Congress*] (LCCP)
**n-us-vt**........ Vermont [*MARC geographic area code*] [*Library of Congress*] (LCCP)
**n-usw--**....... Northwest (United States) [*MARC geographic area code*] [*Library of Congress*] (LCCP)
**n-us-wa**....... Washington [*MARC geographic area code*] [*Library of Congress*] (LCCP)
**n-us-wi**....... Wisconsin [*MARC geographic area code*] [*Library of Congress*] (LCCP)
**n-us-wv**....... West Virginia [*MARC geographic area code*] [*Library of Congress*] (LCCP)
**n-us-wy**....... Wyoming [*MARC geographic area code*] [*Library of Congress*] (LCCP)
**NUSYQ**..... Nuclear Systems [*NASDAQ symbol*] (NQ)
**NUSZ**........ Nucleus Size [*Microscopy*]
**NUT**........... Mauna Loa Macadamia Partners LP [*NYSE symbol*] (SPSG)
**NUT**........... National Union of Teachers [*British*]
**NUT**........... Nautilus Resources Ltd. [*Vancouver Stock Exchange symbol*]
**N-U-T**........ Newcastle-Upon-Tyne [*City in England*]
**NUT**........... Norges Utenrikshandel [*A publication*]
**NUT**........... Number Unobtainable Tone [*Telecommunications*] (TEL)
**NUt**............ Utica Public Library, Utica, NY [*Library symbol*] [*Library of Congress*] (LCLS)
**NUtC**......... Utica College of Syracuse University, Utica, NY [*Library symbol*] [*Library of Congress*] (LCLS)
**NUTEX**..... Nuclear Tactical Exercise
**NUTG**........ National Union of Townswomen's Guilds [*British*]
**NUtGE**...... General Electric Co., Utica, NY [*Library symbol*] [*Library of Congress*] (LCLS)
**NUTGW**.... National Union of Tailors and Garments Workers [*British*]
**NUtHi**........ Oneida Historical Society, Utica, NY [*Library symbol*] [*Library of Congress*] (LCLS)
**NUTI**......... NASCOM User Traffic Interface [*NASA*] (MCD)
**NUTIA**...... Nursing Times [*A publication*]
**Nutida M**... Nutida Musik [*A publication*]
**Nutida Mus**... Nutida Musik [*A publication*]
**NUTK**........ Nu-Tech Industries [*NASDAQ symbol*] (NQ)
**NUtM**........ Munson-Williams-Proctor Institute, Utica, NY [*Library symbol*] [*Library of Congress*] (LCLS)
**NUTM**........ Nutmeg Industries, Inc. [*Tampa, FL*] [*NASDAQ symbol*] (NQ)
**NUtMI**....... Utica Mutual Insurance Co., Utica, NY [*Library symbol*] [*Library of Congress*] (LCLS)
**NUtMM**.... Masonic Medical Research Laboratory, Utica, NY [*Library symbol*] [*Library of Congress*] (LCLS)
**NUtMV**..... Mohawk Valley Community College, Utica, NY [*Library symbol*] [*Library of Congress*] (LCLS)
**NUtMVL**... Mohawk Valley Learning Resource Center, Utica Psychiatric Center, Utica, NY [*Library symbol*] [*Library of Congress*] (LCLS)
**NUtMY**..... Mid-York Library System, Utica, NY [*Library symbol*] [*Library of Congress*] (LCLS)
**NUTN**........ National University Teleconference Network [*Stillwater, OK*] [*Telecommunications*] (TSSD)
**NUTN**........ Nunatext News [*A publication*]
**NUTN**........ Nutrition News [*A publication*]
**NUTP**........ National Uranium Tailings Program [*Canada*]
**NUtP**.......... Utica Psychiatric Center, Utica, NY [*Library symbol*] [*Library of Congress*] (LCLS)
**NUTPW**.... National Union of Tin Plate Workers [*British*]
**NUTR**........ Nutrition (AABC)
**NutrAb**....... Nutrition Abstracts [*A publication*]
**Nutr Abstr Rev**... Nutrition Abstracts and Reviews [*Information service or system*] [*A publication*]
**Nutr Action**... Nutrition Action [*A publication*]
**NUTRAT**.. Nuclear Uses Technology Reaction Analysis Team
**Nutr Behav**... Nutrition and Behavior [*A publication*]
**Nutr Brain**... Nutrition and the Brain [*A publication*]
**Nutr Bromatol Toxicol**... Nutricion Bromatologia Toxicologia [*A publication*]
**Nutr Cancer**... Nutrition and Cancer [*A publication*]
**Nutr Clin Nutr**... Nutrition and Clinical Nutrition [*A publication*]
**Nutr Dent Health**... Nutrition and Dental Health [*A publication*]
**Nutr Dieta**... Nutritio et Dieta [*A publication*]
**Nutr Dieta Eur Nutr Diet**... Nutrio et Dieta. European Review of Nutrition and Dietetics [*A publication*]
**Nutr Food Sci**... Nutrition and Food Science [*A publication*]

**Nutr Food Sci Pres Knowl Util** ... Nutrition and Food Science. Present Knowledge and Utilization [*A publication*]
**Nutr Found Inc Rep** ... Nutrition Foundation, Incorporated. Report [*A publication*]
**Nutr Health** ... Nutrition and Health [*A publication*]
**Nutr Health Dis** ... Nutrition in Health and Disease [*A publication*]
**NUTRI** ...... Nutrition
**NUTRL** ..... Nutritional
**Nutr and MD** ... Nutrition and the MD [*A publication*]
**Nutr Metab** ... Nutrition and Metabolism [*A publication*]
**Nutr Monogr Ser** ... Nutrition Monograph Series [*A publication*]
**Nutr News** ... Nutrition News [*A publication*]
**Nutr Notes** ... Nutrition Notes [*A publication*]
**Nutr Plann** ... Nutrition Planning [*A publication*]
**Nutr R**........ Nutrition Reviews [*A publication*]
**Nutr Rep In** ... Nutrition Reports International [*A publication*]
**Nutr Rep Int** ... Nutrition Reports International [*A publication*]
**Nutr Requir Domest Anim** ... Nutrient Requirements of Domestic Animals [*A publication*]
**Nutr Res**..... Nutrition Research [*A publication*]
**Nutr Res Bull** ... Nutrition Research Bulletin [*A publication*]
**Nutr Rev** .... Nutrition Reviews [*A publication*]
**Nutr Sci**...... Nutrition Sciences [*A publication*]
**Nutr Soc Proc** ... Nutrition Society Proceedings [*British*] [*A publication*]
**Nutr Support Serv** ... Nutritional Support Services [*A publication*]
**Nutr Today** ... Nutrition Today [*A publication*]
**Nutr Update** ... Nutrition Update [*A publication*]
**NUTS** ........ New South Wales University Theatre Society [*Australia*]
**NUTS** ........ New Universal Terminology Subjects
**NUTS** ........ Nutrition World, Inc. [*NASDAQ symbol*] (NQ)
**NUtSC** ....... New York State Supreme Court Law Library, Utica, NY [*Library symbol*] [*Library of Congress*] (LCLS)
**NUTSDT**... Nutrition Sciences [*A publication*]
**NUtSU**....... State University of New York, College at Utica-Rome, Utica, NY [*Library symbol*] [*Library of Congress*] (LCLS)
**NUTT** ........ National Union of Tobacco Trades [*British*]
**NUTX**........ Nucleus Texture [*Microscopy*]
**NUU** .......... New Universal Union (EA)
**NUUSFE**... National Union of United States Forces Employees [*Republic of Korea*]
**NUUT**........ National Union of Uncertified Teachers [*British*]
**NUV**........... Near Ultraviolet
**NUV**........... Nuveen Municipal Value Fund, Inc. [*NYSE symbol*] (SPSG)
**NUVB**........ National Union of Vehicle Builders [*British*]
**NUVI**......... NuVision, Incorporated [*Flint, MI*] [*NASDAQ symbol*] (NQ)
**NUVN** ....... Nuvuk News [*A publication*]
**NUVW**....... National Union of Vehicular Workers [*British*]
**NUW** ......... National Universities Week [*Canada*]
**NUW** ......... Nu-West Group Ltd. [*Toronto Stock Exchange symbol*]
**NUW** ......... Whidbey Island, WA [*Location identifier*] [*FAA*] (FAAL)
**NUWAX**.... Nuclear Weapons Accident Exercises
**NUWC**....... Naval Undersea Warfare Center [*Later, NURDC*]
**NUWEP** .... Nuclear Weapon Employment Policy (MCD)
**NUWEP** .... Nuclear Weapons Effect Planning
**NUWES** .... Naval Undersea Warfare Engineering Station (MCD)
**NUWES** .... Naval Underwater Weapons Evaluation Station
**NUWPNSTRACEN** ... Nuclear Weapons Training Center (MCD)
**NUWPNSUPANX** ... Nuclear Weapons Supply Annex
**NUWPNTRACEN** ... Nuclear Weapons Training Center
**NUWPNTRACENLANT** ... Nuclear Weapons Training Center, Atlantic
**NUWPNTRACENPAC** ... Nuclear Weapons Training Center, Pacific
**NUWRES** ... Naval Underwater Weapons Research and Engineering Station
**NUWS**....... Naval Underwater Weapons Station (MCD)
**NUWSAMBS** ... National United Women's Societies of the Adoration of the Most Blessed Sacrament (EA)
**NUWSEC** ... Naval Underwater Weapons Systems Engineering Center
**NUWT**....... National Union of Women Teachers [*British*] (DAS)
**NUYC**........ Nordic Union of Young Conservatives (EA)
**NV**............. Naamloze Vennootschap [*Limited Company, Corporation*] [*Netherlands*] (GPO)
**NV**............. Naamloze Vennootschap [*A publication*]
**NV**............. Naked Vision
**nV**............. Nanovolt (IEEE)
**NV**............. Nase Veda [*A publication*]
**NV**............. Nastavni Vjesnik [*A publication*]
**N & V** ......... Nausea and Vomiting
**NV**............. Near Vertical [*Aerospace*]
**NV**............. Needle Valve
**NV**............. Neerlands Volksleven [*A publication*]
**NV**............. Net Value
**NV**............. Nevada [*Postal code*]
**Nv**.............. Nevada State Library, Carson City, NV [*Library symbol*] [*Library of Congress*] (LCLS)
**NV**............. New Version [*of the Bible*]
**NV**............. Next Visit [*Medicine*]
**NV**............. Night Vision Device [*Optics*]
**N/V**........... No Value [*Legal term*] (DLA)
**NV**............. Nonvaccinated
**NV**............. Nonvenereal [*Medicine*]
**NV**............. Nonveteran
**NV**............. Nonvintage [*Wine*]
**nv**.............. Nonvirulent [*Pathology*]
**NV**............. Nonvolatile
**NV**............. Nonvoting [*Investment term*]
**NV**............. Nord-Viscount Corp.
**NV**............. Normal Value [*Clinical chemistry*]
**NV**............. Norske Veritas [*Norwegian ship classification society*] (DS)
**NV**............. Northern Executive Aviation Ltd. [*Great Britain*] [*ICAO designator*] (FAAC)
**NV**............. Not Vaccinated [*Medicine*]
**n/v**............ Notre Ville [*Our City*] [*French*] [*Business term*]
**NV**............. Nova et Vetera [*A publication*]
**N & V** ........ Nova et Vetera [*A publication*]
**NV**............. Nozzle Vanes (AAG)
**NV**............. Numizmaticke Vijesti [*A publication*]
**NV1**........... North Anna [*Virginia*] [*Seismograph station code, US Geological Survey*] [*Closed*]
**NV2**........... North Anna [*Virginia*] [*Seismograph station code, US Geological Survey*] [*Closed*] (SEIS)
**NV3**........... North Anna [*Virginia*] [*Seismograph station code, US Geological Survey*] [*Closed*] (SEIS)
**NV4**........... North Anna [*Virginia*] [*Seismograph station code, US Geological Survey*] [*Closed*] (SEIS)
**NV5**........... North Anna [*Virginia*] [*Seismograph station code, US Geological Survey*] [*Closed*] (SEIS)
**NV6**........... North Anna [*Virginia*] [*Seismograph station code, US Geological Survey*] [*Closed*] (SEIS)
**NV7**........... North Anna [*Virginia*] [*Seismograph station code, US Geological Survey*] [*Closed*] (SEIS)
**NVA**........... N-Vinylacetamide [*Organic chemistry*]
**NVA**........... National Variety Artists [*Defunct*] (EA)
**NVA**........... National Velthrow Association (EA)
**NVA**........... National Veterans Association (EA)
**NVA**........... National Vista Alliance (EA)
**NVA**........... Nationale Volksarmee [*National Peoples' Army*] [*Germany*]
**NVA**........... Near Visual Acuity [*Medicine*]
**NVA**........... Negative Vorticity Advection [*Aviation*] (FAAC)
**NVA**........... Neiva [*Colombia*] [*Airport symbol*] (OAG)
**NVA**........... Non-Violent Alternatives [*An association*] (EA)
**NvA**........... Normalized Volt-Ampere
**NVA**........... Norske Videnskaps-Akademi. Aarbok [*A publication*]
**NVA**........... North Vietnamese Army
**Nva**............ Norvaline [*Biochemistry*]
**NVA**........... Nova Corp. of Alberta [*NYSE symbol*] [*Toronto Stock Exchange symbol*] (SPSG)
**NVAC**........ Natal Voluntary Ambulance Corps [*British military*] (DMA)
**NVAC**........ North Vietnamese Army Captured
**NVAC**........ Sunny Von Bulow National Victim Advocacy Center [*Later, NVC*] (EA)
**NVAFB**...... North Vandenberg Air Force Base (NASA)
**NVAL**........ Not Available
**NValHi**...... Columbia County Historical Library, Valatie, NY [*Library symbol*] [*Library of Congress*] (LCLS)
**NValhM** .... Westchester Medical Center, Valhalla, NY [*Library symbol*] [*Library of Congress*] (LCLS)
**NValhW** .... Westchester Community College, Valhalla, NY [*Library symbol*] [*Library of Congress*] (LCLS)
**NVAN**........ Non-Violent Anarchist Network (EA)
**Nv-Ar**......... Nevada State Library, Division of State Archives, Carson City, NV [*Library symbol*] [*Library of Congress*] (LCLS)
**NVARA**..... Naval Architect [*A publication*]
**NVAS** ........ Night Vision Attack System
**NVAS** ........ North Vietnamese Army Suspect
**NVASD** ..... Night Vision Aerial Surveillance Device
**NVASS**...... Night Vision Airborne Surveillance System
**NVATA** ..... National Vocational Agricultural Teachers' Association (EA)
**NVB**........... National Volunteer Brigade [*South African equivalent of the British Home Guard*]
**NVB**........... Navigational Base (KSC)
**NVB**........... Nederlandse Volksbeweging [*Dutch People's Movement*] [*Political party*] (PPE)
**NVB**........... Night Vision Binocular
**NVB**........... Noise and Vibration Bulletin [*A publication*]
**NVBA**........ National Veteran Boxers Association (EA)
**NvBc**.......... Boulder City Library, Boulder City, NV [*Library symbol*] [*Library of Congress*] (LCLS)
**NVBC**........ Napa Valley Bancorp [*Napa, CA*] [*NASDAQ symbol*] (NQ)
**NvBcBM**.... United States Bureau of Mines, Boulder City Metallurgy Research Laboratories, Boulder City, NV [*Library symbol*] [*Library of Congress*] (LCLS)
**NvBcER**..... United States Energy Research and Development Administration, Boulder City Metallurgy Research Laboratories, Boulder City, NV [*Library symbol*] [*Library of Congress*] (LCLS)
**NVBF**......... Nordisk Vetenskapliga Bibliotekarie-Forbundet [*Scandinavian Federation of Research Librarians*] (EA)
**NvBL** ......... Lehman Caves National Monument, Baker, NV [*Library symbol*] [*Library of Congress*] (LCLS)
**NVC**........... Narodopisny Vestnik Ceskoslovensky [*A publication*]
**NVC**........... National Victim Center (EA)
**NVC**........... National Victims of Crime (EA)
**NVC**........... National Video Clearinghouse [*Commercial firm*] (EA)

**NVC**.......... National Video Corporation
**NVC**.......... National Volunteer Center (EA)
**NVC**.......... Nonverbal Communication (ADA)
**NVC**.......... Noverco, Inc. [*Toronto Stock Exchange symbol*]
**NvC**.......... Ormsby Public Library, Carson City, NV [*Library symbol*] [*Library of Congress*] (LCLS)
**NVCA**........ National Valentine Collectors' Association (EA)
**NVCA**........ National Van Conversion Association (EA)
**NVCA**........ National Venture Capital Association [*Arlington, VA*] (EA)
**NVCC**........ Northern Virginia Community College
**NVCF**........ National Victims of Crime Foundation (EA)
**NVCH**........ National Volunteer Clearinghouse for the Homeless (EA)
**NVCO**........ Nodaway Valley Company [*Clarinda, IA*] [*NASDAQ symbol*] (NQ)
**NVCR**........ NovaCare [*NASDAQ symbol*] (NQ)
**NVCT**........ Nonverbal Classification Test
**NVCZ**........ N-Vinylcarbazole [*Organic chemistry*]
**NVD**.......... Nausea, Vomiting, Diarrhea [*Medicine*]
**NVD**.......... Neck Vein Distention [*Medicine*]
**NVD**.......... Nevada, MO [*Location identifier*] [*FAA*] (FAAL)
**NVD**.......... Night Vision Device [*Optics*]
**NVD**.......... No Value Declared [*Business term*] (DCTA)
**NVD**.......... North Vancouver District Public Library [*UTLAS symbol*]
**NVDA**........ National Vitamin Distributors Association (EA)
**NvE**.......... Elko County Library, Elko, NV [*Library symbol*] [*Library of Congress*] (LCLS)
**NVE**.......... Naamloze Vennootschap [*A publication*]
**NVE**.......... Native Valve Endocarditis [*Medicine*]
**NVE**.......... Night Vision Equipment (MCD)
**NVE**.......... Nonviolent Erotica [*Video classification*] [*Australia*]
**NVE**.......... Nonvisual Eyepiece
**NVe**.......... Vestal Public Library, Vestal, NY [*Library symbol*] [*Library of Congress*] (LCLS)
**NVEF**........ National Vocational Educational Foundation (EA)
**NVeGS**....... Church of Jesus Christ of Latter-Day Saints, Genealogical Society Library, Ithaca Branch, Vestal, NY [*Library symbol*] [*Library of Congress*] (LCLS)
**NvEHi**........ Northeastern Nevada Historical Society, Elko, NV [*Library symbol*] [*Library of Congress*] (LCLS)
**NvElGS**..... Church of Jesus Christ of Latter-Day Saints, Genealogical Society Library, Ely Branch, Ely, NV [*Library symbol*] [*Library of Congress*] (LCLS)
**NVEOC**..... Night Vision and Electro-Optics Center [*Fort Belvoir, VA*] [*US Army Communications-Electronics Command*] (RDA)
**NV & EOL**... Night Vision and Electro-Optics Laboratory [*Army*] (RDA)
**NVEOL**..... Night Vision and Electro-Optics Laboratory [*Army*] (GRD)
**NVEPDC**... National Vocational Educational Professional Development Consortium [*Later, NVEPDF*] (EA)
**NVEPDF**... National Vocational Educational Professional Development Foundation [*Later, NVEF*] (EA)
**NVet**.......... Nova et Vetera [*Fribourg*] [*A publication*]
**NVEX**........ Nevex Gold Co., Inc. [*Bellevue, WA*] [*NASDAQ symbol*] (NQ)
**NVF**.......... National Vitamin Foundation (EA)
**NVF**.......... National Vitiligo Foundation (EA)
**NVF**.......... Nordisk Vejteknisk Forbund [*Nordic Association of Road and Traffic Engineering*] (EAIO)
**NVFAAB**... National Vitamin Foundation. Annual Report [*A publication*]
**NVFC**........ National Volunteer Fire Council (EA)
**NvFGS**....... Church of Jesus Christ of Latter-Day Saints, Genealogical Society Library, Fallon Branch, Fallon, NV [*Library symbol*] [*Library of Congress*] (LCLS)
**NVG**.......... National Trust Co. [*Toronto Stock Exchange symbol*]
**NVG**.......... Neoviridogrisein [*Antibacterial*]
**NVG**.......... Night Vision Goggles
**NVGA**........ National Vocational Guidance Association (EA)
**NVGGA**..... Napa Valley Grape Growers Association (EA)
**NVGI**......... National Voluntary Groups Institute (EA)
**NvGM**........ Mormon Station State Park, Genoa, NV [*Library symbol*] [*Library of Congress*] (LCLS)
**NvH**.......... Henderson District Public Library, Henderson, NV [*Library symbol*] [*Library of Congress*] (LCLS)
**NVH**.......... Nitrogen Vent Header [*Nuclear energy*] (NRCH)
**NVH**.......... Noise, Vibration, Harshness [*Automotive technology*]
**NVH**.......... NV Homes Ltd. [*AMEX symbol*] (SPSG)
**NVHA**........ National Voluntary Health Agencies (EA)
**NvHi**.......... Nevada State Historical Society, Reno, NV [*Library symbol*] [*Library of Congress*] (LCLS)
**NVHS**........ Norske Videnskaps-Akademi i Oslo. Hvalradets Skrifter [*A publication*]
**NvHV-A**.... United States Veterans Administration Hospital, Ambulatory Care Service, Henderson, NV [*Library symbol*] [*Library of Congress*] (LCLS)
**NVI**.......... Normalized Vegetation Index [*Meteorology*]
**NVID**........ Network Video, Inc. [*Sarasota, FL*] [*NASDAQ symbol*] (NQ)
**NVII**......... Navy Vocational Interest Inventory (NVT)
**NVIS**......... National Video, Inc. [*Portland, OR*] [*NASDAQ symbol*] (NQ)
**NVIS**......... Nearly Vertical Incident Skywave [*Propagation model*] (MCD)
**NVK**.......... Koeltechniek/Klimaatregeling [*A publication*]
**NVK**.......... Milton, FL [*Location identifier*] [*FAA*] (FAAL)
**NVK**.......... Narvik [*Norway*] [*Airport symbol*] (OAG)
**NvL**.......... Las Vegas Public Library, Las Vegas, NV [*Library symbol*] [*Library of Congress*] (LCLS)
**NVL**.......... National Volleyball League [*Australia*]
**NVL**.......... Night Vision Laboratory [*Army*]
**NVL**.......... Novolazarevskaya [*Antarctica*] [*Seismograph station code, US Geological Survey*] (SEIS)
**NVL**.......... Novolazarevskaya [*Antarctica*] [*Geomagnetic observatory code*]
**NVLA**........ National Vehicle Leasing Association (EA)
**NVLA**........ National Viewers' and Listeners' Association [*British*]
**NVLAP**...... National Voluntary Laboratory Accreditation Program [*National Institute of Standards and Technology*] [*Gaithersburg, MD*]
**NvLBM**..... Basic Magnesium, Inc., Las Vegas, NV [*Library symbol*] [*Library of Congress*] [*Obsolete*] (LCLS)
**NvLC**......... Clark County Library, Las Vegas, NV [*Library symbol*] [*Library of Congress*] (LCLS)
**NVLC**........ National Veterans Law Center [*Defunct*] (EA)
**NvLGS**....... Church of Jesus Christ of Latter-Day Saints, Genealogical Society Library, Las Vegas Branch, Las Vegas, NV [*Library symbol*] [*Library of Congress*] (LCLS)
**NvLN**......... University of Nevada, Las Vegas, NV [*Library symbol*] [*Library of Congress*] (LCLS)
**NVLS**......... Novellus Systems, Inc. [*NASDAQ symbol*] (CTT)
**NVLSA**...... Nauchni Trudove. Vissh Lesotekhnicheski Institut (Sofia) [*A publication*]
**NVM**.......... National Voter Mobilization (EA)
**NVM**.......... Nativity of the Virgin Mary
**NVM**.......... Nonvolatile Matter
**NVM**.......... Nova Marketing Ltd. [*Vancouver Stock Exchange symbol*]
**NVMA**....... Noise and Vibration Monitor Analyzer [*Military*] (CAAL)
**NvMcK**...... Kinnear Public Library, McGill, NV [*Library symbol*] [*Library of Congress*] (LCLS)
**NvMiD**....... Douglas County Library, Minden, NV [*Library symbol*] [*Library of Congress*] (LCLS)
**NVMS**........ Night Visibility Measuring Set
**NvMus**....... Nevada State Museum, Capital Complex, Carson City, NV [*Library symbol*] [*Library of Congress*] (LCLS)
**NVN**.......... Nirvana Industries Ltd. [*Vancouver Stock Exchange symbol*]
**NVN**.......... North Vietnam
**NVN**.......... Noun-Verb-Noun [*Education of the hearing-impaired*]
**NVNAF**..... North Vietnamese Air Force
**NVNN**....... North Vietnamese Navy
**NvNolC**...... Clark County Community College, North Las Vegas, NV [*Library symbol*] [*Library of Congress*] (LCLS)
**NVNTA**..... Night Vision Net Technical Assessment (MCD)
**NVO**.......... Nevada Operations Office [*Department of Energy*] (MCD)
**NVO**.......... Nonverbal Operation
**NVO**.......... Nonvessel Operator [*Shipping*]
**NVO**.......... Nonvolatile Organic [*Residue of thermal processing*]
**NVO**.......... Novo Nordisk A/S ADR [*NYSE symbol*] (SPSG)
**NVOAD**...... National Voluntary Organizations Active in Disaster (EA)
**NVOC**........ Nonvessel-Owning Carrier [*Shipping*] (DS)
**NVOCC**..... Nonvessel Operating Common Carrier [*Shipping*]
**NVOCC**..... Nonvessel-Owning Common Carrier [*Shipping*] (DS)
**NVOI**......... National Voice of Iran [*Clandestine, Soviet-backed radio station*]
**NVOILA**.... National Voluntary Organizations for Independent Living for the Aging (EA)
**NVOO**........ Nevada Operations Office [*Department of Energy*]
**NVOP**........ National Veteran's Outreach Program (EA)
**NVORDCH**... Naval Ordnance Chart
**NVP**.......... Nevada Power Co. [*NYSE symbol*] (SPSG)
**NVPA**........ National Visual Presentation Association (EA)
**NVPO**........ Nuclear Vehicle Projects Office [*NASA*]
**NVPOWG**... NASA [*National Aeronautics and Space Administration*]/ VAFB [*Vandenberg Air Force Base*] Payload Operations Working Group (NASA)
**NVPP**........ National Vehicle Population Profile
**NVP-U**....... Nationale Volkspartij - Unie [*National United People's Party*] [*Netherlands Antilles*] [*Political party*] (PPW)
**NVQ**.......... National Vocation Qualification [*British*]
**NVR**.......... Naval Vessel Register (MCD)
**NVR**.......... No Verification Required (NASA)
**NVR**.......... No Voltage Release [*Electronics*]
**NVR**.......... Nonvolatile Residue (NASA)
**NVR**.......... Norfolk Volunteer Regiment [*British military*] (DMA)
**NVR**.......... NVR Limited Partnership [*AMEX symbol*] (SPSG)
**NVRAM**.... Nonvolatile Random-Access Memory [*Data processing*]
**NvREr**........ United States Energy Research Development Administration, Reno, NV [*Library symbol*] [*Library of Congress*] (LCLS)
**NvRFM**..... Grand Lodge of the Free and Accepted Masons of the State of Nevada, Reno, NV [*Library symbol*] [*Library of Congress*] (LCLS)
**NvRGS**....... Church of Jesus Christ of Latter-Day Saints, Genealogical Society Library, Reno Branch, Reno, NV [*Library symbol*] [*Library of Congress*] (LCLS)
**NvRH**......... Harrah's Automobile Collection and Pony Express Museum, Reno, NV [*Library symbol*] [*Library of Congress*] (LCLS)
**NvRNC**...... National College of the State Judiciary, Law Library, Reno, NV [*Library symbol*] [*Library of Congress*] (LCLS)

**NVROB**..... Nouvelle Revue d'Optique [*A publication*]
**NVRS**........ National Vegetable Research Station [*Research center*] [*British*] (IRC)
**NVRS**........ Night Vision Reconnaissance System
**NVRS**........ Numerical Value Rating System [*Navy*]
**NvRW**........ Washoe County Library, Reno, NV [*Library symbol*] [*Library of Congress*] (LCLS)
**NvRWL**..... Washoe County Law Library, Reno, NV [*Library symbol*] [*Library of Congress*] (LCLS)
**NVs**............ Henry Waldinger Memorial Library, Valley Stream, NY [*Library symbol*] [*Library of Congress*] (LCLS)
**NVS**........... Narrowband Voice Security
**NVS**........... Neurological Vital Signs [*Medicine*]
**NVS**........... Neutron Velocity Selector
**NVS**........... Night Vision System
**NVS**........... Nonvoting Stock [*Investment term*]
**NVS**........... Novosibirsk [*USSR*] [*Seismograph station code, US Geological Survey*] (SEIS)
**NVS**........... Novosibirsk [*USSR*] [*Geomagnetic observatory code*]
**NVS**........... Southeastern Baptist Theological Seminary, Wake Forest, NC [*OCLC symbol*] (OCLC)
**NVSA**........ Ablow [*Vanuatu*] [*ICAO location identifier*] (ICLI)
**NVSA**........ Natuurbestuurvereniging van Suidelike Afrika [*Southern African Wildlife Management Association - SAWMA*] [*Pretoria, South Africa*] (EAIO)
**NVSA**........ Nematologiese Vereniging van Suidelike Afrika [*Nematological Society of Southern Africa*] (EAIO)
**NVSC**......... Sola [*Vanuatu*] [*ICAO location identifier*] (ICLI)
**NVsCSH**.... Central Senior High School, Valley Stream, NY [*Library symbol*] [*Library of Congress*] (LCLS)
**NVSD**........ Lo-Linua [*Vanuatu*] [*ICAO location identifier*] (ICLI)
**NVSD**........ National Vital Statistics Division [*Obsolete*] [*National Center for Health Statistics*]
**NVSD**........ Night Vision System Development [*Military*]
**NVsDE**...... Devet Elementary School, Valley Stream, NY [*Library symbol*] [*Library of Congress*] (LCLS)
**NVSE**......... Emae [*Vanuatu*] [*ICAO location identifier*] (ICLI)
**NVSF**......... Graig Cove [*Vanuatu*] [*ICAO location identifier*] (ICLI)
**NVsFE**....... Forest Elementary School, Valley Stream, NY [*Library symbol*] [*Library of Congress*] (LCLS)
**NVsFH**...... Franklin General Hospital, Valley Stream, NY [*Library symbol*] [*Library of Congress*] (LCLS)
**NVSG**........ Longana [*Vanuatu*] [*ICAO location identifier*] (ICLI)
**NVSH**........ Nonvocal Severely Handicapped
**NVSH**........ Sara [*Vanuatu*] [*ICAO location identifier*] (ICLI)
**NVSI**.......... National Vision Services, Incorporated [*Phoenix, AZ*] [*NASDAQ symbol*] (NQ)
**NVSL**......... Lamap [*Vanuatu*] [*ICAO location identifier*] (ICLI)
**NVSL**......... National Veterinary Services Laboratory [*Department of Agriculture*] [*Ames, IA*] (GRD)
**NVSM**....... Lamen-Bay [*Vanuatu*] [*ICAO location identifier*] (ICLI)
**NVSM**....... Nonvolatile Semiconductor Memory (MCD)
**NVsMJH**.. Memorial Junior High School, Valley Stream, NY [*Library symbol*] [*Library of Congress*] (LCLS)
**NVSN**........ Maewo-Naone [*Vanuatu*] [*ICAO location identifier*] (ICLI)
**NVS Nuus**... Nasionale Versnellersentrum Nuus [*A publication*]
**NVSO**........ Lonorore [*Vanuatu*] [*ICAO location identifier*] (ICLI)
**N-VSOS**.... Non-Verbal Scale of Suffering [*Personality development test*] [*Psychology*]
**NVSP**......... Norsup [*Vanuatu*] [*ICAO location identifier*] (ICLI)
**NVSR**........ Redcliff [*Vanuatu*] [*ICAO location identifier*] (ICLI)
**NVSS**......... Nonvolatile Suspended Solids [*Environmental chemistry*]
**NVSS**......... Normal-Variant Short Stature [*Medicine*]
**NVSS**......... Santo/Pekoa [*Vanuatu*] [*ICAO location identifier*] (ICLI)
**NVsSSH**.... South Senior High School, Valley Stream, NY [*Library symbol*] [*Library of Congress*] (LCLS)
**NVST**......... Tongoa [*Vanuatu*] [*ICAO location identifier*] (ICLI)
**NVSU**........ Ulei [*Vanuatu*] [*ICAO location identifier*] (ICLI)
**NVSV**........ Valesdir [*Vanuatu*] [*ICAO location identifier*] (ICLI)
**NVSW**....... Walaha [*Vanuatu*] [*ICAO location identifier*] (ICLI)
**NVsWE**..... Willow Elementary School, Valley Stream, NY [*Library symbol*] [*Library of Congress*] (LCLS)
**NVsWhE**... Wheeler Elementary School, Valley Stream, NY [*Library symbol*] [*Library of Congress*] (LCLS)
**NVSX**........ South West Bay [*Vanuatu*] [*ICAO location identifier*] (ICLI)
**NVSZ**......... North West Santo [*Vanuatu*] [*ICAO location identifier*] (ICLI)
**NVT**........... Navegantes [*Brazil*] [*Airport symbol*] (OAG)
**NVT**........... Nelson Vending Technology Ltd. [*Toronto Stock Exchange symbol*]
**NVT**........... Network Virtual Terminal
**NVT**........... Nieuw Vlaams Tijdschrift [*A publication*]
**NVT**........... Norton Villiers Triumph [*Automobile manufacturer*] [*British*]
**NvT**............ Novum Testamentum [*Leiden*] [*A publication*]
**NVT**........... Nuisance Valve Tactics
**NVTG**........ Norton Villiers Triumph Group [*Automobile manufacturer*] [*British*]
**NVTHLSS**... Nevertheless (ROG)
**NV-THS**.... National Vocational-Technical Honor Society (EA)
**NVTOC**..... Nonvolatile Total Organic Carbon [*Environmental chemistry*]
**NVTS**......... National Vocational Training Service
**NVTS**......... Null Voltage Test Set (MCD)
**NVTWUGBI**... National Vehicular Traffic Workers' Union of Great Britain and Ireland
**nvu**............. Nevada [*MARC country of publication code*] [*Library of Congress*] (LCCP)
**NvU**............ University of Nevada, Reno, NV [*Library symbol*] [*Library of Congress*] (LCLS)
**NVV**........... Recreatie [*A publication*]
**NVVA**........ Anatom [*Vanuatu*] [*ICAO location identifier*] (ICLI)
**NVVA**........ Napa Valley Vintners Association (EA)
**NVVB**........ Aniwa [*Vanuatu*] [*ICAO location identifier*] (ICLI)
**NVVC**........ National Vietnam Veterans Coalition (EA)
**NVVCCG**.. North Vietnamese and Viet Cong Collecting Group (EA)
**NVVD**........ Dillon's Bay [*Vanuatu*] [*ICAO location identifier*] (ICLI)
**NVVF**........ Futuna [*Vanuatu*] [*ICAO location identifier*] (ICLI)
**NVVI**......... Ipota [*Vanuatu*] [*ICAO location identifier*] (ICLI)
**NVVJ**......... Forari [*Vanuatu*] [*ICAO location identifier*] (ICLI)
**NVVK**........ Lenakel [*Vanuatu*] [*ICAO location identifier*] (ICLI)
**NVVQ**........ Quoin Hill [*Vanuatu*] [*ICAO location identifier*] (ICLI)
**NVVV**........ Port-Vila/Bauerfield [*Vanuatu*] [*ICAO location identifier*] (ICLI)
**NVWA**....... National Volkswagen Association (EA)
**NVWLA**.... Napa Valley Wine Library Association (EA)
**NVX**.......... North American Vaccine [*NYSE symbol*] (SPSG)
**NW**........... Naked Weight
**nW**............ Nanowatt
**NW**........... Narrow Widths [*Construction*]
**NW**........... NASA Waiver (KSC)
**NW**........... Nat-War Alliance (EA)
**NW**........... National Westminster ADS [*NYSE symbol*] (SPSG)
**NW**........... National Women's Conference Committee [*Formerly, CCNWC*] (EA)
**NW**........... Naval Air Systems Command
**NW**........... Net Weight
**NW**........... Net Worth
**NW**........... Network (NASA)
**NW**........... Network Cells [*Botany*]
**NW**........... Neue Weg [*A publication*]
**NW**........... Neue Welt [*A publication*]
**NW**........... Neville and Winther's Acid
**NW**........... New
**NW**........... New Wave [*Style of music*]
**NW**........... New World [*Translation of the Holy Scriptures*] [*A publication*] (BJA)
**NW**........... New Worlds [*A publication*]
**Nw**............ Newsweek [*A publication*]
**NW**........... No Wait [*Industrial engineering*]
**NW**........... No Wind [*Air*] Position [*Navigation*]
**NW**........... Nominal Width (NATG)
**NW**........... Nor-Weberine [*Biochemistry*]
**N & W**........ Norfolk & Western Railway Co.
**NW**........... Norfolk & Western Railway Co. [*AAR code*]
**NW**........... Normal Waste [*Nuclear energy*] (NRCH)
**NW**........... North Wales
**NW**........... North-Western Provinces, High Court Reports [*India*] [*A publication*] (DLA)
**NW**........... North Western Reporter [*National Reporter System*] [*A publication*] (DLA)
**NW**........... Northwest
**NW**........... Northwest Orient Airlines, Inc. [*ICAO designator*]
**NW**........... Northwestern Reporter [*A publication*] (DLA)
**NW**........... Nose Wheel [*Aviation*] (MCD)
**NW**........... Now
**NW**........... Nuclear Warfare
**NW**........... Nuclear Weapon (NG)
**NW**........... Nucleonics Week [*A publication*]
**nw----**........ West Indies [*MARC geographic area code*] [*Library of Congress*] (LCCP)
**NW2**.......... New River [*California*] [*Seismograph station code, US Geological Survey*] (SEIS)
**NWA**.......... Moheli [*Comoro Islands*] [*Airport symbol*] (OAG)
**NWA**.......... Narrogin [*Australia*] [*Seismograph station code, US Geological Survey*] (SEIS)
**NWA**.......... National Water Alliance (EA)
**NWA**.......... National Water Well Association, Worthington, OH [*OCLC symbol*] (OCLC)
**NWA**.......... National Waterfowl Alliance, Waterfowl USA [*Later, WUSA*] (EA)
**NWA**.......... National Weather Association (EA)
**NWA**.......... National Welders Association [*A union*] [*British*]
**NWA**.......... National Wellness Association (EA)
**NWA**.......... National Wine Association (EA)
**NWA**.......... Naval Warfare Analysis (MCD)
**NWA**.......... Naval Weapons Annex
**NWA**.......... Navy Wifeline Association (EA)
**NWA**.......... New Work Authorized (MCD)
**NWA**.......... New World Alliance (EA)
**NWA**.......... New Worlds Science Fiction [*A publication*]
**NWA**.......... Nieuw Europa. Tijdschrift van de Europese Beweging in Nederland [*A publication*]
**NWA**.......... Niggers with Attitude [*Rap recording group*]
**NWA**.......... Northumbrian Water Authority [*British*] (DCTA)

**NWA**.......... Norwich Winterthur Australia
**NWA**.......... Nothin' Worth Askin' [*Rap recording group*]
**NWA**.......... NWA, Inc. [*NYSE symbol*] (SPSG)
**NWAA**....... National Wheelchair Athletic Association (EA)
**NWAA**....... National Women's Automotive Association (EA)
**NWAAF**.... Northwest African Air Forces [*World War II*]
**NWAB**....... Necks with Any Boy [*Slang*]
**NWAC**....... National Weather Analysis Center [*Air Force, Navy*]
**NWAC**....... National Wheelchair Athletic Committee
**NWAC**....... Native Women's Association of Canada
**NWAC**....... Native Women's Association of Canada. Newsletter [*A publication*]
**NWadd**...... Hepburn Library, Waddington, NY [*Library symbol*] [*Library of Congress*] (LCLS)
**NWAFC**.... Northwest and Alaska Fisheries Center [*Department of Commerce*] [*National Marine Fisheries Service*] [*Research center*] (RCD)
**NWAG**....... Naval Warfare Analysis Group
**NWAHACA**... National Warm Air Heating and Air Conditioning Association [*Later, ACCA*] (EA)
**NWAI**........ Nuclear Weapons Acceptance Inspection (NG)
**NWAIAH**... New South Wales. Department of Agriculture. Division of Science Services. Entomology Branch. Insect Pest Survey. Annual Report [*A publication*]
**NWAIB**..... Nuclear Weapon Accident Investigation Board (AABC)
**NWald**....... Josephine-Louise Public Library, Walden, NY [*Library symbol*] [*Library of Congress*] (LCLS)
**NWall**........ Wallkill Public Library, Wallkill, NY [*Library symbol*] [*Library of Congress*] (LCLS)
**NWAN**...... Native Women's Association of the NWT [*Northwest Territories, Canada*]. Newsletter [*A publication*]
**NWan**........ Wantagh Public Library, Wantagh, NY [*Library symbol*] [*Library of Congress*] (LCLS)
**NWanE**...... Wantagh Elementary School, Wantagh, NY [*Library symbol*] [*Library of Congress*] (LCLS)
**NWanFLE**... Forest Lake Elementary School, Wantagh, NY [*Library symbol*] [*Library of Congress*] (LCLS)
**NWanJS**.... Wantagh Junior-Senior High, Wantagh, NY [*Library symbol*] [*Library of Congress*] (LCLS)
**NWanME**... Mandalay Elementary School, Wantagh, NY [*Library symbol*] [*Library of Congress*] (LCLS)
**NWanSPE**... Sunrise Park Elementary School, Wantagh, NY [*Library symbol*] [*Library of Congress*] (LCLS)
**NWAO**...... Narrogin [*Australia*] [*Seismograph station code, US Geological Survey*] (SEIS)
**NWAP**....... National White American Party (BJA)
**NWAPP**..... National Woman Abuse Prevention Project (EA)
**nwaq---**....... Antigua [*MARC geographic area code*] [*Library of Congress*] (LCCP)
**NWAR**....... New Air Flight, Inc. [*NASDAQ symbol*] (NQ)
**N War Coll**... Naval War College [*A publication*]
**NWas**......... Moffat Library Association, Washingtonville, NY [*Library symbol*] [*Library of Congress*] (LCLS)
**NWatfG**..... General Electric Co., Silicone Products Department, Waterford, NY [*Library symbol*] [*Library of Congress*] (LCLS)
**NWatt**........ Roswell P. Flower Memorial Public Library, Watertown, NY [*Library symbol*] [*Library of Congress*] (LCLS)
**NWattJ**...... Jefferson Community College, Watertown, NY [*Library symbol*] [*Library of Congress*] (LCLS)
**NWattJHi**... Jefferson County Historical Society, Watertown, NY [*Library symbol*] [*Library of Congress*] (LCLS)
**NWattKH**... Samaritan Keep Nursing Home, Medical Library, Watertown, NY [*Library symbol*] [*Library of Congress*] (LCLS)
**NWattMH**... Mercy Hospital of Watertown, Watertown, NY [*Library symbol*] [*Library of Congress*] (LCLS)
**NWattN**..... North Country Library System, Watertown, NY [*Library symbol*] [*Library of Congress*] (LCLS)
**NWatvlA**... Watervliet Arsenal Library, Watervliet, NY [*Library symbol*] [*Library of Congress*] (LCLS)
**NWAVL**.... Now Available (NOAA)
**NWAY**....... Norway [*A publication*]
**NWB**.......... National Wiring Bureau [*Defunct*] (EA)
**NWB**.......... Naval Weapons Bulletin
**NWB**.......... New Books and Periodicals [*A publication*]
**NWB**.......... New War Department Building [*Obsolete*]
**NWB**.......... New Worlds (British) [*A publication*]
**NWB**.......... Niedergeschwindigkeitswindkanal Braunschweig [*Federal Republic of Germany*]
**NWB**.......... Nonweightbearing
**NWB**.......... Northwest Towboat Tariff Bureau, Inc., Seattle WA [*STAC*]
**NWBA**....... National Wheelchair Basketball Association (EA)
**nwbb---**....... Barbados [*MARC geographic area code*] [*Library of Congress*] (LCCP)
**NWBB**....... Noumea [*New Caledonia*] [*ICAO location identifier*] (ICLI)
**nwbc---**....... Barbuda [*MARC geographic area code*] [*Library of Congress*] (LCCP)
**NWbC**........ Cardion Electronics, Woodbury, NY [*Library symbol*] [*Library of Congress*] (LCLS)
**NWBC**....... National Wooden Box Council [*Later, NWPCA*] (EA)
**nwbf---**........ Bahamas [*MARC geographic area code*] [*Library of Congress*] (LCCP)
**NWBHI**..... Nuclear Weapon Burst Height Indicator
**NWbN**....... Northwest by North
**NWBW**...... National Women Bowling Writers Association (EA)
**NWbW**...... Northwest by West
**NWbW**...... Waldemar Medical Research Foundation, Woodbury, NY [*Library symbol*] [*Library of Congress*] (LCLS)
**NWC**.......... National Waco Club (EA)
**NWC**.......... National Wage Case [*Australia*]
**NWC**.......... National War College [*Later, UND*] [*DoD*]
**NWC**.......... National Warning Center [*Civil Defense*]
**NWC**.......... National Water Center (EA)
**NWC**.......... National Water Commission [*Terminated, 1973*]
**NWC**.......... National Water Council [*British*] (DCTA)
**NWC**.......... National Waterfowl Council (EA)
**NWC**.......... National Watershed Congress (EA)
**NWC**.......... National Waterways Conference (EA)
**NWC**.......... National Wiretap Commission [*Department of Justice*]
**NWC**.......... National Women's Coalition (EA)
**NWC**.......... National Woodie Club (EA)
**NWC**.......... National Writers Club (EA)
**NWC**.......... Naval War College
**NWC**.......... Naval Weapons Center
**NWC**.......... Net Working Capital
**NWC**.......... New World Club (EA)
**NWC**.......... New World Coalition (EA)
**NWC**.......... North West Community College Library [*UTLAS symbol*]
**NWC**.......... Northwest Cape
**NWC**.......... Northwest College [*Washington*]
**NWC**.......... Nuclear War Capability (AAG)
**NWC**.......... Wingate College, Wingate, NC [*OCLC symbol*] (OCLC)
**NWCA**....... National Water Carriers Association
**NWCA**....... National Woodcarvers Association (EA)
**NWCA**....... National Wrestling Coaches Association (EA)
**NWCA**....... Navy Wives Clubs of America (EA)
**NWCA**....... Northwest Cherry Briners Association
**NWCAA**.... National War College Alumni Association
**NWCAEU**... National Women's Conference of the American Ethical Union (EA)
**NWCC**....... National Water Company Conference [*Later, NAWC*]
**NWCC**....... National Women's Conference Committee (EA)
**NWCC**....... National Women's Consultative Council of Australia
**NWCC**....... Neutron Well Coincidence Counter [*Nuclear energy*] (NRCH)
**NWCC**....... Northwest Christian College [*Oregon*]
**NWCC**....... Noumea/La Tontouta [*New Caledonia*] [*ICAO location identifier*] (ICLI)
**NWCCA**.... Naval Weapons Center, Corona Annex [*California*]
**NWCCL**.... Naval Weapons Center, Corona Laboratories [*California*]
**NWCCS**..... Naval Worldwide Command and Control System (MCD)
**NWCDC**.... North West Cooperative Development Council [*British*]
**NWCG**...... Nuclear Weapons Coordinating Group
**NWCIEP**... Nation-Wide Committee on Import-Export Policy [*Defunct*] (EA)
**nwcj---**........ Cayman Islands [*MARC geographic area code*] [*Library of Congress*] (LCCP)
**NWCME**... National Winter Convention on Military Electronics [*IEEE*] (MCD)
**nwco---**....... Curacao Group [*MARC geographic area code*] [*Library of Congress*] (LCCP)
**NWCP**....... National Wetlands Conservation Project [*Defunct*] (EA)
**NWCR**....... Nuclear Weapons Correction Report [*Army*] (AABC)
**NWCRB**.... Navy War Contracts Relief Board
**NWCS**....... NATO-Wide Communications System (NATG)
**NWCS**....... Nuclear Weapons Control System
**nwcu**........... Cuba [*MARC geographic area code*] [*Library of Congress*] (LCCP)
**NWD**......... Naval Weapons Directory
**NWD**......... Network Wide Directory
**NWD**......... New World Dictionary [*A publication*]
**NWD**......... Northwest Drug Co. Ltd. [*Toronto Stock Exchange symbol*]
**NWD**......... Number of Words (MSA)
**NW 2d**....... North Western Reporter, Second Series [*A publication*] (DLA)
**NWDA**....... National Wholesale Druggists' Association (EA)
**NWDA**....... National Wine Distributors' Association (EA)
**N4WDA**..... National 4 Wheel Drive Association (EA)
**NWDC**....... Northwest Drama Conference (EA)
**NWDC/S**... Navigation/Weapons Delivery Computer/System
**NWDEN**.... Number of Words per Entry (MSA)
**NWDGA**.... National Wholesale Dry Goods Association [*Later, NATAD*]
**nwdq---**....... Dominica [*MARC geographic area code*] [*Library of Congress*] (LCCP)
**nwdr---**....... Dominican Republic [*MARC geographic area code*] [*Library of Congress*] (LCCP)
**NWDS**....... National Water Data System [*US Geological Survey*] [*Reston, VA*]
**NWDS**....... Navigation/Weapons Delivery System
**NWDS**....... Noah Worcester Dermatological Society (EA)
**NWDS**....... Number of Words
**NWDSEN**... Number of Words per Entry
**NWE**.......... New World Entertainment Ltd. [*AMEX symbol*] (SPSG)
**NWE**.......... Newline Resources Ltd. [*Vancouver Stock Exchange symbol*]
**NWE**.......... Nuclear Weapons Effects

**NWe**.......... Westbury Memorial Public Library, Westbury, NY [*Library symbol*] [*Library of Congress*] (LCLS)
**NWEA**....... National Women's Economic Alliance [*Washington, DC*] (EA)
**NWEA**....... National Wood Energy Association (EA)
**NWEB**....... Northwestern Electricity Board [*British*]
**NWeBE**..... Board of Cooperative Educational Services, Nassau Education Resource Center, Westbury, NY [*Library symbol*] [*Library of Congress*] (LCLS)
**NWebPH**... Pilgrim Hospital, West Brentwood, NY [*Library symbol*] [*Library of Congress*] (LCLS)
**NWEC**....... Nuclear Weapons Effects Course (MCD)
**NWED**....... Nuclear Weapon Effects Development
**NWEE**....... National Women's Employment and Education (EA)
**NWEF**....... National Women's Education Fund (EA)
**NWEF**....... Naval Weapons Evaluation Facility [*Kirtland Air Force Base, NM*]
**NWEF**....... New World Education Fund (EA)
**NWEF**....... North Western Expeditionary Force [*Norway*] [*World War II*]
**NWEF**....... Nuclear Weapons Education Fund (EA)
**NWefHi**..... Chautauqua County Historical Society, Westfield, NY [*Library symbol*] [*Library of Congress*] (LCLS)
**NWefMH**.. Westfield Memorial Hospital, Inc., Westfield, NY [*Library symbol*] [*Library of Congress*] (LCLS)
**NWehb**...... Westhampton Free Library, Westhampton Beach, NY [*Library symbol*] [*Library of Congress*] (LCLS)
**NWehbJH**... Westhampton Beach Junior High School, Westhampton Beach, NY [*Library symbol*] [*Library of Congress*] (LCLS)
**NWel**.......... David A. Howe Public Library, Wellsville, NY [*Library symbol*] [*Library of Congress*] (LCLS)
**NWEL**....... Nowsco Well Service Ltd. [*NASDAQ symbol*] (NQ)
**NWEL**....... Nuclear Weapons Effects Laboratory
**NWELA**.... New Electronics [*A publication*]
**NWelH**...... Jones Memorial Hospital, Wellsville, NY [*Library symbol*] [*Library of Congress*] (LCLS)
**NWeM**....... Metco, Inc., Westbury, NY [*Library symbol*] [*Library of Congress*] (LCLS)
**NWEN**....... Northwest Engineering Co. [*Green Bay, WI*] [*NASDAQ symbol*] (NQ)
**NWEO**....... Nuclear Weapon Effects Office [*DoD*] (RDA)
**NWEO**....... Nuclear Weapon Employment Officer (AABC)
**NWEP**....... Nuclear Weapons Effects Panel
**NWER**....... Nuclear Weapons Effects Research [*Army*]
**NWER/T**... Nuclear Weapons Effects Research and Testing [*Army*] (RDA)
**NWES**....... Norwesco, Inc. [*NASDAQ symbol*] (NQ)
**NWES**....... Nuclear Weapons Electronic Specialist (AABC)
**NWes**......... Olive Free Library Association, West Shokan, NY [*Library symbol*] [*Library of Congress*] (LCLS)
**NWESA**..... Naval Weapons Engineering Support Activity (MCD)
**NWesyM**... Suffolk Marine Museum, West Sayville, NY [*Library symbol*] [*Library of Congress*] (LCLS)
**NWET**....... Nuclear Weapon Effects Test
**nweu---**....... Sint Eustatius [*MARC geographic area code*] [*Library of Congress*] (LCCP)
**NWevNS**... West Valley Nuclear Services Co., West Valley, NY [*Library symbol*] [*Library of Congress*] (LCLS)
**NWEX**....... Northwest Explorer. Northwest Territorial Airways [*Yellowknife, NT*] [*A publication*]
**NWF**.......... International Women's Forum [*Acronym is based on former name, National Women's Forum*] (EA)
**NWF**.......... National War Formulary
**NWF**.......... National War Fund
**NWF**.......... National Wildlife Federation (EA)
**NWF**.......... Naval Weapons Factory [*Formerly, NGF*]
**NWF**.......... Naval Working Fund [*Navy, Coast Guard*]
**NWF**.......... New Wilderness Foundation (EA)
**NWF**.......... New World Foundation (EA)
**NWF**.......... Numerical Weather Facility
**NWFA**....... National Wholesale Furniture Association (EA)
**NWFA**....... National Wood Flooring Association (EA)
**NWFA**....... Northwest Farm Managers Association (EA)
**NWFA**....... Northwest Fisheries Association (EA)
**NWFC**....... Nuclear Weapons Freeze Campaign (EA)
**NWFF**....... North West Frontier Fellowship (EA)
**NWFI**........ Non-Woven Fabrics Institute [*Defunct*] (EA)
**NWFMA**... Northwest Farm Managers Association
**NWFN**....... Northwestern Financial [*NASDAQ symbol*] (NQ)
**NWFP**....... North-West Frontier Province [*Pakistan*] (PD)
**NWFP**....... Nuclear Weapons Fire Planning (MCD)
**NWFP**....... Rocky Flats/Nuclear Weapons Facilities Project [*Organization with goal of nuclear disarmament*] (EA)
**NWF Pak**... North West Frontier, Pakistan (ILCA)
**NWFSPCN**... Nahanni National Park, Parks Canada [*Parc National Nahanni, Parcs Canada*] Fort Simpson, Northwest Territories [*Library symbol*] [*National Library of Canada*] (NLC)
**NWFSPCW**... Wood Buffalo National Park, Parks Canada [*Parc National Wood Buffalo, Parcs Canada*] Fort Smith, Northwest Territories [*Library symbol*] [*National Library of Canada*] (NLC)
**NWFST**..... Thebacha College Library, Fort Smith, Northwest Territories [*Library symbol*] [*National Library of Canada*] (NLC)
**NWFWA**... Northwest Forest Workers Association (EA)
**NWFZ**....... Nuclear Weapons-Free Zone
**NWG**......... National Wire Gauge
**NWG**......... New Goliath Minerals Ltd. [*Toronto Stock Exchange symbol*] [*Vancouver Stock Exchange symbol*]
**NWG**......... Niedergeschwindigkeitswindkanal Goettingen [*Federal Republic of Germany*]
**NWG**......... North West Gold Corp. [*AMEX symbol*] (SPSG)
**nwga---**....... Greater Antilles [*MARC geographic area code*] [*Library of Congress*] (LCCP)
**NWGA**....... National Wool Growers Association [*Later, ASIA*] (EA)
**NWGA**....... Northwest Guides Association [*Defunct*]
**NWGB**....... New Writers Group Bulletin [*A publication*]
**nwgd**.......... Grenada [*MARC geographic area code*] [*Library of Congress*] (LCCP)
**NWGDE**.... Nordic Working Group on Development Education [*Nordic Council of Ministers*] [*Copenhagen, Denmark*] (EAIO)
**NWGI**........ N-W Group, Inc. [*NASDAQ symbol*] (NQ)
**nwgp---**....... Guadeloupe [*MARC geographic area code*] [*Library of Congress*] (LCCP)
**NWGP**....... Nuclear War Graphics Project [*Commercial firm*] (EA)
**NWGPA**..... Nachrichten. Gesellschaft der Wissenschaften zu Goettingen. Mathematisch-Physikalische Klasse. Fachgruppe 2. Physik, Astronomie, Geophysik, Technik [*A publication*]
**nwgs---**....... Grenadines [*MARC geographic area code*] [*Library of Congress*] (LCCP)
**NWGS**....... Naval Warfare Gaming System
**NWGWU**.. National Warehouse and General Workers' Union [*British*]
**NWH**......... Lebensmittel Praxis. Unabhangiges Fachmagazin fuer Unternehmensfuehrung, Werbung, und Verkauf im Lebensmittelhandel [*A publication*]
**NWH**......... New Hombre Resources [*Vancouver Stock Exchange symbol*]
**NWH**......... Normal Working Hours
**NWh**.......... West Hempstead Public Library, West Hempstead, NY [*Library symbol*] [*Library of Congress*] (LCLS)
**NWHA**...... National Wholesale Hardware Association (EA)
**NWHC**...... National Women's Health Coalition [*Later, IWHC*]
**NWHC**...... Naval Weapons Handling Center
**NWHF**...... National Wildlife Health Foundation (EA)
**NWHF**...... National Women's Hall of Fame (EA)
**nwhi---**........ Hispaniola [*MARC geographic area code*] [*Library of Congress*] (LCCP)
**NWHI**........ Northwestern Hawaiian Islands
**NWHL**....... National Wildlife Health Laboratory [*Department of the Interior*] (GRD)
**NWHL**....... Naval Weapons Handling Laboratory
**NWHN**...... National Women's Health Network (EA)
**NWHP**....... National Women's History Project (EA)
**NWhp**........ White Plains Public Library, White Plains, NY [*Library symbol*] [*Library of Congress*] (LCLS)
**NWhpG**..... College of White Plains, White Plains, NY [*Library symbol*] [*Library of Congress*] (LCLS)
**NWhpI**....... IBM Library Processing Center, White Plains, NY [*Library symbol*] [*Library of Congress*] (LCLS)
**NWhpNH**... New York Hospital, Westchester Division, White Plains, NY [*Library symbol*] [*Library of Congress*] (LCLS)
**NWhpSC**... New York State Supreme Court Law Library, White Plains, NY [*Library symbol*] [*Library of Congress*] (LCLS)
**NWhpTI**.... Temple Israel Library, White Plains, NY [*Library symbol*] [*Library of Congress*] (LCLS)
**NWhpW**.... Westchester Library System, White Plains, NY [*Library symbol*] [*Library of Congress*] (LCLS)
**NWHRC**.... National Women's Health Resource Center (EA)
**NWHRN**... Northwest Territories Public Library Services, Hay River, Northwest Territories [*Library symbol*] [*National Library of Canada*] (NLC)
**NWHSLC**... Northern Wisconsin Health Science Library Cooperative [*Library network*]
**nwht---**....... Haiti [*MARC geographic area code*] [*Library of Congress*] (LCCP)
**NWI**........... Netherlands West Indies
**NWI**........... Networking and World Information [*Electronic information and communications exchange service*]
**NWI**........... Nieuws uit Zweden [*A publication*]
**NWI**........... Norwich [*England*] [*Airport symbol*] (OAG)
**NWI**........... Nuinsco Resources Ltd. [*Toronto Stock Exchange symbol*]
**NWi**........... West Islip Public Library, West Islip, NY [*Library symbol*] [*Library of Congress*] (LCLS)
**NWIAC**..... Arctic College, Iqualuit, Northwest Territories [*Library symbol*] [*National Library of Canada*] (BIB)
**NWIB**........ National Westminster Investment Bank [*British*]
**NWIB**........ Northwest Illinois Bancorp, Inc. [*Freeport, IL*] [*NASDAQ symbol*] (NQ)
**NWIC**........ National Women's Insurance Center (EA)
**NWICO**..... New World Information and Communications Order [*UNESCO*]
**NWIG**........ Nieuwe West-Indische Gids [*A publication*]
**NWiH**........ Good Samaritan Hospital, West Islip, NY [*Library symbol*] [*Library of Congress*] (LCLS)

**NWII**......... Inuvik Scientific Resource Centre, Indian and Northern Affairs Canada [*Centre Scientifique de Ressources d'Inuvik, Affaires Indiennes et du Nord Canada*], Northwest Territories [*Library symbol*] [*National Library of Canada*] (NLC)
**NWIIE**....... Eastern Arctic Research Laboratory, Indian and Northern Affairs Canada [*Laboratoire de Recherches Arctique de l'Est, Affaires Indiennes et du Nord Canada*], Igloolik, Northwest Territories [*Library symbol*] [*National Library of Canada*] (BIB)
**NWilP**........ Willard Psychiatric Center, Willard, NY [*Library symbol*] [*Library of Congress*] (LCLS)
**NWils**......... Wilson Free Library, Wilson, NY [*Library symbol*] [*Library of Congress*] (LCLS)
**NWilsHi**.... Wilson Historical Society, Wilson, NY [*Library symbol*] [*Library of Congress*] (LCLS)
**NWin**......... Windham Public Library, Windham, NY [*Library symbol*] [*Library of Congress*] (LCLS)
**NWIO**........ New World Information Order [*Term coined by the Nonaligned Countries at their Fifth Summit Meeting in 1976*]
**NWIP**........ Naval Warfare Information Publication
**NWIP**........ Naval Warfare Intercept Procedures (MCD)
**NWIP**........ North Wales Independent Press
**NWIRP**...... Naval Weapons Industrial Reserve Plant (AFM)
**NWIS**......... Naval Weaponeering Information Sheet (MCD)
**NWIYRA**... North West Intercollegiate Yacht Racing Association
**NWJ**.......... New Scientist [*A publication*]
**NWJA**....... National Wholesale Jewelers Association [*Later, AJDA*] (EA)
**Nw J Intl L and Bus**... Northwestern Journal of International Law and Business [*A publication*]
**nwjm**........... Jamaica [*MARC geographic area code*] [*Library of Congress*] (LCCP)
**NWK**.......... Levensmiddelenmarkt [*A publication*]
**NWK**.......... Network Equipment Technologies, Inc. [*NYSE symbol*] (SPSG)
**NWK**.......... Newsweek [*A publication*]
**NWK**.......... Norwalk Public Library, Norwalk, CT [*OCLC symbol*] [*Inactive*] (OCLC)
**NWKLS**...... Northwest Kansas Library System [*Library network*]
**NWL**.......... National Water Lift Co. (MCD)
**NWL**.......... National Women's League of the United Synagogue of America [*Later, AWL*] (EA)
**NWL**.......... Natural Wavelength
**NWL**.......... Naval Weapons Laboratory [*Later, NSWC*]
**NWL**.......... Newell Co. [*NYSE symbol*] (SPSG)
**NWL**.......... Newline Development [*Vancouver Stock Exchange symbol*]
**NWL**.......... Normal Water Leg [*Nuclear energy*] (NRCH)
**NWL**.......... Northwestern University. Law Review [*A publication*]
**nwla---**........ Lesser Antilles [*MARC geographic area code*] [*Library of Congress*] (LCCP)
**NWLA**....... National Women and the Law Association (EA)
**NWLA**....... Northern Woods Logging Association (EA)
**NW Law Rev**... Northwestern Law Review [*A publication*] (DLA)
**NWLB**....... National War Labor Board [*World War II*]
**NWLC**....... National Women's Law Center (EA)
**NWLDYA**... National Wholesale Lumber Distributing Yard Association (EA)
**NWLF**........ National Watermen and Lightermen's Federation [*A union*] [*British*]
**NWLF**........ New World Liberation Front
**nwli---**......... Leeward Islands [*MARC geographic area code*] [*Library of Congress*] (LCCP)
**NWLI**........ National Western Life Insurance Co. [*NASDAQ symbol*] (NQ)
**NWL Rev**... North Western Law Review [*Chicago*] [*A publication*] (DLA)
**NWLS**........ Northwest Wisconsin Library System [*Library network*]
**Nw LS**........ Northwestern University. Law Review. Supplement [*A publication*]
**NWLY**....... Northwesterly [*Meteorology*] (FAAC)
**NWM**........ Morris County Free Library, Whippany, NJ [*OCLC symbol*] (OCLC)
**NWM**........ New Ways Ministry (EA)
**NWM**........ Newfields Minerals Ltd. [*Toronto Stock Exchange symbol*]
**NWM**........ United States Military Academy, West Point, NY [*Library symbol*] [*Library of Congress*] (LCLS)
**NWMA**...... National Woodwork Manufacturers Association [*Formerly, NDMA*] [*Later, NWWDA*] (EA)
**NWMA**...... Northwest Mining Association (EA)
**NWMAF**... National Women's Martial Arts Federation (EA)
**NWMC**...... National Wool Marketing Corporation (EA)
**NWMC**...... Northwest Michigan College
**NWMF**...... National Women's Music Festival (EA)
**NWMF**...... Nuclear Weapons Maintenance Foreman (AABC)
**NWMI**....... Newfields Minerals, Inc. [*NASDAQ symbol*] (NQ)
**nwmj---**....... Montserrat [*MARC geographic area code*] [*Library of Congress*] (LCCP)
**NWMKT**... Newmarket [*Urban district in England*]
**NWML**...... National Women's Mailing List (EA)
**NWMP**...... North-West Mounted Police [*Later, RCMP*] [*Canada*]
**nwmq---**...... Martinique [*MARC geographic area code*] [*Library of Congress*] (LCCP)
**NWMS**...... Nazarene World Mission Society (EA)
**NWMS**...... Nuclear Weapons Maintenance Specialist (AABC)
**NwMSCS**.. Northwest Missouri State College Studies [*A publication*]
**NWN**......... National Workers Network [*Commercial firm*] (EA)
**NWN**......... Newcan Minerals [*Vancouver Stock Exchange symbol*]
**NWN**......... Nonwhite Noise
**NWN**......... Nuclear Waste News [*Business Publishers, Inc.*] [*Information service or system*] [*No longer available online*] (CRD)
**NWN**......... NWNL Companies, Inc. [*NYSE symbol*] (SPSG)
**nwna---**....... Netherlands Antilles [*MARC geographic area code*] [*Library of Congress*] (LCCP)
**NW Newsl**... North Western Newsletter [*A publication*]
**NWNG**...... Northwest Natural Gas Co. [*NASDAQ symbol*] (NQ)
**NWNSA**.... National Women's Neckwear and Scarf Association (EA)
**NW-NW**.... No Work - No Woo [*Slogan adopted by women war workers in Albina shipyards in Portland, Oregon, who agreed not to date men who were absent from work*] [*World War II*]
**NWO**......... NASA Washington Office (KSC)
**NWO**......... New World Order [*Bush administration*]
**NWO**......... Nonwoven Oriented
**NWO**......... Nuclear Weapons Officer
**NWOA**...... National Woodland Owners Association (EA)
**NWOBHM**... New Wave of British Heavy Metal [*Rock music type, 1979-81*]
**NWOFC**.... Numerical Weather and Oceanographic Forecasting Center [*Marine science*] (MSC)
**NW Ohio Q**... Northwest Ohio Quarterly [*A publication*]
**NWOO**...... NATO Wartime Oil Organization (NATG)
**NWOQ**...... Northwest Ohio Quarterly [*A publication*]
**NWOR**....... Neworld Bancorp, Inc. [*NASDAQ symbol*] (NQ)
**NWP**.......... National Water Project [*Later, RCAP*] (EA)
**NWP**.......... National Woman's Party (EA)
**NWP**.......... National Writing Project (EA)
**NWP**.......... Nationwide Outdoor Recreation Plan [*Bureau of Outdoor Recreation*]
**NWP**.......... NATO and Warsaw Pact [*Projects*] (NATG)
**NWP**.......... Naval Warfare Procedures (MCD)
**NWP**.......... Naval Warfare Publications
**NWP**.......... Naval Weapons Plant (AAG)
**NWP**.......... Naval Weapons Publications
**NWP**.......... North-Western Provinces, High Court Reports [*India*] [*A publication*] (DLA)
**NWP**.......... Northwest Passage (ROG)
**NWP**.......... Northwest Provinces
**NWP**.......... Northwestern Pacific Railroad Co. [*AAR code*]
**NWP**.......... Nuclear Waste Project (EA)
**NWP**.......... Numerical Weather Prediction
**NWP**.......... NWP Resources [*Vancouver Stock Exchange symbol*]
**NWp**.......... Williston Park Public Library, Williston Park, NY [*Library symbol*] [*Library of Congress*] (LCLS)
**NWPA**....... Nuclear Waste Policy Act (NRCH)
**NWPAG**.... NATO Wartime Preliminary Analysis Group (NATG)
**NW Paper News**... Northwest Pulp and Paper News [*A publication*]
**NW Pasage**... Northwest Passage [*A publication*]
**NWPC**....... National Women's Political Caucus (EA)
**NWPC**....... Nordic Wood Preservation Council (EAIO)
**NWPC**....... Northwest Provinces Code [*India*] [*A publication*] (DLA)
**NWPCA**.... National Wooden Pallet and Container Association (EA)
**NWPCB**.... Naval Warfare Planning Chart Bases (MCD)
**NWPF**....... National Water Purification Foundation
**NWPH**....... Newport Pharmaceuticals International, Inc. [*NASDAQ symbol*] (NQ)
**NWPHC**.... Northwest Provinces, High Court Reports [*India*] [*A publication*] (DLA)
**NWPL**....... Naval Warfare Publications Library (NVT)
**NWPMA**... National Wooden Pallet Manufacturers Association [*Later, NWPCA*] (EA)
**NWPO**....... Northwest Pacific Oceanographers [*An association*] (NOAA)
**NWPPCA**... Auyuittuq National Park, Parks Canada [*Parc National Auyuittuq, Parcs Canada*] Pangnirtung, Northwest Territories [*Library symbol*] [*National Library of Canada*] (NLC)
**NWPPWM**... National Working Party on Portrayal of Women in the Media [*Australia*]
**NWPR**....... Northwest Prospector. Northwest Miners and Developers Bulletin [*A publication*]
**nwpr---**....... Puerto Rico [*MARC geographic area code*] [*Library of Congress*] (LCCP)
**NWPS**........ National Wilderness Preservation System
**NWPW**...... Naval Weapons Plant, Washington, DC
**NWPYA**.... Sae Mulli [*A publication*]
**NWQ**......... New Worlds. Quarterly [*A publication*]
**NWQ**......... Northwest Digital Ltd. [*Toronto Stock Exchange symbol*]
**NWQI**........ National Water Quality Inventory [*Environmental Protection Agency*]
**NWQL**....... National Water Quality Laboratory
**NWQSS**..... National Water Quality Surveillance System [*Environmental Protection Agency*] [*Dicontinued, 1981*]
**NWR**.......... Navy Weapons Requirement
**NWR**.......... Next Word Request
**NWR**.......... NOAA [*National Oceanic and Atmospheric Administration*] Weather Radio (NOAA)
**NWR**.......... North Western Railway [*India*]

**NWR**.......... North Western Reporter [*Legal*]
**NWR**.......... Northwest Review [*A publication*]
**NWR**.......... Northwestern Reporter [*Commonly cited NW*] [*A publication*] (DLA)
**NWR**.......... Nuclear Weapons Report [*Army*] (AABC)
**NWRA**....... National Water Resources Association (EA)
**NWRA**....... National Waterbed Retailers Association (EA)
**NWRA**....... National Wheel and Rim Association (EA)
**NWRA**....... National Wildlife Refuge Association (EA)
**NWRA**....... National Wildlife Rehabilitators Association (EA)
**NWRA**....... National Women's Rowing Association [*Later, USRA*] (EA)
**NWRBBE** ... Basin Planning Report. New York State Water Resources Commission. Series ENB [*A publication*]
**NWRC**....... National Water Resources Council [*Philippines*] (DS)
**NWRC**....... National Weather Records Center [*Later, National Climatic Center*] [*National Oceanic and Atmospheric Administration*]
**NWRC**....... National Wildflower Research Center (EA)
**NWRC**....... Naval Warfare Research Center (MCD)
**NWRC**....... Nebraska Water Resources Center [*University of Nebraska - Lincoln*] [*Research center*] (RCD)
**NWRC**....... Northeast Watershed Research Center [*University Park, PA*] [*Department of Agriculture*] (GRD)
**NWREDP** ... Water Research Centre. Notes on Water Research [*A publication*]
**NWREL**..... Northwest Regional Educational Laboratory [*Portland, OR*] [*Research center*]
**NW Rep**..... Northwestern Reporter [*Commonly cited NW*] [*A publication*] (DLA)
**NW Repr**.... North Western Reporter [*A publication*] (DLA)
**NW Rev Ord** ... Northwest Territories Revised Ordinances [*Canada*] [*A publication*] (DLA)
**NWRF**....... Naval Weather Research Facility
**NWRI**........ National Water Research Institute [*Environment Canada*] [*Research center*] (RCD)
**NWRK**....... Networks Electronic Corp. [*NASDAQ symbol*] (NQ)
**NWRN**....... Northwestern [*Meteorology*] (FAAC)
**NWRO**....... National Welfare Rights Organization [*Defunct*]
**NWRS**....... North-West Recording Society [*Record label*]
**NWRS**....... Nuclear Weapons Requirements Study (CINC)
**NWRT**....... National Wildlife Rescue Team (EA)
**NWS**.......... National Watercolor Society (EA)
**NWS**.......... National Waterways Study [*Marine science*] (MSC)
**NWS**.......... National Weather Service [*Formerly, US Weather Bureau*] [*Silver Spring, MD*] [*National Oceanic and Atmospheric Administration*]
**NWS**.......... National Winter Sports [*Association*] [*Defunct*] (EA)
**NWS**.......... Naval Weapons Station
**NWS**.......... Navy Weather Service
**NWS**.......... New World Society (EA)
**NWS**.......... [*The*] News Corp. Ltd. [*NYSE symbol*] (SPSG)
**NWS**.......... Nimbus Weather Satellite
**NWS**.......... Normal Water Surface (ADA)
**NWS**.......... North Warning System (MCD)
**NWS**.......... North-West Semitic (BJA)
**NWS**.......... Northwest States (ROG)
**NWS**.......... Norway Station [*South Africa*] [*Later, SNA*] [*Geomagnetic observatory code*]
**NWS**.......... Nose Wheel Steering [*Aviation*]
**NWS**.......... Nowsco Well Service Ltd. [*Toronto Stock Exchange symbol*]
**NWS**.......... Nuclear Weapons State
**NWSA**....... National Water Slide Association (EA)
**NWSA**....... National Welding Supply Association (EA)
**NWSA**....... National Wheelchair Softball Association (EA)
**NWSA**....... National Winter Sports Association
**NWSA**....... National Women's Studies Association (EA)
**NWSA**....... Naval Weapons Support Activity
**NWSA**....... Naval Weather Service Association (EA)
**NWSA**....... Nose Wheel Steering Amplifier [*Aviation*] (MCD)
**NWSA**....... Nuclear Weapons Supply Annex
**NWSAP**..... Naval Weapons Station Acceptance Program (MCD)
**NWSB**....... National Wage Stabilization Board [*Superseded NWLB, 1945; terminated, 1947*]
**NWSB**....... Nuclear Warfare Status Branch (CINC)
**nwsb---**....... Saint-Barthelemy [*MARC geographic area code*] [*Library of Congress*] (LCCP)
**NWSC**....... National Water Safety Congress (EA)
**NWSC**....... National Weather Satellite Center [*Later, National Environmental Satellite Service*]
**NWSC**....... National Weather Service Center (MCD)
**NWSC**....... National Women's Student Coalition (EA)
**NWSC**....... Naval Weapons Support Center (MCD)
**NWSC**....... Naval Weather Service Command
**NWSCC**..... Nuclear Weapons System Control Console (MCD)
**Nw School** ... New Schools Exchange. Newsletter [*A publication*]
**NW Sci**...... Northwest Science [*A publication*]
**NWSD**....... Naval Weather Service Detachment [*or Division*]
**nwsd---**....... Saba [*MARC geographic area code*] [*Library of Congress*] (LCCP)
**NWSED**.... Naval Weather Service Environmental Detachment [*Navy*]
**NWSEO**.... National Weather Service Employees Organization (EA)
**NWSF**........ Northwest Sea Frontier
**NWSF**........ Nuclear Weapons Storage Facility [*Army*] (AABC)
**NWSG**....... Nuclear War Study Group (EA)
**NWSG**....... Nuclear Weapon Systems Surety Group [*Army*]
**NWsH**....... Houghton College, Buffalo Campus, West Seneca, NY [*Library symbol*] [*Library of Congress*] (LCLS)
**NWSH**....... National Weather Service Headquarters
**NWsHeaC** ... Health Care Plan Medical Center, West Seneca, NY [*Library symbol*] [*Library of Congress*] (LCLS)
**NWSIA**...... National Water Supply Improvement Association [*Later, IDA*] (EA)
**NWSIA J**... NWSIA [*National Water Supply Improvement Association*] Journal [*A publication*]
**Nws Lettr**... News and Letters [*A publication*]
**NWSM**...... Nuclear Weapons Stockpile Memorandum
**Nws Nat**..... News National [*A publication*]
**NWSO**....... Naval Weapons Services Office [*Also known as NAVWPNSERVO, WEPSO*]
**NWSO**....... Naval Weather Service Office
**NWSRFS**... National Weather Service River Forecast System (NOAA)
**NWSRS**..... National Wild and Scenic Rivers System
**NWSS**........ National Weather Satellite System (KSC)
**NWSS**........ National Wool Sorters' Society [*A union*] [*British*] (DCTA)
**NWSS**........ Nuclear Weapons Support Section [*Army*] (AABC)
**NWsS**........ West Seneca State School, West Seneca, NY [*Library symbol*] [*Library of Congress*] (LCLS)
**NWSSG**..... Nuclear Weapons System Safety Group
**NWSSGP**.. Nuclear Weapons System Safety Group
**nwst---**........ St. Martin (Sint Maarten) [*MARC geographic area code*] [*Library of Congress*] (LCCP)
**NWSTTC**.. National Weather Service Technical Training Center
**nwsv---**....... Swan Islands [*MARC geographic area code*] [*Library of Congress*] (LCCP)
**NWSY**....... Naval Weapons Station, Yorktown [*Virginia*]
**N WT**......... Net Weight
**NWT**.......... New World Translation (of the Holy Scriptures) [*A publication*] (BJA)
**NWT**.......... Nonwatertight [*Packaging*] (AAG)
**NWT**.......... Northwest Territories [*Canada*]
**NWT**.......... Northwest Territories Reports [*A publication*]
**NWT**.......... Northwestern Terminal R. R. [*AAR code*]
**NWT**.......... Northwestern Utilities Ltd. [*Toronto Stock Exchange symbol*]
**NWT**.......... Nowata [*Papua New Guinea*] [*Airport symbol*] (OAG)
**NWT**.......... Nylon Wire Tie
**NWTA**....... National Waterways Transport Association [*British*]
**NWTA**....... National Woman's Trucking Association [*Defunct*] (EA)
**NWTA**....... National Wool Trade Association [*Defunct*] (EA)
**NWTA**....... North West Territory Alliance (EA)
**NWTB**....... North West Tourist Board [*British*] (DCTA)
**NWTB**....... Northwestern Tariff Bureau
**NWTC**....... National Wetlands Technical Council (EA)
**NWTC**....... Northern Warfare Training Center [*Army*] (MCD)
**NWTC**....... Nuclear Weapons Training Center
**nwtc---**........ Turks and Caicos Islands [*MARC geographic area code*] [*Library of Congress*] (LCCP)
**NWTD**....... Nonwatertight Door (ADA)
**NW Terr**.... Northwest Territories, Supreme Court Reports [*A publication*] (DLA)
**NW Terr (Can)** ... Northwest Territories Reports (Canada) [*A publication*]
**NWTF**....... National Wild Turkey Federation (EA)
**NWTG3**..... NWT [*Northwest Territories, Canada*] Gazette. Part III [*A publication*]
**NWTGII**.... NWT [*Northwest Territories, Canada*] Gazette. Part II [*A publication*]
**NWTI**........ National Wood Tank Institute (EA)
**NWTI**........ Nuclear Weapons Technical Inspections
**NWTK**....... North West Token Kai [*An association*] (EA)
**NWTL**....... Northwest Teleproductions, Inc. [*NASDAQ symbol*] (NQ)
**NWTLR**..... North West Territories Law Reports [*A publication*] (DLA)
**NWTO**....... Network for Work Time Options [*San Francisco, CA*] (EA)
**NWT Ord**.. Northwest Territories Ordinances [*Canada*] [*A publication*] (DLA)
**NWTR**....... North West Territories Reports [*1885-1907*] [*Canada*] [*A publication*] (DLA)
**nwtr---**........ Trinidad and Tobago [*MARC geographic area code*] [*Library of Congress*] (LCCP)
**NWTRCC** ... National War Tax Resistance Coordinating Committee (EA)
**NWT Rep**.. Northwest Territories Reports [*A publication*]
**NWT Rev Ord** ... Northwest Territories Revised Ordinances [*Canada*] [*A publication*] (DLA)
**NWT Rev Ord** ... Revised Ordinances of the Northwest Territories [*A publication*]
**NWTS**....... National Waste Terminal Storage [*For radioactive wastes*]
**NWTS**....... National Wilms' Tumor Study [*Oncology*]
**NWTS**....... Naval Weapons Test Station
**NWT/S**..... Nuclear Weapons Technician/Specialist (AAG)
**NWTSG**.... National Wilms' Tumor Study Group [*Oncology*]
**NWTWN**... NWT [*Northwest Territories, Canada*] Wildlife Notes [*A publication*]
**NWTWSCR** ... NWT [*Northwest Territories, Canada*] Wildlife Service. Completion Reports [*A publication*]

**NWTWSCT** ... NWT [*Northwest Territories, Canada*] Wildlife Service. Contact Reports [*A publication*]
**NWTWSFR** ... NWT [*Northwest Territories, Canada*] Wildlife Service. File Reports [*A publication*]
**NWTWSPR** ... NWT [*Northwest Territories, Canada*] Wildlife Service. Progress Reports [*A publication*]
**NWU** ......... National Writers Union (EA)
**NWU** ......... Nebraska Wesleyan University
**NWU** ......... Northwestern University School of Law (DLA)
**NWU** ......... Nose Wheel Up [*Aviation*]
**NWU** ......... Viewpoint [*A publication*]
**nwuc---** ....... United States Miscellaneous Caribbean Islands [*MARC geographic area code*] [*Library of Congress*] (LCCP)
**NWULR** .... Northwestern University. Law Review [*A publication*]
**NW U L Rev** ... Northwestern University. Law Review [*A publication*]
**NW Univ Law R** ... Northwestern University. Law Review [*A publication*]
**NWUS** ....... Northwestern United States
**NWV** .......... Newcoast Silver Mines [*Vancouver Stock Exchange symbol*]
**NWV** .......... Norfolk, VA [*Location identifier*] [*FAA*] (FAAL)
**nwvb---** ....... Virgin Islands, British [*MARC geographic area code*] [*Library of Congress*] (LCCP)
**nwvi---** ........ Virgin Islands of the US [*MARC geographic area code*] [*Library of Congress*] (LCCP)
**NWVIz** ....... New Visions Entertainment Corp. [*NASDAQ symbol*] (NQ)
**nwvr** ............ Virgin Islands [*MARC geographic area code*] [*Library of Congress*] (LCCP)
**NWvS** ........ Sanders Associates, Inc., Williamsville, NY [*Library symbol*] [*Library of Congress*] (LCLS)
**NWW** ......... New Ways to Work (EA)
**NWW** ......... New World Writing [*A publication*]
**NWW** ......... Newgate Resources [*Vancouver Stock Exchange symbol*]
**NWW** ......... Nose Wheel Well [*Aviation*] (MCD)
**NWWA** ...... National Water Well Association [*Database producer*] (EA)
**NWWA** ...... North-West Water Authority [*British*] (DCTA)
**NWWA** ...... Tiga, Iles Loyaute [*New Caledonia*] [*ICAO location identifier*] (ICLI)
**NWWC** ...... Ile Art/Wala, Iles Belep [*New Caledonia*] [*ICAO location identifier*] (ICLI)
**NWWC** ...... National White Wyandotte Club [*Defunct*] (EA)
**NWWCSS** ... Naval Worldwide Command Support System (MCD)
**NWWD** ...... Kone [*New Caledonia*] [*ICAO location identifier*] (ICLI)
**NWWDA** ... National Wood Window and Door Association (EA)
**NWWE** ...... Ile Des Pins/Moue [*New Caledonia*] [*ICAO location identifier*] (ICLI)
**NWWF** ...... Voh [*New Caledonia*] [*ICAO location identifier*] (ICLI)
**NWWH** ..... Houailou/Nesson [*New Caledonia*] [*ICAO location identifier*] (ICLI)
**NWWI** ....... Hienghene/Henri Martinet [*New Caledonia*] [*ICAO location identifier*] (ICLI)
**nwwi---** ....... Windward Islands [*MARC geographic area code*] [*Library of Congress*] (LCCP)
**NWWJ** ...... Poum [*New Caledonia*] [*ICAO location identifier*] (ICLI)
**NWWK** ...... Koumac [*New Caledonia*] [*ICAO location identifier*] (ICLI)
**NWWL** ...... Lifou/Ouanaham, Iles Loyaute [*New Caledonia*] [*ICAO location identifier*] (ICLI)
**NWWM** ..... Noumea/Magenta [*New Caledonia*] [*ICAO location identifier*] (ICLI)
**NWWN** ..... Noumea [*New Caledonia*] [*ICAO location identifier*] (ICLI)
**NWWO** ..... Ile Ouen/Edmond-Cane [*New Caledonia*] [*ICAO location identifier*] (ICLI)
**NWWQ** ..... Mueo/Nickel [*New Caledonia*] [*ICAO location identifier*] (ICLI)
**NWWR** ...... Mare/La Roche, Iles Loyaute [*New Caledonia*] [*ICAO location identifier*] (ICLI)
**NWWS** ...... NOAA [*National Oceanic and Atmospheric Administration*] Weather Wire Service (NOAA)
**NWWS** ...... Plaine Des Lacs [*New Caledonia*] [*ICAO location identifier*] (ICLI)
**NWWU** ..... Touho [*New Caledonia*] [*ICAO location identifier*] (ICLI)
**NWWV** ...... Ouvea/Ouloup, Iles Loyaute [*New Caledonia*] [*ICAO location identifier*] (ICLI)
**NWWW** ..... Noumea/La Tontouta [*New Caledonia*] [*ICAO location identifier*] (ICLI)
**NWWY** ...... Ouaco/Paquiepe [*New Caledonia*] [*ICAO location identifier*] (ICLI)
**NWX** .......... New Minex Resources Ltd. [*Vancouver Stock Exchange symbol*]
**nwxi---** ........ St. Christopher-Nevis-Anguilla [*MARC geographic area code*] [*Library of Congress*] (LCCP)
**nwxk---** ....... St. Lucia [*MARC geographic area code*] [*Library of Congress*] (LCCP)
**nwxm** .......... St. Vincent [*MARC geographic area code*] [*Library of Congress*] (LCCP)
**NWY** .......... New Penn Energy [*Vancouver Stock Exchange symbol*]
**NWy** ........... Wyoming Free Public Library, Wyoming, NY [*Library symbol*] [*Library of Congress*] (LCLS)
**NWY** .......... Yellowknife Public Library, Northwest Territories [*Library symbol*] [*National Library of Canada*] (NLC)
**NWya** ......... Wyandanch Public Library, Wyandanch, NY [*Library symbol*] [*Library of Congress*] (LCLS)
**NWYC** ....... Court Library, Department of Justice, Yellowknife, Northwest Territories [*Library symbol*] [*National Library of Canada*] (BIB)
**NWYCC** .... National Write Your Congressman [*Also known as National Write Your Congressman Club*] (EA)
**NWYCJ** ..... Cooper-Johnson, Yellowknife, Northwest Territories [*Library symbol*] [*National Library of Canada*] (BIB)
**NWYD** ....... Dene Nation, Yellowknife, Northwest Territories [*Library symbol*] [*National Library of Canada*] (BIB)
**NWYECW** ... Canadian Wildlife Service, Environment Canada [*Service Canadien de la Faune, Environnement Canada*] Yellowknife, Northwest Territories [*Library symbol*] [*National Library of Canada*] (NLC)
**NWYEEP** ... Assessment and Coordination Branch, Environmental Protection Service, Environment Canada [*Direction de l'Evaluation et de la Coordination, Service de la Protection de l'Environnement, Environnement Canada*] Yellowknife, Northwest Territories [*Library symbol*] [*National Library of Canada*] (NLC)
**NWYGI** ..... Government Library, Government of the Northwest Territories, Yellow knife, Northwest Territories [*Library symbol*] [*National Library of Canada*] (NLC)
**NWYIN** ..... Indian and Northern Affairs Canada [*Affaires Indiennes et du Nord Canada*] Yellowknife, Northwest Territories [*Library symbol*] [*National Library of Canada*] (NLC)
**NWYND** .... Northern Region Information System (NORIS), Canada Department of National Defence [*Reseau d'Information de la Region du Nord (NORIS), Ministere de la Defense Nationale*] Yellowknife, Northwest Territories [*Library symbol*] [*National Library of Canada*] (NLC)
**NWYOS** .... Dr. Otto Schaefer Health Resource Centre, Yellowknife, Northwest Territories [*Library symbol*] [*National Library of Canada*] (NLC)
**NWYPC** .... Parks Canada [*Parcs Canada*] Yellowknife, Northwest Territories [*Library symbol*] [*National Library of Canada*] (NLC)
**NWYPW** ... Technical Resource Centre, Department of Public Works and Highways, Government of the Northwest Territories, Yellowknife, Northwest Territories [*Library symbol*] [*National Library of Canada*] (BIB)
**NWYRR** .... Renewable Resources Library, Government of the Northwest Territories, Yellowknife, Northwest Territories [*Library symbol*] [*National Library of Canada*] (NLC)
**NWYWNH** ... Prince of Wales Northern Heritage Centre, Government of the Northwest Territories, Yellowknife, Northwest Territories [*Library symbol*] [*National Library of Canada*] (NLC)
**NWZam** ..... New Writing from Zambia [*A publication*]
**NX** ............. Nantes Aviation [*France*] [*ICAO designator*] (FAAC)
**nx** ............... Norfolk Island [*MARC country of publication code*] [*Library of Congress*] (LCCP)
**NX** ............. Normal to X-Axis (MCD)
**NX** ............. Nose to X-Axis (MCD)
**NX** ............. Not Exceeding
**NX** ............. Not Expendable (MUGU)
**NX** ............. Quanex Corp. [*NYSE symbol*] (SPSG)
**NXA** .......... Norex America [*AMEX symbol*] (SPSG)
**NXA** .......... Wake County Public Library, Raleigh, NC [*OCLC symbol*] (OCLC)
**NXB** .......... Neurotoxin B
**NXCI** ......... National Xeriscape Council, Inc. [*An association*] (EA)
**NXDO** ....... Nike-X Development Office [*Army*] (AABC)
**NXI** ........... Oak Harbor, WA [*Location identifier*] [*FAA*] (FAAL)
**NXL** .......... Napoleon Exploration [*Vancouver Stock Exchange symbol*]
**n-xl---** ......... St. Pierre and Miquelon [*MARC geographic area code*] [*Library of Congress*] (LCCP)
**NXM** .......... Noramex Minerals [*Vancouver Stock Exchange symbol*]
**NXMIS** ...... Nike-X Management Information System [*Army*]
**NXN** .......... Milton, FL [*Location identifier*] [*FAA*] (FAAL)
**NXN** .......... No Christian Name
**NXP** .......... Noxe Resources Corp. [*Vancouver Stock Exchange symbol*]
**NXP** .......... Twentynine Palms, CA [*Location identifier*] [*FAA*] (FAAL)
**NXPM** ....... Nike-X Project Manager [*Army*] (AABC)
**NXPO** ....... Nike-X Program [*or Project*] Office [*Army*]
**NXPRG** ..... Nike-X Program Review Group [*Army*] (AABC)
**NXR** .......... Noncrossing Rule
**NXS** .......... Nexus Resources Corp. [*Vancouver Stock Exchange symbol*] [*Toronto Stock Exchange symbol*]
**NXSM** ....... Nike-X System Manager [*Army*] (AABC)
**NXSMO** .... Nike-X System Manager's Office [*Army*]
**NXSO** ....... Nike-X Support Office [*Army*]
**NXT** .......... Next
**NXW** ......... University of North Carolina, Wilmington, Wilmington, NC [*OCLC symbol*] (OCLC)
**NXX** .......... Willow Grove, PA [*Location identifier*] [*FAA*] (FAAL)
**NY** ............. John Dewey [*Final letters of his first and last name used as a pseudonym*] [*American author, 1859-1952*]
**NY** ............. Navy Yard
**NY** ............. Nelen Yubu [*A publication*] (APTA)
**NY** ............. Net Yield
**NY** ............. New Year
**NY** ............. New York [*A publication*]

**NY**............. New York [*City or state*] [*Postal code*]
**NY**............. New York [*Naval Shipyard*]
**NY**............. New York Airways, Inc. [*ICAO designator*]
**NY**............. New York Court of Appeals Reports [*A publication*] (DLA)
**NY**............. New York Magazine [*A publication*]
**NY**............. New York Reports [*A publication*]
**NY**............. New Yorker [*A publication*]
**NY**............. No Year [*of publication*] [*Bibliography*]
**NY**............. Noorduyn Aviation Ltd. [*Canada*] [*ICAO aircraft manufacturer identifier*] (ICAO)
**NY**............. Normal to Y-Axis (MCD)
**NY**............. Northamptonshire Yeomanry [*British military*] (DMA)
**NY**............. Northumberland Yeomanry [*British military*] (DMA)
**NY**............. Nose to Y-Axis (NASA)
**NY**............. Nuclear Yellow [*A fluorescent dye*]
**NY**............. Nuclear Yield
**NY**............. Nyasaland (ROG)
**NY**............. School Music News [*New York*] [*A publication*]
**NY**............. Yonkers Public Library, Yonkers, NY [*Library symbol*] [*Library of Congress*] (LCLS)
**NYA**.......... National Yogurt Association (EA)
**NYA**.......... National Youth Administration [*Terminated, 1943*]
**NYA**.......... National Youth Alliance (EA)
**NYA**.......... Neighborhood Youth Administration (OICC)
**NYA**.......... New York Airlines, Inc. [*Flushing, NY*] [*FAA designator*] (FAAC)
**NYA**.......... New York Airways, Inc. [*Air carrier designation symbol*]
**NYA**.......... Not Yet Answered
**NyA**.......... Nya Argus [*A publication*]
**nya**............. Nyanja [*MARC language code*] [*Library of Congress*] (LCCP)
**NYAB**........ National Youth Advisory Board [*Environmental Protection Agency*]
**NYAB**........ New York Air Brake Co.
**NYABIC**.... New York Association for Brain Injured Children
**NY Acad Sci Ann** ... New York Academy of Sciences. Annals [*A publication*]
**NY Acad Sci Trans** ... New York Academy of Sciences. Transactions [*A publication*]
**NY Admin Code** ... Official Compilation of Codes, Rules, and Regulations of the State of New York [*A publication*] (DLA)
**NYAES-C** ... New York Agricultural Experiment Station (Cornell University) [*Research center*] (RCD)
**NY Aff**....... New York Affairs [*A publication*]
**NY Ag Dept** ... New York Department of Agriculture. Publications [*A publication*]
**NY Agric Exp Stn (Geneva) Annu Rep** ... New York. Agricultural Experiment Station (Geneva). Annual Report [*A publication*]
**NY Agric Exp Stn (Geneva) Bull** ... New York. Agricultural Experiment Station (Geneva). Bulletin [*A publication*]
**NY Agric Exp Stn (Geneva) Res Circ** ... New York. Agricultural Experiment Station (Geneva). Research Circular [*A publication*]
**NY Agric Exp Stn (Geneva) Tech Bull** ... New York. Agricultural Experiment Station (Geneva). Technical Bulletin [*A publication*]
**NY Agric Exp Stn (Ithaca) Bull** ... New York. Agricultural Experiment Station (Ithaca). Bulletin [*A publication*]
**NY Agric Exp Stn (Ithaca) Mem** ... New York. Agricultural Experiment Station (Ithaca). Memoir [*A publication*]
**NYAIC**....... New York Association of Industrial Communicators [*Later, NY/IABC*] (EA)
**NYAL**........ National Yugoslav Army of Liberation [*World War II*]
**NYAL**........ New York Airlines [*NASDAQ symbol*] (NQ)
**NYALR**...... New Yorkers for Abortion Law Repeal (EA)
**NYAM**....... New York Academy of Medicine
**NYAM**....... New York Academy of Music
**NYAMP**.... New York Advertising Media Planners [*Defunct*] (EA)
**NYANA**..... New York Association for New Americans (EA)
**NY Ann Ca** ... New York Annotated Cases [*A publication*] (DLA)
**NY Ann Cas** ... New York Annotated Cases [*A publication*] (DLA)
**NY Anno Cas** ... New York Annotated Cases [*A publication*] (DLA)
**NY Anno Dig** ... New York Annotated Digest [*A publication*] (ILCA)
**NY Annot Dig** ... New York Annotated Digest [*A publication*] (DLA)
**NYap**.......... Middle Island Central Public Library, Yaphank, NY [*Library symbol*] [*Library of Congress*] (LCLS)
**NYAP**........ New York Assembly Program [*Data processing*]
**NYAP**........ New York Average Price per Share [*Stock market*]
**Nya Perspekt** ... Nya Perspektiv [*A publication*]
**NY App Dec** ... New York Court of Appeals Decisions [*A publication*] (DLA)
**NY App Div** ... New York Supreme Court, Appellate Division Reports [*A publication*] (DLA)
**NY Appl For Res Inst AFRI Misc Rep** ... New York Applied Forestry Research Institute. AFRI Miscellaneous Report [*A publication*]
**NY Appl For Res Inst AFRI Res Note** ... New York Applied Forestry Research Institute. AFRI Research Note [*A publication*]
**NY Appl For Res Inst AFRI Res Rep** ... New York Applied Forestry Research Institute. AFRI Research Report [*A publication*]
**NY Arts J** .. New York Arts Journal
**NYAS**........ New York Academy of Sciences (EA)
**Nyasaland Farmer Forest** ... Nyasaland Farmer and Forester [*A publication*]
**Nyasal Farmer For** ... Nyasaland Farmer and Forester [*A publication*]
**Nyasal Geol Surv Dep Mem** ... Nyasaland Protectorate. Geological Survey Department. Memoir [*A publication*]
**NYB**.......... National Youth Bureau [*British*]
**NYB**.......... New York Bight [*Oceanography*] (MSC)
**NYB**.......... North York Board of Education [*UTLAS symbol*]
**NYBA**........ National Young Buddhist Association [*Defunct*] (EA)
**NY Bank Law** ... New York Banking Law [*A publication*] (DLA)
**NYBC**........ National Yiddish Book Center (EA)
**NYBC**........ New York Bancorp, Inc. [*NASDAQ symbol*] (NQ)
**NYBC**........ New York Business Communicators [*Later, NY/IABC*] (EA)
**NY Bd Agr Mem** ... New York Board of Agriculture. Memoirs [*A publication*]
**NYBE**........ National Yiddish Book Exchange (EA)
**NYBG**........ New York Botanical Garden
**NYB & M** .. New York, Boston & Montreal Railroad
**NYBOS**..... Navy Yard, Boston, Massachusetts [*Obsolete*]
**NY Bot Gard Annu Rep** ... New York Botanical Garden. Annual Report [*A publication*]
**NY Bot Garden B** ... New York Botanical Garden. Bulletin [*A publication*]
**NYBPE**...... New York Business Press Editors [*New York, NY*] (EA)
**NYBS**........ New York Browning Society (EA)
**NYBT**........ Boyce Thompson Institute for Plant Research, Yonkers, NY [*Library symbol*] [*Library of Congress*] (LCLS)
**NYBT**........ New York Board of Trade [*New York, NY*] (EA)
**NYC**.......... Charley [*Nevada*] [*Seismograph station code, US Geological Survey*] [*Closed*] (SEIS)
**NYC**.......... Neighborhood Youth Corps [*Terminated*] [*Department of Labor*]
**NYC**.......... New York Central R. R. [*Later, Penn Central*] [*AAR code*]
**NYC**.......... New York Circus (EA)
**NYC**.......... New York City
**NYC**.......... New York, Motor Carrier Conference [*STAC*]
**NYC**.......... New York [*New York*]/Newark [*New Jersey*] [*Airport symbol*] (OAG)
**NYC**.......... New York, NY [*Location identifier*] [*FAA*] (FAAL)
**NYCA**........ New York Court of Appeals Reports [*A publication*] (DLA)
**NY Cas Err** ... Caines' New York Cases in Error [*A publication*] (DLA)
**NY Cas in Error** ... Caines' New York Cases in Error [*A publication*] (DLA)
**NYCB**........ New York City Ballet
**NYCBA**..... New York City Bar Association. Bulletin [*A publication*] (DLA)
**NYCBA Bull** ... Bulletin. Association of the Bar of the City of New York [*A publication*] (DLA)
**NYCBAN** .. New York Center Beacon Alphanumerics [*FAA*]
**NYC Bd Ed Curric Bul** ... New York City Board of Education. Curriculum Bulletins [*A publication*]
**NYCC**........ New York Candy Club (EA)
**NYCCA**..... New York Cocoa Clearing Association (EA)
**NYCCC**..... New York City Community College
**NYCCD**..... New York Current Court Decisions [*A publication*] (DLA)
**NYCCH**..... New York Advance Digest Service (Commerce Clearing House), Cited by Year [*A publication*] (DLA)
**NYCCI**....... New York Corset Club (EA)
**NYCDC**..... New York Curtain and Drapery Club (EA)
**NYCE**........ New York Cash Exchange [*Automated teller machine network*]
**NYCE**........ New York Cocoa Exchange [*Later, CSCE*]
**NYCE**........ New York Cotton Exchange (EA)
**NYCE**........ New York Curb Exchange [*Later, AMEX*]
**NYCER**...... New York Conference on Electronic Reliability (MCD)
**NY Cert Pub Acct** ... New York Certified Public Accountant [*A publication*]
**NYCFMA** ... New York Credit and Financial Management Association [*New York, NY*] (EA)
**NY Ch**........ Chancery Sentinel [*New York*] [*A publication*] (DLA)
**NYCHA**..... New York Clearing House Association [*New York, NY*] (EA)
**NYCHARL** ... Navy Yard, Charleston, South Carolina
**NYC & HR** ... New York Central & Hudson River Railroad
**NYC & HRR** ... New York Central & Hudson River Railroad (ROG)
**NY Ch Sent** ... New York Chancery Sentinel [*A publication*] (DLA)
**NYCI**......... New York City's First [*First beluga whale born at the New York Aquarium, 1981*] [*Pronounced "Nicky"*]
**NY City Ct** ... New York City Court [*A publication*] (DLA)
**NY City Ct Rep** ... New York City Court Reports [*A publication*] (DLA)
**NY City Ct Supp** ... New York City Court Reports, Supplement [*A publication*] (DLA)
**NY City Hall Rec** ... New York City Hall Recorder [*A publication*] (ILCA)
**NY City H Rec** ... New York City Hall Recorder [*A publication*] (DLA)
**NY Civ Prac Law & R** ... New York Civil Practice Law and Rules [*A publication*] (DLA)
**NY Civ Pro** ... New York Civil Procedure [*A publication*] (DLA)
**NY Civ Proc** ... New York Civil Procedure [*A publication*] (ILCA)
**NY Civ Proc (NS)** ... New York Civil Procedure, New Series [*A publication*] (DLA)
**NY Civ Proc R** ... New York Civil Procedure Reports [*A publication*] (DLA)
**NY Civ Proc Rep** ... Civil Procedure Reports [*New York*] [*A publication*] (DLA)
**NY Civ Proc R NS** ... New York Civil Procedure Reports, New Series [*A publication*] (DLA)
**NY Civ Pro R** ... New York Civil Procedure Reports [*A publication*] (ILCA)
**NY Civ Pro R NS** ... New York Civil Procedure Reports, New Series [*A publication*] (ILCA)
**NY Civ Pr Rep** ... New York Civil Procedure Reports [*A publication*] (ILCA)
**NYCKA**..... Neng Yuan Chi Kan [*A publication*]
**NYCM**....... NYCOM Information Services, Inc. [*NASDAQ symbol*] (NQ)
**NYCMA**.... New York Clothing Manufacturers Association (EA)

**NYCME**.... New York Clothing Manufacturers Exchange [*Later, NYCMA*] (EA)
**NYCN**........ New York Connecting Railroad [*AAR code*]
**NYCO**........ NYCOR, Inc. [*NASDAQ symbol*] (NQ)
**NY Code R**... New York Code Reporter [*A publication*] (DLA)
**NY Code Rep**... New York Code Reporter [*A publication*] (DLA)
**NY Code Rep NS**... New York Code Reports, New Series [*A publication*] (DLA)
**NY Code Report**... New York Code Reporter [*A publication*] (DLA)
**NY Code Report NS**... New York Code Reporter, New Series [*A publication*] (DLA)
**NY Code Reports NS**... New York Code Reports, New Series [*A publication*] (DLA)
**NY Code Reptr**... New York Code Reporter [*A publication*] (DLA)
**NY Code Reptr NS**... New York Code Reporter, New Series [*A publication*] (DLA)
**NY Code R NS**... New York Code Reports, New Series [*A publication*] (DLA)
**NY Comm St Res Niagara An Rp**... New York Commissioners of the State Reservation at Niagara. Annual Report [*A publication*]
**NY Comp Codes R & Regs**... Official Compilation of Codes, Rules, and Regulations of the State of New York [*A publication*]
**NY Cond**.... New York Condensed Reports [*1881-82*] [*A publication*] (DLA)
**NY Co Rem**... New York Code of Remedial Justice [*A publication*] (DLA)
**NY County B Bull**... New York County Lawyers Association. Bar Bulletin [*A publication*]
**NY County Law Ass'n B Bull**... New York County Lawyers Association. Bar Bulletin [*A publication*]
**NYCP**........ Civil Procedure Reports [*New York*] [*A publication*] (DLA)
**NY Cr**......... New York Criminal Reports [*A publication*] (DLA)
**NY Crim**..... New York Criminal Reports [*A publication*] (DLA)
**NY Crim R**... New York Criminal Reports [*A publication*] (DLA)
**NY Crim Rep**... New York Criminal Reports [*A publication*] (DLA)
**NYCRR**..... New York Codes, Rules, and Regulations [*A publication*] (DLA)
**NY Cr R**..... New York Criminal Reports [*A publication*] (DLA)
**NY Cr Rep**... New York Criminal Reports [*A publication*] (DLA)
**NYCS**......... New York Cipher Society (EA)
**NYCS**......... New York City Shoes, Inc. [*Springfield, PA*] [*NASDAQ symbol*] (NQ)
**NYCSA**...... New York Coat and Suit Association (EA)
**NYCSA**...... New York College Stores Association
**NYCSCE**... New York Coffee, Sugar, and Cocoa Exchange
**NYCSE**...... New York Coffee and Sugar Exchange [*Later, CSCE*] (EA)
**NYCSG**...... New York Constitution Study Group (EA)
**NYCSLS**.... New York C. S. Lewis Society (EA)
**NYC & STL**... New York, Chicago & St. Louis Railroad Co.
**NY Ct App**... New York Court of Appeals (DLA)
**NYCTC**...... New York City Technical College
**NYCTCG**... New York Cold Type Composition Group [*Later, TANY*] (EA)
**NYCTNCA**... New York Cotton Exchange, Citrus Associates
**NYCUC**..... New York City Urban Corps (EA)
**NYD**........... Navy Yard
**NYD**........... New York Datum (NRCH)
**NYD**........... New York Dock Railway [*AAR code*]
**NYD**........... Not Yet Diagnosed [*Facetious translation: "Not Yet Dead"*] [*Medicine*]
**NY 2d**......... New York Court of Appeals Reports, Second Series [*A publication*] (DLA)
**NY 2d**......... New York Reports. Second Series [*A publication*]
**NY Daily L Gaz**... New York Daily Law Gazette [*A publication*] (DLA)
**NY Daily L Reg**... New York Daily Law Register [*A publication*] (DLA)
**NY Daily Reg**... New York Daily Register [*A publication*] (DLA)
**NY Daily Tr**... New York Daily Transcript, Old and New Series [*A publication*] (DLA)
**NYDCC**..... New York Drama Critics Circle (EA)
**NY Dep Agric Mark Annu Rep**... New York Department of Agriculture and Markets. Annual Report [*A publication*]
**NY Dep Agric Mark Circ**... New York Department of Agriculture and Markets. Circular [*A publication*]
**NY Dep't R**... New York Department Records [*A publication*] (DLA)
**NY Dep Transp Res Rep**... New York State Department of Transport. Research Report [*A publication*]
**NYDF**........ National Youth Development Foundation (EA)
**NYDLWC Dec**... New York State Department of Labor. Court Decisions of Workmen's Compensation [*A publication*] (DLA)
**NYDP**........ Neighborhood Youth Development Program
**NYDR**........ New York Department Reports [*A publication*] (DLA)
**NY & E**....... New York & Erie Railroad
**Nye**............. Nye's Reports [*18-21 Utah*] [*A publication*] (DLA)
**NYEC**........ National Youth Employment Coalition (EA)
**NY El Cas**... New York Election Cases [*A publication*] (DLA)
**NY Elec Cas**... New York Election Cases [*A publication*] (DLA)
**NY Elect Cas**... New York Election Cases [*A publication*] (DLA)
**Nyelvtudomanyi Dolg Eotvos Lorand TudomEgy**... Nyelvtudomanyi Dolgozatok. Eotvos Lorand Tudomanyegyetum [*A publication*]
**NYEP**........ New York Evening Post [*A publication*]
**NYEPLR**... New York Evening Post Literary Review [*A publication*]
**NYES**......... Elizabeth Seton College, Yonkers, NY [*Library symbol*] [*Library of Congress*] (LCLS)
**NYET LC**.. Not Yet in Library of Congress [*Suggested name for the Library of Congress computer system*]
**NYETR**...... New York Estate Tax Reports [*Prentice-Hall, Inc.*] [*A publication*] (DLA)
**NYEWW**... New York Exchange for Woman's Work [*New York, NY*] (EA)
**NYF**........... National Yeomen F [*Defunct*] (EA)
**NYF**........... New York Foundation
**NYF**........... New York Futures Exchange
**NYF**........... New York Law Forum [*A publication*]
**NY Farms & Markets Dept**... New York State Department of Farms and Markets. Publications [*A publication*]
**NYFBT**...... New York Film Board of Trade [*Defunct*] (EA)
**NYFC**......... New York Film Critics (EA)
**NYFCC**...... New York Futures Clearing Corporation [*New York Futures Exchange*]
**NYFD**........ New York Fashion Designers [*Later, NYFDF*] (EA)
**NYFDF**...... New York Fashion Designers and Foundation (EA)
**NY Fd Life Sci Q**... New York's Food and Life Sciences Quarterly [*A publication*]
**NYFE**......... New York Futures Exchange [*Pronounced "knife"*]
**NYFEA**...... National Young Farmer Educational Association (EA)
**NYFFFBA**... New York Foreign Freight Forwarders and Brokers Association [*New York, NY*] (EA)
**NY Fish Game J**... New York Fish and Game Journal [*A publication*]
**NY Folkl**.... New York Folklore [*A publication*]
**NY Folklore**... New York Folklore [*A publication*]
**NY Folk Q**... New York Folklore. Quarterly [*A publication*]
**NY Food Life Sci Bull**... New York's Food and Life Sciences Bulletin [*A publication*]
**NY Food Life Sci Q**... New York's Food and Life Sciences Quarterly [*A publication*]
**NYFQ**........ New York Folklore. Quarterly [*A publication*]
**NYFRF**...... New York Fertility Research Foundation [*Later, FRF*] (EA)
**NYFUO**..... New York Federation of Urban Organizations
**NYFW**....... New York Film Works, Inc. [*New York, NY*] [*NASDAQ symbol*] (NQ)
**NYFWA**.... New York Financial Writers' Association (EA)
**NYG**........... Geigy Pharmaceuticals, Yonkers, NY [*Library symbol*] [*Library of Congress*] (LCLS)
**NYG**........... New York State Library, Albany, NY [*OCLC symbol*] (OCLC)
**NYG**........... Quantico, VA [*Location identifier*] [*FAA*] (FAAL)
**NYGBS**...... New York Genealogical and Biographical Society (EA)
**NYGC**........ New York Governor's Conference
**NYGJB**...... New York Guild for Jewish Blind [*Later, JGB*]
**NY G S**....... New York Geological Survey [*A publication*]
**NYGZA**..... Nippon Yuketsu Gakkai Zasshi [*A publication*]
**NYH**.......... New York History [*A publication*]
**NY Herald Tribune Bk R**... New York Herald Tribune. Book Review [*A publication*]
**NY Herald Tribune W Bk R**... New York Herald Tribune. Weekly Book Review [*A publication*]
**NY Her Trib Lively Arts**... New York Herald Tribune. Lively Arts Section [*A publication*]
**NYhI**.......... International Business Machines Corp., Thomas J. Watson Research Center, Yorktown Heights, NY [*Library symbol*] [*Library of Congress*] (LCLS)
**NY His**....... New York History [*A publication*]
**NY Hist**..... New York History [*A publication*]
**NY Hist Soc Coll**... New York Historical Society. Collections [*A publication*]
**NY Hist Soc Q**... New York Historical Society. Quarterly [*A publication*]
**NY Hist Soc Quar**... New York Historical Society. Quarterly [*A publication*]
**NYHS**........ New York Historical Society. Quarterly [*A publication*]
**NYHSL**..... New York Health and Safety Laboratory [*Energy Research and Development Administration*]
**NYHSQ**..... New York Historical Society. Quarterly [*A publication*]
**NYHSQB**.. New York Historical Society. Quarterly Bulletin [*A publication*]
**NYHT**........ New York Herald Tribune [*Defunct newspaper*]
**NYHTB**..... New York Herald Tribune. Weekly Book Review [*A publication*]
**NYI**........... Sunyani [*Ghana*] [*Airport symbol*] (OAG)
**NY/IABC**.. New York/International Association of Business Communicators [*New York, NY*] (EA)
**NYIBC**....... New York International Ballet Competition
**NYIBC**....... New York Islanders Booster Club (EA)
**NYIBS**....... New York International Bible Society (EA)
**NYIC**......... New York Iroquois Conference (EA)
**NYICD**...... New York Institute for Child Development (EA)
**NYIDA**...... New York Importers and Distillers Association (EA)
**NYIE**......... New York Insurance Exchange
**NYIF**.......... New York Index - Finance [*Stock market*]
**NYII**.......... New York Index - Industrials [*Stock market*]
**NyIK**.......... Nyelvtudomanyi Intezet Koezlemenyek [*A publication*]
**NYIL**.......... Netherlands Yearbook of International Law [*A publication*] (DLA)
**NYIT**......... New York Index - Transportation [*Stock market*]
**NYIT**......... New York Institute of Technology
**NYIU**......... New York Index - Utilities [*Stock market*]
**NYJ**........... Joshua Tree [*Nevada*] [*Seismograph station code, US Geological Survey*] [*Closed*] (SEIS)

**NYJ** .......... National Young Judaea (EA)
**NY J Dent** ... New York Journal of Dentistry [*A publication*]
**NYJ Int'l & Comp L** ... New York Law School. Journal of International and Comparative Law [*A publication*]
**NY J Med** ... New York State Journal of Medicine [*A publication*]
**NYJO** ........ National Youth Jazz Orchestra [*British*]
**NY Jud Rep** ... New York Judicial Repository [*A publication*] (DLA)
**NY Jud Repos** ... New York Judicial Repository [*A publication*] (DLA)
**NY Jur** ....... New York Jurisprudence [*A publication*] (DLA)
**NY Jur** ....... New York Jurist [*A publication*] (DLA)
**NYK** .......... New York [*City*]
**NYK** .......... North York Public Library [*UTLAS symbol*]
**NyK** .......... Nyelvtudomanyi Koezlemenyek [*A publication*]
**NYKGRP** ... New York Group [*Navy*]
**NYKR** ........ New Yorker Magazine [*NASDAQ symbol*] (NQ)
**NYKZAU** .. Folia Pharmacologica Japonica [*A publication*]
**NYL** .......... Neodymium YAG [*Yttrium Aluminum Garnet*] LASER
**NYL** .......... New York University. Law Review [*A publication*]
**NYL** .......... Nylon (MSA)
**NYL** .......... Yuma, AZ [*Location identifier*] [*FAA*] (FAAL)
**NYLAB** ...... New York Language Association. Bulletin [*A publication*]
**NY Law Bul** ... New York Monthly Law Bulletin [*A publication*] (DLA)
**NY Law Consol** ... New York Consolidated Laws Service [*A publication*]
**NY Law Forum** ... New York Law Forum [*A publication*]
**NY Law Gaz** ... New York Law Gazette [*A publication*] (DLA)
**NY Law J** ... New York Law Journal [*A publication*]
**NY Law (McKinney)** ... McKinney's Consolidated Laws of New York [*A publication*] (DLA)
**NY Law R** .. New York Law Review [*A publication*]
**NY Law Rev** ... New York Law Review [*A publication*]
**NY Laws** .... Laws of New York [*A publication*]
**NYLB** ........ [*The*] New York & Long Branch Railroad Co. [*Absorbed into Consolidated Rail Corp.*] [*AAR code*]
**NYLC** ........ National Young Life Campaign [*British*]
**NYLC Ann** ... New York Leading Cases, Annotated [*A publication*] (DLA)
**NYL Cas** .... New York Leading Cases [*A publication*] (DLA)
**NY Leg N** ... New York Legal News [*1880-82*] [*A publication*] (DLA)
**NY Leg Obs** ... New York Legal Observer (Owen) [*A publication*] (DLA)
**NY Leg Reg** ... New York Legal Register [*A publication*] (DLA)
**NYLE & W** ... New York, Lake Erie & Western Railroad [*Later, EL*] [*Nickname: Now You Lay Easy and Wait*]
**NYLEX USA** ... New York Leather Exposition [*American European Trade and Exhibition Center*] (TSPED)
**NY L F** ....... New York Law Forum [*A publication*]
**NYLG** ........ New York Law Group [*Later, BAHRGNY*] (EA)
**NYL Gaz** .... New York Law Gazette [*A publication*] (DLA)
**NY Lib Assn Bul** ... New York Library Association. Bulletin [*A publication*]
**NY Lit For** ... New York Literary Forum [*A publication*]
**NYLJ** ......... New York Law Journal [*A publication*]
**NYLO** ........ New York Legal Observer [*A publication*] (DLA)
**NYLR** ........ Neodymium YAG [*Yttrium Aluminum Garnet*] LASER Range-Finder
**Ny LR** ........ Nyasaland Law Reports [*South Africa*] [*A publication*] (DLA)
**NYLRB** ...... New York State Labor Relations Board Decisions [*A publication*] (DLA)
**NYLRB Dec** ... New York State Labor Relations Board Decisions and Orders [*A publication*] (DLA)
**NYL Rec** .... New York Law Record [*A publication*] (DLA)
**NYL Rev** .... New York Law Review [*A publication*]
**NylroK** ....... Nyelv-Es Irodalomtudomanyi Koezlemenyek [*A publication*]
**NYLS** ......... New York Law School
**NY L Sch Intl L Socy J** ... New York Law School. International Law Society. Journal [*A publication*]
**NY L Sch J Intl and Comp L** ... New York Law School. Journal of International and Comparative Law [*A publication*]
**NY L Sch L Rev** ... New York Law School. Law Review [*A publication*]
**NYL School Rev** ... New York Law School. Law Review [*A publication*]
**NYLSLR** ... New York Law School. Law Review [*A publication*]
**NY L S L Rev** ... New York Law School. Law Review [*A publication*]
**NYLSMA** ... New York Lamp and Shade Manufacturers Association (EA)
**NYLS Stud L Rev** ... New York Law School. Student Law Review [*A publication*] (DLA)
**NYLTI** ....... National Youth Leadership Training Institute
**NYM** .......... Climax Mine [*Nevada*] [*Seismograph station code, US Geological Survey*] [*Closed*] (SEIS)
**NYM** .......... New York Mercantile Exchange
**NYM** .......... New York Movers Tariff Bureau, Inc., New York NY [*STAC*]
**nym** ........... Nyamwezi [*MARC language code*] [*Library of Congress*] (LCCP)
**NYMA** ....... New York City Metropolitan Area
**NYMA** ....... New York Mounters Association [*New York, NY*] (EA)
**NYMC** ....... New York Medical College [*Valhalla, NY*]
**NYME** ....... New York Mercantile Exchange (EA)
**NY Med** ..... New York Medicine [*A publication*]
**NY Med J** ... New York Medical Journal [*A publication*]
**NY Med Phys J** ... New York Medical and Physical Journal [*A publication*]
**NYMEX** .... New York Mercantile Exchange (EA)
**NYMG** ....... NYMAGIC [*Formerly, New York Marine & General Insurance Co.*], Inc. [*NASDAQ symbol*] (NQ)
**NYMI** ........ Navy Yard, Mare Island, California
**NY Micro Soc J** ... New York Microscopical Society. Journal [*A publication*]
**NY Miner Club B** ... New York Mineralogical Club. Bulletin [*A publication*]
**NY Misc** .... New York Miscellaneous Reports [*A publication*] (DLA)
**NY Misc 2d** ... New York Miscellaneous Reports, Second Series [*A publication*] (DLA)
**NYMM** ...... New York Merchandise Mart
**NYMO** ....... National Youth Ministry Organization (EA)
**NY Mo Law Bul** ... New York Monthly Law Bulletin [*A publication*] (DLA)
**NY Mo L Bul** ... New York Monthly Law Bulletin [*A publication*] (DLA)
**NY Mo LR** ... New York Monthly Law Reports [*A publication*] (DLA)
**NY Mo L Rec** ... New York Monthly Law Record [*A publication*] (DLA)
**NY Month L Bul** ... New York Monthly Law Bulletin [*A publication*] (DLA)
**NY Month LR** ... New York Monthly Law Reports [*A publication*] (DLA)
**NY Month L Rep** ... New York Monthly Law Reports [*A publication*] (DLA)
**NY Monthly Law Bul** ... New York Monthly Law Bulletin [*A publication*] (DLA)
**NYMPH** .... Nymphomaniac (DSUE)
**NYMPHO** ... Nymphomaniac (DSUE)
**NY Mun Gaz** ... New York Municipal Gazette [*A publication*] (DLA)
**NYMZ** ....... Nytt Magasin foer Zoologi [*A publication*]
**NYN** .......... NYNEX Corp. [*NYSE symbol*] (SPSG)
**NYN** .......... Nyngan [*Australia*] [*Airport symbol*] (OAG)
**NY & NE** ... New York & New England Railroad [*Nickname: Now You Are Nearing Eternity*]
**NY New Tech Bks** ... New York Public Library. New Technical Books [*A publication*]
**NYNEX** ..... New York New England Exchange [*Telecommunications*]
**NY & NH** ... New York & New Haven Railroad
**NYNH & H** ... New York, New Haven & Hartford R. R.
**NYNJDDA** ... New York and New Jersey Dry Dock Association (EA)
**NYNOR** ..... Navy Yard, Norfolk, Virginia
**NYNS** ........ New York Naval Shipyards [*Obsolete*]
**NYNYK** ..... Navy Yard, New York, New York
**NYO** .......... New York Observer [*A publication*]
**NYO** .......... New York Oils Ltd. [*Toronto Stock Exchange symbol*]
**NYO** .......... New York Operations [*AEC*] (MCD)
**nyo** ............ Nyoro [*MARC language code*] [*Library of Congress*] (LCCP)
**NYo** ........... Youngstown Free Library, Youngstown, NY [*Library symbol*] [*Library of Congress*] (LCLS)
**NYOD** ....... New York Ordnance District [*Military*] (MUGU)
**NY Off Dept R** ... New York Official Department Reports [*A publication*] (DLA)
**NYOL** ........ New York On-Line [*Information service or system*] (EISS)
**NYoOF** ...... Old Fort Niagara Association, Youngstown, NY [*Library symbol*] [*Library of Congress*] (LCLS)
**NY Op Att Gen** ... Opinions of the Attorneys-General of New York [*A publication*] (DLA)
**NY Ops Atty Gen** ... Opinions of the Attorney General of New York [*A publication*] (DLA)
**N York J Med** ... New York Journal of Medicine [*A publication*]
**N York Med J** ... New York Medical Journal [*A publication*]
**NYOSL** ...... New York Ocean Science Laboratory
**NYO & W** ... New York, Ontario & Western Railway Co.
**NYP** .......... New York-Pennsylvania League [*Baseball*]
**NYP** .......... New York Post [*A publication*]
**NYP** .......... New York Public Library, Serials, New York, NY [*OCLC symbol*] (OCLC)
**NYP** .......... Not Yet Published
**NYPA** ........ New York Port Authority
**NYPAA** ...... National Yellow Pages Agency Association [*Tucson, AZ*] (EA)
**NYP & B** ... New York, Providence & Boston Railroad
**NYPC** ........ New York Pigment Club (EA)
**NYPD** ........ New York Police Department [*Initialism also used as title of TV series*]
**NYPE** ........ New York Port of Embarkation [*Military*]
**NYPE** ........ New York Produce Exchange [*Defunct*] (EA)
**NYPF** ......... National Young Professionals Forum (EA)
**NYPFO** ...... New York Air Force Procurement Field Office
**NYPH** ........ Navy Yard, Pearl Harbor, Hawaii
**NYPHIL** ..... Navy Yard, Philadelphia, Pennsylvania
**NY Phil** ...... New York Philharmonic Program Notes [*A publication*]
**NYPIRG** .... New York Public Interest Research Group
**NYPL** ......... New York Public Library [*New York, NY*]
**NYPL Bull** ... New York Public Library. Bulletin [*A publication*]
**NYPLC** ...... National Youth Pro-Life Coalition (EA)
**NYPLR** ...... New York Prime Loan Rate [*Finance*] (DS)
**NYPM** ....... National Yokefellow Prison Ministry [*Later, YPM*] (EA)
**NYPM** ....... Navy Youth Program Manager (MCD)
**NYPMA** .... New York Paper Merchants Association (EA)
**NYPOE** ..... New York Port of Embarkation [*Military*]
**NYPORT** ... Navy Yard, Portsmouth, New Hampshire
**NYPR** ........ N-Nitrosopyrrolidine [*Also, NO-PYR*] [*Biochemistry, organic chemistry*]
**NYPR** ........ New York Practice Reports [*A publication*] (DLA)
**NY Prod R** ... New York Produce Review and American Creamery [*A publication*]
**NY Prod Rev Am Creamery** ... New York Produce Review and American Creamery [*A publication*]
**NYPRPG** ... New York Publishers Rights and Permissions Group (EA)
**NY Pr Rep** ... New York Practice Reports [*A publication*] (DLA)
**NYPS** ........ National Yellow Pages Service
**NYPS** ........ Navy Yard, Puget Sound [*Bremerton*], Washington

**NYPSO**...... New York Philharmonic Symphony Orchestra
**NY Pub Lib Br Lib Bk News** ... New York Public Library. Branch Library Book News [*A publication*]
**NY Public Lib Bull** ... New York City Public Library. Bulletin [*A publication*]
**NYPYR**...... Nitrosopyrrolidine [*Also, NPYR*] [*Organic chemistry*]
**NYQ**.......... New York Quarterly [*A publication*]
**Nyr**............ Magyar Nyelvor [*A publication*]
**NYR**.......... Neodymium YAG [*Yttrium Aluminum Garnet*] Range-Finder
**NYR**.......... New York Court of Appeals Reports [*A publication*] (DLA)
**NYR**.......... New York Reports [*New York*] [*A publication*]
**NYR**.......... New York Review of Books [*A publication*]
**NYR**.......... Not Yet Reported [*Air Force*]
**NYR**.......... Not Yet Required (MUGU)
**NYR**.......... Not Yet Returned [*Military*]
**NYR**.......... Nuclear Yield Requirement (NATG)
**NYR**.......... Receiver Site [*Nevada*] [*Seismograph station code, US Geological Survey*] [*Closed*] (SEIS)
**NYRA**........ New York Racing Authority [*Cable-television system*]
**NYRAPG**... New York Rights and Permissions Group (EA)
**NYRB**........ New York Review of Books [*A publication*]
**NYR of Bk** ... New York Review of Books [*A publication*]
**NYR Bks**.... New York Review of Books [*A publication*]
**NYRC**........ New York Railroad Commission Reports [*A publication*] (DLA)
**NY Rec**....... New York Record [*A publication*] (DLA)
**NY Reg**...... New York Daily Register [*A publication*] (DLA)
**NY Rep**...... New York Court of Appeals Reports [*A publication*] (DLA)
**NY Reps**..... New York Court of Appeals Reports [*A publication*] (DLA)
**NY Reptr**... New York Reporter [*A publication*] (ILCA)
**NY Rev Bks** ... New York Review of Books [*A publication*]
**NY Rev Book** ... New York Review of Books [*A publication*]
**NY Review** ... New York Review of Books [*A publication*]
**NYRFC**...... New York Rangers Fan Club (EA)
**NYRL**........ New York Revised Laws [*A publication*] (DLA)
**NYRMA**.... New York Raincoat Manufacturers Association (EA)
**NYRRC**..... New York Road Runners Club (EA)
**NYRS**......... New York Revised Statutes [*A publication*] (DLA)
**NYRS**......... New Youth Research Survey [*Religious education test*]
**NYS**.......... New York Shavians (EA)
**NYS**.......... New York State
**NYS**.......... New York State Reporter [*A publication*] (DLA)
**NYS**.......... New York State Union List, Albany, NY [*OCLC symbol*] (OCLC)
**NYS**.......... New York Sun [*A publication*]
**NYS**.......... New York Supplement [*A publication*] (DLA)
**NyS**........... Nydanske Studier. Almen Kommunikationsteori [*A publication*]
**NYS**.......... Syncline Ridge [*Nevada*] [*Seismograph station code, US Geological Survey*] [*Closed*] (SEIS)
**NYS**.......... West's New York Supplement [*A publication*]
**NYS**.......... Yonkers School System, Yonkers, NY [*Library symbol*] [*Library of Congress*] (LCLS)
**NYSA**........ New York Shipping Association (EA)
**NYSASS**.... New York State Association of Service Stations [*Later, NYSASSRS*] (EA)
**NYSASSRS** ... New York State Association of Service Stations and Repair Shops (EA)
**NYSBA Bull** ... New York State Bar Association. Bulletin [*A publication*] (DLA)
**NYSB J**...... New York State Bar Journal [*A publication*]
**NYSC**......... New York Shipbuilding Corporation
**NYSC**......... Thompson and Cook's New York Supreme Court Reports [*A publication*] (DLA)
**NYSCA**...... National Youth Sports Coaches Association (EA)
**NYSCAT**... New York State Union Catalog of Film and Video [*Mid-Hudson Library System*] [*Information service or system*] (IID)
**NYSCS**...... New York State Colonization Society [*Defunct*] (EA)
**NYS Ct**...... New York Superior Court Reports [*A publication*] (DLA)
**NYSD**........ New York Society for the Deaf [*Formerly, JSD*] (EA)
**NYS 2d**...... New York Supplement, Second Series [*A publication*] (DLA)
**NYS 2d**...... West's New York Supplement. Second Series [*A publication*]
**NYSDA**..... New York Security Dealers Association (EA)
**NYSDR**..... New York State Department Reports [*A publication*] (DLA)
**NYSE**......... New York Stock Exchange [*New York, NY*] (EA)
**NYSE**......... New York Stock Exchange Guide [*Commerce Clearing House*] [*A publication*] (DLA)
**NY Sea Grant L and Pol'y J** ... New York Sea Grant Law and Policy Journal [*A publication*]
**NYSE Fact** ... New York Stock Exchange. Fact Book [*A publication*]
**NYSE Guide CCH** ... New York Stock Exchange Guide. Commerce Clearing House [*A publication*]
**NY Sen J**.... New York Senate Journal [*A publication*] (DLA)
**NYSERDA** ... New York State Energy Research and Development Authority
**NYSERDA Rev** ... NYSERDA [*New York State Energy Research and Development Authority*] Review [*A publication*]
**NYSERNet** ... New York State Education and Research Network, Inc. [*Telecommunications service*] (TSSD)
**NYSF**......... National Youth Science Foundation
**NYSFTCA** ... New York State Fruit Testing Cooperative Association (EA)
**NYSGI**....... New York Sea Grant Institute [*Albany, NY*] [*Department of Commerce*] (GRD)
**NYSIIS**...... New York State Identification and Intelligence System
**NYSILL**..... New York State Interlibrary Loan [*Network*]
**NYSNY**..... New York Naval Shipyard (New York)
**NY Soc Exp Study Ed Yrbk** ... New York Society for the Experimental Study of Education. Yearbook [*A publication*]
**NY Spec Term R** ... Howard's New York Practice Reports [*A publication*] (DLA)
**NY Spec Term Rep** ... Howard's New York Practice Reports [*A publication*] (DLA)
**NYSPI**....... New York State Psychiatric Institute [*New York State Office of Mental Hygiene*] [*Research center*] (RCD)
**NYSR**......... New York State Reporter [*A publication*] (DLA)
**Nys S**.......... Nysvenska Studier [*A publication*]
**NYSSA**...... New York Society of Security Analysts [*New York, NY*] (EA)
**NYSSDA**... New York State Safe Deposit Association [*New York, NY*] (EA)
**NYSSNTA J** ... NYSSNTA [*New York State School Nurse-Teachers Association*] Journal [*A publication*]
**NY St**......... New York State Reporter [*A publication*] (DLA)
**NYST**......... Nystagmus [*Medicine*]
**NY St Agr Soc Tr** ... New York State Agricultural Society. Transactions [*A publication*]
**NY State Ag Exp** ... New York State Agricultural Experiment Station. Publications [*A publication*]
**NY State Agric Exp Stn (Geneva) Annu Rep** ... New York State Agricultural Experiment Station (Geneva). Annual Report [*A publication*]
**NY State Agric Exp Stn Seed Res Circ** ... New York State Agricultural Experiment Station. Seed Research Circular [*A publication*]
**NY State Agric Exp Stn Spec Rep** ... New York State Agricultural Experiment Station. Special Report [*A publication*]
**NY State Assoc Milk Food Sanit Annu Rep** ... New York State Association of Milk and Food Sanitarians. Annual Report [*A publication*]
**NY State Assoc Milk Sanit Annu Rep** ... New York State Association of Milk Sanitarians. Annual Report [*A publication*]
**NY State Bar J** ... New York State Bar Journal [*A publication*]
**NY State Coll Ceramics Ceramic Expt Sta Bull** ... New York State College of Ceramics. Ceramic Experiment Station. Bulletin [*A publication*]
**NY State Coll For Syracuse Univ Bull** ... New York State College of Forestry. Syracuse University. Bulletin [*A publication*]
**NY State Conserv** ... New York State Conservationist [*A publication*]
**NY State Dent J** ... New York State Dental Journal [*A publication*]
**NY State Dep Environ Conserv Bull** ... New York State Department of Environmental Conservation. Bulletin [*A publication*]
**NY State Dep Health Div Lab Res Annu Rep** ... New York State Department of Health. Division of Laboratories and Research. Annual Report [*A publication*]
**NY State Dep Health Lab Res Oper Data** ... New York State Department of Health. Division of Laboratories and Research. Operations Data [*A publication*]
**NY State Dep Labor Div Ind Hyg Mon Rev** ... New York State Department of Labor. Division of Industrial Hygiene. Monthly Review [*A publication*]
**NY State Ed** ... New York State Education [*A publication*]
**NY State Flower Growers Bull** ... New York State Flower Growers. Bulletin [*A publication*]
**NY State Horti Soc Proc** ... New York State Horticultural Society. Proceedings [*A publication*]
**NY State J Med** ... New York State Journal of Medicine [*A publication*]
**NY State Mus Bull** ... New York State Museum. Bulletin [*A publication*]
**NY State Mus Circ Handb** ... New York State Museum Circular. Handbook [*A publication*]
**NY State Mus Map Chart Ser** ... New York State Museum. Map and Chart Series [*A publication*]
**NY State Mus Mem** ... New York State Museum. Memoir [*A publication*]
**NY State Mus Sci Serv Bull** ... New York State Museum and Science Service. Bulletin [*A publication*]
**NY State Mus Sci Serv Circ** ... New York State Museum and Science Service. Circular [*A publication*]
**NY State Mus Sci Serv Educ Leafl** ... New York State Museum and Science Service. Educational Leaflet [*A publication*]
**NY State Mus and Sci Service Bull Circ** ... New York State Museum and Science Service. Bulletin. Circular [*A publication*]
**NY State Mus Sci Serv Map Chart Ser** ... New York State Museum and Science Service. Map and Chart Series [*A publication*]
**NY State Mus Sci Serv Mem** ... New York State Museum and Science Service. Memoir [*A publication*]
**NY State Nurse** ... New York State Nurse [*A publication*]
**NY State R** ... New York State Reporter [*A publication*] (DLA)
**NY State Rep** ... New York State Reporter [*A publication*] (DLA)
**NY State Sci Service Rept Inv** ... New York State Science Service. Report of Investigation [*A publication*]
**NY State Sci Serv Univ State NY Report Invest** ... New York State Science Service. University of the State of New York. Report of Investigation [*A publication*]

**NY State Water Resour Comm Basin Plann Rep** ... New York State Water Resources Commission. Basin Planning Report [*A publication*]
**NY St Ba A** ... New York State Bar Association. Bulletin [*A publication*] (DLA)
**NY St BJ** ... New York State Bar Journal [*A publication*]
**NY St Cab An Rp** ... New York State Cabinet of Natural History. Annual Report. Regents University [*A publication*]
**NY St Dept Rep** ... New York State Department Reports [*A publication*] (DLA)
**NYSTDL**... Agricultural Research. Seoul National University [*A publication*]
**NY St G An Rp** ... New York State Geologist. Annual Report [*A publication*]
**NY St His As** ... New York State Historical Association. Proceedings [*A publication*]
**NY St His As Q J** ... New York State Historical Association. Quarterly Journal [*A publication*]
**NY St Hist Assn J** ... New York State Historical Association. Quarterly Journal [*A publication*]
**NYStJ**........ Saint Joseph's Seminary, Dunwoodie, Yonkers, NY [*Library symbol*] [*Library of Congress*] (LCLS)
**NY St J Med** ... New York State Journal of Medicine [*A publication*]
**NY St Mus** ... New York State Museum [*A publication*]
**NY St Mus An Rp** ... New York State Museum of Natural History. Annual Report [*A publication*]
**NY St R**...... New York State Reporter [*A publication*] (DLA)
**NY St Reg** ... New York State Register [*A publication*]
**NY St Rep** ... New York State Reporter [*A publication*] (DLA)
**NY St Repr** ... New York State Reporter [*A publication*] (DLA)
**NY Sup Ct** ... New York Supreme Court Reports [*A publication*] (DLA)
**NY Sup Ct** ... Supreme Court Reports (New York) [*A publication*]
**NY Sup Ct Rep** ... Thompson and Cook's New York Supreme Court Reports [*A publication*] (DLA)
**NY Sup Ct (T & C)** ... Thompson and Cook's New York Supreme Court Reports [*A publication*] (DLA)
**NY Super** ... New York Superior Court Reports [*A publication*] (DLA)
**NY Super Ct** ... New York Superior Court Reports [*Various reporters*] [*A publication*] (DLA)
**NY Super Ct R** ... New York Superior Court Reports [*A publication*] (DLA)
**NY Super Ct Rep** ... New York Superior Court Reports [*A publication*] (DLA)
**NY Supl**..... New York Supplement [*A publication*] (DLA)
**NY Supp**.... New York Supplement [*A publication*] (DLA)
**NY Supp 2d** ... New York Supplement, Second Series [*A publication*] (DLA)
**NY Suppl**... New York Supplement [*A publication*] (DLA)
**NY Supr**..... New York Superior Court Reports [*A publication*] (DLA)
**NY Supr Ct** ... New York Superior Court Reports [*A publication*] (DLA)
**NY Supr Ct R** ... New York Superior Court Reports [*A publication*] (DLA)
**NY Supr Ct Rep** ... New York Superior Court Reports [*A publication*] (DLA)
**NY Supr Ct Repts (T & C)** ... New York Supreme Court Reports, by Thompson and Cook [*A publication*] (DLA)
**NY Suprm Ct** ... New York Supreme Court Reports [*A publication*] (DLA)
**NYSW**....... New York, Susquehanna & Western Railroad Co. [*AAR code*]
**NYSWGGI** ... New York State Wine Grape Growers, Incorporated (EA)
**NYT**........... National Youth Theatre [*British*]
**NYT**........... New Yiddish Theater (BJA)
**NYT**........... New York Testing Laboratories, Inc.
**NYT**........... New York Times [*A publication*]
**NYT**........... New York Times Book Review [*A publication*]
**NYT**........... [*The*] New York Times Co. [*AMEX symbol*] (SPSG)
**NYTA**........ New York Theatre Annual [*A publication*]
**NY Tax Cas** ... New York Tax Cases [*Commerce Clearing House*] [*A publication*] (DLA)
**NYTB**........ New York Theatre Ballet
**NYTB**........ New York Times Book Review [*A publication*]
**NYTBIO**.... [*The*] New York Times Biographical File [*The New York Times Co.*] [*Information service or system*] (CRD)
**NYTBR**...... New York Times Book Review [*A publication*]
**NYTCL**...... New York Temperance Civic League [*Later, AYE*] (EA)
**Ny Tek**....... Ny Teknik [*A publication*]
**NY Theat Cr** ... New York Theatre Critics. Reviews [*A publication*]
**NY Them** ... New York Themis [*New York City*] [*A publication*] (DLA)
**NYTIA**....... New York Times [*A publication*]
**NYT/IB**..... New York Times Information Bank
**NY Times**... New York Times [*A publication*]
**NY Times**... New York Times Book Review [*A publication*]
**NY Times Biog Service** ... New York Times Biographical Service [*A publication*]
**NY Times Bk R** ... New York Times Book Review [*A publication*]
**NY Times Book Rev** ... New York Times Book Review [*A publication*]
**NY Times M** ... New York Times Magazine [*A publication*]
**NY Times Mag** ... New York Times Magazine [*A publication*]
**NY Times N** ... New York Times. National Edition [*A publication*]
**NY Times R** ... New York Times Book Review [*A publication*]
**NYTIS**....... New York Times Information Service, Inc. [*Mead Data Central*] [*Database originator and host*] (IID)
**NYTKB**...... Ny Teknik [*A publication*]
**NYTL**........ New York Testing Laboratories, Inc. [*NASDAQ symbol*] (NQ)
**NYTLS**...... New York Times Literary Supplement [*A publication*]
**NYTM**....... New York Times Magazine [*A publication*]
**NYTMag**... New York Times Magazine [*A publication*]
**NYTMS**..... New York Times Magazine Section [*A publication*]
**NYTNS**...... New York Times News Service
**NYTR**........ New York Term Reports (Caines' Reports) [*A publication*] (DLA)
**NYTRAH**.. Marine Sciences Research Center [*Stony Brook*]. Technical Report [*A publication*]
**NY Trans**... New York Transcript [*Numbers 1-11*] [*1861*] [*New York City*] [*A publication*] (DLA)
**NY Trans App** ... New York Transcript Appeals Reports [*A publication*] (DLA)
**NY Trans NS** ... New York Transcript, New Series [*New York City*] [*A publication*] (DLA)
**NY Trans Rep** ... New York Transcript Reports [*A publication*] (DLA)
**NYT Rep**.... Caines' Term Reports [*New York*] [*A publication*] (DLA)
**NYTS**......... New York Theological Seminary
**NYTS**......... Nytest Environmental, Inc. [*NASDAQ symbol*] (NQ)
**Nytt Mag Bot (Oslo)** ... Nytt Magasin foer Botanikk (Oslo) [*A publication*]
**Nytt Mag Naturvid** ... Nytt Magasin foer Naturvidenskapene [*A publication*]
**Nytt Mag Naturvidensk** ... Nytt Magasin foer Naturvidenskapene [*A publication*]
**Nytt Mag Zool (Oslo)** ... Nytt Magasin foer Zoology (Oslo) [*A publication*]
**NYTTS**...... New York Turtle and Tortoise Society (EA)
**nyu**............ New York [*MARC country of publication code*] [*Library of Congress*] (LCCP)
**NYU**........... New York University
**NYU**........... Nyaung-U [*Burma*] [*Airport symbol*] (OAG)
**NYU Conf on Char Found Proc** ... Conference on Charitable Foundations. Proceedings. New York University [*A publication*] (DLA)
**NYU Conf Charitable** ... New York University. Conference on Charitable Foundations. Proceedings [*A publication*] (DLA)
**NYU Conf Charitable Fdn** ... New York University. Conference on Charitable Foundations. Proceedings [*A publication*] (DLA)
**NYU Conf Lab** ... New York University. Conference on Labor [*A publication*]
**NYU Educ Q** ... New York University. Education Quarterly [*A publication*]
**NYU Eng Res Rev** ... NYU Engineering Research Review [*A publication*]
**NYUEQ**..... New York University. Education Quarterly [*A publication*]
**NYU Inst on Fed Tax** ... New York University. Institute on Federal Taxation [*A publication*]
**NYU Inst Fed Tax** ... New York University. Institute on Federal Taxation [*A publication*]
**NYU Inst Fed Taxation** ... New York University. Institute on Federal Taxation [*A publication*]
**NYU Intra L Rev** ... New York University. Intramural Law Review [*A publication*]
**NYU Intramur L Rev** ... New York University. Intramural Law Review [*A publication*]
**NYUJ Int'l Law & Pol** ... New York University. Journal of International Law and Politics [*A publication*]
**NYU J Int'l L & Pol** ... New York University. Journal of International Law and Politics [*A publication*]
**NYU J Int L & Pol** ... New York University. Journal of International Law and Politics [*A publication*]
**NYU J Int L & Politics** ... New York University. Journal of International Law and Politics [*A publication*]
**NYU Law Q Rev** ... New York University. Law Quarterly Review [*A publication*]
**NYUL Center Bull** ... New York University. Law Center. Bulletin [*A publication*] (DLA)
**NYULQ Rev** ... New York University. Law Quarterly Review [*A publication*]
**NYUL Qu Rev** ... New York University. Law Quarterly Review [*A publication*]
**NYULR**..... New York University. Law Review [*A publication*]
**NYU L Rev** ... New York University. Law Review [*A publication*]
**NYULT**..... New York University School of Continuing Education, Continuing Education in Law and Taxation [*A publication*] (DLA)
**NY Unconsol Laws** ... New York Unconsolidated Laws (McKinney) [*A publication*] (DLA)
**NY Univ J Dent** ... New York University. Journal of Dentistry [*A publication*]
**NY Univ J of Internat L and Polit** ... New York University. Journal of International Law and Politics [*A publication*]
**NY Univ L Rev** ... New York University. Law Review [*A publication*]
**NY Univ Res B** ... New York University. Research Bulletin in Commercial Education [*A publication*]
**NYU Rev Law & Soc** ... New York University. Review of Law and Social Change [*A publication*] (DLA)
**NYU Rev Law & Soc C** ... New York University. Review of Law and Social Change [*A publication*]
**NYU Rev L & Soc** ... New York University. Review of Law and Social Change [*A publication*]
**NYU Rev L and Soc Ch** ... New York University. Review of Law and Social Change [*A publication*]
**NYU Rev L & Soc Change** ... New York University. Review of Law and Social Change [*A publication*]
**NYU Slav P** ... New York University. Slavic Papers [*A publication*]
**NYUTI**...... New York University Tax Institute (DLA)
**NYV**........... Vern [*Nevada*] [*Seismograph station code, US Geological Survey*] [*Closed*] (SEIS)
**NYW**.......... New York World [*A publication*]
**NYWA**....... National Youth Work Alliance (EA)
**NYWASH** ... Navy Yard, Washington, DC [*Obsolete*]

**NY Water Power Control Comm Bull** ... New York State Water Power and Control Commission. Bulletin [*A publication*]
**NY Water Power and Control Comm Bull** ... New York Water Power and Control Commission. Bulletin [*A publication*]
**NY Water Resour Comm Bull** ... New York State Water Resources Commission. Bulletin [*A publication*]
**NYWC**....... New York Wine Council (EA)
**NY Week Dig** ... New York Weekly Digest [*A publication*] (DLA)
**NY Weekly Dig** ... New York Weekly Digest [*A publication*] (DLA)
**NYWF**....... New York World's Fair
**NYWGF**.... New York Wine/Grape Foundation (EA)
**NYWJT**..... New York World Journal Tribune [*A publication*]
**NY Wkly Dig** ... New York Weekly Digest [*A publication*] (DLA)
**NYYP**........ New York Yellow Pages, Inc.
**NYZP**........ New York Zoological Park
**NYZS**......... New York Zoological Society
**NYZZA3** ... Journal. Japan Pharmaceutical Association [*A publication*]
**NZ**............. Air New Zealand Ltd. (Domestic Division) [*ICAO designator*] (ICDA)
**NZ**............. Nasa Zena [*A publication*]
**NZ**............. Neue Zeitschrift fuer Musik [*A publication*]
**NZ**............. Neuphilologische Zeitschrift [*A publication*]
**NZ**............. Neutrality Zone
**NZ**............. New Mexico & Arizona Land Co. [*AMEX symbol*] (SPSG)
**nz**............... New Zealand [*MARC country of publication code*] [*Library of Congress*] (LCCP)
**NZ**............. New Zealand (ADA)
**NZ**............. New Zealand [*ANSI two-letter standard code*] (CNC)
**NZ**............. New Zealand National Airways Corp. [*ICAO designator*]
**NZ**............. New Zealand Reports [*A publication*] (DLA)
**N-Z**............ Nike-Zeus [*Missiles*] (AAG)
**NZ**............. Normal to Z-Axis (MCD)
**NZ**............. Nose to Z-Axis (MCD)
**NZ**............. Novyj Zurnal [*A publication*]
**NZ**............. Nuclear Zone
**NZ**............. Numismatische Zeitschrift [*A publication*]
**NZA**.......... New Zealand Artillery (DMA)
**NZA**.......... Niobium Zinc Alloy
**NZAA**........ Auckland/International [*New Zealand*] [*ICAO location identifier*] (ICLI)
**NZAAC**..... New Zealand Army Air Corps (DMA)
**NZAEC**..... New Zealand Army Educational Corps (DMA)
**NZAF**........ New Zealand Air Force (DAS)
**NZ Agi Sci** ... New Zealand Institution of Agricultural Science. Bulletin [*A publication*]
**NZ Agric Sci** ... New Zealand Agricultural Science [*A publication*]
**NZ Agricst** ... New Zealand Agriculturist [*A publication*]
**NZ Agr Sci** ... New Zealand Agricultural Science [*A publication*]
**NzAGS**....... Church of Jesus Christ of Latter-Day Saints, Genealogical Society Library, Auckland Branch, Auckland, New Zealand [*Library symbol*] [*Library of Congress*] (LCLS)
**NZAK**........ Auckland [*New Zealand*] [*ICAO location identifier*] (ICLI)
**NZAMC**.... New Zealand Army Medical Corps (DMA)
**NZANS**..... New Zealand Army Nursing Service (DMA)
**NZAOC**.... New Zealand Army Ordnance Corps (DMA)
**NZAP**........ Taupo [*New Zealand*] [*ICAO location identifier*] (ICLI)
**NZAPC**..... New Zealand Army Pay Corps (DMA)
**NZ App Rep** ... New Zealand Appeal Reports [*A publication*] (DLA)
**NZAPS**...... Nike-Zeus Automatic Programming System [*Missiles*]
**NZAQ**........ Auckland [*New Zealand*] [*ICAO location identifier*] (ICLI)
**NZAR**........ Ardmore [*New Zealand*] [*ICAO location identifier*] (ICLI)
**NZ Arch**..... New Zealand Architect [*A publication*]
**NZ Archit**.. New Zealand Architect [*A publication*]
**NZASC**...... New Zealand Army Service Corps (DMA)
**NzAU**......... Auckland University, Auckland, New Zealand [*Library symbol*] [*Library of Congress*] (LCLS)
**NZ Awards** ... New Zealand Awards, Recommendations, Agreements, Etc. [*A publication*] (DLA)
**NZB**........... New Zealand Black [*Mice hybrids*]
**NZB**........... Nonzero Binary (NASA)
**NZBC**........ New Zealand Broadcasting Corporation
**NZ Beekeep** ... New Zealand Beekeeper [*A publication*]
**NZ Beekpr** ... New Zealand Beekeeper [*A publication*]
**NZ Beekprs J** ... New Zealand Beekeepers' Journal [*A publication*]
**NZ Bird Banding Scheme Annu Rep** ... New Zealand Bird Banding Scheme. Annual Report [*A publication*]
**NZ Bu Econ** ... New Zealand Building Economist [*A publication*]
**NZ Bu Insp** ... New Zealand Building Inspector [*A publication*]
**NZ Bus Con** ... New Zealand Business Conditions [*A publication*]
**NZC**........... Jacksonville, FL [*Location identifier*] [*FAA*] (FAAL)
**NZC**........... New Zealand Commerce [*A publication*]
**NZC**........... New Zealand Cross (DAS)
**NZCA**........ Campbell Island [*New Zealand*] [*ICAO location identifier*] (ICLI)
**NZ Cartogr J** ... New Zealand Cartographic Journal [*A publication*]
**NZCC**........ New Zealand Cyclist Corps (DMA)
**NZCernU**... Naukovi Zapyski Cernivec'koho Derzavnoho Universyteta [*A publication*]
**NZCerPI**.... Naukovi Zapyski Cerkas'koho Derzavnoho Pedahohicnoho Instytutu [*A publication*]
**NzCGS**....... Church of Jesus Christ of Latter-Day Saints, Genealogical Society Library, Canterbury Branch, Christchurch, New Zealand [*Library symbol*] [*Library of Congress*] (LCLS)
**NZCH**........ Christchurch/International [*New Zealand*] [*ICAO location identifier*] (ICLI)
**NZ Chiro J** ... New Zealand Chiropractic Journal [*A publication*]
**NZCI**......... Chatham Island/Tuuta [*New Zealand*] [*ICAO location identifier*] (ICLI)
**NZCM**....... McMurdo Sound, Antarctica [*New Zealand*] [*ICAO location identifier*] (ICLI)
**NZCO**........ Christchurch [*New Zealand*] [*ICAO location identifier*] (ICLI)
**NZ Coal**.... New Zealand Coal [*A publication*]
**NZ Col LJ** ... New Zealand Colonial Law Journal [*A publication*] (DLA)
**NZ Com**..... New Zealand Commerce [*A publication*]
**NZ Com Grow** ... New Zealand Commercial Grower [*A publication*]
**NZ Commer Grow** ... New Zealand Commercial Grower [*A publication*]
**NZ Conc Constr** ... New Zealand Concrete Construction [*A publication*]
**NZ Concr Constr** ... NZ [*New Zealand*] Concrete Construction [*A publication*]
**NZCS**......... New Zealand Corps of Signals (DMA)
**NZ Ct App** ... New Zealand Court of Appeals (DLA)
**NZ Ct Arb** ... New Zealand Court of Arbitration (DLA)
**NZDC**........ New Zealand Dental Corps (DMA)
**NZ Dent J** ... New Zealand Dental Journal [*A publication*]
**NZ Dep Agric Rep** ... New Zealand. Department of Agriculture. Report [*A publication*]
**NZ Dep Health Spec Rep Ser** ... New Zealand. Department of Health. Special Report Series [*A publication*]
**NZ Dep Intern Aff Wildl Publ** ... New Zealand. Department of Internal Affairs. Wildlife Publication [*A publication*]
**NZ Dep Sci Ind Res Bull** ... New Zealand. Department of Scientific and Industrial Research. Bulletin [*A publication*]
**NZ Dep Sci Ind Res Chem Div Rep** ... New Zealand. Department of Scientific and Industrial Research. Chemistry Division. Report [*A publication*]
**NZ Dep Sci Ind Res Crop Res News** ... New Zealand. Department of Scientific and Industrial Research. Crop Research News [*A publication*]
**NZ Dep Sci Ind Res Discuss Pap** ... New Zealand. Department of Scientific and Industrial Research. Discussion Paper [*A publication*]
**NZ Dep Sci Ind Res Geol Surv Paleontol Bull** ... New Zealand. Department of Scientific and Industrial Research. Geological Survey. Paleontological Bulletin [*A publication*]
**NZ Dep Sci Ind Res Geophys Div Rep** ... New Zealand. Department of Scientific and Industrial Research. Geophysics Division. Report [*A publication*]
**NZ Dep Sci Ind Res Geophys Div Tech Note** ... New Zealand. Department of Scientific and Industrial Research. Geophysics Division. Technical Note [*A publication*]
**NZ Dep Sci Ind Res Inf Ser** ... New Zealand. Department of Scientific and Industrial Research. Information Series [*A publication*]
**NZDF**........ Christchurch/International [*New Zealand*] [*ICAO location identifier*] (ICLI)
**NZDN**........ Dunedin [*New Zealand*] [*ICAO location identifier*] (ICLI)
**NZDnepU** ... Naucnye Zapyski Dnepropetrovskogo Gosudarstvennogo Universiteta [*A publication*]
**NZDonPI**... Naukovi Zapyski Donec'koho Derzavnoho Pedahohicnoho Instytutu [*A publication*]
**NZ Draughtsman** ... New Zealand Draughtsman [*A publication*]
**NZDrohPI** ... Naukovi Zapyski Drohobyc'koho Derzavnoho Pedahohicnoho Instytutu [*A publication*]
**NZE**........... Corps of New Zealand Engineers (DMA)
**NZE**........... Glenview, IL [*Location identifier*] [*FAA*] (FAAL)
**NZE**........... North Zenith East
**N Zealand Lib** ... New Zealand Libraries [*A publication*]
**NZ Ecol Soc Proc** ... New Zealand Ecological Society. Proceedings [*A publication*]
**NZEF**......... New Zealand Expeditionary Force
**NZ Elect**.... New Zealand Electron [*A publication*]
**NZ Elect Rev** ... New Zealand Electronics Review [*A publication*]
**NZ Electr J** ... New Zealand Electrical Journal [*A publication*]
**NZ Electronics** ... New Zealand Electronics. Supplement to Electrical Industry [*A publication*]
**NZ Electron Rev** ... New Zealand Electronics Review [*A publication*]
**NZ Energ J** ... New Zealand Energy Journal [*A publication*]
**NZ Energy J** ... New Zealand Energy Journal [*A publication*]
**NZ Energy Res Dev Comm Newsl** ... New Zealand Energy Research and Development Committee. Newsletter [*A publication*]
**NZ Eng**...... New Zealand Engineering [*A publication*]
**NZ Eng**...... NZ [*New Zealand*] Engineering [*A publication*]
**NZ Eng News** ... New Zealand Engineering News [*A publication*]
**NZ Engng** .. New Zealand Engineering [*A publication*]
**NZ Ent**....... New Zealand Entomologist [*A publication*]
**NZ Entomol** ... New Zealand Entomologist [*A publication*]
**NZ Environ** ... New Zealand Environment [*A publication*]
**NZEP**......... New Zealand Economic Papers [*A publication*]
**NZEVA**..... New Zealand Empire Veterans Association (DMA)
**NZF**........... Near Zero Field
**NZFA**........ New Zealand Field Artillery (DMA)
**NZ Fam Phys** ... New Zealand Family Physician [*A publication*]
**NZ Farmer** ... New Zealand Farmer [*A publication*]

**NZ Fert**...... New Zealand Fertiliser Journal [*A publication*]
**NZ Fert J**... New Zealand Fertiliser Journal [*A publication*]
**NZ Financ Rev**... New Zealand Financial Review [*A publication*]
**NZ Fin Rev**... New Zealand Financial Review [*A publication*]
**NZ Fish Res Div Fish Res Bull**... New Zealand Fisheries. Research Division. Fisheries Research Bulletin [*A publication*]
**NZFL**......... New Zealand Federation of Labor
**NZfM**........ Neue Zeitschrift fuer Musik [*A publication*]
**NZFMCAE**... New Zealand Federated Mountain Clubs Antarctic Expedition [*1962-63*]
**NZ For Affairs R**... New Zealand Foreign Affairs Review [*A publication*]
**NZ Foreign Aff Rev**... New Zealand Foreign Affairs Review [*A publication*]
**NZ For Res Inst For Serv Mapp Ser 6**... New Zealand Forest Research Institute. Forest Service Mapping. Series 6 [*A publication*]
**NZ For Res Notes**... New Zealand Forestry Research Notes [*A publication*]
**NZ For Serv For Res Inst FRI Symp**... New Zealand. Forest Service. Forest Research Institute. FRI Symposium [*A publication*]
**NZ For Serv For Res Inst Tech Pap**... New Zealand. Forest Service. Forest Research Institute. Technical Paper [*A publication*]
**NZ For Serv Inf Ser**... New Zealand. Forest Service. Information Series [*A publication*]
**NZ For Serv Rep Dir-Gen For**... New Zealand. Forest Service. Report of the Director-General of Forests [*A publication*]
**NZ For Serv Rep For Res Inst**... New Zealand. Forest Service. Report of the Forest Research Institute [*A publication*]
**NZ For Serv Res Leafl**... New Zealand. Forest Service. Research Leaflet [*A publication*]
**NZ For Serv Tech Pap**... New Zealand. Forest Service. Technical Paper [*A publication*]
**NZ Fruit and Prod**... New Zealand Fruit and Product Journal [*A publication*]
**NZFSA**...... New Zealand Journal of Forestry Science [*A publication*]
**NZ Furn**..... New Zealand Furniture [*A publication*]
**NZG**........... Near Zero Gravity
**NZG**........... North Carolina School of the Arts, Winston-Salem, NC [*OCLC symbol*] (OCLC)
**NZGA**........ New Zealand Garrison Artillery (DMA)
**NZ Gard**.... New Zealand Gardener [*A publication*]
**NZ Gaz LR**... New Zealand Gazette Law Reports [*A publication*] (DLA)
**NZ Geneal**... New Zealand Genealogist [*A publication*]
**NZ Geochem Group Newsl**... New Zealand Geochemical Group. Newsletter [*A publication*]
**NZ Geogr**... New Zealand Geographer [*A publication*]
**NZ Geol Surv Bull**... New Zealand. Geological Survey. Bulletin [*A publication*]
**NZ Geol Surv Ind Miner Rocks**... New Zealand. Geological Survey. Industrial Minerals and Rocks [*A publication*]
**NZ Geol Surv Misc Ser Map**... New Zealand. Geological Survey. Miscellaneous Series. Map [*A publication*]
**NZ Geol Surv Rep**... New Zealand. Geological Survey. Report [*A publication*]
**NZGG-A**.... New Zealand Geographer [*A publication*]
**NZGLR**..... New Zealand Gazette Law Reports [*A publication*] (DLA)
**NZGS**........ Gisborne [*New Zealand*] [*ICAO location identifier*] (ICLI)
**NZGSAE**... New Zealand Geological Survey Antarctic Expedition [*1957-*]
**NZ He**........ New Zealand Herald [*A publication*]
**NZhi**.......... Nauka i Zhizn' [*Moscow*] [*A publication*]
**NZHK**........ Hokitika [*New Zealand*] [*ICAO location identifier*] (ICLI)
**NZHN**....... Hamilton [*New Zealand*] [*ICAO location identifier*] (ICLI)
**NZHO**....... Wellington [*New Zealand*] [*ICAO location identifier*] (ICLI)
**NZ Home and Bu**... New Zealand Home and Building [*A publication*]
**NZ Home and Build**... New Zealand Home and Building [*A publication*]
**NZ Hosp**.... New Zealand Hospital [*A publication*]
**NZIE Proc Tech Groups**... NZIE [*New Zealand Institution of Engineers*] Proceedings of Technical Groups [*A publication*]
**NZ Ind Arb**... New Zealand Industrial Arbitration Awards [*A publication*] (DLA)
**NZ Inst Eng Proc Tech Groups**... New Zealand Institution of Engineers. Proceedings of Technical Groups [*A publication*]
**NZ Inst Eng Trans**... New Zealand Institution of Engineers. Transactions [*A publication*]
**NZ Inter**..... New Zealand Interface [*A publication*]
**NZ Int Rev**... New Zealand International Review [*A publication*]
**NZIR**.......... Niemeyers Zeitschrift fuer Internationales Recht [*A publication*]
**NZIzmPI**... Naukovi Zapyski Izmail's'koho Derzavnoho Pedahohicnoho Instytutu [*A publication*]
**NZJ**............ Naze [*Ryukyu Islands*] [*Seismograph station code, US Geological Survey*] (SEIS)
**NZJ**............ Santa Ana, CA [*Location identifier*] [*FAA*] (FAAL)
**NZ J Agr**... New Zealand Journal of Agriculture [*A publication*]
**NZ J Agric**... New Zealand Journal of Agriculture [*A publication*]
**NZ J Agric Res**... New Zealand Journal of Agricultural Research [*A publication*]
**NZ J Agr Re**... New Zealand Journal of Agricultural Research [*A publication*]
**NZ J Agr Res**... New Zealand Journal of Agricultural Research [*A publication*]
**NZ J Archaeol**... New Zealand Journal of Archaeology [*A publication*]
**NZ J Bot**.... New Zealand Journal of Botany [*A publication*]
**NZ J Bus**... New Zealand Journal of Business [*A publication*]
**NZ J Crop Hortic Sci**... New Zealand Journal of Crop and Horticultural Science [*A publication*]
**NZ J Dairy**... New Zealand Journal of Dairy Science and Technology [*A publication*]
**NZ J Dairy Sci**... New Zealand Journal of Dairy Science and Technology [*A publication*]
**NZJ Dairy Sci Technol**... New Zealand Journal of Dairy Science and Technology [*A publication*]
**NZ J Dairy Technol**... New Zealand Journal of Dairy Technology [*A publication*]
**NZ J Ecol**.. New Zealand Journal of Ecology [*A publication*]
**NZ J Educ**... New Zealand Journal of Educational Studies [*A publication*]
**NZ J Educ Stud**... New Zealand Journal of Educational Studies [*A publication*]
**NZ J Exp Agric**... New Zealand Journal of Experimental Agriculture [*A publication*]
**NZ J Fam Plann**... New Zealand Journal of Family Planning [*A publication*]
**NZ J For**.... New Zealand Journal of Forestry [*A publication*]
**NZ J For Sci**... New Zealand Journal of Forestry Science [*A publication*]
**NZ J Fr Stud**... New Zealand Journal of French Studies [*A publication*]
**NZ J Geogr**... New Zealand Journal of Geography [*A publication*]
**NZ J Geol**.. New Zealand Journal of Geology and Geophysics [*A publication*]
**NZ J Geol Geophys**... New Zealand Journal of Geology and Geophysics [*A publication*]
**NZ J Hist**.. New Zealand Journal of History [*A publication*]
**NZJHPER**... New Zealand Journal of Health, Physical Education, and Recreation [*A publication*]
**NZ J Ind Relat**... New Zealand Journal of Industrial Relations [*A publication*]
**NZ J Ind Relations**... New Zealand Journal of Industrial Relations [*A publication*]
**NZ Jl Agric**... New Zealand Journal of Agriculture [*A publication*]
**NZ Jl Agric Res**... New Zealand Journal of Agricultural Research [*A publication*]
**NZ Jl Bot**... New Zealand Journal of Botany [*A publication*]
**NZ Jl Sci**... New Zealand Journal of Science [*A publication*]
**NZ Jl Sci Technol**... New Zealand Journal of Science and Technology [*A publication*]
**NZ Jl Zool**... New Zealand Journal of Zoology [*A publication*]
**NZ J Mar Freshwater Res**... New Zealand Journal of Marine and Freshwater Research [*A publication*]
**NZ J Mar Freshw Res**... New Zealand Journal of Marine and Freshwater Research [*A publication*]
**NZ J Mar Res**... New Zealand Journal of Marine and Freshwater Research [*A publication*]
**NZ J Med Lab Technol**... New Zealand Journal of Medical Laboratory Technology [*A publication*]
**NZ Jnl Bus**... New Zealand Journal of Business [*A publication*]
**NZ Jnl D Sci**... New Zealand Journal of Dairy Science and Technology [*A publication*]
**NZJP**......... New Zealand Justice of the Peace [*1876-77*] [*A publication*] (DLA)
**NZ J Phys Educ**... New Zealand Journal of Health, Physical Education, and Recreation [*A publication*]
**NZ J Physiother**... New Zealand Journal of Physiotherapy [*A publication*]
**NZ J Physiotherapy**... New Zealand Journal of Physiotherapy [*A publication*]
**NZ J Pub Admin**... New Zealand Journal of Public Administration [*A publication*]
**NZJ Publ Adm**... New Zealand Journal of Public Administration [*A publication*]
**NZ J Public Admin**... New Zealand Journal of Public Administration [*A publication*]
**NZJSAB**.... New Zealand Journal of Science [*A publication*]
**NZ J Sci**..... New Zealand Journal of Science [*A publication*]
**NZ J Sci Technol**... New Zealand Journal of Science and Technology [*A publication*]
**NZ J Sci Technol Sect A**... New Zealand Journal of Science and Technology. Section A [*A publication*]
**NZ J Sci Technol Sect B**... New Zealand Journal of Science and Technology. Section B [*A publication*]
**NZ J Sports Med**... New Zealand Journal of Sports Medicine [*A publication*]
**NZ J Technol**... New Zealand Journal of Technology [*A publication*]
**NZ Jur**....... New Zealand Jurist [*1873-78*] [*A publication*] (DLA)
**NZ Jur Mining Law**... Jurist Reports, New Series, Cases in Mining Law [*New Zealand*] [*A publication*] (DLA)
**NZ Jur NS**... New Zealand Jurist, New Series [*A publication*] (DLA)
**NZ J Zool**.. New Zealand Journal of Zoology [*A publication*]
**NZKamPI**... Naukovi Zapyski Kam'jancja-Polil's'koho Derzavnoho Pedahohicnoho Instytutu [*A publication*]
**NZKB**........ Wellington/Kilbirnie [*New Zealand*] [*ICAO location identifier*] (ICLI)
**NZKI**......... Kaikoura [*New Zealand*] [*ICAO location identifier*] (ICLI)
**NZKievPIIn**... Naucnye Zapyski Kievskogo Pedagogiceskogo Instytutu Inostrannych Jazykov [*A publication*]
**NZKL**........ Wellington/Kelburn [*New Zealand*] [*ICAO location identifier*] (ICLI)
**NZKT**........ Kaitaia [*New Zealand*] [*ICAO location identifier*] (ICLI)
**NZKX**........ Kaitaia [*New Zealand*] [*ICAO location identifier*] (ICLI)
**NZKyiPI**.... Naukovi Zapyski Kyjivs'koho Derzavnoho Pedahohicnoho Instytutu [*A publication*]
**NZL**........... New Zealand [*ANSI three-letter standard code*] (CNC)

**NZ Law J**... New Zealand Law Journal [*A publication*]
**NZ Law Soc N** ... New Zealand Law Society. Newsletter [*A publication*] (DLA)
**NZLGR** ..... Local Government Reports [*New Zealand*] [*A publication*] (DLA)
**NZ Lib** ....... New Zealand Libraries [*A publication*]
**NZ Libr**...... New Zealand Libraries [*A publication*]
**NZ Lincoln Coll Tech Publ** ... New Zealand Lincoln College. Technical Publication [*A publication*]
**NZ List** ...... New Zealand Listener [*A publication*]
**NZ L J** ....... New Zealand Law Journal [*A publication*]
**NZLJMC** .. New Zealand Law Journal, Magistrates' Court Decisions [*A publication*] (DLA)
**NZLO** ........ New Zealand Liaison Officer
**NZ Local Gov** ... New Zealand Local Government [*A publication*]
**NZ Loc Govt** ... New Zealand Local Government [*A publication*]
**NZLP**......... New Zealand Labour Party [*Political party*] (PPW)
**NZLR** ........ New Zealand Law Reports [*A publication*] (DLA)
**NZLRCA**... New Zealand Law Reports, Court of Appeal [*A publication*] (DLA)
**NZM**.......... Neue Zeitschrift fuer Missionswissenschaft [*A publication*]
**NZM**.......... Neue Zeitschrift fuer Musik [*A publication*]
**NZ Mar Dep Fish Res Div Bull New Ser** ... New Zealand Marine Department. Fisheries Research Division. Bulletin. New Series [*A publication*]
**NZ Mar Dep Fish Tech Rep** ... New Zealand Marine Department. Fisheries Technical Report [*A publication*]
**NZ Mar Dep Rep** ... New Zealand Marine Department. Report [*A publication*]
**NZ Mar News** ... New Zealand Marine News [*A publication*]
**NZMC**....... New Zealand Medical Corps (DMA)
**NZ Meat Prod** ... New Zealand Meat Producer [*A publication*]
**NZ Med J**.. New Zealand Medical Journal [*A publication*]
**NZ Med J Suppl** ... New Zealand Medical Journal. Supplement [*A publication*]
**NZMF** ....... Milford Sound [*New Zealand*] [*ICAO location identifier*] (ICLI)
**NZMGC**.... New Zealand Machine Gun Corps (DMA)
**NZMGS** .... New Zealand Machine Gun Section (DMA)
**NZ Minist Agric Fish Fish Tech Rep** ... New Zealand Ministry of Agriculture and Fisheries. Fisheries Technical Report [*A publication*]
**NZ Minist Agric Fish Rep Fish** ... New Zealand Ministry of Agriculture and Fisheries. Report on Fisheries [*A publication*]
**NZMiss**..... Neue Zeitschrift fuer Missionswissenschaft [*A publication*]
**NZMissWiss** ... Neue Zeitschrift fuer Missionswissenschaft [*Beckenried, Switzerland*] [*A publication*]
**NZMJA**..... New Zealand Medical Journal [*A publication*]
**NZMN**....... New Zealand Merchant Navy (DAS)
**NZMP**....... New Zealand Military Police (DMA)
**NZMR**....... New Zealand Mounted Rifles (DMA)
**NZMUKS** ... Naukovyj Zbirnik Museju Ukranjinskoji Kultury v Sydnyku [*A publication*]
**N Z Musik** ... Neue Zeitschrift fuer Musik [*A publication*]
**NZMW**...... Neue Zeitschrift fuer Missionswissenschaft [*A publication*]
**NZN**........... Niedersachsischer Zeitschriftennachweis [*Deutsches Bibliotheksinstitut*] [*Federal Republic of Germany*] [*Information service or system*] (CRD)
**NZ Natl Radiat Lab Environ Radioact Annu Rep** ... New Zealand. National Radiation Laboratory. Environmental Radioactivity. Annual Report [*A publication*]
**NZ Nat Sci** ... New Zealand Natural Sciences [*A publication*]
**NZNB**........ New Zealand National Bibliography [*A publication*]
**NZNB**........ New Zealand Naval Board [*Wellington*]
**NZNC**........ New Zealand Native Contingent (DMA)
**NZNFC** ..... Norma Zimmer National Fan Club (EA)
**NZNJ** ........ New Zealand Numismatic Journal [*A publication*]
**NZNP**........ New Plymouth [*New Zealand*] [*ICAO location identifier*] (ICLI)
**NZNR**........ Napier [*New Zealand*] [*ICAO location identifier*] (ICLI)
**NZNS**........ Nelson [*New Zealand*] [*ICAO location identifier*] (ICLI)
**NZ Num J** ... New Zealand Numismatic Journal [*A publication*]
**NZ Nurs Forum** ... New Zealand Nursing Forum [*A publication*]
**NZ Nurs J** ... New Zealand Nursing Journal [*A publication*]
**NZNV**........ Invercargill [*New Zealand*] [*ICAO location identifier*] (ICLI)
**NZOC**........ New Zealand Ordnance Corps (DMA)
**NZ Oceanogr Inst Collect Repr** ... New Zealand Oceanographic Institute. Collected Reprints [*A publication*]
**NZ Oceanogr Inst Mem** ... New Zealand Oceanographic Institute. Memoir [*A publication*]
**NZOH** ....... Ohakea [*New Zealand*] [*ICAO location identifier*] (ICLI)
**NZOI** ......... New Zealand Oceanographic Institute
**NZOI Oceanographic Field Report** ... New Zealand Oceanographic Institute. Oceanographic Field Report [*A publication*]
**NZOI Rec** ... NZOI [*New Zealand Oceanographic Institute*] Records [*A publication*]
**NZ Oper Res** ... New Zealand Operational Research [*A publication*]
**NZOR**........ New Zealand Operational Research [*A publication*]
**NZ Ords** .... Ordinances of the Legislative Council of New Zealand [*A publication*] (DLA)
**NZOU** ....... Oamaru [*New Zealand*] [*ICAO location identifier*] (ICLI)
**NZP**........... National Zoological Park [*Smithsonian Institution*]
**NZPA** ........ New Zealand Press Association
**NZ Paint**.... New Zealand Painter and Decorator [*A publication*]
**NZPC** ........ New Zealand Petroleum Company Ltd. [*NASDAQ symbol*] (NQ)
**NZPCC**...... New Zealand Privy Council Cases [*A publication*] (DLA)
**NZPC Cas** ... New Zealand Privy Council Cases [*A publication*] (DLA)
**NZPG** ........ New Zealand Psychic Gazette [*A publication*]
**NZ Pharm** ... New Zealand Pharmacy [*A publication*]
**NZ Plumb**.. New Zealand Plumbers Journal [*A publication*]
**NZPM** ....... Palmerston North [*New Zealand*] [*ICAO location identifier*] (ICLI)
**NZPO**......... New Zealand Post Office [*Telecommunications*] (TEL)
**NZ Pop** ...... New Zealand Population Review [*A publication*]
**NZ Pot** ....... New Zealand Potato Bulletin [*A publication*]
**NZ Potter**... New Zealand Potter [*A publication*]
**NZPP**......... Paraparaumu [*New Zealand*] [*ICAO location identifier*] (ICLI)
**NZPS**......... New Zealand Permanent Staff (DMA)
**NZ Psychol** ... New Zealand Psychologist [*A publication*]
**NZP & TC** ... New Zealand Post and Telegraph Corps (DMA)
**NZ Purch** ... New Zealand Purchasing and Materials Management Journal [*A publication*]
**NZQN**........ Queenstown [*New Zealand*] [*ICAO location identifier*] (ICLI)
**NZR**........... New Zealand Rifles (DMA)
**NZ Railw Obs** ... New Zealand Railway Observer [*A publication*]
**NZRB** ........ New Zealand Rifle Brigade (DMA)
**NZ Real** ..... New Zealand Real Estate [*A publication*]
**NZ Rep** ...... New Zealand Reports, Court of Appeals [*A publication*] (DLA)
**NZ Repr Stat** ... Reprint of the Statutes of New Zealand [*A publication*] (DLA)
**NZRN**........ Raoul Island [*New Zealand*] [*ICAO location identifier*] (ICLI)
**NZRO**........ Rotorua [*New Zealand*] [*ICAO location identifier*] (ICLI)
**NZRR**........ New Zealand Rough Riders [*Military*] (ROG)
**NZR Regs & B** ... Rules, Regulations, and By-Laws under New Zealand Statutes [*A publication*] (DLA)
**NZS** ........... Nonzero Sum [*Genetics*]
**NZSAS**...... New Zealand Special Air Service (DMA)
**NZSC**......... New Zealand Staff Corps (DMA)
**NZSC**......... New Zealand Supreme Court [*A publication*] (DLA)
**NZ Sch Dent Ser Gaz** ... New Zealand School Dental Service. Gazette [*A publication*]
**NZ Sci Rev** ... New Zealand Science Review [*A publication*]
**NZ Sci Teach** ... New Zealand Science Teacher [*A publication*]
**NZSEAFRON** ... New Zealand Sea Frontier
**NZ Ship** ..... New Zealand Shipping Gazette [*A publication*]
**NZSJ** ......... New Zealand Slavonic Journal [*A publication*]
**NZ Slav J**... New Zealand Slavonic Journal [*A publication*]
**NZSM** ....... New Zealand Submarine Mining Volunteers (DMA)
**NZ Soc Earthquake Eng Bull** ... New Zealand Society for Earthquake Engineering. Bulletin [*A publication*]
**NZ Soc Soil Sci Proc** ... New Zealand Society of Soil Science. Proceedings [*A publication*]
**NZ Soil Bur Bull** ... New Zealand. Soil Bureau. Bulletin [*A publication*]
**NZ Soil Bur Sci Rep** ... New Zealand. Soil Bureau. Scientific Report [*A publication*]
**NZ Soil News** ... New Zealand Soil News [*A publication*]
**NZ Soil Surv Rep** ... New Zealand. Soil Survey Report [*A publication*]
**NZ Speech Therapist J** ... New Zealand Speech Therapists' Journal [*A publication*]
**NZ Speech Ther J** ... New Zealand Speech Therapists' Journal [*A publication*]
**NZ Speleol Bull** ... New Zealand Speleological Bulletin [*A publication*]
**NZST**......... Neue Zeitschrift fuer Systematische Theologie [*A publication*]
**NZ Stat**...... Statutes of New Zealand [*A publication*] (DLA)
**NZ Stat Regs** ... New Zealand Statutory Regulations [*A publication*] (DLA)
**NZSThR**.... Neue Zeitschrift fuer Systematische Theologie und Religionsphilosophie [*A publication*]
**NZ Surv** ..... New Zealand Surveyor [*A publication*]
**NZ Sys Th** ... Neue Zeitschrift fuer Systematische Theologie und Religionsphilosophie [*A publication*]
**NZ Syst T**.. Neue Zeitschrift fuer Systematische Theologie und Religionsgeschichte [*A publication*]
**NZSZ**......... Nationalzeitung und Soldatenzeitung [*A publication*]
**NZT** ........... Neue Zurcher Zeitung und Schweizerisches Handelsblatt [*A publication*]
**NZT** ........... Nonzero Transfer
**NZTBA**...... New Zealand Journal of Science and Technology. Section B. General Research [*A publication*]
**NZTBR**...... New Zealand Taxation Board of Review Decisions [*A publication*] (DLA)
**NZTC** ........ New Zealand Tonnage Committee (DS)
**NZTG**........ Tauranga [*New Zealand*] [*ICAO location identifier*] (ICLI)
**NZ Timb**.... New Zealand Timber Worker [*A publication*]
**NZ Timber J Wood Prod Rev** ... New Zealand Timber Journal and Wood Products Review [*A publication*]
**NZ Timb J** ... New Zealand Timber Journal [*A publication*]
**NZTJWG**.. Nike-Zeus Target Joint Working Group [*Missiles*] (MUGU)
**NZTO**........ New Zealand Tourism Office (EA)
**NZ Tob Grow J** ... New Zealand's Tobacco Growers' Journal [*A publication*]
**NZ Tour**..... New Zealand Tourism [*A publication*]
**NZ Tour Res** ... New Zealand Tourism Research Newsletter [*A publication*]
**NZTP**......... New Zealand Tourist and Publicity Office [*Later, NZTO*] (EA)
**NZTS**......... New Zealand Temporary Staff (DMA)

**NZTS**......... New Zealand Treaty Series [*A publication*] (DLA)
**NZTU**......... Timaru [*New Zealand*] [*ICAO location identifier*] (ICLI)
**NzTvGS**..... Church of Jesus Christ of Latter-Day Saints, Genealogical Society Library, Temple View Branch, Temple View, New Zealand [*Library symbol*] [*Library of Congress*] (LCLS)
**NZu**............ Novyj Zurnal [*A publication*]
**NZU**............ Voedingsmiddelen Technologie [*A publication*]
**NZUKCC**.. New Zealand-United Kingdom Chamber of Commerce (DS)
**NZULR**...... New Zealand Universities Law Review [*A publication*]
**NZ U L Rev**... New Zealand Universities Law Review [*A publication*]
**NZ Univ Law Rev**... New Zealand Universities Law Review [*A publication*]
**NZ Univ LR**... New Zealand Universities Law Review [*A publication*]
**NZ Univ L Rev**... New Zealand Universities Law Review [*A publication*]
**NZ Univs Law R**... New Zealand Universities Law Review [*A publication*]
**NZURA**...... Nauchnye Zapiski Gosudarstvennyi Nauchno-Issledovatel'skii i Proektnyi Institut Ugol'noi Promyshlennosti [*A publication*]
**NZV**............ Niederdeutsche Zeitschrift fuer Volkskunde [*A publication*]
**NZ Val**....... New Zealand Valuer [*A publication*]
**NZVC**......... New Zealand Veterinary Corps (DMA)
**NZVC**......... New Zealand Volunteer Corps (DMA)
**NZ Vet J**.... New Zealand Veterinary Journal [*A publication*]
**NZW**........... Neue Zeitschrift fuer Wehrrecht [*A publication*]
**NZW**........... New Zealand White [*Mice hybrids*]
**NZW**........... South Weymouth, MA [*Location identifier*] [*FAA*] (FAAL)
**NZWA**........ Chatham Island/Waitangi [*New Zealand*] [*ICAO location identifier*] (ICLI)
**NZWB**........ Woodbourne [*New Zealand*] [*ICAO location identifier*] (ICLI)
**NZ Wehrr**... Neue Zeitschrift fuer Wehrrecht [*A publication*]
**NZWG**........ Wigram [*New Zealand*] [*ICAO location identifier*] (ICLI)
**NzWGAL**.. General Assembly Library, Wellington, New Zealand, [*Library symbol*] [*Library of Congress*] (LCLS)
**NzWGS**...... Church of Jesus Christ of Latter-Day Saints, Genealogical Society Library, Wellington Stake Branch, Wellington, New Zealand [*Library symbol*] [*Library of Congress*] (LCLS)
**NZ Wheat Rev**... New Zealand Wheat Review [*A publication*]
**NZ Wings**.. New Zealand Wings [*A publication*]
**NZWK**........ Whakatane [*New Zealand*] [*ICAO location identifier*] (ICLI)
**NzWMW**... New Zealand Ministry of Works and Development, Head Office Library, Wellington, New Zealand [*Library symbol*] [*Library of Congress*] (LCLS)
**NZWN**........ Wellington/International [*New Zealand*] [*ICAO location identifier*] (ICLI)
**NzWNA**...... National Archives, Wellington, New Zealand [*Library symbol*] [*Library of Congress*] (LCLS)
**NZ Womans Wkly**... New Zealand Woman's Weekly [*A publication*]
**NZWP**........ Whenuapai [*New Zealand*] [*ICAO location identifier*] (ICLI)
**NZWQ**........ Wellington [*New Zealand*] [*ICAO location identifier*] (ICLI)
**NZWR**........ Whangarei [*New Zealand*] [*ICAO location identifier*] (ICLI)
**NZWRAC**... New Zealand Women's Royal Army Corps (DMA)
**NZWS**........ Westport [*New Zealand*] [*ICAO location identifier*] (ICLI)
**NZWU**........ Wanganui [*New Zealand*] [*ICAO location identifier*] (ICLI)
**NZY**............ San Diego, CA [*Location identifier*] [*FAA*] (FAAL)
**NZYM**........ Synthetech, Inc. [*NASDAQ symbol*] (NQ)
**NZZ**............ Neue Zuericher Zeitung [*A publication*]
**NZZA**......... Auckland [*New Zealand*] [*ICAO location identifier*] (ICLI)
**NZZC**......... Christchurch [*New Zealand*] [*ICAO location identifier*] (ICLI)
**NZZO**......... Auckland [*New Zealand*] [*ICAO location identifier*] (ICLI)
**NZZ/SRWA**... Swiss Review of World Affairs. Neue Zuericher Zeitung [*A publication*]
**NZZW**........ Wellington [*New Zealand*] [*ICAO location identifier*] (ICLI)
**NZZytPI**.... Naukovi Zapyski Zytomyrs'koho Derzavnoho Pedahohicnoho Instytutu [*A publication*]

# O

O ............... An Oige [*The Irish Youth Hostels Association*] [*Founded in 1931*]
O ............... Cleared to the Outer Marker [*Aviation*] (FAAC)
o ............... Deamino [*As substituent on nucleoside*] [*Biochemistry*]
O ............... Hora [*Hour*] [*Latin*]
O ............... Horizontal Opposed [*Aircraft engine*]
O ............... Law Opinions [*A publication*] (DLA)
O ............... New Orleans [*Louisiana*] [*Mint mark, when appearing on US coins*] [*Obsolete*]
O ............... Oasis
O ............... Oath
O ............... Oberst [*Colonel*] [*German military - World War II*]
O ............... Obiit [*He, or She, Died*] [*Latin*]
O ............... Object
O ............... Objective
O ............... Oblast [*Governmental subdivision in USSR corresponding to a province or state*]
O ............... Oboe [*Phonetic alphabet*] [*World War II*] (DSUE)
O ............... Observation Aircraft [*Designation for all US military aircraft*]
O ............... Observer
O ............... Obsolescent (AFIT)
O ............... Occasional [*Concerning occurrence of species*]
O ............... Occidental
O ............... Occiput [*Medicine*]
O ............... Occlusal [*Dentistry*]
O ............... Occupation (ADA)
O ............... Occurrence
O ............... Ocean [*Maps and charts*]
O ............... Octal [*Number system with a base of eight*] [*Data processing*] (BUR)
O ............... Octarius [*Pint*] [*Pharmacy*]
O ............... Octavo [*Book from 20 to 25 centimeters in height*] [*Bibliography*]
O ............... October
O ............... October [*A publication*]
O ............... Oculus [*Eye*] [*Latin*]
O ............... Odericus [*Flourished, 1166-1200*] [*Authority cited in pre-1607 legal work*] (DSA)
O ............... Odetics, Inc. [*AMEX symbol*] (SPSG)
O ............... Off
O ............... Offered [*Stock exchange term*] (SPSG)
O ............... Office [*or Officer*]
O ............... Office of Operations [*Coast Guard*]
O ............... Official
O ............... Official [*Rate*] [*Value of the English pound*]
O ............... Ohio
O ............... Ohio Reports [*A publication*] (DLA)
O ............... Ohio State Library, Columbus, OH [*Library symbol*] [*Library of Congress*] (LCLS)
O ............... Ohm [*Electricity*]
O ............... Ohne [*Antigen*] [*Immunology*]
O ............... Oil
O ............... Oklahoma (DLA)
O ............... Oktjabr [*A publication*]
O ............... Old
O ............... Olivine Subgroup [*Fayalite, forsterite*] [*CIPW classification*] [*Geology*]
O ............... Omicron [*Fifteenth letter of the Greek alphabet*] (NASA)
O ............... Omnipol Foreign Trade Corp. [*Czechoslovakia*] [*ICAO aircraft manufacturer identifier*] (ICAO)
O ............... Omnivore
O ............... Oncovin [*Leurocristine, Vincristine*] [*Also, LCR, V, VC, VCR*] [*Antineoplastic drug*]
O ............... Only
O ............... Ontario (DLA)
O ............... Ontario Reports [*A publication*] (DLA)
O ............... Opacity (MCD)
O ............... Open
O ............... Open [*Dancing position*]
O ............... Open-Air Places [*Parks, pools, etc.*] [*Public-performance tariff class*] [*British*]
O ............... Open Circuit
O ............... Opening
O ............... Operand [*Data processing*]
O ............... Operating Room Attendant [*Ranking title*] [*British Royal Navy*]
O ............... Operation
O ............... Operator
O ............... Operon [*Genetics*]
O ............... Ophthalmology [*Medical Officer designation*] [*British*]
O ............... Opium [*Slang*]
O ............... Optimus [*Best*] [*Latin*]
O ............... Optional Dishes [*School meals*] [*British*]
O ............... Oral [*Medicine*]
O ............... Orange [*Phonetic alphabet*] [*Royal Navy*] [*World War I*] [*Pre-World War II*] (DSUE)
O ............... Orange [*Maps and charts*]
O ............... Orbis [*A publication*]
O ............... Orchid Flowering [*Horticulture*]
O ............... Ordained
o ............... Orden [*Order*] [*Spanish*]
O/ ............... Order [*Order*] [*German*]
O ............... Order
O ............... Orders Group [*British military*] (DMA)
O ............... Ordinance
O ............... Ordinary
O ............... Ordinary Level [*School graduating grade*] [*British*]
O ............... Ordinary Ray [*Direction of*]
O ............... Ordinate [*Mathematics*] (MSA)
O ............... Ordinis [*By the Order Of*] [*Latin*]
O ............... Ordnance
O ............... Ordonnanzoffizier [*Special-Missions Staff Officer*] [*German military - World War II*]
o/ ............... Ordre [*Order*] [*Business term*] [*French*]
O ............... Oregon (ROG)
O ............... Oregon Reports [*A publication*] (DLA)
O ............... Organ
O ............... Organic [*Soil*]
O ............... Organism [*Psychology*]
O ............... Organization
O ............... Organized Naval Reserve
O ............... Organum [*A publication*]
O ............... Orient [*Freemasonry*]
O ............... Oriental
O ............... Origin
O ............... Original
O ............... Orotidine [*One-letter symbol; see Ord*]
o ............... Ortho [*Chemistry*]
O ............... Orthodox [*Judaism*]
O ............... Os [*Bone*] [*Latin*]
O ............... Oscar [*Phonetic alphabet*] [*International*] (DSUE)
O ............... Oscillation or Fluctuation in Behavior [*Psychology*]
O ............... Oscillators [*JETDS nomenclature*] [*Military*] (CET)
O ............... Osphradium [*An organ in mollusks*]
O ............... Osten [*East*] [*German*]
O ............... Osteuropa [*A publication*]
O ............... Ostiole [*Biology*]
O ............... Other
O ............... Otto's United States Supreme Court Reports [*91-107 United States*] [*A publication*] (DLA)
O ............... Ouest [*West*] [*French*]
O ............... Out (NASA)
O ............... Outboard (DS)
O ............... Outfield [*Baseball*]
O ............... Outlet
O ............... Output (BUR)
O ............... Outside Cylinders [*Trains*] [*British*]
O ............... Outside Edge [*Skating*]
O ............... Ovary
O ............... Oven
O ............... Over
O ............... Overall Rating [*Broadcasting*]

**O** ... Overcast
**o** ... Overruled [*Ruling in cited case expressly overruled*] [*Used in Shepard's Citations*] [*Legal term*] (DLA)
**O** ... Overseer
**O** ... Ovule [*Botany*]
**O** ... Owner
**O** ... Oxford [*County borough in England*]
**O** ... Oxygen [*Chemical element*]
**O** ... Shoulder Season [*Airline fare code*]
**O** ... Solicitor's Opinion [*A publication*] (DLA)
**O** ... South African Law Reports, Orange Free State Provincial Division [*1910-46*] [*A publication*] (DLA)
**O1** ... Ensign [*Navy*]
**1/O** ... First Officer [*Women's Royal Naval Service*] [*British*]
**O1** ... Organized Naval Reserve Seagoing
**O1** ... Second Lieutenant [*Air Force, Army, Marine Corps*]
**1-O** ... Selective Service Class [*for Conscientious Objector Available for Alternate Service Contributing to Maintenance of National Health, Safety, or Interest*]
**O²** ... Both Eyes [*Pharmacy*]
**O2** ... First Lieutenant [*Air Force, Army, Marine Corps*]
**O2** ... Lieutenant Junior Grade [*Navy*]
**O2** ... Organized Naval Reserve Aviation
**2/O** ... Second Officer [*British military*] (DMA)
**O3** ... Captain [*Air Force, Army, Marine Corps*]
**O3** ... Lieutenant [*Navy*]
**3/O** ... Third Officer [*British military*] (DMA)
**O4** ... Lieutenant Commander [*Navy*]
**O4** ... Major [*Air Force, Army, Marine Corps*]
**O5** ... Commander [*Navy*]
**O5** ... Lieutenant Colonel [*Air Force, Army, Marine Corps*]
**O6** ... Captain [*Navy*]
**O6** ... Colonel [*Air Force, Army, Marine Corps*]
**O7** ... Brigadier General [*Air Force, Army, Marine Corps*]
**O7** ... Commodore [*Navy*]
**O8** ... Major General [*Air Force, Army, Marine Corps*]
**O8** ... Rear Admiral [*Navy*]
**O9** ... Lieutenant General [*Air Force, Army, Marine Corps*]
**O9** ... Vice Admiral [*Navy*]
**O10** ... Admiral [*Navy*]
**O10** ... General [*Air Force, Army, Marine Corps*]
**OA** ... Almonte Public Library, Ontario [*Library symbol*] [*National Library of Canada*] (NLC)
**OA** ... Oberbayerisches Archiv fuer Vaterlaendische Geschichte [*A publication*]
**O-A** ... Objective Analytic Batteries [*Personality development test*] [*Psychology*]
**OA** ... Objective Aperture [*Microscopy*]
**OA** ... Objective Area [*Military*]
**OA** ... Oblate Sisters of the Assumption [*Roman Catholic religious order*]
**OA** ... Obligation Authority [*Army*]
**O & A** ... Observation and Assessment [*Medicine*]
**OA** ... Occipital Artery [*Anatomy*]
**OA** ... Occiput Anterior [*Medicine*]
**OA** ... Ocean Acre [*Marine science*] (MSC)
**OA** ... Oceanic Abstracts [*A publication*] [*Information service or system*]
**O & A** ... October and April [*Denotes semiannual payments of interest or dividends in these months*] [*Business term*]
**OA** ... Oesterbotten: Aarsbok [*A publication*]
**O/A** ... Offer Accepted (ADA)
**OA** ... Office of Administration [*NASA*]
**OA** ... Office of the Administrator
**OA** ... Office of Applications [*NASA*]
**OA** ... Office Audit [*IRS*]
**OA** ... Office Automation
**OA** ... Office of Operations Analysis [*Arms Control and Disarmament Agency*] (GRD)
**OA** ... Officers Association [*British military*] (DMA)
**OA** ... Official Assignee (ROG)
**OA** ... Ohio Appellate Reports [*A publication*] (DLA)
**OA** ... Oil-Immersed Self-Cooled [*Transformer*] (IEEE)
**OA** ... Old Account [*Banking*]
**OA** ... Old Age
**OA** ... Old Assyrian (BJA)
**OA** ... Olymbiaki Aeroporia [*Olympic Airlines*]
**OA** ... Olympic Airways [*Greece*] [*ICAO designator*] (OAG)
**OA** ... Omniantenna
**OA** ... On or About [*Military*]
**OA** ... On Acceptance [*Business term*]
**OA** ... On Account [*Business and trade*]
**OA** ... On Account Of
**OA** ... On Arrival (ADA)
**OA** ... Open Account
**OA** ... Open Annealed [*Metal industry*]
**OA** ... Opera America [*An association*] (EA)
**OA** ... Operand Address Register [*Data processing*]
**OA** ... Operating Agency
**OA** ... Operating Aircraft
**OA** ... Operating Assemblies [*JETDS nomenclature*] [*Military*] (CET)
**OA** ... Operating Authorization
**OA** ... Operation Appreciation (EA)
**OA** ... Operational Aft (MCD)
**OA** ... Operational Amplifier [*Telecommunications*] (TEL)
**OA** ... Operationally Available (NATG)
**OA** ... Operations Advisor [*NASA*]
**OA** ... Operations Analysis
**OA** ... Operations Area
**OA** ... Opiate Analgesia
**OA** ... Optoacoustic [*Cell*]
**OA** ... Opuscula Archaeologica [*A publication*]
**OA** ... Oral Apparatus [*Zoology*]
**OA** ... Orbit Analyst (MCD)
**OA** ... Orbital Assembly (MCD)
**OA** ... Orbiter Access Arm [*NASA*]
**OA** ... Order of AHEPA [*Also known as American Hellenic Educational Progressive Association*] (EA)
**OA** ... Order of the Alhambra (EA)
**O of A** ... Order of Amaranth (EA)
**OA** ... Order of the Arrow (EA)
**OA** ... Order of Australia
**O/A** ... Order Authority (MCD)
**O/A** ... Ordnance Alteration (MCD)
**OA** ... Ordnance Artificer [*Obsolete*] [*Navy*] [*British*]
**OA** ... Organizational Assessment
**OA** ... Oriens Antiquus [*A publication*]
**OA** ... Oriental Art [*A publication*]
**OA** ... Orientalisches Archiv [*A publication*]
**O/A** ... Original-Abfuellung [*On estate-bottled German wine labels*]
**OA** ... Orlando Aerospace [*Martin Marietta*] (RDA)
**OA** ... Oro Americano [*American Gold*] [*Spanish*] [*Business term*]
**OA** ... Oroems Antiquus [*A publication*]
**OA** ... Osborne Association (EA)
**OA** ... Osteoarthritis [*Medicine*]
**OA** ... Other Appointments
**OA** ... Other Articles
**OA** ... Oudh Appeals [*India*] [*A publication*] (DLA)
**O/A** ... Our Account [*Business term*]
**O/A** ... Outer Anchorage [*Navigation*]
**OA** ... Output Amplitude
**OA** ... Output Axis
**OA** ... Ovalbumin [*Also, OV, OVA, OVAL*] [*Biochemistry*]
**OA** ... Overachievers Anonymous (EA)
**O/A** ... Overall
**OA** ... Overall [*Technical drawings*]
**OA** ... Overeaters Anonymous (EA)
**OA** ... Overfire Airport [*Combustion technology*]
**OA** ... Overhead Approach [*Aviation*] (FAAC)
**OA** ... Overtime Authorization (AAG)
**O-2A** ... Oligodendrocytes and Type 2 Astrocytes [*Neurology*]
**O & A (Date)** ... Oath and Acceptance Date [*Date from which a military officer's commissioned service runs*]
**OAA** ... Hereditary Order of Armigerous Augustans (EA)
**OAA** ... Nora, AK [*Location identifier*] [*FAA*] (FAAL)
**OAA** ... o-Aminoacetanilide [*Organic chemistry*]
**OAA** ... Oesterreichisches Bank-Archiv. Zeitschrift fuer das Gesamte Bankwesen und Sparkassenwesen, Borsenwesen, und Kreditwesen [*A publication*]
**OAA** ... Oeuvres Afro-Asiatiques [*A publication*]
**OAA** ... Office of Aviation Affairs [*Army*]
**OAA** ... Old-Age Assistance [*Superseded by SSI*] [*HEW*]
**OAA** ... Older Americans Act [*1965*]
**OAA** ... Optical Acquisition Aid [*Deep Space Instrumentation Facility, NASA*]
**OAA** ... Opticians Association of America (EA)
**OAA** ... Orbiter Access Arm [*NASA*] (NASA)
**OAA** ... Orbiter Alternate Airfield [*NASA*] (MCD)
**OAA** ... Organic Acidemia Association (EA)
**OAA** ... Organisation des Nations Unies pour l'Alimentation et l'Agriculture [*Food and Agriculture Organization of the United Nations*]
**OAA** ... Organization of Athletic Administrators (EA)
**OAA** ... Orient Airlines Association (EA)
**OAA** ... Oxaloacetic [*or Oxalacetic*] Acid [*Organic chemistry*]
**OAAA** ... Oceania Amateur Athletic Association (EAIO)
**OAAA** ... Order of Americans of Armorial Ancestry (EA)
**OAAA** ... Outdoor Advertising Association of America [*Washington, DC*] (EA)
**OAAB** ... Objective-Analytic Anxiety Battery [*Psychology*]
**OAAC** ... Ocean Affairs Advisory Committee [*Department of State*] (MSC)
**OAAC** ... Older Americans Advocacy Commission [*HEW*]
**OAAD** ... Amdar [*Afghanistan*] [*ICAO location identifier*] (ICLI)
**OAAD** ... Ovarian Ascorbic Acid Depletion [*Test*]
**OAADM** ... Ovarian Ascorbic Acid Depletion Material
**OAAIS** ... Office of Administrative Analysis, Information, and Statistics [*Red Cross*]
**OAAK** ... Andkhoi [*Afghanistan*] [*ICAO location identifier*] (ICLI)
**OAAPS** ... Organization for Afro-Asian Peoples Solidarity
**OAARD** ... Office of the Assistant Administrator for Research and Development [*HEW*]

**OAAS**........ Asmar [*Afghanistan*] [*ICAO location identifier*] (ICLI)
**OAASA**..... Office of the Administrative Assistant to the Secretary of the Army
**OAASN**..... Office of the Administrative Assistant to the Secretary of the Navy
**OAAT**........ Ortho-Aminoazotoluene [*A dye*] [*Organic chemistry*]
**OAAU**........ Organization of Afro-American Unity
**OAAU**........ Orthogonal Array Arithmetic Unit [*Data processing*]
**OAB**.......... Attawapiskat Band Library, Ontario [*Library symbol*] [*National Library of Canada*] (BIB)
**OAB**.......... Moab, UT [*Location identifier*] [*FAA*] (FAAL)
**OAB**.......... Ocean Affairs Board [*National Academy of Sciences*] (MSC)
**OAB**.......... Old-Age Benefits
**OAB**.......... Olive Advisory Board [*Defunct*] (EA)
**OAB**.......... Ordnance Assembly Building (MUGU)
**OAB**.......... Organisation Africaine du Bois [*African Timber Organization*] (EAIO)
**OAB**.......... Overseas Affairs Branch [*Army*]
**OAB**.......... Oxford Annotated Bible [*New York*] [*A publication*] (BJA)
**OABA**........ Burleigh-Anstruther and Chandos Union Public Library, Apsley, Ontario [*Library symbol*] [*National Library of Canada*] (BIB)
**OABA**........ Outdoor Amusement Business Association (EA)
**OABD**........ Behsood [*Afghanistan*] [*ICAO location identifier*] (ICLI)
**OABG**........ Baghlan [*Afghanistan*] [*ICAO location identifier*] (ICLI)
**OABK**........ Bandkamalkhan [*Afghanistan*] [*ICAO location identifier*] (ICLI)
**OABN**........ Bamyan [*Afghanistan*] [*ICAO location identifier*] (ICLI)
**OABP**........ Organic Anion Binding Protein [*Biochemistry*]
**OABR**........ Bamar [*Afghanistan*] [*ICAO location identifier*] (ICLI)
**OABS**........ Sarday [*Afghanistan*] [*ICAO location identifier*] (ICLI)
**OABT**........ Bost [*Afghanistan*] [*ICAO location identifier*] (ICLI)
**OABT**........ Ortho-Aminobenzenethiol [*Organic chemistry*]
**OAC**.......... Acton Public Library, Ontario [*Library symbol*] [*National Library of Canada*] (NLC)
**OAC**.......... Cleveland Institute of Art, Cleveland, OH [*OCLC symbol*] (OCLC)
**OAC**.......... Oceanic Area Control [*Aviation*] (FAAC)
**OAC**.......... Office of Academic Computing [*Research center*] (RCD)
**OAC**.......... Officer Advanced Course [*Army*] (INF)
**OA & C**...... Ohio Circuit Court Decisions [*A publication*] (DLA)
**OAC**.......... On Approved Credit
**OAC**.......... Ontario Agricultural College [*Canada*]
**OAC**.......... Ontario Appeal Cases [*Database*] [*Maritime Law Book Co. Ltd.*] [*Information service or system*] (CRD)
**OAC**.......... Open Air Campaigners, US (EA)
**OAC**.......... Operating Agency Code (AFM)
**OAC**.......... Operation Anti-Christ (EA)
**OAC**.......... Operations Analysis Center
**OAC**.......... Operations Analysis Chief [*Air Force*]
**OAC**.......... Optimal Automatic Control
**OAC**.......... Optimized Aftercooled [*Truck engineering*]
**OAC**.......... Optimum Approach Course [*Navy*] (NVT)
**OAC**.......... Ordnance Ammunition Command [*Merged with Munitions Command*] [*Army*]
**OAC**.......... Ordo ab Chao [*Order Out of Chaos*] [*Latin*] [*Freemasonry*]
**OAC**.......... Outer Approach Channel
**OAC**.......... Overseas Automotive Club (EA)
**OACB**........ Charburjak [*Afghanistan*] [*ICAO location identifier*] (ICLI)
**OACC**........ Chakhcharan [*Afghanistan*] [*ICAO location identifier*] (ICLI)
**OACC**........ Oceanic Area Control Centre
**OACC**........ Older Americans Consumer Cooperative [*Washington, DC*] (EA)
**OACCF**...... Orange Agricultural College Christian Fellowship [*Australia*]
**OACD**........ Office of Agricultural and Chemical Development [*of TVA*]
**OACH**........ Acton High School, Ontario [*Library symbol*] [*National Library of Canada*] (NLC)
**OACI**......... Optical Automatic Car Identification
**OACI**......... Organisation de l'Aviation Civile Internationale [*International Civil Aviation Organization*]
**OACIS**....... Ocean-Atmospheric Climatic Interaction Studies
**OACIS**....... Oregon Advanced Computing Institute [*Research center*] (RCD)
**OACP**........ Canada Publishing Corp., Agincourt, Ontario [*Library symbol*] [*National Library of Canada*] (BIB)
**OACR**........ Office of the Admiral Commanding Reserves [*Navy*] [*British*]
**OAC of S**.... Office of the Assistant Chief of Staff [*Military*]
**OACS**........ Office of the Assistant Chief of Staff [*Military*] (AAG)
**OACSA**...... Office of the Assistant Chief of Staff for Automation and Communications [*Military*] (MCD)
**OACSAC**... Office of the Assistant Chief of Staff for Automation and Communications [*Military*]
**OACSC-E**... Office of the Assistant Chief of Staff for Communications-Electronics (AABC)
**OACSEA**... Older American Community Service Employment Act [*1975*]
**OACSFOR**... Office of the Assistant Chief of Staff for Force Development [*Army*]
**OACSI**....... Office of the Assistant Chief of Staff for Intelligence [*Army*]
**OACSIM**... Office of the Assistant Chief of Staff for Information Management [*Military*]
**OACT**........ Officer, Airman, Civilian, and Total (MCD)
**OACT**........ Ormone Adrenocorticotropina [*Italian*] [*Medicine*]
**OAD**.......... Adria Laboratories, Inc., Columbus, OH [*OCLC symbol*] (OCLC)
**OAD**.......... Obstructive Airway Disease [*Medicine*]
**OAD**.......... Office of Administration
**OAD**.......... Officers' Accounts Division [*Navy*]
**OAD**.......... Officers' Assignment Division, The Adjutant General's Office [*Army*]
**OAD**.......... Opening of Anterior Digestive [*Gland*]
**OAD**.......... Operational Active Data [*Navy*]
**OAD**.......... Operational Analysis Division [*Air Force*]
**OAD**.......... Operational Availability Data [*Military*]
**OAD**.......... Orbiter Atmospheric Drag [*NASA*]
**OAD**.......... Ordered to Active Duty (AABC)
**OAD**.......... Organizations and Agencies Directories Series [*A publication*]
**OAD**.......... Original Air Date [*of program's first telecast*]
**OAD**.......... Overall Absolute Deviation [*Mathematics*]
**OAD**.......... Oxford American Dictionary [*A publication*]
**OA 2d**........ Ohio Appellate Reports, Second Series [*A publication*] (DLA)
**OADAB**..... Office of the Assistant Director of the Army Budget
**OADC**........ Oleic Acid, Albumin, Dextrose, Catalase
**OADD**........ Dawlatabad [*Afghanistan*] [*ICAO location identifier*] (ICLI)
**OADF**........ Darra-I-Soof [*Afghanistan*] [*ICAO location identifier*] (ICLI)
**OADH**........ One-Arm Dove Hunt Association (EA)
**OADH**........ Organization of Advanced Disabled Hobbyists (EA)
**OADMS**.... Office of Automated Data Management Services [*General Services Administration*]
**OAdN**........ Ohio Northern University, Ada, OH [*Library symbol*] [*Library of Congress*] (LCLS)
**OADS**........ Omnidirectional Air Data System
**OADV**........ Devar [*Afghanistan*] [*ICAO location identifier*] (ICLI)
**OADW**........ Wazakhwa [*Afghanistan*] [*ICAO location identifier*] (ICLI)
**OADZ**........ Darwaz [*Afghanistan*] [*ICAO location identifier*] (ICLI)
**OAE**.......... NOAA [*National Oceanic and Atmospheric Administration*]-LISD Seattle Center, Seattle, WA [*OCLC symbol*] (OCLC)
**OAE**.......... Occupational and Adult Education [*Office of Education*] (OICC)
**OAE**.......... Officer of Arms Extraordinary [*College of Arms/Heralds' College*] [*British*]
**OAE**.......... Old Antarctic Explorer
**OAE**.......... Optical Alignment Equipment
**OAE**.......... Optima Energy Corp. [*Vancouver Stock Exchange symbol*]
**OAE**.......... Orchestra of the Age of Enlightenment [*British*]
**OAE**.......... Organization of Architectural Employees
**OAE**.......... Orzeck Aphasia Evaluation [*Psychology*]
**OAEC**........ Essa Centennial Library, Angus, Ontario [*Library symbol*] [*National Library of Canada*] (BIB)
**OAEFT**...... Astorville Branch, East Ferris Township Public Library, Ontario [*Library symbol*] [*National Library of Canada*] (NLC)
**OAEK**........ Keshm [*Afghanistan*] [*ICAO location identifier*] (ICLI)
**OAEM**........ Eshkashem [*Afghanistan*] [*ICAO location identifier*] (ICLI)
**OAEQ**........ Islam Qala [*Afghanistan*] [*ICAO location identifier*] (ICLI)
**OAET**........ Elma Township Public Library, Atwood, Ontario [*Library symbol*] [*National Library of Canada*] (NLC)
**OAF**.......... Occidentale Afrique Francaise [*French West Africa*]
**OAF**.......... Office of Alcohol Fuels [*Department of Energy*]
**OAF**.......... Officer Assignment Folder [*Military*] (AFM)
**OAF**.......... Ontario Ministry of Agriculture and Food [*UTLAS symbol*]
**OAF**.......... Open Air Factor
**OAF**.......... Options for Animals Foundation (EA)
**OAF**.......... Origin Address Field [*Data processing*] (IBMDP)
**OAF**.......... Orthodox and Anglican Fellowship (EA)
**OAF**.......... Osteoclast Activating Factor [*Endocrinology*]
**OAF**.......... Oxygen Alternate Fill
**OAFB**........ Offutt Air Force Base [*Nebraska*] (AAG)
**OAFC**........ Arden Branch, Frontenac County Library, Ontario [*Library symbol*] [*National Library of Canada*] (BIB)
**OAFC**........ Occupational Analysis Field Center
**OAFC**........ Office of Air Force Chaplains
**OAFC**........ Official Aerrage Fan Club (EA)
**OAFD**........ Orbiter Air Flight Deck [*NASA*] (MCD)
**OAFG**........ Khost-O-Fering [*Afghanistan*] [*ICAO location identifier*] (ICLI)
**OA/FI**........ Operational Assurance/Fault Isolation (MCD)
**OAFIE**....... Office of Armed Forces Information and Education
**OAFM**........ On or After Full Moon [*Freemasonry*] (ROG)
**OAFR**........ Farah [*Afghanistan*] [*ICAO location identifier*] (ICLI)
**OAFT**........ Official Air Freight Tariffs
**OAFTO**..... Orbiter Atmospheric Flight Test Office [*NASA*] (NASA)
**OAFZ**........ Faizabad [*Afghanistan*] [*ICAO location identifier*] (ICLI)
**OAG**.......... Oblique Anterior Gauche [*Left Anterior Oblique Position*] [*Medicine*]
**OAG**.......... Office of the Adjutant General [*Military*] (MCD)
**OAG**.......... Official Airline Guide [*A publication*]
**OAG**.......... Official Airline Guides, Inc. [*Information service or system*] (IID)
**OAG**.......... Oil and Gas Journal [*A publication*]
**OAG**.......... Oleoyl(acetyl)glycerol [*Organic chemistry*]
**OAG**.......... Online Airlines Guide [*A publication*]
**OAG**.......... Open Angle Glaucoma [*Ophthalmology*]
**OAG**.......... Opinions of the Attorney General

**OAG**.......... Optical Alignment Group
**OAG**.......... Orange [*Australia*] [*Airport symbol*] (OAG)
**OAGA**........ Ghaziabad [*Afghanistan*] [*ICAO location identifier*] (ICLI)
**OAGB**........ Osteopathic Association of Great Britain
**OAGD**........ Gader [*Afghanistan*] [*ICAO location identifier*] (ICLI)
**OAG-EE**.... Official Airline Guide-Electronic Edition [*Official Airline Guides, Inc.*] [*Database*]
**OAGG**........ Gage Educational Publishing Ltd., Agincourt, Ontario [*Library symbol*] [*National Library of Canada*] (NLC)
**OAGL**........ Gulistan [*Afghanistan*] [*ICAO location identifier*] (ICLI)
**OAGM**....... Ghelmeen [*Afghanistan*] [*ICAO location identifier*] (ICLI)
**OAG Massachusetts** ... Massachusetts Attorney General Reports [*A publication*] (DLA)
**OAGN** ....... Ghazni [*Afghanistan*] [*ICAO location identifier*] (ICLI)
**OAGS**........ Gasar [*Afghanistan*] [*ICAO location identifier*] (ICLI)
**OAG West Virginia** ... West Virginia Attorney General Reports [*A publication*] (DLA)
**OAGZ**........ Gardez [*Afghanistan*] [*ICAO location identifier*] (ICLI)
**OAH**.......... Ancaster High and Vocational School, Ontario [*Library symbol*] [*National Library of Canada*] (NLC)
**OAH**.......... Organization of American Historians (EA)
**OAH**.......... Overhead Air Hoist
**OAHE**........ Hazrat Eman [*Afghanistan*] [*ICAO location identifier*] (ICLI)
**OAHJ**........ Hajigak [*Afghanistan*] [*ICAO location identifier*] (ICLI)
**OAHN**........ Khwahan [*Afghanistan*] [*ICAO location identifier*] (ICLI)
**OAHQ**....... Ohio Archaeological and Historical Quarterly [*A publication*]
**OAHR**........ Herat [*Afghanistan*] [*ICAO location identifier*] (ICLI)
**OAHS**........ O-Acetylhomoserine (thiol)-lyase [*An enzyme*]
**OAI**............ Office of Audit and Inspection [*Energy Research and Development Administration*]
**OAI**............ Office of Audit and Investigation [*United States Geological Survey*]
**OAI**............ Outside Air Intake (NRCH)
**OAIAC**...... Operational Area Industry Advisory Committee [*Civil Defense*]
**OAIDE**...... Operational Assistance and Instructive Data Equipment
**OAIM**........ Office of Aviation Information Management [*Department of Transportation*] [*Information service or system*] (IID)
**OAIP**......... Ontario Assessment Instrument Pool [*Educational test*] [*Canada*]
**OAIP**......... Organic Ablative Insulative Plastic
**OAIS**.......... Opinion, Attitude, and Interest Survey [*Psychology*]
**OAIW**........ International Waxes Ltd., Agincourt, Ontario [*Library symbol*] [*National Library of Canada*] (NLC)
**OAJ**........... Ajax Public Library, Ontario [*Library symbol*] [*National Library of Canada*] (NLC)
**OAJ**........... Jacksonville [*North Carolina*] [*Airport symbol*] (OAG)
**OAJ**........... Jacksonville, NC [*Location identifier*] [*FAA*] (FAAL)
**OAJL**......... Jalalabad [*Afghanistan*] [*ICAO location identifier*] (ICLI)
**OAJS**......... Jabul Saraj [*Afghanistan*] [*ICAO location identifier*] (ICLI)
**OAJW**....... Jawand [*Afghanistan*] [*ICAO location identifier*] (ICLI)
**OAk**........... Akron Public Library, Akron, OH [*Library symbol*] [*Library of Congress*] (LCLS)
**OAK**........... Oak Industries, Inc. [*NYSE symbol*] (SPSG)
**OAK**........... Oakfield [*New York*] [*Seismograph station code, US Geological Survey*] [*Closed*] (SEIS)
**OAK**........... Oakland [*California*] [*Airport symbol*]
**OAK**........... Oakwood College, Huntsville, AL [*OCLC symbol*] (OCLC)
**OAK**........... Oakwood Petroleums Ltd. [*Toronto Stock Exchange symbol*]
**OAK**........... Older Americans Corps [*Proposed*]
**OAK**........... Organization for the Advancement of Knowledge (EA)
**OAK**........... Otcety Archeologiceskoj Komissii [*A publication*]
**OAK**........... Overhaul Alignment Kit (MCD)
**OAK**........... San Francisco [*California*] Oakland [*Airport symbol*] (OAG)
**OAKA**........ Koban [*Afghanistan*] [*ICAO location identifier*] (ICLI)
**OAKB**........ Kabul Ad [*Afghanistan*] [*ICAO location identifier*] (ICLI)
**OAkCh**...... Akron Child Guidance Center, Akron, OH [*Library symbol*] [*Library of Congress*] (LCLS)
**OAKD**........ Kamdesh [*Afghanistan*] [*ICAO location identifier*] (ICLI)
**OAKE**........ Organization of American Kodaly Educators (EA)
**OAkF**......... Firestone Tire & Rubber Co., Akron, OH [*Library symbol*] [*Library of Congress*] (LCLS)
**OAKG**........ Khojaghar [*Afghanistan*] [*ICAO location identifier*] (ICLI)
**OAkGr**....... B. F. Goodrich Co., Akron, OH [*Library symbol*] [*Library of Congress*] (LCLS)
**OAkGy**...... Goodyear Tire & Rubber Co., Akron, OH [*Library symbol*] [*Library of Congress*] (LCLS)
**OAKJ**......... Kajaki [*Afghanistan*] [*ICAO location identifier*] (ICLI)
**OAkk**......... Old Akkadian (BJA)
**OAKL**........ Konjak-I-Logar [*Afghanistan*] [*ICAO location identifier*] (ICLI)
**Oaklnd Bsn** ... Oakland Business Monthly [*A publication*]
**OAKM**....... Kamar [*Afghanistan*] [*ICAO location identifier*] (ICLI)
**OAKN**........ Kandahar [*Afghanistan*] [*ICAO location identifier*] (ICLI)
**OAKR**........ Kaldar [*Afghanistan*] [*ICAO location identifier*] (ICLI)
**OAKR**........ Oakridge Energy, Inc. [*NASDAQ symbol*] (NQ)
**OAKR**........ Oesterreichisches Archiv fuer Kirchenrecht [*A publication*]
**Oak Rept**.... Oak Report. A Quarterly Journal on Music and Musicians [*A publication*]
**Oak Ridge Nat Lab Radiat Shielding Inf Cent Rep** ... Oak Ridge National Laboratory. Radiation Shielding Information Center. Report [*A publication*]
**Oak Ridge Natl Lab Heavy Sect Steel Technol Program Tech Rep** ... Oak Ridge National Laboratory. Heavy Section Steel Technology Program. Technical Report [*A publication*]
**Oak Ridge Natl Lab Rev** ... Oak Ridge National Laboratory. Review [*A publication*]
**OAKS**........ Khost [*Afghanistan*] [*ICAO location identifier*] (ICLI)
**OAKT**........ Kalat [*Afghanistan*] [*ICAO location identifier*] (ICLI)
**OAkU**........ University of Akron, Akron, OH [*Library symbol*] [*Library of Congress*] (LCLS)
**OAkU-L**.... University of Akron, School of Law, Akron, Ohio [*Library symbol*] [*Library of Congress*] (LCLS)
**OAKX**........ Kabul [*Afghanistan*] [*ICAO location identifier*] (ICLI)
**OAKZ**........ Karez-I-Mir [*Afghanistan*] [*ICAO location identifier*] (ICLI)
**OAL**........... Alliston Memorial Public Library, Ontario [*Library symbol*] [*National Library of Canada*] (BIB)
**OAL**........... Coaldale, NV [*Location identifier*] [*FAA*] (FAAL)
**OAL**........... National Oceanic and Atmospheric Administration, Miami Branch, Miami, FL [*OCLC symbol*] (OCLC)
**OAL**........... Office of Arts and Libraries [*British*]
**OAL**........... Operational Applications Laboratory [*Air Force*]
**OAL**........... Order of Ancient Lights
**OAL**........... Ordnance Aerophysics Laboratory
**OAL**........... Overall Level (NASA)
**OALAC**..... Amherstview Branch, Lennox and Addington County Public Library, Ontario [*Library symbol*] [*National Library of Canada*] (NLC)
**OAlB**.......... Babcock & Wilcox Co., Alliance, OH [*Library symbol*] [*Library of Congress*] (LCLS)
**OALC**........ Ogden Air Logistics Center (MCD)
**OALDCE**... Oxford Advanced Learner's Dictionary of Current English
**OALG**........ Logar [*Afghanistan*] [*ICAO location identifier*] (ICLI)
**OALL**........ Allenford Branch, Bruce County Public Library, Ontario [*Library symbol*] [*National Library of Canada*] (NLC)
**OALL**........ Lal [*Afghanistan*] [*ICAO location identifier*] (ICLI)
**OAlM**........ Mount Union College, Alliance, OH [*Library symbol*] [*Library of Congress*] (LCLS)
**OALMA**.... Orthopedic Appliance and Limb Manufacturers Association [*Later, AOPA*]
**OALN**........ Laghman [*Afghanistan*] [*ICAO location identifier*] (ICLI)
**OALS**........ Office of Arid Lands Studies [*University of Arizona*] [*Research center*] (RCD)
**OALS**........ Orbiter Automatic Landing System (MCD)
**OALS Bulletin** ... Office of Arid Lands Studies. Bulletin [*A publication*]
**O ALT HOR** ... Omnibus Alternis Horis [*Every Other Hour*] [*Pharmacy*] (ROG)
**OAM**.......... Oamaru [*New Zealand*] [*Airport symbol*] (OAG)
**OAM**.......... Office of Administration and Management [*Employment and Training Administration*] [*Department of Labor*]
**OAM**.......... Office of Aerospace Medicine [*NASA*] (MCD)
**OAM**.......... Office of Automation and Manpower [*Department of Labor*] [*See also OMAT*]
**OAM**.......... Office of Aviation Medicine [*FAA*]
**OAM**.......... Onze Alma Mater (BJA)
**OAM**.......... OPEC [*Organization of Petroleum Exporting Countries*] Bulletin [*A publication*]
**OAM**.......... Open-Air Mission
**OA & M**..... Operations, Administration, and Maintenance [*Telecommunications*]
**OAM**.......... Operations and Management (MCD)
**OAM**.......... Orbital Assembly Module (MCD)
**OAM**.......... Order of Ancient Maccabees (BJA)
**OAM**.......... Organization and Methods [*Military*] (AFIT)
**OAM**.......... Orthopedic Appliance Mechanic [*Navy*]
**OAM**.......... Oscillator Activity Monitor [*Telecommunications*] (TEL)
**OAMA**....... Office Automation Management Association (EA)
**OAMA**....... Ogden Air Material Area [*AFLC*]
**OAMCE**.... Optical Alignment, Monitoring, and Calibration Equipment
**OAMCE**.... Organisation Africaine et Malgache de Cooperation Economique [*Afro-Malagasy Organization for Economic Cooperation*] [*Later, Common Afro-Malagasy Organization*]
**OAMDG**.... Omnia ad Majorem Dei Gloriam [*All to the Greater Glory of God*] [*Latin*]
**OAME**....... Orbital Attitude and Maneuvering Electronics
**OAMEX**.... Ocean-Atmosphere Exchange Processes [*Marine science*] (MSC)
**OAMF**....... Fort Malden National Historic Park, Amherstburg, Ontario [*Library symbol*] [*National Library of Canada*] (NLC)
**OAMHS**.... Ameliasburgh Historical Society, Ontario [*Library symbol*] [*National Library of Canada*] (BIB)
**OAMK**....... Mukur [*Afghanistan*] [*ICAO location identifier*] (ICLI)
**OAMN**...... Maimama [*Afghanistan*] [*ICAO location identifier*] (ICLI)
**OAMN**...... Operations and Maintenance, Navy (AFIT)
**OAMP**....... Optical Analog Matrix Processing
**OAMS**....... Mazar-I-Sharif [*Afghanistan*] [*ICAO location identifier*] (ICLI)
**OA & MS**... Office of Administration and Management Services [*Employment and Training Administration*] [*Department of Labor*]
**OAMS**....... Office of Administrative and Management Systems [*Social Security Administration*]

**OAMS**....... Optical Angular Motion Sensor
**OAMS**....... Orbital Attitude and Maneuvering System [*NASA*]
**OAMS**....... Organic and Atmospheric Mass Spectrometer (KSC)
**OAMT**....... Munta [*Afghanistan*] [*ICAO location identifier*] (ICLI)
**OAN**.......... Curriculum Resources Centre, Niagara South Board of Education, Allanburg, Ontario [*Library symbol*] [*National Library of Canada*] (BIB)
**OAN**.......... NMFS [*National Marine Fisheries Service*] Southeast Fisheries Center, Beaufort Laboratory, Beaufort, NC [*OCLC symbol*] (OCLC)
**OAN**.......... Ocean Aids to Navigation [*Coast Guard*]
**OAN**.......... Omega Arts Network (EA)
**OANA**........ Organization of Asia-Pacific News Agencies [*Malaysia*] (EY)
**OANAD**..... Online-ADL Nachrichten [*A publication*]
**OANDOS**... Ordnance and Ordnance Stores [*Coast Guard*]
**OANDR**..... Operation and Regulation
**OANDT**..... Organization and Training Division [*Supreme Headquarters Allied Powers Europe*] (NATG)
**OANFE**..... Operational Aircraft Not Fully Equipped (NG)
**OANM**...... On or After New Moon [*Freemasonry*] (ROG)
**OANR**....... Nawor [*Afghanistan*] [*ICAO location identifier*] (ICLI)
**OANS**....... Salang-I-Shamali [*Afghanistan*] [*ICAO location identifier*] (ICLI)
**OANT**....... Normanby Township Community and School Library, Ayton, Ontario [*Library symbol*] [*National Library of Canada*] (NLC)
**OAO**.......... National Oceanic and Atmospheric Administration, Miami, Miami, FL [*OCLC symbol*] (OCLC)
**OAO**.......... Office of Aircraft Operations [*Miami, FL*] [*National Oceanic and Atmospheric Administration*] (GRD)
**OAO**.......... One and Only [*A favorite girl or boy friend*]
**OAO**.......... Orbited Assembly Operation
**OAO**.......... Orbiting Astronomical Observatory [*NASA*]
**OAOB**........ Obeh [*Afghanistan*] [*ICAO location identifier*] (ICLI)
**OAOG**....... Urgoon [*Afghanistan*] [*ICAO location identifier*] (ICLI)
**OAOI**........ On and Off Instruments [*Aviation*]
**OAOO**....... Deshoo [*Afghanistan*] [*ICAO location identifier*] (ICLI)
**OAOP**....... Older Adult Offender Project [*of the Alston Wilkes Society*] (EA)
**OAP**.......... NMFS [*National Marine Fisheries Service*] Northeast Fisheries Center, Woods Hole, MA [*OCLC symbol*] (OCLC)
**OAP**.......... OAPEC [*Organization of Arab Petroleum Exporting Countries*] News Bulletin [*A publication*]
**OAP**.......... Observation Amphibian Plane [*Coast Guard*]
**OAP**.......... Occupational Aptitude Pattern [*US Employment Service*] [*Department of Labor*]
**OAP**.......... Office of Aerial Phenomena [*Air Force*]
**OAP**.......... Office of Air Programs [*Obsolete*] [*Environmental Protection Agency*]
**OAP**.......... Office of Aircraft Production [*World War II*]
**OAP**.......... Office of Alien Property [*World War II*] (DLA)
**OAP**.......... Office of Antarctic Programs [*National Science Foundation*] [*Later, Division of Polar Programs*]
**OAP**.......... Office of Atomic Programs [*DoD*]
**OAP**.......... Office of the Director of Aerospace Programs [*Air Force*]
**OAP**.......... Offset Aiming Point (AFM)
**OAP**.......... Oil Analysis Program [*Military*] (AFIT)
**OAP**.......... Old-Age Pension [*or Pensioner*]
**OAP**.......... Oncovin [*Vincristine*], Ara-C, Prednisone [*Antineoplastic drug regimen*]
**OAP**.......... Operation Angel Plane (EA)
**OAP**.......... Ophthalmic Arterial Pressure [*Medicine*]
**OAP**.......... Optical Augmentation Project
**OAP**.......... Optically Active Polymer
**OAP**.......... Ordinary Alterations Plan [*Navy*] (OAG)
**OAP**.......... Organic Ablative Plastic
**OAP**.......... Orthogonal Array Processor [*Computer*]
**OAP**.......... Outlet Absolute Pressure
**OAP**.......... Outline Acquisition Plan [*Army*]
**OAP**.......... Oxygen at Atmospheric Pressure
**OAPBC**...... Office for Advancement of Public Black Colleges [*of the National Association of State Universities and Land Grant Colleges*] (EA)
**OAPC**........ Office of Alien Property Custodian [*World War II*]
**OAPCA**..... Organotin Antifouling Paint Control Act of 1988
**OAPCB**...... Old-Age-Pensioner CBer [*Experienced citizens band radio operator*]
**OAPEC**...... Organization of Arab Petroleum Exporting Countries [*See also OPAEP*] [*Absorbed by OPEC*] [*Kuwait*]
**OAPEC News Bull**... OAPEC [*Organization of Arab Petroleum Exporting Countries*] News Bulletin [*Kuwait*] [*A publication*]
**OAPEP**...... Organisation Arabe des Pays Exportateurs de Petrole [*Organization of Arab Petroleum Exporting Countries*]
**OAPG**........ Paghman [*Afghanistan*] [*ICAO location identifier*] (ICLI)
**OAPJ**......... Pan Jao [*Afghanistan*] [*ICAO location identifier*] (ICLI)
**OAPM**....... Optimal Amplitude and Phase Modulation
**OAPP**........ Office of Adolescent Pregnancy Programs [*HEW*]
**O App**....... Ohio Appellate Reports [*A publication*] (DLA)
**O App 2d**.... Ohio Appellate Reports, Second Series [*A publication*] (DLA)
**OAPS**......... Orbit Adjust Propulsion Subsystem [*NASA*]
**OAPU**........ Overseas Air Preparation Unit [*British military*] (DMA)
**OAQ**.......... National Climatic Center, Ashville, NC [*OCLC symbol*] (OCLC)
**OAQ**.......... Observatorio Astronomico de Quito [*Ecuador*] [*Seismograph station code, US Geological Survey*] (SEIS)
**OAQD**....... Qades [*Afghanistan*] [*ICAO location identifier*] (ICLI)
**OAQK**........ Qala-I-Nyazkhan [*Afghanistan*] [*ICAO location identifier*] (ICLI)
**OAQM**...... Kron Monjan [*Afghanistan*] [*ICAO location identifier*] (ICLI)
**OAQN**....... Qala-I-Naw [*Afghanistan*] [*ICAO location identifier*] (ICLI)
**OAQPS**...... Office of Air Quality Planning and Standards [*Environmental Protection Agency*]
**OAQQ**....... Qarqin [*Afghanistan*] [*ICAO location identifier*] (ICLI)
**OAQR**........ Qaisar [*Afghanistan*] [*ICAO location identifier*] (ICLI)
**OAR**........... Arnprior Public Library, Ontario [*Library symbol*] [*National Library of Canada*] (NLC)
**OAR**........... Monterey/Fort Ord, CA [*Location identifier*] [*FAA*] (FAAL)
**OAR**........... Offender Aid and Restoration (EA)
**OAR**........... Office of Aerospace Research [*Air Force*]
**OAR**........... Office of Analysis and Review [*Army, Navy*]
**OAR**........... Office of Oceanic and Atmospheric Research [*National Oceanic and Atmospheric Administration*]
**OAR**........... Ohio Appellate Reports [*A publication*] (DLA)
**OAR**........... [*The*] Ohio Art Co. [*AMEX symbol*] (SPSG)
**O-Ar**........... Ohio State Archives, Columbus, OH [*Library symbol*] [*Library of Congress*] (LCLS)
**OAR**........... Ontario Appeal Reports [*A publication*] (DLA)
**OAR**........... Ontario Appeals Report [*A publication*]
**OAR**........... Open Architecture Receiver [*Telecommunications*]
**OAR**........... Operational Availability and Reliability [*Military*]
**OAR**........... Operations Analysis Report
**OAR**........... Operator Authorization Record [*Data processing*] (IBMDP)
**OAR**........... Optical Angle Readout
**OAR**........... Optical Automatic Ranging
**OAR**........... ORDALT [*Ordnance Alterations*] Accomplishment Requirement (NG)
**OAR**........... Order of the Augustinian Recollects [*Roman Catholic men's religious order*]
**OAR**........... Ordnance Allowance Report [*Navy*]
**OAR**........... Ordnance Alteration Reporting
**OAR**........... Ordnance Alteration Requirement (NG)
**OAR**........... Organized Air Reserve
**OAr**............ Orientalisches Archiv [*A publication*]
**OAR**........... Overhaul and Repair
**OAR**........... Overtime Authorization Request (MCD)
**OAR**........... Oxford Applied Research [*Software manufacturer*] [*British*]
**OARAC**...... Office of Air Research Automatic Computer
**OARB**........ Azilda Branch, Rayside-Balfour Public Library, Ontario [*Library symbol*] [*National Library of Canada*] (NLC)
**OARB**........ Oakland Army Base [*California*] (AABC)
**OARBC**..... Boeing of Canada Ltd., Arnprior, Ontario [*Library symbol*] [*National Library of Canada*] (BIB)
**OARC**........ Ordinary Administrative Radio Conference
**O Arch Q**... Ohio Archaeological and Historical Quarterly [*A publication*]
**OARCTA**... 187th Airborne Regimental Combat Team Association (EA)
**OARD**........ Arthur District High School, Arthur, Ontario [*Library symbol*] [*National Library of Canada*] (NLC)
**OARDC**..... Ohio Agricultural Research and Development Center [*Ohio State University*] [*Research center*] (RCD)
**OARG**........ Uruzgan [*Afghanistan*] [*ICAO location identifier*] (ICLI)
**OARID**...... Oesterreichische Abwasser Rundschau. OAR International [*A publication*]
**OARM**....... Dilaram [*Afghanistan*] [*ICAO location identifier*] (ICLI)
**OARM**....... Middlesex County Public Library, Arva, Ontario [*Library symbol*] [*National Library of Canada*] (NLC)
**OARMS**.... Armstrong Community Library, Ontario [*Library symbol*] [*National Library of Canada*] (NLC)
**OAR-N**...... Office of Analysis and Review, Navy (MUGU)
**OARP**........ Office of Advanced Research Programs [*Later, OART*] [*NASA*]
**OARP**........ Operator Accelerated Retraining Program [*Nuclear energy*] (NRCH)
**OARP**........ Rimpa [*Afghanistan*] [*ICAO location identifier*] (ICLI)
**OARS**........ Ocean Area Reconnaissance Satellite [*Antisubmarine warfare*]
**OARS**........ Ocean Atmosphere Response Studies [*Marine science*] (MSC)
**OARS**........ On-Line Automated Reference Service [*Library science*]
**OARS**........ Opening Automated Report Service [*NYSE*]
**OART**........ Oakland Army Terminal [*California*]
**OART**........ Office of Advanced Research and Technology [*Later, OAST*] [*NASA*]
**OARTS**...... Oceanic Air Route Tracking System (FAAC)
**OAS**........... O-Acetylserine (Thiol)-Lyase [*An enzyme*]
**OAS**........... Oasis [*Board on Geographic Names*]
**OAS**........... Occupational Aspiration Scale [*Education*]
**OAS**........... Occupied Areas Section [*Military government*]
**OAS**........... Oesterreich in Amerikanischer Sicht. Das Oesterreichbild im Amerikanischen Schulunterricht [*A publication*]
**OAS**........... Offensive Air Support (MCD)
**OAS**........... Offensive Avionics System
**OAS**........... Office for Advanced Studies (AAG)
**OAS**........... Office of the Assistant Secretary [*Defense*] [*Navy*]
**OAS**........... Office of the Assistant for Study Support [*Air Force*]
**OAS**........... Office Automation System (NASA)

**OAS**.......... Office of Oceanic and Atmospheric Services [*National Oceanic and Atmospheric Administration*] (MSC)
**OAS**.......... Ohio Academy of Science
**OAS**.......... Old-Age Security
**OAS**.......... Olley Air Service Ltd.
**OAS**.......... On Active Service
**OAS**.......... Open-Hearth Acid Steel
**OAS**.......... Optical Alignment Sights [*NASA*]
**OAS**.......... Optical Array Spectrometer
**OAS**.......... Optical Augmentation System
**OAS**.......... Optics and Sensors [*Program*] (MCD)
**OAS**.......... Optoacoustic Spectrometry [*Also, PAS*]
**OAS**.......... Orbiter Aeroflight Simulator [*NASA*] (NASA)
**OAS**.......... Orbiter Atmospheric Simulator [*NASA*] (MCD)
**OAS**.......... Orbiter Avionics System [*NASA*] (NASA)
**OAS**.......... Organisation de l'Armee Secrete [*Secret Army Organization*] [*France*] (PD)
**OAS**.......... Organization of American States (EA)
**OAS**.......... Organization of Arab Students in the USA and Canada (EA)
**OAS**.......... Oriental and African Studies
**OAS**.......... Origin-of-Assembly Sequence [*Genetics*]
**OAS**.......... Other Approved Studies (ADA)
**OA & S**...... Other Arms and Services [*Military*]
**OAS**.......... Output Amplitude Stability
**OAS2**......... Officer Accession/Separation System
**OASAF**....... Office of Assistant Secretary of Air Force
**OASAF**....... Optical Active Surface Approach Fuze
**OASA (FM)**... Office of the Assistant Secretary of the Army (Financial Management) (MUGU)
**OASA (I & L)**... Office of the Assistant Secretary of the Army (Installations and Logistics) (MUGU)
**OASAM**.... Office of the Assistant Secretary for Administration and Management [*Department of Labor*]
**OASA(M & RA)**... Office of the Assistant Secretary of the Army (Manpower and Reserve Affairs)
**OASA (R & D)**... Office of the Assistant Secretary of the Army (Research and Development) (MUGU)
**OASB**........ Sarobi [*Afghanistan*] [*ICAO location identifier*] (ICLI)
**OASBO**..... Office of Asbestos and Small Business Ombudsman [*Environmental Protection Agency*]
**OAsC**......... Ashland College, Ashland, OH [*Library symbol*] [*Library of Congress*] (LCLS)
**OASC**........ Office of Advanced Scientific Computing [*National Science Foundation*]
**OASCB**...... Orbiter Avionics Software Control Board [*NASA*] (NASA)
**OASCMIS**... Operating and Support Costs Management Information System (MCD)
**OASD**........ Office of the Assistant Secretary of Defense
**OASD**........ Shindand [*Afghanistan*] [*ICAO location identifier*] (ICLI)
**OASD(AE)**... Office of the Assistant Secretary of Defense (Applications Engineer) (MCD)
**OASD-C**.... Office of the Assistant Secretary of Defense - Comptroller
**OASDG**..... Alexandria Branch, Stormount, Dundas, and Glengarry County Public Library, Ontario [*Library symbol*] [*National Library of Canada*] (NLC)
**OASDHI**... Old-Age, Survivors, Disability, and Health Insurance [*Program*] [*Social Security Administration*]
**OASDI**....... Old-Age, Survivors, and Disability Insurance [*Program*] [*Social Security Administration*]
**OASD/IL**.. Office of the Assistant Secretary of Defense/Installations and Logistics (MCD)
**OASD/ISA**... Office of the Assistant Secretary of Defense/International Security Affairs (CINC)
**OASD/ISP**... Office of the Assistant Secretary of Defense for International Security Policy (SDI)
**OASD (MRA & L)**... Office of Assistant Secretary of Defense (Manpower-Reserve Affairs and Logistics) (MCD)
**OASD(R & D)**... Office of the Assistant Secretary of Defense (Research and Development) (MCD)
**OASD(SA)**... Office of the Assistant Secretary of Defense (Systems Analysis) (CINC)
**OASD(S & L)**... Office of the Assistant Secretary of Defense (Supply and Logistics) [*Obsolete*] (MCD)
**OASD(T)**... Office of the Assistant Secretary of Defense (Telecommunications)
**OASES**...... Organization for American-Soviet Exchanges (EA)
**OASET**...... Office of the Assistant Secretary for Employment and Training [*Department of Labor*]
**OASF**......... Orbiting Astronomical Support Facility (MCD)
**OASFP**...... Old Alliance Society of French Polishers [*A union*] [*British*]
**OASG**........ Sheberghan [*Afghanistan*] [*ICAO location identifier*] (ICLI)
**OASH**........ Office of the Assistant Secretary for Health [*Department of Health and Human Services*]
**OASHA**..... Operating and Support Hazard Analysis (MCD)
**OAsht**........ Ashtabula County District Library, Ashtabula, OH [*Library symbol*] [*Library of Congress*] (LCLS)
**OAshtK**...... Kent State University, Ashtabula Regional Campus, Ashtabula, OH [*Library symbol*] [*Library of Congress*] (LCLS)
**OASI**......... Office Automation Society International (EA)
**OASI**......... Old-Age and Survivors Insurance [*Program*] [*Social Security Administration*]
**OASIA**....... Office of the Assistant Secretary for International Affairs [*Department of the Treasury*]
**OASIS**....... Occupational Aptitude Survey and Interest Schedule
**OASIS**....... Ocean All-Source Information System
**OASIS**....... Oceanic and Atmospheric Scientific Information System [*National Oceanic and Atmospheric Administration*] (MCD)
**OASIS**....... Office Administration Simulation Study
**OASIS**....... Office Automation and School Information System [*Australia*]
**OASIS**....... Online Automotive Service Information System [*Ford Motor Co.*]
**OASIS**....... Operation Analysis Strategic Interaction Simulator [*Nuclear war games*]
**OASIS**....... Operational Applications of Special Intelligence System (MCD)
**OASIS**....... Operational Automatic Scheduling Information System (MUGU)
**OASIS**....... Optimized Air-to-Surface Infrared Seeker
**OASIS**....... Order and Schedules Input System (MCD)
**OASIS**....... Organization for Applied Science in Society
**OASIS**....... Organized Adoption Search Information Services (EA)
**OASIS**....... Outlook and Situation Information System [*Department of Agriculture*] [*Defunct*] (IID)
**OASIS**....... Outpatient Appointment Scheduling and Information System
**OASIS-AS**... Occupational Aptitude Survey and Interest Schedule - Aptitude Survey [*Vocational guidance test*]
**OASIS-IS**... Occupational Aptitude Survey and Interest Schedule - Interest Schedule [*Vocational guidance test*]
**OASK**........ Serka [*Afghanistan*] [*ICAO location identifier*] (ICLI)
**OASL**......... Salam [*Afghanistan*] [*ICAO location identifier*] (ICLI)
**OASM**....... Office of Aerospace Medicine [*NASA*] (KSC)
**OASM**....... Ohm-Ampere-Second Meter [*System of units*]
**OASM**....... Samangan [*Afghanistan*] [*ICAO location identifier*] (ICLI)
**OASMA**.... Offensive Air Support Mission Analysis (MCD)
**OASMS**..... Ordnance Ammunition Surveillance and Maintenance School [*Army*]
**OASN**........ Office of the Assistant Secretary of the Navy
**OASN**........ Sheghnan [*Afghanistan*] [*ICAO location identifier*] (ICLI)
**OASN(FM)**... Office of the Assistant Secretary of the Navy for Financial Management
**OASN(I & L)**... Office of the Assistant Secretary of the Navy for Installations and Logistics
**OASN(M/RA/L)**... Office of the Assistant Secretary of the Navy (Manpower, Reserve Affairs, and Logistics)
**OASN(P & RF)**... Office of the Assistant Secretary of the Navy for Personnel and Reserve Force
**OASN(R & D)**... Office of the Assistant Secretary of the Navy for Research and Development
**OASP**......... Organic Acid Soluble Phosphorus
**OASP**......... Sare Pul [*Afghanistan*] [*ICAO location identifier*] (ICLI)
**OASPL**...... Overall Sound Pressure Level
**OASR**........ Office of Aeronautical and Space Research [*Later, OART*] [*NASA*]
**OASR**........ Sabar [*Afghanistan*] [*ICAO location identifier*] (ICLI)
**OAss**.......... Old Assyrian (BJA)
**OASS**......... Salang-I-Junubi [*Afghanistan*] [*ICAO location identifier*] (ICLI)
**OASSO**...... Operational Applications of Satellite Snowcover Observations [*NASA*]
**OAsT**......... Ashland Theological Seminary, Ashland, OH [*Library symbol*] [*Library of Congress*] (LCLS)
**OAST**........ Office of Aeronautical and Space Technology [*Formerly, OART*] [*NASA*]
**OAST**........ Order and Shipping Time [*Military*] (AFIT)
**OAST**........ Shur Tepa [*Afghanistan*] [*ICAO location identifier*] (ICLI)
**OASU**........ Oceanographic Air Survey Unit
**OASV**........ Orbital Assembly Support Vehicle
**OASW**....... Office of the Assistant Secretary of War [*World War II*]
**OASYS**...... Office Automation System
**OASYS**...... Order Allocation System
**OAT**........... Atikokan Public Library, Ontario [*Library symbol*] [*National Library of Canada*] (NLC)
**OAT**........... Ocean Acoustic Tomography
**OAT**........... Office for Advanced Technology [*Air Force*]
**OAT**........... One at a Time
**OAT**........... Open-Air Theater
**OAT**........... Operating Ambient Temperature
**OAT**........... Operational Acceptance Test
**OAT**........... Operational Air Traffic (NATG)
**OAT**........... Optical Adaptive Technique
**OAT**........... Ornithineaminotransferase [*An enzyme*]
**OAT**........... Outside Air Temperature [*Aviation*]
**OAT**........... Overall Test
**OAT**........... Quaker Oats Co. [*NYSE symbol*] [*Toronto Stock Exchange symbol*] (SPSG)
**OATA**........ Optical Acquisition and Tracking Aid Assembly
**OATC**........ Oceanic Air Traffic Center
**OATC**........ Overseas Air Traffic Control
**OATD**........ Toorghondi [*Afghanistan*] [*ICAO location identifier*] (ICLI)
**OATG**........ Tashkurghan [*Afghanistan*] [*ICAO location identifier*] (ICLI)
**OATH**........ Atikokan High School, Ontario [*Library symbol*] [*National Library of Canada*] (NLC)

**OAth**........ Opuscula Atheniensia [*A publication*]
**OATK**........ Kotal [*Afghanistan*] [*ICAO location identifier*] (ICLI)
**OATM**........ Atikokan Centennial Museum, Ontario [*Library symbol*] [*National Library of Canada*] (BIB)
**OATM**........ Orbiter Antenna Test Model [*NASA*]
**OATMEAL**... Optimum Allocation of Test and Equipment Manpower Against Logistics
**OATN**........ Tereen [*Afghanistan*] [*ICAO location identifier*] (ICLI)
**OATP**........ On-Aircraft Test Procedure (MCD)
**OATP**........ Operational Acceptance Test Procedure (NRCH)
**OATQ**........ Taluqan [*Afghanistan*] [*ICAO location identifier*] (ICLI)
**OATS**........ Office of Air Transportation Security [*FAA*]
**OATS**........ On-Board Acoustic Tracking System [*Navy*] (CAAL)
**OATS**........ Optimum Aerial Target Sensor
**OATS**........ Original Article Tear Sheets
**OATS**........ Original Article Text Service
**OATS**........ Over Armor Technology Synthesis (RDA)
**OATS**........ Overall Test Set
**OATUU**..... Organisation of African Trade Union Unity [*Formerly, AATUF, ATUC*] [*See also OUSA*] [*Accra, Ghana*] (EAIO)
**OATW**........ Tewara [*Afghanistan*] [*ICAO location identifier*] (ICLI)
**OATZ**........ Tesak [*Afghanistan*] [*ICAO location identifier*] (ICLI)
**OAU**.......... Aurora Public Library, Ontario [*Library symbol*] [*National Library of Canada*] (NLC)
**OAU**.......... Ohio University, Athens, OH [*Library symbol*] [*Library of Congress*] (LCLS)
**OAU**.......... Optical Alignment Unit
**OAUH**........ Aurora Historical Society, Ontario [*Library symbol*] [*National Library of Canada*] (NLC)
**OAUHS**..... PRECIS Project, Aurora High School, Ontario [*Library symbol*] [*National Library of Canada*] (NLC)
**OAULC**..... OAU [*Organization of African Unity*] Liberation Committee [*Addis Ababa, Ethiopia*] (EAIO)
**OAUM**....... Aurora Museum, Ontario [*Library symbol*] [*National Library of Canada*] (BIB)
**OAUS**........ Sterling Drug Ltd., Aurora, Ontario [*Library symbol*] [*National Library of Canada*] (BIB)
**OAU/STRC**... Organization of African Unity Scientific and Technical Research Commission [*Marine science*] (MSC)
**OAUYCE**.. York County Board of Education, Aurora, Ontario [*Library symbol*] [*National Library of Canada*] (NLC)
**OAUZ**........ Kunduz [*Afghanistan*] [*ICAO location identifier*] (ICLI)
**O-A-V**........ Object-Attribute-Value
**OAV**........... Operational Aerospace Vehicle
**OAVCSA**... Office of the Assistant Vice Chief of Staff, Army [*Formerly, OAVC of SA*] (AABC)
**OAVC of SA**... Office of the Assistant Vice Chief of Staff, Army [*Later, OAVCSA*] (AABC)
**OAVE**........ Occupational, Adult, and Vocational Education (OICC)
**OAvG**........ B. F. Goodrich Chemical Co. [*of B. F. Goodrich Co.*], Development Center Library, Avon Lake, OH [*Library symbol*] [*Library of Congress*] (LCLS)
**OAVG**........ Oberbayerisches Archiv fuer Vaterlaendische Geschichte [*A publication*]
**OAVP**........ Older Americans Volunteer Program [*ACTION*]
**OAVSDG**.. Avonmore Branch, Stormont, Dundas, and Glengarry County Public Library, Ontario [*Library symbol*] [*National Library of Canada*] (BIB)
**OAVTME**... Office of Adult, Vocational, Technical, and Manpower Education [*Office of Education*]
**OAW**.......... Oxyacetylene Welding
**OAWCS**.... Overseas Air Weapons Control System
**OAWM**...... Office of Air and Water Measurement [*National Institute of Standards and Technology*]
**OAWOP**.... Ontario Police College, Aylmer West, Ontario [*Library symbol*] [*National Library of Canada*] (NLC)
**OAWP**....... Office of Air and Water Programs (OICC)
**OAWP**....... Operations Analysis Working Paper [*NASA*] (KSC)
**OAW PHKD**... Denkschriften der Oesterreichischen Akademie der Wissenschaften. Philosophisch-Historische Klasse [*A publication*]
**OAW PHKS**... Oesterreichische Akademie der Wissenschaften. Philosophisch-Historische Klasse. Sitzungsberichte [*A publication*]
**OAWR**....... Office of Agricultural War Relations [*World War II*]
**OAWR**....... Office of Atmospheric Water Resources [*Bureau of Reclamation*]
**OAWU**...... Wurtach [*Afghanistan*] [*ICAO location identifier*] (ICLI)
**OAWZ**....... Wazirabad [*Afghanistan*] [*ICAO location identifier*] (ICLI)
**OAX**........... Oaxaca [*Mexico*] [*Airport symbol*] (OAG)
**OAX**........... Oaxaca [*Mexico*] [*Seismograph station code, US Geological Survey*] (SEIS)
**OAY**........... Moses Point, AK [*Location identifier*] [*FAA*] (FAAL)
**OAY**........... NOAA [*National Oceanic and Atmospheric Administration*] Geophysical Fluid Dynamics Laboratory, Princeton, NJ [*OCLC symbol*] (OCLC)
**OAYM**....... Aylmer District Museum, Ontario [*Library symbol*] [*National Library of Canada*] (BIB)
**OAYQ**........ Yangi Qala [*Afghanistan*] [*ICAO location identifier*] (ICLI)
**OAYR**........ Outstanding Airman of the Year Ribbon [*Military decoration*] (AFM)
**OAZB**........ Zebak [*Afghanistan*] [*ICAO location identifier*] (ICLI)
**OAZG**........ Zaranj [*Afghanistan*] [*ICAO location identifier*] (ICLI)
**OB**............. Austrian Airtransport [*ICAO designator*] (FAAC)
**OB**............. Brockville Public Library, Ontario [*Library symbol*] [*National Library of Canada*] (NLC)
**OB**............. Brought Over (ROG)
**Ob**............. Obadiah [*Old Testament book*]
**OB**............. Oberlerchner [*Joseph Oberlerchner Holzindustrie*] [*Austria*] [*ICAO aircraft manufacturer identifier*] (ICAO)
**ob**............. Obese
**OB**............. Obeum [*Nickname for toilets at Cambridge University*] [*Slang*] [*British*] (DSUE)
**OB**............. Obiit [*He, or She, Died*] [*Latin*]
**OB**............. Obituary Notice (DSUE)
**OB**............. Objection (ROG)
**OB**............. Objective [*Microscopy*]
**OB**............. Obligation (ROG)
**ob**............. Obligation [*Obligation*] [*French*] [*Business term*]
**OB**............. Obligation Bond
**OB**............. Obliteration
**OB**............. Oblong
**OB**............. Oboe
**OB**............. Obolus [*Coin*] [*Latin*] (ADA)
**OB**............. O'Brien Energy & Resources Ltd. [*Toronto Stock Exchange symbol*]
**OB**............. Obscure (KSC)
**OB**............. Observed Bearing [*Navigation*]
**OB**............. Observer [*United Kingdom*] [*A publication*]
**OB**............. Obsolete (AABC)
**OB**............. Obstetrics [*Medicine*]
**OB**............. Obtuse Bisectrix [*Crystallography*]
**OB**............. Occult Bleeding [*Medicine*]
**OB**............. Occupational Behavior
**OB**............. Ocean Bottom
**OB**............. Octal-to-Binary [*Data processing*] (BUR)
**OB**............. Octave Band
**OB**............. Offensive Back [*Football*]
**OB**............. Official Bulletin. International Commission for Air Navigation [*A publication*] (DLA)
**OB**............. Oil Bearing (DCTA)
**OB**............. Oil Bomb
**OB**............. Old Babylonian (BJA)
**OB**............. [*The*] Old Bailey [*London court*]
**OB**............. Old Bonded [*Whisky*] (ROG)
**OB**............. Old Boy [*Communications operators' colloquialism*]
**OB**............. Old Buildings [*British Admiralty*]
**OB**............. Oligoclonal Band [*Analytical biochemistry*]
**OB**............. Olive Branch IFR [*Instrument Flight Rules*] Military Training Route [*FAA*] (FAAC)
**OB**............. Ombudsman for Business [*Department of Commerce*]
**OB**............. On Being: the Servant's Servant [*A publication*] (APTA)
**OB**............. On Board
**OB**............. Opening of Books
**OB**............. Operating Base [*Navy*]
**OB**............. Operating Budget (AFM)
**OB**............. Operation Brotherhood
**OB**............. Operational Base [*Navy*]
**OB**............. Or Better [*Business term*]
**OB**............. Ord och Bild [*A publication*]
**OB**............. Order of the Bath
**OB**............. Order of Battle [*Military*]
**OB**............. Order of Burma [*British military*] (DMA)
**OB**............. Ordered Back
**OB**............. Ordnance Battalion [*Navy*]
**OB**............. Ordnance Board [*Navy*]
**OB**............. Orgelbuechlein [*Little Organ Book*] [*Bach*] [*Music*]
**OB**............. Orientalische Bibliographie [*A publication*] (BJA)
**OB**............. Ortsbatterie [*Local Battery*] [*German military - World War II*]
**OB**............. Osvedomitel'nyj Bjulleten' Komissii Ekspedicionnych Issledovanij Akademii Nauk SSSR [*A publication*]
**OB**............. Out-of-Business (OICC)
**OB**............. Outboard
**OB**............. Output Buffer [*Data processing*]
**OB**............. Output Bus [*Data processing*]
**OB**............. Outside Broadcasts (EY)
**OB**............. Outside Bugs [*Nonresident staff at a school*] [*British*] (DSUE)
**OB**............. Outward Bound (EA)
**OB**............. Over Bath [*Classified advertising*] (ADA)
**OB**............. Overboard (AAG)
**OB**............. Overseas Brats [*Commercial firm*] (EA)
**OB**............. Oxford Biographies [*A publication*]
**OB**............. Peru [*Aircraft nationality and registration mark*] (FAAC)
**OBA**........... Barrie Public Library, Ontario [*Library symbol*] [*National Library of Canada*] (NLC)
**OBA**........... Oasis Bungera [*Antarctica*] [*Seismograph station code, US Geological Survey*] [*Closed*] (SEIS)
**OBA**........... Oberbayerisches Archiv fuer Vaterlaendische Geschichte [*A publication*]
**OBA**........... Oberhasli Breeders of America (EA)

**OBA**........... Object Behavior Analysis [*Data processing*]
**OBA**........... Octave Band Analyzer
**OBA**........... Off Boresight Angle (MCD)
**OBA**........... Office of Business Administration [*Later, Office of Administration*] [*NASA*]
**OBA**........... Office of Business Analysis [*Information service or system*] (EISS)
**OBA**........... Open Broadcasting Authority [*Noncommercial TV channel*] [*British*]
**OBA**........... Operating Budget Authority (MCD)
**OBA**........... Optical Base Assembly (KSC)
**OBA**........... Optical Brightening Agents
**OBA**........... Ornithyl-Beta-Alanine [*Biochemistry*]
**OBA**........... Oxygen Breathing Apparatus
**OBAALA**... Organisation for Black Arts Advancement and Learning Activities [*British*]
**Obad**.......... Obadiah [*Old Testament book*]
**OBAD**......... Object Average Optical Density [*Microscopy*]
**OBAD**......... Operating Budget Authority Document [*Military*] (AFIT)
**OBADRS**... Octave Band Automatic Data Reduction System
**OBAG**......... Georgian Bay Regional Library, Barrie, Ontario [*Library symbol*] [*National Library of Canada*] (NLC)
**OBAGC**..... Georgian College of Applied Arts and Technology, Barrie, Ontario [*Library symbol*] [*National Library of Canada*] (NLC)
**OBAL**......... Balmertown Public Library, Ontario [*Library symbol*] [*National Library of Canada*] (NLC)
**OBAN**......... Bancroft Public Library, Ontario [*Library symbol*] [*National Library of Canada*] (NLC)
**OBAN**......... Operating Budget Account Number [*Air Force*]
**OBANU**..... United Public Library, Carlow, Dungannon, and Mayo Townships, Bancroft, Ontario [*Library symbol*] [*National Library of Canada*] (BIB)
**OBAP**......... Organization of Black Airline Pilots (EA)
**O Bar**......... Ohio State Bar Association. Report [*A publication*]
**OBarb**........ Barberton Public Library, Barberton, OH [*Library symbol*] [*Library of Congress*] (LCLS)
**OBarn**........ Barnesville Public Library, Barnesville, OH [*Library symbol*] [*Library of Congress*] (LCLS)
**OBAS**......... Organ Builders' Amalgamated Society [*A union*] [*British*]
**OBAS**......... Simcoe County Co-Op, Barrie, Ontario [*Library symbol*] [*National Library of Canada*] (NLC)
**OBAT**......... Augusta Township Public Library, Brockville, Ontario [*Library symbol*] [*National Library of Canada*] (NLC)
**OBat**.......... Clermont County Public Library, Batavia, OH [*Library symbol*] [*Library of Congress*] (LCLS)
**OBAT**......... Olympic International Bank & Trust Co. [*Boston, MA*] [*NASDAQ symbol*] (NQ)
**OBatC**........ Clermont General and Technical College, Batavia, OH [*Library symbol*] [*Library of Congress*] (LCLS)
**OBatH**........ Clermont Mercy Hospital, Batavia, OH [*Library symbol*] [*Library of Congress*] (LCLS)
**OBAWS**..... On-Board Aircraft Weighing System (MCD)
**O Bay A**..... Oberbayerisches Archiv fuer Vaterlaendische Geschichte [*A publication*]
**OBB**........... Barry's Bay Public Library, Ontario [*Library symbol*] [*National Library of Canada*] (NLC)
**OBB**........... Obbligato [*Essential*] [*Music*]
**OBB**........... Obsidian Butte [*California*] [*Seismograph station code, US Geological Survey*] (SEIS)
**OBB**........... Oesterreichische Bundesbahnen [*Austrian Federal Railways*]
**OBB**........... Old Battleship [*Navy*]
**OBB**........... Operation Better Block
**OBB**........... Oxybisbenzene [*Organic chemistry*]
**OBBB**......... Bahrain [*Bahrain*] [*ICAO location identifier*] (ICLI)
**OBBD**......... Official Board of Ballroom Dancing [*British*]
**OBBFC**...... Official Betty Boop Fan Club (EA)
**OBBI**.......... Bahrain/International [*Bahrain*] [*ICAO location identifier*] (ICLI)
**Obbl**........... Obbligato [*Essential*] [*Music*]
**OBBM**........ Brant County Historical Museum, Brantford, Ontario [*Library symbol*] [*National Library of Canada*] (NLC)
**Obbmo**....... Obbligatissimo [*Your Obedient Servant*] [*Italian*]
**OBBMV**.... Madawaska Valley District High School, Barry's Bay, Ontario [*Library symbol*] [*National Library of Canada*] (NLC)
**OBBO**......... Observation Balloon
**OBC**........... Barwick Community Library, Ontario [*Library symbol*] [*National Library of Canada*] (BIB)
**OBC**........... Obock [*Djibouti*] [*Airport symbol*] (OAG)
**OBC**........... Oceania Basketball Confederation [*Australia*] (EA)
**OBC**........... Off Boresight Correction [*Military*] (CAAL)
**OBC**........... Officer Basic Course [*Military*]
**OBC**........... Ohio Bell Communications, Inc. [*Cleveland*] [*Telecommunications*] (TSSD)
**OBC**........... Old Boys' Corps [*Military*] [*British*]
**OBC**........... On-Board Checkout [*Aircraft*]
**OBC**........... On-Board Computer (MCD)
**OBC**........... On-Board Controller [*Telecommunications*]
**OBC**........... One Big Computer [*Proposed model for automation of the New York and American stock exchanges*]
**OBC**........... Ouachita Baptist College [*Arkadelphia, AR*] [*Later, OBU*]
**OBC**........... Outboard Boating Club of America (EA)
**OBC**........... Overseas Bankers' Club [*British*]
**OBC**........... Overseas Book Centre
**OBC**........... Oxide-Coated Brush Cathode
**OBCA**......... Office of Bank Customer Affairs [*FDIC*]
**OBCAB**...... Albion-Bolton Branch, Town of Caledon Public Libraries, Bolton, Ontario [*Library symbol*] [*National Library of Canada*] (NLC)
**OBCC**......... Olympic Broadcasting Corporation [*Seattle, WA*] [*NASDAQ symbol*] (NQ)
**OBCCL**...... Canada Cement Lafarge Ltd., Belleville, Ontario [*Library symbol*] [*National Library of Canada*] (NLC)
**OBCE**......... Office Belge du Commerce Exterieur [*Belgian Overseas Trade Office*] (GEA)
**OBCE**......... On-Board Checkout Equipment (MCD)
**OBCE**......... Operational Baseline Cost Estimate [*Army*]
**OBCGEH**.. Housewares and Home Entertainment Department, Canada General Electric Co. Ltd., Barrie, Ontario [*Library symbol*] [*National Library of Canada*] (NLC)
**OBCI**.......... Ocean Bio-Chem, Incorporated [*Fort Lauderdale, FL*] [*NASDAQ symbol*] (NQ)
**OBCI**.......... On-Board Controller Interface [*Telecommunications*]
**OBCO**......... On-Board Checkout [*NASA*] (KSC)
**OBCP**......... Ortho-Benzyl-para-chlorophenol [*Disinfectant*]
**OBCS**......... Chromatographic Specialties Ltd., Brockville, Ontario [*Library symbol*] [*National Library of Canada*] (NLC)
**OBCS**......... On-Board Checkout Subsystem [*NASA*] (NASA)
**Obd**............ Obadiah [*Old Testament book*] (BJA)
**OBD**........... Office of Business Development [*Economic Development Administration*]
**OBD**........... Omnibearing Distance
**OBD**........... On-Board Diagnostics [*Chrysler Corp.'s computer system*]
**OBD**........... Operational Base Development (AAG)
**OBD**........... Optical Beam Deflection
**OBD**........... Organic Brain Disease
**OBDD**......... Ordered Bicontinuous Double Diamond [*Phase structure*]
**OBDE**......... Dollman Electronics Canada Ltd., Brampton, Ontario [*Library symbol*] [*National Library of Canada*] (NLC)
**OBDO**......... Oceanographic, Boarding, and Diving Officer [*Navy*] [*British*]
**OBDT**......... Obedient
**Obd Vcelar Prekl**... Obdorne Vcelarske Preklady [*A publication*]
**OBE**........... Belleville Public Library, Ontario [*Library symbol*] [*National Library of Canada*] (NLC)
**OBE**........... Oberlin College, Oberlin, OH [*OCLC symbol*] (OCLC)
**OBE**........... Office of Business Economics [*Later, Office of Economic Analysis*] [*Department of Commerce*]
**OBE**........... Okeechobee, FL [*Location identifier*] [*FAA*] (FAAL)
**OBE**........... On-Board Equipment
**OBE**........... Operating Basis Earthquake [*Nuclear reactor*] (NRCH)
**OBE**........... Operating Basis Event (IEEE)
**OBE**........... Order of the British Empire [*Facetious translations: Old Boiled Egg, Other Buggers' Efforts*]
**OBE**........... Ottawa Board of Education, Library Services Centre [*UTLAS symbol*]
**OBE**........... Out-of-Body Experience [*Parapsychology*]
**OBE**........... Outerback End
**OBE**........... Overcome [*or Overtaken*] by Events
**OBEAB**...... Beaverton Branch, Brock Township Public Library, Ontario [*Library symbol*] [*National Library of Canada*] (BIB)
**OBEAR**..... Beardmore Public Library, Ontario [*Library symbol*] [*National Library of Canada*] (NLC)
**OBEATE**... Beaverton-Thorah Eldon Historical Society, Inc., Ontario [*Library symbol*] [*National Library of Canada*] (NLC)
**Obecna Chem Technol**... Obecna Chemicka Technologie [*A publication*]
**OBECO**..... Outboard Engine Cutoff [*NASA*] (KSC)
**OBED**........ Beamsville District Secondary School, Ontario [*Library symbol*] [*National Library of Canada*] (NLC)
**OBed**.......... Bedford Public Library, Bedford, OH [*Library symbol*] [*Library of Congress*] (LCLS)
**OBedF**........ Ferro Corp., Chemical Library, Bedford, OH [*Library symbol*] [*Library of Congress*] (LCLS)
**Obedin Inst Yad Issled (Dubna USSR) Prepr**... Ob'edinennyi Institut Yadernykh Issledovanii (Dubna, USSR). Preprint [*A publication*]
**OBEDS**...... Deloro Stellite Co., Belleville, Ontario [*Library symbol*] [*National Library of Canada*] (BIB)
**OBEE**......... Beeton Public Library, Ontario [*Library symbol*] [*National Library of Canada*] (BIB)
**OBEGOSC**... Organizational Effectiveness General Officer Steering Committee (MCD)
**OBEH**......... Hastings County Historical Society, Belleville, Ontario [*Library symbol*] [*National Library of Canada*] (BIB)
**OBEHP**..... Hastings and Prince Edward County Health Unit, Belleville, Ontario [*Library symbol*] [*National Library of Canada*] (BIB)
**OBEL**......... Loyalist College of Applied Arts and Technology, Belleville, Ontario [*Library symbol*] [*National Library of Canada*] (NLC)
**OBELF**...... Fleming Branch, Lincoln Public Library, Beamsville, Ontario [*Library symbol*] [*National Library of Canada*] (BIB)

**OBEM**....... Beachville Ye Olde Museum, Ontario [*Library symbol*] [*National Library of Canada*] (BIB)
**OBEM**....... One-Boson Exchange Model
**OBEM**....... Operational Battery Effectiveness Model (MCD)
**O Ben**......... Old Benloe's Reports, English Common Pleas [*1486-1580*] [*A publication*] (DLA)
**OBENFX**... Olive Branch Entry Fix [*FAA*] (FAAC)
**O Benl**........ Old Benloe's Reports, English Common Pleas [*1486-1580*] [*A publication*] (DLA)
**OBEP**......... One-Boson Exchange Potential
**OBEr**.......... OB [*Out-of-the-Body*] Experient [*Parapsychology*]
**OBerB**........ Baldwin-Wallace College, Berea, OH [*Library symbol*] [*Library of Congress*] (LCLS)
**OBERF**...... O'Brien Energy & Resources Ltd. [*NASDAQ symbol*] (NQ)
**Oberflaechentech/Metallprax** ... Oberflaechentechnik/Metallpraxis [*West Germany*] [*A publication*]
**Oberflaeche Surf** ... Oberflaeche Surface [*A publication*]
**Oberlin Coll Mus Bull** ... Oberlin College. Allen Memorial Art Museum. Bulletin [*A publication*]
**Oberoest H Bl** ... Oberoesterreichische Heimatblaetter [*A publication*]
**Oberoest Imker** ... Oberoesterreichische Imker [*A publication*]
**Oberrheinische Geol Abh** ... Oberrheinische Geologische Abhandlungen [*A publication*]
**OBERS**...... Office of Business Economics Research Service (NRCH)
**OBERST**... Oberstimme [*Upper Part*] [*Music*]
**OBERW**.... Oberwerk [*Upper Work*] [*Music*]
**OBES**......... Office of Basic Energy Services [*Department of Energy*]
**OBES**......... Orthonormal Basis of an Error Space [*Statistics*]
**OBESA**...... Stephens-Adamson, Belleville, Ontario [*Library symbol*] [*National Library of Canada*] (NLC)
**Obesity & Bariatric Med** ... Obesity and Bariatric Medicine [*A publication*]
**OBESSU**... Organising Bureau of European School Student Unions (EAIO)
**OBEWS**.... On-Board Electronic Warfare Simulation [*Air Force*]
**OBEXFX**... Olive Branch Exit Fix [*FAA*] (FAAC)
**OBF**.......... Octave Band Filter
**OB & F**....... Ollivier, Bell, and Fitzgerald's Court of Appeal Reports [*1878-80*] [*New Zealand*] [*A publication*] (DLA)
**OBF**.......... Operational Base Facility
**OBF**.......... Organ Blood Flow [*Physiology*]
**OBF**.......... Ottawa Board of Education, Library Services Centre (Films) [*UTLAS symbol*]
**OBFAR**...... Burks Falls, Armour, and Ryerson Union Library, Burks Falls, Ontario [*Library symbol*] [*National Library of Canada*] (NLC)
**OBFC**......... Barriefield Branch, Frontenac County Library, Ontario [*Library symbol*] [*National Library of Canada*] (BIB)
**OBFC**......... O'Leary Brothers Fan Club (EA)
**OB & F (CA)** ... Ollivier, Bell, and Fitzgerald's Court of Appeal Reports [*1878-80*] [*New Zealand*] [*A publication*] (DLA)
**OBFM**....... On or Before Full Moon [*Freemasonry*] (ROG)
**OBFNO**..... Northern Ontario Public School Principals' Association, Burks Falls, Ontario [*Library symbol*] [*National Library of Canada*] (NLC)
**OB & FNZ** ... Ollivier, Bell, and Fitzgerald's New Zealand Reports [*A publication*] (DLA)
**OBFS**......... Octave Band Filter Set
**OBFS**......... Offshore Bulk Fuel System
**OBFS**......... Organization of Biological Field Stations (EA)
**OBFS**......... Overseas Base Facilities Summary [*Navy*]
**OB & F (SC)** ... Ollivier, Bell, and Fitzgerald's Supreme Court Reports [*New Zealand*] [*A publication*] (DLA)
**OBG**.......... Oberg Industries Ltd. [*Vancouver Stock Exchange symbol*]
**Ob G**.......... Obergericht [*Court of Appeal*] [*German*] (DLA)
**OBG**.......... Obigarm [*USSR*] [*Seismograph station code, US Geological Survey*] [*Closed*] (SEIS)
**OBG**.......... Obstetrics-Gynecology [*Medicine*]
**OBG**.......... Oldie but Goodie [*Music*]
**OBGI**......... Orion Broadcasting Group, Incorporated [*NASDAQ symbol*] (NQ)
**OBGNA**..... Obstetrics and Gynecology [*A publication*]
**Ob Gr**........ Ostbairische Grenzmarken [*A publication*]
**OBGS**......... Orbital Bombardment Guidance System
**OBGT**........ Old Babylonian Grammatical Texts [*A publication*] (BJA)
**OBgU**......... Bowling Green State University, Bowling Green, OH [*Library symbol*] [*Library of Congress*] (LCLS)
**OBgU-C**..... Bowling Green State University, Center for Archival Collections, Bowling Green, OH [*Library symbol*] [*Library of Congress*] (LCLS)
**OB-GYN**.... Obstetrics-Gynecology [*Medicine*]
**OBH**.......... Office Busy Hour [*Telecommunications*] (TEL)
**OBH**.......... Oil Bath Heater
**OBH**.......... Old Berkeley Hunt [*British*]
**OBH**.......... Old Berkshire Hounds [*British*]
**OBH**.......... Old Highland Blend [*Whisky*] (ROG)
**OBH**.......... Operational Biomedical Harness
**OBH**.......... Wolbach, NE [*Location identifier*] [*FAA*] (FAAL)
**OBHFC**...... Official Bobby Hart Fan Club (EA)
**OB Hi-Tension News** ... Ohio Brass Hi-Tension News [*A publication*]
**OBHT**........ Tecumseh Township Public Library, Bond Head, Ontario [*Library symbol*] [*National Library of Canada*] (BIB)
**OBI**........... Film [*Amsterdam*] [*A publication*]
**OBI**........... Obihiro [*Japan*] [*Seismograph station code, US Geological Survey*] (SEIS)
**OBI**........... Obligated Involuntary Officer [*Military*]
**OBI**........... Office du Baccalaureat International [*International Baccalaureate Office - IBO*] (EAIO)
**OBI**........... Office of Basic Instrumentation [*National Bureau of Standards*]
**OBI**........... Old Babylonian Inscriptions [*A publication*] (BJA)
**OBI**........... Omnibearing Indicator [*Radio*]
**OBI**........... Open-Back Inclinable Press [*Manufacturing term*]
**OBI**........... Order of British India
**OBI**........... Organisation du Baccalaureat International [*International Baccalaureate Organisation - IBO*] (EAIO)
**O BID**........ Omni Bidus [*Every Two Days*] [*Pharmacy*] (ROG)
**OBIFC**....... Osmond Boys International Fan Club (EA)
**OBIFCO**.... On-Board In-Flight Checkout (MCD)
**OBIG**......... Oesterreichisches Bundesinstitut fuer Gesundheitswesen [*Austrian National Institute for Public Health*] [*Information service or system*] (IID)
**O BIH**........ Omni Bihora [*Every Two Hours*] [*Pharmacy*] (ROG)
**OBIMD**..... Oncodevelopmental Biology and Medicine [*A publication*]
**OBINXTO** ... Obiit in Christo [*Died in Christ*] [*Latin*]
**OBIPS**....... Optical Band Imager and Photometer System [*Aerospace*]
**OBIS**.......... Optimum Burn-In Screening
**OBIS**.......... Outdoor Biology Instructional Strategies [*National Science Foundation project*]
**OBIT**.......... Obiit [*He, or She, Died*] [*Latin*]
**Obit**........... Obiter [*A publication*]
**Oblt**........... Obituary [*A publication*]
**OBIT**.......... Obituary Notice (DSUE)
**OBIWR**..... Whitefish River Band Public Library, Birch Island, Ontario [*Library symbol*] [*National Library of Canada*] (NLC)
**OBJ**........... Intermediate Object Code File [*Data processing*]
**OBJ**........... Object (AAG)
**OBJ**........... Objective
**OBJ**........... Oklahoma Bar Association. Journal [*A publication*] (DLA)
**OBJ**........... Operation Buster-Jangle [*Atomic weapons testing*]
**OBJ**........... Orthodox Black Jews (BJA)
**Obj Monde** ... Objets et Monde [*A publication*]
**OBJN**........ Objection
**OBJV**......... Objective (MSA)
**OBK**.......... Northbrook, IL [*Location identifier*] [*FAA*] (FAAL)
**OBK**.......... Organisation pour l'Amenagement et le Developpement du Bassin de la Riviere Kagera [*Organization for the Management and Development of the Kagera River Basin - KBO*] (EAIO)
**OBL**.......... League of Off-Broadway Theatres and Producers (EA)
**OBL**.......... Oblast [*Governmental subdivision in USSR corresponding to a province or state*]
**OBL**.......... Obligation (ADA)
**OBL**.......... Obligato [*Obbligato*] [*Music*] (ROG)
**OBL**.......... Oblique (AABC)
**OBL**.......... Obliterate (FAAC)
**OBL**.......... Oblong
**OBL**.......... Office of Business Loans [*Economic Development Administration*]
**OBL**.......... Operational Base Launch [*Air Force*]
**OBL**.......... Order Bill of Lading [*Shipping*]
**OBL**.......... Orientalia et Biblica Lovaniensia [*A publication*]
**OBL**.......... Outstanding Balance List [*IRS*]
**OBla**.......... Blanchester Public Library, Blanchester, OH [*Library symbol*] [*Library of Congress*] (LCLS)
**OBLAC**...... Bath Branch, Lennox and Addington County Public Library, Ontario [*Library symbol*] [*National Library of Canada*] (NLC)
**OBLACS** ... Sandburst Branch, Lennox and Addington County Public Library, Bath, Ontario [*Library symbol*] [*National Library of Canada*] (BIB)
**OBLAT**...... Oblatum [*Cachet*] [*Pharmacy*]
**OBLAUTH** ... Obligation Authority [*Army*] (AABC)
**OBlC**.......... Bluffton College, Bluffton, OH [*Library symbol*] [*Library of Congress*] (LCLS)
**OBlC-M**..... Bluffton College, Mennonite Historical Library, Bluffton, OH [*Library symbol*] [*Library of Congress*] (LCLS)
**OBLG**........ Obligate (AABC)
**Ob LGS**...... Entscheidungen des Obersten Bayerischen Landesgerichts in Strafsachen [*A publication*]
**Ob LGZ**..... Entscheidungen des Obersten Bayerischen Landesgerichts in Zivilsachen [*A publication*]
**OBLH**........ Bloomfield-Hallowell Union Library, Bloomfield, Ontario [*Library symbol*] [*National Library of Canada*] (BIB)
**OBLI**.......... Oxford and Bucks Light Infantry [*Military unit*] [*British*]
**OBLIGN**.... Obligation (ROG)
**OBLISERV** ... Obligated Services of [*numbers of months indicated*] Required [*Navy*]
**OBLISERVNATRA** ... Obligated to Serve Three and One-Half Years Following Date of Completion of Training within the Naval Air Training Command
**OBLISERVONEASIX** ... Obligated to Serve on Active Duty One Year for Each Six Months Schooling or Fraction Thereof [*Navy*]
**OBLISERVTHREETIME** ... Obligated to Serve on Active Duty a Period Three Times the Length of Period of Education [*Navy*]

**OBLISERVTWOYR** ... Obligated to Serve on Active Duty a Period of Two Years [*Navy*]
**OBLN** ........ Obligation (AFM)
**OBLR** ........ Blind River Public Library, Ontario [*Library symbol*] [*National Library of Canada*] (NLC)
**OBLu** ........ Old Babylonian Version of Lu [*A publication*] (BJA)
**OBlv** ........ Bliss Memorial Public Library, Bloomville, OH [*Library symbol*] [*Library of Congress*] (LCLS)
**OBM** ........ Morobe [*Papua New Guinea*] [*Airport symbol*] (OAG)
**OBM** ........ Oberlin College, Conservatory of Music, Library, Oberlin, OH [*OCLC symbol*] (OCLC)
**OBM** ........ Optimal Body Mass [*Ecology*]
**OBM** ........ Oriental Boat Mission [*Later, International Missions*] (EA)
**OBM** ........ Ulan Bator [*Mongolia*] [*Seismograph station code, US Geological Survey*] [*Closed*] (SEIS)
**OBMA** ........ Outboard Boat Manufacturers Association [*Later, NMMA*] (EA)
**OBMC** ........ Officers' Basic Military Corps [*Air Force*]
**OBMC** ........ Outbound Midcourse Correction [*NASA*] (KSC)
**OBMP** ........ Bruce Mines and Plummer Additional Union Public Library, Bruce Mines, Ontario [*Library symbol*] [*National Library of Canada*] (NLC)
**OBMR** ........ Occasional Bulletin of Missionary Research [*A publication*]
**OBMS** ........ Objectives-Based Management System (ADA)
**OBN** ........ Oban [*Scotland*] [*Airport symbol*] (OAG)
**OBN** ........ Obninsk [*USSR*] [*Seismograph station code, US Geological Survey*] (SEIS)
**OBN** ........ Office Balancing Network [*Telecommunications*] (TEL)
**OBN** ........ Office of Biochemical Nomenclature [*NAS-NRC*]
**OBN** ........ On-Board Navigation
**OBN** ........ Out-of-Band Noise
**OBND** ........ Outbound (FAAC)
**OBNE** ........ Department 9911, Northern Telecom Ltd., Belleville, Ontario [*Library symbol*] [*National Library of Canada*] [*Obsolete*] (NLC)
**OBNM** ........ On or Before New Moon [*Freemasonry*] (ROG)
**OBNR** ........ Oil Burner Route [*Aviation*] (FAAC)
**OBNR** ........ Olive Branch Route [*FAA*] (FAAC)
**OBNREN** .. Oil Burner Entry Point [*Aviation*] (FAAC)
**OBNREX** .. Oil Burner Exit Point [*Aviation*] (FAAC)
**OBNTC** ..... Old Boys Network Turtle Club (EA)
**OBO** ........ Obihiro [*Japan*] [*Airport symbol*] (OAG)
**OBO** ........ Obock [*Djibouti*] [*Seismograph station code, US Geological Survey*] (SEIS)
**OBO** ........ Official Business Only (AFM)
**OBO** ........ Oil/Bulk/Ore Carrier [*Multipurpose bulk carrier*] (DS)
**OBO** ........ Or Best Offer [*Classified advertising*]
**OBO** ........ Order Book Official [*Investment term*]
**OBO** ........ Order by Order
**O/B/O** ........ Ore/Bulk/Oil [*Bulk carrier vessel*]
**OBO** ........ Organization of Bricklin Owners (EA)
**OBOE** ........ Observed Bombing of Enemy
**OBOF** ........ Old Buffer over Forty [*Elderly recruits*] [*British*] [*World War I*]
**OBOG** ........ On-Board Oxygen-Generation [*For military aviation*]
**Obogashch Briket Uglei** ... Obogashchenie i Briketirovanie Uglei [*A publication*]
**Obogashchenie Briket Uglei** ... Obogashchenie i Briketirovanie Uglei [*USSR*] [*A publication*]
**Obogashch Polezn Iskop** ... Obogashchenie Poleznykh Iskopaemykh [*A publication*]
**Obogashch Rud** ... Obogashchenie Rud [*A publication*]
**Obogashch Rud (Irkutsk)** ... Obogashchenie Rud (Irkutsk) [*A publication*]
**OBOGS** ..... On-Board Oxygen Generating System [*Navy*] (CAAL)
**OBOLC** ..... Caledon Public Libraries, Bolton, Ontario [*Library symbol*] [*National Library of Canada*] (NLC)
**OBOM** ........ Bowmanville Museum, Ontario [*Library symbol*] [*National Library of Canada*] (BIB)
**OBON** ........ Newcastle Public Library Board, Bowmanville, Ontario [*Library symbol*] [*National Library of Canada*] (NLC)
**OBONF** ..... Bonfield Public Library, Ontario [*Library symbol*] [*National Library of Canada*] (NLC)
**OBP** ........ Odorant-Binding Protein [*Biochemistry*]
**OBP** ........ Oil Breather Pressure
**OBP** ........ On-Base Percentage [*Baseball*]
**OBP** ........ On-Board Processor
**OBP** ........ Open Break Position [*Dancing*]
**OBP** ........ Organizational Behavior and Human Performance [*A publication*]
**OBP** ........ Outer (Edge of) Basal Piece
**OBPA** ........ Oxybisphenoxarsine [*Organic chemistry*]
**OBPH** ........ People Helping People, Inc., Brantford, Ontario [*Library symbol*] [*National Library of Canada*] (NLC)
**OBPI** ........ Otisville BioPharm, Incorporated [*Otisville, NY*] [*NASDAQ symbol*] (NQ)
**OBR** ........ Bradford Public Library, Ontario [*Library symbol*] [*National Library of Canada*] (NLC)
**OBR** ........ Office of Budget and Reports
**OBR** ........ One-Button-Recording [*Video technology*]
**OBR** ........ Optical Bar Code
**OBR** ........ Outboard Recorder [*Data processing*] (BUR)
**OBR** ........ Overseas Business Reports [*A publication*]
**OBR** ........ Owens, B. R., Montebello CA [*STAC*]
**OBRA** ........ Brampton Public Library, Ontario [*Library symbol*] [*National Library of Canada*] (NLC)
**OBRA** ........ Office of Business Research and Analysis [*Department of Commerce*]
**OBRA** ........ Omnibus Budget Reconciliation Act [*1987*]
**Obrab Metal Davleniem Mashinostr** ... Obrabotka Metallov Davleniem v Mashinostroenii [*Ukrainian SSR*] [*A publication*]
**Obrab Met Davleniem Mashinostr** ... Obrabotka Metallov Davleniem v Mashinostroenii [*A publication*]
**Obrab Met Davleniem (Rostov-On-Don)** ... Obrabotka Metallov Davleniem (Rostov-On-Don) [*A publication*]
**OBRAC** ..... Bracebridge Public Library, Ontario [*Library symbol*] [*National Library of Canada*] (NLC)
**OBRAM** ..... Chinguacousy Township Public Library, Bramalea, Ontario [*Library symbol*] [*National Library of Canada*] (NLC)
**OBRAMB** ... Bell Northern Research, Bramalea, Ontario [*Library symbol*] [*National Library of Canada*] (NLC)
**OBRANT** .. Northern Telecom, Brampton, Ontario [*Library symbol*] [*National Library of Canada*] (NLC)
**OBRAPA** ... Archives, Region of Peel, Brampton, Ontario [*Library symbol*] [*National Library of Canada*] (BIB)
**OBRASC** ... Brampton Campus, Sheridan College, Brampton, Ontario [*Library symbol*] [*National Library of Canada*] (BIB)
**OBRC** ........ Operating Budget Review Committee [*Military*]
**OBRER** ..... Blind River Refinery, Eldorado Resources Ltd., Ontario [*Library symbol*] [*National Library of Canada*] (NLC)
**OBRET** ..... Old Breton [*Language, etc.*]
**OBrG** ........ B. F. Goodrich Co., Technical Library, Brecksville, OH [*Library symbol*] [*Library of Congress*] (LCLS)
**OBRH** ........ Home Care Program, Brockville, Ontario [*Library symbol*] [*National Library of Canada*] (BIB)
**Obrh Past Bl** ... Oberrheinisches Pastoralblatt [*A publication*]
**OBRI** ........ Belle River Public Library, Ontario [*Library symbol*] [*National Library of Canada*] (NLC)
**O Bridg** ........ Orlando Bridgman's English Common Pleas Reports [*A publication*] (DLA)
**O Bridg (Eng)** ... Orlando Bridgman's English Common Pleas Reports [*A publication*] (DLA)
**O Bridgm** ... Orlando Bridgman's English Common Pleas Reports [*A publication*] (DLA)
**O'Brien** ...... O'Brien's Upper Canada Reports [*A publication*] (DLA)
**OBRIG** ...... Brighton Public Library, Ontario [*Library symbol*] [*National Library of Canada*] (BIB)
**O'Bri Lawy** ... O'Brien's Lawyer's Rule of Holy Life [*A publication*] (DLA)
**O'Bri ML** ... O'Brien's Military Law [*A publication*] (DLA)
**OBRIS** ...... Smith Township Public Library, Bridgenorth, Ontario [*Library symbol*] [*National Library of Canada*] (BIB)
**OBRIT** ...... Britt Area Community Library, Britt, Ontario [*Library symbol*] [*National Library of Canada*] (NLC)
**OBRIT** ...... Old British [*Language, etc.*]
**OBRM** ........ W. Ross MacDonald School, Brantford, Ontario [*Library symbol*] [*National Library of Canada*] (NLC)
**OBRMR** ..... Mississauga Reserve Library, Blind River, Ontario [*Library symbol*] [*National Library of Canada*] (NLC)
**OBRNR** ..... Oil Burner
**OBRO** ........ Oxford-On-Rideau Township Public Library, Burritt's Rapids, Ontario [*Library symbol*] [*National Library of Canada*] (BIB)
**Obrobka Plast** ... Obrobka Plastyczna [*A publication*]
**OBROW** ..... Ochotnicza Brygada Robotnicza Obrony Warszawy [*A publication*] (BJA)
**OBRP** ........ On-Board Repair Parts [*Navy*]
**OBRP** ........ Pauline Johnson College, Brantford, Ontario [*Library symbol*] [*National Library of Canada*] (NLC)
**OBRPH** ..... Library Resources & Information Centre, Brockville Psychiatric Hospital, Ontario [*Library symbol*] [*National Library of Canada*] (NLC)
**OBRT** ........ Brantford Public Library, Ontario [*Library symbol*] [*National Library of Canada*] (NLC)
**OBrV** ........ United States Veterans Administration Hospital, Brecksville, OH [*Library symbol*] [*Library of Congress*] (LCLS)
**OBRWI** ..... [*The*] Woodland Indian Cultural Educational Centre, Brantford, Ontario [*Library symbol*] [*National Library of Canada*] (NLC)
**OBS** ........ Aubenas [*France*] [*Airport symbol*] (OAG)
**OBS** ........ Obligations (ROG)
**OBS** ........ O'Brien Energy Systems, Inc. [*AMEX symbol*] (SPSG)
**OBS** ........ Obscure (ADA)
**OBS** ........ Observation (ROG)
**OBS** ........ Observatory
**OBS** ........ Observe
**Obs** ........ Observer [*A publication*]
**Obs** ........ Obsidian [*A publication*]
**OBS** ........ Obsolete (AAG)
**OBS** ........ Obstacle (AABC)
**OBS** ........ Obstetrics [*Medicine*]
**OBS** ........ Ocean Bottom Seismometer [*California*] [*Seismograph station code, US Geological Survey*] [*Closed*] (SEIS)
**OBS** ........ Ocean Bottom Station
**OBS** ........ Office of Biological Service [*Marine science*] (MSC)

**OBS** .......... Office of Boating Safety [*Coast Guard*]
**OBS** .......... Official Bulletin Station [*Amateur radio*]
**OBS** .......... Old Babylonian Sumerian (BJA)
**OBS** .......... Old Bailey's Sessions Papers [*A publication*] (DLA)
**OBS** .......... Omnibearing Selector [*Radio*]
**OBS** .......... On-Board Spares [*Army*]
**OBS** .......... On-Board System [*Navy*] (CAAL)
**OBS** .......... On-Line Business Systems, Inc. [*Information service or system*] (IID)
**OBS** .......... Open-Back Stationary Press [*Manufacturing term*]
**OBS** .......... Open-Hearth Basic Steel
**OBS** .......... Operational Bioinstrumentation System [*NASA*]
**OBS** .......... Operational Biomedical Sensors (NASA)
**OBS** .......... Operational Biomedical Systems (KSC)
**OBS** .......... Optical Beam Scanner
**OBS** .......... Optical Beam Steering
**OBS** .......... Orange Badge Scheme [*Disabled parking permit*] [*British*]
**OBS** .......... Orbital Bombardment System
**OBS** .......... Organic Brain Syndrome [*Psychiatry*]
**OBS** .......... Oriental and Biblical Studies [*A publication*] (BJA)
**OBS** .......... OSIS [*Ocean Surveillance Information System*] Baseline System [*Navy*]
**OBS** .......... Ottawa Board of Education, Library Services Centre (Software) [*UTLAS symbol*]
**OBS** .......... Sidney Township Public Library, Batawa, Ontario [*Library symbol*] [*National Library of Canada*] (BIB)
**Obs Astronom Univ Nac La Plata Ser Astronom** ... Observatorio Astronomico de la Universidad Nacional de La Plata. Serie Astronomica [*A publication*]
**OBSC**......... Obscure
**OBSC**......... Obscured Light [*Navigation signal*]
**OBSCIS**..... Offender Based State Corrections Information System (OICC)
**Obsc Nauki v Uzbek** ... Obscestvennye Nauki v Uzbekistane [*A publication*]
**Obsc N Uzbek** ... Obscestvennye Nauki v Uzbekistane [*A publication*]
**OBSD** ........ Object Sum Optical Density [*Microscopy*]
**OBSD** ........ Observed
**OBSD** ........ Optical Beam Steering Device
**OBSERV** ... Observatory
**Observer Des Brief** ... Observer Design Brief [*A publication*]
**OBSH** ........ Object Shape [*Microscopy*]
**OBSH** ........ Oxybis(benzenesulfonylhydrazine) [*Organic chemistry*]
**Obs Handb Can** ... Observer's Handbook. Royal Astronomical Society of Canada [*A publication*]
**Obshcha Sravn Patol** ... Obshcha i Sravnitelna Patologiya [*A publication*]
**Obshch Ekol Biotsenol Gidrobiol** ... Obshchaya Ekologiya, Biotsenologiya, Gidrobiologiya [*A publication*]
**Obshch Energ** ... Obshchaya Energetika [*A publication*]
**Obshchest Nauk Uzbek** ... Obshchestvennye Nauki v Uzbekistane [*A publication*]
**Obshchestv Pitan** ... Obshchestvennoe Pitanie [*A publication*]
**Obshch Mashinostr** ... Obshchee Mashinostroenie [*A publication*]
**Obshch Prikl Khim** ... Obshchaya i Prikladnaya Khimiya [*A publication*]
**Obshch Zakonomern Morfog Regener** ... Obshchie Zakonomernosti Morfogeneza i Regeneratsii [*A publication*]
**OBSHT** ..... Obstacle Height
**Obshta Sravnitelna Patol** ... Obshta i Sravnitelna Patologiia [*A publication*]
**OBSL**......... St. Lawrence College [*College Saint-Laurent*], Brockville, Ontario [*Library symbol*] [*National Library of Canada*] (NLC)
**Obs Lt**........ Observer Lieutenant [*British military*] (DMA)
**OBSN** ........ Observation (AAG)
**OBSOL**....... Obsolescent
**OBSP**......... Obiit sine Prole [*Died without Issue*] [*Latin*]
**OBSP**......... Old Bailey's Sessions Papers [*Legal term*] [*British*]
**OBSP**......... Oxford Bibliographical Society. Proceedings [*A publication*]
**OBSP**......... Oxford Bibliographical Society. Publications [*A publication*]
**Obs sur Phys** ... Observations sur la Physique, sur l'Histoire Naturelle, et sur les Arts [*A publication*]
**OBSPL** ...... Octave Band Sound Pressure Level
**OBSPM**..... Obiit sine Prole Masculus [*He, or She, Died without Male Issue*] [*Latin*]
**OBSR**......... Observation
**OBSRON** .. Observation Squadron
**OBSS**......... Ocean Bottom Scanning SONAR
**Obs Spot** .... Observation Spot [*Control point*] [*Nautical charts*]
**OBST**......... Obstacle (AFM)
**OBST**......... Obstetrics [*Medicine*]
**OBST**......... Obstruction (AFM)
**OBSTET** ... Obstetrics [*Medicine*]
**Obstet Ginecol** ... Obstetrica si Ginecologia [*A publication*]
**Obstet Ginecol (Buchar)** ... Obstetrica si Ginecologia (Bucharest) [*A publication*]
**Obstet Ginecol Lat-Am** ... Obstetricia y Ginecologia Latino-Americanas [*A publication*]
**Obstet Gyn** ... Obstetrics and Gynecology [*A publication*]
**Obstet Gynec** ... Obstetrics and Gynecology [*A publication*]
**Obstet Gynecol** ... Obstetrics and Gynecology [*A publication*]
**Obstet Gynecol Annu** ... Obstetrics and Gynecology. Annual [*A publication*]
**Obstet Gynecol Surv** ... Obstetrical and Gynecological Survey [*A publication*]
**Obstet Gynecol Ther** ... Obstetrical and Gynecological Therapy [*Japan*] [*A publication*]
**Obstet Gynecol (Tokyo)** ... Obstetrics and Gynecology (Tokyo) [*A publication*]
**Obstet Gynec Surv** ... Obstetrical and Gynecological Survey [*A publication*]
**Obst Gemuese Verwert Ind** ... Obst- und Gemuese-Verwertungs Industrie [*A publication*]
**Obst Gynec** ... Obstetrics and Gynecology [*A publication*]
**Obst Gynec Surv** ... Obstetrical and Gynecological Survey [*A publication*]
**OBSTN**...... Obstruction (MSA)
**Obstr**.......... Obstruction
**OBSTRN**... Obstetrician [*Medicine*]
**OBSUA** ..... Oberflaeche Surface [*A publication*]
**OBSUED**... Oberbefehlshaber Suedost [*Headquarters, Commander-in-Chief, South*] [*Southern Germany and several army groups on the Eastern Front*] [*German military - World War II*]
**OBSUM** .... Order of Battle Summary [*Military*] (MCD)
**OBSV**......... Observer
**OBSVE**....... Observe (ROG)
**OBSY**........ Observatory (AABC)
**OBSZ**......... Object Size [*Microscopy*]
**OBT**........... Obedient
**OBT**........... Obiit [*He, or She, Died*] [*Latin*]
**OBT**........... Observer Training [*Army*]
**OBT**........... On-Board Trainer [*Navy*] (CAAL)
**OBTAINFUNDISB** ... [*Authorized to*] Obtain Funds in Accordance with NAVCOMPTMAN, to Make Cash Disbursements to Cover Actual Expenses Incurred Account of Recruiting
**OBTD**........ Obtained
**OBTG**........ Obtaining (ROG)
**OBTN**........ Obtain (ROG)
**OBTS**......... Offender Base Transaction Statistical System [*Department of Justice*] [*Database*] [*Information service or system*] (IID)
**OBTS**......... Organizational Behavior Teaching Society (EA)
**OBTVR**....... Office for Battlefield Technical Vulnerability Reduction [*Army*] (RDA)
**OBTX** ........ Object Texture [*Microscopy*]
**OBU**........... Burlington Public Library, Ontario [*Library symbol*] [*National Library of Canada*] (NLC)
**OBU**........... Kobuk [*Alaska*] [*Airport symbol*] (OAG)
**OBU**........... Kobuk, AK [*Location identifier*] [*FAA*] (FAAL)
**OBU**........... Offshore Banking Unit
**OBU**........... Oklahoma Baptist University
**OBU**........... Ombudsman. Tijdschrift voor Klachtrecht Tegen Overheidsoptreden [*A publication*]
**OBU**........... One Big Union [*A reference to Canada*]
**OBU**........... Operational Base Unit [*British military*] (DMA)
**OBU**........... Operative Builders' Union [*British*]
**OBU**........... OSIS [*Ocean Surveillance Information System*] Baseline Upgrade [*Navy*]
**OBU**........... Ouachita Baptist University [*Arkadelphia, AR*] [*Formerly, OBC*]
**OBUC**......... Canada Centre for Inland Waters [*Centre Canadien des Eaux Interieures*], Burlington, Ontario [*Library symbol*] [*National Library of Canada*] (NLC)
**OBUCC** ..... Canadian Canners Ltd., Burlington, Ontario [*Library symbol*] [*National Library of Canada*] (NLC)
**OBUFBL**... Bayfield Laboratory, Ocean Science and Surveys, Fisheries and Oceans Canada [*Laboratoire Bayfield, Science et Leves Oceaniques, Peches et Oceans Canada*] Burlington, Ontario [*Library symbol*] [*National Library of Canada*] (NLC)
**OBUJB**........ Joseph Brant Memorial Hospital, Burlington, Ontario [*Library symbol*] [*National Library of Canada*] (BIB)
**OBUL**........ Lord Elgin High School, Burlington, Ontario [*Library symbol*] [*National Library of Canada*] (NLC)
**OBUR**........ Burford Public Library, Ontario [*Library symbol*] [*National Library of Canada*] (BIB)
**OBur** .......... Burton Public Library, Burton, OH [*Library symbol*] [*Library of Congress*] (LCLS)
**OBUS** ........ Obstetric Ultrasound [*Microcomputer system dealing with results of obstetric ultrasound examinations*]
**OBUTS**...... Organ Builders' United Trade Society [*A union*] [*British*]
**OBv**........... Bellevue Public Library, Bellevue, OH [*Library symbol*] [*Library of Congress*] (LCLS)
**OBV**........... Bobcaygeon Branch, Victoria County Public Library, Ontario [*Library symbol*] [*National Library of Canada*] (BIB)
**OBV**........... Obligated Volunteer Officer [*Military*]
**OBV**........... Obverse
**OBV**........... Ocean Boarding Vessel
**OBV**........... On-Balance Volume [*Measurement devised by stock market technician Joseph Granville*]
**OBV**........... Operation Big Vote (EA)
**OBV**........... Oxidizer Bleed Valve (NASA)
**OBVP** ........ Obiit Vita Patris [*He, or She, Died in the Lifetime of His, or Her, Father*] [*Latin*]
**OBW**.......... Journal fuer Betriebswirtschaft [*A publication*]
**OBW**.......... Oberwerk [*Upper Work*] [*Music*]
**OBW**.......... Observation Window
**OBW**.......... Oxford Bible Warehouse [*British*] (ROG)
**OBWC** ....... Westinghouse Canada, Inc., Burlington, Ontario [*Library symbol*] [*National Library of Canada*] (NLC)
**OBy**........... Old Byblian (BJA)

**OBZ**........... Outer Border Zone [*Geology*]
**Obz Mat Fiz** ... Obzornik za Matematiko in Fiziko [*A publication*]
**Obzornik Mat Fiz** ... Obzornik za Matematiko in Fiziko [*A publication*]
**Obz Otd Proizvod Khim Promsti** ... Obzory po Otdel'nym Proizvodstvam Khimicheskoi Promyshlennosti [*A publication*]
**Obz Veng Lesovod Nauki** ... Obzor Vengerskoi Lesovodstvennoi Nauki [*A publication*]
**OC**............. Cornwall Public Library, Ontario [*Library symbol*] [*National Library of Canada*] (NLC)
**OC**............. Jersey. Ordres du Conseil [*A publication*] (DLA)
**OC**............. Object Class [*Military*]
**O/C**........... Object Classification (NG)
**OC**............. Observation Car [*British*]
**OC**............. Observer-Controller [*Army*] (INF)
**OC**............. Observer Corps [*Became ROC, 1941*] [*British*]
**OC**............. Obstetric Conjugate [*Pelvic measurement*] [*Gynecology*]
**OC**............. Obstruction Chart
**OC**............. Occidental
**Oc**............. Occidente [*A publication*]
**OC**............. Occipital Cortex [*Brain anatomy*]
**OC**............. Occlusocervical [*Dentistry*]
**Oc**............. Occulting Light [*Navigation signal*]
**OC**............. Occurs (MDG)
**OC**............. Ocean
**Oc**............. Oceania [*A publication*]
**OC**............. Oceanographic Devices [*JETDS nomenclature*] [*Military*] (CET)
**O/C**........... O'Clock (ROG)
**Oc**............. Octahedral [*Molecular geometry*]
**OC**............. October (ADA)
**Oc**............. Octyl [*Biochemistry*]
**OC**............. Ocular [*Microscopy*]
**OC**............. Oculentum [*Eye Ointment*] [*Pharmacy*]
**OC**............. Odor Control
**OC**............. Oedipus Coloneus [*of Sophocles*] [*Classical studies*] (OCD)
**O et C**........ Oeuvres et Critiques [*A publication*]
**OC**............. Of Course
**OC**............. Offensive Center [*Football*]
**OC**............. Office Call [*Medicine*]
**OC**............. Office of Censorship [*Terminated, 1945*] [*Military*]
**OC**............. Office of the Commissioner [*Office of Education*]
**OC**............. Office of the Comptroller
**OC**............. Office Copy
**O/C**........... Officer Cadet [*British military*] (DMA)
**OC**............. Officer Candidate [*Military*]
**O/C**........... Officer-in-Charge [*Army*]
**O in C**........ Officer-in-Charge
**OC**............. Officer Commanding [*Military*]
**OC**............. Officer of the Order of Canada
**OC**............. Officers' Cook
**OC**............. Official Circular [*Poor Law Board, etc.*] [*A publication*] (DLA)
**OC**............. Official Classification
**OC**............. Oil Cooler
**OC**............. Old Carthusian
**OC**............. Old Catholic
**O/C**........... Old Charter [*Business and trade*]
**OC**............. Old Cheltonian [*British*] (ROG)
**OC**............. Old Code [*Louisiana Code of 1808*] [*A publication*] (DLA)
**OC**............. Old Cornwall [*A publication*]
**OC**............. Old Crop
**OC**............. On Call (BUR)
**OC**............. On Cards
**OC**............. On Center [*Technical drawings*]
**OC**............. On-Condition (NASA)
**OC**............. On Course [*Navigation*]
**OC**............. Only Child
**O & C**......... Onset and Course [*of a disease*] [*Medicine*]
**OC**............. Ope Consilio [*By Aid and Counsel*] [*Latin*] [*Legal term*] (DLA)
**OC**............. Open Charter [*Business term*]
**OC**............. Open Circuit
**OC**............. Open Circular [*Configuration of DNA*] [*Microbiology*]
**O/C**........... Open/Closed [*Mouth*] [*Doll collecting*]
**OC**............. Open Contract
**OC**............. Open Court [*A publication*]
**O/C**........... Open Cover [*Shipping*]
**OC**............. Open Cup [*Electronics*]
**OC**............. Opera Canada [*A publication*]
**OC**............. Operating Characteristic
**OC**............. Operating Company
**OC**............. Operating Curve (NRCH)
**O & C**......... Operation and Checkout [*NASA*]
**OC**............. Operation CORK [*Joan B. Kroc Foundation*] [*CORK is derived from the foundation name*] [*Defunct*] (EA)
**OC**............. Operation Crossroads [*Atomic weapons testing*]
**OC**............. Operational Capability (AAG)
**OC**............. Operational Check (MCD)
**OC**............. Operational Computer (IEEE)
**OC**............. Operations Center [*Military*]
**OC**............. Operations Chief [*Deep Space Network, NASA*]
**OC**............. Operations Conductor (MUGU)
**OC**............. Operations Control
**O/C**........... Operations Critical (MCD)
**OC**............. Opere Citato [*In the Work Cited*] [*Latin*]
**OC**............. Optic Chiasm [*Anatomy*]
**OC**............. Oracle Series. National Museums of Canada and Department of Indian and Northern Affairs [*A publication*]
**OC**............. Oral Contraceptive [*Endocrinology*]
**OC**............. Orbital Check (MCD)
**OC**............. Order Canceled
**OC**............. Order Card
**OC**............. Order of Cistercians [*Roman Catholic religious order*]
**OC**............. Order in Council [*A publication*] (DLA)
**OC**............. Orderly Corporal [*British*]
**OC**............. Ordinary Capital Account [*Inter-American Development Bank*]
**OC**............. Ordnance Chart (MCD)
**OC**............. Ordnance College [*Military*] [*British*] (ROG)
**OC**............. Ordo Charitatis [*Fathers of the Order of Charity*] [*Roman Catholic religious order*]
**OC**............. Organizational Chart
**OC**............. Organochlorine [*Also, OCL*] [*Organic chemistry*]
**OC**............. Oriens Christianus [*A publication*]
**OC**............. Original Cosmopolitans (EA)
**OC**............. Original Cover
**OC**............. Orion Capital Corp. [*NYSE symbol*] (SPSG)
**OC**............. Orphans' Court (DLA)
**OC**............. Otter Controls Ltd. [*Great Britain*] [*ICAO designator*] (FAAC)
**OC**............. Oudh Cases [*India*] [*A publication*] (DLA)
**O/C**........... Out of Charge [*Customs*]
**OC**............. Out Cold [*Slang*]
**OC**............. Outflow Channels [*A filamentary mark on Mars*]
**OC**............. Outing Club
**OC**............. Outlet Contact
**OC**............. Output Computer
**OC**............. Outside Circumference (MSA)
**OC**............. Outsiders Club (EAIO)
**O/C**........... Over-the-Counter [*Also, OTC*] [*Stock exchange term*]
**OC**............. Over-the-Horizon Compressed (MCD)
**O/C**........... Overcharge
**OC**............. Overcurrent
**OC**............. Overseas Commands [*Air Force*]
**O & C**......... Oxford and Cambridge Schools Examination Board [*British*] (DCTA)
**OC**............. Oxygen Consumed
**OC**............. Oxygen Cutting [*Welding*]
**OC**............. Public Library of Cincinnati and Hamilton County, Cincinnati, OH [*Library symbol*] [*Library of Congress*] (LCLS)
**OCA**........... Campbellford Branch, Northumberland County Public Library, Ontario [*Library symbol*] [*National Library of Canada*] (NLC)
**OCA**........... Cincinnati Art Museum, Cincinnati, OH [*Library symbol*] [*Library of Congress*] (LCLS)
**OCA**........... Creighton University, Alumni Library, Omaha, NE [*OCLC symbol*] (OCLC)
**OCA**........... Obsessive-Compulsive Anonymous (EA)
**OCA**........... O'Casey Annual [*A publication*]
**OCA**........... Ocean Reef Club [*Florida*] [*Airport symbol*] (OAG)
**OCA**........... Oceanic Control Area [*ICAO*]
**OCA**........... Office of Competitive Assessment [*Department of Commerce*]
**OCA**........... Office, Comptroller of the Army
**OCA**........... Office of Computing Activities [*Later, DCR*] [*National Science Foundation*]
**OCA**........... Office of Congressional Affairs [*Energy Research and Development Administration*]
**OCA**........... Office of Consumer Advisor [*USDA*]
**OCA**........... Office of Consumer Affairs [*US Postal Service ombudsman*]
**OCA**........... Officers' Caterer [*Navy*] [*British*]
**OCA**........... Ohio Courts of Appeals Reports [*A publication*] (DLA)
**OCA**........... Old Comrades Association [*British military*] (DMA)
**OCA**........... Oldsmobile Club of America (EA)
**OCA**........... Olympic Council of Asia [*Hawalli, Kuwait*] (EAIO)
**OCA**........... Ontario College of Agriculture
**OCA**........... Ontario College of Art
**OCA**........... Open College of Arts [*British*]
**OCA**........... Opencast Coal Act [*Town planning*] [*British*]
**OCA**........... Operation Crossroads Africa (EA)
**OCA**........... Operational Control Authority [*NATO*]
**OCA**........... Oral Contraceptive Agent [*Endocrinology*]
**OCA**........... Order of the Crown in America [*Later, TOCA*] (EA)
**OCA**........... Organisation Combat Anarchiste [*Anarchist Combat Organization*] [*France*] [*Political party*] (PPW)
**OCA**........... Organizacion de las Cooperativas de America [*Organization of the Cooperatives of America - OCA*] (EAIO)
**OCA**........... Organization of Chinese Americans (EA)
**OCA**........... Orientalia Christiana Analecta [*A publication*]
**OCA**........... Osteopathic Cranial Association [*Later, CA*]
**OCA**........... Otterhound Club of America (EA)
**OCA**........... Outstanding Claims Advance [*Insurance*] (AIA)
**OCA**........... Oxychloride Cement Association [*Defunct*]
**OCAA**......... Oklahoma City-Ada-Atoka Railway Co. [*AAR code*]
**OCAAF**....... Order of the Chief of the Army Air Forces
**OCAB**......... Cannington Branch, Brock Township Public Library, Ontario [*Library symbol*] [*National Library of Canada*] (BIB)

**OCAC**........ Ocean Acre Project [*Marine science*] (MSC)
**OCAC**........ Oceanic Air Traffic Control (FAAC)
**OCAC**........ Office of the Chief of Air Corps [*World War II*]
**OC of AC**... Office of the Chief of Air Corps [*World War II*]
**OCAC**........ Officer Commanding Administrative Centre [*British*] [*World War I*]
**OCACD**...... Oceanologica Acta [*A publication*]
**OCad**.......... Cadiz Public Library, Cadiz, OH [*Library symbol*] [*Library of Congress*] (LCLS)
**OCAE**........ United States Army Engineer Division, Ohio River, Technical Library, Cincinnati, OH [*Library symbol*] [*Library of Congress*] (LCLS)
**OCAFF**...... Office, Chief of Army Field Forces
**OCAJ**......... American Jewish Periodical Center, Cincinnati, OH [*Library symbol*] [*Library of Congress*] (LCLS)
**OCAJA**...... American Jewish Archives, Cincinnati, OH [*Library symbol*] [*Library of Congress*] (LCLS)
**OCal**........... Caldwell Public Library, Caldwell, OH [*Library symbol*] [*Library of Congress*] (LCLS)
**OCAL**........ Online Cryptanalytic Aid Language [*Data processing*]
**OCAL**........ Organization of Communist Action in Lebanon (PD)
**OCAL**........ Overseas Containers Australia Ltd. (DS)
**OCAL**........ [*The*] Oxford Companion to American Literature [*A publication*]
**OCALC**...... Oklahoma City Air Logistic Center [*Formerly, OCAMA*] (MCD)
**O'Callaghan New Neth**... O'Callaghan's History of New Netherland [*A publication*] (DLA)
**OCAM**....... Office, Computing, and Accounting Machinery
**OCAM**....... Organisation Commune Africaine et Mauricienne [*African and Mauritian Common Organization*] [*Formerly, Organisation Commune Africaine et Malgache*]
**OCAMA**.... Oklahoma City Air Materiel Area [*Later, OCALC*]
**OCAMA-SED**... Oklahoma City Air Materiel Area [*later, OCALC*] Service Engineering Division
**OCamd**....... Preble County District Library, Camden Branch, Camden, OH [*Library symbol*] [*Library of Congress*] (LCLS)
**OCAMM**... Organisation Commune Africaine, Malgache, et Mauricienne [*African, Malagasy, and Mauritian Common Organization*] [*Formerly, Organisation Commune Africaine et Malgache*] [*Later, OCAM*]
**OCan**.......... Canton Public Library Association, Canton, OH [*Library symbol*] [*Library of Congress*] (LCLS)
**OCAN**........ Officer Candidate Airman
**OCanK**....... Kent State University, Stark County Regional Campus, Canton, OH [*Library symbol*] [*Library of Congress*] (LCLS)
**OCanM**...... Malone College, Canton, OH [*Library symbol*] [*Library of Congress*] (LCLS)
**OCanS**....... Stark County District Library, Canton, OH [*Library symbol*] [*Library of Congress*] (LCLS)
**OCanW**...... Walsh College, Canton, OH [*Library symbol*] [*Library of Congress*] (LCLS)
**OCAP**........ Capreol Public Library, Ontario [*Library symbol*] [*National Library of Canada*] (NLC)
**OCAP**........ Open Channel Air Preheater [*Heat exchanger*]
**OCAR**........ Cargill Branch, Bruce County Public Library, Ontario [*Library symbol*] [*National Library of Canada*] (NLC)
**OCAR**........ Office of the Chief, Army Reserve (AABC)
**OCARD**..... Cardinal Public Library, Ontario [*Library symbol*] [*National Library of Canada*] (BIB)
**OCareyS**.... Our Lady of Carey Seminary, Carey, OH [*Library symbol*] [*Library of Congress*] (LCLS)
**OCARM**.... Order of Brothers of the Blessed Virgin Mary of Mount Carmel [*Rome, Italy*] (EAIO)
**OCART**..... Cartier Public Library, Ontario [*Library symbol*] [*National Library of Canada*] (NLC)
**OCart**......... Order of Carthusians [*Roman Catholic religious order*]
**OCartSC**.... Saint Charles Seminary, Carthagena, OH [*Library symbol*] [*Library of Congress*] (LCLS)
**OCAS**........ Office of Carrier Accounts and Statistics [*of CAB*]
**OCAS**........ Office of the Chief of Air Service [*World War II*]
**OC of AS**.... Office of the Chief of Air Staff [*World War II*]
**OCAS**........ Office, Coordinator of Army Studies (AABC)
**OCAS**........ Officer-in-Charge of Armament Supply
**OCAS**........ Ohio Casualty Corp. [*NASDAQ symbol*] (NQ)
**OCAS**........ Online Cryptanalytic Aid System [*Data processing*] (IEEE)
**OCAS**........ Ordnance Configuration Accounting System [*Navy*]
**OCAS**........ Organization of Central American States [*See also ODECA*] [*San Salvador, El Salvador*] (EAIO)
**OCAW**....... Oil, Chemical, and Atomic Workers International Union (EA)
**OCAW**....... Organization of Chinese American Women (EA)
**OCB**........... Cache Bay Public Library, Ontario [*Library symbol*] [*National Library of Canada*] (NLC)
**OCB**........... Cincinnati Bible Seminary, Cincinnati, OH [*Library symbol*] [*Library of Congress*] (LCLS)
**OCB**........... Officer Career Brief [*Resume*] [*Military*]
**OCB**........... Officers' Cadet Battalion [*British*]
**OCB**........... Offshore Certification Bureau [*British*] (CB)
**OCB**........... Oil [*Operated*] Circuit Breaker
**OCB**........... Oil Collection Basin (NRCH)
**OCB**........... Oil Control Board [*British*]
**OCB**........... Ol' Country Boy, Inc. [*Tulsa, OK*] [*FAA designator*] (FAAC)
**OCB**........... Operations Coordinating Board [*Terminated, 1961*] [*National Security Council*]
**OCB**........... Outgoing Calls Barred [*Telecommunications*] (TEL)
**OCB**........... Output Current Booster
**OCB**........... Override Control BITS [*Binary Digits*] [*Data processing*]
**OCBC**........ Overseas Chinese Banking Corporation [*Singapore*]
**OCBH**........ Bethesda Base Hospital, Information Resource Center, Cincinnati, OH [*Library symbol*] [*Library of Congress*] (LCLS)
**OC/B/L**..... Ocean Bill of Lading [*Shipping*]
**OCBOA**..... Other Comprehensive Bases of Accounting (ADA)
**OCBR**........ Other than Cost Base Review [*DoD*]
**OCB(S)**..... Oil Control Board, Supply [*British*]
**OcBul**......... Occasional Bulletin of Missionary Research [*A publication*]
**OCC**........... Coca [*Ecuador*] [*Airport symbol*] (OAG)
**OCC**........... Object Class Code [*Military*] (AFM)
**OCC**........... Occasionally
**Occ**............ Occidental [*A publication*]
**OCC**........... Occlusion
**OCC**........... Occultation [*Astronomy*]
**OCC**........... Occulting Light [*Navigation signal*]
**OCC**........... Occupation (AFM)
**OCC**........... Occurrence
**Occ**............ Occurs (ILCA)
**OCC**........... Ocean City College [*Maryland*]
**OCC**........... Ocean Coordinating Committee [*IEEE*] (MSC)
**OCC**........... OCLC [*Online Computer Library Center*] Library, Columbus, OH [*OCLC symbol*] (OCLC)
**OCC**........... Octagon Car Club [*Later, MOCC*] (EAIO)
**OCC**........... Octal Correction Cards [*Data processing*]
**OCC**........... Ocutech Canada [*Vancouver Stock Exchange symbol*]
**OCC**........... Office of the Comptroller of the Currency [*Department of the Treasury*]
**OCC**........... Office of Contract Compliance [*NASA*] (NASA)
**OCC**........... Office of the Director of Command, Control, and Communications [*Air Force*]
**OCC**........... Officers' Chief Cook
**OCC**........... Official Custodian of Charities [*British*]
**OCC**........... Ohio Circuit Reports [*or Decisions*] [*A publication*] (DLA)
**OCC**........... Ohio College of Chiropody
**OCC**........... Ohio Conservation Consortium [*Library network*]
**OCC**........... Olympic Committee Congress
**OCC**........... Omnibus Crime Control and Safe Streets Act [*1968*]
**OCC**........... Open Court (Chicago) [*A publication*]
**OCC**........... Operating Characteristics Curve
**OCC**........... Operational Computer Complex (KSC)
**OCC**........... Operations Control Center [*or Console*] (AFM)
**OCC**........... Operator Control Command (BUR)
**OCC**........... Operator Control Console [*Canadian Navy*]
**OCC**........... Oppenheimer Capital LP [*NYSE symbol*] (SPSG)
**OCC**........... Option Clearing Corporation
**OCC**........... Oral Contraceptive Council (EA)
**OCC**........... Orange Carpet Crowd [*An association*]
**OCC**........... Orange Coast College [*Formerly, OCJC*] [*Costa Mesa, CA*]
**O & CC**...... Order and Change Control (AAG)
**OCC**........... Ordo Carmelitarum Calceatorum [*Carmelites*] [*Roman Catholic religious order*]
**OCC**........... Organic Carbon Cycle
**OCC**........... Organisation Combat Communiste [*Communist Combat Organization*] [*France*] [*Political party*] (PPW)
**OCC**........... Other Common Carrier [*Telecommunications*]
**OCC**........... Outer Critics Circle (EA)
**OCCA**........ Office, Chief of Civil Affairs
**OCCA**........ Officer-in-Charge of Civilian Affairs [*in newly occupied countries*] [*Army*] [*World War II*]
**OCCA**........ Oil and Colour Chemists' Association
**OCCA**........ Omnibus Crime Control Act of 1970 (OICC)
**OCCA**........ Organized Crime Control Act of 1970
**OCCAS**...... Occasional
**Occas**......... Occasional Light [*Navigation signal*]
**Occasional Publ in Math**... Occasional Publications in Mathematics [*A publication*]
**OCCASL**... Occasional
**Occas Newsl Lindsay Club**... Occasional Newsletter. Lindsay Club [*A publication*]
**Occas Pap Aging**... Occasional Papers on Aging [*A publication*]
**Occas Pap BC Prov Mus**... Occasional Papers. British Columbia Provincial Museum [*A publication*]
**Occas Pap Bell Mus Nat Hist Univ Minn**... Occasional Papers. Bell Museum of Natural History. University of Minnesota [*A publication*]
**Occas Pap Bernice Pauahi Bishop Mus**... Occasional Papers. Bernice Pauahi Bishop Museum [*A publication*]
**Occas Pap Buffalo Soc Nat Sci**... Occasional Papers. Buffalo Society of Natural Sciences [*A publication*]
**Occas Pap Calif Acad Sci**... Occasional Papers. California Academy of Sciences [*A publication*]
**Occas Pap C C Adams Cent Ecol Stud West Mich Univ**... Occasional Papers. C. C. Adams Center for Ecological Studies. Western Michigan University [*A publication*]

**Occas Pap Dep Biochem Makerere Univ** ... Occasional Paper. Department of Biochemistry. Makerere University [*A publication*]
**Occas Pap Dep Biol Univ Puget Sound** ... Occasional Papers. Department of Biology. University of Puget Sound [*A publication*]
**Occas Pap Entomol (Sacramento)** ... Occasional Papers in Entomology (Sacramento) [*A publication*]
**Occas Pap Farlow Herb Cryptogam Bot Harv Univ** ... Occasional Papers. Farlow Herbarium of Cryptogamic Botany. Harvard University [*A publication*]
**Occas Pap Fla State Collect Arthropods** ... Occasional Papers. Florida State Collection of Arthropods [*A publication*]
**Occas Pap Geol Surv (New Hebrides)** ... Occasional Paper. Geological Survey (New Hebrides) [*A publication*]
**Occas Pap Inst Min Metall** ... Occasional Papers. Institution of Mining and Metallurgy [*A publication*]
**Occas Pap Mauritius Sugar Ind Res Inst** ... Occasional Paper. Mauritius Sugar Industry Research Institute [*A publication*]
**Occas Pap Minn Mus Nat Hist** ... Occasional Papers. Minnesota Museum of Natural History [*A publication*]
**Occas Pap Mollusks Mus Comp Zool Harv Univ** ... Occasional Papers on Mollusks. Museum of Comparative Zoology. Harvard University [*A publication*]
**Occas Pap Mus Nat Hist Univ Kans** ... Occasional Papers. Museum of Natural History. University of Kansas [*A publication*]
**Occas Pap Mus Nat Hist Univ Puget Sound** ... Occasional Papers. Museum of Natural History. University of Puget Sound [*A publication*]
**Occas Pap Mus Victoria** ... Occasional Papers. Museum of Victoria [*A publication*]
**Occas Pap Mus Zool LA State Univ** ... Occasional Papers. Museum of Zoology. Louisiana State University [*A publication*]
**Occas Pap Mus Zool Univ Mich** ... Occasional Papers. Museum of Zoology. University of Michigan [*A publication*]
**Occas Pap Natl Coll Agric Eng** ... Occasional Paper. National College of Agricultural Engineering [*A publication*]
**Occas Pap Natl Mus Monum Rhod Ser B Nat Sci** ... Occasional Papers. National Museums and Monuments of Rhodesia. Series B. Natural Sciences [*A publication*]
**Occas Pap Natl Speleol Soc** ... Occasional Papers. National Speleological Society [*A publication*]
**Occas Pap R Ont Mus Zool** ... Occasional Papers. Royal Ontario Museum of Zoology [*A publication*]
**Occas Pap San Diego Soc Nat Hist** ... Occasional Papers. San Diego Society of Natural History [*A publication*]
**Occas Pap S Forest Exp Sta US Forest Serv** ... Occasional Papers. Southern Forest Experiment Station. United States Forest Service [*A publication*]
**Occas Pap Trop Sci Cent (San Jose Costa Rica)** ... Occasional Paper. Tropical Science Center (San Jose, Costa Rica) [*A publication*]
**Occas Pap Veg Surv West Aust** ... Occasional Papers. Vegetation Survey of Western Australia. Department of Agriculture [*A publication*] (APTA)
**Occas Pap World Fertil Surv** ... Occasional Papers. World Fertility Survey [*A publication*]
**Occas Publ Cl St** ... Occasional Publications in Classical Studies [*A publication*]
**Occas Publ Inst Health Adm GA State Univ** ... Occasional Publications. Institute of Health Administration. Georgia State University [*A publication*]
**Occas Publ Rowett Res Inst** ... Occasional Publication. Rowett Research Institute [*A publication*]
**Occas Rep VA Div For Dep Conserv Econ Dev** ... Occasional Report. Virginia Division of Forestry. Department of Conservation and Economic Development [*A publication*]
**OCCB** ........ Operational Configuration Control Board (AFM)
**OCCBP**...... Organization for Collectors of Covered Bridge Postcards (EA)
**Occ Bul Miss R** ... Occasional Bulletin of Missionary Research [*A publication*]
**OCCC** ........ Oocyte-Corona-Cumulus Complex
**OCCCA** ..... Office of Congressional, Community, and Consumer Affairs
**OCCCE**...... Organization for Coordination and Cooperation in the Control of Major Endemic Diseases
**OCCD**........ Com Dev Ltd., Cambridge, Ontario [*Library symbol*] [*National Library of Canada*] (NLC)
**OCC-E**....... Office of the Chief of Communications-Electronics [*Army*] (AABC)
**OCCEDCA** ... Organization for Co-Ordination in Control of Endemic Diseases in Central Africa (EA)
**OCCF**......... Operator Communication and Control Facility [*IBM Corp.*]
**OCCGE** ..... Organisation de Coordination et de Cooperation pour la Lutte Contre les Grandes Endemies [*Organization for Co-Ordination and Co-Operation in the Control of Major Endemic Diseases*] (EAIO)
**OCCGERMDL** ... Army of Occupation of Germany Medal [*Military decoration*]
**OCCH**........ Children's Hospital Research Foundation, Research Library, Cincinnati, OH [*Library symbol*] [*Library of Congress*] (LCLS)
**OC of Ch**.... Office, Chief of Chaplains [*Later, OCCH*] [*Army*] (AABC)
**OCCH**........ Office, Chief of Chaplains [*Formerly, OC of Ch*] [*Army*] (AABC)
**Occ Hazards** ... Occupational Hazards [*A publication*]
**Occ Heal ANZ** ... Occupational Health Australia and New Zealand [*A publication*]
**Occ Health Nurs** ... Occupational Health Nursing [*A publication*]
**Occ Health & Sfty** ... Occupational Health and Safety [*A publication*]
**Occid**.......... Occidente [*A publication*]
**Occident Entomol** ... Occidental Entomologist [*A publication*]
**OCCIM** ..... Christ Hospital Institute of Medical Research, Research Library, Cincinnati, OH [*Library symbol*] [*Library of Congress*] (LCLS)
**OCCIN** ...... Process Technology Department, Inco Ltd., Copper Cliff, Ontario [*Library symbol*] [*National Library of Canada*] (BIB)
**OCCIS**....... Operational Command and Control Intelligence System [*Army*] (AABC)
**OCCM**....... Office of Commercial Communications Management (AFM)
**OCCM**....... Optical Counter-Countermeasures
**OCCMDL** ... Army of Occupation Medal [*Military decoration*]
**OCCMED** ... Occupational Medicine (AABC)
**OCCMH**.... Cambridge Memorial Hospital, Ontario [*Library symbol*] [*National Library of Canada*] (BIB)
**OCCMLC** ... Office, Chief, Chemical Corps [*Army*]
**OCCMLO** ... Office of the Chief Chemical Officer [*Military*]
**OCCN**........ Occasion
**Occ N**......... Occasional Notes, Canada Law Times [*A publication*] (DLA)
**OCCN**........ Occidental Nebraska Federal Savings Bank [*Omaha, NE*] [*NASDAQ symbol*] (NQ)
**Occ Newsl** ... Occasional Newsletter [*American Bar Association, Committee on Environmental Law*] [*A publication*] (ILCA)
**OCC NS**..... Ohio Circuit Court Reports, New Series [*A publication*] (DLA)
**OCCO**........ Office Canadien de Commercialisation des Oeufs
**OCCO**........ Office of the Chief Chemical Officer [*Military*] (AAG)
**Occ Outlook Q** ... Occupational Outlook Quarterly [*A publication*]
**OCCP** ........ Octachlorocyclopentene [*Organic chemistry*]
**OCCP** ........ Outside Communications Cable Plant (CET)
**Occ Pap Bur For (Philippines)** ... Occasional Paper. Bureau of Forestry (Manila, Philippines) [*A publication*]
**Occ Pap Bur Trans Eco** ... Occasional Paper. Department of Transport (Bureau of Transport Economics) [*A publication*] (APTA)
**Occ Pap Calif Acad Sci** ... Occasional Papers. California Academy of Sciences [*A publication*]
**Occ Pap Dep Biol Univ Guyana** ... Occasional Papers. Department of Biology. University of Guyana [*A publication*]
**Occ Pap Geol Surv Nig** ... Occasional Papers. Geological Survey of Nigeria [*A publication*]
**Occ Pap Geol Surv Ug** ... Occasional Papers. Geological Survey of Uganda [*A publication*]
**Occ Pap Maurit Sug Ind Res Inst** ... Occasional Paper. Mauritius Sugar Industry Research Institute [*A publication*]
**Occ Pap Univ NSW** ... University of New South Wales. Occasional Papers [*A publication*]
**Occ Pap Vegn Surv West Aust** ... Occasional Paper. Vegetation Survey of Western Australia [*A publication*] (APTA)
**OCCPR**...... Open-Chest Cardiopulmonary Resuscitation
**Occ Publs Aust Conserv Fdn** ... Occasional Publications. Australian Conservation Foundation [*A publication*] (APTA)
**Occ Publ Sci Hort** ... Occasional Publications on Scientific Horticulture [*A publication*]
**OCCR** ........ Cramahe Township Public Library, Castleton, Ontario [*Library symbol*] [*National Library of Canada*] (BIB)
**OCCS**......... Office of Combined Chiefs of Staff [*World War II*]
**OCCS**......... Officer Career Counseling System [*Army*] (RDA)
**OCCS**......... Operational Command and Control System [*Army*] (AABC)
**OCCS**......... Optical Contrast Contour Seeker
**OCCS**......... Ordnance and Chemical Center and School [*Army*] (MCD)
**OCCT** ........ Collingwood Township Public Library, Clarksburg, Ontario [*Library symbol*] [*National Library of Canada*] (NLC)
**OCCULT**... Optical Covert Communications Using LASER Transceivers (MCD)
**OCCULT**... Ordered Computer Collation of Unprepared Literary Texts
**OCCUP** ..... Occupational
**Occupational Outlook Q** ... Occupational Outlook Quarterly [*A publication*]
**Occup Dermatoses** ... Occupational Dermatoses [*A publication*]
**Occup Hazards** ... Occupational Hazards [*A publication*]
**Occup Health Bull (Ottawa)** ... Occupational Health Bulletin (Ottawa) [*A publication*]
**Occup Health (Lond)** ... Occupational Health (London) [*A publication*]
**Occup Health Nurs** ... Occupational Health Nursing [*A publication*]
**Occup Health Nurs (NY)** ... Occupational Health Nursing (New York) [*A publication*]
**Occup Health Rev** ... Occupational Health Review [*A publication*]
**Occup Health and Saf** ... Occupational Health and Safety [*A publication*]
**Occup Health Saf** ... Occupational Health and Safety [*A publication*]
**Occup Hlth** ... Occupational Health [*A publication*]
**Occup Hlth Nurs** ... Occupational Health Nursing [*A publication*]
**Occup Hlth Rev** ... Occupational Health Review [*A publication*]
**Occup Hzrd** ... Occupational Hazards [*A publication*]
**Occup Med** ... Occupational Medicine [*A publication*]
**OCCUPON** ... Occupation (ROG)
**Occup Outl Q** ... Occupational Outlook Quarterly [*A publication*]
**Occup Psych** ... Occupational Psychology [*A publication*]
**Occup Psychol** ... Occupational Psychology [*A publication*]

**Occup Saf Health** ... Occupational Safety and Health [*A publication*]
**Occup Saf Health Ser Int Labour Off** ... Occupational Safety and Health Series. International Labour Office [*A publication*]
**Occup Saf Hlth** ... Occupational Safety and Health [*A publication*]
**Occup Saf Hlth Admin Sub Service Vols 1 & 4** ... Occupational Safety and Health Administration. Subscription Service. Volumes 1 and 4 [*A publication*]
**Occup Ther Health Care** ... Occupational Therapy in Health Care [*A publication*]
**Occup Ther Ment Health** ... Occupational Therapy in Mental Health [*A publication*]
**OCCWC** .... Office of Chief of Counsel, War Crimes [*Allied German Occupation Forces*]
**OCD** .......... Obsessive-Compulsive Disorder [*Psychology*]
**OCD** .......... Occupation Centres for Defectives [*British*]
**OCD** .......... Office of Child Development [*HEW*]
**OCD** .......... Office of Child Development. Publications [*A publication*]
**OCD** .......... Office of Civil Defense
**OCD** .......... Office of Civilian Defense [*Within Office of Emergency Management*] [*World War II*]
**OCD** .......... Office of Community Development [*HUD*]
**OCD** .......... Ohio Circuit Court Decisions [*A publication*] (DLA)
**OCD** .......... Operational Capability Date (AAG)
**OCD** .......... Operational Capability Development (NASA)
**OCD** .......... Ordnance Classification of Defects [*Navy*]
**OCD** .......... Ordo Carmelitarum Discalceatorum [*Order of Discalced, or Barefoot, Carmelites*] [*Roman Catholic religious order*]
**OCD** .......... Osteochondritis Dissecans [*Medicine*]
**O/C/D** ....... Out of Collector's District [*Bookselling*] (ROG)
**OCD** .......... Ovarian Cholesterol Depletion [*Test*]
**OCD** .......... Overhaul Consumption Data
**OCD** .......... Oxford Classical Dictionary [*A publication*]
**OCDD** ........ Octachlorodibenzodioxin [*Organic chemistry*]
**OCDE** ........ Organisation de Cooperation et de Developpement Economiques [*Organization for Economic Cooperation and Development - OECD*] [*French*] (EAIO)
**OCDE** ........ Organizacion de Cooperacion y Desarrollo Economicos [*Organization for Economic Cooperation and Development - OECD*] [*Spanish*] (MSC)
**OCDETF** ... Organized Crime Drug Enforcement Task Force
**Oc Dev and Int L** ... Ocean Development and International Law [*A publication*]
**OCDF** ........ Operations Control and Display Facility [*Military*] (RDA)
**OCDM** ........ Office of Civil and Defense Mobilization [*Merged with Office of Emergency Planning*]
**OCDMS** .... On-Board Checkout and Data Management System (MCD)
**OCDN** ........ Order for Correction of Defect of Nonconformance
**OCDQ** ........ Organizational Climate Description Questionnaire
**OCDr** ......... Drackett Co., Research and Development Library, Cincinnati, OH [*Library symbol*] [*Library of Congress*] (LCLS)
**OCDR** ........ Office of Collateral Development Responsibility (AFM)
**OCDR** ........ Officer Control Distribution Report
**OCDR** ........ Orbiter Critical Design Review [*NASA*] (NASA)
**OCDRE** ..... Organic-Cooled Deuterium Reactor Experiment [*Nuclear energy*]
**OCDS** ........ Overseas College of Defence Studies [*British*]
**OCDS** ........ Secular Order of Discalced Carmelites [*Rome, Italy*] (EAIO)
**OCDU** ........ Optics Coupling Data [*or Display*] Unit [*Guidance and navigation*] (KSC)
**OCE** .......... Edgecliff College, Cincinnati, OH [*Library symbol*] [*Library of Congress*] (LCLS)
**OCE** .......... Ocean City [*Maryland*] [*Airport symbol*] (OAG)
**OCE** .......... Ocean Color Experiment [*NASA*]
**Oce** ............ Oceanic [*Record label*]
**OCE** .......... Office of Career Education [*Office of Education*]
**OCE** .......... Office, Chief of Engineers [*Army*]
**OCE** .......... Office of Coastal Environment [*National Oceanic and Atmospheric Administration*]
**OCE** .......... Office of Cultural Exchange [*Department of State*]
**OCE** .......... Office of the Director of Civil Engineering [*Air Force*]
**OCE** .......... Officer Conducting the Exercise [*Navy, Coast Guard*] [*Military*]
**OCE** .......... Officer Corps Engineers
**OCE** .......... Omega Chi Epsilon [*Honor society*] (EA)
**OCE** .......... OMGUS [*Office of Military Government, United States*] Civilian Employees Association [*Post-World War II, Germany*]
**OCE** .......... Ontario College of Education
**OCE** .......... Oregon, California & Eastern Railway Co. [*AAR code*]
**OCE** .......... Oregon College of Education
**OCE** .......... Oscillating Current Element
**OCEA** ........ Outstanding Civil Engineering Achievement [*Award*] [*American Society of Civil Engineers*]
**OCEAC** ..... Organisation de Coordination pour la Lutte Contre les Endemies en Afrique Centrale [*Organization for Co-Ordination in Control of Endemic Diseases in Central Africa - OCCEDCA*] (EAIO)
**OCEAN** ..... Oceanographic Coordination, Evaluation, and Analysis Network
**OCEAN** ..... Organisation de la Communaute Europeenne des Avitailleurs des Navires [*Ship Suppliers' Organization of the European Community - SSOEC*] [*Hague, Netherlands*] (EAIO)
**OceanAb** .... Oceanic Abstracts [*A publication*]
**OCEANAV** ... Naval Oceanography Command [*Marine science*] (MSC)
**OCEANAV** ... Oceanographer of the Navy
**OCEANAVINST** ... Naval Oceanographic Office Instruction
**Ocean Devel & Int L** ... Ocean Development and International Law [*A publication*]
**Ocean Develop Int Law** ... Ocean Development and International Law [*A publication*]
**Ocean Development and Internat Law** ... Ocean Development and International Law [*A publication*]
**Ocean Dev I** ... Ocean Development and International Law [*A publication*]
**Ocean Dev & Int L** ... Ocean Development and International Law [*A publication*]
**Ocean Dev and Intl LJ** ... Ocean Development and International Law Journal [*A publication*]
**Ocean Eng** ... Ocean Engineering [*A publication*]
**Ocean Eng Inf Ser** ... Ocean Engineering. Information Series [*A publication*]
**Ocean Engng** ... Ocean Engineering [*A publication*]
**OCEANIC** ... Ocean Network Information Center [*Information service or system*] (EISS)
**Ocean Ind** .. Ocean Industry [*A publication*]
**OCEANLANT** ... Ocean Subarea (Atlantic) [*NATO*] (NATG)
**Ocean Ling** ... Oceanic Linguistics [*A publication*]
**Ocean Man** ... Ocean Management [*A publication*] (ILCA)
**Ocean Manage** ... Ocean Management [*A publication*]
**Ocean Mgt** ... Ocean Management [*A publication*]
**OCEANOG** ... Oceanography
**Oceanogr Cruise Rep Inst Mar Res (Djakarta)** ... Oceanographical Cruise Report. Institute of Marine Research (Djakarta) [*A publication*]
**Oceanogrl Cruise Rep Div Fish Oceanogr CSIRO** ... Oceanographical Cruise Report. Division of Fisheries and Oceanography. Commonwealth Scientific and Industrial Research Organisation [*A publication*] (APTA)
**Oceanogrl Stn List Div Fish Oceanogr CSIRO** ... Oceanographical Station List. Division of Fisheries and Oceanography. Commonwealth Scientific and Industrial Research Organisation [*A publication*] (APTA)
**Oceanogr Mag (Tokyo)** ... Oceanographical Magazine (Tokyo) [*A publication*]
**Oceanogr Mar Biol** ... Oceanography and Marine Biology [*A publication*]
**Oceanogr Mar Biol Annu Rev** ... Oceanography and Marine Biology: An Annual Review [*A publication*]
**Oceanogr Res Inst (Durban) Invest Rep** ... Oceanographic Research Institute (Durban). Investigational Report [*A publication*]
**Oceanogr Soc Jap J** ... Oceanographical Society of Japan. Journal [*A publication*]
**Oceanol** ...... Oceanology [*A publication*]
**Oceanol Acta** ... Oceanologica Acta [*A publication*]
**Oceanol Int** ... Oceanology International [*A publication*]
**Oceanol Limnol Sin** ... Oceanologica et Limnologia Sinica [*A publication*]
**Oceanol Limn Sin** ... Oceanologia et Limnologia Sinica [*A publication*]
**Ocean Res (Seoul)** ... Ocean Research (Seoul) [*A publication*]
**OCEANS** ... Omnibus Conference on Experimental Aspects of NMR [*Nuclear Magnetic Resonance*] Spectroscopy (MUGU)
**Ocean Sci Eng** ... Ocean Science and Engineering [*A publication*]
**Ocean & Shoreline Manage** ... Ocean and Shoreline Management [*A publication*]
**Oceans Mag** ... Oceans Magazine [*A publication*]
**Ocean St B** ... Ocean State Business [*A publication*]
**OCEANSYSLANT** ... Ocean Systems, Atlantic
**OCEANSYSPAC** ... Ocean Systems, Pacific
**Ocean Yearb** ... Ocean Yearbook [*A publication*]
**OCEC** ........ Office of the Commissioner for Employees Compensation [*Australia*]
**OCED** ........ Office of Comprehensive Employment Development [*Department of Labor*]
**OCedC** ....... Cedarville College, Cedarville, OH [*Library symbol*] [*Library of Congress*] (LCLS)
**OCEFT** ...... Corbeil Branch, East Ferris Township Public Library, Ontario [*Library symbol*] [*National Library of Canada*] (NLC)
**OCel** ........... Dwyer-Mercer County District Library, Celina, OH [*Library symbol*] [*Library of Congress*] (LCLS)
**OCEL** ........ Overseas Container Europe Ltd. (DS)
**OCELAC** ... Camden East Branch, Lennox and Addington County Library, Ontario [*Library symbol*] [*National Library of Canada*] (NLC)
**OCEleC** ...... Cincinnati Electronics Corporation, Cincinnati, OH [*Library symbol*] [*Library of Congress*] (LCLS)
**OCEmI** ...... Emery Industries, Inc., Research Library, Cincinnati, OH [*Library symbol*] [*Library of Congress*] (LCLS)
**OCEN** ........ Oce-Van der Grinten NV [*Netherlands*] [*NASDAQ symbol*] (NQ)
**OCEP** ........ Office of Community Employment Programs [*Department of Labor*]
**OCEPA** ...... United States Environmental Protection Agency, Cincinnati, OH [*Library symbol*] [*Library of Congress*] (LCLS)
**OCER** ........ Oceaneering International, Inc. [*NASDAQ symbol*] (NQ)
**OCf** ............ Chagrin Falls Public Library, Chagrin Falls, OH [*Library symbol*] [*Library of Congress*] (LCLS)
**OCF** ........... Obsessive Compulsive Foundation (EA)
**OCF** ........... Ocala [*Florida*] [*Airport symbol*] (OAG)

**OCF**........... Ocala, FL [*Location identifier*] [*FAA*] (FAAL)
**OCF**........... Office of the Chief of Finance [*Military*]
**OC of F**...... Office of the Chief of Finance [*Military*]
**OCF**........... Officers' Christian Fellowship of the USA (EA)
**OCF**........... Officiating Chaplain to the Forces [*Military*] [*British*]
**OCF**........... On-Board Computational Facility [*NASA*] (NASA)
**OCF**........... Open Channel Flow
**OCF**........... Operator Console Facility [*Data processing*] (IBMDP)
**OCF**........... Orbiter Computational Facility [*NASA*] (NASA)
**OCF**........... Owens-Corning Fiberglas Corp. [*NYSE symbol*] (SPSG)
**OCF**........... Ozenji Critical Facility [*Nuclear reactor*] [*Japan*]
**OCF & A**.... Office, Chief of Finance and Accounting [*Army*] (AABC)
**OCFC**......... Cloyne Branch, Frontenac County Library, Ontario [*Library symbol*] [*National Library of Canada*] (BIB)
**OCFC**......... Overseas Combined Federal Campaign [*Red Cross*]
**OCFDA**..... United States Food and Drug Administration, Cincinnati, OH [*Library symbol*] [*Library of Congress*] (LCLS)
**OCFMFP**.. Ontario Centre for Farm Machinery and Food Processing Technology, Chatham, Ontario [*Library symbol*] [*National Library of Canada*] (NLC)
**OCF-ML**... Organisation Communiste de France - Marxiste-Leniniste [*Communist Organization of France - Marxist-Leninist*] (PPW)
**OCFNT**..... Occluded Front [*Meteorology*] (FAAC)
**OCFP**......... Office of Commercial and Financial Policy [*Department of Commerce*]
**OCG**........... Cincinnati General Hospital, Medical Library, Cincinnati, OH [*Library symbol*] [*Library of Congress*] (LCLS)
**OCG**........... Occupational Changes in a Generation [*Socioeconomics*]
**OCG**........... Office of the Commanding General [*Army*]
**OCG**........... Optimal Code Generation
**OCG**........... Oral Cholecystography [*or Cholecystogram*] [*Radiology*]
**OCG**........... Osborne & Chappel Goldfields US [*Toronto Stock Exchange symbol*]
**OCG**........... Oxygen Consumption Gauge
**OCGA**........ Official Code of Georgia, Annotated [*A publication*] (DLA)
**OCGH**....... Cornwall General Hospital, Ontario [*Library symbol*] [*National Library of Canada*] (NLC)
**OCGI**......... Omni Capital Group, Inc. [*NASDAQ symbol*] (NQ)
**OCGS**........ Church of Jesus Christ of Latter-Day Saints, Genealogical Society Library, Cincinnati Branch, Cincinnati, OH [*Library symbol*] [*Library of Congress*] (LCLS)
**OCGSH**..... Good Samaritan Hospital, Medical Library, Cincinnati, OH [*Library symbol*] [*Library of Congress*] (LCLS)
**OCGT**........ OCG Technology, Inc. [*NASDAQ symbol*] (NQ)
**OCH**.......... Chesley Branch, Bruce County Public Library, Ontario [*Library symbol*] [*National Library of Canada*] (NLC)
**OCh**........... Chillicothe and Ross County Public Library, Chillicothe, OH [*Library symbol*] [*Library of Congress*] (LCLS)
**OCH**.......... Hebrew Union College - Jewish Institute of Religion, Cincinnati, OH [*Library symbol*] [*Library of Congress*] (LCLS)
**OCH**.......... Nacogdoches, TX [*Location identifier*] [*FAA*] (FAAL)
**OCH**.......... Obedience Champion [*Dog show term*]
**OCH**.......... Ochre [*Philately*] (ROG)
**OCH**.......... Orbiter Common Hardware [*NASA*] (NASA)
**OCH**.......... Order of the Compassionate Heart (EA)
**OCH**.......... Organ Clearing House (EA)
**OCH**.......... Outpatient Clinic (Hospital) [*Veterans Administration*]
**OCHA**....... Chatham Public Library, Ontario [*Library symbol*] [*National Library of Canada*] (NLC)
**O Ch A**....... Orientalia Christiana Analecta [*A publication*]
**OChaG**....... Geauga County Public Library, Chardon, OH [*Library symbol*] [*Library of Congress*] (LCLS)
**OCHAH**.... Chatham Public General Hospital, Ontario [*Library symbol*] [*National Library of Canada*] (NLC)
**OCHAK**..... Chatham-Kent Museum, Chatham, Ontario [*Library symbol*] [*National Library of Canada*] (NLC)
**OCHAKC**.. Kent County Public Library, Chatham, Ontario [*Library symbol*] [*National Library of Canada*] (NLC)
**OCHAMPUS**... Office for the Civilian Health and Medical Program of the Uniformed Services (AABC)
**Ochanomizu Med J**... Ochanomizu Medical Journal [*Japan*] [*A publication*]
**OCHAP**..... Chapleau Public Library, Ontario [*Library symbol*] [*National Library of Canada*] (NLC)
**OCHAT**..... Thames Arts Centre, Chatham, Ontario [*Library symbol*] [*National Library of Canada*] (NLC)
**OCHC**........ Operator Call Handling Center [*Telecommunications*] (TEL)
**OCHCB**..... Huron County Board of Education, Clinton, Ontario [*Library symbol*] [*National Library of Canada*] (NLC)
**OCHDC**..... Hilton Davis Chemical Co., Cincinnati, OH [*Library symbol*] [*Library of Congress*] (LCLS)
**OCHERB**.. Chelmsford Branch, Rayside-Balfour Public Library, Chelmsford, Ontario [*Library symbol*] [*National Library of Canada*] (NLC)
**Ocherki Fiz-Khim Petrol**... Ocherki Fiziko-Khimicheskoi Petrologii [*A publication*]
**Ocherki Geol Sov Karpat**... Ocherki po Geologii Sovetskikh Karpat [*A publication*]
**OCHIN**...... Norton Company Electric, Chippewa, Ontario [*Library symbol*] [*National Library of Canada*] (NLC)
**Ochistka Povtorn Ispol'z Stochnykh Vod Urale**... Ochistka i Povtornoe Ispol'zovanie Stochnykh Vod na Urale [*A publication*]
**Ochistka Vodn Vozdushn Basseinov Predpr Chern Metall**... Ochistka Vodnogo i Vozdushnogo Basseinov na Predpriyatiyakh Chernoi Metallurgii [*A publication*]
**OC-HLTHLB**... Occupational Health Labels [*Army*]
**OCHM**...... Haldimand County Museum Board, Cayuga, Ontario [*Library symbol*] [*National Library of Canada*] (NLC)
**OCHP**........ Cincinnati Historical Society, Cincinnati, OH [*Library symbol*] [*Library of Congress*] (LCLS)
**O Ch P**....... Orientalia Christiana Periodica [*A publication*]
**OCHR**........ Oil Catcher
**O Chr**......... One in Christ [*A publication*]
**Ochr Koroz**... Ochrona Przed Korozja [*A publication*]
**Ochr Ovzdusi**... Ochrana Ovzdusi. Supplement to Vodni Hospodarstvi. Rada B [*A publication*]
**OChrP**....... Orientalia Christiana Periodica [*A publication*]
**Ochr Powietrza**... Ochrona Powietrza [*A publication*]
**Ochr Pr**...... Ochrona Pracy [*A publication*]
**Ochr Przeciwpozarowa Przem Chem**... Ochrona Przeciwpozarowa w Przemysle Chemicznym [*A publication*]
**Ochr Przed Koroz**... Ochrona Przed Korozja [*A publication*]
**Ochr Przyr**... Ochrona Przyrody [*A publication*]
**Ochr Rosl**... Ochrona Roslin [*A publication*]
**Ochr Rostl**... Ochrana Rostlin [*A publication*]
**OCHSDG**.. Chesterville Branch, Stormont, Dundas, and Glengarry County Public Library, Ontario [*Library symbol*] [*National Library of Canada*] (BIB)
**OChU**........ Ohio University, Chillicothe Branch Campus, Chillicothe, OH [*Library symbol*] [*Library of Congress*] (LCLS)
**OCHWL**.... Wollaston and Limerick Public Library, Coe Hill, Ontario [*Library symbol*] [*National Library of Canada*] (BIB)
**OCHZA**..... Oesterreichische Chemiker-Zeitung [*A publication*]
**OCI**........... Integrated Revolutionary Organizations [*Cuba*] (PPW)
**OCI**........... OC [*Overseas Crusades*] International (EA)
**OCI**........... Ocean Color Imager [*Meteorology*] [*NASA*]
**OCI**........... Ocean Industry. Engineering, Construction, and Operations [*A publication*]
**OCI**........... Office of Community Investment [*Federal Home Loan Bank Board*]
**OCI**........... Office of Computer Information [*Department of Commerce*] [*Originator and database*]
**OCI**........... Office of Corollary Interest [*DoD*]
**OCI**........... Office of Current Intelligence (MCD)
**OCI**........... Old Canada Investment Corp. Ltd. [*Toronto Stock Exchange symbol*]
**OCI**........... Ontario Cancer Institute [*UTLAS symbol*]
**OCI**........... Operation Child Identification (EA)
**OCI**........... Optically Coupled Isolator
**OCI**........... Organisation Communiste Internationaliste [*Internationalist Communist Organization*] [*France*] [*Political party*] (PPW)
**OCI**........... Organisation de la Conference Islamique [*Organization of the Islamic Conference - OIC*] [*Jeddah, Saudi Arabia*] (EAIO)
**OCI**........... Organizational Climate Index [*Test*]
**OCI**........... Organized Crime Intelligence Unit [*Law Enforcement Assistance Administration*]
**OCI**........... Outpatient Clinic (Independent) [*Veterans Administration*]
**OCI**........... Oxide Control and Indication (NRCH)
**OCIA**......... Organic Crop Improvement Association (EA)
**OCIAA**...... Office of Coordinator of Inter-American Affairs [*World War II*]
**OCIB**......... Beausoleil Indian Band Library, Christian Island, Ontario [*Library symbol*] [*National Library of Canada*] (BIB)
**OCIC**......... Officer Commanding in Charge [*Facetious acronym*] [*Army*] [*British*] (DSUE)
**OCIC**......... Organisation Catholique Internationale du Cinema et de l'Audiovisuel [*International Catholic Organization for Cinema and Audiovisual*] (EAIO)
**OCIE**......... Organizational Clothing and Individual Equipment [*Military*]
**OCIF**......... Out Card in File
**OCIL**......... Ocilla Industries, Inc. [*NASDAQ symbol*] (NQ)
**OCIMF**...... Oil Companies International Marine Forum [*London, England*] (EAIO)
**OCINFO**... Office of the Chief of Information [*Military*]
**OCIPE**....... Office Catholique d'Information sur les Problemes Europeens [*Catholic European Study and Information Center*] [*Brussels, Belgium*] (EAIO)
**OCirP**........ Pickaway County District Public Library, Circleville, OH [*Library symbol*] [*Library of Congress*] (LCLS)
**OCIS**......... Office for Church in Society (EA)
**OCIS**......... Office of Computing and Information Services [*University of Georgia*] [*Research center*] (RCD)
**OCIS**......... Organized Crime Information System [*Federal Bureau of Investigation*] [*Information service or system*] (IID)
**O CIST**...... Ordinis Cisterciensis [*Cistercian Order*] (ROG)
**OCITA**....... Office of the Chemical Industry Trade Advisor
**OCIU**......... Optical Cable Interface Unit (MCD)
**OCJ**........... Ocho Rios [*Jamaica*] [*Airport symbol*] (OAG)
**OCJ**........... Optional Construction Joint
**OCJC**......... Orange Coast Junior College [*California*] [*Later, OCC*]
**OCJCS**...... Office of the Chairman, Joint Chiefs of Staff (MCD)

**OCJH**........ Jewish Hospital, Medical Library, Cincinnati, OH [*Library symbol*] [*Library of Congress*] (LCLS)
**OCJH-N**.... Jewish Hospital, School of Nursing, Cincinnati, OH [*Library symbol*] [*Library of Congress*] (LCLS)
**OCJP**........ Office of Criminal Justice Program (OICC)
**OCK**.......... Chalk River Public Library, Ontario [*Library symbol*] [*National Library of Canada*] (BIB)
**OCK**.......... Kent State University, Stark County Regional Campus, Canton, OH [*OCLC symbol*] (OCLC)
**OCKA**........ Atomic Energy of Canada [*L'Energie Atomique du Canada*] Chalk River, Ontario [*Library symbol*] [*National Library of Canada*] (NLC)
**OCKE**........ Petawawa National Forestry Institute, Canadian Forestry Service, Environment Canada [*Institut Forestier National Petawawa, Service Canadien des Forets, Environnement Canada*] Chalk River, Ontario [*Library symbol*] [*National Library of Canada*] (NLC)
**OCl**........... Cleveland Public Library, Cleveland, OH [*Library symbol*] [*Library of Congress*] (LCLS)
**OCL**.......... Obstacle [*or Obstruction*] Clearance Limit [*Aviation*] (FAAC)
**OcL**........... Oceanic Linguistics [*A publication*]
**OCL**.......... Ocellus
**OCL**.......... Oil City Lubricants Ltd. [*Vancouver Stock Exchange symbol*]
**OCL**.......... Old Light Cruiser [*Navy symbol*]
**OCL**.......... Operation Control Language [*Computer programming*]
**OCL**.......... Operational Check List (MUGU)
**OCL**.......... Operational Control Level
**OCL**.......... Operators Control Language [*Data processing*] (BUR)
**OCL**.......... Ordnance Circular Letter
**OCL**.......... Organochlorine [*Also, OC*] [*Organic chemistry*]
**OCL**.......... Outgoing Correspondence Log (AAG)
**OCL**.......... Overall Connection Loss [*Telecommunications*] (TEL)
**OCL**.......... Overhaul Cycle Limit
**OCL**.......... Overseas Containers Limited (DS)
**OClA**......... Alcan Aluminum Co., Cleveland, OH [*Library symbol*] [*Library of Congress*] (LCLS)
**OCLA**........ Oregon Compiled Laws Annotated [*A publication*]
**OCLAE**...... Organizacion Continental Latinoamericana de Estudiantes [*Latin American Continental Students' Organization*] (EAIO)
**OClAM**...... Arthur G. McKee & Co., Cleveland, OH [*Library symbol*] [*Library of Congress*] (LCLS)
**OCLaw**...... Cincinnati Law Library Association, Cincinnati, OH [*Library symbol*] [*Library of Congress*] (LCLS)
**OCLB**........ Office Club, Inc. [*NASDAQ symbol*] (CTT)
**OClBE**....... Board of Education, Cleveland, OH [*Library symbol*] [*Library of Congress*] (LCLS)
**OClBHS**.... Benedictine High School, Cleveland, OH [*Library symbol*] [*Library of Congress*] (LCLS)
**OCl-BPH**... Ohio Regional Library, Braille and Talking Books Division, Cleveland Public Library, Cleveland, OH [*Library symbol*] [*Library of Congress*] (LCLS)
**OClBS**....... Blessed Sacrament Seminary, Cleveland, OH [*Library symbol*] [*Library of Congress*] (LCLS)
**OClC**......... Cleveland Clinic Educational Foundation, Cleveland, OH [*Library symbol*] [*Library of Congress*] (LCLS)
**OCLC**........ Online Computer Library Center [*Formerly, Ohio College Library Center. Initialism used in reference to cataloging system it developed*] [*Information service or system*]
**OClCC**....... Cuyahoga Community College, Cleveland, OH [*Library symbol*] [*Library of Congress*] (LCLS)
**OClCh**....... Christian Science Reading Room, Cleveland, OH [*Library symbol*] [*Library of Congress*] (LCLS)
**OClCIM**.... Cleveland Institute of Music, Cleveland, OH [*Library symbol*] [*Library of Congress*] (LCLS)
**OClCo**....... Cuyahoga County Public Library, Cleveland, OH [*Library symbol*] [*Library of Congress*] (LCLS)
**OClD**........ Dyke College, Cleveland, OH [*Library symbol*] [*Library of Congress*] (LCLS)
**OCLD**........ Occlude (FAAC)
**OCLD**........ Oil-Cooled
**OClDe**....... Deaconess Hospital, Medical Library, Cleveland, OH [*Library symbol*] [*Library of Congress*] (LCLS)
**OCLE**........ Continuing Legal Education, University of Oklahoma Law Center (DLA)
**OClFRB**..... Federal Reserve Bank of Cleveland, Cleveland, OH [*Library symbol*] [*Library of Congress*] (LCLS)
**OClG**......... Glidden Co. Research Library, Cleveland, OH [*Library symbol*] [*Library of Congress*] (LCLS)
**OClGC**....... Garden Center of Greater Cleveland, Cleveland, OH [*Library symbol*] [*Library of Congress*] (LCLS)
**OClGI**........ Gould, Incorporated, Gould Information Center, Cleveland, OH [*Library symbol*] [*Library of Congress*] (LCLS)
**OClh**.......... Cleveland Heights-University Heights Public Library, Cleveland Heights, OH [*Library symbol*] [*Library of Congress*] (LCLS)
**OCLI**.......... Curve Lake Indian Band Library, Ontario [*Library symbol*] [*National Library of Canada*] (BIB)
**OCLI**.......... Optical Coating Laboratory, Incorporated [*NASDAQ symbol*] (NQ)
**OClJC**........ John Carroll University, Cleveland, OH [*Library symbol*] [*Library of Congress*] (LCLS)
**OClL**.......... General Electric Co., Light Research Laboratory, Cleveland, OH [*Library symbol*] [*Library of Congress*] (LCLS)
**OCLL**......... Office, Chief of Legislative Liaison [*Military*]
**OClLH**....... Lakeside Hospital, Cleveland, OH [*Library symbol*] [*Library of Congress*] (LCLS)
**OCLloyd**.... Lloyd Library and Museum, Cincinnati, OH [*Library symbol*] [*Library of Congress*] (LCLS)
**OClMA**...... Cleveland Museum of Art, Cleveland, OH [*Library symbol*] [*Library of Congress*] (LCLS)
**OClMGH**.. Cleveland Metropolitan General Hospital, Cleveland, OH [*Library symbol*] [*Library of Congress*] (LCLS)
**OClMN**..... Cleveland Museum of Natural History, Cleveland, OH [*Library symbol*] [*Library of Congress*] (LCLS)
**OClMt**....... Mount Sinai Hospital, Cleveland, OH [*Library symbol*] [*Library of Congress*] (LCLS)
**OCLN**........ Occlusion (FAAC)
**OClNASA**... National Aeronautics and Space Administration, Lewis Research Center, Cleveland, OH [*Library symbol*] [*Library of Congress*] (LCLS)
**OClND**...... Notre Dame College, Cleveland, OH [*Library symbol*] [*Library of Congress*] (LCLS)
**OCLNR**..... Oil Cleaner
**OClP**......... Park Synagogue, Cleveland, OH [*Library symbol*] [*Library of Congress*] (LCLS)
**OCLR**........ Oil Cooler
**OClRC**....... Rowfant Club, Cleveland, OH [*Library symbol*] [*Library of Congress*] (LCLS)
**OClSA**....... Cleveland Institute of Art, Cleveland, OH [*Library symbol*] [*Library of Congress*] (LCLS)
**OClSS**........ Saint Stanislaus Seminary, Cleveland, OH [*Library symbol*] [*Library of Congress*] (LCLS)
**OClStJ**....... Saint John College of Cleveland, Cleveland, OH [*Library symbol*] [*Library of Congress*] (LCLS)
**OClStM**..... Saint Mary's Seminary, Cleveland, OH [*Library symbol*] [*Library of Congress*] (LCLS)
**OClTem**..... Temple Library, Tiffereth Israel Congregation, Cleveland, OH [*Library symbol*] [*Library of Congress*] (LCLS)
**OClU**......... Cleveland State University, Cleveland, OH [*Library symbol*] [*Library of Congress*] (LCLS)
**OClU-L**...... Cleveland-Marshall College of Law, Cleveland State University, Cleveland, OH [*Library symbol*] [*Library of Congress*] (LCLS)
**OClUr**........ Ursuline College, Pepper Pike, OH [*Library symbol*] [*Library of Congress*] (LCLS)
**OCLUS**...... Outside Continental Limits of United States [*Military*]
**OClV**.......... United States Veterans Administration Hospital, Cleveland, OH [*Library symbol*] [*Library of Congress*] (LCLS)
**OClW**......... Case Western Reserve University, Cleveland, OH [*Library symbol*] [*Library of Congress*] (LCLS)
**OClW-H**.... Case Western Reserve University, Cleveland Health Sciences Library, Cleveland, OH [*Library symbol*] [*Library of Congress*] (LCLS)
**OClWHi**.... Western Reserve Historical Society, Cleveland, OH [*Library symbol*] [*Library of Congress*] (LCLS)
**OClWHi-AM**... Western Reserve Historical Society, Frederick C. Crawford Auto-Aviation Museum, Cleveland, OH [*Library symbol*] [*Library of Congress*] (LCLS)
**OClW-LS**.. Case Western Reserve University, School of Library Science, Cleveland, OH [*Library symbol*] [*Library of Congress*] (LCLS)
**OClW-S**..... Case Western Reserve University, Sears Library, Cleveland, OH [*Library symbol*] [*Library of Congress*] (LCLS)
**OClW-SS**... Case Western Reserve University, School of Applied Social Science, Cleveland, OH [*Library symbol*] [*Library of Congress*] (LCLS)
**OCM**.......... Cincinnati Masonic Temple, Cincinnati, OH [*Library symbol*] [*Library of Congress*] (LCLS)
**OCM**.......... Creighton University, Health Sciences Library, Omaha, NE [*OCLC symbol*] (OCLC)
**OCM**.......... Matchedash Public Library, Coldwater, Ontario [*Library symbol*] [*National Library of Canada*] (BIB)
**OCM**.......... Ocean Management [*A publication*]
**OCM**.......... Office of the Commission [*Nuclear energy*] (NRCH)
**OCM**.......... Office of Country Marketing [*Department of Commerce*] (IMH)
**OCM**.......... Oil Content Monitor [*Navy*] (CAAL)
**OCM**.......... On-Camera Meteorologist
**OCM**.......... On Communications [*A publication*]
**OCM**.......... On-Condition Maintenance (AABC)
**OCM**.......... One-Channel Map [*Data processing*] [*NASA*]
**OCM**.......... Optical Countermeasures
**OCM**.......... Ordnance Committee Meeting (AAG)
**OCM**.......... Ordnance Committee Minutes [*Military*]
**OCM**.......... Ordo Constantini Magni [*International Constantinian Order*] (EA)
**OCM**.......... Organic Content Monitor (NASA)
**O & CM**..... Organist and Choir Master (ROG)
**OCM**.......... Origin of Columellar Muscle
**OCM**.......... Oscillator and Clock Module

**OCMAA**.... Oceanographical Magazine [*A publication*]
**OCMCEN**... Occupational Measurement Center [*Air Force*]
**OCMEA**.... Occupational Medicine [*A publication*]
**OCMH**...... Madonna House Library, Combermere, Ontario [*Library symbol*] [*National Library of Canada*] (NLC)
**OCMH**...... Office of the Chief of Military History [*Army*]
**OCMI**........ Officer-in-Charge, Marine Inspection Office [*Coast Guard*]
**OCMil**....... Cincinnati Milacron, Inc., Research Library, Cincinnati, OH [*Library symbol*] [*Library of Congress*] (LCLS)
**OCMil-T**... Cincinnati Milacron, Inc., Technical Information Center, Cincinnati, OH [*Library symbol*] [*Library of Congress*] (LCLS)
**OCM-LP**... Organizacao Comunista Marxista-Leninista Portuguesa [*Portuguese Communist Organization, Marxist-Leninist*] [*Political party*] (PPE)
**OCMLR**.... Organisation Communiste Marxiste-Leniniste de la Reunion [*Reunionese Communist Organization, Marxist-Leninist*] [*Political party*] (PPW)
**OCMM**...... Office of Civilian Manpower Management [*Later, Office of Civilian Personnel*] [*Navy*]
**OCMMINST**... Office of Civilian Manpower Management Instruction [*Navy*]
**OCMM-N**... Office of Civilian Manpower Management - Navy
**OCMN**....... Merrell-National Laboratories, Cincinnati, OH [*Library symbol*] [*Library of Congress*] (LCLS)
**OCMODL**... Operating Cost Model
**OCMR**....... On-Condition Maintenance Rate (MCD)
**OCMR**....... Ontario Centre for Materials Research [*Canada*] [*Research center*] (RCD)
**OCMS**....... On-Board Checkout and Monitoring System [*NASA*] (KSC)
**OCMS**....... Operative Crate Makers' Society [*A union*] [*British*]
**OCMS**....... Optional Calling Measured Service [*Telecommunications*] (TEL)
**OCMS**....... Ordnance Command Management System
**OCMS**....... Ordnance Committee Meeting Standards (AAG)
**OCMSq**..... Occupational Measurement Squadron [*Air Force*]
**OCMU**....... Ocmulgee National Monument
**OCN**........... Canadian Park Service, Environment Canada [*Service Canadien des Parcs, Environnement Canada*], Cornwall, Ontario [*Library symbol*] [*National Library of Canada*] (NLC)
**OCN**........... Ocean Airways, Inc. [*Farmingdale, NJ*] [*FAA designator*] (FAAC)
**OCN**........... Oceanside, CA [*Location identifier*] [*FAA*] (FAAL)
**OCN**........... Oculomotor Nucleus [*Eye anatomy*]
**OC-N**......... Office of the Comptroller of the Navy
**OCN**........... Operation Completion Notice (AAG)
**OCN**........... Orcana Resources Ltd. [*Vancouver Stock Exchange symbol*]
**OCN**........... Order Control Number (NASA)
**OCN**........... Organization Change Notice
**OCN**........... Over Castle Rock [*New York*] [*Seismograph station code, US Geological Survey*] (SEIS)
**OCNA**........ Ouvrages sur la Culture Nord-Africaine [*A publication*]
**OCNAV**..... Office of the Oceanographer of the Navy
**OCNC**........ Coniston Branch, Nickel Centre Public Library, Ontario [*Library symbol*] [*National Library of Canada*] (NLC)
**OCNew**...... New Church Library, Cincinnati, OH [*Library symbol*] [*Library of Congress*] [*Obsolete*] (LCLS)
**OCnf**.......... Canal Fulton Public Library, Canal Fulton, OH [*Library symbol*] [*Library of Congress*] (LCLS)
**OCNGA**..... Officer-in-Charge of National Guard Affairs
**OCNGH**.... Garden Hill Branch, Northumberland County Public Library, Campbellcroft, Ontario [*Library symbol*] [*National Library of Canada*] (BIB)
**OCNGS**..... Oyster Creek Nuclear Generating Station (NRCH)
**OCNHT**..... North Himsworth Township Public Library, Callander, Ontario [*Library symbol*] [*National Library of Canada*] (NLC)
**OCNIOS**... National Institute for Occupational Safety and Health, Cincinnati, OH [*Library symbol*] [*Library of Congress*] (LCLS)
**OCNL**........ Occasional
**OCNLY**..... Occasionally
**OCNO**....... Office of the Chief of Naval Operations
**OCNPP**..... Oyster Creek Nuclear Power Plant (NRCH)
**OCNPR**..... Operation and Conservation of Naval Petroleum Reserves [*Budget appropriation title*]
**OCNWU**.... Organizing Committee for a National Writers Union (EA)
**OCO**.......... Cobourg Public Library, Ontario [*Library symbol*] [*National Library of Canada*] (NLC)
**OCo**........... Columbus Public Library, Columbus, OH [*Library symbol*] [*Library of Congress*] (LCLS)
**OCO**.......... Office of Central Operations [*Bureau of Health Insurance*]
**OCO**.......... Office, Chief of Ordnance [*Army*]
**OCO**.......... Old Cornish [*Language, etc.*]
**OCO**.......... OMS [*Orbital Maneuvering Subsystem*] Cutoff [*NASA*] (NASA)
**OCO**.......... One-Cancels-the-Other Order [*Business term*]
**OCO**.......... Open-Close-Open [*Technical drawings*]
**O & C/O**..... Operation and Checkout [*O & C is preferred*] [*NASA*] (KSC)
**OCO**.......... Operational Capability Objective [*Army*]
**OCO**.......... Operational Checkout (AAG)
**OCO**.......... Operations Console Operator (MUGU)
**OCO**.......... Ordnance Corps Order (AAG)
**OCO**.......... Public Library of Columbus and Franklin County, Columbus, OH [*OCLC symbol*] (OCLC)
**OCOA**........ Art Gallery of Cobourg, Ontario [*Library symbol*] [*National Library of Canada*] (NLC)
**OCoa**......... Columbiana Public Library, Columbiana, OH [*Library symbol*] [*Library of Congress*] (LCLS)
**OCoAC**...... American Ceramic Society, Columbus, OH [*Library symbol*] [*Library of Congress*] (LCLS)
**OCoB**......... Battelle-Columbus Laboratories, Columbus, OH [*Library symbol*] [*Library of Congress*] (LCLS)
**OCOB**........ Cobalt Public Library, Ontario [*Library symbol*] [*National Library of Canada*] (BIB)
**OCOBD**..... Cobden Public Library, Ontario [*Library symbol*] [*National Library of Canada*] (BIB)
**OCoBex**..... Bexley Public Library, Columbus, OH [*Library symbol*] [*Library of Congress*] (LCLS)
**OCoC**......... Capital University, Columbus, OH [*Library symbol*] [*Library of Congress*] (LCLS)
**OCOC**........ Cochrane Public Library, Ontario [*Library symbol*] [*National Library of Canada*] (NLC)
**OCOC**........ Oceans of Canada [*A publication*]
**OCOCC**..... Ontario CAD/CAM Centre, Cambridge, Ontario [*Library symbol*] [*National Library of Canada*] (NLC)
**OCoC-L**..... Capital University, School of Law, Columbus, OH [*Library symbol*] [*Library of Congress*] (LCLS)
**OCoCT**...... Columbus Technical Institute, Columbus, OH [*Library symbol*] [*Library of Congress*] (LCLS)
**OCoD**......... Ohio Dominican College, Columbus, OH [*Library symbol*] [*Library of Congress*] (LCLS)
**OCoE**......... Evangelical Lutheran Theological Seminary, Columbus, OH [*Library symbol*] [*Library of Congress*] (LCLS)
**OCOE**........ Office of the Chief of Engineers [*Army*] (RDA)
**OCoF**......... Franklin University, Columbus, OH [*Library symbol*] [*Library of Congress*] (LCLS)
**OCoG**......... Grandview Heights Library, Columbus, OH [*Library symbol*] [*Library of Congress*] (LCLS)
**OCOGF**..... General Foods Ltd., Cobourg, Ontario [*Library symbol*] [*National Library of Canada*] (NLC)
**OCoGS**...... Church of Jesus Christ of Latter-Day Saints, Genealogical Society Library, Columbus Branch, Columbus, OH [*Library symbol*] [*Library of Congress*] (LCLS)
**OCOKA**..... Observation and Fields of Fire, Cover and Concealment, Obstacles, Key Terrain, Avenues of Approach (MCD)
**OCOL**........ Collingwood Public Library, Ontario [*Library symbol*] [*National Library of Canada*] (NLC)
**OCOLB**..... Colborne Public Library, Ontario [*Library symbol*] [*National Library of Canada*] (BIB)
**OCoLC**....... Ohio College Library Center, Columbus, OH [*Library symbol*] [*Library of Congress*] (LCLS)
**OCOLD**..... Coldwater Memorial Public Library, Ontario [*Library symbol*] [*National Library of Canada*] (BIB)
**OCOM**....... Outlet Communications, Inc. [*NASDAQ symbol*] (NQ)
**OCOMS**.... Office of Community Services [*Military*]
**OCON**....... Northumberland and Newcastle Board of Education, Cobourg, Ontario [*Library symbol*] [*National Library of Canada*] (NLC)
**OCON**....... Orders for Correction of Nonconformance [*Navy*] (NG)
**OCoNC**...... National Center on Educational Media and Materials for the Handicapped, Columbus, OH [*Library symbol*] [*Library of Congress*] (LCLS)
**OCONT**..... Oil Control
**OCONUS**... Outside Continental United States [*Military*]
**OCOO**....... Cookstown Public Library, Ontario [*Library symbol*] [*National Library of Canada*] (BIB)
**OCoO**........ Ohioana Library, Columbus, OH [*Library symbol*] [*Library of Congress*] (LCLS)
**OCOO**....... Osteopathic College of Ophthalmology and Otorhinolaryngology (EA)
**OCoR**......... Riverside Methodist Hospital, Columbus, OH [*Library symbol*] [*Library of Congress*] (LCLS)
**OC of ORD**... Office, Chief of Ordnance [*Army*]
**OCORD**..... Office, Chief of Ordnance [*Army*]
**OCoSH**...... Columbus State Hospital, Columbus, OH [*Library symbol*] [*Library of Congress*] (LCLS)
**OCOT**........ Office, Chief of Transportation [*Army*]
**OCoV**......... Center for Vocational and Technical Education, Ohio State University, Columbus, OH [*Library symbol*] [*Library of Congress*] (LCLS)
**OCoY**......... Young Men's Christian Association, Columbus, OH [*Library symbol*] [*Library of Congress*] (LCLS)
**OCP**........... Carleton Place Public Library, Ontario [*Library symbol*] [*National Library of Canada*] (NLC)
**OCP**........... Occupational Cluster Program (OICC)
**OCP**........... Ocean Culture Product
**OCP**........... Octacalcium Phosphate [*Inorganic chemistry*]
**OCP**........... Ocular Cicatricial Pemphigoid [*Ophthalmology*]
**OCP**........... Office of Civilian Personnel [*Military*]
**OCP**........... Office of Commercial Programs [*NASA*]
**OCP**........... Officer Candidate Programme [*British military*] (DMA)

**OCP**.......... Official Crude Prices [*Petroleum Intelligence Weekly*] [*Information service or system*] (CRD)
**OCP**.......... Ohio CPA [*Certified Public Accountant*] Journal [*A publication*]
**OCP**.......... Onchocerciasis Chemotherapy Project [*WHO*]
**OCP**.......... One-Component Plasma
**OCP**.......... Ontario College of Pharmacy
**OCP**.......... Operating [*or Operational*] Control Procedure (MSA)
**OCP**.......... Operational Capability Plan [*Army*]
**OCP**.......... Operational Checkout Procedure [*NASA*] (KSC)
**OCP**.......... Operational Communications Plan (MCD)
**OCP**.......... Operational Control Panel
**OCP**.......... Operations Control Plan (AAG)
**OCP**.......... Optical Character Printing
**OCP**.......... Orbital Correction Program [*NASA*] (KSC)
**OCP**.......... Order Code Processor [*International Computers Ltd.*]
**OCP**.......... Organizational Competitiveness Program [*Motivational program*]
**OCP**.......... Orientalia Christiana Periodica [*A publication*]
**OCP**.......... Ortho-Chlorophenol [*Organic chemistry*]
**OCP**.......... Ostacalcium Phosphate [*A fertilizer*]
**OCP**.......... Out of Commission for Parts (AFM)
**OCP**.......... Output Control Program
**OCP**.......... Output Control Pulse (NASA)
**OCP**.......... Overland Common Point [*Imported item*] [*Business term*]
**OCP**.......... Overload Control Process [*Telecommunications*] (TEL)
**OCP**.......... Overseas Common Point [*Exported item*] [*Business term*]
**OCP**.......... Owners and Contractors Protective [*Insurance*]
**OCP**.......... Public Library of Cincinnati and Hamilton County, Cincinnati, OH [*OCLC symbol*] (OCLC)
**OCPA**........ Office, Chief of Public Affairs [*Army*]
**OCPA**........ Office of Congressional and Public Affairs [*FCC*] (TSSD)
**OCPA**........ Ortho-Chlorophenoxyacetic Acid [*Organic chemistry*]
**Oc P Anth P**... Occasional Papers in Anthropology. Pennsylvania State University [*A publication*]
**OCPCA**...... Oil and Chemical Plant Constructors' Association [*British*]
**Oc P Dev-A**... Occasional Papers. Centre for Developing-Area Studies [*A publication*]
**Oc P Econ H**... Occasional Papers in Economic and Social History [*A publication*]
**OCPED**..... Office de Commercialisation du Poisson d'Eau Douce [*Freshwater Fish Marketing Corp. - FFMC*]
**OCPG**........ Goodwood Data Systems Ltd., Carleton Place, Ontario [*Library symbol*] [*National Library of Canada*] (NLC)
**OCPG**........ Procter & Gamble Co., Cincinnati, OH [*Library symbol*] [*Library of Congress*] (LCLS)
**Oc P Geog**... Occasional Papers in Geography [*A publication*]
**OCPG-I**..... Procter & Gamble Co., Ivorydale Technical Center, Cincinnati, OH [*Library symbol*] [*Library of Congress*] (LCLS)
**OCPG-Mv**... Procter & Gamble Co., Miami Valley Laboratories, Cincinnati, OH [*Library symbol*] [*Library of Congress*] (LCLS)
**OCPG-Sw**... Procter & Gamble Co., Sharon Woods Technical Center, Technical Library, Cincinnati, OH [*Library symbol*] [*Library of Congress*] (LCLS)
**OCPG-Wh**... Procter & Gamble Co., Winton Hill Technical Center, Cincinnati, OH [*Library symbol*] [*Library of Congress*] (LCLS)
**OCPH**........ Providence Hospital, Medical Library, Cincinnati, OH [*Library symbol*] [*Library of Congress*] (LCLS)
**OCPINST**... Office of Civilian Personnel Instruction [*Navy*] (MCD)
**Oc P Int Af**... Occasional Papers in International Affairs [*A publication*]
**OCPL**......... Leigh Instruments Ltd., Carleton Place, Ontario [*Library symbol*] [*National Library of Canada*] (NLC)
**OCPL**......... Onondaga Library System [*Library network*]
**OCPL**......... Orange County Public Library [*Florida*]
**OCPL**......... Overseas Containers Pacific Ltd. (DS)
**OCPLACS**... Ontario Cooperative Program in Latin American and Caribbean Studies [*Research center*] (RCD)
**OCPNA**..... Ortho-Chloro-para-nitroaniline [*Organic chemistry*]
**OCPO**........ Office of Civilian Personnel Operations [*Air Force*]
**OCPO**........ Office of Computer Processing Operations [*Social Security Administration*]
**OCPP**......... Orbiter Cloud Photopolarimeter [*NASA*]
**OCPP**......... (Ortho-Chlorophenoxy)propionic Acid [*Organic chemistry*]
**OCPPIB**.... Orientalia. Commentarii Periodici Pontificii Instituti Biblici [*A publication*]
**OCPR**........ Office of Claims and Payments Requirements [*Social Security Administration*]
**OCPR**........ Office of Collateral Policy Responsibility (AFM)
**Oc P Rur De**... Occasional Papers. Rural Development Committee [*A publication*]
**OCPS**......... I. P. Sharp Associates Ltd., Carleton Place, Ontario [*Library symbol*] [*National Library of Canada*] (NLC)
**OCPS**......... Office Canadien du Poisson Sale [*Canadian Saltfish Corporation*]
**OCPS**......... Office of Census and Population Studies [*British*]
**OCPS**......... Oxygen Cabin Pressurization Section [*NASA*] (KSC)
**OCQ**.......... Oconto, WI [*Location identifier*] [*FAA*] (FAAL)
**OCQ**.......... Oneida Ltd. [*NYSE symbol*] (SPSG)
**OCQM**....... Office of Chief Quartermaster [*Military*]
**OCR**.......... Creemore Public Library, Ontario [*Library symbol*] [*National Library of Canada*] (BIB)
**OCR**.......... Norcross, GA [*Location identifier*] [*FAA*] (FAAL)
**OCR**.......... Occupational Safety and Health Control Report [*Navy*]
**OCR**.......... Occur (FAAC)
**OCR**.......... O'Connell Ranch [*California*] [*Seismograph station code, US Geological Survey*] (SEIS)
**OCR**.......... Oculocardiac Reflex [*Physiology*]
**OCR**.......... Office for Civil Rights [*Department of Education*]
**OCR**.......... Office of Civilian Requirements [*Division of War Production Board*] [*World War II*]
**OCR**.......... Office of Coal Research [*Energy Research and Development Administration*]
**OCR**.......... Office of Collateral Responsibility (AFM)
**OCR**.......... Office of Coordinating Responsibility [*Air Force*]
**OCR**.......... Oil Circuit Recloser
**O Cr**.......... Oklahoma Criminal Reports [*A publication*] (DLA)
**OCR**.......... Omnicare, Inc. [*NYSE symbol*] (SPSG)
**OCR**.......... Operational Change Report [*Military*] (NVT)
**OCR**.......... Operational Control Record [*Nuclear energy*] (NRCH)
**OC & R**...... Operations, Commitments, and Requirements [*Military*]
**OCR**.......... Operations Control Room [*Military*] (CAAL)
**OCR**.......... Optical Character Reader [*Data processing*]
**OCR**.......... Optical Character Recognition [*Data processing*]
**OCR**.......... Optimum Charge Regulator
**OCR**.......... Oracle Resources [*Vancouver Stock Exchange symbol*]
**OCR**.......... Order of Corporate Reunion [*British*]
**OCR**.......... Order of the Crown of Rumania
**OCR**.......... Ordo Reformatorum Cisterciensium [*Cistercians, Trappists*] [*Roman Catholic men's religious order*]
**OCR**.......... Organisation for the Collaboration of Railways [*See also OSShD*] [*Warsaw, Poland*] (EAIO)
**OCR**.......... Organization Change Request
**OCR**.......... Organized Crime and Racketeering Section [*Department of Justice*] (DLA)
**OCR**.......... Output Control Register
**OCR**.......... Overcurrent Relay (MSA)
**OCR**.......... Overhaul Component Requirement [*NASA*] (KSC)
**OCRA**........ Optical Character Recognition - ANSI Standard (Font A) [*Data processing*]
**OCRB**........ Optical Character Recognition - ANSI Standard (Font B) [*Data processing*]
**OCRBI**....... Organization for Cooperation in the Roller Bearings Industry [*Warsaw, Poland*] (EAIO)
**O Cr C**....... Oudh Criminal Cases [*India*] [*A publication*] (DLA)
**OCRD**........ Office, Chief of Research and Development [*Army*]
**OCRE**........ Optical Character Recognition Equipment [*Data processing*] (AABC)
**OC Register**... Orange County Register [*A publication*]
**oCRF**.......... Ovine Corticotrophin Releasing Factor [*Endocrinology*]
**OCRHA**..... Overseas Command Records Holding Area [*Army*]
**OCRI**......... Office Canadien pour un Renouveau Industriel [*Canadian Office for Industrial Revival*]
**OCRM**....... Officer Commanding Royal Marines [*British military*] (DMA)
**OCRM**....... Orbiter Crash and Rescue Manuals [*NASA*] (NASA)
**Ocrotirea Nat**... Ocrotirea Naturii [*A publication*]
**Ocrotirea Nat Med Inconjurator**... Ocrotirea Naturii si a Mediului Inconjurator [*A publication*]
**OCRR**........ Office of the Coordinator, Regulatory Reform [*Canada*]
**OCRS**......... Ontario Centre for Remote Sensing [*Canada*]
**OCRS**......... Organisation Commune des Regions Sahariennes [*Common Organization of the Saharan Regions*]
**OCRS**......... Organized Crime and Racketeering Section [*Department of Justice*]
**OCRSDG**... Crysler Branch, Stormont, Dundas, and Glengarry County Library, Ontario [*Library symbol*] [*National Library of Canada*] (BIB)
**OCRUA**..... Optical Character Recognition Users Association [*Later, RTUA*] (EA)
**OCRW**....... Raymond Walters General and Technical College, Cincinnati, OH [*Library symbol*] [*Library of Congress*] (LCLS)
**OCRWM**... Office of Civilian Radioactive Waste Management [*Oak Ridge National Laboratory*]
**OCS**.......... Cities Service Co., Technical Center - Energy Resources Group, Research Library, Tulsa, OK [*OCLC symbol*] (OCLC)
**OCS**.......... Obstacle [*or Obstruction*] Clearance Surface [*Aviation*] (FAAC)
**OCS**.......... Ocean Culture System
**OCS**.......... Octachlorostyrene [*Organic chemistry*]
**OCS**.......... Octopine Synthase [*An enzyme*]
**OCS**.......... Office, Chief of Staff [*Army*]
**OCS**.......... Office of the Chief Surgeon [*Military*]
**OCS**.......... Office of Civilian Supply [*Division of War Production Board*]
**OCS**.......... Office Cleaning Service [*Commercial firm*] [*British*]
**OCS**.......... Office of Commercial Services [*Department of Commerce*]
**OCS**.......... Office of Communication Systems [*Air Force*]
**OCS**.......... Office of Community Services [*Bureau of Indian Affairs*]
**OCS**.......... Office of Computing Services [*Georgia Institute of Technology*] [*Research center*] (RCD)
**OCS**.......... Office for Consumer Services [*HEW*]

**OCS** .......... Office of Contract Settlement [*Functions transferred to GSA, 1949; now obsolete*]
**OCS** .......... Officer Candidate School [*Military*]
**OCS** .......... Officers' Chief Steward [*Navy*]
**OCS** .......... Offshore Constitutional Settlement [*Australia*]
**OCS** .......... Old Church Slavonic [*Language, etc.*]
**OCS** .......... On-Board Checkout System [*NASA*]
**OCS** .......... Open Canalicular System [*Hematology*]
**OCS** .......... Open-Circuit-Stable
**OCS** .......... Operational Characteristics (NATG)
**OCS** .......... Operations Control System
**OCS** .......... Optical Character Scanner [*Data processing*]
**OCS** .......... Optical Communicator System (MCD)
**OCS** .......... Optical Contact Sensor
**OCS** .......... Optical Contrasting Seeker (MCD)
**OCS** .......... Orbit Computation System (MCD)
**OCS** .......... Orbit Correction Subsystem (NOAA)
**OCS** .......... Order of the Cross Society (EA)
**OC & S** ....... Ordnance Center and School [*Army*] (RDA)
**OCS** .......... Oriental Ceramic Society (EA)
**OCS** .......... Oriental Chair of Solomon [*Freemasonry*]
**OCS** .......... Oriented Cellular Structure
**OCS** .......... Ornithodoros Coriaceus Spirochete [*Entomology*]
**OCS** .......... Outer Continental Shelf
**OCS** .......... Outpatient Clinic Substation [*Veterans Administration*]
**OCS** .......... Output Control Subsystem
**OCS** .......... Overload Control Subsystem [*Telecommunications*] (TEL)
**OCS** .......... Overspeed Control System (AAG)
**OCS** .......... Saint Thomas Institute, Cincinnati, OH [*Library symbol*] [*Library of Congress*] (LCLS)
**OCSA** ........ Office, Chief of Staff, Army
**OC of SA** .... Office, Chief of Staff, Army (AABC)
**OCSA** ........ Outstanding Civilian Service Award
**OCSAA** ...... Official Committee on Service Attaches and Advisers [*British*]
**OCSAB** ...... Office of Contract Settlement Appeal Board [*Abolished, 1952*]
**OCSAB** ...... Outer Continental Shelf Advisory Board [*Marine science*] (MSC)
**OCSAPB** ... Outer Continental Shelf. Environmental Assessment Program. Arctic Project Bulletin [*A publication*]
**OCSAPSB** ... Outer Continental Shelf. Environmental Assessment Program. Arctic Project Special Bulletin [*United States*] [*A publication*]
**OCSB** ......... Outer Continental Shelf. Environmental Assessment Program. Bering Sea - Gulf of Alaska Newsletter [*A publication*]
**OCSC** ......... Outer Continental Shelf Committee [*Congressional committee*] (MSC)
**OCSDG** ..... Stormont, Dundas, and Glengarry County Public Library, Cornwall, Ontario [*Library symbol*] [*National Library of Canada*] (NLC)
**OCSDGL** ... Stormont, Dundas, and Glengarry Law Association, Cornwall, Ontario [*Library symbol*] [*National Library of Canada*] (BIB)
**OCSE** ......... Office of Child Support Enforcement [*Department of Health and Human Services*]
**OCSEA** ...... Outer Continental Shelf Environmental Assessment [*Marine science*] (MSC)
**OCSEAC** ... Outer Continental Shelf Environmental Studies Advisory Commission [*Department of the Interior*] (MSC)
**OCSEAP** ... Outer Continental Shelf Environmental Assessment Program [*Department of Commerce, Department of the Interior*]
**OCSEF** ...... Outer Continental Shelf Events File [*Department of the Interior*] (MSC)
**OCSEP** ...... Outer Continental Shelf Energy Program [*Marine science*] (MSC)
**OCSF** ......... Office Contents Special Form [*Insurance*]
**OCSIGO** .... Office of the Chief Signal Officer
**OCSL** ......... St. Lawrence College [*College Saint-Laurent*], Cornwall, Ontario [*Library symbol*] [*National Library of Canada*] (NLC)
**OCSLA** ...... Outer Continental Shelf Lands Act
**OCSM** ........ Organization of Canadian Symphony Musicians [*See also OMOSC*]
**OCSO** ........ Office of the Chief Signal Officer
**OCSO** ........ Order of Cistercian Nuns of the Strict Observance [*Roman Catholic religious order*]
**OCSO** ........ Order of Cistercians of the Strict Observance [*Trappists*] [*Roman Catholic men's religious order*]
**OCSOT** ..... Overall Combat Systems Operability Test (NVT)
**OCSP** ......... Office of Cued Speech Programs [*Gallaudet College*] [*Research center*] (RCD)
**OC of SptS** ... Office of the Chief of Support Services [*Army*] (AABC)
**OCSPWAR** ... Office of the Chief of Special Warfare [*Army*]
**OCSR** ......... Optical Cable Signal Repeater (MCD)
**OCSR** ......... Serpent River Band Public Library, Cutler, Ontario [*Library symbol*] [*National Library of Canada*] (NLC)
**OCSS** ......... Office of the Chief of Support Services [*Army*]
**OCSSB9** .... Specialist Periodical Reports. Organic Compounds of Sulphur, Selenium, and Tellurium [*A publication*]
**OCST** ......... Overcast (AABC)
**OCStFH** .... Saint Francis/Saint George Hospital, Cincinnati, OH [*Library symbol*] [*Library of Congress*] (LCLS)
**OCStG** ....... Saint Gregory Seminary, Cincinnati, OH [*Library symbol*] [*Library of Congress*] (LCLS)
**OCSTL** ...... On-Board Checkout System Test Language [*NASA*] (KSC)
**OCT** .......... Cincinnati Technical College, Cincinnati, OH [*Library symbol*] [*Library of Congress*] [*OCLC symbol*] (LCLS)
**OCT** .......... Octagon (AAG)
**OCT** .......... Octal [*Number system with a base of eight*] [*Data processing*] (CET)
**OCT** .......... Octane (AAG)
**Oct** ............ Octanus [*Constellation*]
**OCT** .......... Octarius [*Pint*] [*Pharmacy*]
**OCT** .......... Octave (ADA)
**OCT** .......... Octavo [*Book from 20 to 25 centimeters in height*] [*Bibliography*]
**OCT** .......... October (EY)
**OCT** .......... Octuple (MSA)
**OCT** .......... Office, Chief of Transportation [*Army*]
**OC of T** ...... Office, Chief of Transportation [*Army*]
**OCT** .......... Office of Critical Tables [*NAS-NRC*]
**OCT** .......... Officer Candidate Test [*Army*]
**OCT** .......... Officer Classification Test
**OCT** .......... Operational Climatic Testing (MCD)
**OCT** .......... Operational Cycle Time
**OCT** .......... Operations Control Team [*Deep Space Network, NASA*]
**OCT** .......... Optical Contract Seeker (MCD)
**OCT** .......... Optimal Control Theory
**OCT** .......... Optimal Cutting Temperature [*Material for tissue fixation*]
**OCT** .......... Orbital Circularization Technique
**OCT** .......... Organisation Communiste des Travailleurs [*Communist Organization of Workers*] [*France*] [*Political party*] (PPW)
**OCT** .......... Ornithine Carbamoyltransferase [*Also, OTC*] [*An enzyme*]
**OCT** .......... Ortho-Chlorotoluene [*Organic chemistry*]
**OCT** .......... Overseas Countries and Territories [*Common Market*]
**OCT** .......... Oxford Classical Texts [*A publication*] (OCD)
**OCT** .......... Oxytocin Challenge Test [*Medicine*]
**OCTA** ........ Octanucleotide [*Biochemistry*]
**OCTA** ........ Octapentadiene [*Toxic chemical*]
**OCTA** ........ On-Line Corporation Tax Assessment [*British*]
**OCTA** ........ Ortho-Cyclohexanediaminetetraacetic Acid [*Also, DCTA*] [*Organic chemistry*]
**OCTA** ........ Outsized Cargo Tanker Aircraft
**Octagon Pap** ... Octagon Papers [*A publication*]
**OCTAHDR** ... Octahedral
**OCTANE** .. Operations Control Technique for Actuals Number Extraction (MCD)
**OCTAP** ...... Of Concern to Air Passengers [*Group affiliated with PATCO*] (EA)
**OCTB** ........ Oxford Church Textbooks [*A publication*]
**OCTD** ........ Ornithine Carbamoyltransferase Deficiency [*Medicine*]
**OCTD** ........ Other Connective Tissue Diseases [*Medicine*]
**OCTG** ........ Oil Country Tubular Goods [*Metal industry*]
**OCTH** ........ Town of Haldimand Public Libraries, Caledonia, Ontario [*Library symbol*] [*National Library of Canada*] (NLC)
**OCTHB** ..... Office, Chief of Transportation, Historical Branch [*Army*]
**OCTI** ......... Office Central des Transports Internationaux par Chemins de Fer [*Central Office for International Railway Transport*] (EAIO)
**OCTI** ......... Ordnance Corps Technical Instruction
**OCTL** ........ Octel Communications Corp. [*NASDAQ symbol*] (NQ)
**OCTL** ........ Open-Circuited Transmission Line
**OCTLA** ...... Out of Control Area [*Aviation*] (FAAC)
**Octn** .......... Octanus [*Constellation*]
**OCTO** ........ October Oil Co. [*NASDAQ symbol*] (NQ)
**OCTR** ........ Octoraro Railway, Inc. [*AAR code*]
**O/CTR** ....... Over Center [*Automotive engineering*]
**OCT/RR** .... Off Course Target/Remote Reference Display (NG)
**OCTS** ......... Optical Cable Transmission System (MCD)
**Oct Str** ....... Octavo Strange [*Strange's Select Cases on Evidence*] [*A publication*] (DLA)
**OCTU** ........ Officer Cadet Training Unit [*Military*] [*British*]
**OCTV** ........ Open-Circuit Television
**OCU** .......... Oceanroutes, Inc., Palo Alto, CA [*OCLC symbol*] (OCLC)
**OCU** .......... Oklahoma City University
**OCU** .......... Operational Control Unit
**OCU** .......... Operational Conversion Unit (NATG)
**OCU** .......... Order of Christian Unity [*British*]
**OCU** .......... Orderwire Operator Control Unit (MCD)
**OCU** .......... University of Cincinnati, Cincinnati, OH [*Library symbol*] [*Library of Congress*] (LCLS)
**OCU-B** ....... University of Cincinnati, Biology Library, Cincinnati, OH [*Library symbol*] [*Library of Congress*] (LCLS)
**OCUC** ........ Oxford and Cambridge Universities Club [*British*] (DAS)
**OCU-DA** ... University of Cincinnati, Design, Architecture, and Art Library, Cincinnati, OH [*Library symbol*] [*Library of Congress*] (LCLS)
**OCU-E** ....... University of Cincinnati, Engineering Library, Cincinnati, OH [*Library symbol*] [*Library of Congress*] (LCLS)
**OCUG** ........ Union Gas Ltd., Chatham, Ontario [*Library symbol*] [*National Library of Canada*] (NLC)

**OCUG**........ Union Graduate School, Cincinnati, OH [*Library symbol*] [*Library of Congress*] (LCLS)
**OCU-Geo**... University of Cincinnati, Geology-Geography Library, Cincinnati, OH [*Library symbol*] [*Library of Congress*] (LCLS)
**OCUL**........ Oculo [*To the Eye*] [*Pharmacy*]
**OCU-L**....... University of Cincinnati, Law Library, Cincinnati, OH [*Library symbol*] [*Library of Congress*] (LCLS)
**OCULENT** ... Oculentum [*Eye Ointment*] [*Pharmacy*]
**Ocul Ther Complications Manage** ... Ocular Therapy. Complications and Management [*A publication*]
**OCU-M** ..... University of Cincinnati, School of Medicine, Cincinnati, OH [*Library symbol*] [*Library of Congress*] (LCLS)
**OCU-Math** ... University of Cincinnati, Mathematics Library, Cincinnati, OH [*Library symbol*] [*Library of Congress*] (LCLS)
**OCU-Mu** ... University of Cincinnati, College Conservatory of Music, Cincinnati, OH [*Library symbol*] [*Library of Congress*] (LCLS)
**OCU-N** ...... University of Cincinnati, College of Nursing, Cincinnati, OH [*Library symbol*] [*Library of Congress*] (LCLS)
**OCU-Ph**..... University of Cincinnati, Physics Library, Cincinnati, OH [*Library symbol*] [*Library of Congress*] (LCLS)
**OCUS** ........ Oblate Conference of the United States (EA)
**OCUSI**....... United States Industrial Chemicals Co., Research Center Library, Cincinnati, OH [*Library symbol*] [*Library of Congress*] (LCLS)
**OCV**........... Bering Sea, AK [*Location identifier*] [*FAA*] (FAAL)
**OCV**........... Ocana [*Colombia*] [*Airport symbol*] (OAG)
**OCV**........... Oil Check Valve
**OCV**........... Old Aircraft Carrier [*Navy symbol*]
**OCV**........... Open-Circuit Voltage
**OCV**........... Opimian California Vineyards Corp. [*Toronto Stock Exchange symbol*]
**OCV**........... Ordinary Conversational Voice [*Medicine*]
**OCV**........... Ordre des Chevaliers du Verseau [*Knights of Aquarius Order*] (EAIO)
**OCV**........... Overriding Cam Valve
**OCV**........... United States Veterans Administration Hospital, Cincinnati, OH [*Library symbol*] [*Library of Congress*] (LCLS)
**OCVD**......... Open-Circuit Voltage Decay [*In silicon devices*]
**OCVRA** ...... Overseas Citizens Voting Rights Act
**OCW**.......... Oklahoma College for Women
**OCW**.......... Washington, NC [*Location identifier*] [*FAA*] (FAAL)
**OCW**.......... Waterloo Regional Library, Waterloo, Ontario [*Library symbol*] [*National Library of Canada*] (NLC)
**OCWCIB**... Organizing Committee of the World Congress on Implantology and Bio-Materials [*See also COCMIB*] [*Rouen, France*] (EAIO)
**OCWCT** .... West Carleton Township Public Library, Carp, Ontario [*Library symbol*] [*National Library of Canada*] (BIB)
**OCWFLU** ... Operative Coachmakers' and Wheelwrights' Federal Labour Union [*British*]
**OCX**........... Onex Corp. [*Toronto Stock Exchange symbol*]
**OCX**........... Xavier University, Cincinnati, OH [*Library symbol*] [*Library of Congress*] (LCLS)
**OCXO**........ Oven-Controlled Crystal Oscillator
**OCY**........... Young Men's Mercantile Library Association, Cincinnati, OH [*Library symbol*] [*Library of Congress*] (LCLS)
**OCZ**........... Lincoln, NE [*Location identifier*] [*FAA*] (FAAL)
**OCZM**....... Office of Coastal Zone Management [*National Oceanic and Atmospheric Administration*]
**OD** ............ Aerovias Condor de Colombia Ltda. (AEROCONDOR) [*Colombia*] [*ICAO designator*] (ICDA)
**OD** ............ Delaware County District Library, Delaware, OH [*Library symbol*] [*Library of Congress*] (LCLS)
**OD** ............ Doctor of Optometry
**OD** ............ Dundas Public Library, Ontario [*Library symbol*] [*National Library of Canada*] (NLC)
**OD** ............ Lebanon [*Aircraft nationality and registration mark*] (FAAC)
**OD** ............ Obiter Dicta [*Latin*] [*Legal term*] (DLA)
**OD** ............ Observable Difference
**OD** ............ Observed Drift
**OD** ............ Occupational Disease
**OD** ............ Oceanographic Datastation [*Telecommunications*] (TEL)
**OD** ............ Octal-to-Decimal [*Data processing*] (BUR)
**OD** ............ Ocular Density [*Ophthalmology*]
**OD** ............ Ocular Dominance [*Opthalmology*]
**OD** ............ Oculus Dexter [*Right Eye*] [*Ophthalmology*]
**Od** ............ Odeon [*Record label*] [*Europe, etc.*]
**Od** ............ Odericus [*Flourished, 1166-1200*] [*Authority cited in pre-1607 legal work*] (DSA)
**Od** ............ Odofredus [*Deceased, 1265*] [*Authority cited in pre-1607 legal work*] (DSA)
**Od** ............ Odrodzenie [*A publication*]
**Od** ............ Odyssey [*of Homer*] [*Classical studies*] (OCD)
**OD** ............ Office Decision [*United States Internal Revenue Bureau*] [*A publication*] (DLA)
**OD** ............ Office of the Director
**OD** ............ Officer of the Day [*or Deck*] [*Also, OOD*] [*Navy*]
**OD** ............ Ohio Decisions [*A publication*] (DLA)
**OD** ............ Ohne Dividende [*Without Dividend*] [*German*]
**OD** ............ Oil Desurger
**OD** ............ Oil Drainage
**OD** ............ Old Dutch [*Language, etc.*]
**OD** ............ Olive Drab [*Color often used for military clothing and equipment*]
**OD** ............ Omnes Dies [*Every Day*] [*Pharmacy*]
**O/D**........... On Deck (KSC)
**OD** ............ On Demand [*Business term*]
**O/D**........... On Dock (MCD)
**OD** ............ On Duty
**OD** ............ Onrechtmatige Daad [*Tort or Tortious Act*] [*Netherlands*] (ILCA)
**OD** ............ Open Drop
**OD** ............ Operational Downlink/Downlist (NASA)
**OD** ............ Operations Directive [*or Director*]
**OD** ............ Operations Division
**OD** ............ Optical Density
**OD** ............ Opus Dei (EA)
**OD** ............ Orbit Determination
**OD** ............ Orbiter Operational Downlink (MCD)
**OD** ............ Order of Daedalians (EA)
**OD** ............ Order of DeMolay (EA)
**O/D**........... Order of Deportation
**OD** ............ Order Dienst [*Netherlands first organized resistance group, 1940*] [*World War II*]
**OD** ............ Ordinary Seaman [*British*] (DMA)
**OD** ............ Ordnance Data [*Inspection and test data*]
**OD** ............ Ordnance Department [*or Division*]
**OD** ............ Ordnance Document [*Navy*]
**OD** ............ Ordnance Drawing
**OD** ............ Ordnungsdienst [*Military Police Service*] [*German military - World War II*]
**OD** ............ Organization Development
**OD** ............ Origin and Destination [*Aviation*] (AFM)
**O & D**........ Origin and Destination [*Aviation*]
**OD** ............ Original Design
**OD** ............ Original Dirac [*Vacuum model*] [*Physics*]
**OD** ............ Originally Derived
**OD** ............ Osseous Defect [*Medicine*]
**OD** ............ Other Denomination [*British military*] (DMA)
**OD** ............ Out-of-Date
**OD** ............ Output Data (IEEE)
**OD** ............ Output Disable
**OD** ............ Outside Diameter
**OD** ............ Outside Dimension
**OD** ............ Oven Dry
**OD** ............ Overdose [*of narcotics*]
**OD** ............ Overdraft [*or Overdrawn*] [*Banking*]
**OD** ............ Overdrive (AAG)
**Od** ............ Overdue
**OD** ............ Overload Detection [*Telecommunications*] (TEL)
**OD** ............ Overtly Diabetic [*Medicine*]
**OD** ............ Oxygen Drain (MCD)
**OD3**........... Optical Digital Data Disk
**ODa** .......... Dayton and Montgomery County Public Library, Dayton, OH [*Library symbol*] [*Library of Congress*] (LCLS)
**ODA** .......... Octal Debugging Aid [*Data processing*]
**ODA** .......... Office of Debt [*or Depreciation*] Analysis [*Department of the Treasury*]
**ODA** .......... Office of the Defense Attache [*Foreign Service*]
**ODA** .......... Office Document Architecture [*Telecommunications*] (TSSD)
**ODA** .......... Official Development Aid [*or Assistance*]
**ODA** .......... Omnidirectional Antenna
**ODA** .......... Operational Data Analysis
**ODA** .......... Operational Design and Analysis (IEEE)
**ODA** .......... Optical Diffraction Analysis [*Microscopy*]
**ODA** .......... Oscillating Doublet Antenna
**ODA** .......... Other Design Activity (MSA)
**ODA** .......... Overseas Development Administration [*London, England*] (EAIO)
**ODA** .......... Overseas Development Agency [*British*]
**ODA** .......... Overseas Doctors Association in the United Kingdom [*British*]
**ODA** .......... Oxydianiline [*Organic chemistry*]
**ODAA**......... Aden/International [*People's Democratic Republic of Yemen*] [*ICAO location identifier*] (ICLI)
**ODaA**......... Dayton Art Institute, Dayton, OH [*Library symbol*] [*Library of Congress*] (LCLS)
**ODAA**......... Office of Dependent Area Affairs [*Department of State*]
**ODAB**......... Beihan [*People's Democratic Republic of Yemen*] [*ICAO location identifier*] (ICLI)
**ODAC**......... On Demand Analyzer Computer
**ODACA**...... Original Doll Artists Council of America (EA)
**ODaCox**..... Cox Coronary Heart Institute, Dayton, OH [*Library symbol*] [*Library of Congress*] (LCLS)
**ODaE**......... Engineers' Club of Dayton, Dayton, OH [*Library symbol*] [*Library of Congress*] (LCLS)
**ODAF**......... Aden [*People's Democratic Republic of Yemen*] [*ICAO location identifier*] (ICLI)
**ODAG**......... Al-Gheida [*People's Democratic Republic of Yemen*] [*ICAO location identifier*] (ICLI)

**ODaGH**..... Grandview Hospital, Dayton, OH [*Library symbol*] [*Library of Congress*] (LCLS)
**ODaGL**...... Church of Jesus Christ of Latter-Day Saints, Genealogical Society Library, Dayton Ohio Branch, Dayton, OH [*Library symbol*] [*Library of Congress*] (LCLS)
**ODaGMI**... General Motors Corp., Inland Manufacturing Division, Engineering Library, Dayton, OH [*Library symbol*] [*Library of Congress*] (LCLS)
**ODaGS**...... Good Samaritan Hospital, Dayton, OH [*Library symbol*] [*Library of Congress*] (LCLS)
**ODALC**..... Ogden Air Logistics Center (MCD)
**ODALE**..... Office of Drug Abuse Law Enforcement [*Later, Drug Enforcement Administration*] [*Department of Justice*]
**ODALS**...... Omnidirectional Approach Lighting System [*Aviation*] (FAAC)
**ODAM**....... Mukeiras [*People's Democratic Republic of Yemen*] [*ICAO location identifier*] (ICLI)
**ODaMC**..... Barney Children's Medical Center, Dayton, OH [*Library symbol*] [*Library of Congress*] (LCLS)
**ODaMCo**... Mead Corp., Dayton, OH [*Library symbol*] [*Library of Congress*] (LCLS)
**ODaMNH**... Dayton Museum of Natural History, Dayton, OH [*Library symbol*] [*Library of Congress*] (LCLS)
**ODaMR**..... Monsanto Research Corp., Dayton Laboratory, Dayton, OH [*Library symbol*] [*Library of Congress*] (LCLS)
**ODaMVH**... Miami Valley Hospital, Dayton, OH [*Library symbol*] [*Library of Congress*] (LCLS)
**ODAN**....... Kamaran [*People's Democratic Republic of Yemen*] [*ICAO location identifier*] (ICLI)
**ODaN**........ National Cash Register Co., NCR Library, Dayton, OH [*Library symbol*] [*Library of Congress*] (LCLS)
**ODAN**....... Old Danish [*Language, etc.*]
**ODaNR**...... North Research Stillwater Pioneers, Dayton, OH [*Library symbol*] [*Library of Congress*] (LCLS)
**ODaNT**...... National Cash Register Co., Technical Library, Dayton, OH [*Library symbol*] [*Library of Congress*] (LCLS)
**O-DAP**....... Oncovin [*Vincristine*], Dianhydrogalactitol, Adriamycin, Platinol [*Cisplatin*] [*Antineoplastic drug regimen*]
**ODAP**........ Perim [*People's Democratic Republic of Yemen*] [*ICAO location identifier*] (ICLI)
**ODAPS**...... Oceanic Display and Planning System [*Air traffic control*]
**ODAQ**....... Qishn [*People's Democratic Republic of Yemen*] [*ICAO location identifier*] (ICLI)
**ODAR**........ Riyan [*People's Democratic Republic of Yemen*] [*ICAO location identifier*] (ICLI)
**ODAS**........ Ocean Data Acquisition Systems
**ODAS**........ Ocean Dynamics Advisory Subcommittee [*NASA*] (MSC)
**ODAS**........ Oral Deaf Adults Section [*Later, OHIS*] (EA)
**ODAS**........ Socotra [*People's Democratic Republic of Yemen*] [*ICAO location identifier*] (ICLI)
**ODaSC**...... Sinclair Community College, Dayton, OH [*Library symbol*] [*Library of Congress*] (LCLS)
**ODASD**..... Office of the Deputy Assistant Secretary of Defense
**ODaSR**...... Standard Register Co., Engineering and Research Library, Dayton, OH [*Library symbol*] [*Library of Congress*] (LCLS)
**ODaStE**..... Saint Elizabeth Hospital, Dayton, OH [*Library symbol*] [*Library of Congress*] (LCLS)
**ODaStL**..... Saint Leonard College, Dayton, OH [*Library symbol*] [*Library of Congress*] (LCLS)
**ODAT**........ Ataq [*People's Democratic Republic of Yemen*] [*ICAO location identifier*] (ICLI)
**ODaTS**...... United Theological Seminary, Dayton, OH [*Library symbol*] [*Library of Congress*] (LCLS)
**ODaU**........ University of Dayton, Dayton, OH [*Library symbol*] [*Library of Congress*] (LCLS)
**ODaU-L**..... University of Dayton, Law Library, Dayton, OH [*Library symbol*] [*Library of Congress*] (LCLS)
**ODaUM**.... United Methodist Church, Commission on Archives and History, Dayton, OH [*Library symbol*] [*Library of Congress*] (LCLS)
**ODaU-M**... University of Dayton, Marian Library, Dayton, OH [*Library symbol*] [*Library of Congress*] (LCLS)
**ODaV**......... United States Veterans Administration Center, Library Services, Dayton, OH [*Library symbol*] [*Library of Congress*] (LCLS)
**ODaWU**.... Wright State University, Dayton, OH [*Library symbol*] [*Library of Congress*] (LCLS)
**ODaWU-H**... Wright State University, School of Medicine, Fordham Library, Dayton, OH [*Library symbol*] [*Library of Congress*] (LCLS)
**ODaWU-W**... Wright State University, Western Ohio Branch Campus, Celina, OH [*Library symbol*] [*Library of Congress*] (LCLS)
**ODB**.......... Cordoba [*Spain*] [*Airport symbol*] (OAG)
**ODB**.......... Ocean Data Buoy [*Marine science*] (MSC)
**ODB**.......... Odontoblast
**ODB**.......... Office of Dependency Benefits
**ODB**.......... Oil-Degrading Bacteria
**ODB**.......... Operational Data Book [*NASA*] (KSC)
**ODB**.......... Opiate-Directed Behavior
**ODB**.......... Output Data Buffer
**ODB**.......... Output to Display Buffer [*Data processing*]
**ODB**.......... Oven Dry Basis
**ODB**.......... Overseas Development Bank [*Investors' Overseas Services*]
**ODB**.......... Oxydibenzil [*Organic chemistry*]
**ODBA**........ Ocean Dumping Ban Act [*1988*]
**O'D & Br Eq Dig**... O'Donnell and Brady's Irish Equity Digest [*A publication*] (DLA)
**ODC**.......... Oceanographic Data Center (MCD)
**ODC**.......... Odometer Data Computer [*Developed by Mileage Validator, Inc.*]
**ODC**.......... Office of Deputy Chief of Staff Programs and Resources [*Air Force*]
**ODC**.......... Officer Data Card
**ODC**.......... Ohio Dominican College, Columbus, OH [*OCLC symbol*] (OCLC)
**ODC**.......... Oligodendrocyte [*Also, OLG*] [*Cytology*]
**ODC**.......... Online Data Capture
**ODC**.......... Operation Design Criteria (MCD)
**ODC**.......... Operational Data Center [*Deep Space Network, NASA*]
**ODC**.......... Operational Document Control
**ODC**.......... Orbital Data Collector
**ODC**.......... Order of Discalced Carmelites [*Roman Catholic religious order*]
**ODC**.......... Ordinary Decent Criminal [*British prison slang for other than a political prisoner*]
**ODC**.......... Organization Development Council [*Defunct*] (EA)
**ODC**.......... Original Design Cutoff (AAG)
**ODC**.......... Ornithine Decarboxylase [*An enzyme*]
**ODC**.......... Oscilloscope Digital Control
**ODC**.......... Other Direct Costs [*Accounting*]
**ODC**.......... Output Data Control
**ODC**.......... Overseas Development Council (EA)
**ODC**.......... Oxford Decimal Classification
**ODC**.......... Ozone-Depleting Compound [*Environmental chemistry*]
**ODCA**........ Ocean Dumping Control Act [*Canada*] (MSC)
**ODCA**........ Organizacion Democrata Cristiana de America [*Christian Democratic Organization of America - CDOA*] [*Caracas, Venezuela*]
**ODCC**........ Ohio Decisions, Circuit Court [*Properly cited Ohio Circuit Decisions*] [*A publication*] (DLA)
**ODCC**........ On-Board Digital Computer Control
**ODCC**........ One-Design Class Council (EA)
**ODCC**........ Oxford Dictionary of the Christian Church
**ODCC**........ United States One-Design Class Council (EA)
**ODCM**....... Off-Site Dose Calculation Manual [*Nuclear energy*] (NRCH)
**ODCM**....... Office of Defense and Civilian Mobilization [*See also OCDM*] (MUGU)
**ODCP**........ One-Digit Code Point [*Telecommunications*] (TEL)
**ODCPC**..... Order of Descendants of Colonial Physicians and Chirurgiens (EA)
**ODCR**........ Officer Distribution Control Report [*Navy*] (NG)
**ODCS**........ Office of the Deputy Chief of Staff [*World War II*]
**ODC of S**... Office of the Deputy Chief of Staff [*World War II*]
**ODCSCD**... Office of the Deputy Chief of Staff, Combat Developments [*Army*]
**ODCSI**....... Office of the Deputy Chief of Staff for Intelligence
**ODCSLOG**... Office of the Deputy Chief of Staff for Logistics [*Army*] (AABC)
**ODCSO**..... Office of Data Collection and Survey Operations [*Bureau of Labor Statistics*]
**ODCSOPS**... Office of the Deputy Chief of Staff for Military Operations and Plans [*Army*]
**ODCSOPS**... Office of the Deputy Chief of Staff for Operations and Plans [*Army*]
**ODCSPER**... Office of the Deputy Chief of Staff for Personnel [*Army*]
**ODCSRDA**... Office of the Deputy Chief of Staff for Research, Development, and Acquisition [*Army*] (AABC)
**ODD**.......... Obsessive-Deductive Disorder [*Facetious term for a malady affecting some taxpayers*]
**ODD**.......... Obstacle Detection Device
**ODD**.......... Offboard Deception Device [*Navy*] (CAAL)
**ODD**.......... Old Destroyer [*Navy symbol*]
**ODD**.......... Oodnadatta [*Australia*] [*Airport symbol*] (OAG)
**ODD**.......... Operator Distance Dialing
**ODD**.......... Optical Data Digitizer [*Data processing*]
**ODD**.......... Optical Digital Data Disk
**ODD**.......... Organizing District Delegate [*British labor*]
**ODD**.......... Ouchterlony Double Diffusion Test [*Immunogel assay*]
**ODDA**....... Office of Deputy Director for Administration [*Marshall Space Flight Center*] (KSC)
**ODDD**....... Optical Digital Data Disk
**ODDH**....... On-Board Digital Data Handling
**ODDP**....... Office of the Director of Development Planning [*Air Force*] (MCD)
**ODDRD**..... Office of Deputy Director for Research and Development [*Marshall Space Flight Center*] (KSC)
**ODDR & E**... Office of the Director of Defense Research and Engineering [*Later, Office of the Under Secretary of Defense for Research and Engineering*] [*Army*]
**ODDRE**..... Office of the Director of Defense Research and Engineering [*Later, Office of the Under Secretary of Defense for Research and Engineering*] [*Army*]
**ODDS**....... Oceanographic Digital Data System [*Navy*]

**ODDS**........ Online Data Entry and Display System [*Job Service*] (OICC)
**ODDS**........ Operational Data Delivery Services (MCD)
**ODDS**........ Optional Delivery Dispenser System (MCD)
**ODE**........... Delhi Public Library, Ontario [*Library symbol*] [*National Library of Canada*] (NLC)
**ODE**........... Odense [*Denmark*] [*Airport symbol*] (OAG)
**ODE**........... Odessa [*USSR*] [*Geomagnetic observatory code*]
**ODE**........... Omicron Delta Epsilon [*Fraternity*]
**ODE**........... Online Data Entry (ADA)
**ODE**........... Optical Designation Evaluation (MCD)
**ODE**........... Optimally Designed Experiments
**ODE**........... Orbit Data Editor Assembly [*Space Flight Operations Facility, NASA*]
**ODE**........... Ordinary Differential Equation [*Mathematics*]
**ODE**........... Ortho-Demethylencainide [*Biochemistry*]
**ODEAG**..... Research Station, Agriculture Canada [*Station de Recherches, Agriculture Canada*] Delhi, Ontario [*Library symbol*] [*National Library of Canada*] (NLC)
**O'Dea Med Exp** ... O'Dea's Medical Experts [*A publication*] (DLA)
**ODECA**..... Organizacion de los Estados Centroamericanos [*Organization of Central American States - OCAS*] [*San Salvador, El Salvador*] (EAIO)
**ODECABE** ... Organizacion Deportiva Centroamericana y del Caribe [*Central American and Caribbean Sports Organization*] (EAIO)
**O Dec Rep** ... Ohio Decisions Reprint [*A publication*] (DLA)
**ODEE**........ [*The*] Oxford Dictionary of English Etymology [*A publication*]
**ODef**.......... Defiance Public Library, Defiance, OH [*Library symbol*] [*Library of Congress*] (LCLS)
**ODefC**........ Defiance College, Defiance, OH [*Library symbol*] [*Library of Congress*] (LCLS)
**ODelp**........ Delphos Public Library, Delphos, OH [*Library symbol*] [*Library of Congress*] (LCLS)
**OD-ENDOR** ... Optically Detected Electron Nuclear Double Resonance [*Spectroscopy*]
**Odeneal**...... Odeneal's Reports [*9-11 Oregon*] [*A publication*] (DLA)
**ODEP**........ Office Depot, Inc. [*NASDAQ symbol*] (NQ)
**ODEPA**..... Organizacion Deportiva Panamericana [*Pan American Sports Organization - PASO*] [*Mexico City, Mexico*] (EAIO)
**ODEPA**..... Oxapentamethylenediethylenephosphoramide [*Pharmacology*]
**O Dep Rep** ... Ohio Department Reports [*A publication*] (DLA)
**Oderi**.......... Odericus [*Flourished, 1166-1200*] [*Authority cited in pre-1607 legal work*] (DSA)
**ODES**........ Deseronto Public Library, Ontario [*Library symbol*] [*National Library of Canada*] (NLC)
**ODES**........ Optical Discrimination Evaluation Study [*NASA*] (NASA)
**OD-ESR**..... Optically Detected Electron Spin Resonance [*Spectroscopy*]
**ODESSA**... Ocean Data Environmental Science Services Acquisition [*Buoy*]
**ODESSA**... Organisation der Ehemaligen Schutzstaffel Angehoeriggen [*Organization of Former Members of the Elite Guard*] [*Founded after World War II to smuggle war criminals out of Germany and provide them with false identities*]
**ODESUR**... Organizacion Deportiva Sudamericana [*An association*] (EAIO)
**ODESY**...... Online Data Entry System [*Burroughs Corp.*]
**Odf**............ Odofredus [*Deceased, 1265*] [*Authority cited in pre-1607 legal work*] (DSA)
**ODF**........... One-Dimension Flow
**ODF**........... Opacity Distribution Function [*Spectroscopy*]
**ODF**........... Optimal Decision Function
**ODF**........... Orbit Determination Facility (MCD)
**ODF**........... Orientation Distribution Function
**ODF**........... Output Data File
**ODFFU**..... Organization for Defense of Four Freedoms for Ukraine (EA)
**ODFI**......... Open Die Forging Institute (EA)
**ODFR**........ Oxygen-Derived Free Radicals [*Biochemistry*]
**ODFW**....... Oregon Department of Fish and Wildlife Research and Development Section [*Oregon State University*] [*Research center*] (RCD)
**ODG**.......... Enid, OK [*Location identifier*] [*FAA*] (FAAL)
**ODG**.......... Offline Data Generator
**ODG**.......... Operational Data Group (MCD)
**ODG**.......... Operational Design Group
**ODG**.......... Orbit Data Generator [*NASA*]
**Odgers**....... Odgers on Libel and Slander [*A publication*] (DLA)
**ODGF**........ Osteosarcoma-Derived Growth Factor [*Biochemistry*]
**ODGKA**..... Oita Daigaku Gakugeigakubu Kenkyu Kiyo. Shizenkagaku [*A publication*]
**Odg Lib**...... Odgers on Libel and Slander [*A publication*] (DLA)
**Odg Pl**........ Odgers on Principles of Pleading [*20th ed.*] [*1975*] [*A publication*] (DLA)
**ODGSE**..... Operational Development Ground Support Equipment (AAG)
**ODGSO**..... Office of Domestic Gold and Silver Operations [*Department of the Treasury*]
**ODH**.......... Highland Secondary School, Dundas, Ontario [*Library symbol*] [*National Library of Canada*] (NLC)
**ODH**.......... Octanol Dehydrogenase [*An enzyme*]
**ODH**.......... Octopine Dehydrogenase [*An enzyme*]
**ODHS**........ Dundas Historical Society Museum, Ontario [*Library symbol*] [*National Library of Canada*] (BIB)
**ODHT**....... Hagerman Township Public Library, Ontario [*Library symbol*] [*National Library of Canada*] (NLC)
**ODHWS**.... Office of Defense Health and Welfare Services [*World War II*]
**ODI**........... Nodine, MN [*Location identifier*] [*FAA*] (FAAL)
**ODI**........... Odin Industry Ltd. [*Vancouver Stock Exchange symbol*]
**ODI**........... Office of Director of Intelligence [*Military*]
**ODI**........... Office Document Index
**ODI**........... Open Door International for the Economic Emancipation of the Woman Worker [*Brussels, Belgium*] (EAIO)
**ODI**........... Optical Digital Imagery
**ODI**........... Overseas Development Institute (EA)
**ODIC**......... Outside Diameter of Inner Conductor
**ODID**......... Office of the Director of Industrial Demobilization
**ODIFF**....... Oil Differential
**ODIN**......... Online Dakota Information Network [*Information service or system*] (EISS)
**ODIN**......... Online Dokumentations- und Informationsverbund [*Online Documentation and Information Affiliation*]
**ODIN**......... Operational Display Information Network (MCD)
**ODIN**......... Optimal [*or Orbital*] Design Integration [*Computer program*]
**ODI (Overseas Development Inst) R** ... ODI (Overseas Development Institute). Review [*A publication*]
**ODIRP**....... Office, Director of Personnel [*Air Force*]
**ODIS**......... Ocean Dynamics Information System [*Marine science*] (MSC)
**ODIS**......... Optical Disk Interface System [*Data processing*]
**ODIS**......... Orbital Design Integration System
**ODIS**......... Origin Destination Information System [*US Postal Service*]
**ODISTA**.... Oceanographic Data in Subtrial Areas
**ODIZA**...... Osaka Daigaku Igaku Zasshi [*A publication*]
**ODJB**......... Original Dixieland Jazz Band
**Odjel Teh Nauka** ... Odjeljenje Tehnickih Nauka [*Sarajevo*] [*A publication*]
**ODJS**......... Office of the Director, Joint Staff (MCD)
**ODK**........... Kodiak, AK [*Location identifier*] [*FAA*] (FAAL)
**ODK**........... Omicron Delta Kappa [*Fraternity*]
**ODL**........... Office of Defense Lending [*Department of the Treasury*]
**ODL**........... Office of the Duchy of Lancaster [*British*]
**ODL**........... Officer Deficiency Letter [*Navy*] (NVT)
**ODL**........... Ostwald Dilution Law [*Chemistry*]
**ODL**........... University of Dayton, Law Library, Dayton, OH [*OCLC symbol*] (OCLC)
**ODLAMP** ... One-Dimensional LASER and Mixing Program
**ODLB**......... Dwight Branch, Lake Of Bays Township Public Library, Ontario [*Library symbol*] [*National Library of Canada*] (BIB)
**ODLI**......... Open Data Link Interface [*Data processing*]
**ODLRO**..... Off-Diagonal Long-Range Order [*Physics*]
**ODM**......... Methodist Theological School in Ohio, Delaware, OH [*Library symbol*] [*Library of Congress*] (LCLS)
**ODM**......... Office of Defense Mobilization [*Transferred to Office of Defense and Civilian Mobilization, 1958*]
**ODM**......... Oil Debris Monitor
**ODM**......... One Day Mission [*NASA*] (KSC)
**ODM**......... Operational Data Management (KSC)
**ODM**......... Operational Development Memorandum (AAG)
**ODM**......... Operations Data Message (MCD)
**ODM**......... Optical Diffractogram
**ODM**......... Optical Display Memory [*Data processing*]
**ODM**......... Orbital Determination Module
**ODM**......... Outboard Data Manager [*Data processing*] (BUR)
**ODM**......... Overseas Development Ministry [*British*]
**ODMA**....... Office of the Director of Military Assistance [*Air Force*] (AFM)
**ODMC**....... Office for Dependents' Medical Care [*Army*] (AABC)
**OD and MC** ... Operational Direction and Management Control (NATG)
**ODMD**...... Delcan, Don Mills, Ontario [*Library symbol*] [*National Library of Canada*] (NLC)
**ODMF**....... Ortho-Demethylfortimicin [*Biochemistry*]
**ODMIBM** ... IBM Canada Ltd., Don Mills, Ontario [*Library symbol*] [*National Library of Canada*] (NLC)
**ODMN**...... National Research Council, Don Mills, Ontario [*Library symbol*] [*National Library of Canada*] (NLC)
**ODMO**...... Office of Defense Management and Organization [*Military*]
**ODMR**....... Optically Detected Magnetic Resonance [*Spectroscopy*]
**ODMRJ**.... Rolf Jensen & Associates Ltd., Don Mills, Ontario [*Library symbol*] [*National Library of Canada*] (NLC)
**ODMT**....... Office of the Director of Military Training
**ODMWS**... Wyda Systems Canada, Inc., Don Mills, Ontario [*Library symbol*] [*National Library of Canada*] (NLC)
**ODN**.......... Company of Mary [*Roman Catholic women's religious order*]
**ODN**.......... Dalton-Dalton-Newport, Cleveland, OH [*OCLC symbol*] (OCLC)
**ODN**.......... Long Seridan [*Malaysia*] [*Airport symbol*] (OAG)
**ODN**.......... Ophthalmodynamometry [*Ophthalmology*]
**ODN**.......... Organization Development Network (EA)
**ODN**.......... Overseas Development Network (EA)
**ODN**.......... Own Doppler Nullifier
**ODN**.......... Oxbridge Directory of Newsletters [*A publication*]
**ODNA**....... Operational Data and Notices to Airmen [*FAA*]
**ODNP**....... Ohio Decisions [*A publication*] (DLA)
**ODNR**....... Oxford Dictionary of Nursery Rhymes [*A publication*]
**ODNRI**...... Overseas Development Natural Resources Institute [*Great Britain*] [*Information service or system*] (IID)
**ODNS**........ Operations Division of Naval Staff [*British*]

**Odo** .......... Odofredus [*Deceased, 1265*] [*Authority cited in pre-1607 legal work*] (DSA)
**ODO** .......... Office of Disability Operations [*Social Security Administration*] [*Began in 1979*] (OICC)
**ODO** .......... Opeongo High School, Douglas, Ontario [*Library symbol*] [*National Library of Canada*] (NLC)
**ODO** .......... Operations Duty Officer (MUGU)
**ODO** .......... Outdoor Officer [*Customs*] [*British*]
**ODOB** .......... Dobie Public Library, Ontario [*Library symbol*] [*National Library of Canada*] (BIB)
**OD/OE** .......... Organizational Development/Organizational Effectiveness (MCD)
**ODOF** .......... Dowling Branch, Onaping Falls Public Library, Ontario [*Library symbol*] [*National Library of Canada*] (NLC)
**Odof** .......... Odofredus [*Deceased, 1265*] [*Authority cited in pre-1607 legal work*] (DSA)
**Odofr** .......... Odofredus [*Deceased, 1265*] [*Authority cited in pre-1607 legal work*] (DSA)
**Odofre** .......... Odofredus [*Deceased, 1265*] [*Authority cited in pre-1607 legal work*] (DSA)
**ODOKA** .......... Okayama Daigaku Onsen Kenkyusho Hokoku [*A publication*]
**ODOM** .......... Odometer (AAG)
**ODONA** .......... Odontoiatria [*A publication*]
**Odonel Mercandil** ... Odonellus Mercandilis [*Authority cited in pre-1607 legal work*] (DSA)
**ODONT** .......... Odontology
**Odont Am** .. Odontologia de America [*A publication*]
**Odonto Est Port** ... Odontoestomatologia Portuguesa [*A publication*]
**Odontoiatr Epith** ... Odontoiatrike Epitheoresis [*A publication*]
**Odontoiatr Prat** ... Odontoiatria Pratica [*A publication*]
**Odontol** .......... Odontologie [*A publication*]
**Odontol Atual** ... Odontologia Atual [*A publication*]
**Odontol Bull** ... Odontological Bulletin [*A publication*]
**Odontol Chil** ... Odontologia Chilena [*A publication*]
**Odontol Conserv** ... Odontologie Conservatrice [*A publication*]
**Odontol Din** ... Odontologia Dinamica [*A publication*]
**Odontol Foren Tidskr** ... Odontologiska Foreningens Tidskrift [*A publication*]
**Odontol Mbl** ... Odontologisches Monatsblatt [*A publication*]
**Odontol Peru** ... Odontologia Peruana [*A publication*]
**Odontol Revy** ... Odontologisk Revy [*A publication*]
**Odontol Samf Finl Arsb** ... Odontologiska Samfundft i Finland Arsbok [*A publication*]
**Odontol Tidskr** ... Odontologisk Tidskrift [*A publication*]
**Odontol Ts** ... Odontologisk Tidskrift [*A publication*]
**Odontol Urug** ... Odontologia Uruguaya [*A publication*]
**Odontopr**.... Odontoprotesi [*A publication*]
**Odontostomatol Implantoprotesi** ... Odontostomatologia e Implantoprotesi [*A publication*]
**Odontostomatol Prog** ... Odontostomatological Progress [*A publication*]
**Odontostomatol Proodos** ... Odontostomatologike Proodos [*A publication*]
**ODOP** .......... Offset Doppler
**ODOPA** .......... Publications. Dominion Observatory (Ottawa) [*A publication*]
**ODOR** .......... Dorion Public Library, Ontario [*Library symbol*] [*National Library of Canada*] (NLC)
**Odor Control Assoc J** ... Odor Control Association. Journal [*A publication*]
**Odor Res** .... Odor Research [*A publication*]
**ODOU** .......... Douro Public Library, Ontario [*Library symbol*] [*National Library of Canada*] (BIB)
**O'Dowd Sh** ... O'Dowd's Merchant Shipping Act [*A publication*] (DLA)
**ODP** .......... Ocean Drilling Program [*Texas A & M University*] [*Research center*] (RCD)
**ODP** .......... Octyl Isodecyl Phthalate [*Organic chemistry*]
**ODP** .......... Oekologisch-Demokratische Partei [*Ecological Democratic Party*] [*Federal Republic of Germany*] [*Political party*] (PPW)
**ODP** .......... Office of Defence Production [*Australia*]
**ODP** .......... Office of Defense Planning [*of FRS*]
**ODP** .......... Office of Disability Programs [*Social Security Administration*] (OICC)
**ODP** .......... Officer Distribution Plan [*Army*]
**ODP** .......... Offshore Drilling Platform
**ODP** .......... Open Data Path (MCD)
**ODP** .......... Open Door Policy
**ODP** .......... Open Dripproof
**ODP** .......... Operational Development Plan [*or Program*]
**ODP** .......... Operational Display Procedure (MCD)
**ODP** .......... Optical Data Processing
**ODP** .......... Orbit Determination Program
**ODP** .......... Order of the Sons of Divine Providence
**ODP** .......... Orderly Departure Program [*for Vietnamese refugees*] [*United Nations*]
**ODP** .......... Organized Reservists in Drill Pay Status [*Military*]
**ODP** .......... Original Departure Point
**ODP** .......... Original Document Processing
**ODP** .......... Outline Development Plan [*Army*] (AFIT)
**ODP** .......... Overall Documentation Plan [*NATO*] (NATG)
**ODP** .......... Oviposition-Determining Pheromone
**ODP** .......... Ozone-Depleting [*or Depletion*] Potential [*Environmental science*]
**OD (PA & E)** ... Office of the Director (Program Analysis and Evaluation) (MCD)
**ODPHP** .......... Office of Disease Prevention and Health Promotion [*US Public Health Service*] [*Information service or system*] (IID)
**ODPI** .......... Office of Director Public Information [*Military*]
**ODPP** .......... Open Dripproof Protected
**O'D Pr & Acc** ... O'Dedy's Principal and Accessory [*1812*] [*A publication*] (DLA)
**ODPSK** .......... Oil Dipstick
**ODQ** .......... [*The*] Oxford Dictionary of Quotations [*A publication*]
**ODQM** .......... Office of the Division Quartermaster
**ODR** .......... Dryden Public Library, Ontario [*Library symbol*] [*National Library of Canada*] (NLC)
**ODR** .......... Ocean Drilling & Exploration Co. [*NYSE symbol*] (SPSG)
**ODR** .......... Office of Defense Resources [*Civil Defense*]
**ODR** .......... Office of Dissemination and Resources [*HEW*]
**ODR** .......... Official Discount Rate [*Finance*] (ECON)
**ODR** .......... Omnidirectional Range
**ODR** .......... On Display Racks [*Freight*]
**ODR** .......... Operator Data Register [*Telecommunications*] (TEL)
**ODR** .......... Optical Data Recognition [*Data processing*]
**ODR** .......... ORDALT [*Ordnance Alterations*] Deficiency Review (MCD)
**ODR** .......... Ordnance Difficulty Report (MCD)
**ODR** .......... Original Data Record
**ODR** .......... Output Data Redundancy (MCD)
**ODR** .......... Output Definition Register
**ODR** .......... Roanoke, VA [*Location identifier*] [*FAA*] (FAAL)
**ODRAN** .......... Operational Drawing Revision Advance Notice (NASA)
**OD & RD** ... Overseas Discharge and Replacement Depot
**OD Re** .......... Ohio Decisions Reprint [*A publication*] (DLA)
**OD Rep** .......... Ohio Decisions Reprint [*A publication*] (DLA)
**ODRES** .......... Old Dominion Real Estate [*NASDAQ symbol*] (NQ)
**ODRI** .......... Deep River Public Library, Ontario [*Library symbol*] [*National Library of Canada*] (NLC)
**ODRI** .......... Office of United States Defense Representative, India [*Army*] (AABC)
**ODRL** .......... Delta Branch, Rideau Lakes Union Library, Ontario [*Library symbol*] [*National Library of Canada*] (BIB)
**ODRM** .......... Operations Design Reference Mission (MCD)
**ODRN** .......... Orbiting Data Relay Network
**ODRP** .......... Office of Defense Representative, Pakistan [*Army*]
**ODRS** .......... Orbiting Data Relay System (MCD)
**ODRS** .......... Ore Deposits Research Section [*Pennsylvania State University*] [*Research center*] (RCD)
**ODRSS** .......... Orbiting Data Relay Satellite System (MCD)
**O/DRV** .......... Over Drive [*Automotive engineering*]
**ODS** .......... Occupational Demand Schedule (ADA)
**ODS** .......... Ocean Data Station [*Marine science*] (MSC)
**ODS** .......... Octadecylsilane [*Organic chemistry*]
**ODS** .......... Octadeyl(dimethyl)chlorosilane [*Organic chemistry*]
**ODS** .......... Odessa [*Washington*] [*Seismograph station code, US Geological Survey*] (SEIS)
**ODS** .......... Odessa [*USSR*] [*Airport symbol*] (OAG)
**ODS** .......... Odessa Explorations Ltd. [*Vancouver Stock Exchange symbol*]
**ODS** .......... Office Dialog System [*Data processing*]
**ODS** .......... Office for Domestic Shipping [*Department of Commerce*]
**ODS** .......... Operating-Differential Subsidy [*Authorized by Merchant Marine Act of 1936*]
**ODS** .......... Operational Data Summary (AAG)
**ODS** .......... Optical Docking System
**ODS** .......... Optimal Decisions System
**ODS** .......... Orbiter Dynamic Simulator [*NASA*]
**ODS** .......... Ordbog over det Danske Sprog [*A publication*]
**ODS** .......... Ordnance Delivery Schedule [*Navy*] (NG)
**ODS** .......... Orton Dyslexia Society (EA)
**ODS** .......... Osric Dining Society (EA)
**ODS** .......... Output Data Strobe
**ODS** .......... Overall Distance Standard [*for golf balls*] [*Adopted by the United States Golf Association in 1976*]
**ODS** .......... Oxidative-Desulfurization [*Fuel technology*]
**ODS** .......... Oxide Dispersion Strengthened [*Metallurgy*]
**ODS** .......... Oxygen Depletion Sensor
**ODSAS** .......... Officer Dual Specialty Allocation System
**ODSB** .......... Ocean Data Station Buoy
**ODSD** .......... Oversea Duty Selection Date [*Air Force*]
**ODSDG** .......... Dalkeith Branch, Stormont, Dundas, and Glengarry County Library, Ontario [*Library symbol*] [*National Library of Canada*] (BIB)
**ODSE** .......... Open Door Student Exchange (EA)
**ODS/FRODS** ... Observable Differences/Functionally Related Observable Differences (MCD)
**ODSI** .......... Ocean Data Systems, Incorporated [*Information service or system*] (IID)
**ODSI** .......... Old Dominion Systems, Incorporated [*Gaithersburg, MD*] [*NASDAQ symbol*] (NQ)
**ODSS** .......... Ocean Dumping Surveillance System [*Coast Guard*] (MSC)
**ODSS** .......... Order Delivery Schedule Summary (MCD)
**ODSY** .......... Sayun [*People's Democratic Republic of Yemen*] [*ICAO location identifier*] (ICLI)
**ODT** .......... Ocean Data Transmitter
**ODT** .......... Octal Debugging Technique [*Data processing*] (IEEE)
**ODT** .......... Office of Defense Transportation [*Within Office for Emergency Management*] [*World War II*]

**ODT**........... Omnidirection Transmission (NVT)
**ODT**........... Online Debugging Technique
**ODT**........... Operational Demand Time [*Military*] (CAAL)
**ODT**........... Operational Demonstration Test
**ODT**........... Optical Data Transmission
**ODT**........... Order-Disorder Transformation
**ODT**........... Outside Diameter Tube (MSA)
**ODT**........... Overseas Deployment Training [*Army*]
**ODTAA**..... One Damn Thing After Another [*Title of book by John Masefield*]
**ODTC**........ Optic Display Test Chamber
**ODTF**........ Operational Development Test Facility (AAG)
**ODTM**....... Orbiter Dynamic Test Model [*NASA*]
**ODTS**........ Offset Doppler Tracking System (KSC)
**ODTS**........ Operational Development Test Site (AAG)
**ODTS**........ Optical Data Transmission System
**ODTS**........ Optical Discrimination and Tracking System [*Army*]
**ODTS**........ Organic Dust Toxic Syndrome [*Medicine*]
**ODU**.......... Dunnville Public Library, Ontario [*Library symbol*] [*National Library of Canada*] (NLC)
**ODU**.......... Old Dominion University [*Virginia*]
**ODU**.......... Old Dutch [*Language, etc.*]
**ODU**.......... Optical Density Unit
**ODU**.......... Optical Display Unit [*Data processing*] (MCD)
**ODU**.......... Output Display Unit [*Data processing*]
**ODUB**........ Bibliotheque Publique de Dubreuilville, Ontario [*Library symbol*] [*National Library of Canada*] (NLC)
**ODUC**........ Ohio Data Users Center [*Columbus*] [*Information service or system*] (IID)
**ODUM**...... Association of American Youth of Ukrainian Descent (EA)
**ODUMP**.... Ocean Dumping Permits [*Database*] [*Environment Canada*] [*Information service or system*] (CRD)
**ODUN**....... Dundalk Public Library, Ontario [*Library symbol*] [*National Library of Canada*] (NLC)
**ODUR**........ Durham Public Library, Ontario [*Library symbol*] [*National Library of Canada*] (NLC)
**ODURF**..... Old Dominion University Research Foundation [*Old Dominion University*] [*Research center*] (RCD)
**ODUSD (R & AT)**... Office of the Deputy Under Secretary of Defense for Research and Advanced Technology [*DoD*] (RDA)
**ODUSM**.... Office, Deputy Under Secretary for Manpower [*Navy*]
**ODUSN**..... Office, Deputy Under Secretary of the Navy
**ODV**.......... Eau-de-Vie [*Taken from the French pronunciation and used to refer to brandy*]
**ODVAR**..... Orbit Determination and Vehicle Attitude Reference
**ODVP**........ Optimal Digital Voice Processor (MCD)
**ODW**......... Oak Harbor [*Washington*] [*Airport symbol*] (OAG)
**ODW**......... Office of Drinking Water [*Environmental Protection Agency*]
**ODW**......... Ohio Wesleyan University, Delaware, OH [*Library symbol*] [*Library of Congress*] (LCLS)
**ODW**......... Omega Dropwindsonde [*Meteorology*]
**ODW**......... Oregon Draymen & Warehousemen's Association, Portland OR [*STAC*]
**ODW**......... Organic Dry Weight
**ODW**......... Our Developing World [*An association*] (EA)
**ODW**......... Output Discrete Word (MCD)
**ODW**......... Oven-Dried Weight
**ODW**......... Workers Health and Safety Centre, Don Mills, Ontario [*Library symbol*] [*National Library of Canada*] (BIB)
**ODWC**....... West Carleton Secondary School, Dunrobin, Ontario [*Library symbol*] [*National Library of Canada*] (BIB)
**ODWIN**..... Opening Doors Wider in Nursing [*Project*]
**Od Wiss**..... Ostdeutsche Wissenschaft [*A publication*]
**ODWSA**.... Office of the Directorate of Weapon Systems Analysis [*Army*] (AABC)
**O Dwyer New**... [*Jack*] O'Dwyer's Newsletter [*A publication*]
**ODX**.......... Ord, NE [*Location identifier*] [*FAA*] (FAAL)
**ODXT**........ Omnidentix Systems [*NASDAQ symbol*] (NQ)
**Ody**........... Odyssey [*A publication*]
**ODY**.......... Odyssey Industries, Inc. [*Toronto Stock Exchange symbol*]
**Odyssey**..... Odyssey Review [*A publication*]
**ODYY**........ Odyssey Entertainment Ltd. [*NASDAQ symbol*] (NQ)
**ODZ**.......... Outer Defense Zone
**OE**............. Austria [*Aircraft nationality and registration mark*] [*IYRU nationality code*] (FAAC)
**OE**............. Bedarfsfluqunternehmen Dr. L. Polsterer [*Austria*] [*ICAO designator*] (FAAC)
**OE**............. Exeter Public Library, Ontario [*Library symbol*] [*National Library of Canada*] (NLC)
**O & E**........ Observation and Examination [*Medicine*]
**O/E**........... Observed Versus Expected
**OE**............. OE, Inc. [*Toronto Stock Exchange symbol*]
**Oe**............. Oersted [*Unit of magnetizing intensity*]
**OE**............. Offensive End [*Football*]
**OE**............. Office of Education [*HEW*]
**OE**............. Office of Education. Publications [*A publication*]
**OE**............. Office Equipment
**OE**............. Oil Emulsion [*Microbiology*]
**OE**............. Oil Equivalent
**OE**............. Old English [*Language, etc.*] [*i.e., before 1150 or 1200*]
**OE**............. Old Etonian [*British*]
**OE**............. Omissions Excepted
**OE**............. On Examination [*Medicine*]
**OE**............. Onze Eeuw [*A publication*]
**OE**............. Open End (MSA)
**OE**............. Operating Engineer (NRCH)
**OE**............. Operating Expense
**OE**............. Operation Enterprise [*Hamilton, NY*] (EA)
**OE**............. Operation Enterprise Newsletter [*A publication*]
**OE**............. Operational Evaluation [*Army*]
**OE**............. Operations Engineering (AAG)
**O & E**........ Operations and Engineering
**OE**............. Optical/Electrical Conversion [*Telecommunications*]
**O/E**........... Order/Entry System [*Data processing*] (DHSM)
**OE**............. Ordnance Electrician [*British military*] (DMA)
**OE**............. Ordnance Engineer [*British military*] (DMA)
**OE**............. Oregon Electric Railway Co. [*AAR code*]
**OE**............. Organizational Effectiveness
**OE**............. Organizational Entity
**OE**............. Organo Espressivo [*Swell Organ*] [*Music*]
**OE**............. Oriens Extremus [*A publication*]
**OE**............. Oriental Economist [*A publication*]
**OE**............. Orientalium Ecclesiarum [*Decree on the Eastern Catholic Churches*] [*Vatican II document*]
**OE**............. Original Entry [*Data processing*]
**OE**............. Original Equipment [*Automobile industry*]
**OE**............. Original Error [*Navigation*]
**OE**............. Orthoenstatite [*Mineral*]
**OE**............. Other Essays [*Literature*] (ROG)
**OE**............. Otitis Externa [*Medicine*]
**OE**............. Out Island Airways (OAG)
**OE**............. Output Enable [*Semiconductor memory*] (IEEE)
**OE**............. Over-the-Horizon Expanded (MCD)
**OE**............. Own Exchange [*Telecommunications*] (TEL)
**OEA**........... Archives, City of Etobicoke, Ontario [*Library symbol*] [*National Library of Canada*] (BIB)
**OEA**........... Eastern Oklahoma District Library, Muskogee, OK [*OCLC symbol*] (OCLC)
**OEA**........... Oblate Education Association [*Defunct*] (EA)
**OEA**........... OEA, Inc. [*NYSE symbol*] (SPSG)
**OEA**........... Office of Economic Adjustment [*Air Force*] (AFM)
**OEA**........... Office of Economic Analysis [*Formerly, Office of Business Economics*] [*Department of Commerce*]
**OEA**........... Office Education Association (EA)
**OEA**........... Office of Environmental Analysis [*Oak Ridge National Laboratory*]
**OEA**........... Office of Export Administration [*Formerly, OEC*] [*Department of Commerce*]
**OEA**........... Operational Effectiveness Analysis (MCD)
**OEA**........... Operator Error Analysis
**OEA**........... Optometric Editors Association (EA)
**OEA**........... Ordnance Electrical Artificer [*British military*] (DMA)
**OEA**........... Organizacion de los Estados Americanos [*Organization of American States - OAS*] [*Spanish*]
**OEA**........... Organizational Expense Accounts [*Army*]
**OEA**........... Outdoor Education Association (EA)
**OEA**........... Overseas Education Association (EA)
**OEA**........... Vincennes, IN [*Location identifier*] [*FAA*] (FAAL)
**OEAB**......... Abha [*Saudi Arabia*] [*ICAO location identifier*] (ICLI)
**OEac**.......... East Cleveland Public Library, East Cleveland, OH [*Library symbol*] [*Library of Congress*] (LCLS)
**OEA Communique**... Office Education Association. Communique [*A publication*]
**OEAH**......... Al-Ahsa [*Saudi Arabia*] [*ICAO location identifier*] (ICLI)
**Oe A Kr**...... Oesterreichisches Archiv fuer Kirchenrecht [*A publication*]
**Oe A f KR**.. Oesterreichisches Archiv fuer Kirchenrecht [*A publication*]
**OEal**........... East Liverpool Carnegie Public Library, East Liverpool, OH [*Library symbol*] [*Library of Congress*] (LCLS)
**OEalK**........ Kent State University, East Liverpool Regional Campus, East Liverpool, OH [*Library symbol*] [*Library of Congress*] (LCLS)
**OEA News**... United States Department of Commerce. News. Office of Economic Affairs [*A publication*]
**OEAP**......... Operational Error Analysis Program
**OEAS**......... Orbital Emergency Arresting System [*NASA*] (NASA)
**OEAS**......... Oxygen Enriched Air System (MCD)
**OEASA**...... Outdoor Educators' Association of South Australia
**Oe AW**....... Oesterreichische Akademie der Wissenschaften [*A publication*]
**OEB**........... Officers' Organization for Economic Benefits [*Commercial firm*] (EA)
**OEB**........... Organic Electrolyte Battery
**OEBA**......... El-Baha [*Saudi Arabia*] [*ICAO location identifier*] (ICLI)
**OEBA**......... Office for Economic and Business Affairs [*Department of State*]
**OEBH**......... Bisha [*Saudi Arabia*] [*ICAO location identifier*] (ICLI)
**Oe BL**......... Oesterreichisches Biographisches Lexikon [*A publication*]
**OEBMAL**... Organizacion de los Estados Americanos. Programa Regional de Desarrollo Cientifico y Tecnologico. Serie de Biologia. Monografia [*A publication*]
**Oe Bot Zs**... Oesterreichische Botanische Zeitschrift [*A publication*]
**OEBS**......... Office of Employee Benefits Security [*Department of Labor*]
**OEBS**......... Organic Electrolyte Battery System
**Oe BZ**........ Oesterreichische Botanische Zeitschrift [*A publication*]

**OEC**.......... Odd-Even Check
**OEC**.......... OECD [*Organization for Economic Cooperation and Development*] Economic Outlook [*A publication*]
**Oec**.......... Oeconomica [*of Aristotle*] [*Classical studies*] (OCD)
**Oec**.......... Oeconomicus [*of Xenophon*] [*Classical studies*] (OCD)
**OeC**.......... Oeuvres et Critiques [*A publication*]
**OEC**.......... Office on Educational Credit [*Later, OECC*] (EA)
**OEC**.......... Office of Energy Conservation [*Functions transferred to Federal Energy Administration*]
**OEC**.......... Office of Export Control [*Later, OEA*] [*World War II*]
**OEC**.......... Ohio Edison Company [*NYSE symbol*] (SPSG)
**OEC**.......... Ontario Election Decisions [*A publication*] (DLA)
**OEC**.......... Operational Employment Concept [*Army*] (AABC)
**OEC**.......... Optical Effect Code
**OEC**.......... Opto-Electronics Center (MCD)
**OEC**.......... Orbital Electron Capture
**OEC**.......... Orbiting Experimental Capsule
**OEC**.......... Ordnance Equipment Chart
**OEC**.......... Organizational Effectiveness Consultants (INF)
**OEC**.......... Organizational Entity Code
**OEC**.......... Oriental Economist [*A publication*]
**OEC**.......... Overpaid Entry Certificate (DS)
**OECA**........ Ontario Educational Communications Authority [*Canada*]
**OECC**........ Office on Educational Credit and Credentials (EA)
**OECD**........ Organization for Economic Cooperation and Development [*Formerly, OEEC*]
**OECD Ber Dtsch Landwirtsch Ges Prufungsabt Landmasch** ... OCED Bericht-Deutsche Landwirtschafts-Gesellschaft Prufungsabteilung fuer Landmaschinen [*A publication*]
**OECD/ENC** ... Organization for Economic Cooperation and Development/ Environment Committee [*Marine science*] (MSC)
**OECD Inform** ... OECD [*Organization for Economic Cooperation and Development*] Informatics Studies [*A publication*]
**OECD Observer** ... OECD [*Organization for Economic Cooperation and Development*] Observer [*A publication*]
**OECD Outlk** ... OECD [*Organization for Economic Cooperation and Development*] Economic Outlook [*A publication*]
**OECD Svys** ... Organization for Economic Cooperation and Development. Economic Surveys of Member Countries [*A publication*]
**OECE**........ Organisation Europeenne de Cooperation Economique [*Organization for European Economic Cooperation - OEEC*] [*Later, OECD*] [*See also OCDE*] [*French*] (MSC)
**OECE**........ Organizacion Europea de Cooperacion Economica [*Organization for European Economic Cooperation - OEEC*] [*Later, OECD*] [*Spanish*]
**OECF**........ Overseas Economic Co-Operation Fund [*OECD*] (DS)
**Oe Ch Zg** ... Oesterreichische Chemiker-Zeitung [*A publication*]
**OECO**........ Outboard Engine Cutoff [*NASA*]
**OECO**........ Oxygen Enrichment Company Ltd. [*NASDAQ symbol*] (NQ)
**Oecol Plant** ... Oecologia Plantarum [*A publication*]
**OECON**..... Offshore Engineering Conference (MCD)
**OECON**..... Offshore Exploration Conference
**Oecon Polon** ... Oeconomica Polona [*A publication*]
**Oeco Planta** ... Oecologia Plantarum [*A publication*]
**OECQ**........ Organisation Europeenne pour la Qualite [*European Organization for Quality -EOQC*] [*Switzerland*]
**OECS**........ Organisation of Eastern Caribbean States (EAIO)
**OECS**........ Organization for the Enforcement of Child Support (EA)
**OEC & S**.... Organizational Effectiveness Center and School [*Army*]
**OECSEAS** ... Organisation of Eastern Caribbean States, Economic Affairs Secretariat [*St. Johns, Antigua*] (EAIO)
**OECT**........ Oxford Editions of Cuneiform Texts [*A publication*] (BJA)
**Oecum**........ Oecumenica [*A publication*]
**OED**.......... Ocean Engineering Division [*Coast Guard*]
**OED**.......... Office of Economic Development [*Bureau of Indian Affairs*]
**OED**.......... Operation Effectiveness Demonstration (RDA)
**OED**.......... Operational Engineering Detachment (MCD)
**OED**.......... Operational Engineering Division [*Central Electricity Generating Board*] [*British*] (IRUK)
**OED**.......... Operational Evaluation Demonstration (MCD)
**OED**.......... Orbiting Energy Depot
**OED**.......... Otto Erich Deutsch [*Music cataloger*]
**OED**.......... Oxford English Dictionary [*Information service or system*] [*A publication*]
**OEDA**........ Office of Energy Data and Analysis [*Functions transferred to Federal Energy Administration*]
**OEDC**........ Office of Engineering Design and Construction [*Tennessee Valley Authority*]
**OEDIPUS** ... Oxford English Dictionary Inputting, Proofing, and Updating Service
**OEDO**........ Ordnance Engineering Duty Officer
**OEDP**........ Overall Economic Development Program [*Bureau of Indian Affairs*]
**OEDR**........ Dhahran/International [*Saudi Arabia*] [*ICAO location identifier*] (ICLI)
**OEDS**........ Oxford English Dictionary Supplement
**OEDSF**...... On-Board Experimental Data Support Facility
**OEE**.......... Ernst & Whinney, Cleveland, OH [*OCLC symbol*] (OCLC)
**OEE**.......... Essex County Public Library, Essex, Ontario [*Library symbol*] [*National Library of Canada*] (NLC)
**OEE**.......... Office of Educational Exchange [*Department of State*]
**OEE**.......... Ordre de l'Etoile de l'Europe [*Huy, Belgium*] (EAIO)
**OEE**.......... Outer Enamel Epithelium [*Dentistry*]
**OEEC**........ Organization for European Economic Cooperation [*Later, OECD*]
**OEEO**........ Office of Equal Educational Opportunities [*Office of Education*]
**OEEO**........ Office of Equal Employment Opportunity [*Department of Labor*] (OICC)
**OEER**........ Oceanographic Equipment Evaluation Range (NOAA)
**OEES**........ Interagency Committee on Ocean Exploration and Environmental Services [*Terminated, 1971*] (EGAO)
**OEES**........ Organization for Equal Education of the Sexes (EA)
**OEETD**..... Office of Environmental Engineering and Technology Demonstration [*Washington, DC*] [*Environmental Protection Agency*] (GRD)
**OEF**.......... Ear Falls Public Library, Ontario [*Library symbol*] [*National Library of Canada*] (NLC)
**OEF**.......... Management Totaal [*A publication*]
**OEF**.......... Oceanic Educational Foundation (EA)
**OEF**.......... Officeholders Expense Funds [*Slush money*]
**OEF**.......... Open-End Funds [*Investment term*]
**OEF**.......... Optical Evaluation Facility (RDA)
**OEF**.......... Overseas Education Fund [*Later, OEFI*] (EA)
**OEFD**........ Orbiter Electric Field Detector [*NASA*]
**OEFE**........ Flos-Elmvale Public Library, Elmvale, Ontario [*Library symbol*] [*National Library of Canada*] (BIB)
**Oeff Anz**..... Oeffentlicher Anzeiger fuer das Vereinigte Wirtschaftsgebiet [*A publication*]
**Oeff GD**..... Oeffentliche Gesundheitsdienst [*A publication*]
**Oeff Gesundheitsdienst** ... Oeffentliche Gesundheitsdienst [*West Germany*] [*A publication*]
**Oeff Gesundheitswes** ... Oeffentliche Gesundheitswesen [*A publication*]
**Oeff Verw**... Oeffentliche Verwaltung [*Zeitschrift fuer Verwaltungsrecht und Verwaltungspolitik*] [*A publication*]
**Oeff Verwalt** ... Oeffentliche Verwaltung [*Zeitschrift fuer Verwaltungsrecht und Verwaltungspolitik*] [*A publication*]
**Oe FH**........ Oesterreichs Forst- und Holzwirtschaft [*A publication*]
**OEFI**.......... OEF [*Overseas Educational Fund*] International (EA)
**OEG**.......... Eganville Public Library, Ontario [*Library symbol*] [*National Library of Canada*] (NLC)
**OEG**.......... Operational Exposure Guidance [*Military*] (INF)
**OEG**.......... Operations Evaluation Group [*Military*]
**OEG**.......... Organization and Equipment Guide [*Army*] (AABC)
**OEG**.......... Outdoor Ethics Guild (EA)
**OEG**.......... Public Library of Enid and Garfield County, Enid, OK [*OCLC symbol*] (OCLC)
**OEGCA**..... Old English Game Club of America (EA)
**OEGCMJ**... Officer Exercising General Court-Martial Jurisdiction
**OEGN**........ Gizan [*Saudi Arabia*] [*ICAO location identifier*] (ICLI)
**OEGS**........ Gassim [*Saudi Arabia*] [*ICAO location identifier*] (ICLI)
**OEGT**........ Guriat [*Saudi Arabia*] [*ICAO location identifier*] (ICLI)
**OEGT**........ Observable Evidences of Good Teaching
**OEGT**........ Office of Education for the Gifted and Talented [*HEW*]
**OEGWA**.... Oeffentliche Gesundheitswesen [*A publication*]
**OEH**.......... Baltimore, MD [*Location identifier*] [*FAA*] (FAAL)
**OEH**.......... Orient Express Hotels [*NYSE symbol*] (SPSG)
**OEHL**........ Hail [*Saudi Arabia*] [*ICAO location identifier*] (ICLI)
**OEHL**........ Hoffman-La Roche Ltd., Etobicoke, Ontario [*Library symbol*] [*National Library of Canada*] (NLC)
**OEHL**........ Occupational and Environmental Health Laboratory [*Air Force*] [*Brooks Air Force Base, TX*]
**OEI**.......... Offshore Ecology Investigation [*Oil study*]
**OEI**.......... Oficina de Educacion Iberoamericana [*Ibero-American Bureau of Education - IABE*] [*Madrid, Spain*] (EAIO)
**OEI**.......... One Engine Inoperative [*Aviation*]
**OEI**.......... Options Exchange Index
**OEI**.......... Optoelectronic Isolator
**OEI**.......... Organizacion de Estados Iberoamericanos para la Educacion, la Ciencia, y la Cultura [*Organization of Ibero-American States for Education, Science, and Culture*] (EAIO)
**OEI**.......... Organizational Entity Identity
**OEI**.......... Overall Efficiency Index
**OEIC**........ Ocean Engineering Information Centre [*Memorial University of Newfoundland*] [*Information service or system*] (IID)
**OEIC**........ Open-End Investment Company [*Investment term*]
**OEIC**........ Optoelectronic Integrated Circuit [*Data processing*]
**OEID**........ Office of Engineering Infrastructure Development [*Washington, DC*] [*National Science Foundation*] (GRD)
**OEII**.......... Operation Everest II [*Army*] (RDA)
**OEIO**........ Odds and Ends Input/Output (MCD)
**OEIPS**....... Office of Engineering and Information Processing Standards [*National Bureau of Standards*]
**OEIS**......... Office of Energy Information Services [*Department of Energy*] (IID)
**OEIS**......... Orbiter Electrical Interface Simulator [*NASA*]
**OEIT**......... Open-End Investment Trust [*Investment term*]
**OEITFL**..... Organisation Europeenne des Industries Transformatrices de Fruits et Legumes [*European Organization of Fruit and Vegetable Processing Industries*] [*Common Market*] [*Belgium*]
**OEIU**........ Office Employes International Union [*Later, OPEIU*]
**OEJB**........ Jubail [*Saudi Arabia*] [*ICAO location identifier*] (ICLI)

**OEJD**......... Jeddah [*Saudi Arabia*] [*ICAO location identifier*] (ICLI)
**Oe Jh**......... Jahreshefte. Oesterreichisches Archaeologische Institut in Wien [*A publication*]
**Oe Jh Beibl**... Jahreshefte. Oesterreichisches Archaeologische Institut. Beiblatt [*A publication*]
**OEJN**......... Jeddah/King Abdul Aziz International [*Saudi Arabia*] [*ICAO location identifier*] (ICLI)
**OEKJ**......... Al-Kharj [*Saudi Arabia*] [*ICAO location identifier*] (ICLI)
**OEKM**....... Khamis Mushait [*Saudi Arabia*] [*ICAO location identifier*] (ICLI)
**OEKOA**..... Oel und Kohle [*A publication*]
**Oekonom Unternehmensforsch**... Oekonometrie und Unternehmensforschung [*A publication*]
**Oek S**......... Oekumenische Studien [*A publication*]
**OEL**........... Elliot Lake Public Library, Ontario [*Library symbol*] [*National Library of Canada*] (NLC)
**OEL**........... Eugene Public Library, Eugene, OR [*OCLC symbol*] (OCLC)
**OEL**........... Oakley, KS [*Location identifier*] [*FAA*] (FAAL)
**OEL**........... Occupational Exposure Limit
**OEL**........... Ordnance Equipment List [*Navy*] (NG)
**OEL**........... Organizational Equipment List [*Army*]
**OELB**......... Oertlicher Landwirtschaftsbetrieb [*Local Agricultural Enterprise*] [*German*]
**OELF**......... Fort Hope Band Library, Eabamet Lake, Ontario [*Library symbol*] [*National Library of Canada*] (BIB)
**Oel & Gas Feuerungstech**... Oel und Gas und Feuerungstechnik [*West Germany*] [*A publication*]
**Oelhydraul Pneum**... Oelhydraulik und Pneumatik [*A publication*]
**OELK**......... Elk Lake Public Library, Ontario [*Library symbol*] [*National Library of Canada*] (BIB)
**OELM**....... Elmwood Branch, Bruce County Public Library, Ontario [*Library symbol*] [*National Library of Canada*] (NLC)
**OELMN(A)**... Ordnance Electrical Mechanician (Air) [*British military*] (DMA)
**OELS**......... Elliot Lake Secondary School, Ontario [*Library symbol*] [*National Library of Canada*] (NLC)
**OEly**........... Elyria Library, Elyria, OH [*Library symbol*] [*Library of Congress*] (LCLS)
**OElyL**......... Lorain County Community College, Elyria, OH [*Library symbol*] [*Library of Congress*] (LCLS)
**OEM**.......... Emo Public Library, Ontario [*Library symbol*] [*National Library of Canada*] (NLC)
**OEM**.......... Office of Electronic Machines [*Commercial firm*] [*British*]
**OEM**.......... Office for Emergency Management [*World War II*]
**OEM**.......... Office of Environmental Mediation
**OEM**.......... Office Equipment Maintenance
**OEM**.......... Office of Executive Management
**OEM**.......... On Equipment Materiel [*Army*] (AABC)
**OEM**.......... Open-End Marriage
**OEM**.......... Ordnance Electrical Mechanic [*British military*] (DMA)
**OEM**.......... Organizational Element Model
**OEM**.......... Original Equipment Manufacturer
**OEM**.......... Other Equipment Manufacturers (CMD)
**OEM**.......... Own Equipment Material
**OEM**.......... Oxford English Monographs [*A publication*]
**OEMA**........ Madinah [*Saudi Arabia*] [*ICAO location identifier*] (ICLI)
**OEMA**........ Obras Escohidas de Machado de Assis [*A publication*]
**OEMA**........ Office of Educational and Manpower Assistance (OICC)
**OEMA**........ Office of Export Marketing Assistance [*Department of Commerce*]
**OEMCP**..... Optical Effects Module Electronic Controller and Processor [*NASA*]
**OEMI**........ Office of Energy, Minerals, and Industry [*Environmental Protection Agency*]
**OEMI**........ Office Equipment Manufacturers Institute [*Later, CBEMA*]
**OEMN**....... Ordnance Electrical Mechanician [*British military*] (DMA)
**OEMZ**........ Oesterreichische Musikzeitschrift [*A publication*]
**OEN**........... Ennismore Township Public Library, Ontario [*Library symbol*] [*National Library of Canada*] (BIB)
**OEN**........... Odd-Even Nuclei
**OEN**........... Ohio Environmental Protection Agency Library, Columbus, OH [*OCLC symbol*] (OCLC)
**OEN**........... Old English Newsletter [*A publication*]
**OEN**........... Organizational Entity Name
**OEN**........... Oxford Energy Co. [*AMEX symbol*] (SPSG)
**OEN**........... Oxford English Novels [*A publication*]
**OENCO**..... Organizational Effectiveness Noncommissioned Officer [*Military*]
**OENG**........ Englehart Public Library, Ontario [*Library symbol*] [*National Library of Canada*] (BIB)
**OENG**........ Nejran [*Saudi Arabia*] [*ICAO location identifier*] (ICLI)
**OENLA**...... Enterprise Branch, Lennox and Addington County Library, Ontario [*Library symbol*] [*National Library of Canada*] (NLC)
**OENR**........ Oil-Extended Natural Rubber
**OENR**........ Organization for European Nuclear Research
**OEO**........... OECD [*Organization for Economic Cooperation and Development*] Observer [*A publication*]
**OEO**........... Office of Economic Opportunity [*Functions transferred to other federal agencies, 1973-75*]
**OEO**........... Office of Equal Opportunity [*NASA*]
**OEO**........... Officers' Eyes Only [*Military*] (NVT)
**OEO**........... Ordnance Executive Officer [*Military*] [*British*]
**OEO**........... Osceola, WI [*Location identifier*] [*FAA*] (FAAL)
**OEO**........... Oversea Employment Office [*Air Force*] (AFM)
**OEOB**......... Old Executive Office Building [*Washington, DC*]
**OE/OE**....... Open Entry/Open Exit (OICC)
**OEP**........... Occupational Education Project
**OEP**........... Occupational Exploration Program (OICC)
**OEP**........... Ocean Education Project (EA)
**OEP**........... Odd-Even Predominance [*Organic chemistry*]
**OEP**........... OEP. Office Equipment and Products [*Japan*] [*A publication*]
**OEP**........... Office of Economic Programs [*of BDSA*]
**OEP**........... Office of Emergency Preparedness [*formerly, Planning*] [*Terminated, 1973*]
**OEP**........... Office of Energy Programs [*NASA*]
**OEP**........... Operational Employment Plan [*Army*]
**OEP**........... Osaka Economic Papers [*A publication*]
**OEP**........... Outside Engineering Personnel (MCD)
**OEP**........... Overseas Employment Program [*DoD*]
**OEP**........... Owen Electric Pictures [*Telecommunications service*] (TSSD)
**OEP**........... Oxford Economic Papers [*A publication*]
**OEP**........... Preble County District Library, Eaton, OH [*Library symbol*] [*Library of Congress*] (LCLS)
**OEP**........... United States Environmental Protection Agency, Cincinnati, Cincinnati, OH [*OCLC symbol*] [*Inactive*] (OCLC)
**OEPA**......... Hafr Al-Batin Airport [*Saudi Arabia*] [*ICAO location identifier*] (ICLI)
**OEPER**...... Office of Environmental Processes and Effects Research [*Environmental Protection Agency*] [*Washington, DC*] (GRD)
**OEPF**......... Optometric Extension Program Foundation (EA)
**OEPFC**....... Official Elvis Presley Fan Club (EAIO)
**OEPP**......... Organisation Europeenne et Mediterraneenne pour la Protection des Plantes [*European and Mediterranean Plant Protection Organization - EPPO*] (EAIO)
**OEPR**......... Office of Environmental Project Review [*Department of the Interior*]
**OEPR**......... Office of Extramural Program Review [*Department of Health and Human Services*] (GRD)
**OEPS**......... Office of Educational Programs and Services [*NASA*]
**OEPT**......... Perry Township Public Library Emsdale, Ontario [*Library symbol*] [*National Library of Canada*] (NLC)
**OER**........... Odd-Even Rule
**OER**........... Oersted [*Unit of magnetizing intensity*]
**OER**........... Offensive Efficiency Ratio [*Basketball*]
**OER**........... Office of Economic Research [*Department of Commerce*]
**OER**........... Office of Energy Research [*Department of Energy*] [*Washington, DC*] (GRD)
**OER**........... Office of Energy Research [*University of Illinois*] [*Research center*] (RCD)
**OER**........... Office of Evaluation Research [*University of Illinois at Chicago*] [*Research center*] (RCD)
**OER**........... Office of Exploratory Research [*Environmental Protection Agency*] [*Washington, DC*] (GRD)
**OER**........... Officer Effectiveness Report [*Air Force*] (AFM)
**OER**........... Officer Efficiency Report [*Military*]
**OER**........... Officer Evaluation Report [*Army*]
**OER**........... Officers' Emergency Reserve [*British*]
**OER**........... Operational ELINT Requirements (MCD)
**OER**........... Operational Equipment Requirement (AAG)
**OER**........... Operations Engineering Report (AAG)
**OER**........... Original Equipment Request (AAG)
**OER**........... Ornskoldsvik [*Sweden*] [*Airport symbol*] (OAG)
**OER**........... Osmotic Erythrocyte Resistance
**O'ER**.......... Over (ROG)
**OER**........... Overhead Expenditure Request
**OER**........... Oxygen Enhancement Ratio
**OERA**......... Omnibus Education Reconciliation Act of 1981
**OERAHA**... Organisation Europeenne pour des Recherches Astronomiques dans l'Hemisphere Austral [*European Southern Observatory - ESO*] (EAIO)
**OERC**......... Optimum Earth Reentry Corridor [*Aerospace*]
**OERD**......... Erin District High School, Erin, Ontario [*Library symbol*] [*National Library of Canada*] (NLC)
**OERF**......... Orthodontic Education and Research Foundation (EA)
**OERF**......... Rafha [*Saudi Arabia*] [*ICAO location identifier*] (ICLI)
**OERI**......... Office of Educational Research and Improvement [*Department of Education*] [*Washington, DC*]
**OERI**......... Office of Energy-Related Inventions [*National Institute of Standards and Technology*] [*Gaithersburg, MD*]
**OERK**......... Riyadh/King Khalid International [*Saudi Arabia*] [*ICAO location identifier*] (ICLI)
**OERL**......... Elgin Branch, Rideau Lakes Union Library, Ontario [*Library symbol*] [*National Library of Canada*] (NLC)
**OERL**......... Officer Education Research Laboratory [*Air Force*]
**OERL**......... Overall Echo Return Loss
**Oerlikon Schweissmitt**... Oerlikon Schweissmitteilungen [*A publication*]
**OERP**......... Overseas Expenditure Reduction Program [*Military*] (AFM)
**OERR**......... Arar [*Saudi Arabia*] [*ICAO location identifier*] (ICLI)
**OERS**......... Officer Evaluation Reporting System [*Army*]
**OERS**......... Organisation Europeenne de Recherches Spatiales

**OERT** ........ Succursale d'Embrun, Bibliotheque Publique du Canton de Russell [*Embrun Branch, Russell Township Public Library*] Ontario [*Library symbol*] [*National Library of Canada*] (BIB)
**OERY** ........ Riyadh [*Saudi Arabia*] [*ICAO location identifier*] (ICLI)
**OES** .......... Bureau of Oceans and International Environmental and Scientific Affairs [*Department of State*]
**OES** .......... Espanola Public Library, Ontario [*Library symbol*] [*National Library of Canada*] (NLC)
**OES** .......... IEEE Oceanic Engineering Society (EA)
**OES** .......... Occupational Employment Statistics [*Department of Labor*]
**OES** .......... Occupational Exposure Standard [*Environmental chemistry*]
**OES** .......... Office of Economic Stabilization [*World War II*]
**OES** .......... Office of Emergency Service [*Federal disaster planning*]
**OES** .......... Office of Employment Security [*Department of Labor*]
**OES** .......... Office of Endangered Species [*Department of the Interior*]
**OES** .......... Office of Examinations and Supervision [*Federal Home Loan Bank Board*]
**OES** .......... Official Experimental Station [*Amateur radio*]
**OES** .......... Operations and Engineering Squadron
**OES** .......... Optical Emission Spectroscopy
**OES** .......... Orbital-Escape System [*NASA*]
**OES** .......... Orbiter Emergency Site [*NASA*] (NASA)
**OES** .......... Order of the Eastern Star [*Freemasonry*] (EA)
**OES** .......... Outgoing Echo Suppressor [*Telecommunications*] (TEL)
**OES** .......... Overseas Educational Service [*Defunct*]
**OES** .......... Oxford English Studies [*A publication*]
**OES** .......... San Antonio Oeste [*Argentina*] [*Airport symbol*] (OAG)
**OESA** ........ Office of Earth Sciences Applications [*Department of the Interior*] (GRD)
**OESA** ........ Office of Employment Service Administration [*US Employment Service*] [*Department of Labor*]
**OESCA**...... Old English Sheepdog Club of America (EA)
**OESCAND** ... Old East Scandinavian [*Language, etc.*]
**OESD** ........ Ocean Engineering System Development
**OESE**......... Office of Elementary and Secondary Education [*Department of Education*]
**OES/ENP** ... Bureau of Oceans and International Environmental and Scientific Affairs/Environmental and Population Affairs [*Department of State*] (MSC)
**OESH** ........ Shared Library Services, South Huron Hospital, Exeter, Ontario [*Library symbol*] [*National Library of Canada*] (BIB)
**OESH** ........ Sharurah [*Saudi Arabia*] [*ICAO location identifier*] (ICLI)
**OESK**......... Al-Jouf [*Saudi Arabia*] [*ICAO location identifier*] (ICLI)
**OESK**......... Osteuropeiska Solidaritetskommitten [*East European Solidarity Committee*] (EAIO)
**OESL**......... Oceanographic and Environmental Service Laboratory [*Raytheon Co.*]
**OESL**......... Sulayel [*Saudi Arabia*] [*ICAO location identifier*] (ICLI)
**OESO** ........ Organisation Internationale d'Etudes Statistiques pour les Maladies de l'Oesophage [*International Organization for Statistical Studies on Diseases of the Esophagus*] (EAIO)
**OESO** ........ Organizational Effectiveness Staff Officer [*Military*]
**OESOC** ..... Organizational Effectiveness Staff Officer Course [*Army*]
**OES/OFA** ... Bureau of Oceans and International Environmental and Scientific Affairs/Ocean and Fishery Affairs [*Department of State*] (MSC)
**OESOPH** .. Oesophagus
**OESPCMJ** ... Officer Exercising Special Court-Martial Jurisdiction
**OESS**......... O/ET [*Orbiter/External Tank*] Separation System [*NASA*] (MCD)
**OESS**......... Office of Engineering Standards Services [*National Bureau of Standards*]
**OESS**......... Organizational Effectiveness Survey System [*Army*]
**OES/SCI** ... Bureau of Oceans and International Enviromental and Scientific Affairs/Scientific and Technological Affairs [*Department of State*] (MSC)
**Oest Bank-Arch** ... Oesterreichisches Bank-Archiv [*A publication*]
**Oest Bot Z** ... Oesterreichische Botanische Zeitschrift [*A publication*]
**Oesterr Abwasser Rundsch** ... Oesterreichische Abwasser Rundschau [*A publication*]
**Oesterr Aerzteztg** ... Oesterreichische Aerztezeitung [*A publication*]
**Oesterr Akad Wiss Erdwissenschaftliche Komm Schriftenr** ... Oesterreichische Akademie der Wissenschaften. Erdwissenschaftliche Kommission Schriftenreihe [*A publication*]
**Oesterr Akad Wiss Math Naturwiss Kl Sitzungsber** ... Oesterreichische Akademie der Wissenschaften. Mathematisch-Naturwissenschaftliche Klasse. Sitzungsberichte [*Austria*] [*A publication*]
**Oesterr Akad Wiss Math-Naturwiss Kl Sitzungsber Abt 1** ... Oesterreichische Akademie der Wissenschaften. Mathematisch-Naturwissenschaftliche Klasse. Sitzungsberichte. Abteilung 1. Biologie, Mineralogie, Erdkunde, und Verwandte Wissenschaften [*A publication*]
**Oesterr Akad Wiss Math-Naturwiss Kl Sitzungsber Abt 2** ... Oesterreichische Akademie der Wissenschaften. Mathematisch-Naturwissenschaftliche Klasse. Sitzungsberichte. Abteilung 2. Mathematik, Astronomie, Physik, Meteorologie, und Technik [*A publication*]
**Oesterr Akad Wiss Math Naturwiss Kl Sitzungsber Abt 2A** ... Oesterreichische Akademie der Wissenschaften. Mathematisch-Naturwissenschaftliche Klasse. Sitzungsberichte. Abteilung 2A. Mathematik, Astronomie, Physik, Meteorologie, und Technik [*A publication*]
**Oesterr Akad Wiss Math Naturwiss Kl Sitzungsber Abt 2B** ... Oesterreichische Akademie der Wissenschaften. Mathematisch-Naturwissenschaftliche Klasse. Sitzungsberichte. Abteilung 2B. Chemie [*A publication*]
**Oesterr Akad Wiss Philos-Hist Kl** ... Oesterreichische Akademie der Wissenschaften. Philosophisch-Historische Klasse [*A publication*]
**Oesterr Apoth Ztg** ... Oesterreichische Apotheker Zeitung [*A publication*]
**Oesterr Bot Z** ... Oesterreichische Botanische Zeitschrift [*A publication*]
**Oesterr Chem-Z** ... Oesterreichische Chemie-Zeitschrift [*A publication*]
**Oesterr Chem-Ztg** ... Oesterreichische Chemiker-Zeitung [*A publication*]
**Oesterreich Akad Wiss Math-Natur Kl Denkschr** ... Oesterreichische Akademie der Wissenschaften. Mathematisch-Naturwissenschaftliche Klasse. Denkschriften [*A publication*]
**Oesterreich Akad Wiss Math-Natur Kl S-B 2** ... Oesterreichische Akademie der Wissenschaften. Mathematisch-Naturwissenschaftliche Klasse. Sitzungsberichte. Abteilung 2. Mathematik, Astronomie, Physik, Meteorologie, und Technik [*A publication*]
**Oesterreich Akad Wiss Math-Natur Kl Sitzungsber 2** ... Oesterreichische Akademie der Wissenschaften. Mathematisch-Naturwissenschaftliche Klasse. Sitzungsberichte. Abteilung 2. Mathematik, Astronomie, Physik, Meteorologie, und Technik [*Vienna*] [*A publication*]
**Oesterreich Akad Wiss Math Naturwiss Kl Denkschr** ... Oesterreichische Akademie der Wissenschaften. Mathematisch-Naturwissenschaftliche Klasse. Denkschriften [*A publication*]
**Oesterreich Akad Wiss Math-Naturwiss Kl SB 2** ... Oesterreichische Akademie der Wissenschaften. Mathematisch-Naturwissenschaftliche Klasse. Sitzungsberichte. Abteilung 2. Mathematik, Astronomie, Physik, Meteorologie, und Technik [*A publication*]
**Oesterreich Blasm** ... Oesterreichische Blasmusik [*A publication*]
**Oesterreich Geogr Ges Mitt** ... Oesterreichische Geographische Gesellschaft. Mitteilungen [*A publication*]
**Oesterreichische Zs Berg- u Huettenw** ... Oesterreichische Zeitschrift fuer Berg- und Huettenwesen [*A publication*]
**Oesterr Forst-Holzwirtsch** ... Oesterreichs Forst- und Holzwirtschaft [*A publication*]
**Oesterr Glaserztg** ... Oesterreichische Glaserzeitung [*A publication*]
**Oesterr Ing Arch** ... Oesterreichisches Ingenieur Archiv [*A publication*]
**Oesterr Ing & Archit Z** ... Oesterreichische Ingenieur und Architekten. Zeitschrift [*A publication*]
**Oesterr Ing-Z** ... Oesterreichische Ingenieur-Zeitschrift [*A publication*]
**Oesterr Jb Soziol** ... Oesterreichische Jahrbuch fuer Soziologie [*A publication*]
**Oesterr Krankenpflegez** ... Oesterreichische Krankenpflegezeitschrift [*A publication*]
**Oesterr Kunstst Rundsch** ... Oesterreichische Kunststoff-Rundschau [*A publication*]
**Oesterr Kunstst-Z** ... Oesterreichische Kunststoff-Zeitschrift [*Austria*] [*A publication*]
**Oesterr Landtech** ... Oesterreichische Landtechnik [*Austria*] [*A publication*]
**Oesterr Leder Haeutewirtsch** ... Oesterreichische Leder und Haeuterwirtschaft [*A publication*]
**Oesterr Leder Ztg** ... Oesterreichische Leder-Zeitung [*A publication*]
**Oesterr Mh** ... Oesterreichische Monatshefte [*A publication*]
**Oesterr Milchwirtsch** ... Oesterreichische Milchwirtschaft [*A publication*]
**Oesterr Milchwirtsch Ztg** ... Oesterreichische Milchwirtschaftliche Zeitung [*A publication*]
**Oesterr Mineral Ges Mitt** ... Oesterreichische Mineralogische Gesellschaft. Mitteilungen [*A publication*]
**Oesterr Molk Ztg** ... Oesterreichische Molkerei Zeitung [*A publication*]
**Oesterr Osth** ... Oesterreichische Osthefte [*A publication*]
**Oesterr Papier** ... Oesterreichische Papier [*A publication*]
**Oesterr Papier-Ztg** ... Oesterreichische Papier-Zeitung [*A publication*]
**Oesterr Pap Ztg** ... Oesterreichische Papier-Zeitung [*A publication*]
**Oesterr Schwesternztg** ... Oesterreichische Schwesternzeitung [*Austria*] [*A publication*]
**Oesterr Seifenfachbl** ... Oesterreichisches Seifenfachblatt [*A publication*]
**Oesterr Spirit Ztg** ... Oesterreichische Spirituosen Zeitung [*A publication*]
**Oesterr Studienges Atomenerg** ... Oesterreichische Studiengesellschaft fuer Atomenergie [*A publication*]
**Oesterr Textilz** ... Oesterreichische Textilzeitschrift [*A publication*]
**Oesterr Tierarzt** ... Oesterreichische Tieraerzt [*A publication*]
**Oesterr Tierarzte Ztg** ... Oesterreichische Tieraerzte-Zeitung [*A publication*]
**Oesterr Vierteljahresschr Forstwes** ... Oesterreichische Vierteljahresschrift fuer Forstwesen [*A publication*]
**Oesterr Vrtljschr Wissensch Veterinaerk** ... Oesterreichische Vierteljahresschrift fuer Wissenschaftliche Veterinaerkunde [*A publication*]
**Oesterr Wasserwirtsch** ... Oesterreichische Wasserwirtschaft [*A publication*]
**Oesterr Weidwerk** ... Oesterreichische Weidwerk [*A publication*]
**Oesterr Zahnaerzteztg** ... Oesterreichische Zahnaerzte-Zeitung [*A publication*]
**Oesterr Zahnprothet** ... Oesterreichische Zahnprothetik [*A publication*]

**Oesterr Zahntechnik** ... Oesterreichische Zahntechniker [*A publication*]
**Oesterr Z Aussenpolit** ... Oesterreichische Zeitschrift fuer Aussenpolitik [*A publication*]
**Oesterr Z Berg Huettenwes** ... Oesterreichische Zeitschrift fuer Berg- und Huettenwesen [*A publication*]
**Oesterr Zeits Volksk** ... Oesterreichische Zeitschrift fuer Volkskunde [*A publication*]
**Oesterr Z Elektrizitaetswirtsch** ... Oesterreichische Zeitschrift fuer Elektrizitaetswirtschaft [*A publication*]
**Oesterr Z Erforsch Bekaempf Krebskr** ... Oesterreichische Zeitschrift fuer Erforschung und Bekaempfung der Krebskrankheit [*A publication*]
**Oesterr Z Erforsch Bekaempf Krebskrankheit** ... Oesterreichische Zeitschrift fuer Erforschung und Bekaempfung der Krebskrankheit [*Austria*] [*A publication*]
**Oesterr Z Kinderheilkd Kinderfuersorge** ... Oesterreichische Zeitschrift fuer Kinderheilkunde und Kinderfuersorge [*A publication*]
**Oesterr Z Oeff Recht** ... Oesterreichische Zeitschrift fuer Oeffentliches Recht [*A publication*]
**Oesterr Z Onkol** ... Oesterreichische Zeitschrift fuer Onkologie [*A publication*]
**Oesterr Zool Z** ... Oesterreichische Zoologische Zeitschrift [*A publication*]
**Oesterr Z Polit -Wiss** ... Oesterreichische Zeitschrift fuer Politikwissenschaft [*A publication*]
**Oesterr Z Stomatol** ... Oesterreichische Zeitschrift fuer Stomatologie [*A publication*]
**Oesterr Ztschr Kinderh** ... Oesterreichische Zeitschrift fuer Kinderheilkunde [*A publication*]
**Oesterr Z Volkskd** ... Oesterreichische Zeitschrift fuer Volkskunde [*A publication*]
**Oester Z Pol** ... Oesterreichische Zeitschrift fuer Politikwissenschaft [*A publication*]
**Oest Forschinst Wirt und Pol Ber** ... Oesterreichisches Forschungsinstitut fuer Wirtschaft und Politik. Berichte und Informationen [*A publication*]
**Oest Forschungsinst Sparkassenwesen VJ-Schriftenreihe** ... Oesterreichisches Forschungsinstitut fuer Sparkassenwesen Viertel Jahres-Schriftenreihe [*A publication*]
**Oest Ges Statis und Informatik Mitteilungsbl** ... Oesterreichische Gesellschaft fuer Statistik und Informatik. Mitteilungsblatt [*A publication*]
**Oest Imker** ... Oesterreichische Imker [*A publication*]
**Oest Imkerkal** ... Oester Imkerkalender [*A publication*]
**Oest Mhefte** ... Oesterreichische Monatshefte [*A publication*]
**Oest Osthefte** ... Oesterreichische Osthefte [*A publication*]
**Oest T Ae Zt** ... Oesterreichische Tieraerzte-Zeitung [*A publication*]
**Oest Volkswirt** ... Oesterreichische Volkswirt [*A publication*]
**Oest Wasserw** ... Oesterreichische Wasserwirtschaft [*A publication*]
**Oest Z Aussenpol** ... Oesterreichische Zeitschrift fuer Aussenpolitik [*A publication*]
**Oest Z Oe R** ... Oesterreichische Zeitschrift fuer Oeffentliches Recht [*A publication*]
**Oest Zool Z** ... Oesterreichische Zoologische Zeitschrift [*A publication*]
**Oest Z Politikwiss** ... Oesterreichische Zeitschrift fuer Politikwissenschaft [*A publication*]
**Oest Zs Kinderhk** ... Oesterreichische Zeitschrift fuer Kinderheilkunde und Kinderfuersorge [*A publication*]
**Oest Zs Verm W** ... Oesterreichische Zeitschrift fuer Vermessungswesen [*A publication*]
**Oest Zs Volkskd** ... Oesterreichische Zeitschrift fuer Volkskunde [*A publication*]
**Oest Zs Zahn Hlkd** ... Oesterreichische Zeitschrift fuer Zahnheilkunde [*A publication*]
**OET** .......... Objective End Time
**OET** .......... Office of Emergency Transportation [*FAA*]
**OET** .......... Office of Engineering and Technology [*Washington, DC*] [*FCC*] (GRD)
**OET** .......... Official English Title
**OET** .......... Oldest English Texts
**OET** .......... On Equipment Training (MCD)
**O/ET** .......... Orbiter/External Tank [*NASA*] (NASA)
**OET** .......... Organizacion para Estudios Tropicales [*Organization for Tropical Studies*] (EAIO)
**OET** .......... Oxford English Texts [*A publication*]
**OETA** .......... Occupied Enemy Territory Administration [*World War II*]
**OETA** .......... Township of Armstrong Public Library [*Bibliotheque Publique Canton Armstrong*], Earlton, Ontario [*Library symbol*] [*National Library of Canada*] (BIB)
**OETB** .......... Ocean Economics and Technology Branch [*United Nations*] (MSC)
**OE & TB** .......... Officer Education and Training Branch [*BUPERS*]
**OETB** .......... Offshore Energy Technology Board [*British*]
**OETB** .......... Tabuk [*Saudi Arabia*] [*ICAO location identifier*] (ICLI)
**OETC** .......... Organizational Effectiveness Training Center [*Army*] (MCD)
**OET & E** .......... Operational Employment Testing and Evaluation (AFM)
**OETF** .......... Taif [*Saudi Arabia*] [*ICAO location identifier*] (ICLI)
**OETLC** .......... Office of Economic Trends and Labor Conditions [*Department of Labor*]
**OETP** .......... Orbiter Electron Temperature Probe [*NASA*]
**OETR** .......... Turaif [*Saudi Arabia*] [*ICAO location identifier*] (ICLI)
**OeTV Mag** ... OeTV [*Oeffentliche Dienste. Transport und Verkehr*] Magazin [*A publication*]
**OEu** .......... Euclid Public Library, Euclid, OH [*Library symbol*] [*Library of Congress*] (LCLS)
**OEUNAH** ... Econometrics and Operations Research [*A publication*]
**Oeuvre Crit** ... Oeuvres et Critiques [*A publication*]
**Oe V** .......... Oeffentliche Verwaltung [*A publication*]
**OEV** .......... Oesterreichische Volkswirt [*A publication*]
**Oe VD** .......... Oeffentliche Verwaltung und Datenverarbeitung [*A publication*]
**Oe VE** .......... Oe VE. Oesterreichische Vorschriften fuer die Elektrotechnik [*A publication*]
**Oevers Fin Vetensk Soc Foerh** ... Oeversigt af Finska Vetenskaps-Societetens Foerhandlingar [*A publication*]
**OEW** .......... Office of Economic Warfare [*World War II*]
**OEW** .......... Open-End Wrench
**OEW** .......... Operational Empty Weight [*Aviation*]
**OEW** .......... Ordinary Electromagnetic Wave
**OEW** .......... Osteuropa Wirtschaft [*A publication*]
**OEWG** .......... Open-Ended Working Group (NATG)
**OEWG** .......... Operation, Evaluation Wartime Group (NATG)
**OEWJ** .......... Wejh [*Saudi Arabia*] [*ICAO location identifier*] (ICLI)
**OEX** .......... Office of Educational Exchange [*Department of State*]
**OEX** .......... Oklahoma City, OK [*Location identifier*] [*FAA*] (FAAL)
**OEX** .......... Options Exchange [*Finance*]
**OEX** .......... Orbiter Experiments [*NASA*] (MCD)
**OEXP** .......... Office of Exploration [*NASA*]
**OEYN** .......... Yenbo [*Saudi Arabia*] [*ICAO location identifier*] (ICLI)
**Oe ZE** .......... Oesterreichische Zeitschrift fuer Elektrizitaetswirtschaft [*A publication*]
**Oe Z E Oesterr Z Elek** ... Oe Z E/Oesterreichische Zeitschrift fuer Elektrizitaetswirtschaft [*A publication*]
**Oe ZKD** .......... Oesterreichische Zeitschrift fuer Kunst und Denkmalpflege [*A publication*]
**Oe Z Oeff R** ... Oesterreichische Zeitschrift fuer Oeffentliches Recht [*A publication*]
**Oe Z Oe R** ... Oesterreichische Zeitschrift fuer Oeffentliches Recht [*A publication*]
**Oe Z f Oe R** ... Oesterreichische Zeitschrift fuer Oeffentliches Recht [*A publication*]
**Oe ZV** .......... Oesterreichische Zeitschrift fuer Volkskunde [*A publication*]
**OF** .......... Fast Airways BV [*Netherlands*] [*ICAO designator*] (ICDA)
**OF** .......... Fitted for Oil Fuel [*Ships*]
**OF** .......... Frankford Public Library, Ontario [*Library symbol*] [*National Library of Canada*] (BIB)
**OF** .......... Montana [*Austria*] [*ICAO designator*] (FAAC)
**OF** .......... Occipitalfrontal [*Diameter of skull*]
**OF** .......... Oceanographic Facility
**OF** .......... Odd Fellows [*An association*]
**OF** .......... Official Files
**OF** .......... Offset Printing Program [*Association of Independent Colleges and Schools specialization code*]
**OF** .......... Offshore Funds [*Investment term*]
**OF** .......... Offshore Oil International [*Formerly, Offshore Oil Weekly*] [*A publication*]
**OF** .......... Oil Facility [*International Monetary Fund*]
**OF** .......... Oil Fired (ADA)
**OF** .......... Oil Fuel [*British military*] (DMA)
**OF** .......... Old Face [*Typography*]
**OF** .......... Old Field [*Botany*]
**OF** .......... Old French [*Language, etc.*]
**O/F** .......... On File (FAAC)
**OF** .......... One of the Firm [*Telecommunications*] (TEL)
**OF** .......... Open Forum [*An association*] (EA)
**OF** .......... Open Full [*Container*] (DCTA)
**OF** .......... Operating Forces [*Navy*]
**OF** .......... Operational Fixed
**OF** .......... Operations Following (MCD)
**OF** .......... Ophthalmological Foundation [*Later, NSPB*]
**OF** .......... Optical Frequency
**OF** .......... Optional Form
**O/F** .......... Orbital Flight [*NASA*] (KSC)
**OF** .......... Orbitofrontal
**OF** .......... Order of the Founder [*Salvation Army*]
**O & F** .......... Organizations and Functions (MCD)
**OF** .......... Orphan Foundation [*Later, OFA*] (EA)
**OF** .......... Osfriends (EA)
**OF** .......... Osmotic Fragility Test
**OF** .......... Osteopathic Foundation [*Later, NOF*]
**OF** .......... Outfield [*Baseball*]
**O/F** .......... Outfit [*Doll collecting*]
**OF** .......... Output Factor [*Data processing*] (IEEE)
**OF** .......... Outside Face [*Technical drawings*]
**OF** .......... Overflow
**OF** .......... Overfrequency (MSA)
**O-F** .......... Oxidation-Fermentation [*Growth medium*]
**O/F** .......... Oxidizer-to-Fuel [*Ratio*]
**OF** .......... Oxidizing Flame
**OF** .......... Oxygen Fill (NASA)
**OFA** .......... Fairfield County District Library, Lancaster, OH [*OCLC symbol*] (OCLC)

**OFA** .......... Office of Financial Analysis [*Department of the Treasury*]
**OFA** .......... Oficina Alemania [*Chile*] [*Seismograph station code, US Geological Survey*] (SEIS)
**OFA** .......... Oil-Immersed Forced-Air-Cooled [*Transformer*] (IEEE)
**OFA** .......... Old Farmer's Almanac [*A publication*]
**OFA** .......... Oncofetal Antigen [*Immunology*]
**OFA** .......... Optimized Fuel Assembly [*Nuclear energy*] (NRCH)
**OFA** .......... Order for Assignment [*Military*] (CAAL)
**OFA** .......... Organic Food Alliance (EA)
**OFA** .......... Organized Flying Adjusters (EA)
**OFA** .......... Oronite Fuel Additive
**OFA** .......... Orphan Foundation of America (EA)
**OFA** .......... Orthopedic Foundation for Animals (EA)
**OFA** .......... Overseas Family Allowance [*British military*] (DMA)
**OFA** .......... Oxygenated Fuels Association (EA)
**OFAB** ........ Fort Albany Band Library, Ontario [*Library symbol*] [*National Library of Canada*] (BIB)
**OFACS** ...... Overseas-Foreign Aeronautical Communications Station (MUGU)
**OFAD** ........ Ocean Floor Analysis Division [*Later, Sea Floor Division*] [*NORDA*] (EA)
**OFAED** ..... Organization Forecast Authorization Equipment Data [*Military*] (AFIT)
**OFAF** ......... Metallurgical Research Library, Falconbridge Nickel Mines Ltd., Falconbridge, Ontario [*Library symbol*] [*National Library of Canada*] (NLC)
**OFAGE** ..... Orthogonal-Field-Alternation Gel Electrophoresis [*Analytical biochemistry*]
**OFALF** ...... Omega First Amendment Legal Fund (EA)
**OFAM** ....... Office of Financial and Administrative Management [*Department of Labor*]
**OFANC** ..... Falconbridge Branch, Nickel Centre Public Library, Ontario [*Library symbol*] [*National Library of Canada*] (NLC)
**OFAR** ........ Office of Foreign Agricultural Relations [*Department of Agriculture*]
**OFARS** ...... Overseas-Foreign Aeronautical Receiver Station
**OFAS** ........ Overseas Flight Assistance Service
**OFATS** ...... Overseas-Foreign Aeronautical Transmitter Station
**OFavp** ........ Fairview Park Regional Library, Fairview Park, OH [*Library symbol*] [*Library of Congress*] (LCLS)
**OFB** .......... Operational Facilities Branch [*NASA*] (MCD)
**OFB** .......... Oregon Folklore Bulletin [*A publication*]
**OFC** .......... Conference on Optical Fiber Communication [*Optical Society of America*] [*Washington, DC*] (TSSD)
**OFC** .......... Foleyet Community Library, Ontario [*Library symbol*] [*National Library of Canada*] (NLC)
**OFC** .......... High Court Reports, Orange Free State [*A publication*] (DLA)
**OFC** .......... Occipitofrontal Circumference [*Anatomy*]
**OFC** .......... Oceanography and Fisheries Committee (ASF)
**OFC** .......... Office [*or Officer*] (AFM)
**OFC** .......... Office of Fishery Coordination [*World War II*]
**OFC** .......... Offshore Research Focus [*A publication*]
**OFC** .......... Oil Free Compressor
**OFC** .......... Old Fired Copper [*Initialism once used as brand name for bourbon*]
**OFC** .......... Old French Canadian [*Initialism used in Schenley brand of Canadian whisky*]
**OFC** .......... Operational Flight Control [*NASA*]
**OFC** .......... Opposing Force Component (MCD)
**OFC** .......... Optical File Cabinet [*Data processing*]
**OFC** .......... Optical Frequency Conversion
**OFC** .......... Oxford First Corporation [*NYSE symbol*] (SPSG)
**OFC** .......... Oxyfuel-Gas Cutting [*Welding*]
**OFCA** ........ Offshore Canada. Supplement of Offshore Oil Weekly [*A publication*]
**OFCA** ........ Organisation des Fabricants de Produits Cellulosiques Alimentaires de la CEE [*Organization of Manufacturers of Cellulose Products for Foodstuffs in the European Economic Community*]
**OFC-A** ....... Oxyfuel-Gas Cutting - Acetylene [*Welding*]
**OFCC** ......... Office of Federal Contract Compliance [*Later, OFCCP*] [*Department of Labor*]
**OFCCP** ...... Office of Federal Contract Compliance Programs [*Formerly, OFCC*] [*Department of Labor*]
**OFCCP Fed Cont Compl Man CCH** ... OFCCP [*Office of Federal Contract Compliance Programs*] Federal Contract Compliance Manual. Commerce Clearing House [*A publication*]
**OFCE** ......... Office [*or Officer*]
**OFC-H** ....... Oxyfuel-Gas Cutting - Hydrogen [*Welding*]
**OFCL** ......... Official
**Of Cl Pac** ... Officium Clerici Pacis [*A publication*] (DLA)
**OFCM** ........ Office of the Federal Coordinator for Meteorological Services and Research
**OFC-N** ....... Oxyfuel Cutting - Natural Gas [*Welding*]
**OFCO** ........ Offensive Counterintelligence Operations (MCD)
**OFC-P** ....... Oxyfuel-Gas Cutting - Propane [*Welding*]
**OFCS** ......... Office of Foreign Commercial Services [*Abolished 1970, functions transferred to Bureau of International Commerce*]
**OFCS** ......... Operational Flight Control System [*NASA*] (KSC)
**OFD** .......... Object Film Distance [*Optics*]
**OFD** .......... Objective Force Designator (MCD)
**OFD** .......... Occipitofrontal Diameter [*of the skull*]
**OFD** .......... Ocean Floor Drilling
**Ofd** ............ Offered [*Stock exchange term*]
**OFD** .......... Ohio Federal Decisions [*A publication*] (DLA)
**OFD** .......... One-Function Diagram
**OFD** .......... Oro-Facio-Digital [*Syndrome*] [*Medicine*]
**OFD** .......... Oued Fodda [*Algeria*] [*Seismograph station code, US Geological Survey*] (SEIS)
**OFDA** ........ Office of United States Foreign Disaster Assistance [*Agency for International Development*]
**OFDAP** ...... Office of the Field Directorate of Ammunition Plants
**OFDC** ........ Official First Day Cover [*Canada Post Corp.*]
**OFDC** ........ Ontario Film Development Corp. [*Canada*]
**OFDG** ........ Operator Fractionation Decision Guide [*Process control*]
**OFDI** ......... Office of Foreign Direct Investments [*Department of Commerce*]
**OFDR** ........ Off-Frequency Decoupling Resonance [*Physical chemistry*]
**OFDS** ......... Orbiter Flight Dynamics Simulator [*NASA*] (NASA)
**OFDS** ......... Oxygen Fluid Distribution System [*NASA*] (NASA)
**OFE** ........... Odds for Effectiveness [*Navy*]
**OFE** ........... Office of Federal Elections [*Later, FEC*]
**OFE** ........... Office of Fusion Energy [*Oak Ridge National Laboratory*]
**OFE** ........... Optical Flight Evaluation
**OFE** ........... Order for Engagement [*Military*] (CAAL)
**OFE** ........... Other Further Education
**OFEA** ........ Office of Foreign Economic Administration [*Lend-Lease*] [*World War II*]
**OFEA** ........ Officer Front End Analysis (MCD)
**OFEC** ......... Office of Federal Employees Compensation [*Department of Labor*]
**OFEC** ......... Office of Foreign Economic Coordination [*World War II*]
**OFEC** ......... Wellington County Museum, Fergus, Ontario [*Library symbol*] [*National Library of Canada*] (BIB)
**OFEHM** .... Fort Erie Historical Museum, Ontario [*Library symbol*] [*National Library of Canada*] (BIB)
**OFEN** ........ Offshore Engineer. Incorporating Northern Offshore [*A publication*]
**OFEND** ..... Offshore Engineer [*A publication*]
**OFEP** ......... Fort Erie Public Library, Ontario [*Library symbol*] [*National Library of Canada*] (NLC)
**OFER** ......... Fergus Public Library, Ontario [*Library symbol*] [*National Library of Canada*] (NLC)
**OFER** ......... Ohio Ferro-Alloys Corp. [*NASDAQ symbol*] (NQ)
**OFERC** ...... Centre Wellington District High School, Fergus, Ontario [*Library symbol*] [*National Library of Canada*] (NLC)
**OFERRA** ... Office of Foreign Economic Relief and Rehabilitation Administration
**OFERW** ..... Wellington County Public Library, Fergus, Ontario [*Library symbol*] [*National Library of Canada*] (NLC)
**OFERWM** ... Wellington County Museum and Archives, Fergus, Ontario [*Library symbol*] [*National Library of Canada*] (BIB)
**Off** ............. De Officiis [*of Cicero*] [*Classical studies*] (OCD)
**OFF** ........... Fort Frances Public Library, Ontario [*Library symbol*] [*National Library of Canada*] (NLC)
**OFF** ........... Offensive
**OFF** ........... Offer
**OFF** ........... Offertory
**Off** ............. Office [*A publication*]
**OFF** ........... Office [*or Officer*] (AFM)
**OFF** ........... Office of Facts and Figures [*Later, Office of War Information*] [*Military*]
**OFF** ........... Officers' Family Fund
**OFF** ........... Official
**OFF** ........... Offretite [*A zeolite*]
**OFF** ........... Offshore Engineer [*A publication*]
**OFF** ........... Omaha, NE [*Location identifier*] [*FAA*] (FAAL)
**OFF** ........... Organization for Femininity
**Offa Ber Mitt** ... Offa Berichte und Mitteilungen des Museums Vorgeschichtlicher Altertuemer in Kiel [*A publication*]
**Off Adm Autom** ... Office Administration and Automation [*A publication*]
**Off Air Programs (US) Publ AP Ser** ... Office of Air Programs (United States). Publication. AP Series [*A publication*]
**Off Amer Horseman** ... Official American Horseman [*A publication*]
**OFFAR** ...... Office of Fuel and Fuel Additive Registration [*Environmental Protection Agency*]
**Off Archit Plann** ... Official Architecture and Planning [*A publication*]
**Off Br** ......... Officina Brevium [*1679*] [*A publication*] (DLA)
**Off Brev** ..... Officina Brevium [*1679*] [*A publication*] (DLA)
**OFFC** ......... Office
**Off Dig Fed Paint Varn Prod Clubs** ... Official Digest. Federation of Paint and Varnish Production Clubs [*A publication*]
**Off Dig Fed Soc Paint Technol** ... Official Digest. Federation of Societies for Paint Technology [*A publication*]
**OFFEG** ...... Offshore Fossil-Fueled Electric Generators
**OFFEN** ...... Offensive [*Ammunition*] (AAG)
**Off Eng** ...... Offshore Engineer [*A publication*]
**OFFER** ...... Office of Electricity Regulation [*British*]
**Off Ex** ........ Wentworth's Office of Executors [*A publication*] (DLA)
**Off Exec** ..... Wentworth's Office of Executors [*A publication*] (DLA)
**OFFG** ......... Officiating

**Off Gaz** ...... Official Gazette [*A publication*]
**Off Gaz Pat Off** ... Official Gazette. United States Patent Office [*A publication*]
**Off Gaz Pat Office** ... Official Gazette. United States Patent and Trademark Office [*A publication*] (DLA)
**Off Gaz US Pat Off** ... Official Gazette. United States Patent Office [*A publication*]
**Off Gaz US Pat Off Pat** ... Official Gazette. United States Patent Office. Patents [*A publication*]
**Off Gaz US Pat Trademark Off Pat** ... Official Gazette. United States Patent and Trademark Office. Patents [*A publication*]
**Off Gaz US Pat Trademks Off Pat** ... Official Gazette. United States Patent and Trademark Office. Patents [*A publication*]
**Off Gaz US Pat Trademks Off Trademks** ... Official Gazette. United States Patent and Trademark Office. Trademarks [*A publication*]
**Off Gesundheitswes** ... Oeffentliche Gesundheitswesen [*A publication*]
**OFFI** .......... Official
**OFFI** .......... Old Fashion Foods, Incorporated [*NASDAQ symbol*] (NQ)
**OFFIC** ....... Official
**OFFIC** ....... Officiate
**Offic Board Markets** ... Official Board Markets [*A publication*]
**Office A & A** ... Office Administration and Automation [*A publication*]
**Office Adm & Automation** ... Office Administration and Automation [*A publication*]
**Office Admin** ... Office Administration [*A publication*]
**Office Archit Plann** ... Official Architecture and Planning [*A publication*]
**Office Eqp** ... Office Equipment and Products [*A publication*]
**Office Exec** ... Office Executive [*A publication*]
**Office Int Epizoot Bull** ... Office International des Epizooties. Bulletin [*France*] [*A publication*]
**Office Mgt** ... Office Management [*A publication*]
**Office Nat Etud Rech Aerosp (Fr) Publ** ... Office National d'Etudes et de Recherches Aerospatiales (France). Publication [*A publication*]
**Office Natl Etud Rech Aerosp Rep** ... Office National d'Etudes et de Recherches Aerospatiales. Reports [*A publication*]
**Officer** ........ Officer's Reports [*1-9 Minnesota*] [*A publication*] (DLA)
**Office Sys** .. Office Systems [*A publication*]
**Office Tech People** ... Office: Technology and People [*A publication*]
**Offic Gaz US** ... Official Gazette. United States Patent and Trademark Office [*A publication*]
**Official Gazette USPO** ... United States. Patent Office. Official Gazette [*A publication*]
**Official J Ind Comm Prop** ... Official Journal of Industrial and Commercial Property [*Eire*] [*A publication*] (DLA)
**Official Rep Ill Courts Commission** ... Official Reports, Illinois Courts Commission [*A publication*] (DLA)
**Offic J (Pat) (Gr Brit)** ... Official Journal (Patents) (Great Britain) [*A publication*]
**Off Int Epizoot Bull** ... Office International des Epizooties. Bulletin [*A publication*]
**Off J Eur Communities** ... Official Journal of the European Communities [*A publication*]
**Off J Eur Communities Inf Not** ... Official Journal of the European Communities. Information and Notices. English Edition [*A publication*]
**Off J Inst Art Educ** ... Official Journal. Institute of Art Education [*A publication*] (APTA)
**Off J Jpn Rheum Assoc** ... Official Journal. Japan Rheumatism Association [*A publication*]
**Off Jl (Pat)** ... Official Journal (Patents) [*A publication*]
**Off J (Pat)** ... Official Journal (Patents) [*A publication*]
**Off J Res Inst Med Sci Korea** ... Official Journal. Research Institute of Medical Science of Korea [*A publication*]
**OFFL** ......... Official (AFM)
**OFFM** ........ Fort Frances Museum and Cultural Centre, Ontario [*Library symbol*] [*National Library of Canada*] (BIB)
**Off Mach Guide** ... Office Machine Guide [*A publication*]
**Off Manage** ... Office Management [*A publication*]
**Off Meth Mach** ... Office Methods and Machines [*A publication*]
**Off Nat Etud Rech Aeronaut Note Tech** ... Office National d'Etudes et de Recherches Aeronautiques. Note Technique [*A publication*]
**Off Nat Etud Rech Aeronaut Publ** ... Office National d'Etudes et de Recherches Aeronautiques. Publication [*A publication*]
**Off Nat Etud Rech Aerosp (Fr) Note Tech** ... Office National d'Etudes et de Recherches Aerospatiales (France). Note Technique [*A publication*]
**Off Natl Etud Rech Aerosp (Fr) Tire Part** ... Office National d'Etudes et de Recherches Aerospatiales (France). Tire a Part [*A publication*]
**OFFNAVHIST** ... Office of Naval History [*Also, ONH*]
**Off Nav Res (US) Res Rev** ... Office of Naval Research (United States). Research Review [*A publication*]
**OFFNAVWEASERV** ... Office of Naval Weather Service
**OFFP** ......... Fenelon Falls Public Library, Ontario [*Library symbol*] [*National Library of Canada*] (BIB)
**OFFP** ........ Ovarian Follicular Fluid Peptide [*Endocrinology*]
**Off Patrol**... Offshore Patrol [*A publication*]
**Off Plast Caout** ... Officiel des Plastiques et du Caoutchouc [*A publication*]
**Off Plast Caoutch** ... Officiel des Plastiques et du Caoutchouc [*A publication*]
**Off Print Ink Maker** ... Official Printing Ink Maker [*A publication*]
**Off Proc Amer Ass Feed Micros** ... Official Proceedings. American Association of Feed Microscopists [*A publication*]
**Off Proc Annu Meet Am Assoc Feed Microsc** ... Official Proceedings. Annual Meeting. American Association of Feed Microscopists [*A publication*]
**Off Proc Annu Meet Int Dist Heat Assoc** ... Official Proceedings. Annual Meeting. International District Heating Association [*A publication*]
**Off Proc Natl Dist Heat Assoc** ... Official Proceedings. National District Heating Association [*A publication*]
**Off Publ Assoc Am Plant Food Control Off** ... Official Publication. Association of American Plant Food Control Officials [*A publication*]
**OFFR** ......... Officer
**Off Rech Sci Tech Outre-Mer Trav Doc ORSTOM** ... Office de la Recherche Scientifique et Technique d'Outre-Mer. Travaux et Documents de l'ORSTOM [*A publication*]
**Off Rec WHO** ... Official Records. World Health Organization [*A publication*]
**Off Rep** ...... Official Reports of the High Court of the Transvaal [*A publication*] (DLA)
**Offshore Eng** ... Offshore Engineer [*A publication*]
**Offshore Engr** ... Offshore Engineer [*A publication*]
**Offshore Rep** ... Offshore Report [*A publication*]
**Offshore Res Focus** ... Offshore Research Focus [*A publication*]
**Offshore Serv** ... Offshore Services [*A publication*]
**Offshore Serv Technol** ... Offshore Services and Technology [*A publication*]
**Offshore Technol Conf Proc** ... Offshore Technology Conference. Proceedings [*A publication*]
**OFFSHR** ... Offshore (NVT)
**OFFV** ......... Order of First Families of Virginia, 1607-1624/5 (EA)
**Off Yrbk Cwealth Aust** ... Official Yearbook of the Commonwealth of Australia [*A publication*] (APTA)
**Off Yrbk NSW** ... Official Yearbook of New South Wales [*A publication*] (APTA)
**Off Yrbk Queensland** ... Official Yearbook of Queensland [*A publication*] (APTA)
**Off Yrbk WA** ... Official Yearbook of Western Australia [*A publication*] (APTA)
**OFG** ........... Opferfuersorgegesetz (BJA)
**OFG** ........... Optical Frequency Generator
**OFGAS** ...... Office of Gas Service [*Government body*] [*British*]
**OFGR** ........ Objective Force Gross Requirement [*Army*] (AABC)
**OFH** ........... Odd Fellows Hall (ROG)
**OFH** ........... Oil Field Haulers Association Inc., Austin TX [*STAC*]
**OFH** ........... Rutherford B. Hayes Library, Fremont, OH [*Library symbol*] [*Library of Congress*] (LCLS)
**OFHA** ........ Oil Field Haulers Association (EA)
**OFHC** ........ Oxygen-Free, High-Conductivity [*Copper*]
**OFi** ............ Findlay-Hancock County District Public Library, Findlay, OH [*Library symbol*] [*Library of Congress*] (LCLS)
**OFI** ............ Office of Foreign Investment [*Department of Commerce*]
**OFI** ............ Operational Flight Instrumentation [*NASA*] (NASA)
**OFI** ............ Oxford Forestry Institute [*University of Oxford*] [*British*] (IRUK)
**OFiC** .......... Findlay College, Findlay, OH [*Library symbol*] [*Library of Congress*] (LCLS)
**OFID** ......... OPEC [*Organization of Petroleum Exporting Countries*] Fund for International Development (EAIO)
**O-FID** ........ Oxygen-Flame Ionization Detector
**OFIDA** ....... Office des Douanes et Accises [*Customs and Excise Office*] [*French*]
**OFII** ........... Omni Films International, Inc. [*NASDAQ symbol*] (CTT)
**OFINTAC** ... Offshore Installations Technical Advisory Committee [*British*] [*Marine science*] (MSC)
**OFIV** .......... Our Family. Ilavut. Family Newspaper. Diocese of the Arctic [*A publication*]
**OFJ** ............ Olafsfjordur [*Iceland*] [*Airport symbol*] (OAG)
**OFK** ........... Norfolk [*Nebraska*] [*Airport symbol*] (OAG)
**OFK** ........... Norfolk, NE [*Location identifier*] [*FAA*] (FAAL)
**OFK** ........... Oberfeldkommandantur [*Military government area headquarters*] [*German military - World War II*]
**OFK** ........... Official Flight Kit [*NASA*] (NASA)
**OFK** ........... Optical Flight Kit (NASA)
**OFKSA** ...... Osaka Furitsu Kogyo Shoreikan Hokoku [*A publication*]
**OFKYDA**... Proceedings. Osaka Prefecture Institute of Public Health. Edition of Pharmaceutical Affairs [*A publication*]
**OFL** ........... Flesherton Public Library, Ontario [*Library symbol*] [*National Library of Canada*] (NLC)
**OFL** ........... Official (AABC)
**OFL** ........... Open Fault Locater
**OFL** ........... Optic Fiber Layer
**OFL** ........... Overflow [*Data processing*]
**OFL** ........... Oxidizer Fill Line (AAG)
**OFLAG**...... Offizierslager [*Permanent Prison Camp for Captured Officers*] [*German military - World War II*]
**OFLC** ......... Office of Foreign Liquidation Commission
**OFLD** ........ Off-Load (NVT)
**OFLD** ........ Officeland, Inc. [*Downsview, ON*] [*NASDAQ symbol*] (NQ)
**OFLIC** ....... Office of Foreign Liquidation Commission

**OFLT**......... Office of Foreign Labor and Trade [*Department of Labor*]
**OFLTR**...... Oil Filter
**OFLUSE**... For Official Use Only [*Army*]
**OFM**.......... Observation File Maintenance
**OFM**.......... Office of Financial Management [*Bureau of the Budget; later, OMB*]
**OFM**.......... Office of Flight Missions [*NASA*] (MCD)
**OFM**.......... Office of Foreign Missions [*Department of State*]
**OFM**.......... Optofiber Metric Switch
**OFM**.......... Ordnance Field Manual [*Military*]
**OFM**.......... Ordo Fratrum Minorum [*Order of Friars Minor*] [*Observant Franciscans*] [*Roman Catholic religious order*] (EA)
**OFM**.......... Organization Field Maintenance
**OFM**.......... Oriental Fruit Moth [*Entomology*]
**OFM**.......... Orofacial Malformation
**OFM**.......... Our First Men [*Slang*]
**OFM**.......... Oxygen Fill to Missile (AAG)
**OFMC**....... Order of Friars Minor Conventual [*Conventuals*] [*Roman Catholic religious order*]
**OFM Cap**.. Order of Friars Minor Capuchin [*Capuchins*] [*Roman Catholic religious order*]
**OFM Conv**... Order of Friars Minor Conventual [*Conventuals*] [*Roman Catholic religious order*]
**OFMIS**...... Office of Financial and Management Information Systems (OICC)
**OFMP**....... Organization of Facility Managers and Planners [*Later, OMERF*] (EA)
**OFMS**........ Office of Financial and Management Services [*Department of Labor*]
**O & FN**...... Ordnance and Facilities - Navy
**OFN**........... Organization for Flora Neotropica (EA)
**OFN**........... Overfull Employment [*Economics*]
**OFNPS**....... Outstate Facility Network Planning System [*Telecommunications*] (TEL)
**OFO**........... Office of Field Operations [*Employment and Training Administration*] [*Department of Labor*]
**OFO**........... Office of Flight Operations [*NASA*]
**OFO**........... Orbiting Frog Otolith [*NASA experimental spacecraft*]
**Ofo**............ Orfeo [*Record label*]
**OFOC**......... Old Free Order of Chaldeans [*Freemasonry*] (ROG)
**OFOM**........ Operational Figure of Merit [*Military*] (CAAL)
**OFOS**......... Opening Filled Other State [*Employment*]
**OFP**........... Ashland, VA [*Location identifier*] [*FAA*] (FAAL)
**OFP**........... Occluded Frontal Passage [*Meteorology*] (FAAC)
**OFP**........... Offshore Pipelines [*NYSE symbol*] (SPSG)
**OFP**........... Oil Filter Pack
**OFP**........... On-the-Fly Printer
**OFP**........... Open Fireplace [*Classified advertising*] (ADA)
**OFP**........... Operating Force Plan
**OFP**........... Operational Flight Profile [*NASA*] (NASA)
**OFP**........... Operational Flight Program [*NASA*] (NASA)
**OFP**........... Operational Format Program [*NASA*] (KSC)
**OFP**........... Operative Federal Plasterers [*A union*] [*British*]
**OFP**........... Orbiter Flight Program [*NASA*] (NASA)
**OFP**........... Order of Friars Preachers [*Dominicans*] (ADA)
**OFP**........... Ordnance Field Park [*British*]
**OFP**........... Organizations, Functions, and Programs [*IRS*]
**OFP**........... Original Flight Plan
**OFP**........... Oscilloscope Face Plane
**OFPA**......... Order of the Founders and Patriots of America (EA)
**OFPANA**... Organic Foods Production Association of North America (EA)
**OFPCP**...... Organization of Fitness and Personal Care Professionals (EA)
**OFPM**........ Office of Fiscal Plans and Management [*Bureau of Indian Affairs*]
**OFPP**......... Office of Federal Procurement Policy [*Executive Office of the President*] (MCD)
**OFPU**......... Optical Fiber Production Unit
**OFr**............ Franklin Public Library, Franklin, OH [*Library symbol*] [*Library of Congress*] (LCLS)
**OFR**........... Ocular Following Reflex [*Ophthalmology*]
**OFR**........... Off Frequency Rejection [*Radio communications*]
**OFR**........... Office of the Federal Register
**OFR**........... Office for Recruitment [*American Library Association*]
**OFR**........... Office for Research [*American Library Association*]
**OFR**........... Officer Fitness Report [*Navy*] (NVT)
**OFR**........... Official Failure Rate [*Military*] (AFIT)
**OFR**........... Oil-Filled Resistor
**OFR**........... Old French [*Language, etc.*]
**OFR**........... On-Frequency Repeater (IEEE)
**OFR**........... Open Failure Report [*NASA*] (KSC)
**OFR**........... Open File Report (MCD)
**OFR**........... Operational Fleet Requirements (MCD)
**OFR**........... Ordering Function Register
**OFR**........... Over Frequency Relay
**OFR**........... Overseas Fuel Region (AFIT)
**OFRA**......... O'Dochartaigh Family Research Association (EA)
**OFRF**......... Overland Flow Research Facility [*Army*]
**OFRIS**....... Old Frisian [*Language, etc.*]
**OFRP**......... Overseas Family Residence Program [*Military*] (NVT)
**OFRR**......... Office of Foreign Relief and Rehabilitation [*Obsolete*]
**OFRRO**..... Office of Foreign Relief and Rehabilitation Operation [*Obsolete*]
**OFrS**.......... Franklin City Schools, Franklin, OH [*Library symbol*] [*Library of Congress*] (LCLS)
**OFS**............ Fauquier-Strickland Public Library, Fauquier, Ontario [*Library symbol*] [*National Library of Canada*] (BIB)
**OFS**............ [*Office for*] Oceanographic Facilities and Support [*National Science Foundation*]
**OFS**............ Octave Filter Set
**OFS**............ Office of Field Service [*OSRD*] [*World War II*]
**OFS**............ Office of Field Services [*Later, Bureau of Domestic Commerce*] [*Department of Commerce*]
**OFS**............ Offset (MSA)
**OFS**............ Offshore. The Journal of Ocean Business [*A publication*]
**OFS**............ One-Function Sketch
**O & FS**....... Operations and Flight Support [*NASA*] (NASA)
**OFS**............ Optical Fiber Sensor
**OFS**............ Optical Fuzing System
**OFS**............ Orange Free State [*South Africa*]
**OFS**............ Orange Free State Reports, High Court [*1879-83*] [*South Africa*] [*A publication*] (DLA)
**OFS**............ Orbital [*or Orbiter*] Flight System [*NASA*] (MCD)
**OFS**............ Orbiter Functional Simulator (NASA)
**OFS**............ Ordre Franciscain Seculier
**OFSA**.......... Ordo Fratrum Sancti Augustini [*Order of St. Augustine - OSA*] [*Rome, Italy*] (EAIO)
**OFSB**.......... Fort Severn Band Library, Ontario [*Library symbol*] [*National Library of Canada*] (BIB)
**OFSB**.......... Ordnance Field Service Bulletin [*Military*]
**OFSB**.......... Oriental Federal Savings Bank [*NASDAQ symbol*] (NQ)
**OFSC**.......... Ordnance Field Service Circular [*Military*]
**OFSC**.......... Organization and Finance Subcommittee
**OFSCC**....... Orbiter Functional Simulator Control Center (MCD)
**OFSD**.......... Operating Flight Strength Diagram
**OFSDG**...... Finch Branch, Stormont, Dundas, and Glengarry County Public Library, Ontario [*Library symbol*] [*National Library of Canada*] (BIB)
**OFSHR**...... Offshore (FAAC)
**OFSL**.......... Orange Free State Investment Limited [*New York, NY*] [*NASDAQ symbol*] (NQ)
**OFSO**.......... Overfill Shutoff Sensor (KSC)
**OFSP**.......... Office of Federal Statistical Policy [*Later, OFSPS*] [*Department of Commerce*]
**OFSPS**....... Office of Federal Statistical Policy and Standards [*Formerly, OFSP*] [*Department of Commerce*]
**OFSR**.......... Offshore Resources [*A publication*]
**OFSSA**....... Orange Free State, South Africa (ILCA)
**OFSVA**....... Offshore Services [*A publication*]
**OFT**............ Field Township Public Library, Ontario [*Library symbol*] [*National Library of Canada*] (NLC)
**OFT**............ Observed Fire Trainer [*Army*] (RDA)
**OFT**............ Office of Fair Trading [*British*]
**OFT**............ Often
**OFT**............ Operational Feasibility Testing (MCD)
**OFT**............ Operational Flight Trainer
**OFT**............ Optical Fiber Thermometry [*Instrumentation*]
**OFT**............ Optical Fiber Tube
**OFT**............ Optical Fourier Transform
**OFT**............ Optimal Foraging Theory [*Animal behavior*]
**OFT**............ Orbital Flight Test [*NASA*] (NASA)
**OFT**............ Outfit (MSA)
**OFT**............ Outline Feasibility Test [*Army*]
**OFTA**.......... Operational Flight Transfer Airframe
**Oftalmol Zh**... Oftal'mologicheskii Zhurnal [*A publication*]
**OFTB**.......... Offshore Technology Board [*British*]
**OFTD**.......... Oxygen Furnace Tilt Drive
**OFTDA**....... Office of Flight Tracking and Data Acquisition [*NASA*]
**OFTDS**....... Orbital Flight Test Data System [*NASA*] (MCD)
**OFTEL**....... Office of Telecommunications [*Independent government agency*] [*British*]
**OFTM**......... On-Orbit Flight Technique Meeting [*NASA*] (MCD)
**OFTMS**...... Output Format Table Modification Submodule
**OFTR**.......... Orbital Flight Test Requirement [*NASA*] (NASA)
**OFTS**.......... Operational Flight and Tactics Simulator (MCD)
**OFU**............ Floating Units Division [*Coast Guard*]
**OFU**............ Franklin University, Columbus, OH [*OCLC symbol*] (OCLC)
**OFU**............ Ofu Island [*American Samoa*] [*Airport symbol*] (OAG)
**OFU**............ Ofunato [*Japan*] [*Seismograph station code, US Geological Survey*] (SEIS)
**OFW**........... Off Watch (FAAC)
**OFW**........... Operation Fish Watch [*National Oceanic and Atmospheric Administration*] (MSC)
**OFW**........... Oxyfuel-Gas Welding
**OFWAT**...... Office of Water Services [*British*]
**OFWN**........ Ontario Library Service - Nipigon, Thunder Bay, Ontario [*Library symbol*] [*National Library of Canada*] (NLC)
**OF/WST**.... Operational Flight/Weapons System Trainer (NG)
**OFY**............ Opportunities for Youth Program [*Canada*]
**OFZ**............ Fort Sill, OK [*Location identifier*] [*FAA*] (FAAL)
**OFZ**............ Obstacle Free Zone
**OFZHA**...... Oftal'mologicheskii Zhurnal [*A publication*]

**OG** ............ Guelph Public Library, Ontario [*Library symbol*] [*National Library of Canada*] (NLC)
**OG** ............ Obergericht [*Court of Appeal*] [*German*] (DLA)
**OG** ............ Oberstes Gericht [*Supreme Court*] [*German*]
**OG** ............ Object Glass (MSA)
**OG** ............ Obscure Glass
**OG** ............ Obstetrics-Gynecology [*Medicine*]
**OG** ............ Occlusogingival [*Dentistry*]
**OG** ............ Off-Gas [*Nuclear energy*] (NRCH)
**OG** ............ Offensive Guard [*Football*]
**OG** ............ Office of Geography [*Functions transferred to Geographic Names Division of Army Topographic Command*] [*Department of the Interior*]
**OG** ............ Officer of the Guard [*Army*]
**OG** ............ Official Gazette. United States Patent and Trademark Office [*A publication*]
**OG** ............ Ogasawara Trench
**OG** ............ Ogden Corp. [*NYSE symbol*] (SPSG)
**OG** ............ Ogee [*A molding*] [*Architecture*] (ROG)
**OG** ............ Oh, Gee [*Slang*]
**OG** ............ Oil Gauge
**OG** ............ Oil Glands [*In propeller shaft*]
**OG** ............ Old German [*Language, etc.*]
**OG** ............ Old Girl [*A wife*] [*Slang*]
**OG** ............ Old Greasybeard: Tales from the Cumberland Gap [*A publication*]
**OG** ............ Olympic Games
**OG** ............ On Ground [*Aviation*]
**OG** ............ Ongoing (ADA)
**OG** ............ Operation Greenhouse [*Atomic weapons testing*]
**OG** ............ Operational Group [*World War II*]
**OG** ............ Optic Ganglion
**OG** ............ Or Gate [*Data processing*]
**OG** ............ Orange Green [*Stain*] [*Medicine*]
**OG** ............ Organic Gardening [*A publication*]
**OG** ............ Organisation Gestosis [*Basel, Switzerland*] (EAIO)
**OG** ............ Orientalia Gandensia [*Ghent*] [*A publication*]
**OG** ............ Original Gum [*Philately*]
**OG** ............ Outdoor Girl [*Max Factor cosmetic line*]
**OG** ............ Outer Gimbal
**O/G** ........... Outgoing [*Data processing*]
**OG** ............ Outside Guard
**OG** ............ Outside Guardian [*Freemasonry*] (ROG)
**OG** ............ Oxygen Gauge (NASA)
**OG** ............ Societe Anonyme de Transports Aeriens Air Guadeloupe [*ICAO designator*] (FAAC)
**OGA** .......... Obergurgl [*Austria*] [*Seismograph station code, US Geological Survey*] (SEIS)
**OGA** .......... Oesterreichische Gastgewerbe und Hotel Zeitung [*A publication*]
**OGA** .......... Ogallala, NE [*Location identifier*] [*FAA*] (FAAL)
**O/GA** ......... Oil Gauge [*Automotive engineering*]
**OGA** .......... Ornamental Growers Association (EA)
**OGA** .......... Outer Gimbal Angle (NASA)
**OGA** .......... Outer Gimbal Assembly (NASA)
**OGA** .......... Outer Gimbal Axis
**OGAC** ........ Galt Collegiate Institute, Cambridge, Ontario [*Library symbol*] [*National Library of Canada*] (NLC)
**OGAC** ........ Organizational Governance Advisory Committee [*NERComP*]
**OGAL** ........ Cambridge Public Library, Ontario [*Library symbol*] [*National Library of Canada*] (NLC)
**OGalG** ....... Gallia County District Library, Gallipolis, OH [*Library symbol*] [*Library of Congress*] (LCLS)
**OGALL** ..... Cavendish Public Library (G. Galloway), Ontario [*Library symbol*] [*National Library of Canada*] (BIB)
**OGAMA** .... Ogden Air Material Area [*AFLC*]
**OGAN** ....... Gananoque Public Library, Ontario [*Library symbol*] [*National Library of Canada*] (NLC)
**OGB** .......... Beriault Branch, Gloucester Public Library, Ontario [*Library symbol*] [*National Library of Canada*] (NLC)
**OGB** .......... Orangeburg, SC [*Location identifier*] [*FAA*] (FAAL)
**OGBD** ........ Orbiter Gamma Burst Detecter [*NASA*]
**OGBG** ........ Official Gazette Reports, British Guiana [*A publication*] (DLA)
**OGBH** ........ Blackburn Hamlet Branch, Gloucester Public Library, Ontario [*Library symbol*] [*National Library of Canada*] (NLC)
**OGBKT** ..... Blessed Kateri Tekakwitha School, Gloucester, Ontario [*Library symbol*] [*National Library of Canada*] (NLC)
**OGB-L** ....... Onofhaengege Gewerkschaftsbond-Letzeburg [*Confederation of Independent Trade Unions*] [*Luxembourg*] (EY)
**OGBU** ........ Gore Bay Union Public Library, Ontario [*Library symbol*] [*National Library of Canada*] (NLC)
**OGC** .......... Centennial Collegiate Vocational Institute, Guelph, Ontario [*Library symbol*] [*National Library of Canada*] (NLC)
**OGC** .......... Grove City Public Library, Grove City, OH [*OCLC symbol*] (OCLC)
**OGc** ........... Grove City Public Library, Grove City, OH [*Library symbol*] [*Library of Congress*] (LCLS)
**OGC** .......... Office of General Counsel
**OGC** .......... Order of the Golden Chain (EA)
**OGC** .......... Oregon Graduate Center for Study and Research [*Research center*] (RCD)
**OGCF** ........ Canadian Farm Management Data System, Agriculture Canada [*Systeme Canadien de Donnees sur la Gestion Agricole, Agriculture Canada*] Guelph, Ontario [*Library symbol*] [*National Library of Canada*] (NLC)
**OGCH** ........ College Heights Secondary School, Guelph, Ontario [*Library symbol*] [*National Library of Canada*] (NLC)
**OGC-N** ...... Office of General Counsel - NASA
**OGCV** ........ Guelph Collegiate Vocational Institute, Ontario [*Library symbol*] [*National Library of Canada*] (NLC)
**OGCW** ....... Cairine Wilson Secondary School, Gloucester, Ontario [*Library symbol*] [*National Library of Canada*] (BIB)
**OGD** .......... Ogden, UT [*Location identifier*] [*FAA*] (FAAL)
**Ogd** ............ Ogden's Reports [*12-15 Louisiana*] [*A publication*] (DLA)
**OGD** .......... Ogdensburg [*New Jersey*] [*Seismograph station code, US Geological Survey*] (SEIS)
**OGD** .......... Omega Gamma Delta [*Fraternity*] (EA)
**OGDA** ........ Oyster Growers and Dealers Association (EA)
**OGDD** ........ Outgoing/Delay Dial [*Telecommunications*] (TEL)
**Ogden** ......... Ogden's Reports [*12-15 Louisiana*] [*A publication*] (DLA)
**OGDR** ........ Uniroyal Research Laboratories, Guelph, Ontario [*Library symbol*] [*National Library of Canada*] (NLC)
**OGE** .......... Entomological Society of Ontario, Guelph, Ontario [*Library symbol*] [*National Library of Canada*] (NLC)
**OGE** .......... Office of Government Ethics
**OGE** .......... Oklahoma Gas & Electric Co. [*NYSE symbol*] (SPSG)
**OGE** .......... Omaha Grain Exchange (EA)
**OGE** .......... Ons Geestelijk Erf [*A publication*]
**OGE** .......... Operating [*or Operational*] Ground Equipment
**OGE** .......... Optogalvanic Effect (MCD)
**OGE** .......... Oregon Graduate Center, Beaverton, OR [*OCLC symbol*] (OCLC)
**OGE** .......... Out-of-Ground Effect
**OGEC** ........ Organization of Gas Exporting Countries [*Proposed gas cartel*]
**OGEDJ** ...... E. D. Jones Branch, Gloucester Public Library, Ontario [*Library symbol*] [*National Library of Canada*] (NLC)
**OGEG** ........ Georgetown District High School, Ontario [*Library symbol*] [*National Library of Canada*] (NLC)
**OGEH** ........ Georgetown Branch, Halton Hills Public Libraries, Ontario [*Library symbol*] [*National Library of Canada*] (BIB)
**OGELR** ..... Ecole Secondaire Louis-Riel, Gloucester, Ontario [*Library symbol*] [*National Library of Canada*] (BIB)
**OGEO** ........ Georgetown Public Library, Ontario [*Library symbol*] [*National Library of Canada*] (NLC)
**OGeo** .......... Mary P. Shelton Library, Georgetown, OH [*Library symbol*] [*Library of Congress*] (LCLS)
**OGER** ........ Geraldton Public Library, Ontario [*Library symbol*] [*National Library of Canada*] (NLC)
**OGer** .......... Germantown Public Library, Germantown, OH [*Library symbol*] [*Library of Congress*] (LCLS)
**OGE/RPIE** ... Operating Ground Equipment/Real Property Installed Equipment (AFM)
**OGEV** ........ Varian Canada, Inc., Georgetown, Ontario [*Library symbol*] [*National Library of Canada*] (NLC)
**OGF** .......... Organic Gardening and Farming [*A publication*]
**OGF** .......... Ovarian Growth Factor [*Medicine*]
**OGFC** ........ Official Gumby Fan Club (EA)
**OGFP** ........ Obtaining Goods by False Pretense
**OGFS** ........ Oil and Gas Field Study [*Department of the Interior*]
**OGG** .......... GasTOPS Ltd., Gloucester, Ontario [*Library symbol*] [*National Library of Canada*] (NLC)
**OGG** .......... Kahului [*Hawaii*] [*Airport symbol*] (OAG)
**OGG** .......... Kahului, HI [*Location identifier*] [*FAA*] (FAAL)
**OGG** .......... Organic Geochemistry Group
**OGH** .......... Oberster Gerichtshof [*Supreme Court*] [*German*] (DLA)
**OGHC** ........ Hart Chemicals Ltd., Guelph, Ontario [*Library symbol*] [*National Library of Canada*] (NLC)
**OGHS** ........ Gloucester High School, Ontario [*Library symbol*] [*National Library of Canada*] (BIB)
**OGHS** ........ Orbit Gas Co. [*NASDAQ symbol*] (NQ)
**OGI** ........... Gould Information Center, Cleveland, OH [*OCLC symbol*] (OCLC)
**OGI** ........... Oceanic Gamefish Investigations [*National Oceanic and Atmospheric Administration*] (MSC)
**OGI** ........... Oculogyral Illusion [*NASA*]
**OGI** ........... Off-Gas Isolation [*Nuclear energy*] (NRCH)
**OGI** ........... Oil and Gas Investor [*A publication*]
**OGI** ........... Ontario Government Information [*Database*] [*Ministry of Culture and Communications*] [*Information service or system*] (CRD)
**OGI** ........... Orientis Graeci Inscriptiones Selectae [*A publication*] (OCD)
**OGI** ........... Outer Grid Injection
**OGID** ......... Outgoing/Immediate Dial [*Telecommunications*] (TEL)
**OGIL** ......... [*The*] Ogilvy Group, Inc. [*NASDAQ symbol*] (NQ)
**OGIL** ......... Open General Import Licence [*British*] (DS)
**Ogilvie Dict** ... Ogilvie's Imperial Dictionary of the English Language [*A publication*] (DLA)
**OGIP** ......... Original Gas in Place [*Natural resources*]
**OGIS** ......... Orientis Graeci Inscriptiones Selectae [*A publication*]
**OGJ** .......... Oil and Gas Journal [*A publication*]
**OGJ** .......... Outgoing Junction [*Telecommunications*] (TEL)

**OGJFR** ...... John F. Ross Collegiate Vocational Institute, Guelph, Ontario [*Library symbol*] [*National Library of Canada*] (NLC)
**O & G Jour** ... Oil and Gas Journal. Forecast/Review [*A publication*]
**OGK** .......... Kenyon College, Gambier, OH [*Library symbol*] [*Library of Congress*] (LCLS)
**OGK** .......... Onsei Gakkai Kaiho [*Bulletin of the Phonetic Society of Japan*] [*A publication*]
**OGL** .......... Obscure Glass (AAG)
**OGL** .......... Oesterreich in Geschichte und Literatur [*Wien*] [*A publication*]
**OGL** .......... Open General License [*Import license*] (DS)
**OGL** .......... Oral Glucose Loading [*Endocrinology*]
**OGL** .......... Outgoing Line
**OGLA** ........ Officer Grade Limitations Act of 1954
**OGLE** ........ Oglebay Norton Co. [*NASDAQ symbol*] (NQ)
**OGLE** ........ Organization for Getting Legs Exposed [*Group opposing below-the-knee fashions introduced in 1970*]
**OGLPFC** ... Official Gary Lewis and the Playboys Fan Club (EA)
**OGM** ........ Office of Grants Management [*Public Health Service*]
**OGM** ........ Ontonagon, MI [*Location identifier*] [*FAA*] (FAAL)
**OGM** ........ Optimum Gradient Method
**OGM** ........ Ordinary General Meeting
**OGM** ........ Organic Gaseous Mercury [*Environmental chemistry*]
**OGM** ........ Outgoing Message [*Telecommunications*]
**OGMB** ....... Mattagami Band Public Library, Gogama, Ontario [*Library symbol*] [*National Library of Canada*] (NLC)
**OGMC** ....... Ordnance Guided Missile Center (MCD)
**OGMCAQ** ... Specialist Periodical Reports. Organometallic Chemistry [*A publication*]
**OGMH** ....... Morrison Hershfield Ltd., Guelph, Ontario [*Library symbol*] [*National Library of Canada*] (NLC)
**OGMS** ....... Ordnance Guided Missile School
**OGMSD** .... Glen Morris Branch, South Dumfries Township Public Library, Ontario [*Library symbol*] [*National Library of Canada*] (BIB)
**OGMT** ....... Orbiter Greenwich Mean Time [*NASA*] (MCD)
**OGN** .......... Obstetric, Gynecologic, and Neonatal
**OGN** .......... Yonagunijima [*Japan*] [*Airport symbol*] (OAG)
**OGNC** ........ Garson Branch, Nickel Centre Public Library, Ontario [*Library symbol*] [*National Library of Canada*] (NLC)
**OGNPA** ..... Ogneupory [*A publication*]
**OGO** .......... Abengourou [*Ivory Coast*] [*Airport symbol*] (OAG)
**OGO** .......... City Hall Branch, Gloucester Public Library, Ontario [*Library symbol*] [*National Library of Canada*] (NLC)
**OGO** .......... Gould, Inc., Ocean Systems Information Center, Cleveland, OH [*OCLC symbol*] (OCLC)
**OGO** .......... Officer Grade Objectives
**OGO** .......... Oliver Gold Corp. [*Vancouver Stock Exchange symbol*]
**OGO** .......... Orbiting Geophysical Observatory [*NASA*]
**OG/OB** ...... Office Group/Office Branch [*IRS*]
**OGOG** ....... Gogama Community Library, Ontario [*Library symbol*] [*National Library of Canada*] (NLC)
**OGOH** ....... Huron County Public Library, Goderich, Ontario [*Library symbol*] [*National Library of Canada*] (NLC)
**OGOHC** .... Huron County Pioneer Museum, Goderich, Ontario [*Library symbol*] [*National Library of Canada*] (BIB)
**OGOR** ....... Goulais River Community Library, Ontario [*Library symbol*] [*National Library of Canada*] (NLC)
**OGP** .......... Original Gross Premium [*Insurance*] (AIA)
**OGP** .......... Outgoing Message Process [*Telecommunications*] (TEL)
**OGPA** ........ Office of the General Purchasing Agent [*Military*]
**OG Pat Off** ... Official Gazette. United States Patent Office [*A publication*]
**OGPEC** ...... Officially Guaranteed Private Export Credits
**OGPI** ......... Optical Glide Path Indicator
**OGPS** ........ Office of Grants and Program Systems [*Department of Agriculture*]
**OGPU** ........ Otdelenie Gosudarstvenni Politcheskoi Upravi [*Special Government Political Administration*] [*Former Soviet secret service organization, also known as GPU*] [*Later, KGB*]
**OGR** .......... B. F. Goodrich Co., Information Center, Brecksville, OH [*OCLC symbol*] (OCLC)
**OGr** .......... Greenville Public Library, Greenville, OH [*Library symbol*] [*Library of Congress*] (LCLS)
**OGR** .......... Grimsby Public Library and Art Gallery, Ontario [*Library symbol*] [*National Library of Canada*] (NLC)
**OGR** .......... Official Guide of the Railways [*A publication*]
**OGR** .......... Old Garden Rose [*Pre-1870*] [*Horticulture*]
**OGR** .......... Operation Grass Roots [*Small communities employment service*]
**OGR** .......... Order of the Golden Rule (EA)
**OGR** .......... Ordnance, Gunnery, and Readiness Division [*Coast Guard*]
**OGR** .......... Original Gross Rate [*Insurance*] (AIA)
**OGR** .......... ORNL [*Oak Ridge National Laboratory*] Graphite Reactor
**OGR** .......... Outgoing Repeater
**OGRA** ........ Gravenhurst Public Library, Ontario [*Library symbol*] [*National Library of Canada*] (NLC)
**OGraD** ....... Denison University, Granville, OH [*Library symbol*] [*Library of Congress*] (LCLS)
**OGraO** ....... Owens-Corning Fiberglas Corp., Granville, OH [*Library symbol*] [*Library of Congress*] (LCLS)
**OGRC** ........ Office of Grants and Research Contracts [*NASA*]
**OGRE** ........ Greely Public Library, Ontario [*Library symbol*] [*National Library of Canada*] (NLC)
**OGRE** ........ Organization of Generally Rotten Enterprises [*Evil organization in television cartoon series "The Drak Pack"*]
**OGRM** ....... Grimsby Museum, Ontario [*Library symbol*] [*National Library of Canada*] (BIB)
**OGRV** ........ Grand Valley Public Library, Ontario [*Library symbol*] [*National Library of Canada*] (NLC)
**OGS** .......... Oakland Growth Study [*1932-1964*] [*Sociology*]
**OGS** .......... Obsolete General Supplies [*Military*]
**OGS** .......... Off-Gas System [*Nuclear energy*] (NRCH)
**OGS** .......... Ogdensburg [*New York*] [*Airport symbol*] (OAG)
**OGS** .......... Ogdensburg, NY [*Location identifier*] [*FAA*] (FAAL)
**OGS** .......... Ohio Genealogical Society (EA)
**OGS** .......... Operative Glovers' Society [*A union*] [*British*]
**O-GS** .......... Operator-to-General Support [*Maintenance*] (MCD)
**OGS** .......... Optical Guidance System
**OGS** .......... Oratory of the Good Shepherd [*British*]
**OGS** .......... Original Ground Surface
**OGS** .......... Outer Glide Slope [*Aviation*] (NASA)
**OGS** .......... Oxford German Studies [*A publication*]
**OGS** .......... Oxygen Generation System (NASA)
**OGSE** ........ Operational Ground Support Equipment (AAG)
**OGSEL** ...... Operational Ground Support Equipment List (AAG)
**OGSGS** ...... Orangeburgh German Swiss Genealogical Society (EA)
**OGSM** ....... Office of the General Sales Manager [*Department of Agriculture*]
**OGSM** ....... Stone Shop Museum, Grimsby, Ontario [*Library symbol*] [*National Library of Canada*] (NLC)
**Ogs Med Jur** ... Ogston's Medical Jurisprudence [*1878*] [*A publication*] (DLA)
**OGSt** .......... Entscheidungen des Obersten Gerichts in Strafsachen [*German Democratic Republic*] [*A publication*]
**OGST** ........ Overthread Guide Sleeve Tool [*Nuclear energy*] (NRCH)
**OGSTM** .... St. Matthew High School, Gloucester, Ontario [*Library symbol*] [*National Library of Canada*] (BIB)
**OGT** .......... MIS Division, Turnelle Productions Ltd., Gloucester, Ontario [*Library symbol*] [*National Library of Canada*] (BIB)
**OGT** .......... Office for Gifted and Talented [*Education*]
**OGT** .......... Oppenheimer Multi-Government Trust [*NYSE symbol*] (SPSG)
**OGT** .......... Outgoing Trunk
**OGT** .......... Outlet Gas Temperature (MSA)
**OGTC** ........ Tudor and Cashel Public Library, Gilmour, Ontario [*Library symbol*] [*National Library of Canada*] (BIB)
**OGTM** ....... Official Gazette. United States Patent and Trademark Office [*A publication*] (DLA)
**OGTT** ........ Oral Glucose Tolerance Test [*Medicine*]
**OGU** .......... Occupational Guidance Unit [*Department of Employment*] [*British*]
**OGU** .......... Ogden Bay [*Utah*] [*Seismograph station code, US Geological Survey*] (SEIS)
**OGU** .......... Outgoing Unit
**OGU** .......... University of Guelph, Ontario [*Library symbol*] [*National Library of Canada*] (NLC)
**OGV** .......... Outlet Guide Vane
**OGV** .......... Oxygen Gauge Valve (NASA)
**OGW** ......... Overhead Ground Wire
**OGW** ......... Overload Gross Weight (NG)
**OGWE** ....... Education Library, Wellington County Board of Education, Guelph, Ontario [*Library symbol*] [*National Library of Canada*] (NLC)
**OGWS** ....... Outgoing/Wink Start [*Telecommunications*] (TEL)
**OGX** .......... Ouargla [*Algeria*] [*Airport symbol*] (OAG)
**OGY** .......... OGY Petroleum [*Vancouver Stock Exchange symbol*]
**OGY** .......... O'Gyalla [*Later, HRB*] [*Czechoslovakia*] [*Geomagnetic observatory code*]
**OH** ............ Finland [*Aircraft nationality and registration mark*] (FAAC)
**OH** ............ Hamilton Public Library, Ontario [*Library symbol*] [*National Library of Canada*] (NLC)
**OH** ............ Hospitaller Order of St. John of God [*Roman Catholic men's religious order*]
**OH** ............ Hydroxy [*As substituent on nucleoside*] [*Also, HO*] [*Biochemistry*]
**OH** ............ Oakwood Homes Corp. [*NYSE symbol*] (SPSG)
**OH** ............ Observation Helicopter
**OH** ............ Occipital Horn [*Brain anatomy*]
**OH** ............ Occupational Health
**OH** ............ Occupational History [*Medicine*]
**O-H** ........... Octal-to-Hexadecimal [*Data processing*] (IEEE)
**OH** ............ Off Hook [*Data processing*]
**OH** ............ Office of the Handicapped
**OH** ............ Office Hours
**OH** ............ Ohio [*Postal code*]
**Oh** ............ Ohio Courts of Appeals Reports [*A publication*] (DLA)
**OH** ............ Ohio History [*A publication*]
**OH** ............ Ohmic Heating
**Oh** ............ Oholoth (BJA)
**OH** ............ Olduvai Hominid [*Paleoanthropology*]
**OH** ............ Omni Hora [*Every Hour*] [*Pharmacy*]
**OH** ............ On Hand

**OH**............ Ontario History [*A publication*]
**OH**............ Open Heart Surgery [*Medicine*]
**OH**............ Open Hearth
**OH**............ Operating Hours (MCD)
**OH**............ Operational Handbook [*Marine Corps*] (INF)
**OH**............ Operational Hardware (KSC)
**OH**............ Operator's Handbook
**OH**............ Orah Hayyim Shulhan 'Arukh (BJA)
**OH**............ Originating Hospital [*Aeromedical evacuation*]
**OH**............ Orthostatic Hypotension [*Medicine*]
**OH**............ Osteopathic Hospitals [*A publication*]
**OH**............ Otago Hussars [*British military*] (DMA)
**OH**............ Oud-Holland [*A publication*]
**OH**............ Out Home [*Men's lacrosse position*]
**OH**............ Outlaw HAWK [*Naval Air Development Center*]
**OH**............ Outpatient Hospital [*Medicine*]
**O/H**.......... Over-the-Horizon Transmission
**OH**............ Overhaul
**OH**............ Overhead
**O/H**.......... Overzuche Handels Maatschappij [*Foreign Trade Company*] [*Dutch*] (ILCA)
**OH**............ Ozar Hatorah (EA)
**OH**............ SFO [*San Francisco and Oakland*] Helicopter Airlines, Inc. [*ICAO designator*] (OAG)
**OHA**.......... Chicago, IL [*Location identifier*] [*FAA*] (FAAL)
**OHA**.......... Havelock Public Library, Ontario [*Library symbol*] [*National Library of Canada*] (BIB)
**OHa**.......... Lane Public Library, Hamilton, OH [*Library symbol*] [*Library of Congress*] (LCLS)
**OHA**.......... Occupational Hazards [*A publication*]
**OHA**.......... Office of Hearings and Appeals [*In various federal departments*]
**OHA**.......... Officers' Home Advance (ADA)
**Oha**........... Ohaloth (BJA)
**Oh A**......... Ohio Appellate Reports [*A publication*] (DLA)
**OHA**.......... Operational Hazard Analysis (NASA)
**OHA**.......... Oral History Association (EA)
**OHA**.......... Orbital Height Adjustment Maneuver (MCD)
**OHA**.......... Oscillator Housing Assembly
**OHA**.......... Outside Helix Angle
**OHA**.......... Overseas Housing Allowance
**OHA**.......... Owner Handler Association of America (EA)
**OHaBHi**.... Butler County Historical Society, Hamilton, OH [*Library symbol*] [*Library of Congress*] (LCLS)
**OHAD**....... Dysart Branch, Haliburton County Public Library, Ontario [*Library symbol*] [*National Library of Canada*] (BIB)
**Oh A 2d**..... Ohio Appellate Reports, Second Series [*A publication*] (DLA)
**OHAG**....... Art Gallery of Hamilton, Ontario [*Library symbol*] [*National Library of Canada*] (NLC)
**OHAI**......... Haileybury Public Library, Ontario [*Library symbol*] [*National Library of Canada*] (NLC)
**OHAINC**... Haileybury School of Mines Campus, Northern College of Applied Arts and Technology, Ontario [*Library symbol*] [*National Library of Canada*] (BIB)
**OHAL**........ Haliburton County Public Library, Ontario [*Library symbol*] [*National Library of Canada*] (NLC)
**OHALM**.... Haliburton Highlands Museum, Haliburton, Ontario [*Library symbol*] [*National Library of Canada*] (BIB)
**OHaMH**.... Mercy Hospital, Health Science Library, Hamilton, OH [*Library symbol*] [*Library of Congress*] (LCLS)
**OHAN**....... Hanover Public Library, Ontario [*Library symbol*] [*National Library of Canada*] (NLC)
**Oh Ap**........ Ohio Appellate Reports [*A publication*] (DLA)
**OHARAG**... Research Station, Agriculture Canada [*Station de Recherches, Agriculture Canada*] Harrow, Ontario [*Library symbol*] [*National Library of Canada*] (NLC)
**OHaU**........ Miami University, Hamilton Campus, Hamilton, OH [*Library symbol*] [*Library of Congress*] (LCLS)
**OHB**.......... L'Equilibre Biologique [*France*] [*Research code symbol*]
**OHBC**........ Ohio Bancorp [*NASDAQ symbol*] (NQ)
**OHBC**........ Oregon Highland Bentgrass Commission (EA)
**OHBES**..... Schools, Hamilton Board of Education, Ontario [*Library symbol*] [*National Library of Canada*] (NLC)
**OHBHU**.... Hilton Union Public Library, Hilton Beach, Ontario [*Library symbol*] [*National Library of Canada*] (NLC)
**OHBMS**.... On His [*or Her*] Britannic Majesty's Service
**OHBP**........ Pic Heron Bay Band Public Library, Heron Bay, Ontario [*Library symbol*] [*National Library of Canada*] (BIB)
**OHC**.......... Occupational Health Center (KSC)
**OHC**.......... O'Higgins [*Antarctica*] [*Seismograph station code, US Geological Survey*] (SEIS)
**OHC**.......... On Board Hard Copier (NASA)
**OHC**.......... Optics Hand Controller (KSC)
**OHC**.......... Oral History Collection [*Monash University*] [*Australia*]
**OHC**.......... Order of the Holy Cross [*Episcopalian religious order*]
**OHC**.......... Oriole Homes Corporation [*AMEX symbol*] (SPSG)
**OHC**.......... Ottumwa Heights College [*Iowa*]
**OHC**.......... Outer Hair Cells [*of cochlea*] [*Anatomy*]
**OHC**.......... Overhead Camshaft [*Automotive term*]
**OHC**.......... Overhead Cupboards [*Classified advertising*] (ADA)
**OHCA**........ Otter Hound Club of America [*Later, OCA*] (EA)
**Oh Cir Ct**... Ohio Circuit Court Reports [*A publication*] (DLA)
**Oh Cir Ct NS**... Ohio Circuit Court Reports, New Series [*A publication*] (DLA)
**Oh Cir Dec**... Ohio Circuit Decisions [*A publication*] (DLA)
**OHCU**....... College Universitaire de Hearst, Ontario [*Library symbol*] [*National Library of Canada*] (NLC)
**OHD**.......... Office of Human Development [*Later, OHDS*] [*HEW*]
**OHD**.......... Ohrid [*Yugoslavia*] [*Airport symbol*] (OAG)
**OHD**.......... Old Hickory Dam [*TVA*]
**OHD**.......... Ordinary Hydrodynamic
**OHD**.......... Organic Heart Disease [*Medicine*]
**OHD**.......... Over-the-Horizon Detector [*RADAR*]
**OHDA**........ Hydroxydopamine [*Also, HDA, HDM*] [*Biochemistry*]
**OHD-B**...... Over-the-Horizon Detection RADAR-Backscatter (MCD)
**Oh Dec**....... Ohio Decisions [*A publication*] (DLA)
**Oh Dec Rep**... Ohio Decisions Reprint [*A publication*] (DLA)
**OHDETS**.. Over-the-Horizon Detection System [*RADAR*]
**OHDF**........ Dofasco, Inc., Hamilton, Ontario [*Library symbol*] [*National Library of Canada*] (NLC)
**OHDFR**..... Research Information Center, DOFASCO, Inc., Hamilton, Ontario [*Library symbol*] [*National Library of Canada*] (NLC)
**OHDS**........ Office of Human Development Services [*Formerly, OHD*] [*Department of Health and Human Services*]
**OHE**.......... Hearst Public Library, Ontario [*Library symbol*] [*National Library of Canada*] (NLC)
**OHE**.......... Office of Health Economics [*British*]
**OHE**.......... Office of Higher Education [*New South Wales, Australia*]
**OHE**.......... Office of the Housing Expediter [*Terminated, 1951*] (GPO)
**OHEAT**..... Overheat
**OHEC**........ Dr. Harry Paikin Library, Hamilton Board of Education, Ontario [*Library symbol*] [*National Library of Canada*] (NLC)
**OHEC**........ Hamilton Education Centre, Ontario [*Library symbol*] [*National Library of Canada*] (NLC)
**OHEL**........ Oxford History of English Literature [*A publication*]
**OHEP**........ Hepworth Branch, Bruce County Public Library, Ontario [*Library symbol*] [*National Library of Canada*] (NLC)
**OHER**........ Office of Health and Environmental Research [*Department of Energy*] [*Washington, DC*]
**OHESC**..... Ontario Library Service - Escarpment, Hamilton, Ontario [*Library symbol*] [*National Library of Canada*] (NLC)
**OHET**........ Erin Township Public Library, Hillsburgh, Ontario [*Library symbol*] [*National Library of Canada*] (NLC)
**OHF**.......... Occupational Health Facility [*NASA*] (KSC)
**OHF**.......... Omsk Hemorrhagic Fever [*Medicine*]
**OHF**.......... Ordnance Historical Files [*Military*]
**OHF**.......... Overhead Fire (MCD)
**OHFC**........ Hartington Branch, Frontenac County Library, Hartington, Ontario [*Library symbol*] [*National Library of Canada*] (BIB)
**OHFC**........ Owen Hart Fan Club (EA)
**Oh F Dec**.... Ohio Federal Decisions [*A publication*] (DLA)
**OH/FH**...... Operating Hour/Flight Hour [*Ratio*]
**OHG**.......... Offene Handelsgesellschaft [*General Partnership*] [*German*]
**OHG**.......... Old High German [*Language, etc.*]
**OHGI**........ Over the Hill Gang, International (EA)
**OHGS**........ Omega Hyperbolic Grid System
**OHGVT**..... Orbital Horizontal Ground Vibration Test [*NASA*] (NASA)
**OHH**.......... Herrold Hall Learning Resource Center, Zanesville, OH [*OCLC symbol*] (OCLC)
**OHH**.......... Ohio Household Goods Carriers Bureau Inc., Warren OH [*STAC*]
**OHH**.......... Owen Harrison Harding [*of the James W. Ellison novel, "I'm Owen Harrison Harding"*]
**OHI**........... HUNA International (EA)
**OHI**........... Occupational Health Institute [*Defunct*] (EA)
**OHI**........... Ocular Hypertension Indicator
**OHi**........... Ohio Historical Society, Columbus, OH [*Library symbol*] [*Library of Congress*] (LCLS)
**OHI**........... Oil-Heat Institute of America [*Later, PMAA*]
**OHI**........... Ordnance Handling Instructions
**OHI**........... Organisation Hydrographique Internationale [*International Hydrographic Organization - IHO*] [*Monte Carlo, Monaco*]
**OHI**........... Other Health Impaired [*Education*]
**OHI**........... State Library of Ohio, Columbus, OH [*OCLC symbol*] (OCLC)
**OHIA**......... Oil-Heat Institute of America [*Later, PMAA*] (KSC)
**OHIC**......... ODPHP Health Information Center (EA)
**OHilH**....... Highland County District Library, Hillsboro, OH [*Library symbol*] [*Library of Congress*] (LCLS)
**OHilS**........ South Hillsboro City Schools, Hillsboro, OH [*Library symbol*] [*Library of Congress*] (LCLS)
**Ohio**.......... Ohio Reports [*A publication*]
**Ohio**.......... Ohio Supreme Court Reports [*1821-51*] [*A publication*] (DLA)
**OHIO**........ Over the Hill in October [*Used prior to the bombing of Pearl Harbor to typify a recruit's view of US Army life*]
**Ohio Abs**.... Ohio Law Abstract [*A publication*] (DLA)
**Ohio Abstract**... Ohio Law Abstract [*A publication*] (DLA)
**Ohio Admin Code**... Ohio Administrative Code [*Official compilation published by Banks-Baldwin*] [*A publication*] (DLA)
**Ohio Ag Dept**... Ohio. Department of Agriculture. Bulletins [*A publication*]

**Ohio Ag Exp** ... Ohio. Agricultural Experiment Station. Publications [*A publication*]
**Ohio Agric Exp Stn Res Bull** ... Ohio. Agricultural Experiment Station. Research Bulletin [*A publication*]
**Ohio Agric Exp Stn Res Circ** ... Ohio. Agricultural Experiment Station. Research Circular [*A publication*]
**Ohio Agric Exp Stn Spec Circ** ... Ohio. Agricultural Experiment Station. Special Circular [*A publication*]
**Ohio Agric Res Dev Cent Res Bull** ... Ohio. Agricultural Research and Development Center. Research Bulletin [*A publication*]
**Ohio Agric Res Dev Cent Res Circ** ... Ohio. Agricultural Research and Development Center. Research Circular [*A publication*]
**Ohio Agric Res Dev Cent Res Summ** ... Ohio. Agricultural Research and Development Center. Research Summary [*A publication*]
**Ohio Agric Res Dev Cent Spec Circ** ... Ohio. Agricultural Research and Development Center. Special Circular [*A publication*]
**Ohio Agr Res Develop Cent Res Circ** ... Ohio. Agricultural Research and Development Center. Research Circular [*A publication*]
**OhioanaQ** .. Ohioana Quarterly [*A publication*]
**Ohio App** ... Ohio Appellate Reports [*A publication*] (DLA)
**Ohio App 2d** ... Ohio Appellate Reports, Second Series [*A publication*] (DLA)
**Ohio App 3d** ... Ohio Appellate Reports. Third Series [*A publication*]
**Ohio Apps** ... Ohio Appellate Reports [*A publication*] (DLA)
**Ohio Archael** ... Ohio Archaeologist [*A publication*]
**Ohio Assn Sch Libn Bull** ... Ohio Association of School Librarians. Bulletin [*A publication*]
**Ohio B**........ Ohio Bar Reports [*A publication*]
**Ohio Bar**.... Ohio State Bar Association. Report [*A publication*]
**Ohio Biol Surv Biol Notes** ... Ohio Biological Survey. Biological Notes [*A publication*]
**Ohio Biol Surv Bull** ... Ohio Biological Survey. Bulletin [*A publication*]
**Ohio Biol Surv Inf Circ** ... Ohio Biological Survey. Informative Circular [*A publication*]
**Ohio BTA** .. Ohio Board of Tax Appeals Reports [*A publication*] (DLA)
**Ohio Busn** ... Ohio Business [*A publication*]
**Ohio Bus Tchr** ... Ohio Business Teacher [*A publication*]
**Ohio CA**..... Ohio Courts of Appeals Reports [*A publication*] (DLA)
**Ohio CC**..... Ohio Circuit Court Reports [*A publication*] (DLA)
**Ohio CC Dec** ... Ohio Circuit Court Decisions [*A publication*] (DLA)
**Ohio CC NS** ... Ohio Circuit Court Reports, New Series [*A publication*] (DLA)
**Ohio CCR** .. Ohio Circuit Court Reports [*A publication*] (DLA)
**Ohio CCR NS** ... Ohio Circuit Court Reports, New Series [*A publication*] (DLA)
**Ohio CD**..... Ohio Circuit Decisions [*A publication*] (DLA)
**Ohio C Dec** ... Ohio Circuit Decisions [*A publication*] (DLA)
**Ohio Circ Dec** ... Ohio Circuit Decisions [*A publication*] (DLA)
**Ohio Cir Ct** ... Ohio Circuit Court Decisions [*A publication*] (DLA)
**Ohio Cir Ct (NS)** ... Ohio Circuit Court Reports, New Series [*A publication*] (DLA)
**Ohio Cir Ct R** ... Ohio Circuit Court Reports [*A publication*] (DLA)
**Ohio Cir Ct R NS** ... Ohio Circuit Court Reports, New Series [*A publication*] (DLA)
**Ohio Circuits** ... Ohio Circuit Court Decisions [*A publication*] (DLA)
**Ohio Cir Dec** ... Ohio Circuit Decisions [*A publication*] (DLA)
**Ohio Cond** ... Wilcox's Condensed Ohio Reports [*A publication*] (DLA)
**Ohio Cond R** ... Wilcox's Condensed Ohio Reports [*A publication*] (DLA)
**Ohio Conf Sewage Treat Annu Rep** ... Ohio Conference on Sewage Treatment. Annual Report [*A publication*]
**Ohio Conf Water Purif Annu Rep** ... Ohio Conference on Water Purification. Annual Report [*A publication*]
**Ohio Ct App** ... Ohio Courts of Appeals Reports [*A publication*] (DLA)
**Ohio Dec**.... Ohio Decisions [*A publication*] (DLA)
**Ohio Dec NP** ... Ohio Decisions Nisi Prius [*A publication*] (DLA)
**Ohio Dec R** ... Ohio Decisions Reprint [*A publication*] (DLA)
**Ohio Dec Re** ... Ohio Decisions Reprint [*A publication*] (DLA)
**Ohio Dec Rep** ... Ohio Decisions Reprint [*A publication*] (DLA)
**Ohio Dec Repr** ... Ohio Decisions Reprint [*A publication*] (DLA)
**Ohio Dec Reprint** ... Ohio Decisions Reprint [*A publication*]
**Ohio Dent J** ... Ohio Dental Journal [*A publication*]
**Ohio Dep Nat Resour Div Geol Surv Misc Rep** ... Ohio. Department of Natural Resources. Division of Geological Survey. Miscellaneous Report [*A publication*]
**Ohio Dep't** ... Ohio Department Reports [*A publication*] (DLA)
**Ohio Div Geol Surv Bull** ... Ohio. Division of Geological Survey. Bulletin [*A publication*]
**Ohio Div Geol Surv Inform Circ** ... Ohio. Division of Geological Survey. Information Circular [*A publication*]
**Ohio Div Geol Surv Misc Rep** ... Ohio. Division of Geological Survey. Miscellaneous Report [*A publication*]
**Ohio Div Geol Surv Rep Invest** ... Ohio. Division of Geological Survey. Report of Investigations [*A publication*]
**Ohio Div Water Bull** ... Ohio. Division of Water. Bulletin [*A publication*]
**Ohio Div Water Inform Circ** ... Ohio. Division of Water. Information Circular [*A publication*]
**Ohio Div Water Ohio Water Plan Inventory Rep** ... Ohio. Division of Water. Ohio Water Plan Inventory. Report [*A publication*]
**Ohio Div Water Ohio Water Plan Invent Rep** ... Ohio. Division of Water. Ohio Water Plan Inventory. Report [*A publication*]
**Ohio Div Water Rep Ohio Water Table Surv** ... Ohio. Division of Water. Report on Ohio Water Table Survey [*A publication*]
**Ohio Div Water Tech Rep** ... Ohio. Division of Water. Technical Report [*A publication*]
**Ohio F**........ Ohio Farmer [*A publication*]
**Ohio Farm Home Res** ... Ohio Farm and Home Research [*A publication*]
**Ohio FD**..... Ohio Federal Decisions [*A publication*] (DLA)
**Ohio F Dec** ... Ohio Federal Decisions [*A publication*] (DLA)
**Ohio Fed Dec** ... Ohio Federal Decisions [*A publication*] (DLA)
**Ohio Fish Monogr** ... Ohio Fish Monographs [*A publication*]
**Ohio Fish Wildl Rep** ... Ohio Fish and Wildlife Report [*A publication*]
**Ohio Fm Home Res** ... Ohio Farm and Home Research [*A publication*]
**Ohio Game Monogr** ... Ohio Game Monographs [*A publication*]
**Ohio Gov't** ... Ohio Government Reports [*A publication*] (DLA)
**Ohio G S B** ... Ohio. Geological Survey. Bulletin [*A publication*]
**OhioH**........ Ohio History [*A publication*]
**Ohio Herpetol Soc Spec Publ** ... Ohio Herpetological Society. Special Publication [*A publication*]
**Ohio Hist**... Ohio History [*A publication*]
**Ohio HQ**.... Ohio Historical Quarterly [*A publication*]
**Ohio Jour Sci** ... Ohio Journal of Science [*A publication*]
**Ohio J Rel St** ... Ohio Journal of Religious Studies [*A publication*]
**Ohio J Sci** .. Ohio Journal of Science [*A publication*]
**Ohio Jur**..... Ohio Jurisprudence [*A publication*] (DLA)
**Ohio Jur 2d** ... Ohio Jurisprudence, Second Series [*A publication*] (DLA)
**Ohio L Abs** ... Ohio Law Abstract [*A publication*] (DLA)
**Ohio Law Abs** ... Ohio Law Abstract [*A publication*] (DLA)
**Ohio Law Abst** ... Ohio Law Abstract [*A publication*] (DLA)
**Ohio Law Bull** ... Weekly Law Bulletin [*Ohio*] [*A publication*] (DLA)
**Ohio Law J** ... Ohio Law Journal [*A publication*] (DLA)
**Ohio Law R** ... Ohio Law Reporter [*A publication*] (DLA)
**Ohio Law Rep** ... Ohio Law Reporter [*A publication*] (DLA)
**Ohio Law Repr** ... Ohio Law Reporter [*A publication*] (DLA)
**Ohio Laws** ... State of Ohio: Legislative Acts Passed and Joint Resolutions Adopted [*A publication*] (DLA)
**Ohio LB**..... Weekly Law Bulletin [*Ohio*] [*A publication*] (DLA)
**Ohio L Bull** ... Ohio Law Bulletin [*A publication*] (DLA)
**Ohio Legal N** ... Ohio Legal News [*A publication*] (DLA)
**Ohio Legis Bull** ... Ohio Legislative Bulletin (Anderson) [*A publication*] (DLA)
**Ohio Legis Bull (Anderson)** ... Ohio Legislative Bulletin (Anderson) [*A publication*]
**Ohio Legis Serv** ... Ohio Legislative Service [*A publication*] (DLA)
**Ohio Legis Serv (Baldwin)** ... Baldwin's Ohio Legislative Service [*A publication*]
**Ohio Leg N** ... Ohio Legal News [*A publication*] (DLA)
**Ohio Leg News** ... Ohio Legal News [*A publication*] (DLA)
**Ohio Lib Assn Bul** ... Ohio Library Association. Bulletin [*A publication*]
**Ohio Libr Ass Bull** ... Ohio Library Association. Bulletin [*A publication*]
**Ohio LJ**...... Ohio Law Journal [*A publication*] (DLA)
**Ohio Low Dec** ... Ohio Lower Court Decisions [*A publication*] (DLA)
**Ohio Lower Dec** ... Ohio Lower Court Decisions [*A publication*] (DLA)
**Ohio LR**..... Ohio Law Reporter [*A publication*] (DLA)
**Ohio L Rep** ... Ohio Law Reporter [*A publication*] (DLA)
**Ohio LR & Wk Bul** ... Ohio Law Reporter and Weekly Bulletin [*A publication*] (DLA)
**OHIO M**.... Ohio Magazine [*A publication*] (ROG)
**Ohio Misc** ... Ohio Miscellaneous Reports [*A publication*] (DLA)
**Ohio Misc 2d** ... Ohio Miscellaneous Reports, Second Series [*A publication*] (DLA)
**Ohio Misc 3d** ... Ohio Miscellaneous Reports, Third Series [*A publication*] (DLA)
**Ohio Misc Dec** ... Ohio Miscellaneous Decisions [*A publication*] (DLA)
**Ohio M J** ... Ohio Mining Journal [*A publication*]
**Ohio Monthly Rec** ... Ohio Monthly Record [*A publication*] (DLA)
**Ohio Nat**.... Ohio Naturalist. Ohio State University [*A publication*]
**Ohio (New Series)** ... Ohio State Reports, New Series [*A publication*] (DLA)
**Ohio Nisi Prius** ... Ohio Nisi Prius Reports [*A publication*] (DLA)
**Ohio Nisi Prius (NS)** ... Ohio Nisi Prius Reports, New Series [*A publication*] (DLA)
**Ohio Northern UL Rev** ... Ohio Northern University. Law Review [*A publication*]
**Ohio North L Rev** ... Ohio Northern University. Law Review [*A publication*]
**Ohio North Univ L Rev** ... Ohio Northern University. Law Review [*A publication*]
**Ohio NP**..... Ohio Nisi Prius Reports [*A publication*] (DLA)
**Ohio NP NS** ... Ohio Nisi Prius Reports, New Series [*A publication*] (DLA)
**Ohio NS**..... Ohio State Reports, New Series [*A publication*] (DLA)
**Ohio NUL Rev** ... Ohio Northern University. Law Review [*A publication*]
**Ohio N Univ Law R** ... Ohio Northern University. Law Review [*A publication*]
**Ohio Nurses Rev** ... Ohio Nurses Review [*A publication*]
**Ohio O**....... Ohio Opinions [*A publication*] (DLA)
**Ohio O**....... Ohio Opinions, Annotated [*A publication*] (DLA)
**Ohio O 2d** .. Ohio Opinions, Second Series [*A publication*] (DLA)
**Ohio Op**..... Ohio Opinions [*A publication*] (DLA)
**Ohio Op 2d** ... Ohio Opinions, Second Series [*A publication*] (DLA)
**Ohio Op 3d** ... Ohio Opinions, Third Series [*A publication*] (DLA)
**Ohio Ops** ... Ohio Opinions [*A publication*] (DLA)
**Ohio Prob** .. Ohio Probate Reports, by Goebel [*A publication*] (DLA)
**Ohio Prob Ct** ... Goebel's Probate Reports [*Ohio*] [*A publication*] (DLA)
**Ohio R**........ Ohio Report [*A publication*] (DLA)
**OhioR**........ Ohio Review [*A publication*]

**Ohio R Cond** ... Ohio Reports Condensed [*A publication*] (DLA)
**Ohio Rep**.... Ohio Report [*A publication*]
**Ohio Rep Res Develop** ... Ohio Report on Research and Development (Biology, Agriculture, Home Economics). Ohio Agricultural Experiment Station [*A publication*]
**Ohio Rev**.... Ohio Review [*A publication*]
**Ohio Rev Code Ann** ... Ohio Revised Code, Annotated [*A publication*] (DLA)
**Ohio Rev Code Ann (Anderson)** ... Ohio Revised Code, Annotated (Anderson) [*A publication*] (DLA)
**Ohio Rev Code Ann (Baldwin)** ... Ohio Revised Code, Annotated (Baldwin) [*A publication*] (DLA)
**Ohio Rev Code Ann (Page)** ... Ohio Revised Code, Annotated (Page) [*A publication*] (DLA)
**Ohio S**........ Ohio State Reports [*A publication*] (DLA)
**Ohio SBA Bull** ... Ohio State Bar Association. Bulletin [*A publication*] (DLA)
**Ohio Sch**.... Ohio Schools [*A publication*]
**Ohio S & CP** ... Ohio Superior and Common Pleas Decisions [*A publication*] (DLA)
**Ohio S & CP Dec** ... Ohio Superior and Common Pleas Decisions [*A publication*] (DLA)
**Ohio S L J** ... Ohio State Law Journal [*A publication*]
**Ohio SR**..... Ohio State Reports [*A publication*] (DLA)
**Ohio S Rep** ... Ohio State Reports [*A publication*] (DLA)
**Ohio St**....... Ohio State Reports [*A publication*] (DLA)
**Ohio St Ac Sc An Rp** ... Ohio State Academy of Science. Annual Report [*A publication*]
**Ohio St Ac Sc Pr** ... Ohio State Academy of Science. Proceedings [*A publication*]
**Ohio St Ac Sc Sp P** ... Ohio State Academy of Science. Special Papers [*A publication*]
**Ohio State** ... Ohio State Reports [*A publication*] (DLA)
**Ohio State Archaeol and Hist Quar** ... Ohio State Archaeological and Historical Quarterly [*A publication*]
**Ohio State Law J** ... Ohio State Law Journal [*A publication*]
**Ohio State LJ** ... Ohio State Law Journal [*A publication*]
**Ohio State Med J** ... Ohio State Medical Journal [*A publication*]
**Ohio State Rep** ... Ohio State Reports [*A publication*] (DLA)
**Ohio State R (NS)** ... Ohio State Reports, New Series [*A publication*] (DLA)
**Ohio State Univ Biosci Colloq** ... Ohio State University. Biosciences Colloquia [*A publication*]
**Ohio State Univ Eng Exp Sta Bull** ... Ohio State University. Engineering Experiment Station. Bulletin [*A publication*]
**Ohio State Univ Eng Exp Stn Circ** ... Ohio State University. Engineering Experiment Station. Circular [*A publication*]
**Ohio State Univ Eng Exp Stn News** ... Ohio State University. Engineering Experiment Station. News [*A publication*]
**Ohio State Univ Inst Polar Studies Rept** ... Ohio State University. Institute of Polar Studies. Report [*A publication*]
**Ohio State Univ Inst Polar Stud Rep** ... Ohio State University. Institute of Polar Studies. Report [*A publication*]
**Ohio St BA Rep** ... Ohio State Bar Association. Report [*A publication*]
**Ohio St 2d** ... Ohio State Reports, Second Series [*A publication*] (DLA)
**Ohio St 3d** ... Ohio State Reports, Third Series [*A publication*] (DLA)
**Ohio St Law** ... Ohio State Law Journal [*A publication*]
**Ohio St LJ** ... Ohio State Law Journal [*A publication*]
**Ohio St R** ... Ohio State Reports [*A publication*] (DLA)
**Ohio St Rep** ... Ohio State Reports [*A publication*] (DLA)
**Ohio St Report** ... Ohio State Reports [*A publication*] (DLA)
**Ohio St R (NS)** ... Ohio State Reports, New Series [*A publication*] (DLA)
**Ohio St Univ B** ... Ohio State University. Bulletin [*A publication*]
**Ohio St Univ Coop Ext Serv** ... Ohio State University. Cooperative Extension Service [*A publication*]
**Ohio SU**..... Ohio Supreme Court Decisions, Unreported Cases [*A publication*] (DLA)
**Ohio Sup & CP Dec** ... Ohio Superior and Common Pleas Decisions [*A publication*] (DLA)
**Ohio Supp** ... Ohio Supplement [*A publication*] (DLA)
**Ohio Unrep** ... Ohio Supreme Court Decisions, Unreported Cases [*A publication*] (DLA)
**Ohio Unrep Jud Dec** ... Pollack's Ohio Unreported Judicial Decisions Prior to 1823 [*A publication*] (DLA)
**Ohio Unrept Cas** ... Ohio Supreme Court Decisions, Unreported Cases [*A publication*] (DLA)
**OHIR**......... Operating House of Ill Repute
**OHirC**........ Hiram College, Hiram, OH [*Library symbol*] [*Library of Congress*] (LCLS)
**OHirP**........ Portage County District Library, Hiram, OH [*Library symbol*] [*Library of Congress*] (LCLS)
**OHIS**......... Oral Hearing-Impaired Section [*of the Alexander Graham Bell Association for the Deaf*] (EA)
**OHI-S**........ Oral Hygiene Index-Simplified
**O His**......... Ottawa Hispanica [*A publication*]
**OHJ**.......... Old-House Journal [*A publication*]
**OHJD**........ John Deere Ltd., Hamilton, Ontario [*Library symbol*] [*National Library of Canada*] (NLC)
**Oh J Sci**..... Ohio Journal of Science [*A publication*]
**Oh Jur**........ Ohio Jurisprudence [*A publication*] (DLA)
**OHK**.......... Hawkesbury Public Library, Ontario [*Library symbol*] [*National Library of Canada*] (NLC)
**OHKAC**..... Resource Centre, Algonquin College of Applied Arts and Technology [*Centre de Documentation, College Algonquin des Arts Appliques et de la Technologie*], Hawkesbury, Ontario [*Library symbol*] [*National Library of Canada*] (BIB)
**OHKC**........ CIP Research Ltd., Hawkesbury, Ontario [*Library symbol*] [*National Library of Canada*] (NLC)
**OHKGH**.... Hawkesbury General Hospital, Ontario [*Library symbol*] [*National Library of Canada*] (BIB)
**OHL**........... Ontario Hydro Library [*UTLAS symbol*]
**OHL**........... Overhaul
**OHL**........... Oxford Higher Local Examination [*British*] (ROG)
**OHLA**........ Anthony Pape Memorial Law Library, Hamilton Law Association, Ontario [*Library symbol*] [*National Library of Canada*] (BIB)
**Oh L Bul**.... Ohio Law Bulletin [*A publication*] (DLA)
**Oh L Ct D**.. Ohio Lower Court Decisions [*A publication*] (DLA)
**OHLEG**..... East Gwillimbury Public Libraries, Holland Landing, Ontario [*Library symbol*] [*National Library of Canada*] (NLC)
**Oh Leg N** ... Ohio Legal News [*A publication*] (DLA)
**OHLH**....... Overhead Heavy Load Handling [*Nuclear energy*] (NRCH)
**OHLHA9** .. Osteuropastudien der Hochschulen des Landes Hessen. Reihe I. Giessener Abhandlungen zur Agrar und Wirtschaftsforschung des Europaeischen Ostens [*A publication*]
**Ohlinger Fed Practice** ... Ohlinger's Federal Practice [*A publication*] (DLA)
**Oh LJ**......... Ohio Law Journal [*A publication*] (DLA)
**OHLJ** ........ Osgoode Hall. Law Journal [*A publication*]
**Oh L Rep** ... Ohio Law Reporter [*A publication*] (DLA)
**OHM**......... McMaster University, Hamilton, Ontario [*Library symbol*] [*National Library of Canada*] (NLC)
**OHM**......... Miami University, Hamilton Campus, Hamilton, OH [*OCLC symbol*] (OCLC)
**OHM**......... Office of Hazardous Materials [*Department of Transportation*]
**OHM**......... OHM Corp. [*NYSE symbol*] (SPSG)
**OHM**......... Ohmmeter [*Engineering*] (AAG)
**OHM**......... Oil and Hazardous Materials Incidence
**OHMA**...... Archives and Special Collections Division, McMaster University, Hamilton, Ontario [*Library symbol*] [*National Library of Canada*] (NLC)
**OHMAH**... Department of Art and Art History, McMaster University, Hamilton, Ontario [*Library symbol*] [*National Library of Canada*] (NLC)
**OHMAR** ... Oral History in the Mid-Atlantic Region [*An association*]
**OHMB**...... Health Sciences Library, McMaster University, Hamilton, Ontario [*Library symbol*] [*National Library of Canada*] (NLC)
**OHMC**...... Mohawk College of Applied Arts and Technology, Hamilton, Ontario [*Library symbol*] [*National Library of Canada*] (NLC)
**OHMC**...... OHM Corp. [*NASDAQ symbol*] (NQ)
**OHMCL**.... Library Technician Program, Mohawk College of Applied Arts & Technology, Hamilton, Ontario [*Library symbol*] [*National Library of Canada*] (NLC)
**OHM-CM** ... Ohm-Centimeter (AAG)
**OHMDBA** ... Canadian Baptist Archives, McMaster Divinity College, McMaster University, Hamilton, Ontario [*Library symbol*] [*National Library of Canada*] (NLC)
**Oh Misc**..... Ohio Miscellaneous Reports [*A publication*] (DLA)
**OHMM**..... Map Library, McMaster University, Hamilton, Ontario [*Library symbol*] [*National Library of Canada*] (NLC)
**OHMM**..... Ohmmeter [*Engineering*]
**OHMO**...... Office of Hazardous Materials Operations [*Department of Transportation*] (DLA)
**OHMO**...... Office of Health Maintenance Organization [*Insurance*] (DHSM)
**OHMP**....... Oral Health Maintenance Program [*Army*] (AABC)
**OHMR**...... Office of Hazardous Materials Regulation [*Department of Transportation*] (OICC)
**OHMS**....... On His [*or Her*] Majesty's Service
**OHMS**....... Our Helpless Millions Saved [*Title of early film*]
**OHMS**....... Overhead Machine Screw [*Technical drawings*]
**OHMSB**.... Oil and Hazardous Materials Spills Branch [*Environmental Protection Agency*] (GRD)
**OHMSETT** ... Oil and Hazardous Materials Simulated Environmental Test Tank [*Environmental Protection Agency*] [*Leonardo, NJ*]
**OHM-TADS** ... Oil and Hazardous Materials Technical Assistance Data System [*Environmental Protection Agency*] [*Databank*] (IID)
**OHN**.......... Hastings Branch, Northumberland County Public Library, Ontario [*Library symbol*] [*National Library of Canada*] (BIB)
**OHN**.......... Memphis, TN [*Location identifier*] [*FAA*] (FAAL)
**OHN**.......... Occupational Health Nurse [*Government classification*]
**OHN**.......... OHIONET, Columbus, OH [*OCLC symbol*] (OCLC)
**OHNC**....... Occupational Health Nursing Certificate [*British*]
**OHNN**....... Otorhinolaryngology and Head/Neck Nurses (EA)
**Oh NP**........ Ohio Nisi Prius Reports [*A publication*] (DLA)
**Oh NP (NS)** ... Ohio Nisi Prius Reports, New Series [*A publication*] (DLA)
**Oh NU Intra LR** ... Ohio Northern University. Intramural Law Review [*A publication*] (DLA)

**Oh NULR** ... Ohio Northern University. Law Review [*A publication*]
**OHO** .......... Ohio Resources Corp. [*Vancouver Stock Exchange symbol*]
**Oho** ............ Oholoth (BJA)
**OHO** .......... Order Holding Office
**OHOHS** .... Canadian Centre for Occupational Health and Safety [*Centre Canadien d'Hygiene et de Securite au Travail*] Hamilton, Ontario [*Library symbol*] [*National Library of Canada*] (NLC)
**Ohol** ........... Oholoth (BJA)
**OHP** ........... Oban-Heliport [*Scotland*] [*Airport symbol*] (OAG)
**OHP** ........... Oral History Project [*Macquarie University*] [*Australia*]
**OHP** ........... Order of the Holy Paraclete [*Anglican religious community*]
**OHP** ........... Overhead Projector (ADA)
**OHP** ........... Oxygen at High Pressure [*Also, HBO, HPO*] (MCD)
**OH PED** .... Ohne Pedal [*Without Pedal*] [*Music*]
**OHPO** ....... Organization Health Program Officer (AFM)
**OHPR** ........ Outstanding Hardware Problem Report (MCD)
**Oh Prob** ..... Ohio Probate [*A publication*] (DLA)
**OHPS** ........ Oil Hydraulic Power Switch
**OHQ** .......... Ohio Historical Quarterly [*A publication*]
**OHQ** .......... Oregon Historical Quarterly [*A publication*]
**OHQ** .......... Overseas Headquarters [*British military*] (DMA)
**OHR** .......... Of Human Rights (EA)
**OHR** .......... Office of Health Research [*Environmental Protection Agency*] [*Washington, DC*] (GRD)
**OHR** .......... O'Hara Resources Ltd. [*Vancouver Stock Exchange symbol*]
**OhR** ........... Ohio Review [*A publication*]
**OHR** .......... Ohrid [*Yugoslavia*] [*Seismograph station code, US Geological Survey*] (SEIS)
**OHR** .......... Operational Hazard Report [*Air Force*] (AFM)
**OHR** .......... Over-the-Horizon RADAR
**OHRA** ....... O'Hara Resources Ltd. [*NASDAQ symbol*] (NQ)
**OHRB** ........ Royal Botanical Gardens, Hamilton, Ontario [*Library symbol*] [*National Library of Canada*] (NLC)
**OHRC** ........ Redeemer College, Ancaster, Ontario [*Library symbol*] [*National Library of Canada*] (NLC)
**OHRI** ......... Oral Health Research Institute [*Indiana University*] [*Research center*] (RCD)
**OHRI** ......... Overhaul Recurrent Item (CINC)
**OHRI** ......... Overhaul Removal Interval [*Military*] (AFIT)
**OHRI** ......... Overhaul Removal Item (CINC)
**OHRJ** ......... Orissa Historical Research Journal [*A publication*]
**OHRNA** .... Ontario Hydro-Research News [*A publication*]
**OHRS** ........ Overflow Heat Removal System [*Nuclear energy*] (NRCH)
**OHS** ........... Hamilton Spectator, Ontario [*Library symbol*] [*National Library of Canada*] (NLC)
**OHS** ........... Obesity Hypoventilation Syndrome
**OHS** ........... Occupational Health Services, Inc. [*Secaucus, NJ*] [*Medical databank originator*] [*Information service or system*]
**OHS** ........... Occupational Hearing Service
**OHS** ........... Off-Hook Service [*Telecommunications*] (TEL)
**OHS** ........... Office of Highway Safety [*of BPR*]
**OHS** ........... Open Heart Surgery [*Medicine*]
**OHS** ........... Open-Hearth Steel
**OHS** ........... Optometric Historical Society (EA)
**OHS** ........... Organ Historical Society (EA)
**OHS** ........... Organization Health Survey [*Test*]
**OHS** ........... Organization of Historical Studies (EA)
**OHS** ........... University of Oregon, Health Sciences Library, Portland, OR [*OCLC symbol*] (OCLC)
**OHSAD** ..... Occupational Health and Safety [*A publication*]
**OHSC** ........ Oak Hill Sportswear Corporation [*NASDAQ symbol*] (NQ)
**OHSCC** ..... Steel Company of Canada, Hamilton, Ontario [*Library symbol*] [*National Library of Canada*] (NLC)
**Oh SCD** ..... Ohio Supreme Court Decisions, Unreported Cases [*A publication*] (DLA)
**Oh S & CP** ... Ohio Superior and Common Pleas Decisions [*A publication*] (DLA)
**OHSGT** ..... Office of High-Speed Ground Transportation [*Department of Transportation*]
**OHSI** ......... Oral Health Status Index [*Dentistry*]
**Oh SLJ** ...... Ohio State Law Journal [*A publication*]
**OHS MSDS** ... Occupational Health Services Material Safety Data Sheets [*Database*]
**Oh St** .......... Ohio State Reports [*A publication*] (DLA)
**OHST** ........ Overhead Storage Tank [*Nuclear energy*] (NRCH)
**Oh St LJ** .... Ohio State Law Journal [*A publication*]
**OHT** .......... Hornepayne Township Public Library, Ontario [*Library symbol*] [*National Library of Canada*] (NLC)
**OHT** .......... Ocular Hypertensive [*Ophthalmology*]
**OHT** .......... Office of Housing Technology [*National Bureau of Standards*]
**OHT** .......... Ohio Historical Society, Columbus, OH [*OCLC symbol*] (OCLC)
**OHT** .......... Ohio Tank Truck Carriers Bureau, Worthington OH [*STAC*]
**OHTA** ........ Office of Health Technology Assessment [*HHS*]
**OHTCS** ..... Outer Head Temperature Control System [*Nuclear energy*] (NRCH)
**OHTE** ........ Ohmic Heating Toroidal Experiment [*Nuclear fusion device*]
**OHTR** ........ Theological College of the Canadian Reformed Churches, Hamilton, Ontario [*Library symbol*] [*National Library of Canada*] (NLC)
**OHTS** ........ Oil-Hardened Tool Steel
**OHu** ........... Hubbard Public Library, Hubbard, OH [*Library symbol*] [*Library of Congress*] (LCLS)
**OHU** .......... Huntsville Public Library, Ontario [*Library symbol*] [*National Library of Canada*] (NLC)
**ohu** ............. Ohio [*MARC country of publication code*] [*Library of Congress*] (LCCP)
**OHU** .......... Overseas Homeported Units [*Navy*] (NVT)
**OHUM** ...... Muskoka Pioneer Village, Huntsville, Ontario [*Library symbol*] [*National Library of Canada*] (BIB)
**Oh Univ Rev** ... Ohio University Review [*A publication*]
**OHur** .......... Huron Public Library, Huron, OH [*Library symbol*] [*Library of Congress*] (LCLS)
**OHV** .......... Off-Highway Vehicle
**OHV** .......... Overhead Valve
**OHVE** ........ Hanmer Branch, Valley East Public Library [*Succursale Hanmer, Bibliotheque Publique de Valley-East*], Ontario [*Library symbol*] [*National Library of Canada*] (NLC)
**OHW** ......... Electronic Systems Library, Westinghouse Canada Ltd., Burlington, Ontario [*Library symbol*] [*National Library of Canada*] (NLC)
**OHW** ......... Oak Harbor [*Washington*] [*Seismograph station code, US Geological Survey*] (SEIS)
**OHW** ......... Oxyhydrogen Welding
**OHWL** ....... Wentworth Public Library, Hamilton, Ontario [*Library symbol*] [*National Library of Canada*] (NLC)
**OHWM** ..... Open Heart World Mission (EA)
**OHWS** ....... Overhead Wood Screw [*Technical drawings*]
**OI** ............... Ingersoll Public Library, Ontario [*Library symbol*] [*National Library of Canada*] (NLC)
**OI** ............... O Instituto [*A publication*]
**OI** ............... Odyssey Institute [*Later, OIC*] (EA)
**OI** ............... Office of Information (AFM)
**OI** ............... Office Instruction (AFM)
**OI** ............... Office of Investigations [*Nuclear energy*] (NRCH)
**OI** ............... Ohashi Institute (EA)
**OI** ............... Oil-Immersed
**OI** ............... Oil-Insulated
**OI** ............... Old Irish [*A publication*]
**OI** ............... On Instruments [*Aviation*]
**OI** ............... ONE, Incorporated (EA)
**OI** ............... Opener Inhibitor
**OI** ............... Opening of Intestine
**OI** ............... Operating Income [*Accounting*]
**OI** ............... Operating Instructions
**OI** ............... Operation Identity (EA)
**OI** ............... Operational Instrumentation (NASA)
**OI** ............... Operational Intelligence
**OI** ............... Operational Issue [*Military*]
**O & I** .......... Operations and Intelligence [*Section*] [*Army*] (INF)
**OI** ............... Operations Interface (MCD)
**OI** ............... Operator Input
**OI** ............... Opportunistic Infection [*Medicine*]
**OI** ............... Opsonic Index [*Medicine*]
**OI** ............... Optical Isolator [*Nuclear energy*] (NRCH)
**OI** ............... Optimist International (EA)
**OI** ............... Orbit [*or Orbital*] Insertion
**OI** ............... Orbiter Instrumentation [*NASA*] (NASA)
**OI** ............... Ordinary Interest [*Banking*]
**OI** ............... Organization Integration [*Military*]
**OI** ............... Organizational/Intermediate (MCD)
**OI** ............... Orgasmic Impairment [*Medicine*]
**OI** ............... Orientation Inventory [*Psychology*]
**OI** ............... Orthopedically Impaired
**OI** ............... Osteogenesis Imperfecta [*Medicine*]
**OI** ............... Ote Iwapo [*All That Is Must Be Considered*] [*of OI Committee International, a third-world lobby opposing systematic birth control*] [*Swahili*]
**OI** ............... Ours, Incorporated (EA)
**OI** ............... Output Impedance
**O/I** ............. Overseas Investment [*Economics*]
**OI** ............... Oxygen Income [*or Intake*] [*Medicine*]
**OIA** ............ Office of Inspector and Auditor [*Nuclear Regulatory Commission*] (NRCH)
**OIA** ............ Office of International Activities [*American Chemical Society*]
**OIA** ............ Office of International Administration [*Department of State*]
**OIA** ............ Office of International Affairs [*NASA, HUD*]
**OIA** ............ Oil Import Administration [*Later, Office of Oil and Gas*] [*Department of the Interior*]
**OIA** ............ Oil Insurance Association [*Later, Industrial Risk Insurance*] (EA)
**OIA** ............ Oishiyama A [*Japan*] [*Seismograph station code, US Geological Survey*] (SEIS)
**OIA** ............ Operative Ironmoulders' Association [*A union*] [*British*]
**OIA** ............ Orbiter Interface Adapter [*NASA*] (NASA)
**OIA** ............ Organizacion Internacional del Azucar [*International Sugar Organization - ISO*] (EAIO)
**OIA** ............ Outboard Industry Association [*Later, NMMA*] (EA)
**OIAA** ......... Abadan/International [*Iran*] [*ICAO location identifier*] (ICLI)
**OIAA** ......... Office of Inter-American Affairs [*Later, BIAA*]
**OIAA** ......... Office of International Aviation Affairs [*FAA*]

**OIAB**......... Boostan [*Iran*] [*ICAO location identifier*] (ICLI)
**OIAD**......... Dezful [*Iran*] [*ICAO location identifier*] (ICLI)
**OIAG**......... Aghajari [*Iran*] [*ICAO location identifier*] (ICLI)
**OIAH**......... Gachsaran [*Iran*] [*ICAO location identifier*] (ICLI)
**OIAI**......... Masjed Soleiman [*Iran*] [*ICAO location identifier*] (ICLI)
**OIAI**......... OIA, Inc. [*NASDAQ symbol*] (NQ)
**OIAJ**......... Omidyeh [*Iran*] [*ICAO location identifier*] (ICLI)
**OIAK**......... Haft-Gel [*Iran*] [*ICAO location identifier*] (ICLI)
**OIAL**......... Lali [*Iran*] [*ICAO location identifier*] (ICLI)
**OIAM**......... Bandar Mahshahr [*Iran*] [*ICAO location identifier*] (ICLI)
**OIAN**......... Andimeshk [*Iran*] [*ICAO location identifier*] (ICLI)
**OIAS**......... Observer Impression Assessment Scale
**OIAT**......... Abadan [*Iran*] [*ICAO location identifier*] (ICLI)
**OIATU**...... Office of Industry Affairs and Technology Utilization [*NASA*]
**OIA & TU**... Office of Industry Affairs and Technology Utilization [*NASA*]
**OIAUS**...... 164th Infantry Association of the United States (EA)
**OIAW**......... Ahwaz [*Iran*] [*ICAO location identifier*] (ICLI)
**OIAZ (Oesterreichische In Archit Z)**... OIAZ (Oesterreichische Ingenier und Architekten Zeitschrift) [*A publication*]
**OIB**............ Briggs-Lawrence County Public Library, Ironton, OH [*Library symbol*] [*Library of Congress*] (LCLS)
**OIB**............ Iron Bridge Public Library, Ontario [*Library symbol*] [*National Library of Canada*] (NLC)
**OIB**............ Oceanic Island Basalt [*Geology*]
**OIB**............ Official Information Base
**OIB**............ Oishiyama B [*Japan*] [*Seismograph station code, US Geological Survey*] (SEIS)
**OIB**............ Oligoclonal Immunoglobulin Bands [*Clinical chemistry*]
**OIB**............ Olympic Installations Board
**OIB**............ Operations Integration Branch [*NASA*] (KSC)
**OIB**............ Orbiter Interface Box [*NASA*] (NASA)
**OIB**............ Ortho-Iodobenzoic (Acid) [*Biochemistry*]
**OIBA**......... Abumusa Island [*Iran*] [*ICAO location identifier*] (ICLI)
**OIBB**......... Bushehr/Bushehr [*Iran*] [*ICAO location identifier*] (ICLI)
**OIBD**......... Bandar Deylam [*Iran*] [*ICAO location identifier*] (ICLI)
**OIBF**......... Forouz Island [*Iran*] [*ICAO location identifier*] (ICLI)
**OIBG**......... Ganaveh [*Iran*] [*ICAO location identifier*] (ICLI)
**OIBH**......... Bastak [*Iran*] [*ICAO location identifier*] (ICLI)
**OIBI**......... Golbandi [*Iran*] [*ICAO location identifier*] (ICLI)
**OIBK**......... Kish Island [*Iran*] [*ICAO location identifier*] (ICLI)
**OIBL**......... Bandar Lengeh [*Iran*] [*ICAO location identifier*] (ICLI)
**OIBN**......... Borazjan [*Iran*] [*ICAO location identifier*] (ICLI)
**OIBQ**......... Khark Island [*Iran*] [*ICAO location identifier*] (ICLI)
**OIBS**......... Siri Island [*Iran*] [*ICAO location identifier*] (ICLI)
**OIBT**......... Bushehr [*Iran*] [*ICAO location identifier*] (ICLI)
**OIBV**......... Lavan Island [*Iran*] [*ICAO location identifier*] (ICLI)
**OIBX**......... Tonb Island [*Iran*] [*ICAO location identifier*] (ICLI)
**OIC**............ Norwich, NY [*Location identifier*] [*FAA*] (FAAL)
**OIC**............ Oceanographic Instrumentation Center [*Navy*]
**OIC**............ Octyl Isocyanate [*Organic chemistry*]
**OIC**............ Odyssey Institute Corporation (EA)
**OIC**............ Offer in Compromise [*IRS*]
**OIC**............ Office of Industrial Cooperation [*AEC*]
**OIC**............ Office of International Conferences [*Department of State*]
**OIC**............ Office of International Cooperation [*in CAA*]
**OI & C**....... Office of Investigation and Compliance [*Employment and Training Administration*] [*Department of Labor*]
**OIC**............ Officer-in-Charge
**OIC**............ Ohio Improved Chesters [*Initialism itself now used as name of breed of swine*]
**OIC**............ Oishiyama C [*Japan*] [*Seismograph station code, US Geological Survey*] (SEIS)
**OIC**............ Okinawa Interboard Committee [*Absorbed by Interboard Committee for Christian Work in Japan*] (EA)
**OIC**............ Online Instrument and Control Program [*Data processing*] (NRCH)
**OIC**............ Operational Intelligence Centre [*British military*] (DMA)
**OIC**............ Operations Instrumentation Coordinator [*NASA*] (KSC)
**OIC**............ Operator's Instruction Chart
**OIC**............ Opportunities Industrialization Center (OICC)
**OIC**............ Optical Integrated Circuit (IEEE)
**OIC**............ Orbiter Integrated Checkout [*NASA*] (NASA)
**O-I-C**......... Order-in-Council [*Canada*]
**OIC**............ Organisation Internationale Catholique
**OIC**............ Organisation Internationale du Commerce [*International Organization for Commerce*] [*France*]
**OIC**............ Organization for International Cooperation (EA)
**OIC**............ Organization of the Islamic Conference [*See also OCI*] [*Jeddah, Saudi Arabia*] (EAIO)
**OIC**............ Oriental Institute. Communications [*A publication*]
**OIC**............ Polymers, Paint, and Colour Journal [*A publication*]
**OICA**......... Azna [*Iran*] [*ICAO location identifier*] (ICLI)
**OIC/A**........ Opportunities Industrialization Centers of America (EA)
**OICA**......... Organisation Internationale des Constructeurs d'Automobiles (EAIO)
**OICB**......... Baneh [*Iran*] [*ICAO location identifier*] (ICLI)
**OICC**......... Bakhtaran [*Iran*] [*ICAO location identifier*] (ICLI)
**OICC**......... Office International du Cacoa et du Chocolat [*International Office of Cocoa and Chocolate*] [*Established in 1930*]
**OICC**......... Officer-in-Charge of Construction [*Navy*]
**OICC**......... Operations Interface Control Chart (KSC)
**OICC**......... Organization of Islamic Capitals and Cities (EA)
**OICCFE**.... Officer-in-Charge of Construction, Far East [*Navy*]
**OICD**......... Abdanan [*Iran*] [*ICAO location identifier*] (ICLI)
**OICD**......... Office of International Cooperation and Development [*Department of Agriculture*]
**OICD**......... On-Board Information Compression Device [*Aerospace*]
**OICE**......... Bijar [*Iran*] [*ICAO location identifier*] (ICLI)
**O ICE**......... Old Icelandic [*Language, etc.*] (ROG)
**OICF**......... Naft-E-Shah [*Iran*] [*ICAO location identifier*] (ICLI)
**OICG**......... Ghasre-Shirin [*Iran*] [*ICAO location identifier*] (ICLI)
**OICH**......... Islam Abad [*Iran*] [*ICAO location identifier*] (ICLI)
**OICI**......... Ilam [*Iran*] [*ICAO location identifier*] (ICLI)
**OICI**......... Oficina Internacional Catolica de la Infancia [*International Catholic Child Bureau*]
**OICI**......... Organizacion Ibero-Americana de Cooperacion Intermunicipal [*Ibero-American Municipal Organization*] (EAIO)
**OICI**......... Organizacion Interamericana de Cooperacion Intermunicipal [*Interamerican Municipal Organization*]
**OICJ**......... Boroujerd [*Iran*] [*ICAO location identifier*] (ICLI)
**OICK**......... Khorram Abad [*Iran*] [*ICAO location identifier*] (ICLI)
**OICL**......... Sare Pole Zahab [*Iran*] [*ICAO location identifier*] (ICLI)
**OICM**......... Mehran [*Iran*] [*ICAO location identifier*] (ICLI)
**OICM**......... Organisation Internationale pour la Cooperation Medicale [*International Organization for Medical Cooperation*]
**OICMA**...... Organisation Internationale Contre le Criquet Migrateur Africain [*International African Migratory Locust Organization*] (EAIO)
**OICNA**...... Overseas Indian Congress of North America (EA)
**OICO**......... Office of Integration and Checkout
**OICO**......... OI Corporation [*NASDAQ symbol*] (NQ)
**OICO**......... Songhor [*Iran*] [*ICAO location identifier*] (ICLI)
**OICP**......... Paveh [*Iran*] [*ICAO location identifier*] (ICLI)
**OICQ**......... Takab [*Iran*] [*ICAO location identifier*] (ICLI)
**OICR**......... Dehloran [*Iran*] [*ICAO location identifier*] (ICLI)
**OICR**......... Office of International Commercial Relations [*Department of State*]
**OICRF**....... Office International du Cadastre et Regime Foncier
**OICS**......... Office of Interoceanic Canal Studies [*National Oceanic and Atmospheric Administration*] (NOAA)
**OICS**......... Operational Intelligence Collection System
**OICS**......... Organe International de Controle des Stupefiants [*International Narcotics Control Board*] (EAIO)
**OICS**......... Sanandaj [*Iran*] [*ICAO location identifier*] (ICLI)
**OICT**......... Bakhtaran [*Iran*] [*ICAO location identifier*] (ICLI)
**OICTP**....... Outline Individual and Collective Training Plan [*Army*]
**OICY**......... Malavi [*Iran*] [*ICAO location identifier*] (ICLI)
**OICZ**......... Aligoodarz [*Iran*] [*ICAO location identifier*] (ICLI)
**OID**............ Octal Identifier [*Data processing*] (KSC)
**OID**............ Ofensiva de Izquierda Democratica [*Offensive of the Democratic Left*] [*Bolivia*] (PPW)
**OID**............ Optoelectronic Imaging Device
**OID**............ Order Initiated Distribution
**OID**............ Original Issue Discount [*Business term*]
**OID**............ Outline and Installation Drawing
**OIDA**......... Ordnance Industrial Data Agency
**OIDC**......... Oil Importing and Developing Country
**OIDI**......... Optically Isolated Digital Input
**OIDMM**..... Office Internationale de Documentation de Medecine Militaire [*International Office of Documentation on Military Medicine - IODMM*] (EAIO)
**OIDP**......... Oversea Internal Defense Policy [*Army*] (AABC)
**OIDPS**....... Oversea Intelligence Data Processing System
**OIDS**......... Office of Intellectual Disability Services [*Australia*]
**OIE**............ Central Library, Albright & Wilson Americas, Islington, Ontario [*Library symbol*] [*National Library of Canada*] (NLC)
**OIE**............ Office of Inspection and Enforcement [*Nuclear Regulatory Commission*]
**OIE**............ Office International des Epizooties [*International Office of Epizootics*] [*Research center*] [*France*] (IRC)
**O/I/E**......... Offsites/Infrastructure/Establishment [*Engineering*]
**OIE**............ Operational Independent Evaluator
**OIE**............ Optical Incremental Encoder
**OIE**............ Optical Infrared Equipment
**OIE**............ Organisation Internationale des Employeurs [*International Organization of Employers*]
**OIEC**......... Office International de l'Enseignement Catholique [*Catholic International Education Office - CIEO*] (EAIO)
**OIEFA**....... Oil Engineering and Finance [*A publication*]
**OIEO**......... Ocean Instrumentation Engineering Office [*National Oceanic and Atmospheric Administration*] (MSC)
**OIER**......... Official Intermodal Equipment Register [*Intermodal Publishing Co.*] [*Information service or system*] (IID)
**OIES**......... Oxford Institute for Energy Studies [*British*]
**OIESA**....... Office of International Economic and Social Affairs [*Department of State*]
**OIF**............ American Opportunity Income [*NYSE symbol*] (SPSG)
**OIF**............ Iroquois Falls Public Library, Ontario [*Library symbol*] [*National Library of Canada*] (NLC)
**OIF**............ Office for Intellectual Freedom [*American Library Association*]
**OIF**............ Office of International Finance [*Department of the Treasury*]
**OIF**............ Online Review [*A publication*]

**OIF** ........... Osrodek Informacji Firmowej [*Center of Information on Firms*] [*Poland*] (IMH)
**OIF** ........... Osteogenesis Imperfecta Foundation (EA)
**OIF** ........... Osteoinductive Factor [*Biochemistry*]
**OIF** ........... Other Intelligence File (MCD)
**OIFB**........... Boroujen [*Iran*] [*ICAO location identifier*] (ICLI)
**OIFC**........... Ghamsar [*Iran*] [*ICAO location identifier*] (ICLI)
**OIFC**........... Oil-Insulated, Fan-Cooled
**OIFD** ......... Ardestan [*Iran*] [*ICAO location identifier*] (ICLI)
**OIFF** ......... Soffeh [*Iran*] [*ICAO location identifier*] (ICLI)
**OIFG** ......... Golpaygan [*Iran*] [*ICAO location identifier*] (ICLI)
**OIFH** ......... Esfahan [*Iran*] [*ICAO location identifier*] (ICLI)
**OIFI**........... Semirom [*Iran*] [*ICAO location identifier*] (ICLI)
**OIFIG**........ Official Irish FORTH [*Programming language*] Interest Group (EAIO)
**OIFJ** .......... Najaf Abad [*Iran*] [*ICAO location identifier*] (ICLI)
**OIFK**.......... Kashan [*Iran*] [*ICAO location identifier*] (ICLI)
**OIFL**........... Felavarjan [*Iran*] [*ICAO location identifier*] (ICLI)
**OIFM** ........ Esfahan [*Iran*] [*ICAO location identifier*] (ICLI)
**OIFN** ......... Naein [*Iran*] [*ICAO location identifier*] (ICLI)
**OIFO** ......... Khomeini Shahr [*Iran*] [*ICAO location identifier*] (ICLI)
**OIFR**.......... Ghomsheh [*Iran*] [*ICAO location identifier*] (ICLI)
**OIFS**.......... Shahrekord [*Iran*] [*ICAO location identifier*] (ICLI)
**OIFT**.......... Esfahan [*Iran*] [*ICAO location identifier*] (ICLI)
**OIFU** ......... Fereidan [*Iran*] [*ICAO location identifier*] (ICLI)
**OIFW** ........ Khomein [*Iran*] [*ICAO location identifier*] (ICLI)
**OIFY**.......... Meymeh [*Iran*] [*ICAO location identifier*] (ICLI)
**OIFZ**.......... Natanz [*Iran*] [*ICAO location identifier*] (ICLI)
**OIG**............ Ignace Public Library, Ontario [*Library symbol*] [*National Library of Canada*] (NLC)
**OIG**............ Office of the Inspector General [*Army*]
**OIG**............ Optically Isolated Gate (IEEE)
**OIGA** ......... Astara [*Iran*] [*ICAO location identifier*] (ICLI)
**OIGF** ......... Fouman [*Iran*] [*ICAO location identifier*] (ICLI)
**OIGG** ......... Rasht [*Iran*] [*ICAO location identifier*] (ICLI)
**OIGH**.......... Hashtpar [*Iran*] [*ICAO location identifier*] (ICLI)
**OIGK** ......... Khailkhal [*Iran*] [*ICAO location identifier*] (ICLI)
**OIGL** ......... Langerood [*Iran*] [*ICAO location identifier*] (ICLI)
**OIGM**......... Manjil [*Iran*] [*ICAO location identifier*] (ICLI)
**OIGN**.......... Lahijan [*Iran*] [*ICAO location identifier*] (ICLI)
**OIGP** ......... Bandar Anzali [*Iran*] [*ICAO location identifier*] (ICLI)
**OIGR** ......... Office of Industrial Growth and Research [*of BDSA*]
**OIGR** ......... Office of Intergovernmental Relations [*US Congress*] [*Washington, DC*] (GRD)
**OIGR** ......... Roodsar [*Iran*] [*ICAO location identifier*] (ICLI)
**OIGT** ......... Rasht [*Iran*] [*ICAO location identifier*] (ICLI)
**OIGU**......... Roodbar [*Iran*] [*ICAO location identifier*] (ICLI)
**OIH** ........... Oceanic Institute of Hawaii
**OIH** ........... Office of International Health [*Department of Health and Human Services*]
**OIH** ........... Ovulation-Inducing Hormone [*Endocrinology*]
**OIHA**......... Takestan [*Iran*] [*ICAO location identifier*] (ICLI)
**OIHB**.......... Asad Abad [*Iran*] [*ICAO location identifier*] (ICLI)
**OIHD** ......... Shahzand [*Iran*] [*ICAO location identifier*] (ICLI)
**OIHF** ......... Tafresh [*Iran*] [*ICAO location identifier*] (ICLI)
**OIHG**......... Kharaghan [*Iran*] [*ICAO location identifier*] (ICLI)
**OIHH** ......... Hamadan [*Iran*] [*ICAO location identifier*] (ICLI)
**OIHJ** ......... Avaj [*Iran*] [*ICAO location identifier*] (ICLI)
**OIHM**......... Malayer [*Iran*] [*ICAO location identifier*] (ICLI)
**OIHN** ......... Nahavand [*Iran*] [*ICAO location identifier*] (ICLI)
**OIHP** ......... Office International d'Hygiene Publique [*United Nations*]
**OIHQ** ......... Kangavar [*Iran*] [*ICAO location identifier*] (ICLI)
**OIHR**......... Arak [*Iran*] [*ICAO location identifier*] (ICLI)
**OIHS** ......... Hamadan [*Iran*] [*ICAO location identifier*] (ICLI)
**OIHT**......... Hamadan [*Iran*] [*ICAO location identifier*] (ICLI)
**OIHU** ......... Tooyserkan [*Iran*] [*ICAO location identifier*] (ICLI)
**OII** ............ Office of International Investment [*Department of Commerce*]
**OI & I**......... Office of Invention and Innovation [*Disbanded*] [*National Institute of Standards and Technology*]
**OII** ............ Oil Investment Institute [*Washington, DC*] (EA)
**OII** ............ Operations Integration Instruction [*NASA*] (NASA)
**OII** ............ Ourobourus Institute (EA)
**OIIA** .......... Abe-Ali [*Iran*] [*ICAO location identifier*] (ICLI)
**OIIC**........... Kushke Nosrat [*Iran*] [*ICAO location identifier*] (ICLI)
**OIID** .......... Tehran/Doshan Tappeh [*Iran*] [*ICAO location identifier*] (ICLI)
**OIIE**........... Abyek [*Iran*] [*ICAO location identifier*] (ICLI)
**OIIF** ........... Firouzkouh [*Iran*] [*ICAO location identifier*] (ICLI)
**OIIFDRES** ... Oficina Internacional de Informacion del Frente Democratico Revolucionario de El Salvador [*International Information Office of the Democratic Revolutionary Front of El Salvador - IIODRFES*] [*San Jose, Costa Rica*] (EAIO)
**OIIG** .......... Tehran/Ghaleh Morghi [*Iran*] [*ICAO location identifier*] (ICLI)
**OIIH**.......... Mahallat [*Iran*] [*ICAO location identifier*] (ICLI)
**OIII**........... Tehran/Mehrabad International [*Iran*] [*ICAO location identifier*] (ICLI)
**OIIJ** ........... Karaj [*Iran*] [*ICAO location identifier*] (ICLI)
**OIIK** .......... Ghazvin [*Iran*] [*ICAO location identifier*] (ICLI)
**OIIM** ......... Khoram Dareh [*Iran*] [*ICAO location identifier*] (ICLI)
**OIIN** .......... Delijan [*Iran*] [*ICAO location identifier*] (ICLI)
**OIIQ**.......... Ghom [*Iran*] [*ICAO location identifier*] (ICLI)
**OIIR** .......... Garmsar [*Iran*] [*ICAO location identifier*] (ICLI)
**OIIS**........... Semnan [*Iran*] [*ICAO location identifier*] (ICLI)
**OIIT**........... Tehran [*Iran*] [*ICAO location identifier*] (ICLI)
**OIIU** .......... Damghan [*Iran*] [*ICAO location identifier*] (ICLI)
**OIIV** .......... Seveh [*Iran*] [*ICAO location identifier*] (ICLI)
**OIIW** ......... Varamin [*Iran*] [*ICAO location identifier*] (ICLI)
**OIIX** .......... Tehran [*Iran*] [*ICAO location identifier*] (ICLI)
**OIJ**............. Octarius Duos [*Two Pints*] [*Pharmacy*] (ROG)
**OIJ**............. Organisation Internationale des Journalistes [*International Organization of Journalists - IOJ*] (EAIO)
**OIJSS**........ Octarios Duobus cum Semisse [*Two and a Half Pints*] [*Pharmacy*] (ROG)
**OIK**............ Ocean City, MD [*Location identifier*] [*FAA*] (FAAL)
**OIKA** ......... Shahre Babak [*Iran*] [*ICAO location identifier*] (ICLI)
**OIKB** ......... Bandar Abbas [*Iran*] [*ICAO location identifier*] (ICLI)
**OIKD** ......... Darband/Ravar [*Iran*] [*ICAO location identifier*] (ICLI)
**OIKE** ......... Anar [*Iran*] [*ICAO location identifier*] (ICLI)
**OIKF**.......... Baft [*Iran*] [*ICAO location identifier*] (ICLI)
**OIKI** .......... Bandar Khamir [*Iran*] [*ICAO location identifier*] (ICLI)
**OIKJ**.......... Jiroft [*Iran*] [*ICAO location identifier*] (ICLI)
**OIKK** ......... Kerman [*Iran*] [*ICAO location identifier*] (ICLI)
**OIKM**........ Bam [*Iran*] [*ICAO location identifier*] (ICLI)
**OIKN**......... Narmashir [*Iran*] [*ICAO location identifier*] (ICLI)
**OIKO**......... Minab [*Iran*] [*ICAO location identifier*] (ICLI)
**OIKO**......... Oikos [*A publication*]
**Oikos Suppl** ... Oikos. Supplementum [*A publication*]
**OIKQ**......... Gheshm Island [*Iran*] [*ICAO location identifier*] (ICLI)
**OIKR** ......... Rafsanjan [*Iran*] [*ICAO location identifier*] (ICLI)
**OIKS**.......... Shahdad [*Iran*] [*ICAO location identifier*] (ICLI)
**OIKT** ......... Kerman [*Iran*] [*ICAO location identifier*] (ICLI)
**OIKU**......... Hengam Island [*Iran*] [*ICAO location identifier*] (ICLI)
**OIKW**........ Kahnooj [*Iran*] [*ICAO location identifier*] (ICLI)
**OIKX** ......... Hormoz Island [*Iran*] [*ICAO location identifier*] (ICLI)
**OIKY** ......... Sirjan [*Iran*] [*ICAO location identifier*] (ICLI)
**OIKZ** ......... Zarand [*Iran*] [*ICAO location identifier*] (ICLI)
**OIL** ............ Ocelot Industries Ltd. [*Toronto Stock Exchange symbol*]
**OIL** ............ Oil City, PA [*Location identifier*] [*FAA*] (FAAL)
**OIL** ............ Oklahoma Information Lines [*Oklahoma State Department of Libraries*] [*Oklahoma City*] [*Information service or system*] (IID)
**OIL** ............ Operation Inspection Log (AAG)
**OIL** ............ Orange Indicating Light (MSA)
**OIL** ............ Orbital International Laboratory
**OIL** ............ Ordnance Investigation Laboratory
**OIL** ............ Triton Energy Corp. [*NYSE symbol*] (SPSG)
**OILA** ......... Office of International Labor Affairs [*Department of Labor*]
**OILB**.......... Organisation Internationale de Lutte Biologique Contre les Animaux et les Plantes Nuisibles [*International Organization for Biological Control of Noxious Animals and Plants - IOBC*] (EAIO)
**OILBA**....... Oil Bulletin [*A publication*]
**Oil Bull** ...... Oil Bulletin [*Canada*] [*A publication*]
**OILC**.......... Oil-Dri Corporation of America [*NASDAQ symbol*] (NQ)
**Oil Can**....... Oil in Canada [*A publication*]
**Oil Colour Chem Assoc (Aust) Proc News** ... Oil and Colour Chemists' Association (Australia). Proceedings and News [*A publication*]
**Oil Colour Chemist Assoc J** ... Oil and Colour Chemists' Association. Journal [*A publication*]
**Oil Colour Trades J** ... Oil and Colour Trades Journal [*A publication*]
**OILD** ......... Occupationally Induced Lung Disease
**Oil Eng Finance** ... Oil Engineering and Finance [*England*] [*A publication*]
**Oil Eng Technol** ... Oil Engineering and Technology [*A publication*]
**Oil Fat Ind** ... Oil and Fat Industry [*A publication*]
**Oil Field Eng** ... Oil Field Engineering [*A publication*]
**OILG** ......... Triton Energy Corp. [*NASDAQ symbol*] (NQ)
**Oil Gas**....... Oil and Gas Bulletin [*A publication*] (APTA)
**Oil & Gas**... Oil and Gas Reporter [*A publication*] (DLA)
**Oil Gas Compact Bull** ... Interstate Oil and Gas Compact Commission. Committee Bulletin [*A publication*]
**Oil Gas Compact Bull** ... Oil and Gas Compact Bulletin [*A publication*]
**Oil and Gas Compact Bull** ... Oil and Gas Compact Bulletin [*A publication*]
**Oil Gas Direct** ... Oil and Gas Directory [*A publication*]
**Oil Gas Eur Mag** ... Oil Gas European Magazine [*A publication*]
**Oil Gas Europ Mag** ... Oil Gas European Magazine [*A publication*]
**Oil Gas Geol** ... Oil and Gas Geology [*A publication*]
**Oil Gas Int** ... Oil and Gas International [*England*] [*A publication*]
**Oil Gas J**.... Oil and Gas Journal [*A publication*]
**Oil & Gas J** ... Oil and Gas Journal [*A publication*]
**Oil & Gas LR** ... Oil and Gas Law Review [*A publication*] (DLA)
**Oil Gas Mag (Hamburg)** ... Oil and Gas Magazine (Hamburg) [*A publication*]
**Oil Gas Petrochem Equip** ... Oil, Gas, and Petrochem Equipment [*A publication*]
**Oil Gas Rep** ... Oil and Gas Report [*A publication*]
**Oil & Gas Reptr** ... Oil and Gas Reporter [*A publication*] (DLA)
**Oil & Gas Rptr** ... Oil and Gas Reporter [*A publication*] (DLA)
**Oil Gas Tax Q** ... Oil and Gas Tax Quarterly [*United States*] [*A publication*]
**Oil & Gas Tax Q** ... Oil and Gas Tax Quarterly [*A publication*]
**Oil Geophys Prospect** ... Oil Geophysical Prospecting [*A publication*]
**OILLZ** ....... Ocelot Industries Limited Cl B [*NASDAQ symbol*] (NQ)

**Oil Mill Gazet** ... Oil Mill Gazetteer [*A publication*]
**OILN** ......... Oil International Ltd. [*NASDAQ symbol*] (NQ)
**Oil Paint Drug Rep** ... Oil, Paint, and Drug Reporter [*A publication*]
**Oil Prog** ..... Oil Progress [*A publication*] (APTA)
**OILS** .......... Oil Securities, Inc. [*NASDAQ symbol*] (NQ)
**OILS** .......... Oilsander. Suncor Incorporated Resources Group. Oil Sands Division [*A publication*]
**Oil Shale Relat Fuels** ... Oil Shale and Related Fuels [*A publication*]
**Oil Shale Symp Proc** ... Oil Shale Symposium Proceedings [*A publication*]
**Oils Oilseeds J** ... Oils and Oilseeds Journal [*A publication*]
**Oil Spill Intell Rep** ... Oil Spill Intelligence Report [*A publication*]
**Oil Stat (Paris)** ... Oil Statistics (Paris) [*A publication*]
**Oil Technol** ... Oil Technologist [*A publication*]
**Oil Trade J** ... Oil Trade Journal [*A publication*]
**OILWA** ..... Oil Weekly [*A publication*]
**Oil Wkly** .... Oil Weekly [*A publication*]
**OIM** .......... Office of Industrial Managers [*Navy*]
**OIM** .......... Office of Industrial Mobilization [*of BDSA*]
**OIM** .......... Office of Intergovernmental Management (OICC)
**OIM** .......... Offshore-Installation Manager [*Oil well drilling*]
**OIM** .......... On Its Merits [*British*] (ROG)
**OIM** .......... Orbit Insertion Maneuver
**OIM** .......... Organic Insulating Material
**OIM** .......... Organizational Intermediate Maintenance [*Military*] (AFIT)
**OIM** .......... Oshima Island [*Japan*] [*Airport symbol*] (OAG)
**OIMA** ........ Torbat-E-Jam [*Iran*] [*ICAO location identifier*] (ICLI)
**OIMB** ........ Birjand [*Iran*] [*ICAO location identifier*] (ICLI)
**OIMC** ........ Sarakhs [*Iran*] [*ICAO location identifier*] (ICLI)
**OIMD** ........ Goonabad [*Iran*] [*ICAO location identifier*] (ICLI)
**OIME** ........ Esfarayen [*Iran*] [*ICAO location identifier*] (ICLI)
**OIMF** ........ Ferdous [*Iran*] [*ICAO location identifier*] (ICLI)
**OIMG** ........ Ghaen [*Iran*] [*ICAO location identifier*] (ICLI)
**OIMH** ........ Torbat-E-Heidarieh [*Iran*] [*ICAO location identifier*] (ICLI)
**OIMJ** ........ Emam Shahr [*Iran*] [*ICAO location identifier*] (ICLI)
**OIMK** ........ Nehbandan [*Iran*] [*ICAO location identifier*] (ICLI)
**OIML** ........ Janat Abad [*Iran*] [*ICAO location identifier*] (ICLI)
**OIML** ........ Organisation Internationale de Metrologie Legale [*International Organization of Legal Metrology*] (EAIO)
**OIMM** ....... Mashhad [*Iran*] [*ICAO location identifier*] (ICLI)
**OIMN** ........ Bojnord [*Iran*] [*ICAO location identifier*] (ICLI)
**OIMO** ........ Ghoochan [*Iran*] [*ICAO location identifier*] (ICLI)
**OIMP** ........ Taybad [*Iran*] [*ICAO location identifier*] (ICLI)
**OIMQ** ........ Kashmar [*Iran*] [*ICAO location identifier*] (ICLI)
**OIMR** ........ Fariman [*Iran*] [*ICAO location identifier*] (ICLI)
**OIMS** ........ Orbiter Ion Mass Spectrometer [*NASA*]
**OIMS** ........ Oscillator Instability Measurement System
**OIMS** ........ Sabzevar [*Iran*] [*ICAO location identifier*] (ICLI)
**OIMSJ** ...... Micropower/St. Joseph's High School, Islington, Ontario [*Library symbol*] [*National Library of Canada*] (NLC)
**OIMT** ........ Tabas [*Iran*] [*ICAO location identifier*] (ICLI)
**OIMV** ........ Mashhad [*Iran*] [*ICAO location identifier*] (ICLI)
**OIMW** ....... Shirvan [*Iran*] [*ICAO location identifier*] (ICLI)
**OIMX** ........ Shahr Abad [*Iran*] [*ICAO location identifier*] (ICLI)
**OIMY** ........ Neishaboor [*Iran*] [*ICAO location identifier*] (ICLI)
**OIMYFC** ... Official International Michael York Fan Club (EA)
**OIN** ........... Oberlin, KS [*Location identifier*] [*FAA*] (FAAL)
**OI-N** .......... Office of Information, Navy
**OIN** ........... Organisation Internationale de Normalisation [*International Organization for Standardization*]
**OIN** ........... Organization of International Numismatists
**OIN** ........... Osrodek Informacji Naukowej [*Scientific Information Center*] [*Polish Academy of Sciences*] [*Warsaw*] [*Information service or system*] (IID)
**OINA** ......... Amol [*Iran*] [*ICAO location identifier*] (ICLI)
**OINA** ......... Oyster Institute of North America [*Later, SINA*] (EA)
**OINB** ......... Babolsar [*Iran*] [*ICAO location identifier*] (ICLI)
**OINC** ......... Chalous [*Iran*] [*ICAO location identifier*] (ICLI)
**OINC** ......... Officer-in-Charge [*Navy*]
**OINCABCCTC** ... Officer-in-Charge, Advanced Base Combat Communication Training Center [*Pearl Harbor*] [*Navy*]
**OIND** ......... Minoo Dasht [*Iran*] [*ICAO location identifier*] (ICLI)
**OINE** ......... Kalaleh [*Iran*] [*ICAO location identifier*] (ICLI)
**OInF** .......... Ferro Corp., Independence, OH [*Library symbol*] [*Library of Congress*] (LCLS)
**OING** ......... Gorgan [*Iran*] [*ICAO location identifier*] (ICLI)
**OINH** ......... Behshahr [*Iran*] [*ICAO location identifier*] (ICLI)
**OINI** .......... Ghaem Shahr [*Iran*] [*ICAO location identifier*] (ICLI)
**OINK** ......... Gonbad Ghabous [*Iran*] [*ICAO location identifier*] (ICLI)
**Oink** ........... One Income, No Kids [*Lifestyle classification*]
**OINL** ......... Alamdeh [*Iran*] [*ICAO location identifier*] (ICLI)
**OINM** ........ Mahmood Abad [*Iran*] [*ICAO location identifier*] (ICLI)
**OINN** ......... Noshahr [*Iran*] [*ICAO location identifier*] (ICLI)
**OINO** ......... Noor [*Iran*] [*ICAO location identifier*] (ICLI)
**OINOD** ....... Energy [*South Korea*] [*A publication*]
**OINP** ......... Azad Shahr [*Iran*] [*ICAO location identifier*] (ICLI)
**OINQ** ......... Kelardasht [*Iran*] [*ICAO location identifier*] (ICLI)
**OINR** ......... Ramsar [*Iran*] [*ICAO location identifier*] (ICLI)
**OINS** ......... Sari [*Iran*] [*ICAO location identifier*] (ICLI)
**OINT** ......... Ointment
**OINT** ......... Omni-Intersection [*Aviation*] (FAAC)
**OINV** ......... Tonkabon [*Iran*] [*ICAO location identifier*] (ICLI)
**OINY** ......... Bandar Torkaman [*Iran*] [*ICAO location identifier*] (ICLI)
**OINZ** ......... Dasht-E-Naz [*Iran*] [*ICAO location identifier*] (ICLI)
**OIO** ........... Obligated Involuntary Officers [*Used in movie "Spies Like Us"*]
**OIO** ........... Office of International Operations [*of IRS*]
**OIO** ........... Operations Integration Officer [*NASA*] (MCD)
**OIP** ........... Eastland, TX [*Location identifier*] [*FAA*] (FAAL)
**OIP** ........... Office of Import Programs [*Functions transferred to Domestic and International Business Administration*] [*Department of Commerce*]
**OIP** ........... Office of Industrial Programs [*Department of Energy*]
**OIP** ........... Office of International Programs [*National Science Foundation*]
**OIP** ........... Oil-in-Place
**OIP** ........... Operating Internal Pressure [*Nuclear energy*] (NRCH)
**OIP** ........... Operational Improvement Plan [*or Program*] [*Navy*]
**OIP** ........... Operational Instruction Pamphlet
**OIP** ........... Optical Image Processor
**OIP** ........... Optical Improvement Program [*Army*]
**OIP** ........... Orbital Improvement Program
**OIP** ........... Ordnance Installation Plan (MCD)
**OIP** ........... Organic Insulative Plastic
**OIP** ........... Organisation Internationale de la Paleobotanique [*International Organization of Paleobotany*]
**OIP** ........... Organisation Internationale de Psychophysiologie [*International Organization of Psychophysiology - IOP*] (EAIO)
**OIP** ........... Organizacion Iberoamericana de Pilotos [*Ibero-American Organization of Pilots - IOP*] [*Mexico City, Mexico*] (EAIO)
**OIP** ........... Organizing Interstitial Pneumonia [*Medicine*]
**OIP** ........... Oriental Institute. Publications [*The Oriental Institute of the University of Chicago*] [*A publication*]
**OIPA** ......... Ortho-Isopropylaniline [*Organic chemistry*]
**OIPAAR** .... Office of Industrial Personnel Access Authorization Review [*Army*] (AABC)
**OIPC** ......... Organisation Internationale de Police Criminelle [*International Criminal Police Organization - ICPO*] [*France*]
**OIPC** ......... Organisation Internationale de Protection Civile [*International Civil Defense Organization - ICDO*] (EAIO)
**OIPCFC** .... Official International Peter Coyote Fan Club (EA)
**OIPEEC** .... Organisation Internationale pour l'Etude de l'Endurance des Cables [*International Organization for the Study of the Endurance of Wire Ropes - IOSEWR*] (EAIO)
**Oipi** ........... One Income plus Inheritance [*Lifestyle classification*]
**OIPMT** ...... Optimum Insect Pest Management Trial [*Department of Agriculture*]
**OIPO** ......... Optimum Installation Position Only (MCD)
**OIPOB** ....... Otkrytiya, Izobreteniya, Promyshlennye Obraztsy, Tovarnye Znaki [*Bulletin for Inventions, Designs, and Trademarks*] [*A publication*]
**OIPR** ......... Office of Information, Publications, and Reports [*Department of Labor*]
**OIPS** ......... Optical Image Processing System
**OIQ** ........... Sioux City, IA [*Location identifier*] [*FAA*] (FAAL)
**OIR** ........... Iroquois Public Library, Ontario [*Library symbol*] [*National Library of Canada*] (BIB)
**OIR** ........... Office of Indian Rights [*Department of Justice*]
**OIR** ........... Office of Industrial Relations [*Superseded, 1966, by Office of Civilian Manpower*] [*Navy*]
**OIR** ........... Office of Industrial Research [*University of Manitoba*] [*Canada*] [*Research center*] (RCD)
**OIR** ........... Office of Institutional Relations [*Energy Research and Development Administration*]
**OIR** ........... Office of International Research [*National Institutes of Health*]
**OIR** ........... Office of International Resources [*Department of State*]
**OIR** ........... Oficina Interamericana de Radio [*Inter-American Radio Office*]
**OIR** ........... Okushiri [*Japan*] [*Airport symbol*] (OAG)
**OIR** ........... Old Irish [*Language, etc.*]
**OIR** ........... Online Information Retrieval Ltd. [*Information service or system*] [*Defunct*] (IID)
**OIR** ........... Open Item Review (KSC)
**O & IR** ....... Operation and Inspection Record (KSC)
**OIR** ........... Operations Integration Review (NASA)
**OIR** ........... Orbiter Infrared Radiometer [*NASA*]
**OIR** ........... Organisation Internationale de Radiodiffusion [*International Radio Organization*] [*Later, OIRT*]
**OIR** ........... Oriental Institute. Reports [*A publication*]
**OIR** ........... Other Intelligence Requirements [*Army*] (MCD)
**OIRA** ......... Office of Information and Regulatory Affairs [*Office of Management and Budget*]
**OIRE** ......... Optical Infrared Equipment
**OIRM** ........ Office of Information Resources Management [*General Services Administration*]
**OIR-N** ........ Office of Industrial Relations, Navy [*Superseded, 1966, by Office of Civilian Manpower*]
**OIRS** ......... Occupational Interest Rating Scale [*Vocational guidance test*]
**OIRSA** ....... Organismo Internacional Regional de Sanidad Agropecuaria [*Regional International Organization of Plant Protection and Animal Health*] [*El Salvador*]

**OIRT** ......... Organisation Internationale de Radiodiffusion et Television [*International Radio and Television Organization*] [*Formerly, OIR*] (EAIO)
**OIS** ............ Occupational Information System [*Department of Labor*]
**OIS** ............ Occupational Interest Survey [*Aptitude test*]
**OIS** ............ Office of Industrial Security [*DoD*]
**OIS** ............ Office of Information Services [*Council of State Governments*] [*Lexington, KY*]
**OIS** ............ Office of Information Systems [*Social and Rehabilitation Service, HEW*]
**OIS** ............ Office of International Services [*Red Cross*]
**OIS** ............ Oishiyama [*Japan*] [*Seismograph station code, US Geological Survey*] (SEIS)
**OIS** ............ Oncology Information Service [*University of Leeds*] [*England*] [*Information service or system*] (IID)
**OIS** ............ Operating Information System [*Army*]
**OIS** ............ Operational Insertion System
**OIS** ............ Operational Instrumentation System
**OIS** ............ Operational Intercommunication System [*NASA*] (KSC)
**OIS** ............ Optical Image Sensor
**OIS** ............ Optical Information System [*Data processing*]
**OIS** ............ Orbiter Instrumentation Systems [*NASA*] (MCD)
**OIS** ............ Oxford University. Institute of Economics and Statistics. Bulletin [*A publication*]
**OISA**.......... Abadeh [*Iran*] [*ICAO location identifier*] (ICLI)
**OISA**.......... Office of International Science Activities [*National Science Foundation*]
**OISB**.......... Bavanat [*Iran*] [*ICAO location identifier*] (ICLI)
**OISC**.......... Ardakan-E-Fars [*Iran*] [*ICAO location identifier*] (ICLI)
**OISC**.......... Oil-Insulated, Self-Cooling
**OISCA**....... Organization for Industrial, Spiritual, and Cultural Advancement International[*Tokyo, Japan*] (EAIO)
**OISD** ......... Darab [*Iran*] [*ICAO location identifier*] (ICLI)
**OISDG** ...... Ingleside Branch, Stormont, Dundas, and Glengarry County Library, Ontario [*Library symbol*] [*National Library of Canada*] (BIB)
**OISE**.......... Estahbanat [*Iran*] [*ICAO location identifier*] (ICLI)
**OISE**.......... Office of Industrial Security, Europe [*DoD*]
**OISE**.......... Ontario Institute for Studies in Education [*University of Toronto*] [*Research center*] (RCD)
**Oiseau Rev Fr Ornithol** ... Oiseau et la Revue Francaise d'Ornithologie [*A publication*]
**OISF** .......... Fasa [*Iran*] [*ICAO location identifier*] (ICLI)
**OISH** ......... Farashband [*Iran*] [*ICAO location identifier*] (ICLI)
**OISI**........... Dehbid [*Iran*] [*ICAO location identifier*] (ICLI)
**OISJ** .......... Jahrom [*Iran*] [*ICAO location identifier*] (ICLI)
**OISK**.......... Kazeroun [*Iran*] [*ICAO location identifier*] (ICLI)
**OISL**.......... Lar [*Iran*] [*ICAO location identifier*] (ICLI)
**OISLGR**.... Office of Industry and State and Local Government Relations [*Energy Research and Development Administration*]
**OISM** ........ Mamassani [*Iran*] [*ICAO location identifier*] (ICLI)
**OISN** ......... Neiriz [*Iran*] [*ICAO location identifier*] (ICLI)
**OISP**.......... Overseas Internal Security Program [*Army*]
**OISP**.......... Persepolis/Marvdasht [*Iran*] [*ICAO location identifier*] (ICLI)
**OISQ**.......... Ghir/Karzin [*Iran*] [*ICAO location identifier*] (ICLI)
**OISR**.......... Lamerd [*Iran*] [*ICAO location identifier*] (ICLI)
**OISR**.......... Office of Interstate Sales Registration [*HUD*]
**OISR**.......... Open Item Status Report (NASA)
**OISRU**....... Office of Intergovernmental Science and Research Utilization [*National Science Foundation*]
**OISS**.......... Operational Intelligence Support System (MCD)
**OISS**.......... Organizacion Iberoamericana de Seguridad Social [*Ibero-American Social Security Organization*]
**OISS**.......... Shiraz/International [*Iran*] [*ICAO location identifier*] (ICLI)
**OISSP**........ Office of Interim Space Station Program [*NASA*] (NASA)
**OIS & T**..... Office of Information Systems and Telecommunications [*Veterans Administration*] (TSSD)
**OIST**.......... Operator Integration Shakedown Test
**OIST**.......... Shiraz [*Iran*] [*ICAO location identifier*] (ICLI)
**OISU** ......... Abarghou [*Iran*] [*ICAO location identifier*] (ICLI)
**OISW** ........ Kohkiloyeh [*Iran*] [*ICAO location identifier*] (ICLI)
**OISX**.......... Khonj [*Iran*] [*ICAO location identifier*] (ICLI)
**OISY**.......... Yasouj [*Iran*] [*ICAO location identifier*] (ICLI)
**OISZ**.......... Firouzabad [*Iran*] [*ICAO location identifier*] (ICLI)
**OIT** ............ Object Identification Test
**OIT** ............ Oblique-Incidence Transmission
**OIT** ............ Office of International Trade [*Department of Commerce*]
**OIT** ............ Oil Interceptor Trap
**OIT** ............ Oita [*Japan*] [*Seismograph station code, US Geological Survey*] (SEIS)
**OIT** ............ Oita [*Japan*] [*Airport symbol*] (OAG)
**O IT** ........... Old Italian [*Language, etc.*] (ROG)
**OIT** ............ Ontario Ministry of Industry, Trade, and Technology [*UTLAS symbol*]
**OIT** ............ Operator Interface Terminal (MCD)
**OIT** ............ Orbiter Integrated Test [*NASA*] (NASA)
**OIT** ............ Oregon Institute of Technology, Klamath Falls, OR [*OCLC symbol*] (OCLC)
**OIT** ............ Organic Integrity Test [*Psychology*]
**OIT** ............ Organisation Internationale du Travail [*International Labor Organization - ILO*] (EAIO)
**OITA** ......... Office of International Tax Affairs [*Department of the Treasury*]
**OITA** ......... Sarab [*Iran*] [*ICAO location identifier*] (ICLI)
**OITAF-NACS** ... Organizzazione Internazionale dei Trasporti a Fune [*International Organization for Transportation by Rope*] - North American Continental Section (EA)
**OITB**.......... Mahabad [*Iran*] [*ICAO location identifier*] (ICLI)
**OITC** ......... Sardasht [*Iran*] [*ICAO location identifier*] (ICLI)
**OITD** ......... Marand [*Iran*] [*ICAO location identifier*] (ICLI)
**OITDS**....... Operations and Intelligence Tactical Data Systems (MCD)
**OITF**.......... Office of International Trade Fairs [*Department of Commerce*]
**OITF**.......... Office of International Trade and Finance [*Department of State*]
**OITF**.......... Organisation Intergouvernementale pour les Transports Internationaux Ferroviaires [*Intergovernmental Organization for International Carriage by Rail*] (EAIO)
**OITG** ......... Naghadeh [*Iran*] [*ICAO location identifier*] (ICLI)
**OITH**......... Khaneh/Piranshahr [*Iran*] [*ICAO location identifier*] (ICLI)
**OITI**........... Mianeh [*Iran*] [*ICAO location identifier*] (ICLI)
**OITJ** .......... Julfa [*Iran*] [*ICAO location identifier*] (ICLI)
**OITK** ......... Khoy [*Iran*] [*ICAO location identifier*] (ICLI)
**OITM** ........ Maragheh [*Iran*] [*ICAO location identifier*] (ICLI)
**OITN**......... Meshgin Shahr [*Iran*] [*ICAO location identifier*] (ICLI)
**OITO** ......... Mian Do Ab [*Iran*] [*ICAO location identifier*] (ICLI)
**OITP**.......... Office of International Trade Promotion [*Department of State*]
**OITP**.......... Parsabad/Moghan [*Iran*] [*ICAO location identifier*] (ICLI)
**OITQ** ......... Ahar [*Iran*] [*ICAO location identifier*] (ICLI)
**OITR** ......... Uromiyeh [*Iran*] [*ICAO location identifier*] (ICLI)
**OITS**.......... Saghez [*Iran*] [*ICAO location identifier*] (ICLI)
**OITT**.......... Outpulser, Identifier, Trunk Test
**OITT**.......... Tabriz [*Iran*] [*ICAO location identifier*] (ICLI)
**OITU** ......... Makou [*Iran*] [*ICAO location identifier*] (ICLI)
**OITV** ......... Tabriz [*Iran*] [*ICAO location identifier*] (ICLI)
**OITW** ........ Azar Shahr [*Iran*] [*ICAO location identifier*] (ICLI)
**OITX** ......... Sareskand [*Iran*] [*ICAO location identifier*] (ICLI)
**OITY** ......... Marivan [*Iran*] [*ICAO location identifier*] (ICLI)
**OITZ** ......... Zanjan [*Iran*] [*ICAO location identifier*] (ICLI)
**OIU**............ Operator Interface Unit [*Data processing*]
**OIUC SAOC** ... Oriental Institute. University of Chicago. Studies in Ancient Oriental Civilization [*A publication*]
**OIV**............ Octarios Quatior [*Four Pints*] [*Pharmacy*] (ROG)
**OIV**............ Office International de la Vigne et du Vin [*International Vine and Wine Office*] (EAIO)
**OIV**............ Oxidizer Isolation Valve (MCD)
**OIVA**......... 127th Infantry Veterans Association (EA)
**OIVS**.......... Orbiter Interface Verification Set [*NASA*] (NASA)
**OIW**........... Oceanographic Institute of Washington [*Marine science*] (MSC)
**OIW**........... Oiwake [*Japan*] [*Seismograph station code, US Geological Survey*] [*Closed*] (SEIS)
**OIW**........... Order of the Indian Wars (EA)
**OIWC**........ Oil-Insulated, Water-Cooled
**OIWR**........ Office of Indian Water Rights [*Bureau of Indian Affairs*]
**OIX**............ Ottawa, IL [*Location identifier*] [*FAA*] (FAAL)
**OIYA** ......... Ardakan-E-Yazd [*Iran*] [*ICAO location identifier*] (ICLI)
**OIYB** ......... Bafgh [*Iran*] [*ICAO location identifier*] (ICLI)
**OIYD**......... Dehshir [*Iran*] [*ICAO location identifier*] (ICLI)
**OIYF**.......... Taft [*Iran*] [*ICAO location identifier*] (ICLI)
**OIYK** ......... Khor/Jandagh [*Iran*] [*ICAO location identifier*] (ICLI)
**OIYM**........ Mehriz [*Iran*] [*ICAO location identifier*] (ICLI)
**OIYN**......... Khore Beyabanak [*Iran*] [*ICAO location identifier*] (ICLI)
**OIYQ**......... Khezr Abad [*Iran*] [*ICAO location identifier*] (ICLI)
**OIYT** ......... Yazd [*Iran*] [*ICAO location identifier*] (ICLI)
**OIYY** ......... Yazd [*Iran*] [*ICAO location identifier*] (ICLI)
**OIYZ** ......... Ashkezar [*Iran*] [*ICAO location identifier*] (ICLI)
**OIZA** ......... Jalagh [*Iran*] [*ICAO location identifier*] (ICLI)
**OIZB** ......... Zabol [*Iran*] [*ICAO location identifier*] (ICLI)
**OIZC** ......... Chah Bahar/Konarak [*Iran*] [*ICAO location identifier*] (ICLI)
**OIZD** ......... Dashtyari [*Iran*] [*ICAO location identifier*] (ICLI)
**OIZG** ......... Ghasre Ghand [*Iran*] [*ICAO location identifier*] (ICLI)
**OIZH**......... Zahedan [*Iran*] [*ICAO location identifier*] (ICLI)
**OIZI**........... Iran Shahr [*Iran*] [*ICAO location identifier*] (ICLI)
**OIZJ** .......... Jask [*Iran*] [*ICAO location identifier*] (ICLI)
**OIZK** ......... Khash [*Iran*] [*ICAO location identifier*] (ICLI)
**OIZL**.......... Zabolee [*Iran*] [*ICAO location identifier*] (ICLI)
**OIZM** ........ Mirjaveh [*Iran*] [*ICAO location identifier*] (ICLI)
**OIZN**......... Bazman [*Iran*] [*ICAO location identifier*] (ICLI)
**OIZO** ......... Sarbaz [*Iran*] [*ICAO location identifier*] (ICLI)
**OIZP**.......... Bampoor [*Iran*] [*ICAO location identifier*] (ICLI)
**OIZR** ......... Bask [*Iran*] [*ICAO location identifier*] (ICLI)
**OIZS**.......... Saravan [*Iran*] [*ICAO location identifier*] (ICLI)
**OIZT** ......... Zahedan [*Iran*] [*ICAO location identifier*] (ICLI)
**OIZY** ......... Nik-Shahr [*Iran*] [*ICAO location identifier*] (ICLI)
**OJ** .............. Jackson Public Library, Jackson, OH [*Library symbol*] [*Library of Congress*] (LCLS)
**OJ** .............. Official Journal of the European Communities [*A publication*]
**OJ** .............. Ohne Jahr [*Without Date of Publication*] [*Bibliography*] [*German*]
**OJ** .............. Open-Joisted [*Technical drawings*]
**OJ** .............. Open Web Joist [*Technical drawings*]
**OJ** .............. Opera Journal [*A publication*]

**OJ** ............. Operation Joshua (EA)
**OJ** ............. Opium Joint [*Slang*]
**OJ** ............. Orange Co. [*NYSE symbol*] (SPSG)
**OJ** ............. Orange Juice
**OJ** ............. Order of Jamaica
**OJ** ............. Orenthal James [*Given names of football player O. J. Simpson*]
**OJ** ............. Oriental Pearl Airways Ltd. [*Great Britain*] [*ICAO designator*] (FAAC)
**OJ** ............. Originating Junctor [*Telecommunications*] (TEL)
**OJ** ............. Orthomode Junction [*Electronics*]
**OJ** ............. Oudheidkundig Jaarboek. Bulletijn Uitgegeven door den Nederlandschen Oudkundigen Bond [*A publication*]
**OJ** ............. Outer Jacket
**OJA** ........... Onklos-Jonathan Aramaic (BJA)
**OJA** ........... Weatherford, OK [*Location identifier*] [*FAA*] (FAAL)
**OJAC**........... Amman [*Jordan*] [*ICAO location identifier*] (ICLI)
**OJ Act**........ Ontario Judicature Act [*A publication*] (DLA)
**OJAF** .......... Amman [*Jordan*] [*ICAO location identifier*] (ICLI)
**OJA-G** ........ Office of the Judge Advocate General [*British*]
**OJAI**........... Amman/Queen Alia [*Jordan*] [*ICAO location identifier*] (ICLI)
**OJAJ** .......... October, January, April, and July [*Denotes quarterly payments of interest or dividends in these months*] [*Business term*]
**OJAM** ......... Amman/Marka [*Jordan*] [*ICAO location identifier*] (ICLI)
**OJAQ** .......... Aqaba [*Jordan*] [*ICAO location identifier*] (ICLI)
**OJARS** ....... Office of Justice Assistance, Research, and Statistics [*Department of Justice*]
**OJAY**.......... Orange Julius International, Inc. [*New York, NY*] [*NASDAQ symbol*] (NQ)
**Ojb** ............. Oldenburger Jahrbuch [*A publication*]
**OJBD**.......... Irbid [*Jordan*] [*ICAO location identifier*] (ICLI)
**OJBNOB**... Oudheidkundig Jaarboek. Bulletijn Uitgegeven door den Nederlandschen Oudkundigen Bond [*A publication*]
**OJC** ........... North Central Regional Library, Ojibway Cree Project [*UTLAS symbol*]
**OJC** ........... Occupied Japan Club (EA)
**OJC** ........... Office of Job Corps [*Department of Labor*]
**OJC** ........... Olathe, KS [*Location identifier*] [*FAA*] (FAAL)
**OJC** ........... Orlando Junior College [*Florida*]
**OJC** ........... Otero Junior College [*La Junta, CO*]
**OJC** ........... Overseas Jazz Club (EA)
**OJCE**.......... Orchestre des Jeunes de la Communaute Europeenne [*European Community Youth Orchestra - ECYO*] (EAIO)
**OJCH** ......... Overijssel Jaarboek voor Cultuur en Historie [*A publication*]
**OJCN** ......... Jarvis Branch, City of Nanticoke Public Library, Ontario [*Library symbol*] [*National Library of Canada*] (BIB)
**OJCS** .......... Office of the Joint Chiefs of Staff (AFM)
**OJCS** .......... Organization of the Joint Chiefs of Staff
**OJD** ........... Order of Job's Daughters
**OJDYD** ...... Office of Juvenile Delinquency and Youth Development [*Later, Youth Development Bureau*] [*HEW*]
**OJE**............ Okumenischer Jugendrat in Europa [*Ecumenical Youth Council in Europe - EYCE*] (EAIO)
**OJE**............ On-the-Job Education
**OJE**............ On-the-Job Evaluation (OICC)
**OJE**............ On-the-Job Experience
**OJES** .......... Osmania Journal of English Studies [*A publication*]
**OJ Eur Comm** ... Official Journal of the European Communities [*A publication*]
**OJG** ........... Ordnance Job Guide
**OJHF** ......... Hotel Five [*Jordan*] [*ICAO location identifier*] (ICLI)
**OJHR** ......... Hotel Four [*Jordan*] [*ICAO location identifier*] (ICLI)
**oji** .............. Ojibwa [*MARC language code*] [*Library of Congress*] (LCCP)
**OJI**............. On-the-Job Injuries
**OJJDP** ....... Office of Juvenile Justice and Delinquency Prevention [*Washington, DC*] [*Department of Justice*]
**OJJO**.......... Jericho [*Jordan*] [*ICAO location identifier*] (ICLI)
**OJJR** .......... Jerusalem [*Jordan*] [*ICAO location identifier*] (ICLI)
**OJL**............ Josephine County Library System, Grants Pass, OR [*OCLC symbol*] (OCLC)
**OJMF**......... Mafraq [*Jordan*] [*ICAO location identifier*] (ICLI)
**OJNRF**....... O. J. Noer Research Foundation (EA)
**OJP**............ Office of Justice Programs [*Department of Justice*]
**OJP**............ Orlando, FL [*Location identifier*] [*FAA*] (FAAL)
**OJPR**.......... Office for Jewish Population Research [*Defunct*] (EA)
**OJQ** ........... Objective Judgment Quotient
**OJR** ........... Old Jamaica Rum (ROG)
**OJS**............ Las Oblatas de Jesus Sacerdote [*Oblates of Jesus the Priest*] [*Roman Catholic women's religious order*]
**OJS**............ Optical Jammer Source
**OJSA**.......... Orthomode Junction and Switching Assembly [*Electronics*]
**OJT**............ On-the-Job Training
**OJT**............ Over-Water Jet Transport (MCD)
**OJTA**.......... Officer Job/Task Analysis [*Military*]
**O Judd Farmer** ... Orange Judd Farmer [*A publication*]
**O Judd Ill F** ... Orange Judd Illinois Farmer [*A publication*]
**O Jur**.......... Ohio Jurisprudence [*A publication*] (DLA)
**OJZ** ........... White Plains, NY [*Location identifier*] [*FAA*] (FAAL)
**OJZZ**.......... Amman [*Jordan*] [*ICAO location identifier*] (ICLI)
**OK**............. All Right [*From Oll Korrect; or from Old Kinderhook, a political club that supported the 1840 presidential campaign of Martin Van Buren*]
**OK**............. Ceskoslovenske Aerolinie [*Czechoslovakia*] [*ICAO designator*] (FAAC)
**OK**............. Czechoslovakia [*Aircraft nationality and registration mark*] (FAAC)
**OK**............. Kingston Public Library, Ontario [*Library symbol*] [*National Library of Canada*] (NLC)
**O-K** ........... Object-Kowal [*Object in the solar system*]
**OK**............. Odorless Kerosene
**OK**............. Ohne Kosten [*Without Cost*] [*German*]
**OK**............. Okinawa [*Japan*]
**OK**............. Oklahoma [*Postal code*]
**Ok** ............. Oklahoma Department of Libraries, Oklahoma City, OK [*Library symbol*] [*Library of Congress*] (LCLS)
**OK**............. Oklahoma School Music News [*A publication*]
**OK**............. Ola Kala [*All Is Well*] [*Greek*]
**OK**............. Old Kingdom [*Egyptology*] (ROG)
**OK**............. Onze Kongo [*A publication*]
**OK**............. Order of Knights (ADA)
**OK**............. Oskar Kokoschka [*Austrian painter*] [*1886-1980*]
**OK**............. Outer Keel
**OKA**........... Bethany Nazarene College, Bethany, OK [*OCLC symbol*] (OCLC)
**OKA**........... Kingston Laboratories, Alcan International Ltd., Ontario [*Library symbol*] [*National Library of Canada*] (NLC)
**OKA**........... Okayama [*Japan*] [*Seismograph station code, US Geological Survey*] (SEIS)
**OKA**........... Okinawa [*Japan*] [*Airport symbol*] (OAG)
**OKA**........... Otherwise Known As
**OKA**........... Out-of-Kilter Algorithm [*Mathematics*]
**OKAA**......... Kuwait Directorate General of Civil Aviation [*Kuwait*] [*ICAO location identifier*] (ICLI)
**OKAAN**..... Optokinetic After-After-Nystagmus [*Ophthalmology*]
**OKAB** ........ Beaverbrook Branch, Kanata Public Library, Ontario [*Library symbol*] [*National Library of Canada*] (NLC)
**OKAC** ........ Kuwait [*Kuwait*] [*ICAO location identifier*] (ICLI)
**OkAd** ......... Ada Public Library, Ada, OK [*Library symbol*] [*Library of Congress*] (LCLS)
**OkAdE**....... East Central State College [*Later, East Central Oklahoma State University*], Ada, OK [*Library symbol*] [*Library of Congress*] (LCLS)
**OKAER** ..... Radiochemical Co., Atomic Energy of Canada Ltd., [*Societe Radiochimique, L'Energie Atomique du Canada Ltee.*], Kanata, Ontario [*Library symbol*] [*National Library of Canada*] (NLC)
**OKAF** ........ Kuwait Air Force [*Kuwait*] [*ICAO location identifier*] (ICLI)
**OKAH** ....... Hazeldean Branch, Kanata Public Library, Ontario [*Library symbol*] [*National Library of Canada*] (NLC)
**OKAI** ......... Research & Technology Centre, AMCA International Ltd., Kanata, Ontario [*Library symbol*] [*National Library of Canada*] (NLC)
**Okajimas Folia Anat Jpn** ... Okajimas Folia Anatomica Japonica [*A publication*]
**OKAKS**...... Synod Office, Diocese of Keewatin, Anglican Church of Canada, Kenora, Ontario [*Library symbol*] [*National Library of Canada*] (NLC)
**OkAl**.......... Altus Library, Altus, OK [*Library symbol*] [*Library of Congress*] (LCLS)
**OKAL** ........ Aluminum Co. of Canada Ltd., Kingston, Ontario [*Library symbol*] [*National Library of Canada*] (NLC)
**OkAlS**........ Southern Prairie Library System, Altus, OK [*Library symbol*] [*Library of Congress*] (LCLS)
**OkAlvN** ..... Northwestern State College, Alva, OK [*Library symbol*] [*Library of Congress*] (LCLS)
**OKAN**........ Kanata Public Library, Ontario [*Library symbol*] [*National Library of Canada*] (BIB)
**OKAN**........ Optokinetic After-Nystagmus [*Ophthalmology*]
**OKANA**..... Arctec Canada Ltd., Kanata, Ontario [*Library symbol*] [*National Library of Canada*] (NLC)
**OKAOS** ..... Synod Office, Diocese of Ontario, Anglican Church of Canada, Kingston, Ontario [*Library symbol*] [*National Library of Canada*] (NLC)
**OKAP** ........ Kapuskasing Public Library, Ontario [*Library symbol*] [*National Library of Canada*] (NLC)
**OkArC** ....... Chickasaw Library System, Ardmore, OK [*Library symbol*] [*Library of Congress*] (LCLS)
**OKASG** ..... St. George's Cathedral, Anglican Church of Canada, Kingston, Ontario [*Library symbol*] [*National Library of Canada*] (NLC)
**Okayama Igakkai Zasshi Suppl** ... Okayama Igakkai Zasshi. Supplement [*Japan*] [*A publication*]
**Okayama Univ Inst Therm Spring Res Pap** ... Okayama University. Institute for Thermal Spring Research. Papers [*A publication*]
**OKAYJ**...... A. Y. Jackson High School, Kanata, Ontario [*Library symbol*] [*National Library of Canada*] (BIB)
**OkB**............ Bartlesville Public Library, Bartlesville, OK [*Library symbol*] [*Library of Congress*] (LCLS)
**OKB** ........... Kashechewan Band Library, Ontario [*Library symbol*] [*National Library of Canada*] (BIB)

**OKB**.......... Oesterreichische Kontrollbank [*Export credit agency*] [*Austria*]
**OKB**.......... Oklahoma Baptist University, Shawnee, OK [*OCLC symbol*] (OCLC)
**OKB**.......... Orchid Beach [*Australia*] [*Airport symbol*]
**OkBERDA** ... United States Energy Research Development Administration, Energy Research Center, Bartlesville, OK [*Library symbol*] [*Library of Congress*] (LCLS)
**OkBetC**...... Bethany Nazarene College, Bethany, OK [*Library symbol*] [*Library of Congress*] (LCLS)
**OKBK**........ Kuwait/International [*Kuwait*] [*ICAO location identifier*] (ICLI)
**OkBP**......... Phillips Petroleum Co., Research and Development Department, Bartlesville, OK [*Library symbol*] [*Library of Congress*] (LCLS)
**OkBr**.......... Bristow Public Library, Bristow, OK [*Library symbol*] [*Library of Congress*] (LCLS)
**OKBT**........ Billings Township Public Library, Kagawong, Ontario [*Library symbol*] [*National Library of Canada*] (NLC)
**OkBUSM**.. United States Bureau of Mines, Petroleum Research Center, Bartlesville, OK [*Library symbol*] [*Library of Congress*] [*Obsolete*] (LCLS)
**OKC**.......... Cameron University, Lawton, OK [*OCLC symbol*] (OCLC)
**OKC**.......... Canadian Forces School of Communications and Electronics, Kingston, Ontario [*Library symbol*] [*National Library of Canada*] (BIB)
**OKC**.......... Okanagan College Learning Resources Centre [*UTLAS symbol*]
**OKC**.......... Oklahoma City [*Oklahoma*] [*Airport symbol*] (OAG)
**OKCAA**..... Archives, Archdiocese of Kingston, Catholic Church, Ontario [*Library symbol*] [*National Library of Canada*] (NLC)
**OkChicW**... Oklahoma College of Liberal Arts, Chickasha, OK [*Library symbol*] [*Library of Congress*] (LCLS)
**OKCKT**..... King Township Public Library, King City, Ontario [*Library symbol*] [*National Library of Canada*] (NLC)
**OkCl**.......... Clinton Public Library, Clinton, OK [*Library symbol*] [*Library of Congress*] (LCLS)
**OkClaW**.... Will Rogers Library, Claremore, OH [*Library symbol*] [*Library of Congress*] (LCLS)
**OkClW**...... Western Plains Library System, Clinton, OK [*Library symbol*] [*Library of Congress*] (LCLS)
**OKCM**....... Canadian Marconi Co., Kanata, Ontario [*Library symbol*] [*National Library of Canada*] (NLC)
**OKCO**........ Oakbrook Consolidated [*NASDAQ symbol*] (NQ)
**OKCP**........ OKC Ltd. Partnership [*NASDAQ symbol*] (NQ)
**OKD**.......... Oklahoma Department of Libraries, Oklahoma City, OK [*OCLC symbol*] (OCLC)
**OKD**.......... Research Centre Library, Du Pont Canada, Inc., Kingston, Ontario [*Library symbol*] [*National Library of Canada*] (NLC)
**OKD**.......... Sapporo/Okadama [*Japan*] [*Airport symbol*] (OAG)
**OKDBMS** ... Operations Knowledge Data Base Management System [*NASA*]
**OKDC**........ Du Pont Canada, Inc., Kingston, Ontario [*Library symbol*] [*National Library of Canada*] (NLC)
**OKDIA**...... Osaka Kogyo Daigaku Kiyo. Riko-Hen [*A publication*]
**OkDurS**..... Southeastern State College, Durant, OK [*Library symbol*] [*Library of Congress*] (LCLS)
**OKE**.......... Kenora Public Library, Ontario [*Library symbol*] [*National Library of Canada*] (NLC)
**OKE**.......... Metropolitan Library System, Capitol Hill Branch, Oklahoma City, OK [*OCLC symbol*] (OCLC)
**OKE**.......... Okino Erabu [*Japan*] [*Airport symbol*] (OAG)
**OKE**.......... ONEOK, Inc. [*NYSE symbol*] (SPSG)
**OkE**........... Public Library of Enid and Garfield County, Enid, OK [*Library symbol*] [*Library of Congress*] (LCLS)
**OKEA**........ Kearney and Area Public Library, Kearney, Ontario [*Library symbol*] [*National Library of Canada*] (NLC)
**Okeanol**..... Okeanologiya [*A publication*]
**Okeanol Issled** ... Okeanologicheskie Issledovaniya [*A publication*]
**OkEdT**....... Central State University, Edmond, OK [*Library symbol*] [*Library of Congress*] (LCLS)
**OKEE**........ Keewatin Public Library, Ontario [*Library symbol*] [*National Library of Canada*] (NLC)
**O'Keefe Ord** ... O'Keefe's Order in Chancery [*Ireland*] [*A publication*] (DLA)
**Oke Fish L** ... Oke. Fisher Laws [*4th ed.*] [*1924*] [*A publication*] (DLA)
**OkEG**......... Phillips University, Graduate Seminary, Enid, OK [*Library symbol*] [*Library of Congress*] (LCLS)
**Oke Game L** ... Oke. Game Laws [*5th ed.*] [*1912*] [*A publication*] (DLA)
**OKEH**........ Okehampton [*England*]
**OKEHDW** ... Proceedings. Osaka Prefecture Institute of Public Health. Edition of Public Health [*A publication*]
**OKEM**....... Kemptville Public Library, Ontario [*Library symbol*] [*National Library of Canada*] (NLC)
**OKEMAF** ... Ontario Ministry of Agriculture and Food, Kemptville, Ontario [*Library symbol*] [*National Library of Canada*] (NLC)
**Oke Mag Form** ... Oke. Magisterial Formulist [*19th ed.*] [*1978*] [*A publication*] (DLA)
**Oke Mag Syn** ... Oke. Magisterial Synopsis [*14th ed.*] [*1893*] [*A publication*] (DLA)
**OKEMC**.... Kemptville College of Agricultural Technology, Ontario [*Library symbol*] [*National Library of Canada*] (BIB)
**OKEMS**..... Earl of March Secondary School, Kanata, Ontario [*Library symbol*] [*National Library of Canada*] (NLC)
**OKEN**........ Old Kent Financial Corp. [*NASDAQ symbol*] (NQ)
**OKentU**..... Kent State University, Kent, OH [*Library symbol*] [*Library of Congress*] (LCLS)
**OkEP**......... Phillips University, Enid, OK [*Library symbol*] [*Library of Congress*] (LCLS)
**OKES**......... Georgina Township Public Library, Keswick, Ontario [*Library symbol*] [*National Library of Canada*] (NLC)
**OKET**........ Euphrasia Township Public Library, Kimberley, Ontario [*Library symbol*] [*National Library of Canada*] (NLC)
**OKetH**....... Kettering Memorial Hospital, Kettering, OH [*Library symbol*] [*Library of Congress*] (LCLS)
**OKetK**........ Charles F. Kettering Foundation, Kettering, OH [*Library symbol*] [*Library of Congress*] (LCLS)
**Oke Turn** ... Oke. Turnpike Laws [*2nd ed.*] [*1861*] [*A publication*] (DLA)
**OKF**........... Fort Frontenac Library, Canada Department of National Defence [*Bibliotheque Fort Frontenac, Ministere de la Defense Nationale*] Kingston, Ontario [*Library symbol*] [*National Library of Canada*] (NLC)
**OKFC**........ Frontenac County Library, Kingston, Ontario [*Library symbol*] [*National Library of Canada*] (NLC)
**OKFCSM**.. Frontenac County Schools Museum Association, Kingston, Ontario [*Library symbol*] [*National Library of Canada*] (BIB)
**OKFI**.......... Siltronics Ltd., Kanata, Ontario [*Library symbol*] [*National Library of Canada*] (NLC)
**OkFsAGM** ... United States Army, Artillery and Guided Missile School, Fort Sill, OK [*Library symbol*] [*Library of Congress*] (LCLS)
**OKG**.......... Oak Grove [*Tennessee*] [*Seismograph station code, US Geological Survey*] (SEIS)
**OKG**.......... Okoyo [*Congo*] [*Airport symbol*] (OAG)
**OKG**.......... Phillips University, Graduate Seminary Library, Enid, OK [*OCLC symbol*] (OCLC)
**OKGH**....... Kingston General Hospital, Ontario [*Library symbol*] [*National Library of Canada*] (NLC)
**OkGoP**....... Panhandle State College, Goodwell, OK [*Library symbol*] [*Library of Congress*] (LCLS)
**OkGuC**...... Catholic College of Oklahoma for Women, Guthrie, OK [*Library symbol*] [*Library of Congress*] [*Obsolete*] (LCLS)
**OkGuy**....... Guymon City Library, Guymon, OK [*Library symbol*] [*Library of Congress*] (LCLS)
**OKH**.......... Oberkommando des Heeres [*Army High Command*] [*German military - World War II*]
**OKH**.......... Okha [*USSR*] [*Seismograph station code, US Geological Survey*] (SEIS)
**OKH**.......... University of Oklahoma, Health Science Center Library, Oklahoma City, OK [*OCLC symbol*] (OCLC)
**OKHD**........ Hotel-Dieu Hospital, Kingston, Ontario [*Library symbol*] [*National Library of Canada*] (NLC)
**OKHED4**... Proceedings. Osaka Prefecture Institute of Public Health. Edition of Mental Health [*A publication*]
**OkHenn**..... Hennessey Public Library, Hennessey, OK [*Library symbol*] [*Library of Congress*] (LCLS)
**OkHi**.......... Oklahoma Historical Society, Oklahoma City, OK [*Library symbol*] [*Library of Congress*] (LCLS)
**Okhota Okhot Khoz** ... Okhota i Okhotnich'e Khozyaistvo [*A publication*]
**Okhr Okruzh Sredy Zagryaz Prom Vybrosami** ... Okhrana Okruzhayushchei Sredy ot Zagryazneniya Promyshlennymi Vybrosami [*A publication*]
**Okhr Okruzh Sredy Zagryaz Prom Vybrosami TsBP** ... Okhrana Okruzhayushchei Sredy ot Zagryazneniya Promyshlennymi Vybrosami Tsellyulozno-Bumazhnaya Promyshlennost [*A publication*]
**Okhr Prir** ... Okhrana Prirody [*A publication*]
**Okhr Prir Dal'nem Vostoke** ... Okhrana Prirody na Dal'nem Vostoke [*A publication*]
**Okhr Prir Tsent-Chernozem Polosy** ... Okhrana Prirody Tsentral'no-Chernozemnoi Polosy [*A publication*]
**Okhr Prir Tsentr Chernozemn Polosy** ... Okhrana Prirody Tsentral'no-Chernozemnoi Polosy [*A publication*]
**Okhr Prir Urale** ... Okhrana Prirody na Urale [*A publication*]
**Okhr Prir Vod Urala** ... Okhrana Prirodnykh Vod Urala [*USSR*] [*A publication*]
**Okhr Tr Tekh Bezop Chern Metall** ... Okhrana Truda i Tekhnika Bezopasnosti v Chernoi Metallurgii [*A publication*]
**Okhr Zdor Detei Podrostkov (Kiev)** ... Okhrana Zdorov'ya Detei i Podrostkov (Kiev) [*A publication*]
**OKI**........... Choctaw Nation Multi-County Library, McAlester, OK [*OCLC symbol*] (OCLC)
**OKI**........... Kincardine Branch, Bruce County Public Library, Ontario [*Library symbol*] [*National Library of Canada*] (NLC)
**OKI**........... Ohio-Kentucky-Indiana Regional Planning Authority
**OKI**........... Oki Island [*Japan*] [*Airport symbol*] (OAG)
**OKI**........... Okijuku [*Japan*] [*Seismograph station code, US Geological Survey*] [*Closed*] (SEIS)
**OKIESMO** ... Oklahoma Machismo [*Term coined by author Mark Singer*]
**OKIL**........ Killaloe Public Library, Ontario [*Library symbol*] [*National Library of Canada*] (NLC)
**OKIT**........ Kitchener Public Library, Ontario [*Library symbol*] [*National Library of Canada*] (NLC)

**OKITC**....... Learning Resource Centre, Conestoga College of Applied Arts and Technology, Kitchener, Ontario [*Library symbol*] [*National Library of Canada*] (NLC)
**OKITD**...... Doon Pioneer Village, Kitchener, Ontario [*Library symbol*] [*National Library of Canada*] (BIB)
**Oki Tech Rev**... Oki Technical Review [*A publication*]
**OKITM**..... Ontario Library Service - Saugeen, Kitchener, Ontario [*Library symbol*] [*National Library of Canada*] (NLC)
**OKITW**..... Kitchener-Waterloo Record, Kitchener, Ontario [*Library symbol*] [*National Library of Canada*] (NLC)
**OKITWC**... Waterloo County Board of Education, Kitchener, Ontario [*Library symbol*] [*National Library of Canada*] (NLC)
**OKJ**.......... Okayama [*Japan*] [*Airport symbol*] (OAG)
**OKJ**.......... Oklahoma City Community College, Oklahoma City, OK [*OCLC symbol*] (OCLC)
**OKK**.......... Charles F. Kettering Foundation, Dayton, OH [*OCLC symbol*] (OCLC)
**OKK**.......... Kokomo [*Indiana*] [*Airport symbol*] (OAG)
**OKK**.......... Kokomo, IN [*Location identifier*] [*FAA*] (FAAL)
**OKKBWP**... One Kind Kiss Before We Part [*Slang*]
**OKL**.......... Lake Ontario Regional Library System, Kingston, Ontario [*Library symbol*] [*Obsolete*] [*National Library of Canada*] (NLC)
**OkL**........... Lawton Public Library, Lawton, OK [*Library symbol*] [*Library of Congress*] (LCLS)
**OKL**.......... Oberkommando der Luftwaffe [*Air Force High Command*] [*German military - World War II*]
**Okl**............ Oklahoma (DLA)
**Okl**............ Oklahoma Reports [*A publication*] (DLA)
**OKL**.......... University of Oklahoma, Law Library, Norman, OK [*OCLC symbol*] (OCLC)
**OKLA**........ Oklahoma (AFM)
**Okla**.......... Oklahoma Criminal Reports [*A publication*] (DLA)
**Okla**.......... Oklahoma Supreme Court Reports [*A publication*] (DLA)
**Okla Acad Sci Proc**... Oklahoma Academy of Science. Proceedings [*A publication*]
**Okla Ag Exp**... Oklahoma. Agricultural Experiment Station. Publications [*A publication*]
**Okla Agric Exp Stn Annu Rep**... Oklahoma. Agricultural Experiment Station. Annual Report [*A publication*]
**Okla Agric Exp Stn Bull**... Oklahoma. Agricultural Experiment Station. Bulletin [*A publication*]
**Okla Agric Exp Stn Mimeogr Circ**... Oklahoma. Agricultural Experiment Station. Mimeographed Circular [*A publication*]
**Okla Agric Exp Stn Misc Publ**... Oklahoma. Agricultural Experiment Station. Miscellaneous Publication [*A publication*]
**Okla Agric Exp Stn M P**... Oklahoma. Agricultural Experiment Station. Miscellaneous Publication [*A publication*]
**Okla Agric Exp Stn Processed Ser**... Oklahoma. Agricultural Experiment Station. Processed Series [*A publication*]
**Okla Agric Exp Stn Process Ser**... Oklahoma. Agricultural Experiment Station. Processed Series [*A publication*]
**Okla Agric Exp Stn Prog Rep**... Oklahoma. Agricultural Experiment Station. Progress Report [*A publication*]
**Okla Agric Exp Stn Res Rep**... Oklahoma. Agricultural Experiment Station. Research Report [*A publication*]
**Okla Agric Exp Stn Tech Bull**... Oklahoma. Agricultural Experiment Station. Technical Bulletin [*A publication*]
**Okla Ap Ct Rep**... Oklahoma Appellate Court Reporter [*A publication*] (DLA)
**Okla BA J**... Oklahoma Bar Association. Journal [*A publication*]
**Okla B Ass'n J**... Oklahoma Bar Association. Journal [*A publication*]
**Okla BJ**..... Oklahoma Bar Journal [*A publication*]
**Okla Bsns**.. Oklahoma Business [*A publication*]
**Okla Bus**.... Oklahoma Business [*A publication*]
**Okla Chronicles**... Chronicles of Oklahoma [*A publication*]
**Okla City UL Rev**... Oklahoma City University. Law Review [*A publication*]
**Okla Cr**...... Oklahoma Criminal Reports [*A publication*] (DLA)
**Okla Crim**... Oklahoma Criminal Reports [*A publication*] (DLA)
**Okla CULR**... Oklahoma City University. Law Review [*A publication*] (DLA)
**Okla Curr Farm Econ**... Oklahoma Current Farm Economics [*A publication*]
**Okla Div Water Resour Bull**... Oklahoma. Division of Water Resources. Bulletin [*A publication*]
**Okla Dp G N H Bien Rp**... Oklahoma. Department of Geology and Natural History. Biennial Report [*A publication*]
**Okla Gaz**.... Oklahoma Gazette [*A publication*] (DLA)
**Okla Geol Notes**... Oklahoma Geology Notes [*A publication*]
**Okla Geology Notes**... Oklahoma Geology Notes [*A publication*]
**Okla Geol Surv Bull**... Oklahoma. Geological Survey. Bulletin [*A publication*]
**Okla Geol Surv Circ**... Oklahoma. Geological Survey. Circular [*A publication*]
**Okla Geol Surv Map**... Oklahoma. Geological Survey. Map [*A publication*]
**Okla Geol Surv Miner Rep**... Oklahoma. Geological Survey. Mineral Report [*A publication*]
**Okla G S**.... Oklahoma. Geological Survey [*A publication*]
**Oklahoma**.. Oklahoma Reports [*A publication*] (DLA)
**Oklahoma Acad Sci Proc**... Oklahoma Academy of Science. Proceedings [*A publication*]
**Oklahoma Geology Notes**... Oklahoma Geology Notes. Oklahoma Geological Survey [*A publication*]
**Oklahoma Geol Survey Guidebook**... Oklahoma. Geological Survey. Guidebook [*A publication*]
**Oklahoma Geol Survey Map**... Oklahoma. Geological Survey. Map [*A publication*]
**Oklahoma L Rev**... Oklahoma Law Review [*A publication*]
**Oklahoma Univ Inf Sci Ser Mon**... Oklahoma. University. Information Science Series. Monograph [*A publication*]
**Okla ICR**... Oklahoma Industrial Commission Reports [*A publication*] (DLA)
**Okla Law R**... Oklahoma Law Review [*A publication*]
**Okla Lawy**... Oklahoma Lawyer [*A publication*] (DLA)
**Okla Libn**.. Oklahoma Librarian [*A publication*]
**Okla Librn**... Oklahoma Librarian [*A publication*]
**Okla LJ**...... Oklahoma Law Journal [*A publication*] (DLA)
**Okla LR**..... Oklahoma Law Review [*A publication*]
**Okla L Rev**... Oklahoma Law Review [*A publication*]
**Okla Med Ne J**... Oklahoma Medical News Journal [*A publication*]
**Okla Nurse**... Oklahoma Nurse [*A publication*]
**Okl App**..... Oklahoma Court of Appeals (DLA)
**OKL Arb Osterreichisches Kuratorium Landtech**... OKL-Arbeit-Oesterreichisches Kuratorium fuer Landtechnik [*A publication*]
**Okla SBJ**... Oklahoma State Bar Journal [*A publication*] (DLA)
**Okla Sess Laws**... Oklahoma Session Laws [*A publication*] (DLA)
**Okla Sess Law Serv**... Oklahoma Session Law Service (West) [*A publication*] (DLA)
**Okla Stat**... Oklahoma Statutes [*A publication*] (DLA)
**Okla Stat Ann (West)**... Oklahoma Statutes, Annotated (West) [*A publication*] (DLA)
**Okla State Univ Agric Appl Sci Eng Exp Stn Publ**... Oklahoma State University of Agriculture and Applied Science. Engineering Experiment Station. Publication [*A publication*]
**OkLaU**....... Langston University, Langston, OK [*Library symbol*] [*Library of Congress*] (LCLS)
**Okla Univ Research B**... Oklahoma State University. Research Bulletin [*A publication*]
**Okla Water Res Board Bull**... Oklahoma. Water Resources Board. Bulletin [*A publication*]
**OkLC**......... Cameron University, Lawton, OK [*Library symbol*] [*Library of Congress*] (LCLS)
**Okl City UL Rev**... Oklahoma City University. Law Review [*A publication*] (DLA)
**OkLC-M**.... Cameron College, Medical Library Resource Center, Lawton, OK [*Library symbol*] [*Library of Congress*] (LCLS)
**Okl Cr**........ Oklahoma Criminal Reports [*A publication*] (DLA)
**Okl Cr R**.... Oklahoma Criminal Reports [*A publication*] (DLA)
**OKLEM**.... McMichael Canadian Collection, Kleinburg, Ontario [*Library symbol*] [*National Library of Canada*] (NLC)
**OKLFC**...... Official Kate Linder Fan Club (EA)
**Okl LR**....... Oklahoma Law Review [*A publication*]
**OKLN**........ Northeastern Regional Library, Kirkland Lake, Ontario [*Library symbol*] [*National Library of Canada*] (NLC)
**OKLN**........ Ontario Library Service - James Bay, Kirkland Lake, Ontario [*Library symbol*] [*National Library of Canada*] (NLC)
**OKLNC**..... Kirkland Lake Campus, Northern College, Ontario [*Library symbol*] [*National Library of Canada*] (NLC)
**OK LR**....... Oklahoma Law Review [*A publication*]
**Okl St Ann**... Oklahoma Statutes, Annotated [*A publication*] (DLA)
**OKLT**........ Teck Centennial Public Library, Kirkland Lake, Ontario [*Library symbol*] [*National Library of Canada*] (NLC)
**OKLU**........ Lumonics, Inc., Kanata, Ontario [*Library symbol*] [*National Library of Canada*] (NLC)
**OKM**.......... Mitel Corp., Kanata, Ontario [*Library symbol*] [*National Library of Canada*] (NLC)
**OKM**.......... Oberkommando der Kriegsmarine [*Navy High Command*] [*German military - World War II*]
**OKM**.......... Okmulgee, OK [*Location identifier*] [*FAA*] (FAAL)
**OKM**.......... Pioneer Multi-County Library, Norman, OK [*OCLC symbol*] (OCLC)
**OKMC**....... Miller Communications Systems Ltd., Kanata, Ontario [*Library symbol*] [*National Library of Canada*] (NLC)
**OkMcC**....... Choctaw Nation Multi-County Library, McAlester, OK [*Library symbol*] [*Library of Congress*] (LCLS)
**OkMcO**..... Oscar Rose Junior College, Midwest City, OK [*Library symbol*] [*Library of Congress*] (LCLS)
**OKMD**....... Digital Equipment of Canada Ltd., Kanata, Ontario [*Library symbol*] [*National Library of Canada*] (NLC)
**OKMD**....... Oudheidkundige Mededeelingen [*A publication*]
**OKME**....... Metro Canada Ltd., Kingston, Ontario [*Library symbol*] [*National Library of Canada*] (NLC)
**OKMM**...... Marine Museum of the Great Lakes at Kingston, Ontario [*Library symbol*] [*National Library of Canada*] (NLC)
**OkMu**........ Muskogee Public Library, Muskogee, OK [*Library symbol*] [*Library of Congress*] (LCLS)
**OkMuE**...... Eastern Oklahoma District Library, Muskogee, OK [*Library symbol*] [*Library of Congress*] (LCLS)
**OkMuV**..... United States Veterans Administration Hospital, Muskogee, OK [*Library symbol*] [*Library of Congress*] (LCLS)

**OKN** .......... Northeastern Oklahoma State University, Tahlequah, OK [*OCLC symbol*] (OCLC)
**OKN** .......... Okmulgee Northern Railway Co. [*AAR code*]
**OKN** .......... Okondja [*Gabon*] [*Airport symbol*] (OAG)
**OKN** .......... Optokinetic Nystagmus [*Ophthalmology*]
**OkN** .......... Pioneer Multi-County Library, Norman, OK [*Library symbol*] [*Library of Congress*] (LCLS)
**OKNC** ........ Newbridge Communication Network Corp., Kanata, Ontario [*Library symbol*] [*National Library of Canada*] (BIB)
**OkNNS** ...... National Severe Storms Laboratory, Norman, OK [*Library symbol*] [*Library of Congress*] (LCLS)
**OKNO** ....... Kuwait International NOTAM Office [*Kuwait*] [*ICAO location identifier*] (ICLI)
**OKO** .......... Oral Roberts University, Tulsa, OK [*OCLC symbol*] (OCLC)
**OKOH** ....... Penrose Division, Ongwanada Hospital, Kingston, Ontario [*Library symbol*] [*National Library of Canada*] (NLC)
**OkOk** ......... Oklahoma County Libraries, Oklahoma City, OK [*Library symbol*] [*Library of Congress*] (LCLS)
**OkOkB** ...... Oklahoma Library for the Blind and Physically Handicapped, Oklahoma City, OK [*Library symbol*] [*Library of Congress*] (LCLS)
**OkOkD** ...... Deaconess Hospital, Oklahoma City, OK [*Library symbol*] [*Library of Congress*] (LCLS)
**OkOkFA** .... United States Federal Aviation Administration, Civil Aeromedical Institute, Oklahoma City, OK [*Library symbol*] [*Library of Congress*] (LCLS)
**OkOkGS** ... Church of Jesus Christ of Latter-Day Saints, Genealogical Society Library, Oklahoma City Branch, Oklahoma City, OK [*Library symbol*] [*Library of Congress*] (LCLS)
**OkOkK** ...... Kerr-McGee Corp., Oklahoma City, OK [*Library symbol*] [*Library of Congress*] (LCLS)
**OkOkSO** ... Oklahoma City Community College, Learning Resources Center, Oklahoma City, OK [*Library symbol*] [*Library of Congress*] (LCLS)
**OkOkU** ...... Oklahoma City University, Oklahoma City, OK [*Library symbol*] [*Library of Congress*] (LCLS)
**OkOkU-L** ... Oklahoma City University, Law Library, Oklahoma City, OK [*Library symbol*] [*Library of Congress*] (LCLS)
**OkOkV** ...... United States Veterans Administration Hospital, Oklahoma City, OK [*Library symbol*] [*Library of Congress*] (LCLS)
**Okon og Polit** ... Okonomi og Politik [*A publication*]
**OKOT** ........ Otonabee Township Library, Keen, Ontario [*Library symbol*] [*National Library of Canada*] (NLC)
**OKP** .......... Oksapmin [*Papua New Guinea*] [*Airport symbol*] (OAG)
**OKP** .......... O'Okiep Copper Co. Ltd. [*AMEX symbol*] (SPSG)
**OKP** .......... Optimized Kill Probability
**OKP** .......... Southern Prairie Library System, Altus, OK [*OCLC symbol*] (OCLC)
**OkPo** .......... Ponca City Public Library, Ponca City, OK [*Library symbol*] [*Library of Congress*] (LCLS)
**OkPoC** ....... Continental Oil Co., R and D Technical Information Service, Ponca City, OK [*Library symbol*] [*Library of Congress*] (LCLS)
**OkPot** ........ Buckley Public Library, Poteau, OK [*Library symbol*] [*Library of Congress*] (LCLS)
**OKQ** .......... Okaba [*Indonesia*] [*Airport symbol*] (OAG)
**OKQ** .......... Queen's University, Kingston, Ontario [*Library symbol*] [*National Library of Canada*] (NLC)
**OKQA** ........ Agnes Etherington Art Centre, Queen's University, Kingston, Ontario [*Library symbol*] [*National Library of Canada*] (NLC)
**OKQAR** ..... Archives, Queen's University, Kingston, Ontario [*Library symbol*] [*National Library of Canada*] (NLC)
**OKQCI** ...... Canadian Institute of Guided Ground Transport, Queen's University, Kingston, Ontario [*Library symbol*] [*National Library of Canada*] (NLC)
**OKQG** ........ Department of Geography, Queen's University, Kingston, Ontario [*Library symbol*] [*National Library of Canada*] (NLC)
**OKQGS** ..... Department of Geological Sciences, Queen's University, Kingston, Ontario [*Library symbol*] [*National Library of Canada*] (NLC)
**OKQH** ....... Bracken Library, Queen's University, Kingston, Ontario [*Library symbol*] [*National Library of Canada*] (NLC)
**OKQL** ........ Law Library, Queen's University, Kingston, Ontario [*Library symbol*] [*National Library of Canada*] (NLC)
**OKQM** ...... McArthur College of Education, Queen's University, Kingston, Ontario [*Library symbol*] [*National Library of Canada*] (NLC)
**OKQMA** .... Map Collection, Douglas Library, Queen's University, Kingston, Ontario [*Library symbol*] [*National Library of Canada*] (NLC)
**OKR** .......... Royal Military College of Canada, Kingston, Ontario [*Library symbol*] [*National Library of Canada*] (NLC)
**OKRC** ........ Regiopolis - Notre Dame High School, Kingston, Ontario [*Library symbol*] [*National Library of Canada*] (NLC)
**OKRGI** ...... Rutherford and George Island Township Public Library, Killarney, Ontario [*Library symbol*] [*National Library of Canada*] (NLC)
**OKRK** ........ Okuruk [*A publication*]
**OKRS** ........ Science Engineering Library, Royal Military College of Canada, Kingston, Ontario [*Library symbol*] [*National Library of Canada*] (BIB)
**Okr Tr** ........ Okhrana Truda [*A publication*]
**OKS** .......... Ohio Kache Systems Corp.
**OKS** .......... Okanagan Skeena Group Ltd. [*Vancouver Stock Exchange symbol*] [*Toronto Stock Exchange symbol*]
**OkS** ............ Oklahoma State University, Stillwater, OK [*Library symbol*] [*Library of Congress*] (LCLS)
**OKS** .......... Oklahoma State University, Stillwater, OK [*OCLC symbol*] (OCLC)
**OKS** .......... Old King's Scholars Association [*Canterbury, England*]
**OKS** .......... Oshkosh, NE [*Location identifier*] [*FAA*] (FAAL)
**OKS** .......... Ostkirchliche Studien [*A publication*]
**OkShB** ....... Oklahoma Baptist University, Shawnee, OK [*Library symbol*] [*Library of Congress*] (LCLS)
**OKSL** ......... St. Lawrence College of Applied Arts and Technology, Kingston, Ontario [*Library symbol*] [*National Library of Canada*] (NLC)
**OKSMG** .... Gibson Medical Library, St. Mary's of the Lake Hospital, Kingston, Ontario [*Library symbol*] [*National Library of Canada*] (NLC)
**OkS-T** ........ Oklahoma State University Technical Institute Library, Oklahoma City, OK [*Library symbol*] [*Library of Congress*] (LCLS)
**OkSt** .......... Stillwater Public Library, Stillwater, OK [*Library symbol*] [*Library of Congress*] (LCLS)
**OKT** .......... Oakite Products, Inc. [*NYSE symbol*] (SPSG)
**OKT** .......... [*The*] Oakland Terminal Railway [*Later, OTR*] [*AAR code*]
**Okt** ............ Oktjabr [*A publication*]
**OkT** ........... Tulsa City-County Library System, Tulsa, OK [*Library symbol*] [*Library of Congress*] (LCLS)
**OKT** .......... University of Tulsa, Tulsa, OK [*OCLC symbol*] (OCLC)
**OKT** .......... Yoakum, TX [*Location identifier*] [*FAA*] (FAAL)
**OkTahN** .... Northeastern State College, Tahlequah, OK [*Library symbol*] [*Library of Congress*] (LCLS)
**OkTAm** ...... AMOCO Production Co., Research Center Geology Library, Tulsa, OK [*Library symbol*] [*Library of Congress*] (LCLS)
**OkTC** ......... Ceja Corp., Tulsa, OK [*Library symbol*] [*Library of Congress*] (LCLS)
**OkTCS** ...... Cities Service Co., Energy Resources Group, E & P Library, Tulsa, OK [*Library symbol*] [*Library of Congress*] (LCLS)
**OkTG** ......... Thomas Gilcrease Institute of American History and Art, Tulsa, OK [*Library symbol*] [*Library of Congress*] (LCLS)
**OkTGS** ...... Church of Jesus Christ of Latter-Day Saints, Genealogical Society Library, Tulsa Branch, Tulsa, OK [*Library symbol*] [*Library of Congress*] (LCLS)
**OkTo** .......... Tonkawa Public Library, Tonkawa, OK [*Library symbol*] [*Library of Congress*] (LCLS)
**OkTOR** ...... Oral Roberts University, Learning Resources Center, Tulsa, OK [*Library symbol*] [*Library of Congress*] (LCLS)
**OkTPA** ...... Pan American Oil Corp., Research Library, Tulsa, OK [*Library symbol*] [*Library of Congress*] (LCLS)
**OkTU** ........ University of Tulsa, Tulsa, OK [*Library symbol*] [*Library of Congress*] (LCLS)
**OkTU-L** ..... University of Tulsa, College of Law, Tulsa, OK [*Library symbol*] [*Library of Congress*] (LCLS)
**oku** ............ Oklahoma [*MARC country of publication code*] [*Library of Congress*] (LCCP)
**OKU** .......... Omicron Kappa Upsilon [*Fraternity*]
**OkU** ........... University of Oklahoma, Norman, OK [*Library symbol*] [*Library of Congress*] (LCLS)
**OKU** .......... University of Oklahoma, Norman, OK [*OCLC symbol*] (OCLC)
**OkU-L** ....... University of Oklahoma, Law School, Norman, OK [*Library symbol*] [*Library of Congress*] (LCLS)
**OkU-M** ...... University of Oklahoma, Health Sciences Center, Oklahoma City, OK [*Library symbol*] [*Library of Congress*] (LCLS)
**OkU-P** ....... University of Oklahoma, College of Pharmacy, Norman, OK [*Library symbol*] [*Library of Congress*] (LCLS)
**OKUTD** ..... Urban Transportation Development Corp., Kingston, Ontario [*Library symbol*] [*National Library of Canada*] (NLC)
**OkU-TM** ... University of Oklahoma, Tulsa Medical College, Tulsa, OK [*Library symbol*] [*Library of Congress*] (LCLS)
**OKV** .......... University of Oklahoma, Library School, Norman, OK [*OCLC symbol*] (OCLC)
**OKW** ......... Brookwood, AL [*Location identifier*] [*FAA*] (FAAL)
**OKW** ......... Oberkommando der Wehrmacht [*Armed Forces High Command*] [*German military - World War II*]
**OKW** ......... University of Tulsa, College of Law, Tulsa, OK [*OCLC symbol*] (OCLC)
**OkWeaT** .... Southwestern State College, Weatherford, OK [*Library symbol*] [*Library of Congress*] (LCLS)
**OkWo** ........ Woodward Carnegie Library, Woodward, OK [*Library symbol*] [*Library of Congress*] (LCLS)
**OKX** .......... Central State University, Edmond, OK [*OCLC symbol*] (OCLC)
**OKXS** ........ Xenotech Systems, Inc., Kitchener, Ontario [*Library symbol*] [*National Library of Canada*] (NLC)
**OKY** .......... Oklahoma City University, Law Library, Oklahoma City, OK [*OCLC symbol*] (OCLC)

**OKZ**.......... Phillips University, Zollars Memorial Library, Enid, OK [*OCLC symbol*] (OCLC)
**OKZ**.......... Sandersville, GA [*Location identifier*] [*FAA*] (FAAL)
**OL**............. London Public Library, Ontario [*Library symbol*] [*National Library of Canada*] (NLC)
**OL**............. Occupational Level
**OL**............. Ocean Letter
**OL**............. Oceanic Linguistics [*A publication*]
**OL**............. Oculus Laevus [*Left Eye*] [*Ophthalmology*]
**OL**............. Odd Lot [*Stock exchange term*]
**OL**............. Officer of the Order of Leopold
**OL**............. Official Liquidator [*British*] (ROG)
**OL**............. Ohio Laws [*A publication*] (DLA)
**OL**............. Oil Level (AAG)
**OL**............. Oil Lighter [*Shipping*] [*British*]
**OL**............. Oiseau-Lyre [*Record label*] [*France*]
**OL**............. Old Latin [*Language, etc.*]
**Ol**.............. Oldradus da Ponte de Laude [*Deceased, 1335*] [*Authority cited in pre-1607 legal work*] (DSA)
**OL**............. Oleum [*Oil*] [*Pharmacy*]
**OL**............. Oligoblastic Leukemia [*Oncology*]
**OL**............. Olivary [*Neurology*]
**ol**.............. Olive [*Philately*]
**ol**.............. Olivine [*CIPW classification*] [*Geology*]
**Ol**.............. Olympian [*of Pindar*] [*Classical studies*] (OCD)
**OL**............. Olympic
**OL**............. Olympic Lift [*Sports*]
**OL**............. Online
**OL**............. Open Loop
**OL**............. Operating Level (IEEE)
**OL**............. Operating License
**OL**............. Operating Location [*Army*]
**OL**............. Operating Log
**OL**............. Operating Loss
**OL**............. Operation Liftoff (EA)
**O/L**............ Operations/Logistics
**OL**............. Or Less
**OL**............. Orbis Litterarum [*A publication*]
**OL**............. Orbital Launch
**OL**............. Order of Lafayette (EA)
**OL**............. Ordinary Leave [*Military*] (AFM)
**OL**............. Ordnance Lieutenant [*Navy*] [*British*]
**OL**............. Organization List (MCD)
**OL**............. Original Learning [*Psychometrics*]
**OL**............. Ostfriesische Lufttransport GmbH [*Federal Republic of Germany*] [*ICAO designator*] (ICDA)
**OL**............. Other Line [*Telecommunications*] (TEL)
**OL**............. Outgoing Letter
**OL**............. Output Latch
**OL**............. Outside Left [*Soccer position*]
**OL**............. Overflow Level
**OL**............. Overhead Line
**OL**............. Overlap
**OL**............. Overlay (NASA)
**OL**............. Overload
**OLA**.......... Lakefield Public Library, Ontario [*Library symbol*] [*National Library of Canada*] (NLC)
**OLA**.......... National Oceanic and Atmospheric Administration, Rockville, MD [*OCLC symbol*] (OCLC)
**OLA**.......... Occupiers' Liability Act [*1957*] [*British*] (DCTA)
**OLA**.......... Office of Legislative Affairs
**OLA**.......... Ohio Law Abstract [*A publication*] (DLA)
**OLA**.......... Oligonucleotide Ligation Assay [*Analytical biochemistry*]
**OLA**.......... Optical Laboratories Association (EA)
**OLA**.......... Orbital Lock Assembly
**OLA**.......... Orland [*Norway*] [*Airport symbol*] (OAG)
**OLA**.......... Osteopathic Libraries Association [*Defunct*] (EA)
**OLA**.......... Overview Latin America (EA)
**OL Abs**...... Ohio Law Abstract [*A publication*] (DLA)
**OLAC**........ Offline Adaptive Computer [*Data processing*]
**OLAC**........ Online Audiovisual Catalogers [*An association*] (EA)
**OLADE**..... Organizacion Latinoamericana de Energia [*Latin American Energy Organization*] (EAIO)
**OLAFL**...... Front of Leeds and Lansdowne Public Library, Lansdowne, Ontario [*Library symbol*] [*National Library of Canada*] (NLC)
**OLAFS**...... Orbiting and Launch Approach Flight Simulator
**OLAG**........ London Research Center, Agriculture Canada [*Centre de Recherches de London, Agriculture Canada*] London, Ontario [*Library symbol*] [*National Library of Canada*] (NLC)
**OLAG**........ Oesterreichische Luftverkehrs Aktiengesellschaft [*Austrian Airlines*]
**Olaj Szappan Kozmet**... Olaj, Szappan, Kozmetika [*A publication*]
**OLak**.......... Lakewood Public Library, Lakewood, OH [*Library symbol*] [*Library of Congress*] (LCLS)
**OLakB**....... Lakewood Board of Education, Lakewood, OH [*Library symbol*] [*Library of Congress*] (LCLS)
**OLAL**........ Bibliotheque Publique du Canton d'Alfred [*Alfred Township Public Library*], Lefaivre, Ontario [*Library symbol*] [*National Library of Canada*] (BIB)
**OLAMINE**... Ethanolamine [*Also, EA, Etn*] [*Organic chemistry*] [*USAN*]
**OLAN**........ Landsdowne Public Library, Ontario [*Library symbol*] [*National Library of Canada*] (BIB)
**OLA-N**....... Office of Legislative Affairs, Navy (MUGU)
**O/LAND**... Overland
**O/LANDED**... Overlanded
**OLanF**....... Fairfield County District Library, Lancaster, OH [*Library symbol*] [*Library of Congress*] (LCLS)
**OLanU**....... Ohio University, Lancaster Branch Campus, Lancaster, OH [*Library symbol*] [*Library of Congress*] (LCLS)
**OLAS**......... On-Line Acquisitions Systems [*Brodart, Inc.*] [*Book acquisition system*] [*Information service or system*] (IID)
**OLATN**..... Township of Norfolk Public Library, Langton, Ontario [*Library symbol*] [*National Library of Canada*] (NLC)
**OLAU**........ Lanark Union Public Library, Lanark, Ontario [*Library symbol*] [*National Library of Canada*] (BIB)
**OLB**........... London Board of Education, Ontario [*Library symbol*] [*National Library of Canada*] (NLC)
**OLB**........... Oertlicher Landwirtschaftsbetrieb [*Local Agricultural Enterprise*] [*German*]
**OLB**........... Official Log Book [*Ship's diary*] (DS)
**OLB**........... Ohio Law Bulletin [*A publication*] (DLA)
**OLB**........... Olbia [*Italy*] [*Airport symbol*] (OAG)
**OLB**........... Omaha, Lincoln & Beatrice Railway Co. [*AAR code*]
**OLB**........... Open-Loop Bandwidth [*Also, OLBW*]
**OLB**........... Open Lung Biopsy
**OLB**........... Outer Lead Bond [*Integrated circuit technology*]
**OLB**........... Outside Linebacker [*Football*]
**OLBA**........ Beirut/International [*Lebanon*] [*ICAO location identifier*] (ICLI)
**Ol Ber**........ Bericht ueber die Ausgrabungen in Olympia [*1936-*] [*A publication*]
**OLBGFC**... Official Lane Brody Global Fan Club (EA)
**OLBIEN**.... Olsen's Biomass Energy [*G. V. Olsen Associates*] [*Information service or system*] (CRD)
**OLBR**........ Brescia College, London, Ontario [*Library symbol*] [*National Library of Canada*] (NLC)
**OLBV**........ Beirut [*Lebanon*] [*ICAO location identifier*] (ICLI)
**OLBW**....... Open-Loop Bandwidth [*Also, OLB*]
**OLC**........... Catholic Central High School, London, Ontario [*Library symbol*] [*National Library of Canada*] (NLC)
**OLC**........... Linfield College, McMinnville, OR [*OCLC symbol*] (OCLC)
**OLC**........... Oak Leaf Cluster [*Military decoration*]
**OLC**........... Office of Legal Counsel [*Department of Justice*]
**Olc**............. Olcott's United States District Court Reports, Admiralty [*A publication*] (DLA)
**OLC**........... Olema [*California*] [*Seismograph station code, US Geological Survey*] (SEIS)
**OLC**........... Oneida, TN [*Location identifier*] [*FAA*] (FAAL)
**OLC**........... Online Computer [*System*] [*Data processing*]
**OLC**........... Ontario Ladies College
**OLC**........... Ontario Library Co-Operative [*UTLAS symbol*]
**OLC**........... Operation Load Code (MCD)
**OLC**........... Operator-Level Chart (AFIT)
**OLC**........... Order Location and Control (MCD)
**OLC**........... Oubain-Like Compound [*Biochemistry*]
**OLC**........... Outgoing Line Circuit
**OLC**........... Overseas Liaison Committee [*of the American Council on Education*] [*Later, Division of International Educational Relations of the American Council on Education*] (EA)
**OLCA**........ Online Circuit Analysis [*System*] [*Data processing*]
**Olc Adm**..... Olcott's United States District Court Reports, Admiralty [*A publication*] (DLA)
**OLCC**........ Olympus Capital Corp. [*NASDAQ symbol*] (NQ)
**OLCC**........ Ontario Cancer Clinic, London, Ontario [*Library symbol*] [*National Library of Canada*] (NLC)
**OLCC**........ Our Lady of Cincinnati College [*Ohio*]
**OLCC**........ Overseas Labour Consultative Committee [*British*] (DCTA)
**OLCG**........ Clarkson Gordon, London, Ontario [*Library symbol*] [*National Library of Canada*] (BIB)
**Ol Conv**...... Oliver's Conveyancing [*A publication*] (DLA)
**Olcott**......... Olcott's United States District Court Reports, Admiralty [*A publication*] (DLA)
**Olcott Adm (F)**... Olcott's United States District Court Reports, Admiralty [*A publication*] (DLA)
**Olcott's Adm**... Olcott's United States District Court Reports, Admiralty [*A publication*] (DLA)
**OLCP**......... Oil City Petroleum, Inc. [*NASDAQ symbol*] (NQ)
**OLCPR**...... Canadian Peace Research Institute, London, Ontario [*Library symbol*] [*National Library of Canada*] (NLC)
**OLCR**........ Clark Road Secondary School, London, Ontario [*Library symbol*] [*National Library of Canada*] (NLC)
**OLCR**........ Ordnance Lieutenant-Commander [*Navy*] [*British*]
**OLCR**........ Sisters of Our Lady of Charity of Refuge [*Roman Catholic religious order*]
**OLCSSCP**... Children's Psychiatric Research Institute, Ontario Ministry of Community and Social Services, London, Ontario [*Library symbol*] [*National Library of Canada*] (NLC)
**OLCT**........ Tax Services, Canada Trust Co., London, Ontario [*Library symbol*] [*National Library of Canada*] (BIB)

**OLCV**........ Century Village, Lang, Ontario [*Library symbol*] [*National Library of Canada*] (BIB)
**OLD**........... Odd Lot Dealer
**OLD**........... Office of Legislative Development [*Bureau of Indian Affairs*]
**OLD**........... Ohio Lower Court Decisions [*A publication*] (DLA)
**OLD**........... Old Town, ME [*Location identifier*] [*FAA*] (FAAL)
**Old**............. [*Johannes*] Oldendorpius [*Deceased, 1567*] [*Authority cited in pre-1607 legal work*] (DSA)
**Old**............. Oldradus da Ponte de Laude [*Deceased, 1335*] [*Authority cited in pre-1607 legal work*] (DSA)
**Old**............. Oldright's Nova Scotia Reports [*A publication*] (DLA)
**OLD**........... Open-Loop Damping
**OLD**........... Operations and Liquidations Division [*Federal Savings and Loans Insurance Corporation*]
**OLD**........... Oxford Latin Dictionary [*A publication*]
**OLDB**........ Old National Bancorp [*Evansville, IN*] [*NASDAQ symbol*] (NQ)
**OLDB**........ Online Database [*or Data Bank*]
**Old Bailey Chr** ... Old Bailey Chronicle [*A publication*] (DLA)
**Old Ben**...... Benloe in Benloe and Dalison's English Common Pleas Reports [*A publication*] (DLA)
**Old Benloe** ... Benloe in Benloe and Dalison's English Common Pleas Reports [*A publication*] (DLA)
**OLDC**........ Online Data Collection [*Data processing*] (MCD)
**OLDD**........ Beirut [*Lebanon*] [*ICAO location identifier*] (ICLI)
**Old Dominion J Med and S** ... Old Dominion Journal of Medicine and Surgery [*A publication*]
**OLD ECC** ... Ordinary Linear Differential Equations with Constant Coefficients [*Mathematics*]
**Oldelft Sci Eng Q** ... Oldelft Scientific Engineering Quarterly [*A publication*]
**Olden**......... [*Johannes*] Oldendorpius [*Deceased, 1567*] [*Authority cited in pre-1607 legal work*] (DSA)
**Oldenburg Landwirtschaftsbl** ... Oldenburgisches Landwirtschaftsblatt [*A publication*]
**Old Ent**...... Rastell's Old Entries [*A publication*] (DLA)
**OLDFOS**... Old Established Forces [*Military*] (CINC)
**OLDHM**.... Oldham [*City in England*]
**Old House Jnl** ... Old-House Journal [*A publication*]
**Old Kilkenny Rev** ... Old Kilkenny Review [*A publication*]
**Old Nat Brev** ... Old Natura Brevium [*A publication*] (DLA)
**Oldn Pr**...... Oldnall's Sessions Practice [*A publication*] (DLA)
**Old NW**...... Old Northwest Genealogical Quarterly [*A publication*]
**Oldr**........... Oldradus da Ponte de Laude [*Deceased, 1335*] [*Authority cited in pre-1607 legal work*] (DSA)
**Oldr**........... Oldright's Nova Scotia Reports [*A publication*] (DLA)
**Oldra**......... Oldradus da Ponte de Laude [*Deceased, 1335*] [*Authority cited in pre-1607 legal work*] (DSA)
**Oldra de Lau** ... Oldradus da Ponte de Laude [*Deceased, 1335*] [*Authority cited in pre-1607 legal work*] (DSA)
**Oldr NS**..... Oldright's Nova Scotia Reports [*A publication*] (DLA)
**OLDS**........ Off-Axis LASER Detection System (MCD)
**OLDS**........ Offshore Lease Data System [*Department of the Interior*] [*Information service or system*] (IID)
**OLDS**........ Oldsmobile [*Automotive engineering*]
**OLDS**........ On-Line Detection System [*Nuclear energy*]
**OLDS**........ Online Display System [*Data processing*]
**Old SC**....... Old Select Cases [*Oudh, India*] [*A publication*] (DLA)
**OLDSS**...... Online Database Search Services Directory [*A publication*]
**Old Test Abstr** ... Old Testament Abstracts [*A publication*]
**Old-Time N** ... Old-Time New England [*A publication*]
**Old-Time N E** ... Old-Time New England [*A publication*]
**Old-Time N Eng** ... Old-Time New England [*A publication*]
**Old Vetern** ... Caring for the Older Veteran [*A publication*]
**OLE**........... Lane Community College, Eugene, OR [*OCLC symbol*] (OCLC)
**OLE**........... Leamington Public Library, Ontario [*Library symbol*] [*National Library of Canada*] (NLC)
**OLe**........... Lebanon Public Library, Lebanon, OH [*Library symbol*] [*Library of Congress*] (LCLS)
**OLE**........... Object Linking and Embedding [*Windows*] [*Data processing*]
**OLE**........... Office for Library Education [*American Library Association*]
**OLE**........... Olean, NY [*Location identifier*] [*FAA*] (FAAL)
**OLE**........... On-Line Encyclopedia [*Hypergraphics Corp.*]
**OLE**........... Oral Language Evaluation [*English and Spanish test*]
**OLE**........... Oriole Communication [*Vancouver Stock Exchange symbol*]
**OLE**........... Outside Location Engineer (MCD)
**Oleagineux Rev Int Corps Gras** ... Oleagineux. Revue Internationale des Corps Gras [*A publication*]
**OLeC**......... Lebanon Correctional Institution Library, Lebanon, OH [*Library symbol*] [*Library of Congress*] (LCLS)
**Oleck Corporations** ... Oleck's Modern Corporation Law [*A publication*] (DLA)
**O Legal News** ... Ohio Legal News [*A publication*] (DLA)
**OLEI**......... Point Pelee National Park, Parks Canada [*Parc National de la Pointe-Pelee, Parcs Canada*] Leamington, Ontario [*Library symbol*] [*National Library of Canada*] (NLC)
**OLELB**...... Lyn Branch, Elizabethtown Township Public Library, Ontario [*Library symbol*] [*National Library of Canada*] (BIB)
**Oleodin Pneum** ... Oleodinamica Pneumatica [*A publication*]
**OLEP**........ Office of Law Enforcement Programs [*Federal government*]
**OLEP**........ Organization for the Lifelong Establishment of Paternity (EA)
**OLER**........ Olericulture
**OLERT**...... Online Executive for Real Time [*Data processing*] (IEEE)
**OLeWHi**.... Warren County Historical Society, Lebanon, OH [*Library symbol*] [*Library of Congress*] (LCLS)
**OLF**........... Old Low Franconian [*Language, etc.*]
**OLF**........... Only Living Father [*of Newfoundland's confederation with Canada in 1949*] [*Epithet for Joseph R. Smallwood*]
**OLF**........... Orbital Launch Facility
**OLF**........... Orbiter Landing Facility [*NASA*] (NASA)
**OLF**........... Organ Literature Foundation (EA)
**OLF**........... Oromo Liberation Front [*Ethiopia*] [*Political party*] (PD)
**OLF**........... Outlying Field [*Army*]
**OLF**........... Wolf Point [*Montana*] [*Airport symbol*] (OAG)
**OLF**........... Wolf Point, MT [*Location identifier*] [*FAA*] (FAAL)
**Olfaction Taste Proc Int Symp** ... Olfaction and Taste. Proceedings of the International Symposium [*A publication*]
**OLFC**......... Fanshawe College of Applied Arts and Technology, London, Ontario [*Library symbol*] [*National Library of Canada*] (NLC)
**Ol Forsch**... Olympische Forschungen [*A publication*]
**OLG**........... Oberlandesgericht [*District Court of Appeal*] [*German*] (DLA)
**OLG**........... Ohio Legislative Service Commission, Columbus, OH [*OCLC symbol*] (OCLC)
**OLG**........... Old Low German [*Language, etc.*]
**OLG**........... Oligodendrocyte [*Also, ODC*] [*Cytology*]
**OLG**........... Open-Loop Gain
**OLG**........... Sisters of Guadalupe [*Roman Catholic religious order*]
**OLG**........... Sisters of Our Lady of the Garden [*Roman Catholic religious order*]
**OLGA**........ Olga Co. [*NASDAQ symbol*] (NQ)
**OLGR**........ [*The*] Oilgear Co. [*NASDAQ symbol*] (NQ)
**OLH**........... Huron College, London, Ontario [*Library symbol*] [*National Library of Canada*] (NLC)
**OLH**........... Old Harbor [*Alaska*] [*Airport symbol*] (OAG)
**OLH**........... Old Harbor, AK [*Location identifier*] [*FAA*] (FAAL)
**OLH**........... Orpen's Light Horse [*British military*] (DMA)
**OLH**........... Ovine Luteinizing Hormone [*Endocrinology*]
**OLH**........... Oxfordshire Light Horse [*British military*] (DMA)
**OLHM**....... London Historical Museums, Ontario [*Library symbol*] [*National Library of Canada*] (BIB)
**OLHMIS**... On-Line Hospital Management Information System [*Data processing*]
**Ol Horse**.... Oliphant's Law of Horses [*6th ed.*] [*1908*] [*A publication*] (DLA)
**OLI**........... Lindsay Public Library, Ontario [*Library symbol*] [*National Library of Canada*] (NLC)
**OLI**........... Ocean Living Institute [*Defunct*] (EA)
**OLI**........... Olafsvik [*Iceland*] [*Airport symbol*] (OAG)
**OLI**........... Oliktok, AK [*Location identifier*] [*FAA*] (FAAL)
**OLI**........... Open Learning Institute [*UTLAS symbol*]
**OLI**........... Out-of-Line Igniter [*Military*] (CAAL)
**OLI**........... Out-of-Line Interrupter (MCD)
**OLI**........... Oxfordshire Light Infantry [*Military unit*] [*British*]
**OLiC**......... Columbiana County Court House, Lisbon, OH [*Library symbol*] [*Library of Congress*] (LCLS)
**OLICU**...... Little Current Public Library, Ontario [*Library symbol*] [*National Library of Canada*] (NLC)
**OLICUS**.... Sucker Creek Indian Band Public Library, Little Current, Ontario [*Library symbol*] [*National Library of Canada*] (NLC)
**OLIF**......... Orbiter Landing Instrumentation Facilities [*NASA*] (NASA)
**OLIFLM**... Online Image Forming Light Modulator
**Oli Grassi Deriv** ... Olii, Grassi, Derivati [*A publication*]
**OLIH**......... Lion's Head Branch, Bruce County Public Library, Ontario [*Library symbol*] [*National Library of Canada*] (NLC)
**Olii Miner Grassi Saponi Colori Vernici** ... Olii Minerali. Grassi e Saponi. Colori e Vernici [*A publication*]
**Olii Miner Olii Grassi Colori Vernici** ... Olii Minerali. Olii e Grassi. Colori e Vernici [*A publication*]
**OLIM**........ Olimpiadas [*Ministerio de Cultura*] [*Spain*] [*Information service or system*] (CRD)
**OLima**........ Lima Public Library, Lima, OH [*Library symbol*] [*Library of Congress*] (LCLS)
**OLimaAL**.. Allen County Law Library, Lima, OH [*Library symbol*] [*Library of Congress*] (LCLS)
**OLIP**......... Online Instrument Package [*Data processing*] (NRCH)
**Oliph Hor**.. Oliphant's Law of Horses [*6th ed.*] [*1908*] [*A publication*] (DLA)
**OLIS**......... Listowel Public Library, Ontario [*Library symbol*] [*National Library of Canada*] (NLC)
**OLIS**......... Online Information Services [*Mercer County Community College Library*] (OLDSS)
**OLIS**......... Oregon Legislative Information System [*Information service or system*]
**OLIS**......... Oxide Layer Isolation Structure
**OLISF**....... Frost Campus Library, Sir Sandford Fleming College, Lindsay, Ontario [*Library symbol*] [*National Library of Canada*] (NLC)
**OLISS**....... Online Information Services for Schools [*Australia*]
**OLitW**....... Wagnalls Memorial Library, Lithopolis, OH [*Library symbol*] [*Library of Congress*] (LCLS)

**OLIV** ......... Oleum Olivae [*Olive Oil*] [*Pharmacy*] (ROG)
**OLIV** ......... Victoria County Public Library, Lindsay, Ontario [*Library symbol*] [*National Library of Canada*] (NLC)
**Oliv B & L** ... Oliver, Beavan, and Lefroy's English Railway and Canal Cases [*A publication*] (DLA)
**Oliv Conv** ... Oliver's Conveyancing [*A publication*] (DLA)
**Oliv Prec** .... Oliver's Precedents [*A publication*] (DLA)
**OLIVW** ...... Walden Public Library, Lively, Ontario [*Library symbol*] [*National Library of Canada*] (BIB)
**OLI/ZLW** ... Zeitschrift fuer Lateinamerika (Wien). Oesterreichisches Lateinamerika Institut (Wien) [*A publication*]
**OLJ** ........... Ohio Law Journal [*A publication*] (DLA)
**OLJ** ........... Order of St. Lazarus of Jerusalem [*British*]
**OLJ** ........... Oudh Law Journal [*India*] [*A publication*] (DLA)
**OLJ** ........... Spokane, WA [*Location identifier*] [*FAA*] (FAAL)
**OL Jour** ..... Ohio Law Journal [*A publication*] (DLA)
**OL Jour** ..... Oudh Law Journal [*India*] [*A publication*] (DLA)
**OLK** ........... King's College, London, Ontario [*Library symbol*] [*National Library of Canada*] (NLC)
**OLK** ........... Wolf Lake, IN [*Location identifier*] [*FAA*] (FAAL)
**OLKK** ........ Tripoli [*Lebanon*] [*ICAO location identifier*] (ICLI)
**OLKV** ........ Tripoli [*Lebanon*] [*ICAO location identifier*] (ICLI)
**OLL** ........... Larder Lake Public Library, Ontario [*Library symbol*] [*National Library of Canada*] (BIB)
**OLL** ........... Ollague [*Chile*] [*Seismograph station code, US Geological Survey*] [*Closed*] (SEIS)
**OLL** ........... Organic Liquid LASER
**OLL** ........... Output Logic Level
**OLLA** ........ Office of Lend-Lease Administration [*World War II*]
**OLLA** ........ Oil Lands Leasing Act
**Oll B & F**.... Ollivier, Bell, and Fitzgerald's New Zealand Reports [*A publication*] (DLA)
**OLLC** ......... Our Lady of the Lake College [*Texas*]
**OLLCR** ...... Labatt's Central Research Library, London, Ontario [*Library symbol*] [*National Library of Canada*] (NLC)
**OLLE** ......... Lake Erie Regional Library System, London, Ontario [*Library symbol*] [*National Library of Canada*] (NLC)
**OLLE** ......... Ontario Library Service - Thames, London, Ontario [*Library symbol*] [*National Library of Canada*] (NLC)
**OLLI** ......... Online Library Index [*Western Michigan University*]
**OL LINI SI** ... Oleum Lini sine Igne [*Cold-Drawn Linseed Oil*] [*Pharmacy*] (ROG)
**Olliv B & F** ... Ollivier, Bell, and Fitzgerald's New Zealand Reports [*A publication*] (DLA)
**OLLL** ......... Beirut [*Lebanon*] [*ICAO location identifier*] (ICLI)
**OLLS** ......... Online Logical Simulation System [*Data processing*] (KSC)
**OLM** .......... Lloyd Library and Museum, Cincinnati, OH [*OCLC symbol*] (OCLC)
**OLM** .......... Office for Laboratory Management [*DoD*] (MCD)
**OLM** .......... Olympia, WA [*Location identifier*] [*FAA*] (FAAL)
**OLM** .......... Online Monitor [*Data processing*]
**OLM** .......... Sisters of Charity of Our Lady of Mercy [*Roman Catholic religious order*]
**OLMC** ....... Olivier Management Corporation [*Miami, FL*] [*NASDAQ symbol*] (NQ)
**OLMC** ....... Output Logic Macrocell [*Data processing*]
**OLMR** ....... Organic Liquid Moderated Reactor
**Olms** .......... Decisions of the Judicial Committee of the Privy Council re the British North American Act, 1867, and the Canadian Constitution [*A publication*] (DLA)
**OLMS** ....... Office of Labor-Management Standards [*Department of Labor*]
**OLMS** ....... Osborn Laboratories of Marine Sciences [*New York Zoological Society*] [*Research center*] (RCD)
**Olmsted** ..... Olmsted's Privy Council Decisions [*1867-1954*] [*A publication*] (DLA)
**OLMT** ....... Organizational Level Maintenance Timer
**OLMUG**.... Online Librarian's Microcomputer User Group [*Teleconferencing system*]
**OLMWPR** ... Office of Labor-Management and Welfare-Pension Reports [*Department of Labor*]
**OLN** ........... Lane Public Library, Hamilton, OH [*OCLC symbol*] (OCLC)
**OLN** ........... Ohio Legal News [*A publication*] (DLA)
**OLN** ........... Old Man, AK [*Location identifier*] [*FAA*] (FAAL)
**OLN** ........... Olin Corp. [*NYSE symbol*] (SPSG)
**OLO** ........... Longlac Public Library, Ontario [*Library symbol*] [*National Library of Canada*] (NLC)
**OLO** ........... Olotillo [*Race of maize*]
**OLO** ........... Online Operation [*Data processing*]
**OLO** ........... Oologah [*Oklahoma*] [*Seismograph station code, US Geological Survey*] [*Closed*] (SEIS)
**OLO** ........... Operations Launch Order (MUGU)
**OLO** ........... Orbital Launch Operation
**OLOE** ........ Online Order Entry
**OLOF** ........ Levack Branch, Onaping Falls Public Library, Ontario [*Library symbol*] [*National Library of Canada*] (NLC)
**OLOG**........ Offshore Logistics, Inc. [*NASDAQ symbol*] (NQ)
**OLogC** ....... Logan-Hocking County District Library, Logan, OH [*Library symbol*] [*Library of Congress*] (LCLS)
**OLOGS** ..... Open-Loop Oxygen-Generating System [*Air Force*]
**ol oliv**.......... Oleum Olivae [*Olive Oil*] [*Pharmacy*]
**OLOM**....... Orbiter Lift-Off Mass [*NASA*] (KSC)
**OLor** .......... Lorain Public Library, Lorain, OH [*Library symbol*] [*Library of Congress*] (LCLS)
**OLOS** ........ Oakridge Secondary School, London, Ontario [*Library symbol*] [*National Library of Canada*] (NLC)
**OLOS** ........ Office for Library Outreach Service [*American Library Association*]
**OLOS** ........ Out of Line of Sight (NATG)
**OLou**.......... Loudonville Public Library, Loudonville, OH [*Library symbol*] [*Library of Congress*] (LCLS)
**OLOW**....... Orbiter Lift-Off Weight [*NASA*]
**O Lower D** ... Ohio Lower Court Decisions [*A publication*] (DLA)
**OLP** ........... Lewis and Clark College, Portland, OR [*OCLC symbol*] (OCLC)
**OLP** ........... Missionaries of the Third Order of St. Francis of Our Lady of the Prairies [*Roman Catholic women's religious order*]
**OLP** ........... Observation Landplane [*Coast Guard*]
**OLP** ........... Off-Line Program [*Data processing*]
**OLP** ........... Office of Labor Production [*WPB*] [*World War II*]
**OLP** ........... Olympic Dam [*Australia*] [*Airport symbol*] (OAG)
**OLP** ........... One Liberty Properties, Inc. [*AMEX symbol*] (SPSG)
**OLP** ........... Online Processor (TEL)
**OLP** ........... Online Programming
**OLP** ........... Optical Line Pair
**OLP** ........... Orientalia Lovaniensia Periodica [*A publication*]
**OLP** ........... Outside Left Position [*Dancing*]
**OLP** ........... Oxygen Lime Powder [*Steelmaking process*]
**OLP** ........... Oxygen at Low Pressure (KSC)
**OLP** ........... Sisters of Our Lady of Providence [*Roman Catholic religious order*]
**OLPARS** ... Online Pattern Analysis and Recognition System [*Data processing*] (MCD)
**OLPH** ........ London Psychiatric Hospital, Ontario [*Library symbol*] [*National Library of Canada*] (NLC)
**OLPHS**...... Parkwood Hospital Services, London, Ontario [*Library symbol*] [*National Library of Canada*] (BIB)
**OLPR**......... Office of Library Personnel Resources [*American Library Association*]
**Ol Prec**....... Oliver's Precedents [*A publication*] (DLA)
**OLPS**......... Online Programming System [*Data processing*]
**OLPT**......... Oxford Library of Practical Theology [*A publication*]
**OLPT**......... Pinchas Troester Library, Congregation B'Nai Israel, London, Ontario [*Library symbol*] [*National Library of Canada*] (NLC)
**OLQ**........... Biloxi, MS [*Location identifier*] [*FAA*] (FAAL)
**OLQ**........... Officer-Like Qualities [*British military*] (DMA)
**OLQ**........... Olsobip [*Papua New Guinea*] [*Airport symbol*] (OAG)
**OLR** ........... Oak-Leaf Roller [*Moth*] [*Entomology*]
**OLR** ........... Objective Loudness Rating [*of telephone connections*] (IEEE)
**OLR** ........... Office of Labor Racketeering [*Department of Labor*]
**OLR** ........... Office of Legislative Reference [*Bureau of the Budget; later, OMB*]
**OLR** ........... Offline Recovery [*Telecommunications*] (TEL)
**OLR** ........... Ohio Law Reporter [*A publication*] (DLA)
**O-LR**.......... Ohio Legislative Reference Bureau, Columbus, OH [*Library symbol*] [*Library of Congress*] (LCLS)
**OLR** ........... On-Line Research, Inc. [*Information service or system*] (IID)
**OLR** ........... On Location Repair (MCD)
**OLR** ........... Ontario Law Reporter [*A publication*] (DLA)
**OLR** ........... Ontario Law Reports [*A publication*] (DLA)
**OLR** ........... Ontario Library Review [*A publication*]
**OLR** ........... Open-Loop Receiver [*or Response*]
**OLR** ........... Operator's Local Representative (AIA)
**OLR** ........... Oregon Law Review [*A publication*]
**OLR** ........... Organisation pour la Liberation du Rwanda [*Organization for the Liberation of Rwanda*]
**OLR** ........... Oudh Law Reports [*India*] [*A publication*] (DLA)
**OLR** ........... Outgoing Long-Wave Radiation [*Satellite sensed*]
**OLR** ........... Overload Relay
**OLR** ........... Oxford Literary Review [*A publication*]
**OLR** ........... Robarts School Library, London, Ontario [*Library symbol*] [*National Library of Canada*] (BIB)
**OLRAG** ..... London Regional Art Gallery, Ontario [*Library symbol*] [*National Library of Canada*] (NLC)
**OLRB** ........ Ontario Labour Relations Board Monthly Report [*A publication*] (DLA)
**O/L-RC** ..... Overload-Reverse Current (NASA)
**OL Rep** ...... Ohio Law Reporter [*A publication*] (DLA)
**Ol Res** ....... Oleoresin [*Also, OR*] [*Pharmacy*]
**OLRI**......... Office & Factory, Rochevert Industrie, Inc., Lindsay, Ontario [*Library symbol*] [*National Library of Canada*] (NLC)
**OL RIC**...... Oleum Ricini [*Castor Oil*] [*Pharmacy*] (ROG)
**OLRL**......... Lyndhurst Branch, Rideau Lakes Union Library, Ontario [*Library symbol*] [*National Library of Canada*] (BIB)
**OLRM** ....... Medical Library, Ross Memorial Hospital, Lindsay, Ontario [*Library symbol*] [*National Library of Canada*] (BIB)
**OLRS**......... Optical LASER Ranging System
**OLRT** ........ Online Real Time [*Data processing*]
**OLS** ........... Nogales, AZ [*Location identifier*] [*FAA*] (FAAL)
**O & LS**....... Ocean and Lake Surveys [*Budget appropriation title*] [*Navy*]
**OLS** ........... Office of Legal Services [*of Office of Economic Opportunity*]
**OLS** ........... Olsten Corp. [*AMEX symbol*] (SPSG)

**OLS** .......... Online Scan [*Data processing*] (CAAL)
**OLS** .......... Online System [*Data processing*]
**OLS** .......... Open-Loop System [*Chemical engineering*]
**OLS** .......... Operational Launch Station (AAG)
**OLS** .......... Operational Lines of Succession [*Defense readiness*]
**OLS** .......... Optical Landing System
**OLS** .......... Orbiting Lunar Station [*NASA*]
**OLS** .......... Ordinary Least Squares [*Statistics*]
**OLS** .......... Original Line of Sight
**OLS** .......... Sisters of Our Lady of Sorrows [*Roman Catholic religious order*]
**OLS** .......... Spartan of Canada Ltd., London, Ontario [*Library symbol*] [*National Library of Canada*] (NLC)
**OLSA** .......... Orbiter/LPS [*Launch Processing System*] Signal Adapter [*NASA*] (NASA)
**OLSA** .......... Otolaryngological Society of Australia
**OL'SAM** .......... Online Database Search Assistance Machine [*Franklin Institute*] [*Information service or system*] [*Defunct*] (IID)
**OLSAT** .......... Otis-Lennon School Ability Test [*Education*]
**OLSC** .......... Online Scientific Computer [*Data processing*]
**OLSCA** .......... Orientation Linkage for a Solar Cell Array
**OLSCG** .......... Latchford Senior Citizens Group, Ontario [*Library symbol*] [*National Library of Canada*] (BIB)
**OL Sch VO** ... Verordnung ueber Orderlagerscheine [*A publication*]
**OLSD** .......... Office for Library Service to the Disadvantaged [*American Library Association*]
**OLSDG** .......... Lancaster Branch, Stormont, Dundas, and Glengarry County Library, Ontario [*Library symbol*] [*National Library of Canada*] (BIB)
**OLSE** .......... Ordinary Least-Squares Estimators [*Statistics*]
**OLSF** .......... Olson Farms, Inc. [*NASDAQ symbol*] (NQ)
**OLSF** .......... Online Subsystem Facility [*Data processing*] (MCD)
**OLSH** .......... Our Lady of the Sacred Heart (ADA)
**OLSIDI-F** ... Oral Language Sentence Imitation Diagnostic Inventory - Format Revised [*Educational test*]
**OLSIST-F** ... Oral Language Sentence Imitation Screening Test - Format Revised [*Educational test*]
**OLSJ** .......... St. Joseph's Hospital, London, Ontario [*Library symbol*] [*National Library of Canada*] (NLC)
**OLSN** .......... Olson Industries, Inc. [*Sherman Oaks, CA*] [*NASDAQ symbol*] (NQ)
**OLSP** .......... Oceanic Linguistics. Special Publications [*A publication*]
**OLSP** .......... Office of Life Science Programs [*Obsolete*] [*NASA*]
**OLSP** .......... Operational Logistic Support Plan
**OLSP** .......... Orbiter Logistics Support Plan [*NASA*] (NASA)
**OLSP** .......... St. Peter's Seminary, London, Ontario [*Library symbol*] [*National Library of Canada*] (NLC)
**OLSS** .......... Online Software System [*Data processing*] (IEEE)
**OLSS** .......... Operational Logistic Support Summary [*Military*] (CAAL)
**OLSS** .......... Overseas Limited Storage Site [*Army*]
**OLSSDG** ... Long Sault Branch, Stormont, Dundas, and Glengarry County Public Library, Ontario [*Library symbol*] [*National Library of Canada*] (BIB)
**OLT** .......... Oddity-Learning Task [*Psychology*]
**OLT** .......... Official Latin Title
**OLT** .......... Online Test [*Data processing*]
**OLT** .......... Orange Light
**OLT** .......... Orthotopic Liver Transplantation [*Medicine*]
**OLT** .......... Ostfriesische Lufttransport GmbH [*Airline*] [*Federal Republic of Germany*]
**OL & T** .......... Owners, Landlords, and Tenants [*Liability insurance*]
**OLT** .......... Oxford Library of Translations [*A publication*]
**OLT** .......... United Lodge of Theosophists, London, Ontario [*Library symbol*] [*National Library of Canada*] (NLC)
**OLTE** .......... Organizational Level Test Equipment (MCD)
**Oltenia** .......... Oltenia Studii si Comunicari Istorie [*A publication*]
**OLTEP** .......... On-Line Test Executive Program [*IBM Corp.*] [*Data processing*]
**OLTL** .......... One Life to Live [*Television program*]
**OLTMC** .......... Technical Information Centre, 3M Canada, Inc., London, Ontario [*Library symbol*] [*National Library of Canada*] (NLC)
**OLTP** .......... On-Line Transaction Processing [*Tandem Computers*]
**OLTP** .......... Online Transaction Processing
**OLTS** .......... Online Test System [*Data processing*] (BUR)
**OLTS** .......... Online Time Share [*Data processing*]
**OLTT** .......... Online Teller Terminal
**OLTT** .......... Online Terminal Test [*Data processing*] (IBMDP)
**OLU** .......... Columbus [*Nebraska*] [*Airport symbol*] (OAG)
**OLU** .......... University of Western Ontario, London, Ontario [*Library symbol*] [*National Library of Canada*] (NLC)
**OLUC** .......... Lucknow Branch, Bruce County Public Library, Ontario [*Library symbol*] [*National Library of Canada*] (NLC)
**OLUC** .......... Office of Land Use Coordination [*Abolished, 1944*] [*Department of Agriculture*]
**OLUC** .......... Online Union Catalog [*Online Computer Library Center, Inc.*] [*Information service or system*] (CRD)
**OLuCF** .......... Southern Ohio Correctional Facility, Lucasville, OH [*Library symbol*] [*Library of Congress*] (LCLS)
**OLUD** .......... Online Update (TEL)
**OLUE** .......... Engineering Library, University of Western Ontario, London, Ontario [*Library symbol*] [*National Library of Canada*] (BIB)
**OLUG** .......... Department of Geography, University of Western Ontario, London, Ontario [*Library symbol*] [*National Library of Canada*] (NLC)
**OLUG** .......... Office Landscape Users Group [*Later, OPUG*] (EA)
**OLUH** .......... University Hospital, London, Ontario [*Library symbol*] [*National Library of Canada*] (NLC)
**OLUL** .......... Law Library, University of Western Ontario, London, Ontario [*Library symbol*] [*National Library of Canada*] (NLC)
**OLUM** .......... Online Update Control Module (TEL)
**OLUM** .......... Sciences Library, Natural Sciences Centre, University of Western Ontario, London, Ontario [*Library symbol*] [*National Library of Canada*] (NLC)
**OLUMG** .......... MacIntosh Gallery, University of Western Ontario, London, Ontario [*Library symbol*] [*National Library of Canada*] (NLC)
**OLUNO** .......... Northern Outreach Library Service, University of Western Ontario, London, Ontario [*Library symbol*] [*National Library of Canada*] (BIB)
**OLURC** .......... London Urban Resource Centre, Ontario [*Library symbol*] [*National Library of Canada*] (NLC)
**OLUS** .......... School of Library and Information Science, University of Western Ontario, London, Ontario [*Library symbol*] [*National Library of Canada*] (NLC)
**OLuS** .......... Scioto Technical College, Lucasville, OH [*Library symbol*] [*Library of Congress*] [*Obsolete*] (LCLS)
**OLUVA** .......... Visual Arts Department, University of Western Ontario, London, Ontario [*Library symbol*] [*National Library of Canada*] (NLC)
**OLUWP** .......... Office of Land Use and Water Planning [*Abolished, 1976*] [*Department of the Interior*]
**OLV** .......... Oil and Gas Journal [*A publication*]
**OLV** .......... Olive Branch, MS [*Location identifier*] [*FAA*] (FAAL)
**OLV** .......... Oliver Resources [*Vancouver Stock Exchange symbol*]
**OLV** .......... One-Lung Ventilation [*Medicine*]
**OLV** .......... Open-Frame Low Voltage (IEEE)
**OLV** .......... Orbital Launch Vehicle
**OLVG** .......... Open-Loop Voltage Gain
**OLVH** .......... Medical Library, South Street Campus, Victoria Hospital Corp., London, Ontario [*Library symbol*] [*National Library of Canada*] (NLC)
**OLVL** .......... Oil Level
**OLVM** .......... Our Lady of Victory Missionary Sisters [*Roman Catholic religious order*]
**olvn** .......... Olivine [*Philately*]
**OLVP** .......... Office of Launch Vehicle Programs [*Obsolete*] [*NASA*]
**OLVR** .......... Oliver's Stores, Inc. [*Ridgefield, NJ*] [*NASDAQ symbol*] (NQ)
**OLWE** .......... Oilweek [*A publication*]
**Olwine's LJ (PA)** ... Olwine's Law Journal [*Pennsylvania*] [*A publication*] (DLA)
**OLX** .......... Linn-Benton Community College, Albany, OR [*OCLC symbol*] (OCLC)
**OLY** .......... Olney-Noble, IL [*Location identifier*] [*FAA*] (FAAL)
**OLYM** .......... Olympiad
**OLYM** .......... Olympic National Park
**OLYM** .......... Olympic Solar [*NASDAQ symbol*] (NQ)
**Olym Rev** ... Olympic Review/Revue Olympique [*A publication*]
**Oly Rev** .......... Olympic Review [*A publication*]
**OLZ** .......... Oelwein, IA [*Location identifier*] [*FAA*] (FAAL)
**OLZ** .......... Orientalistische Literaturzeitung [*A publication*]
**OM** .......... Mississauga Public Library, Ontario [*Library symbol*] [*National Library of Canada*] (NLC)
**OM** .......... Monarch Airlines Ltd. [*Great Britain*] [*ICAO designator*] (FAAC)
**OM** .......... Obermanual [*Upper Manual*] [*Music*]
**OM** .......... Objets et Monde [*A publication*]
**OM** .......... Obrazotvorce Mistectvo [*A publication*]
**OM** .......... Observer's Mate [*British military*] (DMA)
**OM** .......... Occipitomental [*Diameter of skull*]
**OM** .......... Occupational Medal [*as used with special reference to Germany or Japan*] [*Military decoration*]
**OM** .......... Occupational Medicine
**OM** .......... Oceanography and Meteorology
**OM** .......... Oduma Magazine [*A publication*]
**OM** .......... Oesterreichische Monatsschrift fuer den Orient (BJA)
**OM** .......... Office Manager
**OM** .......... Office Messenger [*Military*]
**O & M** .......... Ogilvy & Mather [*Advertising agency*]
**OM** .......... Old Man [*Communications operators' colloquialism*]
**OM** .......... Old Measurement
**OM** .......... Olympus Mons [*A filamentary mark on Mars*]
**OM** .......... Oman [*ANSI two-letter standard code*] [*IYRU nationality code*] (CNC)
**OM** .......... Omega. The Journal of Death and Dying [*A publication*]
**om** .......... Omit
**OM** .......... Omni Mane [*Every Morning*] [*Pharmacy*]
**OM** .......... On Margin [*Investment term*]
**OM** .......... Only Music [*A publication*]
**OM** .......... Opaque Media [*X-ray microscopy*]

**OM** ........... Open Market
**OM** ........... Open Matching [*Parapsychology*]
**OM** ........... Open Mouth [*Doll collecting*]
**OM** ........... Opera di Maria [*Work of Mary*] [*An association*] (EAIO)
**OM** ........... Opera Mundi [*Book-packaging firm based in Paris*]
**OM** ........... Operating Memorandum
**OM** ........... Operating Memory (KSC)
**OM** ........... Operation Mainstream (OICC)
**O & M**........ Operation and Maintenance
**OM** ........... Operation Mobilisation [*Religious movement*] [*British*]
**OM** ........... Operation Monkees (EA)
**OM** ........... Operations Maintenance
**O & M**........ Operations and Management
**OM** ........... Operations Manager
**OM** ........... Operator's Manual
**OM** ........... Optical Master (KSC)
**OM** ........... Optical Media [*Computer graphics*]
**OM** ........... Optical Microscopy
**OM** ........... Opticalman [*Navy rating*]
**OM** ........... Optimus Maximus [*Greatest and Best*] [*Latin*]
**OM** ........... Options Market [*Finance*]
**OM** ........... Options for Men [*A publication*]
**OM** ........... Optionsmaeklarna [*Options market*] [*Sweden*]
**OM** ........... Opus Musicum [*A publication*]
**OM** ........... Order of Merit
**OM** ........... Ordnance Mission (AAG)
**OM** ........... Ordo [*Fratrum*] Minimorum [*Minims of St. Francis of Paul*] [*Roman Catholic men's religious order*]
**OM** ........... Organic Matter
**O & M**........ Organization and Management
**O & M**........ Organization and Methods (AABC)
**OM** ........... Organizational Maintenance (MCD)
**OM** ........... Orientalische Miszellen [*A publication*]
**O & M**........ Orientation and Mobility [*for the blind*]
**OM** ........... Oriente Moderno [*A publication*]
**OM** ........... Ostdeutsche Monatshefte [*A publication*]
**OM** ........... Osteomyelitis [*Medicine*]
**OM** ........... Ostmark [*Monetary unit*] [*German Democratic Republic*]
**OM** ........... Otitis Media [*Medicine*]
**OM** ........... Otolitic Membrane [*Otology*]
**OM** ........... Oudheidkundige Mededeelingen uit s'Rijksmuseum van Oudheden te Leiden [*A publication*]
**OM** ........... Our Message
**OM** ........... Out for Maintenance (FAAC)
**OM** ........... Outboard Marine Corp. [*NYSE symbol*] (SPSG)
**OM** ........... Outer Marker [*Part of an instrument landing system*] [*Aviation*]
**OM** ........... Output Module
**OM** ........... Outside Manufacturing
**O/M**........... Outside of Metal (MSA)
**OM** ........... Overall Modernity [*Sociological scale*]
**OM** ........... Overhaul Manual (MCD)
**OM** ........... Overland Monthly [*A publication*] (ROG)
**OM** ........... Overseas Mail [*British*]
**OM** ........... Overseas Minister [*World War I*] [*Canada*]
**OM** ........... Overt Meditation
**OM** ........... Overturning Moment
**OM** ........... Ovulation Method [*Birth control*]
**OM** ........... Oxford Magazine [*A publication*]
**O/M**........... Oxygen-to-Metal [*Ratio*] (NRCH)
**OM1** .......... Opticalman, First Class [*Navy rating*]
**OM2** .......... Opticalman, Second Class [*Navy rating*]
**OM3** .......... Opticalman, Third Class [*Navy rating*]
**OMA**.......... Markham Public Library, Ontario [*Library symbol*] [*National Library of Canada*] (NLC)
**OMA**.......... Office of Management and Administration [*Social Security Administration*] (OICC)
**OMA**.......... Office of Maritime Administration [*Navy*]
**OMA**.......... Office of Military Applications [*Department of Energy*]
**OMA**.......... Office of Military Assistance
**OMA**.......... Office of Multicultural Affairs [*Australia*]
**OMA**.......... Oklahoma Military Academy
**OMA**.......... Omaezaki [*Japan*] [*Seismograph station code, US Geological Survey*] (SEIS)
**OMA**.......... Omaha [*Nebraska*] [*Airport symbol*]
**O & MA**..... Operation and Maintenance Activities (AAG)
**OMA**.......... Operation Medicare Alert
**OMA**.......... Operational Maintenance Activity (NVT)
**OMA**.......... Operations and Maintenance Appopriation [*Army*]
**OMA**.......... Operations Maintenance Area (NASA)
**OMA**.......... Operations and Maintenance, Army
**OMA**.......... Operations Monitor Alarm
**OMA**.......... Optical Manufacturers Association (EA)
**OMA**.......... Optical-Mechanical Assembly [*Apollo*] [*NASA*]
**OMA**.......... Optical Multichannel Analyzer [*Spectrometry*]
**OMA**.......... Orbiter Maintenance Area [*NASA*] (MCD)
**OMA**.......... Orderly Marketing Agreement
**OMA**.......... Organizational Maintenance Activity
**OMA**.......... Oriental Merchants Association [*Commercial firm*] (EA)
**OMA**.......... Outstanding Merchandising Achievement Award
**OMAA**....... Abu Dhabi/International [*United Arab Emirates*] [*ICAO location identifier*] (ICLI)
**OMAA**....... Occupational Medical Administrators' Association (EA)
**OMAA**....... Office of Management Analysis and Audit [*Civil Service Commission*]
**OMAAEEC** ... Organisation Mondiale des Anciens et Anciennes Eleves de l'Enseignement Catholique [*World Organization of Former Pupils of Catholic Schools*] (EAIO)
**OMAB**....... Buhasa [*United Arab Emirates*] [*ICAO location identifier*] (ICLI)
**OMABP** .... Abitibi-Price, Inc., Mississauga, Ontario [*Library symbol*] [*National Library of Canada*] (NLC)
**OMAC**....... Alkaril Chemicals Ltd., Mississauga, Ontario [*Library symbol*] [*National Library of Canada*] (NLC)
**OMAC**....... Asab [*United Arab Emirates*] [*ICAO location identifier*] (ICLI)
**OMAC**....... Online Manufacturing, Accounting, and Control System
**OMAC**....... Operator Measures and Criteria (MCD)
**OMACON** ... Optimized Magnetohydrodynamic Conversion
**OMAD**....... Abu Dhabi/Bateen [*United Arab Emirates*] [*ICAO location identifier*] (ICLI)
**OMAD**....... Madoc Public Library, Ontario [*Library symbol*] [*National Library of Canada*] (BIB)
**OMAD**....... Oncovin [*Vincristine*], Methotrexate, Adriamycin, Dactinomycin [*Actinomycin D*] [*Antineoplastic drug regimen*]
**OMADA**.... Airway Centre, AES Data Ltd., Mississauga, Ontario [*Library symbol*] [*National Library of Canada*] (NLC)
**OMAE**....... Emirates Flight Information Region [*United Arab Emirates*] [*ICAO location identifier*] (ICLI)
**OMAECL** ... AECL International, Mississauga, Ontario [*Library symbol*] [*National Library of Canada*] (NLC)
**OMAF**....... Operations and Maintenance, Air Force
**OMAG**....... Geac Computers International, Markham, Ontario [*Library symbol*] [*National Library of Canada*] (NLC)
**OMAG**....... Orbiter Magnetometer [*NASA*]
**OMAH**...... Al Hamra [*United Arab Emirates*] [*ICAO location identifier*] (ICLI)
**OMAH**...... Markham High School, Ontario [*Library symbol*] [*National Library of Canada*] (NLC)
**OMAH**...... Omaha National Corp. [*NASDAQ symbol*] (NQ)
**Omaha World** ... Omaha World Herald [*A publication*]
**OMAHM**.. Markham District Historical Museum, Ontario [*Library symbol*] [*National Library of Canada*] (BIB)
**OMAI**........ Allelix, Inc., Mississauga, Ontario [*Library symbol*] [*National Library of Canada*] (NLC)
**OMAI**........ Organisation Mondiale Agudath Israel [*Agudas Israel World Organization - AIWO*] (EAIO)
**OMAJ**....... Jebel Dhana [*United Arab Emirates*] [*ICAO location identifier*] (ICLI)
**OMAL**....... Al Ain [*United Arab Emirates*] [*ICAO location identifier*] (ICLI)
**O'Mal & H** ... O'Malley and Hardcastle's Election Cases [*England*] [*A publication*] (DLA)
**OMAM**...... Abu Dhabi/Al Dhafra [*United Arab Emirates*] [*ICAO location identifier*] (ICLI)
**OMAN**...... Manitouwadge Public Library, Ontario [*Library symbol*] [*National Library of Canada*] (NLC)
**O-MAN**..... Overhead Manipulator [*For handling loads in a nuclear environment*]
**OMancAH** ... Alfred Holbrook College, Manchester, OH [*Library symbol*] [*Library of Congress*] [*Obsolete*] (LCLS)
**OMancO**.... Ohio Valley Local District Free Public Library, Manchester, OH [*Library symbol*] [*Library of Congress*] (LCLS)
**OMANO** ... Manotick Public Library, Ontario [*Library symbol*] [*National Library of Canada*] (NLC)
**OMans**....... Mansfield Public Library, Mansfield, OH [*Library symbol*] [*Library of Congress*] (LCLS)
**OMansK**.... Kingwood Center Library, Mansfield, OH [*Library symbol*] [*Library of Congress*] (LCLS)
**OMansU**.... Ohio State University, Mansfield Regional Campus, Mansfield, OH [*Library symbol*] [*Library of Congress*] (LCLS)
**OMAP**....... Object Module Assembly Program
**OMAP**....... Operations and Maintenance Application Part [*Telecommunications*]
**OMAP**....... Vaughan Public Library, Maple, Ontario [*Library symbol*] [*National Library of Canada*] (NLC)
**OMAPC**.... Astra Pharmaceuticals Canada Ltd., Mississauga, Ontario [*Library symbol*] [*National Library of Canada*] (NLC)
**OMAPFW** ... Ontario Ministry of Natural Resources, Maple, Ontario [*Library symbol*] [*National Library of Canada*] (NLC)
**OMAQ**...... Quarmain [*United Arab Emirates*] [*ICAO location identifier*] (ICLI)
**OMAR**....... Arzana [*United Arab Emirates*] [*ICAO location identifier*] (ICLI)
**OMAR**....... Marathon Public Library, Ontario [*Library symbol*] [*National Library of Canada*] (NLC)
**OMAR**....... Office of Medical Applications of Research [*Department of Health and Human Services*] [*National Institutes of Health*] [*Bethesda, MD*]
**OMAR**....... Operations and Maintenance, Army Reserve (AABC)
**OMAR**....... Optical Mark Reader [*Data processing*]

**OMarion**.... Marion Carnegie Public Library, Marion, OH [*Library symbol*] [*Library of Congress*] (LCLS)
**OMarionU** ... Ohio State University, Marion Campus, Marion, OH [*Library symbol*] [*Library of Congress*] (LCLS)
**OMARK**.... Markdale Public Library, Ontario [*Library symbol*] [*National Library of Canada*] (NLC)
**OMARNG** ... Operation and Maintenance, Army National Guard (AABC)
**OMAS**....... Assiginack Public Library, Manitowaning, Ontario [*Library symbol*] [*National Library of Canada*] (NLC)
**OMAS**....... Das Island [*United Arab Emirates*] [*ICAO location identifier*] (ICLI)
**OMas**......... Massillon Public Library, Massillon, OH [*Library symbol*] [*Library of Congress*] (LCLS)
**OMAS**....... Off-Magic-Angle-Spinning [*Spectroscopy*]
**OMAS**....... Operational Miscellaneous Audio Subsystem
**OMAST**..... Massey and Township Public Library, Ontario [*Library symbol*] [*Library network*] (NLC)
**OMAT**....... Matheson Public Library, Ontario [*Library symbol*] [*National Library of Canada*] (NLC)
**OMAT**....... Ocean Measurement and Array Technology [*Navy*] (CAAL)
**OMAT**....... Office of Manpower, Automation, and Training [*See also OAM*] [*Department of Labor*]
**OMATT**.... Mattawa Public Library, Ontario [*Library symbol*] [*National Library of Canada*] (NLC)
**OMAU**...... Magnetawan Area Union Public Library, Magnetawan, Ontario [*Library symbol*] [*National Library of Canada*] (NLC)
**OMAZ**....... Zirku [*United Arab Emirates*] [*ICAO location identifier*] (ICLI)
**OMB**.......... Management in Government [*A publication*]
**OMB**.......... Midhurst Branch Library, Ontario [*Library symbol*] [*National Library of Canada*] (NLC)
**OMB**.......... Office of Management and Budget [*Executive Office of the President*] [*Formerly, Bureau of the Budget*] [*Washington, DC*]
**OMB**.......... Omboue [*Gabon*] [*Airport symbol*] (OAG)
**OMB**.......... Ordnance Maintenance Bulletin
**OMB**.......... Out-of-Home Measurement Bureau [*Later, TABMM*] (EA)
**OMB**.......... Outboard Motorboat
**OMB**.......... Outer Marker Beacon [*Part of an instrument landing system*] [*Aviation*]
**OMBC**....... Beak Consultants, Mississauga, Ontario [*Library symbol*] [*National Library of Canada*] (NLC)
**OMBE**....... Office of Minority Business Enterprise [*Later, MBDA*] [*Department of Commerce*]
**OMBE**....... Oxford Mission Brotherhood of the Epiphany [*Anglican religious community*]
**OMB/FPPO** ... Office of Management and Budget/Federal Procurement Policy Office (OICC)
**OMBI**........ Observation-Measurement-Balancing and Installation [*Production analysis*]
**OMBI**........ Overcoming Mobility Barriers International (EA)
**OMBK**....... OmniBank of Connecticut, Inc. [*NASDAQ symbol*] (NQ)
**OMBR**....... Ontario Municipal Board Reports [*A publication*] (DLA)
**OMBUU**..... Orbiter Midbody Umbilical Unit [*NASA*] (NASA)
**OMBVT**.... Minesing Branch, Vespra Township Public Library, Ontario [*Library symbol*] [*National Library of Canada*] (BIB)
**OMBW**...... Bangor, Wicklow, McClure, and Monteagle Union Public Library, Maynooth, Ontario [*Library symbol*] [*National Library of Canada*] (BIB)
**OMBW**...... OMB [*Office of Management and Budget*] Watch (EA)
**OMC**.......... Chief Opticalman [*Navy rating*]
**OMc**........... Herbert Wescoat Memorial Library, McArthur, OH [*Library symbol*] [*Library of Congress*] (LCLS)
**OMC**.......... Marietta College, Marietta, OH [*Library symbol*] [*Library of Congress*] (LCLS)
**OMC**.......... Mayo Clinic Library, Rochester, MN [*OCLC symbol*] (OCLC)
**OMC**.......... Office of Military Cooperation [*Foreign Service*]
**OMC**.......... Office of Munitions Control [*Department of State*]
**OMC**.......... Official Mail Center [*Air Force*] (AFM)
**OMC**.......... Omnicom Group, Inc. [*NYSE symbol*] (SPSG)
**OMC**.......... Opel Motorsport Club AG (EA)
**OMC**.......... Open Market Committee [*Also, FOMC*] [*Federal Reserve System*]
**OMC**.......... Operating and Maintenance Costs
**OMC**.......... Operations Monitoring Computer
**OMC**.......... Orbiter Maintenance and Checkout [*NASA*] (NASA)
**OMC**.......... Ordnance Missile Command [*Later, Missile Command*]
**OMC**.......... Ordo Minorum Cappucinorum [*Capuchins*] [*Roman Catholic men's religious order*]
**OMC**.......... Ordo Minorum Conventualium [*Conventual Franciscans*] [*Roman Catholic men's religious order*]
**OMC**.......... Organic Molecular Crystal
**OMC**.......... Orion Molecular Cloud [*Astronomy*]
**OMC**.......... Outboard Marine Corporation
**OMC**.......... Oxford Military College (ROG)
**OMC**.......... Oxford Mission to Calcutta [*British*] (ROG)
**OMC1**........ Orion Molecular Cloud 1 [*Astronomy*]
**OMCA**....... Occupational Medical Corp. of America, Inc. [*NASDAQ symbol*] (NQ)
**OMCA**....... Ontario Motor Coach Association
**OMCA**....... Organic-Moderated Critical Assembly [*Nuclear energy*] (NRCH)
**OMCC**....... Open Minded Comics Club (EA)
**OMCF**....... Operations and Maintenance Control File [*NASA*] (NASA)
**OMCF**....... Orbiter Maintenance and Checkout Facility [*NASA*] (NASA)
**OMCG**....... Ciba/Geigy Canada Ltd., Mississauga, Ontario [*Library symbol*] [*National Library of Canada*] (NLC)
**OMCI**........ Organisation Maritime Consultatif Intergouvernementale [*Intergovernmental Maritime Consultative Organization*]
**OMCILCR** ... Chemical Research Laboratory, CIL, Inc., Mississauga, Ontario [*Library symbol*] [*National Library of Canada*] (NLC)
**OMCM**...... Master Chief Opticalman [*Navy rating*]
**OMCO**....... Official Mail Control Officer (MCD)
**OMCO**....... Overmyer Corporation [*NASDAQ symbol*] (NQ)
**OMCR**....... Chippewa Resource Centre, Muncey, Ontario [*Library symbol*] [*National Library of Canada*] (NLC)
**OMCR**....... Organic-Moderated Cooled Reactor
**OMCR**....... Organized Marine Corps Reserve
**OMCS**....... Office of Motor Carrier Standards [*Federal Highway Administration*]
**OMCS**....... Senior Chief Opticalman [*Navy rating*]
**OMCS**....... Sheridan Park Research Community, Cominco Ltd., Mississauga, Ontario [*Library symbol*] [*National Library of Canada*] (NLC)
**OMCSDG** ... Moose Creek Branch, Stormount, Dundas, and Glengarry County Public Library, Ontario [*Library symbol*] [*National Library of Canada*] (NLC)
**OMCSG**.... Canada Systems Group, Mississauga, Ontario [*Library symbol*] [*National Library of Canada*] (NLC)
**OMCT**....... Carnarvon Township Public Library, Mindemoya, Ontario [*Library symbol*] [*National Library of Canada*] (NLC)
**OMCT**....... Office of Motor Carrier Transportation [*Federal Highway Administration*]
**OMCTS**..... Octamethylcyclotetrasiloxane [*Organic chemistry*]
**OMCT/SOST** ... Organisation Mondiale Contre la Torture/SOS-Torture [*World Organization Against Torture/SOS-Torture*] [*Geneva, Switzerland*] (EAIO)
**OM-CVD**... Organometallic Chemical Vapor Deposition [*Also, OM-VPE, MO-CVD, MO-VPE*] [*Semiconductor technology*]
**OMCVH**.... Credit Valley Hospital, Mississauga, Ontario [*Library symbol*] [*National Library of Canada*] (NLC)
**OMD**......... Doctor of Oriental Medicine
**OMD**......... Du Pont Canada, Inc., Maitland, Ontario [*Library symbol*] [*National Library of Canada*] (NLC)
**OMD**......... O-Methyldopa [*Biochemistry*]
**OMD**......... Ocean Margin Drilling [*Program*] [*National Science Foundation*]
**OMD**......... Ocean Movement Designator
**OMD**......... Office of Management Development [*Later, OMPR*] [*NASA*]
**OMD**......... Open Macrodefinition
**OMD**......... Operations and Maintainer Decision
**OMD**......... Operations and Maintenance Documentation [*NASA*] (NASA)
**OMD**......... Orbiter Mating Device [*NASA*] (NASA)
**OMD**......... Orchestral Manoeuvres in the Dark [*Pop music group*]
**OMD**......... Ordnance Medical Department [*British military*] (DMA)
**OMD**......... Ormand Industries, Inc. [*AMEX symbol*] (SPSG)
**O & M-DA** ... Operation and Maintenance, Defense Agencies [*DoD*]
**OMDB**....... Dubai [*United Arab Emirates*] [*ICAO location identifier*] (ICLI)
**OMDC**....... Du Pont Canada, Inc., Mississauga, Ontario [*Library symbol*] [*National Library of Canada*] (NLC)
**OMDCPL** ... Patent & Legal Library, DuPont Canada, Inc., Mississauga, Ontario [*Library symbol*] [*National Library of Canada*] (NLC)
**OMDEAC** ... Dearborn Chemical Co. Ltd., Mississauga, Ontario [*Library symbol*] [*National Library of Canada*] (NLC)
**OMDG**...... Dominion Glass Co. Ltd., Mississauga, Ontario [*Library symbol*] [*National Library of Canada*] (NLC)
**OMDIR**..... Research Library, Duracell, Inc., Mississauga, Ontario [*Library symbol*] [*Obsolete*] [*National Library of Canada*] (NLC)
**OMDL**....... Marmora, Deloro, and Lake Union Public Library, Marmora, Ontario [*Library symbol*] [*National Library of Canada*] (BIB)
**OMDM**..... Optomechanical Display Module
**OMDO**...... Corporate Library, Domglas, Inc., Mississauga, Ontario [*Library symbol*] [*National Library of Canada*] (NLC)
**OMDP**....... Ocean Margin Drilling Program [*National Science Foundation*]
**OMDR**....... Dunlop Research Centre, Sheridan Park, Mississauga, Ontario [*Library symbol*] [*National Library of Canada*] (NLC)
**OMDR**....... Operations and Maintenance Data Record [*NASA*] (KSC)
**OMDR**....... Optic Memory Disk Recorder
**OMDS**....... Delphax Systems, Mississauga, Ontario [*Library symbol*] [*National Library of Canada*] (NLC)
**OMDW**..... Diversey Wyandotte, Inc., Mississauga, Ontario, [*Library symbol*] [*National Library of Canada*] (NLC)
**OME**.......... Erindale College, University of Toronto, Mississauga, Ontario [*Library symbol*] [*National Library of Canada*] (NLC)
**OME**.......... Nome [*Alaska*] [*Airport symbol*] (OAG)
**OME**.......... Object Management Extension
**OME**.......... Office of Management Engineer

**OME**.......... Office of Manpower Economics [*Department of Employment*] [*British*]
**OME**.......... Office of Minerals Exploration [*Functions transferred to Geological Survey*] [*Department of the Interior*]
**OME**.......... Omega [*A publication*]
**Ome**........... Omega [*Record label*] [*Belgium, etc.*]
**OME**.......... Ometepe [*Nicaragua*] [*Seismograph station code, US Geological Survey*] (SEIS)
**OME**.......... Operational Mission Environment (MCD)
**OME**.......... Orbital [*or Orbiter*] Main Engine [*NASA*] (NASA)
**OME**.......... Orbital Maneuvering Engine [*NASA*] (KSC)
**OME**.......... Ordnance Mechanical Engineer [*British military*] (DMA)
**OME**.......... Organisation Mondiale de l'Emballage [*World Packaging Organization - WPO*] (EAIO)
**OME**.......... Ormont Explorations Ltd. [*Vancouver Stock Exchange symbol*]
**OME**.......... Otitis Media with Effusion [*Medicine*]
**OMEA**....... Meaford Public Library, Ontario [*Library symbol*] [*National Library of Canada*] (NLC)
**OMEC**....... Optimized Microminiature Electronic Circuit
**OMEC**....... Organization of Mineral Exporting Countries [*Proposed*]
**OMEF**....... Office Machines and Equipment Federation [*British*] (DIT)
**OMEG**....... Omega. The Journal of Death and Dying [*A publication*]
**OMEG**....... Omega Optical Co. [*NASDAQ symbol*] (NQ)
**OMEGA**.... Off-Road Mobility Evaluation and Generalized Analysis [*Army*]
**OMEGA**.... Operation Model Evaluation Group, Air Force (MCD)
**Omega-Int J** ... Omega - The International Journal of Management Science [*A publication*]
**Omega J Death Dying** ... Omega Journal of Death and Dying [*A publication*]
**OM/EH**..... Occupational Medicine/Environmental Health Evaluation Center [*Emory University*]
**OMEI**........ Office of Minority Economic Impact [*Department of Energy*]
**OMEI**........ Other Major End Item [*Military*] (AFIT)
**OMEN**....... Ohio Medical Education Network [*Ohio State University*] [*Columbus*] (TSSD)
**OMEP**....... Organisation Mondiale pour l'Education Prescolaire [*World Organization for Early Childhood Education*] (EAIO)
**OMER**....... Merrickville Public Library, Ontario [*Library symbol*] [*National Library of Canada*] (NLC)
**OMER**....... Operations Management Education and Research Foundation (EA)
**OMERAD** ... Office of Medical Education Research and Development [*Michigan State University*] [*Research center*] (RCD)
**OMerc**....... Order of Mercedarians [*Also, MMB*] [*Roman Catholic women's religious order*]
**OMERF**..... Operations Management Education and Research Foundation [*Formerly, OFMP*] (EA)
**OMET**....... Orbiter Mission Elapsed Time [*NASA*] (MCD)
**OMET**....... Ordnance Middle East Tasks [*Military*]
**OMET**....... Organization Manning Equipment Table (MCD)
**OMET**....... Orthomet, Inc. [*NASDAQ symbol*] (NQ)
**OMETA**.... Ordnance Management Engineering Training Agency [*Army*]
**OMEW**...... Office of Missile Electronic Warfare [*Army*] (RDA)
**OMEWG**... Orbiter Maintenance Engineering Working Group [*NASA*] (NASA)
**OMF**.......... Moose Factory Library, Ontario [*Library symbol*] [*National Library of Canada*] (BIB)
**OMF**.......... Object Module Format
**OMF**.......... Obzornik za Matematiko in Fiziko [*A publication*]
**OMF**.......... Officer Master File [*Army*] (INF)
**OMF**.......... Old Master File
**OMF**.......... Operation and Maintenance of Facilities [*Army*]
**O & MF**..... Operation and Maintenance Facilities (MUGU)
**OMF**.......... Operational Mission Failure (MCD)
**OMF**.......... Optical Matched Filter
**OMF**.......... Order Materials For
**OMF**.......... Organizational Master File [*Army*]
**OMF**.......... Oscillatory Magnetic Field
**OMF**.......... Overseas Missionary Fellowship, USA Headquarters (EA)
**OMFBAA** ... Operation and Maintenance of Facilities Budget Activity Account [*Army*] (AABC)
**OMFBR**..... Organic-Moderated Fluidized Bed Reactor
**OMFC**....... Overseas Military Forces of Canada [*World War I*]
**OMFCA**.... Operation and Maintenance of Facilities Cost Account [*Army*] (AABC)
**OMFCU**.... Outboard Message Format Conversion Unit (MCD)
**OMFD**....... Mount Forest District High School, Mount Forest, Ontario [*Library symbol*] [*National Library of Canada*] (NLC)
**OMFE**....... Front of Escott Public Library, Mallorytown, Ontario [*Library symbol*] [*National Library of Canada*] (NLC)
**OMFG**....... Optimum Manufacturing, Inc. [*Denver, CO*] [*NASDAQ symbol*] (NQ)
**O & MFH**.. Operation and Maintenance, Family Housing [*Army*] (AABC)
**OMFJ**........ Fujeirah/International [*United Arab Emirates*] [*ICAO location identifier*] (ICLI)
**OMFP**....... Obtaining Money by False Pretense
**OMFP**....... Ortho-Methylfluorescein Phosphate [*Biochemistry*]
**OMFS**........ Office Master Frequency Supply [*Telecommunications*] (TEL)
**OMFS**........ Optimum Metric Fastener System
**OMFSCA**.. Operation and Maintenance of Facilities Summary Cost Account [*Army*] (AABC)
**OMFT**....... Optical Matched Filter Technique
**OMFUG**.... Other Music for Urban Gormandizers [*Acronym used as subtitle to the New York City nightclub name, CBGB*]
**OMFY**....... Front of Yonge Township Public Library, Mallorytown, Ontario [*Library symbol*] [*National Library of Canada*] (BIB)
**OMG**......... Office Machines Group [*Business Equipment Manufacturers Association*]
**OMG**......... Office of Marine Geology [*United States Geological Survey*]
**OMG**......... Office of Military Government
**OMG**......... Older Metamorphic Group [*Geology*]
**OMG**......... Omega [*Namibia*] [*Airport symbol*] (OAG)
**OMG**......... Operational-Maneuver Group [*Military*]
**OMGA**....... Golder Associates, Mississauga, Ontario [*Library symbol*] [*National Library of Canada*] (NLC)
**OMGB**....... Georgian Bay Township Public Library, Mactier, Ontario [*Library symbol*] [*National Library of Canada*] (BIB)
**OMGB**....... Office of Military Government for Bavaria [*US Military Government, Germany*]
**OMGBS**.... Office of Military Government for Berlin Sector [*US Military Government, Germany*]
**OMGCR**.... Research & Development, Gulf Canada Ltd., Mississauga, Ontario [*Library symbol*] [*National Library of Canada*] (NLC)
**OMGCR**.... Technical Library, Petro-Canada Products, Mississauga, Ontario [*Library symbol*] [*National Library of Canada*] (NLC)
**OMGE**....... Organisation Mondiale de Gastroenterologie [*World Organization of Gastroenterology - WOG*] [*Edinburgh, Scotland*] (EAIO)
**OMGH**...... Office of Military Government for Hesse [*US Military Government, Germany*]
**OMGL**....... Gartner Lee Associates Ltd., Markham, Ontario [*Library symbol*] [*National Library of Canada*] (NLC)
**OMGT**....... Overall Missile Guidance Tests (MCD)
**OMGUS**.... Office of Military Government, United States
**OMGWB**... Office of Military Government for Wuerttemberg-Baden [*US Military Government, Germany*]
**OMH**......... Health Sciences Library, Mississauga Hospital, Ontario [*Library symbol*] [*National Library of Canada*] (BIB)
**OMH**......... Omaha Aviation, Inc. [*Omaha, NE*] [*FAA designator*] (FAAC)
**O'M & H** ... O'Malley and Hardcastle's Election Cases [*England*] [*A publication*] (DLA)
**OMH**......... Omega Hydrocarbons Ltd. [*Toronto Stock Exchange symbol*]
**OMH**......... Orumieh [*Iran*] [*Airport symbol*] [*Obsolete*] (OAG)
**O Mh**........ Ostdeutsche Monatshefte [*A publication*]
**O'M & H El Cas** ... O'Malley and Hardcastle's Election Cases [*England*] [*A publication*] (DLA)
**OMHL**....... Occupational Medicine and Hygiene Laboratory [*British*] (IRUK)
**OMHT**...... Hagar Township Public Library, Markstay, Ontario [*Library symbol*] [*National Library of Canada*] (NLC)
**OMI**.......... Middletown Public Library, Middletown, OH [*OCLC symbol*] (OCLC)
**OMI**.......... Midland Public Library, Ontario [*Library symbol*] [*National Library of Canada*] (NLC)
**OMI**.......... Oblats de Marie Immaculee [*Oblates of Mary Immaculate*] [*Rome, Italy*] (EAIO)
**OMI**.......... Office of Management Improvement [*Department of Agriculture*]
**OMI**.......... Office of Management Information [*Military*] (AFIT)
**OMI**.......... Ohio Mechanics Institute
**OMI**.......... Old Myocardial Infarction [*Medicine*]
**OMI**.......... Omnibus Computer Graphics, Inc. [*Toronto Stock Exchange symbol*]
**OMI**.......... Oocyte Maturation Inhibitor [*Endocrinology*]
**OMI**.......... Operating Memorandum - Information
**OMI**.......... Operation Move-In [*New York City*]
**OMI**.......... Operational Maintenance Instruction (AAG)
**OMI**.......... Opinions about Mental Illness [*A questionnaire*]
**OMI**.......... Ordnance Modifications Instructions
**OMI**.......... Organisation Maritime Internationale [*International Maritime Organization - IMO*] (EAIO)
**OMI**.......... Organisation Meteorologique Internationale
**OMI**.......... Organization for Microinformation
**OMI**.......... Organizations Master Index [*A publication*]
**OMI**.......... Other Manufacturing Industries [*Department of Employment*] [*British*]
**OMI**.......... Owens & Minor, Incorporated [*NYSE symbol*] (SPSG)
**OMIA**........ Operating, Maintenance, Interest, and Adaptability
**OMIAA**...... Orientation and Mobility Instructors' Association of Australasia
**OMiabM** ... Monsanto Research Corp., Mound Laboratory, Miamisburg, OH [*Library symbol*] [*Library of Congress*] (LCLS)
**OMiabMM** ... Monarch Marking Systems, Pitney Bowes, Chemical Research and Development Library, Miamisburg, OH [*Library symbol*] [*Library of Congress*] (LCLS)
**OMIBAC**... Ordinal Memory Inspecting Binary Automatic Computer (IEEE)
**OMIBM**.... IBM Canada Ltd., Markham, Ontario [*Library symbol*] [*National Library of Canada*] (NLC)
**OMICA**..... Organized Migrants in Community Action [*Florida*] [*Defunct*]

**OMid** ........ Middletown Public Library, Middletown, OH [*Library symbol*] [*Library of Congress*] (LCLS)
**OMidAR**.... Armco, Inc., Research Center, Technical Library, Middletown, OH [*Library symbol*] [*Library of Congress*] (LCLS)
**OMidU** ...... Miami University, Middletown Campus, Middletown, OH [*Library symbol*] [*Library of Congress*] (LCLS)
**OMIH**........ Huronia Historical Park, Midland, Ontario [*Library symbol*] [*National Library of Canada*] (NLC)
**OMIHM**.... Halton Region Museum, Milton, Ontario [*Library symbol*] [*National Library of Canada*] (BIB)
**OMIHS**..... Institute for Hydrogen Systems, Mississauga, Ontario [*Library symbol*] [*National Library of Canada*] (NLC)
**OMIKE** ..... Orszagos Magyar Izraelita Kozmuvelodesi Egyesuelet [*A publication*]
**OMIKK** ..... Orszagos Muszaki Informacios Kozpont es Konyvtar [*National Technical Information Center and Library*] [*Information service or system*] (IID)
**OMIL** ........ Milton Public Library, Ontario [*Library symbol*] [*National Library of Canada*] (NLC)
**OMILD** ..... Mildmay Branch, Bruce County Public Library, Ontario [*Library symbol*] [*National Library of Canada*] (NLC)
**OMill** ........ Holmes County Public Library, Millersburg, OH [*Library symbol*] [*Library of Congress*] (LCLS)
**OMILL**...... Millbrook Public Library, Ontario [*Library symbol*] [*National Library of Canada*] (BIB)
**OMILV**...... Milverton Public Library, Ontario [*Library symbol*] [*National Library of Canada*] (NLC)
**OMiM** ....... Megis Local School District Public Library, Middleport Branch, Middleport, OH [*Library symbol*] [*Library of Congress*] (LCLS)
**OMiM** ....... Outer Mitochondrial Membrane [*Also, OMM*] [*Cytology*]
**OMIN**........ Inco Ltd., Mississauga, Ontario [*Library symbol*] [*National Library of Canada*] (NLC)
**OMIOM**.... Original Meaning Is the Only Meaning [*Writing term*]
**OMIS** ........ Office of Management Information Systems [*Office of Administration and Management*] [*Department of Labor*]
**OMIS** ........ Omission (AAG)
**OMIS** ........ Operational Management Information System [*Data processing*]
**O Misc**....... Ohio Miscellaneous Reports [*A publication*] (DLA)
**OMISS**...... Operation and Maintenance Instruction Summary Sheet [*NASA*] (MCD)
**OMIT** ........ Mitchell Public Library, Ontario [*Library symbol*] [*National Library of Canada*] (NLC)
**OMIT** ........ Organisation Mondiale Interarmees du Haut Commandement Francais [*French High Command telecommunications system*]
**OMITT**...... Omittatur [*Let It Be Omitted*] [*Pharmacy*] (ROG)
**OMJ** .......... Ohmine [*Japan*] [*Seismograph station code, US Geological Survey*] (SEIS)
**OMJ** .......... Orthomode Junction [*Electronics*]
**OMJAT**..... J. A. Turner Professional Library, H. J. A. Brown Education Centre, Mississauga, Ontario [*Library symbol*] [*National Library of Canada*] (NLC)
**OMK**.......... Omak, WA [*Location identifier*] [*FAA*] (FAAL)
**OMK**.......... Owl Monkey Kidney [*Cell line*]
**OMKDK Modsz Kiad** ... Orszagos Muszaki Konyvtar es Dokumentacios Kozpont. Modszertani Kiadvanyok [*A publication*]
**OMKR**....... Outer Marker [*Part of an instrument landing system*] [*Aviation*]
**OML**.......... Ontario Ministry of Labour Library [*UTLAS symbol*]
**OML**.......... Operations Manual Letter [*National Weather Service*] (NOAA)
**OML**.......... Orbiter Mold Line [*NASA*] (NASA)
**OML**.......... Orbiting Military Laboratory (AAG)
**OML**.......... Order of Merit List [*Army*] (AABC)
**OML**.......... Ordnance Missile Laboratories (KSC)
**OML**.......... Ordnance Muzzle Loading [*British military*] (DMA)
**OML**.......... Organic Materials Laboratory [*Watertown, MA*] [*Army*] (GRD)
**OML**.......... Organizational Maintenanee Level (NVT)
**OML**.......... Outer Mold Line (NASA)
**OML**.......... Outgoing Matching Loss [*Telecommunications*] (TEL)
**OML**.......... Outside Mold Line [*Technical drawings*]
**OML**.......... University of Cincinnati, Marx Law Library, Cincinnati, OH [*OCLC symbol*] (OCLC)
**OMLA**....... Organizational Maintenance Level Activity (MCD)
**OMLCSA** ... Old Mine Lamp Collectors Society of America (EA)
**OMLE**....... Organization of Spanish Marxist-Leninists (PD)
**OM Leiden** ... Oudheidkundige Mededeelingen uit s'Rijksmuseum van Oudheden te Leiden [*A publication*]
**OMLLM** ... Oxford Modern Languages and Literature Monographs [*A publication*]
**OMLP**....... Ohio Midland Light & Power [*AAR code*]
**OMLT**....... [*The*] Learning Tree, Mississauga, Ontario [*Library symbol*] [*National Library of Canada*] (NLC)
**o/m/m**........ A l'Ordre de Moi-Meme [*To Our Own Order*] [*French*] [*Business term*]
**OMM** ........ Miami University, Middletown Campus, Middletown, OH [*OCLC symbol*] (OCLC)
**OMM** ........ Nouvel Officiel de l'Ameublement [*A publication*]
**OMM** ........ Office of Marine Minerals
**OMM** ........ Office of Minerals Mobilization [*Later, OMSF*] [*Department of the Interior*]
**OMM** ........ Officer Message Mail [*Military*]
**OMM** ........ Officer of the Order of Military Merit
**OMM** ........ OMI Corp. [*AMEX symbol*] (SPSG)
**OMM** ........ Ommatidium [*Arthropod eye anatomy*]
**OMM** ........ Operation and Maintenance Manual
**OMM** ........ Organisation Meteorologique Mondiale [*World Meteorological Organization - WMO*] (EAIO)
**OMM** ........ Organizacion Meteorologica Mundial [*World Meteorological Organization - WMO*] [*Spanish*]
**OMM** ........ Organometallic Material
**OMM** ........ Outer Mitochondrial Membrane [*Also, OMiM*] [*Cytology*]
**OMM** ........ Oxford Medical Manuals [*A publication*]
**OMMA**...... Outboard Motor Manufacturers Association [*Later, MEMA*] (EA)
**OMMB**...... Information Centre, Molson Breweries of Canada Ltd., Mississauga, Ontario [*Library symbol*] [*National Library of Canada*] (NLC)
**OMMC**...... Officer Message Mail Center [*Military*]
**O & MMC** ... Operations and Maintenance, Marine Corps
**Om Mer Sh** ... Omond's Merchant Shipping Acts [*1877*] [*A publication*] (DLA)
**OM & MG** ... Organizational Manual and Management Guide
**OMMH**..... Orbiter Maintenance Man-Hours [*NASA*] (NASA)
**OMMI**....... Magna International, Inc., Markham, Ontario [*Library symbol*] [*National Library of Canada*] (BIB)
**OMMIC**.... Ordnance Maintenance Management Information Center [*Navy*]
**OMMI Kiad Sorozat 1** ... OMMI [*Orszagos Mezogazdasagi Minosegvizsgalo Intezet*] Kiadvanyai. Sorozat 1. Genetikus Talajterkepek [*A publication*]
**OMMI (Orsz Mezogazd Minosegvizsgalo Intez) Kiad Sorozat 1** ... OMMI (Orszagos Mezogazdasagi Minosegvizsgalo Intezet) Kiadvanyai. Sorozat 1. Genetikus Talajterkepek [*A publication*]
**OMML**...... Oudheidkundige Mededeelingen uit s'Rjksmuseum van Oudheden te Leiden [*A publication*]
**OMMLT** ... Murchison Lyell Township Community Library, Madawaska, Ontario [*Library symbol*] [*National Library of Canada*] (NLC)
**OMMM** .... Moore Museum, Mooretown, Ontario [*Library symbol*] [*National Library of Canada*] (BIB)
**OMMMSA** ... Oil Mill Machinery Manufacturers and Supply Association (EA)
**OMMS**...... Office of Merchant Marine Safety [*Coast Guard*]
**OMM(S)C** ... Officer Messenger Mail (Sub) Center [*Navy*]
**OMMSQA** ... Office of Modeling, Monitoring Systems, and Quality Assurance [*Environmental Protection Agency*]
**OMN** ......... Mansfield-Richland County Public Library, Mansfield, OH [*OCLC symbol*] (OCLC)
**OMN** ......... Octamethylnaphthalene [*Organic chemistry*]
**OMN** ......... Oman [*ANSI three-letter standard code*] (CNC)
**OMN** ......... Omnivorous
**O & MN**...... Operation and Maintenance, Navy
**OMN** ......... Ormond Beach, FL [*Location identifier*] [*FAA*] (FAAL)
**O & MN**..... Overhaul and Maintenance, Navy (MCD)
**OMNAN** ... Ontario. Ministry of Northern Affairs. News Release [*A publication*]
**OMN BID** ... Omni Bidus [*Every Two Days*] [*Pharmacy*] (ROG)
**OMN BIH** ... Omni Bihora [*Every Two Hours*] [*Pharmacy*]
**OMNCS**.... Office of the Manager National Communications System [*GSA*]
**OMNET**.... Organizational Maintenance New Equipment Training [*Army*] (INF)
**OMNG**...... Operations and Maintenance, National Guard [*Army*]
**OMN H**..... Omni Hora [*Every Hour*] [*Pharmacy*]
**OMN HOR** ... Omni Hora [*Every Hour*] [*Pharmacy*]
**OMNI**........ Omnicorp Ltd. [*NASDAQ symbol*] (NQ)
**OMNI**........ Omnidirectional
**Omnia Med** ... Omnia Medica [*A publication*]
**Omnia Med Suppl** ... Omnia Medica. Supplemento [*A publication*]
**Omnia Med Ther** ... Omnia Medica et Therapeutica [*A publication*]
**Omnia Med Ther Arch** ... Omnia Medica et Therapeutica. Archivio [*A publication*]
**Omnia Ther** ... Omnia Therapeutica [*A publication*]
**Omnibus Mag** ... Omnibus Magazine [*A publication*]
**OMNIRANGE** ... Omnidirectional Radio Range (MSA)
**OMNITAB** ... Omnibus Program with Tabular Numerical Functions [*Programming language*] [*1965*] (CSR)
**OMNITENNA** ... Omnirange Antenna
**OMN MAN** ... Omni Mane [*Every Morning*] [*Pharmacy*]
**OMNMPS** ... Operative Machine Needle Makers' Protection Society [*A union*] [*British*]
**OMN NOCT** ... Omni Nocte [*Every Night*] [*Pharmacy*]
**OMN QUADR HOR** ... Omni Quadrante Horae [*Every Quarter of an Hour*] [*Pharmacy*] (ROG)
**O & MNR** ... Operation and Maintenance, Naval Reserve (NVT)
**OMNRF**.... Omni Resources, Inc. [*NASDAQ symbol*] (NQ)
**OMNT**....... Northern Telecom, Mississauga, Ontario [*Library symbol*] [*National Library of Canada*] (NLC)
**OMNU**...... Orthomolecular Nutrition Institute [*NASDAQ symbol*] (NQ)

**OMNX**....... Omni Exploration, Inc. [*Columbus, OH*] [*NASDAQ symbol*] (NQ)
**OMO**......... Moonbeam Public Library, Ontario [*Library symbol*] [*National Library of Canada*] (BIB)
**OMO**......... Office of the Director of Manpower and Organization [*Air Force*]
**OMO**......... Offshore Mining Organization [*Thailand*] (DS)
**OMO**......... Old Man's Out [*Facetious translation of Omo, a brand of detergent*] [*British*]
**OMO**......... Omoco Holdings [*Vancouver Stock Exchange symbol*]
**OMO**......... One-Man-Operated Bus [*London, England*]
**OMO**......... One Man Operation [*Railroad*] [*British*]
**OMO**......... Open Market Operations [*Economics*]
**OMO**......... Ordinary Money Order
**OMo**.......... Oriente Moderno [*A publication*]
**OMOAM**.. Ontario Agricultural Museum, Milton, Ontario [*Library symbol*] [*National Library of Canada*] (NLC)
**OMOB**....... Offensive Missile Order of Battle (MCD)
**OMODE**.... Ordinary Mode (MCD)
**OMOL**....... Oliver Township Public Library, Murillo, Ontario [*Library symbol*] [*National Library of Canada*] (BIB)
**OMOO**...... Moosonee Public Library, Ontario [*Library symbol*] [*National Library of Canada*] (BIB)
**OMorD**...... Ocerki Mordovskich Dialektov [*A publication*]
**OMorS**....... Salem Township Public Library, Morrow, OH [*Library symbol*] [*Library of Congress*] (LCLS)
**OMORSDG**... Morewood Branch, Stormont, Dundas, and Glengarry County Public Library, Ontario [*Library symbol*] [*National Library of Canada*] (BIB)
**OMOSC**.... Organisation des Musiciens d'Orchestres Symphoniques du Canada [*Organization of Canadian Symphony Musicans - OCSM*]
**OMOSDG**... Morrisburg Branch, Stormont, Dundas, and Glengarry County Public Library, Ontario [*Library symbol*] [*National Library of Canada*] (NLC)
**OMOT**....... Metcalfe Branch, Osgoode Township Library, Ontario [*Library symbol*] [*National Library of Canada*] (BIB)
**OMOTH**... Osgoode Township High School Library, Metcalfe, Ontario [*Library symbol*] [*National Library of Canada*] (BIB)
**OMOV**...... One Member, One Vote [*System to select parliamentary candidates*] [*British*]
**OMP**.......... Espe [*Germany*] [*Research code symbol*]
**OMP**.......... Marion Public Library, Marion, OH [*OCLC symbol*] (OCLC)
**OMP**.......... Office of Metric Programs [*Department of Commerce*]
**OMP**.......... Olfactory Marker Protein [*Biochemistry*]
**OMP**.......... Oligo-N-methylmorpholinopropylene Oxide [*Pharmacology*]
**OMP**.......... Operating Memorandum - Policy
**OMP**.......... Operations and Maintenance Plan [*NASA*] (NASA)
**OMP**.......... Organometallic Polymer (CAAL)
**OMP**.......... Output Makeup
**OMP**.......... Overseas Manpower [*British*]
**OMP**.......... Oxford Medical Publications [*A publication*]
**OMPA**....... Octamethylpyrophosphoramide [*Insecticide*]
**OMPA**....... Office of Marine Pollution Assessment [*National Oceanic and Atmospheric Administration*] (ASF)
**OMPA**....... One-Man Pension Arrangement [*Management*]
**OMPA**....... Operating Memorandum - Personnel Assignment
**OMPA**....... Otitis Media, Purulent, Acute [*Medicine*]
**OMPA**....... Outer Membrane Protein A [*Biochemistry*]
**OMPC**....... Overseas Military Personnel Charter (MCD)
**OMPD**....... Office of Mineral Policy Development [*Department of the Interior*]
**OMPE & R**... Office of Manpower Policy, Evaluation, and Research [*Department of Labor*]
**OMPER**.... Office of Manpower Policy, Evaluation, and Research [*Department of Labor*]
**OMPF**....... Official Military Personnel File [*Army*] (AABC)
**OMPI**........ Ordnance Master Publication Index (MCD)
**OMPI**........ Organisation Mondiale de la Propriete Intellectuelle [*World Intellectual Property Organization - WIPO*] [*Information service or system*] (IID)
**OMPI**........ Oxo(mercaptoethyl)(phenyl)imidazolidine [*Biochemistry*]
**OMPR**....... Office of Management Planning and Review [*Formerly, OMD*] [*NASA*]
**OMPR**....... Operational Maintainability Problem Reporting (NASA)
**OMPR**....... Optical Mark Page Reader [*Data processing*] (AABC)
**OMPRA**..... One-Man Propulsion Research Apparatus [*NASA*]
**OMPS**....... Orbit Maneuvering Propulsion System [*NASA*] (KSC)
**OMPSA**..... Organisation Mondiale pour le Promotion Sociale des Aveugles [*World Council for the Welfare of the Blind - WCWB*] (EAIO)
**OMPT**....... Observed Man [*or Mass*] Point Trajectory [*NASA*] (KSC)
**OMPUS**.... Official Munitions Production United States
**OMPW**...... Pratt & Whitney Aircraft Ltd., Mississauga, Ontario [*Library symbol*] [*National Library of Canada*] (NLC)
**OMR**.......... Midland-Ross Corp., Library, Cleveland, OH [*OCLC symbol*] (OCLC)
**OMR**.......... Office of Marine Resources [*Department of the Interior*] (NOAA)
**OMR**.......... Office Methods Research
**OMR**.......... Officer Master Record [*Air Force*] (AFM)
**OMR**.......... Operation Management Room [*NASA*] (KSC)
**OMR**.......... Operations and Maintenance Requirements (NASA)
**OMR**.......... Operations Manager's Report
**OMR**.......... Optical Mark Reader [*Data processing*]
**OMR**.......... Optical Mark Recognition [*Data processing*] (MCD)
**OMR**.......... Optical Meter Relay
**OMR**.......... Orad [*Romania*] [*Airport symbol*] (OAG)
**OMR**.......... Orbiter Management Review [*NASA*] (NASA)
**OMR**.......... Organic Magnetic Resonance
**OMR**.......... Organic-Moderated Reactor [*Nuclear energy*]
**OMR**.......... Our Material Returned (AAG)
**OMR**.......... Overhaul, Maintenance, and Repair (MCD)
**OMR**.......... Overhead Materials Requirement [*Manufacturing*]
**OMRA**....... 135th Medical Regiment Association (EA)
**OMRB**....... Operating Material Review Board [*NASA*] (NASA)
**OMRC**....... Operational Maintenance Requirements Catalog [*NASA*] (MCD)
**OMRCA**.... Organic-Moderated Reactor Critical Assembly [*Nuclear energy*]
**OMRD**....... Office of Manpower Research and Development [*National Academy of Sciences*]
**OMRE**....... Organic-Moderated Reactor Experiment [*Nuclear energy*]
**OMRF**....... Oklahoma Medical Research Foundation [*University of Oklahoma*] [*Research center*]
**OMRI**........ Oklahoma Medical Research Institute
**OMRK**....... Ras Al Khaimah/International [*United Arab Emirates*] [*ICAO location identifier*] (ICLI)
**OMRL**....... Oudheidkundige Mededeelingen uit s'Rijksmuseum van Oudheden te Leiden [*A publication*]
**OMRM**...... Manitou Library (Ojibway of Manitou Rapids Indian Band), Manitou Rapids, Ontario [*Library symbol*] [*National Library of Canada*] (BIB)
**OMRO**...... Ordnance Materials Research Office [*Army*] [*Later, AMMRC*] (MCD)
**Omron Tech**... Omron Technics [*A publication*]
**OMR-Org Mag**... Organic Magnetic Resonance [*A publication*]
**OMR/P**..... Operations and Maintenance Requirements/Plan [*NASA*] (NASA)
**OMRR**....... Ordnance Material Research Reactor [*Nuclear energy*]
**OMRS**....... Operations and Maintenance Requirements Specifications (NASA)
**OMRS**....... Orders and Medals Research Society (EA)
**OMRSD**.... Operational Maintainability Reporting Systems Document [*NASA*] (NASA)
**OMRSD**.... Operational Maintenance Requirements and Specifications Document [*NASA*] (NASA)
**OMRSD**.... Operations and Maintenance Requirements and Specification Documentation (NASA)
**OMRV**....... Operational Maneuvering Reentry Vehicle (MCD)
**OMRW**...... Optical MASER [*Microwave Amplification by Stimulated Emission of Radiation*] Radiation Weapon (AAG)
**OMS**.......... Ocean Minesweeper
**OMS**.......... Office of Management Services [*Department of Agriculture*]
**OMS**.......... Office of Management Studies (EA)
**OMS**.......... Office of Marketing Services [*of BDSA*]
**OMS**.......... Omsk [*USSR*] [*Airport symbol*] (OAG)
**OMS**.......... One-Minute Superstar [*Actor whose bit part in a television series results in instant stardom*]
**OMS**.......... Operational Maintenance System
**OMS**.......... Operational Meteorological Satellite [*NASA*]
**OMS**.......... Operational Mode Summary
**OMS**.......... Operational Monitoring System (MCD)
**OMS**.......... Oppenheimer Multi-Sector Income Trust [*NYSE symbol*] (SPSG)
**OMS**.......... Optical MASER [*Microwave Amplification by Stimulated Emission of Radiation*] System
**OMS**.......... Optical Modulation System
**OMS**.......... Optimum Mode Selector (CAAL)
**OMS**.......... Oral and Maxillofacial Surgery
**OMS**.......... Orbital Maneuvering System [*or Subsystem*] [*NASA*]
**OMS**.......... Orbital Multifunction Satellite
**OMS**.......... Ordnance Machine Shop
**OMS**.......... Organic Mass Spectroscopy
**OMS**.......... Organisation Mondiale de la Sante [*World Health Organization - WHO*] [*Switzerland*]
**OMS**.......... Organizational Maintenance Shop [*Army*]
**OMS**.......... Organizational Maintenance Squadron [*Air Force*] (MCD)
**OMS**.......... Organizational Maintenance Support
**OMS**.......... Oriental Missionary Society [*Later, OMS International*] (EA)
**OM & S**..... Osteopathic Medicine and Surgery
**OMS**.......... Outdoor Microphone System
**OMS**.......... Output per Man Shift
**OMS**.......... Output Multiplex Synchronizer
**OMS**.......... Overnight Message Service [*Diversified Data Processing and Consulting, Inc.*] [*Oak Park, MI*] [*Telecommunications*] (TSSD)
**OMS**.......... Overseas Mission Society [*Defunct*] (EA)
**OMS**.......... Spectravac Power Conversion Systems, Inc., Mississauga, Ontario [*Library symbol*] [*National Library of Canada*] (NLC)
**OMSA**....... Offshore Marine Service Association [*New Orleans, LA*] (EA)
**OMSA**....... Orders and Medals Society of America (EA)

**OMSA** ....... Otitis Media, Suppurative, Acute [*Medicine*]
**OMSA** ....... Seaman Apprentice, Opticalman, Striker [*Navy rating*]
**OMSA** ....... Simcoe County Archives, Minesing, Ontario [*Library symbol*] [*National Library of Canada*] (NLC)
**OMSAPC** ... Office of Mobile Source Air Pollution Control [*Environmental Protection Agency*]
**OMSC** ....... Organisation Mondiale pour la Systemique et la Cybernetique [*World Organization of Systems and Cybernetics*] (EAIO)
**OMSC** ....... Otitis Media, Suppurative, Chronic [*Medicine*]
**OMSDG** .... Maxville Branch, Stormount, Dundas, and Glengarry County Public Library, Ontario [*Library symbol*] [*National Library of Canada*] (NLC)
**Om Sea** ...... Omond's Law of the Sea [*1916*] [*A publication*] (DLA)
**OMSF** ........ Office of Manned Space Flight [*NASA*]
**OMSF** ........ Office of Minerals and Solid Fuels [*Formerly, OMM*] [*Abolished, 1971*] [*Department of the Interior*]
**OMSG** ....... Official Mail Study Group (EA)
**OMSGM** ... Ottendorfer Memorial Series of Germanic Monographs [*A publication*]
**OMSI** ......... Oregon Museum of Science and Industry
**OMSITE** ... Oral and Maxillofacial Surgery In-Training Examination
**OMSJ** ........ Sharjah/International [*United Arab Emirates*] [*ICAO location identifier*] (ICLI)
**OMSJB** ..... St. Jean Bosco Library, Matachewan, Ontario [*Library symbol*] [*National Library of Canada*] (BIB)
**OMSK** ....... Smith, Kline & French Canada Ltd., Mississauga, Ontario [*Library symbol*] [*National Library of Canada*] (NLC)
**Omsk Inst Inz Zeleznodoroz Transporta Naucn Trudy** ... Omskii Institut Inzenerov Zeleznodoroznogo Transporta. Naucnye Trudy [*A publication*]
**Omsk Med Zhurnal** ... Omskii Meditsinskii Zhurnal [*A publication*]
**OMSLMSq** ... Organizational Missile Maintenance Squadron [*Air Force*]
**OMSM** ...... Medical Library, Syntex, Inc., Mississauga, Ontario [*Library symbol*] [*National Library of Canada*] (NLC)
**OMS/MP** ... Operational Mode Summary/Mission Profiles (MCD)
**OMSMT** ... South Marysburgh Township Public Library, Milford, Ontario [*Library symbol*] [*National Library of Canada*] (BIB)
**OMsn** ......... Mason Public Library, Mason, OH [*Library symbol*] [*Library of Congress*] (LCLS)
**OMSN** ....... Seaman, Opticalman, Striker [*Navy rating*]
**OMS Nouv** ... Nouvelles. Organisation Mondiale de la Sante [*A publication*]
**OMSP** ....... Operational Maintenance Support Plan [*NASA*] (MCD)
**OMSq** ....... Organizational Maintenance Squadron [*Air Force*] (AFM)
**OMSRADS** ... Optimum Mix of Short Range Air Defense Systems
**OMST** ....... Object Manipulation Speed Test
**OMT** .......... McKellar Township Public Library, Ontario [*Library symbol*] [*National Library of Canada*] (NLC)
**OMT** .......... Metropolitan Toronto Library, Multilanguage Service [*UTLAS symbol*]
**OMT** .......... O-Methylthreonine [*Biochemistry*]
**OMT** .......... Ocean Marine Technology [*Vancouver Stock Exchange symbol*]
**OMT** .......... Office of Manufacturing Technology [*DARCOM*] [*Army*] (RDA)
**OMT** .......... Officiating Minister to the Troops [*British*]
**OMT** .......... Ohio Mattress Co. [*NYSE symbol*] (SPSG)
**OMT** .......... Old Merchant Taylors [*School*] [*British*] (ROG)
**OMT** .......... Oleoyl Methyl Taurate [*Organic chemistry*]
**OMT** .......... Ordnance Maintenance Truck [*British*]
**OMT** .......... Organizational Maintenance Technician [*Army*] (AABC)
**OMT** .......... Organizational Maintenance Trainer (MCD)
**OMT** .......... Ortho-Mycaminosyltylonolide [*Antibacterial compound*]
**OMT** .......... Orthomode Transducer [*Electronics*]
**OMT** .......... Orthotropic Multicell Tank
**OMT** .......... Other Military Target
**OMTA** ....... Ovulation Method Teachers Association (EA)
**OMTBP** ..... Octamethyltetrabenzporphyrin [*Organic chemistry*]
**OMTC** ....... Ontario Ministry of Transportation and Communications [*Downsview, ON*] [*Telecommunications*] (TSSD)
**OMTN** ....... Other Military Teletypewriter Network (CET)
**OMTNS** .... Over Mountains [*Meteorology*] (FAAC)
**OMTR** ....... Officer Master Tape Record [*Army*] (AABC)
**OMTS** ....... Organizational Maintenance Test Station [*Army*]
**OMtsjC** ...... College of Mount St. Joseph-On-The-Ohio, Mount St. Joseph, OH [*Library symbol*] [*Library of Congress*] (LCLS)
**OMTSS** ..... Ordnance Multiple-Purpose Tactical Satellite System
**OMtv** ......... Mount Vernon Public Library, Mount Vernon, OH [*Library symbol*] [*Library of Congress*] (LCLS)
**OMtvN** ...... Mount Vernon Nazarene College, Mount Vernon, OH [*Library symbol*] [*Library of Congress*] (LCLS)
**OMU** ......... Operational Mock-Up
**OMU** ......... Operative Mechanics' Union [*British*]
**OMU** ......... Optical Measuring Unit (KSC)
**OMUC** ....... Upper Canada Village, Morrisburg, Ontario [*Library symbol*] [*National Library of Canada*] (NLC)
**OMV** .......... Orbital Maneuvering Vehicle [*NASA*]
**OMV** .......... Oxygen Manual Valve (NASA)
**OMVC** ....... Mattice-Val Cote Public Library, Mattice, Ontario [*Library symbol*] [*National Library of Canada*] (BIB)
**OMVC** ....... Open Mitral Valve Commissurotomy [*Medicine*]
**OMVG** ....... Organisation pour la Mise en Valeur du Fleuve Gambie [*Gambia River Basin Organisation*] (EAIO)
**OM-VPE** ... Organometallic Vapor Phase Epitaxy [*Also, OM-CVD, MO-CVD, MO-VPE*] [*Semiconductor technology*]
**OMVTO** .... Office Motor Vehicle Transportation Officer [*Army*] (AABC)
**OMVUIL** .. Operating Motor Vehicle under the Influence of Liquor [*Traffic offense charge*]
**OMVWI** .... Operating Motor Vehicle while Intoxicated [*Traffic offense charge*]
**OMW** ........ Omak [*Washington*] [*Seismograph station code, US Geological Survey*] (SEIS)
**OMWM** .... Open Marsh Water Managed [*Ecology*]
**OMX** .......... Xerox Research Centre of Canada, Mississauga, Ontario [*Library symbol*] [*National Library of Canada*] (NLC)
**OMZ** .......... Oamaru [*New Zealand*] [*Seismograph station code, US Geological Survey*] (SEIS)
**O Mz** .......... Oesterreichische Musikzeitschrift [*A publication*]
**OMZ** .......... Oxygen-Minimum Zone [*Oceanography*]
**OMZ** .......... Oxymorphonazine [*An analgesic*]
**OMZSA** .... Orszagos Magyar Zsido Segitoe Akcio [*A publication*]
**ON** ............ Air Nauru [*Republic of Nauru*] [*ICAO designator*] (FAAC)
**ON** ............ Central Branch, Nepean Public Library, Ontario [*Library symbol*] [*National Library of Canada*] (NLC)
**ON** ............ McKinley Memorial Library, Niles, OH [*Library symbol*] [*Library of Congress*] (LCLS)
**ON** ............ New Order [*Revolutionary group*] [*Italy*]
**ON** ............ Octane Number [*Fuel terminology*]
**ON** ............ Oculonasal [*Anatomy*]
**ON** ............ Off Normal
**ON** ............ Office Nurse
**ON** ............ Official Number (DS)
**O & N** ........ Old and New [*A publication*]
**ON** ............ Old Norse [*Language, etc.*]
**ON** ............ Old Northwest [*A publication*]
**ON** ............ Oligonucleotide [*Chemistry*]
**ON** ............ Omega Neuron [*Neuroanatomy*]
**ON** ............ Omni Nocte [*Every Night*] [*Pharmacy*]
**ON** ............ Oncology [*Medical specialty*] (DHSM)
**ON** ............ Onions (ROG)
**On** ............ Onoma [*A publication*]
**On** ............ Onomastica [*A publication*]
**ON** ............ Onorevole [*Honorable*] (EY)
**ON** ............ Ontario [*Canadian province*] [*Postal code*]
**ON** ............ Opera News [*A publication*]
**ON** ............ Operation Notice (AAG)
**ON** ............ Optic Nerve [*Anatomy*]
**ON** ............ Orchestra News [*A publication*]
**O/N** ........... Order Notify [*Bill of lading*] [*Shipping*]
**ON** ............ Oregon [*Obsolete*] (ROG)
**ON** ............ Orientalia Neerlandica [*Leiden, 1948*] [*A publication*]
**ON** ............ Original Negative (MCD)
**ON** ............ Orthopedic Nurse
**ON** ............ Our Neighbours [*A publication*]
**O/N** ........... Own Name
**ONA** .......... Nakina Public Library, Ontario [*Library symbol*] [*National Library of Canada*] (BIB)
**ONA** .......... Office of National Assessments [*Australia*] (MCD)
**ONA** .......... Onahama [*Japan*] [*Seismograph station code, US Geological Survey*] (SEIS)
**ONA** .......... Oneita Industries, Inc. [*AMEX symbol*] (SPSG)
**ONA** .......... Open Network Architecture [*Data processing*]
**ONA** .......... Overseas National Airways, Inc.
**ONA** .......... Overseas News Agency
**ONA** .......... Winona, MN [*Location identifier*] [*FAA*] (FAAL)
**ONAC** ........ Office National du Commerce Exterieur [*National Office of External Trade*] [*Burkina Faso*] (EY)
**ONAC** ........ Office of Noise Abatement and Control [*Environmental Protection Agency*]
**ONAC** ........ Operating Network Advisory Committee [*NERComP*]
**ONAIS** ...... Organization of North American Indian Students (EA)
**ONA J** ....... Orthopedic Nurses' Association. Journal [*A publication*]
**ONAL** ........ Off-Net Access Line [*Telecommunications*] (TEL)
**ONAP** ........ Orbit Navigation Analysis Program
**ONAP** ........ Organisation Nationale d'Anti-Pauvrete [*Canada*]
**ONATOUR** ... Office de la Tourbe du Burundi [*Development organization*] [*Burundi*] (EY)
**O-NAV** ...... On-Board Navigation (MCD)
**ONAX** ........ Overseas National Airways, Inc. [*Air carrier designation symbol*]
**ONb** ........... New Breman Public Library, New Breman, OH [*Library symbol*] [*Library of Congress*] (LCLS)
**ONB** ........... North Bay Public Library, Ontario [*Library symbol*] [*National Library of Canada*] (NLC)
**ONB** ........... Octane Number Barrel [*Fuel terminology*]
**ONB** ........... Old Natura Brevium [*A publication*] (DLA)
**ONB** ........... Ortho-Nitrobiphenyl [*Organic chemistry*]
**ONBA** ........ Centre de Ressources, Ecole Secondaire Algonquin, North Bay, Ontario [*Library symbol*] [*National Library of Canada*] (NLC)
**ONBC** ........ Ouachita National Bancshares [*NASDAQ symbol*] (NQ)
**ONBCC** ..... Canadore College, North Bay, Ontario [*Library symbol*] [*National Library of Canada*] (NLC)
**ONBD** ........ On Board (NASA)

**ONBK**........ ONBANCorp, Inc. [*NASDAQ symbol*] (NQ)
**ONBM**........ Belmont and Methuen Township Public Library, Nephton, Ontario [*Library symbol*] [*National Library of Canada*] (BIB)
**ONBNU**.... Nipissing University College, North Bay, Ontario [*Library symbol*] [*National Library of Canada*] (NLC)
**ONBOSUB**... On Board a Submarine [*Navy*]
**ONBOWCOM**... Duty on Board that Vessel when Placed in Commission [*Navy*]
**ONBOWSERV**... Duty on Board that Vessel when Placed in Service [*Navy*]
**ONBP**........ Staff Library, North Bay Psychiatric Hospital, Ontario [*Library symbol*] [*National Library of Canada*] (NLC)
**ONBRDY**.. Ontogenesis of the Brain [*A publication*]
**ONBT**........ Orbiter Neutral Buoyancy Trainer [*NASA*] (MCD)
**ONBWF**.... West Ferris Secondary School, North Bay, Ontario [*Library symbol*] [*National Library of Canada*] (NLC)
**ONC**.......... Confederation High School, Nepean, Ontario [*Library symbol*] [*National Library of Canada*] (NLC)
**ONC**.......... Office of Narcotics Coordinator [*Later, NARCOG*] [*CIA*]
**ONC**.......... Office of New Careers [*HEW*]
**ONC**.......... Olivet Nazarene College [*Kankakee, IL*]
**Onc**............ Oncologia [*A publication*]
**onc**............ Ontario [*MARC country of publication code*] [*Library of Congress*] (LCCP)
**ONC**.......... Operational Navigation Charts [*Air Force*]
**ONC**.......... Optimists National Corps [*British military*] (DMA)
**ONC**.......... Ordinary National Certificate [*British*]
**ONC**.......... Orthopedic Nursing Certificate
**ONC**.......... Overall NATO Command (NATG)
**ONCB**........ Centennial Branch, Nepean Public Library, Ontario [*Library symbol*] [*National Library of Canada*] (NLC)
**ONCF**........ Office National des Chemins de Fer [*Moroccan Railways*]
**ONCFM**.... Office National des Chemins de Fer du Maroc [*Moroccan Railways*] (DCTA)
**ONcM**........ Muskingum College, New Concord, OH [*Library symbol*] [*Library of Congress*] (LCLS)
**ONCMM**... Cosby, Mason, and Martland Public Library, Noelville, Ontario [*Library symbol*] [*National Library of Canada*] (NLC)
**ONCN**....... [*An*] O'Neill Concordance [*A publication*]
**ONCOA**..... Oncologia [*A publication*]
**Oncodev Biol Med**... Oncodevelopmental Biology and Medicine [*Netherlands*] [*A publication*]
**Oncol Nurs Forum**... Oncology Nursing Forum [*A publication*]
**Oncol Radiol**... Oncologia si Radiologia [*A publication*]
**ONCORE**.. On-Command Restartable (MCD)
**ONCR**........ On Campus Review [*A publication*]
**ONCR**........ Oncor, Inc. [*NASDAQ symbol*] (NQ)
**ONCRC**..... Central Resource Centre, Carleton Roman Catholic School Board, Nepean, Ontario [*Library symbol*] [*National Library of Canada*] (NLC)
**ONCS**........ Oncogene Science, Inc. [*NASDAQ symbol*] (NQ)
**ONCU**....... Cumberland Township Library, Navan, Ontario [*Library symbol*] [*National Library of Canada*] (BIB)
**OND**.......... Office National du Ducroire [*Export Credits Guarantee Office*] [*Belgium*] (GEA)
**OND**.......... Office of Neighborhood Development (OICC)
**OND**.......... Office for Network Development [*National Library of Canada*] [*Ottawa, ON*] [*Telecommunications service*] (TSSD)
**OND**.......... Ondangua [*Namibia*] [*Airport symbol*] (OAG)
**OND**.......... Operator Need Date (NASA)
**OND**.......... Ophthalmic Nursing Diploma
**OND**.......... Ordinary National Diploma [*British*]
**OND**.......... Orthopaedic Nursing Diploma [*British*]
**OND**.......... Other Neurological Disorders
**ONDA**....... Norwich and District Archives, Norwich, Ontario [*Library symbol*] [*National Library of Canada*] (BIB)
**ONDE**........ Office of Naval Disability Evaluation (NVT)
**Onde Elec**.. Onde Electrique [*A publication*]
**Onde Electr**... Onde Electrique [*A publication*]
**Onde Electr Suppl**... Onde Electrique. Supplement [*France*] [*A publication*]
**Onderstepoort J Vet Res**... Onderstepoort Journal of Veterinary Research [*A publication*]
**Onderstepoort J Vet Sci**... Onderstepoort Journal of Veterinary Science and Animal Industry [*A publication*]
**Onderstepoort J Vet Sci Anim Ind**... Onderstepoort Journal of Veterinary Science and Animal Industry [*A publication*]
**Onderst J V**... Onderstepoort Journal of Veterinary Research [*A publication*]
**ONDS**........ Dipix Systems Ltd., Nepean, Ontario [*Library symbol*] [*National Library of Canada*] (NLC)
**ONE**.......... Banc One Corp. [*NYSE symbol*] (SPSG)
**ONE**.......... Current Tech [*Vancouver Stock Exchange symbol*]
**ONe**.......... Nelsonville Public Library, Nelsonville, OH [*Library symbol*] [*Library of Congress*] (LCLS)
**ONE**.......... Newmarket Public Library, Ontario [*Library symbol*] [*National Library of Canada*] (NLC)
**ONE**.......... Northeastern Ohio University, College of Medicine, Rootstown, OH [*OCLC symbol*] (OCLC)
**ONE**.......... Office National de l'Energie [*National Energy Board - NEB*] [*Canada*]
**ONE**.......... Office Network Exchange [*Honeywell, Inc.*]
**ONE**.......... Onepusu [*Solomon Islands*] [*Airport symbol*] [*Obsolete*] (OAG)
**ONE**.......... Onerahi [*Whangarei*] [*New Zealand*] [*Seismograph station code, US Geological Survey*] (SEIS)
**ONE**.......... Optimum Nutritional Effectiveness [*Brand name of dog food*] [*Ralston Purina Co.*]
**O'Neal Neg L**... O'Neal's Negro Law of South Carolina [*A publication*] (DLA)
**ONeH**........ Hocking Technical College, Nelsonville, OH [*Library symbol*] [*Library of Congress*] (LCLS)
**ONELAC**... Newburgh Branch, Lennox and Addington County, Ontario [*Library symbol*] [*National Library of Canada*] (BIB)
**ONEMRCM**... BCC Library, CANMET, Energy, Mines, and Resources Canada [*Bibliotheque du CBC, CANMET, Energie, Mines, et Ressources Canada*], Nepean, Ontario [*Library symbol*] [*National Library of Canada*] (NLC)
**ONEO**....... Office of Navajo Economic Opportunity
**ONEP**........ Pickering College, Newmarket, Ontario [*Library symbol*] [*National Library of Canada*] (NLC)
**ONEPI**....... Office National d'Edition, de Presse, et d'Imprimerie [*Publisher*] [*Benin*] (EY)
**ONERA Note Tech**... Office National d'Etudes et de Recherches Aerospatiales. Note Technique [*A publication*]
**ONERA Publ**... Office National d'Etudes et de Recherches Aerospatiales. Publication [*A publication*]
**ONESJ**...... Orient. Report of the Society for Near Eastern Studies in Japan [*A publication*]
**ONEU**........ Neustadt Village Public Library, Ontario [*Library symbol*] [*National Library of Canada*] (NLC)
**ONew**........ Newark Public Library, Newark, OH [*Library symbol*] [*Library of Congress*] (LCLS)
**ONewU**...... Ohio State University, Newark Campus, Newark, OH [*Library symbol*] [*Library of Congress*] (LCLS)
**ONEX**........ Ontario Native Experience [*A publication*]
**ONF**.......... Niagara Falls Public Library, Ontario [*Library symbol*] [*National Library of Canada*] (NLC)
**ONF**.......... Office National du Film du Canada [*National Film Board of Canada - NFB*]
**ONF**.......... Old Norman French [*Language, etc.*]
**ONF**.......... Old Northern French [*Language, etc.*]
**ONF**.......... Optic Nerve Fiber [*Anatomy*]
**ONFA**........ Acres Consulting Services Ltd., Niagara Falls, Ontario [*Library symbol*] [*National Library of Canada*] (NLC)
**ONFCY**..... Cyanamid, Niagara Falls, Ontario [*Library symbol*] [*National Library of Canada*] (NLC)
**ONFJC**...... John Coutts Library Services Ltd., Niagara Falls, Ontario [*Library symbol*] [*National Library of Canada*] (NLC)
**ONFLC**...... Lanmer Consultants Ltd., Niagara Falls, Ontario [*Library symbol*] [*National Library of Canada*] (NLC)
**ONFM**....... On or Nearest Full Moon [*Freemasonry*] (ROG)
**ONFR**........ Old Northern French [*Language, etc.*]
**ONFWM**... Willoughby Historical Museum, Niagara Falls, Ontario [*Library symbol*] [*National Library of Canada*] (BIB)
**ONFWPL**... W. P. London & Associates, Niagara Falls, Ontario [*Library symbol*] [*National Library of Canada*] (NLC)
**ONG**.......... Donalsonville, GA [*Location identifier*] [*FAA*] (FAAL)
**ONG**.......... Mornington Island [*Australia*] [*Airport symbol*] (OAG)
**ONG**.......... Ongar [*England*]
**ONG**.......... Ongoro [*Peru*] [*Seismograph station code, US Geological Survey*] [*Closed*] (SEIS)
**ONGA**....... Overseas Number Group Analysis [*Telecommunications*] (TEL)
**ONGC**........ Office des Normes Generales du Canada
**ONGRT**..... North Gower Branch, Rideau Township Library, Ontario [*Library symbol*] [*National Library of Canada*] (BIB)
**ONGS**........ Office of National Geodetic Survey [*National Ocean Survey*]
**ONH**.......... Office of Naval History [*Also, OFFNAVHIST*]
**ONH**.......... Oneonta [*New York*] [*Airport symbol*] (OAG)
**ONHI**........ Niagara Historical Society, Niagara-On-The-Lake, Ontario [*Library symbol*] [*National Library of Canada*] (NLC)
**ONHIC**...... ODPHP [*Office of Disease Prevention and Health Promotion*] National Health Information Center (EISS)
**ONI**........... Moanamani [*Indonesia*] [*Airport symbol*] (OAG)
**ONI**........... Nipigon Public Library, Ontario [*Library symbol*] [*National Library of Canada*] (NLC)
**ONI**........... Office of Naval Intelligence
**ONI**........... Oficina Nacional de Informacion [*National Information Office*] [*Press agency*] [*Peru*]
**ONI**........... Oni [*USSR*] [*Seismograph station code, US Geological Survey*] (SEIS)
**ONI**........... Operator Number Identification [*Bell System*]
**ONIN**......... Ontario Indian [*A publication*]
**ONIO**......... Office of Naval Inspectors of Ordnance
**ONIP**......... Office of National Industry Promotion [*Bureau of Apprenticeship and Training*] [*Department of Labor*]
**ONIX**......... Onyx + IMI, Inc. [*NASDAQ symbol*] (NQ)
**ONJ**........... Olivia Newton-John [*Singer*]
**ONJSW**..... J. S. Woodsworth Secondary School, Nepean, Ontario [*Library symbol*] [*National Library of Canada*] (NLC)
**On Jug**....... Onomastica Jugoslavica [*A publication*]
**Onk**............ Targum Onkelos (BJA)

**ONKAA**..... Onsen Kagaku [*A publication*]
**ONKIA**...... Onken Kiyo [*A publication*]
**ONKLA**..... Onkologiya [*A publication*]
**ONKOB**..... Onsen Kogakkaishi [*A publication*]
**ONL**........... New Liskeard Public Library, Ontario [*Library symbol*] [*National Library of Canada*] (NLC)
**ONL**........... Office of Naval Liaison [*NASA*] (KSC)
**ONL**........... Ohio Northern University, Law Library, Ada, OH [*OCLC symbol*] (OCLC)
**ONL**........... O'Neill, NE [*Location identifier*] [*FAA*] (FAAL)
**ONL**........... Outer Nuclear Layer [*Anatomy*]
**ONL**........... Overnight Loan (ADA)
**ONLA**........ Our Native Land [*A publication*]
**ONLAC**...... Lennox and Addington Counties Public Library, Napanee, Ontario [*Library symbol*] [*National Library of Canada*] (NLC)
**ONLAH**..... Lennox and Addington Historical Society, Napanee, Ontario [*Library symbol*] [*National Library of Canada*] (BIB)
**ONLAM**.... Lennox and Addington Museum, Napanee, Ontario [*Library symbol*] [*National Library of Canada*] (NLC)
**On-Land Drill News** ... On-Land Drilling News [*A publication*]
**ONLICATS** ... Online Shared Cataloging System [*Data processing*]
**Online**........ Online Review [*A publication*]
**Online Data** ... Online Database Report [*A publication*]
**Online Database Rep** ... Online Database Report [*A publication*]
**Online Rev** ... Online Review [*A publication*]
**On-Line Rv** ... On-Line Review [*A publication*]
**ONlP**.......... Perry County District Library, New Lexington, OH [*Library symbol*] [*Library of Congress*] (LCLS)
**ONLS**........ Sunnidale Township Public Library, New Lowell, Ontario [*Library symbol*] [*National Library of Canada*] (BIB)
**ONLY**........ Online Yield [*Data processing*]
**ONM**......... Office of Naval Material [*Later, NMCOM*]
**ONM**......... Socorro, NM [*Location identifier*] [*FAA*] (FAAL)
**ONMB**....... Merivale Road Branch, Nepean Public Library, Ontario [*Library symbol*] [*National Library of Canada*] (BIB)
**ONMINST** ... Office of Naval Material Publication Type Instruction
**ONMPC**..... Office of Naval Material - Permanent Cadre
**ONMS**....... Orbiter Neutral Mass Spectrometer [*NASA*]
**ONMSS**..... Office of Nuclear Materials Safety and Safeguards [*Nuclear Regulatory Commission*]
**ONN**.......... Enkabe Contact [*A publication*]
**ONN**.......... Fort Meade, MD [*Location identifier*] [*FAA*] (FAAL)
**ONN**.......... O'Nyong-Nyong Virus
**ONNA**....... Ontario Naturalist [*A publication*]
**ONNI**......... Office of National Narcotics Intelligence [*Later, Drug Enforcement Administration*] [*Department of Justice*]
**ONNM**...... On or Nearest New Moon [*Freemasonry*] (ROG)
**ONO**.......... Norwood Public Library, Ontario [*Library symbol*] [*National Library of Canada*] (BIB)
**ONO**.......... Oculus [*A publication*]
**ONO**.......... Office of Naval Operations
**Ono**............ Onomastica [*A publication*]
**ONO**.......... Ontario, OR [*Location identifier*] [*FAA*] (FAAL)
**ONO**.......... Or Nearest Offer [*Business term*] (ADA)
**ONO**.......... Organization of News Ombudsmen (EA)
**ONOC**....... Oceania National Olympic Committees [*Australia*] (EAIO)
**ONocHE**.... Hoover Co., Engineering Division, North Canton, OH [*Library symbol*] [*Library of Congress*] (LCLS)
**ON-OFF**.... Oscillatory, Nonoscillatory Flip-Flop [*Data processing*]
**ONOL**........ Niagara-On-The-Lake Public Library, Ontario [*Library symbol*] [*National Library of Canada*] (BIB)
**Onom**......... Onomastica [*A publication*]
**Onom**......... Onomasticon [*of Eusebius*] (BJA)
**Onomast**.... Onomastica [*A publication*]
**Onomast Slavogerm** ... Onomastica Slavogermanica [*A publication*]
**ONOMAT** ... Onomatopoeia (ROG)
**ONO Meded** ... ONO [*Organisatie voor Natuurwetenschappelijk Onderzoek*] Mededeelingen [*A publication*]
**OnomJug**... Onomastica Jugoslavica [*A publication*]
**Onondaga Ac Sc Pr** ... Onondaga Academy of Science. Proceedings [*A publication*]
**Onondaga Hist As Sc S** ... Onondaga Historical Association. Science Series [*A publication*]
**ONOO**....... Outline NATO Operational Objective (MCD)
**ONOP**........ Office of Naval Officer Procurement
**Onore Angelo Celli 25o An Insegnamento** ... Onore del Professore Angelo Celli nel 25o Anno di Insegnamento [*A publication*]
**ONowdM**... Athenaeum of Ohio, Norwood, OH [*Library symbol*] [*Library of Congress*] (LCLS)
**ONOZ**....... Oil Nozzle
**ONP**........... Newport [*Oregon*] [*Airport symbol*] [*Obsolete*] (OAG)
**ONP**........... Office of National Programs [*Employment and Training Administration*] [*Department of Labor*]
**ONP**........... Ohio Nisi Prius Reports [*A publication*] (DLA)
**ONP**........... Old Newspaper [*Recycling*]
**ONP**........... Onex Packaging, Inc. [*Toronto Stock Exchange symbol*]
**ONP**........... Open Network Provision
**ONP**........... Operating Nursing Procedure
**ONP**........... Original Net Premium [*Insurance*] (AIA)
**ONP**........... Ortho-Nitrophenol [*Organic chemistry*]
**ONPA**......... Office of National Projects Administration [*Department of Labor*]
**ONPG**........ O-Nitrophenyl-beta-D-galactopyranoside [*Test*] [*Microbiology*]
**ONpK**......... Kent State University, Tuscarawas County Regional Campus, New Philadelphia, OH [*Library symbol*] [*Library of Congress*] (LCLS)
**ONPNS**..... Ohio Nisi Prius Reports, New Series [*1903-13*] [*A publication*] (DLA)
**ONPOSR**.. Office of Naval Petroleum and Oil Shale Reserves
**ONPR**......... One Price Clothing Stores, Inc. [*NASDAQ symbol*] (NQ)
**ONR**.......... Oboz Narodowo-Radykalny [*Radical Nationalist Camp*] [*Poland*] [*Political party*] (PPE)
**ONR**.......... Office of Naval Research [*Arlington, VA*]
**ONR**.......... Official Naval Reporter [*British*]
**ONR**.......... Ontario Northland Railway
**ONR**.......... Operational NonRADAR Directed Flights (NATG)
**ONR**.......... Original Net Rate [*Insurance*] (AIA)
**ONR**.......... Phillips Petroleum Co., Exploration and Product Library, Bartlesville, OK [*OCLC symbol*] (OCLC)
**ONR BR**.... Branch Office, Office of Naval Research
**ONRBRO** ... Office of Naval Research Branch Research Office
**ONRC**........ Office of Naval Research, Chicago
**ONRDB**..... Ruth E. Dickinson Branch, Nepean Public Library, Ontario [*Library symbol*] [*National Library of Canada*] (BIB)
**ONRL**........ Office of Naval Research, London
**ONRRR**..... Office of Naval Research Resident Representative
**ONRT**........ Online Real Time [*Data processing*] (ADA)
**ONR Tech Rep** ... ONR [*Office of Naval Research*] Technical Report [*US*] [*A publication*]
**ONRY**........ Ogdensburg Bridge & Port Authority [*AAR code*]
**ONS**........... Northwestern School of Law, Lewis and Clark College, Portland, OR [*OCLC symbol*] (OCLC)
**ONS**........... Oconee Nuclear Station (NRCH)
**ONS**........... Off-Normal Switch
**ONS**........... Omega Navigation System
**ONS**........... Oncology Nursing Society (EA)
**ONS**........... Onslow [*Australia*] [*Airport symbol*] [*Obsolete*] (OAG)
**ONS**........... Operational Needs Statement [*Army*]
**ONS**........... Oriental Numismatic Society [*Reading, Berkshire, England*] (EAIO)
**ONSDG**..... Newington Branch, Stormont, Dundas, and Glengarry County Library, Ontario [*Library symbol*] [*National Library of Canada*] (BIB)
**OnsE**.......... Ons Erfdeel [*A publication*]
**On Serv**...... On Service [*A publication*]
**On SG**........ Onomastica Slavogermanica [*A publication*]
**ONSHR**..... On Shore (FAAC)
**ONSIDIV** ... On-Sight Surveys Division
**Onsl NP**..... Onslow's Nisi Prius [*A publication*] (DLA)
**ONSM**....... Obrazcy Narodnoj Slovesnosti Mongolov [*A publication*]
**ONSMP**.... Obrazcy Narodnoj Slovesnosti Mongol'skich Plemen [*A publication*]
**ONSN**........ Oriental Numismatic Society. Newsletter [*A publication*]
**ONSOD**..... Omega Navigation System Operations Detail
**ONSOP**..... Oriental Numismatic Society. Occasional Paper [*A publication*]
**ONSR**........ Sir Robert Borden High School, Nepean, Ontario [*Library symbol*] [*National Library of Canada*] (BIB)
**ONT**........... Air Ontario Ltd. [*London, ON, Canada*] [*FAA designator*] (FAAC)
**ONT**........... Ontario [*Canadian province*]
**ONT**........... Ontario [*California*] [*Airport symbol*]
**ONT**........... Ontario City Library, Ontario, CA [*OCLC symbol*] (OCLC)
**ONT**........... Ontario Northland Railway [*AAR code*]
**Ont**............ Ontario Reports [*A publication*] (DLA)
**ONT**........... Our New Thread [*Clark thread designation*]
**Ont A**......... Ontario Appeals [*A publication*] (DLA)
**ONTAP**..... On-Line Training and Practice File [*Lockheed*] [*Data processing*]
**Ont App**..... Ontario Appeal Reports [*A publication*] (DLA)
**Ontario Ag Dept** ... Ontario. Department of Agriculture. Publication [*A publication*]
**Ontario Cons Reg** ... Ontario Consolidated Regulations [*Canada*] [*A publication*] (DLA)
**Ontario Dept Mines Geol Rept** ... Ontario. Department of Mines. Geological Report [*A publication*]
**Ontario Dept Mines Indus Mineral Rept** ... Ontario. Department of Mines. Industrial Mineral Report [*A publication*]
**Ontario Dept Mines Map** ... Ontario. Department of Mines. Map [*A publication*]
**Ontario Dept Mines Mineral Resources Circ** ... Ontario. Department of Mines. Mineral Resources Circular [*A publication*]
**Ontario Dept Mines Misc Paper** ... Ontario. Department of Mines. Miscellaneous Paper [*A publication*]
**Ontario Dept Mines Prelim Geochem Map** ... Ontario. Department of Mines. Preliminary Geochemical Map [*A publication*]
**Ontario Dept Mines Prelim Geol Map** ... Ontario. Department of Mines. Preliminary Geological Map [*A publication*]
**Ontario Dept Mines Prelim Map** ... Ontario. Department of Mines. Preliminary Map [*A publication*]
**Ontario Fuel Board Ann Rept** ... Ontario Fuel Board. Annual Report [*A publication*]

**Ontario Hist Soc Papers** ... Ontario Historical Society. Papers and Records [*A publication*]
**Ontario Med Rev** ... Ontario Medical Review [*A publication*]
**Ontario Miner Policy Background Pap** ... Ontario Mineral Policy. Background Paper [*A publication*]
**Ontario R** ... Ontario Review [*A publication*]
**Ontario Research Council Rept** ... Ontario Research Council. Report [*A publication*]
**Ont Bird Banding** ... Ontario Bird Banding [*A publication*]
**Ont Birds** ... Ontario Birds [*A publication*]
**Ont Bur Mines An Rp** ... Ontario. Bureau of Mines. Annual Report [*A publication*]
**Ont Bur Mines B** ... Ontario. Bureau of Mines. Bulletin [*A publication*]
**Ont 2d** ........ Ontario Reports, Second Series [*Canada*] [*A publication*] (DLA)
**Ont Dent** .... Ontario Dentist [*A publication*]
**Ont Dep Agric Food Publ** ... Ontario. Department of Agriculture and Food. Publication [*A publication*]
**Ont Dep Agric Publ** ... Ontario. Department of Agriculture. Publication [*A publication*]
**Ont Dep Mines Annu Rep** ... Ontario. Department of Mines. Annual Report [*A publication*]
**Ont Dep Mines Bull** ... Ontario. Department of Mines. Mines Inspection Branch. Bulletin [*A publication*]
**Ont Dep Mines Geol Circ** ... Ontario. Department of Mines. Geological Circular [*A publication*]
**Ont Dep Mines Geol Rep** ... Ontario. Department of Mines. Geological Report [*A publication*]
**Ont Dep Mines Ind Miner Rep** ... Ontario. Department of Mines. Industrial Mineral Report [*A publication*]
**Ont Dep Mines Miner Resour Circ** ... Ontario. Department of Mines. Mineral Resources Circular [*A publication*]
**Ont Dep Mines Misc Pap** ... Ontario. Department of Mines. Miscellaneous Paper [*A publication*]
**Ont Dep Mines North Aff Geol Rep** ... Ontario. Department of Mines and Northern Affairs. Geological Report [*A publication*]
**Ont Dep Mines North Aff Ind Miner Rep** ... Ontario. Department of Mines and Northern Affairs. Industrial Mineral Report [*A publication*]
**Ont Dep Mines North Aff Misc Pap** ... Ontario. Department of Mines and Northern Affairs. Miscellaneous Paper [*A publication*]
**Ont Dep Mines Rep** ... Ontario. Department of Mines. Report [*A publication*]
**Ont Dig** ...... Digest of Ontario Case Law [*A publication*] (DLA)
**Ont Div Mines Geol Rep** ... Ontario. Division of Mines. Geological Report [*A publication*]
**Ont Div Mines Geosci Rep** ... Ontario. Division of Mines. Geoscience Report [*A publication*]
**Ont Div Mines Ind Miner Rep** ... Ontario. Division of Mines. Industrial Mineral Report [*A publication*]
**Ont Div Mines Misc Pap** ... Ontario. Division of Mines. Miscellaneous Paper [*A publication*]
**Ont Div Mines Prelim Map Geol Ser** ... Ontario. Division of Mines. Preliminary Map. Geological Series [*A publication*]
**Ont Div Mines Prelim Map Geophys Ser** ... Ontario. Division of Mines. Preliminary Map. Geophysical Series [*A publication*]
**Ont Ed** ....... Ontario Education [*A publication*]
**ONTED** ..... Ontario Technologist [*A publication*]
**Ont El Cas** ... Ontario Election Cases [*1884-1900*] [*Canada*] [*A publication*] (DLA)
**Ont Elec** ..... Ontario Election Cases [*1884-1900*] [*Canada*] [*A publication*] (DLA)
**Ont Elec C** ... Ontario Election Cases [*1884-1900*] [*Canada*] [*A publication*] (DLA)
**Ont Elect** .... Ontario Election Cases [*1884-1900*] [*Canada*] [*A publication*] (DLA)
**ONTERIS** ... Ontario Education Resources Information System [*Ontario Ministry of Education*] [*Toronto*] [*Information service or system*] (IID)
**Ont Field Biol** ... Ontario Field Biologist [*A publication*]
**Ont Fish Wildl Rev** ... Ontario Fish and Wildlife Review [*A publication*]
**Ont Fld Biol** ... Ontario Field Biologist [*A publication*]
**Ont For** ...... Ontario Forests [*A publication*]
**ONTG** ........ Oral Nitroglycerine [*Medicine*]
**Ont Geography** ... Ontario Geography [*A publication*]
**Ont Geol Surv Misc Pap** ... Ontario. Geological Survey. Miscellaneous Paper [*A publication*]
**Ont His S** ... Ontario Historical Society. Papers and Records [*A publication*]
**Ont Hist** ..... Ontario History [*A publication*]
**Ont Hortic Exp Stn Prod Lab Rep** ... Ontario. Horticulture Experiment Stations and Products Laboratory. Report [*A publication*]
**Ont Hydro-Res News** ... Ontario Hydro-Research News [*A publication*]
**Ont Hydro-Res Q** ... Ontario Hydro-Research Quarterly [*A publication*]
**Ont Hydro Res Rev** ... Ontario Hydro-Research News. Review [*A publication*]
**Ont Ind Arts Bul** ... Ontario Industrial Arts Association. Bulletin [*A publication*]
**Ont Ind Waste Conf Proc** ... Ontario Industrial Waste Conference. Proceedings [*A publication*]
**Ont J Educ Res** ... Ontario Journal of Educational Research [*A publication*]
**Ont L** .......... Ontario Law Reports [*A publication*] (DLA)
**Ont Lib R** ... Ontario Library Review [*A publication*]
**Ont Libr Rev** ... Ontario Library Review [*A publication*]
**Ont LJ** ....... Ontario Law Journal [*A publication*] (DLA)
**Ont LJ (NS)** ... Ontario Law Journal, New Series [*A publication*] (DLA)
**Ont LR** ....... Ontario Reports [*A publication*] (DLA)
**Ont L Rep** .. Ontario Law Reports [*A publication*] (DLA)
**Ont Math G** ... Ontario Mathematics Gazette [*A publication*]
**Ont Med Rev** ... Ontario Medical Review [*A publication*]
**Ont Minist Agric Food Publ** ... Ontario. Ministry of Agriculture and Food. Publication [*A publication*]
**Ontog Brain** ... Ontogenesis of the Brain [*A publication*]
**Ontog Razvit Zhivotn** ... Ontogeneticheskoe Razvitie Zhivotnykh [*A publication*]
**ONTOLT** .. Onion, Tomato, or Lettuce [*Notation on restaurant checks*]
**Ont Pet Inst Annu Conf Proc** ... Ontario Petroleum Institute. Annual Conference. Proceedings [*Canada*] [*A publication*]
**Ont Pr** ........ Ontario Practice [*A publication*] (DLA)
**Ont PR** ...... Ontario Practice Reports [*A publication*] (DLA)
**Ont Pr Rep** ... Ontario Practice Reports [*A publication*] (DLA)
**Ont R** ......... Ontario Reports [*A publication*] (DLA)
**ONTR** ........ Orders Not to Resuscitate [*Medicine*]
**Ont Reg** ...... Ontario Regulations [*Canada*] [*A publication*] (DLA)
**Ont Regs** .... Ontario Regulations [*Canada*] [*A publication*] (DLA)
**Ont Rev Regs** ... Ontario Revised Regulations [*Canada*] [*A publication*] (DLA)
**Ont Rev Stat** ... Ontario Revised Statutes [*Canada*] [*A publication*] (DLA)
**Ont Rgt** ...... Ontario Regiment [*Canada*] (DMA)
**Ont R & WN** ... Ontario Reports and Ontario Weekly Notes [*Canada*] [*A publication*] (DLA)
**Ont Stat** ..... Ontario Statutes [*Canada*] [*A publication*] (DLA)
**Ont Tax Rep (CCH)** ... Ontario Tax Reporter (Commerce Clearing House) [*A publication*] (DLA)
**Ont Technol** ... Ontario Technologist [*A publication*]
**Ont Vet Coll Rep** ... Ontario Veterinary College. Report [*A publication*]
**Ont Week N** ... Ontario Weekly Notes [*A publication*] (DLA)
**Ont Week R** ... Ontario Weekly Reporter [*A publication*] (DLA)
**Ont Wkly N** ... Ontario Weekly Notes [*A publication*] (DLA)
**Ont Wkly Rep** ... Ontario Weekly Reporter [*A publication*] (DLA)
**Ont WN** ..... Ontario Weekly Notes [*A publication*] (DLA)
**Ont WR** ..... Ontario Weekly Reporter [*A publication*] (DLA)
**Ont WR Op** ... Ontario Weekly Reporter. Opinions of United States Attorneys General [*A publication*] (DLA)
**ONU** .......... Ohio Northern University [*Ada, OH*]
**ONU** .......... Ohio Northern University, Ada, OH [*OCLC symbol*] (OCLC)
**ONU** .......... Ono-I-Lau [*Fiji*] [*Airport symbol*] [*Obsolete*] (OAG)
**ONU** .......... Organisation des Nations Unies [*United Nations*] [*French*]
**ONU** .......... Organizzazione Nazioni Unite [*United Nations*] [*Italian*]
**ONUC** ....... Organisation des Nations Unies au Congo [*United Nations Organization in the Congo*]
**ONUDI** ...... Organisation des Nations Unies pour le Developpement Industriel [*United Nations Industrial Development Organization*]
**ONU Intra LR** ... Ohio Northern University. Intramural Law Review [*A publication*] (DLA)
**ONULP** ..... Ontario New Universities Library Project
**ONU LR** .... Ohio Northern University. Law Review [*A publication*]
**Onuphr De Interp Voc Eccles** ... Onuphrius. De Interpretatione Vocum Ecclesiae [*A publication*] (DLA)
**ONV** .......... Organisations Nationales Volontaires [*Canada*]
**ONW** ......... Office of Naval Weapons
**ONW** ......... On Watch
**ONW** ......... Oregon & Northwestern Railroad Co. [*AAR code*]
**ONWI** ....... Office of Nuclear Waste Isolation (MCD)
**ONWL** ....... Whitefish Lake Band Public Library, Naughton, Ontario [*Library symbol*] [*National Library of Canada*] (NLC)
**ONWS** ....... Office of Naval Weather Service
**ONX** .......... Colon [*Panama*] [*Airport symbol*] (OAG)
**ONX** .......... Mount Olive, NC [*Location identifier*] [*FAA*] (FAAL)
**ONX** .......... Onyx Petroleum Exploration Co. Ltd. [*Toronto Stock Exchange symbol*]
**ONY** .......... Olney, TX [*Location identifier*] [*FAA*] (FAAL)
**OO** ............ Belgium [*Aircraft nationality and registration mark*] (FAAC)
**OO** ............ Naval Oceanographic Office [*Also known as NOO; formerly, HO, NHO, USNHO*]
**OO** ............ Oberlin College, Oberlin, OH [*Library symbol*] [*Library of Congress*] (LCLS)
**OO** ............ Object-Oriented (BYTE)
**OO** ............ Observation Officer [*Military*]
**OO** ............ Ocean Outlook (EA)
**OO** ............ Oceanographic Office
**O/O** ........... Office of Origin (AFM)
**OO** ............ Ohio Opinions [*A publication*] (DLA)
**OO** ............ Ohne Ort [*Without Place of Publication*] [*Bibliography*] [*German*]
**O/O** ........... Oil/Ore [*Ship*] (DS)
**OO** ............ Old Orkney [*Whisky*] (ROG)
**O/O** ........... On Orbit (MCD)
**OO** ............ On Order
**OO** ............ Once Over [*To examine cursorily*] [*Slang*]
**OO** ............ Oophorectomized [*Gynecology*]
**OO** ............ Open Order
**OO** ............ Operation Order [*Military*]

**O & O**......... Operational and Organizational (RDA)
**OO**............ Operations Office [*Energy Research and Development Administration*]
**OO**............ Operations Officer [*Navy*] [*British*]
**O/O**........... Order Of [*Business term*]
**OO**............ Orderly Officer [*British*]
**OO**............ Ordnance Office [*or Officer*]
**O & O**......... Organization and Operation
**OO**............ Orthopaedics Overseas (EA)
**OO**............ Osobyi Otdel [*Counterintelligence surveillance unit in military formation until 1943*] [*USSR*]
**O to O**........ Out to Out [*Technical drawings*]
**OO**............ Own Occupation [*Banking*]
**O & O**......... Owned and Operated
**OO**............ Societe Belge de Transports Aeriens [*Belgium*] [*ICAO designator*] (FAAC)
**O4O**........... October 4th Organization (EA)
**OOA**........... Object of Affections [*Slang*]
**OOA**........... Object-Oriented Analysis [*Data processing*]
**OOA**........... Office of the Americas [*An association*] (EA)
**OOA**........... Office of Ocean Affairs [*Navy*]
**OOA**........... Olive Oil Association (EA)
**OOA**........... Optimum Orbital Altitude (AAG)
**OOA**........... Oskaloosa, IA [*Location identifier*] [*FAA*] (FAAL)
**OOA**........... Out of Action (MCD)
**OOA**........... Out of Area (NVT)
**OOA**........... Owner Operators of America [*Boston, NY*] (EA)
**OOA**........... Public Archives [*Archives Publiques*] Ottawa, Ontario [*Library symbol*] [*National Library of Canada*] (NLC)
**OOAA**.......... Olive Oil Association of America [*Later, OOA*] (EA)
**OOAC**.......... Algonquin College of Applied Arts and Technology, Ottawa, Ontario [*Library symbol*] [*National Library of Canada*] (NLC)
**OOACC**......... Colonel By Campus, Algonquin College of Applied Arts and Technology, Ottawa, Ontario [*Library symbol*] [*National Library of Canada*] (NLC)
**OOACF**......... Alta Vista Branch, Ontario Cancer Foundation, Ottawa, Ontario [*Library symbol*] [*National Library of Canada*] (NLC)
**OOACH**......... Heron Park Campus, Algonquin College of Applied Arts and Technology, Ottawa, Ontario [*Library symbol*] [*National Library of Canada*] (BIB)
**OOACL**......... Library Technician Program, Algonquin College of Applied Arts & Technology, Ottawa, Ontario [*Library symbol*] [*National Library of Canada*] (NLC)
**OOACR**......... Rideau Campus, Algonquin College of Applied Arts and Technology, Ottawa, Ontario, [*Library symbol*] [*National Library of Canada*] (NLC)
**OOADE**......... Archives Deschatelets (Oblats de Marie-Immaculee), Ottawa, Ontario [*Library symbol*] [*National Library of Canada*] (NLC)
**OOAEA**......... Ethnic Archives of Canada, Public Archives [*Archives Ethniques du Canada, Archives Publiques*] Ottawa, Ontario [*Library symbol*] [*National Library of Canada*] (NLC)
**OOAECB**........ Atomic Energy Control Board [*Commission de Controle de l'Energie Atomique*] Ottawa, Ontario [*Library symbol*] [*National Library of Canada*] (NLC)
**OOAER**......... Research Co., Atomic Energy of Canada Ltd. [*Societe de Recherches, L'Energie Atomique du Canada Ltee*] Ottawa, Ontario [*Library symbol*] [*National Library of Canada*] (NLC)
**OOAF**.......... Bibliotheque de l'Ambassade de France, Ottawa, Ontario [*Library symbol*] [*National Library of Canada*] (BIB)
**OOAFN**......... Assembly of First Nations, Ottawa, Ontario [*Library symbol*] [*National Library of Canada*] (NLC)
**OOAG**.......... Libraries Division, Agriculture Canada [*Division des Bibliotheques, Agriculture Canada*] Ottawa, Ontario [*Library symbol*] [*National Library of Canada*] (NLC)
**OOAGA**......... Animal Diseases Research Institute, Agriculture Canada [*Institut de Recherches Veterinaires, Agriculture Canada*] Ottawa, Ontario [*Library symbol*] [*National Library of Canada*] (NLC)
**OOAGAR**........ Animal Research Institute, Agriculture Canada [*Institut de Recherches Zootechniques, Agriculture Canada*] Ottawa, Ontario [*Library symbol*] [*National Library of Canada*] (NLC)
**OOAGB**......... Plant Research Library, Biosystematics Research Institute, Agriculture Canada [*Bibliotheque de Recherches sur les Vegetaux, Institut de Recherches Biosystematiques, Agriculture Canada*] Ottawa, Ontario [*Library symbol*] [*National Library of Canada*] (NLC)
**OOAGCH**........ Neatby Library, Agriculture Canada [*Bibliotheque Neatby, Agriculture Canada*] Ottawa, Ontario [*Library symbol*] [*National Library of Canada*] (NLC)
**OOAGE**......... Entomology Research Library, Biosystematics Research Institute, Agriculture Canada [*Bibliotheque de Recherches Entomologiques, Institut de Recherches Biosytematiques, Agriculture Canada*] Ottawa, Ontario [*Library symbol*] [*National Library of Canada*] (NLC)
**OOAGER**........ Engineering and Statistical Research Centre, Agriculture Canada [*Centre de Recherche Technique et de Statistique, Agriculture Canada*] Ottawa, Ontario [*Library symbol*] [*National Library of Canada*] (NLC)
**OOAGFP**........ Laboratory Services Section, Food Production and Marketing Branch, Agriculture Canada [*Section des Services d'Analyse, Direction de la Production et de la Commercialisation des Aliments, Agriculture Canada*] Ottawa, Ontario [*Library symbol*] [*National Library of Canada*] (NLC)
**OOAGFR**........ Food Research Centre, Agriculture Canada [*Centre de Recherches sur les Aliments,Agriculture Canada*], Ottawa, Ontario [*Library symbol*] [*National Library of Canada*] (BIB)
**OOAGO**......... Research Station, Agriculture Canada [*Station de Recherches, Agriculture Canada*] Ottawa, Ontario [*Library symbol*] [*National Library of Canada*] (NLC)
**OOAGSR**........ Soil Research Institute, Agriculture Canada [*Institut de Recherches sur les Sols, Agriculture Canada*] Ottawa, Ontario [*Library symbol*] [*National Library of Canada*] (NLC)
**OOAI**.......... AMCA International Ltd., Ottawa, Ontario [*Library symbol*] [*National Library of Canada*] (NLC)
**OOAK**.......... Oakville Public Library, Ontario [*Library symbol*] [*National Library of Canada*] (NLC)
**OOAKA**......... Appleby College, Oakville, Ontario [*Library symbol*] [*National Library of Canada*] (NLC)
**OOAKG**......... G. D. Searle Co. of Canada Ltd., Oakville, Ontario [*Library symbol*] [*National Library of Canada*] (BIB)
**OOAKM**......... Oakville Museums, Ontario [*Library symbol*] [*National Library of Canada*] (BIB)
**OOAKS**......... Shell Research Centre, Oakville, Ontario [*Library symbol*] [*National Library of Canada*] (NLC)
**OOAKSC**........ Sheridan College, Oakville, Ontario [*Library symbol*] [*National Library of Canada*] (NLC)
**OOAKSCL**....... Library Techniques, Sheridan College, Oakville, Ontario [*Library symbol*] [*National Library of Canada*] (NLC)
**OOAMA**......... National Map Collection, Public Archives [*Collection Nationale des Cartes et Plans, Archives Publiques*] Ottawa, Ontario [*Library symbol*] [*National Library of Canada*] (NLC)
**OOAMA**......... Office, Ogden Air Material Area [*AFLC*]
**OOAMS**......... Manuscript Division, Public Archives [*Division des Manuscrits, Archives Publiques*] Ottawa, Ontario [*Library symbol*] [*National Library of Canada*] (NLC)
**OOANF**......... National Film Archives, Public Archives [*Archives Nationales du Film, Archives Publiques*] Ottawa, Ontario [*Library symbol*] [*National Library of Canada*] (NLC)
**OOAOA**......... Archives, Diocese of Ottawa, Anglican Church of Canada, Ontario [*Library symbol*] [*National Library of Canada*] (NLC)
**OOAR**.......... Canadian Broadcasting Corp. [*Societe Radio-Canada*] Ottawa, Ontario [*Library symbol*] [*National Library of Canada*] (NLC)
**OOASH**......... Ashbury College, Ottawa, Ontario [*Library symbol*] [*National Library of Canada*] (NLC)
**OOB**........... Bank of Canada [*Banque du Canada*] Ottawa, Ontario [*Library symbol*] [*National Library of Canada*] (NLC)
**OOB**........... OECD [*Organization for Economic Cooperation and Development*] Observer [*A publication*]
**OOB**........... Off-Off Broadway [*Theater*]
**O O B**......... Off Our Backs [*A publication*]
**OOB**........... Opening of Business (MCD)
**OOB**........... Operations Operating Budget [*Military*] (AFIT)
**OoB**........... Ord och Bild [*A publication*]
**OOB**........... Order of Battle [*Military*] (NVT)
**OOB**........... Ordnance Office Bulletin [*Military*]
**OOB**........... Out of Band [*Telecommunications*] (TEL)
**OOB**........... Out of Bed [*Medicine*]
**OOB**........... Out of Body [*Parapsychology*]
**OOBA**.......... Brewers Association of Canada, [*Association des Brasseurs du Canada*], Ottawa, Ontario [*Library symbol*] [*National Library of Canada*] (NLC)
**OOBA**.......... Off Off Broadway Alliance [*Later, ART/NY*]
**OOBC**.......... Bowmar Canada Ltd., Ottawa, Ontario [*Library symbol*] [*National Library of Canada*] (NLC)
**OOBE**.......... Ottawa Board of Education, Ontario [*Library symbol*] [*National Library of Canada*] (NLC)
**OOBE**.......... Out-of-Body Experience [*Parapsychology*]
**OOBH**.......... Information Library, British High Commission, Ottawa, Ontario [*Library symbol*] [*National Library of Canada*] (BIB)
**OOBLA**......... Onset of Blood Lactose Accumulation [*Metabolism*]
**OOBM**.......... Bartonian Metaphysical Society, Ottawa, Ontario [*Library symbol*] [*National Library of Canada*] (NLC)
**OOBMC**......... Bureau of Management Consulting, Department of Supply and Services [*Bureau des Conseillers en Gestion, Ministere des Approvisionnements et Services*] Ottawa, Ontario [*Library symbol*] [*National Library of Canada*] (NLC)
**OOBMI**......... Bell Canada Market Information Centre, Ottawa, Ontario [*Library symbol*] [*National Library of Canada*] (NLC)

**OOBMM**... Medical Library, Bristol-Myers Pharmaceutical Group, Ottawa, Ontario [*Library symbol*] [*National Library of Canada*] (NLC)
**OOBR**........ Buraimi [*Oman*] [*ICAO location identifier*] (ICLI)
**OOC**.......... Junior Optimist Octagon International [*Formerly, Optimist Octagon Clubs*] (EA)
**OOC**.......... Oberlin College, Conservatory of Music, Oberlin, OH [*Library symbol*] [*Library of Congress*] (LCLS)
**OOC**.......... Off-On Control
**OOC**.......... Office of Censorship [*Terminated, 1945*] [*Military*]
**OOC**.......... Operating Vehicle without Owner's Consent [*Traffic offense charge*]
**OOC**.......... Organized Occupational Curricula
**OOC**.......... Ottawa Public Library [*Bibliotheque Publique d'Ottawa*] Ontario [*Library symbol*] [*National Library of Canada*] (NLC)
**OOC**.......... Out of Commission (NVT)
**OOC**.......... Out of Control
**OOC**.......... Over-Ocean Communications
**OOC**.......... Overseas Operating Committee [*World War II*]
**OOCAA**..... Canadian Astronautics, Ottawa, Ontario [*Library symbol*] [*National Library of Canada*] (NLC)
**OOCAAS**.. Canadian Automobile Association, Ottawa, Ontario [*Library symbol*] [*National Library of Canada*] (BIB)
**OOCAB**..... Canadian Association of Broadcasters [*Association Canadienne des Radiodiffuseurs*] Ottawa, Ontario [*Library symbol*] [*National Library of Canada*] (NLC)
**OOCAC**..... Canada Council [*Conseil des Arts du Canada*] Ottawa, Ontario [*Library symbol*] [*National Library of Canada*] (NLC)
**OOCACR**.. Research and Evaluation Section, Canada Council [*Service de Recherche et d'Evaluation, Conseil des Arts du Canada*], Ottawa, Ontario [*Library symbol*] [*National Library of Canada*] (BIB)
**OOCACSW**... Documentation Centre, Canadian Advisory Council on the Status of Women [*Centre de Documentation, Conseil Consultatif Canadien de la Situation de la Femme*] Ottawa, Ontario [*Library symbol*] [*National Library of Canada*] (NLC)
**OOCAM**.... Canadian Association of Medical Radiation Technologists, Ottawa, Ontario [*Library symbol*] [*National Library of Canada*] (BIB)
**OOCANM**... Canadian Museum Association [*Association des Musees Canadiens*], Ottawa, Ontario [*Library symbol*] [*National Library of Canada*] (NLC)
**OOCAR**..... Canadian Arctic Resources Committee, Ottawa, Ontario [*Library symbol*] [*National Library of Canada*] (NLC)
**OOCARE**.. Care Canada, Ottawa, Ontario [*Library symbol*] [*National Library of Canada*] (BIB)
**OOCAS**..... Children's Aid Society of Ottawa-Carleton, Ottawa, Ontario [*Library symbol*] [*National Library of Canada*] (NLC)
**OOCB**....... Colonel By Secondary School, Ottawa, Ontario [*Library symbol*] [*National Library of Canada*] (NLC)
**OOCBC**..... Conference Board of Canada, Ottawa, Ontario [*Library symbol*] [*National Library of Canada*] (NLC)
**OOCBE**..... Carleton Board of Education, Ottawa, Ontario [*Library symbol*] [*National Library of Canada*] (NLC)
**OOCBH**..... Human Resources Department, Canadian Broadcasting Corp. [*Departement des Ressources Humaines, Societe Radio-Canada*], Ottawa, Ontario [*Library symbol*] [*National Library of Canada*] (BIB)
**OOCC**........ Carleton University, Ottawa, Ontario [*Library symbol*] [*National Library of Canada*] (NLC)
**OOCCAH**... Department of Art History, Carleton University, Ottawa, Ontario [*Library symbol*] [*Obsolete*] [*National Library of Canada*] (NLC)
**OOCCFA**... Canadian Centre for Films on Art [*Centre Canadien du Film sur l'Art*] Ottawa, Ontario [*Library symbol*] [*National Library of Canada*] (NLC)
**OOCCG**..... Geography Department, Carleton University, Ottawa, Ontario [*Library symbol*] [*Obsolete*] [*National Library of Canada*] (NLC)
**OOCCJ**...... Church Council on Justice and Correction [*Conseil des Eglises pour la Justice et la Criminologie*], Ottawa, Ontario [*Library symbol*] [*National Library of Canada*] (BIB)
**OOCCL**..... County of Carleton Law Library, Ottawa, Ontario [*Library symbol*] [*National Library of Canada*] (NLC)
**OOCCR**..... Canada Centre for Remote Sensing, Energy, Mines and Resources Canada [*Centre Canadien de Teledetection, Energie, Mines et Ressources Canada*] Ottawa, Ontario [*Library symbol*] [*National Library of Canada*] (NLC)
**OOCCU**..... Canadian Commission for UNESCO, Ottawa, Ontario [*Library symbol*] [*National Library of Canada*] (BIB)
**OOCD**....... Canadian International Development Agency [*Agence Canadienne de Developpement International*] Ottawa, Ontario [*Library symbol*] [*National Library of Canada*] (NLC)
**OOCDA**..... Canadian Dental Association, Ottawa, Ontario [*Library symbol*] [*National Library of Canada*] (NLC)
**OOCDC**..... Computing Devices of Canada, Ottawa, Ontario [*Library symbol*] [*National Library of Canada*] (NLC)
**OOCDP**..... College Dominicain de Philosophie et de Theologie, Ottawa, Ontario [*Library symbol*] [*National Library of Canada*] (NLC)
**OOCEEC**... Delegation of the Commission of the European Communities [*Delegation de la Commission des Communautes Europeennes*], Ottawa, Ontario [*Library symbol*] [*National Library of Canada*] (BIB)
**OOCES**..... Combustion Engineering Superheater Ltd., Ottawa, Ontario [*Library symbol*] [*National Library of Canada*] (NLC)
**OOCESC**... Centre d'Animation Pedagogique, Conseil des Ecoles Separees Catholiques d'Ottawa, Ontario [*Library symbol*] [*National Library of Canada*] (BIB)
**OOCF**........ Canadian Film Institute [*Institut Canadien du Film*] Ottawa, Ontario [*Library symbol*] [*National Library of Canada*] (NLC)
**OOCFB**..... Canadian Forces Base, Ottawa, Ontario [*Library symbol*] [*National Library of Canada*] (BIB)
**OOCHA**.... Canadian Hospital Association [*Association des Hopitaux du Canada*] Ottawa, Ontario [*Library symbol*] [*National Library of Canada*] (NLC)
**OOCHAC**... Catholic Health Association of Canada [*Association Catholique Canadienne de la Sante*], Ottawa, Ontario [*Library symbol*] [*National Library of Canada*] (NLC)
**OOCHC**.... Canadian Horticultural Council [*Conseil Canadien de l'Horticulture*], Ottawa, Ontario [*Library symbol*] [*National Library of Canada*] (BIB)
**OOCHEO**... Children's Hospital of Eastern Ontario [*Hopital pour Enfants de l'Est de l'Ontario*] Ottawa, Ontario [*Library symbol*] [*National Library of Canada*] (NLC)
**OOCHI**...... Chreod International, Ottawa, Ontario [*Library symbol*] [*National Library of Canada*] (NLC)
**OOCHP**..... Common Heritage Programme, Ottawa, Ontario [*Library symbol*] [*National Library of Canada*] (BIB)
**OOCHR**.... Canadian Human Rights Commission [*Commission Canadienne des Droits de la Personne*] Ottawa, Ontario [*Library symbol*] [*National Library of Canada*] (NLC)
**OOCI**......... Department of Consumer and Corporate Affairs [*Ministere de la Consommation et des Corporations*] Ottawa, Ontario [*Library symbol*] [*National Library of Canada*] (NLC)
**OOCIC**...... Documentation Centre, Canadian Intergovernmental Conference Secretariat [*Centre de Documentation, Secretariat des Conferences Intergouvernementales Canadiennes*], Ottawa, Ontario [*Library symbol*] [*National Library of Canada*] (NLC)
**OOCIFE**.... Field Exploration Library, Inco Ltd., Copper Cliff, Ontario [*Library symbol*] [*National Library of Canada*] (NLC)
**OOCIHM**... Canadian Institute for Historical Microreproductions [*Institut Canadien de Microreproductions Historiques*] Ottawa, Ontario [*Library symbol*] [*National Library of Canada*] (NLC)
**OOCIIPS**.. Canadian Institute for International Peace and Security [*Institut Canadien pour la Paix et la Securite Mondiales*] Ottawa, Ontario [*Library symbol*] [*National Library of Canada*] (NLC)
**OOCIRS**.... Canadian Institute for Radiation Safety, Ottawa, Ontario [*Library symbol*] [*National Library of Canada*] (NLC)
**OOCITT**.... Canadian International Trade Tribunal [*Tribunal Canadien du Commerce Exterieur*], Ontario [*Library symbol*] [*National Library of Canada*] (BIB)
**OOCL**........ Capital Library Wholesale, Ottawa, Ontario [*Library symbol*] [*National Library of Canada*] (NLC)
**OOCLA**..... Canadian Library Association, Ottawa, Ontario [*Library symbol*] [*National Library of Canada*] (BIB)
**OOCLC**..... Canadian Labour Congress [*Congres du Travail du Canada*] Ottawa, Ontario [*Library symbol*] [*National Library of Canada*] (NLC)
**OOCLCG**.. Coopers & Lybrand Consulting Group, Ottawa, Ontario [*Library symbol*] [*National Library of Canada*] (BIB)
**OOCLM**.... Canadian Labour Market and Productivity Centre [*Centre Canadien du Marche du Travail et de la Productivite*], Ottawa, Ontario [*Library symbol*] [*National Library of Canada*] (NLC)
**OOCM**....... Canadian Housing Information Centre, Canada Mortgage and Housing Corp. [*Centre Canadien de Documentation sur l'Habitation, Societe Canadienne d'Hypotheques et de Logement*] Ottawa, Ontario [*Library symbol*] [*National Library of Canada*] (NLC)
**OOCMA**.... Canadian Medical Association, Ottawa, Ontario [*Library symbol*] [*National Library of Canada*] (NLC)
**OOCMC**.... Children's Environments Advisory Service, Canada Mortgage and Housing Corp. [*Service Consultatif sur l'Environnement de l'Enfant, Societe Canadienne d'Hypotheques et de Logement*] Ottawa, Ontario [*Library symbol*] [*National Library of Canada*] (NLC)
**OOCMF**.... Office of the Commissioner for Federal Judicial Affairs [*Bureau du Commissaire a la Magistrature Federale*], Ottawa, Ontario [*Library symbol*] [*National Library of Canada*] (BIB)
**OOCN**....... Canadian Nurses' Association [*Association Canadienne des Infirmieres*] Ottawa, Ontario [*Library symbol*] [*National Library of Canada*] (NLC)

**OOCNP**..... CNP Resource Centre, Energy, Mines, and Resources Canada [*Centre d'Information EESP, Energie, Mines, et Ressources Canada*] Ottawa, Ontario [*Library symbol*] [*National Library of Canada*] (NLC)
**OOCO** ....... Department of Communications [*Ministere des Communications*] Ottawa, Ontario [*Library symbol*] [*National Library of Canada*] (NLC)
**OOCOAC** ... Consumer's Association of Canada, Ottawa, Ontario [*Library symbol*] [*National Library of Canada*] (BIB)
**OOCOG** .... COGLA [*Canada Oil and Gas Lands Administration*] Ocean Mining Resource Centre [*Centre de Ressources sur l'Extraction de Minerais Oceaniques, Administration du Petrole et du Gaz des Terres du Canada*], Ottawa, Ontario [*Library symbol*] [*National Library of Canada*] (NLC)
**OOCOI**...... Cognos, Inc., Ottawa, Ontario [*Library symbol*] [*National Library of Canada*] (BIB)
**OOCOL**..... Commissioner of Official Languages [*Commissaire aux Langues Officielles*] Ottawa, Ontario [*Library symbol*] [*National Library of Canada*] (NLC)
**OOCOT**..... Competition Tribunal [*Tribunal de la Concurrence*], Ottawa, Ontario [*Library symbol*] [*National Library of Canada*] (BIB)
**OOCOW** ... Cowater International, Inc., Ottawa, Ontario [*Library symbol*] [*National Library of Canada*] (BIB)
**OOCP**........ Community Planning Association of Canada [*Association Canadienne d'Urbanisme*] Ottawa, Ontario [*Library symbol*] [*National Library of Canada*] (NLC)
**OOCPA**..... Canadian Payments Association, Ottawa, Ontario [*Library symbol*] [*National Library of Canada*] (BIB)
**OOCPB** ..... Planning and Development Library, City of Ottawa, Ontario [*Library symbol*] [*National Library of Canada*] (BIB)
**OOCPR**..... Canadian Public Relations Society [*Societe Canadienne des Relations Publiques*], Ottawa, Ontario [*Library symbol*] [*National Library of Canada*] (BIB)
**OOCRC**..... Canadian Red Cross Society [*Societe Canadienne de la Croix-Rouge*] Ottawa, Ontario [*Library symbol*] [*National Library of Canada*] (NLC)
**OOCRI**...... Canadian Research Institute for the Avancement of Women [*Institut Canadien de Recherches sur les Femmes*] Ottawa, Ontario [*Library symbol*] [*National Library of Canada*] (NLC)
**OOCRLF**... Canadian Rights and Liberties Federation, Ottawa, Ontario [*Library symbol*] [*National Library of Canada*] (NLC)
**OOCRM**.... Canadian Royal Mint [*Monnaie Royale Canadienne*] Ottawa, Ontario [*Library symbol*] [*National Library of Canada*] (NLC)
**OOCS**........ Public Service Commission [*Commission de la Fonction Publique*] Ottawa, Ontario [*Library symbol*] [*National Library of Canada*] (NLC)
**OOCSC** ..... Canada Safety Council [*Conseil Canadien de la Securite*] Ottawa, Ontario [*Library symbol*] [*National Library of Canada*] (NLC)
**OOCT**........ Canadian Teachers Federation, Ottawa, Ontario [*Library symbol*] [*National Library of Canada*] (NLC)
**OOCTI**...... Canadian Textiles Institute [*Institut Canadien des Textiles*], Ottawa, Ontario [*Library symbol*] [*National Library of Canada*] (BIB)
**OOCU** ....... Association of Universities and Colleges of Canada [*Association des Universites et Colleges du Canada*], Ottawa, Ontario [*Library symbol*] [*National Library of Canada*] (NLC)
**OOCUI**...... Canadian Unity Information Office [*Centre d'Information sur l'Unite Canadienne*] Ottawa, Ontario [*Library symbol*] [*National Library of Canada*] (NLC)
**OOCUS**..... CUSO [*Canadian University Service Overseas*], Ottawa, Ontario [*Library symbol*] [*National Library of Canada*] (NLC)
**OOCVB**..... Central Volunteer Bureau of Ottawa-Carleton [*Bureau Central des Benevoles d'Ottawa-Carleton*] Ottawa, Ontario [*Library symbol*] [*National Library of Canada*] (BIB)
**OOCW**....... Canadian Council on Social Development [*Conseil Canadien de Developpement Social*] Ottawa, Ontario [*Library symbol*] [*National Library of Canada*] (NLC)
**OOCWC**.... Canadian Wood Council [*Conseil Canadien du Bois*] Ottawa, Ontario [*Library symbol*] [*National Library of Canada*] (NLC)
**OOCZ**........ Ottawa Citizen, Ontario [*Library symbol*] [*National Library of Canada*] (NLC)
**OOD**.......... Object-Oriented Design [*Data processing*]
**OOD**.......... Office Operations Department
**OOD**.......... Officer of the Day [*or Deck*] [*Also, OD*] [*Navy*]
**OOD**.......... Operations Orientation Director [*NASA*]
**OOD**.......... Orbiter on Dock [*NASA*] (KSC)
**OOD**.......... Woodstown, NJ [*Location identifier*] [*FAA*] (FAAL)
**OO 2d**........ Ohio Opinions, Second Series [*A publication*] (DLA)
**OODB**........ Dominion Bridge Co. Ltd., Ottawa, Ontario [*Library symbol*] [*National Library of Canada*] (NLC)
**OODBMS** ... Object-Oriented Database Management System [*Objectivity, Inc.*] [*Data processing*]
**OODBS**..... DOBIS (Dortmunder Bibliothekssystem), Ottawa, Ontario [*Library symbol*] [*National Library of Canada*] (NLC)
**OODCH**.... DCH Consultants, Inc., Ottawa, Ontario [*Library symbol*] [*National Library of Canada*] (NLC)
**OODE**........ Office of Overseas Dependent Education [*Military*]
**OODEP**..... Owner, Officer, Director, or Executive Personnel (MCD)
**OODLAC**.. Odessa Branch, Lennox and Addington County Library, Ontario [*Library symbol*] [*National Library of Canada*] (NLC)
**OODLC**..... Library Education Services, Data Logic Canada, Ottawa, Ontario [*Library symbol*] [*National Library of Canada*] (NLC)
**OODM**...... Dali Management [*Gestion Dali*], Ottawa, Ontario [*Library symbol*] [*National Library of Canada*] (BIB)
**OODMR** ... DMR Group, Inc., Ottawa, Ontario [*Library symbol*] [*National Library of Canada*] (BIB)
**OODP**........ Department of Supply and Services [*Ministere des Approvisionnements et Services*] Ottawa, Ontario [*Library symbol*] [*National Library of Canada*] (NLC)
**OODP**........ Out-of-Detent Pitch [*Aviation*] (MCD)
**OODPS**..... Superannuation Division, Compensation Services Branch, Department of Supply and Services [*Division des Pensions de Retraite, Direction des Services de Renumeration, Ministere des Approvisionnements et Services*] Ottawa, Ontario [*Library symbol*] [*National Library of Canada*] (NLC)
**OODQ**....... Oliver Organization Description Questionnaire [*Test*]
**OODR**....... Out-of-Detent Roll [*Aviation*] (MCD)
**OODRC**..... Defence Research Establishment Ottawa, Department of National Defence [*Centre de Recherches pour la Defense Ottawa, Ministere de la Defense Nationale*] Ontario[*Library symbol*] [*National Library of Canada*] (NLC)
**OODSIS**.... Directorate of Scientific Information Services, Department of National Defence [*Services d'Information Scientifique, Ministere de la Defense Nationale*] Ottawa, Ontario [*Library symbol*] [*National Library of Canada*] (NLC)
**OODV**....... Orbit-on-Demand Vehicle
**OOE**........... Department of External Affairs [*Ministere des Affaires Exerieures*] Ottawa, Ontario [*Library symbol*] [*National Library of Canada*] (NLC)
**OOE**........... Office of Ocean Engineering [*National Oceanic and Atmospheric Administration*] (MSC)
**OOE**........... Opening of Oesophagus
**OOE**........... Out-of-Ecliptic Mission [*NASA*] (EGAO)
**OOEA**........ Embassy of Argentina, Ottawa, Ontario [*Library symbol*] [*National Library of Canada*] (BIB)
**OOEAB**..... Archaeological Research, Environment Canada [*Recherches Archeologiques, Environnement Canada*] Ottawa, Ontario [*Library symbol*] [*National Library of Canada*] (NLC)
**OOEAPT**... River Road Environmental Technology Centre, Environment Canada [*Centre de Techologie Environnementale de River Road, Environnement Canada*] Ottawa, Ontario [*Library symbol*] [*National Library of Canada*] (NLC)
**OOEB**........ Elisabeth Bruyere Health Center [*Centre de Sante Elisabeth Bruyere*] Ottawa, Ontario [*Library symbol*] [*National Library of Canada*] (NLC)
**OOEC**........ Economic Council of Canada [*Conseil Economique du Canada*] Ottawa, Ontario [*Library symbol*] [*National Library of Canada*] (NLC)
**OOEC**........ Oxford Orthopaedic Engineering Centre [*British*] (IRUK)
**OOECS**..... ECS [*Energy Conversion Systems*] Power Systems, Inc., Ottawa, Ontario [*Library symbol*] [*National Library of Canada*] (NLC)
**OOECW**.... Canadian Wildlife Service, Environment Canada [*Service Canadien de la Faune, Environnement Canada*] Ottawa, Ontario [*Library symbol*] [*National Library of Canada*] (NLC)
**OOECWN** ... National Wildlife Research Centre, Canadian Wildlife Service, Environment Canada [*Centre National de Recherche sur la Faune, Service Canadien de la Faune, Environnement Canada*] Ottawa, Ontario [*Library symbol*] [*National Library of Canada*] (NLC)
**OOEDC**..... Export Development Corp. [*Societe pour l'Expansion des Exportations*] Ottawa, Ontario [*Library symbol*] [*National Library of Canada*] (NLC)
**OOEE**........ Engineering and Economic Research Technologies, Inc., Ottawa, Ontario [*Library symbol*] [*National Library of Canada*] (BIB)
**OOEIB**...... Interpretation Division, Environment Canada - Parks [*Direction de l'Interpretation, Environnement Canada - Parcs*], Ottawa, Ontario [*Library symbol*] [*National Library of Canada*] (NLC)
**OOEK**........ Embassy of Korea, Ottawa, Ontario [*Library symbol*] [*National Library of Canada*] (BIB)
**OOELB**..... Legal Branch, Department of External Affairs [*Direction des Operations Juridiques, Ministere des Affaires Exterieures*] Ottawa, Ontario [*Library symbol*] [*National Library of Canada*] (NLC)
**OOELC**..... Elections Canada, Ottawa, Ontario [*Library symbol*] [*National Library of Canada*] (BIB)

**OOELS**...... Legal Services, Environment Canada [*Services Juridiques, Environnement Canada*] Ottawa, Ontario [*Library symbol*] [*National Library of Canada*] (NLC)
**OOEMB**.... Embassy of Brazil, Ottawa, Ontario [*Library symbol*] [*National Library of Canada*] (BIB)
**OOEN** ....... Cameco Research Center, Ottawa, Ontario [*Library symbol*] [*National Library of Canada*] (NLC)
**Ooe N**......... Oberoesterreichische Nachrichten [*A publication*]
**OOEO** ....... Eastern Ontario Regional Library, Ottawa, Ontario [*Library symbol*] [*National Library of Canada*] (NLC)
**OOEO** ....... Ontario Library Service - Rideau, Ottawa, Ontario [*Library symbol*] [*National Library of Canada*] (NLC)
**OOEOB**..... Conservation Division, Environment Canada [*Division de la Conservation, Environnement Canada*] Ottawa, Ontario [*Library symbol*] [*National Library of Canada*] (NLC)
**OOEPC** ..... Emergency Planning Canada [*Planification d'Urgence Canada*] Ottawa, Ontario [*Library symbol*] [*National Library of Canada*] (NLC)
**OOEPSE**... Socio-Economic Research Division, Parks Canada Program, Environment Canada [*Division de la Recherche Socio-Economique, Programme Parcs Canada, Environnement Canada*] Ottawa, Ontario [*Library symbol*] [*National Library of Canada*] (NLC)
**OOESC** ..... Ecole Secondaire Champlain, Ottawa, Ontario [*Library symbol*] [*National Library of Canada*] (NLC)
**OOEU** ....... Euroline, Ottawa, Ontario [*Library symbol*] [*National Library of Canada*] (BIB)
**OOEY**........ Eyretechnics Ltd., Ottawa, Ontario [*Library symbol*] [*National Library of Canada*] (NLC)
**OOF**........... Department of Finance [*Ministere des Finances*] Ottawa, Ontario [*Library symbol*] [*National Library of Canada*] (NLC)
**OOF**........... Offense Only Fighter (MCD)
**OOFA**........ Documentation Centre, Family Action [*Centre de Documentation, Action Famille*], Ottawa, Ontario [*Library symbol*] [*National Library of Canada*] (NLC)
**OOFC**........ Federal Court of Canada [*Cour Federale du Canada*] Ottawa, Ontario [*Library symbol*] [*National Library of Canada*] (NLC)
**OOFCC** ..... Farm Credit Corp., Ottawa, Ontario [*Library symbol*] [*Obsolete*] [*National Library of Canada*] (NLC)
**OOFD**........ Fahud [*Oman*] [*ICAO location identifier*] (ICLI)
**OOFE**........ Federal Environmental Assessment Review Office [*Bureau Federal d'Examen des Evaluations Environnementales*], Ottawa, Ontario [*Library symbol*] [*National Library of Canada*] (BIB)
**OOFF** ........ Departmental Library, Environment Canada [*Bibliotheque du Ministere, Environnemet Canada*] Ottawa, Ontario [*Library symbol*] [*National Library of Canada*] (NLC)
**OOFI** ......... Fisheries and Oceans Canada [*Peches et Oceans Canada*] Ottawa, Ontario [*Library symbol*] [*National Library of Canada*] (NLC)
**OOFL** ........ Federal Liberal Agency of Canada, Ottawa, Ontario [*Library symbol*] [*National Library of Canada*] (NLC)
**OOFM**....... Mining Library, Falconbridge Ltd., Onaping, Ontario [*Library symbol*] [*National Library of Canada*] (NLC)
**OOFP** ........ Forintek Canada Corp., Ottawa, Ontario [*Library symbol*] [*National Library of Canada*] (NLC)
**OOFQ**........ Firq [*Oman*] [*ICAO location identifier*] (ICLI)
**OOFS** ........ Sport Information Resource Centre [*Centre de Documentation de Reference pour le Sport*] Ottawa, Ontario [*Library symbol*] [*National Library of Canada*] (NLC)
**OOG** .......... Geological Survey of Canada [*Commission Geologique du Canada*] Ottawa, Ontario [*Library symbol*] [*National Library of Canada*] (NLC)
**OOG** .......... Office of Oil and Gas [*Functions transferred to Energy Research and Development Administration*] [*Department of the Interior*]
**OOG** .......... Officer of the Guard [*Navy*] [*British*]
**OOG** .......... Olive Oil Group [*Later, OOA*] (EA)
**OOG** .......... Oscillating Output Geneva
**OOG** .......... Out of Gauge [*Shipping*] (DCTA)
**OOGB**........ Ghaba Central [*Oman*] [*ICAO location identifier*] (ICLI)
**OOGDC**..... Gandalf Data Ltd., Ottawa, Ontario [*Library symbol*] [*National Library of Canada*] (NLC)
**OOGE**........ Canadian Government Expositions Centre, Department of Supply and Services [*Centre des Expositions du Gouvernement Canadien, Ministere des Approvisionnements et Services*] Ottawa, Ontario [*Library symbol*] [*National Library of Canada*] (NLC)
**OOGG** ....... Documentation Centre, Goss, Gilroy & Associates, Ottawa, Ontario [*Library symbol*] [*National Library of Canada*] (BIB)
**OOGGH**.... Grace General Hospital, Ottawa, Ontario [*Library symbol*] [*National Library of Canada*] (NLC)
**OOGH**....... Reference Library, Government House [*Salle de Reference, Residence du Gouverneur-General*] Ottawa, Ontario [*Library symbol*] [*National Library of Canada*] (NLC)
**OOGKS**..... Gottlieb Kaylor & Stocks, Ottawa, Ontario [*Library symbol*] [*National Library of Canada*] (BIB)
**OOGOH**.... Gowling & Henderson, Ottawa, Ontario [*Library symbol*] [*National Library of Canada*] (NLC)
**OOH**.......... Heraldry Society of Canada [*Societe Heraldique du Canada*], Ottawa, Ontario [*Library symbol*] [*National Library of Canada*] (BIB)
**OOH**.......... Occupational Outlook Handbook [*A publication*] (OICC)
**OOH**.......... Oesterreichische Osthefte [*A publication*]
**OOHA**....... Haima [*Oman*] [*ICAO location identifier*] (ICLI)
**OOHC** ....... Heritage Canada Foundation [*Fondation Canadienne pour la Protection du Patrimoine*] Ottawa, Ontario [*Library symbol*] [*National Library of Canada*] (NLC)
**OOHG**....... Ottawa General Hospital [*Hopital General d'Ottawa*] Ontario [*Library symbol*] [*National Library of Canada*] (NLC)
**OOHI** ........ Historical Society of Ottawa Library and the Bytown Historical Museum, Ontario [*Library symbol*] [*National Library of Canada*] (NLC)
**OOH-OOH** ... On the One Hand, On the Other Hand
**OOHUR**.... Huronia Regional Centre, Orillia, Ontario [*Library symbol*] [*National Library of Canada*] (NLC)
**OOI**........... Informetrica Ltd., Ottawa, Ontario [*Library symbol*] [*National Library of Canada*] (NLC)
**OOI**........... Memphis, TN [*Location identifier*] [*FAA*] (FAAL)
**OOI**........... Oxygen/Ozone Indicator
**OOIA**......... Ibra [*Oman*] [*ICAO location identifier*] (ICLI)
**OOIB** ......... Imperial Ballet of Canada, Ottawa, Ontario [*Library symbol*] [*National Library of Canada*] (NLC)
**OOIC**......... Information Centre, Investment Canada [*Centre d'Information, Investissement Canada*] Ottawa, Ontario [*Library symbol*] [*National Library of Canada*] (NLC)
**OOICC** ...... Indian Claims Commission [*Commission d'Etude des Revendications des Indiens*] Ottawa, Ontario [*Library symbol*] [*National Library of Canada*] (NLC)
**OOICCS**.... International Council for Canadian Studies [*Conseil International d'Etudes Canadiennes*], Ottawa, Ontario [*Library symbol*] [*National Library of Canada*] (BIB)
**OOICP** ...... Phototheque, National Film Board [*Phototheque, Office National du Film*] Ottawa, Ontario [*Library symbol*] [*National Library of Canada*] (NLC)
**OOID**......... International Development Research Centre [*Centre de Recherches pour le Developpement International*] Ottawa, Ontario [*Library symbol*] [*National Library of Canada*] (NLC)
**OOIDA**...... Owner-Operator Independent Drivers Association
**OOIHC**...... India High Commission, Ottawa, Ontario [*Library symbol*] [*National Library of Canada*] (BIB)
**OOII** .......... Ibri [*Oman*] [*ICAO location identifier*] (ICLI)
**OOIJC**....... International Joint Commission [*Commission Mixte Internationale*], Ottawa, Ontario [*Library symbol*] [*National Library of Canada*] (NLC)
**OOIL** ......... Osage Energy, Inc. [*NASDAQ symbol*] (NQ)
**OOIN**......... Office of the Superintendent of Financial Institutions Canada [*Bureau du Surintendant des Institutions Financieres Canada*] Ottawa, Ontario [*Library symbol*] [*National Library of Canada*] (NLC)
**OOIP** ......... Original Oil in Place [*Petroleum*]
**OOIPC** ...... Offices of the Information and Privacy Commissioners of Canada [*Bureaux des Commissaires a l'Information et a la Protection de la Vie Privee du Canada*] Ottawa, Ontario [*Library symbol*] [*National Library of Canada*] (NLC)
**OOIRB** ...... Immigration and Refugee Board [*Commission d'Immigration et du Status de Refugie*], Ottawa, Ontario [*Library symbol*] [*National Library of Canada*] (BIB)
**OOIRP** ...... Institute for Research on Public Policy [*Institut de Recherches Politiques*], Ottawa, Ontario [*Library symbol*] [*National Library of Canada*] (NLC)
**OOIRS**....... Irving R. Silver Associates Library [*IRSA*], Ottawa, Ontario [*Library symbol*] [*National Library of Canada*] (NLC)
**OOIT** ......... Inuit Tapirisat of Canada, Ottawa, Ontario [*Library symbol*] [*National Library of Canada*] (NLC)
**OOIZ**......... Izki [*Oman*] [*ICAO location identifier*] (ICLI)
**OOJ** ........... Department of Justice [*Ministere de la Justice*] Ottawa, Ontario [*Library symbol*] [*National Library of Canada*] (NLC)
**OOJ** ........... Obstruction of Justice
**OOJN**........ Jarf North [*Oman*] [*ICAO location identifier*] (ICLI)
**OOK** .......... On-Off Keying [*Data processing*] (IEEE)
**OOK** .......... Toksook [*Alaska*] [*Airport symbol*] (OAG)
**OOKB**........ Khasab [*Oman*] [*ICAO location identifier*] (ICLI)
**OOL**........... Gold Coast [*Australia*] [*Airport symbol*] (OAG)
**OOL**........... Labour Canada [*Travail Canada*] Ottawa, Ontario [*Library symbol*] [*National Library of Canada*] (NLC)
**OOL**........... Oberlin Public Library, Oberlin, OH [*Library symbol*] [*Library of Congress*] (LCLS)
**OOL**........... Object-Oriented Language [*Data processing*] (BYTE)
**OOL**........... Office of Oceanography and Limnology [*Smithsonian Institution*] (MCD)
**OOL**........... Operator-Oriented Language [*Data processing*]
**OOL**........... Optimized Optical Link
**OOL**........... Orient Overseas Line (DS)

**OOLAP**..... Occupational Safety and Health Branch, Labour Canada [*Direction de la Securite et de l'Hygiene, Travail Canada*] Ottawa, Ontario [*Library symbol*] [*National Library of Canada*] (NLC)
**OOLC**........ Labour College of Canada, Ottawa, Ontario [*Library symbol*] [*National Library of Canada*] (NLC)
**OOLHMD**... Optimized Optical Link Helmet-Mounted Display
**OOLK**........ Lekhwair [*Oman*] [*ICAO location identifier*] (ICLI)
**OOLM**....... Computing Department, Loeb's MIS, Ottawa, Ontario [*Library symbol*] [*National Library of Canada*] (BIB)
**OOLML**.... Lang, Michener, Lash & Johnston, Ottawa, Ontario [*Library symbol*] [*National Library of Canada*] (BIB)
**Oologists' Rec**... Oologists' Record [*A publication*]
**OOLR**........ Law Reform Commission [*Commission de Reforme du Droit*] Ottawa, Ontario [*Library symbol*] [*National Library of Canada*] (NLC)
**OOLR**........ Ophthalmology, Otology, Laryngology, Rhinology
**OOLR**........ Overall Objective Loudness Rating [*of telephone connections*] (IEEE)
**OOLRB**..... Canada Labour Relations Board [*Conseil Canadien des Relations de Travail*] Ottawa, Ontario [*Library symbol*] [*National Library of Canada*] (NLC)
**OOLRS**...... Research Library, LRS Trimark Ltd., Ottawa, Ontario [*Library symbol*] [*National Library of Canada*] (BIB)
**OOLWB**.... Women's Bureau, Labour Canada [*Bureau de la Main-d'Oeuvre Feminine, Travail Canada*] Ottawa, Ontario [*Library symbol*] [*National Library of Canada*] (NLC)
**OOM**......... CANMET [*Canada Centre for Mineral and Energy Technology*] Library, Energy, Mines, and Resources Canada [*Bibliotheque CANMET, Energie, Mines, et Ressources Canada*], Ottawa, Ontario [*Library symbol*] [*National Library of Canada*] (NLC)
**OOM**......... Cooma [*Australia*] [*Airport symbol*] (OAG)
**OOM**......... Office of Ocean Management [*Marine science*] (MSC)
**OOM**......... Office of Organization and Management [*NASA*]
**OOM**......... Officers' Open Mess [*Military*] (AFM)
**OOM**......... Oomiya [*Japan*] [*Seismograph station code, US Geological Survey*] [*Closed*] (SEIS)
**OOM**......... Open Ocean Mining
**OOM**......... Open Order Master (MCD)
**OOMA**...... Masirah [*Oman*] [*ICAO location identifier*] (ICLI)
**OOMAD**... Michael A. Dagg Associates [*Michael A. Dagg Associes*], Ottawa, Ontario [*Library symbol*] [*National Library of Canada*] (NLC)
**OOMFC**.... Ompah Branch, Frontenac County Library, Ontario [*Library symbol*] [*National Library of Canada*] (BIB)
**OOMHC**... Malaysia High Commission, Ottawa, Ontario [*Library symbol*] [*National Library of Canada*] (NLC)
**OOMHS**.... Merivale High School, Ottawa, Ontario [*Library symbol*] [*National Library of Canada*] (NLC)
**OOMI**........ Employment and Immigration Canada [*Emploi et Immigration Canada*] Ottawa, Ontario [*Library symbol*] [*National Library of Canada*] (NLC)
**OOMIL**..... MIL Systems Engineering, Inc., Ottawa, Ontario [*Library symbol*] [*National Library of Canada*] (BIB)
**OOMJ**....... Macera & Jarzyna, Ottawa, Ontario [*Library symbol*] [*National Library of Canada*] (BIB)
**OOML**....... Metropolitan Life Insurance Co., Ottawa, Ontario [*Library symbol*] [*National Library of Canada*] (NLC)
**OOMM**..... Muscat [*Oman*] [*ICAO location identifier*] (ICLI)
**OOMM**..... Organizational Operations and Maintenance Manual (NASA)
**OOMNA**... National Air Photo Library, Energy, Mines, and Resources Canada [*Bibliotheque Photographie Aerienne Nationale, Energie, Mines, et Ressources Canada*], Ottawa, Ontario [*Library symbol*] [*National Library of Canada*] (BIB)
**OOMO**...... Oxford Mills Branch, Oxford-On-Rideau Township Public Library [*Library symbol*] [*National Library of Canada*] (BIB)
**OOMP**....... Physical Metallurgy Division, Energy, Mines and Resources Canada [*Division de la Metallurgie Physique, Energie, Mines et Ressources Canada*] Ottawa, Ontario [*Library symbol*] [*National Library of Canada*] (NLC)
**OOMPR**.... Microtel Pacific Research Ltd., Ottawa, Ontario [*Library symbol*] [*National Library of Canada*] (NLC)
**OOMR**...... Headquarters Library, Energy, Mines and Resources Canada [*Bibliotheque Centrale, Energie, Mines et Ressources Canada*] Ottawa, Ontario [*Library symbol*] [*National Library of Canada*] (NLC)
**OOMS**....... Muscat/Seeb International [*Oman*] [*ICAO location identifier*] (ICLI)
**OOMSD**.... Ministry of State for Social Development [*Ministere d'Etat au Developpement Social*] Ottawa, Ontario [*Library symbol*] [*National Library of Canada*] (NLC)
**OOMSS**.... Ministry of State for Science and Technology [*Ministere d'Etat pour les Sciences et la Technologie*], Ottawa, Ontario [*Library symbol*] [*National Library of Canada*] (NLC)
**OON**.......... Canada Institute for Scientific and Technical Information, National Research Council (CISTI) [*Institut Canadien de l'Information Scientifique et Technique, Conseil National de Recherches (ICIST)*] Ottawa, Ontario [*Library symbol*] [*National Library of Canada*] (NLC)
**OON**.......... Odd-Odd Nuclei
**OON**.......... Officer of the Order of Niger
**OONAB**..... Administration Building Library, Canada Institute for Scientific and Technical Information [*Bibliotheque de l'Edifice de l'Administration, Institut Canadien de l'Information Scientifique et Technique*] Ottawa, Ontario [*Library symbol*] [*National Library of Canada*] (NLC)
**OONAM**... Aeronautical and Mechanical Engineering Branch, Canada Institute for Scientific and Technical Information [*Division du Genie Aeronautique et Mecanique, Institut Canadien de l'Information Scientifique et Technique*] Ottawa, Ontario [*Library symbol*] [*National Library of Canada*] (NLC)
**OONAMC**... NABU Manufacturing Corp., Ottawa, Ontario [*Library symbol*] [*National Library of Canada*] (NLC)
**OONBR**..... IRC [*Institute for Research in Construction*] Library, National Research Council Canada [*Bibliotheque IRC (Institut de Recherche en Construction), Conseil National de Recherches Canada*] Ottawa, Ontario [*Library symbol*] [*National Library of Canada*] (NLC)
**OONC**....... Chemistry Library, Canada Institute for Scientific and Technical Information [*Division de Chimie, Institut Canadien de l'Information Scientifique et Technique*] Ottawa, Ontario [*Library symbol*] [*National Library of Canada*] (NLC)
**OONCC**..... National Capital Commission [*Commission de la Capitale Nationale*] Ottawa, Ontario [*Library symbol*] [*National Library of Canada*] (NLC)
**OOND**....... Department of National Defence [*Ministere de la Defense Nationale*] Ottawa, Ontario [*Library symbol*] [*National Library of Canada*] (NLC)
**OONDAT**... Air Technical Library, Department of National Defence [*Bibliotheque Technique de l'Aviation, Ministere de la Defense Nationale*] Ottawa, Ontario [*Library symbol*] [*National Library of Canada*] (NLC)
**OONDC**.... Communications and Electronics Engineering Library, Department of National Defence [*Bibliotheque du Genie Electronique et des Communications, Ministere de la Defense National*] Ottawa, Ontario [*Library symbol*] [*National Library of Canada*] (NLC)
**OONDCP**... Chief, Construction and Properties, Library, Department of National Defence [*Bibliotheque, Chef - Construction et Immeubles, Ministere de le Defense Nationale*] Ottawa, Ontario [*Library symbol*] [*National Library of Canada*] (NLC)
**OONDCS**.. Communications Security Establishment, Department of National Defence [*Centre de la Securite des Telecommunications, Ministere de la Defense Nationale*] Ottawa, Ontario [*Library symbol*] [*National Library of Canada*] (NLC)
**OONDH**.... Directorate of History, Department of National Defence [*Bureau du Service Historique, Ministere de la Defense Nationale*] Ottawa, Ontario [*Library symbol*] [*National Library of Canada*] (NLC)
**OONDIS**... Directorate of Information Services, Department of National Defence [*Services d'Information, Ministere de la Defense Nationale*] Ottawa, Ontario [*Library symbol*] [*National Library of Canada*] (NLC)
**OONDJ**..... Judge Advocate General, Department of National Defence [*Jugeavocat General, Ministere de la Defense Nationale*] Ottawa, Ontario [*Library symbol*] [*National Library of Canada*] (NLC)
**OONDLT**... Land Technical Library, Department of National Defence [*Bibliotheque Technique (Terre), Ministere de la Defense Nationale*] Ottawa, Ontario [*Library symbol*] [*National Library of Canada*] (NLC)
**OONDM**... National Defence Medical Centre, Department of National Defence [*Centre Medical de la Nationale, Ministere de la Defense Nationale*] Ottawa, Ontario [*Library symbol*] [*National Library of Canada*] (NLC)
**OONDMC**... Mapping and Charting Establishment, Department of National Defence [*Service de la Cartographie, Ministere de la Defense Nationale*] Ottawa, Ontario [*Library symbol*] [*National Library of Canada*] (NLC)
**OONDMT**... Maritime Technical Library, Department of National Defence [*Bibliotheque Technique (Mer), Ministere de la Defense Nationale*] Ottawa, Ontario [*Library symbol*] [*National Library of Canada*] (NLC)
**OONDORAE**... Operational Research and Analysis Establishment, Department of National Defence [*Centre d'Analyse et de Recherche Operationnelle, Ministere de la Defense Nationale*] Ottawa, Ontario [*Library symbol*] [*National Library of Canada*] (NLC)
**OONDT**.... Secretary of State Library at National Defence [*Bibliotheque du Secretariat d'Etat a la Defense Nationale*], Ottawa, Ontario [*Library symbol*] [*National Library of Canada*] (NLC)
**OONE**....... National Energy Board [*Office National de l'Energie*] Ottawa, Ontario [*Library symbol*] [*National Library of Canada*] (NLC)

**OONFP**..... National Farm Products Marketing Council [*Conseil National de Commercialisation des Produits Agricoles*], Ottawa, Ontario [*Library symbol*] [*National Library of Canada*] (BIB)

**OONG**....... National Gallery of Canada [*Galerie Nationale du Canada*] Ottawa, Ontario [*Library symbol*] [*National Library of Canada*] (NLC)

**OONH**....... Department of National Health and Welfare [*Ministere de la Sante Nationale et du Bien-Etre Social*] Ottawa, Ontario [*Library symbol*] [*Obsolete*] [*National Library of Canada*] (NLC)

**OONHAC** ... Federal Centre for AIDS [*Acquired Immune Deficiency Syndrome*], Health Protection Branch, Health and Welfare Canada [*Centre Federal du SIDA, Direction Generale de la Protection de la Sante, Sante et Bien-Etre Social Canada*], Ottawa, Ontario [*Library symbol*] [*National Library of Canada*] (BIB)

**OONHBR** ... Banting Research Centre Library, Department of National Health and Welfare [*Bibliotheque du Centre de Recherches Banting, Ministere de la Sante Nationale et du Bien-Etre Social*] Ottawa, Ontario [*Library symbol*] [*National Library of Canada*] (NLC)

**OONHFV** ... National Clearinghouse on Family Violence, Health and Welfare Canada [*Centre National d'Information sur la Violence dans la Famille, Sante et Bien-Etre Social Canada*], Ottawa, Ontario [*Library symbol*] [*National Library of Canada*] (BIB)

**OONHH** ... Environmental Health Directorate, Health Protection Branch, Department of National Health and Welfare [*Direction de l'Hygiene du Milieu, Direction Generale de la Protection de la Sante, Ministere de la Sante Nationale et du Bien-Etre Social*] Ottawa, Ontario [*Library symbol*] [*National Library of Canada*] (NLC)

**OONHHP** ... Library Services Division, Health Protection Branch, Health and Welfare Canada [*Service de Bibliotheque, Direction Generale de la Protection de la Sante, Sante et Bien-Etre Social Canada*] Ottawa, Ontario [*Library symbol*] [*National Library of Canada*] (NLC)

**OONHHS** ... Health Services and Promotion Branch, Department of National Health and Welfare [*Direction Generale des Services et de la Promotion de la Sante, Ministere de la Sante Nationale et du Bien Etre Social*] Ottawa, Ontario [*Library symbol*] [*National Library of Canada*] (NLC)

**OONHL**.... Laboratory Centre for Disease Control, Health Protection Branch, Department of National Health and Welfare [*Laboratoire de Lutte Contre la Maladie, Direction Generale de la Protection de la Sante, Ministere de la Sante Nationale et du Bien-Etre Social*] Ottawa, Ontario [*Library symbol*] [*National Library of Canada*] (NLC)

**OONHP**.... Vanier Reading Room, Place Vanier, Health Protection Branch, Health and Welfare Canada [*Salle de Lecture de Vanier, Place Vanier, Direction Generale de la Protection de la Sante, Sante et Bien-Etre Social Canada*], Ottawa, Ontario [*Library symbol*] [*National Library of Canada*] (NLC)

**OONHPP** ... Library Services, Policy, Communications, and Information Branch, Health and Welfare Canada [*Services de Bibliotheque, Direction Generale de la Politique, des Communications, et de l'Information, Sante et Bien-Etre Social Canada*] Ottawa, Ontario [*Library symbol*] [*National Library of Canada*] (NLC)

**OONIN** ..... National Institute of Nutrition [*Institut National de la Nutrition*], Ottawa, Ontario [*Library symbol*] [*National Library of Canada*] (BIB)

**OONL**........ National Library of Canada [*Bibliotheque Nationale du Canada*] Ottawa, Ontario [*Library symbol*] [*National Library of Canada*] (NLC)

**OONLB**..... Union Catalogue of Books, National Library of Canada [*Catalogue Collectif des Livres, Bibliotheque Nationale du Canada*] Ottawa, Ontario [*Library symbol*] [*National Library of Canada*] (NLC)

**OONLC**..... Canadiana Acquisitions, National Library of Canada [*Acquisitions pour Canadiana, Bibliotheque Nationale du Canada*] Ottawa, Ontario [*Library symbol*] [*National Library of Canada*] (NLC)

**OONLD**..... Information Technology Services, National Library of Canada [*Services de Technologie de l'Information, Bibliotheque Nationale de Canada*], Ottawa, Ontario [*Library symbol*] [*National Library of Canada*] (NLC)

**OONLD**..... Library Systems Centre, National Library of Canada [*Centre des Systemes de Bibliotheque, Bibliotheque Nationale du Canada*] Ottawa, Ontario [*Library symbol*] [*National Library of Canada*] (NLC)

**OONLG**..... Official Publications, National Library of Canada [*Publications Officielles, Bibliotheque Nationale du Canada*] Ottawa, Ontario [*Library symbol*] [*National Library of Canada*] (NLC)

**OONLI**...... ISDS Canada, National Library of Canada [*ISDS Canada, Bibliotheque Nationale du Canada*], Ottawa, Ontario [*Library symbol*] [*National Library of Canada*] (BIB)

**OONLMBS** ... Multilingual Biblioservice, National Library of Canada [*Biblioservice Multilingue, Bibliotheque Nationale du Canada*] Ottawa, Ontario [*Library symbol*] [*National Library of Canada*] (NLC)

**OONLN** .... Newspaper Division, National Library of Canada [*Division des Journaux Bibliotheque Nationale du Canada*] Ottawa, Ontario [*Library symbol*] [*National Library of Canada*] (NLC)

**OONLP**..... Serials Record, National Library of Canada [*Enregistrement des Publications en Serie, Bibliotheque Nationale du Canada*] Ottawa, Ontario [*Library symbol*] [*National Library of Canada*] (NLC)

**OONLR**..... Retrospective Bibliography, National Library of Canada [*Bibliographie Retrospective, Bibliotheque Nationale du Canada*] Ottawa, Ontario [*Library symbol*] [*National Library of Canada*] (NLC)

**OONLS**..... Union Catalogue of Serials, National Library of Canada [*Catalogue Collectif des Periodiques, Bibliotheque Nationale du Canada*] Ottawa, Ontario [*Library symbol*] [*National Library of Canada*] (NLC)

**OONM**...... National Museums of Canada [*Musees Nationaux du Canada*] Ottawa, Ontario [*Library symbol*] [*National Library of Canada*] (NLC)

**OONMA** ... National Aviation Museum [*Musee National de l'Aviation*], Ottawa, Ontario [*Library symbol*] [*National Library of Canada*] (NLC)

**OONMC** ... Canadian War Museum [*Musee de Guerre du Canada*] Ottawa, Ontario [*Library symbol*] [*National Library of Canada*] (NLC)

**OONMCC** ... Canadian Conservation Institute, National Museums of Canada [*Institut Canadien de Conservation, Musees Nationaux du Canada*] Ottawa, Ontario [*Library symbol*] [*National Library of Canada*] (NLC)

**OONMM**.. Canadian Museum of Civilization, National Museums of Canada [*Musee Canadien des Civilisations, Musees Nationaux du Canada*] Ottawa, Ontario [*Library symbol*] [*National Library of Canada*] (NLC)

**OONMNS** ... National Museum of Natural Sciences [*Musee National des Sciences Naturelles*], Ottawa, Ontario [*Library symbol*] [*National Library of Canada*] (NLC)

**OONMS**.... National Museum of Science and Technology [*Musee National des Sciences et de la Technologie*] Ottawa, Ontario [*Library symbol*] [*National Library of Canada*] (NLC)

**OONORE** ... Bell Northern Research, Ottawa, Ontario [*Library symbol*] [*National Library of Canada*] (NLC)

**OONP**........ Division of Physics, Canada Institute for Scientific and Technical Information [*Division de Physique, Institute Canadien de l'Information Scientifique et Technique*] Ottawa, Ontario [*Library symbol*] [*National Library of Canada*] (NLC)

**OONR** ....... Customs and Excise Division, Department of National Revenue [*Division des Douanes et de l'Accise, Ministere du Revenu National*] Ottawa, Ontario [*Library symbol*] [*National Library of Canada*] (NLC)

**OONR** ....... Marmul/Nasir [*Oman*] [*ICAO location identifier*] (ICLI)

**OONRE**..... Electrical Engineering Division, Canada Institute for Scientific and Technical Information [*Division de Genie Electrique, Institut Canadien de l'Information Scientifique et Technique*] Ottawa, Ontario [*Library symbol*] [*National Library of Canada*] (NLC)

**OONRT**..... Taxation Division, Department of National Revenue [*Division de l'Impot, Ministere du Revenu National*] Ottawa, Ontario [*Library symbol*] [*National Library of Canada*] (NLC)

**OONRTC**.. Centre for Career Development, Revenue Canada - Taxation [*Centre de Developpement Professionnel, Revenu Canada - Impot*] Ottawa, Ontario [*Library symbol*] [*National Library of Canada*] (NLC)

**OONS**........ Sussex Library, Canada Institute for Scientific and Technical Information [*Bibliotheque Sussex, Institut Canadien de l'Information Scientifique et Technique*] Ottawa, Ontario [*Library symbol*] [*National Library of Canada*] (NLC)

**OONSE**..... Natural Sciences and Engineering Research Council of Canada [*Conseil de Recherches en Sciences Naturelles et en Genie du Canada*], Ottawa, Ontario [*Library symbol*] [*National Library of Canada*] (NLC)

**OONSF**..... National Science Film Library [*Cinematheque Nationale Scientifique*] Ottawa, Ontario [*Library symbol*] [*National Library of Canada*] (NLC)

**OONSI**...... North-South Institute [*L'Institut Nord-Sud*], Ottawa, Ontario [*Library symbol*] [*National Library of Canada*] (NLC)

**OONU**....... Uplands Library, Canada Institute for Scientific and Technical Information [*Bibliotheque d'Uplands, Institut Canadien de l'Information Scientifique et Technique*] Ottawa, Ontario [*Library symbol*] [*National Library of Canada*] (NLC)

**OONUL** .... Union List of Scientific Serials in Canadian Libraries [*Catalogue Collectif des Publications Scientifiques dans les Bibliotheques Canadiennes*] Ottawa, Ontario [*Library symbol*] [*National Library of Canada*] (NLC)

**OONVRC** ... National Victims Resource Centre [*Centre National de la Documentation sur les Victimes*] Ottawa, Ontario [*Library symbol*] [*National Library of Canada*] (NLC)
**OONZ** ....... Nizwa [*Oman*] [*ICAO location identifier*] (ICLI)
**OOO** .......... Earth Physics Branch, Energy, Mines and Resources Canada [*Direction de la Physique du Globe, Energie, Mines et Resources Canada*] Ottawa, Ontario [*Library symbol*] [*National Library of Canada*] (NLC)
**OOO** .......... Geophysics Collection, Geological Survey of Canada [*Collection de la Geophysique, Commission Geologique du Canada*], Ottawa, Ontario [*Library symbol*] [*National Library of Canada*] (NLC)
**OOO** .......... Grants Pass, OR [*Location identifier*] [*FAA*] (FAAL)
**OOO** .......... O Sapientia, O Radix, O Adonai [*Three anthems sung in Roman Catholic churches before Christmas*] (ROG)
**OOO** .......... Oleum Olivae Optimum [*Best Olive Oil*] [*Pharmacy*] (ROG)
**OOO** .......... Order of Owls (EA)
**OOO** .......... Out of Order [*Telecommunications*] (TEL)
**OOOA** ....... City of Ottawa Archives, Ontario [*Library symbol*] [*National Library of Canada*] (NLC)
**OOOAG** .... Office of the Auditor General [*Bureau du Verificateur General*] Ottawa, Ontario [*Library symbol*] [*National Library of Canada*] (NLC)
**OOOCF** ..... Ottawa Clinic, Ontario Cancer Foundation, Ontario [*Library symbol*] [*National Library of Canada*] (NLC)
**OOOCH** .... Ottawa Civic Hospital, Ontario [*Library symbol*] [*National Library of Canada*] (NLC)
**OOOCM** ... Information Services, Ontario Centre for Microelectronics, Nepean, Ontario [*Library symbol*] [*National Library of Canada*] (NLC)
**OOOF** ........ Onaping Branch, Onaping Falls Public Library, Ontario [*Library symbol*] [*National Library of Canada*] (NLC)
**OOOI** ........ Out-Off-On-In [*Telecommunications*]
**OOOL** ........ Optotek Ltd., Ottawa, Ontario [*Library symbol*] [*National Library of Canada*] (NLC)
**OOOTQFUE** ... Omnipotent Overseer of the Quest for Unsurpassable Excellence [*Rank in the Junior Woodchucks organization mentioned in Donald Duck comic by Carl Barks*]
**OOP** ........... Library of Parliament [*Bibliotheque du Parlement*] Ottawa, Ontario [*Library symbol*] [*National Library of Canada*] (NLC)
**OOP** ........... Object-Oriented Programming [*Data processing*]
**OOP** ........... Oceanographic Observations of the Pacific
**OOP** ........... Office of Organization Planning
**OOP** ........... Optimum Optical Pump
**OOP** ........... Out-of-Phase [*Gynecology*]
**OOP** ........... Out of Plane
**OOP** ........... Out of Plant
**OOP** ........... Out of Position (MCD)
**OOP** ........... Out of Print [*Also, OP*] [*Publishing*]
**OOPA** ........ National Arts Centre [*Centre National des Arts*] Ottawa, Ontario [*Library symbol*] [*National Library of Canada*] (NLC)
**OOPAC** ..... Chaudiere Branch, Departmental Library, Environment Canada [*Succursale Chaudiere, Bibliotheque du Ministere, Environnement Canada*] Ottawa, Ontario [*Library symbol*] [*National Library of Canada*] (NLC)
**OOPART** .. Out of Place Artifact [*Archeology*]
**OOPC** ........ Management Information Centre, Privy Council Office [*Regie Interne de l'Information, Bureau du Conseil Prive*] Ottawa, Ontario [*Library symbol*] [*National Library of Canada*] (NLC)
**OOPC** ........ Office of Operational Planning and Control [*Social Security Administration*]
**OOPCF** ...... Parliamentary Centre for Foreign Affairs and Foreign Trade [*Centre Parlementaire pour les Affaires Etrangeres et le Commerce Exterieur*], Ottawa, Ontario [*Library symbol*] [*National Library of Canada*] (NLC)
**OOPEC** ..... Petro-Canada, Ottawa, Ontario [*Library symbol*] [*National Library of Canada*] (NLC)
**OOPED** ..... Pylon Electronic Development Co. Ltd., Ottawa, Ontario [*Library symbol*] [*National Library of Canada*] (NLC)
**OOPF** ........ Resource Centre, Ottawa Police Force, Ontario [*Library symbol*] [*National Library of Canada*] (BIB)
**OOPH** ....... Perley Hospital, Ottawa, Ontario [*Library symbol*] [*National Library of Canada*] (NLC)
**OOPI** ......... Petroleum Incentives Program, Energy, Mines and Resources Canada [*Programmes d'Encouragement Petrolier, Energie, Mines et Ressources Canada*] Ottawa, Ontario [*Library symbol*] [*National Library of Canada*] (NLC)
**OOPIP** ....... Professional Institute of the Public Service of Canada [*Institut Professionnel de la Fonction Publique du Canada*], Ottawa, Ontario [*Library symbol*] [*National Library of Canada*] (BIB)
**OOPK** ........ Ookpik [*A publication*]
**OOPLFC & A** ... Only Official Peggy Lee Fan Club and Archives (EA)
**OOPM** ....... National Postal Museum [*Musee National des Postes*] Ottawa, Ontario [*Library symbol*] [*National Library of Canada*] (NLC)
**OOPMF** .... Marten Falls Band Library, Ogoki Post, Ontario [*Library symbol*] [*National Library of Canada*] (BIB)
**OOPMP** .... Peat, Marwick & Partners, Ottawa, Ontario [*Library symbol*] [*National Library of Canada*] (NLC)
**OOPO** ........ Canada Post [*Postes Canada*] Ottawa, Ontario [*Library symbol*] [*National Library of Canada*] (NLC)
**OOPOM** .... Meriline Branch, Canada Post [*Postes Canada*], Ottawa, Ontario [*Library symbol*] [*National Library of Canada*] (BIB)
**OOPOR** ..... Ports Canada, Ottawa, Ontario [*Library symbol*] [*National Library of Canada*] (NLC)
**OOPS** ........ Object-Oriented Programming (BYTE)
**OOPS** ........ O'Brien's Oil Pollution Service of New Orleans [*Oil spill cleanup service*]
**OOPS** ........ Off-Line Operating Simulator [*Data processing*]
**OOPS** ........ Office for Operations in Political Systems
**OOPS** ........ Originals on Permanent Sale
**OOPS** ........ Public Service Staff Relations Board [*Commission des Relations de Travail dans la Fonction Publique*] Ottawa, Ontario [*Library symbol*] [*National Library of Canada*] (NLC)
**OOPSAC** ... Public Service Alliance of Canada [*Alliance de la Fonction Publique du Canada*] Ottawa, Ontario [*Library symbol*] [*National Library of Canada*] (NLC)
**OOPSLA** ... Object-Oriented Programming Systems, Languages, and Applications [*Computer conference*]
**OOPW** ....... Public Works Canada [*Travaux Publics Canada*] Ottawa, Ontario [*Library symbol*] [*National Library of Canada*] (NLC)
**OOPWC** .... Capital Region Library, Public Works Canada [*Bibliotheque de la Region de la Capitale, Travaux Publics Canada*] Ottawa, Ontario [*Library symbol*] [*National Library of Canada*] (NLC)
**OOPWR** .... Research and Development Laboratories, Public Works Canada [*Laboratoires de Recherche et de Developpement, Travaux Publics Canada*] Ottawa, Ontario [*Library symbol*] [*Obsolete*] [*National Library of Canada*] (NLC)
**OOQ** .......... Occupational Outlook Quarterly [*A publication*]
**OOQ** .......... Officer of the Quarters
**OOQA** ....... Director-General, Quality Assurance Library, Department of National Defence [*Bibliotheque du Directeur General-Assurance de la Qualite, Ministere de la Defense Nationale*], Ottawa, Ontario [*Library symbol*] [*National Library of Canada*] (NLC)
**OOQC** ....... Queensway-Carleton Hospital, Ottawa, Ontario [*Library symbol*] [*National Library of Canada*] (NLC)
**OOQM** ...... Queen Mary Street School, Ottawa, Ontario [*Library symbol*] [*National Library of Canada*] (BIB)
**OOR** .......... Office for Ordnance Research [*Later, Army Research Office*]
**OOR** .......... Open Ocean Release
**OOR** .......... Operator Override [*Telecommunications*] (TEL)
**OOR** .......... Out-of-Roundness [*Manufacturing term*]
**OOR** .......... Oxygen/Ozone Recorder
**OOR** .......... RCMP Headquarters [*Direction Generale de la GRC*] Ottawa, Ontario [*Library symbol*] [*National Library of Canada*] (NLC)
**OOR** .......... RCMP [*Royal Canadian Mounted Police*] Law Enforcement Reference Centre [*Centre de Documentation Policiere, Gendarmerie Royale du Canada*], Ottawa, Ontario [*Library symbol*] [*National Library of Canada*] (NLC)
**OORA** ........ Orangeville Public Library, Ontario [*Library symbol*] [*National Library of Canada*] (NLC)
**OORCS** ..... Ottawa Roman Catholic Separate School Board, Ontario [*Library symbol*] [*National Library of Canada*] (NLC)
**OORD** ....... Indian and Northern Affairs Canada [*Affaires Indiennes et du Nord Canada*] Ottawa, Ontario [*Library symbol*] [*National Library of Canada*] (NLC)
**OORH** ....... Riverside Hospital, Ottawa, Ontario [*Library symbol*] [*National Library of Canada*] (NLC)
**OORI** ......... Orillia Public Library, Ontario [*Library symbol*] [*National Library of Canada*] (NLC)
**OORIA** ...... J. L. Richard & Associates Ltd., Ottawa, Ontario [*Library symbol*] [*National Library of Canada*] (NLC)
**OORIGC** ... Learning Resources Centre, Georgian College of Applied Arts and Technology, Orillia, Ontario [*Library symbol*] [*National Library of Canada*] (NLC)
**OORIMT** .. Mara Township Public Library, Orillia, Ontario [*Library symbol*] [*National Library of Canada*] (BIB)
**OORISMH** ... OSMH Health Sciences Library, Orillia Soldiers' Memorial Hospital, Ontario [*Library symbol*] [*National Library of Canada*] (NLC)
**OORM** ...... Planning Department Library, Regional Municipality of Ottawa-Carleton, Ottawa, Ontario [*Library symbol*] [*National Library of Canada*] (NLC)
**OORM** ...... Rima [*Oman*] [*ICAO location identifier*] (ICLI)
**OORMT** .... Transportation-Works Department, Regional Municipality of Ottawa-Carleton, Ottawa, Ontario [*Library symbol*] [*National Library of Canada*] (NLC)
**OORO** ....... Royal Ottawa Hospital, Ontario [*Library symbol*] [*National Library of Canada*] (NLC)
**OORORR** ... Royal Ottawa Regional Rehabilitation Centre, Royal Ottawa Hospital, Ontario [*Library symbol*] [*National Library of Canada*] (NLC)

**OORP**........ Rockliffe Park Public Library, Ottawa, Ontario [*Library symbol*] [*National Library of Canada*] (BIB)
**OORPL**..... Communications Research Centre, Department of Communications [*Centre de Recherches sur les Communications, Ministere des Communications*] Ottawa, Ontario [*Library symbol*] [*National Library of Canada*] (NLC)
**OORQ**....... Rostaq [*Oman*] [*ICAO location identifier*] (ICLI)
**OORR**........ Regional Realty Ltd., Ottawa, Ontario [*Library symbol*] [*National Library of Canada*] (BIB)
**OOrrW**...... Wayne General and Technical College, Orrville, OH [*Library symbol*] [*Library of Congress*] (LCLS)
**OORS**........ RCMP Scientific Information Centre [*Centre d'Information Scientifique de la GRC*] Ottawa, Ontario [*Library symbol*] [*National Library of Canada*] (NLC)
**OORSFC**... Only Official Rolling Stones Fan Club (EAIO)
**OORSS**...... CSIS [*Canadian Security Intelligence Service*] Open Information Centre [*Bibliotheque du SCRS (Service Canadien du Renseignement de Securite), Ottawa*] Ontario [*Library symbol*] [*National Library of Canada*] (NLC)
**OORT**........ Canadian Radio-Television and Telecommunications Commission [*Conseil de la Radiodiffusion et des Telecommunications Canadiennes*] Ottawa, Ontario [*Library symbol*] [*National Library of Canada*] (NLC)
**OORTA**..... Roads and Transportation Association of Canada [*Association des Routes et Transports du Canada*] Ottawa, Ontario [*Library symbol*] [*National Library of Canada*] (NLC)
**OOS**........... Office of Operations Support [*Law Enforcement Assistance Administration*]
**OOS**........... On-Orbit Station [*NASA*] (NASA)
**OOS**........... On-Orbit Support
**OOS**........... Operational Operating System [*Telecommunications*] (TEL)
**OOS**........... Orbit-to-Orbit Shuttle [*NASA*]
**OOS**........... Orbit-to-Orbit Stage [*NASA*] (NASA)
**O & OS**...... Ordnance and Ordnance Stores [*Navy*]
**OOS**........... Out of School (OICC)
**OOS**........... Out of Sequence (NRCH)
**OOS**........... Out of Service (NRCH)
**OOS**........... Out-of-Shot [*Photography*] (ADA)
**OOS**........... Statistics Canada [*Statistique Canada*] Ottawa Ontario [*Library symbol*] [*National Library of Canada*] (NLC)
**OOSA**........ National Social Services Consultant and Government Relations Officer, Salvation Army Library, Ottawa, Ontario [*Library symbol*] [*National Library of Canada*] (BIB)
**OOSA**........ Salalah [*Oman*] [*ICAO location identifier*] (ICLI)
**OOSAR**..... Government Relations Office, Spar Aerospace Ltd., Ottawa, Ontario [*Library symbol*] [*National Library of Canada*] (BIB)
**OOSB**........ Smart & Biggar, Ottawa, Ontario [*Library symbol*] [*National Library of Canada*] (BIB)
**OOSC**........ Out-of-Sight Control (MUGU)
**OOSC**........ Supreme Court of Canada [*Cour Supreme du Canada*] Ottawa, Ontario [*Library symbol*] [*National Library of Canada*] (NLC)
**OOSCA**..... Archives des Soeurs de la Charite d'Ottawa, Ontario [*Library symbol*] [*National Library of Canada*] (NLC)
**OOSCAC**... Scanada Consultants Ltd., Ottawa, Ontario [*Library symbol*] [*National Library of Canada*] (NLC)
**OOSCC**..... Science Council of Canada [*Conseil des Sciences du Canada*] Ottawa, Ontario [*Library symbol*] [*National Library of Canada*] (NLC)
**OOSCL**...... Census Library, Statistics Canada [*Bibliotheque du Recensement, Statistique Canada*] Ottawa, Ontario [*Library symbol*] [*National Library of Canada*] (NLC)
**OOSCM**.... Census Map Library, Statistics Canada [*Cartotheque du Recensement, Statistique Canada*] Ottawa, Ontario [*Library symbol*] [*National Library of Canada*] (NLC)
**OOSDP**..... On-Orbit Station Distribution Panel [*NASA*] (MCD)
**OOSG**........ Ministry of the Solicitor General [*Ministere du Solliciteur General*] Ottawa, Ontario [*Library symbol*] [*National Library of Canada*] (NLC)
**OOSGO**..... Osgoode Public Library, Ontario [*Library symbol*] [*National Library of Canada*] (BIB)
**OOSH**........ Oshawa Public Library, Ontario [*Library symbol*] [*National Library of Canada*] (NLC)
**OOSH**........ Sohar [*Oman*] [*ICAO location identifier*] (ICLI)
**OOSHD**..... Durham College of Applied Arts and Technology, Oshawa, Ontario [*Library symbol*] [*National Library of Canada*] (NLC)
**OOSHH**.... Education Resource Centre, Oshawa General Hospital, Ontario [*Library symbol*] [*National Library of Canada*] (BIB)
**OOSHR**..... Robert McLaughlin Gallery, Oshawa, Ontario [*Library symbol*] [*National Library of Canada*] (NLC)
**OOSHT**..... Technical Library, Systemhouse Ltd., Ottawa, Ontario [*Library symbol*] [*National Library of Canada*] (NLC)
**OOSJ**......... La Bibliotheque Deschatelets Peres Oblats [*Closed to the public*] Ottawa, Ontario [*Library symbol*] [*National Library of Canada*] (NLC)
**OOSLM**.... Montfort Hospital [*Hopital Montfort*] Ottawa, Ontario [*Library symbol*] [*National Library of Canada*] (NLC)
**OOSLR**...... S. L. Ross Environmental Research, Ottawa, Ontario [*Library symbol*] [*National Library of Canada*] (BIB)
**OOSM**....... Sahma [*Oman*] [*ICAO location identifier*] (ICLI)
**OOSM**....... Surveying and Mapping Library, Cartographic Information and Distribution Centre, Energy, Mines, and Resources Canada [*Bibliotheque des Leves et de Cartographies, Centre d'Information et de Distribution Cartographiques, Energie, Mines, et Ressources Canada*] Ottawa, Ontario [*Library symbol*] [*National Library of Canada*] (NLC)
**OOSMM**... Map Library, Energy, Mines and Resources Canada [*Cartotheque, Energie, Mines et Ressources Canada*] Ottawa, Ontario [*Library symbol*] [*National Library of Canada*] (NLC)
**OOSN**........ Six Nations Public Library, Ohsweken, Ontario [*Library symbol*] [*National Library of Canada*] (BIB)
**OOSP**........ Patent and Copyright Office, Department of Consumer and Corporate Affairs [*Bureau des Brevets et du Droit d'Auteur, Ministere de la Consommation et des Corporations*] Ottawa, Ontario [*Library symbol*] [*National Library of Canada*] (NLC)
**OOSPX**...... St.-Pius X High School, Ottawa, Ontario [*Library symbol*] [*National Library of Canada*] (BIB)
**OOSQ**........ Saiq [*Oman*] [*ICAO location identifier*] (ICLI)
**OOSR**........ Sur [*Oman*] [*ICAO location identifier*] (ICLI)
**OOSS**........ Department of the Secretary of State [*Secretariat d'Etat*] Ottawa, Ontario [*Library symbol*] [*National Library of Canada*] (NLC)
**OOSS**........ Outpatient Ophthalmic Surgery Society (EA)
**OOSS**........ Overseas Operational Storage Site [*Army*]
**OOSSHRC**... Social Sciences and Humanities Research Council of Canada [*Conseil de Recherches en Sciences Humaines du Canada*] Ottawa, Ontario [*Library symbol*] [*National Library of Canada*] (NLC)
**OOSSTE**... Terminology and Documentation Branch, Translation Bureau, Department of the Secretary of State [*Direction generale de la Terminologie et de la Documentation, Bureau des Traductions, Secretariat d'Etat*] Ottawa, Ontario [*Library symbol*] [*National Library of Canada*] (NLC)
**OOSSTE**... Terminology Library, Information Resource Services Directorate, Secretary of State [*Bibliotheque de la Terminologie, Direction Info-Ressources, Secretariat d'Etat*], Ottawa, Ontario [*Library symbol*] [*National Library of Canada*] (NLC)
**OOSSTM**... Multilingual Services Directorate, Translation Bureau, Department of the Secretary of State [*Direction des Services Multilingues, Bureau des Traductions, Secretariat d'Etat*] Ottawa, Ontario [*Library symbol*] [*National Library of Canada*] (NLC)
**OOSSTR**... Translation Services Branch, Translation Bureau, Department of the Secretary of State [*Direction Generale des Services de Traduction, Bureau des Traductions, Secretariat d'Etat*] Ottawa, Ontario [*Library symbol*] [*National Library of Canada*] (NLC)
**OOST**........ Standards Council of Canada, Ottawa, Ontario [*Library symbol*] [*National Library of Canada*] (BIB)
**OOSTI**....... Scientific and Technical Information Centre, Laboratory and Scientific Services Division, Revenue Canada Customs and Excise [*Centre d'Information Scientifique et Technique, Division du Laboratoire et des Services Scientifiques, Revenu Canada Douanes et Accise*] Ottawa, Ontario [*Library symbol*] [*National Library of Canada*] (NLC)
**OOSTM**.... Careerware Reference Centre, STM Systems Corp., Ottawa, Ontario [*Library symbol*] [*National Library of Canada*] (BIB)
**Oostvlaam Zanten**... Oostvlaamse Zanten. Tijdschrift van de Koninklijke Bond der Oostvlaamse Volkskundigen [*A publication*]
**OostvlZanten**... Oostvlaamse Zanten [*A publication*]
**Oost W**....... Oost en West [*A publication*]
**OOSU**........ St. Paul University [*Universite St-Paul*] Ottawa, Ontario [*Library symbol*] [*National Library of Canada*] (NLC)
**OOSUA**..... Archives, St. Paul University [*Archives, Universite St-Paul*] Ottawa, Ontario [*Library symbol*] [*National Library of Canada*] (NLC)
**OOSV**........ St. Vincent Hospital [*Hopital St-Vincent*] Ottawa, Ontario [*Library symbol*] [*National Library of Canada*] (NLC)
**OOSW**........ Status of Women Canada [*Condition Feminine Canada*] Ottawa, Ontario [*Library symbol*] [*National Library of Canada*] (NLC)
**OOSWH**.... Soloway, Wright & Houston Law Firm, Ottawa, Ontario [*Library symbol*] [*National Library of Canada*] (BIB)
**OOT**........... Oil Out Temperature
**OOT**........... Onotoa [*Kiribati*] [*Airport symbol*] (OAG)
**OOT**........... Ootomari [*USSR*] [*Seismograph station code, US Geological Survey*] [*Closed*] (SEIS)
**OOT**........... Out of Oxygen Tent
**OOT**........... Out of Tolerance (FAAC)
**OOT**........... Out-of-Town [*Word processing*]
**OOT**........... Transport Canada [*Transports Canada*] Ottawa, Ontario [*Library symbol*] [*National Library of Canada*] (NLC)

**OOTA** ........ Airworthiness Library, Transport Canada [*Bibliotheque de la Navigabilite Aerienne, Transports Canada*], Ottawa, Ontario [*Library symbol*] [*National Library of Canada*] (NLC)
**OOTAC** ..... Airports and Construction Services, Transport Canada [*Service des Aeroports et de la Construction, Transports Canada*] Ottawa, Ontario [*Library symbol*] [*National Library of Canada*] (NLC)
**OOTAS** ..... Canadian Aviation Safety Board [*Bureau Canadien de la Securite Aerienne*] Ottawa, Ontario [*Library symbol*] [*National Library of Canada*] (NLC)
**OOTB** ........ Tourism Reference and Documentation, Regional Industrial Expansion [*Centre de Reference et de Documentation Touristique, Expansion Industrielle Regionale*], Ottawa, Ontario [*Library symbol*] [*National Library of Canada*] (NLC)
**OOTC** ........ Department of Regional Industrial Expansion [*Ministere de l'Expansion Industrielle Regionale*] Ottawa, Ontario [*Library symbol*] [*National Library of Canada*] (NLC)
**OOTC** ........ Old Old Timers Club (EA)
**OOTCI** ...... Documentation Centre, Communications and Informatics, Transport Canada [*Centre de Documentation, Communications et Informatique, Transports Canada*], Ottawa, Ontario [*Library symbol*] [*National Library of Canada*] (BIB)
**OOTCO** ..... Telecommunications Library, Transport Canada [*Bibliotheque de Telecommunications, Transports Canada*], Ottawa, Ontario [*Library symbol*] [*National Library of Canada*] (NLC)
**OOTCT** ..... TransCanada Telephone System, Ottawa, Ontario [*Library symbol*] [*National Library of Canada*] (NLC)
**OOTE** ........ Out-of-Town Executive
**OOTEL** ..... Telesat Canada, Ottawa, Ontario [*Library symbol*] [*National Library of Canada*] (NLC)
**OOTFS** ...... Technical Library AAFBAA, Flight Services Directorate, Transport Canada [*Bibliotheque Technique AAFBAA, Direction Generale du Service des Vols, Transports Canada*], Ottawa, Ontario [*Library symbol*] [*National Library of Canada*] (NLC)
**OOTH** ....... Thumrait [*Oman*] [*ICAO location identifier*] (ICLI)
**OOTI** ......... Technical Information Centre, Transport Canada Training Institute [*Centre d'Information Technique, Institut de Formation Transports Canada*], Cornwall, Ontario [*Library symbol*] [*National Library of Canada*] (NLC)
**OOTIR** ...... Traffic Injury Research Foundation of Canada [*Fondation de Recherches sur les Blessures de la Route au Canada*] Ottawa, Ontario [*Library symbol*] [*National Library of Canada*] (NLC)
**OOTN** ....... Trade Negotiations Office, External Affairs Canada [*Affaires Exterieures Canada*] Ottawa, Ontario [*Library symbol*] [*National Library of Canada*] (NLC)
**OOTR** ........ Tax Court of Canada [*Cour Canadienne de l'Impot*] Ottawa, Ontario [*Library symbol*] [*National Library of Canada*] (NLC)
**OOTRAT** .. Les Traductions Tessier SCC (Division de Multiscript International), Ottawa, Ontario [*Library symbol*] [*National Library of Canada*] (BIB)
**OOTRS** ..... Road Safety and Motor Vehicle Regulation Branch, Transport Canada [*Direction de la Securite Routiere et de la Reglementation Automobile, Transports Canada*], Ottawa, Ontario [*Library symbol*] [*National Library of Canada*] (NLC)
**OOTRT** ..... Railway Transportation Directorate, Transport Canada [*Direction du Transport Ferroviaire, Transports Canada*] Ottawa, Ontario [*Library symbol*] [*National Library of Canada*] (NLC)
**OOTSSA** ... St. Lawrence Seaway Authority, Transport Canada [*Administration de la Voie Maritime du Saint-Laurent, Transports Canada*] Ottawa, Ontario [*Library symbol*] [*National Library of Canada*] (NLC)
**OOTT** ........ National Transportation Agency of Canada [*Office National des Transports du Canada*], Ottawa, Ontario [*Library symbol*] [*National Library of Canada*] (NLC)
**OOTTD** ..... Technical Data Resource Centre, Transport Canada [*Centre de la Documentation Technique, Transports Canada*], Ottawa, Ontario [*Library symbol*] [*National Library of Canada*] (NLC)
**OOTTE** ..... Telecommunications and Electronics Directorate, Transport Canada [*Direction des Telecommunications et de l'Electronique, Transports Canada*] Ottawa, Ontario [*Library symbol*] [*Obsolete*] [*National Library of Canada*] (NLC)
**OOU** .......... University of Ottawa [*Universite d'Ottawa*] Ontario [*Library symbol*] [*National Library of Canada*] (NLC)
**OOUA** ....... Archives, Universite d'Ottawa [*Archives, University of Ottawa*], Ontario [*Library symbol*] [*National Library of Canada*] (BIB)
**OOUC** ....... Department of Criminology, University of Ottawa [*Departement de Criminologie, Universite d'Ottawa*] Ontario [*Library symbol*] [*National Library of Canada*] (NLC)
**OOUD** ....... Faculty of Civil Law, University of Ottawa [*Faculte de Droit Civil, Universite d'Ottawa*] Ontario [*Library symbol*] [*National Library of Canada*] (NLC)
**OOUH** ....... Health Sciences Library, University of Ottawa [*Bibliotheque des Sciences de la Sante, Universite d'Ottawa*] Ontario [*Library symbol*] [*National Library of Canada*] (NLC)
**OOUIC** ...... Institute of International Cooperation, University of Ottawa [*Institut de Cooperation Internationale, Universite d'Ottawa*] Ontario [*Library symbol*] [*National Library of Canada*] (NLC)
**OOUM** ...... Vanier Library, University of Ottawa [*Bibliotheque Vanier, Universite d'Ottawa*] Ontario [*Library symbol*] [*National Library of Canada*] (NLC)
**OOUMA** ... Map Library, University of Ottawa [*Cartotheque, Universite d'Ottawa*] Ontario [*Library symbol*] [*National Library of Canada*] (NLC)
**OOURC** ..... Centre de Recherche en Civilisation Canadienne-Francaise, Universite d'Ottawa [*Centre for Research on French Canadian Culture, University of Ottawa*], Ontario [*Library symbol*] [*National Library of Canada*] (BIB)
**OOUSA** ..... United States Information Service, Ottawa, Ontario [*Library symbol*] [*National Library of Canada*] (NLC)
**OOUSC** ..... Unitarian Service Committee of Canada, Ottawa, Ontario [*Library symbol*] [*National Library of Canada*] (BIB)
**OOV** .......... Out of View
**OOV** .......... Out of Vision [*Films, television, etc.*]
**OOVIF** ...... Vanier Institute of the Family [*Institut Vanier de la Famille*] Ottawa, Ontario [*Library symbol*] [*National Library of Canada*] (NLC)
**OOVV** ........ Versatile Vickers Systems, Inc., Ottawa, Ontario [*Library symbol*] [*National Library of Canada*] (NLC)
**OOW** ......... Officer of the Watch [*Navigation*]
**OOW** ......... Owen Sound Public Library, Ontario [*Library symbol*] [*National Library of Canada*] (NLC)
**OOWC** ....... Wordcount, Creative Writing Services, Inc., Ottawa, Ontario [*Library symbol*] [*National Library of Canada*] (NLC)
**OOWD** ...... Western Diversification [*Diversification de l'Ouest*], Ottawa, Ontario [*Library symbol*] [*National Library of Canada*] (BIB)
**OOWGC** .... Georgian College Resource Centre, Owen Sound, Ontario [*Library symbol*] [*National Library of Canada*] (NLC)
**OOWGM** .. Health Sciences Library, General & Marine Hospital, Owen Sound, Ontario [*Library symbol*] [*National Library of Canada*] (NLC)
**OOWGM** .. Health Sciences Library, Grey Bruce Regional Health Centre, Owen Sound, Ontario [*Library symbol*] [*National Library of Canada*] (NLC)
**OOWIC** ..... West Island College of Ontario, Ottawa [*Library symbol*] [*National Library of Canada*] (BIB)
**OOWLS** .... Sir Wilfrid Laurier High School Library, Carleton Board of Education, Ottawa, Ontario [*Library symbol*] [*National Library of Canada*] (BIB)
**OOWM** ..... Owen Sound Museum, County of Grey, Ontario [*Library symbol*] [*National Library of Canada*] (BIB)
**OOWT** ....... Tom Thomson Memorial Gallery, Owen Sound, Ontario [*Library symbol*] [*National Library of Canada*] (NLC)
**OOWU** ...... Briefing Centre, World University Services of Canada [*Centre de Ressources, Entraide Universitaire Mondiale du Canada*], Ottawa, Ontario [*Library symbol*] [*National Library of Canada*] (NLC)
**OOX** .......... XIOS Research Corp., Ottawa, Ontario [*Library symbol*] [*National Library of Canada*] (BIB)
**OOxM** ....... Miami University, Oxford, OH [*Library symbol*] [*Library of Congress*] (LCLS)
**OOxM-S** ... Miami University, Scripps Foundation for Research in Population Problems, Oxford, OH [*Library symbol*] [*Library of Congress*] (LCLS)
**OOYB** ........ Yibal [*Oman*] [*ICAO location identifier*] (ICLI)
**OP** ............. Air Panama International [*ICAO designator*] (FAAC)
**Op** ............. De Opficio Mundi [*Philo*] (BJA)
**OP** ............. Obligated Position [*Civil Service*]
**OP** ............. Observation Plane
**OP** ............. Observation Point [*or Post*]
**OP** ............. Observation Post [*Military*]
**OP** ............. Observed Position [*Navigation*]
**OP** ............. Occiput Posterior [*Medicine*]
**OP** ............. Oceanus Procellarum [*Lunar area*]
**OP** ............. Octapeptide [*Biochemistry*]
**OP** ............. Oelhydraulik und Pneumatik [*A publication*]
**O-P** ............ Off-Price [*A retail outlet selling discounted merchandise*]
**OP** ............. Offering Price
**OP** ............. Office Pass (AAG)
**OP** ............. Office of Pesticides [*Public Health Service*]
**OP** ............. Office of Policy [*NASA*]
**OP** ............. Official Publication (ADA)
**OP** ............. Oil Pressure
**OP** ............. Oil Pump
**OP** ............. Oilproof
**OP** ............. Old Particular [*Marsala*]
**OP** ............. Old [*Previously seen*] Patient
**OP** ............. Old Pattern [*British military*] (DMA)

**OP**............. Old Persian [*Language, etc.*] (OCD)
**OP**............. Old Price [*Riots*] [*Occurred for 67 nights, beginning December 30, 1808, opening night of rebuilt Covent Garden Theatre, London, because of new and higher prices; protestors won*]
**OP**............. Omega Project (EA)
**OP**............. Opaque [*Envelopes*]
**OP**............. Open [*Stock exchange term*]
**O P**............. Open Places [*A publication*]
**OP**............. Open Policy
**OP**............. Open Position [*Dancing*]
**OP**............. Opening Pressure [*Medicine*]
**OP**............. Opening Price [*Stock exchange term*]
**OP**............. Opening Purchase [*Stock exchange term*]
**OP**............. Opera [*A publication*]
**OP**............. Opera
**Op**............. Opera et Dies [*of Hesiod*] [*Classical studies*] (OCD)
**OP**............. Opera News [*A publication*]
**OP**............. Operand [*Data processing*]
**OP**............. Operating Plan [*Management term*] (MCD)
**OP**............. Operating Policy [*Military*]
**OP**............. Operating Procedure [*Management term*] (KSC)
**OP**............. Operating Profit [*DoD*]
**OP**............. Operation (AFM)
**OP**............. Operation Overlord Preparations [*World War II*]
**OP**............. Operation Plans
**OP**............. Operational (CAAL)
**OP**............. Operational Priority
**OP**............. Operational Procedure (MCD)
**OP**............. Operational Project [*Army*] (AABC)
**OP**............. Operations (KSC)
**OP**............. Operations Order (MCD)
**O & P**......... Operations and Procedures (KSC)
**OP**............. Operative Procedure
**OP**............. Operator [*Data processing*]
**OP**............. Ophthalmology
**OP**............. Opinion (ADA)
**O-P**............. Oppenheimer-Phillips [*Process*]
**OP**............. Opposed (NVT)
**OP**............. Opposite
**OP**............. Opposite Prompt [*i.e., the left side*] [*A stage direction*]
**OP**............. Optical Probe (AAG)
**OP**............. Optical Technician Program [*Association of Independent Colleges and Schools specialization code*]
**OP**............. Optime [*Best*] [*Latin*] (ROG)
**OP**............. Optional
**OP**............. Optional Flag [*Navy*] [*British*]
**OP**............. Opus [*Work*]
**Op**............. Opyty [*A publication*]
**OP**............. Orange Pekoe [*Tea*]
**OP**............. Orbital Period (AAG)
**OP**............. Orbital Probe [*NASA*]
**OP**............. Order Policy [*Insurance*]
**OP**............. Order of Preceptors
**OP**............. Ordinis Praedicatorum [*Of the Order of Preachers, or Dominicans*] [*Latin*]
**OP**............. Ordnance Pamphlets
**OP**............. Ordnance Personnel
**OP**............. Ordnance Publications [*Navy*] (MCD)
**OP**............. Ordo Praedicatorum [*Order of Preachers*] [*Dominicans*] [*Roman Catholic religious order*]
**OP**............. Organophosphorus [*Organic chemistry*]
**OP**............. Orient Press [*Press agency*] [*Republic of Korea*]
**OP**............. Original Policy (ADA)
**OP**............. Original Premium [*Insurance*]
**OP**............. Orthomat Plot (MCD)
**OP**............. Osmotic Pressure
**OP**............. Ost-Probleme [*A publication*]
**OP**............. Other Papers (ROG)
**OP**............. Other People's [*Borrowed money, cigarettes, etc.*] [*Slang*]
**OP**............. Other Procurement
**OP**............. Other than Psychotic
**OP**............. Out-of-Press [*Recordings*]
**OP**............. Out of Print [*Also, OOP*] [*Publishing*]
**OP**............. Outer Panel (AAG)
**OP**............. Outpatient [*Medicine*]
**OP**............. Outpost
**OP**............. Output (AAG)
**OP**............. Output Primary [*Electronics*]
**OP**............. Outside Production
**O & P**......... Ova and Parasites [*Medicine*]
**OP**............. Over Pressure (AAG)
**OP**............. Overprint
**OP**............. Overproof [*Distilling*]
**OP**............. Overseas Post (ADA)
**OP**............. Ovine Prolactin [*Endocrinology*]
**O/P**............. Ownership Purpose Code [*Army*] (AABC)
**OP**............. Oxazolinylphenoxy [*Organic radical*]
**OP**............. Oxygen Pressure Process [*Ore leach process*]
**OP**............. Oxygen Purge [*NASA*] (NASA)
**OP**............. Paulding County Carnegie Public Library, Paulding, OH [*Library symbol*] [*Library of Congress*] (LCLS)
**OP**............. Perth Public Library, Ontario [*Library symbol*] [*National Library of Canada*] (NLC)
**OPA**........... Kopasker [*Iceland*] [*Airport symbol*] (OAG)
**OPa**........... Morley Library, Painesville, OH [*Library symbol*] [*Library of Congress*] (LCLS)
**OPA**........... Obscene Publications Act [*British*]
**OPA**........... Office of the Pardon Attorney [*Department of Justice*]
**OPA**........... Office of Petroleum Allocation [*Federal Energy Administration*]
**OPA**........... Office of Population Affairs [*HEW*]
**OPA**........... Office of Price Administration [*World War II*]
**OPA**........... Office of Program Analysis [*Department of Energy*] [*Washington, DC*]
**OPA**........... Office of Program Appraisal [*Navy*]
**OPA**........... Office of Public Affairs [*in various government agencies*]
**OPA**........... Officer Personnel Act
**OPA**........... Onafhankelijke Partij [*Independent Party*] [*Netherlands*] [*Political party*] (PPW)
**OPA**........... Onze Pius-Almanak [*A publication*]
**OPA**........... Opana [*Hawaii*] [*Seismograph station code, US Geological Survey*] (SEIS)
**OPA**........... Opaque [*Type of ice formation*]
**Opa**........... Opera of the Month Club [*Record label*]
**OPA**........... Operations Planning Analysis [*NASA*] (MCD)
**OPA**........... Optical Publishing Association (EA)
**OPA**........... Optoelectronic Pulse Amplifier
**OPA**........... Orbiter Plasma Analyzer [*NASA*]
**OPA**........... Ortho-Phthaldehyde [*Organic chemistry*]
**OPA**........... Ortho-Propylaniline
**OPA**........... Other Procurement, Army (AABC)
**OPA**........... Output Plate Assembly (MCD)
**OPA**........... Ovarian Papillary Adenocarcinoma [*Oncology*]
**OPA**........... Overhead Precautionary Approach
**OPAAER**... Archaeological Survey of Alberta. Occasional Papers [*A publication*]
**OPAAW**.... Organization of Pan Asian-American Women (EA)
**OPAB**........ Abbottabad [*Pakistan*] [*ICAO location identifier*] (ICLI)
**OPAC**........ Online Public Access Catalog [*Silicon Valley Information Center - SVIC*] [*San Jose, CA*] [*Information service or system*] (IID)
**OPAC**........ Resource Centre, School of Lanark County, Algonquin College of Applied Arts & Technology, Perth, Ontario [*Library symbol*] [*National Library of Canada*] (NLC)
**OPACA**..... Optica Acta [*A publication*]
**OPACS**...... Office of Price Administration and Civilian Supply [*Name changed to Office of Price Administration*] [*World War II*]
**OPACS**...... Order Planning and Control System (MCD)
**OPACT**...... Organization of Professional Acting Coaches and Teachers (EA)
**OPaD**......... Diamond Shamrock Corp., Research Library, Painesville, OH [*Library symbol*] [*Library of Congress*] (LCLS)
**OPADEC**... Optical Particle Decoy
**OPAE**........ Office of Program Analysis and Evaluation [*DoD*]
**OPAEP**...... Organisation des Pays Arabes Exportateurs de Petrole [*Organization of Arab Petroleum Exporting Countries*] (EAIO)
**OPAFD7**.... Allan Hancock Foundation. Occasional Papers [*New Series*] [*A publication*]
**Op AG**........ Opinions of the Attorney General [*A publication*] (DLA)
**OPAGY**..... Operating Agency [*Military*]
**OPAH**........ Oil Pump Assembly Housing (MCD)
**OPAI**......... Paisley Branch, Bruce County Public Library, Ontario [*Library symbol*] [*National Library of Canada*] (NLC)
**OPaL**......... Lake Erie College, Painesville, OH [*Library symbol*] [*Library of Congress*] (LCLS)
**OPAL**........ Lakehead University, Thunder Bay, Ontario [*Library symbol*] [*National Library of Canada*] (NLC)
**OPAL**........ Ocean Process Analysis Laboratory [*University of New Hampshire*] [*Research center*] (RCD)
**OPAL**........ Oncovin [*Vincristine*], Prednisolone, Adriamycin, L-Asparaginase [*Antineoplastic drug regimen*]
**OPAL**........ One People of Australia League
**OPAL**........ Operation Alert [*Designed to test ability to recover from an enemy attack*]
**OPAL**........ Operation Plan Analysis Logic [*Search technology*]
**OPAL**........ Operational Performance Analysis Language [*Data processing*]
**OPAL**........ Optical Platform Alignment Linkage
**OPAL**........ Orientation Program in American Law [*of AALS*]
**OPALE**...... Faculty of Education, Lakehead University, Thunder Bay, Ontario [*Library symbol*] [*National Library of Canada*] (NLC)
**OPALG**..... Department of Geography, Lakehead University, Thunder Bay, Ontario [*Library symbol*] [*National Library of Canada*] (NLC)
**Opals**.......... Older People with an Active Lifestyle [*Lifestyle classification*]
**OP AMP**.... Operational Amplifier [*Data processing*]
**OPANAL**.. Operations Analysis [*Navy*] (NG)
**OPANAL**.. Organismo para la Proscripcion de las Armas Nucleares en la America Latina [*Agency for the Prohibition of Nuclear Weapons in Latin America*] (EAIO)
**OPAPE**...... Organisation Pan-Africaine de la Profession Enseignante [*All Africa Teachers' Organization*] (EAIO)

**OPAQ**........ Offer Parent-Adolescent Questionnaire [*Personality development test*] [*Psychology*]
**OPAQUE**.. Optical Atmospheric Quality in Europe (MCD)
**OPAR**........ Paris Public Library, Ontario [*Library symbol*] [*National Library of Canada*] (NLC)
**Op Arch**..... Opuscula Archaeologica [*A publication*] (OCD)
**OPAREA**... Operating Area (CAAL)
**OPARI**....... Occasional Publications. African and Afro-American Research Institute. University of Texas, Austin [*A publication*]
**OPAS**......... Operational Assistance [*United Nations Development Program*]
**OPAS**......... Operational Public Address System
**OPASTCO**... Organization for the Protection and Advancement of Small Telephone Companies (EA)
**OPat**........... Pataskala Public Library, Pataskala, OH [*Library symbol*] [*Library of Congress*] (LCLS)
**Op Ath**....... Opuscula Atheniensia [*A publication*]
**Op Athen**... Opuscula Atheniensia [*A publication*]
**Op Att Gen**... Opinions of the Attorneys-General [*United States*] [*A publication*] (DLA)
**Op Att'y Gen**... Opinions of the Attorney General [*A publication*] (DLA)
**Op Attys Gen**... Opinions of the Attorneys-General [*United States*] [*A publication*] (DLA)
**OPB**........... Occupational Pensions Board [*British*] (DCTA)
**OPB**........... Office of the Publication Board [*Department of Commerce*]
**OPB**........... Old Picked Bumpers [*Choice cigarette butts*] [*Australian slang*]
**Opb**........... Opbouw [*A publication*]
**OPB**........... Open Bay [*Papua New Guinea*] [*Airport symbol*] (OAG)
**OPB**........... Other People's Butts [*Cigarette butts garnered from ash trays*] [*Slang*]
**OPB**........... Outpatient Basis [*Medicine*]
**OPB**........... Oxidizer Preburner (KSC)
**OPB**........... Pikangikum Band Library, Ontario [*Library symbol*] [*National Library of Canada*] (BIB)
**OPBAT**...... Operation Bahamas, Antilles, and Turks [*Air Force*]
**OPBCT**...... Providence Bay Branch, Carnarvon Township Public Library, Ontario [*Library symbol*] [*National Library of Canada*] (NLC)
**OPBDR**..... Office of Program and Budget Development and Review [*Bureau of Apprenticeship and Training*] [*Department of Labor*]
**OPBE**......... Office of Planning, Budgeting, and Evaluation [*National Institute of Education*]
**OPBG**........ Bhagtanwala [*Pakistan*] [*ICAO location identifier*] (ICLI)
**OPBIA**....... Occasional Publications. British Institute of Archaeology at Ankara [*A publication*]
**OPBIDL**.... Memorial University of Newfoundland. Occasional Papers [*A publication*]
**OPBL**......... Bela [*Pakistan*] [*ICAO location identifier*] (ICLI)
**OPBMA**..... Ocean Pearl Button Manufacturers Association [*Defunct*]
**OPBN**........ Bannu [*Pakistan*] [*ICAO location identifier*] (ICLI)
**OPBOV**..... Oxidizer Preburner Oxidizer Valve (NASA)
**OPBR**........ Bahawalnagar [*Pakistan*] [*ICAO location identifier*] (ICLI)
**OPBSDH**... Occasional Papers. Buffalo Society of Natural Sciences [*A publication*]
**OPBU**........ Operating Budget
**OPBW**....... Bahawalpur [*Pakistan*] [*ICAO location identifier*] (ICLI)
**OPC**........... Occult Papillary Carcinoma [*Oncology*]
**OPC**........... Ocean Policy Committee [*Marine science*] (MSC)
**OPC**........... Office of Price Control [*World War II*]
**OPC**........... Office of Primary Concern [*DoD*]
**OPC**........... Office of Private Cooperation [*Department of State*]
**OPC**........... Office de la Protection du Consommateur [*Quebec, PQ*]
**OPC**........... Ogren, Paul C., South Bend IN [*STAC*]
**OPC**........... Oil Policy Committee [*Office of Emergency Preparedness*] [*Obsolete*]
**OPC**........... Oldsmobile Performance Chapter (EA)
**OPC**........... Oligonucleotide Purification Cartridge [*Chromatography*]
**OPC**........... Online Plotter Controller [*California Computer Products, Inc.*]
**OPC**........... Operation Code
**OPC**........... Operational Control [*Aviation*] (FAAC)
**OPC**........... Operator Position Controller [*Telecommunications*]
**OPC**........... Optical Phase Conjugator [*LASER-aiming device*]
**OPC**........... Optical Photo Coupler
**OPC**........... Optional Calling Plans [*Telecommunications*] (TEL)
**OPC**........... Orange Pigment Cell
**OPC**........... Ordinary Portland Cement
**OPC**........... Ordnance Procurement Center [*Army*]
**OPC**........... Organic Photoconductor
**OPC**........... Orion Pictures Corporation [*NYSE symbol*] (SPSG)
**OPC**........... Out of Print, Canceled [*Publishing*]
**OPC**........... Outer Passenger Cabin
**OPC**........... Outpatient Clinic [*Medicine*]
**OPC**........... Overall Performance Category
**OPC**........... Overseas Press Club of America (EA)
**O & PC**...... Owl and the Pussy Cat [*Poem by Edward Lear, 1871*]
**OPC**........... Oxford Pocket Classics [*A publication*] (ROG)
**OPC**........... Perth Courier, Ontario [*Library symbol*] [*National Library of Canada*] (NLC)
**OPCA**........ Occupational Program Consultants Association (EA)
**OPCA**........ Olivopontocerebellar Atrophy [*Neurology*]
**OPCA**........ Opium Poppy Control Act of 1942
**OP-CAL**.... Operation California (EA)
**Op Cal Att'y Gen**... Opinions of the Attorney General of California [*A publication*] (DLA)
**OPCC**........ Optical Product Code Council (EA)
**OPCC**........ Outpatient Psychiatric Care Coverage
**Op CCCG**.. Opinion, Chief Counsel, United States Coast Guard [*A publication*] (DLA)
**OPCE**........ Operator Control Element [*Data processing*] (IBMDP)
**OPCEN**..... Operations Center [*INTELSAT*]
**OPCG**........ Original Print Collectors Group (EA)
**OPCH**........ Chitral [*Pakistan*] [*ICAO location identifier*] (ICLI)
**OP CIT**...... Opere Citato [*In the Work Cited*] [*Latin*]
**OPCL**......... Chilas [*Pakistan*] [*ICAO location identifier*] (ICLI)
**OPCM**....... Operative Plasterers and Cement Masons International Association of the US and Canada
**OPCMAZ**... Specialist Periodical Reports. Organophosphorus Chemistry [*A publication*]
**OPCMIA**... Operative Plasterers and Cement Masons International Association of US and Canada (EA)
**OPCML**..... Township of Muskoka Lakes Public Library Board, Port Carling, Ontario [*Library symbol*] [*National Library of Canada*] (BIB)
**OPCO**........ Operating Plan Change Orders [*Coast Guard publication*]
**OPCO**........ Outside Production Consignment Order
**OPCOCM Symposium**... Symposium on the Occurrence, Prediction, and Control of Outbursts in Coal Mines [*A publication*] (APTA)
**OP-COD**.... Operating Code [*Data processing*]
**OPCODE**.. Operations Code [*Army*] (AABC)
**OP-COM**... Opera-Comique [*Comic Opera*] [*Music*]
**OPCOM**.... Operational Command [*Military*] (MCD)
**OP-COM**... Operations-Communications
**OPCOMCTR**... Operational Command Center [*Navy*] (NVT)
**OPCON**..... Operational Control [*Army*] (NVT)
**OPCON**..... Operator's Console
**OPCON**..... Optimizing Control [*Military*]
**OPCONCEN**... Operational Control Center [*Navy*]
**OPCONCTR**... Operational Control Center [*Navy*] (NVT)
**OPCOSAL**... Optimum Coordinated Shipboard [*or Shorebased*] Allowance List
**OPCPL**...... Port Colborne Public Library, Ontario [*Library symbol*] [*National Library of Canada*] (NLC)
**OPCR**........ Chachro [*Pakistan*] [*ICAO location identifier*] (ICLI)
**OPCR**........ One-Pass Cold-Rolled [*Steel sheets*]
**OPCS**......... Office of Population Censuses and Surveys [*Department of Employment*] [*British*]
**OPCS**......... Operational Planning and Control System [*Department of Labor*] (OICC)
**OPCT**........ Chirat [*Pakistan*] [*ICAO location identifier*] (ICLI)
**OPCTR**...... Operations Center [*Military*]
**OPCV**........ Office of Planning, Control, and Validation [*Social Security Administration*]
**OPD**........... Chemical Marketing Reporter [*A publication*]
**OPD**........... Delayed Opening
**OPD**........... Observed Position Data
**OPD**........... Office of Policy Development [*Executive Office of the President*]
**OPD**........... Office of Program Development [*NASA*]
**OPD**........... Officer Personnel Directorate [*Army*]
**OPD**........... Officer Professional Development [*Military*] (INF)
**OPD**........... Ohio College of Podiatric Medicine, Cleveland, OH [*OCLC symbol*] (OCLC)
**OPD**........... Opened [*Stock exchange term*] (SPSG)
**OPD**........... Opening Posterior Digestive [*Gland*]
**OPD**........... Operand [*Data processing*]
**OPD**........... Operational Programming Department [*Telecommunications*] (TEL)
**OPD**........... Operations Division [*War Department General Staff*] [*World War II*]
**OPD**........... Operations Planning Division [*Manned Spacecraft Center*]
**OPD**........... Optical Particle Detector [*for evaluating film quality*]
**OPD**........... Optical Path Difference (MCD)
**OPD**........... Optical Proximity Detector
**OPD**........... Oral and Pharyngeal Development [*Section*] [*National Institute of Dental Research*]
**OPD**........... Orbiting Propellant Depot [*NASA*]
**OPD**........... Original Pack Dispensing [*For drugs*] [*Packaging*]
**OPD**........... Ortho-Phenylenediamine [*Organic chemistry*]
**OPD**........... 'Osef Piskei Din shel ha-Rabanut ha-Rashit le-'Erets Yisrael (BJA)
**OPD**........... Oto-Palato-Digital [*Syndrome*]
**OPD**........... Outpatient Department [*or Dispensary*] [*Medicine*]
**OPD**........... Overall Program Design (OICC)
**O/PD**......... Overpaid (ROG)
**OPD**........... Overseas Policy Defence Committee [*British*]
**OPD**........... Oxford Paperback Dictionary [*A publication*]
**OPD**........... Port Dover Centennial Public Library, Ontario [*Library symbol*] [*National Library of Canada*] (NLC)
**OPDAC**..... Optical Data Converter (NOAA)
**OPDAR**..... Optical Detection and Ranging

**OPDATS**... Operational Performance Data System
**OPDB**........ Dalbandin [*Pakistan*] [*ICAO location identifier*] (ICLI)
**OPDD**........ Dadu [*Pakistan*] [*ICAO location identifier*] (ICLI)
**OPDD**........ Operational Plan Data Document [*Military*] (AFM)
**OPDEC**..... Operational Deception [*Navy*] (NVT)
**OPDEVFOR**... Operational Development Forces
**OPDF**........ One Percent for Development Fund (EAIO)
**OPDG**........ Dera Ghazi Khan [*Pakistan*] [*ICAO location identifier*] (ICLI)
**OPDI**......... Dera Ismail Khan [*Pakistan*] [*ICAO location identifier*] (ICLI)
**OPDI**......... Operator Please Deliver Immediately
**OP DIAP**... Open Diapason [*Organ stop*] [*Music*]
**OPDIN**...... Ocean Pollution Data and Information Network [*Washington, DC*] [*Department of Commerce*] (GRD)
**OPDK**........ Daharki [*Pakistan*] [*ICAO location identifier*] (ICLI)
**OPDL**........ Office of Production and Defense Lending [*Department of the Treasury*]
**OPDP**........ Officer Professional Development Program [*Pronounced "opey-dopey"*] [*Canadian Navy*]
**OPDPE**...... Office of Policy Development Planning and Evaluation [*Pronounced "opey dopey"*] [*NIMH*]
**OPDR**........ Office of Primary Development Responsibility (AFM)
**OPDU**........ Powassan and District Union Public Library, Powassan, Ontario [*Library symbol*] [*National Library of Canada*] (NLC)
**OPD WDGS**... Operations Division, War Department General Staff [*World War II*]
**OPE**........... Eldorado Nuclear Ltd., Port Hope, Ontario [*Library symbol*] [*National Library of Canada*] (NLC)
**OPE**........... Office of Planning and Evaluation [*Office of Personnel Management*] (GRD)
**OPE**........... Office of Policy Evaluation [*Nuclear energy*] (NRCH)
**OPE**........... Office of Program Evaluation [*Office of Policy, Evaluation, and Research*] [*Department of Labor*]
**OPE**........... One-Pion Exchange [*Nuclear energy*]
**OPE**........... Operational Planning Estimate
**OPE**........... Operations Project Engineer [*NASA*] (KSC)
**OPE**........... Optical Pointing Error
**OPE**........... Optical-Probe Experiment [*Giotto probe of Halley's comet*] [*European Space Agency*]
**OPE**........... Optimized Processing Element
**OPE**........... Orbiting Primate Experiment (MCD)
**OPE**........... Oregon, Pacific & Eastern Railway Co. [*AAR code*]
**OPE**........... Other Plant Equipment [*DoD*]
**OPE**........... Other Project Element (NASA)
**OPE**........... Outer Planets Explorer [*NASA*]
**OPE**........... Topeka, KS [*Location identifier*] [*FAA*] (FAAL)
**OPEAA**..... Outdoor Power Equipment Aftermarket Association (EA)
**OPEB**......... Bruce County Public Library, Port Elgin, Ontario [*Library symbol*] [*National Library of Canada*] (NLC)
**OPEC**........ Oil Producers Equipment [*NASDAQ symbol*] (NQ)
**OPEC**........ Organization of Petroleum Exporting Countries [*Also, OAPEC*] [*Vienna, Austria*]
**OPEC Bull**... OPEC [*Organization of Petroleum Exporting Countries*] Bulletin [*A publication*]
**OPECNA**... OPEC [*Organization of Petroleum Exporting Countries*] News Agency [*See also APOPEC*] [*Vienna, Austria*] (EAIO)
**OPECO**..... Operations Coordinator [*Marine science*] (MSC)
**OPEC (Org Petroleum Exporting Countries) Bul**... OPEC (Organization of Petroleum Exporting Countries) Bulletin [*A publication*]
**OPEC (Org Petroleum Exporting Countries) Pas**... OPEC (Organization of Petroleum Exporting Countries) Papers [*A publication*]
**OPEC (Org Petroleum Exporting Countries) R**... OPEC (Organization of Petroleum Exporting Countries) Review [*A publication*]
**OP-ED**....... Opposite Editorial Page [*in a newspaper*] [*Usually consists of opinion columns by various guest writers or syndicated columnists*]
**OPED**........ Other Pay Entry Date [*Army*] (AABC)
**OPED**........ Point Edward Public Library, Ontario [*Library symbol*] [*National Library of Canada*] (NLC)
**OPEDA**..... Organization of Professional Employees of the United States Department of Agriculture (EA)
**OPEDA**..... Outdoor Power Equipment Distributors Association (EA)
**OPEDC**..... Overseas Private Enterprise Development Corporation [*Proposed successor to Agency for International Development*]
**OPeeO**....... Ohio Valley Local District Free Public Library, Peebles Branch, Peebles, OH [*Library symbol*] [*Library of Congress*] (LCLS)
**OPEF**......... Overall Plume Enhancement Factor [*Space Shuttle*] [*NASA*]
**OPEI**.......... Office of Public Education and Information [*NASA*]
**OPEI**.......... Outdoor Power Equipment Institute (EA)
**OPEIU**....... Office and Professional Employees International Union (EA)
**OPEL**........ Optel Corp. [*NASDAQ symbol*] (NQ)
**OPEM**....... One-Pion Exchange Model [*Nuclear energy*]
**OPEM**....... Pembroke Public Library, Ontario [*Library symbol*] [*National Library of Canada*] (NLC)
**OPEMA**.... Oilfield Production Equipment Manufacturers Association [*Defunct*] (EA)
**OPEMAC**... Upper Ottawa Valley Campus Resource Centre, Algonquin College, Pembroke, Ontario [*Library symbol*] [*National Library of Canada*] (NLC)
**OPEMO**.... Ottawa Valley Historical Society, Pembroke, Ontario [*Library symbol*] [*National Library of Canada*] (BIB)
**OPEN**........ Fund for an Open Society (EA)
**OPEN**........ Open Protocol Enhanced Network [*Northern Telecom communications network*] [*Canada*]
**OPEN**........ Organisation des Producteurs d'Energie Nucleaire [*Paris, France*] (EAIO)
**OPEN**........ Origins of Plasma in the Earth's Neighborhood [*Ad Hoc Advisory Committee terminated, 1981*]
**OPEN**........ Penetanguishene Public Library, Ontario [*Library symbol*] [*National Library of Canada*] (BIB)
**OPENAH**... Operational Evaluation of Armed Helicopters (MCD)
**Openbare Biblioth**... Openbare Bibliotheek [*A publication*]
**OPENE**..... Ecole Secondaire le Caron, Penetanguishene, Ontario [*Library symbol*] [*National Library of Canada*] (BIB)
**Open File Rep Geol Surv North Irel**... Open-File Report. Geological Survey of Northern Ireland [*A publication*]
**Open-File Rep US Geol Surv**... Open-File Report. United States Geological Survey [*A publication*]
**Open Hearth Basic Oxygen Steel Conf Proc**... Open Hearth and Basic Oxygen Steel Conference. Proceedings [*United States*] [*A publication*]
**Open Hearth Proc AIME**... Open Hearth Proceedings. Metallurgical Society of AIME [*American Institute of Mining, Metallurgical, and Petroleum Engineers*]. Iron and Steel Division [*A publication*]
**Open Learn Sys News**... Open Learning Systems News [*A publication*]
**OPENM**.... Mental Health Centre, Penetanguishene, Ontario [*Library symbol*] [*National Library of Canada*] (NLC)
**Open Tech Prog News**... Open Tech Program News [*A publication*]
**OPEO**........ Oakland-Pontiac Enthusiast Organization (EA)
**OPEO**........ Octylphenol Polyethoxylate [*Organic chemistry*]
**OPEOS**...... Outside Plant Planning, Engineering, and Construction Operations System (MCD)
**OPEP**......... Orbital-Plane Experiment Package [*NASA*]
**OPEPB**...... Eastern Pentecostal Bible College, Peterborough, Ontario [*Library symbol*] [*National Library of Canada*] (NLC)
**OPER**........ Coin Phones, Inc. [*White Plains, NY*] [*NASDAQ symbol*] (NQ)
**OPER**........ Office of Policy and Economic Research [*Washington, DC*] [*Federal Home Loan Bank Board*] (GRD)
**OPER**........ Office of Policy, Evaluation, and Research [*Employment and Training Administration*] [*Department of Labor*]
**OPER**........ Operating [*Automotive engineering*]
**OPER**........ Operation [*or Operational*] (KSC)
**Opera**......... Opera and Concert [*A publication*]
**Opera**......... Opera News [*A publication*]
**OPERA**...... Ordnance Pulses Experimental Research Assembly [*Nuclear reactor*]
**OPERA**...... Out-of-Pile Expulsion and Reentry Apparatus [*Nuclear energy*]
**Opera Bot**.. Opera Botanica [*A publication*]
**Opera Can**... Opera Canada [*A publication*]
**Opera Collecta Cent Bosbiol Onderz Bokrijk-Genk**... Opera Collecta. Centrum voor Bosbiologisch Onderzoek. Bokrijk-Genk [*A publication*]
**Opera J**...... Opera Journal [*A publication*]
**Opera N**..... Opera News [*A publication*]
**Operational Res Quart**... Operational Research Quarterly [*A publication*]
**Operation Res**... Operations Research [*A publication*]
**OPERATORS**... Optimization Program for Economical Remote Trunk Arrangement and TSPS [*Traffic Service Positions System*] Operator Arrangements [*Telecommunications*] (TEL)
**Operator Theory Advances and Appl**... Operator Theory. Advances and Applications [*A publication*]
**Operator Theory Adv Appl**... Operator Theory. Advances and Applications [*A publication*]
**Operat Res**... Operations Research [*A publication*]
**Operat Res Q**... Operational Research Quarterly [*A publication*]
**Operat R Q**... Operational Research Quarterly [*A publication*]
**Oper Dent**.. Operative Dentistry [*A publication*]
**OPERG**..... Operating (MDG)
**Oper Miller**... Operative Miller [*A publication*]
**Oper Program Systems Ser**... Operating and Programming Systems Series [*A publication*]
**Oper Res**.... Operations Research [*A publication*]
**Oper Res Lett**... Operations Research Letters [*A publication*]
**Oper Res Q**... Operational Research Quarterly [*A publication*]
**Oper Res Quart**... Operational Research Quarterly [*A publication*]
**OPERSCRS**... Officer Personnel Course [*Air Force*]
**OPersLex**... Old Persian Grammar Texts Lexicon [*A publication*] (BJA)
**Oper Syst Rev**... Operating Systems Review [*A publication*]
**OPES**......... Centre de Documentation, Ecole Secondaire de Plantagenet [*Documentation Centre, Plantagenet Secondary School*], Ontario [*Library symbol*] [*National Library of Canada*] (BIB)
**OPET**......... Organization, Personnel Equipment and Training [*Group*]
**OPET**......... Oriented Polyethylene Terephthalate [*Organic chemistry*]
**OPET**......... Trent University, Peterborough, Ontario [*Library symbol*] [*National Library of Canada*] (NLC)
**OPETA**...... Trent University Archives, Peterborough, Ontario [*Library symbol*] [*National Library of Canada*] (NLC)

**OPETAL** ... Trent Audio Library Services, Trent University, Peterborough, Ontario [*Library symbol*] [*National Library of Canada*] (NLC)
**OPETC** ...... Trent Canal Office, Peterborough, Ontario [*Library symbol*] [*National Library of Canada*] (BIB)
**OPETCG** ... Canadian General Electric Co. Ltd., Peterborough, Ontario [*Library symbol*] [*National Library of Canada*] (NLC)
**OPETCM** ... Peterborough Centennial Museum and Archives, Ontario [*Library symbol*] [*National Library of Canada*] (BIB)
**OPETHS** ... Hutchison House Museum, Peterborough Historical Society, Ontario [*Library symbol*] [*National Library of Canada*] (BIB)
**OPETM** ..... Map Library, Trent University, Peterborough, Ontario [*Library symbol*] [*National Library of Canada*] (NLC)
**OPETP** ...... Peterborough Public Library, Ontario [*Library symbol*] [*National Library of Canada*] (NLC)
**OPETSF** .... Brealy Library, Sir Sandford Fleming College, Peterborough, Ontario [*Library symbol*] [*National Library of Canada*] (NLC)
**OPETSFD** ... Daniel Library, Sir Sandford Fleming College, Peterborough, Ontario [*Library symbol*] [*National Library of Canada*] (BIB)
**OPEV** ........ Petawawa Village and Township Union Public Library, Ontario [*Library symbol*] [*National Library of Canada*] (NLC)
**OPEVAL** ... Operational Evaluation [*Navy*] (NG)
**OPEX** ........ Operational, Executive, and Administrative Personnel Program [*United Nations*]
**OPEX** ........ Operational Extension
**OPF** ........... Miami, FL [*Location identifier*] [*FAA*] (FAAL)
**OPF** ........... Official Personnel File (MCD)
**OPF** ........... Official Personnel Folder [*Military*]
**OPF** ........... Open-Pore Foam [*Plastic*]
**OPF** ........... Optical Propagation Facility
**OPF** ........... Orbiter Processing Facility [*NASA*] (NASA)
**OPF** ........... Overseas Project Fund [*British Overseas Trade Board*] (DS)
**OPF** ........... Public Finance. International Quarterly Journal [*A publication*]
**OPFA** ......... Faisalabad [*Pakistan*] [*ICAO location identifier*] (ICLI)
**OPFAC** ....... Operating Facilities [*Coast Guard publication*]
**OPFAC** ....... Operational Facility (RDA)
**OPFAD** ....... Outer-Perimeter Fleet Air Defense
**OPFAEI** .... Freshwater Biological Association. Occasional Publication [*A publication*]
**OPFB** ......... Optifab, Inc. [*NASDAQ symbol*] (NQ)
**OPFC** ......... Hinchinbrooke Public Library, Frontenac County Library, Parkham, Ontario [*Library symbol*] [*National Library of Canada*] (BIB)
**OPFC** ......... Orbiter Preflight Checklist [*NASA*] (MCD)
**OPFCDN** ... Great Britain. Forestry Commission. Occasional Paper [*A publication*]
**OPFCO** ...... Operational Program Functional Checkout (MCD)
**OPFM** ....... Outlet Plenum Feature Model [*Nuclear energy*] (NRCH)
**OPFOR** ...... Opportunity to Confront the Best Opposing Force [*Army*] (INF)
**OPFOR** ...... Opposing Force [*Military*] (INF)
**OPFRC** ...... Clarendon-Miller Branch, Frontenac County Library, Plevna, Ontario [*Library symbol*] [*National Library of Canada*] (NLC)
**OPG** ........... Oculoplethysmograph [*Instrumentation*]
**OPG** ........... Office of the Postmaster General [*Obsolete*]
**OPG** ........... Opening
**OPG** ........... Operational Performance Goals
**OPG** ........... Operational Planning Grant (OICC)
**OPG** ........... Original Proof Gallon
**OPG** ........... Outside Production Group
**OPG** ........... Overseas Products Group [*Department of Trade*] [*British*]
**OPG** ........... Oxypolygelatin [*Plasma extender*]
**Op GA Att'y Gen** ... Opinions of the Attorney General of Georgia [*A publication*] (DLA)
**Op GCT** ..... Opinion, General Counsel, United States Treasury Department [*A publication*] (DLA)
**OPGD** ........ Gwadar [*Pakistan*] [*ICAO location identifier*] (ICLI)
**OPGE** ........ OEEC [*Organization for European Economic Cooperation*] Petroleum Industry Emergency Group (NATG)
**OP/GSA** .... Office of Preparedness, General Services Administration [*Later, Federal Preparedness Agency*]
**OPGT** ........ Gilgit [*Pakistan*] [*ICAO location identifier*] (ICLI)
**OPGT** ........ Outer Planets Grand Tour [*NASA*]
**OPGUID** ... Optimum Guidance [*Technique*] (NASA)
**OPGW** ....... Optical Groundwire [*Telecommunications*] (TSSD)
**OPH** .......... Obliterative Pulmonary Hypertension [*Medicine*]
**OPH** .......... Old Parliamentary Hand [*Political*] [*British*]
**OPh** .......... Old Phoenician (BJA)
**OPH** .......... Operational Propellant Handling [*NASA*] (AAG)
**OPH** .......... Ophicleide [*Musical instrument*]
**Oph** .......... Ophiuchus [*Constellation*]
**OPH** .......... Ophthalmodynamometry [*Ophthalmology*]
**OPH** .......... Ophthalmology [*or Ophthalmoscopy*]
**OPH** .......... [*The*] Ophthalmoscope [*London*] [*A publication*] (ROG)
**OPH** .......... Opposite Hand [*Technical drawings*]
**OPH** .......... Public Library, Port Hope, Ontario [*Library symbol*] [*National Library of Canada*] (NLC)
**Oph D** ........ Doctor of Ophthalmology
**OPHF** ........ Orbital Polarized Hartree-Fock [*Atomic physics*]
**Ophi** .......... Ophiuchus [*Constellation*]
**OPHIR** ....... Organic Power and Heat Industrial Reactor
**Ophn** .......... Orpheon [*Record label*] [*Poland*]
**OPHQ** ....... Karachi [*Pakistan*] [*ICAO location identifier*] (ICLI)
**OPHS** ........ Operational Propellant Handling System [*NASA*] (AAG)
**OPHTH** ..... Ophthalmology (AABC)
**OPHTHAL** ... Ophthalmology
**Ophthal For** ... Ophthalmic Forum [*A publication*]
**Ophthal Lit** ... Ophthalmic Literature [*A publication*]
**Ophthalmic Nurs Forum** ... Ophthalmic Nursing Forum [*A publication*]
**Ophthalmic Paediatr Genet** ... Ophthalmic Paediatrics and Genetics [*A publication*]
**Ophthalmic Physiol Opt** ... Ophthalmic and Physiological Optics [*A publication*]
**Ophthalmic Res** ... Ophthalmic Research [*A publication*]
**Ophthalmic Semin** ... Ophthalmic Seminars [*A publication*]
**Ophthalmic Surg** ... Ophthalmic Surgery [*A publication*]
**Ophthalmola** ... Ophthalmologica [*A publication*]
**Ophthalmol Ibero Am** ... Ophthalmologia Ibero-Americana [*A publication*]
**Ophthalmol Times** ... Ophthalmology Times [*A publication*]
**Ophthalmol War Years** ... Ophthalmology in the War Years [*A publication*]
**Ophthal Opt** ... Ophthalmic Optician [*A publication*]
**Ophthal Res** ... Ophthalmic Research [*A publication*]
**Ophth Rec** ... Ophthalmic Record [*A publication*]
**Ophth Soc Aust Trans** ... Ophthalmological Society of Australia. Transactions [*A publication*] (APTA)
**OPHTS** ...... Operational Propellant Handling Test Site [*NASA*] (AAG)
**OPHWA** .... Nuclear Products Department, Westinghouse Canada, Inc., Port Hope, Ontario [*Library symbol*] [*National Library of Canada*] (NLC)
**OPI** ............ Bibliotheek en Samenleving [*A publication*]
**OPi** ............ Flesh Public Library, Piqua, OH [*Library symbol*] [*Library of Congress*] (LCLS)
**OPI** ............ Oculoparalytic Illusion [*Ophthalmology*]
**OPI** ............ Off-Site Production Inspection (AAG)
**OP & I** ........ Office of Patents and Inventions
**OPI** ............ Office of Primary Interest
**OPI** ............ Office of Programs Integration [*Energy Research and Development Administration*]
**OPI** ............ Office of Public Information [*NASA*]
**OPI** ............ Office of Public Information [*UNESCO*]
**OP & I** ........ Office of Publications and Information [*Department of Commerce*]
**OPI** ............ Ogden Projects [*NYSE symbol*] (SPSG)
**OPI** ............ Oil Patch Group, Inc. [*Toronto Stock Exchange symbol*]
**OPI** ............ Oil Pressure Indicator
**OPI** ............ Omnibus Personality Inventory [*Psychology*]
**OPI** ............ Open Protocol Interface [*Telecommunications*]
**OPI** ............ Open for Public Inspection [*Patent applications*]
**OPI** ............ Optical Publishing, Inc. [*Information service or system*] (IID)
**OPI** ............ Orbital Position Indicator
**OPI** ............ Orbiter Payload Interrogator [*NASA*] (MCD)
**OPI** ............ Ordnance Procedure Instrumentations (AAG)
**OPI** ............ Ordnance Procurement Instructions [*Army*]
**OPI** ............ Organophosphate Insecticide
**OPI** ............ Output Productivity Index
**OPI** ............ Outside Procurement [*or Purchase*] Inspection (AAG)
**OPI** ............ Overall Performance Index [*Finance*]
**OPI** ............ Picton Public Library, Ontario [*Library symbol*] [*National Library of Canada*] (NLC)
**OPIC** .......... Oficina Permanente Internacional de la Carne [*Permanent International Meat Office*] (EAIO)
**OPIC** .......... Overseas Private Investment Corporation [*US International Development Cooperation Agency*] [*Washington, DC*]
**OPIC** .......... Pickering Public Library, Ontario [*Library symbol*] [*National Library of Canada*] (NLC)
**OPID** .......... Operational Procedures Interface Document (MCD)
**OPIDF** ........ Operational Planning Identification File (MCD)
**OPiE** .......... Edison State Community College, Piqua, OH [*Library symbol*] [*Library of Congress*] (LCLS)
**OPIET** ........ Eco-Tec Ltd., Pickering, Ontario [*Library symbol*] [*National Library of Canada*] (NLC)
**OPIG** .......... Picton Gazette, Ontario [*Library symbol*] [*National Library of Canada*] (NLC)
**OPIL** .......... Opalescent Indicating Light
**Op Ill Att'y Gen** ... Illinois Attorney General's Opinion [*A publication*] (DLA)
**OPIM** ......... Order Processing and Inventory Monitoring [*Data processing*]
**Opin** ........... Opinions of the Attorneys-General [*United States*] [*A publication*] (DLA)
**Opine** ......... Option Income [*Business term*]
**Opin Int Commn Zool Nom** ... Opinions Rendered by the International Commission on Zoological Nomenclature [*A publication*]
**OPINM** ...... North Marysburgh Museum, Picton, Ontario [*Library symbol*] [*National Library of Canada*] (BIB)
**OPINT** ....... Optical Intelligence
**OPINTEL** ... Operational Intelligence
**OPIRL** ....... Operator Interface Rolling Loop
**OPIS** ......... Operational Priority Indicating System (NATG)

**OPIS**.......... Orbiter Prime Item Specification [*NASA*] (NASA)
**OPIS**.......... Pelee Island Public Library, Ontario [*Library symbol*] [*National Library of Canada*] (NLC)
**OP(IT)**....... Operation Overlord Preparations, Inland Transport [*World War II*]
**OPIT**.......... Operator Interface Table (MCD)
**OPiWU**...... Wright State University, Piqua Branch Campus, Piqua, OH [*Library symbol*] [*Library of Congress*] (LCLS)
**OPJA**......... Jacobabad [*Pakistan*] [*ICAO location identifier*] (ICLI)
**Op JAGAF** ... Opinion, Judge Advocate General, United States Air Force [*A publication*] (DLA)
**Op JAGN**.. Opinion, Judge Advocate General, United States Navy [*A publication*] (DLA)
**OPJC**......... Jacobabad [*Pakistan*] [*ICAO location identifier*] (ICLI)
**OPJI**.......... Jiwani [*Pakistan*] [*ICAO location identifier*] (ICLI)
**OPK**.......... Optokinetic
**OPKA**........ Cape Monze [*Pakistan*] [*ICAO location identifier*] (ICLI)
**Op Kan Att'y Gen** ... Opinions of the Attorney General of Kansas [*A publication*] (DLA)
**OPKC**........ Karachi/International [*Pakistan*] [*ICAO location identifier*] (ICLI)
**OPKD**........ Hyderabad [*Pakistan*] [*ICAO location identifier*] (ICLI)
**OPKE**........ Chore [*Pakistan*] [*ICAO location identifier*] (ICLI)
**OPKE**........ Knudsen Engineering Ltd., Perth, Ontario [*Library symbol*] [*National Library of Canada*] (BIB)
**OPKF**......... Gharo [*Pakistan*] [*ICAO location identifier*] (ICLI)
**OPKH**........ Khuzdhar [*Pakistan*] [*ICAO location identifier*] (ICLI)
**OPKK**........ Karachi/Korangi Creek [*Pakistan*] [*ICAO location identifier*] (ICLI)
**OPKL**......... Kalat [*Pakistan*] [*ICAO location identifier*] (ICLI)
**OPKM**....... Opelika Manufacturing Corp. [*NASDAQ symbol*] (NQ)
**OPKN**........ Kharan [*Pakistan*] [*ICAO location identifier*] (ICLI)
**OPKO**........ Kohat [*Pakistan*] [*ICAO location identifier*] (ICLI)
**OPKR**........ Karachi [*Pakistan*] [*ICAO location identifier*] (ICLI)
**OPKT**........ Kohat [*Pakistan*] [*ICAO location identifier*] (ICLI)
**Op KY Att'y Gen** ... Opinion of Attorney General, State of Kentucky [*A publication*] (DLA)
**OPL**........... Oberlin Public Library, Oberlin, OH [*OCLC symbol*] (OCLC)
**OPL**........... Ocean Pressure Laboratory
**OPL**........... Official Publications Library [*The British Library*]
**OPL**........... One-Person Library
**OPL**........... Opelousas, LA [*Location identifier*] [*FAA*] (FAAL)
**OPL**........... Open Problem List (NASA)
**OPL**........... Operational (AFM)
**OPL**........... Operations Plan (KSC)
**OPL**........... Organizer Programming Language [*Data processing*]
**OPL**........... Orient-Pacific Line [*Shipping*] (ROG)
**OPL**........... Osservatore Politico Letterario [*A publication*]
**OPL**........... Ottawa Public Library [*UTLAS symbol*]
**OPL**........... Our Public Lands [*A publication*]
**OPL**........... Out-of-Phase Loading
**OPL**........... Outer Plexiform Layer [*Retina*]
**OPL**........... Outpost Line
**OPL**........... Overpaid Last Account
**OPLA**........ Lahore [*Pakistan*] [*ICAO location identifier*] (ICLI)
**OPLA**........ Our Public Lands [*A publication*]
**Op LA Att'y Gen** ... Opinions of the Attorney General of Louisiana [*A publication*] (DLA)
**OPLAC**...... Argyle Community Library, Port Loring, Ontario [*Library symbol*] [*National Library of Canada*] (NLC)
**OPLAN**..... Operation Plan [*Army*]
**OPLAN SEA** ... Operation Plan, Southeast Asia [*Military*]
**OPLC**......... Organizacion para la Liberacion de Cuba [*Organization for the Liberation of Cuba*] (PD)
**OPLC**......... Overpressure Layer Chromatography
**OPLE**......... Omega Position Location Experiment [*NASA*]
**Op Let**....... Opinion Letter [*A publication*] (DLA)
**OPLF**......... Orbiter Processing and Landing Facility [*NASA*] (MCD)
**OPLG**......... Oil Plug
**OPLH**......... Lahore/Walton [*Pakistan*] [*ICAO location identifier*] (ICLI)
**OPLiLL**..... Occasional Papers in Linguistics and Language Learning [*A publication*]
**OPLing**...... Occasional Papers on Linguistics [*A publication*]
**OPLL**......... Loralai [*Pakistan*] [*ICAO location identifier*] (ICLI)
**OPLLL**...... Occasional Papers in Language, Literature, and Linguistics [*A publication*]
**OPLP**......... Pickle Pat Public Library, Pickle Lake, Ontario [*Library symbol*] [*National Library of Canada*] (NLC)
**OPLR**......... Lahore [*Pakistan*] [*ICAO location identifier*] (ICLI)
**OPLR**......... Outpost Line of Resistance
**OPLSS**....... Optimized Portable Life-Support System [*NASA*]
**OPM**.......... Occult Primary Malignancy [*Oncology*]
**OPM**.......... Office of Personnel Management [*Supersedes Civil Service Commission*]
**OPM**.......... Office, Personnel Manager [*Army*] (MUGU)
**OPM**.......... Office of Planning and Management [*DoD*]
**OPM**.......... Office of Procurement and Materiel [*Army*]
**OPM**.......... Office of Production Management [*Superseded by WPB, 1942*]
**OPM**.......... Office of Program Management [*Unemployment Insurance Service*] [*Department of Labor*]
**OPM**.......... Operating Plane Months [*Navy*] (NG)
**OPM**.......... Operations per Minute [*Performance measure*]
**OPM**.......... Operator Programming Method [*Data processing*]
**OPM**.......... Ophthalmodynamometry [*Ophthalmology*]
**OPM**.......... Optical Power Meter
**OPM**.......... Optically Projected Map
**OPM**.......... Options Pricing Model
**OPM**.......... Organisasi Papua Merdeka [*Papua Independent Organization*] [*Indonesia*] (PD)
**OPM**.......... Organizacion Politico-Militar [*Politico-Military Organization*] [*Paraguay*] (PD)
**OPM**.......... Oscillating Pressure Method
**OPM**.......... Other People's Money
**OPM**.......... Outer Planet Mission
**OPM**.......... Output Processor Module (MCD)
**OPM**.......... Perth Museum, Ontario [*Library symbol*] [*National Library of Canada*] (NLC)
**OPMA**....... Mangla [*Pakistan*] [*ICAO location identifier*] (ICLI)
**OPMA**....... Office Products Manufacturers Association (EA)
**OPMA**....... Open Pit Mining Association (EA)
**OPMA**....... Overseas Press and Media Association [*London, England*] (EAIO)
**OPMACC** ... Operation Military Aid to the Civil Community [*British military*] (DMA)
**OPMARV** ... Operational Maneuvering Reentry Vehicle (MCD)
**OPMC**....... OptimumCare Corporation [*NASDAQ symbol*] (NQ)
**OPMCS**..... Otto Pre-Marital Counseling Schedules [*Psychology*]
**OPMD**....... Officer Personnel Management Directorate [*Military*]
**OPMET**..... Operational Meteorological Information (FAAC)
**OPMF**....... Muzaffarabad [*Pakistan*] [*ICAO location identifier*] (ICLI)
**OPMG**....... Office of the Provost Marshal General [*Army*]
**OPMH**....... Occupations for Patients in Mental Hospitals [*British*]
**OPMI**........ Mianwali [*Pakistan*] [*ICAO location identifier*] (ICLI)
**OPMI**........ Open Perfusion Micro-Incubator
**OPMI**........ Operation Microscope [*Surgery*]
**Op Minn Att'y Gen** ... Opinions of the Attorney General of Minnesota [*A publication*] (DLA)
**OPMJ**........ Moenjodaro [*Pakistan*] [*ICAO location identifier*] (ICLI)
**OPMK**....... Mir Pur Khas [*Pakistan*] [*ICAO location identifier*] (ICLI)
**OPML**....... Occasional Papers in Modern Languages [*A publication*]
**OPMN**....... Miranshah [*Pakistan*] [*ICAO location identifier*] (ICLI)
**OPMN**....... Port McNicoll Public Library, Ontario [*Library symbol*] [*National Library of Canada*] (NLC)
**OPMOPLAN** ... Operation Missouri Plan [*Program for five-day state funeral planned several years in advance for ex-President Harry Truman*] [*Army*]
**OPMR**....... Karachi/Masroor [*Pakistan*] [*ICAO location identifier*] (ICLI)
**OPMS**....... Miranshah [*Pakistan*] [*ICAO location identifier*] (ICLI)
**OPMS**....... Office of Physical Measurement Services [*Gaithersburg, MD*] [*National Institute of Standards and Technology*] (GRD)
**OPMS**....... Officer Personnel Management System [*Army*]
**OPMSO**.... Outside Production Material Sales Order
**OPMT**....... Multan [*Pakistan*] [*ICAO location identifier*] (ICLI)
**OPMW**...... Mianwali [*Pakistan*] [*ICAO location identifier*] (ICLI)
**OPN**.......... Norwell District Secondary School, Palmerston, Ontario [*Library symbol*] [*National Library of Canada*] (NLC)
**OPN**.......... Office of the Chief of Naval Operations
**OPN**.......... Office Productivity Network [*Data processing*]
**OPN**.......... Oil Pan
**OPN**.......... Open (AAG)
**OPN**.......... Operation
**OPN**.......... Opercular Nerve
**OPN**.......... Opinion (ROG)
**OPN**.......... Option (ADA)
**OPN**.......... Ora pro Nobis [*Pray for Us*] [*Latin*]
**OPN**.......... Other Procurement, Navy
**OPNAV**..... Office of the Chief of Naval Operations
**OPNAVINST** ... Office of the Chief of Naval Operations Instruction
**OPNAVO** ... Office of the Chief of Naval Operations
**Op ND Att'y Gen** ... Opinions of the Attorney General of North Dakota [*A publication*] (DLA)
**OPNET**..... Operator's Training New Equipment Training [*Army*] (INF)
**Op Nev Att'y Gen** ... Official Opinions of the Attorney General of Nevada [*A publication*] (DLA)
**Op News**.... Opera News [*A publication*]
**OPNG**......... Opening (AAG)
**OPNH**....... Nawabshah [*Pakistan*] [*ICAO location identifier*] (ICLI)
**OPNJC**...... Ora pro Nobis Jesu Christe [*Pray for Us, Jesus Christ*] [*Latin*] [*Motto of Ernst, Duke of Bavaria (1554-1612)*]
**OPNK**........ Naushki [*Pakistan*] [*ICAO location identifier*] (ICLI)
**OPNL**........ Operational
**OPNML**..... Operations Normal (FAAC)
**OPNOTE**.. Operational Note (MCD)
**OPNS**........ Operations (NASA)
**OPNSEVAL & TNGSq** ... Operational Evaluation and Training Squadron [*Air Force*]
**Opns Res**.... Operations Research [*A publication*]
**Op NY Atty Gen** ... Opinions of the Attorneys-General of New York [*A publication*] (DLA)
**OPo**........... Megis Local School District Public Library, Pomeroy, OH [*Library symbol*] [*Library of Congress*] (LCLS)
**OPO**.......... Office of Personnel Operations [*Army*]

**OPO**.......... Officer of the Post Office [*British*]
**OPO**.......... Oil Pressure Out
**OPO**.......... One-Person Operation [*Slang*] [*Business term*] (DCTA)
**OPO**.......... OPEC [*Organization of Petroleum Exporting Countries*] Review [*A publication*]
**OPO**.......... Ophthalmic and Physiological Optics [*A publication*]
**OPO**.......... Oporto [*Portugal*] [*Airport symbol*] (OAG)
**OPO**.......... Optical Parametric Oscillator [*Tunable LASER device*]
**OPO**.......... Orbiter Project Office [*NASA*] (MCD)
**OPO**.......... Orbiting Planetary Observatory
**OPO**.......... Ordnance Personnel Office [*Army*]
**OPOA**........ Office Products of America, Inc. [*NASDAQ symbol*] (NQ)
**OPOEB**..... Port Elgin Branch, Bruce County Public Library, Ontario [*Library symbol*] [*National Library of Canada*] (NLC)
**Op Off Legal Counsel**... Opinions of the Office of Legal Counsel [*A publication*] (DLA)
**Op Ohio Att'y Gen**... Opinions of the Attorney General of Ohio [*A publication*] (DLA)
**OPOK**........ Okara [*Pakistan*] [*ICAO location identifier*] (ICLI)
**Op Okla Att'y Gen**... Opinions of the Attorney General of Oklahoma [*A publication*] (DLA)
**OPOL**........ Offshore Pollution Liability Association Limited (EA)
**OPOL**........ Optimization-Oriented Language
**Opolsk Roczn Ekon**... Opolskie Roczniki Ekonomiczne [*A publication*]
**OPON**........ Opinion (ROG)
**OPOR**........ Ormara [*Pakistan*] [*ICAO location identifier*] (ICLI)
**Op Or Att'y Gen**... Opinions of the Attorney General of Oregon [*A publication*] (DLA)
**OPORC**..... Port Carling Public Library, Ontario [*Library symbol*] [*National Library of Canada*] (BIB)
**OPORD**..... Operations Order [*Army*]
**OPORPL**... Oppose Replenishment [*Navy*] (NVT)
**OPOS**........ Outside Production Operation Sheet (MCD)
**OPOSENT**... Oppose Entry [*Navy*] (NVT)
**OPosm**....... Portsmouth Public Library, Portsmouth, OH [*Library symbol*] [*Library of Congress*] (LCLS)
**OPosmG**.... Goodyear Atomic Corp., Portsmouth, OH [*Library symbol*] [*Library of Congress*] (LCLS)
**OPosmS**..... Shawnee State College, Portsmouth, OH [*Library symbol*] [*Library of Congress*] (LCLS)
**OPosmU**.... Ohio University, Portsmouth Branch Campus, Portsmouth, OH [*Library symbol*] [*Library of Congress*] [*Obsolete*] (LCLS)
**OPOSORT**... Oppose Sortie [*Navy*] (NVT)
**OPOSS**...... Office of Personnel Operations Standards and Systems Office [*Army*]
**OPOSSMS**... Options to Purchase or Sell Specific Mortgage-Backed Securities [*Merrill Lynch & Co.*] [*Finance*]
**OPOV**........ Oxidizer Preburner Oxidizer Valve (MCD)
**OPowS**....... Scioto Village High School, Powell, OH [*Library symbol*] [*Library of Congress*] (LCLS)
**OPP**........... Octal Print Punch [*Data processing*]
**OPP**........... Office of Pesticide Programs [*Environmental Protection Agency*]
**OPP**........... Office of Polar Programs [*Later, Division of Polar Programs*] [*National Science Foundation*]
**OPP**........... Office of Policy and Planning [*Office of Policy, Evaluation, and Research*] [*Department of Labor*]
**OPP**........... Office of Productivity Programs [*Office of Personnel Management*] (GRD)
**OPP**........... Oncovin [*Vincristine*], Procarbazine, Prednisone [*Antineoplastic drug regimen*]
**OPP**........... Ontario Provincial Police [*UTLAS symbol*]
**OPP**........... Open-Pore Polyurethan [*Plastic*]
**OPP**........... Oppenheimer Industries, Inc. [*AMEX symbol*] (SPSG)
**OPP**........... Opponent
**OPP**........... Opportunity (ADA)
**OPP**........... Opposed To
**OPP**........... Opposite (AAG)
**OPP**........... Oppure [*Otherwise*] [*Music*]
**OPP**........... Organization and Personnel Plan [*Army*]
**OPP**........... [*The*] Organization of Plastics Processors
**OPP**........... Organizational Project Plan [*Civil Defense*]
**OPP**........... Oriented Polypropylene [*Plastics technology*]
**OPP**........... Ortho-Phenylphenol [*Disinfectant*]
**OPP**........... Other Physical Principles [*Defense system*]
**OPP**........... Out of Print at Present [*Publishing*]
**OPP**........... Outer Planet Project
**OPP**........... Oxygen Partial Pressure
**OPPA**........ Octylpyrophosphoric Acid [*Organic chemistry*]
**OPPA**........ Operation Plan Package Appraisal (AFM)
**Op PA Att'y Gen**... Opinions of the Attorney General of Pennsylvania [*A publication*] (DLA)
**OPPAR**...... Orbiter Project Parts Authorization Request [*NASA*] (NASA)
**OPPC**........ Parachinar [*Pakistan*] [*ICAO location identifier*] (ICLI)
**OPPCE**....... Opposite Commutator End (IEEE)
**OPPD**........ Omaha Public Power District
**OPPE**......... Office of Program Planning and Evaluation [*National Institutes of Health*]
**OPPE**......... Operational Propulsion Plant Examination [*Navy*] (NVT)
**OPPE**......... Operations Planning Project Engineer [*Deep Space Instrumentation Facility, NASA*]
**OPPG**........ Panjgur [*Pakistan*] [*ICAO location identifier*] (ICLI)
**OPP HND**... Opposite Hand (MSA)
**OPPI**.......... Organic Preparations and Procedures International [*A publication*]
**OPPI**.......... Pasni [*Pakistan*] [*ICAO location identifier*] (ICLI)
**Opp Int L**... Oppenheim's International Law [*A publication*] (DLA)
**OPPL**......... Orbiter Project Parts List [*NASA*] (NASA)
**OPPLAN**... Operations Plan (KSC)
**OPPN**........ Pishin [*Pakistan*] [*ICAO location identifier*] (ICLI)
**OPPOR**..... Opportunity (AABC)
**Oppor North Can**... Opportunity in Northern Canada [*A publication*]
**OPPORT**... Opportunity (ADA)
**OPPOSIT**... Optimization of a Production Process by an Ordered Simulation and Iteration Technique (IEEE)
**OPPP**......... Office of Program Policy and Planning [*Social Security Administration*] (OICC)
**OPPP**......... Port Perry High School, Ontario [*Library symbol*] [*National Library of Canada*] (NLC)
**OPPR**......... Offset Printing Press
**OPPR**......... Operating Program
**OPPS**......... Office of Planning and Program Services [*Office of Field Operations*] [*Department of Labor*]
**OPPS**......... Overpressurization Protection Switch (IEEE)
**OPPS**......... Overpressurization Protection System (IEEE)
**OPPS**......... Oxygen Partial Pressure Sensor
**OPPS**......... Peshawar [*Pakistan*] [*ICAO location identifier*] (ICLI)
**OPPY**......... Opportunity (ROG)
**OPQ**.......... Occupational Personality Questionnaires [*Employment test*]
**OPQ**.......... Occupying Public Quarters [*Military*]
**OPQS**........ Qasim [*Pakistan*] [*ICAO location identifier*] (ICLI)
**OPQT**........ Quetta/Samungli [*Pakistan*] [*ICAO location identifier*] (ICLI)
**OPR**........... Lifts Operating [*Skiing*]
**OPR**........... Off-Site Procurement Request (NRCH)
**OPR**........... Office of Planning and Research [*International Trade Administration*] (GRD)
**OPR**........... Office of Pre-Claims Requirements [*Social Security Administration*]
**OPR**........... Office of Primary Responsibility [*Air Force*]
**OPR**........... Office of Private Resources [*Department of State*]
**OPR**........... Office of Professional Responsibility [*Department of Justice*]
**OPR**........... Office of Public Relations [*Later, PUBINFO*] [*Navy*]
**OPR**........... Offsite Procurement Request (IEEE)
**OPR**........... Old Prussian [*Language, etc.*]
**OPR**........... Ontario Practice Reports [*A publication*] (DLA)
**OPR**........... OP Resources Ltd. [*Vancouver Stock Exchange symbol*]
**OPR**........... Open Pool Reactor [*Nuclear energy*] (NRCH)
**OPR**........... Opener (MSA)
**OPR**........... Operand [*Data processing*]
**OPR**........... Operate [*or Operator*] (AAG)
**OPR**........... Operational Project Requirements (AABC)
**OPR**........... Operations Planning Review (NASA)
**OPR**........... Operations Procedure (MUGU)
**OPR**........... Operations Research
**OPR**........... Optical Page Reader [*Data processing*]
**OPR**........... Optical Pattern Recognition
**OPR**........... Orbit/Payload Recorder [*NASA*] (MCD)
**OPR**........... Order Point Recognition (ADA)
**OPR**........... Outpatient Rate [*Medicine*] (AFM)
**OPR**........... Outstanding Performance Rating [*Military*] (RDA)
**OPR**........... Overall Pressure Ratio
**OPR**........... Oxygen Pressure Regulator (MCD)
**OPR**........... Port Rowan Public Library, Ontario [*Library symbol*] [*National Library of Canada*] (NLC)
**OPRA**........ Observation Post Royal Artillery [*British military*] (DMA)
**OPRA**........ Office Products Reps Association (EA)
**OPRA**........ Ohio Penal Racing Association (EA)
**OPRA**........ Options Price Reporting Authority [*Information service or system*] (IID)
**OPraem**...... Ordo Canonicorum Regularium Praemonstatenstium [*Order of the Canons Regular of Premontre*] [*Norbertines*] [*Roman Catholic men's religious order*]
**OPRD**........ Office of Production Research and Development
**OPRDY**...... Operationally Ready [*Army*] (AABC)
**OPRE**........ Prescott Public Library, Ontario [*Library symbol*] [*National Library of Canada*] (NLC)
**OPRED**...... Operations Reduction [*Government term*]
**OPREDS**.... Operational Performance Recording and Evaluation Data System [*Military*] (CAAL)
**OPrem**....... Ordre de Premontre [*Order of the Canons Regular of Premontre*] [*Rome, Italy*] (EAIO)
**OPREP**...... Operational Reporting [*Army*]
**OPREPS**.... Operational Reporting System [*Military*]
**Op Res**....... Operations Research [*A publication*]
**Op Res Q**... Operational Research Quarterly [*A publication*]
**OPREX**...... Operational Exercise [*NATO*] (NATG)
**OPRFLT**.... Operator Fault (AAG)
**OPRI**.......... Office de la Propriete Industrielle [*Department of Industrial Property*] [*Ministry of Economic Affairs*] (EISS)
**OPRK**........ Rahimyarkhan [*Pakistan*] [*ICAO location identifier*] (ICLI)
**OPRL**......... Ovine Prolactin [*Endocrinology*]

**OPRL**......... Portland Branch, Rideau Lakes Union Library, Ontario [*Library symbol*] [*National Library of Canada*] (BIB)
**OPRN**......... Islamabad/Chaklala [*Pakistan*] [*ICAO location identifier*] (ICLI)
**OPRNL**..... Operational (AAG)
**OPROM**.... Optical Programmable Read-Only Memory [*Disk*] (BYTE)
**Op Rom**...... Opuscula Romana [*A publication*]
**OPRQ**........ Shorekote/Rafiqui [*Pakistan*] [*ICAO location identifier*] (ICLI)
**OPRR**........ Office for Protection from Research Risks [*Bethesda, MD*] [*National Institutes of Health*] (GRD)
**OPRRB**...... Officer Personnel Record Review Board [*Air Force*] (AFM)
**OPRRE**...... Office of Public Roads and Rural Engineering [*Later, Bureau of Public Roads*]
**OPRS**......... Office of Professional Research Services [*American Occupational Therapy Association*]
**OPRS**......... Oil Pressure
**OPRS**......... Operational Planning and Review Systems [*Employment and Training Administration*] [*Department of Labor*]
**OPRS**......... Risalpur [*Pakistan*] [*ICAO location identifier*] (ICLI)
**OPRT**......... Operator Table
**OPRT**......... Rawalakot [*Pakistan*] [*ICAO location identifier*] (ICLI)
**OPRU**......... Oil Pollution Research Unit [*British*] (ARC)
**OPRV**......... Oxygen Pressure Relief Valve (MCD)
**OPS**........... Oblique Photo Sketcher
**OPS**........... Ocean Platform Station [*National Data Buoy Office*] (NOAA)
**OPS**........... Off-Premise Station [*Telecommunications*] (TEL)
**OPS**........... Office of Pipeline Safety [*Department of Transportation*]
**OPS**........... Office of Population Surveys [*British*]
**OPS**........... Office of Price Stabilization [*Terminated, 1953*]
**OPS**........... Office of Products Safety [*FDA*]
**OPS**........... Office of Program Services [*US Employment Service*] [*Department of Labor*]
**OPS**........... Office of Programmatic Systems [*Social Security Administration*]
**OPS**........... Official Phone Station [*Amateur radio*]
**OPS**........... Official Production System [*Production-system language*]
**OPS**........... Official Public Service Reports [*New York*] [*A publication*] (DLA)
**OPS**........... Offshore Power Systems (NRCH)
**OPS**........... Oil Pressure Switch
**OPS**........... Oil Production Stock
**OPS**........... On-Line Process Synthesis [*Data processing*]
**OPS**........... Open Pan Sulphitation [*Sugar production*]
**OPS**........... Operation and Support (MCD)
**OPS**........... Operational Paging System [*NASA*] (KSC)
**OPS**........... Operational Power Supply
**OPS**........... Operational Protection System [*Nuclear energy*] (NRCH)
**OPS**........... Operational Support (MCD)
**OPS**........... Operations (MCD)
**OPS**........... Operations Division [*NATO*] (NATG)
**OPS**........... Operations Sequence [*NASA*] (MCD)
**OPS**........... Operations Staff [*Military*] [*British*]
**OPS**........... Operator's Subsystem [*Telecommunications*] (TEL)
**OPS**........... Ophthalmic Photographers' Society (EA)
**Ops**............ Opinions [*Legal term*] (DLA)
**OPS**........... Opposite Prompters' Side [*i.e., the left side*] [*Stage direction*] (ROG)
**OPS**........... Opposite Surface [*Technical drawings*]
**OPS**........... OPSEC [*Operations Security*] Professional Society (EA)
**OPS**........... Optical Processing System
**OPS**........... Orbiter Project Schedules [*NASA*] (NASA)
**OPS**........... Orbiting Primate Spacecraft (MCD)
**OPS**........... Organisation Panamericaine de la Sante [*Pan American Health Organization*] (MSC)
**OPS**........... Oriented Polystyrene [*Plastics technology*]
**OPS**........... Ortho-Phosphoserine [*Biochemistry*]
**OPS**........... Out of Print, Searching [*Publishing*]
**OPS**........... Out of Production Spares (MCD)
**OPS**........... Outpatient Service [*Medicine*]
**OPS**........... Overhead Positioning System [*AEC*]
**OPS**........... Overpressure [*or Overpressurization*] Protection System [*Nuclear energy*] (NRCH)
**OPS**........... Oxidizer Particle Size
**OPS**........... Oxygen Purge System [*or Subsystem*] [*NASA*]
**OPS**........... Parry Sound Public Library, Ontario [*Library symbol*] [*National Library of Canada*] (NLC)
**OPS**........... Phillips Petroleum Co., Research and Development Department, Bartlesville, OK [*OCLC symbol*] (OCLC)
**OPSA**......... Algonquin Regional Library, Parry Sound, Ontario [*Library symbol*] [*Obsolete*] [*National Library of Canada*] (NLC)
**Ops AAG POD** ... United States Post Office Department. Official Opinions of the Solicitor [*A publication*] (DLA)
**Ops AG**...... Opinions of the Attorney General [*A publication*] (DLA)
**OP(S)ARMYJAG** ... Opinion(s) of the Army Judge Advocate General
**OPSATCOM** ... Optical Satellite Communications (MCD)
**Ops Atty Gen** ... Opinions of the Attorney General [*A publication*] (DLA)
**Ops Atty Gen Wisc** ... Wisconsin Attorney General Reports [*A publication*] (DLA)
**OPSB**......... Orbiter Processing Support Building [*NASA*] (NASA)
**OPSB**......... Sibi [*Pakistan*] [*ICAO location identifier*] (ICLI)
**OPSC**......... Office of Planning Standards and Coordination [*HUD*]
**OPSCOMM** ... Operations Communications (MCD)
**OPSCON** .. Operations Control [*NASA*] (KSC)
**OPSCOP**... Operations Control [*Monitor*] Program
**OPSCT**...... Christie Township Public Library, Parry Sound, Ontario [*Library symbol*] [*National Library of Canada*] (NLC)
**OPSD**........ Office of Placement Support and Development [*US Employment Service*] [*Department of Labor*]
**OPSD**........ Openside
**OPSD**........ Skardu [*Pakistan*] [*ICAO location identifier*] (ICLI)
**OPSDEP**... Operations Deputy [*In JCS system*] [*Military*]
**OPSEC**...... Operational Security
**OPSEC**...... OPSEC Professionals Society [*Later, OPS*] (EA)
**OPSED**...... Ophthalmic Seminars [*A publication*]
**OPSET**...... Optimal Set [*of Parameters*] [*Hydrology*]
**OPSF**......... Karachi/Shara-E-Faisal [*Pakistan*] [*ICAO location identifier*] (ICLI)
**OP SF**........ Office of Preparedness, General Services Administration [*later, Federal Preparedness Agency*], Special Facility
**OPSF**......... Orbital Propellant Storage Facility (MCD)
**OPSHT**...... Humphrey Township Public Library, Parry Sound, Ontario [*Library symbol*] [*National Library of Canada*] (NLC)
**OPSI**.......... Ordnance Publications for Supply Index [*Military*]
**OPSI**.......... Overwhelming Post-Splenectomy Infection [*Medicine*]
**OPSIM**...... Operational Simulator [*Coast Guard*]
**OPSIMS**.... Operational Simulation Subsystem (MCD)
**Ops JAG**.... Opinions of the Judge Advocate General, United States Army [*A publication*] (DLA)
**OPSK**......... Sukkur [*Pakistan*] [*ICAO location identifier*] (ICLI)
**OPSKS**....... Optimum Phase Shift Keyed Signals [*Telecommunications*]
**OPSMB**..... Organization of Progressive Socialists of the Mediterranean Basin
**OPSO**........ Office of Pipeline Safety Operations [*Department of Transportation*] (DLA)
**Op Sol Dept** ... Opinions of the Solicitor for the Department of Labor [*United States*] [*A publication*] (DLA)
**Op Sol Dept Labor** ... Opinions of the Solicitor for the Department of Labor Dealing with Workmen's Compensation [*A publication*] (DLA)
**Op Solic PO Dep't** ... Official Opinions of the Solicitor for the Post Office Department [*A publication*] (DLA)
**Op Sol POD** ... Opinions of the Solicitor for the Post Office Department [*United States*] [*A publication*] (DLA)
**OPSP**......... Office of Product Standards Policy [*Gaithersburg, MD*] [*Department of Commerce*] (GRD)
**OPSP**......... Shekhupura [*Pakistan*] [*ICAO location identifier*] (ICLI)
**Op Spectra** ... Optical Spectra [*A publication*]
**OPSR**......... Office of Pipeline Safety Regulation [*Department of Transportation*] (OICC)
**OPSR**......... Office of Professional Standards Review [*Medicare and Medicaid*] [*HEW*]
**OPSR**......... Operations Supervisor [*NASA*] (MCD)
**OPSR**......... Sargodha [*Pakistan*] [*ICAO location identifier*] (ICLI)
**OPSRDY**... Operations Readiness (MCD)
**OPSREP**.... Operations Report [*NATO*] (NATG)
**Ops Research** ... Operations Research [*A publication*]
**OPSRO**...... Office of Professional Standards Review [*Medicare and Medicaid*] Organization [*HEW*]
**OPSS**......... Operating and Programming Systems Series [*Elsevier Book Series*] [*A publication*]
**OPSS**......... Orbital Propellant Storage Subsystem (MCD)
**OPSS**......... Saidu Sharif [*Pakistan*] [*ICAO location identifier*] (ICLI)
**OP(ST)**...... Operation Overlord Preparations, Service Leave and Travel [*World War II*]
**OPST**......... Out-of-Pile Systems Test [*Nuclear energy*] (NRCH)
**OPSTAT**... Operational Status [*Navy*] (NVT)
**OPSTATUSREP** ... Operations Status Report (NATG)
**OPSTR**...... Operating Strength [*Army*] (AABC)
**OPSU**........ Sui [*Pakistan*] [*ICAO location identifier*] (ICLI)
**OPSUM**.... Operational Summary [*Navy*] (NVT)
**OPSUPPFAC** ... Operational Support Facility (MCD)
**OPSW**........ Sahiwal [*Pakistan*] [*ICAO location identifier*] (ICLI)
**OPSWL**..... Old Program Status Word Location
**OPS-X**....... Operational Teletype Message
**OPSYS**...... Operating System [*Data processing*]
**OPT**........... Oil Point [*Alaska*] [*Seismograph station code, US Geological Survey*] (SEIS)
**OPT**........... Oil Pressure Transmitter
**OPT**........... Operability Testing [*Military*] (CAAL)
**OPT**........... Operation Prime Time [*Television*]
**OPT**........... Operational Pressure Transducer (MCD)
**OPT**........... Opportunities for Professional Transition [*An association*] (EA)
**OPT**........... Optative [*Grammar*]
**OPT**........... Optical (AAG)
**OPT**........... Optical Point Transfer
**OPT**........... Optician
**OPT**........... Optics
**OPT**........... Optima [*Johannesburg*] [*A publication*]
**OPT**........... Optimization Study [*Nuclear energy*] (NRCH)
**OPT**........... Optimized Production Technology
**OPT**........... Optimum [*A publication*]

**OPT** ........... Optimum (AAG)
**OPT** ........... Optimus [*Best*] [*Latin*]
**OPT** ........... Optional (AAG)
**OPT** ........... Other People's Tobacco [*Slang*]
**OPT** ........... Outpatient Treatment [*Medicine*]
**OPT** ........... Overhead Projection Transparency (MCD)
**OPT** ........... Pakenham Township Public Library, Ontario [*Library symbol*] [*National Library of Canada*] (BIB)
**OPT** ........... Payne Theological Seminary, Wilberforce, OH [*OCLC symbol*] (OCLC)
**OPTA** ........ Optimal Performance Theoretically Attainable (IEEE)
**OPTA** ........ Organ and Piano Teachers Association [*Defunct*] (EA)
**OPTA** ........ Terbela [*Pakistan*] [*ICAO location identifier*] (ICLI)
**OPTACON** ... Optical-to-Tactile Converter [*Electronic reader for the blind*]
**Opt Acta** .... Optica Acta [*A publication*]
**OPTAD** ..... Organisation for Pacific Trade and Development (ADA)
**OPTADS**... Operations Tactical Data Systems [*Army*] (RDA)
**OPTAG** ..... Optical Aimpoint Guidance System [*Weaponry*]
**OPTAN** ..... Operations Target Analysis [*of strike missions in North Vietnam*]
**Opt Appl**.... Optica Applicata [*A publication*]
**OPTAR**...... Operating Target
**OPTAR**...... Optical Automatic Ranging
**OPTARE**... Office of Planning, Technical Assistance, Research, and Evaluation [*Washington, DC*] [*Department of Commerce*] (GRD)
**OPTB**......... Operational Program Time Base [*NASA*] (MCD)
**OPTC** ........ Optelecom, Inc. [*NASDAQ symbol*] (NQ)
**Opt Commun** ... Optics Communications [*A publication*]
**Opt County Gov't** ... Optional County Government [*A publication*] (DLA)
**Opt D** ......... Doctor of Optometry
**Opt Dev**...... Optical Developments [*A publication*]
**OPTE**......... Operational Proficiency Training Equipment [*Roland International Corp.*] (MCD)
**OPTEC**...... Optical Properties Technical Evaluation Center
**Opt-Electron** ... Opto-Electronique [*A publication*]
**OPTEMPO** ... Tempo of Operations (MCD)
**Opt Eng**...... Optical Engineering [*A publication*]
**Opt Engin** .. Optical Engineering [*A publication*]
**Op Tenn Att'y Gen** ... Opinions of the Attorney General of Tennessee [*A publication*] (DLA)
**Opteolektorn and Poluprovodn Tekh** ... Opteolektronika i Poluprovodnikovaya Tekhnika [*A publication*]
**OPTEV**...... Operational Test and Evaluation [*Military*]
**OPTEVFOR** ... Operational Test and Evaluation Force [*Norfolk, VA*] [*Navy*]
**OptEx** ........ Optional Exchange [*Dietetics*]
**Op Tex Att'y Gen** ... Opinions of the Attorney General of Texas [*A publication*] (DLA)
**Opt Fibers Med** ... Optical Fibers in Medicine [*A publication*]
**OPTH**........ Ophthalmic (ROG)
**OPTH**........ Talhar [*Pakistan*] [*ICAO location identifier*] (ICLI)
**OPTI**.......... Office of Productivity, Technology, and Innovation [*Department of Commerce*]
**OPTI**.......... Optimum Holding Corp. [*NASDAQ symbol*] (NQ)
**OPTIC**....... Optical Procedural Task Instruction Compiler
**Optik**.......... Optik. Zeitschrift fuer Licht- und Elektronenoptik [*A publication*]
**Optikomekh Prom** ... Optiko-Mekhanicheskaya Promyshlennost' [*A publication*]
**OPTIM**...... Occupational Projections and Training Information for Michigan [*Information service or system*] (EISS)
**OPTIM**...... Order Point Technique for Inventory Management (BUR)
**OPTIMA**... Organization for the Phyto-Taxonomic Investigation of the Mediterranean Area [*Berlin, Federal Republic of Germany*] (EAIO)
**Optimal Control Appl Methods** ... Optimal Control Applications and Methods [*A publication*]
**Optimal Planirovanie** ... Optimal'noe Planirovanie [*A publication*]
**Optimizacija** ... Akademija Nauk SSSR. Sibirskoe Otdelenie. Institut Matematiki. Optimizacija [*A publication*]
**Optimization** ... Mathematische Operationsforschung und Statistik. Series Optimization [*A publication*]
**OPTIMUM** ... Obtain Increased Productivity through Improved Modernization of Facilities and Updating Maintenance Tools, Equipment, and Methods [*Military*]
**OPTIMUS** ... Office of Public Trustee Information Management User System [*Canada*]
**OPTINT**.... Optical Intelligence (MCD)
**Options Mediterr** ... Options Mediterraneennes [*A publication*]
**OPTK** ........ Optrotech Ltd. [*New York, NY*] [*NASDAQ symbol*] (NQ)
**OPTL**......... Optional (MSA)
**Opt Laser Microlithogr** ... Optical/Laser Microlithography [*A publication*]
**Opt and Lasers Eng** ... Optics and Lasers in Engineering [*A publication*]
**Opt Laser Technol** ... Optics and Laser Technology [*A publication*]
**Opt and Laser Technol** ... Optics and Laser Technology [*A publication*]
**Opt Laser Technol Spec Suppl** ... Optics and Laser Technology. Special Supplement [*A publication*]
**OPTLC**...... Overpressurized Thin-Layer Chromatography
**Opt Lett** ..... Optics Letters [*A publication*]
**OPTM** ....... Optometry
**Opt-Mekh Prom** ... Optiko-Mekhanicheskaya Promyshlennost' [*A publication*]
**Opt-Mekh Prom-St'** ... Optiko-Mekhanicheskaya Promyshlennost' [*A publication*]
**OPTMTRC** ... Optometric
**OPTN**........ [*The*] National Organ Procurement and Transplantation Network [*Information service or system*] (IID)
**Opt News**... Optics News [*A publication*]
**OPTO**........ Opto Mechanik, Inc. [*NASDAQ symbol*] (NQ)
**Opto-Electron** ... Opto-Electronics [*A publication*]
**Optoelektron Poluprovodn Tekh** ... Optoelektronika i Poluprovodnikovaya Tekhnika [*A publication*]
**Optoelektron Spektrosk** ... Optoelektronika i Spektroskopiya [*A publication*]
**Optom**........ Optometry
**OPTOMA** ... Ocean Prediction through Observation, Modeling, and Analysis [*Experimental program*]
**Optom Vision Sci** ... Optometry and Vision Science [*A publication*]
**Opt Pura y Apl** ... Optica Pura y Aplicada [*A publication*]
**Opt Pura Apl** ... Optica Pura y Aplicada [*A publication*]
**Opt Quant E** ... Optical and Quantum Electronics [*A publication*]
**Opt and Quantum Electron** ... Optical and Quantum Electronics [*A publication*]
**Opt Quantum Electron** ... Optical and Quantum Electronics [*A publication*]
**Opt Rev**...... Optical Review [*A publication*]
**OPTS**......... Office of Pesticides and Toxic Substances [*Environmental Protection Agency*]
**OPTS**......... Office of Program and Technical Services [*Employment and Training Administration*] [*Department of Labor*]
**OPTS**......... Online Peripheral Test System
**Opt Soc Am J** ... Optical Society of America. Journal [*A publication*]
**Opt Spectra** ... Optical Spectra [*A publication*]
**Opt and Spectrosc** ... Optics and Spectroscopy [*A publication*]
**Opt Spectrosc (Engl Transl)** ... Optics and Spectroscopy (English Translation of Optika i Spektroskopiya) [*USSR*] [*A publication*]
**Opt Spectrosc (USSR)** ... Optics and Spectroscopy (USSR) [*A publication*]
**Opt Spectry** ... Optics and Spectroscopy [*A publication*]
**Opt Spektro** ... Optika i Spektroskopiya [*A publication*]
**Opt Spektrosk** ... Optika i Spektroskopiya [*A publication*]
**Opt & Spektrosk** ... Optika i Spektroskopiya [*A publication*]
**Opt Spektrosk Akad Nauk SSSR Otd Fiz-Mat Nauk** ... Optika i Spektroskopiya. Akademiya Nauk SSSR. Otdelenie Fiziko-Matematicheskikh Nauk [*USSR*] [*A publication*]
**OPTT**......... Taftan [*Pakistan*] [*ICAO location identifier*] (ICLI)
**Opt Technol** ... Optics Technology [*A publication*]
**OPTU** ........ Turbat [*Pakistan*] [*ICAO location identifier*] (ICLI)
**OPTUL**....... Optical Pulse Transmitter Using LASER
**OPTX** ......... Optek Technology, Inc. [*NASDAQ symbol*] (NQ)
**OPU** ........... Balimo [*Papua New Guinea*] [*Airport symbol*] (OAG)
**OPU**........... Operational Performance Unit (ADA)
**OPU**........... Operations Priority Unit
**OPU**........... Overseas Plexiglas Unit
**OPU**........... Pacific University, Forest Grove, OR [*OCLC symbol*] (OCLC)
**OPUR**........ Object Program Utility Routine
**OPURD7**... Institute of Arctic and Alpine Research. University of Colorado. Occasional Paper [*A publication*]
**OPUS** ........ Octal Program Updating System [*Data processing*]
**OPUS** ........ Offshore Persistent Upwelling Structure
**OPUS** ........ Opus Computer Products, Inc. [*NASDAQ symbol*] (NQ)
**OPUS** ........ Organisation of Professional Users of Statistics
**Opus Arch** ... Opuscula Archaeologica [*A publication*]
**Opus Ath** ... Opuscula Atheniensia [*A publication*]
**OPUSC**...... Opuscula [*Minor Works*] [*Latin*] (ROG)
**Opusc Athen** ... Opuscula Atheniensia. Skrifter Utgivna av Svenska Institutet i Athen - Acta Instituti Atheniensis Regni Sueciae [*A publication*]
**Opusc Ent**.. Opuscula Entomologica [*A publication*]
**Opusc Entomol** ... Opuscula Entomologica [*A publication*]
**Opusc Med** ... Opuscula Medica [*A publication*]
**Opusc Med Suppl** ... Opuscula Medica. Supplementum [*A publication*]
**Opusc Zool (Bpest)** ... Opuscula Zoologica (Budapest) [*A publication*]
**Opusc Zool (Budap)** ... Opuscula Zoologica (Budapest) [*A publication*]
**Opusc Zool (Munich)** ... Opuscula Zoologica (Munich) [*A publication*]
**Opus M**...... Opus Musicum [*A publication*]
**Opus Mus**.. Opus Musicum [*A publication*]
**Opus Ph**..... Opuscula Philologica [*A publication*]
**Opus Rom**.. Opuscula Romana [*A publication*]
**Opus Zool (Muenchen)** ... Opuscula Zoologica (Muenchen) [*A publication*]
**OPV**........... Ohms per Volt
**OPV**........... Oral Polio Virus Vaccine
**Op VA Att'y Gen** ... Opinions of the Attorney General and Report to the Governor of Virginia [*A publication*] (DLA)
**OPW**.......... Oboz Polski Walczacej [*A publication*] (BJA)
**OPW**.......... Ohio Power Co. [*NYSE symbol*] (SPSG)
**OPW**.......... Opawica Explorations, Inc. [*Toronto Stock Exchange symbol*]
**OPW**.......... Open Pilot Warranty [*Insurance*] (AIA)
**OPW**.......... Operating Weight [*Air Force*]
**OPW**.......... Optical Window
**OPW**.......... Opuwa [*Namibia*] [*Airport symbol*] (OAG)
**OPW**.......... Orthogonalized Plane Wave
**OPW**.......... Porter Public Library, Westlake, OH [*OCLC symbol*] (OCLC)

**OPW**.......... Whitney Public Library, Porcupine, Ontario [*Library symbol*] [*National Library of Canada*] (NLC)
**OPWA**....... Official Publications of Western Australia [*A publication*] (APTA)
**Op Wash Att'y Gen** ... Office of the Attorney General (State of Washington) Opinions [*A publication*] (DLA)
**Op Wis Att'y Gen** ... Opinions of the Attorney General of Wisconsin [*A publication*] (DLA)
**OPWN**....... Wana [*Pakistan*] [*ICAO location identifier*] (ICLI)
**OPWS**........ Orbiter Payload Work Station (MCD)
**Op Wyo Att'y Gen** ... Opinions of the Attorney General of Wyoming [*A publication*] (DLA)
**OPX**........... Off-Premise Extension [*Nuclear energy*] (NRCH)
**OPX**........... Orthopyroxene [*A silicate mineral*]
**Opyt Izuch Regul Fiziol Funkts** ... Opyt Izucheniya Regulyatsii Fiziologicheskikh Funktsii [*A publication*]
**Opyt Paseka** ... Opytnaya Paseka [*A publication*]
**Opyt Primen Radioakt Metodov Poiskakh Razved Neradioakt Rud** ... Opyt Primeneniya Radioaktivnykh Metodov pri Poiskakh i Razvedke Neradioaktivnykh Rud [*A publication*]
**Opyt Rab Pchel** ... Opytnaya Rabota Pchelovodov [*A publication*]
**Opyt Rab Peredovogo Sovkhoznogo Proizvod** ... Opyt Raboty Peredovogo Sovkhoznogo Proizvodstva [*A publication*]
**OPZ**........... Opsonized Zymosan [*Biochemistry*]
**OPZB**......... Zhob [*Pakistan*] [*ICAO location identifier*] (ICLI)
**OQ**............. Officers' Quarters [*Military*]
**OQ**............. Ohioana Quarterly [*A publication*]
**OQ**............. Optical Quality
**OQ**............. Tropical Air Services [*ICAO designator*] (FAAC)
**OQA**.......... Operations Quality Assurance [*Nuclear energy*] (NRCH)
**OQA**.......... Reidsville, NC [*Location identifier*] [*FAA*] (FAAL)
**OQAP**........ Oil Quality Assessment Program [*Society of Automotive Engineers, Inc.*]
**OQC**........... Office of Quality Control [*Social and Rehabilitation Service, HEW*]
**OQC**........... Operator Quality Control [*RADAR*]
**OQC**........... Outside Quality Control (KSC)
**OQD**.......... Optical Quantum Detector
**OQDEAN** ... Orquidea [*Mexico City*] [*A publication*]
**OQG**.......... Optical Quantum Generator
**OQI**............ Oil Quantity Indicator
**OQL**........... Observed Quality Level
**OQL**........... Online Query Language
**OQL**........... Outgoing Quality Level
**OQL**........... Outgoing Quality Limit
**OQM**.......... Office of the Quartermaster [*Military*]
**OQMG**....... Office of the Quartermaster General [*Military*]
**OQP**........... Optimum Qualification Procedure
**OQR**........... Officer's Qualification Record [*Army*]
**OQT**........... Officer Qualification Test
**OQTD**........ Operational Qualifications Test Deficiency [*Air Force*]
**OQU**.......... North Kingstown, RI [*Location identifier*] [*FAA*] (FAAL)
**OQW**......... Maquoketa, IA [*Location identifier*] [*FAA*] (FAAL)
**OQZ**........... Union City, TN [*Location identifier*] [*FAA*] (FAAL)
**OR**.............. Air Comoros [*Comoros*] [*ICAO designator*] (FAAC)
**Or**............... Indian Law Reports, Orissa Series [*A publication*] (DLA)
**OR**.............. O-Ring [*Automotive engineering*]
**OR**.............. Objective Reliability (MCD)
**O & R**......... Ocean and Rail [*Shipping*]
**OR**.............. Octane Requirement [*Mechanical engineering*]
**OR**.............. Odds Ratio [*Statistics*]
**OR**.............. Odrodzenie i Reformacja w Polsce [*A publication*]
**OR**.............. Off-Radial (RDA)
**O/R**............ Office of Record (AFM)
**OR**.............. Officer Records [*Military*] (AFM)
**OR**.............. Official Receiver
**OR**.............. Official Records
**OR**.............. Official Referee
**OR**.............. Official Reports, South Africa [*A publication*] (DLA)
**OR**.............. Oil Rehabilitation Committee [*British*]
**OR**.............. Oil and Resource Development Supplement. Fairbanks Daily News Miner [*A publication*]
**OR**.............. Oil Retention [*Enema*] [*Medicine*]
**OR**.............. Oil Ring (MSA)
**OR**.............. Oklahoma Law Review [*A publication*]
**OR**.............. Old Roman (ADA)
**OR**.............. Oleoresin [*Also, Ol Res*] [*Pharmacy*]
**OR**.............. Oligomer Restriction [*Genetics*]
**OR**.............. Omnidirectional Radio Range (MCD)
**O/R**............ On Request
**OR**.............. On Return
**OR**.............. Ontario Reports [*A publication*] (DLA)
**OR**.............. Open Registry [*Flag of convenience*] [*Shipping*] (DS)
**OR**.............. Operating Reactor [*Nuclear energy*] (NRCH)
**OR**.............. Operating Resources (AFM)
**OR**.............. Operating Room [*Medicine*]
**OR**.............. Operation Reach-Out [*Department of Labor*]
**OR**.............. Operation Record
**OR**.............. Operation Rescue (EA)
**OR**.............. Operational Readiness [*Army*]
**OR**.............. Operational Reliability [*Army*] (AABC)
**OR**.............. Operational Report (AAG)
**OR**.............. Operational Requirement
**OR**.............. Operational Research
**OR**.............. Operational Research Quarterly [*A publication*]
**OR**.............. Operationally Ready (MCD)
**OR**.............. Operations Requirements
**OR**.............. Operations Research [*A publication*]
**OR**.............. Operations Research [*Data processing*]
**OR**.............. Operations Review [*NASA*] (MCD)
**OR**.............. Operations Room
**OR**.............. Operculum Ridge
**OR**.............. Ophthalmic Rete [*Bird anatomy*]
**OR**.............. Opponents' Runs [*Baseball*]
**OR**.............. Optical Reader [*Data processing*] (BUR)
**OR**.............. Orange
**Or**............... Oratio [*A publication*] (OCD)
**Or**............... Orationes [*of Dio Chrysostomus*] [*Classical studies*] (OCD)
**Or**............... Orationes [*of Julian*] [*Classical studies*] (OCD)
**OR**.............. Oratorians
**OR**.............. Order Pennant [*Navy*] [*British*]
**OR**.............. Ordered Recorded
**OR**.............. Orderly Room
**OR**.............. Ordnance Report
**OR**.............. Ordnance Requirement
**OR**.............. Oregon [*Postal code*]
**OR**.............. Oregon Music Educator [*A publication*]
**Or**............... Oregon State Library, Salem, OR [*Library symbol*] [*Library of Congress*] (LCLS)
**Or**............... Oregon Supreme Court Reports [*A publication*] (DLA)
**Or**............... Orestes [*of Euripides*] [*Classical studies*] (OCD)
**OR**.............. Organ Recovery (EA)
**OR**.............. Organized Reserves [*Military*]
**OR**.............. Orient
**OR**.............. Orient Review [*A publication*]
**OR**.............. Oriental (ROG)
**Or**............... Orientalia. Commentarii Periodici Pontificii Instituti Biblici [*A publication*]
**OR**.............. Orienting Response [*Psychology*]
**Or**............... Origen [*Deceased circa 254*] [*Authority cited in pre-1607 legal work*] (DSA)
**OR**.............. Original (ADA)
**Or**............... Orizont [*A publication*]
**'Or**.............. 'Orlah (BJA)
**OR**.............. Orosomucoid [*Biochemistry*]
**Or**............... Orpheus. Revista pentru Cultura Clasica [*A publication*]
**or**................ Orthoclase [*CIPW classification*] [*Geology*]
**OR**.............. Orthopedic
**OR**.............. Orthopedic Research [*Medicine*]
**OR**.............. Oswestry Rangers [*British military*] (DMA)
**OR**.............. Other (ROG)
**OR**.............. Other Ranks [*Ranks other than officers*] [*Military*]
**OR**.............. Out of Range
**OR**.............. Outer Roll [*Aviation*] (MCD)
**OR**.............. Output Register (MSA)
**OR**.............. Outside Radius [*Technical drawings*]
**OR**.............. Outside Right [*Soccer position*]
**OR**.............. Overall Report
**O & R**......... Overhaul and Repair
**OR**.............. Overhaul and Repair
**OR**.............. Overload Relay (KSC)
**O/R**............ Overrange [*System or element*] (IEEE)
**O/R**............ Override (KSC)
**OR**.............. Overseas Replacement [*Military*]
**OR**.............. Owasco River [*AAR code*]
**OR**.............. Own Recognizance [*Legal term*]
**OR**.............. Owner's Risk [*Shipping*]
**OR**.............. Oxford Review [*A publication*]
**O-R**............ Oxidation-Reduction
**OR**.............. Oxygen Relief (NASA)
**OR**.............. Renfrew Public Library, Ontario [*Library symbol*] [*National Library of Canada*] (NLC)
**OR**.............. Schweizerisches Obligationenrecht [*A publication*]
**ORA**........... Ocean Reef Airways Club [*Key Largo, FL*] [*FAA designator*] (FAAC)
**ORA**........... Office of Redress Administration [*Department of Justice*]
**ORA**........... Office of Regulatory Analysis [*Federal Energy Regulatory Commission*]
**ORA**........... Office of Research Administration [*North Carolina A & T State University*] [*Research center*] (RCD)
**ORA**........... Office of Research Administration [*St. Louis University*] [*Research center*] (RCD)
**ORA**........... Office of Research Administration [*University of Pennsylvania*] [*Research center*] (RCD)
**ORA**........... Office of Research Administration [*University of Hawaii*] [*Research center*] (RCD)
**ORA**........... Office of Research Analysis [*Air Force*]
**ORA**........... Operating Room Attendant [*British military*] (DMA)
**ORA**........... Operation Response Area (MCD)
**ORA**........... Operational RADAR Directed Flights (NATG)
**ORA**........... Operational Readiness Assessment
**ORA**........... Operations Research Analyst [*Army*] (AABC)

**ORA**.......... Opportunity Resources for the Arts (EA)
**ORA**.......... Optical Reference Axis
**ORA**.......... OR. Journal of the Operational Research Society [*A publication*]
**ORA**.......... Order for Reinforced Alert (NATG)
**Or A**.......... Oregon Court of Appeals Reports [*A publication*] (DLA)
**ORA**.......... Organisation de Resistance de l'Armee [*France*]
**ORA**.......... Organisation Revolutionnaire Anarchiste [*Revolutionary Anarchist Organization*] [*France*] [*Political party*] (PPE)
**ORA**.......... Orifice Rod Assembly [*Nuclear energy*] (NRCH)
**ORA**.......... Outdoor Recreation Action [*A publication*]
**ORA**.......... Output Reference Axis [*Gyro; accelerometer*] (IEEE)
**ORA**.......... Output Register Address
**ORA**.......... Overseas Reports Announcements [*A publication*] (APTA)
**ORA**.......... Ramore Library, Ontario [*Library symbol*] [*National Library of Canada*] (BIB)
**ORA**.......... Ross Laboratory Library, Columbus, OH [*OCLC symbol*] (OCLC)
**ORAAP**..... Outstanding Reserve Airman Appointment Program
**ORACLE**... Oak Ridge Automatic Computer and Logical Engine
**ORACLE**... On-Line Retrieval and Computational Language for Economists [*Data processing*]
**ORACLE**... Optical Reception of Announcements by Coded Line Electronics
**ORACLE**... Optimized Reliability and Component Life Estimate
**ORACLE**... Optimum Record Automation for Court and Law Enforcement
**ORACLE**... Ordnance Rapid Area Clearance [*Military*] (CAAL)
**ORACLE**... Organic Rankine Cycle
**ORACT**..... Operational Readiness and Confidence Test
**ORAD**........ Office of Rural Areas Development [*Later, Rural Community Development Service*] [*Department of Agriculture*]
**ORAD**........ Orbiter RADAR [*NASA*]
**ORAD**........ Outbound Radian [*Aviation*] (FAAC)
**Or Admin R** ... Oregon Administrative Rules [*A publication*] (DLA)
**Or Admin R Bull** ... Oregon Administrative Rules Bulletin [*A publication*] (DLA)
**ORADS**..... Optical Ranging and Detection System
**Or Ad Sh**.... Supreme Court of the State of Oregon Advance Sheets [*A publication*] (DLA)
**ORAE**........ Office de Repartition des Approvisionnements d'Energie [*Canada*]
**ORAE**........ Operational Research and Analysis Establishment (MCD)
**OrAg**.......... Agness Community Library, Agness, OR [*Library symbol*] [*Library of Congress*] (LCLS)
**OrAl**........... Albany Public Library, Albany, OR [*Library symbol*] [*Library of Congress*] (LCLS)
**ORAL**........ Oral Access to Library
**OrAlBM**.... United States Bureau of Mines, Education and Training Center, Albany, OR [*Library symbol*] [*Library of Congress*] (LCLS)
**OrAlC**........ Linn-Benton Community College, Albany, OR [*Library symbol*] [*Library of Congress*] (LCLS)
**Orale Implantol** ... Orale Implantologie [*A publication*]
**OrAlH**........ Albany General Hospital, Albany, OR [*Library symbol*] [*Library of Congress*] (LCLS)
**Oral H**........ Oral History [*A publication*]
**Oral Hyg**.... Oral Hygiene [*A publication*]
**Oral Implantol** ... Oral Implantology [*A publication*]
**Oral Res Abstr** ... Oral Research Abstracts [*A publication*]
**Oral Sci Rev** ... Oral Sciences Reviews [*A publication*]
**Oral Surg** ... Oral Surgery, Oral Medicine, and Oral Pathology [*A publication*]
**Oral Surgery** ... Oral Surgery, Oral Medicine, and Oral Pathology [*A publication*]
**Oral Surg O** ... Oral Surgery, Oral Medicine, and Oral Pathology [*A publication*]
**Oral Surg Oral Med Oral Pathol** ... Oral Surgery, Oral Medicine, and Oral Pathology [*A publication*]
**OrAlT**........ Teledyne-Wah Chang Albany, Albany, OR (LCLS)
**OrAm**......... Amity Public Library, Amity, OR [*Library symbol*] [*Library of Congress*] (LCLS)
**ORAN**........ Orbital Analysis
**ORAN**........ Organisation Regionale Africaine de Normalisation [*African Regional Organization for Standardization - AROS*] (EAIO)
**Or An**......... Oriens Antiquus [*A publication*]
**ORANA**..... Organisme de Recherches sur l'Alimentation et la Nutrition Africaines [*African Food and Nutrition Research Organization*] [*French*]
**Orang C BJ** ... Orange County Business Journal [*A publication*]
**Orange County BJ** ... Orange County Bar Association. Journal [*A publication*]
**Orange County Bus** ... Orange County Business [*A publication*]
**Orange Cty** ... Business Press of Orange County [*A publication*]
**Orange Cty Dent Soc Bull** ... Orange County [*California*] Dental Society. Bulletin [*A publication*]
**ORANS**..... Oak Ridge Analytical Systems
**OrAnt**......... Oriens Antiquus [*Rome*] [*A publication*]
**OrAntBud** ... Oriens Antiquus [*Budapest*] [*A publication*]
**Or App**....... Oregon Reports, Court of Appeal [*A publication*] (DLA)
**OrAr**.......... Arlington Public Library, Arlington, OR [*Library symbol*] [*Library of Congress*] (LCLS)
**Or-Ar**......... Oregon State Archives, Salem, OR [*Library symbol*] [*Library of Congress*] (LCLS)
**ORAR**........ Rainy River Public Library, Ontario [*Library symbol*] [*National Library of Canada*] (NLC)
**Or Art**........ Oriental Art [*United Kingdom*] [*A publication*]
**ORAS**........ Oil Recovery and Separation Technology [*Jastram Werke*]
**OrAshS**...... Southern Oregon College, Ashland, OR [*Library symbol*] [*Library of Congress*] (LCLS)
**OrAst**......... Astor Library, Astoria, OR [*Library symbol*] [*Library of Congress*] (LCLS)
**OrAstC**....... Clatsop Community College, Astoria, OR [*Library symbol*] [*Library of Congress*] (LCLS)
**OrAstM**..... Columbia River Maritime Museum, Astoria, OR [*Library symbol*] [*Library of Congress*] (LCLS)
**Orat**........... Oration [*or Orator or Oratorio*]
**Orat**........... Orator ad M. Brutum [*of Cicero*] [*Classical studies*] (OCD)
**ORAT**......... Oratorical
**ORATE**..... Ordered Random Access Talking Equipment
**ORATMS** ... Off-Route Antitank Mine System (MCD)
**ORATS**...... Operational Readiness Assessment and Training System (MCD)
**ORAU**........ Oak Ridge Associated Universities (EA)
**ORAW**....... Oil Remaining after Waterflooding [*Petroleum technology*]
**OrB**........... Beaverton City Library, Beaverton, OR [*Library symbol*] [*Library of Congress*] (LCLS)
**ORB**.......... Oceanic Ridge Basalts
**ORB**.......... Oceanographic Research Buoy
**ORB**.......... Officer Record Brief [*Army*] (AABC)
**ORB**.......... Omnidirectional Radio Beacon
**ORB**.......... Operational Research Branch [*Canada*]
**ORB**.......... Operations Record Book [*Air Ministry*] [*British*] [*World War II*]
**ORB**.......... Orbe [*Switzerland*] [*Seismograph station code, US Geological Survey*] [*Closed*] (SEIS)
**Orb**............ Orbis [*Record label*] [*Germany, etc.*]
**ORB**.......... Orbit Oil & Gas Ltd. [*Toronto Stock Exchange symbol*]
**ORB**.......... Orbital (KSC)
**ORB**.......... Orbiter [*NASA*] (NASA)
**ORB**.......... Orebro [*Sweden*] [*Airport symbol*] (OAG)
**ORB**.......... Organizational Records Branch [*Army*]
**ORB**.......... Orr, MN [*Location identifier*] [*FAA*] (FAAL)
**ORB**.......... Outer Radiation Belt
**ORB**.......... Outside Reactor Building [*Nuclear energy*] (NRCH)
**ORB**.......... Owner's Risk of Breaking [*Shipping*]
**OrBa**.......... Banks Community Library, Banks, OR [*Library symbol*] [*Library of Congress*] (LCLS)
**ORBA**........ Erbil [*Iraq*] [*ICAO location identifier*] (ICLI)
**OrBak**........ Baker County Public Library, Baker, OR [*Library symbol*] [*Library of Congress*] (LCLS)
**OrBakSE**... Saint Elizabeth Hospital, Baker, OR [*Library symbol*] [*Library of Congress*] (LCLS)
**OrBan**........ Bandon Public Library, Bandon, OR [*Library symbol*] [*Library of Congress*] (LCLS)
**Or Bar Bull** ... Oregon Bar Bulletin [*A publication*] (DLA)
**ORBAT**...... Order of Battle Report [*Military*] (NATG)
**ORBB**........ Sirsenk/Bamarni [*Iraq*] [*ICAO location identifier*] (ICLI)
**ORBC**........ Baghdad/Soica Headquarters [*Iraq*] [*ICAO location identifier*] (ICLI)
**OrBe**.......... Deschutes County Library, Bend, OR [*Library symbol*] [*Library of Congress*] (LCLS)
**OrBeC**........ Central Oregon Community College, Bend, OR [*Library symbol*] [*Library of Congress*] (LCLS)
**OrBeMC**.... Saint Charles Medical Center, Medical Library, Bend, OR [*Library symbol*] [*Library of Congress*] (LCLS)
**OrBFP**....... Floating Point Systems, Inc., Beaverton, OR [*Library symbol*] [*Library of Congress*] (LCLS)
**OrBG**......... Oregon Graduate Center, Beaverton, OR [*Library symbol*] [*Library of Congress*] (LCLS)
**ORB 1-G**.... Orbiter One-G Trainer [*NASA*] (NASA)
**OrBGS**....... Church of Jesus Christ of Latter-Day Saints, Genealogical Society Library, Beaverton Branch, Beaverton, OR [*Library symbol*] [*Library of Congress*] (LCLS)
**ORBI**......... Rocky Band No. 1 Indian Band Library, Ontario [*Library symbol*] [*National Library of Canada*] (BIB)
**OrBiblLov** ... Orientalia et Biblica Lovaniensia [*Louvain*] [*A publication*]
**OrBibLov**... Orientalia et Biblica Lovaniensia [*Louvain*] [*A publication*]
**ORBIFC**.... Oak Ridge Boys International Fan Club (EA)
**ORBIS**....... Orbiting Radio Beacon Ionospheric Satellite [*NASA*]
**ORBIS**....... Ordering and Billing System
**ORBIS**....... Oregon Business Information System [*Oregon State Economic Development Department*] [*Information service or system*] [*Defunct*] (IID)
**Orbis Lit**.... Orbis Litterarum [*A publication*]
**Orbis Mus** ... Orbis Musicae [*A publication*]
**ORBIT**....... Oak Ridge Binary Internal-Translator
**ORBIT**....... On-Line, Real-Time, Branch Information Transmission [*IBM Corp.*] [*Data processing*]
**ORBIT**....... On-Line Reduced Bandwidth Information Transfer [*Data processing*]
**ORBIT**....... On-Line Retrieval of Bibliographic Text [*Search system*] [*Data processing*]

**ORBIT**....... ORACLE Binary Internal Translator [*Algebraic programming system*]
**ORBIT**....... Orbit, Ballistic Impact, and Trajectory [*Computer*] (MUGU)
**ORBM**....... Mosul [*Iraq*] [*ICAO location identifier*] (ICLI)
**ORBN**........ Orbanco Financial Services Corp. [*NASDAQ symbol*] (NQ)
**OrBo**.......... Boardman Public Library, Boardman, OR [*Library symbol*] [*Library of Congress*] (LCLS)
**OrBP**.......... Oregon Regional Primate Research Center, Beaverton, OR [*Library symbol*] [*Library of Congress*] (LCLS)
**Or-BPH**..... Oregon State Library, Services for the Blind and Physically Handicapped, Salem, OR [*Library symbol*] [*Library of Congress*] (LCLS)
**ORBR**........ Baghdad/Rasheed [*Iraq*] [*ICAO location identifier*] (ICLI)
**OrBroo**....... Chetco Community Public Library, Brookings, OR [*Library symbol*] [*Library of Congress*] (LCLS)
**ORBS**......... Baghdad/Saddam International [*Iraq*] [*ICAO location identifier*] (ICLI)
**ORBS**......... Orbis, Inc. [*NASDAQ symbol*] (NQ)
**ORBS**......... Orbital Rendezvous Base System
**ORBT**........ Orbit Instrument Corp. [*NASDAQ symbol*] (NQ)
**OrBT**.......... Tektronix, Inc., Beaverton, OR [*Library symbol*] [*Library of Congress*] (LCLS)
**ORBW**....... Baghdad/Muthenna [*Iraq*] [*ICAO location identifier*] (ICLI)
**ORBZ**........ Ain Zalah [*Iraq*] [*ICAO location identifier*] (ICLI)
**OrC**............ Corvallis Public Library, Corvallis, OR [*Library symbol*] [*Library of Congress*] (LCLS)
**ORC**........... Occupational Research Centre [*Hatfield Polytechnic*] [*British*] (CB)
**ORC**........... Ocean Racing Club [*Australia*]
**ORC**........... Office of the Regional Commissioner [*Social Security Administration*] (OICC)
**ORC**........... Office of Reserve Components [*Army*]
**ORC**........... Officers' Reserve Corps [*Later, Army Reserve*]
**ORC**........... On-Line Reactivity Computer [*Nuclear energy*] (NRCH)
**ORC**........... Operational Readiness Check
**ORC**........... Operational Reports Control [*Military*] (AFM)
**ORC**........... Operational Requirements Committee [*Ministry of Defence*] [*British*]
**ORC**........... Operations Research Center [*Massachusetts Institute of Technology*] [*Research center*] (KSC)
**ORC**........... Opinion Research Center
**ORC**........... Optical Radiation Corp.
**ORC**........... Optical Recording Corporation
**ORC**........... Orange City, IA [*Location identifier*] [*FAA*] (FAAL)
**ORC**........... Orange River Colony [*Later, Orange Free State*] [*South Africa*]
**ORC**........... Orbital Research Centrifuge [*NASA*] (KSC)
**ORC**........... Orcadas Del Sur [*Argentina*] [*Geomagnetic observatory code*]
**ORC**........... Orcatech, Inc. [*Toronto Stock Exchange symbol*]
**ORC**........... Order of the Red Cross
**ORC**........... Orderly Room Corporal [*British*]
**ORC**........... Ordnance Rocket Center (KSC)
**ORC**........... Organization Requirements Clerk [*Defense Supply Agency*]
**ORC**........... Organization Resources Counselors (MCD)
**ORC**........... Organized Reserve Corps [*Later, Army Reserve*]
**ORC**........... Orthogonal Row Computer
**ORC**........... Outbound RADAR Control
**ORC**........... Overrun Clutch
**ORC**........... Overseas Reconstruction Committee [*British*] [*World War II*]
**ORC**........... Overseas Research Center [*Wake Forest University*] [*Research center*] (RCD)
**ORC**........... Owner's Risk of Chafing [*Shipping*]
**ORC**........... Oxidation-Resistant Coating
**ORC**........... Oxidized Regenerated Cellulose [*Hemostatic*] [*Organic chemistry*]
**ORC**........... Ozarks Regional Commission [*Department of Commerce*]
**ORC**........... Reed College, Portland, OR [*OCLC symbol*] (OCLC)
**ORC**........... Reports of the High Court of the Orange River Colony [*South Africa*] [*A publication*] (DLA)
**ORCA**........ Ocean Resource Coordination and Assessment [*National Oceanic and Atmospheric Administration*]
**ORCA**........ Ocean Resources Conservation Association [*British*]
**ORCA**........ Oldtime Radio-Show Collector's Association (EA)
**ORCA**........ Oregon Caves National Monument
**ORCA**........ Organisme Europeen de Recherche sur la Carie [*European Organization for Caries Research*] (EAIO)
**ORCA**........ Organized Resistance to Capture in Alaska (EA)
**OrCan**........ Canby Public Library, Canby, OR [*Library symbol*] [*Library of Congress*] (LCLS)
**OrCanHS**.. Canby Union High School, Canby, OR [*Library symbol*] [*Library of Congress*] (LCLS)
**OrCb**.......... Coos Bay Public Library, Coos Bay, OR [*Library symbol*] [*Library of Congress*] (LCLS)
**ORCB**........ Order of Railway Conductors and Brakemen [*Later, United Transportation Union*] (EA)
**OrCbS**........ Southwestern Oregon Community College, Coos Bay, OR [*Library symbol*] [*Library of Congress*] (LCLS)
**OrCC**......... Corvallis Clinic, Corvallis, OR [*Library symbol*] [*Library of Congress*] (LCLS)
**ORCCA**..... Open Road Camper Clubs of America [*Later, ORSAC*] (EA)
**ORCEN**..... Overseas Records Center [*Military*]
**OrCEPA**.... United States Environmental Protection Agency, Corvallis Environmental Research Laboratory, Corvallis, OR [*Library symbol*] [*Library of Congress*] (LCLS)
**OrCg**.......... W. A. Woodward Memorial Library, Cottage Grove, OR [*Library symbol*] [*Library of Congress*] (LCLS)
**OrCGS**....... Church of Jesus Christ of Latter-Day Saints, Genealogical Society Library, Corvallis Branch, Corvallis, OR [*Library symbol*] [*Library of Congress*] (LCLS)
**OrCGSH**... Good Samaritan Hospital, Corvallis, OR [*Library symbol*] [*Library of Congress*] (LCLS)
**ORCH**........ Orchard
**Orch**........... Orchardist [*A publication*]
**ORCH**........ Orchestra
**Orchardist NZ**... Orchardist of New Zealand [*A publication*]
**Orchard NZ**... Orchardist of New Zealand [*A publication*]
**ORCHD**..... Orchestrated (By) [*Music*]
**Orchid Dig**... Orchid Digest [*A publication*]
**ORCHIS**.... Oak Ridge Computerized Hierarchical Information System [*AEC*] (IID)
**ORCHL**..... Orchestral [*Music*]
**OrChr**........ Oriens Christianus [*A publication*]
**OrChrA**...... Orientalia Christiana Analecta [*A publication*]
**OrChrPer**... Orientalia Christiana Periodica [*Rome*] [*A publication*]
**ORCL**........ Oracle Systems Corp. [*Belmont, CA*] [*NASDAQ symbol*] (NQ)
**OrClS**......... Sunnyside Medical Library, Clackamas, OR [*Library symbol*] [*Library of Congress*] (LCLS)
**OrCMG**..... Mid-Valley Genealogical Society, Corvallis, OR [*Library symbol*] [*Library of Congress*] (LCLS)
**ORCO**........ Central Ontario Regional Library, Richmond Hill, Ontario [*Library symbol*] [*National Library of Canada*] (NLC)
**OrCo**.......... Coquille Public Library, Coquille, OR [*Library symbol*] [*Library of Congress*] (LCLS)
**ORCO**........ Ontario Library Service - Trent, Richmond Hill, Ontario [*Library symbol*] [*National Library of Canada*] (NLC)
**ORCO**........ Optical Radiation Corporation [*NASDAQ symbol*] (NQ)
**ORCODO**... Annual Research Reviews. Oral Contraceptives [*A publication*]
**OrColHS**... Colton High School, Colton, OR [*Library symbol*] [*Library of Congress*] (LCLS)
**OrCon**........ Condon Public Library, Condon, OR [*Library symbol*] [*Library of Congress*] (LCLS)
**ORCON**..... Observation Report Conversion [*Program*]
**ORCON**..... Organic Control
**ORCON**..... Originator Controlled [*Information dissemination*]
**OrCor**......... Cornelius Public Library, Cornelius, OR [*Library symbol*] [*Library of Congress*] (LCLS)
**ORCS**......... Omnitronics Research Corporation [*NASDAQ symbol*] (NQ)
**OrCS**.......... Oregon State University, Corvallis, OR [*Library symbol*] [*Library of Congress*] (LCLS)
**ORCS**......... Organic Rankine Cycle System [*For power generation*]
**ORCS**......... Organic Reactions Catalysis Society (EA)
**ORCSA**...... Orange River Colony, South Africa (ILCA)
**OrCS-Ar**.... Oregon State University Archives, Corvallis, OR [*Library symbol*] [*Library of Congress*] (LCLS)
**OrCS-MB**... Oregon State University, Institute of Marine Biology, Coos Bay, OR [*Library symbol*] [*Library of Congress*] (LCLS)
**ORCUS**..... Operational Research Company, Universal Systems
**ORCV**........ Overriding Cam Valve
**ORD**........... Chicago [*Illinois*] O'Hare Airport [*Airport symbol*] [*Derived from former name: Orchard Field*]
**ORD**........... Off-Range Distance (MCD)
**ORD**........... Office of Regional Development [*Organization of American States*]
**ORD**........... Office of Research and Development [*Washington, DC*] [*Environmental Protection Agency*] (GRD)
**ORD**........... Office of Research Development [*Office of Policy, Evaluation, and Research*] [*Department of Labor*]
**ORD**........... Office of Rubber Director [*WPB*] [*World War II*]
**ORD**........... Ohio River Division [*Army Corps of Engineers*]
**ORD**........... Operational Readiness Date
**ORD**........... Operations Requirement Document
**ORD**........... Optical Reference Device
**ORD**........... Optical Rotary Dispersion
**ORD**........... Orbital Requirements Document
**ORD**........... Ordained
**ORD**........... Order
**ORD**........... Orderly
**ORD**........... Ordinal
**ORD**........... Ordinance
**ORD**........... Ordinary (MSA)
**ORD**........... Ordinary Seaman [*British*]
**ORD**........... Ordnance (AAG)
**ORD**........... Ordovician [*Period, era, or system*] [*Geology*]
**ORD**........... Organizational Dynamics [*A publication*]
**Ord**............. Orotidine [*Also, O*] [*A nucleoside*]
**ORD**........... Overseas Replacement Depot [*Military*]
**ORD**........... Owner's Risk of Damage [*Shipping*]
**ORDA**........ Office of Recombinant DNA Activities [*Bethesda, MD*] [*National Institute of Allergy and Infectious Diseases*]
**ORDAC**..... Overrange Detection and Correction [*Analytical chemistry*]
**OrDal**......... Dallas Public Library, Dallas, OR [*Library symbol*] [*Library of Congress*] (LCLS)

**ORDALT**... Ordnance Alterations
**Ord Amst**... Ordinance of Amsterdam [*A publication*] (DLA)
**Ord Antw**... Ordinance of Antwerp [*A publication*] (DLA)
**Ord Austl Cap Terr**... Ordinances of the Australian Capital Territory [*A publication*] (DLA)
**Ord Bilb**..... Ordinance of Bilboa [*A publication*] (DLA)
**ORDBN**..... Ordnance Battalion
**OrdBrd**....... Ordnance Board [*British*]
**ORDC**........ Ordnance Corps [*Army*]
**ORDC**........ Ordnance Research and Development Center [*Aberdeen Proving Ground, Maryland*] [*Navy*]
**ORDCAL**... Ordnance Calibration [*Navy*] (NVT)
**ORDCAN**... Orders Canceled [*Air Force*]
**ORDCIT**.... Ordnance Department and California Institute of Technology [*Army*] (RDA)
**ORDCONCAN**... Orders Considered Canceled [*Air Force*]
**Ord Con Jer**... Ordres du Conseil Enregistres a Jersey [*A publication*] (DLA)
**Ord Copen**... Ordinance of Copenhagen [*A publication*] (DLA)
**ORDCOR**.. Orders Corrected [*Air Force*]
**ORDCORPS**... Ordnance Corps [*Army*]
**ORDCU**..... Occupational Research and Development Coordinating Unit
**ORDD**........ Office of Research, Development, and Demonstrations [*Federal Railroad Administration*]
**ORDD**........ Ordered (ROG)
**Ord Dept Doc**... Ordinance Department Document [*A publication*]
**ORDDIS**.... Ordinary Discharge [*Military*]
**ORDEAL**... Orbit Rate Display - Earth and Lunar [*NASA*]
**ORDEAL**... Orbital Rate Drive Electronics for Apollo and LM [*NASA*]
**ORDENG**... Ordnance Engineering
**Ordenskunde**... Ordenskunde Beitraege zur Geschichte der Auszeichnungen [*A publication*]
**ORDET**..... Orbit Determination Group
**ORDet**........ Owner's Risk of Deterioration [*Shipping*]
**ORDFAC**... Ordnance Facility
**Ord Flor**..... Ordinance of Florence [*A publication*] (DLA)
**Ord Gen**..... Ordinance of Genoa [*A publication*] (DLA)
**ORDHAC**... Ordnance Systems Command Hydroballistics Advisory Committee [*Obsolete*] [*Navy*]
**Ord Hamb**... Ordinance of Hamburg [*A publication*] (DLA)
**ORDINST**... Ordnance Instruction
**ORDIP**....... Ordnance Alteration Installation Plan [*Navy*]
**ORDIR**...... Omnirange Digital RADAR
**Ord Konigs**... Ordinance of Konigsberg [*A publication*] (DLA)
**ORDL**........ Ohio River Division Laboratory [*Army Corps of Engineers*] (KSC)
**Ord Leg**...... Ordinance of Leghorn [*A publication*] (DLA)
**ORDLIS**.... Ordnance Logistics Information System [*Navy*]
**ORDM**....... Ordnance Corps Manual (AAG)
**Ord Mar**..... Ordonnance de la Marine [*A publication*] (DLA)
**Ord de la Mar**... Ordonnance de la Marine de Louis XIV [*A publication*] (DLA)
**Ord Med Jur**... Ordronaux's Medical Jurisprudence [*A publication*] (DLA)
**ORDMOD**... Orders Modified [*Navy*]
**ORDN**....... Ordnance (KSC)
**ORDNA**..... Organismes de Radiodiffusion des Pays NonAlignes [*Broadcasting Organizations of Non-Aligned Countries - BONAC*] (EAIO)
**ORDO**....... Ordinario [*Ordinarily*] [*Music*] (ROG)
**Ordo Nob Urb**... Ordo Nobilium Urbium [*of Ausonius*] [*Classical studies*] (OCD)
**ORDP**........ Office of Rural Development Policy [*Department of Agriculture*]
**ORDP**........ Ordnance Corps Pamphlet [*Army*] (MCD)
**ORDPDS**... Offender Rehabilitation Division of the Public Defender Service (EA)
**Ord Port**..... Ordinance of Portugal [*A publication*] (DLA)
**Ord Prus**.... Ordinance of Prussia [*A publication*] (DLA)
**ORDRAT**.. Ordnance Dial Reader and Translator
**Ordre des Architectes du Quebec Bull Technique**... Ordre des Architectes du Quebec. Bulletin Technique [*A publication*]
**ORDREV**.. Ordnance Procedures Review [*Military*] (NVT)
**Ordr Jud Ins**... Ordronaux on Judicial Aspects of Insanity [*A publication*] (DLA)
**Ordr Med Jur**... Ordronaux's Medical Jurisprudence [*A publication*] (DLA)
**Ord Rott**..... Ordinance of Rotterdam [*A publication*] (DLA)
**ORDRPT**... Ordnance Report
**ORDS**........ Office of Research, Demonstrations, and Statistics [*Health Care Financing Administration*]
**ORDSER**... Ordnance Support Element Review (NVT)
**Ord Sgt**...... Ordnance Sergeant [*Military*] (DMA)
**Ords NZ**.... Ordinances of the Legislative Council of New Zealand [*A publication*] (DLA)
**ORDSTA**... Ordnance Station
**Ord Swe**..... Ordinance of Sweden [*A publication*] (DLA)
**ORDSYSCOM**... Ordnance Systems Command [*Formerly, Bureau of Naval Weapons; later, Naval Sea Systems Command*]
**ORDT**........ Office of Research, Demonstrations, and Training [*Social and Rehabilitation Service, HEW*]
**Ord Us**....... Ord on Usury [*A publication*] (DLA)
**ORDVAC**.. Ordnance Variable Automatic Computer
**ORDY**........ Ordinary (AABC)
**OrE**........... Eugene Public Library, Eugene, OR [*Library symbol*] [*Library of Congress*] (LCLS)
**ORE**........... Executive Flight Service, Inc. [*Portland, OR*] [*FAA designator*] (FAAC)
**ORE**........... Obtained Radiation Emittance
**ORE**........... Occupational Radiation Exposure (NRCH)
**ORE**........... Oceanographic Research Equipment
**ORE**........... Office of Regional Economics [*Department of Commerce*]
**ORE**........... Office of Research and Evaluation [*Bureau of Labor Statistics*] (GRD)
**ORE**........... Officer Responsible for the Exercise [*Navy*] (NVT)
**ORE**........... On-Orbit Repair Experiment [*NASA*] (NASA)
**ORE**........... Operational Readiness [*Navy*] (NG)
**ORE**........... Operational Readiness Evaluation [*Army*]
**ORE**........... Operational Readiness Exercise (MCD)
**ORE**........... Orange, MA [*Location identifier*] [*FAA*] (FAAL)
**ORE**........... Oregon (AAG)
**ORE**........... Oregon Resources Corp. [*Vancouver Stock Exchange symbol*]
**ORE**........... Oregon State University, Corvallis, Corvallis, OR [*OCLC symbol*] (OCLC)
**ORE**........... Organisation Regionale Europeenne de la CISL
**ORE**........... Ornitologia Rondo Esperantlingva [*Esperantist Ornithologists' Association*] (EAIO)
**ORE**........... Orthophoto Resolution Enhancer [*Army*]
**ORE**........... Overhaul, Rebuild, and Exchange (MCD)
**ORE**........... Overtraining Reversal Effect
**ORE**........... Rekreaksie. Vakblad voor Recreatie Ondernemers [*A publication*]
**Ore Ag Exp**... Oregon. Agricultural Experiment Station. Publications [*A publication*]
**Ore Agric Progr**... Oregon's Agricultural Progress [*A publication*]
**OREALC**... Regional Office for Education in Latin America and the Caribbean [*Acronym is based on foreign phrase*] [*UNESCO*]
**Ore App**..... Oregon Court of Appeals Reports [*A publication*] (DLA)
**OREC**........ Eramosa Community Library, Rockwood, Ontario [*Library symbol*] [*National Library of Canada*] (NLC)
**Or Ec**.......... Oriental Economist [*A publication*]
**ORECHL**.. Centre Hospitalier Le Gardeur, Repentigny, Quebec [*Library symbol*] [*National Library of Canada*] (NLC)
**OrECoAr**... Lane County Archives, Eugene, OR [*Library symbol*] [*Library of Congress*] (LCLS)
**OrECoL**..... Lane County Law Library, Eugene, OR [*Library symbol*] [*Library of Congress*] (LCLS)
**OrEcon**....... Oriental Economist [*A publication*]
**ORE/ERO**... Organisation Regionale de la Federation Internationale Dentaire pour l'Europe [*European Regional Organization of the International Dental Federation*] (EAIO)
**OREG**........ Ordinary Multiple Regression [*Statistics*]
**OREG**........ Oregon (AFM)
**Oreg Agric Exp Stn Bull**... Oregon. Agricultural Experiment Station. Bulletin [*A publication*]
**Oreg Agric Exp Stn Misc Pap**... Oregon. Agricultural Experiment Station. Miscellaneous Paper [*A publication*]
**Oreg Agric Exp Stn Spec Rep**... Oregon. Agricultural Experiment Station. Special Report [*A publication*]
**Oreg Agric Exp Stn Stn Bull**... Oregon. Agricultural Experiment Station. Station Bulletin [*A publication*]
**Oreg Agric Exp Stn Tech Bull**... Oregon. Agricultural Experiment Station. Technical Bulletin [*A publication*]
**Oreg Agr Progr**... Oregon's Agricultural Progress [*A publication*]
**Oreg Bur Mines Min Res Oreg**... Oregon. Bureau of Mines and Geology. Mineral Resources of Oregon [*A publication*]
**Oreg Dep Geol Miner Ind Bull**... Oregon. Department of Geology and Mineral Industries. Bulletin [*A publication*]
**Oreg Dep Geol Miner Ind GMI Short Pap**... Oregon. Department of Geology and Mineral Industries. GMI Short Paper [*A publication*]
**Oreg Dep Geol Miner Ind Misc Pap**... Oregon. Department of Geology and Mineral Industries. Miscellaneous Paper [*A publication*]
**Oreg Dep Geol Miner Ind Misc Paper**... Oregon. Department of Geology and Mineral Industries. Miscellaneous Paper [*A publication*]
**Oregelkunst Vier T**... Orgelkunst. Viermaandelijks Tijdschrift [*A publication*]
**Oreg Fish Comm Contrib**... Oregon. Fish Commission. Contributions [*A publication*]
**Oreg Fish Comm Res Briefs**... Oregon. Fish Commission. Research Briefs [*A publication*]
**Oreg For Prod Lab (Corvallis) Prog Rep**... Oregon. Forest Products Laboratory (Corvallis). Progress Report [*A publication*]
**Oreg For Prod Res Cent Prog Rep**... Oregon. Forest Products Research Center. Progress Report [*A publication*]
**Oreg Hist Q**... Oregon Historical Quarterly [*A publication*]
**Oreg Insect Contr Handb**... Oregon Insect Control Handbook [*A publication*]
**Oreg L Rev**... Oregon Law Review [*A publication*]
**Oreg Min**... Oregon Mineralogist [*A publication*]
**Oreg Nurs**... Oregon Nurse [*A publication*]
**Oreg Nurse**... Oregon Nurse [*A publication*]
**Oregon**....... Oregon Reports [*A publication*] (DLA)
**Oregon Bsn**... Oregon Business [*A publication*]
**Oregon Dep Geol Mineral Ind Oil Gas Invest**... Oregon. Department of Geology and Mineral Industries. Oil and Gas Investigation [*A publication*]

**Oregon Dept Geology and Mineral Industries Bull** ... Oregon. Department of Geology and Mineral Industries. Bulletin [*A publication*]
**Oregon Dept Geology and Mineral Industries Geol Map Ser** ... Oregon. Department of Geology and Mineral Industries. Geological Map Series [*A publication*]
**Oregon Geol** ... Oregon Geology [*A publication*]
**Oregon Hist Q** ... Oregon Historical Quarterly [*A publication*]
**Oreg Rev Stat** ... Oregon Revised Statutes [*A publication*] (DLA)
**OrEGS** ....... Church of Jesus Christ of Latter-Day Saints, Genealogical Society Library, Eugene Branch, Eugene, OR [*Library symbol*] [*Library of Congress*] (LCLS)
**Oreg SB Bull** ... Oregon State Bar Bulletin [*A publication*] (DLA)
**Oreg State Agric Coll Eng Exp Stn** ... Oregon State Agricultural College. Engineering Experiment Station [*A publication*]
**Oreg State Coll Eng Exp Stn Circ** ... Oregon State College. Engineering Experiment Station. Circular [*A publication*]
**Oreg State Dent J** ... Oregon State Dental Journal [*A publication*]
**Oreg State Eng Ground Water Rep** ... Oregon State Engineer. Ground Water Report [*A publication*]
**Oreg State Monogr Stud Bacteriol** ... Oregon State Monographs. Studies in Bacteriology [*A publication*]
**Oreg State Monogr Stud Bot** ... Oregon State Monographs. Studies in Botany [*A publication*]
**Oreg State Monogr Stud Entomol** ... Oregon State Monographs. Studies in Entomology [*A publication*]
**Oreg State Monogr Stud Geol** ... Oregon State Monographs. Studies in Geology [*A publication*]
**Oreg State Monogr Stud Zool** ... Oregon State Monographs. Studies in Zoology [*A publication*]
**Oreg State Univ Biol Colloq** ... Oregon State University. Biology Colloquium [*A publication*]
**Oreg State Univ Eng Exp Sta Circ** ... Oregon State University (Corvallis). Engineering Experiment Station. Circular [*A publication*]
**Oreg State Univ Eng Exp Stn Circ** ... Oregon State University. Engineering Experiment Station. Circular [*A publication*]
**Oreg State Univ For Res Lab Annu Rep** ... Oregon State University. Forest Research Laboratory. Annual Report [*A publication*]
**Oreg State Univ For Res Lab Bull** ... Oregon State University. Forest Research Laboratory. Bulletin [*A publication*]
**Oreg State Univ For Res Lab Prog Rep** ... Oregon State University. Forest Research Laboratory. Progress Report [*A publication*]
**Oreg State Univ For Res Lab Res Bull** ... Oregon State University. Forest Research Laboratory. Research Bulletin [*A publication*]
**Oreg State Univ For Res Lab Res Pap** ... Oregon State University. Forest Research Laboratory. Research Paper [*A publication*]
**Oreg State Univ Sch For For Res Lab Res Note** ... Oregon State University. School of Forestry. Forest Research Laboratory. Research Notes [*A publication*]
**Oreg State Univ Water Resour Res Inst Semin Proc SEMIN WR** ... Oregon State University. Water Resources Research Institute. Seminar Proceedings. SEMIN WR [*A publication*]
**ORE HIS Q** ... Oregon Historical Society. Quarterly [*A publication*]
**Ore Hist Q** ... Oregon Historical Quarterly [*A publication*]
**Ore Hist Soc Quar** ... Oregon Historical Society. Quarterly [*A publication*]
**Orehovo-Zuev Ped Inst Ucen Zap Kaf Mat** ... Orehovo-Zuevskii Pedagogiceskii Institut. Ucenye Zapiski Kafedry Matematiki [*A publication*]
**OreHQ** ....... Oregon Historical Quarterly [*A publication*]
**OrEL** .......... Lane Community College, Eugene, OR [*Library symbol*] [*Library of Congress*] (LCLS)
**ORELA** ...... Oak Ridge Electron Linear Accelerator [*Oak Ridge, TN*] [*Department of Energy*]
**Ore LR** ....... Oregon Law Review [*A publication*]
**Ore L Rev** ... Oregon Law Review [*A publication*]
**OREM** ....... Office of Research and Evaluation Methods [*National Institute of Justice*] (GRD)
**OREM** ....... Oregon Metallurgical Corp. [*NASDAQ symbol*] (NQ)
**OREN** ........ Orthorhombic Enstatite [*Geology*]
**Orenburg Gos Ped Inst Ucen Zap** ... Orenburgskii Gosudarstvennyi Pedagogiceskii Institut Imeni V. P. Ckalova. Ucenye Zapiski [*A publication*]
**OrENC** ...... Northwest Christian College, Eugene, OR [*Library symbol*] [*Library of Congress*] (LCLS)
**O R (English)** ... Osservatore Romano (English) [*A publication*]
**OrEnW** ...... Wallowa County Library, Enterprise, OR [*Library symbol*] [*Library of Congress*] (LCLS)
**OrEnWM** .. Wallowa Memorial Hospital, Burton Carlock Memorial Library, Enterprise, OR [*Library symbol*] [*Library of Congress*] (LCLS)
**OREO** ........ Orbiting Radio Emission Observatory [*Satellite*]
**O Rep** ......... Ohio Reports [*A publication*] (DLA)
**OrEPM** ...... Lane County Museum [*Formerly, Lane County Pioneer Museum*], Eugene, OR [*Library symbol*] [*Library of Congress*] (LCLS)
**ORER** ........ Official Railway Equipment Register [*National Railway Publication Co.*] [*Information service or system*] (IID)
**Ore Rev Stat** ... Oregon Revised Statutes [*A publication*] (DLA)
**ORERP** ...... Off-Site Radiation Exposure Review Project [*Department of Energy*]
**OrEs** .......... Estacada Public Library, Estacada, OR [*Library symbol*] [*Library of Congress*] (LCLS)
**OrESH** ....... Sacred Heart General Hospital, Eugene, OR [*Library symbol*] [*Library of Congress*] (LCLS)
**OrEsHS** ..... Estacada High School, Estacada, OR [*Library symbol*] [*Library of Congress*] (LCLS)
**Ores Met** .... Ores and Metals [*A publication*]
**Ore St B Bull** ... Oregon State Bar Bulletin [*A publication*] (DLA)
**Ore Tax Ct** ... Oregon Tax Court Reports [*A publication*] (DLA)
**O Rev** ......... Occasional Review [*A publication*]
**ORF** ........... Norfolk/Virginia Beach [*Virginia*] [*Airport symbol*] (OAG)
**ORF** ........... Oesterreichischer Rundfunk [*Radio and television network*] [*Austria*]
**ORF** ........... Officers' Recreation Facility
**ORF** ........... Ontario Research Foundation [*Canada*] [*Research center*] (RCD)
**ORF** ........... Open Reading Frame [*Genetics*]
**ORF** ........... Operational Readiness Float (AABC)
**ORF** ........... Oral Rehydration Fluid
**ORF** ........... Oratorum Romanorum Fragmenta [*A publication*] (OCD)
**Orf** ............. Orfeo [*Record label*]
**ORF** ........... Orifice (NASA)
**ORF** ........... Ortho Pharmaceutical Corp. [*Research code symbol*]
**ORF** ........... Overhaul Replacement Factor (MCD)
**ORF** ........... Owner's Risk of Fire [*Shipping*]
**ORF** ........... Owner's Risk of Freezing [*Shipping*]
**OrF** ............ Rogers City Public Library, Forest Grove, OR [*Library symbol*] [*Library of Congress*] (LCLS)
**ORFA** ........ ORFA Corporation of America [*Cherry Hill, NJ*] [*NASDAQ symbol*] (NQ)
**OrFc** .......... Falls City Public Library, Falls City, OR [*Library symbol*] [*Library of Congress*] (LCLS)
**ORFC** ........ Orifice (AAG)
**ORFE** ......... Ornis Fennica [*A publication*]
**OrFFM** ...... Oregon Masonic Grand Lodge, Forest Grove, OR [*Library symbol*] [*Library of Congress*] (LCLS)
**OrFl** ........... Florence Public Library, Florence, OR [*Library symbol*] [*Library of Congress*] (LCLS)
**ORFLS** ...... Oak Ridge Full Matrix Least Squares
**ORFM** ....... Outlet Region Feature Model [*Nuclear energy*] (NRCH)
**Orf ML** ...... Orfila's Medecine Legale [*A publication*] (DLA)
**OrFP** .......... Pacific University, Forest Grove, OR [*Library symbol*] [*Library of Congress*] (LCLS)
**OrFS** .......... Orange Free State (DAS)
**ORG** .......... Glen Robertson Branch, Stormont, Dundas, and Glengarry County Public Library, Ontario [*Library symbol*] [*National Library of Canada*] (BIB)
**ORG** .......... [*The*] Official Recreation Guide [*Applied Information Services, Inc.*] [*Whitefish, MT*] [*Information service or system*] (IID)
**ORG** .......... Olympics Research Group [*University of Calgary*] [*Canada*] [*Research center*] (RCD)
**ORG** .......... Operations Research Group
**org** ............. Orange [*Philately*]
**ORG** .......... Orange, TX [*Location identifier*] [*FAA*] (FAAL)
**ORG** .......... Organ
**ORG** .......... Organic
**ORG** .......... Organism (ADA)
**ORG** .......... Organization (AAG)
**ORG** .......... Organogenesis, Inc. [*AMEX symbol*] (SPSG)
**ORG** .......... Organon [*Netherlands*] [*Research code symbol*]
**ORG** .......... Origin (MDG)
**ORG** .......... Original New York Seltzer of Canada Ltd. [*Vancouver Stock Exchange symbol*]
**org** ............. Originator [*MARC relator code*] [*Library of Congress*] (LCCP)
**ORG** .......... Paramaribo [*Surinam*] Zorg En Hoop Airport [*Airport symbol*] (OAG)
**ORGA** ........ Organizacion Regional Gallega Autonoma [*Regional Galician Autonomy Organization*] [*Spain*] [*Political party*] (PPE)
**ORGALIME** ... Organisme de Liaison des Industries Metalliques Europeennes [*Liaison Group for the European Engineering Industries*] [*Brussels, Belgium*] (EAIO)
**ORGAN** ..... Organisation Regionale Africaine de Normalisation [*African Regional Organization for Standardization - AROS*] (EA)
**ORGAN** ..... Organization
**Organ Afr Unity Sci Tech Res Comm Publ** ... Organization of African Unity. Scientific and Technical Research Commission. Publication [*A publication*]
**Organ Am States Ann** ... Organization of American States. Annals [*A publication*]
**Organ Behav Hum Decis Process** ... Organizational Behavior and Human Decision Processes [*A publication*]
**Organ Behav Hum Perform** ... Organizational Behavior and Human Performance [*A publication*]
**Organ Behavior & Human Perf** ... Organizational Behavior and Human Performance [*A publication*]
**Organ Beh H** ... Organizational Behavior and Human Performance [*A publication*]
**OrGand** ...... Orientalia Gandensia [*A publication*]
**Organ Dyn** ... Organizational Dynamics [*A publication*]
**Organ Dynam** ... Organizational Dynamics [*A publication*]

**Organ Eur Mediterr Prot Plant Publ Ser A** ... Organisation Europeenne et Mediterraneenne pour la Protection des Plantes. Publications. Serie A [*A publication*]
**Organ Eur Mediterr Prot Plant Publ Ser D** ... Organisation Europeenne et Mediterraneenne pour la Protection des Plantes. Publications. Serie D [*A publication*]
**Organ Eur Rech Spat Contract Rep** ... Organisation Europeenne de Recherches Spatiales. Contractor Report [*A publication*]
**Organ Fortschr Eisenbahnwes** ... Organ fuer die Fortschritte des Eisenbahnwesens [*A publication*]
**Organic Gard** ... Organic Gardening [*A publication*]
**Organic Gard & F** ... Organic Gardening and Farming [*A publication*]
**Organic Geochem** ... Organic Geochemistry [*A publication*]
**Organists R** ... Organists Review [*A publication*]
**Organ Mass Spectr** ... Organic Mass Spectrometry [*A publication*]
**Organomet Chem** ... Organometallic Chemistry [*A publication*]
**Organomet Chem Rev** ... Organometallic Chemistry Reviews [*A publication*]
**Organomet Chem Rev Sect A** ... Organometallic Chemistry Reviews. Section A. Subject Reviews [*Netherlands*] [*A publication*]
**Organomet Chem Rev Sect B** ... Organometallic Chemistry Reviews. Section B. Annual Surveys [*A publication*]
**Organomet Chem Synth** ... Organometallics in Chemical Synthesis [*A publication*]
**Organomet React** ... Organometallic Reactions [*A publication*]
**Organomet React Synth** ... Organometallic Reactions and Syntheses [*A publication*]
**Organon**..... Textile Organon [*A publication*]
**Organophosphorus Chem** ... Organophosphorus Chemistry [*A publication*]
**Organ React** ... Organic Reactions [*A publication*]
**Organ Stud** ... Organization Studies [*A publication*]
**Organ Yb** ... Organ Yearbook [*A publication*]
**Organzr**...... Organizer [*A publication*]
**OrGb**.......... Curry Public Library, Gold Beach, OR [*Library symbol*] [*Library of Congress*] (LCLS)
**Org Behav and Hum Perform** ... Organizational Behavior and Human Performance [*A publication*]
**ORgC**......... Rio Grande College, Rio Grande, OH [*Library symbol*] [*Library of Congress*] (LCLS)
**Org Chem Bull** ... Organic Chemical Bulletin [*A publication*]
**Org Chem (New York)** ... Organic Chemistry (New York) [*A publication*]
**Org Chem Ser Monogr** ... Organic Chemistry: A Series of Monographs [*A publication*]
**Org Coat**.... Organic Coatings. Science and Technology [*A publication*]
**Org Coatings Appl Polym Sci Proc** ... Organic Coatings and Applied Polymer Science Proceedings [*A publication*]
**Org Coat Plast Chem** ... Organic Coatings and Plastics Chemistry [*A publication*]
**Org Compd Sulphu Selenium Tellurium** ... Organic Compounds of Sulphur, Selenium, and Tellurium [*A publication*]
**ORGD**........ Organized
**ORGDP**..... Oak Ridge Gaseous Diffusion Plant [*Department of Energy*]
**Org Dyn**..... Organizational Dynamics [*A publication*]
**Org Dynamics** ... Organizational Dynamics [*A publication*]
**ORGEL** ..... Organique et Eau Lourde [*Organic liquid and heavy water nuclear reactor*]
**Org Exp** ..... Organo Espressivo [*Swell Organ*] [*Music*]
**Org Farmer** ... Organic Farmer [*A publication*]
**Org Finish** ... Organic Finishing [*A publication*]
**ORGG-A**.... Oriental Geographer [*A publication*]
**ORGGAH** ... Oriental Geographer [*A publication*]
**Org Gard**.... Organic Gardening [*A publication*]
**Org Gdng Fmg** ... Organic Gardening and Farming [*A publication*]
**Org Geochem** ... Organic Geochemistry [*England*] [*A publication*]
**Org Inst** ..... Organ Institute. Quarterly [*A publication*]
**Org Inst Q** ... Organ Institute. Quarterly [*A publication*]
**OrGl**........... Gladstone Public Library, Gladstone, OR [*Library symbol*] [*Library of Congress*] (LCLS)
**ORGL**........ Organizational (AFM)
**ORGL**........ Overall Reading Grade Level (MCD)
**OrGlHS**..... Gladstone High School, Gladstone, OR [*Library symbol*] [*Library of Congress*] (LCLS)
**ORGM**....... Outdoor Recreation Grants-in-Aid Manual
**Org Magn Resonance** ... Organic Magnetic Resonance [*A publication*]
**Org Mass Sp** ... Organic Mass Spectrometry [*A publication*]
**Org Mass Spectrom** ... Organic Mass Spectrometry [*A publication*]
**ORGN**........ Organization (AFM)
**ORGN**........ Originala Petroleum [*NASDAQ symbol*] (NQ)
**ORGND**..... Organometallics [*A publication*]
**ORGNL**..... Organizational
**ORGO** ....... Organo [*Organ*] [*Music*] (ROG)
**ORGPHC**.. Orographic [*Meteorology*] (FAAC)
**Org Photochem** ... Organic Photochemistry [*A publication*]
**Org Photochem Synth** ... Organic Photochemical Syntheses [*A publication*]
**Org Poluprod Krasiteli** ... Organicheskie Poluprodukty i Krasiteli [*A publication*]
**Org Prep Proced** ... Organic Preparations and Procedures [*A publication*]
**Org Prep Proced Int** ... Organic Preparations and Procedures International [*A publication*]
**OrGR**......... Rogue Community College, Grants Pass, OR [*Library symbol*] [*Library of Congress*] (LCLS)
**OrGrC**........ Mount Hood Community College, Gresham, OR [*Library symbol*] [*Library of Congress*] (LCLS)
**Org React**... Organic Reactions [*A publication*]
**Org React**... Organic Reactivity [*A publication*]
**Org React (Eng Transl)** ... Organic Reactivity (English Translation) [*New York*] [*A publication*]
**Org React Mech** ... Organic Reaction Mechanisms [*A publication*]
**Org React (Tartu)** ... Organic Reactivity (Tartu) [*A publication*]
**Org React (USSR)** ... Organic Reactivity (USSR) [*A publication*]
**ORGREB-Inst Kraftwerke Inf** ... ORGREB [*Organisation fuer Abnahme, Betriebsfuehrung, und Rationalisierung von Energieanlagen*]-Institut fuer Kraftwerke. Informationen [*German Democratic Republic*] [*A publication*]
**OrGrGS**..... Church of Jesus Christ of Latter-Day Saints, Genealogical Society Library, Gresham Branch, Gresham, OR [*Library symbol*] [*Library of Congress*] (LCLS)
**ORGSBS** ... Oak Ridge Graduate School of Biomedical Sciences [*Tennessee*]
**ORGSC**...... Oregon Ryegrass Growers Seed Commission (EA)
**Org Sci**....... Organizational Science [*A publication*]
**Org Scientifique** ... Organisation Scientifique [*A publication*]
**Org Sulfur Compd** ... Organic Sulfur Compounds [*A publication*]
**Org Synt** .... Organic Syntheses [*A publication*]
**ORGT**........ Organist
**Org Techint Bol Informativo** ... Organizacion Techint. Boletin Informativo [*A publication*]
**ORGY**........ Organization for the Rational Guidance of Youth [*Fictitious organization in film, "The Man from ORGY"*]
**ORH** .......... Occupational Role History [*Psychology*]
**ORH** .......... Operational Requirements Handbook
**o-rh**............ Orthorhombic [*Crystallography*]
**ORH** .......... Richmond Hill Public Library, Ontario [*Library symbol*] [*National Library of Canada*] (NLC)
**ORH** .......... Worcester [*Massachusetts*] [*Airport symbol*] (OAG)
**OrHe**.......... Hermiston Public Library, Hermiston, OR [*Library symbol*] [*Library of Congress*] (LCLS)
**ORHEA**..... Orvosi Hetilap [*A publication*]
**OrHeGS** .... Good Shepherd Hospital, Hermiston, OR [*Library symbol*] [*Library of Congress*] (LCLS)
**OrHep**........ Heppner Public Library, Heppner, OR [*Library symbol*] [*Library of Congress*] (LCLS)
**OrHepPM** ... Pioneer Memorial Hospital, Heppner, OR [*Library symbol*] [*Library of Congress*] (LCLS)
**ORHFC** ..... Official Rocky Horror Fan Club (EA)
**OrHi** .......... Oregon Historical Society, Portland, OR [*Library symbol*] [*Library of Congress*] (LCLS)
**OrHil** ......... Hillsboro Public Library, Hillsboro, OR [*Library symbol*] [*Library of Congress*] (LCLS)
**OrHilT**....... Tuality Community Hospital, Hillsboro, OR [*Library symbol*] [*Library of Congress*] (LCLS)
**OrHilW** ..... Washington County Law Library, Hillsboro, OR [*Library symbol*] [*Library of Congress*] (LCLS)
**Or Hlth** ...... Oral Health [*A publication*]
**ORHPB**..... Orthopaede [*West Germany*] [*A publication*]
**OrHQ** ........ Oregon Historical Quarterly [*A publication*]
**OrHr**.......... Hood River County Library, Hood River, OR [*Library symbol*] [*Library of Congress*] (LCLS)
**OrI** ............ Independence Public Library, Independence, OR [*Library symbol*] [*Library of Congress*] (LCLS)
**ORI**............ Octane Requirement Increase [*Mechanical engineering*]
**ORI**............ Office of Research and Inventions
**ORI**............ Office of Road Inquiry [*Later, Bureau of Public Roads*]
**ORI**............ Old Republic International Corp. [*NYSE symbol*] (SPSG)
**ORI**............ Omni Resources, Inc. [*Vancouver Stock Exchange symbol*]
**ORI**............ Operating and Repair Instruction
**ORI**............ Operational Readiness Inspection [*Army*]
**ORI**............ Operational Readiness Instruction [*Military*]
**ORI**............ Operations Research, Incorporated [*Information service or system*]
**ORI**............ Ophthalmic Research Institute (EA)
**ORI**............ Oregon Research Institute
**ORI**............ Orientation Inventory [*Vocational guidance test*]
**Ori**............. Oriole [*Record label*] [*Great Britain*]
**Ori**............. Orion [*Constellation*]
**ori**.............. Oriya [*MARC language code*] [*Library of Congress*] (LCCP)
**ORI**............ Outdoor Recreation Institute (EA)
**ORI**............ Overhaul and Repair Instruction
**ORI**............ Port Lions [*Alaska*] [*Airport symbol*] (OAG)
**Oria**............ [*Lanfrancus de*] Oriano [*Deceased, 1488*] [*Authority cited in pre-1607 legal work*] (DSA)
**ORIA** ......... Oriental Rug Importers Association of America (EA)
**ORIA** ......... Outdoor Recreation in Australia
**ORIADOC** ... Orientation and Access to Information and Documentation Sources in France [*Commission de Coordination de la Documentation Administrative*] [*Database*]
**ORIC** ......... Oak Ridge Isochronous Cyclotron [*Department of Energy*]
**ORIC** ......... Operational Readiness Inspection Committee [*NASA*]
**ORIDE** ...... Override (KSC)
**ORIEN** ...... Orientation (AABC)
**Orient**......... Orientalia. Commentarii de Rebus Assyro-Babylonicis, Arabicis, Aegyptiacis [*Rome*] [*A publication*]
**ORIENT**.... Orientation

**Orientacion Econ** ... Orientacion Economica [*A publication*]
**Oriental Soc Aust J** ... Oriental Society of Australia. Journal [*A publication*] (APTA)
**Orientam Soc** ... Orientamenti Sociali [*A publication*]
**Orient Art** .. Oriental Art [*A publication*]
**Orientat Sc** ... Orientation Scolaire et Professionnelle [*A publication*]
**Orientat Scol Profes** ... Orientation Scolaire et Professionnelle [*A publication*]
**Orient Chr Per** ... Orientalia Christiana Periodica [*A publication*]
**Orient Cult** ... Orientamenti Culturali [*A publication*]
**Oriente Agropecu** ... Oriente Agropecuario [*A publication*]
**Orient Economist** ... Oriental Economist [*A publication*]
**Oriente Crist** ... Oriente Cristiano [*A publication*]
**Oriente Mod** ... Oriente Moderno [*A publication*]
**Orient Geogr** ... Oriental Geographer [*A publication*]
**Orient Geogr (Dacca)** ... Oriental Geographer (Dacca) [*A publication*]
**Orient Insects** ... Oriental Insects [*A publication*]
**Orient Insects Suppl** ... Oriental Insects. Supplementum [*A publication*]
**Orient Lit Ztg** ... Orientalistische Literaturzeitung [*A publication*]
**Orient Lovan** ... Orientalia Lovaniensia Periodica [*A publication*]
**Orient Prof/Voc Guid** ... Orientation Professionnelle/Vocational Guidance [*A publication*]
**Orient Suecana** ... Orientalia Suecana [*A publication*]
**ORIF**.......... Open Reduction with Internal Fixation [*Medicine*]
**Orig**........... Origen [*Deceased circa 254*] [*Authority cited in pre-1607 legal work*] (DSA)
**ORIG**......... Origin [*or Original*] (AAG)
**ORIG**......... Original Italian Pasta Products Co., Inc. [*NASDAQ symbol*] (NQ)
**ORIG**......... Originator (MSA)
**ORIGAN**... Origanum [*Marjoram*] [*Pharmacology*] (ROG)
**ORIGINATG** ... Originating (ROG)
**Origin Tech J** ... Origin Technical Journal [*A publication*]
**ORIGL**....... Original (ROG)
**Orig Life** .... Origins of Life [*A publication*]
**Orig Life Evol Biosph** ... Origins of Life and Evolution of the Biosphere [*A publication*]
**ORIMB** ..... Oral Implantology [*A publication*]
**ORINS**....... Oak Ridge Institute of Nuclear Studies [*Later, ORAU*] (EA)
**Orio**........... Orion [*Constellation*]
**ORION**...... Online Retrieval of Information over a Network
**ORIP**.......... Ripley Branch, Bruce County Public Library, Ontario [*Library symbol*] [*National Library of Canada*] (NLC)
**ORIR** ......... Orion Research, Incorporated [*NASDAQ symbol*] (NQ)
**Oris**............ All India Reporter, Orissa [*A publication*] (DLA)
**ORIS**.......... Office of Regulatory Information Systems [*Energy Regulatory Commission*] (IID)
**ORIS**.......... Officeworker Reader Information Services [*British*]
**ORIS**.......... South Carleton High School, Richmond, Ontario [*Library symbol*] [*National Library of Canada*] (NLC)
**Orissa** ........ All India Reporter, Orissa [*A publication*] (DLA)
**Orissa Vet J** ... Orissa Veterinary Journal [*A publication*]
**ORIT** ......... Operational Readiness Inspection Team [*Air Force*]
**ORIT** ......... Operational Readiness Inspection Test [*Air Force*]
**ORIT** ......... Organizacion Regional Interamericana de Trabajadores [*Inter-American Regional Organization of Workers*] [*Antigua*]
**Orizz Ortop Odie Riabil** ... Orizzonti della Ortopedia Odierna e della Riabilitazione [*Italy*] [*A publication*]
**Orizz Profess** ... Orizzonti Professionali [*A publication*]
**ORJ** ........... Corry, PA [*Location identifier*] [*FAA*] (FAAL)
**ORJ** ........... Oneida Resources, Inc. [*Vancouver Stock Exchange symbol*]
**OrJ**............. Orange Juice
**ORJ** ........... Orinduik [*Guyana*] [*Airport symbol*] (OAG)
**OrJc**........... Junction City Public Library, Junction City, OR [*Library symbol*] [*Library of Congress*] (LCLS)
**OrJe**........... Jefferson Public Library, Jefferson, OR [*Library symbol*] [*Library of Congress*] (LCLS)
**ORJETS**.... On-Line Remote Job Entry Terminal System [*Data processing*]
**OrJM**......... Jacksonville Museum, Jacksonville, OR [*Library symbol*] [*Library of Congress*] (LCLS)
**OrJvHS** ..... Jordan Valley High School, Jordan Valley, OR [*Library symbol*] [*Library of Congress*] (LCLS)
**ORK**........... Cork [*Ireland*] [*Airport symbol*] (OAG)
**OrK** ............ Klamath County Library, Klamath Falls, OR [*Library symbol*] [*Library of Congress*] (LCLS)
**ORK**........... Orbis. A Journal of World Affairs [*A publication*]
**ORK**........... Orkney [*County in Scotland*] (ROG)
**Orkester JL** ... Orkester Journalen [*A publication*]
**Ork J**.......... Orkester Journalen [*A publication*]
**OrKT** ......... Oregon Technical Institute, Klamath Falls, OR [*Library symbol*] [*Library of Congress*] (LCLS)
**ORL**........... Observed Range Limit
**ORL**........... Olivetti Research Laboratory Ltd. [*British*] (IRUK)
**ORL**........... Operations Research Letters [*A publication*] (EAAP)
**ORL**........... Orbital Research Laboratory [*NASA*]
**ORL**........... Ordnance Research Laboratory [*Later, Applied Research Laboratory*] [*Pennsylvania State University*] (MCD)
**ORL** ........... Orient. Deutsche Zeitschrift fuer Politik und Wirtschaft des Orients [*A publication*]
**ORL**........... Orion Resources Ltd. [*Vancouver Stock Exchange symbol*]
**ORL**........... ORL - Journal for Oto-Rhino-Laryngology and Its Borderlands [*A publication*]
**'Orl**............ 'Orlah (BJA)
**ORL**........... Orlando [*Florida*] [*Airport symbol*] (OAG)
**ORL**........... Orlando Public Library, Orlando, FL [*OCLC symbol*] (OCLC)
**ORL**........... Otorhinolaryngology [*Medicine*]
**ORL**........... Overrun Lights [*Aviation*] (FAAC)
**ORL**........... Owner's Risk of Leakage [*Shipping*]
**ORL**........... Red Lake Public Library, Ontario [*Library symbol*] [*National Library of Canada*] (NLC)
**ORLA** ........ Optimum Repair Level Analysis [*Air Force*]
**ORLA** ........ Optimum Repair Level Authorization (MCD)
**ORLA** ........ Orthodox Alaska [*A publication*]
**OrLan** ........ Langlois Public Library, Langlois, OR [*Library symbol*] [*Library of Congress*] (LCLS)
**Orlando Bu J** ... Orlando Business Journal [*A publication*]
**Orland Sen** ... Orlando Sentinel [*A publication*]
**Or Laws** ..... Oregon Laws and Resolutions [*A publication*] (DLA)
**Or Laws Adv Sh** ... Oregon Laws Advance Sheets [*A publication*] (DLA)
**Or Laws Spec Sess** ... Oregon Laws and Resolutions [*A publication*] (DLA)
**Orl Bridg**.... Orlando Bridgman's English Common Pleas Reports [*A publication*] (DLA)
**Orl Bridgman** ... Orlando Bridgman's English Common Pleas Reports [*A publication*] (DLA)
**ORLD** ........ Oriental Review and Literary Digest [*A publication*]
**Orleans App** ... Orleans Court of Appeals [*Louisiana*] (DLA)
**Orleans TR** ... Orleans Term Reports [*1, 2 Martin*] [*Louisiana*] [*A publication*] (DLA)
**OrLg** .......... La Grande Public Library, La Grande, OR [*Library symbol*] [*Library of Congress*] (LCLS)
**OrLgE**........ Eastern Oregon College, La Grande, OR [*Library symbol*] [*Library of Congress*] (LCLS)
**OrLgFS**...... United States Forest Service, Range and Wildlife Habitat Laboratory, La Grande, OR [*Library symbol*] [*Library of Congress*] (LCLS)
**OrLgGRH** ... Grande Ronde Hospital, LaGrande, OR [*Library symbol*] [*Library of Congress*] (LCLS)
**OrLgGS** ..... Church of Jesus Christ of Latter-Day Saints, Genealogical Society Library, La Grande Branch, La Grande, OR [*Library symbol*] [*Library of Congress*] (LCLS)
**ORLIA**....... Oto-Rino-Laringologia Italiana [*A publication*]
**ORLIS** ....... Orts-, Regional-, und Landesplanung Literaturinformationssystem [*Literature Information System for Town and Regional Planning*] [*1974-1978*] [*Database*]
**Or Lit** ......... Orientalistische Literaturzeitung [*A publication*]
**ORLJAH**... ORL [*Oto-Rhino-Laryngology*] [*Basel*] [*A publication*]
**ORL-J Oto R** ... ORL - Journal for Oto-Rhino-Laryngology and Its Borderlands [*A publication*]
**ORLL**......... Operational Reports - Lessons Learned [*Army*] (AABC)
**OrLo** .......... Lake Oswego Public Library, Lake Oswego, OR [*Library symbol*] [*Library of Congress*] (LCLS)
**OrLoHS**..... Lake Oswego High School, Lake Oswego, OR [*Library symbol*] [*Library of Congress*] (LCLS)
**OrLoJS**...... Lake Oswego Junior High School, Lake Oswego, OR [*Library symbol*] [*Library of Congress*] (LCLS)
**OrLoLHS** .. Lakeridge High School, Lake Oswego, OR [*Library symbol*] [*Library of Congress*] (LCLS)
**ORL Oto-Rhino-Laryngol (Basel)** ... ORL. Oto-Rhino-Laryngology (Basel) [*A publication*]
**Orlov Gos Ped Inst Ucen Zap** ... Orlovskii Gosudarstvennyi Pedagogiceskii Institut. Ucenye Zapiski [*A publication*]
**OrLovPer**... Orientalia Lovaniensia Periodica [*A publication*]
**ORLPP**...... Office of Research, Legislation, and Program Policies [*Unemployment Insurance Service*] [*Department of Labor*]
**Or LR**......... Oregon Law Review [*A publication*]
**Or L Rev** .... Oregon Law Review [*A publication*]
**ORLS**......... Selco Mining Corp., Red Lake, Ontario [*Library symbol*] [*National Library of Canada*] (NLC)
**Or LSJ** ....... Oregon Law School Journal [*1902-03*] [*A publication*] (DLA)
**ORLSTJ**.... St. Joseph Township Public Library, Richards Landing, Ontario [*Library symbol*] [*National Library of Canada*] (NLC)
**Orl TR** ....... Orleans Term Reports [*1, 2 Martin*] [*Louisiana*] [*A publication*] (DLA)
**ORLY** ........ Overload Relay (IEEE)
**OrLz**.......... Orientalistische Literaturzeitung [*A publication*]
**ORM**.......... Off-Road Mobility
**ORM**.......... Off-Route Mine
**ORM**.......... Office of Recycled Materials [*National Bureau of Standards*]
**ORM**.......... Office of Regional Management [*Employment and Training Administration*]
**ORM**.......... Optical Reference Manual
**ORM**.......... Opytnyi Reaktivnyi Motor [*Experimental Reaction Motor*] [*USSR*]
**ORM**.......... Overhaul and Repair Manual
**ORM**.......... Overlapping Resolution Mapping [*Data processing*]
**ORMA**....... Office of Refugee and Migration Affairs [*Department of State*]
**OrMaC** ...... Marylhurst College, Marylhurst, OR [*Library symbol*] [*Library of Congress*] (LCLS)
**OrMad** ....... Jefferson County Library, Madras, OR [*Library symbol*] [*Library of Congress*] (LCLS)

**ORMAK**.... Oak Ridge TOKAMAK [*Energy Research and Development Administration*]
**Orm Arast Enst Derg** ... Ormancilik Arastirma Enstituesue Dergisi [*A publication*]
**Orm Arast Enst Muht Yay** ... Ormancilik Arastirma Enstituesue Muhtelif Yayinlar Serisi [*A publication*]
**Orm Arast Enst Tek Buelt** ... Ormancilik Arastirma Enstituesue Teknik Buelten [*A publication*]
**ORMAS**.... Operational Resource Management Assessment System [*Military*]
**OrMc**......... McMinnville Public Library, McMinnville, OR [*Library symbol*] [*Library of Congress*] (LCLS)
**OR/MC**..... Operational Requirements/Military Characteristics (NG)
**OrMcL**....... Linfield College, McMinnville, OR [*Library symbol*] [*Library of Congress*] (LCLS)
**OrMeGS**.... Church of Jesus Christ of Latter-Day Saints, Genealogical Society Library, Medford Branch, Medford, OR [*Library symbol*] [*Library of Congress*] (LCLS)
**OrMeJ**....... Jackson County Library System, Medford, OR [*Library symbol*] [*Library of Congress*] (LCLS)
**OrMf**.......... Milton-Freewater Public Library, Milton-Freewater, OR [*Library symbol*] [*Library of Congress*] (LCLS)
**OrMi**.......... Milwaukie Public Library, Milwaukie, OR [*Library symbol*] [*Library of Congress*] (LCLS)
**ORMI**........ Oak Ridge Military Institute
**OrMiCHS** ... Clackamas High School, Media Center, Milwaukie, OR [*Library symbol*] [*Library of Congress*] (LCLS)
**OrMiD**....... Dwyer Community Hospital, Medical Library, Milwaukie, OR [*Library symbol*] [*Library of Congress*] (LCLS)
**OrMiHS**.... Milwaukie High School, Milwaukie, OR [*Library symbol*] [*Library of Congress*] (LCLS)
**OrMiLHS** ... La Salle High School, Milwaukie, OR [*Library symbol*] [*Library of Congress*] (LCLS)
**OrMiPHS** ... Rex Putnam High School, Milwaukie, OR [*Library symbol*] [*Library of Congress*] (LCLS)
**ORMM**...... Basrah/Magal [*Iraq*] [*ICAO location identifier*] (ICLI)
**ORMOA**.... Office for Relations with Military and Occupation Authorities
**OrMod**....... Oriente Moderno [*Rome*] [*A publication*]
**OrMol**........ Molalla Public Library, Molalla, OR [*Library symbol*] [*Library of Congress*] (LCLS)
**OrMolHS**.. Molalla Senior High School, Molalla, OR [*Library symbol*] [*Library of Congress*] (LCLS)
**OrMon**....... Monmouth Library, Monmouth, OR [*Library symbol*] [*Library of Congress*] (LCLS)
**Ormond**...... Ormond's Reports [*19-107 Alabama*] [*A publication*] (DLA)
**OrMonO**.... Oregon College of Education, Monmouth, OR [*Library symbol*] [*Library of Congress*] (LCLS)
**ORMONS** ... Operational Readiness Monitoring System (MCD)
**OrMp**......... Myrtle Point Public Library (Flora M. Laird Library), Myrtle Point, OR [*Library symbol*] [*Library of Congress*] (LCLS)
**ORMS**....... Basrah/Shaibah [*Iraq*] [*ICAO location identifier*] (ICLI)
**ORMS**....... Operational Readiness Management System
**OR/MS**...... Operations Research or Management Science
**ORMS**....... Operative Roller Makers' Society [*A union*] [*British*]
**ORMT**....... Ormont Drug & Chemical Co., Inc. [*NASDAQ symbol*]
**OrMta**........ Mount Angel Public Library, Mount Angel, OR [*Library symbol*] [*Library of Congress*] (LCLS)
**OrMtaC**..... Mount Angel College [*Later, Cesar Chavez College*], Mount Angel, OR [*Library symbol*] [*Library of Congress*] (LCLS)
**ORMU**....... Orbital Remote Maneuvering Unit
**Orm Vitam** ... Ormoni e Vitamine [*A publication*]
**OrN**............ Newberg Library Association, Newberg, OR [*Library symbol*] [*Library of Congress*] (LCLS)
**ORN** .......... Oak Ridge National Laboratory, Oak Ridge, TN [*OCLC symbol*] (OCLC)
**ORN** .......... Operating Room Nurse [*Medicine*]
**ORN** .......... Oran [*Algeria*] [*Airport symbol*] (OAG)
**ORN** .......... Orange (AAG)
**OR & N**....... Oregon Railroad & Navigation Co.
**ORN** .......... Organization of Revolutionaries of the North [*Lebanon*] (PD)
**ORN** .......... Ornament (MSA)
**Orn**............. Ornithine [*Same as DAV*] [*An amino acid*]
**ORN** .......... Ornithology
**ORN** .......... Orthopedic Nurse
**Orn Abh**..... Ornithologische Abhandlungen [*A publication*]
**ORNAM**.... Ornamental
**Ornamentals Northwest Newsl Coop Ext Serv Oreg State Univ** ... Ornamentals Northwest. Newsletter. Cooperative Extension Service. Oregon State University [*A publication*]
**OrNb**.......... North Bend Public Library, North Bend, OR [*Library symbol*] [*Library of Congress*] (LCLS)
**Orn Ber**...... Ornithologische Berichte [*A publication*]
**OrNbGS**.... Church of Jesus Christ of Latter-Day Saints, Genealogical Society Library, Coos Bay Stake Branch, North Bend, OR [*Library symbol*] [*Library of Congress*] (LCLS)
**OrNep**........ Newport Public Library, Newport, OR [*Library symbol*] [*Library of Congress*] (LCLS)
**OrNGF**...... George Fox College, Newberg, OR [*Library symbol*] [*Library of Congress*] (LCLS)
**Ornis Fenn** ... Ornis Fennica [*A publication*]
**Ornis Scand** ... Ornis Scandinavica [*A publication*]
**ORNITH**... Ornithology
**ORNITHOL** ... Ornithology
**Ornithol Abh** ... Ornithologische Abhandlungen [*A publication*]
**Ornithol Appl** ... Ornithologie Applique [*A publication*]
**Ornithol Beob** ... Ornithologische Beobachter [*A publication*]
**Ornithol Ber** ... Ornithologische Berichte [*A publication*]
**Ornithol Mitt** ... Ornithologische Mitteilungen [*A publication*]
**Ornithol Monatsber** ... Ornithologische Monatsberichte [*A publication*]
**ORNL**........ Oak Ridge National Laboratory [*Oak Ridge, TN*] [*Department of Energy*]
**ORNL TM** ... Oak Ridge National Laboratory. TM [*A publication*]
**ORNLY-NDP** ... Oak Ridge National Laboratory Nuclear Data Project [*Database producer*]
**Orn Mitt**.... Ornithologische Mitteilungen [*A publication*]
**ORNMT**.... Ornament
**ORNRA**..... Oak Ridge National Laboratory. Review [*A publication*]
**OrNS**......... Orientalia. Nova Series [*A publication*]
**OrNyGS**.... Church of Jesus Christ of Latter-Day Saints, Genealogical Society Library, Nyssa Branch, Nyssa, OR [*Library symbol*] [*Library of Congress*] (LCLS)
**OrNyMH**... Malheur Memorial Hospital, J. J. Sarazin Memorial Library, Nyssa, OR [*Library symbol*] [*Library of Congress*] (LCLS)
**ORO** .......... Oak Ridge Operations Office (MCD)
**ORO** .......... Office of Regional Operations [*Office of Field Operations*] [*Department of Labor*]
**ORO** .......... Oil Red O [*A stain*]
**ORO** .......... Operations Research Office
**OrO**............ Oregon City Public Library, Oregon City, OR [*Library symbol*] [*Library of Congress*] (LCLS)
**ORO** .......... Orofino Resources Ltd. [*Toronto Stock Exchange symbol*] [*Vancouver Stock Exchange symbol*]
**ORO** .......... Oropa [*Italy*] [*Seismograph station code, US Geological Survey*] [*Closed*] (SEIS)
**ORO** .......... Oropouche [*An arbovirus*]
**Oro**............ Orotate [*Biochemistry*]
**Oro**............ Orotic Acid [*Biochemistry*]
**ORO** .......... Orthicon Read-Out
**ORO** .......... Rockland Public Library, Ontario [*Library symbol*] [*National Library of Canada*] (NLC)
**OrOa**.......... Oakridge Public Library, Oakridge, OR [*Library symbol*] [*Library of Congress*] (LCLS)
**OROAP**..... Organizacion Regional del Oriente para la Administracion Publica [*Eastern Regional Organization for Public Administration*] (EAIO)
**OrOC**......... Clackamas County Public Library, Oregon City, OR [*Library symbol*] [*Library of Congress*] (LCLS)
**OrOCC**...... Clackamas Community College, Oregon City, OR [*Library symbol*] [*Library of Congress*] (LCLS)
**Or Occ** ....... Orient-Occident [*A publication*]
**OrOHS**...... Oregon City Senior High School, Oregon City, OR [*Library symbol*] [*Library of Congress*] (LCLS)
**OROM** ...... Optical Read-Only Memory [*Data processing*]
**ORom**......... Opuscula Romana [*A publication*]
**ORom**......... Osservatore Romano [*A publication*]
**OrOn**.......... Malheur County Library, Ontario, OR [*Library symbol*] [*Library of Congress*] (LCLS)
**OrOnHR**.... Holy Rosary Hospital, Weise-Biggs Memorial Medical Library, Ontario, OR [*Library symbol*] [*Library of Congress*] (LCLS)
**OrOnT**....... Treasure Valley Community College, Ontario, OR [*Library symbol*] [*Library of Congress*] (LCLS)
**ORootN** ..... Northeastern Ohio Universities, College of Medicine, Basic Medical Sciences Library, Rootstown, OH [*Library symbol*] [*Library of Congress*] (LCLS)
**OROS**........ Optical Read-Only Storage [*Data processing*]
**OROS**........ Oral Osmotic [*System for delivering drugs into the bloodstream*] [*Alza Corp. trademark*]
**OROS**........ Rosseau Public Library, Ontario [*Library symbol*] [*National Library of Canada*] (NLC)
**OrOWH** .... Willamette Falls Community Hospital, Oregon City, OR [*Library symbol*] [*Library of Congress*] (LCLS)
**OrP** ............ Library Association of Portland [*Public Library for Portland and Multnomah County*], Portland, OR [*Library symbol*] [*Library of Congress*] (LCLS)
**ORP**........... Objective Rallying Point [*Military*]
**ORP**........... Objective Release Point [*Army*] (INF)
**ORP**........... Odrodzenie i Reformacja w Polsce [*A publication*]
**ORP**........... Office of Radiation Programs [*Environmental Protection Agency*]
**ORP**........... Office of Regulatory Programs [*Federal Energy Administration*] [*Obsolete*]
**ORP**........... Operational Readiness Panel
**ORP**........... Optical Rotary Power
**ORP**........... Orapa [*Botswana*] [*Airport symbol*] [*Obsolete*] (OAG)
**ORP**........... Orbital Rendezvous Procedure (AAG)
**ORP**........... Organ Recovery Program (EA)
**OrP**............ Orientamenti Pedagogici [*Torino*] [*A publication*]
**ORP**........... Outside Right Position [*Dancing*]
**ORP**........... Oxidation-Reduction Potential
**ORP**........... Oxygen-Regulated Protein [*Biochemistry*]

**ORP**.......... Phelps Community Library, Redbridge, Ontario [*Library symbol*] [*National Library of Canada*] (NLC)
**ORPA**........ Orbiter Retarding Potential Analyzer [*NASA*]
**ORPA**........ Organizacion Revolucionaria del Pueblo en Armas [*Revolutionary Organization of the People in Arms*] [*Guatemala*] [*Political party*] (PD)
**OrP-A**........ Portland City Archives, Portland, OR [*Library symbol*] [*Library of Congress*] (LCLS)
**OrPAA**....... Arthur Anderson & Co., Portland, OR [*Library symbol*] [*Library of Congress*] (LCLS)
**OrPB**.......... Bonneville Power Administration, Portland, OR [*Library symbol*] [*Library of Congress*] (LCLS)
**ORPB**........ Oberrheinisches Pastoralblatt [*A publication*]
**OrPBK**....... Bess Kaiser Foundation Hospital, Medical Library, Portland, OR [*Library symbol*] [*Library of Congress*] (LCLS)
**OrPC**.......... Cascade College, Portland, OR [*Library symbol*] [*Library of Congress*] (LCLS)
**ORPC**........ Office of Rail Public Counsel [*Terminated, 1979*] [*Affiliated with Interstate Commerce Commission*]
**ORPC**........ Old Radio Program Collectors Club (EA)
**ORPC**........ Orion Pictures Corp. [*NASDAQ symbol*] (NQ)
**OrPCA**....... Roman Catholic Archdiocese of Portland in Oregon, Chancery Office, Portland, OR [*Library symbol*] [*Library of Congress*] (LCLS)
**OrPCC**....... Concordia College, Portland, OR [*Library symbol*] [*Library of Congress*] (LCLS)
**OrPCM**...... Cedar Mill Community Library, Portland, OR [*Library symbol*] [*Library of Congress*] (LCLS)
**OrPCNM**... National College of Naturopathic Medicine, Portland, OR [*Library symbol*] [*Library of Congress*] (LCLS)
**OrPCol**....... Columbia Christian College, Portland, OR [*Library symbol*] [*Library of Congress*] (LCLS)
**OrPD**......... Protestant Episcopal Church, Diocesan Library, Portland, OR [*Library symbol*] [*Library of Congress*] (LCLS)
**OrPeB**........ Blue Mountain Community College, Pendleton, OR [*Library symbol*] [*Library of Congress*] (LCLS)
**OrPeCH**..... Pendleton Community Hospital, Pendleton, OR [*Library symbol*] [*Library of Congress*] (LCLS)
**OrPEH**...... Emanuel Hospital, Portland, OR [*Library symbol*] [*Library of Congress*] (LCLS)
**OrPeSA**..... Saint Anthony Hospital, Pendleton, OR [*Library symbol*] [*Library of Congress*] (LCLS)
**OrPeU**........ Umatilla County Library, Pendleton, OR [*Library symbol*] [*Library of Congress*] (LCLS)
**OrPFW**...... United States Fish and Wildlife Service, Portland, OR [*Library symbol*] [*Library of Congress*] (LCLS)
**OrPGE**....... Portland General Electric Co., Portland, OR [*Library symbol*] [*Library of Congress*] (LCLS)
**OrPGF**....... Genealogical Forum of Portland, Portland, OR [*Library symbol*] [*Library of Congress*] (LCLS)
**OrPGH**...... Good Samaritan Hospital and Medical Center, Portland, OR [*Library symbol*] [*Library of Congress*] (LCLS)
**OrPGS**....... Church of Jesus Christ of Latter-Day Saints, Genealogical Society Library, Portland Branch, Portland, OR [*Library symbol*] [*Library of Congress*] (LCLS)
**OrPGSE**.... Church of Jesus Christ of Latter-Day Saints, Genealogical Society Library, Portland East Branch, Portland, OR [*Library symbol*] [*Library of Congress*] (LCLS)
**ORPH**........ Orphan [*or Orphanage*]
**Orph**........... Orpheus. Revista pentru Cultura Clasica [*A publication*]
**Orph Frag**... Orphica Fragmenta [*A publication*] (OCD)
**ORPHIC**.... Organized Projected Hypotheses for Innovations in Curriculum [*Educational planning*]
**OrPHP**...... Holladay Park Hospital, Medical Library, Portland, OR [*Library symbol*] [*Library of Congress*] (LCLS)
**OrPHS-D**.. Oregon Health Sciences University, Dental Library, Portland, OR [*Library symbol*] [*Library of Congress*] (LCLS)
**ORPI**.......... Organ Pipe Cactus National Monument
**ORPICS**.... Orbital Rendezvous Positioning, Indexing, and Coupling System
**OrPK**.......... Bess Kaiser Foundation Hospital, Medical Library, Portland, OR [*Library symbol*] [*Library of Congress*] (LCLS)
**OrPKF**....... Kaiser Foundation Hospitals, Health Services Research Center, Portland, OR [*Library symbol*] [*Library of Congress*] (LCLS)
**OrPL**.......... Lewis and Clark College, Portland, OR [*Library symbol*] [*Library of Congress*] (LCLS)
**ORPL**......... Overseas Replacement [*Military*]
**OrPL-L**....... Northwestern School of Law, Lewis and Clark College, Portland, OR [*Library symbol*] [*Library of Congress*] (LCLS)
**OrPMB**...... Multnomah School of the Bible, Portland, OR [*Library symbol*] [*Library of Congress*] (LCLS)
**OrPML**...... Multnomah County Law Library, Portland, OR [*Library symbol*] [*Library of Congress*] (LCLS)
**OrPNA**...... Northwest Association of Private Colleges and Universities, Microform Center, Portland, OR [*Library symbol*] [*Library of Congress*] (LCLS)
**OrPNR**...... Northwest Regional Educational Laboratory, Information Center Library, Portland, OR [*Library symbol*] [*Library of Congress*] (LCLS)
**OrPO**......... Oregonian Publishing Co. Library, Portland, OR [*Library symbol*] [*Library of Congress*] (LCLS)
**OrPOF**....... Oregon Odd Fellows Grand Lodge, Portland, OR [*Library symbol*] [*Library of Congress*] (LCLS)
**ORPOS**...... Office of Regulatory Policy, Oversight, and Supervision [*Federal Home Loan Bank Board*]
**OrPP**.......... Port of Portland Library, Portland, OR [*Library symbol*] [*Library of Congress*] (LCLS)
**OrPPC**....... Portland Community College, Portland, OR [*Library symbol*] [*Library of Congress*] (LCLS)
**OrPPL**....... Pacific Power & Light Co., Portland, OR [*Library symbol*] [*Library of Congress*] (LCLS)
**OrPPM**...... Providence Medical Center, Portland, OR [*Library symbol*] [*Library of Congress*] (LCLS)
**OrPPS**....... Portland Public School District, Portland, OR [*Library symbol*] [*Library of Congress*] (LCLS)
**OrPr**........... Crook County Library, Prineville, OR [*Library symbol*] [*Library of Congress*] (LCLS)
**OrPR**.......... Reed College, Portland, OR [*Library symbol*] [*Library of Congress*] (LCLS)
**OrPRAM**... Oregon Royal Arch Masons Grand Chapter Archives, Portland, OR [*Library symbol*] [*Library of Congress*] (LCLS)
**OrPRP**....... Riverside Psychiatric Hospital, Portland, OR [*Library symbol*] [*Library of Congress*] (LCLS)
**ORPS**......... Overseas Return Placement System [*Military*]
**OrPS**.......... Portland State University, Portland, OR [*Library symbol*] [*Library of Congress*] (LCLS)
**OrPSMA**... Saint Mary's Academy, Portland, OR [*Library symbol*] [*Library of Congress*] (LCLS)
**OrPStV**...... Saint Vincent Hospital and Medical Center, Portland, OR [*Library symbol*] [*Library of Congress*] (LCLS)
**ORPSU**...... Organized Reserve Port Security Unit [*Military*]
**OrPT**.......... Temple Beth Israel, Portland, OR [*Library symbol*] [*Library of Congress*] (LCLS)
**OrPTC**....... Town Center Library at Tanasbourne, Portland, OR [*Library symbol*] [*Library of Congress*] (LCLS)
**OrPto**......... Port Orford Public Library, Port Orford, OR [*Library symbol*] [*Library of Congress*] (LCLS)
**OrPU**......... University of Portland, Portland, OR [*Library symbol*] [*Library of Congress*] (LCLS)
**Or PUC Ops**... Oregon Office of the Public Utilities Commissioner. Opinions and Decisions [*A publication*] (DLA)
**OrPV**.......... United States Veterans Administration Hospital, Portland, OR [*Library symbol*] [*Library of Congress*] (LCLS)
**OrPW**........ Western Evangelical Seminary, Portland, OR [*Library symbol*] [*Library of Congress*] (LCLS)
**OrPWB**...... Western Conservative Baptist Theological Seminary, Portland, OR [*Library symbol*] [*Library of Congress*] (LCLS)
**OrPWP**...... Warner Pacific College, Portland, OR [*Library symbol*] [*Library of Congress*] (LCLS)
**OrPWS**...... Western States Chiropractic College, Portland, OR [*Library symbol*] [*Library of Congress*] (LCLS)
**OrPWsC**.... West Slope Community Library, Portland, OR [*Library symbol*] [*Library of Congress*] (LCLS)
**ORQ**........... Norwalk, CT [*Location identifier*] [*FAA*] (FAAL)
**ORQMC**.... Orderly Room Quartermaster-Corporal [*British military*] (DMA)
**ORQMS**.... Orderly Room Quartermaster-Sergeant [*British military*] (DMA)
**ORQUA7**... Orquidea [*Rio De Janeiro*] [*A publication*]
**ORR**........... Oak Ridge Research Reactor [*ORNL*] (NRCH)
**ORR**........... Office of Ready Reserve [*Army*]
**ORR**........... Office of Refugee Relief [*Department of Health and Human Services*]
**ORR**........... Operational Readiness Reporting
**ORR**........... Operational Readiness Review (NASA)
**ORR**........... Operational Ready Rate (MCD)
**ORR**........... Operations Requirements Review (NASA)
**ORR**........... Optical Ratio Reflector
**ORR**........... Orbital Rendezvous RADAR (AAG)
**ORR**........... Orroval Valley, Australia, Tracking Station [*NASA*] (NASA)
**ORR**........... Orthographic RADAR Restitutor
**ORR**........... Oudh and Rohilkand Railway Rifles [*British military*] (DMA)
**ORR**........... Owner's Risk Rates [*Shipping*]
**ORR**........... Red Rock Public Library, Ontario [*Library symbol*] [*National Library of Canada*] (NLC)
**ORR**........... Rogue Community College Library, Grants Pass, OR [*OCLC symbol*] (OCLC)
**ORRA**........ Oriental Rug Retailers of America (EA)
**ORRAS**....... Optical Research Radiometrical Analysis System (IEEE)
**ORRBDQ**.. Oxford Reviews of Reproductive Biology [*A publication*]
**ORRCA**..... Organisation for the Rescue and Research of Cetaceans in Australia
**ORRCAT**... Ridgetown College of Agricultural Technology, Ontario [*Library symbol*] [*National Library of Canada*] (NLC)
**OrRed**........ Redmond Public Library, Redmond, OR [*Library symbol*] [*Library of Congress*] (LCLS)
**OrRedDH**.. Central Oregon District Hospital, Medical Library, Redmond, OR [*Library symbol*] [*Library of Congress*] (LCLS)
**Or Rep**....... Oregon Reports [*A publication*] (DLA)
**Or Rev Stat**... Oregon Revised Statutes [*A publication*] (DLA)

**ORRMIS**... Oak Ridge Regional Modeling Information System
**OrRoD**....... Douglas County Library, Roseburg, OR [*Library symbol*] [*Library of Congress*] (LCLS)
**OrRoM**...... Douglas County Museum, Roseburg, OR [*Library symbol*] [*Library of Congress*] (LCLS)
**OrRoMM**.. Mercy Medical Center, Roseburg, OR [*Library symbol*] [*Library of Congress*] (LCLS)
**OrRoU**....... Umpqua Community College, Roseburg, OR [*Library symbol*] [*Library of Congress*] (LCLS)
**OrRoV**....... United States Veterans Administration Hospital, Roseburg, OR [*Library symbol*] [*Library of Congress*] (LCLS)
**ORRR**........ Oak Ridge Research Reactor [*Department of Energy*] (NRCH)
**ORRRC**..... Outdoor Recreation Resources Review Commission [*Terminated, 1962*] [*Department of the Interior*]
**ORRT**........ Operational Readiness and Reliability Test
**ORRV**........ Off-Road Recreation Vehicle
**ORS**........... Obligated Reserve Section [*Air Force*] (AFM)
**ORS**........... Oceanographic Research Ship
**ORS**........... Octahedral Research Satellite [*NASA*]
**ORS**........... Off-Site Repair and Support (MCD)
**ORS**........... Office of Radiation Standards [*AEC*]
**ORS**........... Office of Rent Stabilization [*Functions transferred to Office of Defense Mobilization, 1953*]
**ORS**........... Office of Research and Statistics [*Social Security Administration*]
**ORS**........... Office of Revenue Sharing [*Department of the Treasury*]
**ORS**........... Official Relay Station [*Amateur radio*]
**ORS**........... Oil Recovery System
**ORS**........... Old Red Sandstone
**ORS**........... Online Reference Service [*Thunder Bay Public Library*] [*Canada*] (OLDSS)
**ORS**........... Online Research Systems [*Information service or system*] (IID)
**ORS**........... Operational Research Society [*British*]
**ORS**........... Operational Research Station [*Air Ministry*] [*British*] [*World War II*]
**ORS**........... Optimal Real Storage (CMD)
**ORS**........... Oral Electrolyte Solution [*Nutrition*]
**ORS**........... Oral Rehydration Salts
**ORS**........... Oral Surgeon
**ORS**........... Orbital Refueling System [*NASA*] (NASA)
**ORS**........... Orbiter Relay Simulator [*NASA*]
**ORS**........... Orbiting Research Satellite [*NASA*]
**ORS**........... Orderly Room Sergeant [*British*]
**ORS**........... Organization Rating Scale
**ORS**........... Organization Studies [*A publication*]
**ORS**........... Originating Register Sender
**ORS**........... Orpheus Island [*Australia*] [*Airport symbol*]
**ORS**........... Orsett [*England*]
**ORS**........... Orsina Resources [*Vancouver Stock Exchange symbol*]
**ORS**........... Orthopedic Research Society (EA)
**ORS**........... Orthopedic Surgeon
**ORS**........... Oscillographic Recording System
**ORS**........... Others
**ORS**........... Outboard Rotating Shield
**ORS**........... Oval Ring Seal
**ORS**........... Over Range Station [*Aviation*] (FAAC)
**ORS**........... Overlay Reproducer System
**ORS**........... Owner's Risk of Shifting [*Shipping*]
**ORS**........... Research and Development Library, Shaw Industries, Rexdale, Ontario [*Library symbol*] [*National Library of Canada*] (BIB)
**ORSA**........ Operations Research Society of America (EA)
**OR/SA**....... Operations Research/Systems Analysis [*Army*]
**ORSA**........ Order of Recollects of St. Augustine
**ORSA**........ Oregon Revised Statutes Annotated [*A publication*]
**OrSa**.......... Salem Public Library, Salem, OR [*Library symbol*] [*Library of Congress*] (LCLS)
**OrSaC**........ Chemeketa Community College, Salem, OR [*Library symbol*] [*Library of Congress*] (LCLS)
**ORSAC**...... Oak Ridge Systems Analysis Code
**ORSAC**...... Open Road "See America" Club (EA)
**OR/SAEC**... Operations Research/Systems Analysis Executive Course [*Army*]
**OrSaGS**..... Church of Jesus Christ of Latter-Day Saints, Genealogical Society Library, Salem Branch, Salem, OR [*Library symbol*] [*Library of Congress*] (LCLS)
**OrSaH**....... Salem Hospital, Salem, OR [*Library symbol*] [*Library of Congress*] (LCLS)
**OrSan**........ Sandy Public Library, Sandy, OR [*Library symbol*] [*Library of Congress*] (LCLS)
**ORSANCO**... Ohio River Valley Water Sanitation Commission
**OrSanHS**... Sandy Union High School, Sandy, OR [*Library symbol*] [*Library of Congress*] (LCLS)
**ORSAR**...... Official Reports, South African Republic [*A publication*] (DLA)
**ORSA/TIMS Bull**... ORSA [*Operations Research Society of America*]/TIMS [*The Institute of Management Sciences*] Bulletin [*A publication*]
**OrSaW**....... Willamette University, Salem, OR [*Library symbol*] [*Library of Congress*] (LCLS)
**OrSaWB**.... Western Baptist Bible College, Salem, OR [*Library symbol*] [*Library of Congress*] (LCLS)
**OrSaW-L**... Willamette University, Law Library, Salem, OR [*Library symbol*] [*Library of Congress*] (LCLS)
**Or SB Bull**... Oregon State Bar. Bulletin [*A publication*] (ILCA)
**ORS(BC)**... Operational Research Section (Bomber Command) [*British*] [*World War II*]
**Or-SC**........ Oregon Supreme Court, Salem, OR [*Library symbol*] [*Library of Congress*] (LCLS)
**ORSC**......... Ornis Scandinavica [*A publication*]
**ORSC**......... ORS Corp. [*NASDAQ symbol*] (NQ)
**ORSDI**....... Oak Ridge Selective Dissemination of Information [*Department of Energy*] (NASA)
**ORSE**......... Operational Reactor Safeguard Examination (NVT)
**ORSE**......... Otherwise
**ORSER**...... Office for Remote Sensing of Earth Resources [*Pennsylvania State University*] [*Research center*]
**OrSh**.......... Sherwood Public Library, Sherwood, OR [*Library symbol*] [*Library of Congress*] (LCLS)
**OrShe**......... Sheridan Public Library, Sheridan, OR [*Library symbol*] [*Library of Congress*] (LCLS)
**ORSI**.......... Object Recognition [*NASDAQ symbol*] (NQ)
**OrSi**........... Sisters Public Library, Sisters, OR [*Library symbol*] [*Library of Congress*] (LCLS)
**OrSibyll**..... Sibylline Oracles (Pseudepigrapha) (BJA)
**OrSil**.......... Silverton Public Library, Silverton, OR [*Library symbol*] [*Library of Congress*] (LCLS)
**ORSIP**....... Office of Research, Statistics, and International Policy [*Later, ORS*] [*Social Security Administration*] (IID)
**Orsk Gos Ped Inst Ucen Zap**... Orskii Gosudarstvennyi Pedagogiceskii Institut Imeni T. G. Sevcenko. Ucenye Zapiski [*A publication*]
**ORSL**......... Order of the Republic of Sierra Leone
**ORSON**..... Orient, Spell Out, Nail Down [*Method for organizing and communicating information, proposed by Barry Tarshis in his book "How to Write without Pain"*]
**ORSORT**... Oak Ridge School of Reactor Technology [*Department of Energy*]
**OR & SP**.... Office of Research and Sponsored Programs [*Research center*] (RCD)
**OrSp**.......... Springfield Public Library, Springfield, OR [*Library symbol*] [*Library of Congress*] (LCLS)
**OR Spektrum**... Operations Research Spektrum [*A publication*]
**ORS(S)**...... Operational Research Section (Singapore) [*Military*]
**OrSt**........... Stayton Public Library, Stayton, OR [*Library symbol*] [*Library of Congress*] (LCLS)
**OR St B**...... Operation Rescue Saint Bernard [*Test given to Junior Woodchucks in Donald Duck comic by Carl Barks*]
**Or St B Bull**... Oregon State Bar Bulletin [*A publication*] (DLA)
**OrStbM**..... Mount Angel College, Mount Angel Abbey, St. Benedict, OR [*Library symbol*] [*Library of Congress*] (LCLS)
**OrSthDH**... Columbia District Hospital, Medical Library, St. Helens, OR [*Library symbol*] [*Library of Congress*] (LCLS)
**ORSTOM**... Office de la Recherche Scientifique et Technique d'Outre-Mer [*Office of Overseas Scientific and Technical Research*] [*France*]
**OrSuec**....... Orientalia Suecana [*Uppsala*] [*A publication*]
**Or Surg**...... Oral Surgery, Oral Medicine, and Oral Pathology [*A publication*]
**OrSyr**......... Orient Syrien [*Vernon, France*] [*A publication*]
**Orszagos Mezoegazd Minoesegvizsgalo Intez Evkoen**... Orszagos Mezogazdasagi Minosegvizsgalo Intezet Evkonyve [*A publication*]
**Orsz Husipari Kut Intez Kozl**... Orszagos Husipari Kutato Intezet Kozlemenyei [*A publication*]
**Orsz Met Intez Hivat Kiad**... Orszagos Meteorologiai Intezet Hivatalos Kiadvanyai [*A publication*]
**Orsz Mezogazd Minosegv Intez Evk**... Orszagos Mezogazdasagi Minosegvizsgalo Intezet Evkonyve [*A publication*]
**Orsz Mezogazd Minosegvizsgalo Intez Kiad Sorozat 1**... Orszagos Mezogazdasagi Minosegvizsgalo Intezet Kiadvanyai. Sorozat 1. Genetikus Talajterkepek [*A publication*]
**Orsz Orvost Koenyv Koezl**... Orszagos Orvostoerteneti Koenyvtar Koezlemenyei [*A publication*]
**ORT**........... Northway, AK [*Location identifier*] [*FAA*] (FAAL)
**ORT**........... Oak Ridge [*Tennessee*] [*Seismograph station code, US Geological Survey*] (SEIS)
**ORT**........... Object Relations Technique [*Psychology*]
**ORT**........... Ooty Radio Telescope [*India*]
**ORT**........... Operating Room Technician [*Medicine*]
**ORT**........... Operational Readiness Test
**ORT**........... Operational Readiness Training [*Army*]
**ORT**........... Operationally Ready Time
**ORT**........... Optical Relay Tube (MCD)
**ORT**........... Optical Rotary Table
**ORT**........... Optimum Resolution Technique
**ORT**........... Oral Rehydration Therapy
**ORT**........... Orbit Readiness Test [*NASA*] (NASA)
**ORT**........... Orbital Rendezvous Technique (AAG)
**ORT**........... Order of Railroad Telegraphers [*Later, Transportation-Communication Employees Union*] (EA)

**ORT**.......... Ordnance Repair Truck [*British*]
**ORT**.......... Organization for Rehabilitation through Training [*Acronym is used in names of several Jewish social welfare organizations*]
**ORT**.......... Orientalia Rheno-Traiectina [*A publication*]
**Ort**.......... Ortho Diagnostics
**ORT**.......... Overland RADAR Technology (MCD)
**ORTA**........ Office of Research and Technology Applications [*Gaithersburg, MD*] [*National Institute of Standards and Technology*] (GRD)
**ORTA**........ Office of Research and Technology Applications [*Army*] (RDA)
**ORTA**........ Office of Research and Technology Applications [*Berkeley, CA*] [*Lawrence Berkeley Laboratory*] [*Department of Energy*] (GRD)
**ORTC**........ Organized Reserve Training Center [*Military*]
**ORTEC**....... Oak Ridge Technical Enterprises Corporation
**OR Tech**..... OR Tech: Official Publication of the Association of Operating Room Technicians [*A publication*]
**ORTF**........ Office de la Radio et de la Television Francaise [*State-owned radio and television network*] [*France*]
**ORTH**........ Orthodox
**ORTH**........ Orthography
**ORTH**........ Orthopedic
**Ort Hist**..... Ortolan's History of the Roman Law [*A publication*] (DLA)
**ORTHO**....... American Orthopsychiatric Association (EA)
**ORTHO**....... Orthochromatic [*Photography*] (ROG)
**ORTHO**....... Orthopedic
**Orthod**....... Orthodontics [*A publication*]
**Orthod Fr**... Orthodontie Francaise [*A publication*]
**ORTHOG**... Orthogonal (NASA)
**Orthomol Ps**... Orthomolecular Psychiatry [*A publication*]
**Orthop Clin North Am**... Orthopedic Clinics of North America [*A publication*]
**Orthoped Cl**... Orthopedic Clinics of North America [*A publication*]
**Orthop Lect**... Orthopaedic Lectures [*A publication*]
**Orthop Nurs**... Orthopedic Nursing [*A publication*]
**Orthop Prax**... Orthopaedische Praxis [*A publication*]
**Orthop Surg**... Orthopedic Surgery [*Japan*] [*A publication*]
**Orthop Trans**... Orthopaedic Transactions [*A publication*]
**Orthop Traumatol**... Orthopedics and Traumatology [*Japan*] [*A publication*]
**Orthop Traumatol**... Orthopedie Traumatologie [*A publication*]
**Orthotics Prosthet**... Orthotics and Prosthetics [*A publication*]
**Orthot Pros**... Orthotics and Prosthetics [*A publication*]
**OrTig**........ Tigard Public Library, Tigard, OR [*Library symbol*] [*Library of Congress*] (LCLS)
**Ort Inst**...... Ortolan's Justinian's Institutes [*A publication*] (DLA)
**ORTN**........ Officie Radiodiffusion Television du Niger [*Radio and television network*] [*Niger*]
**ORTO**........ Olympics Radio and Television Organization [*Organisme de Radio-Television des Olympiques*] [*Canada*]
**Ortod**......... Ortodoncia [*A publication*]
**Ortod Clin**... Ortodoncia Clinica [*A publication*]
**Ortop Resp Mezhved Sb**... Ortopediya Respublikanskii Mezhvedomstvennyi Sbornik [*A publication*]
**Ortop Traumatol Appar Mot**... Ortopedia e Traumatologia dell'Apparato Motore [*A publication*]
**Ortop Travmatol Prot**... Ortopediya, Travmatologiya, i Protezirovaniye [*A publication*]
**Ortop Travmatol Protez**... Ortopediya, Travmatologiya, i Protezirovaniye [*A publication*]
**Ortop Travmatol (Sofia)**... Ortopediya i Travmatologiya (Sofia) [*A publication*]
**Ortop Travm Protez**... Ortopedija, Travmatologija, i Protezirovanie [*A publication*]
**ORTP**........ Operational Readiness Training Program [*Military*] (AABC)
**Or TR**........ Oregon Tax Reporter [*A publication*] (DLA)
**Or T Rep**.... Oregon Tax Reporter [*A publication*] (ILCA)
**Or T Rep**.... Orleans Term Reports [*1, 2 Martin*] [*Louisiana*] [*A publication*] (DLA)
**Ort Rom Law**... Ortolan's History of the Roman Law [*A publication*] (DLA)
**ORTS**......... Operational Readiness Test System [*Military*] (CAAL)
**ORTS**......... Optional Residential Telephone Service [*Telecommunications*] (TEL)
**Orts KK**..... Ortskrankenkasse [*A publication*]
**ORTT**........ Operational Readiness Training Test [*Army*] (AABC)
**ORTTDM**... Orthopaedic Transactions [*A publication*]
**ORTU**........ Organized Reserve Training Unit [*Military*]
**OrTua**........ Tualatin Public Library, Tualatin, OR [*Library symbol*] [*Library of Congress*] (LCLS)
**ORTUAG**.. Organized Reserve Training Unit, Vessel Augmentation [*Military*]
**OrTuaM**..... Meridian Park Hospital, Medical Library, Tualatin, OR [*Library symbol*] [*Library of Congress*] (LCLS)
**ORTUAM**... Organized Reserve Training Unit, Administration of Mobilization [*Military*]
**ORTUAV**.. Organized Reserve Training Unit, Aviation Support [*Military*]
**ORTUEL**... Organized Reserve Training Unit, Electronics [*Military*]
**ORTUF**..... Organized Reserve Training Unit, Coastal Force [*Military*]
**Ortung Navig**... Ortung und Navigation [*West Germany*] [*A publication*]
**ORTUPS**... Organized Reserve Training Unit, Port Security [*Military*]
**ORTUPS(O)**... Organized Reserve Training Unit, Port Security (Operational) [*Military*]
**ORTUR**..... Organized Reserve Training Unit, Rescue Coordination Center [*Military*]
**OrTW**........ Wasco County Library, The Dalles, OR [*Library symbol*] [*Library of Congress*] (LCLS)
**ORTX**........ Ortner Air Service [*Air carrier designation symbol*]
**ORU**.......... On-Line Replacement Unit [*Data processing*] (MCD)
**ORU**.......... Operational Readiness Unit
**ORU**.......... Optical Reference Unit
**ORU**.......... Oral Roberts University [*Oklahoma*]
**ORU**.......... Orange & Rockland Utilities, Inc. [*NYSE symbol*] (SPSG)
**oru**............ Oregon [*MARC country of publication code*] [*Library of Congress*] (LCCP)
**ORU**.......... Organization for Rebirth of Ukraine (EA)
**ORU**.......... Russell Branch, Russell Township Public Library, Ontario [*Library symbol*] [*National Library of Canada*] (BIB)
**OrU**........... University of Oregon, Eugene, OR [*Library symbol*] [*Library of Congress*] (LCLS)
**ORU**.......... University of Oregon Library, Eugene, OR [*OCLC symbol*] (OCLC)
**OrU-C**........ University of Oregon, Computing Center, Eugene, OR [*Library symbol*] [*Library of Congress*] (LCLS)
**ORUCC**..... Orpheus. Rivista di Umanita Classica e Cristiana [*A publication*]
**OrU-D**....... University of Oregon, Dental School, Portland, OR [*Library symbol*] [*Library of Congress*] (LCLS)
**ORUEF**..... Oral Roberts University Educational Fellowship (EA)
**ORUFE**..... Operational Research Unit, Far East
**OrU-L**........ University of Oregon, Law Library, Portland, OR [*Library symbol*] [*Library of Congress*] (LCLS)
**OrU-M**...... University of Oregon, Medical School, Portland, OR [*Library symbol*] [*Library of Congress*] (LCLS)
**OrUmH**..... Umatilla Hospital, Umatilla, OR [*Library symbol*] [*Library of Congress*] (LCLS)
**OrUn**.......... Carnegie Public Library, Union, OR [*Library symbol*] [*Library of Congress*] (LCLS)
**O/RUNN**... Overrunning [*Automotive engineering*]
**OrU-Or**...... University of Oregon, Oriental Museum, Portland, OR [*Library symbol*] [*Library of Congress*] (LCLS)
**ORUP**........ Ocean Resource Utilization Program (ASF)
**ORUS**........ Official Register of the United States
**OrU-S**........ University of Oregon, Science Division Library, Eugene, OR [*Library symbol*] [*Library of Congress*] (LCLS)
**OrV**........... Fern Ridge Community Library, Veneta, OR [*Library symbol*] [*Library of Congress*] (LCLS)
**ORV**.......... Noorvik [*Alaska*] [*Airport symbol*] (OAG)
**ORV**.......... Ocean Range Vessel [*Air Force*]
**ORV**.......... Off-Road Vehicle
**ORV**.......... Operations Research Verfahren [*A publication*]
**ORV**.......... Orbital Rescue Vehicle [*NASA*] (KSC)
**ORV**.......... Oroville [*California*] [*Seismograph station code, US Geological Survey*] (SEIS)
**ORVAT**..... Organizational Vehicle Automatic Tester
**ORVC**........ River Valley Community Library, Ontario [*Library symbol*] [*National Library of Canada*] (NLC)
**Orv Hetil**.... Orvosi Hetilap [*A publication*]
**Orv Lap**...... Orvosok Lapja [*A publication*]
**Orv Lapja**... Orvosok Lapja [*A publication*]
**Orvostort Kozl**... Orvostorteneti Koezlemeneyek. Communicationes de Historia Artis Medicinae [*A publication*]
**Orvostud Beszam**... Orvostudomanyi Beszamolo [*A publication*]
**Orv Sz**........ Orvosi Szemle [*A publication*]
**Orv Szle**...... Orvosi Szemle [*A publication*]
**Orv Tech**.... Orvos es Technika [*A publication*]
**ORW**.......... Norwich, CT [*Location identifier*] [*FAA*] (FAAL)
**ORW**.......... Orwell Resources Ltd. [*Vancouver Stock Exchange symbol*]
**ORW**.......... Owner's Risk of Becoming Wet [*Shipping*]
**ORW**.......... Raymond Walters General and Technical College, Blue Ash, OH [*OCLC symbol*] (OCLC)
**OrWel**........ West Linn Public Library, West Linn, OR [*Library symbol*] [*Library of Congress*] (LCLS)
**OrWelH**..... West Linn High School, West Linn, OR [*Library symbol*] [*Library of Congress*] (LCLS)
**OrWi**.......... Willamina Public Library, Willamina, OR [*Library symbol*] [*Library of Congress*] (LCLS)
**ORWISE**... Otherwise (ROG)
**OrWo**......... Woodburn Public Library, Woodburn, OR [*Library symbol*] [*Library of Congress*] (LCLS)
**ORWP**....... Optical Radiation Weapon Program (AAG)
**ORX**.......... Oryx Energy Co. [*NYSE symbol*] (SPSG)
**ORY**.......... Paris [*France*] Orly Airport [*Airport symbol*] (OAG)
**Oryx**.......... Oryx Journal. Fauna Preservation Society [*A publication*]
**Oryx J Fauna Preserv Soc**... Oryx Journal. Fauna Preservation Society [*A publication*]
**Oryx Sci Bibliogr**... Oryx Science Bibliographies [*A publication*]
**Oryza J Assoc Rice Res Work**... Oryza. Journal of the Association of Rice Research Workers [*A publication*]
**ORZ**.......... Omnirange Zone
**ORZ**.......... Orange Walk [*Belize*] [*Airport symbol*] [*Obsolete*] (OAG)
**ORZ**.......... Outer Radiation Zone

**ORZIM** ..... Otkrytija Russkich Zemleprochodcev i Poljarnych Morechodov XVII Veka na Severovostoke Azii [*A publication*]
**OS** ..... Austrian Airlines [*ICAO designator*] (FAAC)
**OS** ..... Obese Strain [*White leghorn*]
**OS** ..... Object-Subject [*Education of the hearing-impaired*]
**OS** ..... Observation-Scouting Plane [*When first two letters in Navy designation*]
**OS** ..... Observing Station [*Marine science*] (MSC)
**OS** ..... Ocean Station [*Maps and charts*]
**OS** ..... Oceanic Society (EA)
**OS** ..... Octavian Society (EA)
**OS** ..... Oculus Sinister [*Left Eye*] [*Ophthalmology*]
**OS** ..... Odd Symmetric
**OS** ..... Oekumenische Studien [*A publication*]
**OS** ..... Off Screen [*or Stage*]
**OS** ..... Office of the Secretary
**OS** ..... Office System
**OS** ..... Office of Systems [*NASA*] (KSC)
**OS** ..... Officers' Steward [*Ranking title*] [*British Women's Royal Naval Service*]
**OS** ..... Official Station
**OS** ..... Ohio State Reports [*A publication*] (DLA)
**OS** ..... Oil Solenoid
**OS** ..... Oil Switch
**OS** ..... Old Saxon [*Language, etc.*]
**OS** ..... Old School
**OS** ..... Old Series
**OS** ..... Old Side
**OS** ..... Old Standard [*Currency*] (ROG)
**OS** ..... Old Style [*Calendar, previous to 1752*]
**OS** ..... Omega Society (EA)
**OS** ..... Omnibus Society [*British*]
**OS** ..... On-Orbit Station [*NASA*] (MCD)
**OS** ..... On Sale
**OS** ..... On Sample
**OS** ..... On Schedule
**O/S** ..... On Sea [*In place names*] [*British*] (ROG)
**OS** ..... On Side
**OS** ..... On Spot (ROG)
**OS** ..... On Station [*Military*]
**OS** ..... On Switch
**OS** ..... One Shot
**OS** ..... One Side
**OS** ..... One-Stop [*Aviation*]
**OS** ..... Only Son
**OS** ..... Opening Snaps [*Cardiology*]
**OS** ..... Operating Schedule [*Field stations*] (MCD)
**OS** ..... Operating Software (MCD)
**OS** ..... Operating System [*Data processing*] (BUR)
**OS** ..... Operation Sandstone [*Atomic weapons testing*]
**OS** ..... Operation Smile (EA)
**OS** ..... Operation Snapper [*Atomic weapons testing*]
**OS** ..... Operation Suburbia (EA)
**O & S** ..... Operation and Support Funds [*DoD*] (RDA)
**O/S** ..... Operational Assist Project/Shipborne Application
**OS** ..... Operational Sequence (KSC)
**OS** ..... Operational Sheets
**OS** ..... Operational Specialist [*Navy*]
**OS** ..... Operational Supplements [*Air Force*] (MCD)
**O & S** ..... Operations and Support (MCD)
**OS** ..... Operator's Set
**OS** ..... Optical Scanning [*Data processing*]
**O & S** ..... Optics and Sensors Program
**OS** ..... Optics Subsystem (NASA)
**OS** ..... Option Spreading [*Investment term*]
**OS** ..... Oral Surgery
**OS** ..... Oral Suspension [*Pharmacy*]
**OS** ..... Orbiter CEI [*Contract End Item*] Specification [*NASA*] (NASA)
**OS** ..... Order of Servites
**OS** ..... Order Sheet
**OS** ..... Ordinary Seaman [*British*]
**OS** ..... Ordnance School [*Army*] (MCD)
**OS** ..... Ordnance Services [*Military*] [*British*]
**OS** ..... Ordnance Specifications [*Navy*]
**OS** ..... Ordnance Survey
**OS** ..... Oregon Steel Mills [*NYSE symbol*] (SPSG)
**OS** ..... Organizational Source [*Online database field identifier*] [*Data processing*]
**OS** ..... Orient Syrien [*A publication*]
**OS** ..... Orientalia Suecana [*Uppsala*] [*A publication*]
**OS** ..... Original Series
**OS** ..... Oro Sellado [*Standard Gold*] [*Business term*] [*Spanish*]
**O/S** ..... Orthopaedic Surgery [*Medical Officer designation*] [*British*]
**OS** ..... Orton Society [*Later, ODS*] (EA)
**OS** ..... Osgood-Schlatter's Disease [*Medicine*]
**Os** ..... Osiris [*A publication*]
**Os** ..... Osmium [*Chemical element*]
**OS** ..... Osmotic Shock
**OS** ..... Osteogenic Sarcoma [*Medicine*]
**OS** ..... Osteosarcoma [*Oncology*]
**OS** ..... Ostkirchliche Studien [*A publication*]
**Os** ..... Osvit [*A publication*]
**OS** ..... Other Side [*A publication*]
**OS** ..... Other Sources
**OS** ..... Otherwise Specified (MSA)
**OS** ..... Oudtestamentische Studien [*Leiden*] [*A publication*]
**O/S** ..... Out of Service (AFM)
**O/S** ..... Out-of-Shot [*Photography*]
**OS** ..... Out Stealing [*Baseball*]
**OS** ..... Out of Stock
**OS** ..... Outer Sheath [*Botany*]
**OS** ..... Outlaw Shark [*RADAR surveillance*] [*Naval Electronic Systems Command*]
**OS** ..... Outline Square Condition [*Vision*]
**OS** ..... Output Secondary [*Electronics*]
**OS** ..... Outside
**OS** ..... Outside Sentinel
**OS** ..... Outsize [*Of clothes*]
**O/S** ..... Outstanding
**OS** ..... Outstation (MCD)
**OS** ..... Over-the-Horizon Targeting System (MCD)
**O & S** ..... Over and Short Account [*Business term*]
**OS** ..... Over the State [*Regarding distribution*]
**OS** ..... Overlong Sentence [*Used in correcting manuscripts, etc.*]
**OS** ..... Overscene [*Films, television, etc.*]
**OS** ..... Oversea [*Military*]
**O/S** ..... Overshipped (MCD)
**OS** ..... Oversize (AAG)
**OS** ..... Overspecificity [*Psychometrics*]
**OS** ..... Own Ship [*Navy*] (CAAL)
**OS** ..... Sarnia Public Library, Ontario [*Library symbol*] [*National Library of Canada*] (NLC)
**OS** ..... Shell Development Co. [*Research code symbol*]
**OS** ..... Test Oscilloscope [*JETDS nomenclature*] [*Military*] (CET)
**OS** ..... Warder Public Library of Springfield and Clark County, Springfield, OH [*Library symbol*] [*Library of Congress*] (LCLS)
**6OS** ..... Somali [*Aircraft nationality and registration mark*] (FAAC)
**OSA** ..... Obstructive Sleep Apnea [*Medicine*]
**OSA** ..... Occupational Safety Aid
**OSA** ..... Office of Savings Associations [*Formerly, FHLIC*]
**OSA** ..... Office of the Secretary of the Army
**OSA** ..... Office of Special Activities (CINC)
**OSA** ..... Office of the Special Assistant to the Ambassador
**OSA** ..... Official Secrets Act [*British*]
**OSA** ..... Offshore Acquisition [*Army*] (AABC)
**OSA** ..... Oklahoma Statutes Annotated [*A publication*] (DLA)
**OSA** ..... Old South Arabic (BJA)
**OSA** ..... Old Style Antique [*British*]
**OSA** ..... Omnibus Society of America (EA)
**OSA** ..... Ontwikkelingsvereniging van Suider-Afrika [*Development Society of Southern Africa*] (EAIO)
**OSA** ..... Open Systems Architecture [*Data processing*]
**OSA** ..... Operation Sciences Appliquees [*Quebec*]
**OSA** ..... Operational Support Aircraft [*or Airlift*]
**OSA** ..... Operational Support Area (NASA)
**OSA** ..... Optical Society of America (EA)
**OSA** ..... Optimization by Simulated Annealing [*Mathematics*]
**OSA** ..... Order of St. Anne [*Anglican religious community*]
**OSA** ..... Order of St. Augustine [*See also OFSA*] [*Rome, Italy*] (EAIO)
**OSA** ..... Order for Simple Alert (NATG)
**osa** ..... Osage [*MARC language code*] [*Library of Congress*] (LCCP)
**OSA** ..... Osaka [*Japan*] [*Seismograph station code, US Geological Survey*] (SEIS)
**OSA** ..... Osaka [*Japan*] [*Airport symbol*] (OAG)
**OSA** ..... Ossa Resources, Inc. [*Vancouver Stock Exchange symbol*]
**OSA** ..... Outfit Supply Activity (MCD)
**OSA** ..... Overseas Supply Agency [*Military*]
**O$A** ..... Overspenders Anonymous (EA)
**OSa** ..... Sabina Public Library, Sabina, OH [*Library symbol*] [*Library of Congress*] (LCLS)
**OSA (ABCMR)** ... Office, Secretary of the Army (Army Board for Correction of Military Records)
**OSAC** ..... Orifice Spark Advance Control [*Valve*] [*Automotive technology*]
**OSAC** ..... Overseas Schools Advisory Council [*Department of State*] [*Washington, DC*] (EGAO)
**OSAC** ..... Overseas Security Advisory Council [*Department of State*] [*Washington, DC*] (EGAO)
**OSA Coop Ext Univ Calif** ... One-Sheet Answers. Cooperative Extension. University of California [*A publication*]
**OS/AEL** ..... Operating Space/Allowance Equipage List
**OSAF** ..... Office of the Secretary of the Air Force
**OSAH** ..... Health Sciences Library, Sudbury Algoma Hospital, Sudbury, Ontario [*Library symbol*] [*National Library of Canada*] (NLC)
**OSAHQ** ..... Ohio State Archaeological and Historical Quarterly [*A publication*]
**OSAHRC** .. Occupational Safety and Health Review Commission [*Department of Labor*]

**OSAI**.......... Office of Systems Analysis and Information [*Department of Transportation*]
**Osaka City Med J** ... Osaka City Medical Journal [*A publication*]
**Osaka City U Econ R** ... Osaka City University. Economic Review [*A publication*]
**Osaka Econ Pap** ... Osaka Economic Papers [*A publication*]
**Osaka J Mat** ... Osaka Journal of Mathematics [*A publication*]
**Osaka J Math** ... Osaka Journal of Mathematics [*A publication*]
**Osaka Mus Nat Hist Bull** ... Osaka Museum of Natural History. Bulletin [*A publication*]
**Osaka Pref Bull** ... Osaka Prefecture. University. Bulletin [*A publication*] (DLA)
**Osaka Prefect Univ Bull Ser A Eng Nat Sci** ... Osaka Prefecture. University. Bulletin. Series A. Engineering and Natural Sciences [*A publication*]
**Osaka ULR** ... Osaka University. Law Review [*A publication*] (DLA)
**Osaka UL Rev** ... Osaka University. Law Review [*A publication*] (DLA)
**Osaka Univ J Geosci** ... Osaka University. Journal of Geosciences [*A publication*]
**Osaka Univ L Rev** ... Osaka University. Law Review [*Osaka, Japan*] [*A publication*] (DLA)
**OSAL**......... Opening of Salivary [*Gland*]
**OSal**.......... Salem Public Library, Salem, OH [*Library symbol*] [*Library of Congress*] (LCLS)
**OSALC**...... Savant Lake Community Library, Ontario [*Library symbol*] [*National Library of Canada*] (NLC)
**OSalK**........ Kent State University, Columbiana Regional Campus, Salem, OH [*Library symbol*] [*Library of Congress*] (LCLS)
**OSALSAA** ... Office, Special Assistant for Logistical Support of Army Aircraft (AABC)
**OSALSTC** ... Office, Special Assistant for Logistical Support of Tactical Communications (AABC)
**OSAM**....... Overflow Sequential Access Method [*Data processing*]
**OSAMM** ... Optimum Supply and Maintenance Model [*Army*] (RDA)
**OSAMS**..... Synod Office, Diocese of Moosonee, Anglican Church of Canada, Schumacher, Ontario [*Library symbol*] [*National Library of Canada*] (NLC)
**OSand**........ Sandusky Library Association, Sandusky, OH [*Library symbol*] [*Library of Congress*] (LCLS)
**OSAP**......... Aleppo/Neirab [*Syria*] [*ICAO location identifier*] (ICLI)
**OSAP**......... Ocean Surveillance Air Patrol (CINC)
**OSAP**......... Ocean Survey Advisory Panel [*Marine science*] (MSC)
**OSAP**......... Office Space Allocation Plan (MCD)
**OSAPI**....... Operating System/Application Program Interface [*Data processing*]
**OSAR**........ Optical Storage and Retrieval [*Data processing*]
**OSarS**........ Southern State Community College, Sardinia, OH [*Library symbol*] [*Library of Congress*] (LCLS)
**OSART**...... Operational Safety Review Team [*International Atomic Energy Agency*]
**OSAS**......... Open Systems Accounting Software [*Data processing*]
**OSAS**......... Overseas Service Aid Scheme
**OSASF**...... Overseas Supply Agency, San Francisco [*Military*] (CINC)
**OSASN**...... Office of Special Assistant, Secretary of the Navy
**OSAT**........ Office of the Special Assistant for Training [*Army*] (RDA)
**OSAT**........ Optical Sensor and Tracker
**OSATA**...... Order of Saint Andrew the Apostle (EA)
**OSAWA8**.. Anzeiger. Oesterreichische Akademie der Wissenschaften. Mathematisch-Naturwissenschaftliche Klasse [*A publication*]
**Osawatom**.. Osawatomie [*A publication*]
**OSB**........... Ocean Sciences Board [*NASA*] (MSC)
**OSB**........... Office of Savings Bonds [*Navy*]
**OSB**........... Officer Selection Battery [*Military*]
**OSB**........... Officer Selection Board
**OSB**........... Operational Status BIT [*Binary Digit*]
**OSB**........... Operations Stations Book [*Navy*]
**OSB**........... Operations Support Building [*NASA*] (KSC)
**OSB**........... Operative Society of Bricklayers [*A union*] [*British*]
**OSB**........... Orangeburg [*South Carolina*] [*Seismograph station code, US Geological Survey*] (SEIS)
**OSB**........... Order of Shepherds of Bethlehem (EA)
**OSB**........... Order of the Stars and Bars [*Later, MOSB*] (EA)
**OSB**........... Ordinis Sancti Bernardi [*Order of St. Bernard*] [*Latin*] (ROG)
**OSB**........... Ordnance Supply Bulletin
**OSB**........... Ordo Sancti Benedicti [*Order of St. Benedict*] [*Benedictines*] [*Roman Catholic religious order*]
**OSB**........... Ordo Sancti Benedicti [*Order of St. Benedict*] [*Anglican religious community*]
**OSB**........... Oriented-Strand Board [*A plywood panel composition*]
**OSB**........... Osage Beach [*Missouri*] [*Airport symbol*] [*Obsolete*] (OAG)
**OSB**........... Sauble Beach Branch, Bruce County Public Library, Ontario [*Library symbol*] [*National Library of Canada*] (NLC)
**OSBA**........ Outlet and Switch Box Association [*Defunct*] (EA)
**OSBA Bull** ... Ohio State Bar Association. Bulletin [*A publication*] (DLA)
**OSBF**......... Damascus [*Syria*] [*ICAO location identifier*] (ICLI)
**OSBIE9**..... Oryx Science Bibliographies [*A publication*]
**OSBK**......... Orange Savings Bank [*NASDAQ symbol*] (NQ)
**OSBL**......... Outside Battery Limits [*Chemical engineering*]
**OSBM**....... Morrison Library Outpost, Severn Bridge, Ontario [*Library symbol*] [*National Library of Canada*] (NLC)
**OSBM**....... Office of Space Biology and Medicine [*Proposed for NASA*]
**OSBM**....... Ordo Sancti Basil Magni [*Order of St. Basil the Great*] [*Roman Catholic religious order*]
**OSBN**........ Osborn Communications Corp. [*NASDAQ symbol*] (NQ)
**OSBR**......... Seeley's Bay Branch, Rideau Lakes Union Library, Ontario [*Library symbol*] [*National Library of Canada*] (BIB)
**OSBRD**...... Office of Small Business Research and Development [*National Science Foundation*] (GRD)
**OSBS**......... Oblate Sisters of the Blessed Sacrament [*Roman Catholic religious order*]
**OSBT**......... Officer Selection Battery Test [*Military*]
**OSBW**....... Olympic Savings Bank [*NASDAQ symbol*] (NQ)
**OSC**........... Canonici Regulares Ordinis Sanctae Crucis [*Canons Regular of the Order of the Holy Cross*] [*Crosier Fathers*] [*Roman Catholic religious order*]
**OSC**........... Clan Grant No. 17, Order of Scottish Clans (EA)
**OSC**........... Clark County Technical Institute, Springfield, OH [*Library symbol*] [*Library of Congress*] (LCLS)
**OSC**........... Complete Operational Software [*Telecommunications*] (TEL)
**OSC**........... Obedience Stewards Club (EA)
**OSC**........... Oblate Spherical Coordinates
**OSC**........... Oblati Sancti Caroli [*Oblate Fathers of St. Charles*] [*Roman Catholic religious order*]
**OSC**........... Occupational Superannuation Commissioner [*Australia*]
**OSC**........... Ocean Science Committee [*National Academy of Sciences/Ocean Affairs Board*] (NOAA)
**OSC**........... Ocean Sciences Center [*Memorial University of Newfoundland*] [*Canada*]
**OSC**........... Office of Special Counsel [*Federal agency*]
**OSC**........... Officer Specialty Code [*Army*] (INF)
**OSC**........... Offshore Survival Centre [*Robert Gordon's Institute of Technology*] [*British*] (CB)
**OSC**........... Ogden [*Utah*] Service Center [*IRS*]
**O-SC**.......... Ohio Supreme Court, Columbus, OH [*Library symbol*] [*Library of Congress*] (LCLS)
**OSC**........... On-Scene Commander [*Navy*] (NVT)
**OSC**........... One Shoe Crew [*An association*] (EA)
**OSC**........... Operational Simulator Console
**OSC**........... Operational Summary Console
**OSC**........... Operational Support Center (NRCH)
**OSC**........... Operational Switching Cabinet
**OSC**........... Operations Sequence Chart (MCD)
**OSC**........... Operator Services Complex [*Telecommunications*] (TEL)
**OSC**........... Optical Sciences Center [*University of Arizona*] [*Research center*] (RCD)
**OSC**........... Optical Signature Code
**OSC**........... Orangeburg [*South Carolina*] [*Seismograph station code, US Geological Survey*] [*Closed*] (SEIS)
**OSC**........... Orbit Shift Coil
**OSC**........... Order of St. Clare [*Roman Catholic women's religious order*]
**OSC**........... Order to Show Cause
**OSC**........... Ordnance Store Corps [*British military*] (DMA)
**OSC**........... Ordnance Systems Command [*Formerly, Bureau of Naval Weapons; later, Naval Sea Systems Command*]
**OSC**........... Oregon State College [*Later, OSU*]
**OSC**........... Organizational Structure Code [*Air Force*] (AFIT)
**OSC**........... Organizational Supply Code [*Army*] (AABC)
**OSC**........... Oscillate [*or Oscillation, Oscillator, Oscillograph, Oscilloscope*] (KSC)
**OSC**........... Oscoda, MI [*Location identifier*] [*FAA*] (FAAL)
**OSC**........... Osmotically Sensitive Cell
**OSC**........... Out, See Copy [*Proofreader's note*]
**OSC**........... Out of Stock, Canceled [*Business term*]
**OSC**........... Outer Space Contact
**OSC**........... Overlap Slotted Container [*Packaging*]
**OSC**........... Overlapping Spreading Centers [*Geology*]
**OSC**........... Overseas Settlement Committee [*British*] [*World War I*]
**OSC**........... Overseas Staff College [*British*]
**OSC**........... Overseas Student Charge [*Australia*]
**OSC**........... Overseas Supply Committee [*World War II*]
**OSC**........... Own Ship's Course [*Navy*]
**OSC**........... Oxidatively Solubilized Coal [*Fuel technology*]
**OSC**........... Oxygenated Sterol Compound [*Biochemistry*]
**OSC**........... Royal Clan, Order of Scottish Clans [*Later, Independent Order of Foresters*] (EA)
**OSC**........... Scugog Public Library, Ontario [*Library symbol*] [*National Library of Canada*] (NLC)
**OSC**........... Southern State Community College, Wilmington, OH [*OCLC symbol*] (OCLC)
**OSCA**........ Office of Saver and Consumer Affairs [*Federal Reserve Board*]
**OSCAA**...... Oil Spill Control Association of America [*Later, SCAA*] (EA)
**OS Cam**..... Order of St. Camillus [*Camillians*] [*Roman Catholic religious order*]
**OSCAND**.. Old Scandinavian [*Language, etc.*]
**OSCAP**...... Operating System Communication Application Program [*Data processing*]
**OSCAR**...... Observation Schedule and Records
**OSCAR**...... On-Site Computer Assisted Research [*Oscar, Inc.*] [*Information service or system*] (IID)
**OSCAR**...... Operating Sequence Control Array [*NASA*]
**OSCAR**...... Operations, Scheduling, Control, and Reporting (MCD)

**OSCAR**...... Optical Submarine Communications by Aerospace Relay
**OSCAR**...... Optically Scanned Character Automatic Reader [*Data processing*] (DIT)
**OSCAR**...... Optimum Survival Containment and Recovery (AAG)
**OSCAR**...... Optimum System for the Control of Aircraft Retardation
**OSCAR**...... Optimum Systems Covariance Analysis Results (IEEE)
**OSCAR**...... Orbiting Satellite Carrying Amateur Radio [*Telecommunications*] (TEL)
**OSCAR**...... Order Status Control and Reporting [*Telecommunications*] (TEL)
**OSCAR**...... Oregon State Conversational Aid to Research [*Data processing*] (CSR)
**OSCAR**...... Organisation for Sickle Cell Anemia Research [*British*]
**OSCAR**...... Organization for Scientific Coordination in AIDS [*Acquired Immune Deficiency Syndrome*] Research, Inc. [*New York, NY*]
**OSCARS** ... Order Status Control and Reporting System [*Telecommunications*]
**OSCB**......... College Bibliocentre, Scarborough, Ontario [*Library symbol*] [*National Library of Canada*] (BIB)
**OSCCB**...... On-Site Change Control Board [*Military*] (CAAL)
**OSCCJA**.... Casimir, Jennings, and Appleby Public Library, St. Charles, Ontario [*Library symbol*] [*National Library of Canada*] (NLC)
**OSCD**........ Ohio Supreme Court Decisions, Unreported Cases [*A publication*] (DLA)
**OSCD**........ Ontario Securities Commission Decisions [*QL Systems Ltd.*] [*Information service or system*] [*Canada*] (CRD)
**OSCE**......... Office Statistique des Communautes Europeennes [*Statistical Office of the European Communities - EUROSTAT*] [*Commission of the European Communities*]
**OSCF**......... Operations Support Computing Facility (MCD)
**OSCG**........ Information Resource Centre, Consumers Gas, Scarborough, Ontario [*Library symbol*] [*National Library of Canada*] (NLC)
**OSCG**........ Oscillating
**OSCG**........ Oscillograph, String
**OSCGRM** ... Oscillogram [*Engineering*]
**OSCH**........ Schreiber Public Library, Ontario [*Library symbol*] [*National Library of Canada*] (NLC)
**OSCILAB** ... Ocean Science Laboratory [*Oceanography*]
**OSCL**......... Own Ship's Centerline [*Navy*]
**O & SCMIS** ... Operating and Support Costs Management Information System
**OSCMIS** ... Operating and Support Costs Management Information System (MCD)
**OSC-MULT** ... Oscillator-Multiplier [*Telecommunications*] (TEL)
**OSCOM**.... Oslo Commission [*London, England*] (EAIO)
**OSCP**......... Ocean Sediment Coring Program [*National Science Foundation*]
**OSCP**......... Oscilloscope (AAG)
**OSCP**......... Oscilloscope Panel
**OS & CP Dec** ... Ohio Superior and Common Pleas Decisions [*A publication*] (DLA)
**OSCPS**...... Oxygen Supply and Cabin Pressurization Section [*Apollo*] [*NASA*]
**OSCR**......... Ocean Surface Current RADAR
**OSCRL**...... Operating System Command and Response Language
**OSCRN** ..... Oil Screen
**OSCUT**...... Oil Spill Clean-Up Technology (ASF)
**Os Cy Med J** ... Osaka City Medical Journal [*A publication*]
**OSD**........... Dow Chemical Co., Sarnia, Ontario [*Library symbol*] [*National Library of Canada*] (NLC)
**OSD**........... Office of the Secretary of Defense
**OSD**........... Office of Standards Development [*Abolished*] [*Nuclear Regulatory Commission*]
**OSD**........... Office of Student Detachment [*Navy*]
**OSD**........... Office of Systems Development [*Social Security Administration*]
**OSD**........... Officer Service Date [*Air Force*] (AFM)
**OSD**........... Officers Service Dress [*British military*] (DMA)
**OSD**........... Online System Drivers [*NCR Corp.*]
**OSD**........... Open Shelter Deck [*Shipping*] (DS)
**OSD**........... Operational Sea Vehicle Diagram (MCD)
**OSD**........... Operational Sequence Diagram (IEEE)
**OSD**........... Operational Support Directive [*Military*] (AFM)
**OSD**........... Operational Systems Development (MCD)
**OSD**........... Optical Scanning Device [*Data processing*]
**OSD**........... Ordinis Sancti Dominici [*Order of St. Dominic*] [*Latin*] (ROG)
**OSD**........... Ordnance Store Department [*British*] (ROG)
**OSD**........... Ordnance Supply Depot
**OSD**........... OSD. Overseas Standards Digest [*A publication*] (APTA)
**OSD**........... Osgood Semantic Differential [*Occupational therapy*]
**OSD**........... Ostersund [*Sweden*] [*Airport symbol*] (OAG)
**OSD**........... Over, Short, and Damaged [*Report*] [*Shipping*] (MCD)
**OS & D** ...... Over, Short, and Damaged [*Report*] [*Shipping*] (MSA)
**OSD**........... Overseas Duty
**OSD**........... Overseas Settlement Department [*British*] [*World War I*]
**OSD**........... Overseas Standards Digest [*A publication*] (ADA)
**OSD**........... Overseas Supply Division [*Military*]
**OSD**........... Own Ship's Distance [*Navy*] (MCD)
**OSD**........... Oxygen Selective Detector [*Chromatography*]
**OS 2d**......... Ohio State Reports, Second Series [*A publication*] (DLA)
**OSDBMC** ... Office of the Secretary of Defense, Ballistic Missile Committee
**OSDBU** ..... Office of Small and Disadvantaged Business Utilization [*See also SDBU/CR*] [*Federal government*]
**OSD/CSD** ... Open Shelter Deck/Closed Shelter Deck [*Shipping*] (DS)
**OSD/DSAA** ... Office of the Secretary of Defense, Defense Security Assistance Agency (MCD)
**OSDH**........ Orbiter System Definition Handbook [*NASA*] (NASA)
**OSDI** ......... Damascus/International [*Syria*] [*ICAO location identifier*] (ICLI)
**OSDIdentBad** ... Office of the Secretary of Defense Identification Badge (AABC)
**OSD/ISA**... Office of the Secretary of Defense for International Security Affairs
**OSDIT**....... Office of Software Development and Information Technology [*General Services Administration*]
**OSDIU** ...... Over-the-Horizon Targeting System Digital Interface Unit
**OSDMT** .... Organization for the Support of Democratic Movement of Taiwan (EA)
**OSDOC** ..... Offshore Discharge of Container-Ships (RDA)
**OSDOC** ..... Over-the-Shore Discharge of Cargo [*Navy*] (CAAL)
**OS/DOS**.... Operating System/Disk Operating System [*Software*]
**OSDP** ........ On-Site Data Processing [*or Processor*] [*NASA*]
**OSDP** ........ Operational System Development Program
**OSD(PA & E)** ... Office of the Secretary of Defense for Program Analysis and Evaluation (MCD)
**OSDR** ........ Oil Slick Detection RADAR
**OS & DR**.... Over, Short, and Damaged Report [*Shipping*]
**OSD-SA** .... Office of the Secretary of Defense - Systems Analysis
**OSDSAC**... Office of the Secretary of Defense, Scientific Advisory Committee
**OSDT** ........ Damascus [*Syria*] [*ICAO location identifier*] (ICLI)
**OSDU**........ Output Signal Distribution Unit (MCD)
**OSDZ** ........ Deir Ez Zor [*Syria*] [*ICAO location identifier*] (ICLI)
**OSE** ........... Bethel, AK [*Location identifier*] [*FAA*] (FAAL)
**OSE** ........... Edwardsburg Township Public Library, Spencerville, Ontario [*Library symbol*] [*National Library of Canada*] (BIB)
**OSE** ........... Occupational Supplies and Equipment [*Red Cross*]
**OSE** ........... Oceanic Society Expeditions (EA)
**OSE** ........... Office of Systems Engineering [*Social Security Administration*]
**OSE** ........... Officer Scheduling the Exercise [*Navy*] (NVT)
**OSE** ........... Olefin Strain Energy [*Organic chemistry*]
**OSE** ........... Omniforce Spatial Environment (AAG)
**OS/E**.......... Operating System/Environment [*Data processing*] (BYTE)
**OSE** ........... Operation Status Equipment
**OSE** ........... Operational Security Evaluation (MCD)
**OSE** ........... Operational Support Equipment
**OSE** ........... Orbiter Support Equipment [*NASA*] (NASA)
**OSE** ........... Order of the Star in the East [*A theosophical organization*]
**OSE** ........... Osaka Stock Exchange [*Japan*]
**OSE** ........... Osec Petroleum [*Vancouver Stock Exchange symbol*]
**OSE** ........... Oslo Studies in English [*A publication*]
**OSE** ........... Overseas Security Eligibility [*DoD*]
**OSE** ........... Salem Public Library, Salem, OR [*OCLC symbol*] (OCLC)
**OSE** ........... Union Mondiale pour la Protection de la Sante des Populations Juives et Oeuvres de Secours aux Enfants
**OSEAP**...... Oil Shale Environmental Advisory Panel [*Department of the Interior*]
**O/SEAS** .... Overseas
**OSEBE3**.... Oxford Surveys in Evolutionary Biology [*A publication*]
**OSEC**......... Office of the Secretary
**OSECCA**... Old Sleepy Eye Collectors' Club of America (EA)
**OSECY**...... Office of the Secretary to the Staff [*NATO*] (NATG)
**OSEDS**...... Operational Support Equipment Design Specification
**OSEE**......... Optically Stimulated Electron Emission [*Also, PEE*] [*Physics*]
**O/SEER** .... Overseer
**OSEH** ........ Order of St. Elizabeth of Hungary [*Anglican religious community*]
**OSEM** ....... Office of Systems Engineering Management [*Department of Transportation*]
**OSEND** ..... Ocean Science and Engineering [*A publication*]
**OSEOS**...... Operational Synchronous Earth Observatory Satellite [*Telecommunications*] (TEL)
**OSEP**......... Office of Scientific and Engineering Personnel [*National Academy of Sciences*] [*Information service or system*] (IID)
**OSEP**......... Office of Special Education Programs [*Also, SEP*] [*Department of Education*]
**OsEP**.......... Osaka Economic Papers [*A publication*]
**OSEQD** ..... Oldelft Scientific Engineering Quarterly [*A publication*]
**OSERS** ...... Office of Special Education and Rehabilitative Services [*Department of Education*]
**OSES**......... Operations Systems Engineering Support (MCD)
**OSESG**...... Oil Sands Environmental Study Group [*Canada*]
**OSF**........... Obtain Service From [*Navy*] (NVT)
**OSF**........... Odd Side Flat
**OSF**........... Office of Space Flight [*NASA*] [*Washington, DC*] (NASA)
**OSF**........... Open Software Foundation
**OSF**........... Orbit Science Fiction [*A publication*]

**OSF**........... Order of St. Francis [*Franciscans*] [*Roman Catholic religious order*]
**OSF**........... Ordnance Storage Facility (KSC)
**OSF**........... Organ System Failure [*Medicine*]
**OSF**........... Osaka Stock Futures [*Japan*] (ECON)
**OSF**........... Out of Stock, To Follow [*Business term*]
**OSF**........... Outer Spiral Fibers [*Ear anatomy*]
**OSF**........... Overgrowth Stimulating Factor [*Cancer cause*]
**OSFA**........ Offshore Shrimp Fisheries Act of 1973
**OSFAR**...... Sturgeon Falls Branch of the Algonquin Regional Library System, Ontario [*Library symbol*] [*National Library of Canada*] (NLC)
**OSFC**......... Fiberglas Canada, Inc., Sarnia, Ontario [*Library symbol*] [*National Library of Canada*] (NLC)
**OSFC**......... Ordinis Sancti Francisci Capuccini [*Franciscan Capuchins*] [*Roman Catholic men's religious order*]
**OSFCSR**.... Rideau Regional Centre, Ministry of Community and Social Services, Smiths Falls, Ontario [*Library symbol*] [*National Library of Canada*] (NLC)
**OSFCW**..... Office of Solid Fuels Coordinator for War [*World War II*]
**OSFD**......... Office of Space Flight Development [*Obsolete*] [*NASA*]
**OSFI**.......... Office of the Superintendent of Financial Institutions [*Department of Insurance*] [*Ottawa, ON*] [*Information service or system*] (IID)
**OSFI**.......... Open Steel Flooring Institute [*Defunct*]
**OSFM**........ Office of Spacecraft and Flight Missions [*NASA*]
**OS & FM**... Office of Systems and Financial Management [*DoD*]
**OSFMA**..... Optika i Spektroskopiya. Akademiya Nauk SSSR. Otdelenie Fiziko-Matematicheskikh Nauk [*A publication*]
**OSFP**......... Office of Space Flight Programs [*Obsolete*] [*NASA*]
**OSFS**......... Oblati Sancti Francisci Salesii [*Oblate Fathers or Sisters of St. Francis of Sales*] [*Roman Catholic religious orders*]
**OSFS**......... Original Science Fiction Stories [*A publication*]
**OSG**........... Occupational Superannuation Group [*Australia*]
**OSG**........... Occupations Study Group [*British*]
**OSG**........... Office of Sea Grant [*National Oceanic and Atmospheric Administration*]
**OSG**........... Office of the Secretary General [*United Nations*]
**OSG**........... Office of the Solicitor General [*Department of Justice*]
**OSG**........... Office of the Surgeon General [*of Public Health Service; later, absorbed by office of Assistant Secretary for Health and Scientific Affairs*]
**OSG**........... Operand Select Gate [*Data processing*]
**OSG**........... Operations Support Group [*Nuclear energy*] (NRCH)
**OSG**........... Organization and Staffing Guide [*Department of Labor*] (OICC)
**OSG**........... Osphradial Ganglion [*In mollusks*]
**OSG**........... Otosclerosis Study Group (EA)
**OSG**........... Overseas Shipholding Group, Inc. [*NYSE symbol*] (SPSG)
**OSG**........... South Gillies Library, Ontario [*Library symbol*] [*National Library of Canada*] (BIB)
**OSGB**........ Orchid Society of Great Britain (EAIO)
**OSGD**........ Office of Sea Grant Development [*National Oceanic and Atmospheric Administration*] (MSC)
**OSGI**......... Otra Securities Group, Inc. [*NASDAQ symbol*] (NQ)
**OSGLI**....... Office of Servicemen's Group Life Insurance
**Osgoode Hall L J**... Osgoode Hall. Law Journal [*A publication*]
**Osgoode Hall LSJ**... Osgoode Hall Law School. Journal [*A publication*]
**OSGP**......... Office of Sea Grant Programs [*National Oceanic and Atmospheric Administration*]
**OSGS**......... Office of the Secretary of the General Staff
**OSGS**......... Stittsville Branch, Goulbourn Township Public Library, Ontario [*Library symbol*] [*National Library of Canada*] (NLC)
**OSH**........... Community Hospital of Springfield, Springfield, OH [*Library symbol*] [*Library of Congress*] (LCLS)
**OSH**........... National Institute for Occupational Safety and Health, Cincinnati, OH [*OCLC symbol*] (OCLC)
**OSH**........... Occupational Safety and Health [*Department of Labor*]
**OSH**........... Office on Smoking and Health Database [*Centers for Disease Control*] [*Information service or system*] (CRD)
**OSH**........... Omni Singula Hora [*Every Hour*] [*Pharmacy*]
**OSH**........... Ordo Sancti Hieronymi [*Hieronymites*]
**OSH**........... Oshawa Group Ltd. [*Toronto Stock Exchange symbol*]
**OSH**........... Oshima [*Japan*] [*Seismograph station code, US Geological Survey*] (SEIS)
**OSH**........... Oshkosh [*Wisconsin*] [*Airport symbol*] (OAG)
**OSH**........... Own Ship's Heading [*Navy*]
**OSh**........... Shaker Heights Public Library, Shaker Heights, OH [*Library symbol*] [*Library of Congress*] (LCLS)
**OSH**........... Shelburne Public Library, Ontario [*Library symbol*] [*National Library of Canada*] (NLC)
**OSHA**........ Occupational Safety and Health Act [*1970*]
**OSHA**........ Occupational Safety and Health Administration [*Department of Labor*] [*Washington, DC*]
**OSHA**........ Office of Special Housing Assistance [*HUD*]
**O & S HA**.. Operating and Support Hazard Analysis
**OSHA Compl Guide CCH**... OSHA [*Occupational Safety and Health Administration*] Compliance Guide. Commerce Clearing House [*A publication*]
**Os Hall LJ**... Osgoode Hall. Law Journal [*A publication*]
**OSHB**........ One-Sided Height Balanced [*Telecommunications*]
**OSHB**........ Sheshegwaning Band Public Library, Ontario [*Library symbol*] [*National Library of Canada*] (NLC)
**OSH Cas**.... Occupational Safety and Health Cases [*A publication*] (DLA)
**OSH Cas BNA**... Occupational Safety and Health Cases. Bureau of National Affairs [*A publication*]
**OSHD**........ Occupational Safety and Health Decisions [*A publication*] (DLA)
**OSH Dec**... Occupational Safety and Health Decisions [*A publication*] (DLA)
**OSH Dec CCH**... Occupational Safety and Health Decisions. Commerce Clearing House [*A publication*]
**OShelS**....... Sacred Heart Seminary, Shelby, OH [*Library symbol*] [*Library of Congress*] (LCLS)
**OSHI**......... Occupational, Safety, and Health Institute [*University of Houston*] [*Research center*] (RCD)
**OSHJ**......... Oblate Sisters of the Sacred Heart of Jesus [*Roman Catholic religious order*]
**OSHM**....... Oshmans Sporting Goods, Inc. [*NASDAQ symbol*] (NQ)
**OSHR**........ Occupational Safety and Health Reporter [*A publication*]
**OSHRC**..... Occupational Safety and Health Review Commission [*Department of Labor*]
**OSH Rep (BNA)**... Occupational Safety and Health Reporter (Bureau of National Affairs) [*A publication*]
**OSHS**......... OSHAP Technologies Ltd. [*Herentalsbaan 55, Belgium*] [*NASDAQ symbol*] (NQ)
**OShS**......... Shaker Heights City School District, Shaker Heights, OH [*Library symbol*] [*Library of Congress*] (LCLS)
**OSHT**......... Grand Lodge Order of the Sons of Hermann in Texas [*San Antonio, TX*] (EA)
**OSHT**......... Sharon Temple, Sharon, Ontario [*Library symbol*] [*National Library of Canada*] (NLC)
**OSI**............ National Institute for Occupational Safety and Health, Rockville, MD [*OCLC symbol*] (OCLC)
**OSI**............ Office of Samoa Information [*Press agency*]
**OSI**............ Office of Scientific Information [*National Science Foundation*] (MCD)
**OSI**............ Office of Scientific Integrity [*National Institutes of Health*]
**OSI**............ Office of Scientific Intelligence [*Fictitious government agency on TV series "The Six Million Dollar Man"*]
**OSI**............ Office of Special Investigation [*Air Force*]
**OSI**............ Office of Strategic Information [*DoD*]
**OSI**............ Office of Systems Integration [*Social Security Administration*]
**OSI**............ Office Systems Interconnection [*Telecommunications*] (TSSD)
**OSI**............ Offshore Islands (CINC)
**OSI**............ On-Line Software International, Inc. [*NYSE symbol*] (SPSG)
**OSI**............ On-Site Inspection
**OSI**............ Open Space Institute (EA)
**OSI**............ Open Standards Interconnection [*International Standards Organisation*]
**OSI**............ Open System Interconnections [*Networking technique*]
**OSI**............ Operating Space Item [*Military*] (CAAL)
**OSI**............ Operating System Interface
**OSI**............ Operating Systems, Incorporated (MCD)
**OSI**............ Operational Status Indicator (MUGU)
**OSI**............ ORDALT [*Ordnance Alterations*]/SHIPALT [*Ship Alteration*] Inspector (MCD)
**OSI**............ Organic Sign Index [*Psychology*]
**OSI**............ Oriental Shorthairs International (EA)
**OSI**............ Osijek [*Yugoslavia*] [*Airport symbol*] (OAG)
**OSI**............ Other Support Items
**OSI**............ Out of Stock, Indefinite [*Business term*]
**OSI**............ Overhead Supply Inventory (MCD)
**OSI**............ Oyster Shell Institute (EA)
**OSI**............ Ozark Society (EA)
**OSI**............ Research Technical Information Centre, ESSO Petroleum Canada, Sarnia, Ontario [*Library symbol*] [*National Library of Canada*] (NLC)
**OSI**............ Woodside, CA [*Location identifier*] [*FAA*] (FAAL)
**OSIA**.......... Office, Services and Information Agency [*Military*] (AABC)
**OSIA**.......... On Site in Alberta [*A publication*]
**OSIA**.......... On-Site Inspection Agency [*DoD*]
**OSIA**.......... Order Sons of Italy in America (EA)
**OSIASL**..... Order Sons of Italy in America Supreme Lodge [*Later, OSIA*] (EA)
**OSIC**.......... Ocean Science Information Center [*University of Hawaii*] (NOAA)
**OSIC**.......... Oil Spill Information Center [*Santa Barbara, CA*]
**OSIC**.......... Optimization of Subcarrier Information Capacity
**OSIC**.......... Osicom Technologies, Inc. [*NASDAQ symbol*] (NQ)
**OSICS**........ Commission Scolaire de Sept-Iles, Quebec [*Library symbol*] [*National Library of Canada*] (NLC)
**OSID**......... Operational System Interface Document (MCD)
**OSIDM**..... Eva Brook Donly Museum, Simcoe, Ontario [*Library symbol*] [*National Library of Canada*] (NLC)
**OSIE**.......... Office of Software Improvement and Engineering [*Social Security Administration*]
**OSIE**.......... Operational Support Integration Engineering
**OS/IES**...... On-Site Integrated Energy System
**OSIGA**....... Ohio State Inventory of Guidance Awareness
**OSIGO**...... Office of the Chief Signal Officer

**Os Ikad Zass** ... Osaka Ikadaigaku Zasshi [*A publication*]
**OSIL** .......... Lynwood Arts Centre, Simcoe, Ontario [*Library symbol*] [*National Library of Canada*] (NLC)
**OSIL** .......... Operating System Implementation Language
**OSINH** ...... Norfolk Historical Society, Simcoe, Ontario [*Library symbol*] [*National Library of Canada*] (NLC)
**OSIP** .......... Operational and Safety Improvement Program (NVT)
**OSIP** .......... Operational Suitability Improvement Program [*Aviation*]
**OSIP** .......... Simcoe Public Library, Ontario [*Library symbol*] [*National Library of Canada*] (NLC)
**OSIPAR** .... Ospedali Italiani - Pediatria e Specialita Chirurgiche [*A publication*]
**OSIQ** ......... Offer Self-Image Questionnaire
**OSIR** .......... Office of Scientific Integrity Review [*US Secretary of Health*]
**OSIR** .......... Out of Service in Reserve [*Military*] (CINC)
**OSIS** .......... Ocean Surveillance Information System [*Navy*] (MCD)
**OSIS** .......... Office of Science Information Service [*National Science Foundation*]
**OSIX** .......... Optical Specialties, Incorporated [*Fremont, CA*] [*NASDAQ symbol*] (NQ)
**OSJ** ............ Oblates of St. Joseph [*Roman Catholic religious order*]
**OSJ** ............ Office of Supervisory Jurisdiction [*Investment term*]
**OSJ** ............ Ordnance Survey of Jerusalem [*A publication*]
**OSJ** ............ Sovereign Order of Saint John of Jerusalem (EA)
**OSJD** .......... Ordinis Sancti Joannis de Deo [*Order of St. John of God*]
**Os Josh Ikad Zass** ... Osaka Joshi Ikadaigaku Zasshi [*A publication*]
**OSK** ........... Osaka [*Takayasuyama*] [*Japan*] [*Seismograph station code, US Geological Survey*] (SEIS)
**OSK** ........... Oskarshamn [*Sweden*] [*Airport symbol*] (OAG)
**OSKAR** ...... Outstanding Superior Kitchen All-Rounder [*Trademark of Sunbeam Corp.*]
**OSKL** ......... Kamishly [*Syria*] [*ICAO location identifier*] (ICLI)
**OSKL** ......... Swastika Branch, Kirkland Lake Public Library, Ontario [*Library symbol*] [*National Library of Canada*] (BIB)
**OSKNC** ..... Skead Branch, Nickel Centre Public Library, Ontario [*Library symbol*] [*National Library of Canada*] (NLC)
**OSKR** ........ One Sky Report [*A publication*]
**OSL** ........... International Order of Saint Luke the Physician (EA)
**OSL** ........... Oil Seal
**OSL** ........... Old [*Church*] Slavonic [*Language, etc.*]
**OSL** ........... Old Style Latin (ADA)
**OSL** ........... Open/Short Locator
**OSL** ........... Operating System Language
**OSL** ........... Optical Storage Ltd.
**OSL** ........... Orbiting Space Laboratory
**OSL** ........... Order of St. Luke the Physician of America (EA)
**OSL** ........... Ordnance Sub-Lieutenant [*British military*] (DMA)
**OSL** ........... Oregon Short Line Railroad [*of Union Pacific Railroad Co.*]
**OSL** ........... Osler Resources, Inc. [*Vancouver Stock Exchange symbol*]
**OSL** ........... Oslo [*Norway*] [*Airport symbol*] (OAG)
**OSL** ........... O'Sullivan Corp. [*AMEX symbol*] (SPSG)
**OSL** ........... Outstanding Leg [*NASA*] (KSC)
**OSL** ........... Sioux Lookout Public Library, Ontario [*Library symbol*] [*National Library of Canada*] (NLC)
**OSL** ........... University of Oregon, School of Librarianship, Eugene, OR [*OCLC symbol*] (OCLC)
**OSLA** .......... Stella Branch, Lennox and Addington County Library, Ontario [*Library symbol*] [*National Library of Canada*] (NLC)
**OSLC** .......... Lambton College of Applied Arts and Technology, Sarnia, Ontaria [*Library symbol*] [*National Library of Canada*] (NLC)
**OSLEAS** .... Association Sectorielle de Fabrication d'Equipement de Transport et de Machines, St.-Leonard, Quebec [*Library symbol*] [*National Library of Canada*] (NLC)
**OSLFC** ...... Sharbot Lake Branch, Frontenac County Library, Ontario [*Library symbol*] [*National Library of Canada*] (BIB)
**OSLI** .......... Office of Servicemen's Life Insurance (OICC)
**OSLJ** ......... Law Journal. Student Bar Association. Ohio State University [*A publication*] (DLA)
**OSLK** ......... Latakia/Latakia [*Syria*] [*ICAO location identifier*] (ICLI)
**OSLM** ........ Operations Shop/Laboratory Manager [*NASA*] (MCD)
**OSLP** ......... Oxford Slavonic Papers [*A publication*]
**OSLT** ......... On-Site Logistics Team (MCD)
**OSM** .......... Office of Spectrum Management [*US National Telecommunications and Information Administration*] (TSSD)
**OSM** .......... Office of Surface Mining Reclamation and Enforcement [*Department of the Interior*]
**OSM** .......... Omnispectra Miniature
**OSM** .......... On Station Mode
**OSM** .......... Operating Service Month
**OSM** .......... Operating System Manual (MCD)
**OSM** .......... Operating System Monitor
**OSM** .......... Operator's Service Manual
**OSM** .......... Opisu Struktur Mikroprogramownych [*Programming language*] (CSR)
**OSM** .......... Optical Section Microscope
**OSM** .......... Orbital Service Module [*NASA*] (MCD)
**OSM** .......... Ordnance Safety Manual [*Military*]
**OSM** .......... Ordo Servorum Mariae [*Order of Servants of Mary*] [*Servites*] [*Roman Catholic religious order*]
**OSM** .......... Oscillating Secondary Mirror [*Telescope*]
**Osm** .......... Osmole [*Physical chemistry*]
**OSM** .......... Osmotic
**OSM** .......... Outside Mail (AFM)
**OSM** .......... Oxygen Steel Making
**OSM** .......... Schumacher Memorial Library, Ontario [*Library symbol*] [*National Library of Canada*] (BIB)
**OSMA** ....... Occidental Society of Metempiric Analysis (EA)
**OSMA** ....... Office of Small Manufacturers Assistance [*FDA*]
**OSMA** ....... Orthopedic Surgical Manufacturers Association (EA)
**OSMA** ....... Overseas Sales and Marketing Association of America [*Lake Bluff, IL*] (EA)
**Osmania J Social Sciences** ... Osmania Journal of Social Sciences [*A publication*]
**Os Math J** ... Osaka Mathematical Journal [*A publication*]
**OSMDAB** ... Osteopathic Medicine [*A publication*]
**OSME** ....... Oral Speech Mechanism Screening Examination [*Educational test*]
**OSME** ....... Ornithological Society of the Middle East (EAIO)
**OSMF** ........ Smith Falls Public Library, Ontario [*Library symbol*] [*National Library of Canada*] (NLC)
**OS/MFT** ... Operating System/Multiprogramming with a Fixed Number of Tasks [*IBM Corp.*] [*Data processing*]
**OSML** ....... McNeil Laboratories (Canada) Ltd., Stouffville, Ontario [*Library symbol*] [*National Library of Canada*] (NLC)
**OSMM** ...... Mercy Medical Center, Springfield, OH [*Library symbol*] [*Library of Congress*] (LCLS)
**OSMM** ...... Office of Safeguards and Materials Management [*AEC*]
**osmo** .......... Osmolality [*Chemistry*]
**OSMO** ........ Osmonics, Inc. [*NASDAQ symbol*] (NQ)
**OSMOS** .... Own Ship's Motion Simulator [*Navy*]
**OSMOS** .... Own Ship's Motion System [*Navy*]
**OSMP** ....... Operational Support Maintenance Plan [*NASA*] (MCD)
**OSMR** ....... Office of Systems Modernization Requirements [*Social Security Administration*]
**OSMRE** ..... Office of Surface Mining Reclamation and Enforcement [*Also, OSM*] [*Department of the Interior*]
**OSMS** ........ Organizational Supply Management System [*Army*] (INF)
**OSMU** ....... Oesterreichische Schuhmusterschau [*Austrian Footwear Exhibition*] [*Wiener Messen und Kongress GmbH*] (TSPED)
**OSMV** ....... One Shot Multivibrator (MSA)
**OS/MVS** ... Operating System/Multiprogramming with Virtual Storage [*Data processing*]
**OS/MVT** ... Operating System/Multiprogramming with a Variable Number of Tasks [*Data processing*]
**OSN** .......... Ocean Science News [*A publication*]
**OSN** .......... Office of the Secretary of the Navy
**OSN** .......... Osphradial Nerve [*In mollusks*]
**OSN** .......... Output Sequence Number
**OSN** .......... Sioux Narrows Public Library, Ontario [*Library symbol*] [*National Library of Canada*] (NLC)
**Osnabr Mitt** ... Osnabruecker Mitteilungen [*A publication*]
**Osnabrueck Mitt** ... Osnabruecker Mitteilungen [*A publication*]
**Osnabrueck Schrift Math** ... Osnabruecker Schriften zur Mathematik [*A publication*]
**OSNAP** ..... Object Snap [*Auto CAD*] [*Data processing*]
**OSNC** ........ Sarnia Northern Collegiate, Ontario [*Library symbol*] [*National Library of Canada*] (NLC)
**Osn Fundam** ... Osnovaniya i Fundamenty [*A publication*]
**Osn Fundam Mekh Gruntov** ... Osnovaniya, Fundamenty, i Mekhanika Gruntov [*USSR*] [*A publication*]
**OSNS** ........ Shedden Public Library, Spanish, Ontario [*Library symbol*] [*National Library of Canada*] (NLC)
**OSO** .......... Ocean Systems Operation [*NASA*]
**OSO** .......... Office of Systems Operations [*Social Security Administration*]
**OSO** .......... Offshore Suppliers Office [*British*]
**OSO** .......... Orbiting Satellite Observer (IEEE)
**OSO** .......... Orbiting Solar Observatory [*A satellite*]
**OSO** .......... Ordnance Supply Office
**O/S/O** ....... Ore/Slurry/Oil [*Supertanker*]
**OSO** .......... Oregon State Library, Salem, OR [*OCLC symbol*] (OCLC)
**OSO** .......... Origination Screening Office [*Telecommunications*] (TEL)
**OSO** .......... Overseas Students Office [*Australia*]
**OSO** .......... Southampton Branch, Bruce County Public Library, Ontario [*Library symbol*] [*National Library of Canada*] (NLC)
**OSOB** ........ Old Senate Office Building [*Also, RSOB*] [*Washington, DC*] (DLA)
**OSOC** ........ Off-Site Originated Change (AAG)
**OSODS** ..... Office of Strategic Offensive and Defensive Systems [*Navy*]
**OSOIPB** .... Ordnance Supply Office Illustrated Parts Breakdown [*Navy*]
**OSol** .......... Odes of Solomon (BJA)
**OSOL** ........ Office of the Solicitor [*Department of Labor*]
**OSOM** ....... Bruce County Museum, Southampton, Ontario [*Library symbol*] [*National Library of Canada*] (BIB)
**OSOP** ........ Orbiter Systems Operating Procedures [*NASA*] (NASA)
**OSOR** ........ Operational Standoff Range (NVT)
**OSoSJ** ........ Saint Joseph's Priory, Somerset, OH [*Library symbol*] [*Library of Congress*] (LCLS)
**OSOT** ........ Oakland Township Public Library, Scotland, Ontario [*Library symbol*] [*National Library of Canada*] (BIB)

**OSOTM** .... Sombra Township Museum, Ontario [*Library symbol*] [*National Library of Canada*] (BIB)
**OSP** .......... Obiit sine Prole [*Died without Issue*] [*Latin*]
**OSP** .......... Oblate Sisters of Providence [*Roman Catholic religious order*]
**OSP** .......... Ocean Survey Plan [*or Program*] [*Navy*]
**OSP** .......... Office of Science Policy [*National Science Foundation*]
**OSP** .......... Office of Scientific Personnel [*NAS-NRC*]
**OSP** .......... Office of Special Technology [*Formerly, Office of Special Projects*] [*Washington, DC*] [*Department of Energy*] (GRD)
**OSP** .......... Office of Staffing Policy [*Office of Personnel Management*] [*Washington, DC*] (GRD)
**OSP** .......... Office of Surplus Property [*Superseded by War Assets Corporation*] [*World War II*]
**OSP** .......... Offshore Procurement [*Army*]
**OSP** .......... Oficina Sanitaria Panamericana [*Pan-American Sanitary Bureau - PASB*] [*Washington, DC*]
**OSP** .......... Oil Suction Pump (MSA)
**OSP** .......... On Station Position (MUGU)
**OSP** .......... Operating Steam Pressure (MSA)
**OSP** .......... Operational Surveillance Program [*Nuclear Regulatory Commission*] (NRCH)
**OSP** .......... Operational Survival Plan [*Civil Defense*]
**OSP** .......... Operations Support Plan [*Navy*] (NG)
**OSP** .......... Optical Signature Program [*Military*] (CAAL)
**OSP** .......... Optimum Sustainable Population [*Marine science*] (MSC)
**OSP** .......... Orbital Support Plan (MCD)
**OSP** .......... Order of St. Paul [*Anglican religious community*]
**OSP** .......... Order of St. Paul the First Hermit [*Pauline Fathers*] [*Roman Catholic religious order*]
**OSP** .......... Original Set Pattern [*Ice dancing*]
**OSP** .......... Outfitting Stock Point
**OSP** .......... Outside Plant [*Telecommunications*] (TEL)
**OSP** .......... Outside Procured Stores (AAG)
**OSP** .......... Own Ship's Position [*Navy*] (MCD)
**OSP** .......... Oxford Slavonic Papers [*A publication*]
**OSP** .......... Polysar Ltd., Sarnia, Ontario [*Library symbol*] [*National Library of Canada*] (NLC)
**OSP** .......... Readi-Air [*Bradenton, FL*] [*FAA designator*] (FAAC)
**OSP** .......... Slupsk [*Poland*] [*Airport symbol*] (OAG)
**OSPA**......... Organisation Sanitaire Panamericaine
**OSPAAAL** ... Organization of Solidarity of the Peoples of Africa, Asia, and Latin America
**OSPADK**... Obshta i Sravnitelna Patologiia [*A publication*]
**OSPCS** ...... Charles M. Shields Centennial Library, South Porcupine, Ontario [*Library symbol*] [*National Library of Canada*] (BIB)
**OSPD** ........ Office of Sponsored Program Development [*State University of New York at Binghamton*] [*Research center*] (RCD)
**OSPE**......... Organizational Spare Parts and Equipment [*Army*]
**Osped Ital Chir** ... Ospedali d'Italia - Chirurgia [*A publication*]
**Osped Psichiat** ... Ospedale Psichiatrico [*A publication*]
**OSPG** ........ Original Society of Painters and Glaziers [*A union*] [*British*]
**OSPIRG** .... Oregon State Public Interest Research Group [*Research center*] (RCD)
**Osp Ital Chir** ... Ospedali d'Italia - Chirurgia [*A publication*]
**Osp Ital Pediatr (Spec Chir)** ... Ospedali Italiani Pediatria (e Specialita Chirurgiche) [*A publication*]
**OSPJ** ......... Offshore Procurement, Japan
**OSpM**........ Mental Health Services for Clark County, Springfield, OH [*Library symbol*] [*Library of Congress*] (LCLS)
**Osp Magg** ... Ospedale Maggiore [*Italy*] [*A publication*]
**Osp Magg Novara** ... Ospedale Maggiore di Novara [*A publication*]
**OSPNC**...... Porcupine Campus, Northern College of Applied Arts and Technology, South Porcupine, Ontario [*Library symbol*] [*National Library of Canada*] (NLC)
**Osp Psichiatr** ... Ospedale Psichiatrico [*A publication*]
**OSPR**......... Palmyra [*Syria*] [*ICAO location identifier*] (ICLI)
**OSPRO**...... Ocean Shipping Procedures
**OSPTM**..... Timmins Museum, South Porcupine, Ontario [*Library symbol*] [*National Library of Canada*] (BIB)
**OSQ**........... San Antonio, TX [*Location identifier*] [*FAA*] (FAAL)
**OSR** ........... Occupational Survey Report
**OSR** ........... Office of Scientific Research [*AFSC*]
**OSR** ........... Office of Security Review [*Obsolete*] [*DoD*]
**OSR** ........... Office of Systems Requirements [*Social Security Administration*]
**OSR** ........... Ohio State Reports [*A publication*] (DLA)
**OSR** ........... Old Style Roman (ADA)
**OSR** ........... Onsite Review [*Military*]
**OSR** ........... Operand Storage Register [*Data processing*]
**OSR** ........... Operational Scanning Recognition
**OSR** ........... Operational Status Release [*Navy*] (NG)
**OSR** ........... Operational Support Readiness
**OSR** ........... Operational Support Requirement [*Military*]
**OSR** ........... Operations Support Room [*NASA*] (KSC)
**OSR** ........... Optical Scanning Recognition [*Data processing*]
**OSR** ........... Optical Solar Reflector
**OSR** ........... Optical Sound Recorder
**OSR** ........... Optical Still Recorder [*LASER-disc technology*]
**OSR** ........... Optimum Ship Routing [*Obsolete*]
**OSR** ........... Ordnance Status Report (NG)
**OSR** ........... Originators Status Report [*Army*]
**OSR** ........... Oscar Resources Ltd. [*Vancouver Stock Exchange symbol*]
**OSR** ........... Ostrava [*Czechoslovakia*] [*Airport symbol*] (OAG)
**OSR** ........... Output Shift Register
**OSR** ........... Output Signal Range
**OSR** ........... Over-the-Shoulder Rating
**OSR** ........... Oversea Returnee [*Military*]
**OSR** ........... Overseas Service Ribbon [*Military decoration*]
**OSR** ........... Own Ship's Roll [*Navy*]
**OSR** ........... Oxide-Stable Resin
**OSRA** ........ Office Systems Research Association [*Cleveland, OH*] (EA)
**OSRAC**....... Ocean Shipping Requirements and Capabilities
**OSR Bull** ... OSR [*Organisation for Scientific Research in Indonesia*] Bulletin [*A publication*]
**OSRC**......... Oil Sands Research Centre [*Alberta*]
**OSRC**......... OSR Corporation [*NASDAQ symbol*] (NQ)
**OSRD** ........ Office of Scientific Research and Development [*World War II*]
**OSRD** ........ Office of Standard Reference Data [*National Institute of Standards and Technology*] [*Gaithersburg, MD*]
**OSRDB**...... Office of Standard Reference Data Bibliography [*National Institute of Standards and Technology*]
**OS Rep**....... Ohio State Reports [*A publication*] (DLA)
**OSREPL**.... Oversea Replacement [*Army*]
**OSRET** ...... Oversea Returnee [*Army*]
**OSRF**......... Smooth Rock Falls Public Library, Ontario [*Library symbol*] [*National Library of Canada*] (NLC)
**OSRL**......... Organizations and Systems Research Laboratory [*Army*] (RDA)
**OSRM** ....... Office of Standard Reference Materials [*National Institute of Standards and Technology*] [*Gaithersburg, MD*] (GRD)
**OSRM** ....... South River-Machar Union Public Library, South River, Ontario [*Library symbol*] [*National Library of Canada*] (NLC)
**Osr Nauk Prod Mater Polprzewodn Pr** ... Osrodek Naukowo-Produkcyjny Materialow Polprzewodnikowych. Prace [*A publication*]
**OSRO** ........ Office for the Sahelian Relief Operation [*UN Food and Agriculture Organization*]
**OSRO** ........ Operations Support Requirements Office [*NASA*] (KSC)
**OSRO** ........ Osrow Products Corp. [*NASDAQ symbol*] (NQ)
**Osrodek Badaw Rozwojowy Elektron Prozniowej (Pr)** ... Osrodek Badawczo-Rozwojowy Elektroniki Prozniowej (Prace) [*A publication*]
**Osrodek Inf Energ Jad Rev Rep** ... Osrodek Informacji o Energii Jadrowej. Review Report [*A publication*]
**OsRom**....... Osservatore Romano [*Vatican City*] [*A publication*]
**OSRPA**...... Offices, Shops, and Railway Premises Act [*1963*] [*British*]
**OSRR** ........ Spanish River Reserve Band Public Library, Ontario [*Library symbol*] [*National Library of Canada*] (NLC)
**OSRS**......... Operational Status Recording Subsystem
**OSRTN** ..... Office of the Special Representative for Trade Negotiations [*Later, Office of the United States Trade Representative*] [*Executive Office of the President*]
**OSS**............ Los Angeles, CA [*Location identifier*] [*FAA*] (FAAL)
**OSS**............ Object Sorting Scales [*Psychology*]
**OSS**............ Ocean Surveillance Satellite (MCD)
**OSS**............ Ocean Survey Ship (NOAA)
**OSS**............ Oceanic Scanning Spectrophotometer
**OSS**............ Oceanic Space Subcommittee [*Congressional committee*] (MSC)
**OSS**............ OEX [*Orbiter Experiments*] Support System [*NASA*] (NASA)
**OSS**............ Office of Safeguards and Security [*Department of Energy*] [*Washington, DC*] (GRD)
**OSS**............ Office of Senate Security [*Congress*]
**OSS**............ Office of Space Science [*NASA*]
**OSS**............ Office of Space Systems [*Air Force*]
**OSS**............ Office of Statistical Standards [*Bureau of the Budget; later, OMB*]
**OSS**............ Office of Strategic Services [*Facetiously translated as "Oh So Social" because some of its staff were socially prominent*] [*World War II*]
**OSS**............ Office of Support Services [*Army*]
**OSS**............ Offshore Surveillance System
**OSS**............ Old Submarine [*Navy symbol*]
**OSS**............ Ontario Secondary School Teachers' Federation [*UTLAS symbol*]
**OSS**............ Operating System Software [*Personal computers*]
**OSS**............ Operating System Supervisor
**OSS**............ Operational Storage Site [*Army*]
**OSS**............ Optical Sensor Subsystem [*Military*] (CAAL)
**OSS**............ Optical Sight System
**OSS**............ Optical Subsystem (KSC)
**OSS**............ Optical Surveillance System (AAG)
**OSS**............ Optimized Systems Software [*San Jose, CA*]
**OSS**............ Orbital Stabilization System (MCD)
**OSS**............ Orbiting Space Station [*NASA*]
**OSS**............ Organised Science Series [*A publication*]
**OSS**............ Organization for Cooperation of Socialist Countries in the Domain of Posts and Telecommunications (EAIO)
**OSS**............ Osisko Lake Mines Ltd. [*Toronto Stock Exchange symbol*]
**oss** ............. Ossetic [*MARC language code*] [*Library of Congress*] (LCCP)
**OSS**............ Ossory [*Ireland*] (ROG)

**OSS**........... Outer Solar System
**OSS**........... Overseas Shipping Services Proprietary Ltd. [*Australia*] (ADA)
**OSS**........... Overseas Switch [*Military*]
**OSS**........... Own Ship's Speed [*Navy*]
**OSS**........... Oxygen Sleep Starvation
**OSS**........... Religious of the Order of the Blessed Sacrament and Our Lady [*Sacramentine Nuns*] [*Roman Catholic religious order*]
**OSS**........... Shawnee State Community College, Portsmouth, OH [*OCLC symbol*] (OCLC)
**OSSA**......... Office of Space Science and Applications [*Washington, DC*] [*NASA*]
**OSSA**......... Order Scheduled Shipment Analysis (MCD)
**OSSA**......... Order Secular of St. Augustine [*See also ASAS*] [*Rome, Italy*] (EAIO)
**OSSC**......... Oblati Sacratissimi Cordis [*Oblate Fathers of the Sacred Heart*] [*Roman Catholic religious order*]
**OSSC**......... Ordnance Storage and Shipment Chart [*Army*] (MCD)
**OSSE**......... Object/Surface/Special Effect
**OSSE**......... Observing Systems Simulation Experiments [*National Center for Atmospheric Research*]
**Osserv**........ Osservatore [*A publication*]
**Osserv Trib** ... Osservatore Tributario [*A publication*]
**OSSF**......... Overseas Services Storage Facility
**OSShD**...... Organisation fur die Zusammenarbeit der Eisenbahnen [*Organisation for the Collaboration of Railways - OCR*] (EAIO)
**OSSJ**......... St. Joseph's Hospital, Sarnia, Ontario [*Library symbol*] [*National Library of Canada*] (BIB)
**OSSKC**...... Operative Society of Spring Knife Cutlers [*A union*] [*British*]
**OSSL**......... Operating System Simulation Language [*1971*] [*Data processing*] (CSR)
**Oss Med**.... Osservatore Medico [*A publication*]
**Oss & Mem Oss Astrofis Arcetri** ... Osservazioni e Memorie. Osservatorio Astrofisico di Arcetri [*A publication*]
**OSSMJ**..... Order of the Societies of Mary and Joseph (ROG)
**OSSN**........ Operational Specialist Supervisor, Night [*Navy*]
**OSSN**........ Other Specialty Serial Numbers [*Air Force*]
**OSSNSS**.... Ordnance Supply Segment of the Navy Supply System
**OSSO**........ Office of State Systems Operations [*Social and Rehabilitation Service, HEW*]
**OSSP**......... Operational Supply Support Plan (MCD)
**OSSP**......... Outer Solar System Probe
**OSSR**......... Oblates [*or Order*] of the Most Holy Redeemer [*Roman Catholic women's religious order*]
**OSSR**......... Own Ship's Speed Repeater [*Navy*]
**OSSRH**...... Orbiter Subsystem Requirements Handbook [*NASA*] (NASA)
**OssRom**..... Osservatore Romano [*Vatican City*] [*A publication*]
**OSSS**......... Damascus [*Syria*] [*ICAO location identifier*] (ICLI)
**OSSS**......... Optical Space Surveillance Subsystem (AAG)
**OSSS**......... Orbital Space Station Study
**OSSS**......... Orbital Space Station System [*of NASA*]
**OSSS**......... Order of the Most Holy Savior [*Bridgettine Sisters*] [*Roman Catholic religious order*]
**OSST**......... Ocean Ship Surveillance Training
**OSST**......... Official Summary of Security Transactions and Holdings
**OSST**......... Offshore Storage Tank
**OSsT**.......... Ordo Sanctissimae Trinitatis Redemptionis Captivorum [*Order of the Most Holy Trinity*] [*Trinitarians*] [*Roman Catholic religious order*]
**OSSTF For** ... OSSTF [*Ontario Secondary School Teachers' Federation*] Forum [*A publication*]
**OSSU**......... Operator Services Switching Unit [*Telecommunications*] (TEL)
**OSSU**......... Sundridge & Strong Union Public Library, Sundridge, Ontario [*Library symbol*] [*National Library of Canada*] (NLC)
**OS Supp**..... Oklahoma Statutes, Supplement [*A publication*] (DLA)
**OST**........... Austria Fund [*NYSE symbol*] (SPSG)
**OST**........... Object Sorting Test [*Psychology*]
**OST**........... Objective Start Time
**OST**........... Objectives, Strategy, and Tactics [*Management system*]
**OST**........... Observation Skills Test
**OST**........... Office of Science and Technology [*Terminated 1973, functions transferred to National Science Foundation*] [*Later, CSTD*]
**OST**........... Office of the Secretary of Transportation [*Department of Transportation*]
**O St**........... Ohio State Reports [*A publication*] (DLA)
**OST**........... On-Shift Test (IEEE)
**OST**........... One-Station Training
**OST**........... Operational Suitability Test [*Aviation*]
**OST**........... Operational System Test (KSC)
**OST**........... Operations Support Team [*NASA*] (MCD)
**OST**........... Optic Support Table
**OST**........... Optical Sensing Trigger
**OST**........... Optical Star Tracker
**OST**........... Orbit Stay Time
**OST**........... Orbiter Support Trolley [*NASA*] (NASA)
**OST**........... Order Ship Time [*DoD*]
**O & ST**....... Order and Shipping Time [*Military*] (MCD)
**OST**........... Ordinary Spring Tides
**OST**........... Ordnance Special Training (AAG)
**OST**........... Ordnance Suitability Test
**OST**........... Organisation Socialiste des Travailleurs [*Socialist Workers' Organization*] [*Senegal*] [*Political party*] (PPW)
**OST**........... Organizacion Socialista de los Trabajadores [*Socialist Workers' Organization*] [*Bolivia*] [*Political party*] (PPW)
**OST**........... Organizacion Socialista de los Trabajadores [*Socialist Workers' Organization*] [*Costa Rica*] [*Political party*] (PPW)
**OST**........... Originating Station Treatment [*Telecommunications*] (TEL)
**OST**........... Ostend [*Belgium*] [*Airport symbol*] (OAG)
**OST**........... Osterhout Free Library, Wilkes-Barre, PA [*OCLC symbol*] (OCLC)
**OST**........... Osteuropa. Zeitschrift fuer Gegenwartsfragen des Ostens [*A publication*]
**OST**........... Out of Stock, Temporary [*Business term*]
**OST**........... Over Stress Testing
**OST**........... Oxford Superconductive Technology [*Manufacturing company*] [*British*]
**OST**........... Stratford Public Library, Ontario [*Library symbol*] [*National Library of Canada*] (NLC)
**OSTA**......... Office of Space and Terrestrial Applications [*NASA*] (GRD)
**OSTA**......... Stayner Public Library, Ontario [*Library symbol*] [*National Library of Canada*] (NLC)
**OSTAC**...... Bibliotheque Publique Cambridge-St.-Albert, St.-Albert, Ontario [*Library symbol*] [*National Library of Canada*] (NLC)
**OSTAC**...... Ocean Science Technology Advisory Committee [*Terminated, 1976*] [*National Security Industrial Association*] (MSC)
**OSTAG**...... Gallery Stratford, Ontario [*Library symbol*] [*National Library of Canada*] (NLC)
**OSTAR**...... Observer Single-Handed Transatlantic Race [*Sailing*]
**OSTARE**... Old Scientific Technical Aerospace Reports Extended
**OSTASDG** ... St. Andrews Branch, Stormount, Dundas, and Glengarry County Library, Ontario [*Library symbol*] [*National Library of Canada*] (BIB)
**O State**....... Ohio State Reports [*A publication*] (DLA)
**Ostb Grenzm** ... Ostbairische Grenzmarken [*A publication*]
**OSTC**......... St. Catharines Public Library, Ontario [*Library symbol*] [*National Library of Canada*] (NLC)
**OStcB**........ Belmont Technical Institute, St. Clairsville, OH [*Library symbol*] [*Library of Congress*] (LCLS)
**OSTCB**...... Brock University, St. Catharines, Ontario [*Library symbol*] [*National Library of Canada*] (NLC)
**OSTCBG**... Department of Geography, Brock University, St. Catharines, Ontario [*Library symbol*] [*National Library of Canada*] (NLC)
**OSTCG**...... Grantham High School, St. Catharines, Ontario [*Library symbol*] [*National Library of Canada*] (NLC)
**OSTCGL**... Genaire Ltd., St. Catharines, Ontario [*Library symbol*] [*National Library of Canada*] (NLC)
**OSTCH**..... Hotel-Dieu Hospital, St. Catharines, Ontario [*Library symbol*] [*National Library of Canada*] (BIB)
**OSTCM**..... St. Catharines Historical Museum, Ontario [*Library symbol*] [*National Library of Canada*] (BIB)
**OSTCMEC** ... Monenco Consultants Ltd., St. Catharines, Ontario [*Library symbol*] [*National Library of Canada*] (NLC)
**OSTCOOP** ... Office of the Secretary of Transportation Continuity of Operations Plan
**OSTCT**...... St. Catharines Teachers' College, Ontario [*Library symbol*] [*National Library of Canada*] (NLC)
**OSTCTR**... St. Catharines Teachers' Reference Library, Ontario [*Library symbol*] [*National Library of Canada*] (NLC)
**OStcU**........ Ohio University, Belmont County Branch Campus, St. Clairsville, OH [*Library symbol*] [*Library of Congress*] (LCLS)
**OSTD**........ Office of Supersonic Transport Development [*Obsolete*] [*Department of Transportation*]
**OSTD**........ Ordnance Standard Technical Directives [*Obsolete*]
**OSTD**........ Ordnance Standards
**OSTDS**...... Office of Space Tracking and Data Systems [*NASA*] (NASA)
**OSte**........... Public Library of Steubenville and Jefferson County, Steubenville, OH [*Library symbol*] [*Library of Congress*] (LCLS)
**OSteC**........ College of Steubenville, Steubenville, OH [*Library symbol*] [*Library of Congress*] (LCLS)
**osteo**........... Osteoarthritis [*Medicine*]
**OSTEO**...... Osteomyelitis [*Medicine*]
**OSTEO**...... Osteopathic
**Osteopath Ann** ... Osteopathic Annals [*A publication*]
**Osteopath Hosp Leadership** ... Osteopathic Hospital Leadership [*A publication*]
**Osteopath Med** ... Osteopathic Medicine [*A publication*]
**Osteopath Prof** ... Osteopathic Profession [*A publication*]
**Osteop Q**.... Osteopathic Quarterly [*A publication*]
**Oster Musik** ... Oesterreichische Musikzeitschrift [*A publication*]
**Osterr Bot Z** ... Oesterreichische Botanische Zeitschrift [*A publication*]
**Osterr Dent Z** ... Oesterreichische Dentisten Zeitschrift [*A publication*]
**Osterreichische Ing Z** ... Oesterreichische Ingenieur Zeitschrift [*A publication*]
**Osterr Hebammenztg** ... Oesterreichische Hebammenzeitung [*A publication*]
**Osterr Krankenpflegez** ... Oesterreichische Krankenpflegezeitschrift [*A publication*]

**Osterr Osth** ... Oesterreichische Osthefte [*A publication*]
**Osterr Z Aussenpolit** ... Oesterreichische Zeitschrift fuer Aussenpolitik [*A publication*]
**Osterr Z Off Recht** ... Oesterreichische Zeitschrift fuer Oeffentliches Recht [*A publication*]
**Osterr Z Polit-Wiss** ... Oesterreichische Zeitschrift fuer Politikwissenschaft [*A publication*]
**OSTEST**.... Operating System Test [*Telecommunications*] (TEL)
**Osteur**........ Osteuropa [*A publication*]
**Osteur Naturwiss** ... Osteuropa Naturwissenschaft [*A publication*]
**Osteuropa Wirtsch** ... Osteuropa Wirtschaft [*A publication*]
**Ost Europ Recht** ... Ost Europa Recht [*Stuttgart, Germany*] [*A publication*] (DLA)
**Osteur Wirt** ... Osteuropa Wirtschaft [*A publication*]
**OSTF**......... Operational Silo Test Facility
**OSTF**......... Operational Suitability Test Facility [*Aviation*]
**OSTF**......... Operational System Test Facility [*Air Force*]
**OSTFC**...... Storrington Branch, Frontenac County Library, Ontario [*Library symbol*] [*National Library of Canada*] (BIB)
**OSTG**........ Ocean Science and Technology Group [*Navy*] (MCD)
**OSTG**........ St. Georges Branch, South Dumfries Public Library, Ontario [*Library symbol*] [*National Library of Canada*] (BIB)
**OSTGU**..... Oriental Society. Transactions. Glasgow University [*A publication*]
**OSTI**.......... Bibliotheque Publique de St.-Isidore, Ontario [*Library symbol*] [*National Library of Canada*] (NLC)
**OSTI**.......... Office of Scientific and Technical Information [*Later, BLR & DD*] [*British Library*]
**OSTI**.......... Office of Scientific and Technical Information [*Department of Energy*] [*Information service or system*] (IID)
**OSTI**.......... Organization for Social and Technical Innovation
**OSTI Newsl** ... Office for Scientific and Technical Information. Newsletter [*A publication*]
**OSTIR**....... Stirling Public Library, Ontario [*Library symbol*] [*National Library of Canada*] (BIB)
**OSTIV**....... Organisation Scientifique et Technique Internationale du Vol a Voile [*International Technical and Scientific Organization for Soaring Flight*]
**OStJ**........... Officer of the Order of St. John of Jerusalem [*British*]
**Ostjydsk Hjemstavn** ... Ostjydsk Hjemstavnforenings Aarsskrift [*A publication*]
**Ostkirch St** ... Ostkirchliche Studien [*A publication*]
**OSTL**......... Operating System Table Loader [*Telecommunications*] (TEL)
**OSTL**......... Ovary Style Length [*Botany*]
**OstM**......... Ostdeutsche Monatshefte [*A publication*]
**OSTM**....... Sault Ste. Marie Public Library, Ontario [*Library symbol*] [*National Library of Canada*] (NLC)
**OSTMA**..... Algoma College, Sault Ste. Marie, Ontario [*Library symbol*] [*National Library of Canada*] (NLC)
**OSTMAAS** ... Synod Office, Diocese of Algoma, Anglican Church of Canada, Sault Ste. Marie, Ontario [*Library symbol*] [*National Library of Canada*] (NLC)
**OStmaC**..... Chatfield College, St. Martin, OH [*Library symbol*] [*Library of Congress*] (LCLS)
**Ostmaerk Milchwirtsch Ztg** ... Ostmaerkische Milchwirtschaftliche Zeitung [*A publication*]
**Ostmaerk Spirit Ztg** ... Ostmaerkische Spirituosen-Zeitung [*A publication*]
**OSTMAS**.. Research Library, Algoma Steel Corp. Ltd., Sault Ste. Marie, Ontario [*Library symbol*] [*National Library of Canada*] (NLC)
**OSTMB**..... Batchewana Indian Band, Sault Ste. Marie, Ontario [*Library symbol*] [*National Library of Canada*] (NLC)
**OSTMEF**.. Sea Lamprey Control Centre, Fisheries and Oceans Canada [*Centre de Controle des Lamproies de Mer, Peches et Oceans Canada*] Sault Ste. Marie, Ontario [*Library symbol*] [*National Library of Canada*] (NLC)
**OSTMF**..... Great Lakes Forest Research Centre, Canadian Forestry Service [*Centre de Recherches Forestieres des Grands Lacs, Service Canadien des Forets*] Sault Ste. Marie, Ontario [*Library symbol*] [*National Library of Canada*] (NLC)
**OSTMFF**... Forest Pest Management Institute, Canadian Forestry Service [*Institut pour la Repression des Ravageurs Forestiers, Service Canadien des Forets*], Sault-Ste.-Marie, Ontario [*Library symbol*] [*National Library of Canada*] (NLC)
**OSTMGH** ... General Hospital, Sault Ste. Marie, Ontario [*Library symbol*] [*National Library of Canada*] (NLC)
**OSTMH**.... Sault Ste. Marie and 49th (SSM) Field Regiment RCA Historical Society, Ontario [*Library symbol*] [*National Library of Canada*] (NLC)
**OSTMM** ... Strathroy Middlesex Museum, Strathroy, Ontario [*Library symbol*] [*National Library of Canada*] (BIB)
**OSTMNA** ... Aviation and Fire Management Centre, Ontario Ministry of Natural Resources, Sault Ste. Marie [*Library symbol*] [*National Library of Canada*] (BIB)
**OSTMPH** ... Plummer Public Hospital, Sault Ste. Marie, Ontario [*Library symbol*] [*National Library of Canada*] (NLC)
**OSTMSC**.. Sault College of Applied Arts and Technology, Sault Ste. Marie, Ontario [*Library symbol*] [*National Library of Canada*] (NLC)
**OSTMY**..... St. Mary's Public Library, Ontario [*Library symbol*] [*National Library of Canada*] (NLC)
**OSTMYM** ... St. Mary's District Museum, St. Mary's, Ontario [*Library symbol*] [*National Library of Canada*] (BIB)
**OSTN**........ Old Stone Corp. [*NASDAQ symbol*] (NQ)
**OSTO**........ Oesterreichische Osthefte [*A publication*]
**OSTO**........ Office of Space Transportation Operations [*NASA*] (NASA)
**OST-ONA** ... Office of the Secretary of Transportation Office of Noise Abatement
**OSTP**......... Office of Science and Technology Policy [*Washington, DC*] [*Executive Office of the President*]
**OSTP**......... On-Site Test Procedure
**OSTP**......... Orbiting System Test Plan [*NASA*] (NASA)
**OSTP**......... Strathroy Public Library, Ontario [*Library symbol*] [*National Library of Canada*] (NLC)
**OSTPA**...... Stratford-Perth Archives Board, Ontario [*Library symbol*] [*National Library of Canada*] (BIB)
**O St R**........ Ohio State Reports [*A publication*] (DLA)
**OSTR**......... Streetsville Public Library, Ontario [*Library symbol*] [*National Library of Canada*] (NLC)
**Ostrava Vys Ak Banska Sb Rada Hornicko-Geol** ... Ostrava. Vysoka Skola Banska. Sbornik. Rada Hornicko-Geologicka [*A publication*]
**OSTRDN**.. Tropical Dental Journal [*A publication*]
**O St Rep**.... Ohio State Reports [*A publication*] (DLA)
**Ostrich Suppl** ... Ostrich. Supplement [*A publication*]
**OSTRO**..... Stroud Branch, Township of Innisfil Public Library, Ontario [*Library symbol*] [*National Library of Canada*] (NLC)
**OSTS**......... Office of Space Transportation Systems [*NASA*] (GRD)
**OSTS**......... Office of State Technical Services [*Also, STS*] [*Abolished, 1970*] [*Department of Commerce*]
**OSTS**......... Operational Suitability Test Site [*Aviation*] (AAG)
**OSTT**......... Damascus [*Syria*] [*ICAO location identifier*] (ICLI)
**OSTT**......... St. Thomas Public Library, Ontario [*Library symbol*] [*National Library of Canada*] (NLC)
**OSTTE**...... Elgin County Public Library, St. Thomas, Ontario [*Library symbol*] [*National Library of Canada*] (NLC)
**OSTTP**...... St. Thomas Psychiatric Hospital, Ontario [*Library symbol*] [*National Library of Canada*] (NLC)
**OSTV**......... Operational Support Television [*Military*] (AFM)
**Ostwalds Klassiker Exakt Wiss** ... Ostwalds Klassiker der Exakten Wissenschaften [*A publication*]
**Ost Zschft Off RNF** ... Oesterreichische Zeitschrift fuer Oeffentliches Recht. Neue Folge [*Vienna, Austria*] [*A publication*] (DLA)
**OSU**........... Columbus, OH [*Location identifier*] [*FAA*] (FAAL)
**OSU**........... Ohio State University [*Columbus*]
**OSU**........... Ohio State University, Columbus, OH [*OCLC symbol*] (OCLC)
**O Su**........... Ohio Supplement [*A publication*] (DLA)
**OSU**........... Ohio Supreme Court Decisions, Unreported Cases [*A publication*] (DLA)
**OSU**........... Oklahoma State University
**OSU**........... Older-Worker Service Unit [*US Employment Service*] [*Department of Labor*]
**OSU**........... Operation Sisters United (EA)
**OSU**........... Operational Switching Unit
**OSU**........... Order of St. Ursula [*Roman Catholic women's religious order*]
**OSU**........... Oregon State University [*Formerly, OSC*]
**OSu**........... Orientalia Suecana [*A publication*]
**OSU**........... Sudbury Public Library, Ontario [*Library symbol*] [*National Library of Canada*] (NLC)
**OsUA**......... Ortnamnssaellskapets i Uppsala Aarsskrift [*A publication*]
**OSUBE**...... Educational Media Centre, Sudbury Board of Education, Ontario [*Library symbol*] [*National Library of Canada*] (NLC)
**OSUC**........ Cambrian College, Sudbury, Ontario [*Library symbol*] [*National Library of Canada*] (NLC)
**OSUCLL**... Ohio State University. Contributions in Language and Literature [*A publication*]
**OSUCS**...... Civic Square, Information and Reference, Sudbury Public Library, Ontario [*Library symbol*] [*National Library of Canada*] (NLC)
**OSUE**........ On-Site User Evaluation (MCD)
**OSU Ext Facts Coop Ext Serv Okla State Univ** ... OSU Extension Facts. Cooperative Extension Service. Oklahoma State University [*A publication*]
**OSUGH**..... Sudbury General Hospital, Ontario [*Library symbol*] [*National Library of Canada*] (NLC)
**OSUK**........ Ophthalmological Society of the United Kingdom
**OSUL**........ Laurentian University [*Universite Laurentienne*] Sudbury, Ontario [*Library symbol*] [*National Library of Canada*] (NLC)
**OSULH**..... Medical Library, Laurentian Hospital, Sudbury, Ontario [*Library symbol*] [*National Library of Canada*] (BIB)
**OSUM**....... Ohio State University Museum of Zoology [*Research center*] (RCD)
**OSUME**.... Ontario Ministry of Education, Sudbury, Ontario [*Library symbol*] [*National Library of Canada*] (BIB)

**OSUN**........ North Central Regional Library, Sudbury, Ontario [*Library symbol*] [*National Library of Canada*] (NLC)
**OSUN**........ Ontario Library Service - Voyageur, Sudbury, Ontario [*Library symbol*] [*National Library of Canada*] (NLC)
**OSUNB**..... Brock Township Public Library, Sunderland, Ontario [*Library symbol*] [*National Library of Canada*] (NLC)
**OSUOP**..... Northeastern Ontario Oncology Program [*Programme d'Oncologie du Nord-Est de l'Ontario*], Sudbury, Ontario [*Library symbol*] [*National Library of Canada*] (NLC)
**O Supp**....... Ohio Supplement [*A publication*] (DLA)
**OSUR**........ Ohio State University Reactor
**OSUREP**... Overseas Unit Replacement System [*Military*] (AFIT)
**OSURF**...... Ohio State University Research Foundation
**OSURO**..... Ohio State University Radio Observatory
**OSUT**........ On-Site User Test
**OSUT**........ On-Site User Training
**OSUT**........ One-Station-Unit Training [*Army*]
**OSUT**........ Ordinary Seamen Under Training [*Canadian Navy*]
**OSUTCB**... Ohio State University. Theatre Collection Bulletin [*A publication*]
**OSUT-COFT**... One-Station-Unit Training - Conduct of Fire Trainer [*Army*] (MCD)
**OSUU**........ University of Subury [*Universite de Sudbury*] Ontario [*Library symbol*] [*National Library of Canada*] (NLC)
**OSV**.......... Ocean Station Vessel
**OSV**.......... Office of Space Vehicles
**OSV**.......... Offscreen Voice [*Films, television, etc.*]
**OSV**.......... On Station Vehicle (MCD)
**OSV**.......... Orbital Support Vehicle
**OSV**.......... Order of St. Vincent (EA)
**OSV**.......... Oriented Space Vehicle
**OSV**.......... Our Sunday Visitor [*A publication*]
**OSV**.......... Output Serving Voltage
**OSVA**........ Off-Site Vital Area (MCD)
**OSVM**....... Our Sunday Visitor Magazine [*A publication*]
**OS/VS**....... Operating Schedule/Virtual System
**OS/VS**....... Operating System/Virtual Storage [*Data processing*] (MDG)
**OS & W**..... Oak, Sunk, and Weathered [*Construction*]
**OSW**.......... Oblique Shock Wave
**OSW**.......... Office of Saline Water [*Later, OWRT*] [*Department of the Interior*]
**OSW**.......... Office of Secretary of War [*Obsolete*]
**OSW**.......... Old Spaghetti Warehouse, Inc. [*AMEX symbol*] (SPSG)
**OSW**.......... Old Swedish [*Language, etc.*]
**OSW**.......... Operational Switching Unit
**OSW**.......... Operations Support Wing [*NASA*]
**OSW**.......... Order of the Sacred Word [*Affiliate of the magical society, Aurum Solis*]
**OSW**.......... Oswego, KS [*Location identifier*] [*FAA*] (FAAL)
**OSW**.......... Oswestry [*British depot code*]
**OSW**.......... Wittenberg University, Springfield, OH [*Library symbol*] [*Library of Congress*] (LCLS)
**OSWA**....... Off-Shift Work Authorization (AAG)
**OSWAC**.... Ordnance Special Weapons Ammunition Command [*Later, Weapons Command*]
**OSWC**....... Ordnance Special Weapons Command [*Merged with Missile Command*] [*Army*]
**OSWD**....... Office of Special Weapons Development [*Army*]
**OSWER**..... Office of Solid Waste and Emergency Response [*Environmental Protection Agency*] [*Washington, DC*]
**OSWG**....... Optical Systems Working Group (MUGU)
**OSWMP**.... Office of Solid Waste Management Programs [*Environmental Protection Agency*]
**OSWS**....... Operating System Workstation [*Data processing*]
**OSWS**....... Whitchurch-Stouffville Public Library, Stouffville, Ontario [*Library symbol*] [*National Library of Canada*] (NLC)
**OSX**.......... Kosciusko, MS [*Location identifier*] [*FAA*] (FAAL)
**OSY**.......... Namsos [*Norway*] [*Airport symbol*] (OAG)
**OSY**.......... National Institute for Occupational Safety and Health, Morgantown, WV [*OCLC symbol*] (OCLC)
**OSY**.......... Odyssey Resources Ltd. [*Vancouver Stock Exchange symbol*]
**OS & Y**....... Outside Screw and Yoke
**OSYC**........ Officer Supervising Yardcraft [*Canadian Navy*]
**OSYFC**...... Sydenham Branch, Frontenac County Library, Ontario [*Library symbol*] [*National Library of Canada*] (BIB)
**OSZ**.......... Koszalin [*Poland*] [*Airport symbol*] (OAG)
**OSZ**.......... Offshore Surf Zone
**OSZ**.......... Washington, DC [*Location identifier*] [*FAA*] (FAAL)
**OSzK**......... Orszagos Szechenyi Konyvtar [*National Szechenyi Library*] [*Information service or system*] (IID)
**OT**............ Linhas Aereas de S Tome e Principe [*Portugal*] [*ICAO designator*] (FAAC)
**OT**............ Objective Test [*Psychology*]
**OT**............ Observer Target [*Army*]
**OT**............ Occipitotransverse [*Obstetrics*]
**OT**............ Occupational Therapist [*or Therapy*] [*Medicine*]
**OT**............ Occupational Therapy Technician [*Navy*]
**OT**............ Occupied Territories (BJA)
**OT**............ Ocean Transportation [*Military*]
**OT**............ Ocular Tension [*Medicine*]
**OT**............ Oedipus Tyrannus [*of Sophocles*] [*Classical studies*] (OCD)
**OT**............ Offensive Tackle [*Football*]
**OT**............ Office of Telecommunications [*Department of Commerce*]
**OT**............ Office of Territories [*Department of the Interior*]
**OT**............ Office of Transportation [*Department of Agriculture*]
**OT**............ Oil-Tight
**OT**............ Old Term
**OT**............ Old Terminology
**OT**............ Old Testament [*of the Bible*]
**OT**............ Old Timer [*Communications operators' colloquialism*]
**OT**............ Old Tom [*British slang term for gin*] (ROG)
**OT**............ Old Top [*Communications operators' colloquialism*]
**OT**............ Old [*or Original*] Tuberculin [*Also, TO*] [*Medicine*]
**OT**............ Olfactory Threshold
**OT**............ Olfactory Tubercle [*Neuroanatomy*]
**OT**............ On Target [*Military*] (CAAL)
**O/T**........... On Thames [*In place names*] [*British*] (ROG)
**OT**............ On Time
**OT**............ On a Track [*Rail*] [*Shipping*] (DCTA)
**O/T**........... On Trent [*In place names*] [*British*] (ROG)
**OT**............ On Truck [*Shipping*]
**OT**............ Once-Through [*Nuclear reactor technology*]
**OT**............ One Time
**OT**............ Onze Taaltuin [*A publication*]
**OT**............ Onze Tijd [*A publication*]
**OT**............ Open Topped [*Container*] [*Packaging*] (DCTA)
**OT**............ Operating Temperature [*Nuclear energy*]
**OT**............ Operating Theater
**OT**............ Operating Time
**OT**............ Operational Technology [*Nuclear energy*] (NRCH)
**OT**............ Operational Test (AFM)
**OT**............ Operational TIROS [*NASA*]
**OT**............ Operational Trajectory [*Aerospace*] (KSC)
**OT**............ Operations Team (MCD)
**O & T**........ Operations and Training [*Military*]
**OT**............ Optatam Totius [*Decree on Priestly Formation*] [*Vatican II document*]
**OT**............ Optic Tectum [*Anatomy*]
**OT**............ Optical Tool
**OT**............ Optical Tracking [*NASA*] (KSC)
**OT**............ Optical-Transient [*Astronomy*]
**OT**............ Oral Testimony (BJA)
**OT**............ Oregon Territory [*Prior to statehood*]
**OT**............ Oregon Trunk Railway [*AAR code*]
**OT**............ Organization Table
**O & T**........ Organization and Training [*Military*]
**OT**............ Organizational Table
**OT**............ Orifice Tube [*Automobile air conditioning system*]
**OT**............ Orotracheal [*Medicine*]
**OT**............ Osmium Tetroxide [*Inorganic chemistry*]
**OT**............ Other Than
**OT**............ Other Time
**OT**............ Otolaryngology [*Medicine*]
**OT**............ Otology [*Medicine*]
**OT**............ O'Toole's Group, Inc. [*Toronto Stock Exchange symbol*]
**Ot**............ Otto Papiensis [*Flourished, 12th century*] [*Authority cited in pre-1607 legal work*] (DSA)
**Ot**............ Otto's United States Supreme Court Reports [*91-107 United States*] [*A publication*] (DLA)
**OT**............ Ought (ROG)
**OT**............ Out Temperature (MCD)
**OT**............ Out of Tolerance
**OT**............ Outer Table (MCD)
**OT**............ Outer Tube
**OT**............ Outfit
**OT**............ Output Terminal
**OT**............ Over There (ADA)
**OT**............ Overall Test (KSC)
**OT**............ Overhead Transparencies
**OT**............ Overland Telegraph [*Australia*] (DSUE)
**OT**............ Overlap Technician
**OT**............ Overlap Telling (MCD)
**OT**............ Overseas Territories (MCD)
**OT**............ Overseas Trade
**O/T**........... Overtemperature (KSC)
**OT**............ Overtime
**OT**............ Overtone
**OT**............ Ovotransferrin [*Biochemistry*]
**OT**............ Oxytocin [*Endocrinology*]
**O & T**........ Oyer and Terminer [*Hear and Determine*] [*Legal term*] (DLA)
**OT**............ Oyer and Terminer [*Hear and Determine*] [*Legal term*] (ROG)
**OT**............ Stations Open Exclusively to Operational Traffic of the Services Concerned [*ITU designation*] (CET)
**OT**............ Tara Branch, Bruce County Public Library, Ontario [*Library symbol*] [*National Library of Canada*] (NLC)
**OT**............ Toledo-Lucas County Public Library, Toledo, OH [*Library symbol*] [*Library of Congress*] (LCLS)
**OTA**.......... Academy of Medicine, Toronto, Ontario [*Library symbol*] [*National Library of Canada*] (NLC)
**OTA**.......... Occupied Territory Administration [*World War II*]
**OTA**.......... Off-the-Air Record Club [*Record label*]
**OTA**.......... Office of Tax Analysis [*Department of the Treasury*]

**OTA** .......... Office of Technology Assessment [*Congressional study group*] [*Washington, DC*]
**OTA** .......... Office of Technology Assistance [*General Services Administration*]
**OTA** .......... Office of Telecommunications Applications [*US National Telecommunications and Information Administration*] (TSSD)
**OTA** .......... Officer Training Allowance [*Naval Reserve*]
**OTA** .......... Oil Trades Association of New York (EA)
**OTA** .......... Old Testament Abstracts [*A publication*] (BJA)
**OTA** .......... Omnidirectional Transmitter Antenna
**OTA** .......... Onze Taal [*A publication*]
**OTA** .......... Open Test Assembly [*Nuclear energy*] (NRCH)
**OTA** .......... Operation Town Affiliations [*An association*] (EA)
**OTA** .......... Operational Transconductance Amplifier (IEEE)
**OTA** .......... Optical Telescope Assembly [*NASA*]
**OTA** .......... Optical Tracking Aid [*Deep Space Instrumentation Facility, NASA*]
**OTA** .......... Organisation Mondiale du Tourisme et de l'Automobile [*World Touring and Automobile Organization*]
**OTA** .......... Ortho-Tolidine Arsenite [*Organic chemistry*]
**OTA** .......... Other than Air (CINC)
**ota** .......... Ottoman Turkish [*MARC language code*] [*Library of Congress*] (LCCP)
**OTA** .......... Outer Transport Area
**OTAA** ........ AASTRA Aerospace, Inc., Downsview, Ontario [*Library symbol*] [*National Library of Canada*] (BIB)
**OTAA** ........ Office of Trade Adjustment Assistance [*Department of Labor*]
**OTAC** ........ Acres Consulting Services Ltd., Toronto, Ontario [*Library symbol*] [*National Library of Canada*] (NLC)
**OTAC** ........ Oceanic Trade Alliance Council International
**OTAC** ........ Ordnance Tank-Automotive Command [*Merged with Weapons and Mobility Command*] [*Army*]
**OTACS** ...... Old Timer Assay Commissioners Society (EA)
**OTAD** ........ Addiction Research Foundation, Toronto, Ontario [*Library symbol*] [*National Library of Canada*] (NLC)
**OTAD** ........ Office of Tributary Area Development [*Tennessee Valley Authority*]
**OTAD** ........ Oversea Terminal Arrival Date [*Army*] (AABC)
**OTADA** ..... Office of Tracking and Data Acquisition [*NASA*]
**OTADL** ..... Outer Target Azimuth Datum Line
**OTAE** ........ Atomic Energy of Canada [*L'Energie Atomique du Canada*] Toronto, Ontario [*Library symbol*] [*National Library of Canada*] (NLC)
**OTAE** ........ [*The*] Old Testament in the Light of the Ancient East [*A publication*] (BJA)
**OTAF** ........ Office of Technology Assessment and Forecast [*Patent and Trademark Office*] [*Washington, DC*]
**OTAF** ........ Ontario Ministry of Agriculture and Food, Toronto, Ontario [*Library symbol*] [*National Library of Canada*] (NLC)
**OTAF** ........ Operating Time at Failure (MCD)
**OTAG** ........ Art Gallery of Ontario, Toronto, Ontario [*Library symbol*] [*National Library of Canada*] (NLC)
**OTAG** ........ Office of the Adjutant General [*Military*]
**OTAGAV** .. Audiovisual Library, Art Gallery of Ontario, Toronto, Ontario [*Library symbol*] [*National Library of Canada*] (NLC)
**Otago Acclim Soc Annu Rep** ... Otago Acclimatisation Society. Annual Report [*A publication*]
**Otago Law Rev** ... Otago Law Review [*A publication*]
**Otago LR** ... Otago Law Review [*A publication*]
**Otago L Rev** ... Otago Law Review [*A publication*]
**Otago Mus Zool Bull** ... Otago Museum of Zoology. Bulletin [*A publication*]
**Otago Pol Gaz** ... Otago Police Gazette [*1861-64*] [*New Zealand*] [*A publication*] (DLA)
**OTAL** ........ Arts and Letters Club, Toronto, Ontario [*Library symbol*] [*National Library of Canada*] (NLC)
**Otal** ........... [*Juan Arze y*] Otalora [*Flourished, 16th century*] [*Authority cited in pre-1607 legal work*] (DSA)
**OTAM** ....... Ozbek Tili va Adabiet Masalalari [*A publication*]
**OTAN** ........ Organisation du Traite de l'Atlantique Nord [*North Atlantic Treaty Organization - NATO*] [*Brussels, Belgium*]
**OTAN** ........ Organizacao do Tratado do Atlantico Norte [*North Atlantic Treaty Organization*] [*Portuguese*]
**OTAN Newsl** ... OTAN [*Organization of Tropical American Nematologists*] Newsletter [*A publication*]
**OTANY** ..... Oil Trades Association of New York (EA)
**OTAP** ........ Alternative Press Centre, Toronto, Ontario [*Library symbol*] [*National Library of Canada*] (NLC)
**OTAQ** ........ Offer Therapist-Adolescent Questionnaire [*Personality development test*] [*Psychology*]
**OTAR** ........ Archives of Ontario, Toronto, Ontario [*Library symbol*] [*National Library of Canada*] (NLC)
**OTAR** ........ Overseas Tariffs and Regulations (DS)
**OTARC** ..... Centennial College of Applied Arts and Technology, Scarborough, Ontario [*Library symbol*] [*National Library of Canada*] (NLC)
**OTAS** ........ Observer Target Acquisition Subsystem (MCD)
**OTAS** ........ On Top and Smooth [*Meteorology*] (FAAC)
**OTASE** ...... Organisation du Traite de Defense Collective pour l'Asie du Sud-Est [*Southeast Asia Treaty Organization*] [*French*]
**OTASO** ..... Organizacao do Tratado da Asia Sul-Oriental [*South-East Asia Treaty Organization*] [*Portuguese*]
**O T AUTIC** ... Other than Automatic [*Freight*]
**OTB** .......... Off the Board [*Investment term*]
**OTB** .......... Off-Track Betting
**OTB** .......... Old Tired Broads
**OTB** .......... On the Bow [*Nautical*]
**OTB** .......... Open to Buy
**OTB** .......... Orbiting Tanker Base [*NASA*] (NASA)
**OTB** .......... Ordnance and Terminal Ballistics
**OTB** .......... Overseas Trust Bank [*Hong Kong*]
**OTB** .......... Waverly Resource Library, Thunder Bay Public Library, Ontario [*Library symbol*] [*National Library of Canada*] (NLC)
**OTBA** ........ Ocean Thermal Boundary Analysis Charts [*Marine science*] (MSC)
**OTBA** ........ Terrace Bay Public Library, Ontario [*Library symbol*] [*National Library of Canada*] (NLC)
**OTBBR** ...... Brodie Resource Library, Thunder Bay, Ontario [*Library symbol*] [*National Library of Canada*] (NLC)
**OTBC** ........ Canadian Broadcasting Corp. [*Societe Radio-Canada*] Toronto, Ontario [*Library symbol*] [*National Library of Canada*] (NLC)
**OTBCC** ...... Confederation College, Thunder Bay, Ontario [*Library symbol*] [*National Library of Canada*] (NLC)
**OTBCG** ..... Blake, Cassels & Graydon, Toronto, Ontario [*Library symbol*] [*National Library of Canada*] (NLC)
**OTBCGC** ... Staff Library, Baycrest Centre for Geriatric Care, Toronto, Ontario [*Library symbol*] [*National Library of Canada*] (BIB)
**OTBCIR** .... Bell Canada Information Resource Centre, Toronto, Ontario [*Library symbol*] [*National Library of Canada*] (NLC)
**OTBCO** ..... Technical Information Facility, Canadien Imperial Bank of Commerce, Toronto, Ontario [*Library symbol*] [*National Library of Canada*] (NLC)
**OTBCP** ...... Program Archives, Canadian Broadcasting Corp. [*Archives des Emissions, Societe Radio-Canada*] Toronto, Ontario [*Library symbol*] [*National Library of Canada*] (NLC)
**OTBD** ........ Doha/International [*Qatar*] [*ICAO location identifier*] (ICLI)
**OTBD** ........ Outboard (ADA)
**OTBDHC** .. Thunder Bay District Health Council, Thunder Bay, Ontario [*Library symbol*] [*National Library of Canada*] (NLC)
**OTBE** ........ Ontario Ministry of Education, Thunder Bay, Ontario [*Library symbol*] [*National Library of Canada*] (NLC)
**OTBGH** ..... General Hospital of Port Arthur, Thunder Bay, Ontario [*Library symbol*] [*National Library of Canada*] (NLC)
**OTBH** ........ Thunder Bay Historical Museum Society, Ontario [*Library symbol*] [*National Library of Canada*] (NLC)
**OTBHS** ..... Hammarskjold High School, Thunder Bay, Ontario [*Library symbol*] [*National Library of Canada*] (NLC)
**OTBLA** ...... Audio Library Services of Northwestern Ontario, Lakehead University, Thunder Bay, Ontario [*Library symbol*] [*National Library of Canada*] (NLC)
**OTBLL** ...... School of Library Technology, Lakehead University, Thunder Bay, Ontario [*Library symbol*] [*National Library of Canada*] (NLC)
**OTBLP** ...... Staff Library, Lakehead Psychiatric Hospital, Thunder Bay, Ontario [*Library symbol*] [*National Library of Canada*] (NLC)
**OTBM** ....... Technical Information Centre, Bank of Montreal, Willowdale, Ontario [*Library symbol*] [*National Library of Canada*] (NLC)
**OTBMB** .... Mary J. L. Black Library, Thunder Bay, Ontario [*Library symbol*] [*National Library of Canada*] (NLC)
**OTBMBI** ... Business Information Centre, Bank of Montreal, Toronto, Ontario [*Library symbol*] [*National Library of Canada*] (BIB)
**OTBMC** .... Medical Library, McKellar General Hospital, Thunder Bay, Ontario [*Library symbol*] [*National Library of Canada*] (NLC)
**OTBML** ..... Music Library, Canadian National Institute for the Blind, Toronto, Ontario [*Library symbol*] [*National Library of Canada*] (BIB)
**OTBNL** ..... National Library Division, Canadian National Institute for the Blind, Toronto, Ontario [*Library symbol*] [*National Library of Canada*] (NLC)
**OTBNR** ..... Learning Resource Centre, BNR Ltd., Toronto, Ontario [*Library symbol*] [*National Library of Canada*] (NLC)
**OTBNS** ...... Bell Northern Software Research, Toronto, Ontario [*Library symbol*] [*National Library of Canada*] (NLC)
**OTBOC** ..... Ontario Cancer Treatment and Research Foundation, Thunder Bay, Ontario [*Library symbol*] [*National Library of Canada*] (NLC)
**Otbor i Peredaca Informacii** ... Otbor i Peredaca Informacii. Akademija Nauk Ukrainskoi SSR. Fiziko-Mehaniceskii Institut [*A publication*]
**Otbor i Peredacha Inf** ... Otbor i Peredacha Informatsii [*A publication*]
**Otbor Pereda Inf** ... Otbor i Peredacha Informatsii [*A publication*]
**OTBP** ......... Blaney, Pasternak, Smela, Eagleson & Watson, Toronto, Ontario [*Library symbol*] [*National Library of Canada*] (NLC)

**OTBR**........ Barringer Research Ltd., Rexdale, Ontario [*Library symbol*] [*National Library of Canada*] (NLC)
**OTBSL**...... Bassel, Sullivan & Leake, Toronto, Ontario [*Library symbol*] [*National Library of Canada*] (NLC)
**OTBSSC**.... Over Thirty but Still Swinging Club
**OTBV**........ Oxidizer Turbine Bypass Valve (KSC)
**OTBV**........ Victoriaville Branch, Thunder Bay Public Library, Ontario [*Library symbol*] [*National Library of Canada*] (BIB)
**OTC**........... Faculty of Education, University of Toronto, Ontario [*Library symbol*] [*National Library of Canada*] (NLC)
**OTC**........... Objective, Time, and Cost
**OTC**........... Office of Technical Cooperation [*United Nations*]
**OTC**........... Office: Technology and People [*A publication*]
**OTC**........... Office of Temporary Controls
**OTC**........... Officer in Tactical Command [*Air Force*]
**OTC**........... Officer Training Center [*Navy*]
**OTC**........... Officers' Training Camp [*World War I*]
**OTC**........... Officers' Training Corps
**OTC**........... Officers Transit Camp [*British military*] (DMA)
**OTC**........... Offshore Technology Conference
**OTC**........... Ohio Motor Freight Tariff Committee Inc., Columbus OH [*STAC*]
**OTC**........... Old Testament Commentary [*A publication*] (BJA)
**OTC**........... Old Timers' Club (EA)
**OTC**........... Once-Through Cooling [*Nuclear energy*] (NRCH)
**OTC**........... One-Stop Tour Charter [*Airline fare*]
**OTC**........... Open Tubular Column [*For gas chromatography*]
**OTC**........... Operador de Transporte Combinado [*Combined Transport Operator*] [*Spanish*] [*Business term*]
**OTC**........... Operating Telephone Company [*Bell System*] (TEL)
**OTC**........... Operational Techniques Conference
**OTC**........... Operational Test Center [*NASA*] (KSC)
**OTC**........... Operational Test Coordinator [*Military*] (CAAL)
**OTC**........... Operational Training Capability [*Air Force*] (AFM)
**OTC**........... Operational Training Command (MCD)
**OTC**........... Operatore di Trasporto Combinato [*Combined Transport Operator*] [*Italian*] [*Business term*]
**OTC**........... Orbiter Test Conductor [*NASA*] (NASA)
**OTC**........... Orbiting Trajectory Computations
**OTC**........... Order of Three Crusades (EA)
**OTC**........... Ordnance Technical Committee [*Military*] (MUGU)
**OTC**........... Ordnance Training Command [*Army*]
**OTC**........... Organization for Trade Cooperation [*GATT*]
**OTC**........... Organize Training Center (EA)
**OTC**........... Original Trenton Cracker Co. [*Maker of Chowder & Oyster Crackers, claimed by some to be the oldest continuously manufactured American food product*]
**OTC**........... Originating Toll Center [*Telecommunications*] (TEL)
**OTC**........... Ornithine Transcarbamoylase [*Also, OCT*] [*An enzyme*]
**OTC**........... Otterbein College, Westerville, OH [*OCLC symbol*] (OCLC)
**OTC**........... Outer Tube Centerline
**OTC**........... Over-the-Capacitor [*Sockets*]
**OTC**........... Over-the-Counter [*Also, O/C*] [*Stock exchange term*]
**OTC**........... Over-the-Counter [*Pharmacy*]
**OTC**........... Overseas Telecommunications Commission [*Australia*] (TEL)
**OTC**........... Oxygen Transfer Compressor
**OTC**........... Oxytetracycline [*Antibiotic*]
**OTCA**........ Olson 30 Class Association (EA)
**OTCA**........ Ontario College of Art, Toronto, Ontario [*Library symbol*] [*National Library of Canada*] (NLC)
**OTCA**........ Oxothiazolidinecarboxylic Acid [*Biochemistry*]
**OTCAG**..... Canada Arctic Gas Study Ltd., Toronto, Ontario [*Library symbol*] [*National Library of Canada*] (NLC)
**OTCAS**...... Canadian Association in Support of the Native Peoples, Toronto, Ontario [*Library symbol*] [*National Library of Canada*] (NLC)
**OTCBS**...... Central Baptist Seminary and Bible College, Toronto, Ontario [*Library symbol*] [*National Library of Canada*] (NLC)
**OTCC**........ Operator Test Control Console (MCD)
**OTCC**........ Organic Thermal Control Coating
**OTCC**........ United Church of Canada Archives, Toronto, Ontario [*Library symbol*] [*National Library of Canada*] (NLC)
**OTCCC**...... Cross Cultural Communication Centre, Toronto, Ontario [*Library symbol*] [*National Library of Canada*] (NLC)
**OTCCC**...... Open Type Control Circuit Contacts (MSA)
**OTCCL**...... Currie, Coopers & Lybrand Ltd., Toronto, Ontario [*Library symbol*] [*National Library of Canada*] (NLC)
**OTCCP**...... Canadian Centre for Philanthropy, Toronto, Ontario [*Library symbol*] [*National Library of Canada*] (NLC)
**OTCCRT**... Technical Standards Division, Ontario Ministry of Consumer and Commercial Relations, Toronto, Ontario [*Library symbol*] [*National Library of Canada*] (NLC)
**OTCE**........ Central Library, North York, Ontario [*Library symbol*] [*National Library of Canada*] (NLC)
**OTCEA**...... [*The*] Canadian Education Association [*L'Association Canadienne d'Education*] Toronto, Ontario [*Library symbol*] [*National Library of Canada*] (NLC)
**OTCF**......... H. Ward Smith Library, Centre of Forensic Sciences, Toronto, Ontario [*Library symbol*] [*National Library of Canada*] (NLC)
**OTCFA**...... Occupational Therapy Comprehensive Functional Assessment
**OTCGL**...... Campbell, Godfrey & Lewtas, Toronto, Ontario [*Library symbol*] [*National Library of Canada*] (NLC)
**OTCGR**..... Canadian Gas Research Institute, Don Mills, Ontario [*Library symbol*] [*National Library of Canada*] (NLC)
**OTCGW**.... Clarkson, Gordon, Woods, Gordon, Toronto, Ontario [*Library symbol*] [*National Library of Canada*] (NLC)
**OTCH**........ Anglican Church House, Toronto, Ontario [*Library symbol*] [*National Library of Canada*] (NLC)
**OTCH**........ Obedience Trial Champion [*Dog training*]
**OTCHA**..... Canadian Hospital Association [*Association des Hopitaux du Canada*] Toronto, Ontario [*Library symbol*] [*National Library of Canada*] (NLC)
**OTCHAR**.. Anglican Church of Canada Archives, Toronto, Ontario [*Library symbol*] [*National Library of Canada*] (NLC)
**Otchery Mezhdunar O-Va Khim Serna** ... Otchery Mezhdunarodnogo Obshchestva po Khimii Serna [*A publication*]
**OTCI**......... OTC [*Overseas Telecommunications Commission*] International Ltd. [*Australia*] [*Telecommunications service*] (TSSD)
**OTCIA**....... Canadian Institute of International Affairs [*Institut Canadien des Affaires Internationales*] Toronto, Ontario [*Library symbol*] [*National Library of Canada*] (NLC)
**OTCIB**....... Canadian Imperial Bank of Commerce, Toronto, Ontario [*Library symbol*] [*National Library of Canada*] (NLC)
**OTCIL**....... Central Library, C-I-L, Inc., North York, Ontario [*Library symbol*] [*National Library of Canada*] (NLC)
**OTCILL**.... Law Library, C-I-L, Inc., North York, Ontario [*Library symbol*] [*National Library of Canada*] (NLC)
**OTCJC**...... Genealogical Society Library, Church of Jesus Christ of Latter-Day Saints, Etobicoke, Ontario [*Library symbol*] [*National Library of Canada*] (NLC)
**OTCL**........ Connaught Laboratories Ltd., Willowdale, Ontario [*Library symbol*] [*National Library of Canada*] (NLC)
**OTCLA**...... Confederation Life Association, Toronto, Ontario [*Library symbol*] [*National Library of Canada*] (NLC)
**OTCLANT** ... Fleet Operational Training Command, Atlantic [*Usually, COTCLANT*]
**OTCLH**..... Research and Information Library, Canadian Life and Health Insurance Association, Toronto, Ontario [*Library symbol*] [*National Library of Canada*] (BIB)
**OTCM**....... Canadian School of Missions and Ecumenical Institute, Toronto, Ontario [*Library symbol*] [*National Library of Canada*] (NLC)
**OTCM**....... Orbiter Thermal Control Model [*NASA*]
**OTCM**....... Ordnance Technical Committee Minutes [*Military*]
**OTCMC**.... Canadian Memorial Chiropractic College, Toronto, Ontario [*Library symbol*] [*National Library of Canada*] (NLC)
**OTCMCC** ... Old Time Country Music Club of Canada (EA)
**OTCMH**.... Saul A. Silverman Library, C. M. Hincks Treatment Centre, Toronto, Ontario [*Library symbol*] [*National Library of Canada*] (BIB)
**OTCMHA** ... Canadian Mental Health Association, Toronto, Ontario [*Library symbol*] [*National Library of Canada*] (BIB)
**OTCMLA** ... Canadian Music Library Association [*Association Canadienne des Bibliotheques Musicales*] Toronto, Ontario [*Library symbol*] [*National Library of Canada*] (NLC)
**OTCMS**..... Operations Training Certification Management System [*NASA*]
**OTCOM**.... Cominco Ltd., Toronto, Ontario [*Library symbol*] [*National Library of Canada*] (NLC)
**OTCOS**..... Concord Scientific Corp., Downsview, Ontario [*Library symbol*] [*National Library of Canada*] (NLC)
**OTCOU**..... Council of Ontario Universities, Toronto, Ontario [*Library symbol*] [*National Library of Canada*] (NLC)
**OTCP**........ Canada Packers Ltd., Toronto, Ontario [*Library symbol*] [*National Library of Canada*] (NLC)
**OTCPAC**... Fleet Operational Training Command, Pacific [*Usually, COTCPAC*]
**OTCPB**...... Toronto City Planning Board Library, Ontario, [*Library symbol*] [*National Library of Canada*] (NLC)
**OTCQM**.... Office of the Theater Chief Quartermaster [*World War II*]
**OTCR**........ Office of Technical Cooperation and Research [*Department of State*]
**OTCR**........ Ontario Ministry of Culture and Communications, Toronto, Ontario [*Library symbol*] [*National Library of Canada*] (NLC)
**OTCRC**...... National Office Library, Canadian Red Cross Society [*Bibliotheque du Siege Social, Societe Canadienne de la Croix-Rouge*] Toronto, Ontario [*Library symbol*] [*National Library of Canada*] (NLC)
**OTCS**......... Ontario Ministry of Correctional Services, Toronto, Ontario [*Library symbol*] [*National Library of Canada*] (NLC)
**OTCS**......... Operational Teletype Communications Subsystem
**OTCS**......... Optical Transient Current Spectroscopy
**OTCSA**...... Canadian Standards Association, Rexdale, Ontario [*Library symbol*] [*National Library of Canada*] (NLC)
**OTCSAO**... Construction Safety Association of Ontario, Toronto, Ontario [*Library symbol*] [*National Library of Canada*] (NLC)
**OTCSC**...... Civil Service Commission of Ontario, Toronto, Ontario [*Library symbol*] [*National Library of Canada*] (NLC)
**OTCSE**...... Canadian Selection, Toronto, Ontario [*Library symbol*] [*National Library of Canada*] (NLC)

**OTCSS**...... CANEBSCO Subscription Service Ltd., Toronto, Ontario [*Library symbol*] [*National Library of Canada*] (NLC)
**OTCT**........ Canadian Tax Foundation [*Association Canadienne d'Etudes Fiscales*] Toronto, Ontario [*Library symbol*] [*National Library of Canada*] (NLC)
**OTCTA**...... Canadian Telebook Agency, Toronto, Ontario [*Library symbol*] [*National Library of Canada*] (NLC)
**OTCTAR**... Division of Records and Archives, City of Toronto (NLC)
**OTCTH**..... Town Hall, Collins Canada, Toronto, Ontario [*Library symbol*] [*National Library of Canada*] (NLC)
**OTCTVN**.. CTV News Research Library, CTV Television Network, Toronto, Ontario [*Library symbol*] [*National Library of Canada*] (NLC)
**OTCW**....... Canada Wire & Cable Co. Ltd., Toronto, Ontario [*Library symbol*] [*National Library of Canada*] (NLC)
**OTCWB**.... Welding Institute of Canada, Oakville, Ontario [*Library symbol*] [*National Library of Canada*] (NLC)
**OTCWT**.... Canadian Waste Technology, Inc., Toronto, Ontario [*Library symbol*] [*National Library of Canada*] (NLC)
**OTD**........... Contadora [*Panama*] [*Airport symbol*] (OAG)
**OTD**........... Ocean Travel Development (DS)
**OTD**........... Official Table of Distances (AFM)
**OTD**........... Offset, Tilted Dipole [*Model of Uranus' magnetic field*]
**OTD**........... Oil Turbine Drive
**OTD**........... On the Deck
**OTD**........... Operational Technical Documentation [*NASA*] (NASA)
**OTD**........... Operational Test Director [*Navy*]
**OTD**........... Operations and Technical Data [*Engineering*]
**OTD**........... Optical Tracking Device
**OTD**........... Oral Temperature Device (MCD)
**OTD**........... Orbiter Test Director [*NASA*] (NASA)
**OTD**........... Organ Tolerance Dose
**OTD**........... Ortho-Toluenediamine [*Organic chemistry*]
**OTDA**........ DSMA Acton Ltd., Toronto, Ontario [*Library symbol*] [*National Library of Canada*] (NLC)
**OTDA**........ Office of Tracking and Data Acquisition [*NASA*]
**OTDAR**..... Alexander Raxlen Memorial Library, Doctors Hospital, Toronto, Ontario [*Library symbol*] [*National Library of Canada*] (NLC)
**OTDC**........ Dominion Colour Ltd., Toronto, Ontario [*Library symbol*] [*National Library of Canada*] (NLC)
**OTDC**........ Observational Test and Development Center [*National Weather Service*] (NOAA)
**OTDC**........ Optical Target Designation Computer
**OTDCB**..... Dictionary of Canadian Biography, Toronto, Ontario [*Library symbol*] [*National Library of Canada*] (BIB)
**OTDD**........ Optical Target Detecting Device
**OTDE**........ Ontario Ministry of Education, Toronto, Ontario [*Library symbol*] [*National Library of Canada*] (NLC)
**OTDH**........ Ontario Ministry of Health, Toronto, Ontario [*Library symbol*] [*National Library of Canada*] (NLC)
**OTDHA**..... De Havilland Aircraft of Canada Ltd., Downsview, Ontario [*Library symbol*] [*National Library of Canada*] (NLC)
**OTDHC**..... Oceanographic Technical Data Handling Committee
**OTDHL**..... Laboratory Services, Ontario Ministry of Health, Toronto, Ontario [*Library symbol*] [*National Library of Canada*] (NLC)
**OTDL**........ Ontario Ministry of Labour, Toronto, Ontario [*Library symbol*] [*National Library of Canada*] (NLC)
**OTDM**....... Mines Library, Ontario Ministry of Natural Resources, Toronto, Ontario [*Library symbol*] [*National Library of Canada*] (NLC)
**OTDO**........ Donwood Institute, Toronto, Ontario [*Library symbol*] [*National Library of Canada*] (BIB)
**OTDR**........ Optical Fiber Time-Domain Reflectometer [*Data processing*]
**OTDR**........ Scientific Information Centre, Defence and Civil Institute of Environmental Medicine, Canada Department of National Defence [*Centre d'Information Scientifique, Institut Militaire et Civil de Medecine de l'Environnement, Ministere de la Defense Nationale*] Downsview, Ontario [*Library symbol*] [*National Library of Canada*] (NLC)
**OTDRE**..... Ontario Ministry of Treasury and Economics, Toronto, Ontario [*Library symbol*] [*National Library of Canada*] (NLC)
**OTDT**........ Ontario Ministry of Transportation and Communications, Toronto, Ontario [*Library symbol*] [*National Library of Canada*] (NLC)
**OTDT**........ Operational Test, Development Test
**OTDT**........ Operations Training Development Team [*Air Force*]
**Otd Tekh**... Otdelochnaya Tekhnika [*A publication*]
**OTDU**........ Ontario Ministry of Colleges and Universities, Toronto, Ontario [*Library symbol*] [*National Library of Canada*] (NLC)
**OTDW**....... Day-Wilson-Campbell, Toronto, Ontario [*Library symbol*] [*National Library of Canada*] (BIB)
**OTE**........... Emmanuel College, Victoria University, Toronto, Ontario [*Library symbol*] [*National Library of Canada*] (NLC)
**OTE**........... Ontario Ministry of Treasury and Economics Library [*UTLAS symbol*]
**OTE**........... Operational Test Equipment [*NASA*] (KSC)
**OT & E**...... Operational Test and Evaluation [*Military*] (AFM)
**OTE**........... Operational Test and Evaluation [*Army*] (AABC)
**OTE**........... Optical Tracking Electronics
**OTE**........... Optically Transparent Electrode
**OTE**........... Organismos Tilepikoinonion Ellados [*Hellenic Telecommunications Organization*] [*Greek*]
**OTE**........... Other Technical Effort
**OTE**........... Outer Tube Equipment
**OTE**........... Oxalyl Thiolester [*Biochemistry*]
**OTEA**........ Operational Test and Evaluation Agency [*Army*]
**OTEA**........ Oval Track Equipment Association (EA)
**OTEAO**..... Atmospheric Environment Service (Ontario Region), Environment Canada [*Service de l'Environnement Atmospherique (Region de l'Ontario), Environnement Canada*] Toronto, Ontario [*Library symbol*] [*National Library of Canada*] (NLC)
**OTEAOW**... Atmospheric Environment Service (ODIT Ontario Weather Centre), Environment Canada [*Service de l'Environnement Atmospherique (Centre Meteorologique de l'Ontario), Environnement Canada*] Toronto, Ontario [*Library symbol*] [*National Library of Canada*] (NLC)
**OTEBE**...... Resource Library, Board of Education for the City of Etobicoke, Ontario [*Library symbol*] [*National Library of Canada*] (NLC)
**OTEC**........ Education Centre, Toronto Board of Education, Ontario [*Library symbol*] [*National Library of Canada*] (NLC)
**OTEC**........ Ocean Thermal Energy Conversion
**OTEC**........ Omnitec, Inc. [*NASDAQ symbol*] (NQ)
**OTEC**........ Osage Tribal Education Committee [*Department of the Interior*] [*Muskogee, OK*] (EGAO)
**OTECA**...... Ocean Thermal Energy Conversion Act of 1980
**OTECS**...... Ocean Thermal Energy Conversion Systems [*Department of Energy*]
**OTECU**..... Colleges and Universitites, Ontario Ministry of Education, Toronto, Ontario [*Library symbol*] [*National Library of Canada*] (NLC)
**OTEE**........ Teeswater Branch, Bruce County Public Library, Ontario [*Library symbol*] [*National Library of Canada*] (NLC)
**OTEF**......... Operational Training and Evaluation Facility
**OTEM**....... ESSO [*Standard Oil*] Minerals of Canada, Toronto, Ontario [*Library symbol*] [*National Library of Canada*] (NLC)
**OTEMAC**... Temagami Community Library, Ontario [*Library symbol*] [*National Library of Canada*] (NLC)
**OTEMAS**... Osaka International Textile Machinery Show (TSPED)
**OTEMC**..... Elizabeth McRae Associates, Toronto, Ontario [*Library symbol*] [*Obsolete*] [*National Library of Canada*] (NLC)
**Otemon Econ Stud**... Otemon Economic Studies [*A publication*]
**OTEMP**..... Overtemperature (NASA)
**OTEMPO**... Operating Temporaries
**OTEMR**..... Conservation and Renewable Energy Office, Energy, Mines, and Resources Canada [*Bureau de la Conservation de l'Energie et de l'Energie Renouvelable, Energie, Mines, et Ressources Canada*] Toronto, Ontario [*Library symbol*] [*National Library of Canada*] (NLC)
**OTEP**......... Office of Transportation Energy Policy [*Department of Transportation*]
**OTEP**......... Operational Test and Evaluation Plan [*Military*] (AFM)
**OTEPL**...... Etobicoke Public Library, Ontario [*Library symbol*] [*National Library of Canada*] (NLC)
**OTEPS**...... Environmental Protection Service, Environment Canada [*Service de la Protection de l'Environnement, Environnement Canada*] Toronto, Ontario [*Library symbol*] [*National Library of Canada*] (NLC)
**OTEPSE**.... Environmental Emergency Library, Environmental Protection Service, Environment Canada [*Bibliotheque des Incidences Environnementales, Service de la Protection de l'Environnement, Environnement Canada*] Toronto, Ontario [*Library symbol*] [*National Library of Canada*] (NLC)
**OTER**........ Ontario Institute for Studies in Education, Toronto, Ontario [*Library symbol*] [*National Library of Canada*] (NLC)
**OTES**......... Optical Technology Experiment System
**OTES**......... Orbiter Thermal Effects Simulator [*NASA*]
**OTET**........ Ontario Educational Communications Authority, Toronto, Ontario [*Library symbol*] [*National Library of Canada*] (NLC)
**OTET**........ TVOntario, Toronto, Ontario [*Library symbol*] [*National Library of Canada*] (NLC)
**OTEU**........ Office and Technical Employees (International) Union
**O TEUT**..... Old Teutonic [*Language, etc.*] (ROG)
**OTEY**........ East York Public Library, Toronto, Ontario [*Library symbol*] [*National Library of Canada*] (NLC)
**OTEYBE**... Professional Library, Board of Education for the Borough of East York, Toronto, Ontario [*Library symbol*] [*National Library of Canada*] (NLC)
**OTF**........... Institute of Environment Studies, University of Toronto, Ontario [*Library symbol*] [*National Library of Canada*] (NLC)
**OTF**........... Octamer Transcription Factor [*Genetics*]
**OTF**........... Off-the-Film Metering [*Olympus cameras*]
**OTF**........... Optical Transfer Function
**OTF**........... Optimum Traffic Frequency [*Radio*]
**OTF**........... Oral Transfer Factor [*Virology*]
**OTF**........... Orbital Test Flight (MCD)

**OTF** ........ Other than Flat [*Freight*]
**OTFC** ........ Official 3 Stooges Fan Club [*Defunct*] (EA)
**OTFC** ........ Ontario Ministry of Consumer and Commercial Relations, Toronto, Ontario [*Library symbol*] [*National Library of Canada*] (NLC)
**OTFC** ........ Over Traffic (FAAC)
**OTFCS** ...... On-Target Fire Control System (MCD)
**OTFE** ........ Optical Terminal Flight Evaluation
**OTFE** ........ OTF Equities, Inc. [*NASDAQ symbol*] (NQ)
**OTFEC** ...... Fenco Consultants Ltd., Toronto, Ontario [*Library symbol*] [*National Library of Canada*] (NLC)
**OTFH** ........ Forest Hill Public Library, Toronto, Ontario [*Library symbol*] [*National Library of Canada*] (NLC)
**OTFM** ........ Fire Marshal of Ontario, Toronto, Ontario [*Library symbol*] [*National Library of Canada*] (NLC)
**OTFN** ........ Information Centre, Falconbridge Nickel Mines Ltd., Toronto, Ontario [*Library symbol*] [*National Library of Canada*] (NLC)
**OT/FOT** .... Operational Test/Follow-On Operational Test
**OTFP** ........ Fisons Corp. Ltd., Markham, Ontario [*Library symbol*] [*National Library of Canada*] (NLC)
**OTFP** ........ Octylthio(trifluoro)propanone [*Biochemistry*]
**OTFP** ........ Other than Full Paid [*IRS*]
**OTFR** ........ Overall Transfer Function Response
**OTFT** ........ Financial Times, Don Mills, Ontario [*Library symbol*] [*National Library of Canada*] (NLC)
**OTFTS** ...... Outfits
**OTG** .......... Information Centre, Glaxo Canada, Inc., Toronto, Ontario [*Library symbol*] [*National Library of Canada*] (BIB)
**OTG** .......... Oil Temperature Gauge (MSA)
**OTG** .......... OPTEVFOR [*Operational Test and Evaluation Force*] Tactics Guide [*Navy*] (CAAL)
**OTG** .......... Option Table Generator
**OTG** .......... Otolith Test Goggles [*NASA*] (KSC)
**OTG** .......... Worthington [*Minnesota*] [*Airport symbol*] (OAG)
**OTGA** ........ Information Centre, Giffels Associates Ltd., Rexdale, Ontario [*Library symbol*] [*National Library of Canada*] (NLC)
**OTGAR** ..... Engineering Library, Garrett Canada, Rexdale, Ontario [*Library symbol*] [*National Library of Canada*] (BIB)
**OTGB** ........ Library and Audio-Visual Services, George Brown College of Applied Arts and Technology, Toronto, Ontario [*Library symbol*] [*National Library of Canada*] (BIB)
**OTGFM** .... Management Science Department, General Foods, Inc., Don Mills, Ontario [*Library symbol*] [*National Library of Canada*] (NLC)
**OTGG** ........ Goodman & Goodman, Toronto, Ontario [*Library symbol*] [*National Library of Canada*] (BIB)
**OTGH** ........ Fudger Medical Library, Toronto General Hospital, Ontario [*Library symbol*] [*National Library of Canada*] (NLC)
**OTGHPP** .. Ocean Thermal Gradient Hydraulic Power Plant
**OTGM** ........ Globe and Mail, Toronto, Ontario [*Library symbol*] [*National Library of Canada*] (NLC)
**OTGMC** .... Gulf Minerals Canada Ltd., Toronto, Ontario [*Library symbol*] [*National Library of Canada*] (NLC)
**OTGOH** .... Gowling & Henderson, Toronto, Ontario [*Library symbol*] [*National Library of Canada*] (NLC)
**OTGS** ........ Gore & Storrie Ltd., Toronto, Ontario [*Library symbol*] [*National Library of Canada*] (NLC)
**OTGS** ........ Ocean Thermal Gradient System [*National Science Foundation*]
**OTGSB** ...... Bibliographic Centre, Ontario Ministry of Government Services, Toronto, Ontario [*Library symbol*] [*National Library of Canada*] (NLC)
**OTGSI** ....... CTS Information Resource Centre, Ontario Ministry of Government Services, Toronto [*Library symbol*] [*National Library of Canada*] (BIB)
**OTH** .......... Independent Institute, NAD, Dublin, OH [*OCLC symbol*] (OCLC)
**OTH** .......... North Bend [*Oregon*] [*Airport symbol*] (OAG)
**OTH** .......... Ontario Hydro, Toronto, Ontario [*Library symbol*] [*National Library of Canada*] (NLC)
**OTH** .......... Optical Time History (MCD)
**Oth** ............ Othello [*Shakespearean work*]
**OTH** .......... Othello [*Washington*] [*Seismograph station code, US Geological Survey*] (SEIS)
**OTH** .......... Other than Hand [*Freight*]
**OTH** .......... Other than Honorable Conditions [*Military*] (AABC)
**OTH** .......... Over-the-Horizon [*RADAR*]
**OTHA** ........ Hatch Associates Ltd., Toronto, Ontario [*Library symbol*] [*National Library of Canada*] (NLC)
**OTHB** ........ Over-the-Horizon Back-Scatter [*RADAR*]
**OTHB** ........ Toronto Historical Society, Ontario [*Library symbol*] [*National Library of Canada*] (BIB)
**OTHC** ........ Humber College of Applied Arts and Technology, Rexdale, Ontario [*Library symbol*] [*National Library of Canada*] (NLC)
**OTH/DA** ... Over-the-Horizon/Damage Assessment [*Navy*] (CAAL)
**OTHDC & T** ... Over-the-Horizon Detection, Classification, and Targeting (NVT)
**OTH-E** ...... Over-the-Horizon - Expanded
**OTHE** ........ Thessalon Union Public Library, Ontario [*Library symbol*] [*National Library of Canada*] (NLC)
**OTH-F** ....... Over-the-Horizon - Forward Scatter
**OTHL** ........ Advanced Technology Centre, Honeywell Ltd., Willowdale, Ontario [*Library symbol*] [*National Library of Canada*] (NLC)
**OTHMC** .... Information Resources, Hay Management Consultants, Toronto, Ontario [*Library symbol*] [*National Library of Canada*] (NLC)
**OTHMH** ... Humber Memorial Hospital, Weston, Ontario [*Library symbol*] [*National Library of Canada*] (NLC)
**OTHO** ....... Thornbury Public Library, Ontario [*Library symbol*] [*National Library of Canada*] (NLC)
**OTHOP** ..... Quebec & Ontario Paper Co. Ltd., Thorold, Ontario [*Library symbol*] [*National Library of Canada*] (NLC)
**OTHOR** ..... Thornhill Public Library, Ontario [*Library symbol*] [*National Library of Canada*] (NLC)
**OTHORF** .. Metallurgical Laboratory, Falconbridge Nickel Mines Ltd., Thornhill, Ontario [*Library symbol*] [*National Library of Canada*] (NLC)
**OTHORO** ... Thorold Public Library, Ontario [*Library symbol*] [*National Library of Canada*] (BIB)
**OTHR** ........ Ontario Hydro Research, Toronto, Ontario [*Library symbol*] [*National Library of Canada*] (NLC)
**OTHR** ........ Over-the-Horizon RADAR (MCD)
**Othr Womn** ... Other Woman [*A publication*]
**OTHSA** ..... Orphan Train Heritage Society of America (EA)
**OTHSC** ..... Hospital for Sick Children, Toronto, Ontario [*Library symbol*] [*National Library of Canada*] (NLC)
**Oth Sce** ...... Other Scenes [*A publication*]
**OTHSSM** ... Over-the-Horizon Ship-to-Ship Missile
**OTHT** ........ Over-the-Horizon Targeting (NVT)
**OTHU** ....... Huntec Ltd., Toronto, Ontario [*Library symbol*] [*National Library of Canada*] (NLC)
**OTI** ........... Morotai Island [*Indonesia*] [*Airport symbol*] (OAG)
**OTI** ........... Newport, RI [*Location identifier*] [*FAA*] (FAAL)
**OTI** ........... Office of Technical Information (MUGU)
**OTI** ........... Official Test Insecticide
**OTI** ........... Ordnance Technical Instructions [*Navy*]
**OTI** ........... Oregon Technical Institute
**OTI** ........... Original Title [*Online database field identifier*]
**OTI** ........... OT Industries, Inc. [*Vancouver Stock Exchange symbol*]
**OTI** ........... Otiai [*USSR*] [*Seismograph station code, US Geological Survey*] [*Closed*] (SEIS)
**OTI** ........... Oxide Throat Insert
**OTI** ........... Timmins Public Library, Ontario [*Library symbol*] [*National Library of Canada*] (NLC)
**OTI** ........... Trend; das Oesterreichische Wirtschaftsmagazin [*A publication*]
**OTIA** ......... Office of Technical Information Agency [*Army*] (MCD)
**OTIA** ......... Ordnance Technical Intelligence Agency (AAG)
**OTIAP** ....... IAPA [*Industrial Accident Prevention Association*] Library, Toronto, Ontario [*Library symbol*] [*National Library of Canada*] (NLC)
**OTIBI** ........ IBI Group, Toronto, Ontario [*Library symbol*] [*National Library of Canada*] (BIB)
**OTIC** ......... Idea Corp., Toronto, Ontario [*Library symbol*] [*National Library of Canada*] (NLC)
**OTIC** ......... Innovation Ontario Corp., Toronto, Ontario [*Library symbol*] [*National Library of Canada*] (NLC)
**OTICA** ....... Institute of Chartered Accountants of Ontario, Toronto, Ontario [*Library symbol*] [*National Library of Canada*] (NLC)
**OTID** ......... Industrial Disease Standards Panel, Toronto, Ontario [*Library symbol*] [*National Library of Canada*] (BIB)
**OTIEP** ....... Office of Technical Information and Educational Programs [*Terminated*] [*NASA*]
**OTIF** ......... Organisation Intergouvernementale pour les Transports Internationaux Ferrovaires [*Intergovernmental Organization for International Carriage by Rail*] (EAIO)
**OTif** ........... Tiffin Seneca Public Library, Tiffin, OH [*Library symbol*] [*Library of Congress*] (LCLS)
**OTifH** ........ Heidelberg College, Tiffin, OH [*Library symbol*] [*Library of Congress*] (LCLS)
**OTIG** ......... Office of the Inspector General [*Army*] (AABC)
**OTIHM** ..... Tillsonburg and District Historical Museum Society, Tillsonburg, Ontario [*Library symbol*] [*National Library of Canada*] (NLC)
**OTII** .......... Our Torah Institutions of Israel (EA)
**OTIL** .......... Tilbury Public Library, Ontario [*Library symbol*] [*National Library of Canada*] (NLC)
**OTIM** ........ Pontifical Institute of Mediaeval Studies, University of Toronto, Ontario [*Library symbol*] [*National Library of Canada*] (NLC)
**OTIN** ......... International Nickel Co. of Canada Ltd., Toronto, Ontario [*Library symbol*] [*National Library of Canada*] (NLC)
**OTINF** ....... Infomart, Toronto, Ontario [*Library symbol*] [*National Library of Canada*] (NLC)
**OTINP** ....... Information Plus Library, Toronto, Ontario [*Library symbol*] [*National Library of Canada*] (BIB)
**OTIO** ......... United Kingdom Information Office, Toronto, Ontario [*Library symbol*] [*National Library of Canada*] (NLC)

**OTIOL** ...... Imperial Oil Ltd., Toronto, Ontario [*Library symbol*] [*National Library of Canada*] (NLC)
**OTIP**.......... Occupational Therapist in Independent Practice
**OTIP**.......... Tillsonburg Public Library, Ontario [*Library symbol*] [*National Library of Canada*] (NLC)
**OTIR** ......... Operational Test Incident Report (MCD)
**OTIS**.......... Occupational Training Information System
**OTIS**.......... Offset Target Indicator System (MCD)
**OTIS**.......... Oklahoma Teletype Interlibrary System [*Library network*]
**OTIS**.......... Once-Through Integral System [*Nuclear energy*] (NRCH)
**OTIS**.......... Online Telecommunications Information Service [*Connections Telecommunications, Inc.*] [*West Bridgewater, MA*] [*Telecommunications service*] (TSSD)
**OTIS**.......... Operational Test Instrumentation Ship [*Navy*]
**OTIS**.......... Ordnance Telemetry Instrumentation Station [*Army*] (AABC)
**OTIS**.......... Oregon Total Information System [*Eugene*] [*Information service or system*] (IID)
**OTIS**.......... Other than Iron or Steel [*Freight*]
**OTIS**.......... Overstayer Tracing and Intelligence System [*British*]
**OTIU** ......... Overseas Technical Information Unit [*Department of Trade*] [*British*]
**OTIV** ......... OT Industries, Inc. [*Vancouver, BC*] [*NASDAQ symbol*] (NQ)
**OTIV** ......... Tiverton Branch, Bruce County Public Library, Ontario [*Library symbol*] [*National Library of Canada*] (NLC)
**OTJ**........... Off-the-Job
**OTJ**........... On the Job
**OTJ**........... Toronto Regional Office, Department of Justice Canada [*Bureau Regional de Toronto, Ministere de la Justice du Canada*] Toronto, Ontario [*Library symbol*] [*National Library of Canada*] (NLC)
**OTJAE** ...... John Arpin Enterprises, Inc., Toronto, Ontario [*Library symbol*] [*National Library of Canada*] (NLC)
**OTJAG**...... Office of the Judge Advocate General [*Army*] (AABC)
**OTJFM** ..... James F. MacLaren Ltd., Willowdale, Ontario [*Library symbol*] [*National Library of Canada*] (NLC)
**OTJL** ......... Judges Library, Ontario Ministry of the Attorney General, Toronto, Ontario [*Library symbol*] [*National Library of Canada*] (NLC)
**OTJPS**....... Sands Pharmaceutical Division, Jerram Pharmaceuticals Ltd., Toronto, Ontario [*Library symbol*] [*National Library of Canada*] (NLC)
**OTJR**......... Occupational Therapy Journal of Research [*A publication*]
**OTJWT** ..... Information Centre, J. Walter Thompson Co. Ltd., Toronto, Ontario [*Library symbol*] [*National Library of Canada*] (NLC)
**OTK**........... Knox College, University of Toronto, Ontario [*Library symbol*] [*National Library of Canada*] (NLC)
**OTK**........... Oil Tank
**OTK**........... Oxidizer Tank (MCD)
**OTKC** ........ Kidd Creek Mines Ltd., Toronto, Ontario [*Library symbol*] [*National Library of Canada*] (NLC)
**OTKDF**...... Other than Knocked Down Flat [*Freight*]
**OTKE** ........ Kilborn Engineering Ltd., Toronto, Ontario [*Library symbol*] [*National Library of Canada*] (NLC)
**Otkrytiya Izobret Prom Obraztsy Tovarnye Znaki** ... Otkrytiya, Izobreteniya, Promyshlennye Obraztsy, Tovarnye Znaki [*Bulletin for Inventions, Designs, and Trademarks*] [*USSR*] [*A publication*]
**Otkryt Izobret** ... Otkrytiya, Izobreteniya, Promyshlennye Obraztsy, Tovarnye Znaki [*Bulletin for Inventions, Designs, and Trademarks*] [*USSR*] [*A publication*]
**OTL**........... Legislative Library of Ontario, Toronto, Ontario [*Library symbol*] [*National Library of Canada*] (NLC)
**OTL**........... Libbey-Owens-Ford Glass Co., Technical Library, Toledo, OH [*Library symbol*] [*Library of Congress*] (LCLS)
**OTL**........... Observer Target Line (NVT)
**OTL**........... Ogden Technology Laboratories [*NASA*] (KSC)
**OTL**........... Ohio Theological Librarians [*Library network*]
**OTL**........... Oil-Tight Light
**OTL**........... [*The*] Old Testament Library [*A publication*] (BJA)
**OTL**........... Online Task Loader
**OTL**........... Operating Temperature Limit
**OTL**........... Operating Time Log (AAG)
**OTL**........... Ordnance Test Laboratory (NASA)
**OTL**........... Out to Lunch
**OTL**........... Outer Tube Limit [*Chemical engineering*]
**OTL**........... Outland Resources [*Vancouver Stock Exchange symbol*]
**OTL**........... Ovine Testicular Lymph [*Endocrinology*]
**OTL**........... Oxidizer Topping Line (AAG)
**OTLAC**...... Tamworth Branch, Lennox and Addington County Library, Ontario [*Library symbol*] [*National Library of Canada*] (BIB)
**OTLC** ........ Information Section, Ontario Ministry of Natural Resources, Toronto, Ontario [*Library symbol*] [*National Library of Canada*] (NLC)
**OTLC** ........ Open Tubular Liquid Chromatography
**OTLC** ........ Orbiter Timeline Constraints [*NASA*] (NASA)
**OTLCC**...... Lummus Co. Canada Ltd., Willowdale, Ontario [*Library symbol*] [*National Library of Canada*] (NLC)
**OTLF**......... Natural Resources Library, Ontario Ministry of Natural Resources, Toronto, Ontario [*Library symbol*] [*National Library of Canada*] (NLC)
**OTLH**........ Laventhol & Horwath, Toronto, Ontario, [*Library symbol*] [*National Library of Canada*] (BIB)
**OTLK** ........ Outlook (FAAC)
**OTLO**........ Libbey-Owens-Ford Glass Co., Corporate Library, Toledo, OH [*Library symbol*] [*Library of Congress*] (LCLS)
**OTLP**......... Ledbury Park Junior High School, Toronto, Ontario [*Library symbol*] [*National Library of Canada*] (NLC)
**OTLR** ........ Otago Law Review [*A publication*]
**OTLR** ........ Research Branch, Ontario Ministry of Natural Resources, Toronto, Ontario [*Library symbol*] [*National Library of Canada*] (NLC)
**OTLS**......... Law Society of Upper Canada, Toronto, Ontario [*Library symbol*] [*National Library of Canada*] (NLC)
**OTLSC** ...... Litton Systems Canada Ltd., Rexdale, Ontario [*Library symbol*] [*National Library of Canada*] (NLC)
**OTLV** ........ Onza, Tigra, y Leon. Revista para la Infancia Venezolana [*A publication*]
**OTM**.......... Atmospheric Environment Service, Environment Canada [*Service de l'Environnement Atmospherique, Environnement Canada*] Downsview, Ontario [*Library symbol*] [*National Library of Canada*] (NLC)
**OTM**.......... Office of Telecommunications Management [*Later, OTP*] [*FCC*]
**OTM**.......... Old Time Music [*A publication*]
**OTM**.......... On the Mark - Mark Hamill Fan Club (EA)
**OTM**.......... Once-through-Methanol [*Fuel technology*]
**OTM**.......... Optical Tool Master (MCD)
**OTM**.......... Ortho-Tolidine Manganese Sulphate
**OTM**.......... Other than Mexican [*Term applied by US Border Patrol to certain illegal immigrants*]
**OTM**.......... Ottumwa [*Iowa*] [*Airport symbol*] (OAG)
**OTM**.......... Timken Co., Research Library, Canton, OH [*OCLC symbol*] (OCLC)
**OTM**.......... Toledo Museum of Art, Toledo, OH [*Library symbol*] [*Library of Congress*] (LCLS)
**OTMA**....... Office Technology Management Association [*Defunct*] (EA)
**OTMA**....... Oilfield Tank Manufacturers Association (EA)
**OTMAG**.... Ontario Ministry of the Attorney General [*Ministere du Procureur-General*], Toronto [*Library symbol*] [*National Library of Canada*] (BIB)
**OTMB** ....... McMillan, Binch, Toronto, Ontario [*Library symbol*] [*National Library of Canada*] (NLC)
**OTMC** ....... Massey College, Toronto, Ontario [*Library symbol*] [*National Library of Canada*] (NLC)
**OTMC** ....... Medical College of Ohio at Toledo, Toledo, OH [*Library symbol*] [*Library of Congress*] (LCLS)
**OTMCL**..... Metropolitan Toronto Library, Ontario [*Library symbol*] [*National Library of Canada*] (NLC)
**OTME** ....... Ontario Ministry of Energy, Toronto, Ontario [*Library symbol*] [*National Library of Canada*] (NLC)
**OTMEN** .... Ontario Ministry of the Environment, Toronto, Ontario [*Library symbol*] [*National Library of Canada*] (NLC)
**OTMENL** ... Laboratory, Ontario Ministry of the Environment, Rexdale, Ontario [*Library symbol*] [*National Library of Canada*] (NLC)
**OTMF** ....... McIntyre-Falconbridge Library, Toronto, Ontario [*Library symbol*] [*National Library of Canada*] (NLC)
**OTMH** ...... Financial Post, Toronto, Ontario [*Library symbol*] [*National Library of Canada*] (NLC)
**OTMI** ........ Royal Canadian Military Institute, Toronto, Ontario [*Library symbol*] [*National Library of Canada*] (NLC)
**OTMIO** ..... Employment and Immigration Canada [*Emploi et Immigration Canada*] Toronto, Ontario [*Library symbol*] [*National Library of Canada*] (NLC)
**OTMIO** ..... Ontario Region Library, Employment and Immigration Canada [*Bibliotheque de la Region de l'Ontario, Emploi et Immigration Canada*], North York, Ontario [*Library symbol*] [*National Library of Canada*] (NLC)
**OTMIS**...... Medical Information Services, Toronto, Ontario [*Library symbol*] [*National Library of Canada*] (BIB)
**OTML** ....... Law Library, Manufacturers Life Insurance Co., Toronto, Ontario [*Library symbol*] [*National Library of Canada*] (BIB)
**OTML** ....... Oatmeal [*Freight*]
**OTMM**...... Mary Manse College, Toledo, OH [*Library symbol*] [*Library of Congress*] (LCLS)
**OTMM**...... McCarthy & McCarthy, Barristers & Solicitors, Toronto, Ontario [*Library symbol*] [*National Library of Canada*] (NLC)
**OTMMB** ... Ontario Milks Marketing Board, Toronto, Ontario [*Library symbol*] [*National Library of Canada*] (NLC)
**OTMML** ... Micromedia Ltd., Toronto, Ontario [*Library symbol*] [*National Library of Canada*] (NLC)
**OTMMM** ... Marshall-Macklin-Monaghan Library, Don Mills, Ontario [*Library symbol*] [*National Library of Canada*] (NLC)
**OTMO**....... Monopros Ltd., Toronto, Ontario [*Library symbol*] [*National Library of Canada*] (BIB)

**OTMOF** .... MacDonald Ophthalmic Foundation, Toronto, Ontario [*Library symbol*] [*National Library of Canada*] (NLC)
**OTMPA** .... Oberflaechentechnik/Metallpraxis [*A publication*]
**OTMS** ....... Mount Sinai Hospital, Toronto, Ontario [*Library symbol*] [*National Library of Canada*] (NLC)
**OTMS** ....... [*The*] Old Testament and Modern Study [*A publication*] (BJA)
**OTMS** ....... Operational Technical Managerial System (NVT)
**OTMSM** ... Management Services Department Library, Municipality of Metropolitan Toronto, Ontario [*Library symbol*] [*National Library of Canada*] (BIB)
**OTMSS** ..... Professional Library, Metropolitan Separate School Board, Willowdale, Ontario [*Library symbol*] [*National Library of Canada*] (NLC)
**OTMT** ....... Monetary Times, Toronto, Ontario [*Library symbol*] [*National Library of Canada*] (NLC)
**OTMTC** .... Economic Development Division, Metro Toronto Chairman's Office, Toronto, Ontario [*Library symbol*] [*National Library of Canada*] (BIB)
**OTMTS** ..... Metropolitan Toronto School Board, Ontario [*Library symbol*] [*National Library of Canada*] (NLC)
**OTMTSS** .. Secondary Schools, Metropolitan Toronto School Board, Ontario [*Library symbol*] [*National Library of Canada*] (NLC)
**OTMW** ...... Department of Works, Municipality of Metropolitan Toronto, Ontario [*Library symbol*] [*National Library of Canada*] (BIB)
**OTN** ........... Newtonbrook Secondary School, Willowdale, Ontario [*Library symbol*] [*National Library of Canada*] (NLC)
**OTN** ........... Oaktown, IN [*Location identifier*] [*FAA*] (FAAL)
**OTN** ........... Octal Track Number [*Data processing*]
**OTN** ........... Operational Teletype Network
**OTN** ........... Operational Test, Non-Major Systems (MCD)
**OTN** ........... Over the Nose [*Aviation*]
**OTNA** ........ Ontario Ministry of Northern Development and Mines, Toronto, Ontario [*Library symbol*] [*National Library of Canada*] (NLC)
**OTNC** ........ International Council for Adult Education, Toronto, Ontario [*Library symbol*] [*National Library of Canada*] (BIB)
**OTNG** ........ Observer Training [*Army*] (AABC)
**OTNGH** .... Health Sciences Library, Northwestern General Hospital, Toronto, Ontario [*Library symbol*] [*National Library of Canada*] (BIB)
**OTNH** ....... National Heritage Ltd., Toronto, Ontario [*Library symbol*] [*National Library of Canada*] (NLC)
**OTNHH** .... Health Protection Branch, Canada Department of National Health and Welfare [*Direction Generale de la Protection de la Sante, Ministere de la Sante Nationale et du Bien-Etre Social*] Toronto, Ontario [*Library symbol*] [*National Library of Canada*] (NLC)
**OTNI** ......... Industrial Development Office, National Research Council Canada [*Bureau du Developpement Industriel, Conseil National de Recherches Canada*], Scarborough, Ontario [*Library symbol*] [*National Library of Canada*] (NLC)
**OTNIMR** .. G. Allan Roeher Institute, Downsview, Ontario [*Library symbol*] [*National Library of Canada*] (NLC)
**OTNIMR** .. National Institute on Mental Retardation [*Institut National pour la Deficience Mentale*] Toronto, Ontario [*Library symbol*] [*National Library of Canada*] (NLC)
**OTNM** ....... Northern Mines, Toronto, Ontario [*Library symbol*] [*National Library of Canada*] (NLC)
**OTNM** ....... Over-Thirty-Never-Married [*Lifestyle classification*]
**OTNR** ........ Survey Records Branch, Ontario Ministry of Natural Resources, Toronto, Ontario [*Library symbol*] [*National Library of Canada*] (BIB)
**OTNS** ........ Bank of Nova Scotia [*Banque de Nouvelle-Ecosse*], Toronto, Ontario [*Library symbol*] [*National Library of Canada*] (NLC)
**OTNY** ........ North York Public Library, Willowdale, Ontario [*Library symbol*] [*National Library of Canada*] (NLC)
**OTNYE** ..... F. W. Minkler Library, North York Board of Education, Willowdale, Ontario [*Library symbol*] [*National Library of Canada*] (NLC)
**OTO** ........... Oil Temperature Out
**OTO** ........... One-Time-Only
**OTO** ........... Operator-to-Operator [*Military*] (CAAL)
**OTO** ........... Optical Tracker Operator (MUGU)
**OTO** ........... Ordo Templi Orientis [*Order of the Oriental Templars*] [*A mystical lodge*] [*Latin*] (ADA)
**Oto** ............. Otolaryngology [*Medicine*]
**OTO** ........... Otology [*Medicine*]
**oto** ............. Otomian [*MARC language code*] [*Library of Congress*] (LCCP)
**OTO** ........... Otorhinolaryngology [*Medicine*] (DHSM)
**OTO** ........... Otto, NM [*Location identifier*] [*FAA*] (FAAL)
**OTO** ........... Out-to-Out (AAG)
**OTO** ........... Owens-Illinois, Inc., Technical Information Service-NTC, Toledo, OH [*Library symbol*] [*Library of Congress*] (LCLS)
**OTO** ........... Tottenham Public Library, Ontario [*Library symbol*] [*National Library of Canada*] (NLC)
**OTOB** ........ Tobermory Branch, Bruce County Public Library, Ontario [*Library symbol*] [*National Library of Canada*] (NLC)
**OTOC** ........ Ontario Cancer Institute, Toronto, Ontario [*Library symbol*] [*National Library of Canada*] (NLC)
**OTOCTA** .. Optimum Technical Operational Concept to Accomplish
**OTOD** ........ Organization of Teachers of Oral Diagnosis (EA)
**OTOE** ........ Omnispace Environments Ltd., Toronto, Ontario [*Library symbol*] [*National Library of Canada*] (NLC)
**OTOEB** ..... Ontario Energy Board, Toronto, Ontario [*Library symbol*] [*National Library of Canada*] (NLC)
**OTOGR** ..... Canadian Geriatrics Research Society, Toronto, Ontario [*Library symbol*] [*National Library of Canada*] (NLC)
**OTOH** ....... Ontario Ministry of Municipal Affairs and Housing, Toronto, Ontario [*Library symbol*] [*National Library of Canada*] (NLC)
**OTOHCR** ... Central Records, Ontario Hydro, Toronto, Ontario [*Library symbol*] [*National Library of Canada*] (NLC)
**OTOL** ........ Ontario Lottery Corporation, Toronto, Ontario [*Library symbol*] [*National Library of Canada*] (BIB)
**OTOL** ........ Otology [*Medicine*]
**Otolar Clin** ... Otolaryngologic Clinics of North America [*A publication*]
**Oto Laring** ... Oto-Laringologia [*A publication*]
**Otolaryngol Clin N Am** ... Otolaryngologic Clinics of North America [*A publication*]
**Otolaryngol Clin North Am** ... Otolaryngologic Clinics of North America [*A publication*]
**Otolaryngol Head Neck Surg** ... Otolaryngology and Head and Neck Surgery [*A publication*]
**Otolaryngol Pol** ... Otolaryngologia Polska [*A publication*]
**Otol Fukuoka** ... Otologia Fukuoka [*A publication*]
**Otol Fukuoka Jibi To Rinsho** ... Otologia Fukuoka Jibi To Rinsho [*A publication*]
**OTOLR** ..... Ontario Labour Relations Board [*Commission des Relations de Travail de l'Ontario*], Toronto, Ontario [*Library symbol*] [*National Library of Canada*] (NLC)
**OTOLRC**... Ontario Law Reform Commission, Toronto, Ontario [*Library symbol*] [*National Library of Canada*] (BIB)
**OTOMA** .... Ontario Medical Association, Toronto, Ontario [*Library symbol*] [*National Library of Canada*] (NLC)
**OTOME** .... Information Resource Centre, Ontario Municipal Employees Retirement Board, Toronto [*Library symbol*] [*National Library of Canada*] (BIB)
**OTOMR** .... Ontario Ministry of Revenue, Toronto, Ontario [*Library symbol*] [*National Library of Canada*] (NLC)
**OTONA** ..... Ontario Nurses Association, Toronto, Ontario [*Library symbol*] [*National Library of Canada*] (NLC)
**Oto Noro Oftalmol** ... Oto-Noro Oftalmoloji [*A publication*]
**OTOPC** ..... Ortho Pharmaceutical Canada Ltd., Don Mills, Ontario [*Library symbol*] [*National Library of Canada*] (NLC)
**OTOPCT**... Planning and Research Library, Technical Services Branch, Ontario Police Commission, Toronto, Ontario [*Library symbol*] [*National Library of Canada*] (NLC)
**Otoplenie Vent Stroit Teplofiz** ... Otoplenie. Ventilyatsiya i Stroitel'naya Teplofizika [*A publication*]
**Oto-Rhino-Laryngol** ... Oto-Rhino-Laryngology [*A publication*]
**Oto-Rhino-Laryngol (Tokyo)** ... Oto-Rhino-Laryngology (Tokyo) [*A publication*]
**Oto-Rino-Laringol Ital** ... Oto-Rino-Laringologia Italiana [*A publication*]
**Oto-Rino-Laringol Oftalmol** ... Oto-Rino-Laringologie si Oftalmologie [*A publication*]
**OTOS** ........ Orbit-to-Orbit Stage [*NASA*] (MCD)
**OTOSC** ..... Ontario Securities Commission, Toronto, Ontario [*Library symbol*] [*National Library of Canada*] (NLC)
**OTOSS** ...... Ontario Secondary School Teachers Federation, Toronto, Ontario [*Library symbol*] [*National Library of Canada*] (NLC)
**OTOW** ....... Resource Centre, Ontario Women's Directorate [*Library symbol*] [*National Library of Canada*] (BIB)
**OTP** ........... Ocean Test Platform [*Marine science*] (MSC)
**OTP** ........... Of This Parish
**OTP** ........... Of True Position (MSA)
**OTP** ........... Office Technology Plus [*General Services Administration*]
**OTP** ........... Office of Telecommunications Policy [*Terminated, 1978*] [*Executive Office of the President*]
**OTP** ........... Office of Trade Promotion [*Department of Commerce*]
**OTP** ........... On Top [*Aviation*]
**OTP** ........... One-Time Pad [*Navy*] [*British*]
**OTP** ........... One-Time Programmable [*Data processing*]
**OTP** ........... Open Top [*Freight*]
**OTP** ........... Operational Test Plan
**OTP** ........... Operational Test Procedure (KSC)
**OTP** ........... Operations Turnaround Plan (NASA)
**OTP** ........... Oscillation Test Point [*British military*] (DMA)
**OTP** ........... Otepa [*Tuamotu Archipelago*] [*Seismograph station code, US Geological Survey*] (SEIS)
**OTP** ........... Other than Portable [*Freight*]
**Ot P** ........... Otto Papiensis [*Flourished, 12th century*] [*Authority cited in pre-1607 legal work*] (DSA)
**OTP** ........... Outline Test Plan [*Army*]
**OTP** ........... Overtime Premium (MCD)
**OTP** ........... Ovine Trophoblast Protein [*Biochemistry*]
**OTP** ........... Oxidizer Tanking Panel (AAG)
**OTP** ........... Ozone Trends Panel [*NASA*]

**OTP**.......... Toronto Public Libraries, Ontario [*Library symbol*] [*National Library of Canada*] (NLC)
**OTPA**........ Institute of Public Administration of Canada [*Institut d'Administration Publique du Canada*] Toronto, Ontario [*Library symbol*] [*National Library of Canada*] (NLC)
**OTPAL**...... PAL Reading Service, Toronto, Ontario [*Library symbol*] [*National Library of Canada*] (NLC)
**OTPEC**...... Officer Training Program Examining Center [*Air Force*]
**OTPFA**...... Fine Arts Library, Northern District, Toronto Public Libraries, Ontario [*Library symbol*] [*National Library of Canada*] (NLC)
**OTPG**........ Polar Gas Library, Toronto, Ontario [*Library symbol*] [*National Library of Canada*] (NLC)
**OTPH**........ History Section, Metropolitan Toronto Library, Ontario [*Library symbol*] [*National Library of Canada*] (NLC)
**OTPHC**..... Prentice Hall Canada, Inc., Scarborough, Ontario [*Library symbol*] [*National Library of Canada*] (NLC)
**OTPHR**..... Resource Centre, Department of Public Health, City of Toronto, Ontario [*Library symbol*] [*National Library of Canada*] (BIB)
**OTPI**.......... On Top Position Indicator [*Navy*] (NG)
**OTPM**....... Peat, Marwick & Partners, Toronto, Ontario [*Library symbol*] [*National Library of Canada*] (NLC)
**OTPMG**.... Office of the Provost Marshal General [*Army*]
**OTPOA**..... Otolaryngologia Polska [*A publication*]
**OTPP**......... Ocean Thermal Power Plant
**OTPP**......... Ontario Provincial Police, Toronto, Ontario [*Library symbol*] [*National Library of Canada*] (NLC)
**Ot Pp**.......... Otto Papiensis [*Flourished, 12th century*] [*Authority cited in pre-1607 legal work*] (DSA)
**OTPPC**...... Ontario Provincial Police College, Toronto, Ontario [*Library symbol*] [*National Library of Canada*] (NLC)
**OTPR**......... Proctor & Redfern Group, Don Mills, Ontario [*Library symbol*] [*National Library of Canada*] (NLC)
**OTP/RS**.... Outline Test Plan/Resume Sheet (MCD)
**OTPRW**..... National Office Library, Price Waterhouse & Co., Toronto, Ontario [*Library symbol*] [*National Library of Canada*] (BIB)
**OTPT**......... Output (KSC)
**OTPW**....... Ontario Ministry of Community and Social Services, Toronto, Ontario [*Library symbol*] [*National Library of Canada*] (NLC)
**OTPWC**..... Ontario Regional Library, Public Works Canada [*Bibliotheque Regionale de l'Ontario, Travaux Publics Canada*] Toronto, Ontario [*Library symbol*] [*National Library of Canada*] (NLC)
**OTQ**........... On the Quarter
**OTQE**........ Queen Elizabeth Hospital, Toronto, Ontario [*Library symbol*] [*National Library of Canada*] (NLC)
**OTQL**........ Quaere Legal Resources Ltd., Toronto, Ontario [*Library symbol*] [*National Library of Canada*] (NLC)
**OTQRM**.... [*The*] Queen's Own Rifles of Canada Regimental Museum, Toronto, Ontario [*Library symbol*] [*National Library of Canada*] (NLC)
**OTQSM**.... Queen Street Mental Health Centre, Toronto, Ontario [*Library symbol*] [*National Library of Canada*] (NLC)
**OTR**........... Coto 47 [*Costa Rica*] [*Airport symbol*] (OAG)
**OTR**........... [*The*] Oakland Terminal Railway [*Formerly, OKT*] [*AAR code*]
**OTR**........... Observed Temperature Rise
**OTR**........... Occupational Therapist, Registered
**OTR**........... Off-the-Road
**OTR**........... Office of Technical Resources
**OTR**........... Old Time Radio
**OTR**........... One Touch Recording
**OTR**........... Open-Tubular Reactor
**OTR**........... Operating Temperature Range
**OTR**........... Operational Time Record (AAG)
**OTR**........... Optical Tracking [*NASA*] (KSC)
**OTR**........... Oregon Tax Reports [*A publication*] (DLA)
**OTR**........... Organic Test Reactor [*Nuclear energy*]
**OTR**........... Orotek Resources Corp. [*Vancouver Stock Exchange symbol*]
**OTR**........... Other (FAAC)
**OTR**........... Outer (MSA)
**OTR**........... Ovarian Tumor Registry [*Medicine*]
**OTR**........... Over-the-Road [*Automotive engineering*]
**OTR**........... Oxygen Transfer Rate [*Chemical engineering*]
**OTR**........... Ryerson Polytechnical Institute, Toronto, Ontario [*Library symbol*] [*National Library of Canada*] (NLC)
**OTr**............ Troy-Miami County Public Library, Troy, OH [*Library symbol*] [*Library of Congress*] (LCLS)
**OTRA**........ Other than Regular Army (AABC)
**OTRA**........ Oversea Theater Requisitioning Authority [*Military*]
**OTRA**........ Royal Astronomical Society [*Societe Royale d'Astronomie*] Toronto, Ontario [*Library symbol*] [*National Library of Canada*] (NLC)
**OTRAC**..... Oscillogram Trace Reader [*Non-Linear Systems, Inc.*] [*Data processing*]
**OTRACO**.. Office des Transports du Congo [*Office of Transportation in the Congo*]
**OTRAG**..... Orbital Transport- und Raketen-Aktiengesellschaft [*Rocket company*] [*West Germany*]
**OTRAL**...... Rio Algom Ltd., Toronto, Ontario [*Library symbol*] [*National Library of Canada*] (NLC)
**OTRAN**..... Ocean Testing Ranges and Instrumentation Conference
**OTRAR**..... Other than Regular Army
**OTRBI**....... Information Resources, Royal Bank of Canada, Toronto, Ontario [*Library symbol*] [*National Library of Canada*] (NLC)
**OTRC**........ Canadian Forces College, Toronto, Ontario [*Library symbol*] [*National Library of Canada*] (NLC)
**OTRCF**...... Royal Commission on the Future of the Toronto Waterfront, Toronto, Ontario [*Library symbol*] [*National Library of Canada*] (BIB)
**OTRCL**...... Reichhold Chemicals Ltd., Weston, Ontario [*Library symbol*] [*National Library of Canada*] (NLC)
**OTRCR**...... Trout Creek Community Library, Ontario [*Library symbol*] [*National Library of Canada*] (NLC)
**OTRCS**...... Canadian Forces Staff School, Canada Department of National Defence [*College d'Etat-Major des Forces Canadiennes, Ministere de la Defense Nationale*] Toronto, Ontario [*Library symbol*] [*National Library of Canada*] (NLC)
**OTRE**........ Ottawa Report. Canadian Wildlife Federation [*A publication*]
**OTRE**........ Trenton Public Library, Ontario [*Library symbol*] [*National Library of Canada*] (NLC)
**OTREC**...... Regis College, Toronto, Ontario [*Library symbol*] [*National Library of Canada*] (NLC)
**OTREN**..... Northumberland County Public Library, Warkworth, Ontario [*Library symbol*] [*National Library of Canada*] (NLC)
**OTREX**...... Canada Department of Regional Industrial Expansion [*Ministere de l'Expansion Industrielle Regionale*] Toronto, Ontario [*Library symbol*] [*National Library of Canada*] (NLC)
**OTRF**......... Ontario Research Foundation, Sheridan Park, Mississauga, Ontario [*Library symbol*] [*National Library of Canada*] (NLC)
**OTRG**........ Office Technology Research Group (EA)
**OTRG**........ Old Testament Reading Guide [*Collegeville, MN*] [*A publication*] (BJA)
**OTRIC**....... Collins Canada Division, Rockwell International, Toronto, Ontario [*Library symbol*] [*National Library of Canada*] (NLC)
**OTRK**........ Oshkosh Truck Corp. [*Oshkosh, WI*] [*NASDAQ symbol*] (NQ)
**OTRL**......... Reed Limited, Toronto, Ontario [*Library symbol*] [*National Library of Canada*] (NLC)
**OTRLAX**... Oto-Rino-Laringologia [*Bucharest*] [*A publication*]
**OTRM**....... Royal Ontario Museum, Toronto, Ontario [*Library symbol*] [*National Library of Canada*] (NLC)
**OTRMC**.... Canadiana Department, Royal Ontario Museum, Toronto, Ontario [*Library symbol*] [*National Library of Canada*] (NLC)
**OTRMF**..... Far Eastern Department, Royal Ontario Museum, Toronto, Ontario [*Library symbol*] [*National Library of Canada*] (NLC)
**OTRO**........ Overhaul Test Requirement Outline
**OTROT**..... Corporate Information Centre, Royal Trust, Toronto, Ontario [*Library symbol*] [*National Library of Canada*] (BIB)
**OTRPM**.... Rothmans of Pall Mall Ltd., Don Mills, Ontario [*Library symbol*] [*National Library of Canada*] (NLC)
**OTRR**........ Operation Test Readiness Review [*Army*]
**OTRS**......... Operational Test Readiness Statement
**OTRT**........ Operating Time Record Tag (AAG)
**OTRT**........ Rose Technology Group Ltd., Toronto, Ontario [*Library symbol*] [*National Library of Canada*] (NLC)
**OTRW**....... Otherwise (FAAC)
**OTS**........... Off the Shelf
**OTS**........... Office of Technical Services [*Later, CFSTI, NTIS*] [*National Institute of Standards and Technology*]
**OTS**........... Office of Technical Support [*US Employment Service*] [*Department of Labor*]
**OTS**........... Office of Thrift Supervision [*Department of the Treasury*] [*Superseded Federal Home Loan Bank Board, 1989*]
**OTS**........... Office of Toxic Substances [*Environmental Protection Agency*]
**OTS**........... Office of Transportation Security [*Department of Transportation*]
**OTS**........... Officers' Tactical School [*Navy*] (NVT)
**OTS**........... Officers' Training School
**OTS**........... Ohio Carriers Tariff Service Inc., Cleveland OH [*STAC*]
**OTS**........... One-Time Source (MCD)
**OTS**........... Operational Test Site (AAG)
**OTS**........... Operational Time Sync
**OTS**........... Operational Training Squadron (MCD)
**OTS**........... Operational Training System [*HAWK*]
**OTS**........... Optical Technology Satellite
**OTS**........... Optical Transport Systems (IEEE)
**OTS**........... Orbital Test Satellite [*Communications satellite*] [*European Space Agency*]
**OTS**........... Orbital Transport Systems (MCD)
**OTS**........... Organization for Tropical Studies (EA)
**OTS**........... Organized Track System [*Aviation*]

**OTS** ........... Ortho-Toluenesulfonamide [*Used in manufacture of saccharin*]
**OTS** ........... Oudtestamentische Studien [*A publication*]
**OTS** ........... Out of Service (FAAC)
**OTS** ........... Over-the-Side [*Navy*] (CAAL)
**OTS** ........... Overseas Telephone Services (DAS)
**OTS** ........... Ovonic Threshold Switch
**OTS** ........... Own Time Switch [*Connection or call*] [*Telecommunications*] (TEL)
**OTS** ........... Oxygen Test Stand (KSC)
**OTS** ........... Statistics Canada [*Statistique Canada*] Toronto, Ontario [*Library symbol*] [*National Library of Canada*] (NLC)
**OTSA** ........ Orthodox Theological Society in America (EA)
**OTSA** ........ Salvation Army, Toronto, Ontario [*Library symbol*] [*National Library of Canada*] (NLC)
**OTSAA**....... Officer Training School Alumni Association (EA)
**OTSAC**...... Sanco Consultants Ltd., Toronto, Ontario [*Library symbol*] [*National Library of Canada*] (NLC)
**OTSAP**...... Spar Aerospace Products, Toronto, Ontario [*Library symbol*] [*National Library of Canada*] (NLC)
**O/TSC**....... Other than Special Consultants [*Military*]
**OTSC**......... Seneca College, Willowdale, Ontario [*Library symbol*] [*National Library of Canada*] (NLC)
**OTSCC**...... Scarborough College, Ontario [*Library symbol*] [*National Library of Canada*] (NLC)
**OTSCI**....... Sulzer Canada, Inc., Toronto, Ontario [*Library symbol*] [*National Library of Canada*] (NLC)
**OTSCL**...... Shell Canada Ltd., Toronto, Ontario [*Library symbol*] [*National Library of Canada*] (NLC)
**OTSCLT** ... Library Techniques, Seneca College of Applied Arts and Technology, Willowdale, Ontario [*Library symbol*] [*National Library of Canada*] (NLC)
**OTSE**......... Toronto Stock Exchange Library, Ontario [*Library symbol*] [*National Library of Canada*] (BIB)
**OTSED**...... Scarborough Borough Board of Education, Toronto, Ontario [*Library symbol*] [*National Library of Canada*] (NLC)
**Otsenka Mestorozhd Poiskakh Razved** ... Otsenka Mestorozhdenii pri Poiskakh i Razvedkakh [*A publication*]
**OTSG** ........ Office of the Surgeon General [*Public Health Service*]
**OTSG** ........ Once-Through Steam Generator [*Nuclear energy*]
**OTSGS**...... Once-Through Steam Generating System [*Nuclear energy*] (IEEE)
**OTSLI** ....... Sun Life of Canada, Toronto, Ontario [*Library symbol*] [*National Library of Canada*] (NLC)
**OTSM** ....... St. Michael's Hospital, Toronto, Ontario [*Library symbol*] [*National Library of Canada*] (NLC)
**OTSMC**..... Sunnybrook Medical Centre, Toronto, Ontario [*Library symbol*] [*National Library of Canada*] (NLC)
**OTSMG** .... St. Mary's General Hospital, Timmins, Ontario [*Library symbol*] [*National Library of Canada*] (NLC)
**OTSML**..... Selco Mining Corp., Toronto, Ontario [*Library symbol*] [*National Library of Canada*] (NLC)
**OTSO** ........ Office of Telecommunications Systems Operations [*Social Security Administration*]
**OTSOA** ..... Overseas Telegraph Superintending Officers' Association [*A union*] [*British*]
**OTSP**......... Office of Technology Support Programs [*Washington, DC*] [*Department of Energy*] (GRD)
**OTSP**......... Office of Transportation Systems and Planning [*Department of Energy*] [*Battelle Memorial Institute*] [*Also, an information service or system*] (IID)
**OTSP**......... Scarborough Public Library, Ontario [*Library symbol*] [*National Library of Canada*] (NLC)
**OTSPA** ...... Albert Campbell Branch, Scarborough Public Library, Ontario [*Library symbol*] [*National Library of Canada*] (NLC)
**OTSPC** ...... Cedarbrae Branch, Scarborough Public Library, Ontario [*Library symbol*] [*National Library of Canada*] (NLC)
**OTSQ** ........ Offer Teacher-Student Questionnaire [*Personality development test*] [*Psychology*]
**OTSR**......... Once-Through Superheat Reactor [*Nuclear energy*]
**OTSR**......... Optimum Track Ship Routing [*Navy*] (NVT)
**OTSS**......... Off-the-Shelf System [*Bell System*]
**OTSS**......... Office of Technical and Special Services [*Office of Field Operations*] [*Department of Labor*]
**OTSS**......... Ontario Regional Library, Secretary of State Canada [*Bibliotheque Regionale de l'Ontario, Secretariat d'Etat*], Toronto, Ontario [*Library symbol*] [*National Library of Canada*] (NLC)
**OTSS**......... Operational Test Support System
**OTSS**......... Optical Tracking Servo
**OTS SB** ..... Office of Technical Service, Selective Bibliographies [*US government*]
**OTST**......... Ontario Science Centre, Toronto, Ontario [*Library symbol*] [*National Library of Canada*] (NLC)
**OTSt**.......... Oudtestamentische Studien [*Leiden*] [*A publication*]
**OTSTA**...... St. Augustine's Seminary, Toronto, Ontario [*Library symbol*] [*National Library of Canada*] (NLC)
**OTSTB** ...... St. Basil's Seminary [*Collection transferred to OTSTM*] Ontario [*Library symbol*] [*National Library of Canada*] (NLC)
**OTSTF** ...... Ontario Film Institute, Ontario Science Centre Library, Don Mills, Ontario [*Library symbol*] [*National Library of Canada*] (NLC)
**OTSTG**...... St. George's College, Toronto, Ontario [*Library symbol*] [*National Library of Canada*] (NLC)
**OTSTJ**....... George Pennal Library, St. Joseph's Health Centre, Toronto, Ontario [*Library symbol*] [*National Library of Canada*] (BIB)
**OTSTM**..... University of Saint Michael's College, Toronto, Ontario [*Library symbol*] [*National Library of Canada*] (NLC)
**OTSZH** ..... Other than Steel or Zinc Heads [*Freight*]
**OTT** ........... Nottingham, MD [*Location identifier*] [*FAA*] (FAAL)
**OTT** ........... Ocean Transport and Trading [*British*]
**OTT** ........... Office of Technology Transfer [*University of Illinois*]
**OTT** ........... One-Time Tape
**OTT** ........... Operational Training Test (NVT)
**OTT** ........... Operator Tactics Trainer [*Patriot air defense system*] (MCD)
**OTT** ........... Optional Team Targeting (MCD)
**OTT** ........... Oral Trade Tests [*Department of Labor*]
**OTT** ........... Ottava [*Octave*] [*Music*]
**OTT** ........... Ottawa [*Ontario*] [*Geomagnetic observatory code*]
**OTT** ........... Ottawa [*Ontario*] [*Seismograph station code, US Geological Survey*] (SEIS)
**OTT** ........... Ottawa [*Canada*]
**OTT** ........... Ottery Saint Mary [*Urban district in England*]
**Ott**............. Otto's United States Supreme Court Reports [*91-107 United States*] [*A publication*] (DLA)
**OTT** ........... Outgoing Teletype
**OTT** ........... Outside Trim Template (MSA)
**OTT** ........... Over-the-Top [*Marshall-MacIntosh knee operation*]
**OTT** ........... Over the Top [*British*] [*Slang*]
**OTT** ........... Technieuws Ottawa. Korte Berichten op Technisch Wetenschappelijk Gebied [*A publication*]
**OTT** ........... Teledyne CAE Engineering Library, Toledo, OH [*Library symbol*] [*Library of Congress*] (LCLS)
**OTT** ........... Toronto Transit Commission, Ontario [*Library symbol*] [*National Library of Canada*] (NLC)
**OTT** ........... University of Ottawa Library [*UTLAS symbol*]
**Ottawa Field Nat Club Tr** ... Ottawa Field Naturalists' Club. Transactions [*A publication*]
**Ottawa Law R** ... Ottawa Law Review [*A publication*]
**Ottawa Lit Sc Soc Tr** ... Ottawa Literary and Scientific Society. Transactions [*A publication*]
**Ottawa LR** ... Ottawa Law Review [*A publication*]
**Ottawa L Rev** ... Ottawa Law Review [*A publication*]
**Ottawa Nat** ... Ottawa Naturalist [*A publication*]
**OTTC** ........ University of Trinity College, Toronto, Ontario [*Library symbol*] [*National Library of Canada*] (NLC)
**OTTCA**...... University of Trinity College Archives, Toronto, Ontario [*Library symbol*] [*National Library of Canada*] (NLC)
**OTTDB** ..... Toronto-Dominion Bank, Toronto, Ontario [*Library symbol*] [*National Library of Canada*] (NLC)
**OTTE** ........ Operational Testing, Training, and Evaluation
**OTTEC**...... Toronto Teachers' College, Ontario [*Library symbol*] [*National Library of Canada*] (NLC)
**OTTER**...... Operational Training, Test, and Evaluation RADAR
**OTTEX**...... Texaco Canada, Inc., Don Mills, Ontario [*Library symbol*] [*National Library of Canada*] (NLC)
**OTTFC**...... Official Tim Topper Fan Club (EA)
**OTTI**.......... Ontario Ministry of Industry and Trade, Toronto, Ontario [*Library symbol*] [*National Library of Canada*] (NLC)
**OTTLE**...... Optically Transparent Thin-Layer Electrode
**Ott LR**........ Ottawa Law Review [*A publication*]
**OTTO**........ Once Through, Then Out [*Fuel management system*]
**Otto**............ Otto's United States Supreme Court Reports [*91-107 United States*] [*A publication*] (DLA)
**OTTOA** ..... Ontario Region, Canadian Air Transportation Administration, Transport Canada [*Region de l'Ontario, Administration Canadienne des Transports Aeriens, Transports Canada*] Toronto, Ontario [*Library symbol*] [*National Library of Canada*] (NLC)
**Otto Graf Inst (Stuttgart) Tech Hochsch Schriftenr** ... Otto-Graf-Institut (Stuttgart). Technische Hochschule. Schriftenreihe [*A publication*]
**Otto-Graf-Inst (Stutt) Tech Hochsch Schriftenr** ... Otto-Graf-Institut (Stuttgart). Technische Hochschule. Schriftenreihe [*A publication*]
**OTTR** ........ Otter Tail Power Co. [*NASDAQ symbol*] (NQ)
**OTTR** ........ Thomson, Rogers, Barristers & Solicitors, Toronto, Ontario [*Library symbol*] [*National Library of Canada*] (NLC)
**OTTRAC**... Travelers Canada, Toronto, Ontario [*Library symbol*] [*National Library of Canada*] (BIB)
**OTTRC**...... Thistletown Regional Centre for Children and Adolescents, Rexdale, Ontario [*Library symbol*] [*National Library of Canada*] (NLC)
**OTTRC**...... Touche Ross & Co., Toronto, Ontario [*Library symbol*] [*National Library of Canada*] (NLC)
**OTTS**......... Operations Training and Technical Services [*Nuclear Regulatory Commission*] (NRCH)
**OTTS**......... Organisation of Teachers of Transport Studies [*British*]
**OTTS**......... Outgoing Trunk Testing System [*Telecommunications*] (TEL)
**OTTST** ...... Toronto School of Theology, Toronto, Ontario [*Library symbol*] [*National Library of Canada*] (NLC)

**Ott's US Sup Ct R** ... Otto's United States Supreme Court Reports [*91-107 United States*] [*A publication*] (DLA)
**OTTT** ........ Tory, Tory, DesLauriers & Binnington, Toronto, Ontario [*Library symbol*] [*National Library of Canada*] (BIB)
**Ott Voronezh Sel-Khoz Inst** ... Ottisk iz Aapisok Voronezhskogo Sel'skokhozyaistvennogo Instituta [*A publication*]
**OTTWH** .... Health Sciences Library, Toronto Western Hospital, Ontario [*Library symbol*] [*National Library of Canada*] (NLC)
**OTU** .......... Office of Technology Utilization [*NASA*]
**OTU** .......... Officers' Training Unit [*Air Force*] [*British*]
**OTU** .......... One-Time Use
**OTU** .......... Operating Time Update
**OTU** .......... Operational Taxonomic Unit [*Numerical taxonomy*]
**OTU** .......... Operational Test Unit (KSC)
**OTU** .......... Operational Training Unit [*Military*]
**OTU** .......... Orthopedic Transcription Unit
**OTU** .......... Otu [*Colombia*] [*Airport symbol*] (OAG)
**OTU** .......... University of Toledo, Toledo, OH [*Library symbol*] [*Library of Congress*] (LCLS)
**OTU** .......... University of Toronto, Ontario [*Library symbol*] [*National Library of Canada*] (NLC)
**OTUA** ........ Institute for Aerospace Studies, University of Toronto, Ontario [*Library symbol*] [*National Library of Canada*] (NLC)
**OTUAN** ..... Department of Anatomy, University of Toronto, Ontario [*Library symbol*] [*National Library of Canada*] (NLC)
**OTUAP** ..... Department of Applied Physics, University of Toronto, Ontario [*Library symbol*] [*National Library of Canada*] (NLC)
**OTUAR** ..... University of Toronto Archives, Ontario [*Library symbol*] [*National Library of Canada*] (NLC)
**OTUAV** ..... Audio-Visual Library, University of Toronto, Ontario [*Library symbol*] [*National Library of Canada*] (NLC)
**OTUB** ........ Department of Biochemistry, University of Toronto, Ontario [*Library symbol*] [*National Library of Canada*] (NLC)
**OTUBP** ..... Banting-Best Physiology Library, University of Toronto, Ontario [*Library symbol*] [*National Library of Canada*] (NLC)
**OTUC** ........ Department of Chemistry, University of Toronto, Ontario [*Library symbol*] [*National Library of Canada*] (NLC)
**OTUCC** ..... Institute of Computer Science, University of Toronto, Ontario [*Library symbol*] [*National Library of Canada*] (NLC)
**OTUCE** ..... Department of Chemical Engineering and Applied Chemistry, University of Toronto, Ontario [*Library symbol*] [*National Library of Canada*] (NLC)
**OTUCI** ...... Department of Civil Engineering, University of Toronto, Ontario [*Library symbol*] [*National Library of Canada*] (NLC)
**OTUCR** ..... Centre of Criminology, University of Toronto, Ontario [*Library symbol*] [*National Library of Canada*] (NLC)
**OTUCS** ...... Institute of Child Study, University of Toronto, Ontario [*Library symbol*] [*National Library of Canada*] (NLC)
**OTUD** ........ David Dunlap Observatory, University of Toronto, Ontario [*Library symbol*] [*National Library of Canada*] (NLC)
**OTUDB** ..... Department of Botany, University of Toronto, Ontario [*Library symbol*] [*National Library of Canada*] (NLC)
**OTUDM** .... Department of Mathematics, University of Toronto, Ontario [*Library symbol*] [*National Library of Canada*] (NLC)
**OTUDP** ..... Clarke Institute of Psychiatry, University of Toronto, Ontario [*Library symbol*] [*National Library of Canada*] (NLC)
**OTUE** ........ Engineering Library, University of Toronto, Ontario [*Library symbol*] [*National Library of Canada*] (NLC)
**OTUEE** ..... Department of Electrical Engineering, University of Toronto, Ontario [*Library symbol*] [*National Library of Canada*] (NLC)
**OTUFA** ..... Department of Fine Art, University of Toronto, Ontario [*Library symbol*] [*National Library of Canada*] (NLC)
**OTUFD** ..... Faculty of Dentistry, University of Toronto, Ontario [*Library symbol*] [*National Library of Canada*] (NLC)
**OTUFM** .... Faculty of Music, University of Toronto, Ontario [*Library symbol*] [*National Library of Canada*] (NLC)
**OTUFP** ...... Faculty of Pharmacy, University of Toronto, Ontario [*Library symbol*] [*National Library of Canada*] (NLC)
**OTUG** ........ Department of Geological Sciences, University of Toronto, Ontario [*Library symbol*] [*National Library of Canada*] (NLC)
**OTUGL** ..... Geophysics Laboratory, University of Toronto, Ontario [*Library symbol*] [*National Library of Canada*] (NLC)
**OTUH** ........ Science and Medicine Library, University of Toronto, Ontario [*Library symbol*] [*National Library of Canada*] (NLC)
**OTUHO** .... Occupational & Environment Health Unit, Science and Medicine Library, University of Toronto, Ontario [*Library symbol*] [*National Library of Canada*] (NLC)
**OTUINC** ... Innis College, University of Toronto, Ontario [*Library symbol*] [*National Library of Canada*] (NLC)
**OTUIRN** ... [*The*] Jean and Dorothy Newman Industrial Relations Library, Center for Industrial Relations, University of Toronto, Ontario [*Library symbol*] [*National Library of Canada*] (NLC)
**OTUL** ........ Faculty of Law, University of Toronto, Ontario [*Library symbol*] [*National Library of Canada*] (NLC)
**OTU-L** ....... University of Toledo, Law Library, Toledo, OH [*Library symbol*] [*Library of Congress*] (LCLS)
**OTULAS** ... UTLAS [*University of Toronto Library Automation System*] International Canada, Toronto, Ontario [*Library symbol*] [*National Library of Canada*] (NLC)
**OTULS** ...... Faculty of Library Science, University of Toronto, Ontario [*Library symbol*] [*National Library of Canada*] (NLC)
**OTUM** ....... Department of Mechanical Engineering, University of Toronto, Ontario [*Library symbol*] [*National Library of Canada*] (NLC)
**OTUMA** .... Map Library, University of Toronto, Ontario [*Library symbol*] [*National Library of Canada*] (NLC)
**OTUME** .... Department of Metallurgical Engineering, University of Toronto, Ontario [*Library symbol*] [*National Library of Canada*] (NLC)
**OTUMI** ..... Department of Mining Engineering, University of Toronto, Ontario [*Library symbol*] [*National Library of Canada*] (NLC)
**OTUMS** .... Faculty of Management Studies, University of Toronto, Ontario [*Library symbol*] [*National Library of Canada*] (NLC)
**OTUN** ........ Faculty of Nursing, University of Toronto, Ontario [*Library symbol*] [*National Library of Canada*] (NLC)
**OTUNC** ..... Union Carbide Canada Ltd., Toronto, Ontario [*Library symbol*] [*National Library of Canada*] (NLC)
**OTUNWC** ... New College, University of Toronto, Ontario [*Library symbol*] [*National Library of Canada*] (NLC)
**OTUP** ........ Department of Physics, University of Toronto, Ontario [*Library symbol*] [*National Library of Canada*] (NLC)
**OTUPA** ..... Department of Pathology, Banting-Best Institute, University of Toronto, Ontario [*Library symbol*] [*National Library of Canada*] (NLC)
**OTUPG** ..... Information Centre, Programme in Gerontology, University of Toronto, Ontario [*Library symbol*] [*National Library of Canada*] (NLC)
**OTUS** ........ Office of the Treasurer of the United States
**OTUSA** ..... School of Architecture, University of Toronto, Ontario [*Library symbol*] [*National Library of Canada*] (NLC)
**OTUSP** ...... School of Physical and Health Education (Women), University of Toronto, Ontario [*Library symbol*] [*National Library of Canada*] (NLC)
**OTUSW** .... School of Social Work, University of Toronto, Ontario [*Library symbol*] [*National Library of Canada*] (NLC)
**OTUTD** ..... Urban Transportation Development Corp., Toronto, Ontario [*Library symbol*] [*National Library of Canada*] (NLC)
**OTUTF** ...... Thomas Fisher Rare Book Library, University of Toronto, Ontario [*Library symbol*] [*National Library of Canada*] (NLC)
**OTUTP** ..... University of Toronto Press, Ontario [*Library symbol*] [*National Library of Canada*] (NLC)
**OTUUC** ..... University College, University of Toronto, Ontario [*Library symbol*] [*National Library of Canada*] (NLC)
**OTUZ** ........ Department of Zoology, University of Toronto, Ontario [*Library symbol*] [*National Library of Canada*] (NLC)
**OTV** .......... Operational Television (KSC)
**OTV** .......... Orbiter Transfer Vehicle [*NASA*]
**OTV** .......... Victoria University, Toronto, Ontario [*Library symbol*] [*National Library of Canada*] (NLC)
**OTVCT** ...... Outer Tube Vertical Centerline Target
**OTVL** ........ V & L Enterprises, Downsview, Ontario [*Library symbol*] [*National Library of Canada*] (NLC)
**OTW** .......... Off the Wall [*Slang*]
**OTW** .......... Out of This World [*A publication*]
**OTW** .......... Over the Wing [*Aircraft*]
**OTW** .......... Owner's Tank Wagons [*Shipping*]
**OTW** .......... Wycliffe College, Toronto, Ontario [*Library symbol*] [*National Library of Canada*] (NLC)
**OTWA** ....... Out of This World Adventures [*A publication*]
**OTWC** ....... Ontario Workmen's Compensation Board, Toronto, Ontario [*Library symbol*] [*National Library of Canada*] (NLC)
**OTWCA** .... Ontario Workers' Compensation Appeals Tribunal, Toronto, Ontario [*Library symbol*] [*National Library of Canada*] (NLC)
**OTWCH** .... Medical Library, Women's College Hospital, Toronto, Ontario [*Library symbol*] [*National Library of Canada*] (NLC)
**OTWE** ....... Tweed Public Library, Ontario [*Library symbol*] [*National Library of Canada*] (BIB)
**OTWEN** .... Ontario Ministry of Northern Development and Mines, Tweed [*Library symbol*] [*National Library of Canada*] (BIB)
**OTWerkSuidA** ... Die Ou Testamentiese Werkgemeenskap in Suid-Afrika [*Pretoria*] [*A publication*]
**OTWFC** ..... Old Time Western Film Club (EA)
**OTWH** ...... Wellesley Hospital, Toronto, Ontario [*Library symbol*] [*National Library of Canada*] (NLC)
**OTWL** ....... William Lyon Mackenzie Collegiate Institute, Downsview, Ontario [*Library symbol*] [*National Library of Canada*] (NLC)
**OTWLC** ..... Warner-Lambert Canada Ltd., Scarborough, Ontario [*Library symbol*] [*National Library of Canada*] (NLC)
**OTWM** ...... William M. Mercer Ltd., Toronto, Ontario [*Library symbol*] [*National Library of Canada*] (NLC)
**OTWR** ....... Oblique Tape Wound Refrasil

**OTWRC** .... Weston Research Centre, Toronto, Ontario [*Library symbol*] [*National Library of Canada*] (NLC)
**OTWSA** ..... Die Ou Testamentiese Werkgemeenskap in Suid-Afrika [*Pretoria*] [*A publication*]
**OTWY** ....... Medical Library, Wyeth Ltd., Downsview, Ontario [*Library symbol*] [*National Library of Canada*] (BIB)
**OTX** ........... Oiltex International Ltd. [*Toronto Stock Exchange symbol*]
**OTXRA** ..... X-Ray Assay Laboratories Ltd., Don Mills, Ontario [*Library symbol*] [*National Library of Canada*] (NLC)
**OTY** ........... Oria [*Papua New Guinea*] [*Airport symbol*] [*Obsolete*] (OAG)
**OTY** ........... York University, Toronto, Ontario [*Library symbol*] [*National Library of Canada*] (NLC)
**OTYA** ........ York University Archives, Toronto, Ontario [*Library symbol*] [*National Library of Canada*] (NLC)
**OTYBE** ...... Professional Library, Board of Education for the City of York, Toronto, Ontario [*Library symbol*] [*National Library of Canada*] (NLC)
**OTYBE** ...... York Borough Board of Education, Toronto, Ontario [*Library symbol*] [*National Library of Canada*] (NLC)
**OTYBES** ... Schools, Board of Education for the City of York, Toronto, Ontario [*Library symbol*] [*National Library of Canada*] (NLC)
**OTYF** ......... Hospital Library, York-Finch General Hospital, Downsview, Ontario [*Library symbol*] [*National Library of Canada*] (BIB)
**OTYL** ........ Law Library, York University, Toronto, Ontario [*Library symbol*] [*National Library of Canada*] (NLC)
**OTYLR** ...... Listening Room, York University, Toronto, Ontario [*Library symbol*] [*National Library of Canada*] (NLC)
**OTYP** ........ City of York Public Library, Toronto, Ontario [*Library symbol*] [*National Library of Canada*] (NLC)
**OTZ** ........... Kotzebue [*Alaska*] [*Airport symbol*] (OAG)
**OTZ** ........... Oesterreichische Textil Zeitung. Zentralblatt fuer die Gesamte Textilwirtschaft [*A publication*]
**OTZ** ........... Ortiz [*New Mexico*] [*Seismograph station code, US Geological Survey*] (SEIS)
**OTZ** ........... Oxothiazolidine [*Biochemistry*]
**OU** ............. Observation Unit
**OU** ............. Oculi Unitas [*Both Eyes Together*] [*Ophthalmology*]
**OU** ............. Oculus Uterque [*Each Eye*] [*Ophthalmology*]
**OU** ............. Odor Unit [*Air pollution*]
**OU** ............. Ohio State University, Columbus, OH [*Library symbol*] [*Library of Congress*] (LCLS)
**OU** ............. Ohio University [*Athens*]
**OU** ............. Oklahoma University
**OU** ............. Open University [*British*]
**OU** ............. Operation Unit
**OU** ............. Oxford University [*England*]
**OU** ............. Sultanate of Oman Air Force [*Airline*] [*ICAO designator*] (FAAC)
**OUA** .......... Office of University Affairs [*NASA*]
**OUA** .......... Organisation de l'Unite Africaine [*Organization of African Unity - OAU*] (EAIO)
**OUA** .......... Ortnamnssaellskapets i Uppsala Aarsskrift [*A publication*]
**OUA** .......... Ouagadougou [*Upper Volta*] [*Airport symbol*] (OAG)
**OUA** .......... Ouanaham [*Loyalty Islands*] [*Seismograph station code, US Geological Survey*] (SEIS)
**OUa** ........... Upper Arlington Public Library, Upper Arlington, OH [*Library symbol*] [*Library of Congress*] (LCLS)
**OUAM** ...... Order of United American Mechanics
**OUAT** ........ Once upon a Time (The Prisoner Fan Club) (EA)
**OUB** ........... Overseas Union Bank [*Singapore*]
**OUB** ........... Parfums, Cosmetiques, Aromes. L'Unique Journal Francais de Son Secteur [*A publication*]
**OUC** ........... Ocracoke, NC [*Location identifier*] [*FAA*] (FAAL)
**OUC** ........... Ohio University, Chillicothe Branch Campus, Chillicothe, OH [*OCLC symbol*] (OCLC)
**OUCA** ........ Chemical Abstracts, Ohio State University, Columbus, OH [*Library symbol*] [*Library of Congress*] (LCLS)
**OUCC** ........ Ohio University Cartographic Center [*Research center*] (RCD)
**OUCH** ....... Occupational-Urgent Care Health Systems, Inc. [*NASDAQ symbol*] (NQ)
**OUCH** ....... Off-Line Universal Command History [*Data processing*] (KSC)
**OUCTA** ..... Order of United Commercial Travelers of America (EA)
**OUD** .......... AMOCO Production Co., Library, Tulsa, OK [*OCLC symbol*] (OCLC)
**OUD** .......... Operational Use Data
**OUD** .......... Oujda [*Morocco*] [*Airport symbol*] (OAG)
**Oud C** ......... Oudh Code [*India*] [*A publication*] (DLA)
**Oudh C** ....... Oudh Code [*India*] [*A publication*] (DLA)
**Oudh LJ** ..... Oudh Law Journal [*India*] [*A publication*] (DLA)
**Oudh LR** .... Oudh Law Reports [*India*] [*A publication*] (DLA)
**Oudh Med** ... Oudheidkundige Mededeelingen [*A publication*]
**Oudh Meded** ... Oudheidkundige Mededeelingen uit s'Rijksmuseum van Oudheden te Leiden [*A publication*]
**Oudh Rev Sel Cas** ... Revised Collection of Selected Cases Issued by Chief Commissioner and Financial Commissioner of Oudh [*A publication*] (DLA)
**Oudh Wkly N** ... Oudh Weekly Notes [*India*] [*A publication*] (DLA)
**Oudh WN** .. Oudh Weekly Notes [*India*] [*A publication*] (DLA)
**OUDP** ........ Officer Undergraduate Degree Program [*Army*] (AABC)
**OudSt** ........ Oudtestamentische Studien [*Leiden*] [*A publication*]
**OUE** ........... National Oceanic and Atmospheric Administration, National Severe Storms Laboratories, Norman, OK [*OCLC symbol*] (OCLC)
**OUE** ........... Operational Utility Evaluation
**OUE** ........... Orbital Uncertainty Estimate
**OUE** ........... Ouesso [*Congo*] [*Airport symbol*] (OAG)
**OUE** ........... Ouvriers Unis de l'Electricite, de la Radio, et de la Machinerie d'Amerique [*United Electrical, Radio, and Machine Workers of America - UE*]
**Ouest Apic** ... L'Ouest Apicole [*A publication*]
**Ouest Med** ... Ouest Medical [*A publication*]
**OUF** ........... Northwestern Oklahoma State University, Library, Alva, OK [*OCLC symbol*] (OCLC)
**OUF** ........... Order of Use File (MCD)
**OUF** ........... Oxygen Utilization Factor
**OUFADI** ... Outdoor Facts [*Fort Collins, CO*] [*A publication*]
**OUG** .......... Oklahoma Children's Memorial Hospital, Library, Oklahoma City, OK [*OCLC symbol*] (OCLC)
**OUG** .......... Organisation de l'Unite Guineenne [*Organization of Guinean Unity*] (PD)
**Ought** ......... Oughton's Ordo Judiciorum [*Order of Judgments*] [*A publication*] (DLA)
**OU-H** ......... Ohio State University, Health Sciences Library, Columbus, OH [*Library symbol*] [*Library of Congress*] (LCLS)
**OUH** .......... Oklahoma College of Osteopathic Medicine and Surgery, Library, Tulsa, OK [*OCLC symbol*] (OCLC)
**OUH** .......... Oudtshoorn [*South Africa*] [*Airport symbol*] (OAG)
**OUI** ............ Office of Unemployment Insurance [*Employment and Training Administration*] [*Department of Labor*]
**OUI** ............ Oklahoma Osteopathic Hospital, Library, Tulsa, OK [*OCLC symbol*] (OCLC)
**OUI** ............ Organisation Universitaire Interamericaine [*Inter-American Organization for Higher Education*] (EAIO)
**OUI** ............ Outdoors Unlimited (EA)
**OUI** ............ Outer Integument [*Botany*]
**OUIL** ......... Operating a Vehicle while under the Influence of Liquor [*Traffic offense charge*]
**OUJ** ........... Oklahoma State University, Technical Institute Library, Oklahoma City, OK [*OCLC symbol*] (OCLC)
**OUK** .......... Operation Upshot-Knothole [*Atomic weapons testing*]
**OUK** .......... Oscar Rose Junior College Library, Midwest City, OK [*OCLC symbol*] (OCLC)
**OU-L** ......... Ohio State University, College of Law, Columbus, OH [*Library symbol*] [*Library of Congress*] (LCLS)
**OUL** ........... Ohio University, Lancaster Branch Campus, Lancaster, OH [*OCLC symbol*] (OCLC)
**OUL** ........... Orbital Utility Light
**OUL** ........... Otonabee Airways Ltd. [*Peterborough, ON*] [*FAA designator*] (FAAC)
**OUL** ........... Oulu [*Finland*] [*Airport symbol*] (OAG)
**OUL** ........... Oulu [*Finland*] [*Seismograph station code, US Geological Survey*] (SEIS)
**Oult Ind** ..... Oulton's Index to Irish Statutes [*A publication*] (DLA)
**Oult Laws Ir** ... Oulton's Laws of Ireland [*A publication*] (DLA)
**Oulun Yliopiston Ydintek Laitoksen Julk** ... Oulun Yliopiston Ydintekniikkan Laitoksen Julkaisuja [*A publication*]
**OUM** ......... Philbrook Art Center Library, Tulsa, OK [*OCLC symbol*] (OCLC)
**OUMC** ....... Otago University Medical Corps [*British military*] (DMA)
**OUN** .......... Norman, OK [*Location identifier*] [*FAA*] (FAAL)
**OUN** .......... Ohio University, Athens, OH [*OCLC symbol*] (OCLC)
**OUNPSA** .. Office of United Nations Political and Security Affairs [*Department of State*]
**OUNS** ........ Office of Urban Neighborhood Services [*HUD*]
**OUNSAF** ... Office of the Under Secretary of the Air Force
**OUO** .......... Official Use Only
**OUO** .......... United States Army, Morris Swett Library, Fort Sill, OK [*OCLC symbol*] (OCLC)
**OUP** ........... Official Unionist Party [*Northern Ireland*] (PPW)
**OU-P** ......... Ohio State University, Pharmacy and Bacteriology Library, Columbus, OH [*Library symbol*] [*Library of Congress*] (LCLS)
**OUP** ........... Operative United Painters [*A union*] [*British*]
**OUP** ........... Operative United Plumbers [*A union*] [*British*]
**OUP** ........... Oxford University Press, Inc. [*New York, NY*]
**OUP** ........... University of Portland, Portland, OR [*OCLC symbol*] (OCLC)
**OUPT** ........ Output (AAG)
**OUQ** .......... United States Army, Nye Library, Fort Sill, OK [*OCLC symbol*] (OCLC)
**OUR** ........... Batouri [*Cameroon*] [*Airport symbol*] (OAG)
**OUR** ........... Ohio University Review [*A publication*]
**OUR** ........... Organizacion de Unidad Revolucionaria [*Organization of Revolutionary Unity*] [*Bolivia*] [*Political party*] (PPW)
**OUR** ........... Oxygen Utilization Rate [*Photosynthesis*]
**OUR** ........... United States Federal Aviation Administration, Aeronautical Center Library, Oklahoma City, OK [*OCLC symbol*] (OCLC)
**OUrC** ......... Urbana College, Urbana, OH [*Library symbol*] [*Library of Congress*] (LCLS)

**OURD**........ [*The*] Ogden Union Railway & Depot Co. [*AAR code*]
**Our Gener** ... Our Generation [*A publication*]
**OURI**......... Oklahoma University Research Institute
**Ouro Preto Esc Minas Rev** ... Ouro Preto. Escola de Minas. Revista [*A publication*]
**OURQ**....... Outer Upper Right Quadrant [*Anatomy*]
**Our Q Mag** ... Our Quarterly Magazine [*A publication*] (APTA)
**OURS**........ Orangutan Recovery Service [*Later, IUCN*]
**OURS**........ Organ of Unemployed, Relief, and Sustenance Workers [*A publication*] (APTA)
**OURTEL**... Our Telegram (NATG)
**Our World W** ... Our World Weekly [*A publication*]
**OUS**.......... Oklahoma Union List of Serials Project, Stillwater, OK [*OCLC symbol*] (OCLC)
**OuS**........... Oudtestamentische Studien [*Leiden*] [*A publication*]
**OUS**.......... Ourinhos [*Brazil*] [*Airport symbol*] (OAG)
**OUS**.......... Outdoor Unit Substation
**OUSA**........ Office of the Under Secretary of the Army
**OUSA**........ Open University Students' Association [*British*]
**OUSA**........ Operation USA [*An association*] (EA)
**OUSA**........ Organisation de l'Unite Syndicale Africaine [*Organisation of African Trade Union Unity - OATUU*] [*Accra, Ghana*] (EAIO)
**OUSAF**...... Office of the Under Secretary of the Air Force
**OUSAIRA** ... Office of the United States Air Attache (CINC)
**OUSARMA** ... Office of the United States Army Attache
**OUSCS**...... Office of Urban Studies and Clearinghouse Services [*HUD*]
**OUSD**........ Office of the Under Secretary of Defense (MCD)
**OUSD(P)**... Office of the Under Secretary of Defense (Policy) (MCD)
**OUSDRE**... Office of the Under Secretary of Defense for Research and Engineering
**OUSE**........ Odense University Studies in English [*A publication*]
**OUSH**........ Uxbridge-Scott Historical Society, Uxbridge, Ontario [*Library symbol*] [*National Library of Canada*] (BIB)
**OUSN**........ Office of the Under Secretary of the Navy
**OUSOFA** .. Office of the Under Secretary of the Army
**OUST**........ Office of Underground Storage Tanks [*Environmental Protection Agency*]
**OUSW**....... Office of the Under Secretary of War [*Obsolete*]
**OUT**.......... Orbiter Utilities Tray [*NASA*] (NASA)
**OUT**.......... Organizacao Unida de Trabalhadores [*United Organization of Workers*] [*Portugal*] [*Political party*] (PPE)
**OUT**.......... Organization for Unemployed Teachers
**OUT**.......... Organization for Use of the Telephone (EA)
**Out**........... Outerbridge's State Reports [*97, 98 Pennsylvania*] [*A publication*] (DLA)
**OUT**.......... Outgoing
**OUT**.......... Outing (ROG)
**Out**........... Outlands [*A publication*]
**OUT**.......... Outlet [*Hawaii*] [*Seismograph station code, US Geological Survey*] (SEIS)
**OUT**.......... Outlet (AAG)
**OUT**.......... Output (NASA)
**Out**........... Outsider [*A publication*]
**OUT**.......... United States Federal Aviation Administration, CAMI Library, Oklahoma City, OK [*OCLC symbol*] (OCLC)
**OUT**.......... Uxbridge Township Public Library, Uxbridge, Ontario [*Library symbol*] [*National Library of Canada*] (NLC)
**OUTA**........ Ouvriers Unis des Textiles d'Amerique [*United Textile Workers of America - UTWA*]
**OUTB**........ Outback Oil and Mineral Exploration Corp. [*NASDAQ symbol*] (NQ)
**OUTBD**..... Outboard (AAG)
**OUTBD**..... Outbound
**OUTBGS**... Outbuildings (ROG)
**OUTC**........ Ordnance Unit Training Center [*Military*]
**Outdoor Am** ... Outdoor America [*A publication*]
**Outdoor Ind** ... Outdoor Indiana [*A publication*]
**Outdoor Okla** ... Outdoor Oklahoma [*A publication*]
**Outd Rec Act** ... Outdoor Recreation Action [*A publication*]
**Outdr Rec**... Selected Outdoor Recreation Statistics [*A publication*]
**OUTG**........ Outage (KSC)
**OUTHO**.... Outhouse (ROG)
**OUTL**........ Outlet
**Outl**........... Outlook [*A publication*]
**Outl Agric** ... Outlook on Agriculture [*A publication*]
**OUTLIM**... Output Limiting Facility [*Data processing*] (MDG)
**Outlook Agr** ... Outlook on Agriculture [*A publication*]
**Outlook Agric** ... Outlook on Agriculture [*A publication*]
**Outlook Bull South Dent Soc NJ** ... Outlook and Bulletin. Southern Dental Society of New Jersey [*A publication*]
**Outlook United Fresh Fruit Veg Assoc** ... Outlook. United Fresh Fruit and Vegetable Association [*A publication*]
**Outok News** ... Outokumpu News [*A publication*]
**OUTPUTM** ... Output Measures for Public Libraries [*Clarion University of Pennsylvania*] [*Information service or system*] (IID)
**OUTR**........ OutRight Industries, Inc. [*Chicago, IL*] [*NASDAQ symbol*] (NQ)
**OUTRAN** ... Output Translator [*IBM Corp.*]
**OUTS**........ Operational Unit Transportable System (MCD)
**Outstate Test Circ Univ Nebr Coll Agr Home Econ Agr Exp Sta** ... Outstate Testing Circular. University of Nebraska. College of Agriculture and Home Economics. Agricultural Experiment Station [*A publication*]
**OUTSTDG** ... Outstanding [*Business term*]
**OUTUS**..... Outside the United States
**OUTWATS** ... Outgoing Wide-Area Telephone Service [*Telecommunications*] (TEL)
**OUTWD**.... Outward (ROG)
**OuTWP**..... Die Ou Testamentiese Werkgemeenskap in Suid-Afrika (Pretoria) [*A publication*]
**OUTXLTR** ... Output Translator [*IBM Corp.*] (MSA)
**OUU**.......... University of Oklahoma, Tulsa Medical College Library, Tulsa, OK [*OCLC symbol*] (OCLC)
**OUUI**......... Decisions Given by the Office of the Umpire (Unemployment Insurance) Respecting Claims to Out-of-Work Donation [*England*] (DLA)
**OUUIBD**... Benefit Decisions of the British Umpire [*A publication*] (DLA)
**OUUID**...... Umpire Decisions, Benefit Claims [*England*] [*A publication*] (DLA)
**OUUISD**... Benefit and Donation Claims, Selected Decisions of Umpire [*England*] [*A publication*] (DLA)
**OUV**.......... Openbare Uitgaven [*A publication*]
**OUV**.......... University of Science and Arts of Oklahoma Libraries, Chickasha, OK [*OCLC symbol*] (OCLC)
**OUVB**........ Oxford University Volunteer Battalion [*British military*] (DMA)
**OUVS**........ Orbiter Ultraviolet Spectrometer [*NASA*]
**OUW**......... Elkins, WV [*Location identifier*] [*FAA*] (FAAL)
**OuW**.......... Ost und West [*A publication*]
**OUW**......... Western Oklahoma State College, Library, Altus, OK [*OCLC symbol*] (OCLC)
**OUZ**........... Zouerate [*Mauritania*] [*Airport symbol*] (OAG)
**OV**............. Offense Variable [*Criminal sentencing*]
**OV**............. Office Visit [*Medicine*]
**OV**............. Office of Volunteers [*Red Cross*]
**OV**............. Ohio Valley
**OV**............. Oil of Vitriol
**OV**............. One Village [*An association*] (EAIO)
**OV**............. One Voice: a Magazine about Church Music [*A publication*] (APTA)
**OV**............. Open Ventilated (MSA)
**OV**............. Operation Venus (EA)
**OV**............. Orbital [*or Orbiter*] Vehicle [*NASA*]
**OV**............. Orphan Voyage (EA)
**OV**............. Output Voltage
**OV**............. Oval
**OV**............. Ovalbumin [*Also, OA, OVA, OVAL*] [*Biochemistry*]
**OV**............. Ovarian Volume [*Gynecology*]
**OV**............. Ovary (ADA)
**OV**............. Ovation
**OV**............. Oven [*Refers to the open space below the stage in a theater*] [*Slang*] (DSUE)
**OV**............. Over (AAG)
**OV**............. Overflow
**OV**............. Overseas National Airways, Inc. [*ICAO designator*] (FAAC)
**OV**............. Overture (ROG)
**OV**............. Overventilation [*Medicine*]
**OV**............. Overvoltage
**OV**............. Ovid [*Roman poet, 43BC-17AD*] [*Classical studies*] (ROG)
**OV**............. Ovum [*Egg*] [*Latin*]
**OV**............. Owner's Vans [*Shipping*]
**OV**............. Oxygen Vent (NASA)
**OVA**.......... Bekily [*Madagascar*] [*Airport symbol*] (OAG)
**OVA**.......... Office of Veterans' Affairs
**OVA**.......... Offshore Valve Association (EA)
**OVA**.......... Organic Vapor Analyzer [*Chromatography*]
**OVA**.......... Ottava [*Octave*] [*Music*]
**OVA**.......... Ovalbumin [*Also, OA, OV, OVAL*] [*Biochemistry*]
**OVA**.......... Overhead Value Analysis (ADA)
**OVAB**........ Orbiting Vehicle Assembly Building [*Later, OVSB*]
**OVAB**........ Ovabloc, Inc. [*Stamford, CT*] [*NASDAQ symbol*] (NQ)
**OVAC**........ Overseas Visual Aids Centre [*British*]
**OVAE**........ Office of Vocational and Adult Education [*Department of Education*] (OICC)
**OVAG**........ Horticultural Research Institute of Ontario Ministry of Agriculture and Food, Vineland Station, Ontario [*Library symbol*] [*National Library of Canada*] (NLC)
**OVAGR**..... Research Station, Agriculture Canada [*Station de Recherches, Agriculture Canada*] Vineland Station, Ontario [*Library symbol*] [*National Library of Canada*] (NLC)
**OVAL**........ Ovalbumin [*Also, OA, OV, OVA*]
**OVAL**........ Overalls [*Freight*]
**OVAM**....... Orbital Vehicle Assembly Mode [*NASA*]
**OVAMS**.... Office of Vulnerability Assessment and Management Services [*Department of Commerce*]
**OVAN**........ Vanier Public Library, Ontario [*Library symbol*] [*National Library of Canada*] (NLC)
**OVAS**........ Offshore Vessels Availability System [*Alpha Asia Systems Pte. Ltd.*] [*Defunct*] [*Information service or system*] (CRD)

**OVATE** ..... Okumenische Vereinigung der Akademien und Tagungzentren in Europa [*Ecumenical Association of Laity Centres and Academies in Europe - EALCAE*] [*Bad Boll, Federal Republic of Germany*] (EAIO)
**OVAX** ........ Ovariectomized [*Gynecology*]
**OVB** .......... Novosibirsk [*USSR*] [*Airport symbol*] (OAG)
**OVB** .......... Overseas Visitors Bureau [*Department of Trade*] [*British*]
**OVBD** ........ Overboard (AAG)
**OVC** .......... Ontario Veterinary College
**OVC** .......... Optimized Valence Configuration [*Air Force*]
**OVC** .......... Overcast
**OVC** .......... Oxidizer Vent Control
**OVC** .......... Valley East Public Library, Val Caron, Ontario [*Library symbol*] [*National Library of Canada*] (NLC)
**OVC** .......... Verwarming en Ventilatie. Maandblad voor Verwarming, Ventilatie, Airconditioning, en Koeling [*A publication*]
**OVCA** ........ Ovarian Carcinoma [*Oncology*]
**OVCO** ........ Operational Voice Communication Office [*NASA*] (MCD)
**OVCP** ........ Orbiting Vehicle Checkout Procedure
**OVCS** ........ Operational Voice Communication Subsystem
**OVCST** ...... Overcast (AFM)
**OVCT** ........ Caldwell Township Public Library, Verner, Ontario [*Library symbol*] [*National Library of Canada*] (NLC)
**OVD** .......... Occlusal Vertical Dimension [*Dentistry*]
**OV/D** ......... Operational Verification/Demonstration
**OVD** .......... Optical Video Disk
**OVD** .......... Optically Variable Device
**OVD** .......... Outer Vapor Phase Deposition [*Coating technology*]
**OVD** .......... Outside Vapor Deposition [*Coating technology*]
**OVD** .......... Overdue (FAAC)
**OVD** .......... Oviedo [*Spain*] [*Airport symbol*] (OAG)
**OVDED** ..... Overdeduction
**OVDR** ........ Observed Vertical Detection Range
**OVE** .......... Ohio Valley Electric Railroad
**OVE** .......... On Vehicle Equipment
**OVE** .......... Optimum Value Engineered (Home)
**OVE** .......... Oroville, CA [*Location identifier*] [*FAA*] (FAAL)
**OVE** .......... Overton [*Nevada*] [*Seismograph station code, US Geological Survey*] [*Closed*] (SEIS)
**OVE** .......... Owen Vapor Engine
**Ove Arup Ptnrship Newsletter** ... Ove Arup Partnership. Newsletter [*A publication*]
**OVER** ........ Overland Express, Inc. [*NASDAQ symbol*] (NQ)
**Over** .......... Overtone [*Record label*]
**Over** .......... Overton's Tennessee Supreme Court Reports [*1791-1816*] [*A publication*] (DLA)
**Overl** .......... Overland [*A publication*]
**Overland** .... Overland Monthly [*A publication*]
**Overland ns** ... Overland Monthly. New Series [*A publication*]
**Overr** .......... Overruled In [*or Overruling*] [*Legal term*] (DLA)
**OVERS** ...... Orbital Vehicle Reentry Simulator [*NASA*]
**Oversea Ed** ... Overseas Education [*A publication*]
**Overseas Bldg Notes** ... Overseas Building Notes [*A publication*]
**Overseas Geol Miner Resour** ... Overseas Geology and Mineral Resources [*Great Britain*] [*A publication*]
**Overseas Geol Miner Resour Suppl Ser Bull Suppl** ... Overseas Geology and Mineral Resources. Supplement Series. Bulletin Supplement [*A publication*]
**Overseas Mem Inst Geol Sci** ... Overseas Memoir. Institute of Geological Sciences [*A publication*]
**Overseas Mem Inst Geol Sci (GB)** ... Overseas Memoir. Institute of Geological Sciences (Great Britain) [*A publication*]
**Overseas Trade Descrip Export & Import Stat** ... Overseas Trade Descriptions. Export and Import Statistics [*A publication*]
**Overseas Trade Stat UK** ... Overseas Trade Statistics of the United Kingdom [*A publication*]
**Overs K Danske Vidensk Selsk Forh** ... Oversigt over det Kongelige Danske Videnskabernes Selskabs. Forhandlinger [*A publication*]
**Overs K Dan Vidensk Selsk** ... Oversigt over Selskabets Virksomhed. Kongelige Danske Videnskabernes Selskab [*A publication*]
**Overs K Dan Vidensk Selsk Forh** ... Oversigt over det Kongelige Danske Videnskabernes Selskabs. Forhandlinger [*A publication*]
**Overt** .......... Overton's Tennessee Supreme Court Reports [*1791-1816*] [*A publication*] (DLA)
**Overt Pr** ..... Overton's Iowa and Wisconsin Practice [*A publication*] (DLA)
**OVEX** ........ Ovex Fertility Corp. [*New York, NY*] [*NASDAQ symbol*] (NQ)
**OVF** .......... Overfill (NASA)
**OVF** .......... Overflow [*Data processing*]
**OVF** .......... Oxygen Vent Fill
**OVFL** ......... Overflow (AAG)
**OVG** .......... Oberverwaltungsgericht [*Provincial Administrative Court of Appeal*] [*German*] (DLA)
**OVGE** ........ Entscheidungen der Oberverwaltungsgerichte fuer das Land Nordrhein-Westfalen in Muenster [*A publication*]
**OVH** .......... Vankleek Hill Public Library, Ontario [*Library symbol*] [*National Library of Canada*] (NLC)
**OVHD** ....... Oval Head
**OVHD** ....... Overhead (AAG)
**OVHDLD** ... Overhandled [*Freight*]
**OVHD PWR CAB** ... Overhead Power Cable [*Nautical charts*]
**OVHG** ........ Overhanging
**OVHL** ........ Overhaul (AAG)
**OVHT** ........ Overheat (NASA)
**OVHT** ........ Tay-Victoria Harbour Union Library, Victoria Harbour, Ontario [*Library symbol*] [*National Library of Canada*] (BIB)
**OVI** ........... Operational Validation Inspection (MCD)
**OVIC** ......... Orbiting Vehicle Integrating Contractor
**OVIR** ......... Office of Visas and Registrations [*USSR*]
**OVIR** ......... Otdel Viz i Registratsii [*A publication*]
**OVIS** .......... Ohio Vocational Interest Survey [*Vocational guidance test*]
**OVL** .......... Office of Volunteer Liaison [*ACTION*]
**OVL** .......... Optically Void Liquid
**OVL** .......... Overlay File [*Data processing*]
**OVLA** ......... Overlay (FAAC)
**OVLAY** ....... Overlay
**OVLBI** ..... Orbital Very-Long Baseline Interferometer [*Communications satellite*] [*Telecommunications*] (IEEE)
**OVLD** ........ Overload (AAG)
**OVLMA** .... Orbiting Vehicle Limited Maintenance Area
**OVLP** ........ Overvoltage Load Protection
**OVLT** ........ Organum Vasculosum of the Lamina Terminalis [*Medicine*]
**OVM** .......... Congregation of the Oblates of the Virgin Mary [*Rome, Italy*] (EAIO)
**OVM** .......... McGarry Public Library, Virginiatown, Ontario [*Library symbol*] [*National Library of Canada*] (BIB)
**OVM** .......... On Vehicle Materiel [*Military*]
**OVM** .......... Orbiting Velocity Meter
**OVNGT** ..... Overnight (FAAC)
**OVNI** ......... Objectos Volantes No Identicados [*Unidentified Flying Objects*] [*Spanish*]
**OVO** .......... North Vernon, IN [*Location identifier*] [*FAA*] (FAAL)
**OVON** ....... Ovonic Imaging Systems, Inc. [*Troy, MI*] [*NASDAQ symbol*] (NQ)
**OVONIC** ... Ovshinsky and Electronic [*Excitation processing term formed by combining name of Stanford Ovshinsky, energy researcher, and "electronic"*]
**OVOR** ........ Overthrust Oil Royalty [*NASDAQ symbol*] (NQ)
**OVOT** ........ Vernon Branch, Osgoode Township Library, Ontario [*Library symbol*] [*National Library of Canada*] (NLC)
**OVP** .......... Oesterreichische Volkspartei [*Austrian People's Party*] [*Political party*] (PPW)
**OVP** .......... Office of the Vice-President
**OVP** .......... Oil-Vapor Pump
**OVP** .......... Outside Vendor Personnel
**OVP** .......... Oval Paint
**OVP** .......... Ovarian Vein Plasma [*Endocrinology*]
**OVP** .......... Overseas Private Investment Corp., Washington, DC [*OCLC symbol*] (OCLC)
**OVP** .......... Overvoltage Protection
**OVPC** ........ Ovary Pubescence - Curly [*Botany*]
**OVPD** ........ Overpaid (AFM)
**OVPG** ........ Ovary Pubescence, Glandular [*Botany*]
**OVPO** ........ Outside Vapor Phase Oxidation [*Glass technology*]
**OVPRESS** ... Overpressurized
**OVPWR** .... Overpower
**OVR** .......... Office of Vocational Rehabilitation [*Later, Vocational Rehabilitation Administration*] [*HEW*]
**OVR** .......... Orbiting Vehicle Requirements
**OVR** .......... Oudtshoorn Volunteer Rifles [*British military*] (DMA)
**OVR** .......... Over (FAAC)
**OVR** .......... Overlay File [*Data processing*]
**OVR** .......... Overvoltage Relay
**OVRD** ........ Override (AAG)
**OVRH** ........ Val Rita-Harty Public Library, Val Rita, Ontario [*Library symbol*] [*National Library of Canada*] (BIB)
**OVRN** ........ Overrun (AFM)
**OVRO** ........ Owens Valley Radio Observatory [*California Institute of Technology*] [*Research center*] (RCD)
**OVRP** ........ Organizacion de Voluntarios para la Revolucion Puertorriquena [*Organization of Volunteers for the Puerto Rican Revolution*] (PD)
**OVRR** ........ Office of Veterans Reemployment Rights [*Department of Labor*]
**OVRS** ........ Operational Voice Recording Subsystem
**OVRS** ........ Overseas Inns SA [*NASDAQ symbol*] (NQ)
**Ov Rspr** ...... Overzicht Rechtspraak [*A publication*]
**OVRT** ........ Overthrust Resources [*NASDAQ symbol*] (NQ)
**OVS** .......... Operational Voice System (MCD)
**OVS** .......... Optical Viewing System
**OVS** .......... Orbiting Vehicle System
**OVS** .......... Ovarian Vein Serum [*Endocrinology*]
**OVS** .......... Overhaul Specification (NG)
**OVS** .......... Oversize
**OVS** .......... Overvoltage Sensing (MCD)
**OVSB** ........ Orbiting Vehicle Support Building [*Formerly, OVAB*]
**OVSP** ........ Overspeed (AAG)
**OVSR** ........ Office of Vehicle Systems Research [*Later, Safety System Laboratory*] [*National Institute of Standards and Technology*]
**OVSTFD** ... Overstuffed [*Freight*]

**OVT** .......... Occupational-Vocational-Technical Training
**OVT** .......... Operational Verification Test
**OVT** .......... Optical Van Trailer
**OVT** .......... Overseas Trading [*A publication*]
**OVTK** ........ Overtake (FAAC)
**OVTR** ........ Operational Video Tape Recorder [*Air Force*] (MCD)
**OVTR** ........ Overtravel
**OVUIL** ...... Operating Vehicle under Influence of Liquor or Narcotic Drugs [*FBI standardized term*]
**OVUREP**... Overseas Unit Replacement [*System*] [*Army*]
**O/V-U/V** ... Over Voltage - Under Voltage (MCD)
**OVV** .......... Optically Violently Variable [*QUASAR*]
**OVV** .......... Overvoltage
**OVV** .......... Ovvero [*Otherwise*] [*Music*]
**OVWD**....... Operating Vehicle while Drunk [*Traffic offense charge*]
**OVWV** ....... One Valley Bancorp of West Virginia, Inc. [*Charleston, WV*] [*NASDAQ symbol*] (NQ)
**OVX** .......... Ovariectomized [*Gynecology*]
**Ow**............ New South Wales Reports [*1-3 Australia*] [*A publication*] (DLA)
**OW** ........... Obere Winkelgruppe [*Angles above 45*] [*German military - World War II*]
**OW** ........... Observation Ward [*British*]
**OW** ........... Ocellus Width
**OW** ........... Offer Wanted
**OW** ........... Officer's Writer [*British military*] (DMA)
**OW** ........... Offshore Oil Weekly [*Later, Offshore Oil International*] [*A publication*]
**OW** ........... Ohne Wert [*Without Value*] [*German*]
**OW** ........... Oil-Immersed Water-Cooled [*Transformer*] (IEEE)
**O/W**.......... Oil in Water
**OW** ........... Old Wellingtonian [*Wellington College*] [*British*]
**OW** ........... Old Welsh [*Language, etc.*]
**OW** ........... Old Woman [*A wife*] [*Slang*]
**OW** ........... Older Worker
**O & W**........ Oldest and Wisest [*Nickname for President Ronald Reagan*]
**OW** ........... One Way [*Fare*]
**O & W**........ Ontario & Western Railroad [*Nickname: Old and Weary*]
**OW** ........... Ontario World Airways [*Canada*] [*ICAO designator*] (FAAC)
**O/W**.......... Ontvangbare Wissels [*Bills Receivable*] [*Business term*] [*Afrikaans*]
**OW** ........... Open Wire (NATO)
**OW** ........... Optical Window (NASA)
**O/W**.......... Optional With [*Automotive engineering*]
**OW** ........... Options for Women [*Later, Options*] (EA)
**OW** ........... Order Wire [*Military*] (AABC)
**OW** ........... Ordinary Warfare
**O-W**.......... Ordinary Wave (MCD)
**OW** ........... Orient/West [*A publication*]
**OW** ........... Ost und West [*A publication*]
**OW** ........... Ostatnie Wiadomosci [*A publication*]
**OW** ........... Ostdeutsche Wissenschaft [*A publication*]
**OW** ........... Other Worlds [*A publication*]
**OW** ........... Out of Wedlock
**OW** ........... Outer Wing
**OW** ........... Over-Achieving Women
**OW** ........... Overseas Writers (EA)
**Ow**............ Owen's English Common Pleas Reports [*A publication*] (DLA)
**Ow**............ Owen's English King's Bench Reports [*1556-1615*] [*A publication*] (DLA)
**OW** ........... Owner's Wagons [*Shipping*]
**OW** ........... Warren Public Library, Warren, OH [*Library symbol*] [*Library of Congress*] (LCLS)
**OW** ........... Windsor Public Library, Ontario [*Library symbol*] [*National Library of Canada*] (NLC)
**OWA**.......... Optical Wholesalers Association [*Later, OLA*] (EA)
**OWA**.......... Organics-in-Water Analyzer [*Instrumentation*]
**OWA**.......... Owase [*Japan*] [*Seismograph station code, US Geological Survey*] (SEIS)
**OWA**.......... Owatonna, MN [*Location identifier*] [*FAA*] (FAAL)
**OWA**.......... University of Windsor, Ontario [*Library symbol*] [*National Library of Canada*] (NLC)
**OWAA**........ Anderson Associates Ltd., Willowdale, Ontario [*Library symbol*] [*National Library of Canada*] (NLC)
**OWAA**........ Outdoor Writers Association of America (EA)
**OWAB**........ Wasaga Beach Public Library, Ontario [*Library symbol*] [*National Library of Canada*] (BIB)
**OWAEC** .... Organization for West African Economic Co-operation
**OWAG**........ Art Gallery of Windsor, Ontario [*Library symbol*] [*National Library of Canada*] (NLC)
**OWAIT** ..... Airy Township Public Library, Whitney, Ontario [*Library symbol*] [*National Library of Canada*] (NLC)
**OWAL** ........ Law Library, University of Windsor, Ontario [*Library symbol*] [*National Library of Canada*] (NLC)
**OWALK** .... Walkerton Branch, Bruce County Public Library, Ontario [*Library symbol*] [*National Library of Canada*] (NLC)
**OWALL**..... Wallaceburg Public Library, Ontario [*Library symbol*] [*National Library of Canada*] (NLC)
**OWaP**........ Pike County Free Public Library, Waverly, OH [*Library symbol*] [*Library of Congress*] (LCLS)
**OWAP**........ Waterford Public Library, Ontario [*Library symbol*] [*National Library of Canada*] (NLC)
**OWAR**........ Warkworth Public Library, Ontario [*Library symbol*] [*National Library of Canada*] (NLC)
**OWARNP** ... Percy Township Branch, Northumberland County Public Library, Warkworth, Ontario [*Library symbol*] [*National Library of Canada*] (BIB)
**OWas**......... Carnegie Public Library, Washington Court House, OH [*Library symbol*] [*Library of Congress*] (LCLS)
**OWASU** .... Old World Archaeological Study Unit (EA)
**OWAT**........ Wainfleet Township Library, Ontario [*Library symbol*] [*National Library of Canada*] (NLC)
**OWAVE** .... Ordinary Wave (MSA)
**OWay**......... Mary L. Cook Public Library, Waynesville, OH [*Library symbol*] [*Library of Congress*] (LCLS)
**OWB**.......... Civis Mundi [*A publication*]
**OWB**.......... Owensboro [*Kentucky*] [*Airport symbol*] (OAG)
**OWB**.......... West Bay Public Library, Ontario [*Library symbol*] [*National Library of Canada*] (NLC)
**OWBC** ....... Health Sciences Library, Bloorview Children's Hospital, Willowdale, Ontario [*Library symbol*] [*National Library of Canada*] (BIB)
**OWBE** ....... Office of Women's Business Enterprise [*Federal government*]
**OWBE** ....... Windsor Board of Education, Ontario [*Library symbol*] [*National Library of Canada*] (NLC)
**OWBL** ....... Beaver Lake Branch, Walden Public Library, Ontario [*Library symbol*] [*National Library of Canada*] (NLC)
**OWBMS** ... Manitoulin Secondary School Library, West Bay, Ontario [*Library symbol*] [*National Library of Canada*] (BIB)
**OWBO**....... Office of Women's Business Ownership [*Small Business Administration*]
**OWBR** ....... Bartlet & Richardes, Windsor, Ontario [*Library symbol*] [*National Library of Canada*] (BIB)
**OWC**.......... Centennial Secondary School, Windsor, Ontario [*Library symbol*] [*National Library of Canada*] (NLC)
**OWC**.......... Officers' Wives Club [*Military*]
**OwC**.......... Omniwest Corporation, Salt Lake City, UT [*Library symbol*] [*Library of Congress*] (LCLS)
**OWC**.......... Ontario Workers' Compensation Appeals Tribunal [*UTLAS symbol*]
**OWC**.......... Ordinary Wave Component
**OWC**.......... Ordnance Weapons Command [*Later, Weapons Command*]
**OWC**.......... Owner Will Carry [*Banking*]
**OWC**.......... Owning Work Center [*Military*] (AFIT)
**OWC**.......... Wood County District Public Library, Bowling Green, OH [*OCLC symbol*] (OCLC)
**OWCA** ....... Canadian Automobile Workers Union, Willowdale, Ontario [*Library symbol*] [*National Library of Canada*] (BIB)
**OWCC** ....... Cape Croker Public Library, Wiarton, Ontario [*Library symbol*] [*National Library of Canada*] (NLC)
**OWCF** ....... Canadian Federation of Independent Business, Willowdale, Ontario [*Library symbol*] [*National Library of Canada*] (BIB)
**OWCL** ....... Octane Weekly Cost Ledger (MCD)
**OWCP** ....... Office of Workers' [*formerly, Workmen's*] Compensation Programs [*Formerly, Bureau of Employees' Compensation*] [*Department of Labor*]
**OWCS** ....... Outer Wing Canted Station (MCD)
**OWCSC**..... Old Water Colour Society's Club (EA)
**OWD** ......... Norwood, MA [*Location identifier*] [*FAA*] (FAAL)
**OWD** ......... Oil-in-Water Dispersion [*Pollution*]
**OWD** ......... On-Line Wholesale Distribution System [*Data processing*] (BUR)
**OWD** ......... One-Way Doppler (MCD)
**OWDC**........ Office of Water Data Coordination [*US Geological Survey*] [*Reston, VA*]
**OWDE**........ One-Way Doppler Extraction
**O & W Dig** ... Oldham and White's Digest of Laws [*Texas*] [*A publication*] (DLA)
**OWE**.......... Eagle, CO [*Location identifier*] [*FAA*] (FAAL)
**OWE**.......... Operating Weight Empty [*of space shuttle*] [*NASA*]
**OWE**.......... Optimum Working Efficiency
**OWE**.......... Outer Window Envelope [*Business stationery*]
**OWE**.......... Welland Public Library, Ontario [*Library symbol*] [*National Library of Canada*] (NLC)
**OWE**.......... Western Plains Library System, Clinton, OK [*OCLC symbol*] (OCLC)
**OWe**.......... Westerville Public Library, Westerville, OH [*Library symbol*] [*Library of Congress*] (LCLS)
**OWEB** ....... Webbwood Public Library, Ontario [*Library symbol*] [*National Library of Canada*] (NLC)
**OWEC** ....... Centennial Secondary School, Welland, Ontario [*Library symbol*] [*National Library of Canada*] (NLC)
**OWel**.......... Sylvester Memorial Wellston Public Library, Wellston, OH [*Library symbol*] [*Library of Congress*] (LCLS)
**OWEL** ....... Wellington Public Library, Ontario [*Library symbol*] [*National Library of Canada*] (BIB)
**OWEN**....... Niagara College of Applied Arts and Technology, Welland, Ontario [*Library symbol*] [*National Library of Canada*] (NLC)

**Owen**.......... Owen's English King's Bench Reports [*1556-1615*] [*A publication*] (DLA)
**Owen Bankr** ... Owen on Bankruptcy [*A publication*] (DLA)
**OWENC**.... Westport-North Crosby Public Library, Westport, Ontario [*Library symbol*] [*National Library of Canada*] (NLC)
**OWENL**.... Library Technician Program, Niagara College of Applied Arts & Technology, Welland, Ontario [*Library symbol*] [*National Library of Canada*] (NLC)
**OWeO**........ Otterbein College, Westerville, OH [*Library symbol*] [*Library of Congress*] (LCLS)
**OWESBC**.. Borden Chemical, Westhill, Ontario [*Library symbol*] [*National Library of Canada*] (NLC)
**OWEST**..... Asphodel Township Public Library, Westwood, Ontario [*Library symbol*] [*National Library of Canada*] (BIB)
**OWF**.......... Oceania Weightlifting Federation [*Australia*] (EA)
**OWF**.......... On Weight of Fiber
**OWF**.......... Optimum Working Frequency [*Telecommunications*]
**OWG**......... Oil, Water, Gas
**OWG**......... Ordnungswidrigkeitengesetz [*A publication*]
**OWG**......... Washington, DC [*Location identifier*] [*FAA*] (FAAL)
**OWGL**....... Obscure Wire Glass
**OWH**......... Herman Collegiate Institute, Windsor, Ontario [*Library symbol*] [*National Library of Canada*] (NLC)
**OWHA**...... Oliver Wendell Holmes Association
**OWHD**...... Medical Library, Hotel-Dieu of St. Joseph Hospital, Windsor, Ontario [*Library symbol*] [*National Library of Canada*] (NLC)
**OWHM**..... Hiram Walker Historical Museum, Windsor, Ontario [*Library symbol*] [*National Library of Canada*] (BIB)
**OWHM**..... Office of Water and Hazardous Materials (OICC)
**OWHP**....... Whitby Public Library, Ontario [*Library symbol*] [*National Library of Canada*] (NLC)
**OWI**........... Ocellus Width Index
**OWI**........... Office of War Information [*World War II*]
**OWI**........... Office of Waste Isolation [*Department of Energy*]
**OWI**........... Open Work Items (KSC)
**OWI**........... Operating Vehicle while Intoxicated [*Traffic offense charge*]
**O Wi**.......... Ostdeutsche Wissenschaft [*A publication*]
**OWI**........... Ottawa, KS [*Location identifier*] [*FAA*] (FAAL)
**OWI**........... Owens-Illinois, Inc., Technical and Business Information Services, Toledo, OH [*OCLC symbol*] (OCLC)
**OWI**........... Wiarton Branch, Bruce County Public Library, Ontario [*Library symbol*] [*National Library of Canada*] (NLC)
**OWIB**........ Wikwemikong Band Public Library, Ontario [*Library symbol*] [*National Library of Canada*] (NLC)
**OWibfC**..... Central State University, Wilberforce, OH [*Library symbol*] [*Library of Congress*] (LCLS)
**OWibfP**..... Payne Theological Seminary, Wilberforce, OH [*Library symbol*] [*Library of Congress*] (LCLS)
**OWibfU**..... Wilberforce University, Wilberforce, OH [*Library symbol*] [*Library of Congress*] (LCLS)
**OWicB**....... Borromeo Seminary of Ohio, Wickliffe, OH [*Library symbol*] [*Library of Congress*] (LCLS)
**OWIFC**...... Wolfe Island Branch, Frontenac County Public Library, Ontario [*Library symbol*] [*National Library of Canada*] (NLC)
**OWIJC**...... International Joint Commission [*Commission Mixte Internationale*] Windsor, Ontario [*Library symbol*] [*National Library of Canada*] (NLC)
**OWil**.......... Willard Memorial Library, Willard, OH [*Library symbol*] [*Library of Congress*] (LCLS)
**OWillo**....... Willoughby-Eastlake Public Library, Willowick, OH [*Library symbol*] [*Library of Congress*] (LCLS)
**OWilm**....... Wilmington Public Library, Wilmington, OH [*Library symbol*] [*Library of Congress*] (LCLS)
**OWilmC**.... Wilmington College, Wilmington, OH [*Library symbol*] [*Library of Congress*] (LCLS)
**OWilmH**.... Clinton Memorial Hospital, Health Resource Center, Wilmington, OH [*Library symbol*] [*Library of Congress*] (LCLS)
**OWilm-O**... Southwestern Ohio Rural Library, Wilmington, OH [*Library symbol*] [*Library of Congress*] (LCLS)
**OWilmS**.... Southern State Community College, Wilmington, OH [*Library symbol*] [*Library of Congress*] (LCLS)
**OWin**......... Adams-Brown County Bookmobile, Winchester, OH [*Library symbol*] [*Library of Congress*] (LCLS)
**OWIN**........ Office of Work Incentive Program [*Office of Comprehensive Employment Development*] [*Department of Labor*]
**OWINF**..... F. E. Madill Secondary School, Wingham, Ontario [*Library symbol*] [*National Library of Canada*] (NLC)
**OWISDG**... Williamstown Branch, Stormount, Dundas, and Glengarry County Library, Ontario [*Library symbol*] [*National Library of Canada*] (NLC)
**OWIU**........ Oil Workers International Union [*Later, OCAW*]
**OWK**.......... Kent State University, Trumbull Regional Campus, Warren, OH [*Library symbol*] [*Library of Congress*] [*OCLC symbol*] (LCLS)
**OWK**.......... Norridgewock, ME [*Location identifier*] [*FAA*] (FAAL)
**OWL**.......... Lowe Technical School, Windsor, Ontario [*Library symbol*] [*National Library of Canada*] (NLC)
**OWL**.......... National Order of Women Legislators (EA)
**OWL**.......... Older Women's League (EA)
**OWL**.......... Older Women's Liberation [*Feminist group*] [*Defunct*]
**OWL**.......... Online without Limits
**OWL**.......... Other Woman Limited [*An association*]
**OWL**.......... Westerville Public Library, Westerville, OH [*OCLC symbol*] (OCLC)
**OWLA**....... Organization of Women for Legal Awareness (EA)
**OWLaw**..... Trumbull County Law Library, Warren, OH [*Library symbol*] [*Library of Congress*] (LCLS)
**OWLB**....... Wunnummin Lake Band Library, Ontario [*Library symbol*] [*National Library of Canada*] (BIB)
**OWL/D**..... Optical Warning Locator/Detector (MCD)
**OWLEF**..... Older Women's League Educational Fund (EA)
**OWlGS**...... Church of Jesus Christ of Latter-Day Saints, Genealogical Society Library, Cleveland Branch, Westlake, OH [*Library symbol*] [*Library of Congress*] (LCLS)
**OWLI**........ Lively Branch, Walden Public Library, Ontario [*Library symbol*] [*National Library of Canada*] (NLC)
**OWLS**........ Office Workers Link Shift [*After-hours production workers*] [*World War II*]
**OWLS**........ Operation Work Load Scheduling (MCD)
**OWLS**........ Outagamie-Waupaca Counties Federated Library System [*Library network*]
**OWLS**........ Overseas Weapons, Logistically Supported (MCD)
**OWLS**........ Oxford Word and Language Service [*A service of the Oxford English Dictionary group*]
**OWM**........ Office of War Mobilization [*Succeeded by OWMR, 1944*]
**OWM**........ Office of Weights and Measures [*National Institute of Standards and Technology*]
**OWMMD**... M. M. Dillon Ltd., Willowdale, Ontario [*Library symbol*] [*National Library of Canada*] (NLC)
**OWMR**...... Office of War Mobilization and Reconversion [*Succeeded OWM, 1944; became part of Office of Temporary Controls, 1946*]
**OWMT**...... Michipicoten Township Public Library, Wawa, Ontario [*Library symbol*] [*National Library of Canada*] (NLC)
**OWN**......... Naughton Branch, Walden Public Library, Ontario [*Library symbol*] [*National Library of Canada*] (NLC)
**OWN**......... Office World News [*A publication*]
**OWN**......... Older Women's Network [*Australia*]
**OWN**......... Ontario Weekly Notes [*A publication*] (DLA)
**OWN**......... Oudh Weekly Notes [*India*] [*A publication*] (DLA)
**OWN**......... Oudtestamentisch Werkgezelschap in Nederland [*A publication*]
**OWN**......... Overwintered Nest [*Ornithology*]
**OWN**......... Owen Ventures Ltd. [*Vancouver Stock Exchange symbol*]
**OWN**......... Owner (MCD)
**OWN**......... Wise, VA [*Location identifier*] [*FAA*] (FAAL)
**OWO**......... On Work Order [*Military*] (AFIT)
**OWo**.......... Wayne County Public Library, Wooster, OH [*Library symbol*] [*Library of Congress*] (LCLS)
**OWO**......... Woodstock Public Library, Ontario [*Library symbol*] [*National Library of Canada*] (NLC)
**OWoA**........ Ohio Agricultural Research and Development Center, Wooster, OH [*Library symbol*] [*Library of Congress*] (LCLS)
**OWOBC**.... J. William Horsey Library, Ontario Bible College, Ontario Theological College, Willowdale, Ontario [*Library symbol*] [*National Library of Canada*] (NLC)
**OWoC**........ College of Wooster, Wooster, OH [*Library symbol*] [*Library of Congress*] (LCLS)
**OWOH**...... Huron Park Secondary School, Woodstock, Ontario [*Library symbol*] [*National Library of Canada*] (NLC)
**OWOL**....... Ontario Library Co-Operative, Wyoming, Ontario [*Library symbol*] [*National Library of Canada*] (NLC)
**OWOM**..... Woodstock Museum, Ontario [*Library symbol*] [*National Library of Canada*] (BIB)
**OWOO**...... Oxford County Public Library, Woodstock, Ontario [*Library symbol*] [*National Library of Canada*] (NLC)
**OWorP**...... Pontifical College Josephinum, Worthington, OH [*Library symbol*] [*Library of Congress*] (LCLS)
**OWoWCL**... Wayne County Law Library, Wooster, OH [*Library symbol*] [*Library of Congress*] (LCLS)
**OWP**.......... Oboz Wielkiej Polski [*Camp of Great Poland*] (PPE)
**OWP**.......... Office of Water Policy [*Department of the Interior*]
**OWP**.......... Office of Water Programs [*Abolished*] [*Environmental Protection Agency*]
**OWP**.......... One-Way Polar [*Telegraph*]
**OWP**.......... Operations Work Procedure [*Nuclear energy*] (NRCH)
**OWP**.......... Orange Washed Pulp [*Citrus processing*]
**OWP**.......... Organization of Wildlife Planners (EA)
**OWP**.......... Outer Wing Panel
**OWP**.......... Warner Pacific College, Portland, OR [*OCLC symbol*] (OCLC)
**OWpAR**..... United States Air Force, Aerospace Research Laboratories, Wright-Patterson Air Force Base, OH [*Library symbol*] [*Library of Congress*] (LCLS)
**OWpDI**...... United States Air Force, Defense Institute of Security Administration Management, Wright-Patterson Air Force Base, OH [*Library symbol*] [*Library of Congress*] (LCLS)
**OWPH**....... Whitby Psychiatric Hospital, Ontario [*Library symbol*] [*National Library of Canada*] (NLC)

**OWpIT** ...... United States Air Force Institute of Technology, Wright-Patterson Air Force Base, OH [*Library symbol*] [*Library of Congress*] (LCLS)
**OWpL** ........ United States Air Force, Air Force Logistics Command, Wright-Patterson Air Force Base, OH [*Library symbol*] [*Library of Congress*] (LCLS)
**OWpM** ...... United States Air Force, Medical Center Library, SGEL, Wright Patterson AFB, OH [*Library symbol*] [*Library of Congress*] (LCLS)
**OWPP** ....... Office of Welfare and Pension Plans [*Department of Labor*]
**OWPR** ....... Ocean Wave Profile Recorder (IEEE)
**OWPS** ........ Offshore Windpower System [*Proposed system to generate electricity by wind turbines mounted on offshore platforms*]
**OWpT** ........ United States Air Force, Wright-Patterson Technical Library, Wright-Patterson Air Force Base, OH [*Library symbol*] [*Library of Congress*] (LCLS)
**OWR** .......... Obligated War Reserves [*Army*] (AABC)
**OWR** .......... Office of Worship Resources [*Later, WRO*] (EA)
**OWR** .......... Omega West Reactor [*Department of Energy*] [*Los Alamos, NM*]
**OWR** .......... Ontario Weekly Reporter [*A publication*] (DLA)
**OWR** .......... Riverside Secondary School, Windsor, Ontario [*Library symbol*] [*National Library of Canada*] (NLC)
**OWR** .......... Worthington Public Library, Worthington, OH [*OCLC symbol*] (OCLC)
**OWRB** ....... RC Reid-Bicknell Eng. Ltd., Woodbridge, Ontario [*Library symbol*] [*National Library of Canada*] (NLC)
**OWRC** ....... Old West Regional Commission [*Department of Commerce*]
**OWRC** ....... White River Community Library, Ontario [*Library symbol*] [*National Library of Canada*] (NLC)
**OWRD** ....... Ratter and Dunnet Public Library, Warren, Ontario [*Library symbol*] [*National Library of Canada*] (NLC)
**OWRM** ...... Office of Weather Research and Modification [*National Oceanic and Atmospheric Administration*] (GRD)
**OWRM** ...... Other War Reserve Materiel
**OWRMR** ... Other War Reserve Materiel Requirement (AFIT)
**OWRMS** ... Other War Reserve Materiel Stocks [*Army*] (AABC)
**OWRR** ....... Office of Water Resources Research [*Later, OWRT*] [*Department of the Interior*]
**OWRRI** ..... Oklahoma Water Resources Research Institute [*Stillwater, OK*] [*Department of the Interior*] (GRD)
**OWRT** ....... Office of Water Research and Technology [*Formerly, OSW, OWRR*] [*Abolished, 1982*] [*Department of the Interior*]
**OWS** .......... Occupational Wage Survey
**OWS** .......... Ocean Weather Ship
**OWS** .......... Ocean Weather Station (MCD)
**OWS** .......... Oil Water Separator [*Navy*] (CAAL)
**OWS** .......... Old West Saxon [*Language, etc.*] (ROG)
**OWS** .......... Oliphant Washington Service [*Information service or system*] (IID)
**OWS** .......... Operational Weather Support
**OWS** .......... Orbital Weapon System (AAG)
**OWS** .......... Orbital Workshop [*NASA*]
**OWS** .......... Ordnance Weapon Systems [*Army*]
**OWS** .......... Outer Wing Station (MCD)
**OWS** .......... Overload Warning System (MCD)
**OWS** .......... Overwear Syndrome [*Of contact lens*]
**OWS** .......... Southwestern Regional Library, Windsor, Ontario [*Library symbol*] [*Obsolete*] [*National Library of Canada*] (NLC)
**OWS** .......... Willamette University, Salem, OR [*OCLC symbol*] (OCLC)
**OWSA** ....... Spar Aerospace Ltd., Weston, Ontario [*Library symbol*] [*National Library of Canada*] (NLC)
**OWSAH** .... Salvation Army Grace Hospital, Windsor, Ontario [*Library symbol*] [*National Library of Canada*] (BIB)
**OWSC** ....... Old West Scandinavian [*Language, etc.*]
**OWSC** ....... St. Clair College, Windsor, Ontario [*Library symbol*] [*National Library of Canada*] (NLC)
**OWSCC** ..... Simon-Carves of Canada Ltd., Willowdale, Ontario [*Library symbol*] [*National Library of Canada*] (NLC)
**OWSCL** ..... Senes Consultants Ltd., Willowdale, Ontario [*Library symbol*] [*National Library of Canada*] (NLC)
**OWSDG** .... Winchester Branch, Stormount, Dundas, and Glengarry County Public Library, Ontario [*Library symbol*] [*National Library of Canada*] (NLC)
**OWSE** ....... Otherwise
**OWSG** ....... Older Worker Specialists Group
**OWSJ** ........ Off the Wall Street Journal [*Parody of the Wall Street Journal*]
**OWSM** ...... Seagram Museum, Waterloo, Ontario [*Library symbol*] [*National Library of Canada*] (BIB)
**OWT** .......... Organic Weather Team
**OWT** .......... Waterloo Public Library, Ontario [*Library symbol*] [*National Library of Canada*] (NLC)
**OWT** .......... Willamette University, Law Library, Salem, OR [*OCLC symbol*] (OCLC)
**OWTA** ....... Kitchener-Waterloo Academy of Medicine, Kitchener, Ontario [*Library symbol*] [*National Library of Canada*] (NLC)
**OWTAI** ..... Airworthiness Library, Ontario Region, Transport Canada [*Bibliotheque de la Navigabilite Aerienne, Region de l'Ontario, Transports Canada*], Willowdale, Ontario [*Library symbol*] [*National Library of Canada*] (NLC)
**OWTG** ....... Kitchener-Waterloo Hospital, Kitchener, Ontario [*Library symbol*] [*National Library of Canada*] (NLC)
**OWTL** ....... Wilfrid Laurier University [*Formerly, Waterloo Lutheran University*] Waterloo, Ontario [*Library symbol*] [*National Library of Canada*] (NLC)
**OWTM** ...... Legal Reference Centre, Manufacturers' Life Insurance Co., Waterloo, Ontario [*Library symbol*] [*National Library of Canada*] (BIB)
**OWTML** ... Corporate Library, Mutual Life of Canada, Waterloo, Ontario [*Library symbol*] [*National Library of Canada*] (BIB)
**OWTO** ....... Ontario Library Services Center, Waterloo, Ontario [*Library symbol*] [*National Library of Canada*] (NLC)
**OWTS** ....... St. Mary's General Hospital, Kitchener, Ontario [*Library symbol*] [*National Library of Canada*] (NLC)
**OWTU** ....... University of Waterloo, Ontario [*Library symbol*] [*National Library of Canada*] (NLC)
**OWTUE** .... Environmental Studies Library, University of Waterloo, Ontario [*Library symbol*] [*National Library of Canada*] (NLC)
**OWU** ......... Office of War Utilities [*War Production Board*]
**OWU** ......... Ohio Wesleyan University [*Delaware, OH*]
**OWU** ......... Ohio Wesleyan University, Delaware, OH [*OCLC symbol*] (OCLC)
**OWU** ......... Open-Window Unit (MSA)
**OWU** ......... Overload Warning Unit (MCD)
**OWU** ......... Woodward, OK [*Location identifier*] [*FAA*] (FAAL)
**OWV** .......... Ocean Weather Vessel [*Shipping*] (AIA)
**OWVM** ...... Vincent Massey Secondary School, Windsor, Ontario [*Library symbol*] [*National Library of Canada*] (NLC)
**OWW** ........ Walkerville Collegiate Institute, Windsor, Ontario [*Library symbol*] [*National Library of Canada*] (NLC)
**OWWA** ...... Waters Branch, Walden Public Library, Ontario [*Library symbol*] [*National Library of Canada*] (NLC)
**OWWH** ..... Whitefish Branch, Walden Public Library, Ontario [*Library symbol*] [*National Library of Canada*] (NLC)
**OWX** .......... Office of the Assistant for Weather [*Air Force*]
**OWX** .......... Ottawa, OH [*Location identifier*] [*FAA*] (FAAL)
**OWY** .......... Owyhee, NV [*Location identifier*] [*FAA*] (FAAL)
**OWYL** ....... Lambton County Public Library, Wyoming, Ontario [*Library symbol*] [*National Library of Canada*] (NLC)
**OX** ............. Oxacillin [*Antibacterial compound*]
**OX** ............. Oxford [*England*]
**Ox** ............. Oxford [*Record label*]
**OX** ............. Oxide [*or Oxidizer*] (AAG)
**OX** ............. Oxymel [*Syrup of vinegar and honey*] [*Pharmacy*]
**OX** ............. Skyline AB [*Sweden*] [*ICAO designator*] (FAAC)
**OXA** .......... Oxalic Acid [*Organic chemistry*]
**OxAbs** ........ Oxford Abstracts [*A publication*]
**OXB** .......... Baldwin-Wallace College, Berea, OH [*OCLC symbol*] (OCLC)
**Ox B Econ S** ... Oxford Bulletin of Economics and Statistics [*A publication*]
**OXBRIDGE** ... Oxford/Cambridge [*England*]
**OXC** .......... Oxford, CT [*Location identifier*] [*FAA*] (FAAL)
**OXCI** ......... Oxford Consolidated, Incorporated [*Denver, CO*] [*NASDAQ symbol*] (NQ)
**OXCO** ........ OXOCO, Inc. [*NASDAQ symbol*] (NQ)
**OXD** .......... Oxford [*England*] [*Seismograph station code, US Geological Survey*] [*Closed*] (SEIS)
**OXD** .......... Oxford, OH [*Location identifier*] [*FAA*] (FAAL)
**OXD** .......... Oxidized (MSA)
**OXDZR** ..... Oxidizer (NASA)
**OXe** ........... Greene County District Library, Xenia, OH [*Library symbol*] [*Library of Congress*] (LCLS)
**Ox Econ Pap** ... Oxford Economic Papers [*A publication*]
**OXeGH** ...... Greene Memorial Hospital, Health Resource Library, Xenia, OH [*Library symbol*] [*Library of Congress*] (LCLS)
**OXEX** ........ Oxford Exploration Co. [*NASDAQ symbol*] (NQ)
**OXF** .......... Oxford [*Mississippi*] [*Seismograph station code, US Geological Survey*] [*Closed*] (SEIS)
**OXF** .......... Oxford [*British depot code*]
**OXF** .......... Oxford [*England*]
**OXF** .......... Oxford Bulletin of Economics and Statistics [*A publication*]
**OXF** .......... Oxford Properties Canada Ltd. [*Toronto Stock Exchange symbol*]
**OXFAM** .... Oxford Committee for Famine Relief [*Acronym is now organization's official name*] [*British*] (EA)
**Oxf Ger Stud** ... Oxford German Studies [*A publication*]
**Oxf Lawy** ... Oxford Lawyer [*1958-61*] [*A publication*] (DLA)
**Oxf Mag** .... Oxford Magazine [*A publication*]
**Oxf Med Sch Gaz** ... Oxford Medical School Gazette [*A publication*]
**Oxford B Econ Statis** ... Oxford Bulletin of Economics and Statistics [*A publication*]
**Oxford Biol Readers** ... Oxford Biology Readers [*A publication*]
**Oxford/Carol Biol Readers** ... Oxford/Carolina Biology Readers [*A publication*]
**Oxford Econ Pa** ... Oxford Economic Papers [*A publication*]
**Oxford Econ Pas** ... Oxford Economic Papers [*A publication*]
**Oxford J Legal Stud** ... Oxford Journal of Legal Studies [*A publication*]
**Oxford Law** ... Oxford Lawyer [*1958-61*] [*A publication*] (DLA)
**Oxford R Educ** ... Oxford Review of Education [*A publication*]
**Oxford Rev Educ** ... Oxford Review of Education [*A publication*]

**Oxford Rev Reprod Biol** ... Oxford Reviews of Reproductive Biology [*A publication*]
**Oxfordshire Rec Soc** ... Oxfordshire Record Society [*A publication*]
**Oxford Slavonic Pa** ... Oxford Slavonic Papers [*A publication*]
**Oxf Phys Ser** ... Oxford Physics Series [*A publication*]
**Oxf R** ......... Oxford Review [*A publication*]
**Oxf Rev Reprod Biol** ... Oxford Reviews of Reproductive Biology [*A publication*]
**Oxf Slav Pap** ... Oxford Slavonic Papers [*A publication*]
**Oxf Surv Evol Biol** ... Oxford Surveys in Evolutionary Biology [*A publication*]
**Oxf Univ Pitt Rivers Mus Occas Pap Technol** ... Oxford University. Pitt Rivers Museum. Occasional Papers on Technology [*A publication*]
**OXH** .......... Oxygen Heat Exchanger (KSC)
**OXI** ........... Knox, IN [*Location identifier*] [*FAA*] (FAAL)
**OXI** ........... Orbex Industries, Incorporated [*Vancouver Stock Exchange symbol*]
**OXID** ......... Oxidizer (AAG)
**OXID** ......... [*The*] Oxidyne Group, Inc. [*NASDAQ symbol*] (NQ)
**Oxid Combust Rev** ... Oxidation and Combustion Reviews [*A publication*]
**Oxid Met** ... Oxidation of Metals [*A publication*]
**OXIDN** ...... Oxidation
**OXIM** ......... Oxide-Isolated Monolith
**OXINE** ...... Oxyquinoline [*Organic chemistry*]
**OXK** .......... Belleville, IL [*Location identifier*] [*FAA*] (FAAL)
**Oxley** ......... Oxley's Railway Cases [*1897-1903*] [*A publication*] (DLA)
**Oxley** ......... Young's Nova Scotia Vice-Admiralty Decisions, Edited by Oxley [*A publication*] (DLA)
**Ox Lit Rev** ... Oxford Literary Review [*A publication*]
**OXM** .......... Oxford Industries, Inc. [*NYSE symbol*] (SPSG)
**OXM** .......... Oxtotitlan [*Mexico*] [*Seismograph station code, US Geological Survey*] (SEIS)
**OXN** .......... Oxin Industries Ltd. [*Vancouver Stock Exchange symbol*]
**OXO** .......... Orbiting X-Ray Observatory [*NASA*]
**OXON** ....... Oxfordshire [*County in England*]
**OXON** ....... Oxonia [*Oxford University*] [*Latin*]
**Oxon** .......... Oxoniensia [*A publication*]
**OXON** ....... Oxoniensis [*Of Oxford University*] [*Latin*]
**OXP** .......... Oxford Poets [*A publication*]
**OXP** .......... Oxprenolol [*Vasodilator*]
**Ox Prize Ess** ... Oxford Prize Essays [*A publication*]
**OXR** .......... Oxnard [*California*] [*Airport symbol*] (OAG)
**OXRB** ........ Oxygen Replacement Bottles
**OXV** .......... Knoxville, IA [*Location identifier*] [*FAA*] (FAAL)
**OXY** .......... Occidental Petroleum Corp. [*NYSE symbol*] [*Toronto Stock Exchange symbol*] (SPSG)
**OXY** .......... Oxley [*British depot code*]
**OXY** .......... Oxygen [*Chemical element*] [*Symbol is O*] (AAG)
**OXY** .......... Oxytocin [*Endocrinology*]
**OXYG** ........ Oxygen [*Chemical element*] [*Symbol is O*]
**OXYM** ....... Oxymel [*Syrup of vinegar and honey*] [*Pharmacy*] (ROG)
**OY** ............. Conair [*Denmark*] [*ICAO designator*] (FAAC)
**OY** ............. Denmark [*Aircraft nationality and registration mark*] (FAAC)
**O & Y** ......... Olympia & York [*Commercial firm*] [*Canada*] (ECON)
**OY** ............. Optimum Yield
**OY** ............. Orange Yellow
**OY** ............. Public Library of Youngstown and Mahoning County, Youngstown, OH [*Library symbol*] [*Library of Congress*] (LCLS)
**OYA** .......... Goya [*Argentina*] [*Airport symbol*] (OAG)
**OYA** .......... Orthodox Youth of America [*Later, SOYO*]
**OYAP** ........ Outstanding Young American Pianist
**OYAS** ........ Abbs [*Yemen*] [*ICAO location identifier*] (ICLI)
**OYBI** ......... Al-Beida [*Yemen*] [*ICAO location identifier*] (ICLI)
**OYBO** ........ Al-Bough [*Yemen*] [*ICAO location identifier*] (ICLI)
**OYBSA** ...... Oyo Butsuri [*A publication*]
**OYBT** ........ Barat [*Yemen*] [*ICAO location identifier*] (ICLI)
**OYC** .......... Corpus Christi, TX [*Location identifier*] [*FAA*] (FAAL)
**OYC** .......... Out Year Costs (MCD)
**OYCA** ........ Ocean Youth Club of Australia
**OYD** .......... Rome, GA [*Location identifier*] [*FAA*] (FAAL)
**OYE** .......... Old Yellow Enzyme [*Biochemistry*]
**OYE** .......... Oyem [*Gabon*] [*Airport symbol*] (OAG)
**OYesA** ....... Antioch College, Yellow Springs, OH [*Library symbol*] [*Library of Congress*] (LCLS)
**OYesF** ........ Fels Research Institute, Yellow Springs, OH [*Library symbol*] [*Library of Congress*] (LCLS)
**OYesK** ....... Charles F. Kettering Foundation, Research Laboratory Library, Yellow Springs, OH [*Library symbol*] [*Library of Congress*] (LCLS)
**OYGK** ........ Okayama Daigaku Hobungakubu Gakujutsu Kiyo [*A publication*]
**OYHD** ....... Hodeidah [*Yemen*] [*ICAO location identifier*] (ICLI)
**OYKM** ....... Kamaran [*Yemen*] [*ICAO location identifier*] (ICLI)
**OYM** .......... Oyama [*Japan*] [*Seismograph station code, US Geological Survey*] (SEIS)
**OYM** .......... St. Mary's, PA [*Location identifier*] [*FAA*] (FAAL)
**OYMB** ....... Marib [*Yemen*] [*ICAO location identifier*] (ICLI)
**OYMC** ....... Mokha [*Yemen*] [*ICAO location identifier*] (ICLI)
**OYMHi** ..... Mahoning Valley Historical Society, Arms Museum, Youngstown, OH [*Library symbol*] [*Library of Congress*] (LCLS)
**OYO** .......... Tres Arroyos [*Argentina*] [*Airport symbol*] (OAG)
**OYP** .......... Office of Youth Programs [*Department of Labor*]
**OYP** .......... Opportunities for Youth Program [*Canada*]
**OYS** .......... Otsar Yehude Sefarad (BJA)
**Oys** ........... Oysters [*Quality of the bottom*] [*Nautical charts*]
**OYS** .......... Yosemite National Park [*California*] [*Airport symbol*] [*Obsolete*] (OAG)
**OYSH** ........ Saada [*Yemen*] [*ICAO location identifier*] (ICLI)
**OYSN** ........ Sanaa/International [*Yemen*] [*ICAO location identifier*] (ICLI)
**OYTZ** ........ Taiz/Ganad [*Yemen*] [*ICAO location identifier*] (ICLI)
**OYU** .......... Youngstown State University, Youngstown, OH [*Library symbol*] [*Library of Congress*] (LCLS)
**OYY** .......... Columbus, OH [*Location identifier*] [*FAA*] (FAAL)
**OYZM** ....... Al-Hazm [*Yemen*] [*ICAO location identifier*] (ICLI)
**OZ** ............. [*A*] programming language [*1975*] (CSR)
**Oz** ............. Ooze [*Quality of the bottom*] [*Nautical charts*]
**OZ** ............. Ounce [*Unit of weight*] (AAG)
**OZ** ............. Ozark Airlines, Inc. [*ICAO designator*] (OAG)
**OZ** ............. Ozone
**OZA** .......... Ozark (MCD)
**OZA** .......... Ozona, TX [*Location identifier*] [*FAA*] (FAAL)
**OZAR** ........ Ozark National Scenic Riverways [*National Park Service designation*]
**OZARC** ..... Ozone ARCAS [*All-Purpose Rocket for Collecting Atmospheric Soundings*] [*Navy*]
**OZav** .......... John McIntire Public Library, Zanesville, OH [*Library symbol*] [*Library of Congress*] (LCLS)
**OZavU** ....... Ohio University, Zanesville Branch Campus, Zanesville, OH [*Library symbol*] [*Library of Congress*] (LCLS)
**OZC** .......... Cleveland Heights-University Heights Public Library, Cleveland Heights, OH [*OCLC symbol*] (OCLC)
**OZC** .......... Ozamis City [*Philippines*] [*Airport symbol*] (OAG)
**OZD** .......... Observed Zenith Distance [*Navigation*]
**OZDP** ........ Oesterreichische Zeitschrift fuer Kunst und Denkmalpflege [*A publication*]
**OZE** .......... Outer Zone Electron
**Ozean Tech** ... Ozean und Technik [*West Germany*] [*A publication*]
**OZEBA** ...... Oesterreichische Zeitschrift fuer Erforschung und Bekaempfung der Krebskrankheit [*A publication*]
**OZE Oesterr Z Elektr** ... Oe Z E/Oesterreichische Zeitschrift fuer Elektrizitaetswirtschaft [*A publication*]
**OZE Oesterr Z fuer Elektrizitaetswirtsch** ... OZE. Oesterreichische Zeitschrift fuer Elektrizitaetswirtschaft [*A publication*]
**OZEP** ......... Outer Zone Electron Precipitation
**OZET** ........ Obshchestvo Remeslennovo i Zemledel'cheskovo Truda [*A publication*]
**OZET** ........ Obshchestvo Zemleistroistva Evreiskikh Trudiashchchikhsia v SSSR [*A publication*]
**OZ-FT** ....... Ounce Foot (AAG)
**OZ/FT²** ...... Ounces per Square Foot
**OZ/GAL** .... Ounces per Gallon
**OZH** .......... Zaporozh'ye [*USSR*] [*Airport symbol*] [*Obsolete*] (OAG)
**OZ-IN** ........ Ounce Inch (AAG)
**OZ/IN²** ...... Ounces per Square Inch
**OZ/IN³** ...... Ounces per Cubic Inch
**OZKDP** ..... Oesterreichische Zeitschrift fuer Kunst und Denkmalpflege [*A publication*]
**OZN** .......... St. George, UT [*Location identifier*] [*FAA*] (FAAL)
**OZO** .......... Orbiting Zoological Observatory to Track Animals
**OZOKAN** ... Austrian Journal of Oncology [*A publication*]
**Ozone Sci Eng** ... Ozone. Science and Engineering [*A publication*]
**OZ/PT** ....... Ounces per Pint
**OZR** .......... Ozark, Fort Rucker, AL [*Location identifier*] [*FAA*] (FAAL)
**OZT** .......... Ounces Troy [*Unit of weight*]
**OZV** .......... Oesterreichische Zeitschrift fuer Volkskunde [*A publication*]
**OZX** .......... Oneonta, NY [*Location identifier*] [*FAA*] (FAAL)
**OZ/YD²** ..... Ounces per Square Yard
**OZZ** .......... Ouarzazate [*Morocco*] [*Airport symbol*] (OAG)
**OZZ** .......... Ozark, AR [*Location identifier*] [*FAA*] (FAAL)